DEBRETT'S HANDBOOK

DEBRETT'S HANDBOOK

1982

Distinguished People in British Life

Comprises short biographies of
The Royal Family, the Peerage, Baronetage,
bearers of courtesy titles, businessmen, industrialists,
and prominent people
with correct forms of epistolary address

Editor
Charles Mosley

Preface by
Sir Iain Moncreiffe of that Ilk, Bt.

Consultant
Peter Townend

DEBRETT'S PEERAGE LIMITED

Published by Debrett's Peerage Limited
73/77 Britannia Road, London SW6 2JR

First published 1981

ISBN 0 905649 38 9

Printed in Great Britain by
Robert MacLehose and Company Limited

CONTENTS

INTRODUCTION

by
The Editor

> 'I was wishing that I came of a more honourable lineage'.
>
> 'You come of the Lord Adam and the Lady Eve,' said Aslan. 'And that is both honour enough to erect the head of the poorest beggar, and shame enough to bow the shoulders of the greatest emperor on earth. Be content.'
>
> C S Lewis - *Prince Caspian*

Debrett's Handbook is the first new general biographical dictionary to appear in the British publishing world for a very long time - possibly a century. Inevitably, such a work excites curiosity as to the criteria for inclusion. Indeed, there may be many people who will feel themselves to be in the position of Carabosse in relation to the Sleeping Beauty's christening. Having snatched only a Napoleonic 3-4 hours rest a night for the last few months while acting as *accoucheur* to the Handbook, I might welcome being plunged into a hundred years of sleep by such persons' resentment at being excluded. Nevertheless, we have written to perhaps thrice the number of people actually in the book. Some of them have not responded; others may be victims of our idiosyncratic national postal system. Yet others may have changed address. To those who have responded and do not see their names in the book, I would stress the large part which that old editor's enemy - cum - stimulant, the deadline, has played in our operations. We confidently expect to expand the number of entries in future years to double or even treble the present total.

Debrett's Handbook, in this its first incarnation, is peculiarly strong in two categories: titled folk and businessmen. The two are not widely featured together in any other general reference work, and their enforced intimacy therefore represents something of a 'scoop' for us. But they have another attribute in common. It is a truth universally acknowledged (incidentally, a collateral descendant of the best known writer of that phrase has an entry in this book) that the British hereditary aristocracy has survived to a degree quite unparalleled in other industrialised countries. Now, despite the taint that trade was traditionally supposed to confer on its practitioner, and the alacrity with which the self-made man abandoned the counting house for the manor, swapping his frock coat worn on 'Change for the frayed tweeds of the squire, the actual practice of the successful upper classes has been to go where the money is. And for the last two hundred years money making has been a fairly intensively urban business. The industrialisation of South Wales by the third Marquess of Bute is sketched in the entry for his successor in this book. But even pre-industrial Britain owed much prosperity to the commercial acumen of some great families, witness the draining of the East Anglian fens by the Earls of Bedford. Other members of the hereditary aristocracy have arrived via trade, rather than ennoblement preceding commerce. The families that, owing success to the hop, make up what Anthony Sampson drew attention to as "The Beerage" are only the most numerous such. In short, the day before yesterday's businessman often became yesterday's Lord or Baronet, and, much more crucially, the founder of a family which stood for more than merely handing down wealth from one generation to another.

The truth seems to be that the dynastic principal is deeply embedded in the human psyche, for we see it reasserting itself, hardy perennial, in that most unpromising of climes - North Korea. Moreover, the constant upward thrust of vigorous families, and the corresponding decline of effete ones, is an important part of social evolution. The reader is referred to the entry for the Duke of St Albans for the most eloquently expressed commentary on this process. There was a time, *temp* King John, when William the Marshal was despised as a parvenu, while there were doubtless die-hards in still earlier centuries who lamented the passing of the Merovingians, and cursed the upstart Carolingians, who had started as mere mayors of the palace, for thrusting themselves forward with such effrontery. Just so did the Jacobite pass his glass defiantly over his finger bowl (the water), anathematise the Hanoverians, and toast the "little gentleman in black velvet". And yet his Stuarts, or Stewarts, had originally been stewards (the more aristocratically perceived spelling with the "u" came about because the French, partners in "The Auld Alliance", had no "w" in their alphabet) to earlier monarchs of Scotland, though their particular position had admittedly gained with time much more prestige than an ordinary steward enjoys today. When viewing matters *sub specie æternitatis*, therefore, the quotation at the head of this Introduction is the only sane credo to adopt in the morass of claims to social superiority arising from birth.

That economically powerful families no longer receive recognition, *qua* families, from the state, despite abundant evidence that the tycoon hankers after seigneurial appurtenances, is the result of the creation of hereditary Peerages lapsing into desuetude. The trenchant pen of Mr Auberon Waugh (who, the reader will see from his entry, is as well connected as any in the land) has fulminated against this state of affairs in several Philippics in The Spectator. We at Debrett's have traditionally adopted a descriptive rather than prescriptive rôle in chronicling the Peerage, but it is obvious that our livelihood may eventually be endangered by the decline of the hereditary, as opposed to the meritocratic, principle.

Collateral members of great families have also scrambled to soil their hands in trade. It was quite astonishing the number of city men we received completed forms from, who turned out to be tucked away among the cousins of the titled. Industrialists, as a class, seem to be rather less well connected - at any rate the editor's in-house genealogical research has not turned up much about most of them. Be that as it may, we welcome future applications from the "wealth creator" sector of the community, whether well connected or no, with as many family and ancestral details as they choose to mention.

The matter of genealogical research needs some amplification. It is obviously a particular stock in trade of Debrett's, and even a Handbook exclusively of the living, with nothing of the stud book in its make-up, would be like Hamlet without the Prince. Accordingly, we have mentioned interesting descents and collateral connections, seasoned from time to time by apposite quotations, glosses and the odd anecdote. For we look up to Dr Johnson as our ideal of a reference book editor, no less for his combining the rôles of commentator and compiler than for his admiration of Countesses, though we part company with him over his reluctance to dispute precedency. Though there may seem to be a certain diffuseness in some entries, there is always, we trust, a justifying connection. For instance, Mr Anthony Powell's kinship with Dr John Dee might seem too remote to warrant space. Yet it is the editor's contention that such information is valuable when contemplating the increasing preoccupation with the occult of the later novels in the "Music of Time" sequence. Again, the Hon William Waldegrave MP's connection with past Prime Ministers is stressed, rather than his father's or his elder brother's, because he has on occasion been tipped as a future Premier himself. Mr Auberon Waugh's family connections are given some emphasis because, as the reader will see, making pronouncements on Ireland is by no means confined, among people with Howard blood in their veins, to his writings about Cardinal O'Fiaich. If some entries are found rather too allusive by the general reader, this is the result of the eternal problems of space. The editor will be glad to clear up any points that are raised by a reader. Quite apart from all this, it is our experience that one of the great English conversational gambits is still, on meeting Mr Fotheringay-Phipps, to enquire "Any relation to the Loamshire Fotheringay-Phippses?" It is precisely this kind of question that we have endeavoured to make redundant by noting the relationships of people to each other.

Meanwhile, we would like to draw attention to another useful feature of our book. From the hundreds of 'phone calls we get a week, we conclude that the very heterogeneous nature of British society means that general rules for forms of address are difficult to grasp, and we know from our own experience that they are hard to formulate with clarity, since each individual case may be *sui generis*. Accordingly, we have inserted the code *"Style"* for each adult entry, followed by the correct form of address for use on an envelope when writing to that person. May it save every reader from the fear of solecism, be he (or she) businessman, hostess or secretary.

Another category of people featured in Debrett's Handbook is the foreign nobility domiciled in, or otherwise linked with, this country. Although all foreigners have for a long time been viewed with patronising amusement by the great mass of the British, it is perhaps the Count (whose Anglo-Saxon equivalent, the Earl, is most redolent in noble terms of sturdy independence of the Continent) who tends to embody popular mistrust of strangers. If one accepts that literature is the most valuable, because spontaneous, reflection of general attitudes in textually recorded form, then Count Dracula is the most obvious example of such xenophobia, for as a presumed beneficiary of the Historic Compromise of 1867 he is subconsciously perceived by the British as symbol of all that was most degenerate in the Habsburg Dual Monarchy. Victorian, and even early twentieth-century, fiction has many other examples of the type, most notably perhaps Wilkie Collins's Count Fosco, villain of *The Woman in White*. It is significant that his accomplice, Sir Percival Glyde, is a petulant cypher in comparison, for he is an epigone to the earlier and more robust portrayal of the Bad Baronet (a "humour" once important as indigenous folk memory of the *jus primae noctis*) by, say, Sir Lucius Grafton in Disraeli's *The Young Duke* or Sir Mulberry Hawk in his odious attentions to Kate Nickleby. (To be fair there is a more benevolent, if insipid, tradition stretching from Sir Hugh Tyrold, through Sir Thomas Bertram, to Sir Leicester Dedlock.) The concept embodied by the Hawks and Graftons was even in the nineteenth century declining into the burlesquing that the character type was to endure in Victorian melodrama.

Lest this analysis seem over-fanciful, I would cite the instance in which we were telephoned recently by a woman of some sophistication, holding a responsible position in a City firm. She assumed *a priori* that a certain mediatised Prince of the Holy Roman Empire was a *rastaquouère*, simply from the sonorousness of his designations. This seems to be adding insult to injury when one contemplates the state to which such beings have come. Thus the Prince of Little Lilliput in Disraeli's *Vivian Grey*: "You have mistaken me for a monarch; I should be one. A curse light on me the hour I can mention it without a burning blush. Oh shame! shame on the blood of my father's son! Can my mouth own that I once was one? Yes, sir! you see before you the most injured, the least enviable of human beings. I am a mediatised prince!" The author goes on to explain this state of affairs by describing how, through the Congress of Vienna, "various petty Princes who exercised absolute sovereignties over little nations of fifty thousand souls...either swelled, by their mediatisation, the territories of some already powerful potentate, or transmuted into a state of importance some more fortunate petty ruler than themselves." The glossator continues "...the mediatised Prince, instead of being an impoverished and uninfluential sovereign, became a wealthy and powerful subject. But so dominant in the heart of man is the love of independent dominion, that even with these temptations few of the petty princes could have been induced to part with their cherished sceptres, had they not been conscious that, in case of contumacy, the resolutions of a Diet would have been enforced by the armies of an emperor." With characteristic perspicacity Disraeli foresaw the mischievous support by such dispossessed *ci-devant* sovereigns for bourgeois demands for a constitution and hinted at the benefits to people like Bismarck. While concern for such beings' plight is less keen than it was, and for lesser nobles such as Counts and Barons virtually non-existent, Debrett's Handbook, though hampered by the widespread destruction of records in two world wars that are in part the outcome of those very mediatisations, has been meticulous in scrutinising antecedents. The greater representation of the foreign nobilities in future editions is planned.

It is only proper to record that the original idea of this book sprang from the head of our Patron (like Minerva out of Jove's, only initially unaccoutred; armouring the concept has taken time). He is of course Sir Iain Moncreiffe of that Ilk, Bt, CVO, QC, DL, who has given constant enthusiastic support for this project. I would like to thank Count d'Angerville, editor of the book "Royalty, Peerage and Nobility of the World", published by L'Annuaire de Noblesse de France, for permission to reproduce Sir Iain's counsel's opinion on the use of foreign titles. I would also like to thank A D Peters & Co for permission to quote from the late Evelyn Waugh's "Men at Arms" and Messrs Collins for permission to quote from C S Lewis's "Prince Caspian". The process of producing this book has been the unstinting work of Chris Jarman. Count Adam Zamoyski and Count d'Angerville have given valuable help and advice on foreign nobilities, while Charles Kidd, editor of Debrett's Peerage, has been generous with information on native titles. Without what it is not too strong to call the genius and application (cybernetic) of Cahal Dallat and (marketing) of Mr A H Mian, this project would be nothing. Cahal's co-director on the board of Briter Business Systems, Brian Rogers, has also been of great service. Finally I must express my gratitude to my able and diligent Lieutenant, Suzie Duke, also to Alice Hyde, Helen Kearney and Isabella Szredski for their help. While every care is taken to ensure accuracy, neither the publishers nor the printers can admit liability for any loss incurred through misprint or other circumstances.

73-77 Britannia Road
London SW6

CHARLES MOSLEY

PREFACE

by

Sir Iain Moncreiffe of that Ilk, Bt, CVO, QC, DL
Patron of Debrett

Debrett's Handbook is the successor to Kelly's Handbook, which was originally the quickest and most useful way in which to look up members of the 'Titled, Landed and Official Classes', together with their addresses, telephone numbers and careers. Unfortunately, Kelly's was discontinued after it omitted courtesy titles, which had been one of its most useful functions.

Debrett's Handbook, on the other hand, includes, among many other prominent people, British hereditary titles both courtesy and substantive. It's scarcely necessary to look up the Duke of Norfolk, but often useful to discover at a glance (on learning that she's coming to dinner) who the Hon Mrs John Smith is. Moreover, it's not always understood that every Hon Mrs Smith would automatically take precedence before even Lady Bacon, wife of the Premier Baronet of England. Indeed, "Honourables before Baronets" is rightly the constant cry of my old buddy Mr Bobby Corbett (alias the Hon Robert Corbett, youngest son of the late Lord Rowallan), as he hurries through doorways ahead of me.

For our British system of precedence, so puzzling to earnest foreigners but set out for your beguilement at the beginning of this useful Handbook, is organic: an amusing and harmless medley of the evolving pageant of our national history coupled with real importance, that helps to restrain what Churchill (a Duke's grandson) called civil servants from becoming "no longer servants and no longer civil," softens the harsh realities of power without entirely excluding it, and blunts the cruel edge of Iron Curtain-Style precedence, where one is immediately preceded on all occasions by that Dirty Dick who as one's deadly rival has repeatedly pipped one to the post.

We are happily a realm, and a popular one: most of the world has heard favourably of our Queen, but would be hard put to it - like you, gentle reader - to name the present Presidents of West Germany, Greece, and Italy. And like such other constitutional monarchies as Sweden, Denmark, Belgium, the Netherlands and Spain, we have hereditary titles: forming (at no expense to the community) living memorials to their founders. They add to the fun and colour of life, and are a highly civilised concept: it's doubtful if rabbits or even chimpanzees could think of anything as colourful as a Duke of Northumberland or a Knight of Kerry. But very few people realise that our Peerage is quite unlike a Continental aristocracy.

Many great historic families, like Berkeley of Berkeley, Giffard of Chillingham, Scrope of Danby or Cameron of Lochiel, are not peers at all. On the other hand, our actual hereditary peerage families may be divided roughly into three fairly equal parts: respectively of working class, middle class and upper class origin. An analysis I made for my late friend Nancy Mitford revealed that about a third of the Peerage descend from the able middle or lower class peerages conferred on the advice of successive Liberal or Labour premiers in the twentieth century - for example, the Hon Colin Moynihan, recent President of the Union at Oxford, is grandson of the late 1 Lord Moynihan, one of the most eminent surgeons of his time (first promoted to a Baronetcy by *Earl* Lloyd George) and whose working class father Sergeant Andrew Moynihan won a Victoria Cross and a commission; and the present Lord Macpherson of Drumochter's father was a kindly working class Trades Unionist leader who became Minister of War Transport during the Second World War and was recommended for a peerage by *Earl* Attlee. About another third of our peerage belong to the talented families like Cecil Marquess of Salisbury and Wellesley Duke of Wellington who between Tudor and Victorian times made us the greatest and most respected country in the world. Only about the remaining third in fact belong to the ancient historic families, like Nevill Marquess of Abergavenny or Lindsay Earl of Crawford, who are what would be called immemorial nobility abroad. Thus entry into our peerage has always hitherto been open to merit, and it would be sad if it were ever to be made into a completely closed order.

This almost unnoticed mixture of all classes in our modern Peerage has led us to an enviable constitutional position, not always fully appreciated. For our unwritten Constitution is organic too, and for a long time has saved us from Aristotle's dread cycle that "autocracy begets tyranny, remedied by aristocracy which begets oligarchy, remedied by democracy which begets demagogy, remedied by autocracy" and so full circle back to Square One. We have so far managed to avoid all three traps during the past few generations. An absolute democracy, allied to no moral principle, must logically lead to the arbitrary selfishness of the passing majority, but in Britain we have evolved historic safeguards in our constitutional monarchy and a senate who are bred to a sense of duty and are not swayed by the fears and ambitions of election.

Some ancient Greek city-state democracies, faced with the divisive rivalries of election, chose their officials by lot, rather as we choose a jury of average citizens. We choose our own Upper House as a sort of jury by the lot of birth, from a group of families, originating in all classes, who have shown some sense of responsibility in advance and are of all ages and both sexes. It's of course the proper purpose of any upper house of parliament to be carefully conservative with a small "c", since it's for the elected lower house to initiate reformative or revolutionary legislation and for the Lords, I repeat, to act as a sort of uncommitted national jury (leavened by the advice of Life Peer experts) to reconsider and restrain awhile the only too well-known dangers that would arise from a completely unfettered single chamber parliament.

Debrett's Handbook, therefore, includes first of all the holders of those Peerages (and those peers, such as Irish peers, who are not members of the House of Lords) together with the titled members of their families, and also the Baronets. It is our intention also to include all knights, so that every holder of a British title can be looked up at a glance; at the moment, in this pioneer work, we have been able to track down a majority of them, but not all have been good at answering enquiries. Those knights who already belong to Peerage or Baronetage families are more easily traced, of course, and we also include British knights of the Sovereign Military Order of Malta.

We have also included, for readiness of social reference, a number of the principal holders of foreign titles normally resident in this country. The principles governing our social recognition of such historic names, out of natural politeness, whatever the vicissitudes that have befallen them in the crises of Western Civilisation, are set out in a Counsel's Opinion that I wrote some years ago and which is appended to this Preface.

As for our predecessor Kelly's original "Landed and Official Classes", changes in British society since the Second World War have been such that Kelly itself had already abandoned so exact a definition. As befits Debrett, we include most of the great untitled landowners of the old "landed gentry", also the Scottish chiefs and Irish chieftains - and a great number of socially distinguished people, such as members of both British and European Parliaments, ambassadors, high government officials, church leaders, and important members of Her Majesty's Services and the legal and medical professions.

Of its nature, Debrett's Handbook is obviously more akin to the French *Bottin Mondain* or the American *Social Register* than to the more academic emphasis of *Who's Who*. But it has seemed to us proper to stress more especially the social significance of prominent people in business and industry, on whom the prosperity of our country so largely depends. The world's two greatest constitutional monarchies are Britain and Japan, heavily populated islands at opposite ends of the Eurasian land mass. They have to live by their wits and industry, and therefore resemble dynamos of activity. New ideas have constantly to be tested against old ones, and this would lead to bitter disunity were it not for the unifying force of a Royalty that stands outside politics. So the industrialists and businessmen whose interaction powers this dynamo are therefore vital to our survival. The rural Lord of the Manor has to a great extent been replaced by the urban Head of the Firm; and indeed many family firms are rather like industrialised manors today.

THE SOCIAL RECOGNITION OF TITLES OF HONOUR

by

Sir Iain Moncreiffe of that Ilk, Bt
Advocate - Albany Herald

We now consider from an international point of view and in the light of a common-sense combination of law, history and social practice, the question of titles of honour.

These fall broadly into two categories: those that are officially recognised, and those that are *socially* recognised by courtesy.

Titles recognised Officially

First, there are titles of honour that are valid officially throughout the world, because they are conferred or recognised by a Sovereign who is universally significant: such as the Queen of the United Kingdom or the King of the Belgians or the Pope. This includes of course the Swedish titled families such as Bielke or Bonde although no new creations have been made for many years, and the historic houses of Denmark and the Netherlands. Among the rarest of *official* (as opposed to *courtesy*) titles is that of "Master" when applied to the heir apparent of a Peerage of Scotland created before 1707: eg the Master of Lovat. Similarly, there are valid titles of honour where the reigning dynasty has been deposed without the abolition of titles formerly granted by it, and where there is still officially recognised machinery for regulating their succession. (An example is Spain where the Government* employed the late Duke of Alba under that title as their Ambassador at the Court of St James's. Another example is Portugal where the Duke of Palmella as such was employed by the Republic of Portugal as their Ambassador at St James's.)

The above are qualified where a subject or citizen of a Sovereign State, which does not recognise foreign titles among its own subjects, nevertheless accepts a foreign title himself - or else possessed one before being naturalised a subject, or later inherits one. In this case the title can still be valid *officially* in its country of origin or perhaps elsewhere abroad and usually be accepted by courtesy in Society.

Examples of the foregoing would be where an American citizen inherited a Scottish title (Earldom of Lindsay or Dunbar Baronetcy), a Spanish Duke** by inheritance with large estates in Spain was a British subject by birth (Ciudad Rodrigo *alias* Wellington) or when the Dutch Baron Mackay van Ophemert was naturalised a British subject on succeeding to the Scottish peerage of Reay. And is a Scottish royal officer-of-arms going to refuse to recognise officially the Countess of Newburgh as a Peeress of Scotland in her own right, simply because she is a citizen of the Italian Republic which purports to have abolished titles but which has no jurisdiction whatsoever in Scotland?

Thus it is seen how easily titles of honour can fail to be distinguished clearly between the *official* and the *social* categories.

Titles accepted Socially

In this category there are a number of groupings, some merging with each other, others half linked with Category One above.

First, there are the descendants of the Sovereigns who lost their thrones in the past, such as the Duke of Bavaria, the Margrave of Baden or the Prince of Prussia - more especially those

**Written before Juan Carlos's accession. **The Duke of Ciudad Rodrigo is not recognised as such in England - but he is in Spain. He might also be so recognised say, if visiting Sweden.*

whose ancestors never legally abdicated. Into this grouping merge the great mediatised families such as Leiningen and Lobkowicz, Schwarzenberg and Esterházy - who for a short time after the dissolution of the Holy Roman Empire exercised immediate sovereign powers, often including the maintenance of their own troops and coinage or even the creation of their own orders of knighthood.* In this "mediatised" grouping one may include the great Indian princes, like the Maharaja of Udaipur and the Nizam of Hyderabad and the Maharao Raja of Bundi, who for a short time after the dissolution of the British Empire in India also exercised immediate sovereign powers: the Maharaja Sriraj of Dhrangadhra, who already had his own troops, then founding his own Order of Knighthood (named after His Highness's legendary ancestress-goddess).

Another grouping that again merges into the foregoing are the immemorial dynastic Princes of the Houses of Rurik of Russia and Guédimine of Lithuania - such as Czartoryski or Galitzine or Obolensky - never "created" but undoubtedly strengthened when recognised by Poland after the Treaty of Lublin in 1569, or by Muscovy during the Romanoff expansion. This also applies to the immemorial Armenian and Georgian dynastic princely houses, like Amilakhvari and Toumanoff and - above all - Bagration, whose dynasty had reigned in the male line as Kings from 886 until the 19th century, before the 17th century boyar family of Romanoff dispossessed them. Both Bagration and Romanoff are now equally dispossessed: which needs the official recognition of which? Prince Bagration's social recognition is as assured as that of the Grand Duke Vladimir of Russia in modern international Society. In this context, a subsequent Tsarist confirmation is hardly required for the social recognition as princes of the imperial house of Genghis Khan (such as the Guirey dynasty, ruling Khans of the Crimea until their accession to Catherine the Great) who in the days of the Golden Horde were themselves paramount over all the Russian rulers.

Almost merging into this group, too, are such Romanian houses as Cantacuzène or Sturdza who formerly furnished Reigning Princes to Moldavia or Wallachia.

Then there are the great Austro-German, Bohemian and Hungarian also Italian names - like Thun and Bismarck, Clary and Batthyány and Orsini. They remain listed in the *Annuaire*** and similar works of reference, although their countries have supposedly abolished titles "officially", because no gentleman in his senses would regard them as false. So they continue to use their historic titles socially through such legalistic concepts as "they are part of the surname". In Great Britain, where an anointed Sovereign still reigns there is an official rule which is the law. Moreover, it is the duty of a herald or courtier to see the law observed in the course of legalistic formalities. If, for political reasons, Her Majesty's Government feel obliged to recognise a régime which has abolished titles, we cannot enforce such titles officially. Thus Prince Johannes Schwarzenberg, recent Austrian Ambassador at the Court of St James's, had to be received by officials as "Dr Johannes Schwarzenberg". But nobody in Society calls him anything but "prince".

There may be persons who derive a sense of self-importance by calling Archduke Otto, "Dr Habsburg". And this brings us back to the doctrine of "courtesy": the manners of a Court as opposed to those of the uneducated. It is not the power that is respected, but the sense of history. And there is no reason why one should not apply the courteous social custom "commonly called..." to an officially disqualified nobleman of a State which for political reasons our country can no longer recognise as a realm. The most difficult grouping within titles of honour that are socially though perhaps not always officially acceptable, is that which consists of honours conferred by illegally deposed Sovereigns who have not abdicated, and in

**Such as the Hohenlohe Order of the Phoenix.* ** Annuaire de Noblesse - *for which this opinion was originally written.*

some cases by their heirs.*

For the purposes of simplicity it is proposed to confine the study of this final grouping to three cases: those of the Jacobite "Kings over the Water", of the late King of Yugoslavia, and of King Umberto. The exiled King James II and VII and his son, the Old Chevalier (James III and VIII) conferred a number of titles of honour, which are listed in Ruvigny's *Jacobite Peerage*.

Ruvigny rightly observes of James III and VIII that it is difficult to see on what grounds the kingly style can be refused him, when it is remembered that he was recognised as a sovereign by the Continental powers, and that his ambassadors were received and the titles he conferred recognised by them. Moreover, these exiled Stuarts lived exclusively on ground accorded full diplomatic privilege by sovereigns (the King of France or the Pope) who recognised them as Kings, and it was at the Stuart Court maintained *extra finem terræ* that Jacobite titles of honour were conferred. Indeed nobody in Scotland would have referred to James Drummond, Esquire, as anything but the Duke of Perth; nor does any historian of the '45 Rising call him anything but the Duke of Perth. One of the most popular of Scottish country dances is called the "Duke of Perth", and nobody is so foolish as to suggest that there never was such a person.

With the exception of such great chiefs as Lochiel, Clanranald and The Mackintosh, who have no need of titles, most Jacobite titles are vested in people who have officially recognised titles anyway: thus the Jacobite Duke of Rannoch is the present Duke of Atholl. This includes our present Lord Chamberlain: Lord Maclean. The last Jacobite title known to have been used was that of Earl Walsh, which became extinct in 1881. No British herald can recognise a Jacobite title "officially", but I cannot see why a Club of the highest standing in Paris should not do so socially.

We now come to the case of the late King of Yugoslavia, which realm, of course, also included Montenegro. The late King Peter II's grandmother was Princess Zorka of Montenegro, whose cousin, the last independent King of Montenegro, created several titles of Duke, Prince and Count, whilst in exile. I understand that some of these were recognised by the Foreign Office in London (prior to 1930), and appear in the register of *Foreign Arms* at the College of Arms, London.

Dr Ranko M Brashich, a counsellor on International Law, and Mr Deyan Brashich, attorney-at-law, an authority on Yugoslav Law practising in the USA, prepared a memorandum for the King in 1966. They were of the opinion, with which I agree, that the Serbian Constitution falls to be interpreted as meaning the King of Serbia was empowered to confer a title on any foreigner. Moreover, after the First World War, Croatia, and the Kingdom of Montenegro, together with territories in Macedonia, etc, were amalgamated with the Kingdom of Serbia to form Yugoslavia. In the constitutions of this new Kingdom of Yugoslavia, the Brashich Memorandum points out, "there does not exist the slightest restriction or negation on the Monarch's right to bestow titles of nobility" (on foreigners). Titles of honour have often been conferred by Sovereigns on foreigners, as witness Charles I's creation of the Dutch Ambassador Boreel a Baronet, the Holy Roman Emperor's creation of

**In its simplest form, this can be seen in the case of family Orders. Otto of Habsburg awards the Golden Fleece, and no nobleman in his senses would decline that honour. Yet he does not claim to be Emperor of Austria. Nor is he the effective Duke reigning in Burgundy, where his forefathers first instituted that order which - with the Garter - is the most coveted in Europe. He is not even the heir male nor the heir female of its Founder. Yet the circumstances are such that nobody worthy of serious consideration doubts that he is the Sovereign of the Austrian branch of the Golden Fleece.*

Arundell of Wardour a Count, the King of Denmark's creation of the French Duc Decazes a Danish Duke, and the Dutch King's creation of the Duke of Wellington "Prince of Waterloo". Whether or not they are "officially" recognised, they are certainly socially recognised internationally.

When the Communists seized power in Yugoslavia, the King did not abdicate, and continued to be recognised by some countries: as he had been during the German occupation, when His Majesty continued to issue postage stamps bearing his own portrait at least until 1943. After the unilateral seizure of power by the Communists, he continued to keep his own consulate in Monaco, under the direction of General T K Militchevitch, a royal Yugoslav officer. In 1950, His Majesty visited General Franco for the purpose of changing his Ambassador to Spain; and upon the death of this ambassador some dozen years or so ago, he was replaced by a Royal Yugoslav Consul-General. King Peter in exile, like the Jacobite monarch, still therefore had royal territory *extra finem terrae*; and travelled on his own passport, made up at his consulate in Monte Carlo and signed by himself.

The position of titles conferred by King Umberto in exile may now be considered. Although he may perhaps have no diplomatic representatives abroad, for the *de facto* régime in Italy is officially recognised everywhere, he is still *de jure* a King because his father, the late King Vittorio Emanuele, abdicated in his favour and King Umberto himself has never abdicated. Indeed he is still regarded in Jacobite fashion as their King by very many Italians. Moreover, there was never any Constitutional limitation on his power to confer honours.

A king who has not abdicated remains a king, even though his power may not extend *de facto* over a former realm. When I acted as an usher at the Requiem Mass for the late King of Spain, he was neither referred to officially as "ex-King" nor as "King of Spain" (since he had never abdicated *de jure* but since Her Majesty's Government had recognised the Caudillo's Government *de facto*), but was simply called in our orders "King Alfonso XIII, KG."*

The styles to which King Umberto succeeded from his father, and which he has never abdicated, include some of almost purely historic interest: yet they represent unabdicated claims none of which are bogus. His Majesty is styled, for example, King of Italy, Sardinia, Cyprus, Jerusalem and Armenia. Obviously if a Palaeologue were to appear today styling himself Emperor of Byzantium and claiming to grant titles of honour, he would be making a fool of himself: as no Palaeologue claim to Byzantium has been made since 1453. But the House of Savoy, as heirs of the Luisgnan Crusader-Kings of Cyprus and Jerusalem, have never relinquished that claim: one which might be accepted as still giving them some legitimist authority among the social heirs of some of the crusader knightly bodies. Yet another paradox appears: for another of the styles inherited by King Umberto is that of Duke of Savoy and Sovereign of the Order of the Annunziata. It would be a surly or churlish Italian nobleman from Sardinia or Piedmont who refused to accept that Order at His Majesty's hands: and the late King-Emperor George V himself accepted it from the then King of Italy. But Savoy was ceded by the then Head of the House of Savoy to France in 1860: so it seems there has been no internationally social (and for a long time no internationally official) objection to the Italian royal family continuing to be Dukes of Savoy and conferring its family Order: without any actual possession of Savoy itself. (The situation is in some respects analogous to the Burgundian Order of the Golden Fleece.)

**Indeed the dignity of king appears to have originally been personal rather than territorial in some ancient realms, especially in early Scandinavia with its roving "sea-kings". This system continued perhaps longest among the Rurikid princes of Russia, all of whom bore the kingly style of knaes.*

But King Umberto is not just the remote descendant or pretender to any thrones save the romantic crusader kingdoms. He is the actual *de jure* King of Italy and Sardinia who duly succeeded his father and has reigned but never abdicated.

Since the Republic of Italy has purported to abolish former titles of honour, its fundamentally unconstitutional edicts have been ignored by the whole of Italian society - and in what way is a title granted by King Umberto *now* less valid *socially* than one granted by His Majesty *before* the political but quite illegal change of his kingdom into a republic? He was never a usurper but a lawful King who reigned lawfully and never abdicated. Who then is sovereign aboard His Majesty's yacht on the high seas outside all territorial waters? His villa in Portugal has tacit extra-territorial rights, as has the palace of the Grand Master of the Knights of Malta in Rome, and he travels on a special type of passport and is treated by civilised governments as an international personage. And so, although Her Majesty's Government cannot recognise his status officially for reasons of practical politics, it is my firm opinion that his power to confer socially accepted honours is in no whit abated.

In most western countries a man may call himself what he wishes, provided he does not do so for purposes of fraud. Genuine titles were or are usually conferred for relationship or special service to a Sovereign: occasionally, as with our original baronetcies, that service being provided in the form of much needed finance in time of difficulty. In certain countries, some feudal estates even carried titles that could pass by purchase, it being supposed that the purchaser might be expected to be in a better financial position to carry out the accompanying duties. A celebrated example was the Dauphiné of Viennois. False titles in general are those that are self-assumed, though even in this case I would not necessarily deny a self-assumed style to a genuine member of some ancient dynasty. Unassailable titles are those still recognised officially in their own country. Thus the reigning Prince of Liechtenstein created the Count de Bendern and our own Queen created Lord George-Brown. Other titles must be regarded as socially acceptable and only a little less firm than British courtesy titles: the Duke of Devonshire's son Peregrine Cavendish is "commonly called" Marquess of Hartington by "courtesy", and no Court Circular would call him anything else. The historic names in the *Annuaire* and the *Almanach de Gotha* are firmly enough established socially although many are no longer recognised officially. "Socially recognised" titles of honour, therefore, fall into a number of categories irrespective of "official recognition", including those created by illegally deposed Sovereigns who have never abdicated their legal right to be a fountain of honour.

[NB Since this opinion was first published the Countess of Newburgh has died and been succeeded by a kinsman; since he is also an Italian citizen, the statement is as valid in principal as before - Ed]

PRECEDENCE OF PEERAGES

In reading the list of precedence among Peers, it is helpful to understand the principal behind it. The ranking among Peers according to degree is: Dukes, Marquesses, Earls, Viscounts, Barons. Assuming Eugène de Tournon's hypothetical case, whereby all twenty-six Dukes are invited to dinner (and accept), the order of their placing would be: Dukes in the English Peerage according to date of creation (Bedford before Devonshire), followed by Dukes in the Peerage of Scotland in chronological order of creation (Montrose before Roxburghe), then Dukes in the Peerage of Great Britain according to the same criteria, The Duke of Leinster (sole Duke in the Peerage of Ireland), and finally Dukes in the Peerage of the United Kingdom, again in order of date of creation. Were this hypothetical dinner party to take place North of the (Anglo-Scottish) Border, the Duke of Argyll, as Hereditary Master of the Queen's Household in Scotland, would take precedence of all his fellow Dukes. (NB The Earl of Erroll, as Hereditary Lord High Constable of Scotland, would, if present, and again provided the function were to take place in that country, have precedence over all other holders of hereditary honours after the Blood Royal, including all Dukes - even Argyll - and Marquesses).

Each Marquess takes his turn in the taxis according to the same order: those of the Peerage of England, then of Scotland, Great Britain, Ireland, and United Kingdom. This follows the concentration into one Crown marked by the Act of Union of the English and Scottish Crowns of 1707 and the Act of Union of the British and Irish Parliaments of 1800, so that English and Scottish Peerage creations antedate 1707, GB creations antedate 1800 and postdate 1707, while UK creations postdate 1800; some Irish Peerages were created after 1800 but count for purposes of precedence as UK ones, whether Marquess, Earl, Viscount or Baron. Of Marquessates created in the same year (the specific date may be looked up under the entry for that individual), the order is:-
Salisbury then Bath;
Waterford then Downshire;
Headfort then Sligo;
Ely then Exeter;
Northampton then Camden;
Anglesey then Cholmondeley (unless the latter is in official fulfilment of his post of Lord Great Chamberlain of England, when he takes precedence over all other Marquesses);
Londonderry before Conyngham.

The same order obtains with Earls, except that with the four senior Scottish ones (Crawford, Erroll, Mar, and Sutherland) the Decreet of Ranking of 1606 laid down the exact order of precedence of various Scottish Peerages, notwithstanding a differing chronology of creation. Every so often years of creation have been inserted to help the reader. Of Earldoms created in or around the same year, the order is:-
(E 1661) Essex then Carlisle;
Albemarle then Coventry then Jersey;
(S c 1458) Rothes then Morton;
Moray then Mar and Kellie (not to be confused with Mar);
Home then Perth;
(S 1633) Lindsay, Loudoun, Kinnoull, Elgin, Southesk, Wemyss, then Dalhousie;
Dundee then Newburgh;
Kintore then Breadalbane;
(S 1703) Stair, Rosebery, then Glasgow;
(GB 1711) Ferrers then Dartmouth;
Tankerville then Aylesford;

Brooke (and Warwick) then Buckinghamshire;
Radnor then Spencer;
Clarendon then Mansfield and Mansfield;
Mount Edgcumbe then Fortescue;
(GB 1800) Cadogan then Malmesbury;
(I 1756) Shannon then Lanesborough;
Arran then Courtown;
Mexborough then Winterton;
Lisburne then Clanwilliam;
(I 1785) Antrim, Longford, Portarlington, then Mayo;
Annesley, Enniskillen, then Erne;
(I 1800) Bandon, Castle Stewart, Donoughmore, Caledon;
(UK 1801) Rosslyn, Craven, Onslow, Romney, Chichester, Wilton;
Limerick then Clancarty;
Gosford, Rosse, Normanton, then Grey;
(UK 1815) Verulam, St Germans, Morley, then Bradford;
Eldon, Howe, then Stradbroke;
Temple of Stowe, Kilmorey, Dunraven and Mountearl, then Listowel;
Norbury then Cawdor;
(UK 1831) Munster, Ranfurly, then Lichfield;
Durham then Granville;
Effingham, Ducie, Yarborough, then Leicester;
(UK 1861) Russell then Cromartie;
Lytton then Sondes;
Cranbrook then Ancaster (unless the latter is in the official performance of his duty as Lord Great Chamberlain, when he would take precedence of all other Earls);
(UK 1905) Plymouth then Liverpool;
Beatty, Haig, then Iveagh;
Balfour, Ypres, then Birkenhead;
(UK 1925) Oxford and Asquith, then Jellicoe;
Inchcape then Peel;
(UK 1945) Gowrie then Lloyd George of Dwyfor;
Swinton then Attlee;
(UK 1961) Avon then Snowdon.

Viscounts follow exactly the same rules. For creations of the same year the order is:
(I 1622) Valentia then Dillon;
(I 1717) Chetwynd then Boyne;
Barrington then Gage;
(I 1776) Southwell then De Vesci;
Lifford, Bangor, then Clifden;
Gort (I 1816) then Exmouth (UK 1816);
(UK 1900) Goschen then Ridley;
Colville of Culross then Churchill;
Knollys, Allendale, Chilston, then Scarsdale;
Mersey then Chaplin;
(UK 1917) Cowdray, Devonport, then Astor;
Furness, Wimborne, then St Davids;
Rothermere then Allenby;
Chelmsford, Long, then Ullswater;
Bridgeman, Hailsham, then Brentford;
(UK 1935) Bledisloe then Monsell;
Hanworth then Trenchard;

Greenwood, Samuel, Runciman of Doxford, then Davidson;
Weir then Stonehaven;
(UK 1945) Addison, Lambert, Kemsley, then Marchwood;
Portal of Hungerford, Alanbrooke, Montgomery of Alamein, then Hall;
Waverley, Thurso, Brookeborough, then Norwich;
(UK 1954) Leathers, Soulbury, Chandos, then Simonds;
De L'Isle then Ingleby;
Monckton of Brenchley, Tenby, then Mackintosh of Halifax;
Dunrossil then Stuart of Findhorn;
(UK 1960) Rochdale, Slim, Head, Boyd of Merton, then Ward of Witley
Radcliffe then Mills
Eccles, Watkinson, Muirshiel, then Dilhorne.

Barons are so numerous that, once again, every so often a date of creation has been placed to act as a pointer. The reader need only look up the date of creation of a Barony in the entry for that Peer, then run the eye up or down from the nearest date in the margin, to find the relative order of precedence. Recently there have been some very numerous creations. Nineteen sixty-four, for example, might stand comparison with 69, the Year of the Four Emperors, and be known as the Year of the Fifty-five Peerages. It is curious to reflect that the contemplated creation of only five more than that number in 1832 was sufficient to cowe the opponents of Parliamentary Reform in the Lords. For Barons (whether Life or Hereditary) of the same year of creation, the order is:-
(E 1295) Furnivall then FitzWalter;
(E 1313) Audley then Strabolgi;
(E 1529) Burgh then Bray;
(E 1603) Petre then Saye and Sele;
Scottish Lordship of Lovat *after* all other Scottish Lordships arranged chronologically up to and including Elphinstone, but before Torphichen;
(S 1627) Napier then Fairfax of Cameron;
Rollo then Ruthven of Freeland;
(GB 1776) Hawke, Brownlow, then Foley;
Dynevor, Walsingham, Bagot, then Southampton;
Grantley then Rodney;
Somers then Sherborne;
Kenyon then Braybrooke;
(GB 1797) Carrington, Bolton, then Lilford;
(I 1461) Trimlestown then Dunsany;
Dunboyne then Louth;
(I 1776) Macdonald, Kensington, Newborough, then Massy;
Huntingfield then Rossmore;
Hotham then Headley;
Teignmouth, Crofton, then ffrench;
(I 1800) Langford, Henniker, Ventry, Dunalley, Clanmorris, then Ashtown;
(UK 1802) Ellenborough then Sandys;
Castlemaine then Decies;
(UK 1821) Ravensworth, Delamere, Forester, then Rayleigh;
Heytesbury then Skelmersdale;
Talbot de Malahide, Kilmarnock, Poltimore, Mostyn, Templemore, then De Saumarez;
Denman then Carew;
Abinger, Ashburton, then Hatherton;
Stratheden and Campbell, then Oranmore and Browne;
(UK 1838) De Mauley, Wrottesley, Sudeley, then Methuen;
Leigh, Lurgan, then Monteagle of Brandon;

Vivian then Congleton;
(UK 1852) St Leonards then Raglan;
Belper then Fermoy;
Chesham then Churston;
Leconfield then Lyveden;
Romilly, Northbrook, Hylton, then Penrhyn;
Ormathwaite, O'Neill, Napier of Magdala, then Rathdonnell;
Lawrence, Acton, Wolverton, then Greville;
(UK 1874) Moncreiff, Coleridge, Cottesloe, then Hampton;
Harlech, Tollemache, Gerard, then Sackville;
Trevor then Brabourne;
Ampthill, Derwent, then Hothfield;
(UK 1884) Tennyson, Strathspey, Monk Bretton, then Northbourne;
Rothschild, Revelstoke, Monkswell, Ashbourne, St Oswald, Deramore, then Montagu of Beaulieu;
Herschell, Hillingdon, Hindlip, Grimthorpe, then Hamilton of Dalzell;
St Levan, Basing, De Ramsey, Addington;
Ashcombe, Crawshaw, Amherst of Hackney, Newton, then Dunleath;
(UK 1897) Holm Patrick then Burton;
Glanusk then Cranworth;
Avebury, Killanin, then Strathcona and Mount Royal;
Kinross, Shuttleworth, Allerton, Grenfell, then Redesdale;
Burnham, Biddulph, then Armstrong;
Ritchie of Dundee then Michelham;
Hemphill, Joicey, then Nunburnholme;
(UK 1907) Airedale, Swaythling, then Blyth;
Pentland, Gorell, Fisher, then Kilbracken;
Hardinge of Penshurst then de Villiers;
Glenconner, Aberconway, St Audries, Merthyr, Rowallan, Ashton of Hyde, then Ravensdale;
Parmoor, Cozens-Hardy, Lyell, then Cunliffe;
Faringdon, Shaughnessy, Rathcreedan, Somerleyton, Carnock, then Glentanar;
(UK 1917) Gainford, Forteviot, Colwyn, Gisborough, then Southborough;
Morris, Cawley, Terrington, Glenarthur, then Phillimore;
Inverforth, Sinha, Cochrane of Cults, Wyfold, Clwyd, Russell of Liverpool, Swinfen, then Meston;
Ailwyn, Glenavy, then Trevethin;
Glendyne, Manton, Barnby, Forres, Vestey, Borwick, Maclay, then Bethell;
Jessel, Darling, then Banbury of Southam;
Merrivale, Bradbury, then Lloyd;
(UK 1927) Greenway, Hayter, Cornwallis, then Daresbury;
Wraxall, Melchett, Remnant, then Ebbisham;
Moynihan, Fairhaven, Craigmyle, Dulverton, Luke, Alvingham, Amulree, then Baden-Powell;
Marley, Ponsonby of Shulbrede, Dickinson, Noel-Buxton, then Howard of Penrith;
Selsdon, Moyne, Essendon, Davies, then Rankeillour;
Brocket, Horder, Milne, Rennell, Mottistone, Iliffe, then Palmer;
Rockley, Elton, then Wakehurst;
Hesketh, Tweedsmuir, Sysonby, Wigram, Blackford, Riverdale, May, St Just, then Kennet;
Strathcarran, Catto, then Wardington;
(UK 1937) Windlesham, Mancroft, McGowan, Denham, Rea, Chatfield, Cadman, Kenilworth, then Pender;
Roborough, Birdwood, Brassey of Apethorpe, Belstead, Stamp, then Bicester;

Milford, Hankey, Harmsworth, Rotherwick, Glentoran;
Tryon, Croft, Teviot, Nathan;
Kindersley, Ironside;
Latham, Wedgwood, Geddes, Bruntisfield, Brabazon of Tara;
Keyes, Hemingford, Moran, Killearn, then Dowding;
Gretton, then Westwood;
(UK 1945) Hazlerigg, Hacking, Balfour of Inchrye, Chetwode, Sandford, Altrincham, Lyle of Westbourne, Broadbridge, Broughshane, Henderson, Mountevans, Lindsay of Birker, Piercy, Morrison, Chorley, then Calverley;
Tedder, Colgrain, Inman, Darwen, Wilson, Lucas of Chilworth, Shepherd, Citrine, Newall, then Fraser of North Cape;
Layton, Simon of Wythenshawe, Kershaw, Trefgarne, Rugby, MacDermott, Crook, Amwell, then Milverton;
Boyd-Orr, Macdonald of Gwaenysgor, then Archibald;
(UK 1950) Bilsland, Burden, Haden-Guest, Douglas of Barloch, Ogmore, Hives, Greenhill, then Morris of Kenwood;
Milner of Leeds, Kirkwood, then Wise;
Rathcavan, Baillieu, then Grantchester;
Strang, Coleraine, then Harvey of Tasburgh;
(1955) Gridley, Adrian, Strathalmond, Strathclyde, Clitheroe, then McNair;
Colyton then Astor of Hever;
Sinclair of Cleeve, Bridges, Denning, then Norrie;
Birkett, Harding of Petherton, Poole, Fraser of Lonsdale, Taylor, Wootton of Abinger, Shackleton, Boothby, Ferrier, then Elliot of Harwood;
(UK 1960) Morris of Borth-y-Gest, Nelson of Stafford, Howick of Glendale, Gladwyn, Hodson, then Cobbold;
Summerskill, Hughes, Walston, Alport, Molson, Robens of Woldingham, Robertson of Oakridge, then Marks of Broughton;
Leighton of Saint Mellons, Brain, Aldington, Inchyra, Burton of Coventry, Todd, Sainsbury, Franks, Champion, then Williamson;
Silsoe, Chelmer, Hill of Luton, Balerno, Drumalbyn, then Wakefield of Kendal;
(UK 1964) Gardiner, Llewelyn-Davies, Bowden, Willis, Tangley, Gaitskell, Thomson of Fleet, Martonmere, Sherfield, Inglewood, Glendevon, Wilberforce, Oakshott, Bourne, Erskine of Rerrick, Rhodes, Murray of Newhaven, Caradon, Chalfont, Brooke of Ystradfellte, Grimston of Westbury, Collison, Blyton, Leatherland, Brockway, Beswick, Segal, Erroll of Hale, Wynne-Jones, Phillips, Brown, Byers, Renwick, Wade, Arwyn, Fraser of Allander, then St Helens;
(UK 1965) Margadale, Hinton of Bankside, Butler of Saffron Walden, Wells-Pestell, Caccia, Soper, Lloyd of Hampstead, Winterbottom, Kings Norton, Kahn, Beeching, Annan, Goodman, then Hylton-Foster;
(UK 1966) Campbell of Eskan, Fulton, Nugent of Guildford, Taylor of Mansfield, Kilmany, Stow Hill, Pargiter, Redmayne, Maelor, McFadzean, Hunt, Ritchie-Calder, Cooper of Stockton Heath, Brooke of Cumnor, Sharp;
(UK 1967) Platt, Morris of Grasmere, Woolley, Serota, MacLeod of Fuinary, Redcliffe-Maud, Penney, Heycock, Evans of Hungershall, Mais, Llewelyn-Davies of Hastoe, Hirshfield, Granville of Eye, Birk, Aylestone, Delacourt-Smith, Donaldson of Kingsbridge, Wigg, Foot, Thorneycroft, Beaumont of Whitley;
(UK 1968) Pilkington, Hartwell, Taylor of Gryfe, Trevelyan, Balogh, Black, Energlyn, Jacques, Grey of Naunton, Diplock;
(UK 1969) Stokes, Garner, Wilson of Langside, Gore-Booth, Bernstein, Clark, Roberthall;
(UK 1970) Ardwick, O'Neill of the Maine, Kearton, Masham of Ilton (but as Countess of Swinton she takes higher precedence), Shinwell, Janner, Hailsham of St Marylebone (but as Lord High Chancellor takes higher precedence), Reigate, Boyle of Handsworth, Fletcher,

(UK 1970 continued) Wheatley, Burntwood, Greenwood of Rossendale, Diamond, Davies of Leek, White, Bacon, Lee of Ashridge, George-Brown;
(UK 1971) Simon of Glaisdale, Maclean, Maybray-King, Olivier, Cross of Chelsea, Orr-Ewing, Harvey of Prestbury, Blake, Seear, Tanlaw, Young, Macleod of Borve, Zuckerman, Moyola;
(UK 1972) Salmon, Adeane, Seebohm, Hale, Boyd-Carpenter, Elles, Elworthy, Watkins, Samuel of Wych Cross;
(UK 1973) O'Brien of Lothbury, Sharples, Hunt of Fawley, Lloyd of Kilgerran, Darling of Hillsborough, Ashby, Crowther-Hunt;
(UK 1974) Greenhill of Harrow, Trend, Elwyn-Jones, Harris of Greenwich, Duncan-Sandys, Glenkinglas, Geoffrey-Lloyd, Chelwood, Tranmire, Mackie of Benshie, Hornsby-Smith, Robson of Kiddington, Pike, Fraser of Kilmorack, Fisher of Camden, Houghton of Sowerby, Harvington, Stedman, Lovell-Davies, Kissin, Wallace of Campsie, Lee of Newton, Fisher of Rednal, Delacourt-Smith of Alteryn, Davies of Penrhys, Kaldor, Allen of Fallowfield, Falkender, Alexander of Potterhill, Edmund-Davies, Ramsey of Canterbury, Home of the Hirsel;
(UK 1975) Paget of Northampton, Barber, Banks, Cudlipp, Campbell of Croy, Harmar-Nicholls, Fraser of Tullybelton, Wilson of Radcliffe, Stewart of Alvechurch, Briginshaw, Wallace of Coslany, Bruce of Donington, Greene of Harrow Weald, Pritchard, Vickers, Gibson, Pitt of Hampstead, Gregson, Ryder of Eaton Hastings, Jacobson, Kirkhill, then Russell of Killowen;
(UK 1976) Brookes, Carr of Hadley, McCarthy, Northfield, Parry, Oram, Winstanley, Faithfull, Schon, Brimelow, Bullock, Grade, Vaizey, Stone, Weidenfeld, Boston of Faversham, Delfont, Allen of Abbeydale, Briggs, Rayne, Peart, McCluskey;
(UK 1977) Keith of Kinkel, Baker of Windrush, Glenamara, St Brides, Thomson of Monifieth, Carver, Chitnis, Wedderburn of Charlton, Noel-Baker, Roll of Ipsden, Scarman;
(UK 1978) the only *relative* placings for this year available at time of going to press are: Charteris of Amisfield, Croham, McGregor of Durris, Lockwood, Young of Dartington.

READER'S GUIDE

1. Double/multi-barrelled names are indexed under the first barrel, unless the owner styles him/herself otherwise.

2. Some owners of a double/multi-barrelled family name use hyphens; others, even when close relations (eg siblings) do not.

3. Entries are indexed by the forenames they use and are therefore known by. First forenames that are not used do not count for indexation purposes, eg (Ethel) Margaret Dumont is indexed as Margaret Dumont.

4. All addresses with a street followed by a postal district refer to London.

5. Some counties that are strictly speaking obsolete (eg Worcestershire, Herefordshire; also the old Welsh and Scottish ones) have been given in addresses. In view of the strength of local nostalgia for the old counties and the feeling of outrage in some quarters at the 1974 and 1975 changes, this slight idiosyncrasy, if on the part of the subject of the entry, has been respected.

6. At the time of going to press the Bath Club's future is uncertain. Members have been listed as such, nevertheless.

7. For brevity's sake (and for reasons concerned with our data input technology) a bar to a medal is denoted by an asterisk (*), 2 bars by ** etc. To be punctilious when addressing an envelope, one should write: Captain Miserrimus Doleful, MC and bar/two bars etc (for MC*/ MC** etc). We have assumed that most users of our code for correct style on an envelope will be typing. However, some sticklers for propriety maintain that military rank should be written in full when in longhand.

8. Where the entry heading in bold typeface differs as to name from the code marked "Style" it reflects the fact of a person being known professionally by one name and socially by another, eg Miss Rosie M Banks, the popular novelist, is also Mrs Bingo Little, the giver of mouth-watering dinner parties. Common sense suggests that it is a matter of context which appellation one uses.

9. Ordinal numbers, when given in Arabic numerals, are represented as cardinal ones, eg 10 Duke of Omnium equals the tenth Duke etc.

10. Mac's and Mc's, whether followed by capital letters (MacHeath) or small ones (Macheath) are regarded as identical for indexation purposes. A name which starts with Mac- coincidentally is indexed along with Mac's and Mc's (eg the distinctly un-Celtic Maccabaeus would be sandwiched between Macbeth and Macduff).

11. Indexation of identical names is along the lines of the London Telephone Directory as regards forenames and initials.

ABBREVIATIONS

A

(MC etc)*	and Bar
A&AEE	Aeroplane and Armament Experimental Assoc
AA	Automobile Assoc; Anti-Aircraft
AACCA	Associate of Assoc of Certified & Corporate Accountants
AAF	Auxiliary Air Force
AAFCE	Allied Air Forces Central Europe
AAG	Assist Adjutant-General
AA & QMG	Assist Adj & Quarter-Master-General
AAI	Assoc of Chartered Auctioneers' and Estate Agents' Institute
AALPA	Associate of Incorporated Auctioneers & Landed Property Agents
AAMC	Australian Army Medical Corps
AASA	Associate of Australian Society of Accountants
AASC	Australian Army Service Corps
AASF	Advanced Air Striking Force
AB	Bachelor of Arts (USA); Able-bodied Seaman
ABA	Associate of British Archaeological Assoc / Antiquarian Booksellers' Assoc
ABIM	Associate of British Institute of Management
ABOD	Advance Base Ordnance Depot
AC	Companion of the Order of Australia
ACA	Associate of the Institute of Chartered Accountants
Acad	Academy
ACAS	Advisory, Conciliation and Arbitration Service
ACBSI	Associate, Chartered Building Societies Institute
ACCS	Associate of the Corporation of Secretaries
Acct	Accountant
ACDS	Assistant Chief of Defence
ACF	Army Cadet Force
AGG	Assist Chaplain General
ACGI	Associate of City & Guilds of London Institute
ACGS	Assist Chief of General Staff
ACIS	Associate of Chartered Institute of Secretaries
ACMA	Associate, Institute of Cost and Management Accountants
ACNS	Assist Chief of Naval Staff
ACommA	Associate, Society of Commercial Accountants
ACOS	Assist Chief of Staff
ACSEA	Allied Command SE Asia
ACT	Australian Capital Territory; Australian College of Theology
Actg	Acting
ACWA	Associate of Institute of Cost and Works Accountants
ADAS	Agricultural Development and Advisory Service (MAFF)
ADC	Aide-de-Camp
AD Corps	Army Dental Corps
ADGB	Air Defence of Great Britain
ADGMS	Assist Director-General of Medical Services
Adj(t)	Adjutant
Adj-Gen	Adjutant-General
Adm	Admiral
Admin	Administration
Adminr	Administrator
Adminve	Administrative
ADMS	Assist Director of Medical Services
Admty	Admiralty
ADNI	Assist Director of Naval Intelligence
ADOS	Assist Director of Ordnance Services
ADPR	Assist Dir Public Relations
ADS&T	Assist Dir of Supplies and Transport
Adv-Gen	Advocate-General
Adv(s)r	Adviser
Advsy	Advisory
ADVS	Assistant Director of Veterinary Services
AE	Air Efficiency Award (see AEA)
AEA	Air Efficiency Award; Atomic Energy Authority
AEAF	Allied Expeditionary Force
AEC	Agricultural Executive Committee
AED	Air Efficiency Decoration
AEF	Amalgamated Union of Engineering and Foundry Workers
AEM	Air Efficiency Medal
aet	aged (Ætatis)
AERE	Atomic Energy Research Establishment
AEU	Amalgamated Engineering Union
AFAIM	Assoc Fellow of the Australian Institute of Management

AFC	Air Force Cross; Association Football Club
Affs	Affairs
AF	Air Force
AFHQ	Allied Force Headquarters
AFI	Associate of the Faculty of Insurance
AFM	Air Force Medal
AFRAeS	Fellow of the Royal Aeronautical Society
AFS	Auxiliary Fire Service
AFV	Armoured Fighting Vehicles
Ag	Agricultural
AG	Attorney-General
Agent-Gen	Agent-General
Ag, Fish & Food	(Ministry) of Agriculture, Fisheries, and Foods
AHA	Area Health Authority
AHQ	Army Head Quarters
AIAC	Associate of the Institute of Company Accountants
AIB	Associate of Institute of Bankers
AI(nst)CE	Associate of the Institution of Civil Engineers
AICS	Associate of the Institute of Chartered Shipbuilders
AIEE	Associate of the Institution of Electrical Engineers
AIF	Australian Imperial Forces
AIG	Adjutant-Inspector-General
AIIA	Associate of the Institute of Industrial Administration
AIM	Associate of the Institution of Metallurgists
AIMarE	Associate of the Institute of Marine Engineers
AINA	Associate of the Institute of Naval Architects
AInstM	Associate Member of the Institute of Marketing
AInstP	Associate of the Institute of Physics
Air Cdre	Air Commodore
aka	Also known as
ALAS	Associate Member of Chartered Land Agents' Society
Ald	Alderman
ALFSEA	Allied Land Forces South East Asia
ALI	Argyll Light Infantry
Alta	Alberta (Canada)
AM	Member of the Order of Australia; Albert Medal; Master of the Arts (USA); Alpes Maritimes
Ambass	Ambassador
AMBIM	Associate Member of the British Institute of Management
AMEME	Association of Mining Electrical and Mechanical Engineers
AMF	Australian Military Forces
AMGOT	Allied Military Government Occupied Territory
AMIBE	Associate Member of the Institution of British Engineers
AMICE	Associate Member of the Institution of Civil Engineers
AMIChemE	Associate Member of the Institution of Chemical Engineers
AMIED	Associate Member of the Institution of Engineering Designers
AMIEE	Associate Member of the Institution of Electrical Engineers
AMIMechE	Associate Member of the Institution of Mechanical Engineers
AMIMinE	Associate Member of the Institution of Mining Engineers
AMInstNA	Associate Member of the Institution of Naval Architects
AMIPE	Associate Member of the Institution of Production Engineers
AMPC	Auxiliary Military Pioneer Corps
AMS	Army Medical Service; Assistant Military Secretary
AMTPI	Associate of the Town Planning Institution
AO	Air Officer; Officer of the Order of Australia
AOA	Air Officer in Charge of Administration
AOC	Air Officer Commanding
AOC-in-C	Air Officer Commanding-in-Chief
AOD	Army Ordnance Department
AOER	Army Officers' Emergency Reserve
AOM	Air Officer Maintenance
APEX	Association of Professional, Executive, Clerical and Computer Staffs
APM	Assist Provost Marshal
AQ	Administration and Quartering
AQMG	Assist Quarter-Master-General
ARA	Associate of the Royal Academy of the Arts
ARAeS	Associate of the Royal Aeronautical Society
ARAM	Associate of the Royal Academy of Music
ARBA	Associate of the Royal Society of British Artists
ARBS	Associate of the Royal Society of British Sculptors
ARC	Agricultural Research Council
ARCA	Associate of Royal College of Art
ARCA (Lond)	Associate of the Royal Academy of Arts
Archbp	Archbishop

Archdn	Archdeacon
ARCM	Assoc of the Royal College of Music
ARCO	Assoc of the Royal College of Organists
ARCS	Assoc of the Royal College of Science
ARCVS	Assoc of the Royal College of Veterinary Surgeons
ARIBA	Assoc of the Royal Institute of British Artists
ARIC	Assoc of the Royal College of Chemistry
ARICS	Assoc of the Royal Institution of Chartered Surveyors
ARINA	Assoc of the Royal Institution of Naval Architects
Armd	Armoured
ARP	Air Raid Precautions
ARPS	Associate of the Royal Photographic Society
ARRC	Assoc of the Royal Red Cross
ARSA	Assoc of the Royal Scottish Academy
ARSM	Assoc of the Royal School of Mines
ARTC	Assoc of the Royal Technical College
ARWS	Assoc of the Royal Society of Painters in Water Colours
ASA	Assoc Member of the Society of Actuaries; Australian Society of Accountants
ASAA	Assoc of the Society of Incorporated Accountants
ASC	ArmyService Corps
ASD	Armament Supply Department
ASF	Associate of the Institute of Shipping and Forwarding Agents
ASLIB	Assoc of Special Libraries and Information Bureaux
ASO	Air Staff Officer (in C-in Chief)
assas	assassinated
Assist	Assistant
Assoc(n)	Association
Assoc InstT	Associate of the Institute of Transport
Assur	Assurance
ATA	Air Transport Auxiliary
ATAF	Allied Tactical Air Force
ATC	Air Training Corps
ATD	Art Teachers' Diploma
ATII	Associate Member, Institute of Taxation
ATS	Auxiliary Territorial Service
au	author (of)
AUEW	Amalgamated Union of Engineering Workers
Aux	Auxiliary
Av(e)	Avenue
AVR	Army VolunteerReserve
AWRE	Atomic Weapons Research Establishment

B

b	Born
BA	Bachelor of Arts; British Airways
BAC	British Aircraft Corporation
BAFO	British Air Forces Occupation
BAFSEA	British Air Forces South East Asia
BAFTA	British Academy of Film and Television Arts
BAO	Bachelor of Obstetrics
BAOR	British Army of the Rhine
BARC	British Automobile Racing Club
BArch	Bachelor of Architecture
Barr	Barrister
Bart's	St Bartholomew's Hospital
BAS	Bachelor in Agricultural Science
BASc	Bachelor of Applied Science
Batty	Battery
BBA	British Bankers' Association
BBC	British Broadcasting Corporation
BC	British Columbia
BCh or BChir	Bachelor of Surgery
BCL	Bachelor in Civil Law
BCOF	British Commonwealth Occupation Force in Japan
BCom	Bachelor of Commerce
BCS	Bengal Civil Service
Bd	Board
Bdcast(ing)	Broadcast(ing)
BD	Bachelor in Divinity
Bde	Brigade
BE	Bachelor of Engineering
BEA	British European Airways Corporation
BEd	Bachelor of Education
BEF	British Expeditionary Force
BEM	British Empire Medal
BEng	Bachelor of Engineering

BETRO	British Export Trade Organisation
BFME	British Forces Middle East
BFPO	British Forces Post Office
BGGS	Brig-General General Staff
BGS	Brigadier, General Staff
BHS	British Horse Society
BHy	Bachelor of Hygiene
BIM	British Institute of Management
BJSM	British Joint Service Mission
Bker	Broker
BL	Bachelor of Law; British Leyland
BLA	British Army of Liberation
Bldgs	Buildings
BLitt	Bachelor of Letters
BM	Bachelor of Medicine (Oxford); Brigade Major
BMA	British Medical Association
BMus	Bachelor of Music
Bn	Battalion
BNAF	British North Africa Force
BNC	Brasenose (College)
BOAC	British Overseas Airways Corporation
BOT	Board of Trade
Bp	Bishop
Br	British
BRCS	British Red Cross Society
BRDC	British Racing Drivers' Club
Brig(-Gen)	Brigadier(-General)
bro	brother
BS	Bachelor of Surgery
BSc	Bachelor of Science
Bt	Baronet
BTA	British Troops in Austria; British Tourist Authority
Bt-Col	Brevet-Colonel
Btcy	Baronetcy
Btss	Baronetess
BWI	British West Indies
BWM	British War Medal

C

c	child(ren); circa
(C)	Conservative
CA	Chartered Accountant; County Alderman
CACTM	Central Advisory Council of Training for the Ministry
CAMC	Canadian Army Medical Corps
CAMRA	Campaign for Real Ale
Cantab	Of Cambridge University
Capt	Captain
CAS	Chief of Air Staff
Cav	Cavalry
CB	Companion of the Order of Bath
CBE	Commander of the Order of the British Empire
CBI	Confederation of British Industry
CBIM	Companion, British Institute of Management
CC	County Council(lor); Companion of the Order of Canada; Cricket Club
CCA	County Councils' Association
CCC	Corpus Christi College; County Cricket Club
CCG(BE)	Control Commission, Germany (British Element)
CCllr	County Councillor
CCRE	Commander, Corps of Royal Engineers
CCRA	Commander Corps, Royal Artillery
CCRSigs	Commander Corps of Royal Signals
CD	Civil Defence; Candian Forces Decoration
Cdr	Commander
Cdre	Commodore
CDS	Chief of Defence Staff
CE	Chief Engineer
CEGB	Central Electricity Generating Board
CEng	Chartered Engineer
Centl	Central
CERN	Conseil (now Organisation) Européenne pour la Recherche Nucléaire
CF	Chaplain to the Forces
CFM	Canadian Forces Medal

ChCh	Christ Church (Oxford)
Chem	Chemical
Chev	Chevalier
Chllr	Chancellor
Chm	Chairman
ChM	Mastery of Surgery
ChStJ	Chaplain of the Order of St John of Jerusalem
CI	Order of the Crown of India; Channel Islands
CIC	Commander-in-Chief
CID	Criminal Investigation Bureau
CIEE	Companion of the Order of the Indian Empire
CIGS	Chief of the Imperial General Staff
CIMarE	Companion of the Institute of Marine Engineers
CIMechE	Companion of the Institution of Mechanical Engineers
C-in-C	Commander-in-Chief
CJ	Chief Justice
Cl	Class
CLA	Country Landowners' Assoc
CLitt	Companion of the Royal Society of Literature
CLJ	Commander of the Order of Lazarus of Jerusalem
CLP	Constituency Labour Party
CM	Member of the Order of Canada; Master of Surgery
Cmd	Commanded
Cmdg	Commanding
Cmdt	Commandant
CMF	Commonwealth Military Forces; Central Mediterranean Force
CMG	Companion of the Order of St Michael and St George
Cmmn	Commission
Cmmnd	Commissioned
Cmmr	Commissioner
CMO	Chief Medical Officer
CMP	Corps of Military Police
CMS	Church Missionary Society
Cncl	Council
Cncllr	Councillor
Cnsllr	Counsellor
Co	Company, County
CO	Commanding Officer
COD	Communications and Operations Department (FO)
Co dir	Company Director
C of C	Chamber of Commerce
C of E	Church of England
C of S	Chief of Staff
COI	Central Office of Information
Col	Colonel
Co L	Coalition Liberal
Coll	College
(Com)	Communist
Comd	Commanded
Con(s)	Conservative
Conf(ce)	Conference
Confedn	Confederation
Conn	Connecticut
Conslt	Consultant
Co-op	Co-Operative
Corpn	Corporation
Corr	Correspondent
COS	Chief of Staff
COSIRA	Council for Smaller Industries in Rural Areas
cous	cousin
CPM	Colonial Police Medal
CPRE	Council for the Protection of Rural England
CPS	Canadian Pacific Steamships
cr	created
CRA	Commander Royal Artillery
CRD	Conservative Research Department
CRE	Commanding Royal Engineers
CRMP	Corps of Royal Military Police
CRO	Commonwealth Relations Office
CS	Civil Service
CSD	Civil Service Department
CSERB	Computer Systems and Electronics Requirements Board
CSI	Companion of the Order of the Star of India
CSIRO	Commonwealth Scientific and Industrial Research Organization

CSO	Chief Signal Officer; Chief Staff Officer; Chief Scientific Officer
CStJ	Commander of the Order of St John of Jerusalem
CSV	Community Service Volunteers
ct	court
Ct(t)ee	Committee
CText	Chartered Textile Technologist
Cter	Computer
Ctory	Consistory (Court)
ctr	creator
CU	Cambridge University
CUP	Cambridge University Press
CVO	Commander of the Royal Victorian Order
C'wlth	Commonwealth

D

d	Died; death
da	Daughter
DA	Diploma in Anaesthetics
DAAG	Deputy-Assist-Adjutant-General
DAA & QMG	Dep Assist-Adjutant and Quartermaster-General
DACG	Dep Asst Chaplain General
DAD	Deputy-Asst Director
DADS	Dep Asst Director of Supplies
DAG	Dep-Adj-General
DA & QMG	Dep-Adj & Quartermaster-General
DADGMS	Dep-Assist Director General of Medical Services
DADMS	Dep-Assist-Director Medical Services
DADR	Dep-Assist Director of Remounts
DAPS	Director of Army Postal Services
DAQMG	Dep-Assist-Quartermaster-General
DBA	Doctor of Business Administration
DBE	Dame Commander of the British Empire
DC	District Council
DCAS	Deputy Chief of Air Staff
DCB	Dame Commander Order of the Bath
DCGS	Dep Chief of General Staff
DCH	Diploma in Child Heath
DCL	Doctor of Civil Law
DCLI	Duke of Cornwall's Light Infantry
DCllr	District Councillor
DCM	Distinguished Conduct Medal
DCMG	Dame Commander of Order of St Michael and St George
DCMS	Dep Commissioner Medical Services
DCVO	Dame Commander Royal Victorian Order
DD	Doctor in Divinity
DDDS	Dep Director of Dental Services
DDME	Dep Dir Mechanical Engineering
DDMS	Dep Dir of Medical Services
DDOS	Dep Dir of Ordnance Services
DDPS	Dep Dir of Personal Services
DDR	Dep Dir of Remounts
DDS	Doctor of Dental Surgery; Director of Dental Services
DDSD	Dep Dir of Staff Duties
DDS & T	Dep Dir Supplies and Transport
DDVS	Dep-Dir of Veterinary Services
decd	deceased
Def	Defence
Del	Delegate
DEME	Dir of Electrical and Mechanical Engineering
DEng	Doctor of Engineering
Dep(y)	Deputy
Dep-Adv-Gen	Deputy-Advocate-General
Dep-Sec	Deputy Secretary
Dept	Department
DèsL	Docteur ès Lettres
DES	Department of Education and Science
DesRCA	Designer of the Royal College of Art
Devpt	Development
DFC	Distinguished Flying Cross
DGAMS	Dir-Gen of Army Medical Services
DGCStJ	Dame Grand Cross of the Order of St John of Jerusalem
DGMS	Director-General of Medical Services

DGStJ	Dame of Grace of the Order of St John of Jerusalem
DHQ	District Headquarters
DHSS	Department of Health and Social Security
DHy	Doctor of Hygiene
DIC	Diploma of the Imperial College
DIH	Diploma in Industrial Health
Dioc	Diocese
Dip	Diploma; Diplomatic
dir(ship)	director(ship)
dis	dissolved (marriage)
Dis(t)	District
Div(nl)	Division(al)
DJAG	Deputy Judge, Advocate General
DJStJ	Dame of Justice of the Order of St John of Jerusalem
DL	Deputy-Lieutenant for the County of
DLC	Diploma Loughborough College
DLI	Durham Light Infantry
DLit(t)	Doctor of Literature; Doctor of Letters
DLJ	Dame of Justice of the Order of St Lazarus of Jerusalem
DM	Doctor of Medicine
DM & Q	Director of Movements and Quartering
DMD	Doctor in Dental Medicine
DME	Director Mechanical Engineering
DMGO	Divisional Machine Gun Officer
DMI	Director Military Intelligence
DMO & I	Dir Military Operations and Intelligence
DMRE	Diploma in Medical Radiology and Electrology
DMS	Dir of Medical Services
DMSI	Dir of Management and Support Intelligence
DMT	Dir of Military Training
DMus	Doctor of Music (Oxford)
DNI	Director of Naval Intelligence
DNO	Director of Naval Ordnance
DO	Diploma in Opthalmology
DOC	District Officer Commanding
DOE	Department of Environment
DOI	Dept of Industry
DOMS	Diploma in Opthalmic Medicine
DOR	Dir of Operational Requirements
DOS	Dir of Ordnance Services
DPA	Diploma in Public Administration
DPH	Diploma in Public Health
DPhil	Doctor of Philosophy
DPL	Dir of Pioneers and Labour
DPM	Diploma in Psychological Medicine
DPR	Dir of Public Relations
DPS	Dir of Personal Services
DQMG	Deputy Quartermaster-General
DSAO	Diplomatic Service Administration Office
DSc	Doctor of Science
DSC	Distinguished Service Cross
DSD	Director of Staff Duties
DSM (USA)	Distinguished Service Medal (United States of America)
DSO	Companion of the Distinguished Service Order
dsp	*decessit sine prole*
DSP	Docteur en Sciences Politiques (Montreal)
DStJ	Lady of the Order of St John of Jerusalem
DS & T	Dir of Supplies and Transport
DTh	Doctor of Theology
DTI	Dept of Trade and Industry
DTM & H	Diploma in Tropical Medicine and Hygiene
Dve	Drive
Dvn	Division
Dvpt	Development
DVS	Director of Veterinary Services

E

E	East; Earl
Ec	Economic
Ed	Editor
ED	Efficiency Decoration; European Democratic (Group)
EDC	Economic Development Committee

edn	edition
educn(l)	education(al)
EETPU	Electrical, Electronic, Telecommunication and Plumbing Union
EFTA	European Free Trade Association
EIU	Economist Intelligence Unit
eld	eldest
empld	employed
EMS	Emergency Medical Service
Eng	English; England
Engr	Engineer
Engrg	Engineering
ENSA	Entertainments National Services Association
er	elder
ERD	Emergency Reserve Decoration
Estab	Established
ESU	English-Speaking Union
Exec	Executive
Expdn	Expedition
Ext	Extinct

F

f	father
FA	Football Association
FAA	Fellow of the Australian Academy of Science
FACCA	Fell of the Assoc of Certified and Corporate Accountants
FACOG	Fell, American College of Obstetricians and Gynaecologists
FACP	Fell, American College of Physicians
FACS	Fell, American College of Surgeons
FAES	Fell of the Audio Engineering Society
FAI	Fell of the Chartered Auctioneers' and Estate Agents' Institute
FAIM	Fell of the Australian Institute of Management
FALPA	Fell of the Incorporated Auctioneers and Land Property Agents
FAMS	Fell of the Ancient Monuments Society
FANY	First Aid Nursing Yeomanry
FAO	Food and Agricultural Organisation
FARELF	Far East Land Forces
FAS	Fell, Antiquarian Society
FASA	Fell of the Australian Society of Accountants
FBA	Fell of the British Academy
FBHI	Fell of the British Horological Institute
FBI	Federation of British Industries
FBIM	Fell of the British Institute of Management
FBIS	Fell of the British Interplanetary Society
FBKSTS	Fellow, British Kinematograph, Sound and Television Society
FBOA	Fell of the British Optical Association
FBSI	Fell of the Boot and Shoe Industry
FCA	Fell of the Institute of Chartered Accountants
FCAI	Fell of the Canadian Aeronautical Institute
FCCA	Fell of the Assoc of Certified and Corporate Accountants
FCCS	Fell of the Corporation of Certified Secretaries
Fce(s)	Force(s)
FCGI	Fell of of City
FCIArb	Fell, Chartered Institute of Arbitrators
FCIB	Fell of the Corporation of Insurance Brokers
FCII	Fell of the Chartered Insurance Institute
FCIS	Fell of the Chartered Institute of Secretaries
FCIT	Fell of the Chartered Institute of Transport
FCO	Foreign and Commonwealth Office
FCOG	Fell of the College of Obstetrics and Gynaecology
FCommA	Fell of the Society of Commercial Accountants
FCMA	Fell of the Institute of Cost and Management Accountants
FCPS	Fell of the College of Physicians and Surgeons
FCS	Fell of the Chemical Society
FCWA	Fell of the Institute of Cost and Works Accountants
FD	Field (Regiment)
FDSRCS	Fell in Dental Surgery Royal College of Surgeons of England
FEAF	Far East Air Force
Fed	Federal
Fedn	Federation
FEIS	Fell of the Educational Institute of Scotland
Fell	Fellow
FEng	Fell, Fellowship of Engineering

FES	Fell of the Entomological Society
FFA	Fell of the Faculty of Actuaries
FFARCS	Fell of the Faculty of Anaesthetists, Royal College of Surgeons
FFAS	Fell of the Faculty of Architects and Surveyors
FFB	Fell of the Faculty of Building
FFHom	Fell of the Faculty of Homeopathy
FFR	Fell of the Faculty of Radiologists
FGA	Fell of the Gemmological Association
FGS	Fell of the Geological Society
FGSM	Fell, Guildhall School of Music
FIA	Fell, Institute of Actuaries; Fédération Internationale de L'Automobile
FIAeS	Fell of the Institute of Aeronautical Sciences
FIArb	Fell of the Institute of Arbitration
FIAA	Fell Architect Member of the Incorporated Assoc of Architects and Surveyors
FIAC	Fell of the Institute of Company Accountants
FIAM	Fell International Academy of Management
FIB	Fell of the Institute of Bankers
FICA	Fell of the Institute of Chartered Accountants in England and Wales
FICD	Fell of the Institute of Civil Defence
FICE	Fell of the Institution of Civil Engineers
FIChemE	Fell of the Institution of Chemical Engineers
FICS	Fell of the Institute of Chartered Shipbrokers
FID	Fell of the Institute of Directors
FIEE	Fell of the Institution of Electrical Engineers
FIERE	Fell of the Institution of Electronics and Radio Engineers
FIFor	Fell Institute of Forestry
FIEST	Fell of Food Science and Technology
FIIM	Fell, Institute of Industrial Managers
FILA	Fell of the Institute of Landscape Architects
FIMA	Fell of the Institute of Mathematics and its Applications
FIMarE	Fell, Institute of Marine Engineers
FIMechE	Fell of the Institution of Mechanical Engineers
FIMinE	Fell, Institute of Mining Engineers
FIMT	Fell of the Institute of the Motor Trade
FIMTA	Fell of the Institute of Municipal Treasures & Accountants
Fin	Financial
FInstD	Fell Institute of Directors
FInstF	Fell of Institute of Fuel
FInstHE	Fell, Institution of Highway Engineers
FIInst	Fell of the Imperial Institute
FInstM	Fell Institute of Marketing
FInstMSM	Fell of the Institute of Marketing and Sales Management
FInstP	Fell of the Institute of Physics
FInstPet	Fell of the Institute of Petroleum
FInstPI	Fell, Institute of Patentees (Incorporated)
FIOB	Fell, Institute of Building
FIOP	Fell of the Institute of Printing
FIOSc	Fell of the Institute of Optical Science
FIPA	Fell of the Institute of Public Administration
FIPHE	Fell of the Institution of Public Health Engineers
FIPM	Fell, Institute of Personnel Management
FIPR	Fell of the Institute of Public Relations
FIProdE	Fell of the Institute of Production Engineers
FIRE	Fell of the Institution of Radio Engineers
FIRI	Fell of the Institution of the Rubber Industry
FISE	Fell of the Institute of Sanitary Engineers
FIStructE	Fell, Institution of Structural Engineers
FJI	Fell of the Institute of Journalists
FKC	Fell of the King's College, London
Fl	Flight
FLA	Fell of the Library Association
FLCM	Fell of the London College of Music
Fl Lt	Flight Lieutenant
FLS	Fell of the Linnean Society
FM	Field Marshal
FMA	Fell of the Museums' Assoc
FMS	Fell, Institute of Management Services; Fell, Inst of Medical Society; Fell, Manorial Society
Fndn	Foundation
Fndr	Founder
FNI	Fell, Nautical Institute
FO	Foreign Office
For	Foreign
FPCA	Fell of Practising and Commercial Accountants

FPCA . . Fell of Practising and Commercial Accountants
FPS . . Fell of Philological Society of Great Britain
FPhS(Eng) . . Fell of the Philosophical Society of England
Fr . . France
FRACP . . Fell of the Royal Australasian College of Physicians
FRACS . . Fell of the Royal Australasian College of Surgeons
FRAI . . Fell of the Royal Anthropological Institute
FRAM . . Fell of the Royal Academy of Music
FRAS . . Fell of the Royal Astronomical Society
FRAeS . . Fell of the Royal Aeronautical Society
FRBS . . Fell of the Royal Botanic Society; Fell of the Royal Society of British Sculptors
FRCAA . . Fell of the Royal Cambrian Academy of Art
FRCGP . . Fell of the Royal College of General Practitioners
FRCI . . *see* FRCS
FRCM . . Fell of the Royal College of Music
FRCO . . Fell of the Royal College of Organists
FRCOG . . Fell of the Royal College of Obstetricians and Gynaecologists
FRCP . . Fell of the Royal College of Physicians
FRCPE . . Fell of the Royal College of Physicians of Edinburgh
FRCPS . . Fell of the Royal College of Physicians and Surgeons (Glasgow)
FRCS . . Fell of the Roy College of Surgeons; Fell of the Roy C'wlth Society (formerly Roy Empire Soc)
FRCSE(d) . . Fell, Royal College of Surgeons of Edinburgh
FRCSI . . Fell, Royal College of Surgeons in Ireland
FREconS . . Fell of the Royal Economic Society
FREntS . . Fell of the Royal Entomological Society
FRGS . . Fell of the Royal Geographical Society
FRHistS . . Fell of the Royal Historical Society
FRHS . . Fell of the Royal Horticultural Society
FRIAS . . Fell of the Royal Incorporation of Architects in Scotland
FRIBA . . Fell of the Royal Institute of British Architects
FRIC . . Fell of the Royal Institute of Chemistry
FRICS . . Fell of the Royal Institution of Chartered Surveyors
FRIN . . Fell of the Royal Institute of Navigation
FRINA . . Fell of the Roy Institution of Naval Architects
FRIPH . . Fell of the Royal Institute of Public Health
FRMetS . . Fell of the Royal Meteorological Society
FRMS . . Fell of the Royal Microscopical Society
FRNS . . Fell of the Royal Numismatic Society
FRPS . . Fell of the Royal Photographic Society
FRPSL . . Fell of the Royal Philatelic Society, London
FRS . . Fell of the Royal Society
FRSA . . Fell of the Royal Society of Arts
FRSAIre . . Fell of the Royal Society of Antiquaries of Ireland
FRSC . . Fell of the Royal Society of Canada
FRSE . . Fell of the Royal Society of Edinburgh
FRSGS . . Fell of the Royal Scottish Geographical Society
FRSH . . Fell of the Royal Society of Health
FRSL . . Fell of the Royal Society of Literature
FRSM . . Fell of the Royal Society of Medicine
FRVA . . Fell of the Rating and Valuation Association
FRZS Scot . . Fell of the Royal Zoological Society of Scotland
FSA . . Fell of the Society of Antiquaries
FSAA . . Fell of the Society of Incorporated Accountants
FSAS . . Fell of the Society of Antiquaries, Scotland
FSE . . Fell of Society of Engineers
FSF . . Fell of the Institute of Shipping and Forwarding Agents
FSG . . Fell of the Society of Genealogists
FSI . . Fell Royal Institution of Chartered Surveyors (*see also* FRICS)
FSIA . . Fell of the Society of Industrial Artists
FSS . . Fell of the Royal Statistical Society
FSScA . . Fell of the Society of Science and Art, of London
FTCL . . Fell of Trinity College of Music, London
FTI . . Fell of the Textile Institute
FTII . . Fellow, Institute of Taxation
Fus . . Fusiliers
FZS . . Fell of the ZoologicalSociety

G

g . . great
Ga . . Georgia (USA)
G&MWU . . General and Municipal Workers' Union

GB . . Great Britain
GBE . . Knight of the Grand Cross of the British Empire
GC . . George Cross; Grand Cross; Golf Club
GCB . . Knight Grand Cross of the Bath
GCHQ . . Government Communications Headquarters
GCIE . . Knight Grand Commander of the Indian Empire
GCMG . . Knight and Dame Grand Cross of St Michael and St George
GCON . . Grand Cross, Order of the Niger
GCSI . . Knight Grand Commander of the Star of India
GCStJ . . Bailiff or Dame Grand Cross of the Order of St John of Jerusalem
GCVO . . Knight or Dame of the Grand Cross of the Royal Victorian Order
gda . . grandaughter
gdns . . gardens
gf . . grandfather
ggda . . great grandaughter (and so forth)
ggs . . great grandson (and so forth)
Gds . . Guards
Gen . . General
gen man . . general manager
GHQ . . General Headquarters
GLC . . Greater London Council
GM . . George Medal
GMB . . Great Master of the Bath
GMIE . . Grand Master of the Indian Empire
GMMG . . Grand Master of St Michael and St George
GMSI . . Grand Master of the Star of India
gn . . greatnephew
GO . . Grand Officier (de la Légion d'Honneur)
GOC(IC) . . General Officer Commanding(-in-Chief)
Gov(r) . . Governor
Govt . . Government
GP . . General Practitioner
Gp . . Group
Gp Capt . . Group Captain
GPO . . General Post Office
gr . . grove
GRCM . . Graduate of the Royal College of Music
GRSM . . Graduate of the Royal Schools of Music
gs . . grandson
GS . . General Staff
G S . . Grammar School
GSM . . General Service Medal
GSO . . General Staff Officer
Gt . . Great
Gt(e)r . . Greater
Guy's . . Guy's Hospital

H

h . . heir
ha . . heir apparent
HA . . Historical Association
HAA . . Heavy Anti-Aircraft
HAC . . Honourable Artillery Co
HBM . . His / Her Britannic Majesty
HCF . . Hon Chaplain to the Forces
HE . . His Excellency
HG . . Homeguard
HH . . His / Her Highness
HHA . . Historic Houses Association
High Cmmr . . High Commissioner
HIH . . His / Her Imperial Highness
HIllH . . His / Her Illustrious Highness
HIM . . His / Her Imperial Majesty
Hist . . Historical
Hldgs . . Holdings
HLI . . Highland Light Infantry
HMHS . . Her Majesty's Hospital Ship
HMS . . Her Majesty's Ship
HMSO . . Her Majesty's Stationery Office
Ho . . House
Hon . . Honourable; Honour (Judges)ı Honorary
Hons . . Honours
Hort . . Horticultural

Hosp	Hospital
hp	heir presumptive
HRE	Holy Roman Empire
HRH	His/Her Royal Highness
HRI	Hon Member of the Royal Institute of Painters in Water Colours
HRSA	Hon Member Royal Scottish Academy
H S	High School
HSH	His/Her Serene Highness
husb	husband

I

IA	Indian Army
IAF	Indian Air Force; Indian Auxiliary Force
IAMC	Indian Army Medical Corps
IAOC	Indian Army Ordnance Corps
IAPS	Incorporated Assoc of Preparatory Schools
IARO	Indian Army Reserve of Officers
IAS	Indian Administrative Service
IASC	Indian Army Service Corps
IBA	Independent Broadcasting Authority
IBRD	International Bank for Reconstruction and Dvpt (World Bank)
i/c	in charge of
ICA	Institute of Contemporary Arts
ICFC	Industrial and Commercial Finance Corporation
ICI	Imperial Chemical Industries
ICL	International Computers Ltd
ICS	Indian Civil Service
IDC	Imperial Defence College
idc	has completed a course at, or served for a year on the staff of, The Imperial Defence Coll
IEE	Institution of Electrical Engineers
IEF	Indian Expeditionary Force
IFC	International Finance Corporation
ILEA	Inner London Education Authority
ILO	International Labour Office
ILP	Independent Labour Party
IMA	International Music Association
IMS	Indian Medical Service
IMechE	Institution of Mechanical Engineers
IMF	International Monetary Fund
Imp	Imperial
IMS	Indian Medical Service
inc(l)	including
Inc	Incorporated
Ind	Independent
Indust	Industry/Industrial
Industs	Industries
Inf	Infantry
info	information
INSEAD	Institut Européen d'Administration des Affaires
Insp(r)	Inspector
Inst	Institute
Inst	Institution
Insur	Insurance
Int(ernat)	International
Invest(s)	Investment(s)
IOD	Institute of Directors
IOM	Isle of Man
IOW	Isle of Wight
IPM	Institute of Personnel Management
IProdE	Institution of Production Engineers
IPS	Indian Political Service
Ir	Irish
IRA	Irish Republican Army
IRE	Indian Corps of Royal Engineers
Is	Island(s)
ISC	Indian Staff Corps; Imperial Service College
ISCO	Independent Schools Careers Organisation
ISIS	Independent Schools Information Service
ISM	Imperial Service Medal
ISO	Imperial Service Order
IStructE	Institution of Structural Engineers

ITA	Independent Television Authority
IY	Imperial Yeomanry

J

JAG	Judge Advocate General
JCD	Doctor of Canon Law (Juris Canonici Doctor)
JP	Justice of the Peace
jr	junior
JSSC	Qualified at Joint Services Staff College
Jt	Joint

K

k(a)	killed (in action)
KAR	King's African Rifles
KBE	Knight Commander Order of the British Empire
KC	King's Counsel
KCB	Knight Commander Order of the Bath
KCH	King's College Hospital
KCIE	Knight Commander of the Order of the Indian Empire
KCMG	Knight Commander of the Order of St Michael and St George
KCS	King's College School
KCSG	Knight Commander of St Gregory
KCSI	Knight Commander of the Star of India
KCVO	Knight Commander of the Royal Victorian Order
KDG	King's Dragoon Guards
KEG	King Edward's Horse Regiment
KG	Knight of the Order of the Garter
KGStJ	Knight of Grace, Order of St John of Jerusalem (see also KSEJ)
KGV'sO	King George V's Own
KHC	Hon Chaplain to the King
KHDS	Hon Dental Surgeon to the King
KHP	Hon Physician to the King
KHS	Hon Surgeon to the King
KJStJ	Knight of Justice, Order of St John of Jerusalem
KLJ	Knight of Justice of the Order of St Lazarus of Jerusalem
KORR	King's own Royal Regiment
KOSB	King's own Scottish Borderers
KOYLI	King's own Yorkshire Light Infantry
KP	Knight of the Order of St Patrick
KPM	King's Police Medal
KRRC	King's Royal Rifle Corps
KSG	Knight of St Gregory
KSLI	King's Shropshire Light Infantry
KStJ	Knight of the Order of St John of Jerusalem
kt	knighted (Knight Bachelor)
KT	Knight of the Order of the Thistle

L

(L)	Labour (MP)
La/LA	Louisiana/Los Angeles(USA)
LAA	Light Anti-Aircraft
Lab	Labour
LAH	Licentiate of Apothecaries Hall, Dublin
LBC	London Broadcasting Co
LCC	London County Council
LCJ	Lord Chief Justice
LCP	Licentiate of the College of Preceptors
Ld(-Lt)	Lord(-Lieutenant)
Ldr	Leader
LDS	Licentiate in Dental Surgery
LDV	Local Defence Volunteers
LEA	Local Educational Authority
lectr	lecturer
Legve	Legislative
LèsL	Licencié ès Lettres
LG	Life Guards
LH	Light Horse
LI	Light Infantry

Lib	Liberal
Lieut	Lieutenant
LittD	Doctor of Letters (Cambridge & Dublin)
LLA	Lady Literate in Arts
LLB	Bachelor of Laws
LLCM	Licentiate London College of Music
LLD	Doctor of Laws
LLM	Master of Laws
LM	Licentiate in Midwifery
LMH	Lady Margaret Hall (Oxford)
LMSSA	Licentiate in Medicine and Surgery, Society of Apothecaries
LMTPI	Legal Member of the Town Planning Institute
LPTB	London Passenger Transport Board
LRAM	Licentiate of the Royal Academy of Music
LRCP	Licentiate of the Royal College of Physicians
LRFPS	Licentiate of the Royal Faculty of Physicians and Surgeons (Glasgow)
LRIBA	Licentiate of the Royal Institute of British Architects
LSA	Licentiate of the Society of Apothecaries
LSE	London School of Economics
LSO	London Symphony Orchestra
Lt(-Col)	Lieutenant(-Colonel)
Ltcy	Lieutenancy
Lt-Gen	Lieutenant-General
(LU)	Liberal Unionist

M

m	married, marriage
MA	Master of Arts; Military Assistant
MAAF	Mediterranean Allied Forces
MAFF	Ministry of Agriculture, Fisheries and Food
MAI	Master of Engineering
Maj(-Gen)	Major(-General)
man	manager
Mans	Mansions
MAOT	Member of the Association of Occupational Therapists
MAP	Ministry of Aircraft Production
MArch	Master of Architecture
Marq	Marquess
Mass	Massachusetts (US)
MB	Bachelor of Medicine
MBA	Master of Business Administration
MBE	Member of the Order of the British Empire
MBHI	Member of the British Horological Institute
MBIM	Member of the British Institute of Management
MBOU	Member, British Ornithologist's Union
MC	Military Cross
MCB	Master of Clinical Biochemistry
MCC	Marylebone Cricket Club; Metropolitan County Council
MCIT	Member of the Chartered Institute of Transport
MChir	Master in Surgery
MCom	Master of Commerce
MConsE	Association of Consulting Engineers
MCP	Member of Colonial Parliament
MCPath	Member of the College of Pathologists
MCSP	Member of the Chartered Society of Physiotherapy
md	managing director
MD	Doctor of Medicine
(m dis)	marriage dissolved
ME, M East	Middle East
MEC	Member, Executive Council
MEd	Master of Education
Med	Medical
MEF	Mediterranean Expeditionary Force
MEIC	Member of the Engineering Institute of Canada
MELF	Middle East Land Forces
memb	member
MEP	Member of the European Parliament
Met	Metropolitan
MFA	Ministry of Foreign Affairs
MFARCS	Member of the Faculty of Anaesthetists, Roy Coll of Surgeons
MFH	Master of Fox Hounds
mfr/mfrg	manufacturer/manufacturing

MGC	Machine Gun Corps
MGGS	Major-General General Staff
Mgmnt	Management
Mgr	Monsignor
MGRA	Major-General Royal Artillery
MHK	Member of the House of Keys (IOM)
MHR	Member of the House of Representatives
MIAeE	Member of the Institute of Aeronautical Engineers
MIBE	Member of the Institution of British Engineers
MIChemE	Member of the Institution of Chemical Engineers
MICE	Member of the Institution of Civil Engineers
MICEI	Member of the Institution of Civil Engineers of Ireland
MIEA	Member of the Institution of Engineers, Australia
MIEE	Member of the Institution of Electrical Engineers
MIEI	Member of the Institute of Engineering Inspection
MIERE	Member of the Institution of Electronic and Radio Engineers
MIES	Member of the Institution of Engineers and Shipbuilders in Scotland
MIEx	Member of the Institute of Export
Mil	Military
MILE	Member of the Institution of Locomotive Engineers
MIM	Member, Institution of Metallurgists
MIMarE	Member of the Institute of Marine Engineers
MIMC	Member of the Institute of Management Consultants
MIMCE	Member of the Institute of Municipal and County Engineers
MIME, MInstME	Member of the Institution of Mining Engineers
MIMechE	Member of the Institution of Mechanical Engineers
MIMI	Member of the Institute of the Motor Trade Industry
MIMM	Member of the Institution of Mining & Metallurgy
Min	Minister
Miny	Ministry
MInstGasE	Member of the Institution of Gas Engineers
MInstHE	Member of the Institution of Highway Engineers
MInstMet	Member of the Institute of Metals
MInstPet	Member of the Institute of Petroleum
MInstW	Member of the Institution of Welding
MINucE	Member of the Institution of Nuclear Engineers
MIOB	Member of the Institute of Building
MIPA	Member of the Institute of Practitioners in Advertising
MIPHE	Member of the Institute of Public Health Engineers
MIPM	Member of the Institute of Personnel Management
MIPR	Member of the Institute of Public Relations
MIProdE	Member of the Institution of Production Engineers
MIQ	Member, Institute of Quarrying
MIRE	Member of the Institution of Royal Engineers
MISI	Member of the Iron and Steel Institute
Miss	Mississippi (USA)
MIStructE	Member of the Institution of Structural Engineers
MIT	Massachusetts Institute of Technology (USA)
MIWE	Member of the Institution of Water Engineers
MJI	Member of the Institute of Journalists
MJInstE	Member of the Junior Engineers Institute
Mkt(g)	Market(ing)
MLA	Memb, Legislative Assembly; Modern Language Assoc; Master in Landscape Architecture
MLC	Member of the Legislative Council
MLO	Military Liaison Officer
MM	Military Medal
MMechE	Master of Mechanical Engineering
MN	Merchant Navy
MNZIE	Member of the New Zealand Institution of Engineers
Mo	Missouri (USA)
MO	Medical Officer
MOD	Ministry of Defence
MOH	Medical Officer of Health
MOI	Ministry of Information
MP	Member of Parliament
MPBW	Ministry of Public Building and Works
MPS	Member of the Pharmaceutical Society of Great Britain
MR	Master of the Rolls
MRAC	Member of the Royal Agricultural College
MRAS	Member of the Royal Asiatic Society
MRC	Medical Research Council
MRCGP	Member, Royal College of General Practitioners
MRCOG	Member of the Royal College of Obstetricians and Gynaecologists

MRCP . . Member of the Royal College of Physicians
MRCS . . Member of the Royal College of Surgeons
MRCVS . . Member of the Royal College of Veterinary Surgeons
MRCVS . . Member of the Royal College of Veterinary Surgeons
MRI . . Member Royal Institution
MRIA . . Member of the Royal Irish Academy
MRIC . . Member, Royal Institute of Chemistry
MRICS . . Member of the Royal Institution of Chartered Surveyors
MRIN . . Member of the Royal Institute of Navigation
MRINA . . Member of the Royal Institution of Naval Architects
MRO . . Member of the Register of Osteopaths
MRSH . . Member of the Royal Society of Health
MRST . . Member of the Royal Society of Teachers
MRTPI . . Member of the Royal Town Planning Institute
MRUSI . . Member of the Royal United Service Institution
MS . . Master of Surgery; Manuscript
MSc . . Master of Science
MSE . . Member of the Society of Engineers
MSIA . . Member of the Society of Industrial Artists
MSIAD . . Member of the Society of Industrial Artists and Designers
MSM . . Meritorious Service Medal
MSST . . Member of the Society of Surveying Technicians
MTh . . Master of Theology
MTPI . . Member, Town Planning Institute
MusB . . Bachelor of Music
MusD . . Doctor of Music (Cambridge and Durham)
MusM . . Master of Music
MV . . Motor Vessel
Mvmnt . . Movement
MVO . . Member, Royal Victorian Order
MWB . . Metropolitan Water Board
MY . . Motor Yacht

N

(N), (Nat) . . Nationalist
n . . nephew
N . . North
NA . . Naval Attaché
NAAFI . . Navy, Army and Air Force Institutes
NABC . . National Association of Boys' Clubs
NAG . . Northern Army Group
NALGO . . National and Local Government Officers' Association
NATCS . . National Air Traffic Control Services
Nat'nl . . National
NATO . . North Atlantic Treaty Organisation
NBL . . National Book League
NBPI . . National Board for Prices and Incomes
NC . . Nautical College
NCA . . National Certificate of Agriculture
NCB . . National Coal Board
NCCL . . National Council for Civil Liberties
NCLC . . National Council of Labour Colleges
NDA . . National Diploma in Agriculture
NEAC . . New English Art Club
NEAF . . Near East Air Force
NEC . . National Executive Committee
NEDC . . National Economic Development Council
NEDO . . National Economic Development Office
NERC . . Natural Environment Research Council
NFS . . National Fire Service
NFWI . . National Federation of Women's Institutes
NFU . . National Farmers' Union
NHS . . National Health Service
NI . . Northern Ireland
NICS . . Northern Ireland Civil Service
NID . . Naval Intelligence Department
NIESR . . National Institute of Economic and Social Research
NILP . . Northern Ireland Labour Party
NJ . . New Jersey (USA)
N(at) Lib . . National Liberal
NFL . . National Liberal Federation
N'mberland . . Northumberland

NRA	National Rifle Association
NRDC	National Research Development Corporation
NS	Nova Scotia
ns	Graduate of the Royal Naval Staff College, Greenwich
NSW	New South Wales
NTDA	National Trade Development Association
NUGMW	National Union of General and Municipal Workers
NUJ	National Union of Journalists
NUR	National Union of Railwaymen
NUT	National Union of Teachers
NWFP	North West Frontier Province
NY	New York
NYC	New York City
NZ	New Zealand Expeditionary Force

O

o	only
O & O	Oriental and Occidental Steamship Co
OA	Officier d'Académie
OBE	Officer of the Order of British Empire
OC	Officer Commanding, Officer of the Order of Canada
OCF	Officiating Chaplain to the Forces
OCS	Officer Cadet School
OCTU	Officer Cadet Training Unit
ODA	Overseas Development Administration
ODI	Overseas Development Institute
ODM	Ministry of Overseas Development
OECD	Organisation for Economic Co-operation and Development
OEEC	Organisation for European Economic Co-operation
OER	Officers' Emergency Reserve
Off(r)	Office(r)
OFS	Orange Free State
OIC	Officer in Charge
OM	Order of Merit
OMC	Oxford Military College
Ops	Operations
Ord	Ordained
Org	Organisation
OSB	Order of St Benedict
OSNC	Orient Steam Navigation Company
OSRD	Office of Scientific Research and Development
OstJ	Officer of the Order of St John of Jerusalem
OTC	Officers' Training Corps
OUDS	Oxford University Dramatic Society
OUP	Oxford University Press

P

pa	per annum
Pa	Pennsylvania (USA)
pac	Passed final exam of advanced class Mil Coll of Science
Paiforce	Palestine and Iraq Force
P&OSNCo	Peninsular and Oriental Steam Navigation Co
Parl	Parliament
Parly	Parliamentary
PC	Privy Councillor; Peace Commissioner (Ireland)
PDSA	People's Dispensary for Sick Animals
PEP	Political and Economic Planning
Perm	Permanent
PhD	Doctor of Philosophy
PIRA	Paper Industries Research Orgtanisation
pla	place
PLA	Port of London Authority
PLP	Parliamentary Labour Party
PM	Prime Minister
PMO	Principal Medical Officer
PMRAFNS	Princess Mary's Royal Air Force Nursing Service
PNEU	Parents' National Educational Union
PNG	Papua New Guinea
PO	Pilot Officer; Post Office
POD	Personnel Operations Department

Poly	Polytechnic
POUNC	Post Office Users' National Council
Pncpl; princ	Principal
POW	Prisoner of War
PPE	Philosophy, Politics and Economics (Oxford University)
PPS	Parliamentary Private Secretary
PRA	President of the Royal Academy
PRE	President of the Royal Society of Painters, Etchers and Engravers
Preb	Prebendary
Pres	President
prev	previously
princ	principal
PRO	Public Relations Officer; Public Records Office
Prod	Producer
Prods	Products; Productions
Prof	Professor
Prov	Provost; Provincial
PRS	President of Royal Society
PSA	President of the Society of Antiquaries; Property Services Agency
psa	Graduate of RAF Staff College
psc	Staff College Graduate
psm	Certificate of the Royal Military School of Music
PSNC	Pacific Steam Navigation Society
pt	part
PT	Physical Training
PTE	Passenger Transport Executive
ptnr	partner
Pty	Proprietary; Party
Pub	Public
Pubns	Publications
PUS	Permanent Under-Secretary
PUSD (FCO)	Permanent Under-Secretary's Department
PWD	Public Works Department
PWO	Prince of Wales's Own

Q

QAIMNS	Queen Alexandra's Imperial Military Nursing Service
QALAS	Qualified Associate of Land Agents' Society
QARANC	Queen Alexandra's Royal Army Nursing Corps
QC	Queen's Counsel
QFSM	Queen's Fire Service Medal for Distinguished Service
QGM	Queen's Gallantry Medal
QHC	Hon Chaplain to the Queen
QHDS	Honorary Dental Surgeon to the Queen
QHNS	Hon Nursing Sister to the Queen
QHP	Hon Physician to the Queen
QHS	Hon Surgeon to the Queen
Qld	Queensland
QMAAC	Queen Mary's Army Auxiliary Corps
QMC	Queen Mary College (London)
QMG	Quartermaster-General
QOH	Queen's Own Hussars
QPM	Queen's Police Medal
QS	Quarter Sessions
QSM	Queen's Service Medal (NZ)
QSO	Queen's Service Order (NZ)
qv	Quod Vide (which see)
qqv	Qua Vide (which see-plural)

R

(R)	Reserve
R	Rector; Royal
R & A	Royal and Ancient (St Andrews) Club
R & D	Research and Development
RA	Royal Artillery; Royal Academician
RAAF	Royal Australian Air Force
RAC	Roy Armoured Corps; Roy Automobile Club; Roy Agricultural College
RAAMC	Royal Australian Army Medical Corps
RACGP	Royal Australian College of General Practitioners
RACP	Royal Australasian College of Physicians
RACS	Royal Australasian College of Surgeons

RADA	Royal Academy of Dramatic Art
RADC	Royal Army Dental Corps
RAE	Royal Australian Engineers
RAEC	Royal Army Educational Corps
RAeS	Royal Aeronautical Society
RAF	Royal Air Force
RAFA	Royal Air Force Association
RAFO	Reserve of Air Force Officers
RAFRO	Royal Air Force Reserve of Officers
RAFVR	Royal Air Force Volunteer Reserve
RAI	Royal Anthropological Institute
RAIA	Royal Australian Institute of Architects
RAIC	Royal Architectural Institute of Canada
RAM	(member of) Royal Academy of Music
RAMC	Royal Army Medical Corps
RAN	Royal Australian Navy
RANR	Royal Australian Naval Reserve
RANVR	Royal Australian Naval Volunteer Reserve
RAOC	Royal Army Ordnance Corps
RAPC	Royal Army Pay Corps
RARO	Regular Army Reserve of Officers
RASC	Royal Army Service Corps (now RCT)
RASE	Royal Agricultural Society of England
RAUXAF	Royal Auxiliary Air Force
RAVC	Royal Army Veterinary Corps
RB	Rifle Brigade
RBA	Royal Society of British Artists
RBC	Royal British Colonial Society of Artists
RBS	Royal Society of British Sculptors
RC	Roman Catholic
RCA	Royal College of Art
RCAC	Royal Canadian Armoured Corps
RCAF	Royal Canadian Air Force
RCAMC	Royal Canadian Army Medical Corps
RCDS	Royal College of Defence Studies
RCGP	Royal College of General Practitioners
RCHA	Royal Canadian Horse Artillery
RCM	Royal College of Music
RCN	Royal Canadian Navy
RCNC	Royal Corps of Naval Constructors
RCNR	Royal Canadian Naval Reserve
RCNVR	Royal Canadian Naval Volunteer Reserve
RCOG	Royal College of Obstetricians and Gynaecologists
RCP	Royal College of Physicians, London
RCPath	Royal College of Pathologists
RCPE(d)	Royal College of Physicians, Edinburgh
RCPGlas	Royal College of Physicians and Surgeons, Glasgow
RCPI	Royal College of Physicians in Ireland
RCS	Roy Coll of Surgeons of England; Roy Corps of Signals; Royal Coll of Science
RCSE(d)	Roy College of Surgeons of Edinburgh
RCSI	Royal College of Surgeons in Ireland
RCT	Royal Corps of Transport
rd	road
RD	Royal Naval Reserve Officers' Decoration; Rural Dean
RDA	Royal Defence Academy
RCD	Rural District Council
RDF	Royal Dublin Fusiliers
RDI	Royal Designer for Industry (RSA)
RE	Royal Engineers
Rear-Adm	Rear-Admiral
Rec	Recorder
Rect	Rector
Regnl	Regional
Regt	Regiment
Rels	Relations
REME	Royal Electrical and Mechanical Engineers
RERO	Royal Engineers Reserve of Officers
Rep	Representative
Repub	Republic(an)
Res	Reserve; Research; Resident
ret	retired
Rev	Reverend
RFA	Royal Field Artillery
RFC	Royal Flying Corps
RGA	Royal Garrison Artillery
RGS	Royal Geographic Society
RHA	Royal Horse Artillery; Royal Hibernian Academy

RHF	Royal Highland Fusiliers
RHG	Royal Horse Guards
RHR	Royal Highland Regiment
RI	Royal Institute of Painters in Water Colours; Rhode Island
RIASC	Royal Indian Army Service Corps
RIBA	Royal Institute of British Architects
RIC	Royal Irish Constabulary
RIF	Royal Irish Fusiliers
RIIA	Royal Institute of International Affairs
RIM	Royal Indian Marine
RIN	Royal Indian Navy
RINVR	Royal Indian Navy Volunteer Reserve
RLSS	Royal Life Saving Society
RLYC	Royal Lymington Yacht Club
RM	Royal Marines
RMC	Royal Military College, Sandhurst (now Roy Military Academy)
RMCS	Royal Military College of Science
RMFVR	Royal Marine Forces Volunteer Reserve
RMLI	Royal Marine Light Infantry
RMS	Royal Meteorological Society
RN	Royal Navy
RNAS	Royal Naval Air Service
RNC	Royal Nautical College
RND	Royal Naval Division
RNLI	Royal National Lifeboat Institution
RNR	Royal Naval Reserve
RNSA	Royal Naval Sailing Association
RNVR	Royal Naval Volunteer Reserve
RNVSR	Royal Naval Volunteer Supplementary Reserve
RNZN	Royal New Zealand Navy
RNZNVR	Royal New Zealand Naval Volunteer Reserve
ROC	Royal Observer Corps
ROI	Royal Institute of Painters in Oils
R of O	Reserve of Officers
Roy	Royal
RP	Member of the Royal Society of Portrait Painters
RPC	Royal Pioneer Corps
RPO	Royal Philharmonic Orchestra
RRAF	Royal Rhodesian Air Force
RRC	Royal Red Cross
RSA	Royal Scottish Academician
RSAC	Royal Scottish Automobile Club
RSC	Royal Shakespeare Co; Roy Society of Canada
RSE	Royal Society of Edinburgh
RSF	Royal Scots Fusiliers
RSL	Royal Society of Literature
RSM	Royal Society of Medicine
RSPB	Royal Society for the Protection of Birds
RSPCA	Royal Society for the Prevention of Cruelty to Animals
RSW	Royal Scottish Water Colours' Society
Rt Hon	Right Honourable
RTO	Railway Transport Officer
RTR	Royal Tank Regiment
Rt Rev	Right Reverend
RUFC	Rugby Union Football Club
RUI	Royal University of Ireland
RUKBA	Royal United Kingdom Beneficent Association
RUR	Royal Ulster Regiment
RUSI	Royal United Services Institute
RVC	Royal Veterinary College
RWAFF	Royal West African Frontier Force
RWF	Royal Welch Fusiliers
RWS	Member, Royal Society of Painters in Water Colours
Ry	Railway
RYA	Royal Yachting Association
RZS	Royal Zoological Society

S

s	son
S	South; Scotland / Scottish (Peerages)
(S)	Paymaster (Navy)
SA	South Africa; South Australia; Société Anonyme

SAAF	South African Air Force
sac	Qualified at a Small Arms Technical Long Course
SACEUR	Supreme Allied Commander Europe
SACLANT	Supreme Allied Commander Atlantic
SACSEA	Supreme Allied Command, S E Asia
Salop	(formerly) Shropshire
SAS	Special Air Service
Sask	Saskatchewan
SASO	Senior Air Staff Officer
SBAC	Society of British Aircraft Constructors
SBNO	Senior British Naval Officer
SBStJ	Serving Brother of the Order of St John of Jerusalem
SC	Sailing Club
ScD	Doctor of Science (Cambridge and Dublin)
SCF	Senior Chaplain to the Forces
SCGB	Ski Club of Great Britain
sch	school
Sci	Science
SCL	Student in Civil Law
SCM	State Certified Midwife
Sco(t)	Scottish; Scotland
SEAC	South East Asia Command
Sec	Secretary
Secdy	Secondary
Sec-Gen	Secretary-General
Sen	Senator
Serv	Service
SF	Science fiction
SG	Solicitor-General
SGM	Sea Gallantry Medal
Sgt	Sergeant
SHAEF	Supreme Headquarters, Allied Expeditionary Force
SHAPE	Supreme Headquarters, Allied Powers Europe
sis	sister
SJ	Society of Jesus (Jesuits)
SKGB	Ski Club of Great Britain
slr	solicitor
SM	Service Medal of the Order of Canada; Master of Science (USA)
SME	School of Military Engineering
SMO	Senior Medical Officer; Sovereign Military Order
SMOM	Sovereign Military Order of Malta
SNO	Senior Naval Officer
SNP	Scottish Nationalist Party
SO	Scottish Office
Soc	Society
Socl	Social
SOE	Special Operations Executive
SOGAT	Society of Graphical and Allied Trades
Som	Somerset
Sov	Sovereign
sp	Sine Prole (without issue)
Sp	Spain; Spanish
SPCK	Society for Promoting Christian Knowledge
SPG	Society for the Propagation of the Gospel
SPSO	Senior Personnel Staff Officer
sq	square
Sqdn	Squadron
Sqdn-Ldr	Squadron Leader
sr	senior
SR	Special Reserve; Southern Railway; Southern Region
SRN	State Registered Nurse
SRO	Supplementary Reserve of Officers
SS & AFA	Soldiers', Sailors', and Airmen's Families' Association
SSC	Solicitor, Supreme Court (Scotland)
SSStJ	Serving Sister of the Order of St John of Jerusalem
St Cat's	St Catherine's; Catharine's (Cambridge)
STC	Senior Training Corps
STD	Doctor of Theology (America)
STL	Licenciate of Sacred Theology
STSO	Senior Technical Staff Officer
Subs	Submarines (RN)
Subst	Substitute
suc	succeeded
Sup	Supérieure

Supp	Supplementary
Supt	Superintendent
Surgn	Surgeon
Surv(g)	Surviving

T

TA	Territorial Army
TAA	Territorial Army Association
TAF	Tactical Air Force
TANS	Territorial Army Nursing Service
Tas	Tasmania
TA & VR	Territorial and Army Volunteer Reserve
TA & VRA	Territorial and Army Volunteer Reserve Association
Tbnl	Tribunal
TC	Order of Trinity Cross (Trinidad and Tobago)
TD	Territorial Officers' Decoration; Teachta Dala (member of the Dail Parliament of Eire)
Tdes	Trades
Temp	Temporary
Tech	Technical
Technol	Technology; Technological
TF	Territorial Force
TGWU	Transport and General Workers' Union
Theo	Theological
T'ning	Training
T'port	Transport
Transfd	Transferred
Treasy	Treasury
Tres	Treasurer
Trg	Training
Trin	Trinity College
Tst(ee)	Trust(ee)
TUC	Trades Union Congress

U

(U)	Unionist
U	University
UAR	United Arab Republic
UC	University College
UCCA	Universities Central Council on Admissions
UCH	University College Hospital
UCL	University College London
UCLA	University of California at Los Angeles
UCNW	University College of North Wales
UCS	University College School
UCW	University College of Wales
UDC	Urban District Council
UDF	Union Defence Force; Ulster Defence Force
UDR	Ulster Defence Regiment
UEA	University of East Anglia
UFO	Unidentified Flying Object
UHS	University High School
UK	United Kingdom
UKAEA	United Kingdom Atomic Energy Authority
UKLF	United Kingdom Land Forces
UN	United Nations
unc	uncle
Und-Sec	Under-Secretary
UNESCO	United Nations Educational, Scientific and Cultural Organisation
UNFAO	United Nations Food and Agricultural Organisation
UNICEF	United Nations International Children's Emergency Fund
Univ	University
UNO	United Nations Organisation
UNRRA	United Nations Relief and Rehabilitation Organisation
UP	Uttar Pradesh; United Provinces; United Presbyterian
UPNI	Unionist Party of Northern Ireland
Us	Universities
US	United States
USA	United States of America
USAF	United States Air Force

USN	United States Navy
USNR	United States Naval Reserve
USSR	Union of Soviet Socialist Republics
UTC	University Training Corps
Utd	United
(UU)	Ulster Unionist

V

v	versus (against)
V	Vicar; Vice
V & A	Victoria and Albert (Museum)
Va	Virginia
VA	Lady of the Order of Victoria and Albert
VAD	Voluntary Aid Detachment
VAT	Value Added Tax
VC	Victoria Cross
VCAS	Vice-Chief of the Air Staff
VD	Volunteer Officers' Decoration (now VRD)
VDC	Volunteer Defence Corps
Ven	Venerable
Very Rev	Very Reverend
Vet	Veterinary
V(ice) Adm	Vice Admiral
Vice Lieut	Vice Lieutenant
Vice-Pres	Vice-President
Visc	Viscount
VM	Victory Medal
VMH	Victoria Medal of Honour (Royal Horticultural Society)
Vol	Volunteer
VP	Vice-President
VRD	Volunteer Reserve Officers' Decoration

W

w	wife
W	West
WA	Western Australia
WAAF	Women's Auxiliary Air Force (now WRAF)
WEA	Workers' Educational Association
WEU	Western European Union
WFTU	World Federation of Trade Unions
WG	Welsh Guards
WHO	World Health Organisation
WI	West Indies
wid	widow
Wing-Cdr	Wing-Commander
Wm	William
WNO	Welsh National Opera
WO	War Office
WR	West Riding
WRAC	Women's Royal Army Corps
WRAF	Women's Royal Air Force
WRNR	Women's Royal Naval Reserve
WRNS	Women's Royal Naval Service
WRVS	Women's Royal Voluntary Service (formerly WVS)
WS	Writer to the Signet
WVS	Women's Voluntary Service
WW I	First World War
WW II	Second World War

Y

Yeo	Yeomanry
YC	Yacht Club
YHA	Youth Hostels' Association
YMCA	Young Men's Christian Association
yr	younger
yst	youngest
YWCA	Young Women's Christian Association

ADDENDA AND CORRIGENDA

ALEXANDER OF TUNIS, 2 Earl; m 1981, Hon Davina Woodhouse, da of 4 Baron Terrington

ASTOR, Hon Fiona, for Fiona read Flora

AUSTIN, Lady Lilian, died 1981

BARNARD, Sir Henry, died 1981

BETHELL, Hon William Alexander, 2 s of 4 Baron Bethell; b 18 March 1969; *Style* - The Hon William Bethell

BLADES, Hon Catherine, m 1981, Charles J, s of Kenneth Spencer, of Zeals, Wilts; *Style* The Hon Mrs Spencer

CAYZER, Lady (Beatrice Eileen), OBE, widow of Sir Charles Cayzer, 3 Bt; died 1981

CHISHOLM, Sir Henry, died 1981

CORY, Christopher Gordon, MVO, DL; died 1981

CRICHTON-STUART, Lord Anthony, 2 s of 6 Marquess of Bute, JP; b 14 May 1961; *Style* - Lord Anthony Crichton-Stuart

CRICHTON-STUART, Lady Eileen Caroline, 2 da of 6 Marquess of Bute, JP; b 21 Feb 1957; *Style* - Lady Eileen Crichton-Stuart

CRICHTON-STUART, Lord James Charles, 3 s (but 2 surviving) of 5 Marquess of Bute, JP, by Lady Eileen Forbes (yr da of 8 Earl of Granard); b 17 Sept 1935; *Educ* Ampleforth, Trin Cambridge; m 1, 1959 (m dis 1968), Sally (Sarah) Frances, da of Lt-Col Arthur Croker Poole (d 1981), of Kensington (she m 2, HH The Aga Khan, *qv*); m 2, 1970, Anna Rose, da of late Maj H Bramwell, of Co Cork; 2 s (William b 1971, Hugh b 1973); *Career* Lt Scots Gds Reserve; ADC to Govr-Gen Fedn Rhodesia & Nyasaland 1957-58; dir Coutts & Co, Coutts Finance, Fidelity American Assets, Disability Press Ltd, Fidelity Internat Funds, Fidelity Pacific Fund, Fidelity World Fund, William Lawson Distillers; chm Intel Funds (Management) Ltd; *Club* Turf; *Style* - Lord James Crichton-Stuart, Upton Grey House, Upton Grey, Basingstoke, Hants (☎ Long Sutton (025 681) 659)

DICK-LAUDER, Sir George Andrew, 12 Bt, died 1981; er s Piers succeeds as 13 Bt (*Style* Sir Piers Dick-Lauder, Bt); hp is now Sir Piers's yr bro, Mark Andrew D-L, b 1951, m 1970 Jeanne, nee Mullineaux, of Bolton; 1 s (Martin); *Style* - Mark Dick-Lauder Esq

DONOUGHMORE, 7 Earl of, died 1981; er s, Viscount Suirdale, succeeds as 8 Earl (Style as for his late father); Lord Donoughmore's h is his eldest s, formerly Hon John Hely-Hutchinson, now Viscount Suirdale; Style for 7 Earl's widow becomes: The Rt Hon Dorothy, Countess of Donoughmore, MBE

DOUGLAS, Mrs Kingman, died 1981

DUTT, Hon Mrs (Bijoli), da of 1 Baron Sinha; b 1900; m 1918, Runge Lall Dutt; 2 da; *Style* - The Hon Mrs Dutt

GALBRAITH, Hon Norman Dunlop Galloway, s of 1 Baron Strathclyde; b 1925; *m* 1950, Susan, da of Cdr J Galloway; 1 s, 2 da; *Style* - The Hon Norman Galbraith

DUTTON, Ralph Stawell, s of Henry Dutton, JP (himself gs of 2 Baron Sherborne); hp of 2 cous once removed, 7 Baron Sherborne (since death of Hon George Dutton, the 7 Baron's bro, in 1981); b 25 Aug 1898; *Educ* Eton, Ch Ch Oxford; *Career* author, FSA; High Sheriff Hants 1944; *Style* - Ralph Dutton Esq; Hinton Ampner House, Alresford, Hants (☎ Bramdean (096 279) 222)

EATON, Vice-Adml Sir John, died 1981

EDWARDS, Hon Robin Ernest, s of Baron Chelmer, MC, TD (Life Peer); b 1940; m 1967, Carol Mayes; children; *Style* - The Hon Robin Edwards; 14 Augustin Way, Bicknacre, Danbury Way, Essex (☎ 024 541 4321)

FAIRFAX, Hon Hugh Nigel Thomas, 2 s of 13 Lord Fairfax of Cameron and hp of bro, 14 Lord; b 29 March 1958; *Style* - The Hon Hugh Fairfax

FRASER, Rt Hon Sir Hugh Charles Patrick Joseph, MBE (1945), PC (1962), MP (C) Stafford and Stone 1950-; 2 s of 14 Lord Lovat, KT, GCVO, KCMG, CB, DSO, and bro of 15 Lord; b 23 Jan 1918; *Educ* Ampleforth, Balliol Oxford, Sorbonne; *m* 1956 (m dis 1977), Lady Antonia Pakenham (*see* Lady Antonia Fraser); *Career* MP Staffs Stone 1945-50; Parly Under Sec State (& Fin Sec) War Off 1958-60, Colonies 1960-62, Sec State Air 1962-64, Pres W Midlands Con Assoc 1967; dir Sun Alliance, Aird Motors, A I Welders, Alliance Assur, London Assur; kt 1980 *Style* - The Rt Hon Sir Hugh Fraser MBE PC MP; Eilean Aigas, Beauly, Inverness (☎ 046 374 203); House of Commons, SW1

HEBBLETHWAITE, Richard Jeremy, TD; s of Lt-Col R V Hebblethwaite, MC; b 5 Dec 1933; *Educ* Wellington, Nottingham U; *m* 1966, Sara Elisabeth, da of James Stucker Offutt, of Clearwater, Florida; 2 children; *Career* CA; md Save & Prosper Gp; *Recreations* sailing, golf; *Clubs* New, City; *Style* - Richard Hebblethwaite Esq; 25 Hazlewell rd, SW15

HEGINBOTHAM, Stafford, s of Stafford Heginbotham, of Oldham; b 12 Sept 1933; *Educ* Greenhill G S Oldham; *m* 1963, Lorna, da of Alfred Silverwood, of Leeds; 2 s (Simon b 1965, James b 1967); *Career* served RAF; chm & md Tebro Toys Ltd 1966-, chm Bradford AFC 1965-73; dir: Carlton Diecasters 1976-80, Douglas Plastics 1976-80; *Recreations* racing (racehorses: 'Cutler Heights', 'Tebro Teddy'), golf, international travel; *Style* - Stafford Heginbotham Esq, The Pastures, Tong Village, Bradford, W Yorks (☎ 0532 853661)

HELY-HUTCHINSON, Hon John Michael James, became Viscount Suirdale on death of his gf, 7 Earl of Donoughmore, and succession of f as 8 Earl 1981; his da became The Hon Marie-Pierre Hely-Hutchinson; *Style* - Viscount Suirdale

HOBSON, Alfred Collingwood, MC (1944); s of Alfred Hobson; b 2 March 1917; *Educ* Marlborough; *m* 1946, Priscilla Ruth, da of Maj Harry Thorold, of Cranford Hall, Kettering; 3 da; *Career* slr, late sr ptnr Druces & Attlee; *Recreations* field sports, skiing; *Club* Boodle's; *Style* - Alfred Hobson Esq MC; Hascombe Grange, Loxhill, Godalming, Surrey (☎ 048 632 227)

KEEVIL, Ambrose Clement Arthur, s of Col Sir Ambrose Keevil KBE MC DL; b 21 Sept 1919; *Educ* Tonbridge, Queen's Oxford; *m* 1945, Olwen Marjorie Enid, da of John Gibbins; 2 s (Philip m Augusta McGrail, Julian m Mary Harrison), 1 da (Harriet Anne); *Career* dep chm Fitch Lovell Ltd; Master Worshipful Co of Poulterers 1966-67; *Recreations* painting; *Clubs* Army & Navy, MCC; *Style* - Ambrose Keevil Esq, Buckwell Place, Herstmonceux, Sussex (☎ 032 181 2157); c/o Fitch Lovell Ltd, 1 West Smithfield, London EC1A 9LA (☎ 01 248 6431)

KENSINGTON, 7 Baron, died 1981; nephew (Hugh Ivor Edwardes) succeeded as 8 Baron (*Style* - as for predecessor); Lord Kensington's 2 s & 1 da are now: The Hon William (er s & h; b 1964) & Hon Hugh Edwardes (b 1967), The Hon Amanda Edwardes (b 1962)

KRAUSHAR, Christopher Arthur Anthony, s of Casimir Kraushar; b 8 Feb 1940; *Educ* St Paul's, Christ's Cambridge; *m* 1963, Alison Margaret, da of Alexander Graham, of Peterborough; 1 s (Anthony b 1967), 1 da (Alison b 1964); *Career* chartered engr; md Gaskell & Chambers Ltd 1980-; dir: MKR Hldgs 1980-, Perkins Engines Gp 1978-80; *Recreations* badminton, squash; *Style* - Christopher Kraushar Esq; 16 Fairways, Hayes Lane, Kenley, Surrey (☎ 01 668 3104)

LAVINGTON, Michael Richard, Richard Lavington; b 21 Feb 1943; *Educ* Whitgift, Cambridge, Columbia U New York, Lancaster U; *m* 1966, Clarie June, da of James Watford; 2 da (Susan b 1969, Victoria b 1970); *Career* Pres Black Starr & Frost (New York), Kay Jewelers (Alexandria, Va); late dir Bowater-Ralli America (1971-74), Ralli Australia (1970-71); *Recreations* theatre, chess, bridge, travel; *Style* - Michael Lavington Esq; 501 South Fairfax st, Alexandria, Va 22314, USA (☎ business (703) 683 3800)

LEEPER, Thomas William Brian, s of Richard Leeper, of W Byfleet; b 16 June 1927; *Educ* Downside, Magdalene Cambridge; *m* 1951, Edreen Diana, da of Capt Edric Lyte; 4 s (Patrick, Michael, James m 1980 Valerie Bird, Timothy b 1965), 2 da (Elizabeth m 1975 Andrew Bruce, Jennifer); *Career* dir Lep Gp 1970-; *Recreations* horticulture, herbalism, photography; *Club* Cavalry & Guards; *Style* - Thomas Leeper Esq, Kingsmead, Blackdown ave, Pyrford, Woking, Surrey

LINDESAY-BETHUNE, Hon Caroline, m 1981 George, s & h of Sir Castel Wrey, 14 Bt; *Style* - The Hon Mrs Wrey

McCANN, Keith, s of George McCann; b 27 Sept 1931; *Educ* Queen Mary Coll London U; *m* 1955, Ina Lucy, da of Samuel Rostrow; 2 da (Corrie Lyndis, Kirstie Philippa); *Career* chm F D Sims, Kent Electric Wire, Winding Wires (Pty) Ltd; md London Electric Wire Co & Smiths Ltd; *Recreations* flying; *Club* Stapleford; *Style* - Keith McCann Esq; Holmlea House, Chipping Ongar, Essex

MAFFEY, Hon John, died 1981; h to Barony of Rugby now Hon Robert Maffey

MUNDY, Lady Bridget, *née* Elliot-Murray-Kynynmound; da of 5 Earl of Minto; b 1921; *m* 1, 1944, Lt-Col James Clark, Jr, DFC, USAF; 1 s (Christopher); m 2, 1954 (m dis 1963), Maj Henry Garnett, CBE; m 3, 1966 (m dis 1970), Maj Peter Mundy, MC; *Style* - Lady Bridget Mundy

NUTTALL, Richard Wardleworth, s of Henry Nuttall, FRCS; b 20 Oct 1927; *Educ* Marlborough, St John's Cambridge, Geneva U (MBA); *m* 1953, Veryll Bambury, da of William Sever; 1 s (David b 1964), 3 da (Fiona, Veronica m -- Strawbridge, Heather); chm & md Devon Boats Ltd; late md RTZ Metals Stockholding Ltd, dep md RTZ Metals; *Recreations* sailing (yacht: 'Volunteer of Clyde'); *Style* - Richard Nuttall Esq; Pitt Court, Nymet Rowland, nr Crediton, Devon; Haven House, Haven rd, Exeter (☎ 0392 50970/ 32676)

SHIVELY, William Jerome, s of Robert Shively; b 3 Jan 1929; *Educ* Hamilton H S Hamilton New York, Deerfield Acad Mass, Colgate U Hamilton New York, Harvard Business Sch; *m* 1953, Eleanor, da of Dr William Jackson; 4 children; *Career* served USAF 2 Lt; advertising and marketing executive; chm and md McCann & Co London 1981-; regional dir McCann-Erickson Internat 1980-; formerly exec v-pres Johnson Wax, exec v-pres McCann-Erickson 1980-; *Recreations* scuba diving, skiing, flying, shooting, fishing; *Clubs* Annabel's, White Elephant, American; *Style* William Shively Esq; 1 The Vale, SW3 (☎ 01 351 4850); Avalon, Old Barn Lane, Churt, Surrey (☎ Hindhead 4686)

SIEMENS, Herman Werner, s of Prof Dr Herman Siemens, of Leiden; b 21 May 1925; *Educ* Leiden Gymnasium Sch, Delft Technology U (MSc Nuclear Physics), Universidad Del Valle (MBA); *m* 1955, Cornélie, da of Count Herman Schimmelpenninck, of The Hague; 1 s, 4 da; *Career* res engr Centre à l'Energie Atomique, Paris 1953; chm & ch exec Alcan Aluminium of Nigeria Ltd and Alcan Aluminium Products Ltd (both in Lagos) 1978-; previously exec with various Aluminium Cos; *Recreations* music, riding, sailing, squash; *Clubs* Lansdowne, Roy Overseas League, IOD, Metropolitan (Lagos); *Style* - Herman Siemens Esq, 12 Wilton st, SW1 (☎ 01 235 2772); 108 Riouwstraat, The Hague, The Netherlands (☎ (070) 632793); 16 Akin Olugbade st, Victoria Island, Lagos, Nigeria (☎ 611499)

SNEDDEN, David King, s of David Snedden; b 23 Feb 1933; *Educ* Daniel Stewart's Coll Edinburgh; *m* 1958, Jean, da of Edward Goldie Smith; 2 s (David b 1961, Stuart b 1963), 1 da (Ann); *Career* CA 1956; jt md Thomson Regional Newspapers Ltd 1980- (dir 1974-, gp assist md 1979-80); dir: Scotsman Publications 1970-, Belfast Telegraph Newspapers 1979; formerly memb Press Cncl, dir Radio Forth Ltd, investment advsr Guinness Mahon Ltd; *Recreations* golf, shooting, fishing; *Clubs* Caledonian, Bruntisfield Links Golfing Soc, Roy Wimbledon Golf; *Style* - David Snedden Esq; 82a Ashley Gardens, London SW1 (☎ 01 828 0965)

SOPHER, Ivan, b 27 Aug 1949; *m* Helen; 1 s, 1 da; *Career* CA, sole proprietor Ivan Sopher & Co Chartered Accountants; FCA, ATII, MBIM; *Recreation* sport; *Style* - Ivan Sopher Esq, c/o Administration Building, EMI Elstree Studios, Borehamwood, Herts, WD6 1JG (☎ 01 207 0602)

THOMAS, Douglas Ronald, s of Harry Thomas; b 15 Feb 1925; *m* Shirley Edith Frances, da of Archibald Dixon; 1 s (David Malcolm), 2 da (Susan m Peter Taylor 1979, Sally Frances); *Career* FCIS, FBIM; served Sergeant RAF; md Rank Advertising Films Ltd; Pres Cinema Advertising Assoc; *Style* - Douglas Thomas Esq; 98 Oakwood rd, Hampstead Garden Suburb, NW11 (☎ 01 458 4131)

TROUBRIDGE, Pamela, Lady, died 1981

WAKELY, Leonard John Dean, CMG (1965), OBE (1945), s of Sir Leonard Wakely, KCIE, CB; b 18 June 1909; *Educ* Westminster, Ch Ch Oxford; *m* 1938, Margaret, da of Lt-Cdr Charles Tinson, OBE, RN; 2 s; *Career* ICS 1932-47; Dep High Commissioner Madras 1953-57, Ghana 1957-60, Canada 1962-65; Ambass to Rangoon 1965-67; *Style* - Leonard Wakely Esq CMG OBE; Long Meadow, Forest rd, East Horsley, Leatherhead, Surrey (☎ E Horsley 3152)

WARDELL, Lady Antonia, m 1981 Charles William Beckwith; *Style* - Lady Antonia Beckwith

WEBSTER, Colin, s of Robert Webster, of Loughton, Essex; b 15 March 1924; *Educ* Loughton Sch, London U; *m* 1949, Sylvia, da of Hedley Baker; 2 children; *Career* served WW II as Lt N Africa, NW Europe, Italy; Pres & Ch Exec Offr B&B Finance Hldgs 1980-; dir internat finance Benton & Bowles Gp 1967-; *Recreations* golf, gardening, charity; *Club* Carlton; *Style* - Colin Webster Esq; High Wood, Steeds Way, Loughton, Essex (☎ 01 508 1975 home; 01 589 1444 office)

WENNERSTROM, Bruce Kent, s of John Wennerstrom; b 20 Dec 1926; *Educ* Pratt Inst; *m* 1955, Genia Catherine, da of Bronislaw Walukanis; 3 s (Nord Rohlf b 1960, Lief Anders b 1962, Kirk Lars b 1967), 1 da (Bria Christa b 1967); *Career* served US Army Signal Corps Asia-Pacific theatre; Pres Previews Inc; *Recreations* sailing (sabre-class sloop: 'Preview'), skiing, motor sports; *Clubs* Madison Avenue Sports Car Driving, Chowder Soc *Style* - Bruce Wennerstrom Esq; Sumner rd, Greenwich, Connecticut 06830, USA (☎ 203 661 1669)

WHITE, Peter Awbery, s of Sidney White, of Wimbledon; b 22 Aug 1934; *Educ* Rutligh Sch Merton, Law Soc's Sch of Law; *m* 1966, Angela, da of Thomas Davies (Capt Merchant Navy); 1 s (Lawrence b 1972), 1 da (Eleanor b 1968); *Career* slr 1959-, Commissioner for Oaths 1973-; *Recreations* lay lector (C of E), calligraphy; *Club* Wig and Pen; *Style* - Peter White Esq; 8 Otterwood Paddock, Stamford Bridge, York YO4 1BA

WIDGERY, Baron, died 1981

WRIGHT, Hon Mrs (Alison Elizabeth); da of Baron Franks (Life Peer); b 1945; *m* 1974, Stanley Wright; *Style* The Hon Mrs Wright; 6 Holly Place, Holly Walk, NW3

WYLIE, Hon Lord; Norman Russell, s of William Wylie; b 26 Oct 1923; *Educ* Paisley G S, St Edmund Hall Oxford, Glasgow and Edinburgh Us; *m* 1963, Gillian, da of Dr Richard Verney, of Edinburgh; 3 s (Julian b 1964, Russell b 1966, Philip b 1968); *Career* Lt-Cdr RNR, served Fleet Air Arm and Russian and Atlantic Convoys; advocate 1952, Standing Counsel to Air Ministry Scotland 1956-59, Crown Counsel 1959-64, QC 1964; Slr-Gen Scotland 1964 (April-Oct); MP (C) Edinburgh Pentlands 1964-74, PC 1970; Scottish Lord of Session (Senator of the Coll of Justice) 1974-; *Recreations* shooting, sailing (yacht: 'Juneph'); *Clubs* New, Roy Highland Yacht, RNSA; *Style* - The Hon Lord Wylie VRD PC; 30 Lauder rd, Edinburgh EH9 2JF (☎ 031 667 8377)

YOCKLUNN, Sir John Soong Chung, KCVO (1977); s of Charles Yocklunn; b 5 May 1933; *Educ* Northam H S, U of W Australia, Australian Nat U, Sheffield U; *m* 1981, Patricia, da of Douglas Swann, of Tasmania; *Career* Asst Sec (Library Servs) Dept Educn Papua New Guinea 1978-; kt 1975 *Recreations* book collecting, languages; *Style* - Sir John Yocklunn KCVO; PO Box 1821, Boroko, Papua New Guinea (☎ Port Moresby 25 8998)

MACLEOD MATTHEWS, Alistair Francis; OBE (1970); s of Reginald Macleod Matthews; b 12 April 1921; *Educ* St Paul's, Ch Ch Oxford; *m* 1955, Elizabeth Marina Addenbrooke, da of Gordon Spenser Marston DSO MC, of Chalfont St Giles; 2 s; *Career* served as Lt-Col Gen Staff Mediterranean; former asst gen man BP; dir British Gas Corpn 1975-, memb Scottish Devpt Bd 1972-, chm New Court Natural Resources Ltd 1973-; JP Bucks 1971; companion Inst Gas Engrs; *Recreation* fishing, historical research; *Club* Roy Scottish Automobile; *Style* - Alistair Macleod Matthews Esq OBE JP; Achnacarnin, Culkein, Sutherland (☎ Stoer 262); The Manor House, Chenies, Bucks (☎ Little Chalfont 2888); 29 Carlisle Place, SW1

HARLOCK, Maj-Gen H G F, died 1981

BRADFORD, 11 Earl of; died 1981; s, Viscount Newport, succeeded (*Style* - as for predecessor minus TD); Hon Alexander Bridgeman became Viscount Newport

LASCELLES, Hon Alexander; 2 s (but h to courtesy Viscountcy since b in wedlock) of Viscount Lascelles; b 13 May 1980

THE ROYAL FAMILY

The Royal Family Section is numbered in order of succession, with six exceptions: The Queen herself; The Duke of Edinburgh, who, though in line to the throne, would otherwise appear rather far down a much lengthened list; The Queen Mother; Princess Alice Duchess of Gloucester;The Duchess of Windsor; and Prince Michael of Kent, whose marriage to a Roman Catholic disqualified him (though his children, to whose upbringing in the Anglican faith their parents have consented, remain in line of succession). The Duke of Edinburgh was in any case placed in precedence next to Her Majesty by Royal Warrant of 18 Sept 1952. These six exceptions are not, therefore, numbered. For foreign and Commonwealth decorations and military ranks see *Debrett's Peerage*. The Civil List Act 1972, periodically reviewed, provides varying sums for the Royal Family's maintenance.

ELIZABETH II (Elizabeth Alexandra Mary, *née* Windsor, now Windsor-Mountbatten), by the Grace of God, of the United Kingdom of Great Britain and Northern Ireland and of her other realms and territories Queen, Head of the Commonwealth, Defender of the Faith; er da of His late Majesty King George VI and HM Queen Elizabeth the Queen Mother, *qv*; b 21 April 1926, at 17 Bruton st, Mayfair, London W1; *Educ* privately; *m* 1947, HRH The Prince Philip, Duke of Edinburgh, *qv*; 3 s (HRH The Prince of Wales, HRH Prince Andrew, HRH Prince Edward), 1 da (HRH The Princess Anne, Mrs Mark Phillips), *qqv*; *Heir* s, Prince of Wales;
suc f 6 Feb 1952, proclaimed Queen 8 Feb 1952, crowned at Westminster Abbey 2 June 1953;
Sovereign of: all Br Orders of Knighthood, OM, Roy Order of Victoria & Albert, CI, CH, DSO, Imperial Serv Order, OC, Sov Head Order of St John of Jerusalem, OA;
Military titles and ranks: Lord High Admiral of UK, Col-in-Ch: Life Gds, Blues & Royals, Roy Scots Dragoon Gds, 16/5 Queen's Roy Lancers, Roy Tank Regt, RE, Gren, Coldstream, Scots, Irish, and Welsh Gds, Roy Welch Fusiliers, Queen's Lancashire Regt, Argyll & Sutherland Highlanders, Roy Green Jackets, RAOC, Queen's Own Mercian Yeo, Duke of Lancaster's Own Yeo, Corps of Roy Mil Police; Air Cdre-in-Ch: RAuxAF, RAF Regt, Roy Observer Corps; Hon Air Cdre RAF Marham, Cmmdt-in-Ch RAF Coll Cranwell;
Academic distinctions: Oxford: Hon DCL; London: Hon BMus, Hon LLD; Edinburgh: Hon LLD; Wales: Hon MusD; FRS; Hon FRCS, FRCOG;
Miscellaneous: Master of Merchant Navy and Fishing Fleets, Head Civil Def Corps, Head Nat Hosp Serv Reserve, Patron Roy Coll Physicians Edinburgh;
Civil List: £3,260,200 (as of March 1981; 1980 figure: £2,900,500; HM had returned £285,073 by March 1981);
Style - (see *Debrett's Correct Form* for further details for HM and other members of the Royal Family) Her Majesty The Queen *or* The Private Secretary to Her Majesty The Queen; Buckingham Palace, London SW1 (☎ 01 930 4832); Windsor Castle, Berkshire; Balmoral Castle, Aberdeenshire; Sandringham, Norfolk

EDINBURGH, HRH The Prince Philip, 1 Duke of (UK 1947); KG (1947), KT (1952), OM (1968), GBE (1953, Grand Master and First Knight of Order), PC (GB 1951, Canada 1957); also Earl of Merioneth and Baron Greenwich (both UK 1947); granted style and titular dignity of Prince of the UK and NI 1957; only s of HRH Prince Andrew of Greece, GCVO (himself 4 s of George I, King of the Hellenes, who in his turn was 2 s of Christian IX, King of Denmark), by Alice (at time of her marriage HSH Princess Alice of Battenberg, from 1917 notionally the former Lady Alice Mountbatten), er da of 1 Marquess of Milford Haven (formerly HSH Prince Louis of Battenberg), sis of late Earl Mountbatten of Burma, and maternally ggda of Queen Victoria and niece of last Tsarina (Alix, later Alexandra) of Russia; b 10 June 1921, at 'Mon Repos', Corfu; *Educ* Cheam Sch, Salem (Baden), Gordonstoun, RNC Dartmouth; took surname Mountbatten *vice* Oldenburg and naturalised a Br subject

28 Feb 1947; *m* 20 Nov 1947, HM Queen Elizabeth II, *qv*; *Heir* s, Prince of Wales;
Career served WW II Mediterranean Fleet (Home Waters) and with Br Pacific Fleet SE Asia and Pacific;
Military ranks and titles: Adm of the Fleet, Field Marshal, Marshal of the RAF, Capt Gen RM, Col-in-Ch: Queen's Roy Irish Hussars, Duke of Edinburgh's Roy Regt, Queen's Own Highlanders, REME, Intelligence Corps, Army Cadet Force; Col Gren Gds, Hon Col Edinburgh & Heriot Watt Us OTC, Air Cdre-in-Ch ATC, Hon Air Cdre RAF Kinloss, Cmmdt-in-Ch & Extra Master Merchant Navy;
Academic distinctions: Chllr Us of Wales 1948-, Edinburgh 1952-, Cambridge 1977- (Salford 1967-71); Visitor Manchester Coll Sci & Technol 1959-, Life Govr King's Coll London 1954-; Hon LLD: Wales, London, Edinburgh, Cambridge, Karachi, Malta, California; Hon DCL: Durham, Oxford; Hon DSc: Delhi, Reading, Salford, Southampton; Hon Degree Engrg Lima; Hon FRCP London, Hon FRCSE, Hon FRCS; Hon Fellow Univ Oxford;
Sports: Pres Br Amateur Athletic Bd 1952-, C'wlth Games Fedn 1955-, Br Sportsman's Club 1958-, Centl Cncl Physical Recreation 1951-;
Sailing: Adm House of Lords Yacht Club, Roy Motor Yacht Club, RN Sailing Assoc, Roy Southern Yacht Club, Bar Yacht Club, Roy Dart Yacht Club, Roy Gibraltar Yacht Club, Roy Yacht Club of Victoria (Australia), Great Navy of State of of Nebraska;
Miscellaneous (selection only): memb Cncl Duchy of Cornwall 1952-, Ranger Windsor Great Park 1952-, Lord High Steward Plymouth 1960-, Elder Bro Trin House 1952- and Master 1969-; Pres: Guards' Polo Club 1955-, Roy Ag Soc of C'wlth, Roy Household Cricket Club 1953-, PRSA 1952-, Third Pres Internat Wild Life Fund 1981-, V-Pres Soc Friends St George's & Descendants of KGs 1948-, FRS, Hon Fellow RZS Scotland, Tstee Nat Maritime Museum Greenwich, Tstee Roy Ag Soc England; Patron Inst Navigation, Lord's Taverners, Grand Master Guild Air Pilots & Air Navigators; *Club* White's;
Also: Patron & Tstee Duke of Edinburgh's Award, chm Duke of Edinburgh's Ctee for Queen's Awards to Industry 1965-;
Civil List: £160,000 (as of March 1981; 1980 figure: £141,950);
Style - His Royal Highness The Prince Philip, The Duke of Edinburgh, KG, KT, OM, GBE, PC *or* The Private Secretary to His Royal Highness etc; address as for HM The Queen

1. WALES, HRH The Prince of; Charles Philip Arthur George; KG (1958), KT (1977), GCB (1975, Great Master), PC (1977); Prince of Wales and Earl of Chester (cr 1958, titles declared inseparable 1398; invested 1969), Duke of Cornwall (in Peerage of E; succeeded 1952, on his mother's ascending the throne, according to charter of 1337, although Dukedom recreated 1399 and 1471) and Duke of Rothesay (S 1398, perhaps recreated 1404, automatic succession of Monarch's eldest s regulated by Act of 1469), Earl of Carrick (S 1368, perhaps recreated 1404, succession regularised 1469) and Baron of Renfrew (S, succession regularised 1469), Lord of the Isles and Great Steward of Scotland; s and h of both HM Queen Elizabeth II and HRH Prince Philip, Duke of Edinburgh; b 14 Nov 1948 (at Buckingham Palace); *Educ* Cheam Sch, Gordonstoun, Geelong G S (Melbourne), Trin Cambridge (Polo half-blue), Univ Coll Aberystwyth; *m* 29 July 1981 (in St Paul's Cathedral), his 7 cous once removed (common descent from 3 Duke of Devonshire) Lady Diana Spencer (b 1 July 1961; *Educ* Riddlesworth Hall, West Heath, Switzerland; *Career* formerly kindergarten teacher; *Style* HRH The Princess of Wales), 3 da of 8 Earl Spencer by his 1 w, now Hon Mrs Shand Kydd; served RAF Coll Cranwell 1971 & RN 1972-78, Cdr 1976; barr Gray's Inn 1974; Personal ADC to HM 1973-; author of *The Old Man of Lochnagar*;
Military appointments: Col-in-Ch: Roy Regt of Wales, Cheshire Regt, Gordon Highlanders, Lord Strathcona's Horse Regt, The Parachute Regt; Col Welsh Gds; Wing Cdr RAF, Hon Air Cdre RAF Brawdy;
Other: Pres Soc of St George's & Descendants of KGs, Cdre Roy Thames Yacht Club, High Steward Roy Borough Windsor & Maidenhead; chm Queen's Silver Jubilee Tst 1978-, Prince

of Wales's Tst, Prince of Wales's Ctee for Wales; Pres United World Colleges, Chllr U of Wales, memb Bd C'wlth Devpt Corpn; *Clubs* White's, Turf, Oxford & Cambridge, RAF, New (Edinburgh), Cornish, Norfolk, Naval, Roy Yacht Sqdn, Island Sailing, Roy London Yacht, Roy Dart Yacht, Cowes Corinthian Yacht;
Civil List: nil; HRH receives half net revenues of Duchy of Cornwall in lieu; the other half is voluntarily remitted to the Exchequer *Style* - His Royal Highness The Prince of Wales, KG, KT, GCB, PC *or* The Private Secretary to His Royal Highness etc; Highgrove House, nr Tetbury, Glos; Kensington Palace, W8

HM QUEEN ELIZABETH THE QUEEN MOTHER; Lady Elizabeth Angela Marguerite, *née* Bowes-Lyon; Lady of Order of the Garter (1936), Lady of Order of the Thistle (1937), CI (1931), GCVO (1937), GBE (1927); 4 da of 14 Earl of Strathmore and Kinghorne, KG, KT, GCVO, TD, JP, DL, by his w Nina, GCVO, herself da of Rev Charles Cavendish-Bentinck (in his turn gs of 3 Duke of Portland, KG, twice PM during George III's reign); b 4 Aug 1900; *m* 1923, HRH The Duke of York, subsequently HM George VI (d 1952); 2 da (HM The Queen, HRH The Princess Margaret);
Military titles and ranks: Col-in-Ch 1 Queen's Roy Dragoon Gds, Queen's Own Hussars, 9/12 Roy Lancers, King's Regt, Roy Anglian Regt, Light Infantry, Black Watch, RAMC; Hon Col Roy Yeo, Gordon Highlanders (TA), London U Contingent OTC; Cmmdt-in-Ch WRNS, WRAC, RAF Centl Flying Sch, WRAF;
Academic distinctions: Hon LLD Queen's U Belfast, St Andrews, Glasgow, Edinburgh, Cape Town, Cambridge, Manchester, Leeds, Columbia (New York), Melbourne, Liverpool, Auckland, Halifax Nova Scotia, Dundee; Hon DCL Oxford; Hon DLitt London, W Indies; Hon LittD Keele; Hon DMus Sheffield; Hon FRCOG, Hon FRCS, Hon FRCP (Edinburgh), FRCP, FRS; Chllr Dundee U, Hon Fellow London U;
Miscellaneous (selection): Cmmdt-in-Ch Nursing Corps & Divs St John Ambulance Bde, Hon memb Lloyd's, Dep Pres Br Red Cross, GCStJ; Lord Warden and Adml Cinque Ports and Constable Dover Castle 1978-; Roy Victorian Chain 1937;
Civil List: £286,000 (as of March 1981; 1980 figure: £253,900);
Recreations National Hunt racing, fishing;
Style - Her Majesty Queen Elizabeth The Queen Mother *or* The Private Secretary to Her Majesty Queen Elizabeth The Queen Mother; Clarence House, SW1; Royal Lodge, Windsor Great Park, Berks; Castle of Mey, Caithness

2. HRH Prince Andrew Albert Christian Edward; CVO (1979); 2 s of HM; b 19 Feb 1960; *Educ* Gordonstoun, Lakefield Coll Ontario, RNC Dartmouth; got his RAF 'Wings' April 1981; *Civil List* £20,000 (as of March 1981; 1980 figure: £20,000); *Recreations* shooting; *Style* His Royal Highness The Prince Andrew, CVO *or* The Private Secretary to His Royal Highness etc; Buckingham Palace, SW1

3. HRH Prince Edward Antony Richard Louis; 3 s of HM; b 10 March 1964; *Educ* Gordonstoun; *Recreations* riding; *Style* - His Royal Highness The Prince Edward *or* The Private Secretary to His Royal Highness etc; Buckingham Palace, SW1

4. HRH Princess Anne Elizabeth Alice Louise; GCVO (1974); only da of HM; b 15 Aug 1950; *Educ* Benenden; *m* 1973, Capt Mark Anthony Peter Phillips, CVO, ADC (P), s of Maj Peter Phillips, MC, late 1 King's Dragoon Gds (himself s of John Phillips, of Oldbury Grange, Nuneaton) by the Major's w Anne (da of Brig John Tiarks and 3 cous of Marchioness of Tavistock); 1 s, 1 da (*see below*);
Military ranks and titles: Col-in-Ch: 14/20 King's Hussars, Worcs and Sherwood Foresters Regiment; Chief Commandant Women's Royal Naval Service, Honorary Air Commodore RAF Lyneham;

Charities and Benevolent Institutions: Pres WRNS Benevolent Tst, Save The Children Fund, Roy Sch for Daughters of Offrs of RN and RM, Riding for Disabled Assoc, Jersey Wildlife Tst, Roy Corps of Signals Assoc, Roy Corps of Signals Inst, Breast Cancer Res Tst, Horse of the Year Ball, Benenden Ball, Save the Children Fund Action Gp; Cmmdt-in-Ch St John Ambulance and Nursing Cadets; Life Memb Roy Br Legion Women's Section, Hon Life Memb RNVR Offrs' Assoc, Hon Memb Br Equine Veterinary Assoc;
Miscellaneous (selection): Pres BAFTA, Windsor Horse Trials; Patron Army & RA Hunter Trials, Gloucester & N Avon Fedn of Young Farmers' Clubs; V-Patron Br Show Jumping Assoc, Freedom City of London 1976, Chllr London U 1981-;
Civil List: £100,000 (as of March 1981; 1980 figure: £88,450);
Style - Her Royal Highness The Princess Anne, Mrs Mark Phillips, GCVO *or* The Private Secretary to Her Royal Highness etc; Gatcombe Park, Cirencester, Glos

5. **PHILLIPS, Peter Mark Andrew**; s of HRH The Princess Anne by Capt Mark Phillips, CVO; b 15 Nov 1977; *Style* - Peter Phillips

6. **PHILLIPS, Zara Anne Elizabeth**; da of HRH The Princess Anne by Capt Mark Phillips, CVO; b 15 May 1981 (christened 27 July 1981; sponsors: Prince Andrew, Countess of Lichfield, Mrs Jackie Stewart, Lt-Col Andrew Parker-Bowles, Hugh Thomas); the name Zara appears to be either of Hebrew or Arabic origin (the original suggestion that it was Greek, made at the time the choice of forename was announced, remained unsubstantiated) and to mean "dawning" or "the morning star"; *Style* - Miss Zara Phillips

7. **SNOWDON, HRH Princess Margaret, Countess of; Margaret Rose**; CI (1947), GCVO (1953); yr da of His late Majesty George VI by Queen Elizabeth The Queen Mother; b 21 Aug 1930 (at Glamis Castle); *Educ* privately; *m* 1960 (in Westminster Abbey, m dis 1978), 1 Earl of Snowdon, *qv*; 1 s (Viscount Linley), 1 da (Lady Sarah Armstrong-Jones);
Military ranks and titles: Col-in-Ch: Roy Highland Fusiliers, 15/19 King's Roy Hussars, Princess Louise Fusiliers; Dep Col-in-Ch Roy Anglian Regt; Hon Air Cdre RAF Coningsby;
Academic distinctions: Chllr Keele U; Hon DMus London, Hon LLD Cambridge, Hon DLitt Keele, Hon FRIBA, Hon FRSM, Hon FRCS, Hon FRCOG, Hon Life FZS;
Charities and Benevolent Institutions: Pres: Barnardo's, Scottish Children's League, Victoria League, Sunshine Homes and Schs for Blind Children (RNIB), NSPCC, Dockland Settlements, Friends of the Elderly and Gentlefolks Help, Invalid Children's Aid Assoc (also Chm Cncl), Horder Centres for Arthritics, Girl Guides Assoc, Chorleywood Coll for Girls with Little or No Sight; Jt-Pres Lowland Bde Club; Patron-in-Ch Barristers' Benevolent Assoc, Bristol Roy Workshops for Blind, Br Sailors' Soc Guild, Friends of Southwark Cathedral, Friends of St John's, Mary Hare G S for the Deaf, Princess Margaret Rose Hosp (Edinburgh), Services Kinema Corpn, Roy Coll Nursing and Nat Cncl Nurses of UK, The Mathilda and Terence Kennedy Inst of Rheumatology, St Margaret's Chapel Guild Edinburgh Castle, Scottish Assoc Youth Clubs, Suffolk Regimental Assoc, Union of Schs for Soc Serv, Architects' Benevolent Assoc, Tenovus (Inst Cancer Research), Migraine Tst, Zebra Tst, St Pancras Housing Assoc in Camden; temp Patron Roy Caledonian Ball 1956-; Grand Pres St John Ambulance Assoc & Bde; Life Memb Br Legion Women's Section, Hon Memb Coventry Cathedral Ten Year Devpt Plan;
Miscellaneous (selection): Pres: English Folk Dance and Song Assoc, Sadlers Wells Fndn, Roy Ballet, Roy Ag Soc of England 1966; Patron-in-Ch: English Harbour Repair Fund, Light Industry Club, Scottish Community Drama Association, London University Choir, London Festival Ballet; CStJ; Honorary Membership: Automobile Association, Royal Automobile Club, Sealyham Terrier Breeders' Association; Freedom City of London 1966; Honorary Member and Patron of Grand Antiquity Society of Glasgow;
Civil List: £98,000 (as of March 1981; 1980 figure: £87,750);

Style Her Royal Highness The Princess Margaret, Countess of Snowdon, CI, GCVO *or* The Private Secretary to Her Royal Higness etc; Kensington Palace, W8

8. LINLEY, Viscount; David Albert Charles Armstrong-Jones; s and h of 1 Earl of Snowdon by his 1 w, HRH The Princess Margaret; b 3 Nov 1961; *Educ* Ashdown House, Bedales; *Style* Viscount Linley

9. ARMSTRONG-JONES, Lady Sarah Frances Elizabeth; da of HRH Princess Margaret by her former husb 1 Earl of Snowdon; b 1 May 1964; *Educ* Ashdown House, Bedales; *Style* Lady Sarah Armstrong-Jones; Kensington Palace, W8

10. GLOUCESTER, HRH 2 Duke of (UK 1928); Prince Richard Alexander Walter George; GCVO (1974); also Earl of Ulster and Baron Culloden (both UK 1928); 2 (but only surviving) s of late HRH Prince Henry, 1 Duke of Gloucester (d 1974, himself 3 s of George V), by his w HRH Princess Alice, Duchess of Gloucester, *qv*; b 26 Aug 1944; *Educ* Eton, Magdalene Cambridge; *m* 1972, Birgitte Eva (da of Asger Preben Wissing Henriksen, of Odense, Denmark; b 20 June 1946, Odense; *Educ* Odense, Brillantmont Lausanne, a Cambridge Language Sch, Niels Brock Commercial Coll Copenhagen, a London Language Coll; formerly sec Royal Danish Embassy London; adopted surname van Deurs prior to marriage; DStJ, Col-in-Ch Roy Army Educnl Corps, Pres London Regn WRVS, Roy Alexander & Albert Sch, Cambridge House; *Style* Her Royal Highness The Princess Richard, Duchess of Gloucester *or* The Private Secretary to Her Royal Highness Princess Richard etc); *Heir* s, Earl of Ulster;
Career: RIBA, FSA, KStJ; Pres Inst Advanced Motorists 1976-, Cancer Res Campaign 1973-, Nat Assoc Boys' Clubs 1974-, Br Consultants Bureau 1978-, V-Pres Br Leprosy Relief Assoc 1971-; Patron ASH 1974-, Victorian Soc 1976-, Bulldog Manpower Servs 1976-; Ranger Epping Forest 1975-, Queen's Tstee Br Museum 1973-, Pres E England Ag Soc 1979-, FRSA; Grand Prior Order of St John of Jerusalem 1975-;
Military titles and rank: Col-in-Ch: Gloucestershire Regt, Roy Pioneer Corps; Hon Col Roy Monmouthshire RE (Militia);
Civil List: £78,000 (as of March 1981; 1980 figure: £70,500);
Clubs Bath, Cavalry, Buck's, Roy Ulster Yacht;
Style - His Royal Highness The Duke of Gloucester, GCVO *or* The Private Secretary to His Royal Highness etc; Kensington Palace, W8; Barnwell Manor, Peterborough

11. ULSTER, Earl of; Alexander Patrick Gregers Richard Windsor; s and h of 2 Duke of Gloucester GCVO; b 24 Oct 1974; *Style* - Earl of Ulster;

12. WINDSOR, Lady Davina Elizabeth Alice Benedikte; er da of 2 Duke of Gloucester GCVO; b 19 Nov 1977; *Style* - Lady Davina Windsor

13. WINDSOR, Lady Rose Victoria Birgitte Louise; 2 da of 2 Duke of Gloucester GCVO; b 1 March 1980; *Style* - Lady Rose Windsor

GLOUCESTER, HRH Princess Alice, Duchess of; Lady Alice Christabel *née* Montagu Douglas Scott; GCB (1975), CI (1937), GCVO (1948), GBE (1937); 3 da of 7 Duke of Buccleuch and Queensberry, KT, GCVO, JP, by his wife Lady Margaret Alice, *née* Bridgeman (2 daughter of 4 Earl of Bradford by his wife, Lady Ida Frances Annabella Lumley, DGStJ, Extra Lady of the Bedchamber to Her late Majesty Queen Mary and 2 daughter of 9 Earl of Scarbrough); b 25 Dec 1901; *Educ* St James's School West Malvern, Paris; *m* 1935, HRH Prince Henry, 1 Duke of Gloucester, KG, KT, KP, GCB, GCMG, GCVO, PC, (d 1974, himself 3 s of His late Majesty King George V); 2 s (Prince William, killed in an aeroplane accident 1972; HRH Prince Richard, 2 Duke of Gloucester, GCVO);

Military titles and ranks: Air Marshal WRAF; Col-in-Ch: KOSB, Roy Hussars, RCT; Dep Col-in-Ch Roy Anglian Regt; memb Cncl Br Red Cross Soc; Dep CIC Nursing Corps & Divs St John Ambulance Bde;
Miscellaneous: GCStJ; Freedom: City of Edinburgh, City of Gloucester, City of Belfast;
Civil List: £40,000 (as of March 1981; 1980 figure: £35,000);
Style - Her Royal Highness Princess Alice, Duchess of Gloucester, GCB, CI, GCVO, GBE *or* The Private Secretary to Her Royal Highness etc; 1 Kensington Palace, W8; Barnwell Manor, Peterborough

14. KENT, HRH 2 Duke of; Edward George Nicholas Paul Patrick Windsor; GCMG (1967), GCVO (1960); also Earl of St Andrews and Baron Downpatrick (both UK 1934); er s of HRH 1 Duke of Kent, KG, KT, GCMG, GCVO, PC (4 s of HM George V; k active serv 1942), by his w HRH Princess Marina, CI, GCVO, GBE (d 1968, yst da of HRH late Prince Nicholas of Greece and 1 cous to HRH Prince Philip, Duke of Edinburgh); b 9 Oct 1935 (at 3 Belgrave sq, London); *Educ* Eton, Le Rosey Switzerland, Sandhurst; *m* 1961, Katharine Lucy Mary, GCVO (1977), only da of late Sir William Worsley, 4 Bt (*see* Sir Marcus Worsley, 5 Bt, for ancestry; b 22 Feb 1933; *Educ* in Yorks, finishing sch Oxford; Controller-Cmmdt WRAC (Hon Maj-Gen), Col-in-Ch Army Catering Corps, Hon Col Yorks Volunteers TAVR; Chllr Leeds U; *Style* Her Royal Highness The Duchess of Kent GCVO *or* The Private Secretary to Her Royal Highness etc); 2 s (Earl of St Andrews, Lord Nicholas Windsor), 1 da (Lady Helen Windsor);
Military rank and titles: Lt-Col (ret) Roy Scots Dragoon Gds; Col-in-Ch: Roy Regt of Fusiliers, Devonshire & Dorset Regt; Col Scots Gds, GSO II E Cmmd 1966-68, Coy Instructor Sandhurst 1968-70, Cmmd C Sqdn Roy Scots Greys 1970-71;
Miscellaneous: Hon DCL Durham 1961; Grand Master Utd Grand Lodge Freemasons England & Grand Master Order St Michael & St George; Pres: Wellington Coll, C'wlth War Graves Cmmn, Scout Assoc; V-Chm Br Overseas Tde Bd; Chllr Surrey U; Pres Technician Educn Cncl 1981-, dir BICC 1981-;
Civil List: £106,000 (as of March 1981; 1980 figure: £94,500);
Clubs White's, St James's, Boodle's, Travellers', Buck's, Naval and Military, Cavalry, RAF, RAC, Union, New (Edinburgh), Roy Thames Yacht, Br Racing Drivers;
Style - His Royal Highness The Duke of Kent, GCMG, GCVO *or* The Private Secretary to His Royal Highness etc; York House, SW1; Anmer Hall, Kings Lynn, Norfolk

15. ST ANDREWS, Earl of; George Philip Nicholas Windsor; er s and h of HRH 2 Duke of Kent GCMG GCVO; b 26 June 1962 (at Coppins, Iver, Bucks); *Educ* Eton End Datchet, Heatherdown Ascot, Eton; *Style* - Earl of St Andrews

16. WINDSOR, Lord Nicholas Charles Edward Jonathan; 2 s of HRH 2 Duke of Kent GCMG GCVO; b 25 July 1970 (at Coppins); Page to HRH Princess of Wales at her m 1981 *Style* - Lord Nicholas Windsor

17. WINDSOR, Lady Helen Marina Lucy; da of HRH 2 Duke of Kent GCMG GCVO; b 28 April 1964 (Coppins); *Educ* Eton End Datchet, St Paul's Prep Sch London; *Style* - Lady Helen Windsor

KENT, HRH Prince Michael (George Charles Franklin) of; 2 s of HRH 1 Duke of Kent (k on active serv 1942); b 4 July 1942 (Coppins; sponsor: late Franklin D Roosevelt, sometime Pres USA); *Educ* Eton, Sandhurst; *m* 1978, as her 2 husb, Baroness Marie Christine, da of Baron Günther Hubertus von Reibnitz (and formerly w of Tom (Thomas), yr bro of Sir Peter Troubridge, 6 Bt); 1 s (Lord Frederick Windsor), 1 da (Lady Ella Windsor); *Career* Maj Roy Hussars to 1981, ret; For Attaché Liaison Sec MOD 1968-70, UN Force Cyprus 1971, Def Intelligence Serv 1974-76, Army Recruiting Directorate 1976-78, GSO Def Intelligence Staff

1978-81;
Miscellaneous: Pres Br Bobsleigh Assoc, Soc Genealogists, Inst Motor Industry; C'wlth Pres Roy Lifesaving Soc; memb RAC Br Motor Sports Cncl, Br Olympic Assoc, HAC;
Recreations riding, squash, music, motorcycling, windsurfing; *Club* Roy Yacht Sqdn (Hon Memb);
Style - His Royal Highness Prince Michael of Kent *or* The Private Secretary to His Royal Highness etc; Kensington Palace, W8; Nether Lypiatt Manor, Stroud, Glos

18. WINDSOR, Lord Frederick Michael George David Louis; only s of HRH Prince Michael of Kent; b 6 April 1979; *Style* - Lord Frederick Windsor

19. WINDSOR, Lady Ella (Gabriella) Marina Alexandra Ophelia; only da of HRH Prince Michael of Kent; b 23 April 1981 (godparents: King Constantine of the Hellenes, Prince Hugo Windisch-Graetz, Miss Marina Ogilvy, Marchioness of Douro, Lady Elizabeth Shakerley); *Style* - Lady Ella Windsor

20. HRH Princess Alexandra (Helen Elizabeth Olga Christabel, *née* Windsor); GCVO (1960); da of HRH 1 Duke of Kent (k on active serv 1942); b 25 Dec 1936 (3 Belgrave sq, London); *Educ* Heathfield, Paris; *m* 1963 (Westminster Abbey), Hon Angus Ogilvy, 2 s of 12 Earl of Airlie, KT, GCVO, MC; 1 s (James), 1 da (Marina);
Military rank and titles: Col-in-Ch 17/21 Lancers, King's Own Border Regt, Dep Col-in-Ch LI, Dep Hon Col Roy Yeo TAVR, Air Ch Cmmdt Princess Mary's RAF Nursing Serv, Hon Cmmdt Gen Roy Hong Kong Police Force and Roy Hong Kong Aux Police Force;
Miscellaneous: Pres Roy C'wlth Soc for Blind, Children's Country Holidays Fund, Queen Alexandra's House Assoc, Star & Garter Home, Alexandra Day, Br Sch at Rome, Roy Humane Soc, V-Pres Br Red Cross Soc;
Civil List: £101,000 (as of March 1981; 1980 figure: £89,800);
Style - Her Royal Highness Princess Alexandra, the Hon Mrs Angus Ogilvy, GCVO *or* The Private Secretary to Her Royal Highness etc; Thatched House Lodge, Richmond Park, Surrey; (Office) 22 Friary Court, St James's Palace, SW1

21. OGILVY, James Robert Bruce; only s of HRH Princess Alexandra by her husb Hon Angus Ogilvy; b 29 Feb 1964 (at Thatched House Lodge); *Style* - James Ogilvy Esq

22. OGILVY, Marina Victoria Alexandra; only da of HRH Princess Alexandra by her husb Hon Angus Ogilvy; b 31 July 1966 (at Thatched House Lodge); *Style* - Miss Marina Ogilvy

WINDSOR, Duchess of; (Bessie) Wallis ; da of Teackle Wallis Warfield (d 1896), of Baltimore Md, by his w Alice (da of William Montague, of Virginia); b 19 June 1896, Monterey Pa; *m* 1, 1916 (m dis 1927), Lt Earl Spencer, Jr (USN), of Chicago; m 2, 1928, as his 2 w, Ernest Simpson (m dis 1936), of New York; m 3, 1937, HRH The Duke of Windsor, KG (d 1972, eldest s and originally h of HM George V); served WW II with French Red Cross; First Woman Govr American Hosp Paris 1972; *Style* - Her Grace The Duchess of Windsor; 4 Route du Champ d'Entrainement, Bois de Boulogne, Paris XVI, France

CLUBS REFERRED TO IN THE WORK,

WITH THE ADDRESSES OF THE CLUB HOUSES.

Ladies' Clubs are marked *.

All England Lawn Tennis.—Wimbledon.
Alpine.—74, South Audley Street, W.1.
American.—95, Piccadilly, W.1.
Army and Navy.—36, Pall Mall, S.W.1.
Arts.—40, Dover Street, W.1.
Arts Theatre—6/7 Great Newport Street, W.C.2.
Athenæum.—107, Pall Mall, S.W.1.
Authors'.—40, Dover St., W.1.

Bath.—43, Brook Street, W.1.
Beefsteak.—9, Irving Street, W.C.2.
Boodle's.—28, St. James's Street, S.W.1.
Brooks's.—60, St. James's Street, S.W.1.
Buck's.—18, Clifford Street, W.1.

Caledonian.—9, Halkin St., S.W.1.
Caledonian.—32, Abercromby Pl., Edinburgh.
Canning.—42, Half Moon St., W.1.
Carlton.—69, St. James's Street, S.W.1.
Cavalry and Guards'.—127, Piccadilly, W.1.
Calloner.—59, Pont St., S.W.1.
City Livery.—Sion College, Victoria Embankment, E.C.4.
City of London.—King William St. House, Arthur St., E.C.4.
City University.—50, Cornhill, E.C.3.
Civil Service.—13, Great Scotland Yard, S.W.1.
Constitutional.—c/o The Naval & Military Club, 94, Piccadilly, W.1.
Crockford's.—16, Carlton House Terrace, S.W.1.

East India, Devonshire, Sports and Public Schools.—16, St. James's Square, SW1Y 4LH.
* *Empress.*—28, Berkeley Sq., W.1.
English Speaking Union.—37, Charles St., W.1.
Europe House.—1, Whitehall Place, SW1A 2HA.

Farmers'.—3 Whitehall Court, S.W.1.
Flyfishers'.—43, Brook St., W.1.

Garrick.—15, Garrick Street, W.C.2.
Gresham.—15, Abchurch Lane, E.C.4.

Hibernian United Service.—8, St. Stephen's Green North, Dublin.
Highland.—39, High St., Inverness.
Hurlingham.—Ranelagh Gdns, S.W.6.

Jockey.—High Street, Newmarket.

Kildare Street and University, 17 St. Stephen Green, Dublin 2.

* *Ladies' Caledonian.*—29, Queensferry St., 2.
* *Ladies' V.A.D.*—44, Great Cumberland Place, W.1.
Lansdowne.—9, Fitzmaurice Place, Berkeley Sq., W.1.
Leander.—Henley-on-Thames, and Putney, S.W

Manchester.—50, Spring Gardens, Manchester.
Marylebone Cricket Club (MCC).—St. John's Wood, NW8.

National.—c/o Carlton Club.
National Liberal.—Whitehall Place, S.W.1.
Naval.—38, Hill Street, W.1.
Naval and Military.—94, Piccadilly, W.1.
New.—86, Princes Street, Edinburgh.

Oriental.—Stratford House, Stratford Place, W.1.
Overseas.—Overseas House, Park Place, St. James's Street, S.W.1.

Phyllis Court.—Henley-on-Thames.
Portland.—42, Half Moon St., W1.
Pratt's.—14, Park Place, St. James's, S.W.1.
Press.—76, Shoe Lane, EC4.
Puffin's.—c/o The Edinburgh Wine Bar, 110 Hanover St., Edinburgh.

Queen's.—Palliser Road, W. Kensington, W.14.

Reform.—104, Pall Mall, S.W.1.
Roehampton.—Roehampton Lane, S.W.15.
Royal Air Force.—128, Piccadilly, W.1.
Royal Air Force Reserve.—38 Hill St., W.1.
Royal Air Force Yacht.—Hamble, Southampton.
Royal and Ancient.—St. Andrews.
Royal Automobile.—89, Pall Mall, S.W.1.
Royal Burnham Yacht—Burnham-on-Crouch.
Royal Channel Islands Yacht.—Jersey.
Royal Cinque Ports Yacht.—Waterloo Cres., Dover.
Royal Commonwealth Society.—18, Northumberland Avenue, W.C.2.
Royal Corinthian Yacht.—Burnham-on-Crouch, Essex.
Royal Dorset Yacht.—6, Charlotte Row, Weymouth.
Royal Irish Automobile.—55, South Mall, Dublin.
Royal Lymington Yacht.—Bath Rd., Lymington, Hants'
Royal Munster Yacht.—Crosshaven, co. Cork.
Royal Naval and Royal Albert Yacht.—Pembroke Road, Portsmouth.
R.N.V.R.—Now the Naval Club.
Royal Ocean Racing.—20, St. James's Place, S.W.1.
Royal Over Seas League.—Over Seas House, Park Place, St. James's, S.W.1.
Royal Scottish Automobile.—11, Blythswood Sq., Glasgow.
Royal Southern Yacht.—Hamble, Southampton.
Royal Thames Yacht.—60, Knightsbridge, S.W.1.
Royal Torbay Yacht.—Torquay.
Royal Ulster Yacht.—Bangor, co. Down.
Royal Victoria Yacht.—91, Fishbourne Lane, Fishbourne, Isle of Wight.
Royal Western Yacht.—The Hoe, Plymouth.
Royal Yacht Squadron.—Cowes, Isle of Wight.

St. James'.—7, Charlotte St., Manchester.
St. John House.—50, Eaton Place, S.W.1.
St. Stephen's.—34, Queen Anne's Gate, S.W.1.
Savage.—9, Fitzmaurice Place, Berkeley Square, W.1.
Saville.—69, Brook Street, W.1.
Sesame, Pioneer and Lyceum.—49, Grosvenor Street, W.1.
Ski Club of Great Britain.—118, Eaton Sq., S.W.1.
Special Forces.—8, Herbert Cres., S.W.1.
Stephen's Green.—9, St. Stephen's Green North, Dublin.

Travellers'.—108, Pall Mall, S.W.1.
Turf.—5, Carlton House Terr., S.W.1.

Ulster.—48, High St., Belfast.
Ulster Reform.—4, Royal Avenue, Belfast.
* *United Nursing Services.*—40, South Street, W.1.
United Service and Royal Aero.—116, Pall Mall, S.W.1.
United Sports.—4, Whitehall Court, S.W.1.
United Oxford and Cambridge University.—71–7, Pall Mall, S.W.1.
* *University Women's.*—2, Audley Sq., South Audley St., W.1.

**V.A.D.*.—44, Great Cumberland Place, W.1.
Victoria League.—38, Chesham Place, S.W.1.

West Indian.—4, Whitehall Court, S.W.1.
Western.—32, Royal Exch. Sq., G1.
White's.—27, St. James's Street, S.W.1.

Yorkshire.—17, Museum St., York.

Finance, Investment & Insurance

Advertisers' Index overleaf

Advertisers' Index

If you're looking for an investment which consistently outpaces inflation, look to Britain's timber resources. Today you'd be hard pressed to find a better place to put your money.
The world's timber supplies are being rapidly depleted and substantial price increases are forecast.
The tax incentives, particularly with regard to income and capital transfer, make it a most attractive asset. Fountain Forestry has many years experience in this specialised field and the knowledge to handle every aspect, including land purchases and forest management. As part of Stewart Wrightson, a publicly quoted group, it enjoys the confidence of the City. In addition to the nationwide network of professional forest management teams it has strong overseas connections and an operating management company in the U.S.A. Fountain Forestry clients have enjoyed returns substantially above inflation since 1957.
Isn't it time you moved into this prosperous avenue? If you're interested in knowing more facts, phone Brian Howell on 01-623 7511. It could be the most profitable move you make.
MOVE INTO THIS PROSPEROUS AVENUE.

Florida
discover the suncoast
We've located our select communities in the heart of Florida's Best Coast. From Port Richey south to Clearwater, from Tarpon Springs west to Tampa, we've selected the most desirable locations available for our Minieri Communities.
Our list of desirable addresses begins with Regency Park U.S.A., our most successful and largest community. Ideally located in Port Richey, Regency Park is close to all shopping and offers fun-filled days drenched in a sunny Florida lifestyle. Dove Hollow and Orchid Lake are two of our Prestige lifestyle communities, offering spacious homes full of custom features. Country Villas South, in Clearwater, was selected specifically for its central location. And our newest address, The Cove, is situated in the fast growing metropolitan Tampa market. Close to commerce and country, The Cove is well on its way to the same kind of popular reception we've enjoyed in the past.
We've got a lifestyle and location to fit your needs, from retirement retreat to a prestigious executive home. Minieri Communities . . . more than an address, they're a way of life.
Minieri Communities, George Street West, Luton, Beds. LU1 2BT
Tel. Luton (0582) 412301 (10 lines) Evenings (05257) 3082
Building a Florida Tradition Since 1959
Minieri
COMMUNITIES

Healey & Baker
Your link with the property market in the City of London
When dealing in the international property market the vital expertise and understanding required can only come from a local presence.
Qualified surveyors at Healey & Baker, 118 Old Broad St., EC2 are able to offer a wide range of professional services with a complete understanding of The City's commercial property market.
HB
Healey & Baker
Established 1820 in London
118 Old Broad Street, London EC2N 1AR
Telephone 01-628 4361
Also at 29 St. George Street, Hanover Square, London W1A 3BG
Amsterdam Brussels Glasgow Jersey New York Paris

Executive World

Advertisers' Index overleaf

Advertisers' Index

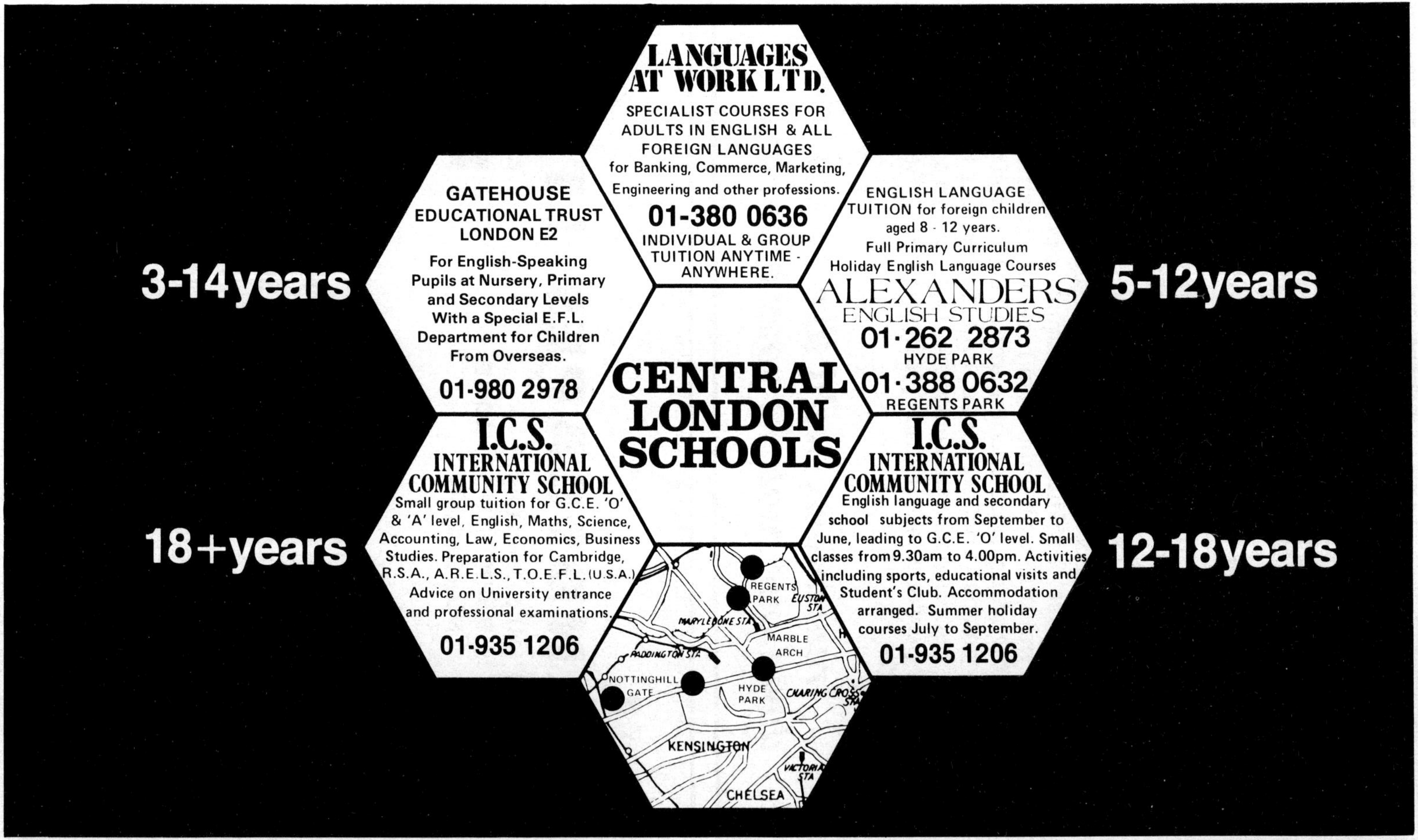
3-14years
5-12years
18+years
12-18years
LANGUAGES AT WORK LTD.
SPECIALIST COURSES FOR ADULTS IN ENGLISH & ALL FOREIGN LANGUAGES
for Banking, Commerce, Marketing, Engineering and other professions.
01-380 0636
INDIVIDUAL & GROUP TUITION ANYTIME - ANYWHERE.
GATEHOUSE EDUCATIONAL TRUST LONDON E2
For English-Speaking Pupils at Nursery, Primary and Secondary Levels With a Special E.F.L. Department for Children From Overseas.
01-980 2978
ENGLISH LANGUAGE TUITION for foreign children aged 8 - 12 years.
Full Primary Curriculum
Holiday English Language Courses
ALEXANDERS ENGLISH STUDIES
01·262 2873
HYDE PARK
01·388 0632
REGENTS PARK
CENTRAL LONDON SCHOOLS
I.C.S. INTERNATIONAL COMMUNITY SCHOOL
Small group tuition for G.C.E. 'O' & 'A' level, English, Maths, Science, Accounting, Law, Economics, Business Studies. Preparation for Cambridge, R.S.A., A.R.E.L.S., T.O.E.F.L. (U.S.A.) Advice on University entrance and professional examinations.
01-935 1206
I.C.S. INTERNATIONAL COMMUNITY SCHOOL
English language and secondary school subjects from September to June, leading to G.C.E. 'O' level. Small classes from 9.30am to 4.00pm. Activities including sports, educational visits and Student's Club. Accommodation arranged. Summer holiday courses July to September.
01-935 1206
REGENTS PARK
EUSTON STA
MARYLEBONE STA
MARBLE ARCH
PADDINGTON STA
NOTTINGHILL GATE
HYDE PARK
CHARING CROSS
KENSINGTON
VICTORIA STA
CHELSEA

Their future is your choice.

Some of the finest American Universities have accepted four or more ASL graduates over the past four years, including:- Brown, Bucknell, Cornell, Harvard, Purdue, Texas A. & M., Tufts, Tulane, Vanderbilt, Yale, University of California – Berkeley, University of Michigan, University of Notre Dame, University of Texas, Queens University, Ontario, Canada.

ASL offers a complete, high quality American curriculum to 1600 students. It includes extensive art, music, drama and sports programs as well as a wide range of extracurricular activities.

The American School in London

THE OLDEST ESTABLISHED AMERICAN SCHOOL IN THE UNITED KINGDOM

It also holds American accreditation from the Middle States Association, awarded in 1976 after a rigorous evaluation by a team of American educators.

The school is an independent, non profit making educational trust administered by a Board of Trustees.

For our brochure or further information, please contact:
The American School in London,
2-8 Loudoun Rd,
London NW8 0NP.
Telephone: 01-722 0101.
Cables: Amschool London NW8.

Elm Farm Health & Beauty Clinic

Fulbrook, Burford, Oxfordshire

Set in the beautiful Cotswolds, our sophisticated Clinic offers a comprehensive range of treatments by highly qualified and experienced Staff.

Facials,
Eyelash Tinting,
Depilatory Wax, Electrolysis
Manicure, Pedicure,
Suntan,
Separate Hair Salon,

Sauna, Steam Bath
Massage,
Slimming Courses, Kwik Slim,
Wax Bath,
Osteopathy,
Relaxation Lounge.

TOP-TO-TOE all-day treatment
Free Consultations

For Brochure and Appointments: Tel: BURFORD 3387

PRIVATE CAR PARK *Residential Arrangements Available*

Member of British Association of Beauty Therapy and Cosmetology

Hotels, Restaurants Food & Drink

Advertisers' Index overleaf

Advertisers' Index

COME AND ENJOY A MEAL AT

The Old School House Restaurant

Ockley, Surrey *(South of Dorking on A29, Stane Street)*

Open for Lunch: Tuesday — Sunday *(Table d'Hote and a la Carte)*
Sunday: Traditional Sunday Lunch: Choice of 5 Roasts
Dinner: extensive a la Carte Menu only
★*Special Parties and Business Lunches*★ also catered for
For Reservations: Tel: Oakwood Hill 430

BARBON INN

Nestling between the Lakes and North Dales

This early 17th Century coaching inn is situated in delightful countryside, near Kirkby Lonsdale, Cumbria, only 20 minutes from the M6. Enjoying quiet and seclusion it is ideally placed for visits to the Lakes and North Yorkshire or the Scottish Borders. The open log fires in all public rooms ensure, even in cold weather a warm welcome and enhance the friendly atmosphere.

The Barbon Inn enjoys a fine reputation for its cuisine and now under the supervision of the Whitlock Family the Barbon is recommended by Egon Ronay, Ashley Courtnay, Signpost and is AA – RAC 2 star rated.

Bargain breaks of a minimum of two nights are available from mid-October and for further details and current tariff contact Mr Keith Whitlock, Barbon 233.

300 years of catering excellence will guarantee success at your next major function.

Whatever you're planning — a conference or banquet; major product launch or cocktail party; sophisticated presentation or business luncheon — turn to the unequalled expertise and service of Ring and Brymer for catering to perfection.

Ring and Brymer can offer a number of outstanding venues, including the rugged HMS Belfast, the historic City livery halls or tranquil Kempton Manor. Alternatively, we can cater at any location of your choice or at your own premises.

With care and attention to detail, Ring and Brymer provide everything you may require, leaving you free to get on with your business in the sure knowledge that the organisation of your function is in the hands of the experts.

Call Nikky Coombs on 01-377 2552 for further details or information regarding your function catering.

LONDON OFFICE
30/32 Sun Street, London EC2
Telephone: 01-377 2552

Ring and Brymer
CATERERS SINCE 1690

FOUR SEASONS RESTAURANT

Avening near Tetbury Gloucestershire

A warm welcome awaits you at our family run restaurant nestled in the Cotswold village of Avening, situated near Minchinhampton, Nailsworth and Tetbury.

Our menu is completely changed every two weeks and we use only fresh seasonal ingredients.

FOR RESERVATIONS PLEASE TELEPHONE
NAILSWORTH (045-383) 3070

We are also able to cater for private parties on request

THE
CHURCHILL

★★★★★

- 489 Luxury rooms and suites, fully air-conditioned, colour T.V. direct dial telephones and 24 hour full Room Service
- The Number 10 Restaurant with International Cuisine
- The Greenery Coffee Shop
- The Lounge, for Refreshments and Afternoon tea
- The Churchill Bar
- Private Banqueting and meeting facilities for 10 to 200 persons

The Churchill,
Portman Square, London, W.1., England.
Telephone: 01-486 5800. Telex: 264831.

A Loews Hotel

A Choice of Excellence

With a discreet air of elegance and sumptuous furnishings the Montcalm offers . . .

- 100 Luxury rooms, 12 duplex suites and 3 Penthouse suites all air-conditioned with colour T.V. direct dial telephone and 24 hour Room Service
- La Varenne Restaurant with International Cuisine
- The Montcalm Lounge Bar

The Montcalm,
Great Cumberland Place,
London, W.1., England.
Telephone: 01-402 4288. Telex: 28710.

A Loews Hotel

THE
MONTCALM

★★★★★

Relax in the luxurious comfort of

BUCKLAND-TOUT-SAINTS HOTEL

Nr. Kingsbridge, S. Devon. England's Best Weather Area

Set in six acres of glorious rolling park land. Buckland is one of the finest Queen Anne Country House Hotels in Britain and the ideal tranquil centre to enjoy beautiful South Devon. Famed for its cuisine, comprehensive wine list and personal service, the hotel is privately owned and managed by the Shephard family.

All rooms have private baths, G.P.O. telephones and some have colour TV. For the Honeymoon or Second Honeymoon the sumptuous Regency Room is available with its canopied four poster.

Best Western

for free colour brochure telephone Mine Host
Victor Shephard (0548) 3055 or write
BUCKLAND-TOUT-SAINTS HOTEL
Nr. KINGSBRIDGE S. DEVON TQ7 2DS

AA ★★ Red Star Hotel

RAC ★★★

Plough & Harrow Hotel

From a drawing on stone by J. Brandard and presented to Lord Calthorpe in 1859.

French Cuisine • 41 Luxury Bedrooms • Conference Facilities
Private Car Parking • 1 Mile City Centre
General Manager: Thomas Perez
Hagley Road, Edgbaston, Birmingham, B16 8LS, England.
Telephone: (021) 454 4111. Telex No. 338074 CREST G.

PENGETHLEY

COUNTRY HOUSE HOTEL AND RESTAURANT

Come and experience a stay at this elegantly restored Georgian Country House. Let us look after you while you sample our award winning Restaurant and take advantage of our 7 acres of attractively landscaped gardens and heated outdoor swimming pool.

Explore the natural beauty and history of Herefordshire or walk in the Malvern Hills and Black Mountains. We are also an ideal centre for fishing, riding and golf (16 courses nearby) as well as other activity holidays.

Let us help you on HAREWOOD END (098987) 211

PENGETHLEY HOTEL & RESTAURANT
NR ROSS-ON-WYE, HEREFORDSHIRE HR9 6LL

*AA *** RAC, Egon Ronay, Ashley Courtenay*
BTA Commended Country House Hotel

Harbour thoughts of Cornwall

An idyllic holiday at any time of the year with the romance of yesteryear and the comforts of today

- 40 bedrooms with bath or shower
- Panoramic harbour views
- Superb food and wine

Write for brochure and tariff to

Greenbank Hotel

Harbourside, Falmouth TR11 2ST Tel: (0326) 312440 Telex 45240

MIDDLE TAR As defined in H.M. Government Tables.
NGER: H.M. Government Health Departments' WARNING:
THINK FIRST – MOST DOCTORS DON'T SMOKE

The North Lodge
Hotel & Restaurant

2 North Road The Park Nottingham
Tel (0602) 45215

North Lodge is a discretely located Hotel situated in the centre of Nottingham on the edge of the original Castle Park with easy access from the M1 (junction 25) and approximately 20 minutes from East Midlands Airport.

We have superbly appointed bedrooms each having private bathroom/shower suites, colour T.V., GPO telephone together with full room service.

Sauna, solarium and heated outdoor swimming pool.

Conference suites, Exhibition and Meeting rooms, and interview rooms, with most types of video/slide/projection cine equipment.

Private car park & garages.

THE RESTAURANT (Open to Non-Residents)

We invite you to step into the luxury and comfort of our lounge where you may enjoy a cocktail or aperitif whilst you choose from our exciting international à la carte menu, featuring delightful new dishes, as well as the best of your old favourites. You will be delighted with the warmth and excellence of the service in the restaurant, complimenting the high standard of the food, relaxing afterwards with your friends over coffee and Liquers.

CROWN HOTEL

The Crown Hotel is located in the centre of Boroughbridge, only one mile from the A1 and ideally situated for touring the Yorkshire Dales, Teeside and the North East, or for visiting the historic towns of York, Harrogate, Ripon and Thirsk.

Boroughbridge is also geographically suited for racing enthusiasts and guests are within easy reach of eight Racecourses – at Ripon, Thirsk, Wetherby, York, Catterick, Doncaster, Pontefract and Redcar.

In addition the immediate area offers a variety of sporting activities (including golf, shooting, riding and fishing) and there are many major annual events held within close proximity.

The hotel itself caters especially for those who seek excellence in cuisine and comfort, and each of the 45 bedrooms is luxuriously and elegantly appointed – including private bathroom, colour television, radio and telephone.

The kitchen is one of the most up-to-date in Europe, capable of producing the very best in English and International fare, and the hotel's superb 'Helena' restaurant, seating over 100 people, is equipped to the highest standard.

For further details, including a copy of our colour brochure, please telephone:
BOROUGHBRIDGE (090 12) 2328

CROWN HOTEL

Boroughbridge · North Yorkshire YO5 9LB

The hotel grounds are beautifully kept and have an abundance of trees, including some particularly fine Cedars. There is a lovely topiary – not often seen these days – and a terrace by the lawns for relaxing outdoors. Leisure facilities within the grounds include tennis courts, croquet lawn and putting green.

Situated in eight acres of beautiful parkland, Green End Park Hotel is the ideal place for a quiet weekend away or for commercial travellers and businessmen looking for a reasonably-priced short stay.

Green End Park Hotel was originally an 18th century manor and we have taken great care to preserve its historic character in the overall decor, combining traditional elegance with a warm, inviting atmosphere.

The Cedar Room has a magnificent open fire and a lovely view of the garden. Seating up to 80 people it is ideally suited for banqueting functions, weddings, receptions, business conferences, private parties and dinner dances. Our restaurant is open to non-residents and offers superb cuisine at very reasonable prices.

If you wish to make a reservation or need any further information, please do not hesitate to ring us on Dane End 344 or 780.

GREEN END PARK HOTEL

Dane End, Ware, Herts SG12 0NY Tel: Dane End 344 or 780

The Palace Hotel Torquay

In the elegant charm of a Bishop's former home, the Palace is proud to halt history and offer you the near-forgotten courtesies of yester-years.

Relaxed atmosphere * Personal service * Unseen attention * Superb food * Wines from the world * Majority of Bedrooms overlooking 25 acres of Italian gardens, and private woodland walks to the edge of the sea.

Plus a very modern bonus of FREE

- **Nine-hole Golf Course**
- **Two Swimming Pools (indoors and outdoors)**
- **Six Tennis Courts (indoors and outdoors)**
- **Squash Courts**
- **Sauna**
- **Double Snooker Room**
- **Putting Green**
- **Table Tennis**
- **Private Card Rooms**
- **T.V. Lounges**
- **Ballroom with resident Trio**
- **Children's Play Area with a Hotel Nanny**

For your pleasure — and ours —

Write or phone for brochure to:—
PALACE HOTEL
BABBACOMBE ROAD, TORQUAY TQ1 3TG
Tel. 0803-22271. Telex: 42606

Ristorante La Pavona

5/7 Blandford Street, W1

01 486 9696 01 486 9256

The most prestigious Italian restaurant in London specialises in Fish and offers from the best catches a varied and interesting selection of Sea Food, together with a cuisine and service geared to please the most demanding of its patrons.

Specially selected meat dishes are available including game when in season.

Our pasta is freshly made.

A good choice of international wines complements the menu.

Open:

Monday to Friday from noon to 2.30pm
Monday to Saturday from 7pm to 12.30am
Last order 11.15pm
Air conditioned

Intimate Continental Restaurant under the WAYSIDE HOTEL

Warwick Road
Stratford-upon-Avon

Wine Bar, Gourmet Week-ends accepted.
Accommodation available in the Wayside Hotel.

EGON RONAY, A.A. Recommended

Telephone (0789) 292550

Travel & Leisure

Advertisers' Index overleaf

Advertisers' Index

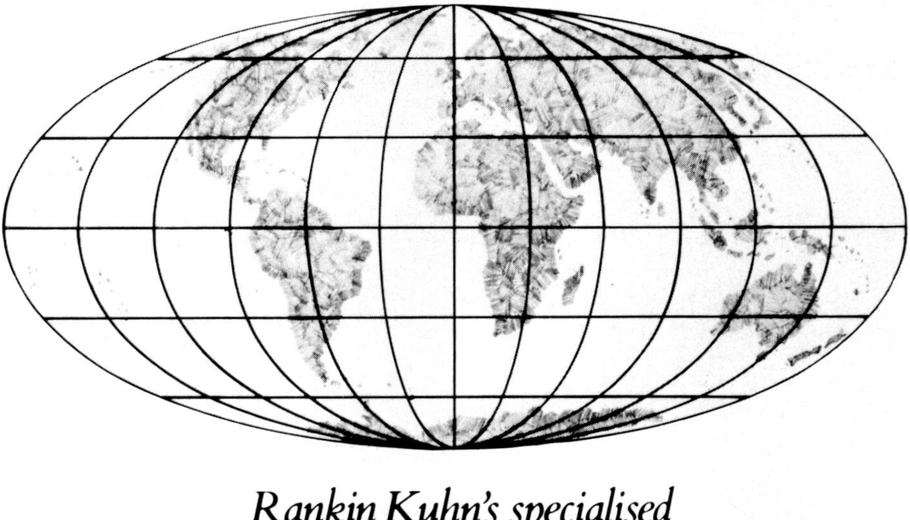

BEDROOMS
All bedrooms have colour televisions and telephones.
BILLIARD ROOM
The full size billiard table and table tennis table are available for guests to play on. Other facilities for guests include croquet, tennis and squash. The squash courts are completed. It is also possible to arrange roe deer stalking, riding, shooting and fishing (Don and Deveron), if enough notice is given.
PRIVATE DINING ROOM
The library is available for private dinners.

Pittodrie House is situated in the heartof the fertile Aberdeenshire countryside with Bennachie providing a dramatic backdrop. The house dates back to 1480. There is very little left of the original building which was burnt down by the Marquis of Montrose. (He was eventually executed in 1650). The main building is a Z plan castle which was rebuilt in 1675. Substantial Victorian additions were completed in 1850. The architect was Archibald Simpson who was famous for many buildings in Aberdeen. The hotel was opened in May 1977 after extensive alterations which made it not only very comfortable but also incorporated all the necessary fire precautions for guests safety. The property was originally owned by the Erskines, a branch of the family of the Earls of Mar. It was purchased by the grandfather of the present owner in 1900. The pictures and antique furniture have been retained in all the reception rooms and bedrooms so as to retain the atmosphere of a family home rather than a hotel.

The **PITTODRIE HOUSE** *Hotel*

Pittodrie House Hotel
Pitcaple Aberdeenshire AB5 9HS
Telephone Pitcaple (04676) 202.

TOWN AND GOWN TRAVEL

40/41 South Parade, Summertown
Oxford OX2 7JP: Tel. Oxford (0865) 511341

Bonded

IATA

Atol No. 275

Have established over the last eighteen years in both City and University (as the name implies) an unrivalled reputation for all travel services. All locations (branches at Headington and Bicester) are fully licenced for IATA ticketing and are ABTA approved. In addition there are these special facilities:—

1. **Instant Computer Access to all the World Major Airlines** via a Travicom II installation. This will be extended to Inclusive Holidays, Continental Rail, Ferry, Hotel and Car Hire. Reservations as the system develops.

2. **A Special Business Travel Unit.** Has an elite staff headed by a manager at Diploma Level for Air ticketing and route planning.

3. **A Conference Unit.** Already an enviable record for arrangements in most of the world's major cities and also in secluded winter resorts such as Agios Nikolaos, Crete.

4. **Peregrine Holidays. Special Interest Tours** (Botany, Ornithology, Archaeology) with eleven years experience of tours to *Greece, Italy, France, Spain, Sicily, Crete; N. and S. America, Hawaii, Turkey, Tunisia, Israel, Zaire, Galapagos, India, Nepal, Malaysia.*

All this experience (and efficiency to go with it) is immediately available.

Directors: Raymond Hodgkins MA (Oxon); Patricia Hodgkins MTAI; Neville Wykes FAAI ACEA.

THE MEN WHO TURNED THE ATLANTIC INTO A POND.

Capt. Alcock and Lt. Brown.

Charles Lindbergh.

Sir Frank Whittle.

Sir Freddie Laker.

Back in 1919, flying the Atlantic non-stop was a dream that turned into a nightmare for many.

Alcock and Brown proved it could be done – just. Lindbergh showed it could be done safely. And Whittle enabled it to be done quickly by ushering in the jet age.

But it was only in 1977 that everyone realised they could make the trip – because all of a sudden everyone could afford it.

That was when the first Laker Skytrain service took off for New York and trimmed hundreds of pounds off the standard fare.

We've been 'taking off' ever since. So much so that trans-Atlantic air-fares are one of the few costs to have gone down as inflation has soared up.

And with such success that in three years we have flown 1½ million passengers across the Pond.

If we carry on at this rate it's going to seem more like a puddle.

Full details of our scheduled service to New York, Los Angeles and Florida from your travel agent, or by phoning 01-668 9300 or Horley (02934) 5511.

LAKER Skytrain Trade mark SCHEDULED AIR SERVICE

Nobody OutLakers Laker.

The pleasure of saunas— spa baths and UVA sun tan equipment in your home.

SuperSun have the range of products to make your leisure time more enjoyable

8 MODELS TO CHOOSE FROM

TYLO Saunas

- 8 Sizes to choose from 4′ x 4′ to a huge 10′ x 8′.
- Constructed to your own design and size if required
- Installed complete, by experts in a few hours.
- Incorporating the world famous TYLO Heater control panel.
- Guaranteed 3 years.

Spa Baths—

Simply replaces your existing bath, installed complete. You and your family can enjoy the pleasures of spa-bathing in your own home from under £700. Single/double/multiple models available.

5 MODELS TO CHOOSE FROM

18 MODELS TO CHOOSE FROM

UVA SUN TANNING EQUIPMENT

- 18 months guarantee
- One of the world's leading makers
- Certificates of safety and approval from – TUV–Germany SEV–Switzerland CSA–Canada SEL–Iceland

SuperSun

Supersun, Freepost, Wigan, Lancs. WI 597

Branches:

78 Camberwell Church Street SE5
703 4077

240/2 Kennington Park Road SE11
735 5176

By Appointment to Her Majesty The Queen Suppliers of Mopeds

Registered Office:

248 Camberwell Road SE5

EDWARDES (CAMBERWELL) LTD. LONDON

221-223-225-248 CAMBERWELL ROAD, LONDON, SE5
Telephone: 01-703 3676 and 01-703 5720

We Supply and Maintain

Mopeds to the Royal Household

We are the Biggest Moped and Cycle dealers in London:

We can Supply all makes of Mopeds & Cycles

Also maintain and repair all makes and at competitive prices

We supply Foreign Embassies & Local Councils with Mopeds & Cycles!

So come to us for a Fair Deal

The Country Gentleman

Advertisers' Index overleaf

Advertisers' Index

The two most likely home disasters. And how to intercept them.

● You come home and find that someone has broken into your home.

He hasn't taken much of value.

But he's left a disgusting mess.

Your home will never quite be the same again.

● You wake up in the middle of the night.

The room is full of smoke.

Maybe you can get your family out in time. Maybe not.

This is why you need Intercept, the world's first computerised home security system.

If an intruder tries to get in an alarm goes off inside and outside the house.

It sounds a little like a French police siren.

Except that it's slightly louder than Concorde taking off.

It scares the hell out of intruders.

The fire alarm has its own distinct sound. It wakes you up at once.

In time to get out.

● Your Intercept system not only warns you against intruders or fire.

It can give you a level of home security that's never been possible before.

DISASTER ONE: VANDALISM
He's 16 years old. He's good to his mum. He'd very much like to smash up your home.

DISASTER TWO: FIRE
Over 85% of fires start when the family is at home. Often when they're in bed. Think about it.

It can even monitor freezers, greenhouses, aquariums.

You don't have to fit it.

It fits you.

How it works.

Even though it does so much, the Master Control Unit is no bigger than a portable radio.

It's connected by narrow gauge wiring to tiny contacts embedded in the door frames and windows.

And wired to unobtrusive smoke and heat detector units.

It's operated by a specially made security key issued only to you and your family.

Today, you, your family and your home are under greater risk than ever before.

Intercept has been specially developed to fight today's risks.

In a way no other home security system can.

Intercept alarms

The world's first computerised security system.

The Chalfont Greenhouse

by BACO®

size 10′ 5″ x 12′ 8″

Special Features included as standard

- **Automatically controlled ridge ventilation**
- **Cord-operated base ventilation**
- **Locking double door**
- **Sun shading both sides**
- **Bar cap glazing – no overlapping glass**
- **Plant watering system**

Staging and shelves optional extras

The Gardeners Dreamhouse

DELIVERY AND ERECTION INCLUDED IN PRICE!

Please send me details of your prestigious Greenhouses

Name . . . .

Address . . . .

. . . . DB82

BACO® LEISURE PRODUCTS LTD.

Baco is the registered trade mark of the British Aluminium Company Limited.

Windover Road, HUNTINGDON, CAMBS. PE18 7EH Tel: 0480 55141

Specialist Shops & Services

Advertisers' Index overleaf

Advertisers' Index

You need never lose the comfort of your own home.

Knowing that you don't have to leave home when you need nursing care brings real peace of mind. BNA can provide just the help you need.

Trained nurses are available 24 hours a day, 7 days a week How long you have the services of your nurse depends entirely on you — but it could be for as little as an hour a day.

Private nursing isn't a luxury when it allows you to stay in the place where you most want to be.

Our nationwide network of offices means that we almost certainly have a branch close to you. See Yellow Pages for your local branch or contact our Head Office:

BNA

British Nursing Association,
470 Oxford Street, London W1N 0HQ.
Telephone: 01-629 9030

EDINBURGH NURSING HOME COMPANY

MEMBER OF REGISTERED NURSING HOME ASSOCIATION

PRINCIPALS MR & MRS E.H. BERRY

Head Office: 8 Chalmers Crescent, Edinburgh

031-667 2244

MEDICAL GERIATRIC AND CONVALESCENT
MALE – FEMALE LONG AND SHORT STAY
HIGH STANDARD OF NURSING CARE
TELE-NURSE SYSTEM . TV LOUNGE

BUPA ACCEPTED

FINDHORN NURSING HOME
15 Findhorn Place
Edinburgh
Tel: 031-667 3148

MILFORD NURSING HOME
58 Duddingston Road
Edinburgh EH15 1SG
Tel: 031-669 8551

GLENCAIRN TOWERS NURSING HOME
8 Chalmers Crescent
Edinburgh
Tel: 031-667 3548

LEVEN HOUSE
Care & Rest Home
14 Hope Place
Musselburgh EH21 7QD
Tel: 031-665 4478

NUCLEAR ATTACK!!

Protect your family with the Newbridge Shelter.

Sectional view of Newbridge Nuclear Blast & Fall Out Shelter

The Newbridge Nuclear Blast and Fallout Shelter is designed and built to the highest specification to provide contamination free accommodation for 4 to 5 people for a period of three weeks following a nuclear attack or accident.

The tensile steel construction will withstand 3 atmospheres, equal to the blast and radiation from a 1 megaton bomb dropped at a distance of 1½ miles away.

After installation only the hatch cover, similar to a drainage inspection cover, and the air intake and exhaust are visible.

Experts in filtration, lighting and other safety equipment were consulted at all stages of the shelter's manufacture, then in the full glare of national publicity we chose the 'Farmer' family to spend two weeks in the shelter as final proof of a family's ability to live comfortably for an extended period of time under simulated nuclear war conditions.

The protection offered by the Newbridge shelter is in excess of that suggested by Government agencies and we believe it to be one of the strongest, most carefully developed shelters available in Britain.

Unlike many shelters you can have confidence in the Newbridge shelter as it has been proven under actual living conditions.

The Farmer family said "the test itself, was an unqualified success, proving that apart from offering all the necessary protection needed in the event of a nuclear war that the shelter itself can be 'lived in' for the necessary period following an attack by an ordinary family having no specialised knowledge."

Newbridge Nuclear Engineering Ltd.

Newbridge Lane, Old Whittington, Chesterfield, Derbyshire.
Telephone (0246) 453031. Telex 547643.

BY APPOINTMENT
TO H. M. THE QUEEN
ECCLESIASTICAL ROBE MAKERS

ESTABLISHED 1851

THOMAS PRATT & SONS, LTD.

ROBEMAKERS

to the Church and Clergy

Clergy Cassocks and Surplices etc

Choir Robes

Special Rates for RSCM affiliated Choirs

**34 SOUTHAMPTON STREET,
STRAND LONDON, WC2E 7HH
Telephone: 01-836 5718**

ROYAL ARMS

For Warrant Holders Civic Arms for Local Authorities, Service Arms and Badges and FAMILY COATS OF ARMS are beautifully emblazoned by Britain's Heraldic craftsmen

For details ask…

YORK INSIGNIA Ltd

Minster Gates, York YO1 2HL
Telephone YORK (0904) 25522

JOSEPH KNIGHT LAMPS

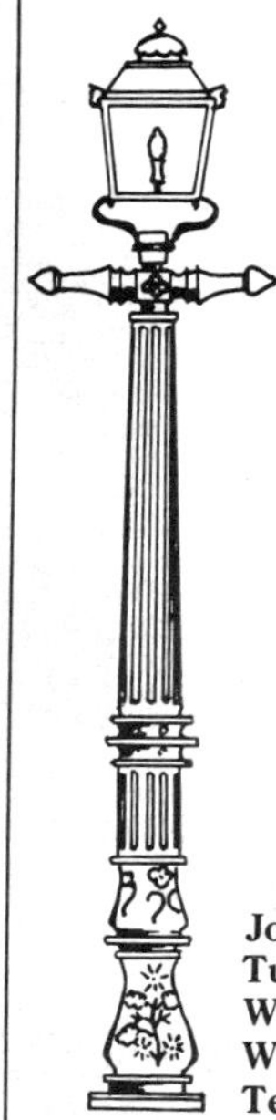

Joseph Knight brings to you the romance, artistry and craftsmanship of the Victorian and Edwardian era. Standards of the gas light age, dating back to 1882 have been faithfully reproduced, using the same casting and forming techniques. They are still assembled by hand. Lantern heads are still 100% copper and the range represents the finest now available in the world.

Please send for our illustrated brochure.

**Joseph Knight Lamp Co. Ltd.,
Turpin's, Charles Street,
Willenhall,
West Midlands.
Tel: (0902) 62231/68060**

Antiques & Fine Art

Advertisers' Index overleaf

Advertisers' Index

A FINE PAIR OF 'ROMAYNE HEADS'. CARVINGS PROBABLY OF GERMAN ORIGIN, IN FRUIT WOOD. 1550-70

Touchwood Antiques

Touchwood Antiques has been run by a family of antiquarians, for over seven generations, specializing in period oak furniture from the pre-middle ages to the beginning of the 18th Century, and Persian rugs both antique and semi-antique.

Touchwood Antiques offer a complete furnishing service from restoration of buildings to period interior design. Renowned for quality pieces, Touchwood are used by stately homes, museums and collectors as an antique finding service as well as disposing of pieces in what has become a very specialised market place.

Before a Touchwood Antique is ready for sale it is thoroughly treated for worm and waxed with Touchwood's own formula polish. This polishing service – 2nd to none – is now generally available.

Touchwood Antiques Wax Polish is the result of years of use and research by the family. Used by selective collectors worldwide to preserve and protect. It is a blend of the finest honey wax and produces a superb patination, unparrelled by modern "antique" waxes.

Connoisseurs will find an unrivalled selection of magnificent pieces and a warm welcome at Touchwood Antiques.

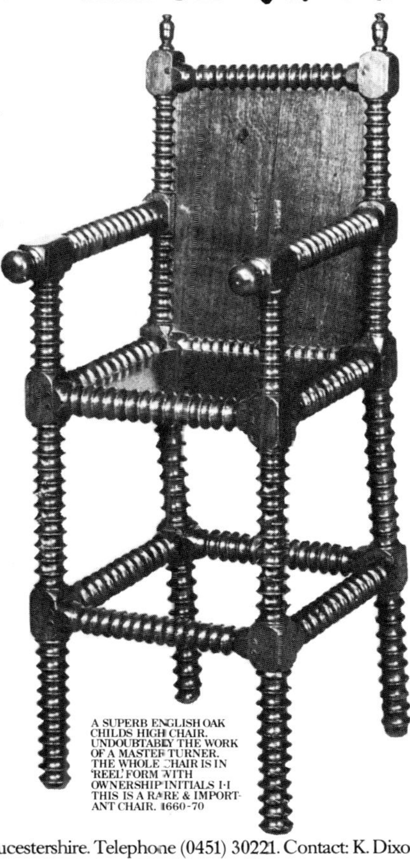

A SUPERB ENGLISH OAK CHILDS HIGH CHAIR. UNDOUBTABLY THE WORK OF A MASTER TURNER. THE WHOLE CHAIR IS IN 'REEL' FORM WITH OWNERSHIP INITIALS I·I THIS IS A RARE & IMPORTANT CHAIR. 1660-70

Touchwood Antiques

Period and Country Furniture.

Touchwood Antiques Ltd., 9 Park Street, Stow-on-the-Wold, Gloucestershire. Telephone (0451) 30221. Contact: K. Dixon

Asi Termina La Metaphysica

D. A. Hernandez-Purnell
Oil on canvas 1981

Commission and other enquiries to the artist's agent
A. Hadden
19 Tedworth Square
Chelsea
London

Photograph Ashcroft Hawkins & Company Ltd, Cubitts Yard, James Street, Covent Garden, London W.C.2.

PRIESTS

ANTIQUES AND FINE ARTS

56 North Street Thame Oxfordshire Telephone Thame 4461

We specialize in high quality English Antique Furniture of the 17th and 18th centuries, and fine Victorian oil paintings.

Dimensions:
Height: $34\frac{1}{4}$".
Width: $38\frac{1}{2}$".
Depth: $22\frac{1}{4}$".

William & Mary Olive-wood Oyster/Chest of two short and three long drawers of beautiful colour and patination. Circa 1690

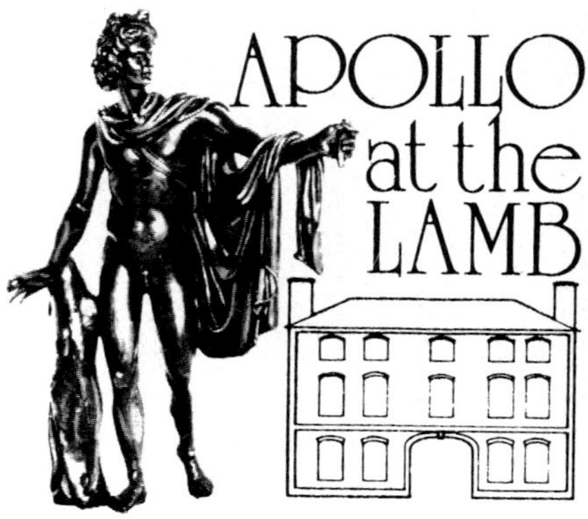

WALLINGFORD OXFORDSHIRE
Telephone: Wallingford (0491) 35009

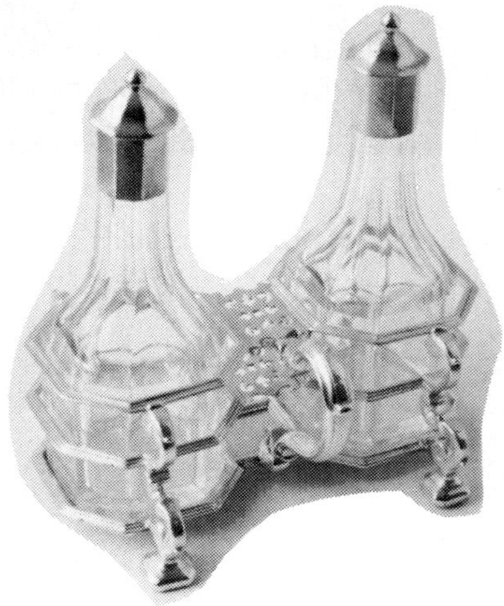

Reign:	Queen Anne
Assay:	London
Date:	1702
Maker:	David Willaume
Silver Weight:	21ozs 11dwts

DOVERIDGE HOUSE OF NEACH HILL

For Universally Good Taste

The Blue Room

DOVERIDGE HOUSE ANTIQUES,
NEACH HILL, LONG LANE, Nr. TONG,
SHROPSHIRE TF11 8PJ
Telephone (Code 090-722) 3131/2 Cables: Antiques, Shifnal, England

LOCATION: 8 Miles from Wolverhampton on A41. 45 minutes Birmingham International Airport. 1 hour 50 minutes Inter-city Euston/ Wolverhampton. All clients personally collected.

ROAD DIRECTIONS: M6 Exit 12. A5 towards Telford. At A41 roundabout left Wolverhampton/RAF Cosford. 3 miles see **NEACH HILL** signpost; right into Long Lane. Entrance clearly indicated.

Gracious Living

Advertisers' Index overleaf

Advertisers' Index

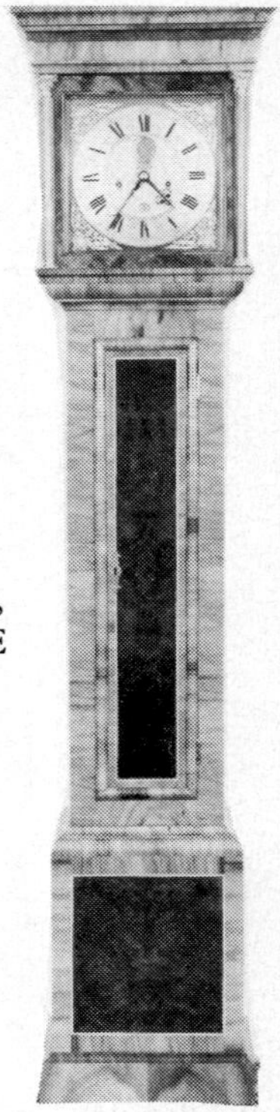

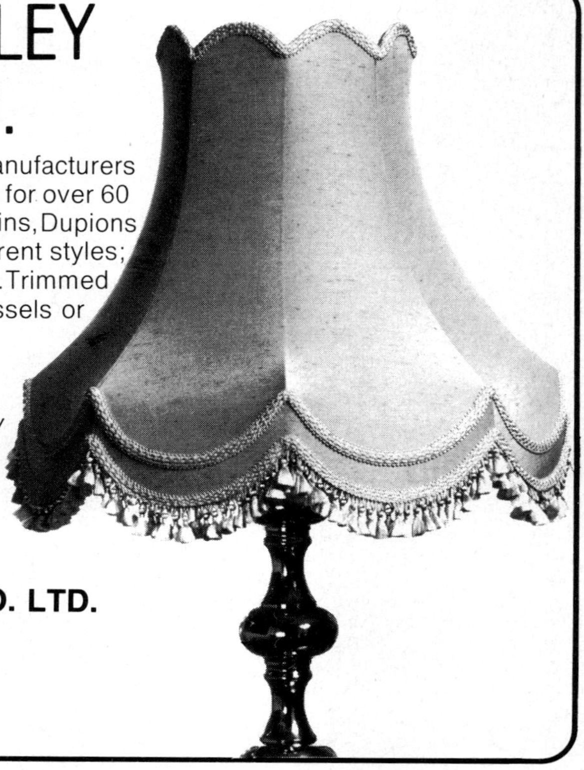

BOEHM
Creators of porcelain art
Grace de Monaco Rose
As presented to Her Serene Highness the Princess Grace to commemorate the occasion of 1er Salon International de la Rose held in Monte Carlo 12th/14th June 1981
Limited Edition: 350
An Investment in Beauty. . .
Boehm of Malvern England Limited,
Tanhouse Lane, Malvern WR14 1LG, England. Telephone: Leigh Sinton (0886) 32111 Telex: 338759
Boehm Porcelain Gallery, 225 Fifth Avenue, Suite 104, New York, New York 10010 U.S.A.

shoes forever
Manolo Blahnik®
49-51 OLD CHURCH STREET LONDON SW3
PHONE 352 8622 AND 352 3863

Brushing the Mason Pearson way does so much to beautify your hair.

Hair beauty and regular brushing go hand in hand. And, to help you condition your hair to shining loveliness, there's no brush quite like a Mason Pearson with its original and perfected pneumatic design and functionally spired tufts – an unbeatable combination. These bristles stimulate the scalp and – very important indeed – distribute the natural oil that conditions the hair and gives it suppleness and sheen. Every genuine Mason Pearson brush has the name on the handle – and it's well worth looking for. Because no other brush is made with such regard for quality and durability as well as effectiveness. So to care for your hair – beautifully – make Mason Pearson a 'must'!

MASON PEARSON

– the great original.

Recommended prices from £2.68 to £15.84 at top chemists and stores. Or write for the name of your nearest stockist and a free Hair Care leaflet to: 37 Old Bond Street, London W1X 3AE.

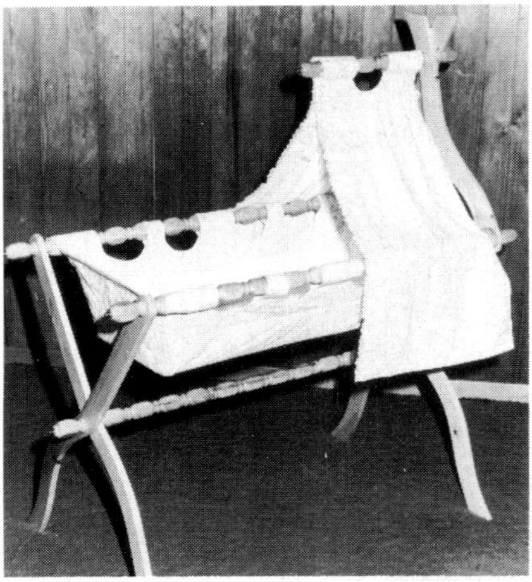

Reproduction Victorian Cribs

Handmade in Sussex by craftsmen, to a Victorian design. Made of kiln dried Pine and Maple, Dark Oak is available to special order. Overall dimensions are 36″ long, 22″ wide, 30″ high plus canopy, and the Crib is suitable for infants up to the age of at least six months. The Crib may be gently rocked and is easily folded for transport. It also dismantles completely for storage.

The Drapes may be made in the material of your choice, otherwise available in Dolly Mixture, pink or blue, or in Ecru, these materials being 100% cotton and machine washable. Matching sheets, pillowcases and quilts are also available.

For further information please write or telephone:
Main Marketing,
Brambletye, Fairwarp, Uckfield, East Sussex.
Tel: Nutley 2674

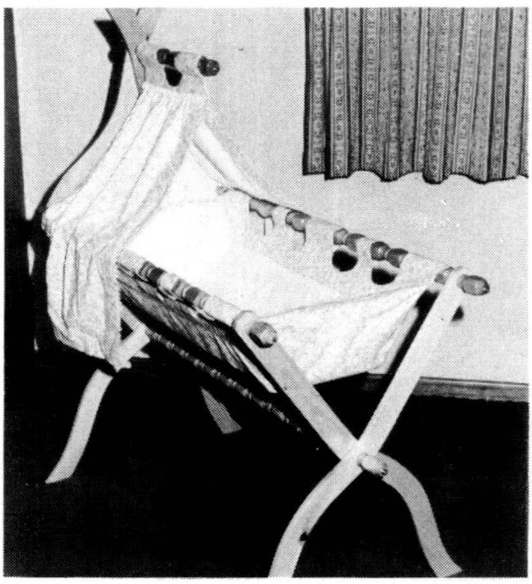

DEBRETT'S
Fine Books

The English Gentleman's Wife

BY DOUGLAS SUTHERLAND

Foreword by Diana Duchess of Newcastle
Introduction by Lady Windlesham (Prudence Glynn)

Following the tremendous success of 'The English Gentleman', Debrett asked Douglas Sutherland to do a similar disservice for the English Lady. The result is a worthy companion to his hilarious exposé of the English Gentleman and will certainly cause a good deal more controversy. This new volume is again illustrated with Timothy Jacques' charming and witty drawings and makes an ideal present for any Wife, Sister, Mother, Aunt or Grandmother; in short any 'English Gentleman's Wife'. **Price £3.95** (plus 25p post).

The English Gentleman

BY DOUGLAS SUTHERLAND

FOREWORD BY SIR IAIN MONCREIFFE OF THAT ILK, BART.

Is the "English Gentleman" a disappearing species? In his book, Douglas Sutherland examines the creature's habits and habitats in a light-hearted but penetrating way, and provides an amusing insight into the world of this endangered species. **Price £3.95** (plus 25p post).

Published by Debrett's Peerage Ltd.
Available from all good bookshops or from Debrett's
73/77 Britannia Road, London SW6

Read by three-quarters of a million
influential men and women every month.
For the style,
the wit,
the elegance and the information.

3
Joseph Knox Ltd.
4
JOSEPH
KNOX

Charities

Advertisers' Index overleaf

Advertisers' Index

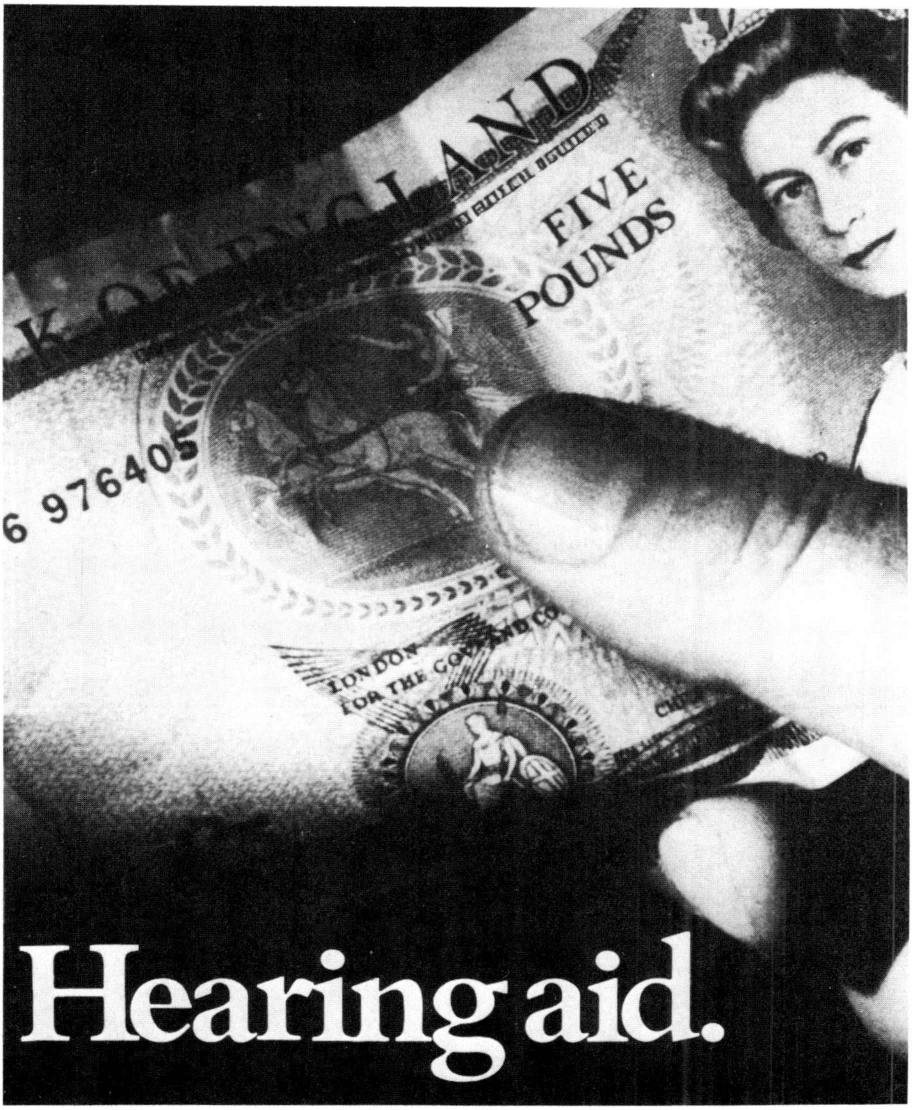

Can you place a value on your hearing?

It costs a lot to be deaf: not only in terms of the loss of the faculty most crucial for communication and education, but in hard cash.

The RNID, Britain's leading voluntary organisation in the field of deafness, is hard at work. But, because we receive no direct government aid, we must ask for your help.

We need to do a lot more, and we could, with your support.

19 81
International Year of Disabled People

RNID. The Royal National Institute for the Deaf.

Send your donations to RNID, Room PC, 105 Gower Street, London WC1E 6AH. For details telephone 01-387 8033.

King Edward VII's Hospital for Officers

Beaumont House, Beaumont Street, London W.1.

(Sister Agnes's) Patron: Her Majesty the Queen

King Edward VII's Hospital for Officers, affectionately known as Sister Agnes's, provides the best medical and surgical facilities at the lowest possible cost to officers of all three services (including women officers) serving or retired, who have held a permanent or temporary commission in the Armed Forces. This facility also extends to officers' wives, widows and dependent children of not less than 4 years of age.

The hospital has both private rooms and small wards, and well-equipped X-Ray and Physiotherapy Departments.

Serving officers are entitled to free nursing and maintenance in the shared rooms. Other patients are asked to pay at the rate of £245 per week for a private room and £210 for a shared room or ward bed. If, however a patient can pay a sum nearer to the actual cost of his maintenance (now over £450 per week) this is much appreciated as it helps others. Consultant's fees are a matter for personal arrangement between patient and Consultant. There is a generously administered Benevolent Fund for those in straitened circumstances.

BUPA give friends of the Hospital a 15% reduction on their BUPACARE subscriptions and PPP and Western Provident a 25% reduction on their Family Masterplan subscriptions and Super cover policies respectively, if payment is made by direct debit.

The hospital is currently handling over 2300 in-patients and 700 out-patients a year. It is not part of the NHS and is therefore reliant on voluntary aid via subscriptions, donations and legacies for which there is an increasing need as the number of patients grows.

If you would like to receive information or become a subscriber please write to the Appeals Secretary, (DH82), 6 Buckingham Place, London, SW1E 6HR, or phone 01-828 4454. Applications for admission should be made to the Matron on 01-486 4411.

Thank God you're not in their situation.

Like a number of young soldiers trying to keep the precarious peace in Ireland, he was killed. His wife and child were still in married quarters in Germany, his former posting.

They were flown back to England. SSAFA organised an escort to accompany them from the airport to a London station where the train took them to Scotland. SSAFA had booked a sleeper and, at the end of this long journey, another SSAFA representative had arranged for their relatives to meet them at the station.

This could be the end of the story. Except that SSAFA will continue to watch over them. For once a man or woman has served in war, or in any of the Regular Armed Forces, their dependants can turn to SSAFA for the rest of their lives. But the demand for our help is increasing as a growing number of ex-Service men and women of two world wars reach retirement age. We need both funds and voluntary helpers, especially in urban areas. You can play your part by giving some of your time as a SSAFA representative, signing a deed of covenant or remembering SSAFA in your will.* Offers of help will be welcomed by the Secretary, SSAFA, on 01-222 9221.

* Legacies up to £200,000 are now exempt from Capital Transfer Tax.

SSAFA

Soldiers', Sailors' & Airmen's Families Association,
27 Queen Anne's Gate, London SW1H 9BZ.

Meet Chris Gallagher. After a serious accident in Canada resulted in total paralysis of his limbs, he was confined to a wheelchair. His career was in ruins, but thanks to specialist help at Queen Elizabeth's Training College, including typing and writing with a mouth stick, and aided by his own incredible determination, he is now a management accounts clerk. His courage, our facilities and your help have made him useful, independent and happy.

A heartwarming story like Chris's requires a financial commitment from people who really care – people like you. The more you can give, the more we can do.

Queen Elizabeth's Foundation comprises three other units apart from the Training College: Dorincourt, a residential sheltered workshop; Benstead Place, an assessment centre for handicapped young people; and Lulworth Court, a holiday home for those who are severely paralysed.

Please write for further details to –

Queen Elizabeth's Foundation for the Disabled

Leatherhead, Surrey KT22 0BN.

Patron: Her Majesty Queen Elizabeth The Queen Mother.

For 16 years Marjorie and Wyndham Sargeant lived happily in their cottage. They worked hard to make it one of the prettiest in the Highlands and had no intention of moving. But when the savage inflation of recent years bit into their savings, and Marjorie's health started to fail, they realised they couldn't stay. At the age of 80, they faced a desperate situation: dwindling funds, ill health, and the prospect of being homeless.

Then a friend suggested the D.G.A.A. The Sargeants explained their predicament and, to their immense relief, they were offered rooms in The Grove, one of the Association's residential homes. Understandably, they felt nothing

"We dreaded leaving our lovely cottage, until the D.G.A.A. found us a home from home."

could replace their cottage. But once they had settled in they realised how wrong they were.

"It's a real home", says Wyndham, and Marjorie adds, "The Staff are so kind and there is always a doctor on call. We're so happy now."

In fact, the majority of people helped by the D.G.A.A. are those who want to stay in their own homes. The Association through its visitors helps in every way it can.

The Sargeant's happiness only comes from a sense of security; perhaps that's the only form of happiness money can buy. For that reason the D.G.A.A. desperately needs the generous support of individuals, through donations, covenants and, most important of all, legacies.

Perhaps you are lucky enough to look forward to a secure old age. If so, please help those who, through no fault of their own, cannot help themselves.

To find out how much more the D.G.A.A. does for old people please write to the Appeals Secretary who will be pleased to send you information.

THE DISTRESSED GENTLEFOLK'S AID ASSOCIATION, VICARAGE GATE HOUSE, VICARAGE GATE, KENSINGTON, LONDON W8 4AQ.

Please send me more information about the D.G.A.A.

Name __________

Address __________

Replies to Appeals Secretary, D.G.A.A. CBH

MIND

National Association for Mental Health

Mental illness is too big a problem to forget

Over 5 million of us who are now fit, will need psychiatric help at some point in our lives. And yet mental illness is still the poor relation of health care.

MIND is the national charity that works for those who suffer by providing facilities (homes, hostels, social clubs etc), by researching into methods of care, and by campaigning for the legal and welfare rights of mental patients.

CARE TAKES CASH – MIND NEEDS YOUR HELP.

Please send a donation to:
MIND, Room D1,
22 Harley Street,
London W1N 2ED.

PARKINSON'S DISEASE...

Where there's a Will There's a Way...

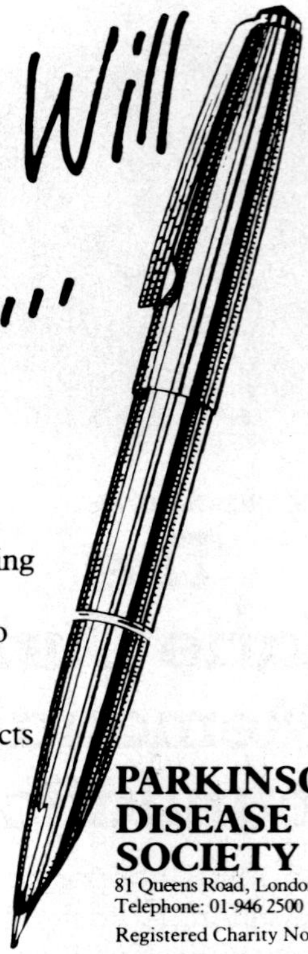

. . . to help us find new and improved ways of helping sufferers and their families

. . . to help us, with the support of our Branches, to intensify our welfare activity and the sponsoring of research

. . . to help us find medications with fewer side effects

. . . to help us eradicate Parkinson's Disease totally by finding the cure.

To do all this will cost money.
We need your clients' help.

Please help them to help us.

PARKINSON'S DISEASE SOCIETY
81 Queens Road, London, SW19 8NR.
Telephone: 01-946 2500
Registered Charity No. 258197

CYSTIC FIBROSIS DESTROYS LUNGS, DIGESTION AND LIFE

PLEASE HELP US DESTROY CYSTIC FIBROSIS

Thousands of British children are born with **CYSTIC FIBROSIS.** There is no cure, they depend for their lives on drugs, daily physiotherapy, complex breathing exercises and a devoted family.

CYSTIC FIBROSIS is the most common genetically determined disorder, which seriously affects the lungs and digestive system. Early diagnosis enables proper treatment and care, but it is **STILL A MAJOR CAUSE OF DEATH IN CHILDHOOD.**

RESEARCH PROMISES NEW HOPE.

Donations, Legacies and Covenants *VERY WELCOME.*

CYSTIC FIBROSIS RESEARCH TRUST
5 Blyth Road, Bromley, Kent BR1 3RS
Tel: 01-464 7211/2

The Cystic Fibrosis Research Trust

Patron: H.R.H. Princess Alexandra, the Hon Mrs Angus Ogilvy

Since its foundation in 1964 the Trust has pursued through its national network of Branches and support Groups, a dual policy of sponsoring medical research and providing welfare advice to CF families.

Today the Trust is financing over 49 major research projects by skilled doctors and scientists in hospitals and universities throughout the country in an attempt to find a cure for this life-threatening condition.

The Trust's welfare function involves helping parents to cope with the many problems that arise in caring for the CF child.

In spite of ever increasing costs, our research programme **MUST** be extended if a cure is to be found. So please help us to **CONQUER CYSTIC FIBROSIS.**

Reg. Charity No. 281287

HOW YOU CAN HELP
Since 1921 the Musicians Benevolent Fund has assisted musicians and their dependants in a wide variety of ways. These include providing financial support during illness, old-age or other misfortunes, advice and the management of residential homes for the elderly. It is our proud claim that no bona fide request for help has ever been refused. Help us to maintain that record.
● Tell musicians about the fund
● Let us know about musicians in need
● Make a donation or mention us in your Will
Write for further details and an informative leaflet about the work of the Fund to:—Room A, Musicians Benevolent Fund, 16 Ogle Street, London W1P 7LG. Telephone: 01-636 4481
MUSICIANS BENEVOLENT FUND

A

AARONS, Sir Daniel Sidney; OBE (1966), MC and Bar (1918); s of Solomon Aarons and Hannah Hart; *b* 1 Aug 1885; *Educ* North Broken Hill Public Sch; *m* 1925, Jessie Stronach; *Career* gen man NSW Vacuum Oil Co 1935-47, founder memb Liberal Pty of Australia 1945 kt 1970; *Style* - Sir Daniel Aarons, OBE, MC*; Australian Club, 165 Macquarie st, Sydney NSW 2000, Australia (☎ 221 1533)

AARONSON, Edward John; *Career* dir Equity Recoveries Ltd, Shawfield Greyhound Racing Co Ltd, Wanborough Studios Ltd, chm and ch exec G R A Property Trust Ltd; FCA, memb IOD; *Style* - Edward Aaronson, Esq; c/o Equities Recoveries Ltd, Bushey House, Upper Wanborough, nr Swindon, Wilts

AARONSON, Henry; *Career* dir Aaronson Bros Ltd, Aroveneer (Pty) Ltd Australia, Laconite Ltd, Stratton Estates Ltd; *Style* - Henry Aaronson, Esq; Aro House, 18-19 Long Lane, EC1

AARVOLD, His Honour Sir Carl Douglas; OBE (1945), TD (1950), DL (Surrey 1973); s of late O P Aarvold; *b* 7 June 1907; *Educ* Durham Sch, Emmanuel Cambridge; *m* 1934, Noeline Etrenne Hill, of Denton Park, Yorks; 3 s ; *Career* Recorder of London 1964-75, Chm Home Sec's Advsy Bd on Restricted Patients 1978-, RAC 1978-81, Pres Lawn Tennis Assoc 1962- kt 1968; *Style* - His Honour Sir Carl Aarvold, OBE, TD, DL; Foxbury, Westhumble, Dorking, Surrey (☎ 2771)

ABALKHAIL, His Excellency Sheikh Mohammed; *Career* chm Al-Bank Al-Saudi Al-Alami Ltd; *Style* - H E Sheikh Mohammed Abalkhail; c/o Al-Bank Al-Saudi Al-Alami Ltd, 99 Bishopsgate, EC2

ABAYOMI, Sir Kofo Adekunle; s of Joseph Davies; *b* 10 July 1896; *Educ* Edinburgh U; *m* 1932, Oyinkan Morenikeji, MBE, da of Sir Kitoyi Ajasa, OBE; 5 s, 1 da; *Career* kt 1951, MD, ChB, DTM&H, DOMS (Eng), FRSA, memb Privy Cncl Nigeria 1951, Chief Ona Ishokun off Oyo 1949-, Chief Baba Isale of Lagos 1952-, chm Lagos Exec Dvpt Bd; dir Barclays Bank DCO (Nigeria), ICI (Nigeria), P&Z Co Ltd; v-chm British Bata Shoe Co (Nigeria); *Style* - Sir Kofo Abayomi; 2 Keffi St, PO Box 300, Lagos , Nigeria

ABBA, Rev Dr Raymond; s of Rev Herbert Abba, of York (d 1963); *b* 11 Oct 1910; *Educ* Beverley G S, Cambridge; *m* 1940, Hilda, nee Blackham; 1 s, 1 da; *Career* head of dept Religious Studies Swansea Coll of Educn U of Wales 1958-76, consultant Commn on Liturgy Uniting Church in Australia, Sr Min St John's Uniting Ch Essendon Melbourne; *Recreations* walking, swimming, music; *Style* - The Rev Dr Raymond Abba; 853 Mt Alexander rd, Essendon, Vict 3040, Australia (☎ 03 375 1065)

ABBADO, Claudio; *b* 26 June 1933; *Educ* Conservatorio G Verdi Milan, Musical Acad Vienna; *Career* Principal Conductor Vienna Philharmonic 1971-, LSO 1979-, Musical Dir European Community Youth Orchestra 1977-; *Style* - Claudio Abbado, Esq; Piazzetta Bossi 1, 20121 Milano, Italy; 27 Jubilee Place, SW3

ABBEY, Henry William; *Career* dir Wm Hill Org Ltd, E J Riley & Co Ltd, Family Entertainments Ltd, Golf Centres Ltd, Tele Circuit Ltd, Viewsport Ltd; ACIS; *Style* - Henry Abbey, Esq; Hill House, Blackfriars rd, SE1

ABBEY, Lady Ursula Helen; da of late 4 Earl Cairns; *b* 1899; *m* 1921, Maj John Roland Abbey (d 1969); 2 da; *Style* - Lady Ursula Abbey; Mansby, Fittleworth, Sussex

ABBOT, Dermot Charles Hyatt; CB (1959); s of late Reginald Abbot; *b* 8 Sept 1908; *Educ* Newcastle-under-Lyme and Southend-on-Sea, UCL; *m* 1947, Dame Elsie Abbot, DBE; *Career* assist und-sec of state DHSS 1968-69; *Style* - Dermot Abbot

Esq, CB; 4 Constable Close, NW 11 (☎ 01 455 9413)

ABBOT, Dame Elsie Myrtle; DBE (1966, CBE 1957); da of Leonard Tostevin; *b* 3 Sept 1907; *Educ* Clapham County Secdy Sch, St Hugh's Oxford; *m* 1, 1938, E A Arnott; 1 s, 1 da; m 2, 1947, Dermot Abbot, CB; *Career* 3 Sec HM Treasury 1958-67; *Style* - Dame Elsie Abbot, DBE; 4 Constable Close, NW11 (☎ 01 455 9413)

ABBOTT, Clifford; *Career* dir Service Finance Corp Ltd; *Style* - Clifford Abbott, Esq; Winston Hall, East Park rd, Blackburn, Lancs

ABBOTT, Hon Douglas Charles; PC (Canada 1945), QC (1939); s of Lewis Abbott; *b* 29 May 1899; *Educ* McGill U, Dijon U France; *m* 1925, Mary Chisholm; 2 s, 1 da; *Career* Justice of Canadian Supreme Court 1954-73, , Min of Finance Canada 1946-54 (MP from 1940); *Style* - Hon Douglas Abbott, PC, QC; 124 Springfield rd, Ottawa, Canada (☎ 745 6250)

ABBOTT, Rev Eric Symes; KCVO (1966); s of William Abbott; *b* 26 May 1906; *Educ* Nottingham H S, Jesus Cambridge; *Career* Dean of King's Coll London 1945-55, Warden of Keble Coll Oxford 1956-60, Chaplain to King George VI 1948-52 and to HM The Queen 1952-59; DD, MA; Dean of Westminster 1959-74; *Style* - The Rev Eric Abbott, KCVO; 17 Vincent sq, SW1

ABBOTT, Lt-Col Graham Sharrah; TD, JP (Surrey 1963); s of Stanley Abbott (d 1953); *b* 17 July 1915; *Educ* King's Coll Sch Wimbledon; *m* 1938, Sybil, da of John Dunster Furneaux, of Fulham; 3 da; *Career* CO 381 (E Surrey) Light Regt RA (TA) 1946; *Style* - Lt-Col Graham Abbott, TD, JP; Joust End, Mizen Way, Cobham, Surrey (☎ 3886)

ABBOTT, John Mackie; *Career* dir and gen man NSF Ltd; *Style* - John Abbott, Esq; c/o NSF Ltd, Ingrow Bridge, Keighley, Yorks

ABBOTT, John Sutherland; JP (Ayrshire 1942); s of George Sutherland Abbott, JP (d 1940), of Middleton House, Ayr; *b* 1900; *Educ* Bedales, Pembroke Cambridge; *m* 1928, Winifred, da of George Thomas; 1 s, 2 da; *Career* late dir Bank of Scotland & Roy Exchange Assur; *Style* - John Abbott, Esq, JP; 25b Rutland Gate, SW7; 3 Admiral's Walk, West Cliff, Bournemouth

ABBOTT, Sir Myles John; s of Edmund Abbott, Slr; *b* 27 Feb 1906; *Educ* King's Sch Canterbury; *m* 1, 1932, Grace Jeffrey; 1 da; m 2, 1960, Dorothy, w of Robert Campbell; *Career* Ch Justice Bermuda 1961-71 kt 1964; *Style* - Sir Myles Abbott; High Ferry, Harbour rd, Warwick, Bermuda (☎ 23521)

ABDELA, His Honour Judge; Jack Samuel Ronald; TD (1948), QC (1966); s of Joseph Abdela; *Educ* Manchester G S, Milton Sch Bulawayo, Fitzwilliam House Cambridge; *m* 1942, Enid Hope Russell; 1 s (and 1 s decd); *Career* barr 1935, Liveryman Worshipful Co of Painter-Stainers, Circuit Judge Central Criminal Court 1970-; *Style* - His Honour Judge Abdela, TD, QC; 4 South sq, Gray's Inn, WC1 (☎ 01 405 3627); Goldingtons, Sarratt, Herts

ABDULRAHMAN-AL-HELAISSI; Hon GCVO; *Style* - Abdulrahman-Al-Helaissi, Hon GCVO; c/o Ministry of Foreign Affairs, Riyadh, Saudi Arabia

ABDY, Robert Etienne Eric; s and h of Sir Valentine Abdy, 6 Bt, and Mathilde Coche de la Ferté; *b* 22 Feb 1978; *Style* - Robert Abdy Esq

ABDY, Sir Valentine Robert Duff; 6 Bt (UK 1850) of Albyns Essex; s of Sir Robert Abdy, 5 Bt (d 1976), and Lady Diana (d 1967), nee Bridgeman, da of 5 Earl of Bradford; *b* 11 Sept 1937; *Educ* Eton; *m* 1971, Mathilde Coche de la Ferté; 1 s; *Heir* s Robert Abdy; *Style* - Sir Valentine Abdy, Bt; Newton Ferrers, Callington, Cornwall; 9 Rue de Turenne, 75003 Paris, France

ABEL SMITH, Vice-Adm Sir (Edward Michael) Connolly; GCVO (1958, KCVO 1954, CVO 1946), CB (1951); s of Eustace Abel Smith and Ailleen, da of Col John Connolly, VC; *b* 3 Dec 1899; *Educ*

RNCs Osborne and Dartmouth; *m* 1932, Lady Mary Carnegie, da of 10 Earl of Southesk; 1 s, 1 da; *Career* RN ret, HM Lt for Selkirk 1958-74, Extra Equerry to HM The Queen 1952-; *Recreations* hunting, shooting; *Clubs* Buck's, Naval & Military; *Style* - Vice-Adm Sir Connolly Abel Smith, GCVO, CB, RN, Ashiestiel, Galashiels, Scotland (☎ Clovenfords 214)

ABEL SMITH, Col Sir Henry; KCMG (1961), KCVO (1950), DSO (1945), DL (Berks 1953); s of late Francis Abel Smith and Madeline, da of late Rev Henry Seymour; *b* 8 March 1900; *Educ* Sandhurst; *m* 1931, Lady May Cambridge, da of Earl of Athlone, KG, GCB, GCMG, GCVO, DSO, PC (d 1957) and Princess Alice, Countess of Athlone (d 1981); 1 s, 2 da; *Career* KStJ; ADC to Earl of Athlone when Gov-Gen S Africa 1928-31, Gov Qld 1958-66, Adminr Australian C'wlth 1965; *Recreations* hunting, shooting, fishing, polo; *Clubs* Turf; *Style* -Col Sir Henry Abel Smith, KCMG, KCVO, DSO, DL; Barton Lodge, Winkfield, Windsor, Berks (☎ Winkfield Row 2632)

ABEL SMITH, Lady; Henriette Alice; DCVO (1977, CVO 1964), JP (Tunbridge Wells 1955, Glos 1971); da of late Cdr Francis Cadogan, RN; *b* 6 June 1914; *m* 1, 1939, Sir Anthony Palmer, 4 Bt (ka 1941); 1 s, 1 da; m 2, 1953, Sir Alexander Abel Smith, TD, JP (d 1980); 1 s, 1 da; *Career* Lady-in-Waiting to HM The Queen 1949-; *Style* - Lady Abel Smith, DCVO, JP; Quenington Old Rectory, Cirencester, Glos (☎ Coln StAldwyns 231)

ABEL SMITH, Lady Mary Elisabeth; *née* Carnegie; da of late 10 Earl of Southesk; *b* 1899; *m* 1932, Vice-Adm Sir (Edward Michael) Conolly Abel Smith, GCVO, CB; 1 s, 1 da; *Style* - Lady Mary Abel Smith; Ashiestiel, Galashiels, Selkirkshire

ABEL SMITH, Richard Francis; s of Col Sir Henry Abel Smith, KCMG, KCVO, DSO, DL, *qv*; *b* 11 Oct 1933; *Educ* Eton, Sandhurst, RAC Cirencester; *m* 1960, Marcia, da of Maj-Gen Sir Douglas Kendrew, KCMG, CB, CBE, DSO, of Islip Manor, Islip, Northants; 1 da ; *Career* farmer, High Sheriff Notts 1978; *Recreations* shooting, fishing, riding; *Style* - Richard Abel Smith, Esq; Blidworth Dale, Ravenshead, Notts

ABELES, Sir (Emil Herbert) Peter; s of late Alexander Abel and Mrs Anna Deakin; *b* 25 April 1914; *Educ* Budapest; *m* 1969, Katalin, nee Fischer; 2 da; *Career* dep chm and md Thomas Nationwide Transport Ltd Australia 1967-, md Alltrans Gp (Aust) Pty Ltd, dir Bulkships Ltd, Seatainer Terminals Ltd, Tricontinental Corp Ltd, Union Steamship Co of NZ Ltd, Tasman Union Ltd, Ansett Transport Industs Ltd kt 1972; *Style* - Sir Peter Abeles; TNT Management Pty Ltd, Tower 1, 10th Floor, TNT Plaza, Redfern, NSW, Australia

ABELL, (John) David; s of Leonard Abell; *b* 15 Dec 1942; *Educ* Leeds U, LSE; *m* 1967, Anne Priestley (m diss 1977); 3 s; *Career* former md BL Commercial Vehicles, former chm and md Leyland Vehicles Ltd; chm and ch exec Suter Electrical 1981-; *Style* - David Abell Esq; The Old Rectory, Branston-by-Belvoir, Grantham, Lincs

ABELL, Sir George Edmond Brackenbury; KCIE (1947, CIE 1946), OBE (1943); s of George Foster Abell, of Foxcote Manor, Andoversford, Glos (d 1946); *b* 22 June 1904; *Educ* Marlborough, CCC Oxford; *m* 1928, Susan, da of Arthur Norman-Butler (d 1970), of Chelsfield House, Chelsfield, Kent; 2 s, 1 da ; *Career* ICS, Priv Sec to Viceroy 1945-47, dir Bank of England 1952-64, 1st CS Cmmr 1964-67, chm Rhodes Tst 1969-74; *Clubs* Oriental, MCC; *Style* - Sir George Abell, KCIE, OBE; Whittonditch House, Ramsbury, nr Marlborough, Wilts (☎ 449)

ABERCONWAY, 3 Baron (1911 UK); Sir Charles Melville McLaren; 3 Bt (UK 1902), JP (Denbigh 1946); s of 2 Baron Aberconway, CBE (d 1953), and Christabel (d 1974), da of Sir Melville Macnaghten, CB; *b* 16 April 1913; *Educ* Eton, New Coll Oxford; *m* 1, 1941, Deirdre Knewstub (m diss 1949); 1 s, 2 da; m 2, 1949, Ann, da of Mrs A L Aymer, of New York, and formerly w of Maj Robert

Bullard III; 1 s; *Heir* s Hon Henry McLaren, *qv*; *Career* barr 1937, pres John Brown & Co Ltd (chm 1953-78), chm Sheepbridge Engineering Ltd, English China Clays Ltd, dep chm Sun Alliance & London Insurance Ltd 1978-, Westland Aircraft Ltd 1979-, pres Roy Hort Soc 1961-, dir National Westminster Bank Ltd; High Sheriff Denbighshire 1955; *Style* - The Rt Hon The Lord Aberconway, JP; 25 Egerton ter, SW3 (☎ 01 589 4369); Bodnant, Tal-y-Cafn, N Wales

ABERCORN, 5 Duke of (I 1868); Sir James Hamilton; 15 Bt (I 1660), DL (Co Tyrone); also Lord Paisley (S 1578), Lord Abercorn (S 1603), Earl of Abercorn and Lord Paisley, Hamilton, Mountcastell, and Kilpatrick (S 1606), Baron of Strabane (I 1617), Baron Mountcastle and Viscount Strabane (I 1701), Viscount Hamilton (GB 1785), Marquess of Abercorn (GB 1790, which title he sits as in House of Lords), and Marquess of Hamilton (I 1868); s of 4 Duke of Abercorn (d 1979) and Lady Mary Crichton, DCVO, sis of 5 Earl of Erne (*see* Abercorn, Dowager Duchess of); *b* 4 July 1934; *Educ* Eton, RAC Cirencester; *m* 1966, Alexandra, sis of Duchess of Westminster & da of Lt-Col Harold Phillips and gda through her m, Georgina, of Sir Harold Wernher, 3 Bt, GCVO, TD, DL, by his w, Lady Zia, CBE, nee Countess Anastasia Mikhailovna (er da of HIH Grand Duke Mikhail Mikhailovitch of Russia, himself gs of Tsar Nicholas I); 2 s, 1 da; *Heir* s, Marquess of Hamilton; *Career* formerly 2 Lt Grenadier Gds; MP (UU) Fermanagh & S Tyrone 1964-70; High Sheriff Co Tyrone 1970; Pres RUKBA 1979-; co dir; *Recreations* shooting, water skiing; *Clubs* Turf, Ulster; *Style* - His Grace The Duke of Abercorn DL; Barons Court, Omagh, Co Tyrone, N Ireland (☎ Newtownstewart 61470)

ABERCORN, Dowager Duchess of; Lady Mary Kathleen; *née* Crichton; DCVO (1969); da of Viscount Crichton, MVO, DSO (ka 1914, eld s and h of 4 Earl of Erne, KP, PC, sometime MP Enniskillen), and Lady Mary Grosvenor, da of 1 Duke of Westminster, raised to rank of Earl's da 1920; *b* 8 July 1905; *m* 1928, 4 Duke of Abercorn (d 1979); 2 s, 1 da; *Career* Mistress of the Robes to HM The Queen Mother 1964-; *Style* - Her Grace The Dowager Duchess of Abercorn, DCVO; Barons Court, Omagh, Co Tyrone, N Ireland

ABERCROMBY, Eleanor Lady; Eleanor; da of late Sir Arthur Anderson, CIE, CBE, of Roffey Place, Horsham; *m* 1935, Col Sir George Abercromby, 8 Bt, DSO (d 1964); *Style* - Eleanor, Lady Abercromby; 202 Cranmer Court, Sloane av, SW3; East Wing, Leith Hall, Kennethmount, Aberdeenshire

ABERCROMBY, Sir Ian George; 10 Bt (NS 1636), of Birkenbog, Banffshire; s of Robert Ogilvie Abercromby, gs of 5 Bt; suc kinsman 1972; *b* 30 June 1925; *Educ* Lancing, Bloxham Sch; *m* 1, 1950 (m dis 1957), Joyce Beryl, da of Leonard Griffiths; m 2, 1959, Fanny Mary Udale (Molly), da of Dr Graham Udale-Smith, of Sitio Litre, Puerto de la Cruz, Tenerife; 1 da; m 3, 1976, Diana Marjorie, da of Horace Geoffrey Cockell, and wid of Capt Ian Charles Palliser; *Style* - Sir Ian Abercromby, Bt; c/o Nat West Bank, 224 King's rd, SW3

ABERDARE, 4 Baron (UK 1873); Morys George Lyndhurst Bruce; PC (1974); s of 3 Baron Aberdare, GBE (d 1957); *b* 16 June 1919; *Educ* Winchester, New Coll Oxford; *m* 1946, Maud, da of Sir John Dashwood, 10 Bt, CVO; 4 s; *Heir* s, Hon Alastair Bruce; *Career* chm Ctees House of Lords 1976-, Prior Wales, Order of St John; takes Con Whip, Min of State DHSS 1970-74, Min Without Portfolio 1974; chm Albany Life Assur 1975-; *Recreations* real tennis, rackets; *Clubs* Lansdowne, MCC; *Style* - The Rt Hon The Lord Aberdare, PC; 107 Hazlebury rd, SW6 (☎ 01 736 0825)

ABERDEEN AND TEMAIR, 5 Marquess of (UK 1916); Sir Archibald Victor Dudley Gordon; 13 Bt (S 1642); also 11 Earl of Aberdeen (S 1682), Lord Haddo, Methlic, Tarves, and Kellie (S 1682), Viscount Formartine (S 1682), Viscount Gordon (UK 1814), and Earl of Haddo (UK 1916); s of 3 Marquess of Aberdeen and Temair, DSO, by his 1 w, Cecile (da of George Drummond by his w, Elizabeth, da of Rev Frederick Norman and Lady Adeliza, nee Manners, da of 5 Duke of Rutland; George Drummond was ggggs of Andrew Drummond, founder of Messrs Drummond, the bankers, and yr bro of 4 Viscount Strathallan); suc er bro, 4 Marquess of Aberdeen and Temair, CBE, TD, 1974; *b* 9 Jul 1913; *Educ* Harrow; *Heir* bro, Lord Alastair Gordon; *Career* writer and broadcaster, with BBC 1940-72; *Style* - The Most Hon The Marquess of Aberdeen and Temair; The Grange, Haughley, Stowmarket, Suffolk

ABERDEEN AND TEMAIR, Marchioness of; (Beatrice Mary) June Gordon; MBE (1971), DL (Aberdeenshire 1971); da of late Arthur Paul Boissier; *b* 29 Dec 1913; *Educ* Southlands Sch Harrow, RCM; *m* 1939, 4 Marquess of Aberdeen and Temair, CBE, TD (d 1974); 2 adopted s, 2 adopted da; *Career* GRSM, ARCM; musical dir & conductor Haddo House Choral Soc 1945-, also dir Haddo House Arts Centre; FRCM 1967, DStJ 1977; chm Scottish Children's League 1969; *Style* - The Most Hon The Marchioness of Aberdeen and Temair, MBE, DL; Haddo House, Aberdeen (☎ Tarves 216)

ABERDEEN AND TEMAIR, Margaret, Marchioness of; Margaret Gladys; ARRC (1941), JP, DL (E Sussex); da of late Lt-Col Reginald Munn, CMG; *b* 26 April 1907; *m* 1949, as his 2 w, 3 Marquess of Aberdeen and Temair, DSO (d 1972); *Career* chm E Grinstead UDC 1953-54 and 1960-61, pres Sussex Counties Branch Br Red Cross Soc 1975-80, chm Soc of Friends of Ashdown Forest, gov Ardingly Coll; *Clubs* Roy Ashdown Forest Golf; *Style* - The Most Hon Margaret, Marchioness of Aberdeen and Temair ARRC JP DL; Sycamore Cottage, Forest Row, Sussex

ABERDOUR, Lord; John Stewart Sholto Douglas; s and h of 21 Earl of Morton; *b* 17 Jan 1952; *Educ* Dunrobin Castle Sch, Aberdeen U; *Style* - Lord Aberdour; Haggs Farm, Kirknewton, Midlothian

ABERGAVENNY, 5 Marquess of (UK 1876); John Henry Guy Nevill; KG (1974), OBE (1945), JP (Sussex 1948); also Baron Abergavenny (E 1450 as Baron Bergavenny; the 14 Baron, who held the title 1724-45, was the first to be styled Lord Abergavenny), Viscount Nevill, Earl of Abergavenny (both GB 1784), and Earl of Lewes (UK 1876); s of 4 Marquess of Abergavenny (d 1954); *b* 8 Nov 1914; *Educ* Eton, Trin Cambridge; *m* 1938, Mary, CVO, da of Maj John Harrison, JP, and Hon Margert, nee Lawson, da of 3 Baron Burnham, DSO; 3 da (and 1 s and 1 da decd); *Heir* bro, Lord Rupert Nevill, JP, DL; *Career* Ld-Lt E Sussex 1974- (Vice-Lt 1970-74, DL 1955); Chllr Order of the Garter 1977-; KStJ 1976 (Pres Cncl Order of St John Sussex 1975); served WW II with Life Gds, ret as Lt-Col 1946; memb Nat Hunt Cttee 1942- (Sr Steward 1955 and 1963); Tstee Ascot Authority 1952-, HM The Queen's Rep at Ascot 1972-; dir Massey-Ferguson Hldgs, Massey-Ferguson (Toronto), Lloyds Bank, Lloyds Bank UK Management, Lloyds Bank SE Regnl Bd (chm), Whitbread Investment Co; *Clubs* White's; *Style* - The Most Hon The Marquess of Abergavenny, KG, OBE, JP; Eridge Park, Tunbridge Wells, E Sussex (☎ 27378); Flat 2, 46 Pont st, SW1 (☎ 01 581 3967)

ABERTAY, Baroness; Ethel; da of Sir James Broom; *m* 1926, 1 & last Baron Abertay (d 1940); 2 da (Hon Mrs Fordham, Hon Mrs Maitland); *Style* - The Rt Hon Lady Abertay; Mansfield, Callander, Perths

ABINGER, 8 Baron (UK 1835); James Richard Scarlett; DL (Essex 1968); s of 7 Baron Abinger, DSO (d 1943); *b* 28 Sept 1914; *Educ* Eton, Magdalene Cambridge; *m* 1957, Isla, niece of Sir Henry Rivett-Carnac, 7 Bt, and da of late Vice-Adm J W Rivett-Carnac, CB, CBE, DSC; 2 s; *Heir* s Hon James Scarlett; *Career* farmer and businessman, chm Keats Shelley Mem Assoc, KStJ; *Style* - The Rt Hon The Lord Abinger, DL; Clees Hall, Bures, Suffolk (☎ 227 227)

ABNEY-HASTINGS, Hon Amanda Louise; da of Lord Mauchline; *b* 1969; *Style* - The Hon Amanda Abney-Hastings

ABNEY-HASTINGS, Lady Clare Louise; da of Countess of Loudoun by her 3 husb, Peter Abney-Hastings, né Griffiths;

b 8 Dec 1958; *Style* - Lady Clare Abney-Hastings

ABNEY-HASTINGS, Hon Frederick James; s of Countess of Loudoun by her 2 husb, Capt Gilbert Greenwood (d 1951); *b* 29 Jan 1949; *Style* - The Hon Frederick Abney-Hastings

ABNEY-HASTINGS, Hon Lisa; da of Lord Mauchline; *b* 1971; *Style* - The Hon Lisa Abney-Hastings

ABNEY-HASTINGS, Lady Mary Joy; da of Countess of Loudoun by her 3 husb, Peter Abney-Hastings, né Griffiths; *b* 18 March 1957; *Style* - Lady Mary Abney-Hastings

ABNEY-HASTINGS, Lady Margaret Maud; da of Countess of Loudoun by her 3 husb, Peter Abney-Hastings, né Griffiths; *b* 10 Feb 1956; *Style* - Lady Margaret Abney-Hastings

ABNEY-HASTINGS, Hon Rebecca; twin da of Lord Mauchline; *b* 1974; *Style* - Hon Rebecca Abney-Hastings

ABNEY-HASTINGS, Hon Simon; s and h of Lord Mauchline; *b* 1974; *Style* - The Hon Simon Abney-Hastings

ABOYNE, Earl of; Granville Charles Gomer Gordon; s and h of 12 Marquess of Huntly, by his 1 w, Hon Pamela, nee Berry, da of 1 Viscount Kemsley; *b* 4 Feb 1944; *Educ* Gordonstoun; *m* 1972, Jane Elizabeth Angela, da of late Lt-Col Alistair Gibb by his w, Hon Daisy Pearson (da of 2 Viscount Cowdray, DL, and Agnes, yr da of Lord Edward Spencer Churchill, DL, 5 s of 6 Duke of Marlborough); Hon Daisy Pearson had m as her 1 husb Lt Hon Robert Brampton Gurdon (s of 2 Baron Cranworth) and after Lt-Col Gibb's death (1955) m (1962) 1 Baron McCorquodale of Newton, PC; 1 s, 2 da; *Heir* s, Lord Strathavon and Glenlivet; *Style* - Earl of Aboyne; Aboyne Castle, Aberdeenshire (☎ Aboyne 2118)

ABRAHAM, Sir Edward Penley; CBE (1973); s of Albert Abraham; *b* 10 June 1913; *Educ* King Edward VI Sch S'thampton, Queen's Oxford; *m* 1939, Asbjorg Harung, of Norway; 1 s; *Career* kt 1980, FRS 1958, MA DPhil, fellow Lincoln Coll Oxford 1948-, Prof Clinical Pathology 1964-; *Style* - Sir Edward Abraham, CBE; Badger's Wood, Bedwells Heath, Boars Hill, Oxford (☎ 735395)

ABRAHAM, Lady (Rosemary Eustace); da of Louis H King, of Berrow Somerset; *m* 1966, Maj-Gen Sir William Abraham, CBE, as his 2 w, (d 1980); *Style* - Lady Abraham; Kencot Manor, Lechlade, Glos (☎ Filkins 212)

ABRAHAM, Maj-Gen Sutton Martin O'Heguerty; CB (1973), MC and bar (1942 1943); s of Capt E Abraham, CB, late ICS; *b* 26 Jan 1919; *Educ* Eton, Trin Cambridge; *m* 1950, Iona, da of Sir John Stirling, KT, MBE; 2 s, 1 da; *Career* chief Jt Servs Liaison Org BAOR 1971-74, sec Bedford Coll, London U 1976; *Style* - Maj-Gen Sutton Abraham, CB, MC*; c/o Hoare & Co, 37 Fleet st, EC4 (☎ 01 353 4522)

ABRAHAMS, Allan Rose; CMG (1962); s of late Frank Abrahams; *b* 29 Nov 1908; *Educ* Jamaica Coll Jamaica; *m* 1948, Norma Neita; 1 s, 2 da; *Career* civil servant 1927-64, company dir; *Style* - Allan Abrahams Esq, CMG; 20 Widcombe rd, Kingston 6, Jamaica (☎ 78214)

ABRAHAMS, Sir Charles Myer; KCVO (1970); s of late Isidor Abrahams; *b* 25 April 1914; *Educ* Westminster; *m* 1940, Luisa, nee Kramer; 2 da; *Career* dep chm and jt md Aquascutum and assoc cos; *Style* - Sir Charles Abrahams, KCVO; 188 Coombe Lane West, Kingston-upon-Thames, Surrey (☎ 01 942 3379)

ABRAHAMS, Gerald Milton; CBE (1967); s of Isidor Abrahams (d 1943); *b* 20 June 1917; *Educ* Westminster; *m* 1, 1946, Doris, da of Mark Cole, of Brookline Mass; 2 da; m 2, 1972, Marianne, nee Kay; *Career* chm and md Aquascutum & Assoc Cos ltd, FRSA, FBIM; *Style* - Gerald Abrahams Esq CBE; Aquascutum ltd, 100 Regent st, W1 (☎ 01 734 6090)

ABRAHAMS, Ian Charles; s of John Abrahams, of Tatsfield; *b* 15 April 1950; *Educ* Borden G S Sittingbourne, Bradford

U; *m* 1974, Janet, da of Frank Gilling, of Plumstead; 2 da; *Career* CA; fin dir Salter Plastic; *Recreations* motorcycling; *Style* - Ian Abrahams Esq; 334 Burnt Oak Lane, Sidcup, Kent (☎ 01 302 6651)

ABSE, Leo; MP (L) Pontypool 1958-; s of Rudolph Abse; *b* 22 April 1917; *Educ* LSE; *m* 1955, Marjorie, nee Davies; 1 s, 1 da; *Career* slr, chm Welsh PLP 1976; *Style* - Leo Abse Esq, MP; Merchaviah, 396 Cyncoed rd, Cardiff (☎ 751844 and 23252); Beulah, 13 Cavendish av, NW8 (☎ 01 286 7440)

ACHESON, Lady Isabella Augusta; da of 6 Earl of Gosford, OBE; *b* 17 Jan 1950; *Style* - Lady Isabella Acheson; 14 De Vere gdns, W8

ACHESON, Hon Patrick Bernard Victor Montagu; s of 5 Earl of Gosford, MC (d 1954); unc and hp of 7 Earl of Gosford; *b* 4 Feb 1915; *Educ* Harrow, Trin Cambridge, Harvard (MBA); *m* 1946, Judith, da of Mrs F Bate, of Virginia; 3 s, 2 da; *Career* with Internat Bank for Reconstruction & Devpt 1947-65, Pres Culligan Water Conditioning Corpn of N Virginia 1966-80; *Recreations* golf, tennis, gardening; *Clubs* Loudoun Golf; *Style* - The Hon Patrick Acheson; Box 71, Waterford, Va 22190, USA (☎ 703 882 3259)

ACKERMAN, Myron; CBE (Hon 1972); s of late Simon Ackerman; *b* 21 Sept 1913; *Educ* Yale; *m* 1954, Marjorie Jacob; *Career* chm Tuscan Clothing Co ltd, dir Atlas Avenue ltd, d'Avenza spa Carrara Italy; *Style* - Myron Ackerman Esq, Hon CBE; Henhull Cottage, Acton, Nantwich, Cheshire (☎ 65782)

ACKNER, Hon Mr Justice; Hon Sir Desmond James Conrad Ackner; s of Dr Conrad Ackner; *b* 18 Sept 1920; *Educ* Highgate Sch, Clare Cambridge; *m* 1946, Joan, da of late John Evans, JP, and wid of K Spence; 1 s, 2 da; *Career* High Court Judge (Queen's Bench), kt 1971, barr 1945, QC 1961 Pres Senate of Inns of Court and the Bar 1980; *Style* - The Hon Mr Justice Ackner; 7 Rivermill, 151 Grosvenor rd, SW1 (☎ 01 821 8068); Browns House, Sutton, Petworth, W Sussex (☎ Sutton 206)

ACKROYD, Dame (Dorothy) Elizabeth; DBE (1970); da of late Maj Charles Ackroyd, MC; *Educ* St Hugh's Oxford; *Career* chm Patients Assoc 1978-, ind memb Eggs Authority 1970-, chm SE Electricity Consultative Cncl 1972-, memb Seeboard 1972-, Horserace Totalisator Bd 1975-; *Style* - Dame Elizabeth Ackroyd, DBE; 73 St James's st, SW1 (☎ 01 493 6686)

ACKROYD, Sir John Robert Whyte; 2 Bt (UK 1956), of Dewsbury, W Riding of Yorks; s of 1 Bt (d 1973); *b* 2 March 1932; *Educ* Bradfield, Worcester Coll Oxford; *m* 1956, Jennifer Eileen McLeod, da of Henry Stokes Bishop; 2 s, 2 da; *Heir* s, Timothy Ackroyd; *Career* memb Lloyd's, chm and md Ackroyd Underwriting Agencies Ltd 1978-, Freeman of City of London, Liveryman Carpenters' Co; *Style* - Sir John Ackroyd, Bt; 43 Lansdowne cres, Holland Park, W11 (☎ 01 727 5465)

ACLAND, Sir Antony Arthur; KCVO (1976), CMG (1976); s of Brig P Acland, *qv*; *b* 12 March 1930; *Educ* Eton, Ch Ch Oxford; *m* 1956, Clare Verdon; 2 s, 1 da; *Career* HM Diplomatic Serv, Ambass to Spain 1977-80; dep Und-Sec FCO 1980-; *Recreations* reading, shooting, gardening; *Clubs* Travellers'; *Style* - Sir Antony Acland, KCVO, CMG; c/o FCO, SW1

ACLAND, Sir Antony Guy; 5 Bt (UK 1890), of St Mary Magdalen Oxford; s of 4 Bt (d 1978); *b* 17 Aug 1916; *Educ* Winchester, RMA Woolwich; *m* 1, 1939, Avriel Ann (d 1943), da of late Capt Mervyn Edward John Wingfield-Stratford, WS; 1 da; m 2, 1944, Margaret Joan, da of late Maj Nelson Rooke, HLI; 1 s, 1 da; *Heir* s, Maj Christopher Acland; *Style* - Sir Antony Acland, Bt; Sunny Bank, Totland Bay, Isle of Wight (☎ Freshwater 2085)

ACLAND, John Dyke; s and h of Sir Richard Acland, 15 Bt; *b* 13 May 1939; *Educ* Clifton, Magdalene Cambridge, U of West Indies; *m* 1961, Virginia, da of Roland Forge, of The Grange, Barnold-le-Beck, Lincs; 2 s, 1 da; *Style* - John Acland Esq; 15 Canynge sq, Clifton, Bristol 8

ACLAND, Maj-Gen Sir John Hugh Bevil; KCB (1980), CBE (1978); s of Brig Peter Acland,*qv*, and bro of Sir Antony Acland, KCVO, CMG; *b* 26 Nov 1928; *Educ* Eton; *m* 1953, Myrtle, da of Brig Alastair Crawford, of Stirlingshire; 1 s, 1 da; *Career* GOC SW Dist 1978-; *Style* - Maj-Gen Sir John Acland, KCB, CBE; HQ SW District, Bulford Camp, Salisbury, Wilts; Feniton Court, Honiton, Devon

ACLAND, Lady; Katherine; *m* 1935, Sir John Acland, KBE (d 1981); 3 s, 3 da; *Style* - Lady Acland; Mount Peel, Peel Forest, S Canterbury, New Zealand

ACLAND, Martin Edward; JP (Herts 1964); s of Lt-Col Arthur Acland, OBE, MC, of Cowes; *b* 31 July 1932; *Educ* Eton; *m* 1956, Anne, da of Stanley Runton, of Pine Lodge, Ilkley; 3 s; *Career* formerly 2 Lt 11 Hussars; dir Mercantile Credit; High Sheriff Herts 1978-79; *Recreations* shooting, sailing; *Clubs* Roy Yacht Sqdn, Seaview Yacht; *Style* - Martin Acland Esq, JP; Standon Green End, Ware, Herts (☎ Dane End 233)

ACLAND, Brig Peter Bevil Edward; OBE (1945), MC (1941), TD, JP (Devon 1962), DL (1948); s of Col A Acland, CBE; *b* 9 July 1902; *Educ* Eton, Ch Ch Oxford; *m* 1927, Susan, da of late Canon H Barnett; 2 s (Sir Antony Acland, KCVO, CMG, and Maj-Gen Sir John Acland, KCB, CBE, *qqv*); *Career* farmer 1946-80; Vice-Lt of Devon 1962-78, High Sheriff 1961, JP 1962, DL 1948; *Style* - Brig Peter Acland OBE MC TD JP DL; Little Court-,Feniton, Honiton, Devon

ACLAND, Sir Richard Thomas Dyke; 15 Bt (E 1678, with precedency from 1644), of Columb-John, Devon; s of Rt Hon Sir Francis Dyke Acland, 14 Bt, PC, MP (Richmond, N Yorks), JP, DL (d 1939); *b* 26 Nov 1906; *Educ* Rugby, Balliol Oxford; *m* 1936, Anne, da of R Alford, of Chelsea; 3 s; *Heir* s, John Dyke Acland; *Career* formerly Lance Bombardier AA Artillery; MP (Lib and subsequently C'wlth) Barnstaple 1939-45, MP (L) Gravesend 1947-55; schoolmaster 1955-59, lecturer St Luke's Coll Exeter 1960-74; *Recreations* riding; *Style* - Sir Richard Acland, Bt; Sprydon, Broadclyst, Exeter (☎ 82412)

ACLOQUE, Hon Mrs (Camilla Anne Bronwen); *née* Scott-Ellis; da of 9 Baron Howard de Walden and 5 Baron Seaford by his 1 w, Countess Irene Harrach; *b* 1 April 1947; *m* 1971, Guy Acloque; 1 s, 2 twin da; *Career* co-heiress to Barony of Howard de Walden; *Style* - The Hon Mrs Acloque; Alderley Grange, Wotton-under-Edge, Glos (☎ 2161)

ACTON, 3 Baron (UK 1869); Sir John Emerich Henry Lyon-Dalberg-Acton; 10 Bt (E 1644), CMG (1963), MBE (1945), TD (1949); also Hereditary Duke of Dalberg (through the m of Sir Ferdinand Acton, 7 Bt, f of the 1 Baron, with Marie, only child and h of Emerich Joseph, Duke de Dalberg, by his w, Pellina, da of Marchese Brignole-Sale of Genoa) and a Patrician of Naples; s of 2 Baron Acton, KCVO (d 1924); *b* 15 Dec 1907; *Educ* Downside, Sandhurst, Trin Cambridge; *m* 1931, Hon Daphne Strutt, da of 4 Baron Rayleigh, JP, DL, by his 1 w, Lady Mary Clements, 2 da of 4 Earl of Leitrim; 5 s, 5 da; *Heir* s, Hon Richard Lyon-Dalberg-Acton; *Career* served WW II as Maj Shropshire Yeomanry; chm Br Continental Hldgs (Insur Bkers), Wood Acton Ltd; Tstee Cold Comfort Farm Soc 1967-; was co dir & agriculturist in Rhodesia (now Zimbabwe) 1947-67; was co dir in Swaziland 1967-71; patron of one living (but being Roman Catholic cannot present); *Clubs* Shrewsbury, British American (Palma); *Style* - The Rt Hon The Lord Acton, CMG MBE TD; Ca-Na Rosalinda, Pollensa, Majorca (☎ 531071)

ACTON, Hon Edward David Joseph Lyon-Dalberg-; s of 3 Baron Acton, CMG, MBE, TD; *b* 1949; *Educ* York U; *m* 1972, Stella Marie, da of Henry Conroy, of 8 Stirling rd, Bolton; 2 da; *Style* - The Hon Edward Lyon-Dalberg-Acton; 170 Mather av, Allerton, Liverpool 18

ACTON, Sir Harold Mario Mitchell; CBE (1965); s of Arthur Acton and Hortense Mitchell; *b* 5 July 1904; *Educ* Eton, Ch Ch Oxford; *Career* author, kt 1974; *Style* - Sir Harold Acton, CBE; La Pietra, Florence, Italy (☎ 496 156)

ACTON, Rev Hon John Charles Lyon-Dalberg-; s of 3 Baron Acton, CMG, MBE, TD; *b* 1943; *Educ* Gregorian U, Rome; *Career* Prof of Dogmatic Theology, Westminster Diocesan Seminary; *Style* - The Reverend the Hon John Lyon-Dalberg-Acton;Westminster Diocesan. Seminary, 28Beaufort st, SW3

ACTON, Hon Joan Henrica Josepha Mary Clare Lyon-Dalberg-; da of 2 Baron Acton, KCVO (d 1924); *b* 1915; *Style* - The Hon Joan Lyon-Dalberg-Acton; 1 Churchgate, Southport

ACTON, Hon Margaret Mary Teresa Lyon-Dalberg-; da of 2 Baron Acton, KCVO (d 1924); *b* 1919; *Style* - The Hon Margaret Lyon-Dalberg-Acton; 602 Park West, W1

ACTON, Hon Peter Hedley Lyon-Dalberg-; s of 3 Baron Acton, CMG, MBE, TD; *b* 1950; *Educ* Cirencester Agric Coll; *Style* - The Hon Peter Lyon-Dalberg-Acton; c/o Tirling Place, Chelmsford, Essex

ACTON, Hon Richard Gerald Lyon-Dalberg-; s and h of 3 Baron Acton, CMG, MBE, TD; *b* 30 July 1941; *Educ* St George's Coll Salisbury, Rhodesia, and Trin Oxford; *m* 1, 1965, Hilary Juliet Sarah (d 1973), da of Dr L O C Cookson, of Perth, WA; 1 s; m 2, 1974, Judith Garfield, da of the Hon R S Garfield Todd, of Hokonu Ranch, P O Dadaya, Rhodesia (formerly PM of S Rhodesia); *Career* barr Inner Temple 1976, dir Coutts & Co 1971-74; *Style* - The Hon Richard Lyon-Dalberg-Acton; 95 Ebury st, SW1

ACTON, Hon Robert Peter Lyon-Dalberg-; s of 3 Baron Acton, CMG, MBE, TD; *b* 1946; *m* 1974, Michele, da of Henri Laigle, France; 2 s; *Style* - The Hon Robert Lyon-Dalberg-Acton; National Stud, Newmarket, Suffolk

ACTON, William Antony; s of late William Acton; *b* 8 April 1904; *Educ* Eton, Trin Cambridge; *m* 1932, Joan, da of Hon Francis Pearson; 1 da; *Career* served with Treasury 1939-45, thereafter banker, High Sheriff London 1955; *Style* - William Acton Esq; Poste Restante, Corfu, Greece (☎ 91 236)

ACUTT, Sir Keith Courtney KBE (1962, CBE 1957); s of late Guy Acutt; *b* 6 Oct 1909; *Career* dep chm Anglo-American Corp of S Africa ltd, dir De Beers Consolidated Mines ltd; *Style* - Sir Keith Acutt, KBE; 44 Main st, Johannesburg, S Africa (☎ 838 8111)

ADAIR, Maj-Gen Sir Allan Henry Shafto; 6 Bt (UK 1838), of Flixton Hall, Suffolk, GCVO (1974, KCVO 1967, CVO 1957), CB (1945), DSO (1940), MC* (1918), JP (Suffolk), DL (Co Antrim); s of Sir Shafto Adair, 5 Bt, JP, DL (d 1949); *b* 3 Nov 1897; *Educ* Harrow; *m* 1919, Enid, da of William Dudley Ward (s of Hon Humble Dudley Ward, 2 s of 10 Baron Ward and bro of 1 Earl of Dudley) and Hon Eugénie, da of 1 Viscount Esher; (1 s, ka 1943) 3 da; *Heir* none; *Career* Maj-Gen (former Cdr Gds Armoured Division NW Europe), Col Grenadier Gds 1961-74 Lt HM Bodyguard of the Yeomen of the Guard 1951-67; *Recreations* gardening; *Clubs* Turf, Guards & Cavalry; *Style* - Maj-Gen Sir Allan Adair, Bt, GCVO, CB, DSO, MC*, JP, DL; Holy Hill, Strabane, Co Tyrone, N Ireland (☎ 882279); 53 Green st, W1 (☎ 01 629 3860)

ADAIR, (Arthur) Robin; CVO (1961), MBE (1947); s of Francis Adair, MBE; *b* 10 Feb 1913; *Educ* abroad, Emmanuel Cambridge; *m* 1952, Diana, da of Neville Synnott, of Rickmansworth; 1 s; *Career* High Commissioner Brunei 1968-72 (ret 1972); *Recreations* flying, painting; *Clubs* Naval & Military, Tiger (Redhill), Kilkenny Flying; *Style* - Robin Adair Esq, CVO, MBE; Grove House, Youghal, Co Cork, Eire (☎ 2930)

ADAM, Hon Sir Alistair (Alexander Duncan Grant) ; s of late Rev and Prof Adam; *b* 30 Nov 1902; *Educ* Scottish Coll Melbourne, Melbourne U; *m* 1930, Nora Laver; 1 s. 2 da; *Career* kt 1970, Judge Supreme Court of Victoria 1957-74, QC 1950; *Style* - Hon Sir Alistair Adam; 39 Walsh st, Balwyn, Vic 3103, Australia (☎ 801524)

ADAM, Christopher Eric Forbes; s of Eric Forbes Adam, CMG (2 s of Sir Frank

Forbes Adam, 1 Bt, CB, CIE, JP, DL); hp of unc, Gen Sir Ronald Forbes Adam, 2 Bt, GCB, DSO, OBE; *b* 12 Feb 1920; *Educ* Abinger Hill Sch Surrey and privately; *m* 1957, Patricia, da of John Wreford Brown; *Style* - Christopher Adam Esq; 46 Rawlings st, SW3

ADAM, Colin Gurdon Forbes; CSI (1924); Sir Frank Forbes Adam, 1 Bt; *b* 18 Dec 1899; *Educ* Eton, King's Cambridge; *m* 1920, Hon Irene Lawley, da of 3 Baron Wenlock; 2 s, 1 da (and 1 s decd); *Style* - Colin Adam Esq, CSI; The Grange, Elvington, Yorks (☎ 493)

ADAM, David Lionel; TD (1950); s of Cdr Lionel Stuart Moncrieffe Adam, RN, of Hythe, Kent; *b* 15 Oct 1915; *Educ* Christ's Hosp; *m* 1945, Marjorie, da of Gerald Sharpe, of Charlwood, Surrey; 2 s; *Career* Maj Middle East 1940-45; CA, man ptnr Mann Judd & Co 1968-75; *Recreations* walking; *Clubs* Naval & Military; *Style* - David Adam Esq, TD; The Grange, Ruckinge, Ashford, Kent (☎ 023373 2400)

ADAM, Gordon Johnston; MEP (L) Northumbria 1979-; s of John Adam; *b* 28 March 1934; *Educ* Leeds U; *m* 1973, Sarah Seely; 1 s; *Career* Mining engnr NCB 1959-79; *Style* - Gordon Adam Esq, MEP; 2 Queens rd , Whitley Bay, Tyne and Wear (☎ 528616)

ADAM, Robin (Robert Wilson); s of R Adam; *b* 21 May 1923; *Educ* Fettes; *m* 1957, Marion Scott; *Career* md BP 1975-; *Style* - Robin Adam Esq; 25 Onslow sq, SW 7

ADAM, Gen Sir Ronald Forbes; 2 Bt (UK 1917), of Hankelow Court, Co Chester, GCB (1946, KCB 1941, CB 1939), DSO (1918), OBE (1919); s of Sir Frank Forbes Adam, 1 Bt, CB, CIE, JP, DL (d 1926); *b* 30 Oct 1885; *Educ* Eton, RMA Woolwich; *m* 1915, Anna, da of Frederick Pitman, of Twyford; 3 da (and 1 da decd); *Heir* n, Christopher Forbes Adam; *Career* Gen, served 1914-18 France, 1939-40 France; Pres UN Assoc; Dep-CIGS 1938-39, GOC-in-C N Cmmd 1940-41, Adj-Gen to Forces 1941-46; chm & Dir-Gen Br Cncl 1946-54, chm exec bd UNESCO 1952-54; *Clubs* Athenaeum, Naval & Military; *Style* - Gen Sir Ronald Adam, Bt, GCB, DSO, OBE; Carylls Lea, Faygate, Horsham (☎ Faygate 213)

ADAMS, Allen; MP (L) Paisley 1979-; *b* Feb 1946; *Educ* Camphill H Sch, Reid-Kerr Tech Coll Paisley; *Style* - Allen Adams Esq, MP; 76 Murray st, Paisley

ADAMS, Air Vice-Marshal Alexander Annan; CB (1957), DFC (1944); s of Capt Norman Adams; *b* 14 Nov 1908; *Educ* Beechmont Sevenoaks, Switzerland, Austria; *m* 1933, Eileen O'Neill; 1 s; *Career* Ch of Staff Far E Air Fce 1957-59, Hawker Siddeley Aviation 1961-66; *Style* - Air Vice-Marshal Alexander Adams, CB, DFC; Pound Cottage, Loders, Dorset

ADAMS, Hon Lady - Hon (Mary) Elizabeth; *née* Lawrence; da of 3 Baron Trevethin and 1 Oaksey, DSO, TD, PC (d 1971); *b* 1922; *m* 1954, Sir Philip George Doyne Adams, KCMG; 2 s, 2 da; *Style* - The Hon Lady Adams; 78 Sussex sq, W2

ADAMS, Hon Mrs (Eileen Esther); *née* Handcock; da of late 7 Baron Castlemaine; *b* 1931; *m* 1959, Flight-Lt Terence Frank Adams, RAF; 2 s, 1 da; *Style* - The Hon Mrs Adams; c/o National Westminster Bank, 851 Gleadless rd, Sheffield 12

ADAMS, Ernest Malcolm; s of Hastings Adams (d 1942); *b* 25 Jan 1933; *Educ* Montfort H S Yercaud, Loyola Coll Madras; *m* 1958, Frances, da of Francis Stephens, of W Australia; 1 s, 2 da; *Career* Racing Man & Assist Sec W Australia Turf Club 1966-; dir Fairplay Newspapers & Printing Works Pty 1977; *Recreations* boating, water skiing, fishing, electronics; *Clubs* W Australian Cricket Assoc, Fremantle Sailing, W A Masonic; *Style* - Ernest Adams Esq; 27 Links rd, Applecross, W Australia 6153 (☎ 09 364 3121)

ADAMS, Sir John Bertram; CMG (1962); s of John Adams; *b* 24 May 1920; *Educ* Eltham Coll; *m* 1943, Renie Warburton; 1 s, 2 da; *Career* kt 1980, FRS 1963, Exec Dir-Gen CERN 1976-; *Style* - Sir John Adams, CMG; Champ Rosset, 1297 Founex VD, Switzerland

ADAMS, Rear-Adm John Harold; CB (1967), MVO (1957); *b* 19 Dec 1918; *Educ* Glenalmond; *m* 1, 1943, Mary Parker (m diss 1961); 1 s (decd); m 2, 1961, Ione Eadie, MVO; 2 s, 2 da; *Career* Asst Chf Naval Staff (Policy) 1966-68, Dir Gen Br Paper and Board Indust Fedn 1974-; *Style* - Rear-Adm John Adams, CB, MVO; The Oxdrove House, Burghclere, Newbury, Berks (☎ Burghclere 385)

ADAMS, John Kenneth; s of late Thomas Adams; *b* 3 June 1915; *Educ* City of Oxford Sch, Balliol Oxford; *m* 1944, Margaret, nee Fortescue; *Career* ed Country Life 1958-73; *Style* - John Adams Esq; 95 Alleyn Pk, W Dulwich, SE 21

ADAMS, Rt Hon John Michael Geoffrey Manningham; PC (1977), QC (1980); s of Sir Grantley Adams, of Barbados; *b* 24 Sept 1931; *Educ* Harrison Coll Barbados, Magdalen Oxford; *m* 1962, Genevieve, da of Philip Turner, CBE, of Ewell; 2 s; *Career* BBC producer 1959-62, barr 1963-76, MP (Barbados) 1966- (Leader Oppn 1971-76); PM 1976-; *Recreations* boating, gardening, stamp collecting, Freemasonry, watching cricket; *Clubs* Union (Barbados); *Style* - The Rt Hon John Adams, PC, QC; 14 Walkers Ter, Gun Hill, St George 5, Barbados (☎ 809 42 63179)

ADAMS, Murray; s of Frank Adams, of Mansfield Vict Australia; *b* 15 July 1919; *Educ* Trin G S Melbourne; *m* 1946, Ethne Margot Maplesden; 1 s, 2 da; *Career* state dir Nat Safety Cncl of Australia, Qld Dvn, 1973-; *Recreations* tennis; *Style* - Murray Adams Esq; 16 Lone st, Indooroopilly, Qld 4068, Australia (☎ 07 3702816)

ADAMS, Sir Maurice Edward; KBE (1958, OBE 1943); s of Herbert Adams; *b* 20 Aug 1901; *m* 1924, Hilda Williams; 1 s, 1 da; *Career* Admty Engnr 1927-46 and 1954-59, FICE, company dir, consultant to Brian Colquhoun & Ptnrs 1971-; *Style* - Sir Maurice Adams, KBE; 12 Melvill Lane, Willingdon, Eastbourne, E Sussex

ADAMS, Hon Mrs (Marjorie Heather); *née* Davies; JP (Barry); da of late 1 Baron Darwen; *b* 27 Oct 1923; *Educ* Queen Mary's Sch Lytham, Ayton Sch & The Mount Sch York; *m* 1944, Frederick Joseph Adams, CBE; 1 s; *Recreations* painting, tennis; *Clubs* Roy Overseas League; *Style* - The Hon Mrs Adams, JP; Ynysdawel, Llancarfan, Barry, S Glam (☎ Bonvilston 292)

ADAMS, Sir Philip George Doyne; KCMG (1969, CMG 1959); s of late George Adams; *b* 7 Dec 1915; *Educ* Lancing, Ch Ch Oxford; *m* 1954, Hon Elizabeth Lawrence, da of 3 Baron Trevethin and (1) Oaksey; 2 s, 2 da; *Career* dir Ditchley Fndn 1977-, ambass to Egypt 1973-75; *Style* - Sir Philip Adams, KCMG; 78 Sussex sq, W2; Ditchley Park, Enstone, Oxon

ADAMS, (John) Roland; QC (1949); late Alfred Adams; s of 24 July 1900; *b* Charterhouse, New Coll Oxford; *m* 1, 1924, Ruth, nee Schlivek (m dis 1946); m 2, 1946, Violet, da of Sir Francis Hanson; *Career* barr 1925; *Style* - Roland Adams Esq, QC; Little Gubbions, Gubbions Hall, Great Leighs, Chelmsford (☎ Gt Leighs 248)

ADAMS, Richard Borlase; s of James Adams; *b* 9 Sept 1921; *Educ* Winchester, Trin Oxford; *m* 1951, Susan Lambert; 2 s, 1 da; *Career* md P&O 1979-, chm British India Steam Navigation Co ltd 1970, dir Clerical Medical & General Life Assurance Soc 1975; *Style* - Richard Adams Esq; Beacon House, Bethersden, Ashford, Kent (☎ Bethersden 247)

ADAMS, Richard George; s of Evelyn Adams, FRCS; *b* 10 May 1920; *Educ* Bradfield, Worcester Coll Oxford; *m* 1949, Barbara Acland; 2 da; *Career* author; Books *Watership Down 1972 (filmed 1978)*; *Style* - Richard Adams Esq; Knocksharry House, Lhergy-Dhoo, nr Peel, IOM

ADAMS, Mrs Vyvyan (Mary Grace); OBE (1953); da of late Edward and Catherine Campin; *Educ* Godolphin Sch, U Coll Cardiff, Newnham Cambridge; *m* 1925, Vyvyan Adams (d 1951), sometime MP W Leeds; 1 da; *Career* with BBC 1930-58, chm Telephone Users Assoc; *Style* - Mrs Vyvyan Adams, OBE; 10 Regent's Pk rd, NW1 (☎ 01 485 8324)

ADAMSON, Sir (William Owen) Campbell; s of late John Adamson; *b* 26 June 1922; *Educ* Rugby, CCC Cambridge; *m* 1945, Gilvray, nee Allan; 2 s, 2 da; *Career* chm Abbey Nat Bldg Soc 1978-, Revertex Chemicals 1978-, dir Imperial Gp, Renold Ltd 1976-, Lazard Bros, Doulton & Co 1977-, dir-gen CBI 1969-76 kt 1976; *Style* - Sir Campbell Adamson; 11 St Augustine's House, Bloomburg st, SW1; Birchamp House, Newland, Glos

ADAMSON, Norman Joseph; QC (Scot 1979); s of Joseph Adamson; *b* 29 Sept 1930; *Educ* Glasgow U; *m* 1961, Patricia, nee Guthrie; 4 da; *Career* Legal Sec to Lord Advocate and First Parly Draftsman for Scotland 1979-, barr Gray's Inn 1959; *Style* - Norman Adamson Esq, QC; 6 Wildoaks, Acacia rd, Staines, Middx (☎ 50319)

ADAMSON, Lt-Col William John Campbell; TD, JP (1951), DL (Angus 1971); s of Capt W Adamson (k 1915; gn through his m, Norah, da of Rt Hon James Campbell, PC, MP, of Rt Hon Sir Henry Campbell-Bannerman, Liberal PM 1905-08), of Careston Castle, Brechin; *b* 13 March 1914; *Educ* Eton, Trin Oxford; *m* 1947, Margaret, da of James Helme; 2 s, 3 da; *Career* memb Roy Co of Archers (Queen's Bodyguard for Scotland); md Careston Estates; CC Angus for 24 years, Hon Sheriff Angus; *Recreations* farming, shooting, fishing; *Style* - Lt-Col William Adamson, TD, JP, DL; Careston Castle, Brechin, Angus (☎ 242); Craig Lodge, Glenposen (☎ Cortachy 314); Nathro Lodge, Lethnot

ADCOCK, Sir Robert Henry; CBE (1941); s of late Henry Adcock; *b* 27 Sept 1899; *Educ* Atherstone Warwicks; *m* Mary, da of R Wadsworth, of Handforth Hall Cheshire; 1 s, 2 da; *Career* kt 1950, Clerk of CC Lancs 1944-60, Clerk of the Peace Lancs and Lancs Ltcy, solr; *Style* - Sir Robert Adcock, CBE; Summer Place, Rock End, Torquay, Devon (☎ 22775)

ADCOCK, Robert Wadsworth; DL (Essex 1978); s of Sir Robert Adcock; *b* 29 Dec 1932; *Educ* Rugby; *m* 1957, Valerie Robins; 1 s, 1 da; *Career* ch exec and clerk Essex CC 1976-; *Style* - Robert Adcock Esq, DL; The Christmas Cottage, Gt Sampford, Saffron Walden, Essex (☎ Gt Sampford 363)

ADDERLEY, Hon James Nigel Arden; s and h of 7 Baron Norton, OBE; *b* 2 June 1947; *m* 1971, Jacqueline Julie, da of Guy W Willett; 1 da; *Style* - The Hon James Adderley; 50 Adam and Eve Mews, Kensington High st, W8 6UJ

ADDERLEY, Hon Michael Charles; OBE (1960), AFC; s of 6 Baron Norton (d 1961); *b* 1917; *Educ* Radley and Sidney Sussex, Cambridge; *m* 1953, Margrethe Ann, MRCVS, da of Karl Gerhardt Ornbo; 3 s, 1 da; *Career* Group Capt RAF (ret); 1939-45 War (AFC and Bar), Malaya 1949-51 (King's Commendation), Korea 1951-52 (American DFC, Bronze Star and Air Medal); *Style* - The Hon Michael Adderley OBE AFC*; 23 Welham rd, Norton, Malton, Yorks YO17 9DS

ADDERLEY, Hon Nigel John; s of 7 Baron Norton, OBE; *b* 1950; *Career* Capt, Life Gds; *Style* - The Hon Nigel Adderley

ADDINGTON, 5 Baron (UK 1887); James Hubbard; s of Lt-Col John Hubbard, OBE (eldest s of Hon Cecil Hubbard, 3 s of 1 Baron Addington, PC, sometime MP for Buckingham and City of London; Cecil's mother was Hon Maria, da of 9 Lord Napier); *b* 3 Nov 1930; *Educ* Eastbourne Coll, Chadacre Ag Inst; *m* 1961, Alexandra, da of Norman Ford Millar; 2 s, 2 da; *Heir* s, Hon Dominic Hubbard; *Career* served with Br S Africa Police S Rhodesia (now Zimbabwe) 1955-58; *Style* - The Rt Hon The Lord Addington; c/o Peter Hubbard Esq, Folly Farm, Bramfield, Halesworth

ADDINGTON, Hon Christopher John; s and h of 7 Viscount Sidmouth; *b* 10 April 1941; *Educ* Downside, BNC Oxford; *m* 1963, Clio Mona, da of John Peristiany; *Style* - The Hon Christopher Addington; April Cottage, 15 Church st, Kidlington, Oxon

ADDINGTON, Hon Elizabeth Clare; da of late 6 Viscount Sidmouth; *b* 1928; *Style* - The Hon Elizabeth Addington; Coachmans Cottage, Pewsey, Wilts

ADDINGTON, Hon Gurth Louis Francis; s of late 6 Viscount Sidmouth; *b* 1920; *Educ* Downside, BNC Oxford; *m* 1950, Patience Gillian, da of late Col L E Travers, RE; 3 s, 6 da (inc twins); *Career* RAF 1939-45; *Style* - The Hon Gurth Addington; 47 Clarence st, Devonport, Auckland, NZ

ADDINGTON, Hon Hiley William Dever; s of late 6 Viscount Sidmouth; *b* 1917; *m* 1942, Brenda Swanney, da of late Robert Charles Wallace, CMG, Princ of Queen's U Kingston Canada; 2 s, 1 da; *Career* Lt-Cdr RD (ret), MIMechE; *Style* - The Hon Hiley Addington; 1688 Mills st, Sarnia, Ontario, Canada

ADDINGTON, Hon Jeremy Francis; s of 7 Viscount Sidmouth; *b* 1947; *Educ* Ampleforth; *m* 1970, Grete, nee Henningsen of Randers, Denmark; 1 s, 1 da; *Style* - The Hon Jeremy Addington; Herskind Sondergaard, Praestbrovej 14, Herskind, 8464 Galten, Denmark

ADDINGTON, Hon Leslie Richard Bagnall; DFC (1951); s of 6 Viscount Sidmouth; *b* 20 Sept 1923; *Educ* Downside; *m* 1955, Anne, da of Capt Trevor Hume and Sybil, sis of Sir Maurice Lacy, 2 Bt; 2 s, 2 da; *Career* served RA 1941-71 Far East, ret as Lt-Col, CO Essex Yeo 1965-66 and 100 (Yeomanry) FD Regt 1967-68; *Clubs* Army & Navy; *Style* - Lt-Col The Hon Leslie Addington DFC; Polebridge, Sutton Veny, Warminster, Wilts (☎ Sutton Veny 202)

ADDINGTON, Hon Thomas Raymond Casamajor; MC; s of late 6 Viscount Sidmouth; *b* 1919; *Educ* Downside; *m* 1947, Veronique (d 1970), da of Emile Wirtz of Antwerp, Belgium; 3 s, 4 da; *Career* Maj (ret) RHA, War with Commandos (MC) 1939-45; *Style* - The Hon Thomas Addington MC; Highway Farm, nr Calne, Wilts

ADDINGTON, Hon Veronica Mary; da of 7 Viscount Sidmouth; *b* 1944; *Style* - The Hon Veronica Addington; 67 East st, Thame, Oxon

ADDIS, Sir John Mansfield; KCMG (1973, CMG 1959); s of late Sir Charles Addis; *b* 11 June 1914; *Educ* Rugby, Ch Ch Oxford; *Career* Ambass to China 1972-74, memb adv cncl V&A Museum 1977-, Trustee British Museum 1977-, Sr Res Fell Contemporary Chinese Studies Wolfson Coll Oxford 1975-; *Recreations* Chinese porcelain, gardening; *Clubs* Boodle's; *Style* - Sir John Addis, KCMG; Wolfson College, Oxford (☎ 55605); 7D Pont st, SW1; Woodside, Frant, Tunbridge Wells (☎ Frant 202)

ADDISON, 3 Viscount (UK 1945); Michael Addison; s of 1 Viscount Addison, KG, PC, MD, FRCS, sometime MP Shoreditch and Swindon (d 1951); suc er bro, 2 Viscount Addison, 1976; *b* 12 April 1914; *Educ* Hele's Sch Exeter, Balliol Oxford; *m* 1936, Kathleen, da of late Rt Rev & Rt Hon Bishop John Wand, KCVO, DD, formerly 110 Bp of London; 1 s, 2 da; *Heir* s, Hon William Addison; *Career* Civil Serv 1935-65, Polytechnic Lecturer 1966-76; memb Roy Inst Public Admin, Assoc of Teachers of Management; *Style* - The Rt Hon The Viscount Addison; Old Stables, Maplehurst, Horsham, W Sussex (☎ Lower Beeding 298)

ADDISON, Dorothy, Viscountess; Beatrice Dorothy; da of F Percy Low, of Staines; *b* 1896; *m* 1937, as his 2 w, 1 Viscount Addison, KG, PC, MD, FRCS (d 1951); *Style* - The Rt Hon Dorothy, Viscountess Addison; 6 Edgecote House, Amersham Hill, High Wycombe, Bucks

ADDISON, Joseph; CBE (1967); s of Francis Addison; *b* 30 May 1912; *Educ* Eton, Trin Cambridge; *m* 1938, Wendy, da of Cecil Payn, of Durban; 1 s, 1 da; *Career* Maj Queen's Roy Regt WW II; slr 1936; chm London Policy Gp, Internat Oil Indust 1971; *Style* - Joseph Addison Esq, CBE; The Weir House, Alresford, Hants (☎ 2320)

ADDISON, Kenneth George; OBE (1978); s of Herbert Addison; *b* 1 Jan 1923; *Educ* Felixstowe G S; *m* 1945, Maureen Newman; 1 s, 1 da; *Career* dep ch gen man Sun Alliance & London Insurance Gp 1976- (dir 1971-76), FCIS, FCII, FIArb; *Style* - Kenneth Addison Esq, OBE;

Ockley, 13 Hillcroft av, Purley, Surrey (☎ 01 660 2793)

ADDISON, Hon William Matthew Wand; s and h of 3 Viscount Addison; *b* 13 June 1945; *Educ* King's Sch Bruton, Essex Inst of Ag; *m* 1970, Joanna Mary, da of John Dickinson, of Blyborough Grange, Lincs; 1 s, 2 da; *Style* - The Hon William Addison; Kingersby Hall, Market Rasen, Lincs

ADDISON, Sir William Wilkinson; JP (1949), DL (Essex 1973); s of Joseph Addison; *b* 4 April 1905; *m* 1929, Phoebe, nee Dean; *Career* chm Cncl Magistrates Assoc 1970-76, Verderer Epping Forest 1957-, FSA, FRHistS, kt 1974; *Style* - Sir William Addison, JP, DL; Ravensmere, Epping, Essex (☎ 73439)

ADDLESHAW, His Hon John Lawrence; s of Harold Addleshaw; *b* 30 Oct 1902; *Educ* Shrewsbury, Univ Oxford; *Career* Circuit Judge 1960-75; *Style* - His Hon John Addleshaw; 3 College House, Southdowns rd, Bowdon, Altrincham, Cheshire (☎ 061 928 2139)

ADEANE, Baron (Life Peer UK 1972); Michael Edward Adeane; GCB (1968, KCB 1955, CB 1947), GCVO (1962, KCVO 1951, MVO 1946), PC (1953), Royal Victorian Chain (1972); s of Capt Harry Adeane, late Coldstream Gds (ka 1914; s of Adm Edward Stanley Adeane, CMG, JP, DL, by his w, Lady Edith Dalzell, da of 11 Earl of Carnwath), and Hon Victoria Eugenie, nee Bigge, da of 1 and last Baron Stamfordham, GCB, GCIE, GCVO, KCSI, KCMG, ISO, DCL (Private Sec to HM George V); *b* 30 Sept 1910; *Educ* Eton, Magdalene Cambridge (Hon Fellow 1971); *m* 1939, Helen, da of Richard Chetwynd-Stapleton (ggggs of 3 Viscount Chetwynd) and Vera (da of Andrew Maitland-Makgill-Crichton, gggs of 6 Earl of Lauderdale); 1 s, 1 da; *Career* Lt-Col Coldstream Gds NW Europe 1944-45 & reg commission 1931-53; Equerry & Assist Priv Sec to King George VI 1937-52 & HM The Queen 1952-53, Priv Sec to HM The Queen & Keeper of HM's Archives 1953-72; chm Roy Commission on Hist Monuments 1972-; dir Roy Bank of Canada 1972-, Banque Belge Ltd 1972-, The Diners Club Ltd 1976-; memb Br Library Bd 1972-; *Recreations* fishing, shooting; *Clubs* Brooks's, Beefsteak, Pratt's; *Style* - The Rt Hon The Lord Adeane, GCB, GCVO PC; Mosshead Cottage, Kildrummy, Alford, Aberdeenshire (☎ Kildrummy 260); 22 Chelsea sq, SW3 (☎ 01 352 3080)

ADEANE, Hon (George) Edward; s of Baron Adeane, GCB, GCVO, PC (Life Peer); *b* 4 Oct 1939; *Educ* Eton, Magdalene Cambridge; *Career* Private Sec to HRH The Prince of Wales 1979-, barr 1962; *Style* - The Hon Edward Adeane; B4 Albany, Piccadilly, W1 (☎ 01 734 9410)

ADEBO, Simeon Olaosebikan; CFR (1979), CMG (1959); The Okanlomo of Egbaland; s of late Chief Adebo, the Okanlomo of Itoko, Abeokuta; *b* 5 Oct 1913; *Educ* King's Coll Lagos; *m* 1941, Regina Abimbola, da of Chief D Majekodunmi, Abẹokuta; 3 s, 1 da; *Career* chm Nat U Cmmn Nigeria 1975-77, barr 1949, permanent sec Treasury & head Nigerian CS 1958, Nigerian Perm Rep to UN and Cmmr-Gen for economic affairs 1962-67; *Style* - Chief Simeon Adebo CFR CMG; c/o Box 139, Abeokuta, Nigeria

ADEMOLA, Rt Hon Sir Adetokunbo Adegboyega; GCON (1972), CFR (1963), KBE (1963), PC (1963); s of late Sir Ladapo Ademola, Alake of Abeokuta, KBE, CMG; *b* 1 Feb 1906; *Educ* King's Coll Lagos; *m* 1939, Kofoworola, da of late Eric Olawolu Moore, CBE; 3 s, 2 da; *Career* Chllr U of Nigeria 1975-, Ch Justice of Nigeria 1958-72, chm Commonwealth Foundation 1978- kt 1957; *Style* - The Rt Hon Sir Adetokunbo Ademola, GCON, CFR, KBE, PC; The Close, Adetokunbo, Ademola st, Victoria Island, Lagos, Nigera (☎ 52219)

ADEY, (Arthur) Victor; s of Arthur Adey; *b* 2 May 1912; *Educ* Wolverhampton Secdy Sch; *m* 1936, Kathleen Lewis; 1 s, 1 da; *Career* chm Mercantile Credit 1977-, dir Barclays Bank Internatnl 1979-, Ampex Corp (US) 1973-; *Style* - Victor Adey Esq; Rosemount, Burtons Lane, Chalfont St Giles, Bucks (☎ Little Chalfont 2160)

ADLER, John James; s of Cdr Alan Adler, RNVR; *b* 16 Sept 1935; *Educ* Felsted; *m* 1962, Hilary, da of Reginald Drew, of Essex; 2 s, 2 da; *Career* chm A Oppenheim 1979, Cadogan Investments 1970, Tobacco Trade Benevolent Assoc 1977; *Recreations* squash, sailing (yacht Phee Anna - Albacore), rugby; *Clubs* City Livery, Thorpe Bay Yacht; *Style* - John Adler Esq; 4 Green Close, Springfield, Chelmsford, Essex (☎ 0245 59531 home, 01 606 9121 work)

ADLER, Larry (Lawrence Cecil); s of Louis Adler and Sadie Hack; *b* 10 Feb 1914; *Educ* Baltimore City Coll; *m* 1, 1938, Eileen Walser (m diss 1961); 1 s, 2 da; m 2, 1969, Sally Cline (m diss 1977); 1 da; *Career* mouth organist; *Style* - Larry Adler Esq; c/o Michael Bakewell, 118 Tottenham Ct rd, W1

ADLEY, Robert James; MP (C) Christchurch and Lymington 1974-; s of Harry Adley; *b* 2 March 1935; *Educ* Uppingham; *m* 1961, Jane Pople; 2 s; *Career* MP (C) Bristol NE 1970-74, mktng dir Cwlth Holiday Inns of Canada ltd, fndr and 1 chm Brunel Soc, patron SS Great Britain Project; *Style* - Robert Adley Esq, MP; Woodend House, Lymington, Hants

ADRIAN, 2 Baron (UK 1955); Richard Hume Adrian; s of 1 Baron Adrian, OM (d 1955), and Hester, nee Pinsent, DBE, BEM (d 1966); *b* 16 Oct 1927; *Educ* Westminster, Trin Cambridge; *m* 1967, Lucy, da of Alban Caroe, of Campden Hill; *Heir* none; *Career* FRS, Prof of Cell Physiology Cambridge 1978-; *Style* - The Rt Hon The Lord Adrian; Umgeni, Cley, Norfolk; 3 Adams rd, Cambridge (☎ 352090)

AGA KHAN (IV), H H The; Prince Karim; s of late Prince Aly Khan and Hon Joan, nee Yarde-Buller, da of 3 Baron Churston, MVO, OBE, and gs of HH Rt Hon the Aga Khan (III), GCSI, GCIE, GCVO (d 1957); *b* 13 Dec 1936; *Educ* Le Rosey, Harvard; *m* 1969, Sally (Sarah), da of Lt-Col A Croker Poole, and former w of Lord James Crichton-Stuart, s of 5 Marq of Bute; 1 s, 1 da; *Career* spiritual leader and Imam of Ismaili Muslims, granted title HH by HM The Queen 1957, and HRH by late Shah of Iran 1959; *Style* - His Highness the Aga Khan; Aiglemont, 60270 Gouvieux, France (☎ 457 40 22; Telex AKADM 150054 F)

AGAR, Lady Caroline Amy Cora; da of 4 Earl of Normanton (d 1933); *b* 11 July 1899; *Style* - Lady Caroline Agar; Little Park, Ibsley, Ringwood, Hants BH24 3PP

AGAR, Lady Marisa Charlotte; 2 da of 6 Earl of Normanton; *b* 9 Oct 1979; *Style* - Lady Marisa Agar

AGAR, Hon Mark Sidney Andrew; s of 5 Earl of Normanton (d 1967); hp of bro, 6 Earl; *b* 2 Sept 1948; *Educ* Gordonstoun; *m* 1973, Rosemary, da of Maj Philip Marnham; *Career* Lt Blues & Royals; *Style* - The Hon Mark Agar; Fosse Farm, Brokenborough, Malmesbury, Wilts

AGAR, Lady Portia Caroline; eld da of 6 Earl of Normanton; *b* 26 Dec 1976; *Style* - Lady Portia Agar

AGLEN, Anthony John; CB (1957); s of Sir Francis Aglen, GCMG, KBE; *b* 30 May 1911; *Educ* Marlborough, Trin Cambridge; *m* 1946, Audrey, da of Andrew Murray, WS, of Edinburgh; 1 s, 1 da; *Career* entered Scottish Off 1934; dep Sec Scottish Home Dept 1959-60 and Dept of Ag & Fish Scotland 1960-71, memb UK Delegation to 3 UN Conference on Law of the Sea; *Recreations* gardening; *Clubs* New (Edinburgh); *Style* - Anthony Aglen Esq, CB; Birkhill, Earlston, Berwickshire (☎ 307)

AGLIONBY, His Hon Judge; Francis John; s of Francis Aglionby; *b* 17 May 1932; *Educ* Charterhouse, CCC Oxford; *m* 1967, Susan Vaughan; 1 s, 1 da; *Career* barr 1956, Recorder of Crown Court 1975-, Circuit Judge (SE) 1980-; *Style* - His Hon Judge Aglionby; 36 Bark Place, W2 (☎ 01 229 7303)

AGNEW, Dr Andrew David Quentin; s of Col David Agnew (d 1975, s of Col Quentin Agnew, DSO, MVO, JP, DL, 4 s of Sir Andrew Agnew, 8 Bt, MP, DL, by Lady Louisa Noel, eld da of 1 Earl of Gainsborough); hp of cous, Sir Crispin Agnew of Lochnaw, 11 Bt; *b* 31 Dec 1929;

Educ Trin Coll Glenalmond, Edinburgh U, Univ Coll Bangor; *m* 1957, Shirley, nee Smithson; 3 s; *Career* PhD Bangor 1957, univ lectr- Bagdad U 1957-63, Nairobi U 1963-69, sr lectr U of Wales 1969-; *Recreations* ecology, cruising under sail; *Style* - Dr Andrew Agnew; 5/6 Clarach rd, Borth, Dyfed (☎ Borth 314)

AGNEW, Hon Mrs (Agneta Joanna Middleton); da (by 1st marr) of Baron Campbell of Eskan (Life Peer); *b* 1944; *m* 1966, Jonathan Geoffrey William Agnew; 1 s, 2 da; *Style* - The Hon Mrs Agnew; 6 Brompton sq, SW3

AGNEW, Sir (John) Anthony Stuart; 4 Bt (UK 1895), of Great Stanhope St, St George, Hanover Sq, Co London; s of Maj Sir John Stuart Agnew, 3 Bt (d 1957); *b* 25 July 1914; *Heir* bro, Maj George Agnew; *Style* - Sir Anthony Agnew, Bt; c/o Backthorpe Farm, Rougham, Bury St Edmunds, Suffolk

AGNEW OF LOCHNAW, Sir Crispin Hamlyn; 11 Bt (NS 1629), of Lochnaw, Wigtownshire; Chief of the Name of Agnew (recognised by Lyon Court 1976); s of Sir Fulque Melville Gerald Noel Agnew, 10 Bt (d 1975); *b* 13 May 1944; *Educ* Uppingham, Sandhurst; *m* 1980, Susan, da of Jock Strang Steel (2 s of Sir Samuel Strang Steel, 1 Bt, TD, DL, and Hon Vere Cornwallis, 2 da of 1 Baron Cornwallis) and Lesley (da of Lt-Col Sir John Graham, 3 Bt, VC, OBE, by Rachel, 5 da of Col Sir Alexander Sprot, 1 Bt, CMG); *Heir* cous, Dr Andrew Agnew; *Career* Maj RHF (ret 1981); Slains Pursuivant at Arms to the Lord High Constable of Scotland (The Earl of Erroll) 1978-; leader of expeditions to Greenland, Antarctica, Patagonia and Everest; *Recreations* mountaineering, yachting (yacht- 'Oran Na Mara'), heraldry, genealogy; *Clubs* Army & Navy, Puffin's (Edinburgh), Alpine, Alpine Ski; *Style* - Sir Crispin Agnew of Lochnaw, Bt; 3 Lonsdale ter, Edinburgh EH3 9HN (☎ 031 229 7942)

AGNEW, Hon Lady; Hon Doreen Maud; da of 1 Baron Jessel, CB, CMG, TD (d 1950); *b* 1909; *Educ* Univ Coll London, Courtauld Inst London U; *m* 1934, Sir Geoffrey William Gerald Agnew, s of late Charles Gerald Agnew; 2 s, 1 da; *Career* Admin Asst Offices of War Cabinet 1942-43 and 1944-45; *Style* - The Hon Lady Agnew; Flat 3, 6 Onslow sq, SW7; Egmere Farm House, Walsingham, Norfolk

AGNEW, Sir (William) Godfrey; KCVO (1965, CVO 1953), CB (1975); s of late Lennox Agnew; *b* 11 Oct 1913; *Educ* Tonbridge; *m* 1, 1939, Ruth (d 1962), da of late Charles Moore, CVO, MC, and late Lady Dorothie, da of 9 Earl of Denbigh and Desmond, GCVO, and Hon Cecilia Clifford (da of 8 Baron Clifford of Chudleigh); 3 s, 3 da; m 2, Lady (Nancy) Tyrwhitt, widow of Adm Sir St John Tyrwhitt, 2 Bt, KCB, DSO, DSC; 2 step s, 1 step da ; *Career* chm Lady Clare Ltd 1970-, dir Sun Life Assur Soc 1974-, Seaway Shipping Agencies Ltd 1971-, Seaway Holdgs Ltd 1971-, Artagen Properties 1976-; solr 1935, Dep Sec Cabinet Office 1972-74; *Style* - Sir Godfrey Agnew, KCVO, CB; Pinehurst, S Ascot, Berks (☎ Ascot 20036)

AGNEW, Maj George Keith; TD, JP; s of Maj Sir John Stuart Agnew, 3 Bt (d 1957); hp of bro, Sir (John) Anthony Stuart Agnew, 4 Bt; *b* 25 Nov 1918; *Educ* Rugby, Trin Cambridge; *m* 1948, Baroness Anne Merete Louise, da of Baron Schaffalitzky de Muckadell, of Rodkilde, Fyn, Denmark; 2 s; *Career* Maj Suffolk Yeo (Res); *Style* - Maj George Agnew, TD, JP; Blackthorpe Farm, Rougham, Bury St Edmunds

AGNEW, Sir Geoffrey William Gerald; s of late Charles Agnew; *b* 11 July 1908; *Educ* Eton, Trin Cambridge; *m* 1934, Hon Doreen, da of 1 Baron Jessel, CB, CMG; 2 s, 1 da; *Career* chm Thos Agnew & Son 1965-, kt 1973; *Style* - Sir Geoffrey Agnew; 3/6 Onslow sq, SW7 (☎ 01 589 8536); Egmere Farm House, Walsingham, Norfolk (☎ 247)

AGNEW, Jonathan Geoffrey William; s of Sir Geoffrey Agnew and Hon Doreen, da of 1 Baron Jessel, CB, CMG; *b* 30 July 1941; *Educ* Eton, Trin Cambridge; *m* 1966, Hon Agneta Joanna Middleton, da of Baron Campbell of Eskan; 1 s (and 1 s decd), 2 da; *Career* md Morgan Stanley & Co Inc (New York) and Morgan Stanley Int (London) 1977-; *Clubs* Turf, Automobile (Paris); *Style* - Jonathan Agnew Esq; 6 Brompton sq, SW3 (☎ 01 584 8098)

AGNEW, Peter Graeme; MBE (1946); s of late Alan Agnew; *b* 7 April 1914; *Educ* Stowe, Trin Cambridge; *m* 1937, Mary, nee Hervey; 2 s, 2 da; *Career* dep chm Bradbury Agnew & Co (proprietors of Punch) 1969-, ; *Style* - Peter Agnew Esq MBE; Roscaddon, Manaccan, nr Helston, Cornwall (☎ 223)

AGNEW, Sir Peter Garnett; 1 Bt (UK 1957), of Clendry, Co Wigtown; s of Charles Agnew, of Knutsford (n of Sir William Agnew, 1 Bt, JP, of London, *see Sir Anthony Agnew, 4 Bt*); *b* 9 July 1900; *Educ* Repton; *m* 1928, Enid, da of Henry Boan, of Perth W Australia; 1 s; *Heir* s, Quentin Agnew-Somerville; *Career* Cdr RN; MP (C) Camborne 1931-50 and S Worcs 1955-66; ADC to Gov Jamaica 1927-28, Con Whip 1945-50; trustee Historic Churches Preservation Trust 1968-; *Recreations* travel; *Clubs* Carlton, Buck's; *Style* - Sir Peter Agnew, Bt; 2 Smith sq, SW1 (☎ 01 222 7179)

AGNEW, Rudolph Ion Joseph; s of Rudolph Agnew; *b* 12 March 1934; *Educ* Downside; *m* 1, 1957, Tessa Longley (m diss 1965); 1 s; m 2, 1965, Hon Clare, da of 2 Baron Glentoran, KBE, and Lady Diana Wellesley (da of 3 Earl Cowley); 1 s, 1 da; *Career* dep chm and gp ch exec Consolidated Gold Fields Ltd 1978-, FBIM, Fell Game Conservancy; *Style* - Rudolph Agnew Esq; 49 Moorgate, EC2

AGNEW, Lady Teresa Jane; *née* Fox-Strangways; da of 7 Earl of Ilchester (d 1964); *b* 1932; *m* 1, 1953, 9 Viscount Galway (d 1971); m 2, 1972, (Richard) Mark Walter Agnew; *Style* - Lady Teresa Agnew; Melbury House, Dorchester, Dorset; Bishopfield House, Bawtry, Doncaster, Yorks

AGNEW-SOMERVILLE, Hon Mrs (Margaret April Irene); *née* Drummond of Megginch; da and co-heiress presumptive of 15 Baron Strange; *b* 3 April 1939; *m* 1963, Quentin Charles Somerville Agnew-Somerville, *qv*; *Style* - The Hon Mrs Agnew-Somerville; Somerville, Navan, Co Meath

AGNEW-SOMERVILLE, Quentin Charles Somerville; s and h of Sir Peter Agnew, 1 Bt (assumed by Roy Licence 1950 additional surname of Somerville after that of Agnew, and the arms of Somerville quarterly with those of Agnew, on succeeding to the Somerville estate of his maternal unc by m, 2 and last Baron Athlumney, who d 1929, leaving a widow, Margery, da of Henry Boan and sis of Enid, Quentin's mother); *b* 8 March 1929; *m* 1963, Hon Margaret Drummond, da of 15 Baron Strange and Violet (da of Sir Robert Buchanan-Jardine, 2 Bt); 1 s, 2 da; *Career* Sub-Lt RN to 1950, when invalided from service; *Style* - Quentin Agnew-Somerville Esq

AH-CHUEN, Sir Jean Etienne Moilin; *Career* kt 1980; *Style* - Sir Jean Ah-Chuen

AICKIN, Hon Mr Justice; Hon Sir Keith Arthur; KBE (1976); s of J Aickin, of Belfast; *b* 1 Feb 1916, in Melbourne; *Educ* C of E G S Melbourne, Melbourne U; *m* 1952, Elizabeth, nee Gullett; 1 s, 1 da; Career *Justice of Australian High Ct 1976-, QC Vict 1957, Tas 1959, NSW 1967; Style* - Hon Mr Justice Aickin; 41 Marne st, S Yarra, Vic 3141, Australia

AIKEN, Air Chief Marshal Sir John Alexander Carlisle; KCB (1973, CB 1976); s of Thomas Aiken; *b* 22 Dec 1921; *Educ* Birkenhead Sch; *m* 1948, Pamela, nee Bartlett; 1 s, 1 da; *Career* Dir Gen Intell MOD 1978-; *Style* - Air Chief Marshal Sir John Aiken, KCB; MOD, Main Building, SW1

AILESBURY, 8 Marquess of (UK 1821); Sir Michael Sydney Cedric Brudenell-Bruce; 14 Bt (E 1611); also Baron Brudenell (E 1628), Earl of Cardigan (E 1661), Baron Bruce (GB 1746), Earl of Ailesbury (GB 1776), and Earl Bruce and Viscount Savernake (both UK 1821); 30 Hereditary Warden of Savernake Forest; s of 7 Marquess of Ailesbury (d 1974); *b* 31 March 1926; *Educ* Eton; *m* 1, 1952, Edwina (m dis

1961), da of Lt-Col Sir Edward Wills, 4 Bt; 1 s, 2 da; m 2, 1963 (m dis 1974), Juliette, da of Hilary Kingsford; 2 da; m 3, 1974, Caroline, da of Cdr Owen Wethered, JP, DL, RN (ret), and former w of Simon Romilly; *Heir* s, Earl of Cardigan; *Career* memb London Stock Exchange 1954-, late Lt RHG (reserve); *Style* - The Most Hon The Marquess of Ailesbury; Avebury Manor, Marlborough, Wilts (☎ Avebury 203)

AILESBURY, Jean, Marchioness of; Jean Frances Margaret; da of John Addison Wilson, of Banbury; *m* 1, Sqdn-Ldr Richard Williamson, MBE, RAFVR (decd); m 2, 1950, as his 3 w, 7 Marquess of Ailesbury (d 1974); 1 s (Lord Charles Brudenell-Bruce, *qv*); *Style* - The Most Hon Jean, Marchioness of Ailesbury; Bel au Vent, St Lawrence, Jersey CI

AILSA, 7 Marquess of (UK 1831); Archibald David Kennedy; OBE (1968), DL (Ayrshire); also Lord Kennedy (S 1452), Earl of Cassillis (S 1509), and Baron Ailsa (UK 1806); s of Capt 6 Marquess of Ailsa (d 1957); *b* 3 Dec 1925; *Educ* Pangbourne Nautical Coll; *m* 1954, Mary, da of late John Burn, of Amble, Northumberland; 2 s, 1 da; *Heir* s, Earl of Cassillis; *Career* formerly Lt Scots Gds, Lt-Col Roy Scots Fusiliers (TA), Hon Col Ayrshire Bn ACF 1980-, Patron IOM Rly Soc 1978-, chm Scottish Assoc of Boys Clubs 1973-; *Clubs* New (Edinburgh); *Style* - The Most Hon The Marquess of Ailsa, OBE, DL; Cassillis House, Maybole, Ayrshire

AILWYN, 4 Baron (UK 1921); Carol Arthur Fellowes; TD (1946); 4 s of 1 Baron Ailwyn, KCVO, KBE, PC (2 s of 1 Baron de Ramsey, JP, DL, sometime MP Huntingdon), and Hon Agatha Jolliffe (da of 2 Baron Hylton, JP, DL, by his 1 w, Lady Agnes Byng, da of 2 Earl of Strafford, PC); suc bro, 3 Baron Ailwyn, CBE, 1976; *b* 23 Nov 1896; *Educ* RNCs Osborne & Dartmouth; *m* 1936, Caroline, da of Maynard Cowan, of Br Columbia, and former w of Charles Cudemore; *Heir* none; *Career* served WW I & II, formerly fruit farmer and agent to Earl of Strafford; Assist Sec Roy Ag Soc 1952-59; *Style* - The Rt Hon The Lord Ailwyn, TD; The Cottage, Gissing, Diss, Norfolk (☎ Tivetshall 221)

AINLEY, Sir (Alfred) John; MC (1940); s of late Rev A Ainley; *b* 10 May 1906; *Educ* St Bees Sch, CCC Oxford; *m* 1935, Mona Wood (d 1981); 1 s, 2 da; *Career* barr 1928, Ch Justice Kenya 1963-68, kt 1957, chm Industl Tbnls 1972-76; *Style* - Sir John Ainley, MC; Horrock Wood, Watermillock, Penrith, Cumbria

AINSWORTH, Anita, Lady; Anita Margaret Ann; da of Harold Arthur Lett, of Co Wexford; *m* 1946, as his 2 w, Sir John Ainsworth, 3 Bt (d 1981); *Style* - Anita, Lady Ainsworth; Carraphuca, Shankill, Co Dublin, Eire

AINSWORTH, Anthony Thomas Hugh; s and h of Sir David Ainsworth, 4 Bt; *b* 30 March 1962; *Style* - Anthony Ainsworth Esq

AINSWORTH, Sir (Thomas) David; 4 Bt (UK 1916); s of Sir Thomas Ainsworth, 2 Bt, by his 2 w, Marie, da of Compton Domvile; suc half-bro, Sir John Ainsworth, 3 Bt, 1981; *b* 22 Aug 1926; *Educ* Eton; *m* 1957, Sarah, da of Lt-Col Hugh Walford, 17/21 Lancers; 2 s, 2 da; *Heir* s, Anthony Ainsworth; *Career* farmer; late Lt 11 Hussars; *Recreations* shooting, fishing; *Style* - Sir David Ainsworth, Bt; 80 Elm Pk gdns, SW10; Ballyneale House, Ballingarry, Co Limerick (☎ 069 68187)

AIRD, Capt Alastair Sturgis; CVO (1977, MVO 1969); s of Col Malcolm Aird; *b* 14 Jan 1931; *Educ* Eton, Sandhurst; *m* 1963, Fiona, da of Lt-Col Ririd Myddelton, *qv*; 2 da; *Career* Comptroller to Queen Elizabeth The Queen Mother 1974-; *Style* - Capt Alastair Aird, CVO; 31B St James's Palace, SW1

AIRD, Sir John George; 4 Bt (UK 1901), of Hyde Park Terrace, Paddington, Co London; s of Col Sir John Aird, 3 Bt, MVO, MC, JP, DL (d 1973), sometime Extra Equerry to King George VI and to HM The Queen, of Forest Lodge, Windsor Great Park, by his w, Lady Priscilla, nee Heathcote-Drummond-Willoughby, yr da of 2 Earl of Ancaster; *b* 31 Jan 1940; *Educ* Eton, Ch Ch Oxford, Harvard; *m* 1968, Margaret, da of Sir John Muir, 3 Bt, TD, DL; 1 s, 2 da; *Heir* s, James Aird; *Career* chm Sir John Aird & Co 1969-; engr; Page of Honour to HM 1955-57; *Recreations* skiing, farming; *Clubs* White's; *Style* - Sir John Aird, Bt; Grange Farm, Evenlode, Moreton-in-Marsh, Glos (☎ 0608 50607)

AIRD, James John; s and h of Sir John Aird, 4 Bt, by his w Margaret, da of Sir John Muir, 3 Bt, TD; *b* 12 June 1978; *Style* - James Aird

AIREDALE, 4 Baron (UK 1907); Sir Oliver James Vandeleur Kitson; 4 Bt (UK 1886); s of 3 Baron Airedale, DSO, MC (d 1958); *b* 22 April 1915; *Educ* Eton, Trin Cambridge; *Heir* none; *Career* barr 1941, dep chm Cttees House of Lords 1961-, dep Speaker 1962-; Maj The Green Howards; *Style* - The Rt Hon The Lord Airedale; Ufford Hall, Stamford, Lincs

AIREY OF ABINGDON, Baroness (Life Peer UK 1979); Diana Josceline Barbara Neave Airey; da of Thomas Giffard, MBE, JP, 27th of his line of Chillington, Staffs (descended from Osbern de Bolebec, Sire de Longueville, *temp* Richard 'Sans Peur' Duke of Normandy, who d 960 and whose sister-in-law, Aveline, Osbern married) and Angela, eld da and co-heir of Sir William Trollope, 10 Bt; *b* 7 July 1919; *m* 1942, Airey Neave, DSO, OBE, MC, TD, MP (assassinated 1979; gggs of Sir Thomas Neave, 2 Bt); 2 s, 1 da; *Career* with Foreign Office and Polish Miny of Info London WW II, thereafter supported husb politically; *Style* - The Rt Hon Baroness Airey of Abingdon; c/o NEI Ltd, Tavistock House East, Woburn Walk, WC1

AIREY, Sir Lawrence; KCB (1978, CB 1976); s of late Lawrence Airey; *b* 10 March 1926; *Educ* Newcastle Roy G S, Peterhouse Cambridge, Nuffield Coll Oxford; *m* 1953, Patricia, nee Williams; 2 s, 1 da; *Career* 2 Perm Sec (Domestic Economy), HM Treasury 1977- chm Bd of Inland Revenue 1980-; *Recreations* collecting books, music; *Style* - Sir Lawrence Airey, KCB; 263 Mill rd, Cambridge (☎ 45858); 41 Fairdene rd, Coulsdon, Surrey (☎ Downland 54191)

AIREY, Lt-Gen Sir Terence Sydney; KCMG (1951), CB (1944), CBE (1943, OBE 1941); s of late Sydney Airey; *b* 9 July 1900; *m* 1934 (m diss 1947), Constance Hedley; 1 s; m 2, 1947, Bridget, da of late Col Hon Thomas Vesey, bro of 5 Viscount de Vesci, and Lady Cecily Browne, da of 5 Earl of Kenmare; *Career* Cdr Br Forces Hong Kong 1952-54; *Style* - Lt-Gen Sir Terence Airey, KCMG, CB, CBE; Fritton Old Rectory, nr Norwich, Norfolk (☎ Hempnall 214)

AIRLIE, 13 Earl of (S 1639); David George Coke Patrick Ogilvy; DL (Angus 1964); also Lord Ogilvy of Airlie (S 1491) and Lord Ogilvy of Alyth and Lintrathen (S 1639); s of 12 Earl of Airlie, KT, GCVO, MC (d 1968), and Lady Alexandra Coke, da of 3 Earl of Leicester; bro-in-law of HRH Princess Alexandra; *b* 17 May 1926; *Educ* Eton; *m* 1952, Virginia, da of John Ryan, of Newport RI; 3 s, 3 da; *Heir* s, Lord Ogilvy; *Career* Capt Scots Gds Reserve; ADC to CIC 2 Bn Germany 1945 and High Commr Austria 1947-48; Tres Scout Assoc; Ensign Roy Co of Archers (Queen's Bodyguard for Scotland) 1975-; chm Schroders 1977-, Ashdown Investment Trust; dep chm Gen Accident Fire & Life Assur Corpn 1975-; dir J Henry Schroder Wagg & Co 1961-, Scottish & Newcastle Breweries, Roy Bank of Scotland 1980- CStJ 1981; *Style* - The Rt Hon The Earl of Airlie DL; Cortachy Castle, Kirriemiuir, Angus (☎ Cortachy 231); Airlie Castle, Kirriemuir, Angus; 3 St Leonard's ter, SW3 (☎ 01 730 8741)

AIRLIE, Dowager Countess of; Lady Alexandra Maria Bridget; *née* Coke; da of 3 Earl of Leicester, GCVO, CMG, TD, and Hon Alice White, DBE, da of 2 Baron Annaly, KP; *b* 1891; *m* 1917, 12 Earl of Airlie, KT, GCVO, MC (d 1968); 3 s, 3 da; *Style* - The Rt Hon Dowager Countess of Airlie; Airlie Castle, Kirriemuir, Angus

AISHER, Sir Owen A(rthur) ; s of late Owen Aisher; *b* 28 May 1900; *m* 1921, Ann Allingham; 2 s, 2 da; *Career* chm Marley Tile Companies, Yachtsman of the Year 1958, Pres RYA 1970-75; kt 1981; *Style* - Sir Owen Aisher

AITCHISON, Sir Charles Walter de Lancey; 4 Bt (UK 1938), of Lemmington, Co Northumberland; s of 3 Bt (d 1958); *b* 27 March 1951; *Heir* bro, (Stephen)

Edward Aitchison; *Career* late Lt 15/19 KRH; *Style* - Sir Charles Aitchison, Bt; Howden Dene, Corbridge, Northumberland

AITHRIE, Viscount; Andrew Victor Arthur Charles Hope; s and h of Earl of Hopetoun and gs of 3 Marquess of Linlithgow; *b* 22 May 1969; *Heir* bro, Hon Alexander Hope; *Style* - Viscount Aithrie

AITKEN, Jonathan William Patrick; MP (C) Thanet E 1974-; s of late Sir William Aitken, KBE, MP (d 1964), and Hon Lady Aitken, MBE,*qv*; is great nephew of 1 Baron Beaverbrook and bro of Maria Aitken, the actress and ex-wife of Nigel Davenport, the actor; *b* 30 Aug 1942; *Educ* Eton, Ch Ch Oxford; *m* 1979, Lolicia Olivera, da of O A Azucki, of Zurich; *Career* Priv Sec to Selwyn Lloyd 1964-66, for corresp Evening Standard 1966-71, md Slater Walker (M East) 1973-75, chm R Sanbar Consultants Ltd 1976-; *Books* The Young Meteors (1967) Turf, Pratt's; *Style* - Jonathan Aitken Esq, MP; 47 Phillimore gdns, W8 (☎ 01 937 0438)

AITKEN, Hon Laura; da of Sir Max Aitken, 2 Bt, DSO, DFC, by his 3 w, Violet, da of Sir Humphrey de Trafford, 4 Bt, MC; *b* 18 Nov 1953; *Style* - The Hon Laura Aitken

AITKEN, Sir (John William) Max(well); 2 Bt (UK 1916), DSO (1942), DFC (1940); s of 1 Baron Beaverbrook, ED, CD, PC (d 1964); suc as 2 Baron Beaverbrook 9 June 1964, disclaimed his peerage for life 12 June 1964; *b* 15 Feb 1910; *Educ* Westminster, Pembroke Coll Cambridge; *m* 1, 1939 (m dis 1944), Cynthia H G, da of Col Hugh Glencairn Monteith, DSO, OBE; m 2, 1946 (m dis 1950), Mrs Ursula Jane Lindsay, da of late Maj Robert Orlando Rudolph Kenyon-Slaney, gggs of 1 Baron Kenyon, KB; 2 da; m 3, 1951, Violet, da of late Sir Humphrey Edmund de Trafford, 4 Bt, MC; 1 s, 1 da; *Heir* (to disclaimed Barony as well as Btcy) s, Hon Maxwell Aitken; *Career* Gp Capt Aux Air Force; chm Beaverbrook Newspapers (now Express) 1968-77, Life Pres 1977-, MP (C) Holborn 1945-50, former dir ATV Ltd; *Style* - Sir Max Aitken, Bt, DSO, DFC; 46 Chelsea sq, SW3 (☎ 01 351 0116)

AITKEN, Maria Penelope Katharine; da of Sir William Aitken, KBE, MP Bury St Edmunds 1950-64 (d 1964, s of Joseph Aitken, 2 s of Rev William Aitken and eld bro of 1 Baron Beaverbrook; Sir William's yr sis Margaret Annie was a Canadian MP in the early 1970s), and Hon Lady Aitken, *qv*; *b* 12 Sept 1945; *Educ* privately, Riddlesworth Hall Norfolk, Sherborne Girls' Sch, St Anne's Oxford; *m* 1, 1968 (m dis), Mark Durden-Smith, yst s of A J Durden-Smith, FRCS, of Kensington; m 2, 1972 (m dis 1980), Nigel Davenport, the actor, *qv*; 1 s, 1 da (Laura); *Career* actress; roles include Amanda in a 1980 production of Noel Coward's 'Private Lives'; played during 1981 in Shaw's 'The Doctor's Dilemma' and previously at the Regent's Park open air theatre in 'The Man of Destiny'; has also been in 'Travesties' at the RSC, 'A Little Night Music' and 'Blithe Spirit' (at the National); *Recreations* pig-breeding, goose-rearing; *Style* - Miss Maria Aitken; c/o Leading Artists, 60 St James's st, SW1 (☎ 01 491 4400)

AITKEN, Hon Maxwell William Humphrey; s and h of Sir Max Aitken, 2 Bt, DSO, DFC, (also h to Barony of Beaverbrook, which Sir Max Aitken disclaimed for life 1964, having suc as 2 Baron 1964) by his 3 w, Violet, da of Sir Humphrey de Trafford, 4 Bt, MC, and Hon Cynthia Cadogan (3 da of Viscount Chelsea, DL, who, dying 1908, predeceased his f, 5 Earl Cadogan, KG, PC); *b* 29 Dec 1951; *Educ* Ampleforth; *m* 1974, Susan Angela, da of Francis More O'Ferrall and Angela (niece of Sir George Mather-Jackson, 5 Bt, and da of Anthony Mather-Jackson, JP, DL, by his w, Evelyn, da of Lt-Col Sir Henry Stephenson, 1 Bt, DSO); 2 s; *Style* - The Hon Maxwell Aitken; 21 Margaretta ter, SW3

AITKEN, Sir Peter (Arthur Percival Hay) ; s of late Canon R Aitken; *b* 2 Oct 1905; *Educ* Norwich G S, Trin Oxford; *m* 1937, Ursula, da of Dr Herbert Wales; 1 s, 1 da; *Career* chm Textile Machinery Makers 1960, dep chm Stone-Platt Industs; dir Norwich Gen Trust (chm), Norwich Union Insurance and Life

Insurance Gp, Scottish Union and Nat Insurance Co, Maritime Insurance Co; kt 1968; *Style* - Sir Peter Aitken; Roefield, Alde Lane, Aldeburgh, Suffolk (☎ 3450)

AITKEN, Hon Lady - Hon Penelope Loader; *née* Maffey; MBE (1955); da of 1 Baron Rugby, GCMG, KCB, KCVO, CSI, CIE (d 1969); *b* 1910; *m* 1938, Sir William Aitken, KBE, MP (d 1964); 1 s, 1 da; *Style* - The Hon Lady Aitken MBE; 47 Phillimore gdns, W8

AITKEN, Gp Capt Russell Faulkner; CBE (1958, OBE 1943), AFC (1941); s of Robert Aitken, of Lower Hutt; *b* 15 Sept 1913; *Educ* schs in Gore & Timaru NZ; *m* 1939, Rhoda Ruth, da of Edward Bransome; 1 da; *Career* RAF Gp Capt WW II, served Europe, Burma, Cyprus, Palestine; dir Nat Safety Assoc of NZ 1962-75, Accident Compensation Commn 1975-78; *Recreations* music, reading; *Clubs* Wellington Rotary; *Style* - Gp Capt Russell Aitken, CBE, AFC; Rixlade, 64 Seaview rd, Paremata, N Zealand (☎ Plimmerton 338 487)

AITKEN, Sir Robert Stevenson; DL (Warwicks 1967); s of late Rev James Aitken; *Educ* Otago U, NZ; Oxford; *m* 1929, Margaret Kane; 1 s, 2 da; *Career* MD, DPhil, FRCP, FRACP, Regius Prof of Medicine, Aberdeen U 1939-48, V-Chllr Birmingham U 1953-68; *Style* - Sir Robert Aitken, DL; 6 Hintlesham av, Birmingham, B15 2PH

AITKEN, Ronald William; s of Brig William Aitken; *b* 20 Sept 1933; *Educ* Wellesley House, Cheltenham; *m* 1962, Frances, da of Edward Wharton Farmer; 6 da; *Career* FCA; chm Barker & Dobson Gp, Landcrest Ltd, Queen Street Warehouse Hldgs, Ronnie Aitken & Assocs, Saville & Milne; Pres Barker & Dobson (USA); jt-chm Belhaven Brewery Gp; dir- Ashpoint Ltd, Belhaven Finance, Brewinson Ltd, Dallas Mining & Exploration (PTY) and Holdings (Guernsey), Dvpt Pubns, Etam Ltd, Footner & Co Inc (UK), John Crowther Gp, Charles Letts Hldgs, Lichfield Laundry Gp, Melora Industrial Ltd, Morclair Ltd, N Brown Investments Ltd, Norton Warburg Investments, Seaway Hldgs; special adviser to Lonrho; *Recreations* golf, bridge, backgammon; *Clubs* Brooks's, Berkshire Golf; *Style* - Ronald Aitken Esq; 212 Ashley gdns, SW1 (☎ 01 834 3110)

AITKEN, Air Vice-Marshal (Robert) Stanley; CB (1945), CBE (1942, OBE 1938), MC (1917), AFC (1918); s of late Robert Aitken; *b* 4 April 1896; *Educ* Highgate, Wiesbaden; *m* 1, 1925, Jeanie Allison (d 1963), da of late Rev David Tweedie; 1 s (and 1 decd); m 2, 1964, Laura; *Career* ASO in C, HQ, MAAF, 1944-45, ret 1946; *Style* - Air Vice-Marshal Stanley Aitken, CB; CBE, MC, AFC, Rose Cottage, Shalfleet, IoW (☎ Calbourne 337)

AITKEN, Thomas Patrick Howie; s of James Aitken (d 1962); *b* 2 July 1925; *Educ* Munro Coll Jamaica; *m* 1953, Rosemary, da of Michael Decosmo; 1 s, 2 da; *Career* Pres Gill & Duffus Hldgs 1980-; *Recreations* usual country pastimes; *Clubs* India House (New York), Nat Golf Links of America (S'thampton NY); *Style* - Thomas Aitken Esq; 9 Southway, Bronxville, New York, NY 10708 (☎ 914 779 1909/6626)

AIZLEWOOD, John Aldam; MC and Bar (1917 and 1918), DL (Glos 1960); s of G Aizlewood, of Whirlow Grange, Parkhead, Sheffield; *b* 4 Jan 1895; *Educ* Uppingham, Sandhurst; *m* 1920, Margaret Delia (Meta, d 1977), da of Col M Dennis, CB, JP, DL, of Fortgranite, Baltinglass, Co Wicklow, by his w, Hon Alice, yst da of 4 Baron Castlemaine; 1 s, 1 da; *Career* joined Roy Irish Dragoons 1914, served in France 1914-18 and India, Persia, UK 1939-45; Lt-Col Cmmdg Essex & Suffolk Dist 1943-44, ret 1945, Col 4/7 Roy Dragoon Gds 1948-58; *Recreations* country sports; *Clubs* Guards & Cavalry; *Style* - Lt-Col John Aizlewood, MC*, DL; Paxford Manor, Chipping Campden, Glos (☎ Paxford 216)

AKERS-DOUGLAS, Alastair George; s of late Capt Ian Stanley Akers-Douglas, by his 2 w, Phyllis Rosemary; hp of kinsman, 3 Viscount Chilston; *b* 6 Sept 1946; *m* 1971, Juliet A, da of Lt-Col Nigel Lovett, of The Old Rectory, Inwardleigh,

Okehampton, Devon; 3 s; *Style* - Alastair Akers-Douglas Esq; Crofton House, Latchingdon, Chelmsford, Essex

AL-SABAH, Shaikh Saud Nasir; *b* 3 Oct 1944; *m* 1962, Shaikha Awatif Al-Sabah; 2 s, 2 da; *Career* Kuwaiti Ambass to UK 1975-81, to US 1981-; barr Gray's Inn; *Style* - HE Shaikh Saud Nasir Al-Sabah

AL-SHAWI, His Excellency Hisham Ibrahim; s of Ibrahim Al-Shawi; *b* 16 March 1931; *Educ* Baghdad, American U Beirut; *m* 1966, Hadia Al-Atia; 1 s, 1 da; *Career* Iraqi Ambass to UK 1978-, Dean Coll of Law and Politics Mustansyria U 1970-72; *Style* - H E Hisham Ibrahim Al-Shawi; Embassy of the Republic of Iraq, 21 Queen's Gate, SW7 (☎ 01 584 7141); 15 Kensington Palace gdns, W8

AL-TAJIR, His Excellency Mohamed Mahdi; *b* 26 Dec 1931; *Educ* Al Tajir Sch Bahrain, Preston G S Lancs; *m* 1956, Zohra Al-Tajir; 5 s, 1 da; *Career* United Arab Emirates Ambass to UK 1972-, and France 1972-77, dir Nat Bank of Dubai 1963-, Dubai Petroleum Co 1963-, Dubai Nat Air Travel Agency 1966-, United Arab Emirates Currency Bd 1973-, Dubai Dry Dock Co 1973-, chm S E Dubai Drilling Co 1968-; *Style* - HE Mr Mohamed Mahdi Al-Tajir; Embassy of the United Arab Emirates, 30 Prince's Gate, SW7

ALAM, Hon Anthony Alexander; *b* 23 Jan 1898; *Educ* De La Salle Coll Armidale NSW; *Career* dir Alam Homes Pty Ltd, Alam Stores Pty Ltd, Mala Homes Pty Ltd, Latec Ltd, memb Legve Cncl 1925-59 and 1963-73; *Style* - Hon Anthony Alam; 69 Bradleys Head rd, Mosman, NSW 2088, Australia

ALANBROOKE, 3 Viscount (UK 1946); Alan Victor Harold Brooke; s of 1 Viscount Alanbrooke, KG, GCB, OM, GCVO, DSO, by his 2 w, Benita, da of Sir Harold Pelly, 4 Bt, JP, and wid of Sir Thomas Lees, 2 Bt; suc half-bro, 2 Viscount, 1972; *b* 24 Nov 1932; *Educ* Harrow, Bristol U; *Heir* none; *Career* served army 1952-72, Capt RA ret; qualified teacher 1975; *Style* - The Rt Hon The Viscount Alanbrooke; Fernley Close, Hartley Wintney, Hants

ALBEMARLE, 10 Earl of (E 1696); Rufus Arnold Alexis Keppel; s of Viscount Bury (d 1968, eld s of 9 Earl of Albemarle, MC) by his 2 w, Marina, da of late Lt-Cdr Count Serge Orloff-Davidoff, RNVR, and late Hon Elisabeth, nee Scott-Ellis (2 da of 8 Baron Howard de Walden and 4 Baron Seaford); through his paternal grandmother he is 2 cous once removed of Lord Carrington, the For Sec, and 1 cous once removed of Marchioness of Donegall; suc gf 1979; *b* 16 July 1965; *Heir* unc, Hon Walter Keppel, DSC; *Style* - The Rt Hon The Earl of Albemarle; Piazza di Bellosguardo 10, Florence 50124, Italy

ALBEMARLE, Countess of; Dame Diana Cicely; DBE (1956); da of Maj John Grove; *b* 6 Aug 1909; *Educ* Sherborne Sch for Girls; *m* 1931, as his 2 w, 9 Earl of Albemarle, MC (d 1979); 1 da (Lady Anne-Louise Hamilton-Dalrymple, *qv*); *Career* chm Dvpt Cmmn 1948-74, Drama Bd 1964-78; V-Chm Br Cncl 1959-74; chm Carnegie UK Trust 1977-; Trustee The Observer to 1977, Glyndebourne Arts Trust 1968-; *Style* - The Rt Hon Countess of Albemarle DBE; Seymours, Melton, Woodbridge, Suffolk (☎ 2151)

ALBERT, Sir Alexis François; CMG (1967), VRD (1942); s of late M Albert; *b* 15 Oct 1904; *Educ* Sydney U; *m* 1934, Elsa Lundgren (decd); 3 s; *Career* chm and gov dir J Albert & Son Pty Ltd 1962-, chm Australian B'dcasting Co Pty Ltd, CStJ 1981, kt 1972; *Style* - Sir Alexis Albert, CMG, VRD; 25 Coolong rd, Vaucluse, NSW 2030, Australia

ALBERY, Sir Donald Arthur Rolleston; s of late Sir Bronson Albery; *b* 19 June 1914; *Educ* Alpine Coll Switzerland; *Career* former chm and md Wyndham Theatres Ltd, Donmar Prodns Ltd, Piccadilly Theatre Ltd, kt 1977; *Style* - Sir Donald Albery; 31 Av Princesse Grace, Monte Carlo, Monaco (☎ 507082)

ALBROW, Desmond; s of Frederick Albrow; *b* 22 Jan 1925; *Educ* St Bede's G S Bradford, Keble Oxford; *m* 1950, Aileen

Jennings; 1 s, 3 da; *Career* assist ed Sunday Telegraph 1976-; *Style* - Desmond Albrow Esq; Totyngton Cottage, Victoria rd, Teddington, Middx (☎ 01 979 4220)

ALBU, Sir George; 3 Bt (UK 1912), of Grosvenor Place, City of Westminster, and Johannesburg, Province of Transvaal, Union of S Africa; s of 2 Bt (d 1963); *b* 5 June 1944; *m* 1969, Joan Valerie, da of late Malcolm Millar; 2 da; *Heir* none; *Style* - Sir George Albu, Bt; Glen Hamish Farm, PO Box 62, Richmond 3780, Natal, S Africa

ALBUM, Edward Jonathan Corcos; s of Harry Album, of London N3; *b* 8 Sept 1936; *Educ* Emanuel Sch, Ch Ch Oxford; *m* 1970, Elizabeth, da of Lancelot Ezra, of London NW6; 1 s, 1 da; *Career* Capt Reserve TA 1962-70; slr; dir- Leopold Lazarus Ltd, American Medical (Europe) Ltd, Harley Street Clinic Ltd, Windsor Hospital Ltd, Francis Sumner Hldgs, Tretol Ltd, Int House Assoc; *Style* - Edward Album Esq; Sanderling House, High Street, Cley, Norfolk; 47 Lyndale av, NW2

ALCE, Henry Thomas; AM (1980); s of John Alce, master mariner (d 1918); *b* 8 Sept 1915; *Educ* Canterbury H S, Sydney; *m* 1940, Johnann Rae, da of William Bannatyne, accountant; 1 s, 3 da; *Career* mentioned in despatches 1946 serving in S Pacific; Queen's Silver Jubilee Medal 1977; dir Penfolds Wines, Wright Heaton Ltd, Roy N Shore Hosp 1979-; memb Sydney Cricket Ground Tst 1979-; md Tooth & Co 1975-80; *Recreations* riding, tennis, reading; *Clubs* Union, American, Tattersalls (all Sydney); *Style* - Henry Alce, Esq, AM; Banool, Nangus, 2722 NSW, Australia (☎ 069 447 292); 18 Dalmeny rd, Northbridge 2063, NSW Australia (☎ 95 6495)

ALCHIN, Hon Mrs (Juliet Alers); da of 2 Baron Hankey, KCMG, KCVO; *b* 1931; *m* 1957, Peter, s of His Hon Judge Gordon Alchin, AFC (d 1947); 1 s, 2 da; *Style* - The Hon Mrs Alchin; Parkstone, Clenches Farm rd, Sevenoaks, Kent (☎ 57 188)

ALDENHAM (AND HUNSDON OF HUNSDON), 5 (& 3) Baron (UK 1896 & 1923) respectively; Antony Durant Gibbs; s of 4 (& 2) Baron Aldenham (& Hunsdon of Hunsdon), himself s of 1 Baron Hunsdon of Hunsdon (a keen bimetallist, whose work 'A Bimetallic Primer' convinced many of the soundness of his doctrines; he was also n of 'GEC' (George Cokayne), the prime compiler of 'The Complete Peerage') by his w, Beatrix, da of Herbert Paul; suc f 1969; *b* 18 May 1922; *Educ* Eton, Ch Ch Oxford; *m* 1947, Mary, da of Walter Tyser; 2 s (and 1 s decd), 1 da; *Heir* s, Hon Vicary Gibbs; *Career* dir Antony Gibbs & Sons 1951-80 formerly Lt RNVR; *Recreations* shooting, fishing, sailing; *Clubs* MCC, Roy Yacht Sqdn, Pratt's; *Style* - The Rt Hon Lord Aldenham; Rimpton Manor, Yeovil, Somerset (☎ 0935 850151); 3, 37 Portland Place, W1 (☎ 01 580 2766)

ALDER, Keith Frederick; Frederick Alder; s of 4 Sept 1921; *b* Scotch Coll Melbourne, Melbourne U; *Educ* 1947, Pauline, da of Rev J Gray Robertson, OBE; 3 s; *Career* metallurgist, Commr (1968) and Gen Man Australian Atomic Energy Commn; *Recreations* tennis, sailing; *Clubs* Roy Prince Alfred Yacht; *Style* - Keith Alder Esq; 60 Ku-ring-gai av, Turramurra, NSW, Australia (☎ 44 3438)

ALDER, Michael; s of late Thomas Alder; *b* 3 Nov 1928; *Educ* Rutherford Coll Newcastle; *m* 1955, Freda, nee Hall; 2 da; *Career* Controller English Regnl TV BBC 1977-; *Style* - Michael Alder Esq; Ingleford, 14 Danford Lane, Solihull, W Midlands (☎ 021 705 1537)

ALDERSON, John Cottingham; QPM (1974); s of late Ernest Alderson; *b* 28 May 1922; *Educ* Barnsley; *m* 1948, Irene Stirling; 1 s; *Career* Ch Constable Devon and Cornwall 1973-, barr; *Style* - John Alderson Esq, QPM; Devon & Cornwall Constabulary, Middlemoor, Exeter, Devon

ALDERTON, John; s of Gordon Alderton; *b* 27 Nov 1940; *Educ* Kingston H S Hull; *m* 1, Jill Browne (m diss); m 2, Pauline Collins; 2 s, 1 da; *Career* actor; *Style* - John Alderton Esq; c/o Nems Management Ltd, 29-31 King's rd, SW3

ALDINGTON, 1 Baron (UK 1962); Toby Austin Richard William Low; KCMG (1957), CBE (1945, MBE 1944), DSO (1941), TD* (1950), PC (1954), DL (Kent 1973); s of Col Stuart Low, DSO (d on active serv 1942; s of Sir Austin Low, CIE, JP), and Hon Lucy Atkin, da of Baron Atkin, PC (Life Peer, d 1944), by his 2 w; *b* 25 May 1914; *Educ* Winchester, New Coll Oxford; *m* 1947, Araminta, da of Sir Harold MacMichael, GCMG, DSO, and former w of Capt Paul Bowman; 1 s, 2 da; *Heir* s, Hon Charles Low; *Career* barr 1939; served WW II as Brig BGS 5 Corps; MP (C) Blackpool N 1945-62, Min of State BOT 1954-57; dep chm Con Pty Organisation 1959-63; formerly chm PLA, BBC Gen Advsy Cncl; chm Sun Alliance & London Insur, Westland Aircraft; dep chm GEC; dir- Citicorp, Lloyds Bank; Warden Winchester Coll 1979-; *Recreations* golf; *Clubs* Carlton, Beefsteak, Roy St George's Golf; *Style* - The Rt Hon The Lord Aldington, KCMG, CBE, DSO, TD*, PC, DL; Knoll Farm, Aldington, Kent (☎ 292); Flat R, 45 Eaton sq, SW1 (☎ 01 235 3425)

ALDINGTON, Sir Geoffrey William; KBE (1965, OBE 1946), CMG (1958); s of late Henry Aldington; *b* 1 June 1907; *Educ* City of London Sch, Magdalen Oxford; *m* 1932, Roberta Finch; 2 da; *Career* ambass to Luxembourg 1961-66; *Style* - Sir Geoffrey Aldington, KBE, CMG; Rustlings, 4 Tudor Close, Barnmeadow Lane, Surrey

ALDISS, Brian Wilson; s of Stanley Aldiss; *b* 18 Aug 1925; *Educ* Framlingham Coll, W Buckland Sch; *m* 1965, Margaret Manson; 1 s, 1 da (and 1 s, 1 da by prev m); *Career* sf writer and critic; *Style* - Brian Aldiss Esq; 11 Charlbury rd, Oxford

ALDOUS, Guy Travers; QC (1956); s of H Aldous, of Gedding Hall, Suffolk; is bro of Brig James Aldous, CBE, MC, DL; *b* 30 Aug 1906; *Educ* Harrow, Trin Cambridge; *m* 1932, Elizabeth, da of Stuart Paul, of Freston Lodge nr Ipswich; 4 s, 1 da; *Career* barr ret 1967, dir Showerings 1968-, MFH Suffolk 1958-60, Essex & Suffolk 1967-76; legal advsr Allied Breweries; *Style* - Guy Aldous Esq, QC; 5 Queens Bench, Temple, EC4 (☎ 01 353 4659); Freston House, nr Ipswich, Suffolk (☎ 0473 84 243)

ALDOUS, Brig James Robert Travers; CBE (1946), MC (1918), DL (Suffolk 1964); s of Hugh Aldous, of Gedding Hall, Suffolk; is bro of Guy Aldous, QC; *b* 5 Oct 1898; *Educ* Cheltenham, RMA Woolwich, Magdalene Cambridge; *m* 1925, Nancy Corona, JP (Suffolk 1951), only da of Sir George Morse (d 1931), of Beech Hill, Thorpe St Andrew, Norfolk; 1 s (Lt-Col James Aldous), 2 da (Pamela, m, 1956, Henry, yst s of Lt-Col Edward Lillingston, DSO; Dr Inez Aldous); *Career* Cmd BGS N Cmd 1944-47, 161 Ind Infantry Bde Gp (TA) 1947-50; chm W Suffolk CC 1965-71, High Sheriff Suffolk 1969; Hon Lay Canon St Edmundsbury Cathedral 1970, Emeritus 1976; farmer; *Recreations* horses, mountaineering; *Clubs* Army & Navy; *Style* - Brig James Aldous CBE MC DL; Chelsworth, Ipswich, Suffolk (☎ Bildeston 740320)

ALDOUS, Lucette; da of Charles Aldous; *b* 26 Sept 1938; *Educ* Toronto Pub Sch NSW, Brisbane Pub Sch Qld, Randwick Girls' H S NSW; *m* 1972, Alan Alder; *Career* prima Ballerina Australian Ballet 1971-; *Style* - Miss Lucette Aldous; 66 Grange rd, Toorak, Victoria 3142, Australia (☎ 269 2198)

ALDOUS, William; QC (1976); s of Guy Aldous,*qv*; *b* 17 March 1936; *Educ* Harrow, Trin Cambridge; *m* Gillian Henson; 1 s, 2 da; *Career* barr 1960; *Style* - William Aldous Esq, QC; Layham Lodge, Layham, nr Ipswich, Suffolk (☎ Hadleigh 3143)

ALDRICH, Michael John; s of the late Charles Albert Aldrich; *b* 22 Aug 1941; *Educ* Clapham Coll, Hull U; *m* 1962, Sandra Kay, nee Hutchings; 4 c; *Career* md Rediffusion Computers Ltd 1980-, adviser to HM Government for information technology 1981-; *Recreations* gardening, reading; *Clubs* Rediffusion Sports; *Style* - Michael Aldrich Esq; Woodside, Colgate, Horsham, Sussex

ALEC-SMITH, Rupert Alexander; TD (1950); s of late Alexander Alec-Smith, OBE, of Wawne Lodge, Hull; *b* 5 Sept

1913; *Educ* Malvern; *m* 1952, Suzette, da of James Watson, of Holyrood House, Hedon, Yorks; 1 da; *Career* Ld-Lt Humberside 1980-, KStJ 1980, pres Georgian Soc for E Yorks (fndr 1937), JP (1950), DL (E Yorks and Kingston on Hull 1973), JP and DL Humberside 1974, High Sheriff 1975, FSA 1975; *Style* - Rupert Alec-Smith Esq, TD, JP, DL, HM Lord-Lieut for Humberside; Winestead, Hull (☎ Patrington 30297)

ALEXANDER OF TUNIS, 2 Earl (UK 1962); Shane William Desmond Alexander; also Viscount Alexander of Tunis (UK 1946) and Baron Rideau (UK 1952); s of Field-Marshal 1 Earl Alexander of Tunis, KG, GCB, OM, GCMG, CSI, DSO, MC, PC (3 s of 4 Earl Caledon, through whom the present Earl is hp to Earldom of Caledon) and Lady Margaret Bingham, GBE, JP, da of 5 Earl of Lucan (gs of the Crimean War Commander and gf of the fugitive); *b* 30 June 1935; *Educ* Harrow, Ashbury Coll Ottawa; *m* 1, 1971 (m dis 1976), Hilary, da of John van Geest, of Lincs; *Heir* bro, Hon Brian Alexander; *Career* Lt Irish Gds (res); Liveryman Mercers' Co; Ld in Waiting to HM 1974; *Style* - Rt Hon Earl Alexander of Tunis; Winkfield Lodge, Windsor Forest, Berks (☎ Winkfield Row 2240)

ALEXANDER OF POTTERHILL, Baron (Life Peer UK 1974); William Picken Alexander; s of Thomas Alexander, of Paisley; *b* 13 Dec 1905; *Educ* Paisley G S, Glasgow U; *m* 1949, Joan, da of Robert Williamson, of Sheffield; 1 s (Hon Thomas Alexander, b 1951); *Career* Gen Sec Assoc Educn Cttees England & Wales 1944-, kt 1960; *Style* - Rt Hon Lord Alexander of Potterhill; 3 Moor Pk Gdns, Pembroke rd, Moor Pk, Herts

ALEXANDER, Sir Alex (Alexander Sandor); *b* 21 Nov 1916; *Educ* Charles U Prague; *m* 1946, Margaret Irma; 2 s, 2 da; *Career* kt 1974, chm J Lyons 1979-, dir Allied Breweries 1979-, Inchcape Insur Holdgs 1978-, Marchwiel Ltd 1978-, Tate & Lyle 1978-, Unigate Ltd 1978-, dep chm Br United Trawlers, FBIM, FRSA, also dir- Nat West Bank S Regn, Ransomes Sims & Jefferies; Trustee and V-Chm Glyndebourne Arts Trust; *Style* - Sir Alex Alexander; Westwick Hall, Westwick, Norwich (☎ Swanton Abbot 664)

ALEXANDER, Hon Brian James; s of 1 Earl Alexander of Tunis, KG, GCB, OM, GCMG, CSI, DSO, MC, PC (d 1969 - 3 s of 4 Earl of Caledon); hp of bro, 2 Earl; *b* 31 July 1939; *Educ* Harrow; *Career* Lt Irish Gds (Reserve); *Style* - The Hon Brian Alexander

ALEXANDER, Sir Charles Gundry; 2 Bt (UK 1945), of Sundridge Park, Co Kent; s of Sir Frank Alexander, 1 Bt, JP (d 1959), by his w, Elsa, da of Sir Charles Collett, 1 Bt; *b* 5 May 1923; *Educ* Bishop's Stortford Coll, St John 's Cambridge; *m* 1, 1944, Mary, da of S Richardson, of Lyndhurst; 1 s, 1 da; m 2, 1979, Eileen, da of Gordon Stewart, of Inveresk, Finchampstead; *Heir* s, Richard Alexander; *Career* formerly Lt RN N Atlantic & Far East; chm Alexander Shipping Co, gov Care Ltd, dep chm Houlder Bros & Co, dir Furness-Houlder Insur Ltd and Reinsurance Service Ltd, Inner London Regn, Nat W Bank; *Clubs* RAC; *Style* - Sir Charles Alexander, Bt; Bells Farm, E Sutton, Maidstone, Kent (☎ Sutton Valence 2410)

ALEXANDER, Sir Claud Hagart-; 3 Bt (UK 1886), of Ballochmyle, co Ayr; s of late Wilfred Archibald Alexander (2 s of 2 Bt); suc gf 1945; *b* 6 Jan 1927; *Educ* Sherborne, Corpus Christi Cambridge; *m* 1959, Hilda Etain, da of Miles Malcolm Acheson, late Chinese Maritime Customs Ser; 2 s, 2 da; *Heir* s, Claud Hagart-Alexander; *Career* DL Ayrshire 1973; additional surname of Hagart recognised by decree of Lord Lyon 1948; *Clubs* New (Edinburgh); *Style* - Sir Claud Hagart-Alexander, Bt, DL; Kingencleuch House, Mauchline, Ayrshire

ALEXANDER, Claud Hagart-; s and h of Sir Claud Hagart-Alexander, 3 Bt, DL; *b* 5 Nov 1963; *Style* - Claud Hagart-Alexander Esq

ALEXANDER, Sir Darnley Arthur Raymond; CBE (1963); s of Pamphile Joseph Alexander; *b* St Lucia 28 Jan 1920; *Educ* St Mary's Coll St Lucia, UCL; *m* 1943, Mildred, nee King; 1 s, 1 da; *Career*

barr 1942, Ch Justice Nigeria 1975-, kt 1974; *Style* - Sir Darnley Alexander, CBE; Supreme Court of Nigeria, Lagos, Nigeria

ALEXANDER, Maj-Gen David Crichton; CB (1976); s of James Alexander; *b* 28 Nov 1926; *Educ* Edinburgh Acad, Staff Coll Camberley, Roy Coll of Defence Studies; *m* 1957, Diana, da of Sydney Fisher, CVO (d 1980); 1 s, 2 da; *Career* Cmdt Scottish Police Coll 1979- served RM 1944-77 and as Equerry and Actg Tres to HRH Duke of Edinburgh 1957-60; *Recreations* fishing, golf; *Clubs* Army & Navy; *Style* - Maj-Gen David Alexander, CB; Tulliallan Castle, Kincardine, Fife (☎ 0259 30333)

ALEXANDER, Sir Douglas Hamilton; 2 Bt (UK 1921), of Edgehill, Stamford, Connecticut, USA; s of 1 Bt (d 1949); *b* 6 June 1900; *Educ* Princeton U; *Heir* n, Prof Douglas Alexander; *Career* formerly with Singer Co, ret; *Style* - Sir Douglas Alexander, Bt; Palmers Hill, Stamford, Conn 06902, USA

ALEXANDER, Lady (Elizabeth) Jane; da of 6 Earl of Caledon (d 1980) by 1 w, Ghislaine, da of Cornelius Dresselhuys, of Long Island, USA; *b* 1962; *Style* - Lady Jane Alexander

ALEXANDER, John Osmond Macdonald; DSO (1944), MC (1940), TD, DL (Northumberland 1968); s of James Alexander, of Belfast; *b* 29 March 1916; *Educ* Rugby, Clare Cambridge; *m* 1947, Joanna, da of Rev John Twells Poole, of Norfolk; 2 da; *Career* Col (late RE), served RE (TA) 1937-60; dir Procter & Gamble 1955-75, chm Cncl U of Newcastle 1965-; *Recreations* hunting; *Clubs* Army & Navy, Northern Counties (Newcastle); *Style* - Col John Alexander, DSO, MC, TD, DL; Greenfield, Wall, Hexham, Northumberland (☎ Humshaugh 335)

ALEXANDER, Kenneth Alston; s of Brig-Gen Sir William Alexander, KBE, CB, CMG, DSO, MP (d 1954); *b* 21 Nov 1928; *Educ* Winchester, Trin Cambridge; *m* 1957, Linda, da of Edward Lefevre, of Cochin and Gargrave, Yorks; 1 s, 3 da; *Career* chemical merchant and manufacturer; chm Tennants Consolidated Ltd 1972- (previously holding various directorships within the Tennant Group); *Recreations* tennis, shooting, music; *Clubs* RAC; *Style* - Kenneth Alexander Esq; 69 Grosvenor st, W1 (☎ 01 493 5451)

ALEXANDER, Prof Sir Kenneth John Wilson; s of late William Alexander; *b* 14 March 1922; *Educ* George Heriot's Sch Edinburgh, Dundee Sch of Economics; *m* 1949, Angela-May, da of late Capt G Lane, RN; 1 s, 4 da; *Career* chm Highlands and Islands Dvpt Bd 1976-, prof of Economics Strathclyde U 1963-, FBIM, FRSE, kt 1978; *Style* - Prof Sir Kenneth Alexander; Woodhill, Brae of Balnabeen, Conon Bridge, Ross-shire (☎ Culbokie 653)

ALEXANDER, Sir (John) Lindsay; s of Ernest Alexander; *b* 12 Sept 1920; *Educ* Alleyn's Sch, Brasenose Oxford; *m* 1944, Maud, nee Collard; 2 s, 1 da; *Career* chm Ocean Transport & Trading 1971-80, Overseas Container Holdgs 1976-, Lloyds Bank Internat 1980-, dir Lloyds Bank 1970-, BP 1975-, FCIT, FBIM, kt 1975; *Recreations* gardening, music, photography; *Clubs* Brooks's; *Style* - Sir Lindsay Alexander; Corton Denham House, Corton Denham, Sherborne, Dorset (☎ 205)

ALEXANDER, Michael Charles; s of late Rear-Adm Charles Alexander and Antonia Geermans; *b* 20 Nov 1920; *Educ* Stowe, Sandhurst; *m* 1963, Sarah Wignall (m diss); 1 da; *Career* writer, explorer, dir Acorn Prodns Ltd, Wildlife Pubns Ltd, FZS, FRGS, FRAI; *Style* - Michael Alexander Esq; 48 Eaton Pla, SW1 (☎ 01 235 2724)

ALEXANDER, Maurice Lionel; s of the late Abraham Alexander; *b* 23 Aug 1916; *Educ* Manchester Central H S, Manchester U; *m* 1947, Irene, da of the late Robert Cohen, JP; 2 s, 1 da; *Career* Major NW Europe, slr and sr ptnr for Alexander, Tatham & Co; *Clubs* Manchester Football, Dunham Forest Golf; *Style* - Maurice Alexander Esq

ALEXANDER, Michael O'Donel Bjarne; s of late Col Hugh Alexander, CMG, CBE; *b* 19 June 1936; *Educ* Foyle

Coll Londonderry, St Paul's, King's Cambridge; *m* 1960, Traute Krohn; 2 s, 1 da; *Career* Priv Sec to PM (Overseas Affs) 1979-, Head POD FCO 1978-79; *Style* - Michael Alexander Esq; 19 Spencer Pk, SW18 (☎ 01 870 1964)

ALEXANDER, Sir Norman Stanley; CBE (1959); s of Charles Monrath Alexander, of NZ; *b* 25 Oct 1906; *Educ* Hamilton H S NZ, U Coll Auckland, Trin Cambridge; *m* 1, 1935, Frances, da of Kenneth Caldwell; 1 s, 2 da; m 2, 1959, Constance, da of Henry Geary; *Career* formerly Prof Physics Malaya U and Ibadan U Coll Nigeria; V-Chllr Ahmadu Bello U Nigeria 1961-66; advr on Higher Educn Miny Overseas Dvpt, kt 1966; *Recreations* gardening; *Style* - Sir Norman Alexander, CBE; Yew Tree Cottage, Redisham, Beccles, Suffolk (☎ Brampton 256)

ALEXANDER, Peter Charles; CMG (1980), OBE (1970); s of Charles Alexander, of London (ka 1915); *b* 19 Jan 1915; *Educ* Sydney U; *m* 1953, Rita, da of Frank Williams, of Chesterfield; 3 da; *Career* FCA, FICS; chm Australian Branch Assoc Certified Accountants 1974-, Kenya-Australia Soc 1971-, V-Pres World Veterans Fedn 1979-, Fedl Sec Air Force Assoc 1960-; formerly with Dept of Productivity; *Recreations* cricket, journalism; *Clubs* Air Force (Sydney); *Style* - Peter Alexander Esq, CMG, OBE; 46 Hawthorn av, Chatswood, NSW 2067, Australia (☎ 419 5024)

ALEXANDER, Richard; s and h of Sir Charles Alexander, 2 Bt, by his 1 w, Mary, da of Stanley Richardson; *b* 1 Sept 1947; *Educ* Bishop's Stortford Coll; *m* 1971, Lesley, da of Frederick Jordan, of Bishop's Stortford; 2 s; *Style* - Richard Alexander Esq; Squirrel Court, 262 Chislehurst rd, Petts Wood, Kent

ALEXANDER, Rear-Adm Robert Love; CB (1964), DSO (1943), DSC (1944); s of Capt R Alexander; *b* 29 April 1913; *Educ* Merchiston, RNC Dartmouth; *m* 1936, Margaret, nee Spring; 1 s, 4 da; *Career* Vice Naval Dep to Supreme Allied Cdr Europe 1962-65; *Style* - Rear-Adm Robert Alexander, CB, DSO, DSC; Beeches Croft, Fyning Lane, Rogate, Petersfield, Hants (☎ Rogate 368)

ALEXANDER, Robert Scott; QC (1973); s of late Samuel Alexander; *b* 5 Sept 1936; *Educ* Brighton Coll, King's Cambridge; *m* 1978, Elizabeth, da of Col C Norman; *Career* barr 1961; *Style* - Robert Alexander Esq, QC; 1 Brick Court, Temple EC4 (☎ 01 353 0777)

ALEXANDER, Richard Thain; MP (C) Newark 1979-; s of Richard Alexander; *b* 29 June 1934; *Educ* Dewsbury G S, UCL; *m* 1966, Valerie; 1 s, 1 da; *Career* slr, sr ptnr Jones Alexander & Co Retford 1964-; *Recreations* tennis, swimming, squash, golf; *Clubs* Farmers, Newark Conservative; *Style* - Richard Alexander Esq, MP; 6 W Markham, Newark, Notts; 809 Hood House, Dolphin sq, SW1

ALEXANDER-SINCLAIR, Maj-Gen David Boyd; CB (1980); s of Cdr M Alexander-Sinclair, RN; *b* 2 May 1927; *Educ* Eton; *m* 1958, Ann, da of Lt-Col Graeme Daglish; 2 s, 1 da; *Career* Ch of Staff UKLF 1978-; *Style* - Maj-Gen David Alexander-Sinclair, CB; c/o Midland Bank ltd, 69 Pall Mall, SW1

ALEXANDER-SINCLAIR, John Alexis Clifford Cerda; s of Col C Alexander and Donna Lyta Alexander dei Marchesi della Cerda; *b* 22 Feb 1906; *Educ* Charterhouse, Goettingen and Munich Us; *m* 1, 1927, Baroness von Gottberg (decd); 1 da; m 2, 1933, Stella Tucker; 1 s, 1 da; m 3, 1950, Simonne de Rougemont, nee Vion; m 4, 1965 Maureen Dover, nee Wood; 1 step s; *Career* chm Human Rights Tst 1974-; *Style* - John Alexander-Sinclair Esq; 5 Aysgarth rd, Dulwich Village, SE21 (☎ 01 733 1666); The Clink, Goodings, Woodlands St Mary, Newbury (☎ Gt Shefford 450)

ALFORD, Lady; Eileen Mary, formerly Riddell; *m* 1967, as his 2 wife, Sir Robert Edmund Alford, KBE, CMG, sometime Gov and CIC St Helena (d 1979); *Style* - Lady Alford, The Barn, Staplecross, Near Battle, East Sussex (☎ Staplecross 363)

ALFRED, Arnold Montague; s of Reuben Alfred and Bessie, nee Arbesfield; *b* 21 March 1925; *Educ* Imp Coll London, LSE; *m* 1947, Sheila Gold; 3 s; *Career* dir BPC 1969-, chm BPC ltd 1971-, Caxton Publishing Holdgs 1971-; *Style* - Arnold Montague Esq; 44 Gt Queen st, WC2 (☎ 01 240 3411)

ALINGTON, Charles Francis; DL (Cambs 1968); s of Walter Hildebrand Alington; *b* 8 March 1919; *Educ* Elstree Sch, RNC Dartmouth; *m* 1944, Anne, da of Lt-Col Alexander Maclean, 16 Chieftain and Laird of Ardgour, JP, DL, of Ardgour House, Ardgour, Argyll, by his w, Hon Muriel Burns, OBE, JP, yr da of 3 Baron Inverclyde; 1 s, 2 da; *Career* Cdr RN, served 1932-58; nurseryman 1960-; High Sheriff Huntingdon & Peterborough 1967; *Recreations* fishing; *Style* - Charles Alington Esq, DL; Little Barford Dower House, St Neots, Huntingdon, Cambs (☎ Huntingdon 217294)

ALISON, Michael James Hugh; MP (C) Barkston Ash 1964-; *b* 27 June 1926; *Educ* Eton, Wadham Oxford; *m* 1958, Sylvia Haigh; 2 s, 1 da; *Career* Min of State NI Off 1979-; *Style* - Michael Alison Esq, MP; Flat 7, Sheridan Court, Barkston gdns, SW5

ALLAIRE, Paul Arthur; s of Arthur Allaire; *b* 21 July 1938; *Educ* Worcester Polytechnic Inst, Carnegie Mellon U; *m* 1963, Kathleen, da of Thomas Buckley, of New York; 1 s, 1 da; *Career* md Rank Xerox, bd memb American Chamber Commerce; *Recreations* riding, tennis; *Style* - Paul Allaire Esq; 9 Chester ter, NW1

ALLAN, Andrew Garth; s of Andrew Allan, of Middx; *b* 9 Sept 1936; *Educ* King's Coll London; *m* 1959, Ann, da of Patrick O'Callaghan; 3 s (of whom 2 are twins); *Career* md James Burn Bindings Ltd 1971-, James Burn Overseas, James Burn Eynsham; Pres James Burn International Ltd 1980-; *Recreations* water colour painting, bee keeping, the Church choir; *Style* - Andrew Allan Esq; 2 Gateways, Epsom rd, Guildford, Surrey (☎ 67088)

ALLAN, Sir Colin Hamilton; KCMG (1977, CMG 1968), OBE (1959); s of late John Allan; *b* 23 Oct 1921; *Educ* Hamilton H S NZ, Magdalene Cambridge; *m* 1955, Betty, nee Evans; 3 s; *Career* Gov Solomon Is, High Commr W Pacific 1976-78; *Style* - Sir Colin Allan, KCMG, OBE; 26 Alpha st, Cambridge, New Zealand

ALLAN, Ian; s of George Allan, OBE; *b* 29 June 1922; *Educ* St Paul's; *m* 1947, Mollie, nee Franklin; 2 s; *Career* chm Ian Allan Gp 1962-, Dart Valley Light Ry 1976-; *Style* - Ian Allan Esq; The Jetty, Middleton-on-Sea, Bognor Regis, W Sussex (☎ M-0n-S 3378)

ALLAN, James Nicholas; CBE (1976); s of Morris Allan and Joan Bach; *b* 22 May 1932; *Educ* Gresham's, LSE; *m* 1961, Helena Susara Crouse; 1 s, 1 da; *Career* High Commr Mauritius 1980-; *Style* - James Allan Esq CBE; c/o FCO, SW1

ALLAN, William Roderick Buchanan; s of James Allan; *b* 11 Sept 1945; *Educ* Stowe, Trin Cambridge; *m* 1973, Gillian Colgan; 1 s; *Career* ed The Connoisseur 1976-80; *Style* - William Allan Esq; Swiss Cottage, The Street, Albury, Surrey (☎ Shere 3383)

ALLANBRIDGE, Hon Lord; William Ian Stewart; s of late John Stewart, FRIBA; *b* 8 Nov 1925; *Educ* Loretto, Edinburgh and Glasgow Us; *m* 1935, Naomi, da of late Sir James Douglas, CBE, of Barstibly, Castle Douglas; 1 s, 1 da; *Career* barr 1951, advocate depute 1959-64, memb Criminal Injuries Compensation Bd 1969-70, home adv dep 1970-71, slr gen for Scotland 1972-74, Sen of College of Justice in Scotland (Scottish Ld of Session) 1977-, QC (Scot) 1965; *Style* - Hon Lord Allanbridge; 60 Northumberland st, Edinburgh EH3 6JE (☎ 031 556 2823)

ALLANBY, Lady Anne Sarah Elizabeth; *née* Savile; da of 7 Earl of Mexborough (d 1980); *b* 1938; *m* 1964, Charles Hynman Allanby; 1 s; *Style* - Lady Anne Allanby; Balblair, Nairn

ALLANSON-WINN, Hon Mrs John - Barbara Muriel; da of late Owen Sparks, of Bridgetown, W Australia; *m* 1942, the

Hon John Valentine Allanson-Winn (d 1972); *Style* - The Hon Mrs John Allanson-Winn; Flat 2, 37 Hastie st, Bunbury, W Australia 6230

ALLANSON-WINN, Hon John Rowland; s and h of 7 Baron Headley; *b* 14 Oct 1934; *Educ* Canford Sch; *Style* - The Hon John Allanson-Winn; 37 Lytchett Way, Poole, Dorset

ALLANSON-WINN, Hon Owain Gwynedd; s of 6 Baron Headley (d 1969); *b* 1906; *Educ* Bedford Sch; *m* 1938, Ruth (Pearson), da of late Cecil Orpin, of Strand House, Youghal, co Cork; *Style* - The Hon Owain Allanson-Winn; Gwydyr, Witfontein rd, George, Cape Province, S Africa

ALLANSON-WINN, Hon Susan Ethel; da of 7 Baron Headley; *b* 1936; *Style* - The Hon Susan Allanson-Winn

ALLARD, Sir Gordon Laidlaw; Kt (1981); s of late G Allard; *b* 7 Aug 1909; *m* 1935, Cherry, da of S R E Singleton; 1 s; *Career* pres Roy Victorian Eye and Ear Hosp 1964-; *Style* - Sir Gordon Allard; 4 St Martins close, Kootyong, Vic 3144, Australia

ALLARD, Gen Jean Victor; CC (1968), CBE (1946), DSO** (1943 1944 1945), ED (1946), CD (1958); s of late Ernest Allard and Victorine Trudel; *b* 12 June 1913; *Educ* St Laurent Coll Montreal, St Jerome Coll Kitchener Ont; *m* 1939, Simone, da of Gustave Piche, OBE; 2 da; *Career* Ch Canadian Def Staff 1966-69, Quebec Rep in New York 1969-70, business consultant; *Style* - General Jean Allard CC CBE DSO** ED CD; 3265 Blvd du Carmel, Trois Rivières, Quebec, Canada

ALLARDICE, His Hon Judge; William Arthur Llewellyn Allardice; DL (1980); s of late W Allardice, MD, FRCSEd, JP; *b* 18 Dec 1924; *Educ* Stonyhurst, Univ Oxford; *m* 1956, Jennifer, nee Jackson; 1 s, 1 da; *Career* Circuit Judge (Midland & Oxford) 1972-, barr 1950; *Style* - His Hon Judge Allardice, DL; c/o Courts Administrator, Stafford (☎ 55219)

ALLASON, Lt-Col James Harry; OBE (1953); s of late Brig-Gen Walter Allason, DSO; *b* 6 Sept 1912; *Educ* Haileybury, RMA Woolwich; *m* 1946 (m dis 1974), Nuala Elveen; 2 s; *Career* MP (C) Hemel Hempstead 1959-74, PPS to Sec of State for War 1960-64; *Also* White's, Roy Yacht Sqdn; *Style* - Lt-Col James Allason, OBE; 82 Ebury Mews, SW1 (☎ 01 730 1576)

ALLAUN, Frank; MP (L) E Salford 1955-; s of Harry and Hannah Allaun; *b* 27 Feb 1913; *Educ* Manchester G S; *m* 1941, Lilian Ball; 1 s, 1 da; *Career* chm Lab Nat Exec 1978-79; *Style* - Frank Allun Esq, MP; 1 South Drive, Manchester M 21 2DX

ALLAWAY, Percy Albert; CBE (1973); s of Albert Allaway; *b* 22 Aug 1915; *Educ* Southall Tech Coll; *m* 1959, Margaret Petyt; *Career* dir EMI 1965-, chm EMI Electronics 1968-, dir Nuclear Enterprises, RDL (EMI), SE Labs (EMI); FRSA; *Style* - Percy Allaway Esq, CBE; Kroller, 54 Howards Wood dve, Gerrards Cross, Bucks (☎ 85028)

ALLCOCK, John Gladding Major; CB (1964); s of Rev William Allcock; *b* 20 July 1905; *Educ* St Paul's, Jesus Cambridge; *m* 1936, Eileen, da of Dr Ll Baiss, OBE; 1 s, 1 da; *Career* asst master Exeter Sch 1927-28, Liverpool Coll 1928-35, HM Inspector of Sch 1935, Div Insp (NW Div) 1949, Ch Insp Educn Dvpts 1959-66, ret; *Style* - John Allcock Esq, CB; Russet Cottage, Corfe Castle, Dorset (☎ 574)

ALLDAY, Coningsby; CBE (1971); s of late Esca Allday; *b* 21 Nov 1920; *Educ* Solihull Sch; *m* 1945, Iris Adams; 1 s, 1 da; *Career* md Br Nuclear Fuels 1971-; *Style* - Coningsby Allday Esq, CBE; Br Nuclear Fuels Ltd, Risley, Warrington, Cheshire

ALLDAY, Michael William; s of Percy Allday, of Solihull; *b* 30 April 1919; *Educ* Clifton; *m* 1940, Mary, da of Robert David Roberts, JP (High Sheriff Merioneth 1923), of Bryndedwydd, N Wales; 2 da; *Career* formerly Capt RE, served with 1 Assault Bde RE NW Europe; chm William Allday & Co 1959-; *Recreations* shooting, fishing; *Clubs* Naval & Military; *Style* - Michael Allday Esq; Bryndedwydd,

Corwen, Clwyd (☎ Maerdy 308); The Shrubbery, Hartlebury, Worcs (☎ 304)

ALLDIS, John; s of William Alldis; *b* 10 Aug 1929; *Educ* Felsted, King's Cambridge; *m* 1960, Ursula Mason; 2 s; *Career* conductor London Philharmonic Choir 1969-, Groupe Vocale de France 1979-; FGSM 1976; *Style* - John Alldis Esq; 3 Wool rd, Wimbledon, SW20 (☎ 01 946 4168)

ALLEBONE, Alan; TD (1949); s of Arthur Allebone, JP, CA, of Rushden; *b* 28 July 1915; *Educ* Kimbolton Sch and Switzerland; *m* 1938, Muriel, da of Frederick Sibley, of Wales; 1 s, 2 da; *Career* formerly Lt-Col N Africa, France, Germany; chm & md Allebone & Sons 1970; *Recreations* travel; *Clubs* RSAC; *Style* - Alan Allebone Esq, TD; Erskine House, 264 Wellingborough rd, Rushden, Northants (☎ 09 334 2765)

ALLEGRO, John Marco; s of late John Allegro and Mabel, nee Perry; *b* 17 Feb 1923; *Educ* Wallington Co G S, Manchester U; *m* 1948, Joan Lawrence; 1 s, 1 da; *Career* author; *Books* The Sacred Mushroom and the Cross 1970; *Style* - John Allegro Esq; Craigmore, Ballasalla, IOM (☎ Castletown 2345)

ALLEN OF FALLOWFIELD, Baron (Life Peer UK 1974); Alfred Walter Henry Allen; CBE (1967); s of Walter Allen, of Bristol; *b* 7 July 1914; *Educ* E Bristol Centl Sch; *m* 1940, Ruby, da of Albert Hounsell; 1 s (Hon Lionel Allen, b 1943), 1 da; *Career* Gen Sec USDAW 1962-, Crown Estate Commr 1965-, memb Gen Cncl TUC & NEDC, dir Industl T'ning Servs; memb Bd Govs BBC 1977-, dir BAA 1977-; served WW II RAF; *Style* - Rt Hon Lord Allen of Fallowfield CBE; 83 Manley rd, Sale, Cheshire

ALLEN OF ABBEYDALE, Baron (Life Peer UK 1976); Philip Allen; GCB (1970, KCB 1964, CB 1954); s of Arthur Allen, of Sheffield; *b* 8 July 1912; *Educ* King Edward VII Sch Sheffield, Queens' Cambridge; *m* 1938, Marjorie, da of Thomas Colton Coe; *Career* 2 Sec Treasury 1963-66, PUS Home Off 1966-72; memb Security Commission 1973-, chm Gaming Bd for GB 1977-; memb Tbnl of Enquiry into Crown Agents 1978-; *Clubs* Brooks's; *Style* - Rt Hon Lord Allen of Abbeydale GCB; Holly Lodge, Englefield Green, Surrey (☎ Egham 32291)

ALLEN, Hon Alfred Ernest; CMG (1973), JP; s of Ernest Allen; *b* 20 May 1912; *Educ* Auckland G S; *m* 1935, Nancy, nee Cutfield; 1 s, 3 da; *Career* pres Assoc Tstee Savings Banks of NZ 1976-78, Speaker NZ House of Representatives 1972 (MP 1957-72) ; *Style* - Hon Alfred Allen, CMG, JP; 32 Carlton cres, Maraetai Beach, Auckland, New Zealand (☎ Beachlands 6595)

ALLEN, His Hon Judge; Anthony Kenway Allen; OBE (1946); s of Charles Allen; *b* 31 Oct 1917; *Educ* St George's Coll Weybridge, St John's Cambridge, Freiburg and Grenoble Us; *m* 1975, Maureen Murtough; *Career* Circuit Judge 1978-, barr 1947; *Style* - His Hon Judge Allen OBE; 73 Downswood, Epsom Downs, Surrey (☎ Burgh Heath 50017)

ALLEN, Arnold Millman; CBE (1977); s of Wilfrid Millman & Edith Allen; *b* 30 Dec 1924; *Educ* Hackney Downs Secondary Sch, Peterhouse Cambridge; *m* 1947, Beatrice Whitaker; 3 s, 1 da; *Career* dep chm UKAEA 1981-, memb for fin & admin 1976-81; served Treasury 1945-55; *Style* - Arnold Allen Esq, CBE; Duntish Cottage, Duntish, Dorchester, Dorset (☎ Buckland Newton 258)

ALLEN, Antony William; s of William Allen; *b* 2 Oct 1926; *Educ* Haileybury, Merton Oxford; *m* 1953, Hazel, da of Dr Paul King; 2 s, 2 da; *Career* FCA, sr ptnr Gilbert Allen & Co; chm Municipal Properties Ltd; *Recreations* gardens, books; *Style* - Antony Allen Esq; West Wind, Wadhurst, Sussex

ALLEN, Sir (William) Denis; GCMG (1969, KCMG 1958, CMG 1950), CB (1955); s of John Allen; *b* 24 Dec 1910; *Educ* New Zealand, Cambridge; *m* 1939, Elizabeth, nee Watkin Williams; 1 s; *Career* Ambass to Turkey 1963-67, Dep Under-Sec FO 1967-69; *Style* - Sir Denis Allen, GCMG, CB; Stockland, Honiton,

Devon

ALLEN, Sir Donald Richard; OBE (1944), MC* (1917); s of Thomas Allen; *b* 31 Aug 1894; *Educ* Wm Morris Sch Walthamstow; *m* 1918, Irene Andrews (d 1965); 1 s, 1 da; *Career* kt 1954, Clerk to Tstees of London Parochial Charities 1930-65; *Style* - Sir Donald Allen, OBE, MC*; Sprigg's Court, Epping, Essex

ALLEN, Prof Sir Geoffrey; s of John Allen; *b* 29 Oct 1928; *Educ* Leeds U; *m* 1973, Valerie Duckworth; 1 da; *Career* kt 1979, Phd, FRS 1976, FInstP, prof of Clinical Technology Imperial Coll 1976-, chm Social Science Res Cncl 1977-81; *Style* - Prof Sir Geoffrey Allen; 16 Burghley rd, SW19 (☎ 01 947 7459)

ALLEN, George Oswald Browning; CBE (1962), TD (1945); s of late Sir Walter Allen, KBE; *b* 31 July 1902; *Educ* Eton, Trin Cambridge; *Career* cricketer, Capt England XI *v* India 1936, *v* Australia 1936-37, *v* W Indies 1948; *Club* White's; *Style* - George Allen Esq, CBE, TD; 4 Grove End rd, NW8 (☎ 01 286 4601)

ALLEN, Harry; s of Harry Allen; *b* 30 May 1931; *Educ* High Pavement Sch Nottingham; *m* 1954, Patricia Mary; 2 s; *Career* CA; md Polaroid UK 1971-; *Recreations* music, swimming; *Style* - Harry Allen Esq; 64 Harmer Green Lane, Digswell, Herts (☎ Welwyn 5459)

ALLEN, Hon John Douglas; s of Baron Croham (Life Peer), *qv*; *b* 1945; *m* 1969, Sheila Ward; *Style* - The Hon John Allen

ALLEN, Hon Mrs (Joan Elizabeth); *née* Platt; da of Baron Platt (Life Peer and 1 Bt) (d 1978); *b* 1927; *m* 1952, John Bunting Allen; 3 s; *Style* - The Hon Mrs Allen; 2 Highfield rd, Torkington, Hazel Grove, Cheshire

ALLEN, Maj-Gen John Geoffrey Robyn; CB (1976); s of R Allen; *b* 19 Aug 1923; *Educ* Haileybury; *m* 1959, Ann, nee Morford; 1 s, 1 da; *Career* sr Army Directing Staff RCDS 1976-78, ret 1979, Lay Observer attached to Lord Chancellor's Dept 1979-; *Style* - Maj-Gen John Allen, CB; Waney Edges, Fitzroy rd, Fleet, Hants

ALLEN, Janet Rosemary; da of John Allen; *b* 11 April 1936; *Educ* Cheltenham Ladies' Coll, U Coll Leicester, Hughes Hall Cambridge; *Career* Headmistress Benenden Sch 1976-; *Style* - Miss Janet Allen; Benenden School, Cranbrook, Kent (☎ Benenden 592)

ALLEN, Sir (William) Kenneth (Gwynne); DL (Beds 1978); s of Harold Allen; *b* 23 May 1907; *Educ* Westminster, Neuchatel U Switzerland; *m* 1931, Eleanor, nee Eeles; 1 s, 1 da; *Career* kt 1961, FIMarE, MRINA, MIBritishE, chm W H Allen Sons & Co 1955-70; *Style* - Sir Kenneth Allen, DL; Manor Close, Aspley Guise, Milton Keynes, Beds (☎ Woburn Sands 583161)

ALLEN, Kenneth Radway; s of Alexander Allen; *b* 12 Feb 1911; *Educ* Manchester G S, Cambridge; *m* 1938, Rosa Mary, da of Harry Bullen; *Career* biologist; ch Divn of Fisheries & Oceanography CSIRO, Cronulla NSW 1972-77; *Style* - Kenneth Allen Esq; 192 Ewos Pde, Cronulla, NSW 2230, Australia

ALLEN, Hon Lionel Paul; s of Baron Allen of Fallowfield, CBE; *b* 1943; *Style* - The Hon Lionel Allen; 103 Old rd, Tintwistle, Hadfield, Hyde, Cheshire

ALLEN, Sir Milton Pentonville; OBE (1964); *b* 22 June 1888, St Kitts; *m* 1937, Annie, nee Locker, MBE (d 1979); *Career* kt 1972, Gov St Kitts/Nevis/Anguilla 1972-75, formerly tailor; *Style* - Sir Milton Allen, OBE; The Fortlands, Basseterre, St Kitts, W Indies

ALLEN, Sir Peter Christopher; s of late Sir Ernest Allen, CBE, and Florence, nee Gellatly; *b* 8 Sept 1905; *Educ* Harrow, Trin Oxford; *m* 1, 1931, Violet (d 1951), da of Sir Ernest Wingate-Saul; 2 da; m 2, 1952, Consuelo Rivas; *Career* chm ICI 1968-71; dir Bank of Montreal 1968-75, Br Insulated Callender's Cables 1971-, FBIM, FInstD, advsy dir New Perspective Fund of Los Angeles 1973; Gov Harrow Sch; kt 1967; *Recreations* writing, golf, transport history; *Clubs* Carlton, Roy & Ancient St Andrews, Augusta National;

Style - Sir Peter Allen; Telham Hill House, nr Battle, E Sussex (☎ 042 46 3150)

ALLEN, Hon Richard Anthony; s of Baron Croham (Life Peer), *qv*; *b* 1950; *m* 1980, Karen, nee Hughes; *Style* - The Hon Richard Allen

ALLEN, Sir Roy George Douglas; CBE (1954, OBE 1946); s of G Allen; *b* 3 June 1906; *Educ* Roy G S Worcester, Sidney Sussex Cambridge; *m* 1936; 2 s, 1 da; *Career* Prof of Statistics London U 1944-73, Prof Emeritus Consultant Roy Cmmn on Civil Liability 1974-78, MA, DSc, FBA; kt 1966; *Style* - Sir Roy Allen, CBE; 11 The Limes, Linden gdns, W2 (☎ 01 727 9979); Greyfriars (South), South Green, Southwold, Suffolk (☎ 723307)

ALLEN, Sir Richard Hugh Sedley; KCMG (1960, CMG 1953); s of late Sir Hugh Allen, GCVO; *b* 3 Feb 1903; *Educ* RNCs Osborne and Dartmouth, New Coll Oxford; *m* 1945, Juliet Thomson; 1 s (and 1 step s); *Career* Br Ambass to Burma 1956-62; *Style* - Sir Richard Allen, KCMG; 18 Radnor Walk, SW3 (☎ 01 352 9602); 9 Cawley rd, Chichester, Sussex (☎ 89133)

ALLEN, Sir William Guilford; *Career* honoured for service to broadcasting and pastoral industry; kt 1981; *Style* - Sir William Allen

ALLENBY, 2 Viscount (UK 1919); Dudley Jaffray Hynman Allenby; s of Capt Frederick Allenby, CBE, JP, RN (ret), yr bro of Field Marshal 1 Viscount Allenby, GCB, GCMG, GCVO (d 1933), by the Capt's w Edith, niece of Sir William Jaffray, 2 Bt, and da of John J by his w Edith, nee Franklyn, whereby Lord Allenby is kin to Lord Thorneycroft, *qv*; suc unc (by special remainder) 1933; *b* 8 Jan 1903; *Educ* Eton; *m* 1, 1930 (m dis 1949), Gertrude, da of Edward Champneys, of Otterpool Manor, Sellindge, Kent; 1 s; m 2, 1949, Mrs Daisy Neame, CStJ, da of Charles Hancox, and formerly w of Col Lionel Neame and prior to him of Carl Bendix; *Heir* s, Hon Michael Allenby; *Career* Lt-Col (ret) 11 Hussars, served WW II Europe; *Style* - The Rt Hon Viscount Allenby; Parsonage Farm, Westwell, Ashford, Kent

ALLENBY, Hon Michael Jaffray Hynman; s and h of 2 Viscount Allenby; *b* 20 April 1921; *Educ* Eton; *m* 1965, Sara Margaret, da of Lt-Col Peter Milner Wiggin; 1 s; *Career* Lt-Col Roy Hussars; appointed CO Roy Yeo 1974; *Clubs* Cavalry and Guards; *Style* - The Hon Michael Allenby; Newnham Lodge, Newnham, Basingstoke, Hants

ALLENDALE, 3 Viscount (UK 1911); Wentworth Hubert Charles Beaumont; DL (Northumberland); also Baron Allendale (UK 1906); s of 2 Viscount Allendale, KG, CB, CBE, MC (d 1956), and Violet, da of Sir Charles Seely, 2 Bt; *b* 12 Sept 1922; *Educ* Eton; *m* 1948, Hon Sarah Ismay, da of Gen 1 Baron Ismay, KG, GCB, CH, DSO, PC; 3 s; *Heir* s, Hon Wentworth Beaumont; *Career* Fl Lt RAFVR, Hon Air Cdre 3508 N'mberland; Pres N'mberland & Durham Assoc Bldg Socs; OStJ; Steward Jockey Club 1963-65; ADC to Viceroy India 1946; served WW II, POW; *Style* - Rt Hon Viscount Allendale, DL; Allenheads Hall, Allenheads, Northumberland; Bywell Hall, Stocksfield-on-Tyne, Northumberland

ALLENDALE, Viscountess; Hon Sarah Field; da of 1 Baron Ismay (d 1965); *b* 1928; *m* 1948, 3 Viscount Allendale; *Style* - The Rt Hon the Viscountess Allendale; Bywell Hall, Stocksfield-on-Tyne, Northumberland; Allenheads Hall, Allenheads, Northumberland

ALLERTON, 3 Baron (UK 1902); George William Lawies Jackson; s of 2 Baron (d 1925); *b* 23 July 1903; *Educ* Eton; *m* 1, 1926 (m dis 1934), Joyce (d 1953), da of John Hatfeild, of Thorp Arch Hall, Yorks; 1 s; m 2, 1934, Hope (m dis 1947), da of Allan Havelock-Allan (2 s of Sir Henry Havelock-Allan, 1 Bt, VC, GCB, DL, himself s of the hero of the siege of Lucknow during the Indian Mutiny; the 1 Bt m Lady Alice Moreton, da of 2 Earl of Ducie) and sis of Sir Anthony Allan, 4 Bt, the film producer; m 3, 1947, Anne, da of James Montagu; 1 da; *Heir* s, Hon Edward Jackson; *Career* Sqdn Ldr AAF ret; late Lt

Coldstream Gds Reserve; *Style* - The Rt Hon Lord Allerton; Loddington Hall, Leics

ALLEYNE, Capt Sir John Meynell; 4 Bt (GB 1769), of Four Hills, Barbados, DSO (1918), DSC (1916), RN; s of Reynold Alleyne (er s of Sir John Alleyne, 3 Bt, JP, by his w, Augusta, da of Sir Henry FitzHerbert, 3 Bt) and Susanna, 3 da of John Meynell, of Meynell Langley, Derbys; suc gf 1912; *b* 11 Aug 1889; *Educ* HMS Britannia RNC; *m* 1920, Alice, da of James Campbell, of Cornwall Gdns, SW; 1 s, 2 da; *Heir* s, Rev John Alleyne; *Career* served WW I & II in RN; *Recreations* riding; *Clubs* Naval & Military; *Style* - Capt Sir John Alleyne Bt DSO DSC RN; South Lynch, Hursley, Winchester, Hants (☎ Hursley 239)

ALLEYNE, Rev John Olpherts Campbell; s and h of Capt Sir John Alleyne, 4 Bt, DSO, DSC, RN; *b* 18 Jan 1928; *Educ* Eton, Jesus Cambridge; *m* 1968, Honor, da of William Irwin, of Belfast; 1 s, 1 da; *Career* Rector of Weeke, Winchester; *Recreations* sailing, mountain walking, astronomy; *Style* - The Rev John Alleyne; The Rectory, Cheriton rd, Winchester, Hants (☎ 4849)

ALLFREY, Hon Mrs (Julian Mary); *née* Russell; da of Baron Russell of Killowen, PC; *b* 1935; *m* 1, 1955 (m dis 1974), Anthony Allfrey, s of Lady Holman, *qv*, by her 1 husb Capt Basil Allfrey; 1 s, 2 da; *Style* - The Hon Mrs Allfrey

ALLHUSEN, Hon Mrs (Claudia Violet); *née* Betterton; da of 1 Baron Rushcliff by his 1 w; *b* 11 Oct 1917; *m* 1937, Maj Derek Allhusen, s of Lt-Col Frederick Allhusen, CMG, DSO (d 1957); 1 s (Timothy Frederick m 1965 Annabel Morris) also 1 s decd, 1 da (Rosemary Claudia m 1973 Capt Jeremy Groves, 17/21 Lancers); *Recreations* riding; *Style* - The Hon Mrs Allhusen; Flat 1, 22 St James's sq, SW1 (☎ 01 839 3390); The Manor House, Claxton, Norwich (☎ Thurton 228)

ALLHUSEN, Maj Derek Swithin; DL (Norfolk 1969); s of late Lt-Col F Allhusen, CMG, DSO, of Fulmer House, Fulmer, Bucks; *b* 9 Jan 1914; *Educ* Eton, Chillon Coll Switzerland, Trin Cambridge; *m* 1937, Hon Claudia Betterton, da of 1 and last Baron Rushcliffe, GBE, PC (d 1949); 1 s, 1 da (and 1 s decd); *Career* farmer, Standard Bearer Hon Corps of Gentlemen-at-Arms 1981-, High Sheriff Norfolk 1958; *Style* - Maj Derek Allhusen Esq, DL; Flat 1, 22 St James's sq, SW1 (☎ 01 839 3390); Manor House, Claxton, Norwich, Norfolk (☎ Thurton 228)

ALLINSON, Sir (Walter) Leonard; KCVO (1979, MVO 1961), CMG (1976); s of Walter Allinson; *b* 1 May 1926; *Educ* Friern Barnet G S, Merton Oxford; *m* 1951, Margaret Watts; 3 da (including twins); *Career* High Commr Lusaka 1978-80, Assist Under Sec (Africa) FCO 1980-; *Recreations* Br Indian history & fiction, rough gardening, tennis; *Clubs* Travellers', Nairobi; *Style* - Sir Leonard Allinson, KCVO, CMG; c/o FCO, SW1

ALLINSON, Air Vice-Marshal Norman Stuart; CB (1946), DL (Essex 1964); s of late Rev H Allinson; *b* 19 April 1904; *Educ* Trent Coll, RAF Cranwell; *m* 1928, Florence Hall (d 1975); 1 s, 1 da; *Career* AO i/c Admn, Flying Training Cmmd 1954-56; *Style* - Air Vice-Marshal Norman Allinson CB DL; Dene House, Layer de la Haye, Colchester, Essex

ALLIOTT, John Downes; QC (1973); s of late Alexander Alliott; *b* 9 Jan 1932; *Educ* Charterhouse, Peterhouse Cambridge; *m* 1957, Patsy, nee Willson; 2 s, 1 da; *Career* Recorder of Crown Court 1972-, barr 1955; *Style* - John Alliott Esq, QC; Park Stile, Love Hill Lane, Langley, Slough, Bucks (☎ Iver 652745)

ALLISON, Ralph Victor; CMG (1967); s of late Albert Allison; *b* 20 Feb 1900; *m* 1923, Myrtle Birch; 2 da; *Career* sometime chm Finlayson Ltd Adelaide, memb S Australia Dairy Bd 1957-, dir Australian Export Promotions Ltd to 1966; *Style* - Ralph Allison Esq, CMG; 18 Taylor Ter, Rosslyn Pk, SA 5072, Australia (☎ 31 2538)

ALLISON, Ronald William Paul; CVO (1978); s of Percy Allison; *b* 26 Jan 1932; *Educ* Weymouth G S, Taunton's Sch

S'thampton; *m* 1956, Maureen Macdonald; 2 da; *Career* md Ronald Allison & Assocs 1978-, BBC reporter 1957-73, Press Sec to HM The Queen 1973-78, presenter Thames TV 1978-; *Style* - Ronald Allison Esq, CVO; 36 Ormond dve, Hampton, Middx (☎ 01 979 1912)

ALLOTT, Air Cdre Molly Greenwood; CB (1975); da of late Gerald Allott; *b* 28 Dec 1918; *Educ* Sheffield H S for Girls; *Career* Dir WRAF 1973-76, MBIM, Nat Chm Girls' Venture Corps 1977-; *Style* - Air Cdre Molly Allott, CB; c/o Midland Bank, Chapeltown, Sheffield s, S30 4XE

ALLPORT, Denis Ivor; s of late A Allport and E M, nee Mashman; *b* 20 Nov 1922; *Educ* Highgate; *m* 1949, Diana, nee Marler; 2 s, 1 da; *Career* chm (ch exec 1977-) Metal Box 1979-, FBIM; *Style* - Denis Allport Esq; Elm Place, Mumbery Hill, Wargrave, Berks (☎ 3007)

ALLSOP, Peter Henry Bruce; s of late Herbert Allsop; *b* 22 Aug 1924; *Educ* Haileybury, Caius Cambridge; *m* 1950, Patricia Bown; 2 s, 1 da; *Career* barr 1948; chm Sweet & Maxwell 1974- (ed 1950-59, dir 1960-64, md 1965-73); md Associated Book Publishers 1968-76 (dir 1963, assist man 1965-67); memb cncl Publishers' Assoc (tres 1973-75, 1979-; pres 1975-77, v pres 1977-78), chm Software Scis Teleordering Ltd 1978-; *Style* - Peter Allsop Esq; Manor Farm, Charlton Mackrell, Somerton, Somerset (☎ C M 650)

ALLSOPP, (Harold) Bruce; s of Henry Allsopp; *b* 4 July 1912; *Educ* Manchester G S, Liverpool Sch of Architecture; *m* 1935, Florence Woodroffe; 2 s; *Career* chm Oriel Press Ltd 1962-, dir Routledge & Kegan Paul Books 1974-, ARIBA, AMTPI, FRIBA, FSA, Reader in Architecture Newcastle U 1973-77; *Style* - Bruce Allsopp Esq; Woodburn, 3 Batt House rd, Stocksfield, Northumberland (☎ 2323)

ALLSOPP, Hon Charles Henry; s and h of 5 Baron Hindlip; *b* 5 Aug 1940; *Educ* Eton; *m* 1968, Fiona Victoria Jean Atherley, da of late Hon William Johnston McGowan, 2 s of 1 Baron McGowan; 1 s, 2 da; *Career* dir Christie's; late Lt Coldstream Gds; *Style* - The Hon Charles Allsopp; Totterdown House, Inkpen, Berks (☎ Inkpen 402); 47 Cathcart rd, SW10 (☎ 01 352 7599)

ALLSOPP, Hon Elizabeth Tulla; da of 4 Baron Hindlip (d 1966); *b* 1942; *Style* - The Hon Elizabeth Allsopp

ALLSOPP, Hon John Peter; s of 5 Baron Hindlip; *b* 1942; *Educ* Eton; *m* 1976, Daryl, da of Leonard Shawzin, of Huisinbois, Constantia, CP, S Africa; 1 s, 1 da; *Style* - The Hon John Allsopp

ALLSOPP, Hon Mrs - Hon Norah Hyacinthe; *née* Littleton; da of 4 Baron Hatherton (d 1944); *b* 1899; *m* 1923, Samuel Ranulph Allsopp, CBE (d 1975); *Style* - The Hon Mrs Allsopp; Alsa Lodge, Stansted, Essex

ALMENT, Sir Edward Anthony John; s of Edward Alment; *b* 3 Feb 1922; *Educ* Marlborough, Bart's; *m* 1946, Elizabeth Bacon; *Career* kt 1980, FRCOG, gynaecologist, MRCS, LRCP, ; *Style* - Sir Edward Alment; Winston House, Boughton, Northampton (☎ 842317)

ALMISMARI, Mohamed Younis; *b* 3 July 1937; *Educ* Camberley Staff Coll; *m* 1959, Khadija Gargoum; 3 s, 2 da; *Career* late Libyan Ambass to UK, army Colto 1969, min of Foreign Affairs 1969-; *Style*- Mohamed Almismari Esq; 31 Phillimore gdns, W8

ALPEN, John Elliott; s of John Alpen, of Leeton NSW; *b* 31 Oct 1912; *Educ* Leeton H S, C'wlth Inst of Accountants; *m* 1938, Barbara, da of William Mould, of Cooma NSW; 1 s, 1 da; *Career* retired banker (assist gen man & ch man Victoria, Commercial Banking Co of Sydney, 1973-75); Fellow Australian Soc of Accountants, Australian Inst of Management; *Recreations* gardening (Nat Tres Aust Camellia Res Soc, ed Internat Camellia Soc), bowls; *Clubs* Union, Sydney, Roy Prince Alfred Yacht (all Sydney), Athenaeum (Melbourne), Newport Bowling; *Style* - John Alpen Esq; Newport Beach, NSW 991588, Australia

ALPORT, Baron (Life Peer UK 1961); Cuthbert James McCall Alport; TD (1949), PC (1960), DL (Essex 1974); s of Prof Arthur Alport, MD, FRCP; *b* 22 March 1912; *Educ* Haileybury, Pembroke Cambridge; *m* 1945, Rachel, da of Lt-Col Ralph Bingham, CVO, DSO (s of Hon Cecil Bingham, 2 s of 4 Earl of Lucan, KP, JP, by his - Hon Cecil Bingham's - 1 w); 1 s, 2 da; *Career* barr; formerly Lt-Col WW II (GSO 1 E Africa 1944-45); MP (C) Colchester 1950-61, Min of State CRO 1959-61, High Commr Fedn of Rhodesia & Nyasaland 1961-63; Dep Speaker House of Lords 1971-; High Steward Colchester 1967-; advsr to Home Sec 1974-; *Clubs* Pratt's, Farmers; *Style* - Rt Hon Lord Alport, TD, PC, DL; The Cross House, Layer de la Haye, Colchester, Essex (☎ 34207)

ALSTON, Albert Edward Constable; TD (1947), DL (Essex 1958); s of Edward Alston, of Wingfield Hall, Suffolk; *b* 22 Jan 1912; *Educ* St Paul's; *m* 1955, Betty, da of Charles Muggridge, of Thornton Heath; 1 s, 1 da; *Career* served in WW II as Col W Desert; pension consultant; *Recreations* gardening; *Style* - Albert Alston Esq, TD, DL; Foxgloves, The Ridge, Little Baddow, Essex (☎ 0245 41 3205)

ALSTON, James Douglas; CBE (1967); s of James Alston, of Uphall, Norfolk; *b* 6 May 1913; *Educ* Thetford G S, Midland Ag Coll; *m* 1943, Gale, da of Edward Lewis, of Manitoba; 2 s, 2 da; *Career* chm Eastern Counties Farmers Ltd 1954-68 (Pres 1973-); V-Chm Roy Norfolk Ag Assoc 1963-, Norfolk Ag Assoc 1973-; chm Plant Breeding Inst Cambridge 1971-; *Recreations* shooting; *Clubs* Farmers, Norfolk; *Style* - James Alston, Esq, CBE; South Lopham Hall, Diss, Norfolk (☎ Bressingham 286)

ALTAMONT, Earl of; Jeremy Ulick Browne; s and h of 10 Marq of Sligo; *b* 4 June 1939; *Educ* St Columba's Coll Eire, RAC Cirencester; *m* 1961, Jennifer, da of Maj Derek Cooper, of Co Donegal, and Mrs C Heber Percy; 4 da; *Style* - Earl of Altamont; Westport House, Co Mayo, Eire

ALTHAM, Hon Mrs (Elizabeth Oona); *née* McNair; da of 1 Baron McNair, CBE, QC, LLD (d 1975); *b* 1913; *m* 1939, Group Capt John Barrett Altham, CBE; 2 s, 2 da; *Style* - The Hon Mrs Altham; Ivy Cottage, Little Shelford, Cambridge

ALTHAM, John Barrett; CBE (1955); s of Capt Edward Altham, CB, RN; *b* 17 March 1909; *Educ* Eton, Trin Cambridge; *m* 1939, Hon Elizabeth Oona, eldest da of 1 Baron McNair, CBE (d 1975); 2 s, 2 da; *Career* Gp Capt RAF WW II and 1932-62, commanded Communications Gp Allied Forces Central Europe 1959-62; *Recreations* sailing, golf, landscape gardening; *Clubs* Aldeburgh Yacht; *Also* owns foxcub cruiser- 'Flying Fox'; *Style* - Gp Capt John Altham, CBE; Ivy Cottage, Little Shelford, Cambridge (☎ 842182)

ALTHORP, Viscount; Charles Edward Maurice Spencer; s (by 1 m) and h of 8 Earl Spencer, MVO, JP, DL, *qv*; bro of HRH The Princess of Wales (*see* Royal Family); *b* 20 May 1964; *Career* appointed a Page of Honour to HM 1977; *Style* - Viscount Althorp

ALTON, David Patrick; MP (Lib) Liverpool Edge Hill March 1979-; s of Frederick Alton; *b* 15 March 1951; *Educ* Christ's Coll of Educn Liverpool; *Career* Nat Pres Nat League of Young Liberals 1979; *Style* - David Alton Esq, MP; 45 Onslow rd, Edge Hill, Liverpool (☎ 051 260 8792)

ALTRINCHAM; Barony of, *see* Grigg, John Edward Poynder

ALTRINCHAM, Baroness; Hon Joan Alice Katherine; *née* Dickson-Poynder; da of 1 and last Baron Islington (d 1936); *m* 1923, 1 Baron Altrincham (d 1955); *Style* - The Rt Hon the Lady Altrincham; Tormarton Court, Badminton, Glos

ALUN-JONES, John Derek; s of Thomas Alun-Jones; *b* 6 June 1933 *Educ* Lancing, St Edmund Hall Oxford; *m* 1960, Gillian, da of Ian Palmer; 2 s, 3 da; *Career* ch exec Ferranti 1975-; *Recreations* shooting, fishing, riding; *Style* - John Alun-Jones Esq; The Willows, Effingham Common, Surrey (☎ Bookham 58158)

ALVINGHAM, 2 Baron (UK 1929); Robert Guy Eardley Yerburgh; CBE (1977, OBE 1972); s of 1 Baron Alvingham (d 1955); *b* 16 Dec 1926; *Educ* Eton; *m* 1952, Beryl, da of William Wiliams, of Hindhead; 1 s, 1 da; *Heir* s, Hon Robert Yerburgh; *Career* Maj-Gen late Coldstream Gds; Dir Army Quartering MOD 1978; *Style* - Maj-Gen Rt Hon Lord Alvingham CBE; Bix Hall, Henley-on-Thames, Oxon

ALY KHAN, Princess Joan - Hon Joan Barbara; *née* Yarde-Buller; da of 3 Baron Churston, MVO, OBE (d 1930); *b* 1908; *m* 1, 1927, Loel Guinness, OBE (m diss 1936); m 2, 1936 (m diss 1949), Prince Aly Khan, s of HH The Aga Khan (III); 2 s; *Style* - Princess Joan Aly Khan; 8 Hobart Place, SW1

AMBLER, Eric; s of Alfred Percy and Amy Madeleine Ambler; *b* 28 June 1909; *Educ* Colfe's G S, London U; *m* 1, 1939, Louise Crombie; m 2, 1958, Joan Harrison; *Career* author and scriptwriter; *Style* - Eric Ambler Esq; Av Eugene Rambert, 1815 Clarens, Switzerland

AMERY, Rt Hon Julian; PC (1960), MP (C) Brighton Pavilion 1969-; s of late Rt Hon Leopold Amery, CH, PC; *b* 27 March 1919; *Educ* Eton, Balliol Oxford; *m* 1950, Catherine, da of Rt Hon Harold Macmillan; 1 s, 3 da; *Career* MP (C) Preston N 1950-66, Min of Aviation 1962-64, Public Building and Works 1970, Min for Housing and Construction DOE 1970-72, Min of State FCO 1972-74; *Clubs* White's, Beefsteak, Carlton, Buck's; *Style* - The Rt Hon Julian Amery, PC, MP; 112 Eaton sq, SW1 (☎ 01 235 1543/7409); Forest Farm House, Chelwood Gate, Sussex

AMHERST OF HACKNEY, 4 Baron (UK 1892); (William) Hugh Amherst Cecil; s of 3 Baron Amherst of Hackney, CBE (d 1980), and Margaret, Baroness Amherst of Hackney, *qv*; *b* 28 Dec 1940; *Educ* Eton; *m* 1965, Elisabeth, da of Hugh Merriman, DSO, MC, TD, DL; 1 s, 1 da; *Heir* s, Hon Hugh Cecil; *Career* dir E A Gibson (shipbrokers); *Recreations* sailing (yacht- 'Marelanja'); *Clubs* Roy Yacht Sqdn, Roy Ocean Racing; *Style* - Rt Hon Lord Amherst of Hackney; Hazel Hall, Peaslake, Surrey (☎ Shere 3363)

AMHERST, 5 Earl (UK 1826); Jeffrey John Archer Amherst; MC (1918); also Baron Amherst (GB 1788) and Viscount Holmesdale (UK 1826); s of 4 Earl Amherst (d 1927, gs of the 1 Earl, Ambassador to China 1816 and Gov-Gen of Bengal 1822-28; his impious refusal to perform the *ko-tou* ceremony to the Celestial Occupant of the Dragon Throne delayed the acceptance of his credentials and, with Lord Macartney's refusal of twenty years earlier, gave a new phrase (kow-tow) to the English language; his chastisement of the King of Burma, whose insolent pretensions had caused him to invade Bengal, added Assam, Tenasserim and Arracan to Britain's Indian possessions; his 1 w, grandmother of the 4 Earl, gave her name to the ornamental bird known as Amherst's pheasant) and Hon Eleanor St Aubyn, da of 1 Baron St Levan; *b* 13 Dec 1896; *Educ* Eton, Sandhurst; *Heir* none; *Career* ret Maj Coldstream Gds & Hon Wing Cdr RAF; former man BEA and journalist; served WW I & II; former commercial air pilot; *Style* - The Rt Hon Earl Amherst MC

AMHERST OF HACKNEY, Margaret, Baroness; Margaret Eirene Clifton; da of Brig-Gen Howard Brown, sometime MP Newbury, JP, DL (gs of Sir William Brown, 1 Bt, sometime MP S Lancs, JP, DL); *b* 23 Feb 1921; *m* 1939, 3 Baron Amherst of Hackney, CBE (d 1980); 2 s (4 Baron and Hon Anthony Cecil), 1 da (Hon Mrs Reid); *Style* - Rt Hon Margaret, Lady Amherst of Hackney; Rudge House, Crondall, Farnham, Surrey (☎ 0252 850450)

AMIES, (Edwin) Hardy; CVO (1977); s of late Herbert Amies; *b* 17 July 1909; *Career* Dressmaker by appointment to HM The Queen, dir Hardy Amies Ltd 1946, design consultant to J Hepworth & Son 1960-, FRSA; *Style* - Hardy Amies Esq, CVO; 17b Eldon rd, W8 (☎ 01 734 2436)

AMIS, Kingsley; s of William Amis; *b* 16 April 1922; *Educ* City of London Sch, St John's Oxford; *m* 1, 1948, Hilary, nee Bardwell; 2 s, 1 da; m 2, 1965, Elizabeth

Jane Howard,*qv*; *Career* novelist; *Books* Lucky Jim (1954), That Uncertain Feeling (1955, filmed as Only Two Can Play 1962), One Fat Englishman (1963), The Green Man (1969); *Style* - Kingsley Amis Esq; c/o Jonathan Clowes, 19 Jeffrey's Pla, NW1

AMMON, Hon Ada Mary; *née* Ammon; MBE (1950); da of 1 and last Baron Ammon, PC, JP, DL (d 1960); *b* 5 Oct 1900; *Educ* St Saviour's & St Olave's Sch, Kent Coll, London U (extra mural); *Career* Mayoress Camberwell 1950-51; *Style* - The Hon Ada Ammon; Midland Bank, The Broadway, Haywards Heath, W Sussex

AMOS, Roy; s of Leonard Amos, of Birmingham; *b* 8 Sept 1934; *Educ* King Edward 's Sch Birmingham, Birmingham Coll of Commerce; *m* 1956, Marjorie, da of Arnold Hall, of Birmingham; *Career* chm & md Lightning International Ltd 1961-74, exec gp dir IMI 1974-; *Recreations* tennis, golf; *Clubs* Four Oaks; *Style* - Roy Amos Esq; The Lodge, Roman rd, Little Aston Park, Sutton Coldfield, W Midlands (☎ 021 353 5373)

AMPTHILL, 4 Baron (UK 1881); Geoffrey Denis Erskine Russell; s of 3 Baron Ampthill, CBE, by his 1 w, Christabel, da of Lt-Col John Hart, by his w, Blanche, 4 da of Capt David Erskine (2 s of Sir David Erskine, 1 Bt); suc 1973 and petitioned HM The Queen for a Writ of Summons as Baron Ampthill on death of 3 Baron, the House of Lords Cttee on Privileges deciding in his favour 1976; *b* 15 Oct 1921; *Educ* Stowe; *m* 1, 1946 (m dis 1971), Susan, da of Hon Charles Winn (2 s of 2 Baron St Oswald, JP, DL) by his 1 w, Hon Olive Paget (da of 1 and last Baron Queenborough, GBE, JP, gs of 1 Marquess of Anglesey by his 2 w); 2 s (and 1 s decd), 1 da; m 2, 1972, Elisabeth (who runs a catering firm Mallon Ltd, based in Battersea, which cooks official meals for the For Sec at Carlton Gardens), da of Claude Mallon, of Paris; *Heir* s, Hon David Russell; *Career* gen man Fortnum & Mason 1947-51, former md of Theatre Owning Cos; served WW II as Capt Irish Gds; *Style* - The Rt Hon The Lord Ampthill; 20 Cathcart rd, SW10 (☎ 01 352 4666)

AMPTHILL, Adeline, Baroness; Adeline Mary Constance; da of Rev Canon Henry Hone, late Vicar of Godalming; *m* 1948, as his 3 w, 3 Baron Ampthill (d 1973); 1 s, 1 da; *Style* - The Rt Hon Adeline, Lady Ampthill; Flat 3, 75 Holland Park, W 11

AMULREE, 2 Baron (UK 1929); Basil William Sholto Mackenzie; KBE (1977); s of 1 Baron Amulree, CBE (d 1966); *b* 25 July 1900; *Educ* Lancing, Gonville & Caius Cambridge; *Heir* none; *Career* MD, MB, BCh, MRCS, LRCP, MRCP, FRCP; Ch Lib Whip Ho of Lds 1955-77; *Style* - The Rt Hon Lord Amulree KBE; Cranbrook Lodge, Cranbrook, Kent

AMWELL, 2 Baron (UK 1947); Frederick Norman Montague; s of 1 Baron Amwell, CBE (d 1966); *b* 6 Nov 1912; *Educ* Northampton Coll of Advanced Educn; *m* 1939, Kathleen, da of Arthur Fountain; 1 s, 1 da; *Heir* s, Hon Keith Montague; *Career* ret aircraft design engr; *Recreations* gardening, model railways; *Style* - Rt Hon Lord Amwell; 34 Halliford rd, Sunbury-on-Thames, Middx (☎ 85413)

ANCASTER, 3 Earl of (UK 1892); Sir Gilbert James Heathcote-Drummond-Willoughby; 8 Bt (GB 1733), KCVO (1971), TD (1945), JP (1937), DL (Lincs 1977); also 26 Baron Willoughby de Eresby (E 1313) and 4 Baron Aveland (UK 1856); s of 2 Earl of Ancaster, GCVO, TD, JP, DL (d 1951); *b* 8 Dec 1909; *Educ* Eton, Magdalene Cambridge; *m* 1933, Hon Nancy Astor (d 1975), da of 2 Viscount Astor, DL, by his w, Nancy, nee Witcher, CH and the first woman MP; (1 s decd), 1 da; *Heir* to Barony of Willoughby de Eresby da, Lady Nancy Heathcote-Drummond-Willoughby; to Baronetcy, Simon Heathcote, CBE; to Earldom of Ancaster and Barony of Aveland, none; *Career* Ld-Lt Lincs 1950-75; served WW II Leics Yeomanry & RA (Maj); MP (C) Rutland and Stamford 1933-50; Lord Gt Chamberlain of England 1950-52; Nat Pres BLESMA 1956-; KStJ 1957; co dir; *Recreations* shooting, golf; *Style* - The Rt Hon The Earl of Ancaster, KCVO TD, JP,

DL; Drummond Castle, Crieff (☎ Muthill 321); Grimsthorpe, Bourne, Lincs (☎ Edenham 222)

ANCRAM, Earl of; Michael Andrew Foster Jude Kerr; MP (C) Edinburgh S 1979-; s and h of 12 Marq of Lothian; *b* 7 July 1945; *Educ* Ampleforth, Ch Ch Oxford; *m* 1975, Lady Jane Fitzalan-Howard, da of 16 Duke of Norfolk, KG, GCVO, GBE, TD, PC (d 1975), and Lavinia, Duchess of Norfolk; 2 da; *Heir* bro, Lord Ralph Kerr; *Career* advocate (Scot) 1970, MP (C) Berwickshire and E Lothian Feb-Sept 1974, V-Chmn Con Pty in Scotland 1975-; *Style* - Earl of Ancram, MP; 6 Ainslie Pla, Edinburgh (☎ 031 226 3147); Monteviot, Jedburgh, Scotland

ANDERSON, Barry John; CBE (1959), JP (Torbay 1974), DL (Devon 1974); s of Hugh Anderson; *b* 5 April 1914; *Educ* George Watson's Coll Edinburgh, Nautical Colls; *m* 1972, Gwendoline, da of Ronald Raine; 2 s; *Career* Cdre RN, served WW II and 1 Cod War; yr bro Trin House 1958, Hon Sec Torbay Life Boat RNLI 1975; *Recreations* watercolour painting; *Clubs* Brixham Yacht; *Style* - Barry Anderson Esq, CBE, JP, DL; 2 Hanover Close, Brixham, S Devon (☎ 51065)

ANDERSON, Lt-Col Charles Groves Wright; VC (1942), MC (1914-18 War); s of A Anderson; *b* 12 Feb 1897, Capetown; *m* 1931, Edith Tout; 2 s, 2 da; *Career* memb House of Representatives Hume NSW 1949-51, grazier; *Style* - Lt-Col Charles Anderson, VC, MC; Springfield, Young, NSW 2594, Australia

ANDERSON, Donald; MP (L) Swansea E 1974-; s of David Anderson and Eva, nee Mathias; *b* 17 June 1939; *Educ* Swansea G S, U Coll of Swansea; *m* 1963, Dr Dorothy Trotman; 3 s; *Career* barr 1969, memb of FCO 1960-64, lecturer in politics U Coll Swansea 1964-66, MP (L) Monmouth 1966-70, PPS Min of Defence 1969-70, PPS to Attorney Gen 1974-79, chm Welsh Lab Gp 1977-78; *Style* - Donald Anderson Esq, MP; Lamb Bldg, Temple, EC4

ANDERSON, David Colville; VRD (1947) and Clasp (1958), QC (Scot 1957); s of late J Anderson; *b* 8 Sept 1916; *Educ* Trin Coll Glenalmond, Pembroke Oxford, Edinburgh U; *m* 1948, Juliet, da of Hon Lord Hill Watson, MC; 2 s, 1 da; *Career* advocate 1946, MP (C) Dumfries Dec 1963-Sept 1964, Slr-Gen Scotland 1960-64; *Style* - David Anderson Esq, VRD and Clasp, QC; 8 Arboretum rd, Edinburgh EH3 5PD (☎ 031 552 3003)

ANDERSON, Douglas Kinloch; s of William Anderson, of Edinburgh; *b* 19 Feb 1939; *Educ* George Watson's Coll Edinburgh, St Andrews & Edinburgh Us; *m* 1962, Deirdre, da of Leonard Loryman, of Dorking; 2 s, 1 da; *Career* chm & md Kinloch Anderson Ltd; *Recreations* fishing, golf, tennis, skiing, reading; *Clubs* New (Edinburgh), Caledonian; *Style* - Douglas Anderson Esq; 7 Barnton Park, Edinburgh EH4 6JF

ANDERSON, Lady; Doris Norah; da of Lt-Col J Wyburgh; *b* 5 Aug 1916; *m* 1942, Lt-Gen Sir Richard Nevill Anderson (d 1979), s of Lt-Col Sir Neville Anderson, CBE; 2 s; *Recreations* horse breeding, whippet breeding, coursing, judging show ponies; *Style* - Lady Anderson; Tarrant Keynston House, Blandford, Dorset (☎ 52138)

ANDERSON, Lady - Edens Alcyone; da of Wallace McMullen; *m* 1947, Sir Duncan Anderson, KBE, TD (d 1980); *Style* - Lady Anderson; Flat 7, 14 Melbury rd, Holland Pk, W14 (☎ 01 602 3434)

ANDERSON, (William) Eric Kinloch; s of W Kinloch Anderson; *b* 27 May 1936; *Educ* George Watson's Coll, St Andrew's U, Balliol Oxford; *m* 1960, Anne Elizabeth, da of William Mattock Mason, of Yorks; 1 s, 1 da; *Career* Headmaster Eton 1980- (Shrewsbury 1975-80); *Recreations* golf, studying Sir Walter Scott; *Style* - Eric Anderson Esq; Eton College, Windsor, Berks

ANDERSON, Prof Sir (William) Ferguson; OBE (1961); s of James Anderson (ka 1917); *b* 8 April 1914; *Educ* Merchiston, Glasgow Acad, Glasgow U; *m* 1940, Margaret Gebbie; 1 s, 2 da; *Career* physician in Geriatric medicine Stobhill Gen Hospital and Advr in Diseases of old age and chronic sickness W Region Hosp Bd Scotland 1952-74, David Cargill Prof of Geriatric Medicine Glasgow U 1965-79, FRFPSG, FRCPE, FRCP, FRCPI; kt 1974; *Recreations* golf, tennis; *Clubs* Caledonian; *Style* - Prof Sir Ferguson Anderson, OBE; Strathallan, Blanefield, Glasgow G63 9AY

ANDERSON, Lady Flavia Joan Lucy; *née* Giffard; da of 2 Earl of Halsbury, KC; *b* 20 Sept 1910; *Educ* Queen's Gate Sch; *m* 1933, James Alasdair Anderson of Tullichewan; 1 s- Douglas Hardinge Anderson, portraitist, m 1, 1962, Mary Jenkins, m 2, 1974, Veronica Markes; 1 da- Margaret Minette Rohais, m, 1961, Sir Ilay Campbell, 7 Bt; *Career* author of five books; *see Campbell, Sir Ilay Mark, 7 Bt* ; *Style* - Lady Flavia Anderson; 39 Royal Terrace, Edinburgh 7

ANDERSON, George David; CMG (1967); s of George Anderson; *b* 11 Sept 1913; *Educ* King Edward VII G S King's Lynn, Emmanuel Cambridge; *m* 1950, Audrey, da of Frederick Cowslade Money, of Newbury; 1 da; *Career* High Commissioner Botswana 1969-73; *Recreations* gardening, music; *Clubs* Roy C'wlth Soc; *Style* - George Anderson Esq, CMG; 45a Hayes Way, Beckenham, Kent (☎ 01 650 4613)

ANDERSON, Dame Judith; DBE (1960); Dame Frances Margaret Anderson; da of James Anderson and Jessie Saltmarsh; *b* 10 Feb 1898; *Educ* Norwood H S, S Australia; *m* 1, 1937, Prof B H Lehman (m diss 1939); m 2, 1946, Luther Greene (m diss 1950); *Career* actress; *Style* - Dame Judith Anderson, DBE; 808 San Ysidro Lane, Santa Barbara, Calif 93103, USA

ANDERSON, Gen Sir John D'Arcy; GBE (1967, CBE 1945), KCB (1961, CB 1957), DSO (1940), DL (Co Down 1969); s of late Maj Reginald Anderson; *b* 23 Sept 1908; *Educ* Winchester, New Coll Oxford; *m* 1937, Elizabeth, nee Walker; *Career* Pro-Chllr Queen's U Belfast 1969-, Cmmdt IDC 1966-68, ADC Gen to HM The Queen 1966-68, High Sheriff Co Down 1964; *Style* - Gen Sir John Anderson, GBE, KCB,; Ballyhosset, Downpatrick, Co Down, N Ireland (☎ Ardglass 841227)

ANDERSON, Hon John Desmond Forbes; s and h of 2 Viscount Waverley; *b* 31 Oct 1949; *Educ* Malvern; *Style* - The Hon John Anderson

ANDERSON, Maj-Gen Sir John Evelyn; KBE (1971, CBE 1963); s of Lt-Col John Anderson, of Christchurch NZ; *b* 28 June 1916; *Educ* King's Sch Rochester, RMA Woolwich; *m* 1944, Jean, nee Tait; 1 s, 1 da; *Career* CEng, FIEE, FBIM, Dir-Gen NATO Integrated Communications System Management Agency 1977-; *Style* - Maj-Gen Sir John Anderson, KBE; 18 Av du Capricorne, 1410 Waterloo, Belgium (☎ 354 1180)

ANDERSON, Sir John Muir; CMG (1957); s of John Anderson; *b* 14 Sept 1914; *Educ* Brighton G S, Melbourne U; *m* 1949, Audrey Jamieson; 1 s, 1 da; *Career* kt 1969, Commr State Savings Bank Victoria 1962-, ch Commrs 1967, founder John M Anderson & Co Pty Ltd 1951, md King Oscar Fine Foods Pty Ltd, Pres Liberal and Country Pty Victoria 1952-56; *Style* - Sir John Anderson, CMG; 25 Cosham st, Brighton, Vic 3186, Australia (☎ 92 4790)

ANDERSON, Sir Kenneth; KBE (1962, CBE 1946), CB (1955); s of Walter Anderson; *b* 5 June 1906; *Educ* Swindon Sec Sch, Wadham Oxford; *m* 1932, Helen Grose; 1 s, 1 da; *Career* Comptroller and Accountant-Gen GPO 1952-66; *Style* - Sir Kenneth Anderson, KBE, CB; 7 Milton Close, N2 (☎ 01 455 8701)

ANDERSON, Hon Sir Kenneth McColl; KBE (1972); *b* 11 Oct 1909; *m* m; 1 da; *Career* kt 1970, Sen NSW 1953-75, Govt Ldr in Senate 1968-72, C'wlth Min for Health 1971-72; *Style* - Hon Sir Kenneth Anderson, KBE; 80 E Parade, Eastwood, NSW, Australia

ANDERSON, Hon Mr Justice; Hon Sir Kevin Victor Anderson; *b* 4 Sept 1912; *Educ* Xavier Coll Melbourne, Melbourne U; *m* 1942, Claire, nee Murphy; 6 da; *Career* kt 1980, barr 1939, QC Vict 1952, Supreme Court Judge (Vict) 1969-; *Style* -

Hon Mr Justice Anderson; 12 Power av, Toorak, Vict 3142, Australia

ANDERSON, Lindsay Gordon; s of late Maj-Gen A Anderson; *b* 17 April 1923; *Educ* Cheltenham, Wadham Oxford; *Career* film dir- This Sporting Life (1963), If . . . . . (1968, Grand Prix Cannes 1969), O Lucky Man (1963) , also theatre producer; *Style* - Lindsay Anderson Esq; 9 Stirling Mans, Canfield gdns, NW6

ANDERSON, Lady - Lorna Ticehurst; *m* 1974, as his 2 w, Sir David Anderson (d 1981); *Style* - Lady Anderson; Braehead, Helensburgh, Dunbartonshire (☎ 2227)

ANDERSON, Michael Arthur; JP (Chester 1979); s of Alexander Anderson; *b* 23 March 1928; *Educ* LSE; *m* 1954, Anne, da of Joseph Benyon; 2 s, 2 da; *Career* FCA, FCMA; fin dir Mersey Docks & Harbour Co 1975; Gp Fin Dir Tillotson & Son 1970-71, sr fin appts BLMC 1972-75; *Recreations* genealogy, walking, opera, classical music; *Style* - Michael Anderson Esq, JP; Kintrave, Meadow Court, Mollington, Chester (☎ 0244 851652)

ANDERSON, Lady - Morna Campbell; da of Sir Alexander MacCormick, KCMG; *m* 1932, Sir Colin Anderson, KBE (d 1980); 2 da (and 1 da decd); *Style* - Lady Anderson; Le Val House, St Brelade, Jersey, CI

ANDERSON, Prof Sir (James) Norman Dalrymple; OBE (1945, MBE 1943), QC (1974); s of late William Anderson; *b* 29 Sept 1908; *Educ* St Lawrence Coll Ramsgate, Trin Cambridge; *m* 1933, Patricia, nee Givan; 1 s and 2 da decd; *Career* barr, Prof Oriental Laws London U 1954-75, Dir Inst Advanced Legal Studies London U 1959-76, LLB, LLD, FBA; kt 1975; *Style* - Prof Sir Norman Anderson, OBE, QC; 9 Larchfield, Gough Way, Cambridge (☎ 58778)

ANDERTON, (Cyril) James; QPM (1977); s of late James Anderton; *b* 24 May 1932; *Educ* Wigan G S; *m* 1955, Joan Baron; 1 da; *Career* Ch Constable Gter Manchester Police Force 1976-, FBIM, OStJ 1978; *Style* - James Anderton Esq, QPM; Gter Manchester Police Force, Police HQ, Southmill st, Manchester M60 2NH

ANDOVER, Viscount; Alexander Charles Michael Winston Robsahm Howard; s and h of 21 Earl of Suffolk and Berkshire; *b* 17 Sept 1974; *Style* - Viscount Andover

ANDREW, Geoffrey Harry Langdon; s of Henry Andrew; *b* 1 Oct 1919; *Educ* Merton Coll Oxford; *m* 1, 1946, Prudence Hastings (m dis 1976); 2 da; m 2, 1976, Lilias Jean; *Career* chm Colloids (Widnes) Ltd; *Recreations* golf, squash, industrial archaeology; *Style* - Geoffrey Andrew Esq; 85 Woodlands rd, Liverpool 17 (☎ 051 727 1545)

ANDREW, Rev Sir (George) Herbert; KCMG (1963), CB (1956); s of James Andrew; *b* 19 March 1910; *Educ* Godley Sch, Manchester G S, CCC Oxford; *m* 1936, Irene Jones; 2 s, 2 da; *Career* assist curate Edenbridge, Perm Under-Sec of State Educn and Science 1964-70; *Style* - The Rev Sir Herbert Andrew, KCMG, CB; 18 Stangrove rd, Edenbridge, Kent (☎ 862569)

ANDREW, Lady Serena Mary; *née* Bridgeman; da of 6 Earl of Bradford, TD, JP, DL; *b* 1 July 1949; *Educ* Benenden; *m* 1978, Richard Andrew; *Style* - Lady Serena Andrew

ANDREWES, Sir Christopher Howard; s of late Sir Frederick Andrewes, MD, FRS, and Phyllis Hamer; *b* 7 June 1896; *Educ* Highgate, Bart's; *m* 1927, Kathleen Lamb; 3 s; *Career* dep dir Nat Inst for Med Research 1952-61, MRCS, LRCP, MRCP, FRCP, FRS; kt 1961; *Style* - Sir Christopher Andrewes; Overchalke, Coombe Bissett, Salisbury, Wilts (☎ C B 201)

ANDREWES, Edward David Eden; s of Edward Andrewes; *b* 4 Oct 1909, Portmadoc; *Educ* Repton, Oriel Oxford; *m* 1935, Katherine, da of Brig W Barne, CBE, DSO; 1 s, 2 da; *Career* slr 1935, dep chm and md Tube Investments Ltd 1972-75, Tstee Cheshire Fndn 1976-, dir Maen Offeren Slate Quarry Co; *Recreations* gardening, riding, fishing; *Club* Boodle's; *Style* - Edward Andrewes Esq; Stockton House, Worcester (☎ Eardiston 272)

ANDREWS, David Roger Griffith; CBE (1980); s of C Andrews; *b* 27 March 1933; *Educ* Abingdon Sch, Pembroke Oxford; *m* 1963, Dorothy Campbell; 2 s, 1 da; *Career* exec v-chm BL 1977-, ACMA; *Recreations* sailing, photography; *Style* - David Andrews Esq, CBE; Gainford, Mill Lane, Gerrards Cross, Bucks

ANDREWS, Eamonn; CBE (Hon 1970); s of William Andrews; *b* 19 Dec 1922; *Educ* Irish Christian Brothers Synge st Dublin; *m* 1951, Grainne Bourke; 1 s, 2 da; *Career* TV compere, writer; host of *This Is Your Life*; *Style* - Eamonn Andrews Esq, Hon CBE; Windsor House, Heathfield gdns, Chiswick, W4

ANDREWS, Edgar Harold; s of Richard Andrews; *b* 16 Dec 1932; *Educ* Dartford G S, London U; *m* 1961, Thelma, da of Selbie John Walker, of Watford; 1 s, 1 da; *Career* FIP, FIM; Prof of Materials Queen Mary Coll London U 1968-; dir Denbyware Ltd 1971-; *Recreations* writing, music, Church work; *Style* - Prof Edgar Andrews; 87 Harmer Green Lane, Welwyn, Herts (☎ Bulls Green 376)

ANDREWS, Harry Fleetwood; CBE (1966); *b* 10 Nov 1911; *Educ* Tonbridge, Wrekin; *Career* actor; *Style* - Harry Andrews Esq, CBE; Church Farm Oast, Salehurst, Robertsbridge, E Sussex; Flat 7, 1 Bryanston sq, W1

ANDREWS, Harry Thomson; s of late H Andrews, of Capetown; *b* 11 Dec 1897; *Educ* in Capetown, Pretoria U; *m* 1926, R Williams; *Career* dir Welkom GM Co (Anglo-American Corp of S Africa), advocate Transvaal 1927, SA Rep to League of Nations 1936-40, Perm Rep to UN 1945-49, Ambass to France 1949-57; *Style* - Harry Andrews Esq; 214 Bretton Woods, Killarney, Johannesburg, S Africa

ANDREWS, Julie Elizabeth; *b* 1 Oct 1935; *Educ* Woodbrook Girls' Sch Beckenham and private governess; *m* 1, Anthony Walton (m dis 1968); 1 da; m 2, 1969, Blake Edwards; 1 step s, 1 step da, 2 adopted da; *Career* actress; films include *The Sound of Music* and *Mary Poppins*; *Style* - Miss Julie Andrews; Chasin-Park-Citron Agency, 9255 Sunset Bvd, Los Angeles, Calif 90069, USA

ANDREWS, Rt Hon Sir John Lawson Ormrod; KBE (1974), PC (NI 1957), DL (Co Down 1961); s of late Rt Hon John Andrews, CH, DL, MP; *b* 15 July 1903; *Educ* Shrewsbury; *m* 1928, Marjorie (d 1980), da of Alfred James; 3 s, 1 da; *Career* NI Sen 1964-72, Min and Sen Leader NI 1964-72, Dep PM 1970-72 and MP (U) Mid-Down 1953-64; *Style* - The Rt Hon Sir John Andrews; KBE, PC, DL, Maxwell Court, Comber, Co Down

ANDREWS, Air Vice-Marshal John Oliver; CB (1942), DSO (1917), MC*; s of John Andrews; *b* 20 July 1896; *m* 1923, Bertha, nee Bisdee; 2 s; *Career* RAF 1919-45*Style* - Air Vice-Marshal John Andrews CB DSO MC*

ANDREWS, Lady Patricia Ann; *née* Le Poer Trench; da of late 6 Earl of Clancarty; *b* 1928; *m* 1, 1946, Eugene Szpiganowicz (d 1965); m 2, 1977, Alan Sidney Andrews; *Style* - Lady Patricia Andrews; Flat 9, Eyol House, D'Oyly Carte Island, Weybridge, Surrey

ANDREWS, Stuart Morrison; s of William Andrews; *b* 23 June 1932; *Educ* Newton Abbot G S, Sidney Sussex Cambridge; *m* 1962, Marie van Wyk; 2 s; *Career* Head Master Clifton 1975-; *Style* - Stuart Andrews Esq; Headmaster's House, Clifton College, Bristol (☎ 35613)

ANDREWS, William Denys Cathcart; WS; s of Eugene Andrews; *b* 3 June 1931; *Educ* Girvan H S, Worksop Coll, Edinburgh U; *m* 1955, May O'Beirne; 2 s, 2 da; *Career* ptnr Shepherd & Wedderburn, WS, Edinburgh and Kirkwall 1962-, Pres Law Soc of Scotland 1978-79; *Style* - William Andrews Esq, WS; Hillend House, Lothianburn, Edinburgh EH10 (☎ 031 445 2767)

ANDRUS, Francis Sedley; s of late Brig-Gen Thomas Andrus, CMG, JP; *b* 26 Feb 1915; *Educ* Wellington, St Peter's Oxford; *Career* Lancaster Herald of Arms 1972-; *Style* - Francis Andrus Esq; 8 Oakwood

Rise, Longfield, nr Dartford, Kent (☎ 5424; office 01 248 2762)

ANGEL, Richard Reeve; s of Edward Angel, of Cranford Northants; *b* 4 Aug 1928; *Educ* Oundle, Edinburgh U; *m* 1951, Margaret, da of William Warren, of Somerset; 2 da; *Career* dir Whatman Reeve Angel Ltd 1974, Reeve Angel Internat Ltd 1959; Pres Br Laboratory Ware Assoc 1970-72; *Recreations* reading, gardening; *Style* - Richard Reeve Esq; Melrose, Broad Oak, Brenchley, Kent (☎ 3328)

ANGELL-JAMES, John; CBE (1967); s of Dr John Angell-James, of Bristol; *b* 23 Aug 1901; *Educ* Bristol G S, Bristol U; *m* 1930, Evelyn, da of Francis Everard, of Devon; 2 s, 1 da; *Career* formerly RAMC; otolaryngologist; Hon Consulting Surgn Utd Bristol Hosps 1966-; Pres Br Assoc of Otolaryngology 1966, Otological Res Soc 1977-; MD, BS, MBChB, FRCP, FRCS; farmer 1950-; *Recreations* shooting, sailing, gardening; *Clubs* Sesame (London); *Style* - Dr John Angell-James, CBE; (Consulting Room) Litfield House, Clifton Down, Bristol (☎ 33483); Sundayshill House, Falfield, Wotton-under-Edge, Glos (☎ Falfield 351)

ANGGARD, Hon Mrs (Adele Beryl Alers); da of 2 Baron Hankey, KCMG, KCVO; *b* 1933; *m* 1964, Dr Erik Anggard; 2 s, 1 da; *Style* - The Hon Mrs Anggard; Strandragan, 67, Stockholm, Sweden

ANGLESEY, 7 Marquess of (UK 1815); Sir George Charles Henry Victor Paget; 10 Bt (I 1730), DL (Anglesey 1960); also Lord Paget of Beaudesert (E 1552) and Earl of Uxbridge (GB 1784); s of 6 Marquess of Anglesey (d 1947) and Lady Victoria Manners, da of 8 Duke of Rutland; *b* 8 Oct 1922; *Educ* Eton; *m* 1948, Elizabeth, CBE, da of Charles Morgan, the writer (*see Anglesey, Marchioness of*); 2 s, 3 da; *Heir* s, Earl of Uxbridge; *Career* memb Nat Heritage Memorial Fund 1980-; formerly Maj RHG; dir for Wales Nationwide Bldg Soc 1973-; Pres Anglesey Con Assoc; chm Historic Bldgs Soc Wales 1977-; JP 1959-68; Tstee Nat Portrait Gallery 1979-; FSA, FRHistsS, FRSL, Hon FRIBA; patron of four livings and Lord of the Manor of Burton-on-Trent; *Style* - The Most Hon The Marquess of Anglesey DL; Plâs Newydd, Llanfairpwll, Gwynedd (☎ 714330); 5/3 Walpole st, SW3 (☎ 01 730 4140)

ANGLESEY, Marchioness of; (Elizabeth) Shirley Vaughan Paget; CBE (1977); da of late Charles Morgan (the novelist); *b* 4 Dec 1924; *Educ* Francis Holland Sch, St James' Sch W Malvern, Kent Place Sch USA; *m* 1948, 7 Marq of Anglesey; 2 s, 3 da; *Career* chm Welsh Arts Cncl 1975-81, dep chm Prince of Wales Cttee 1970-, memb IBA 1976-; *Style* - The Most Hon The Marchioness of Anglesey CBE; 5/3 Walpole st, SW3 (☎ 01 730 4140)

ANGLISS, Dame Jacobena Victoria Alice; DBE (1975, CBE 1949); da of Francis Grutzner, of Vict Australia; *b* 23 May 1897; *m* 1919, Hon Sir William Angliss (d 1957); *Career* chm Bluff Downs Pastoral Co, Miranda Downs Pty Ltd, Wm Angliss Charitable Tst; dir Investors Pty Ltd; *Style* - Dame Jacobena Angliss, DBE; Harcourt st, Hawthorne, Melbourne, Vic 3122, Australia

ANNALY, 5 Baron (UK 1863); Luke Robert White; s of 4 Baron Annaly, MC (d 1970), and Lady Lavinia Spencer, da of 6 Earl Spencer, KG, GCVO, VD, PC; is 1 cous once removed of HRH Princess of Wales; *b* 15 March 1927; *Educ* Eton, Trin Cambridge; *m* 1, 1953 (m dis 1957), Lady Marye Pepys (d 1958), da of 7 Earl of Cottenham and Lady Angela Nevill (da of 4 Marquess of Abergavenny); 1 s; m 2, 1960 (m dis 1967), Jennifer, da of Rupert Sausmarez Carey, OBE, of East Hoe Manor, Hambledon, Hants; 2 da; *Heir* s, Hon Luke White; *Career* served RAF 1944-48, RAuxAF 1948-53; ptnr W Greenwell & Co (Stockbrokers); Freeman City of London; *Clubs* Turf, Beefsteak, Pratt's; *Style* - The Rt Hon The Lord Annaly; Welches, Bentley, Farnham, Surrey (☎ Bentley 2107)

ANNAMUNTHODO, Sir Harry; s of George Annamunthodo and Rosaline, nee Viapree; *b* 26 April 1920; *Educ* Queen's Coll Guyana, London Hosp Med Sch; *m* 1953, Margaret Pullman; 1 s, 3 da; *Career* Prof and Head Dept Clinical Surgery, U of

WI 1961-, FRCS, FACS, MB, BS, DTM&H, Hunterian Prof Roy Coll of Surgeons 1960; *Style* - Sir Harry Annamunthodo; 44 Hope Blvd, Kingston 6, Jamaica (☎ 70716)

ANNAN, Baron (Life Peer UK 1965); Noel Gilroy Annan; OBE (1946); s of late James Annan; *b* 25 Dec 1916; *Educ* Stowe, King's Cambridge; *m* 1950, Gabriele, nee Ullstein, of Berlin; 2 da; *Career* Provost King's Cambridge 1956-66, UCL 1966-78; Vice-Chllr London U 1978-81 (Prof Randolph Quirk succeeded), chm Cttee on Future of B'dcasting 1974-77, Tstee Nat Gallery 1978-, FRHistS; *Clubs* Brooks's; *Style* - Rt Hon The Lord Annan, OBE; 16 St John's Wood rd, NW8 (☎ 01 289 2555)

ANNAN, John Christopher; s of Alexander Annan; *b* 4 Sept 1926; *Educ* Gordonstoun; *m* 1956, Margaret, da of Albert Marlow (d 1943); 1 s, 1 da; *Career* chm A & J C Annan Ltd; Lloyd's Underwriter; *Recreations* golf, shooting, fishing, sailing (yacht- 'Raku'); *Clubs* Lloyd's Yacht; *Style* - John Annan Esq; Marindin House, Chesterton, Bridgnorth, Salop (☎ Ackleton 224)

ANNAND, Richard Wallace; VC (1940), DL (Co Durham 1956); s of Lt-Cdr Wallace Annand (k 1915); *b* 5 Nov 1914; *Educ* Pocklington, E Yorks; *m* 1940, Shirley Osborne, JP; *Career* Personnel Offr Finchale Abbey T'ning Centre for Disabled 1948-; *Style* - Richard Annand Esq, VC, DL; Springwell House, Whitesmocks, Durham City

ANNENBERG, Walter H; KBE (Hon 1976); s of Mo Annenberg; *b* 13 March 1908; *Educ* Pennsylvania U; *m* 1951, Leonore Cohn; 1 da; *Career* US Ambass to UK 1969-74, Pres Triangle Pubns, publisher; *Style* - Walter Annenberg Esq, Hon KBE; 250 King of Prussia rd, Radnor, Pa 19088, USA

ANNESLEY, 10 Earl (I 1789); Patrick; also Baron Annesley (I 1758) and Viscount Glerawly (I 1766); s of 9 Earl Annesley (d 1979); *b* 12 Aug 1924; *Educ* Strode's G S Egham; *m* 1947, Catherine, da of John Burgess; 4 da; *Heir* bro, Hon Philip Annesley; *Career* formerly in RN; *Style* - The Rt Hon The Earl Annesley; 35 Spring Rise, Egham, Surrey

ANNESLEY, Gerald Francis; s of Cdr Gerald Sowerby, RN, and Lady Mabel Annesley (da of 5 Earl Annesley); assumed name of Annesley when m inherited Castlewellan estates on d of her bro, 6 Earl Annesley; *b* 5 Nov 1904; *Educ* Wellington; *m* 1, 1927, as her 1 husb, Lady Elizabeth Jocelyn (m dis 1940), da of 8 Earl of Roden; 2 da; m 2, 1941 (m dis 1954), Mary, da of Maj Donald Ramsey MacDonald, DSO, MC, RA; 2 s (yr of whom, Richard, m 1968 Haidée, da of Rt Hon Lord Rawlinson, QC, sometime MP & Attorney Gen); m 3, Lily Cromwell; twin s; *Style* - Gerald Annesley Esq; 78 Bryansford rd, Newcastle, Co Down (☎ 23511)

ANNESLEY, Hon Mrs (Haidée Marylin Antonina); da of Rt Hon Baron Rawlinson of Ewell, PC, QC (Life Peer), by his 1 w; *b* 9 May 1948; *m* 1968, William Annesley, yr s of Gerald Annesley, *qv*, by his 2 w, Mary, nee MacDonald; 1 s, 1 da; *Recreations* riding, golf; *Clubs* Royal Co Down; *Style* - The Hon Mrs Annesley; Corriewood, Castlewellan, Co Down, N Ireland

ANNESLEY, Nora, Countess; Nora; da of Walter Harrison, of Sapperton, Glos; *b* 5 Nov 1900; *Educ* Sapperton C of E Sch; *m* 1922, 9 Earl Annesley (d 1979); 3 s; *Career* teacher; *Recreations* gardening, knitting, sewing; *Style* - Rt Hon Nora, Countess Annesley; 67 Vegal cres, Englefield Green, Surrey (☎ Egham 3 2162)

ANNESLEY, Hon Philip Harrison; s of 9 Earl Annesley (d 1979), and hp of bro, 10 Earl; *b* 1927; *Educ* Strode's G S Egham; *m* 1951, Florence Eileen, da of late John Arthur Johnston, of Gillingham, Kent; *Career* late REME; *Style* - The Hon Philip Annesley; 48 Shackleton rd, Tilgate, Crawley, Sussex

ANNESLEY, Hon Richard John Dighton; s and h of 14 Viscount Valentia, MC, MRCS, LRCP; *b* 15 Aug 1929; *Educ* Marlborough; *m* 1957, Anita Phyllis, da of W A Joy, of Bristol; 3 s, 1 da; *Career* Capt RA (ret); *Style* - The Hon Richard

Annesley; Shumba Farm, Sinoia, Zimbabwe

ANNIS, Francesca; *b* 1945; *Career* theatre, film and TV actress; *Style* - Miss Francesca Annis; c/o Dennis Selinger, ICM, 22 Grafton st, W1

ANSELL, Sir Michael Picton; CBE (1951), DSO (1944), DL (Devon 1966); s of Lt-Col G Ansell; *b* 26 March 1905; *Educ* Wellington, Sandhurst; *m* 1, 1936, Victoria Fuller (d 1969); 2 s, 1 da; m 2, 1970, Eileen, nee Stanton, widow of Maj-Gen Roger Evans, CB, MC; *Career* Pres Cncl St Dunstan's 1977-, High Sheriff Devon 1967, Pres/chm Br Equestrian Fedn 1972-76; kt 1968; *Style* - Sir Michael Ansell, CBE, DSO, DL; Pillhead House, Bideford, N Devon (☎ 2574)

ANSETT, Sir Reginald Myles; KBE (1969); s of late Charles Ansett; *b* 13 Feb 1909; *Educ* Swinburne Tech Coll Vict Australia; *m* 1944, Joan Adams; 3 da; *Career* chm and md Ansett Transport Industs and subsids-, Ansett Airlines of Australia, Ansett Airlines of NSW, Ansett Airlines of S Australia, MacRobertson Miller Airline Servs, Ansett Freight Express, Aviation Engineering Supplies, NIC Instrument Co, Ansett-Pioneer, Mildura Bus Lines, Ansett Hotels, Ansair, Ansett Motors, Provincial Motors, Ansett Gen Aviation, Ansett TV Films, Wridgways, Kalamunda T'port, P E Power (Wagga) T'port, Cooper Airmotive, Austarama TV Pty Ltd, Universal Telecasters (Qld) Ltd, Ansett Hotels, Ansett Niugini Enterprises, Ansett Brewarrana Holdgs, T'port Industs Insurance , Sist Constructions Pty, Avis Rent a Car System Pty, Nat'nl Rent a Car System Pty, Diners Club Ltd; *Style* - Sir Reginald Ansett, KBE; Gunyong Valley, Mount Eliza, Vic 3930, Australia (☎ Melbourne 3453144); (business) 489 Swanston st, Melbourne, Vic 3000, Australia

ANSON, Rear-Adm Edward Rosebery; s of Ross Anson; *b* 11 May 1929; *Educ* Nairobi, RNC Dartmouth; *m* 1960, Rosemary Radcliffe; 1 s, 1 da; *Career* Flag Offr Naval Air Cmmd 1979-; *Style* - Rear-Adm Edward Anson; Thornhill Fields, Passfield, Liphook, Hants (☎ Passfield 242)

ANSON, John; CB (1980); s of Sir Edward Anson, 6 Bt, and Frances, da of Hugh Pollock (gs of Sir George Pollock, 1 Bt, GCB, GCSI); *b* 3 Aug 1930; *Educ* Winchester, Magdalene Cambridge; *m* 1957, Myrica Fergie-Woods; 2 s, 2 da; *Career* Ec Min and Head UK Treas and Supply Delegn Washington, UK Exec Dir IMF and IBRD 1980-, Dep Sec Treasury 1977-79; *Style* - John Anson Esq, CB; 76 Kalorama Circle NW, Washington DC 20008, USA (☎ 202 462 6212); 18 Church rd, Barnes, SW13 (☎ 01 748 5079)

ANSON, James William; CBE (1969); s of Lt-Col George Anson, OBE; *b* 9 Jan 1915; *Educ* Fettes, Gonville & Caius Cambridge; *m* 1940, Barbara, da of Gordon Peace, OBE; 1 s, 1 da; *Career* Hon Sec Br Italian Soc 1977-; chm & md P & O Steam Navigation Gp 1964-69, now with Mackinnon Mackenzie & Co; *Recreations* golf, gardening; *Clubs* MCC, Roy St George's (Sandwich); *Style* - James Anson Esq, CBE; Courtlands, Pilgrim's Way, Wrotham, Kent (☎ 0732 822400)

ANSON, Malcolm Allinson; s of Sir Wilfrid Anson, MBE, MC; *b* 23 April 1924; *Educ* Winchester, Trin Oxford; *m* 1950, Isabel Lothian; 3 s, 1 da; *Career* chm Imperial Gp Ltd 1980-81 (salary £100,000 pa; formerly dep chm), Careers Advsy Bd Bristol U; dir Ullswater Outward Bound Mountain Sch, INSEAD, Centre Européen d'Education Permanente; High Sheriff Avon 1977-78; *Recreations* shooting, sailing, skiing, golf; *Clubs* Cavalry & Guards; *Style* - Malcolm Anson Esq; Hill Court, Congresbury, Bristol (☎ Yatton 832117)

ANSON, Rear-Adm Sir Peter; 7 Bt (1831), CB (1974); s of Sir Edward Anson, 6 Bt (d 1951), and Alison, da of Hugh Pollock (gs of Sir George Pollock, 1 Bt, GCB, GCSI); bro of John Anson, CB; *b* 31 July 1924; *Educ* RNC Dartmouth; *m* 1955, Elizabeth, da of late Rear-Adm Sir Philip Clarke, KBE, CB, DSO; 2 s, 2 da; *Heir* s Philip Anson; *Career* CEng, FIERE, Divn Man Satellites (dir 1975-) Marconi Space and Defence Systems Ltd 1977-, ret from

RN 1975; *Recreations* shooting, sailing, gardening; *Style* - Rear-Adm Sir Peter Anson, Bt, CB; Rosefield, Rowledge, Farnham, Surrey (☎ Frensham 2724)

ANSON, Philip Roland; s and h of Rear-Adm Sir Peter Anson, 7 Bt, CB; *b* 4 Oct 1957; *Educ* Charterhouse, Chelsea Coll London; *Career* pharmacist, MPS 1980, MIPM 1980, with Boots 1979-; *Recreations* photography; *Style* - Philip Anson Esq; Rosefield, Rowledge, Farnham, Surrey (☎ Frensham 2724)

ANSON, Viscount; Thomas William Robert Hugh Anson; s and h of 5 Earl of Lichfield by his w, Lady Leonora Grosvenor, er da of 5 Duke of Westminster; *b* 19 July 1978; *Style* - Viscount Anson

ANSTEY, Lady Evelyn Frances; *née* Courtenay; da of late 16 Earl of Devon; *b* 1908; *m* 1936, Thomas Anstey; 2 s, 2 da; *Style* - Lady Evelyn Anstey; 8 Green Leaves, Clyst St George, Devon

ANSTEY, Brig Sir John; CBE (1946), TD, DL (Notts 1970); s of late Maj Alfred Anstey, of Matford House, Exeter; *b* 3 Jan 1907; *Educ* Clifton, Trin Oxford; *m* 1935, Elizabeth, nee Garnett; 1 s, 1 da; *Career* kt 1975, Pres and chm Nat Savings Cttee 1975-78, formerly chm John Player & Co; *Style* - Brig Sir John Anstey, CBE, TD, DL; West Wing, Norwood Park, Southwell, Notts

ANSTRUTHER, Sir Ralph Hugo; 7 Bt (NS 1694), KCVO (1976, CVO 1967), MC (1943), DL (Fife 1960, Caithness 1965); s of late Capt Robert Anstruther, MC, and Marguerite (da of Hugo de Burgh, 3 s of Thomas de Burgh, senior male representative of the de Burghs of Oldtown, Co Kildare, who descend from William de Burgh, bro of Hubert de Burgh, Earl of Kent and the putative murderer of Prince Arthur *temp* King John); suc gf, Sir Ralph Anstruther, 6 Bt, JP, DL, 1934; *b* 13 June 1921; *Educ* Eton, Magdalene Cambridge; *Heir* cous, Ian Anstruther; *Career* Equerry to HM Queen Elizabeth The Queen Mother 1959- & Treasurer 1961-, memb Roy Co of Archers (Queen's Bodyguard for Scotland); *Style* - Sir Ralph Anstruther, Bt, KCVO, MC, DL; Balcaskie, Pittenweem, Fife; Watten Mains, Caithness

ANSTRUTHER-GOUGH-CALTHORPE, Lady Mary Gaye Georgiana Lorne; *née* Curzon; da of 6 Earl Howe, CBE; *b* 1947; *m* 1, 1971 (m dis 1976), (Kevin) Esmond (Peter) Cooper-Key; m 2, 1977, John Austin Anstruther-Gough-Calthorpe, s of Sir Richard Hamilton Anstruther-Gough-Calthorpe, CBE, 2 Bt; *Style* - Lady Mary Anstruther-Gough-Calthorpe; Shroner Wood, Martyr Worthy, Winchester, Hants

ANSTRUTHER-GOUGH-CALTHORPE, Euan Hamilton; s (by 1 m) of late Niall Hamilton Anstruther-Gough-Calthorpe and h to Baronetcy of grandfather, Brig Sir Richard Anstruther-Gough-Calthorpe, 2 Bt; *b* 22 June 1966; *Style* - Euan Anstruther-Gough-Calthorpe Esq

ANSTRUTHER-GOUGH-CALTHORPE, Sir Richard Hamilton; 2 Bt (UK 1929), CBE (1946, OBE 1940), JP (Hants 1950), DL (1955); s of Sir Fitzroy Anstruther-Gough-Calthorpe, 1 Bt (d 1957); *b* 28 March 1908; *Educ* Harrow, Magdalene Cambridge; *m* 1939, Nancy Moireach, nee Malcolmson (d 1976); 2 s; *Heir* gs, Euan Anstruther-Gough-Calthorpe; *Career* Brig (ret) RSG, Dir Mil Ops War Office 1944-47; CC 1949, CA 1956; dir Lloyds Bank Ltd 1972-78; *Style* - Brig Sir Richard Anstruther-Gough-Calthorpe, Bt, CBE, JP, DL; Elvetham Farm House, Hartley Wintney, Hants

ANTHONY, Archbishop; Andre Borisovich Bloom; s of Boris Edwardovich Bloom, Russian Imperial Diplomatic Serv, and Xenia Nikolaevna Scriabina (sis of the composer Alexander Scriabin); *b* 19 June 1914, in Lausanne; *Educ* Lycee Condorcet, Sorbonne; *Career* Metropolitan of Sourozh 1965-, Head of Russian Orthodox Patriarchal Ch in UK, Exarch of Patriarch of Moscow and All Russia in W Europe 1965-74 ; *Style* - The Most Reverend Anthony; Metropolitan of Sourozh, Russian Orthodox Cathedral, Ennismore gdns, SW7

ANTHONY, Rt Hon (John) Douglas; PC (1971), MP (Australian) 1975-; s of late H Anthony; *b* 31 Dec 1929; *Educ* King's Sch Parramatta, Qld Ag Coll; *m* 1957, Margot Budd; 2 s, 1 da; *Career* Leader Nat Country Pty of Australia 1971-, Dep PM and Min Overseas Trade and Nat Resources 1975-; *Style* - The Rt Hon Douglas Anthony, PC, MP; Parliament House, Canberra ACT 2600, Australia (☎ 733296)

ANTICO, Sir Tristan; s of Terribile Antico and Erminia Bertin; *b* 25 March 1923; *Educ* Sydney H S; *m* 1950, Dorothy Shields; 3 s, 4 da; *Career* md Pioneer Concrete Servs Ltd, kt 1973; *Style* - Sir Tristan Antico; 161 Raglan st, Mosman, NSW 2088, Australia (☎ 969 4070)

ANTRIM, 9 Earl of (I 1785); Alexander Randal Mark McDonnell; also Viscount Dunluce (I 1618), which has continued to be known as despite succeeding f; s of 8 Earl of Antrim, KBE (d 1977), and Angela, da of Col Sir Mark Sykes, 6 Bt, & sis of Christopher Sykes; *b* 3 Feb 1935; *Educ* Downside, Ch Ch Oxford, Ruskin Sch of Art; *m* 1, 1963 (m dis 1974), Sarah, 2 da of St John Harmsworth (nephew of 2 Viscounts, 1 Baron and 2 Baronets, *videlicet* the First Viscounts Northcliffe and Rothermere, the First Baron Harmsworth, and Sir Robert and Sir Hildebrand Harmsworth, both 1 Bts; also 1 cous of Cecil King) and Jane, gggda of Sir William Boothby, 8 Bt; 1 s, 2 da; m 2, 1977, Elizabeth, da of Michael Moses Sacher; 1 da; *Heir* s, Hon Randal McDonnell; *Career* Keeper of Conservation Tate Gallery 1975- (Restorer Grade II 1965, Grade I 1968), Restorer The Ulster Museum 1969-71; *Style* - Viscount Dunluce; Glenarm Castle, Glenarm, Co Antrim, N Ireland (☎ 229); (☎ in office hours 01 821 1313); 35 Durand Gardens, SW9

ANTROBUS, Maurice Edward; CMG (1943), OBE (1938); s of late Sir Reginald Antrobus and late Dame Edith Antrobus, DBE; *b* 20 July 1895; *Educ* Winchester, Trin Cambridge; *m* 1929, Betty, da of late Sir Llewelyn Dalton; 2 s; *Career* Assist Sec C'wlth Rels Office 1945-55; *Style* - Maurice Antrobus Esq, CMG, OBE; Quorndon, Forest Row, E Sussex (☎ 2159)

ANTROBUS, Sir Philip Coutts; 7 Bt (UK 1815), of Antrobus, Cheshire; s of Geoffrey Antrobus (gn of Sir Edmund Antrobus, 2 Bt, and gn through his m, Mary nee Shakerley, of Sir Charles Shakerley, 1 Bt); suc cous, Sir Philip Antrobus, 6 Bt, MC, 1968; *b* 10 April 1908; *m* 1, 1937, Dorothy (d 1973), da of Rev William Davis, of Grahamstown S Africa; 2 s, 1 da; m 2, 1975, Doris, da of Harry Watts and widow of Thomas Dawkins; *Heir* s, Edward Antrobus; *Career* served WW II (POW); Lord of the Manor of Amesbury; *Style* - Sir Philip Antrobus, Bt; West Amesbury House, Amesbury, Wilts

ANWYL-DAVIES, His Hon Judge; Marcus John Anwyl-Davies; QC (1967); s of late Thomas Anwyl-Davies; *b* 11 July 1923; *Educ* Harrow, Ch Ch Oxford; *m* 1954, Eva Paulson (m dis 1974); 1 s, 1 da; *Career* Circuit Judge 1972-, barr 1949; *Style* - His Hon Judge Anwyl-Davies, QC

AP ROBERT, His Hon Judge; Hywel Wyn Jones; s of Rev Robert Jones; *b* 19 Nov 1923; *Educ* Cardiff H S, CCC Oxford; *m* 1956, Elizabeth Davies; 2 da; *Career* barr 1950, Recorder of the Crown Court 1972-75, Circuit Judge 1975-; hon memb of the Gorsedd of Bards 1972; *Style* - His Hon Judge Ap Robert; Law Courts, Cardiff

APPLEBY, Brian John; QC (1971); s of Ernest Joel and Gertrude Appleby; *b* 25 Feb 1930; *Educ* Uppingham, St John's Cambridge; *m* 1958, Rosa, nee Flitterman; 1 s, 1 da; *Career* barr 1953, Recorder of Crown Court 1972-; *Style* - Brian Appleby Esq, QC; The Poplars, Edwalton Village, Notts (☎ Nottingham 223814)

APPLEBY, Douglas Edward Marrison; s of late Robert Appleby and Muriel, nee Surtees; *b* 17 May 1929; *Educ* Nottingham U; *m* 1952, June; 1 s, 1 da; *Career* CA, md Boots 1973- (fin dir 1968-72); memb Cncl Inst of CA 1971-75 and CBI 1977-; *Style* - Douglas Appleby Esq; Pond Farm, Upper Broughton, Melton Mowbray, Leics

APPLEBY, Maj-Gen David Stanley; CB

(1979), MC (1943), TD (1950); s of Stanley Appleby; *b* 4 Dec 1918; *Educ* St Peter's Sch; *m* 1942, Prudence Chisholm; 1 s, 1 da (and 1 s decd); *Career* Dir Army Legal Servs 1976-78; *Style* - Maj-Gen David Appleby, CB, MC, TD; Two Acres, Beechwood Lane, Burley, Ringwood, Hants

APPLEBY, Lesley Elizabeth; QC (1979); Mrs Michael Collins; da of Arthur Appleby; *b* 12 Aug 1942; *Educ* Wolverhampton Girls' H S, Manchester U; *m* 1978, Michael Collins; *Career* barr 1965; *Style* - Miss Lesley Appleby, QC; 32 Pembroke rd, W8 (☎ 01 602 4141)

APPLETON, George Fortnam; OBE (1946), TD (1947), JP (1954), DL (Lancs 1971); s of James Appleton, JP, of Ainsdale Lancs and Wetwood Staffs; *b* 23 July 1913; *Educ* Warwick Sch; *m* 1940, Patricia, da of Henry Dunlop, of Lancs; 1 s, 1 da; *Career* Lt-Col served WW II; ret co dir & farmer; chm N Sefton Petty Sessional Division, chm Merseyside Branch Magistrates Assoc; High Sheriff Merseyside 1977-78; *Style* - Lt-Col George Appleton OBE TD JP DL; Shore House, Shore rd, Ainsdale, Southport, Lancs (☎ 78211)

APPLEYARD-LIST, Hon Mrs (Caroline Elizabeth); *née* Arbuthnot; da of Baroness Wharton (*see* Hon Mrs Robertson for story) by David Arbuthnot; *b* 28 Aug 1935; *m* 1970, Cdr Jonathon Appleyard-List, RN; 1 da; *Style* - The Hon Mrs Appleyard-List; Birches, Stanford Corner, Pirbright, Surrey

APSLEY, Lord; Allen Christopher Bertram Bathurst; s and h of 8 Earl Bathurst; *b* 11 March 1961; *Style* - Lord Apsley

ARBUTHNOT, Andrew Robert Coghill; s of Robert Wemyss Arbuthnot; *b* 14 Jan 1926; *Educ* Eton; *m* 1952, Audrey Dutton-Barker; 1 s, 1 da; *Career* chm Arbuthnot Latham Holdgs 1974-, dir Sun Alliance and London Insurance 1970-, contested Houghton-le-Spring 1959 (C), ordained priest 1975; *Style* - Andrew Arbuthnot Esq; Monksfield House, Tilford, Farnham, Surrey (☎ Runfold 2233)

ARBUTHNOT, Sir Hugh Fitzgerald; 7 Bt (UK 1823), of Edinburgh; s of late Brig-Gen Sir Dalrymple Arbuthnot, 5 Bt, CMG, DSO; suc bro 1944; *b* 2 Jan 1922; *Educ* Eton; *m* 1949, Elizabeth Kathleen (d 1972), da of late Sqdn-Ldr G G A Williams; 2 s, 1 da; *Heir* s, Keith Arbuthnot; *Career* formerly Capt Welsh Gds, MFH Jedforest (formerly of Duke of Buccleuch's); *Style* - Sir Hugh Arbuthnot, Bt; Brundeanlaws, Jedburgh, Roxburghshire

ARBUTHNOT, Sir John Sinclair-Wemyss; 1 Bt (UK 1964), of Kittybrewster, Aberdeen, MBE (1944), TD (1951); s of late Maj Kenneth Wyndham Arbuthnot, Seaforth Highlanders; *b* 11 Feb 1912; *Educ* Eton, Trin Cambridge; *m* 1943, Margaret Jean, da of Alexander G Duff; 2 s; *Heir* s, William Reierson Arbuthnot; *Career* underwriting memb Lloyd's, chm Ecclesiastical Insurance Office Ltd, chm of Folkestone and Dist Water Co, a Nat V-Pres of Tstee Savings Bank Assoc 1962-76, Jt Hon Sec of Assocn of British Chambers of Commerce 1953-59, PPS to Min of Pensions 1952-55, to Min of Health 1956-57, Chm of Ctees and Temp Chm of House of Commons 1958-64, Second Church Estates Cmmr 1962-64, former tstee Lambeth Palace Library, memb Church Assembly and Gen Synod of C of E 1955-75, Church Cmmr for England 1962-77, MP (C) Dover 1950-64; *Style* - Sir John Arbuthnot, Bt, MBE, TD; 7 Fairholt st, SW7 (☎ 01 589 1727); Poulton Manor, Ash, Canterbury, Kent (☎ Ash 812516)

ARBUTHNOT, Keith Robert Charles; s and h of Sir Hugh Arbuthnot, 7 Bt; *b* 23 Sept 1951; *Style* - Keith Arbuthnot Esq

ARBUTHNOT, William Reierson; s and h of Sir John Arbuthnot, 1 Bt, MBE, TD; *b* 2 Sept 1950; *Educ* Eton; *Career* employed Arbuthnot Latham Hldgs Ltd 1970-76, memb Lloyd's; *Style* - William Arbuthnot Esq; 14 Ashburn gdns, SW7

ARBUTHNOTT, 16 Viscount of (S 1641); John Campbell Arbuthnott; DSC (1945); also Lord Inverbervie (S 1641); s of

15 Viscount of Arbuthnott (d 1966) and Ursula, Viscountess of Arbuthnott; *b* 26 Oct 1924; *Educ* Fettes, Gonville & Caius Cambridge; *m* 1949, Mary, da of Cdr Christopher Oxley, DSC, RN; 1 s, 1 da; *Heir* s, Master of Arbuthnott; *Career* dir N Area Clydesdale Bank 1975-, Aberdeen & N Marts 1973-, Scottish Widows & Life Assur 1978-, Scottish N Investment Tst 1979-; Pres Wildfowlers' Assoc of GB & Ireland 1973-, RZS Scotland 1976-; FRSA; FRICS; Ld-Lt Grampian Regn 1977-; served WW II Fleet Air Arm Far East & Pacific; chm Nature Conservancy Cncl 1980-; *Style* - The Rt Hon Viscount of Arbuthnott DSC, HM Lord-Lieut for Grampian Region; Arbuthnott House, by Laurencekirk, Kincardineshire (☎ Inverbervie 226)

ARBUTHNOTT, Master of; Hon John Keith Oxley Arbuthnott; s and h of 16 Viscount of Arbuthnott, DSC; *b* 18 July 1950; *Educ* Fettes, Aberdeen U; *m* 1974, Jill Mary, da of Capt Colin Farquharson, *qv*; 1 s, 2 da; *Style* - Master of Arbuthnott; Kilternan, Arbuthnott, Laurencekirk, Kincardineshire (☎ Inverbervie 203)

ARBUTHNOTT, Hon Mrs (Louisa Nina); *née* Hughes-Young; da of late 1 Baron St Helens, MC; *b* 1949; *m* 1974, Maj James Francis Arbuthnott, Black Watch (gggs of 8 Viscount Arbuthnott); 1 s; *Style* - The Hon Mrs Arbuthnott; Stone House Cottage, Kidderminster, Worcs

ARBUTHNOTT, Robert; MBE (1945), TD (1941), DL (Dunbartonshire 1961); s of Hugh Arbuthnott; *b* 22 Sept 1900; *Educ* Cheltenham; *Career* HM Ld-Lt Co of Dunbarton 1968-75, memb Roy Co of Archers (Queen's Bodyguard for Scotland), CEng, FICE, FIMechE; *Style* - Robert Arbuthnott Esq, MBE, TD, DL; Ardmoy , Rhu, Dunbartonshire (☎ 230)

ARCHDALE, Sir Edward Folmer; 3 Bt (UK 1928), of Riversdale, Co Fermanagh, DSC (1943), RN; s of Vice-Adm Sir Edward Archdale, 2 Bt, CBE (d 1955), and Gerda, da of Frederik Sievers, of Copenhagen; *b* 8 Sept 1921; *Educ* RNC Dartmouth; *m* 1954 (m dis 1978), Elizabeth, da of Maj-Gen William Lukis, CBE; 1 s, 2 da; *Heir* s, Nicholas Archdale; *Career* Capt RN (ret), served WW II; now defence consultant; *Recreations* civilisation; *Style* - Sir Edward Archdale, Bt, DSC; 11 West Hill Park, Winchester, Hants (☎ 69551)

ARCHDALE, Nicholas Edward; s and h of Sir Edward Archdale, Bt, DSC; *b* 2 Dec 1965; *Style* - Nicholas Archdale Esq

ARCHER, Archibald; CMG (1961); s of late Robert Archer; *b* 10 Jan 1902; *Educ* C of E G S Sydney; *m* 1930, Sarah, nee Crombie; 1 s, 2 da; *Career* grazier and co dir; *Style* - Archibald Archer Esq, CMG; 23 Sefton av, Clayfield, Qld 4011, Australia

ARCHER, Sir Clyde Vernon Harcourt; *b* 12 Nov 1904; *Educ* Harrison Coll Barbados, Cambridge; *Career* kt 1962, Judge of Court of Appeal Bahamas 1971-75, Fedl Justice WI 1958-62; *Style* - Sir Clyde Archer; Belleville, St Michael, Barbados

ARCHER, Gen Sir (Arthur) John; KCB (1976), OBE (1964); s of Alfred Archer; *b* 12 Feb 1924; *Educ* King's Sch Peterborough, St Cat's Cambridge; *m* 1950, Cynthia, da of Col Alexander Allan; 2 s; *Career* CIC UKLF 1978-79; *Style* - Gen Sir John Archer, KCB, OBE; Royal Hong Kong Jockey Club, Sports rd, Happy Valley, Hong Kong

ARCHER, John Francis Ashweek; QC (1975); s of late George Archer, FRCSE; *b* 9 July 1925; *Educ* Winchester; *m* 1960, Doris Hennessey; *Career* Crown Court Recorder 1974-, barr 1950; *Style* - John Archer Esq, QC; 22a Connaught sq, W2 (☎ 01 262 9406)

ARCHER, Jeffrey Howard; s of William Archer and Lola, nee Cook; *b* 15 April 1940; *Educ* Wellington Sch Somerset, Brasenose Oxford; *m* 1966, Mary Weeden; 2 s; *Career* author, politician, MP (C) Louth 1969-74, FRSA; *Style* - Jeffrey Archer Esq; 93 Albert Embankment, SE1

ARCHER, Rt Hon Peter Kingsley; PC (1977), QC (1971), MP (L) Warley W 1974-; s of Cyril Archer; *b* 20 Nov 1926; *Educ* LSE, UCL; *m* 1954, Margaret, nee

Smith; 1 s; *Career* barr 1952, MP (L) Rowley Regis and Tipton 1966-74, Slr Gen 1974-79; *Style* - The Rt Hon Peter Archer, PC, QC, MP; 5 Penn Close, Chorleywood, Herts

ARCHIBALD, Barony of (UK 1949); *see* Archibald, George Christopher

ARCHIBALD, Brig Brian Mortimer; CBE (1945), DSO (1944); s of Thomas Dickson Archibald; *b* 1906; *Educ* Trinity Coll Sch, Port Hope, Ontario, RMC Canada, Cambridge; *m* 1 1934, Margaret Olivia, (m dis 1948) da of Charles Illingworth (d 1961); 1 da; m 2, 1950, Daphne Frances, da of Capt Sir Claude Morrison-Bell, 2 Bt; 1 da; *Career* Lt 1926, Lt-Col 1941, Col 1942, Brig 1944, served 1942-45 (N Africa and Italy), retired 1948; *Clubs* Naval and Military Club; *Style* - Brig Brian Archibald, CBE, DSO; Wadge Head, Tarset, Hexham, Northumberland (☎ Greenhaugh 231)

ARCHIBALD, Baroness; Catherine Edith Mary; da of Rt Hon Andrew Bonar Law, MP; *m* 1, Kent Colwell; m 2, 1961, as his 2 w, 1 Baron Archibald (d 1975); *Style* - The Rt Hon The Lady Archibald; 29 Hampstead Hill gdns, NW3

ARCHIBALD, George Christopher; s of 1 Baron Archibald, CBE (d 1975); *b* 30 Dec 1926; *Educ* Phillips Exeter Acad USA, King's Cambridge; *m* 1, 1951, Liliana Barou (m dis 1965); m 2, 1971, Daphne May Vincent; *Career* disclaimed peerage for life 1975, FRSC, Prof of Economics U of BC 1970-; *Style* - Prof George Archibald; c/o Dept of Economics, University of Br Columbia, Vancouver 8, BC, Canada

ARCHIBALD, James Montgomery; MBE (1945), JP (Inner London 1967); s of Brig Gordon Archibald, DSO; *b* 3 April 1920; *Educ* Westminster, Merton Oxford; *m* 1956, Sheila Stafford; 2 s; *Career* chm and md James Archibald & Assocs 1963-, film producer, writer and dir, FRAI, FRSA, OStJ 1977; *Style* - James Archibald Esq, MBE, JP; 35 Morpeth Mans, Morpeth Ter, SW1 (☎ 01 828 9691); 1 The Coastguards, Thorpeness, Leiston, Suffolk (☎ Aldeburgh 2922)

ARCHIBALD, Liliana; da of late Noah Barou; *b* 25 May 1928; *Educ* Kingsley Sch, Geneva U; *m* 1951, George Archibald (m dis 1965); *Career* EEC advr to Lloyd's 1978-, dir Adam Bros Contingency Ltd 1970-, memb Lloyd's 1973-; *Style* - Mrs Liliana Archibald; 21 Langland gdns, NW3

ARCULUS, Sir Ronald; KCVO (1980), KCMG (1979, CMG 1968); s of late Cecil Arculus; *b* 11 Feb 1923; *Educ* Solihull, Exeter Oxford; *m* 1953, Sheila Faux; 1 s, 1 da; *Career* Min (Economic) Paris 1973-77, Ambass and Perm Ldr UK Delegn to UN Confnce on Law of Sea 1977-79, Ambass to Italy 1979-; *Style* - Sir Ronald Arculus, KCVO, KCMG; c/o Lloyds Bank Ltd, Guards and Cavalry Section, 6 Pall Mall, SW1

ARDEE, Lord; John Anthony Brabazon; s and h of 14 Earl of Meath; *b* 11 May 1941; *Educ* Harrow; *m* 1973, Xenia Goudime; 1 s, 2 da; *Heir* s Hon Anthony Brabazon; *Career* Page of Honour to HM The Queen 1956-57, Gren Gds 1959-62; *Style* - Lord Ardee; Furnace House, Rathdrum, Co Wicklow, Eire

ARDEN, George Philip; s of William Arden (d 1954), whose f sold Longcroft, which had been in the family 11 generations (from *temp* Elizabeth I); Simon Arden, the original purchaser, was yr bro of William, whose gggs Robert, was the last of Park Hall, Curdworth, and owned the Warwick Roll (now at the Coll of Arms); Park Hall had been held by an Arden since 1373, when Sir Henry de Arden had it confirmed to him by Sir John de Botetourt for no service but a red rose; the Ardens descend from Guy de Warwick (d 929), being of Saxon origin and of considerable consequence before (and for some time after) The Conquest - Thurkill of Arden's properties took up more space in Domesday Book than any other Englishman's; Shakespeare's mother was an Arden (George, the present sr male rep, is 3 cous twelve times removed of the dramatist); the Bard's membership of perhaps the oldest English family plus both his birth and death on St George's Day (April 23) make a curious coincidence; *b* 4 June 1913; *Educ* Roy G S High Wycombe,

UCL; *m* 1944, Kathleen, da of Edward McCaffrey, of Virginia Water; 4 da; *Heir* the next sr male reps live in Alberta; *Career* served RAF Med Serv Wing Cdr in M East; ret orthopaedic surgn (Wexham Pk Hosp Slough 1966-78) MB, BS, FRCS, MRCS, LRCP; *Recreations* golf, sailing, travel; *Clubs* Berks Golf, Swinley Golf, Island Sailing, RAF Yacht; *Style* - George Arden Esq; 'Longcroft', Portnall Rise, Virginia Water, Surrey (☎ Wentworth 2525)

ARDEN, John; s of C Arden; *b* 26 Oct 1930; *Educ* Sedbergh Sch, King's Cambridge, Edinburgh Coll of Art; *m* 1957, Margaretta D'Arcy; 4 s (and 1 decd); *Career* playwright; works include *Sergeant Musgrave's Dance* (1959); *Style* - John Arden Esq; c/o Margaret Ramsay Ltd, 14 Goodwin's Court, WC2

ARDWICK, Baron (Life Peer UK 1970); John Cowburn Beavan; s of late Silas Beavan and Alderman Emily Beavan, JP; *b* 19 April 1910; *Educ* Manchester G S; *m* 1934, Gladys, nee Jones; 1 da; *Career* MEP 1975-79, London Editor Manchester Guardian 1946, ed Daily Herald 1960-62; *Style* - The Rt Hon The Lord Ardwick; 10 Chester Close, SW13 (☎ 01 789 3490)

ARGENT, Eric William; s of Eric Argent; *b* 5 Sept 1923; *Educ* Chiswick G S; *m* 1949, Pauline Grant; 2 da; *Career* FCA, FBS, dir and jt gen man Anglia Hastings and Thanet Bldg Soc 1978-; *Style* - Eric Argent Esq; New House, Whiston, Northampton (☎ 891342)

ARGYLE, His Hon Judge; Maj Michael Victor Argyle; MC (1945); s of late Harold Argyle; *b* 31 Aug 1915; *Educ* Westminster, Trin Cambridge; *m* 1951, Ann, nee Newton; 3 da; *Career* barr 1938, Recorder of Northampton 1962-65 and Birmingham 1965-70, dep chm Holland Quarter Sessions 1965-71, lay Judge Arches Court Canterbury 1968-, Circuit Judge 1970- (formerly Judge of the Central Criminal Ct); *Style* - His Hon Judge Argyle, MC; The Red House, Fiskerton, nr Southwell, Notts

ARGYLL, 12 Duke of (S 1701); Sir Ian Campbell; 14 Bt (NS 1627); also Lord Campbell (S 1445), Earl of Argyll (S 1457), Lord Lorne (S 1470), Marquess of Kintyre and Lorne, Earl of Campbell and Cowal, Viscount Lochow and Glenilla, and Lord Inverary, Mull, Morvern and Tiry (all S 1701), Baron Sundridge (GB 1766), Baron Hamilton (GB 1776), Hereditary Master of HM's Household in Scotland, Keeper of the Great Seal of Scotland, Keeper of Dunoon, Carrick, Dunstaffnage and Tarbert Castles, Admiral of the Western Isles, and Hereditary Sheriff of Argyll; s of 11 Duke of Argyll (d 1973) by his 2 w Louise, da of Henry Clews; briefly (1962-63) half-bro-in-law to Norman Mailer, the writer; *b* 28 Aug 1937; *Educ* Le Rosey, Trin Coll Glenalmond, McGill U Canada; *m* 1964, Iona, da of Capt Sir Ivar Iain Colquhoun of Luss, 8 Bt; 1 s, 1 da; *Heir* s, Marquess of Lorne; *Career* late Capt Argyll & Sutherland Highlanders; memb Roy Co of Archers (Queen's Bodyguard for Scotland); KStJ 1975; *Clubs* White's, New (Edinburgh); *Style* - His Grace The Duke of Argyll; Inveraray Castle, Inveraray, Argyll (☎ 2275); 3 Lamont rd, SW10 (☎ 01 352 8075)

ARGYLL, Margaret, Duchess of; Margaret; da of George Hay Whigham, chm & fndr Celanese Corpns of Britain, America & Canada & who liaised in the merger between Courtaulds and Celanese (his gf, Robert, m Jane, da of Sir Robert Dundas, 1 Bt, of Beechwood and memb of a cadet branch of the Dundas's who became Viscounts Melville; George's brothers were Gen Sir Robert Whigham, sometime Dep CIGS, James, sometime ed 'Town and Country' magazine, Charles, sometime dir Morgan Grenfell, Gilbert, sometime md Burmah Oil, and Walter, sometime dir Bank of England & md LNER) and Helen, da of Douglas Hannay; *Educ* Miss Hewitt's Classes (New York), Miss Wolff's S Audley st, Heathfield, Paris; *m* 1, 1933 (m dis 1947), Charles, s of Robert Sweeny (of the Charterhouse Investment Tst); 1 s (Brian), 1 da (Frances m 1958, as his 2 w, 10 Duke of Rutland); m 2, 1951 (m dis 1963), as his 3 w, 11 Duke of Argyll (d 1973); *Career* Pres Bleakholt Animal Sanctuary Lancs; helped organise campaign to save Argyll & Sutherland Highlanders 1968; *Books* Forget Not (autobiography 1975); *Recreations* animal and child welfare, photography, travel, writing; *Style* - Margaret, Duchess of Argyll; Grosvenor House, W1 (☎ 01 499 6363)

ARIAS, Roberto Emilio; s of Harmodio Arias; *b* 1918; *Educ* Peddie Sch NJ USA, St John's Cambridge; *m* 1955, Margot Fonteyn; *Career* barr (Panama) 1939, ed El Panama-America 1942-46, publisher La Hora 1948-, Panamanian Ambass to UK 1955-58 and 1960-62, dep Panamanian Assembly 1964-68; *Style* - Roberto Arias Esq; Apartado 6399, Panama 5, Republic of Panama

ARKELL, John Heward; CBE (1961), TD; s of Rev H Arkell; *b* 20 May 1909; *Educ* Radley, Ch Ch Oxford; *m* 1, 1940, Helen Huitfeldt; 2 s, 1 da; m 2, 1956, Meta Bachke Grundtvig (m dis); 1 s; *Career* dir Boots 1970-, chm Air T'port and Travel Indust T'ning Bd 1970-, dir UK Provident Inst 1971-, with BBC 1949-70, management consultant, chm Cncl BIM 1972-74 (dir BIM Fndn 1976-), memb Cncl CBI 1973-75; *Style* - John Arkell Esq, CBE, TD; Pinnocks, Fawley, nr Henley-on-Thames, Oxon (☎ Henley 3017)

ARKELL, Lady; Olive Arscott; *née* Quick; *m* 1919, Sir Noel Arkell, DL (d 1981); 2 s (and 1 s ka), 3 da; *Style* - Lady Arkell; Hillcrest, Highworth, nr Swindon, Wilts (☎ 762216)

ARLOTT, (Leslie Thomas) John; OBE (1970); s of late William Arlott; *b* 25 Feb 1914; *Educ* Queen Mary's Sch Basingstoke; *m* 1, Dawn Rees; 1 s (and 1 s decd); m 2, Valerie France (d 1976); 1 s; m 3, 1977, Patricia Hoare; *Career* author, wine writer, broadcaster, topographer; worked as detective, BBC producer, clerk in mental hosp; contested Epping 1955 and 1959 (Lib), Pres Cricketers' Assoc 1968-; *Style* - John Arlott Esq, OBE; c/o The Guardian, 119 Farringdon rd, EC1

ARMAGH, Archbishop of, and Primate of All Ireland (1977-), His Eminence Cardinal Thomas Seamus O'Fiaich; s of Patrick Fee; *b* 3 Nov 1923; *Educ* St Patrick's Coll Armagh, St Patrick's Coll Maynooth, St Peter's Coll Wexford, U Coll Dublin, Catholic U of Louvain; *Career* ord 1948, lectr Mod History Maynooth 1953-59, prof 1959-74, Cardinal 1979; *Style* - His Eminence The Cardinal Archbishop of Armagh; Ara Coeli, Armagh, Ireland (☎ 0861 522045)

ARMAGH, Archbishop of, and Primate of All Ireland (1980-); Most Rev John Armstrong ; s of John Armstrong; *b* 30 Sept 1915;*Educ* Belfast Roy Acad, Trin Dublin; *m* 1941, Doris Harrison; 2 s, 2 da; *Career* ordained 1938, Bp Cashel & Ossory 1977-80; *Style* - The Most Rev The Archbishop of Armagh; The See House, Cathedral Close, Armagh (☎ 522851)

ARMER, Sir (Isaac) Frederick; KBE (1954), CB (1945), MC (1918); s of William Armer; *b* 1891; *Educ* U Coll. S Wales and Monmouth; *m* 1925, Elsie Maude Neale; 1 s, 2 da; *Career* chm Bd of Control 1952-60; *Style* - Sir Frederick Armer, KBE, CB, MC; Picketston Cottage, Flemingston, Barry, S Glam

ARMITAGE, Sir Arthur Llewellyn; *b* 1 Aug 1916; *Educ* Oldham Hulme G S, Queens' Cambridge; *m* 1940, Joan Marcroft; 2 da; *Career* barr 1940, V-Chllr and Prof of Common Law Victoria U Manchester 1970-80; kt 1975; *Style* - Sir Arthur Armitage; Rowley Lodge, Kermincham, Cheshire

ARMITAGE, Maj-Gen Geoffrey Thomas Alexander; CBE (1968, MBE 1945); s of late Lt-Col H Armitage; *b* 5 July 1917; *Educ* Haileybury, RMA Woolwich; *m* 1949, Monica, nee Poat, and wid of Mr Kent; 1 s, 1 step da; *Career* dir CLA Game Fair 1974-, GOC Northumbrian Dist 1970-72; *Style* - Maj-Gen Geoffrey Armitage, CBE; Clyffe, Tincleton, nr Dorchester, Dorset

ARMITAGE, Prof John Vernon; s of Horace Armitage; *b* 21 May 1932; *Educ* Rothwell G S, UCL, Cuddesdon Oxford; *m* 1963, Sarah Clay; 2 s; *Career* PhD, Pncpl Coll of St Hild and St Bede Durham 1975-, mathematician; *Style* - Prof John Armitage; The Principal's House, Leazes Lane, Durham (☎ 63741)

ARMITAGE, Air Vice-Marshal Michael John; CBE (1975); *b* 25 Aug 1930; *Educ* Newport G S, RAF Cranwell; *m* 1970, Gretl Steinig; 2 s; *Career* Dep Cdr RAF Germany 1978-80, RCDS 1980-; *Style* - Air Vice-Marshal Michael Armitage, CBE; Roy College of Defence Studies, 37 Belgrave sq, SW1

ARMITAGE, Sir Robert Perceval; KCMG (1954, CMG 1951), MBE (1944); s of Frank Armitage, CIE (d 1955); *b* 21 Dec 1906; *Educ* Winchester, New Coll Oxford; *m* 1930, Gwladys, da of late Lt-Col Hugh Mowbray Meyler, CBE, DSO, MC; 2 s; *Career* Gov Nyasaland 1956-61, KStJ 1954, Tstee Beit Tst 1963-; *Style* - Sir Robert Armitage, KCMG, MBE, ; Suite 24, Gt Maytham Hall, Rolvenden, Kent (☎ 279)

ARMSTRONG, 3 Baron (UK 1903); William Henry Cecil John Robin Watson-Armstrong; s of 2 Baron Armstrong (d 1972) and Zaida Cécile, da of Cecil Drummond Wolff, of Pau, France (himself paternal gs of Lady Georgiana Walpole, da of 2 Earl of Orford of the 2 cr); *b* 6 March 1919; *Educ* Eton, Trin Cambridge; *m* 1947, Contessa Maria-Teresa, formerly w of Baron Jean Marie Ghislain Colette Alphonse Jules du Four, and da of late Gen Conte (Fabrizio) Chiodelli-Manzoni (originally Chirurgo Chiodelli, cr of Victor Emmanuel II of Italy) by his w Condesa Isabella Salazar y Muñatones (who m 2 Paul Ruegger, Swiss Minister to UK 1944-48, and d 1969); 1 s decd and 1 s & 1 da (both adopted); Lady Armstrong's paternal grandmother was niece of Manzoni, the father of the modern Italian novel and author of 'I Promessi Sposi'; she is thought to be the last of his family extant; *Heir* none; *Career* Lloyd's underwriter; served WW II as Capt Scots Gds (wounded); *Clubs* Brooks's; *Style* - The Rt Hon Lord Armstrong; Bamburgh Castle, Northumberland; 1 Mount Vernon, NW3 (☎ 01 794 9749)

ARMSTRONG, Andrew Clarence Francis; CMG (1959); s of late Edmund Armstrong, Bluemantle Pursuivant of Arms, gs of 1 Bt; hp of kinsman, Sir Andrew St Clare Armstrong, 5 Bt; *b* 1 May 1907; *Educ* St Edmund's Coll Old Hall Ware, Christ's Cambridge; *m* 1, 1930, Phyllis Marguerite (d 1930), da of Lt-Col Roland Henry Waithman, DSO; m 2, 1932, Laurel May, da of late A W Stuart; 1 s (and 1 s decd); *Career* Colonial Admin Serv- Perm Sec Miny of Mines and Power of Federation of Nigeria, ret 1961; *Style* - Andrew Armstrong Esq, CMG; 15 Ravenscroft rd, Henley-on-Thames, Oxon (☎ 2752)

ARMSTRONG, Sir Andrew St Clare; 5 Bt (UK 1841), of Gallen Priory, King's Co; s of Sir Nesbitt William Armstrong, 4 Bt (d 1953); *b* 20 Dec 1912; *Educ* Waitaki, Wellesley Coll Wellington New Zealand; *Heir* kinsman, Andrew Clarence Francis Armstrong; *Career* Australian Imperial Force WW II; *Style* - Sir Andrew Armstrong, Bt

ARMSTRONG, Rt Hon Ernest; PC (1979), MP (L) NW Durham 1964-; s of John Armstrong; *b* 12 Jan 1915; *Educ* Wolsingham G S; *m* 1941, Hannah Lamb; 1 s, 1 da; *Career* Parly Under-Sec of State DES (1974-75), DOE (1975-79); *Style* - The Rt Hon Ernest Armstrong, PC, MP; Penny Well, Witton-le-Wear, Bishop Auckland, Co Durham (☎ W-le-W 397)

ARMSTRONG, Hon Mrs - Hon (Marion) Kathleen; *née* Napier; da of 4 Baron Napier of Magdala (d 1948); *b* 1901; *m* 1930, James Robert Bargrave Armstrong, DL, JP; 2 s, 2 da; *Style* - The Hon Mrs Armstrong; Fellows Hall, Killylea, Co Armagh

ARMSTRONG, Sir Robert Temple; KCB (1978, CB 1974), CVO (1975); s of Sir Thomas Armstrong; *b* 30 March 1927; *Educ* Eton, Ch Ch Oxford; *m* 1953, Serena, da of Sir Roger Chance, 3 Bt; 2 da; *Career* Sec of the Cabinet 1979-, Sec Bd of Dirs Royal Opera House Covent Gdn 1968-; *Style* - Sir Robert Armstrong, KCB, CVO; Cabinet Office, SW1

ARMSTRONG, Sheila Ann; *b* 13 Aug 1942; *Educ* Hirst Pk Girls' Sch Northumberland, RAM; *Career* soprano, FRAM; *Style* - Miss Sheila Armstrong

ARMSTRONG, Sir Thomas Henry

Wait; s of A Armstrong; *b* 15 June 1898; *Educ* Choir Sch Chapel Royal, King's Sch Peterborough, Keble Oxford, RCM; *m* 1926, Hester, da of late Rev W Draper; 1 s, 1 da; *Career* Organist of Ch Ch Oxford 1933-55, Pncpl RAM 1955-69, FRCM, kt 1958; *Style* - Sir Thomas Armstrong; The Old Rectory, Newton Blossomville, nr Turvey, Beds

ARMSTRONG-JONES, Lady Frances; da (by 2 m) of 1 Earl of Snowdon; *b* 1979; *Style* - Lady Frances Armstrong-Jones

ARMYTAGE, Capt Sir John Lionel; 8 Bt (GB 1738), of Kirklees, Yorkshire; s of Brig-Gen Sir George Armytage, 7 Bt, CMG, DSO (d 1953), and Aimée (d 1935), da of Sir Lionel Milborne Swinnerton-Pilkington, 11 Bt; *b* 23 Nov 1901; *Educ* Eton, Sandhurst; *m* 1, 1927, Evelyne (m dis 1946), da of Edward Fox, of Adbury Park, Newbury; 1 s, 1 da; m 2, 1949, Maria, nee Tenhaeff; 1 da; *Heir* s John Armytage; *Career* served King's Roy Rifle Corps 1921-40; *Style* - Capt Sir John Armytage, Bt; Kirklees Park, Brighouse, W Yorks (☎ 713016)

ARMYTAGE, John Martin; s and h of Capt Sir John Armytage, 8 Bt; *b* 26 Feb 1933; *Style* - John Armytage Esq

ARMYTAGE, Rear-Adm Reginald William; GC (AM 1928), CBE (1959); s of Sir George Armytage, 7 Bt, CMG, DSO, of Kirklees Park, Brighouse, W York; *b* 18 May 1903; *Educ* RNCs Osborne and Dartmouth; *m* 1928, Sylvia Staveley; 3 s; *Career* RN 1917-62, ret; Pres Ordnance Bd 1961-62 (Ch Insp Naval Ordnance 1956, V Pres 1959); *Style* - Rear Adm Reginald Armytage, GC, CBE; The Malt House, Downton, Wilts

ARNOLD, Hon Mr Justice; Hon Sir John Lewis Arnold; s of late A Arnold; *b* 6 May 1915; *Educ* Wellington; *m* m 1, 1940, Alice, nee Cookson (m dis 1963); 1 s, 1 da; m 2, 1963, Florence, nee Hague, of Montreal; 1 s, 2 da; *Career* barr 1937, High Court Judge (Family Dvn) 1972-, Pres Family Dvn 1979-, QC 1958; *Style* - The Hon Mr Justice Arnold, QC; Little Horse Leas, Bradfield, Berks (☎ 442); 8 Mimosa st, SW6 (☎ 01 736 8686)

ARNOLD, Malcolm; CBE (1970); s of William Arnold; *b* 21 Oct 1921; *Educ* RCM; *m* m; 2 s, 1 da; *Career* composer; pncpl trumpet LPO 1941-44 and 1945-48; *Style* - Malcolm Arnold Esq, CBE; 26 Homefield ct, Belsize Grove, NW3

ARNOLD, Thomas Richard; MP (C) Hazel Grove 1974-; s of Thomas Arnold; *b* 25 Jan 1947; *Educ* Bedales, Le Rosey, Pembroke Oxford; *Career* theatre producer; *Style* - Thomas Arnold Esq, MP; House of Commons, SW1 (☎ 01 219 4096)

ARNOLD, Vere Arbuthnot; CBE (1970), MC (1945), TD (1953), JP (Co of Chester 1949), DL (Cheshire 1969); s of Rev H Arnold; *b* 23 May 1902; *Educ* Haileybury, Jesus Cambridge; *m* 1928, Joan, nee Tully; 1 s, 1 da; *Career* chm Ross T Smythe & Co 1957-, dir D T Russell & Baird (Ireland), chm Liverpool Grain Storage and Transit Co, Alexandra Silos, High Sheriff Cheshire 1955; *Style* - Vere Arnold Esq, CBE, MC, TD, JP, DL; Ardmore, Great Barrow, nr Chester (☎ Tarvin 40257)

ARNOLD-BAKER, Charles; OBE (1966); s of Baron Albrecht von Blumenthal and Alice, nee Hainsworth; *b* 25 June 1918; *Educ* Winchester, Magdalen Oxford; *m* 1943, Edith, nee Woods; 1 s, 1 da; *Career* dep chm Eastern Traffic Commrs, consultant lectr City U 1978-; *Style* - Charles Arnold-Baker Esq, OBE; Top Floor, 2 Paper Bldgs, Inner Temple, EC4 (☎ 01 353 3490)

ARNOLD-FORSTER, Hon Mrs (Valentine Harriet Isobel Dione); *née* Mitchison; da of Baron Mitchison, CBE, QC (Life Peer) (d 1970); *m* Mark Arnold-Forster; *Style* - The Hon Mrs Arnold-Forster; 50 Clarendon rd, W11

ARNOTT, Andrew John Eric; 2 s of Sir John Arnott, 5 Bt (d 1981); hp to bro, Sir Alexander Arnott; *b* 20 June 1978; *Style* - Andrew Arnott

ARNOTT, Sir Alexander John Maxwell; 6 Bt (UK 1896); s of Sir John Arnott, 5 Bt (d 1981); *b* 18 Sept 1975; *Heir* bro, Andrew Arnott; *Style* - Sir Alexander Arnott, Bt; Ashtown House, Castleknock, Co Dublin, Eire

ARNOTT, Lady; Ann Margaret; da of Terence Alphonsus Farrelly, of Kilcar, Co Cavan; *m* 1974, Sir John Arnott, 5 Bt (d 1981); 2 s; *Style* - Lady Arnott; Ashtown House, Castleknock, Co Dublin, Eire

ARNOTT, Sir (William) Melville; TD and Clasps (1944); s of Rev Henry Arnott; *b* 14 Jan 1909; *Educ* George Watson's Coll Edinburgh, Edinburgh U; *m* 1938, Dorothy, nee Hill; 1 s; *Career* MD, FRCP, FRCPE, FRSE, FRCPath, Br Heart Fndn Prof Cardiology Birmingham U 1971-74, now Emeritus, consultant advsr research to W Midlands RHA; kt 197l; *Style* - Sir Melville Arnott; 40 Carpenter rd, Edgbaston, Birmingham B15 2JJ (☎ 021 440 2195)

ARRAN, 8 Earl of (I 1762); Sir Arthur Kattendyke Strange David Archibald Gore; 10 Bt (I 1662); also Viscount Sudley, Baron Saunders (both I 1758), and Baron Sudley (UK 1884, which sits as); s of 6 Earl of Arran, KP, JP, DL, PC (d 1958), by his 1 w, Mathilde, da of 3 Baron (Frederik Johan) Huyssen van Kattendijke (Netherlands cr by King William I 1828; the Baron descended from Hugo Adrianse Huyssen, pensionary (roughly 'town clerk' but with far more prestige and influence than the English variety; Dutch pensionaries, at least Grand ones, at one time virtually ruled Holland) of Rotterdam in 1578) by his w Mathilda, da of Rev Thomas Rathborne; suc bro, 7 Earl, 1958; *b* 5 July 1910; *Educ* Eton, Balliol Oxford; *m* 1937, Fiona (set world record of 102 mph for Class II powerboats on Lake Windermere in Aug 1980, and was awarded (1981) Segrave Trophy 'for outstanding courage on water, land or in the air'), da of Sir Iain Colquhoun, 7 Bt, KT, DSO, and aunt of Duchess of Argyll; 1 s (and 1 s decd); *Heir* s, Viscount Sudley; *Career* attaché Br Legation Berne 1940-41, Br Embassy Lisbon 1941-42, with Min of Info 1942-45 & COI 1945-49; dir Daily Mail, Gen Tst Ltd; chm Children's Country Holidays Fund; Hon Treasurer Moorfields Eye Hosp; journalist; *Clubs* Turf, Beefsteak; *Style* - The Rt Hon Earl of Arran; Pimlico House, Hemel Hempstead, Herts (☎ King's Langley 62240/63350)

ARROWSMITH, Sir Edwin Porter; KCMG (1959, CMG 1950); s of late Edwin Arrowsmith; *b* 23 May 1909; *Educ* Cheltenham, Trin Oxford; *m* 1936, Clondagh, da of late Dr W Connor; 2 da; *Career* Gov and CIC Falkland Islands 1957-64, High Commissioner Br Antarctic Territory 1962-64, chm Roy C'wlth Soc for Blind 1970-; *Style* - Sir Edwin Arrowsmith, KCMG; 25 Rivermead Court, SW6 (☎ 01 736 4757)

ARTHINGTON-DAVY, Humphrey Augustine; MVO (1977), OBE (1965); *b* 1920; *Educ* Eastbourne Coll, Trin Cambridge; *Career* High Commissioner Tonga 1973- and W Samoa 1973-77; *Style* - Humphrey Arthington-Davy Esq, MVO, OBE; c/o FCO, SW1

ARTHUR, Allan James Vincent; MBE (1948), DL (Essex 1974); s of Col Sir Charles Arthur, MC, VD (d 1953); *b* 16 Sept 1915; *Educ* Rugby, Magdalene Cambridge; *m* 1949, Dawn Rosemary Everil, da of late Col Francis Drake, CBE, MC, DL; 2 s, 2 da; *Career* Indian CS 1938-47, Sudan Political Serv 1949-54, J V Drake and Co Ltd Sugar Brokers 1954-60, Woodhouse Drake and Carey Ltd 1960-75 (chm 1972-75); High Sheriff Essex 1971-72, Mayor Chelmsford 1977-78, V Ld-Lt of Essex 1978; *Recreations* swimming, shooting, gardening; *Clubs* Oriental, Hawks (Cambridge); *Style* - Allan Arthur Esq, MBE, DL

ARTHUR, Hon Sir Basil Malcolm; 5 Bt (UK 1841), of Upper Canada, MP (L) Timaru, New Zealand 1962-; s of Sir George Malcolm Arthur, 4 Bt (d 1949); *b* 18 Sept 1928; *m* 1950, Elizabeth Rita, da of Alan Mervyn Wells, of Wakefield, Nelson, New Zealand; 1 s, 2 da; *Heir* s, Stephen Arthur; *Career* Min of Transport and Min in Charge of State Insurance Office New Zealand 1973-75; *Style* - The Hon Sir Basil Arthur, Bt, MP; Seadown, No 3 RD, Timaru, New Zealand

ARTHUR, Hon Edward Alexander; s and h of 4 Baron Glenarthur; *b* 9 April 1973; *Style* - The Hon Edward Arthur

ARTHUR, Hon Emily Victoria; da of 4 Baron Glenarthur; *b* 1975; *Style* - The Hon Emily Glenarthur

ARTHUR, Sir Geoffrey George; KCMG (1971, CMG 1963); s of G Arthur; *b* 19 March 1920; *Educ* Ashby de la Zouch G S, Ch Ch Oxford; *m* 1946, Margaret, da of late T Woodcock, OBE; *Career* Master Pembroke Coll Oxford 1975-, Dep Under-Sec of State FCO 1973-75, dir Br Bank of M East 1975-; *Style* - Sir Geoffrey Arthur, KCMG; Master's Lodgings, Pembroke College, Oxford (☎ 43482)

ARTHUR, His Hon Judge; John Rhys Arthur; DFC (1944), JP (Lancs 1970); s of late John Arthur; *b* 29 April 1923; *Educ* Mill Hill, Christ's Cambridge; *m* 1951, Joan Pickering; 2 s, 1 da; *Career* Circuit Judge 1975-, barr 1949-; *Style* - His Hon Judge Arthur, DFC, JP; Orovales, Caldy, Wirral, Merseyside (☎ 051 625 8624)

ARTHUR, Hon Matthew Richard; s of 3 Baron Glenarthur, OBE, DL, by his 2 w; *b* 6 March 1948; *Educ* Eton; *m* 1974, Veronica, yr da of Michael Hall, of Kilternan, Co Dublin; *Style* - The Hon Matthew Arthur; Blackhill Farm, Wark on Tyne, Hexham, Northumberland

ARTHUR, Peter Bernard; s of Charles Arthur; *b* 29 Aug 1923; *Educ* Oundle; *m* 1954, Irene, nee Schupbach; 1 s, 2 da; *Career* Lloyd's underwriter 1954-, dir Bolton Steam Shipping Co 1958-, dep chm and chm subcttees of classification Lloyd's Register of Shipping 1976-; *Style* - Peter Arthur Esq; Oak Lodge, Peter av, Oxted, Surrey (☎ 2962)

ARTHUR, Stephen John; s and h of Hon Sir Basil Arthur, 5 Bt, MP; *b* 1 July 1953; *Style* - Stephen Arthur Esq

ARTHURTON, Hon Mrs (Phillipa Susan); *née* Mills; da of 2 Viscount Mills; *b* 1950; *m* 1970, Russell Scott Arthurton; *Style* - The Hon Mrs Arthurton; 96 Pannal Ash rd, Harogate, N Yorks

ARTUS, Ronald Edward; s of Ernest Artus; *b* 8 Oct 1931; *Educ* Sir Thos Rich's Sch Gloucester, Magdalen Oxford; *m* 1956, Brenda, da of late Sir Norman Touche, 2 Bt (d 1977); 3 s, 1 da; *Career* dir Keyser Ullmann Hldgs 1972-, jt sec & ch investment man Prudential Assurance Co 1975-, jt sec and gp ch investment man Prudential Corp 1979-; *Style* - Ronald Artus Esq; Lidde Hill Farm, London rd, Henfield, W Sussex (☎ 2910)

ARUNDEL, Earl of; Edward William Fitzalan Howard; s and h of 17 Duke of Norfolk, CB, CBE, MC, DL; the eldest sons and heirs of the 14 and 15 Dukes were styled Earl of Arundel and Surrey *b* 2 Dec 1956; *Educ* Ampleforth, Lincoln Coll Oxford; *Heir* bro, Lord Gerald Fitzalan Howard; *Style* - Earl of Arundel; Bacres House, Hambleden, Henley-on-Thames (☎Hambleden 350); Arundel Castle, Arundel, Sussex (☎ 882173); Carlton Towers, Yorks (☎ Goole 860 243)

ARUNDELL, Brig Sir Robert Duncan Harris; KCMG (1950, CMG 1947), OBE (1943); s of Constantine Harris Arundell (d 1934); *b* 22 July 1904; *Educ* Blundell's, Brasenose Oxford; *m* 1929, Joan, da of late Capt J Ingles, RN; 1 s; *Career* colonial serv Tanganyika and Uganda 1927-40, gov and CIC Windward Islands 1948-53, Barbados 1953-59, acting Gov-Gen and CIC W Indies 1959, KStJ 1952; *Recreations* tennis,shooting; *Clubs* E India and Sports; *Style* - Brig Sir Robert Arundell, KCMG, OBE; Wakehill, Ilminster, Somerset

ARUNDELL, Reginald John Richard; s of late Reginald John Arthur Arundell (d 1953, having assumed by Roy licence 1945 the surname of Arundell in lieu of Talbot, and the arms of Arundell); *b* 9 Jan 1931; *m* 1955, Laura Duff, JP, da of late Group Capt Edward John Tennant, DSO, MC; 1 s, 4 da; *Career* OStJ; hp to Barony of cous, 9 Baron Talbot of Malahide; *Style* - Reginald Arundell Esq; Hook Manor, Donhead St Andrew, nr Shaftesbury, Dorset

ARUP, Sir Ove Nyquist; CBE (1953); s of Jens Arup; *b* 16 April 1895; *Educ* Hamburg, Copenhagen U; *m* 1925, Ruth Soerensen; 1 s, 2 da; *Career* kt 1971, FEng, FICE, FIStructE, MICEI, MSAICE, fndr Ove Arup ptnrships, dir Arup Designs Ltd, Arup & Arup Ltd; *Style* - Sir Ove Arup, CBE; 6 Fitzroy Pk, Highgate, N6 (☎ 01 340 3388)

ASBURY, Gordon Albert George; *Career* dir Stratstone Ltd, Stratstone (Virginia Water) Ltd; *Style* - Gordon Asbury Esq; 40 Berkeley st, W1 (☎ 01 629 4404/499 4666/629 0264)

ASFA WOSSEN HAILE SELLASSIE, HIH Merd Azmatch; GCMG (Hon 1965), GCVO (Hon 1930), GBE (Hon 1932); Crown Prince of Ethiopia 1930-; s and h of late Emperor Haile Sellassie, KG, and Empress Menen; *b* 27 July 1916; *Educ* privately, Liverpool U; *m* 1, Princess Wallatta Israel; 1 da (decd); m 2, Princess Madfariash Wark Abebe; 1 s, 3 da; *Heir* s Prince Zara Yacob; *Style* - HIH Asfa Wossen Haile Sellassie, Hon GCMG, Hon GCVO, Hon GBE; 82 Portland Place, W1

ASH, Graham Baron; s of Alfred Ash, OBE; *b* 18 Aug 1889; *Educ* Radley; *Career* High Sheriff Warwicks 1938-39; *Style* - Graham Ash Esq; Wingfield Castle, Diss, Norfolk

ASH, Rear-Adm William Noel; CB (1977), MVO (1959); s of late H Ash, MRCS, LRCP; *b* 6 March 1921; *Educ* Merchant Taylors'; *m* 1951, Pamela, nee Davies; 1 s, 1 da; *Career* dir Serv Intelligence 1974-77; *Style* - Rear-Adm William Ash, CB, MVO; 7 Wonford rd, Exeter, Devon (☎ 58751)

ASH, Rear-Adm Walter William Hector; CB (1962); s of Hector Ash; *b* 2 May 1906; *Educ* RNC Greenwich; *m* 1932, Louisa Salt; 3 da; *Career* CEng, FIEE, Ship Dept Directorate Admty to 1963; *Style* - Rear-Adm Walter Ash, CB; Saltash, 14 Beacon Dve, Highcliffe-on-Sea, Christchurch, Dorset(☎H-on-S 5261)

ASHBOURNE, 3 Baron (UK 1885); Edward Russell Gibson; CB (1950), DSO (1943); s of Hon Edward Gibson, JP, by his 1 w Mary; suc unc, 2 Baron, 1942; *b* 1 June 1901; *Educ* RNC Dartmouth, Gonville & Caius Cambridge; *m* 1929, Reta, er da of Ernest Manning Hazeland, of Hong Kong; 1 s, 1 da; *Heir* s, Hon Barry Gibson; *Career* Vice-Adm ret; served HMS 'Superb', 'Dreadnought', 'Monarch' WW I; commanded HMS 'Ariadne' WW II; Flag Offr & Adm Suptdt HM Dockyard Gibraltar 1950-52; Pres Devon St John Ambulance Bde 1963; OStJ, JP Devon 1955; *Clubs* Army & Navy; *Style* - Vice-Adm The Rt Hon Lord Ashbourne CB DSO JP; 56 Chiltley Way, Liphook, Hants

ASHBROOK, 10 Viscount (I 1751); Desmond Llowarch Edward Flower; KCVO (1977), MBE (1945), DL (Cheshire 1949); also Baron Castle Durrow (I 1733); s of 9 Viscount Ashbrook, DL (d 1936), and Gladys, da of Gen Sir George Higginson, GCB, GCVO; *b* 9 July 1905; *Educ* Eton, Balliol Oxford; *m* 1934, Elizabeth, sis of Lady Newton (w of 4 Baron) and da of Capt John Egerton-Warburton by his w Hon Lettice Legh, JP, eldest da of 2 Baron Newton (the Capt's f, Piers, was gn of Sir John and Philip Egerton, 8 & 9 Bts, while his mother was Hon Antoinette Saumarez, da of 3 Baron de Saumarez); 2 s, 1 da; *Heir* s, Hon Michael Flower; *Career* JP Cheshire 1946-67, V-Lt 1961-67; memb Cncl Duchy of Lancaster 1957-77; late CA; chm CGA 1955-62; served WW II as Maj RA; *Style* - Rt Hon Viscount Ashbrook KCVO MBE DL; Arley Hall, Northwich, Cheshire (☎ Arley 204)

ASHBURNHAM, Capt Sir Denny Reginald; 12 Bt (E 1661), of Broomham, Sussex; s of Sir Fleetwood Ashburnham, 11 Bt (d 1953); co-heir to Barony of Grandison (abeyant since 1328); *b* 24 March 1916; *m* 1946, Mary Frances, da of Maj Robert Pascoe Mair, of Wick, Udimore, Sussex; 1 s, 2 da; *Heir* s, John Anchitel Fleetwood Ashburnham; *Career* Capt S Staffs Regt; *Style* - Capt Sir Denny Ashburnham, Bt; Little Broomham, Guestling, Hastings, E Sussex

ASHBURNHAM, John Anchitel Fleetwood; s and h of Capt Sir Denny Ashburnham, 12 Bt; *b* 25 June 1951; *m* 1975, Corinne, da of D W J O'Brien, of

Nutley, Sussex; *Style* - John Ashburnham Esq

ASHBURTON, 6 Baron (UK 1835); Alexander Francis St Vincent Baring; KG (1969), KCVO (1961), JP (Hants 1951), DL (1973); s of 5 Baron Ashburton (d 1938) by his 1 w, Hon Mabel Hood (da of 4 Viscount Hood); *b* 7 April 1898; *Educ* Eton, Sandhurst; *m* 1924, Hon Doris Harcourt (d 1981), da of 1 Viscount Harcourt; 2 s; *Heir* s, Hon John Baring; *Career* Ld-Lt & Custos Rotulorum Hants & IOW 1960-73 (V-Lt 1951-60), High Steward Winchester 1967-78; Receiver-Gen Duchy Cornwall 1961-74; served as Lt The Greys 1917-23, as Fl Lt AAF 1939, Capt 1944 (ret); former md Baring Bros & co dir; Tstee Chantrey Bequest; KStJ; *Clubs* Lansdowne; *Style* - Rt Hon Lord Ashburton KG KCVO JP DL; Itchen Stoke House, Alresford, Hants (☎ 2479)

ASHBY, Baron (Life Peer UK 1973); Eric Ashby; s of Herbert Charles Ashby, of Shortlands, Kent; *b* 24 Aug 1904; *Educ* City of London Sch, Imperial Coll of Sci London; *m* 1931, Elizabeth, da of Francis Farries, of Castle Douglas, Scotland; 2 s; *Career* V-Chllr Cambridge U 1967-69, Master Clare Cambridge 1959-75, V-Chllr Queen's U Belfast 1950-59; kt 1956, FRS, OStJ; *Recreations* music; *Style* - Rt Hon Lord Ashby; Norman Cottage, Manor rd, Brandon, Suffolk

ASHCOMBE, 4 Baron (UK 1892); Henry Edward Cubitt; s of 3 Baron Ashcombe (d 1962, ggs of Thomas Cubitt, who started life as a ship's carpenter and built the vast Westminster and Lowndes estates that still comprise much of Belgravia and Pimlico; he also constructed the East side of Buckingham Palace and designed Osborne; his privately circulated pamphlet on sewage was for a time the last word on the subject) by his 1 w, Sonia (da of Lt-Col Hon George Keppel, MVO, 3 s of 7 Earl of Albemarle); *b* 31 March 1924; *Educ* Eton; *m* 1, 1955 (m dis 1968), Ghislaine, da of Cornelius Dresselhuys, of Long Island and formerly w of late Maj Denis Alexander (afterwards 6 Earl of Caledon); m 2, 1973 (m dis 1979), Hon Virginia Carington, yr da of 6 Baron Carrington (For Sec 1979-); m 3, 1979, Elizabeth, da of Dr Henry Chipps, of Lexington Kentucky, and widow of Geoffrye Dent-Brocklehurst, of Sudeley Castle, Glos; *Heir* 1 cous, Alick Cubitt; *Career* served WW II RAF; Consul-Gen for Monaco in London 1961-68; *Clubs* White's; *Style* - The Rt Hon Lord Ashcombe; Denbies, Dorking, Surrey (☎ Dorking 2655)

ASHCOMBE, Virginia, Baroness - Hon Virginia; *née* Carington; da of 6 Baron Carrington; *b* 1946; *m* 1973 (m dis 1979), 4 Baron Ashcombe; *Style* - Virginia, Lady Ashcombe

ASHCROFT, Dame Peggy (Edith Margaret Emily); DBE (1956, CBE 1951); da of William Ashcroft and Violet Bernheim; *b* 22 Dec 1907; *m* 1, 1929, Rupert (later Sir Rupert) Hart-Davis; m 2, 1934, Theodore Komisarjevsky (m dis); m 3, 1940, Jeremy Hutchinson, QC (later Lord Hutchinson of Lullington, m dis 1966); 1 s, 1 da; *Career* Best Actress Award 1981 Monte Carlo TV Festival actress, dir Roy Shakespeare Co 1968-; *Style* - Dame Peggy Ashcroft, DBE; Manor Lodge, Frognal Lane, NW3

ASHDOWN, Baroness; Lillian Nell; CBE (1971); da of Ralph King, of Rhodesia (now Zimbabwe) and London; *b* 19 May 19--; *Educ* St Margaret's Harrow, Paris, King's Coll London; *m* 1937, Arnold Silverstone, kt 1964, cr Baron Ashdown (Life Peer) 1974 and d 1977; *Career* chm SE Area Con Pty 1971-75, Nat Union 1963-79, Con Pty Policy Cttee 1975-79; Fndr Memb Women's Nat Cancer Campaign (V-Chm 1967-70), Gov St George's Hosp 1971-75; chm Friends of Moorfield Hosp 1979; served WW II Mech T'port Corps; Conservator Ashdown Forest, Pres E Sussex DGAA 1974-78; Westminster City Cllr 1955-65; *Recreations* amateur politics, reading; *Style* - The Rt Hon Lady Ashdown, CBE; c/o Barclays Bank, 8 W Halkin st, SW1

ASHE, Sir Derick Rosslyn; KCMG (1978, CMG 1966); s of Frederick Charles Allen Angelo Patrick Donnelly Ashe (d 1930); *b* 20 Jan 1919; *Educ* Bradfield, Trin Oxford; *m* 1957, Rissa Guinness, da of late Capt Hon Trevor Parker, DSC, RN (s of Baron Parker of Waddington of the 1 cr); 1

s, 1 da; *Career* HM Diplomatic Serv 1947, cnclr British Embassy Addis Ababa 1962-64, Havana 1964-66, head of Security Dept FO 1966-69, minister British Embassy Toyko 1969-71, HM Ambass Romania 1972-75, Argentina 1975-77, ambass and permanent delegate to Disarmament Conference Geneva 1977-79, ret 1979; *Recreations* gardening, fine arts; *Clubs* Travellers', Beefsteak; *Style* - Sir Derick Ashe, KCMG; Dalton House, Hurstbourne Tarrant, Andover, Hants (☎ Hurstbourne Tarrant 276)

ASHE, Hon Mrs (Estelle Emily Spencer); *née* de Courcy; da of 28 Baron Kingsale (d 1931); *b* 1889; *m* 1916, Wellesley St George Ashe (d 1958); 2 s, 1 da; *Style* - The Hon Mrs Ashe; Crinan House, Charlbury, Oxon

ASHENHEIM, Sir Neville Noel; CBE (1958); s of Lewis Ashenheim and Estelle Lillian de Cordova; *b* 18 Dec 1900; *Educ* Jamaica Coll, Munro Coll, Wadham Oxford; *m* 1926, Leonie Delavante; 3 s; *Career* slr 1926, chm 'The Gleaner' Co 1946-67 (Caribbean newspaper founded by ancestors 1834), leader Govt Business in Senate and Min without Portfolio Jamaica 1967-72, Jamaican Ambass to US 1962-67; dir Lascelles de Merado & Co, formerly dir many cos; kt 1963; *Style* - Sir Neville Ashenheim, CBE; Apartment B5, Roxdene, Pitts Bay rd, Pembroke, Bermuda

ASHFORD, George Francis; OBE (1945); s of G Ashford; *b* 5 July 1911; *Educ* Malvern, Trin Hall Cambridge; *m* 1950, Eleanor Alexander; 2 s; *Career* slr 1937, md BP 1969-73, dir Albright and Wilson Ltd 1973-, memb Monopolies and Mergers Commn 1973-; *Style* - George Ashford Esq, OBE; The Old House, Sonning, Berks (☎ Reading 692122); 13 Cheyne gdns, SW3 (☎ 01 352 1754)

ASHLEY, Lord; Anthony Nils Christian Ashley-Cooper; s and h of 10 Earl of Shaftesbury by his 2 wife Christina, nee Montan *b* 24 June 1977; *Style* - Lord Ashley; St Giles's House, Wimborne, Dorset, BH21 5NH (☎Cranborne 312)

ASHLEY, Rt Hon Jack; CH (1975), PC (1979), MP (L) Stoke-on-Trent S 1966-; s of John Ashley; *b* 6 Dec 1922; *Educ* Ruskin Coll Oxford, Gonville and Caius Cambridge; *m* 1951, Pauline Crispin; 3 da; *Career* former labourer, shop steward convenor (Chem Workers' Union), BBC producer, PPS to Sec of State DHSS 1974-76; *Style* - The Rt Hon Jack Ashley, CH, PC, MP; House of Commons, SW1

ASHLEY, Maurice Percy; CBE (1978); s of Sir Percy Ashley, KBE; *b* 4 Sept 1907; *Educ* St Paul's, New Coll Oxford; *m* 1935, Phyllis Griffiths; 1 s, 1 da; *Career* historian, res assist to Sir Winston Churchill 1929-33, journalist with Guardian and The Times 1933-39, ed Britain Today 1939-40, author of many books on 17th century; *Style* - Maurice Ashley Esq, CBE; 34 Wood Lane, Ruislip, Middx (☎ 35993)

ASHLEY-COOPER, Lady Frances Mary Elizabeth; da of late Lord Ashley (s of 9 Earl of Shaftesbury); sis of 10 Earl, *qv*; raised to the rank of an Earl's daughter 1962; *b* 1940; *Style* - Lady Frances Ashley-Cooper; La Combe, 30126 Tavel, Gard, France

ASHLEY-COOPER, Hon (Anthony) John Percy Hugh Michael; s of late 9 Earl of Shaftesbury and unc of 10 Earl, *qv*; *b* 1915; *Educ* Eton, Trin Oxford; *m* 1946, Julian, da of late Capt George Petherick; 4 da; *Career* Maj Life Gds (Reserve), CStJ; *Style* - The Hon John Ashley-Cooper; Nine Yews House, Wimborne, Dorset

ASHLEY-COOPER, Lady Lettice Mildred Mary; da of late 9 Earl of Shaftesbury and aunt of 10 Earl, *qv*; *b* 1911; *Career* OStJ, late Flight Officer WAAF (despatches) 1939-45; *Style* - Lady Lettice Ashley-Cooper; Butts Close, Wimborne St Giles, Dorset

ASHLEY-COOPER, Hon Nicholas Edmund Anthony; s of 10 Earl of Shaftesbury; *b* 1979; *Style* - The Hon Nicholas Ashley-Cooper

ASHMOLE, Michael Achille; s of Harold Ashmole; *b* 10 Feb 1939; *Educ* Bemrose G S Derby; *m* 1961, Jean, da of

Samuel Higginbottom; 2 s, 2 da; *Career* dir Fountain Forestry Ltd, Fountain Forestry Inc; MIFor; exec dir Internat Union of Socs of Foresters; *Recreations* field sports, philately; *Clubs* Catenian Assoc; *Style* - Michael Ashmole Esq; 111 Burghmuir rd, Perth (☎ 27622)

ASHMORE, Adm of the Fleet Sir Edward Beckwith; GCB (1974, KCB 1971, CB 1966), KCVO (1980), DSC (1942); s of Vice-Adm L Ashmore, CB, DSO and late Tamara Vasilevna Shutt, of Petrograd; *b* 11 Dec 1919; *Educ* RNC Dartmouth; *m* 1942, Elizabeth, da of late Rear-Adm Sir Lionel Sturdee, 2 Bt, CBE; 1 s, 1 da (and 1 da decd); *Career* dir Racal Electronics Ltd, Ch Defence Staff Feb-Aug 1977, First and Principal Naval ADC to HM The Queen 1974-77, First Sea Lord 1974-77; *Style* - Adm of the Fleet Sir Edward Ashmore GCB KCVO DSC; South Cottage, Headley Down, Hants

ASHMORE, Vice-Adm Sir Peter William Beckwith; KCB (1972, CB 1968), MVO (4 Class 1948), DSC (1942); s of late Vice-Adm L Ashmore, CB, DSO and late Tamara Vasilevna Shutt, of Petrograd; *b* 4 Feb 1921; *Educ* Yardley Court, RNC Dartmouth; *m* 1952, Patricia, da of late Adm Sir Henry Buller, GCVO, CB, and Lady Hermione, nee Stuart, da of 17 Earl of Moray; 1 s, 3 da; *Career* Master of HM's Household 1973-, Extra Equerry to HM The Queen 1952-, Ch Allied Staff NATO Naval HQ S Europe 1970-72; *Style* - Vice-Adm Sir Peter Ashmore, KCB, MVO, DSC; c/o Westminster Bank, 26 Haymarket, SW1

ASHTON OF HYDE, 2 Baron (UK 1911); Thomas Henry Raymond Ashton; JP (Glos 1944), DL (1957); s of 1 Baron (d 1933); *b* 2 Oct 1901; *Educ* Eton, New Coll Oxford; *m* 1925, Marjorie Nell, JP, da of Hon Marshall Brooks (2 s of 1 Baron Crawshaw) and Florence, sis of 1 Marquess of Willingdon; 1 s (2 da decd); *Heir* s, Hon Thomas Ashton; *Career* late Maj Roy Glos Hussars (RAC TA); Jt Master Heythrop 1934-36, Master 1936-38, Joint Master 1948-52; *Clubs* Boodle's; *Style* - Rt Hon Lord Ashton of Hyde JP DL; Broadwell Hill, Moreton-in-Marsh, Glos (☎ Stow-on-the-Wold 30626)

ASHTON, Anthony Southcliffe; s of late Prof Thomas Ashton, FBA; *b* 5 July 1916; *Educ* Manchester G S, Hertford Coll Oxford; *m* 1939, Katharine Vivian; 2 da; *Career* dir Provincial Insurance Co 1974-, tstee PO Pension Fund 1975-, Tyzack Employee Tst 1979-; *Style* - Anthony Ashton Esq; Quarry Field, Stonewall Hill, Presteigne, Powys

ASHTON, Sir Frederick William Mallandaine; OM (1977), CH (1970), CBE (1950); s of George Ashton and Georgiana Fulcher; *b* 17 Sept 1904, in Ecuador; *Educ* Lima, Dover Coll; *Career* kt 1962, Fnder-Choreographer Royal Ballet (Principal Choreographer 1933-70, Dir 1963-70); *Style* - Sir Frederick Ashton, OM, CH, CBE; Royal Opera House, Covent Garden, WC2

ASHTON, Gilbert; MC (1916), JP (1934), DL (Worcs 1968); s of Hubert Ashton and Victoria, da of Maj-Gen Sir John Inglis, KCB; *b* 27 Sept 1896; *Educ* Winchester, Trin Cambridge; *m* 1921, Joan, da of Rev H Huband; 4 da; *Career* Headmaster Abberley Hall prep sch nr Worcester 1921-61, Lloyd's underwriter 1936, chm IAPS 1937 and 1946; *Style* - Gilbert Ashgton Esq, MC, JP, DL; Abberley Lodge, nr Worcester (☎ Gt Witley 305)

ASHTON, Hubert Gaitskell; s of Sir Hubert Ashton, KBE, MC, of Brentwood (d 1979); *b* 27 Jan 1930; *Educ* Winchester, Trin Cambridge; *m* 1956, Anna-Brita, da of Gustav Rylander, of Sweden; 3 s, 1 da; *Career* formerly 2 Lt Irish Gds; CA Peat Marwick Mitchell 1953-61, now with J Henry Schroder Wagg & Co (1961-); dir The Housing Corpn; *Recreations* shooting, eating, drinking; *Clubs* MCC; *Style* - Hubert Ashton Esq; Wealdside, S Weald, Brentwood, Essex (☎ 0277 73406); 32 Garrick House, Carrington st, W1 (☎ 01 499 3989)

ASHTON, Joe (Joseph William); MP (L) Bassetlaw 1968-; s of Arthur Ashton; *b* 9 Oct 1933; *Educ* High Storrs G S, Rotherham Tech Coll; *m* 1957, Margaret Lee; 1 da; *Career* journalist, PPS to Sec of State Energy 1975-76, Assist Govt Whip

1976-77; *Style* - Joe Ashton Esq, MP; 16 Ranmoor Pk rd, Sheffield (☎ 301763)

ASHTON, Ken (Kenneth Bruce); s of late Harry Ashton; *b* 9 Nov 1925; *Educ* Latymer Upper; *m* 1955, Amy, nee Sidebotham; 4 s; *Career* Gen Sec NUJ 1977- (Pres 1975), former sub-editor Daily Express and Daily Mail; *Style* - Ken Ashton Esq; Acorn House, 314 Gray's Inn rd, WC1 (☎ 01 278 7916)

ASHTON, Sir (Arthur) Leigh (Bolland); s of late A Ashton, KC, Recorder of Manchester; *b* 20 Oct 1897; *Educ* Winchester, Balliol Oxford; *m* 1952, Mrs Madge Garland; *Career* dir and sec V & A Museum 1945-55, authority on Chinese and Indian art; kt 1948; *Style* - Sir Leigh Ashton

ASHTON, Rt Rev Leonard James; CB (1970); s of late Henry Ashton; *b* 27 June 1915; *Educ* Tyndale Hall Bristol; *Career* Bp in Cyprus and The Gulf 1976-, Episcopal Church in Jerusalem and the Middle East, ChStJ 1976; *Style* - The Rt Rev Leonard Ashton, CB; Bishop in Cyprus and The Gulf, 60 Lowndes av, Chesham, Bucks (☎ 2952)

ASHTON, Hon Thomas John; TD, JP (Oxon); s and h of 2 Baron Ashton of Hyde; *b* 19 Nov 1926; *Educ* Eton, New Coll Oxford; *m* 1957, Pauline Trewlove, da of Lt-Col Robert Henry Langton Brackenbury, OBE, of Yerdley House, Long Compton, Shipston on Stour; 2 s, 2 da; *Career* formerly Lt 11 Hussars, Maj Roy Gloucestershire Hussars; *Clubs* Boodle's; *Style* - The Hon Thomas Ashton, TD, JP; Ashton Grange, nr Chester

ASHTON-BOSTOCK, David Ashton; s of Cdr John Bostock DSC; *b* 17 Feb 1933; *Educ* Wellington, Maidstone Coll of Art, Byam Shaw Art Sch; *m* 1965, Victoria Rosamond, da of Capt Richard White DSO RN (ret); 1 da (1 s decd); *Career* interior designer, v-pres Alexandra Rose Day, memb Lloyd's; *Style* - David Ashton-Bostock Esq; Danes Bottom place, Worms Hill, Sittingbourne, Kent (☎ Worms Hill 476); 49 Gloucester st, SW1 (☎ 834 1696)

ASHTOWN, 6 Baron (I 1800); Christopher Oliver Trench; s of Algernon Trench (himself s of Hon William Trench, yr bro of 3 Baron); through his paternal grandmother, Frances, Lord Ashtown is great nephew to Desmond Shawe-Taylor, music critic of The Sunday Times; suc 5 Baron (1 cous once removed) 1979; *b* 23 March 1931; *Heir* 2 cous once removed, Cosby Patrick Musgrave Trench (gs of Hon Cosby Trench, 2 s of 2 Baron Ashtown; Hon Cosby's w was Maria, da of Sir Richard Musgrave, 4 Bt), b 14 Jan 1915, educ Eton & Trin Coll Dublin, m 1956 Julia, da of Frank Porch & widow of Frank Whiting; *Style* - Rt Hon Lord Ashtown; Sopwell Hall, Cloughjordan, Co Tipperary, Eire (T Ballingarry 7); 131 Stinson st, Hamilton, Ontario, Canada

ASHWELL, Maj Arthur Lindley; DSO (1916), OBE (1946), TD (1926), DL (1941 Notts); s of Arthur Ashwell, slr; *b* 19 Jan 1886; *Educ* Winchester; *m* 1932, Sylvia, nee Scratchley and wid of Harold Gallatly, MC; *Style* - Maj Arthur Ashwell, DSO, OBE, TD, DL; Flat 3, 19 The Vale, SW3

ASHWORTH, Sir Herbert; s of Joseph Ashworth; *b* 30 Jan 1910; *Educ* Burnley G S, London U; *m* 1936, Barbara, nee Henderson; 2 s, 1 da; *Career* chm Nationwide Bldg Soc 1970-, dir The Builder Ltd 1975, chm Surrey E and W Sussex Ag Wages Cttee 1974-; kt 1972; *Style* - Sir Herbert Ashworth; 8 Tracery, Park rd, Banstead, Surrey (☎ Burgh Heath 52608)

ASHWORTH, Brig John Blackwood; CBE (1962), DSO (1944), DL (1972 Sussex); s of Lt-Col H Ashworth (ka 1917); *b* 7 Dec 1910; *Educ* Wellington, Sandhurst; *m* 1946, Eileen, da of late Maj H Gifford and Lady Gooch; 1 da; *Career* OStJ 1950, Cdt Jt Sch Chem Warfare 1954, Cdr 133 Inf Bde (TA) 1957, Dir Mil T'ning War Office 1962-65; *Style* - Brig John Ashworth, CBE, DSO, DL; West Common Drive, Hayward's Heath, W Sussex (☎ 52371)

ASHWORTH, Piers; QC (1973); s of Tom Ashworth; *b* 27 May 1931; *Educ* Christ's Hosp, Pembroke Cambridge; *m* 1959, Iolene, nee Foxley; 3 s, 1 da; *Career*

Recorder of Crown Court 1974-, barr 1956; *Style* - Piers Ashworth Esq, QC; 14 Heaton dve, Edgbaston, Birmingham, B15 3LW (☎ 021 454 3069); 2 Harcourt Bldgs, Temple, EC4 (☎ 01 353 4746)

ASHWORTH, Peter Anthony Frank; s of Peter Ashworth; *b* 24 Aug 1935; *Educ* Leeds G S; *m* 1964, Elisabeth Crompton; 1 s, 1 da; *Career* dir Leeds Perm Bldg Soc 1971- (Pres 1978), ptnr Weatherall Hollis & Gale Chatered Surveyors, FRICS, AIArb; *Style* - Peter Ashworth Esq; The Spinney, Garth av, Collingham, Wetherby (☎ Collingham Bridge 72172)

ASIROGLU, H E Vahap; *b* 1916; *Educ* Istanbul U; *m* m; 1 child; *Career* Turkish Ambass to UK; *Style* - H E Vahap Asiroglu; 43 Belgrave sq, SW1 (☎ 01 235 5252)

ASKE, Rev Sir Conan; 2 Bt (UK 1922), of Aughton, East Riding of Yorkshire; s of Sir Robert Aske, 1 Bt, TD, QC, JP (d 1954), by his 2 w Edith; *b* 22 April 1912; *Educ* Rugby, Balliol Oxford; *m* 1965, Rebecca, da of Hugh Fraser Grant, of Wick; *Heir* bro, Robert Aske; *Career* served M East 1941-51 Maj E Yorks Regt, Sudan Def Force; schoolmaster 1952-69, assist curate Hagley 1970-72, St John's Worcester 1972-80, chaplain to Mayor of Worcester 1979-80; *Style* - The Rev Sir Conan Aske, Bt; 167. Malvern rd, Worcester (☎ 422817)

ASKE, Robert Edward; 2 s of Sir Robert Aske, 1 Bt, TD, QC, JP, sometime MP Newcastle E; hp to bro, Rev Sir Conan Aske, 2 Bt; *b* 21 March 1915; *m* 1940, Joan, da of Capt Bingham Ackerley, of Cobham; 1 s; *Style* - Robert Aske Esq

ASKEW, Herbert Royston; QC (1955); s of late Leonard Askew; *Educ* Alleyn's Sch Dulwich, London U; *m* 1, 1919, Christiana, nee Dixon (decd); 1 da (and 1 s k 1942)); m 2, 1948, Dorothy, da of late J Gale Wilson; *Career* BSc, MICE, barr 1926, Master of the Bench 1963; *Style* - Herbert Askew Esq, QC; 24 Palace Court, W2 (☎ 01 727 6033)

ASKEW, Ian Voase; MC (1945), DL (E Sussex 1975); s of Sidney Bruce Askew (d 1955); *b* 9 May 1921; *Educ* Charterhouse, Christ's Cambridge; *Career* Capt Italy WW II, Jt MFH Southdown 1956-66, high sheriff Sussex 1969; *Recreations* foxhunting; *Clubs* Cavalry and Guards; *Style* - Ian Askew Esq, MC, DL; Wellington House, Lewes, E Sussex (☎ Ringmer 812357)

ASKEW, Brig John Marjoribanks; CBE (1974), JP; s of William Haggerston Askew (d 1942); *b* 22 Sept 1908; *Educ* Eton, Magdalene Cambridge; *Career* maj Gren Gds, WW II, brig Roy Co of Archers (Queen's Bodygd for Scotland), covenor Berwicks Co Cncl 1961 and Border Regional Cncl 1974; *Clubs* Boodle's, Pratt's; *Style* - Brig John Askew, CBE, JP; Ladykirk, Berwick on Tweed; (☎ 82229) Castle Hills, Berwick on Tweed

ASKEW, John Marjoribanks Eskdale; CBE (1974); s of late William Haggerston Askew, JP, of Ladykirk Berwicks and Castle Hills Berwick-on-Tweed; *b* 22 Sept 1908; *Educ* Eton, Magdalene Cambridge; *m* 1, 1933 (m dis 1966), Lady Susan Egerton, da of 4 Earl of Ellesmere, MVO; 1 s, 1 da; m 2, 1976, Priscilla, da of late Algernon Ross-Farrow; *Career* Lt 2 Bn Grenadier Gds 1932, Capt 1940, Maj 1943, Roy Co of Archers (Queen's Body Guard for Scotland); *Clubs* Boodle's, New; *Style* - John Askew Esq, CBE; Ladykirk, Berwicks (☎ Norham 229); Castle Hills, Berwick-on-Tweed

ASKEW, Lady Susan Alice; *née* Egerton; da of late 4 Earl of Ellesmere, MVO and Lady Violet, nee Lambton, da of 4 Earl of Durham; sis of 6 Duke of Sutherland; *b* 1913; *m* 1933 (m dis 1966), Maj John Marjoribanks Askew, Gren Gds; 1 s, 1 da (m 3 Baron Faringdon, *qv*); *Style* - Lady Susan Askew; Stone House, Sprouston, Kelso, Roxburghshire

ASKEY, Arthur Bowden; CBE (1980, OBE 1969); s of Samuel Askey, of Liverpool; *b* 6 June 1900; *Educ* Liverpool Inst; *m* 1925, Elizabeth Swash (d 1974); 1 da; *Career* comedian

ASKIN, Hon Sir Robert William; GCMG (1975, KCMG 1972); s of William Askin; *b* 4 April 1909; *Educ* Sydnet Tech

H S, Central Coaching Coll; *m* 1937, Mollie Underhill; *Career* Premier NSW 1965-75; *Style* - Hon Sir Robert Askin, GCMG; 86 Bower st, Manly, NSW 2095, Australia (☎ 977 1844)

ASKWITH, Hon Betty Ellen; (Hon Mrs Jones); da of 1 and last Baron Askwith, KCB, KC (d 1942) and late Baroness Askwith, CBE; *b* 26 June 1909; *Educ* Lycee Francais London; *m* 1950, Keith Jones (d 1978); *Career* FRSL, poetess and authoress; *Style* - The Hon Mrs Jones; 9/105 Onslow sq, SW7 (☎ 01 589 7126)

ASPDEN, Hon Mrs - Hon Judith Ann; *née* Nicholls; da of Baron Harmar-Nicholls, JP (Life Peer and 1 Bt); *Style* - The Hon Mrs Aspden

ASPIN, Peter; s of Thomas Aspin (d 1955); *b* 3 Jan 1933; *Educ* Quarry Bank Sch Liverpool, Kings Coll Cambridge; *m* Maureen; 2 children; *Career* engr, md Allbook & Hashfield Ltd (formerly Giltspur Precision Industries Ltd), md Giltspur Motor Industries Ltd; *Recreations* shooting; *Style* - Peter Aspin Esq; Scylla House, Whatton-in-the-Vale, Notts

ASPINALL, Lady Sarah Marguerite; *née* Curzon; da of 5 Earl Howe, CBE, VD, PC (d 1964); *b* 1945; *m* 1, 1966, Piers Raymond Courage (d 1970); 2 s; m 2, 1972, John Victor Aspinall; 1 child; *Style* - Lady Sarah Aspinall; 1 Lyall st, SW1

ASPINWALL, Jack Heywood; MP (C) Kingswood 1979-; *b* Feb 1933; *Educ* Prescot G S Lancs, Marconi Coll Chelmsford; *m* Brenda Jean Aspinwall; *Career* RAF 1949-56; co dir; memb Avon Co Cncl; *Style* - Jack Aspinwall Esq, MP; House of Commons, SW1

ASPRAY, Rodney George; JP; *b* 1934; *Career* FCA 1960, memb Monopolies and Mergers Commn 1975-, ch exec offr Norwest Co-Op Soc 1969-; *Style* - Rodney Aspray Esq, JP; c/o Monopolies and Mergers Commn, New Court, 48 Carey st, WC2 (☎ 01 831 6111)

ASPREY, Algernon; s of George Asprey; *b* 2 June 1912; *Educ* Charterhouse, Sch of Art Regent St Polytechnic; *m* 1939, Beatrice, nee Bryant; 1 s, 2 da; *Career* chm Algernon Asprey Ltd 1971-, Pres Bond St Assoc 1968-; *Style* - Algernon Asprey Esq; 34 Trevor sq, SW7 (☎ 01 589 2465)

ASPREY, Edward Algernon; s of George Kenneth Asprey (d 1946); *b* 2 June 1912; *Educ* Charterhouse; *m* 1939, Beatrice, nee Bryant; 1 s, 1 da (and 1 da decd); *Career* Capt Scots Guards 1940-46, artist and designer, chm- Algernon Asprey Ltd 1971-80, Purchase Tax Ctee post war years to disbandment, Guards Club 1960-65, pres Bond St Assoc 1968-81 (chm 1965-68), memb ctee Friends of Roy Acad, prime warden Worshipful Co of Goldsmiths 1977-78; *Recreations* painting, sailing, gold; *Clubs* Buck's, Cavalry and Guards; *Style* - Edward Asprey Esq; 34 Trevor sq, Knightsbridge, SW7 (☎ 01 589 2465)

ASQUITH, Lady (Mary) Annunziata; da of 2 Earl of Oxford and Asquith, KCMG; *b* 1948; *Educ* Oxford; *Career* formerly with Daily Telegraph Magazine, also model; writer, author of 'Marie Antoinette' (biography, 1974); *Style* - Lady Annunziata Asquith; c/o The Manor House, Mells, Frome

ASQUITH, Lady Clare Perpetua Frances; da of 2 Earl of Oxford and Asquith, KCMG; *b* 1955; *Style* - Lady Clare Asquith; c/o The Manor House, Mells, Frome

ASQUITH, Hon Dominic Anthony Gerard; s of 2 Earl of Oxford and Asquith, KCMG; *b* 1957; *Style* - The Hon Dominic Asquith; c/o The Manor House, Mells, Frome

ASQUITH, Lady Helen Frances; OBE (1965); da of late Raymond Asquith (s of 1 Earl of Oxford and Asquith) and sis of 2 Earl; *b* 1908; *Educ* Somervill Coll, Oxford; *Style* - Lady Helen Asquith OBE; Tynts Hill, Mells, Frome, Somerset

ASQUITH, Hon Mark Julian; s and h of Viscount Asquith; *b* 13 May 1979; *Style* - The Hon Mark Asquith

ASQUITH, Viscount; Raymond

Benedict Bartholomew Michael Asquith; s and h of 2 Earl of Oxford and Asquith, KCMG; *b* 24 Aug 1952; *Educ* Ampleforth, Balliol Oxford; *m* 1978, Clare, da of Francis Pollen and Marie-Therese (da of His Hon Sir Joseph Sheridan) and gda of late Arthur Pollen (gn of Sir Richard Pollen, 3 Bt) by his w Hon Daphne Baring, da of 3 Baron Revelstoke; 1 s; *Heir* s Hon Mark Asquith; *Style* - Viscount Asquith; Manor House, Mells, Frome, Somerset

ASSHETON, Hon Nicholas; s of 1 Baron Clitheroe, KCVO, PC, and Hon Sylvia Hotham, da of 6 Baron Hotham; *b* 23 May 1934; *Educ* Eton, Ch Ch Oxford; *m* 1960, Jacqueline, da of Marshal of the RAF Sir Arthur Harris, 1 Bt, GCB, OBE, AFC, of Goring-on-Thames, by his 2 w; 1 s, 2 da; *Career* formerly Lt Inns of Court Regt & 2 Lt Life Gds; memb Stock Exchange (Cncl 1969), sr ptnr Montagu Loebl Stanley & Co; dir Nat Mutual Life Assoc of Australasia; Liveryman Vintners' Co; Lord of the Manor and Liberty of Slaidburn, Grindleton and Bradford; *Clubs* City of London, Pratt's; *Style* - The Hon Nicholas Assheton; 5 Astell st, SW3 (☎ 01 352 9131)

ASSHETON, Hon Ralph John; s and h of 1 Baron Clitheroe, KCVO, PC, by his w, Hon Sylvia Hotham, da of 6 Baron Hotham; *b* 3 Nov 1929; *Educ* Eton, Ch Ch Oxford; *m* 1961, Juliet, da of Lt-Col Christopher Lionel Hanbury, MBE, TD; 2 s, 1 da; *Career* Lord of the Honor of Clitheroe and Hundred of Blackburn, dir Rio Tinto Zinc Corpn Ltd, dir Borax Holdings Ltd, Liveryman Skinners' Co; late 2 Lt Life Gds; *Clubs* Royal Automobile; *Style* - The Hon Ralph Assheton; Burners Cottage, Wexham, Stoke Poges, Bucks

ASTAIRE, Edgar; s of Max Astaire; *b* 23 Jan 1930; *Educ* Harrow; *m* 1958 (m dis 1975); 3 s; *Career* stockbroker, chm Astaire & Co; *Style* - Edgar Astaire Esq; 11 Lowndes Close, Lowndes place, SW1 (☎ 235 5757); Cold Comfort Farm, Wendover, Bucks (☎ 0296 623172)

ASTBURY, Sir George; JP (Cheshire 1938); s of Thomas Astbury; *b* 10 May 1902; *Educ* St James's Longton; *m* 1930, Nellie, nee Bagnall (decd); 2 s; *Career* kt 1966, Co-Op Soc Insurance Agent ret, former memb Nat Wages Bd of Co-Op Union; *Style* - Sir George Astbury, JP; West Winds, Strawberry Roundabout, Backford, nr Chester

ASTLEY, Hon Delaval Thomas Harold; s and h of 22 Baron Hastings; *b* 25 April 1960; *Style* - The Hon Delaval Astley

ASTLEY, Sir Francis Jacob Dugdale, 6 Bt (UK 1821), of Everleigh, Wilts; s of late Rev Anthony Aylmer Astley, 6 s of 2 Bt; suc kinsman, Capt Sir Francis Henry Rivers Astley-Corbett, 5 Bt, 1943; *b* 26 Oct 1908; *Educ* Marlborough, Trin Oxford; *m* 1934, Brita Margareta Josefina Nyström, of Stockholm; 1 da; *Heir* none; *Career* sr lectr Univ Coll Ghana 1948-62, head of Classics Dept Atlantic Coll St Donat's Castle 1962-69; *Style* - Sir Francis Astley, Bt; 21a Lindfield gdns, NW3 (☎ 01 435 9945)

ASTLEY, Hon Harriet Marguerite; da of 22 Baron Hastings; *b* 15 March 1958; *Style* - The Hon Harriet Astley

ASTLEY, Hon Justin Edward; s of 22 Baron Hastings; *b* 22 April 1968; *Style* - The Hon Justin Astley

ASTON, Sir Kit (Christopher) Southcote; KCVO (1981); s of Maj-Gen Sir George Aston, KCB, RM (d 1938); *b* 9 Jan 1920; *Educ* Marlborough, Southampton U; *m* 1949, Eileen, da of John Bell McNair; 1 s (James), 2 da (Mrs Sergio Martinuzzi, Harriet); *Career* served RN WW II Petty Offr, St Nazaire 1942; chm Powell Duffryn 1978-81, Internat Year Disabled 1981, Windsor Theatre Royal Ltd, Tree Cncl 1977-; fndr chm Queen's Trees Tst, Prince Philip Tst Fund, Silver Jubilee Medal 1977; dir Ready Mixed Concrete 1968-, Rolls-Royce Motors 1972-; *Recreations* natural history, music, theatre; *Style* - Sir Kit Aston KCVO; Longfield, Wraysbury, Berks (☎ 2470)

ASTON, Lt-Col Stanley Collin; OBE (1973), TD and clasps, DL (Cambs 1960);

s of Alfred Ernest Aston (d 1961); *b* 4 Sept 1915; *Educ* City Sch, Lincoln, and St Catherine's Cambridge; *m* 1940, Rosalind Molly, nee Fairfax; 1 s, 2 da; *Career* WW II Suffolk Regt, dep hon Col (TA) Roy Anglian Regt 1972-80, chm Cambs TA 1967-77, bye-fell Magdalene Cambridge 1938-43, fell St Catherine's Cambridge 1943, dean 1946-57, tutor 1957-59, bursar 1961-79, pres 1980, U lectr Cambridge 1946-, visiting prof Ohio State U 1955-56 and 1961, pres Modern Humanities Research Assoc 1970, sec-gen Int Fedn for Modern Languages and Literatures, pres UNESCO 1979-; *Recreations* sports, music, philately; *Clubs* Assoc Football, Nat Liberal; *Style* - Lt-Col Stanley Aston, OBE, TD, DL; 22 Topcliffe Way, Cambridge (☎ 47414); 108 Rasen lane, Lincoln

ASTON, Hon Sir William John; KCMG (1970), JP (NSW 1954); s of Harold Aston; *b* 19 Sept 1916; *m* 1941, Beatrice Delaney Burrett; 1 s, 2 da; *Career* Speaker House of Representatives Australia 1967-73, MP 1955-61 and 1963-72, chm Kolotex Hldgs, dir Neilson McCarthy & Ptnrs; *Style* - Hon Sir William Aston, KCMG, JP; 55 Olola av, Vaucluse, NSW 2030, Australia (☎ 337 5992)

ASTOR OF HEVER, 2 Baron (UK 1956); Gavin Astor; s of 1 Baron Astor of Hever (2 s of 1 Viscount Astor, whereby Gavin is 1 cous once removed to 4 Viscount Astor, *qv*) and Lady Violet Elliot, da of 4 Earl of Minto and widow of Lord Charles Mercer-Nairne, CVO, (2 s of 5 Marquess of Lansdowne); suc f 1971; *b* 1 June 1918; *Educ* Eton, New Coll Oxford; *m* 1945, Lady Irene Haig, da of 1 Earl Haig; 2 s, 3 da; *Heir* s, Hon John (Jacob) Astor; *Career* Ld-Lt & Custos Rotulorum Kent 1972-; dir Alliance Assur 1954; Pres C'wlth Press Union 1972-81; former co-owner of The Times; served in Life Gds 1940-46; late dir Reuters; Pres Kent CLA; Seneschal Canterbury Cathedral 1973-; High Sheriff Kent 1955-56, DL 1966 (DL Sussex 1956); FRSA, KStJ; *Clubs* White's, Hurlingham; *Style* - Rt Hon Lord Astor of Hever DL; Hever Castle, Edenbridge, Kent (☎ 862204)

ASTOR, 4 Viscount (UK 1917); William Waldorf Astor; also Baron Astor (UK 1916); s of 3 Viscount Astor (d 1966, whose mother was the celebrated Nancy Astor, first woman MP) by his 1 w, Hon Sarah Norton, da of 6 Baron Grantley; Lord Astor is 1 cous once removed of Lord Astor of Hever and 1 cous to Lord Ancaster's da and (as far as the Barony of Willoughby de Eresby goes) hp, Lady Nancy Heathcote-Drummond-Willoughby; *b* 27 Dec 1951; *Educ* Eton; *m* 1976, Annabel, da of Timothy Jones (s of Sir Roderick Jones, KBE, chm Reuters, and Enid Bagnold) by Pandora Clifford (niece of 11 & 12 Barons Clifford of Chudleigh and sis of present Lady Norwich, John Julius's w) and former w of Reginald (now Sir) Sheffield (now 8 Bt); 2 s, 1 da; *Heir* s, Hon William Astor; *Career* chm Ancroft Tractors Ltd; farmer; *Recreations* fishing, shooting; *Clubs* White's, Turf; *Style* - The Rt Hon Viscount Astor; Ginge Manor, Wantage, Oxon (☎ East Hendred 228)

ASTOR, Hon (Francis) David Langhorne; s of 2 Viscount Astor (d 1952), and Nancy, Viscountess Astor, CH, MP (d 1964); *b* 5 March 1912; *Educ* Eton, Balliol Oxford; *m* 1, 1945, Melanie Hauser; 1 da; m 2, 1952, Bridget Wreford; 2 s, 3 da; *Career* ed The Observer 1948-75, dir 1976-; *Style* - The Hon David Astor; 9 Cavendish av, St John's Wood, NW8 (☎ 01 286 0223/4); Manor House, Sutton Courtenay, Oxon (☎ 221)

ASTOR, Hon Emily Mary; da of 3 Viscount Astor (d 1966) by his 2 w, Philippa, da of Lt-Col Henry Hunloke (only s of Maj Sir Philip Hunloke, GCVO) and Lady Anne Cavendish, MBE, JP, 5 da of 9 Duke of Devonshire, KG, GCMG, GCVO, PC, JP, DL; *b* 9 June 1956; *Educ* Francis Holland Sch; *Career* Photographer; *Style* - The Hon Emily Astor; 16 Pleasant st, San Francisco, Calif 94108 (☎ 415 7750676); 2 St Albans Grove, W8 (☎ 01 937 3964)

ASTOR, Hon Fiona Katherine; da of 4 Viscount Astor; *b* 1976; *Style* - The Hon Fiona Astor

ASTOR, Hon Hugh Waldorf; JP (Berks

1953); s of 1 Baron Astor of Hever; *b* 20 Nov 1920; *Educ* Eton, New Coll Oxford; *m* 1950, Emily, da of Sir Alexander Kinloch, 12 Bt; 2 s, 3 da; *Career* chm Cncl THF 1971-, dir Hambro's Bank, Phoenix Assurance, Hutchinson Ltd, Winterbottom Tst, dep chm The Times 1959-67, chm Times Tst 1967, High Sheriff Berks 1963; *Recreations* shooting, sailing (Motor Yacht- 'Toravia III'), flying (Beechcraft Travelair); *Clubs* Brooks's, Buck's, Pratt's, Roy Yacht Sqdn, Roy Ocean Racing; *Style* - The Hon Hugh Astor, JP; 14 Culross st, W1 (☎ 01 629 4601); Folly Farm, Sulhamstead, Berkss (☎ Reading 302326)

ASTOR OF HEVER, Baroness - Lady Irene Violet Freesia Janet Augusta; da of 1 Earl Haig; *b* 1919; *see* Astor of Hever, 2 Baron; *Style* - The Rt Hon The Lady Astor of Hever

ASTOR, Hon John; 3 s of 1 Baron Astor of Hever; *b* 26 Sept 1923; *Educ* Eton; *m* 1950, Diana Drummond; 2 s (Richard m 1977 Katherine , da of Brig Sir Jeffrey Darell, 8 Bt, MC; 1 da; David), 1 da (Elizabeth); *Career* Fl Lt RAFVR; Berks CCllr 1953, Alderman 1960-67; dir TPC Invests, MP (C) 1964-74 Newbury; *Clubs* Buck's, Roy Yacht Sqdn; *Style* - The Hon John Astor; Kirby House, Inkpen, Berks (☎ 284)

ASTOR, Maj Hon Sir John Jacob; MBE (1945), DL (Cambs 1962); s of 2 Viscount Astor; *b* 29 Aug 1918; *Educ* Eton, New Coll Oxford; *m* 1, 1944, Ana Inez (m dis 1972), da of Señor Dr Don Miguel Carcano, (Hon) KCMG, (Hon) KBE, sometime Argentine Ambass to UK; 1 s (Michael Ramon Langhorne m 1979 Daphne Warburg), 1 da (Stella m 1974 Martin Wilkinson); m 2, 1976, Susan, da of Maj Michael Eveleigh, of Luffenham Court, Luffenham, Rutland; *Career* served WW II as Maj; former JP Cambs; chm Educn for Ag Indust 1978-, Ag Res Cncl 1968-78; Steward Jockey Club 1968-71; kt 1978, MP (C) 1951-59 Plymouth Sutton, PPS to Fin Sec Treasury 1951-52, memb Horserace Betting Levy Bd 1976- *Clubs* White's, RAC; *Style* - Maj The Hon Sir John Astor, MBE, DL; Hatley Park, Hatley St George, Sandy, Beds (☎ Gamlingay 50266)

ASTOR, Hon John Jacob; s and h of 2 Baron Astor of Hever by his w, Lady Irene Haig, da of 1 Earl Haig, KT, GCB, OM, GCVO, KCIE; *b* 16 June 1946; *Educ* Eton; *m* 1970, Fiona, da of Capt Roger Harvey, JP, DL, Scots Gds, and Diana (da of Sir Harry Mainwaring, 5 and last Bt, by his w Generis, eldest da of Sir Richard Williams-Bulkeley, 12 Bt, KCB, VD, JP, and Lady Magdalen Yorke, da of 5 Earl of Hardwicke); 3 da; *Career* formerly Lt Life Gds, served Malaysia, Hong Kong, N Ireland; dir Terre Blanches Servs Sarl 1975-, Valberg Plaza Sarl 1977-; *Clubs* White's; *Style* - The Hon John Astor; Le Galion, Cannes Marina, 06210 Mandelieu, France (☎ 93 49 34 82)

ASTOR, Hon James Jacob; 2 s of 4 Viscount Astor; *b* 4 March 1981; *Style* - The Hon James Astor

ASTOR, Michael Ramon Langhorne; s of Hon Sir John Astor, MBE, DL, sometime MP Plymouth Sutton (4 s of 2 Viscount Astor), by his 1 w, Ana (herself da of late Senor Dr Don Miguel Carcano, KBE, sometime Argentine Ambass to UK); *b* 29 Sept 1946; *Educ* Eton; *m* 1979, Daphne, da of Edward Warburg, of Westport, Connecticut, USA; *Style* - Michael Astor Esq; Hatley Park, Hatley St George, Sandy, Beds

ASTOR, Hon William Waldorf; s and h of 4 Viscount Astor; *b* 1979; *Style* - The Hon William Astor

ASTWOOD, Lt-Col Sir Jeffrey Carlton; CBE (1966, OBE mil 1946), ED (1942); s of late Jeffrey Burgess Astwood, of Neston, Bermuda; *b* 5 Oct 1907; *Educ* Saltus G S Bermuda; *m* 1928, Hilda, nee Onions; 1 s, 1 da; *Career* Speaker House of Assembly Bermuda 1968-72, Min of Ag Immigration and Labour, and of Health; Pres Atlantic Investment and Development Ltd, J B Astwood & Son Ltd, Belfield-in-Somerset Ltd and Brewer Distributors Ltd; kt 1972; *Style* - Lt-Col Sir Jeffrey Astwood, CBE, ED; Greenfield, Somerset, Bermuda (☎ 4 1729)

ASTWOOD, Hon Mr Justice; Hon James Rufus; Jr, JP; s of James Astwood Sr; *b* 4 Oct 1923; *Educ* Berkeley Inst Bermuda, Toronto U; *m* 1952, Gloria Norton; 1 s, 2 da; *Career* Ch Just Bermuda 1977-, barr Gray's Inn 1956, actg Attorney Gen Bermuda 1976-77, actg Dep Gov 1977; *Style* - Hon Mr Justice Astwood, JP; Clifton, Middle rd, Devonshire, Bermuda

ATCHERLEY, Sir Harold Winter; s of L Atcherley; *b* 30 Aug 1918; *Educ* Gresham's, Heidelberg and Geneva Us; *m* 1946 (separated 1978), Anita, nee Leslie & widow of Sub-Lt W Eves, RN; 1 s, 2 da; *Career* with Roy Dutch Shell Gp 1946-70, recruitment adv to Miny of Defence 1970-7l, dir British Home Stores Ltd 1973-memb Cttee of Inquiry into Remuneration of Members of Local Authorities 1977-, kt 1977; *Style* - Sir Harold Atcherley; Conduit House, The Green, Long Melford, Suffolk (☎ 8197)

ATHERTON, John Bryan; s of John Atherton; *b* 17 Feb 1938; *Educ* Arnold Sch, Sheffield U; *m* 1965, Valerie, da of Guy Easton; *Career* md London Works Steel Co, dir Duport Steels Ltd; *Recreations* golf, music; *Clubs* Enville; *Style* - John Atherton Esq; Loneacre, Feiashill rd, Trysull, nr Wolverhampton, W Midlands (☎ Wombourne 896500)

ATHOLL, 10 Duke of (S 1703); George Iain Murray; also Lord Murray of Tullibardine (S 1604), Earl of Tullibardine (S 1606), Earl of Atholl (S 1629), Marquess of Atholl (S 1676), Marquess of Tullibardine (S 1703), Earl of Strathtay and Strathardle (S 1703), Viscount of Balwhidder, Glenalmond and Glenlyon (S 1703), and Lord Murray, Balvenie, and Gask (S 1703); s of Lt-Col George Murray OBE RA (ka 1945, s of Sir Evelyn Murray, KCB, himself gggs of Rt Rev Lord George Murray, DD, sometime Bishop of St David's and 2 s of 3 Duke of Atholl, KT), by his w, Hon Angela Pearson (later Hon Mrs Campbell-Preston, d 1981), da of 2 Viscount Cowdray; suc kinsman, 9 Duke of Atholl, 1957; *b* 19 June 1931; *Educ* Eton, Ch Ch Oxford; *Heir* 1 cous twice removed, Brig Stewart Murray; *Career* Rep Peer for Scotland 1958-63; chm Westminster Press 1974- (dir 1963-), RNLI 1979-; dir BPM Hldgs, Pearson Longman 1975-; V-Pres Nat Tst for Scotland 1977-; memb exec cttee Red Deer Commission; *Recreations* golf, bridge, shooting, stalking; *Clubs* Turf, White's, New (Edinburgh); *Style* - His Grace The Duke of Atholl; Blair Castle, Blair Atholl, Perthshire (☎ 212); 31 Marlborough Hill, NW8 (☎ 01 586 2291)

ATKIN, Alec Field; CBE (1978); s of Alec Atkin; *b* 26 April 1925; *Educ* Riley H S, Hull Tech Coll, Hull U; *m* 1948, Nora Darby; 2 s, 1 da; *Career* FEng, FIMechE, FRAes, md (Military) Aircraft Gp Br Aerospace, chm Warton, Kingston-Brough and Manchester Dvns 1978-, assist md BAC 1976-77, FRSA; *Style* - Alec Atkin Esq, CBE; Dinglehead, Foregate, Fulwood, Preston, Lancs (☎ 719670)

ATKINS, Rt Hon Humphrey Edward; PC (19730, MP (C) Spelthorne 1970-; s of late Capt E Atkins, of Kenya; *b* 12 Aug 1922; *Educ* Wellington; *m* 1944, Margaret, da of Sir Robert Spencer-Nairn, 1 Bt; 1 s, 3 da; *Career* Sec of State for NI 1979-, MP (C) Merton and Morden Surrey 1955-70, Parly Sec to Treasury and Govt Ch Whip 1973-74, Oppn Ch Whip 1974-79; *Clubs* Brooks's; *Style* - The Rt Hon Humphrey Atkins, MP; 3 North Court, Gt Peter st, SW1; Tuckenhams, Waltham St Lawrence, Berks

ATKINS, Prof Sir Hedley John Barnard; KBE (1967); s of Col Sir John Atkins, KCMG, KCVO, FRCS; *b* 30 Dec 1905; *Educ* Rugby, Trin Oxford, Guy's Hosp; *m* 1933, Gladwys, nee Jones; 2 s; *Career* DM, MCh, FRCS, FRCP, Emeritus Prof of Surgery London U, former Dir Dept of Surgery Guy's; *Style* - Prof Sir Hedley Atkins, KBE; Down House, Downe, Kent

ATKINS, John Spencer; DSO (1945), TD, DL (Leics 1946); s of late Col E Atkins, CB, DL; *b* 28 Oct 1905; *Educ* Uppingham; *m* 1936, Monica Standish; 1 s, 2 da; *Career* Pres Atkins Bros; *Style* - John Atkins Esq, DSO, TD, DL; White House, Ullesthorpe, Lutterworth, Leics (☎ Leire 209274)

ATKINS, Robert James; MP (C)

Preston N 1979-; s of Reginald Atkins, of Chequers Cottage, S Heath, Gt Missenden; *b* 5 Feb 1946; *Educ* Highgate; *m* 1969, Dulcie, da of Frederick Moon Chaplin, of Bexley; 1 s, 1 da; *Career* jt sec Con Parly Def & Aviation Cttees; Nat V-Pres Con Trade Unionists; *Recreations* wine, cricket, old churches; *Style* - Robert Atkins Esq, MP; 29c Haringey Park, Hornsey, N8 (☎ 01 348 5316); 15 St Andrew's rd, Preston, Lancs (☎ 55477)

ATKINS, Sir William Sydney Albert; CBE (1966); s of Robert Atkins; *b* 6 Feb 1902; *Educ* London U; *m* 1928, Elsie, nee Barrow; 2 da; *Career* chm W S Atkins & Ptnrs 1951-, W S Atkins & Ptnrs (Ethiopia) Ltd 1963-, W S Atkins Gp 1971-, W S Atkins & Assocs Pty 1971-, W S Atkins (Overseas Projects) 1973-, W S Atkins International 1973-, Sir William Atkins & Ptnrs 1977-; kt 1976; *Style* - Sir William Atkins, CBE; Chobham Place, Chobham, Surrey (☎ 8867)

ATKINSON, Sir Alec (John Alexander); KCB (1978, CB 1976), DFC (1943); s of late Rev R Atkinson; *b* 9 June 1919; *Educ* Queen's Oxford; *m* 1945, Marguerite Pearson; 1 da; *Career* 2 Perm Sec DHSS 1977-79; *Style* - Sir Alec Atkinson KCB DFC; Bleak House, The Drive, Belmont, Sutton, Surrey (☎ 01 642 6479)

ATKINSON, Colin Ronald Michael; s of R Atkinson; *b* 23 July 1931; *Educ* Durham U, Queen's U Belfast, Nottingham U, Loughborough Coll of Educn, Bath U; *m* 1957, Shirley Angus; 2 s, 1 da; *Career* Headmaster Millfield 1971- *Style* - Colin Atkinson Esq; Millfield School, Street, Somerset

ATKINSON, David Anthony; MP (C) Bournemouth E 1977-; s of Arthur Atkinson and Joan, nee Zink; *b* 24 March 1940; *Educ* St George's Coll Weybridge, Coll of Automobile and Aeronautical Engineering Chelsea; *m* 1968, Susan, da of Dr Roy Pilsworth, of Benfleet Essex; 1 s, 1 da; *Career* md David Graham Ltd 1972-, dir Chalkwell Motor Co Westcliff-on-Sea 1963-72; PPS to Paul Channon (Min of Arts) 1981-; *Recreations* mountaineering, art, architecture, travel; *Style* - David Atkinson Esq, MP; 20 Keswick rd, Boscombe, Bournemouth (☎ 0202 301731)

ATKINSON, Sir Fred (Frederick John); KCB (1979, CB 1971); s of George Atkinson; *b* 7 Dec 1919; *Educ* Dulwich, Jesus Oxford; *m* 1947, Margaret Gibson; 2 da; *Career* Ch Ec Advsr to Treasury and Head of Govt Ec Serv 1977-; *Style* - Sir Fred Atkinson, KCB; 26 Lee ter, Blackheath, SE3 (☎ 01 852 1040); Tickner Cottage, Aldington, Kent (514)

ATKINSON, Col Francis Cuthbert; DL (Norfolk 1968); s of John Atkinson, of Morland Hall Westmorland and Sheringham Norfolk; *b* 25 Nov 1912; *Educ* Bradfield, Sandhurst; *m* 1941, Susan, da of Lt-Cdr John de Burgh Jessop, DSO, RN, of Overton Hall, Derbys; 2 da (and 2 da decd); *Career* served NW Frontier, WW II (NW Europe), M East; Cmmd Depot Roy Norfolk Regt 1948-50, subsequently Malaya, Germany; memb N Norfolk DC 1979-; CStJ 1973; *Recreations* looking back on memories of polo, pig-sticking, shooting, hunting, winter sports, athletics; *Clubs* Naval & Military, Norfolk; *Style* - Col Francis Atkinson, DL; Kettleby Lodge, Sheringham, Norfolk (☎ 822652)

ATKINSON, Sir (John) Kenneth; s of late James Atkinson; *b* 21 May 1905; *Educ* The Leys Sch Cambridge; *m* 1930, Ellen Dod (d 1975); 1 da; *Career* Ch Valuer Valuation Office Inland Revenue 1951-66, kt 1953; *Style* - Sir Kenneth Atkinson; Clouds, High Park av, E Horsley, Leatherhead (☎ E Horsley 3103)

ATKINSON, Leslie; CMG (1965), OBE (1961); s of J Atkinson; *b* 11 Jan 1913; *Educ* Wollongong Tech Sch; *m* 1935, Ellen, nee Kinsey; 1 s, 1 da; *Career* md Leslie Atkinson Pty 1960; *Style* - Leslie Atkinson Esq CMG OBE; 11 Kyle Parade, Kyle Bay, NSW 2221, Australia

ATKINSON, Maj-Gen Sir Leonard Henry; KBE (1966, OBE 1945); s of A Atkinson; *b* 4 Dec 1910; *Educ* Wellington, UCL; *m* 1939, Jean, da of C Atchley, OBE; 1 s, 3 da; *Career* Cmdt REME Training Centre and Cdr Berkshire Dist 1958-63, dir Bespoke Securities 1974-, Emray 1978-, chm Christopher Gold Assocs 1976-, vice-chm S Regnl Cncl Further Educn 1978-, FIMechE, FIEE, FIGasE, FIERE; *Style* - Maj-Gen Sir Leonard Atkinson, KBE; Pound Cottage, Silchester, Reading, Berks (☎ Bramley Green 220)

ATKINSON, Lady (Margaret Mary); da of James Edward and Mary Roy, of Radlett; *m* 1929, Rt Hon Sir Fenton Atkinson, PC (d 1980); 1 s, 2 da; *Style* - Lady Atkinson; Dalbeathie House, Dunkeld, Perthshire (☎ 230)

ATKINSON, Norman; MP (L) Haringey 1974-; s of George Atkinson, of Manchester; *b* 25 March 1923; *m* 1948, Irene Parry; *Career* MP Tottenham 1964-74, Tres Labour Party 1976-; *Style* - Norman Atkinson Esq, MP; House of Commons, SW1

ATKINSON, Robert; DSC (1941, and 2 Bars), RD (1947); s of Nicholas Atkinson; *b* 7 March 1916; *Educ* London U; *m* 1, 1941, Joyce, nee Forster (d 1972); 1 s, 1 da; m 2, 1977, Margaret Hazel Walker; *Career* served 1939-45 War, MIMechE, CEng, md- Wm Doxford 1957-61, Tube Investments (Eng) 1961-67, Unicorn Industries 1967-72, Aurora Holdings Sheffield 1972-, chm Br Shipbuilders 1980- (salary £48,000 pa as of June 1981); *Recreations* salmon fishing, walking; *Clubs* Royal Thames Yacht; *Style* - Robert Atkinson Esq, DSC*, RD; c/o British Shipbuilders Ltd, 243 Knightsbridge, SW7 (☎ 01 589 3488/581 1393/4511); 16 Ivy Park ct, Sheffield; 3 Whitehall ct, SW1

ATKINSON, Rowan Sebastian; s of Eric Atkinson; *b* 6 Jan 1955; *Educ* Durham Cathedral Choristers' Sch, St Bees Cumbria, Newcastle & Oxford Us; *Career* actor and writer; voted TV Personality of 1980 by Variety Club of GB; Pres Young Liberals 1981-; *Style* - Rowan Atkinson Esq; c/o Richard Armitage-Noel Gay Org, 24 Denmark st, WC2 (☎ 01 836 3941)

ATTENBOROUGH, David Frederick; CBE (1974); s of late Frederick Levi Attenborough; *b* 8 May 1926; *Educ* Wyggeston G S for Boys Leicester, Clare Cambridge; *m* 1950, Jane Oriel; 1 s, 1 da; *Career* traveller, broadcaster and writer; *Style* - David Attenborough Esq, CBE; 5 Park rd, Richmond, Surrey (☎ 01 940 5055)

ATTENBOROUGH, Philip John; s of John Attenborough, CBE; *b* 3 June 1936; *Educ* Rugby, Trin Oxford; *m* 1963, Rosemary, da of Dr W Littler, CB; 1 s, 1 da; *Career* chm Hodder & Stoughton Ltd and Hodder & Stoughton Hldgs 1975-, Lancet Ltd 1977-, memb Cncl Publishers Assoc 1976-; *Style* - Philip Attenborough Esq; Coldhanger, Seal Chart, Sevenoaks, Kent (☎ 61516)

ATTENBOROUGH, Sir Richard Samuel; CBE (1967); s of late Frederick Levi Attenborough; *b* 29 Aug 1923; *Educ* Wyggeston G S for Boys Leicester, RADA; *m* 1945, Sheila Sim; 1 s, 2 da; *Career* actor, producer and director; Gov Nat Film Sch 1970-, chm RADA 1970-, Pro-Chllr Sussex U 1970-, Capital Radio 1973-, Tstee Tate Gall 1976-, dir Chelsea Football Club 1969-; kt 1976; *Style* - Sir Richard Attenborough, CBE; Old Friars, Richmond Green, Surrey

ATTERTON, David Valentine; s of Frank Atterton; *b* 13 Feb 1927; *Educ* Bishop Wordsworth's Sch Salisbury, Peterhouse Cambridge; *m* 1948, Sheila McMahon; 2 s, 1 da; *Career* chm Foseco Minsep 1979-, dep chm Associated Engrg 1979-; dir Fin Corp for Industry Ltd 1974-, and IMI Ltd 1976-; *Style* - David Atterton Esq; The Tan House, Lapworth, Solihull, W Midlands (☎ Lapworth 2902)

ATTLEE, 2 Earl (UK 1955); Martin Richard Attlee; also Viscount Prestwood (UK 1955); s of 1 Earl ('Clem'(-ent)) Attlee, KG, OM, CH, PC, PM (L) 1945-51 (d 1967), and Violet (yst da of Henry Millar and 2 cous of 1 Baron Inchyra); *b* 10 Aug 1927; *Educ* Millfield, Southampton U; *m* 1955, Anne, da of James Henderson, CBE, of Bath; 1 s, 1 da; *Heir* s, Viscount Prestwood; *Career* late Merchant navy; assist PRO BR (S Regn) 1970-76; MIPR, proprietor of Prestwood Publicity 1967-; *Style* - The Rt Hon Earl Attlee; 125 Hendon Lane, N3 (☎ 01 346 7306)

ATTLEE, Hon Mrs; Hon Rosemary; da of late 1 Baron Elton; *b* 1925; *m* 1, 1946 (m dis 1955), William Yates; 2 da; m 2, 1955,

David Charles Attlee; 1 s, 1 da; *Style* - The Hon Mrs Attlee; Greenhill, Egerton, Ashford, Kent

ATWELL, Sir John William; CBE (1970); s of William Atwell; *b* 24 Nov 1911; *Educ* Hyndland Secondary Sch Glasgow, Roy Tech Coll Glasgow, Cambridge; *m* 1945, Dorothy, nee Baxter; *Career* kt 1976, CEng, FIMechE, FRSE, memb BR Scot Regnl Advsy Bd 1975-, Bd of Roy Ordnance Factories 1974-, chm Scot Offshore Ptnrship 1975-, dir Govan Shipbuilders 1975-; *Style* - Sir John Atwell, CBE; Elmfield, Buchanan dve, Rutherglen, Glasgow (☎ 041 647 1824)

ATWILL, Sir (Milton) John Napier; s of Milton Atwill; *b* 16 Jan 1926; *Educ* Geelong G S, Jesus Cambridge; *m* 1955, Susan Playfair; 2 da; *Career* barr 1953, dep chm David Jones Ltd 1975-, D J's Properties Ltd 1976-; dir Waugh & Josephson Hldgs 1965-, Nat Mutual Life Assoc of Australasia (NSW) 1973-, Brooke Bond Australia Pty 1979-; Fed Pres Liberal Party 1975-; kt 1979; *Style* - Sir John Atwill; 5 Fullerton st, Woolahra, NSW 2025, Australia (☎ 02 32 1570)

AUBREY-FLETCHER, Lt-Col Edward Henry Lancelot; s of Maj Sir Henry Lancelot Aubrey-Fletcher, 6 Bt, CVO, DSO; *b* 6 May 1930; *Educ* Eton, New Coll Oxford; *m* 1, 1953, Bridget (d 1977), da of Brig Sir Henry Floyd, 5 Bt, CB, CBE, DL, and Hon Kathleen, da of 1 Baron Gretton, CBE, VD, TD, PC; 2 s, 1 da; m 2, 1981, Hon Penelope Verney-Cave, da and h of 7 Baron Braye, DL; *Career* serving with Gren Gds; *Style* - Lt-Col Edward Aubrey-Fletcher; Gatherum Farm, Ryehurst Lane, Binfield, Berks

AUBREY-FLETCHER, Henry Egerton; s and h of Sir John Aubrey-Fletcher, 7 Bt; *b* 27 Nov 1945; *Educ* Eton; *m* 1976, Sara Roberta, da of Maj Robert Buchanan, of Evanton, Ross-Shire; 2 s; *Style* - Henry Aubrey-Fletcher Esq; Town Hill Farm, Chilton, Aylesbury, Bucks

AUBREY-FLETCHER, Sir John Henry Lancelot; 7 Bt (GB 1782), of Clea Hall, Cumberland, JP (Bucks); s of Maj Sir Henry Lancelot Aubrey-Fletcher, CVO, DSO (d 1969); *b* 22 Aug 1912; *Educ* Eton, New Coll Oxford; *m* 1939, Diana Fynvola, da of late Lt-Col Arthur George Edward Egerton, Coldm Gds; 1 s (and 1 da decd); *Heir* s, Henry Egerton Aubrey-Fletcher; *Career* barr 1937, Dep Chm of Quarter Sessions 1959-71, a Metropolitan Magistrate 1959-71, Recorder of Crown Court 1972-74, High Sheriff of Bucks 1961; *Style* - Sir John Aubrey-Fletcher, JP; The Gate House, Chilton, Aylesbury, Bucks (☎ Long Crendon 347)

AUBREY-FLETCHER, Hon Mrs (Penelope Mary); *née* Verney-Cave; da and h of 7 Baron Braye, DL; *b* 29 Sept 1941; *Educ* Assumption Convent, Hengrave Hall; *m* 1981, Lt-Col Edward Henry Lancelot Aubrey-Fletcher Gren Gds, s of Maj Sir Henry Lancelot Aubrey-Fletcher, 6 Bt, CVO, DSO, JP, DL; *Style* - The Hon Mrs Aubrey-Fletcher; Gatherum Farm, Ryehurst Lane, Binfield, Berks

AUCKLAND, 9 Baron (I 1789 & GB 1793); Ian George Eden; s of 8 Baron Auckland, MC (d 1957), and Evelyn, 3 da of Col Arthur Hay-Drummond of Cromlix (nephew of 12 Earl of Kinnoull), whose mother Arabella was maternal gda of 1 Duke of Cleveland; His Grace's wine glasses were without bases, forcing guests to drain their wine in one go; though a pluralist in rotten boroughs (6), he supported the Reform Bill (it was said 'he bought his boroughs to be made a Marquess, and gave them up to be made a Duke'); his paternal grandmother Grace was gda of Barbara, cr Duchess of Cleveland, by whom Lord Auckland is ninth in descent from Charles II; others to whom Her Grace granted her favours ('If she were as beautiful as Helen, she had as many lovers as Messalina' - Jesse) were Wycherley, Churchill, Lord Chesterfield, and the Duke of Montagu; she dissipated her vast wealth in gambling, Pepys noting that she won £15,000 in one night and lost £25,000 in another; Newton himself could scarce compute such sums in today's money; *b* 23 June 1926; *Educ* Blundell's; *m* 1954, Dorothy, JP (Surrey), da of Henry Manser, of Eastbourne; 1 s, 2 da; *Heir* s, Hon Robert Eden; *Career* insur consultant; non-exec dir C J Sims & Co;

served Roy Signals 1945-48 & London Yeo Sharpshooters TA 1948-53; Lloyd's Underwriter 1956-64; V-Pres Roy Soc Prevention Accidents; *Clubs* City Livery; *Style* - The Rt Hon Lord Auckland; Tudor Rose House, 30 Links rd, Ashtead, Surrey (☎ 74393)

AUDLEY, 25 Baron (E 1312-13); Richard Michael Thomas Souter; s of Sir Charles Souter, KCIE, CSI, and Charlotte Jesson (sis of Thomas Tuchet-Jesson, f of 23 Baron & the 23 Baron's sis who as Baroness Audley was 24 holder of that title; Charlotte and Thomas were children of Charlotte, da of John Thicknesse-Tuchet, bro of 21 Baron Audley, by her husb Thomas Jesson); suc cous 1973; *b* 31 May 1914; *Educ* Uppingham; *m* 1941, Pauline, da of Dallas Louis Eskell; 3 da; *Heir* all 3 da as coheiresses presumptive- Hon Mrs Mackinnon, Hon Jennifer Souter, Hon Amanda Souter, *qqv*; *Career* Capt RA WW II; fellow Chartered Inst of Loss Adjusters; dir Graham Miller & Co; *Recreations* shooting, gardening; *Style* - The Rt Hon The Lord Audley; Friendly Green, Cowden, nr Edenbridge, Kent (☎ Cowden 682)

AUERBACH, Frank Helmuth; s of Max Auerbach; *b* 29 April 1931; *Educ* privately, St Martin's Sch of Art; *m* 1958, Julia Wolstenholme; 1 s; *Career* painter and draughtsman; *Style* - c/o Marlborough Fine Art; 6 Albemarle st, W1

AULD, Robin Ernest; QC (1975); s of Ernest Auld; *b* 19 July 1937; *Educ* Brooklands Coll, King's Coll London; *m* 1963, Catherine, nee Pritchard; 1 s, 1 da; *Career* barr 1959 (NI bar 1973), Recorder of Crown Court 1977-; *Style* - Robin Auld Esq, QC; Lamb Bldg, Temple, EC4 (☎ 01 353 6701)

AUSTEN, David James; s of Albert Austen; *b* 19 July 1925; *Educ* Margate Coll; *m* 1951, Margaret (decd), da of Hewel Morgan Owen; 1 s; *Career* CA; ch exec & dir ITS Rubber; dir Charles Colston Gp, Tallent Engrg Ltd; *Recreations* photography, painting, ornithology, music, reading; *Style* - David Austen Esq; Netherbury, Burtons Lane, Chalfont St Giles, Bucks (☎ Little Chalfont 2269)

AUSTEN-SMITH, Air Marshal Sir Roy David; KBE (1979), CB (1975), DFC (1953); *b* 28 June 1924; *Educ* Hurstpierpoint; *m* 1951, Ann, nee Alderson; 2 s; *Career* Head Br Def Staff Washington and Def Attache 1978-; Cdr Br Forces Cyprus, AOC Air HQ Cyprus and Administrator Sovn Base Areas Cyprus 1967-78; *Style* - Air Marshal Sir Roy Austen-Smith; KBE, CB, DFC, c/o Nat West Bank, Swanley, Kent

AUSTIN, Hon Jack (Jacob); QC (Canada 1970); s of Morris Austin and Clara, nee Chetner; *b* 2 March 1932; *Educ* BC U, Harvard; *m* 1 (m dis); 3 da; m 2, 1978, Natalie Freeman; *Career* barr & slr BC and Yukon Territory; Dep Min Dept of Energy, Mines and Resources Ottawa 1970-74, Principal Sec to PM Ottawa 1974-75, memb Senate, Canadian Parliament 1975-; *Style* - Hon Jack Austin, QC; Room 668-5, The Senate, Ottawa, Ontario, Canada (☎ 613 992 1437)

AUSTIN, John; s of John Austin, of Chesterfield; *b* 13 April 1927; *Educ* St George's Sch Harpenden, Glasgow U; *m* 1959, Shirley, da of Maj G Proctor, of Tullydoey, Co Tyrone; 1 s, 1 da; *Career* formerly Capt RASC; MIProdE; dir Howard Machinery; dir & ch exec J Mann & Son; chm Lehman Power Corpn (USA) and Lehman Power Ltd; *Recreations* walking, swimming; *Clubs* RAC; *Style* - John Austin Esq; The White Cottage, Woodbridge, Suffolk (☎ Woodbridge 3044)

AUSTIN, Sir John Byron Fraser; 3 Bt (UK 1894), of Red Hill, Castleford, W Riding of York; s of Sir William Michael Byron Austin, 2 Bt (d 1940); *b* 14 July 1897; *Educ* Downside; *m* 1, 1953 (m dis 1958), Sheila Jean, da of Duncan McNaught, and formerly w of Col Harry Carlisle Boyce, CBE, RA; m 2, 1960, Rhoda Noreen, da of Herbert Lloyd Pinches, of Eastbourne, and wid of Col C Rose; *Heir* bro, William Ronald Austin; *Career* late Lt 7 Hussars, Maj Indian Army, served with Somaliland Camel Corps and King's African Rifles

Tanganyika, Fl-Cdr RFC and RAF Burma and E Frontier of India, commanding Bn of Indian Army (despatches) 1939-44; dir Austin Properties Ltd, St Anthony's Properties Ltd, Baronetcy Properties Ltd; *Style* - Sir John Austin, Bt; Pax, St George's lane, Hurstpierpoint, Sussex

AUSTIN, James David Sharwood; s of Douglas Austin; *b* 8 March 1954; *Educ* Harrow, Caen U France; *Career* dir E Austin & Sons (London)- warehousing, oil recycling, fork lift truck hire, transport, oil distribution, non-woven paper products, rag recycling, oil tank cleaning; *Recreations* sailing, driving, squash, cricket, water skiing; *Clubs* Lansdowne; *Style* - James Austin Esq; Bradley Springs, Codicote, Hitchin, Herts (☎ 0483 820274); The Bungalow, Dedham, nr Colchester, Essex; 15 Canonbury Grove, Islington, N1 (☎ 01 226 6304)

AUSTIN, Sir John Worroker; s of late J Austin; *Educ* Sydney H S, Sydney U; *m* 1948, Doris, nee Jenkins; 1 s; *Career* CA, chm Blue Metal Industs 1952-, TRW (Aust) Ltd 1968-, dir Rank Industs Aust Pty 1974-, Gter Union Orgn Pty 1974-, George Kent (ANZ) Pty, Allied Polymer Gp (Hldgs) Pty, Ready Mixed Concrete; kt 1971; *Style* - Sir John Austin; Toft Monks, 95 Elizabeth Bay rd, NSW 2011, Australia

AUSTIN, Vice-Adm Sir Peter Murray; KCB (1976); s of late Vice-Adm Sir Francis Austin, KBE, CB; *b* 16 April 1921; *Educ* RNC Dartmouth; *m* 1959, Josephine Shutte-Smith; 3 s, 1 da; *Career* Ops Dir Mersey Docks and Harbour Co 1976-, FBIM, Flag Offr Naval Air Cmmd 1973-76; *Style* - Vice-Adm Sir Peter Austin, KCB; 111 Banks rd, W Kirby, Wirral

AUSTIN, William James; s of John Austin, of Chelmsford; *b* 8 Feb 1913; *Educ* UCL; *m* 1943, Ann, da of Sir Ronald Matthews, of Doncaster; 1 s, 4 da; *Career* served WW II, Lt-Col 1943 (RAOC 1936 42, REME 1942-53); co dir; *Recreations* sailing, winter sports; *Clubs* Army & Navy; *Style* - Lt-Col William Austin; Seawards, 7 Winchester rd, Frinton-on-Sea, Essex (☎ 2852); Hatfield Place, Hatfield Peverel, Chelmsford, Essex (☎ 380363)

AUSTIN, William Ronald; s of Sir William Austin, 2 Bt (d 1940); hp of bro, 3 Bt; *b* 20 July 1900; *m* 1, 1926, Dorothy Mary (d 1957), da of late L A Bidwell, FRCS; 2 s; m 2, 1958, Mary Helen Farrell; *Style* - William Austin Esq; Holeland House, Dunsford, Devon

AUSWILD, Sir James Frederick John; CBE (1970); s of late James Auswild; *b* 12 April 1908; *Educ* Temora H S; *m* 1933, Kathleen, nee Conway; 2 da; *Career* FCA, FAIM, kt 1974, Commissioner Rural Bank NSW 1961-, governing dir Auswild Orgn (130 assoc cos), chm Austwide Corp Pty, jt chm and md Preston Motor Hldgs; dir Boyded Pty, C V Holland Pty, Finance & Guarantee Co, Rossfield House Pty, Auswild Securities, Embassy Motel, Statesman Hotel Pty, ACT Motors, Holden Dealers Canberra, Ambassador Hotel Canberra, Mentone Motors Gp, Cooma-Monaro Express Pty, Canberra Publishing and Printing Co, J F J Auswild (Hldgs) Pty, Auswild Properties, Mindaribba Vineyards, Roxburgh Vineyards; *Style* - Sir James Auswild, CBE; 609 New South Head rd, Rose Bay, Sydney, NSW 2029 (☎ 36 1711)

AVEBURY, 4 Baron (UK 1900); Sir Eric Reginald Lubbock; 7 Bt (UK 1806); s of Hon Maurice Fox Pitt Lubbock (yst s of 1 Baron Avebury) and Hon Mary Stanley (eldest da of 5 Baron Stanley of Alderley and sis of the actress Pamela Stanley), whereby Lord Avebury is 3 cous of Nancy Mitford and her siblings; suc 3 Baron (1 cous) 1971; *b* 29 Sept 1928; *Educ* Upper Canada Coll, Harrow, Balliol Oxford; *m* 1953, Kina-Maria, da of Count Joseph O'Kelly de Gallagh (a yr s of the family whose head is a Count of the Holy Roman Empire by Imperial Letters Patent of 1767); 2 s, 1 da; *Heir* s, Hon Lyulph Lubbock; *Career* late Lt Welsh Gds; MP (Lib) Orpington 1962-70, Lib Ch Whip 1963-70; with Rolls Royce as engr 1951-56; managemnet consultant Charterhouse Gp 1960, consultant Morgan-Grampian 1970-; chm Digico Ltd; dir C L Projects; Pres Fluoridation Soc 1972-, Conservation Soc 1973-; MIMechE; late memb Cncl Inst Race Rels; *Style* - The Rt Hon Lord Avebury; House of Lords, SW 1; Combe House, Sundridge, Kent

AVERY, Gillian Elsie (Mrs A Cockshut); da of Norman and Grace Avery; *b* 1926; *Educ* Dunottar Sch Reigate; *m* 1952, A O J Cockshut; 1 da; *Career* writer, authoress of children's books and non-fiction; *Books* A Likely Lad (Guardian Award 1972); *Style* - Miss Gillian Avery; 32 Charlbury rd, Oxford

AVERY, Marshall Angus; s of Maj N Avery, MC; *b* 6 May 1933; *Educ* Loretto, Sandhurst; *m* 1975, Penelope, da of Alan Berners-Price; 1 s; *Career* formerly army Capt (Gordon Highlanders 1953-62); md Irish Vintners 1958-70, dir Waverley Vintners 1974-; *Recreations* sailing, skiing, shooting, squash; *Clubs* Naval & Military; *Style* - Marshall Avery Esq; Costerton Mains, Pathhead, Midlothian

AVES, Dame Geraldine Maitland; DBE (1977, CBE 1963, OBE 1946); da of Ernest Aves; *b* 22 Aug 1898; *Educ* Frognal, Newnham Cambridge; *Career* Min of Health 1941-63 (Ch Welfare Offr and Head Welfare Dvn); seconded UNRRA Ch Child Care Consultant (Europe) 1945-46; chm Highgate Cemetery Tst 1977-; *Style* - Dame Geraldine Aves, DBE; 24 North Grove, Highgate Village, N6 (☎ 01 340 1685)

AVON, 2 Earl of (UK 1961); Nicholas Eden; OBE (1970), TD (1965), DL (Gter London 1973); also Viscount Eden (UK 1961); s of 1 Earl of Avon, KG, MC (Sir Anthony Eden, For Sec 1935-38 & 1940-45, PM 1955-57, d 1977; s of Sir William Eden, 7 & 5 Bt), by his 1 w, Beatrice (da of Hon Sir Gervase Beckett, 1 Bt, bro of 2 Baron Grimthorpe, by his w Hon Mabel Duncombe, da of Viscount Helmsley and sis of 2 Earl of Feversham); *b* 3 Oct 1930; *Educ* Eton; *Heir* none; *Career* late 2 Lt KRRC, ADC Gov-Gen Canada 1952-53; Lord-in-Waiting to HM 1980-; V-Chm Gter London TAVR Assoc, Capt Queen Victoria Rifles (TA) 1953-61, Maj then Lt-Col Queen's R Rifles (TA) 1961-65 & 1965-70; Col TAVR 1972-75 (Col RARO 1945-); Govt Spokesman Arts, Environment, T'port 1980-; ADC (TAVR) to HM 1978-, Oppn Whip 1978-79, Parly Delegate to N Atlantic Assembly 1979-; *Style* - The Rt Hon Earl of Avon OBE TD DL; House of Lords, SW1; 6 Boyne ter Mews, W11

AVONSIDE, Rt Hon Lord; Ian Hamilton Shearer; PC (1962); s of Andrew Shearer, OBE; *b* 6 Nov 1914; *Educ* Dunfermline H S, Glasgow U, Edinburgh U; *m* 1, 1942; 1 s, 1 da; m 2, 1954, Janet Sutherland Murray (*see* Avonside, Lady); *Career* Scottish Lord of Session (Senator of the Coll of Justice in Scotland) 1964-; LLB Edinburgh 1937, advocate 1938, QC (Scot) 1952, Sheriff Renfrew and Argyll 1960-62, Lord Advocate 1962-64; *Style* - The Rt Hon Lord Avonside, PC; The Mill House, Samuelston, E Lothian (☎ Haddington 2396)

AVONSIDE, Lady - Janet Sutherland Shearer; OBE (1956); da of William Murray, MB, ChB; *b* 31 May 1917; *Educ* St Columba's Sch Kilmacolm, Erlenhaus Baden Baden, Edinburgh U; *m* 1953, as his 2 w, Rt Hon Lord Avonside, PC; *Career* Scottish Govr BBC 1971-76; contested (C) Glasgow Maryhill 1950, Dundee E 1951, Leith 1955; *Style* - Lady Avonside, OBE; The Mill House, Samuelston, E Lothian (☎ Haddington 2396)

AWAD, HE Muhammad Hadi; *b* 5 May 1934; *Educ* Murray House Coll of Educn; *m* 1956, Adla; 1 s, 3 da; *Career* PDRY Ambass to UK 1973-, Sweden and Spain 1974-, Denmark Portugal and The Netherlands 1975-; *Style* - HE Mr Muhammad Hadi Awad; PDRY Embassy, 57 Cromwell rd, SW7 (☎ 01 584 6607)

AWAK, His Excellency Mr Alhaji Shehu; *Career* Nigerian High Commissioner to UK 1981-; *Also* ('Alhaji' signifies that HE has made the pilgrimage to Mecca); *Style* - HE Mr Alhaji Shehu Awak; The Nigerian High Commission, Nigeria House, 9 Northumberland Avenue, WC2 (☎ 01 839 1244)

AWDRY, Daniel Edmund; TD, DL (Wilts 1979); s of late Col Edmund Awdry, MC, TD, DL, and Mrs Awdry, JP, nee French; *b* 10 Sept 1924; *Educ* Winchester, Sandhurst; *m* 1950, Elizabeth Cattley; 3 da; *Career* slr 1950, MP (C) Chippenham 1962-79, PPS to Slr Gen 1973-74; dir- BET

Omnibus Servs 1966-, Sheepbridge Engineering 1968-, Rediffusion 1973-; *Style* - Daniel Awdry Esq, TD, DL; Old Manor, Beanacre, nr Melksham, Wilts (☎ Melksham 2315)

AXTON, Henry Stuart; s of Wilfrid Axton; *b* 6 May 1923; *Educ* Rock Ferry, Sandhurst; *m* 1947, Constance, da of Lycurgus Godefroy; 1 da; *Career* served WW II N Africa & NW Europe Roy Tank Regt and Fife & Forfar Yeomanry respectively; FCA, dep chm Brixton Estate Ltd 1971 (md 1963-), chm Investment Cos in Australia, Belgium, France and Germany; *Recreations* music, sailing (yacht- 'Alpha II'); *Clubs* Roy Thames Yacht, Roy Ocean Racing; *Style* - Henry Axton Esq; Invermark, Oxted, Surrey (☎ 2935)

AYCKBOURN, Alan; s of Horace Ayckbourn; *b* 12 April 1939; *Educ* Haileybury; *m* 1959, Christine, nee Roland; 2 s; *Career* playwright, Dir of Productions Stephen Joseph Theatre in the Round Scarborough; *Style* - Alan Ayckbourn Esq; c/o Margaret Ramsay ltd, 14a Goodwin's Court, St Martin's Lane, WC2 (☎ 01 240 0691)

AYER, Sir Alfred Jules; s of late Jules Louis Cyprien Ayer; *b* 29 Oct 1910; *Educ* Eton, Ch Ch Oxford; *m* 1960, Alberta Chapman (Dee Wells); 1 s; *Career* philosopher, Wykeham Prof of Logic Oxford, FBA; kt 1970; *Style* - Sir Alfred Ayer; 10 Regent's Park ter, NW1 (☎ 01 485 4855)

AYKROYD, Bertram; s of late Sir Frederic Aykroyd, 1 Bt; hp of bro, Sir Cecil Aykroyd, 2 Bt; *b* 17 Sept 1915; *Educ* Charterhouse, Trin Cambridge; *m* 1, 1938 (m dis 1947), Margot, da of late L Graham Brown, FRCS; 1 s, 1 da; m 2, 1949, Catalina, da of late Henry Marchington, of Hope Green, Addington, Cheshire; 2 s, 1 da; *Career* Capt King's Own LI (despatches) WW II; *Style* - Bertram Aykroyd Esq; Treyford Manor, Midhurst, Sussex

AYKROYD, Sir Cecil William; 2 Bt (UK 1929), of Birstwith Hall, Hampsthwaite, Co York; s of Sir Frederic Alfred Aykroyd, 1 Bt (d 1949) and Lily, da of Sir James Roberts, 1 Bt; *b* 23 April 1905; *Educ* Charterhouse, Jesus Cambridge; *Heir* bro, Bertram Aykroyd; *Career* former dir Nat Provincial Bank; *Style* - Sir Cecil Aykroyd, Bt; Birstwith Hall, nr Harrogate, N Yorks (☎ Harrogate 770250)

AYKROYD, Michael David; s of late George Hammond Aykroyd, TD, s of Sir William Henry Aykroyd, 1 Bt; hp of cous, Sir William Aykroyd, 3 Bt, MC; *b* 14 June 1928; *m* 1952, Oenone Gillian Diana, da of Donald George Cowling, MBE, of Leeds; 1 s, 3 da; *Style* - Michael Aykroyd Esq; The Homestead, Killinghall, Harrogate, Yorks

AYKROYD, Sir William Miles; 3 Bt (UK 1920), of Lightcliffe, W Riding, Co of York, MC (1944); s of Sir Alfred Hammond Aykroyd, 2 Bt (d 1965); *b* 24 Aug 1923; *Career* Lt 5 Roy Inniskilling Dragoon Gds, former dir Hardy Amies; *Style* - Sir William Aykroyd, Bt, MC; Buckland Newton Place, Dorchester, Dorset (☎ Buckland Newton 259)

AYLESFORD, 11 Earl of (GB 1714); Charles Ian Finch-Knightley; JP (Warwicks 1948); also Baron Guernsey (GB 1702); s of 10 Earl of Aylesford (d 1958, seventh in descent from 1 Earl, who was 2 s of 1 Earl of Nottingham) by his w Aileen, nee Boyle; *b* 2 Nov 1918; *Educ* Oundle; *m* 1946, Margaret, da of Maj Austin Tyer, MVO, TD; 1 s, 2 da; *Heir* s, Lord Guernsey; *Career* Ld-Lt W Midlands 1974-; served WW II, Capt Black Watch; memb Water Space Amenity Commission 1973-; V-Lt Warwicks 1964-74; KStJ 1974; Patron Warwicks Boy Scouts Assoc 1974- Pres Warwicks CC 1980-; *Style* - The Rt Hon Earl of Aylesford JP; Diddington Hall, Coventry; Packington Hall, Coventry, W Midlands (☎ Meriden 22274)

AYLESTONE, Baron (Life Peer UK 1967); Herbert William Bowden; CH (1975), CBE (1953), PC (1962); s of Herbert Henwood Bowden, of Cardiff, by Henrietta, nee Gould; *b* 20 Jan 1905; *m* 1928, Louisa, nee Brown; 1 da; *Career* chm IBA 1967-75, MP (L) Leicester S 1945-50 (SW 1950-67), Ch Oppn Whip 1955-64, Sec of State for C'wlth Affairs 1966-67,

SDP Leader in House of Lords 1981-; *Style* - The Rt Hon The Lord Aylestone CH, CBE, PC; House of Lords, SW1

AYLMER, 12 Baron (I 1718); Sir Hugh Yates Aylmer; 15 Bt (I 1662); s of Arthur Aylmer by his 1 w Georgina, da of Lt-Col James Sweeney; Arthur was s of Henry Aylmer (gggs of 2 Baron Aylmer) and Henry's cous Hon Isabella Aylmer, da of 7 Baron Aylmer; suc kinsman (11 Baron) 1977; *b* 5 Feb 1907; *Educ* Minneapolis; *m* 1939, Althea, da of Lt-Col John Talbot; 1 da; *Heir* 2 cous, Michael Anthony Aylmer; *Career* late 2 Lt 5 BC Coast Bde Canadian Artillery; ret businessman; *Style* - The Rt Hon Lord Aylmer; 601-1159 Beach dve, Victoria BC, Canada

AYLMER, Sir Fenton Gerald; 15 Bt (I 1622), of Donadea, Co Kildare; s of Sir Gerald Arthur Evans-Freke Aylmer, 14 Bt (d 1939); *b* 12 March 1901; *m* 1928, Rosalind Boultbee, da of J Percival Bell, of Hamilton, Ontario; 1 s, 1 da; *Heir* s, Richard John Aylmer; *Style* - Sir Fenton Aylmer, Bt; 29 Church Hill, Westmount, Quebec H3Y 2Z8, Canada

AYLMER, Dr Gerald Edward; s of late Capt E Aylmer, RN; *b* 30 April 1926; *Educ* Winchester, Balliol; *m* 1955, Ursula Nixon; 1 s, 1 da; *Career* FBA, Master St Peter's Coll Oxford 1978-, historian; *Style* - Dr Gerald Aylmer; Canal House, St Peter's College, Oxford (☎ 48436, 40554)

AYLMER, Michael Anthony; s of Christopher Aylmer (whose mother Constance, nee Grenfell, was sis of 1 & last Baron Desborough); hp to 2 cous 12 Baron Aylmer; *b* 27 March 1923; *Educ* privately, Trin Hall Cambridge; *m* 1950, Contessa Maddalena, da of Count Arbeno Attems di Santa Croce (conceivably of the family formed by the union of 9 Count (Heinrich) von Attems (Countship of Holy Roman Empire cr 1603) with Countess Maria, da of 1 Count (Aloys) Ceschi a Santa Croce (Austrian cr of 1874) at Trento in 1896), of Aiello del Friuli, Italy, whose w was Sofie (da of Prince Maximilian zu Lowenstein-Wertheim-Freudenberg); 1 s (Julian b 10 Dec 1951, educ Westminster & Trin Hall Cambridge, slr 1976), 1 da (Gioia Francesca b 14 Sept 1953); *Career* slr 1948; *Style* - Michael Aylmer Esq; 42 Brampton Grove, NW4 (☎ 01 202 8300)

AYLMER, Richard John; s and h of Sir Fenton Aylmer, 15 Bt; *b* 23 April 1937; *m* 1962, Lise, da of Paul Demers, of Montreal; 1 s, 1 da; *Style* - Richard Aylmer Esq; 464 Argyle av, Westmount, Quebec H3Y 2B4, Canada

AYLWEN, Lady; Elena Ingraa; da of late Prof Alexander Bulgarides (s of late diplomat Constantine Bulgarides); *m* 1951, as his 2 w, Sir George Aylwen, 1 Bt (d 1967, when title became extinct); *Style* - Lady Aylwen; 39 Green st, W1

AYRE, Lady Margaret Isabel; *née* Lane; da of Charles Lane, CSI (gs of Lady Frances Erskine, sis of 27 Earl of Mar) and sis of 30 Earl of Mar; *b* 28 March 1921; *m* 1943, Maj John Bulley Bray Ayre, late RA; 1 s, 1 da; *Career* raised to rank of Earl's da 1967; *Style* - Lady Margaret Ayre; 1 Penhurst Park, Pointe Claire, PQ Canada

AZIKIWE, Rt Hon Nnamdi; PC (1960); Ndichie Chief Owelle of Onitsha 1973; s of Obededom Chukwuemeka and Rachel Chinwe Azikiwe; *b* 16 Nov 1904; *Educ* Lagos, Storer Coll Harpers Ferry USA, Howard U Washington DC, Lincoln U Pa, Pennsylvania U; *m* 1936, Flora Ogbenyeanu Ogoegbunam, da of Chief Ogoegbunam, the Adazia of Onitsha; 3 s, 1 da; *Career* Pres Fed Republic of Nigeria 1963-66, Gov-Gen and CIC Nigeria 1960-63; *Style* - The Rt Hon Nnamdi Azikiwe, PC; Onuiyi Haven, PO Box 7, Nsukka, Nigeria

B

BABER, Hon Mr Justice; Hon Ernest George; s of late Walter Averette Baber and Kate Marion, nee Pratt; *b* 18 July 1924; *Educ* Brentwood School, Emmanuel College Cambridge; *m* 1960, Dr Flora Marion, younger daughter of Dr Raymond Bisset Smith by his wife Jean Gemmell, nee Howie; 1 s, 2 da; *Career* served RN WW II and to 1947 as Lieutenant; Judge of Supreme Court Hong Kong 1973- (District Judge 1967-73), barr (Lincolns Inn) 1951, Resident Magistrate Uganda 1954-62; *Style* - The Hon Mr Justice Baber; Supreme Court, Hong Kong

BABINGTON, His Honour Judge; Anthony Patrick Babington; s of late Oscar Babington; *b* 4 April 1920; *Educ* Reading Sch; *Career* barr 1948, Circuit Judge 1972-; *Style* - His Hon Judge Babington; 3 Gledhow gdns, SW5 (☎ 01 373 4014); Thydon Cottage, Chilham, nr Canterbury, Kent (☎ 300)

BABINGTON SMITH, Michael James; CBE (1945), TD; s of Sir Henry Babington Smith, GBE, KCB, CH, and Lady Elisabeth, nee Bruce, da of 9 Earl of Elgin and 13 Earl of Kincardine, KG, GCSI, GCIE, PC (d 1917), and Lady Constance Carnegie (da of 9 Earl of Southesk, KT); *b* 20 March 1901; *Educ* Eton, Trin Cambridge; *m* 1943, Jean, da of late Adm Hon Sir Herbert Meade-Fetherstonhaugh, GCVO, CB, DSO (bro of 5 Earl of Clanwilliam); 1 s, 2 da; *Career* chm London Ctee Ottoman Bank 1975-, dir Bank of England 1949-69, Sheriff of London 1953 and 1962, dir Grindlays Bank, Grindlays Hldgs; *Recreations* sketching; *Clubs* Boodle's; *Style* - Michael Babington Smith Esq, CBE, TD,; Flat 6, 20 Embankment gdns, SW3 (☎ 01 352 2854)

BACCHUS, James; s of Cecil Bacchus, of Billericay; *b* 11 July 1941; *Educ* St Clement Danes London; *m* 1964, Marion, da of Thomas Victor Stratton (d 1970); 3 children; *Career* accountant, fin dir Jessups Hldgs and subsids 1973-; *Recreations* golf; *Clubs* Anglo-American Sporting; *Style* - James Bacchus Esq; 147 Western rd, Billericay, Essex

BACK, Frederick Charles Douglas; s of Herbert Back (d 1931); *b* 12 Feb 1919; *Educ* Queen's Oxford; *m* 1953, Bernadette, da of Michael Anthony (d 1965); 2 s; *Career* dir Glaxo Hldgs and various subsids including Glaxo Inc (USA) and Nippon Glaxo Japan (Jt Pres); *Recreations* music, reading; *Style* - Frederick Back Esq; Orrong, Oval Way, Gerrards Cross, Bucks

BACK, Kenneth John Campbell; s of J Back; *b* 13 Aug 1925; *Educ* Sydney H S, Sydney U; *m* 1950, Patricia, nee Cummings; 2 da; *Career* Vice-Chllr James Cook U of N Qld 1970-; *Style* - Kenneth Back Esq; 15 Yarrawonga dve, Townsville, Qld 4810, Australia

BACK, Patrick; QC (1970); s of late Ivor Back, FRCS; *b* 23 Aug 1917; *Educ* Marlborough, Trin Hall Cambridge; *Career* barr 1940, dep chm Devon QS 1968; *Style* - Patrick Back Esq, QC; Flat 3, Marquess House, 74 Marquess rd, N1 (☎ 01 226 0991)

BACKHOUSE, Jonathan; s of late Lt-Col M Backhouse, DSO, TD; *b* 16 March 1907; *Educ* RNC Dartmouth; *m* 1934, Alice Woodroffe; 2 s, 1 da; *Career* ret merchant banker; *Style* - Jonathan Backhouse Esq; Breewood Hall, Great Horkesley, Colchester, Essex (☎ 271260)

BACKHOUSE, Sir Jonathan Roger; 4 Bt (UK 1901), of Uplands, Darlington, Co Durham, and The Rookery, Middleton Tyas, North Riding of Yorkshire; s of Maj Sir John Backhouse, 3 Bt, MC (d 1944); *b* 30 Dec 1939; *Educ* Ampleforth, BNC Oxford; *Heir* bro, Oliver Backhouse; *Career* dir W H Freeman & Co Ltd, publishers; *Style* - Sir Jonathan Backhouse, Bt; c/o Lloyds Bank, 39 Piccadilly, W1

BACKHOUSE, Oliver Richard; s of late Maj Sir John Backhouse, 3 Bt, MC; hp of bro, Sir Jonathan Backhouse, 4 Bt; *b* 18

July 1941; *Educ* Ampleforth; *m* 1970, Gillian Irene, da of L W Lincoln, of Northwood, Middx; *Style* - Oliver Backhouse Esq; 34 Briarwood dve, Northwood Hill, Middx

BACON, Baroness (Life Peeress UK 1970); Alice Martha Bacon; CBE (1953), PC (1966), DL (W Yorks 1974); *Educ* Normanton Girls' H S, London U (external); *Career* schoolmistress, MP (L) NE Leeds (1945-55), SE Leeds (1955-70) Min of State DES 1967-70, chm Labour Party 1950-51; *Style* - The Rt Hon Lady Bacon, CBE, PC, DL; 53 Snydale rd, Normanton, W Yorks (☎ Wakefield 893229)

BACON, Sir Edmund Castell; 13 Bt (E 1611, of Redgrave) and 14 Bt (E 1627, of Mildenhall), KG (1970), KBE (1965, OBE 1945), TD, JP (Norfolk); Premier Baronet of England; s of Sir Nicholas Bacon, 12 and 13 Bt (d 1947), and Constance, CBE (d 1962), da of late A Leslie Melville; *b* 18 March 1903; *Educ* Eton, Trin Cambridge; *m* 1936, Priscilla, da of Col Sir Charles Ponsonby, 1 Bt, TD, and Hon Winifred Gibbs (da of 1 Baron Hunsdon); 1 s, 4 da; *Heir* s, Nicholas Bacon; *Career* HM Ld-Lt Norfolk 1949-78, chm Br Sugar Corpn 1956-68, dir Lloyds Bank 1949-73, High Steward Norwich Cathedral 1956-79, Gt Yarmouth 1968-; *Clubs* Carlton, Pratt's; *Style* - Sir Edmund Bacon, Bt, KG, KBE, TD, JP; Raveningham Hall, Norwich (☎ Raveningham 206)

BACON, Francis; *b* 1909 Dublin; *Career* artist, portraitist; *Style* - Francis Bacon Esq; c/o Marlborough Fine Art, 6 Albemarle st, W1

BACON, Nicholas Hickman Ponsonby; s and h of Sir Edmund Bacon, 13 and 14 Bt, KG, KBE, TD, JP, by his w Priscilla, da of Col Sir Charles Ponsonby, 1 Bt, TD, and Hon Winifred Gibbs (da of 1 Baron Hunsdon); *b* 17 May 1953; *Educ* Eton, Dundee U; *Career* Page of Honour to HM The Queen 1966-69; *Style* - Nicholas Bacon Esq; Raveningham Hall, Norwich (☎ Raveningham 206)

BACON, Sir Ranulph Robert Maunsell; KPM (1953); s of late Arthur Bacon; *b* 6 Aug 1906; *Educ* Tonbridge, Queens' Cambridge; *m* 1932, Alfreda, nee Annett; 1 da (decd); *Career* kt 1966; dir Securicor 1966-, Int Intelligence Inc USA 1970-, assist cmmr Met Police 1961-66; *Style* - Sir Ranulph Bacon, KPM; 3 Royal Court, 8 King's gdns, Hove, Sussex (☎ Brighton 732396)

BACON, Sir Sidney Charles; CB (1971); s of Charles Bacon; *b* 11 Feb 1919; *Educ* Woolwich Poly, London U; *Career* kt 1977, md Roy Ordnance Factories 1972-79; *Style* - Sir Sidney Bacon, CB; 228 Erith rd, Bexleyheath, Kent

BADDELEY, Sir John Wolsey Beresford; 4 Bt (UK 1922), of Lakefield, Parish of St Mary Stoke Newington, Co London; s of Sir John Beresford Baddeley, 3 Bt (d 1979); *b* 27 Jan 1938; *Educ* Bradfield; *m* 1962, Sara, nee Crofts; 3 da; *Heir* kinsman, Mark Baddeley; *Career* chartered accountant, fin dir Spillers Internat Ltd 1978-; *Recreations* tennis, squash, inland waterways; *Style* - Sir John Baddeley, Bt; 41 School Hill, Storrington, Sussex (☎ 09066 2423)

BADDELEY, Lady; Katharine Angela; MBE (1920); da of Maj-Gen Sir Reginald Thynne, KCB (d 1926, s of Rev Lord John Thynne, DD, s of 2 Marq of Bath, KG); *b* 20 April 1893; *m* 1933, Sir Vincent Wilberforce Baddeley, KCB (d 1961); *Career* in War Office 1914-19; *Style* - Lady Baddeley, MBE; 77 Melton Court, SW7 (☎ 01 589 0288)

BADDELEY, Mark David; s of late Mark Badeley (d 1930), gs of Sir John Baddeley, 1 Bt, and hp of kinsman Sir John Wolsey Baddeley, 4 Bt; *b* 1921; *Educ* Cliftonville Coll; *Style* - Mark Baddeley Esq; Woodberry, King George's av, Margate, Kent

BADDELEY, Nancy, Lady; Nancy Winifred; da of late Thomas Wolsey, of Smallburgh Hall Norfolk; *m* 1929, Sir John Baddeley, 3 Bt (d 1979); 1 s, 2 da; *Style* - Nancy, Lady Baddeley; Street Cottage, Bury, W Sussex

BADDILEY, Prof Sir James; s of late

James Baddiley and Ivy Cato; *b* 15 May 1918; *Educ* Manchester G S, Manchester U; *m* 1944, Hazel, da of Wesley Townsend and Ann, nee Kilner; 1 s; *Career* kt 1977, FRS, FRSE, Phd, DSc, prof of Chemical Microbiology 1977- and dir Microbiological Chem Res Lab Newcastle U 1975-; *Style* - Prof Sir James Baddiley; 26 Woolsington Pk, Woolsington, Newcastle on Tyne (☎ 860229)

BADEN-POWELL, 3 Baron (UK 1929); Sir Robert Crause Baden-Powell; 3 Bt (UK 1922); s of 2 Baron Baden-Powell (d 1962); *b* 15 Oct 1936; *Educ* Bryanston; *m* 1963, Patience, da of Maj Douglas Batty, of Rhodesia (now Zimbabwe); *Heir* bro, Hon David Baden-Powell; *Career* RN 1955-57, Ch Scouts Commissioner Scout Assoc; *Style* - The Rt Hon the Lord Baden-Powell; Chapel Farm, Ripley, Surrey (☎ 2262)

BADEN-POWELL, Carine, Baroness; Carine; da of late Clement Hamilton Crause Boardman, of Johannesburg; *m* 1936, 2 Baron Baden-Powell (d 1962); 2 s, 1 da; *Style* - The Rt Hon Carine, Lady Baden-Powell; Turnstones, Old Bursledon, nr Southampton, Hants

BADEN-POWELL, Hon David Michael; s of 2 Baron Baden-Powell (d 1962); hp of bro, 3 Baron Baden-Powell; *b* 11 Dec 1940; *Educ* Pierrepont House; *m* 1966, Joan, da of Horace Berryman, of Melbourne; 3 s; *Career* insurance consultant, agent with Australian Mutual Provident Soc 1972-, Freeman City of London, memb Worshipful Co of Mercers; *Style* - The Hon David Baden-Powell; 18 Kalang rd, Camberwell, Vict 3124, Australia (☎ 29 5009)

BADEN-POWELL, Hon Wendy Dorothy Lilian; da of 2 Baron Baden-Powell (d 1962); *b* 16 Sept 1944; *Educ* St Cyprian's Sch Cape Town, The Sorbonne; *Style* - The Hon Wendy Baden-Powell; Turnstones, Old Bursledon, Southampton, Hants

BADENI, Count (Austria 1845 by Emperor Ferdinand I); Jan; s of Count Stefan Badeni (d 1961, whose f Count Stanislaus was Head of the Autonomous State of Galicia while his bro Count Casimir was Premier of Austria-Hungary under Franz Josef around the turn of the nineteenth and twentieth centuries); Count Badeni became head of the family on the death of his unc and would be a hereditary member of the Upper House of Austria were such an institution still to exist; *b* 15 Feb 1921; *Educ* privately; *m* 1956, June (author, notably of a biography of Alice Meynell published 1981, and local historian of Wilts), da of Maj Noel Wilson, JP, of Norton Manor, Malmesbury; 1 s (Count Michael Stefan Noel), 1 da (Countess Mary Sophie Teresa Matilda); *Heir* s, Count Michael Badeni; *Career* High Sheriff Wilts 1978-79, Kt of Honour & Devotion (Polish Assoc) Sov Mil Order Malta; served WW II Sqdn Ldr RAF, M East, Coastal Cmmd, also Malayan Emergency 1954-57; Queen's Commendation for valuable servs in the air 1962; *Recreations* reading, social & charitable activities; *Style* - Count Badeni; Norton Manor, Malmesbury, Wilts (☎ 066 63 253)

BADER, Gp Capt Sir Douglas Robert Steuart; CBE (1956), DSO (1940), DFC (1940), DL (Gter London 1977); s of Frederick Bader; *b* 21 Feb 1910; *Educ* St Edward's Sch Oxford, RAF Coll Cranwell; *m* 1, 1933, Olive Edwards (d 1971); m 2, 1973, Mrs Joan Murray; *Career* kt 1976, FRAeS, fighter pilot in WW II, md Shell Aircraft Ltd 1958-69, led first post war Battle of Britain fly-past 15 Sept 1945; *Style* - Gp Capt Sir Douglas Bader, CBE, DSO, DFC, DL; 5 Petersham Mews, Gloucester rd, SW7 (☎ 01 584 0902)

BADGER, Sir Geoffrey Malcolm; AO (1975); s of J Badger; *b* 10 Oct 1916; *Educ* Geelong Coll, Gordon Inst of Technology, Melbourne U, London U, Glasgow U; *m* 1941, Edith, nee Chevis; *Career* kt 1979, PhD, DSc, FRIC, FRACI, FACE, FAIM, FTS, FAA, Res Prof Adelaide U 1977-, Vice-Chllr 1967-77, Pres Australian Acad of Sci 1974-78, chm Australian Sci and Technology Cncl 1977-, former res chemist; *Style* - Sir Geoffrey Badger, AO; 240 Childers st, N Adelaide, SA 5006, Australia (☎ 08 267 3029)

BADHAM, Douglas George; CBE (1975), JP (Glam 1962), DL (Mid Glam 1975); s of late David Badham, JP; *b* 1 Dec 1914; *Educ* Leys Sch Cambridge; *m* 1939, Doreen Spencer Phillips; 2 da; *Career* chm Dvpt Corp for Wales 1971-, memb Wales and Marches Telecommunications Bd 1973-, Br Gas Corpn 1974-, Welsh Cncl 1971-, Welsh Dvpt Agency 1978-, High Sheriff Mid Glam 1976, co dir; *Style* - Douglas Badham Esq, CBE, JP, DL; Plas Watford, Caerphilly, Mid Glam (☎ 882094)

BADHAM, Leonard; s of John Badham; *b* 10 June 1923; *Educ* Wandsworth G S; *m* 1944, Joyce Lowrie; 2 da; *Career* md J Lyons & Co 1977-, dir Allied Breweries 1978-, FIAM, FHCIMA, FBIM; *Style* - Leonard Badham Esq; 26 Vicarage dve, E Sheen, SW14 (☎ 01 876 4373)

BAER, Jack Mervyn Frank; s of late Frank Baer; *b* 29 Aug 1924; *Educ* Bryanston, Slade Sch of Fine Art, UCL; *m* 1, 1952, Jean St Clair (m dis 1969, she d 1973); 1 da; m 2, 1970, Diana Downes Baillieu, da of Aubrey Clare Robinson and Mollie Panter-Downes; 2 step da; *Career* chm Hazlitt Gallery 1960-, md Hazlitt Gooden & Fox 1973-, chm Soc of London Art Dealers 1977-; *Clubs* Brooks's, Buck's, Beefsteak; *Style* - Jack Baer Esq; 9 Phillimore ter, W8 (☎ 01 937 6899)

BAGGE, Sir John Alfred Picton; 6 Bt (UK 1867), ED (1946), DL (Norfolk 1978); s of Sir Picton Bagge, 5 Bt, CMG (d 1967), and Muriel, da of late Samuel Mendel; *b* 27 Oct 1914; *Educ* Eton and abroad; *m* 1939, Elizabeth, da of late Daniel Davies, CBE, Commissioner for Newfoundland; 3 s, 3 da; *Heir* s, Jeremy Bagge; *Career* landowner and farmer, High Sheriff Norfolk 1977, v-chm and chm W Norfolk DC 1974-77, KStJ 1975; *Recreations* shooting; *Style* - Sir John Bagge, Bt, ED, DL; Stradsett Hall, King's Lynn, Norfolk (☎ Fincham 215)

BAGGE, (John) Jeremy Picton; s and h of Sir John Bagge, 6 Bt, ED, DL; *b* 21 June 1945; *Educ* Eton; *m* 1979, Sarah, da of late Maj James Armstrong, Agent-Gen for Ontario; 1 s; *Career* FCA; *Style* - Jeremy Bagge Esq

BAGIER, Gordon Alexander Thomas; MP (L) Sunderland S 1964-; *b* July 1924; *Educ* Pendower Secdy Tech Sch Newcastle; *m* 1949, Violet Sinclair; 2 s, 2 da; *Career* PPS to Home Sec 1968-69; *Style* - Gordon Bagier Esq, MP; Rahana, Whickham Highway, Dunston, Gateshead, Co Durham

BAGNALL, Frank Colin; CBE (1950); s of late Francis Bagnall, OBE; *b* 6 Nov 1909; *Educ* Repton, BNC Oxford; *m* 1, 1933, Ethel, nee Robertson (k 1941); m 2, 1941, Rona, nee Rooker Roberts (m dis 1975); 1 s, 1 da; m 3, 1975, Christine, nee Gerrard; *Career* commercial dir ICI 1965-70 (fin dir 1967-68), non-exec dir ICI 1964, OStJ; *Style* - Frank Bagnall Esq, CBE; Vermont, Budleigh Salterton, Devon (☎ 3068)

BAGNALL, Kenneth Reginald; QC (1973); s of Reginald Bagnall; *b* 26 Nov 1927; *Educ* King Edward VI Sch Birmingham, Birmingham U; *m* 1, 1955, Margaret Wall; 1 s, 1 da; m 2, 1963, Rosemary Hearn; 1 s, 1 da; *Career* Dep Judge Crown Court 1975-, barr 1950, chm Hurstwood Timber Co 1972-; *Style* - Kenneth Bagnall Esq, QC; 11 King's Bench Walk, Temple, EC4 (☎ 01 353 2484)

BAGNALL, Lt-Gen Sir Nigel Thomas; KCB (1980), CVO (1978), MC (1950) and Bar (1953); s of Lt-Col Harry Bagnall; *b* 10 Feb 1927; *Educ* Wellington; *m* 1959, Anna Church; 2 da; *Career* Col Cmmdt Army Physical T'ning Corps 1981-, Assist Ch Def Staff (Policy) MOD 1978-, Cdr 1 Br Corps 1980-; *Style* - Lt-Gen Sir Nigel Bagnall, KCB, CVO, MC*; Blackwell Lodge, Chesham, Bucks

BAGNALL, Richard Maurice; MBE (1945); s of late Francis Bagnall, OBE; *b* 20 Nov 1917; *Educ* Repton; *m* 1946, Irene Pickford; 1 s, 1 da; *Career* dep chm Tube Investments 1976-, chm Round Oak Steel Works Ltd 1976-; *Style* - Richard Bagnall Esq, MBE; Oak House Farm, Himbleton, Droitwich, Worcs

BAGOT, 9 Baron (GB 1780); Sir Heneage Charles Bagot; 14 Bt (E 1627); s of late Charles Frederick Heneage Bagot, ggs of 1 Baron; suc half-bro 1979; *b* 11 June 1914; *Educ* Harrow; *m* 1939, Muriel Patricia, da of late Maxwell James Moore Boyle; 1 s, 1 da; *Heir* s, Hon Charles Bagot; *Career* late Maj Indian Army; *Style* - The Rt Hon The Lord Bagot; Hillcott House, Bitterley, Ludlow, Shropshire

BAGOT, Charles Henry; s of Oliver Robin Bagot, JP, DL (s of Henry Melville Gaskell, JP, (Oliver assumed name Bagot *vice* Gaskell 1936) by Dorothy, da of Lt-Col Josceline Bagot, who was nominated a Bt 1913 but d before the patent passed the Great Seal; the Col's s Alan was cr a Bt, but the title died with him; the Col was gs of Rt Hon Sir Charles Bagot, GCB, PC, MP, 2 s of 1 Baron Bagot and sometime Under Sec State For Affairs, Ambass to St Petersburg, The Hague & Vienna and Gov-Gen Canada); *b* 16 Feb 1946; *Educ* Eton, RAC Cirencester; *m* 1975, Susan, da of Ian Alexander Ross, of Ards Cottage, Gullane, E Lothian; 2 children; *Career* FRICS 1980; High Sheriff Cumbria 1980; hp to Levens Hall, one of the most celebrated houses in the North of England, its famous topiary vying with its Elizabethan architecture, interior plaster work, panelling and furniture; *Recreations* fishing, horology; *Clubs* Brooks's; *Style* - Charles Bagot Esq; Levens Hall, Kendal, Cumbria (☎ 0448 60321)

BAGOT, Hon Charles Hugh Shaun; s and h of 9 Baron Bagot; *b* 23 Feb 1944; *Educ* Abbotsholme; *Style* - The Hon Charles Bagot; 3 Callow st, SW3

BAGSHAWE, Francis Ernest Gisborne; s of Ernest Bagshawe, of Ford Hall, Chapel-en-le-Frith, Derbys (d 1936); *b* 19 Sept 1893; *Educ* Harrow, Hertford Coll Oxford; *m* 1922, Albinia Marian Dolben, da of Capt Gilbert Dolben Paul, of Theale Berks (d 1938); 2 s (and 1 s decd); *Career* md Bagshawe Estate Co 1947-76; *Style* - Francis Bagshawe Esq; Snitterton Hall, Matlock, Derbys (☎ 3840)

BAILEY, Sir Donald Coleman; OBE (1944), JP (Bournemouth 1946); s of J Bailey; *b* 15 Sept 1901; *Educ* The Leys Cambridge, Sheffield U; *m* Phyllis, nee Andrew (d 1971); 1 s; *Career* kt 1946, engineer ret; *Style* - Sir Donald Bailey, OBE, JP; 14 Viking Close, Southbourne, Bournemouth (☎ 49181)

BAILEY, Lady Daphne Magdalene; *née* Cadogan; da of 7 Earl Cadogan by his 1 w Primrose; *b* 23 Oct 1939; *m* 1961, David, s of Ronald Bailey; 2 s, 1 da; *Style* - Lady Daphne Bailey; The Manor House, Dry Sandford, Abingdon, Oxford (☎ Frilford Heath 390 834)

BAILEY, His Honour Desmond Patrick; s of Alfred Bailey; *b* 6 May 1907; *Educ* Brighton Coll, Queens' Cambridge, *Career* barr 1931, Circuit Judge 1965-79; *Style* - His Hon Desmond Bailey; Chaseley, Bowdon, Cheshire (☎ 061 928 0059)

BAILEY, David Royston; s of William Bailey; *b* 2 Jan 1938; *m* 1, 1960, Rosemary Bramble; m 2, 1967, Catherine Deneuve; m 3, 1975, Marie Helvin; *Career* photographer, proprietor and co-editor Ritz newspaper 1976-; *Style* - David Bailey Esq; 177 Gloucester av, NW1 (☎ 01 722 6615/4221)

BAILEY, Sir Derrick Thomas Louis; 3 Bt (UK 1919), of Cradock, Province of Cape of Good Hope, Union of South Africa, DFC; s of late Sir Abe Bailey, 1 Bt, KCMG; suc half-bro, Sir John Milner Bailey, 2 Bt (d 1946); *b* 15 Aug 1918; *Educ* Winchester, Ch Ch Oxford; *m* 1, 1946, Katharine Nancy, da of Robert Stormonth Darling, of Kelso, Scotland; 4 s, 1 da; m 2, 1980, Mrs Jean Roscoe; *Heir* s, John Richard Bailey; *Career* Capt S African Air Force, formerly 2 Lt S African Irish; farmer; *Style* - Sir Derrick Bailey, Bt, DFC; De Poort, Colesberg, Cape, S Africa; Bluestones, Alderney, CI

BAILEY, Harry; s of Joseph Bailey, of Doncaster (d 1955); *b* 28 March 1928; *Educ* Thorne G S Yorks, Rotterdam Coll of Technol Yorks; *m* 1961, Sheila, nee Dance; 3 s; *Career* md Matthew Hall Engineering (S E Asia) Pty Ltd 1980-, dir Matthew Hall Engrg London 1974-, Matthew Hall Engrg Internat 1977-; *Recreations* swimming, reading, music; *Clubs* Les Ambassadeurs, Tanglin (Singapore); *Style* - Harry Bailey Esq; 13

Nonsuch Walk, Cheam, Surrey (☎ 01 393 5454); 1704 Lucky Tower, 57 Grange rd, Singapore 1204 (☎ 7376186)

BAILEY, Sir Harold Walter; *b* 16 Dec 1899; *Career* Prof of Sanskrit Cambridge 1936-67, kt 1960, FBA, DPhil, Prof Emeritus 1967; *Style* - Sir Harold Bailey; Queens' Coll, Cambridge

BAILEY, Jack Arthur; s of Horace Bailey; *b* 22 June 1930; *Educ* Christ's Hosp, Univ Oxford; *m* 1957, Julianne Squier; 1 s, 2 da; *Career* sec MCC 1974-, sec Int Cricket Conf 1974-; *Style* - Jack Bailey Esq; 20 Elm Tree rd, NW8 (☎ 01 228 6246)

BAILEY, John Richard; s (by 1 m) and h of Sir Derrick Bailey, Bt, DFC; *b* 11 June 1947; *Educ* Winchester, Christ's Cambridge; *m* 1977, Philippa Jane, da of John Sherwin Mervyn Pearson Gregory, of Monnington-on-Wye, Herefords; *Style* - John Bailey Esq

BAILEY, Keith Anthony; s of William Bailey, of Masons Court, Solihull; *b* 2 Dec 1934; *Educ* Saltley G S, Aston U; *m* 1957, Sylvia, da of William Garland, of Sutton Coldfield; 1 s, 1 da; *Career* md White-BSA Tools Ltd 1980-, dir Alfred Herbert 1976-80 (md Birmingham Plant); *Recreations* yachting (yacht called 'Silent Tide'); *Style* - Keith Bailey Esq; 82 Heathcroft rd, Four Oaks, Sutton Coldfield, W Midlands (☎ 021 308 2497)

BAILEY, Keith Cyril Austin; s of James Bailey (d 1944) of Swansea; *b* 8 July 1919; *Educ* Wycliffe Coll; *m* 1948, Joan, da of Capt John Thomas (d 1979), of Southampton; 1 s; *Career* chm Bailey Carpets, Bailey Carpets Int, Redlands Flooring Distributors (Bristol); dir Mandina Properties, local dir Bristol & West Bldg Soc, High Sheriff W Glam 1979-80, memb IOD Cncl for Wales; *Recreations* walking, countryside; *Clubs* Bristol Channel Yacht, City and County (Swansea); *Style* - Keith Bailey Esq; Ailsa Craig, Caswell Bay, Swansea, W Glam (☎ 0792 66836)

BAILEY, Oswald Nigel; OBE (1953); s of Lt-Col Frederick George Glyn Bailey; *b* 19 June 1913; *Educ* RNCs Dartmouth and Greenwich; *Career* Cdre RN to 1963, dir Inchcape & Co 1963-68, farmer 1970-; *Recreations* fishing, shooting; *Clubs* White's, Roy Yacht Sqdn, Pratt's; *Style* - Oswald Bailey Esq, OBE; Lake House, Lake, Salisbury, Wilts (☎ 0980 22138 and 22752)

BAILEY, Ronald William; CMG (1961); s of William Bailey, of Southampton (d 1956); *b* 14 June 1917; *Educ* King Edward VI Sch Southampton, Trin Hall Cambridge; *m* 1946, Joan Hassall, da of Albert Gray, JP (d 1959); 1 s, 1 da; *Career* UK Ambass to Bolivia 1967-71, Morocco 1971-75; *Recreations* gardening; *Clubs* Oriental; *Style* - Ronald Bailey Esq, CMG; Redwood, Tennyson's Lane, Haslemere, Surrey (☎ 2800)

BAILEY, Stanley Ernest; QPM (1975); *b* 30 Sept 1926; *m* 1954, Marguerita Whitbread; *Career* Ch Constable Northumbria 1975-, SBStJ 1969; *Style* - Stanley Bailey Esq, QPM; Police HQ, Morpeth rd, Ashington, Northumberland (☎ 814511)

BAILIE, Rt Hon Robin John; PC (NI 1971); *b* 6 March 1937; *Educ* Queen's U Belfast; *m* 1961, Margaret, nee Boggs; 1 s, 3 da; *Career* slr Supreme Court of Judicature NI 1961-, MP (NI) Newtownabbey 1969-72, Min of Commerce NI 1971-72; *Style* - The Rt Hon Robin Bailie, PC; 39a Malone Pk, Belfast (☎ 668085)

BAILLIE, Adrian Louis; s and h of Sir Gawaine Baillie, 7 Bt; *b* 26 March 1973; *Style* - Adrian Baillie Esq

BAILLIE, Hon Evan Michael Ronald; s and h of 3 Baron Burton by his 1 w Elizabeth; *b* 19 March 1949; *Educ* Harrow; *m* 1970, Lucinda, da of Robin Law, of Haverhill; 2 s, 1 da; *Clubs* Brooks's; *Style* - The Hon Evan Baillie; Greenhill House, Redcastle, Muir of Ord, Ross-shire (☎ 420)

BAILLIE, Hon Fiona Mary; da of 3 Baron Burton by 1 w Elizabeth; *b* 31 Oct 1957; *Educ* West Heath Sevenoaks; *Recreations* riding, stalking; *Style* - The

Hon Fiona Baillie; Dochfour, Inverness (☎ 046 386 252)

BAILLIE, Hon Georgina Frances; da of 3 Baron Burton by 1 w Elizabeth; *b* 11 May 1955; *Educ* West Heath Sevenoaks; *Recreations* fishing; *Style* - The Hon Georgina Baillie; 5 Coltbridge av, Murrayfield, Edinburgh (☎ 031 346 1546)

BAILLIE, Sir Gawaine George Hope; 7 Bt (UK 1923); s of Sir Adrian Baillie, 6 Bt (d 1947), and Hon Olive, nee Paget, da of 1 and last Baron Queenborough, GBE, JP (gs of 1 Marq of Anglesey); *b* 8 March 1934; *Educ* Eton, Cambridge; *m* 1966, Lucile Margot, da of Hon Louis Beaubien (Senator) of Ottawa; 1 s, 1 da; *Heir* s, Adrian Baillie; *Career* co dir; *Recreations* golf, tennis, skiing; *Clubs* St George's Golf, Berkshire Golf; *Style* - Sir Gawaine Baillie, Bt; Freechase, Warninglid, Sussex (☎ 296)

BAILLIE, Dame Isobel; DBE (1978, CBE 1951); *Educ* Dover St H S for Girls Manchester; *m* 1918, H Wrigley; 1 da; *Career* singer; *Style* - Dame Isobel Baillie, DBE; 524 Stretford rd, Manchester (☎ 061 872 1731)

BAILLIE, Maj Hon Peter Charles; JP (Hants 1968); s of Brig Hon George Baillie, MC, TD (d 1941), of Ballindarroch, Scaniport, Inverness; bro of 3 Baron Burton; *b* 26 June 1927; *Educ* Eton; *m* 1955, Jennifer, da of Harold Newgass, GC, of Winterbourn Dorset; 4 da; *Career* late Maj Life Gds; raised to rank of Baron's s 1964; *Recreations* deer, shooting; *Style* - Maj The Hon Peter Baillie, JP; Wootton Hall, New Milton, Hants (☎ 0425 613722)

BAILLIE, Hon Philippa Ursula Maud; da of 3 Baron Burton by 1 w Elizabeth; *b* 30 Aug 1951; *Educ* West Heath Sevenoaks; *Recreations* riding; *Style* - The Hon Philippa Baillie; 9 Foxmore st, SW11 (☎ 01 223 5277)

BAILLIEU, 3 Baron (UK 1953); James William Latham Baillieu; s of 2 Baron Baillieu (d 1973); *b* 16 Nov 1950; *Educ* Radley, Monash U Melbourne; *m* 1974, Cornelia, da of W Ladd; 1 s; *Heir* s, Hon Robert Baillieu; *Career* 2 Lt Coldstream Gds 1970-73; *Clubs* Boodle's; *Style* - The Rt Hon The Lord Baillieu; c/o Mutual Trust Pty Ltd, 360 Collins st, Melbourne, Vict 3000 (☎ Australia)

BAILLIEU, Delia, Baroness; Delia Muriel; *m* 1, Champion; m 2, 1962, as his 2 w, 2 Baron Baillieu (d 1973); *Style* - The Rt Hon Delia, Lady Baillieu

BAILLIEU, Hon Edward Latham; s of 1 Baron Baillieu, KBE, CMG (d 1967); *b* 17 Oct 1919; *Educ* Winchester, BNC Oxford; *m* 1942, Betty, nee Taylor; 2 s, 1 da; *Career* stockbroker, jr ptnr Hoare Govett, dir NMLA London Bd, Wogen Resources, RTZ 1967-77, ANZ Bank 1967-80; *Recreations* shooting, golf; *Clubs* Boodle's, Leander, Melbourne, MCC; *Style* - The Hon Edward Baillieu; Tangle Copse, West Drive, Sunningdale, Berks (☎ Wentworth 2301)

BAILLIEU, Hon Robert Latham; s and h of 3 Baron Baillieu; *b* 2 Feb 1979; *Style* - The Hon Robert Baillieu

BAILWARD, Hon Mrs; Hon Diana Penelope Florence; *née* Sclater-Booth; da of 3 Baron Basing, TD; *b* 29 Jan 1925; *Educ* Downham Bishops Stortford; *m* 1946, James Tennant, s of Cdr Maurice Bailward, RN (ret); 1 s, 1 da; *Career* served WW II FANY Lance-Corpl; *Recreations* music (principally singing); *Style* - The Hon Mrs Bailward; Causeway House, Radipole, Weymouth, Dorset (☎ 783916)

BAINBRIDGE, Beryl; da of Richard Bainbridge; *b* 21 Nov 1934; *Educ* Merchant Taylors' Sch Liverpool, Arts Educational Schs Tring; *m* 1954, Austin Davies (m dis); 1 s, 2 da; *Career* actress, writer, FRSL; *Books* The Bottle Factory Outing 1974 (Guardian Fiction Award), Injury Time 1977 (Whitbread Award) *Style* - Miss Beryl Bainbridge; 42 Albert st, NW1 (☎ 01 387 3113)

BAINES, Leslie Henry; OBE (1974); s of Henry Eaton Baines (d 1965); *b* 23 Sept 1909; *Educ* Bedford Sch, BNC Oxford; *m* 1943, Irvina, da of Rev Frank Kent (d 1969); 1 s, 1 da (and 1 s decd); *Career* slr 1934, Clerk of the Peace & CC IOW 1946-

74, chm Health Educn Cncl 1979; *Recreations* sailing, swimming; *Style* - Leslie Baines Esq, OBE; Downside, Collyer's Rise, Fontmell Magna, Dorset (☎ 0747 811803)

BAINS, Lawrence Arthur; DL (Gter London 1978); s of late Arthur Bains; *b* 11 May 1920; *Educ* Stationers' Co's Sch; *m* 1954, Margaret, da of Sir William Grimshaw; 2 s, 1 da; *Career* chm GLC 1977-78, dir Bains Bros Ltd, Crowland Leasings, Tower Plywood & Boards, D R S Beers Ltd, memb Lloyd's, FCII; *Style* - Lawrence Bains Esq, DL; Crowland Lodge, 100 Galley Lane, Arkley, Barnet, EN5 4AL (☎ 01 440 3499)

BAINS, Malcolm Arnold; DL (Kent 1976); s of Herbert Bains; *b* 12 Sept 1921; *Educ* Hymers Coll, Durham U; *m* 1, 1942, Winifred Davies (m dis 1961); 3 s; m 2, 1968, Margaret Hunter; *Career* Clerk of Kent CC and Clerk to Lieutenancy of Kent 1970-74, FRSA 1976; *Style* - Malcolm Bains Esq, DL; 55 Mill st, Harbury, Leamington Spa, Warwicks

BAINTON, Richard Leslie; s of Richard Bainton (d 1970); *b* 4 March 1923; *Educ* Ch Ch Cathedral G S; *m* 1954, Ruth; 1 s, 3 da; *Career* md Portland Gp of Cos 1977- (exec dir 1969-); *Recreations* golf, youth and church work; *Clubs* Badgemore Golf; *Style* - Richard Bainton Esq; Apnagar, 139 Wilderness rd, Earley, Berks (☎ Reading 83156 (home), 84671 (work))

BAIRAMIAN, Sir Váhe Robert; s of Dr Bairamian, of Cyprus; *b* 30 Nov 1900; *Educ* English Sch Nicosia, UCL; *m* 1934, Eileen Connelly; 1 s; *Career* barr 1923, Justice Supreme Court Nigeria, kt 1959; *Style* - Sir Váhe Bairamian; 36 The Crescent, Sandgate, Folkestone, Kent (☎ 38240)

BAIRD, Hon Alexander David; s of 12 Earl of Kintore; *b* 1946; *Style* - The Hon Alexander Baird

BAIRD, Sir Dugald; s of David Baird; *b* 16 Nov 1899; *Educ* Greenock Acad, Glasgow U, Strasbourg U; *m* 1928, May Tennent; 2 s, 2 da; *Career* kt 1959, MD, FRCOG, BSc, DPH, Regius Prof of Midwifery Aberdeen U 1937-65; *Style* - Sir Dugald Baird; 21 Russell Place, Edinburgh

BAIRD, James Andrew Gardiner; s and h of Sir James Baird, 10 Bt, MC; *b* 2 May 1946; *Educ* Eton; *Style* - James Baird Esq

BAIRD, Lt-Gen Sir James Parlane; KBE (1973); s of Rev David Baird; *b* 12 May 1915; *Educ* Bathgate Acad, Edinburgh U; *m* 1948, Anne Anderson; 1 s, 1 da; *Career* MD, FRCP, FRCPEd, Med Adviser Nat Advice Center for Postgrad Educn 1977-, Dir Gen AMS 1973-77, QHP 1969; *Style* - Lt-Gen Sir James Baird, KBE; 30 Stonehills Court, College rd, Dulwich, SE21 (☎ 01 693 2735)

BAIRD, Sir James Richard Gardiner; 10 Bt (NS 1695), MC; s of late Capt William Frank Gardiner Baird, 2 s of 8 Bt; suc unc, Maj Sir James Hozier Gardiner Baird, 9 Bt, MC, 1966; *b* 12 July 1913; *Educ* Eton, Univ Coll Oxford; *m* 1941, Mabel Ann Tempest, da of Algernon Gill, of Toronto; 2 s, 1 da; *Heir* s, James Andrew Gardiner Baird; *Career* formerly Capt Kent Yeo; *Style* - Sir James Baird, Bt, MC; 11 St Mary Abbots ct, W14 (☎ 01 603 7356)

BAIRD, Lady; May Deans; CBE (1962); da of Matthew Tennent; *b* 14 May 1901; *Educ* Glasgow H S for Girls, Glasgow U; *m* 1928, Sir Dugald Baird; 2 s, 2 da; *Career* Nat Gov BBC in Scotland 1966-70, MB, ChB; *Style* - Lady Baird, CBE; 21 Russell Place, Edinburgh

BAIRD, Vice-Adm Sir Thomas Henry Eustace; KCB (1980); s of Geoffrey; *b* 17 May 1924; *Educ* RNC Dartmouth; *m* 1953, Angela Paul; 1 s, 1 da; *Career* Flag Offr Scotland and NI 1979-; *Style* - Vice-Adm Sir Thomas Baird, KCB; Admiralty House, N Queensferry, Fife; Craigrethill, Symington, Ayrshire (☎ 830339)

BAIRD, William Stanley; TD; s of Brig-Gen Edward Baird, CBE (d 1956), of Duns Berwicks, and Forse, Caithness; *b* 19 Aug 1903; *Educ* Eton, Edinburgh Acad, Ch Ch Oxford; *m* 1, 1944, Johanna Elizabeth (m dis 1964), da of Barthold,

Jonkheer Mackay, of The Hague; m 2, 1968, Sigrid Wootton, da of John Jacob Egeland, of Durban; *Career* served with Roy Hussars (Bt Col 1951), memb Roy Co of Archers (Queen's Bodyguard in Scotland), DL Caithness 1946-68; *Clubs* New (Edinburgh); *Style* - William Baird Esq, TD; 11 Nuttall gdns, Durban, S Africa (☎ 337357)

BAIRSTO, Air Marshal Sir Peter Edward; KBE (1981, CBE 1973), AFC (1957); s of late Arthur Bairsto; *b* 3 Aug 1926; *Educ* Rhyl G S; *m* 1947, Kathleen, nee Clarbour; 2 s, 1 da; *Career* Dep CIC Strike Cmmd, Dep CIC UKAF, Air Marshal 1981-; *Recreations* gardening, shooting, fishing, controversy; *Clubs* RAF, New (Edinburgh); *Style* - Air Marshal Sir Peter Bairsto, KBE AFC; Bendameer House, Burntisland, Fife (☎ 873266)

BAKER, Baron (Life Peer UK 1977); John Fleetwood Baker; OBE (1941); s of J Baker; *b* 19 March 1901; *Educ* Rossall, Clare Cambridge; *m* 1928, Fiona MacAlister (d 1979); 2 da; *Career* kt 1961, FRS, dir R & D IDC Gp, dep chm IDC Consultants Ltd, dir IDC Project Management Consultants Ltd, Prof of Engineering Cambridge 1943-68 (Emeritus 1968); *Clubs* Athenaeum; *Style* - The Rt Hon The Lord Baker, OBE; 100 Long rd, Cambridge (☎ 840152)

BAKER, Andrew Joseph; s of Joseph Baker, FCA (d 1980); *b* 4 Aug 1943; *Educ* Greenmore Coll; *m* 1971, Hilary, da of John Jones, of Coventry; 2 da; *Career* dir Williams & Farmer Hldgs, timber importer and merchant; *Recreations* golf; *Style* - Andrew Baker Esq; Woodreeves, Chartwell Close, Hempsted, Gloucester

BAKER, Colin Lewis Gilbert; CBE (1974); *b* 24 Aug 1913; *Educ* Queen's Coll Taunton; *m* 1942, Pauleen Hartley; 2 s, 2 da; *Career* FCA, memb Cos Consultative Gp (DOT) 1972-, chm N regional bd Lloyds Bank 1979-, dir Lloyds Bank UK Management, chm Jobling Purser, commissaris Bos Kalis Westminster Gp NV, Gen Cmmr Income Tax 1965-; *Style* - Colin Baker Esq, CBE; Lynton, Apperley rd, Stocksfield, Northumberland (☎ 3454)

BAKER, Christopher Paul; s of Roland Baker, of Clifton (d 1949); *b* 31 Oct 1925; *Educ* Marlborough; *m* 1956, Jane, da of Maj-Gen Sir Charles Dunphie, CB, CBE, DSO, of Wincanton; 2 s, 1 da; *Career* Insurance broker, dir Glanvill Enthoven & Co and various subsids, dir Mid-Southern Water Co; *Recreations* gardening, steam trains; *Style* - Christopher Baker Esq; Broad Oak House, Odiham, Hants (☎ 025 671 2482)

BAKER, His Honour Judge Geoffrey; QC (1970); s of late Sidney Baker; *b* 5 April 1925; *Educ* Bradford G S, Leeds U; *m* 1948, Sheila, nee Hill; 2 s, 1 da; *Career* barr 1947, Circuit Judge 1978-; *Style* - His Honour Judge Geoffrey Baker, QC; 246 Lidgett Lane, Leeds (☎ 685181)

BAKER, Rt Hon Sir George Gillespie; OBE (1945), PC (1971); s of late Capt John Baker; *b* 25 April 1910; *Educ* Glasgow Acad, Strathallan Sch Perthshire, BNC Oxford; *m* 1935, Jessie McCall Findlay; 3 s; *Career* kt 1961, Pres Family Div High Court of Justice 1971-79, barr 1932, contested (C) Southall 1945, QC 1952; *Style* - The Rt Hon Sir George Baker, OBE, PC; Camrie, Overstream, Loudwater, Rickmansworth, Herts (☎ 77296)

BAKER, George William; CBE (1977, OBE 171), VRD (1952, Clasp 1979); s of the late George William Baker; *b* 7 July 1917; *Educ* Chigwell Sch, Hertford Coll Oxford; *m* 1942, Audrey Martha Elizabeth, nee Day; 2 da; *Career* Lt Cdr RNR, British High Commissioner to Papua New Guinea 1974-77, London Division RNVR 1937-62, War Service RN 1939-45, Colonial Admin Service Tanganyika 1946-62, assistant Colonial Attaché Washington 1957, Defence Secretary Tanganyika 1959, head of Tanganyika Government Information Dept 1959-62, First Secretary and Director of British Information Services, British High Commission Freetown 1962-65, served in FCO 1965-69, First Secretary and head of Chancery, British Embassy Kinshasa 1969-72, dep British Government Representative St Vincent and Grenada 1972-74, A Vice-Pres. Royal African Society 1970-; *Recreations* photography, cabinet making, fishing, sailing, cricket, flying, Rugby Union, tennis; *Clubs* MCC, SES; *Style* - George Baker Esq, CBE, VRD; Siggswood, Waldron, nr Heathfield, Sussex (☎ 043 52 2847)

BAKER, Sir (Allan) Ivor; CBE (1944), JP (Cambridgeshire 1954), DL (Cambridgeshire 1973); s of late Allan Baker; *b* 2 June 1908; *Educ* Bootham York, King's Cambridge, Harvard; *m* 1935, Josephine, da of late A Harley, KC; 3 s, 1 da; *Career* kt 1972, chm Baker Perkins Hldgs 1944-75, dir Mitchell Construction Hldgs 1963-; *Style* - Sir Ivor Baker, CBE, JP, DL; 26 Cherry Orton rd, Orton Waterville, Peterborough (☎ 233482)

BAKER, Maj-Gen Ian Helstrip; CBE (1977, MBE 1965); s of Henry Baker; *b* 26 Nov 1927; *Educ* St Peter's Sch York, St Edmund Hall Oxford; *m* 1956, Susan, da of Maj Henry Lock; 1 s, 1 da (and 1 s decd); *Career* GOC NE Dist 1980-, Col Cmdt Roy Tank Regt 1981-; *Recreations* skiing, sailing, outdoor pursuits; *Clubs* Army and Navy; *Style* - Maj-Gen Ian Baker, CBE; Owen's Farm, Hook, Hants

BAKER, Sir (Stanislaus) Joseph; CB (1947); s of Henry Baker; *b* 7 March 1898; *Educ* St Francis Xavier Sch, Liverpool U; *m* 1920, Eleonora White; 1 da (and 1 da decd); *Career* kt 1958, Receiver Met Police Dist and Courts 1952-60; *Style* - Sir Joseph Baker, CB; Grenfields, Grenofen, Tavistock, Devon (☎ 2702)

BAKER, Dame Janet Abbott; DBE (1976, CBE 1970); da of Robert Abbott Baker; *b* 21 Aug 1933; *Educ* The Coll for Girls York; *m* 1957, James Shelley; *Career* singer; *Style* - Dame Janet Baker, DBE; c/o Ibbs & Tillett ltd, 124 Wigmore st, W1

BAKER, His Honour Judge; John Arnold Baker; s of late William Baker, MC; *b* 5 Nov 1925 Calcutta; *Educ* Plymouth Coll, Wellington Sch Somerset, Wadham Oxford; *m* 1954, Edith Heward; 2 da; *Career* Circuit Judge 1973-, slr 1951, barr 1960, contested (Lib) Richmond 1959 and 1964, Dorking 1970, chm Lib Party Exec 1969-70; *Style* - His Honour Judge Baker; 1 Rosemont rd, Richmond, Surrey (☎ 01 940 6983)

BAKER, His Honour Judge John Burkett; QC (1975); s of Philip Baker; *b* 17 Sept 1931; *Educ* Finchley Catholic G S, U Coll Exeter; *m* Margaret, nee Joseph; 3 s, 7 da; *Career* barr 1957, Circuit Judge 1978-; *Recreations* marriage counselling; *Style* - His Hon Judge John Baker, QC; 43 The Ridgeway, Enfield, Middx

BAKER, Kenneth Wilfred; MP (C) St Marylebone 1970-; s of late W Baker, OBE; *b* 3 Nov 1934; *Educ* St Paul's, Magdalen Oxford; *m* 1963, Mary Gray-Muir; 1 s, 2 da; *Career* Min of State Indust 1981-, industl consultant, MP (C) Acton 1968-70, PPS to Leader of Opposition 1974-75, memb exec 1922 Ctee, chm Hansard Soc 1978-; *Style* - Kenneth Baker Esq, MP; House of Commons, SW1

BAKER, Lady; Mary Caroline; *m* 1, Lt-Col Frank Preedy (decd); m 2, 1955, as his 2 wife, Sir Randolf Littlehales Baker, 4 and last Bt, DSO (d 1959); *Style* - Lady Baker; Bessels Cottage, Shroton, Blandford, Dorset

BAKER, Mary Elizabeth; da of William Gray Muir, WS (d 1959); *b* 5 Feb 1937; *Educ* St Mary's Wantage, St Andrew's U; *m* 1963, Kenneth Baker, MP; 1 s, 2 da; *Career* dir Thames TV 1975-, Gov Bedford Coll 1980-, chm London Tourist Bd 1980-; *Style* - Mrs Kenneth Baker; 31 Sussex st, SW1

BAKER, Nicholas Brian; MP (C) N Dorset 1979-; *b* 23 Nov 1938; *Educ* Clifton, Exeter Coll Oxford; *m* 1970, Penelope d'Abo, gggda of 3 Baron Suffield; 1 s; *Career* ptnr Frere Cholmeley slrs 1973-; *Clubs* Blandford Constitutional, Wimborne Conservative, Carlton; *Style* - Nicholas Baker Esq, MP; 28 Lincoln's Inn Fields, WC2 (☎ 01 405 7878)

BAKER, Peter Maxwell; QC (1974); s of late Harold Baker; *b* 26 March 1930; *Educ* King Edward VII Sch Sheffield, Exeter Coll Oxford; *m* 1954, Jacqueline Marshall; 3 da; *Career* Crown Court Recorder 1972-, barr 1956; *Also* yacht- Susajo II (seamaster 30 TSDY); *Style* - Peter Baker

Esq, QC; 28 Snaithing Lane, Sheffield, S10 3LG

BAKER, Paul Vivian; QC (1972); s of Vivian Baker; *b* 27 March 1923; *Educ* City of London Sch, Univ Oxford; *m* 1957, Stella Eadie; 1 s, 1 da; *Career* barr 1950, ed Law Quarterly Review 1971-; *Style* - Paul Baker Esq, QC; 9 Old sq, Lincoln's Inn, WC2 (☎ 01 405 0846); 27 Peaks Hill, Purley, Surrey (☎ 01 660 5465)

BAKER, Sir Rowland; OBE (1946); s of Isaac Baker; *b* 3 June 1908; *Educ* RNC Greenwich; *m* 1, 1931, Frances Cornish; 1 s, 3 da; m 2, 1972, Barabara Comley; *Career* kt 1968, dir Balrena Gp; *Style* - Sir Rowland Baker, OBE; Newfield, Entry Hill, Bath (☎ 22452)

BAKER, Richard Douglas James; OBE (1976); s of Albert Baker; *b* 15 June 1925; *Educ* Kilburn G S, Peterhouse Cambridge; *Career* broadcaster and author, BBC TV newsreader 1954-, TV Newscaster of the Year (Radio Industs Club) 1972 and 1974; *Style* - Richard Baker Esq, OBE; Hadley Lodge, 12 Watford rd, Radlett, Herts (☎ 01 637 5541)

BAKER, Stephen; s of late Arthur Baker; *b* 27 March 1926; *Educ* Epsom Coll, Clare Cambridge; *m* 1950, Margaret Wright; 1 s, 2 da; *Career* md Br Electricity Int 1978-, dir Davy Ashmore 1963, chm and ch exec Davy Utd Engrg, Ashmore Benson Pease Ltd and Loewy Robertson Engrg 1968, md Kearney & Trecker Ltd 1970; *Style* - Stephen Baker Esq; 43a Heathfield rd, SW18 (☎ 01 870 1115)

BAKER, Hon Mrs; Hon Sarah; *née* Ward; also known as Lalla Ward; da of 7 Viscount Bangor by 4 w Marjorie; *b* 1951; *m* 1980, Tom Baker, the actor (b 20 Jan 1936, educ Rose Bruford Drama Sch; formerly a novice monk for seven years, a suitable training for his first big rôle as Rasputin in 'Nicholas and Alexandra'; best known for his portrayal of Dr Who, also played Oscar Wilde in 1974 Oxford & 1981 Chichester productions of 'Feasting with Panthers'); *Style* - The Hon Mrs Baker; c/o Tom Baker Esq, c/o London Management, 235 Regent st, W1 (☎ 01 734 4192)

BAKER, Tom; *Career see* Hon Mrs Baker

BAKER, Thomas Scott Gillespie; QC (1978); s of Rt Hon Sir George Baker, OBE; *b* 10 Dec 1937; *Educ* Haileybury, BNC Oxford; *m* 1973, Margaret Strange; 2 s, 1 da; *Career* barr 1961, Crown Court Recorder 1976-; *Style* - Thomas Baker Esq, QC; Fern House, Jordans Lane, Jordans, Bucks (☎ Chalfont St Giles 4566); Craigenholly Cottage, Glenluce, Wigtownshire

BAKER, Lady; Valerie; da of late Maj J Lockhart; *m* 1946, Field-Marshal Sir Geoffrey Baker, GCB, CMG, CBE, MC (d 1980); 2 s, 1 da; *Style* - Lady Baker; Broomden Oast, Ticehurst, Sussex

BAKER, Willfred Harold Kerton; TD; s of late W Baker; *b* 6 Jan 1920; *Educ* Hardye's Sch, Edinburgh U, Cornell; *m* 1945, Kathleen, nee Murray Bisset; 1 s, 2 da (and 1 step da); *Career* MP (C) Banffshire 1964-74, co dir; *Style* - Willfred Baker Esq, TD; Plancoet, Alderney, CI (☎ Alderney 2232)

BAKER WILBRAHAM, Randle; s and h of Sir Richard Baker Wilbraham, 8 Bt,*qv* *b* 1963; *Style* - Randle Baker Wilbraham Esq

BAKER WILBRAHAM, Sir Richard; 8 Bt (GB 1776); s of Sir Randle John Baker Wilbraham, 7 Bt, JP, DL (d 1980); *b* 5 Feb 1934; *Educ* Harrow; *m* 1962, Anne Christine Peto, da of late Charles Peto Bennett, OBE, of Jersey; 1 s, 3 da; *Heir* s, Randle Baker Wilbraham; *Career* late Lt Welsh Gds, md J Henry Schroder Wagg & Co, Tstee Grosvenor Estate 1981-; *Style* - Sir Richard Baker Wilbraham, Bt; 41 Carlyle sq, SW3 (☎ 01 352 5069); Rode Hall, Scholar Green, Cheshire (☎ Alsager 3237)

BAKER-CARR, Air Marshal Sir John Darcy; KBE (1962, CBE 1951), CB (1957), AFC (1944); s of late Brig-Gen C Baker-Carr, CMG, DSO, and Sarah Quinan; *b* 13 Jan 1906; *m* 1934, Margery Dallas; *Career* Controller Engrg and Equipment Air Miny 1962-64; *Style* - Air Marshal Sir John Baker-Carr, KBE CB,

AFC; Thatchwell Cottage, King's Somborne, Hants

BAKER-CRESSWELL, Addison Joe; DSO (1941); s of Maj Addison Baker-Cresswell, of Cresswell Hall and Harehope Hall Northumberland (d 1921); *b* 2 Feb 1901; *Educ* Gresham's; *m* 1926, Rona, nee Vaile, of Auckland NZ; 1 s, 2 da; *Career* served RN 1919-51, Dep Dir Naval Intelligence Div 1948-51; *Style* - Addison Baker-Cresswell Esq; Budle Hall, Bamburgh, Northumberland (☎ 297)

BAKER-CRESSWELL, Thomas Henry; JP (Northumberland 1959), DL (N'mberland 1971); s of Henry Gilfrid Baker-Cresswell (d 1956); *b* 13 March 1917; *Educ* Westminster; *m* 1946, Anne (who m, 1938, Maj Gilfrid Edward Baker-Cresswell, RE, ka 1942, and had by him 1 s, 1 da), da of Sir John Charrington (d 1978); 2 da; *Career* Offr Roy Marines 1935-57; *Clubs* Army and Navy; *Style* - Thomas Baker-Cresswell Esq, JP, DL; Preston Tower, Chathill, Northumberland (☎ 227)

BAKEWELL, Joan Dawson; da of John Rowlands; *b* 16 April 1933; *Educ* Stockport H S for Girls, Newnham Coll Cambridge; *m* 1, 1955, Michael Bakewell (m dis 1972), 1 s, 1 da; m 2, 1975, Jack Emery; *Career* broadcaster and writer; *Style* - Miss Joan Bakewell; c/o AD Peters & Co Ltd, 10 Buckingham St, WC2 (☎ 01 839 2556)

BALCAZAR-MONZON, Gustavo; *b* 10 Aug 1927; *Educ* Javeriana U Bogota; *m* 1952, Bolivia Ramos de Balcazar; 2 da; *Career* Colombian Ambassador to UK 1979-, Pres House of Representatives 1960, Senator 1962-, Min of Ag 1964-65, Pres Senate 1975, Pres Designate Colombia 1978; *Style* - HE Mr Gustavo Balcazar-Monzon; The Colombian Embassy, 76 Chester sq, SW1 (☎ 01 730 1625)

BALCOMBE, Hon Mr Justice; Hon Sir (Alfred) John; s of Edwin Balcombe; *b* 29 Sept 1925; *Educ* Winchester, New Coll Oxford; *m* 1950, Jacqueline, nee Cowan; 2 s, 1 da; *Career* kt 1977, High Court Judge (Family Div) 1977-, barr 1950, QC 1969; *Style* - The Hon Mr Justice Balcombe; 6 Highbury rd, Wimbledon, SW19 (☎ 01 947 0980)

BALCON, Hon Mrs; Hon Sarah Patricia; *née* Mills; da of 5 Baron Hillingdon, MC, TD; *b* 1933; *m* 1955, Maj Jonathan Michael Henry Balcon, TD; 3 da; *Style* - The Hon Mrs Balcon; The Grey House, Seal, Sevenoaks, Kent

BALCON, Lady; Aileen Freda; *née* Leatherman; MBE; da of late Mrs Leatherman, of Johannesburg ; *m* 1924, Sir Michael Balcon (d 1977); 1 s, 1 da; *Style* - Lady Balcon, MBE ; Upper Parrock, Hartfield, E Sussex

BALDING, R C; *Career* chm United Friendly Insurance Co; *Style* - R C Balding Esq

BALDOCK, John Markham; VRD (1949); s of late Capt W Baldock; *b* 19 Nov 1915; *Educ* Rugby, Balliol Oxford; *m* 1949, Pauline Gauntlett; 2 s; *Career* chm Lenscrete Ltd 1949, dir CIBA-GEIGY (UK) Ltd; MP (C) Harborough Leics 1950-59; *Style* - John Baldock Esq, VRD; 17 Aylesford st, SW1 (☎ 01 821 8759); Hollycombe House, Liphook, Hants (☎ 723233)

BALDREY, Frank William; s of William Baldrey, of London (d 1960); *b* 7 Jan 1921; *Educ* City of London Sch, King's Coll London; *m.* 1974, Patricia, da of Francis Clements, of Droitwich (d 1974); 2 s, 2 da; *Career* md Stanley Bridges Ltd to 1967, chm Garringtons Ltd to 1976, ch exec IP & SD BOC Ltd; *Recreations* sport, administration; *Also* race-horse- National Hunt mare 'No Gold'; *Style* - Frank Baldrey Esq; Deancroft, Cookham Dean, Berks (☎ Marlow 6699)

BALDWIN OF BEWDLEY, 4 Earl (UK 1937); Edward Alfred Alexander Baldwin; also Viscount Corvedale (UK 1937); s of 3 Earl (d 1976, 2 s of 1 Earl, otherwise Stanley Baldwin, thrice PM and 1 cous of Rudyard Kipling); *b* 3 Jan 1938; *Educ* Eton, Trin Cambridge; *m* 1970, Sarah MacMurray, da of Evan James, of Upwood Park, Abingdon, Berks; 3 s; *Heir* s, Viscount Corvedale; *Style* - The Rt Hon The Earl Baldwin of Bewdley; Dunlea,

Otmoor lane, Beckley, Oxon

BALDWIN, Hon --; 3 s of 4 Earl Baldwin of Bewdley; *b* 1980

BALDWIN, Hon Mrs; Hon Alison Mary; *née* Sandilands; da of 14 Lord Torphichen; *b* 1944; *m* 1966, David Maurice Baldwin; 2 da; *Style* - The Hon Mrs Baldwin; 30 Rochford Ave, Shenfield, Essex

BALDWIN, Claude Rosemary; da of Archibald Walter Dickson Dove, of Kingston Hill, Surrey (d 1960); *b* 22 Sept 1917; *Educ* Eton Rectory Beverley, St John's Bexhill, Château d'Oex; *m* 1, 1938, Peter George Calvert, of Ockley Court, Dorking; 3 da (Amanda, Hon Mrs (Jinty) Money-Coutts, Mrs Blake (Victoria) Tyler); m 2, 1947, Hon 'Taffy' (Gustaf) Rodd (4 s of 1 Baron Rennell and yr bro of Peter, sometime husb of (Hon) Nancy Mitford, *see* Hon Mrs Treuhaft); m 3, 1962, Ken Baldwin, of Kusadasi, Turkey; *Career* tour guide; *Recreations* lying on a bed of thyme under an olive tree; *Clubs* Cotton House; *Style* - Mrs Ken Baldwin; c/o Coutts & Co, 440 The Strand, WC2

BALDWIN, D A; *Career* jt md Hewlett-Packard Ltd; *Style* - D A Baldwin Esq; c/o Hewlett-Packard Ltd, King st Lane, Winnersh, Wokingham, Berks

BALDWIN, Hon James Conrad; s of 4 Earl Baldwin of Bewdley, *qv*; *b* 1976; *Style* - The Hon James Baldwin

BALDWIN, Sir Peter (Robin); KCB (1977, CB 1973); s of Charles Baldwin; *b* 10 Nov 1922; *Educ* City of London Sch, CCC Oxford; *m* 1951, Margaret Moar; 2 s; *Career* Perm Sec Dept of T'port 1976-; *Style* - Sir Peter Baldwin, KCB; Sanders, 21 Crescent rd, Beckenham, Kent (☎ 01 658 6956)

BALDWIN, Maj-Gen Peter Alan Charles; s of Alec Baldwin; *b* 19 Feb 1927; *Educ* King Edward VI G S, Chelmsford; *m* 1953, Judith Elizabeth Mace; *Career* Chief Signal Officer, HQ BAOR 1977; *Style* - Maj-Gen Peter Baldwin ; c/o Lloyds Bank Ltd, 6 Pall Mall, SW1

BALERNO, Baron (Life Peer UK 1963); Alick Drummond Buchanan-Smith; CBE (1945, OBE 1939), TD (1938), DL (Midlothian 1975); s of late Very Rev Sir George Adam Smith, DD, Principal of Aberdeen U, and late Lilian, da of Sir George Buchanan, LLD, FRS; *b* 9 Oct 1898; *Educ* Glasgow Acad, Aberdeen U, Iowa State U; *m* 1926, Mary (d 1947), da of late Capt George Smith; 4 s, 1 da; *Career* kt 1956, MA, DSc, MSA Iowa, FRSE, FRSGS, lecturer Animal Genetics Edinburgh U 1925-60, chm Edinburgh Lothians and Peebles TA & AFA 1953-57, Pres Scottish Unionist Assoc 1955-56; *Style* - The Rt Hon The Lord Balerno, CBE, TD, DL; House of Cockburn, Balerno, Midlothian (☎ 031 449 3737)

BALES, Edward; *Career* dep chm J and J Dyson Ltd, manufacturers of fire resisting goods; FCA; *Style* - Edward Bales Esq ; c/o J and J Dyson Ltd, Griffs Works, Stannington, Nr Sheffield

BALFE, Richard Andrew; MEP (L) London S Inner 1979-; s of Dr Richard Balfe, of Yorks; *b* 14 May 1944; *Educ* Brook Secondary Sch Sheffield, LSE; *m* 1978, Vivienne, nee Job; 1 s; *Career* Corpl London Irish Rifles (TA); *Recreations* walking, reading, music; *Clubs* Peckham Labour; *Also* part share in yacht 'Brittania' (*sic*); *Style* - Richard Balfe Esq, MEP; 259 Barry rd, SE21 (☎ 01 299 0858)

BALFOUR, 4 Earl of (UK 1922); Gerald Arthur James Balfour; JP (E Lothian 1970); also Viscount Traprain (UK 1922); s of 3 Earl (d 1968, nephew of 1 Earl, otherwise Arthur Balfour, PM (C) 1902-05) and Jean Lily, da of late Rev John James Cooke-Yarborough; *b* 23 Dec 1925; *Educ* Eton; *m* 1956, Natasha Georgina Lousada, da of late Capt George Anton; *Heir* kinsman, Eustace Balfour; *Career* Master Mariner, CCllr E Lothian, Merchant Navy WW II; *Style* - The Rt Hon The Earl of Balfour, JP; Whittingehame Tower, Haddington, E Lothian

BALFOUR OF INCHRYE, 1 Baron (UK 1945); Harold Harington Balfour; MC & Bar (1914-18), PC (1941); s of Col N Balfour; *b* 1 Nov 1897; *Educ* Chilverton

Elms Dover, RNC Osborne; *m* 1, 1921, Diana (m dis 1946), da of Sir Robert Harvey, 2 Bt; 1 s; m 2, 1947, Mary, da of late Baron Profumo, KC, and sis of John Profumo, CBE; 1 da; *Heir* s Hon Ian Balfour; *Career* MP (C) Isle of Thanet 1929-45, Parly Under-Sec of State for Air 1938-44, chm BEA Helicopters Ltd 1964-66; *Style* - The Rt Hon The Lord Balfour of Inchrye, MC*, PC; End House, St Mary Abbot's Place, W8 (☎ 01 603 6231)

BALFOUR OF BURLEIGH, 8 (de facto and 12 but for the attainder) Lord (S 1607); Robert Bruce; s of 7 (11 but for the attainder) Lord (d 1967); *b* 6 Jan 1927; *Educ* Westminster; *m* 1971, Jennifer, da of late E S Manasseh and formerly w of John Brittain-Catlin; 2 da; *Heir* (hp) da, Hon Victoria Bruce; *Career* foreman supt English Electric Co Ltd Stafford & Liverpool 1952-57, gen man of Eng Electric Co India Ltd 1957-64, of Eng Electric Netherton Works 1964-66, of D Napier & Son Ltd 1967-68; dir Bank of Scotland 1968-, of Scottish Investment Tst 1971-, chm Scottish Arts Cncl 1971-80, Viking Oil Ltd 1971-80, chm Fedn of Scottish Bank Employers, tresr Roy Scottish Corpn, CEng, FIEE; *Style* - The Rt Hon The Lord Balfour of Burleigh; Brucefield, Clackmannan

BALFOUR, Alastair Norman; DL (Tweeddale 1954); s of Frederick Balfour, CVO, DL (d 1945); *b* 20 March 1909; *Educ* Stowe, Oxford; *m* 1942, Elizabeth, da of Horace Cowell, of Abington Park, nr Cambridge; 1 s, 1 da; *Career* co dir, memb Roy Co of Archers (Queen's Bodyguard for Scotland) 1930-; *Recreations* gardening, shooting; *Clubs* New (Edinburgh), Brooks's, Pratt's; *Style* - Alastair Balfour Esq, DL; Dawyck House, Stobo, Peebles, Tweeddale (☎ Stobo 242)

BALFOUR, Hon Christopher Patrick; s and h of 4 Baron Kinross, OBE, TD, DL, by his 2 w, Helen; *b* 1 Oct 1949; *Educ* Eton, St Andrews and Edinburgh Us; *m* 1974, Susan Jane Pitman; 1 s; *Career* WS; *Style* - The Hon Christopher Balfour; 11 Belford Place, Edinburgh

BALFOUR, David Mathers; CBE (1970); s of late George Balfour, MP; *b* 11 Jan 1910; *Educ* Shrewsbury, Pembroke Cambridge; *m* 1938, Elisabeth, nee Beddall; 2 s, 1 da; *Career* CEng, MICE, dir R M Douglas Construction 1975-, chm Balfour Beatty & Co 1971-74; *Style* - David Balfour Esq, CBE; Little Garnstone Manor, Seal, Sevenoaks, Kent (☎ 61221)

BALFOUR, Hon David Rowland; s of 2 Baron Riverdale DL, *qv*, and Christian Mary, nee Hill; *b* 1938; *Educ* Harrow and Queens' Coll, Cambridge; *Style* - The Hon David Balfour

BALFOUR, Eustace Arthur Goschen; s of late Lt-Col Francis Cecil Campbell Balfour, CIE, CVO, CBE, MC and great nephew of 1 Earl of Balfour, KG, OM, PC (d 1930); Francis m Hon Phyllis (d 1975), da of 2 Viscount Goschen; hp to Earldom of Balfour; *b* 26 May 1921; *Educ* Eton; *m* 1 1946, Anne, nee Yule, (m dis 1971); 2 s; m 2, 1971, Mrs Paula Susan Cuene-Grandidier, nee Davis; *Career* with Mather and Platt Ltd (France); *Style* - Eustace Balfour Esq; 8 Avenue des Pages, 78110, Le Vesinet, France

BALFOUR, Lady Evelyn Barbara; da of 2 Earl of Balfour, PC (d 1945); *b* 1898; *Educ* Reading U; *Career* consultant, the Soil Reserach Association; *Style* - Lady Evelyn Balfour; 4 Rattla Corner, Theberton, Leiston, Suffolk

BALFOUR, Lady; Frances; CVO (1969); da of Prof Alexander van Millingen, DD; *m* 1933, Sir John Balfour, GCMG, GBE, *qv*; *Career* Lady-in-Waiting to HRH Princess Marina Duchess of Kent 1961-68; *Style* - Lady Balfour, CVO; 38 Onslow sq, SW7 (☎ 01 584 1970)

BALFOUR, Hon Frances Christian; da of 2 Baron Riverdale, DL, and Christian Mary, nee Hill; *b* 1946; *Style* - The Hon Frances Balfour

BALFOUR, Hon Francis Henry; TD; s of 1 Baron Riverdale, GBE, (d 1957); *b* 1905; *Educ* Oundle; *m* 1, 1932, Muriel Anne (d 1970), da of late Eng Rear-Adm Ralph Berry; 2 s, 2 da; m 2, 1971, Daphne Cecelia, nee Moss; *Career* Vice-Consul for Denmark 1946-50, kt of Order of

Dannebrog of Denmark; *Style* - The Hon Francis Balfour, TD; The Barn, Mill Lane, Bathampton, Bath

BALFOUR, Hon Ian; s and h of 1 Baron Balfour of Inchrye, MC, PC; *b* 21 Dec 1924; *Educ* Eton and Magdalen Coll, Oxford; *m* 1953, Josephine Maria Jane, nee Bernard; 1 da; *Style* - The Hon Ian Balfour; 10 Limerston st, SW10

BALFOUR, (Elizabeth) Jean; CBE (1980), JP (Fife 1963); da of late Maj-Gen Sir James Syme Drew, KBE, CB, DSO, MC; *b* 4 Nov 1927; *Educ* Edinburgh U; *m* 1950, John Balfour; 3 s; *Career* FIFor, chm Countryside Commission Scotland 1972-, dir A & J Bowen & Co, memb Nature Conservancy Cncl 1973-; *Style* - Mrs John Balfour, CBE, JP; Kirkforthar House, Markinch, Fife (☎ Glenrothes 752233); Scourie, by Lairg, Sutherland

BALFOUR, Sir John; GCMG (1954, KCMG 1947, CMG 1941), GBE (1959); s of Charles Balfour, CB, of Newton Don, Kelso, and Balfour House, Balgonie, and Lady Nina, nee McDonnell, da of 5 Earl of Antrim; *b* 26 May 1894; *Educ* Eton, New Coll Oxford; *m* 1933, Frances, da of Prof Alexander van Millingen (*see Balfour, Lady*); *Career* Ambass to Spain 1951-54, chm Br and French Bank 1959-69, Utd Bank for Africa 1961-69; *Style* - Sir John Balfour, GCMG, GBE; 38 Onslow sq, SW7 (☎ 01 584 1970)

BALFOUR, John Charles; OBE (1978), MC (1943), JP (Fife 1957), DL (Fife 1958); s of late Brig Edward Balfour, CVO, DSO, OBE, MC, and Lady Ruth, CBE (d 1967), nee Balfour, da of 2 Earl of Balfour (d 1945) and Lady Elizabeth Bulwer-Lytton, da of 1 Earl of Lytton; *b* 28 July 1919; *Educ* Eton, Trin Cambridge; *m* 1950, Jean, nee Drew; 3 s; *Career* memb Roy Co of Archers (Queen's Bodyguard for Scotland) 1949-; *Style* - John Balfour Esq, OBE, MC, JP, DL; Kirkforthar House, Markinch, Glenrothes, Fife (☎ 752233)

BALFOUR, Dowager Countess of; Jean Lily; da of late Rev John James Cooke-Yarborough; *m* 1925, 3 Earl of Balfour (d 1968); 1 s, 2 da; *Style* - The Rt Hon The Dowager Countess of Balfour; West Roundel, Broxmouth Park, Dunbar

BALFOUR, Lady; (Catherine) Marjorie; da of Sir Charles Rugge-Price, 7 Bt (d 1953); *b* 1904; *m* 1930, Lt-Gen Sir Philip Maxwell Balfour, KBE, CB, MC (d 1977); *Style* - Lady Balfour; Little Wincombe House, Donhead St Mary, Shaftesbury, Dorset

BALFOUR, Hon Mark Robin; s and h of 2 Baron Riverdale; *b* 16 July 1927; *Educ* Aysgarth Sch Yorks, Trin Coll Sch Port Hope Canada; *m* 1959, Susan Ann, da of R P Phillips, of Sheffield; 1 s, 2 da; *Career* pres Nat Fedn of Engineer's Tool Manufacturers 1974-76, chm Sheffield Rolling Mills Ltd 1969-75, and of Balfour Darwins Ltd 1971-75, memb Exec Ctee of BISPA 1967-75, and of Economic Devt Council for Machine Tools 1975-78, Master of Cutlers' Co 1969-70, dir Overseas Operations Edgar Allen Balfour Ltd, chm of Eagle & Globe Steel Ltd Aust, Eagle & Globe Products Pty Ltd Aust, Eagle & Globe (Hong Kong) Ltd Hong Kong, Arthur Balfour Ltd Canada, Light Trades House Ltd, and Export Year Ctee for S Yorks, pres Sheffield Chamber of Commerce, memb Aust British Trade Assocn Council, and Aust and NZ Trade Adv Ctee, a Vice-Consul for Finland, memb Blacksmiths' Co and Freeman of City of London; *Clubs* Sheffield; *Style* - The Hon Mark Balfour; The White House, Hollow Meadows, Sheffield

BALFOUR, Nancy; OBE (1965); da of Alexander Balfour and Ruth Macfarland Balfour; *b* 1911; *Educ* Wycombe Abbey, LMH Oxford; *Career* chm Contemporary Art Soc 1976-; *Style* - Miss Nancy Balfour, OBE; 36E Eaton sq, SW1 (☎ 01 235 7874)

BALFOUR, Neil Roxburgh; MEP (C) N Yorks 1979-; s of Archibald Roxburgh Balfour (d 1958); *b* 12 Aug 1944; *Educ* Ampleforth, The Sorbonne, Univ Coll Oxford; *m* 1, 1969, HRH Princess Elizabeth of Yugoslavia; 1 s; m 2, 1978, Serena Mary Churchill, nee Russell; 1 da, (and 2 stepchildren); *Career* barrister 1969; executive dir European Banking Co Ltd 1979-; *Clubs* Turf, Pratt's, Royal St George's Golf; *Style* - Neil Balfour Esq, MEP; 24 The Little Boltons, SW10 (☎ 01

373 8092); Studley Royal House, Ripon, Yorks (☎ Ripon 2535)

BALFOUR, Peter Edward Gerald; s of late Brig Edward Balfour, CVO, DSO, OBE, MC, and Lady Ruth, CBE (d 1967), nee Balfour, da of 2 Earl of Balfour (d 1945) and Lady Elizabeth Bulwer-Lytton, da of 1 Earl of Lytton; *b* 9 July 1921; *Educ* Eton; *m* 1, 1948 (m dis 1967), Lady Grizelda, nee Ogilvy, da of 7 (12 but for attainder) Earl of Airlie, KT, GCVO, MC (d 1968); 2 s, 1 da; m 2, 1968, Diana Wainman; 1 s, 1 da; *Career* chm Scottish and Newcastle Breweries, dir Roy Bank of Scotland 1971-, Br Assets Tst, Edinburgh American Assets Tst 1962- (chm 1978-), Nat and Commercial Banking Gp 1978-; *Style* - Peter Balfour Esq; Scadlaw House, Humbie, E Lothian (☎ 252)

BALFOUR, Richard Creighton; MBE (1945); s of Donald Creighton Balfour and Muriel Fonceca; *b* 3 Feb 1916; *Educ* St Edward's Sch Oxford; *m* 1943, Adela Rosemary Welch; 2 s; *Career* dir Datasaab Ltd 1975-; chm The Year of the Rose 1976-; *Style* - Richard Balfour Esq MBE; Albion House, Little Waltham, Chelmsford, Essex (☎ Chelmsford 360410)

BALFOUR, Lady Tessa Mary Isobel; *née* Fitzalan Howard; da of 17 Duke of Norfolk, CB, CBE, MC, DL, *qv* ; *b* 1950; *m* 1971, Roderick Francis Arthur Balfour, s of Eustace Arthur Goschen Balfour, *qv*; *Style* - Lady Tessa Balfour; 41 Napier Ave, SW6

BALFOUR, William Harold St Clair; s of the late Francis Edmund Balfour; *b* 29 Aug 1934; *Educ* Edinburgh Academy, Edinburgh U; *m* 1961, Patricia, nee Waite; 1 s, 2 da; *Career* solicitor; *Recreations* sailing, walking; *Clubs* New (Edinburgh), Royal Forth Yacht; *Style* - William Balfour Esq; 58 Frederick st, Edinburgh (☎ 031 225 8291)

BALFOUR-LYNN, Dr Stanley; s of John Balfour-Lynn; *b* 21 June 1922; *Educ* City of London Sch, Guy's Hospital London; *m* 1952, Valerie Eker; 3 s, 1 da; *Career* Lloyd's underwriter 1977-; dir American Medical International Inc 1977- & ch exec American Medical (Europe) Ltd 1969-; *Style* - Dr Stanley Balfour-Lynn; Flat F, 19 Hyde Park gdns, W2 (☎ 01 723 3960); Hush Heath Manor, Goudhurst, Kent (☎ Goudhurst 312)

BALGONIE, Lord; David Alexander Leslie Melville; s and h of 14 Earl of Leven and (13 of) Melville, DL; *b* 26 Jan 1954; *Educ* Eton; *m* 1981, Julia Clare, yr da of Col I R Critchley, of Lindores, Muthill, Perths; *Heir* bro Hon Archibald Leslie Melville; *Career* Lt Queen's Own Highlanders, RARO 1979; *Style* - Lord Balgonie; Glenferness House, Nairn

BALINT, George; *Career* md Agricultural Holdings Co; *Style* - George Balint Esq

BALL, Anthony George; s of Harry Ball, of Bridgwater; *b* 14 Nov 1934; *Educ* Dr Morgan's G S Bridgwater; *m* 1957, Ruth Parry, nee Davies; 2 s, 1 da; *Career* chm BL Europe and Overseas 1979-, dir Austin-Morris, Rover-Triumph, BL Cars, BL Internat; *Recreations* military history, theatre, golf; *Clubs* Oriental; *Style* - Anthony Ball Esq; Marywood, Compton Way, Moor Pk, Farnham, Surrey (☎ Runfold 2660)

BALL, Alan Hugh; s of late Sir George Joseph Ball, KBE; *b* 8 June 1924; *Educ* Eton; *m* 1948, Eleanor Turner; 2 s, 1 da; *Career* dir Lonrho Ltd and Associated Cos (chm and joint md 1961-72); *Style* - Alan Ball Esq; The Old Mill, Ramsbury, Wilts (☎ Ramsbury 266)

BALL, Air Marshal Sir Alfred Henry Wynne; KCB (1976, CB 1967), DSO (1943), DFC (1942); s of Capt J Ball, MC; *b* 18 Jan 1921; *Educ* Campbell Coll Belfast, RAF Coll Cranwell; *m* 1942, Nan McDonald; 3 s, 1 da; *Career* Dep CIC RAF Strike Cmmd 1977-78, ret 1979; *Style* - Air Marshal Sir Alfred Ball, KCB, DSO DFC; Tarshyne, Lambridge Wood rd, Henley-on-Thames, Oxon

BALL, Hon Mrs; Hon Ann Marguerite *née* Gordon-Walker; da of late Baron Gordon-Walker, CH, PC; *b* 1944; *Educ* N London Collegiate Sch, Queen's Coll Dundee, St Andrews U, Oxford; *m*

1968, Laurence Andrew Ball; *Style* - The Hon Mrs Ball

BALL, Sir Charles Irwin; 4 Bt (UK 1911); s of Sir Nigel Ball, 3 Bt (d 1978); *b* 12 Jan 1924; *Educ* Sherborne; *m* 1950, Alison, da of Percy Bentley (d 1979); 1 s, 1 da; *Heir* s, Richard Ball; *Career* chartered accountant, chm Barclays Merchant Bank 1976-77; dir Telephone Rentals 1971-, Avenue Close Ltd 1981-, Sun Alliance & London Insurance 1971-, Tunnel Hldgs 1976-, Rockware Gp 1978-, Peachey Property Corpn 1978-, memb Br T'port Docks Bd 1971- chm Telephone Rentals 1981-; *Style* - Sir Charles Ball, Bt; Downlands, Seale, Farnham, Surrey (☎ Runfold 2415)

BALL, Christopher John Elinger; s of late Laurence Elinger Ball, OBE; *b* 22 April 1953; *Educ* St George's Sch Harpenden, Merton Coll Oxford; *m* 1958, Wendy Ruth Colyer; 3 s, 3 da; *Career* Warden, Keble Coll, Oxford 1980-; *Style* - Christopher Ball Esq; Keble Coll, Oxford, (☎ Oxford 59201)

BALL, Edmund Bruce; CBE (1953), DL (Salop 1979); s of Edmund Ball, of Prestwick (1944); *b* 6 Nov 1903; *Educ* St Paul's, Sidney Sussex Cambridge; *m* 1930, Mona, nee Stewart; 2 s; *Career* Vice-Pres Ironbridge Gorge Museum Tst 1977- (md Lilleshall Co 1957-68); *Recreations* golf, orchids; *Style* - Edmund Ball Esq, CBE, DL; The Sheiling, Haughton Lane, Shifnal, Salop

BALL, Florine, Lady - Florine Isabel; da of late Col Herbert Edwardes Irwin; *m* 1922, Sir Nigel Gresley Ball, 3 Bt (d 1978); *Style* - Florine, Lady Ball; 19 Bernard rd, W Worthing, Sussex

BALL, Nigel; s of Thomas Ball (d 1951); *b* 22 March 1934; *Educ* Alleyne's, Stone, and W Ham; *m* 1957, Maureen, nee Gibbens; 1 s, 1 da; *Career* md Steetley Refractories 1980-; *Recreations* squash; *Style* - Nigel Ball Esq; Westwind, N Wheatley, Retford, Notts (☎ 0742 880376)

BALL, Lady; Pamela; da of late Capt William Eaton Caldbeck, of Dublin; *m* 1938, Air Vice Marshal Sir Ben Ball, KBE, CB (d 1977); 3 s; *Style* - Lady Ball

BALL, Richard Bentley; s and h of Sir Charles Irwin Ball, 4 Bt,*qv*; *b* 29 Jan 1953; *Style* - Richard Ball Esq

BALL, Prof Robert James; s of Arnold Ball; *b* 15 July 1933; *Educ* St Marylebone G S; Queen's Coll, Oxford; *m* 1, 1954, Patricia Mary Hart Davies (m dis 1970); 1 s, 3 da (and 1 da decd); m 2, 1970, Lindsay Jackson, nee Wonnacott; 1 step s; *Career* chm Legal and General Assurance Society 1980-; principal London Business Sch 1972-; dir Barclays Bank Trust Co, Tube Investments, IBM UK Holdings, IBM UK; *Style* - Prof Robert Ball; 1 Sussex pla, Regent's Park, NW1 (☎ 01 723 8777); Cross Trees, Beacon rd, Kingswear, Devon

BALL, Tony; *b aet* 46 as of June 1981; *Career* chm & md BL Europe and Overseas (responsible for launch of Mini Metro 1980-81), Freeman City of London, FIM; *Style* - Tony Ball Esq; c/o BL Europe & Overseas Ltd, Austin Morris House, Bickenhill Lane, Birmingham 37 (☎ 021 779 6525)

BALL-GREENE, Brian Goldsworthy; *Career* chm Unicorn Industries Ltd; *Style* - Brian Ball-Greene Esq; Castle Hill House, Windsor, Berks

BALLANTRAE, Baroness; Laura Margaret; da of Lt-Col Arthur Grenfell, DSO (d 1958), and Hilda, OBE, da of Gen Rt Hon Sir Neville Lyttelton, GCB, GCVO (s of 4 Baron Lyttelton, KCMG, PC); *b* 14 April 1920; *m* 1950, Baron Ballantrae, KT, GCMG, GCVO, DSO, OBE (Life Peer, d 1980); 1 s; *Style* - The Rt Hon The Lady Ballantrae; Auchairne, Ballantrae, Ayrshire (☎ 344)

BALLANTYNE, Alexander Hanson; CVO (1957), CBE (1962); s of Dr Harold Ballantyne, of Midlothian (d 1955); *b* 27 Feb 1911; *Educ* Rugby, Christ's Cambridge; *m* 1944, Helene, nee Contoroussi; 1 s, 1 da; *Career* For Serv 1934-80, Consul-Gen Frankfurt 1964-69, consultant OECD Paris 1971-80; *Style* - Alexander Ballantyne Esq, CVO, CBE; 2 Ave Marie-Christine, 06000 Nice, France (☎ 88 39 30)

BALLANTYNE, Colin Sandergrove; CMG (1971); s of James Ballantyne, of Adelaide; *b* 12 July 1908; *Educ* Adelaide H S; *m* 1934, Gwenneth Richmond; 1 s, 2 da; *Career* Pres Arts Cncl of Australia 1974-, chm Bd of Govrs SA Theatre Co 1972-; *Style* - Colin Ballantyne Esq, CMG; 77 Kingston ter, N Adelaide, SA 5006, Australia (☎ 267)

BALLANTYNE, Henry; CBE (1968), JP (Peeblesshire 1943), DL (Peeblesshire 1953); s of Lt-Col David Ballantyne, OBE, of Barns Kirkton Manor, Peeblesshire; *b* 27 Nov 1912; *Educ* Cheltenham, Pembroke Cambridge; *m* 1938, Barbara, nee Gavin; 1 s, 3 da; *Career* chm Henry Ballantyne & Sons 1977-, memb Roy Co of Archers (Queen's Bodyguard for Scotland), chm Scottish Woollen Publicity Cncl 1974-; *Style* - Henry Ballantyne Esq, CBE, JP, DL; Caerlee House, Innerleithen, Peeblesshire (☎ 392)

BALLARD, Geoffrey Horace; CBE (1978), JP (Worcs 1967); s of Horace Ballard; *b* 21 May 1927; *Educ* Hanley Castle Grammar Sch; *m* 1948, Dorothy Sheila Bache; 2 s, 1 da,; *Career* md GH Ballard (Farms) Ltd, GH Ballard (Leasing) Ltd; chm MSF (Meats) Ltd; vice chm MSF Ltd, Woodbury Growers; *Style* - Geoffrey Ballard Esq, CBE, JP; Old Yates, Abberley, Worcester (☎ Great Witley 307)

BALLIN, Hon Mrs; Hon Rose Griselda; *née* Eden; da of 7 Baron Henley (d 1977); *b* 1957; *m* 1976, Stuart Ballin; *Style* - The Hon Mrs Ballin; Bourg-Dessous 7, 1814 La Tour de Peilz, Vaud, Switzerland

BALME, David Mowbray; CMG (1955), DSO (1943), DFC (1943); s of Harold Balme, FRCS (d 1953); *b* 8 Sept 1912; *Educ* Marlborough, Clare Cambridge; *m* 1936, Beatrice, da of Lt-Col Arthur Rice (d 1965); 2 s; *Career* Prof of Classics Queen Mary Coll London 1964-78; *Recreations* music, hunting; *Style* - David Balme Esq, CMG, DSO, DFC; Gumley, Market Harborough, Leics (☎ Kibworth 2762)

BALMER, Sir Joseph Reginald; JP; s of Joseph Balmer; *b* 22 Sept 1899; *Educ* King Edward's G S Birmingham; *m* 1927, Dora, nee Johnson; *Career* kt 1965; Nat Chm Guild of Insurance Officials 1943-47; *Style* - Sir Joseph Balmer, JP; 26 Stechford Lane, Ward End, Birmingham (☎ 021 783 3198)

BALNIEL, Lord; Anthony Robert Lindsay; s and h of 29 Earl of Crawford and (12 of) Balcarres, PC; *b* 24 Nov 1958; *Educ* Eton; *Style* - Lord Balniel; 107 Frognal, NW3

BALOGH, Baron (Life Peer UK 1968); Thomas Balogh; s of Emil Balogh; *b* 2 Nov 1905; *Educ* Gymnasium of Budapest U, Budapest U, Berlin U, Harvard; *m* 1, 1945 (m dis 1970), Penelope, da of Rev Henry Tower and widow of Oliver Gatty; 2 s, 1 da, 1 step da; m 2, 1970, Catherine Storr, MRCS, LRCP; 3 step da; *Career* Ec Advr BNOC 1978-, Fellow Balliol Oxford 1945-73, Min of State Dept of Energy 1974-75, memb Ec and Financial Ctee Labour Party 1971-, Ec Advr Cabinet 1964-67, PM's Consultant 1968, Chm Fabian Soc 1970; *Style* - The Rt Hon The Lord Balogh; Old Bank House, 14 Hampstead High st, NW3 (☎ 01 435 9275); The Cottage, Christmas Common, Watlington, Oxon (☎ 2735)

BALOGH, Hon Christopher Thomas; s of Baron Balogh; *b* 1948; *Educ* Westminster, King's Cambridge ; *Style* - The Hon Christoper Balogh

BALOGH, Hon Penelope Kathryn Teresa; da of Baron Balogh; *b* 1957; *Style* - The Hon Penelope Balogh

BALOGH, Hon Stephen Bernard; s of Baron Balogh ; *b* 1946; *Educ* Westminster, Balliol Oxford; *Style* - The Hon Stêphen Balogh;

BAMBERG, Harold Rolf; CBE (1968); *b* 17 Nov 1923; *Educ* Fleet Sch and William Ellis Sch Hampstead; *m* 1957, June Winifred Clarke; 1 s, 2 da (and 1 s, 1 da of a former m) ; *Career* chm Bamberg Group Ltd, Eagle Aircraft Services Ltd; *Style* - Harold Bamberg Esq, CBE; Harewood Park, Sunninghill, Berks

BAMBOROUGH, John Barnard; s of

John George Bamborough; *b* 3 Jan 1921; *Educ* Haberdasher's Aske's Hampstead Sch and New Coll Oxford; *m* 1947, Anne, nee Indrehus; 1 s, 1 da; *Career* fell and tutor Wadham Oxford 1947-62 (univ lectr in English 1951-62); Princ Linacre Oxford 1962-, Pro-Vice-Chancellor Oxford 1966-; *Style* - John Bamborough Esq; 40 St Giles, Oxford

BAMFIELD, Clifford; CB (1980); s of G Bamfield; *b* 21 March 1922; *Educ* Wintringham G S; *Career* Under Sec CSD 1974-; *Style* - Clifford Bamfield Esq, CB; 15 The Linkway, Sutton, Surrey (☎ 01 642 5377)

BAMFORD, Anthony Paul; s of Joseph Cyril Bamford *qv*; *b* 23 Oct 1945; *Educ* Ampleforth and Grenoble Univ; *m* 1974, Carole Gray Whitt; 1 s, 1 da ; *Career* chm and md J C Bamford Gp 1976; Young Businessman of the Year 1979; *Style* - Anthony Bamford Esq; J C Bamford Excavators, Rocester, Uttoxeter, Staffs (☎ Rocester 590312)

BAMFORD, Joseph Cyril; CBE (1969); *b* 21 June 1916; *Educ* St John's Alton Staffs, Stonyhurst; *m* 1941, Marjorie Griffin; 2 s; *Career* chm and md J C Bamford Excavators 1945-76; *Style* - Joseph Bamford Esq, CBE; 16 Rue de Bourg, CH 1003 Lausanne, Switzerland

BAMFORD, Brig Percy Geoffrey; CBE (1959, OBE 1951), DSO (1944); s of Lt-Col Percy Bamford (d 1951); *b* 23 May 1907; *Educ* Cranleigh Sch, Sandhurst; *m* 1930, Betty Fallding, nee Crossley; 1 s, 1 da; *Career* Brig, Cdr 150 Infantry Brigade 1954-56; *Recreations* hunting; *Clubs* Army and Navy; *Style* - Brig Percy Bamford, CBE, DSO; The Square, Swalcliffe, Banbury, Oxon (☎ Swalcliffe 240)

BAMPFYLDE, Hon David Cecil Warwick; s of 6 Baron Poltimore (d 1978) and Margret Mary, da of 4 Marquis de la Pasture (cr France 1768); hp to Barony of nephew 7 Baron Poltimore, *qv*; *b* 3 March 1924 ; *Educ* Eton; *m* 1950, Jean Margaret, nee Campbell; 3 s; *Style* - The Hon David Bampfylde; Coombe Lea, Malmesbury, Wilts

BANBURY OF SOUTHAM, 3 Baron (UK 1924); Sir Charles William Banbury; 3 Bt (UK 1902); s of 2 Baron, DL (d 1981), by his w Hilda, nee Carr (m dis 1958, she m 2 Maj R Gardner, MC); *b* 29 July 1953; *Style* - The Rt Hon The Lord Banbury of Southam; Stratton Cleeve, Cirencester, Glos

BANCROFT, Sir Ian Powell; GCB (1979, KCB 1975, CB 1971); s of A Bancroft; *b* 23 Dec 1922; *Educ* Coatham Sch, Balliol Oxford; *m* 1950, Jean Swaine; 2 s, 1 da; *Career* Head of Home CS and Perm Sec CSD 1978-; *Style* - Sir Ian Bancroft, GCB; 4 Melrose rd, West Hill, SW18

BANCROFT, John; MBE (1957), TD (1951), DL (E Yorks 1969, Humberside 1974); s of Edward Bancroft (d 1950); *b* 23 Dec 1910; *Educ* Waterloo H S Oldham; *Career* co dir (ret), chm SSAFA Hull Dist; *Style* - John Bancroft Esq, MBE, TD, DL; 11 Woodland End, Anlaby Pk, Hull (☎ 0482 54068)

BAND, His Honour Judge; Robert Murray Niven Band; MC (1944), QC (1974); s of Robert Band; *b* 23 Nov 1919; *Educ* Trin Coll Glenalmond, Hertford Oxford; *m* 1948, Nancy Redhead; 2 da; *Career* barr 1947, Circuit Judge 1978-; *Style* - His Honour Judge Band, MC, QC; Well Farm, Banstead, Surrey (☎ Burgh Heath 52288)

BANDON, Countess of; Lois; da of Francis Russell, of Victoria, Australia ; *m* 1, Mr White; m 2, 1946, as his 2 w, Air Ch Marshal 5 & last Earl of Bandon GBE CB CVO DSO (d 1979); *Style* - The Rt Hon The Countess of Bandon

BANERJEE, Rabindra Nath; CSI (1938); s of late Haradhan Banerjee; *b* 1 Feb 1895; *Educ* Calcutta U, Emmanuel Cambridge; *m* 1953, Manisha, da of late Lt-Col Upendra Nath Mukerjee, IMS; 1 s, 1 da ; *Career* chm, Union Public Service Commission, India 1949-55; ret; *Style* - Rabindra Banerjee Esq, CSI; 17 Friends' Colony, Mathura rd, New Delhi, India (☎ New Delhi 640220)

BANGERT, Bruce Antony; s of Cecil Bangert; *b* 31 Aug 1935; *Educ* Brentwood Sch, Christ's Cambridge; *m* 1963, Patricia, da of Kenneth Jackson; 1 s, 3 da; *Career* dir Petrochemicals Div ICI 1976-; *Recreations* sailing, skiing; *Style* - Bruce Bangert Esq; 67 The Grove, Marton, Middlesbrough, Cleveland (☎ 316139)

BANGOR, 7 Viscount (I 1781); Edward Henry Harold Ward; also Baron Bangor (I 1770); s of 6 Viscount Bangor, PC, OBE; *b* 5 Nov 1905; *Educ* Harrow, RMA Woolwich; *m* 1, 1933 (m dis 1937), Elizabeth, da of Thomas Balfour, JP, of Wrockwardine Hall, Wellington, Salop; m 2, 1937, May Kathleen (d 1969), da of W Middleton, of Shanghai; m 3, 1947 (m dis 1951), Leila Mary (d 1959) da of David Rimington Heaton, DSO; 1 s; m 4, 1951, Mrs Marjorie Alice Simpson, da of late Peter Banks; 1 s, 1 da (Hon Mrs (Sarah) Baker); *Heir* s, Hon William Ward; *Career* broadcaster and journalist, sometime Reuter's correspondent in China and Far East, BBC news observer Libya 1941; *Clubs* Savile, Garrick; *Style* - The Rt Hon The Viscount Bangor; 59 Cadogan sq, SW1 (☎ 01 235 3202)

BANISTER, John Michael; s of Frederick Banister (d 1963); *b* 30 Nov 1924; *Educ* St Peter's Sch York, BNC Oxford; *m* 1960, Thelma, da of William Smart, of Solihull; 1 s, 1 da; *Career* chm Toon & Heath (ad agency) 1972- (md 1961-72) MA, MCAM, FIPA; *Recreations* philately, bridge; *Clubs* Rotary; *Style* - John Banister Esq; 102 Ladbroke rd, Solihull, W Midlands (☎ 021 705 3332)

BANK-ANTHONY, Sir Mobolaji; KBE (1963, OBE 1956); s of Alfred Bank-Anthony; *b* 11 June 1907; *Educ* Lagos; *m* 1935, Olamide Adeshigbin; *Career* FRSA, FInstD, co dir; *Style* - Sir Mobolaji Bank-Anthony, KBE; Executive House, 2a Oil Mill st, Lagos, Nigeria (☎ 24660)

BANKES, Henry John Ralph; JP (Dorset 1936); s of Walter Bankes, of Corfe Castle and Kingston Lacy; *b* 14 July 1902; *Educ* Eton, Magdalen Oxford; *m* 1935, Hilary (d 1966), da of late Lt-Col F Strickland-Constable, of Wassand Hall Yorks; 1 s, 1 da; *Career* barr 1925, High Sheriff Dorset 1939; *Style* - Henry Bankes Esq, JP; Kingston Lacy, Wimborne, Dorset

BANKES, Hon Mrs; Hon Juliet Anne; *née* Williamson; da of 3 Baron Forres (d 1978) and Gillian Ann Maclean, nee Grant *b* 1949; *m* 1972, Nigel John Eldon Bankes; 1 s; *Style* - The Hon Mrs Bankes

BANKS, Baron (Life Peer UK 1974); Desmond Anderson Harvie Banks; CBE (1972); s of James Banks, OBE; *b* 23 Oct 1918; *Educ* U Coll Sch Hampstead; *m* 1948, Barbara, da of Richard Taylor Wells; 2 s; *Career* life assur broker, dir Tweddle French & Co (Life & Pensions) Ltd 1973-; chm Lib Pty Exec 1961-63 & 1969-70, Pres Lib Pty 1968-69, memb For Affrs & Soc Securities Panel 1961-, Lib Spokesman soc servs 1977-, Dep Lib Whip Ho Lds 1977-, Pres Lib European Action Gp 1971-; stood (Lib) for Parl 1950 Harrow E, 1955 St Ives, 1959 SW Herts; served WW II M East & Italy KRRC & RA as Maj (Ch PRO Allied Mil Govt Trieste 1946); V-Chm European Atlantic Gp 1979-, Br Cncl European Movement 1979-; Elder of the Utd Reformed Church; *Style* - The Rt Hon Lord Banks CBE; 58 The Ridgeway, Kenton, Middx (☎ 01 907 7369)

BANKS, Hon Alistair Richard Harvie; s of Baron Banks, CBE, *qv*; *b* 1950; *m* 1977, Loretta Ann Owen; *Style* - The Hon Alistair Banks

BANKS, Colin; s of William Banks; *b* 1 Jan 1932; *Educ* Rochester Tech Sch; *m* 1961, Caroline Grigson; 1 s, 1 da (decd); *Career* Fndr Banks and Miles (graphic designers) 1958, dir John Marshbanks Ltd (publishers); co-editor Which? 1964-; *Style* - Colin Banks Esq; 1 Tranquil Vale, Blackheath, SE3 (☎ 01 318 1131)

BANKS, Hon Mrs; Hon Caroline Veronica; *née* Hamilton-Russell; da of 10 Viscount Boyne, JP, DL; *b* 1957; *m* 1975, David George Fothergill Banks; 1 s; *Style* - The Hon Mrs Banks; Martley Court, Martley, Worcester

BANKS, Donald Robert Butler; *Career* chm Cyanamid of Great Britain, manufacturers of pharmaceuticals; *Style* - Donald Banks Esq; Cyanamid of Great Britain Ltd, Fareham rd, Gosport, Hants

BANKS, Frank David; s of Samuel Banks; *b* 11 April 1933; *Educ* Liverpool Collegiate Sch, Carnegie Mellon U; *m* 1, 1955, Catherine Jacob; 1 s, 2 da; m 2, 1967, Sonia Coleman; 1 da; *Career* FCA, dir Constructors John Brown Ltd 1974-; *Style* - Frank Banks Esq; The Castle Inn, Benson, Oxon

BANKS, Hon Graham Thornton Harvie; s of Baron Banks CBE;*b* 1953; *Style* - The Hon Graham Banks

BANKS, Sir Maurice Alfred Lister; s of Alfred Banks, FRCS; *b* 11 Aug 1901; *Educ* Westminster, Manchester U; *m* 1933, Ruth Hall, of Philadelphia; 1 s, 2 da; *Career* kt 1971, chm Laird Gp 1970-75; *Style* - Sir Maurice Banks; Beech Coppice, Kingswood, Surrey (☎ Mogador 2270)

BANKS, Michael Charles; *Career* man dir Sidney C Banks Ltd (grain merchants and seed specialists) ; *Style* - Michael Banks Esq; c/o Sidney C Banks Ltd, 29 St Neots rd, Sandy, Beds

BANKS, Robert George; MP (C) Harrogate 1974-; s of George Banks, MBE; *b* 18 Jan 1937; *Educ* Haileybury; *m* 1967, Diana Crawfurd; 4 s, 1 da; *Career* Ptnr Breckland Securities, Jt Sec Con Parly Def Cttee; *Style* - Robert Banks Esq, MP; Bretteston Hall, Stanstead, Sudbury, Suffolk; Cow Myers, Galphay, Ripon, Yorks

BANKS, Richard Lewin; *Career* md Sidney C Banks Ltd; *Style* - Richard Banks Esq; 29 St Neots rd, Sandy, Beds

BANKS, Charles George Edmond; *Career* chm and ch exec Thomas De La Rue and Co Ltd; *Style* - Charles Banks Esq; De La Rue House, PO Box 10, Basingstoke, Hants

BANNATYNE, Capt Charles Gordon; s of Arthur Bannatyne (d 1932); *b* 2 June 1925; *Educ* Loretto, Mil Coll of Science; *m* 1952, Christina, da of Ernesto Herman Mallmann (d 1964); 2 s, 1 da; *Career* reg soldier to 1956, chm Wiggins Teape (Ireland) Hldgs and subsids, Pres EUGROPA 1981-, dir Hovat Ltd, Hovat (Europe) Ltd, Samuel Jones & Co; *Recreations* skiing, sailing, fishing, reading; *Style* - Capt Charles Bannatyne; c/o Nat West Bank, 63 Piccadilly, W1

BANNENBERG, Jon; s of Henryk Bannenberg; *b* 8 July 1929; *Educ* Canterbury H S Sydney, Sydney Conservatorium of Music; *m* 1960, Beaupre Robinson; 2 s; *Career* RDI AMRINA, boat designer; *Style* - Jon Bannenberg Esq; 35 Carlyle sq, SW3 (☎ 01 352 6129)

BANNERMAN, Alexander Patrick; s and h of Sir Donald Arthur Gordon Bannerman, 13 Bt, *qv*; *b* 5 May 1933; *Educ* Gordonstoun and Royal Agricultural Coll, Cirencester; *m* 1977, Joan Mary, da of late John Henry Wilcox of Tadcaster, Yorks; *Career* formerly with Queen's Own Cameron Highlanders and at Queen Elizabeth's Training Coll for The Disabled; *Style* - Alexander Bannerman Esq; 24 Rathgar Close, Redhill, Surrey

BANNERMAN, Hon Calum Ruairi Mundell ; s of Baron Bannerman of Kildonan (Life Peer, d 1969); *b* 1936; *Educ* Cambridge; *Style* - The Hon Calum Bannerman

BANNERMAN, Lt-Col Sir Donald Arthur Gordon; 13 Bt (NS 1682); s of Lt-Col Sir Arthur Bannerman, 12 Bt, KCVO, CIE (d 1955); *b* 2 July 1899; *Educ* Harrow, Sandhurst; *m* 1932, Barbara, da of Lt-Col Alick Cameron, OBE (d 1932); 2 s, 2 da; *Heir* s, Alexander Bannerman; *Career* Army Offr 1918-47 (Mil Govt Germany 1945-48 as PRO and SCO), Housemaster Gordonstoun 1948-52, Fettes 1952-69; *Recreations* writing, gardening; *Style* - Lt-Col Sir Donald Bannerman, Bt; 11 Learmonth pla, Edinburgh EH4 1AX (☎ 031 332 1076)

BANNERMAN, George Gordon; s of George Bannerman Jr (CA), of Glasgow (d 1964); *b* 25 Feb 1932; *Educ* Glasgow H S, Glasgow Acad, Sidney Sussex, Cambridge;

m 1959, Ann, da of James Gemmell, of Milngavie (d 1977); 1 s, 1 da; *Career* actuary (FFA, AIA, ASA, FPMI); dir and actuary C T Bowring & Layborn Ltd 1972; *Style* - George Bannerman Esq; 37 Westbury rd, N12 (☎ 01 445 1795)

BANNERMAN, Joan, Lady; Joan Mary; *née* Harford, da of the late Frederic Dundas Harford, CVO, JP, DL; *m* 1920, Lt-Col Sir Alexander Bannerman, 11 Bt (d 1934); *Style* - Joan, Lady Bannerman; 28 Melton ct, SW7

BANNERMAN, Hon John Walter MacDonald; s of Baron Bannerman of Kildonan (Life Peer, d 1969); *b* 1932; *Educ* Cambridge; *Style* - The Hon John Bannerman

BANNERMAN OF KILDONAN, Baroness; Ray; *née* Mundell; da of late Walter Mundell, of Swordale, Evanton, Ross-shire; *m* 1931, Baron Bannerman of Kildonan (Life Peer, d 1969); *Style* - The Rt Hon Lady Bannerman of Kildonan; The Old Manse, Balmaha, Stirlingshire

BANNISTER, Sir Roger Gilbert; CBE (1955); s of late Ralph Bannister; *b* 23 March 1929; *Educ* U Coll Sch, Exeter and Merton Colls Oxford; *m* 1955, Moyra, da of Per Jacobsson, chm IMF; 2 s, 2 da; *Career* Consultant- Nat Hosp Nervous Diseases, Dept Nervous Diseases St Mary's, Western Ophthalmic Hosp, FRCP; kt 1975; 1st man to run four minute mile; *Style* - Sir Roger Bannister, CBE; 16 Edwardes sq, W8 (☎ 01 603 9903); Churchfield, Lyminster, Sussex

BANWELL, Sir (George) Harold; s of late Edward Banwell; *b* 11 Dec 1900; *Educ* Tankerton Coll Kent; *m* 1924, Kate Bull; 2 s, 3 da; *Career* kt 1955, Pres Lincoln Civic Tst; *Style* - Sir Harold Banwell; 2 Vicars' Court, Lincoln (☎ 28869)

BARBARY, Lady Pamela Joan; *née* Nugent; da of 12 Earl of Westmeath; *b* 1921; *m* 1950, Lt-Col Peter John Barbary, OBE, GM, TD, DL, (d 1969); 1 s, 1 da ; *Career* Sometime Section Officer WAAF ; *Style* - Lady Pamela Barbary; Briar Rose Cottage, 17 Landeryon Gdns, Penzance, Cornwall

BARBER, Baron (Life Peer UK 1974); Anthony Perrinott Lysberg Barber; TD, PC (1963); s of John Barber, CBE; *b* 4 July 1920; *Educ* Retford G S, Oriel Oxford; *m* 1950, Jean, da of Milton Asquith, of Wentbridge; 2 da; *Career* chm Standard Chartered Bank 1974-, barr 1948, MP (C) Doncaster 1951-64 and Altrincham and Sale 1965-74, Chllr of Exchequer 1970-74, Chm Con Party Orgn 1967-70; *Style* - The Rt Hon The Lord Barber, TD, PC; Standard Chartered Bank, 10 Clement's Lane, EC4 (☎ 01 623 7500); 15 Montpelier sq, SW7; Wentbridge, Pontefract, W Yorks

BARBER, David Stewart; s of Jack Barber (d 1961); *b* 21 Sept 1931; *Educ* Rossendale G S; *m* 1965, Hazel Valerie; 1 s, 1 da; *Career* sr consultant PA Management Consultants Ltd 1960-71; chm and md Halma Ltd 1972-; *Recreations* Golf, Squash; *Style* - David Barber Esq; Ballinger House, Ballinger, Bucks (☎ Gr Missenden 2345)

BARBER, Hon Sir (Edward Hamilton) Esler; s of late Rev John Barber; *b* 26 July 1905; *Educ* Hamilton Coll Vict, Scots Coll Sydney, Scotch Coll Melbourne, Melbourne U; *m* 1954, Constance, da of Capt C Palmer; 1 s, 1 da; *Career* barr 1929, Puisne Judge Vict Supreme Court Australia 1965-77, QC (Vict) 1955; kt 1976; *Style* - Hon Sir Esler Barber; 1 St George's Court, Toorak, Vict 3142, Australia (☎ 24 5104)

BARBER, Eric Edward; *Career* chm Sterling-Winthrop Gp Ltd; *Style* - Eric Barber Esq; Sterling-Winthrop House, Surbiton, Surrey

BARBER, John Norman Romney; s of George Barber; *b* 22 April 1919; *Educ* Westcliff; *m* 1941, Babette, da of Louis Chalu (d 1975); 1 s; *Career* chm Aberhurst Ltd 1976-, A C Edwards Engrg 1977-; dep chm John E Wiltshire & Co 1980-, Cox & Kings Ltd 1980-; dir- Acrow Ltd 1977-, Amalgamated Metal Corpn 1980-, Spear & Jackson Int 1980-; memb Investment Bd Wiltshire Gp 1979-, FBIM; *Style* - John Barber Esq; High Walls, Claremont ave, Esher, Surrey

BARBER, Hon Louise Patricia Lysberg; da of Baron Barber, TD, PC, *qv*; *b* 1951; *Style* - The Hon Louise Barber

BARBER, Thomas David; s and h of Sir William Barber, 2 Bt, TD, *qv*; *b* 18 Nov 1937; *Educ* Eton, Trin Cambridge; *m* 1, 1972, Amanda Mary, nee Rabone (m dis 1976); 1 s; m 2, 1978, Jeannine Mary, nee Gurney; *Style* - Thomas Barber Esq; Windrush House, Inkpen, Berks

BARBER, Sir William Francis; 2 Bt (UK 1960), of Greasley, Co Nottingham, TD, JP (Notts); s of Col Sir (Thomas) Philip Barber, 1 Bt, DSO, TD, JP, DL (d 1961); *b* 20 Nov 1905; *m* 1, 1936 (m dis 1978), Diana Constance, da of late Lt-Col Thomas Owen Lloyd, CMG; 1 s, 1 da; m 2, 1978, Jean Marie, wid of Dr Harry Carew Nott, of Adelaide, S Australia; *Heir* s, Thomas David Barber; *Career* Hon Col S Notts Hussars Yeo 1961-66, High Sheriff Notts 1964-65, Lt-Col RHA 1947; *Style* - Sir William Barber, Bt, TD, JP; Lamb Close, Eastwood, Notts; Dunmaglass, Aberarder, Inverness-shire

BARBER, Hon Josephine Julia Asquith; da of Baron Barber, TD, PC, *qv*; *b* 1952; *Style* - The Hon Josephine Barber

BARBIERI, Margaret Elizabeth; da of Ettore Barbieri and Lea Barbieri; *b* 2 March 1947; *Educ* Durban, Roy Ballet Senior Sch; *Career* Senior Pncpl Sadler's Wells Royal Ballet 1974-; *Style* - Miss Margaret Barbieri; 19 Merton av, W4 (☎ 01 995 6554)

BARBOUR, Hon Mrs; Hon Helen Victoria; *née* Hepburne-Scott; da of 9 Lord Polwarth and Edith Frances, da of Sir Thomas Fowell Buxton, 3 Bt ; *b* 1891; *m* 1919, George Freeland Barbour (d 1946); 2 s, 3 da; *Style* - The Hon Mrs Barbour; Fincastle, Pitlochry, Perthshire

BARCLAY, Sir Colville Herbert Sanford; 14 Bt (NS 1668); s of late Rt Hon Sir Colville Adrian de Rune Barclay, KCMG, 3 s of 11 Bt; suc unc, Sir Robert Cecil de Belzim Barclay, 13 Bt, 1930; *b* 7 May 1913; *Educ* Eton, Trin Oxford; *m* 1949, Rosamond Grant Renton, da of late Dr W Armstrong Elliott, of Chandler's Ford, Hants; 3 s; *Heir* s, Robert Colraine Barclay; *Career* 3 Sec Diplomatic Serv 1938-41, Lt-Cdr RNVR WW II; RBA; *Style* - Sir Colville Barclay, Bt; Pitshill, Petworth, W Sussex (☎ Lodsworth 341)

BARCLAY, David William; s of Theodore Barclay, of Desnage Lodge, Bury St Edmunds; *b* 29 Nov 1942; *Educ* Harrow, Trin Cambridge; *m* 1967, Celia, da of Maj Hugh Cairns, MC, of St Boswell's, Roxburghshire; 1 s, 1 da; *Career* local dir Barclays Bank Pall Mall 1973-79, Ipswich 1979-; *Recreations* shooting, fishing, hunting; *Clubs* Boodle's, Pratt's; *Style* - David Barclay Esq; Lodge Farm, Higham, Bury St Edmunds, Suffolk (☎ 810429)

BARCLAY, Joseph Gurney; s of Sir Roderick Barclay, GCVO, KCMG; *b* 17 Jan 1946; *Educ* Harrow, St Edmund Hall Oxford; *m* 1978, Joanna, da of Brig A Brindley, CBE; 1 da; *Career* local dir Barclays Bank Birmingham 1978-; *Recreations* shooting, travel; *Style* - Joseph Barclay Esq; c/o Barclays Bank, 63 Colmore Row, Birmingham B3

BARCLAY, Hon Mrs; Hon Phyllis Patty; *née* Crossley; MBE (1942), JP (Norfolk); da of 1 Baron Somerleyton, GCVO, PC, ; *b* 1890; *m* 1917, Capt Evelyn Hugh Barclay (d 1956); 2 da; *Career* sometime Subaltern ATS; *Style* - The Hon Mrs Barclay, MBE, JP; Glebe House, Somerleyton, Lowestoft, Suffolk

BARCLAY, Robert Colraine; s and h of Sir Colville Herbert Sanford Barclay, 14 Bt, *qv*; *b* 12 Feb 1950; *m* 1980, Lucilia Saboia, da of Senhor Carlos Saboia de Albuquerque, of Ipanema, Rio de Janeiro; *Style* - Robert Barclay Esq

BARCLAY, Sir Roderick Edward; GCVO (1966, KCVO 1957, CVO 1953), KCMG (1955, CMG 1948); s of late J Gurney Barclay; *b* 22 Feb 1909; *Educ* Harrow, Trin Cambridge; *m* 1934, Jean, da of late Sir Hugh Gladstone; 1 s, 3 da; *Career* dir Barclays Bank SA 1969- (chm 1970-74), Slough Estates 1969-, Ambass to Belgium 1963-69; *Style* - Sir Roderick Barclay, GCVO, KCMG; Great White

End, Latimer, Bucks (☎ Little Chalfont 2050)

BARCLAY-HARVEY, Lady Muriel Felicia Vere; *née* Bertie; da of 12 Earl of Lindsey, JP, DL; *b* 1893; *m* 1, 1922, Capt Henry Liddell-Grainger, DL, Scots Gds, of Ayton Castle, Berwicks (d 1935); 1 s (David Liddell-Grainger, DL, *qv*); m 2, 1938, as his 2 w, Col Sir Charles Barclay-Harvey, KCMG (d 1969); *Career* DJStJ; served WW I; *Style* - Lady Muriel Barclay-Harvey; Dinnet Aberdeenshire; Uffington House, Stamford, Lincs

BARD, Dr Basil Joseph Asher; CBE (1968); s of Abram Bard; *b* 20 Aug 1914; *Educ* Owen's Sch, RCS (Imperial Coll); *m* 1942, Ena Birk; 3 s; *Career* chm New Product Management (NPM) Gp 1977-, Birmingham Mint Ltd 1977-, Transcan Video Ltd 1978-, barr 1938, Pres Anglo-Jewish Assoc 1977-; *Style* - Dr Basil Bard, CBE; 23 Mourne House, Maresfield gdns, NW3 (☎ 01 435 5340, business 01 404 5414)

BARDSLEY, Lady Rose; *née* Fane; da of 14 Earl of Westmorland (d 1948) and Diana, Countess of Westmorland, *qv*; *b* 1930; *m* Capt John Macdonald-Buchanan, MC (m dis 1969); m 2, 1972, John V Bardsley; *Style* - Lady Rose Bardsley ; St Mary's House, Tormarton, Glos

BARENBOIM, Daniel; s of Enrique Barenboim and Aida, nee Schuster; *b* 15 Nov 1942 Buenos Aires; *Educ* Santa Cecilia Acad Rome, coached by Edwin Fischer, Nadia Boulanger and Igor Markevitch; *m* 1967, Jacqueline du Pre; *Career* pianist and conductor, Musical Dir Orchestre de Paris 1975-; *Style* - Daniel Barenboim Esq; c/o Harold Holt Ltd, 134 Wigmore st, W1

BARFETT, Ven Thomas; s of Rev Thomas Barfett (d 1968); *b* 2 Oct 1916; *Educ* St John's Leatherhead, Keble Oxford; *m* 1945, Edna, nee Toy; 1 s, 1 da; *Career* Archdeacon Hereford and Canon Residentiary H Cathedral 1977-, Chaplain to HM The Queen 1975-; *Recreations* genealogy, heraldry; *Clubs* Oxford & Cambridge; *Style* - The Ven The Archdeacon of Hereford; The Archdeacon's House, The Close, Hereford (☎ 0432 2873)

BARFORD, Clive Julian Stanley; s of Maj E Barford, MC (d 1979), and Hon Grace Lowrey Stanley, da of 1 and last Baron Ashfield; *b* 11 May 1933; *Educ* Eton; *m* 1961, Helen, da of Hon Mr Justice Foster, MBE, TD; 1 s, 3 da; *Career* chm and md Aldworth Investments Ltd and Abex Ltd, memb of Lloyd's; *Recreations* shooting, golf, gardening; *Clubs* Buck's; *Style* - Clive Barford Esq; Pibworth House, Aldworth, Berks (☎ Compton 495)

BARFORD, Sir Leonard; s of William Barford; *b* 1 Aug 1908; *Educ* Dame Alice Owen's Sch, St Cat's Cambridge; *m* 1939, Betty Crichton; 2 s; *Career* kt 1967, dep chm Horserace Totalisator Bd 1974-77, Ch Inspector Taxes Bd of Inland Revenue 1964-73; *Style* - Sir Leonard Barford; Harley House, 79 Sutton rd, Seaford, E Sussex (☎ 893364)

BARFORD, Hon Mrs Marian; Hon Marian Woodruff; *née* Stanley; da of 1 Baron Ashfield; *m* 1, 1927, James Hart Rutland (m dis 1934); 1 s; m 2, 1934, James Henry Royds (m dis 1940); 1 da; m 3, 1940, Ralph Arthur Hubbard (m dis 1954); 2 da; m 4, 1964, Edward James Barford, MC, (m dis 1971); *Style* - The Hon Mrs Marian Barford; 1 Pine Acre, Charters rd, Sunningdale, Berks

BARGE, Ronald Mansfield; DSC (1942), VRD (1950), DL (Dunbartonshire 1972); s of Lt-Col Kenneth Barge, DSO, MC (d 1971); *b* 10 Nov 1920; *Educ* Glasgow Art Sch, Munich and Durham Us, RCA; *m* 1950, Elizabeth, da of Col John Lamberton, DSO, MC; 3 s, 2 da; *Career* salmon farmer, chm Otter Ferry Salmon Ltd, V-Chm Bitmac Ltd, chm Barworth (Haulage) Ltd, dir Lamberton Hldgs; *Recreations* art, gardening, fishing; *Clubs* Roy Northern Yacht, Midhook Yacht; *Style* - Ronald Barge Esq, DSC, VRD, DL; Whistler's Hill, Rhu, Dunbartonshire (☎ 820 285); Evanaghan, Otterferry, Argyll (☎ Kilfinan 284)

BARING, Hon Anne; da of 4 Baron Northbrook (d 1947); *b* 1917; *Style* - The Hon Anne Baring; Woodlands Farm,

Bramdean, Alresford, Hants

BARING, Hon Alexandra Grace; da of 5 Baron Northbrook, *qv*; *b* 4 Feb 1957; *Style* - The Hon Alexandra Baring

BARING, Hon Angela Mildred; da of 5 Baron Ashburton (d 1938); *b* 1893; *Style* - The Hon Angela Baring; Itchen Stoke Manor, Itchen Stoke, Alresford, Hants (☎ Alresford 2440)

BARING, Hon Alice Olivia; da of 2 Baron Howick of Glendale, *qv*; *b* 1971; *Style* - The Hon Alice Baring

BARING, Hon Catherine Margaret; da of 5 Baron Northbrook; *b* 12 May 1965; *Style* - The Hon Catherine Baring

BARING, Hon David Evelyn Charles; s and h of 2 Baron Howick of Glendale, *qv*; *b* 26 Mar 1975; *Style* - The Hon David Baring

BARING, Hon Francis Thomas; s and h of 5 Baron Northbrook, *qv*; *b* 21 Feb 1954; *Educ* Winchester; *Style* - The Hon Francis Baring

BARING, Hon John; s and h of 4 Baron Revelstoke, *qv*; *b* 2 Dec 1934; *Educ* Eton; *Style* - The Hon John Baring; Passenham Manor, Stony Stratford, Bucks (☎ 2150)

BARING, Hon James Cecil; s of 4 Baron Revelstoke, *qv*; *b* 1938; *Educ* Eton; *m* 1968, Aneta, da of late Erskine Fisher; 2 s; *Style* - The Hon James Baring; 105 Elgin cres, W11

BARING, Hon John Francis Harcourt; CVO (1980); s and h of 6 Baron Ashburton, KG, KCVO; *b* 2 Nov 1928; *Educ* Eton, Trin Cambridge; *m* 1955, Hon Susan, da of 1 Baron Renwick, KBE; 2 s, 2 da; *Career* chm Baring Bros & Co 1974-, Receiver-Gen Duchy of Cornwall 1974-, chm Accepting Houses Ctee 1977-, dir Pye Hldgs 1966-, dep chm Roy Insur Tst 1968-memb Cncl CBI 1976, Tstee Nat Gallery 1981-; *Style* - The Hon John Baring, CVO; Flat 7, 34 Bryanston sq, W1; Lake House, Northington, Alresford, Hants (☎ 4293)

BARING, Hon Jessica Mary Clare; da of 2 Baron Howick of Glendale, *qv*; *b* 1969; *Style* - The Hon Jessica Baring

BARING, Hon Laura Anne; da of 5 Baron Northbrook, *qv*; *b* 12 June 1952; *Style* - The Hon Laura Baring; Shawlands Farm, Hursley, Hants

BARING, Sir Mark; KCVO (1980, CVO 1970), JP (Inner London 1963); s of late Hon Windham Baring, s of 1 Earl of Cromer, GCB, OM, and Lady Gweneth, JP, nee Ponsonby, da of 8 Earl of Bessborough (who m as her 2 husband, Col Ralph Cavendish, CBE, MVO, DL); *b* 9 June 1916; *Educ* Eton, Trin Cambridge; *m* 1949, Victoria, da of late Col R Russell, CVO, CBE, DSO; 2 da- Lavinia Gweneth (m 1974, Hon Vivian John Baring, *qv*), Juliet Victoria; *Career* Gen Commissioner Income Tax 1966-, exec chm King Edward VII's Hosp for Officers 1969-, High Sheriff Gter London 1975, Chm Assoc Ind Hosps; *Recreations* real tennis, bridge, swimming; *Clubs* Brooks's, White's; *Style* - Sir Mark Baring KCVO JP; 18 Thurloe sq, SW7 (☎ 01 589 8485)

BARING, (Charles) Peter; s of Capt Raymond Alexander Baring (2 s of Sir Godfrey Baring, 1 Bt, KBE, who d 1967) and Margaret Fleetwood, nee Campbell-Preston; h to Btcy of unc, Sir Charles Christian Baring, 2 Bt, JP, DL, *qv*; *b* 24 May 1939; *Educ* Eton; *m* 1, 1964, Sarah, nee Withycombe (m dis 1974); 2 da; m 2, 1976, Susannah Jane, nee Smith; 1 da; *Style* - Peter Baring Esq; Av Insurgenties Sur 1377, Mexico City, Mexico

BARING, Hon Robin Alexander; s of 6 Baron Ashburton, KG, KCVO, JP, DL, *qv*; *b* 1931; *Educ* Eton; *m* 1960, Anne Caroline Thalia, nee Gage; 1 da; *Career* late Sub-Lt RNVR; *Style* - The Hon Robin Baring; 142 Hamilton terrace, NW8

BARING, Lady Rose Gwendolen Louisa; *née* DCVO (1972, CVO 1964); da of 12 Earl of Antrim and Margaret, da of late Rt Hon J G Talbot; *b* 23 May 1909; *m* 1933, Francis Baring (s of Hon Hugo Baring, OBE, and Lady Evelyn, nee Ashley-Cooper, da of 8 Earl of Shaftesbury, and gs of 1 Baron Revelstoke; ka 1940); 2 s, 1 da; *Career* Woman of the

Bedchamber to HM The Queen 1953-73, Extra Woman of the Bedchamber 1973-; *Style* - Lady Rose Baring, DCVO; 43 Pembroke sq, W8

BARING, Hon Rachel Monica; da of 2 Baron Howick of Glendale, *qv*; *b* 1967; *Style* - The Hon Rachel Baring

BARING, Hon Mrs; Hon Sarah Katharine Elinor; da of 6 Baron Grantley (d 1954); *m* 1, 1945, 3 Viscount Astor (m dis 1953 and who d 1966); 1 s; m 2, 1953, Thomas Michael Baring (m dis 1965); 1 s (adopted); *Style* - The Hon Mrs Baring; 23 Scarsdale Villas, W8; Ginge Manor, Wantage, Berks

BARING, Hon Vivian John Rowland; s of 3 Earl of Cromer, KG, GCMG, MBE, PC, *qv*; *b* 12 June 1950; *Educ* Stanbridge Earls Sch, Romsey Royal Farms Windsor, RAC Cirencester; *m* 1974, Lavinia Gweneth, da of Mark Baring, CVO; 2 s; *Style* - The Hon Vivian Baring; Frenchstreet Farm, Westerham, Kent

BARKE, James Allen; s of James E Barke; *b* 16 April 1903; *Educ* Birley st Central Sch and Manchester Coll of Technology; *m* 1, 1937, Doris Bayne (d 1952); 2 s, 1 da; m 2, 1953, Marguerite Amy Sutcliffe, nee Williams (d 1968); 1 step da; *Career* dir Falcon Engineering Co 1972-, V-Chm Ford 1965-68; *Style* - James Barke Esq; Thurlestone, Mill Green, Ingatestone, Essex

BARKER, Sir Alwyn Bowman; CMG (1962); s of late A Barker; *b* 5 Aug 1900; *Educ* St Peter's Coll Adelaide, Geelong G S, Adelaide U; *m* 1926, Isabel, da of late Sir Edward Lucas; 1 da (and 1 s decd); *Career* kt 1969, BSc, BE, FIEAust, chm Kelvinator Australia Ltd 1967-, Tecalemit (Australia) Pty Ltd; *Style* - Sir Alwyn Barker, CMG; 51 Hackney rd, Hackney, SA 5069, Australia (☎ 42 2838)

BARKER, Hon Adam Campbell; s of Baroness Trumpington, JP (Life Peeress), *qv*, and William Alan Barker; *b* 1955; *Style* - The Hon Adam Barker

BARKER, David; QC (1976); s of Frederick Barker; *b* 13 April 1932; *Educ* UCL, Michigan U; *m* 1957, Diana, nee Duckworth; 1 s, 3 da; *Career* Crown Court Recorder 1974-, barr 1954, contested (L) Runcorn 1955; *Style* - David Barker Esq, QC; Nanhill, Woodhouse Eaves, Leics (☎ 890224; office 01 351 7881)

BARKER, Dennis Albert; QC (1968); s of J Barker; *b* 9 June 1926; *Educ* Nottingham H S, Queen's Oxford; *m* 1949, Daphne, nee Ruffle; 1 s, 1 da (and 1 da decd); *Career* Crown Court Recorder 1972-, barr 1950; *Style* - Dennis Barker Esq, QC; Heathlands, Gt Brickhill, Milton Keynes (☎ Gt Brickhill 251; office 01 353 0375)

BARKER, Denis William Knighton; *b* 21 Aug 1908; *Educ* Holgate G S, Barnsley; Sheffield U; *m* 1938, Esmee Doris Marsh; 2 da; *Career* md BP 1967-72; *Style* - Denis Barker Esq; Stable Cottage, Upper House lane, Shamley Green, Guildford, Surrey (☎ Cranleigh 2726)

BARKER, Gen Sir Evelyn Hugh; KCB (1950, CB 1944), KBE (1945, CBE 1940), DSO (1918), MC; s of late Maj-Gen Sir George Barker, KCB, and late Hon Lady Barker (Hon Clemency Hubbard, da of 1 Baron Addington); *b* 22 May 1894; *Educ* Wellington, Sandhurst; *m* 1923, Violet, da of T Thornton, of Brockhall, Northants; 1 s; *Career* GOC-in-C E Cmmd 1947-50, ADC Gen to the King 1949-50, DL Beds 1952-67; *Style* - Gen Sir Evelyn Barker, KCB, KBE, DSO, MC; Park House, Bromham, Bedford (☎ Oakley 2332)

BARKER, Sir Harry Heaton; KBE (1978, CBE 1972, OBE 1964), JP; s of J Barker; *b* 18 July 1898; *Educ* Wellington and Auckland, New Plymouth Boys' High School; *m* 1926, Anita, MBE, daughter of H Greaves; *Career* served with New Zealand Expeditionary Force in World War I 1917-19; journalist, ed Gisborne Herald 1935-43 (formerly sub-editor, leader writer and associate editor); Mayor of Gisborne 1950, 1953, 1956, 1959, 1962, 1965, 1968, 1971, 1974; *Style* - Sir Harry Barker, KBE, JP; 218 Harris Street, Gisborne, New Zealand (☎ 6405)

BARKER, Hugh Purslove; s of Arthur Henry Barker and Florence, nee Saich; *b* 11 March 1909; *Educ* Oundle; *m* 1935, Joyce Frances Higgs; 2 s, 1 da; *Career* v-pres BIM 1962-; chm Boosey and Hawkes Ltd 1974-79; *Style* - Hugh Barker Esq; Flat 18, 22 St James's sq, SW1 (☎ 01-930 2618); Rose Cottage, Elkstone, Buxton, Derbys (☎ Blackshaw 287)

BARKER, James; JP; *Career* md London and Northern Securities Ltd; *Style* - James Barker Esq, JP; Bamburgh House, Market st, Newcastle upon Tyne

BARKER, Air Vice-Marshal John Lindsay; CB (1963), CBE (1946), DFC (1945); s of Dr Abraham Barker (d 1972); *b* 12 Nov 1910; *Educ* Trent Coll, BNC Oxford; *m* 1948, Eleanor; 1 s; *Career* Air Attaché Rome 1955-58, Cdr Roy Ceylon Air Force 1958-63, barr; *Recreations* sailing, golf, photography; *Clubs* RAF, Roy Dart Yacht; *Style* - Air Vice-Marshal John Barker, CB, CBE DFC; Ravensbourne, Stoke Fleming, Dartmouth (☎ S Fleming 271)

BARKER, Hon Mrs; Hon Olwen Gwynne; *née* Philipps; JP; da of 1 and last Baron Kylsant (d 1937); *b* 1905; *m* 1, 1925 (m dis 1937), 7 Baron Suffield; m 2, 1937, Lt-Col Frank Richard Peter Barker (d 1974); 1 s; *Style* - The Hon Mrs Barker, JP; Lund Court, Nawton, York

BARKER, Ronnie (Ronald William George Barker); OBE (1978); s of Leonard Barker; *b* 25 Sept 1929; *Educ* Oxford H S; *m* 1957, Joy Tubb; 2 s, 1 da; *Career* actor, jt winner with Ronnie Corbett 1980 Variety Club of GB Award Showbusiness Personality of the Year; *Style* - Ronnie Barker Esq, OBE; c/o Peter Eade Ltd, 9 Cork st, W1

BARKER, Sir William; KCMG (1967, CMG 1958), OBE (1949); s of Alfred Barker; *b* 19 July 1909; *Educ* Liverpool and Prague Us; *m* 1939, Margaret Beirne; 1 s, 1 da; *Career* Bowes Prof of Russian Liverpool U 1969-76, Br Ambass to Czechoslovakia 1966-68; *Style* - Sir William Barker, KCMG, OBE; 53 Eshe rd N, Liverpool L23 8UE

BARKES, Neville Rogerson; TD; s of W Barkes, of Northumberland; *b* 11 July 1924; *Educ* Sedbergh Sch; *m* 1952, Gillian, da of Col C Cookson, DSO, of Morpeth; 2 s, 1 da; *Career* dir Br Electrical & Mfg Co, TSB Hldgs 1980-; chm TSB NE, TSB Computer Servs 1973, memb TSB Central Bd 1980; *Recreations* shooting, gardening; *Clubs* Northern Counties; *Style* - Neville Barkes Esq, TD; Muckleridge, Matfen, Northumberland (☎ Stamfordham 230)

BARKWORTH, Peter Wynn; s of Walter Barkworth; *b* 14 Jan 1929; *Educ* Stockport Sch, RADA; *Career* actor; *Style* - Peter Barkworth Esq; 47 Flask Walk, NW3 (☎ 01 794 4591)

BARLAS, Sir Richard Douglas; KCB (1977, CB 1968), OBE (1943); s of E Barlas; *b* 19 May 1916; *Educ* Westminster, Ch Ch Oxford; *m* 1940, Ann, da of Canon R Porter; 3 s; *Career* Clerk of House of Commons 1976-79; *Style* - Sir Richard Barlas, KCB, OBE; Walnut House, Ticehurst, E Sussex

BARLOW, Sir Christopher Hilaro; 7 Bt (UK 1803), of Fort William, Bengal; s of Sir Richard Barlow, 6 Bt, AFC (d 1946); *b* 1 Dec 1929; *Educ* Eton, McGill U; *m* 1952, Jacqueline, da of John Audley (d 1980); 2 s, 2 da; *Heir* s, Crispian Barlow; *Career* architect; *Recreations* sailing (owner of ketch 'Phoebe'); *Style* - Sir Christopher Barlow, Bt; 18 Winter av; St Johns, Newfoundland, Canada

BARLOW, Crispian John Edmund Audley; s and h of Sir Christopher Hilaro Barlow, 7 Bt, *qv*; *b* 20 April 1958; *Career* inspector Royal Hong Kong Police; *Style* - Crispian Barlow Esq

BARLOW, Hon Lady; Hon Diana Helen; *née* Kemp; da of 1 Baron Rochdale, CB (d 1945), and Lady Beatrice Egerton, MBE, da of 3 Earl of Ellesmere (Earldom now held by Duke of Sutherland, *qv*); *b* 19 July 1904; *m* 1928, Sir John Barlow, 2 Bt, *qv*; *Style* - The Hon Lady

Barlow; Bradwall Manor, Sandbach, Cheshire

BARLOW, Erasmus Darwin; s of Sir Alan Barlow, 2 Bt, GCB, KBE (d 1968); *b* 15 April 1915; *Educ* Marlborough, Trin Cambridge; *m* 1938, Brigit, da of Ladbroke Black, of Wendover; 1 s, 2 da; *Career* Sec Zoological Soc of London 1980-, chm and dep chm Cambridge Instrument Co 1964-79; *Clubs* Athenaeum, Savile; *Style* - Erasmus Barlow Esq; Elbrook House, Aswell, Baldock, Herts

BARLOW, James Alan; s and h of Sir Thomas Barlow, 3 Bt, DSC, DL, *qv*; *b* 10 July 1956; *Style* - James Barlow Esq

BARLOW, Sir John Denman; 2 Bt (UK 1907); s of Sir John Emmott Barlow, 1 Bt (d 1932), and Hon Anna Maria Heywood Denman (d 1965), sis of 3 Baron Denman, GCMG, KCVO, PC; *b* 15 June 1898; *m* 1928, Hon Diana Helen Kemp, da of 1 Baron Rochdale, CB, and sis of 1 Viscount Rochdale; 3 s, 1 da; *Heir* s, John Kemp Barlow; *Career* ptnr, now consultant Thomas Barlow and Brother, of Manchester and London, chm several Rubber and Tea Producing cos; MP (Nat) Eddisbury Div of Cheshire 1945-50, and (C) for Middleton and Prestwich Div of Lancs 1951-56; *Style* - Sir John Barlow, Bt; Bradwall Manor, Sandbach, Cheshire (☎ Sandbach 2036)

BARLOW, John Kemp; s and h of Sir John Denman Barlow, 2 Bt, *qv*; *b* 22 April 1934; *Educ* Winchester and Trin Cambridge; *m* 1962, Susan, da of Col Sir Andrew Horsbrugh Porter, 3 Bt, DSO; 4 s; *Style* - John Barlow Esq; Bulkeley Grange, Malpas, Cheshire

BARLOW, Nora, Lady; (Emma) Nora; da of late Sir Horace Darwin, KBE; *m* 1911, Sir (James) Alan (Noel) Barlow, 2 Bt, GCB, KBE (d 1968); *Style* - Nora, Lady Barlow; Sellenger, Sylvester rd, Cambridge

BARLOW, Roy Oxspring; s of George Barlow; *b* 13 Feb 1927; *Educ* King Edward VII Sch Sheffield, Queen's Oxford, Sheffield U; *m* 1957, Kathleen Roberts; 2 s, 1 da; *Career* slr, Crown Court Recorder 1975; *Style* - Roy Barlow Esq; The Cottage, Oxton Rakes, Barlow, Sheffield (☎ 890652)

BARLOW, Thomas Bradwell; s of Sir John Barlow, 1 Bt, and Hon Anna, sis of 3 Baron Denman, GCMG, KCVO, PC; *b* 7 March 1900; *m* 1943, Elizabeth, da of Hon Bertrand Sackville-West (bro of 3 and 4 Barons Sackville); 1 s, 1 da; *Career* merchant banker, chm Br Assoc of Malaysia 1965, Highlands and Lowlands Para Rubber Co, Chersonese (FMS) Estates; *Style* - Thomas Barlow Esq; Thornby House, Northampton (☎ Guilsborough 214)

BARLOW, Sir Thomas Erasmus; 3 Bt (UK 1902), DSC (1945), DL (Bucks 1976); s of Sir Alan Barlow, 2 Bt, GCB, KBE (d 1968); *b* 23 Jan 1914; *Educ* Winchester; *m* 1955, Isabel, nee Body; 2 s, 2 da; *Heir* s, James Barlow; *Career* RN 1932, Capt, ret 1964; farmer, Pres Chiltern Hills Ag Assoc, Berks Bucks and Oxon Naturalists' Tst; *Recreations* birdwatching, wildlife conservation; *Clubs* Athenaeum, Savile; *Style* - Sir Thomas Barlow, Bt, DSC, DL; Boswells, Wendover, Bucks (☎ 622119)

BARLOW, Sir (George) William; s of Albert Barlow; *b* 8 June 1924; *Educ* Manchester G S, Manchester U; *m* 1948, Elaine, nee Adamson; 1 s, 1 da; *Career* kt 1977, chm Post Office 1977-80, chm Thorn EMI 1980-, Roy Worcester 1976-, BSc, FEng, FIMechE, FIEE; *Style* - Sir William Barlow; 23 Howland st, W1

BARNARD, 11 Baron (E 1698); Harry John Neville Vane; TD (1960), JP (Durham 1961); s of 10 Baron Barnard, CMG, OBE, MC, TD, JP (d 1964); *b* 21 Sept 1923; *Educ* Eton; *m* 1952, Lady Davina, nee Cecil, da of 6 Marq of Exeter; 1 s, 4 da; *Heir* s, Hon Henry Vane; *Career* landowner, Ld-Lt and Custos Rotulorum Co Durham 1970-, KStJ 1971, patron of ten livings, Pres N of Eng TAVR Assoc 1974-, Pres Farmway Ltd 1965, Jt MFH Zetland Hounds 1963-65; *Clubs* Brooks's, Durham County, Northern County (Newcastle); *Style* - The Rt Hon The Lord Barnard, TD, JP; Selaby Hall, Gainford, Darlington, Co Durham (☎ 0325 76 206);

Raby Castle, Staindrop, Darlington, Co Durham (☎ 0833 60202)

BARNARD, Baroness; Lady Davina Mary; *née* Cecil; da of 6 Marquess of Exeter by his 1 w, Lady Mary Montagu Douglas Scott, da of 7 Duke of Buccleuch; *b* 1931; *m* 1952, 11 Baron Barnard, *qv*; *Career* OStJ; *Style* - The Rt Hon The Lady Barnard; Selaby, Gainford, Darlington, Co Durham

BARNARD, Capt Sir George Edward; s of Michael Barnard; *b* 11 Aug 1907; *m* 1940, Barbara Hughes (d 1976); 1 s; *Career* kt 1968, Dep Master Trin House 1961-72, FRSA; *Style* - Capt Sir George Barnard; Warden, Station rd, Much Hadham, Herts (☎ 3133)

BARNARD, Hon Lance Herbert; s of Hon H Barnard; *b* 1 May 1919; *Educ* Launceston Tech Coll; *m* 1; 1 da; m 2, 1962, Jill, da of Senator H Cant; 1 s, 2 da (and 1 da decd); *Career* State Pres Tasmanian Branch Australian Lab Party, Min for Defence 1973-75, Australian Ambass to Sweden, Norway and Finland 1975-78; *Style* - Hon Lance Barnard; 8 Lantana av, Launceston, Tasmania 7250, Australia

BARNARD, Dowager Baroness; Sylvia Mary; da of Herbert Straker, formerly of Hartforth Grange, Richmond, Yorks; *m* 1920, 10 Baron Barnard (d 1964); 2 s, 1 da; *Career* late Chief Commander ATS; *Style* - The Rt Hon Dowager Lady Barnard; The White House, Gainford, Darlington

BARNARD, Sir (Arthur) Thomas; CB (1954), OBE (1946); s of late Arthur Barnard; *b* 28 Sept 1893; *Educ* Erith Tech Coll; *m* 1921, Grace, nee Magerkorth; *Career* kt 1958, Dir-Gen Inspection Min of Supply 1956-58; *Style* - Sir Thomas Barnard, CB, OBE; Kentmere, 26 Heathfield, Chislehurst, Kent

BARNARD, Thomas Theodore; MC; s of late T Barnard; *b* 31 Aug 1898; *Educ* Eton, Ch Ch Oxford; *m* 1924, Gillian (d 1961), da of late Lt-Col Hon Anthony Schomberg Byng, DSO, s of 5 Earl of Strafford; 1 s, 2 da; *Career* Coldstream Gds 1917-19 and 1940-45, Prof of Socl Anthropolgy and Dir Sch of African Life and Langs Cape Town U 1926-34; *Style* - Thomas Barnard Esq, MC; Furzebrook, Wareham, Dorset

BARNBY, 2 Baron (UK 1922); Francis Vernon Willey; CMG (1918), CBE (1919), MVO (1918); s of 1 Baron (d 1929); *b* 29 Sept 1884; *Educ* Eton, Magdalen Oxford; *m* 1940, Banning, da of William Drayton Grange, of Pennsylvania, USA; *Heir* none; *Career* Lord of the Manors of Blyth and Barnby Moor, formerly Lt-Col Cmdg Notts Yeo, MP (C U) S Div of Bradford 1918-22, Controller of Wool Supplies Min of Munitions Supply 1916-20, Assist Dir RAOC 1918; Pres Fedn of British Industries 1925-26, memb Central Electricity Bd 1927-46; former dir Lloyds Bank Ltd, Commercial Union Assur Co Ltd, Past Master of Woolmen's Co; *Style* - The Rt Hon The Lord Barnby CMG CBE MVO; 35-37 Grosvenor sq, W1 (☎ 01 499 2112); Hillthorpe, Ashtead, Surrey

BARNE, Lady Elizabeth Beatrice; *née* Montgomerie; da of 17 Earl of Eglinton and Winton (d 1966) and Ursula Joan, da of Hon Ronald Bannatyne Watson; *b* 1945; *m* 1976, Maj Christopher Miles Barne; 1 s; *Style* - Lady Elizabeth Barne; Culeaze, Wareham, Dorset

BARNE, Hon Mrs; Hon Janet Elizabeth; *née* Maclean; da of Baron Maclean, KT, GCVO, KBE, PC (Life Peer and 11 Bt); *b* 1944; *m* 1974, Maj Nicholas M L Barne, Scots Guards; 1 s; *Style* - The Hon Mrs Barne; Blofield House, Blofield, Norwich

BARNEBY, Lt-Col Henry Habington; TD (1946), DL (Herefordshire 1958); s of Richard Barneby, of Longworth Hall, Hereford; *b* 19 June 1909; *Educ* Radley, Sandhurst; *m* 1, 1935, Evelyn Heywood; m 2, 1944, Angela Campbell; 4 s, 1 da (and 1 s decd); *Career* chm Hereford RDC 1964-67, High Sheriff Herefs 1972, Vice-Lt 1973-74, Maj KSLI 1947-55, JP Herefs 1960-79; *Style* - Lt-Col Henry Barneby, TD, DL; Llanerch-y-Coed, Dorstone, Herefordshire (☎ Clifford 215)

BARNES, Sir Denis Charles; KCB (1967, CB 1964); s of Frederick Barnes; *b* 15 Dec 1914; *Educ* Hulme G S Manchester, Merton Oxford; *m* 1938, Patricia Abercrombie; *Career* dir Glynwed Ltd, Gen Accident Fire & Life Assur Corpn 1976-, Pres Manpower Soc 1976-, FIPM, Perm Sec Dept of Emp 1968-73; *Style* - Sir Denis Barnes, KCB; The Old Inn, 30 The Street, Wittersham, Kent (☎ 528)

BARNES, Daniel Sennett; CBE (1977); s of John Barnes; *b* 13 Sept 1924; *Educ* Dulwich, Battersea Poly; *m* 1955, Jean Steadman; 1 s; *Career* md Sperry Gyroscope 1971-, dir Sperry Rand, CEng, FIEE; *Style* - Daniel Barnes Esq, CBE; Zenda, 9 Eastwick rd, Burwood Pk, Walton-on-Thames, Surrey (☎ 28042)

BARNES, Donald Tom; *Career* md Fine Art Developments Ltd; *Style* - Donald Barnes Esq; Fine Art House, Queen st, Burton on Trent, Staffs

BARNES, Edward Campbell; s of Hubert Barnes; *b* 8 Oct 1928; *Educ* Wigan Coll; *m* 1950, Dorothy Smith; 1 s, 2 da; *Career* Head Children's Progs BBC TV 1978-; *Style* - Edward Barnes Esq; 50 Hill House rd, SW16 (☎ 01 769 0323); Carn Mallows, Rinsey, Cornwall (☎ Germoe 3381)

BARNES, Francis Walter Ibbetson; s of Rev Walter Barnes (d 1959); *b* 10 May 1914; *Educ* Mill Hill, Balliol Oxford; *m* 1, 1948, Heather, nee Tamplin; 2 s; m 2, 1955, Sonia, nee Higginbottom; 2 s, 1 da; *Career* barr 1938, Crown Court Recorder 1972-76, Chm Industl Tribunals; *Recreations* music, gardening, swimming; *Style* - Francis Barnes Esq; 42 St Martin's Approach, Ruislip, Middx (☎ 37326); Southernhay, Diptford, S Devon

BARNES, Sir (Harry) Jefferson; CBE (1971); s of Prof Alfred Barnes, FRCP; *b* 3 April 1915; *Educ* Repton, The Slade; *m* 1941, Joan, da of Prof Randolph Schwabe, RWS; 2 da (and 1 s decd); *Career* kt 1980, dir Glasgow Sch of Art 1964-80; *Style* - Sir Jefferson Barnes, CBE; 11 Whittingehame dve, Glasgow (☎ 041 339 1019)

BARNES, Sir James George; MBE, JP; s of Richard Barnes; *Educ* King Edward Tech H S; *m* 1938, Elsie, nee Clark; 1 da; *Career* kt 1967, Mayor of Dunedin NZ 1968-77, sharebroker; *Style* - Sir James Barnes, MBE, JP; 11 Cavell st, Dunedin, New Zealand

BARNES, Dame (Alice) Josephine Mary Taylor; DBE (1974); Dame Josephine Warren; da of late Rev Walter Barnes, MA (Oxon), and Alice Ibbetson, FRCO, ARCM; *b* 18 Aug 1912; *Educ* Oxford H S, LMH Oxford, U Coll Hosp Med Sch; *m* 1942, Sir Brian Warren (m dis 1946); 1 s, 2 da; *Career* FRCP, FRCS, FRCOG, Consulting Obstetrician and Gynaecologist, Charing Cross Hosp and Elizabeth Garrett Anderson Hosp, Pres Women's Nat Cancer Control Campaign 1974-; *Style* - Dame Josephine Barnes, DBE; 8 Aubrey Walk, W8 (☎ 01 727 9832)

BARNES, Sir (Ernest) John Ward; KCMG (1974), MBE (1946); s of Rt Rev Ernest Barnes, Bp of Birmingham (d 1953), and Adelaide, da of Sir Adolphus Ward, Master of Peterhouse Cambridge; *b* 22 June 1917; *Educ* Winchester, Trin Cambridge; *m* 1948, Cynthia Margaret Ray, da of Sir Herbert Stewart, CIE; 2 s, 3 da; *Career* Lt-Col RA WW II; HM Diplomatic Serv 1946-77, Ambass to Israel 1969-72, to The Netherlands 1972-77; dir Alliance Investment Co 1977-, Esperanza Ltd 1979-, Whiteaway Laidlaw & Co, dir Wolfson Foundation 1980-; *Clubs* Athenaeum, Beefsteak, Brooks's, MCC; *Style* - Sir John Barnes, KCMG, MBE; Hampton Lodge, Hurstpierpoint, Sussex (☎ 0273 833247); 20 Thurloe Pla Mews, SW7 (☎ 01 584 9652)

BARNES, Sir Kenneth; KCB (1977, CB 1970); s of Arthur Barnes; *b* 26 Aug 1922; *Educ* Accrington G S, Balliol Oxford; *m* 1948, Barbara Ainsworth; 1 s, 2 da; *Career* permanent sec Dept of Employment 1976-; *Style* - Sir Kenneth Barnes, KCB; Hill House, 35 Pilgrim's Way, Reigate, Surrey (☎ 45237)

BARNES, Peter Robert; s of Robert Stanley Barnes; *b* 1 Feb 1921; *Educ* Eton and Trin Cambridge; *m* 1955, Pauline Hannen; 2 s, 1 da; *Career* dep dir Public

Prosecutions 1977-; *Style* - Peter Barnes Esq; 12 Queen Anne's gate, SW1 (☎ 01-763 5110)

BARNES, Dr Robert Sandford; s of William Barnes; *b* 8 July 1924; *Educ* Manchester U; *m* 1952, Julia Grant; 1 s, 3 da; *Career* princ Queen Elizabeth Coll London U 1978-, metallurgist, FIM, FInstP; *Style* - Dr Robert Barnes; Pigeon Forge, Daneshill, The Hockering, Woking (☎ 61529)

BARNETSON, Hon Julia Claire Denholm; da of Baron Barnetson, (d 1981); *b* 1963; *Style* - The Hon Julia Barnetson

BARNETSON, Baroness; Joan Fairley; da of late William Fairley Davidson; *m* 1940, Baron Barnetson (Life Peer 1975, kt 1972, d 1981); 1 s, 3 da; *Style* - The Rt Hon The Lady Barnetson; Flat 5, 12 Charles st, W1 (☎ 01 493 0309); Broom, Chillies Lane, Crowborough, E Sussex (☎ 5748)

BARNETSON, Hon Louise Jane Denholm; da of Baron Barnetson, (d 1981); *b* 1952; *Style* - The Hon Louise Barnetson

BARNETSON, Hon William Denholm; s of Baron Barnetson, (d 1981); *b* 1955; *Style* - The Hon William Barnetson

BARNETT, Brian; *Career* exec chm Augustus Barnet Ltd; *Style* - Brian Barnett Esq; Augustus Barnett Ltd, Barnett House, Backchurch lane, London E1

BARNETT, Brian Alex; *Career* md Ellis and Goldstein Holdings Ltd; *Style* - Brian Barnett Esq; Ellis and Goldstein Holdings Ltd, 3 London Wall Buildings, London Wall, EC2

BARNETT, Benjamin George; MBE (1945), TD; s of Col George Barnett, CMG, DSO (d 1942), of Glympton Park, Oxon; *b* 5 Dec 1912; *Educ* Malvern; *m* 1943, Delia, da of Maj Sir Algernon Peyton, 7 Bt (d 1962); 2 s, 1 da; *Career* retired memb of Stock Exchange; *Recreations* shooting, fishing; *Style* - Benjamin Barnett Esq, MBE, TD; Swifts House, nr Bicester, Oxon (☎ Fritwell 288)

BARNETT, Correlli Douglas; s of D Barnett; *b* 28 June 1927; *Educ* Trin Sch Croydon, Exeter Coll Oxford; *m* 1950, Ruth Murby; 2 da; *Career* Keeper of Archives and Fellow Churchill Coll Cambridge 1977-, FRSL, writer and historian; *Style* - Correlli Barnett Esq; Catbridge House, E Carleton, Norwich (☎ Mulbarton 410)

BARNETT, Air Chief Marshal Sir Denis Hensley Fulton; GCB (1964, KCB 1957, CB 1956), CBE (1945), DFC (1940); s of late Sir Louis Barnett; *b* 11 Feb 1906; *Educ* Christ's Coll NZ, Clare Cambridge; *m* 1939, Pamela, da of Sir Allan Grant; 1 s, 2 da; *Career* RAF ret, AOC-in-C RAF T'port Cmmd 1959-62, RAF Near East, Cdr Br Forces Cyprus and Admin Sovereign Base Area 1962-64, memb Weapons R & D AEA 1965-72; *Style* - Air Chief Marshal Sir Denis Barnett GCB, CBE, DFC; River House, Rushall, Pewsey, Wilts

BARNETT, (Nicholas) Guy; MP (L) Greenwich 1971-; s of late B Barnett; *b* 23 Aug 1928; *Educ* Highgate, St Edmund Hall Oxford; *m* 1967, Daphne, da of Geoffrey Hortin, JP; 1 s, 1 da; *Career* former teacher, MP (L) Dorset S 1962-64, Sec of State DOE 1976-79, MEP 1975-76, memb Gen Advsy Cncl BBC 1973-76; *Style* - Guy Barnett Esq, MP; 32 Westcombe Pk rd, SE3

BARNETT, Dame (Mary) Henrietta; DBE (1958, CBE 1956, OBE 1950); da of Col George Barnett, 60th Rifles, of Glympton Park, Woodstock; *b* 16 Feb 1905; *Educ* Heathfield Ascot; *Career* Dir WRAF 1956-60; *Style* - Dame Henrietta Barnett, DBE; Hoggrove House, Park st, Woodstock, Oxon (☎ 811502)

BARNETT, Rt Hon Joel; PC (1975), JP (Lancs 1960), MP (L) Lancs Heywood and Royton 1964-; s of Louis Barnett; *b* 14 Oct 1923; *Educ* Derby st Jewish Sch, Manchester Centl H S; *m* 1949, Lillian Goldstone; 1 da; *Career* Ch Sec to Treasury 1974-79 (Cabinet memb 1977-79); *Style* - The Rt Hon Joel Barnett,

PC, JP, MP; Flat 92, 24 John Islip st, SW1; 10 Park Lane, Whitefield, Lancs

BARNETT, Hon Mrs; Hon Kathleen Irene Mary; *née* Hennessy; da of 1 Baron Windlesham, OBE (d 1914); *m* 1947, Wilfred Ernest Barnett; 2 s; *Style* - The Hon Mrs Barnett; Pullington Cottage, Benenden, Kent

BARNETT, Hon Mrs; Hon Laura Miriam Elizabeth; da of Baron Weidenfeld (Life Peer), by his 1 w; *b* 1953; *m* 1976, Christopher Andrew Barnett; 2 s; *Style* - The Hon Mrs Barnett; Forge Cottage, Bradfield, Berks

BARNETT, Sir Oliver Charles; CBE (1954, OBE 1946), QC (1956); s of Charles Barnett (ka 1915); *b* 7 Feb 1907; *Educ* Eton; *m* 1945, Joan, da of Capt W Eve (ka 1917) and gda of Rt Hon Sir Harry Eve (High Court Judge); *Career* kt 1968, barr 1928, Judge Advocate Gen 1963-68; *Style* - Sir Oliver Barnett, CBE, QC; Zinch Cottage, Stogumber, nr Taunton, Somerset (☎ 264)

BARNETT, Hon Mrs; Hon Vera Kate; *née* Churchman; da of 1 Baron Woodbridge; *b* 1913; *m* 1936, Peter William Barnett; 1 s, 1 da; *Style* - The Hon Mrs Barnett; Campsie Hill, Guildtown, nr Perth

BARNEWALL, Hon Anthony Edward; s and h of 19 Baron Trimlestown, *qv*; *b* 2 Feb 1928; *Educ* Ampleforth; *m* 1, 1963, Lorna Margaret Marion, nee Ramsay; m 2, 1977, Mary Wouderley, da of late Judge Thomas McAllister, of Ada, Michigan; *Career* late Irish Gds; *Style* - The Hon Anthony Barnewall; Ada, Grand Rapids, Michigan, USA

BARNEWALL, Peter Joseph; s and h of Sir Reginald Robert Barnewall, 13 Bt, *qv*; *b* 26 Oct 1963; *Style* - Peter Barnewall Esq

BARNEWALL, Hon Raymond Charles; s of 19 Baron Trimlestown, *qv*; *b* 1930; *Educ* Ampleforth; *Style* - The Hon Raymond Barnewall; Tigley, Dartington, Totnes, Devon

BARNEWALL, Sir Reginald Robert; 13 Bt (I 1623); s of Sir Reginald John Barnewall, 12 Bt (d 1961); *b* 1 Oct 1924; *Educ* Xavier Coll Melbourne; *m* 1, 1946, Elsie Muriel (d 1962), da of Thomas Matthews Frederick, of Brisbane, Queensland; 3 da; m 2, 1962, Maureen Ellen, da of William Daly, of S Caulfield, Victoria; 1 s; *Heir* s, Peter Joseph Barnewall; *Career* wool grower, cattle breeder, orchardist; former dir Island Airways Pty Ltd (Pialba, Qld), operator and owner Coastal-Air Co (Qld) 1971-76, former dir and v-chm J Roy Stevens Pty Ltd; *Style* - Sir Reginald Barnewall, Bt; Mount Tamborine, Queensland 4272, Australia

BARNSLEY, Thomas Edward; OBE (1975); s of Alfred Barnsley; *b* 10 Sept 1919; *Educ* Wednesbury Boys' H S; *m* 1947, Margaret Llewellin; 1 s, 1 da; *Career* FCA, md Tube Investments 1974-; *Style* - Thomas Barnsley Esq; Old Rectory, Cossington, nr Leicester (☎ Sileby 2623)

BARNWELL, Hon Mrs; Hon Elizabeth Mary; *née* Shore; da of 6 Baron Teignmouth (d 1964); *b* 1916; *m* 1942, Maj Charles John Patrick Barnwell; 1 s; *Style* - The Hon Mrs Barnwell; Wick Manor, Curry Rivel, Somerset

BARR, John Malcolm; *Career* chm and md Barr and Wallace Arnold Trust Ltd; pres Leeds Permanent Building Society; *Style* - John Barr Esq; 21 The Calls, Leeds 2;

BARR, Kenneth Glen; s of Rev Gavin Barr; *b* 20 Jan 1941; *Educ* Ardrossan Acad, Roy H S, Edinburgh U; *m* 1970, Susanne Keir; *Career* Sheriff S Strathclyde Dumfries and Galloway 1976-; *Style* - Kenneth Barr Esq; Sheriff Court House, Dumfries

BARR, Prof Murray Llewellyn; OC (1968); *b* 20 June 1908; *Educ* W Ontario U; *m* 1934, Ruth King; 3 s, 1 da; *Career* FRS, Prof of Anatomy W Ontario U 1949-79 (now Emeritus); *Style* - Prof Murray Barr, OC; 452 Wonderland rd, London, Ontario, Canada (☎ 471 5618)

BARR, His Honour Judge; Reginald Alfred Barr; s of Alfred Barr; *b* 21 Nov

1920; *Educ* Christ's Hosp, Trin Oxford; *m* 1946, Elaine, nee Morris; *Career* barr 1954, Circuit Judge 1970; *Style* - His Hon Judge Barr; 42 Bathurst Mews, Hyde Pk, W2 (☎ 01 262 5731)

BARR, Robert Zbigniew; MBE (1944); s of Stanislaw Bachurzewski; *b* 2 Nov 1920; *Educ* Stefan Bathory U Vilno (Poland); *m* 1947, Ewa, da of Capt Evgraf Cutjev (d 1979); 1 s; *Career* Capt Polish Army WW II, engineer, export dir Head Wrightson & Co 1971-76, md Head Wrightson Process Engrg 1976-80 VM (Polish Decoration) 1944; *Recreations* sailing (has yacht-'Punia'); *Style* - Robert Barr Esq; 37 Ladbroke sq, W11 (☎ 01 727 4616)

BARR, Stuart Alan; s of Robert Barr, of Leeds; *b* 18 Nov 1930; *Educ* Shrewsbury; *m* 1 (m dis 1964); 2 s; m 2, 1969, Karin Johanne, da of Col Donald Smiley; 2 da; *Career* Maj Queen's Own Yorks Dragoons (TA), dep chm Barr & Wallace Arnold Tst, tres Leeds Con Assoc; Pres W Yorks Youth Assoc, St John's Ambulance Bde (Knaresborough Div); dir American Sightseeing Tours, Charing Cross Tourist Agency, Data Sciences Internat, Embankment Motor Co, Euroways Express Coaches, Evan Evans Tours, Feather Bros (Tours), Fenchurch (Northern) Ltd, Garnetts (Nottingham) Ltd, Hardwick's Servs, Highfield's Travel Bureau, J W Kitchens & Sons, Leeds Autocars Sales & Servs, Lismore Coaches, Manchester Computer Centre, Northern Computer Centre, Oswald's Hotel Ltd, Robert Sibbald Travel Agents, Roseway Vehicle Contracts, Scottish Transit Tst, Skellys (Dumbarton, Glasgow and Motherwell) Ltd, The Tidebank Ltd, Trust Motors (Bradford and Leeds), Wallace Arnold, Wardways Ltd, Waverley Motor Coach Tours, Wilks & Meade, Woburn Garages (London) Ltd; *Recreations* racing, shooting, farming; *Clubs* Cavalry & Guards, Carlton; *Style* - Stuart Barr Esq; Loftus Hill, Knaresborough, N Yorks (☎ Copegrove (09014) 301)

BARR, William Greig; DL (Oxon 1974); s of late William Barr; *b* 10 June 1917; *Educ* Sedbergh Sch, Magdalen Oxford; *m* 1954, Helen Georgopoulos; 2 s; *Career* Rector Exeter Coll Oxford 1972-, Pro-Vice-Chllr Oxford 1980-, historian; *Style* - William Barr Esq, DL; Exeter College, Oxford (☎ 44681)

BARRACK, William S; s of William S Barrack; *b* 26 July 1929; *Educ* Univ of Pittsburgh, Dartmouth College; *m* 1953, Evelyn Irene; 1 s, 1 da; *Career* Cdr USNR; chm & ch exec offr Texaco Ltd; Gov Foreign Policy Association (USA); *Recreations* golf, fishing, shooting, sailing; *Clubs* Ox Ridge (Connecticut), Woodway Country (Connecticut); *Style* - William Barrack Esq; care of Texaco Ltd, 1 Knightsbridge Green, SW1 (☎ 01 584 5000)

BARRACLOUGH, Geoffrey; s of late Walter Barraclough; *b* 10 May 1908; *Educ* Bootham Sch York, Oriel Oxford, Munich U; *Career* historian, Chichele Prof of Mod History and Fellow of All Souls Oxford 1970-73, Pres Historical Assoc 1964-67; *Books* The Mediaeval Papacy 1968, (ed) Times Atlas of World History 1978; *Style* - Geoffrey Barraclough Esq

BARRACLOUGH, Henry; CVO (1976, MVO 1958); s of late Thomas Barraclough, shipowner, of W Hartlepool; *b* 10 Aug 1894; *Educ* Giggleswick Sch; *m* 1922, Ethel, da of Wilkinson Dix Sunderland; 2 s; *Career* dir Dene Shipping Co to 1970, memb Lloyd's; *Style* - Henry Barraclough Esq, CVO, Cotehow, Martindale, Penrith, Cumbria (☎ Pooley Bridge 521)

BARRACLOUGH, Air Chief Marshal Sir John; KCB (1970, CB 1969), CBE (1961), DFC (1942), AFC (1941); s of late Horatio Barraclough; *b* 2 May 1918; *Educ* Cranbrook Sch; *m* 1946, Maureen, nee McCormack, niece of George Noble Count Plunkett; 1 da; *Career* FIPM, MBIM, MIPR, Cmmdt Roy Coll Defence Studies 1974-76, Air-Sec 1972-74 V-Chm C'wlth War Graves Commission 1981-; *Style* - Air Chief Marshal Sir John Barraclough, KCB, CBE, DFC, AFC; c/o Barclays Bank, 11 Newgate st, EC1

BARRACLOUGH, Brig Sir John Ashworth; CMG (1950), DSO (1941),

OBE (1941), MC (1918), DL (Warwicks 1962); *Career* chm Engineering Employers' Assoc 1950-67, Dep Reg Cdr Land N Rhine-Westphalia 1946-50, KStJ 1964, kt 1962; *Style* - Brig Sir John Barraclough, CMG, DSO, OBE, MC, DL; 6 Devonshire Mews South, W1 (☎ 01 935 3680)

BARRACLOUGH, Sir Kenneth James Priestley; CBE (1967, OBE 1945), TD, JP (Hants 1957); s of Herbert Barraclough; *b* 1907; *Educ* Oundle, Clare Cambridge; *m* 1931, Gladys, nee Henderson; 2 s, 1 da; *Career* Ch Met Magistrate 1975-78, barr 1929, kt 1978; *Style* - Sir Kenneth Barraclough, CBE, TD, JP; 18 Fitzroy rd, Fleet, Hants

BARRAN, Sir David Haven; s of Sir John Barran, 2 Bt; *b* 23 May 1912; *Educ* Winchester, Trin Cambridge; *m* 1944, Jane, da of Nicholas Macaskie, QC; 4 s, 3 da; *Career* chm Midland Bank 1980-, dir Shell T'port and Trading 1961-73, Gen Accident Insurance, BICC, Glaxo Hldgs, Standard Chartered Bank 1977-, chm CBI Ctee on Inflation Accounting 1973-74, kt 1971; *Style* - Sir David Barran; 36 Kensington sq, W8 (☎ 01 937 5664); Brent Eleigh Hall, Suffolk (☎ Lavenham 247202)

BARRAN, Dowager Lady; Esther Frances; da of late Hon F M B Fisher, of Rotorua, New Zealand; *m* 1946, as his 2 w, Sir John Nicholson Barran, 2 Bt (d 1952); *Style* - Dowager Lady Barran; 2 Phillimore pla, W8

BARRAN, Sir John Napoleon Ruthven; 4 Bt (UK 1895); s of Sir John Leighton Barran, 3 Bt (d 1974), and Hon Alison (d 1973), da of 9 Lord Ruthven of Freeland, CB, CMG, DSO; nephew of Sir David Barran, chm of the Midland Bank and ex-chm Shell; *b* 14 Feb 1934; *Educ* Heatherdown Ascot, Winchester; *m* 1965, Jane, da of Sir Stanley Hooker, CBE, by his w Hon Margaret Bradbury, da of 1 Baron Bradbury; 1 s, 1 da (Susannah Margaret b 22 April 1981, godparents include Lady Jane Seth-Smith and Mrs David Tomlinson); *Heir* s, John Ruthven Barran (b 10 Nov 1971); *Career* Head Viewdata Unit COI 1978-, in advertising 1956-63; *Style* - Sir John Barran, Bt; 17 St Leonard's ter, SW3 (☎ 01 730 2801); The Hermitage, E Bergholt, Suffolk

BARRAN, John Ruthven; s and h of Sir John Barran, 4 Bt, *qv*; *b* 10 Nov 1971; *Style* - John Barran Esq

BARRATT, Eric George; s of Frank Barratt, of Stokenchurch, Bucks; *b* 15 April 1938; *Career* CA, ptnr Arthur Anderson & Co, memb Bucks CC; dir Automotive Products, Callwittin Ltd, Camway Investments Jersey, E S Hldgs Jersey, Esthwaite Estate Ltd, Ely Place Registrars, The Emmott Fndn, G F H Investments Jersey, Pinion Investments Jersey; *Clubs* Carlton, City of London; *Style* - Eric Barratt Esq; Stockfield, Stokenchurch, Bucks (☎ 024 026 2284); 1 Surrey st, WC2 (☎ 01 836 1200)

BARRATT, Francis Russell; CB (1975); s of Frederick Barratt (d 1957); *b* 16 Nov 1924; *Educ* Durban H S, Clifton, Univ Oxford; *m* 1, 1949, Janet, nee Sherborne; 3 s; m 2, 1979, Josephine, da of Brig D McCririck (d 1947); *Career* Dep Sec HM Treasury; *Recreations* reading, music, golf; *Style* - Francis Barratt Esq, CB; 8 Arlington av, N1 (☎ 01 359 1747)

BARRATT, Lawrence Arthur; *b* 14 Nov 1927; *Career* chm and md Barratt Developments Ltd; *Style* - Lawrence Barratt Esq; Wingrove House, Ponteland rd, Newcastle-upon-Tyne (☎ 0632 866811)

BARRATT, Michael Fieldhouse; s of Wallace Barratt; *b* 3 Jan 1928; *Educ* Rossall, Paisley G S; *m* m 1, 1952, Joan Warner (m dis); 3 s, 3 da; m 2, 1977, Dilys Morgan; 1 s; *Career* broadcaster (Panorama, Nationwide, 24 Hours); *Style* - Michael Barratt Esq; 108 Park st, W1 (☎ 01 491 4872)

BARRATT-BOYES, Sir Brian Gerald; KBE (1971, CBE 1966); s of Gerald Boyes and Edna, nee Barratt; *b* 13 Jan 1924; *Educ* Wellington, Otago U; *m* 1949, Norma Thompson; 5 s; *Career* surgn in charge Cardio-Thoracic Surgical Unit

Greenlane Hosp Auckland 1964-, FRACS, FACS; *Style* - Sir Brian Barratt-Boyes, KBE; 27 Rahiri rd, Auckland 4, N Zealand (☎ 689 414)

BARRAUD, Hon Mrs; Hon Jane; *née* King-Hall; da of Baron King-Hall (Life Peer, d 1966); *b* 1930; *m* 1951, Yves Barraud; *Style* - The Hon Mrs Barraud; Les Saules, Les Cullayes, Vaud, Switzerland

BARRERO, Lady Katherine Lucy; *née* Lambart; da of 12 Earl of Cavan, TD; *b* 1955; *m* 1978, Don Lorenzo Ruiz Barrero, of Madrid; *Style* - Lady Katherine Barrero; Ground Floor Flat, 5 Waldemar ave, SW6

BARRETT, Anthony Frank; s of Percy Barrett (d 1970); *b* 26 Feb 1926; *Educ* Dunstable Sch; *m* 1952, Mary, da of Arthur Hignett (d 1964); 1 s, 1 da; *Career* dir Barclays Bank UK Ltd 1979- (local dir Darlington 1969, London NW 1973, Luton 1978); *Recreations* music, golf; *Clubs* Ashridge Golf; *Style* - Anthony Barrett Esq; West Lodge, Bulstrode Way, Gerrards Cross, Bucks

BARRETT, Sir Arthur George; s of A O Barrett; *b* 7 May 1895; *Educ* Melbourne C of E G S; *m* 1922, Jean , nee Mair; 2 da; *Career* kt 1942, Ld Mayor Adelaide 1937-41; *Style* - Sir Arthur Barrett; 210 Stanley st, N Adelaide, SA 5006, Australia (☎ 267 1171)

BARRETT, David; *b* 2 Oct 1930; *Educ* Britannia H S Vancouver, Seattle U, St Louis U; *m* 1953, Shirley Hackman; 2 s, 1 da; *Career* Leader Oppn Br Columbia 1976- and New Democratic Party 1970-; *Style* - David Barrett Esq; Legislative Bldgs, Victoria, BC, Canada (☎ 387 5571)

BARRETT, Dennis Frederick Frank; *Career* gp md Howard Tenens Services Ltd; *Style* - Dennis Barrett Esq; Howard Tenens Services Ltd, Parsonage rd, Stratton St Margaret, Swindon, Wilts

BARRETT, Ernest; s of Ernest Barrett; *b* 8 April 1917; *Educ* Charterhouse; *m* 1940, Eileen Peel; 1 da; *Career* jt md Henry Barrett & Sons 1968-, chm Steel Stockholding Dvn Henry Barrett & Sons 1967-, John France & Co 1969-, Henry Lindsay Ltd 1974-; *Style* - Ernest Barrett Esq; West Ghyll, Victoria ave, Ilkley, W Yorks (☎ 609294)

BARRETT, Jack Wheeler; CBE (1971); s of John Barrett; *b* 13 June 1912; *Educ* Cheltenham G S, Imperial Coll London; *m* 1935, Muriel Read; 2 s, 2 da; *Career* chm Info-line 1976-, dir R H Cole Ltd 1978-, FRIC, FIChemE; *Style* - Jack Barrett Esq, CBE; 195 Latymer Court, Hammersmith rd, W6 (☎ 01 748 7080); West Manor House, Bourton-on-the-Water, Glos (☎ 20296)

BARRETT, Kenneth Ronald; *Career* md Britannia Lead Co; *Style* - Kenneth Barrett Esq; Britannia Lead Co, Adelaide House, King William st, EC4

BARRETT, R J; s of chm Barretts and Baird (Wholesale) Ltd; *Style* - R J Barrett Esq; The Abattoir, Harvil's Hawthorn, West Bromwich, West Midlands

BARRETT-LENNARD, Lady; (Kathleen) Finora; da of late Hon John Donohoe FitzGerald, KC, s of late Baron FitzGerald (Life Peer); *m* 1, 1922, Sir (Thomas) Richard Fiennes Barrett-Lennard, 5 Bt, OBE (d 1977); *Style* - Lady Barrett-Lennard ; Bolham House, Tiverton, Devon

BARRETT-LENNARD, Rev Sir Hugh Dacre; 6 Bt (UK 1801); s of Sir Fiennes Cecil Arthur Barrett-Lennard, gggs of 1 Bt; suc kinsman, Sir (Thomas) Richard Fiennes Barrett-Lennard, 5 Bt, OBE, 1977; *b* 27 June 1917; *Educ* Radley, Pontifical Beda Coll Rome; *Heir* cous, Roy Barrett-Lennard; *Career* priest London Oratory 1950-; *Style* - Rev Sir Hugh Barrett-Lennard, Bt; The Oratory, S Kensington, SW7 (☎ 01 589 4811)

BARRETT-LENNARD, Richard Fynes; s of Roy Barrett-Lennard (d 1979); hp of kinsman, Rev Sir Hugh Barrett-Lennard, 6 Bt; *b* 6 Apr 1942; *Style* - Richard Barrett-Lennard Esq

BARRIE, Derek Stiven Maxwelton; OBE (1969, MBE 1945); s of John Barrie;

b 8 Aug 1907; *Educ* Tonbridge; *m* 1936, Kathleen Collins; 1 s, 1 da; *Career* dir Derwent Valley Railway Co, formerly chm BR Eastern Bd, OStJ; *Style* - Derek Barrie Esq, OBE; 1 Norman Close, Castlegate, Pickering, N Yorks (☎ 73580)

BARRIE, Sir Walter; s of late Rt Hon H Barrie, JP, DL, MP; *b* 31 May 1901; *Educ* Merchiston, Gonville and Caius Cambridge; *m* 1927, Noele, da of G Furness, JP; 2 s; *Career* chm Lloyd's 1953-54 and 57-58, dir Jos W Hobbs Ltd kt 1958; *Style* - Sir Walter Barrie; Compton Elms, Pinkneys Green, Maidenhead, Berks (☎ 27151)

BARRINGER, Hon Mrs; Hon Diana Dorothy; *née* Latham; da of 1 Baron Latham (d 1970); *b* 1925; *m* -- Barringer; *Style* - The Hon Mrs Barringer

BARRINGTON, 11 Viscount (I 1720); Patrick William Daines Barrington; also Baron Barrington (I 1720), Baron Shute (UK 1880); sits as Baron Shute; s of Hon Walter Barrington (d 1959), suc unc 1960; *b* 29 Oct 1908; *Educ* Eton, Magdalen Oxford; *Heir* cous, Eric Barrington; *Career* barr 1940, formerly Hon Attaché Berlin; *Style* - The Rt Hon The Viscount Barrington; c/o House of Lords, SW1

BARRINGTON, Capt Sir Alexander Fitzwilliam Croker; 7 Bt (UK 1831); 2 s of Sir Charles Barrington, 5 Bt, MBE (d 1943), and Mary (da of Sir Henry Bacon, 10 and 11 Bt); bro of Sir Charles Barrington, 6 Bt (d 1980); *b* 19 Nov 1909; *Heir* kinsman, John Barrington; *Style* - Capt Sir Alexander Barrington, Bt; 11 Tedworth sq, SW3; Linhay Farm, Bramshaw, Hants

BARRINGTON, Lady; Constance Doris; da of E J Elkington; *m* 1930, Sir Charles Barrington, 6 Bt (d 1980); 2 da; *Style* - Lady Barrington; Barrihurst, Cranleigh, Surrey

BARRINGTON, Hon Mrs; Hon Elizabeth Florence Marion; *née* Cholmondeley; da of 4 Baron Delamere (d 1979); *b* 1925; *m* 1, 1947, Sir Evelyn Delves Broughton, 12 Bt (m dis 1953); m 2, 1953, Peter Alexander Barrington; *Style* - The Hon Mrs Barringer; 36a Gratton Road , W 14

BARRINGTON, Eric Rupert Walter; s of Hon Rupert Edward Selborne Barrington, DSO and hp of kinsman, 11 Viscount Barrington; *b* 13 Dec 1904; *Educ* Lancing; *m* 1, 1929, Hester Maude Vere, nee Campbell, CBE (m dis 1938); m 2, 1941, Mabel Susannah, nee Taylor; *Style* - Eric Barrington Esq; Hyne, Corfe, Taunton, Somerset

BARRINGTON, John William; s of John Barrington, DSO, and gggs of Sir Joseph Barrington, 1 Bt; hp to Baronetcy of cous, Sir Alexander Barrington, 7 Bt; *b* 28 Oct 1917; *Educ* Stowe, Sandhurst; *m* 1948, Annie, nee Wetten, of Switzerland; 2 s, 1 da; *Career* served WWII 1939-45 and Palestine 1945-48; *Style* - John Barrington Esq; 2216 7th st, SW Calgary, Canada

BARRINGTON, Sir Kenneth Charles Peto; s of C Barrington; *b* 27 Aug 1911; *Educ* St Paul's; *m* 1938, Eileen Stone; 1 da; *Career* kt 1973, FCA, V-Chm United Biscuits, dep chm BICC, Baker Perkins dir- Canada Life Assurance Co of GB, Canada Life Unit Tst Managers, Computer Leasings, English and New York Tst Co, Ultramar Co; *Recreations* bridge; *Style* - Sir Kenneth Barrington; Hall Land, Slinfold, Horsham, W Sussex (☎ Slinfold 790250); Flat 12, 20 Hyde Park Place, W2 (☎ 01 262 6914)

BARRINGTON, Hon Priscilla May; da of Hon Walter Barrington (d 1959) & sis of 11 Visc Barrington; *b* 1907; *Style* - The Hon Priscilla Barrington

BARRINGTON, R N; *Career* md Manesty Machines Ltd, winner Queen's Award for Export Achievement; *Style* - R N Barrington Esq; c/o Manesty Machines Ltd, Speke, Liverpool

BARRITT, Sir David Thurlow; s of late David Barritt; *b* 17 Oct 1903; *Educ* Newcastle-under-Lyme H S, N Staffs Poly; *m* 1931, Hilda Creyke; 1 s; *Career* kt 1969, FIChemE, chm Cammell Laird 1971-79; *Style* - Sir David Barritt; 7 Castle Rise, Prestbury, Cheshire (☎ 829716)

BARRON, Sir Donald James; DL (N Yorks 1971); s of Albert Barron; *b* 17 March 1921; *Educ* George Heriot's Sch Edinburgh, Edinburgh U; *m* 1956, Gillian, nee Saville; 3 s, 2 da; *Career* kt 1972, chm Rowntree Mackintosh 1966-81, dir Midland Bank 1972- (vice-chm 1981-), BIM Fndn 1977-, memb Cncl BIM, Tstee Josph Rowntree Meml Tst, memb Cncl CBI dir- Finance for Indust Ltd 1979-, ICFC Ltd 1980-, Fin Corpn for Indust Ltd 1979-, Finance for Industry (UK Finance) Ltd 1980-, Clifton Estate Ltd 1961-, Canada Life Assurance Co of GB Ltd 1980-, Canada Life Unit Tst Managers Ltd 1980-; *Recreations* golf, tennis, boating, gardening; *Clubs* Athenaeum, Yorkshire (York); *Style* - Sir Donald Barron, DL; Greenfield, Sim Balk Lane, Bishopthorpe, York (☎ 705675)

BARROW, Anthony John Grenfell; s and h of Capt Sir Richard John Uniacke Barrow, 6 Bt; *b* 24 May 1962; *Style* - Anthony Barrow Esq

BARROW, Rt Hon Errol Walton; PC (1969), MP (Democratic Labour) Barbados; s of Reginald Barrow, LTh, DD; *b* 21 Jan 1920; *Educ* Harrison Coll Barbados, LSE; *m* 1945, Carolyn Plaskett; 1 s, 1 da; *Career* barr 1949, PM Barbados 1966-76; *Style* - The Rt Hon Errol Barrow, PC, MP; PO Box 125, Bridgetown, Barbados

BARROW, Hon Mrs; Hon Hilary Ann Evans; da of Baron Evans of Hungershall (Life Peer); *b* 22 July 1931; *m* 1954, William John Barrow (m dis 1963); 2 s, 1 da; *Style* - The Hon Mrs Barrow; Brandon, Sandown Park, Tunbridge Wells, Kent

BARROW, Julian Gurney; s of Erskine Barrow (d 1979); *b* 28 Aug 1939; *Educ* Harrow; *m* 1971, Serena Catherine Lucy, nee Harington; 2 da; *Career* landscape and portrait painter; *Style* - Julian Barrow Esq; 33 Tite st, SW3 (☎ 01 352 4337)

BARROW, Capt Sir Richard John Uniacke; 6 Bt (UK 1835); s of Maj Sir Wilfrid Barrow, 5 Bt (d 1960); *b* 2 Aug 1933; *Educ* Beaumont; *m* 1961, Alison, da of late Capt Russell Grenfell, RN; 1 s; 2 da; *Heir* s, Anthony Barrow; *Career* served Irish Gds 1952-60, with International Computers and Tabulators Ltd to 1973; *Style* - Capt Sir Richard Barrow, Bt; 36 South Vale, SE19 (☎ 01 771 0905)

BARROWCLOUGH, Anthony Richard; QC (1974); *b* 24 June 1924; *Educ* Stowe, New Coll Oxford; *m* 1949, Mary Pery-Knox-Gore; 1 s, 1 da; *Career* barr 1949, Crown Court Recorder 1972-; *Style* - Anthony Barrowclough Esq, QC; 13 Hillgate Place, W8; The Old Vicarage, Winsford, nr Minehead, Somerset

BARRY, Anthony James; s of Edmund Barry, of Douglas IOM (decd); *b* 31 July 1931; *Educ* Old Swan Inst, Liverpool Coll of Bldg; *m* 1958, Margaret, da of William Foulkes; 1 s, 1 da; *Career* chm Bd of Bldg Educn CIOB; md J M Jones & Sons; dir Berks, Bucks & Oxon Trading Co, Herbert & Lascelles, Markham Devpts, Southern Heating Ltd; *Recreations* swimming, reading; *Clubs* Sonning Working Men's, RAC, The Livery; *Style* - Anthony Barry Esq; Sonning Mead, Sonning-on-Thames, Berks (☎ 0734 690657)

BARRY, Sir (Lawrence) Edward Anthony Tress; 5 Bt (UK 1899); Baron de Barry of Portugal, Lord of the Manors of Ockwells and Lillibrooke, Berks; s of Maj Sir Rupert Barry, 4 Bt, MBE (d 1977); *b* 1 Nov 1939; *Educ* Haileybury; *m* 1968, Fenella Hoult; 1 s, 1 da; *Heir* s, William Barry; *Career* former Capt Gren Gds; *Style* - Sir Edward Barry, Bt, 3 Sunnyside Cottages, Warehorne rd, Ham st, Kent (☎ 2454)

BARRY, Lady Margaret; *née* Pleydell-Bouverie; da of 6 Earl of Radnor, CIE, CBE (d 1930); *b* 1903; *m* 1923, Lt-Col Gerald Barry, MC (d 1977); 1 s, 5 da; *Style* - Lady Margaret Barry; Lake House, Great Witchingham, Norfolk

BARRY, Rev Noel Patrick; OSB; s of Dr T Barry; *b* 6 Dec 1917; *Educ* Ampleforth, St Benet's Hall Oxford; *Career* Headmaster Ampleforth 1964-; *Style* - The Rev Noel Barry, OSB; Ampleforth College, York (☎ 224)

BARRY, Sheila, Lady; Sheila Georgina Veronica; da of Maj George Joseph

Francis White, MBE; *m* 1951, as his 2 w, Maj Sir Rupert Barry, 4 Bt, MBE (d 1977); *Style* - Sheila, Lady Barry; Brisley Rise, Willesborough Lees, Ashford, Kent

BARRY, Lady Sarah Sue; *née* Stanhope; da of 11 Earl of Harrington; *b* 1951; *Educ* Lawnside; *m* 1970, Robert John Barry; 3 s; *Style* - Lady Sarah Barry; Stone Park, Bruff, Co Limerick, Eire

BARRY, William Rupert Philip Tress; s and h of Sir Edward Barry, 5 Bt; *b* 13 Dec 1973; *Style* - William Barry Esq; 3 Sunnyside Cottages, Warehorne rd, Hanstreet, Ashford, Kent

BART, Lionel; *b* 1 Aug 1930; *Career* songwriter and playwright; *Style* - Lionel Bart Esq; c/o Patricia McNaughton, MLR, 194 Old Brompton rd, SW5 (☎ 01 373 1161)

BARTELL, Lt-Col (Hon) Kenneth George William; CBE (1977); s of William Bartell; *b* 5 Dec 1914; *Educ* Cooper's Co's Sch; *m* 1955, Lucie George; *Career* FIB, Pres Cncl Br Chambers of Commerce in Europe 1977-, dir ICL (France), Wimpey France; *Style* - Lt-Col Kenneth Bartell, CBE; 5 Ave St Honore d'Eylau, Paris 75116, France (☎ 553 69 48)

BARTER, John Wilfred; JP (Gter London 1974); s of late W Barter; *b* 6 Oct 1917; *Educ* Roy Pinner Sch; *m* 1, 1941, Joan Mackay (d 1973); 2 s, 1 da; m 2, 1974, Jessica Crabtree; *Career* chm Ealing and Acton Bldg Soc 1975-, MP (C) Ealing N 1955-64, last chm Middx CC; *Style* - John Barter Esq, JP

BARTFELD, A; *Career* chm Arthur Bartfeld Gp Ltd (preparation of furs and skins); *Style* - A Bartfeld Esq; Brooks Wharf, 48 Upper Thames st, EC4

BARTFELD, P N; *Career* md Arthur Bartfeld Gp Ltd; *Style* - P N Bartfeld Esq; Brooks Wharf, 48 Upper Thames st, EC4

BARTHOLOMEW, Hon Mrs - Hon Noreen; da of 3 Visc Long, TD, DL (1967); *b* 1921; *m* 1947, Capt John Cairns Bartholomew, TD; 2 s, 1 da; *Style* - The Hon Mrs Bartholomew; Poulshot House, Poulshot, Devizes, Wilts

BARTLETT, Lt-Col Sir Basil Hardington; 2 Bt (UK 1913); s of late Hardington Bartlett and gs of Sir Herbert Bartlett, 1 Bt (d 1921); *b* 15 Sept 1905; *Educ* Repton, CCC Cambridge; *m* 1937, Mary (m dis 1960), da of late Sir Ian Malcolm of Poltalloch, KCMG; 2 da; *Heir* bro, Henry Bartlett, MBE; *Career* Drama Script Supervisor BBC TV 1952-55, dramatist; *Style* - Lt-Col Sir Basil Bartlett, Bt; 33c Holland Park, W11

BARTLETT, Henry David Hardington; MBE (1944); s of late Hardington Bartlett; bro and hp of Sir Basil Bartlett, 2 Bt; *b* 18 March 1912; *Educ* Stowe, CCC Cambridge; *m* 1, 1936 (m dis), Kathlene Rosemond, da of Lt-Col W H Stanbury, of Putney; 3 s; m 2; *Career* Lt-Col RA (TA); *Style* - Henry Bartlett Esq, MBE; Harpers, Bledlow Ridge, High Wycombe, Bucks

BARTLETT, John Vernon; CBE (1976); s of late Vernon Bartlett and Olga, nee Testrup; *b* 18 June 1927; *Educ* Stowe, Trin Cambridge; *m* 1951, Gillian, da of late Philip Hoffmann, of Sturmer Hall, Essex; 4 s; *Career* FEng, FICE, FASCE, FIE Aust, consulting engr, sr ptnr and chm Mott Hay & Anderson; *Style* - John Bartlett Esq, CBE; c/o Mott Hay & Anderson, 20/26 Wellesley rd, Croydon, Surrey (☎ 01 686 5041)

BARTLETT, Vernon; CBE (1956); s of late T Bartlett; *b* 30 April 1894; *Educ* Blundell's; *m* 1, Marguerite van den Bemden (d 1966); 2 s; m 2, 1969, Eleanor Ritchie; *Career* writer, formerly journalist with Times, Daily Mail, Daily Herald, News Chronicle, Guardian, MP (Ind) Somerset Bridgwater 1938-50; *Style* - Vernon Bartlett Esq, CBE; Middle Barn, Rimpton, Yeovil, Somerset (☎ Marston Magna 850708)

BARTON, Sir Charles Newton; OBE, ED; s of J Barton; *b* 5 July 1907; *Educ* Maryborough Boys' G S, Qld U; *m* 1935, Enid, nee Wetherell; *Career* kt 1974, chm Brisbane Port Authority, Qld Local Govt Grants Commission; *Recreations*

gardening; *Style* - Sir Charles Barton, OBE, ED; 78 Jilba st, Indooroopilly, Qld 4068, Australia

BARTON, Sir Derek Harold Richard; s of William Barton; *b* 8 Sept 1918; *Educ* Tonbridge, Imperial Coll London; *m* 1, 1944, Jeanne Wilkins; 1 s; m 2, 1969, Christiane Cognet; *Career* organic chemist, kt 1972, FRS, FRSE, Directeur Inst de Chimie des Substances Naturelles, Gif-sur-Yvette 1978-; *Style* - Sir Derek Barton; Institut de Chimie des Substances Naturelles, 91190 Gif-sur-Yvette, France

BARTON, Hon Mrs; Hon Elizabeth Joan Boyd; *née* Orr; da of 1 and last Baron Boyd-Orr, CH, DSO, MC (d 1971); *b* 1916; *m* 1944, Lt-Col Kenneth Alfred John Barton; 2 s, 1 da; *Style* - The Hon Mrs Barton; Brathinch, Brechin, Angus

BARTON, Hugh David MacEwen; CBE (1965, MBE 1944); s of Sir Sidney Barton, GBE (d 1945); *b* 17 Jan 1911; *Educ* Charterhouse, Trin Cambridge; *m* 1937, Rose-Marie, da of Wilhelm Meyer (d 1935); 1 da; *Career* chm and md Jardine Matheson 1955-63, dep chm E H C Penta Hotels N V 1970-; dir Internat Pacific Securities Tst; *Recreations* golf, fishing, shooting; *Clubs* Roy St George's Golf, Berkshire Golf; *Style* - Hugh Barton Esq, CBE; 2 Pelham Place, SW7

BARTON, Lady Mary Gwynedd; da of Maj-Gen Charles William Campbell of Boreland (d 1894); sis of 9 Earl of Breadalbane, MC, and aunt of 10 Earl; *b* 1893; *m* 1925, Cdr Reginald Victor Barton, RN (ret, he d 1967); 1 da; *Career* raised to rank of Earl's da 1924; *Style* - Lady Mary Barton; Stone Cottage, Gellifor, nr Ruthin, Denbighshire

BARTOSIK, Rear-Adm Josef C; CB (1968), DSC (1943); *b* 20 July 1917, Poland; *Educ* in Poland; *m* 1, 1943, Cynthia, da of late Humphrey Bowman, CMG, CBE; 3 s, 1 da; m 2, 1969, Mrs Jeannine Scott, nee Bridgeman; *Career* dir Australia NZ Europe Container Serv 1977-, Assist Ch Naval Staff (Ops) 1966-68 (RN); *Style* - Rear-Adm Josef Bartosik, CB, DSC; 78 Leadenhall st, EC3

BARTTELOT, Maj Sir Brian Walter de Stopham; 5 Bt (UK 1875); s of Lt-Col Sir Walter Barttelot, 4 Bt, (d 1944), and Sara, da of late Lt-Col Herbert Ravenscroft, JP, of The Abbey, Storrington, Sussex; *b* 17 July 1941; *Educ* Eton, Sandhurst; *m* 1969, Hon Fiona Weld Forester, da of late 7 Baron Forester and Marie, da of Sir Herbert Perrott, 6 Bt, CH, CB; 4 da; *Heir* bro, Robin Barttelot; *Career* Mil Sec to Maj-Gen Commanding London Dist and Household Dvn 1978-, Equerry to HM The Queen 1970-71; *Style* - Maj Sir Brian Barttelot, Bt; Keepers, Stopham, Pulborough, W Sussex (☎ Fittleworth 347)

BARTTELOT, Hon Lady - Hon (Mary Angela) Fiona; *née* Weld-Forester; da of 7 Baron Forester; *b* 1944; *m* 1969, Capt Sir Brian Walter de Stopham Barttelot, 5 Bt, *qv*; *Style* - The Hon Lady Barttelot; Keeper's, Stopham, Pulborough, W Sussex

BARTTELOT, Robin Ravenscroft; s and h of Sir Brian Barttelot, 5 Bt, and Hon Fiona Weld Forester, da of late 7 Baron Forester; *b* 15 Dec 1943; *Educ* Seaford Coll; Perth U, W Australia; *Style* - Robin Barttelot Esq

BARWELL, Hon Mrs; Hon Sheila Margaret Ramsay; *née* McNair; da of 1 Baron McNair, CBE, QC; *b* 1918; *m* 1946, John Barwell; 1 s, 3 da; *Style* - The Hon Mrs Barwell; 13 Cranmer rd, Cambridge

BARWICK, Lady - Denise; da of late Alexander Reginald Pole, of Walton-on-Thames; *m* 1, Hugh Christian Radcliffe, barr (decd); m 2, 1968, as his 2 w, Sir Richard Barwick, 3 and last Bt (d 1979); *Style* - Lady Barwick; Thimbleby Hall, Northallerton, Yorks

BARWICK, Rt Hon Sir Garfield Edward John; GCMG (1965), PC (1964), QC (Australia 1958); s of late Jabez Barwick; *b* 22 June 1903; *Educ* Fort St Boys' H S Sydney, Sydney U; *m* 1929, Norma Mountier Symons; 1 s, 1 da; *Career* kt 1953, barr NSW 1927, KC 1941, barr Vict 1945 (KC 1945), QC Qld 1958, Ch Justice Australia 1964-; *Style* - The Rt Hon Sir Garfield Barwick, GCMG, PC, QC;

Mundroola, 133 George st, Careel Bay, Sydney, Australia

BASARAH, Air Chief Marshal Saleh; *b* 14 Aug 1928; *Educ* Air Force Staff and Command Coll; *m* 1955, Sartini Kartina; 2 s, 3 da; *Career* Indonesian Ambass to UK 1978-, CoS Air Force 1973-77; *Style* - H E Air Chief Marshal Saleh Basarah; Nusantara, Bishops Grove, The Bishop's av, N2 (☎ 01 455 8154)

BASHFORD, (John) Patrick; s of Roderick Fleming O'Nolan Bashford (d 1959); *b* 15 Nov 1929; *Educ* St Paul's, Guildhall Sch of Music and Drama, Mannes Sch of Music New York; *m* 1962, Ana-Raquel, da of Alvaro Satre Sanjurjo y Ramirez de Arellano (d 1971); 1 s; *Career* Prof RCM, guitarist; *Style* - Patrick Bashford Esq; c/o Coutts & Co, 1 Cadogan Place, SW1

BASING, 4 Baron (UK 1887); George Lutley Sclater-Booth; s of Hon Charles Sclater-Booth (d 1931); suc cous 1957; *b* 7 Dec 1903; *Educ* Winchester; *m* 1, 1938 (m dis 1944), Jeanette (d 1957), da of late Neil MacKelvie, of New York; 1 s; m 2, 1951, Cynthia, da of late Charles Hardy, of Salt Lake City and widow of Carl Beal of Los Angeles; *Heir* s, Hon Neil Sclater-Booth; *Style* - The Rt Hon The Lord Basing; PO Box 301, Pebble Beach, Calif, USA

BASNETT, David; *b* 9 Feb 1924; *Educ* Quarry Bank H S Liverpool; *m* 1956, Kathleen Molyneaux; 2 s; *Career* Gen Sec GMWU 1973-, chm TUC Gen Cncl 1977-78 (memb 1966-), memb NEDC 1973-, NEB 1975-; *Style* - David Basnett Esq; Thorne House, Ruxley Ridge, Claygate, Esher, Surrey (☎ 62081)

BASS, Harry Godfrey Mitchell; CMG (1972); s of Rev Arthur Bass (d 1966); *b* 26 Aug 1914; *Educ* Marlborough, Gonville and Caius Cambridge, St John's Oxford; *m* 1948, Monica, da of Rev Frederick Burroughs (d 1957); 2 s, 1 da; *Career* High Cmmr Lesotho 1970-73; *Recreations* birdwatching; *Clubs* Roy C'wlth Soc; *Style* - Harry Bass Esq, CMG; Tyler's Mead, Dereham rd, Reepham, Norfolk (☎ 252)

BASS, John Charles; s of Charles Bass (d 1939); *b* 29 July 1929; *Educ* Farnham G S, London U, Sheffield U; *m* 1954, Jean, da of Herbert Stark (d 1975); 2 s; *Career* dir of res Plessey Co, md Allen Clark Res Centre; *Recreations* cabinet making, clock making, gardening; *Style* - John Bass Esq; 10 Thorburn rd, Weston Favell, Northampton

BASS, Robert Olin; *Career* chm Borg-Warner Ltd; *Style* - Robert Bass Esq; PO Box 18, Letchworth, Herts

BASSET, Lady Carey Elizabeth; *née* Coke; da of 5 Earl of Leicester; *b* 1934; *m* 1960, Bryan Ronald Basset; 3 s; *Style* - Lady Carey Basset; 10 Stack House, Cundy st, SW1 (☎ 01 730 2785)); Quarles, Wells-next-Sea, Norfolk

BASTIN, David Terence; CBE (1943, OBE 1942), TD, DL (Surrey 1968); s of Edward Bastin (d 1908), of Exmouth; *b* 20 July 1904; *Educ* Sherborne; *m* 1938, Margaret, da of Alexander Stewart, of Tonbridge; 2 s; *Career* chm Surrey CC 1975-78, High Sheriff Surrey 1969, Master Worshipful Co of Ironmongers 1967; *Recreations* hunting, fishing, shooting, skiing; *Clubs* Fly Fishers; *Style* - David Bastin Esq, CBE, TD, DL; Crooksbury Cottage, Tilford, nr Farnham (☎ Runfold 2010)

BASTYAN, Lady - Victoria Eugenie Helen; *née* Bett; *m* 1944, Lt-Gen Sir Edric Bastyan, KCMG, KCVO, KBE, CB (d 1980); 1 s; *Career* DStJ 1969; *Style* - Lady Bastyan; Flat 42, 52 Brougham Place, N Adelaide, SA 5006, Australia

BASUALDO, Hon Mrs Lucy; *née* Pearson; da of 3 Visc Cowdray; *b* 11 April 1954; *Educ* Daneshill Basingstoke; *m* 1972, Hector Luis Juan Sosa Basualdo (m dis 1978); 1 s, 1 da; *Style* - The Hon Mrs Lucy Basualdo; 135 E 54th st, New York, NY 10022, USA

BATA, Thomas J; *Career* chm Br Bata Shoe Co, dir Bata Overseas Trading Corpn, memb IOD; *Style* - Thomas Bata Esq; c/o British Bata Shoe Co, E Tilbury, Essex RM18 8RL

BATCHELOR, Prof Sir Ivor Ralph

Campbell; CBE (1976); s of Ralph C L Batchelor; *b* 29 Nov 1916; *Educ* Edinburgh Academy, Edinburgh U; *m* 1941, Honor Wallace Williamson; 1 s, 3 da; *Career* consultant psychiatrist to Dundee General and Phychiatric Hosp; author, kt 1981; *Style* - Prof Sir Ivor Batchelor, CBE; Dept of Psychiatry, Ninewells Hosp, Dundee

BATCHELOR, Keith; s of George Batchelor (d 1941); *b* 25 April 1922; *Educ* Haberdashers' Aske's; *m* 1956, Jean, da of Ernest Brown; 2 da; *Career* memb Lloyd's 1948-, dep chm C T Bowring (Insurance) Hldgs 1978-, chm Terra Nova Insurance Co 1975-79; dir Intercontinental Reinsurance Co Bermuda, Winchester Bowring & Co; *Recreations* golf, gardening; *Clubs* MCC, Highgate Golf, Pilgrims; *Style* - Keith Batchelor Esq; Cardinals, Totteridge Village, Herts (☎ 01 445 4718)

BATE, Sir David Lindsay; KBE (1977, CBE 1968); s of Thomas Bate (d 1964); *b* 3 March 1916; *Educ* Marlborough, Trin Cambridge; *m* 1948, Thadeen, da of Robert Peet (d 1977); 2 s; *Career* barr, Slr-Gen N Nigeria 1956, High Court Judge N Nigeria 1957-73 (Ch Judge Plateau State 1973-77); *Recreations* fishing, gardening; *Clubs* Fly Fishers; *Style* - Sir David Bate, KBE; 4029 Lanchaster rd, RR2 Duncan, BC, Canada (☎ 7484400)

BATE, Sir (Walter) Edwin; OBE (1955); s of Peter Bate (d 1967), of Wellington NZ; *b* 12 March 1901; *Educ* Napier Boys' H S, Victoria U Wellington; *m* 1925, Louise, da of James Jordan; 2 s, 1 da; *Career* barr and slr 1922, Pres Hosp Bds Assoc of NZ 1953-74, Tstee Savings Banks Assoc of NZ 1967-69, kt 1969, OStJ 1957; *Recreations* gardening; *Style* - Sir Edwin Bate, OBE; 38 Busby Hill, Havelock North, New Zealand (☎ 777448); 53 Rainbow dve, Taupo

BATE, Rex; OBE (1980); s of Ferdinand Bate, of Solihull (d 1958); *b* 18 June 1911; *Educ* West Bridgford Sch, Loughborough U; *m* 1937, Peggie, da of James Heron Watt, of Ealing (d 1955); 1 s, 2 da; *Career* md Renold Ltd 1959-73, dir Renold, chartered electrical and mechanical engr, chm London Assoc for the Blind; *Recreations* music, rowing, fishing; *Clubs* East India and Sports, Leander; *Style* - Rex Bate Esq, OBE; The Dial House, Chobham, Surrey (☎ 8176)

BATE, Maj-Gen William; CB (1974), OBE (1963), DL (Surrey 1960); s of S Bate, of Warrington; *b* 6 June 1920; *m* 1946, Veronica, nee Quinn; 2 s, 2 da; *Career* Sec to Cncl TAVR Assocs 1975-, Dir Movements (Army) MOD 1971-73, FCIT; *Recreations* cricket, tennis; *Style* - Maj-Gen William Bate, CB, OBE, DL; Netherbury, Belton rd, Camberley, Surrey (☎ 63529)

BATEMAN, Sir Geoffrey Hirst; s of William Bateman (d 1959); *b* 24 Oct 1906; *Educ* Epsom Coll, Univ Oxford; *m* 1931, Margaret, da of Sir Samuel Turner (d 1955); 3 s, 1 da; *Career* surgeon St Thomas's 1938-71, memb Cncl Roy Coll of Surgeons 1963-67, kt 1972; *Recreations* golf, fishing; *Style* - Sir Geoffrey Bateman; Thorney, Graffham, Petworth, W Sussex (☎ 314)

BATES, Allan Frederick; CMG (1958); s of John Bates (d 1954); *b* 15 July 1911; *Educ* Woolwich Centl Sch, London U; *m* 1937, Ena, da of John Boxall (d 1944); 3 s; *Career* md Dvpt Bank Mauritius 1964-70, IMF Fin Advsr Bahamas Govt 1971-74 and Lesotho 1975-76; *Recreations* painting, carving; *Clubs* Roy C'wlth Soc, IOD; *Style* - Allan Bates Esq, CMG; 5 Redford av, Coulsdon, Surrey (☎ 01 660 7421)

BATES, Sir (John) Dawson; 2 Bt (UK 1937), MC (1943); s of Rt Hon Sir Dawson Bates, 1 Bt, OBE (d 1949), and Muriel (d 1972), da of late Sir Charles Cleland, KBE, MVO, LLD; *b* 21 Sept 1921; *Educ* Winchester, Balliol Oxford; *m* 1953, Mary, da of late Lt- Col Joseph Hoult; 2 s, 1 da; *Heir* s, Richard Bates; *Career* Area Land Agent for Nat Tst, FRICS, Maj Rifle Brigade WWII; *Style* - Sir Dawson Bates, Bt, MC; Eaton Hastings Grange, Faringdon, Berks

BATES, Sir (Julian) Darrell; CMG (1956), CVO (1954); s of E Stuart Bates (author, d 1944); *b* 10 Nov 1913; *Educ* Sevenoaks Sch, Keble Oxford; *m* 1944,

Susan, da of F Sinclair; 2 s, 1 da; *Career* Colonial Serv 1936-68, Perm Sec Gibraltar 1964-68, kt 1966; *Style* - Sir Darrell Bates, CMG, CVO; Mellindons, St Buryan, Cornwall (☎ 485)

BATES, Sir David Robert; s of Walter Bates (d 1937), of Co Tyrone; *b* 18 Nov 1916; *Educ* Roy Belfast Academical Inst, Queen's U Belfast, UCL; *m* 1956, Barbara, da of John Bailey, DSO, of Qld; 1 s, 1 da; *Career* kt 1978, FRS 1955, Prof Theoretical Physics Queen's U Belfast 1968-73, Res Prof 1973-; *Recreations* reading (history, biography, thrillers); *Style* - Sir David Bates; 6 Deramore Pk, Belfast BT9 5JT (☎ 665640)

BATES, Edward Robert; s and h of Sir Geoffrey Bates, 5 Bt, MC; *b* 4 July 1946; *Educ* Gordonstoun; *Style* - Edward Bates Esq; Gyrn Castle, Llanasa, Holywell, Clwyd (☎ Prestatyn 3500)

BATES, Sir Geoffrey Voltelin; 5 Bt (UK 1880), MC (1942); s of late Maj Cecil Bates, DSO, MC, and Hylda, da of Sir James Heath, 1 Bt; suc (1946) unc, Sir Percy Bates, 4 Bt, GBE; *b* 2 Oct 1921; *Educ* Radley; *m* 1, 1945, Kitty (d 1956), da of Ernest Kendall-Lane, of Saskatchewan; 2 s; m 2, 1957, Hon Olivia FitzRoy (d 1969), da of 2 Visc Daventry; 1 da (and 1 da decd); m 3, 1971, Mrs Juliet Eleanor Hugolyn Whitelocke-Winter, da of late Cdr G Whitelocke, RN, and widow of Edward Winter; *Heir* s, Edward Bates; *Career* High Sheriff Flintshire 1969, Maj (ret) Cheshire Yeomanry; *Recreations* hunting, shooting, fishing; *Style* - Sir Geoffrey Bates, Bt, MC; Gyrn Castle, Llanasa, Holywell, Clwyd (☎ Prestatyn 3500)

BATES, Sir (Edward) John Hunter; KBE (1969), CB (1965), MC (1944); s of Ernest Bates, FRIBA (d 1954), of Bournemouth; *b* 5 Dec 1911; *Educ* Wellington, CCC Cambridge; *m* 1947, Sheila, da of Maj Herbert Norman (d 1962); 2 s, 2 da; *Career* Dir RA 1961-64, Roy Def Acad 1967-69, Personnel Dir Thomson Regnl Newspapers 1969-78, Master Worshipful Co Haberdashers 1978-79; *Recreations* fishing, shooting; *Clubs* Army & Navy, Rye Golf; *Style* - Sir John Bates, KBE, CB, MC; Seymours Oast, Leeds, nr Maidstone, Kent (☎ 861275)

BATES, Lady - Margaret; da of late Rev J H Clarke; *m* 1925, Sir Alfred Bates, MC, DL (d 1979); 3 s, 1 da; *Style* - Lady Bates; 191 Coleherne Court, SW5 (☎ 01 373 4799)

BATES, Martin Colin; s of Harry Bates, CSI, of Milford-on-Sea; *b* 24 March 1927; *Educ* Uppingham, St Cat's Cambridge; *m* 1955, Patricia, da of George Percival Simon (d 1963); 1 s, 1 da; *Career* FCA, md Getty Marine Servs 1968-, dir Sutton Place Property Co; *Recreations* tennis, golf, walking, reading; *Clubs* Leatherhead Golf; *Style* - Martin Bates Esq; Brackenhurst, Wonham Way, Gomshall, Surrey (☎ Shere 2953)

BATES, Hon Mrs; Hon Margaret Eleanor; *née* Shepherd; da of 1 Baron Shepherd, PC; *b* 1922; *m* 1949, Theodore Leonard Bates; 1 s, 1 da; *Style* - The Hon Mrs Bates; 45 Whyteleafe Hill, Whyteleafe, Surrey

BATES, Malcolm Rowland; s of Rowland Bates, of Waterlooville Hants; *b* 23 Sept 1934; *Educ* Portsmouth G S, Warwick U, Harvard Grad Sch of Business Admin; *m* 1960, Lynda, da of Maurice Price, of Bristol; 3 da; *Career* dir GEC 1980-, jt md Wm Brandt's & Sons 1974-; dir Custodian Hldgs, Custodian Properties, HEC-Hitachi TV, Greenwood Airvac Ventilation, Stanhope Pension Tst; *Recreations* classical music, reading, tennis; *Style* - Malcolm Bates Esq; The Woodlands, 77 Kidmore rd, Caversham, Berks (☎ 0734 471715)

BATES, Richard Dawson Hoult; s and h of Sir Dawson Bates, 2 Bt, MC; *b* 12 May 1956; *Style* - Richard Bates Esq; Eaton Hastings Grange, Faringdon, Berks

BATH, 6 Marquess of (GB 1789); Sir Henry Frederick Thynne; 9 Bt (GB 1641), ED, JP (Wilts 1938); also Viscount Weymouth and Baron Thynne of Warminster (GB 1682); s of 5 Marquess, KG, CB, PC (d 1946) and Violet, da of Sir Charles Mordaunt, 10 Bt; *b* 26 Jan 1905;

Educ Harrow, Ch Ch Oxford; *m* 1, 1927 (m dis 1953), Hon Daphne, da of 4 Baron Vivian, DSO; 2 s, 1 da; m 2, 1953, Virginia Penelope, da of late Alan Parsons and formerly w of Hon David Francis Tennant; 1 da; *Heir* s, Viscount Weymouth; *Career* formerly Maj Roy Wilts Yeo, memb of Cncl of HRH The Prince of Wales 1933-36, sat as MP for Frome Div of Somerset (C) Oct 1931-Oct 1935; *Style* - The Most Hon The Marquess of Bath ED JP; Job's Mill, Crockerton, Warminster, Wilts (2279); Longleat, Warminster, Wilts

BATH AND WELLS, 75 Bishop of (cr 909) 1975-; Rt Rev John Monier Bickersteth; s of Rev Canon Edward Bickersteth (d 1976); *b* 6 Sept 1921; *Educ* Rugby, Ch Ch Oxford; *m* 1955, Jane, da of Edward Cleveland-Stevens (d 1976); 3 s, 1 da; *Career* ordained 1951, Bp of Warrington 1970-75, Chaplain and Sub-Prelate Order of St John 1977-, Clerk of the Closet to HM The Queen 1979-; *Recreations* calligraphy, country pursuits; *Clubs* Roy C'wlth Soc; *Style* - The Rt Rev The Lord Bishop of Bath and Wells; The Palace, Wells, Somerset (☎ 72341)

BATHO, Sir Maurice Benjamin; 2 Bt (UK 1928); s of Sir Charles Batho, 1 Bt (d 1938); *b* 14 Jan 1910; *Educ* Uppingham and in Belgium; *m* 1934, Antoinette, da of Baron d'Udekem d'Acoz, of Ghent; 2 s, 2 da; *Heir* s, Peter Batho; *Career* chm and md Ridgley (Huntingdon) Ltd and assoc cos, md Reed Paper 1959-65; *Style* - Sir Maurice Batho, Bt; Carlton Hall, Saxmundham, Suffolk (☎ 2505)

BATHO, Peter Ghislain; s and h of Sir Maurice Batho, 2 Bt, by his w, Antoinette, da of Baron d'Udekem d'Acoz, of Ghent; *b* 9 Dec 1939; *Educ* Ampleforth; *m* 1966, Lucille Mary, da of late Wilfrid Williamson, of Saxmundham; 3 s; *Style* - Peter Batho Esq; Park Farm, Saxmundham, Suffolk

BATHURST, 8 Earl (GB 1772); Henry Allen John Bathurst; DL (Glos 1960); also Baron Bathurst (GB 1711) and Baron Apsley (GB 1771); s of Lt-Col Lord Apsley, DSO, MC, TD, MP (k on active serv 1942) and late Lady Apsley, CBE; suc gf (7 Earl) 1943; *b* 1 May 1927; *Educ* Eton, Ch Ch Oxford; *m* 1, 1959, Judith (m dis 1976), da of late A Nelson, of Fosse Corner Cirencester; 2 s, 1 da; m 2, 1978, Gloria, da of Harold Clarry, of Vancouver, and widow of David Rutherston; *Heir* s, Lord Apsley; *Career* Lord in Waiting 1957-61, Jt Parly Under-Sec Home Off 1961-62, Gov Roy Ag Coll, Pres Glos Branch CPRE, Chllr Primrose League 1959-61, memb CLA Cncl; *Clubs* White's; *Style* - The Rt Hon The Earl Bathurst, DL; Cirencester Park, Glos (☎ Cirencester 3412)

BATHURST, Lady (Elizabeth) Ann; da of Capt Hon Chandos Graham Temple-Gore-Langton (d 1921); sis of 7 Earl Temple of Stowe; *b* 1908; *m* 1927, Gp-Capt Peter Bathurst (d 1970); 2 s; *Career* raised to rank of Earl's da 1941; *Style* - Lady Ann Bathurst; Tolzey Cottage, Queen Charlton, Bristol

BATHURST, Hon Alexander Edward Seymour; s of 8 Earl Bathurst, DL; *b* 8 Aug 1965; *Style* - The Hon Alexander Bathurst

BATHURST, Hon David Charles Lopes; s of 2 Visc Bledisloe, QC (d 1979); *b* 15 Dec 1937; *Educ* Eton, Magdalen Oxford; *m* 1967, Cornelia, da of A K McCosh, of Biggar Lanarks; 3 da; *Career* 2 Lt 12th Roy Lancers 1956-58, dir Christie Manson & Woods; *Clubs* Boodle's, Garrick; *Style* - The Hon David Bathurst; South Lodge, E Heath rd, London NW3 (☎ 01 794 6999)

BATHURST, Hon George Bertram; TD; s of Lt-Col Lord Apsley, DSO, MC, TD, MP (k on active serv 1942); bro of 8 Earl Bathurst, DL; *b* 1929; *Educ* Eton, Trin Oxford; *m* 1973, Susan, nee Messer; *Career* late Capt Roy Wilts Yeomanry, late Lt 10 Hussars; *Style* - The Hon George Bathurst, TD; Hullasey House, Tarlton, Cirencester, Glos

BATHURST, Lady Henrietta Mary Lilias; da of 8 Earl Bathurst, DL; *b* 17 Oct 1962; *Style* - Lady Henrietta Bathurst; Cirencester Park, Cirencester, Glos (☎ 3412)

BATHURST, Hon Rupert Edward Ludlow; s and h of 3 Viscount Bledisloe,

QC; *b* 13 March 1964; *Style* - The Hon Rupert Bathurst

BATLEY, Lawrence; s of John Arthur Batley, of Huddersfield (d 1958); *b* 15 Feb 1911; *Educ* Hillhouse Centl Sch Huddersfield; *m* 1937, Dorothie, nee Boothroyd; 1 da; *Career* chm Batleys of Yorkshire; opened first cash and carry warehouse in UK 1955; *Style* - Lawrence Batley Esq; Heaton Pk House, Heaton rd, Huddersfield; 456 Queen's Promenade, Blackpool

BATSFORD, Sir Brian Caldwell Cook; s of Arthur Cook; took mother's name of Batsford; *b* 18 Dec 1910; *Educ* Repton; *m* 1945, Joan, da of Norman Cunliffe, of Oxford (d 1964); 2 da; *Career* chm B T Batsford (Publishers) 1952-74, pres 1974-76; contested Chelmsford for Nat Govt 1945, MP (C) Ealing S 1958-74, kt 1974, assist Govt Whip 1962-64, oppn dep ch whip 1964-67, chm House of Commons Library Ctee 1970-74; chm RSA 1973-75 (v-pres 1975-); *Club* Pratt's; *Style* - Sir Brian Batsford; Lamb House, Rye, E Sussex (☎ 07973 3763)

BATT, Hon Mrs; Hon Elisabeth Noel; da of Hon Charles Henry Stanley Monck (d 1914); sis of 6 Visc Monck, OBE, JP, DL; *b* 1908; *m* 1928, William Batt, MBE, JP, DL; 1 s, 2 da (and 1 s decd); *Also* raised to rank of Viscount's da 1928; *Style* - The Hon Mrs Batt; Chaucer's Farm, Gresham, Norwich

BATT, William Frederic; MBE (Mil 1945); s of Lt-Col Reginald Batt, CBE, MVO, of Gresham Hall, Norwich (d 1952); *b* 4 April 1904; *Educ* Winchester, Sandhurst; *m* 1928, Hon Elisabeth, da of Capt Hon Charles Monck (d 1914) and sis of 6 Visc Monck; 1 s, 2 da (and 1 s decd); *Career* Maj Coldstream Gds 1924-29 and 1939-45 (served NW Europe); High Sheriff Norfolk 1963, memb Gen Synod C of E, retired landowner and farmer; *Clubs* Cavalry and Guards; *Style* - William Batt Esq, MBE, JP, DL; Chaucer's Farm, Gresham, Norwich (☎ Matlase 223)

BATTEN, John Charles; s of Raymond Batten (d 1978); *b* 11 March 1924; *Educ* Mill Hill, London U, Bart's; *m* 1950, Anne, da of John Oriel (d 1968); 1 s, 2 da; *Career* formerly Surgn-Capt Roy Horse Gds, consultant physician, Physician to HM The Queen 1974- (to HM Roy Household 1970-74); *Recreations* sailing; *Style* - John Batten Esq; 7 Lion Gate gdns, Richmond, Surrey (☎ 01 940 3282)

BATTLE, Derrick Bisdee; *Career* md Bullough Ltd, chm B & B Trailers, Beanstalk Shelving, Druce & Co, Gauges Bourdon, Newman Granger Industs, Project Office Furniture; dir Bayroe Engineering, Bredon Hydraulics, Hagley Industl Tst, Hago Products, John Pring & Son, Johnson Precision Ltd, Metallifacture Ltd, M H H Engineering, Midland Electro Plating, Morley Electrical Engineering, Newton Derby Ltd, Small Electric Motors Ltd BSc (Eng); *Style* - Derrick Battle Esq; 85 East St, Epsom, Surrey KT17 1ED

BATTY, Sir William Bradshaw; TD (1946); s of Rowland Batty; *b* 15 May 1913; *Educ* Hulme G S Manchester; *m* 1946, Jean Brice; 1 s, 1 da (and 1 s decd); *Career* kt 1973, chm Ford Motor Co 1972-75, now ret, FBIM, Pres SMMT 1975-76; *Recreations* golf, sailing, gardening; *Clubs* Roy Western Yacht; *Style* - Sir William Batty, TD; Glenhaven Cottage, Riverside rd West, Newton Ferrers, S Devon

BATTYE, Maj-Gen Stuart Hedley Molesworth; CB (Mil 1960); s of Lt-Col Walter Battye, DSO, CStJ, LRCP; *b* 21 June 1907; *Educ* Marlborough, RMA Woolwich, Sidney Sussex Cambridge; *m* 1940, Evelyn Desirée, da of Capt George Hartford, DSO and Bar, RN; 1 s, 2 da; *Career* served 1937-61 (Dir of Movements Army 1958-61), Dir Roy Industs Bureau 1963-68, COSIRA 1968-73; *Recreations* fly fishing, painting; *Clubs* Army and Navy; *Style* - Maj-Gen Stuart Battye, CB; Fensacre House, Ascot, Berks

BAUCHER, Stanley Esmond; *Career* chm Norwest Holst Ltd, dir Joseph Thompson & Co (Liverpool), Norwest Pensions, FIOB, memb IOD; *Style* - Stanley Baucher Esq; 35 Chesham Place, SW1

BAUGHAN, Michael Christopher; s of

Prof Edward Baughan, CBE; *b* 25 April 1942; *Educ* Westminster; *m* 1975, Moira, da of Percy Levy; 2 's; *Career* exec dir Lazard Bros & Co, memb Bd of Govrs-Roy Hosp and Home for Incurables, Westminster Sch; *Recreations* philately; *Style* - Michael Baughan Esq; 21 Moorfields, EC2

BAVIN, Alfred Robert Walter; CB (1966); s of Alfred Bavin (d 1918); *b* 4 April 1917; *Educ* Christ's Hosp, Balliol Oxford; *m* 1947, Helen, da of Percival Mansfield (d 1919); 1 s, 3 da; *Career* Dep Under Sec DHSS 1968-73; *Recreations* reading, watching cricket; *Clubs* Athenaeum, MCC; *Style* - Alfred Bavin Esq, CB; 7 First av, Felpham, Bognor Regis, W Sussex (☎ Middleton-on-Sea 3073)

BAX, His Honour Judge; Rodney Ian Shirley Bax; QC (1966); s of Rudolph Bax (d 1969); *b* 16 Sept 1920; *Educ* Bryanston, RCM; *m* 1953, Patricia Anne, da of Martin Turner, MC; 1 s, 1 da; *Career* barr 1947, Circuit Judge 1973-; *Recreations* music, books; *Style* - His Hon Judge Bax, QC; 4 Jocelyn rd, Richmond, Surrey (☎ 01 940 3395); 3 Le Bourgage, Alderney, CI

BAXENDALE, Lady Elizabeth Joan; *née* Fortescue; da of 5 Earl Fortescue, KG, PC, CB, OBE, MC, (d 1958); *b* 1926; *m* 1946, Maj William Lloyd Baxendale, JP; 2 s, 1 da; *Style* - Lady Elizabeth Baxendale; Hailwell House, Framfield, Uckfield, E Sussex (☎ Framfield 256)

BAXENDELL, Sir Peter Brian; CBE (1972); s of Lesley Baxendell; *b* 28 Feb 1925; *Educ* St Francis Xavier's Liverpool and Royal Sch of Mines; *m* 1949, Rosemary, nee Lacey; 2 s, 2 da; *Career* md Royal Dutch/Shell gp of companies 1973, kt 1981; *Style* - Sir Peter Baxendell, CBE; Shell Centre, SE1 (☎ 01 934 2772)

BAXTER, Hon Mrs; Hon Helen Margaretta; *née* Maude; da of 7 Viscount Hawarden (d 1958); *b* 1921; *m* 1947, Walter Peter Baxter (d 1977) 1 s, 3 da; *Style* - The Hon Mrs Baxter; Milton Old House, Gillingham, Dorset

BAXTER, John Walter; CBE (1974); s of late J G Baxter; *b* 4 June 1917; *Educ* Westminster City Sch; City and Guilds Engineering Coll; *m* 1941, Jessie, nee Pimblott; 1 da; *Career* senior partner G Maunsell and Ptnrs 1959-; *Style* - John Baxter Esq, CBE; 17 Chislehurst rd, Bickley, Kent (☎ 01 467 1985)

BAXTER, Raymond; s of Frederick Garfield Baxter; *b* 25 Jan 1922; *Educ* Ilford County High Sch; *m* 1945, Sylvia Kathryn, nee Johnson, of Boston, Mass; 1 s, 1 da; *Career* broadcaster and writer; *Style* - Raymond Baxter Esq; The Old Rectory, Denham, Bucks

BAXTER, W G; OBE; *Career* md Baxter's Scottish Game Ltd, winner of Queen's Award for Export Achievement 1979; *Style* - W G Baxter Esq, OBE; Baxter's Scottish Game Ltd, Fochabers, Morayshire

BAYFORD, Hon Mrs; Hon Hilda Elizabeth Mary; *née* Croft; da of 1 Baron Croft, CMG, TD (d 1947); 1 s, 2 da; *Style* - The Hon Mrs Bayford; Upper Bowden, nr Pangbourne, Berks

BAYHAM, Viscount; James William John Pratt; s and h of Earl of Brecknock (s and h of 5 Marquess Camden) *b* 11 Dec 1965; *Style* - Viscount Bayham

BAYLIS, Clifford Henry; CB (1973); s of late Arthur Baylis; *b* 20 March 1915; *Educ* Alcester G S, Keble Oxford: *m* 1, 1939, Phyllis Clark; 2 s; m 2, 1979, Margaret Hawkins; *Career* 1947-74 Home CS, Controller HMSO 1969-74; dir Harland & Wolff, Clerk Worshipful Co of Shipbuilders 1977-; *Clubs* RAC; *Style* - Clifford Baylis Esq, CB; 38 Cleaver st, SE11 (☎ 01 587 0817)

BAYLISS, Col George Sheldon; CB (1966), OBE (1945, MBE 1939), TD (1941), DL (Staffs 1953); s of Francis Bayliss (d 1945); *b* 26 Dec 1900; *Educ* Shrewsbury; *m* 1935, Margaret (d 1962), da of Joseph Harker (d 1914), of Penrith, and widow of Dr K Williamson, MC (d 1929); 1 s, 1 step s; *Career* chm Staffs TA Assoc 1958-65, md S B & N Ltd, Walsall, 1930-76; *Style* - Col George Bayliss, CB,

OBE, TD, DL; The Bungalow, Littlefield House, Wall, Staffs (☎ Shenstone 480024)

BAYLISS, J; *Career* gen man of Abbey National Building Society; *Style* - J Bayliss Esq; Abbey National Building Society, Abbey House, Baker st, NW1

BAYLISS, Hon Mrs (Mary Selina); da of 2 Viscount Bridgeman; *b* 1940; m 1962, Jeremy Bayliss; 3 s; *Style* - The Hon Mrs Bayliss; Sheepbridge Court, Swallowfield, nr Reading, Berks

BAYLISS, Sir Noel Stanley; CBE (1960); s of Henry Bayliss (d 1948), of NSW; *b* 19 Dec 1906; *Educ* Melbourne H S, Melbourne U, Lincoln Coll Oxford, U of Calif Berkeley; *m* 1933, Nellie, da of Arthur Banks, of Los Angeles; 2 s; *Career* Prof Chem W Australia U 1938-71 (Emeritus 1972) kt 1979; *Recreations* music, golf; *Clubs* Weld (Perth), Roy Perth Yacht, Nedlands Golf (WA); *Style* - Sir Noel Bayliss, CBE; 104 Thomas st, Nedlands, W Australia 6009 (☎ 09 386 1453)

BAYLISS, Sir Richard (Ian Samuel); KCVO (1978); s of late Frederick Bayliss; *b* 2 Jan 1917; *Educ* Rugby; Clare Cambridge; St Thomas' Hospital, London; *m* 1, 1941, Margaret Hardman (m dis 1956); 1 s, 1 da; m 2, 1957, Constance Ellen, nee Frey, of Connecticut; 2 da; m 3, 1979, Marina, widow of Charles Rankin; *Career* MD, FRCP; physician to HM The Queen 1970- and head of HM Medical Household 1973-; *Style* - Sir Richard Bayliss, KCVO; 9 Park sq West, NW1 (☎ 01 935 2071)

BAYNE, John; *Career* advocate; Sheriff of Glasgow and Strathkelvin 1975-79; *Style* - John Bayne Esq; Winsford, 7 Milrig rd, Rutherglen

BAYNES, Christopher Rory; s and h of Sir John Baynes, 7 Bt, *qv*; *b* 1956; *Style* - Christopher Baynes Esq

BAYNES, Sir John (Christopher Malcolm); 7 Bt (UK 1801); s of Sir Rory Baynes, 6 Bt (d 1979); *b* 24 April 1928; *Educ* Sedbergh Sch; Sandhurst; Edinburgh U; *m* 1955, Shirley Maxwell, nee Dodds; 4 s; *Career* Lt-Col (ret) QOH, Cameronians (Scottish Rifles) 1948-68; proprietor Lake Vyrnwy Hotel; *Style* - Sir John Baynes, Bt; The Cottage, Lake Vyrnwy Hotel, via Oswestry, Salop (☎ Llanwddyn 244)

BAYNES, Pauline Diana; da of Frederick Baynes, CIE; *b* 9 Sept 1922; *Educ* Beaufront Sch Camberley, Farnham Sch of Art, Slade Sch of Art; *m* 1951, Fritz Otto Gasch; *Career* designer and book illustrator; *Style* - Miss Pauline Baynes; Rock Barn Cottage, Dockenfield, Farnham, Surrey (☎ Headley Down 713306)

BAZALGETTE, Rear-Adm Derek Willoughby; CB (1976); s of Harry Bazalgette (d 1953); *b* 22 July 1924; *Educ* RNC Dartmouth; *m* 1947, Angela, da of Sir Henry Hinchcliffe (d 1980); 4 da; *Career* RN 1938-76, princ Netley Waterside House 1977- (Local Govt), Cmmr Scout Assoc HQ 1977-; *Clubs* Lansdowne; *Style* - Rear-Adm Derek Bazalgette, CB; The Glebe House, Newtown, Fareham, Hants (☎ Wickham 833138)

BAZLEY, Thomas John Sebastian; s and h of Sir Thomas Bazley, 3 Bt, *qv*; *b* 31 Aug 1948; *Style* - Thomas Bazley Esq

BAZLEY, Sir Thomas Stafford; 3 Bt (UK 1869); s of late Gardner Sebastian Bazley, only s of 2 Bt; suc gf, Sir Thomas Sebastian Bazley, 2 Bt, 1919; *b* 5 Oct 1907; *Educ* Harrow, Magdalen Oxford; *m* 1945, Carmen, da of J Tulla; 3 s, 2 da; *Heir* s, Thomas John Bazley; *Style* - Sir Thomas Bazley, Bt; Eastleach Folly, nr Hatherop, Cirencester, Gloucester

BEACH, Gen Sir (William Gerald) Hugh; GBE (1980, OBE 1966), KCB (1976), MC (1944); s of Maj-Gen William Beach, CB, CMG, DSO; *b* 20 May 1924; *Educ* Winchester, Peterhouse Cambridge; *m* 1951, Estelle, da of Gordon Henry; 3 s, 1 da; *Career* Master Gen Ordnance MOD 1977-, Col Cmdt RE 1977-, Dep CIC UKLF 1976-77; *Recreations* sailing (yacht- 'Gay Gannet V'), skiing; *Clubs* Farmers', Roy Lymington Yacht; *Style* - Gen Sir Hugh Beach, GBE, KCB, MC;

The Ropeway, Beaulieu, Hants (☎ 612269)

BEACH, Surgn Rear-Adm William Vincent; CB (1961), OBE (1949), QHS (1960); s of William Beach; *b* 22 Nov 1903; *Educ* Seaford Coll, Guy's; *m* 1931, Daphne, da of Eustace Joseph (d 1953); 2 da; *Career* RN Medical Serv 1928-63, Sr Surgn Shaw Savill Line 1966-75; *Recreations* shooting, fishing; *Clubs* Naval and Military; *Style* - Surgn Rear-Adm William Beach, CB, OBE QHS; Cherry Tree Cottage, Easton, Winchester, Hants (☎ Itchen Abbas 222)

BEADLE, Rt Hon Sir (Thomas) Hugh (William); CMG (1957), OBE (1946), PC (1964), QC (1946); s of late A W Beadle, OBE; *b* 6 Feb 1905; *Educ* Salisbury Boys' High Sch, Diocesan Coll Rondebosch, Cape Town U, Queen's Oxford; *m* 1, 1934, Leonie Barry (d 1953); 2 da; m 2, 1954, Olive Staley Jackson (d 1974); m 3, 1976, Pleasance Johnson; *Career* ch justice Rhodesia 1961-77, kt 1961; *Style* - The Rt Hon Sir Hugh Beadle CMG OBE PC QC; Leander av, Hillside, Bulawayo, Zimbabwe

BEAKBANE, Henry Renault; s of Henry Beakbane, of Stourport-on-Severn (d 1953); *b* 28 April 1923; *Educ* Leighton Pk, Leeds U, LSE; *m* 1951, Joan, da of Henry Epton Hornby, OBE, FRCVS, DVSM, of Zimbabwe (d 1976); 2 s, 1 da; *Career* Colonial Serv Tanganyika 1944-50, chm Beakbane Ltd, Master Worshipful Co of Glovers 1979; Quaker BSc, CBIM, FRSA; *Recreations* riding (horse-'Figeac'); *Clubs* City Livery; *Style* - Henry Beakbane Esq; Jacob's Ladder, Low Habberley, Kidderminster, Worcs (☎ 0562 745125/745061)

BEAL, Anthony Ridley; s of Harold Beal; *b* 28 Feb 1925; *Educ* Haberdashers' Aske's Hampstead Sch; Downing Cambridge; *m* 1958, Rosemary Howarth; 3 da; *Career* chm Heinemann Educational Books 1979-; md Heinemann Educational Books (International) 1979-; *Style* - Anthony Beal Esq; 24 Loom lane, Radlett, Herts (☎ Radlett 4567)

BEALE, Evelyn Martin Lansdowne; s of Evelyn Stewart Landsdowne Beale (d 1972) and Muriel Rebecca, OBE, nee Slade (ggda of Gen Sir John Slade, 1 Bt, GCH); *b* 8 Sept 1928; *Educ* Winchester and Trin Cambridge; *m* 1953, Violette Elizabeth Anne, nee Lewis; 2 s, 1 da; *Career* FRS 1979; technical dir Scicon Consultancy International Ltd 1968-, tech dir Scicon Computer Servs 1975-, chm Mathematical Programming Soc 1974-76, V-Pres Roy Statistical Soc 1978-80, Operational Res Soc Silver Medallist 1980; *Style* - Evelyn Beale Esq; Brick Close, Kiln Farm, Milton Keynes, Bucks (☎ 565656)

BEALE, Thomas Edward; CBE (1966), JP (Inner London 1950); s of Thomas Beale; *b* 5 March 1904; *Educ* City of London Sch; *m* 1932, Beatrice, da of William McLaughlin, JP, of Enniskillen; 1 s; *Career* FRSA, FRSH, chm Beale's Ltd; *Recreations* arboriculture; *Clubs* Carlton; *Style* - Thomas Beale Esq, CBE, JP; West Lodge Park, Hadley Wood, Herts (☎ 01 440 8311)

BEALE, Sir William Francis; OBE (1945); s of late George Beale; *b* 27 Jan 1908; *Educ* Downside Sch, Pembroke Coll Cambridge; *m* 1934, Deva, nee Zaloudek; 1 s, 1 da; *Career* chm NAAFI 1953-61, dep chm Randall Group British West Africa Corpn 1964-78, chm Staple Green, dir Radio Rentals NCR 1964-78, MFH Tedworth Foxhounds 1972-81; kt 1956; *Recreations* hunting, shooting; *Clubs* Bath, Hawks; *Style* - Sir William Beale, OBE; The Grange, All Cannings, Devizes, Wilts (☎ Cannings 686)

BEAMENT, Sir James William Longman; s of late T Beament; *b* 17 Nov 1921; *Educ* Crewkerne G S, Queens' Cambridge, London Sch of Tropical Medicine; *m* 1962, Juliet, da of late Prof Sir Ernest Barker; 2 s; *Career* ScD, FRS (1964); Draper's Prof of Agriculture and head of dept of Applied Biology Cambridge; kt 1980; *Style* - Sir James Beament; 19 Sedley Taylor rd, Cambridge (☎ 46045)

BEAMISH, Hon Andrea Tufton; da of Baron Chelwood, MC, DL, *qv*; *b* 1955; *Style* - The Hon Andrea Beamish

BEAMISH, Hon Claudia Hamilton; da of Baron Chelwood, MC, DL, *qv*; *b* 1952; *Style* - The Hon Claudia Beamish

BEAN, Lady; Constance Mary; da of William Greenlees, of Adelaide; *m* 1927, Sir Edgar Bean, CMG (d 1977); 2 s; *Clubs* Ormskirk G S; *Style* - Lady Bean; 51 Godfrey terrace, Leabrook, S Australia

BEARD, Allan Geoffrey; s of Maj Henry Beard (d 1969); *b* 18 Oct 1919; *Educ* Ormskirk G S; *m* 1945, Ellen Matthews, nee McDonagh; 1 da; *Career* under-sec DHSS to 1979; *Style* - Allan Beard Esq; 51 Rectory Park, Sanderstead, Surrey (☎ 01 657 4197)

BEARDMORE, Brian John; *Career* chm Crown House Engineering Ltd; *Style* - Brian Beardmore Esq; Crown House Engineering Ltd, 2 Lygon pla, SW1

BEARSTED, 3 Viscount (UK 1925); Sir Marcus Richard Samuel; 3 Bt (UK 1903), TD (1945), DL (Warwicks 1950); s of 2 Viscount Bearsted, MC (d 1948); *b* 1 June 1909; *Educ* Eton, New Coll Oxford; *m* 1, 1947, Elizabeth (m dis 1966), da of G Firmston-Williams, of Hans Place, SW; 1 da (and 1 da decd); m 2, 1968, Jean (d 1978), da of R Wallace, of Edinburgh, and formerly w of -- Somerville; *Heir* bro, Hon Peter Samuel; *Career* chm Hill Samuel Gp 1948-66, Nineteen Twenty-Eight Investment Tst 1948-, Tanker Finance Ltd 1957-, Samuel Properties & subsids 1961-, Negit SA Luxembourg & Subsids 1966-; dir Philip Hill Investment Tst 1965-81; Pres Jewish Home & Hosp Tottenham 1948-, Nat Soc for Epileptics, Chalfont Colony, 1960-, Jt-Pres Barkingside Jewish Youth Club 1969-; chm Warwicks Hunt 1960-69; *Recreations* fishing, tapestry; *Clubs* White's; *Style* - The Rt Hon The Viscount Bearsted TD DL; Upton House, Banbury, Oxon (☎ 029 587 242); 3 Netherton Grove, SW 10 (☎ 01 730 2026)

BEASLEY, Lady Alexandra Mariota Flora Egerton; da of 6 Earl of Wilton (d 1927); *b* 9 Nov 1919; *m* 1939, Patrick Beasley (m dis); 1 da; *Style* - Lady Alexandra Beasley; Chimney Cottage, Gressenhall, East Dereham, Norfolk

BEASLEY, Alan Walter; s of Frederick Beasley (d 1980); *b* 10 Feb 1935; *Educ* King Edward VI G S Nuneaton; *m* 1960, Margaret, nee Payne; 3 s; *Career* CA 1958, dir Charrington Industl Hldgs 1974 to takeover by Coalite Gp 1977, dir Coalite Main Bd 1979-; *Recreations* sport, reading, theatre, home and garden, travelling, family; *Style* - Alan Beasley Esq; 694 Chatsworth rd, Brookside, Chesterfield, Derbys (☎ 0246 68785)

BEASLEY, John Telford; *Career* md William R Warner & Co; *Style* - John Beasley Esq; Chestnut ave, Eastleigh, Hants

BEATON, Ch Insp James Wallace; GC (1974); s of J A Beaton; *b* 16 Feb 1943; *Educ* Peterhead Academy, Aberdeenshire; *m* 1965, Anne Ballantyne; 2 da; *Career* ch inspector Metropolitan Police 1979-; *Style* - Ch Insp James Beaton, GC; 12 Embry Way, Stanmore, Middx (☎ 01 954 5054)

BEATTIE, Hon Sir David Stuart; GCMG (1980); *Career* gov gen of New Zealand; *Style* - The Hon Sir David Beattie, GCMG

BEATTIE, Hon Mrs; Hon Jane Katherine; *née* Herbert; da of Baron Tangley, KBE (Life Peer, d 1973); *b* 1938; *m* 1964, George Beattie, RD; 3 da; *Style* - The Hon Mrs Beattie; Big Oak, Churt, Surrey (☎ Headley Down 3163)

BEATTY, 3 Earl (UK 1919); David Beatty; also Viscount Borodale and Baron Beatty (UK 1919); s of 2 Earl, DSC (d 1972); *b* 21 Nov 1946; *Educ* Eton; *m* 1971, Ann, da of A Please, of Wokingham; 1 s; *Heir* s, Viscount Borodale; *Style* - The Rt Hon The Earl Beatty; Keepers Combe, Over Stowey, Somerset; House of Lords, SW1

BEATTY, Lady Diana Adrienne; da of 2 Earl Beatty, DSC (d 1972); *b* 13 Sept 1962; *Educ* St Paul's Girls' Sch, London; *Style* - Lady Diana Beatty; Chicheley Hall, Newport Pagnell, Bucks

BEATTY, Lady Miranda Katherine; da of 2 Earl Beatty, DSC (1972); *b* 18 Feb 1963; *Style* - Lady Miranda Beatty

BEATTY, Lt-Col Michael Philip Kenneth; TD (1971), DL (Staffs 1980); s of Col George Beatty, MC, MRCS, LRCP, of Upland Grange, Kidderminster (d 1962); *b* 9 June 1941; *Educ* St Edward's Sch Oxford; *m* 1969, Frances, JP, da of Richard Nathaniel Twisleton-Wykeham-Fiennes (ggs of 15 Baron Saye and Sele by his 1 w, Hon Emily Wingfield, da of 4 Visc Powerscourt; also gs of Rev Hon Wingfield Twisleton-Wykeham-Fiennes by his w, Alice, da of Very Rev Hon Grantham Munton Yorke, bro of 4 Earl of Hardwicke, PC); 1 s, 2 da; *Career* Lt-Col (TA); dir Glynwed Screws and Fastenings 1977, Glynwed Overseas Ltd 1979-; *Recreations* restoring ruined old houses; *Style* - Lt-Col Michael Beatty TD, DL; The Old Vicarage, Gt Haywood, Stafford

BEATTY, Hon Nicholas Duncan; s of 2 Earl Beatty, DSC (d 1972); *b* 1 Apr 1961; *Style* - The Hon Nicholas Beatty

BEAUCHAMP, Countess; Else; MBE; da of late Viggo Schiwe; *m* 1, Dornonville de la Cour, of Copenhagen (died); m 2, 1936, 8 and last Earl Beauchamp, JP, DL (d 1979); *Career* DstJ; Grand Cdr, Order of Dannebroy of Denmark; *Style* - The Rt Hon The Countess Beauchamp; Madresfield Court, Malvern, Worcs

BEAUCHAMP, Sir Peter (Douglas Clifford); 2 Bt (UK 1918); s of Sir Frank Beauchamp, 1 Bt, CBE (d 1950); *b* 11 March 1903; *Educ* Eton; *m* 1, 1926 (m dis 1933), Nancy Esther, da of Laurence E Moss, of Sydney, N S Wales; m 2, 1933, Pamela Dorothy May Chandor (d 1971); m 3, 1972, Mary Elizabeth, da of late Guy Harrop Haslewood, of Bridgnorth, and wid of J H Tilbury; *Heir* none; *Style* - Sir Peter Beauchamp, Bt; The Pebbles, Fore st, Budleigh Salterton, Devon

BEAUCLERK, Lady Emma Caroline de Vere; da of Earl of Burford; *b* 1963; *Educ* Rodean; *Style* - Lady Emma Beauclerk

BEAUCLERK, Lord James Charles Fesq de Vere; s of 13 Duke of St Albans, OBE; *b* 1949; *Educ* Eton; *Style* - Lord James Beauclerk

BEAUCLERK, Lord John William Aubrey de Vere; s of 13 Duke of St Albans, OBE; *b* 1950; *Educ* Eton; *Style* - Lord John Beauclerk; 399 Blas Cercena, Lima 27, Peru

BEAUCLERK, Lord Peter Charles de Vere; s of 13 Duke of St Albans, OBE; *b* 13 Jan 1948; *m* 1972, Beverley June, nee Bailey, of California; 1 da; *Style* - Lord Peter Beauclerk; Beauclerk Ranch, Evans Ridge rd, Anapolis, Calif, USA

BEAUCLERK-DEWAR, Peter de Vere; RD (1980); s of James Dewar, MBE, GM, and Hermione (d 1969), yr da and co-heir of Maj Aubrey Beauclerk, of Little Grimsby Hall, Lincs (d 1916, heir-in-line to Dukedom of St Albans); *b* 19 Feb 1943; *Educ* Ampleforth; *m* 1967, Sarah, da of Maj Lionel Rudder, of Bibury Glos; 1 s, 2 da; *Career* Lt-Cdr RNVR, kt Sovereign Mil Order of Malta 1971 (Dep Tres Br Assoc 1979-); genealogist- Falkland Pursuivant Extraordinary 1975; Silver Stick Usher Silver Jubilee Thanksgiving Serv 1977; Hon Tres Inst of Heraldic and Genealogical Studies 1979-; FAAI, MIBM; *Clubs* Puffins and New (Edinburgh); *Style* - Peter Beauclerk-Dewar Esq, RD; 45 Airedale av, W4 (☎ 01 995 6770)

BEAUFORT, 10 Duke of (E 1682); Henry Hugh Arthur FitzRoy Somerset; KG (1937), GCVO (1930), PC (1936), JP (Glos 1927); also Baron Botetourt (E 1305), Lord Herbert (E 1461), Baron Herbert of Raglan, Chepstow and Gower (E 1506), Earl of Worcester (E 1513), Marquess of Worcester (E 1642), and Hereditary Keeper of Raglan Castle; s of 9 Duke of Beaufort (d 1924) and Louise, JP, da of William Harford, JP, DL, and widow of Baron Charles van Tuyll van Serooskerken (d 1893); *b* 4 April 1900; *Educ* Eton, Sandhurst; *m* 1923, Lady Mary, da of 1 Marquess of Cambridge, GCB, GCVO, CMG, JP, DL (*see Whitley, Lady Mary*); *Heir* to Baronies of Botetourt and Herbert- Samantha Cope (gda of Lady Rosemary Eliot, da of Lady Blanche Somerset, sis of 10 Duke), Alexandra Peyronel (gda of Lady Blanche), and Lady Cathleen Hudson (da of Lady Blanche) all as coheiresses presumptive; to Dukedom and other Peerages- 1 cous twice removed, David Somerset; *Career* Roy Victorian Chain 1953; late Capt RHG, Dep Hon Col A & C Sqdns Wessex Yeomanry RAC TAVR 1972-; Master of the Horse to HM The Queen 1936-78; Ld-Lt Bristol and Gloucester 1931-74 and Glos 1974-78; KStJ; High Steward Bristol & Gloucester 1925, Tewkesbury 1948; Freedom of City of Gloucester; *Books* Fox Hunting (1980) *Clubs* Turf; *Style* - His Grace The Duke of Beaufort, KG, GCVO, PC, JP; Badminton House, Glos (☎ Badminton 202)

BEAUFORT, Duchess of; Lady (Victoria Constance) Mary; da of late 1 Marquess of Cambridge; *b* 1897; *m* 1923, 10 Duke of Beaufort; *Career* CStJ; *Style* - Her Grace the Duchess of Beaufort,; Badminton, Glos

BEAUMAN, Christopher Bentley; s of Wing-Cdr Eric Beauman, of Chester Row, SW; *b* 12 Oct 1944; *Educ* Winchester, Trin Cambridge, Harkness Fellow at Johns Hopkins Sch of Advanced Internat Studies & Columbia U; *m* 1, 1966 (m dis 1976), Sally Kinsey-Miles; m 2, 1976, Nicola, da of Dr Francis Mann, of Addison av, W8; 1 da, 3 step children; *Career* corporate fin exec Hill Samuel 1968-72, dir Guinness Mahon 1973-76, advsr to chm BSC 1976-81, with Centl Policy Review Staff 1981- dir FMC Ltd 1975-81; *Recreations* reading, walking; *Style* - Christopher Beauman Esq; 35 Christchurch Hill, NW3 (☎ 01 435 1975)

BEAUMONT OF WHITLEY, Baron (Life Peer UK 1967); Timothy Wentworth Beaumont; s of late Maj Michael Wentworth Beaumont, TD (gs of 1 Baron Allendale) by 1 w, Hon Faith Muriel, nee Pease, da of 1 Baron Gainford; *b* 22 Nov 1928; *Educ* Eton, Gordonstoun, Ch Ch Oxford; *m* 1955, Mary Rose, da of Lt-Col Charles Edward Wauchope, MC; 1 s, 2 da; *Career* vicar of Ch Ch Kowloon Hong Kong 1957-59, resigned Holy Orders 1973, proprietor various periodicals including Time & Tide, New Christian 1960-70, Pres Liberal Pty 1969-70 (Head of Org 1965-66), delegate to Parly Assembly Cncl of Europe and Western European Union 1974-77, chm Albany Tst 1969-71, pres Br Fedn of Film Socs 1974-79, chm Studio Vista Books Ltd 1963-68, proprietor and ed New Outlook 1972-74, md Holystone Productions Ltd; *Style* - The Rt Hon The Lord Beaumont of Whitley; 1 Hampstead sq, NW3 (☎ 01 435 7080)

BEAUMONT, Hon Atalanta Armstrong; da of Baron Beaumont of Whitley (Life Peer); *b* 3 Apr 1961; *Educ* St Margaret's Bushy; *Career* personal assist with slrs; *Recreations* riding, swimming, ping pong, theatre; *Style* - The Hon Atalanta Beaumont; 1 Hampstead sq, NW3

BEAUMONT, Hon Ariadne Grace; da of Baron Beaumont of Whitley (Life Peer); *b* 22 Apr 1963; *Style* - The Hon Ariadne Beaumont

BEAUMONT, Bryan Kenneth; s of Cyril Beaumont (d 1918); *b* 16 July 1918; *Educ* Firth Pk Sch Sheffield; *m* 1940, Kathleen, da of Henry Greaves (d 1948); 1 da; *Career* CA, fin dir Express Dairy 1980, Express Dairy Foods 1975, chm Luncheon Vouchers Ltd 1970; *Recreations* reading, gardening; *Style* - Bryan Beaumont Esq; 20 York av, E Sheen, SW14 (☎ 01 876 4270)

BEAUMONT, Christopher; s and h of Michael Beaumont, Seigneur of Sark, *qv*; *b* 4 Feb 1957; *Style* - Christopher Beaumont Esq

BEAUMONT, Hon Charles Richard; s of 3 Viscount Allendale; *b* 8 March 1954; *m* 1979, Charlotte Sybil, da of Lt-Col Richard Ian Griffith Taylor, DSO, MC, JP, DL; *Style* - The Hon Charles Beaumont; Bywell Hall, Stocksfield-on-Tyne, Northumberland (☎ 3169); Allenheads, Hexham, Northumberland (☎ Allenheads 205)

BEAUMONT, Ernest George; *Career* dep chm and jt md Bunzl Pulp and Paper Ltd; *Style* - Ernest Beaumont Esq; 21-24 Chiswell st, EC1

BEAUMONT, Sir George Howland Francis; 12 Bt (E 1661); s of Sir George Arthur Hamilton Beaumont, 11 Bt (d 1933); *b* 24 Sept 1924; *Educ* Stowe; *m* 1, 1949 (m annulled 1951), Barbara, da of

William Singleton; m 2, 1963, Henrietta Anne, da of late Dr Arthur Waymouth; 2 da (twins); *Heir* none; *Career* formerly warrant offr Australian Army; Coldstream Gds, Lt 60 Rifles WW II; patron of one living; *Style* - Sir George Beaumont, Bt; Duntrune Nurseries, Deddington Mill, Deddington, Oxon

BEAUMONT, His Honour Judge; Herbert Christopher Beaumont; MBE (1948); s of Gerald Beaumont, MC and Bar (d 1923); *b* 3 June 1912; *Educ* Uppingham, Worcester Coll Oxford; *m* 1940, Helen, da of William Smail; 1 s, 2 da; *Career* formerly ICS and FO; barr 1951-72, Circuit Judge 1972-; *Recreations* European travel; *Clubs* Brooks's, Yorkshire (York); *Style* - His Hon Judge Beaumont, MBE; Minskip Lodge, Boroughbridge, N Yorks (☎ 2365)

BEAUMONT, Hon Hubert Wentworth; s of Baron Beaumont of Whitley (Life Peer); *b* 12 Apr 1956; *Educ* Gordonstoun, S Bank Polytechnic; *m* 1980, Katherine Emma Abel Smith; *Career* chartered surveyor; *Recreations* shooting; *Clubs* MCC; *Style* - The Hon Hubert Beaumont; 9 Elm Pk Mans, Park Walk, SW10 (☎ 01 352 0739)

BEAUMONT, (John) Michael; s of late Lionel (Buster) Beaumont and Enid Beaumont, nee Ripley; *b* 20 Dec 1927; *Educ* Loughborough Coll; *m* 1956, Diana, nee La Trobe-Bateman; 2 s; *Heir* s, Christopher Beaumont, *qv*; *Career* aircraft design engineer to 1975; Seigneur of Sark (cr 1565) 1974-; *Style* - Michael Beaumont Esq; La Seigneurie, Sark, C I (☎ Sark 2017)

BEAUMONT, Hon Mark Henry; s of 3 Viscount Allendale; *b* 21 July 1959; *Educ* Eton; *Style* - The Hon Mark Beaumont; Bywell Hall, Stocksfield-on-Tyne, Northumberland (☎ 3169); Allenheads, Hexham, Northumberland (Allenheads 205)

BEAUMONT, Hon Matthew Henry; s of 1 Viscount Allendale, KG, CB, CBE, MC (d 1956); *b* 1933; *Educ* Bradfield; *m* 1, 1959, Anne C Margaret, da of Gerald Hamilton (m dis 1972); 1 s, 1 da; m 2, 1973, Belinda Jane Elizabeth, da of late Harold David Cuthbert, of Beaufront Castle, Hexham, Northumberland; *Career* underwriting memb of Lloyd's 1960; *Clubs* Boodle's; *Style* - The Hon Matthew Beaumont; 71 South Side, Clapham Common, SW4

BEAUMONT, Hon Richard Blackett; s of 2 Viscount Allendale, KG, CB, CBE, MC (d 1956); *b* 13 Aug 1926; *Educ* Eton; *m* 1971, Lavinia Mary (sometime Governess to HRH Prince Edward), da of late Lt-Col Arnold Keppel (gggs of Rt Rev Hon Frederick Keppel, sometime Bp of Exeter & 4 s of 2 Earl of Albemarle); *Career* chm James Purdey & Sons 1970-, Master Gunmakers' Co 1969; joined RNVR 1944, sub-lt 1946; *Recreations* shooting; *Clubs* White's, Turf; *Style* - The Hon Richard Beaumont; Flat 1, 58 South Audley st, W1 (☎ 01 499 5845)

BEAUMONT, Hon Wentworth Peter Ismay; s and h of 3 Viscount Allendale; *b* 13 Nov 1948; *Educ* Harrow; *m* 1975, Theresa Mary More O'Ferrall; 1 s, 1 da; *Style* - The Hon Wentworth Beaumont; Bywell Hall, Stocksfield-on-Tyne, Northumberland (☎ 3169); Allenheads, Hexham, Northumberland (Allenheads 205)

BEAUMONT-DARK, Anthony Michael; MP (C) Birmingham Selly Oak 1979-; s of Leonard Dark; *b* 11 Oct 1932; *Educ* Birmingham Coll of Arts and Crafts, Birmingham U; *m* 1959, Sheelagh Irene, nee Cassey; 1 s, 1 da; *Career* investment analyst and company director; *Style* - Anthony Beaumont-Dark Esq MP; House of Commons, SW1

BEAVAN, William Franklin; OBE (1961), JP (Flintshire 1945), DL (Clwyd 1953); s of the late William Franklin Beavan, JP; *b* 10 Sept 1898; *Educ* Sedbergh, RMC Sandhurst; *m* 1925, Dorothy Esme Bentley, nee Mellor; 2 da; *Career* High Sheriff (Flintshire) 1954, Fellow of RICS 1921, Pres of Chartered Auctioneers & Estate Agents Institute 1960-61, now consultant to Beavan Maples & Co, Surveyors; *Recreations* shooting, fishing, gardening; *Style* - William Beavan

Esq, OBE, JP, DL; The Paddocks, Eccleston, Chester, Cheshire

BEAVERBROOK, Barony of (UK 1917), disclaimed 1964; *see* Aitken, 2 Bt, Sir (John William) Max(well)

BEAVERBROOK, Baroness; Marcia Anastasia; da of John Christoforides, of Leyswood, Groombridge, Sussex; *m* 1, Sir James Hamet Dunn, 1 Bt, QC (d 1956); m 2, 1963, as his 2 w, 1 Baron Beaverbrook, CD, PC (d 1964); *Style* - The Rt Hon The Lady Beaverbrook; Saint Andrews, New Brunswick, Canada

BEAVIS, Air Marshal Sir Michael Gordon; KCB (1981), CBE (1977, OBE 1969), AFC (1962); s of Walter Beavis, of Haverhill (d 1972); *b* 13 Aug 1929; *Educ* Kilburn G S; *m* 1950, Joy, da of Arthur Jones; 1 s, 1 da; *Career* joined RAF 1947, AOCIC RAF Support Cmmd 1981-, Actg Air Marshal 1981; *Recreations* golf; *Clubs* RAF; *Style* - Air Marshal Sir Michael Beavis, KCB, CBE, AFC; 5 Heathfield Gate, Midhurst, Sussex (☎ 3434)

BEAZLEY, Peter George; MEP (C) Beds 1979-; s of late Thomas Alfred Beazley; *b* 9 June 1922; *Educ* Highgate Sch, St John's Oxford; *m* 1945, Joyce Marion, nee Sulman; 1 s, 2 da (1 decd); *Career* dir- ICI Europa Fibres, ICI Italia 1947-78, Res Fell Roy Inst Int Affairs 1977-78; *Clubs* Oriental, Willingdon Golf; *Style* - Peter Beazley Esq, MEP; Rest Harrow, The Coombe, Ratton, Eastbourne (☎ Eastbourne 54460); 4 Bridgewater Court, Little Gaddesden, Herts (☎ 3548)

BECCARI, Hon Mrs (Bridget Mary); 3 da of 1 Visc Chelmsford, GCSI, GCMG, PC (d 1933); *b* 1900; *m* 1, 1919, Maj Richard Hasell Sheepshanks, DSO, MVO, (m dis 1937 and who d 1951), 1 s; m 2, 1938, Nello Beccari (d 1957); *Style* - The Hon Mrs Beccari; Villa Beccari, Bandino, Florence, Italy (☎ 63507)

BECHMANN, Hon Mrs (Elizabeth Suzanne); da of 2 Baron Merrivale, OBE; *b* 1921; *m* 1, 1942 (m dis 1953), Capt Jean Pompei; 1 s, 1 da; m 2, 1955, Jacques Bechmann (s of René Bechmann, b 20 Nov 1918, ret banker, memb Chantilly Golf Club); 1 s; *Style* - The Hon Mrs Bechmann; La Charité, 60 Vineuil, St Firmin, Oise, France (☎ 4 457 0169)

BECK, Clive; s of Sir Edgar Beck, CBE; *b* 12 April 1937; *Educ* Ampleforth; *m* 1960, Philippa, da of Dr Philip Flood (d 1968); 6 children; *Career* dep chm and jt md SGB Gp; chm Scaffolding (GB) Ltd; md Harduns (Contractors Tools) Ltd; dir Basingdown Investments, Scafco Ltd Eire, Scarab Computer Servs, Zetland Hotel Co; memb IOD; *Recreations* fishing, shooting; *Clubs* Swinley Forest Golf; *Style* - Clive Beck Esq; 23 Willow Lane, Mitcham, Surrey

BECK, Hon Mrs - Hon Celia Yvonne Lovett; da of 3 Baron de Villiers, of Wynberg, Cape Town, S Africa; *b* 7 Nov 1942; *Educ* Herschel, Claremont, Cape Town, U of Cape Town and Royal Northern Hospital, London; *m* 1968, Robin Hastings Sancroft Beck, s of (Harold) Hastings Beck, of St James, S Africa and Mrs A M A Struben, of Rondebosch, Cape Town, SA; 2 s, 1 da; *Style* - The Hon Mrs Beck; Timber Cottage, Private Bag No 438, Stellenbosch, Cape, S Africa (Stellenbosch 4178)

BECK, Baron Rolf (Rudolph); s of Baron Dr Otto Beck; *b* 25 March 1914; *Educ* Theresanium Mil Acad, Geneva U, Lausanne U, Vienna U; *m* 1, 1944 (m dis), Elizabeth Lesley Brenchley, da of Capt Fletcher, RN; 1 s (Stephen b 1948); m 2, 1979, Countess Mariana von Rosen, da of Count Mörner, of Sweden; *Career* petrochemical engr and researcher, founded various companies, chm and md Slip and Molyslip Gp of Companies 1939-; *Clubs* RAC, Roy Scottish Automobile, Royal Harwich Yacht, West Mersey Yacht, Hurlingham, Union Interalliée (Paris); *Style* - Baron Rolf Beck; Layham Hall, nr Hadleigh, Suffolk (☎ Hadleigh 822137); 19 Empire House, Thurloe pl, SW7 (☎ 01 589 7570)

BECKER, Basil George Christie; VRD (1964); s of Leslie Becker, of Frinton; *b* 17 May 1928; *Educ* Shrewsbury; *m* 1952, Gillian, nee Dawson; 1 s, 1 da; *Career* chm and ch exec Phonotas Gp, chm Contract Cleaning & Maintenance Assoc 1972-74;

dir Eastern Contract Packers, G S Chemicals, Kent Chemical Co, Wealden Computer Servs; *Recreations* golf, gardening, sailing, livery co; *Clubs* City Livery, RAC; *Style* - Basil Becker Esq, VRD; Coppers Hill, Burwash, E Sussex (☎ 882332)

BECKER, Edward Lionel; s of Isaac (Jack) Becker (d 1956); *b* 5 Jan 1926; *Educ* King George V Sch Southport, Manchester U; *m* 1979, Deborah Ann, da of Dr Sydney Hepworth (d 1980); 1 s, 4 da; *Career* chartered accountant Isle of Man, md Apollo Leisure Group Ltd 1977-, fellow of Institute of Chartered Accountants 1950; *Recreations* golf, fishing; *Style* - Edward Becker Esq; Ballasherlogue, Colby, Isle of Man (☎ 0624 834252)

BECKER, Lady (Gladys Sarah); da of Percival Duggan, of Adelaide; *m* 1928, Sir Ellerton Becker (d 1980); *Style* - Lady Becker; Palomera, Fairylands, Pembroke, Bermuda

BECKETT, Maj-Gen Denis Arthur; CB (1971), DSO (1944), OBE (1960); s of Archibald Beckett; *b* 19 May 1917; *Educ* Forest Sch, Chard Sch; *m* 1, 1946, Elizabeth, nee Edwards; 1 s; m 2, 1978, Nancy, nee Hitt, of Grosse Pointe USA; *Career* HAC 1939, Ch of Staff Far East Land Forces 1966-68, Dir Personal Servs Army 1968-71, ret 1971; *Style* - Maj-Gen Denis Beckett, CB, DSO, OBE; 12 Wellington House, Eton rd, NW3

BECKETT, Hon Edward John; s and h of 4 Baron Grimthorpe, OBE; *b* 29 Nov 1954; *Educ* Hawtreys and Harrow; *Style* - The Hon Edward Beckett

BECKETT, Hon Harriet Lucy; 4 Baron Grimthorpe, OBE; *b* 18 Feb 1961; *Style* - The Hon Harriet Beckett

BECKETT, John Michael; s of H Beckett, MBE; *b* 22 June 1929; *Educ* Wolverhampton G S, Magdalen Oxford; *m* 1955, Joan, nee Rogerson; 5 da; *Career* barr 1954-55, ch exec Br Sugar Corpn 1975-; dir Br Sugar Allied Prods, Tarmac Ltd; chm Br Sugar Bureau 1978-, UK Sugar Industs Assoc 1978-; *Style* - John Beckett Esq; Belton House, Uppingham, Leics (☎ Belton 682)

BECKETT, Sir Martyn Gervase; 2 Bt (UK 1921), MC; s of Hon Sir William Gervase Beckett, 1 Bt (d 1937, bro of 2 Baron Grimthorpe), and Lady Marjorie (d 1964), da of 5 Earl of Warwick and wid of 2 Earl of Feversham; *b* 6 Nov 1918; *Educ* Eton, Trin Cambridge; *m* 1941, Hon Priscilla Léonie Helen Brett, da of 3 Viscount Esher; 2 s, 1 da; *Heir* s, Richard Gervase Beckett; *Career* Capt Welsh Gds; RIBA; *Style* - Sir Martyn Beckett, Bt, MC; 3 St Alban's grove, W8 (☎ 01 937 7834); Kirkdale Farm, Nawton, Yorks

BECKETT, Hon Oliver Ralph; s of 7 Baron Grimthorpe (d 1963); *b* 1918; *Educ* Eton and Cambridge U; *m* 1944, Mrs Helene Agnes Tasker-Evans, da of Constantine Fessas; 2 da; *Style* - The Hon Oliver Beckett; Old Elm Farm, Crouch lane, Goffs Oak, Herts (☎ Cuffey 4866)

BECKETT, Hon Lady; Hon Priscilla Léonie Helen; *née* Brett; da of 3 Viscount Esher, GBE (d 1963); *b* 1921; *m* 1941, Sir Martyn Beckett, 2 Bt, MC, *qv*; *Style* - The Hon Lady Beckett; 3 St Alban's Grove, W8

BECKETT, Hon Ralph Daniel; s of 4 Baron Grimthorpe, OBE; *b* 11 Apr 1957; *Style* - The Hon Ralph Beckett

BECKETT, Richard Gervase; s and h of Sir Martyn Beckett, 2 Bt, MC, *qv*; *b* 27 March 1944; *m* 1976, Elizabeth Ann, nee Waterhouse; *Style* - Richard Beckett Esq

BECKETT, Samuel; *b* 1906; *Educ* Portora Roy Sch, Trin Coll Dublin; *Career* author and playwright; *Style* - Samuel Beckett Esq; c/o Faber and Faber Ltd, 24 Russell sq, WC1

BECKETT, Sir Terence Norman; CBE (1974); s of Horace Norman Beckett, MBE; *b* 13 Dec 1923; *Educ* Secondary Sch Wolverhampton, S Staffs Tech Coll, LSE; *m* 1950, Sylvia Gladys Asprey; 1 da; *Career* md Ford Motor Co Ltd 1974, chm 1976-80 (joined 1950), dir-gen CBI 1980-; kt 1978; *Style* - Sir Terence Beckett, CBE; CBI, Centre Point, New Oxford st, WC1

BECKETT, Hon William Ernest; s of 3 Baron Grimthorpe (d 1963); *b* 30 June 1945; *Educ* Eton; *m* 1968, Virginia, da of Alan Michael Clark Hutchison, MP; 1 s, 1 da; *Career* computer sales man; short service commission in 9/12 Royal Lancers (POW) 1964-68; *Recreations* sailing, shooting, skiing, windsurfing, hunting; *Clubs* Mytton's, Annabel's; *Style* - The Hon William Beckett; 8 Elthiron rd, SW6 (☎ 01 736 3205)

BECKMAN, Hon Mrs; Hon Angela Clare; da of Baron Mais, GBE, ERD, TD, JP, DL (Life Peer); *b* 1946; *Educ* St Margaret's Bushey, and House of Citizenship; *m* 1976, Robert Beckman, of Washington DC; *Style* - The Hon Mrs Beckman; Suite 235, 1001 Connecticut av NW, Washington DC, 20036, USA

BECTIVE, Earl of; Thomas Michael Ronald Christopher Taylour; s and h of 6 Marquess of Headfort; *b* 10 Feb 1959; *Style* - Earl of Bective

BEDBROOK, Sir George Montario; OBE (1963); s of Arthur Bedbrook; *b* 8 Nov 1921; *Educ* University High School Melbourne, Med Sch Melbourne U; *m* 1946, Jessie, nee Page; 2 s, 3 da; *Career* kt 1978, FRCS, FRACS, DPRM, OStJ; Sr Surgn Spinal Unit, Dept Paraplegia Roy Perth Rehabilitation Hosp 1979-; *Recreations* reading; *Style* - Sir George Bedbrook, OBE; 29 Ulster rd, Floreat Pk, W Australia 6014 (☎ 387 3582)

BEDDALL, Hugh Richard Muir; s of Herbert Muir Beddall; *b* 20 May 1922; *Educ* Stowe and Ecole de Commerce Neuchatel; *m* 1946, Monique, nee Haefliger; 3 s, 1 da; *Career* chm Muir Beddall and Co Ltd 1964-, C T Bowring (Continental) Ltd; memb of Lloyd's; *Style* - Hugh Beddall Esq; Iver Lodge, Iver, Bucks (☎ 653007)

BEDDOES, Air Vice-Marshal John Geoffrey Genior; CB (1980); s of Algernon Beddoes; *b* 21 May 1925; *Educ* Wirral G S; *m* 1947, Betty, nee Kendrick; 3 s; *Career* Dir Gen Aircraft (2) MOD Procurement Exec 1978-81, ret; *Recreations* gardening, DIY, cricket, golf; *Clubs* RAF, MCC; *Style* - Air Vice-Marshal John Beddoes, CB; White Stables, Stow Bedon, Norfolk (☎ Caston 524)

BEDDOW, Raymond Percival; CBE (1956); s of late Percival Bonwick Beddow; *b* 24 May 1903; *Educ* St Anselm's Sch Croydon, Mill Hill Sch; *m* 1, 1926, Elizabeth Jean Hanbury-Williams; m 2, 1969, Edna May Niessen, nee Riley; *Career* formerly exec dir of The British Electric Traction Co Ltd, ret 1968; *Style* - Raymond Beddow Esq, CBE; 22 The Gateway, Marine Parade, Dover, Kent

BEDFORD, 13 Duke of (E 1694); John Robert Russell; also Baron Russell (E 1539), Earl of Bedford (E 1550), Baron Russell of Thornhaugh (E 1603), Marquess of Tavistock (E 1694), Baron Howland (E 1695); s of 12 Duke (d 1953); *b* 24 May 1917; *m* 1, 1939, Mrs Clare Gwendolen Hollway, da of late John Bridgman; 2 s; m 2, 1947 (m dis 1960), Hon Lydia Yarde-Buller, da of 3 Baron Churston and late Duchess of Leinster, and widow of Capt Ian Archibald de Hoghton Lyle, Black Watch; 1 s; m 3, 1960, Mme Nicole Milinaire, da of Paul Schneider, of Paris; *Heir* s, Marquess of Tavistock; *Career* Coldstream Gds WW II (invalided out); *Style* - His Grace The Duke of Bedford; 22 Boulevard des Moulins, Monte Carlo

BEDFORD, Lydia, Duchess of - Hon Lydia; *née* Yarde-Buller; da of late 3 Baron Churston; *b* 1917; *m* 1, 1938, Capt Ian Archibald de Hoghton Lyle, Black Watch (d 1942); m 2 (m dis 1960) 13 Duke of Bedford; *Style* - Lydia, Duchess of Bedford; Little Ribsden, Windlesham, Bagshot, Surrey

BEDFORD, Hon Mrs - Hon Sarah; *née* Lyttelton; twin da of 10 Visc Cobham, KG, GCMG, GCVO, TD, PC (d 1977); *b* 10 June 1954; *Educ* The Abbey Sch Malvern Wells; *m* 1976, C Nicholas Bedford; 1 da; *Style* - The Hon Mrs Bedford; 9 Burnsall st, SW3 (01 352 7654)

BEEBEE, Meyrick Frederick Legge; JP (Radnorshire 1966), DL (1962); s of Meyrick Beebee (d 1956); *b* 16 July 1910; *Educ* RNC Dartmouth; *m* 1962, Angela, da of Santos Diego (d 1924); 8 children; *Career* V-Chm Welsh Conservatives 1975-80, Powys Magistrates' Cttee 1974-80; *Clubs* Army and Navy; *Style* - Meyrick Beebee Esq, JP, DL; Womaston House, Presteigne, Powys (☎ 0544 230543)

BEECH, D A E; *Career* chm Hecht Hetworth & Alcan Ltd; *Style* - D A E Beech Esq; Myrtil House, 70 Clifton st, EC2

BEECHAM, Sir Adrian Welles; 3 Bt (UK 1914); s of Sir Thomas Beecham, 2 Bt, CH, the composer and conductor (d 1961), and Utica (d 1977), da of Dr Charles Welles, of New York; *b* 4 Sept 1904; *Educ* privately; *m* 1939, Barbara, da of late Edward Cairn; 2 s, 1 da; *Heir* s, John Beecham; *Career* composer, MusB Durham; *Style* - Sir Adrian Beecham, Bt; Compton Scorpion Manor, Shipston-on-Stour, Warwicks (☎ 61482)

BEECHAM, John Stratford Roland; s and h of Sir Adrian Beecham, 3 Bt; *b* 21 April 1940; *Educ* Winchester, Oxford; *Career* minister Pentecostal Church; *Recreations* walking, gardening; *Style* - John Beecham Esq; Shalom, Station rd, Shipston-on-Stour, Warwicks

BEECHING, Baron (Life Peer UK 1965); Richard Beeching; s of Hubert J Beeching, of Maidstone; *b* 21 April 1913; *Educ* Maidstone G S, Imperial Coll of Science and Technol; *m* 1938, Ella Margaret, da of William J Tiley; *Career* joined ICI 1948, dir 1957-61 and 1965, dep chm 1966-68, v-pres ICI Canada 1953-55, chm of Metals Div 1955-57, memb Special Advsy Gp on British Transport Cmmn 1960, and of Nat Economic Dvpt Cnc 1962-64, chm British Transport Cmmn 1961-62, of Br Railways Bd 1962-65, chm Redland Ltd 1970-77, of Furness Withy & Co Ltd 1972-75, chm Economic Insur Co Ltd, dir Lloyds Bank; *Recreations* golf; *Style* - The Rt Hon The Lord Beeching; Little Manor, E Grinstead, W Sussex

BEECK, Sir Marcus Truby; s of Gustav Edwin Beeck and Martha, nee Keast; *b* 28 Dec 1923; *Educ* State Correspondence Sch, W Australia; Katanning State Sch, W Australia; *m* 1950, Leonie Pamela Dale Robertson; 1 s, 2 da; *Career* farmer, co dir; kt 1979; *Style* - Sir Marcus Beeck; Coyrecup, PO Box 110, Katanning, W Australia (☎ E Katanning 222224)

BEER, Ernest Trevor; CBE (1946, OBE 1945); s of Alfred Beer (d 1952); *b* 12 Jan 1906; *Educ* Highgate Sch, Neuchatel U Switzerland; *m* 1939, Eleonore, da of Count Paul Szubinski, of Poland; 2 s, 2 da; *Career* chm I Beer & Sons 1963-; *Recreations* shooting, fishing; *Clubs* RAF; *Style* - Ernest Beer Esq, CBE; Upeke House, Thorverton, Devon (☎ Exeter 860448)

BEER, James Edmund; s of Edmund Huxtable Beer; *b* 17 March 1931; *Educ* Torquay G S; *m* 1953, Barbara, nee Tunley; 2 s, 1 da; *Career* dir Short Loan and Mortgage Co, Shortloan (Leasing) Ltd; *Style* - James Beer Esq; 48 High Ash av, Alwoodley, Leeds LS17 8RG (☎ 683907)

BEER, Michael John; *Career* md B Elliott & Co, dir GIC Servs S Africa, Goldfields Industl Corpn S Africa; *Style* - Michael Beer Esq; B E C House, 167 Imperial dve, Harrow, Middx

BEESON, Prof Paul Bruce; Hon KBE (1973); s of John Beeson, of Montana; *b* 18 Oct 1908; *Educ* Washington U, McGill U Med Sch; *m* 1942, Barbara Neal, of Buffalo; 2 s, 1 da; *Career* FRCP, Prof Medicine Washington U 1974-; *Style* - Prof Paul Beeson, Hon KBE; US Veterans' Admin Hospital, Seattle, Washington, USA

BEETHAM, Lady (Eileen Joy); da of late A L Parkinson, of Polegate; *m* 1933, Sir Edward Beetham, KCMG, CVO, OBE (d 1979); *Style* - Lady Beetham; Millstream, Hambleden, Henley-on-Thames, Oxon

BEEVOR, Antony Romer, s of Miles Beevor, of Welwyn; *b* 18 May 1940; *Educ* Winchester, New Coll Oxford; *m* 1970, Cecilia, da of John Hopton (d 1969); 1 s, 1 da; *Career* dir Hambros Bank 1974-; *Style* - Antony Beevor Esq; 84 Cambridge st, SW1 (☎ 01 821 0120)

BEEVOR, John Grosvenor; OBE (Mil 1945); s of Henry Beevor, of Newark Notts; *b* 1 March 1905; *Educ* Winchester, New Coll Oxford; *m* 1, 1933, Carinthia (m dis 1956), da of Aubrey Waterfield; 3 s; m 2, 1957, Mary, da of Hamilton Grepe; *Career* dir Nat and Commercial Devpt Capital 1971-, formerly slr; *Recreations* golf, travel; *Clubs* Roy St George's (Sandwich), Special Forces; *Style* - John Beevor Esq, OBE; 51 Eaton sq, SW1 (☎ 01 235 7987)

BEEVOR, Sir Thomas Agnew; 7 Bt (GB 1784); s of Cdr Sir Thomas Beevor, 6 Bt (d 1943); *b* 6 Jan 1929; *Educ* Eton, Magdalene Cambridge; *m* 1, 1957 (m dis 1965), Barbara, da of Capt Robert Cunliffe, CBE, RN (ret); 1 s, 2 da; m 2, 1966 (m dis 1975), Carola, da of His Hon Judge Herbert, MC, QC; m 3, 1976, Mrs Sally Bouwens, da of Edward Madoc, of White Hall, Thetford; *Heir* s, Thomas Beevor; *Style* - Sir Thomas Beevor, Bt; Hargham Hall, Norwich

BEEVOR, Thomas Hugh Cunliffe; s and h of Sir Thomas Beevor, 7 Bt; *b* 1 Oct 1962; *Style* - Thomas Beevor Esq; Hargham Hall, Norwich

BEGBIE, Hon Mrs - Hon Joyce; *née* Taylor; da of Baron Taylor of Gryfe (Life Peer); *b* 14 March 1948; *Educ* Hutcheson's Girls' G S Glasgow, Strathclyde U; *m* 1969, Alan Begbie; *Style* - The Hon Mrs Begbie; 51 Spiers rd, Bearsden, Glasgow

BEGG, John Alexander Sutherland; s of Daniel Begg, of Wick; *b* 2 July 1938; *Educ* Wick H S, Aberdeen U, Edinburgh U; *m* 1978, Lesley, da of Donald Nichol, of The Wirral; 1 child; *Career* md S Reece (Liverpool) Ltd 1979-, Lewis's Ltd (dept store) 1981-; *Style* - John Begg Esq; Croft End, Neston rd, Willaston, S Wirral (☎ 051 327 5215)

BEGG, Robert William; CBE (1977); s of David Begg, CA, FCA (d 1968); *b* 19 Feb 1922; *Educ* Glasgow U; *m* 1948, Sheena, da of Archibald Boyd, slr, of Largs (d 1958); 2 s; *Career* CA, sr ptnr Mann Judd Gordon CA; dir Hay Nisbett & Miller, Marine Repair Bases; tres Roy Glasgow Inst of Fine Arts 1976-, chm Nat Galleries of Scotland; *Recreations* painting; *Clubs* Glasgow Art; *Style* - Robert Begg Esq, CBE; 3 Colquhoun dve, Bearsden, Glasgow (☎ 041 942 2436)

BEHAR, A; *Career* md Hardy & Co (Furnishers) Ltd; *Style* - A Behar Esq; Hardy House, 112-114 High st, Croydon, Surrey

BEHRENS, Lady (Beatrice Mary); da of Dr W Sandham Symes; *m* 1920, Sir Leonard Behrens, CBE, JP (d 1978); 2 da; *Style* - Lady Behrens; 119 Barlow Moor rd, Didsbury, Manchester (☎ 061 445 3600)

BEHRENS, E M; *Career* chm Ionian Securities; *Style* - E M Behrens Esq; 1 Crown Court, Cheapside, EC2

BEICKLER, F; *Career* md Vauxhall Motors; *Style* - F Beickler Esq; c/o Vauxhall Motors, Luton, Beds

BEILBY, Owen John; CBE (1973); s of Hubert Beilby (d 1954); *b* 8 July 1913; *Educ* Glasgow Acad, Exeter Coll Oxford; *m* 1944, Norma, da of Ernest Thompson (d 1942); 3 da; *Career* ch ag Economist Dept of Ag Scotland 1950-74; *Recreations* gardening, island visiting (Scotland); *Style* - Owen Beilby Esq, CBE; 33 Gillespie rd, Edinburgh 13 (☎ 031 441 3432)

BEIT, Sir Alfred Lane; 2 Bt (UK 1924); s of Sir Otto (John) Beit, KCMG (d 1930); *b* 19 Jan 1903; *Educ* Eton, Ch Ch Oxford; *m* 1939, Clementine Mabell Kitty, da of late Maj Hon Clement Bertram Ogilvy Freeman-Mitford, DSO, s of late 1 Baron Redesdale; *Heir* none; *Career* tstee Beit Tst, dir Nyasaland Hotels & Brewery Ltd, former memb Advsy Ctee of Tanganyika Concessions Ltd; Sqdn RAFVR (ret); PPS (unpaid) to Fin Sec to War Office 1935-38, Sec of State for Colonies 1944-45, contested S E Div of St Pancras (C) May 1929, MP there Oct 1931 to June 1945; *Style* - Sir Alfred Beit, Bt; Russborough, Blessington, Co Wicklow, Eire; Beach rd, Gordon's Bay, S Africa

BEITH, Sir John; KCMG (1969, CMG 1959); s of William Beith (d 1922), of Qld; *b* 4 April 1914; *Educ* Eton, King's Cambridge; *m* 1949, Diana, da of Sir John Gilmour, 2 Bt; 1 s, 1 da (and 1 da decd), 1

step s, 1 step da; *Career* Ambass to Belgium 1969-74; *Recreations* music, racing, books; *Clubs* White's; *Style* - Sir John Beith, KCMG; Dean Farm House, Sparsholt, Hants (☎ 326)

BEKEN, A; *Career* chm Agfa-Gevaert; *Style* - A Beken Esq; c/o Agfa-Gevaert, Great West Road, Brentford, Middx

BELAIEFF, Lady Mary; *née* Pelham-Clinton-Hope; da of 8 Duke of Newcastle (d 1941); *b* 1910; *m* 1, 1930 (m annulled on her petition 1933), Charles Kenneth Horne; m 2, 1939, Romain Stemmer (m dis 1946); m 3, 1947, William Serge Belaieff (m dis); *Style* - Lady Mary Belaieff; Clumber Cottage, Sutton Veny, Warminster, Wilts

BELDAM, Robert Geoffrey; CBE (1975); s of late Ernest Asplan Beldam; *b* 3 Jan 1914; *Educ* Repton, Corpus Christi Cambridge; *Career* FCA (chartered), chm and md Beldam Asbestos Co Ltd and Auto-Klean Strainers Ltd,memb CBI council 1965-, memb CBI Smaller Firms Council 1965-79 (chm until 1974), memb CBI London Regional Council 1952-80, memb SE Economic Planning Council 1966-73 (acting chm 1971), memb Woking UDC 1947-70 (chm 1954-55); *Recreations* travel and gardening; *Clubs* MCC, Bath; *Style* - Robert Beldam Esq, CBE; Rocombe, Grange rd, Horsell, Woking (☎ 04862 61400)

BELFAST, Earl of; Arthur Patrick Chichester; s and h of 7 Marquess of Donegall; *b* 9 May 1952; *Educ* Harrow; *Career* Lt Coldstream Gds; *Style* - Earl of Belfast

BELFIELD, Eversley Michael Gallimore; s of late Frederick Bruce Belfield; *b* 10 Sept 1918; *Educ* Ampleforth, Pembroke Coll Oxford; *m* 1950, Felicity Ann, nee Hellaby; 3 s, 2 da; *Career* lecturer 1950, senior lecturer Adult Education Dept Southampton Univ 1966, military historian; *Style* - Eversley Belfield Esq; Beauchamp, Sark, C I (☎ 0481 83 2011)

BELFIELD, Gervase Richard; s of Eversley M G Belfield, *qv*; *b* 24 Aug 1953; *Educ* Ampleforth Coll, Southampton U; *Career* barr, genealogist (Debrett's Ancestry Research); *Recreations* reading, travel, tennis; *Clubs* Chelsea Arts; *Style* - Gervase Belfield Esq; 75 Greenside rd, W12 (☎ 749 6645)

BELFRAGE, Leif Axel Lorentz; Hon GBE; s of J K E Belfrage; *b* 1 Feb 1910; *Educ* Stockholm U; *m* 1937, Greta Jering; 1 s, 3 da; *Career* Swedish Ambass to UK 1967-72; *Style* - Leif Belfrage Esq, Hon GBE; Sturegaten 14, 11436 Stockholm, Sweden

BELHAVEN, Master of; Hon Frederick Carmichael Arthur Hamilton; s and h of 13 Lord Belhaven and Stenton; *b* 27 Sept 1953; *Educ* Eton; *m* 1981, Elizabeth Anne, da of S V Tredinnick, of Naldretts Court, Wisborough Green, W Sussex; *Style* - The Master of Belhaven

BELHAVEN AND STENTON, 13 Lord (S 1647); Robert Anthony Carmichael Hamilton; s of 12 Lord (d 1961); *b* 27 Feb 1927; *Educ* Eton; *m* 1, 1952, Elizabeth, da of late Col Arthur Moseley, DSO, of NSW (m dis 1972); 1 s, 1 da; m 2, 1973, Rosemary, da of Sir Herbert Williams, 1 Bt, MP (d 1954), and formerly w of Sir Ian Mactaggart, 3 Bt; 1 adopted da; *Heir* s, Master of Belhaven; *Career* army 1945-48, farmer 1950-72, cook 1972-80; *Recreations* writing children's stories, growing vegetables; *Clubs* Army and Navy; *Style* - The Rt Hon The Lord Belhaven and Stenton; Tighcargaman, Isle of Islay, Argyll (☎ 04962345)

BELHAVEN AND STENTON, Ann, Lady; (Elizabeth) Ann; da of late Col Arthur Moseley, of Hastings rd, Warrawee, NSW; *m* 1952, 13 Lord Belhaven and Stenton (m dis 1972); 1 s, 1 da; *Style* - Ann, Lady Belhaven and Stenton; 15 Duke st, Sydney, Australia

BELL, Hon Mrs - Hon Astrid Signe; *née* Williamson; da of 3 Baron Forres (d 1978) and Gillian Ann Maclean, nee Grant; *b* 1951; *m* 1976, Peter Karl Dobree Bell; *Style* - The Hon Mrs Bell; Conifer Cottage, Aldermaston, Berks

BELL, Christopher John; TD; s of Alfred Bell (d 1979); *b* 11 Jan 1929; *Educ* Worksop Coll; *m* 1951, Margaret, da of Thomas Beaumont (d 1938); 2 children; *Career* chm M M Bell & Sons (cardboard box mfrs), Pres Packaging Employers Confed 1980-, Regnl Cncl CBI 1979-; *Recreations* gardening, scouting; *Style* - Christopher Bell Esq, TD; 529 Fulwood rd, Sheffield (☎ 305272)

BELL, David Hugh; s of Sir Hugh Bell, 4 Bt (d 1970); bro and hp of Sir John Lowthian Bell, 5 Bt; *b* 8 Oct 1961; *Style* - David Bell Esq

BELL, (William) Ewart; CB (1978); s of Rev Dr Frederick Bell and Margaret Jane Ewart; *b* 13 Nov 1924; *Educ* Methodist Coll Belfast, Wadham Oxford; *m* 1957, Kathleen Ross Boucher; 2 da; *Career* school master Cheltenham 1946-48; NI Civ Serv 1948-81 (Head 1979-81), Dep PUS NI Off 1981-; *Style* - Ewart Bell Esq, CB; Stormont Castle, Belfast, N Ireland (☎ 63011)

BELL, George Douglas Hutton; CBE (1965), FRS (1965); s of the late George Henry Bell; *b* 18 Oct 1905; *Educ* Bishop Gore's G S, Univ Coll Bangor, Cambridge; *m* 1934, Eileen Gertrude, nee Wright; 2 da; *Career* Demonstrator and University lecturer Cambridge 1932-47, dir Plant Breeding Institute Cambridge 1947-71; *Recreations* walking, gardening, natural history; *Style* - George Bell Esq, CBE, FRS; 6 Worts Causeway, Cambridge (☎ 47449)

BELL, Sir Gawain Westray; KCMG (1957), CBE (1955, MBE 1942); s of late William Westray Bell; *b* 21 Jan 1909; *Educ* Winchester, Oxford; *m* 1945, Silvia, da of the late Maj Adrian Cornwell-Clyne; 3 da; *Career* KStJ 1959, Sudan Political Service 1931, 2 Lt TA 1929-32, Military Service Middle East 1941-45, District Comr Sudan Political Service 1945-49, dep Sudan Agent Cairo 1949-51, HM Political Agent Kuwait 1955-57, Governer Northern Nigeria 1957-62, Sec Gen Council Middle East Trade 1963-64, chm exec Ctee LEPRA, part-time chm CS Selection Body London Univ 1971-; *Recreations* walking, riding, gardening; *Clubs* Bath; *Style* - Sir Gawain Bell, KCMG, CBE; Hidcote Bartrim Manor, Chipping Campden, Glos (☎ Mickleton 305)

BELL, Hon Mrs (Heather Doreen); *née* Parnell; da of 6 Baron Congleton (d 1932) and Hon Edith Mary Palmer Howard, MBE (d 1980, da of Baroness Strathcona and Mount Royal in her own right); *b* 1929; *m* 1960, Robert Peter Mangin Bell, *qv*; 2 s, 1 da; *Style* - The Hon Mrs Bell; Bindon House, St Cross, Winchester, Hants (☎ 65320)

BELL, Ian; *Career* assist gen man Leeds Permanent Bldg Soc; *Style* - Ian Bell Esq; Permanent House, The Headrow, Leeds

BELL, John; *Career* pres Bellway Ltd, dir Cramlington Dvpts and others; *Style* - John Bell Esq; Dobson House, The Regent Centre, Gosforth, Newcastle-on-Tyne NE3 3LT

BELL, Lady Jean; *née* Douglas-Hamilton; da of 13 Duke of Hamilton and (10 of) Brandon (d 1940); *b* 1904; *m* 1, 1927, Charles Mackintosh (m dis 1946); 2 s, 2 da; m 2, 1947, Maj Leo Zinovieff (d 1951); m 3, 1972, Wing Cdr Vivian Bell (d 1978); *Style* - Lady Jean Bell; Hacienda, Montevideo, Alhaurin el Grande Malaga, Spain

BELL, Rear-Adm John Anthony; CB (1977); s of Mathew Bell (d 1948); *b* 25 Nov 1924; *Educ* St Ignatius Coll, U Coll of SW; *m* 1946, Eileen, nee Woodman; 3 da; *Career* Educn Sec BBC 1979-, Dir Naval Educn 1975-79; *Recreations* walking, swimming, travelling; *Style* - Rear-Adm John Bell, CB; The Beild, Conifer av, Hartley, Kent (☎ Longfield 2485)

BELL, Sir John Lowthian; 5 Bt (UK 1885); s of Sir Hugh Francis Bell, 4 Bt (d 1970); *b* 14 June 1960; *Style* - Sir John Bell, Bt; Arncliffe Hall, Ingleby Cross, Northallerton, Yorks

BELL, Kenneth; *Career* md Bellway Holds Ltd, dir Bellway Gp of Cos and many others; *Style* - Kenneth Bell Esq; Dobson House, Regent Centre, Gosforth, Newcastle-on-Tyne NE3 3LT

BELL, Hon Mrs (Lydia Joyce); *née* Sclater-Booth; da of 2 Baron Basing, CB (d 1919); *b* 1898; *m* 1921, Maj Anthony Harley Mark Bell, MC (d 1964); 2 s, 1 da; *Style* - The Hon Mrs Bell; Rose Cottage, Broughton, Stockbridge, Hants (☎ Broughton 344)

BELL, Lady - Mary; JP (Yorks); da of late George Howson, MC, of Hambledon Bucks; *m* 1959, as his 2 w, Sir Hugh Francis Bell, 4 Bt (d 1970); *Career* MB, ChB, DObst, RCOG; *Style* - Lady Bell, JP; Arncliffe Hall, Ingleby Cross, Northallerton, N Yorks

BELL, P T; *Career* jt md Forth Wines Ltd; *Style* - P T Bell Esq; c/o Forth Wines, Crawford Place, Milnathort, Tayside

BELL, Robert Peter Mangin; s of Rev Robert Bell (d 1940), of Stamfordham Vicarage Northumberland; *b* 11 Sept 1918; *Educ* Durham Sch, Jesus Cambridge; *m* 1960, Hon Heather, nee Parnell, da of 6 Baron Congleton (d 1932); 2 s, 1 da; *Career* slr; *Clubs* Oxford & Cambridge, Roy Lymington Yacht; *Style* - Robert Bell Esq; Bindon House, St Cross, Winchester, Hants (☎ 0962 65320)

BELL, Hon Mrs; Hon Serena Frances; *née* Fairfax; da of 13 Lord Fairfax of Cameron (d 1964); *b* 12 Dec 1952; *m* 1976, W Robert G Bell; *Style* - The Hon Mrs Bell

BELL, William Edwin; CBE (1980); s of Cuthbert Bell (d 1961); *b* 4 Aug 1926; *Educ* Birmingham U, Roy Sch of Mines; *m* 1952, Angela, da of Fl-Lt E Vaughan, MC (d 1931); 2 s, 2 da; *Career* exec Roy Dutch Shell Gp, dir Shell Internat 1980-, CBIM, FInstPetroleum; *Recreations* golf, sailing (yacht- 'Bel Esprit'); *Clubs* Chichester Yacht; *Style* - William Bell Esq, CBE; Nevill Court, Tunbridge Wells, Kent

BELLAMY, Richard Anthony; s of Maj Roland Cecil Bellamy, OBE, TD, JP, DL, *qv*; *b* 21 March 1939; *Educ* Shrewsbury; *m* 1965, Wendy, nee Hopwood; 2 s, 1 da; *Career* chm Avia Fuels (UK) Ltd; dir Avia Internat of Zurich; md Bell Oil Operations, Bell Gas Products; High Sheriff Humberside 1980-81; *Recreations* shooting; *Style* - Richard Bellamy Esq; Parklands, Barnoldby-Le-Beck, Great Grimsby, S Humberside (☎ 0472 823630)

BELLAMY, Maj Roland Cecil; OBE (1974), TD (1950), JP (1943), DL (Humberside 1974); s of William Bellamy (d 1945); *b* 17 May 1902; *Educ* Rossall; *m* 1927, Kathleen, da of Edwin Beacock; 1 s, 2 da; *Career* C Eng, MIMechE; High Sheriff Lincs 1971, chm Bell Petroleum; *Recreations* country pursuits; *Clubs* Army & Navy; *Style* - Maj Roland Bellamy, OBE, TD, JP, DL; West Park, Barnoldby-Le-Beck, nr Grimsby, S Humberside (☎ 0472 823150)

BELLEW, 6 Baron (I 1848); Sir Bryan Bertram Bellew; 12 Bt (I 1688), MC (1916); s of late Hon Richard Eustace Bellew (4 s of 2 Baron); suc bro, 1975; *b* 11 June 1890; *Educ* Stubbington, Trin Hall Cambridge; *m* 1918, Jeanie Ellen Agnes (d 1973), da of late James Ormsby Jameson; 1 s; *Heir* s, Hon James Bellew; *Career* late Lt Cav Special Res, served WW I; *Style* - The Rt Hon The Lord Bellew; Barmeath Castle, Togher, Drogheda, Co Louth, Eire

BELLEW, Hon James Bryan; s and h of 6 Baron Bellew; *b* 1920; *Educ* Malvern; *m* 1, 1942, Mary Elizabeth, da of Rev Eustace Hill, of West Malling, Kent; 2 s, 1 da; m 2, 1978, Mrs Gwendoline Bellew, da of late Charles Redmond Clayton-Daubeny, of Bridgwater, Som, and Bihar, India; *Career* Irish Gds 1940-46; *Style* - The Hon James Bellew; Barmeath Castle, Dunleer, Co Louth, Eire

BELLEW, Hon Patrick Herbert; s of Hon Richard Eustace Bellew (d 1933) and bro of 5 Baron Bellew, MBE (d 1975); *b* 1905; *Educ* privately and Cambridge U; *m* 1, 1936, Hon Catherine Môya de la Poer Beresford (m dis 1946 and who d 1967), da of 5 Baron Decies, DSO, PC (d 1944); 1 s; m 2, 1954, Helen Carol, da of late Walter Clinton Louchheim of New York; *Career* granted 1935 rank, title and precedence of a Baron's son which would have been his had his father survived to succeed to the title; Lt RNVR 1938; *Style* - The Hon Patrick Bellew; Litchfield, Connecticut, USA

BELLINGHAM, Anthony Edward Norman; s of Sir Roger Bellingham, 6 Bt (d 1973); bro and hp of Sir Noel Bellingham, 7 Bt; *b* 24 March 1947; *Educ* Rossall; *Style* - Anthony Bellingham Esq

BELLINGHAM, Mary, Lady; Mary; da of late William Norman; *m* 1941, Sir Roger Bellingham, 6 Bt (d 1973); 2 s; *Style* - Mary, Lady Bellingham; 1 Adswood Lane West, Cale Green, Stockport, Cheshire

BELLINGHAM, Sir Noel Peter Roger; 7 Bt (GB 1796); s of Sir Roger Bellingham, 6 Bt, MB, ChB, DA (d 1973); *b* 4 Sept 1943; *Educ* Lindisfarne Coll; *m* 1977, Jane, da of Edwin Taylor, of Sale, Cheshire; *Heir* bro, Anthony Bellingham; *Career* accountant; *Style* - Sir Noel Bellingham, Bt; 20 Davenport Pk rd, Davenport, Stockport, Cheshire (☎ 061 483 7168)

BELLOW, Hon Stephen Jeremy; s of Baron Bellwin, JP (Life Peer); *b* 1953; *m* 1974, Marilyn Stern; *Style* - The Hon Stephen Bellow; 10 Shadwell Pk Court, Leeds 17

BELLWIN, Baron (Life Peer UK 1979); Irwin Norman Bellow; JP (Leeds 1969); s of Abraham Bellow; *b* 7 Feb 1923; *Educ* Leeds Roy G S, Leeds U; *m* 1948, Doreen Saperia; 1 s, 2 da; *Career* Parly Under-Sec Dept of Environment 1979-, leader Leeds City Cncl, Alderman Leeds CC 1968-; *Style* - The Rt Hon The Lord Bellwin, JP; Woodside Lodge, Ling Lane, Scarcroft, Leeds LS14 3HX (☎ 892908)

BELLWOOD, Raymond Lee; TD (1950), DL (Tyne and Wear 1980); s of Norman Arthur Bellwood (d 1953); *b* 19 Dec 1913; *Educ* privately, Durham U; *m* 1939, Moyra Lindores, nee Reid; 1 s, 3 da (and 1 decd); *Career* Maj RA (TA) ret, solicitor, KStJ 1969, memb Chapter General Order of St John 1969-, chm St John Cncl for Northumbria 1963-, cdr St John Ambulance Northumbria 1970-81; *Clubs* Northern Counties (Newcastle on Tyne); *Style* - Raymond Bellwood Esq, TD, DL; Low Hawkwell, Stamfordham, Northumberland (☎ 06616 254)

BELMORE, 8 Earl (I 1797); John Armar Lowry-Corry; also Baron Belmore (I 1781) and Viscount Belmore (I 1789); s of 7 Earl Belmore, JP, DL (d 1960); *b* 4 Sept 1951; *Educ* Ashdown House Sussex, Lancing, RAC Cirencester; *Career* landowner, conservationist; *Recreations* fishing; *Clubs* Kildare Street, Travellers'; *Style* - The Rt Hon The Earl Belmore; Castle Coole, Enniskillen, N Ireland (☎ 22368/4255)

BELOFF, Baron (Life Peer UK 1981); Max Beloff; s of Simon and Mary Beloff; *b* 2 July 1913; *Educ* St Paul's, CCC Oxford; *m* 1938, Helen Dobrin; 2 s; *Career* kt 1980; FBA, FRHistS, FRSA; Emeritus Fellow All Souls 1980-; Pncpl U Coll of Buckingham 1974-79; historian; *Style* - The Rt Hon Lord Beloff; c/o St Anthony's Coll, Oxford

BELPER, 4 Baron (UK 1856); (Alexander) Ronald George Strutt; s of 3 Baron (d 1956) by 1 w, Hon Dame Eva Bruce, DBE, JP, da of 2 Baron Aberdare; bro of Lavinia, Duchess of Norfolk; *b* 23 April 1912; *Educ* Harrow; *m* 1940 (m dis 1949), Zara Sophie Kathleen Mary, da of Sir Harry Mainwaring, 5 Bt; 1 s; *Heir* s, Hon Henry Strutt; *Career* formerly Maj Coldstream Gds; *Style* - The Rt Hon The Lord Belper; Kingston Hall, Nottingham

BELSON, Dorrien Berkeley Euan; s of Frederick Belson (d 1952); *b* 10 Feb 1917; *Educ* St Edmund's Sch Canterbury; *m* 1948, Mary, da of Charles Deane Cowper (d 1956); 3 s, 1 da; *Career* chm IDV (Export) Ltd 1969-78, High Sheriff Bucks 1981, Kt Sov Mil Order of Malta 1978; *Recreations* fishing, wine, gardening, photography; *Clubs* Leander, Army & Navy; *Style* - Dorrien Belson Esq; Stayes, Northend, Henley-on-Thames, Oxon (☎ Heath 381)

BELSTEAD, 2 Baron (UK 1938); Sir John Julian Ganzoni; 2 Bt (UK 1929), JP (Ipswich), DL (Suffolk 1979); s of 1 Baron (d 1958); *b* 30 Sept 1932; *Educ* Eton, Ch Ch Oxford; *Career* Parly Under-Sec of State Dept of Education and Science 1970-73, and Parly Under-Sec of State for N Ireland 1973-74, Home Office 1979-, chm Governing Bodies Assoc 1974; *Style* - The Rt Hon The Lord Belstead, JP, DL; The Old Rectory, Great Bealings, Woodbridge,

Suffolk (☎ Grundisburgh 278); 42 Pelham Court, Fulham rd, SW3 (☎ 01 584 6714)

BEMROSE, Esmond Clive; OBE (1971); s of late H H Bemrose, JP; *b* 6 July 1902; *Educ* Abbotsholme Sch Derbyshire, Clare Cambridge; *m* 1946, Enid Marjorie, da of the late Major Ian Ainslie; 1 s, 2 da (1 da decd); *Career* Squadron Leader RAF, dir Bemrose & Sons Ltd, High Sheriff Derbyshire 1967, chm St Christophers Home for children of railwaymen 1947-65, past pres Derby and Derbyshire Chamber of commerce, chm Abbotsholme Sch Exec 1947-74, pres of Duke of Edinburgh Award Scheme 1969-79; *Recreations* riding, music, freemasonry, literature; *Style* - Esmond Bemrose Esq, OBE; Ithersey, Windley lane, Weston Underwood, Derbyshire (☎ Brailsford 422)

BENCE, John Douglas; *Career* md MacMillan Bloedel Containers Ltd; dir The British Paper (Waste) Ltd, Pakfast Ltd, Scotpack Ltd; *Style* - John Bence Esq; 24-30 King st, Watford, Herts

BENCE, Hon Mrs - Hon Patricia Mary; *née* Dent; da of Baroness Furnivall (d 1968, herself da of 14 Baron Petre and co-heir with Lord Mowbray, Segrave and Stourton to the Baronies of Strange de Blackmere, Talbot, Howard, and others; the Barony of Furnivall, abeyant since the death of the 9 Duke of Norfolk (who was also 18 Baron Furnivall) in 1777, was called out in her favour by Letters Patent 1913) and co-heiress to the Barony of Furnivall, abeyant since 1968; *b* 4 Apr 1935; *m* 1, 1956, Capt Thomas Hornsby (m dis 1963; he d 1967); 1 s (Francis Walton Petre b 21 April 1958), 1 da (Clare Mary Petre b 25 Jan 1957); m 2, 1970, Roger Thomas John Bence; 1 s (Richard William Petre b 1976), 1 da (Katharine Rosamond Petre b 1971); *Style* - The Hon Mrs Bence; Trotwood, 11 Gresham rd, Limpsfield, Oxted, Surrey (☎ Oxted 4062)

BENDALL, David Vere; CMG (1946), MBE (1945); s of John Bendall (d 1970); *b* 27 Feb 1920; *Educ* Winchester, King's Cambridge; *m* 1941, Eve, da of Charles Galpin (d 1928); 1 da; *Career* dep chm Morgan Grenfell Internat 1971-, For Serv 1946-71; *Recreations* tennis, shooting; *Clubs* Boodle's; *Style* - David Bendall Esq, CMG, MBE; 3 Eaton Terrace Mews, SW1 (☎ 01 730 4229); Ashbocking Hall, Ipswich, Suffolk (☎ Helmingham 262)

BENDALL, Vivian Walter Hough; MP (C) Redbridge 1978-; s of Cecil Bendall (d 1963); *b* 14 Dec 1938; *Educ* Broad Green Coll Croydon; *m* 1969, Ann, da of Henry Jarvis; *Career* surveyor and valuer; *Recreations* cricket, golf; *Clubs* Carlton, Ilford Golf, Exec County Cricket; *Style* - Vivian Bendall Esq, MP; The Old House, Bletchingley, Surrey (☎ 088384 3657)

BENDING, M E J; *Career* gen man Anglia Hastings & Thanet Bldg Soc; *Style* - M E J Bending Esq; c/o Anglia Hastings & Thanet Building Soc, Moulton Park, Northampton

BENDIX, Michael; DL (Essex 1977); s of Carl Bendix (d 1944) and Daisy, da of late Charles Hancox, who m 2, Col Lionel Neame and m 3, (as his 2 w), 2 Visc Allenby; *b* 9 Feb 1925; *Educ* Eton, Magdalene Cambridge; *m* 1951, Ingrid, da of Ivan de Rehren, of Brussels (d 1966); 1 s, 1 da; *Career* dir Barclays Bank UK 1973-, sr dir Barclays Bank Chelmsford Dist 1968- OStJ 1966, FIOB, Fell Linnaean Soc; *Recreations* shooting, botany, ornithology, music; *Clubs* Boodle's, Army & Navy; *Style* - Michael Bendix Esq, DL; Wallops, Gt Waltham, Chelmsford, Essex (☎ 0245 360219)

BENHAM, Peter Carr; MBE (Mil 1945), TD (1946); s of Gerald Carr Benham, MC, TD (d 1962); *b* 17 June 1917; *Educ* Uppingham; *m* 1940, Eileen Mary, nee Adams; 1 s; *Career* maj N Africa Field Artillery, Normandy, slr 1947, coroner for Borough of Colchester 1958-74, chm Colchester Permanent Building Soc 1977-80; *Recreations* golf, sea fishing (owner m/v 'Pescador'); *Clubs* Colchester Garrison Officers, Walton and Frinton Yacht; *Style* - Peter Benham Esq MBE TD; 21 Queens rd, Colchester, Essex (☎ 72019)

BENJAMIN, (Isaac) Louis; s of Benjamin Benjamin; *b* 17 Oct 1922; *Educ* Highbury County Secondary Sch; *m* 1954, Vera Ketteman; 2 da; *Career* dir ATV gp of cos, dir PYE gp of cos, dep chm

Associated Communications Corpn Ltd, dir Theatre Royal Drury Lane Ltd, and other cos; *Style* - Louis Benjamin Esq; 17 Gt Cumberland Place, W1 (☎ 01 262 5502)

BENN, Hon David Julian Wedgwood; s of 1 Viscount Stansgate, DSO, DFC, PC (d 1960); bro of Tony Benn, MP; *b* 28 Dec 1928; *Educ* Balliol Oxford; *m* 1959, June, da of late Ernest Barraclough; 1 s, 1 da; *Style* - The Hon David Benn; 4 Liskeard gdns, Blackheath, SE3 (☎ 01 858 0912); Stansgate Cottage, nr Steeple, Southminster, Essex

BENN, Hilary James Wedgwood; s of Rt Hon Tony Benn, PC, MP (disclaimed Viscountcy of Stansgate for life 1963); *b* 1953; *Educ* Holland Pk Sch; *m* Rosalind (d 1979); *Style* - Hilary Benn Esq

BENN, Sir John Andrews; 3 Bt (UK 1914); s of Sir Ernest John Pickstone Benn, 2 Bt, CBE (d 1954); *b* 28 Jan 1904; *Educ* Harrow, Princeton U, Gonville and Caius Cambridge; *m* 1929, Hon Ursula Helen Alers Hankey, da of 1 Baron Hankey; 2 s, 3 da; *Heir* s, James Jonathan Benn; *Career* chm English-Speaking Union of the Commonwealth 1969-72, chm Cincinnati Milacron Ltd 1969-76, consultant Benn Bros Ltd and Ernest Benn Ltd; author; *Style* - Sir John Benn, Bt; High Field, Limpsfield, Surrey

BENN, James Jonathan; s and h of Sir John Andrews Benn, 3 Bt, *qv*; *b* 27 July 1933; *Educ* Harrow, Clare Coll Camb; *m* 1960, Jennifer, nee Howells; 1 s, 1 da; *Style* - James Benn Esq; Fielden Lodge, Ightham, Kent

BENN, Joshua William Wedgwood; s of Rt Hon Tony Benn, PC, MP (disclaimed Viscountcy of Stansgate for life 1963); *b* 1958; *Educ* Holland Pk Sch; *Style* - Joshua Benn Esq

BENN, Melissa Anne Wedgwood; da of Rt Hon Tony Benn, PC, MP (disclaimed Viscountcy of Stansgate for life 1963); *b* 1957; *Educ* Holland Pk Sch; *Style* - Miss Melissa Benn

BENN, Capt Sir Patrick Ion Hamilton; 2 Bt (UK 1920); s of late Col Ion Bridges Hamilton Benn, s of 1 Bt; suc gf, Capt Sir (Ion) Hamilton Benn, 1 Bt, CB, DSO, TD, RNVR, 1961; *b* 26 Feb 1922; *Educ* Rugby; *m* 1959, Edel Jorgine, da of late Col W S Loback, formerly Roy Norwegian Army; *Career* Capt Reserve of Offrs late Duke of Cornwall's Light Infantry, Maj Norfolk Army Cadet Force; tstee and Gov E Anglian Tstee Savings Bank, cmmr Gt Yarmouth Port and Haven; *Style* - Capt Sir Patrick Benn, Bt; Rollesby Hall, nr Gt Yarmouth, Norfolk

BENN, Stephen Michael Wedgwood; s of Rt Hon Tony Benn, PC, MP and h to Viscountcy of Stansgate, which was disclaimed by his father for life 1963; *b* 21 Aug 1951; *Educ* Holland Pk Sch, Keele U; *Style* - Stephen Benn Esq

BENN, Timothy John; s of Sir John Benn, 3 Bt, and Hon Ursula, da of 1 Baron Hankey, GCB, GCMG, GCVO, PC, FRS; *b* 27 Oct 1936; *Educ* Harrow, Princeton, Clare Cambridge; *m* 1, 1959, Valerie (m dis 1973), da of late Capt P Davie; 3 s; m 2, 1973, Susan, da of George Hodges, of Florida; *Career* chm Benn Bros (publishers), Ernest Benn Ltd; *Recreations* fishing, writing, toymaking; *Clubs* Flyfishers'; *Style* - Timothy Benn Esq; Hickens Cottage, Chiddingstone, Edenbridge, Kent (☎ 0892 870 346)

BENN, Rt Hon Tony (Anthony) Neil Wedgwood; PC (1964), MP (L) Bristol South-East 1950-60 and 1963-; s of 1 Visc Stansgate, DSO, DFC, PC (d 1960); suc as 2 Visc 1960, but made it known that he did not wish to claim the Viscountcy; disclaimed his peerage for life 31 July 1963, having unsuccessfully attempted to renounce his right of succession 1955 and 1960; *b* 3 April 1925; *Educ* Westminster, New Coll Oxford; *m* 1949, Caroline Middleton, da of late James Milton De Camp, of Cincinnati, USA; 3 s, 1 da; *Career* Postmaster General 1964-66, Min of Technology and Min of Power 1969-70, memb Nat Exec Ctee of Lab Party 1962-, chm Lab Party 1971-72, Sec of State for Energy 1975-79; *Style* - Rt Hon Tony Benn, MP; 12 Holland pk, W11

BENN, Hon Lady - Hon Ursula Helen

Alers; da of 1 Baron Hankey, GCB, GCMG, GCVO, PC (d 1963); *b* 1909; *m* 1929, Sir John Benn, 3 Bt, *qv*; 2 s, 3 da; *Style* - The Hon Lady Benn; High Field, Limpsfield, Surrey

BENNARD, Hon Mrs - Hon Edith Ellen; JP (Parts of Lindsay Lincs); da of 1 and last Baron Quibell (d 1962); *b* 1904; *m* 1954, Eric Bennard Cuthbert, who took name of Bennard by deed poll 1962; *Career* dir Quibell and Hardy Ltd; pres RSPCA, Scunthorpe; Mayoress of Scunthorpe 1953-54; *Style* - The Hon Mrs Bennard, JP; 3 Hobart pla, Eaton sq, SW1

BENNET, Lady Alexandra Katherine; da of 9 Earl of Tankerville (d 1980); *b* 1955; *Style* - Lady Alexandra Bennet

BENNET, Rev the Hon George Arthur Grey; s of 8 Earl of Tankerville (d 1971) and hp of n, 10 Earl of Tankerville; *b* 12 March 1925; *Educ* Radley, CCC Cambridge; *m* 1957, Hazel (Jane) G, da of late Ernest W G Judson, of Bishopswood, Chard, Somerset; 2 s, 1 da; *Career* Vicar in Shaston Team Min 1973-; *Books* Electricity and Modern Physics (1965) *Style* - The Reverend the Hon George Bennet; The Rectory, Harleston, Norfolk

BENNET, Hon Mrs George - Constance Clare; da of Cyril Wace, of Victoria, BC, Canada; *m* 1929, Hon George William Bennet (d 1981); *Style* - The Hon Mrs George Bennet; Polwarth, Greenlaw, Berwicks

BENNET, Hon Ian; s of 8 Earl of Tankerville (d 1971); *b* 1935; *Educ* Radley, CCC Cambridge; *Career* Lt RNR; *Style* - The Hon Ian Bennet; Estate House, Chillingham, Chatton, Northumberland

BENNETT, Alan; s of Walter Bennett; *b* 9 May 1934; *Educ* Leeds Modern Sch, Exeter Coll Camb; *Career* actor and dramatist; *Style* - Alan Bennett Esq; c/o Chatto and Linnit Ltd, Globe Theatre, Shaftesbury ave, W1 (☎ 01 439 4371)

BENNETT, (Frederick Onslow) Alexander (Godwyn); TD; s of Alfred Bennett and Marjorie Muir Bremner; *b* 21 Dec 1913; *Educ* Winchester and Trin Cambridge; *m* 1942, Rosemary, da of Sir Malcolm Perks, 2 Bt; 1 s, 4 da; *Career* chm Whitbread and Co Ltd 1972-77; *Style* - Alexander Bennett Esq TD; Grove House, Selling, Faversham, Kent (☎ Selling 250)

BENNETT, Arthur James; s of Harry Bennett (1973); *b* 28 Aug 1922; *Educ* Perse Sch, Malvern, Queens' Cambridge; *m* 1945, Jean, da of Ernest Baynham (d 1967); 2 da; *Career* dir Transmission Engrg 1977-; *Recreations* sailing (boat- 'White Rose'); *Style* - Arthur Bennett Esq; 44 Thornton Close, Girton, Cambridge (☎ 0223 276175)

BENNETT, Sir Arnold Lucas; QC (Qld 1947, Vict 1952, NSW 1953); s of George Bennett (d 1958); *b* 12 Nov 1908; *Educ* Brisbane G S, Qld U; *m* 1932, Nancy, da of Eric Mellor (d 1978); 3 s, 5 da; *Career* barr, chm Qld Bar Bd 1957-79; *Recreations* farming, golf, aviation; *Clubs* Brisbane Rotary; *Style* - Sir Arnold Bennett, QC; 52 Dunmore ter, Auchenflower, Brisbane (☎ 371 3313 and 370 8485)

BENNETT, Hon Mrs (Catharine Jacobine); *née* Sackville-West; da (by 1 m) of 6 Baron Sackville; *b* 1956; *m* 1980, Stuart Cooper Bennett; *Style* - The Hon Mrs Bennett; Pasadena, California, USA

BENNETT, Francis Ernest Herman; CBE (1963); s of Sir Ernest Bennett (d 1947); *b* 5 Nov 1916; *Educ* Westminster, New Coll Oxford; *m* 1947, Ruth Gordon, da of 1 Baron Catto (d 1959); 2 s, 1 da; *Career* 2 Lt RA 1939-46, 3 sec to HM Legation Bucharest 1947-49, sec-gen Liberal International 1951-52, barr 1953, ch whip Con LCC 1959, alderman & ch whip Con GLC 1965- (dep chm 1975-76), gov London Festival Ballet, memb Court & Cncl Brunel U, chm W J Cox Ltd 1959-74, gen cmmr Income Tax 1978-, chm MMBS Ltd 1979; *Recreations* skiing, shooting, travelling, entomology; *Clubs* Reform, Carlton; *Style* - Francis Bennett Esq, CBE; C Hoare & Co, 37 Fleet st, EC4

BENNETT, George Colin; s of Rowland Bennett, OBE (d 1973); *b* 10 May 1924; *Educ* Rydal Sch, Trin Cambridge; *m* 1953, Mary Christina Barron, nee Jones; 2 s, 1

da; *Career* slr, notary public, Clerk to Corby Justices 1959-74; *Recreations* sport, jazz, photography; *Clubs* MCC; *Style* - George Bennett Esq; Colwyn, Woodlands lane, Gt Oakley, Corby, Northants (☎ Gt Oakley 743475)

BENNETT, Jeremy James Balfe; s of Arthur Bennett (d 1965); *b* 20 Jan 1934; *Educ* Repton; *m* 1965, Shelagh, da of Robert Jones; 3 da; *Career* chm London Wine Importers, S Cole Ltd, Winecash Ltd; dir Grants of St James's, Herman Jung; *Recreations* interior design, music, reading, walking; *Clubs* Cavalry & Guards; *Style* - Jeremy Bennett Esq; 18 Portland rd, Holland Pk, W11 (☎ 01 221 0731)

BENNETT, John Michael; *Career* gp md Tecalemit Ltd; BSc, CEng, FIMechE, MSAE, FBIM, FRAeS; *Style* - John Bennett Esq; Old Court, Cox Green, Maidenhead, Berks

BENNETT, James Ultan; s of Augustus Bennett, of Dublin (d 1966); *b* 19 May 1919; *Educ* U Sch Dublin; *m* 1943, Mary, da of David O'Callaghan, of Port Talbot (d 1930); 1 s, 1 da; *Career* md Buckley's Brewery Ltd 1977-; *Recreations* rugby, racing, walking; *Clubs* Conservative (Llanelli); *Style* - James Bennett Esq; Kilcreene, 1A Swiss Valley, Llanelli, Dyfed (☎ 59199, office 58441)

BENNETT, Dowager Lady - Leopoldine; da of Leopold Armata, of Vienna; *m* 1938, as his 2 w, Sir Albert Bennett, 1 Bt (d 1945); *Style* - Dowager Lady Bennett; c/o 46 High Point, Weybridge, Surrey

BENNETT, Michael; s of late Frank Carlton Bennett (d 1973); h to Btcy of cousin, Sir Ronald Bennett, Bt, *qv*; *b* 15 Feb 1924; *m* 1952, Janet Hazel Margaret, da of Brig Edward Todhunter, TD; 1 s, 2 da; *Style* - Michael Bennett Esq; Flat 70, Albert Hall Mansions, SW7

BENNETT, Marion, Lady - (Agnes) Marion Dawes; OBE (1953); da of late James Somervell, of Sorn Castle, Ayrshire; *m* 1927, Sir (Charles) Wilfrid Bennett, 2 Bt, TD (d 1952); *Style* - Marion, Lady Bennett, OBE; 63 Cheyne Court, Flood st, SW3

BENNETT, Mrs John; Mary Letitia Somerville; da of Rt Hon H A L Fisher, OM; *b* 9 Jan 1913; *Educ* Oxford High Sch, Somerville Oxford; *m* 1955, John Sloman Bennett, CMG; *Career* principal St Hilda's Coll, Oxford; *Style* - Mrs John Bennett; St Hilda's College, Oxford

BENNETT, Nigel Jack; DFC; *Career* chm Tecalemit Ltd; FCA, FBIM; *Style* - Nigel Bennett Esq DFC; Tecalemit Ltd, Old Court, Cox Green, Maidenhead, Berks

BENNETT, Peter Ward; OBE; *Career* chm W H Smith and Son Ltd 1977-; dir Lloyds and Scottish Ltd, Thorn Electrical Industries Ltd; *Style* - Peter Bennett Esq OBE; W H Smith and Son Ltd, Strand House, 10 New Fetter lane, EC4 (☎ 01 353 0277)

BENNETT, Sir Reginald Frederick Brittain; VRD (1944); s of Samuel Bennett (d 1965); *b* 22 July 1911; *Educ* Winchester, New Coll Oxford; *m* 1947, Henrietta, da of Capt Henry Crane, CBE, RN; 1 s, 3 da; *Career* MP (C) Gosport and Fareham 1950-79, PPS to Iain Macleod 1954-63, chm R Yachting Assoc 1980-, kt 1979; *Recreations* yacht racing, foreign travel, basking; *Clubs* White's, Imperial Poona Yacht (Cdre); *Style* - Sir Reginald Bennett, VRD; 37 Cottesmore Court, W8 (☎ 01 937 0777)

BENNETT, Roy Grissell; CMG (1971); s of Charles Bennett (d 1962); *b* 21 Nov 1917; *Educ* Sandhurst; *Career* dir Vosper Private Ltd Singapore, Union Rubber Brokers; chm Pilkington SE Asia, Beder Malaysia, Beder Interńat, Racehorse Spelling Station; *Recreations* polo, riding, shooting, swimming, tennis, squash, gardening, travelling; *Style* - Roy Bennett Esq, CMG; Oak Tree House, S Holmwood, Surrey (☎ Dorking 6414)

BENNETT, Richard Rodney; CBE (1977); s of H Rodney Bennett; *b* 29 Mar 1936; *Educ* Leighton Park and Royal Academy of Music; *Career* composer and memb Gen Council, Performing Right

Society 1975-; *Style* - Richard Rodney Bennett Esq CBE; c/o Mrs Keys, London Management, Regent House, 235 Regent st, W1

BENNETT, Sir Ronald Wilfred Murdoch; 3 Bt (UK 1929); s of Sir (Charles) Wilfrid Bennett, 2 Bt, TD (d 1952); *b* 25 March 1930; *Educ* Wellington, Trin Oxford; *m* 1, 1953, Audrey Rose-Marie Patricia, da of Maj A L J H Aubépin, of France and of Co Mayo, Ireland; 2 da; *Heir* kinsman, Michael Bennett; *Style* - Sir Ronald Bennett, Bt

BENNETT, Hon William Richards; PC (Can); s of late Hon William Bennett, PC (Can); *b* 1932; *m* Audrey; 4 s; *Career* Premier of British Columbia 1975-; *Style* - The Hon William Bennett PC; Provincial House of Legislature, Victoria, BC, Canada

BENSON, Baron (Life Peer UK 1980); Henry Alexander Benson; GBE (1971, CBE 1946); s of Alexander Benson; *b* 2 Aug 1909; *Educ* Johannesburg; *m* 1939, Anne, da of Charles Macleod; 2 s, 1 da; *Career* FCA; kt 1964; former ptnr Coopers & Lybrand; advsr Bank of England 1975-; Pres Inst Chartered Accountants England & Wales 1966; Tstee Times Tst 1967-; *Recreations* shooting, golf, sailing (sloop-'Drover'); *Clubs* Brooks's, Roy Yacht Sqdn, Jockey; *Style* - Rt Hon Lord Benson, GBE; 9 Durward House, 31 Kensington Court, W8 (☎ 01 937 4850)

BENSON, Christopher John; s of late Charles Woodburn Benson; *b* 20 July 1933; *Educ* Worcester Cathedral Kings Sch, The Incorporated Thames Nautical Training Coll; *m* 1960, Margaret Josephine; 2 s; *Career* sub-Lt RN, dir Arndale Developments Ltd, 1965-69, founder chm Dolphin Developments and Dolphin Property Ltd 1969-72, assistant md The Law Lane Co Ltd 1972-74, dir MEPC Ltd 1974-, md MEPC Ltd 1976-, dir Sun Alliance and London Insurance Group 1978-, senior v-pres British Property Federation, chm Commercial Property Ctee 1978-, underwriting memb Lloyds 1979-, adviser to Investment Ctee BP Pension Fund 1979-, Freeman Guild of Air Pilots and Air Navigators 1980-, v-pres and md MEPC Ltd 1977-; *Recreations* farming, aviation, swimming; *Clubs* City Livery, Naval, RAC; *Style* - Christopher Benson Esq; Pauls Dene House, Castle rd, Salisbury, Wilts (☎ 0722 22187); Flat 2, 50 South Audley st, W1 (☎ 01 499 3570)

BENSON, David Holford; s of Lt-Col Sir Rex Benson, DSO, MVO, MC (d 1968), of Cucumber Farm Sussex; *b* 26 Feb 1938; *Educ* Eton, Madrid U; *m* 1964, Lady Elizabeth, nee Charteris, da of 12 Earl of Wemyss and (8 of) March, KT, JP; 1 s, 2 da; *Career* merchant banker, dir Kleinwort Benson, Wemyss & March Estate Co, Campbell Soups; *Recreations* painting; *Clubs* White's, ESU; *Style* - David Benson Esq; 11 Brunswick gdns, W8 (☎ 01 727 4949); Cucumber Farm, Singleton, Sussex (☎ 222)

BENSON, Maj-Gen Edward Riou; CB (1952), CMG (1950), CBE (1945); s of Brig-Gen Riou Benson, CB, CMG (d 1969); *b* 4 April 1903; *Educ* Cheltenham, RMA Woolwich; *m* 1931, Isolda, da of Gen Sir John Shea, GCB, KCMG, DSO (d 1966); 1 s (and 1 da decd); *Career* Ch of Staff MELF 1954-57; *Style* - Maj-Gen Edward Benson, CB, CMG, CBE; Well House, Aldermaston, Berks (☎ Woolhampton 3347)

BENSON, Prof Frank Atkinson; DL (South Yorks 1979); s of late John Benson; *b* 21 Nov 1921; *Educ* Ulverston G S and Liverpool U; *m* 1950, Kathleen Paskell; 2 s; *Career* B Eng, M Eng, PhD, D Eng, FIEE, FIEEE, FCIBS; prof and head of dept of Electronic and Electrical Engineering, Sheffield U 1967-; *Style* - Prof Frank Benson DL; 64 Grove rd, Sheffield (☎ 363493)

BENSON, James; s of Henry Benson; *b* 17 July 1925; *Educ* Bromley G S, Emmanuel Cambridge; *m* 1950, Honoria, nee Hurley, of Dublin; 1 da; *Career* v-chm Ogilvy & Mather International 1970-; *Recreations* travelling, fishing; *Style* - James Benson Esq; 9 E 79th st, NYC, NY 10021, USA (☎ 212 472 0450)

BENSON, Lt-Col John Elliott; JP (Northumberland 1954); s of late Walter John Benson; *b* 15 Jan 1915; *Educ* Eton, Sandhurst; *m* 1948, Alice Elisabeth

Kalmia, da of Capt Alexander Milne Keith; 1 s, 3 da; *Career* 2 Lt Black Watch 1935, command 2 Bn 1945-47, High Sheriff Northumberland 1973-74; *Recreations* shooting, fishing, golf; *Style* - Lt-Col John Benson, JP; Chesters, Humshaugh, Hexham, Northumberland

BENSON, Lady Jane Helen Harbord; *née* Lowther; da of 7 Earl of Lonsdale; *b* 1947; *m* 1, 1969, Gary Hunter Wooten, of Cal, USA; m 2, 1978, Robert Charles Benson; 1 da; *Style* - Lady Jane Benson; c/o Westminster Bank, 41 King st, Penrith, Cumberland

BENSON, Hon Michael D'Arcy; s of Baron Benson, GBE (Life Peer); *b* 1943; *m* 1969, Rachel Woods; *Style* - Hon Michael Benson; 34 St John 's av, SW15

BENSON, Hon Peter Macleod; s of Baron Benson, GBE (Life Peer); *b* 1940; *m* 1970, Hermione Boulton; *Style* - The Hon Peter Benson; 22 Larpent av, SW15

BENSON, Stephen; s of A Benson; *b* 7 June 1943; *Educ* Highgate, Magdalen Oxford; *m* 1966, Jacqueline, nee Russell; 3 da; *Career* dir Davidson Pearce (ad agency) 1974-; *Recreations* music, running; *Style* - Stephen Benson Esq; 8 Laurel rd, NW5 (☎ 01 485 0287)

BENSON, Maj William Arthur; TD, DL (Northumberland 1953); s of Walter Benson (d 1923); *b* 27 June 1905; *Educ* Eton; *m* 1948, Adela (d 1980), da of Maj William Standish (d 1922); *Career* Maj with Northumberland Hussars, served Greece, W Desert, Normandy WW II; High Sheriff Northumberland 1951, memb Cncl Roy Ag Soc of England 1949, hon show dir 1955-62, dep pres 1963; *Clubs* Cavalry; *Style* - Maj William Benson, TD, DL; Newbrough Hall, Hexham, Northumberland (☎ 043 474 202)

BENTALL, (Leonard Edward) Rowan; DL (Gter London 1977); s of Leonard Bentall, JP (d 1942), of Leatherhead; *b* 27 Nov 1911; *Educ* Eastbourne Coll; *m* 1937, Adelia, da of David Hawes; 3 s, 2 da; *Career* pres Bentalls 1978- (dir 1936-) pres IOD Surrey Branch 1981, dir Bentalls Pension Tstees; *Recreations* ornithology, farming, gardening, shooting; *Clubs* RAC, Constitutional (St Stephens); *Style* - Rowan Bentall Esq, DL; Hill House, Broughton, Stockbridge, Hants (☎ Broughton 551)

BENTHALL, Sir (Arthur) Paul; KBE (1950); s of Rev Charles Benthall, of Teignmouth (d 1936); *b* 25 Jan 1902; *Educ* Eton, Ch Ch Oxford; *m* 1932, Mary, da of John Pringle (d 1952); 4 s; *Career* FLS, former co dir; *Clubs* Oriental, Lansdowne; *Style* - Sir Paul Benthall, KBE; Benthall Hall, Broseley, Salop (☎ Telford 882254)

BENTINCK, Count (HRE 1732 by Charles VI); Henry Noel Aldenburg-Bentinck; s of Capt 5 Count Bentinck (Robert Charles Aldenburg-Bentinck, d 1932, ggggs of 1 Count, who was in turn half-bro of 1 Duke of Portland and s (by his 2 w) of 1 Earl of Portland), by the Count's w Lady Norah Noel (da of 3 Earl of Gainsborough); hp to Earldom of Portland, Viscountcy of Woodstock, and Barony of Cirencester, at present held by kinsman, 9 Duke of Portland, CMG; *b* 2 Oct 1919; *Educ* Harrow; *m* 1, 1940, Pauline Ursula (d 1967), da of Frederick William Mellowes, of Penn House, Reynolds Close, Hampstead; 1 s (Count Timothy Robert Charles Noel b 1953), 2 da (Mrs John (Sorrel) Lister-Kaye, da-in-law of Sir John L-K, 7 Bt; Mrs Nicholas (Anna) Vester); m 2, 1974, Jenifer, da of late Reginald Hopkins, of London; *Career* 1939-45 War (twice wounded), formerly Lt Coldstream Gds; a Mediatised Count of the Holy Roman Empire (Decree of the German Diet 1845); Queen Victoria permitted the 4 Count's descendants to bear title of Count in England 1888; *Style* - Count Bentinck; Wigham, Morchard Bishop, Crediton, Devon (☎ Morchard Bishop 350)

BENTLEY, John; *b* 19 Feb 1940; *Educ* Harrow; *m* 1960 (m dis 1969); 1 s, 1 da; *Career* chm Bentley Securities, Weston Hldgs 1973, Lion Internat 1973, Bardsey Ltd 1980-81 (L Stopford Sackville suc), remains dir Bardsey Gp; *Style* - John Bentley Esq; c/o Bardsey Gp Ltd

BENTLEY, Hon Mrs (Victoria Elizabeth); *née* Mansfield; da of 5 Baron

Sandhurst, DFC; *b* 30 Jan 1957; *Educ* Benenden, Bordeaux U; *m* 1978, Charles, s of Kenneth Bentley, of Balmuir Angus; *Recreations* skiing, riding, tennis, windsurfing; *Style* - The Hon Mrs Bentley

BENTON, Kenneth Carter; CMG (1966); s of William Benton (d 1944); *b* 4 March 1909; *Educ* Wolverhampton G S, London U; *m* 1938, Winifred, da of Maj-Gen Charles Pollock, CB, CBE, DSO (d 1928); 1 s, 2 step s; *Career* Counsellor Rio 1966-68, HM Foreign Serv ret; *Recreations* enamelling, writing; *Clubs* Authors', Detection; *Style* - Kenneth Benton Esq, CMG; Vine House, Appledore, Ashford, Kent (☎ 023363 260)

BENYON, Thomas Yates; MP (C) Abingdon 1979-; s of Capt Thomas Yates Benyon (d 1958, s of Hon Christina, da of 11 Baron North, JP); *b* 13 Aug 1942; *Educ* Wellington Sch Somerset, Sandhurst; *m* 1968, Jane, da of Humphrey Scott Plummer by his w, Hon Pamela, nee Balfour, da of 2 Baron Kinross, KC; 2 s, 2 da; *Career* commodity broker, former Lt Scots Gds, served Kenya, Muscat; *Recreations* hunting, reading, swimming; *Clubs* Brooks's; *Style* - Thomas Benyon Esq, MP; 33 Marsham Court, SW1 (☎ 01 828 6628); The Old Rectory, Adstock, nr Winslow, Bucks

BENYON, William Richard; JP (Berks 1962), DL (1970), MP (C) Buckingham 1970-; s of Vice-Adm Richard Benyon, CB, CBE (d 1968, né Shelley, 2 s of Sir John Shelley, 9 Bt, JP, DL, a distant cous of the Shelley Bts who produced the poet, and Marion, da of Richard Benyon) and Eve (twin da of Rt Rev Lord William Cecil, sometime Bp of Exeter and 2 s of 3 Marquess of Salisbury); the Adm changed his name to Benyon by Deed Poll on inheriting the Benyon estates of his cous Sir Henry Benyon, Bt; William is hence ggs of a man (Lord Salisbury) who is generally regarded as one of the ablest Conservative PMs, also great nephew of Lords Robert & Hugh Cecil, the High Church Unionist Free Traders opposed to Joe Chamberlain; he is also 2 cous once removed to his fellow (C) MP Viscount Cranborne; *b* 17 Jan 1930; *Educ* RNC Dartmouth; *m* 1957, Elizabeth, da of Vice-Adm Ronald Hallifax, CB, CBE (d 1941); 2 s (Richard; Edward, to whom HM Queen Anne Marie of the Hellenes was sponsor), 3 da (Catherine Rose Ingrid, to whom HM Queen Ingrid of Denmark stood sponsor; Mary, Susannah); *Career* PPS to Paul Channon as Min Housing 1972-74, Oppn Whip 1974-77; *Clubs* Boodle's, Pratt's, White's; *Style* - William Benyon Esq, JP, DL, MP; Englefield House, Englefield, Reading, Berks (☎ 0734 302221)

BERE, Rennie Montague; CMG (1957); s of Rev Montague Bere (d 1947); *b* 28 Nov 1907; *Educ* Marlborough, Selwyn Cambridge; *m* 1936, Anne, da of Charles Barber (d 1962); *Career* Dir and Ch Warden Uganda Nat Parks 1955-60, author of wildlife books; *Recreations* mountaineering, cricket, watching wildlife; *Clubs* Alpine, Climbers, Roy C'wlth Soc; *Style* - Rennie Bere Esq, CMG; West Cottage, Bude, N Cornwall (☎ 2082)

BERENDT, Lady Frances Virginia Susan; *née* Ryder; da of 6 Earl of Harrowby; *b* 1926; *Educ* St Hugh's Oxford; *m* 1949, Frank Ernest Berendt; 1 s, 1 da; *Style* - Lady Frances Berendt; 34 The Marloes, Boundary rd, NW8

BERESFORD, Lady Alice Rose de la Poer; da of 8 Marquess of Waterford; *b* 1970; *Style* - Lady Alice Beresford

BERESFORD, Lord Charles Richard de la Poer; 2 s of 8 Marquess of Waterford; *b* 18 Jan 1960; *Style* - Lord Charles Beresford

BERESFORD, Lord James Patrick de la Poer; 3 s of 8 Marquess of Waterford; *b* 10 Dec 1965; *Style* - Lord James Beresford

BERESFORD, Lord Patrick Tristram de la Poer; s of 7 Marquess of Waterford (d 1934); *b* 16 June 1934; *Educ* Eton, Sandhurst; *m* 1964, Mrs Julia Carey (m dis 1971), da of Col Thomas Cromwell Williamson, DSO; 1 s, 1 da; *Career* bloodstock agent, formerly Capt RHG; *Clubs* White's; *Style* - Lord Patrick Beresford; Fairview Cottage, Wicks Green, Binfield, Berks (☎ Bracknell 20562)

BERESFORD-PEIRSE, Sir Henry Grant de la Poer; 6 Bt (UK 1814), of Bagnall, Waterford; s of Sir Henry Beresford-Peirse, 5 Bt, CB (d 1972); *b* 7 Feb 1933; *Educ* Eton, Guelph Coll Toronto U; *m* 1966, Jadranka, da of Ivan Njerš, of Zagreb; 2 s; *Heir* s, Henry Beresford-Peirse; *Career* Scots Gds reservist; banker (European rep Fiduciary Co of New York); *Recreations* tennis, golf, country homes in Yorkshire & Portugal; *Style* - Sir Henry Beresford-Peirse Bt; Bedall Manor, Bedale, N Yorks (☎ 0677 22811); 34 Cadogan sq, SW1 (☎ 01 589 1134)

BERESFORD-PEIRSE, Henry Njerš de la Poer; s and h of Sir Henry Grant de la Poer Beresford-Peirse, 6 Bt; *b* 25 March 1969; *Style* - Henry Beresford-Peirse Esq; c/o Bedall Manor, Bedale, Yorks

BERESFORD-PEIRSE, Margaret, Lady - Margaret; da of Frank Morison Seafield Grant; *m* 1932, Sir Henry Campell de la Poer Beresford-Peirse, 5 Bt, CB (d 1972); *Style* - Margaret, Lady Beresford-Peirse; Bedall Manor, Bedale, Yorks

BERESFORD-STOOKE, Sir George; KCMG (1948, CMG 1945); s of Rev Charles Stooke, of Bath (d 1955); *b* 3 Jan 1897; *Educ* Fulneck Sch Leeds, King Edward's Sch Bath; *m* 1931, Creenagh, da of Sir Henry Richards, KBE, KC, of Durban, formerly Ch Just Allahabad; 1 s, 1 da; *Career* Gov Sierra Leone 1948-53, Crown Agent 1953-55, Gentleman Usher of the Blue Rod 1959-72 KStJ 1951; *Recreations* foreign travel, bird watching; *Style* - Sir George Beresford-Stooke, KCMG; Little Rydon, Hillfarrance, Taunton, Somerset (☎ Bradford-on-Tone 640)

BERESFORD-WEST, Michael Charles; QC (1975); s of Arthur Charles West; *b* 3 June 1928; *Educ* Portsmouth G S, BNC Oxford; *m* 1956, Patricia Eileen, nee Beresford; 2 s, 1 da; *Career* Serv Intelligence Middle East, barr 1952, Western Circuit 1953-65, South Eastern Circuit 1965, chm Independent Schs Tribunal 1974; *Recreations* tennis, music, swimming; *Style* - Michael Beresford-West Esq, QC; Chilterns, 4 Furze Hill, Purley, Surrey (☎ 01 660 3293); 9 King's Bench Walk, Temple, EC4

BERGER, Vice-Adm Sir Peter Egerton Capel; KCB (1979), MVO (1960), DSC (1949); s of Capel Colquhoun Berger (d 1941); *b* 11 Feb 1925; *Educ* Harrow; *m* 1956, June, da of Cdr F Pigou, RN (d 1979); 2 da; *Career* RN 1943; Ch of Staff to CIC Fleet 1976-78; Flag Offr Plymouth, Port Adm Devonport, Cdr Centl Sub Area E Atlantic, Cdr Plymouth Sub Area Channel, all 1979-81; *Recreations* reading history, shooting, fishing; *Style* - Vice-Adm Sir Peter Berger, KCB, MVO, DSC; Pincotts, Meadow Way, W Horsley, Surrey

BERGIN, Kenneth Glenny; s of Dr Frank Bergin, of Clifton; *b* 10 June 1911; *Educ* Clifton, Queens' Cambridge; *m* 1938, Joan, da of George Simmott, of Clifton; 2 s, 1 da; *Career* dir Medical Servs BOAC 1963-64, gp personnel dir Cunard 1969-71, FRSM, FRAeS, OStJ, MD; *Recreations* country pursuits; *Clubs* Athenaeum, Oxford & Cambridge, Boodle's, RAF; *Style* - Kenneth Bergin Esq; 99 Harley st, W1 (☎ 01 935 7501); The Mill House, Kintbury, Berks (☎ 292)

BERKELEY, Baroness (E 1421); Mary Lalle Foley Berkeley; da of Col Frank Wigram Foley, CBE, DSO (d 1949), and Eva Mary Fitz-Hardinge, Baroness Berkeley (d 1964, da of Maj-Gen Gustavus Milman and Louisa Mary, Baroness Berkeley, title confirmed by Roy Warrant 1893, she being da of Hon Craven Berkeley and gda of 5 Earl of Berkeley); abeyance of Barony terminated 1967; *b* 9 Oct 1905; *Heir* sis, Hon Mrs Gueterbock; *Career* assumed additional surname of Berkeley 1951; *Style* - The Rt Hon The Lady Berkeley; Pickade Cottage, Gt Kimble, Aylesbury, Bucks (☎ Princes Risborough 3051)

BERKELEY, Frederic George; s of Dr Augustus Frederic Millard Berkeley (d 1952); *b* 21 Dec 1919; *Educ* Aldenham Sch, Pembroke Cambridge; *m* 1964, Gillian Eugenie Louise, nee Willis; 1 s, 2 da; *Career* Maj WW II, slr, ptnr Lewis and Lewis 1951-70, v-chm and chm Legal Aid Area Ctee 1964-70, master of the

Supreme Ct 1971; *Recreations* reading, gardening, travel; *Style* - Frederic Berkeley Esq; Tyrells End Farm, Eversholt, Bletchley, Bucks (☎ Ridgmont 308)

BERKELEY, Sir Lennox Randal; CBE (1957); s of Capt Hastings Berkeley, RN (d 1934); *b* 12 May 1903; *Educ* Gresham's, Merton Oxford; *m* 1946, Freda, da of Isaac Bernstein (d 1926), of London; 3 s; *Career* composer, kt 1974, Pres Performing Rights Soc 1975-; *Recreations* reading; *Style* - Sir Lennox Berkeley, CBE; 8 Warwick av, W2 (☎ 01 262 3922)

BERKELEY, (Augustus Fitzhardinge) Maurice; CB (1975); s of Augustus Berkeley, of Kennington; *b* 26 Feb 1903; *Educ* Aldenham, Pembroke Cambridge; *m* 1931, Elaine, nee Simmonds; *Career* barr 1927, Ch Registrar High Court Bankruptcy 1966-75; *Recreations* watching cricket, travel, reading; *Clubs* Garrick, MCC; *Style* - Maurice Berkeley Esq, CB; 3 Dr Johnson's Bldgs, Temple, EC4 (☎ 01 353 2448); Freshwell Cottage, Little Sampford, Saffron Walden, Essex (☎ Gt Sampford 244)

BERKELEY, Robert John Grantley; TD, JP (Glos 1960); s of Capt Robert Berkeley (d 1969) and Hon Myrtle, da of 14 Baron Dormer; *b* 24 July 1931; *Educ* Oratory Sch, Magdalen Oxford; *m* 1967, Georgina, da of Maj Andrew Drummond Moray (d 1971), of Easter Ross, Comrie, Perthshire; 1 s, 1 da; *Career* High Sheriff Worcs 1967, Jt Master Berkeley Hunt 1960-, Maj Queen's Own Warwicks Yeomanry 1963; *Clubs* Cavalry & Guards; *Style* - Robert Berkeley Esq, TD, JP; Berkeley Castle, Glos (☎ Dursley 810202); Spetchley Park, nr Worcester (☎ Spetchley 224)

BERNARD, Sir Dallas Edmund; 2 Bt (UK 1954); s of Sir Dallas Gerald Mercer Bernard, 1 Bt (d 1975); *b* 14 Dec 1926; *Educ* Eton, CCC Oxford; *m* 1, 1959 (m dis 1978), Sheila Mary, da of Arthur Gordon Robey; 3 da (Juliet b 1961, Alicia b 1964, Sarah Jane b 1968); m 2, 1979, Mrs Monica J Montford; 1 da (b 19??, christened Olivia Louise 11 July 1981; godparents include Sir Robert Armstrong and Catherine, Lady Brougham and Vaux); *Heir* none; *Career* dir Morgan Grenfell and Co Ltd 1964-77, dir Italian International Bank Ltd 1978-; *Style* - Sir Dallas Bernard, Bt; 7 Cresswell gdns, SW5 (☎ 01 373 9412)

BERNARD, Jeffrey Joseph; s of Maj Oliver Bernard, OBE, MC, FRIBA (d 1939); *b* 27 May 1932; *Educ* Pangbourne; *m* 1978, Susan; 1 da (by previous mar); *Career* journalist (Spectator and Private Eye), columnist formerly with New Statesman, Daily Mirror, Pacemaker; feature writer Sunday Times Mag, reviewer Punch, racing columnist Harpers & Queen; *Recreations* cooking, music, racing, drinking with friends; *Clubs* Colony Room, Chelsea Arts, Gerry's; *Style* - Jeffrey Bernard Esq; Cranes Farm, E Garston, Newbury, Berks (☎ Gt Shefford 359)

BERNERS, Baroness (15 in line, E 1455); Vera Ruby Williams; da of Maj the Hon Rupert Tyrwhitt, 5 s of Emma Harriet, Baroness Berners (12 holder of title *de jure* and seventeenth in descent from Edward III; also eleventh in descent from the 2 Baron, who translated Froissart and who, if his anticipation of Lyly's Euphues is less than certain, may in some sense be said to have pre-empted Hemingway in describing bull fights from Spain); suc 1 cous once removed, 14 Baron Berners (the author, painter, producer of ballets and composer, whose dyed pigeons at Faringdon House were immortalised in Nancy Mitford's novels, where he features as Lord Merlin) 1950; *b* 25 Dec 1901; *m* 1927, Harold Williams, JP; 2 da; *Co-Heiresses* daughters, Hon Mrs (P V) Kirkham and Hon Mrs (R T) Pollock, *qqv*; *Style* - The Rt Hon The Lady Berners; Ashwellthorpe, Charlton lane, Cheltenham, Glos (☎ 519595)

BERNEY, Sir Julian Reedham Stuart; 11 Bt (E 1620), of Parkehall in Redham, Suffolk; s of Lt John Berney (k on active serv Korea 1952) and Hon Jean (who m 2, P Jesson), da of 1 Visc Stuart of Findhorn, CH, MVO, MC, PC; suc gf 1975; *b* 26 Sept 1952; *Educ* Wellington, NE London Poly; *m* 1976, Sheena, da of Ralph Day, of Danbury Essex; 1 s; *Heir* s, William

Berney; *Career* chartered surveyor, ARICS; *Recreations* sailing, hill walking; *Clubs* Roy Ocean Racing; *Style* - Sir Julian Berney, Bt; 4 St John's av, Chelmsford, Essex (☎ 0245 84359)

BERNEY, William Reedham John; s and h of Sir Julian Berney, 11 Bt; *b* 29 June 1980

BERNSTEIN, Baron (Life Peer UK 1969); Sidney Lewis Bernstein; s of Alexander Bernstein, of Swansea; bro of late Cecil Bernstein (jt fndr with him of Granada) and unc of Alex Bernstein, chm Granada Gp; *b* 30 Jan 1899; *m* 1954, Sandra, da of Charles Malone, of Toronto; 1 s, 2 da; *Career* fndr Film Soc 1924, films advr Miny of Information 1940-45, ch Film Section AFHQ N Africa 1942-43, ch Film section SHAEF 1943-45, chm Granada Gp Ltd 1934-79, pres 1979-, formerly chm Granada TV Ltd, chm Granada Theatres Ltd, Granada Publishing Ltd, Granada TV Rental Ltd; *Style* - The Rt Hon The Lord Bernstein; Coppings Farm, Leigh, Kent; 36 Golden sq, W1 (☎ 01 734 8080)

BERNSTEIN, Alexander; s of Cecil Bernstein, of Grosvenor Sq London W; *b* 15 March 1936; *Educ* Stowe, St John's Cambridge; *m* 1962, Vanessa, da of Alwyn Mills; 1 s, 1 da; *Career* chm Granada Gp 1979-; dir Granada TV Rental 1964-, Granada TV Ltd 1970- and other Granada subsids; Tstee Civic Tst for NW; memb Court of Salford U; dir Roy Exchange Theatre; *Recreations* modern art, skiing; *Style* - Alexander Bernstein Esq; 22 Kingston House, Prince's Gate, SW7

BERRIDGE, Donald Roy; CBE (1980); s of Alfred Berridge (d 1966), of Peterborough; *b* 24 March 1922; *Educ* King's Sch Peterborough; *m* 1945, Marie, da of Ernest Kinder (d 1958), of Leicester; 1 da; *Career* chm SSEB 1977-; *Style* - Donald Berridge Esq, CBE; Whinfell, Broom rd, Newton Mearns, Glasgow G77 5DN (☎ 041 639 1091)

BERRIMAN, David; s of the late Algernon Edward Berriman, OBE; *b* 20 May 1928; *Educ* Winchester, New Coll Oxford; *m* 1, 1954, Margaret Lloyd, nee Owen (m dis 1970), 2 s; m 2, 1976, Shirley Elizabeth, nee Wright; *Career* Citibank 1952-56, Ford Motor Co UK 1956-60, fin planning manager AEI Hotpoint 1960-63, PMD course Harvard Business School 1961, set up United Leasing Corpn UK 1963, dir Morgan Grenfell, later of Morgan Grenfell Holdings, joined Guiness Mahon as md 1973, md Guiness Peat Overseas Ltd 1975-77, returned Guiness Mahon in 1977, non exec dir Cable & Wireless Ltd and The National Film School, dep chm Bunzl Textile Holdings Ltd, chm of Governers MacIntyre Schools Ltd, memb Interim Action Ctee on Future of British Film Industry, memb Government Ctee on Harland and Wolff Diversification, Fellow of Inst of Bankers, Companion of British Inst of Management; *Books* XYZ Case *Recreations* golf, tennis; *Clubs* RAC; *Style* - David Berriman Esq

BERRY, Hon Anthony George; JP (Cardiff 1961), MP (C) Enfield, Southgate 1974-; s of 1 Viscount Kemsley, GBE (d 1968); *b* 12 Feb 1925; *Educ* Eton, Ch Ch Oxford; *m* 1, 1954 (m dis 1966), Hon Mary Cynthia Burke Roche, da of 4 Baron Fermoy (d 1955); 1 s, 3 da; m 2, 1966, Sarah Anne, da of Raymond Clifford-Turner; 1 s, 1 da; *Career* Lt Welsh Gds 1943-47, dir Kemsley Newspapers 1954-59, md Western Mail and Echo Ltd 1955-59, dep chm Leopold Joseph & Sons Ltd 1962-79, MP (C) Southgate 1964-74, PPS to Rt Hon Peter Walker, Sec of State for the Environment 1970-72, for Trade and Industry 1972-74, Opposition Whip 1975-79; High Sheriff Glamorgan 1962; Vice-Chamberlain HM Household 1979; CStJ; *Clubs* Portland, White's, Cardiff and County (Cardiff); *Style* - The Hon Anthony Berry, JP, MP; 1 Graham Terrace, SW1 (☎ 01 235 3801)

BERRY, Hon Adrian Michael; s of Baron Hartwell, MBE, TD (Life Peer); *b* 15 June 1937; *Educ* Eton and Ch Ch Oxford; *m* 1967, Marina Beatrice, da of Cyrus Sulzberger, of Paris; 1 s, 1 da; *Style* - The Hon Adrian Berry; 11 Cottesmore gdns, W8

BERRY, Hon Mrs - Hon Bride Faith Louisa; *née* Fremantle; da of 3 Baron Cottesloe, CB, VD, TD (d 1956); *b* 1 July 1910; *Educ* PNEU Sch Burgess Hill,

Girton Cambridge; *m* 1936, John Berry, CBE, DL, *qv*; *Style* - The Hon Mrs Berry; Tayfield, Newport-on-Tay, Fife (☎ 08264 3118)

BERRY, Hon Denis Gomer; TD, DL (Hants); s of 1 Viscount Kemsley, GBE (d 1968), and hp of bro, 2 Viscount; *b* 11 July 1911; *Educ* Marlborough; *m* 1, 1934 (m dis 1942), Rosemary Leonora, da of late Lionel de Rothschild; 2 da; m 2, 1947, Pamela (Grant), da of late Capt Lord Richard Wellesley (2 s of late 4 Duke of Wellington); 1 s, 1 da; *Career* Cllr Hants and of New Forest RDC 1968-73, pres Hants Fedn of Young Farmers' Clubs 1970, pres New Forest Assocn, formerly a dir of Kemsley Newspapers Ltd, Master of Coachmakers' and Coach Harness Makers' Co 1959-60, 1939-45 War as Capt RA and Maj Gren Gds; KStJ; *Clubs* White's, Pratt's, Roy Yacht Sqdn; *Style* - The Hon Denis Berry, TD, DL; Brockenhust Park, Hants SO4 7QP

BERRY, Hon Eleanor Agnes; da of Baron Hartwell, MBE, TD (Life Peer); *b* 1950; *Educ* Wycombe Abbey; *Style* - The Hon Eleanor Berry; 21 Rivermill Flats, 151 Grosvenor rd, SW1 (☎ 01 821 7993)

BERRY, John; CBE (1968), DL (Fife 1969); s of William Berry, OBE (d 1954), of Tayfield Fife; *b* 5 Aug 1907; *Educ* Eton, Trin Cambridge, St Andrews U; *m* 1936, Hon Bride, *qv* nee Fremantle, da of 3 Baron Cottesloe, CB, VD, TD (d 1956); 2 s, 1 da; *Career* advsr and consultant on environmental conservation and fisheries N of Scot Hydro-Board, S Scot Electricity Bd and other authorities in UK and abroad 1968-; *Recreations* natural history (especially wild geese), music; *Clubs* New (Edinburgh); *Style* - John Berry Esq, CBE, DL; Tayfield, Newport-on-Tay, Fife (☎ 0382 543118)

BERRY, Hon Julian; OBE (1959), JP (Hants 1966), DL (1975); s of 1 Visc Camrose (d 1954), of Hackwood Park Hants; *b* 14 May 1920; *Educ* Eton; *m* 1946, Janet, da of Maj J Leslie Rowan-Thomson; 1 s, 1 da; *Career* farmer, Steward of The Jockey Club 1970-72, Col Commanding Household Cavalry and Silver Stick in Waiting 1960-64; *Clubs* White's, Jockey, Roy Yacht Sqdn; *Style* - The Hon Julian Berry, OBE, JP, DL; Old Rectory, Tunworth, Basingstoke, Hants (☎ Long Sutton 436); Ardtalnaig, By Aberfeldy, Perthshire (☎ Killin 427)

BERRY, Michael Francis; s of Charles Berry, of Newnham Manor, Baldock (d 1946); *b* 17 Oct 1906; *Educ* Eton, Hertford Coll Oxford; *m* 1939, Prudence, da of Charles Gurney Atha, of Haverbrack House Westmorland (d 1943); 1 da; *Career* banker, dir Robert Fleming & Co Ltd 1937-76, dir Westminster Bank Ltd 1946-68, Nat West Bank 1968-76, a Crown Estate Cmmr 1956-65, High Sheriff Northants 1973; *Recreations* farming, hunting; *Clubs* Boodle's; *Style* - Michael Berry Esq; Benefield House, nr Peterborough (☎ Benefield 219)

BERRY, Hon (William) Neville; s of 1 Viscount Kemsley, GBE (d 1968); *b* 1914; *Educ* Harrow, Magdalen Oxford; *m* 1951, Christobel (Norrie), da of late John Wallis More-Molyneux; *Career* dir Kemsley Newspapers 1938-59 and London Assurance 1950-59, 1939-45 War as Capt Gren Gds; *Clubs* White's, Turf, Pratt's, Royal Yacht Sqdn, Travellers' (Paris) and The Brook (New York); *Style* - The Hon Neville Berry; Bermuda 49, Av Hector Otto, Monaco; Château St Georges, 06320, Cap d'Ail, France

BERRY, Hon Nicholas William; s of Baron Hartwell, MBE, TD (Life Peer); *b* 1942; *Educ* Eton and Ch Ch Oxford; *m* 1977, Evelyn, nee Prouvost; 1 s; *Style* - The Hon Nicholas Berry

BERRY, Peter Fremantle; s of John Berry, CBE, DL, PhD, FRSE, of Fifeshire; *b* 17 May 1944; *Educ* Eton, Lincoln Coll Oxford; *m* 1972, Paola, da of Giovanni Padovani (d 1951); 1 s, 2 da; *Career* dir Anglo-Indonesian Corpn, dir Walker Sons & Co Ltd, Sri Lanka, Walker Sons & Co (UK) Ltd, dir Mau Forest Hldgs Ltd, Central Province Ceylon Tea Co Ltd, Central Province Ceylon Tea Hldgs Ltd, and others; *Recreations* travel, wildlife, country pursuits; *Clubs* Gresham; *Style* - Peter Berry Esq; 58 Pyrland rd, N5

BERRY, William; WS; s of John Berry, CBE, DL, *qv* of Tayfield; *b* 26 Sept 1939; *Educ* Eton, St Andrews U, Edinburgh U; *m* 1973, Elizabeth, da of Sir Edward Warner, KCMG, OBE, of Bockley Glos; 2 s; *Career* dir- Scottish American Investment Co, Castle Street Nominees, Cockburn Conservation Tst, Dalscot Ltd, Edinburgh Festival Soc, Largie Estate Ltd, McNeill Pearson Ltd, New Town Concerts Soc, Scottish Life Assur, Scotworld Servs; memb Roy Co of Archers (Queen's Bodyguard for Scotland); *Recreations* music, shooting; *Clubs* New (Edinburgh); *Style* - William Berry Esq, WS; 27 Saxe Coburg Place, Edinburgh; Tayfield, Newport-on-Tay, Fife

BERRYMAN, Lady; Muriel Whipp; CBE; *m* 1925, Lt-Gen Sir Frank Berryman, KCVO, CB, CBE, DSO (d 1981); 1 s, 1 da; *Style* - Lady Berryman, CBE; 17 Wentworth st, Point Piper, Sydney, NSW 2027, Australia

BERTELSEN, Aage; s of Jens Bertelsen (d 1947), of Denmark; *b* 2 Sept 1921; *Educ* engineering sch Denmark; *m* 1958, Dorthe, da of August Hald, of Denmark (d 1960); 1 s, 1 da; *Career* md Celcon Ltd 1956-, chm 1979-; *Recreations* bridge, gardening; *Clubs* Danish, Norwegian; *Style* - Aage Bertelsen Esq; Chalford, Traps Hill, Loughton, Essex (☎ 01 508 1778)

BERTHON, Vice-Adm Sir Stephen Ferrier; KCB (1979); s of Rear-Adm Charles Berthon, CBE (d 1965), of Deddington Oxon; *b* 24 Aug 1922; *Educ* RNC Dartmouth; *m* 1948, Elizabeth, da of Henry Leigh-Bennett; 2 s, 2 da; *Career* RN WW II; Dep Ch Def Staff (Operational Requirements) 1978-80, ret 1981; *Recreations* riding, hunting, gardening, walking; *Clubs* Army & Navy; *Style* - Vice-Adm Sir Stephen Berthon, KCB; Stert House, Devizes, Wilts (☎ 3713)

BERTIE, Hon Alexander Michael Richard; s of 14 Earl of Lindsey and 9 of Abingdon; hp of bro, Lord Norreys of Rycote; *b* 8 Apr 1970; *Style* - The Hon Alexander Bertie

BERTIE, Lady Jean; *nee* Crichton-Stuart; da of 4 Marquess of Bute, KT; *b* 1908; *m* 1928, Hon James Willoughby Bertie (d 1966); 2 s; *Style* - Lady Jean Bertie; Casa De Piro, Attard, Malta, GC

BERTIE, Hon Mrs Arthur - Lillian Isabel; da of late Charles Cary-Elwes; *m* 1, Lt-Cdr Francis Crackanthorpe, RN (decd); m 2, 1949, as his 2 wife, Lt-Col Hon Arthur Michael Cosmo Bertie, DSO, MC, 2 s of 7 Earl of Abingdon, and who d 1957; *Style* - The Hon Mrs Arthur Bertie; 2 The Albany, Main st, St Julians, Malta

BERTLIN, Dennis Percy; s of Percy Bertlin (d 1953); *b* 18 May 1911; *Educ* Manchester G S, Liverpool U; *m* 1954, Patricia, da of Dr Ashley Daly (d 1977); 2 s, 3 da; *Career* sr ptnr Bertlin & Ptnrs 1960-; *Recreations* chess, yachting; *Clubs* Savile, Roy Thames Yacht, Roy Cruising, Roy Ocean Racing; *Style* - Dennis Bertlin Esq; Castle Place, Bletchingley, Surrey (☎ 0883 843186)

BERWICK, Lady Elizabeth; *née* Harris; da of 5 Earl of Malmesbury (d 1950); *b* 1906; *m* 1, 1926, Lt-Col Hon John Fremantle, s of 3 Baron Cottesloe (m dis 1944); m 2, 1944, Lt-Col Edward Berwick; 1 da ; *Style* - Lady Elizabeth Berwick; 17 Montpelier Villas, Brighton, Sussex

BERWICK, Lt-Col Edward Walter Hall; s of Walter Berwick (d 1929), of Toronto; *b* 2 Aug 1908; *Educ* Ridley Coll, St Catherine's Ontario, Staff Coll Camberley; *m* 1944, as her 2 husb, Lady Elizabeth, nee Harris, da of 5 Earl of Malmesbury; 1 da; *Career* 2 Lt Canadian Regular Army (Roy Canadian Dragoons) 1930, GSO (1) HQ Australian Mil Forces (Melbourne) 1949-51, Col (Ch of Staff) UN Mil Org India/Pakistan (Kashmir) 1957-58; *Clubs* Cavalry & Guards; *Style* - Lt-Col Edward Berwick; 17 Montpelier Villas, Brighton, Sussex (☎ 29645)

BESHOFF, Hon Mrs - Hon Pamela Jean; *née* Allanson-Winn; da of 7 Baron Headley; *b* 1928; *m* 1948, Ivan Beshoff; 1 s; *Style* - The Hon Mrs Beshoff

BESSBOROUGH, 10 Earl of (I 1739, UK 1937); Frederick Edward Neuflize Ponsonby; DL (W Sussex 1977); also Baron Bessborough (I 1721), Viscount

Duncannon (I 1723), Baron Ponsonby of Sysonby (GB 1749); s of 9 Earl, GCMG, PC (d 1956) and Roberte, JP (GCStJ), da of Baron Neuflize, of Paris; *b* 29 March 1913; *Educ* Eton, Trin Cambridge; *m* 1948, Mary, da of Charles A Munn, of New York and Paris; 1 da; *Heir* (to Irish Earldom and UK Barony only) cous, Arthur Ponsonby; *Career* First Sec Br Embassy Paris 1944-48 (formerly 2 Sec), merchant banker Robert Benson, Lonsdale & Co Ltd 1950-56, dir ATV Ltd 1955-63 and other cos; Parly Sec for Science 1963-64, Jt Parly Under-Sec of State for Education and Science 1964, dep chm Metrication Bd 1969-70, Min of State Miny of Tech 1970, MEP 1972-79, v-pres and dep leader Con Gp 1973-77; author of plays and other publications, pres Chichester Festival Theatre Trust; OStJ, FRGS, Chevalier of Legion of Honour; *Style* - The Rt Hon Earl of Bessborough DL; Stansted Park, Rowland's Castle, Hants (☎ Rowland's Castle 2223); 4 Westminster gdns, SW1 (☎ 01 828 5959)

BEST, Edward Wallace; CMG (1971), JP; s of Edward Best; *b* 11 Sept 1917; *Educ* Trinity G S and Wesley Coll, Melbourne; *m* 1940, Joan Ramsay; 3 da; *Career* former Lord Mayor of Melbourne, dep chm Melbourne and Metropolitan Board of Works 1975-; *Style* - Edward Best Esq CMG JP; Eildon Park, Kerrie, Via Romsey, Victoria, Australia (☎ 054 270230)

BEST, Henry Nicholas; s of Hon J W Best, OBE, VD (d 1960, s of 5 Baron Wynford) and Florence (da of Sir Elliott Lees, 1 Bt, DSO); *b* 3 May 1930; *Educ* Wellington; *m* 1963, Elizabeth, nee Druchenbrodt; 2 s, 1 da; *Career* MBIM; dir and gen man Anglo Blackwells Ltd, winner of Queen's Award for Export Achievement 1979; *Recreations* hill walking, gardening, reading, local affairs; *Style* - Henry Best Esq; Viewmount, Alkington rd, Whitchurch, Salop (☎ 0948 2312)

BEST, Hon John Philip Robert; s and h of 8 Baron Wynford, MBE; *b* 23 Nov 1950; *Educ* Radley, Keele U, Cirencester Agric Coll; *Style* - The Hon John Best; Wynford House, Maiden Newton, Dorset

BEST, John Robert Hall; s of Robert Dudley Best; *b* 11 Feb 1929; *Educ* Leighton Pk, Christ's Cambridge; *m* 1961, Avril; 2 s; *Career* md Best & Lloyd 1970-, chm 1975-; *Clubs* Savile, Thames Hare and Hounds; *Style* - John Best Esq; Edgbaston, Birmingham B 15

BEST, Keith Lander; MP (C) Anglesey 1979-; s of Peter Edwin Best, of Hurstpierpoint; *b* 10 June 1949; *Educ* Brighton Coll, Keble Oxford; *Career* Capt RA (TA), barr 1971; *Recreations* walking, photography; *Style* - Keith Best Esq, MP; 7 Alderley ter, Holyhead, Anglesey (☎ 2972)

BEST, Hon Patrick George Matthew; s of 7 Baron Wynford (d 1943); *b* 5 Oct 1923; *Educ* Wellington; *m* 1947, Heather Elizabeth, da of Hamilton Gardner, of London and Assam; 4 s (1 decd); 1 da; *Career* Lt RNVR; chm Wiggins Teape Gp 1979-; FRSA; dir BAT Industs 1979-, BAT US Inc 1980-; Court Memb Ironmongers Co; *Recreations* skiing, shooting, spectator sports, theatre/arts, golf, squash; *Clubs* Boodle's; *Style* - The Hon Patrick Best; Monk's House, Durford Wood, Petersfield, Hants (☎ Liss 3176)

BEST, Rear-Adm Thomas William; CB (Mil 1966), DL (Dorset 1977); s of James Best, CBE (d 1960); *b* 1 Sept 1915; *Educ* RNCs Dartmouth and Greenwich; *m* 1943, Brenda, nee Hellaby; 2 s, 1 da; *Career* Flag Offr Gibraltar 1964-66, ret 1967, chm Dorset Branch NFU 1976; Dir Norton Cider Growers' Assoc 1978-; *Recreations* beekeeping, fruit growing, forestry; *Clubs* Naval & Military; *Style* - Rear-Adm Thomas Best, CB, DL; Hincknowle, Melplash, Bridport (☎ Netherbury 221)

BEST-SHAW, Sir John James Kenward; 9 Bt (E 1665), of Eltham, Kent; s of Rev Sir Charles Shaw, 8 Bt (d 1922), and Elizabeth, da of James Whatman Bosanquet, JP, by his w Emily, nee Best; assumed by Roy Licence for himself and his issue additional name and arms of Best 1956; *b* 11 June 1895; *Educ* Cheam Sch, RNCs Dartmouth and Osborne; *m* 1921, Elizabeth, da of Sir Robert Hughes, 12 Bt; 3 s, 4 da; *Heir* s, John

Best-Shaw; *Career* a Lay Guardian of The Sanctuary of Our Lady of Walsingham 1931-78, High Sheriff Kent 1961, OStJ; *Clubs* Naval & Military; *Style* - Sir John Best-Shaw, Bt; Boxley Abbey, Sandling, Maidstone, Kent (☎ 52910)

BEST-SHAW, John Michael Robert; s and h of Cdr Sir John Best-Shaw, 9 Bt, RN; *b* 28 Sept 1924; *Educ* Lancing, Hertford Coll Oxford, London U; *m* 1960, Jane, da of Alexander Guthrie; 2 s, 1 da (& 1 child decd); *Career* late Capt Queen's Own Roy W Kent Regt, served WW II NW Europe; with Fedn Malaya Police 1950-58, church work 1959-71, teaching 1972-; *Recreations* gardening, wine & beer making; *Clubs* Roy C'wlth Soc; *Style* - John Best-Shaw Esq; The Stone House, Boxley, Maidstone, Kent (☎ 57524)

BESWICK, Baron (Life Peer UK 1964); Frank Beswick; PC (1968), JP (Co of London 1963); s of Jesse Beswick, of Hucknall, Notts; *b* 1912; *m* 1936, Dora, da of Edward Plumb, of Kettering; 1 s, 1 da; *Career* Flight-Lt RAF 1942, Actg Capt BOAC 1945, MP (L) Middx Uxbridge Div 1945-59; a Lord in Waiting 1964-65, Parly Under-Sec of State Commonwealth Affairs and Colonies 1965-67, Capt Hon Corps of Gentlemen-at-Arms and Govt Ch Whip House of Lords 1967-70, Oppn Ch Whip 1970-74, Min of State Dept of Industry and Dep Leader House of Lords 1974-76, special advr to chm of BAC 1970-74, former pres Br Air Line Pilots Assoc; *Style* - The Rt Hon The Lord Beswick, PC, JP; 27 Margin dve, SW19 (☎ 01 946 2088); House of Lords, SW1

BESWICK, Hon Frank Jesse; s of Baron Beswick, PC (Life Peer); *b* 12 May 1949; *Educ* Latymer Upper Sch; *Style* - The Hon Frank Beswick; 28 Skeena Hill, SW18

BETHELL, 4 Baron (UK 1922); Sir Nicholas William Bethell; 4 Bt (UK 1911), MEP (C) London NW 1979-; s of Hon William Gladstone Bethell (d 1964), 3 s of 1 Baron Bethell; suc cous 1967; *b* 19 Feb 1938; *Educ* Harrow, Pembroke Cambridge; *m* 1964, Cecilia (m dis 1961, she d 1977), da of Prof Alexander Honeyman; 2 s; *Heir* s, Hon James Bethell; *Career* sub-ed TLS 1962-64; script ed BBC Radio Drama 1964-67; nominated MEP 1975-79, 1980 Jewish Chronicle HH Wingate Award (Non-Fiction) *The Palestine Triangle*; *Recreations* poker, cricket; *Clubs* Pratt's, Garrick, Carlton, MCC; *Style* - The Rt Hon The Lord Bethell, MEP; 73 Sussex sq, W2 (☎ 01 402 6877)

r ø1**BETHELL, Lady Jane**; *née* Pleydell-Bouverie; da of 7 Earl of Radnor (d 1968); *b* 1923; *m* 1945, Richard Bethell, JP; 2 s, 2 da; *Style* - Lady Jane Bethell; Rise Park, Hull (☎ Skirlaugh 241)

BETHELL, Hon James David William; s of 5 Baron Westbury, MC; *b* 22 Feb 1952; *Educ* Harrow; *m* 1974, Emma, da of Malise Nicolson, of Frog Hall, Tilston, Malpas, Cheshire; 2 da; *Career* racehorse trainer; *Recreations* shooting; *Style* - The Hon James Bethell; Manor Farm House, Whitsbury, Fordingbridge, Hants (☎ Rockbourne 220)

BETHELL, Hon James Nicholas; s and h of 4 Baron Bethell; *b* 1 Oct 1967; *Style* - The Hon James Bethell

BETHELL, Richard Anthony; s of Capt William Adrian Vincent Bethell (d 1941) and Cicely, da of Sir John Richard Geers Cotterell, 4 Bt, by his w, Lady Evelyn Gordon-Lennox (da of 7 Duke of Richmond, KG); *b* 22 March 1922; *Educ* Eton; *m* 1945, Lady Jane, nee Pleydell-Bouverie, da of 7 Earl of Radnor, KG, KCVO (d 1968); 2 s, 2 da; *Career* landowner and farmer; *Recreations* racing, shooting, hunting; *Style* - Richard Bethell Esq; Rise Park, Hull, Humberside (☎ Skirlaugh 62241)

BETHELL, Hon Richard Nicholas; MBE (1979); s and h of 5 Baron Westbury, MC; *b* 29 May 1950; *Educ* Harrow; *m* 1975, Caroline, da of Richard Palmer, JP, of Swallowfield, Berks; 1 da; *Career* Maj Scots Gds; Esq Order of St John; *Style* - The Hon Richard Bethell MBE; Barton Cottage, Malton, Yorks

BETHUNE, Hon Sir (Walter) Angus; s of Frank Bethune; *b* 10 Sept 1908; *m* 1936, Alexandra, nee Pritchard; 1 s, 1 da; *Career* Premier of Tasmania 1969-72; pastoralist; *Style* - The Hon Sir Angus Bethune; Dunrobin, Ouse, Tasmania 7461

BETHUNE, Sir Alexander Maitland Sharp; 10 Bt (NS 1683); s of Sir Alexander Sharp Bethune, 9 Bt, JP (d 1917), by Elisabeth, da of Frederick Maitland-Heriot; *b* 28 March 1909; *Educ* Eton, Magdalene Cambridge; *m* 1955, (Ruth) Mary, da of James Hayes; 1 da; *Heir* none; *Career* managing director Contoura Photocopying Ltd, Copytec Servs; *Recreations* golf, nature; *Style* - Sir Alexander Bethune, Bt; 21 Victoria Grove, W8 (☎ 01 584 0983)

BETHWAITE, Cyril Forrester; s of Albert Henry Bethwaite (d 1954); *b* 23 July 1920; *Educ* Leeds U; *m* 1944, Hylda Mollie, da of Leslie Bexon (d 1946); 2 s; *Career* divnl dir Br Aerospace (Aircraft Gp) 1978-, exec dir Hawker Siddeley Aviation 1970-78; *Recreations* music; *Style* - Cyril Bethwaite Esq; 5 Dale av, Gustard Wood, Wheathampstead, Herts (☎ Kimpton 832553)

BETJEMAN, Sir John; CBE (1960); s of late E E Betjeman; *b* 1906; *Educ* Marlborough, Magdalen Oxford; *m* 1933, Hon Penelope, *qv*; 1 s, 1 da; *Career* gov Pusey House Oxford, memb Historic Monuments Cmmn, Poet Laureate 1972-, Queen's Gold Medal for Poetry 1960, kt 1969; *Style* - Sir John Betjeman, CBE; c/o John Murray Ltd, 50 Albemarle st, W1 (☎ 01 493 4361)

BETJEMAN, Hon Lady - Hon Penelope Valentine; da of 1 Baron Chetwode, GCB, OM, GCSI, KCMG, DSO (d 1950); *b* 1910; *m* 1933, Sir John Betjeman, CBE *qv*; 1 s, 1 da; *Style* - The Hon Lady Betjeman

BETTINSON, John Richard; s of Richard Bettinson, of Edgbaston; *b* 27 June 1932; *Educ* Haileybury, Birmingham U; *m* Margaret, da of Richard Good; 1 s, 1 da; *Career* slr 1955; sr ptnr Bettinsons; chm Birmingham AHA; chm Concentric Ltd 1981-; dir Birmingham Specialities Ltd, N T Frost Ltd, Newhall Business Dvpts, Samuel Groves & Co; *Recreations* theatre, reading, woodwork; *Clubs* Cavalry & Guards; *Style* - John Bettinson Esq; Storey House, 4 Pritchatts rd, Edgbaston, Birmingham B15 2QT (☎ 021 454 4298)

BEVAN, Andrew David Gilroy; MP (C) Yardley (Birmingham) 1979-; s of Rev Thomas Bevan; *b* 10 Apr 1928; *Educ* King Edward VI Sch, Birmingham; *m* 1967, Cynthia Boulstridge; 1 s, 3 da; *Career* principal, A Gilroy Bevan, Incorporated Valuers and Surveyors; *Style* - Andrew Bevan Esq MP; The Cottage, 12 Wentworth rd, Four Oaks Park, Sutton Coldfield, W Midlands (☎ 021 308 3292

BEVAN, Rear-Adm Christopher Martin; CB (1978); s of Humphrey Bevan; *b* 22 Jan 1923; *Educ* Stowe; Victoria U, Wellington, NZ; *m* 1948, Patricia Bedford; 1 s, 3 da; *Career* RN 1942, ADC to HM The Queen 1976, Flag Offr Medway and Port Adm Chatham 1976-78, Under Treasurer Gray's Inn 1980-; *Style* - Rear-Adm Christopher Bevan, CB; 18 Upper Cheyne Row, SW3

BEVAN, Cecil Wilfrid Luscombe; CBE (1965); s of Benjamin Bevan; *b* 2 Apr 1920; *Educ* University Colleges of Wales and London; *m* 1944, Elizabeth Bondfield; 4 s; *Career* former prof of Chemistry U of Ibadan, former dep v-chllr and v-chllr U of Wales, principal University Coll of Cardiff 1966; *Style* - Cecil Bevan Esq CBE; University College of Cardiff, Cathays Park, Cardiff

BEVAN, Dr Edward Vaughan; TD (1946), DL (Cambs 1969); s of Prof Penry Vaughan Bevan; *b* 3 Nov 1907; *Educ* Bedford Sch, Trin Cambridge, St Mary's Hosp London; *m* 1937, Joan, da of Reginald Goddard (d 1946), of Chessington; 2 s, 1 da; *Career* formerly Lt-

Col RAMC, doctor; *Recreations* dining, philately; *Clubs* Pitt, Hawks, First & Third Trin Boat (Hon Tres), Cambridge U Boat (Hon Tres), Rob Roy Boat, Leander; *Style* - Dr Edward Bevan, TD, DL; Storey's End, 76 Storey's Way, Cambridge (☎ 50410)

BEVAN, Hon Mrs - Hon Hilary Evelyn Spicer; *née* Pakington; da of 5 Baron Hampton, OBE; *b* 1914; *m* 1938, David John Vaughan Bevan, TD; 3 s, 2 da; *Style* - The Hon Mrs Bevan; Kingsland, Bledington, Oxford

BEVAN, Timothy Hugh; s of late Hugh Bevan; *b* 24 May 1927; *Educ* Eton; *m* 1952, Pamela, nee Smith; 2 s, 2 da; *Career* chm Barclays Bank U,K Management from 1972; dep chm Barclays Bank Ltd from 1973 ; *Style* - Timothy Bevan Esq

BEVERIDGE, John Caldwell; QC (1979); s of Prof William Beveridge, of Geneva; *b* 26 Sept 1937; *Educ* privately and Jesus Cambridge; *m* 1973, Frances, da of Dr John Sutherland, of Edinburgh; *Career* barr, Crown Court Recorder 1975-, Freeman City of London 1965; Jt Master Westmeath Foxhounds; *Recreations* hunting, shooting; *Clubs* Turf, Brooks's, Travellers' (Paris); *Style* - John Beveridge Esq, QC; 28 Arlington House, St James's, SW1 (☎ 01 493 3945); Flat 2, 9th Floor, The Astor, Maquarie st, Sydney, Australia

BEVINS, Kenneth Milton; CBE (1973), TD (1951); s of John Bevins (d 1928), of Liverpool; *b* 2 Nov 1918; *Educ* Liverpool Collegiate Sch; *m* 1, 1940, Joan Harding (d 1969); 2 da; m 2, 1971, Diana, da of Godfrey Sellers, of Keighley; *Career* dir Roy Insurance 1970-, Br Aerospace 1980-; *Recreations* travel, gardening, reading, photography, handiwork; *Clubs* Army & Navy, Oriental; *Style* - Kenneth Bevins Esq, CBE, TD; Linton, The Drive, Sevenoaks, Kent (☎ 0732 56909)

BEVIR, Lady; Noel Sidney; da of Dominick Browne, of Mayo; *m* 1935, Sir Anthony Bevir, KCVO, CBE (d 1977); *Style* - Lady Bevir

BEWICKE-COPLEY, Hon Anne Elizabeth; da of 6 Baron Cromwell; *b* 1955; *Style* - The Hon Anne Bewicke-Copley

BEWICKE-COPLEY, Hon Davina Mary; da of 6 Baron Cromwell; *b* 1958; *Style* - The Hon Davina Bewicke-Copley

BEWICKE-COPLEY, Hon Godfrey John; s and h of 6 Baron Cromwell; *b* 4 March 1960; *Style* - The Hon Godfrey Bewicke-Copley

BEWICKE-COPLEY, Hon Thomas David; s of 6 Baron Cromwell; *b* 1964; *Style* - The Hon Thomas Bewicke-Copley

BEXON, Michael Laurence; MC (1945); s of MacAlister Bexon, CBE, of High Wycombe (d 1976); *b* 28 June 1923; *Educ* Denstone Coll, St John's Oxford; *m* 1949, Joan, da of Joseph Austin (d 1938), of Wadhurst; 2 s; *Career* dir Dunlop Hldgs (formerly Dunlop Rubber) 1967-; *Style* - Michael Bexon Esq, MC; 14a Ashley gdns, SW1 (☎ 01 834 7362)

BEYFUS, Drusilla Norman; da of late Norman Beyfus; *Educ* Royal Naval Sch, Channing Sch; *m* 1956, Milton Shulman; 1 s, 2 da; *Career* assoc ed British Vogue Magazine from 1979, ed Brides Magazine 1971-79, assoc ed Queen Magazine 1958-63, Daily Telegraph Colour Supplement 1964-70, home ed The Observer 1963-64, contributor to The Sunday Times; *Style* - Miss Drusilla Beyfus; 51G Eaton square, SW1 (☎ 01 235 7162)

BIBBY, Derek James; MC (1945); s and h of Sir Harold Bibby, 1 Bt, DSO, DL; *b* 29 June 1922; *Educ* Rugby, Trin Oxford; *m* 1961, Christine, da of Rt Rev Frank Okell, Bp of Stockport (d 1950); 4 s, 1 da; *Career* chm Bibby Line Ltd 1969-; *Recreations* gardening, shooting; *Clubs* Roy C'wlth Soc; *Style* - Derek Bibby Esq, MC; Willaston Grange, Hadlow rd, Willaston, S Wirral (☎ 051 327 4913); 401 Norwich House, Water st, Liverpool L2 8UW (☎ 051 236 0492)

BIBBY, Maj Sir (Arthur) Harold; 1 Bt (UK 1959), DSO (1917), DL (Chester 1937); s of late Arthur Wilson Bibby, of Woolton, Liverpool; *b* 18 Feb 1889; *Educ*

Rugby; *m* 1920, Marjorie Guthrie, da of late Charles James Williamson, JP; 1 s, 3 da; *Heir* s, Derek James Bibby, MC; *Career* Maj late RA (TA); sr ptnr Bibby Bros & Co 1935-73, chm Bibby Line Ltd 1935-69, Hon Freeman of Liverpool, gov Rugby Sch; kt 1956; *Style* - Maj Sir Harold Bibby, Bt, DSO, DL; Tilstone Lodge, Tarporley, Cheshire

BIBBY, John Benjamin; JP (Liverpool 1975); s of J P Bibby; *b* 19 April 1929; *Educ* Oundle, St Catherine's Cambridge; *m* 1956, Susan Patterson; 2 s, 1 da; *Career* chm J Bibby and Sons Ltd 1970-78; *Style* - John Bibby Esq, JP; Kirby Mount, Warwick drive, West Kirby, Wirral, Merseyside (☎ 051 625 8071)

BIBICA ROSETTI, Princess Raoul; Dorothy; da of Henry Acton (ggs of Lt-Gen Joseph Acton, bro of Sir John Acton, 6 Bt, by his w, Eleanora Countess Berghe von Trips) and Elly, da of Prince Cleon Rize Rangabe, of Greece; *b* 20 April 1893; *m* 1921, Prince Raoul Bibica Rosetti (d 1967), sometime Greek Ambass to Canada and s of Prince Salvator Bibica Rosetti; 1 da- Princess Lobanov-Rostovsky, *qv*; *Style* - Princess Raoul Bibica Rosetti; 243 Goldstone Cres, Hove 4, Sussex

BICESTER, 3 Baron (UK 1938); Angus Edward Vivian Smith; s of late Lt-Col the Hon Stephen Edward Vivian Smith, 2 s of 1 Baron by Lady Sybil McDonnell (da of 6 Earl of Antrim); 4 cous once removed to Lord Carrington, the For Sec; suc unc 1968; *b* 20 Feb 1932; *Educ* Eton; *Heir* bro, Hugh Charles Vivian Smith; *Style* - The Rt Hon The Lord Bicester; House of Lords, SW1

BICKERTON, P W; *Career* dep chm Sime Darby (London); *Style* - P W Bickerton Esq; Sime Darby, Portland House, 18b Charles st, W1

BICKET, Henry Brussel; JP (1961), DL (Merseyside 1976); s of Alexander Bicket, of Birkenhead; *b* 1 June 1922; *Educ* Radley, BNC Oxford; *m* 1956, Katharine, da of Clarence Young, of Connecticut; 2 s, 2 da; *Career* Lt-Cdr RNVR; *Recreations* sailing; *Clubs* Roy Yacht Sqdn, Naval & Military; *Style* - Henry Bicket Esq, JP, DL; 21 Fulwood Pk, Liverpool; The Old Rectory, Rhoscolyn, Anglesey

BICKFORD SMITH, John Roger; TD (1950); s of late Leonard Bickford Smith; *b* 31 Oct 1915; *Educ* Eton and Hertford Oxford; *m* 1, 1939, Cecilia Heath (m dis); 2 s; m 2, 1972, Baronin Joaise Miranda et Omnes Sancti von Kirchberg-Hohenheim; *Career* Master of Supreme Court, Queen's Bench Division 1967-; *Style* - John Bickford Smith Esq TD; Royal Courts of Justice, Strand, WC2

BICKFORD-SMITH, Hon Mrs (Joan Angel Allsebrook); da (by 1 m) of late 1 Viscount Simon, GCSI, GCVO, OBE, PC, QC; *b* 1901; *m* 1924, Capt John Allan Bickford-Smith, RN (ret), who d 1970, 1 s, 2 da; *Style* - The Hon Mrs Bickford-Smith; Younghouse, Liss, Hants

BICKMORE, Laurence Hyde Neild; OBE (Mil 1945); s of Harry Bickmore, JP, of Edwardes Sq, W8; *b* 29 March 1905; *Educ* City of London Sch; *m* 1, 1932, Audrey (m dis 1937), da of Vivian Dampier-Palmer, OBE, JP; m 2, 1941, Anne (m dis 1947), da of Vice-Adm Hon Rupert Drummond, CB, CVO (s of 16 Earl of Perth and 10 Viscount Strathallan, GCMG, CB, PC, by his w, Hon Angela, nee Constable-Maxwell, da of 11 Lord Herries of Terregles), and Lady Evelyn, nee Butler, da of 4 Marquess of Ormonde; 1 s; m 3, 1949, Elizabeth, da of Frederick Smith, of Calif; 1 s, 1 da; *Career* chm Hobbs Savill & Bradford Ltd Pension Consultants, ret 1970; *Recreations* golf, bridge; *Clubs* American, Roy St George's Golf (Sandwich); *Style* - Laurence Bickmore Esq, OBE; 6 Campden House Court, 42 Gloucester Walk, W8 (☎ 01 937 0701)

BIDDULPH, 4 Baron (UK 1903); Robert Michael Christian Biddulph; s of 3 Baron (d 1972) and Lady Amy Louise Agar, da of 4 Earl of Normanton; *b* 6 Jan 1931; *Educ* Canford, RMA Sandhurst; *m* 1958, Lady Mary Maitland, da of Viscount Maitland, s of 15 Earl of Lauderdale; 2 s, 1 da; *Heir* s, Hon Anthony Maitland Biddulph; *Career* late Lt 16/5 Queen's Roy Lancers; *Style* - The Rt Hon The Lord

Biddulph; Makerstoun, Kelso, Roxburghshire

BIDDULPH, Maj Anthony; TD; s of Hon Claude William Biddulph (d 1954, s of 1 Baron Biddulph); *b* 18 Aug 1910; *Educ* Eton, Ch Ch Oxford; *m* 1939, Mary Dearman, da of late Maj Sir John Birchall, MP; 2 s, 1 da; *Career* WW II 1 Roy Glos Hussars TA, High Sheriff Glos 1960; *Style* - Maj Anthony Biddulph, TD; Rodmarton Manor, Cirencester, Glos (☎ Rodmarton 219)

BIDDULPH, Amy, Lady - Lady Amy Louise Agar; da of 4 Earl of Normanton; *b* 1905; *m* 1925, 3 Baron Biddulph (d 1972); 2 s, 2 da; *Style* - The Rt Hon Amy, Lady Biddulph; Under Down, Ledbury, Herefordshire, (☎ 2669)

BIDDULPH, Hon Edward Sidney; s of 3 Baron Biddulph; *b* 16 Nov 1934; *Educ* Eton; *Career* Lt RHG 1955, ret; *Recreations* hunting, shooting, gardening; *Clubs* White's; *Style* - The Hon Edward Biddulph; Under Down, Ledbury, Herefordshire (☎ 2669)

BIDDULPH, Hon Fiona Mary; da of 4 Baron Biddulph; *b* 1961; *Style* - The Hon Fiona Biddulph

BIDDULPH, Ian D'Olier; s and h of Sir Stuart Royden Biddulph, 10 Bt, *qv*; *b* 28 Feb 1940; *m* 1967, Margaret, da of late John Gablonski, of Oxley, Brisbane; 1 s, 2 da; *Style* - Ian Biddulph, Esq; 24 Currey st, Roma, Queensland, Australia

BIDDULPH, Hon Susan Louise; da of 3 Baron Biddulph (d 1972); *b* 1929; *Educ* Lawnside Sch Malvern; *Style* - The Hon Susan Biddulph; Under Down, Ledbury, Herefordshire

BIDDULPH, Sir Stuart Royden; 10 Bt (E 1664); s of Sir Francis Henry Biddulph, 9 Bt (d 1980); *b* 24 June 1908; *m* 1939 Muriel, nee Harkness; 1 s, 2 da; *Heir* s, Ian D'Olier Biddulph; *Style* - Sir Stuart Biddulph, Bt; 140 Galatea st, Charleville, Queensland 1470, Australia

BIDE, Sir Austin Ernest; s of Ernest Bide (d 1918); *b* 11 Sept 1915; *Educ* Acton County Sch, London U; *m* 1941, Irene, da of Ernest Ward (d 1953); 3 da; *Career* chm and ch exec Glaxo Hldgs 1973-; non-exec dep chm BL 1980-; chm CBI Res & Tech Cttee 1977, kt 1980; *Recreations* fishing, handicrafts; *Clubs* Hurlingham; *Style* - Sir Austin Bide; Clarges House, 6-12 Clarges st, W1 (☎ 01 493 4060)

BIDGOOD, John Claude; s of Edward Bidgood (d 1967); *b* 12 May 1914; *Educ* London Choir Sch, Woodhouse Tech Sch; *m* 1945, Sheila, da of Dr James Walker-Wood (d 1968); 1 s, 2 da; *Career* chm Anglo-Dominion Finance Co, A-D Construction, A-D Trading; dir- Bidgood Hldgs, Edward Bidgood & Co, Bidgood Larsson Ltd, Wright & Summerhill, R Horsfield & Co, Constructional Erection Ltd; MP (C) Bury and Radcliffe 1955-64; *Recreations* music, walking, flying; *Clubs* Naval & Military, City Livery, Leeds; *Style* - John Bidgood Esq; The Old Joinery, Walton, Wetherby, W Yorks (☎ 0937 844028)

BIDWELL, Hugh Charles Philip; s of Edward Bidwell; *b* 1 Nov 1934; *Educ* Stonyhurst; *m* 1962, Jenifer, nee Webb; 2 s, 1 da; *Career* chm Pearce Duff Holdings Ltd 1970-; *Recreations* golf, tennis, fishing; *Clubs* Boodle's, City of London, Roy St George's (Sandwich), MCC; *Style* - Hugh Bidwell Esq; Waterlane Farm, Bovingdon, Herts (☎ Hemel Hempstead 832179)

BIGGS, Sir Norman Parris; s of John Biggs; *b* 23 Dec 1907; *Educ* John Watson's Sch Edinburgh; *m* 1936, Peggy Stammwitz; 2 s, 1 da; *Career* dir Banco de Bilbão 1981-, dep chm Privatbanken Ltd 1980-; former dir Roy Bank Scotland, Gillett Bros Discount; chm Williams and Glyn's Bank Ltd 1972-76; kt 1977; *Style* - Sir Norman Biggs; Northbrooks, Danworth lane, Hurstpierpoint, Sussex (☎ 832022)

BIGGS-DAVISON, Sir John Alec; MP (C) Epping Forest 1974-; s of Maj John Biggs-Davison; *b* 7 June 1918; *Educ* Clifton, Magdalen Oxford; *m* 1948, Pamela, da of Ralph Hodder-Williams, MC; 2 s, 4 da; *Career* chm Con Parly NI Cttee (Oppn Front Bench Spokesman NI

1976-78), V-Chm Con Parly For & C'wlth Affrs Cttee, V-Chm Monday Club to 1981 (but remains memb); MP Chigwell 1955-74 (as Ind C 1957-58); late ICS, kt 1981; *Recreations* reading, walking, riding, tennis; *Clubs* Carlton, Special Forces'; *Style* - Sir John Biggs-Davison, MP; House of Commons, SW1

BIGHAM, Hon Andrew; s of 3 Viscount Mersey and Lady Nairne; *b* 26 June 1941; *Educ* Eton and Worcester Oxford; *Career* short service commission Irish Gds 1964-66; *Style* - The Hon Andrew Bigham; Bignor Park, Pulborough, Sussex (☎ Sutton (Sussex) 214)

BIGHAM, Hon David; s of 3 Viscount Mersey and Lady Nairne; *b* 14 Apr 1938; *Educ* Eton; *m* 1965, Anthea Rosemary, da of Leo Seymour, of Little Hadham Place, Much Hadham, Herts; 3 s, 1 da; *Style* - The Hon David Bigham; 24 Argyll rd, W8 (☎ 01 937 8944); Bignor Park, Pulborough, Sussex (☎ Sutton (Sussex) 214)

BIGHAM, Hon Lady - Edith Ellen; da of Lt-Col David Drysdale; *m* 1931, as his 2 wife, Hon Sir (Frank) Trevor Roger Bigham, KBE, CB (d 1954); *Style* - The Hon Lady Bigham; 188 Cranmer ct, SW3

BIGHAM, Hon Edward John Hallam; s and h of 4 Viscount Mersey; *b* 23 May 1966; *Style* - The Hon Edward Bigham

BIGHAM, Hon Ralph John; s of 2 Viscount Mersey, PC (d 1956); *b* 1913; *Educ* Eton; *m* 1954, Cicely Ruth, da of Mrs C E Johnson, of Douglas, IOM *Career* OStJ; *Style* - The Hon Ralph Bigham; 22 Eaton pla, SW1 (☎ 01 235 5508)

BIGLAND, Ernest Frank; MBE (1945), TD (1946); s of late Robert Taylor Bigland; *b* 7 Dec 1913 *Educ* St Edward's Sch, Oxford; *m* 1936, Mary, nee Dalzell; 2 s, 1 da; *Career* Lt Col RA, Europe, dep chm Guardian Royal Exchange Assurance Ltd 1978-, md Guardian Assurance Co Ltd 1965, v-chm 1975; *Recreations* shooting, fishing; *Clubs* Bath, Leander; *Style* - Ernest Bigland Esq, MBE, TD; Lucas Green Manor, West End, Woking, Surrey (☎ Brookwood 2234); Flat 11, 49 Rutland Gate, London SW7 (☎ 01 584 4565)

BILLAM, John Bertram Hardy; CB (1979), DFC (1944); s of late John Billam; *b* 29 Oct 1920; *Educ* Merchant Taylors'; King's London; *m* 1944, Mary, nee Armitage; 1 s, 1 da; *Career* barr 1947-, legal adviser and dep sec Dept of Employment; *Style* - John Billam Esq, CB, DFC; 32 St James's sq, SW1 (☎ 01 214 8734)

BILLINGHAM, Hon Mrs - Hon Brenda Dolores Bowden; da of Baron Aylestone, CBE, PC (Life Peer); *b* 1929; *m* 1951, John Leonard Billingham; 1 s, 1 da; *Style* - The Hon Mrs Billingham; 67 Kingsmead av, Worcester Park, Surrey

BILLINGTON, J; *Career* chm Edward Billington and Son; *Style* - J Billington Esq; Cunard Building, Liverpool, L3 1EL

BILLINGTON, Lady Rachel Mary; *née* Pakenham; da of 7 Earl of Longford, KG, PC, & sis of Lady Antonia Pinter (*see* Lady Antonia Fraser); *b* 11 May 1942; *Educ* London U; *m* 1967, Kevin, s of Richard Billington of Warrington, Lancs; 1 s, 1 da; *Style* - Lady Rachel Billington; 30 Addison ave, W11; The Court House, Poynington, nr Sherborne, Dorset

BILTON, Percy; s of Christopher Bilton and Hannah Dunlop; *b* 28 Nov 1896; *m*; 3 s, 2 da; *Career* chm Percy Bilton Ltd; *Style* - Percy Bilton Esq; Percy Bilton Ltd, Bilton Towers, W1

BILTON, Roland Fisher; TD; s of Cyril Bilton (d 1957), of Cottingham, E Yorks; *b* 9 July 1904; *Educ* Hymers Coll Hull; *m* 1928, Sybil, da of George Dixon, of Coniston, E Yorks (d 1950); 2 s; *Career* ret industrialist; farmer and co dir; *Clubs* Army & Navy; owner of race horse (hurdler) 'Arram Still Waters' (trainer M W Easterly); *Style* - Roland Bilton Esq, TD; 73 Cromwell rd, SW7; Rolston Hall, Hornsea, N Humberside

BIN YEOP, Tan Sri Abdul Azis Al-Haj; PSM (Malaysia), Hon GCVO (1972); *b* 5 Oct 1916; *Educ* King Edward VII Sch, Perak, Malaysia; *m* 1942, Puan Sri Hamidah Aziz; 6 s, 3 da; *Career* member Malaysian Parliament; partner in Aziz and Mazlan, solicitors

1973-; *Style* - Tan Sri Abdul Azis Al-Haj bin Yeop PSM GCVO, 17 Jalan Klyne, Kuala Lumpur, Malaysia

BINDMAN, Geoffrey Lionel; s of Dr Gerald Bindman (d 1974); *b* 3 January 1933; *Educ* Royal G S Newcastle-on-Tyne, Oriel Oxford; *m* 1961, Lynn Janice; 3 children; *Career* solicitor; legal adviser Commission for Racial Equality 1977-, chm Legal Action Gp 1976-78, councillor London Borough of Camden 1971-74, deputy leader London Borough of Camden 1973-74; *Recreations* book collecting, music, walking; *Clubs* Law Society, Royal Commonwealth Society; *Style* - Geoffrey Bindman Esq; 26 Hillway, Highgate, London N6 (☎ 348 0941)

BING, Hon Mrs (Christian Keith); da of 15 Viscount of Arbuthnott CB CBE DSO MC (d 1966); *b* 1933; *Educ* Edinburgh U; *m* 1954, Cdr Peter John Bing, OBE, RN; 3 s, 1 da; *Style* - The Hon Mrs Bing; The Cottage, Hillside, Montrose, Angus

BING, Peter John; OBE (1974); s of William Bing, of Crowborough; *b* 30 Aug 1925 *Educ* Felsted, RN Engrg Coll Plymouth; *m* 1954, Hon Christian, da of 15 Viscount of Arbuthnott, CB, CBE, DSO, MC; 3 s, 1 da; *Career* Cdr RN (ret 1974), man Offshore T'ning Centre Montrose Angus 1977-; CEng, FIMechE, FCIS, FBIM, FInstPet; *Recreations* restoring furniture and houses; *Clubs* Army & Navy; *Style* Cdr Peter Bing OBE RN; - The Cottage, Hillside, Montrose, Angus (☎ 0674 83 267)

BINGHAM, Lady Camilla; da of 7 Earl of Lucan; *b* 24 Oct 1970

BINGHAM, Lady Frances; da of 7 Earl of Lucan; *b* 30 June 1964; *Style* - Lady Frances Bingham

BINGHAM, Lord; George Charles Bingham; s and h of 7 Earl of Lucan; *b* 21 Sept 1967; *Style* - Lord Bingham

BINGHAM, Hon Hugh; s of 6 Earl of Lucan, MC (d 1964); *b* 1939; *Educ* Charterhouse and Hertford Oxford; *Style* - The Hon Hugh Bingham; 6 Gledhow gdns, SW5 (☎ 01 373 1855)

BINGHAM, Hon John Edward; TD; s of 5 Earl of Lucan, GCVO, KBE, CB, TD, PC (d 1949); *b* 1904; *Educ* Eton, Trin Cambridge; *m* 1942, Dorothea, da of late Rev John Kyrle Chatfield; 3 s; *Career* late Derbyshire Yeo and 2nd SAS regt; 1939-45 War in N Africa; *Clubs* Pratt's and ESU; *Style* - The Hon John Bingham; Hayes Farm, Peasmarsh, Rye, Sussex

BINGHAM, Stephen Denis; s of Commander Francis Bingham, RN (ret); *b* 28 June 1934; *Educ* Ampleforth, St Catherine's Cambridge; *m* 1962, Elizabeth, nee Paine; 3 s, 2 da; *Career* md Sodastream Ltd 1974-; *Style* - Stephen Bingham Esq; Geeston, Ketton, Stamford, Lincs (☎ 720135)

BINGHAM, Hon Simon John Ward; s and h of 7 Baron Clanmorris; *b* 25 Oct 1937; *Educ* Downside and Queens' Cambridge; *m* 1971, Gizella Maria, da of Sandor Zverkó, of Budapest; 1 da; *Career* CA; Capt 13/18 Royal Hussars (QMO) 1956-58; *Recreations* skiing, sailing; *Style* - The Hon Simon Bingham; 28 Norfolk Mansions, Prince of Wales dve, SW11 (☎ 01 622 1503)

BINGHAM, Hon Mr Justice; Hon Sir Thomas Henry Bingham; s of Dr Thomas Bingham; *b* 13 Oct 1933; *Educ* Sedbergh Sch, Balliol Oxford; *m* 1963, Elizabeth, da of Peter Loxley (d 1945); 2 s, 1 da; *Career* barr 1959, jr counsel Dept of Employment 1968-72, QC (1972), High Court Judge (Queen's Bench Div) 1980, kt 1980; Leader Investigation into Supply of Petroleum and Petroleum Products to Rhodesia 1977-78; *Clubs* Brooks's; *Style* - The Hon Mr Justice Bingham; 74 Lansdowne rd, W11 (☎ 01 727 8891)

BINKS, Edward; *Career* md Cawoods Holdings Ltd; *Style* - Edward Binks Esq; Cawoods Holdings Ltd, Southlands, Harrogate, Yorks

BINNEY, H(arry) A(ugustus) Roy; CB (1950); s of Harry Binney (d 1960) of Devon; *b* 18 May 1907; *Educ* Roy Dockland Sch Devonport, London U; *m* 1944, Barbara, da of Jeffrey Poole (d 1952);

3 s, 1 da (and 1 da decd); *Career* UN Advr on Standards Cyprus 1974-77, Dir-Gen Br Standards Inst 1950-72, Civ Servant at BOT 1929-50; *Recreations* gardening; *Style* - Roy Binney Esq, CB; Hambutts Orchard, Painswick, Glos

BINNEY, Hector Danneskiold Brudenell; s of Richard Christian Cecil James Binney (d 1935) and Lady Marjory Brudenell-Bruce (d 1923), da of 5 Marquess of Ailesbury; *b* 15 Dec 1919; *m* 1; 1 da; m 2; 1 da; *Style* - Hector Binney Esq; Pampisford Hall, Cambs

BINNEY, Marcus; s of late Lt-Col Francis Crofton Simms, MC, and Lady (Sonia) Binney,*qv*; *m* 1, 1966, Hon Sarah Anne Vanneck (m dis); m 2, 1981, Anne, da of Dr T H Hills, of Church Hill House, Merstham, Surrey; *Career* chm SAVE, architectural writer; *Style* - Marcus Binney Esq; 21 Cambridge Mansions, SW1

BINNEY, Lady - Sonia; da of late Paymaster Rear-Adm Sir William Marcus Charles Beresford-Whyte, KCB, CMG; *m* 1, Lt-Col F C Simms, MC (decd); m 2, 1955, as his 2 w, Cdr Sir (Frederick) George Binney, DSO, RN (d 1972); *Style* - Lady Binney; Domaine des Vaux, St Lawrence, Jersey, CI

BINNING, Lord; John George Baillie-Hamilton; s and h of 12 Earl of Haddington; *b* 21 Dec 1941; *Educ* Ampleforth; *m* 1975, Prudence Elizabeth, da of Andrew Rutherford Hales, of Bowerchalke, Wilts; *Style* - Lord Binning; Mellerstain, Gordon, Berwickshire; Tyninghame, Prestonkirk, E Lothian

BINNING, Lady Nora; da of 10 Earl Annesley; *b* 1950; *m* 1969, John Binning; 2 s, 2 da; *Style* - Lady Nora Binning; 6 Baron's Way, Egham, Surrey

BINNS, Prof Howard Reed; CMG (1958), OBE (1948); s of Cuthbert Binns; *b* 3 Aug 1909; *Educ* Bootham Sch, York; St John's Cambridge; *m* 1935, Katharine Vroom Lawson; 1 s, 1 da; *Career* MA, BSc, MRCVS; hon prof of Veterinary Science in U of E Africa; *Style* - Prof Howard Binns; San Diego, Estepona, Malaga, Spain

BINNS, J H; *Career* chm Armstrong Cork Co; *Style* - J H Binns Esq; Armstrong Cork Co, Armstrong House, Chequers sq, Uxbridge, Middx

BINNY, Brig Robert Angus Graham; CBE (1961, OBE 1946); s of Graham Binny (d 1929); *b* 26 Nov 1908; *Educ* Cheltenham and Trinity Hall Cambridge; *m* 1934, Joanna, da of Maj-Gen Sir Philip Grant, KCB, CMG (d 1943); 1 s, 3 da; *Style* - Brig Robert Binny CBE; Pitt Farmhouse, Skilgate, Taunton, Somerset (☎ Bampton 346)

BIOBAKU, Dr Saburi Oladeni; CMG (1961); s of late Chief S O Biobaku, Aré of Iddu, Abeokuta; *b* 16 June 1918; *Educ* Trinity Cambridge; *m* 1949, Muhabat Folasade, da of Alhaji L B Agusto; 1 s; *Career* research prof and dir Institute of African Studies, Ibadan U 1976-; *Style* - Dr Saburi Biobaku CMG; PO Box 7741, Lagos, Nigeria (☎ 31430)

BIRCH, Henry; MBE (1944), TD, JP (Chester 1955), DL (Cheshire 1966); s of Arthur Birch (d 1967) of Chester; *b* 7 March 1915; *Educ* Charterhouse, Oriel Oxford; *m* 1948, Helen Margaret, da of Capt Harvey Blease (ka 1915); 1 da; *Career* Lt-Col (Hon Col) TA; solicitor; *Style* - Henry Birch Esq, MBE, TD, JP, DL; Lion House, Tattenhall, Chester

BIRCH, Philip; *Career* chm and md Ward White Gp; FBIM; *Style* - Philip Birch Esq; Ward White Group, Midland rd, Higham Ferrers, Wellingborough, Northants

BIRCH, Reginald; s of Charles Birch; *b* 7 June 1914; *m* 1942, Dorothy; 3 s; *Career* chm Communist Party of Great Britain (Marxist-Leninist) 1968-; *Style* - Reginald Birch Esq; 29 Langley park, NW7 (☎ 01 959 7058)

BIRCH, Hon Mrs; Vera Benedicta; da of 5 Viscount Gage (d 1912); *b* 29 April 1899; *Educ* 1919, Francis Lyall Birch, CMG, OBE (d 1956); *Style* - The Hon Mrs Birch; 40 Pont st, SWI (☎ 01 584 0196)

BIRCH-REYNARDSON, William Robert Ashley; s of the late Lt Col Henry

Thomas Birch-Reynardson; *b* 7 Dec 1923; *Educ* Eton, Ch Ch Oxford; *m* 1950, Pamela Matnika, da of Lt Gen Sir Edward Thomas Humphreys, KCB, DSO; 1 s, 2 da; *Career* barrister, ptnr Thos R Miller & Son, Hon secretary British Maritime Law Assoc, V-Pres Comité Maritime Int, High Sheriff Oxfordshire 1974-75; *Recreations* hunting, shooting, gardening; *Clubs* Cavalry & Guards, City University, City of London, Pratt's; *Style* - William Birch-Reynardson Esq; Adwell House, Tetsworth, Oxford (☎ Tetsworth 204); 66 Gloucester Terrace, London W2 (☎ 01 262 2951)

BIRD, Lt-Gen Sir Clarence August; KCIE (1943), CB (1940), DSO (1917); s of Clarence Bird (d 1917); *b* 5 Feb 1885; *Educ* Cheltenham, RMA Woolwich, Staff Coll Quetta; *m* 1919, Dorothea, da of Maj William Nichols; 1 s (and 1 s d on act serv); *Career* late RE, Army Offr 1904-44, Regnl Food Offr India 1944-47 and Min of Food UK 1947-48; chm Rhodesia Railways 1948-53; *Recreations* music; *Style* - Lt-Gen Sir Clarence Bird, KCIE, CB, DSO, Polesden Lacey, Dorking, Surrey

BIRD, Hon Mrs (Catherine Mary); da of 15 Baron Dormer (d 1975); *b* 1950; *m* 1973, Christopher J G Bird; *Style* - The Hon Mrs Bird; 45 Addison av, W11

BIRD, John Andrew; s and h of Sir Richard Bird, 4 Bt; *b* 19 Jan 1964

BIRD, John Lovis; s of Sydney Bird; *b* 18 Jan 1929; *m* 1950, Mary Arnold; 1 s, 1 da; *Career* md Communications Systems and Services, Cable and Wireless Ltd 1977-; *Style* - John Bird Esq; 109 Woodland av, Watford, Herts

BIRD, Michael Gwynne; s of Edward Bird; *b* 16 Aug 1921; *Educ* Harrow, St Catharine's Cambridge; *m* 1944, Frances Townley; 1 s, 1 da; *Career* md Massey-Ferguson Holdings Ltd 1978-; *Style* - Michael Bird Esq; 12 Acacia gdns, NW8 (☎ 01 722 6069)

BIRD, Sir Richard Geoffrey Chapman; 4 Bt (UK 1922); s of Sir Donald Geoffrey Bird, 3 Bt (d 1963); *b* 3 Nov 1935; *Educ* Beaumont; *m* 1, 1957, Gillian Frances (d 1966), da of Bernard Haggett; 2 s, 4 da; *m* 2, 1968, Helen Patricia, da of Frank Beaumont, of Pontefract; *Heir* s, John Andrew Bird; *Style* - Sir Richard Bird, Bt; 12 Hampton lane, Solihull, W Midlands

BIRD, (George William) Terence; s of George Webber Bird and Jane, nee Houkin; *b* 27 July 1914; *Educ* Prescot G S and Imperial College of Science and Technology; *m* 1942, Hylda Owen Craven; 1 da (and 1 s, decd); *Career* dir Pilkington Brothers Ltd 1962-; *Style* - Terence Bird Esq; 21 Grange drive, Eccleston Hill, St Helens, Merseyside

BIRDWOOD, 3 Baron (UK 1938); Sir Mark William Ogilvie Birdwood; 3 Bt (UK 1919); s of 2 Baron, MVO (d 1962) and (Elizabeth) Vere Drummond, CVO, da of Lt-Col Sir George Drummond Ogilvie, KCIE, CSI; *b* 23 Nov 1938; *Educ* Radley, Trin Cambridge; *m* 1963, Judith Helen, da of Reginald Gordon Seymour Roberts; 1 da; *Career* V-Pres Inst of Sales & Mktng Management 1981-; late 2 Lt RHG; *Style* - The Rt Hon The Lord Birdwood; Russell House, Broadway, Worcs; 5 Holbein Mews, SW1

BIRDWOOD, Dowager Lady - Joan Pollock; da of Christopher Graham; *m* 1954, as his 2 w, 2 Baron Birdwood, MVO (d 1962); *Style* - The Rt Hon Dowager Lady Birdwood; 100 Philbeach gdns, SW5

BIRDWOOD, Lt-Col Richard Douglas Davis; MC (1942), JP (Devon 1964), DL (1964); s of Lt-Col Gordon Birdwood (d 1945); *b* 5 Jan 1905; *Educ* Clifton, Peterhouse Cambridge; *m* 1930, Phyllis, JP, da of Lt-Col Sir Thomas Bilbe-Robinson, GBE, KCMG (d 1939); 2 s, 1 da; *Career* High Sheriff Devon 1962, Mayor Bideford 1963, Pres Torrington Farmers' Hunt; *Recreations* fishing, golf; *Style* - Lt-Col Richard Birdwood, MC, JP, DL; Horwood House, Horwood, Bideford, Devon (☎ Newton Tracey 231)

BIRDWOOD, Hon Sophie Frederika; da of 3 Baron Birdwood; *b* 29 July 1964

BIRDWOOD, Vere, Baroness; (Elizabeth) Vere Drummond; CVO

(1972, MVO 1958); da of Lt-Col Sir George Drummond Ogilvie, KCIE, CSI (d 1966); *b* 7 Aug 1909; *m* 1931 (m dis 1954), 2 Baron Birdwood, MVO; 1 s, 1 da; *Career* administrator King Edward VII's Hosp for Officers 1950-72; ed Public Record Office 1972-; V-Chm Provident Assoc for Medical Care 1977- (bd memb 1958-); *Style* - Vere, Lady Birdwood, CVO; 95 Cadogan gdns, SW3

BIRK, Baroness (Life Peeress UK 1967); Alma Lillian Birk; JP (Highgate 1952); da of late Barnett Wilson; *Educ* S Hampstead H S, LSE; *m* 1939, Ellis Samuel Birk; 1 s, 1 da; *Career* assoc ed Nova 1965-69, a Baroness-in-Waiting to HM 1974, Under-sec of State DOE 1974-79, Min of State Privy Cncl Office 1979; contested (L) Ruislip-Northwood 1950 and Portsmouth West 1951 and 1955, memb Fabian Soc 1946-, memb London Pregnancy Advsy Service 1968-, former lectr and visitor Holloway Prison; *Style* - The Rt Hon The Lady Birk, JP; 13 Hanover ter, NW1

BIRK, Hon David Barry Wilson; s of Baroness Birk (Life Peeress) and Ellis Samuel Birk; *b* 25 June 1943; *Educ* Clifton Coll Bristol, Cambridge U, U of Hull, Univ Coll London and Australian National U Canberra; *m* 1969, Kate, da of Joseph Green, of London NW8; 2 da; *Style* - The Hon David Birk; The Oaks, 12 Planetree rd, Hale, Cheshire

BIRKBECK, Capt Henry; s of Maj Henry Birkbeck (d 1956), of Westacre High House; *b* 15 Nov 1915; *Educ* Eton, Magdalene Cambridge; *m* 1939, Nadine, da of Maj Francis Gore-Langton (d 1931), of Tingewick, Buckingham; 1 s, 4 da; *Career* Capt Gren Gds, landowner and farmer; *Recreations* hunting, shooting, fishing; *Clubs* Guards & Cavalry; *Style* - Capt Henry Birkbeck; Westacre High House, Castleacre, King's Lynn, Norfolk (☎ 076 05 203)

BIRKBECK, Hon Mrs - Hon Mary; *née* Crossley; JP; da of 2 Baron Somerleyton, MC (d 1959); *b* 1926; *m* 1950, Maj William Birkbeck, DL; 1 s, 3 da; *Style* - The Hon Mrs Birkbeck, JP; Bainton House, Stamford, Lincs, (☎ 227)

BIRKBECK, William; DL (Huntingdon and Peterborough 1965, subsequently Cambs); s of Maj Henry Birkbeck, of Westacre Norfolk (d 1956); *b* 13 April 1922; *Educ* Eton; *m* 1950, Hon Mary, JP, nee Crossley, da of 2 Baron Somerleyton, MC; 1 s, 3 da; *Career* Coldstream Gds 1941-57, Maj; banker- dir Barclays Bank 1970-, Bank of Scotland 1971-; *Recreations* country sports; *Clubs* Army & Navy; *Style* - Maj William Birkbeck, DL; Bainton House, Stamford, Lincs (☎ 740227)

BIRKENHEAD, 3 Earl of (UK 1922); Sir Frederick William Robin Smith; 3 Bt (UK 1918); also Baron Birkenhead (UK 1919), Viscount Birkenhead (UK 1921), Viscount Furneaux (UK 1922); s of 2 Earl, TD (d 1975, himself s of 1 Earl, better known as F E Smith, who as an orator rivalled Lloyd George and took the Commons by storm in his maiden speech, whose cross-examination as a lawyer was deadly whether appearing for Ethel Le Neve in the Crippen trial or against Lord Alfred Douglas in a case generated by the Wilde scandal, and who was Lord Chancellor and Sec of State for India) and Hon Sheila Berry, da of 1 Viscount Camrose; n of Lady Hartwell (formerly Lady Pamela Berry); *b* 17 April 1936; *Educ* Eton, Ch Ch Oxford; *Heir* none; *Career* memb Cncl of Roy Soc of Literature 1975-; author; *Style* - The Rt Hon The Earl of Birkenhead; The Cottage, Charlton, Banbury, Oxon (☎ King's Sutton 224); 48 Arthur rd, Wimbledon, SW19 (☎ 01 947 3983)

BIRKENHEAD, Countess of; Hon Sheila; *née* Berry; DL (Northants 1979); da of 1 Visc Camrose; *b* 3 May 1913; *m* 1935, 2 Earl of Birkenhead, TD; 1 s, 1 da; *Career* authoress, Lady-in-Waiting to HRH Princess Marina Duchess of Kent 1949-53, chm Northants Branch CPRE 1975-, V-Pres RSL 1975-, chm Keats-Shelley Assoc 1977-; *Recreations* reading, gardening, watching tennis; *Style* - The Rt Hon The Countess of Birkenhead DL; 24 Wilton st, SW1 (☎ 01 235 4111); Charlton, Banbury, Oxon (☎ 0295 811224)

BIRKETT, 2 Baron (UK 1958); Michael Birkett; s of 1 Baron Birkett (d

1962); *b* 22 Oct 1929; *Educ* Stowe, Trin Cambridge; *m* 1, 1960, Mrs Junia Crawford (d 1973), da of Harold Elliott; m 2, 1978, Gloria, da of Thomas Taylor, of Queens Gate SW; *Heir* none; *Career* Dir Recreation and Arts GLC 1979-, previously film producer and Dep Dir Nat Theatre; *Recreations* the arts; *Style* - The Rt Hon The Lord Birkett; House of Lords, SW1

BIRKETT, Brig John Brian; OBE (1958); s of John Guy Giberne Birkett, Cambrian House, Burgess Hill, Sussex (d 1967); *b* 2 Oct 1916; *Educ* Marlborough, RMA Woolwich; *m* 1941, Emily Margaret, nee Higginson; 1 s (and 1 s decd), 1 da; *Career* Served in Second World War in France, Belgium and Germany; Lt-Col 1958; Brigadier 1966; Brigadier General Staff Ministry of Defence 1966-69; Director of Trade Association 1969-, Master of Worshipful Co of Ironmongers 1974; *Recreations* active outdoor occupations; *Clubs* Army & Navy, Boodle's, Harlequin FC, MCC; *Style* - Brigadier John Birkett, OBE; West Tillingham House, Upper Hartfield, Sussex

BIRKIN, Sir Charles Lloyd; 5 Bt (UK 1905); s of late Col Charles Wilfrid Birkin, CMG, 4 s of 1 Bt; suc unc, Sir Alexander Russell Birkin, 4 Bt, 1942; *b* 24 Sept 1907; *Educ* Eton; *m* 1940, Janet, da of Peter Johnson; 1 s, 2 da; *Heir* s, John Christian William Birkin; *Style* - Sir Charles Birkin, Bt; West Kella, Sulby, Isle of Man

BIRKIN, John Christian William; s and h of Sir Charles Birkin, 5 Bt; *b* 1 July 1953; *Educ* Eton; *Style* - John Birkin Esq

BIRKIN, John Derek; *Career* chm and man dir Tunnel Holdings Ltd; *Style* - John Birkin Esq; 16 Old Queen st, SW1

BIRKIN, Air Cdre James Michael; CB (1956), DSO (1944), OBE (1951), DFC (1944), AFC (1942), AE (1947), DL (IOW 1978); s of Maj Harry Birkin, TD (d 1951), of Lincoln House, The Park, Nottingham; *b* 23 April 1912; *Educ* Harrow, Trin Cambridge; *m* 1, 1956, Antonia (m dis 1977), da of Lt-Col A Stanley Clarke; 1 s, 1 da; m 2, 1980, Susan, da of Edward Mitchell (d 1966), of Wellington Salop; *Career* dir Birkin & Co (lace mfrs), stockbroker to 1939, RAFVR 1938-47, RAuxAF 1947-63, High Sheriff IOW 1977; *Clubs* Roy Yacht Sqdn, MCC, Pathfinder; *Style* - Air Cdre James Birkin, CB, DSO, OBE, DFC, AFC, AE, DL; Little Burneston, Ashlake Copse, Fishbourn, Ryde, IOW (☎ 0983 882437)

BIRKIN, Jane Mallory; da of Lt-Cdr David Birkin, DSC (1 cous of Sir Charles Birkin, 5 Bt, and Winifred, Marquesa de Casa Maury, *qqv*), by Judy Campbell, the actress (da of John Gamble, OBE); *b* 14 Dec 1946; *m* 1965 (m dis 1969), John Barry, a composer; 1 da; *Career* actress; *Style* - Miss Jane Birkin

BIRKMYRE, Archibald; s and h of Sir Henry Birkmyre, 2 Bt; *b* 12 Feb 1923; *Educ* Radley; *m* 1953, Gillian, nee Downes; 1 s, 2 da; *Career* Capt RA Burma, memb Stock Exchange London; *Recreations* golf, shooting; *Clubs* Boodle's; *Style* - Archibald Birkmyre Esq; Hebron Cottage, W Ilsley, Newbury, Berks (☎ East Ilsley 210)

BIRKMYRE, Sir Henry; 2 Bt (UK 1921), of Dalmunzie, Co Perth; s of Sir Archibald Birkmyre, 1 Bt, CBE (d 1935); *b* 24 March 1898; *Educ* Wellington; *m* 1922, Doris, da of late Col Herbert Austen Smith, CIE (d 1949); 1 s, 1 da; *Heir* s, Archibald Birkmyre; *Career* former co dir; *Recreations* golf; *Clubs* Rye Golf, Cooden Beach Golf; *Style* - Sir Henry Birkmyre, Bt; Springbank, Cooden, Bexhill-on-Sea, Sussex (☎ 04243 2214)

BIRKS, Dr Jack; CBE (1975); s of Herbert Birks (d 1950); *b* 1 Jan 1920; *Educ* Ecclesfield G S, Leeds U; *m* 1948, Vere, da of Barnard Burrell-Davis (d 1960); 2 s, 2 da; *Career* engineer; md BP 1978-; memb SRC 1976-, Meteorological Ctee 1977-; *Recreations* tennis, cricket, golf; *Clubs* Athenaeum; *Style* - Dr Jack Birks, CBE; 1a Alwyne rd, Canonbury, London N1 (☎ 01 226 4905); Cliff House, Cromer rd, Trimingham, Norfolk (☎ Southrepps 338)

BIRLEY, Anthony Addison; CB (1979); s of Charles Birley; *b* 28 Nov 1920; *Educ* Winchester and Christ Church Oxford; *m* 1951, Jane Ruggles-Brisė; 2 da; *Career* Clerk of Public Bills, House of Commons 1973-; *Style* - Anthony Birley, Esq; Holtam House, Paxford, Chipping Campden, Gloucestershire (☎ Paxford (STD Code 038 678) 318)

BIRLEY, Mark Oswald; s of Sir Oswald Birley (d 1952); *Educ* Eton and Univ Coll Oxford; *m* m 1954 (m dis 1975), Lady Annabel Vane-Tempest-Stewart (now Goldsmith, *qv*), da of 8 Marquess of Londonderry; 2 s, 1 da; *Clubs* White's, Travellers' (Paris), Jockey (Paris), The Brook (New York); *Style* - Mark Birley Esq; 24 Pelham st, SW7 (☎ 01 589 3743)

BIRMINGHAM, 6 Bishop of (cr 1905), 1978-; Rt Rev Hugh William Montefiore; s of late Charles Sebag-Montefiore, OBE (whose f, Arthur, was paternally gs of Sarah, sis of Sir Moses Montefiore, 1 & last Bt, and a philanthropist); *b* 12 May 1920; *Educ* Rugby, St John's Cambridge (MA, BD); *m* 1945, Elisabeth Paton; 3 da; *Career* patron of 61 livings and part patron of others, and patron of the Archdeaconries of Birmingham and Aston, and of 24 Hon Canonries; ordained priest 1950, Bp Suffragan of Kingston-upon-Thames 1970-78; *Recreations* walking, water colour painting; *Clubs* Roy C'wlth Soc; *Style* - The Rt Rev the Lord Bishop of Birmingham; Bishop's Croft, Birmingham, West Midlands (☎ 021 427 2062)

BIRMINGHAM, 7 Archbishop of (RC, 1911 by Pius X's Letters Apostolic 'Si qua est') 1965-; Most Rev George Patrick Dwyer; s of John William Dwyer; *b* 25 Sept 1908; *Educ* St Bede's Coll Manchester, Eng Coll & Gregorian U Rome, Christ's Cambridge; *Career* Bp of Leeds 1957-65, ordained 1932; *Recreations* history; *Style* - Most Rev Archbishop Dwyer; Archbishop's House, St Chad's Queensway, Birmingham, West Midlands B4 6EX (☎ 021 445 1467)

BIRNIE, Lady Marguerite Kathleen; *née* Courtenay; da of Rev 16 Earl of Devon; *b* 15 Feb 1911; *m* 1933, Col Eugene St John Birnie, OBE (d 1976); 2 da (Mrs Jasper (Marguerite) Clutterbuck, of Mottisfont House, Romsey; Mrs Michael (Angela Patricia) Joly de Lotbinière, da-in-law of Sir Edmond, *qv*, Rougham House, Bury St Edmunds); *Style* - Lady Marguerite Birnie; The Cottage, Longparish, Hants (☎ 346)

BIRTWISTLE, Hon Mrs - Hon Diana; *née* Barnewall; da of 19 Baron Trimlestown; *b* 1929; *m* 1954, Anthony Gerard Astley Birtwistle; 4 da; *Style* - The Hon Mrs Birtwistle; Hatch Hill House, Hindhead, Surrey (☎ 388)

BIRTWISTLE, Harrison; *b* 1934; *Educ* Royal Manchester Coll of Music; RAM; *m* Sheila; 1 s; *Career* composer; associate dir National Theatre 1975-; *Style* - Harrison Birtwistle Esq; c/o Allied Artists Agency, 36 Beauchamp Place, SW3

BISHOP, David Broughton Gibson; s of Col A W G Bishop MC (d 1979); *b* 1 Feb 1933; *Educ* Wellington, Jesus Cambridge; *m* 1974, Judith, nee Brown; 1 s, 1 da; *Career* solicitor, sr ptnr Baileys Shaw & Gillett, chm Wyvern Property Unit Tst 1962, dir (now exec) California Companies Inc UK & Europe 1975; *Recreations* cricket, skiing, shooting, gardening, antiques; *Clubs* Bath, Sunningdale Golf; *Style* - David Bishop Esq; Rosemary, Phoenix Green, Hartley Wintney, Hants

BISHOP, Lady; Daphne Rhea; da of J W Gillert, of Adelaide, S Australia; *m* 1, W R Birks, of Echunga, S Australia (decd); m 2, 1968, late Sir William Poole Bishop, CMG; *Style* - Lady Bishop; 67 Tusmore av, Tusmore, S Australia

BISHOP, James Drew; s of Sir Patrick Bishop, MP (d 1972); *b* 18 June 1929; *Educ* Haileybury, CCC Cambridge; *m* 1959, Brenda, da of George Pearson; 2 s; *Career* foreign corresp The Times 1957-64, foreign news ed 1964-66, assist ed features 1966-70; ed Illustrated London News 1971-; memb Advsy Bd Annual Register

1970-; *Books* A Social History of Edwardian Britain (1977) *Recreations* reading, walking; *Clubs* Oxford & Cambridge, MCC; *Style* - James Bishop Esq; 11 Willow rd, NW3 (☎ 01 435 4403)

BISHOP, Michael David; *aet* 38 in 1981; joined BR Midland 1965 as station man Manchester; chm and md Br Midlands Airways Ltd; chm Br Midland (Acceptances) Ltd, Br Midland (Travel) Ltd, Glendon Brook Hldgs; *Style* - Michael Bishop Esq; c/o Br Midland Airways, E Midlands Airport, Castle Donington, Derby

BISHOPSTON, Baron (Life Peer UK 1981); Edward Stanley Bishop; PC (1977), JP (Notts 1973); s of Frank Bishop; *b* 3 Oct 1920; *Educ* Merchant Venturers' Tech Coll Bristol, Bristol U (extra-mural subjs); *m* 1945, Winifred, JP, da of Frank Bryant, of Bristol; 4 da; *Career* aeronautical designer to 1964; MP (L) Newark 1964-79, Assist Govt Whip 1965-66, UK Parly Del N Atlantic Assembly 1966-72, Min of State Ag & Fish 1974-79; Church Commissioner 1968-, memb Cncl Nat Tst 1980-; *Style* - The Rt Hon Lord Bishopston, PC, JP; 59 London rd, Newark-on-Trent, Notts (☎ 0636 702443)

BISS, Godfrey Charles d'Arcy; *b* 2 Sept 1909; *Educ* St Paul's Sch, Worcester Coll Oxford; *m* 1946, Margaret Ellis; 2 s; *Career* chm Siebe Gorman and Co Ltd, dir other cos; *Style* - Godfrey Biss Esq; Black House Farm, St Lawrence, nr Southminster, Essex (☎ Tillingham 361)

BISSETT, Thomas Melville; *Career* man dir FJC Lilley; chartered accountant; *Style* - Thomas Bissett Esq; 331 Charles st, Glasgow

BISSILL, Hon Mrs - Hon Charmiane Elizabeth Violet Cecilia; *née* Wilson; da of 3 Baron Nunburnholme; *b* 1930; *m* 1957, William Rippon Bissill; 2 s, 1 da; *Style* - The Hon Mrs Bissill; Cranmer House, Aslockton, Notts (☎ Whatton 226)

BJELKE-PETERSEN, Hon Johannes; s of late C G Bjelke-Petersen, of Denmark; *b* 13 Jan 1911, New Zealand; *Educ* Taabinga Valley Sch and privately; *m* 1952, Florence Isabel, nee Gilmour; 1 s, 3 da; *Career* premier of Queensland 1968-; *Style* - The Hon Johannes Bjelke-Petersen; Bethany, Kingaroy, Queensland 4610

BJORNSSON, Henrik Sveinsson; Hon KBE; s of Sveinn Bjornsson, First Pres of Iceland, and Georgia Hoff-Hansen; *b* 2 Sept 1914; *Educ* Reykjavik G S, Iceland U; *m* 1941, Gróa Torfhildur Jónsdóttir; 1 s, 2 da; *Career* Icelandic Ambass to EEC and permanent representative to NATO 1979-; *Style* - Henrik Bjornsson Esq, Hon KBE; Ministry for Foreign Affairs, Reykjavik, Iceland

BLACK, Baron (Life Peer UK 1968); William Rushton Black; s of James Black, of Barrow in Furness; *b* 12 Jan 1893; *Educ* Barrow Secdy Sch, Barrow Tech; *m* 1917, Patricia Margaret (d 1976), da of James Dallas, of Dundee; (1 s missing 1944-), 1 da; *Career* JP Middx 1950-58; engr; Pres SMMT 1953, formerly chm NRDC and Leyland Motor Corpn kt 1958; *Recreations* golf, gardening; *Clubs* RAC; *Style* - The Rt Hon The Lord Black; Birchwood Grange, Ruxley cres, Claygate, Esher (☎ 62823)

BLACK, Sir Cyril Wilson; JP (London 1942), DL (Surrey 1957-66, Gter London 1966); s of Robert Black (d 1951); *b* 8 April 1902; *Educ* King's Coll Sch Wimbledon; *m* 1930, Dorothy, da of Thomas Birkett (d 1962); 1 s, 2 da; *Career* surveyor, FRICS; chm Beaumont Properties to 1980, London Shop Property Tst to 1979; kt 1959, MP (C) Wimbledon 1950-70; mayor Wimbledon 1945-47 and Merton 1966-67; chm Surrey CC 1956-59; *Recreations* reading, music, public work; *Clubs* Carlton, Inner London Justices'; *Style* - Sir Cyril Black, JP, DL; Rosewall, Calonne rd, SW19 (☎ 01 946 2588); Windmill Cottage, Sea Way, Middleton-on-Sea, Sussex (☎ 024 369 2288)

BLACK, Sir Douglas Andrew Kilgour; s of Rev Walter Black (d 1951); *b* 29 May 1913; *Educ* Forfar Acad, St Andrews U; *m* 1948, Mollie, da of Edward Thorn (d 1962); 1 s, 1 da; *Career* kt 1973, Prof of Medicine Manchester U 1959-78, ch scientist DHSS 1973-77, Pres Roy Coll of Physicians 1977-; *Recreations* reading, writing; *Clubs* Athenaeum; *Style* - Sir Douglas Black; c/o Royal College of Physicians, 11 St Andrews pla, Regent's Pk, NW1

BLACK, His Honour Judge; George Joseph Black; DSO (1944), DFC (1942) and Bar (1944); s of Tom Black, of Cardiff; *b* 24 Jan 1918; *Educ* Queen's Coll Taunton; *Career* Sqdn-Ldr RAF 1941-46; slr 1946; sr legal assist New Scotland Yard; Crown Court Judge 1977-; *Recreations* sailing; *Style* - His Hon Judge Black, DSO, DFC*; 11 Sealawns, The Knap, Barry, S Glam

BLACK, Sir Harold; s of Alexander Black (d 1946) of Belfast; *b* 9 April 1914; *Educ* Roy Belfast Academical Institution; *m* 1940, Margaret, da of John Milton Saxton (d 1951); 1 s, 1 da; *Career* Dep Sec NI Off 1972-74, kt 1970; *Recreations* sailing, photography; *Clubs* Strangford Lough Yacht; *Style* - Sir Harold Black; 19 Rosepark, Belfast (☎ Dundonald 215)

BLACK, John Alexander; s of Arthur Alexander Black (d 1958); *b* 8 July 1923; *Educ* Cheltenham, Birmingham U; *m* 1950, Joan, da of Henry Knight (d 1954); 2 da; *Career* chm- Charles Barker Black & Gross Ltd 1976-, Charles Barker Cross Courtenay Ltd 1978-, Charles Barker Scotland Ltd 1980-, Solihull AHA 1977-; *Recreations* gardening, woodturning, walking, photography; *Style* - John Black Esq; 36 Hampton Lane, Solihull, W Midlands (☎ 021 705 4131)

BLACK, Lady; Joan Edna; da of George Fairbrother, of Birkenhead; *m* 1955, Sir Misha Black, OBE (d 1977); 2 s, 1 da; *Style* - Lady Black; 160 Gloucester rd, SW7 (☎ 01 373 0040); Thistley Common, Boyton End, Halstead, Essex (☎ Ridgewell 203)

BLACK, John Kennedy; s of Maj C Kennedy Black, of W Hoathly Sussex; *b* 22 April 1922; *Educ* Malvern; *m* 1955, Barbara, da of Capt H Johnson, of Westcott Surrey; 1 s, 2 da; *Career* CA, sr ptnr Kidsons; Master Worshipful Co of Makers of Playing Cards 1980; v-chm Mornington Bldg Soc 1978-; dir Abuk Investments Ltd; *Recreations* gardening, shooting, the ridiculous; *Clubs* Br Sportsman's, Carlton, Richmond Football (Rugby); *Style* - John Black Esq; Dunsfold Grange, Dunsfold, Surrey (☎ 236)

BLACK, John Nicholson; s of Harold Black, FRCP; *b* 28 June 1922; *Educ* Rugby and Exeter Coll Oxford; *m* 1, 1952, Mary Webb (d 1966); 1 s, 1 da; m 2, 1967, Wendy Waterston; 2 s; *Career* principal Bedford Coll London U 1971-; *Style* - John Black Esq; Westholm, Orchehill av, Gerrards Cross, Bucks

BLACK, Lady Moorea; *née* Hastings; da of 15 Earl of Huntingdon by his 1 w, Cristina, da of Marchese Casati; *b* 4 March 1928; *m* 1, 1957 (m dis 1966), Woodrow Wyatt, MP, *qv*; 1 s (Pericles Plantagenet James Casati, b 1963); m 2, 1967, Brinsley Black; 1 s (Orlando Irvine Casati, b 1968); *Style* - Lady Moorea Black; 17 Lansdowne Walk, W11 (☎ 01 727 3528)

BLACK, Hon Mrs Moira Violet Maria; da of 5 Baron Plunket; *b* 1897; *m* 1, 1923, Lt-Col Herbert Frederick Edgar Smith, DSO (d on active service 1940); 1 da; m 2, 1944 (m dis 1952), Capt Ian Reddie Hamilton Black, CBE, RN (ret); *Style* - The Hon Mrs Moira Black; Flat 20, 34 Sloane Court West, SW3

BLACK, Sir Robert Brown; GCMG (1962, KCMG 1955, CMG 1953), OBE (1949, MBE 1948); s of Robert Black (d 1929), of Blair Lodge, Stirlingshire; *b* 3 June 1906; *Educ* George Watson's Coll Edinburgh, Edinburgh U; *m* 1937, Elsie, da of Alan Stevenson; 2 da; *Career* Pres Internat Socl Serv of GB 1973-; Govr and CIC Hong Kong 1958-64; KStJ; dir C'wlth War Graves Cmmn 1964-; *Recreations* fishing, walking, books; *Clubs* E India Devonshire Sports and Public Schools; *Style* - Sir Robert Black, GCMG, OBE; Mapletons House, Ashampton Common, Berks (☎ Hermitage 201254)

BLACK, Sir Robert David; 3 Bt (UK 1922); s of Sir Robert Andrew Stransham Black, 2 Bt, ED, (d 1979); *b* 29 March 1929; *Educ* Eton; *m* 1, 1953 (m dis 1972), Rosemary Diana, da of Sir Rupert John Hardy, 4 Bt; 3 da; m 2, 1973, (Dorothy)

Maureen, da of Maj Charles Robert Eustace Radclyffe, and wid of Alan Roger Douglas Pilkington; *Heir* none; *Career* formerly Maj Royal Horse Guards and Maj Berks and Westminster Dragoon Yeomanry (1964-67); Joint MFH Garth and S Berks Hunt 1964-73; *Style* - Sir Robert Black, Bt; Ford Farm, Aldbourne, Marlborough, Wilts

BLACK, Sheila Psyche; da of Clement Black; *b* 6 May 1920; *Educ* Dorset, Switzerland and RADA; *m* 1 1939 (m dis 1951), Geoffrey Davien, sculptor; 1 da (and 1 s decd); m 2, 1951 (m dis 1973), L A Lee Howard; *Career* special feature writer for The Times 1973-, dir Cole Black and Ptnrs 1975-; *Style* - Miss Sheila Black; 34 Hesper Mews, SW5

BLACKBURN, 5 Bp of (cr 1926) 1972-; Rt Rev Robert Arnold Schürhoff Martineau; s of late Prof C E Martineau, MA, MCom, FCA (sixth in descent from Gaston Martineau, who started life as a surgeon in Bergerac, in the Dordogne, but was forced by the Revocation of the Edict of Nantes (1685) to flee to England , where he settled at Norwich; also gn of Harriet Martineau, the novelist, political economist, sociologist, propagator of Auguste Comte's positivism, adviser to the Cabinet, friend of Wordsworth and unitarian, who left her head to the Phrenological Society); *b* 22 Aug 1913; *Educ* King Edward's Sch Birmingham, Trin Hall Cambridge, Westcott House Cambridge; *m* 1941, Elinor Gertrude, da of late Rev Keinion Ap-Thomas; 1 s, 2 da; *Career* curate of Melksham 1938-41; Bp Suffragan of Huntingdon 1966-72, Residentiary Canon of Ely 1966-72; patron of 65 livings, the Archdeaconries of Lancaster and Blackburn, and 18 Hon Canonries; *Style* - The Rt Rev The Lord Bishop of Blackburn; Bishop's House, Clayton-le-Dale, Blackburn, Lancs (☎ 48234)

BLACKBURN, Cdr (David) Anthony (James); MVO (1978), RN; s of late Lieut J Blackburn, DSC, RN; *b* 18 Jan 1945; *Educ* Taunton Sch and RNC Dartmouth; *m* 1973, Elizabeth Barstow; 2 da; *Career* Equerry-in-Waiting to HRH the Duke of Edinburgh 1976-78; Executive Officer HMS Antrim 1978; *Style* - Cdr Anthony Blackburn, MVO, RN; Greystones, Selborne, Alton, Hants (☎ Selborne 385)

BLACKBURN, George Alexander Peskett; OBE (1981); s of late G C Blackburn; *b* 26 Oct 1920; *Educ* Birkenhead Inst; *m* 1965, Betty Rigby, nee Machell; 1 da; *Career* chartered marine engineer, presently technical dir Cammell Laird Shipbuilders, previously technical manager 1971-74, chief marine engineer 1967-71; *Recreations* swimming, dancing, walking; *Clubs* White's; *Style* - George Blackburn Esq, OBE; 67 Thingwall rd, Irby, Merseyside

BLACKBURN, John Graham; MP (C) Dudley W 1979-; s of Charles Blackburn (d 1969); *b* 2 Sept 1934; *Educ* Liverpool Collegiate Sch, Liverpool U; *m* 1958, Marjorie, da of George Thompson (d 1974), of Wigan; 1 s, 2 da; *Career* formerly police offr Liverpool; sales dir Solway Engrg 1965-; memb POUNC 1972-; Freeman Cities of London and Tel Aviv; *Recreations* yachting (yacht 'Tobermory'); *Clubs* Wolverhampton and Bilston Athletic, Traeth Coch Yacht (Anglesey); *Style* - John Blackburn Esq, MP; 159 Ashley gdns, SW1; Canterbury House, Canterbury rd, Penn, Wolverhampton (☎ 36222)

BLACKBURN, Thomas; s of Thomas Blackburn, of Penrith; *b* 22 July 1932; *Educ* Oundle; *m* 1955, Diana, da of William Lillico, of Barnet; 1 s, 2 da; *Career* engr; dir- C Seward & Co Hldgs 1960, Citrus Products (St Annes) Ltd 1978, Shard Bridge Co 1980; jt md C Seward & Co 1967; *Recreations* shooting, fishing; *Style* - Thomas Blackburn Esq; Hill Top Farm, Thornley with Wheatley, Longridge, Preston, Lancs (☎ 077478 3353)

BLACKBURNE, Lady - Bridget Senhouse Constant; da of James Mackay Wilson, DL (d 1934), of Currygrane, Co Longford; *m* 1935, Sir Kenneth Blackburne, GCMG, GBE, (d 1980); 1 s, 1 da; *Style* - Lady Blackburne; Garvagh, Ballasalla, Isle of Man (☎ Castletown 3640)

BLACKBURNE, Rt Rev Hugh Charles; s of late Very Rev Harry William Blackburne, Dean of Bristol; *b* 4 June 1912; *Educ* Marlborough, Clare Cambridge, Westcott House; *m* 1944, Doris Freda, widow of Pilot Officer H L N Davis; 2 s, 1 da; *Career* Deacon 1937, Priest 1938, Curate of Almondbury Yorks, Chaplain to the Forces 1939-47, served with 1 Guards Brigade, 11 Armoured Division, HQ AA command and as Chaplain RMC Sandhurst, Rector of New Milton Hants 1947-53, Vicar St Mary's Harrow 1953-61, Rector of Hilborough Group 1961-72, Vicar of Ranworth and Chaplain for Norfolk Broads 1972-77, Bishop of Thetford 1977-80, Chaplain to HM The Queen 1962-77; *Recreations* sailing, birdwatching; *Style* - The Rt Rev Hugh Blackburne; 39 Northgate, Beccles, Suffolk (☎ Beccles 716374)

BLACKER, Gen Sir Cecil Hugh; GCB (1975, KCB 1969, CB 1967), OBE (1960), MC (1944); s of Col Norman Blacker; *b* 4 June 1916; *Educ* Wellington, Sandhurst; *m* 1947, Felicity, da of Ivor Buxton, DSO (d 1968); 2 s; *Career* 2 Lt Roy Inniskilling Dragoon Gds 1936; GOCIC Northern Command 1969-70, V-Ch of General Staff 1970-73, Adj-Gen 1973-76, ret 1976; FBIM 1973; ADC to HM The Queen 1962-64, ADC (Gen) to HM The Queen 1974-76; *Clubs* Jockey, Cavalry & Guards; *Style* - Gen Sir Cecil Blacker, GCB, OBE, MC; Whitchurch House, Whitchurch, Bucks (☎ 212)

BLACKER, Hon Mrs - Hon Caroline Susan Dean; da of Rev Baron Soper; *b* 11 Aug 1946; *Educ* Queenswood, Hatfield; Exeter U; *m* 1975, Terence Blacker, s of Gen Sir Cecil Hugh Blacker, KCB, OBE, MC, *qv*; 2 children; *Style* - The Hon Mrs Blacker; 91 Wendell rd, W12 (☎ 01 743 8746)

BLACKER, Lady Doris; da of 1 Earl Peel, GCSI, GBE, PC (d 1937); *b* 25 Mar 1900; *m* 1927, Lt-Col Latham Valentine Stewart Blacker OBE TD (d 1964); 2 s, 2 da; *Career* JP (1939) Co of London, (1948) Sussex; *Style* - Lady Doris Blacker JP; Little Cold Hayes, Liss, Hants (☎ 2299)

BLACKETT, Baroness; Costanza; da of late Eugenio Bayon; *m* 1924, Baron Blackett, OM, CH (Life Peer, d 1974); 1 s, 1 da; *Style* - The Rt Hon Lady Blackett; Pen Parc, Llanfrothen, Penrhyndeudraeth, Gwynedd

BLACKETT, Francis Hugh; s of Sir Hugh Douglas Blackett, 8 Bt (d 1960); hp to Btcy of bro, Sir George Blackett, 10 Bt; *b* 16 Oct 1907; *Educ* Eton; *m* 1950, Elizabeth Eily, da of late Howard Dennison, of Valparaiso, Chile; 2 s, 2 da; *Style* - Francis Blackett Esq; Halton Castle, Corbridge, Northumberland

BLACKETT, Sir George William; 10 Bt (E 1673); s of late Sir Hugh Blackett, 8 Bt; suc bro, Sir Charles Douglas Blackett, 9 Bt, 1968; *b* 26 April 1906; *m* 1, 1933, Euphemia Cicely (d 1960), da of late Maj Nicholas Robinson, of Frankton Grange, Salop; m 2, 1964, Daphne Laing, da of late Maj Guy Laing Bradley, TD, of Bridge End House, Hexham; *Heir* bro, Maj Francis Hugh Blackett; *Career* Shropshire Yeo and CMP WW II; *Style* - Sir George Blackett, Bt; Colwyn, Corbridge-on-Tyne, Northumberland (☎ Corbridge 2252)

BLACKETT, Hon Nicolas Maynard; s of Baron Blackett, OM, CH (Life Peer, d 1974); *b* 25 May 1928; *Educ* U Coll Sch London and U of Bristol; *m* 1951, Patricia Kathleen Tankins, of Bristol; *Career* research scientist, Institute of Cancer Research, London 1954-; *Style* - The Hon Nicolas Blackett; 32 Woodstock rd, Carshalton, Surrey

BLACKETT, Ursula, Lady - Ursula Mary; da of late Maj Maurice Fearing Cely-Trevilian, of Midelney Manor, Drayton, Somerset; *m* 1935, Sir Charles Douglas Blackett, 9 Bt (d 1968); *Style* - Ursula, Lady Blackett; The Estate House, Matfen, Newcastle upon Tyne

BLACKETT-ORD, His Honour Vice-Chancellor; Andrew James Blackett-Ord; s of John Blackett-Ord, of Northumberland; *b* 21 Aug 1921; *Educ* Eton, New Coll Oxford; *m* 1945, Rosemary, da of Edward Bovill, of Brook House, Ongar; 3 s, 1 da; *Career* V-Chllr County Palatine of Lancaster 1973-,

Circuit Judge 1972-, Chllr Diocese of Newcastle-on-Tyne 1971-; *Recreations* country life, books; *Clubs* Garrick, Lansdowne, St James's (Manchester); *Style* - His Hon Vice-Chancellor Blackett-Ord; Welbeck Hall, Brough, Kirkby Stephen, Cumbria (☎ Brough 323)

BLACKETT-ORD, John Christopher; JP (1960); s of John Reginald Blackett-Ord, of Whitfield Hall, Hexham (d 1967); *b* 30 Sept 1918; *Educ* Eton, New Coll Oxford; *m* 1941, Elisabeth Hamilton (d 1977), da of Charles Mitchell, DSO, OBE (d 1958), of Pallinsburn, Cornhill on Tweed; 1 s, 2 da; *Career* FRICS 1949; *Recreations* shooting, fishing; *Clubs* Lansdowne; *Style* - John Blackett-Ord Esq, JP; Whitfield Hall, Hexham, Northumberland (☎ Whitfield 273)

BLACKFORD, 4 Baron (1935 UK), Sir William Keith Mason; 4 Bt (1918 UK); s of 3 Baron Blackford, DFC (d 1977), and Sarah, da of Judge Sir Shirley Worthington-Evans, 2 Bt; *b* 27 Mar 1962; *Educ* Harrow; *Style* - The Rt Hon the Lord Blackford; 135 Cranmer Court, SW1 (☎ 01 235 3071)

BLACKHAM, Rear-Adm Joseph Leslie; CB (1965), DL (Hants & IOW 1970); s of Dr Walter Blackham, of Birmingham; *b* 29 Feb 1912; *Educ* W House Sch Birmingham, RNC Dartmouth; *m* 1938, Coreen, da of Paymaster-Capt William Skinner, RN, of Blackheath; 1 s, 1 da; *Career* Adm Supt Portsmouth Dockyard 1964-66; chm IOW CC 1975-77; v-chm IOW AHA 1974-; High Sheriff IOW 1975; *Style* - Rear-Adm Joseph Blackham, CB, DL; Downedge, The Mall, Brading, IOW (☎ 218)

BLACKIE, John Walter Graham; s of Walter Graham Blackie (d 1972); *b* 2 October 1946; *Educ* Uppingham, Cambridge U, Harvard U, Merton Coll Oxford, Edinburgh U; *m* 1972, Jane; *Career* advocate 1974, lecturer in Scots Law U of Edinburgh 1975, visiting lecturer U of Göttingen 1981, dir Blackie & Son Ltd (Publishers) 1970; *Recreations* singing, playing wind instruments; *Style* - John Blackie Esq; The Old Coach House, 23a Russell Place, Trinity, Edinburgh EH5 (☎ 031 552 3103)

BLACKIE, Dr Margery Grace; CVO; da of Robert Blackie; *Educ* Royal Free Hospital and Medical Sch; *Career* physician to HM The Queen 1969-80; *Style* - Dr Margery Blackie CVO; 18 Thurloe st, SW7 (☎ 01 589 2776); Hedingham Castle, Halstead, Essex (☎ 60261)

BLACKLEY, John Lorimer; JP; s of John Blackley (d 1951); *b* 22 Nov 1915; *Educ* Sedbergh Sch; *m* 1940, Christina Ferrier, da of Robert Stepford, of Dumfries; 1 s; *Career* farmer; chm W Cumberland Farmers' Ltd 1976-, EFG (New Lands) Ltd 1976-; *Recreations* angling, shooting, gardening; *Clubs* Farmers'; *Style* - John Blackley Esq, JP; Berscar, Closeburn, Thornhill, Dumfriesshire (☎ Closeburn 246)

BLACKMORE, Courtenay Thomas Gardner; s of Rev Canon Alfred Blackmore; *b* 16 Oct 1922; *Educ* Oakham Sch, Keble Oxford; *m* 1957, as her 2 husb, Lady Pamela, *qv*, da of 1 and last Earl of Kilmuir (d 1967); 1 s, 2 da; *Career* FIPM; formerly with ICI; Head of Admin Lloyd's 1975-; memb Cncl Sail T'ning Assoc 1978-; memb Exec Cttee Industl Soc; *Recreations* gardening, reading, photography, painting; *Clubs* Architecture, Carlton, MCC, 1900; *Style* - Courtenay Blackmore Esq; 55a Lee rd, Blackheath, SE3 (☎ 01 852 7001)

BLACKMORE, Lady Pamela Maxwell; *née* Fyfe; JP (Inner London); da of 1 and last Earl of Kilmuir, GCVO, PC (d 1967); *b* 14 Oct 1928; *Educ* Crofton Grange, LMH Oxford; *m* 1, 1950, Clive Wigram (d 1956); 1 da; m 2, 1957, Courtenay Thomas Gardner Blackmore, *qv*; 1 s, 2 da; *Career* Dep Chm Greenwich & Woolwich Div Inner London Bench; memb exec cttee & chm Appeals Cttee Peckham Settlement; *Clubs* Roy C'wlth Soc; *Style* - Lady Pamela Blackmore JP; 55a Lee rd, Blackheath, SE3 (☎ 01 852 7001)

BLACKSHAW, Ian Stewart; s of William Pakington Blackshaw, of Derbys; *b* 18 Dec 1944; *Educ* King Edward VII Sch Lytham St Annes, Coll of Law

London, Madrid U; *m* 1970, Christine, da of Thomas Haworth, FCA, of Lytham St Annes; 2 s; *Career* sec of bd & legal advr Monsanto Ltd 1980-, formerly in priv practice and with Coca-Cola and GKN; *Recreations* music, travel, family pursuits; *Clubs* Travellers'; *Style* - Ian Blackshaw Esq; 4 Yewens, Chiddingfold, nr Godalming, Surrey (☎ Wormley 3073)

BLACKSTONE, Geoffrey Vaughan; CBE (1956, OBE 1947), GM (1941), QFSM (1964); s of Harold Vaughan Blackstone; *b* 10 May 1910; *Educ* Uppingham; *m* 1941, Joanna, da of Major Stanley Vosper; 2 s, 2 da; *Career* OStJ 1945, Div Officer London Fire Brigade 1938-41, Fire Force Comdr National Fire Service 1941-43, chief Regional Fire Officer NFS 1943-48, chief officer Hertfordshire Fire Brigade 1948-71; *Style* - Geoffrey Blackstone Esq, CBE, GM QFSM; Dassels Bury, Ware, Herts (☎ Great Hormead 330)

BLACKSTONE, Stanley Ernest; CBE (1972); s of late Ernest Edward Blackstone; *b* 17 June 1908; *Educ* Uppingham, Clare Coll Cambridge; *m* 1945, Barbara Helen, nee Bleckly; 1 s (step), 2 da; *Career* industrial consultant; md P E Consulting Group Companies to 1959, founder chm Management Consultants Assoc 1954-55, chief industrial adviser ICFC Ltd 1959-66, chm and dir various companies to 1979, chm Industrial Training Foundation; *Recreations* farming, music; *Clubs* RAC, Hawks (Cambridge); *Style* - Stanley Blackstone Esq, CBE; The Malt House, Frensham, Nr Farnham, Surrey (☎ Frensham 2133)

BLACKWELL, Basil Davenport; s of late Alfred Blackwell; *b* 8 Feb 1922; *Educ* Leeds G S; St John's Cambridge; London U; *m* 1948, Betty Meggs; 1 da; *Career* MA, BSc (Eng), FEng; vice-chm and ch exec, Westland Gp of Cos 1974-; *Recreations* gardens, gardening; *Style* - Basil Blackwell Esq; High Newland, Sherborne, Dorset (☎ 3516)

BLACKWELL, Richard; DSC (1944); s of Sir Basil Blackwell; *b* 5 Jan 1918; *Educ* Winchester and New Coll Oxford; *m* 1942, Marguerite, nee Holliday; 2 s; *Career* chm B H Blackwell Ltd 1969-; Basil Blackwell, Publisher 1976-; *Style* - Richard Blackwell Esq DSC; Tubney House, nr Abingdon, Oxon (☎ Frilford Heath 390444)

BLACKWELL, Thomas Francis; MBE (Mil 1945), DL (Suffolk 1975); s of Thomas Blackwell, OBE, of Northchurch Herts; *b* 31 July 1912; *Educ* Harrow, Magdalene Cambridge; *m* 1948, Joan, da of Alan Pilkington; 1 s, 1 da; *Career* chm Turf Newspapers, Colne Valley Water Co, dir Rickmansworth and Uxbridge Water Co, Sr Steward Jockey Club 1966; *Recreations* racing, golf, shooting; *Clubs* Jockey, White's, Pratt's; *Style* - Thomas Blackwell Esq, MBE, DL; Flat E, 3/4 Balfour Place, W1 (☎ 01 499 3360); Langham Hall, Bury St Edmunds, Suffolk (☎ 03598 271); 55 Curzon st, W1 (☎ 01 499 4391)

BLACKWOOD, Sir Francis George; 7 Bt (UK 1814); s of late Capt Maurice Baldwin Raymond Blackwood, DSO, RN (d on active service 1941) and Dorothea (d 1967), da of late Hon G Bertrand Edwards of Huon Park Sydney, NS Wales; suc to cousin's Btcy 1979; hp to Barony of Dufferin and Clandeboye and Btcy of Ballyleidy (cr 1763); *b* 20 May 1916; *m* 1941, Margaret, nee Kirkpatrick; 2 s, 1 da; *Heir* s, John Francis Blackwood; *Style* - Sir Francis Blackwood, Bt; Uaimbi, 408 Bobbin Head rd, N Turramurra, NSW 2074 Australia

BLACKWOOD, Wing Cdr George Douglas; s of late James Blackwood; *b* 11 Oct 1909; *Educ* Eton and Clare Cambridge; *m* 1936, Phyllis Marion, da of Sir John Caulcutt, KCMG; 1 s, 1 da; *Career* chm William Blackwood and Sons Ltd 1948-; *Style* - Wing Cdr George Blackwood; 32 Thistle st, Edinburgh (☎ 031 225 3411); Airhouse, Oxton, Berwickshire

BLACKWOOD, John Francis; s and h of Sir Francis George Blackwood, 7 Bt; *b* 1944; *Educ* U of N S Wales (BArch); *m* 1971, Kay Greenhill, of Seaforth, Sydney, NSW; *Style* - John Blackwood Esq

BLACKWOOD, Lily, Lady - Lily Margaret; da of late Fulton J MacGougan, of Vancouver; *m* 1921, Sir Francis Elliot Temple Blackwood, 6 Bt (d 1979); *Style* - Lily, Lady Blackwood; c/o Riverside Convalescent Hospital, 1090 Rio lane, Sacramento, California, USA

BLACKWOOD, Lady Perdita Maureen Hamilton-Temple-; da of 4 Marquess of Dufferin and Ava (k in action 1945); *b* 1934; *Style* - Lady Perdita Blackwood; Cavalls Stud Farm, Newtownards, Co Down, N Ireland (☎ 2603)

BLADES, Hon Catherine Anne; da of 2 Baron Ebbisham; *b* 3 Dec 1955; *Educ* St Mary's Sch Calne, Prior's Field, Wye Coll London; *Career* agricultural tech advr; *Recreations* sailing, hill walking, motor sport; *Style* - The Hon Catherine Blades; The Old Rectory, Bletchingley, Surrey (☎ 843388)

BLAIR, David Arthur; MBE (1943), MC (1944); s of Brig-Gen A Blair, DSO; *b* 25 Aug 1917; *Educ* Harrow, Sandhurst; *m* 1947, Elizabeth Adela Morton; 2 s, 1 da (and 1 da decd); *Career* dir The Distillers Co Ltd; chm United Glass Ltd, Export Committee (Scotch Whisky); *Clubs* White's, New (Edinburgh) and Royal and Ancient St Andrews (Capt 1978-79); *Style* - David Blair Esq, MBE, MC; Lilliesleaf House, Lilliesleaf, Roxburghshire

BLAIR, Edward Thomas Hunter; s and h of Sir James Hunter Blair, 7 Bt; *b* 15 Dec 1920; *Educ* Eton and Balliol Oxford; *m* 1956, Norma, nee Harris (d 1972); *Career* memb Kirkcudbright CC 1970; *Style* - Edward Blair Esq; Parton House, Castle Douglas, Kirkcudbrightshire

BLAIR, Henry Gordon; CBE (1951), DL (Berks 1975); s of Henry Blair, of Manchester; *b* 2 July 1909; *Educ* privately; *m* 1937, Margaret, da of James Kelly, of Edinburgh; 1 da (and 1 s, ka Ulster 1979); *Career* Air Cdre RAF ret 1960, memb Berks CC 1970-, Newbury RDC 1964-70; *Recreations* gardening, local govt, birds (memb RSPB); *Style* - Air Cdre Henry Blair CBE DL; Upover, Cold Ash, Newbury, Berks (☎ Thatcham 61322)

BLAIR, Thomas Alexander; QC (NI 1958); s of late John Blair; *b* 12 Dec 1916; *Educ* Queen's U, Belfast; *m* 1947, Ida Irvine Moore; 2 s, 1 da; *Career* Chief National Insurance Commissioner (NI) 1969-; *Style* - Thomas Blair Esq QC; 10 Knockdene Park, Belfast (☎ 655182)

BLAIR-KERR, Sir Alastair (William Alexander); s of William Milne Kerr; *b* 1 Dec 1911; *Educ* McLaren H S Perthshire, Edinburgh U; *m* 1942, Esther, da of Sydney Wright; 1 s, 1 da; *Career* Pres Court of Appeal Bahamas 1978, Bermuda 1979, Belize 1979, kt 1973; *Recreations* music, walking; *Clubs* Roy Overseas League; *Style* - Sir Alastair Blair-Kerr; Gairn, Kinbuck by Dunblane, Perthshire (☎ 0786 823377)

BLAKE, Baron (Life Peer UK 1971); Robert Norman William Blake; FBA (1967), JP (Oxford); s of William Joseph Blake, of Brundall, Norfolk; *b* 23 Dec 1916; *Educ* King Edward VI Sch Norwich, Magdalen Oxford; *m* 1953, Patricia Mary, da of Thomas Richard Waters; 3 da; *Career* politics tutor and student Christ Church Coll Oxford 1947-68 (formerly lectr), Censor 1950-55, Sr Proctor 1969-60, Ford's Lectr in Eng History 1967-68, Provost of Queen's Coll Oxford 1968-, Pro-Vice-Chancellor Oxford U 1971-; author, books include *Disraeli* 1966, *The Conservative Opportunity* ed with John Patten 1976, *A History of Rhodesia* 1977; *Style* - The Rt Hon The Lord Blake, JP; Riverview House, Brundall, Norfolk; Queen's College, Oxford

BLAKE, Anthony Teilo Bruce; s of Maj Charles Anthony Howell Bruce Blake (ka 1951); hp to Btcy of kinsman, Sir Richard Valentine Blake, 17 Bt; *b* 5 May 1951; *Educ* Wellington; *Style* - Anthony Blake Esq

BLAKE, Hon Deborah Cicelie; da of Baron Blake (Life Peer); *b* 1955; *Style* - The Hon Deborah Blake; Riverview House, Brundall, Norfolk

BLAKE, Francis Julian; s and h of Sir Francis Michael Blake, 3 Bt; *b* 17 Feb 1971

BLAKE, Sir Francis Michael; 3 Bt (UK 1907); s of Sir (Francis) Edward Colquhoun Blake, 2 Bt (d 1950); *b* 11 July

1943; *Educ* Rugby; *m* 1968, Joan Ashbridge, da of F C A Miller, of Ramsay Lodge, Kelso; 2 s; *Heir* s, Francis Julian Blake; *Style* - Sir Francis Blake, Bt; The Dower House, Tillmouth Park, Cornhill-on-Tweed, Northumberland (☎ Coldstream 2443)

BLAKE, John; s of Frederick Blake; *b* 4 Jan 1936; *Educ* The Leiston Sch; *m* 1961, Beryl, da of Jack English; 1 child; *Career* chartered sec; dir- W S Cowell Ltd, Archon Press, Utd Greeting Card Co (UK), Utd Greeting Card (Ireland), Gloucester Press Inc (USA); *Recreations* photography, walking, caravanning; *Style* - John Blake Esq; Brackendale, Bromeswell, Woodbridge, Suffolk

BLAKE, Hon Letitia Lindley; da of Baron Blake (Life Peer); *b* 1960; *Style* - The Hon Letitia Blake

BLAKE, Quentin Saxby; s of William Blake; *b* 16 Dec 1932; *Educ* Downing Cambridge; *Career* freelance artist and illustrator; Head of Dept of Illustration, RCA 1978-; *Style* - Quentin Blake Esq; 30 Bramham gdns, SW5 (☎ 01 373 7464)

BLAKE, Sir Thomas Richard Valentine; 17 Bt (I 1622); s of Sir Ulick Temple Blake, 16 Bt (d 1963); *b* 7 Jan 1942; *Educ* Bradfield; *m* 1976, Jacqueline, da of late Desmond E Daroux, and formerly w of Peter Alers Hankey; *Heir* kinsman, Anthony Teilo Bruce Blake; *Style* - Sir Thomas Blake, Bt

BLAKELY, Colin George Edward; s of Victor Blakely; *b* 23 Sept 1930; *Educ* Sedbergh Sch; *m* 1961, Margaret Whiting; 3 s; *Career* actor and (from 1975) director; *Style* - Colin Blakely Esq; c/o Leading Artists, 60 St James's st, SW1 (☎ 01 491 4400)

BLAKENEY, Frederick Joseph; CBE (1968); s of Frederick Blakeney; *b* 2 July 1913; *m* 1943, Marjorie, nee Martin; 1 da; *Career* Australian Ambassador and Permanent Representative to UNO, Geneva; *Style* - Frederick Blakeney Esq CBE; 19 Grey st, Deakin, Canberra, ACT, Australia

BLAKENHAM, 1 Viscount (UK 1963); Hon John Hugh Hare; OBE (Mil 1945, MBE Mil 1943), PC (1955), DL (Suffolk 1968); s of 4 Earl of Listowel (d 1931) and Hon Freda, nee Vanden-Bempde-Johnstone, da of 2 Baron Derwent; *b* 22 Jan 1911; *Educ* Eton; *m* 1934, Hon Beryl Nancy, nee Pearson, da of 2 Viscount Cowdray and Agnes, da of Lord Edward Spencer-Churchill (5 s of 5 Duke of Marlborough); 1 s, 2 da; *Heir* s, Hon Michael Hare; *Career* MP (C) E Suffolk Woodbridge Div 1950-63, v-chm Cons Pty 1951-55, Min of State for Colonial Affairs 1955-56, Sec of State for War 1956-58, Min of Ag Fish and Food 1958-60, Min of Labour 1960-63, Chllr Duchy of Lancaster and Dep Leader of House of Lords 1963-64, chm Cons Pty Org 1963-65, memb Governing Body Peabody Tst 1967-, Tresr Roy Horticultural Soc 1971-, VMH 1974; *Style* - The Rt Hon The Viscount Blakenham, OBE, PC, DL; 10 Holland pk, W 11 (☎ 01 727 0159); Cottage Farm, Little Blakenham, nr Ipswich, Suffolk (☎ Ipswich 830344)

BLAKENHAM, Viscountess; Hon (Beryl) Nancy; *née* Pearson; da of late 2 Visc Cowdray and Agnes, da of Lord Edward Spencer-Churchill; *b* 1908; *m* 1934, 1 Viscount Blakenham OBE PC DL *qv*; *Style* - The Rt Hon The Viscountess Blakenham; 10 Holland pk, W11; Cottage Farm, Little Blakenham, nr Ipswich

BLAKER, Sir John; 3 Bt (UK 1919); s of Maj Sir Reginald Blaker, 2 Bt, TD (d 1975); *b* 22 March 1935; *m* 1, 1960 (m dis 1965), Catherine Ann, da of late Francis John Anselm Thorold; m 2, 1968, Elizabeth Katherine, da of Col John Russell, DSO; *Style* - Sir John Blaker, Bt; Barton Hill Farm, Barton-on-the-Heath, Moreton-in-Marsh, Glos

BLAKER, His Honour Judge; Nathaniel Robert Blaker; QC (1972); s of Maj Herbert Blaker, of Anstye Place, Sussex; *b* 31 Jan 1921; *Educ* Winchester, Univ Oxford; *m* 1951, Celia, da of Walter Hedley, DSO, KC, of Westminster; 1 da; *Career* barr 1948, Circuit Judge 1976-; *Recreations* photography; *Style* - His Hon Judge Blaker, QC; 16 Embankment gdns, SW3 (☎ 01 352 0792)

BLAKER, Peter Allan Renshaw; MP (C) Blackpool S 1964-; s of Cedric Blaker, CBE, MC; *b* 4 Oct 1922; *Educ* Shrewsbury, Trin Coll Toronto, New Coll Oxford; *m* 1953, Jennifer, da of Sir Pierson Dixon, GCMG, CB ; 1 s, 2 da; *Career* slr 1948, barr 1952; For Serv 1953-64; Parly Under Sec Army 1972-74 and FCO 1974, Min of State FCO 1979-81, Armed Forces (MOD) admin 1981-; V-Chm Con Pty For and C'wlth Affrs Ctee 1974-79, V-Chm Three Services Bd 1981-, Min of State for Armed Forces 1981-; *Recreations* tennis, sailing, swimming, opera; *Style* - Peter Blaker Esq, MP; Woodsland Farm, Lindfield, Sussex (☎ 2381)

BLAKER, Sheila, Lady - Sheila Kellas; da of Alexander Cran, of Little Court, Merrow, nr Guildford; *m* 1930, Maj Sir Reginald Blaker, 2 Bt, TD (d 1975); *Style* - Sheila, Lady Blaker; Knowles, Ardingly, Sussex

BLAKEWAY, John Denys; s of late Sir Denys Blakeway, CIE; *b* 27 May 1918; *Educ* Rugby and Magdalen Oxford; *m* 1946, Jasmine Iremonger; 1 s, 2 da; *Career* HM Consul-General Istanbul 1975-78; *Style* - John Blakeway Esq; Row Farm, Zeals, Warminster, Wilts (☎ Bourton 209)

BLAKISTON, Ann, Lady - Ann Hope Percival; da of late Purcell Cooke Jeans; *m* 1954, as his 2 w, Sir Arthur Frederick Blakiston, 7 Bt, MC (d 1974); *Style* - Ann, Lady Blakiston; Corton, Warminster, Wilts

BLAKISTON, Sir Ferguson Arthur James; 9 Bt (GB 1763); s of Sir (Arthur) Norman Hunter Blakiston, 8 Bt (d 1977); *b* 19 Feb 1963; *Heir* bro, Norman John Balfour Blakiston,*qv*; *Style* - Sir Ferguson Blakiston Bt; 28 McKenzie st, Geraldine, S Canterbury, New Zealand

BLAKISTON, Mary, Lady - Mary Ferguson; da of late Alfred Ernest Gillingham, of Cave, S Canterbury; *m* 1962, Sir (Arthur) Norman Hunter Blakiston, 8 Bt (d 1977); *Style* - Mary, Lady Blakiston; 28 McKenzie st, Geraldine, S Canterbury, New Zealand

BLAKISTON, Norman John Balfour; s of Sir Norman Blakiston 8 Bt (d 1977); hp of bro, Sir Ferguson Blakiston, 9 Bt; *b* 1964; *Style* - Norman Blakiston Esq

BLAKISTON-HOUSTON, Lt-Col John Matthew; DL (Co Down); s of Richard Blakiston-Houston and gggs of Sir Matthew Blakiston, 2 Bt; *b* 31 Aug 1898; *Educ* Eton, Sandhurst; *m* 1931, Lettice, da of Henry Stobart; 1 s, 5 da; *Career* Lt-Col 11 Hussars, High Sheriff Co Tyrone 1954 & Co Down 1944; *Recreations* shooting, fishing, riding; *Clubs* Cavalry & Guards; *Style* - Lt-Col John Blakiston-Houston, DL; Beltrim Castle, Gortin, Co Tyrone, N Ireland

BLAKSTAD, Nigel Henry; s of Erick Blakstad (d 1978); *b* 8 Apr 1929; *Educ* Warwick Sch; *m* 1956, Patricia, nee Hall; 1 s, 2 da; *Career* gp md Renold Ltd 1979-; *Style* - Nigel Blakstad Esq; Greenmeadows, Withilee rd, Prestbury, Cheshire (☎ 829 106)

BLAMEY, Glendenning; CBE (1945); s of late Glendenning Blamey; *b* 10 July 1906; *Educ* Plymouth Coll; *m* 1931, Una, nee Hamley; 2 da; *Career* Captain, secretary to 2 Sea Lord 1940-41, joined RN as Paymaster Cadet 1923, Commander 1942, Captain 1952, chm memb of various Civil Service Interview Boards 1965-76; *Recreations* gardening, reading; *Style* - Glendenning Blamey Esq, CBE; Hill Cross, Swanmore, Hants (☎ Droxford 04897 534)

BLAMIRE-BROWN, John; DL (Staffs 1974); s of Rev Frederick Blamire-Brown; *b* 16 April 1915; *Educ* Cheam Sch, St Edmund's Canterbury; *m* 1945, Joyce, da of Harry Pearson, of Newcastle; 2 s; *Career* slr 1937, Ch Exec Staffs CC 1973-78; Clerk to Staffs Ltcy 1972-78; chm St Giles Home Ltd 1979-; memb Beth Johnson Fndn Cncl 1978-; *Recreations* beagling, gardening, painting; *Style* - John Blamire-Brown Esq, DL; The Mount, Codsall Wood, Wolverhampton (☎ Codsall 2044)

BLANCH, John William; s of Lt-Col John Blanch, of Betchworth Surrey; *b* 10 May 1933; *Educ* Dulwich; *m* 1959, Nikola, da of William Thompson, of Dorking; 1 s, 1 da; *Career* dir Wasey Campbell-Ewald

1978-, in advertising; *Recreations* travel, theatre, photography; *Style* - John Blanch Esq; Mid-Holmwood Lane, Dorking, Surrey (☎ 0306 6127)

BLANCHARD, George Herbert; CBE (1972), JP (1958); s of Edward Blanchard; *b* 17 Jan 1912; *Educ* privately, Nottingham U Coll; *m* 1940, Edith, da of George Housley; 1 s, 1 da; *Career* chm and md Blanchards Ltd 1956-73, chm Red Blanchard Motors Ltd 1968; *Clubs* Nottingham and County Constitutional; *Style* - George Blanchard Esq, CBE, JP; Manor Court, Kilburn, Derbyshire (☎ Derby 880315)

BLANCO WHITE, Thomas Anthony; QC (1969); s of George Blanco White, QC; *b* 19 Jan 1915; *Educ* Gresham's, Trin Cambridge; *m* 1950, Anne, da of James Ironside Smith, ICS; 2 s, 1 da; *Career* barr 1937; *Recreations* gardening, photography; *Style* - Thomas Blanco White Esq, QC; Mants, Bedham, Fittleworth, Pulborough, Sussex

BLAND, Francis Christopher Buchan; s of James Bland, of Co Down; *b* 29 May 1938; *Educ* Sedbergh Sch, Queen's Oxford; *Career* chm Sir Joseph Causton & Sons 1977-, Bow Gp 1970; dir Nat Provident Inst; *Recreations* fishing, skiing; *Clubs* Beefsteak, Flyfishers; *Style* - Francis Bland Esq; 10 Catherine pla, SW1 (☎ 01 834 0021)

BLAND, Lt-Col Simon Claud Michael; CVO (1973, MVO 1967); s of Sir Nevile Bland, KCMG, KCVO (d 1972); *b* 4 Dec 1923; *Educ* Eton; *m* 1954, Beatrice, da of William Blackett, of Dumfries; 1 s, 3 da; *Career* Comptroller and Priv Sec to Duke and Duchess of Gloucester 1972-, CStJ 1978; *Recreations* shooting; *Clubs* Buck's; *Style* - Lt-Col Simon Bland, CVO; Tower Flat, Kensington Palace, W8 (☎ 01 937 6374); Gabriels Manor, Edenbridge, Kent (☎ 2340)

BLANDFORD, Marquess of; Charles James Spencer-Churchill; s and h of 11 Duke of Marlborough, JP, DL; *b* 24 Nov 1955; *Educ* Pinewood, Harrow; *Career* insurance broker and helicopter pilot; *Recreations* skiing, flying, shooting; *Clubs* Turf, Annabel's; *Style* - Marquess of Blandford; 38 Seymour Walk, SW10 (☎ 01 352 4444)

BLANK, Herbert; s of Alfred Blank; *b* 18 Dec 1923; *Educ* Dorking G S, Edinburgh U; *m* 1952, Joyce, da of Alfred Pulfer; 1 s, 1 da; *Career* md and dep chm Polymark International Ltd; *Recreations* chess, bridge, tennis, squash, skiing; *Style* - Herbert Blank Esq; 10 Greenway Close, Totteridge, N20 (☎ 01 445 2293)

BLANKENHORN, Herbert; GCVO (Hon 1965); s of Erich Blankenhorn; *b* 15 Dec 1904; *Educ* Gymnasiums in Strasbourg, Berlin and Karlsruhe and Munich; London, Heidelberg and Paris Us; *m* 1944, Gisela Krug; 2 s, 2 da; *Career* German Ambassador to London 1965-70; consultant to Dir-Gen UNESCO 1977-; *Style* - Herbert Blankenhorn Esq, Hon GCVO; 7847 Badenweiler, Hintere Au 2, Germany

BLAUHORN, Karl Max; s of Dr Josef Blauhorn; *b* 6 May 1912; *Educ* Realgymnasium Vienna, Fed Inst of Technol Zurich; *m* 1938, Kate, da of Julius Steiner; 1 da; *Career* formerly md J B Jackson & Ptnrs; consulting engr 1967-; chm Product Search & Dvpt Ltd 1968-; chm Inst of Int Licensing Practitioners 1980-; *Recreations* reading; *Clubs* RAC; *Style* - Karl Blauhorn Esq; 4 Wellington House, Eton rd, NW3 (☎ 01 586 1814)

BLAUSTEN, Cyril; JP; *b* 1916; *m* 1944, Norma Cinnamon; 4 s; *Career* Lloyd's Underwriter; Commissioner of Taxes, V-Pres Jewish Welfare Bd and Maccabi Assoc; Freeman City of London; *Clubs* City Livery, United University, MCC; *Style* - Cyril Blausten Esq, JP; 5 Linnell Close, Meadway, NW11; 52 Brook st, W1

BLAUTH-MUSZKOWSKI, Peter Christopher; s of Dr Jan Muszkowski (d 1953); *b* 18 Sept 1919; *Educ* Grenoble U; *m* 1948, Izabella, da of Tadeusz Blauth (d 1951); 2 s; *Career* awarded Polish Cross of Valour, former Capt Polish Army, subst Flying Offr with RAF; Lloyd's broker, dir Bain Dawes (reinsurance brokers) 1970-, Gil Carvajal & Ptnrs 1980-; *Recreations* writing, music; *Clubs* City of London;

Style - Peter Blauth-Muszkowski Esq; 45 Meadvale rd, W5 (☎ 01 997 8970)

BLAXTER, Sir Kenneth (Lyon); s of Gaspard Blaxter; *b* 19 June 1919; *Educ* Reading and Illinois U; *m* 1957, Mildred Hall; 2 s, 1 da; *Career* dir Rowett Research Institute, consultant dir Commonwealth Bureau of Nutrition 1965-; FRS (1967), FRSE (1965), kt 1977; *Style* - Sir Kenneth Blaxter; Wardenhill, Bucksburn, Aberdeen, (☎ 712751)

BLEAKLEY, Rt Hon David Wylie; PC (1971); s of John Bleakley, of Belfast; *b* 11 Jan 1925; *Educ* Ruskin Coll Oxford, Queen's U Belfast, Oxford U; *m* 1949, Winifred, da of Alfred Wason; 3 s; *Career* MP (L) Victoria (Belfast) NI Parl 1958-65; memb NI Assembly 1973-75, NI Convention 1975-76; Min Community Rels NI Govt 1971; *Style* - The Rt Hon David Bleakley, PC; 8 Thornhill, Bangor, Co Down, N Ireland (☎ 0247 4898)

BLEASE, Baron (Life Peer UK 1978); William John Blease; JP (Belfast 1974); s of late William Blease; *b* 28 May 1914; *Educ* Belfast Tech, New U of Ulster; *m* 1939, Sarah Caldwell; 3 s, 1 da; *Career* industl rels consultant, former union official; memb IBA 1974-79; *Recreations* reading, DIY; *Clubs* Sloane; *Style* - The Rt Hon Lord Blease JP; 27 Ferguson drive, Belfast (☎ 654 327)

BLEASE, Leslie; *Career* dep chm Nationwide Building Society, New Oxford House; FRIBA, FRICS; *Style* - Leslie Blease Esq; Nationwide Building Society, New Oxford House, High Holborn, WC1

BLEASE, Hon Maurice Caldwell; s of Baron Blease, JP; *b* 1944; *m* 1967, Mary, da of Philip Carol; *Style* - The Hon Maurice Blease; 26 Ormiston Park, Belfast 4

BLEASE, Hon Paul Charles; s of Baron Blease, JP; *b* 1953; *Style* - The Hon Paul Blease

BLEASE, Hon William Victor; s of Baron Blease, JP; *b* 1942; *m* 1969, Rose Mary, da of Alan Seaton; *Style* - The Hon William Blease; 6 Ormiston Cres, Belfast 4

BLECH, Harry; OBE (1962); *b* 2 Mar 1910; *Educ* Trinity Coll of Music; Manchester Coll of Music; *m* 1, 1935, Enid Lessing (d 1977); 1 s, 2 da; m 2, 1957, Marion Manley, pianist; 1 s, 3 da; *Career* musical dir Haydn-Mozart Society; founder and conductor London Mozart Players 1949-; *Style* - Harry Blech Esq OBE; The Owls, 70 Leopold Road, Wimbledon, SW19 (☎ 01 946 8135)

BLEDISLOE, 3 Viscount (1935 UK); Christopher Hiley Ludlow Bathurst; QC (1978); s of 2 Viscount Bledisloe, QC (d 1979); *b* 24 June 1934; *Educ* Eton and Trinity Oxford; *m* 1962, Elizabeth, da of Sir Edward Thompson, *qv*; 2 s (Hon Rupert Edward Ludlow Bathurst, Hon Otto Benjamin Charles Bathurst), 1 da (Hon Matilda Blanche Bathurst); *Heir* s, Hon Rupert Bathurst, *qv*; *Career* barrister 1959-; *Style* - The Rt Hon The Viscount Bledisloe, QC; Fountain Court, Temple, London, EC4; 4 Essex Villas, Kensington, London W8

BLEDISLOE, Joan, Viscountess - Joan; da of late Otto Krishaber; *m* 1933, 2 Viscount Bledisloe, QC (d 1979); 2 s (3 Viscount, Hon David Bathurst); *Style* - The Rt Hon Joan, The Viscountess Bledisloe; Lydney Park, Lydney, Gloucestershire (☎ Dean (STD Code 0594) 42566); 14 Mulberry Walk, Chelsea, SW3

BLEICHROEDER, Rudolf P J; s of Dr Fritz Bleichroeder, of Berlin (d 1938); *b* 9 March 1914; *Educ* Berlin and Holzminden (W Germany), Berlin and Madrid Us; *m* 1940, Wera, da of Gustav Fuerstenberg, of Berlin (d 1931); 2 da; *Career* dep chm Samuel Montagu 1979-; dir- City & Commercial Investment Tst, Drayton Commercial Investment Co, Drayton Consolidated Tst, Drayton Premier Investment Tst, Dualvest Ltd, Fundinvest Ltd, Montagu Boston Investment Tst, Triplevest Ltd, G T Investment Fund S A; *Recreations* bridge, swimming, walking; *Clubs* Brooks's; *Style* - Rudolf Bleichroeder Esq; 58 Avenue Close, Avenue rd, NW8 (☎ 01 722 9933); 70 Les Oliviers, Beaulieu s/m, France (☎ 93

011342)

BLENKINSOP, Henry Gerald; DL (1970 Warwickshire); s of late Henry Maxwell Blenkinsop; *b* 31 Jan 1925; *Educ* Marlborough; *m* 1957, Tessa Susan, da of Dr Eric Leonard Edmondson; 1 s, 2 da; *Career* solicitor 1951, Undersheriff Warwickshire 1951, Undersheriff part West Midlands 1972; *Recreations* sailing, (yacht 'Callooh'); *Clubs* Island Sailing; *Style* - Henry Blenkinsop Esq, DL; 45 Mill st, Warwick

BLENKINSOPP, Robert John; s of Capt John Blenkinsopp, JP, of Sheriff Hutton Hall, York; *b* 12 May 1948; *Educ* Ampleforth; *Career* dir Owen & Robinson Ltd 1975-, Henry Hardcastle Ltd 1975-, Murgatroyd & Horsfall Ltd 1975-, goldsmiths, silversmiths, jewellers and diamond merchants; *Recreations* fishing, shooting, travel, theatre, exhibitions; *Clubs* Yorkshire (York); *Style* - Robert Blenkinsopp Esq; 15 Bedford Gdns House, Bedford gdns, W8 (☎ 01 727 8588); Valley House, Scackleton, Hovingham, York (☎ 065382 339); Sheriff Hutton Hall, York (☎ 03477 442)

BLENNERHASSETT, Sir (Marmaduke) Adrian Francis William; 7 Bt (UK 1809); s of Lt Sir Marmaduke Charles Henry Joseph Casimir Blennerhassett, 6 Bt, RNVR (d 1940); *b* 25 May 1940; *Educ* McGill U, Imperial Coll London (MSc), Cranfield Business Coll (MBA); *m* 1972, Carolyn Margaret, da of late Gilbert Brown; 1 s, 1 da; *Heir* s, Charles Blennerhassett; *Style* - Sir Adrian Blennerhassett, Bt; 41 Park rd, Chiswick, W4

BLENNERHASSETT, Charles Henry Marmaduke; s & h of Sir Adrian Blennerhassett 7 Bt; *b* 18 July 1975; *Style* - Charles Blennerhassett

BLENNERHASSETT, His Honour Judge; Francis Andrew Blennerhassett; QC (1965); s of John Blennerhassett, of Knowle, Warwicks; *b* 7 July 1916; *Educ* Solihull Sch; *m* 1946, Betty, da of Rex Bray, of Sheffield; 2 da; *Career* barr 1946, Circuit Judge 1978-; *Recreations* golf; *Clubs* Copt Heath Golf; *Style* - His Hon Judge Blennerhassett, QC; 106 Old Station rd, Hampton in Arden, Solihull, Warwicks (☎ Hampton 2660)

BLEWITT, Maj Shane Gabriel Basil; s of late Col Basil Blewitt; *b* 25 Mar 1935; *Educ* Ampleforth and Ch Ch Oxford; *m* 1969, Julia, nee Calvert, widow of Maj Morrogh-Bernard, Irish Guards; 1 s, 1 da (1 step s, 1 step da); *Career* assistant keeper of the Privy Purse 1975-; *Style* - Maj Shane Blewitt; South Corner House, Duncton, nr Petworth, W Sussex (☎ 42143)

BLIGH, Lady Harriet Esme Ghislaine; da of 9 Earl of Darnley (d 1955); *b* 27 April 1949; *Educ* Cobham Hall, Somerville Oxford; *Style* - Lady Harriet Bligh; Meadow House, Cobham, nr Gravesend, Kent (☎ 0474 814 355)

BLIGH, Lady Katherine Amanda; da of 11 Earl of Darnley; *b* 1971

BLIGH, Lt-Col Hon Noel Gervase; DSO (1918); s of 8 Earl of Darnley; *b* 1888; *Educ* Eton, Sandhurst; *m* 1, 1912, Mary Jack (m dis 1934, she d 1940), da of late Capt G Frost; 2 da; m 2, 1934, Dorothy Millicent (d 1972), da of Hubert Lee Bevan; m 3, 1973, Mrs Kathleen Weatherill Strickland; *Career* Capt Rifle Brigade 1914, Lt-Col 1919-21, temp Lt-Col Pioneer Corps 1944; *Style* - Lt-Col The Hon Noel Bligh DSO; 3 Sloane Gate Mans, D'Oyly st, SW1

BLOCH, (Andrew Charles) Danby; s of Prof Moishe Rudolf Bloch; *b* 19 Dec 1945; *Educ* Tonbridge Sch, Wadham Coll Oxford; *m* 1968, Sandra, nee Wilkinson; 1 s (Adam Danby b 1972), 1 da (Hester Mary b 1974); *Career* researcher Oxford Centre for Management Studies 1968-70, dir Grosvenor Advisory Services Ltd 1971-74, dir Oxford Fine Arts Ltd 1975-, dir Raymond Godfrey & Ptnrs Ltd 1974-, dir Taxbriefs Ltd 1975-, regular weekly column on taxation The Times 1979-; *Style* - Danby Bloch Esq; Highfield Farmhouse, Highfield av, Headington, Oxford

BLOCK, Maj-Gen Adam Johnstone Cheyne; CB (1962), CBE (1959, OBE 1951), DSO (1945); s of the late Col Arthur

Hugh Block; *b* 13 June 1908; *Educ* Blundell's, RMA Woolwich; *m* 1945, Pauline Bingham, da of the late Norman Kennedy, CBE, DSO, TD, DL; 3 da (1 decd); *Career* WW II 1939-45, France, UK, N Africa, Italy, Co 24 Field Regt RA 1943-45, GSO1 RA and AMS, GHQ 1945-47, AQMG and GSO1 Trg AA Command 1947-50, sen dir staff Joint Services Staff Coll 1950-53, CRA 6 Armd Div 1953, Cdr Sch of Artillery Larkhill 1956, GOC Troops Malta and Libya 1959-62, Col Cmdt Royal Regt of Artillery 1965-73, retd 1963; *Recreations* all country pursuits, golf; *Clubs* Army & Navy; *Style* - Maj-Gen Adam Block, CB, CBE, DSO; St Cross House, Whitchurch, Hants (☎ Whitchurch 2344)

BLOCK, Simon Anthony Allen; s of Gerald Allen Block; *b* 19 July 1935; *Educ* Marlborough, Pembroke Coll Cambridge; *m* 1958, Patricia Ann, da of Gen Sir Rodney Moore, GCVO, KCB, CBE, DSO; 3 s; *Career* solicitor, master Broderers Co 1979-80; *Recreations* fine wine, field sports; *Clubs* Leander, Justinians, The Grannies; *Style* - Simon Block Esq; Brissenden House, East Sutton, nr Maidstone, Kent (☎ 062786 3191)

BLOFELD, John Christopher Calthorpe; QC (1975); s of Thomas Blofeld, CBE, JP, High Sheriff Norfolk 1953 & Chm CGA, of Hoveton House, Wroxham, Norfolk; *b* 11 July 1932; *Educ* Eton, King's Cambridge; *m* 1961, Judith, da of Dr Mohun & adopted da of James Mitchell, of Malta; 2 s, 1 da; *Career* barr; Recorder 1975; Chllr Diocese St Edmundbury 1973; chm CGA 1977; *Recreations* gardening, antiques, pottering; *Clubs* Boodle's, Norfolk; *Style* - John Blofeld Esq, QC; Harlequin House, Ickleton, Saffron Walden, Essex

BLOFELD, Thomas Robert Calthorpe; CBE (1959), JP (1954); s of John Blofeld; *b* 10 Sept 1903; *Educ* Eton, King's Cambridge; *m* 1928, Grizel Blanche, da of Christopher Rede Turner, of Postwick Lodge Norfolk; 2 s, 1 da; *Career* farmer and landowner; High Sheriff Norfolk 1953; *Recreations* shooting, country sports, collecting, art history; *Clubs* Boodle's, MCC; *Style* - Thomas Blofeld Esq, CBE, JP; Hoveton House, Norfolk (☎ Wroxham 2202)

BLOIS, Andrew Charles David; s and h of Sir Charles Blois, 11 Bt, *qv*; *b* 7 Feb 1971

BLOIS, Lady (Elizabeth) Caroline Elinor Evelyn; *née* Giffard; da of 3 Earl of Halsbury; *b* 1939; *m* 1968, Rodney John Derek Blois, s of Capt Sir Gervase Blois, 10 Bt, MC (d 1968); 2 da; *Style* - Lady Caroline Blois; Cockfield Hall, Yoxford, Suffolk

BLOIS, Sir Charles Nicholas Gervase; 11 Bt (E 1686), of Grundisburgh Hall Suffolk; s of Capt Sir Gervase Blois, 10 Bt, MC (d 1968); *b* 25 Dec 1939; *Educ* Harrow, Trin Coll Dublin; *m* 1967, Celia, da of Cyril Pritchett, CBE, of Mayfield Sussex; 1 s, 1 da; *Heir* s, Andrew Blois; *Career* farmer and landowner; *Recreations* yacht cruising (owner of yacht- 'Caleta'), travel, shooting; *Style* - Sir Charles Blois, Bt; Red House, Westleton, Saxmundham, Suffolk (☎ Blythburgh 456)

BLOIS, Margaret, Lady - Margaret Lucia; da of Maj Hon Charles White (3 s of 2 Baron Annaly); *m* 1948, as his 2 w, Capt Sir Gervase Blois, 10 Bt (d 1968); *Style* - Margaret, Lady Blois; The Vicarage, Ballyhooly, Co Cork, Eire

BLOMEFIELD, His Honour Judge; Peregrine Maitland Blomefield; s of Lt-Col Wilmot Blomefield, OBE (s of Sir Thomas Blomefield, 4 Bt, CB, JP); *b* 25 Oct 1917; *Educ* Repton, Trin Oxford; *m* 1941, Angela, da of Maj G Crofton; 1 s; *Career* Circuit Judge 1972-; *Recreations* music, living in the country; *Style* - His Hon Judge Blomefield; The Coach House, Frilsham, Newbury, Berks (☎ 0635 201421)

BLOMEFIELD, Thomas Charles Peregrine; s and h of Sir Thomas Edward Peregrine Blomefield, 5 Bt,*qv*; *b* 24 July 1948; *Educ* Wellington and Mansfield Oxford; *m* 1975, Georgina, nee Over; 1 da; *Style* - Thomas Blomefield Esq; 21b Parsons Green, SW6

BLOMEFIELD, Sir Thomas Edward Peregrine; 5 Bt (UK 1807), of

Attleborough co Norfolk; s of Cdr Thomas Blomefield, RN (ka 1915); suc gf, Sir Thomas Blomefield, 4 Bt, CB, JP (whose w, Lilias, was da of Maj Hon Charles Napier, s of 8 Baron Napier); *b* 31 May 1907; *Educ* Wellington, Trin Oxford; *m* 1947, Ginette, da of Dr Raphael Massart, of Paris; 1 s; *Heir* s, Thomas Blomefield; *Career* dir Whitehall Securities Corpn 1965-72; *Clubs* Army & Navy; *Style* - Sir Thomas Blomefield, Bt; 1 Gt Lane, Shaftesbury, Dorset (☎ 3788)

BLOMFIELD, Brig John Reginald; OBE (1957), MC (1945); s of late Douglas John Blomfield, CIE; *b* 10 Jan 1916; *Educ* Clifton Coll, RMA Woolwich, Peterhouse Cambridge; *m* 1939, Patricia Mary, nee McKim; 2 da; *Career* Royal Engineers 1936-69, manager commission for New Towns Hemel Hempstead 1969-78; *Recreations* cruising, ocean racing (yacht-'Trefoil'); *Clubs* Royal Ocean Racing, Royal Engineers Yacht, Royal Lymington Yacht; *Style* - Brig John Blomfield, OBE, MC; 9 Armstrong close, Brockenhurst, Hants (☎ Brockenhurst 2164)

BLOOM, Claire; da of late Edward Bloom; *b* 15 Feb 1931; *Educ* Badminton, USA and privately; *m* 1, 1959, Rod Steiger (m dis 1969); 1 da; m 2, 1969, Hillard Elkins (m dis 1976); *Career* actress; has appeared in theatre, film and television productions; *Style* - Miss Claire Bloom; c/o Michael Linnitt, Globe Theatre, W1

BLOOM, G(eorge) Cromarty; CBE (1974); s of late George Bloom; *b* 8 June 1910; *Educ* privately and Keble Oxford; *m* 1, 1940, Patricia Ramplin (d 1957); 2 s; m 2, 1961, Sheila Curran; 1 s; *Career* dep chm LBC; *Style* - G C Bloom Esq CBE; 1 Tivoli Court, Tivoli rd, Cheltenham, Glos (☎ 39413)

BLOOR, Hon Mrs - Hon Giovanna; da of Baron Blackett, OM, CH (Life Peer); *b* 1926; *m* 1950, Kenneth Bloor; *Style* - The Hon Mrs Bloor; 9 Queenston rd, West Didsbury, Manchester 20

BLOSS, Hon Mrs - Hon Caroline Juliet; *née* Boyd; da of 6 Baron Kilmarnock, MBE (d 1975); *b* 1939; *Educ* Doune House, Newbury, Murray House, Edinburgh and Strasbourg Us; *m* 1969, Allan Bloss; *Style* - The Hon Mrs Bloss; Wakehurst, Cranleigh, Surrey

BLOUNT, Hon Mrs - Hon Susan Victoria; da of 1 Baron Cobbold, GCVO, PC, DL, *qv*; *b* 1933; *m* 1957, Sqdn-Ldr Christopher Charles Blount, MVO (b 6 Feb 1925, educ Harrow, Trin Cambridge; Serv Equerry to HM 1954-57, with Hambros Bank 1961-79, Lazards Bank 1980-); 2 s, 2 da; *Style* - The Hon Mrs Blount; Manor Farm, Barkway, Herts (☎ 076384 550)

BLOUNT, Sir Walter Edward Alpin (Jasper); 12 Bt (E 1642), DSC; s of Sir Edward Blount, 11 Bt (d 1978); *b* 31 Oct 1917; *Educ* Beaumont Coll, Sidney Sussex Coll Cambridge; *m* 1954, Eileen Audrey, da of late Hugh B Carritt; 1 da; *Heir* none; *Career* Lt RNVR; *Style* - Sir Walter Blount, Bt, DSC; 19 St Ann's ter, St John's Wood, NW8 (☎ 01 722 0802)

BLUMER, Lady (Ella) Mary; da of Rev Hon Sydney George William Maitland (d 1946) and sister of 17 Earl of Lauderdale; *b* 1906; *m* 1932, John Alder Cripps Blumer; 3 s, 2 da; raised to rank of Earl's daughter 1953; *Style* - Lady Mary Blumer; 19 Queen's rd, Cheltenham

BLUNDELL, Brig Richard Victor; CBE (1953); s of late Walter Blundell; *b* 20 June 1908; *Educ* Newport County Secondary Sch I of W, Army; *m* 1928, Mable Violet Lydia, nee Southee; 1 s, 3 da (1 decd); *Career* enlisted RAOC 1924, Lt 1933, instr OCTU 1941-42, chief instr 1942-43, ADOS 1943-44, Lt Col 1951, Temp Col and Dep Inspr RAOC War Office 1951-52, dep command COD Bicester 1953-55, Col 1954, Cmdt 15 ABOD BAOR 1956-59, temp Brig and DDOS Eastern Command 1959-63, ret 1963; *Recreations* competition shooting rifle and revolver; *Clubs* Island Sailing (Cowes I of W); *Style* - Brig Richard Blundell, CBE; 2 Bryntirion, Pound Green, Freshwater, Isle of Wight (☎ 098 383 2427)

BLUNDEN, George; s of late George Blunden and Floren Holder; *b* 31 Dec

1922; *Educ* City of London Sch; Univ Coll Oxford; *m* 1949, Anne, nee Bulford 2 s, 1 da; *Career* exec dir Bank of England 1976-; *Style* - George Blunden Esq; Bank of England, Threadneedle st, EC2 (☎ 01 601 4444)

BLUNDEN, Philip Overington; s of Sir John Blunden, 5 Bt (d 1923); bro and hp of Sir William Blunden, 6 Bt; *b* 27 Jan 1922; *Educ* Repton; *m* 1945, Jeanette Francesca (WRNS), da of Capt D Macdonald, RNR, of Portree, Isle of Skye; 2 s, 1 da; *Style* - Philip Blunden Esq

BLUNT, Sir David Richard Reginald Harvey; 12 Bt (GB 1720); s of Sir Richard David Harvey Blunt, 11 Bt (d 1975); *b* 8 Nov 1938; *m* 1969, Sonia Tudor Rosemary, da of late Albert Edward Day; 1 da; *Heir* kinsman, Robin Anthony Blunt; *Style* - Sir David Blunt, Bt; 74 Kirkstall rd, SW2

BLUNT, Margaret, Lady; Margaret; da of John Dean; *m* 1943 (as his 2 w), Sir Richard Blunt, 11 Bt (d 1975); 2 da (Georgina b 1945, m 1981 Martin Trotter; Caroline b 1947); *Style* - Margaret, Lady Blunt; Westside House, Cherington, Tetbury, Glos

BLUNT, Robin Anthony; s of late Charles Blunt, 3 s of 8 Bt; hp of kinsman, Sir David Blunt, 12 Bt; *b* 23 Nov 1926; *Educ* Wellington; *m* 1, 1949 (m dis 1962), Sheila Stuart, da of C Stuart Brindley; 1 s; m 2, 1962, June Elizabeth, da of Charles Wigginton; 1 s; *Career* CEng, MIMechE; *Style* - Robin Blunt Esq; Edge Hill Cottage, Eaton Bank, Duffield, Derby

BLYTH, 4 Baron (1907 UK); Sir Anthony Audley Rupert Blyth; 4 Bt (1895); s of 3 Baron Blyth (d 1977); *b* 3 June 1931; *Educ* St Columba's Coll, Dublin; *m* 1, 1954, Elizabeth, nee Sparrow (m dis 1962); 1 s, 2 da; m 2, 1963, Oonagh, nee Conway; 1 s, 1 da; *Heir* s, Hon Riley Blyth; *Style* - The Rt Hon the Lord Blyth; Blythwood Estate, Athenry, Co Galway, Eire

BLYTH, Hon Alexandra; da of 4 Baron Blyth; *b* 1957; *Style* - The Hon Alexandra Blyth

BLYTH, Hon Anne Shelagh Jennifer; 1936; da (twin) of 3 Baron Blyth; *Style* - The Hon Anne Blyth; Athenry, Co Galway, Eire

BLYTH, Hon Adrian Ulrick Christopher David; s of 3 Baron Blyth; *b* 1944; *Educ* Sebright Sch, Northants Coll of Ag; *m* 1966, Patricia Maureen, SRN, da of Desmond Southey; 1 da; *Style* - The Hon Adrian Blyth; Rockfield House, Athenry, Co Galway, Eire

BLYTH, Hon Barbara Patricia Edna; da (twin) of 3 Baron Blyth; *b* 1936; *Educ* Alexandra Sch Dublin, Moreton Hall Oswestry; *Style* - The Hon Barbara Blyth; Rockfield House, Athenry, Co Galway, Eire

BLYTH, Hon James Audley Ian; s of 4 Baron Blyth; *b* 1970; *Style* - The Hon James Blyth

BLYTH, Hon Lucinda Audley Jane; da of 4 Baron Blyth; *b* 1966; *Style* - The Hon Lucinda Blyth

BLYTH, Hon Marcia Edna Dorothea; da of 4 Baron Blyth; *b* 1956; *Style* - The Hon Marcia Blyth

BLYTH, Hon Riley Audley John; s and h of 4 Baron Blyth; *b* 4 Mar 1955; *Style* - The Hon Riley Blyth

BLYTH, Hon Tanya Ormonde Audley; da of 3 Baron Blyth; *b* 1929; *Educ* Alexandra Sch Dublin, Moreton Hall Oswestry; *Career* SRN; *Style* - The Hon Tanya Blyth; Rockfield House, Athenry, Co Galway, Eire

BLYTH CURRIE, J M; *Career* md Blyth, Green, Jourdain and Co Ltd; *Style* - J M Blyth Currie Esq; Blyth, Green, Jourdain and Co Ltd, Plantation House, Fenchurch st, EC3

BLYTHE, Hon Mrs - Hon Rachel Georgiana; da of 2 Baron Rennell; *b* 1935; *m* 1964, Richard Douglas Blythe; 2 s; *Style* - The Hon Mrs Blythe; Kordabup, Denmark, W Australia

BLYTON, Baron (Life Peer UK 1964);

William Reid Blyton; s of Charles Blyton; *b* 2 May 1899; *Educ* elementary schs S Shields; *m* 1919, Jane, da of Edward Ord; 3 da; *Career* coal miner 1913-45, MP (L) Houghton-le-Spring 1945-64; *Recreations* gardening; *Clubs* White Leas and Simonside Working Men's; *Style* - The Rt Hon The Lord Blyton; 139 Brockley av, S Shields, Tyne & Wear

BOARDLEY, Hon Mrs - Hon Katherine Susan; *née* FitzRoy; da of 2 Viscount Daventry; *b* 1923; *m* 1 1945, Phil John Turner (m dis 1958); m 2, 1958, Anthony Woodington Boardley (d 1967); 1 s; *Career* late Cadet Ensign First Aid Nursing Yeo; *Style* - The Hon Mrs Boardley; 47 Four Gables, Sandown Park, Sandown, Johannesburg, S Africa

BOARDMAN, Baron (Life Peer UK 1980); Thomas Gray Boardman; MC (1944), TD (1952), DL (Northants 1977); s of John Boardman; *b* 12 Jan 1919; *Educ* Bromsgrove Sch; *m* 1948, Norah, da of Hubert Gough, of Pangbourne, and widow of John Chaworth-Musters; 2 s, 1 da; *Career* MP (C) Leicester SW 1967-74 & Leicester S Feb-Sept 1974; Min Indust 1972-74, Ch Sec Treasury 1974; served WW II Northants Yeo, Cmmdg 1956; High Sheriff Northants 1979; chm Steetley Co 1978-, dir Nat West Bank 1979-, MEPC Ltd 1980-; *Style* - The Rt Hon Lord Boardman, MC, TD, DL; The Manor House, Welford, Northants (☎ 235); 29 Tufton Court, Tufton st, SW1 (☎ 01 222 6793)

BOARDMAN, Alan; *Career* ch exec Adams Foods; *Style* - Alan Boardman Esq; Adams Foods, Springfields rd, Leek, Staffs

BOARDMAN, Hon Anthony Hubert Gray; s of Baron Boardman; *b* 6 May 1949; *Educ* Ampleforth; *m* 1977, Catherine, da of Thomas Penn, of Manor Farm, Northampton; 1 da; *Style* - The Hon Anthony Boardman; Meadow Farm Cottage, Bourton-on-the-Water, Glos

BOARDMAN, Sir Kenneth Ormrod; *Career* kt 1981 for political and public service; *Style* - Sir Kennth Boardman

BOARDMAN, Hon Nigel Patrick Gray; s of Baron Boardman; *b* 1950; *m* 1975, Sarah, nee Coslett; *Style* - The Hon Nigel Boardman; 107 Huddlestone rd, Tufnell Park, N7

BOAST, Roy Stanley; CBE (1964, OBE 1960), DFC; s of Henry Boast (d 1932); *b* 21 Dec 1920; *Educ* Southend H S for Boys; *m* 1943, Maureen, née Ratcliffe; 1 s, 1 da; *Career* Gp Capt Bomber Cmmd and Far East RAF; Exec V-Pres Br Scrap Metal Fedn 1968-; *Recreations* gardening, reading; *Clubs* RAF; *Style* - Roy Boast Esq, CBE, DFC; Breckland, Sheringwood, Sheringham, Norfolk (☎ 822869)

BOCKETT, Herbert Leslie; CMG (1961); s of C F Bockett; *b* 29 June 1905; *Educ* Seddon Memorial Technical Coll; *m* 1932, Constance Ramsay; 2 da; *Career* accountant; memb, shipping industry tribunal 1972-; *Style* - Herbert Bockett Esq CMG; 189 The Parade, Island Bay, Wellington, New Zealand (☎ 838 549)

BOCKSTOCE, Lady Romayne Bryony; *née* Grimston; da of 6 Earl of Verulam; *b* 1946; *m* 1973, John Roberts Bockstoce; 1 s; *Style* - Lady Romayne Bockstoce; 1 Hill st, S Dartmouth, Mass, USA

BODDEN, John; s of Harry Bodden (d 1954); *b* 15 May 1923; *Educ* Felsted Sch, Manchester U, Wadham Oxford; *Career* slr and notary public; sr ptnr Platt Bodden & Co, dir Ernest Broadbelt Investments Ltd; tstee Oldham Foundation, cncl memb Manchester Statistical Soc; *Recreations* golf; *Clubs* St James's (Manchester), Manchester Tennis and Racquet Club, Prestbury Golf; *Style* - John Bodden Esq; 10 Woodhead dve, Park rd, Hale, Ches (☎ 061 980 4969); Kensham, Moat Hill, Totnes, S Devon (☎ Tones 86349)

BODEN, John Hewetson; *Career* chm and ch exec Metal Closures Gp Ltd; *Style* - John Boden Esq; 40 Brook st, W1

BODY, Lady Julia Frances; da of Victor Montagu (10 Earl of Sandwich, who disclaimed his peerages for life 1964); *b* 1947; *m* 1, 1972, Martin Lee Oakley (m dis 1976); m 2, 1976, Peter Gerald Edward Body; *Style* - Lady Julia Body

BODY, Richard Bernard Frank Stewart; MP (C) Holland with Boston 1966-; s of Lt-Col Bernard Body, of Donnington Beds; *b* 18 May 1927; *Educ* Reading Sch; *m* 1959, Doris, da of Maj Harold Graham, OBE; 1 s, 1 da; *Career* barr 1949, MP (C) Billericay 1955-59, Lloyd's Underwriter 1979-; *Recreations* hunting with own pack of bloodhounds; *Clubs* Carlton, Reform; *Style* - Richard Body Esq, MP; Jewell's Farm, Stanford Dingley, Berks (☎ Bradfield 295)

BOEHM, Hugo; OBE (Mil 1946), TD (1949), JP (Bucks 1953), DL (1952); s of Frederick Boehm, of Harrow; *b* 24 July 1911; *Educ* Oundle; *m* 1934, Nancy, da of Dr Cecil Golding; 1 s, 2 da; *Career* co dir ret 1971; *Recreations* archery; *Clubs* Roy Toxophilite Soc; *Style* - Hugo Boehm Esq, OBE, TD, JP, DL; Hampden Lodge, Parslows Hillock, Princes Risborough, Bucks (☎ Hampden Row 371)

BOGERT, Maj-Gen Mortimer Patrick; CBE (1953), DSO (1944), CD (1952); s of Mortimer Bogert, of Montreal; *b* 17 March 1908; *Educ* Ashbury Coll Ottawa, Roy Mil Coll of Canada; *m* 1, 1946, Pauline (m dis 1955), da of Philip Martin, of Dorset; 1 s; m 2, 1964, Gertrude, da of Hugh MacPhee, of Ottawa; *Career* GOC E Cmmd Canada 1958-62; *Recreations* shooting, bridge; *Clubs* Boodle's, Army & Navy; *Style* - Maj-Gen Mortimer Bogert, CBE, DSO, CD; Grove Cottage, Donnington, Newbury, Berks (☎ 40631)

BOGGIS-ROLFE, Hume; CB (1971), CBE (1962); s of Douglass Boggis-Rolfe, of The Grange, Wormingford, Colchester; *b* 20 Oct 1911; *Educ* Westminster, Freiburg U, Trin Cambridge; *m* 1941, Annie, da of Capt Eric Noble, of Henley; 2 s, 1 da; *Career* barr 1935, Dep Clerk of the Crown & Dep Perm Sec Ld Chancellor's Off 1968-75; farmer; *Recreations* gardening, travel; *Clubs* Athenaeum; *Style* - Hume Boggis-Rolfe Esq, CB, CBE; The Grange, Wormingford, Colchester, Essex (☎ Bures 227303)

BOGIE, Dr David James; TD (1945); s of David Bogie; *b* 28 Nov 1905; *Educ* Strathallan Sch, Edinburgh U; *m* 1945, Eirene May, da of George Miller; 1 s, 1 da; *Career* CA, ptnr Deloitte Haskin & Sells, Edinburgh, 1933-74; dir- Waverley Cameron Ltd; chm Wemyss Investment Co; *Recreations* golf, fishing, curling; *Clubs* Caledonian, Bruntisfield Golfing Soc (late Capt); *Style* - Dr David Bogie, TD; Woodley, 34 Southerton Road, Kirkcaldy, Fife, Scotland (☎ Kirkcaldy (STD Code 0592) 4110)

BOILEAU, Mary, Lady - Catherine; da of late Lawrence Riordan; *m* 1941, as his 2 w, Maj Sir Gilbert Boileau, 6 Bt (d 1978); *Style* - Mary, Lady Boileau; Minto Lodge, 1480 Heatherston rd, Dandenong, Victoria, Australia

BOILEAU, Lt-Col Sir Guy Francis; 8 Bt (UK 1838); s of Sir Edmond Charles Boileau, 7 Bt (d 1980); *b* 23 Feb 1935; *Educ* Xavier Coll Melbourne, RMC Duntroon Australia; *m* 1962, Judith Frances, da of Senator George Conrad Hannan, of Glen Iris, Canberra; 2 s, 3 da; *Heir* s, Nicolas Boileau; *Career* Lt-Col Australian Army; company dir; *Style* - Lt-Col Sir Guy Boileau, Bt; 14 Faircroft av, Glen Iris, Victoria 3146, Australia

BOILEAU, Nicolas Edmond George; s and h of Lt-Col Sir Guy Boileau, 8 Bt; *b* 1964; *Style* - Nicolas Boileau Esq; c/o Lt-Col Sir Guy Boileau, Bt, 14 Faircroft Avenue, Glen Iris, Victoria 3146, Australia

BOLES, Lady Anne Hermione; *née* Waldegrave; fourth daughter of 12 Earl Waldegrave, KG, TD, JP, DL, and sister of Hon William Waldegrave, MP; *b* 24 December 1937; *m* 1971, John Dennis Boles; *Style* - Lady Anne Boles; The Old Rectory, Englefield, nr Reading, Berks

BOLES, John Dennis; MBE (1960); s of late Cdr Geoffrey Boles; *b* 25 June 1925; *Educ* Winchester; *m* 1, Benita, nee Wormald (d 1969); 2 s, 3 da; m 2, 1971, Lady Anne Hermione, da of 12 Earl Waldegrave; *Career* dir gen National Trust 1975-; *Style* - John Boles Esq MBE; The Old Rectory, Englefield, nr Reading, Berks (☎ Reading 302 497)

BOLES, Sir Jeremy John Fortescue; 3 Bt (UK 1922); s of Capt Sir Gerald

Fortescue Boles, 2 Bt (d 1945); *b* 9 Jan 1932; *Educ* Stowe; *m* 1, 1955 (m dis 1970), Dorothy Jane, da of J A Worswick; 2 s, 1 da; m 2, 1970, Elisabeth Gildroy, da of E P Shaw, of Englefield Green, Surrey, and wid of Oliver Simon Willis Fleming; 1 da; *Heir* s, Richard Boles; *Style* - Sir Jeremy Boles, Bt; Lime House, Tilford, Farnham, Surrey

BOLES, Richard Fortescue; s and h of Sir Jeremy Boles, 3 Bt; *b* 12 Dec 1958; *Style* - Richard Boles Esq

BOLINGBROKE AND ST JOHN, 7 Viscount (GB 1712); Sir Kenneth Oliver Musgrave St John; 11 Bt (E 1611); also Baron St John of Lydiard Tregoze (GB 1712), Viscount St John and Baron St John of Battersea (GB 1716); s of Capt Geoffrey St John, MC (d 1972), gggs of 3 Viscount, by his 2 w Katharine; suc kinsman 1974; *b* 22 March 1927; *Educ* Eton; *m* 1, 1953 (m dis 1972), Patricia Mary, da of B J McKenna, of Christchurch, NZ; 1 s; m 2, 1972, Jainey Anne, da of late Alexander Duncan McRae, of Timaru, NZ; 2 s; *Heir* s, Hon Henry St John; *Career* patron of one living; Fell of Australian Inst of Travel, Pres of Travel Agents Assoc of NZ 1966-68, dir of World Assoc of Travel Agencies 1967-75, chm Australian Cncl of Tour Wholesalers 1972-75, chm Atlantic & Pacific Travel Gp of Cos 1958-76, dir Bolingbroke and Ptnrs Ltd 1976-; *Style* - The Rt Hon The Viscount Bolingbroke and St John; 32 Andover st, Christchurch, New Zealand

BOLITHO, Maj Simon Edward; MC (1945), JP (Cornwall 1959); s of Col Sir Edward Bolitho, KBE, CB, DSO; *b* 13 March 1916; *Educ* RNC Dartmouth, Sandhurst; *m* 1953, Elizabeth, da of Rear-Adm G Creswelll, CB, DSO; 2 s, 2 d; *Career* dir Barclays Bank 1959-, English China Clays 1966-, High Sheriff Cornwall 1956-57, Vice-Lt Cornwall 1970-, DL 1964; *Recreations* shooting, fishing, sailing; *Clubs* Army & Navy, Pratt's, MCC, Roy Yacht Sqdn; *Style* - Maj Simon Bolitho MC JP, HM Vice-Lt for Cornwall; Trengwainton, Penzance, Cornwall (☎ 3106)

BOLLAND, Sir Edwin; KCMG (1981, CMG 1971); *b* 20 Oct 1922; *Educ* Morley G S, Univ Coll Oxford; *m* 1948, Winifred Mellor; 1 s, 3 da; *Career* HM Ambass Belgrade; formerly head British Delegation to Reductions of Forces and Armaments in Central Europe; *Style* - Sir Edwin Bolland, KCMG; c/o Foreign and Commonwealth Office, SW1

BOLLOM, Philip; s of Ivor Bollom; *b* 30 March 1926; *Educ* Wycliffe Coll; *m* 1947, Patricia, da of Walter Vincent Carr Sweeting; 2 s, 2 da; *Career* chm of Bollom Ltd 1977-, Hartonclean Ltd 1977-, Jas Smith and Sons Ltd 1977-, John Crockatt Ltd 1977-, J Pullar & Sons 1977-, Stevenson Bros (Dundee) 1977-, Zernys Ltd 1977-, Joseph Harris Ltd 1979-; md Johnson Group Cleaners Ltd; dep chm Johnson Gp Cleaners Properties 1977-; dir-Capital & County Laundries 1979-, James Hayes & Sons 1979-, Winter Gardens Hotel (Bournemouth) Ltd 1980-; *Style* - Philip Bollom Esq; Mildmay rd, Bootle, Merseyside L20 5EW

BOLT, Frederick William George; *Career* chm and md Biro Bic; ACMA; *Style* - Frederick Bolt Esq; Biro Bic, Whitby ave, NW10

BOLTE, Dame Edith (Lilian); *née* DBE (1973, CBE 1959); da of D F M Elder; *m* 1943, Hon Sir Henry Bolte, GCMG, late Premier of Victoria; *Career* Girl Guide Movement; *Style* - Dame Edith Bolte, DBE; Kialla, Meredith, Victoria 3333, Australia

BOLTON, 7 Baron (GB 1797); Richard William Algar Orde-Powlett; JP (N Riding of Yorks 1957); s of 6 Baron Bolton (d 1963) and Victoria, da of late Henry Montagu Villiers, MVO, gn of 4 Earl of Clarendon; *b* 11 July 1929; *Educ* Eton, Trin Cambridge; *m* 1, 1951 (m dis 1981), Hon Christine Helena Weld-Forester, da of 7 Baron Forester and Marie, CStJ, da of Sir Herbert Perrott, 6 Bt, CH, CB; 2 s, 1 da; m 2, 1981, Masha Anne, da of Maj F E Hudson, of Winterfield House, Hornby, Bedale, Yorks; *Heir* s, Hon Harry Orde-Powlett; *Career* chm Yorks Branch Roy Forestry Soc 1963-64, dir Yorks General Life, chm Waterers Gp and Yorks Soc of Agric, FRICS; *Style* - The Rt Hon The Lord Bolton, JP; Bolton Hall, Leyburn, N Yorks (☎ Wensleydale 22303)

BOLTON, Anthony Hale; s of Eric Bolton, of New Barnet; *b* 8 Aug 1942; *Educ* St Albans Sch; *m* 1962, Olive, da of Thomas O'Loughlin; 1 s, 1 da; *Career* ch exec Aviation Div C T Bowring & Co; chm Bowring Space Projects Ltd, ATISV (all 1980); dir Marsh & McLennan Inc (USA) 1981-; memb exec ctee Lloyd's Insur Brokers; *Recreations* golf, tennis, soccer; *Style* - Anthony Bolton Esq; 19 Friern Mount dve, N20

BOLTON, Baroness; Hon Christine Helena; *née* Weld-Forester; da of late 7 Baron Forester; *b* 1932; *m* 1951, 7 Baron Bolton, *qv*; *Style* - Christine, Lady Bolton

BOLTON, Sir Frederic Bernard; MC (1945); s of Louis Bolton; *b* 9 March 1921; *Educ* Rugby; *m* 1, 1950, Valerie Barwick (d 1970); 2 s; m 2, 1971, Vanessa, da of Lt-Col Anthony Robarts; 2 s, 2 da; *Career* chm F Bolton Gp 1953-, Atlantic Steam Navigation Co 1960-71; dir BP Tanker Co, Sealink UK Ltd; Pres Internat Shipping Fedn 1973-, kt 1976; *Recreations* country sports; *Clubs* City of London; *Style* - Sir Frederic Bolton, MC; Pudlicote, Charlbury, Oxon; Corn Exchange Bldg, 52/57 Mark Lane, EC3 (☎ 01 709 0722)

BOLTON, Sir Ian Frederick Cheney; 2 Bt (UK 1927), of West Plean, co Stirling., KBE (1957, OBE 1946); s of Sir Edwin Bolton, 1 Bt, MBE, DL (d 1931), and Elinor (da of Sir John Hatt Noble Graham, 1 Bt); *b* 29 Jan 1889; *Educ* Eton; *Heir* none; *Career* CA ret, Ld-Lt Stirlingshire 1940-54, Past Pres CAs of Scotland; *Recreations* boy scouts; *Clubs* Western (Glasgow); *Style* - Sir Ian Bolton, Bt, KBE; West Plean, Stirling (☎ Bannockburn 812208)

BOLTON, Sir John Brown; OBE (1973); s of Richard Bolton; *b* 20 Jan 1902; *Educ* Hull G S, Keighley Trade & G S; *m* 1930, Mary, da of Harrington Smith; 1 s, 1 da; *Career* CA, memb House of Keys 1946-67, memb Legislative Cncl IOM 1967-79, chm IOM Finance Bd 1967-77 kt 1977; *Recreations* gardening; *Clubs* Douglas Golf; *Style* - Sir John Bolton, OBE; Amberley, Woodlands Close, Douglas, IOM (☎ 21267)

BOLTON, James Douglas; TD (1962), DL (Herts 1968); s of Percy Bolton, of Hitchin; *b* 4 Feb 1921; *Educ* Oundle, King's Cambridge; *m* 1959, Margaret, nee Forsyth; 1 s, 1 da; *Career* slr, memb Cncl Law Soc 1975-; *Recreations* tennis, swimming; *Style* - James Bolton Esq, TD, DL; Cox's, 23 Park Ave South, Harpenden, Herts (☎ 2222)

BOLTON, Hon Mrs (Lavinia Valerie); *née* Woodhouse; da of 4 Baron Terrington; *b* 29 Aug 1943; *Educ* Downham Herts, Montesano Gstaad; *m* 1974, Nicholas George Bolton, s of Sir George Lewis French Bolton, KCMG; 2 da; *Recreations* antique collecting; *Style* - The Hon Mrs Bolton; Sevenhampton House, Sevenhampton, Highworth, Wilts

BOLTON, Martin Alfred Butts; JP (Staffs 1959), DL (1969); s of Francis Bolton, JP, CA, of Moor Court, Oakmoor, Staffs; *b* 27 June 1923; *Educ* Shrewsbury, Magdalene Cambridge; *m* 1946, Margaret, da of C Kennaway, WS, of Kenwood Park, Auchterarder, Perthshire; 2 s, 3 da; *Career* farmer, memb CLA Cncl 1962-; chm Cmmn of Income Tax Staffs 1972-, W Midlands Ag Land Tbnl 1974-; Pres Staffs Ag Soc 1971, High Sheriff Staffs 1960-61; *Recreations* shooting, golf, tennis; *Clubs* Farmers'; *Style* - Martin Bolton Esq, JP, DL; Croxden Abbey, Uttoxeter, Staffs (☎ 088 926 225)

BOMPAS, Donald George; CMG (1966); s of Rev Edward Bompas; *b* 20 Nov 1920; *Educ* Merchant Taylors', Oriel Oxford; *m* 1946, Freda, da of Fred Milner Smithyman, of Malawi; 1 s, 1 da; *Career* Sec Guy's Med and Dental Sch 1969-, Liveryman Merchant Taylors' Co 1951-; formerly with Overseas Audit Serv; *Clubs* Roy C'wlth Soc; *Style* - Donald Bompas Esq, CMG; 8 Birchwood rd, Petts Wood, Kent (☎ Orpington 21661)

BONALLACK, Michael Francis; OBE (1971); s of Sir Richard Bonallack, *qv*; *b* 31 Dec 1934; *Educ* Chigwell and Haileybury; *m* 1958, Angela Ward; 1 s, 3 da; *Career* md Miller Buckley Golf Services Ltd 1974-; dir Buckley Investments Ltd 1976-; *Style* - Michael Bonallack Esq OBE; The Old Rectory, North Fambridge, Chelmsford,

Essex (☎ Maldon 740397)

BONALLACK, Sir Richard Frank; CBE (1955, OBE Mil 1945); s of Francis Bonallack; *b* 2 June 1904; *Educ* Haileybury; *m* 1930, Winifred, da of James Esplen, OBE; 2 s, 1 da; *Career* kt 1957, dir Alcan T'port Products 1979, Pres Freight Bonallack Ltd 1977-; chm Bonallack Gp 1955-71; *Recreations* golf; *Style* - Sir Richard Bonallack, CBE; 4 The Willows, Thorpe Bay, Essex (☎ Southend 588180)

BONAPARTE WYSE, William Lucien; s of Andrew Bonaparte Wyse (gs of Rt Hon Sir Thomas Wyse, KCB, PC, DL, of a family settled in Waterford since *temp* Richard Earl of Pembroke and which provided Waterford with 36 Mayors & High Sheriffs 1452-1690; Sir Thomas m HH Laetizia, Princess Bonaparte, da of HIH Lucien Bonaparte, the maverick bro of the Emperor, who nonetheless played a vital role in the 19 Brumaire coup and who was the last to support Napoleon during the tail end of the Hundred Days in 1815); Andrew m Countess Marie, da of Count Dmitri Chiriponov, of Orel province, Russia; *b* 13 March 1908; *Educ* Downside, Pembroke Cambridge; *m* 1, 1933 (m annulled 1946), Benedicta, da of Charles Chichester, of Jersey; m 2, 1954, Olga, da of Henry Rollason, of Southsea; 1 s (Henry, b 11 July 1950), 1 da (Frances, b 28 Jan 1948); *Career* served WW II Lt Free Fr Navy, ADC to Adm Auboyneau (CIC 1942-45); *Style* - William Bonaparte Wyse Esq; Beaumarchais, 22690 Pleudihen-sur-Rance, France

BONAS, I G; *Career* md Bonas Machine Co Ltd; *Style* - I G Bonas Esq; Bonas Machine Co Ltd, Sunderland, Tyne and Wear

BOND, Edward; *b* 18 July 1934; *m* 1971, Elisabeth Pable; *Career* playwright and director; George Devine Award 1968, John Whiting Award 1968; *Style* - Edward Bond Esq; c/o Margaret Ramsay, 14a Goodwins Court, St Martin's lane, WC2

BOND, Maurice Francis; CB (1978), MVO (1976), OBE (1955); s of William Bond; *b* 29 Oct 1916; *Educ* Windsor G S and Selwyn Cambridge; *m* 1954, Shelagh, nee Lewis (d 1973); *Career* clerk of the records 1946-; principal clerk information services House of Lords 1974-; *Style* - Maurice Bond Esq, CB, MVO, OBE; 19 Bolton Crescent, Windsor, Berks (☎ 65132)

BOND-WILLIAMS, Noel Ignace; CBE (1979); s of late W H Williams; *b* 7 Nov 1914; *Educ* Oundle and Birmingham U; *m* 1939, Mary Tomey; 1 s, 2 da; *Career* dir National Exhibition Centre Ltd 1970-; vice-chm Lucas Ltd 1979-; chm Remploy Ltd 1979-; Pro-Chancellor, U of Aston in Birmingham 1970-; *Style* - Noel Bond-Williams Esq CBE; Kiftsgate, Weston Subedge, Chipping Campden (☎ Evesham 840 088)

BONE, Geoffrey William; *Career* chm Ransomes Sims and Jeffries Ltd; *Style* - Geoffrey Bone Esq; Ransomes Sims and Jeffries Ltd, Nacton Works, Ipswich

BONEFELD, Kresten; *Career* joint-chm Danish Bacon Co Ltd; *Style* - Kresten Bonefeld Esq; Danish Bacon Co Ltd, Howards gate, Welwyn Garden City, Herts

BONHAM, Sir Antony Lionel Thomas; 4 Bt (UK 1852); s of Maj Sir Eric Bonham, 3 Bt, CVO, JP (d 1937), and Ethel, da of Lt-Col Leopold Seymour (s of Rt Hon Sir George Seymour, GCB, GCH, PC, and Hon Gertrude, da of 21 Baron Dacre; Sir George Seymour was s of Lord George Seymour, MP, s of 1 Marquess of Hertford); *b* 21 Oct 1916; *Educ* Eton, Sandhurst; *m* 1944, Felicity, da of Col Frank Pardoe, DSO, of Bartonbury, Cirencester; 3 s; *Heir* s, George Bonham; *Career* dir wine business to 1970, ret; *Style* - Sir Antony Bonham, Bt; Ash House, Ampney Crucis, Cirencester, Glos (☎ Poulton 391); Beach Cottage, Bembridge, IOW (☎ 2252)

BONHAM, Hon Mrs - Hon Caroline; *née* Hamilton; da of 2 Baron Holmpatrick, DSO, MC (d 1942); *b* 21 Oct 1926; *Educ* Lawnside Malvern, Froebel Inst Roehampton; *m* 1951, Maj John Henry Hamilton Bonham; 3 s; *Career* teacher Miss Ironside's Sch Elvaston Place SW7 1948-50; *Recreations* reading, craftwork, languages; *Style* - The Hon Mrs Bonham; Trumroe, Castlepollard, Co Westmeath, Eire (☎ Mullingar 61132)

BONHAM, (George) Martin Antony; s and h of Sir Antony Bonham, 4 Bt; *b* 18 Feb 1945; *Educ* Eton, Aston U; *m* 1979, Nenon Baillieu, da of Robert Ruttan Wilson, of Petersfield; 1 s; *Career* retail sales man Calor Gas Ltd; *Recreations* sailing, golf, tennis, squash, riding; *Clubs* RAC; *Style* - Martin Bonham Esq; 8 Campana rd, SW6 (☎ 01 731 0278)

BONHAM CARTER, Hon Mark Raymond; s of Sir Maurice Bonham Carter, KCB, KCVO (d 1958), and Baroness Asquith of Yarnbury, DBE (d 1969; she was Lady Violet Asquith, da of 1 Earl of Oxford and Asquith, KG); *b* 11 Feb 1922; *Educ* Winchester, Balliol Oxford; *m* 1955, Leslie, da of Condé Nast, of New York, and formerly w of 2 Baron St Just; 3 da; *Career* chm Outer Circle Policy Unit 1976-, V-Chm BBC 1975-81, MP (Lib) Torrington 1958-59, chm Race Rels Bd 1966-70; *Clubs* Brooks's, MCC; *Style* - The Hon Mark Bonham Carter; 49 Victoria rd, W8 (☎ 01 937 4142)

BONHAM CARTER, Richard Erskine; s of late Capt A E Bonham Carter; *b* 27 Aug 1910; *Educ* Clifton; Peterhouse Cambridge; St Thomas' Hospital; *m* 1946, Margaret, nee Stace; 3 da; *Career* physician to Hospital for Sick Children, Gt Ormond st; *Style* - Richard Bonham Carter Esq; 18 Doughty Mews, WC1 (☎ 01 405 3062); Castle Sweyn Cottage, Achnamara, Argyll

BONHAM CARTER, Hon Raymond Henry; s of Sir Maurice Bonham Carter, KCB, KCVO, and Lady Violet Bonham Carter, DBE (later Baroness Asquith of Yarnburg); *b* 19 June 1929; *Educ* Winchester; Magdalen Oxford; Harvard Business Sch; *m* 1958, Elena Propper de Callejon; 2 s, 1 da; *Career* on secondment as dir, Industrial Development Unit Dept of Industry 1977-; *Style* - The Hon Raymond Bonham Carter; 7 West Heath ave, NW11 (☎ 01 455 8434)

BONHAM-CARTER, Sir Arthur Desmond; TD (1942); s of Gen Sir Charles Bonham-Carter, GCB, CMG, DSO (d 1955), and Beryl, nee Codrington; *b* 15 Feb 1908; *Educ* Winchester, Magdalene Cambridge; *m* 1, 1933, Ann Parker (d 1972), da of George Hazelwood; 1 s; m 2, 1973, Diane, da of Mervyn Madden; *Career* dir Unilever 1953-68, kt 1969, memb Roy Cmmn Pay of Doctors and Dentists 1957-60, Tstee Nightingale Fund 1961-; *Recreations* gardening, racing; *Style* - Sir Arthur Bonham-Carter, TD; 15 Ashfield Close, Midhurst, Sussex (☎ 2109)

BONHAM-CARTER, Lady; Charlotte Helen; *née* Ogilvy; da of Col William Ogilvy, CB (gs of Rear-Adm Sir William Ogilvy, 8 Bt), by his w Lucy, JP (Hants), da of William Wickham, DL, MP (descended from William Wickham, PC, MP, sometime Ch Sec for Ireland and envoy to Swiss cantons and Austrian & Russian armies during Napoleonic Wars); *b* 1893; *m* 1926, Sir Edgar Bonham-Carter KCMG CIE (d 1956, 5 s of Henry Bonham Carter and unc of Mark and Raymond Bonham Carter and Mrs Jo (Laura) Grimond); *Style* - Lady Bonham-Carter; Wyck Place, Alton, Hants; 5 Connaught sq, W2 (☎ 01 723 4980)

BONHAM-CARTER, Victor; 4 s of Gen Sir Charles Bonham-Carter, GCB, CMG, DSO (d 1955) by his 2 w Gabrielle and is 1 cous of Hon. Mark Bonham Carter the first chm of the Race Relations Bd; *b* 13 Dec 1913; *Educ* Winchester, Magdalene Cambridge; *m* 1, 1938, Audrey Edith Stogdon (m dis 1979); 2 s; m 2, 1979, Cynthia Claire Sanford, nee Young; *Career* author, publications offr Soc of Authors 1965- (joint-sec 1971-78, consultant 1978-) sec Royal Literary Fund 1966-; *Recreations* listening to *good* music; *Clubs* Authors'; *Style* - Victor Bonham-Carter Esq; The Mount, Milverton, Taunton

BONNAR, Douglas Kershaw; s of Thomas Bonnar; *b* 3 July 1931; *Educ* Edinburgh Acad, Melville Coll Edinburgh; *m* 1960, Suzanne, da of Charles Bettinson; 3 s, 1 da; *Career* memb ICA Scotland; dir Chase Manhattan Bank 1969-; *Recreations* bridge, snooker, golf; *Clubs* Caledonian,

United (Jersey), Victoria (Jersey); *Style* - Douglas Bonnar Esq; Westward, Rue de Pont Marquet, St Brelade, Jersey (☎ 0534 42020)

BONNER, Paul Max; s of Frank Max Bonner; *b* 30 May 1934; *Educ* Felsted School; *m* 1956, Nora Jenifer; 3 s; *Career* channel controller Channel Four TV Co Ltd; formerly head of science BBC TV; documentary producer with BBC; *Recreations* walking, photography and sailing; *Clubs* BAFTA; *Style* - Paul Bonner Esq; Wimbledon Common, London SW19

BONNOR-MAURICE, Edward Arthur Trevor; s of Trevor Bonnor-Maurice; *b* 24 April 1928; *Educ* Winchester; *m* 1958, Lavinia, da of Sir Richard Leighton, 10 Bt, TD; 2 da; *Career* served Coldstream Gds 1946-61, Maj; MFH Tanatside Foxhounds 1971-, memb CC Montgomeryshire 1961-74, High Sheriff 1975-76; *Clubs* Guards & Cavalry, MCC; *Style* - Edward Bonnor-Maurice Esq; Bodynfoel Hall, Llanfechain, Montgomeryshire (☎ 069 184 486)

BONSER, Air Vice-Marshal Stanley Haslam; CB (1969), MBE (1941); s of Sam Bonser; *b* 17 May 1916; *Educ* High Storrs G S, Sheffield U; *m* 1941, Margaret, da of William Howard; 2 s; *Career* Dep Controller Aircraft (C) MOD 1971-72, dir Easams Ltd 1972-; *Recreations* scout movement, gardening; *Clubs* RAF; *Style* - Air Vice-Marshal Stanley Bonser, CB, MBE; Chalfont, Waverley av, Fleet, Hants (☎ 5835)

BONSOR, (Alexander) Cosmo; s and h of Sir Nicholas Bonsor, 4 Bt, MP; *b* 8 Sept 1976; *Style* - Cosmo Bonsor

BONSOR, Elizabeth, Lady - Elizabeth; da of Capt Angus Valdimar Hambro, of Milton Abbas, Dorset; *m* 1942, Maj Sir Bryan Cosmo Bonsor, 3 Bt, MC, TD (d 1977); *Style* - Elizabeth, Lady Bonsor; Liscombe Park, Leighton Buzzard, Beds

BONSOR, Sir Nicholas Cosmo; 4 Bt (UK 1925), MP (C) Nantwich 1979-; s of Sir Bryan Bonsor, 3 Bt, MC, TD (d 1979) and Elizabeth, nee Hambro, *see Bonsor, Elizabeth, Lady*; *b* 9 Dec 1942; *Educ* Eton and Keble Oxford; *m* 1969, Hon Nadine Marisa Lampson, da of 2 Baron Killearn,*qv*; 1 s, 1 da; *Heir* s, Cosmo Bonsor; *Career* FRSA 1970; *Clubs* White's, Potters, Royal Yacht Squadron; *Style* - Sir Nicholas Bonsor, Bt, MP; Liscombe Park, Leighton Buzzard, Beds; Calverley, Bunbury, Cheshire

BONSOR, Hon Lady; Hon Nadine Marisa; *née* Lampson; JP (Beds); da of 2 Baron Killearn; *b* 1948; *m* 1969, Sir Nicholas Cosmo Bonsor, 4 Bt; 1 s, 1 da; *Style* - The Hon Lady Bonsor, JP; Liscombe Park, Leighton Buzzard, Beds

BONYNGE, Richard; CBE (1977); s of C A Bonynge; *b* 29 Sept 1930; *Educ* Sydney Conservatorium; *m* 1954, Dame Joan Sutherland,*qv*; 1 s; *Career* artistic dir, Vancouver Opera Association 1975-; *Style* - Richard Bonynge Esq CBE; c/o Australian Opera, PO Box J194, Brickfield Hill, NSW 2000, Australia

BOOBBYER, Hon Mrs (Juliet Honor); *née* Rodd; da of 2 Baron Rennell, KBE, CB (d 1978); *b* 28 Oct 1930; *Educ* Westonbirt; *m* 1957, Brian Boobbyer; 2 s; *Career* moral rearmament, writer; *Recreations* painting; *Style* - The Hon Mrs Boobbyer; 4 Victoria rd, Oxford (☎ 58624)

BOODLE, John Victor; s of Rev John Boodle (d 1971); *b* 28 Oct 1926; *Educ* Wadham Oxford; *m* 1957, Lorna, da of John Vincent (d 1970); 1 child; *Career* md British Fermentation Products 1981- (dir 1957-); *Style* - John Boodle Esq; 26 Graham rd, Ipswich, Suffolk (☎ 54647)

BOOKER, Christopher John Penrice; s of John Booker; *b* 7 Oct 1937; *Educ* Shrewsbury, CCC Cambridge; *m* 1, 1963 (m dis), Emma (*see* Hon Mrs Cockburn); m 2, 1979, Valerie, nee Patrick; 1 s; *Career* author, journalist and broadcaster; *Style* - Christopher Booker Esq; The Old Shop, Lamyatt, Somerset (☎ Bruton 2401)

BOOLELL, Sir Satcam; s of Sahadewoo Boolell; *b* 11 Sept 1920; *Educ* LSE; *m* 1946, Kissoondaye Indurjeet, da of Bappoo Indurjeet, of Quatre Bornes; 2 s, 1 da; *Career* barr, Min Ag & Nat Resources & Environment Mauritius 1968-, kt

1959; *Recreations* farming, travel, travel books; *Style* - Sir Satcam Boolell; 4 bis, Bancilhon st, Port Louis, Mauritius (☎ 080079)

BOON, John Trevor; CBE (1968); s of Charles Boon; *b* 21 Dec 1916; *Educ* Felsted and Trinity Hall Cambridge; *m* 1943, Felicity, nee Logan; 4 s; *Career* chm Mills and Boon Ltd 1972-; *Style* - John Boon Esq CBE; c/o Williams and Glyn's Bank Ltd, Kirkland House, Whitehall, SW1

BOON, Sir Peter Coleman; s of Frank Boon; *b* 2 Sept 1916; *Educ* Felsted; *m* 1940, Pamela; 1 s, 1 da; *Career* chm Hoover Administrative Servs Brussels 1978-, kt 1979; *Style* - Sir Peter Boon; c/o Hoover Ltd, PO Box 22, Perivale, Greenford, Middx

BOORD, Antony Andrew; s of Sqdn-Ldr Sir Richard Boord, 3 Bt (d 1975), and bro and hp of Sir Nicholas Boord, 4 Bt; *b* 21 May 1938; *m* 1960, Anna Christina von Krogh; 1 s, 1 da; *Career* dir Staplefords Kaye Ltd, memb IOD; *Clubs* Carlton, Special Forces; *Style* - Antony Boord Esq; 18 Morden rd, SE3

BOORD, Sir Nicolas John Charles; 4 Bt (UK 1896); s of Sqdn-Ldr Sir Richard William Boord, 3 Bt (d 1975); *b* 10 June 1936; *Educ* Eton, Sorbonne, Societa Dante Alighieri (Italy), U of Santander (Spain); *m* 1, 1960 (m dis 1965), Françoise, da of Giuseppe Tempra; m 2, 1965, Françoise Renée, da of Marcel Clovis Mouret, of Marseilles; *Heir* bro, Antony Andrew Boord; *Career* scientific translator/English training specialist; jt translator of *The History of Physics and The Philosophy of Science* 1972, and numerous scientific papers; *Style* - Sir Nicholas Boord, Bt; Résidence Les Aloadès, Bâtiment L, 94 Traverse Prat, 13008 Marseilles, France

BOORMAN, Maj-Gen Derek; s of late N R Boorman, MBE; *b* 13 Sept 1903; *Educ* Sandhurst; *m* 1956, Jennifer Skinner; 1 s, 2 da; *Career* dir Military Operations 1980-; *Style* - Maj-Gen Derek Boorman; c/o Lloyds Bank Ltd, Cox's and King's Branch, Pall Mall, SW1

BOORMAN, Edwin Roy Pratt; *b* 7 Nov 1935; *Educ* Queens' Cambridge; *m* Merrilyn Pettit; 4 da; *Career* md Kent Messenger Gp 1965-; chm South Eastern Newspapers Ltd; South Eastern Magazines Ltd; Apricot Investments; Moadford Ltd; Seacoast Newspapers Ltd; Union Motors Ltd; md Messenger Print Ltd, Kentish Express Ltd; *Style* - Edwin Boorman Esq; The White Lodge, Linton, Maidstone, Kent (☎ 43129)

BOORMAN, Henry Roy Pratt; CBE (1966, MBE 1945), DL (1968 Kent); s of late Barham Pratt Boorman, JP; *b* 21 Sept 1900; *Educ* Leys Sch, Queens' Cambridge; *m* 1, 1933, Enid, nee Starke; 1 s; m 2, 1947, Evelyn Mary, nee Clinch; 1 da; *Career* Major 1944, JP 1962-63, Mayor of Maidstone 1962-63, editor Kent Messenger 1928-52, chm Kent Messenger Ltd 1952-70, chm Kent Messenger Group of Co 1970-, FJI 1936, pres Newspaper Society 1960-61; *Recreations* travel; *Clubs* City Livery, Royal Commonwealth Society, Press, United Wards; *Style* - Henry Boorman Esq, CBE, DL; St Augustine's Priory, Bilsington, Ashford, Kent (☎ Aldington 252)

BOOT, David Henry; *Career* dep chm Henry Boot and Sons; *Style* - David Boot Esq; Henry Boot and Sons, Banner Cross Hall, Sheffield, S11 9PD

BOOT, Edward Hamer; *Career* chm and joint md Henry Boot and Sons; *Style* - Edward Boot Esq; Henry Boot and Sons, Banner Cross Hall, Sheffield S11 9PD

BOOTE, Charles Richard Michael; TD and Clasp (1971 and 1978); s of Col Charles Boote, of Inverness-shire; *b* 7 Aug 1939; *Educ* Cheltenham; *m* 1965, Alison, da of Charles Stott, of Tixall Lodge, Staffs; 1 s, 2 da; *Career* Maj TA, FCAA, ACMA; corporate devpt dir Armitage Shanks Gp 1978; *Recreations* salmon fishing, stalking, pedigree Suffolk sheep farming; *Clubs* Trentham Golf; *Style* - Charles Boote Esq, TD and Clasp; Enson Moor House, Sandon, Staffs (☎ 08897 223)

BOOTH, His Honour Judge Alan; Alan Shore Booth; QC (1975); s of Parkin Booth; *b* 20 Aug 1922; *Educ* Shrewsbury, Liverpool U; *m* 1954, Mary, da of John

Hilton; 1 s, 1 da; *Career* barr 1949, Circuit Judge 1976-; *Recreations* golf; *Clubs* Roy Liverpool Golf, Roy and Ancient (St Andrews); *Style* - His Hon Judge Alan Booth, QC; Little Paddocks, Croft Drive East, Caldy, Wirral, Merseyside (☎ 051 625 5796)

BOOTH, Charles Leonard; CMG (1979), MVO (1961); s of Charles Booth; *b* 7 Mar 1925; *Educ* Pembroke Oxford; *m* 1958, Mary Emms; 2 s, 2 da; *Career* HM Diplomatic Service; Ambassador to Burma 1978-; *Style* - Charles Booth Esq CMG, MVO; c/o Foreign & Commonwealth Office, SW1

BOOTH, Sir Douglas Allen; 3 Bt (UK 1916); s of Sir Philip Booth, 2 Bt (d 1960); *b* 2 Dec 1949; *Educ* Gaspar de Portolà Junior High Sch, Beverly Hills High Sch California, Harvard U; *Heir* bro, Derek Blake Booth; *Career* television and film writer; *Style* - Sir Douglas Booth, Bt; 1255 Daniels dve, Los Angeles, Calif 90035, USA

BOOTH, Derek Blake; s of Sir Philip Booth, 2 Bt (d 1960); hp of bro, Sir Douglas Booth, 3 Bt,*qv*; *b* 7 Apr 1953; *Educ* Hampshire Coll and U of California; *Style* - Derek Booth Esq

BOOTH, D H; *Career* gen man Burnley Building Society; *Style* - D H Booth Esq; 12 Grimshaw st, Burnley, Lancs

BOOTH, David Hugh; s of Hugh Booth, of Battle; *b* 18 Jan 1926; *Educ* Eastbourne G S, Queen Mary Coll London; *m* 1949, Joan, nee Thompson; 1 s, 2 da; *Career* Gp Dir BICC Cables Ltd 1978-, dir BICC Research & Engrg Ltd 1978-, memb NW Regnl Cncl CBI, FIEE; *Recreations* hill walking, cooking, photography; *Style* - David Booth Esq; Flat 1, Maple Lodge, 53 Roe Green av, Worsley, Gter Manchester; Flamborough Rigg Cottage, Stape, nr Pickering, N Yorks

BOOTH, John Sebastian Macaulay; *Career* md Booth (International Holdings) Ltd; *Style* - John Booth Esq; Trent Bridge Leather Works, Nottingham NG2 3BT

BOOTH, Richard George William Pitt; *b* 12 Sept 1938; *Educ* Rugby and Oxford; *m* (m dis); *Career* chm Richard Booth (Booksellers) Ltd 1961-; *Style* - Richard Booth Esq; Hay Castle, Hay-on-Wye, Herefordshire

BOOTHBY, Baron (Life Peer UK 1958); Robert John Graham Boothby; KBE (1953); s of late Sir Robert Tuite Boothby, KBE; 1 cous once removed (through his f's sis who m 1 Baron) of 3 Baron Cunliffe; *b* 12 Feb 1900; *Educ* Eton, Magdalen Oxford; *m* 1, 1935 (m dis 1937), Diana, da of late Col the Rt Hon Lord Richard Frederick Cavendish, CB, CMG, PC, bro of 9 Duke of Devonshire; m 2, 1967, Wanda, da of Giuseppe Sanna, of Sardinia; *Career* Rector of St Andrews U 1958, PPS to Chllr of the Exchequer 1926-29, Parly Sec to Min of Food 1940-41, Radnor Lectr Colombia U New York 1960, chm Roy Philharmonic Orchestra 1961-63 and Hon Life Memb, MP (C) E Div of Kincardineshire 1924-55 and for E Div of Aberdeenshire 1955-58; *Style* - The Rt Hon The Lord Boothby, KBE; 1 Eaton sq, SW1

BOOTHBY, Brooke Charles; s and h of Sir Hugo Boothby, 15 Bt, JP; *b* 6 Apr 1949; *Educ* Eton and Trin Cambridge; *m* 1976, Georgiana Alexandra, da of Sir John Wriothesley Russell, GCVO, CMG; 1 da; *Style* - Brooke Boothby Esq

BOOTHBY, Sir Hugo Robert Brooke; 15 Bt (E 1660), of Broadlow Ash, Derbyshire, JP (Glam 1950); s of Sir Seymour Boothby, 14 Bt (d 1951); *b* 10 Aug 1907; *Educ* Lancing, Hertford Coll Oxford; *m* 1938, Evelyn Ann, da of Herbert Homfray, of Penllyn Castle, Glam; 1 s, 2 da; *Heir* s, Brooke Boothby; *Career* HM Ld-Lt for S Glam 1974-81 (V-Lt Glam 1957, DL 1953), High Sheriff 1953; dir Divnl Bd Wales Nationwide Bldg Soc 1971; chm HHA Wales 1974; *Recreations* shooting, gardening; *Clubs* Brooks's, Cardiff County; *Style* - Sir Hugo Boothby, Bt, JP; Fonmon Castle, Barry, S Glam (☎ Rhoose 710206)

BOOTLE-WILBRAHAM, Hon Andrew; s and h of 7 Baron Skelmersdale; *b* 9 Aug 1977; *Style* - The Hon Andrew Bootle-Wilbraham

BOOTLE-WILBRAHAM, Hon Carolyn Ann; da of 7 Baron Skelmersdale; *b* 1974; *Style* - The Hon Carolyn Bootle-Wilbraham

BOREEL, Jonkheer Sir Francis David; 13 Bt (E 1645); s of Jonkheer Sir Alfred Boreel, 12 Bt (d 1964); *b* 14 June 1926; *m* 1964, Suzanne, da of Willy Campagne, of Paris; 3 da; *Heir* kinsman, Jonkheer Stephen Boreel; *Career* consul Netherlands For Serv; *Style* - Jonkheer Sir Francis Boreel, Bt; Netherlands Embassy, Strässchensweg 10, 5300 Bonn 1, Germany

BOREEL, Jonkheer Stephen Gerard; s of Jonkheer Gerard Lucas Cornelis Boreel (d 1970); h to Btcy of kinsman, Jonkheer Sir Francis Boreel, 13 Bt; *b* 9 Feb 1945; *m* Francien P Kooyman; 1 s; *Style* - Jonkheer Stephen Boreel; Elzenoord, 30, Vaassen, Holland

BOREHAM, Sir Arthur John; KCB (1980); s of Ven Frederick Boreham, Archdeacon of Cornwall; *b* 30 July 1925; *Educ* Marlborough, Trin Oxford; *m* 1948, Heather, da of Harold Horth; 3 s, 1 da; *Career* Dir Centl Statistical Off and Head Govt Statistical Serv 1978-; *Recreations* music, golf; *Clubs* Knole Park Golf; *Style* - Sir Arthur Boreham, KCB; Piperscroft, Brittains Lane, Sevenoaks, Kent (☎ 54678)

BORGES, Thomas William Alfred; s of Arthur Borges; *b* 1 Apr 1923; *Educ* Luton Technical Coll; *m* 1, (m dis); m 2, 1966, Serena, nee Jamieson; 2 s; *Career* md Thomas Borges and Sons 1949-; chm Smith Whitworth Ltd 1974-; *Style* - Thomas Borges Esq; 50 Aubrey Walk, W8 (☎ 01 221 4397)

BORINGDON, Viscount; Mark Lionel Parker; s and h of 6 Earl of Morley; *b* 22 Aug 1956; *Educ* Eton; *Career* 2 Lt Roy Green Jackets; *Style* - Viscount Boringdon; Pound House, Yelverton, S Devon

BORLAND, David Morton; s of David Borland; *b* 17 Jan 1911; *Educ* Glasgow Academy and Brasenose Oxford; *m* 1947, Nessa Helwig; 1 s, 1 da; *Career* dir Cadbury Schweppes Ltd and UBM Gp Ltd 1976-; *Style* - David Borland Esq; Cotswold Lodge, Hollymead lane, Stoke Bishop, Bristol (☎ 683978)

BORLEY, Lester; s of Edwin Borley; *b* 7 Apr 1931; *Educ* London U; *m* Mary, nee Pearce; 3 da; *Career* ch exec English Tourist Board 1975-; *Style* - Lester Borley Esq; 27 Blandy rd, Henley-on-Thames, Oxon (☎ 6613)

BORODALE, Viscount; Sean David Beatty; s and h of 3 Earl Beatty; *b* 12 June 1973; *Style* - Viscount Borodale

BORRIE, Gordon Johnson; s of Stanley Borrie; *b* 13 Mar 1931; *Educ* Manchester U; *m* 1960, Dorene, nee Toland, of Toronto; *Career* barrister 1952; dir gen of Fair Trading 1976-; *Style* - Gordon Borrie Esq; Manor Farm, Abbots Morton, Worcestershire (☎ Inkberrow 792330); 33 Sloane gdns, SW1 (☎ 01 730 5443)

BORTHWICK, Antony Thomas; s and h of Sir John Borthwick, 3 Bt, MBE; *b* 12 Feb 1941; *Educ* Eton; *m* 1966, Gillian Deirdre Broke, twin da of late Nigel Vere Broke Thurston, RN; 1 s, 2 da; *Style* - Antony Borthwick Esq; 13 Lansdowne cres, W11

BORTHWICK OF BORTHWICK YR, John Hugh; s and h of Maj John Borthwick of Borthwick, TD, JP, DL,*qv*; *b* 14 Nov 1940; *m* 1974, Adelaide, da of Archy Birkmyre, of Overdale, Crieff, Perthshire; 2 da; *Style* - John Borthwick of Borthwick yr; The Neuk, nr Gilston, by Heriot, Midlothian

BORTHWICK OF BORTHWICK, Maj John Henry Stuart; TD (1943), JP (Midlothian 1938), DL (1965); Baron (territorial) of Heriotmuir, Borthwick and Lockerwart; The Borthwick of Borthwick; s of Henry Borthwick of Borthwick (d 1937); is fourteenth in descent from Hon John Borthwick (2 s of 1 Lord Borthwick); claims to be heir male and 24 Lord Borthwick (S Lordship 1452); *b* 13 Sept 1905; *Educ* Fettes, King's Coll Newcastle; *m* 1938, Margaret, da of Alexander Campbell Cormack, of Leith; 2 s (twins); *Heir* s, John Borthwick the Younger; *Career* chm Heriotmuir Properties Ltd 1965-, Heriotmuir Exporters 1972-; dir

Ronald Morrison & Co 1972-; memb Lothians Area Cttee NFU Mutual Insur Soc 1969-; chm Monitoring Cttee Scottish Tartans 1976; memb Standing Cncl Scottish Chiefs, GCLJ; *Recreations* shooting, travel, history; *Clubs* New and Puffin's (Edinburgh); *Style* - Maj John Borthwick of Borthwick, TD, JP, DL; Crookston, Heriot, Midlothian (☎ 087 535 232)

BORTHWICK, Hon Mrs James; Irene Evangeline; da of late George Wise, JP, of Roslyn House, Croydon, NSW; *m* 1912, Hon James Alexander Borthwick (d 1961), s of 1 and last Baron Whitburgh (d 1967); 1 s; *Style* - The Hon Mrs James Borthwick; 86 Eaton Place, SW1 (☎ 01 235 1624)

BORTHWICK, (William) Jason (Maxwell); DSC (1942); s of Hon William Borthwick (d 1958), bro of 1 and last Baron Borthwick (their f, Thomas, chm and sr ptnr Thos Borthwick & Sons, was nominated a Peer 1912 but d before the patent passed the Great Seal); *b* 1 Nov 1910; *m* 1937, Elizabeth Cleveland, nee Elworthy (d 1978); 1 s, 3 da; *Career* barr 1932, Thos Borthwick & Sons Ltd 1933 (dir 1946-76), Int Commodity Clearing House 1952-, Central Cncl of Physical Recreation 1950-, C'wlth Dvpt Corpn 1971-77; *Recreations* shooting, sailing; *Clubs* United Oxford and Cambridge, Roy Thames Yacht; *Style* - Jason Borthwick Esq, DSC; North House, Brancaster Staithe, King's Lynn, Norfolk (☎ Brancaster 475)

BORTHWICK, Sir John Thomas; 3 Bt (UK 1908), MBE (1945); s of late Hon James Alexander Borthwick, 2 s of 1 Bt; suc to Btcy of unc, 1 Baron Whitburgh, formerly Sir Thomas Banks Borthwick, 2 Bt, who d 1967, when Barony became extinct; *b* 5 Dec 1917; *Educ* Eton, Trin Oxford; *m* 1, 1939 (m dis 1961), Irene, da of Joseph Heller; 3 s; m 2, 1962, Irene, da of late Leo Fink, of Paris XVI; 2 s; *Heir* s, Antony Borthwick; *Career* late Maj Rifle Bde (TA); dir Thomas Borthwick & Sons Ltd, v-chm 1979-; *Style* - Sir John Borthwick, Bt, MBE; 23 Lennox gdns, SW1; The Foxhills Dower House, Longcross, Surrey

BORTHWICK, Kenneth W; JP, DL (1980 Edinburgh); s of Andrew Borthwick; *b* 4 Nov 1915; *Educ* George Heriot Sch, Edinburgh; *m* 1942, Irene Wilson; 2 s, 1 da; *Career* Ld Provost (and Ld Lt City & County) of Edinburgh 1977-80; family business, confectionery mfrs; *Style* - Kenneth Borthwick Esq JP DL; 7 Duddingston cres, Edinburgh EH15 3A5 (☎ 031 669 0600)

BORWICK, 4 Baron (UK 1922); Sir James Hugh Myles Borwick; 4 Bt (UK 1916), MC (1945); s of 3 Baron (d 1961) by his 1 w Irene; *b* 12 Dec 1917; *Educ* Eton, RMC Sandhurst; *m* 1954, Hyllarie Adalia Mary, da of late Lt-Col William Hamilton Hall Johnston, DSO, MC, DL, of Bryn-y-Groes, Bala, N Wales; 4 da; *Heir* half-bro, Hon George Borwick; *Career* Maj (ret) Highland Light Infantry; *Style* - The Rt Hon The Lord Borwick, MC; Knap Farm, Owermoigne, Dorchester, Dorset (☎ Warmwell 852365)

BORWICK, Hon Amanda Gwyneth Rosemary; da of 4 Baron Borwick, MC; *b* 24 Jan 1965; *Style* - The Hon Amanda Borwick

BORWICK, Hon Angela Jane; da of 4 Baron Borwick, MC; *b* 12 July 1955; *Style* - The Hon Angela Borwick; Keeping, Beaulieu, Hants (☎ Bucklers Hard 243)

BORWICK, Hon Diana; da of 4 Baron Borwick, MC; *b* 28 June 1959; *Style* - The Hon Diana Borwick

BORWICK, Hon George Sandbach; s of 3 Baron Borwick (d 1961); bro and hp of 4 Baron Borwick, MC; *b* 18 Oct 1922; *Educ* Eton; *Clubs* Garrick, Bath; *Style* - The Hon George Borwick; 18 Kinnerton st, SW1 (☎ 01 235 5742)

BORWICK, Hon Mary-Anne; da of 4 Baron Borwick, MC; *b* 11 July 1957; *Style* - The Hon Mary-Anne Borwick

BORWICK, Hon Robin Sandbach; s of 3 Baron Borwick (d 1961); *b* 22 March 1927; *Educ* Eton; *m* 1950, Hon Patricia Garnett, da of Baron McAlpine of Moffat, of Benhams, Fawley Green, Bucks; 2 s (James, m 1981 Victoria, da of Roger

Poore; Richard, educ Eton; address for both- 40 Bernard st WC1 T 01 837 3377), 1 da (Mrs Curry-Towneley-O'Hagan, 5 Carpenter rd, Edgbaston T 021 454 1943); *Career* memb Lloyd's 1959-; Lt Life Gds 1946-52; *Recreations* horses, donkeys, all equines; *Clubs* Cavalry, Casino Maltese; *Style* - The Hon Robin Borwick; 303 Main st, Zebbug, Malta (☎ 27742)

BOSANQUET, Charles Ion Carr; DL (Northumberland 1971); s of Prof Robert Bosanquet, of Alnwick; *b* 19 April 1903; *Educ* Winchester, Trin Cambridge; *m* 1931, Barbara, da of William Schieffelin, of New York; 1 s, 3 da; *Career* High Sheriff Northumberland 1948-49, V-Chllr Newcastle U 1963-68; *Recreations* archaeology, travel; *Clubs* Farmers', N Counties (Newcastle); *Style* - Charles Bosanquet Esq, DL; Rock Moor, Alnwick, Northumberland (☎ 066 579 224)

BOSANQUET, Lady Katherine Ethel; *née* Carnegie; da of 10 Earl of Southesk and Ethel, da of Sir Alexander Bannerman, 9 Bt; *b* 1892; *m* 1917, Maj Arthur Rivers Bosanquet, MC (m dis 1940, he d 1971); 1 s, 2 da; *Style* - Lady Katherine Bosanquet; High Street House, Watlington, Oxon (☎ 332)

BOSANQUET, Reginald; ITN news reader to 1980; rector Glasgow U 1980- *Style* - Reginald Bosanquet Esq

BOSANQUET, Samuel Anthony John Pierre; s of Samuel John Anson Bosanquet (k on active serv 1944); *b* 11 Jan 1944; *Educ* Eton, Oxford; *m* 1975, Helen, da of William Hanbury Saumarez Smith; 2 s; *Career* landowner; *Style* - Samuel Bosanquet Esq; Dingestow Court, Monmouth, Gwent (☎ Dingestow 238)

BOSCAWEN, Hon Charles Richard; s of 9 Visc Falmouth; *b* 10 Oct 1958; *Style* - The Hon Charles Boscawen

BOSCAWEN, Hon Evelyn Arthur Hugh; s and h of 9 Visc Falmouth; *b* 13 May 1955; *Educ* Eton, Roy Ag Coll Cirencester; *m* 1977, Lucia Caroline, da of Ralph Vivian-Neal, of Poundisford Park, Somerset; 1 s; *Career* farmer; dir Goonvean & Rostowrack China Clay Co 1979-; *Recreations* shooting, sailing; *Style* - The Hon Evelyn Boscawen; Graythwaite, Mereworth, Maidstone, Kent

BOSCAWEN, Hon Henry Edward; s of 8 Visc Falmouth (d 1962); *b* 4 Oct 1921; *Educ* Eton, Peterhouse Cambridge; *m* 1951, Anne Philippa, da of Sir Edward Warner, 2 Bt, DSO, MC; 1 s, 2 da; *Career* Lt RE WWII; chartered civil engr; High Sheriff W Sussex 1979-80; *Recreations* sailing, gardening; *Style* - The Hon Henry Boscawen; The High Beeches, Handcross, Sussex

BOSCAWEN, Hon Nicholas John; s of 9 Visc Falmouth; *b* 1957; *Style* - Hon Nicholas Boscawen

BOSCAWEN, Hon Vere George; s of 9 Visc Falmouth; *b* 18 Sept 1964; *Style* - The Hon Vere Boscawen

BOSE, A K; JP; *Career* md Electrical Dvn Newage Engineers Ltd, winner of Queen's Award for Export Achievement 1980; *Style* - A K Bose Esq, JP; c/o Newage Engineers Ltd, Stamford, Lincs

BOSSOM, Bruce Charles; s and h of Hon Sir Clive Bossom, 2 Bt; *b* 22 Aug 1952; *Style* - Bruce Bossom Esq

BOSSOM, Lady Barbara Joan; *née* North; da of Maj Lord North (d 1940), and sis of 9 Earl of Guilford, JP, DL; *b* 1928; *m* 1951, Maj The Hon Sir Clive Bossom, 2 Bt, *qv*; *Career* OStJ, raised to rank of Earl's da 1950; *Style* - Lady Barbara Bossom; 3 Eaton Mans, SW1; Parson's Orchard, Eastnor, Ledbury, Herefs

BOSSOM, Hon Sir Clive; 2 Bt (UK 1953), of Maidstone, Kent; s of Baron Bossom (Life Peer and Bt; Sir Clive suc (1965) to Btcy only) by his 1 w Emily; *b* 4 Feb 1918; *Educ* Eton; *m* 1951, Lady Barbara, *qv*, nee North, da of late Lord North & sis of 9 Earl of Guilford; 3 s, 1 da; *Heir* s, Bruce Bossom; *Career* Maj Europe and Far East (regular soldier 1939-48), Kent Co Cllr 1949-51, MP (C) Leominster 1959-74, PPS to Home Sec 1970-72; chm Europe Assistance Ltd, dir Vosper Ltd; chm Ex-Servs War Disabled Help Cttee 1973-, Br Motor Sports Cncl 1975-, V-Pres

FIA 1975-; Pres Anglo-Netherlands Soc 1978-; KStJ; *Recreations* travel; *Clubs* Carlton, RAC, MCC, BRDC; *Style* - The Hon Sir Clive Bossom Bt; Parsons Orchard, Eastnor, Ledbury, Herefordshire (2318); 3 Eaton Mans, Cliveden Place, SW1 (☎ 01 730 1108)

BOSTELMANN, Michael John; s of Martin Horst Bostelmann; *b* 16 Nov 1947; *Educ* Bradfield; *m* 1973, Gillian, da of Allan Vickery; 1 s; *Career* CA, ptnr Arnold Hill; dir Quadrem Hope Ltd, Br Paper Co, Br Paper (Waste) Ltd, Frogmore Mill Ltd; *Recreations* long distance running, squash, tennis; *Clubs* Thames Hare and Hounds, Hurlingham; *Style* - Michael Bostelmann Esq; 18 Wayside, SW14

BOSTOCK, Edward; CBE (1975); s of Geoffrey Bostock, of Hampstead; *b* 21 Aug 1908; *Educ* Charterhouse, Queen's Oxford; *m* 1934, Alice, da of George Smale; 3 s, 1 da; *Career* CA, sr ptnr Anna Dexter & Co 1961-71, Dearden & Co 1972-75; *Recreations* gardening, opera, motoring; *Style* - Edward Bostock Esq, CBE; Norfolk Lodge, Park rd, Teddington, Middx (☎ 01 977 1121)

BOSTOCK, Godfrey Stafford; s of late Henry John Bostock, CBE, JP; *b* 23 June 1915; *Educ* Uppingham, Switzerland; *m* 1940, Diana, nee Heywood; 2 s 1 da; *Career* dir- The Claverley Co, Midland News Assoc Ltd, R F Kershaw Ltd, The Economic Estate Planning Co Ltd, High Sheriff Staffordshire 1958; *Recreations* shooting, gardening; *Clubs* Boodle's; *Style* - Godfrey Bostock Esq; Tixall, Stafford (☎ Stafford 661039); The Moor House, Dallowgill, Ripon, Yorks (☎ Kirkby Malzeard 371 /491)

BOSTON OF FAVERSHAM, Baron (Life Peer UK 1976); Terence George Boston; s of George Thomas Boston; *b* 21 March 1930; *Educ* Woolwich Polytechnic Sch, King's Coll London U; *m* 1962, Margaret Joyce, da of Rowley Henry Jack Head; *Career* Fl-Lt RAF 1950-52, barr Inner Temple 1960, Gray's Inn 1973, former BBC News Sub-Ed External Servs, Sr BBC Producer (Current Affairs) 1960-64, MP (L) Faversham Kent 1964-70, PPS to Min of Public Bldg and Works 1964-66, to Min of Power 1966-68, to Min of Transport 1968-69, Assist Govt Whip 1969-70, Min of State Home Office 1979, Oppn Front Bench Spokesman on Home Office Affairs 1979-; *Style* - The Rt Hon The Lord Boston of Faversham; 27 Capstan sq, Isle of Dogs, E14

BOSTON, 10 Baron (GB 1761); Sir Timothy George Frank Boteler Irby; 11 Bt (E 1704); s of 9 Baron, MBE (d 1978), by his 2 w Erica; *b* 27 March 1939; *Educ* Clayesmore Sch Dorset, Southampton U; *m* 1967, Rhonda Anne, da of R A Bate, of Balgowlah, NSW; 2 s, 1 da; *Heir* s, Hon George Irby; *Style* - The Rt Hon The Lord Boston; 33 Cloncurry st, SW6 (☎ 01 731 1936)

BOSTON, Erica, Baroness; Erica Nelly; da of T H Hill; *m* 1936, as his 2 w, 9 Baron Boston (d 1978); *Style* - The Rt Hon Erica, Lady Boston; Flat 11, Gunters Mead, Copse Lane, Esher

BOSTON, Irene, Baroness; Irene Frances; da of Francis Holt (d 1942), of Ewell, Surrey; *m* 1, 1925, Harry Mills (d 1949); m 2, 1954, as his 2 w, 7 Baron Boston (d 1958); *Style* - The Rt Hon Irene, Lady Boston; 155 Oakwood Court, W14 (☎ 01 937 2576)

BOSVILLE MACDONALD OF SLEAT, Sir Ian Godfrey; 17 Bt (NS 1625); also 25 Chief of Sleat; s of Sir Somerled Bosville Macdonald of Sleat, 16 Bt, MC (24 Chief of Sleat) (d 1958), and Mary, Lady Bosville Macdonald of Sleat, *qv*; *b* 18 July 1947; *Educ* Pinewood Sch and Eton; Royal Agricultural Coll, Cirencester; *m* 1970, Juliet Fleury, only da of Maj-Gen John Ward-Harrison, OBE, MC; 1 s, 1 da; *Heir* s, Somerled Bosville Macdonald, yr of Sleat, *qv*; *Career* chartered surveyor 1972, memb Roy Soc of Health 1972, Ec Res Cncl 1979; *Recreations* ornithology, hunting, fishing; *Clubs* Brooks's; *Style* - Sir Ian Bosville Macdonald of Sleat Bt; Thorpe Hall, Rudston, Driffield, Yorks (☎ Kilham 239); Upper Duntulm, Isle of Skye (☎ Duntulm 206)

BOSVILLE MACDONALD OF SLEAT, Mary, Lady - Mary Elizabeth;

da of Lt-Col Ralph Crawley-Boevy Gibbs (1 cous of 1 Baron Wraxall); *b* 5 June 1919; *m* 1946, Sir (Alexander) Somerled Angus Bosville Macdonald of Sleat, 16 Bt, MC (d 1958); *Style* - Mary, Lady Bosville Macdonald of Sleat; Thorpe Hall, Rudston, Driffield, Yorks (☎ Kilham 239)

BOSVILLE MACDONALD, YOUNGER OF SLEAT, Somerled Alexander; s and h of Sir Ian Bosville Macdonald of Sleat, 17 Bt, *qv*; *b* 30 Jan 1976; *Style* - Somerled Bosville Macdonald, yr of Sleat

BOTNAR, Octav; *Career* chm Datsun (UK) Ltd; *Style* - Octav Botnar Esq; 109 Gloucester pla, W1

BOTTOMLEY, Brian Rogers; s of Harry Bottomley, of Sale Cheshire; *b* 14 Dec 1927; *Educ* Sale Centl Sch; *m* 1950,; *Heir* Kathleen, da of Thomas Neville, of Altrincham; 1 s; *Career* tech dir Churchill Machine Tool Co 1968-72, dir of mfrg (ch exec) T I Machine Tools 1980-; *Recreations* sailing, shooting, motoring, reading, music, travel; *Style* - Brian Bottomley Esq; 84 Riverside dve, Solihull, W Midlands (☎ 021 704 4948)

BOTTOMLEY, Peter James; MP (C) Greenwich, Woolwich W 1975-; s of Sir James Bottomley; *b* 30 July 1944; *Educ* Westminster, Trin Cambridge; *m* 1967, Virginia, da of John Garnett, CBE, of IOW; 1 s, 1 da; *Career* chm Family Forum 1980-, Sec Con Foreign Affrs Cttee 1979-, bd memb Christian Aid 1978-; *Recreations* children; *Clubs* TGWU; *Also* pt owner yacht- 'Division Bell'; *Style* - Peter Bottomley Esq, MP; 2 St Barnabas Villas, SW8 (☎ 01 720 4282); Horestone Point, Seaview, IOW (☎ 098371 3220)

BOUCHER, Arthur James Kinnear; s of Frederick Boucher, OBE; *b* 3 Oct 1934; *Educ* Campbell Coll, Queen's U Belfast; *m* 1962, Karen, da of William Leitch, CB; 4 da; *Career* FCA Ireland, dep chm Morton Gp Ltd and subsids; dir Francis Curley Ltd, DSB Photographic Servs Ltd; *Style* - Arthur Boucher Esq; 9 Tweskard Park, Belfast BT4 2JY (☎ 63153)

BOUCHIER, Lady; Isabella Dorothy Guyver; daughter of Frank Guyver Britton, of Yokohama (d 1934); *b* 14 Feb 1922; *Educ* Claremont School England, Mills College California, San Francisco Conservatory of Music; *m* 1968, late Air Vice-Marshal Sir Cecil Arthur Bouchier, KBE, CB, DFC, s of Arthur Couch Bouchier, Chichester (d 1904); 1 step s; *Career* composer, writer (under maiden name); principal works include orchestral suites 'Tokyo Impressions', 'Yedo Fantasy' (Los Angeles 1957); cantata 'And Certain Women' (New York 1957); publications- 'A Haiku Journey' (Tokyo 1975); 'National Parks of Japan' (Tokyo 1980); own television programme NHK, Tokyo 1960-1970; *Recreations* chess, shell collecting, watercolour painting; *Clubs* Royal Air Force, International House of Japan; *Style* - Lady Bouchier; 2275 Isshiki, Hayama, Kanagawa-ken 240-01, Japan (☎ 0468 75 1217)

BOUGHEY, Lady - Gillian Claire; da of late Maj Robert Moubray, DL, late 16 Lancers, of Kelso, Roxburghshire; *m* 1976, as his 2 w, Sir Richard Boughey, 10 Bt, JP, DL (d 1978); *Style* - Lady Boughey; The Old Rectory, Quarley, Andover, Hants (☎ Grately 245)

BOUGHEY, Sir John George Fletcher; 11 Bt (GB 1798); s of Sir Richard Boughey, 10 Bt, JP, DL (d 1978); *b* 12 Aug 1959; *Heir* bro, James Richard Boughey; *Style* - Sir John Boughey, Bt; 11 Rutland gate, SW7

BOUGHEY, James Richard; s of Sir Richard Boughey, 10 Bt, JP, DL (d 1978); h to Btcy of bro, Sir John Boughey, 11 Bt; *b* 29 Aug 1960; *Style* - James Boughey Esq

BOULT, Sir Adrian Cedric; CH (1969); s of Cedric Boult; *b* 8 April 1889; *Educ* Westminster, Ch Ch Oxford, Leipzig Konservatorium; *m* 1933, Ann, da of Capt F Bowles, RN, JP; *Career* V-Pres Cncl RCM, conductor- Birmingham City Orchestra 1924-30, BBC 1930-51, LPO 1951-57, kt 1937; *Clubs* Athenaeum, Roy

C'wlth Soc, Leander; *Style* - Sir Adrian Boult, CH; Fox Yard Cottage, West st, Farnham, Surrey (☎ 715881)

BOULT, David Luard; s of Maj Peter Boult, MC, of Hoylake; *b* 6 Dec 1924; *Educ* Shrewsbury; *m* 1957, Elizabeth Anne, da of David Collett, of Rickmansworth; 2 s, 1 da; *Career* dir BICC Cables 1980-; chm Brookside Metal 1980-, Prescot Rod Rollers 1980-, Merseyside Playing Fields Assoc 1981-; *Recreations* golf, gardening, Rugby Union Admin; *Clubs* Delamere Forest Golf, Liverpool RUFC; *Style* - David Boult Esq; Manor House, Norley, Cheshire (☎ 092888382)

BOULTER, Hereward Emanuel; CBE (1965), DSO (1945); s of Edward Boulter, of Chelmsford; *b* 12 June 1911; *Educ* Brentwood Sch, Sandhurst; *m* 1949, Dorothy, da of Robert Owen-Swaffield, of Dorset; 1 s, 2 da; *Career* Army Offr to 1964, ret as Brig; Sec Roy Patriotic Fund Corpn 1965-79; *Recreations* racing, golf, bird watching; *Clubs* Army & Navy, Thorndon Pk Golf; *Style* - Brig Hereward Boulter, CBE, DSO; Upper Herons, Flyfield, Ongar, Essex (☎ 027785 362)

BOULTING, Roy; s of Arthur Boulting; *b* 21 Nov 1913; *Educ* HMS Worcester and Reading Sch; *Career* producer and joint man dir (with bro John), Chartered Film Productions Ltd 1973-; *Style* - Roy Boulting Esq; Charter Film Productions Ltd, 8a Glebe place, SW3

BOULTON, Maj Sir Edward John; 2 Bt (UK 1944); s of Sir William Whytehead Boulton, 1 Bt (d 1949); *b* 11 April 1907; *Educ* Eton, Trin Cambridge; *Heir* bro, Sir William Whytehead Boulton, CBE, TD; *Career* late Maj Staffs Yeo; contested S Div of Ilford (C) July 1945; Lord of the Manors of Alresford, Great Braxted, and Kelvedon Hall; *Style* - Maj Sir Edward Boulton, Bt; Ouaisné Lodge, Portelet, Jersey, CI (☎ Jersey 42935)

BOULTON, Sir Harold Hugh Christian; 4 Bt (UK 1905); s of Sir (Denis Duncan) Harold (Owen) Boulton, 3 Bt (d 1968); *b* 29 Oct 1918; *Educ* Ampleforth; *m* 1944, Patricia Mary, OBE (who re-assumed by deed poll 1951 her maiden name of Maxwell-Scott), da of late Maj-Gen Sir Walter Joseph Constable-Maxwell-Scott, 1 Bt, CB, DSO; *Career* late Capt Irish Gds (Sup Reserve); *Style* - Sir Harold Boulton, Bt; c/o Bank of Montreal, City View Branch, 1481 Merivale rd, Ottawa 5, Ontario, Canada

BOULTON, Louise, Lady - Louise; da of late Hugh McGowan, of USA; *m* 1918, Sir (Denis Duncan) Harold (Owen) Boulton, 3 Bt (d 1968); *Style* - Louise, Lady Boulton; c/o National Westminster Bank, Stanhope gate, W1

BOULTON, Sir William Whytehead; CBE (1958), TD (1949); s of late Sir William Boulton, 1 Bt and hp of bro, Sir Edward Boulton, 2 Bt; *b* 21 June 1912; *Educ* Eton, Trin Cambridge; *m* 1944, Margaret Elizabeth, da of late Brig Henry Noel Alexander Hunter, DSO; 1 s, 2 da; *Career* barr 1936; Hon Lt-Col RHA Essex Yeo (TA), sec to Gen Cncl of the Bar 1950-74, and to Senate of the Inns of Court and the Bar 1974-75; kt 1975; *Style* - Sir William Boulton, CBE, TD; 53 Montpelier Walk, SW7 (☎ 01 589 1663); The Quarters House, Alresford, nr Colchester, Essex (☎ Wivenhoe 2450)

BOURKE, Hon Corinne Mary Jane; da of Lord Naas; *b* 1975

BOURKE, Hon Geoffrey John; s of 8 Earl of Mayo (d 1939); *b* 1900; *Educ* Repton; *m* 1926, Nancy Lisette, da of late Douglas Thring, estates bursar of Merton Coll Oxford; 2 da (1 decd); *Career* FRICS, Pres Land Agents' Soc 1947-48; *Clubs* Farmers'; *Style* - The Hon Geoffrey Bourke; 167 Russell Court, Woburn Place, WC1 (☎ 01 837 0663)

BOURKE, Hon Harry Richard; s of 10 Earl of Mayo; *b* 23 Sept 1960; *Style* - The Hon Harry Bourke; Doon House, Maam, Co Galway, Eire

BOURKE, Brig Henry Sackville Joynt; DSO (1946), OBE (1941), MC, DL (Worcs 1953); s of Col E A Bourke RAMC (d 1954); *b* 25 Aug 1900; *Educ* Cheltenham Coll, RMC Woolwich; *m* 1935, Phebe Elizabeth, nee Slater; 1 s, 1

da; *Career* Maj and Lt-Col Middle East, Maj Syria and Eritrea, Brig (India, Assam, Burma, Germany), sec Worcs Territorial Assoc 1946-65, gen cmmr Income Tax Worcs Div 1960 (chm 1964-75), dir Herefordshire Red Cross 1969-75; *Recreations* gardening; *Clubs* Army and Navy; *Style* - Brig Henry Bourke DSO, OBE, MC, DL; White House, Aylton, nr Ledbury, Herefs (☎ Trumpet 349)

BOURKE, John Oliver Paget; s of Sir Paget Bourke, of Dublin; *b* 19 Feb 1937; *Educ* Clongowes Wood Coll, Univ Coll Dublin; *m* Margaret, da of Joseph Paffrath, of Dublin; 2 s, 2 da; *Career* chm Br Credit Tst Ltd; dir Bank of Ireland 1978-, Hibernian Insurance; *Recreations* sailing, golf, music; *Clubs* Roy St George Yacht, Milltown Golf, Roy Yacht Sqdn; *Also* owner of yacht- 'Shemite'; *Style* - John Bourke Esq; Albert House, Victoria rd, Dalkey, Dublin, Eire (☎ 858355)

BOURKE, J P; *Career* chm British Credit Trust; *Style* - J P Bourke Esq; Essex House, Manor st, Hull

BOURKE, Hon Patrick Antony; s of 10 Earl of Mayo; *b* 16 Dec 1955; *Educ* St Aubyn's Rottingdean; *Style* - The Hon Patrick Bourke; Donn House, Maam, Co Galway, Eire

BOURNE, Baron (Life Peer UK 1964); Geoffrey Kemp Bourne; GCB (1960, KCB Mil 1957, CB Mil 1949), KBE (1954, CBE Mil 1947, OBE Mil 1942) CMG (1952); s of late Col Walter Kemp Bourne, OBE, of Sway, Hants; *b* 5 Oct 1902; *Educ* Rugby; *m* 1928, Agnes Evelyn, da of late Sir (William) Ernest Thompson; 1 s, 1 da; *Career* RA 1923, Maj-Gen 1948, GOC Berlin (British Sector) 1949-51, and 16 Airborne Div (TA) 1951-53, GOCIC E Command 1953-54, Dir of Ops Malaya 1954-56, CIC MELF 1957, Cmdt Imperial Defence Coll 1958-59, Col Cmdt RA 1954-67, Hon Col 10 Bn Parachute Regt TA 1960-65, chm National Building Agency 1967; *Style* - Maj-Gen The Rt Hon The Lord Bourne, GCB, KBE, CMG; Drove House, Cranborne, Wimborne, Dorset (☎ Cranborne 321)

BOURNE, Lady - Heather Frances; (Kaisar-i-Hind gold medal); da of Lt-Col F W Burbury, of Barnsley; *m* 1918, Sir Frederick Bourne, KCSI, CIE (d 1977); *Style* - Lady Bourne; Eachen Hill, Buxted, Sussex (☎ 3108)

BOURNE, Lady Hester Margaret; da of 4 Earl Cairns (d 1946); *b* 1895; *m* 1917, Capt Rt Hon Robert Croft Bourne, PC, JP, MP (d 1938); 2 s, 1 da; *Career* vice-chm Conservative Party Organization 1939-43; *Style* - Lady Hester Bourne; Old Mill House, Bradford Abbas, Sherborne, Dorset (☎ Yeovil 4733)

BOURNE, Henry Roland; *Career* MA Cantab; chm S Hoffnung and Co Ltd; *Style* - Henry Bourne Esq; 1-2 Finsbury sq, EC2

BOURNE, Hon Michael Kemp; s of Baron Bourne, GCB, KBE, CMG (Life Peer); *b* 9 June 1937; *Educ* Harrow; *m* 1963, Penelope Jane, da of H W Blyth, of Melgund Glen, Minto, Hawick, Roxburghshire; 1 s, 2 da; *Clubs* Cavalry; *Style* - The Hon Michael Bourne; Chrishall Grange, Heydon, Royston, Herts (☎ Chrishall 215)

BOURNE, (Rowland) Richard; s of Arthur Bourne; *Educ* Uppingham and Brasenose Oxford; *m* 1966, Juliet, nee Attenborough; 2 s, 1 da; *Career* founder ed Learn Magazines; man dir Torrens Publications Ltd 1979-; *Style* - Richard Bourne Esq; 65 Lee rd, SE3 (☎ 01 852 9645)

BOUSFIELD, Eric Gilroy; *Career* MA Cantab; man dir Associated Dairies Ltd; *Style* - Eric Bousfield Esq; Craven House, Kirkstall rd, Leeds LS3 1JE

BOWATER, Euan David Vansittart; s and h of Sir Noël Vansittart Bowater, 2 Bt, GBE, MC; *b* 9 Sept 1935; *Educ* Eton and Trin Cambridge; *m* 1964, Susan Mary Humphrey, da of A R O Slater; 3 s, 1 da; *Style* - Euan Bowater Esq; Coombe Farmhouse, Chagford, Devon

BOWATER, Dowager Lady - Jessie Faithfull; da of W J Frampton, of Stone Kent; *m* 1, Norman Vansittart Bowater (bro of 1 Bt); m 2, 1948, as his 2 w, Sir

(Thomas) Dudley (Blennerhassett) Bowater, 3 Bt (d 1972); *Style* - Dowager Lady Bowater; Flat 6, Elmfield court, Tenterden, Kent

BOWATER, Sir John Vansittart; 4 Bt (UK 1914); s of late Capt Victor Spencer Bowater, 3 s of 1 Bt; suc unc, Sir (Thomas) Dudley (Blennerhassett) Bowater, 3 Bt, 1972; *b* 6 April 1918; *m* 1943, Joan Kathleen, da of late Wilfrid Ernest Henry Scullard, of Boscombe; 1 s, 1 da; *Heir* s, Michael Bowater; *Style* - Sir John Bowater, Bt; 214 Runnymede av, Bournemouth, Dorset (☎ Northbourne 71782)

BOWATER, Michael Patrick; s and h of Sir John Vansittart Bowater, 4 Bt; *b* 18 July 1949; *m* 1968, Alison, da of Edward Wall of Knowle; 1 da; *Style* - Michael Bowater Esq; 8 Rosehill ave, Whittington, Oswestry, Shropshire

BOWATER, Sir Noël Vansittart; 2 Bt (UK 1939), GBE (1954), MC (1917); s of Sir Frank H Bowater, 1 Bt (d 1947); *b* 25 Dec 1892; *Educ* Rugby; *m* 1921, Constance Heiton, da of David Gordon Bett, of Woodbridge, Suffolk; 1 s, 2 da; *Heir* s, Euan Bowater; *Career* past v-chm Bowater Corpn, Alderman City of London 1944-70, Sheriff 1948-49, Lord Mayor 1953-54, Master of Vintners' Co 1954-55, KStJ; *Style* - Sir Noël Bowater, Bt, GBE, MC; Conifers, St George's Hill, Weybridge, Surrey (☎ Weybridge 42744)

BOWATER, Hon Lady - Hon Ursula Margaret; *née* Dawson; da of 1 and last Viscount Dawson of Penn, GCVO, KCB, KCMG, PC (d 1945); *b* 1907; *m* 1927, Lt-Col Sir Ian Bowater, GBE, DSO; 1 s, 2 da; *Style* - The Hon Lady Bowater; Hasker House, Woolley Firs, Maidenhead Thicket, Berks

BOWDEN, Baron (Life Peer UK 1963); Bertram Vivian Bowden; s of B Bowden, of Chesterfield; *b* 18 Jan 1910; *Educ* Chesterfield G S, Emmanuel Cambridge; *m* 1, 1937, Marjorie Browne (m dis 1954, she d 1956); 1 s, 2 da; m 2, 1967, Mary Maltby (d 1971); m 3, Phyllis, da of Stanley Myson and widow of John James; *Career* Pncpl U of Manchester Inst of Science and Technology 1964-76, Min of State DES 1964-65, formerly schoolmaster (physics); with Ferranti Ltd 1950-53; chm Electronics Res Cncl Min Aviation 1960-64; *Recreations* music; *Clubs* Athenaeum; *Style* - The Rt Hon The Lord Bowden; Pine Croft, Stanhope rd, Bowdon, Cheshire (☎ 061 928 4005)

BOWDEN, Andrew; MBE (1961), MP (C) Brighton Kemp Town 1970-; s of Victor Bowden, slr; *b* 8 April 1930; *Educ* Ardingly; *m* 1970, Benita, da of B Napier, of Brighton; 1 s, 1 da; *Career* personnel consultant 1967-; jt chm All-Party Parly Gp for Pensioners 1971-, memb Employment Select Cttee 1979-; *Recreations* fishing, chess, golf; *Clubs* Carlton; *Style* - Andrew Bowden Esq, MBE, MP; Flat 11, 19/20 Sussex sq, Brighton, Sussex (☎ 01 219 5047)

BOWDEN, Maj Aubrey Henry; DSO (1918); s of Henry Bowden; *Educ* Oundle; *m* 1, 1918, Helen, nee Moderra (d 1939); 1 s, 1 da; m 2, 1941, Andrée July; 1 s, 2 da; *Career* chm Bowden Bros Ltd. *Style* - Maj Aubrey Bowden DSO; 28 Berkeley ct, Baker st, NW1

BOWDEN, Sir Frank Houston; 3 Bt (UK 1915); s of Sir Harold Bowden, 2 Bt (d 1960); *b* 10 Aug 1909; *Educ* Rugby, Merton Oxford; *m* 1, 1934 (m dis 1936), Marie, da of Charles Stiénon, of Paris, and Comtesse Laure de Messey; 1 s; m 2, 1937, Lydia, da of Jean Manovolici, of Bucharest; 3 s; *Heir* s, Nicholas Bowden; *Career* industrialist and landowner; V-Chm Japan Soc 1979-; Hon V-Pres World Kendo Championships 1976; *Recreations* collecting arms and armour, particularly Japanese swords; *Clubs* White's, Carlton, Bath, Roy Thames Yacht; *Style* - Sir Frank Bowden, Bt; Thame Park, Oxon (☎ Thame 2637)

BOWDEN, Geoffrey Anthony; s of James Noble Bowden; *b* 5 June 1939; *Educ* Farnborough; *m* 1; m 2, 1973, Wendy, da of Alfred Powell, of Richmond Surrey; 1 s, 3 da *Career* md Siebe Gorman & Co 1977-, dep chm Merryweather & Sons 1979-, John Morris & Sons 1979-; *Recreations* golf, squash, theatre; *Clubs* Roehampton, RAC; *Style* - Geoffrey Bowden Esq; Belair,

Bryn Rhedyn Close, Llanfrechfa, Cwmbran, Gwent (☎ Gwent 063 33 60849)

BOWDEN, Nicholas Richard; s and h of Sir Frank Houston Bowden, 3 Bt; *b* 13 Aug 1935; *Educ* Millfield; *Career* late trooper Life Guards; farmer; *Recreations* riding; *Style* - Nicholas Bowden Esq; Hensting Farm, Fishers Pond, Eastleigh, Hants (☎ Owslebury 260)

BOWDEN, Baroness; Phyllis Bertha Mabel; da of Stanley Myson; *b* 19 June 1918; *Educ* Wimbledon High Sch; Newnham Cambridge; *m* 1, 1941, John James (d 1961); 1 da; m 2, 1974, Baron Bowden, *qv*; *Career* pres, Lucy Cavendish Coll, Cambridge 1979-; memb, local govt boundary commission for England 1977-; West Midlands Committee, National Trust 1976-; *Style* - The Rt Hon Lady Bowden; Pinecroft, Stanhope rd, Bowdon, Altrincham, Cheshire; 18 Trafalgar rd, Cambridge

BOWDER, Kenneth William; OBE *Career* vice-chm Leicester Building Soc; *Style* - Kenneth Bowder Esq, OBE; Oadby, Leicester

BOWEN, Mark Edward Mortimer; s and h of Sir Thomas Frederic Charles Bowen, 4 Bt; *b* 17 Oct 1958; *Style* - Mark Bowen Esq

BOWEN, Hon Sir Nigel Hubert; KBE (1976); s of Otway Bowen; *b* 26 May 1911; *Educ* King's Sch Parramatta NSW, St Paul's Coll, Sydney U; *m* 1947, Eileen, da of Francis Mullens; 3 da; *Career* Ch Judge Fedl Court of Australia 1976-; barr NSW 1936, Victoria 1954, QC (Australia) 1953; memb House of Reps (Lib) Parramatta 1964-73, Attorney-Gen Australia 1966-69 and 1971, Min Educn & Science 1969-71, Min For Affrs 1971-72; *Recreations* swimming, music; *Clubs* Union (Sydney); *Style* - Hon Sir Nigel Bowen, KBE; 43 Grosvenor st, Wahroonga, NSW 2076, Australia (☎ 48 1899)

BOWEN, Sir Thomas Frederick Charles; 4 Bt (UK 1921); s of 2 Bt (d 1937); suc bro, Sir John Edward Mortimer Bowen, 3 Bt, 1939; *b* 11 Oct 1921; *Educ* Eton; *m* 1947, Jill Claude, da of Cyril Lloyd Evans, of Prestea, Ghana, W Africa; 1 s, 1 da; *Heir* s, Mark Edward Mortimer Bowen; *Style* - Sir Thomas Bowen, Bt; 1 Barford close, Fleet, Hants

BOWEN, Col Thomas Jim; MC (1941); s of Thomas Oliver Bowen (d 1941); *b* 21 Jul 1917; *Educ* The Leys Sch Cambridge, St John's Cambridge; *m* 1950, Kathleen Bowen (cousin); 2 s, 1 da; *Career* High Sheriff Hereford and Worcester 1980; *Style* - Col Thomas Bowen MC; Little Blakes, Shelsley Beauchamp, Worcs (☎ 08 865261)

BOWEN, Timothy James Glyn; s of John Glyn Bowen, FRCS; *b* 15 March 1946; *Educ* Harrow; *m* 1979, Suzanne, da of Griffith Eaton Jeffreys, of Swansea; *Career* FCA; dir Chesterfield Properties Ltd; *Recreations* cricket; *Style* - Timothy Bowen Esq; 4 Thornton rd, Wimbledon Common, SW19 (☎ 01 947 9798)

BOWEN-GOTHAM, Arthur; MBE (1962), VRD and Bar (1970) CFM and 2 Bars (1977), DL (1981); s of Arthur Bowen-Gotham (d 1952); *b* 27 Aug 1915; *Educ* Aston G S; *m* 1954, Estelle Amelia Fry; 1 c; *Career* MRIN (1981), Lt-Cdr Atlantic, English Channel, N Africa, Malta, Italy, Yugoslavia, consultant; *Recreations* sailing; *Clubs* RYA, RNSA; *Style* - Arthur Bowen-Gotham Esq, MBE, VRD* CFM**, DL; 79 Lake drive, Hamworthy, Poole, Dorset (☎ Poole 3855); 13, Old Broadway, Withington, Manchester (☎ 434 2989)

BOWER, Hon Lady - Hon Catherine Muriel; da of late Capt Henry Edward Hotham and aunt of 8 Baron Hotham; *b* 1908; *m* 1939, Lt-Gen Sir Roger Bower, KCB, KBE; 1 s (adopted), 1 da; raised to rank of Baron's da 1924; *Style* - Hon Lady Bower; Ash House, St Mary Bourne, Andover, Hants

BOWER, Sir Frank; CBE (1948); s of Austin Bower; *b* 25 Aug 1894; *Educ* Lancaster G S, St Cat's Cambridge; *m* 1920, Ethel, da of Henry Shaw; 1 s, 2 da; *Career* kt 1960, tax inspector 1920-24, Taxation Offr Unilever 1924-60; *Style* - Sir Frank Bower, CBE; Flat 3 Highwood, 13

Sunset av, Woodford Green, Essex (☎ 01 505 7030)

BOWER, Air Marshal Sir Leslie; KCB (1962, CB 1954), DSO (1945), DFC (1943); s of William Bower; *b* 11 July 1909; *Educ* Harvey G S, RAF Coll Cranwell; *m* 1, 1963, Clare (d 1971), da of H Etkins, OBE, of Cornwall; m 2, 1980, Patricia Winifred, da of William Beresford Mortimore; *Career* UK Rep Perm Mil Deps Gp (Ankara) CENTO 1962-65; *Recreations* cricket, squash, sailing; *Clubs* RAF; *Style* - Air Marshal Sir Leslie Bower KCB DSO DFC; c/o Lloyds Bank, Cox's & King's Branch, 6 Pall Mall, SW1

BOWERMAN, Ian Nicholas; s of Duncan Bowerman; *b* 21 June 1921; *Educ* privately; *Career* dir- Dreyfus Louis & Co 1972-, Internatnl Trade Dvpt Co 1969-; Freeman City of London; *Recreations* collecting china and ceramics; *Clubs* Roehampton, Roy Overseas; *Style* - Ian Bowerman Esq; 6 Phoenix Lodge Mans, Brook Green, W6

BOWERS, A G; *Career* gen man Anglia Hastings and Thanet Building Soc; *Style* - A G Bowers Esq; Moulton Park, Northampton

BOWERS, Frederick John; s of Frederick Bowers (d 1971); *b* 23 Sept 1941; *Educ* Pembroke G S; *m* 1964, Sheila May, da of Hector Macdonald (d 1963); 2 s; *Career* dir Johnston Construction, Samuel Johnston Ltd (Sri Lanka), Hadsphaltic International (W Indies) Ltd, quantity surveyor; *Recreations* sailing, walking, scouting; *Clubs* Commonwealth; *Style* - Frederick Bowers Esq; 13 St Johns Meadow, Blindley Heath, Lingfield, Surrey (☎ 0342 833201)

BOWES LYON, Simon Alexander; s of late Hon Sir David Bowes Lyon, KCVO; *b* 17 June 1932; *Educ* Eton, Magdalen Oxford; *m* 1966, Caroline Mary Victoria, nee Pike; 3 s, 1 da; *Career* dir Financial Asssurance Co Ltd, Electro-Pneumatic Equipment Ltd, WRVS Trustees Ltd, joint Treasurer Council for Protection of Rural England; *Recreations* gardening, plant collecting, music, shooting; *Clubs* White's, Brooks's; *Style* - Simon Bowes Lyon Esq; St Paul's, Walden Bury, Hitchen, Herts (☎ Whitwell 218); 12 Morpeth Mansions, London SW1 (☎ 01 834 8057)

BOWES-LYON, Lady Diana Evelyn; da of 17 Earl of Strathmore and Kinghorne; *b* 1966; *Style* - Lady Diana Bowes-Lyon

BOWES-LYON, David James; s of Maj-Gen Sir James Bowes-Lyon, KCVO, CB, OBE, MC (d 1977); *b* 21 July 1947; *Educ* Ampleforth; *m* 1976, Elizabeth, da of Sir John Colville, CB, CVO, of the Old Rectory, Stratfield Saye, Hants; 1 s, 1 da; *Career* with The Union Discount Co of London 1979-; *Clubs* Turf, Guards and Cavalry, Puffin's; *Style* - David Bowes-Lyon Esq; Heriot Water, Heriot, Midlothian (☎ 281)

BOWES-LYON, Lady Elizabeth Mary Cecilia; da of 17 Earl of Strathmore and Kinghorne; *b* 1959; *Style* - Lady Elizabeth Bowes-Lyon

BOWES-LYON, Hon Michael Albemarle; s of late Hon Michael Claude Hamilton Bowes-Lyon, 5 s of 14 Earl of Strathmore and Kinghorne; bro of 17 Earl; raised to the rank of Earl's son 1974; *b* 1940; *Educ* Eton; *Style* - The Hon Michael Bowes-Lyon

BOWES-LYON, Hon Lady; Rachel Pauline; da of late Col the Rt Hon Herbert Spender-Clay CMG MC PC MP by Hon Pauline, JP, da of 1 Viscount Astor and sis of 1 Baron Astor of Hever; *m* 1929, Hon Sir David Bowes-Lyon, KCVO (d 1961), s of 14 Earl of Strathmore and Kinghorne; 1 s, 1 da (*see* 13 Earl of Stair, KCVO, MBE); *Style* - The Hon Lady Bowes-Lyon; St Paul's Waldenbury, Hitchin, Herts

BOWETT, Derek William; QC (1978); s of Arnold Bowett; *b* 20 Apr 1927; *Educ* Downing Cambridge; *m* 1953, Betty Northall; 2 s, 1 da; *Career* barrister 1953; pres, Queens' Coll, Cambridge; *Style* - Derek Bowett Esq QC; President's Lodge, Queens' College, Cambridge (☎ 65511)

BOWIE, Norman Walter; s of Walter Bowie, of Beckenham; *b* 10 Oct 1914; *Educ* Stationers' Co's Sch; *m* 1947, Kathleen, da of John Hannigan, of Highgate; *Career* FRICS; property consultant Jones Lang Wootton 1974, Br Land Co 1974-, Crown Agents 1976-, Nat Water Cncl Superannuation Fnd 1974-; dir Imry Property Hldgs 1965-; chm European Gp of Valuers of Fixed Assets 1977-; *Recreations* rowing; *Clubs* Ibis Rowing; *Style* - Norman Bowie Esq; 1 Uplands Close, SW14 (☎ 01 876 1434); White Horses, Coastal rd, W Kingston, Littlehampton, W Sussex

BOWLBY, Sir Anthony Hugh Mostyn; 2 Bt (UK 1923); s of Sir Anthony Alfred Bowlby, 1 Bt, KCB, KCMG, KCVO, FRCS (d 1929); *b* 13 Jan 1906; *Educ* Wellington, New Coll Oxford; *m* 1930, Dora Evelyn, da of late John Charles Allen, of York; 2 da; *Heir* bro, (Edward) John Bowlby; *Style* - Sir Anthony Bowlby, Bt; The Old Rectory, Ozleworth, nr Wotton-under-Edge, Glos

BOWLBY, Lady Ann Lavinia Maud, *née* Montagu-Stuart-Wortley-Mackenzie; da of 3 Earl of Wharncliffe (d 1953); *b* 1919; *m* 1939, as his 2 w, Cdr Vivian Russell Salvin Bowlby, RN (d 1972); 1 s; *Style* - Lady Ann Bowlby; Sutton Stables, Felixkirk rd, Sutton-under-Whitestonecliffe, Thirsk, Yorks

BOWLBY, Hon Mrs (Dorothy Anne); da of Hon Dudley North, MC, JP (d 1936); sis and co-heiress of 13 Baron North (E 1554), ka 1941, since when the Barony has been in abeyance; *b* 4 May 1915; *m* 1, 1937, William Graham, Lt Sherwood Foresters (m dis 1950); 1 da; m 2, 1950, Maj John Bowlby, 1 Roy Dragoons; 1 da; *Style* - The Hon Mrs Bowlby; 51 Shawfield st, SW3 (☎ 01 352 0573)

BOWLBY, (Edward) John Mostyn; CBE (1972); s of Sir Anthony Alfred Bowlby, 1 Bt, KCB, KCMG, KCVO (d 1929); hp to Btcy of bro, Sir Anthony Bowlby, 2 Bt; *b* 26 Feb 1907; *Educ* RNC Dartmouth, Trin Cambridge; *m* 1938, Ursula, nee Longstaff; 2 s, 2 da; *Career* psychiatrist, MD, FRCP, FRCPsych; author; consultant Tavistock Clinic 1946-72; *Recreations* natural history, field sports; *Style* - John Bowlby Esq CBE; Wyldes Close Corner, Hampstead Way, NW11 (☎ 01 455 9380); Ullinish, Struan, Isle of Skye (☎ 047 072 237)

BOWLBY, Hon Mrs - Hon Penelope Isobel; da of 7 Viscount Portman (d 1948); *b* 1913; *m* 1, 1934, Brig Archer Francis Lawrence Clive, DSO, MC (m dis 1949); 1 s, 1 da; m 2, 1949, David Bowlby; *Career* breeding racehorses; *Style* - The Hon Mrs Bowlby; Inverinate, Kyle of Lochalsh, Ross-shire; The Manor, Healing, Grimsby

BOWLER, Geoffrey; s of James Bowler; *b* 11 July 1924; *Educ* Sloane Sch, Chelsea; *Career* FCIS; ch gen man Sun Alliance and London Insurance Gp 1977-; *Style* - Geoffrey Bowler Esq; 13 Green lane, Purley, Surrey (☎ 01 660 0756)

BOWLER, Ian John; CBE (1971, OBE 1957); s of Maj John Bowler; *b* 1920; *Educ* King's Sch Worcester, Oxford U; *m* 1963, Hamideh, da of Prince Yadollah Azodi, GCMG; 2 da; 1 step s, 1 step d; *Career* pres Iranian Management and Engineering Gp Ltd 1965-; chm International Management and Engineering Gp Ltd 1973-; Kinhill/IMEG, Australia 1971-; *Style* - Ian Bowler Esq, CBE; 4 Kucheh, Bagh Bank, Golhak, Tehran, Iran; 28 Mallord st, SW3 (☎ 01 351 3322)

BOWMAN, David Anthony Paget; s and h of Sir John Paget Bowman, 4 Bt; *b* 16 Oct 1935; *m* 1968, Valerie Winifred, da of Reginald Cyril Tatham, FRCS; *Style* - David Bowman Esq; Sherwood, Boar's Hill, Oxford

BOWMAN, Sir George; 2 Bt (UK 1961); s of Sir James Bowman, 1 Bt, KBE (d 1978); *b* 2 July 1923; *m* 1960, Olive, nee Case; 3 da; *Heir* none; *Style* - Sir George Bowman Bt; Parkside, Killingworth drive, Killingworth Station, Newcastle-upon-Tyne

BOWMAN, Jean, Lady - Jean; da of Henry Brooks, of Ashington, Northumberland; *m* 1922, Sir James Bowman, 1 Bt, KBE (d 1978); 1 s, 1 da; *Style* - Jean, Lady Bowman; Woodlands, Killingworth Station, Forest Hall, Newcastle-upon-Tyne

BOWMAN, Sir John Paget; 4 Bt (UK 1884); s of Rev Sir Paget Mervyn Bowman, 3 Bt (d 1955); *b* 12 Feb 1904; *Educ* Eton; *m* 1, 1931, Countess Cajetana Hoyos (d 1948), da of Count Edgar Hoyos, of Schloss Soss, Lower Austria; 1 s, 1 da; m 2, 1948, Frances Edith Marian, da of late Sir (James) Beethom Whitehead, KCMG; *Heir* s, David Anthony Paget Bowman; *Career* formerly 2 Lt 98 (Surrey and Sussex Yeo, Queen Mary's) Army Field Bde, RA (TA); *Style* - Sir John Bowman, Bt; Bishops Green House, Greenham Common, nr Newbury, Bucks

BOWMAN, James Thomas; s of Benjamin Bowman; *b* 6 Nov 1941; *Educ* Ely Cathedral Choir Sch; King's Sch, Ely; New Coll Oxford; *Career* counter-tenor; *Style* - James Bowman Esq; 19a Wetherby gdns, SW5

BOWMAN, Thomas Patrick; s of Thomas Marshall Bowman; *b* 25 Sept 1915; *Educ* Oundle and Hertford Oxford; *m* 1950, Norman Deravin; 1 s; *Career* chm PA Management Consultants Ltd 1966-75; *Style* - Thomas Bowman Esq; 9 Clements rd, Wimbledon, SW19 (☎ 01 946 3828)

BOWMAN-SHAW, George Neville; s of George Bowman-Shaw; *b* 4 Oct 1930; *Educ* Caldicott Prep Sch and privately; *m* 1962, Georgina, da of G Blundell; 3 s, 1 da; *Career* chm Lancer Boss Rentals 1971-, Lancer Boss France 1967-, Lancer Boss Austria 1966-, Lancer Boss Ireland 1966-, Lancer Boss Gp 1966-, Lancer Boss Ltd 1967-, Boss Trucks & Equipment 1959-, Lancer Boss Internatnl SA Lausanne 1962-, Boss Engrs 1961-, Potters Ltd 1979-; *Recreations* shooting, wildlife, rare breeds and vintage tractors collections; *Clubs* Cavalry & Guards, Hurlingham, Constitutional; *Style* - George Bowman-Shaw Esq; Toddington Manor, Toddington, Beds (☎ 2576)

BOWMONT AND CESSFORD, Marquess of; Charles Robert George Innes-Ker; s and h of 10 Duke of Roxburghe by Lady Jane Grosvenor, da of 5 Duke of Westminster; *b* 18 Feb 1981; *Style* - Marquess of Bowmont and Cessford

BOWNESS, Alan; CBE (1976); s of George Bowness; *b* 11 Jan 1928; *Educ* UCS; Downing Cambridge; Courtauld Inst of Art; *m* 1957, Sarah, da of Ben Nicholson and late Dame Barbara Hepworth, DBE; 1 s, 1 da; *Career* dir Tate Gallery 1980-; *Style* - Alan Bowness Esq CBE; 91 Castelnau, SW13 (☎ 01 748 9696); 16 Piazza, St Ives, Cornwall (☎ 5444)

BOWRING, Edgar Rennie Harvey; MC (1945); s of Arthur Bowring, of Goudhurst; *b* 5 Nov 1915; *Educ* Eastbourne Coll, Clare Cambridge, Berkeley Coll Yale; *m* 1940, Margaret, da of John Grant Brook, of Goudhurst; 2 s, 1 da; *Career* slr 1949-; dir Marsh & McLennan Cos USA 1980-, C T Bowring & Co 1963-; *Recreations* golf, gardening; *Clubs* City University, Piltdown Golf; *Style* - Edgar Bowring Esq, MC; 18 Denbigh House, Hans Place, SW1 (☎ 01 584 0781); Leopards Mill, Horam, Heathfield, Sussex (☎ Horam Road 2687)

BOWRING, Peter; s of Frederick Bowring (d 1965); *b* 22 Apr 1923; *Educ* Shrewsbury; *m* 1, 1946, Barbara Brewis (m dis); 1 s, 1 da; m 2, 1979, Carol Hutchings; *Career* chm C T Bowring and Co Ltd 1978-; *Style* - Peter Bowring Esq; Flat 5, 69 Onslow sq, SW7 (☎ 01 584 8946); Flash Corner, Theberton, Leiston, Suffolk (☎ 830477)

BOWSER, David Stewart; JP (Perthshire 1956); s of David Charles Bowser, CBE; *b* 11 March 1926; *Educ* Harrow, Trin Cambridge; *m* 1951, Judith Crabbe; 1 s, 4 da; *Career* forestry commissioner 1974-, landowner 1947-; *Style* - David Bowser Esq, JP; Argaty and the King's Lundies, Doune, Perthshire (☎ 287)

BOWSER, H; *Career* chm Thomas Witter & Co; *Style* - H Bowser Esq; Thomas Witter & Co, Water st, Chorley, Lancs

BOWSHER, Peter Charles; QC (1978); s of Charles and Ellen Bowsher; *b* 9 Feb 1935; *Educ* Ardingly, Oriel Oxford; *m* 1960, Deborah, nee Wilkins, of Vancouver; 2 s; *Career* barr 1959; *Style* - Peter

Bowsher Esq, QC; 10 South sq, Gray's Inn, WC1 (☎ 01 242 2902)

BOWYER, Hon George Philip Paul; s of 2 Baron Denham; *b* 13 Dec 1964

BOWYER, Hon Henry Martin Mitford; s of 2 Baron Denham; *b* 9 May 1963 *Style* - The Hon Henry Bowyer

BOWYER, Hon Jocelyn Jane; da of 2 Baron Denham; *b* 18 Oct 1957; *Educ* Riddlesworth Hall; *Style* - The Hon Jocelyn Bowyer; The Laundry Cottage, Weston Underwood, Olney, Bucks

BOWYER, Hon Richard Grenville George; s and h of 2 Baron Denham; *b* 8 Feb 1959; *Style* - The Hon Richard Bowyer

BOWYER-SMYTH, Sir Thomas Weyland; 15 Bt (E 1661); s of Capt Sir Philip Weyland Bowyer-Smyth, 14 Bt, RN (d 1978); *b* 25 June 1960; *Heir* kinsman, John Windham; *Style* - Sir Thomas Bowyer-Smyth, Bt; La Provençale, Plascassier, France, AM

BOWYER-SMYTH, Lady - Veronica Mary; da of Capt C W Bower, DSC, RN (ret), of Fordwich, Kent; *m* 1951, as his 2 w, Capt Sir Philip Bowyer-Smyth, 14 Bt, RN (d 1978); *Style* - Lady Bowyer-Smyth; La Provençale, 06870 Plascassier, France, AM

BOXALL, Richard George; s of Thomas Boxall, OBE, of Appleby Magna Leics; *b* 23 May 1936; *Educ* Bedford Sch, Christ's Cambridge; *m* 1960, Dorothy, da of Samuel Breeze, of Folkestone; 2 s, 1 da; *Career* mechanical engr; ops dir Ibstock Johnsen Ltd; *Recreations* sailing, gardening; *Clubs* Naval; *Style* - Richard Boxall Esq; Holme Leys Farm, Appleby Magna, Burton-on-Trent, Staffs (☎ 0530 70504); Rue du Commandant Charcot, Jard sur Mer, France 85520

BOXER, Lady Arabella; *née* Stuart; da of 18 Earl of Moray (d 1943); *b* 11 July 1934; *m* 1956, (Charles) Mark Edward Boxer (Marc the cartoonist); 1 s, 1 da; *Career* author; *Style* - Lady Arabella Boxer; 174 Ebury st, SW1

BOYCE, John Leslie; s of late Sir (Harold) Leslie Boyce, 1 Bt, KBE; hp of nephew, Sir Robert Boyce, 3 Bt; *b* 16 Nov 1934; *m* 1957, Finola Mary, da of late James Patrick Maxwell, of Bansha, Co Tipperary; 1 s, 3 da; *Style* - John Boyce Esq; 182 Huntingdon rd, Mt Waverley, Victoria 3149, Australia

BOYCE, Sir Robert (Charles) Leslie; 3 Bt (UK 1952); s of Sir Richard (Leslie) Boyce, 2 Bt (d 1968); *b* 2 May 1962; *Heir* unc, John Leslie Boyce; *Style* - Sir Robert Boyce, Bt; The Barn House, Ascott Earl, Ascott under Wychwood, Oxon

BOYD OF MERTON, 1 Viscount (UK 1960); Alan Tindal Lennox-Boyd; CH (1960), PC (1951), DL (Cornwall 1965); s of Alan Lennox-Boyd; *b* 18 Nov 1904; *Educ* Sherborne, Ch Ch Oxford; *m* 1938, Lady Patricia Guinness, da of 2 Earl of Iveagh, KG, CB, CMG, and aunt of Marchioness of Douro & Paul Channon, MP & Min for the Arts; Lady Patricia's mother was Lady Gwendolen, CBE, da of 4 Earl of Onslow; 3 s; *Heir* s, Hon Simon Lennox-Boyd; *Career* jt V-Chm Arthur Guinness Son & Co 1967-79; dir ICI 1967-75; MP (C) Beds 1931-60, Sec of State for Colonies 1954-59; Pres Roy C'wlth Soc 1965-, memb Cncl IOD 1962-; *Clubs* Carlton, Pratt's, Buck's, Naval, RAC, Roy C'wlth Soc, Roy Yacht Sqdn, Roy Western Yacht; *Style* - The Rt Hon The Viscount Boyd of Merton, CH, PC, DL; 58 Jermyn st, SW1 (☎ 01 409 2604); Ince Castle, Saltash, Cornwall (☎ 2274)

BOYD, Sir Alexander Walter; 3 Bt (UK 1916); s of late Maj Cecil Anderson Boyd, MC, MD, late RAMC, 2 s of 1 Bt; suc unc, Sir Walter Herbert Boyd, 2 Bt, 1948; *b* 16 June 1934; *m* 1958, Molly Madeline, da of late Ernest Arthur Rendell, of Vernon, British Columbia; 2 s, 3 da; *Heir* s, Ian Walter Rendell Boyd; *Style* - Sir Alexander Boyd, Bt; RR3, Vernon, British Columbia, Canada

BOYD, Ian Walter Rendell; s and h of Sir Alexander Boyd, 3 Bt; *b* 14 March 1964; *Style* - Ian Boyd Esq

BOYD, Hon Jonathan Aubrey Lewis; 3 s of 6 Baron Kilmarnock, MBE (d 1975); *b*

1 Oct 1956; *Style* - The Hon Jonathan Boyd ; 28 Eaton ter, SW1 (☎ 01 730 8393)

BOYD OF MERTON, Viscountess; Lady Patricia Florence Susan; *née* Guinness; da of Viscount Elveden (ka 1945), and sis of 3 Earl of Iveagh; *b* 1918; *m* 1938, 1 Viscount Boyd of Merton; *Style* - The Rt Hon the Viscountess Boyd of Merton; Ince Castle, Saltash, Cornwall; Flat 12, 5 Carlton gdns, SW1

BOYD, Hon Robin Jordan; 2 s of 6 Baron Kilmarnock, MBE (d 1975) and hp of bro, 7 Baron; *b* 6 June 1941; *Educ* Eton, Strasbourg U, Keble Oxford; *Career* Page to Lord High Constable of Scotland at Coronation of HM the Queen 1953; MB, BS, LRCP, MRCS, DCH; *Style* - The Hon Robin Boyd; Flat 5, 2 Brondesbury Road, NW6

BOYD, Prof Robert Lewis Fullarton; CBE (1972); s of Dr William Boyd, of Sanderstead; *b* 19 Oct 1922; *Educ* Whitgift Sch, London U, Heriot Watt U; *m* 1949, Mary, da of John Higgins; 2 s, 1 da; *Career* FRS (1969), Tstee Nat Maritime Museum 1980-, memb SRC 1977-, Prof of Astronomy Roy Inst 1961-67; Dir Mullard Space Science Lab UCL 1952-; *Recreations* elderly Rolls Royce motor cars; *Style* - Prof Robert Boyd, CBE; Ariel House, Holmbury St Mary, Dorking, Surrey (☎ Ewhurst 478); Roseneath, 41 Church st, Littlehampton, Sussex (☎ 09064 4438)

BOYD, Robert Nathaniel; CBE (1971); s of Peter Boyd; *b* 17 Nov 1918; *Educ* Boys' G S Suva Fiji, Churchers' Coll Petersfield; *m* 1947, Carrie, da of Harry Squires; 2 s; *Career* FCIS, FCIArb, FBIM; Auditor-Gen Zambia 1966-68; Sec/Financial Controller Air T'port and Travel Indust T'ning Bd 1969-77; *Recreations* bowls; *Clubs* Hurst Bowling, Roy C'wlth Soc; *Style* - Robert Boyd Esq, CBE; Clare Lodge, Glebelands rd, Wokingham, Berks (☎ 781122)

BOYD, Hon Timothy Iain; s of 6 Baron Kilmarnock, MBE (d 1975); *b* 5 April 1959; *Style* - The Hon Timothy Boyd

BOYD-CARPENTER, Baron (Life Peer UK 1972); John Archibald Boyd-Carpenter; PC (1954), DL (Gter London 1973); s of Maj Sir Archibald Boyd-Carpenter, MP (d 1937); *b* 2 June 1908; *Educ* Stowe, Balliol Oxford; *m* 1937, Margaret, da of Lt-Col George Hall, OBE, by his w, Dorothy, nee Coventry, ggggda of 6 Earl of Coventry; 1 s, 2 da (of which the yr, Hon Sarah, m Hon Douglas Hogg, MP, s of Baron Hailsham of St Marylebone); *Career* barr 1934, MP (C) Kingston-upon-Thames 1945-72, Ch Sec Tres 1962-64, Chm CAA 1972-77, chm Rugby Portland Cement 1976-; *Recreations* swimming, tennis, walking, gardening; *Clubs* Carlton (Chm 1979-); *Style* - The Rt Hon Lord Boyd-Carpenter PC DL; 12 Eaton ter, SW1 (☎ 01 730 7765); Crux Easton House, Crux Easton, Highclere, Berks (☎ 0635 253037)

BOYD-CARPENTER, Hon Anne Mary; da of Baron Boyd-Carpenter, PC, DL (Life Peer); *b* 1942; *Style* - The Hon Anne Boyd-Carpenter

BOYD-CARPENTER, Col Hon Thomas Patrick John; MBE (Mil 1973); s of Baron Boyd-Carpenter, PC, DL (Life Peer); *b* 1938; *m* 1971, Jean, nee Duffield; 3 children; *Career* Scots Gds, Col GSAT3 MOD 1981-; *Style* - Col Hon Thomas Boyd-Carpenter, MBE; Sun Hill Farm, Chieveley, Newbury, Berks

BOYER, John Leslie; *Career* chm Antony Gibbs Hldgs 1981-, dep chm Hongkong & Shanghai Banking Corpn to 1981; chm Wardley Ltd to 1981; dir-Eastern Asia Navigation Ltd, Far Eastern Economic Review Ltd, Hakone Hldgs SA, Mass Transit Railway Corpn, Mercantile Bank Ltd, Regent Shipping Investment Hldgs, Swire Pacific Ltd, Wardley Investment Servs, Wardley Nikko Management, WHS Investments, World Shipping & Investment Co; chm Lion Corpte Servs, S China Morning Post, Wayhong Investment Ltd; *Style* - John Boyer Esq; c/o Antony Gibbs Hldgs, 3 Frederick's Place, Old Jewry, EC2 (☎ 01 588 4111)

BOYES, Roland; MEP (L) Durham 1979-; *b* 12 Feb 1937; *Career* memb GMWU; *Clubs* Peterlee Labour; *Style* -

Roland Boyes Esq, MEP; 12 Spire Hollin, Peterlee, Co Durham (☎ 863917)

BOYLE OF HANDSWORTH, Baron (Life Peer UK 1970); Sir Edward Charles Gurney Boyle; 3 Bt (UK 1904), CH (1981), PC (1962); s of Sir Edward Boyle, 2 Bt, JP (d 1945); *b* 31 Aug 1923; *Educ* Eton, Ch Ch Oxford; *Heir* to Btcy only- bro, Richard Boyle; *Career* Tstee Br Museum 1970-81, chm Top Salaries Review Body 1971-81; MP (C) Birmingham Handsworth 1950-70, Min of Educn 1962-64 & Min of State DES 1964; V-Chllr Leeds U 1970-; *Clubs* Carlton; *Style* - Rt Hon Lord Boyle of Handsworth CH PC; Vice-Chancellor's Lodge, Grosvenor rd, Leeds LS6 2DZ

BOYLE, Hon Mrs (Rebecca Juliet) ; *née* Noble; da of Baron Glenkinglas, PC; *b* 1950; *m* 1973, Lt-Comdr John Richard Boyle, RN; *Style* - The Hon Mrs Boyle; Hawthorn Cottage, Newtown, Fareham, Hants

BOYLE, Brian; s of Peter Joseph Boyle; *b* 24 Nov 1952; *Educ* Winchmore Sch; *Career* AV photographer/jt ptnr photographic company; *Recreations* photography, music, sport, driving; *Style* - Brian Boyle Esq; 2 Haslemere rd, Winchmore Hill, N21 (☎ 886 2026)

BOYLE, Lady Caroline Mary Victoria; yr da of 9 Earl of Shannon; *b* 12 Oct 1965

BOYLE, Hon David Michael Douglas; s & h of Viscount of Kelburn; *b* 15 Oct 1978; *Style* - The Hon David Boyle

BOYLE, Lady Geraldine Lilian ; da of Col Gerald Edmund Boyle (d 1927) and half sis of 12 Earl of Cork and Orrery, GCB, GCVO; *b* 1899; *Career* granted rank, title and precedence of an Earl's da which would have been hers had her father survived to succeed to the title ; *Style* - Lady Geraldine Boyle; 38 Strand Court, Topsham, Exeter, Devon

BOYLE, Lady Georgina Susan; da of 9 Earl of Shannon; *b* 7 Feb 1961; *Style* - Lady Georgina Boyle

BOYLE, Hon John William; DSC; s of Hon Reginald Courtenay Boyle MBE, MC (d 1946), and bro of 13 Earl of Cork and Orrery; *b* 12 May 1916; *Educ* Harrow and King's Coll, London; *m* 1943, Mary Leslie, da of Gen Sir Robert Gordon-Finlayson, KCB, CMG, DSO (d 1956); 3 s ; *Career* Served in Second World War (despatches 2), Lt-Cdr, RNVR, granted 1967, title, rank and precedence of an Earl's son ; *Clubs* Royal Thames Yacht Club; *Style* - The Hon John Boyle, DSC; Craigantaggart, Dunkeld, Perthshire

BOYLE, Sir Lawrence; JP (Glasgow 1970); s of Hugh Boyle; *b* 31 Jan 1920; *Educ* Holy Cross Acad Leith, Edinburgh U; *m* 1952, Mary, da of Andrew McWilliam; 1 s, 3 da; *Career* kt 1979, chm Scot Nat Orchestra 1980-; dir Short Loan & Mortgage Co, Pension Fund Property Unit Tst, Scot Mutual Assur Soc; ch exec Strathclyde Regnl Cncl 1974-80; visiting prof Strathclyde U Business Sch; *Recreations* music; *Style* - Sir Lawrence Boyle, JP; 24 Broomburn dve, Newton Mearns, Glasgow G77 5JF (☎ 041 639 3776)

BOYLE, Michael Patrick Radcliffe; s of Patrick Boyle (s of late Capt Hon Edward Boyle, RN, 5 s of 5 Earl of Shannonnby his 2 w, Julia, da of Sir William Hartopp, 3 Bt); *b* 25 Jan 1934; *Educ* Eton; *m* 1962, Lady Nell, nee Harris, da of 6 Earl of Malmesbury, TD, JP, and Hon Diana Carleton, da of 2 Baron Dorchester; 2 s, 1 da; *Career* High Sheriff Hants 1976-77, memb Hants CC 1970-, chm Hants Police Authority 1976- CStJ; *Recreations* shooting, sailing; *Clubs* Boodle's, White's, Pratt's, Roy Yacht Sqdn; *Style* - Michael Boyle Esq; Ashe Hill, Ashe, Basingstoke, Hants (☎ 0256 770368)

BOYLE, Lady Nell Carleton *née* Harris; da of 6 Earl of Malmesbury; *b* 1950; *m* 1962, Capt Michael Boyle, Irish Guards; 2 s, 1 da; *Style* - Lady Nell Boyle; Ashe Hill House, Basingstoke, Hants

BOYLE, Capt Richard Courtenay; DSC (1940), DL (Herts 1975), RN; s of Col Lionel Richard Cavendish Boyle, CMG, MVO; *b* 20 May 1902; *Educ* RNCs Osborne and Dartmouth; *m* 1926, Gwendolen, da of Lt-Col E Griffith; 2 s, 1 da; *Career* sometime Dir Boom Defence and Capt HM Dockyard Chatham, assist man BAC Luton; *Recreations* gardening; *Style* - Capt Richard Boyle, DSC, DL, RN; Pegsdon Barns, Pegsdon, Hitchin, Herts (☎ Luton 881334)

BOYLE, Richard Gurney; s and h of Sir Edward Boyle, 2 Bt, and bro of Baron Boyle of Handsworth, PC; *b* 14 May 1930; *m* 1961, Elizabeth Anne, nee Dennes; *Style* - Richard Boyle Esq; Paris Hall Cottage, Hastingwood, Harlow, Essex

BOYLE, Viscount; Richard Henry John Boyle; s (by 2 m) and h of 9 Earl of Shannon; *b* 19 Jan 1960; *Educ* Northease Manor Sch; *Career* in catering business; *Style* - Viscount Boyle; Old Loose Court, Maidstone, Kent

BOYLE, Ranald Hugh Montgomerie; DSC (1944); s of David Boyle, CMG; *b* 19 Aug 1970; *Educ* Wellington, Exeter Coll Oxford; *m* 1957, Norma, da of Alexander Gray, of Calcutta and London; 5 s, 2 da; *Career* dir Hambro Bank 1974-, Sr Rep (London) Arab Banking Corpn 1981-, formerly with For and Colonial Servs; *Recreations* fishing, shooting, tennis, squash, sailing; *Style* - Ranald Boyle Esq, DSC; 901 Beatty House, Dolphin sq, SW1 (☎ 01 821 8028); Downcraig Ferry, Millport, Isle of Cumbrae, Scotland (Millport 550)

BOYNE, 10 Viscount (I 1717); Gustavus Michael George Hamilton-Russell; JP (Salop 1961), DL (1965); also Baron Hamilton of Stackallen (I 1715) and Baron Brancepeth (UK 1866); sits as Baron Brancepeth; s of Hon Gustavus Hamilton-Russell (ka 1940, s and h of 9 Visc Boyne, JP, DL, by his w, Lady Margaret Lascelles, CBE, da of 5 Earl of Harewood) and Joan, da of Sir Harry Lloyd Verney, GCVO (gs of Sir Harry Verney, 2 Bt), by his w, Lady Joan Cuffe (da of 5 and last Earl of Desart, KP); suc gf 1942; *b* 10 Dec 1931; *Educ* Eton, Sandhurst, Roy Ag Coll Cirencester; *m* 1956, Rosemary, da of Sir Denis Stucley, 5 Bt, JP, DL, and Hon Sheila Bampfylde, da of 4 Baron Poltimore; 1 s, 3 da; *Heir* s, Hon Gustavus Hamilton-Russell; *Career* Lord in Waiting to HM 1981-; formerly Lt Life Gds (ret 1956); dir Nat West Bank 1976- (chm W Midland & Wales Regnl Bd), CStJ, dep chm Telford Devpt Corpn 1976-; *Recreations* skiing, shooting, fishing; *Clubs* Turf, Roy Overseas League; *Style* - The Rt Hon The Viscount Boyne, JP, DL; 54 Montagu sq, W1 (☎ 01 402 4976); Burwarton House, Bridgnorth, Salop (☎ Burwarton 203)

BOYNE, Sir Harry (Henry Brian); CBE (1969); s of late Lockhart Boyne; *b* 29 July 1910; *Educ* High Sch and Roy Acad Inverness; *m* 1935, Margaret Little Templeton; 1 da; *Career* kt 1976, dir Communications Conservative Centl Off 1980-, political corr Daily Telegraph 1956-76; *Recreations* reading, playgoing; *Clubs* Press, Victory, Western (Dundee); *Style* - Sir Harry Boyne, CBE; 11 Marsham Court, SW1 (☎ 01 834 8803)

BRABAZON OF TARA, 3 Baron (UK 1942); Ivon Anthony Moore-Brabazon; s of 2 Baron Brabazon of Tara, CBE (d 1974, whose f the 1 Baron was Min of Aircraft Production just after Beaverbrock and much involved with civil aviation & aeronautics; the mighty Bristol-Brabazon airliner (a cross between Howard Hughes's 'Spruce Goose' in that it needed the largest hangar in the UK and 'Concorde' in that it cost the taxpayer £12,000,000 (in 1940s money) before being scrapped) was named after him; he was ggs of Barbara, nee Brabazon, gda of 7 Earl of Meath); *b* 20 Dec 1946; *Educ* Harrow; *m* 1979, Harriet, da of Mervyn de Courcy Hamilton, of Salisbury Zimbabwe; *Heir* none; *Career* memb Stock Exchange 1972-; *Recreations* sailing; *Clubs* White's, Roy Yacht Sqdn; *Style* - The Rt Hon The Lord Brabazon of Tara; 26 Coulson st, SW3 (☎ 01 589 9019)

BRABAZON, Hon Anthony Jaques; s and h of Lord Ardee; *b* 20 Jan 1977; *Style* - The Hon Anthony Brabazon

BRABAZON, Hon Corinna Lettice; da of Lord Ardee; *b* 1974

BRABAZON, Hon David Geoffrey Normand; s of 14 Earl of Meath; *b* 1948; *Educ* Tabley House; *m* 1972, Gay, da of late Cdr William Whitworth, RN, 1 s, 1 da; *Style* - The Hon David Brabazon; West

Wing, Killruddery, Bray, Co Wicklow, Ireland

BRABAZON OF TARA, Dowager Lady - Henrietta Mary; da of Sir Rowland Clegg; *m* 1, Ivor Krabbe (decd); m 2, 1939, 2 Baron Brabazon of Tara (d 1974); *Style* - The Rt Hon The Dowager Lady Brabazon of Tara; The Watch House, Bembridge, IOW

BRABAZON, Hon Serena Alexandra; da of Lord Ardee; *b* 1979

BRABHAM, Sir Jack; OBE 1966 ; *b* 2 April 1926; *Educ* Hurstville Technical Coll, Sydney; *m* 1951 Betty Evelyn; 3 s; *Career* Racing Driver ret 1970; md- Jack Brabham (Motors) Ltd, Jack Brabham (Worcester Park) Ltd, Brabham Racing Org Ltd, Engine Dev Ltd; *Style* - Sir Jack Brabham, OBE; c/o 248 Hook Rd, Chessington, Surrey (☎ 01 397 4343)

BRABOURNE, 7 Baron (UK 1880); Sir John Ulick Knatchbull; 16 Bt (E 1641); s of 5 Baron Brabourne, GCSI, GCIE, MC, JP, MP, sometime Actg Gov-Gen India, by his w, Lady Doreen Browne, da of 6 Marquess of Sligo; suc er bro, 6 Baron, (shot by the Germans after escaping from a prison train in Italy and recaptured 1943); *b* 9 Nov 1924; *Educ* Eton, BNC Oxford; *m* 1946, Lady Patricia Edwina Mountbatten (now Countess Mountbatten of Burma), da of 1 Earl Mountbatten of Burma; 4 s (and 1 s decd), 2 da; *Heir* s, Lord Romsey; *Career* dir (non-exec) Thorn EMI 1981-; served WW II Capt Coldstream Gds; film producer; films include 'Sink the Bismarck', 'Murder on the Orient Express' and 'Tales of Beatrix Potter'; dir Thames TV 1978-, Gov BFI 1979-; *Style* - The Rt Hon Lord Brabourne; Newhouse, Mersham, Ashford, Kent (☎ 0233 23466); 39/41 Montpelier Walk, SW7 (☎ 01 589 8829)

BRABOURNE, Dowager Baroness; Lady Doreen Geraldine; *née* Browne; CI (1937); da of late 6 Marquess of Sligo; *b* 1896; *m* 1919, 5 Baron Brabourne (d 1939); *Career* DStJ, dep v-chm Overseas League 1953-56; *Style* - The Rt Hon The Dowager Lady Brabourne, CI; 64 Kingston House North, SW7

BRACEWELL SMITH, Charles; s of Sir George Bracewell Smith, 2 Bt (d 1976); *b* 13 October 1955; *Career* hp of bro, Sir Guy Bracewell Smith, 3 Bt; *Style* - Charles Bracewell Smith Esq

BRACEWELL SMITH, Sir Guy; 3 Bt (1947); s of Sir George Bracewell Smith, 2 Bt, MBE (d 1976); *b* 12 December 1952; *Heir* bro, Charles Bracewell Smith; *Style* - Sir Guy Bracewell Smith, Bt; Park Lane Hotel, Piccadilly, W1

BRACKENBURY, Ian Mills; s of Charles Brackenbury; *b* 18 Aug 1930; *Educ* Uppingham; *m* 1961, Clare, da of Rex Phillips, of Guernsey; 2 s, 1 da; *Career* chm Redlac Engrg Gp and subsids, R G S Attenborough (Tools), Vacuum Engrg Industs; dir Rudolf Wolff & Co, Starkey's Technicast Ltd; memb IOD; *Recreations* shooting, skiing; *Clubs* Cavalry & Guards; *Style* - Ian Brackenbury Esq; Fullers Farm, West Horsley, Surrey

BRACKFIELD, Peter; s of Julius Brackfield; *b* 26 Sept 1922; *Educ* Berkhamsted, Trin Cambridge; *m* 1954, Odile (m dis), da of Louis de Koenigswarter, of Paris; 1 s; *Career* merchant banker; dep chm Singer & Friedlander Ltd 1976- (md 1956-76); dir C T Bowring & Co 1971-80; *Recreations* riding, tennis, skiing, gardening; yacht- 'Gioconda'; *Style* - Peter Brackfield Esq; Flat 6, 58 Rutland Gate, SW7; Priory Stones, Lurgashall, Petworth, W Sussex

BRADBURN, Stephen Ernest; s of Ernest Bradburn, of Sheffield; *b* 24 Sept 1947; *Educ* Abbeydale Boys' G S Sheffield; *m* 1969, Geraldine, da of Albert Britton, of Woodley Berks; 1 s; *Career* dir Hargreaves T'port Ltd 1976-, Hargreaves Vehicle Distributors Ltd 1978-; *Style* - Stephen Bradburn Esq; 10 Cottesmore gdns, Hale Barns, Altrincham, Cheshire

BRADBURY, 2 Baron (UK 1925); John Bradbury; s of 1 Baron, GCB (d 1950); *b* 7 Jan 114; *Educ* Westminster, BNC Oxford; *m* 1, 1939, Joan, da of W D Knight, of Darley, Addlestone, Surrey; 1 s, 1 da; m 2, 1946, Gwerfyl, da of late E Stanton Roberts, of Gellifor, Ruthin, Denbighshire; 1 da; *Heir* s, Hon John

Bradbury; *Style* - The Rt Hon The Lord Bradbury; Sunridge, Downsway, Merrow, Guildford, Surrey (☎ Cobham 7757)

BRADBURY, Hon John; s and h of 2 Baron Bradbury ; *b* 17 March 1940; *Educ* Gresham's and Bristol U; *m* 1968 Susan, nee Liddiard; 2 s ; *Style* - The Hon John Bradbury; 3 Ashchurch Park Villas, London W12 (☎ 01 743 4909)

BRADBURY, Hon Paul; s of 1 Baron Bradbury, GCB (d 1950); *b* 28 Nov 1915; *Educ* Westminster and BNC Oxford; *m* 1940, Margaret Amy, da of John William Stammers; 3 s; *Career* co dir (ret); *Style* - The Hon Paul Bradbury; Chelvey Batch, Brockley, Somerset (☎ 027 583 2813)

BRADBURY, Rear-Adm Thomas Henry; CB (1979); s of Thomas Bradbury (d 1970); *b* 4 Dec 1922; *Educ* Christ's Hospital; *m* 1, 1945, Beryl Evans (m dis 1979); 1 s, 1 da; m 2, 1979, Sarah, nee Hillier; *Career* Gp personnel dir Inchcape Gp 1979- Flag Offr Admlty Interview Bd 1977-79; *Recreations* sailing, gardening; *Clubs* Oriental; *Style* - Rear-Adm Thomas Bradbury, CB; Churches Green, Dallington, Heathfield, Sussex (☎ Rushlake Green 657)

BRADEN, Bernard; s of Rev Edwin Braden *b* 1916 *Educ* Canada *m* 1942, Barbara Kelly; 1 s, 2 da *Career* TV presenter; Hon Chancellor LSE 1955; *Style* - Bernard Braden Esq

BRADFIELD, John Harvey; s of Godfrey Bradfield (d 1970); *b* 11 April 1928; *Educ* Merchant Taylors'; *m* 1956, Mary, da of Reginald Cole Parsons, of Williton Lodge, St Audries, Somerset; 1 s, 2 da; *Career* CA 1952; chm Bishop's Stores 1967-, md Harvey Bradfield & Toyer 1960-73, dir Makro UK 1971-, chm Allied Grocery Distributors 1977-, pres Nat Fedn Wholesale Grocers 1980-; memb Executive Planning Grp Comité International des Entreprises à Succursales 1978-; *Recreations* golf, philately; *Clubs* Moor Park Golf; *Style* - John Bradfield Esq; c/o Barclays Bank, Ruislip, Middlesex

BRADFORD, 6 Earl of (UK 1815); Sir Gerald Michael Orlando Bridgeman; 11 Bt (E 1660), TD (1945), JP (Salop 1949), DL (1951); also Baron Bradford (GB 1794) and Viscount Newport (UK 1815); s of 5 Earl of Bradford (d 1957) and Hon Margaret, née Bruce, da of 2 Baron Aberdare; *b* 29 Sept 1911; *Educ* Harrow, Trin Cambridge; *m* 1946, Mary, da of Lt-Col Thomas Montgomery, DSO, of Cadogan House, Shrewsbury; 2 s, 2 da; *Heir* s, Viscount Newport; *Career* landowner, farmer, forester; Pres CLA 1955-57, Crown Estate Commissioner 1956-67, Pres Timber Growers' Org 1962-64 and Soil Assoc 1951-70; chm Nat Tst (NW Midlands Regn) 1972-80, Forestry Cttee of GB 1964-66; Vice-Lt Salop 1970-74; patron of five livings; *Recreations* travel, field sports, dendrology; *Clubs* MCC; *Style* - The Rt Hon The Earl of Bradford, TD, JP, DL; 61d Eaton sq, SW1 (☎ 01 235 4942); Weston Park, Shifnal, Salop (☎ Weston-under-Lizard 218)

BRADFORD, Hon Mrs (Alice Tattersall); *née* Whiteley; da of 2 Baron Marchamley (d 1949); *b* 1917; *m* 1946, as his 2 w, Robert Danby Bradford; 2 s (Robert b 1947; Andrew b 1949, m 1980 Janice Diverty); *Career* sometime Jr Cdr ATS; *Style* - The Hon Mrs Bradford; Membland, Haddington, East Lothian, Scotland EH41 4JH

BRADFORD, Donald Clifton; s of late Col Sir Evelyn Bradford, 2 Bt; hp of nephew, Sir Edward Bradford, 5 Bt; *b* 22 May 1914; *m* 1949, Constance, nee Morgan; 3 da; *Style* - Donald Bradford Esq; Woodside, Seal, Sevenoaks, Kent

BRADFORD, (Sir) Edward Alexander Slade; (5 Bt, UK 1902); s of 3 Bt (d 1952); suc half-bro, Sir John Ridley Evelyn Bradford, 4 Bt, 1954, but does not use title; *b* 18 June 1952; *Heir* unc, Donald Bradford; *Style* - Edward Bradford Esq; Faith Cottage, Pett, Sussex

BRADFORD, 6 Bishop of (cr 1920) 1980-; Rt Rev Geoffrey Paul; s of Robert Paul; *b* 4 Mar 1921; *Educ* Queens' Cambridge; King's Coll, London; *Career*

deacon 1948; *Style* - The Rt Rev the Bishop of Bradford; Bishopscroft, Ashwell rd, Bradford, W Yorks

BRADFORD, Lady - Marjorie (Chapman); da of Samuel Bere; *m* 1950, as his 2 w, Maj Sir Edward Bradford, 3 Bt (d 1952); *Style* - Lady Bradford; Faith Cottage, Pett, Sussex

BRADFORD, Hon Mrs (Tatiana Sonia); da of 1 Baron Lucas of Chilworth (d 1967); *b* 1933; *m* 1964, Kenneth Bradford; 2 s; *Style* - The Hon Mrs Bradford; c/o POB 199, 99 Bishopsgate, EC2

BRADLAW, Prof Sir Robert Vivian; CBE (1950); s of Philip Bradlaw, of Blackrock, Dublin; *b* 14 April 1905; *Educ* Cranleigh, Guy's; *Career* kt 1965; chm Advsy Cncl Misuse of Drugs Home Off 1976-; Emeritus Prof Oral Medicine London U 1970-; *Recreations* golf, fishing, orchids, oriental ceramics; *Clubs* Athenaeum; *Style* - Prof Sir Robert Bradlaw, CBE; The Manse, Stoke Goldington, Bucks (☎ 0908 55281)

BRADLEY, Hon Mrs (Caroline Agnes Morgan); *née* Thomson; da of Baron Thomson of Monifieth, PC; *b* 1954; *m* 1977, Ian C Bradley; *Style* - The Hon Mrs Bradley

BRADLEY, Hon Mrs (Elizabeth Mary Jean); *née* Annesley; da of 14 Viscount Valentia, MC; *b* 1926; *m* 1948, Maj James Terence Ralph Sylvester Bradley; 1 s, 3 da; *Style* - The Hon Mrs Bradley; Knighton Manor, Durweston, Blandford, Dorset

BRADLEY, Joe; *Career* gen man Nationwide Building Soc; *Style* - Joe Bradley Esq; New Oxford House, High Holborn, WC1

BRADMAN, Godfrey Michael; s of William Isadore Bradman; *b* 9 Sept 1936; *m* 1975, Susan, da of George Bennett; 2 s, 3 da; *Career* FCA; chm and ch exec Rosehaugh Co, and London Mercantile Gp of Cos; *Recreations* riding; *Style* - Godfrey Bradman Esq; 53 Queen Anne st, W1 (☎ 01 486 7100)

BRADSHAW, Hon Mrs (Alison Margaret); *née* Herbert; da of Baron Tangley, KBE (Life Peer, d 1973); *b* 1943; *m* 1965, John Michael Bradshaw; c; *Career* LRAM, ARCM; *Style* - The Hon Mrs Bradshaw; Cherrydale, W Clandon, Surrey

BRADSHAW, Hon Mrs (Diana Mary); *née* Hepburne-Scott; da of 10 Lord Polwarth, TD; *b* 1946; *m* 1977, Richard James Bradshaw; 1 da; *Style* - The Hon Mrs Bradshaw; c/o San Francisco Opera, War Memorial Opera House, San Francisco, Calif 94012, USA

BRADY, Hon Mrs (Charlotte Mary Thérèse); *née* Bingham; da of 7 Baron Clanmorris; *b* 29 June 1942; *Educ* The Priory Hayward's Heath; The Sorbonne; *m* 1964, Terence Brady; 1 s, 1 da; *Career* playwright & novelist as Charlotte Bingham; *Style* - The Hon Mrs Brady; 111 East Sheen ave, SW14

BRAGG, Henry John; s of Henry Bragg, of Torquay; *b* 28 Nov 1929; *Educ* Torquay G S, London U; *m* 1972, Anthea, da of Kew Shelley, QC; 3 children; *Career* md Calor Gas Hldg Co 1980-, Calor Gp 1978-; dir Imperial Continental Gas Ltd 1980; FCIT 1979; *Recreations* golf, hunting; *Clubs* Roy St George's Golf; *Style* - Henry Bragg Esq; 22 Thamespoint, Fairways, Teddington, Middx (☎ 01 977 9852); Hideway House, St George's rd, Sandwich, Kent (☎ 12364)

BRAGG, Melvyn; s of Stanley Bragg; *b* 6 Oct 1939; *Educ* Wadham Oxford; *m* 1, 1961, Marie-Elisabeth Roche (decd); 1 da; m 2, 1973, Catherine Haste; 1 da; *Career* presenter and ed Southbank Show for ITV 1978-; *Style* - Melvyn Bragg Esq; 9 Gayton rd, NW3

BRAGG, Stephen Lawrence; s of Sir Lawrence Bragg, CH, MC (d 1971); *b* 17 Nov 1923; *Educ* Rugby and Trinity Cambridge; MIT; *m* 1951, Maureen, nee Roberts; 3 s; *Career* scientist; V-Chllr Brunel U 1971-; *Style* - Stephen Bragg Esq; Brunel University, Uxbridge, Middx (☎ 37188)

BRAGGINS, Lt-Col Charles Willison;

TD (1945), JP (1959 Beds), DL (1961); s of E Braggins, of Bedford; *b* 27 June 1910; *Educ* Mill Hill; *m* 1936, Hilda, da of John Heys (d 1966), of Cornwall; 2 s, 1 da; *Career* Cmmr Inland Revenue 1960- Lt-Col Cmmding Beds Yeomanry RA 1954-57; *Clubs* Army & Navy, Bedford; *Style* - Lt-Col Charles Braggins, TD, JP, DL; 29 Pemberley av, Bedford (☎ 53711); Arden Close, Overstrand, Norfolk

BRAHMS, Caryl; *Educ* RAM; *Career* critic, novelist, script-writer; *Style* - Caryl Brahms Esq; 3 Cambridge gate, Regent's park, NW1 (☎ 01 935 6439)

BRAIN, 2 Baron (UK 1962); Sir Christopher Langdon Brain; 2 Bt (UK 1954); s of 1 Baron, DM, FRCP, FRCPI, FRCPE (d 1966); *b* 30 Aug 1926; *Educ* Leighton Park Sch, New Coll Oxford; *m* 1953, Susan Mary, da of George Philip Morris; 3 da; *Heir* bro, Hon Michael Brain; *Career* Liveryman and formerly Upper Warden Worshipful Co of Weavers; *Style* - The Rt Hon The Lord Brain; 52 Bove Town, Glastonbury, Somerset

BRAIN, Hon Michael Cottrell; s of 1 Baron Brain (d 1966), and hp of bro, 2 Baron; *b* 6 Aug 1928; *Educ* Leighton Park Sch, New Coll Oxford, London Hospital; *m* 1960, Hon Elizabeth Ann, da of Baron Tangley, KBE (Life Peer); 1 s, 2 da; *Career* Capt RAMC 1956-58, physician Hammersmith Hospital 1966-69, Prof of Medicine, McMaster U Canada 1969-MA, DM, BCh, FRCP, DTM & H; *Style* - The Hon Michael Brain; 131 North Shore, Blvd E, Bulington, Ontario, Canada

BRAIN, Sir (Henry) Norman; KBE (1963, OBE 1947), CMG (1953); s of Bert Brain, of Rushall Staffs; *b* 19 July 1907; *Educ* King Edward's H S Birmingham, Queen's Oxford; *m* 1939, Nuala, da of Capt Archibald Butterworth, of Ryde IOW; 1 s (and 1 s decd); *Career* Ambass Cambodia 1956-58 and Uruguay 1961-66; Pres British-Uruguayan Soc 1973-; *Recreations* music, golf; *Clubs* Canning; *Style* - Sir Norman Brain, KBE, CMG; St Andrews, Abney Court, Bourne End, Bucks (☎ 20509)

BRAIN, Hon Nicola Dorothy; da of 2 Baron Brain; *b* 1955; *Style* - The Hon Nicola Brain; 12 Kingsley pla, N6 5EA

BRAIN, Hon Naomi Melicent; da of 2 Baron Brain; *b* 1960 *Style* - The Hon Naomi Brain

BRAIN, Stella Lady - Stella; da of Reginald Langdon-Down, MB (d 1955), of Teddington, Middlesex; *b* 1896; *m* 1920, 1 Baron Brain, DM, FRS, FRCP (d 1966); 2 s, 1 da; *Style* - The Rt Hon Stella, Lady Brain; 9 Fairways, Broom rd, Teddington, Middx (☎ 01 977 7668)

BRAINE, Sir Bernard Richard; DL (Essex 1978), MP (C) Essex SE 1955-; s of Arthur Braine, of Kew Gdns; *b* 24 June 1914; *Educ* Hendon County G S; *m* 1935, Kathleen, da of Herbert Faun; 3 s; *Career* MP Billericay 1950-55, Parly Under-Sec Pensions and Nat Insur 1960-61, C'wlth Rels 1961-62, Min of Health 1962-64; Con Front Bench spokesman C'wlth Affrs & Overseas Aid 1967-70, chm Nat Cncl on Alcoholism, Soc for Internat Dvpt; FRSA; kt 1972 CStJ; *Recreations* gardening, reading; *Clubs* Carlton, Beefsteak, Essex; *Style* - Sir Bernard Braine, MP, DL; King's Wood, Rayleigh, Essex (☎ 743643)

BRAINE, John (Gerard); s of Fred Braine; *b* 13 Apr 1922; *Educ* St Bede's G S, Bradford; *m* 1955, Helen Wood; 1 s, 3 da; *Career* writer; *Books* Room at the Top *Style* - John Braine Esq; Pentons, Onslow crescent, Woking, Surrey

BRAININ, Norbert; OBE (1960); s of Adolph Brainin; *b* 12 Mar 1923; *Educ* High Sch, Vienna; *m* 1948, Kathe Kottow; 1 da; *Career* leader of Amadeus String Quartet; *Style* - Norbert Brainin Esq OBE; 19 Prowse ave, Bushey Heath, Herts (☎ 01 950 7379)

BRAITHWAITE, His Honour Judge; Bernard Richard Braithwaite; s of Bernard Braithwaite, of Great House, Newchurch, Mon; *b* 20 Aug 1917; *Educ* Clifton, Peterhouse Cambridge; *Career* barr 1946, Circuit Judge 1972-; *Recreations* hunting, sailing; *Clubs* Boodle's; *Style* - His Hon Judge Braithwaite; Summerfield House, Owlpen, Uley, Glos

BRAITHWAITE, Sir (Joseph) Franklin (Madders); s of Sir John Braithwaite (d 1973); *b* 6 Apr 1917; *Educ* Bootham Sch, King's Cambridge; *m* 1939, Charlotte, nee Baker, of NYC; 1 s (Peter Franklin Braithwaite b 1942, m 1968 Patricia Neville-O'Brien), 1 da (Virginia Louise b 1940, m 1966 Comte Geoffroi de Vitry d'Avaucourt); *Career* chm (dir 1950-, md 1971-79) Baker Perkins Holdings Ltd 1980-, kt 1980, Pres Process Plant Assoc 1977-79, dir Lloyds Bank (E Counties Regnl Bd) 1979-; *Recreations* music, golf; *Style* - Sir Franklin Braithwaite; 21 Westwood Park rd, Peterborough (☎ 1733 54238); 2 Golf Course rd, Old Hunstanton, Norfolk (☎ 04853 2616)

BRANCKER, Sir John Eustace Theodore; QC (1961); s of Jabel Brancker; *b* 9 Feb 1909; *Educ* Harrison Coll Barbados; *m* 1967, Esmé, da of Victor Walcott, of Barbados; *Career* barr, Pres Barbados Senate 1971-76; *Recreations* chess, classical music, drama; *Clubs* Rotary Barbados, Empire Barbados, Challoner (London), Bridgetown Barbados; *Style* - Sir John Brancker, QC; Valencia, St James, Barbados (☎ 04138)

BRAND, Cedric; *Career* md Tilbury Contracting Gp Ltd; *Style* - Cedric Brand Esq; Tilbury Contracting Gp Ltd, Tilbury House, Rusper rd, Horsham, W Sussex

BRAND, Lady - Doris Elspeth; da of H McNeill, of Arrino, W Australia; *m* 1944, Hon Sir David Brand, KCMG (d 1979); 2 s, 1 da; *Style* - Lady Brand; 24 Ednah st, Como, W Australia

BRAND, Hon Lord; David William Robert Brand; s of James Brand, advocate, of Dumfries; *b* 21 Oct 1923; *Educ* Stonyhurst, Edinburgh U; *m* 1, 1948, Rose, da of James Devlin, of Co Tyrone; 4 da; m 2, 1969, Brigid, da of Garrett Russell, of Co Limerick, and widow of Thomas Lynch; *Career* advocate 1948, QC (Scot) 1959, Sheriff Dumfries & Galloway 1968-70, Slr Gen Scotland 1970-72, Senator Coll of Justice Scotland (Lord of Session) 1972-; *Recreations* golf; *Clubs* New (Edinburgh), Hon Co of Edinburgh Golfers; *Style* - The Hon Lord Brand; Gospatric House, Dalmeny, S Queensferry, W Lothian (☎ 031 331 1224)

BRAND, Hon Francis Anthony; s and h of 6 Viscount Hampden, *qv*; *b* 17 Sept 1970; *Style* - The Hon Francis Brand

BRAND, Hon Jonathan Claud David Humphrey; s of 6 Viscount Hampden, *qv*; *b* 1975; *Style* - The Hon Jonathan Brand

BRAND, Hon Mrs (Laura Caroline Beatrice); *née* Smith; da of 3 Visc Hambleden and Lady Patricia Herbert, da of 15 Earl of Pembroke; *b* 1931; *m* 1953, Michael Charles Brand; 1 s, 2 da; *Style* - The Hon Mrs Brand; 10 Upper Phillimore gdns, W8

BRAND, Hon Mrs Roger - Muriel H L; da of H B Montgomery; *m* 1913, Brig-Gen Hon Roger Brand, CMG, DSO (d 1945); 1 da; *Style* - The Hon Mrs Roger Brand; 10 Dorchester ct, Sloane st, SW1

BRAND, Hon Saracha Mary; da of 6 Viscount Hampden; *b* 1973

BRANDEBERRY, J E; *Career* md National Semiconductor (UK) Ltd, a winner of Queen's Award for Technological Achievement 1980; *Style* - J E Brandeberry Esq; Larkfield Industrial Estate, Greenock, Renfrewshire

BRANDER, Lady Evelyn Jean Blanche; da of 3 Earl of Balfour (d 1968); *b* 1929; *m* 1948, Michael William Brander; 1 s, 2 da; *Style* - Lady Evelyn Brander; Whittingehame Mains, Haddington, E Lothian

BRANDLER, Hon Mrs (Rebecca Moraigh Eveleigh); *née* Leith; da of 7 Baron Burgh; *b* 17 Dec 1959; *m* 1978, David K O Brandler; *Style* - The Hon Mrs Brandler

BRANDON, (Oscar) Henry; *b* 9 Mar 1916; *Educ* Prague and Lausanne Us; *m* 1970, Mabel Wentworth; 1 da; *Career* associate ed and chief American correspondent Sunday Times; *Style* - Henry Brandon Esq; 814 National Press Building, Washington DC 20004, USA (☎ 628 4310)

BRANDON, Rt Hon Lord Justice; Rt Hon Sir Henry Vivian; MC (1942), PC (1978); s of Capt Vivian Brandon, CBE, RN; *b* 3 June 1920; *Educ* Winchester, King's Cambridge; *m* 1955, Jeanette, da of Julian Janvrin; 3 s, 1 da; *Career* Ld Justice of Appeal 1978-; High Court Judge (Probate, Divorce and Admlty Div 1966-71 and Family Div 1971-78); barr 1946; QC 1961; *Recreations* watching cricket, travel, bridge *Club* MCC *Style* - The Rt Hon Lord Justice Brandon MC PC; 6 Thackeray Close, SW19 (☎ 01 947 6344)

BRANDON, Hon Mrs - Hon Signe Evelyn; *née* Gully; da of 2 Viscount Selby (d 1923); *b* 1909; *m* 1938, Max Brandenstein, who assumed the name Mark Leslie Brandon; 1 s, 1 da; *Style* - The Hon Mrs Brandon; 2 Tyrawley rd, SW6

BRANDRAM, Lady Katherine; HRH Princess Katherine of Greece and Denmark; da of His late Majesty King Constantine of the Hellenes, and sister of Their late Majesties King George II and King Paul I of the Hellenes; *b* 4 May 1913; *m* 1947, Maj Richard Campbell Andrew Brandram, MC, TD; 1 s; *Career* granted style, title and precedence as da of Duke by Royal Warrant 1947; *Style* - Lady Katherine Brandram; Croft Cottage, Marlow, Bucks (☎ 3974)

BRANDRETH, Gyles Daubeney; s of Charles Brandreth, of San Diego Calif; *b* 8 Mar 1948; *Educ* Lycée Français, Bedales, New Coll Oxford; *m* 1973, Michèle, da of Alec Brown; 1 s, 2 da; *Career* writer, broadcaster, theatrical producer, publisher, chm Victorama Ltd 1974-; *Style* - Gyles Brandreth Esq; Victorama Ltd, 2 Campden Hill gdns, W8 7AU

BRANDT, Peter Augustus; s of Walter Brandt, of Saffron Walden; *b* 2 July 1931; *Educ* Eton, Trin Cambridge; *m* 1962, Elisabeth, da of Frans ten Bos, of Holland; 2 s, 1 da; *Career* chm Atkins Fulford Ltd 1977-, ch exec Wm Brandt's Sons & Co 1966-; dir Wm Brandt's Sons & Co, London Life Assoc, Corpn of Argentine Meat Producers' London Cos, Edward Bates Sons & Co; *Recreations* rowing, sailing; *Clubs* Carlton, Leander, Roy Harwich Yacht; *Style* - Peter Brandt Esq; 13 Kensington Place, W8 (☎ 01 727 8449); Spout Farm, Boxford, Colchester, Essex (☎ 0787 210297)

BRANIGAN, Sir Patrick Francis; QC (Gold Coast 1949); s of Daniel Branigan; *b* 30 Aug 1906; *Educ* Newbridge Coll Co Kildare, Trin Coll Dublin; Downing Cambridge; *m* 1935, Ruth, da of Dr Arthur Avent; 1 s, 1 da; *Career* barr; Colonial Serv 1931-54; Chm Pension Appeal Tbnl, Ag Land Tbnl, Med Appeal Tbnl, Mental Health Review Tbnl, ret 1978; *Style* - Sir Patrick Branigan, QC; Willhayne, nr Colyton, Devon (☎ 0297 52435)

BRANSOM, Harold Ian; CBE (Mil 1965), DSO (1942), TD (1947), DL (Northumberland 1968); s of George Bransom, of Newcastle; *b* 29 Aug 1912; *Educ* Ackworth Sch; *m* 1945, Sonia, da of George Tinn (dentist), of Newcastle; 2 da; *Career* slr 1936-, Dep Ld Mayor Newcastle 1959; chm N Cons 1975-78, Utd Europe Assoc (NE) 1962-72; chm DHSS Tbnl 1967-; *Recreations* golf, politics, bridge; *Club* Northumberland Golf; *Style* - Harold Bransom Esq, CBE, DSO, TD, DL; 29 Moor Court, Gosforth, Newcastle-upon-Tyne (☎ Gosforth 853264)

BRANSON, Sir Douglas Stephenson; KBE (1954), CB (1950), DSO (1918) and two Bars, MC (1917), TD, DL (W Yorks 1934); s of Col George Branson, of Sheffield; *b* 25 July 1893; *Educ* Marlborough, New Coll Oxford; *m* 1, 1930, Edith, da of Joseph Bradbury (she d 1959); m 2, 1961, Ailie (d 1981), da of Sir William Bell and widow of Brig John Fisher; *Career* slr 1920, consultant to Branson, Bramley & Co; addnl ADC to the King 1927-52 and HM The Queen 1952-60; chm W Riding Yorks T&AF Assoc 1947-58; High Sheriff Hallamshire 1963; *Style* - Sir Douglas Branson KBE CB DSO** MC TD DL; 385 Fulwood rd, Sheffield S10

BRANSON, Lady Noreen; da of late Lt-Col Lord Alfred Browne, DSO, s of 5 Marquess of Sligo; *b* 1910; *m* 1931, Clive Ali Chimmo Branson (k in action 1944); 1 da; *Style* - Lady Noreen Branson; 46 Southwood ave, N6

BRANT, Colin Trevor; CVO (1979); *b* 2 June 1929; *Educ* Christ's Hospital; Sidney Sussex Cambridge; *m* 1954, Jean Walker; 1 s, 2 da; *Career* HM Diplomatic Service; Ambassador to Qatar 1978-81; *Style* - Colin Brant Esq, CVO; Wethersfield Manor, Braintree, Essex

BRASH, Robert; CMG (1980); s of Frank Brash; *b* 30 May 1924; *Educ* Trin Cambridge; *m* 1954, Barbara Clarke; 3 s, 1 da; *Career* Foreign Serv 1949-; Consul Gen Düsseldorf 1979-81, Ambass Jakarta 1981-; *Style* - Robert Brash Esq, CMG; c/o FCO, SW1

BRASHER, Christopher William; s of William Brasher, CBE; *b* 21 Aug 1928; *Educ* Rugby and St John's Cambridge; *m* 1959, Shirley Bloomer; 1 s, 2 da; *Career* Sports Ed The Observer 1957-61, BBC TV reporter 'Tonight' 1961-65; ed Time Out and Man Alive 1964-65; Head Gen Features TV 1969-72; Columnist and Olympic Corr The Observer 1972-; Olympic Gold Medallist 1956; *Recreations* mountains, orienteering, social running; *Clubs* Alpine, Hurlingham, Ranelagh Harriers; *Style* - Christopher Brasher Esq; The Navigator's House, River Lane, Richmond, Surrey (☎ 01 940 0296/8822)

BRASS, John; CBE (1968); s of John Brass, of New Hall, Ardsley, Yorks; *b* 22 Oct 1908; *Educ* Oundle, Birmingham U; *m* 1934, Jocelyn, da of Lionel Cape; 3 s, 1 da; *Career* chm Amalgamated Construction 1977-, memb NCB 1971-73; *Recreations* gardening; *Style* - John Brass Esq, CBE; 2 Fledborough rd, Wetherby, W Yorks

BRASSEY OF APETHORPE, 3 Baron (UK 1938); Sir David Henry Brassey; 3 Bt (UK 1922), JP (Northants 1970), DL (1972); s of 2 Baron Brassey of Apethorpe, MC, TD (d 1967, whose maternal grandfather was 7 Duke of Richmond & Gordon); *b* 16 Sept 1932; *Educ* Stowe; *m* 1, 1958, Myrna (d 1974), da of Lt-Col John Baskervyle-Glegg, of Withington Hall, Cheshire; 1 s; m 2, 1978, Caroline, da of Lt-Col Godfrey Evill, of Chepstow; 1 da; *Heir* s, Hon Edward Brassey; *Career* farmer; *Clubs* White's; *Style* - The Rt Hon The Lord Brassey of Apethorpe, JP, DL; The Manor House, Apethorpe, Peterborough (☎ Kingscliffe 231)

BRASSEY OF APETHORPE, Barbara, Baroness; Barbara; da of late Leonard Jorgensen, of West Tytherley; *b* 19 Dec 1911; *m* 1934, Lt-Col Herbert Campbell Westmorland, DSO, MC (m dis 1948); m 2, 1963, 2 Baron Brassey of Apethorpe, MC, TD (d 1967); *Style* - The Rt Hon Barbara, Lady Brassey of Apethorpe; Bridge House, Blatherwyke, Peterborough

BRASSEY, Hon Edward; s and h of 3 Baron Brassey of Apethorpe; *b* 9 Mar 1964; *Style* - The Hon Edward Brassey

BRASSEY, Col Hugh Trefusis; OBE (1959), MC (1944), JP (Wilts 1951); s of Lt-Col Edgar Brassey, MVO, of Dauntsey Park, Chippenham; *b* 5 Oct 1915; *Educ* Eton, Sandhurst; *m* 1939, Joyce, da of Capt Maurice Kingscote, of Kingscote Park, Dursley, Glos; 2 s, 2 da (and 1 da decd); *Career* Vice-Ld-Lt Wilts 1968- (DL 1955); High Sheriff 1959; Lt Queen's Bodyguard of Yeomen of the Guard 1978; Pres Chippenham Con Assoc 1968-80; Regnl Dir Lloyds Bank Salisbury 1964; *Recreations* hunting, shooting, wondering why; *Clubs* Guards & Cavalry; *Style* - Col Hugh Brassey, OBE, MC, JP; Manor Farm, Little Somerford, Wilts (☎ Malmesbury 2255)

BRASSEY, Lt-Col Hon Peter Esmé; JP (1947); s of 1 Baron Brassey of Apethorpe (d 1958) and Lady Violet Gordon-Lennox, da of 7 Duke of Richmond and Gordon; *b* 5 Dec 1907; *Educ* Eton, Magdalene Cambridge; *m* 1944, Lady Romayne, nee Cecil, da of 5 Marquess of Exeter, KG, CMG, TD, and Hon Myra Orde-Powlett (da of 4 Baron Bolton); 2 s, 1 da; *Career* barr 1930; dep chm Essex Water Co; High Sheriff Huntingdon and Peterborough 1966; Ld-Lt Cambs 1975-; *Recreations* shooting, fishing; *Clubs* Carlton, Farmers'; *Style* - Lt-Col Hon Peter Brassey, JP; Close House, Barnack, Stamford, Lincs (☎ 740238)

BRASSEY, Lady Romayne Elizabeth Algitha; *née* Cecil; da of 5 Marquess of Exeter (d 1956); *b* 1915; *m* 1944, Lt-Col Hon Peter Brassey, ARRC; *Style* - Lady

Romayne Brassey; Close House, Barnack, Stamford, Lincs

BRASSEY, Hon Thomas Ian; s of 2 Baron Brassey of Apethorpe, MC, TD (d 1967); *b* 1934; *Educ* Stowe; *m* 1960, Valerie Christine Finlason, da of Mrs F F Powell (d 1964) and step da of F F Powell, of Great Maytham Hall, Rolvenden, Kent; 1 s, 3 da; *Career* Lt Grenadier Guards 1953-58; *Style* - The Hon Thomas Brassey; Manor close, Oving, nr Aylesbury, Bucks (☎ 029 664 257)

BRASSEY, Hon Mrs - Hon Victoria Ivy Louise; *née* Spencer; da of 1 Viscount and 3 Baron Churchill, GCVO (d 1934) and Lady Verena Maud (d 1938), da of 3 Earl of Lonsdale; *b* 1897; *m* 1920, Capt Hon Cecil Henry Brassey (d 1949), s of 1 Baron Brassey of Apethorpe; *Style* - The Hon Mrs Brassey; Worton, Devizes, Wilts

BRASSEY, Hon Zara; da of 3 Baron Brassey of Apethorpe JP, DL; *b* 1980

BRAY, Denis Campbell; CMG (1977), CVO (1975); s of Rev Arthur Bray; *b* 24 Jan 1926; *Educ* Chefoo Sch China, Kingswood Sch Bath, Jesus Cambridge; *m* 1952, Marjorie, da of John Bottomley; (1 s decd), 4 da; *Career* Home Affrs Sec Hong Kong 1973-77 and 1980-; H K Cmmr London 1977-80; *Recreations* ocean cruising; *Clubs* Travellers', Roy Ocean Racing, Roy Hong Kong Yacht; *Style* - Denis Bray Esq, CMG, CVO; c/o Govt Secretariat, Hong Kong

BRAY, Derek William; s of Charles Bray, of Stratford House, Milford Haven; *b* 20 Sept 1926; *Educ* U of Wales; *m* 1948, Christina, da of Minard Hooper; 1 s, 1 da; *Career* dir and gen man Thomas Bolton & Sons 1964; chm- Uttley Ingham & Co 1979, Elsy & Gibbons 1979, BNF Metals Technology Centre 1981; dir BICC Industl Products 1980; *Recreations* work, golf; *Style* - Derek Bray Esq; Third Acre, Mottram rd, Alderley Edge, Cheshire (☎ 0625 582609)

BRAY, Hon Dr John Jefferson; QC; s of Harry Bray; *b* 16 Sept 1912; *Educ* St Peter's Coll, Adelaide; Adelaide U; *Career* barr 1933; Chancellor of Adelaide U 1968-; *Style* - The Hon Dr John Bray QC; 39 Hurtle sq, Adelaide, South Australia 5000

BRAY, Ronald William Thomas; s of William Bray; *b* 5 Jan 1922; *Educ* Edward Latymer Upper Sch; *m* 1944, Margaret, da of James Parker; *Career* md & chm Langstroth Hldgs, Lloyd's Underwriter; memb N Yorks CC 1977-; farmer 1962-79; MP (C) Rossendale 1970-74; *Recreations* gardening; *Clubs* RAC; *Style* - Ronald Bray Esq; Hallbeck, Beckermonds, Buckden, Skipton, N Yorks (☎ 075 676 832)

BRAY, William Neil; s of Brig-Gen Robert Bray, CMG, DSO; *b* 11 Oct 1909; *Educ* Gresham's, Emmanuel Cambridge; *m* 1938, Mabel, da of George Gorham; 3 s (and 1 s decd); *Career* chm Loughborough Consultants Ltd 1972-; v-chm and md Br Utd Shoe Machinery Co 1971-74 (dir 1954-71); *Recreations* sailing (ketch- 'Nichola Jane'), shooting, fishing; *Clubs* Leicestershire, Cruising Assoc; *Style* - William Bray Esq; Whitcroft, Ulverscroft, Markfield, Leics (☎ 05305 2942)

BRAYBON, Richard Harry; MBE, TD; *Career* dep chm Alliance Building Society; *Style* - Richard Braybon Esq MBE, TD; Alliance Building Society, Alliance House, Hove Park, Hove, Sussex

BRAYBROOKE, 9 Baron (GB 1788); Henry Seymour Neville; JP (Saffron Walden 1953); Hereditary Visitor Magdalene Coll Cambridge; s of Rev Hon Grey Neville (d 1920, descended from a yr branch of the Nevilles who were Lords Abergavenny, also from the Lords Howard de Walden, Grenville Marquesses of Buckingham and Marquesses Cornwallis); suc cous, 8 Baron (ka 1943); *b* 5 Feb 1897; *Educ* Shrewsbury, Magdalene Cambridge; *m* 1, 1930, Muriel (d 1962), da of William Manning and widow of Euan Cartwright; 1 s; m 2, 1963, Angela, da of late W Hollis and widow of John Ree; *Heir* s, Hon Robin Neville; *Career* ADC and Assist Priv Sec to Lord Weir and Winston Churchill (Secs of State for Air 1918-19); with BP 1919-29, Shell 1935-44; chm Diocesan Bd of Finance 1950-68; DL 1950-75; *Also* patron of three livings; *Style* - The Rt Hon The Lord

Braybrooke, JP; Bruncketts, Wendens Ambo, Saffron Walden, Essex (☎ 40200)

BRAYE, 7 Baron (E 1529); Thomas Adrian Verney-Cave; DL (Leics 1954); s of Cdr 6 Baron Braye (d 1952) and Ethel, da of Capt Edward Bouverie Pusey (ggs of Hon Philip Bouverie-Pusey by his w, Lady Lucy, da of 4 Earl of Harborough; Hon Philip was 3 s of 1 Viscount Folkestone, whose eldest s was cr 1 Earl of Radnor); *b* 26 July 1902; *Educ* Eton; *m* 1934, Dorothea, da of Daniel Donoghue, of Philadelphia USA; 1 da; *Heir* da, Hon Mrs Aubrey-Fletcher, *qv*; *Career* formerly Maj 13/18 Roy Hussars; farmer; dir George Spencer Ltd 1969-77; JP Leics 1953-77; is heir-gen of Earls Verney of Claydon (ext 1791); *Clubs* Cavalry; *Style* - The Rt Hon The Lord Braye, DL; Stanford Hall, Lutterworth, Leics (☎ Swinford 250)

BRAYLEY, Hon Avril Gay; da of Baron Brayley (Life Peer, d 1977)

BRAYLEY, Hon Tessa Ann; da of Baron Brayley (Life Peer, d 1977)

BRAYNEN, Sir Alvin Rudolph; JP (Bahamas 1975); s of William Braynen; *b* 6 Dec 1904; *Educ* in the Bahamas; *m* 1969, Ena, nee Elden; (1 s, 1 da by a previous m); *Career* consultant to Shell Bahamas 1969-, Bahamas High Cmmr in London 1973-77; kt 1975; *Style* - Sir Alvin Braynen JP; PO Box N42, Nassau, Bahamas

BRAZIER-CREAGH, Maj-Gen Sir (Kilner) Rupert; KBE (1962, CBE 1947), CB (1954), DSO (1944); s of Lt-Col Kilner Brazier-Creagh, TD; *b* 12 Dec 1909; *Educ* Rugby, RMA Woolwich; *m* 1, 1938, Elizabeth (d 1967), da of Edward Magor; 1 s, 2 da; m 2, 1968, Marie, da of Edward O'Keeffe; *Career* Assist Cmdt Staff Coll 1955-57, Ch of Staff E Cmmd 1957-59, Dir Staff Duties War Off 1959-61; Sec Horse Race Betting Levy Bd 1961-65; *Style* - Maj-Gen Sir Rupert Brazier-Creagh, KBE, CB, DSO; Travis Corners rd, Garrison, NY, USA 10524

BREACH, Andrew; CBE *Career* chm Bristol and West Building Society; *Style* - Andrew Breach Esq, CBE; GPO Box 27, Broad Quay, Bristol 1

BREADALBANE AND HOLLAND, 10 Earl of (S 1677); Sir John Romer Boreland Campbell; 14 Bt (NS 1625); also Viscount of Tay and Paintland (S 1677), and Lord Glenorchy, Benederaloch, Ormelie and Weick (S 1677); s of 9 Earl, MC (d 1959); *b* 28 April 1919; *Educ* Eton, RMC Sandhurst, Edinburgh U; *m* 1949 (m dis), Coralie, da of Charles Archer; *Heir* none known; *Career* formerly Lt Black Watch, served in France 1939-42 (despatches, invalided); *Style* - The Rt Hon The Earl of Breadalbane and Holland; 29 Mackeson rd, NW3

BREADALBANE AND HOLLAND, Armorer, Countess of - Armorer Romer; da of Romer Williams, JP, DL (d 1942), of Newnham Hall, Daventry, Northants; *m* 1, Capt Eric Nicholson (decd); 1 s (decd); m 2, 1918, 9 Earl of Breadalbane and Holland (d 1959); 1 s; *Style* - The Rt Hon Armorer, Countess of Breadalbane and Holland; Invereil House, Dirleton, East Lothian

BREAM, Hon Mrs (Catherine Frances Lilian) *née* Berry; da of 2 Viscount Kemsley; *b* 9 June 1944; *m* 1969, Richard Douglas Fowler Bream; 1 s, 1 da; *Style* - The Hon Mrs Bream; Long Folly Farm, Peatling Parva, Lutterworth, Leics

BREAM, Julian; OBE (1964); s of Henry Bream; *b* 15 July 1933; *Educ* RCM; *Career* guitarist and lutenist; *Style* - Julian Bream Esq, OBE; c/o Harold Holt Ltd, 122 Wigmore st, W1

BREARE, William Robert Ackrill; s of Robert Breare; *b* 5 July 1916; *Educ* Charterhouse, Wadham Oxford; *m* 1942, Sybella, da of John Annan; 1 s, 2 da; *Career* chm Ackrill Gp; memb Press Cncl, Cncl of Newspaper Soc; *Recreations* music, sailing; *Style* - William Breare Esq; Harrison Hill House, Starbeck, Harrogate, N Yorks (☎ 883302)

BREARLEY, (John) Michael ; OBE (1978); s of Horace Brearley; *b* 28 April 1942; *Educ* City of London Sch, St John's Cambridge; *Career* lecturer in Philosophy Newcastle U 1968-71; cricketer, Capt England XI 1977; *Style* - Michael Brearley Esq, OBE

BRECHIN, Bishop of; Rt Rev Lawrence Edward Luscombe; s of Reginald John Luscombe (d 1970); *b* 10 Nov 1924; *Educ* Torquay G S, Kelham Theological Coll, Kings Coll London; *m* 1946, Doris Carswell, da of Andrew Morgan; 1 da; *Career* formerly chartered accountant, ptnr in Watson Galbraith CA Glasgow; ordained deacon 1963, priest 1964, rector St Barnabas Paisley 1966-71, provost of St Paul's Cathedral Dundee 1971-75, Bishop of Brechin 1975-; *Style* - The Rt Rev the Bishop of Brechin; Tordarroch Lodge, Balmoral rd, Blairgowrie (☎ 3823); Bishops House, Shaftesbury rd, Dundee (☎ 644215)

BRECHIN, Lady - Jane Richmond Cameron, ; JP; *m* 1934, Sir Herbert Brechin, KBE, (d 1979); 2 s; *Style* - Lady Brechin, JP; 13 Great King st, Edinburgh (☎ 031 556 5441)

BRECKNOCK, Earl of; David George Edward Henry Pratt; s (by 1 m) and h of 5 Marquess Camden; *b* 13 Aug 1930; *Educ* Eton; *m* 1961, Virginia Ann, da of late F H Finlaison, of Windsor, Berks; 2 s (1 decd); *Heir* s, Viscount Bayham; *Career* late Lt Scots Gds, former co dir; *Style* - Earl of Brecknock; Cowdown Farm House, Andover, Hants (☎ 2085)

BRECKNOCK, Marjorie, Countess of; Marjorie Minna; DBE (1967); da of Col Atherton Jenkins, of Wherwell Priory Andover; *b* 28 March 1900; *Educ* Heathfield; *m* 1920, as his 1 w, Earl of Brecknock (now 5 Marquess Camden; m dis 1941); 1 s (Earl of Brecknock, *qv*), 1 da (Lady Mary Pawle, *qv*); *Career* Supt-in-Ch St John Ambulance Bde 1960-70, Ch Pres 1972; GCStJ 1971; Lady-in-Waiting to Princess Marina, Duchess of Kent 1937-39; Sr ATS Offr SHAEF 1944-45; *Recreations* gardening, fishing, shooting; *Style* - Marjorie, Countess of Brecknock, DBE; 2 Kinnerton st, SW1 (☎ 01 235 0081); Wherwell Priory, Andover, Hants (☎ Chilbolton 388)

BRECON, Baroness; Mabel Helen; CBE (1964), JP; da of John McColville, of Abergavenny; *m* 1933, 1 & last Baron Brecon (d 1976); 2 da; *Career* High Sheriff Breconshire 1971-72; *Style* - The Rt Hon Lady Brecon CBE JP; Greenhill, Cross Oak, Powys

BREDIN, Brig Alexander Edward Craven; DSO (1945), MC (1944), DL (Devon 1966); s of Lt-Col Alexander Bredin, of Canterbury; *b* 6 Jan 1911; *Educ* Sandhurst; *m* 1950, Desirée, da of Robert Mills, of Co Kildare; 1 s (1 da decd); *Career* served UK 1956-63 OC 156 Lowland Infantry Bde TA & Inspector PT War Off, Col Devonshire & Dorset Regt 1967-77, Pres Dorset Regt Assoc 1962-; D-Day or Normandy Fellowship 1978-; V-Pres Devon Emergency Volunteers (E Devon Branch); *Recreations* shooting, beagling, cricket, fishing, writing on military subjects; *Clubs* Army & Navy; *Style* - Brig Alexander Bredin, DSO, MC, DL; Castle House, Hawkchurch, nr Axminster, Devon (☎ 02977 237)

BREDIN, James John; s of John Bredin; *b* 18 Feb 1924; *Educ* London U; *m* 1958, Virginia Meddowes; 1 s, 2 da; *Career* md Border Television Ltd 1964-; *Style* - James Bredin Esq; The Old Vicarage, Crosby-on-Eden, Carlisle (☎ Crosby-on-Eden 672)

BREEDEN, David Lucas; *Career* chm and jt md Wilmot Breeden (Holdings) Ltd; *Style* - David Breeden Esq; Tyseley, Birmingham B25 8EW

BREEN, Dame Marie Freda; DBE (1979, OBE 1958); da of Frederick and Jeanne Chamberlin; *b* 3 Nov 1902; *Educ* St Michael's C of E Girls' Grammar Sch; *m* 1928, Robert Breen (d 1968); 3 da; *Career* senator for Victoria 1962-68; *Style* - Dame Marie Breen, DBE; 51 Carpenter st, Brighton, Victoria 3186, Australia (☎ 592 2314)

BREESE, Brig Charles Fred Osborne; CBE (1963), DSC (US 1945); s of Sqdn-Ldr George Breese, DSC, of St Andrews; *b* 1 Jan 1916; *Educ* Magdalen Coll Sch Brackley, Sandhurst; *m* 1939, Mhora, da of Capt A Campbell-Colquhoun, of Ballaig, Perthshire; 1 s, 3 da; *Career* Assist Cmmdt Joint Warfare Establishment 1964-66; md Western Foods 1967-78; *Recreations* golf, fishing, philately; *Clubs* Army & Navy, Roy & Ancient Golf; *Style* - Brig Charles

Breese CBE DSC; Greenbanks, Rillington, Malton, N Yorks (☎ Rillington 303)

BREMRIDGE, John Henry; OBE; *Career* chm Swire Gp to 1980, dir- Hong Kong & Shanghai Banking Corpn, Mercantile Bank Ltd, S China Morning Post Ltd, Hong Kong Fin Soc 1981-; *Style* - John Bremridge Esq, OBE

BRENDEL, Alfred; s of Albert Brendel; *b* 5 Jan 1931; *Educ* London U; *m* 1, 1960, Iris Heymann-Gonzala (m dis 1972); 1 da; m 2, 1975, Irene, nee Semler; 1 s, 2 da; *Career* pianist and writer, concert career since 1949, recordings for Vox, Turnabout, Vanguard, Philips; *Books* Musical Thoughts and Afterthoughts 1976 *Recreations* reading, theatre, films, unintentional humour, kitsch; *Style* - Alfred Brendel Esq; Ingpen & Williams, 14 Kensington court, W8

BRENT, Allan Arthur; s of Lawrence Arther Brent (d 1975); *b* 10 August 1931; *Educ* Woodhouse Sch, City of London Coll; *m* 1963, Sheila Moira, da of James Patrick Caird MacKinlay (m dis 1980); 3 s, 1 da; *Career* md Grendon Tst Ltd 1969-71, chm Camco (Machinery) Ltd 1975-80, sr consultant Alpha Beta Consultants Ltd 1975-; FCIS (memb of cncl 1974-80), FCIArb, FTII (memb of cncl 1966-8l, pres 1969-70); *Recreations* tennis, sailing, bridge, travel; *Clubs* Athenaeum, City Livery Club, Balboa Bay Club (USA); *Style* - Allan Brent Esq, Moate Thorpe & Co, CA, 40 Curzon st, W1; 1221 W Coast Hwy, Newport Beach, CA 92660 USA; 10 Old Burlington St London W 1

BRENT, Lucy Elizabeth; da of Allan Brent (d 1978); *b* 7 Jan 1947; *Educ* Oak Hall; *Career* dep chm Trimite Ltd; *Recreations* skiing, bridge, golf, water skiing, theatre, opera, ballet, shooting; *Clubs* Wentworth Golf; *Style* - Miss Lucy Brent; c/o Midland Bank, 28 High st, PO Box 41, Uxbridge, Middx

BRENT, Michael Hamilton; s of Allan Brent; *b* 18 March 1943; *Educ* Charterhouse; *m* 1973, Janet, da of Irvine McBeath; 1 child; *Career* FCA 1967; chm & md Trimite Ltd 1974-; *Recreations* bridge, chess, golf, sailing, skiing, tennis; *Clubs* Carlton, Wentworth Golf; *Style* - Michael Brent Esq; c/o Midland Bank, 28 High st, PO Box 41, Uxbridge, Middx

BRENTFORD, 3 Viscount (UK 1929); Sir Lancelot William Joynson-Hicks; 3 Bt of Holmbury (UK 1919), 1 Bt of Newick (UK 1956), DL (E Sussex 1977); s of late 1 Viscount, PC, DL (who as Sir William Joynson-Hicks, Home Sec 1924-29, was an energetic prosecutor of morally subversive literature); suc bro 1958; *b* 10 April 1902; *Educ* Winchester, Trin Oxford; *m* 1931, Phyllis (d 1979), da of late Maj Herbert Allfrey, of Newnton House, Tetbury, Glos; 1 s; *Heir* s, Hon Crispin Joynson-Hicks; *Career* cr Baronet of Newick 1956; slr 1926, Parly Sec Min of Fuel and Power 1951-55, Lt-Cdr RNVR WW II, sr ptnr Joynson-Hicks & Co 1938-66, chm AA 1957-74, MP (C) Chichester Div of W Sussex 1942-58, memb Church Assembly 1934-70; *Style* - The Rt Hon The Viscount Brentford, DL; Newick Park, Sussex (☎ Newick 2915)

BRENTFORD, Grace Viscountess - Grace Esther Amelia; da of A E A Tothill, of Cape Town; *m* 1, D S T McNellan (decd) of Johannesburg; m 2, 1955, as his 2 w, 1 Viscount Brentford (d 1958); *Style* - The Rt Hon Grace Viscountess Brentford; 216 Cradock Heights, Cradock ave, Rosebank, Johannesburg, S Africa

BRETT, Hon Christopher Lionel Baliol; s of 4 Viscount Esher; *b* 23 Dec 1936; *Educ* Eton, Magdalen Oxford; *m* 1, 1962, Camilla Charlotte (m dis 1970), da of Sir Horace Anthony Claude Rumbold, 10 Bt, KCMG, CB; 1 s, 2 da; m 2, 1971, F Valerie, da of Maxwell Maurice Harrington; 1 s, 2 da; *Style* - The Hon Christopher Brett; Watlington Park, Watlington, Oxon, (☎ 2302)

BRETT, Hon Guy Anthony Baliol; s of 4 Viscount Esher; *b* 1942; *Educ* Eton; *Style* - The Hon Guy Brett; Watlington Park, Oxon (☎ 2302)

BRETT, Leonard; AE (1955); s of Alfred Brett (d 1966); *b* 20 March 1923; *Educ* St George's Sch London; *m* 1950, Vera, da of

Reginald Corlett; 1 s, 1 da; *Career* md Medens Tst 1975- (gen man 1967-75); *Recreations* flying; *Clubs* RAF, Isle of Wight County; *Style* - Leonard Brett Esq, AE; 3 Hillside Walk, Haywards Heath, W Sussex (☎ 53005)

BRETT, Hon Michael Jeremy Baliol; s of 4 Viscount Esher; *b* 1939 *Educ* Eton, Architectural Assoc London; *m* 1971, Sarah Calloway; *Career* ARIBA; *Style* - The Hon Michael Brett; Shelbyville, Kentucky, USA

BRETT, Michael John Lee; s of John Brett; *b* 23 May 1939; *Educ* King's Coll Sch Wimbledon, Wadham Oxford; *Career* dir Throgmorton Publications and Financial Times Business Publishing Div; ed Investors Chronicle 1977-; *Style* - Michael Brett Esq; 134 Offord rd, N1 (☎ 01 609 2362)

BRETT, Hon Maurice Sebastian Baliol; s of 4 Viscount Esher; *b* 1944; *Educ* Eton, Trinity Oxford; *m* 1968, Pauline, da of Lt-Cdr Paul Murray-Jones, RN (ret); *Style* - The Hon Maurice Brett; Cordwainers, Titchfield, Hants

BRETT, Hon Olivia Clare Teresa; da of 4 Viscount Esher; *b* 1947; *Style* - The Hon Olivia Brett; Watlington Park, Oxon (☎ 302)

BRETT, Hon Stephen Patrick Baliol; s of 4 Viscount Esher; *b* 1952; *Educ* Bryanston Sch; *Style* - The Hon Stephen Brett; Watlington Park, Oxon

BRETT, Hon Virginia Charlotte Anne; da of 3 Viscount Esher, GBE (d 1963); *b* 1916; *Style* - The Hon Virginia Brett; Watlington Park, Oxon (☎ 302)

BRETTEN, George Rex; QC (1980); s of Horace Bretten (d 1954); *b* 21 Feb 1942; *Educ* Cambridge; *m* 1965, Maureen, nee Crowhurst; 1 da; *Career* barr 1970; *Style* - George Bretten Esq, QC; Church Farm, Great Everden, Cambs (☎ 022 026 3538)

BREW, William Raymond Thomas; s of William Brew; *b* 27 March 1915; *Educ* Palmers Coll Essex; *m* 1940, Peggy, da of William Farmer; 1 s; *Career* md Moody Gp 1975-80; co dir 1980-, consultant oil indust; *Recreations* philately, racing; *Clubs* Directors', Eccentric, Wig & Pen, Oil Industry; *Style* - William Brew Esq; 4 Coombe Bank, Kingston-upon-Thames, Surrey (☎ 01 942 3178)

BREWER, Douglas Morton; *Career* md Nairn Floors Ltd, winner of a Queen's Award for Export Achievement 1979; *Style* - Douglas Brewer Esq; Kirkcaldy, Fife

BREWER, Dr Derek Stanley; s of Stanley Brewer; *b* 13 July 1923; *Educ* The Crypt G S, Magdalen Oxford; *m* 1951, Lucie Hoole; 3 s, 2 da; *Career* FSA 1977; academic publisher; Master of Emmanuel College Cambridge 1977-, reader in Medieval English 1976-; *Style* - Dr Derek Brewer; The Master's Lodge, Emmanuel College, Cambridge (☎ 50484)

BREWIS, Lady Anne Beatrice Mary; *née* Palmer; da of 3 Earl of Selborne CH PC (d 1971); *b* 26 March 1911; *Educ* Queen's Coll Harley st, Somerville Oxford; *m* 1935, Rev John Salusbury Brewis, MA (d 1972); 2 s, 2 da; *Recreations* nature conservation, botany; *Style* - Lady Anne Brewis; Benham's House, Benham's lane, Blackmoor, Hants (☎ Blackmoor 348)

BREWIS, Henry John; DL (Wigtownshire 1966); s of Lt-Col Francis Brewis, of Norton Grove, Yorks; *b* 8 April 1920; *Educ* Eton, New Coll Oxford; *m* 1949, Faith, da of Sir Edward MacTaggart-Stewart, 2 and last Bt (d 1948); 3 s, 1 da; *Career* barr 1946; MP (C) Galloway 1959-74, PPS to Ld Advocate 1960-61, MEP nominee 1973-75, Regnl Chm Scottish Landowners' Fedn 1978-80, Chm Scottish Woodland Owners 1980; md Ardwell Estates Stranraer, dir Border TV Ltd 1977-; *Recreations* shooting, golf; *Clubs* Caledonian, New (Edinburgh); *Style* - Henry Brewis Esq, DL; Ardwell House, Stranraer (☎ Ardwell 227)

BREWIS, Peter Norman Godfrey; s of Eric Brewis, of Orpington; *b* 7 Oct 1941; *Educ* Bromley G S; *m* 1966, Margaret, da of Frederick Strong; 2 s, 1 da; *Career* dep chm Alexander Howden Insur Brokers (Lloyd's) 1981, ch exec Aviation Div 1975, md 1975-81; *Recreations* tennis, golf, football; *Style* - Peter Brewis Esq; 15 Buckingham Close, Petts Wood, Orpington, Kent

BREYER, Hon Mrs - Hon Joanna Freda; da of 1 Viscount Blakenham, OBE, PC, and Hon Beryl Nancy, nee Pearson, da of 2 Viscount Cowdray; *b* 1942; *m* 1967, Stephen Breyer, assist prof Harvard Law School 1967-; *Style* - The Hon Mrs Breyer; 9 Maynard pla, Cambridge, Mass, USA

BRIANCE, John Albert; CMG (1960); s of Albert Briance; *b* 19 Oct 1915; *Educ* King Edward VII Sch Lytham, London U; *m* 1950, Prunella, da of Col Eric Chapman; 1 s, 1 da; *Career* Foreign Serv 1950-70; Dep Supt Palestine (Colonial Police) 1936-48; *Recreations* tennis, walking, reading; *Clubs* Bath, Hurlingham; *Style* - John Briance Esq, CMG; 14 Pitt st, W8 (☎ 01 937 4140)

BRIARS, Colin Hubert; s of Hubert Alfred Briars (d 1958); *b* 8 July 1926; *Educ* Christ's Hosp; *m*; m 2, 1975, Susan, da of James Frail CBE; 1 s, 1 da; *Career* chartered engr, dir- Ottermill Ltd and Westinghouse Electric MK Ltd, Allenwest Ltd 1970-79, Brush Switchgear Ltd 1960-70, chm Control & Automation Mfrs Assoc; *Recreations* squash, tennis, skiing; *Clubs* RAC; *Style* - Colin Briars Esq; Shannon House, Kings rd, Sunninghill, Berks (☎ Ascot 22448)

BRICE, Edward St John; s of W Brice, OBE, TD, DL, of Highover Hoo, Rochester; *b* 15 Feb 1936; *Educ* Tonbridge, Clare Cambridge; *m* 1960, Elizabeth, da of G Grieve; 1 s, 1 da; *Career* farmer, Lloyd's Underwriter; memb Kent CC 1977; High Sheriff Kent 1980-81; *Recreations* golf, tennis; *Clubs* Roy & Ancient, Roy St George's Golf; *Style* - Edward Brice Esq; Hoo Lodge, Hoo, Rochester, Kent

BRICKWOOD, Sir Basil Greame; 3 Bt (UK 1927); s of Sir John Brickwood, 1 Bt; suc half bro, Sir Rupert Brickwood, 2 Bt, 1974; *b* 21 May 1923; *Educ* King Edward's Grammar Sch Stratford-upon-Avon, Clifton; *m* 1956, Shirley, da of Wallace Brown; 2 da; *Heir* none; *Recreations* bird watching *Style* - Sir Basil Brickwood, Bt, c/o RAF Club, 128 Piccadilly, W1

BRIDGE OF HARWICH, Baron (Life Peer UK 1980); The Rt Hon Nigel Cyprian Bridge; PC (1975); s of Cdr Cyprian Bridge, RN; bro of Dean of Guildford; *b* 26 Feb 1917; *Educ* Marlborough; *m* 1944, Margaret, da of Leonard Heseltine Swinbank, of Weybridge; 1 s, 2 da; *Career* barr 1947-68; High Court Judge 1968-75, Ld Justice of Appeal 1975-80, Ld of Appeal in Ordinary 1980-, kt 1968; *Style* - The Rt Hon Lord Bridge of Harwich PC; The Old Rectory, Dowdeswell, Cheltenham, Glos

BRIDGE, Hon Charles Cyprian; s of Rt Hon Baron Bridge of Harwich, PC; *b* 26 Mar 1951; *m* 1971, Sheila Marie Street; *Style* - The Hon Charles Bridge

BRIDGE, Christopher Charles Cyprian; s of Brig Charles Bridge, CMG, DSO, MC, of Kensington; *b* 23 Oct 1918; *Educ* Eton, Trin Cambridge; *m* 1953, Hon Dinah, da of 1 and last Baron Brand, CMG (d 1963, s of 2 Visc Hampden), of Eydon Hall, Daventry; 1 s, 1 da (and 1 step s, 1 step da); *Career* Maj Coldstream Gds 1939-45; ptnr Akroyd & Smithers 1953-66; md Seccombe Marshall & Campion 1967-79, dir Hambros Investment Tst 1979-; High Sheriff E Sussex 1979-80; *Recreations* shooting, fishing, gardening, racing; *Clubs* White's, Pratt's, Beefsteak, MCC; *Style* - Christopher Bridge Esq; Old Vicarage, Firle, Lewes, E Sussex (☎ Glynde 279); Stream Farm, Chiddingly, E Sussex (☎ 256); 71 Cadogan gdns, SW3 (☎ 01 584 6023)

BRIDGE, Hon Mrs - Hon Dinah; da of 1 and last Baron Brand, CMG (d 1963); *b* 1920; *m* 1, 1943, Lyttleton Fox (m dis 1950); 1 s, 1 da; m 2 1953, Christopher Charles Cyprian Bridge; 1 s, 1 da; *Style* - The Hon Mrs Bridge; The Old Vicarage, Firle, Sussex

BRIDGE, Walter John Blencowe; s of Walter Bridge (d 1969); *b* 8 Mar 1920; *Educ* Repton; *m* 1948, Susan, da of Robert Basil Wyndham Rushbrooke (d 1972); 2 s, 1 da; *Career* chm Greene King and Sons 1979-; *Style* - Walter Bridge Esq

BRIDGEHOUSE, Edward; s of Edward Bridgehouse (d 1965); *b* 19 May 1939; *Educ* Audenshaw G S; *m* 1, 1962, Brenda Elizabeth (d 1979); 1 s, 1 da; m 2, 1981, Muriel Winifred; *Career* CA; Managing ptnr Boardman Woolrich 1964-, co sec United Engrg Industries Ltd 1970-; *Recreations* golf; *Style* - Edward Bridgehouse Esq; Trefin, Hilda Road, Gee Cross, Hyde, Cheshire (☎ 061 368 3649)

BRIDGEMAN, 2 Viscount (UK 1929); Robert Clive Bridgeman; KBE (1954), CB (1944), DSO (1940), MC, JP (Salop 1951); s of 1 Viscount (d 1935, himself gs of 2 Earl of Bradford) and Caroline, DBE, da of Hon Cecil Parker (s of 6 Earl of Macclesfield by Lady Mary Grosvenor, da of 2 Marquess of Westminster); *b* 1 April 1896; *Educ* Eton; *m* 1930, Hon Mary Lane Fox, JP (d 1981), da of 1 and last Baron Bingley, PC, and niece of Baroness Lane Fox; 3 da; *Heir* n, Robin Bridgeman; *Career* V-Chm THF Cncl 1971-; Col late Rifle Brig (Prince Consort's Own), Hon Maj-Gen; Hon Col 4 Bn King's Shropshire LI (TA) 1949-59, Lord-Lt for Co Salop 1951-69, Brig Maj 7 Inf Bde 1932-34, and GSO War Office 1935-37, Private Sec to father when Parly Sec to Min of Labour 1918, Dir-Gen Home Gd 1941-44, Dep Adjutant-Gen 1944-45; *Style* - The Rt Hon The Viscount Bridgeman KBE CB DSO MC JP; Leigh Manor, Minsterley, Salop (☎ Worthen 210)

BRIDGEMAN, Hon Alexander Michael Orlando; s and h of Viscount Newport; *b* 1980

BRIDGEMAN, Hon Charles Gerald Orlando; s of 6 Earl of Bradford; *b* 25 June 1954; *Educ* Harrow, Warwick U; *Style* - The Hon Charles Bridgeman; Weston Park, Shifnal, Salop

BRIDGEMAN, Hon Mrs Henry - Joan; da of late Hon Bernard Constable-Maxwell; *m* 1930, Col Hon Henry George Orlando Bridgeman, DSO, MC (d 1972); 2 s, 2 da; *Style* - The Hon Mrs Henry Bridgeman; 50 Lennox gdns, SW1

BRIDGEMAN, John Stuart; s of James Bridgeman, of Cardiff; *b* 5 Oct 1944; *Educ* Whitcurch Sch Cardiff, U Coll Swansea; *m* 1967, Lindy, da of Sidney Fillmore, of Romford; 3 da; *Career* commercial dir Alcan Lynemouth; v-pres Alcan Trading; dir Alcan Enfield Alloys and Saguenay Shipping (UK); advsr Aluminium Fedn; Tstee and memb Magnesium Indust Cncl; memb Br Airways Consumer Cncl; *Recreations* TA (REME), genealogy, swimming, shooting, squash, skiing, running, church affairs, golf, natural history; *Style* - John Bridgeman Esq; Khymar, Morwick rd, Warkworth, Northumberland (☎ 364)

BRIDGEMAN, Robin John Orlando; s of Hon Geoffrey John Orlando Bridgeman, MC (d 1974, s of 1 Visc Bridgeman) and Mary, da of late Rt Hon Sir George Talbot; hp of kinsman 2 Visc Bridgeman, KBE, CB, DSO, MC; *b* 5 Dec 1930; *Educ* Eton; *m* 1966, Victoria, da of Ralph Turton, of Kildale Hall, Whitby; 3 s; *Career* Lt Roy Green Jackets; CA 1958; ptnr Henderson Crosthwaite & Co Stockbrokers; *Recreations* gardening, shooting, music; *Clubs* MCC; *Style* - Robin Bridgeman Esq; 19 Chepstow rd, W2

BRIDGEMAN, Richard Lynedoch Orlando; s of Maj Roger Bridgeman (d 1975, ggs of 2 Earl of Bradford by his w, Georgina, da of Sir Thomas Moncreiffe, 5 Bt) and Marjorie, da of late Lt-Gen Hon Sir Richard Montagu-Stuart-Wortley, KCB, KCMG, DSO (yr bro of 2 Earl of Wharncliffe) by his w, Hon Maud, née Winn (da of 1 Baron St Oswald); *b* 23 June 1931; *Educ* Harrow; *m* 1965, Romayne, da of Ingram Ord Capper, of Suffolk; 2 s, 1 da; *Career* wine merchant; dir Justerini and Brooks 1959-; tennis and rackets correspondent for Country Life; chm Tennis and Rackets Assoc, Pres Army Rackets Assoc; *Recreations* tennis, rackets, embroidery, verse; *Clubs* Boodle's, MCC, Queen's; *Style* - Richard Bridgeman Esq; 123 Castelnau, SW13 (☎ 01 748 6479)

BRIDGER, Colin Henry; *Career* md Davy Powergas Ltd; memb IOD, FCA; *Style* - Colin Bridger Esq; 8 Baker st, W1

BRIDGES, 2 Baron (UK 1957); Thomas Edward Bridges; CMG (1975); s of 1 Baron Bridges, KG, GCB, GCVO,

MC, FRS (d 1969) and Hon Katharine, da of 2 Baron Farrer (*see* Bridges, Katharine, Baroness); *b* 27 Nov 1927; *Educ* Eton, New Coll Oxford; *m* 1953, Rachel, da of Sir Henry Bunbury, KCB; 2 s, 1 da; *Heir* s, Hon Mark Bridges; *Career* For Serv 1951-, Dep Sec FCO 1979-; *Style* - The Rt Hon The Lord Bridges, CMG; c/o FCO, SW1

BRIDGES, Katharine, Lady - Hon Katharine Dianthe; da of 2 Baron Farrer; *b* 1896; *m* 1922, 1 Baron Bridges, KG, GCB, GCVO, MC, PC (d 1969); 2 s, 2 da; *Style* - The Rt Hon Katharine, Lady Bridges; Goodman's Furze, Headley, Surrey (☎ 265)

BRIDGES, Dame Mary Patricia; DBE (1981); da of Austin Edward Fawkes, of Retford; *b* 6 June 1930; *Educ* Retford H S; *m* 1951, Bertram, s of Bertram Bridges; 1 s (1 da decd); *Recreations* cricket; *Style* - Dame Mary Bridges, DBE; Walton House, Fairfield Close, Exmouth, Devon (☎ 5317 03952)

BRIDGES, Hon Mark Thomas; s and h of 2 Baron Bridges, CMG, and Rachel, da of Sir Henry Bunbury, KCB; *b* 25 July 1954; *Educ* Eton, Corpus Christi Cambridge; *m* 1978, Angela Margaret, da of J P Collinson of Mansfield, Notts; *Career* slr with Farrer & Co; *Recreations* walking, sailing (yacht- 'Bitter Sweet'), reading; *Style* - The Hon Mark Bridges; 2 Benbow rd, W6 (☎ 01 747 4779)

BRIDGES, Hon Nicholas Edward; s of 2 Baron Bridges, CMG; *b* 1956; *Educ* Eton, Bath U; *Style* - The Hon Nicholas Bridges

BRIDGES, Hon Sir Phillip Rodney; CMG (1967); s of Capt Sir Ernest Bridges, of Bedford; *b* 9 July 1922; *Educ* Bedford Sch; *m* 1, 1951, Rosemary Streeten (m dis 1961); 2 s, 1 da; m 2, 1962, Angela, da of Frederick Dearden, of Appledore; *Career* kt 1973, slr 1951, barr 1954, QC (Gambia 1964), Slr Gen 1961 and Attorney Gen 1964 (both The Gambia), Ch Justice The Gambia 1968; *Clubs* Travellers'; *Style* - Hon Sir Phillip Bridges, CMG; Supreme Court, Banjul, The Gambia (☎ 380)

BRIDGES, Ven Peter Sydney Godfrey; *Career* ARIBA, ordained 1958, Archdeacon of Southend (Diocese of Chelmsford) and priest i/c St John's, Southend 1972-; *Style* - The Ven the Archdeacon of Southend; St John's Vicarage, 144 Alexander rd, Southend, Essex SS1 1HB

BRIDGES, Hon Robert Oliver; s of 1 Baron Bridges KG GCB GCVO MC PC (d 1969); *b* 18 Aug 1930; *Educ* Eton, Magdalen Oxford, Archtectural Assoc Sch of Architecture; *m* 1963, Rosamund Theresa, da of late Roger de Wesselow, of York House W8; 2 s; *Career* MA, ARIBA, AADip; *Style* - The Hon Robert Bridges; 12 Hillside, SW19 (☎ 01 946 0481)

BRIDGES, Hon Mrs - Hon Susan Constance; da of 6 Baron Auckland (d 1941); *b* 1918; *m* 1, 1942, Jose Diaz de Rivera (m dis 1956); 1 s; m 2, 1957, Guillermo Pakenham Bridges, MBE, HM Hon Vice-Consul at Rio Grande, Argentina; *Style* - The Hon Mrs Bridges; Estancia Viamonte, Rio Grande, Tierra del Fuego, Argentina

BRIDLE, Rear-Adm Gordon Walter; CB (1977), MBE (1952); s of Percy Bridle; *b* 14 May 1923; *Educ* in Birmingham and Portsmouth; Imperial Coll, London; *m* 1944, Phyllis Page; 3 s; *Career* assistant controller of the Navy 1974-77; *Style* - Rear-Adm Gordon Bridle CB MBE; 25 Heatherwood, Midhurst, Sussex (☎ 2838)

BRIDPORT, 4 Viscount (UK 1868); Alexander Nelson Hood; also Baron Bridport (I 1794) and 7 Duke of Bronte in Sicily (cr 1799 by Ferdinand IV, the 'Lazzarone' King of the Two Sicilies, largely for Nelson's role in exterminating the Parthenopean Republic); s of 3 Viscount (d 1969, fourth in descent from the union of 2 Baron Bridport (2 s of 2 Viscount Hood) and Lady Charlotte Nelson, da of 1 Earl and niece of the great Admiral); *b* 17 March 1948; *Educ* Eton and the Sorbonne; *m* 1, 1972 (m dis 1979), Linda Jacqueline, da of Lt-Col Vincent Rudolph Paravicini, of Nutley Manor, Basingstoke; 1 s; m 2, 1979, Mrs Nina Rindt-Martyn; *Heir* s, Hon Peregrine Hood; *Style* - The Rt Hon The Viscount Bridport; Castello di Maniace, 95030 Maniace di Bronte,

Catania, Sicily

BRIDPORT, Sheila Viscountess - Sheila Jeanne Agatha; da of Johan Hendrik van Meurs, of London; *m* 1, Wing-Cdr J H Little DFC (decd); m 2, 1946, 3 Viscount Bridport (d 1969); 1 s; *Style* - The Rt Hon Sheila, Viscountess Bridport; Via del Plebiscito 107, Rome, Italy

BRIEN, Alan; s of Ernest Brien; *b* 12 Mar 1925; *Educ* Bede G S, Sunderland, Jesus Oxford; *m* 1, 1947, Pamela Jones; 3 da; m 2, 1961, Nancy Ryan; 1 s, 1 da; m 3, 1973, Jill Tweedie; *Career* Punch columnist 1972-; Sunday Times film critic 1976-; *Style* - Alan Brien Esq; 14 Falkland rd, NW5 (☎ 01 485 9074)

BRIERLEY, Hon Mrs - Hon Caroline; da of Baron Gordon-Walker, CH, PC; *b* 1937; *m* 1960, David Brierley; *Style* - The Hon Mrs Brierley; Old Farm, Harthall Lane, King's Langley, Hertfordshire (☎ 40 62507)

BRIERLEY, John David; CB (1978); s of late Walter Brierley; *b* 16 Mar 1918; *Educ* Whitgift Sch Croydon, Lincoln Oxford; *m* 1956, Frances Davis; 1 s, 1 da (both adopted); *Career* Under-Secretary DES 1969-77; Dean of Studies, Working Men's Coll, 1978-; *Style* - John Brierley Esq, CB; 98 Arundel ave, Sanderstead, Surrey (☎ 01 657 7508)

BRIERLEY, Zachry; CBE (1978, MBE 1969); s of late Zachry Brierley, of Rhos; *b* 16 April 1920; *Educ* Rydal School, Colwyn Bay, North Wales; *m* 1946, Iris, da of Arnold Macara; 1 da; *Career* chm Z Brierley Ltd 1972- (chm and md 1957, dir 1952-) and Australia Pty (1973-); Pres Z Brierley USA Inc (1972-); memb- CBI Centl Cncl 1970-, Design Cncl 1976-, Welsh Devpt Agency 1975-, National Broadcasting Cncl Wales 1981-; Pres Conservative Political Centre (Wales) 1980-, chm Conway Conservative and Unionist Assoc 1980-; v-chm Mostyn Art Gallery 1979-; *Recreations* philately, travel, reading, sketching; *Clubs* Carlton; *Style* - Zachry Brierley Esq, CBE; West Point, Gloddaeth Avenue, Llandudno, Gwynnedd (☎ 0492 76970)

BRIGGS, Baron (Life Peer UK 1976); Asa Briggs; s of William Briggs; *b* 7 May 1921; *Educ* Keighley G S, Sidney Sussex Cambridge, LSE; *m* 1955, Susan, da of Donald Banwell; 2 s, 2 da; *Career* historian; Tstee Glyndebourne Arts Trust 1966-, International Broadcasting Inst 1968-; chm Heritage Education Group 1976-, Civic Trust 1976-;Provost Worcester Coll Oxford 1976-, Chllr OU 1979-; Prof of History Sussex U 1961-76, V-Chllr 1967-76; *Recreations* travel; *Clubs* Beefsteak; *Style* - The Rt Hon The Lord Briggs; The Provost's Lodgings, Worcester College, Oxford (☎ 0865 47251); The Caprons, Keere Street, Lewes, East Sussex (☎ 07916 4704)

BRIGGS, Hon Daniel Nicholas; s of Baron Briggs; *b* 1958; *Style* - The Hon Daniel Briggs

BRIGGS, Hon Sir Francis Arthur; s of William Briggs, of Ringwood; *b* 9 July 1902; *Educ* Charterhouse, Trin Oxford; *m* 1953, Edna, da of William Keylock; *Career* barr, Puisne Judge 1948 Malaya; Fedl Justice Supreme Court Fedn Rhodesia & Nyasaland 1958-62 kt 1961; *Style* - Hon Sir Francis Briggs; Shillingford, La Brecque Philippe, Alderney, Channel Islands (☎ 0481 82 2019)

BRIGGS, Frederick John; s of Frederick Briggs; *b* 24 Oct 1923; *Educ* Wm Hulme G S Manchester; *m* 1949, Margaret, da of Maj Percy Libbis Smout, MC; 3 s; *Career* Pres Inst of Marketing 1978-; dir- Blagden & Noakes 1980-, Bunzl 1978-, Norcros 1966-, Willliams & James (Engrs) 1981; chm Manston Dvpt Gp 1978-, BIM Reading Branch; memb BR Western Bd 1981-; *Recreations* soccer, tennis; *Clubs* Carlton, City Livery, HAC, Phyllis Court (Henley), RAF (dep chm), RAC, MCC; *Style* - Frederick Briggs Esq; Huish Cross, Finchampstead, Berks (☎ 0734 733156)

BRIGGS, Wing Cdr Geoffrey Harry; DFC (1944), DL (Sussex 1970); s of Henry Briggs, of Holton Park, Oxon; *b* 22 March 1918; *Educ* Eton, Sandhurst, RAC Cirencester; *m* 1947, Elizabeth, da of Crossley Swithinbank, of Newbury; 3 s, 1

da; *Career* ret farmer; County Ch Warden Civ Def 1964, Cmmdt Special Constabulary W Sussex 1967, High Sheriff W Sussex 1974; *Recreations* shooting, fishing, sailing (yacht- 'Soubrette'); *Clubs* Household Division Yacht, Itchenor Sailing; *Style* - Wing Cdr Geoffrey Briggs, DFC, DL; The Farm House, Strettington, Chichester, W Sussex (☎ Halnaker 331)

BRIGGS, H J; *Career* Sec of Leeds Permanent Building Society; *Style* - H J Briggs Esq; Permanent Building Society, Permanent House, The Headrow, Leeds LS1 INS

BRIGGS, John; s of John Briggs, of Bolton; *b* 30 May 1933; *Educ* Stowe, Selwyn Cambridge; *m* 1960, Celia Rosalind, da of Henry Wild, of Bury; 1 s, 2 da; *Career* slr 1960, notary public 1965-; sr ptnr Owen & Briggs and also Cartwright Cliffe & Co; *Recreations* shooting, fell walking, stock-breeeding; *Style* - John Briggs Esq; Thorpe House, Almondbury, Huddersfield HD5 8TU

BRIGGS, Hon Judith Susanna; da of Baron Briggs; *b* 1961

BRIGGS, Hon Katharine Jane; da of Baron Briggs; *b* 1956

BRIGGS, Hon Matthew William Banwell; s of Baron Briggs; *b* 1964

BRIGGS, Gp Capt Nelson; CBE (Mil 1968), AFC (1946); s of Nelson Briggs; *b* 15 Aug 1915; *Educ* Swanwick Hall; *m* 1941, Linda, da of Herbert Hunt; 1 s, 1 da; *Career* admin man Beecham Gp 1968-69; dir admin 1969-73, employee servs 1973-78, centl servs 1978-79 Borough of Hammersmith & Fulham; *Clubs* RAF; *Style* - Gp Capt Nelson Briggs, CBE, AFC; Lime Tree Cottage, West st, Marlow, Bucks (☎ 3465)

BRIGGS, Robert Keith; s of Alfred Briggs; *b* 29 Aug 1926; *Educ* Cheltenham, Queen's Oxford; *m* 1959, Jill, da of Charles Chapman; 1 s, 3 da; *Career* jt md Holden Surface Coatings; dir Arthur Holden & Sons; *Recreations* squash; *Clubs* RAC; *Style* - Robert Briggs Esq; Greybrook, 25 Alderbrook rd, Solihull, W Midlands (☎ 021 705 3353)

BRIGGS, Rear-Adm Thomas Vallack; CB (1958), OBE (1945); s of Adm Sir Charles Briggs (d 1951); *b* 6 April 1906; *Educ* Imperial Service Coll Windsor, RNC Greenwich, Imperial Defence Coll, US Naval War Coll Rhode Island; *m* 1947, Estelle Burland, nee Willing; 1 s (step); *Career* joined RN 1924, chief of staff Home Fleet and Eastern Atlantic 1956-7, assistant controller of Navy 1957-8; *Recreations* golf, shooting *Clubs* RN Sailing, RN Ski, White's; *Style* - Rear-Adm Thomas Briggs, CB, OBE; Kings Legend, Aldeburgh, Suffolk

BRIGHT, Graham Frank James; MP (C) Luton East 1979-; s of Robert Bright; *b* 2 Apr 1942; *Educ* Hassenbrook County Sch, Thurrock Technical Coll; *m* 1972, Valerie Woolliams; *Career* chm Dietary Foods (Bletchley) Ltd 1977-; *Style* - Graham Bright Esq, MP; House of Commons, SW1

BRIGINSHAW, Baron (Life Peer UK 1974); Richard William Briginshaw; *m*; *Career* gen sec Nat Soc of Operative Printers, Graphical and Media Personnel 1951-75, memb General Cncl TUC 1965-75, memb ACAS 1974-76, former memb British National Oil Corpn; *Style* - The Rt Hon The Lord Briginshaw; House of Lords, SW1

BRIGSTOCKE, Mrs Geoffrey - Heather Renwick; da of Sqdn-Ldr John Renwick Brown, DFC; *b* 2 Sept 1929; *Educ* The Abbey Sch Reading, Girton Cambridge; *m* 1952, Geoffrey Brigstocke (d 1974); 2 s, 1 da; *Career* High Mistress, St Paul's Girls' Sch 1974-; *Style* - Mrs Geoffrey Brigstocke; 48 Rowan rd, W6

BRIMELOW, Baron (Life Peer UK 1976); Thomas Brimelow; GCMG (1975, KCMG 1968, CMG 1959), OBE (1954); s of late William Brimelow, of New Mills, Derbys; *b* 25 Oct 1915; *Educ* New Mills G S, Oriel Oxford; *m* 1945, Jean, da of late John William Underwood Cull, of Glasgow; 2 da; *Career* FO 1938, counsellor Washington 1960-63, Min Br Embassy Moscow 1963-66, Ambass to Poland 1966-69, Dep Under-Sec of State FCO 1969-73,

Perm Under-Sec of State FO and Head of Diplomatic Service 1973-75, MEP 1977-78, chm Occupational Pensions Bd 1978-; *Style* - The Rt Hon The Lord Brimelow, GCMG OBE; 12 West Hill ct, Millfield lane, N6 (☎ 01 340 8722)

BRIMELOW, Hon Alison Jane; da of Baron Brimelow GCMG OBE; *b* 1949 *Style* - The Hon Alison Brimelow

BRIMELOW, Hon Elizabeth Anne; da of Baron Brimelow GCMG OBE; *b* 1951 *Style* - The Hon Elizabeth Brimelow

BRINCKMAN, Col Sir Roderick (Napoleon); 5 Bt, DSO (1940), MC (1941); s of late Col Sir Theodore Brinckman, 3 Bt, CB; suc bro, Maj Sir Theodore Ernest Warren Brinckman, 4 Bt, 1954; *b* 27 Dec 1902; *Educ* RNCs Osborne and Dartmouth; *m* 1, 1931, Margaret Wilson, da of Wilson Southam, of Rockliffe, Ottawa, Canada; 2 s; m 2, 1942, Rosemary Marguerite Gilbey, da of late Lt-Col James Hope-Vere and gggggda of 1 Earl of Hopetoun; 1 da; *Heir* s, Theodore Brinckman; *Career* Col (ret) Gren Gds; former ADC to Gov-Gen of Canada, Ch of Staff Mil Mission to Moscow 1944-45, Head of Liaison Mission to Netherlands 1945; *Style* - Col Sir Roderick Brinckman Bt DSO MC; 7 Mallord st, SW3 (☎ 01 352 9935); Crosskeys, Sandwich, Kent

BRINCKMAN, Theodore George Roderick; s and h of Sir Roderick Brinckman, 5 Bt, DSO, MC; *b* 20 Mar 1932; *Educ* Millfield, Trin Coll Sch Port Hope Ontario, Ch Ch Oxford, Trinity Coll Toronto U; *m* 1958, Helen, nee Cooke; 2 s, 1 da; *Style* - Theodore Brinckman Esq; 1 Dale ave, Toronto, Canada; St Helena, St James, Barbados

BRINDLE, Hon Mrs - Hon Joan Kathleen; *née* Davies; da of 1 Baron Darwen (d 1950); *b* 1917; *m* 1940, Walter Higham Brindle, MBE, TD; 1 s, 1 da; *Style* - The Hon Mrs Brindle; Cottonwood, 20 Firs rd, Edwalton, Nottingham

BRINTON, Michael Ashley Cecil; s of Sir Tatton Brinton, DL, of Kyrewood House, Tenbury Wells, Worcs; *b* 6 Oct 1941; *Educ* Eton, Vienna, Perugia, Aix-en-Provence; *m* 1966, Angela, da of John Ludlow, of High Wycombe; 2 s, 1 da; *Career* dir Brintons Ltd 1970-, export sales man 1965-; *Style* - Michael Brinton Esq; Park Hall, nr Kidderminster, Worcs (☎ 0562 700268)

BRINTON, Maj Sir (Esmé) Tatton Cecil; DL (Worcs 1968); s of Col Cecil Brinton, JP; *b* 4 Jan 1916; *Educ* Eton, Caius Cambridge, Vienna, Paris; *m* 1, 1938, Mary Fahnestock (d 1960); 4 s, 1 da; m 2, 1961, Mrs Irene Borthwick (d 1978); m 3, Mrs Mary Cappel; *Career* MP (C) Kidderminster 1964-74 (mayor 1953-54), High Sheriff Worcs 1961-62, High Steward Kidderminster 1978, jt tres Con Pty 1966-67; OStJ; kt 1964; *Clubs* Carlton, Bath; *Style* - Maj Sir Tatton Brinton, DL; 35d Queens gte, SW7

BRINTON, Timothy Denis; MP (C) Gravesend 1979-; s of Dr Denis Brinton; *b* 24 Dec 1929; *Educ* Eton, Geneva U, Central Sch of Speech and Drama; *Style* - Timothy Brinton Esq MP; House of Commons, SW1

BRISBANE, Lady Marguerite Mary Chetwynd-Talbot; da of 21 Earl of Shrewsbury (d 1980); *b* 1950; *m* 1970, Guy William Brisbane; *Style* - Lady Marguerite Brisbane; 228 Meadvale rd, Ealing W5 (☎ 01 997 5527)

BRISCO, Sir Donald Gilfrid; 8 Bt (GB 1782), JP (1967); s of Sir Hylton Musgrave Campbell Brisco, 7 Bt (d 1968); *b* 15 Sept 1920; *Educ* Wairapa Coll New Zealand; *m* 1945, Irene, da of Henry John Gage, of Ermine Park, Brockworth, Glos; 3 da; *Heir* unc, Oriel Brisco; *Career* sheep farmer (ret); former pilot RNZAF and RAF WW II; *Style* - Sir Donald Brisco, Bt, JP; Longworth, PO Box 165, Havelock North, Hawke's Bay, New Zealand

BRISCO, Kathleen, Lady - Kathleen; da of W Fenwick McAllaum, of NZ; *m* 1914, Sir Hylton Brisco, 7 Bt (d 1968); *Style* - Kathleen, Lady Brisco; 208 Windsor ave, Hastings, Hawke's Bay, New Zealand

BRISCO, Oriel Arthur; s of Arthur Hylton Brisco (d 1927); h to Btcy of n, Sir Donald Brisco, 8 Bt; *b* 26 June 1892; *m* 1, 1921, Lilian Frederica, nee Saunderson; m

2, 1960, Sarah Louise (d 1971), nee Clark; *Style* - Oriel Brisco Esq; 136 Fraser st, Tauranga, NZ

BRISCOE, John James; s and h of Sir John Leigh Charlton Briscoe, 4 Bt, DFC; *b* 15 July 1951

BRISCOE, Sir John Leigh Charlton; 4 Bt (UK 1910), of Bourn Hall, Bourn, Co of Cambridge, DFC (1945); s of Sir John Briscoe, 3 Bt, MD, FRCP (d 1960), of Lakenheath Hall, Suffolk; *b* 3 Dec 1911; *Educ* Harrow, Magdalen Oxford; *m* 1948, Teresa, da of Brig-Gen Sir Archibald Home KCVO CB CMG DSO; 2 s, 1 da; *Heir* s, John Briscoe; *Career* ACA 1937, dir ops BAA 1966-73; *Recreations* old cars; *Clubs* RAF, Roy Ocean Racing; *Style* - Sir John Briscoe, Bt, DFC; Little Acres, Stoke Poges, Bucks (☎ Farnham Common 2394)

BRISTOL, 53 Bishop of (cr 1541) 1976-; Rt Rev Ernest John Tinsley; s of Ernest William Tinsley (d 1955); *b* 22 March 1919; *Educ* St John's Coll Durham U, Westcott House Cambridge; *m* 1947, Marjorie Dixon (d 1977); 2 da; *Career* patron of 98 livings, of 6 with joint patronage, and of the archdeaconries of Bristol and Swindon (the See of Bristol is one of the 6 Bishoprics created by Henry VIII in 1541); Bp of Sheffield 1963-75, Prof of Theology Leeds 1962-75, Hon Canon of Ripon 1966-75, Special Lectr in Theology Bristol U 1976-; *Style* - The Rt Rev The Lord Bishop of Bristol; Bishop's House, Clifton Hill, Bristol (☎ Bristol 30222)

BRISTOL, 6 Marquess of (UK 1826); Victor Frederick Cochrane Hervey; also Baron Hervey of Ickworth (E 1703), Earl of Bristol (GB 1714) and Earl Jermyn (UK 1826); Hereditary High Steward of the Liberty of St Edmund; s of 5 Marquess of Bristol (d 1960, fourth in descent from the 4 Earl of Bristol, also Bp of Derry, whose magnificence and love of travel to Italy is commemorated in the large number of Hotels which bear his name; his opposition to the Union of GB & Ireland was allegedly motivated more by vanity than conviction; the Earl-Bishop's f was the Lord Hervey satirised as Sporus by Pope) and Lady Jean Cochrane, da of 12 Earl of Dundonald; *b* 6 Oct 1915; *Educ* Eton, Sandhurst; *m* 1, 1949 (m dis 1959), Pauline, da of late Herbert Bolton; 1 s; m 2, 1960 (m dis 1972), Lady Anne, da of 8 Earl Fitzwilliam, DSC, and Olive (da of Most Rev Hon Benjamin Plunket, sometime Bp of Meath and s of 4 Baron Plunket, by his w Dorothea, da of Sir Thomas Butler, 10 Bt); 1 s; m 3, 1974, Yvonne, da of Anthony Sutton, of Florida Court, Bromley; 1 s, 1 da; *Heir* s, Earl Jermyn; *Career* Chllr and Ambassador-at-Large The Monarchist League 1971-, V-Pres Tax Payers Union 1968-; memb W India Cttee 1965-, Monday Club 1970-, European Atlantic Gp 1966-; patron of thirty livings; Hereditary Lord High Interrogator; chm- Sleaford Investments, Eastern Caravan Parks, Bristol Publishing Co, Br International Airways, Bristol Powersport Co, Dominica Paradise Ltd, Marquis of Bristol & Co, VLC Associated, Atlantis Project Cyprus, Jersey & Co (Finland); dir of thirty other cos; *Recreations* yachting, shooting, antiques; *Clubs* Hurlingham, Eccentric, House of Lords Yachting, House of Lords Motoring, Guards Polo, Clermont, Roy Worlington Golf, East Hill (Nassau), Monte Carlo Yacht; fast motor yacht- 'Isabella' (type 'Super America 48', maker Riva); *Style* - The Most Hon The Marquess of Bristol; Le Formentor, Av Princesse Grace, Monte Carlo, Monaco

BRISTOL, Hon Mrs (Lavinia Mary); da of 9 Baron Hawke; *b* 15 June 1945; *Educ* Hatherop Castle, Queensgate London; *m* 1965, Maj Nicholas Maclean Verity Bristol; 3 s; *Career* administrator Project Tst 1973-; *Recreations* Army & Navy, New (Edinburgh); *Style* - The Hon Mrs Bristol; Breacachadh Castle, Isle of Coll, Argyll (☎ 08793378)

BRISTOW, Alan Edgar; OBE (1966); *b* 3 Sept 1923; *Educ* Portsmouth G S; *m* 1945, Jean Catherine; 1 s, 1 da; *Career* chm Bristow Helicopter Gp Ltd 1967-; FRAeS 1967; *Recreations* flying, shooting, sailing, farming, four-in-hand driving; *Style* - Alan Bristow Esq, OBE; Meadowfield, Barhatch rd, Cranleigh, Surrey (☎ 4674)

BRISTOW, Hon Mrs - Hon Caroline

Jean; da of 2 Baron Luke, KCVO, TD, JP, DL; *b* 1935; *m* 1958, James Bristow; 3 s, 1 da; *Style* - The Hon Mrs Bristow; Biddenham Close, Bedford (☎ 52088)

BRISTOW, James; s of James Percy Bristow; *b* 25 May 1934; *Educ* Oakham Sch; *m* 1958, Hon Caroline Jean, da of 2 Baron Luke, KCVO, TD, DL; 3 s, 1 da; *Career* dir Charleswells Ltd (Brewery); md London Brick Co; *Recreations* music, sailing; *Clubs* Seaview Yacht; *Style* - James Bristow Esq; Biddenham Close, Bedford (☎ 52088)

BRITTAN, Samuel; s of late Joseph Brittan and Riva, nee Lipetz; *b* 29 Dec 1933; *Educ* Kilburn G S; Jesus Cambridge; *Career* princ economic commentator 1966- and assist ed Financial Times 1977-; *Style* - Samuel Brittan Esq; Flat 10, The Lodge, Kensington Park gdns, W11

BRITTEN, C H; *Career* assist gen man Anglia Hastings and Thanet Building Soc; *Style* - C H Britten Esq; Moulton Park, Northampton

BRITTENDEN, (Charles) Arthur; s of late Tom Brittenden and Caroline, nee Scrivener; *b* 23 Oct 1924; *Educ* Leeds G S; *m* 1, 1953, Sylvia Cadman (m dis 1960); m 2, 1966, Ann Kenny (m dis 1972); m 3, 1975, Valerie Arnison; *Career* dep ed The Sun 1972-; *Style* - Arthur Brittenden Esq; 6Strathearn pla, W2; 42 Oxford st ,Woodstock, Oxon

BRITTON, Sir Edward Louis; CBE (1967); s of George Britton; *b* 4 Dec 1909; *Educ* Bromley G S; Trinity Cambridge; *m* 1936, Nora Arnald; *Career* sr res fell Educn Div Sheffield U 1975; kt 1975; *Style* - Sir Edward Britton, CBE; 40 Nightingale rd, Guildford, Surrey

BROACKES, Nigel; s of late Donald Broackes; *b* 21 July 1934; *Educ* Stowe; *m* 1956, Joyce Horne; 2 s, 1 da; *Career* chm Trafalgar House Ltd; trustee, Royal Opera House Trust; dir Horserace Totalisator Bd 1976-, Guardian Young Businessman of the Year 1978; *Style* - Nigel Broackes Esq; 41 Chelsea sq, SW3; The Deanery, Thames st, Sonning, Berks

BROAD, Harold Peter; CBE (1946), DFC (1940); s of Harold Broad, of Duncton, Sussex; *b* 1 Oct 1909; *Educ* Lancing, RAF Cranwell; *m* 1942, Margaret, da of Dr Bertram Lambert, OBE, DSC, Fellow of Merton Coll Oxford (invented gas masks used by forces in WWI and II; d 1963); *Career* served RAF 1940-57, OC RAF Kuala Lumpur 1954-57; assist to tech dir Hunting Aircraft 1957-65, BAC assist to chm 1965-74; *Recreations* hunting, shooting, fishing, reading, roses; *Clubs* Flyfishers; *Style* - Harold Broad Esq, CBE, DFC; 28 Fishpool st, St Albans, Herts (☎ 53736)

BROAD, Sidney Thomas; CBE (1972); s of Francis Broad, JP, sometime MP Edmonton; *b* 12 Nov 1911; *Educ* Latymer, Queen's Oxford; *m* 1944, Mary, da of Peter Johnston; 2 s, 1 da; *Career* first pres Soc Educn Offrs 1971, sometime pres County Educn Offrs Soc; County Educn Offr Herts 1958-74; *Style* - Sidney Broad Esq, CBE; The Manor House, Ugborough, S Devon (☎ Ivybridge 2279)

BROADBENT, George Walter; s of John Broadbent (d 1967); hp to Btcy of kinsman Sir William Broadbent, 3 Bt; *b* 23 Apr 1935; *m* 1962, Valerie, nee Ward; 1 s, 1 da; *Career* Fl-Lt RAF; *Style* - George Broadbent Esq; c/o Lloyds Bank, Fairford, Glos

BROADBENT, William Benedict; ERD (1959); s of William Broadbent, of Huddersfield; *b* 10 Jan 1924; *Educ* Rugby; *m* 1954 (m dis 1980), Joy, da of Ernest Wilkinson, CBE; 4 da; *Career* chm Severn Valley Railway Hldgs 1975-; dir Festiniog Ry Co 1954-; md Br Salt Ltd 1966-71; engr and management consultant; *Recreations* hill climbing, cruising; *Clubs* Mountain Rangers Assoc; *Style* - William Broadbent Esq, ERD; 20 St Mary's Steps, Bridgnorth, Salop (☎ 07462 4148)

BROADBENT, Sir William Francis; 3 Bt (UK 1893); s of Sir John Francis Harpin Broadbent, 2 Bt, MD, FRCP, MRCS (d 1946); *b* 29 Nov 1904; *Educ* Winchester, Trin Oxford; *m* 1935, Veronica Pearl (d 1951), da of late Benjamin F Eustace, of Glasnevin, Dublin; *Heir* kinsman, George Walter Broadbent;

Career slr 1933; *Style* - Sir William Broadbent, Bt; Flat 43, Ritchie Court, 380 Banbury rd, Oxford

BROADBRIDGE, 3 Baron (UK 1945); Sir Peter Hewett Broadbridge; 3 Bt (UK 1937); s of 2 Baron (d 1972); *b* 19 Aug 1938; *Educ* Hurstpierpoint, St Cat's Oxford; *m* 1967, Mary, da of Wilhelm Otto Busch; 2 da; *Heir* unc, Hon Ralph Broadbridge; *Career* directorships within Ravendale Gp of Cos; formerly consultant Coopers & Lybrand, Peat Marwick Mitchell & Co; mktng appts with Gallaher, Colgate-Palmolive, Unilever; *Recreations* early English watercolours, old English silver, silversmithing, tennis, squash; *Style* - The Rt Hon The Lord Broadbridge; Cross House, East Meon, Petersfield, Hants (☎ 87203)

BROADBRIDGE, Hon Howard Eustace; s of 1 Baron Broadbridge, KCVO (d 1952); *b* 1904; *m* 1935, Margaret A M, da of Capt H H Witherington, of St Michaels, Natal; 1 da; *Style* - The Hon Howard Broadbridge; 12 Texel, Alexandra rd, Pietermaritzburg, Natal, S Africa

BROADBRIDGE, Hon Hugh Trevor; s of 1 Baron Broadbridge, KCVO (d 1952); *b* 1903; *Educ* Shoreham G S; *m* 1927, Anne Marjorie, da of late J Locke Elfick, of Purley, Surrey; 1 s, 1 da; *Career* regional works advr to Regional Cmmr Midland Region 1939-42, employed Miny of Supply 1942-44; *Style* - The Hon Hugh Broadbridge; 19 Hanover Close, Sturminster, Newton, Dorset

BROADBRIDGE, Hon Jemima Louise; da of 3 Baron Broadbridge; *b* 1970

BROADBRIDGE, Hon Rupert Guy; s of 1 Baron Broadbridge, KCVO (d 1952); *b* 1906; *m* 1948, Margaret, nee Cumming; 1 da; *Career* served 1939-45 (Abyssinia, Libya and Tripoli); *Style* - The Hon Rupert Broadbridge; 199 Kingsway, Warner Beach, Natal, S Africa

BROADBRIDGE, Hon Ralph George Cameron; s of 1 Baron Broadbridge, KCVO (d 1952); hp to Barony; *b* 20 Nov 1901; *Educ* Shoreham G S; *m* 1925, Emma Rose Hancock, da of Harry Van der Weyden; 3 da; *Career* dentist; *Style* - The Hon Ralph Broadbridge; Old School House, Church Walk, Sturminster Newton, Dorset

BROADBRIDGE, Hon Sophie Mary; da of 3 Baron Broadbridge; *b* 1972

BROADHURST, Brig Ronald Joseph Callender; s of Capt Joseph F Broadhurst (d 1964), of Felpham, Sussex; *b* 25 Dec 1906; *Educ* English Coll Jerusalem, King's Cambridge; *m* 1934, Annie Doreen, da of John B Morrison, of Ballydrain, Dunmurry, Co Antrim; 1 s; *Career* entered Colonial Service 1926, Dep Cmdt Arab Legion 1939, equerry to HM King Abdullah of Jordan 1942, resigned as Brig, Assist Ch of Staff Arab Legion, returned to UK 1948; raised and commanded no 31 gp Roy Observer Corps, dir of Ceremonies, Commandery of Ards; chm Forces Help Soc and Lord Roberts Workshops, N Ireland; chm Outward Bound Trust N Ireland; pres Amateur Fencing Union N Ireland; memb N Ireland Legislative Assembly June 1973; oriental historian; OStJ; KStJ; *Style* - Brig Ronald Broadhurst; Belvedere, Ballyaughlis, Co Down, N Ireland (☎ Drumbo 220)

BROADLEY, Sir Herbert; KBE (1947, CBE 1943); s of Stephenson Broadley; *b* 23 Nov 1892; *Educ* King Edward VI G S Louth, Birkbeck Coll London; *m* 1927, Kathleen, nee Moore; *Career* Dep Sec Min of Food 1939-48, UK rep UN Children's Fund 1958-68; *Recreations* gardening, reading; *Clubs* Naval & Military; *Style* - Sir Herbert Broadley, KBE; Hollingsworth, Redlands Lane, Ewshot, Farnham, Surrey (☎ 0252 850437)

BROCAS, Viscount; Patrick John Bernard Jellicoe; s (by 1 m) and h of 2 Earl Jellicoe, DSO, MC, PC; *b* 29 Aug 1950; *Educ* Eton; *m* 1971, (m dis 1980), Geraldine Ann Jackson; 2 .s; *Style* - Viscount Brocas; Pantglas, Llanwoda, Dyfed

BROCK, Baroness; Chrissie Palmer; da of John Alfred Jones, of Leeds; *m* 1979, as his 2 w, Baron Brock (d 1980); 2 da;

Style - The Rt Hon the Lady Brock; 28 Westminster gdns, Marsham st, SW1

BROCK, Michael George; s of Sir Laurence Brock; *b* 9 Mar 1920; *Educ* Wellington, CCC Oxford; *m* 1949, Eleanor Morrison; 3 s; *Career* historian; FRHistS 1965; warden Nuffield Oxford 1978-, Pro-V-Chllr Oxford 1980-; *Style* - Michael Brock Esq; Nuffield College, Oxford

BROCKBANK, (James) Tyrrell; DL (Durham 1970); s of James Brockbank, of York; *b* 14 Dec 1920; *Educ* St Peter's York, St John's Cambridge; *m* 1950, Pamela, da of Lt-Col John Parker, of Essex; 4 s; *Career* memb Local Govt Boundary Commission England 1976-, Clerk to Durham Ltcy 1964-; *Recreations* fishing, shooting, golf; *Clubs* Travellers', Durham County; *Style* - Tyrrell Brockbank Esq, DL; The Orange Tree, Shincliffe, Durham (☎ 0385 65569)

BROCKET, 3 Baron (UK 1933); Sir Charles Ronald George Nall-Cain; 3 Bt (UK 1921); s of late Hon Ronald Charles Manus Nall-Cain, er s of 2 Baron; suc gf 1967; *b* 12 Feb 1952; *Educ* Eton; *Heir* bro, Hon Richard Nall-Cain; *Career* late 14/20 King's Hussars; *Style* - The Rt Hon The Lord Brocket; Brocket Hall, Welwyn, Herts

BROCKHOFF, Sir Jack Stuart; s of Douglas Brockhoff; *b* 1908; *Educ* Wesley Coll, Victoria; *Career* kt 1979, chm & md Brockhoff's Biscuits Pty Ltd; Arnott-Brockhoff-Guest Pty Ltd; dir Arnotts Ltd; *Style* - Sir Jack Brockhoff; 113 Beach rd, Sandringham, Victoria 3191, Australia (☎ 598 9227)

BROCKLEBANK, Sir Aubrey (Thomas); 6 Bt (UK 1885); s of Maj Sir John Montague Brocklebank, 5 Bt, TD, 1974; *b* 29 Jan 1952; *Educ* Eton, Univ Coll Durham; *m* 1979, Anna-Marie, da of Dr William Dunnet, of Woldingham, Surrey; *Heir* s, Aubrey Brocklebank; *Career* dir Augill Castle Antiques Ltd; *Style* - Sir Aubrey Brocklebank, Bt; 78 Overstrand Mansions, Prince of Wales dve, SW11

BROCKLEBANK, Aubrey William; s and h of Sir Aubrey Brocklebank, 6 Bt; *b* 15 Dec 1980

BROCKLEBANK, Pamela, Lady - Pamela Sue; da of late William Harold Pierce OBE, of Bidston, Cheshire; *m* 1, Maj Leslie Forshaw-Wilson; m 2, 1950, Maj Sir John Brocklebank, TD, 5 Bt (d 1974); *Style* - Pamela, Lady Brocklebank; Il Palazz, Zejtun, Malta, GC

BROCKLEBANK-FOWLER, Christopher; MP (stood as C 1979 but joined SDP 1981) Norfolk NW 1974-; s of Sidney Brocklebank-Fowler; *b* 13 Jan 1934; *Educ* Perse Cambridge; *m* 1, 1957 (m dis 1975), Joan, nee Nowland; 2 s; m 2, 1975, Mrs Mary Berry; *Career* MP King's Lynn 1970-74; Gov Inst Dvpt Studies 1978-, memb Bow Gp 1961-; dir Creative Consultants Ltd; chm SOS Children's Villages 1978-; *Recreations* swimming, shooting, fishing, painting; *Clubs* Carlton; *Style* - Christopher Brocklebank-Fowler Esq MP; The Long Cottage, Flitcham, King's Lynn, Norfolk (☎ Hillington 255)

BROCKMAN, Vice-Adm Sir Ronald; KCB (1965), CSI (1947), CIE (1946), CVO (1979), CBE (1943), DL (Devon 1968); s of Rear-Adm Henry Brockman, CB; *b* 8 March 1909; *Educ* Weymouth Coll; *m* 1932, Marjorie, da of Charles Butt; 1 s, 3 da; *Career* Extra Gentleman Usher to HM The Queen 1979- (Gentleman Usher 1967-79); Priv Sec to Gov Gen India 1947-48; Pncpl Staff Offr to Adm of the Fleet Earl Mountbatten of Burma as CDS 1959-65; CStJ; *Recreations* sailing; *Clubs* White's, Army & Navy, MCC, Roy Western Yacht of England, Coastal Forces Sailing (Cdre); *Style* - Vice-Adm Sir Ronald Brockman, KCB, CSI, CIE, CVO, CBE, DL; 3 Court House, Basil st, SW3 (☎ 01 584 1023); Glenholme, West Hill, Budleigh Salterton, Devon (☎ 0395 42687)

BROCKWAY, Baron (Life Peer UK 1964); (Archibald) Fenner Brockway; s of Rev Wotham Brockway, of Calcutta; *b* 1 Nov 1888; *Educ* Sch for Sons of Missionaries, Blackheath (now Eltham Coll); *m* 1914, Lilla (m dis 1946), da of Late Rev W Harvey-Smith; 2 da; m 2, 1946, Edith, da of late Archibald King; 1 s; *Career* MP (L) Leyton 1929-31, Eton & Slough 1950-64; chm ILP 1931-33, Gen Sec 1928 and 1933-39, Political Sec 1939-46; Pres Br Campaign for Peace in

Vietnam 1970-; Co-Chm (with Ld Noel-Baker) World Disarmament Campaign 1979-; journalist; *Recreations* watching sport on TV; *Style* - The Rt Hon The Lord Brockway; 67 Southway, N20 (☎ 01 445 3054)

BROCKWAY, Hon Chris Fenner; s of Baron Brockway (Life Peer); *b* 1946; *Style* - The Hon Chris Brockway; 67 Southway, N20

BRODIE, Sir Benjamin David Ross; 5 Bt (UK 1834); s of Sir Benjamin Collins Brodie, 4 Bt, MC (d 1971); *b* 29 May 1925; *Educ* Eton; *Style* - Sir Benjamin Brodie, Bt

BRODIE, Colin Alexander; s of Sir Benjamin Collins Brodie, MC 4 Bt (d 1971); hp to Baronetcy of bro, Sir Benjamin David Ross Brodie, 5 Bt; *b* 19 April 1929; *Educ* Eton, Magdalen Oxford; *m* 1955, Julia, nee Wates; 2 s; *Career* barr 1953; *Style* - Colin Brodie Esq; 24 Old Buildings, Lincoln's Inn, WC2

BRODIE, Lady - Fanny; da of Jacob Levine, of London; *m* 1946, Very Rev Rabbi Sir Israel Brodie, KBE (d 1979); *Style* - Lady Brodie; 82 Portland pla, W1

BRODIE, Air Cdre Ian Eustace; OBE (1940), DL (Bucks 1964); s of William Brodie; *b* 17 Sept 1898; *Educ* Oundle, St John's Cambridge; *m* 1925, Mary Gonville, da of William Coates, JP, sometime High Sheriff Co Kildare; 3 da; *Career* ret as Air-Cdre 1951; *Recreations* sailing; *Clubs* Roy Solent Yacht; *Style* - Air Cdre Ian Brodie, OBE, DL; Briar Well, Moons Hill, Freshwater, IOW (☎ 2835)

BRODIE OF BRODIE, (Montagu) Ninian Alexander; JP (Morayshire 1958), DL (Nairn 1970); s of Ian Brodie of Brodie (d 1943); *b* 12 June 1912; *Educ* Eton; *m* 1939, Helena, da of Janssen Budgen, of Wendover; 1 s, 1 da; *Heir* Alastair Brodie, Younger of Brodie; *Career* 25 Chief of Clan Brodie; market gardener and landowner 1953-; professional actor 1935-40 and 1945-50; *Recreations* shooting, bridge, backgammon, bird watching; *Style* - Ninian Brodie of Brodie, JP, DL; Brodie Castle, Forres, Moray

BRODIE, YOUNGER OF BRODIE, Alastair Ian Ninian; s and h of Ninian Brodie of Brodie, JP, DL; *b* 7 Sept 1943; *m* 1968, Mary Louise Johnson; 2 s, 1 da; *Style* - Alastair Brodie, yr of Brodie

BRODRICK, Alan Henry; s of Alan Rupert Brodrick (d 1972), and hp of uncle, 11 Viscount Midleton; *b* 4 Aug 1949; *m* 1978, Julia Helen, da of Michael Pitt, of Lias Cottage, Compton Durdon, Somerton, Som; *Style* - Alan Brodrick Esq; Elder Cottage, Forest rd, Onehouse, Stowmarket, Suffolk

BRODRICK, Hon Mrs - Hon Hester Winifred; *née* Astley; da of 20 Baron Hastings; *b* 1899; *m* 1923, Alan Houghton Brodrick (d 1973); 1 s; *Style* - The Hon Mrs Brodrick; Connecticut, USA

BROGAN, Lt-Gen Sir Mervyn Francis; KBE (1972, CBE 1964, OBE 1944), CB (1970); s of Bernard Brogan, of NSW; *b* 10 Jan 1915; *Educ* Sydney Tech H S, Sydney U; *m* 1941, Sheila, da of David Jones, of Canberra; 2 s; *Career* Ch Gen Staff 1971-73 (ret); *Recreations* surfing, tennis; *Clubs* Union, Tattersalls (both Sydney), Australian Jockey, Roy Sydney G C; *Style* - Lt-Gen Sir Mervyn Brogan, KBE, CB; 71/53 Ocean av, Double Bay, NSW 2028, Australia (☎ 32 9509)

BROKE, Maj George Robin Straton; MVO (1977); s of Maj-Gen R S Broke; *b* 31 Mar 1946; *Educ* Eton; *m* 1978, Patricia Shann; *Career* Equerry-in-waiting to HM The Queen 1974-77; *Style* - Maj George Broke, MVO; Holme Hale Hall, Thetford, Norfolk (☎ Holme Hale 225)

BROKE, Robert Straton; CB (1967), OBE (1946), MC (1940); s of Rev Horatio George Broke (d 1931); *b* 15 Mar 1913; *Educ* Eton, Magdalene Cambridge; *m* 1939, Ernine Susan Margaret, da of Rev William Henry Bonsey (d 1951); 2 s; *Career* farmer; dir Wellman Engrg Corpn Ltd 1968-, pres Metallurgical Plantmakers Fedn 1977-79; Col Cmdt Roy Artillery 1968-78; *Recreations* country sports; *Clubs* Army & Navy, MCC; *Style* - Robert Broke Esq, CB, OBE, MC; Holme Hale Hall, Thetford, Norfolk (☎ Holme Hale (0760) 440225)

BROMHEAD, Sir John Desmond Gonville; 6 Bt (UK 1806), of Thurlby Lincs; s of Sir Benjamin Bromhead, 5 Bt, OBE (d 1981); *b* 21 Dec 1943; *Educ* Wellington; *Heir* cous, John Bromhead; *Style* - Sir John Bromhead, Bt

BROMHEAD, John Edmund de Gonville; s of late Lt-Col Edmund de Gonville Hosking Bromhead (d 1973) and Joan, da of late Brig Sir Henry Scott, CB, DSO, MC; 1 cous and hp of Sir John Bromhead, 6 Bt; *b* 10 Oct 1939; *Educ* St Andrew's Coll Grahamstown S Africa, RAF Coll Cranwell; *m* 1965, Janet, da of Henry Brotherton, of Moreton-in-Marsh Glos; 1 s, 1 da; *Career* Capt Br Airways, served RAF to 1964 (when ret); *Style* - John Bromhead Esq; Duiker House, Fencott, Islip, Oxford

BROMHEAD, Lady; Nancy Mary; da of late T S Lough, of Buenos Aires; *m* 1938, Sir Benjamin Bromhead, 5 Bt, OBE (d 1981); 1 s, 2 da; *Style* - Lady Bromhead; Thurlby Hall, Aubourn, Lincoln (☎ Bassingham 386)

BROMILOW, Denis; TD (1944); s of John Henry Bromilow (d 1948); *b* 15 Aug 1910; *Educ* Wrekin Coll Wellington, Birmingham U; *m* 1939, Vivien Mary da Brig-Gen Alfred Huggins CMG DSO; 1 s, 1 da; *Career* Maj RA 1941-45, solicitor 1934-76; *Clubs* The Birmingham; *Style* - Denis Bromilow Esq, TD; 'Eversleigh', 54 St Agnes rd, Moseley, Birmingham

BROMLEY, Charles Howard; s and h of Sir Rupert Bromley, 10 Bt; *b* 31 July 1963; *Style* - Charles Bromley Esq

BROMLEY, Sir Rupert Charles; 10 Bt (GB 1757), of East Stoke, Nottinghamshire; s of Maj Sir Rupert Bromley, 9 Bt, MC (d 1966, fifth in descent from Sir George Bromley, 2 Bt, who changed his name to Bromley from Smith; Sir George's unc, Abel Smith, was the ancestor of Lord Carrington; the 1 Bt, Sir George Smith, m Mary Howe, whose paternal grandmother, Ruperta, was love child of Prince Rupert of the Rhine; Ruperta's husb was Lt-Gen Emmanuel Scrope Howe, whose mother Annabella was natural da and testamentary coheir of Emmanuel Scrope, Earl of Sunderland); *b* 2 April 1936; *Educ* Rhodes U, Ch Ch Oxford; *m* 1962, Priscilla, da of Maj Howard Bourne, HAC; 3 s; *Heir* s, Charles Howard Bromley; *Career* co exec Murray & Roberts Ltd; *Recreations* squash; *Clubs* Western Province Sports; *Style* - Sir Rupert Bromley, Bt; Brendon House, Selwyn rd, Kenilworth 7700, S Africa

BROMLEY-MARTIN, Hon Mrs (Anne Elizabeth); *née* Walsh; da of 5 Baron Ormathwaite, MVO (d 1944); *b* 1911; *m* 1948, as his 2 w, Peter Edward Bromley-Martin (d 1968); *Style* - The Hon Mrs Bromley-Martin; The Pheasantry, Builth Wells, Powys BLD 3NP

BRON, Eleanor; da of Sydney and Fagah Bron; *Educ* North London Collegiate Sch; Newnham Cambridge; *Career* actress and writer; *Style* - Miss Eleanor Bron; c/o Jenne Casarotto, 28 Charing Cross rd, WC1 (☎ 01 836 3903)

BROOK, Eric Armitage; s of Harold Brook, of Holywell N Wales; *b* 27 Nov 1921; *Educ* Holywell G S, Liverpool U; *m* 1947, Audrey, da of Harold Garside, of Huddersfield; *Career* md Robert Marriott Gp Ltd and chm/md of all subsids (1961-81); dir Briggs & Forrester Hldgs 1974-; *Recreations* travel, photography; *Clubs* City Livery, Northampton & County; *Style* - Eric Brook Esq; The Old Vicarage, Easton Maudit, nr Wellingborough, Northants (☎ 0933 663260)

BROOK, Lady - Helen; da of John Knewstub; *b* 12 Oct 1907; *Educ* Convent of Holy Child Jesus, Mark Cross, Sussex; *m* 1937, Sir Robin Brook, CMG, OBE; 2 da (and 1 da of previous m); *Career* founder (1963) and pres Brook Advisory Centre for Young People; *Style* - Lady Brook; 31 Acacia rd, NW8 (☎ 01 722 5844); Claydene Garden Cottage, Cowden, Kent

BROOK, Leopold; s of Albert Brook; *b* 2 Jan 1912; *Educ* Univ Coll, London; *m* 1, 1940, Susan, nee Rose (d 1970); 2 s; m 2, 1974, Mrs Elly Rhodes; 2 step s, 1 step da; *Career* FICE, FIMechE; chm Associated

Nuclear Services Ltd 1977-; Sanders and Forster Ltd 1978-; dir Chamberlain Gp Ltd 1978-; *Style* - Leopold Brook Esq; 55 Kingston House North, Prince's gate, SW7 (☎ 01 584 2041)

BROOK, (Gerald) Robert; s of Charles Brook; *b* 19 Dec 1928; *Educ* King James G S Knaresborough; *m* 1957, Joan Oldfield; 2 s, 1 da; *Career* dep chm National Bus Co 1978-; *Style* - Robert Brook Esq; 25 New st sq, EC4 (☎ 01 583 9177)

BROOK, Sir Robin; CMG (1954), OBE (1945); s of Francis Brook, of Harley st; *b* 19 June 1908; *Educ* Eton, King's Cambridge; *m* 1937, Helen, da of John Knewstub; 2 da; *Career* kt 1974, chm Leda Investment Tst, Carlco Ltd; dir Utd City Merchants; memb City and E London HA 1974-; High Sheriff London 1950; Br Sabre Champion 1936 (Olympic Games 1936 and 1948); *Style* - Sir Robin Brook, CMG, OBE; 31 Acacia rd, NW8 (☎ 01 722 5844); Claydene, nr Edenbridge, Kent (☎ Cowden 367 1412)

BROOK, Assist Chief Constable Vivian; *aet* 52 in 1981 *Career* Dep-Ch Supt to 1981, head S Wales CID 1974-81, S Wales Assist Ch Constable 1981 *Style* - Assistant Ch Constable Vivian Brook

BROOKE OF YSTRADFELLTE, Baroness (Life Peeress 1964); Barbara Muriel Brooke; DBE (1960); da of late Rev Canon Alfred Augustus Mathews, of Llanwern, Gwent; *b* 14 Jan 1908; *Educ* Queen Anne's Sch Caversham, Glos Training Coll of Domestic Science; *m* 1933, Baron Brooke of Cumnor, CH, PC, *qv*; *Career* memb Hampstead Boro' Cncl 1948-65, v-chm Cons Pty Org 1954-64, memb N W Metropolitan Regional Hosp Bd 1955-66, chm Governing Body of Godolphin and Latymer Sch 1960-78, chm Exec Ctee Queen's Inst of Dist Nursing 1961-71, memb Management Ctee King Edward's Hosp Fund for London 1967-70; *Style* - The Rt Hon The Lady Brooke of Ystradfellte, DBE; The Glebe House, Mildenhall, Marlborough, Wilts

BROOKE OF CUMNOR, Baron (Life Peer UK 1966); Henry Brooke; CH (1964), PC (1955); s of late L Leslie Brooke; *b* 9 April 1903; *Educ* Marlborough, Balliol Oxford; *m* 1933, Barbara Muriel (Baroness Brooke of Ystradfellte, DBE, *qv*); 2 s, 2 da; *Career* former cllr and alderman Boro' of Hampstead, Co Cllr for London 1945-55 (Leader Con Pty 1945-52), Fin Sec to Treasury 1954-57, Min of Housing and Local Govt, and Min for Welsh Affairs 1957-61, Ch Sec to Treasury and Paymaster-Gen 1961-62, Home Sec 1962-64, MP (C) W Lewisham 1938-45 and Hampstead 1950-66; *Style* - The Rt Hon The Lord Brooke of Cumnor CH PC; The Glebe House, Mildenhall, Marlborough, Wilts

BROOKE, Capt Hon Alan Henry; s and h of 2 Viscount Brookeborough, PC, DL; *b* 30 June 1952; *Educ* Harrow and Millfield; *m* 1980, Janet, da of John Cooke, of Ballyvoy Lodge, Doagh, Co Antrim; *Career* Capt UDR; farmer; *Recreations* riding, fishing, shooting, skiing; *Style* - Capt The Hon Alan Brooke; Colebrooke, Brookeborough, Co Fermanagh, N Ireland (☎ 402)

BROOKE, Alistair Weston; s and h of Sir John Weston Brooke, 3 Bt; *b* 12 Sept 1947; *Educ* Repton; *Style* - Alistair Brooke Esq

BROOKE, Lt Hon Christopher Arthur; s of 2 Viscount Brookeborough; *b* 1954; *Educ* Gordonstoun; *Career* served 5 Inniskilling Dragoon Gds *Style* - Lt The Hon Christopher Brooke

BROOKE, David; s of Alec Brooke, of Huddersfield; *b* 18 Dec 1940; *Educ* Uppingham, Leeds U; *m* 1967, Margaret, da of William Stork, of Kirkburton Yorks; 1 s, 1 da; *Career* dir C & J Hirst & Sons 1977; *Style* - David Brooke Esq; Hazelhurst, Arkenley Lane, Almondbury, Hudersfield, Yorks

BROOKE, (Richard) David Christopher; s and h of Sir Richard Neville Brooke, 10 Bt, by his 1 w, Lady Mabel, nee Jocelyn, da of 8 Earl of Roden; *b* 23 Oct 1938; *Educ* Eton; *m* 1963 (m dis 1978), Carola Marion, da of Sir Robert Erskine-Hill, 2 Bt; 2 s; *Style* - David Brooke Esq; Cedar House, Shurlock Row, Twyford, Berks

BROOKE, Lord; David Robin Francis Guy Greville; JP (Warwicks); s (by 1 m) and h of 7 Earl of Warwick; *b* 15 May 1934; *Educ* Eton; *m* 1956 (m dis 1976), Sarah Anne, da of Alfred Chester Beatty; 1 s, 1 da; *Heir* s, Hon Guy Greville; *Career* late Life Gds, Warwicks Yeo (TA) 1954, gov Roy Shakespeare Theatre, v-pres Midland Assoc of Bldg Socs; *Clubs* White's; *Style* - Lord Brooke, JP; 43 Rue du Colisée, Paris VIII, France; Apt 210, Mermaid Beach, Warwick, Bermuda

BROOKE, Francis George Windham; s and h of Sir George Brooke, 3 Bt, MBE; *b* 15 Oct 1963; *Style* - Francis Brooke Esq

BROOKE, Sir George Cecil Francis; 3 Bt (UK 1903), MBE (1949); s of Sir Francis Brooke, 2 Bt (d 1954), by Mabel, da of Sir John Arnott, 1 Bt; *b* 30 March 1916; *Educ* Stowe; *m* 1959, Lady Melissa, *qv*; 1 s, 1 da; *Heir* s, Francis George Windham Brooke; *Career* formerly Maj 17/21 Lancers; *Style* - Sir George Brooke, Bt, MBE; Glenbevan, Croom, Co Limerick

BROOKE, Hon Henry; s of Baron Brooke of Cumnor, CH, PC (Life Peer), and Baroness Brooke of Ystradfellte, DBE (Life Peeress); *b* 19 July 1936; *Educ* Marlborough and Balliol Coll, Oxford; *m* 1966, Bridget Mary, da of W G Kalaugher, of Appledene, Marlborough, Wilts; 3 s, 1 da; *Career* barr Inner Temple 1963, Jr Cncl to the Crown (Common Law) 1978; *Style* - The Hon Henry Brooke; 1 Dynevor rd, Richmond, Surrey (☎ 01 940 4418)

BROOKE, Sir John Weston; 3 Bt (UK 1919), JP (Ross-shire 1960), DL (Ross and Cromarty 1964); s of Maj Sir Robert Weston Brooke, 2 Bt, DSO, MC (d 1942); *b* 26 Sept 1911; *Educ* Repton, Trin Cambridge; *m* 1, 1945 (m dis 1963), Rosemary, da of late Percy Llewelyn Nevill; 2 s; m 2, 1966, Phoebe Napier Harvey, MB, ChB (d 1977), da of late G A Harvey, of Edinburgh, and wid of Capt Sir Peter Drummond Macdonald, KBE, FRS; *Heir* s, Alistair Weston Brooke; *Career* Maj (ret) Lovat Scouts; *Style* - Sir John Brooke, Bt, JP, DL; Midfearn, Ardgay, Ross-shire (☎ Ardgay 250)

BROOKE, Lady - (Mary Louisa) Mabel; da of Sir John Arnott, 1 Bt; *m* 1951, Sir Francis Hugh Brooke, 2 Bt (d 1954); 1 s, 1 da; *Style* - Lady Brooke; Pickering Forest, Celbridge, Co Kildare, Eire

BROOKE, Hon Melinda Charlotte; da of 2 Viscount Brookeborough; *b* 1958 *Style* -The Hon Melinda Brooke

BROOKE, Lady Melissa Eva Caroline; *née* Wyndham-Quin; da of 6 Earl of Dunraven, CB, MBE, MC (d 1965); *b* 1935; *m* 1959, Maj Sir George Cecil Francis Brooke, 3 Bt, MBE; 1 s, 1 da; *Style* - Lady Melissa Brooke; Glenbevan, Croom, Co Limerick, Eire

BROOKE, Martin Montague; s of Montague Brooke; *b* 25 Aug 1923; *Educ* Eastbourne Coll, Magdalene Cambridge; *m* 1950, Judith, da of Rev Truman Tanqueray; 2 s, 1 da; *Career* banker; dir Guinness Mahon 1963-72, chm Druidale Securities 1972-; *Recreations* gardening; *Clubs* Naval; *Style* - Martin Brooke Esq; Duxbury House, Chantry View rd, Guildford, Surrey (☎ 0483 504777)

BROOKE, Hon Mrs - Hon Nancy Marion; *née* Allsopp; da of 3 Baron Hindlip (d 1931); *b* 1910; *m* 1936, Peter Geoffrey Brooke; 1 s; *Style* - The Hon Mrs Brooke; Dial House, Chilmark, Wilts

BROOKE, Hon Peter Leonard; MP (C) City of London & Westminster S 1977-; s of Baron Brooke of Cumnor, CH, PC; *b* 3 March 1934; *Educ* Marlborough, Balliol Oxford, Harvard Business Sch (MBA); *m* 1964, Joan, da of Frederick Smith of São Paulo; 3 s (and 1 s decd); *Career* former RE (invalided out); Res Assoc IMEDE Lausanne & Swiss correspondent Financial Times 1960-61; Chm Spencer Stuart Management Consultants 1974-79; Assist Govt Whip 1979-; *Recreations* cricket, walking; *Clubs* Brooks's, City Livery, I Zingari, MCC, St George's (Hanover Sq) Constitutional, St Stephen's Constitutional; *Style* - The Hon Peter Brooke MP; 110a Ashley gdns, SW1 (☎ 01 834 1563)

BROOKE, R; *Career* md EMI; *Style* - R

Brooke Esq; EMI, Group Head Office, EMI House, Manchester sq, W1

BROOKE, Sir Richard Neville; 10 Bt (E 1662); s of Sir Richard Christopher Brooke, 9 Bt (d 1981); *b* 1 May 1915; *Educ* Eton; *m* 1937 (m dis 1959), Lady Mabel Kathleen Jocelyn, da of 8 Earl of Roden; 2 s; m 2, 1960, Jean Evison, da of late Lt-Col Arthur Cecil Corfe, DSO, and formerly w of Sir Nicolas John Cheetham, KCMG; *Heir* s, (Richard) David Christopher Brooke; *Career* formerly Lt Scots Gds; *Style* - Sir Richard Brooke, Bt; Parc Residentiel de L'Esterel, par les Adrets, Var, France

BROOKE, Hon Susanna Cynthia; da of 2 Viscount Brookeborough; *b* 1962 *Style* - The Hon Susanna Brooke

BROOKE-HITCHING, Hon Mrs (Emma Caroline); *née* Blades; da of 2 Baron Ebbisham, TD; *b* 1954; *m* 1977, Franklin Brooke-Hitching; *Style* - The Hon Mrs Brooke-Hitching

BROOKE-LITTLE, John Philip Brooke; MVO (1969); s of Raymond Brooke-Little, late of Unicorns House, Swalcliffe, Oxon; *b* 6 April 1927; *Educ* Clayesmore Sch, New Coll Oxford; *m* 1960, Mary, da of John Pierce; 3 s, 1 da; *Career* Norroy and Ulster King of Arms 1980-; Librarian, Registrar and Tres Coll of Arms 1975; Bluemantle Pursuivant 1956-67; Richmond Herald 1967-80, KStJ 1976, Kt Grand Cross of Grace & Devotion Order of Malta 1975; *Clubs* Carlton, City Livery, Chelsea Arts; *Style* - John Brooke-Little Esq, MVO; Heyford House, Lower Heyford, Oxford (☎ Steeple Aston 40337); College of Arms, Queen Victoria st, EC4 (☎ 01 248 1310)

BROOKEBOROUGH, 2 Viscount (UK 1952); Sir John Warden Brooke; 6 Bt (UK 1822), PC (NI 1972), DL (Co Fermanagh 1967); s of 1 Viscount, KG, CBE, MC, PC (d 1973) by his 1 w, Dame Cynthia, DBE, da of late Capt Charles Warden Sergison (whose w Florence was da of 4 Baron Sudeley); *b* 9 Nov 1922; *Educ* Eton; *m* 1949, Rosemary Hilda, da of late Lt-Col Arthur O'Neil Cubitt Chichester, OBE, MC, ggggs of John Chichester, bro of 2 Earl of Donegall; 2 s, 3 da; *Heir* s, Hon Alan Henry Brooke; *Career* late Capt 10 Hussars, on personal staff of Field Marshal Viscount Alexander of Tunis, KG, and Gen Sir Brian Robertson, Bt, GBE; ADC to Field Marshal Earl Wavell, GCB, PC, as Viceroy of India 1946; MP for Lisnaskea (U) NI 1968-72, Min of State for Finance NI and Govt Ch Whip 1971-72, memb of NI Assembly (UPNI) 1973-74, and of NI Convention 1975-76; chm Fermanagh CC 1961-73, High Sheriff 1955; *Style* - Rt Hon Viscount Brookeborough PC DL; Ashbrooke, Brookeborough, Co Fermanagh

BROOKEBOROUGH, Eileen, Viscountess - Sarah Eileen Bell; da of Henry Healey, of Belfast; *m* 1, Cecil Armstrong Calvert, FRCS; m 2, 1971, as his 2 w, 1 Viscount Brookeborough, KG, PC, CBE, MC (d 1973); *Style* - The Rt Hon Eileen, Viscountess Brookeborough; Carnbeg, Spa, Ballynahinch, Co Down, Northern Ireland

BROOKES, Baron (Life Peer UK 1975); Raymond Percival Brookes; s of William Percival Brookes, of W Bromwich; *b* 10 April 1909; *Educ* Kenrick Tech Coll W Bromwich; *m* 1937, Florence Edna, da of Isaac William Sharman; 1 s; *Career* kt 1971, chm and ch exec Guest Keen & Nettlefold Ltd 1965-74, life pres 1975-, dir The Plessey Co Ltd, former memb cncl CBI; *Style* - The Rt Hon The Lord Brookes; Mallards, Stanton, Isle of Man

BROOKES, Beata; MEP (C) N Wales 1979-; *b* 1931; *Educ* U of Wales, Bangor; Alliance Francaise, Paris; *Style* - Miss Beata Brookes, MEP; The Cottage, Wayside Acres, Bodelwyddan, New Rhyl, N Wales

BROOKES, Hon John David; s of Baron Brookes (Life Peer); *b* 22 Sept 1940; *Educ* Malvern, Oriel Oxford; *m* 1970, Faith, da of John Redman, of Bidford on Avon Warwicks; 2 s; *Career* dir Business Dvpt GKN Automotive Components (USA) 1978- (md GKN Transmissions 1974-78); *Recreations* fishing, conflict simulation; *Style* - The Hon John Brookes; 30425 S Greenbriar, Franklin, Mich 48025, USA

(☎ 313 626 7738)

BROOKES, Sir Wilfred Deakin; CBE (1972), DSO (1944), AEA (1945); s of Herbert Brookes; *b* 17 Apr 1906; *Educ* Melbourne G S; Melbourne U; *m* 1928, Betty, nee Heal (d 1968); 1 s; *Career* chm- Electrolytic Refining and Smelting Co of Australia Ltd, Apsonor Pty Ltd, Collins Wales Pty Ltd 1978-; dir of various mining Cos; kt 1979; *Style* - Sir Wilfred Brookes CBE, DSO, AEA; 20 Heyington pla, Toorak, Victoria 3142, Australia (☎ 20 4553)

BROOKS OF TREMORFA, Baron (Life Peer UK 1979); John Edward Brooks; s of Edward Brooks; *b* 12 Apr 1927; *m* 1, 1948 (m dis 1956); 1 s, 1 da; m 2, 1958, Margaret Pringle; 2 s; *Career* parliamentary agent to Rt Hon James Callaghan, MP, 1970 and 1979 gen elections; *Style* - The Rt Hon the Lord Brooks of Tremorfa; 57 Janet st, Slott, Cardiff (☎ 40709)

BROOKS, Hon Mrs - Hon Ann; *née* Fremantle; da of 4 Baron Cottesloe, GBE, TD, by his 1 w, Lady Elizabeth Harris, da of 5 Earl of Malmesbury; *b* 21 Oct 1930; *m* 1951, Timothy Gerald Martin Brooks, JP, s of Hon Herbert Brooks (s of 2 Baron Crawshaw by his w, Mary, da of Sir Michael Hicks Beach, 8 Bt); 3 s, 2 da; *Style* - The Hon Mrs Brooks; Wistow Hall, Leicester (☎ Great Glen 2000)

BROOKS, Charles Attfield; OBE (1959), TD (1946), JP 1946, DL (Essex 1957); s of Charles Norman Brooks JP (d 1925); *b* 8 April 1905; *Educ* Charterhouse, Caius Coll Cambridge; *m* 1932, Rhoda, da of Frank Radcliffe MD, JP (d 1925); 2 s (John, Richard), 2 da (Elizabeth, Carol); *Career* Lt-Col Essex Regt; chm Brooks (Mistley) Ltd (Maltsters, Seedsmen, Animal Food Mfrs, Corn Merchants & Farmers) 1962-71 (dir 1928-); pres Nat Assoc of Corn & Agric Merchants 1952-53, master Worshipful Co of Farmers; *Recreations* gardening, travel, study of John Constable's scenes; *Clubs* Farmers; *Style* - Charles Brooks Esq, OBE, TD, JP, DL; The Lecture House, Dedham, Colchester, Essex (☎ (0206) 323 170)

BROOKS, Douglas; s of Oliver James Brooks (d 1977); *b* 3 Sept 1928; *Educ* Newbridge G S, Univ Coll Cardiff; *m* 1952, June Anne, nee Branch; 1 s, 1 da; *Career* assoc dir Hoover Ltd 1972-78, dir Walker Brooks and Ptnrs 1980-, ch personnel exec Tarmac Ltd 1979-80; *Recreations* talking, cooking, music, gardening; *Clubs* Reform; *Style* - Douglas Brooks Esq; Bull Farm House, Park Lane, Beaconsfield, Bucks (☎ Beaconsfield 5253)

BROOKS, Hon David Gerald; s of 3 Baron Crawshaw (d 1946); hp of bro, 4 Baron; *b* 14 Sept 1934; *Educ* Eton; Royal Agricultural Coll, Cirencester; *m* 1970, Belinda Mary, da of G P H Burgess, of Sandringham, Melbourne, Australia; 1 da; *Style* - The Hon David Brooks; Little Rise, Long Whatton, Loughborough, Leics (☎ Hathern 392)

BROOKS, David Read; *Career* chm and md WGI Ltd; FCA; *Style* - David Brooks Esq; Lloyds House, Alderley rd, Wilmslow, Cheshire

BROOKS, Hon John Patrick; s of 3 Baron Crawshaw (d 1946); *b* 1938; *Educ* Loughborough Coll; *m* 1967, Rosemary Vans Agnew, da of C V A Frank; 1 s, 1 da; *Style* - The Hon John Brooks; 25 Cadogan st, SW3

BROOKS, Hon Mary Altheia; da of 3 Baron Crawshaw (d 1946); *b* 1931; *Style* - The Hon Mary Brooks; Whatton, Nr Loughborough, Leics

BROOKS, Oliver; s of Perry Brooks (d 1978); *b* 22 Jan 1920; *Educ* Wandsworth Commercial Sch; *m* 1944, Lillian, nee Reeve; 1 da; *Career* md P and O Steam Navigation Co Ltd 1979-; dir Burmah Oil 1975-; *Style* - Oliver Brooks Esq; 98 Sandy lane, Cheam, Surrey (☎ 01 642 9915)

BROOKS, William Donald Wykeham; CBE (1956); s of Arthur Brooks, of Maidenhead; *b* 3 Aug 1905; *Educ* Reading Sch, St John's Oxford; *m* 1934, Phyllis, da of Frank Juler, CVO, of Harley st; 2 s, 2 da; *Career* consultant St Mary's and Brompton Hosps 1935-70; *Recreations* gardening, golf, bridge, shooting; *Style* -

William Brooks Esq, CBE; Two Acres, Fryern rd, Storrington, Sussex

BROOKS-BAKER, 'Brookie' (Harold B); s of Charles Silas Brooks Baker (d 1943); *b* 16 Nov 1933; *Educ* Trin Sch (Hartford), Virginia Law Sch; *m* 1963, Comtesse Irène Marie Aude, da of Comte Robert-Elliot du Luart de Montsaulnin (d 1952, of a Maine family ennobled *par charge* 1589; a member of it was cr Marquis by Louis XV 1726) & Elisabeth (da of Edouard, 10 Duc de Bisaccia, cr of Ferdinand II of the Two Sicilies 1851 (also entered in Bavarian nobility by Maximilian II 1855); as the Sicilian Dukedom is transmissible through the female, Natasha and Nadia (*vide infra*) would be in remainder to it; Edouard's f was also 4 Duc de Doudeauville (cr of Charles III of Spain with Grandeeship of the 1 Class 1782, also Dukedom of Louis XVIII of France 1817) and descended from Louis de La Rochefoucauld, yr s of François, cr Comte de La Rochefoucauld 1515 by his godfather François I; Mrs Harold Brooks-Baker is approx 5 cous six or so times removed of the Duc de La Rochefoucauld famous as author of the 'Maxims', *frondeur*, and lover of Mesdames de Chevreuse & de Longueville); 2 da (Natasha, Nadia); *Career* foreign correspondent American Observer 1960-63, V-Pres Securities Management 1963-74; md Debrett's Peerage Ltd 1976-81, jt md 1981-; *Recreations* history, philately, travel; *Clubs* Jockey (Paris), Metropolitan (Washington), Chevy Chase (Maryland), Gibson Island (Maryland); *Style* - H B Brooks-Baker Esq; 1700 H st, Washington DC, USA; 46 Royal Avenue, SW3 (☎ (Fridays) 0962 69067; (other days) 01 730 2342/01 736 6524)

BROOKSBANK, Hon Mrs - Hon Emma Myrtle Mary Anne; *née* Wood; da of Baron Holderness, PC, DL (Life Peer); *b* 1949; *m* 1970, Capt Edward Nicholas Brooksbank, *qv*; *Style* - The Hon Mrs Brooksbank

BROOKSBANK, Edward Nicholas; s and h of Sir William Brooksbank, 2 Bt, TD, JP, DL; *b* 4 Oct 1944; *Educ* Eton; *m* 1970, Hon Emma, da of Baron Holderness, PC, DL; *Career* Capt Blues & Royals *Style* -Edward Brooksbank Esq

BROOKSBANK, Sir Edward William; 2 Bt (UK 1919), TD, JP (E R Yorks 1962), DL (1959); s of Lt-Col Edward York Brooksbank, 2 s of 1 Bt; suc gf, Sir Edward Clitherow Brooksbank, 1 Bt, 1943; *b* 15 June 1915; *Educ* Eton; *m* 1943, Ann, da of Lt-Col Thomas Claud Clitherow, DSO, of Hotham Hall, Brough, Yorkshire; 1 s; *Heir* s, Edward Brooksbank; *Career* Lt-Col Queen's Own Yorkshire Yeo (Hon Col 1963-71); Lord of the Manor of Healaugh; *Style* - Sir Edward Brooksbank, Bt, TD, JP, DL; Menethorpe Hall, Malton, N Yorks

BROOM, Sir Ivor Gordon; KCB (1975, CB 1972), CBE (1969), DSO (1945), DFC and two Bars (1942, 1944 and 1945 respectively), AFC (1956); s of Alfred Broom, of Southport; *b* 2 June 1920; *Educ* W Monmouth Sch, Pontypridd G S; *m* 1942, Jess, da of William Cooper, of Ipswich; 2 s, 1 da; *Career* bomber pilot in WW II, Cmdt Central Flying Sch 1968-70, memb CAA 1974-77, with RAF to 1977; int aerospace consultant 1977-; *Recreations* golf; *Clubs* RAF, Moor Park Golf; *Style* - Sir Ivor Broom, KCB, CBE, DSO, DFC**, AFC; Cherry Lawn, Bridle Lane, Loudwater, Rickmansworth, Herts (☎ 78878)

BROOMAN, John Cresswell; *Career* chm Black and Decker Ltd; *Style* - John Brooman Esq; Black and Decker Ltd, Cannon lane, Maidenhead, Berks

BROOME, Viscountess; Adela Mary Evelyn; da of John Monins, of Ringwould House, Dover; *m* 1916, Viscount Broome (d 1928, s of 2 Earl Kitchener of Khartoum); 2 s (including 3 Earl), 1 da (Lady Kenya Tatton-Brown) *Style* - Viscountess Broome; 56 Elm Park rd, SW3 (☎ 01 352 5468)

BROOME, David; OBE (1970); s of Fred Broome; *b* 1 Mar 1940; *Educ* Monmouth G S; *m* 1976, Elizabeth, nee Fletcher; 1 s; *Career* show jumper and farmer; World Show Jumping Champion 1970; MFH;

Style - David Broome Esq, OBE; Mount Ballan Manor, Crick, Chepstow, Gwent (☎ Caldicot 42077)

BROPHY, Brigid Antonia; *b* 12 June 1929; *Educ* St Paul's Girls' Sch; St Hugh's Coll, Oxford; *m* 1954, Michael Levey; 1 da; *Career* FRSL; author and playwright; *Style* - Miss Brigid Brophy; Flat 3, Old Brompton rd, SW5 (☎ 01 373 9335)

BROTHERTON, Ian Dryhurst; TD (1964), DL (Middx 1964, Gter London 1967); s of Thomas Brotherton, of Hampton, Middx; *b* 16 Nov 1920; *Educ* Hampton Sch, London U; *m* 1943, Margaret, da of Sidney Ponting, of Shepperton; 3 da; *Career* ADC (TAVR) to HM The Queen 1968-73; Col Middx Regt 1939-46; md S Daval & Sons 1968-69, Br American Optical Co 1970-72, Hadley Co 1972-; *Recreations* photography, gardening, yachting (yacht- 'Jimpa'); *Clubs* Army & Navy, Roy Lymington Yacht; *Style* - Ian Dryhurst Esq, TD, DL; 5 Chestnut Walk, Shepperton, Middx (☎ Sunbury 85367)

BROTHERTON, Michael Lewis; MP (C) Louth 1974-; s of Capt John Brotherton; *b* 26 May 1931; *Educ* RNC Dartmouth; *m* 1968, Julia, da of Austin King; 3 s, 1 da; *Career* Lt-Cdr RN to 1964; with Times Newspapers 1967-74; Pres Hyde Pk Tories 1975; *Recreations* cricket, cooking; *Clubs* Carlton; *Style* - Michael Brotherton Esq, MP; The Old Vicarage, Wrangle, Boston, Lincs (☎ 020583 688)

BROUGH, Edward; s of late Hugh Brough; *b* 28 May 1918; *Educ* Berwick G S; Edinburgh U; *m* 1941, Peggy Jennings; 2 s; *Career* chm Adriaan Volker (UK) Ltd 1974-; FBIM 1967-; *Style* - Edward Brough Esq; Far End, The Great Quarry, Guildford, Surrey (☎ 504064); St John's, Chagford, Devon

BROUGHAM, Hon Mrs; da of Baron von Hengervar, late Austro-Hungarian Ambass to US *m* 1 Baron Hengelmüller; m 2, 1923, as his 2 w, Capt Hon Henry Brougham (d 1927), s of 3 Baron Brougham & Vaux *Style* - The Hon Mrs Brougham

BROUGHAM, Hon Charles William; s and h of 5 Baron Brougham and Vaux; *b* 9 Nov 1971; *Style* - The Hon Charles Brougham

BROUGHAM, Hon David Peter; s of 4 Baron Brougham and Vaux (d 1967); *b* 1940; *Educ* Sedbergh; *m* 1, 1969 (m dis 1976), Moussie, da of Mrs Marianne Hallstrom of Stockholm; 1 s; m 2, 1977, Caroline Dixon; 1 s; *Style* - The Hon David Brougham; 85 Addison rd, W 14

BROUGHAM, Hon Henrietta Louise; da of 5 Baron Brougham and Vaux; *b* 1965

BROUGHAM AND VAUX, 5 Baron (UK 1860); Michael John Brougham; s of 4 Baron (d 1967, ggn of Henry Brougham, 1 Baron (full title *Brougham and Vaux of Brougham and of Highhead Castle*), the polymath (but principally lawyer) who defended George IV's Queen Caroline in her trial 1820; he also much busied himself in the Diffusion of Useful Knowledge (of the Society for which he was founder, being much ridiculed for it in Peacock's 'Crotchet Castle') and the abolition of slavery and trade therein; the brougham carriage is named after him) by his 2 w, Jean, da of late Brig-Gen Gilbert Follett, DSO, MVO, and Lady Mildred, nee Murray (da of 7 Earl of Dunmore, DL, by his w, Lady Gertrude Coke, 3 da of 2 Earl of Leicester, KG); *b* 2 Aug 1938; *Educ* Lycée Jaccard Lausanne, Millfield, Northampton Inst of Ag; *m* 1, 1963 (m dis 1967), Olivia, da of Rear-Adm Gordon Seccombe Gray, DSC, of Midhurst; 1 da; m 2, 1969, Catherine, da of William Gulliver; 1 s; *Heir* s, Hon Charles Brougham; *Career* sr mkting exec and co dir; *Recreations* rugger, tennis, photography; *Clubs* Turf; *Style* - The Rt Hon Lord Brougham and Vaux; c/o Lloyds Bank Ltd, 84 Park Lane, London W1

BROUGHAM AND VAUX, Edith, Baroness; Edith Ellaline; da of Leonard Teichman; *m* 1, Richard Hart-Davis; m 2, 1942, as his 3 w, 4 Baron Brougham and Vaux (d 1967); *Style* - The Rt Hon Edith, Lady Brougham and Vaux

BROUGHSHANE, 2 Baron (UK 1945); Patrick Owen Alexander Davison; s of

1 Baron, KBE (d 1953), by his 1 w, Beatrice, da of Sir Owen Roberts, DL; *b* 18 June 1903; *Educ* Winchester, Magdalen Oxford; *m* 1929, Bettine, da of late Sir Arthur Russell, 6 Bt; 1 s; *Heir* s, Hon Alexander Davison; *Career* barr 1926, Irish Gds 1939-42, Assist Sec (Mil) War Cabinet 1942-45; American Legion of Merit; *Style* - The Rt Hon The Lord Broughshane; 21 Eaton sq, SW1 (☎ 01 235 4663); 28 Fisher st, Sandwich, Kent

BROUGHTON, Hon Charles Leander; s of 3 Baron Fairhaven, JP; *b* 1973

BROUGHTON, Hon Diana Cara; da of 3 Baron Fairhaven JP; *b* 1961 *Style* - The Hon Diana Broughton

BROUGHTON, David Delves; s of Lt-Cdr Peter John Delves Broughton, RN (d 1963); hp to Btcy of kinsman, Sir Evelyn Delves Broughton 12 Bt; *b* 7 May 1942; *Style* - David Broughton Esq

BROUGHTON, Sir Evelyn Delves; 12 Bt (E 1660), of Broughton, Staffs; s of Sir John Delves Broughton, 11 Bt (d 1942); *b* 2 Oct 1915; *Educ* Eton, Trin Cambridge; *m* 1, 1947, Hon Elizabeth Cholmondeley (m dis 1953), da of 4 Baron Delamere, JP, by his 1 w, Phyllis (da of late Lord George Montagu-Douglas-Scott, OBE, 3 s of 6 Duke of Buccleuch, KG, KT, PC); m 2, 1955 (m dis 1974), Helen, da of J Shore, of Wilmslow; 3 da (and 1 s decd); m 3, 1974, Rona, da of E Clifford Johns, of Wargrave, and previously w of -- Crammond; *Heir* kinsman, David Delves Broughton; *Career* farmer and landowner for 37 years; former 2 Lt Irish Gds; *Recreations* shooting, travel; *Clubs* Brooks's; *Style* - Sir Evelyn Delves Broughton, Bt; 37 Kensington sq, W8 (☎ 01 937 8883); Doddington Park, Nantwich, Cheshire

BROUGHTON, Hon Huttleston Rupert; s of 3 Baron Fairhaven, JP; *b* 1970

BROUGHTON, Hon Henry Robert; s of 3 Baron Fairhaven, JP; *b* 1978

BROUGHTON, Lady - Joyce; da of late H S Denton, of Leeds; *m* 1923, as his 2 w, Sir Alfred Broughton, MP (d 1979); *Style* - Lady Broughton; Stockwell Shaw Farm, Batley, W Yorks (☎ 4321)

BROUGHTON, Hon James Henry Ailwyn; s & h of 3 Baron Fairhaven; *b* 25 May 1963 *Style* - Hon James Broughton

BROUGHTON, Hon Melanie Frances; da of 3 Baron Fairhaven, JP; *b* 1966

BROUN, Lady - Georgie; da of late Henry Law, of NSW; *m* 1925, Sir (James) Lionel Broun, 11 Bt (d 1962); *Style* - Lady Broun; Colstoun, Gunnedah, Pottinger, NSW, Australia

BROUN, Sir Lionel John Law; 12 Bt (NS 1686), of Colstoun, Haddingtonshire; s of Sir Lionel Broun, 11 Bt (d 1962, gn of Sir Richard Broun, 8 Bt, who before succeeding demanded to be knighted as a Bt's eldest s; on being refused he dubbed himself *eques auratus*; he was allegedly the model for Sir Vavasour Firebrace in Disraeli's 'Sybil', where his supposed ideas on the Baronetage as institution are quoted- 'Picture us for a moment, to yourself, going down in procession to Westminster, for example, to hold a chapter. Five or six hundred baronets in dark green costume, - the appropriate dress of *equites aurati*; each not only with his badge, but with his collar of SS; belted and scarfed; his star glittering; his pennon flying; his hat white, with a plume of white feathers; of course the sword and the gilt spurs. In our hand,the thumb-ring and signet not forgotten, we hold our coronet of two balls.' After having the Barony of Bardolf called out of abeyance in his favour, this 'former champion of the Baronetage...never mentioned the order'); *b* 25 April 1927 *Heir* see below *Style* - Sir Lionel Broun, Bt; 89 Penshurst st, Willoughby, NSW 2068, Australia

BROUN, William Windsor; s of William Arthur Broun (d 1925); hp to Btcy of kinsman, Sir Lionel Broun, 12 Bt; *b* 1917; *m* 1952, D'Hrie, da of Frank King, of Bingara, NSW; 2 da; *Style* - William Broun Esq; 23 Clanalpine st, Mosman, NSW, Australia

BROWN, Baron (Life Peer UK 1964); Wilfred Banks Duncan Brown; MBE (1944), PC (1970); s of late Peter Brown, of Greenock; *b* 29 Nov 1908; *Educ* Rossall; *m*

1, 1935, Barbara (d 1937), da of Cuyler Findlay; m 2, 1939, Marjorie Hershell, da of J H Skinner, of Ealing; 3 s; *Career* chm Glacier Metal Co 1939-65, formerly dir Associated Engineering Ltd, Min of State Bd of Trade 1965-70; *Style* - The Rt Hon The Lord Brown, MBE, PC; 9 Blenheim rd, NW8 (☎ 01 624 1446)

BROWN, A; JP; *Career* assist gen man, Anglia Hastings and Thanet Building Society; *Style* - A Brown Esq, JP; Moulton Park, Northampton

BROWN, Hon Mrs - Hon Alison de Bois; da of 2 Baron Clwyd, JP; *b* 1939; *m* 1 1965, George Stricevic (m dis 1972); 1 s; m 2, 1972, Anthony H Brown; 2 s; *Style* - The Hon Mrs Brown; 9 Royal terrace, Glasgow G3 7NT

BROWN, Anthony Cecil; *Career* chm and man dir Spirax-Sacro Engrg Ltd; AGGI, FCIBS; *Style* - Anthony Brown Esq; 130-132 St Georges rd, Cheltenham, Glos

BROWN, Brig Athol Earle; CMG (1964), OBE (1956); s of late W J C Brown of NSW Australia; *b* 2 Jan 1905; *Educ* Armidale Sch, Roy Australian Naval Coll, Sydney U; *m* 1928, Millicent Alice, da of late HM Heesh of Sydney; 2 s, 1 da; *Career* WW II Roy Australian Artillery, Lt-Col 1944, Brig 1946, sec-gen Commonwealth War Graves Cmmn (Pacific Regn) 1960-69,sec-gen British Commonwealth-Japanese Jt Ctee 1957-69; *Clubs* RAC; *Style* - Brig Athol Brown, CMG, OBE; 351 Belmore rd, N Balwyn, Victoria 3104, Australia (☎ 857 7544)

BROWN, Hon Angus John Duncan; s of Baron Brown, PC, MBE (Life Peer); *b* 13 Jan 1951; *Educ* Bryanston Sch; *m* 1974, Polonca, da of Janez Baloh, of Ljubljana; *Style* - The Hon Angus Brown; Flat 13, 23 Prince Albert rd, NW1

BROWN, Arnold Kingsmill; MBE (Mil 1945); s of Douglas Brown; *b* 16 Nov 1905; *Educ* Marlborough; *m* 1, 1932, Doris, da of Cyril Attenborough, of Harrow Weald; 1 s, 1 da; m 2, 1946, Nina, da of Frank Randell, of Shamley Green; m 3, 1968, Marianne, da of Pastor Peter Bang; 1 da; *Career* London Discount Mkt 1924-65, chm Ryders Discount Co 1958-60; dep chm Cater Ryder & Co 1960-65; farmer 1946-; *Recreations* cricket, hockey, squash, golf; *Clubs* Norfolk (Norwich); *Style* - Arnold Brown Esq, MBE; Ash Tree Farm, Attlebridge, Norwich (☎ 860222)

BROWN, Alan Thomas; CBE (1978), DL (Oxon 1978); s of Thomas Brown, of Cromer; *b* 18 April 1928; *Educ* Wyggeston G S, Leicester; Sidney Sussex Cambridge; *m* 1962, Marie, da of Hubert York East, late of Blackburn; 2 da; *Career* ch exec Oxon CC 1973-; *Recreations* reading, chess, cliff walking; *Clubs* Nat Liberal; *Style* - Alan Brown Esq, CBE, DL; 7 Field House dve, Oxford

BROWN, Lt-Col Sir Charles Frederick Richmond; 4 Bt (UK 1863), TD, DL (N R Yorks 1962); s of late Frederick Richmond Brown, 2 s of 2 Bt; suc unc, Sir Melville Richmond Brown, 3 Bt, 1944; *b* 6 Dec 1902; *Educ* Eton; *m* 1, 1933 (m dis 1948), Audrey, da of late Brig-Gen Hon Everard Baring CVO CBE (3 s of 1 Baron Revelstoke); 1 s, 2 da; m 2, 1951 (m dis 1968), Hon Gwendolen Meysey-Thompson, da of 1 Baron Knaresborough; m 3, 1969, Pauline Emily Gwyneth Mansel, da of late Arden Llewelyn Morgan, and widow of Edward Westgarth Hildyard, FSA, FRES, of Middleton Hall, Pickering, Yorks; *Heir* s, George Brown; *Career* Capt (ret) Welsh Gds, and Lt-Col Cmdg 7 Bn Green Howards (TA); *Style* - Lt-Col Sir Charles Brown, Bt, TD, DL; Stonely Woods, Fadmoor, York

BROWN, Charles Michael; s of Richard Brown, of Minchinhampton Glos; *b* 11 June 1930; *Educ* Clifton; *m* 1, 1954, Sonia, da of Harvey Valency Schwalm; 3 s, 1 da; m 2, 1977, Pauline, da of John Robinson, of Allanton Berwicks (d 1981); *Career* FCA 1959; chm Butterley Co 1968- and Vinten Gp 1975-; md West of England Sack Hldgs 1968-; *Recreations* shooting, flying; *Style* - Charles Brown Esq; The Old Forge, Risby, Bury St Edmunds, Suffolk (☎ 0284 810197); Fort Fredrick, Port Royal, Roatan Island, Honduras

BROWN, David John Bowes; s of Matthew Brown (d 1977); *b* 2 Aug 1925; *Educ* King James Sch Knaresborough, Leeds Coll of Technology; *m* 1954, Patricia; 2 s, 2 da (and 1 s, 1 da by prev m); *Career* md DJB Engineering Ltd & Archer components Ltd; *Style* - David Brown Esq; The Abbey, Knaresborough, N Yorks (☎ 0423 863148); Brentwood, Castle Eden, Co Durham (☎ 0429 81408)

BROWN, Hon Mrs; Hon Edna; da of 1 & last Baron Lawson (d 1965); *b* 1912; *m* D Brown; 1 s *Style* - The Hon Mrs Brown

BROWN, Hon George Arthur; CMG; s of Samuel Brown; *b* 25 July 1922; *Educ* in Jamaica and LSE; *m* 1964, Leila Gill; 2 da (and 1 s, 1 da by prev m); *Career* dep administrator UN Devpt Programme 1978 *Style* - The Hon George Brown CMG; c/o UN Development Programme, UN, New York, NY 10017,

BROWN, Hon Lady - Hon Gwendolen Carlis Meysey-Thompson; da of 1 and last Baron Knaresborough (d 1929); *b* 1903; *m* 1951, as his 2 w, Lt-Col Sir Charles Frederick Richmond Brown, 4 Bt (m dis 1968); *Career* a lady in waiting to HRH Duchess of Gloucester 1938-45; *Style* - The Hon Lady Brown; Estate Office House, Birdsall, Malton, N Yorks

BROWN, George Francis Richmond ; s and h of Sir Charles Brown, 4 Bt; *b* 3 Feb 1938; *Career* Lt Welsh Guards, Extra Equerry to HRH Duke of Edinburgh 1961-63, ADC to Gov of Queensland 1963-5; *Style* - George Brown Esq

BROWN, George Frederick William; CMG (1974); s of late G Brown; *b* 12 April 1908; *Educ* Phahran Technical Coll, Royal Melbourne Inst of Technology; *m* 1933, Catherine Mills, 1 da (and 1 da decd); *Career* memb Melbourne Underground Railway Loop Authority 1971-; *Style* - George F W Brown Esq, CMG; Unit 1, 10 Lucas st, East Brighton, Victoria 3187, Australia

BROWN, Hon Mrs - Hon Gweneth Mary; da of 1 and last Baron Williams (d 1966); *b* 1927; *m* 1, 1947, Hugh Sharp Eadie (m dis 1958); 1 s, 1 da; m 2, 1961, Donald Brown; *Style* - The Hon Mrs Brown; 39 Blenheim gdns, Aveley, S Ockendon, Essex

BROWN, Harold Arthur Neville; CMG (1963), CVO (1961); s of Stanley Brown, of Penarth; *b* 13 Dec 1914; *Educ* Cardiff H S, U Coll Cardiff; *m* 1939, Mary, da of Alan Urquhart; 1 s, 1 da; *Career* Foreign Serv ret; Min Cape Town/Pretoria 1973-74; *Style* - Harold Brown Esq, CMG, CVO; 14 Embassy Court, King's rd, Brighton, Sussex (☎ 0273 734623)

BROWN, Hon Mrs (Helen Jean); da of Baron Todd, OM; *b* 13 July 1941; *Educ* Perse Sch for Girls Cambridge, Westonbirt, Somerville Oxford; *m* 1963, Philip Brown; 2 s, 1 da ; *Style* - The Hon Mrs Brown; 124 Edge Hill, Darras Hall, Pontiland, Newcastle-upon-Tyne (☎ 4533)

BROWN, Jack; JP (Manchester 1967); s of Maurice Brown; *b* 10 Nov 1929; *Educ* Primary and Secondary Sch in Leigh, Lancs; *m* 1952, Alice Brown; 1 s; *Career* gen sec Amalgamated Textile Workers Union 1976-; *Style* - Jack Brown Esq, JP; 11 Thomas st, Atherton, Manchester, M29 9DP (☎ 870218)

BROWN, James; s of Alexander Brown, of Edinburgh; *b* 15 Oct 1925; *Educ* Leith Acad, Broughton Sch Edinburgh; *m* 1948, Elsie, da of Charles Paterson, of Grantham; 1 s, 2 da; *Career* md Br Fuel Co 1966-; dir- AHH Ltd, Allied Coal & Shipping, David G Allan & Co, McGruther & Marshall, Smith Hood & Co, Walker Muir Hldgs, Castlefield Oil, Walter Whiteman (Kenilworth), Ernest J Henry Ltd, Kinnell de Putron Ltd, Smith Parkinson & Cole, Grimsby Express Packet Co, Manor Hardware, Watts Bros (Beverley), R Dennison & Sons, Arkwright Glass Works, Fred W Davies (Midlands), K & M Hauliers, W S Lewitt & Son, J R Mitchell & Co, Parsons Bros & Snape, Singleton Flint & Co, A Suthrell Haulage, Clayton Chambers Ltd, Br Holland Fuel Co, Sandermans T'port Belgium, TSC Hldgs, Br Anthracite Sales, Castleton Oil Swansea, Colman Pipework Supplies, P H Coward & Sons, Sir James German & Son, J Rees-Jones & Co, Daniel Roberts

(Llanelly), Williams Bros (Cross Hands), Henry Nicholls Ltd, Banbury Glass Co; *Recreations* golf, swimming, church, Gideons International; *Clubs* RAC, Southcliffe Golf (Lincoln); *Style* - James Brown Esq; 4 Grange Close, Canwick, Lincoln (☎ 0522 25622)

BROWN, John Granger; s of Frank Brown, of Birkenhead; *b* 24 Nov 1939; *Educ* Birkenhead Sch, Birmingham U; *m* 1964, Averil, da of Arthur Jones, of Norwich; 2 da; *Career* CA; fin dir/sec Bernard Matthews Ltd 1977-; *Recreations* squash, cricket, golf, bridge; *Style* - John Brown Esq; 4 The Glade, Old Costessey, Norwich (☎ 0603 744477)

BROWN, Sir John Gilbert Newton; CBE (1966); s of John Brown, of Milton Lodge, Gt Milton, Oxford; *b* 16 July 1916; *Educ* Lancing, Hertford Oxford; *m* 1946, Helen, da of Darcy Braddell, of Holland Pk W11; 1 s, 2 da; *Career* publisher OUP 1956-80; chm B H Blackwell 1980-; kt 1974; *Clubs* Garrick; *Style* - Sir John Brown, CBE; 8 Lansdowne rd, W11 (☎ 01 727 7987); Milton Lodge, Milton, Oxford (☎ 08446 217)

BROWN, Joseph Lawler; CBE (1977), TD (1953), DL (W Midlands 1975); s of Neil Brown, of Peebles; *b* 22 March 1921; *Educ* Peebles, Heriot-Watt Coll Edinburgh; *m* 1950, Mabel, da of Alderman Pearson Smith, BEM; 1 s, 1 da; *Career* dir BPM Hldgs 1971-, Reuters 1972-75; Pres Newspaper Soc 1976-77; chm & md Birmingham Post and Mail 1971-77; *Recreations* trout fishing, Japanese woodcuts; *Style* - Joseph Brown Esq, CBE, TD, DL; 37 Mearse Lane, Barnt Green, Birmingham B45 8HH (☎ 021 445 1234)

BROWN, Hon Mrs (Jennifer Mary); *née* Bethell; da of 2 Baron Bethell (d 1965); *b* 26 Aug 1930; *Educ* St Mary's Convent Ascot; *m* 1954, Edward Peter Moncrieff Brown (sr ptnr Simon & Coates stockbrokers); 4 s; *Style* - The Hon Mrs Brown; Wotton, Grove Lane, Petworth, Sussex (☎ 43146)

BROWN, Jack Reginald Valentine; s of Reginald Brown; *b* 14 Feb 1922; *Educ* Taunton Sch; *m* 1945, Margaret, nee Mustard; 2 s, 1 da; *Career* slr, now sec and slr Stone-Platt Industs Ltd; *Recreations* golf; *Clubs* Frinton-on-Sea Golf, RAF; *Style* - Jack Brown Esq; 4 Inner Court, 48 Old Church st, SW3

BROWN, Kenneth Edward Lindsay; s of Col Thomas Pyne Brown, OBE; *b* 17 Oct 1940; *Educ* Sherborne; *m* 1968, Mary, da of Thomas Forrester; 2 s; *Career* FCA; chm A R Brown McFarlane & Co; *Recreations* sailing, skiing; *Clubs* Roy Ocean Racing; *Style* - Kenneth Brown Esq; 65 St Andrews dve, Glasgow G41 (☎ 041 423 8381)

BROWN, Leslie; s of late WH Brown and late Eliza J Fiveash; *b* 20 Oct 1902; *Educ* Selhurst GS; *m* 1930, Frances, nee Lever; 2 s, 1 da; *Career* dir, Prudential Assurance Co Ltd 1965-77 (chm 1970-74); *Style* - Leslie Brown Esq; 12 Park View, Christchurch rd, Purley, Surrey

BROWN, Mervyn; CMG (1975), OBE (1963); s of William Brown; *b* 24 Sept 1923; *Educ* Ryhope G S Sunderland, St John's Oxford; *m* 1949, Elizabeth, da of Harry Gittings; *Career* Foreign Serv 1949-; High Cmmr Nigeria 1979-; *Recreations* music, tennis, history; *Clubs* Roy C'wlth Soc, Hurlingham; *Style* - Mervyn Brown Esq, CMG, OBE; 3 Queen's dve, Ikuyi, Lagos, Nigeria; c/o FCO, SW1

BROWN, Hon Michael Colin Duncan; s of Baron Brown, MBE, PC (Life Peer); *b* 11 July 1944; *Educ* Bryanston Sch and Architectural Association; *m* 1970, Fenella, da of Peter Barnard, of Dorking; *Style* - The Hon Michael Brown; 23 Leighton cres, Kentish Town, NW1 (☎ 01 485 2071)

BROWN, Hon Mrs (Marjorie Elizabeth); da of 2 Baron Palmer (d 1950); *b* 1910; *m* 1945, Frederick Richard Brown, MBE; 3 s, 1 da; *Style* - The Hon Mrs Brown; Kintore, Newton Green, Sudbury, Suffolk

BROWN, Hon (Marjorie Elizabeth); *née* Palmer; da of 2 Baron Palmer (d 1950); *b* 24 April 1910; *m* 1945, Frederick, s of Roger Grounds Brown; 3 s, 1 da; *Style* -

The Hon Mrs Brown; Kintore, Rectory Lane, Newton Green, Sudbury, Suffolk

BROWN, Lady Margaret Nicola; *née* Sinclair; da of 19 Earl of Caithness, CVO, CBE, DSO, JP (d 1956); *b* 1937; *m* 1959, Capt David Brown; 2 da; *Style* - Lady Margaret Brown; 38 Settrington rd, SW6

BROWN, Sir (Cyril) Max(well) Palmer; KCB (1969, CB 1965), CMG (1957); s of Cyril Brown, of New Zealand; *b* 30 June 1914; *Educ* Wanganui Collegiate Sch, Victoria U NZ, Clare Cambridge; *m* 1940, Margaret, da of Edward Gillhespy; 3 s, 1 da; *Career* 2 Perm Sec BOT 1968-70, DTI 1970-74; dir John Brown & Co, Ransome Hoffman Pollard, Era Technology Ltd (all 1975-); dep chm Monopolies & Mergers Commission 1976-; *Style* - Sir Max Brown, KCB, CMG; 20 Cottenham Pk rd, SW20 (☎ 01 946 7237)

BROWN, Michael Russell; s of Frederick Brown; *b* 3 July 1951; *Educ* Littlehampton, York U; *Career* MP(C) Brigg and Scunthorpe from 1979; *Style* - Michael Brown, Esq, MP; House of Commons, SWI

BROWN, Ron; s of James Brown; *b* 1940; *Educ* Edinburgh; *m* 1963, May Smart; 2 s; *Career* MP (L) Edinburgh, Leith from 1979; *Style* - Ron Brown Esq, MP; House of Commons, SWI

BROWN, Hon Richard Banks Duncan; s of Baron Brown, MBE (Life Peer); *b* 31 May 1942; *Educ* Bryanston Sch, Brunel Coll; *m* 1968, Gillian Mary, da of John Kennedy Carter; 1 da; *Style* - The Hon Richard Brown; 30 Mount ave, Ealing W5 (☎ 01 997 3759)

BROWN, Sir Raymond Frederick; OBE (1966); s of Frederick Brown; *b* 19 July 1920; *Educ* Morden Terr LCC Sch, SE London Tech, Morley Coll; *m* 1, 1942 (m dis 1949), Evelyn Jennings; 1 da; m 2, 1953, Carol, da of H Sprinks, of Paris; 2 s, 1 da; *Career* jt founder Racal Electronics 1950 (chm, md and Pres 1950-66); chm Racecourse Tech Servs 1970-, indust advr to NEDC 1976-; dir Nat Westminster Bank Outer London Region 1978-; kt 1964; *Recreations* polo, farming, shooting, golf; *Clubs* Sunningdale Golf, Guards Polo, Swinley Forest Golf, City Livery, Travellers' (Canada, Australia), Ends of the Earth; *Style* - Sir Raymond Brown, OBE; Westcroft Park, Windlesham rd, Chobham, Surrey (☎ 09905 7758)

BROWN, Hon Mr Justice; Hon Sir Stephen; s of Wilfrid Brown, of Staffs; *b* 3 Oct 1924; *Educ* Malvern, Queens' Cambridge; *m* 1951, Patricia, da of Richard Good; 2 s, 3 da; *Career* barr; High Court Judge 1975-; kt 1975; *Recreations* sailing; *Clubs* Garrick, Naval; *Style* - The Hon Mr Justice Brown; 3 King's Bench Walk, Temple, EC4; 78 Hamilton av, Harborne, Birmingham B17 8AR (☎ 021 427 1313)

BROWN, Air Cdre Sir Vernon Sydney; CB (1944), OBE (1937); s of Ernest Brown, of Blackheath; *b* 10 Jan 1889; *Educ* Eastbourne Coll, Jesus Cambridge; *m* 1, 1914, Constance (d 1967), da of E Duckham, of Blackheath; 1 da; m 2, 1971, Sheila, da of T Rigby, of Effingham; *Career* ch insp Accidents Air Miny 1937-46, Min Civil Aviation 1946-52; dir Gravinor (Fire Protection), Gravatom Ltd of Gosport; kt 1952; *Recreations* hockey, cricket; *Clubs* United Serv, Roy Aero, Naval & Military; *Style* - Air Cdre Sir Vernon Brown, CB, OBE; Eastholme, Station rd, Yarmouth, IOW (☎ 0983 760189)

BROWN, William;CBE (1971); s of Robert Brown; *b* 24 June 1929; *Educ* Ayr Acad, Edinburgh U; *m* 1955, Nancy, nee Hunter, of Edmonton, Alberta; 1 s, 3 da; *Career* dir Ind Television Publications Ltd 1968- (md from 1966), dep chm Scottish Television Ltd, 1974; *Style* - William Brown Esq, CBE; 90 Drymen rd, Bearsden, Glasgow (☎ 041 942 0115)

BROWN, William Anthony Bartlett; *Career* chm and md Rose Forgrove Ltd; CEng, FIMech E, FBIM; *Style* - William Brown Esq; Seacroft, Leeds, W Yorks

BROWN, William Ernest; s of William Brown (d 1941); *b* 9 Dec 1923; *Educ* Christ's Hospital and Grocers' Company Sch ; *m* 1950, Catherine, nee McColgan; 1 s, 1 da ; *Career* md E G Cornelius and Co

Ltd, dir Cornelius Chemical Co Ltd; *Style* - William Brown Esq; 8 Elm Grove, Hornchurch, Essex

BROWN, William Paterson; s of William Brown, of Cambuslang; *b* 18 March 1948; *Educ* Lenzie Acad, Glasgow U; *m* 1948, Nancy, da of William Palmer, of Cambuslang; 1 s, 1 da; *Career* dir Thomas Meadows UK Hldgs and subsids; *Recreations* golf, reading; *Clubs* RAF, Directors'; *Style* - William Brown Esq; 38 Cuckoo Hill rd, Pinner, Middx (☎ 01 866 8973)

BROWN, William Michael; *Career* jt md Thomson British Holdings; *Style* - William Brown Esq; 4 Stratford pl, W1

BROWNE, Maj Alexander Simon Cadogan; JP (Northumberland 1946), DL (1961); s of Alexander Browne, of Callaly Castle, Alnwick; *b* 22 July 1895; *Educ* Eton, Sandhurst; *m* 1918, Dorothy, da of Maj Francis Howard, 8 Roy Hussars; 1 da (and 1 da decd); *Career* served in BEF 1915-18 and 1940 and Br Liberation Army 1945; Hon County Alderman Northumberland 1974, High Sheriff 1958; Sec Duke of Beaufort's Foxhounds 1928-38, Jt-Master Percy Foxhounds 1938-46, chm Rothbury RDC 1950-55, Pres Berwick-on-Tweed Con Assoc 1970-78; *Clubs* Cavalry, Northern Counties (Newcastle); *Style* - Maj Alexander Browne, JP, DL; Callaly Castle, Alnwick, Northumberland (☎ 0665 4663)

BROWNE, Coral Edith; *née* Browne; da of Leslie Browne; *b* 23 July 1913; *Educ* Claremont Ladies' Coll Melbourne; *m* 1, 1950, Philip Westrope Pearman (d 1964); m 2, 1974, Vincent Price; ; *Career* actress; *Style* - Miss Coral Browne; 16 Eaton Pl, SW1

BROWNE, Hon Dominick Geoffrey Thomas; s and h of 4 Baron Oranmore and Browne; *b* 1 July 1929; *m* 1957 (m dis 1974), Sara Margaret, da of late Dr Herbert Wright, of 59 Merrion sq, Dublin; *Style* - The Hon Dominick Browne; Leckenagh, Burtonport, Letterkenny, Co Donegal

BROWNE, Donald John Woodthorpe; JP (1977); s of Harold Browne; *b* 1 Dec 1924; *Educ* Dulwich, Hertford Oxford; *m* 1965, Dinah, da of Arthur Gurling, MC, of London W1; 1 s, 2 da; *Career* Sub-Lt RNVR; chm Hays Oils & Chemicals and Assoc Cos 1980-; *Recreations* penal matters, country living; *Clubs* Western, Ulster; *Style* - Donald Browne Esq, JP; Watch Hill, Reagh Island, Comber, Co Down, N Ireland (☎ 0238 541585)

BROWNE, Lady Enid Doreen Grace; da of Hon Evelyn Scudamore-Stanhope (d 1925) and gda of 9 Earl of Chesterfield ; *b* 25 Jan 1899; *m* 1926, as his 2 w, Maj Alexander Browne (d 1961); 1 s; *Career* raised to the rank of an Earl's da 1938; *Style* - Lady Enid Browne; c/o Barclay's Bank, 36 Curzon St , W1

BROWNE, Lady Ulick - Fiona; *née* Glenn; *m* 1962, as his 2 w, Lord Ulick Browne, s of late Lt-Col Lord Alfred Eden Browne, DSO, s of 5 Marquess of Sligo, who was raised to the rank of a Marquess' son (1953) and who d 1980; 1 s, 1 da,; *Style* - Lady Ulick Browne; 32 The Little Boltons, SW10

BROWNE, Hon Geoffrey Charles Myles; s of 3 Baron Oranmore and Browne, KP, PC, (d 1927); *b* 1912; *Educ* Eton, CCC Cambridge, Trin Coll Dublin; *m* 1946, Kathleen Mary (m dis 1959), da of late Arland Ussher, of Eastwell, Co Galway; *Style* - The Hon Geoffrey Browne; 72 Fellows rd, NW3

BROWNE, Hon Garech Domnagh; s of 4 Baron Oranmore and Browne; *b* 25 June 1939; *Educ* Castle Park (Dublin) and Le Rosey (Switzerland); *Style* - The Hon Garech Browne; Woodtown Manor, Rathfarnham, Dublin 14 (☎ 804855); Luggala, Rundwood, Co Wicklow, Eire

BROWNE, Sir (Edward) Humphrey; CBE (1952); s of James Browne; *b* 7 April 1911; *Educ* Repton, Magdalene Cambridge; *m* 1934, Barbara, da of Thomas Stone, of Liverpool (High Sheriff Lancs 1935); 2 s; *Career* kt 1964; chm Br T'port Docks Bd 1971-, John Thompson Ltd, Woodall Duckham Ltd, Bestobel Ltd 1967-79; *Recreations* shooting, fishing, music; *Clubs* Brooks's; *Style* - Sir

Humphrey Browne, CBE; Beckbury Hall, Shifnal, Salop (☎ Ryton 207); 71 Chiltern Court, Baker st, NW1 (☎ 01 935 8958)

BROWNE, Hablot Robert Edgar; CMG (1955), OBE (1942); s of Hablot John Moxon Browne (gs of the Victorian illustrator Hablot Browne, better known as 'Phiz', whose pictures in Dickens's novels are for many virtually inseparable from the characters in the books themselves); *b* 11 Aug 1905; *Educ* St George's Harpenden, Christ's Cambridge; *m* 1933, Petra; 1 da; *Career* Colonial Serv Nigeria 1928 & 1951-55; CRO 1959-68; *Recreations* watching cricket; *Clubs* Travellers', MCC; *Style* - Hablot Browne Esq, CMG, OBE; 85 Bishops Mans, Bishops Pk rd, SW6 (☎ 01 731 3209)

BROWNE, John Ernest Douglas de la Valette; MP (C) Winchester 1979-; s of Col Ernest Coigny de la Valette Browne, OBE; *b* 17 Oct 1938; *Educ* Malvern, Sandhurst, Cranfield Inst of Technol, Harvard Business Sch; *m* 1965, Elizabeth Garthwaite; *Career* advsr Barclays bank 1978-, man dir Falcon Rose Ltd 1978-; *Recreations* riding, sailing, skiing, shooting, squash; *Clubs* Boodle's, Turf; *Style* - John Browne Esq, MP; House of Commons, SW1

BROWNE, Hon John Nixon; s (by 1 m) of Baron Craigton (Life Peer), CBE, PC, *qv*; *b* 1937; *Educ* Kelvinside Acad; *m* 1964 (m dis 1978), Mrs Jean Athalie van Blommenstein, da of late Eben Alec Hendry; 1 da; *Career* TV producer; *Style* - The Hon John Browne; RR1, Terra Cotta, Ontario, Canada

BROWNE, Lady Karen Lavinia; da of Earl of Altamont; *b* 1964

BROWNE, Lady Lucinda Jane; da of Earl of Altamont; *b* 18 May 1969

BROWNE, Hon Martin Michael Dominick; s of 4 Baron Oranmore and Browne by his 1 w, Mildred (da of Hon Thomas Egerton, s of 3 Earl of Ellesmere, JP, DL; the 3 Earl of Ellesmere was ggs of 1 Duke of Sutherland, KG, PC); *b* 27 Oct 1931; *Educ* Eton; *m* 1958, Alison, nee Bradford; 1 s, 1 da; *Career* stockbroker; *Clubs* White's; *Style* - The Hon Martin Browne; Berghane Hall, Castle Camps, Cambridge CB2 6TN

BROWNE, Hon Mrs - Noreen Anne; da of Sean MacSherry, of Co Down; *m* 1963, Hon Tara Browne (d 1966), s of 4 Baron Oranmore and Browne; 2 s; *Style* - The Hon Mrs Tara Browne; 19 Eaton Row, SW1

BROWNE, Peter Kilmaine; s of Noel Francis Howe Browne (d 1943), and hp of 7 Baron Kilmaine; *b* 1920; *m* 1948, Grace Dorothy Robson, of Nakuru, Kenya; 2 da; *Style* - Peter Browne Esq; Morningside Farm, P O Box 692, Rustenburg, Transvaal

BROWNE, Lady Sheelyn Felicity; da of Earl of Altamont; *b* 1 June 1963

BROWNE, Sheila Jeanne; CB (1977); da of Edward Browne; *b* 25 Dec 1924; *Educ* Lady Margaret Hall Oxford, Ecole des Chartes Paris; *Career* Senr Ch Inspector, DES, 1974-; *Style* - Miss Sheila Browne, CB; 9 Rossmore Court, Park rd, NW1 (☎ 01 402 9931)

BROWNE-WILKINSON, Hon Mr Justice; Hon Sir Nicolas Christopher Henry Browne-Wilkinson; s of Canon Arthur Browne-Wilkinson; *b* 30 March 1930; *Educ* Lancing, Magdalen Oxford; *m* 1955, Ursula, da of Cedric de Lacy Bacon; 3 s, 2 da; *Career* QC 1972; Judge of Court of Appeal Jersey & Guernsey 1976-77, High Court Judge (Chancery) 1977; kt 1977; *Recreations* gardening, music; *Style* - Hon Mr Justice Browne-Wilkinson; Royal Courts of Justice, The Strand, WC2

BROWNING, Michael Lovelace; s of Harold Browning, of Exmouth; *b* 18 March 1937; *Educ* Kelly Coll Tavistock; *m* 1965, Anna, da of Clifford White, of Sampford Peverell; 3 da; *Career* FCA; fin dir HAT Gp 1976-; *Style* - Michael Browning Esq; Elm Tree Farm, Harts Lane, Hallatrow, Bristol BS 18 5EA (☎ 0761 52218)

BROWNLOW, 7 Baron (UK 1776); Sir Edward John Peregrine Cust; 10 Bt (E 1677); s of 6 Baron

Brownlow (d 1978) by his 1 w, Katherine, da of Brig-Gen Sir David Kinloch, 11 Bt, CB, MVO; *b* 25 March 1936; *Educ* Eton; *m* 1964, Shirlie, nee Yeomans; 1 s; *Heir* s, Hon Peregrine Cust; *Career* md Harrison and Dixon Ltd (Underwriters) 1976-; High Sheriff of Lincs 1978-79; *Clubs* White's; *Style* - The Rt Hon the Lord Brownlow; The Mill, Manthorpe, Grantham, Lincs (☎ 5244)

BROWNLOW, Air Cdre Bertrand; OBE (1967), AFC (1962); s of Robert Brownlow; *b* 13 Jan 1939; *Educ* Beaufort Lodge Sch; *m* 1958, Kathleen Shannon; 2 s, 1 da; *Career* Cmdt Aeroplane and Armament Experimental Establishment Boscombe Down 1977-; *Style* - Air Cdre Bertrand Brownlow, OBE, AFC; The Baulk House, 66 Bromham rd, Biddenham, Beds (☎ Bedford 65595)

BROWNLOW, John Desmond Cavendish; OBE (1950); s of late Capt the Hon Francis Cecil Brownlow (3 s of 2 Baron Lurgan); hp to 1 cous, 4 Baron Lurgan; *b* 29 June 1911; *Educ* Eton; *Career* Lt-Col (ret) Gren Gds; *Style* - John Brownlow Esq OBE

BROWNLOW, Leila, Baroness; Leila Joan; da of late Maj Philip Reynolds, DSO; *m* 1, John Player; m 2, 1938, as his 2 w, 2 Baron Manton (d 1968); m 3, 1969, as his 3 w, 6 Baron Brownlow (d 1978); *Style* - The Rt Hon Leila, Lady Brownlow; 16 Farm st, W1 (☎ 01 491 4405)

BROWNLOW, Maj William Stephen; JP (Co Down 1956), DL (1961); s of Col Guy Brownlow, DSO, DL; *b* 9 Oct 1921; *Educ* Eton; *m* 1961, Eveleigh, da of Lt-Col George Panter, MBE, of Newcastle Co Down; 1 s, 2 da; *Career* Maj Rifle Bde WW II, Hon Col 4 Bn Roy Irish Rangers TAVR 1973-78; High Sheriff Co Down 1959, memb N Ireland Assembly 1973-75; Irish Nat Hunt Cttee 1956, Master E Down Foxhounds 1959-62, chm Downpatrick Race Club 1960-, NI Regn Br Field Sports Soc; *Recreations* field sports; *Clubs* Army & Navy; *Style* - Maj William Brownlow, JP, DL; Ballywhite House, Portaferry, Co Down, N Ireland

BROWNRIGG, Michael Gawen; s & h of Sir Nicholas Brownrigg, 5 Bt; *b* Oct 1961 *Style* - Michael Brownrigg Esq

BROWNRIGG, Sir Nicholas Gawen; 5 Bt (UK 1816); s of late Gawen Egremont Brownrigg, 2 s of 4 Bt; suc gf, Rear-Adm Sir Douglas Egremont Robert Brownrigg, 4 Bt, CB, 1939; *b* 22 Dec 1932; *m* 1, 1959 (m dis 1965), Linda Louise, da of Jonathan B Lovelace, of Beverly Hills, California, USA; 1 s, 1 da; m 2, 1971, Valerie Ann, da of Julia A Arden, of Livonia, Michigan, USA; *Heir* s, Michael Gawen Browrigg; *Style* - Sir Nicholas Brownrigg, Bt; PO Box 548, Ukiah, Calif 95482, USA

BROWNRIGG, Philip Henry Akerman; CMG (1964), DSO (1945), OBE (1953), TD (1945); s of Charles Edward Brownrigg (d 1942); *b* 3 June 1911; *Educ* Eton, Oxford; *m* 1936, Marguerite Doreen, da of Capt C R Otley (d 1935); 3 da; *Career* Lt Col Reconnaissance Corps RAC North West Europe, journalist 1934-52, editor Sunday Graphic 1952, Anglo-American Corporation of South Africa 1953, dir in Rhodesia 1961-63, Zambia 1964-65, dir Nchanga Consolidated Copper Mines Ltd and Roan Consolidated Mines Ltd 1969; *Style* - Philip Brownrigg Esq, CMG, DSO, OBE,; Wheeler's, Checkendon, Reading (☎ Checkendon 680328)

BRUCE OF DONINGTON, Baron (Life Peer UK 1974); Donald William Trevor Bruce; s of late W T Bruce, of Norbury, Surrey; *b* 3 Oct 1912; *Educ* The Grammar School Donington Lincs; *m* 1939 (m dis 1980), Joan Letitia, da of late H C Butcher; 1 s, 3 da; *Career* chartered accountant, economist, author; MP (L) Portsmouth N 1945-50, PPS to Min of Health 1945-50, MEP 1975-79; *Style* - The Rt Hon The Lord Bruce of Donington, 24/27 Thayer st, W1 (☎ 01 486 7188)

BRUCE, Sir Arthur Atkinson; KBE (1943), MC (1917); s of John Bruce; *b* 26 March 1895; *Educ* Jarrow Sch, Cambridge; *m* 1928, Kathleen, da of John Houldey; 3 da; *Career* dir Wallace Bros 1947-65, Chartered Bank of India 1950-70; dir Centl Bd of Reserve Bank India 1935-46; *Recreations* gardening; *Clubs* Oriental; *Style* - Sir Arthur Bruce, KBE,

MC; Little Tylers, Warwicks Bench, Guildford, Surrey (☎ 73136)

BRUCE, Hon Alastair John Lyndhurst; s and h of 4 Baron Aberdare, PC, DL; *b* 2 May 1947; *Educ* Eton, Ch Ch Oxford; *m* 1971, Elizabeth Mary Culbert, da of John Foulkes; 1 s, 1 da; *Style* - The Hon Alistair Bruce; 34 Lillian rd, SW13 (☎ 748 4957)

BRUCE, Lady Antonia Katherine; da of 11 Earl of Elgin and Kincardine; *b* 1964; *Style* - Lady Antonia Bruce

BRUCE, Hon Adam Robert; s of 11 Earl of Elgin and Kincardine; *b* 1968

BRUCE, Hon Alexander Victor; s of 11 Earl of Elgin; *b* 31 Mar 1971; *Style* - The Hon Alexander Bruce

BRUCE, Hon Bernard; MC (1943); s of 9 Earl of Elgin and Kincardine; *b* 1917; *Educ* Eton, New Coll Oxford; *m* 1, 1958, Mary Coxe (m dis 1968) (who m 1, Humphrey Humphreys, m dis 1957), da of Philippus Miller; m 2, 1970, Georgina, da of Philip Argenti, of Rome; *Career* Pilot Offr RAFVR 1937-39; Lt 1940, Maj 1944; *Clubs* Brooks's, Pratt's, City of London and MCC; *Style* - The Hon Bernard Bruce MC; 35 Brompton sq, SW3; Cauldhame, Dunblane, Perthshire

BRUCE, Lord; Charles Edward Bruce; s and h of 11 Earl of Elgin (and Kincardine); *b* 19 Oct 1961; *Career* a Page of Honour to HM Queen Elizabeth, The Queen Mother 1975-77; *Style* - Lord Bruce

BRUCE, Hon Mrs David - Jennet; OBE (1974); da of Rt Rev Atherton Gwillym Rawsthorne, DD, Suffragan Bp of Whalley; *m* 1919, Col the Hon David Bruce (d 1964), s of late 9 Earl of Elgin and (13 of) Kincardine, KG, GCSI, GCIE, PC and Lady Constance Carnegie, CI, da of 9 Earl of Southesk, KT; 1 da; *Style* - The Hon Mrs David Bruce, OBE; Ballamor, Brora, Sutherland

BRUCE, Hon Edward David; s of 10 Earl of Elgin (d 1968); *b* 1936; *Educ* Eton, Balliol Oxford; *m* 1960, Sara Elizabeth Wallop; 1 s, 1 da; *Career* formerly Lt Intelligence Corps; *Style* - The Hon Edward Bruce; Blairhill, Rumbling Bridge, Kinross

BRUCE, Hon George John Done; s and h of 11 Baron Balfour of Burleigh (d 1967); *b* 28 Mar 1930; *Educ* Westminster; trained at Byam Shaw Sch of Drawing and Painting; *Career* hon sec Roy Soc of Portrait Painters (memb 1959-); *Style* - The Hon George Bruce; 6 Pembroke Walk, Kensington W8 (☎ 01 937 1493); Brucefield, Clackmannan, Kincardine (Fife 228)

BRUCE, Lady Georgina Mary; da of 11 Earl of Elgin and Kincardine; *b* 1960; *Style* - Lady Georgina Bruce

BRUCE, Hon Henry Adam Francis; s of 4 Baron Aberdare, PC, DL; *b* 5 Feb 1962; *Style* - The Hon Henry Bruce

BRUCE, Sir Hervey James Hugh; 7 Bt (UK 1804); s of Sir Hervey John William Bruce, 6 Bt (d 1971); *b* 4 Sept 1952; *Educ* Eton; *m* 1979, Charlotte, da of John Temple Gore (s of late Capt Christopher Gore and Lady Barbara, da of 16 Earl of Eglinton); *Heir* unc, Ronald Cecil Juckes Bruce; *Career* Capt Gren Gds; *Style* - Sir Hervey Bruce, Bt; 3 Halford rd, SW6

BRUCE, Hon James Henry Morys; s of 4 Baron Aberdare; *b* 28 Dec 1948; *Educ* Eton; *m* 1977, Grace, da of Allen Jao Wu; 1 da; *Style* - The Hon James Bruce; 99 Eaton ter, SW1 (☎ 01 7306873)

BRUCE, Hon Mrs John - Helen Rachel; da of late Henry Feilden Rawstorne of Roche Court, Fareham, Hants; *m* 1923, Capt the Hon John Bernard Bruce, RN (d 1971), s of late 9 Earl of Elgin and (13 of) Kincardine, KG, GCSI, GCIE, PC and Lady Constance Carnegie, CI, da of 9 Earl of Southesk; 4 s, 2 da; *Style* - The Hon Mrs John Bruce; Larchwood, Itchen Abbas, Winchester; Clunel Cottage, Sallachy, Lairg

BRUCE, Hon James Michael Edward; JP (1962 Perthshire); s of 10 Earl of Elgin (d 1968); *b* 1927; *Educ* Eton, RMC and RAC Cirencester; *m* 1950, Hon

(Margaret) Jean Dagbjort, da of 2 Baron Glentanar, KBE (d 1971); 3 s, 1 da; *Career* served Scots Gds; chm Scottish Woodland Owners Assoc (Commercial) Ltd; memb Home Grown Timber Advisory Ctee; *Clubs* New (Edinburgh) Club; *Style* - The Hon James Bruce, JP; Flat 15, 35 Bryanston sq, W1 (☎ 01 262 4866); Blamanno Castle, by Perth (☎ Bridge of Earn 263)

BRUCE, Hon Mrs Katherine Gordon; *née* Bruce; da of late 7 Lord Balfour of Burleigh; *b* 1922; *m* 1946 (m dis 1961), Thomas Riviere Bland, MC; 1 s, 2 da; reverted by deed poll 1975 to surname of Bruce; *Style* - The Hon Mrs Katherine Bruce; 25 Kew Green, Kew, Richmond, Surrey

BRUCE, Sir (Francis) Michael Ian; 12 Bt (NS 1628); s of Sir Michael William Selby Bruce, 11 Bt (d 1957); discontinued use of Christian name Francis; *b* 3 April 1926; *m* 1, 1947 (m dis 1957), Barbara Stevens, da of Francis J Lynch; 2 s; m 2, 1961 (m dis 1963), Frances Keegan; m 3, 1966, Marilyn Anne, da of Carter Mullaly; *Heir* s, Michael Ian Richard Bruce; *Career* US Marine Corps 1943-46, memb Sqdn A 7 Regt NY 1948 (ret); Master's Ticket 1968; *Style* - Sir Michael Bruce, Bt; c/o Newport National Bank, Westcliff & Dover, Newport, Calif, USA

BRUCE, Michael Ian Richard; s (by 1 m) and h of Sir (Francis) Michael Bruce, 12 Bt; *b* 10 Dec 1950; *Style* - Michael Bruce Esq

BRUCE, Lady Martha Veronica; OBE (1958), TD, JP (Fife); da of late 10 Earl of Elgin and (14 of) Kincardine, KT, CMG, TD, CD, by Hon Dame Katherine Cochrane, DBE, da of late 1 Baron Cochrane of Cults and Lady Gertrude Boyle, OBE, da of 6 Earl of Glasgow; *b* 1921; *Career* Gov HM Prison, Cornton Vale, Stirling; Lady-in-Waiting to HRH the late Princess Royal Jan to March 1965; *Style* - Lady Martha Bruce, OBE, TD, JP; 17 Coxburn Bae, Bridge of Allan, Stirling

BRUCE, Robert Alister Peel; AFC (1943); s of Col K Bruce, DSO, of Trevereux House, Limpsfield; *b* 27 Aug 1915; *Educ* Eton; *m* 1941, Monica, da of Richard Jeff, of Kuala Lumpur; 3 da; *Career* FCA; dir Country & New Town Properties, London & St Lawrence Investments, Practical Investment Co, Tst of Property Shares; *Recreations* tennis, golf, shooting, fishing; *Clubs* Army & Navy, City of London; *Style* - Robert Bruce Esq, AFC; Abbots Leigh, Haywards Heath, Sussex (☎ 0444 54411)

BRUCE, Ronald Cecil Juckes; s of late Sir Hervey Bruce, 5 Bt; hp of nephew, Sir Hervey Bruce, 7 Bt; *b* 22 Aug 1921; *m* 1960, Jean, da of Lewis James William Murfitt; 1 s; *Style* - Ronald Bruce Esq; 24 Fairfax rd, Teddington, Middx

BRUCE, Hon Mrs Robert - Mary Katherine; da of late Maj-Gen the Hon John Lindley (s of Baron Lindley, Life Peer, d 1921); *m* 1910, Maj the Hon Robert Bruce, CBE (d 1959), s of late 9 Earl of Elgin and (13 of) Kincardine, KG, GCSI, GCIE, PC, by Lady Constance Carnegie, CI, da of 9 Earl of Southesk, KT; 2 da; *Style* - The Hon Mrs Robert Bruce; Glenerney, Dunphail, Morayshire

BRUCE, Hon Victoria; da and hp of 8 (12 but for the attainder) Lord Balfour of Burleigh; *b* 5 April 1973; *Style* - The Hon Victoria Bruce

BRUCE, William Henry; s of William Bruce, of Grangewood, Ellon; *b* 17 Sept 1933; *Educ* Ellon Acad; *m* 1957, Margaret, da of Albert Wyness; 1 s, 2 da; *Career* dep chm Barratt Dvpts, chm Barratt Dvpts (Scotland) Ltd; *Recreations* riding, golf, badminton, shooting; *Clubs* Roy Aberdeen Golf; *Style* - William Bruce Esq; Logie House, Ellon, Aberdeenshire (☎ 0358 20531)

BRUCE-GARDNER, Bryan Charles; s of Sir Charles Bruce-Gardner, 1 Bt (d 1960); bro of Sir Douglas Bruce-Gardner, 2 Bt; *b* 4 July 1924; *Educ* Uppingham, Trin Cambridge; *m* 1952, Helen, da of Digby Sowerby; 4 s; *Career* md Patent Shaft Steel Works 1961-; dir Laird Gp 1963-; *Recreations* golf; *Style* - Bryan Bruce-Gardner Esq; Stedefield, Church Lane, Flyford Flavell, Worcester (☎ 038 682 451)

BRUCE-GARDNER, Sir Douglas Bruce; 2 Bt (UK 1945); s of Sir Charles Bruce-Gardner, 1 Bt (d 1960); *b* 27 Jan 1917; *Educ* Uppingham, Trin Cambridge; *m* 1, 1940, Monica Flumerfelt (m dis 1964), da of Prof Sir Geoffrey Jefferson, CBE, FRS; 1 s, 2 da; m 2, 1964, Sheila, da of Roger Stilliard, of Seer Green, Bucks; 1 s, 1 da; *Heir* s, Robert Bruce-Gardner; *Career* chm GKN Steel 1965-67, GKN Rolled and Bright Steel 1968-72, GKN (S Wales), Miles Druce & Co 1974-77; dep chm GKN Gp 1974-77; dir BHP GKN Hldgs 1977-78, GKN Ltd 1960-, Iron Tdes Employers Insur Assoc, Iron Tdes Mutual Insur Co 1977-; *Clubs* Carlton; *Style* - Sir Douglas Bruce-Gardner, Bt; Bishopwood Grange, Ross-on-Wye, Herefs (☎ Lydbrook 60444)

BRUCE-GARDNER, Robert Henry; s and h of Sir Douglas Bruce-Gardner, 2 Bt; *b* 10 June 1943; *Educ* Uppingham, Reading U; *m* 1979, Veronica Hand-Oxborrow, da of Rev W E Hand; *Style* - Robert Bruce-Gardner Esq

BRUCE-GARDYNE, Jock (John); MP (C) Knutsford 1979-; s of Capt E Bruce-Gardyne, DSO, RN ret; *b* 12 April 1930; *Educ* Winchester, Magdalen Oxford; *m* 1959, Sarah, da of Sir John Maitland, of Harrington Hall, Spilsby, Lincs; 2 s, 1 da; *Career* MP S Angus 1964-74, columnist Sunday Telegraph; consultant Northern Engrg Industs; For Serv 1953-56; PPS to Sec of State Scotland 1970-72; *Recreations* fishing; *Clubs* Garrick, St James's (Manchester); *Style* - Jock Bruce-Gardyne Esq, MP; Illidge Green Farm, Brereton, Cheshire; 13 Kelso Place, W8 (☎ 01 937 6953)

BRUCKHEIMER, Nathan Robert; s of Simon Bruckheimer; *b* 6 Nov 1933; *Educ* Alleyne's Stevenage, Holloway Sch London, Edinburgh U; *Career* exec dir Brookside Metal Watford (BICC Gp); *Recreations* theatre, music (particularly opera); *Style* - Nathan Bruckheimer Esq; 9 Eveline Court, Connaught gdns, Muswell Hill, N 10 (☎ 01 883 7040)

BRUDENELL, Edmund Crispin Stephen James George; DL (Northants 1977); s of George Brudenell (2 s of Cdr Lord Robert Brudenell-Bruce, RN, 4 s of 3 Marquess of Ailesbury); *b* 24 Oct 1928; *Educ* Harrow, RAC Cirencester; *m* 1955, Hon Marian, JP, nee Manningham-Buller, da of 1 Viscount Dilhorne, PC; 2 s, 1 da; *Career* landowner, farmer; *Recreations* shooting, deer stalking, travelling; *Clubs* Carlton, Pratt's, Beefsteak; *Style* - Edmund Brudenell Esq, DL; 18 Laxford House, Ebury st, SW1 (☎ 01 730 8715); Deene Park, Corby, Northants (☎ Bulwick 223)

BRUDENELL, Hon Mrs (Marian Cynthia); da of late 1 Viscount Dilhorne; *b* 1934; *m* 1955, Edmund Crispin Stephen James George Brudenell; 2 s (twins), 1 da; *Style* - The Hon Mrs Brudenell; 18 Laxford House, Ebury st, SW1; Deene Park, Corby, Northants

BRUDENELL-BRUCE, Lord Charles Adam; s of 7 Marquess of Ailesbury (d 1974) by his 3 w, Jean, nee Wilson; *b* 23 March 1951; *Educ* Eton; *Career* late Lt Roy Hussars, with COI 1976; currently with Chestertons (estate agents); *Recreations* tennis, squash, shooting; *Clubs* Cavalry; *Style* - Lord Charles Brudenell-Bruce; Little Lye Hill, Savernake Forest, Marlborough, Wilts (☎ 0672 810261)

BRUDENELL-BRUCE, Lady Carina Doune; da of 8 Marquess of Ailesbury; *b* 13 Jan 1956; *Educ* Lawnside; *Style* - Lady Carina Brudenell-Bruce; Sturmy House, Savernake Forest, Marlborough, Wilts

BRUDENELL-BRUCE, Lady Kathryn Juliet; da of 8 Marquess of Ailesbury; *b* 24 Aug 1965; *Style* - Lady Kathryn Brudenell-Bruce

BRUDENELL-BRUCE, Lady Louise; da of 8 Marquess of Ailesbury; *b* 13 July 1964; *Style* - Lady Louise Brudenell-Bruce

BRUDENELL-BRUCE, Lady Piers; Nelida Garcia Otero; da of Mariano Garcia Villalba, of Madrid; *m* 1958, as his 2 w, Lord (Chandos Gerald) Piers Brudenell-Bruce (d 1980; 2 s of 7 Marquess of Ailesbury); 2 da; *Style* - Lady Piers Brudenell-Bruce; Cortijo de la Plata, Zahara de los Atunes, Cadiz, Spain

BRUDENELL-BRUCE, Lady Rosemary Enid; da of 6 Marquess of Ailesbury, DSO, TD; *b* 9 Feb 1907; *Style* - Lady Rosemary Brudenell-Bruce; The Kennels, Savernake, Marlborough, Wilts

BRUDENELL-BRUCE, Lady Sylvia Davina; da of 8 Marquess of Ailesbury; *b* 19 June 1954; *Educ* Lawnside and Redlynch ' Park; *Style* - Lady Sylvia Brudenell-Bruce; Sturmy House, Savernake Forest, Marlborough, Wilts

BRUFORD-DAVIES, Edmund Robin; s of Brig Edmund Davies; *b* 29 June 1928; *Educ* Radley, Sandhurst; *m* 1969, Sheelagh, da of Dr Norman Patterson; *Career* dir Wm Bruford & Sons, Gowland Bros; *Recreations* tennis, skiing; *Clubs* Special Forces; *Style* - Edmund Bruford-Davies Esq; Higher Bootham, Brampford Speke, Exeter

BRUNNER, Sir Felix John Morgan; 3 Bt (UK 1895); s of Sir John Fowler Brunner, 2 Bt (d 1929); *b* 13 Oct 1897; *Educ* Cheltenham Coll, Trin Oxford; *m* 1926, Dorothea Elizabeth, OBE, JP, da of late Henry Brodribb Irving; 3 s; *Heir* s, John Brunner; *Career* Lt RFA WW I; former chm Brunner Investment Tst Ltd, and other cos; chm Henley Rural Dist Cncl 1954-57, pres Liberal Party Org 1962-63; *Style* - Sir Felix Brunner, Bt; Greys Court, Henley-on-Thames, Oxon (☎ Rotherfield Greys 296)

BRUNNER, John Henry Kilian; s and h of Sir Felix Brunner, 3 Bt; *b* 1 June 1927; *Educ* Eton, Trin Oxford; *m* 1955, Jasmine Cicely, da of late John Wardrop-Moore; 2 s, 1 da; *Career* formerly Lt RA; *Style* - John Brunner Esq; 13 Glyndon av, Brighton, Victoria, Australia 3186

BRUNTISFIELD, 1 Baron (UK 1942); Sir Victor Alexander George Anthony Warrender; 8 Bt (GB 1715), MC (1918); s of Sir George John Scott, 7 Bt, KCB, KCVO (d 1945), and Lady Ethel Maud Ashley-Cooper, da of 8 Earl of Shaftesbury; *b* 23 June 1899; *Educ* Eton; *m* 1, 1920 (m dis 1946), Dorothy Etta (d 1975), da of late Col Richard Hamilton Rawson, MP, by the Col's w Lady Beatrice, nee Anson (da of 2 Earl of Lichfield); 3 s; m 2, 1948, Tania, da of Dr M Kolin, of St Jacob, Dubrovnik, Yugoslavia; 1 s, 1 da; *Heir* s, Hon John Warrender, OBE, MC, TD; *Career* Private Sec to Sir Robert S Horne, GBE, KC, MP 1920-22, chm Young Conservative's Union 1929-30, PPS (unpaid) to Parly Under-Sec of State for India 1924, an Assist Cons Whip 1928-31, Jr Lord of the Treasury 1931-32, V-Chamberlain of the Household 1932-35, Comptroller of HM's Household 1935, Parly and Fin Sec to Admiralty 1935, Fin Sec to War Dept and memb Army Cncl 1935-40, Parly Sec to Admiralty 1940-45, sat as MP (C) for Kesteven and Rutland Grantham Div Dec 1923-Feb 1942; *Style* - The Rt Hon The Lord Bruntisfield, MC; Chalet les Pommiers, 3780 Gstaad, Switzerland

BRUNTON, Gordon Charles; s of Charles Brunton; *b* 27 Dec 1921; *Educ* Cranleigh Sch, LSE; *m* 1, 1944, Nadine Sohr (m dis 1965); 1 s, 2 da (and 1 s decd); m 2, 1966, Gillian, da of Howard Kirk; 1 s, 1 da; *Career* Pres Periodical Publishers Assoc 1981-; publisher; joined Tothill Press 1947, exec dir Tothill 1956; md Tower Press Gp 1958, exec dir Odhams 1961; Thomson Org 1961- (dir 1963), md Thomson Publications 1961, md & ch exec Thomson Br Hldgs and Thomson Org 1968-; Pres Int Thomson Org, History of Advertising Tst 1981-; *Recreations* books, horse breeding; *Clubs* Garrick; *Style* - Gordon Brunton Esq; North Munstead, Godalming, Surrey (☎ 04868 6313)

BRUNTON, James Lauder; s and h of Sir (Edward Francis) Lauder Brunton, 3 Bt; *b* 24 Sept 1947; *m* 1967, Susan, da of Charles Hons; 1 s, 1 da; *Style* - James Brunton Esq; Apt 104, 1000 McGregor st, Montreal 112, Canada

BRUNTON, Sir (Edward Francis) Lauder; 3 Bt (UK 1908); s of Sir (James) Stopford (Lauder) Brunton, 2 Bt (d 1943); *b* 10 Nov 1916; *Educ* Trin Coll Sch Port Hope Ontario, Bryanston Sch, McGill U; *m* 1946, Marjorie Grant, da of David Sclater Lewis; 1 s, 1 da; *Heir* s, James Brunton; *Career* Hon Attending Physician Roy Victoria Hosp Montreal, Fell of

Internat Soc of Hematology and of American Coll of Physicians, memb American Soc of Hematology; *Style* - Sir Lauder Brunton, Bt; PO Box 140, Guysborough, Nova Scotia, Canada

BRUSH, Lt-Col Edward James Augustus Howard; CB (1966), DSO (1945), OBE (1946); s of Maj George Brush, of Drumnabreeze, Co Down; *b* 5 March 1901; *Educ* Clifton, Sandhurst; *m* 1937, Susan, da of Maj F Torbett, of Bridge House, Britford, Salisbury; 1 da; *Career* V-Lt Co Down 1957-64, JP & DL 1953-74, High Sheriff 1953; chm T&AFA 1954-65; memb N Ireland Convention 1975-76; memb Irish Nat Hunt Steeplechase Cttee; *Style* - Lt-Col Edward Brush, CB, DSO, OBE; Drumnabreeze, Magheralin, Craigavon, N Ireland (☎ 0846 611284)

BRYAN, Sir Arthur; s of William Bryan; *b* 4 March 1923; *Educ* Longton H S, Stoke on Trent; *m* 1947, Betty Ratford; 1 s, 1 da; *Career* chm Wedgwood 1968- (joined Wedgwood 1947, md 1963), chm N Amer Advsy Gp Br Overseas Trade Bd 1977-, dir Phoenix Assurance Co 1976-; FBIM, KStJ, FRSA; HM Ld-Lt Staffs 1968; kt 1966; *Recreations* walking, tennis, reading; *Style* - Sir Arthur Bryan, HM Lord-Lieut for Staffs; Parkfields Cottage, Tittensor, Stoke-on-Trent, Staffs (☎ Barlaston 2686)

BRYAN, Sir Andrew Meikle; s of John Bryan; *b* 1 March 1893; *Educ* Hamilton Acad, Glasgow U; *m* 1922, Henrietta Paterson, da of George Seater Begg; 1 s (and 1 da decd); *Career* kt 1950; CEng, FIMinE, FICE, FRSE; mining engr 1920-65-, HM Inspector Mines, Prof Mining Glasgow U, memb NCB 1951-57, chm Mining Qualifications Bd; Pres- Mining Inst Scotland 1949-50, Nat Assoc Colliery Mans 1949-50, Inst Mining Engrs; *Clubs* Caledonian; *Style* - Sir Andrew Bryan; 3 Hounslow gdns, Hounslow, Middx (☎ 01 894 5115)

BRYANT, Sir Arthur Wynne Morgan; CH (1964), CBE (1949); s of Sir Francis Bryant, CB, CVO, CBE; *b* 18 Feb 1899; *Educ* Harrow, Queen's Oxford; *m* 1, 1924, Sylvia (m dis 1939), da of Sir Walter Shakerley, 3 Bt, CBE, and Lady Shakerley, CBE, DGStJ (Hilda, nee Hodgson); m 2, 1941, Anne (m dis 1976), da of Bertram Brooke, HH Tuan Muda of Sarawak, and Gladys (da of Sir Walter Palmer, 1 Bt); *Career* historian, journalist, barr; writer of 'Our Note Book' in Illustrated London News 1936-; Pres Friends of the Vale of Aylesbury, Common Market Safeguards Campaign; *Clubs* Athenaeum, Beefsteak, Pratt's, Grillion's, MCC; *Style* - Sir Arthur Bryant CH CBE; Myles Place, The Close, Salisbury, Wilts

BRYANT, John Beaton; TD (1963 and 1975), JP (Bristol 1979), DL (Avon 1974); s of Arthur Bryant, of Bristol; *b* 9 July 1930; *Educ* Bristol G S; *m* 1960, Shirley, da of Henry Hopley, of Bristol; 2 s; *Career* dir Joseph Bryant Ltd 1956, Blacks Camping & Leisure Ltd 1978; *Recreations* fishing, shooting, hill walking; *Clubs* Army & Navy; *Style* - John Bryant Esq, TD, JP, DL; Aelbryn, Bancyffordd, Llandyssul, Dyfed; 11 Sion Hill, Clifton, Bristol, Avon (☎ 0272 311868)

BRYANT, Jonathan Nicholas; JP (1979); s of Basil Stuart Bryant (d 1976); *b* 12 July 1944; *Educ* Cheltenham; *m* 1966, Sandra Anne, da of Alexander Kendrich, of Tunbridge Wells; 2 s, 1 da; *Career* md Brymor Ltd and Bryant Estates Ltd 1969-; memb of Lloyd's 1981, memb Livery of Curriers Co and Leathersellers Co; *Style* - Jonathan Bryant Esq, JP; Greenwood, Frant, E Sussex (☎ 089 275 462)

BRYDEN, Hon Mrs; Hon (Monica) Deborah; *née* Morris; da of 3 Baron Killanin, MBE, TD; *b* 24 Feb 1950; *Educ* Convent of the Assumption Hengrave, Byam Shaw Sch of Drawing and Painting; *m* 1970, William Bryden, *qv*; 1 s, 1 da; *Style* - The Hon Mrs Bryden

BRYDEN, William Campbell Rough; s of George Bryden; *b* 12 April 1942; *Educ* Greenock H S, Glasgow U; *m* 1970, Hon Deborah, nee Morris, da of 3 Baron Killanin, MBE, TD, and Mary, MBE, da of Rev Canon Douglas Dunlop; 1 s, 1 da; *Career* theatre dir; *Style* - William Bryden Esq; c/o National Theatre, S Bank, SE1 (☎ 01 928 2033)

BRYDEN, Sir William James; CBE

(1970), QC (Scot 1973); s of James Bryden, JP, of Scone; *b* 2 Oct 1909; *Educ* Perth Acad, BNC Oxford; *m* 1937, Christina, da of Thomas Bannatyne Marshall, CBE, of Gaskhill, Perth; 2 s, 1 da; *Career* barr 1933 (Inner Temple); advocate Scot 1935; Sheriff Lothians & Peebles 1973-75, Lothians & Borders 1975-78, ret 1978; kt 1978; *Recreations* books, countryside; *Clubs* New (Edinburgh); *Style* - Sir William Bryden, CBE, QC; Whinneyknowe, Peebles (☎ 21243)

BRYSON, Col James Graeme; OBE (Mil 1954), TD (1949), JP (Liverpool 1956), DL (1968); s of John Bryson, slr Liverpool; *b* 4 Feb 1913; *Educ* St Edward's Coll Liverpool, Liverpool U; *m* 1938, Jean, da of Walter Cook Glendinning; 2 s (and 1 s decd), 4 da; *Career* slr 1935; dep Circuit Judge 1978-; chm Medical Appeal Tbnl 1978-; HM V-Ld-Lt Merseyside 1979-; kt of Holy Sepulchre 1974; *Recreations* ex-service interests, local history, boating; *Clubs* Athenaeum (Liverpool, Pres 1969); *Style* - Col James Bryson OBE TD JP DL, HM Vice-Lord-Lieut for Merseyside; Sunwards, Thirlmere rd, Hightown, Liverpool L38 3RQ (☎ 051 929 2652)

BUCCLEUCH AND QUEENSBERRY, 9 and 11 Duke of (S 1663 & 1684); Walter Francis John Montagu Douglas Scott; KT (1978), VRD (1970), JP (Roxburgh 1975); also Lord Scott of Buccleuch (S 1606), Lord Scott of Whitchester and Eskdaill, Earl of Buccleuch (both S 1619), Earl of Dalkeith (S 1663), Earl of Doncaster, Baron Scott of Tynedale (both E 1663), Lord Douglas of Kinmont, Middlebie and Dornoch, Viscount of Nith, Thorthorwald and Ross, Earl of Drumlanrig and Sanquhar, and Marquess of Dumfriesshire (all S 1706); s of 8 & 10 Duke of Buccleuch & Queensberry, KT, GCVO, TD, PC (d 1973), and Mary, da of Maj William Lascelles (s of Sir Frank Lascelles, GCB, GCMG, GCVO, PC - himself s of Hon William Lascelles, PC, MP, by his w, Lady Caroline Howard, da of 6 Earl of Carlisle; Hon William Lascelles was 3 s of 2 Earl of Harewood) and Lady Sybil Beauclerk (2 da of 10 Duke of St Albans); *b* 28 Sept 1923; *Educ* Eton, Ch Ch Oxford; *m* 1953, Jane, da of John McNeill, QC, Drumavuic, Argyllshire; 3 s, 1 da; *Heir* s, Earl of Dalkeith; *Career* MP (C) Edinburgh N 1960-73, PPS Sec of State Scotland 1961-64; chm Con Forestry Cttee; Ld-Lt Roxburghshire 1974-75, Selkirk 1975, Roxburgh, Ettrick and Lauderdale 1975-; Pres E of England Ag Soc 1976, Roy Scot Ag Benevolent Inst, Scot Nat Inst for War Blinded; chm C'wlth Forestry Assoc 1979; Capt Roy Co Archers (Queen's Bodyguard for Scotland); *Recreations* music, painting, fishing, shooting; *Clubs* New (Edinburgh); *Style* - His Grace The Duke of Buccleuch and Queensberry, KT, VRD, JP; Drumlanrig Castle, Thornhill, Dumfriesshire (☎ 30248); Boughton House, Kettering, Northants; 46 Bedford gdns, W8 (☎ 01 727 4358); Bowhill, Selkirk (☎ 20732)

BUCCLEUCH AND QUEENSBERRY, Mary, Duchess of; (Vreda Esther) Mary; da of Maj William Frank Lascelles (gn of 3 Earl of Harewood) and Lady Sybil de Vere Beauclerk (2 da of 10 Duke of St Albans); *b* 17 Sept 1900; *m* 1921, 8 Duke of Buccleuch and (10 of) Queensberry, KT, GCVO, TD, PC; 1 s (9 Duke), 2 da (Duchess of Northumberland, w of 10 Duke; Lady Caroline Gilmour, w of Sir Ian G, 3 Bt, Ld Privy Seal); *Career* held the Queen's (now HM Queen Elizabeth The Queen Mother) canopy at the Coronation 1937; *Style* - Her Grace Mary, Duchess of Buccleuch and Queensberry; Boughton Manor, Kettering, Northants

BUCHAN, 16 Earl of (S 1469); Donald Cardross Flower Erskine; also Lord Auchterhouse (S 1469), Lord Cardross (S 1610), and Baron Erskine (UK 1806); s of late 6 Baron Erskine; suc father as Baron Erskine 1957 and kinsman as Earl of Buchan 1960; *b* 3 June 1899; *Educ* Charterhouse, RMC; *m* 1927, Christina, da of late Hugh Woolner and adopted da of late Lloyd Harry Baxendale, JP; 1 s, 2 da; *Heir* s, Lord Cardross; *Career* Lt-Col (ret) 9 Lancers; *Style* - Lt-Col The Rt Hon The Earl of Buchan; Little Orchard, Moreton-in-Marsh, Glos (☎ 50274)

BUCHAN, Hon Mrs Alastair; Hope; da of late David Gordon Gilmour, of Ottawa,

Canada; *m* 1942, Prof the Hon Alastair Francis Buchan, CBE (d 1976); 2 s, 1 da; *Style* - The Hon Mrs Alastair Buchan; Waterloo House, Brill, Bucks

BUCHAN OF AUCHMACOY, YR, (John) Charles Augustus David; s and h of Capt David Buchan of Auchmacoy, JP, by his w, Hon Susan, nee Scott-Ellis, da of 9 Baron Howard de Walden, to which Barony he is in remainder through his mother; *b* 1 March 1963; *Style* - Charles Buchan of Auchmacoy, yr

BUCHAN OF AUCHMACOY, Capt David William Sinclair; JP (Westminster 1959); s of Capt Stephen Lloyd Trevor, JP (d 1959), and Lady Olivia, née Sinclair, da of 18 Earl of Caithness, CBE (d 1947); suc maternal gf (18 Earl) as Chief of the Name of Buchan and recognised as such by Lord Lyon 1949; *b* 18 Sept 1929; *Educ* Eton, Sandhurst; *m* 1961, Hon (Blanche) Susan Fionodhbar, nee Scott-Ellis, da and coheiress of 9 Baron Howard de Walden; 4 s, 1 da; *Heir* s, Charles Buchan of Auchmacoy, yr; *Career* Capt Gordon Highlanders (ADC to GOC-in-C) Singapore 1951-53; memb London Stock Exchange, sr ptnr Gow & Parsons 1961-68; Freeman City of London, fell IOD; *Recreations* cricket, tennis, squash; *Clubs* White's, Turf, City of London, RAC, MCC, Puffin's (Edinburgh); *Style* - Capt David Buchan of Auchmacoy, JP; Auchmacoy House, Ellon, Aberdeenshire (☎ 20229); 28 Little Boltons, SW10 (☎ 01 373 0654)

BUCHAN OF AUCHMACOY, Hon Mrs; Hon (Blanche) Susan Fionodbhar; *née* Scott-Ellis; da of 9 Baron Howard de Walden and 5 Baron Seaford; *b* 6 Oct 1937; *m* 1961, Capt David William Sinclair Buchan of Auchmacoy; 4 s, 1 da; *Career* co-heiress to Barony of Howard de Walden; *Style* - The Hon Mrs Buchan of Auchmacoy; Auchmacoy House, Ellon, Aberdeenshire; 28 The Little Boltons, SW10

BUCHAN, Hon William De L'Aigle; s of 1 Baron Tweedsmuir, GCMG, GCVO, CH (d 1940), and hp of bro, 2 Baron Tweedsmuir, CBE, CD; *b* 10 Jan 1916; *Educ* Eton, New Coll Oxford; *m* 1, 1939 (m dis 1946), Nesta, da of Lt-Col C D Crozier; 1 da; m 2, 1946 (m dis 1960, she d 1969), Barbara Howard, da of E N Ensor; 3 s, 3 da (of whom 2 da are twins); m 3, 1960, Sauré Cynthia Mary, da of late Maj G E Tatchell; 1 s; *Career* Sqdn-Ldr RAF Vol Reserve; *Clubs* Travellers'; *Style* - The Hon William Buchan; 47 Cardigan st, SE11

BUCHAN-HEPBURN, John Alistair Trant Kidd; s of late John Trant Buchan-Hepburn and hp of kinsman, Sir Ninian Buchan Archibald Buchan-Hepburn, 6 Bt; *b* 27 June 1931; *Educ* Charterhouse, St Andrews U; *m* 1957, Georgina Elizabeth, SRN, da of late Oswald Morris Turner, MC; 1 s, 3 da; *Career* Capt (ret) late 1 King's Dragoon Gds, ADC to Gen Officer Cmdg Malaya 1956-57; *Clubs* New (Edinburgh); *Style* - John Buchan-Hepburn Esq; Castle House, Grosmont, Abergavenny, Gwent; Chagford, St Andrews, Fife

BUCHAN-HEPBURN, Sir Ninian Buchan Archibald; 6 Bt (UK 1815); s of Sir John Karslake Thomas Buchan-Hepburn, 5 Bt (d 1961); *b* 8 Oct 1922; *Educ* St Aubyn's Rottingdean Sussex, Canford Sch Wimborne Dorset; *m* 1958, Bridget (d 1976), da of late Sir Louis (Leisler) Greig, KBE, CVO; *Heir* kinsman, John Buchan-Hepburn; *Career* Burma 1943-45 with Queen's Own Cameron Highlanders; painter (RA Exhibitor), memb Roy Co of Archers (Queen's Bodyguard for Scotland); *Clubs* New (Edinburgh), Puffin's (Edinburgh); *Style* - Sir Ninian Buchan-Hepburn, Bt; Logan, Port Logan, Wigtownshire

BUCHANAN, Most Rev Alan Alexander; *Educ* Trinity College Dublin; *m* 1935, Audrey Kathryn, da of W A Crone, of Knock, Belfast, Northern Ireland; 2 da; *Career* deacon 1930, ordained priest 1931; Rural Dean Mid-Belfast 1951-55, Archbishop of Dublin & Primate of Ireland 1969-77; *Style* - The Most Rev Alan Buchanan; Kilbride, Castleknock, Co Dublin

BUCHANAN, Andrew George; s and h of Major Sir Charles Buchanan, 4 Bt; *b* 21 July 1937; *Educ* Eton, Trin Camb, Wye

Coll London; *m* 1966, Belinda Jane Virginia, da of Donald Colquhoun Maclean, KStJ, of Thurloe sq, SW, and widow of Gresham Vaughan (d 1964); 1 s, 1 da (and 1 step s, 1 step da); *Career* 2 Lt Coldstream Guards 1956-58, Major Cmding A Sqdn Sherwood Rangers Yeo (TA) 1971-74; farmer and land agent; High Sheriff of Nottinghamshire 1976-77; *Recreations* skiing, shooting; *Clubs* Farmers; *Style* - Andrew Buchan Esq; Hodsock Priory, Blyth, Worksop, Notts (☎ 090976 204)

BUCHANAN, Maj Sir Charles James; 4 Bt (UK 1878), JP (Notts 1952), DL (1954); s of Sir Eric Buchanan, 3 Bt (d 1926); *b* 16 April 1899; *Educ* Harrow; *m* 1932, Barbara, da of Lt-Col Rt Hon Sir George Stanley, GCSI, GCIE, CMG, PC (6 s of 16 Earl of Derby and Lady Constance Villiers, da of 4 Earl of Clarendon, KG) and Lady Beatrix Taylour, CI, CBE, da of 3 Marquess of Headfort; 2 s, 2 da; *Heir* s, Andrew Buchanan; *Career* memb Roy Co of Archers (Queen's Bodyguard for Scotland); Maj Highland Light Infantry, served BEF France and Russia 1919 and France 1939 and AMG Staff Italy; ADC to Gov Madras 1928-32; High Sheriff Notts 1962; *Recreations* gardening; *Clubs* Lansdowne; *Style* - Sir Charles Buchanan, Bt, JP, DL; St Anne's Manor, Sutton Bonington, Loughborough, Leics (☎ Kegworth 2280)

BUCHANAN, George Henry Perrott; s of Rev Charles Buchanan, of Co Antrim; *b* 9 Jan 1904; *Educ* Campbell Coll Belfast, Belfast U; *m* 1, 1938, Winifred Corn (m dis 1945, she d 1971); m 2, 1949, Noel Ritter (d 1951); m 3, 1952, Hon Janet (d 1968), da of 1 Viscount Margesson; 2 da; m 4, 1974, Sandra McCloy, of Vancouver; *Career* poet; editorial staff The Times 1930-35, critic News Chronicle 1935-38; Pres London Centre European Soc of Culture 1954-80; novelist; *Clubs* Savile, Athenaeum; *Style* - George Buchanan Esq; 27 Ashley gdns, SW1 (☎ 01 834 5722)

BUCHANAN, Vice-Adm Sir Peter William; KBE (1980); s of Francis Buchanan; *b* 14 May 1925; *Educ* Malvern; *m* 1953, Audrey, da of Dr Dunstan Edmondson, of Huddington Court, Droitwich; 3 s, 1 da; *Career* RN 1943-; Ch Staff Allied Naval Forces S Europe 1979-; *Recreations* sailing, walking; *Clubs* Caledonian; *Style* - Vice-Adm Sir Peter Buchanan, KBE; 30 The Square, Titchfield, Fareham, Hants (☎ 42146)

BUCHANAN-DUNLOP, Brig (Archibald) Ian; CBE (1959), DSO (1944); s of Col Archibald Buchanan-Dunlop, 18 Laird of Drumhead, Dunbartonshire (d 1947); *b* 3 March 1908; *Educ* Loretto, Sandhurst, Imperial Defence Coll; *m* 1938, Renée, da of John Serjeant, of Hextable, Kent; 1 s, 1 da; *Career* cmd 6 Cameronians 1944-45, DAG Far East LF 1956-8, Col Roy Scots Fusiliers 1958-59, Princ Scottish Off 1960-75; *Recreations* painting, gardening; *Clubs* Army & Navy; *Style* - Brig Ian Buchanan-Dunlop, CBE, DSO; Broughton Place, Broughton, Peeblesshire (☎ 379)

BUCHANAN-JARDINE, Sir Andrew Rupert John; 4 Bt (UK 1885), MC (1945), JP (Dumfriesshire 1957), DL (1978); s of Sir John Buchanan-Jardine, 3 Bt, JP (d 1969), by his 1 w, Jean, da of Lord Ernest Hamilton, sometime MP N Tyrone (7 s of 1 Duke of Abercorn, KG, PC, and Lady Louisa Russell, 2 da of 6 Duke of Bedford, KG); *b* 2 Feb 1923; *Educ* Harrow, RAC Cirencester; *m* 1950, Jane (m dis 1975), da of Sir Archibald Edmonstone, 6 Bt, and Gwendolyn (da of Marshall Field, of Chicago); 1 s, 1 da; *Heir* s, John Buchanan-Jardine; *Career* farmer and landowner, formerly Maj RHG; Master Dumfriesshire Foxhounds 1950-; *Recreations* country pursuits; *Clubs* MCC; *Style* - Sir Andrew Buchanan-Jardine, Bt, MC, JP, DL; Dixons, Lockerbie, Dumfriesshire (☎ 2508)

BUCHANAN-JARDINE, John Christopher Rupert; s and h of Sir Andrew Buchanan-Jardine, 4 Bt, MC, JP, DL; *b* 20 March 1952; *Educ* Harrow; *m* 1975, Pandora, da of Peter Murray Lee; 1 s, 1 da; *Style* - John Buchanan-Jardine Esq

BUCHANAN-JARDINE, Prudence, Lady; Prudence Audrey; da of William Haggie, of Knayton, Thirsk, Yorks; *m* 1944, as his 2 wife, Capt Sir John William

Buchanan-Jardine, 3 Bt (d 1969); *Style* - Prudence, Lady Buchanan-Jardine; Moulin de la Mourachonne, 06370 Mouans Sartoux, France AM

BUCK, (Philip) Antony Fyson; QC (1974), MP (C) Colchester 1961-; s of A Buck, of Ely; *b* 19 Dec 1928; *Educ* King's Sch Ely, Trin Hall Cambridge; *m* 1955, Judy, da of Dr C Grant, of Perth W Australia; 1 da; *Career* Min for RN 1972-74; chm Con Pty Def Cttee; *Recreations* most sports, reading; *Clubs* Oxford & Cambridge; *Style* - Antony Buck Esq, QC, MP; Pete Hall, Langenhoe, Colchester, Essex (☎ Peldon 230)

BUCK, Charles Gerard; JP (1966); s of Walter Buck; *b* 21 Sept 1910; *Educ* Trent Coll; *m* 1946, Georgette, da of John Raeside; 1 da (and 1 da decd); *Career* CA 1934-; chm Buck & Lloyd (Sheffield) and Sheffield Brick Gp 1975-80; Gen Cmmr Taxes 1970-; High Sheriff S Yorks 1980-81; *Recreations* cricket, hockey, golf; *Clubs* MCC (Sheffield), Sheffield Amateur Sports Club; *Style* - Charles Buck Esq, JP; The Grange, Bradway rd, Sheffield S17 4PF (☎ 0742 363585)

BUCK, Harry Grant; s of Harry Buck, OBE, JP, of Newmarket; *b* 17 June 1921; *Educ* Perse Sch, Clare Cambridge; *m* 1950, Nancy, da of Frederick Taylor, of Dullingham House, Newmarket; 3 da; *Career* dir Shell Venezuela (with Roy Dutch Shell Gp 1947-79); now int oil consultant & memb bd advsrs Northville Industl Corpn US; *Recreations* travel, working, racing; *Style* - Harry Buck Esq; Ickleton Place, nr Saffron Walden, Essex (☎ 0799 30266)

BUCK, Michael Bernard Langdale; s of Horace Kitchen Buck (d 1953); *b* 25 May 1923; *Educ* Cockburn H S; *m* 1956, Brenda, da of Harry Simpson (d 1977); 3 s; *Career* CA, assist md finance Hargreaves Gp (dir 1971-); *Recreations* gardening, bird watching, short walks; *Style* - Michael Buck Esq; Langdale, 55 Breary Lane E, Bramhope, Leeds

BUCKHURST, Lord; William Herbrand Sackville; s and h of 10 Earl De La Warr; *b* 10 April 1948; *Educ* Eton; *m* 1978, Anne, nee Leveson, former w of Earl of Hopetoun (s of 3 Marq of Linlithgow); 2 s; *Career* stockbroker, Mullens & Co; *Style* - Lord Buckhurst; 49 Smith st, SW3 (☎ 01 352 1317)

BUCKINGHAMSHIRE, 9 Earl of (GB 1746); Sir Vere Frederick Cecil Hobart-Hampden; 13 Bt (E 1611); Baron Hobart (GB 1728); s of late Arthur Ernest Hobart-Hampden, gs of 6 Earl (himself ggs of Mary, da of John Hampden, the opponent of Charles I's Ship Money and one of the leading Parliamentarian opponents of the Monarchy in the 1640s and early Civil War); suc kinsman 1963; *b* 17 May 1901; *Educ* in Switzerland and at St Lawrence Coll Ramsgate; *m* 1972, Margot Macrae, da of John Storey Rodger, of NSW, Australia, & widow of F C Bruce Hittman, MD, FRACS, of Sydney, Australia; *Heir* kinsman, (George) Miles Hobart-Hampden; *Career* sheep farmer Australia 1919-49, served 1942-46 RAAF; *Style* - The Rt Hon The Earl of Buckinghamshire; 21a Hanover sq, W1

BUCKLEY, Hon Colin Burton; s of 1 Baron Wrenbury, PC, QC, sometime Ld Justice of Appeal; *b* 16 Oct 1899; *Educ* Eton, King's Cambridge; *m* 1925, Evelyn, da of Sir Hugh Webster; 1 s, 4 da (and 1 da decd); *Career* MB, BCh; *Style* - The Hon Colin Buckley; Greenstead, Windermere, Westmorland

BUCKLEY, Rt Hon Lord Justice; Rt Hon Sir Denys Burton Buckley; MBE (Mil 1945), PC (1970); s of 1 Baron Wrenbury, PC, QC (Lord Justice of Appeal 1906-15, d 1935); *b* 6 Feb 1906; *Educ* Eton, Trin Oxford; *m* 1932, Gwendolen, da of Sir Robert Armstrong-Jones, CBE, JP, DL; 3 da; *Career* barr 1928; High Ct Judge (Chancery) 1960-70, Lord Justice of Appeal 1970-; CstJ ; kt 1960; *Clubs* Brooks's, Beefsteak; *Style* - Rt Hon Lord Justice Buckley, MBE, PC; Stream Farm, Dallington, Sussex (☎ Rushlake Green 223); Plâs Dinas, nr Caernarvon, Gwynedd (☎ Llanwnda 830274); 105 Onslow sq, SW7 (☎ 01 584 4735)

BUCKLEY, Hon Elizabeth Margaret; da of 3 Baron Wrenbury by his 2 w

Penelope; *b* 21 May 1964; *Style* - The Hon Elizabeth Buckley

BUCKLEY, Hon Joyce Burton; da of 1 Baron Wrenbury, PC, QC; *b* 10 Feb 1889; *Style* - The Hon Joyce Buckley; Caldicote, Lindfield, Sussex (☎ 3115)

BUCKLEY, Hon Katherine Lucy; 2 da of 3 Baron Wrenbury by his 2 w Penelope; *b* 13 Nov 1968; *Style* - The Hon Katherine Buckley

BUCKLEY, Hon Dame Ruth Burton; DBE (1959), JP (Sussex 1935); 4 da of 1 Baron Wrenbury, PC, QC; *b* 12 July 1898; *Educ* Cheltenham Ladies' Coll; *Career* barr 1926; alderman Sussex 1946-74, chm Sussex CC 1952-55; *Style* - The Hon Dame Ruth Buckley DBE JP; Toll Wood Cottage, Netherfield, Battle, E Sussex (☎ Brightling 222)

BUCKLEY, Hon William Edward; s and h of 3 Baron Wrenbury by his 2 w Penelope; *b* 19 June 1966; *Style* - The Hon William Buckley

BUCKLEY, Maj William Kemmis; MBE (1959), DL (Carmarthenshire, latterly Dyfed 1969); s of Lt-Col William Buckley, DL, of Castell Gorfod, Dyfed; *b* 18 Oct 1921; *Educ* Radley, New Coll Oxford; *Career* Lt-Col Welsh Gds, served WW II and Suez 1956, Mil Assist to Vice-CIGS 1958-59; chm Buckley's Brewery 1972; High Sheriff Carmarthenshire 1966-67; dir Felinfoel Brewery 1975, Rhymney Brewery (now Whitbread) 1962; *Recreations* gardening; *Clubs* Brooks's, Cardiff & County; *Style* - Maj William Buckley, MBE, DL; Briar Cottage, Ferryside, Dyfed (☎ 359)

BUCKMAN, Hon Mrs Griselda Rosalind; *née* Eden; da of 6 Baron Henley (d 1962); *b* 1917; *m* 1939 (m dis 1964), John Buckman, late Sqdn-Ldr RAFVR; 1 s, 1 da; *Style* - The Hon Mrs Griselda Buckman; 8 High st, W Haddon, Northampton

BUCKMASTER, 3 Viscount (UK 1933); Martin Stanley Buckmaster; OBE (1979); also Baron Buckmaster (UK 1915); s of 2 Viscount (d 1974), by 1 w, Joan, da of Dr Garry Simpson; *b* 11 April 1921; *Educ* Stowe; *Heir* bro, Hon Colin Buckmaster; *Career* FO 1946, First Sec Br High Cmmn Kampala 1969-71, Beirut 1971-73, FCO 1973-77, Head of Chancery Yemen Arab Republic 1977-, FRGS; *Style* - The Rt Hon The Viscount Buckmaster OBE; 8 Redcliffe sq, SW10

BUCKMASTER, Hon Colin John; s of late 2 Viscount Buckmaster, by 1 w, Joan, da of Dr Garry Simpson; hp of bro, 3 Viscount; *b* 17 April 1923; *Educ* Winchester; *m* 1946, May, da of Charles Henry Gibbon; 3 s, 2 da; *Career* late Fl-Lt RAF; *Style* - The Hon Colin Buckmaster; Ryece Hall, Brettenham, Ipswich, Suffolk

BUCKMASTER, Viscountess; Diana Constance; da of Maj Kenneth Seth-Smith; *m* 1, 1948 (m dis 1956), Charles Vane-Tempest (gggs of 3 Marquess of Londonderry); 1 s, 1 da; m 2, 1961, as his 2 w, 2 Viscount Buckmaster (d 1974); *Style* - The Rt Hon The Viscountess Buckmaster; 74 Cheyne Court, Royal Hospital rd, SW3 (☎ 01 352 2593)

BUCKWORTH-HERNE-SOAME, Sir Charles John; 12 Bt (E 1697) of Sheen, Surrey; s of Sir Charles Burnett Buckworth-Herne-Soame, 11 Bt (d 1977); *b* 28 May 1932; *m* 1958, Eileen Margaret Mary, da of Leonard Minton, of Caughley, Salop; 1 s; *Heir* s, Richard Buckworth-Herne-Soame; *Style* - Sir Charles Buckworth-Herne-Soame, Bt; Sheen Cottage, Coalbrookdale, Telford, Salop

BUCKWORTH-HERNE-SOAME, Richard John; s of Sir Charles Buckworth-Herne-Some, 12 Bt; *b* 17 Aug 1970

BUDGEN, Hon Mrs - Hon (Anne) Patricia Rosamund; *née* Wynn; da of 7 Baron Newborough, DSC; *b* 1947; *m* 1970, Anthony George Budgen; 1 s, 1 da; *Style* - The Hon Mrs Budgen; Boreaton House, Baschurch, Salop SY4 2EP

BULFIELD, Peter William; s of Wilfred Bulfield, of Midhurst; *b* 14 June 1930; *Educ* Beaumont; *m* 1958, Pamela, da of Arthur Beckett, of Buenos Aires; 2 da; *Career* CA Scotland 1953; dir J Henry

Schroder Wagg 1966, Darling Hldgs Australia 1973, jt dep chm Schroder Int 1978, v-chm MTBC & Schroder Bank SA Brussels 1976; Crown Agent for Overseas Govts & Admins 1978; *Recreations* music, sailing (yacht- 'Keiko IV'), shooting, painting *Clubs* Kildare Street & University *Style* - Peter Bulfield Esq; 16 Coldharbour Lane, Hildenborough, Tonbridge, Kent (☎ Hildenborough 832231); Flat 3, 48 Lower Sloane st, SW1

BULGIN, Ronald Arthur; s of Wing Cdr Arthur Bulgin, OBE, of Essex; *b* 20 Aug 1935; *Educ* Westminster, Merton Oxford; *m* 1, 1958, Margaret Gray (m dis); 2 s, 1 da; m 2, 1969, Elaine Harvey; 1 s, 1 da; *Career* chm Bulgin Gp; *Recreations* riding, golf; *Clubs* Essex Farmers Hunt, Chigwell Golf, RAC; *Style* - Ronald Bulgin Esq; Norton Manor, Norton Mandeville, Blackmore, Essex (☎ 822211)

BULL, Sir George; 3 Bt (UK 1922), of Hammersmith Co London; s of Rt Hon Sir William Bull, 1 Bt, PC, sometime MP Hammersmith (d 1931); suc bro, Sir Stephen Bull, 2 Bt, 1942; *b* 19 June 1906; *Educ* RNCs Osborne and Dartmouth, Paris, Vienna; *m* 1933, Gabrielle, da of late Bramwell Jackson, MC, of Bury St Edmunds; 1 s, 1 da; *Heir* s, Simeon Bull; *Career* formerly Cdr RNVR; slr 1929, sr ptnr legal firm of Bull & Bull; chm Standing Cncl Baronetage 1979-; *Clubs* Arts, MCC; *Style* - Sir George Bull, Bt; 3 Hammersmith ter, W6 (☎ 01 748 2400)

BULL, George Jeffrey; s of Michael Bull; *b* 16 July 1936; *Educ* Ampleforth; *m* 1960, Fleur, da of Patrick Freeland; 4 s; *Career* formerly Lt Coldstream Gds; dep md IDV Ltd; *Recreations* golf, photography *Clubs* Roy Worlington Golf, Newmarket Golf; *Style* - George Bull Esq; The Old Vicarage, Arkesden, Saffron Walden, Essex (☎ Clavering 445)

BULL, Sir Graham MacGregor; s of Dr Arthur Bull; *b* 30 Jan 1918; *Educ* Diocesan Coll Capetown, Capetown U; *m* 1947, Megan, da of Thomas Jones; 3 s, 1 da; *Career* kt 1976, dir Med Res Cncl's Clin Res Centre Northwich Park Hosp Harrow 1966-78; *Style* - Sir Graham Bull; 29 Heath dve, NW3 (☎ 01 435 1624)

BULL, Hon Mrs (Judith Florence); *née* Gurdon; DL (1980 Suffolk); da of late 2 Baron Cranworth, KG, MC; *b* 1914; *m* 1943, Thomas Henry Bull, late Lt RA; *Style* - The Hon Mrs Bull, DL; Park Farm, Grundisburgh, Suffolk

BULL, Lady; Megan Patricia; da of Thomas Jones; *b* 17 March 1922, S Africa; *Educ* Good Hope Seminary Cape Town, Cape Town U; *m* 1947, Sir Graham Bull; 3 s, 1 da *Career* Gov Holloway Prison 1973-, MB, ChB, MRCP; *Style* - Lady Bull; HM Prison, Holloway, Parkhurst rd, N7 (☎ 01 607 0231)

BULL, Hon Mrs Noreen Madeleine; *née* Hennessy; da of 1 Baron Windlesham, OBE, JP; *b* 1910; *m* 1931 (m dis 1948), Michael Bull; 2 s; *Style* - The Hon Mrs Noreen Bull; Belgravia Court, 33 Ebury st, SW1

BULL, Simeon George; s and h of Sir George Bull, 3 Bt; *b* 1 Aug 1934; *Educ* Eton, Innsbruck, Paris (Ecole de Notariat); *m* 1961, Annick Elizabeth Renée Geneviève, da of Louis Bresson, of Château des Masselins, Chandai, Orne, France; 1 s, 2 da; *Career* slr; ptnr legal firm of Bull & Bull; *Recreations* sailing, gardening; *Clubs* Roy Thames Yacht, MCC; *Style* - Simeon Bull Esq; Kerlan, Pont L'Abbé, Finistère 5, France; Oakwood, Sturry, Kent

BULLEN, William Alexander; s of Francis Bullen; *b* 22 Sept 1918; *Educ* Merchant Taylors, London Hosp; *m* 1, 1949, Phyllis (m dis 1955), da of George Leeson; 3 da; m 2, 1956, Beatrice, da of Rev William Crutchley; *Career* Pres Pfizer Canada 1962, chm Coty (England) 1965, md Scribbans Kemp 1966, dep chm Borthwicks 1974, chm Freshbake Foods 1975, chm Thomas Borthwick & Sons 1975-, chm Whitburgh Investments; dir Nat Bank of NZ; *Recreations* sailing (auxiliary ketch- 'Sal Volatile'), reading, music; *Clubs* Roy Thames Yacht; *Style* - William Bullen Esq; The Baye House, Ickham, Canterbury, Kent (☎ Littlebourne 224)

BULLER, Lady Hermione (Moray); *née* Stuart; da of 17 Earl of Moray (d 1930); *b*

1899; *m* 1919, Adm Sir Henry Tritton Buller, GCVO, CB (d 1960); 1 s, 1 da; *Style* - Lady Hermione Buller; Netherwood, Southwater, Horsham, Sussex

BULLOCK, Baron (Life Peer UK 1976); Alan Louis Charles Bullock; FBA (1967); s of Rev Frank Allen Bullock, of Bradford, Yorks; *b* 13 Dec 1914; *Educ* Bradford G S, Wadham Oxford (MA, DLitt); *m* 1940, Hilda Yates, da of Edwin Handy, of Bradford; 3 s, 1 da; *Career* kt 1972, historian and writer; author of *Hitler, A Study in Tyranny* 1952, *The Life and Times of Ernest Bevin* Vol I 1960, Vol II 1967, Fellow, Dean and Tutor of New Coll Oxford 1945-52, Censor St Catherine's Soc Oxford 1960-, V-Chllr Oxford U 1969-73; *Style* - The Rt Hon The Lord Bullock; Master's Lodgings, St Catherine's College, Oxford (☎ 49541)

BULLUS, Wing Cdr Sir Eric Edward; s of Thomas Bullus, of Leeds; *b* 20 Nov 1906; *Educ* Leeds Modern Sch, Leeds U; *m* 1949, Joan, da of Capt Hector Denny, of Herne Bay; 2 da; *Career* kt 1964, journalist; MP (C) Wembley N 1950-74, PPS Min Overseas Tde, Aviation and to Sec of State Def 1953-64; *Recreations* swimming; *Clubs* MCC; *Style* - Wing Cdr Sir Eric Bullus; Westway, Herne Bay, Kent

BULMAN, Arthur Denis; s of H Bulman, of Morwick Hall; *b* 18 June 1919; *Educ* RNCs Dartmouth & Greenwich; *m* 1940, Katharine, da of Col D McVean; 2 da; *Career* Cdr RN (1937-61); with Texaco 1961-, dir Texaco and Assist V-Pres Marine Dept; md Regent Oil; *Recreations* sailing, shooting, fishing; *Clubs* Brooks's, RN Sailing Assoc; *Style* - Cdr Arthur Bulman; South Court, Finchampstead, Berks (☎ 0734 733230)

BULSTRODE, David Wilton; s of Norman Wilton Bulstrode; *b* 22 Sept 1940; *Educ* Haberdashers' Aske's; *m* 1965, Maria Sylvia; 1 s, 1 da; *Career* AIB; dir-Lazard Bros (Jersey) 1976, Marler Estates 1978, Jersey European Airways 1980, London Equitable Estates 1980, Jersey New Waterworks 1981; *Recreations* rugby, cricket; *Clubs* IOD; *Style* - David Bulstrode Esq; Le Nid Solitaire, Rue des Charrières, St Martin, Jersey, CI (☎ 0534 54626)

BUNBURY, Michael William; s and h of Sir (John) William Bunbury, 12 Bt; *b* 29 Dec 1946; *Educ* Eton, Trin Cambridge; *m* 1976, Caroline Anne, da of Col A D S Magnall, OBE, of Bradley Court, Chieveley, Berks; 1 s, 1 da; *Style* - Michael Bunbury Esq; Naunton Hall, Rendlesham, Woodbridge, Suffolk

BUNBURY, Sir (John) William Napier; 12 Bt (E 1681); s of Sir Charles Henry Napier Bunbury, 11 Bt (d 1963); *b* 3 July 1915; *Educ* Eton, Jesus Cambridge; *m* 1940, Margaret Pamela, da of late Thomas Alexander Sutton (gs of Sir Richard Sutton, 4 Bt); 3 s; *Heir* s, Michael William Bunbury; *Career* Capt KRRC WW II; High Sheriff of Suffolk 1972-73; *Style* - Sir William Bunbury, Bt; Hollesley House, Hollesley, Woodbridge, Suffolk (☎ Shottisham 250)

BUNCH, Austin Wyeth; CBE (1978, MBE 1974); s of Horace William Bunch (d 1953); *b* 20 March 1918; *Educ* Christ's Hosp; *m* 1944, Joan Mary, nee Peryer; 4 da; *Career* Lt Essex Regt 1941-44, chm The Electricity Cncl 1981- (dep chm 1976-81, salary as chm £48,000 pa as of June 1981), S Electricity Bd 1949-76, Deloite Plender Griffiths 1935-48; *Recreations* sports for the disabled; *Clubs* Victory (Services); *Style* - Austin Bunch Esq, CBE; Somner, School lane, Cookham, Berks (☎ Bourne End 21551)

BUNDEY, Ian Oliver; s of Rev Stanley Bundey, of Alvanley, Cheshire; *b* 7 July 1939; *Educ* St John's Leatherhead; *m* 1966, Gwenda, da of Haydn Carrington, of Wrexham; *Career* financial dir Capper Neill Int 1972-; *Recreations* golf; *Clubs* Sandiway Golf (Cheshire); *Style* - Ian Bundey Esq; 1 Wayside Close, Lymm, Cheshire (☎ 092575 4568)

BUNFORD, (Max Adolph) Edward; s of late (Adolph) John Tassillo Bunford; *b* 10 Nov 1920; *Educ* Theresianum Vienna, Univ of Vienna, LSE; *m* 1, 1946; m 2, 1967, (Marie) Claude (Blanche), da of late

André Elysée Bidoire (gynaecologist and prof of Medicine Paris University); 2 s, 1 da; *Career* chm Layford Gp of Cos 1962, dir Comotor SA Luxembourg 1964, v-chm Gestam Inc New York (USA) 1976, chm Gestam Guinness Peat Int Realty Ltd London 1980; *Recreations* riding, yachting (yacht- 'Amalia'); *Clubs* Royal Thames Yacht, Automobile Club de France, Club Interallié (Paris), Lyford Cay Club (Nassau Bahamas); *Style* - Edward Bunford Esq

BUNKER, Peter John; s of Leslie John Daniel Bunker; *b* 26 Feb 1928; *Educ* Brighton Hove & Sussex G S, Gonville & Caius Coll Cambridge; *m* 1952, Angela Elizabeth, nee Higham; 2 s, 2 da; *Career* slr (Broderip & Mellersh Prizes); pres Sussex Law Society 1979-80; *Recreations* gardening, skiing, listening to music; *Style* - Peter Bunker Esq; 38 Shirley drive, Hove, East Sussex (☎ Brighton 503729)

BUNNEY, John Herrick; *b* 2 June 1945; *m* 1970, Pamela Anne Simcock; 1 s, 1 da; *Career* 2 Sec FCO 1971, MECAS 1971, 1 Sec Damascus 1974-78, Consul Sana'a 1981-; *Style* - John Bunney Esq; c/o FCO, SW1

BUNZL, Thomas F; s of Dr Max Bunzl; *b* 13 Dec 1934; *Educ* Bembridge Sch (IOW), Glasgow U, U of Calif; *m* 1959, Marian, da of Walter Strauss; 2 da; *Career* md Electrautom Ltd 1965-; MIEE, MIEEE, FISM, FIPM; *Style* - Thomas Bunzl Esq; 126 West Heath rd, NW3 (☎ 01 458 2691)

BURBIDGE, Sir Herbert Dudley; 5 Bt (UK 1916); s of late Herbert Edward Burbidge, 2 s of 1 Bt; suc kinsman, Sir John Richard Woodman Burbidge, 4 Bt, 1974; *b* 13 Nov 1904; *Educ* University Sch Victoria BC Canada; *m* 1933, Ruby, da of Charles Ethelbert Taylor, of Comox, Vancouver 1, BC; 1 s; *Heir* s, Peter Burbidge; *Career* man Silverwood Industries (Vancouver) 1931-70; *Style* - Sir Herbert Burbidge, Bt; 12549, 27th Avenue, Surrey, British Columbia, Canada

BURBIDGE, Peter Dudley; s and h of Sir Herbert Burbidge, 5 Bt; *b* 20 June 1942; *m* 1967, Peggy Marilyn, da of Kenneth Anderson, of Ladner, BC; 1 s, 1 da; *Style* - Peter Burbidge Esq; 3809 West 24th av, Vancouver, BC, Canada

BURBURY, Hon Mrs (Sarah Dingle); *née* Foot; da of Baron Caradon (Life Peer); *b* 1939; *m* 1961, Maj Timothy Nicholas Percival Winter Burbury, The Blues & Royals; *Style* - Hon Mrs Burbury

BURDEN, 2 Baron (UK 1950); Philip William Burden; s of 1 Baron Burden, CBE (d 1970); *b* 21 June 1916; *Educ* Raines Foundation Sch; *m* 1951, Audrey Elsworth, da of Maj Wilfred Elsworth Sykes, of Kirk Ella, Hull; 3 s, 3 da; *Heir* s, Hon Andrew Burden; *Style* - The Rt Hon The Lord Burden; North Down House Farm, Churchinford, Taunton, Somerset

BURDEN, Augusta, Baroness; Augusta; da of David Sime, of Aberdeen; *m* 1910, 1 Baron Burden (d 1970); 1 s (2 Baron); *Style* - The Rt Hon Augusta, Lady Burden; North Down House Farm, Churchinford, Taunton, Somerset

BURDEN, Hon Andrew Philip; s and h of 2 Baron Burden; *b* 20 July 1959; *Style* - The Hon Andrew Burden

BURDER, Sir John Henry; ED; s of Henry Burder; *b* 30 Nov 1900; *Educ* Eton; *m* 1929, Constance, da of Maj Gilbert Bailey (k 1915); 2 da; *Career* Lt-Col; Pres Imperial Bank of India 1945-47, Assoc'd with Chambers of Commerce India 1943; memb Cncl of State India 1943; kt 1944; *Clubs* Oriental; *Style* - Sir John Burder, ED; Pytts Piece, Burford, Oxon (☎ 2287)

BURDETT, Crispin Peter; s and h of Sir Savile Burdett, 11 Bt; *b* 8 Feb 1967; *Style* - Crispin Burdett Esq

BURDETT, Sir Savile Aylmer; 11 Bt (E 1665); s of Sir Henry Aylmer Burdett, 10 Bt, MC (d 1943); *b* 24 Sept 1931; *Educ* Wellington, Imperial Coll London; *m* 1962, June Elizabeth Campbell, da of late Dr J M Rutherford, of Knowl Hill, Woking, Surrey; 1 s, 1 da; *Heir* s, Crispin Burdett; *Career* late temporary Sub-Lt RNVR; *Style* - Sir Savile Burdett, Bt;

Farthings, 35 Park av, Solihull, W Midlands

BURFORD, Earl of; Murray de Vere Beauclerk; s (by 1 m) and h of 13 Duke of St Albans, OBE; *b* 19 Jan 1939; *Educ* Tonbridge; *m* 1, 1963 (m dis 1974), Rosemary Frances, da of Francis Scoones, MRCS, LRCP, JP; 1 s, 1 da; m 2, 1974, Cynthia Theresa Mary, da of Lt-Col William James Holdsworth Howard DSO and former w of Sir Anthony Robin Maurice Hooper, 2 Bt; *Heir* s, Lord Vere of Hanworth; *Career* CA, Freeman of the City of London, Liveryman Drapers' Co; *Clubs* MCC, Hurlingham; *Style* - Earl of Burford; 3 St George's ct, Gloucester rd, SW7 (☎ 01 589 1771)

BURGEN, Sir Arnold Stanley Vincent; s of Peter Burgen; *b* 20 March 1922; *Educ* Christ's Coll Finchley, London U; *m* 1946, Judith, da of Frederick Browne; 2 s, 1 da; *Career* medical scientist, dir Inst Med Res 1971-; FRS 1964; kt 1976; *Recreations* sculpture, music; *Style* - Sir Arnold Burgen; Penshurst, Hill Crescent, Totteridge, N20 (☎ 01 959 3666)

BURGES, Maj-Gen Rodney Lyon Travers; CBE (1962), DSO (1946); s of Dr Richard Burges (d 1948); *b* 19 March 1914; *Educ* Wellington, RMA Woolwich; *m* 1946, Sheila Marion Lyster, nee Goldby; 1 s, 1 da; *Career* Maj-Gen RA; Lt 1934, Burma Assam Java 1939-45, CO Berkshire Yeomanry 1945-46, CO 3rd RHA 1955-58, GCO Cyprus 1964-66, VQMG MoD 1966-67; Grieveson Grant & Co 1968-78, ptnr and memb of the Stock Exchange 1971-78, consultant Pat Simon Wines Ltd 1978-; *Recreations* racing, drinking wine in the sun; *Clubs* Buck's, Army and Navy; *Style* - Maj-Gen Rodney Burges CBE, DSO; Freemantle, Over Wallop, Hampshire (☎ Wallop 469), Flat 8, 74 St George's sq, SW1 (☎ 821 8769)

BURGES, Maj Ynyr Alfred; JP (1936), DL (1933); s of Ynyr Richard Patrick Burges, of Queensberry Place, SW; *b* 16 April 1900; *Educ* Eton, Sandhurst; *m* 1930, Christine, da of Lt-Col George O'Shee, JP, of Elm Pk gdns, SW; 1 s, 2 da; *Career* Maj, served Army of The Black Sea 1922-23 and WW II; High Sheriff Co Tyrone 1939 and Co Armagh 1951; *Recreations* formerly cricket, tennis, squash, shooting; *Clubs* Army & Navy, Eton Ramblers Cricket; *Style* - Maj Ynyr Burges, JP, DL; Catsfield Manor, Battle, Sussex (☎ Ninfield 892339)

BURGESS, Alfred Leslie; JP (Westminster 1976); s of Alfred James Burgess (d 1967); *b* 7 Jan 1925; *Educ* Archbishop Tenison's Sch Croydon; *m* 1947, Mabel Millicent, nee Davis; 2 s, 1 da; *Career* CA, sr ptnr Barker Hibbert & Co (qualified 1952, admitted to ptnrship 1962); *Recreations* music, reading; *Clubs* City of London; *Style* - Alfred Burgess Esq, JP; 175, Amesbury ave, Streatham Hill, SW2 (☎ 674 0050)

BURGESS, Sir John Lawie; OBE (Mil 1945), TD (1945), JP (Carlisle 1952), DL (Cumberland 1955); s of Robert Burgess, of Carlisle; *b* 17 Nov 1912; *Educ* Trin Coll Glenalmond; *m* 1948, Alice, da of Frederic Gillieron, of Elgin; 2 s, 1 da; *Career* Lt-Col (Hon Col) WW II and Hon Col 4 Bn Border Regt 1955-68; chm- Cumbria Newspapers Gp 1945-, Border TV, Press Assoc 1955; kt 1972; *Clubs* Army & Navy, Garrick; *Style* - Sir John Burgess, OBE, TD, JP, DL; The Limes, Cavendish ter, Carlisle (☎ 37450)

BURGH, 7 Baron (E 1529); Alexander Peter Willoughby Leith; s of 6 Baron (d 1959); *b* 20 March 1935; *Educ* Harrow, Magdalene Cambridge; *m* 1957, Anita Lorna, da of Frederick Eldridge, of Gillingham, Kent; 2 s, 1 da (The Hon Mrs Brandler); *Heir* s, Hon Alexander Leith; *Career* formerly RAF Pilot Officer; *Style* - The Rt Hon The Lord Burgh; 174 Chesterton road, Cambridge

BURGHERSH, Lord; David Anthony Francis Fane; s and h of 15 Earl of Westmorland, KCVO; *b* 1 Aug 1951; *Educ* Eton; *Heir* brother, The Hon Harry Fane; *Style* - Lord Burghersh; 20 West London Studios, 402 Fulham rd, SW6 (☎ 01 381 1785); Kingsmead, Didmarton, Badminton, Avon (☎ Didmarton (STD Code 045 423) 634)

BURGHLEY, Lady Mary Theresa; *née* Montagu Douglas Scott; da of 7 & 9 Duke of Buccleuch & Queensberry, KT, GCVO, and Lady Margaret Bridgeman (da of 4 Earl of Bradford by his w, Lady Ida Lumley, 2 da of 9 Earl of Scarbrough); *b* 4 March 1904; *m* 1929 (m dis 1946), Lord Burghley, KCMG (now 6 Marquess of Exeter); 3 da; *Career* CStJ; *Style* - Lady Mary Burghley; 21 Hyde Park Gdns Mews, W2 (☎ 01 262 3355)

BURGIN, Peter Brinton; s of George Burgin, of Huddersfield; *b* 3 Aug 1934; *Educ* Holme Valley G S Holmfirth; *m* 1960, Jean, da of Donovan Hartshorne, of Tamerton Foliat; 1 s, 1 da; *Career* ACMA, MBCS, MInstM; mktng dir Crittall Windows 1974-78, dir & sec Dow-Mac Concrete 1978-; *Recreations* golf, gardening; *Style* - Peter Burgin Esq; 13 Robins Wood, Wansford, Peterborough (☎ 0780 783018)

BURKE, James Stanley Gilbert; s and h of Sir Thomas Burke, 8 Bt; *b* 1 July 1956; *Style* - James Burke Esq

BURKE, Sir Thomas Stanley; 8 Bt (I 1797), of Marble Hill, Galway; s of Capt Sir Gerald Burke, 7 Bt, DL (d 1954); *b* 20 July 1916; *Educ* Harrow, Trin Cambridge; *m* 1955, Susanne, da of Otto Salvisberg, of Thun, Switzerland; 1 s, 1 da; *Heir* s, James Burke; *Career* translation agent; *Style* - Sir Thomas Burke, Bt; 18 Elmcroft av, NW11 (☎ 01 455 9407)

BURLINGHAM, Richard Geoffrey; OBE (1977), TD (1944), JP (1960), DL (Hereford & Worcester 1976); s of Capt Richard Burlingham, of Pershore; *b* 11 Nov 1912; *Educ* Malvern; *m* 1939, Evelyn, da of Theodore Armstrong, of Rudgewick; 1 s, 3 da; *Career* Lt-Col WW II; ag & builders merchant; *Recreations* music, genealogy, gardening; *Style* - Richard Burlingham Esq, OBE, TD, JP, DL; The Mill House, Chadbury, Evesham, Worcs (☎ 6541)

BURLINGTON, Earl of; William Cavendish; s of Marquess of Hartington; *b* 6 June 1969 *Style* - Earl of Burlington

BURMAN, Sir (John) Charles; JP (Birmingham 1942), DL (Warwicks 1967); s of Sir John Burman, JP, of Tibbington House, Edgbaston; *b* 30 Aug 1908; *Educ* Rugby; *m* 1936, Ursula, JP, da of John Hesketh-Wright, of Bournemouth; 2 s, 2 da; *Career* chm Tarmac Ltd 1961-71; High Sheriff Warwicks 1958-59, chm Birmingham Con Assoc 1963-72, memb Roy Cmmn on Police 1960, Govt Ctee on Administrative Tbnls 1955; Lord Mayor Birmingham 1947-49; *Recreations* gardening; *Clubs* Birmingham; *Style* - Sir Charles Burman, JP, DL; Little Bickerscourt, Danzey Green, Tamworth-in-Arden, Warwicks (☎ 2711)

BURN, Hon Mrs (Anne Catherine); *née* Wilberforce; da of Baron Wilberforce, CMG, OBE, PC; *b* 5 Sept 1948; *m* 1975, Lindsay Stuart Burn; *Style* - The Hon Mrs Burn

BURNABY-ATKINS, Hon Mrs - Hon (Anne) Jennifer; *née* Lawrence; da of 3 Baron Trevethin and 1 Oaksey, DSO, TD, PC (d 1971); *b* 1926; *m* 1951, Lt-Col Frederick John Burnaby-Atkins; 1 s, 3 da; *Style* - The Hon Mrs Burnaby-Atkins; 14 Woodsfords sq, W14; 3 The Street, Oaksey, Malmesbury, Wilts

BURNELL, Digby McLaren; s of Charles Burnell; *b* 25 Feb 1920; *Educ* Harvard; *m* 1958, Maureen, da of Dr Moray Melvin, FRCP; 3 s; *Career* chm-AAA Industs, Anglo-American Asphalt Ltd 1970-, Metrotect Ltd, Airoil-Flaregas, Agil Hldgs, W J Glossop Ltd; *Recreations* reading, music; *Clubs* Army & Navy, NY Athletic (New York); *Style* - Digby Burnell Esq; 44 Boscobel Place, Eaton sq, SW1 (☎ 01 235 4715)

BURNETT, Charles David; s and h of Sir David Burnett, 3 Bt, MBE, TD; *b* 18 May 1951; *Educ* Harrow, Lincoln Oxford; *Style* - Charles Burnett Esq

BURNETT, Sir David Humphrey; 3 Bt (UK 1913), MBE (1945), TD; s of Col Sir Leslie Trew Burnett, 2 Bt, CBE, TD (d 1955); *b* 27 Jan 1918; *Educ* Harrow, St John's Cambridge; *m* 1948, Geraldine Elizabeth Mortimer, da of late Sir Godfrey Arthur Fisher, KCMG; 2 s; *Heir* s, Charles David Burnett; *Career* FRICS, FBIM;

chm Proprietors of Hay's Wharf Ltd 1965-80 (now consultant), dir Guardian Roy Exchange Assurance Ltd; memb Port of London Authority 1962-75, chm S London Botanical Inst 1964-, chm London Wharfingers Assoc 1964-71, Master of Co of Watermen and Lightermen 1964; one of HM Lts of City of London; *Style* - Sir David Burnett, Bt, MBE, TD, HM Lt of City of London; Tandridge Hall, nr Oxted, Surrey; Tillmouth Park, Cornhill-on-Tweed, Northumberland

BURNETT, Prof George Murray; s of George Burnett; *b* 12 July 1921; *Educ* Robert Gordon's Coll Aberdeen, Aberdeen U, Birmingham U; *m* 1946, Anne, da of Sidney Bow, of Aberdeen; 1 s, 3 da; *Career* Prof Chemistry Aberdeen U 1955-74; Princ & V-Chllr Heriot-Watt U 1974-; *Clubs* Caledonian, New (Edinburgh); *Style* - Prof George Burnett; Hermiston House, Hermiston, Calder rd, Edinburgh EH14 4AQ (☎ 031 449 5595)

BURNETT, Dr John Harrison; s of Rev T Harrison Burnett; *b* 21 Jan 1922; *Educ* Kingswood Sch Bath, Merton Oxford; *m* 1945, Enid, da of Rev Dr Edgar Bishop; 2 s; *Career* Princ & V-Chllr Edinburgh U 1979-; Sibthorpian Prof Rural Economy & Fell St John's Oxford 1970-79; Regius Prof Botany Glasgow 1968-70; *Recreations* writing, walking, gardening; *Clubs* New (Edinburgh), Caledonian (London); *Style* - Dr John Burnett; Old College, South Bridge, Edinburgh EH8 9YL (☎ 031 667 1011)

BURNETT, Lt-Col Maurice John Brownless; DSO (1944), JP (N Yorks 1957), DL (1958); s of Ernest Burnett, MBE, JP, OStJ; *b* 24 Sept 1904; *Educ* Rugby, RMA Woolwich, Staff Coll Camberley; *m* 1930, Crystal, da of Col Henry Deschamps Chamier, The Connaught Rangers; 1 s; *Career* Lt-Col, Regular Offr 1924-48, Sec N Riding Yorks TA 1950-68, chm Richmond RDC 1967-69, memb N Riding and N Yorks CC 1962-; *Recreations* formerly hunting, shooting, polo, swimming; *Clubs* Army & Navy; *Style* - Lt-Col Maurice Burnett, DSO, JP, DL; Dunsa Manor, Dalton, Richmond, N Yorks (☎ East Layton 251)

BURNEY, Sir Cecil Denniston; 3 Bt (UK 1921), of Preston House, Preston Candover, Co Southampton; s of Sir Charles Burney, 2 Bt, CMG (d 1968); *b* 8 Jan 1923; *Educ* Eton, Trin Cambridge; *m* 1957, Mrs Hazel de Hamel, da of Thurman Coleman; 2 s; *Heir* s, Nigel Burney; *Career* formerly Lt Special Branch RNVR; chm Hampton Tst; memb Legve Cncl N Rhodesia 1959-64 and MP Zambia 1964-68, chm Public Accounts Cttee Zambia 1964-68; *Recreations* tennis, skiing; *Clubs* Turf, Carlton, Buck's, Leander, Salisbury, Ndola; *Style* - Sir Cecil Burney, Bt; 5 Lyall st, SW1 (☎ 01 235 4014)

BURNEY, Gladys, Lady; Gladys; da of George Henry High, of Lake Shore Drive, Chicago; *m* 1921, Cdr Sir Dennistoun Burney, 2 Bt, CMG (d 1968); 1 s; *Style* - Gladys, Lady Burney; Huntley Towers, Paget, Bermuda

BURNEY, Nigel Dennistoun; s and h of Sir Cecil Burney, 3 Bt; *b* 6 Sept 1959; *Style* - Nigel Burney Esq

BURNHAM, 5 Baron (UK 1903); Sir William Edward Harry Lawson; 5 Bt (UK 1892), JP (Bucks 1970), DL (1977); s of Maj-Gen 4 Baron Burnham, CB, DSO, MC, TD (d 1963, ggs of Joseph Moses Levy, fndr proprietor of The Daily Telegraph as the first London penny daily), and Marie Enid, nee Robson, CBE; *b* 22 Oct 1920; *Educ* Eton; *m* 1942, Anne, da of Maj George Petherick, of St Cross Hants; (1 s decd), 3 da; *Heir* bro, Hon Hugh Lawson; *Career* landowner; served Roy Bucks Yeomanry 1939-41, Scots Gds 1941-68 (commanded 1 Bn 1959-62); chm Sail T'ning Assoc 1977-, Masonic Housing Assoc 1979-; *Recreations* sailing, shooting; *Clubs* Roy Yacht Sqdn, Turf, Garrick; *Style* - The Rt Hon The Lord Burnham, JP, DL; Hall Barn, Beaconsfield, Bucks (☎ 3315)

BURNIER, Hon Mrs; Hon Kamala; da of late 1 Baron Sinha (*see Sinha, Hon Tarun*); *b* 1892; *m* 1, 1910 (m dis 1943), Ashoke Chandra Gupta, OBE, Accountant-Gen (ret) Central Revenue India; 1 s; m 2, 1943, J Burnier; *Style* - The Hon Mrs Burnier; Paris

BURNS, Hon Mrs; Hon Dorothy; da of 1 and last Baron Duveen (d 1939); *m* 1, 1931 (m dis 1937), Lt-Cdr William Francis Cuthbert Garthwaite, DSC, RNVR (afterwards 2 Bt); m 2, 1938, Bryan Hartopp Burns, FRCS; *Style* - The Hon Mrs Burns; 6 Chesterfield Hill, W1

BURNS, Sir John Crawford; s of William Burns; *b* 29 Aug 1903; *Educ* Glasgow H S; *m* 1941, Eleanor, da of Rev Montague James; 1 s, 3 da; *Career* Capt in WW II; dir James Finlay & Co 1957-74; kt 1957; *Recreations* golf, fishing; *Clubs* Oriental; *Style* - Sir John Burns; Glenorchard, Dunblane, Perthshire (☎ 0786 822367)

BURNS, Hon Mrs (Mary Margaret); *née* Addington; da of 7 Viscount Sidmouth; *b* 1956; *m* 1978, James Alexander Burns; *Style* - The Hon Mrs Burns; Travessa da Portugesa No 5, Lisbon, Portugal

BURNS, Sir Wilfred; CB (1972), CBE (1967); s of Bertram Burns; *b* 11 April 1923; *Educ* Ulverston G S, Liverpool U, Newcastle U; *m* 1945, Edna, da of George Price; 1 s, 1 da; *Career* kt 1980; Ch Planner (1968-) & Dep Sec DOE 1971-; *Style* - Sir Wilfred Burns, CB, CBE; 29a Sydenham Hill, SE 26 (☎ 01 670 3525)

BURNTWOOD, Baron (Life Peer UK 1970); Julian Ward Snow; s of late Henry Martin Snow, CVO, of Eltham, Kent; *b* 24 Feb 1910; *Educ* Haileybury; *m* 1948, Flavia Ria Joan (d 1980), da of late Sir Ralph Barrett Macnaughten Blois, 9 Bt; 1 da; *Career* with Dunlop Rubber Co 1928-37, John Lewis & Co Ltd 1938-39, Capt RA WW II, MP (L) Portsmouth Central 1945-50, for Lichfield and Tamworth Staffs 1950-70, V-Chamberlain to Roy Household 1945-50, a Lord Cmmr of HM Treasury and a Govt Whip 1946-50, Parly Sec Miny of Aviation 1966-67, Miny of Health 1967-68, Parly Under-Sec of State Dept of Health and Social Security 1968-69, V-Pres British-Japanese Parl Gp; *Style* - The Rt Hon The Lord Burntwood; 2/37 Chester Way, SE11 (☎ 01 735 6760)

BURRELL, Hon Lady; Hon Anne Judith; OBE (1947); da of late 3 Baron Denman; *b* 1907; *Educ* Cambridge U; *m* 1931, Lt-Col Sir Walter Raymond Burrell, 8 Bt, CBE, TD, DL; 2 s, 2 da; *Career* former Chm of Women's Land Army W Sussex, V-Pres Family Planning Assoc; *Style* - The Hon Lady Burrell, OBE; Knepp Castle, Horsham

BURRELL, John Raymond; s and h of Sir Walter Burrell, 8 Bt, CBE, TD, DL, by his w, Hon Anne, OBE, da of 3 Baron Denman, GCMG, KCVO, PC; *b* 20 Feb 1934; *Educ* Eton; *m* 1, 1959, Rowena (m dis 1971), da of Michael Pearce; 1 s; m 2, 1971, Margot, da of F Thatcher, of Sydney; 1 s, 1 da; *Style* - John Burrell Esq; Foreglen, Armidale, NSW, Australia

BURRELL, Lt-Col Sir Walter Raymond; 8 Bt (GB 1774), of Valentine House, Essex, CBE (1956, MBE Mil 1945), TD (1942), DL (Sussex 1937); s of Lt-Col Sir Merrik Burrell, 7 Bt, CBE, JP (d 1957); *b* 11 Dec 1903; *Educ* Eton; *m* 1931, Hon Anne, OBE, da of 3 Baron Denman, GCMG, KCVO, PC, JP, and Hon Gertrude Pearson, GBE, JP (da of 1 Viscount Cowdray); 2 s, 2 da; *Heir* s, John Burrell; *Career* landowner and farmer; Pres CLA 1952-53, Roy Ag Soc of England 1964; v-chm W Sussex CC 1953; Lt-Col Washington 1943; *Recreations* shooting, fishing; *Clubs* Boodle's; *Style* - Lt-Col Sir Walter Burrell, Bt, CBE TD DL; Knepp Castle, W Grinstead, Horsham, Sussex (☎ Coolham 247)

BURROWS, Sir (Robert) John Formby; s of Rev Canon Francis Burrows, of Ashton-under-Lyne; *b* 29 May 1901; *Educ* Eton, Trin Cambridge; *m* 1926, Mary, da of Rev Robert Salmon, of Chiddingstone, Kent; 1 s, 1 da; *Career* slr ret; Pres Law Soc 1964-65; kt 1965; *Recreations* small scale forestry; *Clubs* United Oxford & Cambridge, Buck's; *Style* - Sir John Burrows; Ridlands Cottage, Limpsfield Chart, Surrey (☎ 3288)

BURROWS, John Henry; ERD (1946), JP (Essex 1939), DL (1961); s of John Burrows, JP, FSA; *b* 16 July 1908; *Educ* Gresham's, Trin Hall Cambridge; *m* 1937, Agnes, da of William Brown, of Isle of Arran; 4 s; *Career* Maj WW II; chm Southend-on-Sea Justices 1955-64;

formerly md John H Burrows & Sons Ltd; *Recreations* fishing, shooting; *Clubs* Farmers' (Whitehall), Sydney, United Services (Brisbane); *Style* - John Burrows Esq, ERD, JP, DL; c/o Harden Grazing Co, Bundorah, Tenterfield, NSW 2372; 26 The Lido, Isle of Capri, Surfers Paradise, Qld, Australia

BURROWS, Robert David; s of Sir Robert Burrows (d 1961); *b* 12 May 1929; *Educ* Shrewsbury; *m* 1973, Erica, da of Louis Simonds; 1 s, 3 da; *Career* formerly 2 Lt 9 Lancers; md Br Moulded Fibre, chm Br Moulded Fibre (Engrg) Ltd; *Recreations* shooting; *Style* - Robert Burrows Esq; Field Grove House, Bitton, Bristol

BURROWS, Timothy John; s of Sir John Burrows, *qv*; *b* 18 Dec 1927; *Educ* Eton, Trin Cambridge; *m* 1952, Catherine, da of Dr Samuel Russell Foster, MC, of Belfast; 3 s, 1 da; *Career* slr 1953, ptnr Currey & Co, London; dir Halifax Bldg Soc 1968, Moorside Tst 1979-; *Recreations* swimming, shooting, stalking, chess; *Clubs* MCC, Jesters, Oxford & Cambridge; *Style* - Timothy Burrows Esq; Hilders Farm, Bough Beech, Edenbridge, Kent

BURTON OF COVENTRY, Baroness (Life Peeress UK 1962); Elaine Frances Burton; da of late Leslie Aubrey Burton, of Harrogate; *b* 2 March 1904; *Educ* Leeds Modern Sch, Leeds Training Coll; *Career* teacher Leeds 1924-35, memb S Wales Cncl of Social Welfare 1935-37, of Nat Fitness Cncl 1938-39, MP (L) Coventry S 1950-59; former consultant John Waddington Ltd, Courtaulds Ltd; memb ITA 1964-69, Cncl of Industrial Design 1963-68, Sports Cncl 1965-71, chm Mail Order Publishers' Authority 1970, pres Inst of Travel Managers in Industry and Commerce; *Style* - The Rt Hon The Lady Burton of Coventry; 47 Molyneux st, W1 (☎ 01 262 0864)

BURTON, 3 Baron (UK 1897); Michael Evan Victor Baillie; s of Brig Hon George Evan Michael Baillie, MC, TD (s of Baroness Burton, to whom Barony passed from 1 Baron by special remainder, and her 1 husband, Col James Baillie, MVO, JP, DL, sometime MP Inverness-shire), by his w, Lady Maud, nee Cavendish, CBE, JP, widow of Capt Angus Mackintosh, RHG, and da of 9 Duke of Devonshire, KG; through Lady Maud Lord Burton is 1 cous to Maurice Macmillan, MP, and 2 Viscount Stuart of Findhorn; suc grandmother 1962; *b* 27 June 1924; *Educ* Eton; *m* 1, 1948 (m dis 1977), Elizabeth, da of late Capt Anthony Wise; 2 s, 4 da; m 2, 1978, Coralie, da of Claude Cliffe, of S Africa; *Heir* s, Hon Evan Baillie; *Career* landowner & farmer; memb Inverness CC 1948-75, JP 1961-75, DL 1963-65; formerly Lt Lovat Scouts & Scots Gds; *Recreations* stalking, shooting, fishing, hunting; *Clubs* Cavalry & Guards, Brooks's, Pratt's, New (Edinburgh); *Style* - The Rt Hon The Lord Burton; Dochfour, Inverness (☎ 046 386 252)

BURTON, Granville George; s of Clifford Burton; *b* 24 May 1929; *Educ* Norwich Commercial Sch; *m* 1953, Vera, da of Stanley Parker; 1 s, 2 da; *Career* local dir & branch man Graham-Ford Ltd Norwich 1981-, FInstBM, MBIM; *Recreations* travel, photography; *Clubs* Norwich Rotary; *Style* - Granville Burton Esq; 21 Hill rd, New Costessey, Norwich (☎ 0603 742460)

BURTON, Sir George Vernon Kennedy; CBE (1972, MBE Mil 1945); s of George Burton; *b* 21 April 1916; *Educ* Charterhouse, Weimar U; *m* 1, 1945, Sarah (m dis) Tcherniavsky; 2 s; m 2, 1975, Priscilla, da of Cecil King *qv*, and formerly w of Francis Gore *qv*; *Career* formerly Maj RA WW II; chm Fisons 1973-, dir Barclays Bank Int, Thomas Tilling 1976-, Rolls-Royce 1976-; memb Cncl CBI 1970-, chm CBI Overseas Ctee 1975-; memb BOTB European Trade Ctee 1972-, NEDC 1975-, Assoc Br Sponsorship of the Arts 1978-; FRSA; kt 1977; *Recreations* music; *Clubs* Farmers; *Style* - Sir George Burton, CBE; Aldham Mill, Hadleigh, Suffolk

BURY, Lady Mairi (Elizabeth); *née* Vane-Tempest-Stewart; da of 7 Marquess of Londonderry, KG, MVO, TD, PC (d 1949); *b* 1921; *m* 1940 (m diss 1958), Lt-Col Viscount Bury (who d 1968), s of 9 Earl of Albemarle; *Career* JP Co Down;

Style - Lady Mairi Bury, JP; Mount Stewart, Newtownards, Co Down

BURY, Viscountess; Countess Marina; *née* Orloff-Davidoff; da of Count Serge Orloff-Davidoff and Hon Elisabeth, nee Scott-Ellis, da of 8 Baron Howard de Walden and 4 Baron Seaford; *b* 30 Dec 1937; *m* 1964, Viscount Bury (d 1968, s and h of 9 Earl of Albemarle, MC, who d 1979); 1 s (10 Earl of Albemarle, *qv*); *Career* ARIBA, AA Dip; *Style* - Viscountess Bury; Palazzo di Bellosguardo 10, Florence 50124, Italy

BUSBY, (Thomas Samuel) Charles; CBE, AE, DL (Kent 1981); *Career* FSVA; *Style* - Thomas Busby Esq CBE, AE, DL; 16 High st, Tenterden, Kent (☎ 3636)

BUSH, Adm Sir John Fitzroy Duyland; GCB (1970, KCB 1965, CB 1963), DSC and two Bars (1941, 1941 and 1944); s of Fitzroy Bush; *b* 1 Nov 1914; *Educ* Clifton; *m* 1938, Ruth, da of Capt Herbert Horsey, RN; 3 s, 2 da; *Career* CIC Western Fleet, Allied CIC Channel, Allied CIC E Atlantic 1967-70; Vice-Adm of UK & Lt of the Admiralty 1979-; *Recreations* fishing, gardening; *Style* - Adm Sir John Bush, GCB, DSC**; Becksteddle House, Colemore, nr Alton, Hants (☎ Tisted 367)

BUSSE, Hon Mrs (Susan Anne); da of Baron Trevelyan (Life Peer); *b* 1941; *m* 1961, Harald Busse; 2 s, 1 da; *Style* - The Hon Mrs Busse; c/o Ministry of Foreign Affairs, Bonn, W Germany

BUSWELL, Hon Mrs; Hon Barbara; da of late 2 Baron Fisher; *b* 1925; *m* 1961, Leslie Charles Croft Buswell; 1 s, 1 da; *Style* - The Hon Mrs Buswell; St Peter's House, Jersey, CI; Seaton Farm, Stellenbosch, S Africa

BUTE, 6 Marquess of (GB 1796); Sir John Crichton-Stuart; 11 Bt (S 1627), JP (Bute 1967); Lord Crichton (S 1488), Earl of Dumfries, Viscount of Air, Lord Crichton of Sanquhar and Cumnock (S 1633), Earl of Bute, Viscount Kingarth, Lord Mountstuart, Cumra(e) and Inchmarnock (S 1703), Baron Mountstuart of Wortley (GB 1761), Baron Cardiff of Cardiff Castle (GB 1776), Earl of Windsor and Viscount Mountjoy (GB 1796); Hereditary Sheriff and Coroner of Co Bute, Hereditary Keeper of Rothesay Castle; patron of 9 livings (but being a Roman Catholic cannot present); s (twin) of 5 Marquess (d 1956, himself gs of the 3 Marquess, whose conversion to Catholicism was regarded as a great *coup* for Rome and allegedly inspired Disraeli's 'Lothair'; Lord Bute's development of his Cambrian estates virtually created industrial S Wales, while kindlier results were the Transylvanian splendour of Cardiff Castle and the vineyards of Castel Coch; the latter produced a distinctive red (whether Claret or Burgundy is not recorded) till His Lordship's death, tho' its commercial success is thought to have owed more to the dictates of fashion than the sterner touchstone of potability) and Lady Eileen, nee Forbes, da of 8 Earl of Granard; *b* 27 Feb 1933; *Educ* Ampleforth, Trin Cambridge; *m* 1, 1955 (m dis 1977), (Beatrice) Nicola Grace, da of late Lt-Cdr Wolstan Beaumont Charles Weld-Forester, CBE, RN, gs of 5 Baron Forester; 2 s, 2 da; m 2, 1978, Jennifer, da of J B Home-Rigg and former w of Gerald Percy (of the family of the Duke of Northumberland); *Heir* s, Earl of Dumfries; *Career* Lord-Lt for Bute 1967-75 (DL 1961); chm Nat Trust for Scotland Exec Ctee 1969, memb Countryside Cmmn for Scotland 1970, memb Oil Devpt Cncl for Scotland 1973; *Clubs* Turf, White's, New, Puffin's (last two both Edinburgh); *Style* - The Most Hon Marquess of Bute JP DL; Mount Stuart, Rothesay, Isle of Bute (☎ Rothesay 2730)

BUTE, Dowager Marchioness of; Lady Eileen Beatrice; *née* Forbes; da of 8 Earl of Granard; *b* 1 July 1912; *m* 1932, 5 Marquess of Bute (d 1956); 3 s (including 6 Marquess), 1 da; *Style* - The Most Hon The Dowager Marchioness of Bute; Dumfries House; Cumnock, Ayrshire

BUTLAND, Sir Jack Richard; KBE (1966); s of Henry Butland, of NZ; *Educ* Hokitika H S, NZ; *m* Gretta Taylor (d 1962); 2 s, 1 da; *Career* fnder & chm J R Butland Pty 1922-, Butland Tobacco 1936- New Zealand Cheese 1926-79, Butland Industs 1949-79; chm Rothmans (NZ) 1956-, NZ Honey Control Bd 1933-38; dir

Rothmans Industs 1971-, Butland Industs 1949-; *Style* - Sir Jack Butland, KBE; J R Butland Pty Ltd, Queen st, Auckland 1, New Zealand; 542 Remuera rd, Remuera, Auckland 5, New Zealand

BUTLER OF SAFFRON WALDEN, Baron (Life Peer UK 1965); Richard Austen Butler; KG (1971), CH (1954), PC (1939), DL (Essex); s of late Sir Montagu Sherard Dawes Butler, KCSI, CB, CIE, CVO, CBE, through whom Lord Butler is ggs of one Headmaster of Harrow, great nephew of another and a Head Master of Haileybury, and 1 cous once removed to an assistant master at Harrow and the wife of an assistant master; *b* 9 Dec 1902; *Educ* Marlborough, Pembroke Coll Cambridge; *m* 1, 1926, Sydney Elizabeth (d 1954), da of late Samuel Courtauld; 3 s, 1 da; m 2, 1959, Mollie, da of late Frank Douglas Montgomerie, of Castle Hedingham, Essex, and Esmé, ggda of 8 Lord Napier, and widow of Augustine Courtauld; *Career* architect of the Butler Education Act 1944, twice nearly chosen Leader of the Conservative Party (and hence PM); fellow CCC Cambridge 1925-29 & Master Trin 1965-78, MP (U) Saffron Walden 1929-65, Min Educn 1941-45, of Labour 1945, Leader House of Commons 1955-61, Home Sec 1957-62, First Sec of State 1962-63, Dep PM 1962-63, Min in Charge of Central African Office 1962-63, Sec of State for Foreign Affairs 1963-64, former chm Conservative Pty Org; FRSL, FRGS; Rector Glasgow U 1956-59, Chllr Sheffield U 1960-78, Chllr Essex U 1962-; *Style* - The Rt Hon The Lord Butler of Saffron Walden, KG, CH, PC, DL; Flat 142, Whitehall Court, SW1 (☎ 01 930 3160); Spencers, Gt Yeldham, Essex (☎ Gt Yeldham 237255)

BUTLER, Hon Adam Courtauld; MP (C) Bosworth 1970-; s of Baron Butler of Saffron Walden, KG, CH, PC, by his 1 w, Sydney, da of Samuel Courtauld; *b* 11 Oct 1931; *Educ* Eton, Pembroke Cambridge; *m* 1955, Felicity, da of Guy Molesworth-St Aubyn (s of Sir Hugh Molesworth-St Aubyn, 13 Bt, JP, by his w, Emma, da of Adm Charles Wake, 2 s of Sir Charles Wake, 10 Bt; Adm Charles Wake m Emma, da of Sir Edward St Aubyn, 1 Bt, and sis of 1 Baron St Levan); 2 s, 1 da; *Career* Con Whip 1974-75, PPS to Margaret Thatcher 1975-79, Min of State Indust 1979-; dir- Kayser Bondor 1966-73, Aristoc Ltd 1966-73, Capital & Counties Property Co Ltd 1973-79; *Recreations* field sports; *Style* - The Hon Adam Butler, MP; The Old Rectory, Lighthorne, Warwick (☎ Moreton Morrell 214)

BUTLER, Hon Arion Thomas Piers Hamilton; s of Viscount Ikerrin; *b* 1 Sept 1975

BUTLER, Hon Betty Quenelda; da of 28 Baron Dunboyne; *b* 1956; *Educ* Benenden, Girton Cambridge; *Style* - The Hon Betty Butler

BUTLER, Hon Edmund Henry Richard; s of 17 Viscount Mountgarret; *b* 1962 *Style* - The Hon Edmund Butler

BUTLER, Col Eric Langton; OBE (1957), MC (1945), TD (1953), DL (Staffs 1956); s of Samuel Butler, of Wolverhampton; *b* 18 July 1915; *Educ* Bromsgrove Sch; *Career* Col (TA) S Staffs 1957, ADC to HM The Queen 1960-65; dir Bass Charrington to 1975; *Style* - Col Eric Butler, OBE, MC, TD, DL; Mere Oak Farm, Hollies Lane, Pattingham, Wolverhampton (☎ Pattingham 700 292)

BUTLER, Hon Mrs (Elizabeth Olson); *née* Erskine; da of 1 Baron Erskine of Rerrick, GBE (d 1980); *b* 1923; *m* 1944, Gilbert Butler; 2 s, 1 da; *Career* Subaltern ATS 1939-45; *Style* - The Hon Mrs Butler; The Croft, 8 Churchfields av, Weybridge, Surrey

BUTLER, Hon Godfrey Claud Somerset Pierce; s of late 7 Earl of Carrick; *b* 1907; *Educ* Stowe; *Career* late Pilot Officer RAF Vol Reserve; *Style* - The Hon Godfrey Butler; 106 Divinity rd, Oxford

BUTLER, Hon Guy Somerset Lionel; s of late 7 Earl of Carrick; *b* 1905; *Educ* Tonbridge; *m* 1, 1939, Patricia Anne, nee Dunne; 2 s; m 2, 1961, Mrs Janet Frances Parker, nee Preston; *Career* late Lt Indian Army (Reserve), Maj Roy Canadian Dragoons (Canadian Army Reserve); md

Guy Butler & Co Ltd; *Style* - The Hon Guy Butler; Red Acres, Wivelsfield Green, Sussex

BUTLER, Hubert Arthur James; s of Charles Butler, MBE, of Newport Essex; *b* 24 Sept 1937; *Educ* Eton, RAC Cirencester; *m* 1968, Anne, da of Capt Peter Robert Churchward, of Devon; 1 s, 2 da; *Career* formerly Lt 17/21 Lancers; ARICS; chm- Winchmore Ltd 1973, Swifts of Exmouth 1979; *Recreations* shooting, cricket; *Clubs* Cavalry & Guards, Farmers; *Style* - Hubert Butler Esq; le Pavillon, Newport, Essex (☎ Saffron Walden 40225)

BUTLER, Maj-Gen Hew Dacres George; CB (1975), DL (Hants 1980); s of Maj-Gen S Butler, CB, CMG, DSO, of Bury Lodge, Hambledon; *b* 12 March 1922; *Educ* Winchester; *m* 1954, Joanna, da of G Puckridge, CMG, ED, of Worton, Wilts; 2 s, 1 da; *Career* Lloyd's underwriter; Sec Beit Tst 1978-; GOC Near East Land Force 1972-74; *Recreations* shooting, racing, skiing, horticulture; *Clubs* Boodle's, Roy C'wlth Soc, MCC; *Style* - Maj-Gen Hew Butler, CB, DL; Bury Lodge, Hambledon, Hants (☎ 070 132 507)

BUTLER, Hon Henrietta Elizabeth Alexandra; da of 17 Viscount Mountgarret; *b* 1964

BUTLER, Ian Geoffrey; s of Hubert Desrameaux Butler, of Cumbria; *b* 12 April 1925; *Educ* Stowe, Trin Oxford; *m* 1973, Anne, da of James Robertson, of Dunbartonshire; 2 da; *Career* Lt Coldstream Gds 1945-47; ptnr Tansley Witt 1951-55; md 1973- & chm 1976- Lead Industs Gp; *Recreations* yachting (National Swallow- 'Dart'), skiing; *Clubs* Roy Yacht Sqdn, Roy Thames Yacht, Itchenor Sailing; *Style* - Ian Butler Esq; Wyke House, Ellanore Lane, W Wittering, Sussex (☎ 0243 663269); 105 Abingdon rd, W8 (☎ 01 937 5220)

BUTLER, (Percy) James; CBE (1980); s of Percy Butler; *b* 15 March 1929; *Educ* Marlborough, Clare Cambridge; *m* 1954, Margaret, da of Percy Copland; 1 s, 2 da; *Career* CA, ptnr i/c London Off Peat Marwick Mitchell & Co 1981-; dir (Govt apptmnt) Mersey Docks & Harbours 1972-; memb Lloyd's; *Recreations* farming, tennis, bridge; *Clubs* Carlton; *Style* - James Butler Esq, CBE; East Lymden, Ticehurst, E Sussex (☎ 0580 200397); 28 Eaton Mews North, SW1 (☎ 01 235 1120)

BUTLER, Hon John Fitzwalter; s and h of 28 Baron Dunboyne; *b* 31 July 1951; *Educ* Winchester, Trin Cambridge; *m* 1975, Diana Caroline, da of Sir Michael Sanigear Williams, KCMG; 1 da; *Style* - The Hon John Butler

BUTLER, James Morris; s of Frederick Thomas Butler; *b* 15 June 1926; *Educ* Hull G S, Cambridge; *m* 1950, Freda; 1 s, 2 da; *Career* dep chm & ch exec McKechnie Bros; Pres Br Non-Ferrous Metals Fedn; *Recreations* golf; *Style* - James Butler Esq; 2 Old Hall, Whittington, Staffs (☎ 0543 432323)

BUTLER, Lady Juliana Mary Philomena; da of 9 Earl of Carrick and Belinda, da of Maj David Turville-Constable-Maxwell, TD (s of Hon Bernard Constable-Maxwell, 4 s of 10 Lord Herries of Terregles, by his 2 w, Hon Alice, nee Fraser, da of 15 Lord Lovat), by his w, Mary, da of Lt-Col Oswald Turville-Petre, TD, JP, DL (gggs of 9 Baron Petre); *b* 20 Dec 1960; *Career* nurse; *Style* - Lady Juliana Butler; 10 Netherton Grove, SW10

BUTLER, Hon Lindsay Simon Turville Somerset; s (twin) of Viscount Ikerrin; *b* 1979

BUTLER, Sir Michael Dacres; KCMG (1979, CMG 1975); s of T Butler, of Blandford, Dorset; *b* 27 Feb 1927; *Educ* Winchester, Trin Oxford; *m* 1951, Margaret, da of Rt Hon Lord Clyde, PC, KC, JP, sometime Ld Justice-Gen Scotland (d 1944); 2 s, 2 da; *Career* For Serv 1950-; UK Perm Rep to EEC 1979-; *Recreations* collecting Chinese porcelain, tennis, skiing; *Style* - Sir Michael Butler, KCMG; The Old Rectory, Almer, Blandford, Dorset

BUTLER, Hon Mary Synolda; da of 28 Baron Dunboyne; *b* 1954; *Educ* Benenden,

Girton Cambridge; *Style* - The Hon Mary Butler

BUTLER, Sir (Reginald) Michael Thomas; 3 Bt (UK 1922), QC (Can 1967); s of Sir (Reginald) Thomas Butler, 2 Bt (d 1959); *b* 22 April 1928; *m* 1, 1952 (m dis 1967), Marja Margaret Elizabeth, da of Ewen H McLean, of Toronto; 3 s; m 2, 1968 (m dis 1974), Barbara Anne, da of Kevin Cahill, of Dublin; *Heir* s, (Reginald) Richard Michael Butler; *Career* barr and slr Ontario 1954 and BC 1967; ptnr Messrs Farris & Co (Vancouver); *Style* - Sir Michael Butler, Bt, QC; Box 381, Brentwood Bay, BC, Canada

BUTLER, Hon Mrs Pierce - Dorothea; *née* Bennett; *m* 1957, as his 2 w, Maj the Hon Pierce Alan Somerset David Butler (s of late 7 Earl of Carrick and who died 1964); *Style* - The Hon Mrs Pierce Butler; 11 Rushfield, Sawbridgeworth, Herts

BUTLER, Hon Piers Edmund Theobald Lismalyn Butler; s (twin) of Viscount Ikerrin; *b* 1979

BUTLER, Hon Piers James Richard; s and h of 17 Viscount Mountgarret; *b* 15 April 1961; *Style* - The Hon Piers Butler

BUTLER, Hon Sir Richard Clive; DL (Essex 1972); s of Baron Butler of Saffron Walden, KG, CH, PC (Life Peer) by his 1 w, Sydney, da of Samuel Courtauld; *b* 12 Jan 1929; *Educ* Eton, Pembroke Cambridge; *m* 1952, Susan, da of Maj Patrick Walker, MBE (s of Sir James Walker, 3 Bt); 2 s, 1 da; *Career* 2 Lt RHG BAOR 1948-49; farmer; Pres NFU 1979-, memb NFU Cncl 1962-; kt 1981; *Recreations* hunting, shooting, tennis; *Clubs* Farmers; *Style* - The Hon Sir Richard Butler, DL; Penny Pot, Halstead, Essex (☎ 07874 2828)

BUTLER, Richard Pierce; s and h of Sir Thomas Butler, 12 Bt, CVO, DSO, OBE; *b* 22 July 1940; *Educ* Eton; *m* 1965, Diana, da of Col S J Borg, of The Palms, St Julians, Malta; 3 s, 1 da; *Career* MBA, FCA; *Style* - Richard Butler Esq

BUTLER, Terence Brinsley John Danvers; DL (Pembrokeshire 1964); s of late Capt the Hon Francis Almeric Butler (3 s of 6 Earl of Lanesborough) and hp of cous, 9 Earl; *b* 7 March 1913; *m* 1, 1937 (m dis 1947), Hermione, da of late Cdr Thomas Williams, MVO, RN; 1 da; m 2, 1947 (m dis 1970), Beryl Axten, da of late George Trotter and formerly w of Frederick Kennedy Axten; 4 da; m 3, 1972, Mrs Jacqueline Balmer, da of late Winthrop Greene, of Washington, DC; *Career* Cdr (ret) RN; late HM's Harbour Master, Pembroke Dock; 1939-45 War (prisoner); *Style* - Cdr Terence Butler DL, RN; c/o Nat Westminster Bank, Meyrick st, Pembroke Dock

BUTLER, Col Sir Thomas Pierce; 12 Bt (I 1628), CVO (1970), DSO (1944), OBE (1954); s of Lt-Col Sir Richard Pierce Butler, 11 Bt, OBE (d 1955); *b* 18 Sept 1910; *Educ* Harrow, Trin Cambridge; *m* 1937 (m dis 1972), Rosemary Liège Woodgate, whom he re-married 1973, da of late Maj James Hamilton Davidson-Houston, of Pembury Hall, Kent and of Thurloe Sq, SW7; 1 s, 2 da; *Heir* s, Richard Pierce Butler; *Career* Col, Lt-Col Cmdg Grenadier Gds 1955-59, Mil Advr to High Cmmr for UK in New Zealand 1959-61, Maj and Resident Gov of HM Tower of London 1961-71, Keeper of Jewel House Tower of London 1968-71, pres of London (Prince of Wales's) Dist St John Ambulance Bde 1967-70; CStJ, FRGS, former JP Co London; *Style* - Col Sir Thomas Butler, Bt, CVO, DSO, OBE; 7 Thurloe sq, SW7 (☎ 01 584 1225); Ballin Temple, Ardattin, Co Carlow

BUTLER, Hon Victoria Morina; da of 28 Baron Dunboyne; *b* 1959; *Educ* Benenden, St Andrew's U; *Style* - The Hon Victoria Butler

BUTLER-COLE, Hon Mrs (Jane Elizabeth); *née* Napier; da of 5 Baron Napier of Magdala, OBE; *b* 1942; *Educ* 1964, Christopher Thomas Butler-Cole; 1 s, 1 da; *Style* - The Hon Mrs Butler-Cole; The Old Manse, Carlops, Penicuik, Midlothian

BUTLER-HENDERSON, Edward; s of Hon Eric Butler-Henderson, of Faccombe Manor, Andover (6 s of 1 Baron Faringdon, CH, JP), and Hon Sophia

Massey (2 da of 5 Baron Clarina, DL); *b* 9 June 1916; *Educ* Eton, Trin Cambridge; *m* 1939, Elizabeth, da of Henry Dacres Dixon, of Eire; 1 s, 1 da; *Career* formerly Lt-Col 99 Bucks Yeomanry RA (TA); chm Naydale Servs, dir Electric & Gen Investment Co, md Henderson Admin 1951-69; *Recreations* shooting, escapism; *Clubs* City of London; *Style* - Edward Butler-Henderson Esq; 43 Lowndes sq, SW1 (☎ 01 235 5888)

BUTLER-HENDERSON, Kenneth; s of Capt Hon Eric Butler-Henderson (6 s of 1 Baron Faringdon, CH, JP) and Hon Sophia Massey (da of 5 Baron Clarina, DL); *b* 19 May 1929; *Educ* Eton; *m* 1952, Phyllis, da of Lt-Col Alfred Cartmel, CIE, MM, of Hertford; 1 s, 2 da; *Career* memb Stock Exchange; dir Strauss Turnbull & Co, The Cronite Gp; *Clubs* City of London, Farmers; *Style* - Kenneth Butler-Henderson Esq; 11 Egerton Place, SW3 (☎ 01 589 2648)

BUTLER-SLOSS, Joseph William Alexander; s of Francis Alexander Sloss (d 1952); *b* 16 Nov 1926; *Educ* Bangor G S Co Down, Hertford Coll Oxford; *m* 1958, Dame Ann Oldfield DBE, da of Sir Cecil Robert Havers; 2 s, 1 da; *Career* Sub Lt RNVR, barr 1952, Recorder of The Crown Court 1972-; *Recreations* violin, hunting; *Clubs* Carlton; *Style* - Joseph Butler-Sloss Esq; 10 King's Bench Walk, Temple, EC4 (☎ 583 4649); Higher Marsh Farm, Marsh Green, Rockbeare, nr Exeter, Devon (☎ Whimple)

BUTT, Sir (Alfred) Kenneth Dudley; 2 Bt (UK 1929), of Westminster, Co London; s of Sir Alfred Butt, 1 Bt (d 1962); *b* 7 July 1908; *Educ* Rugby, BNC Oxford; *m* 1, 1938, Kathleen (m dis 1948), da of E Farmer, of Shanklin IOW; m 2, 1948, Marie, da of John Bain, of Wadhurst and widow of Lt-Col Ivor Birts; *Heir* none; *Career* bloodstock breeder, md Brook Stud Co 1962-; chm Thoroughbred Breeders Assoc 1973; farmer, Pres Aberdeen Angus Cattle Soc 1967-68; Lloyd's Underwriter 1931-74; *Recreations* shooting, paintings, racing; *Clubs* Carlton; *Style* - Sir Kenneth Butt, Bt; Wheat Hill, Sandon, Buntingford, Herts (☎ 076 387 203); Flat 29, 1 Hyde Park sq, W2 (☎ 01 262 3988)

BUTT, Michael Acton; s of late Gp-Capt Leslie Butt; *b* 25 May 1942; *Educ* Rugby, Cambridge U, INSEAD Fontainebleau France (MBA); *m* 1965, Diana Lorraine, da of Sir Robin Brook; 2 s; *Career* Lloyd's insurance broker, chm Sedgwick International Ltd, dir Sedgwick Gp, Sedgwick Ltd, Sedgwick Overseas Gp Ltd, chm United Kingdom Insurance Brokers Association 1980; *Clubs* Mark's, Annabel's; yacht- 'Tunku'; *Style* - Michael Butt Esq; 34 St Anne's ter, NW8 (☎ 01 722 2046); The Garden Cottage, Claydene, Cowden, Kent (☎ Cowden 412)

BUTTENSHAW, Brig Cedric George; CBE (1967, OBE 1953, MBE 1943), DSO (1945); s of Brig Alfred Buttenshaw; *b* 17 June 1912; *Educ* Sherborne, RMA Woolwich; *m* 1939, Barbara, da of Hubert de Burgh Wooldridge; 3 da; *Career* served WW II, CO 142 Field Regt Roy Devon Yeomanry 1944-45; Provost Marshal 1962-65, commanded Salisbury Plain Sub-Dist 1965-67; *Recreations* following hounds, gardening; *Style* - Brig Cedric Buttenshaw, CBE, DSO; The Coach House, Worton, Devizes, Wilts

BUTTER, Neil McLaren; QC (1976); s of Andrew Butter, of London N22; *b* 10 May 1933; *Educ* The Leys Sch, Queens' Cambridge; *m* 1974, Claire, da of A Miskin, of Ifield Court Farm, Ifield, Kent; *Career* barr 1955, assist & dep Recorder Bournemouth 1971, Crown Court Recorder 1972-; Tstee Kingdon-Ward Speech Therapy Tst 1980-; *Recreations* holidays, motoring; *Clubs* Oxford & Cambridge, Hampshire (Winchester); *Style* - Neil Butler Esq, QC; Carpmael Bldg, Temple, EC4 (☎ 01 353 5537); 54 Linton st, N1 (☎ 01 359 8939)

BUTTERFIELD, John David; s of Leslie John Butterfield; *b* 20 Jan 1930; *Educ* Glengyle Prep Sch, Kings College Sch Wimbledon, Nautical Coll Pangbourne; *m* 1981, Anita Marie, da of late Edward Marek; *Career* assist sales man Raithby Lawrence & Co 1948-54, print buyer Lonsdale-Hands Org 1954-56; owner & md The Norman Press Ltd 1956-61, world wide dir of printing Ambassador Press (Los Angeles) 1961-73, owner and md The Euroweb Gp of Cos Rickmansworth 1973-;

Recreations boating; *Style* - John Butterfield Esq; 3a Fernhills, Kings Langley, Herts, WD4 8PT

BUTTERFIELD, Prof Sir William John Hughes; OBE (1953); s of William Butterfield, of Hampton-in-Arden, Warwicks; *b* 28 March 1920; *Educ* Solihull Sch, Exeter Coll Oxford, Johns Hopkins U USA; *m* 1950, Isabel-Ann, nee Foster-Kennedy, of New York; 3 s, 1 da; *Career* kt 1978; Master of Downing Cambridge 1978-; Regius Prof of Physics (Cambridge) 1975-; chm Medicines Commission 1976-; *Recreations* real tennis, cricket; *Clubs* Athenaeum, MCC, Queen's; *Style* - Prof Sir William Butterfield, OBE; The Master's Lodge, Downing College, Cambridge (☎ 0223 59491)

BUTTERICK, Peter Stephen; s of Stephen Butterick, of Epsom; *b* 1 Dec 1933; *Educ* Ealing G S; *m* 1958, Audrey, da of Raymond Bates, of Ealing; 2 s; *Career* FCA; dir & sec Macmillan Bloedel Containers Ltd 1975-; *Recreations* church, gardening, motoring, DIY, scouting; *Style* - Peter Butterick Esq; Openfields, Love Lane, King's Langley, Herts (☎ 64085)

BUTTERWICK, Hon Mrs (Agnes Désirée); OBE (1966), JP; da of late 1 Baron Dickinson, KBE; *b* 1892; *m* 1922, James Cyril Butterwick (d 1966); 3 s, 1 da; *Style* - The Hon Mrs Butterwick, OBE, JP; Parkside, Beaconsfield, Bucks

BUTTERWICK, John Newton; TD (1961); s of James Butterwick, of Old Park, Beaconsfield; *b* 3 March 1923; *Educ* Eton, Trin Oxford; *m* 1956, Marcia, da of John Scott, of Pittsburgh; 3 s, 1 da; *Career* Capt NW Europe WW II 1944-45, TA 1949-62, ret with rank Bt-Col; V-Chm Lazard Bros & Co 1981- (dir 1972-80); dir Glyn Mills (later Williams & Glyn) Bank 1959-72; *Recreations* golf. gardening; *Clubs* Roy West Norfolk Golf; *Style* - John Butterwick Esq, TD; The Gables, Brancaster, King's Lynn, Norfolk (☎ Brancaster 245); Danyells, Sandon, Buntingford, Herts (☎ 0763 87 312)

BUXTON OF ALSA, Baron (Life Peer UK 1978); Aubrey Leland Oakes Buxton; MC (1943), DL (Essex 1975); s of late Leland William Wilberforce Buxton, s of Sir Thomas Fowell Buxton, 3 Bt, GCMG, DL, JP; *b* 15 July 1918; *Educ* Ampleforth, Trin Cambridge; *m* 1946, Pamela Mary, da of Sir Henry Ralph Stanley Birkin, 3 Bt, and widow of Maj Samuel Luckyn Buxton, MC, 17/21 Lancers; 2 s, 4 da; *Career* Maj Sup Reserves, ch exec Anglia TV (dir 1958-), tres London Zoological Soc 1977-, v-pres World Wildlife Fund 1968-, pres Roy Television Soc 1973-77, chm ITV News Ltd 1981-, dir Survival Anglia Ltd; producer of television and wildlife films; Queen's Award for Industry 1974, High Sheriff of Essex 1972; Extra Equerry to Duke of Edinburgh 1964; *Style* - The Rt Hon The Lord Buxton of Alsa MC, DL; Stiffkey, Wells-next-the-Sea, Norfolk (☎ Binham 347)

BUXTON, Adrian Clarence; CMG (1978); s of Clarence Buxton; *b* 12 June 1925; *Educ* Christ's Hosp, Trin Cambridge; *m* 1958, Leonora, da of Timothy Cherkas; 3 s; *Career* formerly S/Lt RNVR E Indies; Foreign Serv 1947-, Ambass to Bolivia 1977-81, to Ecuador 1981-; *Clubs* Travellers'; *Style* - Adrian Buxton Esq, CMG; c/o FCO, SW1; 7 Grove rd, Guildford, Surrey

BUXTON, Andrew Edward; s of Desmond Gurney Buxton, of Hoveton Hall, Norfolk, and gggs of Sir Edward Buxton, 2 Bt, MP; *b* 3 March 19356; *Educ* Eton, Magdalene Cambridge; *m* 1967, Barbara, da of Capt Cyril Gascoigne Lloyd; 2 s, 1 da; *Career* finance dir Rio Tinto Zinc; *Recreations* shooting, tennis, cricket; *Clubs* Boodle's; *Style* - Andrew Buxton Esq; 36 Burnsall st, SW3

BUXTON, Andrew Robert Fowell; s of Capt Joseph Gurney Fowell Buxton, Gren Gds (ka 1943, gggs of Sir Thomas Buxton, 1 Bt), by Elizabeth (da of late Maj Robert Barbour, of Bolesworth Castle, Tattenhall, Chester); she m subsequently (1946) Alexander Grant, TD, JP, DL, thereby becoming great aunt to Andrew, her son's, future w; *b* 5 April 1939; *Educ* Winchester, Pembroke Oxford; *m* 1965, Jane, da of Lt-Col Peter Grant of Rothiemurchus, MBE, and Lady Katherine Grant, *qv*; 2 da; *Career* late 2 Lt Gren Gds; *Style* - Andrew

Buxton Esq; Bentley Park, Ipswich, Suffolk

BUXTON, Desmond Gurney; DL (Norfolk 1961); s of Edward Gurney Buxton (s of Samuel Gurney Buxton, 2 s of Sir Edward Buxton, 2 Bt, MP), of Catton Hall, Norfolk; *b* 4 Jan 1898; *Educ* Eton, Sandhurst; *m* 1930, Rachel, da of Col Arthur Morse, of Norwich; 2 s, 3 da (and 1 da decd); *Career* formerly Maj King's Roy Rifle Corps, served France 1917-18 and 1945; local dir Barclays Bank Norwich 1929-58; Sheriff Norwich 1936; High Sheriff Norfolk 1960, Cdr St John's Ambulance Bde 1961; *Recreations* forestry, bridge, chess; *Clubs* Lansdowne; *Style* - Desmond Buxton Esq, DL; Hoveton Hall, Wroxham, Norwich

BUXTON, John Burns; s of Alan Thomas Buxton, of NZ; *b* 31 Oct 1933; *Educ* Takapuna G S, Massey U, Lincoln Coll; *m* 1961, Helen, da of Sir George Robb; 1 s, 3 da (and 1 s decd); *Career* Pres NZ Soc 1980-81, V-Pres Imported Meat Trade Assoc 1977-; exec chm Towers & Co 1972-; gen man W Richmond Ltd (NZ) 1968-72; *Recreations* gardening, music, sport, art; *Clubs* RAC; *Style* - John Buxton Esq; 37 Ducks Hill rd, Northwood, Middx

BUXTON, Jocelyn Charles Roden; VRD; s of late Capt Roden Buxton, CBE, RN, 2 s of 4 Bt, by 1 w, Dorothy, da of late Col Charles St John, RE; hp of kinsman, Sir Thomas Buxton, 6 Bt; *b* 8 Aug 1924; *m* 1960, Ann Frances, da of Frank Smitherman, MBE; 3 da; *Career* Lt-Cdr RNVR, despatches WW II; *Style* - Jocelyn Buxton Esq VRD; Eastlands, West Wellow, Romsey, Hants

BUXTON, Hon Jane Elizabeth Noel; da of 1 Baron Noel-Buxton, PC (d 1948); *b* 1925; *Career* relinquished surname of Noel by Public Declaration, 1957; *Style* - The Hon Jane Buxton; 27 Redington rd, Hampstead, NW3

BUXTON, Hon (Aubrey) James Francis; 2 s of Baron Buxton of Alsa; *b* 20 March 1956; *m* 1981, Melinda D M, da of Peter Samuelson, of Ugley Hall, Ugley, Essex; *Style* - The Hon James Buxton

BUXTON, James Geoffrey Pease; s of Peter Stapleton Buxton (ka 1944; s of Maj Geoffrey Buxton, TD, by his w, Clare, da of Sir Francis Stapleton, 8 Bt; Maj Geoffrey Buxton was s of Geoffrey Buxton CB JP DL by his w, Mary, da of Rev Hon John Harbord, 5 s of 3 Baron Suffield; Geoffrey sr was s of Thomas Buxton, himself 2 s of Sir Thomas Buxton, 1 Bt); *b* 24 Oct 1939; *Educ* Eton, Trin Cambridge; *m* 1970, Meriel, da of Maj Denis Cowen, of East Farndon Hall, Market Harborough; 1 s, 1 da; *Career* local dir Barclays Bank; *Recreations* hunting, stalking, swimming; *Style* - James Buxton Esq; The Grange, New Buckenham, Norwich (☎ 321)

BUXTON, Jonathan James; s of Cdr Michael Buxton (s of Henry Fowell Buxton by his 1 w, Katharine, da of Rt Hon James Round, of Birch Hall, Essex; Henry Buxton was 1 s of John Henry Buxton, DL, by his w, Emma, da of Capt Richard Pelly, DL, RN, 5 s of Sir John Pelly, 1 Bt; John Henry Buxton was 1 s of Thomas Buxton, JP, 2 s of Sir Thomas Buxton, 1 Bt); *b* 2 July 1943; *Educ* Harrow; *m* 1972, Rosaleen, da of Sir John Bagge, 6 Bt; 3 da; *Career* formerly Maj 17/21 Lancers; co dir; *Recreations* sailing, shooting, skiing; *Clubs* Cavalry; *Style* - Jonathan Buxton Esq; 62 Endlesham rd, SW12 (☎ 01 675 4242)

BUXTON, Hon Lucinda Catherine; 2 da of Baron Buxton of Alsa; *b* 21 Aug 1950; *Style* - The Hon Lucinda Buxton; The Old House, Langham, Holt, Norfolk

BUXTON, Hon Mrs (Margaret Evelyn); *née* Bridges; da of 1 Baron Bridges, KG, GCB, GCVO, MC, FRS (d 1969), and Hon Katharine, da of 2 Baron Farrer; *b* 1932; *m* 1, 1954 (m dis 1969), Trevor Aston; m 2, 1971, as his 2 w, Paul William Jex Buxton (gggs of Sir Thomas Buxton, 1 Bt); 2 da; *Style* - The Hon Mrs Buxton; Castle House, Ongar, Essex

BUXTON, Hon Richard Christopher; s of 2 Baron Noel-Buxton (d 1980); *b* 1950; *Educ* Bryanston; *Style* - The Hon Richard Buxton

BUXTON, Hon Simon Campden; s of 2

Baron Noel-Buxton (d 1980); *b* 1943; *Educ* Bryanston and Balliol, Oxford; *Style* - The Hon Simon Buxton

BUXTON, Sir Thomas Fowell Victor; 6 Bt (UK 1840); s of Sir Thomas Fowell Buxton, 5 Bt (d 1945) and late Hon Dorothy, da of 1 Baron Cochrane of Cults; *b* 18 Aug 1925; *Educ* Eton, Trin Cambridge; *m* 1955, Mrs Doris Mary Chisenhale-Marsh (d 1965), da of Peter Randall Johnson; *Heir* kinsman, Jocelyn Buxton, VRD; *Career* Scots Gds 1943-48; *Style* - Sir Thomas Buxton, Bt

BUXTON, Hon Timothy Leland; er s of Baron Buxton of Alsa; *b* 20 Nov 1948; *Educ* Ampleforth; *m* 1972, Julie, da of Lt-Cdr Michael Parker, CVO; 1 s (Edward b 1976), 1 da (Alexandra b 1973); *Style* - The Hon Timothy Buxton; Alsa Wood House, Stansted, Essex

BUXTON, Hon Victoria Jane; 4 da of Baron Buxton of Alsa; *b* 4 June 1960; *Style* - The Hon Victoria Buxton

BUZZARD, Sir Anthony Farquhar; 3 Bt (UK 1929), of Munstead Grange, Godalming, Co Surrey; s of Rear-Adm Sir Anthony Wass Buzzard, 2 Bt, CB, DSO, OBE (d 1972), and Margaret, da of Sir Arthur Knapp, KCIE, CSI, CBE; *b* 28 June 1935; *Educ* Charterhouse, Ch Ch Oxford; *m* 1970, Barbara, da of Gordon Arnold, of Michigan; 2 da; *Heir* bro, Timothy Buzzard; *Career* modern languages teacher at American School in London 1974-; *Recreations* music; *Style* - Sir Anthony Buzzard, Bt; Robin Hill, Amersham rd, Chalfont St Giles, Bucks (☎ 2136)

BUZZARD, Hon Mrs (Ann Sophia Madeline); *née* Whitfield; da of 1 Baron Kenswood (d 1963); *b* 1928; *m* 1948, Richard Bethune Buzzard, BM, BCh; 1 s, 3 da; *Style* - The Hon Mrs Buzzard; 40 Arlington rd, NW1

BUZZARD, Timothy Macdonnell; s of Rear-Adm Sir Anthony Wass Buzzard, 2 Bt, CB, DSO, OBE (d 1972); hp of bro, Sir Anthony Buzzard, 3 Bt; *b* 28 Jan 1939; *Educ* Roy Coll of Music; *m* 1970, Jennifer, da of Peter Patching; 1 s, 1 da; *Career* LRAM; *Style* - Timothy Buzzard Esq; Great Walstead, Lindfield, Haywards Heath, Sussex

BYATT, Hugh Campbell; CMG (1979); s of Sir Horace Byatt, GCMG; *b* 27 Aug 1927; *Educ* Gordonstoun, New Coll Oxford; *m* 1954, Fiona, da of Ian Pountney Coats, DL; 2 s, 1 da; *Career* served RN 1945-48; HMOCS 1952-57, latterly CRO, subsequently FCO; Ambass to Angola 1978-81, Lisbon 1981-; *Clubs* Roy Ocean Racing, Leander; *Style* - Hugh Campbell Esq, CMG; c/o FCO, SW1

BYERS, Baron (Life Peer UK 1964); Charles Frank Byers; OBE (1944), PC (1972), DL (Surrey 1974); s of late Charles Cecil Byers, of Lancing, Sussex; *b* 24 July 1915; *Educ* Westminster, Ch Ch Oxford; *m* 1939, Joan Elizabeth, da of late William Oliver; 1 s, 3 da; *Career* MP (Lib) Dorset N 1945-50, Lib Ch Whip 1946-50, chm Lib Pty 1950-52 and 1965-67 (v-pres 1954-65), exec dir Rio Tinto Co Ltd 1951-63, Rio Tinto-Zinc Corpn Ltd 1962-73, chm Co Pensions Information Centre 1973-, Lib Leader House of Lords 1967-; Lt-Col RA WWII, GSOI 8 Army and 21 Army Gp (despatches 3 times); *Style* - The Rt Hon The Lord Byers, OBE PC, DL; Hunters Hill, Blindley Heath, Lingfield, Surrey

BYNG, Lady (Florence) Elizabeth Alice; *née* Byng; da of late 6 Earl of Strafford and Mary, da of Sir Thomas Colebrooke, 4 Bt; resumed surname Byng in lieu of that of Lafone by deed poll 1952; *b* 1897; *m* 1928 (m dis 1931), Michael William M Lafone; 1 s; *Style* - Lady Elizabeth Byng; Wrotham Park, Barnet, Herts

BYNG, Hon Georgia Mary Caroline; da of Viscount Enfield; *b* 1965

BYNG, Hon Harriet Clare Tara; da of Viscount Enfield; *b* 1967

BYNG, Hon Henrietta Rose; da of 11 Viscount Torrington; *b* 1977; *Style* - The Hon Henrietta Byng

BYNG, Hon James Edmund; s of Viscount Enfield; *b* 1969

BYNG, John Launcelot; MC; s of late Capt Launcelot Alfred Cranmer Byng; hp of kinsman, 11 Viscount Torrington; *b* 18 March 1919; *m* 1955, Margaret Ellen, da of R H Hardy, of Sevenoaks, Kent; 1 s, 2 da; *Career* 1939-45 War as Major Airborne Forces; Prof of History Toronto University, formerly Lecturer in History Hong Kong University; *Style* - John Byng Esq, MC; 190 Glengrove av, Toronto, Ontario, Canada

BYNG, Hon William Robert; s of Viscount Enfield; *b* 1964; *Style* - The Hon William Byng; c/o Viscount Enfield, 23 Lamont Road, London SW10; Abbotts Worthy House, Abbotts Worthy, near Winchester, Hampshire (☎ Winchester (STD Code 0962) 881333)

BYRNE, Hon Mrs (Nona Georgette); *née* Lawrence; da of 3 Baron Lawrence; *b* 10 Sept 1922; *Educ* Francis Holland Sch; *m* 1945, Wing Cdr Vincent Byrne (d 1978); 5 s, 4 da (and 1 da decd); *Career* chm Catholic Bldg Soc; *Clubs* RAF; *Style* - The Hon Mrs Byrne; Raughmere Rise, Lavant, Chichester, West Sussex (☎ Chichester (STD Code 0243) 527460); 7 Allestree Road, London SW6

BYRON, 11 Baron (E 1643); Rupert Frederick George Byron; s of late Col Wilfrid Byron, s of Rev the Hon William Byron, 4 s of 7 Baron (who succeeded his cousin, the poet, 6 Baron); suc kinsman 1949; *b* 13 Aug 1903; *Educ* Gresham's Sch Holt; *m* 1931, Pauline Augusta, da of late T J Cornwall, of Wagin, W Australia; 1 da; *Heir* kinsman, Richard Byron, DSO; *Career* Lt RANVR WW II; farmer and grazier; *Style* - The Rt Hon The Lord Byron; 16 Barnsley rd, Mt Claremont, W Australia

BYRON, Richard Geoffrey Gordon; DSO (1944); s of late Col Richard Byron, DSO, ggggs of 4 Baron Byron; hp of kinsman, 11 Baron; *b* 3 Nov 1939; *Educ* Eton; *m* 1, 1926 (m dis 1946), Margaret Mary, da of F G Steuart; m 2, 1946, Dorigen, da of P Kennedy Esdaile; 2 s; *Career* Lt-Col 4/7 Roy Dragoon Gds; *Style* - Lieutenant-Colonel Richard Byron DSO; 52 Eresby House, Rutland Gate, London SW7

BYSTRAM, Charles Anthony; s of Baron Cyprian Bystram, sometime Col in Polish Army (d 1961); *b* 23 Dec 1929; *Educ* Douai Sch, Cambridge; *m* 1958, Jean, da of Col Ian Hardie, DSO, RA; 1 s, 2 da; *Career* dir Utd Biscuits Hldgs 1972-, md UB Int 1978-, Gp Corporate Dvpt dir 1980-; chm ORTIZ SA 1975-; *Recreations* travel, food and wine, various sports; *Style* - Charles Bystram Esq; Wolmer Wood, Marlow Common, Bucks (☎ Marlow 4223)

BYWATER, James Edward; s of Elam Bywater; *b* 22 May 1921; *Educ* Morley G S Yorks; *m* Margaret, da of Leonard Fry; 1 da; *Career* engrg; dir Ford of Britain 1965, chm & ch exec Sime Darby Hldgs 1975, chm Thermal Syndicate 1980; dir Associated Biscuits 1979; *Recreations* archaeology, prehistory; *Clubs* Oriental; *Style* - James Bywater Esq; 15 Hamsey Lane, Seaford, E Sussex

C

CABBELL MANNERS, Hon Richard Neville; s of 4 Baron Manners, MC (d 1972); *b* 4 April 1924; *Educ* Eton; *m* 1945, Juliet Mary, eld da of Lt-Col Sir Edward Hulton Preston, 5 Bt, DSO, MC, (d 1963) of Beeston Hall, Neatishead, Norwich; 3 s, 1 da; *Career* farmer; *Recreations* hunting; *Also* adopted additional surname 'Cabbell'; *Style* - The Hon Richard Cabbell Manners; Cromer Hall, Cromer, Norfolk (☎ 2506)

CABLE, Sir James Eric; KCVO (1976), CMG (1967); s of Eric Grant Cable; *b* 15 Nov 1920; *Educ* Stowe, CCC Cambridge; *m* 1954, Viveca Hollmerus; 1 s; *Career* entered Foreign Office 1947, Asst Under-Sec of State FCO 1972-75, Ambassador to Finland 1975-; *Style* - Sir James Cable, KCVO, CMG; c/o FCO, SW1

CABLE-ALEXANDER, Sir Desmond William Lionel; 7 Bt (UK 1809); s of Maj Sir Lionel Alexander, 6 Bt, DSO (d

1956); *b* 4 Oct 1910; *Educ* Harrow, Oxford; *m* 1, 1935 (m dis 1941), Mary Jane, nee O'Brien; 1s; m 2, 1976, Margaret Wood, nee Burnett; 2 da; *Heir* s, Patrick Desmond William Cable-Alexander, b 19 April 1936; *Career* assumed by deed poll 1931 additional name of Cable before that of Alexander; *Style* - Sir Desmond Cable-Alexander, Bt; c/o Barclays Bank, 16 Whitehall, SW1

CABLE-ALEXANDER, Lt-Col Patrick Desmond William; s and h of Sir Desmond William Lionel Cable-Alexander, 7 Bt, by his 1 w Mary; *b* 19 April 1936; *Educ* Downside Sch, RMA Sandhurst; *m* 1, 1961 (m dis 1976), Diana Frances, da of Col Paul Rogers; 2 da (Melanie b 1963, Louise b 1967), m 2, 1976, Jane Mary, da of Dr Anthony Lewis; 1 s (Fergus William Antony b 19 June 1981); *Career* Lt-Col Royal Scots Dragoon Guards, cmmnd 1956, served BAOR, UK, Aden, Army Staff Coll 1967, Asst Military Attache Saigon 1968-70, BAOR, MOD, Nat Defense Coll 1975-6, cmd Duke of Lancaster's Own Yeomanry 1978-80, GSO HQ NW Dist 1981-; *Recreations* the arts, painting, animal husbandry, cricket, reading; *Clubs* St James's, Manchester Racquets and Real Tennis Club; *Style* - Lt-Col Patrick Cable-Alexander; c/o Barclays Bank Ltd, 63 Terminus rd, Eastbourne, East Sussex

CABORN, Richard George; MEP(L) Sheffield, 1979-; s of George Caborn; *b* 6 Oct 1943; *Educ* Hurlfield Comprehensive Sch, Granville Coll of Further Education, Sheffield Polytechnic; *m* 1966, Margaret; 1 s, 1 da; *Career* engineer; Convenor of Shop Stewards, Firth Brown Ltd, 1967-79; *Style* - Richard Caborn Esq, MEP; 29 Quarry Vale rd, Sheffield (☎ 3933802)

CABOT, Richard Murray de Quetteville; s of Dr Philippe de Quetteville Cabot; *b* 20 June 1936; *Educ* Dartington Hall Sch, Cambridge U; *m* 1960, Janet, nee MacGibbon; 1 s, 2 da; *Career* v-chm W & A Gilbey Ltd, James Catto Ltd, 1976-; dir International Distillers and Vintners Ltd, 1976-; *Style* - Richard Cabot Esq; 44 Courthope rd, NW3 (☎ 01 485 2755)

CACCIA, Baron (Life Peer UK 1965) Harold Anthony Caccia; GCMG (1959, KCMG 1950, CMG 1945), GCVO (1961, KCVO 1957); s of late Anthony Mario Felix Caccia, CB, MVO (s of Fabio Caccia, of Florence, of a Florentine family long politically active (they are mentioned in Dante's Purgatory canto 29); Count Alessandro Caccia, whose arms were recorded 1576, was an ancestor of Lord Caccia) by his w and 1 cous, Fanny Birch (da of Azim Birch, of Erewhon, NZ, an area from which Samuel Butler derived the setting for his homonymous novel); *b* 21 Dec 1905; *Educ* Eton, Trinity Oxford, Queen's Oxford; *m* 1932, Anne Catherine, da of late Sir George Barstow, KCB; 1 s, 2 da; *Career* joined Foreign Office, 1929; Dep Under-Sec of State, 1949 and 1954-56; Ambassador to Austria, 1951-54, to Washington, 1956-61; Perm Under-Sec, FO, 1962-65; Head of Diplomatic Service, 1964-65, ret; Provost of Eton, 1965-77; dir ITT (UK) Ltd, Prudential Assurance Co Ltd; Lord Prior of the Order of St John of Jerusalem, 1969-; GCStJ; *Style* - The Rt Hon Lord Caccia, GCMG, GCVO; 1 Chester pl, Regent's pk, NW1 (☎ 01 935 0302); Abernat, Builth-Wells, Breconshire (☎ Erwood 233)

CACCIA, Hon David Anthony Lawrence; s of Baron Caccia (Life Peer); *b* 4 Aug 1936; *Educ* Eton, Trinity Oxford; *m* 1962 (m dis 1973), Angela Margaret, nee Read; c; *Style* - The Hon David Caccia; c/o Hoare & Co, 37 Fleet st, EC4

CADBURY, Sir (George) Adrian Hayhurst; s of Laurence John Cadbury; *b* 15 April 1929; *Educ* Eton, King's Cambridge; *m* 1956, Gillian Mary, nee Skepper; 2 s, 1 da; *Career* memb advsy editorial bd Personnel Management (jnl of IPM) 1981-; chm Cadbury Schweppes Ltd, 1975- (formerly jt md 1970-73, exec dep chm 1974); dir Cadbury gp of cos, IBM (UK) Ltd, IBM (UK) Hldgs Ltd, Jeyes Gp Ltd, Bank of England; chm Financial Policy Cmtee, CBI, 1974-; kt 1977; Hon Fellow Inst Sales & Mktg 1981- *Style* - Sir Adrian Cadbury; Rising Sun House, Baker's la, Knowle, Solihull, W Midlands (☎ Knowle 2931)

CADBURY, Jocelyn Benedict Laurence; MP (C) Birmingham Northfield, 1979-; s of Laurence Cadbury; *b* 3 March 1946; *Educ* Eton, Trinity Cambridge; *Career* former industrial relations official, foreman Cadbury Ltd 1974-76, production man Cadbury's Bournville factory 1976-79; *Style* - Jocelyn Cadbury Esq, MP; The Davids, Northfield, Birmingham B31 2AN (☎ 021 475 1441)

CADBURY, Kenneth Hotham; CBE (1974), MC (1944); s of Joel Hotham Cadbury; *b* 19 Feb 1919; *Educ* Bootham Sch York, Birmingham U; *m* 1, 1944 (m dis 1964), Margaret Rosamund King; 1 s, 1 da; m 2, Marjorie Iris Lilley; 3 da; *Career* assist princ Post Office 1946, princ Cabinet Office 1950-53, sr dir Planning and Purchasing Post Office 1970, assist md Telecommunications 1976- *Style* - Kenneth Cadbury Esq, CBE, MC; Post Office Telecommunications, 2-12 Gresham st, EC1 (☎ 01 432 4596); Pendle, Burdenshott Hill, Worplesdon, Surrey (☎ Worplesdon 2084)

CADBURY, Michael Hotham; DL (W Midlands 1975); s of Joel Cadbury; *b* 16 Dec 1946; *Educ* Leighton Park Sch Reading, Munich and Freiburg Us; *m* 1939, Margaret Heather, nee Chambers; 2 s, 1 da; *Career* former dir Cadbury Bros Ltd; High Sheriff (1974) W Midlands; chm National Trust Regional Ctee; *Style* - Michael Cadbury Esq, DL; 54 Ramsden Close, Selly Oak, Birmingham

CADBURY, Peter Egbert; s of Sir Egbert Cadbury DSC DFC DL (d 1968); *b* 6 Feb 1918; *Educ* Leighton Park Sch, Trin Coll Cambridge; *m* 1, 1947 (m dis 1965), Eugenie Benedicta, da of late Maj Ewen Bruce DSO MC; 1 s (Justin b 1951), 1 da (Felicity); m 2, 1970 (m dis 1975), Mrs Jennifer Morgan-Jones, da of Maj Michael Hammond-Maude; 1 s (Joel b 1972); m 3, 1976, Mrs Angela Jane Meade; 2 s (George b 1978, James b 1979); *Career* experimental test pilot 1941-45, barr (Inner Temple) 1946-54, stood for Stroud (Lib) 1945, exec chm of various cos since 1954- Keith Prowse Ltd, Ashton & Mitchell Alfred Hays, Westward Television, Air Westward, Prowest Ltd, Preston Estates, freeman of the City of London, Curriers Livery Co; *Recreations* flying (Cessna 340 'G-Pete', Helicopter (Squirrell) 'G-Jany'), sailing (express 55' motor cruiser 'Colinette VI'), golf, tennis, shooting, travelling; *Also* owns racehorses 'Cool Million', 'Egbert'; *Style* - Peter Cadbury Esq; Armsworth Hill, Alresford, Hampshire (☎ 096 273 4656); 9 Cheyne Gardens, SW3 (☎ 01 352 6061)

CADBURY, Paul Strangman; CBE (1948); s of Barrow Cadbury; *b* 3 Nov 1895; *m* 1919, Rachel Eveline, nee Wilson; 2 s, 2 da; *Career* formerly chm and md Cadbury Bros Ltd, J S Fry & Sons Ltd, British Cocoa and Chocolate Co Ltd; *Style* - Paul Cadbury Esq, CBE; 32 St Mary's rd, Harborne, Birmingham 17

CADDICK, Col Godfrey Armstrong; OBE (1952), TD (1948), DL (Staffs 1953, W Midlands 1974); s of Charles Frederick Caddick (d 1939); *b* 31 May 1912; *Educ* Malvern, Emmanuel Cambridge; *m* 1941, Kathleen Marcelle; 1 da; *Career* slr, 1937; private practice, 1937-77; *Style* - Col Godfrey Caddick, OBE, TD, DL; Rydal, 62 Streetly lane, Sutton Coldfield (☎ 021 353 7585)

CADELL, Colin Simson; CBE (1944); s of late Lt-Col J M Cadell, DL, of Foxhall, Kirkliston, W Lothian; *b* 7 Aug 1905; *Educ* Merchiston, Edinburgh U, Ecole Supérieur de l'Electricité Paris; *m* 1939, Rosemary, nee Pooley; 2 s, 1 da; *Career* Air Cdre RAF ret, V-Lt for W Lothian 1972-, memb Roy Company of Archers (HM Queen's Bodyguard for Scotland), DL Linlithgowshire 1963-72, chm Edinburgh Airport Consultative Ctee 1972; *Style* - Colin Cadell Esq CBE, HM Vice-Lieut for W Lothian; Whinmill Brae, Coltbridge gdns, Edinburgh

CADELL, Ian Victor; s of Air Cdre Colin S Cadell, CBE; *b* 3 July 1940; *Educ* Eton; *m* 1966, Teresa, nee Ribon; 2 s, 1 da; *Career* dir Carron Company Hldgs Ltd 1976-, dir MCP Holdings Ltd 1979-, memb Roy Co of Archers (Queen's Body Guard for Scotland); *Style* - Ian Cadell Esq; Whinmill Brae, Coltbridge gdns, Edinburgh 12

CADGE, Christopher Rawlinson; OBE

(1917); s of late Edward Cadge; *b* 1 June 1890; *Educ* Haileybury; *m* 1930, Elizabeth Rio, nee Pratten; 2 s, 2 da (1 decd); *Career* 8 Bn E Surrey Regt 1914-18, Lt-Col Royal Norfolk Regt TA 1935, BT-Col 1939, slr, DL (1954) Norfolk; *Style* - Col Christopher Cadge OBE DL; Ballygate House, Beccles, Suffolk (☎ Beccles 712869)

CADIEUX, Hon Leo; PC (1965), QC (1975); s of Joseph Cadieux; *b* 28 May 1908; *m* 1962, Monique, da of Placide Plante; 1 s; *Career* journalist 1930-44, Canada MP 1962-70, Min of National Defence 1967-70, ambass to France 1970-75; *Style* - Hon Leo Cadieux, PC, QC; 20 Driveway, Appt 1106, Ottawa, Canada

CADMAN, 3 Baron (1937 UK); John Anthony Cadman; s of 2 Baron Cadman (d 1966); *b* 3 July 1938; *Educ* Harrow, Selwyn Cambridge, RAC Cirencester; *m* 1975, Janet, da of Arthur Hayes, of Morecambe; 2 s; *Heir* s Hon Nicholas Cadman; *Career* farmer; *Style* - The Rt Hon The Lord Cadman; Eakley Manor Farm, Stoke Goldington, Newport Pagnell, Bucks (☎ 0908 55 249)

CADMAN, Hon Arthur Denys; s of late 1 Baron Cadman; *b* 1911; *Educ* Harrow, Harvard; *m* 1933, Cary, nee Baker; 2 s, 3 da; *Style* - The Hon Arthur Cadman; 115 Fifth av, New York, NY 19028, USA

CADMAN, Surgn Rear-Adm Albert Edward; CB (1977); *b* 14 Oct 1918; *Educ* Dover G S, Guy's Dental Sch; *m* 1, 1946, Margaret Henrietta Tomkins-Russell (d 1974); 1 s , 1 da; m 2, 1975, Mary Croil Macdonald, Superintendent, WRNS; *Career* LDS RCS 1941, Surg Lt (D) RNVR 1942, RN 1947, dir of Naval Dental Services 1974-77, QHDS 1974-77, dep county dir for Hants, St John Ambulance Assoc 1978-; *Style* - Surgn Rear-Adm Albert Cadman, CB; Solent House, 2 Solent Way, Alverstoke, Hants (☎ Gosport 86648)

CADMAN, Hon Giles Oliver Richard; 2 s of 3 Baron Cadman; *b* 5 Feb 1979; *Style* - The Hon Giles Cadman

CADMAN, Hon James Rupert; s of late 2 Baron Cadman; *b* 9 June 1944; *Educ* Harrow; *Style* - The Hon James Cadman; Overlands, 157 Church rd, Combe Down, Bath, Somerset

CADMAN, Marjorie, Baroness; Marjorie Elizabeth; *née* Bunnis; da of Byron Bunnis; *m* 1936, 2 Baron Cadman (d 1966); 2 s (3 Baron, Hon James Cadman); *Style* - The Rt Hon Marjorie, Lady Cadman; Overlands, 157 Church rd, Combe Down, Bath, Somerset

CADMAN, Hon Nicholas Anthony James; s and h of 3 Baron Cadman; *b* 18 Nov 1977; *Style* - The Hon Nicholas Cadman

CADMAN, Hon Mrs (Sybil Mary); da of late 1 Baron Cadman; *b* 1916; *m* 1, 1938, Maj-Gen William Pat Arthur Bradshaw, CB, DSO, late Scots Gds (d 1966); 2 s, 2 da; m 2, 1968, her 1 cous James Simon Cadman (whose 1 w was Kathleen, da of Sir John Ferguson, KBE, MP); *Style* - The Hon Mrs Cadman; Rhagatt Hall, Corwen, Merionethshire

CADOGAN, 7 Earl (GB 1800); William Gerald Charles Cadogan; MC (1943), DL (County of London 1958); also Baron Cadogan (GB 1718), Viscount Chelsea (GB 1800), and Baron Oakley (UK 1831); s of 6 Earl (d 1933) and Lilian (d 1973), nee Coxon, who m 2, 1941, Lt-Col H E Hambro, CBE; *b* 13 Feb 1914; *Educ* Eton, Sandhurst ; *m* 1, 1936 (m dis 1959), Hon Primrose Yarde-Buller, da of 3 Baron Churston and sis of Princess Joan Aly Khan, Denise Lady Ebury (ex-w of 5 Baron) and Lydia Duchess of Bedford (ex-w of 13 Duke); 1 s, 3 da; m 2, 1961, Cecilia, da of Lt-Col H K Hamilton-Wedderburn, OBE; *Heir* s Viscount Chelsea; *Career* landowner, Mayor of Chelsea 1964, chm Cadogan Estates Ltd and subsidiaries 1935-; *Style* - The Rt Hon The Earl Cadogan, MC, DL; 28 Cadogan sq, SW1 (☎ 01 584 2335); Snaigow, Dunkeld, Perthshire (☎ Caputh 223)

CADOGAN, Hon Anna-Karina; da of Viscount Chelsea (s and h of 7 Earl Cadogan); *b* 1964

CADOGAN, Hon Edward Charles; s of

Viscount Chelsea (s and h of 7 Earl Cadogan); *b* 10 May 1966

CADOGAN, Lady Mary Veronica; *née* Lambart; da of late 11 Earl of Cavan; *b* 1908; *m* 1934, Col Edward Henry Cadogan, CBE, late Roy Welch Fusiliers; 3 s; *Style* - Lady Mary Cadogan; Shallows House, Boldre, Lymington, Hants

CADOGAN, Hon William John; s of Viscount Chelsea (s and h of 7 Earl Cadogan); *b* 1973

CADWALLADER, Air Vice-Marshal Howard George; CB (1974); *b* 16 March 1916; *Educ* Hampton Sch Middx; *m* 1950, Betty Samuels; *Career* RAF ret, dir Purchasing Post Office 1974-79; *Style* - Air Vice-Marshal Howard Cadwallader, CB; 3 Greenway Close, Totteridge, N20

CADWALLADER, Sir John; *b* 25 Aug 1902; *Educ* Sydney C of E G S, NSW; *m* 1935, Helen Moxham; 2 s, 1 da; *Career* chm & md Allied Mills Ltd 1949-, kt 1967; *Style* - Sir John Cadwallader; 27 Marian st, Killara, NSW 2071 Australia (☎ 498 1974)

CAESAR, Rev Canon Anthony Douglass; s of Harold Caesar; *b* 3 April 1924; *Educ* Cranleigh Sch, Magdalene Cambridge, St Stephen's House Oxford; *Career* Residentiary Canon of Winchester Cathedral, 1976-79 (formerly Precentor and Sacrist and Hon Canon); Sub-Almoner and Domestic Chaplain to HM the Queen, Sub-Dean of Her Majesty's Chapels Royal and Deputy Clerk of the Closet, 1979-; *Style* - The Rev Canon Anthony Caesar; Marlborough Gate, St James's Palace, SW1 (☎ 01 930 6609)

CAFFIN, A(rthur) Crawford; s of Charles Caffin; *b* 10 June 1910; *Educ* King's Sch Rochester; *m* 1933, Mala Pocock; 1 da; *Career* slr 1932, former ptnr R L Frank & Caffin Truro (now consultant), Recorder of the Crown Court 1972-; *Style* - Crawford Caffin Esq; Cotna House, Gorran, St Austell, Cornwall

CAFFIN, Albert Edward; CIE (1947), OBE (1946); s of Claud Carter and Lilian Caffin; *b* 16 June 1902; *m* 1929, Hilda Elizabeth Wheeler; *Career* joined Indian Police, 1922; Asst Inspector General, Poona, 1939; Commr of Police, Bombay, 1947 (formerly Dep Commr); *Style* - Albert Caffin Esq, CIE, OBE; C22 San Remo Towers, Sea rd, Boscombe, Bournemouth

CAFFYN, Brig Sir Edward Roy; KBE (1963, CBE 1945, OBE 1942), CB (1955), TD (1950), DL (Sussex 1956); s of Percy Caffyn; *b* 27 May 1904; *Educ* Eastbourne and Loughborough Colls; *m* 1, 1929, Elsa , nee Nurse; 2 s; m 2, 1946, Delphine, da of Maj William Chilton-Riggs; *Career* dir Mech Eng Field Marshal Montgomery's Staff 1943-45, v-chm E Sussex CC 1967, chm Sussex Police Authority 1971-74, JP Eastbourne 1948, E Sussex 1960, chm Sussex TAFA 1947-67, v-chm Cncl TAFA 1961-66; chm Caffyns to 1981, pres 1981-; *Style* - Brig Sir Edward Caffyn, KBE, CB, TD, JP, DL; Norman Norris, Vines Cross, Heathfield, E Sussex (☎ Horam Road 2674)

CAFFYN, Robert James Morris; s of late Sir Sydney Caffyn; *b* 1 June 1935; *Educ* Eastbourne Coll, Peterhouse Cambridge; *m* 1961, Gillian Mabel Ann, nee Bailey; 1 s, 2 da; *Career* jt md Caffyns Ltd 1972-, Hon treasurer Free Church Federal Council 1976, FCA; *Style* - Robert Caffyn Esq; Field House, Old Willingdon rd, Friston, nr Eastbourne, E Sussex (☎ E Dean 3100)

CAHN, Sir Albert Jonas; 2 Bt (UK 1934), of Stanford-upon-Soar, Co Nottingham; s of Sir Julien Cahn, 1 Bt (d 1944); *b* 27 June 1924; *Educ* Harrow; *m* 1948, Malka, nee Bluestone; 2 s, 2 da; *Heir* s Julien Cahn; *Career* company dir, marriage guidance cnsllr; *Style* - Sir Albert Cahn, Bt; 10 Edgecombe Close, Warren rd, Kingston-upon-Thames, Surrey (☎ 01 942 6956)

CAHN, Julien Michael; s and h of Sir Albert Cahn, 2 Bt; *b* 15 Jan 1951; *Educ* Harrow *Style* - Julien Cahn Esq

CAIN, Lady (Enid Bertha Willoughby); *née* Glasgow; *m* 1923, Col Sir Ernest Cain, 2 and last Bt (d 1969); 3 da; *Style* - Lady Cain; White House,

Ferry Lane, Wargrave, Berks

CAIN, Sir Edward Thomas; CBE (1966); s of Edward Cain; *b* 7 Dec 1916; *Educ* Nudgee Coll Qld, Qld U; *m* 1942, Marcia, nee Parbery; 1 s, 1 da ; *Career* Commissioner of Taxation Australia 1964-76, kt 1972; *Style* - Sir Edward Cain, CBE; 99 Buxton st, Deakin, Canberra Australia (☎ 811462)

CAINE, Michael (né Maurice Micklewhite); s of late Maurice Micklewhite; *b* 14 March 1933 ; *Educ* Wilson's G S Peckham; *m* 1, 1955, Patricia Haines (m dis); 1 da; m 2, 1973, Shakira Baksh; 1 da; *Career* actor in TV, theatre, films; *Style* - Michael Caine, Esq; Clewer, Berks

CAINE, Michael Harris; s of Sir Sydney Caine, KCMG, of Buckland House, Hindhead, Surrey; *b* 17 June 1927; *Educ* Bedales, Lincoln Coll Oxford, George Washington U Washington DC; *m* 1952, Janice, nee Mercer; 1 s, 1 da; *Career* chm 1979- (ch exec 1975-, dir 1964-) Booker McConnell Ltd, dir Acklands Ltd (Canada); *Recreations* reading, walking; *Clubs* Reform; *Style* - Michael Caine, Esq; 23 Upper Wimpole st, W1 (☎ 01 935 4044); Wilton House, 33 High st, Hungerford, Berks (☎ 2861)

CAINE, Sir Sydney; KCMG (1947, CMG 1945); s of Harry Caine; *b* 27 June 1902; *Educ* Harrow County Sch, LSE; *m* 1, 1925, Muriel (d 1962), nee Harris; 1 s (Michael Caine, *qv*); m 2, 1965, Doris Folkard (d 1973); m 3, 1975, Elizabeth, da of late J Crane Nicholls and wid of Sir Eric Bowyer, KCB, KBE; *Career* dir LSE 1957-67, served Colonial Off 1940-48, Treasury 1948-51; *Style* - Sir Sydney Caine, KCMG; Buckland House, Tarn rd, Hindhead, Surrey

CAIRNCROSS, Sir Alec (Alexander Kirkland); KCMG (1967, CMG 1950); s of Alexander Cairncross (d 1948); *b* 11 Feb 1911; *Educ* Hamilton Acad, Glasgow U, Cambridge (PhD 1936); *m* 1943, Mary, da of Maj Edward Glynn, TD, of Ilkley (d 1948); 3 s, 2 da; *Career* Chllr Glasgow U 1972-, master St Peter's Coll Oxford 1969-78, head Govt Ec Serv 1964-69, Ec Advsr to HM Govt 1961-64; *Recreations* travelling, writing; *Clubs* Oxford & Cambridge; *Style* - Sir Alec Cairncross, KCMG; 14 Staverton rd, Oxford (☎ 52358)

CAIRNCROSS, Neil Francis; CB (1971); s of late James Cairncross; *b* 29 July 1920; *Educ* Charterhouse, Oriel Oxford; *m* 1947, Eleanor Elizabeth Leisten; 2 s, 1 da; *Career* barr 1948, Private Sec to Prime Minister 1955-58, Dep Under-Sec of State Home Office 1972- *Style* - Neil Cairncross Esq, CB; 28 Cassiobury Park av, Watford, Herts (☎ 23856)

CAIRNS, 5 Earl (1878 UK); David Charles Cairns; GCVO (1972, KCVO 1969), CB (1960), DL (Suffolk 1973); also Baron Cairns (UK 1867) and Viscount Garmoyle (UK 1878); s of 4 Earl (d 1946) and Olive (d 1952), da of late J P Cobbold, MP; *b* 3 July 1909; *Educ* RNC Dartmouth; *m* 1936, Barbara, da of Sydney Burgess, of Heathfield, Bowdon, Cheshire; 2 s, 1 da; *Heir* s Visc Garmoyle; *Career* served RN, Rear-Adm ret, Pres Navy League 1966-77, HM Marshal of Diplomatic Corps 1962-71, Extra Equerry to HM The Queen 1972-; *Style* - Rear-Adm The Rt Hon The Earl Cairns, GCVO, CB, DL; The Red House, Clopton, nr Woodbridge (☎ 262)

CAIRNS, Hon Alistair Benedict; s of Viscount Garmoyle, *qv*; *b* 1969

CAIRNS, Rt Hon Sir David Arnold Scott; PC (1970); s of David Cairns, JP (d 1955); *b* 3 March 1902; *Educ* Bede Sch Sunderland, Pembroke Cambridge; *m* 1932, Irene, nee Teacher; 1 s, 2 da; *Career* kt 1955, QC (1952-60), barr, Lord Justice of Appeal 1970-77; *Recreations* swimming, gardening; *Style* - Rt Hon Sir David Cairns, PC; Applecroft, Ashtead, Surrey (☎ 74132)

CAIRNS, Hon David Patrick; s of Viscount Garmoyle, *qv* ; *b* 1967

CAIRNS, Hon Hugh Andrew David; s of 5 Earl Cairns; *b* 1942; *Educ* Wellington, Dublin U; *m* 1966, Elizabeth, da of Lt-Col F C L Bell; 1 s, 1 da; *Style* - The Hon Hugh Cairns; 75 Lee rd, Blackheath, SE3

CAIRNS, Hon Hugh Sebastian; s of Viscount Garmoyle, *qv*; *b* 26 March 1965

CAIRNS, Sir Joseph Foster; s of Frederick Cairns; *b* 27 June 1920; *m* 1944, Helena McCullough; 1 s, 1 da; *Career* md J Cairns Ltd 1945-, Lord Mayor of Belfast 1969-72, Member of the Senate of Northern Ireland 1969-72, JP (1963), High Sheriff (1963) Belfast, kt 1972; *Style* - Sir Joseph Cairns, JP; Amaranth, Craigdarragh rd, Helens Bay, Northern Ireland (☎ (Helens Bay 852813)

CAIRNS, Dr James Ford; MHR (L) Lalor 1969- (formerly for Yarra 1955-69); s of James Cairns and Letitia Ford; *b* 4 Oct 1914; *Educ* Melbourne U; *m* 1939, Gwendolyn Olga Robb; 2 s; *Career* Memb of House of Representatives, former Min for Overseas Trade and Treasurer of Australia, Dep Prime Minister, 1974-75, Min for the Environment 1975; *Style* - Dr James Cairns, MHR; 21 Wattle rd, Hawthorn, Victoria 3122, Australia (☎ 819-1929)

CAIRNS, Peter Granville; s of Maj H W Cairns MC; *b* 3 Sept 1940; *Educ* Eton; *Career* banker, dir Cater Ryder & Co Ltd; *Style* - Peter Cairns Esq; 11 St Mary Abbots ct, W14 (☎ 01 603 7356)

CAITHNESS, 20 Earl of (S 1455); Malcolm Ian Sinclair; 15 Bt (S 1631); also Lord Berriedale (S 1592); s of 19 Earl of Caithness (James Roderick Sinclair, CVO, CBE, DSO, d 1965) by his 2 w Madeleine; *b* 3 Nov 1948; *Educ* Marlborough, RAC Cirencester; *m* 1975, Diana Caroline, da of Maj Richard Coke (gs of 2 Earl of Leicester); 1 s, 1 da; *Heir* s, Lord Berriedale, b 26 March 1981; *Career* ARICS; *Style* - The Rt Hon the Earl of Caithness; Finstock Manor, Finstock, Oxford; Girnigoe Castle, Caithness

CAKEBREAD, Frank Ingram; s of late Alfred George Watson; *b* 15 March 1919; *Educ* Aldenham; *m* 1960, Berenice Mary, nee Mortimer; 2 s, 2 da; *Career* joined Cakebread Robey & Co Ltd of Enfield dep chm 1962-, chm Princes Electric Theatres Co 1950-, memb Lloyd's, memb Worshipful Co of Builders Merchants, Freeman of the City of London; *Style* - Frank Cakebread Esq; 318-326 Southbury rd, Enfield, Middx

CAKOBAU, Ratu Sir George (Kadavulevu); GCMG (1973), GCVO (1977), OBE (1953); s of Ratu Popi Epeli Seniloli Cakobau; *b* 1911; *Educ* Newington Coll Australia, Wanganui Technical Coll, NZ; *m* Adi Lelea Balekiwai ; *Career* memb of Legislative Council of Fiji 1951-70, Min Fijian Affairs and Local Govt 1970-71, Min without Portfolio 1971-72, Gov-Gen of Fiji 1973-, KStJ 1973; *Style* - His Excellency Ratu Sir George Cakobau, GCMG, GCVO, OBE; Government House, Suva, Fiji

CALCUTT, David Charles; QC (1972); s of late Henry Calcutt; *b* 2 Nov 1930; *Educ* Cranleigh, Ch Ch Oxford, King's Cambridge; *m* 1969, Barbara Ann, nee Walker; *Career* barr 1955, with The Times 1957-66, Chancellor of the Diocese of Exeter and of Bristol 1971-, Recorder of the Crown Court 1972-, Judge of the Court of Appeal of Jersey and of Guernsey 1978-, Dep Judge of the High Court of Justice 1978-79, Master of Bench Middle Temple 1980-; *Style* - David Calcutt Esq, QC; Lamb Building, Temple, EC4; 5 Essex ct, EC4; Colebrook House, Winchester

CALDECOTE, 2 Viscount (UK 1939); Robert Andrew Inskip; DSC (1941); s of 1 Viscount Caldecote (Rt Hon Sir Thomas Walker Hobart Inskip, CBE, d 1947); *b* 8 Oct 1917; *Educ* Eton, King's Cambridge ; *m* 1942, Jean Hamilla, da of late Rear-Adm Hugh Dundas Hamilton; 1 s, 2 da; *Heir* s, Hon Piers James Hampden Inskip; *Career* dir Lloyd's Bank and Lloyds Bank International, dir Delta Metal Col 1969- (formerly chm), Consolidated Goldfields Ltd 1969-, Legal and General Assurance Soc 1976-, Pro-Chancellor Cranfield Inst of Technology, Memb Advisory Council for Applied Research and Dvpt 1981-; *Clubs* Pratt's, Boodle's, Royal Yacht Sqdn, Royal Ocean Racing, Athenaeum; *Style* - The Rt Hon the Viscount Caldecote; Orchard Cottage, South Harting, Petersfield, Hants (☎ Harting 264)

CALDER, The Hon Allan Graham Ritchie; s of Baron Ritchie-Calder, CBE, Philpstoun Hse, West Lothian, Scotland; *b*

4 Jan 1944; *Educ* Ewell Technical College; Birbeck Coll, University of London; *m* ; 1 s; *Career* Mathematician and Commercial Balloon Pilot, Assistant Professor Carleton Univ Ottawa 1970-71, Louisiana State U 1971-2, University of Missouri 1975-6, Lecturer in Mathematics Univ of Essex 1972-3, Birbeck College 1972-, Associate Professor New Mexico State Univ 1979-81, Freelance Commercial Balloonist 1980-; *Recreations* Sailing, Classic Cars (131/own Cameron V77 Hot Air Balloon); *Clubs* Savile, Bentley Drivers, Porsche GB, British Balloon and Airship; *Style* - The Hon Allan Calder; Ormond Hse, Boswell st, London, WCI (☎ 01 242 5816)

CALDER, John; DL (West Lothian 1976); s of late John Calder; *b* 11 July 1914; *Educ* Morgan Acad Dundee, Univ Coll Dundee, Edinburgh U; *m* 1940, Vida Campbell, nee Carmichael; 1 s, 1 da; *Career* slr, County Clerk W Lothian CC 1950-75; *Style* - John Calder Esq, DL; Woodlands, Dundas st, Bo'ness, W Lothian (☎ 2311)

CALDER, John Mackenzie; s of James Calder; *b* 25 Jan 1927; *Educ* McGill U, Sir George Williams Coll, Zurich U; *m* 1, 1949, Mary Ann Simmonds; 1 da; m 2, 1960 (m dis 1975), Bettina Jonic; 1 da; *Career* publisher, editor, author; founder and md John Calder (Publishers) Ltd, later Calder & Boyars Ltd; contested (L) Kinross and W Perthshire, 1970, Hamilton, 1974; *Style* - John Calder Esq; Calder & Boyars Ltd, 18 Brewer st, W1

CALDER, Air Vice-Marshal Malcolm Frederick; CB (1957), CBE (1947) ; s of Andrew Calder; *b* 1907; *Educ* Christ Church Boys' H S NZ, Univ Coll Canterbury NZ; *m* 1935, Margaret Emily, nee Mandeno; 1 s, 1 da ; *Career* NZ Sr Air Liaison Officer London 1954-56, served Malaya 1957-58, Chief of Air Staff RNZAF 1958, former chm NZ Chiefs of Staff Ctee; *Style* - Air Vice-Marshal Malcolm Calder, CB, CBE; Herekiekie st, Turangi, New Zealnd

CALDER, Hon Nigel David Ritchie; s of Baron Ritchie-Calder, CBE; *b* 2 Dec 1931; *Educ* Merchant Taylors', Sidney Sussex Cambridge; *m* 1954, Elisabeth, da of Alfred Palmer; 2 s, 3 da; *Career* writer with New Scientist 1956- (ed 1962-66), freelance author & TV scriptwriter 1966-; *Recreations* sailing (ketch-'Charmed'); *Clubs* Athenaeum, Cruising Assoc; *Style* - The Hon Nigel Calder; 8 The Chase, Furnace Green, Crawley, W Sussex (☎ 26693)

CALDICOTT, Hon Sir John Moore; KBE (1963), CMG (1955); *b* 1900; *Educ* Shrewsbury; *m* 1945, Evelyn Macarthur; 1 s, 2 da (step); *Career* farmer Rhodesia, MP Rhodesia Parliament Mazoe 1948, Min of Economic Affairs 1958-62, then of the Common Market and of Finance, Fedn of Rhodesia and Nyasaland; *Style* - The Hon Sir John Caldicott, KBE, CMG; 24 Court rd, Greendale, Salisbury, Rhodesia

CALDWELL, Surgn Vice-Adm Sir (Eric) Dick; KBE (1969), CB (1965); s of Dr John Caldwell; *b* 6 July 1909; *Educ* Edinburgh Acad, Edinburgh U; *m* 1942, Margery Lee Abbott; *Career* medical dir-gen of Royal Navy 1966-69, former exec dir Medical Cncl on Alcoholism, CStJ; *Style* - Surgeon Vice-Admiral Sir Dick Caldwell, KBE, CB; 9a Holland Park rd, Kensington, W14

CALDWELL, Maj-Gen Frank Griffiths; OBE (1953, MBE 1945), MC (1941 and Bar 1942); s of William Caldwell; *b* 26 Feb 1921; *Educ* Elizabeth Coll Guernsey, RMC Woolwich; *m* 1945, Betty, da of Capt Charles Palmer Buesden; 1 s, 1 da; *Career* commissioned RE 1940, Col 1965, Brig 1966, Assist Ch Gen Staff 1972-74, ret 1974, dir Thomas Storey (Engineers) Ltd and consultant 1974-; *Style* - Maj-Gen Frank Caldwell, OBE, MC; The Eighteenth, Pond rd, Hook Heath, Woking, Surrey (☎ Woking 4706)

CALEDON, 7 Earl of (I 1800); Nicholas James Alexander; also Baron & Viscount Caledon (I 1790 & 1797); s of 6 Earl (d 1980) by his 2 w, Anne (d 1963), da of Baron de Graevenitz (cr by Duke of Schwerin 1847, Tsar Nicholas I of Russia 1851); *b* 6 May 1955; *Educ* Gordonstoun; *m* 1979, Wendy Catherine, nee Coumantaros; *Heir* kinsman, 2 Earl Alexander of Tunis; *Style* - The Rt Hon the Earl of Caledon; Caledon Castle, co Tyrone, Ireland (☎ 232)

CALEDON, Elisabeth, Countess of; Marie Elisabeth Burton; da of Maj Richard Burton Allen; *m* 1, Maj the Hon Iain Maxwell Erskine, later 2 Baron Erskine of Rerrick; *m* 2, 1964, as his 3 w, 6 Earl of Caledon (d 1980); *Style* - The Rt Hon Elisabeth, Countess of Caledon; Caledon Castle, Co Tyrone

CALLAGHAN, Sir Allan Robert; CMG (1945); s of late Phillip George Callaghan; *b* 24 Nov 1903; *Educ* St Paul's Coll Sydney U, St John's Oxford; *m* 1, 1928, Zillah May Sampson (decd); 2 s, 1 da; m 2, 1965, Doreen Rhys Draper; *Career* dir of Agriculture South Australia 1949-59, Commercial Counsellor Australian Embassy Washington DC 1959-65, former chm Australian Wheat Bd 1965-71, agricultural consultant, kt 1972; *Style* - Sir Allan Callaghan, CMG; Tralee, 22 Murray st, Clapham, SA 5062, Australia (☎ 276-6524)

CALLAGHAN, Sir Bede Bertrand; CBE (1968); s of Stanislaus K Callaghan (d 1950); *b* 16 March 1912; *Educ* Newcastle H S, Newcastle U (Aust); *m* 1940, Mollie, nee Brewer; 3 da; *Career* gen man Commonwealth Dvpt Bank of Australia 1959-65, md Commonwealth Banking Corpn 1965-76, Chllr Newcastle U 1977- (Dep Chllr 1973-77), kt 1976; *Style* - Sir Bede Callaghan, CBE; 69 Darnley st, Gordon, NSW 2072, Australia (☎ 498 7583)

CALLAGHAN, Rear-Adm Desmond Noble; CB (1970); s of Edmund Callaghan and Kathleen, nee Noble ; *b* 24 Nov 1915; *Educ* RNC Dartmouth; *m* 1948, Patricia Munro Geddes; 1 s, 2 da; *Career* joined RN 1929, Capt 1958, Rear-Adm 1968, pres Ordnance Bd 1968-71, ret 1978, Dir-Gen National Supervisory Council for Intruder Alarms 1971-77, FRSA; *Style* - Rear-Adm Desmond Callaghan, CB; Willand, Boyn Hill rd, Maidenhead, Berks (☎ 26840)

CALLAGHAN, James; MP (L) Middleton and Prestwich, 1974-; s of James Callaghan; *b* 28 Jan 1927; *Educ* Manchester U, London U; *Career* lectr St John's Coll Manchester 1959-74, former Borough Councillor Middleton; *Style* - James Callaghan Esq, MP; 139 Hollin la, Middleton, Manchester M24 3LA (☎ 061 643 8108)

CALLAGHAN, Rt Hon (Leonard) James; PC (1964), MP (L) South Cardiff, 1945-50, S E Cardiff, 1950-; s of James Callaghan; *b* 27 March 1912; *Educ* Portsmouth Northern Secondary Sch; *m* 1938, Audrey Elizabeth Moulton; 1 s, 2 da; *Career* joined Civil Service, 1929; Asst Sec Inland Revenue Staff Fedn, 1936-47; Parly Sec Min of Transport, 1947-50; Parly and Financial Sec, Admiralty, 1950-51; Chancellor of the Exchequer, 1964-67; Home Sec, 1967-70; Sec of State for Foreign and Commonwealth Affairs, 1974-76; Min of Overseas Devpt, 1975-76; Prime Minister and First Lord of the Treasury, 1976-79; *Style* - The Rt Hon James Callaghan, MP; House of Commons, London SW1

CALLAN, Maj-Gen Michael; CB (1979); s of Maj John Callan; *b* 27 Nov 1925; *Educ* Farnborough G S; *m* 1948, Marie Evelyn, nee Farthing; 2 s; *Career* Indian Army (1 Gurkhas) 1944-47, Cdr Rhine Area BAOR 1975-76, dir gen Ordnance Services (MOD) 1976-1980, Col-Commandant RAOC 1981-, dir IDC Ltd Stratford-upon-Avon; *Clubs* Army & Navy; *Style* - Maj-Gen Michael Callan, CB; 7 Hands Paddock, Newbold on Stour, Stratford-upon-Avon, Warwicks; c/o Williams & Glyns Bank Ltd, Kirkland House, Whitehall, SW1

CALLANDER, Lady Mary (Pamela); *née* Douglas; da of 21 Earl of Morton; *b* 1950; *m* 1973, Richard Callander; 1 da; *Style* - Lady Mary Callander; Saughland House, Pathhead, Midlothian

CALLARD, Sir Jack (Eric John); s of late Frank Callard; *b* 15 March 1913; *Educ* St John's Cambridge; *m* 1938, Pauline Mary, nee Pengelly; 3 da; *Career* chartered mechanical engr, chm- ICI Ltd 1971-75, British Home Stores Ltd 1976-; dir- Midland Bank Ltd 1971-, Commercial Union Assurance Ltd 1975-, Ferguson Industl Hldgs 1975-, kt 1974; *Style* - Sir Jack Callard; Crookwath Cottage, High Row, Dockray, nr Penrith, Cumbria

CALLEY, Sir Henry Algernon; DSO

(1945), DFC (1943), DL (Wilts 1968); s of Rev A Langton; *b* 9 Feb 1914; *Educ* St John's Sch Leatherhead; *Career* former teacher, stud owner and manager; with Metropolitan Police 1938-41; late chm Cncl & Finance Ctee Wilts CC, Wessex Area Con Assoc; kt 1964; adopted mother's name of Calley 1974 *Style* - Sir Henry Calley, DSO, DFC, DL; Overtown House, Wroughton, Swindon, Wilts (☎ Wroughton 812208)

CALLINAN, Sir Bernard James; CBE (1971), DSO (1945), MC (1943); s of late Michael Joseph Callinan; *b* 2 Feb 1913; *Educ* Melbourne U; *m* 1943, Naomi Marian, nee Cullinan; 5 s; *Career* chm and md Gutteridge, Haskins & Davey Pty Ltd 1971-78 (now consultant) dir- BP Co of Australia Ltd 1969-, CSR Ltd 1978-, kt 1977; *Style* - Sir Bernard Callinan, CBE, DSO, MC; 111 Sackville st, Kew Victoria, Australia 3101 (☎ 03 80 1230)

CALLINAN, Raymond Clive; s of Jeremiah Callinan (d 1959); *b* 13 Mar 1934; *Educ* Clifton Coll, BNC Oxford; *m* 1962 (m dis 1977), Gita, da of Satish Gore of Calcutta; 1 s, 1 da; *Career* banker, md Singer & Friedlander Ltd 1970-; *Recreations* cricket, motor racing, reading; *Style* - Raymond Callinan Esq; 19 Westbourne st, W2

CALLINICOS, Hon Mrs (Aedgyth Bertha Milburg Mary Antonia Frances); *née* Lyon-Dalberg-Acton; da of 2 Baron Acton, KCVO; *b* 15 Dec 1920; *m* 1949, John Callinicos, of Ithaca; 2 s; *Style* - The Hon Mrs Callinicos; Villa Ithaki, Hatfield, Salisbury, Zimbabwe (☎ 50065)

CALLMAN, His Hon Judge; Clive Vernon Callman; s of Felix Callman; *b* 21 June 1927; *Educ* Ottershaw, St George's Coll Weybridge, LSE; *m* 1967, Judith Helen, da of Gus Hines, OBE, JP, of Adelaide; 1 s, 1 da; *Career* called to Bar Middle Temple 1951, Circuit Judge (SE) 1973-; *Style* - His Hon Judge Callman; 11 Constable Close, NW11 (☎ 01 458 3010)

CALLOW, Hon Mrs (Sophia Margaret); *née* Watson; da of Baron Thankerton (Life Peer d 1948); *b* 1907; *m* 1936, Michael John Callow; *Style* - The Hon Mrs Callow; Relf House, Rockshaw rd, Merstham, Surrey

CALNE AND CALSTONE, Viscount; Simon Henry George Petty-Fitzmaurice; s and h of Earl of Shelburne and gs of 8 Marq of Lansdowne, PC; *b* 24 Nov 1970; *Style* - Viscount Calne and Calstone

CALTHORPE, 10 Baron (1796 GB), Sir Peter Waldo Somerset Gough-Calthorpe; 11 Bt (1728); s of late Hon Frederick Gough-Calthorpe (d 1935) and Dorothy, nee Vernon-Harcourt; suc bro, 9 Baron, 1945; *b* 13 July 1927; *Educ* Stowe; *m* 1, 1956 (m dis 1971), Saranne nee Alexander; m 2, 1979, Elizabeth, nee Young; *Heir* none; *Career* late Lt Welsh Gds; *Style* - The Rt Hon The Lord Calthorpe; c/o IOM Bank ltd, 2 Athol st, Douglas, IOM

CALVER, Gordon Anthony; s of late Ernest Walter Calver; *b* 12 Jan 21; *Educ* Sutton Valence Sch; *m* 1959, Yvonne Margaret, nee Burnside; 2 da; *Career* international banker, gen man and dir British Bank of the Middle East 1970-77 (dir 1977-79), London Advisory Cmtee 1979-, FIB; *Style* - Gordon Calver Esq; Darband House, Blackdown av, Pyrford, nr Woking, Surrey (☎ Byfleet 47602)

CALVERLEY, 3 Baron (UK 1945); Charles Rodney Muff; s of 2 Baron Calverley (George Raymond Orford Muff, d 1971); *b* 2 Oct 1946; *Educ* Moravian Fulneck Sch for Boys, Pudsey; *m* 1972, Barbara Ann, nee Brown; 1 s; *Heir* s, Jonathan Edward Muff, b 16 April 1975; *Career* Member of City of Bradford Police; *Style* - The Rt Hon the Lord Calverley; 10 Briarwood grove, Wibsey, Bradford

CALVERLEY, Mary Baroness; Mary; da of Arthur Farrar; *m* 1940, 2 Baron Calverley (d 1971); 2 s; *Style* - The Rt Hon Mary, Lady Calverley

CALVERT, Mrs Barbara Adamson ; QC (1975); da of Albert Parker; *b* 30 April 1926; *Educ* LSE; *m* 1948, John Thornton Calvert, CBE; 1 s, 1 da; *Career* called to Bar Middle Temple 1959, part-time chm Industrial Tribunals, 1974-; *Style* - Mrs J

T Calvert, QC; 158 Ashley gdns, SW1 (☎ 01 828 0530); Parknasilla, Rushden, nr Buntingford, Herts (0776 388 249)

CALVERT, Capt Michael John; JP (1972), DL (Surrey 1974); s of late John Charles Calvert; *b* 15 Sept 1930; *Educ* Eton, Sandhurst; *m* 1963, Sally Noel, nee Cannon; 3 da; *Career* 60 Rifles BAOR 1949-62, Adjt Queen's Royal Rifles 1962-64, farmer 1964-; *Style* - Capt Michael Calvert, JP, DL; Ockley Court, Ockley, nr Dorking, Surrey (☎ Dorking 711160)

CALVOCORESSI, Hon Mrs (Barbara Dorothy); *née* Eden; da of 6 Baron Henley (d 1962); *b* 1915; *m* 1938, Peter Calvocoressi; 2 s; *Style* - The Hon Mrs Calvocoressi; Guise House, Aspley Guise, Bedfordshire; 33 Regency House, Osnaburgh st, NW1

CALVOCORESSI, Maj Ion Melville; MBE (1945), MC (1942); s of Matthew Calvocoressi and Agnes, da of late Judge Robert Melville, of Sussex and Salop; *b* 12 April 1919; *Educ* Eton, Magdalen Oxford; *m* 1947, Katherine, da of Capt Edward Kennedy, RN (d on active serv 1939, ggs of Hon Robert Kennedy, bro of 1 Marquess of Ailsa and 3 s of 11 Earl of Cassillis), and Rosalind, da of Sir Ludovic Grant, 11 Bt; 3 s, 1 da; *Career* memb London Stock Exchange; late Maj Scots Gds; High Sheriff Kent 1978; *Style* - Maj Ion Calvocoressi, MBE, MC; Court Lodge, Westerham, Kent

CALVOCORESSI, Peter John Ambrose; s of late Pandia John Calvocoressi; *b* Karachi, 17 Nov 1912; *Educ* Eton, Balliol Coll; *m* 1938, Hon Barbara Dorothy Eden, da of late 6 Baron Henley; 2 s; *Career* barr Inner Temple 1935, served 1939-45 War as Wing Cdr RAFVR (Air Intelligence), contested (Lib) Warwicks (Nuneaton Div) 1945, author, dir Chatto & Windus Ltd and The Hogarth Press Ltd 1954-65, reader in International Relations Sussex U 1966-71, editorial dir and ch exec Penguin Books 1972-76, memb Council of Roy Inst of Int Affairs; *Clubs* Garrick; *Style* - Peter Calvocoressi Esq; Guise House, Aspley Guise, Bletchley, Bucks

CAMARA, His Excellency Monsieur Ousmane; *Career* Senegalese Ambass to UK 1981-; *Style* - HE Monsieur Ousmane Camara; Embassy of Republic of Senegal, 11 Phillimore gdns, W8 (☎ 01 937 0925)

CAMBELL, Rear-Adm Dennis Royle Farquharson; CB (1960), DSC (1940); s of Dr Archibald Cambell; *b* 13 Nov 1907; *Educ* Westminster Sch; *m* 1933, Dorothy Elinor Downes; 2 da; *Career* joined RN, 1925; First Capt, HMS Ark Royal IV, 1955-56; Flag Officer Flying Training, 1957-60, ret; *Style* - Rear-Adm Dennis Cambell, CB, DSC; The Old School House, Colemore, Alton, Hants

CAMBRIDGE, Marchioness of; Dorothy Isabel Westenra; *née* Hastings; da of late Capt the Hon Osmond William Toone Westenra Hastings, 2 s of 13 Earl of Huntingdon; *b* 18 May 1899; *m* 1923, 2 and last Marquess of Cambridge, GCVO (d 1981), whereby she is sis-in-law of the Duchess of Beaufort; 1 da (*see Lady Mary Whitley*); *Style* - The Most Hon The Marchioness of Cambridge; The Old House, Little Abington, Cambs

CAMBRIDGE, Sydney John Guy; CMG (1979), CVO (1979); s of Jack Cambridge; *b* 5 Nov 1928; *Educ* Marlborough, King's Cambridge; *Career* joined HM Diplomatic Service, 1952; First Sec UK Mission New York, 1960; Head of Chancery Jakarta, 1964; Counsellor Rome, 1970, Nicosia, 1975; Ambassador to Kuwait, 1977-; *Style* - Sydney Cambridge Esq, CMG, CVO; c/o Foreign and Commonwealth Office, SW1

CAMDEN, 5 Marquess (UK 1812); John Charles Henry Pratt; JP, DL (Kent); also Baron Camden (GB 1765), Earl Camden and Viscount Bayham (GB 1786), and Earl of Brecknock (UK 1812); s of 4 Marquess Camden, GCVO, TD (d 1943), and Lady Joan Nevill (da of 3 Marquess of Abergavenny); *b* 12 April 1899; *Educ* Eton, Sandhurst; *m* 1, 1920 (m dis 1941), Marjorie Minna, DBE; 1 s, 1 da; m 2, 1942, Averil (d 1977), da of Col Henry Streatfeild, DSO, by whom she was ggda of 2 Earl of Lichfield (by her mother she was gda of Sir Daniel Cooper, 2 Bt); 1 s; m 3, 1978, Rosemary Cecil, da of late

Brig Gen Hanbury Pawle, CBE, TD, and former wife of (1) Gp Capt Peter Townsend, CVO, DSC, DFC, and (2) of John de Laszlo; *Heir* s, Earl of Brecknock; *Career* Maj Reserve of Officers late Scots Gds; ADC to Gen Officer Comdg London Dist, 1920-24; War Comdg 45 Battery (which he raised), 16 Light Anti-Aircraft Regt, RA and with Scots Gds, 1939-45; dir Dirracq Motor Engineering Co, Bayard Cars Ltd, RAC Buildings Co Ltd, RAC Travel Service Ltd, RAC Country Club; DL and JP Kent ; *Clubs* MCC, Roy Yacht Sqdn, Pratt's, Turf, RAC, Guards & Cavalry; *Style* - The Most Hon Marquess Camden JP DL; 42 Limerston st, SW10 (☎ 01 352 7838); Bayham Manor, Lamberhurst, Kent (☎ 500)

CAMDEN, John; s of late Joseph Camden; *b* 18 Nov 1925; *Educ* Worcester Royal G S, Birmingham U; *m* m; 1 s, 2 da; m 1972, Diane Mae Yarbrough; 2 da; *Career* md Ready Mixed Concrete Ltd, 1966-; *Style* - John Camden Esq; Westbourn, Wentworth, Surrey

CAME, William Gerald; CIE (1944); s of late John Mathew Came; *b* 8 Dec 1899; *m* 1, 1916, Ada Coombs; 1 s, 1 da; m 2, 1937, Gertrude Marie Farmer; 1 s ; *Career* civil engineer; Chief Engineer and Sec to Indian Govt, 1942-48; *Style* - William Came Esq, CIE; Somerley View, Ringwood, Hants (☎ 3733)

CAMERON, Lt-Col Angus Ewen; MC, DL (Inverness-shire 1967); s of late Capt Allan George Cameron of Lochiel; *b* 20 Jan 1914; *Educ* Eton, Cambridge U; *m* 1949, Hon Judith Evelyn Maud, da of Brig Hon George Evan Michael Baillie, MC, TD and granted rank of a baron's daughter, 1964; 1 s, 1 da; *Career* 2 Lt Scots Gds, 1936; Lt-Col, 1950, ret; *Style* - Lt-Col Angus Cameron, MC, DL; Aldourie Castle, Inverness

CAMERON, Maj Allan John; s of Col Sir Donald Cameron of Lochiel, KT, CMG, by Lady Hermione Cameron (d of 5 Duke of Montrose); *b* 25 March 1917; *Educ* Harrow, Sandhurst; *m* 1945, Mary Elizabeth Vaughan-Lee; 2 s, 2 da; *Career* Vice Lord-Lt Ross and Cromarty, Highland Region, 1977-; *Style* - Major Allan Cameron, HM Vice Lord-Lieutenant for Ross and Cromarty; Allangrange, Munlochy, Ross-shire (☎ Munlochy 249)

CAMERON, Lt-Gen Sir Alexander Maurice; KBE (1952), CB (1945), MC; s of late Maj Sir Maurice Alexander Cameron, KCMG; *b* 30 May 1898; *Educ* Wellington; *m* 1922, Loveday, nee Thomson (d 1965); *Career* Maj-Gen, 1943; SHAEF, 1944-45; Dep QMG, 1945-48; MGA, Middle East, 1948-51; GOC, E Africa, 1951-53, ret; *Style* - Lt Gen Sir Alexander Cameron, KBE, CB, MC; c/o Lloyds Bank, 6 Pall Mall, SW1

CAMERON, Lady Cecil (Nennella Therese); *née* Kerr; da of 12 Marquess of Lothian; *b* 1948; *m* 1974, Donald Angus Cameron of Lochiel, yr, s of Sir Donald Hamish Cameron of Lochiel; 1 s, 1 da; *Style* - Lady Cecil Cameron

CAMERON, Lt-Col Charles Alexander; MC (1944), TD (1947), JP (1961), DL (1956); s of late Sir Donald Walter Cameron of Lochiel, KT, CMG; *b* 29 Sept 1920; *Educ* Loretto; *m* 1953, Felicia Margaret, nee Macdonald; 1 s; 1 da; *Career* served 1939-45 Cameron Highlanders TA, Maj 1944, Lt-Col 1957, CC 1952-75 (Inverness-shire); *Style* - Lt-Col Charles Cameron, MC, TD, JP, DL; The Cottage, Ardersier, Inverness

CAMERON, Catherine Mary; da of Donald Cameron of Lochiel, yr , and Lady Cecil, nee Kerr, da of 12 Marquess of Lothian, DL (*qqv*); *b* 1975; *Career* bridesmaid to Lady Diana Spencer at her marriage to HRH The Prince of Wales 1981; *Style* - Miss Catherine Cameron

CAMERON OF LOCHIEL, YR, Donald Angus; s and h to chieftainship of Col Sir Donald Cameron of Lochiel, KT, CVO, TD; *b* 2 Aug 1946; *Educ* Harrow; *m* Lady Cecil, nee Kerr, da of 12 Marquess of Lothian, DL; 1 s, 2 da (*see* Cameron, Catherine); *Style* - Donald Cameron of Lochiel, yr; Achnacarry, Spean Bridge, Inverness-shire (☎ Gairlochy 208)

CAMERON OF LOCHIEL, Col Sir Donald Hamish; KT (1973), CVO (1970), TD (1944); 26 Chief of the Clan Cameron; s of Col Sir Donald Walter Cameron of Lochiel, KT, CMG, 25 Chief of the Clan of Cameron (d 1951) and Lady Hermione Graham (d 1978, da of 5 Duke of Montrose); *b* 12 Sept 1910; *Educ* Harrow, Balliol Oxford; *m* 1939, Margaret, da of Lt-Col Hon Nigel Gathorne-Hardy, DSO, JP (himself 4 s of 2 Earl of Cranbrook, JP, DL); 2 s, 2 da; *Heir* s Donald Angus Cameron of Lochiel, yr; *Career* chartered accountant; dir Royal Bank of Scotland, 1954- (former chm and vice-chm); dir Scottish Widows Life Assurance Soc, 1955-; chm Scotbits Securities Ltd, 1968-; Lord-Lt of County of Inverness, 1971- (formerly Vice-Lt); JP; *Clubs* Boodle's; *Style* - Col Sir Donald Cameron of Lochiel, KT, CVO, TD, HM Lord-Lieutenant for Inverness-shire; Achnacarry, Spean Bridge, Inverness-shire (☎ Gairlochy 208)

CAMERON, George Edmund; CBE (1970); s of William Cameron; *b* 1911; *Educ* Ballymena Acad; *m* 1939, Winifred Audry, nee Brown; *Career* sr ptnr Wright Fitzsimmons and Cameron (CA); chm Northern Ireland Carriers Ltd; dir Cameron Investments Ltd, Lombard & Ulster Banking Ltd, Ulster Bank Unit Trust Managers Ltd; *Style* - George Cameron Esq, CBE; Ardavon, Glen rd, Craigavad, Co Down, N Ireland

CAMERON, Hugh Forbes; MC, TD; s of late James Cameron; *b* 27 Dec 1917; *Educ* Edinburgh Acad, Sidney Sussex Cambridge, Edinburgh U; *m* 1941, Jean Robertson, nee Kydd; 1 s, 1 da; *Career* Writer to the Signet Edinburgh; former v-chm Fraser Westfield Motor Gp; dir The Edinburgh and Dundee Investment Co Ltd 1964-77; dir The Appleyard Gp of Cos Ltd 1969-80; *Style* - Hugh Cameron Esq, MC, TD; Laighfield, New Galloway, Castle Douglas, Kirkcudbrightshire (☎ New Galloway 336)

CAMERON, Sir (Eustace) John; CBE (1970); s of Eustace Noel Cameron; *b* 8 Oct 1913; *Educ* Geelong G S, Victoria, Australia, Trinity Cambridge; *m* 1934, Nancie Ailsa, nee Summers; 1 da; *Career* pastoralist, 1946-; State President, Liberal Party, 1948-52; Depy Chancellor, Tasmania U, 1964-72, Chancellor, 1973-; knighted 1977; *Style* - Sir John Cameron, CBE; Lochiel, Ross, Tasmania, Australia (☎ Ross 81523)

CAMERON, Lt-Col John; OBE (1954), TD (1945); s of John Cameron, JP; *b* 21 Jan 1911; *Educ* Oundle; *m* 1935, Jean McNaughton, nee Wallace; 2 s, 2 da; *Career* former chm Trustee Savings Bank of Kirkintilloch, 1956; DL (1957) Stirlingshire; *Style* - Lt-Col John Cameron, OBE, TD; Leddriegreen, Strathbane, Stirlingshire (☎ Blanefield 292)

CAMERON, Hon Lord - Sir John Cameron; KT (1978), DSC; s of John Cameron; *b* 8 Feb 1900; *Educ* Edinburgh Acad and U; *m* 1, 1927, Eileen Dorothea, nee Burrell (d 1943); 1 s, 2 da; m 2, 1944, Iris Shepherd; *Career* advocate, Scotland, 1924; KC 1936; appointed a Lord of Session with title Lord Cameron, 1955; former Sheriff of Inverness, Elgin and Nairn and of Inverness, Moray, Nairn and Ross and Cromarty; DL (1953) Edinburgh; knighted 1954; *Style* - The Hon Lord Cameron KT DSC DL; 28 Moray Place, Edinburgh (☎ 031 225 7585)

CAMERON, Sir James Clark; CBE (1979), TD (1947); s of Malcolm Clark Cameron; *b* 8 April 1905; *Educ* Perth Acad, St Andrews U; *m* 1933, Irene, nee Ferguson; 1 s, 2 da; *Career* chm Merton, Sutton and Wandsworth Medical Ctee, memb Standing Medical Advisory Ctee, Central Health Services Cncl and Cncl for Postgraduate Medical Education; memb Advisory Ctee on Medical Education, Cmmn of the European Communities; former chm General Medical Services Ctee and of Council British Medical Assoc; kt 1979; *Style* - Sir James Cameron, CBE, TD; 201 Croydon rd, Wallington, Surrey (☎ 01 647 6123)

CAMERON, John Taylor; QC (Scot, 1973); s of John Reid Cameron; *b* 24 April 1934; *Educ* Fettes Coll, CCC Oxford,

Edinburgh U; *m* 1964, Bridget Deirdre Sloan; *Career* advocate, 1960; lectr Edinburgh U, 1960-64; Advocate-Depute, 1977-79; Keeper of the Advocates' Law Library, 1977-; *Style* - John Taylor Esq, QC; 17 Moray pl, Edinburgh (☎ 031 225 7695)

CAMERON, (Mark) James (Walter); CBE (1979); s of William Ernest Cameron *b* 17 June 1911; *m* 1, 1938, Eleanor Mara Murray (decd); 1 da; m 2, 1944 (m dis) Elizabeth O'Conor; 2 s (1 step); m 3, 1971, Moneesha Sarkar; 1 step s, 1 step da; *Career* journalist; Journalist of the Year Granada Award, 1965; TV film producer; author; *Style* - James Cameron Esq, CBE; 3 Eton College rd, NW3 (☎ 01 586 5340)

CAMERON, Sir John Watson; *Career* kt 1981 for political service, northern area; *Style* - Sir John Cameron

CAMERON, Kenneth John; QC (1972); s of Hon Lord Cameron, DSC; *b* 11 June 1931; *Educ* Edinburgh Acad, Oxford and Edinburgh Us; *m* 1964, Jean Pamela, da of Col Granville Murray; 2 da; *Career* advocate, 1958; *Style* - Kenneth Cameron Esq, QC; 10 Bedford ter, Edinburgh 4 (☎ 031 332 6636)

CAMERON, Marshal of the Royal Air Force Sir Neil; GCB (1976, KCB 1975, CB 1971), CBE (1967), DSO (1945), DFC (1944); s of Neil Cameron; *b* 8 July 1920; *Educ* Perth Acad; *m* 1947, Patricia Louise, nee Asprey; 1 s, 1 da; *Career* joined RAF, 1939; Asst Chief Defence Staff (Policy), 1968-70; Air Marshal, 1974; Air Memb for Personnel, 1974-76; Chief of Air Staff, 1976-77; Air ADC to HM the Queen, 1976-77; Chief of the Defence Staff, 1977-79; Principal King's Coll London, 1980-; *Style* - Marshal of the Royal Air Force, Sir Neil Cameron, GCB, CBE, DSO, DFC; MOD, Whitehall, SW1

CAMERON, Waverley Blair; s of late Duncan Cameron; *b* 21 Aug 1903; *Educ* Edinburgh Acad; *m* 1941, Josephine G; 2 c; *Career* chm and md Waverley Cameron Ltd; dir Oban Times Ltd; *Style* - Waverley Cameron Esq; 4 Grosvenor st, Edinburgh 12 (☎ 337 2034)

CAMERON-HEAD OF INVERAILORT, Mrs (Lucretia Pauline Rebecca Ann); *née* Farrell; CBE *m* 1942, Francis Somerville Cameron-Head of Inverailort (decd); *Career* DL (1974), JP Inverness-shire; *Style* - Mrs Cameron-Head of Inverailort CBE JP DL; Inverailort, Lochailort, Inverness

CAMILLERI, His Honour Sir Luigi, s of notary Giuseppe Camilleri; *b* 7 Dec 1892 *Educ* Gozo Seminary, Malta U; *m* 1914, Erminia, nee Cali'; 5 s, 3 da; *Career* Malta Legislative Assembly, 1921-24; Magistrate, 1924-30; one of HM Judges in Malta, 1930-52; Chief Justice and Pres of the Court of Appeal, 1952-57; Examiner in Civil, Criminal and Roman Law Malta U 1931-70; knighted 1954; *Style* - His Honour Sir Luigi Camilleri; 27 Victoria av, Malta (☎ 513532)

CAMM, John Sutcliffe; s of Thomas Camm; *b* 18 Jan 1925; *Educ* Wycliffe Coll, Bristol U; *m* 1956, Barbara Kathleen Small; 3 s, 3 da; *Career* former schoolmaster; chm and chief exec Dickinson Robinson Group Ltd, 1978-; dir Dickinson Robinson Group of Cos; *Style* - John Camm Esq; 19 Old Aust rd, Almondsbury, Bristol (☎ Almondsbury 613207)

CAMOYS, 7 Baron (E 1264; called out of abeyance 1839); Ralph Thomas Campion George Sherman Stonor; s of 6 Baron Camoys (d 1976); although the Camoys's inherited the Barony through a Mary Biddulph who m Thomas Stonor 1732, the present Lord C is also seventeenth in descent from the union of Thomas Stonor and Jeanne, love child of John de la Pole, Duke of Suffolk, whereby he is descended from Geoffrey Chaucer, the poet; *b* 16 April 1940; *Educ* Eton, Balliol Oxford; *m* 1966, Elisabeth Mary Hyde, da of Sir William Hyde Parker, 11 Bt; 1 s, 3 da; *Heir* s, Hon (Ralph) William (Robert Thomas) Stonor; *Career* md Barclays Merchant Bank Ltd, 1978-; dir Barclays Bank International Ltd, Mercantile Credit Co Ltd; chm Robert Jackson & Co Ltd, 1968-; *Style* - The Rt Hon the Lord Camoys; Stonor Park, Henley-on-Thames, Oxon (☎ Turville Heath 644)

CAMOYS, Dowager Baroness; Mary Jeanne; da of late Capt Herbert Marmaduke Joseph Stourton, OBE (gs of 19 Baron Stourton); *m* 1938, 6 Baron Camoys (d 1976); 2 s, 3 da; *Career* Dame of Honour and Devotion, Soveriegn Order of Malta; Order of Gorkha-Dakshina-Bahu of Nepal; OStJ; *Style* - The Rt Hon the Dowager Lady Camoys; The Dower House, Stonor, Henley-on-Thames (☎ Oxon)

CAMPBELL OF ALLOWAY, Baron (Life Peer UK 1981); Alan Robertson Campbell; QC (1965); s of John Campbell; *b* 24 May 1917; *Educ* Aldenham, Trin Hall Cambridge; *m* 1957, Vivien, da of Cdr A H de Kantzow, DSO, RN; *Career* late Lt RA supp reserve, BEF France WW II; Crown Court Recorder 1976-, consultant to Legal Ctee Cncl of Europe on industrial espionage 1965-74; chm Legal Res Ctee, Soc Con Lawyers 1968-80; memb Law Advsy Cttee Br Cncl 1974-, Management Ctee Assoc for European Law 1975-; barr; *Clubs* Carlton, Pratt's, Beefsteak; *Style* - Rt Hon Lord Campbell of Alloway QC; 1 Harcourt Bldgs, Temple, EC4 (☎ 01 353 2214)

CAMPBELL OF CROY, Baron (UK Life Peer 1974); Gordon Thomas Calthrop Campbell; MC (1944 and Bar 1945), PC (1970); s of late Maj-Gen J A Campbell, DSO and Bar; *b* 8 June 1921; *Educ* Wellington; *m* 1949, Nicola Elizabeth Gina, nee Madan; 2 s, 1 da; *Career* HM Diplomatic Service, 1946-57; MP Moray and Nairn, 1959-74; Opposition Spokesman on Defence and Scottish Affairs, 1966-70; Sec of State for Scotland, 1970-74; chm Alliance Building Soc, Scottish Bd; *Style* - The Rt Hon the Lord Campbell of Croy, MC*, PC; Holme Rose, Cawdor, Nairnshire

CAMPBELL OF ESKAN, Baron (Life Peer UK 1966); Jock (John) Middleton Campbell; s of late Colin Algernon Campbell; *b* 8 Aug 1912; *Educ* Eton, Exeter Coll Oxford; *m* 1, 1938 (m dis 1948), Barbara Noel, nee Roffey; 2 s, 2 da; m 2, 1948, Phyllis Jacqueline Gilmour (Taylor), nee Boyd; *Career* former chm Booker McConnell Ltd and Statesman and Nation Publishing Co Ltd; former dir London Weekend TV Ltd; chm Commonwealth Sugar Exporters' Assoc, 1950; dir Commonwealth Dvpt Corpn, 1968-; kt 1957; *Style* - The Rt Hon Lord Campbell of Eskan,; 15 Eaton sq, SW1 (☎ 01 235 5695); Lawers, Crocker End, Nettlebed, Oxon (☎ Nettlebed 641202)

CAMPBELL, Archibald; CMG (1966); s of late Archibald Campbell; *b* 10 Dec 1914; *Educ* Berkhamsted Sch, Hertford Oxford; *m* 1939, Peggy Phyllis, nee Hussey; 2 s, 1 da; *Career* barr, 1947; joined Colonial Service, 1936; Colonial Attache Washington, 1952-56; Chief Sec Malta, 1959-62; Asst Sec Colonial Office, 1956-67; Asst Under-Sec MOD, 1970-74, ret ; *Style* - Archibald Campbell Esq, CMG; Bransbury, Long Park, Chesham Bois, Bucks (☎ Amersham 7727)

CAMPBELL, Archibald; CBE (1951); s of Archibald Campbell; *b* 1891; *m* 1916, Jane, nee Russell; *Career* in Office of Crown Agents for Overseas Govts and Administrations, 1914-59 (Asst Engineer, 1921, Dep Chief Engineer, 1935, Chief Mechanical Engineer, 1948, Consultant, Railways, 1956); *Style* - Archibald Campbell Esq CBE; Flat 17, 208 Woodcote rd, Wallington, Surrey

CAMPBELL, Hon Alastair Colin Leckie; s (by 1 m) and h of 3 Baron Colgrain; *b* 16 Sept 1951; *Educ* Eton, Trin Cambridge; *m* 1979, Annabel Rose, da of Hon Robin Hugh Warrender (s of 1 Baron Bruntisfield, MC); *Style* - The Hon Alastair Campbell

CAMPBELL, Arnold Everitt; CMG (1966); s of Fernly Campbell; *b* 13 Aug 1906; *Educ* Palmerston North Boys' H S, Victoria U Wellington; *m* 1934, Louise Annie, nee Livingstone; 1 s, 2 da; *Career* dir New Zealand Council for Educational Research, 1939-52; joined Dept of Education, 1952, dir-gen of Education, 1960-66; *Style* - Arnold Campbell Esq CMG; 13 Pitt st, Wellington, New Zealand (☎ 45-438)

CAMPBELL, Sir Alan Hugh; GCMG (1979, KCMG 1976, CMG 1964); s of late Hugh Elphinstone Campbell; *b* 1 July 1919; *Educ* Sherborne Sch, Gonville and

Caius Cambridge; *m* 1947, Margaret Jean, nee Taylor; 3 da; *Career* HM Diplomatic Service, 1946; Ambassador to Ethiopia, 1969-72; Dep Under-Sec of State Foreign Office, 1973-76; Ambassador to Italy, 1976-79, ret; Foreign Affairs Adviser Rolls Royce Ltd, 1979-; *Style* - Sir Alan Campbell, GCMG; 45 Carlisle Mansions, Carlisle place, SW1

CAMPBELL, Hon Mrs Andrew - Helen Christina; da of late Hon Douglas Halyburton Cairns (s of late 1 Earl Cairns); *b* 1909; *m* 1935, Maj the Hon Andrew Charles Campbell (s of late 4 Earl Cawdor and who d 1976); *Style* - The Hon Mrs Andrew Campbell; Baile-na-Coille, Cawdor, Nairn

CAMPBELL, Alan Johnston; CMG (1973); s of late Charles Campbell; *b* 31 July 1895; *Educ* Toowoomba G S and privately; *m* 1965, Barbara Jane, nee Dunn; *Career* owner and controller of sheep and cattle stations SW Queensland, 1920-50, ret; chm Charles Campbell & Sons Pty Ltd, 1933-1950 and Countryman Newspaper Pty Ltd, 1947-68; memb Royal Society of Queensland; former pres Australian Country Party; *Style* - Alan Campbell Esq, CMG; 24 Dusk st, Kenmore, Q 4069, Australia (☎ Brisbane 378 1477)

CAMPBELL, Hon Mrs Angus - Joan Esther Sybella; JP (Cheshire); da of late Col Hercules Arthur Pakenham, CMG; *b* 1904; *m* 1926, Hon Angus Dudley Campbell, CBE, JP, s of late 1 Baron Colgrain and who d 1967; 3 da; *Style* - The Hon Mrs Angus Campbell, JP; Doddington Cottage, Nantwich, Cheshire

CAMPBELL, Alastair Lorne; s of Brig Lorne Campbell of Airds, VC, DSO, OBE, TD; *b* 11 July 1937; *Educ* Eton, Sandhurst; *m* 1960, Mary Ann, da of Lt-Col Patrick Campbell-Preston MBE; 4 c; *Career* md Waverley Vintners Ltd, 1977-; chm Christopher & Co Ltd, 1975-; *Style* - Alastair Campbell Esq; Rosehill, Inveresk, by Musselburgh, Scotland

CAMPBELL, Agnes, Lady - Agnes Louise; da of late William Henry Gerhardi and widow of Victor Vsevolod Watson, MBE; *m* 1942, Sir Ian Campbell, 7 Bt, CB (d 1977); 1 s; *Style* - Agnes, Lady Campbell; Balcardine Castle, Ledaig, Argyllshire; White Rose, Hawkhurst, Kent

CAMPBELL, Group Capt Archibald Patrick; CBE (1944); s of late Lt-Col Duncan Frederick Campbell, DSO, MP; *b* 1903; *Educ* Trinity Coll Sch, RMC Canada; *m* 1930, Sylvie, nee Eby; 2 da; *Career* joined RCAF 1924, transfd RAF 1944, Group Capt 1946, SASO Burma 1947, Station Cdr Changi Singapore 1948-49, Acting Air Cdre 1951, Air Attaché Cairo and Addis Ababa 1951, ret 1953; *Style* - Group Capt Archibald Campbell, CBE; Perrot Farm, Graffham, Petworth, W Sussex

CAMPBELL OF ACHALADER, Brig Archibald Pennant; DSO (1945), OBE (1939); 9 Chief of Baronial House of Achalader (suc bro, 1963); s of late Brig-Gen J C L Campbell of Achalader ; *b* 26 Jan 1896; *Educ* Malvern, RMA; *m* 1, 1926, Phyllis (d 1953), da of Sir Henry Bax-Ironside, KCMG; 1 da; m 2, 1961, Elsie, nee Thompson; *Career* 2 Lt RFA, 1914; Bt Lt-Col, 1939; Brig, 1941; Col, 1943; Cdr Suez Canal, 1946-47, ret; Consular Agent Moji Japan, 1957-58; *Style* - Brig Archibald Campbell of Achalader, DSO, OBE; 6 Rockley rd, South Yarra, Victoria 3141, Australia (☎ Melbourne 248300)

CAMPBELL, Alida, Lady - Alida Virginia (Allan); da of Augustus Peeters van Nieuwenrode; *m* 1955, as his 2 wife, Maj Sir Guy Colin Campbell, 4 Bt (d 1960); *Style* - Alida, Lady Campbell; 49 Hill st, W1; Pilmour pl, St Andrews, Fife

CAMPBELL, His Honour Judge; (Keith) Bruce; QC (1964); s of Walter Henry Pearson Campbell; *b* 25 Oct 1916; *Educ* Christchurch Technical H S New Zealand, New Zealand and London Us; *m* 1939, Betty Joan, nee Muffett; 2 s, 4 da; *Career* barr, 1947; MP (C) Oldham West, 1968-70; Recorder of the Crown Court, 1972-76; a Circuit Judge, 1976-; *Style* - His Honour Judge Campbell, QC; 2 King's Bench Walk, Temple, EC4

CAMPBELL, Sir Bruce Colin Patrick; 3 Bt (UK 1913, with precedence of 1804), of Ardnamurchan, Argyllshire; s of Lt-Col

Sir John Campbell, 2 Bt, DSO (d 1943); *b* 1904; *Educ* Edinburgh Acad, Glenalmond, Pangbourne Nautical Coll; *Style* - Sir Bruce Campbell, Bt

CAMPBELL, Hon Brigid Mary; da of 3 Baron Glenavy (Patrick Campbell, the raconteur and wit, d 1980) by his 2 w, Cherry, da of Maj George Monro; *b* 8 May 1948; *Educ* Godstowe, Pipers Corner Sch Naphill, E Berks Coll of Further Educn Windsor; *Style* - The Hon Brigid Campbell

CAMPBELL, Sir Clifford Clarence; GCMG (1962), GCVO (1966); s of late James Campbell; *b* 28 June 1892; *Educ* Mico Training Coll Jamaica; *m* 1920, Alice Esthephene, CStJ, nee Jolly; 2 s, 2 da; *Career* former headmaster, MHR Jamaica 1944-45, Speaker of the House of Representatives 1950-55, Pres of the Senate 1962, Gov-Gen of Jamaica 1962-73, KStJ; *Style* - Sir Clifford Campbell, GCMG, GCVO; 8 Cherry gdns av, Kingston 8, Jamaica

CAMPBELL, Cochrane Highet; CBE (1967); s of late James Campbell; *b* 23 June 1912; *Educ* Edinburgh Acad; *m* 1946, Lesley Margaret Frances, nee Graham; 3 da; *Career* Maj 19 King George V Own Lancers (Indian Armoured Corps) Second World War; dir James Finlay & Co Ltd ; *Style* - Cochrane Campbell Esq, CBE; Hellenic House, 87 Bath st, Glasgow G2 (☎ 041 332 6972)

CAMPBELL, Hon Colin Ian Calthrop; s of Baron Campbell of Croy (Life Peer); *b* 1950; *Style* - The Hon Colin Campbell

CAMPBELL, Colin John; DL (Sutherland 1959); s of Ian M Campbell, CBE; *b* 6 March 1925; *Educ* Loretto; *m* 1947, Susan Helen Hindley; 3 s; *Career* Fleet Air Arm Pilot 1942-46, farmer; *Style* - Colin Campbell Esq, DL; Balbair, Ardgay, Ross-shire (☎ Ardgay 259)

CAMPBELL, Sir Colin Moffat; 8 Bt (NS *c* 1668), of Aberuchill, Perthshire, MC (1945); s of late Sir John Campbell, 7 Bt; *b* 4 Aug 1925; *Educ* Stowe; *m* 1952, Mary Anne Chichester, da of Brig George Bain, OBE; *Heir* James Moffat Campbell *Career* dir James Finlay & Co Ltd and associated cos 1971-, chm 1975-; *Style* - Sir Colin Campbell, Bt, MC; Kilbryde Castle, Dunblane, Perthshire (☎ Dunblane 823104)

CAMPBELL, Maj-Gen Charles Peter; CBE (1977); s of late Charles Alfred Campbell; *b* 25 Aug 1926; *Educ* Emmanuel Cambridge; *m* 1949, Lucy Kitching; 2 s; *Career* Royal Engineers 1945, Command 12 Engineer Bde 1973, RCDS 1974, Ch of Staff HQ Northern Ireland 1975-77, Engineer-in-Chief (Army) 1977-; *Style* - Maj-Gen Charles Campbell CBE; c/o Lloyds Bank Ltd, Cox's & King's Branch, 6 Pall Mall, SW1

CAMPBELL, Donald le Strange; MC (1944); s of Donald Fraser Campbell; *b* 16 June 1919; *Educ* Winchester, Clare Cambridge; *m* 1952, Hon Shona Catherine Greig, da of late 1 Baron Macpherson of Drumochter; 1 s, 2 da (1 decd); *Career* dir Project Services Overseas Ltd, Rolair Systems (UK) Ltd; memb Blacksmiths' Co, 1960; *Style* - Donald Campbell Esq, MC; Bagnor Manor, Newbury, Berks (☎ 40930)

CAMPBELL, Lady Elizabeth; da of 6 Earl Cawdor; *b* 1959; *Style* - Lady Elizabeth Campbell

CAMPBELL, Lady Emma Clare; da of 6 Earl Cawdor; *b* 1958; *Style* - Lady Emma Campbell

CAMPBELL, Hon Mrs; Hon Elisabeth Joan; *née* Adderley; da of 6 Baron Norton (d 1961); *b* 1919; *m* 1943, Professor (Alexander) Colin Patton Campbell, MB, ChB, MSc, FRCP, FRCPath; 2 s, 1 da; *Style* - The Hon Mrs Campbell; The Priory House, Ascott-under-Wychwood, Oxon

CAMPBELL, Lady Fiona; *née* Erskine; da of 13 Earl of Mar and 15 of Kellie; *b* 5 April 1956 (twin with Hon Michael Erskine); *m* 1980, Capt Andrew P W Campbell, Argyll & Sutherland Highlanders; *Style* - Lady Fiona Campbell

CAMPBELL, Hon Fiona; da (by 1 m) of 4 Baron Campbell, CBE; *b* 1932; *Style* - The Hon Fiona Campbell

CAMPBELL, Hon Frederick William; s of 6 Earl Cawdor; *b* 1965; *Style* - The Hon Frederick Campbell

CAMPBELL, George; s of late William Campbell; *b* 25 Sept 1918; *Educ* Dalry H S, Glasgow U, Strathclyde U; *m* 1950, Mary Miller Scott; 2 da; *Career* assist md The British Aluminium Co Ltd 1973-81; chm Magnesium Elektron Co Ltd, Magnesium Elektron Inc (USA); *Style* - George Campbell Esq; 86 St George's av, Northampton (☎ 0604 713864)

CAMPBELL, Hon Gavin; s of late Capt the Hon John Beresford Campbell, DSO, s of 3 Baron Stratheden and Campbell; raised to the rank of a Baron's son 1921; hp of bro, 4 Baron, CBE; *b* 28 Aug 1901; *Educ* Eton; *m* 1933, Evelyn Mary Austen, da of late Col Herbert Austen Smith, CIE; 1 s; *Career* Maj (ret) King's Roy Rifle Corps and Lt-Col 19 (Kenya) Bn King's African Rifles WW II; *Style* - The Hon Gavin Campbell; 7 Denway Grove, S Norwood, Launceston, Tas 7250, Australia

CAMPBELL, Col Sir Guy Theophilus Halswell; 5 Bt (UK 1815), OBE (1954), MC (1941); s of Maj Sir Guy Colin Campbell, 4 Bt (d 1960); *b* 18 Jan 1910; *Educ* Eton, St Andrews U; *m* 1956, Lizbeth Webb, nee Holton; 2 s; *Heir* s, Lachlan Philip Kemeys Campbell; *Career* Col late 60 Rifles, Camel Corps, Sudan Defence Force; commanded Kenya Regt, 1952-56; Head of British Mil Mission to Libya, 1956-60; *Style* - Col Sir Guy Campbell, Bt, OBE, MC

CAMPBELL, Maj-Gen Sir Hamish Manus; KBE (1963), CB (1961); s of late Arthur Campbell; *b* 6 Jan 1905; *Educ* Downside, New Coll Oxford; *m* 1929, Marcelle Amelie Alice, nee Ortlieb; 1 s; *Career* commissioned Argyll and Sutherland Highlanders 1927, transfd RAPC 1937, Maj-Gen 1959, Paymaster-in-Chief 1959-63, ret 1963, Col Cmdt RAPC 1963-70; *Style* - Maj-Gen Sir Hamish Campbell, KBE, CB; 27 Honey Park rd, Budleigh Salterton, Devon (☎ 3818)

CAMPBELL, Ian; MP (L) Dunbartonshire (West Div), 1970-; s of John Campbell; *b* 26 April 1926; *Educ* Dumbarton Acad, Royal Technical Coll; *m* 1950, Mary, nee Millar; 2 s, 3 da; *Career* electrical power engineer; Provost of Dumbarton, 1962-70; Parly Private Sec to Sec of State for Scotland, 1976-79; *Style* - Ian Campbell Esq, MP; 20 McGregor drive, Dumbarton (☎ 63612)

CAMPBELL, Col Ian Clement; OBE (1962), DFC (1944), TD (1951), DL (Renfrewshire 1970); s of S Campbell, MC; *b* 26 April 1922; *Educ* Hurst Grange and The Leys Sch; *m* 1, 1945, Nadine Lilian (decd), da of H Wesley Steel; 3 da; m 2, 1972, Kathleen Mary, nee Bagot; *Career* RAF 1940-46, TA 1947-48, dir Scotcros Ltd; *Style* - Col Ian Campbell, OBE, DFC, TD, DL; Scotcros Ltd, Fitzpatrick House, Cadogan st, Glasgow (☎ 041 248 5822); Barcapel Holm Farm, Newton Mearns, Renfrewshire (☎ 041 639 3735)

CAMPBELL, Ian George Hallyburton; TD, QC (1956); s of late Hon Kenneth Campbell; *b* 19 July 1909; *Educ* Charterhouse, Trinity Cambridge; *m* 1949, Betty Yolande, nee Maclean; 1 s, 1 da (both adopted); *Career* barr, 1932; Lord Chancellor's Legal Visitor, 1963-79 ; *Style* - Ian Campbell Esq, TD, QC; Chancery House, Hill Brow, Liss, Hants (☎ Liss 3141)

CAMPBELL, Ian Macdonald; CVO (1977); s of late John Campbell; *b* 13 July 1922; *Educ* Univ Coll London U; *m* 1946, Hilda Williams; 1 s, 3 da; *Career* joined British Rail, 1953; former chm BR Engineering; Chief Exec Railways BR Board, 1978-; Exec Memb Engineering and Research, 1977-; chm Transportation Systems and Market Research Ltd ; *Style* - Ian Campbell Esq CVO; 222 Marylebone rd, NW1

CAMPBELL, Sir Ilay Mark; 7 Bt (UK 1808), of Succoth, Dunbartonshire; s of Capt Sir George Ilay Campbell, 6 Bt (d 1967); *b* 29 May 1927; *Educ* Eton, Ch Ch Oxford; *m* 1961, Margaret Minette Rohais, nee Anderson; 2 da; *Career* Scottish Agent for Christie Manson & Woods, 1968, jt Scottish Agent, 1973-; pres Assoc for the Protection of Rural Scotland; memb Council, Exec Ctee and Public Relations Ctee Scottish Landowners Fedn;

Scottish Rep Nat Arts Collection Fund; *Style* - Sir Ilay Campbell, Bt; Lennel, Coldstream, Berwickshire (☎ Coldstream 2254); Crarae Lodge, Inveraray, Argyll (☎ Minard 274)

CAMPBELL, Air Vice-Marshal Ian Robert; CB (1976), CBE (1964), AFC (1948); s of late Maj Duncan Elidor Campbell, DSO; *b* 5 Oct 1920; *Educ* Eton, RAF Coll Cranwell; *m* 1953, Beryl Evelyn, nee Newbigging; 1 s; *Career* joined RAF, 1939; Air Attaché Bonn, 1968-70; DMSI MOD, 1970-72; Air Cdre, 1965; Air Vice-Marshal, 1970; Chief of Staff No 18 (Maritime) Gp, 1973-75; *Style* - Air Vice-Marshal Ian Campbell, CB, CBE, AFC; Poulton House, Cirencester, Glos (☎ Poulton 237)

CAMPBELL, Hon James Alexander; s of late 5 Earl Cawdor; *b* 1942; *Educ* Eton, Royal Coll of Art; *m* 1, 1964 (m dis) Brigid, da of late Capt Patrick Owen Lyons; 2 da; m 2, 1973, Ann Elizabeth, da of late Col Argyle Henry Gillmore, OBE; 2 da; *Career* ARCA; *Style* - The Hon James Campbell; Archer's Mill, Cradley, Malvern, Worcs

CAMPBELL, James Alexander Moffat Bain; s and h of Sir Colin Moffat Campbell, 8 Bt; *b* 23 Sept 1956; *Educ* Stowe; *Career* Lt Scots Gds; *Style* - James Campbell Esq

CAMPBELL, Hon John Charles Middleton; s of (by 1st m) Lord Campbell of Eskan (Life Peer); *b* 1940; *Educ* Eton; *m* 1965, Patricia Ann, nee Webster; c; *Style* - The Hon John Campbell

CAMPBELL, John Davies; CVO (1980), MBE (1957), MC (1945) and Bar; s of late William Campbell and Hon Mrs Campbell, da of 14 Baron Louth; *b* 11 Nov 1921; *Educ* Cheltenham Coll, St Andrews U; *m* 1959, Shirley Bouch; 1 s, 2 da; *Career* joined HM Diplomatic Service, 1961 (formerly with Colonial Service); Counsellor Ottawa, 1972-77; Consul-Gen Naples, 1977-; *Style* - John Campbell Esq, CVO, MBE, MC*; c/o FCO, SW1

CAMPBELL, James Grant; CMG (1970); s of John Kay Campbell; *b* 8 June 1914; *Educ* Mount Allison U, Canada; *m* 1941, Alice Dougall; 1 da; *Career* chemical engineer; overseas rep Alcan International Ltd, 1977-, also consultant (formerly v-pres); *Style* - James Campbell Esq, CMG; 45 Eaton sq, SW1

CAMPBELL, Sir John Johnston; s of late William Campbell; *b* 11 Dec 1897; *Educ* Stewart Secondary Sch; *m* 1927, Margaret Fullerton, nee Brown; 1 s, 1 da; *Career* dir Clydesdale Bank Ltd, 1958-75 (formerly gen man); Pres Inst of Bankers in Scotland, 1953-55; kt 1957 ; *Style* - Sir John Campbell; 22 Saffrons Court, Compton Place Road, Eastbourne, East Sussex (☎ Eastbourne (STD Code 0323) 29271)

CAMPBELL OF CANNA, John Lorne; s of Lt-Col Duncan Campbell of Inverneill (d 1954) by his 1 w Ethel; *b* 1 Oct 1906; *Educ* Rugby, abroad, St John's College Oxford; *m* 1935, Margaret Fay, da of Henry Shaw, of Pennsylvania; *Career* owns and farms Isle of Canna; author and editor; President Folklore Institute of Scotland 1947-51; Chairman Inverness Gaelic Society 1965; *Recreations* entomology, chamber music, sea fishing; *Clubs* Oxford Union; *Style* - John Campbell of Canna; Canna House, Isle of Canna, Inner Hebrides, Scotland

CAMPBELL, Hon Mrs; Hon Jennet Parker; da of 1 Baron Adrian, OM; *b* 16 Oct 1927; *m* 1953, Peter Campbell; 1 s (Richard John b 1956), 2 da (Sally Anne b 1958; Emma Jane b 1960); *Style* - The Hon Mrs Campbell; 16 Stonehill rd, SW 14 (☎ 01 876 7205)

CAMPBELL, Dame Kate Isabel; DBE (1971); da of Donald Campbell; *b* 1899; *Educ* Hawthorn State Sch, Methodist Ladies' Coll Melbourne, Melbourne U; *Career* specialist in children's diseases; General Practitioner and Paediatrician, 1937-76; Hon Physician Queen Victoria Hospital Children's Dept Melbourne, 1926-60; former lectr Melbourne U; *Style* - Dame Kate Campbell, DBE; 1293 Burke rd, Kew, Melbourne, Victoria 3101, Australia (☎ 80 2536)

CAMPBELL, Louis Auchinbreck; s and h of Sir Robin Auchinbreck Campbell, 15 Bt; *b* 17 Jan 1953; *Style* - Louis Campbell Esq

CAMPBELL, Lady Laura Jane; da of 6 Earl Cawdor; *b* 1966; *Style* - Lady Laura Campbell

CAMPBELL OF AIRDS, Brig Lorne Maclaine; VC (1943), DSO (1940), OBE (1968), TD (1941); s of late Col Ian Maxwell Campbell, CBE, TD; *b* 22 July 1902; *Educ* Dulwich Coll, Merton Oxford; *m* 1935, Amy Muriel Jordan (d 1950); 2 s; *Career* 8 Bn Argyll and Sutherland Highlanders, 1921-42 (later Hon Col); commanded 7 Bn and 13 Inf Bde; wineshipper; Master of Vintners Co, 1958-68; Lt City of London, 1958-68; *Style* - Brig Lorne Campbell of Airds, VC, DSO, OBE, TD; 95 Trinity rd, Edinburgh 5 (☎ 031 552 6851)

CAMPBELL, Lachlan Philip Kemeys Campbell; s and h of Sir Guy Campbell, 5 Bt, OBE, MC; *b* 9 Oct 1958; *Style* - Lachlan Campbell Esq

CAMPBELL, Sir Matthew; KBE (1963), CB (1959); s of late Matthew Campbell; *b* 23 May 1907; *Educ* Hamilton Acad, Glasgow U; *m* 1939, Isabella, nee Wilson; 2 s; *Career* entered Civil Service, 1928; Under-Sec Dept of Agriculture and Fisheries, 1953-58; Sec, 1958-68; dep chm White Fish Authority, 1968-78; *Style* - Sir Matthew Campbell, KBE, CB; 10 Craigleith view, Edinburgh (☎ 031 337 5168)

CAMPBELL, Mungo; CBE (1946); *b* 5 June 1900; *Educ* Loretto, Pembroke Cambridge; *m* 1, 1944, Esther Helen (d 1971), nee Armstrong; m 2, 1976, Betty Kirkpatrick; *Career* dir of Ship Repair Div Min of War Transport, 1942-46; former local dir Barclays Bank Ltd Newcastle; *Style* - Mungo Campbell Esq CBE; Rothley Lake House, Morpeth, Northumberland

CAMPBELL, Hon Mrs; Hon Mary; *née* Adderley; da of 6 Baron Norton (d 1961); *b* 1922; *m* 1950, Hugh Montgomery Campbell, s of the Rt Rev and Rt Hon Bishop Henry Colville Montgomery Campbell, KCVO, MC, PC, DD, formerly Lord Bishop of London; 1 s, 2 da; *Style* - The Hon Mrs Campbell; 16 Ashworth rd, W9

CAMPBELL, Michael David Colin Craven; s of late Bruce Colin Campbell; *b* 12 Dec 1942; *Educ* Radley; *m* 1967, Linda Frances, nee Brownrigg; 1 s, 2 da; *Career* md The Ellis Campbell Gp, Arundell House Securities Ltd; *Style* - Michael Campbell Esq; 21 Duchess Mews, Portland pl, W1 (☎ 01 580 3617); Shalden, Alton, Hants (☎ Herriard 307); Ely Place, Swains rd, Bembridge, IOW (☎ 4168)

CAMPBELL, Margaret, Lady (Margaret Elizabeth Patricia); *née* Campbell; *m* 1920, Sir Louis Hamilton Campbell, 14 Bt (d 1970); 1 s; *Style* - Margaret, Lady Campbell; 15 Jacksons rd, Fendalton, Christchurch, New Zealand

CAMPBELL, Hon Moyra Jean; da (by 1 m) of 4 Baron Stratheden and Campbell, CBE; *b* 1924; *Style* - The Hon Moyra Campbell

CAMPBELL OF DUNSTAFFNAGE, Michael John Alexander; 22 Hereditary Capt of Dunstaffnage (in Argyllshire), also Marnycht (roughly 'Steward', though there is some controversy about the exact meaning and the term originally had less servile connotations than now) of Duke of Argyll; suc f 1980; s of Michael Eaden Campbell of Dunstaffnage; *b* 22 Nov 1953; *Educ* Stowe; *m* 1977, Anne Ingrid, da of Charles Arthur McIntyre; *Career* yacht Capt 1973-77; dir Halway House Enterprises Ltd, chm Bencamp Ltd; *Recreations* sailing, shooting; *Style* - Michael Campbell of Dunstaffnage; Dunstaffnage House, Connel, Argyll, Scotland (☎ 0631 71 269)

CAMPBELL, Margaret Letitia; da of John Campbell; *b* 13 July 1947; *Educ* Newnham Cambridge, Manchester Business Sch; *m* 1973, John Sinclair Gillespie; *Career* v-pres Morgan Guaranty Trust Co of New York; *Style* - Miss

Margaret Campbell; 5 Red Post hill, Dulwich, SE21 (☎ 01 693 6614); Aldavhu, Garelochhead, Scotland (☎ 810221)

CAMPBELL OF AIRDS BAY, Michael McNeil; yr twin s of Rear-Adm Keith McNeil Campbell-Walter, CB (d 1976); *b* 2 March 1941; *Educ* Wellington, Sandhurst; *m* 1963, Anne Catriona, nee Tait; 1 s, 2 da; *Career* 2 Lt Scots Gds 1961, Maj 1970; recognized by Lord Lyon 1954 as representor of family of Campbells of Airds Bay and matriculated as successor to and representor to his uncle Sir Duncan Campbell of Airds Bay, 2 and last Bt (d 1954); *Style* - Michael Campbell of Airds Bay; Maison de Bas, rue d'Egypt, Trinity, Jersey, CI (☎ North 474)

CAMPBELL, Hon Mrs Margaret Taylor Young; *née* Westwood; da of 1 Baron Westwood, OBE; *b* 1913; *m* 1, 1934, William Lynn; m 2, 1945 (m dis 1974), John Campbell; 1 s, 1 da; *Style* - The Hon Mrs Margaret Campbell; 7 S Park Court, Gerrards Cross, Bucks

CAMPBELL, Sir Niall Alexander Hamilton; 8 Bt (UK 1831), of Barcaldine and Glenure, Argyllshire; 15 Chieftain, Hereditary Keeper of Barcaldine Castle; s of Sir Ian Campbell, 7 Bt, CB (d 1978); *b* 7 Jan 1925 *Educ* Cheltenham, CCC Oxford *m* 1, 1949 (m dis 1956) Patricia Turner; m 2, 1957, Norma Joyce, nee Wiggin; 2 s, 2 da; *Heir* s, Roderick Campbell; *Career* barr 1951, Hospital Administrator 1953-70, Dep Chief Clerk Inner London Magistrates' Courts 1970-76, Clerk to Justices of Barnstaple, Bideford and Great Torrington and S Molton (N Devon Divs) 1976-; *Style* - Sir Niall Campbell, Bt; The Old Mill, Milltown, Muddiford, Barnstaple, Devon (☎ Shirwell 341); The Law Courts, Civic Centre, Barnstaple, Devon (☎ Barnstaple 72511); Barcaldine Castle, Benderloch via Connel, Argyllshire

CAMPBELL, Hon Neil Donald; DSC; s of late 2 Baron Colgrain; *b* 1922; *m* 1951, Angela Louise Vereker, da of Rt Hon Sir Ronald Hibbert Cross, 1 Bt, KCMG, KCVO; 3 s, 1 da; *Career* late Lt RN; *Style* - The Hon Neil Campbell DSC; Yorks Hill Farm, Ide Hill, Sevenoaks, Kent

CAMPBELL OF STRACHUR, Niall Macarthur; 24 Chief of the Macarthur Campbells of Strachur and Representer of Baronial House of Campbell of Strachur; s of late Lt-Col Kenneth John Campbell of Strachur; *b* 23 Nov 1916; *Educ* Beaumont; *m* 1947, Diana Susan, da of Ernest Albert Sursham, JP, Lord of the Manor of Markyate, Herts; 1 s, 1 da; *Heir* s, David Campbell *Career* 2 Lt Black Watch 1939-45, Maj 1945; Hon Local Sec for Berwicks and Edinburgh City British Field Sports Soc; *Style* - Niall Campbell of Strachur; Spottiswoode, Gordon, Berwicks (☎ Westruther 210)

CAMPBELL, Hon Mrs; Hon Phyllis Audrey; *née* Thomson; da of 1 Baron Thomson of Fleet, GBE (d 1976); *b* 1917; *m* 1947, Clarence Elwood Campbell; 3 da; *Style* - The Hon Mrs Campbell; c/o Thomson Organisation Ltd, PO Box 4YG, 4 Stratford Place, W1A 4YG

CAMPBELL, Hon Peter Mark Middleton; s (by 1st marr) of Baron Campbell of Eskan (Life Peer); *b* 1946; *Educ* Eton; *m* 1972, Anne Susan, nee Cuthbert; c; *Style* - Hon Peter Campbell

CAMPBELL, Sir Ralph Abercromby; s of Maj William Orr Campbell, MC; *b* 16 March 1906; *Educ* Winchester, Univ Coll Oxford; *m* 1, 1936 (m dis 1967), Joan, nee Blake; 1 s, 1 da; m 2, 1968, Mrs Shelagh Moore; *Career* barr, 1928; Res Magistrate Kenya, 1945; Chief Justice Aden, 1952-60, Bahamas, 1960-70; kt 1961; *Style* - Sir Ralph Campbell; Lomans Hill, Hartley Wintney, Hants (☎ 3283)

CAMPBELL, Sir Robin Auchinbreck; 15 Bt (NS 1628), of Auchinbreck; s of late Sir Louis Campbell, 14 Bt; *b* 7 June 1922; *Educ* Eton; *m* 1, 1948, Rosemary (Sally), nee Dean, (d 1978); 1 s, 2 da; m 2, 1978, Mrs Elizabeth Gunston, da of Sir Arthur Colegate, MP, and formerly w of Richard Wellesley Gunston; *Heir* s, Louis Auchinbreck Campbell; *Career* late Lt (A) RNVR; *Style* - Sir Robin Campbell, Bt; Glen Dhu, Motunau, Scargill, N Canterbury, New Zealand

CAMPBELL, Hon Robert (Robin) Dudley; s of late 2 Baron Colgrain; *b* 1921; *m* 1954 (m dis 1978), Cecilia Barbara, da of late Cdr Alexander Leslie RN (ret); 2

da; *Career* late Scots Gds, md Baltic Investments (London) Ltd; *Style* - The Hon Robert Campbell; Sharp's Place, Boughbeech, Edenbridge, Kent

CAMPBELL, Roderick Duncan Hamilton ; s and h of Sir Niall Campbell, 8 Bt; *b* 24 Feb 1961; *Style* - Roderick Campbell Esq

CAMPBELL, Robin Francis; CBE (1978), DSO (1943); s of Rt Hon Sir Ronald Hugh Campbell, GCMG (d 1953); *b* 1912; *Educ* Wellington, Oxford U; *m* 1, 1936 (m dis 1945), Hon Mary Hermione, nee Ormsby-Gore, da of 4 Baron Harlech, KG, GCMG, PC; 2 s; m 2, 1946 (m dis 1959), Lady Mary Sybil, nee St Clair-Erskine, da of 5 Earl of Rosslyn; m 3, 1959, Susan, nee Benson; 2 s; *Career* Arts Council, 1960-78, dir of Art, 1969-78; *Style* - Robin Campbell Esq, CBE, DSO; 6 Noel rd, N1 (☎ 01 226 1009)

CAMPBELL, Sir Ronald Ian; GCMG (1947, KCMG 1941, CMG 1932), CB (1937), PC (1950); s of Sir Guy Campbell, 3 Bt; *b* 7 June 1890; *Educ* Eton, Magdalen Oxford; *Career* For Serv 1914-50, former Min Paris, Belgrade, Washington; Dep to For Sec on Cncl of For Mins 1945-46; Ambass Egypt 1946-50; dir Roy Bank Scotland 1950-65 *Style* - The Rt Hon Sir Ronald Campbell GCMG CB PC; 20 Sidegate,Haddington, East Lothian (☎ 062 082 3353)

CAMPBELL, Hon Rosalind Leonora Middleton; da (by 1 m) of Baron Campbell of Eskan (Life Peer); *b* 8 July 1942; *Educ* Down House Newbury; *Career* bookbinder and restorer; *Style* - The Hon Rosalind Campbell; Lawers, Crocker End, Nettlebed, Oxon (☎ Nettlebed 641 202)

CAMPBELL, Hon Mrs Ralph - Marjorie Edith; da of Horace George Devas; *m* 1914, as his 2 w, Lt-Col the Hon Ralph Alexander Campbell, CBE (s of late 3 Earl Cawdor and who d 1945); *Style* - The Hon Mrs Ralph Campbell; Manor House, Padworth, Reading, Berks

CAMPBELL, Hon Mrs (Shona Catherine Greig); *née* Macpherson; da of 1 Baron Macpherson of Drumochter (d 1965); *b* 1929; *m* 1952, Donald le Strange Campbell, MC; 1 s, 1 da; *Style* - The Hon Mrs Campbell; Bagnor Manor, Newbury, Berks

CAMPBELL, Maj-Gen Victor David Graham; CB (1956), DSO (1940), OBE (1946), JP (1962), DL (Devon 1962); s of late Gen Sir David Campbell, GCB; *b* 9 March 1905; *Educ* Rugby, Sandhurst; *m* 1947, Dulce Beatrix, wid of Lt-Col J A Goodwin; *Career* 2 Lt Cameron Highlanders, 1924; Lt-Col Cmding 1 Bn Gordon Highlanders, 1949; Brig Commdg 31 Lorried Inf Bde, 1951-52, Chief of Staff HQ Scottish Command, 1954-57; Maj-Gen 1955; ret 1957; High Sheriff, Devon, 1968; *Style* - Maj-Gen Victor Campbell, CB, DSO, OBE, JP, DL; Beggars Bush, South Brent, South Devon

CAMPBELL, Hon Mr Justice; Hon Sir Walter Benjamin; QC (1960); s of late Archie Eric Gordon Campbell; *b* 4 March 1921; *Educ* Downlands Coll, Queensland U Australia; *m* 1942, Georgina Margaret, nee Pearce; 2 s (1 decd), 1 da; *Career* barr 1948, Judge of the Supreme Court of Queensland 1967-, Chancellor Queensland U 1977-, kt 1978; *Style* - The Hon Mr Justice Campbell; 71 Enderley rd, Clayfield, Brisbane, Queensland, Australia 4011 (☎ 07 2623849)

CAMPBELL, Maj-Gen William Tait; CBE (1945, OBE 1944); s of late Robert Campbell; *b* 8 Oct 1912; *Educ* Fettes Coll, Sandhurst; *m* 1942, Rhoda Alice, da of Adm Algernon Walker-Heneage-Vivian, CB, MVO; 2 da; *Career* 2 Lt R Scots Gds, 1933; Brig 1962; DQMG MOD Army Dept, 1964-67, Maj-Gen 1964, ret 1967; Col R Scots Gds Royal Regt, 1964-74; dir The Fairbridge Soc, 1969-78; *Style* - Maj-Gen William Campbell CBE; Ashwood, Boarhills, St Andrews, Fife (☎ Boarhills 394)

CAMPBELL, Hon Alastair James Calthrop; s of Baron Campbell of Croy (Life Peer); *b* 1952; *Style* - The Hon Alastair Campbell

CAMPBELL-GROVE, Lady Moyra Kathleen; *née* Hamilton; CVO (1963); da of 4 Duke of Abercorn; *b* 22 July 1930; *m*

1966, Cdr Peter Campbell-Grove, MVO, RN, *qv*, s of Maj-Gen Sir Douglas Campbell, KBE, CB, DSO, MC; 2 s; *Career* Maid of Honour to HM at her Coronation 1953, Lady-in-Waiting (temp) to HRH Princess Alexandra of Kent 1954-64, Lady-in-Waiting 1964-66, Extra L-i-W 1966-69; *Style* - Lady Moyra Campbell-Grove, CVO; Hollybrook House, Randalstown, Co Antrim, N Ireland

CAMPBELL-GROVE, Peter Colin Drummond; MVO (1960); s of Maj-Gen Sir Douglas Campbell, KBE, CB, DSO, MC (d 1980); *b* 24 Oct 1927; *Educ* Cheltenham, RNC Dartmouth; *m* 1966, Lady Moyra Hamilton, da of 4 Duke of Abercorn (*see* Lady Moyra Campbell-Grove); 2 s; *Career* late Cdr RN, served Med & Far East; farmer; Equerry to HM 1957-60; Ireland Rep The Hon The Irish Soc 1974-; *Recreations* field sports; *Clubs* Army & Navy, Ulster (Belfast); *Style* - Cdr Peter Campbell-Grove, MVO, RN; Hollybrook Farm, Randalstown, Co Antrim, N Ireland (☎ Randalstown 72224); Castle Grove, Letterkenny, Co Donegal, Eire (☎ Ramelton 9)

CAMPBELL-JOHNSON, Alan; CIE (1947), OBE (1946); s of late Lt-Col J A Campbell-Johnson; *b* 16 July 1913; *Educ* Westminster, Ch Ch Oxford; *m* 1938, Imogen Fay, nee Dunlap; 1s (decd), 1 da; *Career* former Political Sec to Rt Hon Sir Archibald Sinclair, Leader Liberal Party 1937-39; contested (Lib) Salisbury and S Wilts, 1945 and 1950; Press Attaché to Viceroy and Gov-Gen of India, 1947-48; author; chm Campbell-Johnson Ltd (PR Consultants); *Style* - Alan Campbell-Johnson, CIE, OBE; 21 Ashley gdns, SW1 (☎ 01 834 1532)

CAMPBELL-ORDE, Eleanor, Lady; Eleanor Hyde; da of late Col Humphrey Watts, OBE, TD; *m* 1938, Maj Sir Simon Campbell-Orde, 5 Bt, TD (d 1969); 2 s, 1 da; *Style* - Eleanor, Lady Campbell-Orde; Westgate House, Dedham, Colchester, Essex

CAMPBELL-ORDE, Sir John Alexander; 6 Bt (GB 1790); s of Maj Sir Simon Arthur Campbell-Orde, 5 Bt, TD (d 1969); *b* 11 May 1943; *Educ* Gordonstoun; *m* 1973, Lacy Ralls, nee Gallant; 2 da; *Heir* bro, Peter Humphrey Campbell-Orde; *Style* - Sir John Campbell-Orde, Bt; 228 West Hillwood drive, Nashville, Tennessee, USA

CAMPBELL-ORDE, Peter Humphrey s of Sir Simon Campbell-Orde, 5 Bt, TD and hp of bro, Sir John Campbell-Orde, 6 Bt; *b* 18 June 1946; *Educ* Gordonstoun; *m* 1976, Mrs Perdita Bennett, nee Watt; *Style* - Peter Campbell-Orde Esq; 228 West Hillwood drive, Nashville, Tennessee, USA

CAMPBELL-PRESTON, Robert Modan Thorne; OBE (1955), MC (1943), JP (Argyll 1950); s of Col Robert Campbell-Preston, JP, DL; *b* 7 Jan 1909; *Educ* Eton, Ch Ch Oxford; *m* 1950, Hon Angela, nee Pearson (d 1981), da of 2 Visc Cowdray & widow of Lt-Col George Murray; 1 da; *Career* Lt-Col L Scottish Horse 1945; Hon Col Fife & Forfar Yeo/Scot Horse 1962-67; memb Roy Co of Archers (Queen's Bodyguard for Scotland), Vice Ld-Lt Argyll 1976- (DL 1951); *Style* - Col Robert Campbell-Preston OBE MC JP, HM Vice Lord-Lieut for Argyll; 31 Marlborough Hill, NW8 (☎ 01 586 2291); Ardchattan Priory, Connel, Argyll (☎ Bonawe 274)

CAMPBELL-SAVOURS, Dale Norman; MP (L) Workington Cumbria, 1979-; s of John Lawrence Campbell-Savours; *b* 23 Aug 1943; *Educ* Keswick Sch, Sorbonne; *m* 1970, Gudrun Runolfsdottir; 2 s; *Career* former co dir; contested Darwen Lancs, 1974, Workington, 1976; *Style* - Dale Campbell-Savours Esq, MP; House of Commons, SW1

CAMPDEN, Viscount (Anthony Baptist Noel); s and h of 5 Earl of Gainsborough; *b* 16 Jan 1950; *Educ* Ampleforth, RAC Cirencester; *m* 1972, Sarah Rose, nee Winnington; 1 s; *Heir* s, Hon Henry Noel; *Style* - Viscount Campden; 105 Earls Court rd, W8 (☎ 01 370 5650); Top House, Exton, Rutland, Leics (☎ Oakha 812587)

CAMPION, David Bardsley; s of Norman Campion; *b* 20 March 1938; *Educ*

Shrewsbury; *m* 1, 1962; 1 s, 1 da; m 2, 1979, Sally Manning, nee Arkle; *Career* dir Linfood Hldgs, BAF Securities Ltd, Wheatsheaf Distribution & Trading Ltd; *Style* - David Campion Esq; Frogs Hole, Rogate, Petersfield, Hants

CAMPION, Sir Harry; CB (1949), CBE (1945); s of John Henry Campion; *b* 20 May 1905; *Educ* Farnworth G S, Manchester; *Career* former dir Central Statistical Office, Cabinet Office; Pres International Statistical Inst, 1963-67; kt 1957; *Style* - Sir Harry Campion, CB, CBE; Rima, Priory close, Stanmore, Middx (☎ 01 954 3267)

CAMPION, Baroness; Hilda Mary; *née* Spafford; *m* 1920, 1 Baron Campion (d 1958, when title became extinct); *Style* - The Rt Hon the Lady Campion; Little Bowes, Abinger Hammer, Surrey

CAMPLING, Stanley John; CBE (1952); s of George Parry; *b* 1894; *Educ* London U; *m* 1921, May Gwendoline, nee Holloway (d 1975); 1 s, 1 da; *Career* former Under-Sec and Princ Finance Offr Board of Trade; former chm British Film Fund Agency and Pay Television Levy Ltd; *Style* - Stanley Campling Esq, CBE; 31 Malpas drive, Pinner, Middx

CAMPOS, Roberto de Oliveira; Hon GCVO; *b* 17 April 1917; *Educ* Brazil, George Washington U; *Career* Brazilian Ambassador to the Court of St James's, 1975-; *Style* - HE Mr Roberto de Oliveira Campos, GCVO; Brazilian Embassy, 32 Green Street, Mayfair, W1 (☎ 01 629 0155)

CAMPS, William Anthony; s of P W L Camps; *b* 28 Dec 1910; *Educ* Marlborough, Pembroke Cambridge; *m* 1953, Miriam, da of Prof Burton H Camp; *Career* lectr in Classics Cambridge 1939-, Fell Pembroke Coll 1933-, Sr Tutor 1947-62, Master 1970-; *Style* - William Camps Esq; Pembroke College, Cambridge (☎ 52241)

CAMROSE, 2 Viscount (UK 1941); Sir (John) Seymour Berry; 2 Bt (UK 1921), TD; also Baron Camrose (UK 1929); s of late 1 Viscount Camrose (d 1954); *b* 12 July 1909; *Educ* Eton, Ch Ch Oxford; *Heir* bro, Baron Hartwell; *Career* served WW II Maj City London Yeo; MP (C) Hitchin, 1941-45; dep chm Daily Telegraph; a Younger Brother of Trinity House; *Clubs* White's, Buck's, Beefsteak, MCC, Roy Yacht Sqdn; *Style* - The Rt Hon the Viscount Camrose, TD; Hackwood Park, Basingstoke, Hants (☎ 64630)

CANAVAN, Dennis Andrew; MP (L) W Stirlingshire, 1974-; s of Thomas Canavan; *b* 8 Aug 1942; *Educ* St Columba's H S Cowdenbeath, Edinburgh U; *m* 1964, Elnor Stewart; 3 s, 1 da; *Career* former Maths teacher; Treasurer Scottish Parly Labour Gp, 1976-; *Style* - Dennis Canavan Esq, MP; House of Commons, SW1

CANDLISH, Thomas Tait; s of late John Candlish; *b* 26 Nov 1926; *Educ* Perth Acad, Glasgow U; *m* 1964, Mary, nee Trinkwon; 2 s; *Career* md Geo Wimpey Ltd; chm Wimpey International Ltd, Wimpey M E & C Ltd, Wimpey Marine Ltd; dir Brown and Root-Wimpey Gp of Cos; *Style* - Thomas Candlish Esq; 10 Cheveley gdns, Burnham, Bucks (☎ 61893)

CANDY, Air Vice-Marshal Charles Douglas; CB (1963), CBE (1957); s of late Charles Henry Candy; *b* 17 Sept 1912; *Educ* Caulfield G S Melbourne, RMC Duntroon; *m* 1938, Eileen Cathryn Mary, nee Poole-Ricketts; 1 da; *Career* joined RAF 1929; Air Vice-Marshal 1957; AOC Support Command RAAF 1962; Air Memb for Personnel Dept of Air 1966-69, ret; *Style* - Air Vice-Marshal Charles Candy, CB, CBE; Unit 43, Giles st, Kingston, ACT 2604, Australia; PO Box 128, Kingston, ACT

CANET, Maj-Gen Lawrence George; CB (1964), CBE (1956); s of late Albert Canet; *b* 1 Dec 1910; *Educ* RMC Duntroon, Sydney U; *m* 1940, Mary Elizabeth Clift, nee Jones; 1 s; *Career* 7 Australian Div Brig 1953, Maj-Gen 1957; GOC Southern Command 1960-64; Master-Gen of the Ordnance 1964-66; *Style* - Major-General Lawrence Canet, CB, CBE; 37 The Corso, Isle of Capri, Surfers Paradise, Qld 4217, Australia

CANNING, Hon Spencer George Stratford de Redcliffe; s and h of 5 Baron Garvagh; *b* 12 Feb 1953; *m* 1979, Julia, da of Col F Bye, of Twickenham; *Style* - The Hon Spencer Canning; 24 Cobbold rd, W12 (☎ 01 749 4360)

CANNING, Victor; *b* 16 June 1911; *m* 1976, Mrs Adria Irving Bell; *Career* author; *Style* - Victor Canning Esq; The Bridge House, Pembridge, Herefordshire (☎ Pembridge 355)

CANNON, Air Vice-Marshal Leslie William; CB (1952), CBE (1945); s of late Capt W E Cannon; *b* 9 April 1904; *Educ* Hertford G S, Cranwell; *m* 1930, Beryl, nee Heyworth; *Career* joined RAF 1920, Air V-Marshal 1953, Dir-Gen of Organization Air Min 1955-58, ret; C'wlth Relations Office 1959, rep Rolls Royce Ltd India 1959-65; *Style* - Air Vice-Marshal Leslie Cannon, CB, CBE; 6 Stockwells, Berry hill, Taplow, Maidenhead, Berks (☎ Maidenhead 30684)

CANNON, Richard Walter; s of Richard Cannon; *b* 7 Dec 1923; *m* 1949, Dorothy; 2 da; *Career* md (Telecommunications) Cable and Wireless Ltd 1977-; dir Cable & Wireless Gp of Cos; dir Eastern Telegraph Co Ltd, Mercury House Ltd; *Style* - Richard Cannon Esq; Elm Cottage, Birch Grove, Horsted Keynes, W Sussex (☎ Chelwood Gate 235)

CANT, Robert Bowen; MP (L) Stoke on Trent (Central) 1966-; s of Robert Cant; *b* 24 July 1915; *Educ* Middlesbrough H S, LSE; *m* 1940, Rebecca, nee Watt; 1 s, 2 da; *Career* memb Stoke-on-Trent City Council 1953-76; CC Staffs 1974; *Style* - Robert Cant Esq, MP; 119 Chell Green av, Tunstall, Stoke-on-Trent, Staffs (☎ 88272)

CANTERBURY, 102 Archbishop of; Most Rev and Rt Hon Robert Alexander Kennedy Runcie; MC (1945), PC (1980); Primate of all England and Metropolitan; s of Robert Dalziel Runcie; *b* 2 Oct 1921; *Educ* Merchant Taylors' Crosby, Brasenose Oxford, Westcott House Cambridge; *m* 1957, Angela Rosalind, nee Turner; 1 s, 1 da; *Career* Freedom of City of London 1981; ordained 1950; Fell and Dean of Trinity Hall Cambridge 1956-60; Vicar of Cuddesdon and Principal of Cuddesdon Theol Coll 1960-69; Bishop of St Albans 1970-80; Archbishop of Canterbury 1980-; Anglican Chm Anglican-Orthodox Joint Doctrinal Cmmn 1973-; Hon DD Oxford patron 179 livings, Archdeaconries of Canterbury and Maidstone (each of which is endowed with a canonry), the Archdeaconry of Croydon, and 6 Cathedral Preacherships; province (contains 29 sees) founded by St Augustine (under Ethelbert King of Kent) 597; *Style* - The Most Rev and Rt Hon Lord Archbishop of Canterbury MC PC; Lambeth Palace, SE1 (☎ 01 928 8282); Old Palace, Canterbury

CANTLAY, George Thomson; CBE (1973); s of G Cantlay; *b* 2 Aug 1907; *Educ* H S Glasgow; *m* 1934, Sibyl Gwendoline Alsop, nee Stoker; 1 s, 1 da; *Career* chm London & Cardiff Hotels Ltd, United Capitals Investment Trust Ltd, Athenaeum Investments Ltd; dir Newport Precision Engineering Co Ltd, Welsh National Opera Co; ptnr Murray & Co; *Style* - George Cantlay Esq, CBE; 9 Park rd, Penarth

CANTLEY, Hon Mr Justice; Hon Sir Joseph Donaldson; OBE (1945); s of late Joseph Cantley; *b* 8 Aug 1910; *Educ* Manchester G S, Manchester U; *m* 1966, Hilda Goodwin, nee Jones, former w of Sir Denis Gerrard; *Career* barr 1933, Recorder of Oldham 1959-60, a Judge of the High Court of Justice (Queen's Bench Div) 1965-, Judge of Appeal IOM 1962-65, Presiding Judge of the Northern Circuit 1970-74; kt 1965; *Style* - The Hon Mr Justice Cantley, OBE; Royal Courts of Justice, Strand, WC2

CAPE, Donald Paul Montagu Stewart; CMG (1977); s of late John Scarvell Cape; *b* 6 Jan 1923; *Educ* Ampleforth, Brasenose Oxford; *m* 1948, Cathune Agnes, nee Johnston; 4 s, 1 da; *Career* entered Foreign Office 1945; Counsellor Washington 1970-73, Brasilia 1973-75, Ambass to Laos 1976-78; Ambass and UK Permanent Rep Cncl of Europe 1978-; *Style* - Donald Cape Esq, CMG; c/o FCO, SW1

CAPE, Maj-Gen Timothy Frederick; CB (1972), CBE (1966), DSO; s of C S Cape, DSO; *b* 5 Aug 1915; *Educ* Cranbrook Sch Sydney, RMC Duntroon; *m* 1961, Elizabeth, da of Brig R L R Rabett, CMG; 1 da; *Career* 1st Heavy Brigade RAA Sydney 1938, Dir of Staff Duties Army HQ Canberra 1962-63, Cdr C Command Adelaide 1964, GOC Northern Command Brisbane 1965-68, Master-Gen of the Ordnance 1968-72, ret; md Lawarra Liaison Pty Ltd Canberra; *Style* - Maj-Gen Timothy Cape CB CBE DSO; 10 Scarborough st, Red Hill, ACT 2603,Australia

CAPEL CURE, George Nigel; TD, JP (1947), DL; s of late Maj George Capel Cure, JP; *b* 28 Sept 1908; *Educ* Eton, Trinity Cambridge; *m* 1935, Nancy Elizabeth, nee Barry; 2 s, 1 da; *Career* insurance broker (ret), landowner and farmer, High Sheriff of Essex; V Ld-Lt Essex 1958-78; *Style* - George Capel Cure Esq, TD, JP, DL; Blake Hall, Ongar, Essex (☎ 362652)

CAPEL CURE, George Ronald; s of George Nigel Capel Cure; *b* 21 Oct 1936; *Educ* Eton; *m* 1968, Caroline Ann, nee Mills; 3 s; *Career* dir Hogg Robinson Gp 1981-, dep chm Hogg Robinson Overseas Ltd 1980-; *Style* - George Capel Cure Esq; Blake Hall, Ongar, Essex

CAPLAN, Leonard; QC (1954); s of late Henry Caplan; *b* 28 June 1909; *m* 1, 1942, Tania (d 1974); 2 da; m 2, 1977, Korda; *Career* barr 1935, contested (C) Kensington N 1950 and 1951; Master of the Bench Gray's Inn 1964, Treasurer 1979, Memb of Senate of Inns of Court 1975-; *Style* - Leonard Caplan Esq, QC; 1 Pump ct, Temple, EC4 (☎ 01 353 9332); 40 East 66th st, New York, USA

CAPLAN, Philip Isaac; QC (1970, Scot); s of late Hyman Caplan; *b* 24 Feb 1929; *Educ* Eastwood Secondary, Glasgow U; *m* 1, 1953; 2 s, 1 da; m 2, 1974, Joyce, nee Stone; 1 da; *Career* admitted Faculty of Advocates 1957-, former Standing Jr Counsel to the Accountant of Ct; Sheriff of Lothian and Borders at Edinburgh 1978-; *Style* - Philip Caplan Esq, QC; The Green, Duddingston Village, Edinburgh 15 (☎ 031 661 4254)

CAPLAT, Moran Victor Hingston; CBE (1968); s of Roger Caplat; *b* 1 Oct 1916; *m* 1943, Diana Murray Downton; 1 s, 2 da; *Career* former actor; General Administrator Glyndebourne Festival Opera 1949-; *Style* - Moran Caplat Esq CBE; The Yew Tree House; Barcombe, nr Lewes, E Sussex (☎ Barcombe 400202)

CAPRON, Hon Mrs (Edith Christian); *née* Hepburne-Scott; da of 9 Lord Polwarth (d 1944); *b* 1901; *m* 1926, Lt-Col George Theodore Herbert Capron, RE (d 1970); 1 s, 3 da; *Style* - The Hon Mrs Capron; Southwick Hall, Oundle, Peterborough

CAPSTICK, Brian Eric; QC (1973); s of Norman Eric Capstick; *b* 12 Feb 1927; *Educ* Sedbergh, Queen's Oxford; *m* 1960, Margaret Elizabeth, nee Harrison; 1 s, 1 da; *Career* barr 1952, Recorder of the Crown Court 1980-; dir Hartley Main Farms Ltd 1950-; *Style* - Brian Capstick Esq, QC; 2 Crown Office Row, Temple, EC4 (☎ 01 583 2681); 71 South End rd, NW3 (☎ 01 435 3540)

CAPSTICK, Charles William; CMG (1972); s of William Capstick; *b* 18 Dec 1934; *Educ* King's Coll Durham U, Kentucky U; *m* 1962, Joyce Alma Dodsworth; 2 s; *Career* former und-sec Milk and Milk Products Miny of Ag Fish and Food; Dir Economics and Statistics 1977-; *Style* - Charles Capstick Esq, CMG; 7 Dellfield clo, Radlett, Herts (☎ Radlett 7640)

CARADON, Baron (Life Peer UK 1964); Hugh Mackintosh Foot; GCMG (1957, KCMG 1951, CMG 1946), KCVO (1953), OBE (1939), PC (1968); s of late Rt Hon Isaac Foot, PC; bro of Lord Foot and Michael Foot, Ldr of Oppn; *b* 8 Oct 1907; *Educ* Leighton Park Sch, St John's Cambridge; *m* 1936, Florence Sylvia, nee Tod; 3 s, 1 da; *Career* Colonial Service Palestine Cyprus and Jamaica; Ambassador to United Nations 1962, Min of State for Foreign and Commonwealth Affairs and Perm UK Representative to UN 1964-70; *Style* - The Rt Hon the Lord Caradon, GCMG, KCVO, OBE, PC;

Trematon Castle, Saltash, Cornwall (☎ 3778)

CARBERRY, Sir John Edward Dobson; s of D A Carberry; *b* 20 Aug 1893; *Educ* Wesley Hall Grenada, McGill U; *m* 1920, Georgina Emily Isabella, nee Jackson; 1 s, 1 da; *Career* barr 1925; Puisne Judge Jamaica 1946, Chief Justice 1954-58; kt 1956 *Style* - Sir John Carberry; 8 East King's House rd, Kingston 6, Jamaica

CARBERRY, (Hon) Juanita Virginia Sistare; *née* (Evans-Freke); da of late 10 Baron Carbery; *b* 7 May 1925; *Educ* Rhodean Johannesburg, Wickham Piettermaritzburg, Switzerland; *Career* late Corpl WTS (FANY) 1942-46; served as seaman in Br & Norwegian Merchant Navy; *Recreations* many & varied, travel; *Style* - Ms Juanita Carberry; Anchorage, PO Box 96094, Likoni, via Mombasa, Kenya (☎T Mombasa 451238)

CARBERY, 11 Baron (I 1715); Sir Peter Ralfe Harrington Evans-Freke; 7 Bt (I 1768); s of Maj the Hon Ralfe Evans-Freke, MBE, 2 s of 9 Baron (d 1969); suc unc, 10 Baron, 1970; *b* 20 March 1920; *Educ* Downside; *m* 1941, Joyzelle Mary, nee Binnie; 3 s, 2 da *Heir* s, Hon Michael Evans-Freke; *Career* MICE; former memb London Stock Exchange; *Style* - The Rt Hon the Lord Carbery; Baskings House, Selsfield, East Grinstead, W Sussex (☎ 810761)

CARBERY, June, Baroness; June Weir Mosley; *m* 1930, as his 3 w, 10 Baron Carbery (d 1970); *Style* - The Rt Hon June, Lady Carbery; Saxondale, Johannesburg, S Africa

CARBONELL, William Leycester Rouse; CMG (1956); s of John Carbonell; *b* 14 Aug 1912; *Educ* Shrewsbury, St Catharine's Cambridge; *m* 1937, Elsa Agnes, nee Curdie; 2 s; *Career* entd Colonial Police Service 1935; Asst Cmmr 1952, Cmmr of Police Fedn of Malaya 1953-58; OStJ; *Style* - William Carbonell Esq, CMG; Amery End, Tanhouse lane, Alton, Hants

CARD, Gp Capt Leslie Thomas; CBE (1957); s of Herbert Henry Card; *b* 1905; *Educ* Reigate G S; *m* 1946, Evelyn Maud; 1 da; *Career* Gp Capt RAF 1939-45, ret; *Style* - Gp Capt Leslie Card, CBE; 88 Riverview rd, Ewell, Surrey

CARDEN, Christopher Robert; s (by 1 m) and h of Sir Henry Carden, 4 Bt, OBE; *b* 24 Nov 1946; *Educ* Eton; *m* 1972 (m dis 1979), Sainimere Rokotuibau, of Fiji; *Style* - Christopher Carden Esq; Creg Ny Baa, Little Glebe Farm, Little Rissington, Cheltenham, Glos

CARDEN, Derrick Charles; CMG (1974); s of late Rev Canon Henry Craven Carden, gs of Sir John Craven Carden, 4 Bt; hp of kinsman, Sir John Carden, 7 Bt; *b* 30 Oct 1921; *Educ* Marlborough, Ch Ch Oxford; *m* 1952, Elizabeth Anne, da of Capt Alfred Spalding Russell, DSO, RN; 2 s, 2 da; *Career* entd HM Diplomatic Service 1954; Consul-Gen Muscat 1965-69, Ambass to Yemen Arab Repub 1973-76 and to Sudan 1977-; *Style* - Derrick Carden Esq, CMG; Wistaria Cottage, Castle st, Portchester, Hants (☎ Cosham 375458)

CARDEN, Dowager Lady (Dorothy Mary); da of Charles Luckraft McKinnon; *m* 1925, as his 2 wife, Sir John Valentine Carden, 6 Bt, MBE (d 1935); 1 s; *Style* - Dowager Lady Carden

CARDEN, Lt-Col Donald Stapleton; CBE (1969); s of Reginald W Carden (d 1948); *b* 1914; *Educ* Sherborne, Clare Cambridge; *m* 1947, Heather, da of late Lt-Col Harold Morgan Chandler, RE; 1 s, 3 da; *Career* Mil Attaché Baghdad 1963-66; cmmd Advanced Base Belgium 1966-69; Col late R Leics Regt; *Style* - Lt-Col Donald Carden, CBE; c/o National Westminster Bank Ltd, Lower Sloane st, SW1

CARDEN, Sir Henry Christopher; 4 Bt (UK 1887), of Wimpole St, Middlesex, and of Mole Lodge, Surrey, OBE (1945); s of Sir Frederick H W Carden, 3 Bt (d 1966); *b* 16 Oct 1908; *Educ* Eton, Sandhurst; *m* 1, 1943 (m dis 1960), Jane St Clare, da of late Thomas Edward St Clare Daniell, OBE, MC; 1 s, 1 da; m 2, 1962, Gwyneth Emerson, nee Acland, wid of Flight-Lt Roderick Stanley Emerson (ka

1944); *Heir* s, Christopher Robert Carden; *Career* Capt 17/21 Lancers 1934, Lt-Col 1943; Mil Attaché Stockholm 1951-55, ret 1956; *Style* - Sir Henry Carden, Bt, OBE; Moongrove, East Woodhay, nr Newbury, Berks (☎ Highclere 253661)

CARDEN, Sir John Craven; 7 Bt (I 1787), of Templemore, Tipperary; s of Capt Sir John V Carden, 6 Bt (d 1935) ; *b* 11 March 1926; *Educ* Eton; *m* 1947, Isabel Georgette, da of Robert de Hart; 1 da; *Heir* kinsman, Derrick Charles Carden; *Style* - Sir John Carden, Bt; PO Box N7776, Lyford Cay, Nassau, Bahamas

CARDIFF, Archbishop of (RC); John Aloysius Murphy; s of John Murphy; *b* 21 Dec 1905; *Educ* St Francis Xavier Coll, English Coll Lisbon; *Career* ordained 1931; Coadjutor Bishop of Shrewsbury 1948, Bishop of Shrewsbury 1949-61, Archbishop of Cardiff 1961-; ChStJ 1974; *Style* - His Grace the Archbishop of Cardiff; The Archbishop's House, Westbourne cres, Whitchurch, Cardiff (☎ Cardiff 66063)

CARDIFF, Brig Ereld Botelier Wingfield; CB (1963), CBE (1958, OBE 1943); s of late Col R H W Cardiff; *b* 5 March 1909; *Educ* Eton; *m* 1932, Margaret Evelyn, nee Pope; 2 da; *Career* 2 Lt Scots Gds 1930, Brig 1956, DQMG FARELF 1955-58, SHAPE 1958, ret 1963; *Style* - Brig Ereld Cardiff, CB, CBE; Easton Court, Little Hereford, Ludlow, Salop (☎ 0584 810475)

CARDIFF, Maurice Henry; CBE (1973); s of Lt-Col Richard Henry Wingfield Cardiff; *b* 1915; *Educ* Eton, Worcester Coll Oxford; *m* 1939, Leonora Rachel, nee Freidman; 3 s; *Career* British Cncl Rep 1952-, Belgium 1963-67, Thailand 1968-71, France 1971-73; author under pseudonym John Lincoln; *Style* - Maurice Cardiff Esq, CBE; Stone House, Little Haseley, Oxford

CARDIGAN, Earl of; David Michael James Brudenell-Bruce; s and h of 8 Marq of Ailesbury; *b* 12 Nov 1952; *Educ* Eton, RAC Cirencester; *m* 1980, Rosamond Jane, nee Winkley; *Heir* half-unc, Lord Charles Brudenell-Bruce; *Career* estate manager, Savernake Forest; *Style* - Earl of Cardigan; Leigh Hill Cottage, Savernake Forest, Marlborough, Wilts

CARDROSS, Lord; Malcolm Harry Erskine; s and h of 16 Earl of Buchan; *b* 4 July 1930; *Educ* Eton; *m* 1957, Hilary Diana Cecil, da of late Sir Ivan McLannahan Power, 2 Bt; 2 s, 2 da; *Heir* s, Hon Henry Thomas Alexander Erskine; *Career* JP Westminster; *Style* - Lord Cardross, JP; Newnham House, Newnham, Basingstoke, Hants

CARDWELL, Sir David; KCB (1981, CB 1974); s of late George Cardwell; *b* 27 Nov 1920; *Educ* Dulwich Coll, City and Guilds Coll London; *m* 1948, Eileen Tonkin Kitt; 1 s, 1 da; *Career* dep controller R & D Establishment and Res B, and Ch Scientist (Army) 1976-78; dir Atomic Weapons Res Establishment MOD 1978-; ch of defence procurement Miny of Defence; *Style* - Sir David Cardwell, KCB; Carn Lea, 5 Grove rd, Camberley, Surrey (☎ 22636)

CARE, Henry Clifford; CB (1948); s of late William John Care; *b* 1892; *Educ* Univ Coll School Hampstead, St John's Cambridge; *m* 1923, Helen Ivy May, nee Cameron; *Career* entd Civil Service 1915; dir finance War Office 1945-54, ret; *Style* - Henry Care Esq, CB; Old Orchard, Little Bedwyn, Marlborough, Wilts (☎ Great Bedwyn 288)

CARELESS, Col William Paget; DSO, JP (1963), DL (Salop 1962); *b* 1907; *m* 1937, Beatrice Delitia; 1 da; *Career* former Cmmr St John's Ambulance, CStJ; High Sheriff Radnorshire 1964; *Style* - Col William Careless, DSO, JP, DL; 3 Russell Ridge, Shrewsbury, Salop

CAREW, 6 Baron (I 1834 & UK 1838); William Francis Conolly-Carew; CBE (1966); s of 5 Baron Carew (d 1927); *b* 23 April 1905; *Educ* Wellington, Sandhurst; *m* 1937, Lady Sylvia Gwendoline Eva Maitland, da of 15 Earl of Lauderdale; 2 s, 2 da; *Heir* Hon Patrick Thomas Conolly-Carew; *Career* assumed by Deed Poll 1938 additional surname of Conolly; Maj Duke of Cornwall's LI (ret); former ADC to

Govr and CIC of Bermuda; former National Chm British Legion; CStJ; *Style* - The Rt Hon the Lord Carew, CBE; Mount Armstrong, Donadea, Co Kildare, Kildare (☎ Naas 68196)

CAREW, Hon Gavin George; MBE (1945), TD; s of late 5 Baron Carew; *b* 1906; *Educ* Clifton; *m* 1932, Aileen Hilda Frances (d 1974), da of late Ean Francis Cecil; 1 da; *Career* late Maj Co London Yeo; *Style* - The Hon Gavin Carew, MBE, TD; Gellillyndu, Llanio, Tregaron, Dyfed

CAREW, Gerald de Redvers; s and h of Sir Rivers Carew, 11 Bt; *b* 24 May 1975

CAREW, Sir Rivers Verain; 11 Bt (E 1661), of Haccombe, Devonshire; s of Sir Thomas Palk Carew, 10 Bt (d 1976); *b* 17 Oct 1935; *Educ* St Columba's Coll, Dublin U; *m* 1968, Susan Babington, nee Hill; 1 s, 2 da; *Heir* s, Gerald de Redvers Carew; *Career* stud farmer; editor, journalist, author; journalist Irish Television 1967-; *Style* - Sir Rivers Carew, Bt; Killyon Manor, Hill of Down, Co Meath (☎ Castlerickard 115)

CAREW, William James; CBE (1937); s of late James Carew; *b* 28 Dec 1890; *m* 1920, Mary Channing (decd); 1 s, 3 da; *Career* former Sec Prime Minister's Office, Dep Min for External Affairs 1932, Clerk of Exec Cncl and Dep Min of Provincial Affairs Newfoundland, ret; *Style* - William Carew Esq, CBE; 74 Cochrane st, St John's, Newfoundland

CAREW POLE, Col Sir John Gawen; 12 Bt (E 1628), DSO (1944), TD, JP (Cornwall 1939), DL (1947); s of late Lt-Gen Sir Reginald Pole-Carew KCB CVO & Lady Beatrice Pole-Carew, nee Butler, da of 3 Marquess of Ormonde; suc kinsman Sir Frederick Arundell de la Pole, 11 Bt, 1926; assumed by deed poll 1926 the name of John Gawen Carew Pole in lieu of John Gawen Pole-Carew; *b* 4 March 1902; *Educ* RMC Sandhurst; *m* 1, 1928, Cynthia Mary, OBE (d 1977), da of Walter Burns; 1 s, 2 da; M 2, 1979, Joan, wid of Lt-Col Anthony Fulford; *Heir* s (John) Richard (Walter Reginald) Carew Pole; *Career* Coldstream Gds 1923-39, Col Second Army 1944-45, raised and commanded post-war TA Bn 4/5 Bn DCLI 1946-47, Hon Col 4/5 Bn DCLI (TA) 1958-60, Hon Col DCLI (TA) 1960-67, CA 1954-66 Cornwall, High Sheriff 1947-48, Vice-Lt 1950-62, Ld-Lt 1962-77, a Gentleman of HM Bodyguard of the Hon Corps of Gentlemen-at-Arms 1950-72, Standard Bearer 1968-72, Memb of the Prince of Wales's Council 1952-68, Steward Nat Hunt Ctee 1953-56, memb Jockey Club 1969-; KStJ 1972, Hon LLD Exeter 1979; *Clubs* Army and Navy, Pratt's, MCC; *Style* - Col Sir John Carew Pole Bt DSO TD JP DL; Antony House, Torpoint, Cornwall PL11 2QA (☎ Plymouth 812406)

CAREW POLE, (John) Richard Walter Reginald; s and h of Sir John Gawen Carew Pole, DSO, TD, 12 Bt; *b* 2 Dec 1938; *Educ* Eton and RAC Cirencester; *m* 1, 1966 (m dis 1973), the Hon Victoria Marion Ann Lever, da of 3 Visc Leverhulme; m 2, 1974, Mary, da of Lt-Col Ronald Dawnay; 2 s; *Career* late Coldstream Gds, a Liveryman of Fishmongers' Co; CC for Cornwall, Devon and Cornwall Ctee, Nat Trust 1978-; *Style* - Richard Carew Pole Esq; Erth Barton, Saltash, Cornwall

CAREY, Gp Capt Alban Majendie; CBE (1943); s of Henry N Carey; *b* 18 April 1906; *Educ* Bloxham; *m* 1934, Enid Morton, nee Bond; 1 s; *Career* Gp Capt RAF 1942; chm Maden Park Property Investment Co Ltd and Chirit Investment Co Ltd; *Style* - Gp Capt Alban Carey, CBE; Shaway House, Lower Sydenham, SE26; Town Green Farm, Englefield Green, Surrey (☎ Egham 213)

CAREY, Hon Mrs (Ivy Felicia); *née* Somerset; da of 3 Baron Raglan, GBE, CB, and Lady Ethel Ponsonby, da of 7 Earl of Bessborough; *b* 30 March 1897; *m* 1947, as his 2 w, Raymond Marwood-Elton Carey, FRIBA (d 1976); *Style* - The Hon Mrs Carey; 43 Cadogan Place, SW1 (☎ 01 235 4259)

CAREY, Sir Peter Willoughby; KCB (1976, CB 1972); s of Jack Delves Carey; *b* 26 July 1923; *Educ* Portsmouth G S, Oriel Oxford; *m* 1946, Thelma, nee Young; 3 da; *Career* Dep Sec Cabinet Office 1971, Dep

Sec of Dept of Trade and Industry 1972-73, Dep Sec Dept of Industry 1974, Perm Sec 1976-; *Style* - Sir Peter Carey, KCB; 19 Leeward gdns, Wimbledon, SW19 (☎ 01 947 5530)

CAREY JONES, Norman Stewart; CMG (1965); s of late Samuel Carey-Jones; *b* 11 Dec 1911; *Educ* Monmouth Sch, Merton Oxford; *m* 1946, Stella, da of Maj Claud Myles of Capetown; 2 s; *Career* Colonial Audit Service 1934-54; Perm Sec Miny of Lands and Settlement Kenya 1962-65; Dir Dvpt Administration Leeds U 1965-77; *Style* - Norman Carey Jones Esq, CMG; Mawingo, Welsh St Donats, nr Cowbridge, S Glam

CAREY-EVANS, *see* Evans

CAREY-FOSTER, George Arthur; CMG (1952), DFC (1944), AFC (1941); s of late George Muir Foster; *b* 18 Nov 1907; *Educ* Clifton; *m* 1936, Margaret Aloysius, nee Egan; 1 da; *Career* entered Foreign Office 1946; Consul-Gen Hanover 1959-61, Counsellor British Embassy The Hague 1961-64, Asst Under-Sec Foreign Office 1965-68, ret; *Style* - George Carey-Foster Esq CMG DFC AFC; Kilkeran, Castle Freke, Co Cork

CARGILL, Lady; Margaret Eileen, formerly Gonzalez; *m* 1978, as his 3 w, Sir Peter Cargill, MBE, late V-Pres Internat Bank for Reconstruction & Dvpt (d 1981); *Style* - Lady Cargill; 1701 North Kent st, Arlington, Va 22209, USA

CARINGTON, Hon Rupert Francis John; s and h of 6 Baron Carrington; *b* 2 Dec 1948; *Educ* Eton, Bristol U; *Style* - The Hon Rupert Carington

CARLESS, Hugh Michael; CMG (1976); s of Henry Alfred Carless (d 1975); *b* 22 April 1925; *Educ* Sherborne Sch, Sch of Oriental and African Studies London, Trinity Hall Cambridge; *m* 1957, Rosa Maria, nee Frontini; 2s; *Career* joined Diplomatic Service 1950; Consul-Gen Luanda 1967-70, Counsellor Bonn 1970-73, Head of Latin America Dept FCO 1973-77, Chargé d'Affaires Buenos Aires 1977-80; *Style* - Hugh Carless Esq, CMG; 5 Bryanston sq, W1

CARLESTON, Hadden Hamilton; CIE (1947), OBE (1944); s of late Hadden Hamilton Carleston; *b* 25 July 1904; *Educ* St Olave's Sch, Trinity Hall Cambridge; *m* 1946, Eirene Leslie, nee Stevens; 2 s, 1 da; *Career* Indian Civil Service 1927-47 (Bangalore, Vizagapatam, The Nilgiris); Admin Sec Cambridge U Sch of Veterinary Medicine 1952-71; *Style* - Hadden Carleston Esq, CIE, OBE; 4 High Green, Great Shelford, Cambs (☎ Cambridge 842096)

CARLETON-SMITH INGLIS, Lt-Col Dudley Guy; DL (Ayrshire 1972); s of Lt-Col Dudley Lancelot Guy Carleton-Smith; *b* 8 Sept 1918; *Educ* Lancing, Sandhurst and Camberley; *m* 1947, Barbara Anne, da of Air Cdre Henry Le Marchant Brock, CBE (d 1964); 1 s, 1 da; *Career* commissioned Roy Scots Fusiliers 1939, Lt-Col Madagascar, N Africa, Sicily Italy and Palestine; served 2 and 4/5 Bns RSF and on staff XIII Corps HQ 8 Army, War Office and MOD as memb personal staff of Chief of Defence Staff; commanded 4/5 Bn RSF (TA) 1960-62; Councillor Royal Burgh of Ayr 1967, Baillie 1968, ret 1972; *Style* - Lt-Col Dudley Carleton-Smith Inglis DL; Dooncroft, Doonfoot, Ayrshire

CARLEY, James; s of Arthur William John Carley, of Leyton, London (d 1972); *b* 2 Oct 1913; *Educ* Leyton County High Sch; *m* 1938, Helen; 1 s, 1 da; *Career* WW II RASC Middle East and Western Command (despatches 1942); Lt in Home Guard circa 1953; chartered accountant; Chm of Meopham Parish Council 1973-; Chm of Meopham Historical Society 1976- *Recreations* country walking; writing history of the parish; writing guided walks leaflets; gardening; *Clubs* Gravesend Conservative; *Style* - James Carley Esq; Wrenbury, Wrotham rd, Meopham Kent (☎ 812110)

CARLILE, Thomas; CBE (1975); s of late James Carlile; *b* 9 Feb 1924; *Educ* Minchenden County Sch, City & Guilds Coll London; *m* 1955, Jessie Davidson Clarkson; 3 da; *Career* dep chm and md Babcock International Ltd; dir Babcock Gp of Cos, Chubb & Son Ltd, Rolls Royce & Associates Ltd ; *Style* - Thomas Carlile

Esq, CBE; 8 Aldenham grove, Radlett, Herts (☎ 6881)

CARLILL, Vice-Adm Sir Stephen Hope; KBE (1957), CB (1954), DSO (1942); s of late Harold Flamank Carlill; *b* 23 Dec 1902; *Educ* RN Colls Osborne and Dartmouth; *m* 1928, Hildegarde Rahlenbeck; 2 s; *Career* joined RN 1916, Cdr 1937, Capt 1942, Rear-Adm 1952, Flag Officer Home Fleet Training Squadron 1954-55, Vice-Adm 1954, Chief of Naval Staff Indian Navy 1955-58, ret 1959; West Africa Cmtee Rep Ghana 1960, Adviser to West Africa Cmtee 1966-67; *Style* - Vice-Adm Sir Stephen Carlill, KBE, CB, DSO; 22 Hamilton Court, Milford on Sea, Lymington Hants (☎ 2958)

CARLISLE, 12 Earl of (E 1661); Charles James Ruthven Howard; MC (1945); also Viscount Howard of Morpeth and Baron Dacre of Gillesland (both E 1661); s of 11 Earl (d 1963, whose ancestor, 1 Earl, was gggs of 4 Duke of Norfolk) and Lady Ruthven of Freeland; ha to Lordship of Ruthven of Freeland (*see* Dowager Viscountess Monckton of Brenchley); *b* 21 Feb 1923; *Educ* Eton; *m* 1945, Hon Ela, nee Beaumont, da of late 2 Visc Allendale, KG; 2 s, 2 da; *Heir* Viscount Morpeth; *Career* FRICS; late Lt Rifle Bde; former forestry commissioner; chartered surveyor; *Style* - The Rt Hon the Earl of Carlisle, MC; Naworth Castle, Brampton, Cumberland (☎ Brampton 2621)

CARLISLE, 64 Bishop of (1133); Rt Rev Henry David Halsey; Patron of 63 Livings, the Archdeaconries of Carlisle, Westmorland and Furness and W Cumberland and the Canonries in his Cathedral; s of late George Halsey, MBE; *b* 27 Jan 1919; *Educ* King's Coll Sch Wimbledon, London U, Wells Theo Coll; *m* 1947, Rachel Margaret Neil Smith; 4 da; *Career* Hon Canon of Rochester 1964-68, Rural Dean of Bromley 1965-66, Archdeacon of Bromley 1966-68, Lord Bp Suffragan of Tonbridge 1968-72, Bp of Carlisle 1972-; *Style* - The Rt Rev the Lord Bishop of Carlisle; Rose Castle, Dalston, Carlisle, Cumbria (☎ Raughton Head 274)

CARLISLE, Brian Apcar; CBE (1974), DSC (1945); s of late Capt Frederick Montagu Methven Carlisle; *b* 27 Dec 1919; *Educ* Harrow, CCC Cambridge; *m* 1953, Elizabeth Hazel Mary, nee Binnie; 1 s, 3 da; *Career* former regional co-ordinator Oil & Gas Middle East, ret 1974; consultant Lloyds Bank 1975-; dir Home Oil UK Ltd 1977-; *Style* - Brian Carlisle Esq, CBE, DSC; Heath Cottage, Hartley Wintney, Hants (☎ 2224)

CARLISLE, Hon Mrs (Elizabeth Mary); *née* McLaren; da of 2 Baron Aberconway; *b* 1911; *m* 1938, Maj Kenneth Carlisle; 1 s, 3 da (including twins, one of whom is w of Sir James Watson, 5 Bt); *Style* - The Hon Mrs Carlisle; 9 Steele's rd, NW3

CARLISLE, Esmé, Countess of; Esmé Mary Shrubb; da of Charles Iredell *m* 1947, as his 2 w, 11 Earl of Carlisle (d 1963); 1 da ; *Style* - The Rt Hon Esmé, Countess of Carlisle; 17 Sheffield ter, W8 (☎ 01 727 8770)

CARLISLE, Hugh Bernard Harwood; QC (1978); s of W H Carlisle; *b* 14 March 1937; *Educ* Oundle, Downing Coll; *m* 1964, Veronica, nee Worth; 1 s, 1 da; *Career* barr 1961; former jr treasury counsel Personal Injuries; *Style* - Hugh Carlisle Esq, QC; 18 Ranelagh av, SW6 (☎ 01 736 4238)

CARLISLE, John Russell; MP (C) Luton W 1979-; s of Andrew Russell Carlisle; *b* 28 Aug 1942; *Educ* Bedford, St Lawrence Coll Ramsgate, London U; *m* 1964, Anthea Jane Lindsay, nee May; 2 da; *Career* dir Granfin Agriculture Ltd 1979-, memb London Corn Exchange 1970-; *Style* - John Carlisle Esq, MP; Meadow Cottage, Henlow, Beds (☎ 0462 812268)

CARLISLE, Kenneth Melville; MP (C) Lincoln 1979-; s of Kenneth Ralph Malcolm Carlisle; *b* 21 March 1941; *Educ* Harrow, Magdalen Oxford; *Career* barr 1965; farmer; *Style* - Kenneth Carlisle Esq, MP; Wyken Hall Farm, Stanton, Bury St Edmunds, Suffolk (☎ Stanton 50240)

CARLISLE, Kenneth Ralph Malcolm (Peter); TD; s of late Kenneth Methven

Carlisle; *b* 28 March 1908; *Educ* Harrow, Magdalen Oxford; *m* 1938, Hon Elizabeth Mary, nee McLaren, da of 2 Baron Aberconway; 1 s, 3 da; *Career* Maj Rifle Bde, ret 1945; dir Tribune Investment Trust Co Ltd; *Style* - Kenneth Carlisle Esq, TD; Laurie House, 16 Airlie gdns, W8 (☎ 01 229 1714); Wyken Hall Farm, Stanton, Bury St Edmunds, Suffolk (☎ Stanton 50240)

CARLISLE, Mark; PC (1979), QC (1971), MP (C) Runcorn 1964- ; s of Philip E Carlisle; *b* 7 July 1929; *Educ* Radley, Manchester U; *m* 1959, Sandra Joyce, nee Des Vœux; 1 da; *Career* barr 1954; Parly Under-Sec of State Home Office 1970-72, Min of State Home Office 1972-74, Recorder of the Crown Court 1976-, Sec of State for Education and Science 1979-; *Style* - The Rt Hon Mark Carlisle, QC, MP; 3 Bench Walk, Temple, EC4 (☎ 01 353 0431); Newstead, Mobberley, Cheshire (☎ Mobberley 2275)

CARLOW, Viscount; Charles George Yuill Seymour Dawson-Damer; s and h of 7 Earl of Portarlington; *b* 6 Oct 1965; *Career* Page of Honour to HM the Queen 1981-; *Style* - Viscount Carlow

CARLYON, Thomas Symington; CMG (1968), OBE (1942); s of late Thomas Symington Carlyon; *b* 27 April 1902; *Educ* Geelong G S; *m* 1950, Marie Pichoir, nee de Launay; 1 s, 1 da (by previous m) *Career* md T S Carlyon & Co Pty Ltd 1950-; *Style* - Thomas Carlyon Esq, CMG, OBE; 82/390 Toorak rd, South Yarra, Vic 3141, Australia

CARMAN, George Alfred; QC (1971); s of Alfred George Carman; *b* 6 Oct 1929; *Educ* St Joseph's Coll Blackpool, Balliol Oxford; *m* 1, 1960 (m dis 1976), Cecilia Sparrow; 1 s; m 2, 1976, Frances Elizabeth Venning; *Career* barr 1953, Recorder of the Crown Court 1972; *Style* - George Carman Esq, QC; 5 Essex Court, Temple, EC4; Dalhousie, Oldfield rd, Altrincham, Cheshire

CARMICHAEL, Hon Mrs (Diana Heather Marion); *née* Wynn; da of 7 Baron Newborough, DSC; *b* 1951; *m* 1979, Capt Ralph Peter Kinloch Carmichael, R Scots Dragoon Gds; *Style* - The Hon Mrs Carmichael

CARMICHAEL, Ian; s of Arthur Carmichael; *b* 18 June 1920; *Educ* RADA; *m* 1943, Jean MacLean; 2 da; *Career* film, theatre and television actor; TV performances include *The World of Wooster, Lord Peter Wimsey*; *Style* - Ian Carmichael Esq; c/o London Management, 235/241 Regent st, W1

CARMICHAEL, Sir John; KBE (1955); s of late Thomas Carmichael; *b* 22 April 1910; *Educ* Madras Coll St Andrews, St Andrews and Michigan Us; *m* 1940, Cecilia MacDonald, nee Edwards; 1 s, 3 da; *Career* entd Sudan Civil Service 1936, Under-Sec Min of Finance Sudan Govt 1955-59; former dir Fison's, chm Sidelaw Industries Ltd 1970-; dir Abbey National Bdg Soc 1968-, Royal Bank of Scotland 1966-; memb Scottish Development Bd 1972-; *Style* - Sir John Carmichael, KBE; Hayston Park, Balmullo, Fife (☎ 268)

CARMICHAEL, Dr James Armstrong Gordon; CB (1978); s of Dr Donald Carmichael; *b* 28 July 1913; *Educ* Epsom Coll, Guy's Hosp; *m* 1936, Nina Betty Ashton, nee Heape; 2 s; *Career* Chief Medical Adviser DHSS 1973-78 (formerly Dep Chief); FRCP, MRCS; *Style* - Dr James Carmichael, CB; Hassets, Stockton, Fleet, Hants (☎ Fleet 4675)

CARMICHAEL, Hon Mrs (Margaret Beaufort); da (by 1 m) of late 18 Baron St John of Bletso; *b* 1909; *m* 1934, Charles Somerville Carmichael; 1 da; *Style* - The Hon Mrs Carmichael; Old Mill House, Newton Blossomville, Bedford

CARMICHAEL, Neil George; MP (L) Glasgow Kelvingrove 1974-; s of James Carmichael (former MP Glasgow Bridgeton); *b* 1921; *Educ* Eastbank Secondary Sch Glasgow, Royal Coll of Science and Technology Glasgow; *m* 1948, Catherine, nee Rankin; 1 da; *Career* memb Glasgow Corp 1962; MP (L) Glasgow Woodside 1962-74; Parly Sec Min of Technology and Power 1969-70, Parly Under-Sec of State DOE 1974-75, Dept of Industry 1975-76; *Style* - Neil Carmichael

Esq, MP; 53 Partick Hill rd, Glasgow G11 5AB (☎ 041 334 1718)

CARMICHAEL, Maj Peter Oliphant; s of late Col James Louis Carmichael, TD, JP; *b* 25 Aug 1921; *Educ* Stowe, Peterhouse Cambridge, RAC Cirencester; *m* 1948, Pamela Muriel, nee Wilson; 3 s, 1 da; *Career* served with 79 (Scottish Horse) Medium Regt RA 1942-45, with Scottish Horse RAC TA 1951-61; DL Perthshire 1966, JP 1962; *Style* - Maj Peter Carmichael, JP, DL; Arthurstone, Meigle, Perthshire (☎ 217)

CARMONT, Lady; Barbara Wilson Campbell; da of late D Russell Malloy; *m* 1929, John Francis Carmont, a Lord of Session with title of Lord Carmont, and Privy Chamberlain to the Pope (d 1965); *Career* Dame of Br Assoc, Sov Mil Order of Malta; *Clubs* University Women's; *Style* - Lady Carmont; The Avenue, Greenhill gdns, Edinburgh

CARNARVON, 6 Earl of (GB 1793); Lt-Col Henry George Alfred Marius Victor Francis Herbert; also Baron Porchester (GB 1780); s of 5 Earl (d 1923, the excavator (vicariously), though not provenly the victim of the curse, of Tutankhamun; possessor, through gggf (5 s of 8 Earl of Pembroke) and grandmother (niece of 12 Duke of Norfolk), of one of the oldest pedigrees in the kingdom (though a shade less ancient than the Pharaohs'); and half great uncle of Auberon Waugh); *b* 7 Nov 1898; *Educ* Eton, RMC; *m* 1, 1922 (m dis 1936), Anne Catherine Tredick, nee Wendell; 1 s, 1 da; m 2, 1939 (m dis 1947), Ottilie (d 1975), nee Losch (Tillie Losch the actress, former w of Edward James, *qv*); *Heir* Lord Porchester; *Career* Lt-Col 7 QOH, served India, Mesopotamia, Constantinople 1914-19, re-empld 1939; landowner; *Clubs* White's, Portland; *Style* - The Rt Hon the Earl of Carnarvon; Highclere Castle, Newbury, Berks (☎ Highclere 253204)

CARNE, Col James Power; VC (1953), DSO (1951), DL (Glos 1960); s of late G N Carne; *b* 11 April 1906; *Educ* Imperial Service Coll, Sandhurst; *m* 1946, Jean, nee Ferguson, widow of Lt-Col J T Gibson; 1 step s; *Career* 2 Lt Gloster Regt 1925, comd 1 Bn Gloster Regt in Korea 1950-51, Cmdt Army Apprentices' Sch Harrogate 1954-57, Col 1954, ret 1957; Hon Col 5 Bn Gloster Regt 1956-61; Hon Freeman of Gloucester and Falmouth; *Style* - Col James Carne, VC, DSO, DL; Stonebank, Cranham, Glos

CARNE, Capt William Power; CBE (1955); s of late G N Carne; *b* 1898; *Educ* RN Colls Osborne and Dartmouth; *m* 1923, Valentine Grace Naudin, nee Tweedy; 4 s; *Career* Capt RN (ret); Cdre Cmdg 30 Aircraft Carrier Sqdn British Pacific Fleet 1944-45, Cdre Superintendent Contract Built Ships 1952-57; *Style* - Capt Willaim Carne, CBE; Tresahor Vean, Constantine, Cornwall

CARNEGIE, Hon Alexander Bannerman; s of late 10 Earl of Southesk; *b* 1894; *m* 1, 1919, Susan Ottilia (d 1968), da of late Maj Ernest Rodakowski; 1 s (*see* Carnegie, Raymond); m 2, 1969, Cynthia Averil Gurney, da of late Brig Harold Vincent Spencer Charrington, DSO, MC; *Career* Cdr (ret) RN; *Style* - The Hon Alexander Carnegie; Vann Farm, Hawkley, Hants

CARNEGIE, Lady Alexandra Clare; da of 3 Duke of Fife; *b* 20 June 1959; *Style* - Lady Alexandra Carnegie

CARNEGIE, Hon Alexander Robert MacRae; s and h of Lord Rosehill and gs of 13 Earl of Northesk; *b* 16 Nov 1980; *Style* - The Hon Alexander Carnegie

CARNEGIE, Hon James Duthac; TD; s of late 10 Earl of Southesk; *b* 1910; *Educ* Eton, Trin Cambridge; *m* 1935, Claudia Katharine Angela, da of late Hon Lord Blackburn; 1 s (Robin, *see* Selina, Marchioness of Lansdowne); *Career* Maj 4/5 Bn Black Watch (TA); *Style* - The Hon James Carnegie, TD; Balloch, Alyth, Perths

CARNEGIE, Hon Jocelyn Jacek Alexander Bannerman; s of Countess of Erroll (d 1978) and 2 husband, Maj Raymond Alexander Carnegie, gs of late 10 Earl of Southesk; half-bro of Earl of Erroll; *b* 1966; *Style* - The Hon Jocelyn Carnegie

CARNEGIE, Maj Raymond Alexander; s (by 1 m) of Hon Alexander Carnegie, *qv*, s of late 10 Earl of Southesk; *b* 1920; *m* 1, 1943 (m dis 1953), Patricia Elinor Trevor, da of Cdr Sir Hugh Trevor Dawson, 2 Bt (cr 1920), RN (ret); 2 da; m 2, 1964, Diana Denyse Hay, Countess of Errol (who m 1, Capt Sir (Rupert) Iain Kay Moncreiffe of that Ilk, 11 Bt, and who d 1978); 1 s (*see* Carnegie, Hon Jocelyn); *Career* late Scots Gds, wounded 3 times and despatches WW II; *Style* - Maj Raymond Carnegie; Crimonmogate, Lonmay, Aberdeenshire

CARNEGIE, Sir Roderick Howard; s of Douglas Howard Carnegie; *b* 27 Nov 1932; *Educ* Geelong G S, Trinity Coll Melbourne U, New Coll Oxford, Harvard Business Sch; *m* 1959, Carmen Sandra, nee Clarke; 3 s; *Career* former dir McKinsey & Co, md Conzinc Riotinto of Australia Ltd 1971-, chm 1974-; dir Comalco Ltd, Hamersley Hldgs, Bougainville Copper Ltd; kt 1978; *Style* - Sir Roderick Carnegie; 55 Collins st, Melbourne, Victoria, Australia (☎ 658 3311)

CARNEGIE, Lt-Gen Robin Macdonald; OBE (1968); s of late Sir Francis Carnegie; *b* 22 June 1926; *Educ* Rugby; *m* 1955, Iona, da of Sir John Sinclair, KCMG, CB, OBE; 1 s, 2 da; *Career* comd Queen's Own Hussars 1967-69, comd 11 Armoured Bde 1971-72, GOC 3 Div (Maj-Gen) 1974-76, Chief of Staff HQ BAOR 1976-78; Mil Sec 1978-80; Dir-Gen Army Training MOD 1980-; *Style* - Lt-Gen Robin Carnegie, OBE; Coombe Bank West, Uckfield, Sussex

CARNEGY, Derek Francis; s of Francis Anthony Roberts Carnegy; *b* 23 Aug 1928; *Educ* Pangbourne Coll; *m* 1961, Judith Frances; 2 s; *Career* former submarine specialist RN; joined Hambros Bank 1977, dir Allied Hambro Ltd; *Style* - Derek Carnegy Esq; 14 Ranelagh rd, Winchester, Hants (☎ 66077)

CARNEGY-ARBUTHNOTT, Brevet Col David; TD (1969); s of late Wilmot Boys Carnegy-Arbuthnott; *b* 17 July 1925; *Educ* Stowe; *m* 1949, Helen Adamson, nee Lyell; 2 s, 2 da; *Career* Black Watch 1943, Bt Col 1969; memb Royal Co of Archers (Queen's Bodyguard for Scotland) 1959-; chartered accountant Dundee 1956-; DL City of Dundee 1973; *Style* - Brevet Col David Carnegy-Arbuthnot TD; Meadowburn, Balnamoon, Brechin, Angus (☎ Menmuir 208)

CARNEY, Adm Robert Bostwick; Hon CBE (1946), DSM (1942 US); s of Robert Carney; *b* 26 March 1895; *Educ* Naval Acad US; *m* 1918, Grace Craycroft; 1 s, 1 da; *Career* Adm US Navy, CIC Allied Forces S Europe NATO 1951-53, Chief of Naval Operations 1953-55, ret; *Style* - Admiral Robert Carney, CBE, DSM; 2801 New Mexico av (NW), Washington, DC 2007, USA

CARNOCK, 3 Baron (UK 1916); Capt Sir Erskine Arthur Nicolson; 13 Bt (NS 1637), DSO (1919); s of 1 Baron (d 1928); suc bro, 2 Baron, 1952; yet another bro was (Hon Sir) Harold Nicolson, the author; his sis m 3 Baron St Levan; *b* 26 March 1884; *Educ* HMS Britannia; *m* 1919, Hon Katharine Frederica Albertha, nee Lopes (d 1968), da of 1 Baron Roborough; 2 s (1 decd), 1 da (decd); *Heir* s, Hon David Nicolson; *Career* Capt RN, ret 1924; JP Devon 1937; *Style* - The Rt Hon the Lord Carnock, DSO, JP; Beechfield Nursing Home, Harrowbeer Lane, Yelverton, nr Plymouth, Devon

CARNWATH, Sir Andrew Hunter; KCVO (1975); s of late Dr Thomas Carnwath, DSO; *b* 26 Oct 1909; *Educ* Eton; *m* 1, 1939, Kathleen Marianne, nee Armstrong (d 1968); 5 s, 1 da; m 2, 1973, Joan, widow of D S Wetherell-Pepper; *Career* merchant banker; former md Baring Bros & Co Ltd, chm Save & Prosper Gp Ltd, dir Equity and Law Life Assurance Society; Treasurer London Philharmonic Orchestra; High Sheriff of Essex 1965, DL 1972, CC 1973; *Style* - Sir Andrew Carnwath, KCVO, DL; Coachman's Cottage, 33 Grove rd, Barnes, SW13 (☎ 01 876 5338)

CAROE, Sir (Einar) Athelstan Gordon; OBE (1958); s of late J F Caroe; *b* 6 Oct 1903; *Educ* Eton, Trinity Cambridge; *m* 1, 1934, Mary (d 1947), da of Brig-Gen C H

Lyon; 2 s; m 2, 1952, Jane, nee Sandland; 1 s, 1 da; *Career* Consul for Iceland 1947-; pres Trustee Savings Banks 1976-, Minton Ltd 1970-; knighted 1972; *Style* - Sir Athelstan Caroe, OBE; Anthonys Close, Caldy rd, Caldy, West Kirby, Wirral, W Merseyside (☎ 051 625 7089)

CAROE, Sir Olaf Kirkpatrick; KCIE (1944), KCSI (1946); s of William Douglas Caroe; *b* 15 Nov 1892; *Educ* Winchester, Magdalen Oxford; *m* 1920, Frances Marion, da of Rt Rev A G Rawstorne; 2 s; *Career* Indian Civil Service and Political Service, Foreign Sec to Viceroy 1939-45, Govr N-W Frontier Province 1946-47; former first pres Tibet Soc of the UK; author; *Style* - Sir Olaf Caroe, KCIE, KCSI; Newham House, Steyning, Sussex (☎ 812241)

CARPENTER, Very Rev Edward Frederick; s of Frederick Carpenter; *b* 27 Nov 1910; *Educ* Strodes Sch Egham, King's Coll London U; *m* 1951, Lilian Betsy Wright; 3 s, 1 da; *Career* ordained 1935, Archdn of Westminster 1963-75, Dean of Westminster 1975-; *Style* - The Very Rev Edward Carpenter; The Deanery, Westminster, SW1 (☎ 01 222 2953)

CARPENTER, Herbert Franklin; CBE (1955); s of late Herbert Carpenter; *b* 1891; *Educ* Bancroft's Sch; *m* 1, 1915, Elsie, nee Edwards; 2 da; m 2, 1947, Vera Gertrude, nee Boilard; *Career* electricity consultant; chm Cyprus Electricity Authority 1953-60; adviser to Jamaican Govt 1958-59, to Jordanian Govt 1963-67; *Style* - Herbert Carpenter Esq, CBE; 12 Bulkington av, Worthing, W Sussex

CARPENTER, Maj-Gen (Victor Harry) John; CB (1975), MBE (1945); s of Harry Carpenter; *b* 21 June 1921; *m* 1946, Theresa McCulloch; 1 s, 1 da; *Career* 2 Lt RASC 1939, Transport Officer in Chief MOD 1971-73, Maj-Gen 1971, Dir of Movements (Army) MOD 1973-75, ret; chm Traffic Commissioners Yorks Traffic Area 1975-; *Style* - Maj-Gen John Carpenter, CB, MBE; Traffic Commrs, Yorkshire Traffic Area, 386 Harehills Lane, Leeds

CARPENTER, Joan; CBE (1943); da of H G Carpenter; *b* 1895; *Career* joined WRNS 1939, organized Women's Royal Canadian Naval Service 1942; dep dir Welfare WRNS 1944; *Style* - Miss Joan Carpenter, CBE; 1 Sloncombe House, Moretonhampstead, Newton Abbot, Devon

CARPENTER, James Montagu; s of late Edward Harry Osmund Carpenter; *b* 28 Dec 1924; *Educ* Eton; *m* 1961, Mary Morris, da of Brig G W Auten, OBE; 3 s; *Career* chm Carpets International Ltd and dir Carpets International Group of Cos; chm Debron Carpets Ltd; dir BCMA Services Ltd; *Style* - James Carpenter Esq; Eardington Manor, nr Bridgnorth, Salop (☎ 2397)

CARPENTER, Leslie Arthur; s of William Carpenter; *b* 26 June 1927; *Educ* Hackney Tech Coll; *m* 1952, Stella Louise Bozza; 1 da; *Career* chm and chief exec International Publishing Corp Ltd, dir Reed Gp of Cos, IPC Investments (Pty) Ltd; *Style* - Leslie Carpenter Esq; 22 Wickliffe av, N3 (☎ 01 346 2139)

CARPENTER-GARNIER, Col Leonard George; OBE (1949); s of late George William Carpenter; *b* 1 Nov 1911; *Educ* Radley, Sandhurst; *m* 1937, Eileen Florence Turnell; 1 da; *Career* commd Devonshire Regt 1932, Col 1958, ret; memb City of Winchester Council 1974-; High Sheriff Hants 1968, DL 1971; *Style* - Col Leonard Carpenter-Garnier OBE DL; Beverley, Wickham, Fareham, Hants (☎ Wickham 833125)

CARR OF HADLEY, Baron (Life Peer UK 1975); (Leonard) Robert Carr; PC (1963); s of late Ralph Edward Carr; *b* 11 Nov 1916; *Educ* Westminster Sch, Gonville and Caius Cambridge; *m* 1943, Joan Kathleen, nee Twining; 2 da; *Career* former PPS to Sir Anthony Eden; Sec of State for Employment 1970-72, Lord Pres of the Council and Leader of the House of Commons 1972, Sec of State for Home Affairs 1972-74; MP (C) Mitcham 1950-74, Sutton (Carshalton) 1974-75; dir S Hoffnung & Co, Securicor Ltd, SGB Group Ltd, Prudential Assurance Co; *Style* - The Rt Hon the Lord Carr of

Hadley, PC; Monkenholt, Hadley Green, Barnet, Herts

CARR, Charles Francis; CBE (1973); s of Edward Crossley Carr; *b* 1913; *Educ* Nottingham H S, Hertford Oxford; *m* 1951, Florian, nee Winslow; *Career* Dep Ch Inspector of Factories DOE 1965, Sr Dep Ch Inspector of Factories Dept of Employment; *Style* - Charles Carr Esq, CBE; 64 Marlborough pla, NW8

CARR, Edward Hallett; CBE (1920); *b* 28 June 1892; *Educ* Merchant Taylors' Sch London, Trin Cambridge; *Career* Foreign Office 1916, Temp Sec British Embassy 1920-21; First Sec 1933; former Wilson Prof of International Politics Univ Coll Aberystwyth; Asst Ed The Times 1941-46; Tutor Balliol Oxford 1953-55; Fellow Trin Cambridge 1955-; author; *Style* - Edward Carr Esq, CBE; Trinity College, Cambridge; Dales Barn, Barton, Cambs

CARR, Frank George Griffith; CB (1967), CBE (1954); s of late Frank Carr; *b* 23 April 1923; *Educ* Perse Sch, Trin Hall Cambridge; *m* 1932, Ruth, nee Burkitt; *Career* former dir National Maritime Museum Greenwich; chm Cutty Sark Ship Management Cmtee 1953-72; international chm American Ship Trust Cmtee 1978-, chm World Ship Trust Action Gp 1980-; *Style* - Frank Carr Esq, CB, CBE; 10 Park Gate, Blackheath, SE3 (☎ 01 852 5181)

CARR, Frank Henry; CBE (1963); s of F L Carr; *b* 1904; *Educ* Portsmouth G S, Univ Coll London; *m* 1934, Christine Violet, nee Ortling; 3 s; *Career* Maj RE (despatches) 1939-45; Miny of Housing & Local Govt 1947-68; *Style* - Frank Carr Esq, CBE; No 1 Tellisford, Esher, Surrey

CARR, Henry Lambton; CMG (1945), MVO (1957); s of late Archibald Lambton; *b* 28 Nov 1899; *Educ* Haileybury Coll; *m* 1924, Winifred Luba Nicolson, nee Eveleigh; 2 s; *Career* entd Foreign Service 1920, First Sec Copenhagen 1955-58, FO 1958, ret 1961; *Style* - Henry Carr Esq, CMG, MVO; The Links, Forest Row, E Sussex (☎ 2091)

CARR, Ian Cufaude; s of late Laurence Carr; *b* 12 Aug 1928; *Educ* Rugby; *m* 1, 1952 (m dis 1976), Doreen; 2 s, 2 da; m 2, 1976, Rilla, nee Carr; *Career* chm Carr's Milling Industries Ltd Gp of Cos 1964-; trustee Trustee Savings Bank for Lancs and Cumbria 1971-; *Style* - Ian Carr Esq; Brown Hill, Walton, Brampton, Cumbria (☎ Brampton 2540)

CARR, Brig James Gouinlock; CBE (1965); s of George Carr; *b* 1 Sept 1911; *Educ* Upper Canada Coll, RMC Canada, Cambridge U; *m* 1941, Joyce Ranicar; 3 s; *Career* 2 Lt RE 1931, NWEF and 7 Armd Div 1939-45, Brig 1960, CE Northern Command 1959-62, Cmdt Roy Sch of Mil Engineering 1962-65, ADC to HM the Queen 1963-65; *Style* - Brig James Carr, CBE; Wicks Field, Yateley, Camberley, Surrey

CARR, Rear-Adm Lawrence George; CB (1971), DSC (1954); s of late George Henry Carr; *b* 31 Jan 1920; *Educ* Wellington Tech Coll New Zealand; *Career* Cdre Auckland 1966-68, 2 Naval Memb NZ Naval Board 1968-69, Ch of Naval Staff NZ 1969, ret 1972; *Style* - Rear-Adm Lawrence Carr, CB, DSC; 57 Pigeon Mountain rd, Half Moon Bay, Auckland, New Zealand

CARR, Roy Lancelot; s of Lancelot John Carr (d 1951); *b* 30 June 1909; *Educ* privately; *m* 1943, Evelyn Muriel; 2 s, 1 da; *Career* Maj RA Europe, memb of the Stock Exchange; *Recreations* golf; *Clubs* Army & Navy, MCC, Royal St George's (Sandwich); *Style* - Roy Carr Esq; Swan House, Preston, Canterbury, Kent

CARR, (Albert) Raymond (Maillard); s of Reginald Carr; *b* 11 April 1919; *Educ* Brockenhurst Sch, Ch Ch Oxford; *m* 1950, Sara Strickland; 3 s, 1 da; *Career* former Fellow of All Souls' and New Coll Oxford; Prof of Latin American History Oxford 1967-68; Warden of St Anthony's Coll Oxford 1968-, Fellow 1964-; author; *Style* - Raymond Carr Esq; St Anthony's College, Oxford; 29 Charlbury rd, Oxford (☎ 58136); Woolhanger Manor, Parracombe, Devon (☎ 379)

CARR, Dr Thomas Ernest Ashdown; CB (1977); s of late Laurence Carr; *b* 2[illegible]

June 1915; *Educ* County H S Altrincham, Victoria U Manchester (MB, ChB); *m* 1940, Mary Sybil, nee Dunkley; 1 s, 2 da; *Career* Princ Medical Officer DHSS 1966, Sr Princ Medical Officer GP and Regional Medical Service 1967-79, part-time medical referee 1979-; *Style* - Dr Thomas Carr, CB; Tollgate House, 2 Pilgrims Way, Guildford, Surrey (☎ 63012)

CARR, Hon Virginia Sarah; da of Baron Carr of Hadley (Life Peer); *b* 1957; *Style* - The Hon Virginia Carr

CARR, Air Cdre William George; CBE (1968); s of late William George Carr; *b* 12 Nov 1916; *Educ* Southampton; *m* 1949, Marion Ethel, nee Hislop; 1 s, 1 da; *Career* Dir of Movements RAF 1969-72, ret; British Transport Hotels 1972-; *Style* - Air Cdre William Carr, CBE; High Oaks, Wonersh Park, nr Guildford, Surrey

CARR, Brig William Greenwood; CVO (1971), DSO (1941) & Bar (1942), JP (Norfolk 1953), DL (1961); s of William Carr, JP, DL, and Margaret, nee Bright (whose 3 sisters m (1) Sir Henry Newbolt's bro, Sir Francis (2) 1 Baron Aldenham's bro, Rev John Gibbs and (3) Rt Rev Hubert Burge, sometime Bp of Oxford); *b* 10 March 1901; *Educ* Eton, Univ Coll Oxford; *m* 1928, Donna Nennella, formerly w of late Maj-Gen Sir Foster Newland, KCMG, CB, and yr da of late Gen Count Michele Salazar, of Rome, and gda of Duke Dusmet de Smours; 1 da (Annabel, b 20 May 1930, m 13 Earl Ferrers, *qv*); *Career* in Br Olympic Riding Team 1936; formerly with 12 Roy Lancers, raised and commanded 4 London Yeo 1939-41, later Brig British Staff GHQ South West Pacific Area 1944-45, ret 1946; an Exon of HM's Bodyguard of Yeomen of the Guard 1950, Ensign 1955-70, Lt 1970-71; *Clubs* Cavalry & Guards, Roy Yacht Sqdn; *Style* - Brig William Carr, CVO, DSO*, JP, DL; 3 Chesterfield st, Mayfair, W1 (☎ 01 629 5725); Ditchingham Hall, Norfolk (☎ Woodton 226)

CARR-ELLISON, Sir Ralph Harry; TD (1962); s of late John Campbell Carr-Ellison; *b* 8 Dec 1925; *Educ* Eton; *m* 1951, Mary Clare, da of Maj Arthur McMorrough Kavanagh, MC; 3 s, 1 da; *Career* TAVR Col Northumbrian District 1969-72, Dep Cdr NE District 1973, ADC (TAVR) to HM the Queen 1970-75; former Pres Northern Area Conservative Assocs; chm Tyne Tees Television Ltd 1974-, Northumbrian Water Authority 1973-; dep chm Trident Television 1976-; former JP Northumberland, High Sheriff 19722; kt 197; *Style* - Sir Ralph Carr-Ellison, TD; Hedgeley Hall, Powburn, Alnwick, Northumberland (☎ Powburn 273;(office) Powburn 272)

CARREL, Philip; CMG (1960), OBE (1954); s of late Louis Raymond Carrel; *b* 23 Sept 1915; *Educ* Blundell's, Balliol Oxford; *m* 1948, Eileen Mary, nee Hainworth; 1 s, 1 da; *Career* entd Colonial Admin Service (Zanzibar) 1938, Admin Officer Somaliland 1947, Chief Sec 1959-60, ret; *Style* - Philip Carrel Esq, CMG, OBE; Lych Gates, Chiltley Lane, Liphook, Hants (☎ 722150)

CARRERAS, Sir James; MBE (1944); s of Henry Carreras; *b* 30 Jan 1909; *m* 1927, Vera St John; 1 s; *Career* former chm and chief exec Hammer Film Productions Ltd; dir Studio Film Laboratories Ltd, National Screen Service; special adviser EMI Gp of Cos; kt 1970; *Style* - Sir James Carreras, MBE; The White House, Bolney av, Shiplake, Oxon

CARRICK, 9 Earl of (I 1748); Brian Stuart Theobald Somerset Caher Butler; also Viscount Ikerrin (I 1629) and (sits as) Baron Butler of Mount Juliet (UK 1912); s of 8 Earl (d 1957) by his 1 w Marion; *b* 17 Aug 1931; *Educ* Downside; *m* 1951 (m dis 1976) (Mary) Belinda, da of Maj David Constable-Maxwell, TD; 1 s, 1 da; *Heir* s, Viscount Ikerrin; *Career* dir The Bowater Gp Ltd, Reynolds & Gibson (Cotton) Ltd, The Bacup Warehousing Co Ltd, Maclaine Wasson Ltd and others; chm Ralli Bros & Coney Ltd; *Style* - The Rt Hon the Earl of Carrick; 10 Netherton grove, SW10 (☎ 01 352 6328)

CARRICK, Ruth, Countess of - Ruth; *née* McEnery; *m* 1954, as his 3 w, 8 Earl of Carrick (d 1957); *Style* - The Rt Hon Ruth, Countess of Carrick; Box 1190, Pinehurst,

N Carolina 28374, USA

CARRICK, Maj-Gen Thomas Welsh; OBE (1959); s of late George Carrick; *b* 19 Dec 1914; *Educ* Glasgow Acad, Glasgow U, London Sch of Hygiene and Tropical Medicine; *m* 1948, Nan Middleton Allison; 1 s; *Career* Prof of Army Health Royal Army Medical Coll 1970-71, Dir of Army Health and Research MOD 1971-73, Cmdt Post-Graduate Dean Royal Army Medical Coll 1973, ret; specialist in Community Medicine (Medical Staffing) Camden and Islington Area Health Authority; QHS (1973), OStJ (1947); *Style* - Maj-Gen Thomas Carrick, OBE, QHS; Little Chantry, Gillingham, Dorset

CARRICK-BUCHANAN, Lt-Col David Richard; s of late Lt-Col Arthur L H Buchanan, MP; *b* 1906; *Educ* Eton, Trin Cambridge; *m* 1937, Cinderella Beatrix, nee Staveley; 1 s, 1 da; *Career* Lt 2 Bn Gordon Highlanders 1929, Capt 1938, Lt-Col 1945; DL Wigtownshire 1949, JP 1952; *Style* - Lt-Col David Carrick-Buchanan JP DL; Corsewall, Stranraer, Wigtownshire (☎ Kircolm 209)

CARRINGTON, 6 Baron (I 1796, GB 1797); Peter Alexander Rupert Carington; KCMG (1958), MC (1945), PC (1959), JP (Bucks 1948), DL (1951); s of 5 Baron (d 1938, n of 3 Baron who was also 1 & last Marquess of Lincolnshire; the 1 Baron, gggf to the present For Sec, was only ennobled after long resistance by George III, who objected to his being in trade; the family name, originally Smith, was changed by the 2 Baron to Carrington and by the 3 Baron to Carington; a member of the family, one Augustus Smith, decisively demolished any pretensions to a link with the Smyth/Smith cr Viscount Carrington of Burford 1643, calling his own ancestors' origins 'altogether plebeian'; however, through the 2 Baron's m with Charlotte, da of 21 Baron Willoughby de Eresby, Lord C not only descends from that ancient line but the de Vere Earls of Oxford, de Ufford Earls of Suffolk, Lords Strange of Knockyn, and Barons Bec of Eresby, which more than compensates for any deficiency of blood through the male ancestry) and Hon Sybil, da of 2 Visc Colville of Culross; four cous once removed to 3 Baron Bicester; *b* 6 June 1919; *Educ* Eton, Sandhurst; *m* 1942, Iona, da of Sir Francis McClean; 1 s, 2 da (Hon Mrs de Bunsen; Virginia, Lady Ashcombe); *Heir* s, Hon Rupert Carington; *Career* formerly dir RTZ, Hambros, Cadbury Schweppes, Barclays Bank, Br Metal Corpn; Parly Sec Min Agriculture and Fisheries 1951-54, to MOD 1954-56, High Cmmr for UK in Australia 1956-59, Min without Portfolio and Leader of the House of Lords 1963-64, Leader of the Opposition of House of Lords 1964-70 and 1974-79, Sec of State for Defence 1970-74, Sec of State Dept of Energy 1974, Min of Aviation Supply 1971, chm Conservative Party 1972-74, Sec of State for Foreign and Commonwealth Affairs and Min of Overseas Devpt 1979-; dir Barclays Bank International 1975-; Fellow of Eton 1966; *Style* - The Rt Hon Lord Carrington KCMG MC PC JP DL; 32a Ovington sq, SW3 (☎ 01 584 1476) The Manor House, Bledlow, nr Aylesbury, Bucks (☎ Princes Risborough 3499)

CARROLL, Maj-Gen Derek Raymond; OBE (1958); s of late Raymond Carroll; *b* 2 Jan 1919; *m* 1946, Bettina Mary Gould; 1 s, 1 da; *Career* Cdr 12 Engineer Bde 1966-67, Dir MOD (Army) 1969-70, Chief Engineer BAOR 1970-73; bus driver/conductor E Kent Road Car Co Canterbury 1974; with Family Coach Firm 1975; *Style* - Maj-Gen Derek Carroll, OBE; c/o Barclays Bank Ltd, Wimbledon Broadway, SW19

CARRON, Baroness; Mary Emma; da of John McGuire; *m* 1931, Baron Carron (Life Peer, d 1969); 2 da (Hon Mrs Weidemann, Hon Mrs Hull); *Style* - The Rt Hon the Lady Carron; The Gables, 27 Bromley rd, SE6

CARS, Ernest; *b* 14 July 1923; *Career* CEng, FIMechE, FIProdE, chm and md Moss Engineering Gp Ltd, chm Holbrook Engrg Ltd, chm J & T Engrg Ltd, chm Jackson Bros Ltd, chm Moss Engrg Gp Services Ltd, chm The Moss Gear Co Ltd, chm Stevens & Bullivant Ltd & assoc companies, chm Wallwin (Pumps) Ltd & assoc companies, chm Welded Presswork Ltd, chm William E Farrer Ltd & assoc companies; *Style* - Ernest Cars Esq;

Shenstone Hall, Shenstone, Lichfield, Staffs

CARSE, William Mitchell; CBE (1953); s of late Robert Carse; *b* 23 Aug 1889; *Educ* Glasgow H S, Glasgow U, Wellington Mil Coll Madras, St John's Cambridge, Sandhurst; *m* 1928, Helen Knox (d 1976), nee Beaton; 1 s; *Career* joined HM Consular Service 1923, Consul-Gen Tabriz 1946-47, Ahwaz 1948, Dep High Cmmr for UK in Peshawar Pakistan 1948-51, Consul-Gen Sao Paulo 1951-56; Distillers Ltd 1957; *Style* - William Carse Esq, CBE; Little Dene, St Alban's rd, Reigate, Surrey

CARSLAKE, Maj John; DL (Warwicks 1973); *Style* - Maj John Carslake, DL; The Old Rectory, Preston Bagot, nr Henley-in-Arden, Warwicks

CARSON, Charles Young; CB (1968), CMG (1950); s of late George Carstairs; *b* 30 Oct 1910; *Educ* Glasgow Acad, George Watson's Boys' Coll Edinburgh, Edinburgh U; *m* 1939, Frances Mary, nee Coode; 1 s, 1 da; *Career* entd Civil Service 1934, Under-Sec Min of Public Building and Works 1965, Special Adviser Expenditure Cmtee House of Commons 1971, Clerk to Select Cmtee on Commodity Prices House of Lords 1976-77; *Style* - Charles Carson Esq, CB, CMG; St Kea, 9 Ridgegate close, Reigate, Surrey

CARSON, Hon Edward; s of Baron Carson (Life Peer, d 1935); *b* 1920; *Educ* Eton, Trin Hall Cambridge; *m* 1943, Heather, nee Sclater; 1 s, 1 da; *Career* Lt Life Gds; MP (C) Isle of Thanet Div Kent 1945-53; *Style* - The Hon Edward Carson

CARSON, George Lefroy; CBE (1965); s of late George Moffat Carson, MM; *b* 1914; *Educ* Victoria Coll Jersey, Edinburgh U, Exeter Oxford; *m* 1946, Rosemary Eileen, nee Le Messurier; 1 da; *Career* conservator of Forests HM Overseas Forest Service Sabah Malaysia 1954-67, Park Warden Kinabalu National Park Sabah 1967-69; *Style* - George Carson Esq, CBE; 1 Le Feugeral, La Moye, Jersey, CI

CARSON, Air Cdre Robert John; CBE (1974), AFC (1964); s of Robert Carson; *b* 3 Aug 1924; *Educ* Regent House Sch Newtownards; *m* 1945, Jane, nee Bailie; 3 da; *Career* Air Adviser British Cmmn Ottawa 1974-75, Defence Adviser British High Cmmr Canada 1975-78; man Grumman Aerospace Corp Bethpage (Panavia Office) 1978-; Queen's Commendation (Air) 1962; *Style* - Air Cdre Robert Carson, CBE, AFC; 20 Meadow drive, Scruton, nr Northallerton, N Yorks (☎ Kirkby Fleetham 656)

CARSWELL, John Patrick; CB (1977); s of Donald Carswell; *b* 30 May 1918; *Educ* Merchant Taylors' Sch, St John's Oxford; *m* 1944, Ianthe Elstob; 2 da; *Career* Miny National Insurance 1946-56; Under-Sec DES 1964-74; Sec University Grants Cmtee 1974-77; Sec British Acad 1978-; author; *Style* - John Carswell Esq, CB; 5 Prince Arthur rd, NW3 (☎ 01 794 6527)

CARTE, Brian Addison; TD (1976); s of late James Carte; *b* 7 Aug 1943; *Educ* St Lawrence Coll Ramsgate; *m* 1969, Shirley Anne, da of Lt-Col W H Brinkley; 2 da; *Career* Co Command Queen's Regt TA, Maj GSO II HG London Dist; dir and head of Banking Div County Bank Ltd; *Style* - Brian Carte Esq, TD; Linden Lea, Leys rd, Oxshott, Surrey (☎ 01 638 6000)

CARTER, Hon Mrs (Brenda Ruby); *née* Pearson; da of late 2 Visc Cowdray and Agnes, da of Lord Edward Spencer-Churchill; *b* 1912; *m* 1, 1934 (m dis 1948), Group-Capt Paul Willert, RAF; 2 da (Pauline m John, s of Sir Maurice Dorman, *qv*); m 2, 1948, Hugh Carter; 1 s; *Style* - The Hon Mrs Carter; Wakeham, Rogate, Petersfield, Hants

CARTER, Sir Charles Frederick; s of late Frederick William Carter; *b* 15 Aug 1919; *Educ* Rugby, St John's Cambridge; *m* 1944, Janet, nee Shea; 1 s, 2 da; *Career* former lectr in Statistics Cambridge U; Prof of Economics Queen's U Belfast 1950-59, Manchester U 1959-63; Vice-Chancellor Lancaster U 1963-79; Exec Chm Policy Studies Inst 1978-; kt 1978; *Style* - Sir Charles Carter; Bank Head, The Banks, Seascale, Cumbria (☎ 09402 8050)

CARTER, Douglas; CB (1969); s of late

Albert Carter; *b* 4 Dec 1911; *Educ* Bradford G S, St John's Cambridge; *m* 1935, Alice Mary Clare, nee Le Mesurier; 3 s, 1 da; *Career* entd Bd of Trade 1934, Under-Sec 1963-71, ret; Under-Sec Dept of Trade and Industry 1969-71; *Style* - Douglas Carter Esq, CB; 12 Garbrand Walk, Ewell Village, Epsom, Surrey (☎ 01 394 1316)

CARTER, David Alexander; CBE (1968); s of late John Howard Carter, JP; *b* 1901; *Educ* Repton, Reading U; *Career* chm Herts Branch NFU 1953, chm Herts and Middlesex Branch Country Landowners Assoc 1955-57; JP Herts 1944, CC 1954-61; Chm of Magistrates Buntingford Court 1959; *Style* - David Carter Esq CBE JP; Bancroft Farm, Cottered, Buntingford, Herts (☎ Cottered 253)

CARTER, Sir Derek Hunton; TD (1952); s of late Dr Arthur Hunton Carter; *b* 7 April 1906; *Educ* Haileybury, St John's Cambridge; *m* 1, 1933, Phyllis, nee Best; 1 s, 1 da; m 2, 1948, Madeline, da of Col Denis Moriarty O'Callaghan, CMG, DSO; 1 da; *Career* 2 Lt 27 (LEE) Bn RE (TA), Lt-Col RA 1942; chm Mond Div ICI Ltd 1963-67, Remploy Ltd 1972-76; kt 1975; *Style* - Sir Derek Carter, TD; Withington House, Withington, Cheltenham, Glos

CARTER, Hon Sir Douglas Julian; KCMG (1977); s of Walter Carter; *b* 5 Aug 1908; *Educ* Palmerston North H S, Waitaki Boys' H S; *m* Mavis Miles; *Career* Min of Agriculture 1969-72, MP (Nat) Raglan 1957-75, New Zealand High Commissioner to UK 1976-79; *Style* - The Hon Sir Douglas Carter, KCMG; Orini, RD 2, Taupiri, New Zealand

CARTER, Frederick Brian; s of late Arthur Carter; *b* 11 May 1933; *Educ* Stretford G S, King's Coll London; *m* 1960, Elizabeth, nee Hughes; 1 s, 3 da; *Career* barr 1955, Inland Revenue N Circuit 1973-, a Recorder of the Crown Court 1978-; *Style* - Frederick Carter Esq; 55 Ogden rd, Bramhall, Stockport, Cheshire (☎ 061 439 3637)

CARTER, Frank Ernest Lovell; CBE (1956); s of late E C Carter; *b* 1909; *Educ* Chigwell Sch, Hertford Oxford; *Career* former Dir-Gen of Overseas Audit Service, ret 1972; *Style* - Frank Carter Esq CBE; 8 The Leys, N2

CARTER, Frank Jackson; CMG (1954), CVO (1963), CBE (1946); s of late Francis Henry Carter; *b* 9 Sept 1899; *Educ* Hobart H S, Tasmania U; *m* 1926, Margaret Flora, nee Walker; 2 s, 1 da; *Career* State Under-Sec and Perm Head of Premier's Dept Tasmania 1952-64, Official Sec for Tasmania in London 1949-50; chm Fire Brigades Cmmn of Tasmania 1946-70; former Grand Master Freemasons Grand Lodge of Tasmania; *Style* - Frank Carter Esq, CMG, CVO, CBE; Tavistock, 568 Churchill av, Sandy Bay, Hobart, Tasmania (☎ 252382)

CARTER, Air Cdre Gerald Paul Halliley; CBE (1946); s of late William Fowler Carter; *b* 1900; *Educ* Bromsgrove Sch, St Catharine's Cambridge; *m* 1930, Esther Mary Douglas, da of Sir H J M MacAndrew, KCB, DSO; 2 da; *Career* joined RAF 1918, Air Cdre 1944, Commanding RAF Base Seletar 1946-49, ret 1950; Bursar Ardingly Coll 1953-65; *Style* - Air Cdre Gerald Carter, CBE; Pryor House, East Hanney, Wantage, Oxon (☎ West Hanney 233)

CARTER, Sir John; QC (Guyana 1962); s of Kemp R Carter; *b* 27 Jan 1919; *Educ* Queen's Coll Guyana, London U; *m* 1959, Sara Lou, nee Harris; 2 s, 2 da; *Career* barr 1942; Pro-Chancellor U of British Guyana 1962-66; High Cmmr for Guyana in UK 1970-76; Ambassador of Guyana to China 1976-; kt 1966; *Style* - Sir John Carter, QC; Embassy of Guyana, No 1 Hsui Hsueh Tung Chieh, Chien Kuo Men Wai, China

CARTER, Jeffrey Alan; s of George Thomas Carter; *b* 9 April 1938; *Educ* Whitgift Sch, Imperial Coll London U, Harvard Graduate Sch; *m* 1962, Diana Shirley, nee Aukett; 1 s, 2 da; *Career* chartered engineer; md Babcock Woodall Duckham Ltd 1978-, Babcock Engineering Contractos (Pty) Ltd Johannesburg SA 1980-, dir Coal Processing Consultants Ltd 1980-, Fluidised Combustion Contractors Ltd 1979-, Babcock Contractors Ltd 1979-;

MIMechE; *Style* - Jeffrey Carter Esq; 36 Hurst View rd, Croham Hurst, South Croydon, Surrey (☎ 01 688 6203); Briardene, Loch rd, Bryanston 8, Johannesburg, S Africa (☎ Johannesburg 833 4311)

CARTER, Maj-Gen James Norman; CB (1958), CBE (1955); s of late Capt N H Carter, RN; *b* 26 June 1906; *Educ* Charterhouse, Sandhurst; *m* 1929, Barbara, nee Bovill; 2 da; *Career* 2 Lt Dorset Regt 1926, Asst Chief of Staff (Organisation and Training) SHAPE 1955-57, Maj-Gen 1957, Cdr British Army Staff and Mil Memb British Joint Services Mission Washington 1958-60, Mil Attaché Washington 1960; *Style* - Maj-Gen James Carter, CB, CBE; Fold Farm House, Austwick, via Lancaster

CARTER, John Stanley; CBE (1960); s of Walter Carter; *b* 1900; *Educ* Leeds U; *m* 1926, Doris, nee Harrison; *Career* former Chief Alkali Inspector Min of Housing and Local Govt; *Style* - John Carter Esq, CBE; 21 Glenbuck court, Surbiton, Surrey

CARTER, Lt-Col Maurice Fitzgerald; TD (1952); s of Maurice Frederic Carter; *b* 1 Aug 1913; *Educ* Cheltenham; *Career* Maj 43 Recce Regt NW Europe (despatches); CO Royal Glos Hussars 1958; solicitor; DL Glos 1960; *Style* - Lt-Col Maurice Carter Esq TD DL; The Castle House, Newnham, Glos

CARTER, Malcolm Ogilvy; CIE (1943), MC (1918); s of late Reginald Carter; *b* 2 July 1898; *Educ* Edinburgh Acad, Bedford, Balliol Oxford; *m* 1, 1921, Gwyneth Elaine, nee Platts; 1 da; m 2, 1944, Iris Cowgill, nee Thomson; *Career* entd Indian Colonial Service 1921, Cmmr Chittagong Div and Liaison Officer to 14 Army and 3 TAF 1943-47; Sec South-Western Regional Hospital Bd 1947-63, ret; *Style* - Malcolm Carter Esq, CIE, MC; The Stile House, Vicarage lane, Haselmere, Surrey

CARTER, Air Cdre North; CB (1948), DFC (1935); s of late Lt-Col G L Carter, CIE, IA; *b* 26 Nov 1902; *Educ* Wellington, RAF Coll Cranwell; *m* 1931, Kathleen Graham, nee Machattie; 1 s, 1 da; *Career* joined RAF 1921, Air Cdre 1948, SASO No 205 Group MEAF 1951, Provost Marshal and Chief of Air Force Police 1953, ret 1954; Admin Officer in Public Service N Region Nigeria 1955-63; *Style* - Air Cdre North Carter, CB, DFC; Gould's Bay, Hawkesbury River, PMB Brooklyn, NSW 2253, Australia

CARTER, Air Vice-Marshal Oliver Eric; CBE (1944); s of late Oliver Edward Carter; *b* 1898; *Educ* St Albans; *m* 1919, Gertrude Victoria, nee James; 2 s, 1 da; *Career* RAF Wing-Cdr 1938, Air Cdre 1942, Chief Maintenance Officer S E Asia Air Command to 1944, Dir-Gen Aircraft Supply Govt of India (Air Vice-Marshal) 1944, ret 1946; *Style* - Air Vice-Marshal Oliver Carter, CBE; c/o National and Grindlays Bank Ltd, 13 St James's sq, SW1

CARTER, Peter Anthony; CMG (1970); s of late Thomas Birchall Carter; *b* 16 Jan 1914; *Educ* Charterhouse, Sidney Sussex Cambridge; *m* 1946, Mary Hutchinson, nee Heard; 1 s, 1 da; *Career* Colonial Office Principal 1947-60; Head of British Residual Mission Salisbury 1968-69, British High Cmmr Mauritius 1970-73, FCO 1973, ret 1974; Sr Clerk House of Commons 1974-76; *Style* - Peter Carter Esq, CMG; Forth House, Beech Drive, Kingswood, Surrey (☎ Mogador 2647)

CARTER, Peter Basil; s of late Albert Carter; *b* 10 April 1921; *Educ* Loughborough, Oriel Oxford; *m* 1960, Elizabeth Maxwell (decd); *Career* barr 1947; Fell Wadham Coll Oxford 1949-; JP 1959-; former Visiting Prof various Commonwealth and United States Us; dir University Life Assurance Soc 1969-, chm 1980-; *Style* - Peter Carter Esq, JP; Wadham College, Oxford (☎ 42564)

CARTER, Peers Lee; CMG (1965); s of late Peers Owen Carter; *b* 5 Dec 1916; *Educ* Radley, Ch Ch Oxford; *m* 1940, Joan Eleanor, nee Lovegrove; 1 s; *Career* entd HM Foreign Service 1939, Head of UK Perm Mission Geneva 1961-63, Chief Inspector of HM Diplomatic Service 1966-68, Ambassador to Afghanistan 1968-72, Asst Under-Sec of State FO and Ministerial Interpreter 1973, ret; *Style* -

Peers Carter Esq, CMG; Holgate, Balcombe, Sussex (☎ Balcombe 205)

CARTER, Air Cdre Robert Alfred Copsey; CB (1956), DSO (1942), DFC (1943); s of late Sidney Herbert Carter; *b* 15 Sept 1910; *Educ* Portsmouth G S, RAF Cranwell; *m* 1947, Sarah Ann, nee Peters; 2 s, 1 da; *Career* joined RAF 1927, Air Cdre 1956, SASO Transport Command 1955-58, DPS (A) Air Min 1958-61, AOA RAF Germany 1961-64, ret; *Style* - Air Commodore Robert Carter, CB, DSO DFC; The Old Cottage, Castle Lane, Whaddon, Salisbury, Wilts

CARTER, Robert Owen; CBE (1970); s of Joseph Charles William Carter; *b* 1906; *Educ* Bancroft's Sch, London U; *Career* Research Branch GPO Eng Dept 1933-65, Asst Dir (Res and Dvpt) Communications Electronic Security Dept 1965-70; FIEE; *Style* - Robert Carter Esq, CBE; 8 Grange av, Woodford Green, Essex

CARTER, Robert William Bernard; CMG (1964); s of late William Joseph Carter; *b* 19 Dec 1913; *Educ* St Bees Sch, Trin Oxford; *m* 1945, Joan Violet, nee Magnus; 1 s, 2 da; *Career* former Trade Cmmr Calcutta, Delhi, Accra, Colombo (Princ); Sr Trade Cmmr Karachi 1961-66, Min FCO 1966, Dep High Cmmr Karachi 1966-68, Melbourne 1969-73, ret 1974; *Style* - Robert Carter Esq; The Old Parsonage, Heywood, Westbury, Wilts (☎ Westbury 822194)

CARTER, Air Vice-Marshal Wilfred; CBE (1963), DFC (1943); s of late Samuel Carter; *b* 5 Nov 1912; *Educ* Witney G S; *m* 1950, Margaret Enid, nee Bray; 1 s, 1 da; *Career* joined RAF 1929, Air Cdre 1960, AOA Bomber Command 1965-67, Air Vice-Marshal 1965, ret 1967; dir National Emergency Services Coll Australia; *Style* - Air Vice-Marshal Wilfred Carter, CBE, DFC; Blue Range, Macedon, Vic 3440, Australia

CARTER, William Henry Newton; CBE (1964); s of William Henry Carter; *b* 1903; *Educ* Dean Close Sch, Nottingham U; *m* 1936, da of J West; 2 s; *Career* Princ Inspector of Mines & Quarries Miny of Power 1954, Pres S Cos Instn of Mining Engineers 1954-65; *Style* - William Carter Esq, CBE; 21 Clifton rd, Chesham Bois, Bucks

CARTER, His Honour Sir Walker Kelly; QC (1951); s of late Walter Carter, CBE; *b* 7 July 1899; *Educ* Repton, Sidney Sussex Cambridge; *m* 1925, Phyllis Irene, nee Clarke; 1 da; *Career* barr 1924, bencher 1965; Chm Quarter Sessions Lincs (Parts of Lindsey) 1945-67, (Parts of Kesteven) 1960-67; Official Referee Supreme Court of Judicature 1954-71, Chm Criminal Injuries Compensation Bd 1964-75; kt 1965; *Style* - His Honour Sir Walker Carter, QC; 65 Bedford gdns, W8 (☎ 01 727 9862)

CARTER, Sir William Oscar; s of late Oscar Carter; *b* 12 Jan 1905; *Educ* Swaffham G S, City of Norwich Sch; *m* 1934, Winifred Rose, nee Thompson; *Career* solicitor 1931; consultant partner Hill & Perks (Slrs) Norwich, partner Bird Hill & Co (Slrs) Amsterdam; memb Criminal Injuries Compensation Bd and Law Panel of British Council; former Pres Law Society; dir Mann Egerton & Co Ltd and Tibbenham Hldgs Ltd; liveryman of Glaziers' Co; kt 1972; *Style* - Sir William Carter; 83 Newmarket rd, Norwich (☎ 53772)

CARTER, William Stovold; CMG (1970), CVO (1956); s of late R S Carter; *b* 10 Oct 1915; *Educ* Bec Sch Tooting, Christ's Cambridge; *m* 1944, Barbara Alice Kathleen, nee Dines; 2 s, 1 da; *Career* Colonial Administrative Office (Nigeria) 1939-57; Colonial Office 1959, Commonwealth Office 1966, FCO 1967, Head of Hong Kong Dept 1965-70, Sec Council on Tribunals 1970, ret 1976; *Style* - William Carter Esq, CMG, CVO; Broad Oak Farm, Chiddingly, nr Lewes, E Sussex (☎ Chiddingly 267)

CARTER-JONES, Lewis; MP (L) Eccles 1964-; s of late Tom Jones; *b* 17 Nov 1920; *Educ* Kenfig Hill Council Sch, Bridgend County Sch, Univ Coll of Wales Aberystwyth; *m* 1945, Patricia Hylda, nee Bastiman; 2 da; *Career* former Head of Business Studies Dept Yale Grammar/Technical Sch Denbighshire; contested Chester 1956 (by-election) and 1959; chm Student Finance Cmtee Univ

Coll of Wales; *Style* - Lewis Carter-Jones Esq, MP; Cader Idris, 5 Cefn rd, Rhosnessney, Wrexham, N Wales

CARTLAND, Barbara (Hamilton); da of late Maj Bertram Cartland; *b* 9 July 1901; *m* 1, 1927 (m dis 1932), Alexander George McCorquodale (d 1964); 1 da (Countess Spencer); m 2, 1936, Hugh McCorquodale (d 1963); 2 s; *Career* authoress of over 170 novels; has also published plays, poems, biography and autobiography; former chm St John Ambulance Exhibition Ctee; founder Barbara Cartland Onslow Romany Gypsy Fund; pres Nat Assoc of Health 1966; DStJ 1972; *see* also Ian McCorquodale; *Style* - Miss Barbara Cartland; Camfield Place, Herts (☎ Potters Bar 42612)

CARTLAND, Sir George Barrington; CMG (1956); s of late William Arthur Cartland; *b* 22 Sept 1912; *Educ* Manchester H S, Manchester U, Hertford Oxford; *m* 1937, Dorothy, nee Rayton; 2 s; *Career* Colonial Service (Gold Coast) 1935; Colonial Officer 1944-49; Min of Social Services Uganda 1955, of Education Labour and Information 1958, Chief Sec 1960, Dep Govr 1961-62; Registrar Birmingham U 1963-67, Vice-Chancellor Tasmania U 1968-77; chm Australian National Accreditation Authority for Translators and Interpreters 1977-; KStJ 1971, kt 1963; *Style* - Sir George Cartland, CMG; 5 Aotea rd, Sandy Bay, Hobart, Tasmania 7005

CARTLEDGE, Trevor; s of Albert Cartledge; *b* 26 April 1931; *Educ* Rotherham G S; *m* 1956, Anne Margaret, nee Powell; 2 da; *Career* dir and company sec Advance Tapes (UK) Ltd; *Style* - Trevor Cartledge Esq; 5 St Michael's Close, Ashby de la Zouch, Leics (☎ Ashby 413616)

CARTLIDGE, Hon Mrs (Mary Cecilia); da of Baron Wigg, PC; *b* 1930; *m* 1958, Robert Cartlidge; *Style* - The Hon Mrs Cartlidge; 9 Grigor dve, Inverness

CARTMELL, John; CBE (1960); s of late John Cartmell; *b* 1913; *Educ* Keswick Sch, Pembroke Coll Oxford; *m* 1942, Evelyn Gruffydd, nee Jones; 1 s; *Career* Colonial Audit Dept 1936-61; Princ Miny Pensions and National Insurance 1961-68, Asst Sec Dept of Health and Social Security 1968-74; *Style* - John Cartmell Esq, CBE; Flat 8, Regent House, Lansdown rd, Cheltenham, Glos

CARTWRIGHT, Lady Elizabeth (Betty) Constance; *née* Bertie; OBE (1938); da of 7 Earl of Abingdon (decd); *b* 1895; *m* 1 1914, Maj Sigismund William Joseph Trafford (d 1953); 1 s, 3 da; m 2 1956, Col Henry Antrobus Cartwright, CMG, MC (d 1957); *Career* sr Cmdt ATC 1938-44; *Style* - Lady Betty Cartwright, OBE; 30 Lennox gdns, SW1

CARTWRIGHT, (William) Frederick; CBE (1977); s of late Rev William Digby Cartwright; *b* 13 Nov 1906; *Educ* Rugby; *m* 1937, Sally Chrystobel, nee Wyndham; 2 s, 1 da; *Career* engineer; former dep chm British Steel Corporation; former md Steel Co of Wales Ltd; dir Davy Corp Ltd, BSC (International) Ltd; DL Glamorganshire 1946, High Sheriff 1961; OStJ; *Style* - Frederick Cartwright Esq, CBE, DL; Castle-upon-Alun, St Brides Major, Bridgend, Mid Glam (☎ Southerndown 298)

CARTWRIGHT, Harry; CBE (1979); s of Edwin Harry Cartwright; *b* 16 Sept 1919; *Educ* William Hulme's G S, St John's Cambridge; *m* 1950, Catharine Margaret Carson Bradbury; 2 s; *Career* Dept of Atomic Energy 1949, Chief Engineer 1955; dir Water Reactors 1964-70, Fast Reactor Systems 1970-73, Atomic Energy Establishment Winfrith 1973-; *Style* - Harry Cartwright Esq, CBE; Tabbit's Hill House, Corfe Castle, Wareham, Dorset (☎ Corfe Castle 480 582)

CARTWRIGHT, John Cameron; MP (L) Greenwich Woolwich E 1974-; s of late Aubrey Cartwright; *b* 29 Nov 1933; *Educ* Woking County G S; *m* 1959, Iris June Tant; 1 s, 1 da; *Career* Labour Party Agent 1955-67; political sec Royal Arsenal Co-operative Soc Ltd 1967-72, dir 1972-74; PPS to Sec of State for Education and Science 1976-77; *Style* - John Cartwright Esq, MP; 17 Commonwealth Way, SE2 (☎

01 311 4394)

CARTWRIGHT, Brig John Mael Fox; CBE (1946); s of Rev G F Cartwright; *b* 1904; *Educ* King's Sch Canterbury, RMA; *m* 1940, Pamela, da of Lt-Col Wellesley Hutcheson; 1 s, 2 da; *Career* 2 Lt RA 1924, Staff Coll 1950, Brig 1954, ret 1956; Bursar Welbeck Coll 1957-67; *Style* - Brig John Cartwright, CBE; Barn House, Kingston, Cambridge

CARTWRIGHT, Dame Mary Lucy; DBE (1969); da of late Rev William Cartwright; *b* 17 Dec 1900; *Educ* Godolphin Sch Salisbury, St Hugh's Oxford; *Career* lectr Mathematics 1935-59, Reader 1959-68, Emeritus Reader Cambridge U 1968, Mistress of Girton 1946-68 (and former Staff Fellow), Life Fellow 1968; *Style* - Dame Mary Cartwright, DBE; 38 Sherlock close, Cambridge (☎ 52574)

CARTWRIGHT, Ronald Casper; s of late Joseph William Cartwright; *b* 21 Nov 1919; *Educ* King's Coll Sch Wimbledon; *m* 1, 1947, Ella Margaret, nee Trinnear (d 1978); 1 s, 1 da; m 2, 1980, Isobel Andrews, nee Parrack; *Career* chartered secretary; chm and md Martonair International Ltd and dir subsidiaries; *Style* - Ronald Cartwright Esq; Meriton, Copsem lane, Esher, Surrey

CARVER, Baron (Life Peer 1977); Field-Marshal (Richard) Michael (Power) Carver; GCB (1970, KCB 1966, CB 1957), CBE (1945), DSO (1943) and Bar (1943), MC (1941); s of late Harold Power Carver; *b* 24 April 1915; *Educ* Winchester, Sandhurst; *m* 1947, Edith, da of Lt-Col Sir Henry Lowry-Corry, MC (gs of 3 Earl Belmore); 2 s, 2 da; *Career* 2 Lt R Tank Corps 1935, Command 4 Armoured Bde 1944-47, Lt-Col 1942, Brig 1944; GOC 3 Div (Maj-Gen) 1962-64, Dep Cdr UN Force in Cyprus 1964, Dir Army Staff Duties MOD 1964-66, GOCIC Southern Command 1969-71, CGS 1971-73, Chief of Defence Staff 1973-76, Field-Marshal 1973, Col Cmdt REME 1966-76, Col Cmdt RAC 1973-77; British Resident Commr in Rhodesia 1977-78; *Style* - The Rt Hon the Lord Carver GCB CBE DSO* MC; Wood End House, Wickham, Fareham, Hants (☎ Wickham 832143)

CARVER, Hon Andrew Richard; s of Baron Carver (Life Peer); *b* 1950; *m* 1973, Anne Rosamunde, nee Stewart; *Style* - The Hon Andrew Carver; 18 Hayter rd, SW2

CARVER, James; CB (1978); s of late William Carver; *b* 29 Feb 1916; *Educ* Wigan Mining and Tech Coll; *m* 1944, Elsie, nee Sharrock; 1 s (twin); 2 da; *Career* former asst mine manager; inspector of Mines and Quarries from 1943, HM Chief Inspector of Mines and Quarries 1975-77, memb Health and Safety Exec 1976-77; *Style* - James Carver Esq, CB; 196 Forest rd, Tunbridge Wells, Kent (☎ 26748)

CARVER, Hon John Anthony; s of Baron Carver (Life Peer); *b* 1961; *Style* - The Hon John Carver

CARVER, Hon Susanna Mary; da of Baron Carver (Life Peer); *b* 1948; *Style* - The Hon Susanna Carver; 16 Kelso pla, W8

CARY, Hon Mrs (Clare Louise Katharine); da of Baron Elworthy, KG, GCB, CBE, DSO, MVO, DFC, AFC (Life Peer); *b* 1950; *m* 1975, Anthony Joyce Cary, s of Sir (Arthur Lucius) Michael Cary, KCB; children; *Style* - The Hon Mrs Cary

CARY, Nicolas Robert Hugh; s and h of Sir Roger Cary, 2 Bt; *b* 17 April 1955; *Educ* St Paul's, London U (BA Archaeology); *m* 1979, Pauline Jean, da of Dr Thomas Boyd, MB, ChB, of Grays, Essex; *Career* production assist Sotheby's catalogue dept 1979- (joined Sotheby's 1977); *Recreations* book collecting, typography, cookery; *Style* - Nicolas Cary Esq; 33 Corrance rd, SW2 (☎ 01 733 0321)

CARY, Sir Roger Hugh; 2 Bt (UK 1955); s of Sir Robert Cary, 1 Bt, sometime MP Eccles, Leader of the House 1951-55 and noted for having accumulated more directorships than any other MP (d 1979, twelfth in descent from Robert Cary, MP Barnstaple 1553, who was himself ggs of Philip Cary, MP Devon 1433, whose f m, as his 1 w, Elizabeth, da of Sir Philip

Courtenay, of Powderham; tho' it is not clear whether Philip was the product of the 1 or 2 m, the facts of his birth being c 1400, while his f Sir Robert's was c 1380 and the 2 w d 1448, combine to imply cousinship, albeit remote, between the present Bt and the Earls of Devon; Philip's s, Sir William (beheaded after Tewkesbury), m, as his 1 w, Elizabeth, da of Sir William Powlett, of Heanton St George Somerset, presumably identical with that Sir William Paulett knighted by Henry VI; if so, Sir Roger is distant kin to the Marquesses of Winchester and Earls Poulett) and Hon Lady Cary, *qv*; *b* 8 Jan 1926; *Educ* Ludgrove, Eton, New Coll Oxford; *m* 1, 1948 (m dis 1951), Marilda, da of Maj Philip Pearson-Gregory, MC; 1 da; m 2, 1953, Ann Helen Katharine, nee Brenan; 2 s, 1 da; *Heir* s, Nicolas Cary; *Career* former sub-ed and leader writer The Times and Dep Ed The Listener; Sr Asst 1972-74, Special Asst (Public Affairs) BBC 1974-77 and to md BBC TV 1977-; late Gren Gds; *Clubs* Pratt's; *Style* - Sir Roger Cary, Bt; 23 Bath rd, W4 (☎ 01 994 7293)

CARY, Hon Lady - Hon Rosamond Mary; da of late Col the Hon Alfred Nathaniel Curzon and sis of late 2 Visc Scarsdale; *b* 1893; *m* 1924, Sir Robert Cary, 1 Bt (d 1979); 1 s (present Bt); *Career* raised to the rank of a Viscount's da 1930; *Style* - The Hon Lady Cary; Wrotham Water, Wrotham, Kent

CASE, Air Vice-Marshal Albert Avion; CB (1964), CBE (1957, OBE 1943); s of late Gp-Capt Albert Edward Case; *b* 5 April 1916; *Educ* Imperial Service Coll; *m* 1949, Brenda Margaret, nee Andrews; 1 s, 1 da; *Career* joined RAF 1934, Gp Capt 1953, Air Cdre 1959, Air Vice-Marshal 1962, AOC No 22 Gp Tech Training 1963-66, SASO HQ Coastal Command 1967-69, ret; Gen Sec Hospital Saving Assoc 1969-, Hon Sec British Hospitals Contributory Schemes Assoc 1972-; *Style* - Air Vice-Marshal Albert Case, CB, CBE; 25 Kewferry rd, Northwood, Middx

CASE, David Charles; s of Charles Kendal Case; *b* 18 Oct 1943; *Educ* Oakham Sch, Oxford U; *m* 1967, Anthea Fiendley, nee Stones; 1 da; *Career* art dealer and publisher, dir Christies Publications Ltd; *Style* - David Case Esq; 41 Gibson sq, N1 (☎ 01 607 6898)

CASE, Humphrey John; s of late George Reginald Case; *b* 26 May 1918; *Educ* Charterhouse, St John's Cambridge; *m*; 2 s; m 2, 1979, Jocelyn, nee Herickx; *Career* Keeper Dept of Antiquities Ashmolean Museum Oxford 1973-; chm Charles Case & Son Ltd 1959-; *Style* - Humphrey Case Esq; Pitts Cottage, 187 Thame rd, Warborough, Oxford

CASEY, Hon (Richard Charles) Donn; s of Baron Casey (Life Baron, d 1976); *b* 1931; *Style* - The Hon Donn Casey; 141 Newmarket rd, Cambridge

CASEY, Hon Mrs (Diana Sybil); *née* Eyres Monsell; da of 1 Viscount Monsell, GBE (d 1969); *b* 1907; *m* 1935, Lt-Col Alan Stuart Casey (d 1958); 1 s, 2 da; *Style* - The Hon Mrs Casey; Nutmeadow House, Dumbleton, Evesham, Worcs

CASEY, Baroness - Ethel Marian (Maie) Sumner; da of late Maj-Gen Sir Charles Snodgrass Ryan, KBE, CB, CMG; *m* 1926, Baron Casey (Life Peer, d 1976); 1 s, 1 da; *Style* - The Rt Hon the Lady Casey; Edrington, Berwick, Vic, Aust; 159 Gipps st, E Melbourne, Australia

CASEY, Terence Anthony; CBE (1977); s of Daniel Casey; *b* 6 Sept 1920; *Educ* Holycross nr Ramsgate, Camden Coll, London U; *m* 1944, Catherine Wills; 2 s, 3 da; *Career* former headmaster St Joseph's Sch London; Gen Sec National Assoc of Schoolmasters 1975-; Pres National Fedn of Professional Workers; *Style* - Terence Casey Esq, CBE; 22 Upper Brook st, W1 (☎ 01 629 3916)

CASEY, Thomas William; CBE (1950), MC (1918); s of late Thomas Worrall Casey; *b* 1896; *Educ* Mexborough G S; *m* 1922, Mabel Elise, nee Ray; 1 s, 1 da; *Career* Royal Fusiliers 1914-18; Asst Sec Miny of Pensions & National Insurance 1945-61; *Style* - Thomas Casey Esq, CBE; Flat 8, Lavington ct, 77 Putney Hill, SW15

CASH, Sir Gerald Christopher; KCVO (1977), OBE (1964), JP (1940); s of late

Wilfred Gladstone Cash; *b* 28 May 1917; *Educ* HS Nassau; *m* Dorothy, nee Long; 2 s, 1 da; *Career* barr 1948; memb House of Assembly of Bahamas 1949-62; former member and Pres of Senate; Gov-Gen Bahamas 1979- (Actg 1976-79); *Style* - Sir Gerald Cash, KCVO, OBE, JP; Government House, PO Box N 8301, Nassau, Bahamas (☎ 809 21875)

CASHEL AND EMLY, Archbishop of (RC) 1960-; Most Rev Thomas Morris; s of James Morris; *b* 16 Oct 1914; *Educ* Christian Bros Thurles and Maynooth Coll; *Career* ordained 1939; former Prof of Theology and Vice-Pres St Patrick's Coll Thurles; *Style* - The Most Rev Archbishop Morris; Archbishop's House, Thurles, Co Tipperary, Ireland (☎ 21512)

CASHEL AND OSSORY, Bishop of (901) - Rt Rev John Ward Armstrong; 57 Bp of Cashel (901), 88 Bp of Emly (441), 62 Bp of Waterford (1096), 69 Bp of Lismore (631); s of John Armstrong; *b* 30 Sept 1915; *Educ* Belfast Royal Acad, Trin Coll Dublin; *m* 1941, Doris Winifred, nee Harrison; 2 s, 2 da; *Career* ordained 1938, Dean of St Patrick's Cathedral Dublin 1958-68, Bishop of Cashel, Waterford, Lismore, Ossory, Ferns and Leighlin 1968- (Cashel and Emly, Waterford and Lismore until 1977 when diocese reorganised); *Style* - The Rt Rev the Bishop of Cashel and Ossory; The Palace, Kilkenny, Ireland (☎ 21560)

CASS, Edward Geoffrey; CB (1974), OBE (1951); s of Edward Charles Cass; *b* 10 Sept 1916; *Educ* St Olave's, Univ Coll London, Queen's Oxford; *m* 1941, Ruth Powley; 4 da; *Career* economist and statistician; Asst Under-Sec of State MOD 1965-72, Dep Under-Sec of State 1972-76; Govr Reserve Bank of Rhodesia 1978-; *Style* - Edward Cass Esq, CB, OBE; 60 Rotherwick rd, NW11 (☎ 01 455 1664)

CASS, Sir John Patrick; OBE (1960); s of Philip Cass; *b* 7 May 1909; *Educ* Christian Bros Coll NSW; *m* 1932, Velma Mostyn; 2 s; *Career* former sr vice-pres Australian NFU; dir Farmers and Graziers Co-op Co 1962-; kt 1978; *Style* - Sir John Cass, OBE; Stoney Ridge, Crowther, NSW 2692, Australia

CASSAB, Judy; CBE (1969); da of late Imre Kaszab; *b* 15 Aug 1920; *Educ* Budapest and Prague; *m* 1939, John Kampfner; 2 s; *Career* artist; one-man shows 1953-76; works in galleries in UK, Hungary and Australia; *Style* - Miss Judy Cassab, CBE; 156 Victoria rd, Bellevue Hill, NSW 2023, Australia (☎ 389 4466)

CASSEL, His Honour Judge Sir Harold Felix; 3 Bt (1920 UK), TD (1975), QC (1970); s of Sir Felix Cassel, 1 Bt, PC, QC (d 1953); suc bro, Sir Francis Cassel, 2 Bt 1969; *b* 8 Nov 1916; *Educ* Stowe, CCC Oxford; *m* 1, 1940 (m dis 1963), Ione Jean, nee Barclay; 3 s, 1 da; m 2, 1963, Mrs Eileen Elfrida Smedley, nee Faulkner; *Heir* s, Timothy Cassel; *Career* barr 1946, Dep Chm Herts Quarter Sessions 1959-62, Recorder of Great Yarmouth 1968-71, a Recorder of the Crown Court 1972-76, a Circuit Judge 1976-; JP Herts 1959-62; *Style* - His Hon Judge Sir Harold Cassel Bt TD QC; 49 Lennox gdns, SW1 (☎ 01 584 2721)

CASSEL, Timothy Felix Harold; s and h of His Hon Judge Sir Harold Cassel, Bt, TD, QC; *b* 30 April 1942; *Educ* Eton; *m* 1971 (m dis 1977), Mrs Jenifer Samuel, nee Puckle; 1 s, 1 da; *Career* barr 1965; *Style* - Timothy Cassel Esq; 15 Kildare gdns, W2

CASSELS, His Honour Francis Henry; TD (1945); s of late Sir James Dale Cassels; *b* 3 Sept 1910; *Educ* Sedbergh, CCC Cambridge; *m* 1939, Evelyn Dorothy, nee Richardson (d 1979); 1 s, 1 da; *Career* barr 1932, Dep Chm County of London Sessions 1954-65, Chm SW London Quarter Sessions 1965-72, Sr Circuit Judge Inner London Crown Court 1972-79; *Style* - His Honour Francis Cassels, TD; 14 Buckingham House, Courtlands, Richmond, Surrey (☎ 01 940 4180)

CASSELS, Gervase de la Poer; CBE (1971); s of late Walter Seton Cassels; *b* 1915; *Educ* Marlborough, St John's Oxford; *m* 1947, Mary Edith, nee Cresswell; 2 s, 1 da; *Career* Colonial Admin Service 1938-60, British Mil Admin in Cyprus 1953-60; with UNRWA for Palestine Refugees in Near East 1960-71, dir 1967-71; *Style* - Gervase de la Poer

Cassels Esq, CBE; 17 Five Mile Drive, Oxford

CASSELS, Field-Marshal Sir (Archibald) James (Halkert); GCB (1961, CB 1950), KBE (1952, CBE 1944), DSO (1944); s of late General Sir Robert A Cassels, GCB, GCSI, DSO; *b* 28 Feb 1907; *Educ* Rugby, Sandhurst; *m* 1, 1935, Joyce (d 1978), da of late Brig-Gen Henry Kirk; 1 s; m 1978, Mrs Kenneth Dickson; *Career* 2 Lt Seaforth Highlanders 1926 (Col 1957-61), Adjt-Gen to the Forces 1963-64, CGS 1965-68, Field-Marshal 1968, Col Queen's Own Highlanders (Seaforth and Camerons) 1961-66, Col Cmdt Army Physical Training Corps 1961-66, Corps of Royal Mil Police 1957-68, ADC (Gen) to HM the Queen 1960-63; *Style* - Field-Marshal Sir James Cassels, GCB, KBE, DSO; Pitearn, Alves, Forres, Moray

CASSELS, John Seton; CB (1978); s of Alastair Cassels; *b* 10 Oct 1928; *Educ* Sedbergh Sch Yorks, Trin Cambridge; *m* 1956, Mary Whittington; 2 s, 2 da; *Career* Miny of Labour 1954, late Under-Sec National Bd for Prices and Incomes, ch exec Training Services Agency 1972-75, dir Manpower Services Cmmn 1975-; *Style* - John Cassels Esq CB; 10 Beverley rd, Barnes, SW 13 (☎ 01 876 6270)

CASSELS, Vice-Adm Simon Alastair Cassillis; CBE (1976); s of late Cdr A G Cassels, RN; *b* 5 March 1928; *Educ* RNC Dartmouth; *m* 1962, Jillian Kannreuther; 1 s, 1 da; *Career* Midshipman 1945, Commanding Officer HMS Tiger 1976-78, Rear-Adm 1978, Asst Chief of Naval Staff (Operational Requirements) 1978-, Vice-Adm 1980-; *Style* - Vice-Admiral Simon Cassels, CBE; The Old Rectory, Exton, Southampton

CASSIDI, Adm Sir (Arthur) Desmond; KCB (1978); s of late Cdr Robert Alexander Cassidi; *b* 26 Jan 1925; *Educ* RNC Dartmouth; *m* 1950, Dorothy Sheelagh Marie, nee Scott (d 1974); 1 s, 2 da; *Career* Midshipman and Sub-Lt 1942-45, Flag Officer Carriers and Amphibious Ships 1974-75, Dir-Gen Naval Manpower Training 1975-77, Flag Officer Naval Air Command 1978-79, Chief of Naval Personnel and Second Sea Lord 1979-; *Style* - Adm Sir Desmond Cassidi, KCB; 15 Roupell st, SE1 (☎ 01 928 2955)

CASSIE, Arnold Blatchford David; CBE (1955); s of late D A Morris Cassie; *b* 17 May 1905; *Educ* Edinburgh U, Christ's Cambridge, London U; *m* 1939, Catherine Dufour, nee Halahan; 1 s, 2 da; *Career* former ch physicist Wool Industries Res Assoc, dir of Research 1950-67; *Style* - Arnold Cassie Esq, CBE; White Heather, Crescent Walk, Ferndown, Dorset (☎ 873705)

CASSIE, William Fisher; CBE (1966); *b* 29 June 1905; *Educ* Grove Acad Dundee, St Andrews U; *m* 1933, Mary Robertson Reid; *Career* engineer; lectr Queen's U Belfast, Univ Coll Cardiff, Univ Coll London 1940-70, Prof of Civil Engineering Newcastle U 1943-70, now Emeritus; consultant partner Waterhouse & Partners 1970-74; *Style* - William Cassie Esq, CBE; Benachie, Lochinver, by Lairg, Sutherland (☎ Lochinver 302)

CASSILLIS, Earl of; Archibald Angus Charles Kennedy; s and h of 7 Marquess of Ailsa, OBE, DL; *b* 13 Sept 1956; *m* 1979, Dawn Leslie Anne, da of David Keen, of Paris; 2 da (Lady Rosemary Kennedy, Lady Alicia-Jane Kennedy b 11 July 1981); *Heir* bro, Lord David Kennedy; *Recreations* shooting, skiing, youth work; *Clubs* New (Edinburgh); *Style* - Earl of Cassillis; Cassillis House, Maybole, Ayrshire (☎ Dalrymple 310)

CASSON, Sir Hugh Maxwell; KCVO (1978); s of late Randal Casson; *b* 23 May 1910; *Educ* Eastbourne Coll, St John's Cambridge; *m* 1938, Margaret MacDonald, nee Troup (designer and architect); 3 da; *Career* dir of Architecture Festival of Britain 1948-51, Prof Royal Coll of Art 1953-75, Pres Roy Academy 1976-; kt 1952; *Style* - Sir Hugh Casson, KCVO; 35 Victoria rd, W8; (office) 35 Thurloe pla, SW7 (☎ 01 584 4581)

CASSTLES, Lt-Col David Stewart; TD; s of Joseph Cecil Casstles (d 1956); *b* 5 Mar 1936; *Educ* Brentwood Sch, Cambridge U; *m* 1964, Lynne Frances, nee

Alexandre; 1 s (Andrew b 1969), 1 da (Amanda b 1966); *Career* Lt-Col cmding 7 (Yeomanry) Signal Regt, investment banker; *Recreations* opera going, dining, shooting, volunteer soldiering; *Clubs* Army and Navy; *Style* - Lt-Col David Casstles, TD; Glovers, Little Leighs, Chelmsford, Essex (☎ Great Leighs 258)

CASSWELL, Hon Mrs (Helen Jennifer Frances); *née* Annesley; da of 14 Viscount Valentia, MC, MRCS, LRCP; *b* 1935; *m* 1957, Simon FitzRoy Casswell; 1 s, 2 da; *Style* - The Hon Mrs Casswell; The Limes Farm, Smarden, nr Ashford, Kent

CASTELFRANCO AND MARANO, Prince (Naples 1628 by Philip IV of Spain); Renato Carlos José Sersale di Cerisano; also Duke of Cerisano; s of Prince Luigi Sersale di Cerisano, Dr, of Buenos Aires; *b* 21 March 1950; *Educ* State U Buenos Aires, Salvador U Argentina; *m* 1978, Liliana, da of Col Cosme Scocozza; 1 s; *Heir* s, Prince Francisco (b 23 Sept 1980); *Career* late ec consultant Chas T Main & Assoc in Argentina; with Argentine For Serv 1977-, Consul-Adjoint Argentine Republic at Hong Kong 1981; *Recreations* reading; *Clubs* Jockey (Buenos Aires); *Style* - Prince Renato di Castelfranco and Marano (Duke di Cerisano); Flat A, I Olympian Mansion, 9 Conduit rd, Hong Kong; Juncal 1284, 9 Piso A (1062), Buenos Aires; 5-11 S Bay Close, Kingly Court 1B, Repulse Bay, Hong Kong

CASTLE, Rt Hon Barbara Anne; PC (1964), MEP (L) Gtr Manchester N 1979-; Baroness Castle; da of Frank Betts; *b* 6 Oct 1911; *Educ* Bradford Girls' G S, St Hugh's Oxford; *m* 1944, Edward Cyril Castle (d 1979), later Baron Castle (Life Peer 1974); *Career* MP (L) Blackburn 1945-50, Blackburn E 1950-55, Blackburn 1955-79, memb National Exec Cmtee of Labour Party 1950-79, Min of Transport 1965-68, First Sec of State and Sec of State for Employment and Productivity 1968-70, Opposition Spokesman on Social Security 1971, Sec of State for Social Services 1974-76, v-chm Socialist Gp European Parlt 1979-; *Style* - The Rt Hon Barbara Castle, PC, MEP; House of Commons, SW1

CASTLE, Norman Henry; s of Hubert Castle; *b* 1 Sept 1913; *Educ* Ludlow G S; *m* 1939, Ivy Olive Watson; 1 da; *Career* chm Wace Gp Ltd, Condale Investments Ltd, Smith Castle & Co Ltd, Hookcastle Ltd; Underwriting Memb Lloyd's; dir Ashbourne Investments Ltd, Incentive Investments Ltd, E S Schwab & Co Ltd, Chelton Hldgs Ltd; *Style* - Norman Castle Esq; The Penthouse, 39 Courcels, Black Rock, Brighton, E Sussex

CASTLE STEWART, 8 Earl (I 1800); Sir Arthur Patrick Avondale Stuart; 15 Bt (S 1628); also Baron Castle Stuart (I 1619) and Viscount Castle Stuart (I 1793); s of 7 Earl Castle Stewart, MC (d 1961), and Eleanor, da of Solomon Guggenheim; *b* 18 Aug 1928; *Educ* Eton, Trin Cambridge; *m* 1952, Edna, nee Fowler; 1 s, 1 da; *Heir* s, Viscount (Castle) Stuart (tho' Castle Stuart is the full title in the patents, the habit seems to have grown up since 1880 of designating the s & h Viscount Stuart); *Career* late Lt Scots Gds; farmer; MBIM; *Style* - The Rt Hon the Earl Castle Stewart; Stone House, East Pennard, nr Shepton Mallet, Somerset (☎ Ditcheat 240); Stuart Hall, Stewartstown, Co Tyrone (☎ Stewartstown 208)

CASTLE STEWART, Eleanor, Countess - Eleanor May; da of Solomon R Guggenheim; *m* 1920, 7 Earl Castle Stewart (d 1961); 2 s; *Style* - The Rt Hon Eleanor, Countess Castle Stewart; Old Lodge, Nutley, Sussex

CASTLEMAINE, 8 Baron (I 1812); Roland Thomas John Handcock; s of late 7 Baron (1973); *b* 22 April 1943; *Educ* Campbell Coll Belfast; *m* 1969, Pauline Anne, nee Bainbridge; *Heir* cous, Clifford Handcock; *Career* Maj Army Air Corps; *Style* - The Rt Hon the Lord Castlemaine; c/o Lloyds Bank, Aldershot, Hants

CASTLEMAN, Christopher Norman Anthony; s of late M S Phillips; *b* 23 June 1941; *Educ* Harrow, Clare Cambridge; *m* 1, 1965, Sarah Victoria, nee Stockdale (d 1979); 1 s, 1 da; m 2, 1980, Caroline Clare, nee Westcott; *Career* merchant banker; joined M Samuel & Co 1963, md Hill Samuel Gp (SA) Ltd 1978-80, ch exec Hill Samuel Gp Ltd 1980-; *Style* - Christopher

Castleman Esq; 39 Compton rd, N1 (☎ 01 226 0078)

CASTLEREAGH, Viscount; Frederick Aubrey Vane-Tempest-Stewart; s (by 2 m) and h of 9 Marq of Londonderry; *b* 6 Sept 1972; *Style* - Viscount Castlereagh

CASWELL, Rear-Adm Arthur Frederick; CBE (1971); s of F J Caswell; *b* 25 June 1915; *Educ* Kings Sch Rochester; *m* 1940, Eileen Margaret, nee Tonkin; 3 s; *Career* joined RN 1940, Capt 1961, Asst Ch of Staff (Logistics) on staff of SACEUR 1969, Rear-Adm 1969, ret 1971; *Style* - Rear-Admiral Arthur Caswell, CBE; 67 Portchester rd, Fareham, Hants (☎ 2461)

CASWELL, Rev Canon Colin Douglas Charles; CBE (1974); s of Colin George Caswell; *b* 7 Nov 1909; *Educ* Wanganui Collegiate Sch and Coll House Christchurch NZ; *m* 1941, Nellie Frances Creed Meredith; 1 s, 1 da; *Career* ordained 1940, Rural Dean of Westland 1946, City Missioner (diocese of Auckland) 1946-67, dir Selwyn Foundation 1967-73, Hon Canon St Mary's Cathedral Auckland 1964, ret; *Style* - The Rev Canon Colin Caswell, CBE; 22a Tui Glen rd, Auckland 10, New Zealand (☎ 488 683)

CASWELL, Donald; s of late George Clement Caswell; *b* 17 April 1926; *Educ* Wilsons G S; *m* 1, Margaret Sheila (d 1969); 1 s, 1 da; m 2, 1970, Susan Ann, nee Thompson; *Career* chartered accountant; gp dep dir of finance and treasurer Inchcape Gp 1953-; FICA, FCT; *Style* - Donald Caswell Esq; Old Linkfield, Hatchlands rd, Redhill, Surrey

CATER, Sir Jack; KBE (1979, CBE 1973, MBE 1956); s of Alfred Cater; *b* 21 Feb 1922; *Educ* Sir George Monoux G S Walthamstow; *m* 1950, Peggy Gwenda Richards; 1 s, 2 da; *Career* Colonial Admin Service Hong Kong 1946, Dir Commerce and Industry 1970-72, Sec for Information 1972, for Home Affairs and Information 1973, Chief Secretary 1978-; *Style* - Sir Jack Cater, KBE; Victoria House, Hong Kong (☎ 5 96696)

CATER, John Robert; s of late Sir John Cater; *b* 25 April 1919; *Educ* George Watson's Coll Edinburgh, Jesus Cambridge; *m* 1946, Isobel Calder Ritchie; 1 da; *Career* chm The Distillers Co 1976-, chm The Scotch Whisky Assoc 1976-; *Style* - John Cater Esq; 20 St James's sq, SW1 (☎ 01 930 1040)

CATHCART, 6 Earl (UK 1814); Alan Cathcart; CB (1973), DSO (1945), MC (1944); also 15 Lord Cathcart (S *c* 1447), Baron Greenock and Viscount Cathcart (both UK 1807); s of 5 Earl (d 1927); *b* 22 Aug 1919; *Educ* Eton, Magdalene Cambridge; *m* 1946, Rosemary Clare Marie Gabrielle (d 1980), da of late Air-Cdre Sir Henry Smyth-Osborne, CMG, CBE; 1 s, 2 da; *Heir* s, Lord Greenock; *Career* 2 Lt Scots Gds 1939; Brig Operations Div SHAPE 1967-69, Maj-Gen 1969, GOC Yorks Dist 1969-70, GOC Berlin (British Sector) 1970-73, ret; Brig Roy Co Archers (Queen's Body Guard for Scotland); *Style* - The Rt Hon the Earl Cathcart CB DSO MC; 2 Pembroke gdns, W8 (☎ 01 602 4535); Auchindoune, Cawdor, Nairn

CATHERWOOD, Sir (Henry) Frederick (Ross); MEP (C) Cambridgeshire 1979-; s of late Harold Matthew Stuart; *b* 30 Jan 1925; *Educ* Shrewsbury, Clare Cambridge; *m* 1954, Elizabeth, nee Lloyd-Jones; 2 s, 1 da; *Career* chartered accountant; chm British Inst of Management 1974-76, chm British Overseas Trade Bd 1975-79, chm European Parly Cmtee on External Economic Relations 1979-; chm Wittenborg Automat Ltd, dir John Laing Ltd, The Goodyear Tyre and Rubber Co (GB) Ltd; kt 1971; *Style* - Sir Frederick Catherwood, MEP; 25 Woodville gdns, W5 (☎ 01 997 4117); Sutton Hall, Balsham, Cambridgeshire

CATLING, Sir Richard Charles; CMG (1956), OBE (1951); s of late William Catling; *b* 22 Aug 1912; *Educ* Leiston and Bungay G S; *m* 1951, Mary Joan (d 1974), da of Rev R W M Lewis; *Career* entd Colonial Service 1935, Cmmr of Police Kenya 1954-63 (despatches), Inspr-Gen Kenya Police 1963-64; kt 1964, OStJ; *Style* - Sir Richard Catling, CMG, OBE; Hall Fen House, Irstead, Norfolk

CATO, Hon Sir Arnott Samuel; PC (1976 Barbados); *b* 24 Sept 1912; *Educ* St Vincent G S, Edinburgh U; *Career* formerly surgeon in private practice; Memb and Pres Senate of Barbados 1976-; kt 1977; *Style* - The Hon Sir Arnott Cato, PC; Senate House, Bridgetown, Barbados

CATOR, Lady (Wilhelmina) Joan Mary; *née* Fitz-Clarence; da of late Maj the Hon Harold Edward Fitz-Clarence MC and sis of 5 Earl of Munster (d 1975); *b* 1904; *m* 1, 1928, Oliver Birkbeck (d 1952); 2 s, 1 da; m 2, 1961, Lt-Col Henry John Cator, MC (d 1965); *Career* raised to the rank of an Earl's da 1928; *Style* - Lady Joan Cator; Little Massingham House, King's Lynn, Norfolk

CATOR, Lady Penelope Anne; *née* Rous; da of 4 Earl of Stradbroke; *b* 1932; *m* 1, 1950 (m dis 1960), Cdr Ian Dudley Stewart Forbes, DSC, RN, s of late Lt-Col James Stewart Forbes (gs of late Sir Charles Forbes, 3 Bt) by his 1 w Angela, nee St Clair-Erskine, da of 4 Earl of Rosslyn; 1 s, 2 da; m 2, 1961 (m dis 1969), John Cator, s of late Col Henry Cator, MC, JP, DL, of Woodbastwick Hall, Norfolk; *Style* - Lady Penelope Cator; 26 Cambridge st, SW1

CATTELL, George Bernard; s of late Harold William Kingston Cattell; *b* 23 March 1920; *Educ* Royal G S Colchester, Camberley, Royal Mil Coll of Science; *m* 1951, Agnes Jean, nee Hardy; 3 s, 1 da; *Career* with Rootes Gp and Chrysler Organisation 1960-68 (former dir of manufacturing UK Chrysler); dir of Manpower and Productivity Services Dept of Employment and Producitivity 1968-70; gp md FMC Ltd, ch exec NFU Hldgs Ltd; *Style* - George Cattell Esq; Little Cheveney, Yalding, Kent (☎ Hunton 365)

CATTO, 2 Baron (1936 UK); Sir Stephen Gordon Catto; 2 Bt (1921 UK); s of 1 Baron (d 1959); *b* 14 Jan 1923; *Educ* Eton, Trin Cambridge; *m* 1, 1948 (m dis 1965), Josephine Innes, nee Packer; 2 s, 2 da; m 2, 1966, Margaret, nee Forrest; 1 s, 1 da; *Heir* s, Hon Innes Catto; *Career* chm Morgan Grenfell & Co, Yule Catto & Co Ltd, London Bd Australian Mutual Provident Soc; dir GEC Co Ltd, News International Ltd, Anglo-American Securities Corp; dir Times Newspaper Hldgs 1981- *Style* - The Rt Hon Lord Catto; Flat 6, 12 Charles st, W1; Morgan Grenfell & Co Ltd, 23 Great Winchester St, EC2

CATTO, Hon Alexander Gordon; 2 s of 2 Baron Catto by his 1 w Josephine; *b* 22 June 1952; *Educ* Westminster; *m* 1981, Elizabeth Scott, da of Maj T P Boyes, of Brookvale Cottage, Whitford, Devon: *Style* -The Hon Alexander Catto

CATTO, Hon Ariane Madeleine Gordon; da (by 1 m) of 2 Baron Catto; *b* 1960; *Style* - The Hon Ariane Catto

CATTO, Hon Christina Victoria Gordon; da (by 1 m) of 2 Baron Catto; *b* 1955; *Style* - The Hon Christina Catto

CATTO, Hon Georgina Lucinda Gordon; da (by 2 m) of 2 Baron Catto; *b* 1969

CATTO, Hon Innes Gordon; s (by 1 m) and h of 2 Baron Catto; *b* 7 Aug 1950; *Educ* Grenville Coll; *Style* - The Hon Innes Catto

CATTO, Hon Isabel Ida Gordon; OBE (1952); da of late 1 Baron Catto; *b* 1912; *Career* Govr of PNEU Schs; World Pres YWCA 1955-63, Pres YWCA of Gt Britain 1966-72; *Style* - The Hon Isabel Catto, OBE; 61 Cadogan gdns, SW3

CATTO, Hon James Stuart Gordon; s (by 2 m) of 2 Baron Catto; *b* 1966

CAUGHEY, Sir Thomas Harcourt Clarke; KBE (1972); s of James Marsden Caughey; *b* 4 July 1911; *Educ* King's Coll Auckland; *m* 1939, Patricia Mary, da of Hon Sir George Finlay; 1 s, 2 da; *Career* dep chm British Insurance Co Ltd 1978-, chm Smith & Caughey Ltd 1975- (md 1962-); former chm Auckland Hosps Bd, pres Auckland Medical Foundation 1978-; CStJ; *Style* - Sir Thomas Caughey, KBE; 7 Judges Bay rd, Auckland, New Zealand

CAULFIELD, Hon Mr Justice; Hon Sir Bernard; QC (1961); s of late John Caulfield; *b* 24 April 1914; *Educ* St Francis Xavier's Coll, Liverpool U; *m* 1953, Sheila

Mary, nee Herbert; 3 s, 1 da; *Career* solicitor 1940, barr 1947; a Recorder of Coventry 1964-68, a Judge of the High Court of Justice (Queen's Bench Div) 1968-, Presiding Judge N Circuit 1976-80; kt 1968; *Style* - The Hon Mr Justice Caulfield, QC; Royal Courts of Justice, WC2

CAULFIELD, John Day; s of late Eric St George Caulfield and h of uncle, 13 Viscount Charlemont; *b* 19 March 1934; *m* 1, 1964, Judith Ann, nee Dodd (d 1971); 1 s, 1 da; m 2, 1972, Janet Evelyn, nee Nancekivell; *Style* - John Caulfield Esq; 39 Rossburn drive, Etobicoke, Ontario M9C 2P9, Canada

CAULFIELD, Hon Patricia St George; da of late 9 Visc Charlemont; *b* 1920; *Career* 3 Officer WRNS 1939-45; *Style* - The Hon Patricia Caulfield; 55 New rd, Lewes, E Sussex

CAUSLEY, Charles; s of Charles Causley; *b* 24 Aug 1917; *Educ* Launceston National Sch, Horwell G S, Launceston Coll, Peterborough Training Coll; *Career* poet; former literary ed Signature and Apollo BBC W Region Radio; Queen's Gold Medal for Poetry 1967; *Style* - Charles Causley Esq; 2 Cyprus Well, Launceston, Cornwall (☎ Launceston 2731)

CAUTE, (John) Caute; *b* 16 Dec 1936; *Educ* Edinburgh Acad, Wellington, Wadham Oxford; *m* 1, 1961 (m dis 1970), Catherine Shuckburgh; 2 s; m 2, 1973, Martha Bates; 2 da; *Career* former Fellow All Souls Oxford and Reader in Social and Political Theory Brunel U; literary ed New Statesman 1979-; playwright and author; *Style* - David Caute Esq; 41 Westcroft sq, W6

CAVAN, 12 Earl of (I 1647); Michael Edward Oliver Lambart; TD; also Lord Lambart and Baron of Cavan (I 1617), and Viscount Kilcoursie (I 1647); s of 11 Earl (d 1950) and Audrey (gda of Sir Robert Loder, 1 Bt); *b* 29 Oct 1911; *Educ* Radley; *m* 1947, Essex Lucy, da of late Henry Cholmondeley (gs of 1 Baron Delamere); 2 da; *Heir* cous, Roger Cavan; *Career* Lt-Col (ret) Shropshire Yeo (Cmdg 1955-58); Hon Col C Sqdn Queen's Own Mercian Yeo TAVR 1974-77; Vice Lord-Lt Salop 1975- (DL 1959); *Style* - The Rt Hon the Earl of Cavan TD, HM Vice Lord-Lieut for Salop; The Glebe House, Stockton, Shifnal, Shropshire (☎ Norton 236)

CAVAZZA, Lady Charlotte Sarah Alexandra; *née* Chetwynd-Talbot; da (by 1 m) of late 21 Earl of Shrewsbury and Waterford; *b* 1938; *m* 1965, Camillo Cavazza dei Conti Cavazza; 2 s, 1 da; *Style* - Lady Charlotte Cavazza; S Felice del Benaco, Brescia, Italy

CAVE, Sir Charles Edward Coleridge; 4 Bt (UK 1896), JP (Devon 1972), DL (1977); s of Sir Edward Cave, 3 Bt (d 1946); *b* 28 Feb 1927; *Educ* Eton; *m* 1957, Mary Elizabeth, da of John Francis Gore, CVO; 4 s; *Heir* s, John Cave; *Career* formerly Lt Devonshire Regt; High Sheriff of Devon 1969; FRICS; *Style* - Sir Charles Cave, Bt, JP, DL; Sidbury Manor, Sidmouth, Devon (☎ Sidbury 207)

CAVE, John Arthur; s of Ernest Cave; *b* 30 Jan 1915; *Educ* Loughborough G S; *m* 1937, Peggy, nee Browne; 2 s, 2 da; *Career* dir Midland Bank 1975-; chm Forward Trust Ltd, Midland Bank Finance Corp Ltd, Midland Montagu Leasing Ltd 1975-; FIB; *Style* - John Cave Esq; Dolphin House, Centre Cliff, Southwold, Suffolk (☎ Southwold 722232)

CAVE, John Charles; s and h of Sir Charles Cave, 4 Bt; *b* 8 Sept 1958; *Style* - John Cave Esq

CAVE, Sir Richard Guy; MC (1944); s of William Cave; *b* 16 March 1920; *Educ* Tonbridge, Gonville and Caius Cambridge; *m* 1957, Dorothy Fry; 2 s, 2 da; *Career* dir Tunnel Hldgs Ltd, Tate & Lyle Ltd; chm Thorn Electrical Industries Ltd 1976-, kt 1976; *Style* - Sir Richard Cave, MC; Thamescote, Chiswick Mall, W4 (☎ 01 994 8017)

CAVE, Sir Richard Philip; KCVO (1977, MVO 1969), CB 1975; s of late Charles John Philip Cave; *b* 26 April 1912; *Educ* Ampleforth, Trin Cambridge, Herts Inst of Agriculture, Coll of Estate

Management; *m* 1936, Margaret Mary, nee Perceval; 1 s; *Career* Taxing Officer of Judicial Costs House of Lords 1957-77, Sec Assoc of Lieutenants of Counties and Custodes Rotulorum 1946-59 and 1964-77, Crown Examiner in Peerage Cases 1953-77, Princ Clerk Judicial Dept House of Lords 1959-77, Fourth Clerk at the Table (Judicial) House of Lords 1959-77; founder and pres Multiple Sclerosis Soc of Great Britain and N Ireland (former chm); DL Greater London 1973; *Style* - Sir Richard Cave, KCVO, CB, DL; Watergate, 34 Ham Common, Richmond, Surrey (☎ 01 940 8014)

CAVE-BROWN-CAVE, Dorothea, Lady - Dorothea Plewman; da of Robert Greene Dwen; *m* 1923, Sir Clement Charles Cave-Brown-Cave, 15 Bt (d 1945); 1 s; *Style* - Dorothea, Lady Cave-Brown-Cave

CAVE-BROWN-CAVE, John Robert Charles; s and h of Sir Robert Cave-Brown-Cave, 16 Bt; *b* 22 June 1957

CAVE-BROWN-CAVE, Sir Robert; 16 Bt (E 1641); s of Sir Clement Cave-Brown-Cave, 15 Bt (d 1945); *b* 8 June 1929; *Educ* St George's Sch Vancouver, Univ Sch Victoria, British Columbia U; *m* 1954, Lois Shirley, nee Huggard; 1 s, 1 da; *Heir* s, John Cave-Brown-Cave; *Career* pres Cave & Co Ltd, Seaboard Chemicals Ltd *Style* - Sir Robert Cave-Brown-Cave, Bt; 6087 Wiltshire st, Vancouver, British Columbia, Canada

CAVENAGH-MAINWARING, Rafe Gordon Dutton; s of late Maj James Gordon Cavenagh-Mainwaring; *b* 20 July 1906; *Educ* Cheltenham Coll; *m* 1931, Rosemary Mainwaring, nee Cudmore; 1 s; *Career* landowner; JP Staffs 1932-35, High Sheriff 1954-55, Patron of the Living of Whitmore, 33 Hereditary Lord of the Manors of Whitmore and Biddulph; *Style* - Rafe Cavenagh-Mainwaring Esq; Whitmore Hall, Whitmore, nr Newcastle, Staffs (☎ Whitmore 680235); 22 Lakeman st, N Adelaide, S Australia 5006 (☎ Adelaide 267 4294)

CAVENAGH-MAINWARING, Guy; s of Rafe Gordon Cavenagh-Mainwaring; *b* 22 Feb 1934 *Educ* privately; *m* 1961, Margery Christine Rachel, nee Robbins; 1 s, 3 da; *Career* landowner and farmer; High Sheriff of Staffs 1977-78; *Style* - Guy Cavenagh-Mainwaring Esq; Hillside Farm, Whitmore, Staffs (☎ Whitmore 680478)

CAVENAGH-MAINWARING, Maurice Kildare; DSO (1940); s of late Maj James Gordon Cavenagh-Mainwaring; *b* 13 April 1908; *Educ* Dartmouth; *m* 1933, Iris Mary, da of Col Carles Denaro, OBE; 1 s; *Career* Capt RN 1951, Naval Attaché Paris 1957-60, ret; ADC to HM the Queen 1960; joined Simpson (Piccadilly) Ltd 1961; *Style* - Maurice Cavenagh-Mainwaring Esq, DSO; 47 Cadogan gdns, SW3 (☎ 01 584 7870); Apollo Court, St Julians, Malta (☎ 512712)

CAVENDISH, Anthony John; s of George Henry Frederick Cavendish (d 1932); *b* 20 July 1927; *Educ* Lyceum Alpinum, London U (BA); *m* 1980, Elspeth Gail, da of Montague Frank MacDonald; *Career* HM Foreign Service 1948-1953, for correspondent UPI, France, Poland, Hungary, M East 1953-1960, banker, dir Brandts 1972-1975, Hong Kong Shanghai Bank 1975-78, pres and chm Ovin Industries A G 1978-, dir Caparo Group Ltd 1978-; *Recreations* cooking, music, winter sports; *Clubs* Carlton, Cavalry and Guards, Special Forces, Roy Southern Yacht, Travellers Paris, St Moritz Tobogganing; *Style* - Anthony Cavendish Esq; Lowfields, Hartley Wintney, Hants (☎ 3124)

CAVENDISH, Lady Celina; da of Marquess of Hartington, *qv*; *b* 1971

CAVENDISH, Hon Caroline Laurence Patricia; da of 7 Baron Waterpark; *b* 3 March 1952; *Style* - The Hon Caroline Cavendish

CAVENDISH, Lady Elizabeth Georgiana Alice; MVO (1976); da of late 10 Duke of Devonshire, KG, MBE, TD; *b* 1926; *Career* JP London 1961; appointed an Extra Lady-in-Waiting to HRH Princess Margaret 1960; *Style* - Lady Elizabeth Cavendish, MVO, JP; 19

Radnor walk, SW3 (☎ 01 352 0774); Moor View, Edensor, Bakewell, Derbyshire (☎ Baslow 2204)

CAVENDISH, Lady Gweneth Frida; *née* Ponsonby; JP; da of late 9 Earl of Bessborough, GCMG, PC, by Roberte, da of Baron de Neuflize, of Paris; *b* 1888 *m* 1, 1913, Hon Windham Baring (d 1922), s of 1 Earl of Cromer; 2 s; m 2, 1926, Col Ralph Henry Voltelin Cavendish, CBE, MVO, DL (d 1968); *Career* has Order of Mercy; *Style* - Lady Gweneth Cavendish, JP; Yaldham Manor, Kemsing, Kent

CAVENDISH, Lady Jasmin; da of Marquess of Hartington; *b* 1973

CAVENDISH, Hon John Charles Gregory; s of 5 Baron Chesham; *b* 23 Nov 1952; *Educ* Eton, Jesus Cambridge; *m* 1976, Lucinda Mary, da of Richard Hugh Corbett (d 1974); *Career* shipbroker; with Tradax England Ltd (grain shippers) 1974-81, E D & F Man Ltd (sugar shippers) 1981-; *Recreations* motor sports, country life and sports; *Style* - The Hon John Cavendish; Hall Farm, Farringdon, Alton, Hants (☎ Tisted 275)

CAVENDISH, Hon Juliet Enid; da of 7 Baron Waterpark; *b* 17 Oct 1953; *Style* - The Hon Juliet Cavendish

CAVENDISH, Hon Nicholas Charles; s and h of 5 Baron Chesham; *b* 7 Nov 1941; *Educ* Eton; *m* 1, 1965 (m dis), Susan Donne, nee Beauchamp; m 2, 1973, Suzanne Adrienne, nee Byrne; 2 s; *Career* ACA; *Style* - The Hon Nicholas Cavendish; Woollahra, Sydney, NSW 2025, Australia

CAVENDISH, Maj-Gen Peter Boucher; OBE (1969); s of late Brig R V C Cavendish, OBE, MC; *b* 26 Aug 1925; *Educ* Abberley Hall Worcester, Winchester, New Coll Oxford; *m* 1952, Marion, nee Constantine; *Career* Royal Dragoons 1945, 3 King's Own Hussars 1946 (CO 14/20 1966-69 and Col 1976-81); Sec to Mil Ctee International Mil Staff HQ NATO 1975-78, Dir Armaments Standardisation and Interoperability Div 1978- and Chm Mil Agency for Standardisation 1978-; *Style* - Maj-Gen Peter Cavendish, OBE; Avenue des Cerfs 24, Kraainem 1950, Brussels, Belgium; The Rock Cottage, Middleton-by-Youlgrave, Bakewell, Derby (☎ Youlgrave 225)

CAVENDISH, Hon Roderick Alexander; s and h of 7 Baron Waterpark; *b* 10 Oct 1959; *Style* - The Hon Roderick Cavendish

CAVENDISH-BENTINCK, Lady Alexandra Margaret Anne; da of 7 Duke of Portland, KG (d 1977); *b* 1916; *Career* CStJ; *Style* - Lady Alexandra Cavendish-Bentinck; Welbeck Abbey, Worksop, Notts; Welbeck Woodhouse, Worksop, Notts; Langwell, Berriedale, Caithness; Bothal Castle, Northumberland; Culnaha, Easter Ross

CAVENDISH-BENTINCK, Lady Venetia Barbara; da of (William George) Frederick Cavendish-Bentinck (gs of Maj-Gen Lord Frederick Cavendish-Bentinck, CB, MP, 4 s of 3 Duke of Portland) and sis of 9 Duke of Portland, CMG; *b* 1902; *Style* - Lady Venetia Cavendish-Bentinck; 140 Chiltern Court, NW1

CAVENDISH-TRIBE, Hon Mrs; Hon Winifred; *née* Cavendish; da of 6 Baron Waterpark by 2 w, May; *b* 1 June 1909; *m* 1929, Capt Albert Tribe, who later assumed additional surname of Cavendish; 1 s; *Style* - The Hon Mrs Cavendish-Tribe; Ragstone Cottage, Meadow Close, Bridge, Canterbury, Kent

CAWDOR, 6 Earl (1827 UK); Hugh John Vaughan Campbell; also 24 Thane of Cawdor, Baron Cawdor (GB 1796), and Viscount Emlyn (UK 1827); s of late 5 Earl (d 1970) by his 1 w Wilma nee Vickers; *b* 6 Sept 1932; *Educ* Eton, Magdalen Oxford, RAC Cirencester; *m* 1, 1957 (m dis 1979), Cathryn, da of Maj-Gen Sir Robert Hinde, KBE, CB, DSO; 2 s, 3 da; m 2, 1979, Countess Angelika Lazansky (presumably of the family granted title of Count (Reichsgraf) of the Holy Roman Empire by Emperor Ferdinand III 1631, though a subsequent grant of Count to a cadet was made by the King of Hungary in 1681); *Heir* s, Viscount Emlyn; *Career* High Sheriff of

Carmarthenshire 1964; FRICS; *Style* - The Rt Hon the Earl Cawdor; Cawdor Castle, Nairn

CAWDOR, Elizabeth, Countess - Elizabeth; da of J Topham Richardson; *m* 1, 1924, Maj Sir Alexander Gordon-Cumming, 5 Bt, MC (d 1939); 1 s (Sir William G-C, 6 Bt), 2 da (Countess of Woolton, w of 2 Earl; Mrs David Innes); m 2, 1961, as his 2 w, 5 Earl Cawdor (d 1970); *Style* - The Rt Hon Elizabeth, Countess Cawdor

CAWDOR, Wilma, Countess; Wilma Mairi; da of late Vincent C Vickers; *m* 1929 (m dis 1961), 5 Earl (d 1970); 2 s (see 6 Earl); *Style* - Wilma, Countess Cawdor; c/o Lloyds Bank, 68 Warwick sq, SW1

CAWLEY, 3 Baron (UK 1918); Sir Frederick Lee Cawley; 3 Bt (UK 1906); s of 2 Baron (d 1954); *b* 27 July 1913; *Educ* Eton, New Coll Oxford; *m* 1944, Rosemary Joan, nee Marsden; 6 s, 1 da; *Heir* s, Hon John Cawley; *Career* barr 1938, practised 1946-73; Dep Chm of Cmtees House of Lords 1958-67; farmer; *Style* - The Rt Hon the Lord Cawley; Bircher Hall, Leominster, Herefordshire (☎ Yarpole 218); Berrington Hall, Leominster

CAWLEY, Hon Charles Michael; s of 3 Baron Cawley; *b* 9 Feb 1955; *Educ* Milton Abbey, Manchester U; *m* 1980, Justine J, nee Parry; *Style* - The Hon Charles Cawley

CAWLEY, Sir Charles Mills; CBE (1957); s of late John Cawley; *b* 17 May 1907; *Educ* Sir Joseph Williamson's Mathematical Sch Rochester, Imperial Coll of Science and Technology; *m* 1934, Florence Mary Ellaline, nee Shepherd; 1 da; *Career* empld Fuel Research Station DSIR 1929-53, dir DSIR HQ 1953-59, Ch Scientist Miny of Power 1959-67, a Civil Service Cmmr 1967-69; kt 1965; *Style* - Sir Charles Cawley, CBE; 8 Glen gdns, Ferring-by-Sea, Worthing, W Sussex

CAWLEY, Hon John Francis; s and h of 3 Baron Cawley; *b* 28 Sept 1946; *Educ* Eton; *m* 1979, Regina, da of Marqués de Hazas (Sp cr of King Amadeus I 1873); 1 da; *Style* - The Hon John Cawley; Castle Grounds, Ashton, Leominster, Herefs

CAWLEY, Hon Justin Robert; s of 3 Baron Cawley; *b* 15 June 1953; *Educ* Milton Abbey; *Style* - The Hon Justin Cawley

CAWLEY, Hon Mark Andrew; s of 3 Baron Cawley; *b* 3 Nov 1957; *Educ* Eton; *Style* - The Hon Mark Cawley

CAWLEY, Hon Richard Kenneth; s of 3 Baron Cawley; *b* 14 April 1949; *Educ* Eton, Durham U (BA); *m* 1976, Tsugumi, da of S Ota of Takarazuka Japan; *Style* - The Hon Richard Cawley

CAWLEY, Hon Stephen Robert; s of late 2 Baron Cawley; *b* 22 Oct 1915; *Educ* Eton, New Coll Oxford (BA, BSc, MA); *m* 1952, Iris Edrica, da of Reginald Marsden and Hon Vera, aunt of late 20 Viscount Dillon; 3 s, 1 da; *Career* War with Roy Signals; JP Surrey 1955-74 & Hereford & Worcester 1978-; Lib Candidate Gen Election 1950 (Stretford), 1951, 1955, 1959 (High Peak), 1964, 1966 (Esher); Chemical Plant dir; Prime Warden of the Dyers' Co 1970-71; *Recreations* fruit growing, maintaining property; *Style* - The Hon Stephen Cawley; The Woodlands, Eardiston, Tenbury Wells, Worcs

CAWLEY, Hon William Frederick; s of 3 Baron Cawley; *b* 1947; *Educ* Eton, New Coll Oxford; *m* 1979, Philippa J, nee Hoare; *Style* - The Hon William Cawley

CAWSTON, (Edwin) Richard; CVO (1972); s of late Edwin Cawston; *b* 31 May 1923; *Educ* Westminster Sch, Oriel Oxford; *m* 1951, Elisabeth Anne, da of Canon R L Rhys; 2 s; *Career* joined BBC TV 1947, documentary producer 1954-; Head of Documentary Programmes 1965-79, Special Projects Dir Video Arts Ltd 1979-, documentary consultant to BBC TV 1979-; *Style* - Richard Cawston Esq, CVO; 25 Lower Addison gdns, W14; Willow Cottage, Chalfont Lane, Chorleywood, Herts (☎ 2333)

CAWTHRA, Rear-Adm Arthur James; CB (1966); s of J H Cawthra; *b* 30 Sept 1911; *Educ* abroad; *m* 1959, Adrien Eleanor Lakeman, nee Tivy; *Career* joined RN 1930, Capt 1955, Dir Underwater Weapons Admiralty 1960-63, Adm Supt

HM Dockyard Devonport 1964, Rear-Adm 1964, ret 1967; *Style* - Rear-Admiral Arthur Cawthra, CB; Lower Island, Blackawton, Totnes, Devon

CAYFORD, Dame Florence Evelyn; DBE (1965); da of late George Bunch; *b* 14 June 1897; *Educ* County Secondary Sch St Pancras, Paddington Tech Inst; *m* 1923, John, s of Alfred Cayford; 2 s; *Career* chm London CC 1960-61, memb GLC 1964-67, Mayor of London Borough of Camden 1969, JP Co of London 1941, Freeman of Hampstead; chm Metropolitan Water Bd 1966-67; *Style* - Dame Florence Cayford, DBE; 26 Hemstal rd, Hampstead, NW6 (☎ 01 624 6181)

CAYLEY, Sir Digby William David; 11 Bt (UK 1661); s of late Digby Leonard Arthur Cayley, gs of 7 Bt; suc his kinsman Maj Sir Kenelm Cayley, 10 Bt, 1967; *b* 3 June 1944; *Educ* Malvern, Downing Cambridge; *m* 1969, Christine Mary, nee Gaunt; 2 da; *Heir* kinsman, George Paul Cayley; *Career* asst classics master Stonyhurst Coll 1973-; *Style* - Sir Digby Cayley, Bt; Homestead, Eastham st, Clitheroe, Lancs

CAYLEY, George Paul; s of late Capt Charles Cayley, ggs of 7 Bt; hp of kinsman, Sir Digby Cayley, 11 Bt; *b* 23 May 1940; *Educ* Felsted; *m* 1967, Shirley Southwell, da of Frank Woodward Petford, of Kirby Cane, Norfolk; 2 s; *Style* - George Cayley Esq; Applegarth, Brewers Green, Roydon, Diss, Norfolk

CAYZER, Hon Avon Arthur; s of 2 Baron Rotherwick; *b* 13 Sept 1968; *Style* - The Hon Avon Cayzer

CAYZER, Hon (Michael) Anthony (Rathborne); s of late 1 Baron Rotherwick; *b* 28 May 1920; *Educ* Eton, Sandhurst; *m* 1952, Hon Patricia Browne (d 1981), da of 4 Baron Oranmore and Browne by his 1 w Mildred (now Hon Mrs Hew Dalrymple); 3 da; *Career* chm British Island Airways Gp of Cos, Servisair Ltd, Air UK Ltd and others; dir Cayzer Irvine & Co Ltd, Bristow Helicopters Gp of Cos, Caledonia Investments Ltd, Scottish Lion Insurance Gp of Cos; *Style* - The Hon Anthony Cayzer; Great Westwood, Kings Langley, Herts

CAYZER, Lady - Beatrice Eileen; OBE (1963); da of late James Meakin; *m* 1919, Sir Charles William Cayzer, 3 Bt, MP (d 1940); *Style* - Lady Cayzer, OBE; Kinpurnie Castle, Newtyle, Angus

CAYZER, Bernard Gilbert Stancomb; s of late Lt Cdr Sir August Bernard Tellefsen Cayzer, 3 s of 1 Bt; hp of bro, Sir (William) Nicholas Cayzer, 2 Bt; *b* 14 March 1914; *Educ* Eton, Magdalene Cambridge; *Career* dep chm British & Commonwealth Shipping Co Ltd and Union Castle Mail S S Co Ltd; dir Cayzer Irvine & Co Ltd, Clan Line Steamers Ltd; *Style* - Bernard Cayzer Esq; 64 Kingston House North, SW7; Parish's House, Timsbury, nr Bath, Avon

CAYZER, Hon Charles William; s of 2 Baron Rotherwick; *b* 26 April 1957; *Style* - The Hon Charles Cayzer

CAYZER, Hon Herbert Robin; s and h of 2 Baron Rotherwick; *b* 12 March 1954; *Educ* Harrow; *Style* - The Hon Herbert Cayzer

CAYZER, Sir James Arthur; 5 Bt (UK 1904), of Gartmore, Co Perth; s of Sir Charles William Cayzer, 3 Bt, MP (d 1940); suc his bro, 4 Bt, 1943; *b* 15 Nov 1931; *Educ* Eton; *Heir* kinsman, Sir (William) Nicholas Cayzer, 2 Bt; *Style* - Sir James Cayzer, Bt; Kinpurnie Castle, Newtyle, Angus (☎ Newtyle 207)

CAYZER, Sir (William) Nicholas; 2 Bt (UK 1921), of Roffey Park, Horsham, Co Sussex; s of late Sir August Cayzer, 1 Bt (d 1943) & hp of kinsman Sir James Cayzer, 5 Bt; *b* 21 Jan 1910; *Educ* Eton, CCC Cambridge; *m* 1935, Elizabeth Catherine, nee Williams; 2 da; *Heir* bro, Maj Bernard Cayzer; *Career* chm Clan Line Steamers Ltd, Cayzer Irvine & Co Ltd, Caledonia Investments Ltd, Union-Castle Mail Steamship Co Ltd, British and Commonwealth Shipping Co Ltd, Scottish Lion Insurance Co Ltd; *Style* - Sir Nicholas Cayzer, Bt; 95j Eaton sq, SW1 (☎ 01 235 5551); The Grove, Walsham-le-Willows, Suffolk (☎ 263)

CAZALET, Hon Mrs (Camilla Jane); *née* Gage; da of 6 Viscount Gage, KCVO, by his 1 w, Hon Alexandra Grenfell; *b* 12 July 1937; *Educ* Benenden; *m* 1965, Edward Cazalet, s of Peter Cazalet, JP, DL, the race horse trainer, by his 1 w, Leonora, nee Rowley, step da of late (Sir) P(elham) G Wodehouse; 2 s, 1 da; *Career* dir Lumley Cazalet 1967-; Tstee Glyndebourne Arts Tst 1978-; *Recreations* tennis, music; *Clubs* Queen's; *Style* - The Hon Mrs Cazalet; Shaw Farm, Plumpton Green, Lewes, Sussex; 58 Seymour Walk, SW10 (☎ 01 352 0401)

CAZALET, Edward Stephen; QC (1980); s of Peter Cazalet; *b* 26 April 1936; *Educ* Eton, Oxford; *m* 1965, Camilla Jane, da of Viscount Gage, KCVO; 2 s, 1 da; *Career* barrister; chm Horse Race Betting Levy Appeal Tribunal 1979-; *Style* - Edward Cazalet Esq, QC; 58 Seymour Walk, SW10 (☎ 01 352 0401)

CAZALET, Peter Grenville; s of Vice-Adm Sir Peter Grenville Cazalet, KBE, CB, DSO, DSC; *b* 26 Feb 1929; *Educ* Uppingham Sch, Magdalene Cambridge; *m* 1957, Jane Jennifer, nee Rew; 3 s; *Career* md British Petroleum Co Ltd; *Style* - Peter Cazalet Esq; c/o BP Co Ltd, Britannic House, Moor lane, EC2 (☎ 01 920 8000)

CAZALET, Vice-Adm Sir Peter Grenville Lyon; KBE (1955), CB (1952), DSO (1945) and Bar (1949), DSC (1940); s of Grenville Cazalet; *b* 29 July 1899; *Educ* Dulwich; *m* 1928, Elise, nee Winterbotham; 4 s; *Career* Midshipman HMS Princess Royal 1918, Rear-Adm 1950, Allied Ch of Staff to CIC Mediterranean 1953-55, Vice-Adm 1953, Flag Offr Cmmdg Reserve Fleet 1955-56, ret 1957; former ADC to the King 1950; v-pres Assoc of Royal Navy Officers; *Style* - Vice-Admiral Sir Peter Cazalet, KBE, CB, DSO*, DSC; 16 High Hurst Close, Newick, Lewes, E Sussex (☎ Newick 2396)

CAZALET, Raymond Percival St George; s of Vice Adm Sir Peter Cazalet, KBE, CB, DSO*, DSC; *b* 23 April 1931; *Educ* Uppingham Sch; *m* 1962, Deborah Caroline, nee Fuggles-Couchman; 3 s; *Career* ch accountant Marshall-Andrew & Co Ltd 1959-61, chm Henderson Administration Ltd 1961-, ACA, FCA; *Recreations* tennis; *Clubs* City of London; *Style* - Raymond Cazalet Esq. 4 Kelso pla, W8 (☎ 01 937 6446)

CAÑEDO, Lady Rosemary Millicent; *née* Ward; da (twin, by 1 m) of 4 Earl of Dudley; *b* 1955; *m* 1980, Castor Cañedo; *Style* - Lady Rosemary Cañedo

CECIL, Hon Anthony Henry Amherst; s of 3 Baron Amherst of Hackney, CBE (d 1980); *b* 1947; *Educ* Eton; *m* 1, 1969 (m dis 1974), Fenella Jane, da of David George Crichton, MVO; m 2, 1974, Jane Elizabeth, da of Philip Holbrook; 1 s; *Style* - The Hon Anthony Cecil; Church Cottage, Greywell, Odiham, Basingstoke, Hants

CECIL, Hon Aurelia Margaret Amherst; da of 4 Baron Amherst of Hackney; *b* 19 July 1966; *Educ* Queensgate and Prior's Field; *Style* - The Hon Aurelia Cecil

CECIL, Hon Anthony Robert; s and h of 3 Baron Rockley by Lady Sarah Cadogan, da of 7 Earl Cadogan, MC; *b* 29 July 1961; *Educ* Eton, Cambridge; *Career* student as of summer 1981; *Recreations* rugby, squash, tennis; *Style* - The Hon Anthony Cecil; Lytchett Heath, Poole, Dorset (☎ 0202 622228)

CECIL, Hon Caroline Anne; da of 3 Baron Rockley; *b* 27 March 1960; *Style* - The Hon Caroline Cecil

CECIL, Hon Charles Evelyn; 2 s of 2 Baron Rockley; *b* 15 Nov 1936; *Educ* Eton; *m* 1965, Jennifer, da of Duncan Mackinnon and Pamela, da of Capt Robert Brassey, JP, DL (nephew of 1 Earl Brassey, JP, DL, and 1 cous of 1 Baron Brassey of Apethorpe, JP, DL; Pamela's mother was the Capt's 1 w, Violet Lowry-Corry, great niece of 3 Earl Belmore; the Capt's mother was Hon Matilda Bingham, OBE, da of 4 Baron Clanmorris) and 2 cous of the writer Charlotte Bingham; 1 s, 2 da; *Style* - The Hon Charles Cecil; Wilcote House, Charlbury, Oxon (☎ 099 386 355)

CECIL, Lord Charles Edward Vere (Gascoyne); s of 6 Marquess of Salisbury; *b* 13 July 1949; *Educ* Eton, Ch Ch Oxford; *Career* merchant banker; *Clubs* Turf, Beefsteak; *Style* - Lord Charles Cecil; 21 Hollywood rd, SW 10 (☎ 01 352 1169)

CECIL, Hon Camilla Sarah; da of 3 Baron Rockley; *b* 8 Feb 1965; *Style* - The Hon Camilla Cecil

CECIL, Lord (Edward Christian) David (Gascoyne); CH (1949), CLit (1972); s of 4 Marq of Salisbury, KG, GCVO; *b* 9 April 1902; *Educ* Eton, Ch Ch Oxford; *m* 1932, Rachel, da of Sir Desmond MacCarthy; 2 s, 1 da; *Career* former Fellow of Wadham Coll Oxford, of New Coll 1939-69; Goldsmiths' Prof of English Literature Oxford 1948-69; author; books include *Early Victorian Novelists* 1934, *A Portrait of Jane Austen* 1978; *Style* - Lord David Cecil, CH; Red Lion House, Cranborne, Wimborne, Dorset (☎ Cranborne 244)

CECIL, Hon Elizabeth Ann (Gascoyne); da of Viscount Cranborne; *b* 1972

CECIL, Hon Georgiana; da (twin) of Viscount Cranborne; *b* 1977

CECIL, Hon Hugh William Amherst; s and h of 4 Baron Amherst of Hackney; *b* 17 July 1968; *Educ* Ludgrove; *Style* - The Hon Hugh Cecil

CECIL, Hon James Richard (Gascoyne); s of Viscount Cranborne; *b* 1973

CECIL, Hon Katherine; da (twin) of Viscount Cranborne; *b* 1977

CECIL, Lord (William) Martin Alleyne; s of late 5 Marq of Exeter KG CMG and hp of 6 Marq of Exeter; *b* 27 April 1909; *Educ* RNC Dartmouth; *m* 1, 1934, Edith Lilian De Csánady (d 1954); 1 s; m 2, 1954, Lillian Jane Johnson; 1 da (and 1 decd); *Career* author; *Style* - Lord Martin Cecil; 100 Mile House, PO Box 8, British Columbia, Canada (☎ 604 395 2323)

CECIL, Lord Michael Hugh (Gascoyne); s of 6 Marquess of Salisbury; *b* 1960; *Career* commissioned Gren Gds 1980; *Style* - Lord Michael Cecil

CECIL, Rear-Adm Sir (Oswald) Nigel Amherst; KBE (1979), CB (1978); s of Cdr the Hon Henry Cecil, OBE, RN; *Educ* 11 Nov 1925; *m* 1961, Annette, nee Barclay; 1 s; *Career* joined Navy 1939, Capt 1966, Naval ADC to HM the Queen 1975, Cdr British Forces Malta and Flag Officer Malta 1975-79, Cdr NATO S Eastern Mediterranean 1975-77, Rear-Adm 1975; OStJ 1971, KStJ 1980; *Style* - Rear-Admiral Sir Nigel Cecil, KBE, CB; Greenoaks, Bishop's Waltham, Hants

CECIL, Lady Rose Alice Elizabeth (Gascoyne); da of 6 Marquess of Salisbury; *b* 1956; *Style* - Lady Rose Cecil

CECIL, Hon Robert Edward William (Gascoyne); s and h of Viscount Cranborne; *b* 1970; *Style* - Hon Robert Cecil

CECIL, Lord Valentine William (Gascoyne); s of 6 Marquess of Salisbury; *b* 1952; *Career* a Page of Honour to HM Queen Elizabeth The Queen Mother 1966-67, Capt Gren Gds; *Style* - Lord Valentine Cecil

CECIL, Hon Mrs; Hon Yvonne; da of late 1 Baron Cornwallis; *b* 1896; *m* 1923, Cdr the Hon Henry Mitford Amherst Cecil, OBE, RN (s of Mary Rothes Margaret, Baroness Amherst of Hackney, and who d 1962); 1 s, 2 da; *Style* - The Hon Mrs Cecil; Greenoaks, Bishop's Waltham, Hants

CECIL-WRIGHT, Air Commodore John Allan Cecil; AFC, TD, AE; s of late Alfred Cecil Wright; *b* 28 Aug 1886; *Educ* Winchester; *m* 1946, Ethne Monica, nee Falconar; 2 s (by previous m); *Career* adopted surname of Cecil-Wright by deed poll; joined 1 Vol Bn T Warwicks Regt 1905; RFC 1916; Regional Cdmt Air Training Corps for Midlands 1941-45, Gp Capt 1942, Hon Air Cdre No 605 (County of Warwicks) Sqdn AAF 1946-55; MP (C) Birmingham Erdington Div 1936-45; former chm and company dir; *Style* - Air

Commodore John Cecil-Wright, AFC, TD, AE; 33 Ennismore gdns, SW7; 14 Richmond ct, Milford-on-Sea

CENTNER, Hon Mrs (Anne Catherine); da of 2 Viscount Leathers; *b* 1944; *m* 1977, Arthur Sydney Centner; *Style* - The Hon Mrs Centner

CHACKSFIELD, Air Vice-Marshal Sir Bernard; KBE (1968, OBE 1945), CB (1961); s of Edgar Chacksfield; *b* 13 April 1913 *Educ* Ilford Co H S, RAF Halton & Cranwell; *m* 1937, Myrtle, nee Matthews; 2 s, 2 da; *Career* joined RAF 1928, Gp Capt 1951, Air Cdre 1956, SASO Tech Training Command (Acting Air Vice-Marshal) 1960, AOC No 22 Group 1960-62, Cmdt-Gen RAF Regt and Inspr of Ground Defence 1963-68, ret; *Style* - Air Vice-Marshal Sir Bernard Chacksfield, KBE, CB; Windwhistle, Bourne End, Bucks (☎ Bourne End 20829)

CHADBON, Hon Mrs (Deborah Elspeth); da of 2 Viscount Leathers; *m* 1966, Thomas Richard Chadbon; 2 s; *Style* - The Hon Mrs Chadbon; 83 Elm Bank gdns, Barnes, SW13

CHADWICK, Sir Albert Edward; CMG (1967); s of Andrew Chadwick; *b* 15 Nov 1897; *Educ* Victoria; *m* 1924, Thelma, nee Crawley; 1 s, 1 da; *Career* engineer; former gen man and chm Gas and Fuel Corp of Victoria; chm Overseas Telecommunications Commission Australia 1962-68; kt 1974; *Style* - Sir Albert Chadwick, CMG; 413 Toorak rd, Toorak, Vic 3142, Australia (☎ Melbourne 24-1163)

CHADWICK, (Gerald William St) John; CMG (1961); s of late John F Chadwick; *b* 28 May 1915; *Educ* Lancing, St Catharine's Cambridge; *m* 1938, Madeleine Boucheron; 2 s; *Career* Colonial Office 1938, Dominions Office 1940; Commonwealth Relations Office Asst Under-Sec of State 1960-66 (formerly Asst Sec); Govr Commonwealth Inst 1967-; First Dir Commonwealth Foundn 1966-; author; *Style* - John Chadwick Esq, CMG; 11 Cumberland House, Kensington rd, W8

CHADWICK, Sir John Edward; KCMG (1967, CMG 1957); s of late John Chadwick; *b* 17 Dec 1911; *Educ* Rugby, CCC Cambridge; *m* 1945, Audrey Lenfestey; 1 s, 2 da; *Career* HM Ambassador to Romania 1967-68, UK Rep to OECD Paris 1969-71; special adviser to Asian Devpt Bank 1973-; *Style* - Sir John Chadwick, KCMG; Larkfields, Woodstock rd, Charlbury, Oxon

CHADWICK, Joshua Kenneth; s (by 2 m) and h of Sir Robert Chadwick, 2 Bt; *b* 1 Feb 1954; *Style* - Joshua Chadwick Esq

CHADWICK, John Murray; ED (1979), QC (1980); s of late Capt H G Chadwick; *b* 20 Jan 1941; *Educ* Rugby, Magdalene Cambridge; *m* 1975, Diana Mary, nee Blunt; 2 da; *Career* Maj (TAVR); barrister *Style* - John Chadwick Esq ED QC; Queen Elizabeth Building, Temple, EC4 (☎ 01 353 9076)

CHADWICK, Prof (William) Owen; s of late John Chadwick; er bro of the Regius Prof of Divinity at Cambridge (Rev Prof Henry C), yr bro of Sir John Chadwick, KCMG (sometime Ambass to Romania), and bro-in-law of Vice-Adm Sir Alan McNicoll, KBE, CB, GM, late Australian Ambass to Turkey; *b* 20 May 1916; *Educ* Tonbridge, St John's Cambridge; *m* 1949, Ruth, nee Hallward; 2 s, 2 da; *Career* Pres Br Acad 1981-82; former Dean and Fellow of Trin Hall Cambridge; Regius Prof of Modern History Cambridge U 1968-, Master of Selwyn Coll 1956-; *Style* - Prof Owen Chadwick; Master's Lodge, Selwyn College, Cambridge

CHADWICK, Sir Robert (Peter) Burton; 2 Bt (UK 1935), of Bidston, Co Palatine of Chester; s of Sir Robert Burton-Chadwick, 1 Bt (d 1951); *b* 22 June 1911; *Educ* St George's Sch Harpenden; *m* 1, 1937 (m dis 1949), Rosalind, nee Stott; 2 da; m 2, 1950, Beryl Joan, nee Brailsford; 1 s, 1 da; *Heir* s, Joshua Chadwick; *Career* New Zealand Force in N Africa and Italy 1942-45; *Style* - Sir Robert Chadwick, Bt; 102 Meadowbank rd, Remuera 5, Auckland, New Zealand

CHADWYCK-HEALEY, Sir Charles Arthur; 4 Bt (UK 1919), OBE (1945),

TD; s of Sir Gerald Edward Chadwyck-Healey, MC, 2 Bt (d 1955); suc bro, Sir Edward Randal Chadwyck-Healey, 3 Bt, 1979; *b* 27 May 1910; *Educ* Eton, Trin Oxford (BA, MA); *m* 1939, Viola, da of late Cecil Lubbock; 3 s, 2 da; *Heir* s, Charles Chadwyck-Healey; *Career* Lt-Col RA (TA); 1939-45 War in N Africa, Sicily and Italy (despatches twice, OBE); *Clubs* Brooks's; *Style* - Sir Charles Chadwyck-Healey, Bt, OBE, TD; Old Middleton, Westmeston, Hassocks, Sussex

CHADWYCK-HEALEY, Charles Edward; s and h of Sir Charles Chadwyck-Healey, Bt; *b* 13 May 1940; *Educ* Eton, Trin Oxford (MA); *m* 1967, Angela Mary, nee Metson; 1 s, 2 da; *Style* - Charles Chadwyck-Healey Esq; Manor Farm, Bassingbourn, Cambridge

CHAGRIN, Hon Mrs (Elizabeth Constance); *née* Mackintosh; da of 2 Viscount Mackintosh of Halifax, OBE, BEM (d 1980), by his 1 w, Bronda; *b* 4 May 1950; *m* 1, 1972, Timothy Cutting; m 2, 1980, Nicholas Chagrin; *Style* - The Hon Mrs Chagrin

CHALFONT, Baron (Life Peer UK 1964); (Alun) Arthur Gwynne Jones; OBE (1961), MC (1957), PC (1964); s of Arthur Gwynne Jones; *b* 5 Dec 1919; *Educ* West Monmouth Sch; *m* 1948, Dr Mona, nee Mitchell MB ChB,; *Career* Pres Roy Nat Inst for Deaf; Brevet Lt-Col (ret) S Wales Borderers (Regular Army Officer 1940-61); former defence and mil correspondent The Times; Min of State Foreign Office 1964-70, British Perm Rep to WEU 1969-70; former foreign ed New Statesman; dir IBM UK Holdings Ltd, IBM United Kingdom Ltd; *Style* - The Rt Hon the Lord Chalfont, OBE, MC, PC; 65 Ashley gdns, SW1 (☎ 01 834 5485)

CHALK, Hon Sir Gordon (William Wesley); KBE (1971); *b* 1913; *Educ* Queensland; *m* 1937, Ellen Grant; 1 s, 1 da; *Career* MP Queensland Australia 1947-76, Leader Australian Liberal Party (Queensland) 1965-76, Dep Premier and Treasurer Queensland State Govt 1965-76, ret; *Style* - The Hon Sir Gordon Chalk, KBE; 277 Indooroopilly rd, Indooroopilly, Queensland 4068, Australia (☎ Brisbane 3711598)

CHALKER, Mrs Lynda; MP (C) Wallasey Feb 1974-; da of Sidney Bates; *b* 29 April 1942; *Educ* Roedean, Heidelberg U, Westfield Coll London, Central London Polytechnic; *m* 1967 (m dis 1973), Eric Chalker; *Career* late statistician; Parly Under-Sec of State DHSS 1979-; *Style* - Mrs Lynda Chalker, MP; House of Commons, SW1 (☎ 01 219 5098)

CHALLIS, George Hubert; s of late Hubert Challis; *b* 26 May 1921; *Educ* King Edward VI Sch Stourbridge; *m* 1946, Margaret Beatrice, nee Bonner; 1 s, 1 da; *Career* banker; joined Lloyds Bank 1938, head of Premises Div 1974- (formerly empld at Head Office); dir Lloyds Bank Property Co Ltd; *Style* - George Challis Esq; 77 West Hill av, Epsom, Surrey (☎ Epsom 21705)

CHALMERS, Hon Mrs (Lydia Elizabeth Palmer); *née* MacDermott; da of Baron MacDermott, MC, PC (Life Peer) (d 1979); *b* 1939; *Educ* Wycombe Abbey Sch and Belfast Coll of Art; *m* 1964, Capt David McKenzie Chalmers, RAF (ret); *Style* - The Hon Mrs Chalmers; Old School House, Beech Hill, Reading, Berks RG7 2BE

CHALMERS, William John; CB (1973), CVO (1979), CBE (1954); s of late William Chalmers; *b* 20 Oct 1914; *Educ* Inverness Royal Acad, Edinburgh U; *m* 1942, Jessie, nee McGregor; 1 s, 1 da; *Career* Sec and Dir-Gen Commonwealth War Graves Cmmn 1956-75, Hon Sec Imperial War Graves Endowment Fund Trustees 1952-75; Appeal Sec HM's Silver Jubilee Appeal 1975-78; *Style* - William Chalmers Esq, CB, CVO, CBE; Holy Well House, Luston, Leominster, Herefordshire (☎ Yarpole 455)

CHALONER, Hon Robert Toby Long; s of 3 Baron Gisborough; *b* 13 July 1966; *Style* - The Hon Robert Chaloner

CHALONER, Hon Thomas Peregrine Long; s and h of 3 Baron Gisborough; *b* 17 Jan 1961; *Style* - The Hon Thomas Chaloner

CHALONER, Hon Ursula Violet; da of 1 Baron Gisborough, JP, DL, sometime MP W Wilts and Liverpool Abercromby; *Career* ambulance driver in Stepney 1939-40; served 1940-45 as Section Offr WAAF Bomber Cmmd Honeybourne; *Recreations* hunting, riding; *Style* - The Hon Ursula Chaloner; Wood Cottage, Earls Common, Droitwich, Worcs (☎ Himbleton 236/211)

CHAMBERLAIN, Lady Catharine Laura; *née* Chetwynd-Talbot; da (by 1 m) of late 21 Earl of Shrewsbury and Waterford; *b* 1945; *m* 1966, Richard Sebastian Endicott Chamberlain; 1 s, 2 da; *Style* - Lady Catharine Chamberlain; Blanchards, Barnes lane, Milford-on-Sea, Hants

CHAMBERLAIN, Air Vice-Marshal George Philip; CB (1946), OBE (1941); s of George Chamberlain; *b* 18 Aug 1905; *Educ* Denston Coll, RAF Cranwell; *m* 1930, Alfreda Rosamond Kedward; 1 s, 1 da; *Career* commissioned RAF 1925, AOA Fighter Command 1954-57, Air Vice-Marshal 1955, Dep Controller of Electronics Miny of Supply 1957, Miny of Aviation 1959-60, ret; md Collins Radio Co of England Ltd 1962, aviation and electronics consultant and non-exec dir 1966-75; *Style* - Air Vice-Marshal George Chamberlain, CB, OBE; Little Orchard, Adelaide close, Stanmore, Middx

CHAMBERLAIN, Sir Henry Wilmot; 5 Bt (UK 1828), of London; s of Sir Henry Chamberlain, 4 Bt (d 1936); *b* 17 May 1899; *Style* - Sir Henry Chamberlain, Bt; c/o Church Adams & Co, 23/25 Bell st, Reigate, Surrey

CHAMBERLAIN, Hon Sir (Reginald) Roderic (St Clair); QC (1945); s of late Henry Chamberlain; *b* 17 June 1901; *Educ* St Peter's Coll, Adelaide U; *m* 1929, Leila Macdonald Haining; 1 da; *Career* former Crown Solicitor and Crown Prosecutor; Judge of the Supreme Court of South Australia 1959-71; kt 1970; *Style* - The Hon Sir Roderic Chamberlain, QC; 72 Moseley st, Glenelg South, SA 5045, Australia (☎ 95 2036)

CHAMBERLAIN, William Richard; s of late Lt-Cdr Richard Chamberlain; *b* 13 April 1925; *Educ* Uppingham Sch; *m* 1960, Gillian Diarmid, nee Castle; 1 s, 1 da; *Career* chm Chamberlain Phipps Ltd 1972-, Chamberlain Phipps International 1976-, chm Salpa Kay Ltd 1979-, chm Phipps & Son Hldgs Ltd; dir Crane & Percival Ltd, Ferrersflex Ltd and others; *Style* - William Chamberlain Esq; Manor House, Swineshead, Bedford (☎ Riseley 283)

CHAMBERLEN, Nicholas Hugh; s of Rev Leonard Chamberlen; *b* 18 April 1939; *Educ* Sherborne, Lincoln Coll Oxford; *m* 1962, Jane Mary, nee Lindo; 3 s, 1 da; *Career* bill broker; chm Clive Discount Hldgs 1977-; *Style* - Nicholas Chamberlen Esq; Costells, Scaynes Hill, Haywards Heath, Sussex (☎ Scaynes Hill 258)

CHAMBERS, Sir (Stanley) Paul; KBE (1965), CB (1944), CIE (1941); s of late Philip Chambers; *b* 2 April 1904; *Educ* City of London Coll, LSE; *m* 1, 1926 (m dis 1955), Dorothy, nee Copp; m 2, 1955, Mrs Edith Pollack, nee Lamb; 2 da; *Career* former chm ICI, Royal Insurance Co Ltd 1968-74, London & Lancs Insurance Co Ltd 1968-74, Liverpool & London & Globe Insurance Co Ltd 1968-74; *Style* - Sir Paul Chambers, KBE, CB, CIE; 1a Frognal gdns, Hampstead, NW3

CHAMPION, Baron (Life Peer UK 1962); Arthur Joseph Champion; PC (1967); s of late William Champion; *b* 26 July 1897; *m* 1930, Mary Emma, nee Williams; 1 da; *Career* railwayman; MP (L) S Derbys 1945-50 and for SE Derbys 1950-59; dir British Sugar Corp 1960-64 and 1967-68; Min without Portfolio and Dep Leader of the House of Lords 1964-67; Dep Speaker and Dep Chm of Cmtees House of Lords 1967; JP Glamorgan; *Style* - The Rt Hon Lord Champion, PC, JP; 22 Lanelay ter, Pontypridd, Mid Glam (☎ Pontypridd 402349)

CHAMPION, Rev Sir Reginald Stuart; KCMG (1946, CMG 1944), OBE (1934); s of late Philip Champion; *b* 21 March 1895; *Educ* Sutton Valence Sch; *m* 1920, Margaret, da of late Very Rev W M Macgregor; 2 s, 1 da; *Career* Colonial Service 1920-1951 (Govr and CIC Aden

1944-51), ret; ordained 1952, Vicar of Chilham 1953-61, ret; *Style* - The Rev Sir Reginald Champion, KCMG, OBE; 46 Chancellor House, Mount Ephraim, Tunbridge Wells, Kent (☎ 20719)

CHANCE, Lady (Hilda) Ava Fiona Nancy; *née* Baird; da of 1 Viscount Stonehaven, GCMG, DSO, PC (d 1941) and Countess of Kintore (d 1974); *b* 1919; *m* 1945, Lt-Col Ronald Fulton Lucas Chance, MC; 1 s, 1 da; *Style* - Lady Ava Chance; Lower Moor Farm, Charlton, Malmesbury, Wilts

CHANCE, George Jeremy ffolliott; s and h of Sir Roger Chance, 3 Bt, MC; *b* 24 Feb 1926; *m* 1950, his cousin, Cecila Mary Elizabeth, da of Sir Hugh Chance, CBE; 1 s; *Career* late Lt RNVR, former dir Massey-Ferguson Ltd Coventry; *Style* - George Chance Esq; Rhosgyll Fawr, Chwilog, Pwllheli, Gwynedd

CHANCE, Sir Roger James Ferguson; 3 Bt (UK 1900), of Grand Avenue, Hove, Co Sussex, MC; s of George Ferguson Chance (s of 1 Bt); *b* 26 Jan 1893; *Educ* Eton, Trin Cambridge, London U; *m* 1921, Mary Georgina, da of Col William Rowney; 1 s, 2 da; *Heir* s, George Chance; *Career* formerly Capt 4 Dragoon Guards and Rifle Bde; Press Attaché British Embassy Berlin 1938, Sqdn-Ldr RAF Vol Reserve 1940-41; author; *Style* - Sir Roger Chance, Bt, MC; 9 Eaton sq, SW1

CHANCELLOR, Alexander Surtees; s of Sir Christopher Chancellor, CMG, and Sylvia, eldest da of Sir Richard Paget, 2 Bt, by Sir Richard's 1 w, Lady Muriel Finch-Hatton, CBE (only da of 12 Earl of Winchilsea and Nottingham); Mr Chancellor is n of Sir John Paget, 3 Bt, and (by m) of 2 Baron Glenconner and Sir Piers Debenham, 2 Bt; also 1 cous of Hon Mrs Emma Cockburn (nee Tennant, who m, as her 2 husb and his 1 w, Christopher Booker, *qv*) and Hon Colin Tennant; Mr Chancellor's er bro, John, was 1 husb of Hon Mrs Windsor-Clive (da of 4 Baron Hylton), while his sis Teresa m Edward Gatacre, one of the Gatacres of Gatacre, Salop, and gs through his m, Alice, of Jonkheer Victor Eugène Louis de Stuers; *b* 4 Jan 1940; *Educ* Eton, Trin Hall Cambridge; *m* 1964, Susanna, da of Martin Debenham, JP (3 s of Sir Ernest Debenham, 1 Bt, JP, by Cecily, niece of Rt Hon Joseph Chamberlain), Mr Chancellor's aunt Angela's bro-in-law; 2 da; *Career* Reuters News Agency 1964-74, ed The Spectator 1975-; *Style* - Alexander Chancellor Esq; The Spectator, 56 Doughty st, WC1

CHANCELLOR, Sir Christopher (John); CMG (1948); s of late Sir John Chancellor, GCMG, GCVO, GBE, DSO; *b* 29 March 1904; *Educ* Eton, Trin Cambridge; *m* 1926, Sylvia Mary, OBE, da of Sir Richard Paget and Lady Muriel Finch-Hatton, da of 12 Earl of Winchelsea and Nottingham; 2 s, 2 da; *Career* Reuters 1930-59, then trustee, former chm Odhams Press Ltd, chm and ch exec The Bowater Paper Corp Ltd 1962-69, kt 1951; *Style* - Sir Christopher Chancellor, CMG; The Priory, Ditcheat, Shepton Mallet, Somerset

CHANDLER, Charles Henry; s of late Charles Chandler; *b* 6 March 1940; *Educ* Highgate Sch; *m* 1965, Christine Elizabeth, nee Dunn; 2 c; *Career* md (Promotions) GRA Property Trust Ltd 1972-, md Greyhound Racing Assoc Ltd 1972-, chm Walthamstow Stadium Ltd 1976-; *Style* - Charles Chandler Esq; Mymfield, Kentish lane, Brookmans Park, Herts (☎ office 01 743 0152, home Potters Bar 52478)

CHANDOS, 3 Viscount (1954 UK); Thomas Orlando Lyttelton; s of late 2 Viscount (d 1980, ggs of 4 Baron Cobham) and Caroline (da of Sir Alan Lascelles, himself gs of 4 Earl of Harewood); Lord C is nephew of Lady (w of 3 Visc) Chaplin; *b* 12 Feb 1953; *Educ* Eton, Worcester Oxford; *Heir* bro, Hon Matthew Lyttelton; *Style* - The Rt Hon the Viscount Chandos; The Vine, Sherborne St John, Basingstoke, Hants (☎ Bramley Green 227)

CHANDOS, Viscountess; Caroline Mary; da of Sir Alan Frederick Lascelles, GCVO, KCB, CMG, MC, PC; *b* 1928; *m* 1949, 2 Viscount Chandos (d 1980); 2 s, 2 da; *Style* - The Rt Hon Viscountess Chandos; The Vine, Sherborne St John,

Basingstoke, Hants

CHANDOS-POLE, Lt-Col John; CVO (1979), OBE (1951); s of late Brig-Gen Harry Anthony Chandos-Pole, CBE; *b* 20 July 1909; *Educ* Eton, Magdalene Cambridge; *m* 1952, Josephine Sylvia, da of Brig-Gen Cyril Crofton, CBE; *Career* Lt Coldstream Gds 1933, command 2 Bn 1950-52, ret 1953, a Gentleman-at-Arms 1956-66 (Harbinger 1966-), Lord-Lt Northants 1967- (DL 1965), JP 1957; KStJ 1975; *Style* - Lt-Col John Chandos-Pole CVO OBE JP, HM Lord-Lieut of Northamptonshire; Newnham Hall, Daventry, Northants (☎ 2711)

CHANDOS-POLE, John Walkelyne; s of late Col Reginald Walkelyne Chandos-Pole, TD, JP; *b* 4 Nov 1913; *Educ* Eton, RMC; *m* 1947, Ilsa Jill, nee Barstz; 1 da (and 1 s decd); *Career* Maj late Grenadier Gds, ADC to Viceroy of India 1938-39; JP Derbyshire 1951, DL 1961, High Sheriff 1959; *Style* - John Chandos-Pole Esq, JP, DL; Radburne Hall, Kirk Langley, Derby (☎ Kirk Langley 246)

CHANNING-WILLIAMS, Maj-Gen John William; CB (1963), DSO (1944), OBE (1951); s of late W A Williams; *b* 14 Aug 1908; *Educ* Trent Coll, Sandhurst; *m* 1936, Margaret Blachford, nee Wood; 3 s; *Career* 2 Lt Staffs Regt 1929, Brig Gen Staff (Operations and Plans) Gen HQ Middle East Land Forces 1955-58, Maj-Gen 1960, dir War Office (Quartering) 1960-61, dir (Movements) 1961-63, ret; *Style* - Maj-Gen John Channing-Williams, CB, DSO, OBE; Hayes Well, Inkpen, Newbury, Berks

CHANNON, Derek French; s of John French Channon; *b* 3 April 1939; *Educ* Eastbourne G S, U Coll London (BSc), Manchester U (MBA), Harvard Grad Sch of Business Admin (DBA); *m* 1963, Ann Lesley; 1 s, 1 da; *Career* formerly with Roy Dutch Shell Gp, md Evode Hldgs 1976-77, Prof of Marketing Manchester Business Sch 1978, dir Centre for Business Research, company dir; *Style* - Prof Derek Channon; White Lodge, Leicester rd, Knutsford, Cheshire; 509N University dve, Plantation, Florida

CHANNON, (Henry) Paul (Guinness); MP (C) Southend W 1959-; s of late Sir Henry Channon, MP and late Lady Honor Svejdar (nee Guinness); *b* 9 Oct 1935; *Educ* Eton, Ch Ch Oxford; *m* 1963, Ingrid Guinness, nee Wyndham; 1 s, 2 da; *Career* Min of State CSD 1979-80, Spokesman for the Arts and Min of State Dept of Educn and Science 1980-; *Style* - Paul Channon Esq, MP; 96 Cheyne walk, SW10 (☎ 01 351 0293); Kelvedon Hall, Brentwood, Essex (☎ Ongar 2180)

CHANT-SEMPILL, Hon Ian David Whitemore; s (by 2 m) of Lady Sempill; *b* 1951; *Educ* Oratory Sch; *m* 1980, Amanda, nee Dallas; *Career* Capt Gordon Highlanders; *Style* - The Hon Ian Chant-Sempill

CHANTLER, Philip; CMG (1963); s of Tom Chantler; *b* 16 May 1911; *Educ* Manchester Central H S, Manchester U; *m* 1938, Elizabeth Margaret Pentney; 1 da; *Career* Under-Sec Electricity Div Miny of Power 1961-65, chm N W Economic Planning Bd 1965-69, Dir of Economic Planning Cyprus 1969-70, Swaziland 1970-71, dir Salford U Appeal Fund 1971-; *Style* - Philip Chantler Esq, CMG; 1 Fingal pla, Edinburgh 9 (☎ 031 667 2657)

CHAPIN, Hon Mrs (Deirdre Jane Frances); *née* O'Brien; da of 16 Baron Inchiquin (d 1968); *b* 1924; *m* 1954, Horace Beecher Chapin, MD; *Style* - The Hon Mrs Chapin; 136 East 54th st, New York 21, USA; Quinville Abbey, Quin, Co Clare

CHAPLIN, 3 Viscount (1916 UK); Anthony Freskyn Charles Hamby Chaplin; s of 2 Viscount (d 1949, whose f, the 1 Viscount, had m Lady Florence Leveson-Gower, er da of 3 Duke of Sutherland; before that he had been affianced to Lady Florence Paget, but in 1864 she made a sensational elopement with the 4 Marquess of Hastings (great great unc of the present Lady Loudoun) via the Oxford Street entrance of Marshall & Snelgrove; three years later Lord Chaplin (as he then wasn't) had the satisfaction of winning the Derby (at 66-1) with his horse 'Hermit', thereby vicariously ruining Lord Hastings, who had wagered £100,000 on a different result) and Hon Gwladys, 4 da of 1 Baron Nunburnholme; *b* 14 Dec 1906; *Educ* Radley; *m* 1, 1933 (m dis 1951, she m 2 James Lees Milne), Alvilde, da of late Lt-Gen Sir Tom Bridges, KCB, KCMG; 1 da; m 2, 1951, Rosemary, da of 1 Visc Chandos, KG, DSO, MC, PC; 2 da; *Heir* none; *Career* Flight Lt RAF 1939-45; zoologist and musician; former Hon Sec Zoological Soc of London; *Style* - The Rt Hon the Viscount Chaplin; Wadstray House, Blackawton, nr Totnes, Devon

CHAPLIN, Hon Christina Susanna; da (by 2 m) of 3 Visc Chaplin; *b* 1958; *Style* - The Hon Christina Chaplin

CHAPLIN, Hon Miranda Amadea; da (by 2 m) of 3 Visc Chaplin; *b* 1956; *Style* - The Hon Miranda Chaplin

CHAPLIN, Hon Mrs Niall - Angela Marjory; da of late Hon Claud Lambton (d 1945), s of 2 Earl of Durham; *m* 1961, as his 2 w, Hon Niall Greville Chaplin (d 1963); *Style* - The Hon Mrs Niall Chaplin; Flat 4, 34 Ennismore gdns, SW7

CHAPLIN, Viscountess - Hon Rosemary; *née* Lyttelton; da of late 1 Visc Chandos; *b* 1922; *m* 1951, as his 2 w, 3 Viscount Chaplin; *Style* - The Rt Hon the Viscountess Chaplin; Wadstray House, Blackawton, Totnes, S Devon

CHAPLIN, William John Montague; s of late Rev Canon William Robert Moffett Chaplin; *b* 28 Feb 1932; *Educ* Shrewsbury, St Edmund Hall Oxford; *m* 1957, Claire Mary, nee Pedder; 3 s, 1 da; *Career* farmer and company director; chm Titus Wilson & Sons Ltd 1975-, dir Hawker Marris Ltd 1966-, Thomas Reed Ltd 1969-; *Style* - William Chaplin Esq; Finsthwaite House, nr Ulverston, Cumbria (☎ Newby Bridge 31339)

CHAPMAN, Brian Henry Gowland; s of Henry Chapman; *b* 27 March 1935; *Educ* Bradfield Coll, Clare Cambridge; *m* 1963, Anne Nicola Willoughby, nee Burton; 2 s; *Career* md GKN Crompton Ltd; *Style* - Brian Chapman Esq; Cherry Yate, Stoneygate lane, Ribchester, Preston, Lancs (☎ 0254 84 224)

CHAPMAN, (Anthony) Colin (Bruce); CBE (1970); s of late S F Kennedy Chapman; *b* 19 May 1928; *Educ* Stationers' Co's Sch, London U (BScEng); *m* 1954, Hazel Williams; 1 s, 2 da; *Career* former RAF pilot; car designer; chm Group Lotus Car Cos Ltd 1961- (founder Lotus Cars 1955), FRSA; *Style* - Colin Chapman Esq CBE; Lotus Cars Ltd, Norwich, Norfolk

CHAPMAN, His Honour Judge; Cyril Donald; QC (1965); s of Cyril Chapman; *b* 17 Sept 1920; *Educ* Roundhay Sch Leeds, BNC Oxford; *m* 1, 1950 (m dis 1959), Audrey Margaret Fraser, nee Gough; 1 s; m 2, 1960, Muriel Falconer Bristow; 1 s; *Career* barr 1947, contested (C) E Leeds 1955, Goole 1964, Brighouse and Spenborough 1966, Recorder of Huddersfield 1965-69, Bradford 1969-71, a Circuit Judge 1972-; *Style* - His Honour Judge Chapman, QC; Hill Top, Collingham, Wetherby, W Yorks (☎ Collingham Bridge 2813)

CHAPMAN, David Robert Macgowan; s and h of Sir Robin Chapman, 2 Bt, CBE, TD and Bar; *b* 16 Dec 1941; *Educ* Marlborough, McGill U Montreal; *m* 1965, Maria Elizabeth de Gosztony-Zsolnay, da of Dr N de Mattyasovsky-Zsolnay, of Montreal, Canada; 1 s, 1 da; *Career* dir North Eastern Investment Trust Ltd, John W Pratt Ltd and others; partner Wise Speke & Co Stock and Share Brokers, Newcastle; *Style* - David Chapman Esq; Rosemont, 2 West Meadows rd, Cleadon, Sunderland, Tyne and Wear

CHAPMAN, Hon Mrs; Hon (Catharine) Fiona; *née* Robertson; da of 1 Baron Robertson of Oakridge, GCB, GBE, KCMG, KCVO, DSO, MC; *b* 13 Aug 1939; *m* 1965, Allan Chapman; 2 da (twins); *Style* - The Hon Mrs Chapman; Sillwood, Apsley Guise, Bucks

CHAPMAN, (Francis) Ian; s of late Rev Peter Chapman; *b* 26 Oct 1925; *Educ* Shawlands Acad Glasgow, Royal Scottish Acad of Music; *m* 1953, Marjory Stewart, nee Swinton; 1 s, 1 da; *Career* book publisher; chm William Collins Publishers Ltd, Harvill Press Ltd, Hatchards Ltd,

Radio Clyde Ltd, dep chm William Collins (Hldgs) Ltd, dir Pan Books Ltd; Pres Publishers Assocn 1979-8; *Clubs* Brooks's; *Style* - Ian Chapman Esq; Kenmore, 46 The Avenue, Cheam, Surrey (☎ 01 642 1820)

CHAPMAN, Kenneth Herbert; s of Herbert Chapman; *b* 9 Sept 1908; *Educ* St Peter's York; *m* 1937, Jean Mahring; 1 s; *Career* solicitor 1931, former md Thomas Tilling Ltd, chm Goodliffe Garages Ltd, dir British Steam Specialities Gp Ltd, dir Ready Mixed Concrete Ltd; *Style* - Kenneth Chapman Esq; Cumberland House, Thakeham, nr Pulborough, Sussex (☎ W Chiltington 2103)

CHAPMAN, Sir Robin (Robert Macgowan); 2 Bt (UK 1958), of Cleadon, Co Durham, CBE (1961), TD and Bar (1947), JP (1946), DL (1952); s of 1 Bt (d 1963); *b* 12 Feb 1911; *Educ* Marlborough, CCC Cambridge; *m* 1941, Barbara May, nee Tonks; 2 s, 1 da; *Heir* s, David Chapman; *Career* chartered accountant, partner Chapman Hilton & Dunford, S Shields; chm Commercial Union Assurance Co Ltd (Newcastle Bd), James Hogg & Sons (North Shields) Ltd, North Eastern Investment Trust Ltd; dir Shields Commercial Building Soc, John W Pratt Ltd; Vice Lord-Lt Tyne and Wear 1974- High Sheriff Co Durham 1960; *Style* - Sir Robin Chapman Bt CBE TD* JP DL, HM Vice Lord-Lt for Tyne and Wear; Cherry Tree House, Cleadon, nr Sunderland (☎ Boldon 367451)

CHAPMAN, Roy de Courcy; s of Edward Chapman; *b* 1 Oct 1936; *Educ* St Andrews U, Moray House Coll of Educn Edinburgh; *m* 1959, Valerie Small; 2 s, 1 da; *Career* Rector of Glasgow Academy 1975-; *Style* - Roy Chapman Esq; 11 Kirklee ter, Glasgow G12 OTH

CHAPMAN, Hon Mrs (Rhiannon Elisabeth); *née* Philipps; da (by 1 m) of 2 Viscount St Davids; *b* 1946; *m* 1974, Donald Hudson Chapman; *Style* - The Hon Mrs Chapman; The Old School House, Odsey, Ashwell, Herts

CHAPMAN, Sir Stephen; s of late Sir Sydney Chapman, KCB, CBE, and Lady Chapman, JP; *b* 5 June 1907; *Educ* Westminster, Trin Coll Cambridge; *m* 1963, Mrs Pauline Niewiarowski, nee Allcard; *Career* barr 1931, former Recorder of Rochester and Cambridge, a Recorder of the Crown Court 1963-66, Recorder of Liverpool 1963-66, a Judge of the High Court of Justice Queen's Bench Div 1966-81 (ret), kt 1966; *Style* - Sir Stephen Chapman; Royal Courts of Justice, Strand, WC2; 72 Thomas More House, Barbican, EC2 (☎ 01 628 9251); The Manor House, Ware, Herts (☎ 2123)

CHAPPELL, (Edwin) Philip; CBE (1976); s of late Rev C R Chappell; *b* 12 June 1929; *Educ* Marlborough, Ch Ch Oxford; *m* 1962, Julia Clavering, nee House; 1 s, 3 da; *Career* chm ICL to 1981; dir Equity & Law Life Assurance, Guest Keen & Nettlefolds, Fisons; v-chm Morgan Grenfell Hldgs 1975-, dir 1964-; *Style* - Philip Chappell Esq CBE; 22 Frognal lane, NW3 (☎ 01 435 8627)

CHAPPLE, Frank Joseph; *b* 1921; *m* ; 2 s; *Career* electrician; memb TUC Gen Council 1971, gen sec Electrical, Electronic, Telecommunication and Plumbing Union 1966-, dir National Nuclear Corp 1980-; *Style* - Frank Chapple Esq; EETPU, Hayes Court, West Common rd, Bromley, Kent

CHARLEMONT, 13 Viscount (I 1665); Charles Wilberforce Caulfield; also Lord Caulfield and Baron of Charlemont (I 1620); s of late Charles Hans Caulfield; suc cousin, 12 Visc, 1979; *b* 10 March 1899; *m* 1930, Dorothy Jessie, nee Johnston; *Heir* nephew, John Day Caulfield; *Career* Civil Service, ret; *Style* - The Rt Hon the Viscount Charlemont; RR2, Cumberland, Ontario, Canada

CHARLES, Claude Roger; s of René G Charles; *b* 21 March 1937; *Educ* Wharton Sch of Finance & Commerce Pennsylvania U, Graduate Sch of Business Columbia U; *m* 1973, Gillian Rosemary; 2 s; *Career* merchant banker; exec dir S G Warburg & Co Ltd; *Style* - Claude Charles Esq; 3 Grosvenor Studios, Eaton ter, London SW1 (☎ 01 730 0602)

CHARLES, Lady - Gipsy Joan; *m* 1957, as his 2 w, Sir Noel Hughes Havelock Charles, 3 Bt, KCMG, MC (d 1975, when title became extinct); *Style* - Lady Charles; St Christophe, Châteauneuf-de-Grasse, France, AM

CHARLES, Sir John Pendrill; KCVO (1975), MC (1945); *b* 3 May 1914; *Educ* Tonbridge, Magdalene Cambridge; *m* 1, 1939 (m dis), Mary Dudley; m 2, 1959, Winifred Marie Heath; 2 da; *Career* solicitor 1938, ptnr Allen & Overy 1947-78; *Style* - Sir John Charles, KCVO, MC; 3 Wilton Row, Belgrave sq, SW1 (☎ 01 235 5792)

CHARLES, Rev Canon Sebastian; s of Gnanamuthu Charles; *b* 31 May 1932; *Educ* Madras and Serampore Us, Lincoln Theol Coll; *m* 1967, Frances Challen; 2 s, 2 da; *Career* former Vicar St Barnabas' Pendleton and chaplain Salford U, asst gen sec and sec British Council of Churches (Community Affairs) 1974-78, Residentiary Canon Westminster Abbey 1978-; *Style* - The Rev Canon Sebastian Charles; Westminster Abbey, SW1 (☎ 01 222 6939)

CHARLESWORTH, David Anthony; s of David Harold Charlesworth, MBE (d 1970); *b* 19 July 1936; *Educ* Haileybury, ISC; *m* 1970 (m dis 1975), Carol Ann, nee Green; *Career* Capt RA, underwriting memb of Lloyd's 1975, dir- Surban Trading Co Ltd 1968-, Michael Ashby Fine Arts Ltd 1978-, Johnson & Avon Ltd 1978-, SGB Gp 1973-76; *Recreations* bridge, listening to Mozart, walking; *Clubs* Institute of Directors; *Style* - David Charlesworth Esq; 4 Shaftesbury Mews, Stratford rd, W8 (☎ 01 937 3550)

CHARLTON, (Frederick) Noel; CB (1961), CBE (1946); s of late Frederick Charlton; *b* 4 Dec 1906; *Educ* Rugby, Hertford Oxford; *m* 1932, Maud Helen Rudgard; *Career* solicitor 1932, Solicitor's Dept Treasury 1946, Princ Asst Slr (Litigation) 1956-71, sec Lord Chancellor's Ctee on Defamation 1971-74, employed Dept of Energy 1975-78; *Style* - Noel Charlton Esq, CB, CBE; Windyridge, 11 Hillcroft av, Purley, Surrey (☎ 01 660 2802)

CHARLTON, Sir William Arthur; DSC (1943); s of William Charlton; *b* 25 Feb 1893; *m* 1919, Eleanor Elcoat (d 1978); 2 s; *Career* General Marine Superintendent New York, Furness Withy & Co SS Lines to 1960, Liveryman Hon Co of Master Mariners, Younger Brother Trinity House, kt 1946; *Style* - Sir William Charlton, DSC; Apt 419, 81 Linden av, Rochester, NY 14610, USA

CHARNLEY, Sir John; CBE (1970); *b* 29 Aug 1911; *Educ* Bury G S Lancs, Manchester U (BSc, MB, ChB); *m* 1957, Jill Margaret, nee Heaver; 1 s, 1 da; *Career* surgeon; consultant orthopaedic surgeon and dir Wrightington Hosp Centre for Hip Surgery, Wigan; Prof of Orthopaedic Surgery Manchester U 1972-76, now Emeritus; kt 1977; *Style* - Sir John Charnley, CBE; Birchwood, Moss lane, Mere, Knutsford, Cheshire (☎ Knutsford 2267)

CHARNLEY, Sir William John; CB (1973); s of George Charnley; *b* 4 Sept 1922; *Educ* Oulton H S Liverpool, Liverpool U; *m* 1945, Mary Paden; 1 s, 1 da; *Career* aerodynamic scientist; ch scientist RAF 1973-77, dep controller R & D Establishments and controller Research MOD 1975-77, controller R & D Establishments and Research 1977-; kt 1980; *Style* - Sir William Charnley, CB; Kirkstones, Brackendale close, Camberley, Surrey (☎ 22547)

CHARNWOOD, Baroness - Beryl Joan; da of late Percy Cuthbert Quilter; *m* 1933, 2 Baron Charnwood (d 1955, when title became extinct); *Style* - The Rt Hon the Lady Charnwood; Court Lodge Farm, East Brabourne, Kent

CHARRINGTON, Gerald Anthony; DL (Essex 1977); s of Brig Harold Vincent Spencer Charrington, DSO, MC; *b* 14 July 1926; *Educ* Eton, Sandhurst, Staff Coll; *m* 1957, Susannah Elizabeth, da of Brig Ord Henderson Tidbury, MC, of The Greate House, Layer de la Haye; 3 s, 1 da; *Career* farmer 1969-, High Sheriff of Essex 1981-82, Church Cmmr 1978-, memb Gen Synod 1970-; *Recreations* shooting, beagling, Tudor brickwork, church architecture; *Clubs* Roy Commonwealth;

Style - Gerald Charrington Esq, DL; Layer Marney Tower, Colchester, Essex (☎ 0206 330202)

CHARTERIS OF AMISFIELD, Baron (Life Peer UK 1977); Martin Michael Charles Charteris; GCB (1977, KCB 1972, CB 1958), GCVO (1976, KCVO 1962, MVO 1953), OBE 1946, QSO (1978), PC (1972); s of late Capt Hugh Francis Charteris, Lord Elcho, and bro of 12 Earl of Wemyss and March; *b* 7 Sept 1913; *Educ* Eton, Sandhurst; *m* 1944, Hon (Mary) Gay Hobart Margesson, da of 1 Viscount Margesson; 2 s, 1 da; *Career* Asst Private Sec to HM the Queen 1952-72, Private Sec to HM the Queen and Keeper of HM's Archives 1972-77, a Permanent Lord in Waiting to HM the Queen 1978-, dir De La Rue Co 1978-, Rio Tinto Zinc Corp, Claridge's and Connaught Hotels, Provost of Eton 1978-; *Style* - The Rt Hon the Lord Charteris of Amisfield GCB GCVO OBE QSO PC; Provost's Lodge, Eton College, Windsor, Berks (☎ 66304); Wood Stanway House, Wood Stanway, Cheltenham, Glos

CHARTERIS, Hon Andrew Martin; s of Baron Charteris of Amisfield (Life Peer); *b* 1947; *Educ* Milton Abbey; *Style* - The Hon Andrew Charteris

CHARTERIS OF AMISFIELD, Baroness; Hon (Mary) Gay Hobart; da of late 1 Visc Margesson; *b* 1919; *m* 1944, Baron Charteris of Amisfield GCB, GCVO, OBE, QSO, PC; *Style* - The Rt Hon The Lady Charteris of Amisfield

CHARTERIS, Hon Harold Francis; s of Baron Charteris of Amisfield; *b* 1950; *Educ* Eton, Pembroke Coll Cambridge; *Style* - The Hon Harold Charteris

CHARTERIS, Hon Mrs Guy; Violet; da of Alfred Masterton Porter, of Dundee; *m* 1945, as his 2 w, Capt Hon Guy Charteris (d 1967), 2 s of 11 Earl of Wemyss and (7 of) March; *Style* - The Hon Mrs Guy Charteris; The Old House, Didbrook, Winchcombe, Glos

CHATAWAY, Rt Hon Christopher John; PC (1970); s of late J D P Chataway; *b* 31 Jan 1931; *Educ* Sherborne, Magdalen Oxford; *m* 1, 1959 (m dis 1975), Anna Lett; 2 s, 1 da; m 2, 1976, Carola Walker; 1 s; *Career* Olympic runner 1952 and 1956 (world record holder 5,000 metres 1954); former TV News reporter; MP (C) Lewisham N 1959-66, Chichester 1969-74; Min of Posts & Telecommunications 1970-72, for Industrial Dvpt 1972-74; chm London Broadcasting Co 1981-, dir Dorchester Hotel, British Electric Traction Co, md Orion Bank 1974-; *Style* - The Rt Hon Christopher Chataway; 40 Addison rd, W14

CHATER, Dr Anthony Philip John; *b* 21 Dec 1929; *Educ* Northampton G S, Queen Mary Coll London; *m* 1954, Janice, nee Smith; 3 s; *Career* biochemist; former teacher and lectr; contested Luton (Com) 1963, 1964, 1966, 1970; National Chm Communist Party 1967-69; ed Morning Star 1974-; *Style* - Dr Anthony Chater; 8 Katherine drive, Dunstable, Beds (☎ 64835)

CHATFIELD, 2 Baron (1937 UK); Ernle David Lewis Chatfield; s of 1 Baron, GCB, OM, KCMG, CVO, PC (Admiral of the Fleet, d 1967); *b* 2 Jan 1917; *Educ* Dartmouth, Trin Cambridge; *m* 1969, (Felicia Mary) Elizabeth, da of Dr John Bulman *Heir* none *Career* ADC to Govr-Gen Canada 1940-44; *Style* - The Rt Hon the Lord Chatfield; RR2, Williamstown, Ontario, Canada

CHATTEN, Harold Raymond Percy; CB (1975); s of Walter Chatten, CBE; *b* 1 Oct 1919; *Educ* Dulwich Coll, Clare Cambridge; *m* Eileen Mary Grindell; *Career* former gen man HM Dockyard Rosyth, ch exec Royal Dockyards MOD (Navy) 1975-79, head of Royal Corps of Naval Constructors 1979; *Style* - Harold Chatten Esq, CB; MOD (Navy), Carpenter House, Broad Quay, Bath (☎ 28391)

CHAU, Hon Sir Sik-Nin; CBE (1950), JP (1940); s of late Cheuk-Fan Chau; *b* 13 April 1903; *Educ* St Stephen's Coll Hong Kong; Hong Kong, London, Vienna State U; *m* 1927, Ida Hing-Kwai; 2 s; *Career* memb Hong Kong Exec Council 1947-62, company director, pres Firecrackers and Fireworks Co Ltd (Taiwan), State Trading

Corp (Far East) Ltd, hon chm Hong Kong Chinese Bank Ltd, kt 1960; *Style* - Hon Sir Sik-Nin Chau, CBE, JP; IL 3547 Hatton rd, Hong Kong (☎ 433695)

CHAUVEL, Jean; Hon GCMG (1960), Hon GCVO (1957); s of Ferdinand Chauvel; *b* 16 April 1897; *Educ* Paris University; *m* 1926, Diane de Warzee d'Hermalle; 2 s, 2 da; *Career* diplomat; former French Ambassador to Berne, Austria, London (1955-62); author; *Style* - Monsieur Jean Chauvel GCMG GCVO; 123 Rue de la Tour, 75016 Paris, France; Le Ruluet, Combrit, Finistère

CHAVASSE, His Honour Judge - Michael Louis Maude; QC (1968); s of late Christopher Chavasse, former Bishop of Rochester; *b* 5 Jan 1923; *Educ* Shrewsbury, Trin Oxford; *m* 1951, Rose Ethel, da of late Vice-Adm Arthur Read, CB; 3 da; *Career* barr 1950, Recorder of the Crown Court 1972-77, a Circuit Judge 1977-; *Style* - His Honour Judge Chavasse, QC; 2 Paper Buildings, Temple, EC4; Park House, Chevening, Sevenoaks, Kent (☎ Knockholt 2271)

CHAYTOR, (Herbert) Gordon; s of Herbert Chaytor (d 1979); hp of cous, Sir George Chaytor, 8 Bt; *b* 1922; *m* 1947, Mary Alice, nee Craven; 3 s; *Style* - Gordon Chaytor Esq; Honeymoon Bay, British Columbia, Canada

CHAYTOR, Sir George Reginald; 8 Bt (UK 1831), of Croft, Yorkshire, and Witton Castle, Durham; s of late William Chaytor, gs of 2 Bt; suc kinsman, Sir William Chaytor, 7 Bt, 1976; *b* 28 Oct 1912; *m* 1970, Mrs Elsie Magdeline Rogers; *Heir* cousin, (Herbert) Gordon Chaytor; *Career* patron (alternately) of living of Witton-le-Wear *Style* - Sir George Chaytor, Bt; 32 Bonny av, Chilliwack, British Columbia, Canada

CHAYTOR, Patricia, Lady - Patricia Nora; da of Loftus Joseph McCaffry and former w of George Walkley Alderman; *m* 1947, Sir William Henry Clervaux Chaytor, 7 Bt (d 1976); *Style* - Patricia, Lady Chaytor; Nowat, No 3, Tower pla, York

CHEADLE, Sir Eric Wallers; CBE (1973); s of Edgar Cheadle; *b* 14 May 1908; *Educ* Farnworth G S; *m* 1938, Pamela, nee Hulme; 2 s; *Career* joined Evening Chronicle and Daily Dispatch 1924, md Thomson Organisation 1959-74, ret; dir Thomson International Press Consultancy Ltd, Macclesfield Press Ltd, Lancs and Cheshire County Newspapers Ltd, North Western Newspaper Co Ltd, Burnley Buidling Soc, Stockport Express Ltd; kt 1978; *Style* - Sir Eric Cheadle, CBE; The Old Church House, 172 Fishpool st, St Albans, Herts (☎ 59639)

CHEALES, Maxwell Bellingham; s of late Lt-Cdr Ralph Cheales; *b* 4 Nov 1929; *Educ* Michaelhouse S Africa, Pembroke Coll Cambridge; *m* 1960, Hermione Ann, nee Hogarth; 1 s, 2 da; *Career* dir Hill Samuel & Co Ltd 1965-77, chm 1978- and md 1971- Hogarth Shipping Co Ltd Glasgow, FICA; *Style* - Maxwell Cheales Esq; 44 Nella rd, W6 (☎ 01 385 4134); Blenburton Hall, Aston Upthorpe, Didcot, Oxon (☎ 0235 850772)

CHECKETTS, Sqdn Ldr Sir David John; KCVO (1979, CVO 1969, MVO 1966); s of late Reginald Checketts; *b* 23 Aug 1930; *m* 1958, Rachel Leila Warren Herrick; 1 s, 3 da; *Career* 3 Sqdn Germany 1960-61, Equerry to HRH the Duke of Edinburgh 1961-66, Equerry to HRH the Prince of Wales 1967-70 and Extra Equerry 1979-, Private Sec 1970-78; dir Phoenix Lloyd Ltd, Neilson McCarthy Co; *Style* - Squadron Leader Sir David Checketts, KCVO; Church Cottage, Winkfield, Windsor, Berks

CHEDLOW, Barry William; QC (1969); *b* 8 Oct 1921; *Educ* Burnage H S, Manchester U; *m* Anne Sheldon; 1 s, 1 da; *Career* Flight-Lt RAF 1943, barr 1947, a Recorder of the Crown Court 1974-; *Style* - Barry Chedlow Esq, QC; 12 King's Bench Walk, Temple, EC4 (☎ 01 583 0811); Little Kimblewick Farm, Finch lane, Amersham, Bucks (☎ Little Chalfont 2156)

CHEETHAM, John Frederick Thomas; CB (1978); s of late James Cheetham; *b* 27 March 1919; *Educ* Penarth G S, Wales U; *m* 1943, Yvonne Marie Smith; 1 s, 1 da;

Career former dep sec Exchequer and Audit Dept, sec 1975-79; *Style* - John Cheetham Esq, CB; 70 Chatsworth rd, Croydon, Surrey (☎ 01 688 3740)

CHEETHAM, Lady Mabel Kathleen; *née* Jocelyn; da of 8 Earl of Roden; *b* 25 March 1915; *m* 1, 1937 (m dis 1959), Richard Brooke (now Sir Richard Brooke, 10 Bt), late Lt Scots Gds; 2 s (Richard, h to Btcy; Piers); m 2, 1960, Sir Nicholas Cheetham, KCMG, *qv*; *Style* - Lady Mabel Cheetham; 50 Cadogan sq, SW1

CHEETHAM, Sir Nicolas John Alexander; KCMG (1964, CMG 1953); s of late Sir Milne Cheetham; *b* 8 Oct 1910; *Educ* Eton, Ch Ch Oxford; *m* 1, 1937 (m dis 1960), Jean Evison Corfe; 2 s; m 2, 1960, Lady Mabel Brooke, nee Jocelyn; *Career* joined HM Diplomatic Service 1934, Min to Hungary 1959-61, Asst Under-Sec FO 1961-64, Ambass to Mexico 1964-68; *Style* - Sir Nicolas Cheetham, KCMG; 50 Cadogan sq, SW1; 83122 Claviers, France

CHEGWIDDEN, Sir Thomas Sidney; CB (1943); s of late Thomas Chegwidden; *b* 7 Feb 1895; *Educ* Plymouth Coll, Maidstone G S, Worcester Coll Oxford; *m* 1, 1919, Kathleen Muriel, nee Breeds; m 2, 1934, Beryl Sinclair, nee Nicholson (d 1980); *Career* joined Civil Service 1919, Under-Sec Miny of Production 1942-46, Civilian Dir of Studies Imperial Defence Coll 1946-47, chm S Rhodesia Public Services Bd and Police Advisory Bd 1947-53, former pres Assoc of Rhodesian Industries and Council memb Rhodesia U, kt 1955; *Style* - Sir Thomas Chegwidden, CB; Greathed Manor, Lingfield, Surrey

CHEKE, Hon Lady (Constance Elizabeth); *née* Lopes; da of 1 Baron Roborough, JP, DL, and Lady Albertha, da of 4 Earl of Mount Edgcumbe; *b* 24 Aug 1901; *m* 1939, Sir Marcus John Cheke, KCVO, CMG (d 1960), sometime Minister to the Holy See and s of Col Edward Cheke; *Career* sometime temp Lady in Waiting to HRH Duchess of Gloucester c 1963; *Style* - The Hon Lady Cheke; The Rock Hotel, Yelverton, S Devon

CHELMER, Baron (Life Peer UK 1963); Eric Cyril Boyd Edwards; MC (1944), TD, JP (Essex 1950), DL (1971); s of Col C E Edwards, DSO, MC, TD, DL, JP; *b* 9 Oct 1914; *Educ* Felsted Sch; *m* 1939, Enid, nee Harvey; 1 s; *Career* solicitor 1937; former chm National Union of Conservative Assocs, treasurer Conservative Party 1965-77 dir NEM Gp of Cos 1977-, chm Provident Financial Gp 1977-, chm Greycoats Estates Ltd; kt 1954; *Style* - Rt Hon Lord Chelmer MC TD JP DL; 5 John st, WC1; Peacocks, Margaretting, Essex

CHELMSFORD, 3 Viscount (UK 1921); Frederic Jan Thesiger; also Baron Chelmsford (UK 1858); s of 2 Viscount (d 1970) and Gilian Lubbock (great niece of 1 Baron Avebury); 1 cous once removed of Wilfrid Thesiger, the Arabist and traveller; *b* 7 March 1931; *m* 1958, Clare, nee Rendle; 1 s, 1 da; *Heir* Hon Frederic Thesiger; *Career* late Lt Inns of Court Regt, Lloyd's Insurance broker; *Style* - The Rt Hon the Viscount Chelmsford; 26 Ormonde Gate, SW3 (☎ 01 352 5636); Hazelbridge Court, Chiddingfold, Surrey

CHELMSFORD, 6 Bishop of (cr 1914) 1971-; Rt Rev Albert John Trillo; s of late Albert Trillo; *b* 4 July 1915; *Educ* The Quintin Sch, King's Coll London U (MTh); *m* 1942, Patricia Eva, da of Rev Canon Gilbert Hemming Williams; 2 s, 1 da; *Career* Curate Ch Ch Fulham 1938-41, Bp of St Albans 1963-71, Bedford 1963-68, Hertford 1968-71; *Style* - The Rt Rev the Lord Bishop of Chelmsford; Bishopscourt, Chelmsford, Essex (☎ 353053)

CHELSEA, Viscount; Charles Gerald John Cadogan; s and h of 7 Earl Cadogan; *b* 24 March 1937; *Educ* Eton; *m* 1963, Lady Philippa Wallop, da of 9 Earl of Portsmouth; 2 s, 1 da; *Heir* s, Hon Edward Cadogan; *Style* - Viscount Chelsea; 7 Smith st, SW3 (☎ 01 730 2465); Marndhill, Ardington, Wantage, Oxon (☎ E Hendred 273)

CHELSEA, Viscountess - Lady Philippa Dorothy Bluett; *née* Wallop; da of 9 Earl of Portsmouth; *b* 1937; *m* 1963, Charles Gerald John, Viscount Chelsea, s of 7 Earl Cadogan; *Style* - Viscountess

Chelsea; 7 Smith Street, SW3; Marndhill, Ardington, Wantage, Oxon

CHELWOOD, Baron (Life Peer UK 1974); Tufton Victor Hamilton Beamish; MC (1940); s of late Rear-Adm T P H Beamish, CB; *b* 27 Jan 1917; *Educ* Stowe, Sandhurst; *m* 1, 1950 (m dis 1973), Janet McMillan, nee Stevenson (d 1975); 2 da; m 2, 1975, Mrs Pia McHenry, nee Baroness Maria Pia von Roretz; *Career* MP (C) Lewes 1945-74, Hon Col 411 (Sussex) Coast Regt RA (TA) 1951-57, Opposition defence spokesman 1965-67, jt v-chm 1922 Cmtee 1958-74, chm of Cons Gp for Europe 1970-73, jt dep ldr British Delegation to European Parlt 1973-74, company director, author, DL E Sussex 1970, kt 1961; *Clubs* White's; *Style* - The Rt Hon Lord Chelwood MC DL; Plover's Meadow, Uckfield, Sussex

CHERMONT, Jayme Sloan; Hon KCVO (1968); s of Ambassador E L Chermont; *b* 5 April 1903; *Educ* Law Sch, Rio de Janeiro U; *m* 1928, Zaide Alvim de Mello Franco (decd); *Career* Brazilian Foreign Office 1928, Ambass to Netherlands 1963-66, to the Court of St James's 1966-68, ret; *Style* - Jayme Chermont Esq, Hon KCVO

CHESHAM, 5 Baron (UK 1858); John Charles Compton Cavendish; PC (1964); s of 4 Baron (d 1952), himself ggs of 1 Baron (4 s of 1 Earl of Burlington); *b* 18 June 1916; *Educ* Eton, Zuoz Coll Switzerland, Trin Cambridge; *m* 1937, Mary Edmunds, nee Marshall; 2 s, 2 da; *Heir* s, Hon Nicholas Cavendish; *Career* former JP Bucks, a Lord-in-Waiting to HM 1955-59, Parly Sec Miny of Transport 1959-64, exec v-chm RAC 1966-70, v-pres British Road Fedn 1972-76 (formerly pres); *Style* - The Rt Hon the Lord Chesham, PC; Manor Farm, Preston Candover, nr Basingstoke, Hants (☎ Preston Candover 230)

CHESHIRE, Hon Elizabeth Diana; da of Baroness Ryder of Warsaw and Gp Capt Leonard Cheshire, *qqv*; *b* 1962; *Style* - The Hon Elizabeth Cheshire

CHESHIRE, Hon Mrs (Isobel Gray); da of 1 Viscount Addison, KG, PC, MD, FRCS; *b* 1907; *m* 1932, Nicholas, s of Francis Augustus Cheshire, of St Petersburg (now Leningrad); 1 s, 2 da; *Style* - The Hon Mrs Cheshire; Ballinger, Gt Missenden, Bucks

CHESHIRE, Hon Jeremy Charles; s of Baroness Ryder of Warsaw and Gp Capt Leonard Cheshire, *qqv*; *b* 1960; *Style* - The Hon Jeremy Cheshire

CHESHIRE, Group Captain (Geoffrey) Leonard; VC (1944), OM (1981), DSO (1940), DFC (1941), RAF Retd; s of late Geoffrey Cheshire; *b* 7 Sept 1917; *Educ* Stowe, Merton Oxford; *m* 2, 1959, Susan Ryder (Baroness Ryder of Warsaw, *qv*); 1 s, 1 da; *Career* joined Oxford U Sqdn 1936, RAFR 1937, Pilot Officer RAF 1939, Wing Cdr 1944, Group Capt 1944, ret 1946; founder Leonard Cheshire Foundation, co-founder Mission for the Relief of Suffering (with Baroness Ryder of Warsaw); *Style* - Group Capt Leonard Cheshire, VC, OM, DSO, DFC; Cavendish, Suffolk

CHESTER, 38 Bishop of (1541) 1974-82; Rt Rev Hubert Victor Whitsey; s of Samuel Whitsey; *b* 21 Nov 1916; *Educ* Queen Elizabeth's G S Blackburn, Tech Coll Blackburn, St Edmund Hall Oxford, Westcott House Cambridge; *m* 1950, Jean Margaret, da of Silas Bellinger; 2 s, 1 da; *Career* Bishop of Chester 1974 to Dec 31 1981; patron of 114 livings, the Canonries of the Cathedral, The Archdeaconries of Chester and Macclesfield, and the Chllrship of the Diocese; Asst Curate Chorley Lancs 1949-51, Hon Canon Manchester Cathedral 1963, Emeritus 1968, Bp Suffragan of Hertford 1971-74; *Style* - The Rt Rev the Lord Bishop of Chester; Bishop's House, Chester

CHESTER, Sir (Daniel) Norman; CBE (1951); s of Daniel Chester; *b* 27 Oct 1907; *Educ* Manchester U; *m* 1936, Eva, nee Jeavons (d 1980); *Career* Official Fellow Nuffield Coll Oxford 1945-54, Warden 1954-78, former memb Oxford City Council and chm Oxford Centre for Management Studies, kt 1974; *Style* - Sir Norman Chester, CBE; 136 Woodstock rd, Oxford

CHESTERFIELD, Arthur Desborough; CBE (1962); s of Arthur Chesterfield; *b* 21 Aug 1905; *Educ* Hastings G S; *m* 1932, Betty, nee Downey; 2 s, 3 da; *Career* joined Westminster Bank 1923, dir 1963-69; dir Singer & Friedlander (Hldgs) Ltd 1967-, Singer & Friedlander Ltd 1967-, Percy Bilton Ltd 1977-, Clifford Property Co Ltd, v-chm Woolwich Equitable Building Soc 1976-; *Style* - Arthur Chesterfield Esq, CBE; Coaters, Shirleys, Ditchling, Sussex (☎ Hassocks 3514)

CHESTERMAN, Sir Ross; s of late Dudley Chesterman; *b* 27 April 1909; *Educ* Hastings G S, Imperial Coll of Science London; *m* 1938, Audrey Mary Horlick; 1 s, 1 da; *Career* former headmaster (Meols Cop Secondary Sch Southport) and school inspector; Warden of Goldsmiths' Coll London U 1953-74, Dean of the Coll of Craft Educn 1958-60, Master 1960-; Freeman and Liveryman Goldsmiths' Co; kt 1970; *Style* - Sir Ross Chesterman; Greenacre, 27 Greenhill rd, Otford, Sevenoaks, Kent

CHESTERTON, Sir Oliver Sidney; MC (1943); s of Frank Chesterton; *b* 28 Jan 1913; *Educ* Rugby; *m* 1944, Violet Ethel, nee Jameson; 2 s, 1 da; *Career* chartered surveyor 1934, sr ptnr Chesterton & Sons, chm Woolwich Equitable Building Soc 1976- (formerly v-chm); kt 1969; *Style* - Sir Oliver Chesterton, MC (1943); 7 York House, Kensington Church st, W8

CHETWODE, 2 Baron (UK 1945); Sir Philip Chetwode; 8 Bt (E 1700); s (by 1 m) of Capt Hon Roger Chetwode (s of 1 Baron) and Hon Molly, nee Berry, da of 1 Visc Camrose; suc grandfather 1950; nephew of w of Sir John Betjeman; *b* 26 March 1937; *Educ* Eton; *m* 1967 (m dis 1979), Mrs Susan Dudley Smith, da of Capt Voltelin James Howard Van der Byl, DSC, RN (ret); 2 s, 1 da; *Heir* s, Hon Roger Chetwode; *Career* Capt (ret) Royal Horse Guards; *Clubs* White's; *Style* - The Rt Hon the Lord Chetwode; 31 Moore st, SW3 (☎ 01 584 6300); Crowood House, Ramsbury, Wilts (☎ 242)

CHETWODE, Hon Alexander; s of 2 Baron Chetwode; *b* 1969

CHETWODE, Hon Christopher Roger; s of late Capt Roger Charles George Chetwode and bro of 2 Baron Chetwode; *b* 1940; *Educ* Eton; *m* 1961, Hon Philippa Mary Imogen, nee Brand, da of 5 Visc Hampden; 5 s; *Career* raised to the rank of a Baron's son 1951; *Style* - The Hon Christopher Chetwode; Hill House, Cheriton, Alresford, Hants

CHETWODE, Hon Miranda; da of 2 Baron Chetwode; *b* 1974

CHETWODE, Hon Roger; s and h of 2 Baron Chetwode; *b* 29 May 1968; *Style* - The Hon Roger Chetwode

CHETWODE, Lady Willa; *née* Elliot; da of 5 Earl of Minto (d 1975); *b* 1924; *m* 1946, Maj George David Chetwode, MBE; 1 s, 5 da; *Style* - Lady Willa Chetwode; The Mantles, Blyth, Worksop, Notts

CHETWYND, 10 Viscount (I 1717); Adam Richard John Casson Chetwynd; also Baron Rathdown (I 1717); s of 9 Viscount (d 1965); *b* 2 Feb 1935; *Educ* Eton; *m* 1, 1966 (m dis 1974), Celia Grace, da of Cdr Alexander Robert Ramsay, DSC, RNVR; 2 s, 1 da; m 2, 1974, Angela May, nee McCarthy; *Heir* s, Hon Adam Chetwynd; *Career* Lt Queen's Own Cameron Highlanders, now business man Prudential Assurance Co of SA Ltd, Harland House Branch, Johannesburg; *Style* - The Rt Hon the Viscount Chetwynd; c/o J G Ouvry Esq, Lee Bolton & Lee, 1 The Sanctuary, Westminster, SW1

CHETWYND, Audrey, Lady - (Frances) Audrey; da of late Dr Thomas Smith; *m* 1956, as his 3 w, Sir (Arthur Henry) Talbot Chetwynd, 7 Bt, OBE, MC (d 1972); *Style* - Audrey, Lady Chetwynd; Firs Cottage, 63 Belmore lane, Lymington, Hants

CHETWYND, Hon Adam Douglas; s (by 1 m) and h of 10 Viscount Chetwynd; *b* 26 Feb 1969; *Style* - The Hon Adam Chetwynd

CHETWYND, Sir Arthur Ralph Talbot; 8 Bt (GB 1795), of Brocton Hall, Staffordshire; s of late William Chetwynd, MC, bro of 7 Bt; suc unc 1972; *b* 28 Oct 1913; *Educ* British Columbia U; *m* 1940, Marjory May MacDonald, nee Lang; 2 s; *Heir* s, Robin Talbot; *Career* former rancher and physical education instructor; chm Chetwynd Films Ltd Toronto, pres Brocton Hall Communications Ltd Toronto; *Style* - Sir Arthur Chetwynd, Bt; 95 Thorncliffe Park drive, Leaside Towers, Apt 402, Toronto, Ontario, Canada

CHETWYND, Hon Catherine Sophia Marianne; da (by 2 m) of late 9 Visc Chetwynd; *b* 1956; *Style* - The Hon Catherine Chetwynd

CHETWYND, Dorothea, Viscountess - Dorothea Marianne; MBE (1974); da of late Lt-Col Angus Colin Duncan-Johnstone, MBE, ED; *m* 1952, as his 2 w, 9 Visc Chetwynd (d 1965); 2 da (Hon Catherine Sophia Marianne b 5 Oct 1956; Hon Frances Diana Dorothea b 19 Jan 1959); *Career* OStJ; *Style* - The Rt Hon Dorothea, Viscountess Chetwynd, MBE; Daniel's Lane, Stype, Hungerford, Berks

CHETWYND, Hon (Mary Diana) Eve; da of late 8 Visc Chetwynd; *b* 1908; *Style* - The Hon Eve Chetwynd; 6 Hulton drive, Emberton, Olney, Bucks

CHETWYND, Hon Emma Grace; da (by 1 m) of 10 Viscount Chetwynd; *b* 1967; *Style* - The Hon Emma Chetwynd

CHETWYND, Hon Frances Diana Dorothea; da (by 2 m) of late 9 Visc Chetwynd; *b* 1959; *Style* - The Hon Frances Chetwynd

CHETWYND, Hon Mrs John - Margaret Agnes; da of late Maj-Gen Hugh Clement Sutton, CB, CMG; *m* 1937, Hon John Julian Cetwynd (s of late 8 Visc Chetwynd and who d 1966); 2 s; *Style* - The Hon Mrs John Chetwynd; 3 Cadogan sq, SW1

CHETWYND, Hon Robert Duncan; twin s (by 1 m) of 10 Visc Chetwynd; *b* 26 Feb 1969; *Style* - The Hon Robert Chetwynd

CHETWYND, Robin John Talbot; s and h of Sir Arthur Chetwynd, 8 Bt; *b* 21 Aug 1941; *m* 1967, Heather Helen, nee Lothian; 1 s, 1 da; *Style* - Robin Chetwynd Esq; 20 Cockburn drive, Scarborough, Ontario M1C 2T2, Canada

CHETWYND-TALBOT, Hon Paul Alexander Anthony Bueno; s (by 1 m) of late 21 Earl of Shrewsbury and Waterford; *b* 1957; *Style* - The Hon Paul Chetwynd-Talbot

CHETWYND-TALBOT, His Honour Judge - Richard Michael Arthur; s of late Rev Arthur Talbot (s of Rev Hon Arthur Chetwynd-Talbot, 3 s of 2 Earl Talbot); 2 cous twice removed of 21 Earl of Shrewsbury and Waterford, the Premier Earl (on the Roll) of England and Ireland; *b* 28 Sept 1911; *Educ* Harrow, Magdalene Cambridge; *Career* barr 1936, bencher Middle Temple 1962, former Recorder of Banbury, Dep Chm Salop Quarter Sessions 1950-67, Chm 1967-71, a Circuit Judge 1972-; *Style* - His Honour Judge Chetwynd-Talbot; 7 St Leonard's close, Bridgnorth, Salop (☎ Bridgnorth 3619)

CHETWYND-TALBOT, Lady Victoria Jane; da of 22 Earl of Shrewsbury and Waterford; *b* 1975

CHEWTON, Viscount; James Sherbrooke Waldegrave; s and h of 12 Earl Waldegrave, KG, GCVO, TD; *b* 8 Dec 1940; *Educ* Eton, Trin Cambridge; *Style* - Viscount Chewton; West End Farm, Chewton Mendip, Bath

CHEYNE, Major Sir Joseph Lister Watson; 3 Bt (UK 1908), OBE (1976); s of Col Sir Joseph Cheyne, 2 Bt, MC (d 1957); *b* 10 Oct 1914; *Educ* Stowe, CCC Cambridge; *m* 1, 1938 (m dis 1955, she d 1959), da of late Vice-Adm J D Allen, CB; 1 s, 1 da; m 2, 1955, Cicely, nee Metcalfe; 2 s, 1 da; *Heir* s, Patrick Cheyne; *Career* former First Sec British Embassy Rome, curator Keats Shelley Memorial House Rome 1976-; *Style* - Major Sir Joseph Cheyne, Bt, OBE; Leagarth, Rome, Italy (☎ 5778835); Leagarth, Fetlar, Shetland

CHEYNE, Patrick John Lister; s (by 1 m) and h of Sir Joseph Cheyne, 3 Bt, OBE; *b* 2 July 1941; *Educ* Lancing; *m* 1968, Helen Louise Trevor, nee Smith; 1 s, 3 da; *Style* - Patrick Cheyne Esq; 5 Avereng rd, Folkestone, Kent

CHIBBETT, Geoffrey John; s of late Ernest Chibbett; *b* 2 Sept 1928; *Educ* Stowe, Liverpool U; *m* 1977, Diana Leslie, nee Green; 1 s, 1 da; *Career* chartered accountant, chm Dobson Park Industries Ltd (Midlands Div), chm Dobson Park Properties Ltd; *Style* - Geoffrey Chibbett Esq; 8 Old Manor close, Woodborough, nr Nottingham (☎ Nottingham 652236)

CHICHESTER, 9 Earl of (UK 1801); Sir John Nicholas Pelham; 14 Bt (E 1611); also Baron Pelham of Stanmer (GB 1762); s of 8 Earl of Chichester (ka 1944); *b* (posthumously) 14 April 1944; *Educ* Standbridge Earls Sch; *m* 1975, Mrs June Marijke Hall, da of Gp-Capt E D Wells, DSO, DFC, of Marbella; *Heir* kinsman, Richard Pelham; *Career* farmer; *Recreations* music, theatre, tennis, riding; *Style* - The Rt Hon the Earl of Chichester; 53 Shawfield st, SW3 (☎ 01 352 1516); Little Durnford Manor, Salisbury, Wilts

CHICHESTER, Hon Lady - Hon Anne Rachel Pearl; *née* Douglas-Scott-Montagu; da of 2 Baron Montagu of Beaulieu, KCIE, CSI (d 1929); *b* 1921; *m* 1, 1946, Maj Howel Joseph Morre-Gwyn (d 1947); 1 s; m 2, 1950, Sir (Edward) John Chichester, 11 Bt; 2 s, 3 da; *Style* - The Hon Lady Chichester; Battramsley Lodge, Boldre, Nr Lymington, Hants

CHICHESTER, Lord Desmond Clive; MC; s of late 4 Baron Templemore and bro of 7 Marquess of Donegall; raised to the rank of a Marquess's son 1977; *b* 1920; *Educ* Harrow, Ch Ch Oxford; *m* 1, 1946, Lorna Althea (d 1948), da of Capt Montagu Ravenhill and wid of Capt Richard Twining, Welsh Guards; 1 s; m 2, 1951, Felicity Stella, da of Maj John Harrison; 1 s; *Career* Maj Coldstream Gds (ret), ADC to Gov-Gen of Canada 1948-50; *Style* - Lord Desmond Chichester, MC; Preston Hill, Preston, Hitchin, Herts

CHICHESTER, 99 Bishop of (680) 1974-; Rt Rev Eric Waldram Kemp; s of Tom Kemp; *b* 27 April 1915; *Educ* Brigg G S Lincs, Exeter Coll Oxford, St Stephen's House Oxford; *m* 1953, Leslie Patricia, da of late Rt Rev K E Kirk, former Bp of Oxford; 1 s, 4 da; *Career* Deacon 1939, DD Oxford 1961, Fellow and Chaplain of Exeter Coll Oxford 1946-69, Dean of Worcester 1969-74; patron of 96 livings and 9 alternately, the Archdeaconries of Chichester, Hastings and Lewes and the Prebends (including the three residentaries) in the Cathedral; author; bishopric founded in Isle of Selsey by Wilfrid 2 ArchBp of York, removed to Chichester by Stigand 1071; *Style* - The Rt Rev the Lord Bishop of Chichester; The Palace, Chichester, Sussex (☎ 782161)

CHICHESTER, Sir (Edward) John; 11 Bt (E 1641), of Raleigh, Devonshire; s of Cdr Sir Edward Chichester, 10 Bt, RN (ret, d 1940); *b* 14 April 1916; *Educ* Radley, Sandhurst; *m* 1950, Hon Anne Rachel Pearl Douglas-Scott-Montagu, da of 2 Baron Montagu of Beaulieu; 2 s, 3 da; *Heir* s, James Chichester; *Career* late Capt Roy Scots Fusiliers, Lt RNVR, King's Foreign Service Messenger 1947-50, ICI Ltd 1950-60; Patron of one living; *Style* - Sir John Chichester, Bt; Battramsley Lodge, Boldre, Lymington, Hants

CHICHESTER, Lady Juliet Clare; da of 7 Marquess of Donegall; *b* 1954; *Style* - Lady Juliet Chichester

CHICHESTER, James Henry Edward; s and h of Sir (Edward) John Chichester, 11 Bt; *b* 15 Oct 1951; *Style* - James Chichester Esq

CHICHESTER, Hon Lady; Hon Moira Faith Lilian; *née* de Yarburgh-Bateson; da of late 3 Baron Deramore; *b* 1898; *m* 1, 1919 (m annulled 1923), John Robert Rankin Fullerton, sometime Lt 19 Hussars; m 2, 1924 (m dis 1935), Sir Edward George Chichester, 10 Bt (d 1940); *Style* - The Hon Lady Chichester; 3 Metropole ct, Regency sq, Brighton, Sussex

CHICHESTER-CLARK, Hon Fiona; da of Baron Moyola (Life Peer); *b* 1960; *Style* - The Hon Fiona Chichester-Clark

CHICHESTER-CLARK, Hon Tara Olivia; da of Baron Moyola (Life Peer); *b* 1962; *Style* - The Hon Tara Chichester-Clark

CHICK, Charles Richard; s of Edgar Percy Chick; *b* 6 April 1941; *Educ* Sir Robert Pattinson Sec Mod, Lincoln Tech Coll; *m* 1963, Janet Yvonne; 2 da; *Career* dir Howard Tenens Ltd 1976-79, dir Mansill Booth Ltd 1979-; *Style* - Charles Chick Esq; 423 Lichfield rd, Four Oaks, Sutton Coldfield, W Midlands (☎ 021 308 2533)

CHILD, Alan Arthur; s of late Walter Child; *b* 7 July 1912; *Educ* Alleyns Sch; *m* 1941, Olive Ella, nee Wood; 1 s, 1 da; *Career* insurance and pension fund consultant; former ch exec dir C T Bowring & Layborn Ltd, chm 1974-78; chm Hospital Saving Assoc 1975-, memb Occupational Pensions Bd 1973-; *Style* - Alan Child Esq; 30 Upfield, Croydon, Surrey (☎ 01 654 6715)

CHILD, Sir (Coles John) Jeremy; 3 Bt (UK 1919), of Bromley Palace, Bromley, Kent; s of Sir John Child, 2 Bt (d 1971); *b* 20 Sept 1944; *Educ* Eton, Poitiers U; *m* 1, 1971 (m dis 1976), Deborah Jane, nee Snelling; 1 da; m 2, 1978, Jan, nee Todd; *Career* actor; films include Oh What a Lovely War (1967), TV appearances include Glittering Prizes, Edward and Mrs Simpson; *Style* - Sir Jeremy Child, Bt; 48 Sydney st, SW3 (☎ 01 351 1498)

CHILD-VILLIERS, Hon Charles Victor; s of 9 Earl of Jersey; *b* 1952; *m* 1975, Brigitte Elisabeth Germaine, da of Robert Jean Rolland Marchand; 2 da (Eleanor Monica b 1979, Barbara Beatrice b 18 June 1981); *Style* - The Hon Charles Child-Villiers

CHILD-VILLIERS, Hon George Francis William; s and h of Viscount Villiers; *b* 5 Feb 1976; *Style* - The Hon George Child-Villiers

CHILD-VILLIERS, Hon Helen Katherine Luisa; da of Viscount Villiers; *b* 1978; *Style* - The Hon Helen Child-Villiers

CHILD-VILLIERS, Hon Luciana Dorothea; second daughter of Viscount Villiers by his 2 w, Sacha; *b* 23 July 1981; *Style* - The Hon Luciana Child-Villiers

CHILD-VILLIERS, Hon Sophia Georgiana; da of Viscount Villiers (s and h of 9 Earl of Jersey) by his 1 wife, Verna, nee Stott; *b* 1971; *Style* - The Hon Sophia Child-Villiers; c/o Viscount Villiers, Bel Respiro, Trinity Hill, St Helier, Jersey, Channel Islands

CHILSTON, 3 Viscount (UK 1911); Eric Alexander Akers-Douglas; also Baron Douglas of Baads (UK 1911); s of 2 Viscount (d 1947); *b* 17 Dec 1910; *Educ* Eton, Trin Oxford; *m* 1955, Marion (d 1970), da of late Capt Charles Howard, RE; *Heir* cousin, Alastair Akers-Douglas; *Career* late Fl-Lt RAFVR; patron of one living; *Style* - The Rt Hon the Viscount Chilston; Chilston Park, Maidstone, Kent (☎ Lenham 214); Craigs, Dumfries

CHILTON, Air Marshal Sir (Charles) Edward; KBE (1959, CBE 1945), CB (1951), RAF (ret); s of J C Chilton; *m* 1, 1929, Betty Ursula (d 1963), nee Wrinch; 1 s; m 2, 1964, Joyce Carnforth; *Career* Air Cdre 1950, Air Marshal 1959, AOCIC Coastal Command and Maritime Air Cdr E Atlantic Area and Cdr Maritime Air Channel and S North Sea 1959-62; former consultant and director IBM, Defence Systems and Data Processing international consultant; *Style* - Air Marshal Sir Edward Chilton, KBE, CB; 11 Charles House, Phyllis Court Drive, Henley-on-Thames, Oxfordshire (☎ Henley-on-Thames (STD Code 049 12) 3836)

CHILTON, Brig Sir Frederick Oliver; CBE (1963, OBE 1957), DSO (1941) and Bar (1944); s of Fred Chilton; *b* 23 July 1905; *Educ* Sydney U; *Career* solicitor NSW 1929, chm Australian Repatriation Cmmn 1958-70, kt 1969; *Style* - Brig Sir Frederick Chilton, CBE, DSO*; Clareville Beach, NSW, Australia

CHILTON, James Richard; s of Col

Richard Chilton; *b* 2 Jan 1941; *Educ* Winchester; *m* 1964, Margaret Ann, nee McKay; 1 s, 3 da; *Career* 1 The Royal Dragoons, Arabian Peninsular 1960, Malaysia 1961-62, dir McKay Securities Ltd 1973-; *Recreations* ski-ing, plantsmanship, vinousness; *Clubs* Cavalry and Guards; *Style* - James Chilton Esq; Hyde House, Great Missenden, Bucks; Maufant Manor, Jersey, CI

CHILVER, Sir (Amos) Henry; s of Amos Chilver; *b* 30 Oct 1926; *Educ* Southend H S, Bristol U; *m* 1959, Claudia M B Grigson, da of Sir Wilfrid Grigson; 3 s, 2 da; *Career* former engineering lecturer Bristol and Cambridge Us, Chadwick Prof of Civil Engineering UCL 1961-69; dir SKF (UK) Ltd 1972-, English China Ltd 1973-, De La Rue Company 1973-, Delta Metal Co 1977-, SE Region National Westminster Bank 1975-, Chancellor Cranfield Inst of Technology 1970-, kt 1978; *Style* - Sir Henry Chilver; Cranfield Institute of Technology, Cranfield, Bedford (☎ Bedford 750111)

CHILVER, Richard Clementson; CB (1952); s of Arthur Chilver; *b* 1912; *Educ* Winchester, New Coll Oxford; *m* 1937, Elizabeth Chilver, nee Graves (Princ of Lady Margaret Hall Oxford 1971-79); *Career* Civil Service 1934-72, admin dir Insurance Technical Bureau 1972-; *Style* - Richard Chilver Esq, CB; 108 Clifton Mews, NW8 (☎ 01 624 2702)

CHINNERY, Charles Derek; s of Percy Chinnery; *b* 27 April 1925 *Educ* Gosforth G S; *m* 1953, Doreen Grace Clarke; *Career* Controller BBC Radio 1 1978-; *Style* - Charles Chinnery Esq; c/o BBC Broadcasting House, Portland pla, W1

CHIPPINDALE, Hon Mrs (Margaret Ruth); *née* Ritchie; da of 2 Baron Ritchie of Dundee and sis of 3, 4 and 5 Barons; *b* 13 Nov 1913; *m* 1943, Maj Martin Chippindale; 1 s, 1 da; *Style* - The Hon Mrs Chippindale; Wintons, Peasmarsh, Rye, Sussex

CHISHOLM, Hon Mrs (Annabel Jane); *née* Hennessy; da of 2 Baron Windlesham; *b* 20 Dec 1937; *m* 1963, Dr Ian Chisholm, MRCP, DPM; 4 s; *Style* - The Hon Mrs Chisholm; Bourton House, Flax Bourton, Somerset (☎ 2250)

CHISHOLM, Hon Mrs (Caroline Elizabeth); *née* Wyndham; da of late 6 Baron Leconfield and (1) Egremont, and Pamela Wyndham-Quin, gda of 5 Earl of Dunraven and Mount-Earl; *b* 1951; *m* 1976, Colin Chisholm; 2 s, 1 da; *Style* - The Hon Mrs Chisholm

CHISHOLM, Lady; Margaret Grace; *née* Brantom; m 1, -- Crofton-Atkins; m 2, 1956, Sir Henry Chisholm, CBE, FCA, first chm Corby Devpt Corpn (d 1981); *Style* - Lady Chisholm; Scott's Grove House, Chobham, Woking, Surrey (☎ Chobham 8660)

CHITNIS, Baron (Life Peer UK 1977); Pratap Chidamber Chitnis; s of late Chidamber Chitnis; *b* 1 May 1936; *Educ* Penryn Sch, Stonyhurst Coll, Birmingham and Kansas Us; *m* 1964, Anne, nee Brand; 1 s (decd); *Career* Head of Liberal Party Organisation 1966-69, ch exec Rowntree Social Service Trust 1974, dir 1975, memb Community Relations Cmmn 1970-77; *Style* - The Rt Hon the Lord Chitnis; Beverley House, Shipton rd, York (☎ 25744)

CHITTENDEN, Keith Alan; s of Norman Jack Chittenden, St Kitts, Saltwood, Kent; *b* 26 March 1934; *Educ* Nottingham High Sch; Imperial College London; *m* 1959, Sylvia June; 1 s, 1 da; *Career* chartered engineer, general man Marconi Space & Defence Systems, Frimley, Surrey 1981-; *Recreations* riding, golf, theatre; *Clubs* Royal Commonwealth Society; *Style* - Keith Chittenden Esq; 19 Glebe court, Fleet, Hampshire (☎ 02514 4863)

CHITTY, Andrew Edward Willes; s and h of Sir Thomas Chitty, 3 Bt; *b* 20 Nov 1953; *Style* - Andrew Chitty Esq

CHITTY, (Thomas) David; s of late Joseph Chitty; *b* 4 Feb 1922; *Educ* Haileybury Coll; *m* 1944, Patricia Pamela, nee Magrath; 1 da; *Career* dir Barclays Unicorn Gp Ltd 1977-, Barclays Unicorn Ltd 1977-, gen man Barclays Life Assurance Co Ltd 1974-, dir 1977-; *Style* -

David Chitty Esq; Pippins Mount Close, Hook Heath, Woking, Surrey (☎ 04862 63773)

CHITTY, Sir Thomas Willes; 3 Bt (UK 1924), of The Temple; s of Sir (Thomas) Henry Willes Chitty, 2 Bt (d 1955); *b* 2 March 1926; *Educ* Winchester, Univ Coll Oxford; *m* 1951, Susan Elspeth Russell, nee Glossop (author); 1 s, 3 da; *Heir* Andrew Chitty; *Career* served RN 1944-47, Granada Arts Fellow York U 1964-65, Visiting Prof Boston U 1969-70; novelist; *Style* - Sir Thomas Chitty, Bt; Bow Cottage, West Hoathly, Sussex

CHOLMELEY, Cecilia, Lady - Cecilia; da of W H Ellice; *m* 1931, Lt-Col Sir Hugh Francis Sibthorp Cholmeley, 5 Bt, CB, DSO; 1 s; *Style* - Cecilia, Lady Cholmeley; The Dower House, Easton, Grantham, Lincs

CHOLMELEY, Hugh John Frederick Sebastian; s and h of Sir Montague Cholmeley, 6 Bt; *b* 3 Jan 1968; *Style* - Hugh Cholmeley Esq

CHOLMELEY, Sir Montague John; 6 Bt (UK 1806), of Easton, Lincolnshire; s of Lt-Col Sir Hugh Cholmeley, 5 Bt, CB, DSO (d 1964); *b* 27 March 1935; *Educ* Eton; *m* 1960, Juliet Auriol Sally, da of Maj-Gen Sir Eustace Nelson, KCVO, CB, DSO, MC; 1 s, 2 da; *Heir* s, Hugh Cholmeley; *Career* Grenadier Gds 1954-64; *Style* - Sir Montague Cholmeley, Bt; Church Farm, Burton le Coggles, Grantham, Lincs (☎ Corby Glen 329); Easton Hall, Grantham

CHOLMONDELEY, 6 Marquess of (UK 1815); Sir George Hugh Cholmondeley; Bt (I 1611), GCVO (1977), MC (1943), DL (Chester 1955); also Viscount Cholmondeley of Kells (I 1661), Baron Cholmondeley of Namptwich (E 1689), Viscount Malpas and Earl of Cholmondeley (GB 1706), Baron Newborough (I 1715), Baron Newburgh (GB 1716), and Earl of Rocksavage (UK 1815); s of 5 Marquess of Cholmondeley, GCVO (d 1968), and Sybil, da of Sir Edward Sassoon, 2 Bt, by his w Aline (da of Baron Gustave de Rothschild); *b* 24 April 1919; *Educ* Eton, Magdalene Cambridge; *m* 1947, Lavinia Margaret, da of Col John Leslie, DSO, MC; 1 s, 3 da; *Heir* s, Earl of Rocksavage; *Career* 1 Royal Dragoons Middle East, Italy, France, Germany 1939-45, ret Hon Maj 1949, Joint Hereditary Lord Chamberlain of England 1966-; *Clubs* Turf, Cavalry & Guards; *Style* - The Most Hon the Marquess of Cholmondeley GCVO MC DL; Cholmondeley Castle, Malpas, Cheshire (☎ Cholmondeley 202)

CHOLMONDELEY, Lady Aline Caroline; da of late 5 Marq of Cholmondeley, GCVO; *b* 1916; *Style* - Lady Aline Cholmondeley; Flat 5, 6 Strathearn pla, W2

CHOLMONDELEY, Lady Caroline Mary; da of 6 Marq of Cholmondeley, GCVO, MC; *b* 1952; *Style* - Lady Caroline Cholmondeley

CHOLMONDELEY, Lord (George) John; s of late 5 Marq of Cholmondeley, GCVO, MC; *Educ* Eton, Magdalene Cambridge; *m* 1957, Cristina, da of late Giorgio Solari; 1 s, 1 da; *Career* Lt (A) RNVR, ret; *Style* - Lord John Cholmondeley; 22 Hyde Park gdns, W2

CHOLMONDELEY, Lady Rose Aline; da of 6 Marq of Cholmondeley, GCVO, MC; *b* 1948; *Style* - Lady Rose Cholmondeley

CHOLMONDELEY, Dowager Marchioness of - Sybil Rachel Betty Cecile; CBE (1946); da of Sir Edward Albert Sassoon, 2 Bt; *b* 1894; *m* 1913, 5 Marquess of Cholmondeley (d 1968); 2 s, 1 da; *Career* Assist Prin WRNS 1914-18, Sup WRNS 1939-45; *Style* - The Most Hon The Dowager Marchioness of Cholmondeley, CBE; 12 Kensington Palace gdns, W8; Houghton Hall, King's Lynn, Norfolk

CHOPE, His Honour Judge - Robert Charles; s of Leonard Chope; *b* 26 June 1913; *Educ* St Paul's Sch, UCL; *m* 1946, Pamela, nee Durell; 1 s, 2 da; *Career* barr 1938, Dep Chm Cornwall Quarter Sessions 1966-71, a Circuit Judge 1965-; *Style* - His Honour Judge Chope; 12 King's Bench Walk, Temple, EC4; Carclew House,

Perranarworthal, Truro, Cornwall

CHORLEY, 2 Baron (UK 1945); Roger Richard Edward Chorley; s of 1 Baron Chorley, QC (d 1978); *b* 14 Aug 1930; *Educ* Stowe, Gonville and Caius Cambridge; *m* 1964, Ann, nee Debenham; 2 s; *Heir* s, Hon Nicholas Chorley; *Career* partner Coopers & Lybrand (CA) 1967-, FCA; *Style* - The Rt Hon the Lord Chorley; 69 Bedford gdns, W8 (☎ 01 727 8992); Borwick Fold, Ambleside, Cumbria

CHORLEY, Hon Christopher Robert Hopkinson; s of 2 Baron Chorley; *b* 1968; *Style* - The Hon Christopher Chorley

CHORLEY, Katharine, Baroness - Katharine Campbell; da of Edward Hopkinson; *m* 1925, 1 Baron Chorley, QC (d 1978); 2 s, 1 da; *Style* - The Rt Hon Katharine, Lady Chorley; 90 Campbell Hill Court, Campden Hill rd, W8 (☎ 01 937 8663)

CHORLEY, Hon Nicholas Rupert Debenham; s and h of 2 Baron Chorley; *b* 15 July 1966; *Style* - The Hon Nicholas Chorley

CHORLEY, Hon (Geoffrey) Patrick Hopkinson; s of late 1 Baron Chorley, QC; *b* 1933; *Educ* Stowe, New Coll Oxford; *m* 1, 1955 (m dis 1972), Daria Antonia Maria, da of the Marquis de Merindol (she m subsequently Count Alexander Schouvaloff, presumably of the Russian family granted the title of Count by the Empress Elizabeth 1746; their residence- 59 Lyndhurst Grove, SE15, T 01 703 3671); 2 da (Alexandra b 1956, m 1981 Hugh Bett; Elizabeth b 1961); m 2, 1975, Mary Amaryllis, da of Prof A Ashmore; *Style* - The Hon Patrick Chorley; 28 Sibella rd, SW4 (☎ 01 720 4298)

CHOULARTON, Stephen Derek; s of Cyril Choularton; *b* 29 March 1949; *Educ* Hollingbourne; *m* 1975, Sandra, nee Graveley; 1 s, 1 da; *Career* banker; employed Williams & Deacons Bank Ltd 1965, md C P Choularton, Sons & Partners Ltd (dir 1970-79); *Style* - Stephen Choularton Esq; The Avenue, Hale, Cheshire (☎ 061 928 9011)

CHRISTENSEN, Jens; s of Christian Christensen; *b* 30 July 1921; *Educ* Copenhagen U; *m* 1950, Tove, nee Jensen; 1 s, 2 da; *Career* Danish Foreign Service 1945, former State Sec Foreign Economic Affairs and Danish Govr Asian Dvpt Bank, Danish Ambassador to the Court of St James's 1977-, Cdr 1 Class Order of the Dannebrog; *Style* - HE Mr Jens Christensen; The Royal Danish Embassy, 55 Sloane st, SW1 (☎ 01 235 1255)

CHRISTIAN, Hon Mrs (Margaret Anne); *née* Mackay; da of 13 Lord Reay; *b* 13 March 1941; *m* 1977, Allen Leslie Christian, of Berwicks and Florida; *Style* - The Hon Mrs Christian; Buttonwood Bay AA8, Key Largo, Florida, USA; Upper Huntlywood, Earlston, Berwicks

CHRISTIE, George William Langham; s of John Christie, CH, MC; *b* 1934; *Educ* Eton; *m* 1958, Patricia Nicolson; 3 s, 1 da; *Career* founder chm London Sinfonietta, chm Glyndebourne Productions; *Style* - George Christie Esq; Glyndebourne, Lewes, E Sussex (☎ Ringmer 812250)

CHRISTIE, Lady Jean Agatha; *née* Dundas; da of 2 Marquess of Zetland; *b* 4 May 1916; *m* 1939, Capt Hector Lorenzo Christie, MBE (d 1969), s of William Christie, JP, of Jervaulx Abbey; 1 s, 1 da; *Style* - Lady Jean Christie; Seven Springs, Upper Lambourn, Berks

CHRISTIE, Julie Frances; *b* 14 April 1940; *Career* actress, films include Dr Zhivago (1965), Far from the Madding Crowd (1966), The Go-Between (1971), Don't Look Now (1973); *Style* - Miss Julie Christie; c/o ICM Ltd, 22 Grafton st, W1

CHRISTIE, Hon Sir Vernon Howard Colville; s of C Christie; *b* 17 Dec 1909; *m* 1936, Joyce, nee Hamlin; 1 s, 2 da; *Career* Memb Legislative Assembly (Lib) Ivanhoe Victoria Australia 1955-73, Speaker 1967-73, kt 1972; AASA, FCIS, AFAIM; *Style* - The Hon Sir Vernon Christie; Gray st, Redlands Bay, Queensland 4165, Australia

CHRISTIE, Sir William; KCIE (1947, CIE 1941), CSI (1945), MC (1917); s of late Rev Alexander Christie; *b* 29 Feb 1896; *Educ* Perth Acad, Bell Baxter Sch Cupar, St Andrews U, Clare Cambridge; *m* 1922, Marjorie Haughton, nee Stobbs; 1 s, 1 da; *Career* Indian Civil Service 1920, Ch Cmmr Delhi 1945-47; former dir Thomas Tilling Ltd, former chm Bailey Meters & Controls Ltd and Cornhill Insurance Ltd; *Style* - Sir William Christie, KCIE, CSI, MC; 3 Hartley ct, East Common, Gerrards Cross, Bucks (☎ Gerrards Cross 82246)

CHRISTIE, Sir William; MBE (1970), JP (Belfast 1951), DL (Belfast 1977); s of Richard Christie; *b* 1 June 1913; *Educ* Ward Sch Bangor N Ireland; *m* 1935, Selina, nee Pattison; 1 s, 2 da (and 1 s decd); *Career* High Sheriff of Belfast 1964-65, Lord Mayor 1972-75 (Dep 1969), alderman 1973-77; company director; kt 1975; *Style* - Sir William Christie, MBE, JP, DL; 96 Warren rd, Donaghadee, Co Down

CHRISTIE, Walter Henry John; CSI (1948), CIE (1946), OBE (1943); s of late H G F Christie; *b* 17 Dec 1905; *Educ* Eton, King's Cambridge; *m* 1934, Elizabeth Louise, nee Stapleton; 2 s, 2 da; *Career* Indian Civil Service 1928, Jt Private Sec to Viceroy 1947, adviser in India to Central Commercial Ctee 1947-52; with Commonwealth Dvpt Finance Co Ltd 1959-68, adviser E African Dvpt Bank 1969-70; *Style* - Walter Christie Esq, CSI, CIE, OBE; Quarry Ridge, Oxted, Surrey

CHRISTISON, Gen Sir (Alexander Frank) Philip; 4 Bt (UK 1871), of Moray Place, Edinburgh, GBE (1948, KBE 1944), CB (1943), DSO (1945), MC and Bar, DL (Roxburghshire 1956); s of late Sir Alexander Christison, 2 Bt; suc half-bro, 3 Bt 1945; *b* 17 Nov 1893; *Educ* Edinburgh Acad, Oxford U; *m* 1, 1916, Betty (d 1974), da of late Rt Rev A Mitchell; 1 s (ka 1942), 2 da (and 1 decd); m 2, 1974, Vida Wallace Smith, MBE; *Career* 2 Lt Cameron Highlanders 1914, Lt-Col Duke of Wellington's Regt 1937 (Col 1947-57), Brig Gen Staff 1941, Gen 1947, ADC Gen to HM the King 1947-49, Hon Col Coast Regt Royal Artillery 1950-57; chm Alban Timber Ltd 1953-78; fruit farmer and ornithologist; *Style* - General Sir Philip Christison, Bt, GBE, CB, DSO, MC*, DL; The Croft, Melrose, Roxburghshire (☎ Melrose 2456)

CHRISTOFAS, Kenneth Cavendish; CMG (1969), MBE (1944); s of late Edwin Goodwin and Lillian Christofas, step s of late Alexander Christofas; *b* 18 Aug 1917; *Educ* Merchant Taylors', UCL; *m* 1948, Jessica, nee Sparshott; 2 da; *Career* joined Foreign Service 1948, Min and Dep Head UK Delegation to the European Communities 1969-72, Dir-Gen Secretariat of Council of Ministers 1973-; *Style* - Kenneth Christofas Esq, CMG, MBE; Rue de la Loi 170, 1048 Brussels, Belgium (☎ 736 7900); 3 The Ridge, Bolsover rd, Eastbourne, Sussex (☎ 22384)

CHRISTOPHERSON, Sir Derman Guy; OBE (1946); s of late Derman Christopherson; *b* 6 Sept 1915; *Educ* Sherborne, Univ Coll Oxford (DPhil); *m* 1940, Frances Edith, nee Tearle; 3 s, 1 da; *Career* Prof of Mechanical Engineering Leeds U 1949-55, of Applied Science Imperial Coll of Science and Technology 1955-60, FRS 1960, Vice-Chancellor and Warden Durham U 1960-78, Master of Magdalene Coll Cambridge 1979- (former Fellow and Bursar), kt 1969; *Style* - Sir Derman Christopherson, OBE, FRS; Magdalene College, Cambridge

CHRISTOPHERSON, Hon Mrs (Griselda Ethelreda Clodagh); *née* O'Brien; da of 15 Baron Inchiquin (d 1929); *b* 1906; *m* 1953, David Clifford Christopherson, DSO; *Style* - The Hon Mrs Christopherson; Cherry Tree Cottage, Holmwood, Dorking, Surrey

CHUBB, Hon Mrs - Hon Barbara; da of Baron Champion (Life Peer); *m* 1957, Trevor Chubb; *Style* - The Hon Mrs Chubb; 10 Salisbury rd, Redland, Bristol

CHUBB, Hon Charles Henry Thomas; s of 3 Baron Hayter, KCVO, CBE; *b* 1949; *Educ* Marlborough, King's Cambridge; *m* 1979, Ann Nicola, da of Charles Manning, of Herts; *Style* - The Hon Charles Chubb; 26 Orde Hall st, WC1

CHUBB, Hon David William Early; s of 2 Baron Hayter (d 1967); *b* 1914; *m*

1939, Veronica, da of W Clifton, of Shanghai; 1 s; *Career* Cdr RN (ret), Far East 1939-45 (despatches, prisoner); *Style* - The Hon David Chubb; 117 New Kings rd, SW6; St Mary's Cottage, Broughton, Hants

CHUBB, Hon George William Michael; s and h of 3 Baron Hayter, KCVO, CBE; *b* 9 Oct 1943; *Educ* Marlborough, and Nottingham U (BSc); *Style* - The Hon George Chubb

CHUBB, Hon John Andrew; s of 3 Baron Hayter, KCVO, CBE; *b* 1946; *Educ* Marlborough, and Southampton U; *m* 1975, Sandra, da of late A E Brereton; 1 s, 1 da; *Style* - The Hon John Chubb; 117 New King's rd, SW6

CHUNG, Sir Sze-yuen; CBE (1975, OBE 1968), JP (Hong Kong 1964); *b* 3 Nov 1917; *Educ* Hong Kong U, Sheffield U (PhD); *m* 1942, Nancy Cheung (d 1977); 1 s, 2 da; *Career* engineer; chm Sonca Industries 1978- (formerly md), Memb Hong Kong Exec Council 1972-, Chm Hong Kong Polytechnic 1972-, kt 1978; *Style* - Sir Sze-yuen Chung, CBE, JP; 128 Argyle st, Kowloon, Hong Kong (☎ Hong Kong 3-013604)

CHURCH, Dan Ernest; *Career* chm H J Enthoven & Sons Ltd 1981-; dir EGM Solders, Billiton (UK) Ltd and others, FCA; *Style* - Dan Church Esq; c/o Billiton Ltd, 3/4 Lincoln's Inn Fields, WC2 (☎ 01 831 7252)

CHURCH, Ian Berkeley; s of late L H Church, DSO; *b* 23 Jan 1927; *Educ* Stowe; *m* 1956, Elizabeth Anne Linley, da of late Lt-Col Linley Messel; 1 s, 1 da; *Career* chm Church & Co Ltd, dir Chandler Henderson Financial Services Ltd, Lloyd's underwriter; *Style* - Ian Church Esq; 12 Cranley Mews, SW7 (☎ 01 373 8278)

CHURCHER, Maj-Gen John Bryan; CB (1952), DSO (1944) and Bar (1946); s of late Lt-Col B T Churcher; *b* 2 Sept 1905; *Educ* Wellington, Sandhurst; *m* 1937, Rosamond Hildegarde Mary, nee Parkin; 1 s, 2 da; *Career* 2 Lt DCLI 1925, command 43 Wessex Div 1946, Maj-Gen 1947; dir Mil Training War Office 1957, ret 1959, ADC to HM the King 1949-52 and to HM the Queen to 1952, dir and sec Independent Stores Assoc, ret 1971; *Style* - Maj-Gen John Churcher, CB, DSO*; Tudor Barn, Stanway, nr Colchester, Essex (☎ 210294)

CHURCHILL, 3 Viscount (UK 1902); Victor George Spencer; also Baron Churchill (UK 1815); s (by 2 m) of 1 Viscount Churchill, GCVO (d 1934), by his 2 w Christine; suc half-bro 1973; *b* (posthumous) 31 July 1934; *Educ* Eton, New Coll Oxford; *Heir* (to Barony only) kinsman, Richard Spencer; *Career* Lt Scots Gds 1953-55, employed Morgan Grenfell & Co Ltd 1958-74; *Style* - The Rt Hon the Viscount Churchill; 6 Cumberland Mansions, George st, W1 (☎ 01 262 6223)

CHURCHILL, John George Spencer; s of John Strange Spencer Churchill, DSO, TD, (yr bro of Sir Winston and 2 s of Lord Randolph Churchill) and Lady Gwendeline Bertie (da of 7 Earl of Abingdon); 2 cous of 10 Duke of Marlborough; bro of Countess of Avon, *qv*; *b* 31 May 1909; *Educ* Harrow, RCA, Centl Sch Art, Pembroke Oxford, Ruskin Sch of Art; *m* 1, 1934 (m dis 1938), Angela (*see* Rauf, Beyan), da of Capt George Culme-Seymour (3 s of Sir Michael Culme-Seymour, 3 Bt, GCB, GCVO, by his w Mary, herself da of Hon Richard Watson, of Rockingham Castle, Northants, 4 s of 2 Baron Sondes); 1 da (Sarah, b 26 March 1935, m 1957 James, s of late Maj Hugh Crewe, né Dodds, CMG, and Lady Annabel Crewe-Milnes, da of 1 and last Marquess of Crewe by his 1 w Sibyl; James's bro is Quentin Crewe, *qv*; 1 s, 2 da); m 2, 1941 (m dis 1953), Mary, da of Kenneth Cookson (*see* Mrs Jacob Huizinga); m 3, 1953, Mrs Kathlyn Tandy (d 1957), da of Maj-Gen Walter Beddall, CB, OBE; m 4, 1958, Anna, da of Johan Janson, of Kristianstad, Sweden, and widow of Granger Boston; *Career* served WW II Maj GSO2; artist; *Recreations* music, travel; *Style* - John Churchill Esq; Place du Cros, Grimaud 83360, France (☎ 94 43 21); Oscar Court, 17a Tite st, SW3 (☎ 01 352 2352)

CHURCHILL, Maj-Gen Thomas Bell Lindsay; CB (1957), CBE (1949), MC; s of late Alec Fleming Churchill; *b* 1 Nov 1907; *Educ* Magdalen Coll Sch Oxford, Sandhurst; *m* 1, Gwendolen Janie, nee Williams (d 1962); 1 s, 1 da; m 2, 1968 (m dis 1974), Penelope Jane Ormiston; *Career* 2 Lt Manchester Regt 1927, Col 1952-58, Col King's Regt 1958-62; Vice-Quartermaster-Gen to Forces 1957-60, Dep Ch of Staff Allied Land Forces Central Europe 1960-62, ret; *Style* - Maj-Gen Thomas Churchill, CB, CBE, MC; Lower Minchingdown Farm, Black Dog, nr Crediton, Devon

CHURCHILL, Winston Spencer; MP (C) Stretford 1970-; s of Randolph Churchill (& gs of Sir Winston) by Randolph's 1 w, Hon Pamela (da of 11 Baron Digby), now Mrs Averell Harriman; *b* 10 Oct 1940; *Educ* Eton, Ch Ch Oxford; *m* 1964, May Caroline, da of late Sir Gerard d'Erlanger, CBE; 2 s, 2 da; *Career* former war correspondent, with The Times 1969-70; contested Manchester (Gorton Div) 1967, PPS to Min of Housing and Construction 1970-72, to Min of State FCO 1972-72, former Conservative Spokesman on Defence; author; *Style* - Winston Churchill Esq, MP; Broadwater House, Chailey, Sussex

CHURSTON, 4 Baron (UK 1858); Sir Richard Francis Roger Yarde-Buller; 6 Bt (GB 1790), VRD; s of 3 Baron (d 1930); bro of Princess Joan Aly Khan, Denise Lady Ebury, Lydia Duchess of Bedford and late Primrose Countess Cadogan; *b* 12 Feb 1910; *Educ* Eton; *m* 1, 1933 (m dis 1943) da of Lt-Col William Baring Du Pre, JP, DL; 1 s, 1 da; m 2, 1949, Sandra (d 1979), nee Needham and former w of Jack Dunfee; *Heir* s, Hon John Yarde-Buller; *Career* Lt-Cdr RNVR, ret; patron of two livings; bore one of the Golden Spurs at Coronations of King George VI and Queen Elizabeth II; *Style* - The Rt Hon the Lord Churston, VRD; Woodcote, St Andrews, Guernsey, Channel Islands

CIECHANOWIECKI, Andrew Stanislaus; s of George Ciechanowiecki (d 1930), Polish diplomat; *b* 28 Sept 1924; *Educ* Lycée S Batory Warsaw, Krakow (BA Higher Sch Ec Studies), Jagiellonian U Krakow, Karl Eberhard U Tübingen (PhD); *Career* anti-Nazi Resistance in Poland 1942-45, former lectr Krakow U, former museum curator in Poland; md Heim Gallery (London) Ltd 1965-; dir other companies; OM Senegal, Cdr Polonia Restitua, Chev Légion d'Honneur, Grosses Silbernes Ehrenzeichen (Austria), Kt of Hon and Dev and Kt Cdr Order of Merit SMOM, Kt Cdr Order of Merit (Italy), Gr Cross of Justice Constantinian Order of St George, Bundesverdienstkreuz (1 Class) Germany; *Recreations* reading, travelling; *Clubs* Brooks's; *Style* - Andrew Ciechanowiecki Esq; 44 Sydney st, SW3 (☎ 01 352 1395)

CILENTO, Sir Raphael West; s of Raphael Ambrose Cilento; *b* 2 Dec 1893; *Educ* Adelaide H S, Prince Alfred Coll S Australia, Adelaide U (MD, BS); *m* 1920, Phyllis Dorothy, nee McGlew; 3 s, 3 da; *Career* barr Queensland Supreme Court 1939, former Dir-Gen of Health and Medical Services Queensland, kt 1935, Hon Prof of Tropical and Social Medicine Queensland U 1934-45, former Pres National Trust of Queensland; *Style* - Sir Raphael Cilento; Alta Villa, 56 Glen rd, Toowong, Queensland 4066, Australia

CITRINE, 1 Baron (UK 1946); Walter McLennan Citrine; GBE (1958, KBE 1935), PC (1940); s of Alfred Citrine; *b* 22 Aug 1887; *m* 1913, Doris Helen (d 1973), nee Slade; 2 s; *Heir* s, Hon Norman Citrine; *Career* former Asst Gen Sec Electrical Trades Union, Gen Sec TUC 1926-46, dir Daily Herald 1929-46, Pres Int Fedn of Trade Unions 1928-45, of World Fedn 1945-46, former Pres British Electrical Devpt Assoc and Electrical Res Assoc, former chm Central Electricity Authority; *Style* - The Rt Hon the Lord Citrine, GBE, PC; 13 Lower Rea rd, Brixham, Devon

CITRINE, Hon Norman Arthur; s and h of 1 Baron Citrine, GBE, PC; *b* 27 Sept 1914; *Educ* Univ Coll Sch, LLB London 1938; *m* 1939, Kathleen Alice, da of late George Chilvers; 1 da; *Career* Lt RNVR 1940-45, solicitor 1937, legal author, legal adviser to Trades Union Congress 1946-51; *Style* - The Hon Norman Citrine; Gorse Cottage, Berry Head, Brixham, S

Devon

CITRINE, Hon Ronald Eric; s of 1 Baron Citrine; *b* 1919; *Educ* Univ Coll Sch, UCL; *m* 1945, Mary, nee Williams; *Career* MRCS, LRCP; *Style* - The Hon Ronald Citrine; Paihia, Bay of Islands, North Islands, New Zealand

CLABBY, Brig John; CBE (1964, OBE 1958, MBE 1941); s of W G Clabby, late of the Indian Police; *b* 11 June 1911; *Educ* Taunton Sch and Royal Veterinary Coll London *m* 1939, Emily Celia, da of W Lancaster, of Yorks; 1 da; *Career* served WW II M East, Greece, Eritrea; dir Army Veterinary & Remount Servs 1959-63, Col Cmmdt RAVC 1965-76; ch exec offr Animal Health Tst 1966 *Style* - Brigadier John Clabby, CBE

CLAGUE, Col Sir (John) Douglas; CBE (1946, OBE 1943), MC (1942), QPM (1968), CPM (1966), TD (1954), JP (Hong Kong 1952); s of Alfred Ernest Clague; *b* 13 June 1917; *Educ* King William's Coll Isle of Man; *m* 1947, Margaret Isolin Cowley; 1 s, 2 da; *Career* chm Hutchinson Int Ltd Gp 1952-76, memb (unofficial) Hong Kong Exec Council 1961-74, kt 1971; *Style* - Col Sir Douglas Clague CBE MC QPM CPM TD JP; Kam Tsin Lodge, Kam Tsin, New Territories, Hong Kong (☎ Hong Kong 12-900325)

CLANCARTY, 8 Earl of (I 1803); William Francis Brinsley Le Poer Trench; also (sits as) Viscount Clancarty (UK 1823), Baron Kilconnel (I 1793), Viscount Dunlo (I 1801), Baron Trench (UK 1815), Marquess of Heusden in the Netherlands (1818); s of late 5 Earl of Clancarty; suc his half-bro 1975; *b* 18 Sept 1911; *Educ* Nautical Coll Pangbourne; *m* 1, 1940 (m dis 1947), Diana Joan, da of Sir William Younger, Bt; m 2, 1961 (m dis 1969), Mrs Wilma Dorothy Millen Belknap, nee Vermilyea; m 3, 1974, Mrs Mildred Alleyn Spong (d 1975); m 4, 1976, May, nee Radonicich, widow of Cdr Frank Beasley, RN; *Heir* nephew, Nicholas Le Poer Trench; *Career* V-Pres Br UFO Assoc; *Style* - The Rt Hon the Earl of Clancarty; 6 Lyall st, SW1 (☎ 01 235 2673)

CLANCARTY, Cora, Countess of - Cora Marie Edith; *née* Spooner; *m* 1919, as his 2 w, 6 Earl (d 1971); *Style* - The Rt Hon Cora, Countess of Clancarty; Croft Cottage, Wheathampstead, Herts

CLANFIELD, Viscount; Ashton Robert Gerard Peel; s and h of 3 Earl Peel; *b* 16 Sept 1976; *Style* - Viscount Clanfield

CLANMORRIS, 7 Baron (I 1800); John Michael Ward Bingham; s of 6 Baron (d 1960); *b* 3 Nov 1908; *Educ* Cheltenham; *m* 1934, Madeleine Mary, nee Ebel; 1 s, 1 da; *Heir* s, Hon Simon Bingham; *Career* author under name John Bingham; *Style* - The Rt Hon the Lord Clanmorris; Windyridge, 11 Hillcroft av, Purley, Surrey (☎ 01 660 2802)

CLANRANALD, The Captain of (c 1380); Ranald Alexander Macdonald of Clanranald; 24 Chief of Clanranald; s of Capt Kenneth Macdonald of Inch-Kenneth and Gribune, DSO (d 1938); suc kinsman Angus Macdonald, Captain of Clanranald, 1944; *b* 27 March 1934; *Educ* Christ's Hospital; *m* 1961, Jane, da of Ivar Campbell-Davys, of Llandovery; 2 s (Ranald b 1963, Andrew b 1966), 1 da (Catriona b 1972); *Heir* s, Ranald (Og Angus) Macdonald, yr of Clanranald, b 17 Sept 1963; *Career* fndr chm & md Tektura Wallcoverings, chm Br Contract Furnishing Assoc 1975-76, memb Standing Cncl Scottish Chiefs 1957-; dir Highland Soc London 1959-80, V-Pres Caledonian Catholic Assoc London; Exec Chm Clan Donald Lands Tst 1978-80; *Recreations* off-shore sailing, fishing; *Clubs* Turf, Puffin's; *Style* - The Captain of Clanranald; 74 Upper st, Islington Green, N1 (☎ 01 226 3034)

CLANWILLIAM, 6 Earl of (I 1776); Sir John Charles Edmund Carson Meade; 9 Bt (I 1703); also (sits as) Baron Clanwilliam (UK 1828), Viscount Clanwilliam and Baron Gillford (I 1766); s of 5 Earl (d 1953); *b* 6 June 1914; *Educ* Eton, Sandhurst; *m* 1948, Catherine, nee Loyd; 6 da; *Heir* cousin, John Meade; *Career* OStJ; HM Ld-Lt Co Down 1975-79 (formerly HM Lt); Maj Coldstream Gds (ret); *Style* - The Rt Hon the Earl of

Clanwilliam; Rainscombe Park, Oare, Marlborough, Wilts (☎ Pewsey 3491); Montalto, Ballynahinch, Co Down

CLAPHAM, His Honour Judge - Brian Ralph; s of late Isaac Bleazard Clapham; *b* 1 July 1913; *Educ* Tonbridge, Wadham Oxford, UCL, Open U; *m* 1961, Renata Margaret, da of Dr Rudolph Pius Warburg; 2 s; *Career* barr 1936, contested (L) Tonbridge 1950, Billericay 1951 and 1955, Chelmsford 1959, a Circuit Judge 1974-, Freeman of the City of London; *Style* - His Honour Judge Clapham; 10 Bounds Oak Way, Southborough, Tunbridge Wells, Kent (☎ Tunbridge Wells 31969)

CLAPHAM, Hon Lady (Elisabeth Russell); JP (1956, supp 1981-); da of 1 Baron Rea, PC (d 1948); *b* 2 May 1911; *Educ* Newnham Cambridge; *m* 1935, Sir Michael Clapham, KBE, *qv*; 3 s, 1 da; *Style* - The Hon Lady Clapham, JP; 26 Hill st, W1

CLAPHAM, Sir Michael John Sinclair; KBE (1973); s of late Sir John Clapham, CBE; *b* 17 Jan 1912; *Educ* Marlborough, King's Cambridge; *m* 1935, Hon Elisabeth Russell Rea, da of 1 Baron Rea, PC; 3 s, 1 da; *Career* former dep chm ICI, dir Lloyds Bank Ltd 1971- (dep chm 1974-79), Grindlays Bank Ltd 1975-, chm BPM Hds Ltd 1974-, IMI Ltd 1974-; *Style* - Sir Michael Clapham, KBE; 26 Hill st, W1 (☎ 01 499 1240)

CLAPPERTON, Alexander Wallace Ford; s of late Alexander Clapperton; *b* 22 July 1934; *Educ* Charterhouse; *m* 1965, Catherine Anne, da of Lady and step da of Sir Henry Horsman; 1 s, 1 da; *Career* chartered accountant 1956, memb of the Stock Exchange, ptnr de Zoete & Bevan, chm Amisford Investment Co Ltd 1973-; *Style* - Alexander Clapperton Esq; Broomfield House, Great Missenden, Bucks (☎ 02406 2559); Chalet Waldegg, 3903 Wiler, Valais, Switzerland (☎ 028 491225)

CLARE, Hon Mrs (Pauline Rosemary); *née* Addington; da of 7 Viscount Sidmouth; *b* 1951; *m* 1973, Paul Christopher Clare; *Style* - The Hon Mrs Clare; Glenarth, Abernarth, Aberaeron, Dyfed

CLARENDON, 7 Earl of (GB 1776); George Frederick Laurence Hyde Villiers; also Baron Hyde (GB 1756); s of late Lord Hyde and Hon Marion, nee Glyn, da of 4 Baron Wolverton; suc gf 1955; *b* 2 Feb 1933; *Educ* Eton; *m* 1974, Jane Diana, nee Dawson; 1 s, 1 da; *Heir* s, Lord Hyde; *Career* md Seccombe Marshall & Campion 1962-; Page of Honour to HM King George VI 1948-49, Lt RHG 1951-53; *Style* - The Rt Hon the Earl of Clarendon; 8 Chelsea sq, SW3 (☎ 01 352 6338)

CLARFELT, Hon Mrs (Christina Marjorie); da of Baron Campbell of Croy (Life Peer); *b* 1953; *m* 1980, Mark M Clarfelt; *Style* - The Hon Mrs Clarfelt

CLARFELT, Jack Gerald; s of Barnett Clarfelt; *b* 7 Feb 1914; *Educ* Grocers' Co Sch, Sorbonne U; *m* 1948, Baba Fredman; 1 s, 1 da; *Career* exec dep chm FMC Ltd, dir Ulster Leather Co Ltd, A J Macpherson Ltd, Macpherson Train & Co Ltd and others; *Style* - Jack Clarfelt Esq; 37a Queen's grove, NW8 (☎ 01 722 3345)

CLARIDGE, Hon Mrs (Fabienne Jose); *née* Evans-Freke; da of late 10 Baron Carbery; *b* 1916; *m* 1, 1936 (m dis 1946), Cdr John Dudley Dowse-Finnemor, RN (d 1971), who assumed by Roy Licence 1938 additional surname and arms of Finnemor; m 2, 1947, Philip Claridge; *Style* - The Hon Mrs Claridge; Cloonagh, Monkstown, Co Cork

CLARINGBULL, Sir (Gordon) Frank; s of William Claringbull; *b* 21 Aug 1911; *Educ* Finchley G S, Queen Mary Coll, London U; *m* 1, 1938, Grace Helen Mortimer (d 1953); 1 s, 1 da; m 2, 1953, Enid Dorothy Phyllis, nee Lambert; *Career* joined British Museum 1935, Keeper of Mineralogy 1953-68, Dir 1968-76, kt 1975; *Style* - Sir Frank Claringbull; Padfield House, West Bradley, Glastonbury, Somerset (☎ Baltonsborough 557)

CLARK, Baron (Life Peer UK 1969); Kenneth McKenzie Clark; OM (1976),

CH (1959), KCB (1938); s of late Kenneth McKenzie Clark; *b* 13 July 1903; *Educ* Winchester, Trin Oxford; *m* 1, 1927, Elizabeth Martin (d 1976); 2 s, 1 da; m 2, 1977, Nolwen, da of Frederic, Comte de Janzé and former w of Edward Rice; *Career* TV presenter (notably of 'Civilisation'); former dir of National Gallery and Surveyor of HM the King's Pictures; Slade Prof of Fine Art Oxford 1946-58 and 1961-62, chm ITA 1954-57, chm Arts Council of Great Britain 1953-60, Chancellor of York U 1969-, FBA; *Style* - The Rt Hon the Lord Clark, OM, CH, KCB; The Garden House, Castle rd, Saltwood, nr Hythe, Kent

CLARK, Hon Mrs; Hon Anna; da of late 2 Baron Fisher; *b* 1916; *m* 1936, Thomas Williams Clark, MD; 2 s, 2 da; *Style* - The Hon Mrs Clark; 44 West Highland av, Philadelphia, Pa, USA 19118

CLARK, Hon Alan Kenneth McKenzie; MP (C) Plymouth Sutton Feb 1974-; s (by 1 m) of Baron Clark (Life Peer); *b* 13 April 1928; *Educ* Eton, Ch Ch Oxford; *m* 1958, Caroline Jane, nee Beuttler; 2 s; *Career* barr 1955, gov St Thomas's Hosp; military historian; *Style* - The Hon Alan Clark, MP; Saltwood Castle, Hythe, Kent (☎ Hythe 67190); Town Farm, Bratton-Clovelly, Devon (☎ Bratton-Clovelly 252)

CLARK, His Honour Judge Albert - Albert William; s of William Clark; *b* 23 Sept 1922; *Educ* Christ's Coll Finchley; *m* 1951, Frances Philippa, nee Hart; 1 s, 1 da; *Career* barr 1949, Metropolitan Magistrate 1970, Dep Circuit Judge 1972, Circuit Judge (SE) 1981-; *Style* - His Honour Judge Albert Clark; Coombe Cottage, Renfrew rd, Kingston Hill, Surrey (☎ 01 942 8100)

CLARK of Herriotshall, Arthur Melville; s of James Clark; *b* 20 Aug 1895; *Educ* Stewart's Coll Edinburgh, Edinburgh U; *Career* Reader Eng Lit Edinburgh University 1946-60 studies); FRSE, FRSA, *Style* - Arthur Clark of Herriotshall, 3 Woodburn Ter, Edinburgh 10 (☎ 031 447 1240)

CLARK, Colin Douglas; MC; s of late Sir George Clark, 2 Bt and hp of bro, 3 Bt; *b* 20 July 1918; *Educ* Eton, Cambridge U; *m* 1946, Margaret Coleman, da of Maj-Gen Sir Charlton Spinks, KBE, DSO, and widow of Maj G W Threlfall, MC; 1 s, 2 da; *Career* Maj RE; *Style* - Colin Clark Esq, MC; Cillenamara, Ringhaddy, Killinchy, Co Down

CLARK, Hon Colette Elizabeth Dickson; twin da (by 1 m) of Baron Clark; *b* 1932; *Educ* Cheltenham Coll, LMH Oxford (BA); *Style* - The Hon Colette Clark

CLARK, Hon Colin MacArthur; s (by 1 m) of Baron Clark (Life Peer); *b* 1932; *Educ* Eton, Ch Ch Oxford; *m* 1, 1961 (m dis 1969), Violette Verdy; m 2, 1971, Mrs Faith Shuckburgh; *Style* - The Hon Colin Clark

CLARK, Col Charles Willoughby; DSO (1918), OBE (1945), MC (1916), DL (Warwicks 1965); s of John J Clark; *b* 6 April 1888; *Educ* Atherstone G S; *m* 1916, Athie, nee Thompson; 1 s; 1 da (decd); *Career* former dir Alfred Herbert Ltd Coventry, Freeman of the City of London; *Style* - Col Charles Clark, DSO, OBE, MC, DL; Flat 41, Regency House, Newbold ter, Leamington Spa, Warwicks (☎ 24004); Brooklands close, Ablington, nr Bibury, Glos (☎ Bibury 326)

CLARK, Dennis; *b* 19 Dec 1946; *m* 1966, Sylvia; 2 s; *Career* dir William Press Production Systems, P & W Offshore Services, OTN Ltd, Press (Gt Yarmouth) Ltd, Anglia Oil and Gas Services, Thomas Tannahill Ltd; quantity surveyor; *Style* - Dennis Clark Esq; 9 Warkworth drive, Hartlepool, Cleveland (☎ H'Pool 71586)

CLARK, David George; MP (L) S Shields 1979-; s of George Clark; *b* 19 Oct 1939; *Educ* Manchester and Sheffield U (PhD); *m* 1970, Christine Kirkby; 1 da; *Career* former University lectr; MP Colne Valley 1970-74 (which contested again Oct 1974); Opposition Spokesman (Agric and Food) 1973-74; *Style* - David Clark Esq, MP; House of Commons, SW1

CLARK, Elenita, Lady - Ellen Mary; da of late Francis Drake; *m* 19[illegible]4, Sir Thomas

Clark, 3 Bt (d 1977); *Style* - Elenita, Lady Clark; 23 Wester Coates av, Edinburgh 12

CLARK, Sir (Thomas) Fife; CBE (1949); *b* 29 May 1907; *Educ* Middlesbrough H S; *m* 1945, Joan (d 1977), da of late Capt James Mould, DSO, MC; 2 s, 1 da; *Career* former newspaper reporter; Dir Gen Central Office of Information 1954-71, kt 1965; *Style* - Sir Fife Clark, CBE; Wave Hill, Nevill rd, Rottingdean, Sussex (☎ Brighton 33020)

CLARK, Francis Drake; s of late Sir Thomas Clark, 3 Bt and hp of bro, 4 Bt; *b* 16 July 1924; *Educ* Edinburgh Acad; *m* 1958, Mary, nee Andrews; 1 s; *Career* RN 1939-45; *Style* - Francis Clark Esq; 1 Charlwood pla, SW1

CLARK, Sir George Anthony; 3 Bt (UK 1917), of Dunlambert, City of Belfast, DL (Belfast 1961); s of Sir George Clark, 2 Bt (d 1950); *b* 24 Jan 1914; *Educ* Canford; *m* 1949, Nancy Catherine, da of George W N Clark; 1 da; *Heir* bro, Colin Clark, MC; *Career* Capt Res of Officers Black Watch 1939-64, MP (U) Dock Div Belfast, N Ireland Parl, Senator 1951-69, High Sheriff Co Antrim 1954; *Style* - Sir George Clark, Bt, DL; Tullygirvan House, Ballygowan, Newtownards, Co Down (☎ Ballygowan 267)

CLARK, Prof (John) Grahame (Douglas); CBE (1971); s of Lt-Col Charles Douglas Clark; *b* 28 July 1907; *Educ* Marlborough, Peterhouse Cambridge; *m* 1936, Gwladys Maude, nee White; 2 s, 1 da; *Career* MA, PhD, ScD (Cantab), FBA (1951); Disney Prof of Archaeology Cambridge U 1952-74, Head of Dept of Archaeology and Anthropology 1956-61, Master of Peterhouse 1973- (Fell 1950-); *Style* - Prof Grahame Clark, CBE; The Master's Lodge, Peterhouse, Cambridge (☎ 50256)

CLARK, Henry Wallace Stuart; MBE (1969), DL (1962); s of late Maj H F Clark, MBE, JP; *b* 20 Nov 1926; *Educ* Shrewsbury; *m* 1956, June Elisabeth Lester, nee Deane; 2 s; *Career* md William Clark & Sons Ltd N Ireland; *Style* - Henry Clark Esq, MBE, DL; Gorteade Cottage, Upperlands, Co Derry, N Ireland (☎ 0648 42737)

CLARK, Ian Robertson; CBE (1979); s of Alexander Clark; *b* 18 Jan 1939; *Educ* Dalziel H S Motherwell; *m* 1961, Jean Scott Waddell, nee Lang; 1 s, 1 da; *Career* exec memb British National Oil Corpn 1976-, former co tres Zetland County Council, ch exec Shetlands Islands Council 1974-76; *Recreations* reading, writing, walking; *Clubs* Roy Scottish Automobile; *Style* - Ian Robertson Esq, CBE; British National Oil Corpn, 150 Vincent st, Glasgow G2 5LJ

CLARK, Sir John Allen; s of late Sir Allen Clark; *b* 14 Feb 1926; *Educ* Harrow, Cambridge; *m* 1, 1952 (m dis 1962), Deirdre Kathleen, nee Waterhouse; 1 s, 1 da; m 2, 1970, Olivia, nee Pratt; 2 s (twin), 1 da; *Career* joined Plessey Int Ltd 1949, chm and ch exec Plessey Compay Ltd 1970-, dir Banque Internationale de Paris Ltd 1976-, International Computers Ltd, kt 1971; *Style* - Sir John Clark; The Plessey Co Ltd, Millbank Tower, SW1 (☎ 01 834 9641)

CLARK, Sir John Douglas; 4 Bt (UK 1886), of Melville Crescent, Edinburgh; s of Sir Thomas Clark, 3 Bt (d 1977); *b* 9 Jan 1923; *Educ* Gordonstoun, Edinburgh U; *m* 1969, Anne, nee Gordon; *Heir* bro, Francis Clark; *Career* publisher, former ptnr T & T Clark Publishers Edinburgh; *Style* - Sir John Clark, Bt; 23 Wester Coates av, Edinburgh 12 (☎ 031 337 1913)

CLARK, His Honour Judge Leo - (Francis) Leo; QC (1972); s of Sydney Clark; *b* 15 Dec 1920; *Educ* Bablake Sch, St Peter's Oxford; *m* 1, 1957, Denise Jacqueline Rambaud; 1 s; m 2, 1967, Dr Daphne Margaret Humphreys; *Career* barr 1947, Recorder of the Crown Court 1972-76, a Circuit Judge 1976-; *Style* - His Honour Judge Leo Clark QC; The Ivy House, Charlbury, Oxon (☎ 810242)

CLARK, Sir (Gordon Colvin) Lindesay; AC (1975), KBE (1968), CMG (1961), MC; s of late Lindesay C Clark; *b* 7 Jan 1896; *Educ* G S Launceston Tasmania, Tasmania and Melbourne Us; *m* 1922, Barbara, nee Walch; 1 s, 2 da; *Career* former chm Central

Norseman Gold Corp NL, West Mining Corp Ltd, BH South Ltd, ret; engineer; *Style* - Sir Lindesay Clark, AC, KBE, CMG, MC; 8 Moralla rd, Kooyong, Victoria 3144, Australia; Western Mining Corp, 360 Collins st, Melbourne, Victoria 3144, Australia

CLARK, Leslie Joseph; CBE (1977), BEM (1942); s of late Joseph George Clark; *b* 21 May 1914; *Educ* Stationers Company's Sch, King's Coll London U; *m* 1940, Mary Myfanwy, da of Robert Peacock; 1 s, 1 da; *Career* engineer; chm Northern Gas Bd 1967-75, chm Victor Products (Wallsend) Ltd 1976-79, former pres International Gas Union; *Style* - Leslie Clark Esq, CBE, BEM; Hillway, New Ridley rd, Stocksfield, Northumberland

CLARK, Hon Mrs (Moira Muriel); da of Baron Sorensen (Life Peer, d 1971); *b* 1917; *m* 1951, Derek Gerald Clark, JP; children; *Style* - The Hon Mrs Clark; 15 Crossing rd, Epping, Essex

CLARK, Michael William; CBE (1977); s of late Sir Allen Clark; *b* 7 May 1927; *Educ* Harrow; *m* 1955, Shirley, nee MacPhadyen (d 1974); 2 s, 2 da; *Career* joined Plessey Co 1950, dep chm and dep ch exec Plessey Co Ltd, founder and chm Plessey Electronic Systems Ltd; *Style* - Michael Clark Esq, CBE; Braxted Park, Witham, Essex

CLARK, Petula; da of Leslie Clark; *b* 15 Nov 1934; *m* 1961, Claude Wolff; 1 s, 2 da; *Career* singer and actress, films include Goodbye Mr Chips 1969; *Style* - Miss Petual Clark; c/o PROGENAR, 82 rue de Lausanne, Fribourg 1701, Switzerland

CLARK, His Honour Reginald; QC (1949); s of J T Clark; *b* 18 March 1895; *Educ* Trin Hall Cambridge; *m* 1923, Joan Marguerite, nee Shiers; 3 da; *Career* barr 1920, former Judge of High Court Madras, Judge of Clerkenwell 1955-66, ret; *Style* - His Honour Reginald Clark, QC; 4 Trumpeters House, Old Palace Yard, Richmond, Surrey (☎ 01940 2829)

CLARK, Sir Robert Anthony; DSC (1944); s of John Clark; *b* 6 Jan 1924; *Educ* Highgate Sch, King's Cambridge; *m* 1949, Andolyn Marjorie Lewis; 2 s, 1 da; *Career* ptnr Slaughter & May Slrs 1953, joined Hill Samuel & Co Ltd (then Philip Hill, Higginson, Erlangers Ltd) 1961, chm 1974-, dir British Leyland Ltd, kt 1976, chm IMI 1981-, dir United Drapery Stores Gp 1981-; *Style* - Sir Robert Clark, DSC; Hill Samuel & Co Ltd, 100 Wood st, EC2 (☎ 01 628 8011); Munstead Wood, Godalming, Surrey (☎ 7867)

CLARK, Russell John; s of late Albert Clark; *b* 18 March 1915; *Educ* Bancrofts, London U; *m* 1940, Bernice Priscilla; 2 c; *Career* bank economist; former economic adviser Westminster Bank and National Westminster Bank Gp, international economic consultant Northern Trust Co of Chicago (London) 1975-80, dir Foreign and Colonial Investment Trust Co Ltd 1975-, Visiting Fellow City U 1979-; *Style* - Russell Clark Esq; Old School, Wingfield, Diss, Norfolk (☎ Stradbroke 537)

CLARK, Hon Mrs; Hon Sarah *née* Chubb; da of 3 Baron Hayter, KCVO, CBE; *b* 1941; *m* 1963, the Rev David Humphrey Clark, Priest in charge of St George, Colegate, and Industrial Chaplain; 1 s, 1 da; *Style* - The Hon Mrs Clark; St Pauls Vicarage, Mill Lane, Norwich NOR 55P

CLARK, Terence George; OBE (1980); s of late George Cyril Clark; *b* 6 March 1922; *Educ* Southampton Polytechnic, Regent Polytechnic; *m* 1946, Patricia Eve, nee Careford; 2 s; *Career* md Engineering Lab Equipment Ltd, dir Protective Materials Ltd, Corrosion Technical Services Ltd; *Style* - Terence Clark Esq, OBE; St James House, Park rd, Toddington, Beds (☎ 052 55 2060)

CLARK, Sir William Gibson; MP (C) S Croydon 1974-; s of Hugh Clark; *b* 18 Oct 1917; *m* 1944, Irene Dorothy Dawson Rands; 3 s, 1 da; *Career* contested Northampton 1955, MP Nottingham S 1959-66, E Surrey 1970-74, kt 1979; *Style* - Sir William Clark, MP; 3 Barton st, SW1 (☎ 01 222 5759); The Clock House, Box End, Bedford (☎ 852361)

CLARK, (Henry) Wallace (Stuart); MBE (1970), DL (1963); s of Maj Harry Francis Clark, MBE, JP (d 1977); *b* 20 Nov 1926; *Educ* Shrewsbury; *m* 1956, June Elisabeth Lester, da of James Lester Deane of Belfast; 2 s; *Career* Maj Ulster Defence Regt (NI), Lt RNVR Bomb and Mine Disposal UK, District Cmdt Ulster Special Constabulary, dir William Clark & Sons Ltd (Est 1940) Linen Mfrs 1970-; *Recreations* sailing (yacht- 'Wild Goose of Royle' 10 Ton Yawl); *Clubs* Roy Cruising, Irish Cruising; *Style* - Wallace Clark Esq, MBE, DL; Gorteade Cottage, Upperlands, Maghera, Co Londonderry (☎ 0648 4237)

CLARKE, Sir (Henry) Ashley; GCMG (1962, KCMG 1952, CMG 1946), GCVO (1961); s of H H R Clarke, MD; *b* 26 June 1903; *Educ* Repton, Pembroke Cambridge; *m* 1, 1937 (m dis 1960), Virginia, nee Bell; m 2, 1962, Frances, nee Molyneux; *Career* joined Diplomatic Service 1925, Ambass to Italy 1953-62, ret; dir Royal Acad of Music 1973-, V-Chm Venice in Peril Fund 1970-; *Style* - Sir Ashley Clarke, GCMG, GCVO; Fondamenta Bonlini 1113, Dorsoduro, 30123 Venice, Italy

CLARKE, Arthur C(harles); s of Charles Clarke; *b* 16 Dec 1917; *Educ* Taunton, King's Coll London; *m* 1953 (m dis 1964), Marilyn Mayfield; *Career* scientist; author of books on the Space Age, also science-fiction novelist, *2001- A Space Odyssey*, 1968, *The Mysterious World of Arthur C Clarke* 1980, (also TV series); *Style* - Arthur C Clarke Esq; c/o David Higham Associates, 5 Lower John st, Golden sq, W1; 25 Barnes pla, Colombo 7, Sri Lanka

CLARKE, Lady Betty (Jocelyne); *née* Bourke; da of 8 Earl of Mayo (d 1939); *b* 1917; *m* 1, 1943, Capt Ronald Banon (d 1943); m 2, 1953, Samuel Clarke; 2 da; *Style* - Lady Betty Clarke; Cnoc-Na-Curra, Oughterard, Co Galway

CLARKE, Prof Sir Cyril Astley; KBE (1974, CBE 1969), FRS (1970); s of Astley Clarke, MD, JP; *b* 22 Aug 1907; *Educ* Oundle, Gonville and Caius Cambridge, Guy's London; *m* 1935, Frieda Margaret Mary, nee Hart; 3 s; *Career* MD, ScD; prof of Medicine Liverpool U Nuffield Unit of Medical Genetics 1965-72, dir 1963-72 (now Emeritus Prof and Hon Res Fell); consultant physician Royal Infirmary, Broadgreen Hosp and United Liverpool Hosps; *Style* - Prof Sir Cyril Clarke, KBE, FRS; Nuffield Unit of Medical Genetics, The University, Crown st, PO Box 147, Liverpool L69 3BX (☎ 051 709 6022)

CLARKE, Maj-Gen Desmond Alexander Bruce; CB (1965), CBE (1961, OBE 1944); s of late R T Clarke, ICS, LLD; *b* 15 July 1912; *Educ* Stonyhurst Coll, RMA Woolwich; *m* 1944, Madeleine, da of Rear-Adm Walter Glyn Petre, DSO; 3 s, 2 da; *Career* commissioned RA 1932, dir of Personal Services War Office 1962-64, dir of Personal Services (Army) MOD 1964-66, ret; *Style* - Maj-Gen Desmond Clarke, CB, CBE; Huntington Place, Great Orton, nr Carlisle, Cumbria

CLARKE, Donald Roberts; s of late Harold Leslie; *b* 14 May 1933; *Educ* Ealing G S, Queen's Oxford; *m* 1959, Susan Charlotte, da of Col J C Cotton; 1 s, 3 da; *Career* FCA, FCT, gen man (fin) Finance for Industry Ltd; *Style* - Donald Clarke Esq; 67 Cottenham Park rd, SW20 (☎ 01 947 3213)

CLARKE, His Honour Judge - Edward; QC (1960); s of William Francis Clarke; *b* 21 May 1908; *Educ* Sherborne, King's Coll London; *m* 1948, Dorothy May, nee Leask; 3 s, 1 da; *Career* barr 1935, Dep Chm London Quarter Sessions 1963-64, Judge of the Central Criminal Court 1964-; *Style* - His Honour Judge Clarke, QC; Central Criminal Court, EC4; 2 Addisland ct, Holland Villas rd, W14 (☎ 01 603 8140)

CLARKE, Sir Ellis Emmanuel Innocent; TC (1969), GCMG (1972, CMG 160); s of late Cecil Clarke; *b* 28 Dec 1917; *Educ* St Mary's Coll Trinidad, London U; *m* 1952, Eyrmyntrude, nee Hagley; 1 s, 1 da; *Career* barr 1940, in private practice to 1954; former Permanent Rep to UN for Trinidad and Tobago, Ambass to US 1962-73, to Mexico 1966-73, Gov Gen and CIC Repub of Trinidad and Tobago 1973-76, President 1976-, kt 1963 (does not use title in Trinidad and Tobago), KStJ 1973; *Style* - Ellis Clarke Esq, TC, GCMG; President's House, Port of Spain, Trinidad

CLARKE, Hon Mrs Eleanor Geraldine; *née* de Courcy; da of 29 Baron Kingsale, DSO (d 1969); *b* 1919; *m* 1940 (m dis 1947), John Campbell Clarke; 1 s; *Style* - The Hon Mrs Eleanor Clarke; 48 Fore st, North Tawton, Devon

CLARKE, Sir Frederick Joseph; s of late R G H Clarke; *b* 21 May 1912; *Educ* St Vincent G S, Edinburgh Sch of Medicine; *m* 1944, Phyliss, nee Lunn; 1 s, 2 da; *Career* GP UK 1945, former medical officer, Gov St Lucia 1967-73, kt 1967; *Style* - Sir Frederick Clarke; PO Box 391, Castries, St Lucia, W Indies

CLARKE, Graham Staward; TD (1971); s of Douglas Staward Clarke (d 1949); *b* 16 March 1937; *Educ* St Bees Sch Cumberland, Emmanuel Coll Cambridge; *m* 1964, Rita Elisabeth Karoline, da of Oskar Becker (d 1961); 1 s, 1 da; *Career* Maj Roy Artillery, European theatre; MA, FCA; Gp Financial Dir Telex Computers Ltd 1973-75, Coles Cranes Ltd 1976-81, Fairey Holdings Ltd; *Style* - Graham Clarke Esq, TD; Bourn Reach, Montrose Gdns, Oxshott, Surrey, KT22 0UU (☎ Oxshott 3655)

CLARKE, Sir Jonathan Dennis; s of late Dennis Robert Clarke (Master of the Supreme Court); *b* 19 Jan 1930; *Educ* Kidstones Sch, Univ Coll London; *m* 1956, Susan Margaret Elizabeth Ashworth; 1 s, 3 da; *Career* a recorder of the Crown Court 1972-; ptnr Townsends 1959-; pres Law Soc; kt 1981; *Style* - Sir Jonathan Clarke; West Lodge, Westlecot rd, Swindon, Wilts

CLARKE, John Neil; s of George Philip Clarke (d 1969); *b* 7 Aug 1934; *Educ* Rugby, King's Coll London; *m* 1958, Sonia Heather, nee Beckett; 3 s; *Career* CA, FCA, ch exec Charter Consolidated Ltd 1980-; *Style* - John Clarke Esq; High Willows, 18 Park av, Farnborough Park, Kent (☎ Farnborough 51651); The Cottage, Hall lane, Thornham, Norfolk (☎ Thornham 269)

CLARKE, Kenneth Harry; MP (C) Rushcliffe Notts 1970-; s of Kenneth Clarke; *b* 2 July 1940; *Educ* Nottingham H S, Gonville and Caius Cambridge *m* 1964, Gillian Mary Edwards; 1 s, 1 da; *Career* former Pres Cambridge Union, barr 1963, former opposition spokesman on Social Services and Industry, Parly Sec Dept of Transport 1979-; *Style* - Kenneth Clarke Esq, MP; House of Commons, SW1

CLARKE, Michael John Marshal; s of late Adm Sir Marshal Clarke, KBE, CB, DSC; *b* 3 Feb 1927; *Educ* St Edward's Sch Oxford, Trin Oxford; *m* 1954, Flavia Dorothea, da of Sir Alec Coryton, KCB, KBE, MVO, DFC; 1 s, 1 da; *Career* Capt Rifle Bde, dir Personnel Services British Steel Corpn; *Recreations* shooting, landscape painting; *Style* - Michael Clarke Esq; Osbaston House, Monmouth, Gwent (☎ Monmouth 3596)

CLARKE, Orme Roosevelt; s of late Sir Humphrey Clarke, 5 Bt; half-bro and hp of Sir Tobias Clarke, 6 Bt; *b* 30 Nov 1947; *Educ* Eton; *m* 1971, Joanna Valentine, nee Schuster; 1 s; *Style* - Orme Clarke Esq; 28 Marville rd, SW6

CLARKE, Maj Peter Cecil; CVO (1969), JP (Hants 1971); s of late Capt E D Clarke, CBE, MC; *b* 9 Aug 1927; *Educ* Eton, Sandhurst; *m* 1950, Rosemary Virginia Margaret Harmsworth, nee Durham; 1 s, 2 da; *Career* Maj (ret) 3 then 14/20 King's Hussars 1945-64, Asst Priv Sec then Comptroller to HRH Princess Marina, Duchess of Kent 1961-68, Comptroller to HRH Princess Alexandra, the Hon Mrs Angus Ogilvy 1964-69, Extra Equerry and Ch Clerk Duchy of Lancaster 1969-; *Style* - Major Peter Clarke, CVO, JP; 6 Gordon pla, W8 (☎ 01 937 0356)

CLARKE, His Honour Judge Paul - Paul Henry Francis; s of Dr Richard Clarke; *b* 14 Oct 1921; *Educ* Clifton Coll, Exeter Coll Oxford; *m* 1955, Eileen Sheila, da of Lt-Col J K B Crawford; 2 s, 1 da; *Career* barr 1949, practised to 1974, a Circuit Judge 1974-; *Style* - His Honour Judge Paul Clarke; Saffron close, Chudleigh, Devon

CLARKE, Rupert Grant Alexander; s and h of Maj Sir Rupert Clarke, 3 Bt, MBE; *b* 12 Dec 1947; *m* 1973, Susannah, nee Law-Smith; 1 s; *Style* - Rupert Clarke Esq

CLARKE, Roger Simon Woodchurch; s of late Charles Samuel Clarke; *b* 29 June 1903; *Educ* RN Colls Osborne and Dartmouth, Bristol U; *m* 1936, Nancy Lingard, nee Martin (d 1980); *Career* joined Imperial Tobacco Co 1922, dir 1944-66, chm 1959-64, JP Bristol 1964, Pro-Chllr Bristol U 1975-; *Style* - Roger Clarke Esq, JP; The Little Priory, Bathwick Hill, Bath (☎ Bath 63103)

CLARKE, Maj Sir Rupert William John; 3 Bt (UK 1882), of Rupertswood, Colony of Victoria, MBE (1943); s of Sir Rupert Turner Havelock Clarke, 2 Bt (d 1926); *b* 5 Nov 1919; *Educ* Eton, Magdalen Oxford; *m* 1947, Kathleen Grant, nee Hay; 2 s, 1 da; *Heir* s, Rupert Clarke; *Career* late Maj Irish Guards, chm Cadbury Schweppes Australia Ltd, Bain Dawes Australia Ltd, v-chm Bank of Australasia, dir Cozinc Riotinto of Australia Ltd and others; *Style* - Major Sir Rupert Clarke, Bt, MBE; Bolinda Vale, Clarkfield, Vic 3430, Australia

CLARKE, Sir (Charles Mansfield) Tobias; 6 Bt (UK 1831), of Dunham Lodge, Norfolk; s of Sir Humphrey Orme Clarke, 5 Bt (d 1973); *b* 8 Sept 1939; *Educ* Eton, Ch Ch Oxford, Sorbonne, New York U; *m* 1971 (m dis 1979), Charlotte, nee Walter; *Heir* half-bro, Orme Clarke; *Career* V-Pres London Branch of Bankers Trust Co New York; adopted name Tobias 1962; *Style* - Sir Tobias Clarke, Bt; 80a Campden Hill rd, W8 (☎ 01 937 6213); The Church House, Bibury, Glos (☎ 225)

CLARKE, William Malpas; CBE (1976); *b* 1922; *Career* Dir Gen & Dep Chm Cttee Invisible Exports 1976- *Style* - William Clarke Esq, CBE; 37 Park Vista, SE10 (☎ 01 858 0979)

CLARKSON, His Honour Judge - Derek Joshua; QC (1969); s of late Albert Clarkson; *b* 10 Dec 1929; *Educ* Pudsey G S, King's Coll London; *m* 1960, Peternella Marie-Luise Ilse, nee Canenbley; 1 s, 1 da; *Career* barr 1951, Recorder of the Crown Court 1977, Circuit Judge (SE) 1977-; *Style* - His Honour Judge Clarkson, QC; 24 John Islip st, SW1; 26 Cornwall rd, Harrogate, N Yorks

CLASEN, Andrew Joseph; Hon GCVO (1968); s of late Bernard Clasen; *b* 5 Sept 1906; *Educ* Beaumont Coll; Oxford, London and Aix-la-Chapelle Us; *m* 1944, Joan Mary Luke; 1 s, 1 da; *Career* Luxembourg Ambass to London 1955-71; *Style* - Andrew Clasen Esq, GCVO; The Manor House, Rotherfield, Sussex

CLAXTON, Maj-Gen Patrick Fisher; CB (1972), OBE (1946); s of late Rear-Adm Ernest Claxton; *b* 13 March 1915; *Educ* Sutton Valence Sch, St John's Cambridge; *m* 1941, Jóna Gudrún Gunnarsdóttir (d 1980); 2 da; *Career* Cdt Sch of Transport and ADC to HM the Queen 1966-68, Transport Offr-in-Ch (Army) 1969-71, ret, gen man Regular Forces Employment Assoc 1971-; *Style* - Maj-Gen Patrick Claxton, CB, OBE; The Lodge, Beacon Hill pk, Hindhead, Surrey (☎ Hindhead 4437)

CLAY, Sir Henry Felix; 6 Bt (UK 1841), of Fulwell Lodge, Middlesex; s of Sir Felix Clay, 5 Bt (d 1941); *b* 8 Feb 1909; *Educ* Gresham's Sch, Trin Cambridge; *m* 1933, Phyllis Mary, nee Paramore; 1 s, 2 da; *Heir* s, Richard Clay; *Career* sr consultant to McLellan and Ptnrs Consulting Engrs; *Style* - Sir Henry Clay, Bt; Wheelwrights, Cocking, Midhurst, Sussex

CLAY, His Honour Judge - John Lionel; TD (1961); s of late Lionel Clay; *b* 31 Jan 191; *Educ* Harrow, CCC Oxford; *m* 1952, Elizabeth, nee Ponsonby; 1 s, 3 da; *Career* barr 1947, Recorder 1975-77, Circuit Judge 1977-; *Style* - His Hon Judge Clay TD; Newtimber Place, Hassocks, Sussex (☎ Hurstpierpoint 833104)

CLAY, John Martin; s of late Sir Henry Clay; *b* 20 Aug 1927; *Educ* Eton, Magdalen Oxford; *m* 1952, Susan, da of Lt-Gen Sir Euan Miller; 4 s; *Career* dep chm and dir Hambros Bank Ltd, chm Hambro Life Assurance, dir Bank of England; *Style* - John Clay Esq; Farningham House, Farningham,

Dartford, Kent (☎ Farningham 862266)

CLAY, John Peter; s of late Harold Clay; *b* 26 Nov 1934; *Educ* St Paul's Sch, Queen's Oxford (BA); *m* 1972, Jennifer Mary Ellen, da of Dr William Ernest Coutts, MD; *Career* joined Vickers da Costa Ltd 1957, dep chm 1976-, memb Council of the Stock Exchange 1974-77; *Style* - John Clay Esq; 54 Ebury Mews, SW1 (☎ 01 730 5368); 9167 Phyllis av, Los Angeles CA 90069 (213 276 4097); Maison de la Voûte, Place de l'Amour, La Garde-Freinet, 83310 Var, France

CLAY, Richard Henry; s and h of Sir Henry Clay, 6 Bt; *b* 2 June 1940; *m* 1963, Alison Mary, nee Fife; 3 s, 2 da; *Style* - Richard Clay Esq; 18 De Freville av, Cambridge

CLAYDEN, Rt Hon Sir (Henry) John; PC (1963); s of Harold Clayden; *b* 26 April 1904; *Educ* Diocesan Coll Capetown, Charterhouse, BNC Oxford; *m* 1948, Gwendoline Edith Lawrance; *Career* barr 1926 and advocate S Africa, former chief justice, chm Industrial Tribunals 1967-77, Actg Gov-Gen Fedn of Rhodesia and Nyasaland May-June 1961, kt 1958; *Style* - The Rt Hon Sir John Clayden; 8 Walton st, SW3 (☎ 01 589 1300)

CLAYSON, Sir Eric Maurice; DL (W Midlands 1975); s of late Harry Clayson; *b* 17 Feb 1908; *Educ* Woodbridge Sch; *m* 1933, Pauline Audrey Wright; 2 s; *Career* chartered accountant 1941, former dir Reuters Ltd, Sun Alliance & London Insurance Gp, ATV Network, former chm The Press Assoc, chm Sun Alliance & London Insurance Gp Ltd Birmingham Area Bd, kt 1964; *Style* - Sir Eric Clayson, DL; The Poor's Piece, Linthurst rd, Barnt Green, Birmingham B45 8JJ

CLAYTON, Sir Arthur Harold; 11 Bt (GB 1732), of Marden Park, Surrey, DSC (1945); s of Sir Harold Clayton, 10 Bt (d 1951); *b* 14 Oct 1903; *Educ* Haileybury; *m* 1, 1927, Muriel Edith (d 1929), da of Arthur John Clayton; m 2, 1931 (m dis 1954), Alexandra, nee Andreevsky; 1 s, 1 da; m 3, 1954, Mrs Dorothy (Jill) Hamer, nee Greenhalgh (d 1964); m 4, Mrs Diana Bircham, da of late Capt Charles Grazebrook, 60 Rifles; *Heir* s, David Clayton; *Career* Lt-Cdr RNR; *Style* - Sir Arthur Clayton, Bt; Colonsay Kingswear, Dartmouth, Devon (☎ Kingswear 243)

CLAYTON, David Robert; s (by 2 m) and h of Sir Arthur Clayton, 11 Bt, DSC; *b* 12 Dec 1936; *m* 1971, Julia Louise, nee Redfearn; 1 s; *Career* Capt MN; *Style* - David Clayton Esq; Rock House, Kingswear, Devon

CLAYTON, Air Marshal Sir Gareth Thomas Butler; KCB (1970, CB 1962), DFC (1940) and Bar (1944); s of Thomas Clayton; *b* 13 Nov 1914; *Educ* Rossall Sch; *m* 1938, Elisabeth Marian Keates; 3 da; *Career* entered RAF 1936, Dir-Gen RAF Personal Services 1966-69, Ch of Staff HQ RAF Strike Command 1969-70, Air Sec MOD 1970-72, ret, chm RAFA 1978-; *Style* - Air Marshal Sir Gareth Clayton, KCB DFC*; c/o Lloyds Bank Ltd, 263 Tottenham Court rd, W1

CLAYTON, John Pilkington; MVO (1975); s of late Brig-Gen Sir Gilbert Clayton, KCMG, KBE, CB; *b* 13 Feb 1921; *Educ* Wellington, Gonville and Caius Cambridge; *Career* Surgn-Apothecary to HM's Household at Windsor and to the Household of HM Queen Elizabeth the Queen Mother at Royal Lodge 1965-; *Style* - John Pilkington Esq, MVO; Town End House, Eton College, Windsor (☎ 62257)

CLAYTON, John Robert; s of late John Clayton; *b* 29 March 1922; *Educ* Highgate Sch, LSE; *m* 1958, Aileen Bowen, nee Morris; 1 s; *Career* ptnr John Tyzack & Partners Ltd 1961-69, gp md Pauls & Whites Ltd 1970-, dir Richard Clay & Co Ltd 1977-, memb CBI Regnl Council. *Style* John Clayton Esq; Berrishill, Burstall, Ipswich (☎ Hintlesham 264)

CLAYTON, Michael Aylwin; s of Aylwin Goff Clayton; *b* 20 Nov 1934; *Educ* Bournemouth G S; *m* 1, Mary; 1 s, 1 da; m 2, 1979, Barbara Jane, da of Prof A G W Whitfield, CBE; *Career* journalist, author and broadcaster, BBC News correspondent Radio and TV 1965-73, ed Horse and Hound 1973-; *Style* - Michael Clayton Esq; Waldley, Doveridge, Derbys

CLAYTON, Michael Thomas Emilius; CB (1976), OBE (1958); s of Lt-Col Emilius Clayton, OBE (ggs of George Clayton, who was gs of Sir William Clayton, 1 Bt; George's mother (his father William's 3 w) was Lady Louisa Fermor, da of 1 Earl of Pomfret by Henrietta, gda of Judge Jeffreys); *b* 15 Sept 1917; *Educ* Bradfield; *m* 1942, Mary, da of Dr John Pate, of Oxford; 1 da (Amanda, m 1976 Peter Hobson); *Career* attached War Off 1939-64, MOD 1964-76; *Recreations* philately, country pursuits; *Style* - Michael Clayton Esq, CB, OBE; Hillside Cottage, Marshwood, Bridport, Dorset (☎ 029 77 452)

CLAYTON, Sir Robert James; CBE (1970); *b* 30 Oct 1915; *Educ* Cambridge U; *m* 1949, Joy Kathleen King; *Career* tech dir GEC Co Ltd (formerly md research), memb NEB 1980-, memb British Library Bd, kt 1980; *Style* - Sir Robert Clayton, CBE; Drumness, Church rd, Stanmore, Middx (☎ 01 954 0329)

CLAYTON, Adm Sir Richard Pilkington; GCB (1980, KCB 1978); s of late Rear-Adm John Clayton; *b* 9 July 1925; *Educ* Horris Hill Newbury, RNC Dartmouth; *Career* Midshipman HMS Cumberland 1942-43, cmmd HMS Kent and HMS Hampshire 1968-69, MOD 1970-72, Flag Offr 2 Flotilla 1973-74, Sr Naval Memb Directing Staff RCDS 1975, Controller of the Navy 1976-79, CIC Naval Home Command 1979-May 1981; *Style* - Admiral Sir Richard Clayton, GCB; c/o Coutts & Co, 1 Cadogan pla, Sloane st, SW1

CLAYTON, Prof Sir Stanley George; s of Rev George Clayton; *b* 13 Sept 1911; *Educ* Kingswood Sch, King's Coll Hosp Medical Sch; *m* 1936, Kathleen Mary Willshire; 1 s, 1 da; *Career* MD, MS, kt 1974, Prof of Obstetrics and Gynaecology King's Coll Hosp Medical Sch 1967-76, now Emeritus, hon consulting surgeon King's Coll Hosp, Queen Charlotte's Hosp, Chelsea Hosp for Women; *Style* - Prof Sir Stanley Clayton; Fir Tree Lodge, Fir Tree rd, Leatherhead, Surrey

CLEAVER, Air Vice-Marshal Peter Charles; CB (1971), OBE (1945); s of William Cleaver; *b* 6 July 1919; *Educ* Warwick Sch, Coll of Aeronautics, Staff Coll Haifa; *m* 1948, Jean, nee Fairclough; 2 s; *Career* Air Offr Engrg HQ FEAF 1967-69, Air Support Command 1969-72, ret, sec Cranfield Inst of Technol 1973-78; *Style* - Air Vice-Marshal Peter Cleaver, CB, OBE; Willow House, Watling st, Little Brickhill, Milton Keynes, Bucks

CLEDWYN OF PENRHOS, Baron (Life Peer UK 1979); Cledwyn Hughes; CH (1977), PC (1966); s of Rev Henry Hughes; *b* 14 Sept 1916; *Educ* Holyhead G S, Univ Coll of Wales Aberystwyth; *m* 1949, Jean Beatrice Hughes; 1 s, 1 da; *Career* slr 1940, MP (L) Anglesey 1951-79 (also candidate 1945 and 1950), Min of Ag, Fish and Food 1968-70, Oppn Spokesman on Ag, Fish and Food 1970-72, Cmmr of House of Commons 1979; former chm Welsh Parly Pty and Parly Labour Pty, dir Shell UK Ltd 1980-; *Style* - The Rt Hon The Lord Cledwyn of Penrhos, CH, PC; Swynol Le, Trearddur, Holyhead, Gwynedd (☎ Trearddur 544)

CLEESE, John Marwood; s of Reginald Cleese; *b* 27 Oct 1939; *Educ* Downing Cambridge; *m* 1, 1968 (m dis 1978), Connie Booth; 1 da; m 2, 1981, Barbara Trentham; *Career* comedian, actor, writer; TV series include Monty Python's Flying Circus, Fawlty Towers; films include *Life of Brian*, *Time Bandits* (1981); *Style* - John Cleese Esq; c/o David Wilkinson, 8 Waterloo pla, SW1

CLEGG, Sir Alec (Alexander) Bradshaw; s of Samuel Clegg; *b* 13 June 1909; *Educ* Long Eaton G S, Bootham Sch York, Clare Cambridge, King's Coll London; *m* 1940, Jessie Coverdale Phillips; 3 s; *Career* former master St Clement Dane's G S, ch education offr W Riding County Council 1945-74, kt 1965; *Style* - Sir Alec Clegg; Saxton, Tadcaster, N Yorks (☎ Barkston Ash 288)

CLEGG, Sir Cuthbert Barwick; TD, JP (Lancs 1946); s of Edmund Clegg, JP, DL; *b* 9 Aug 1904; *Educ* Charterhouse, Trin Oxford; *m* 1930, Helen Margaret, nee Jefferson, MD; 1 s; *Career* Sheriff of Lancs 1955, of Westmorland 1969, former chm Martins Bank Ltd and former dir Barclays

Bank Ltd, v-chm Halifax Building Soc 1971-76, kt 1950; *Style* - Sir Cuthbert Clegg, TD, JP; Willow Cottage, Arkholme, Carnforth, Lancs (☎ Hornby 21205)

CLEGG, Nicholas Peter; s of Hugh Anthony Clegg, CBE; *b* 24 May 1936; *Educ* Bryanston Sch, Trin Cambridge; *m* 1959, Eulalie, da of Herman van den Wall Bake; 3 s, 1 da; *Career* banker, with Royal Netherlands Blast Furnaces & Steelworks 1960-62, Proctor & Gamble Brussels 1962-64, dir Hill Samuel & Co Ltd 1970; *Recreations* gardening, ski-ing, listening to music; *Style* - Nicholas Clegg Esq; Hay Lane Cottage, Hay Lane, Fulmer, Bucks (☎ Fulmer 2993)

CLEGG, Sir Walter; MP (C) N Fylde 1966-; s of Edwin Clegg; *b* 18 April 1920; *Educ* Bury G S, Arnold Sch Blackpool, Manchester U Law Sch; *m* 1951, Elise Margaret Hargreaves; *Career* solicitor 1947, practising to 1961; a Lord Cmmr HM Treasury 1970-72, V-Chamberlain HM Household 1972-73, Comptroller 1973-74, Opposition Whip 1967-69 and 1974, kt 1980; *Style* - Sir Walter Clegg, MP; Beech House, Raikes rd, Little Thornton, nr Blackpool (☎ Cleveleys 76131)

CLEGG-HILL, Hon Mrs Frederick - Alice Dorothy; da of late Rear-Adm Cuthbert Godfrey Chapman, MVO; *m* 1938, Maj Hon Frederick Clegg-Hill (ka 1945, s of 6 Visc Hill); 1 s; *Style* - The Hon Mrs Frederick Clegg-Hill; The Old Forge, Stone in Oxney, nr Tenterden, Kent

CLEGG-HILL, Peter David Raymond Charles; s of Major the Hon Frederick Raymond Clegg-Hill (ka 1945; 2 s of 6 Viscount Hill); hp to Viscountcy of cous, 8 Viscount Hill; *b* 17 Oct 1945 (posthumous); *m* 1973, Sharon Ruth Deane, of Kaikohe, NZ; 2 da; *Style* - Peter Clegg-Hill Esq

CLEMENT, Hon Mrs (Diana Benda); *née* Richards; da of 1 Baron Milverton, GCMG (d 1978); *b* 1928; *Educ* Havergal Coll, Toronto; Cheltenham Ladies' Coll; London U; Sorbonne, Paris; *m* 1960, Sqdn-Ldr Glyn John Clement, RAF; 1 s, 1 da; *Style* - The Hon Mrs Clement; The Bell House, Kewstoke rd, Worle, Weston-super-Mare, Somerset

CLEMENT, John; *Career* chm and jt ch exec Unigate Gp 1977-, dir Unigate Gp of Cos and others; *Style* - John Clement Esq; Home Farm, Heveningham, nr Halesworth, Suffolk (☎ Ubbeston 487)

CLEMENTI, Air Vice-Marshal Cresswell Montagu; CB (1973), CBE (1968, OBE 1946); s of late Sir Cecil Clementi, GCMG; *b* 30 Dec 1918; *Educ* Winchester, Magdalen Oxford; *m* 1940, Susan, da of late Sir Henry Pelham, KCB; 2 s, 1 da; *Career* joined RAF 1939, Air Vice-Marshal 1968, Sr RAF Memb RCDS 1969-71, AOA Air Support Command RAF Upavon 1972, AOA Strike Command 1972-74, ret, administrator Sion Coll 1979-; *Style* - Air Vice-Marshal Cresswell Clementi, CB, CBE; 8 Chiswick Staithe, W4 (☎ 01 995 9532)

CLEMENTS, Sir John Selby; CBE (1956); s of late Herbert Clements; *b* 25 April 1910; *Educ* St Paul's Sch, St John's Cambridge; *m* 1, 1936 (m dis 1946), Inga Maria Lillemor Ahlgren; m 2, 1946, Dorothy Katharine (Kay Hammond, actress, d 1980), da of late Sir Guy Standing, KBE; *Career* actor and director; founder and dir The Intimate Theatre Palmers Green, dir Chichester Festival Theatre 1966-73, kt 1968, FRSA; *Style* - Sir John Clements, CBE; 109 Marine Parade, Brighton, E Sussex (☎ 63026)

CLEMINSON, James Arnold Stacey; MC (1945); s of late Arnold Cleminson; *b* 31 Aug 1921; *Educ* Rugby; *m* 1950, Helen, da of Charles Measor; 1 s, 2 da; *Career* chm Reckitt & Colman Ltd 1977-, ch exec 1973-1973-; memb CBI Council 1978, Pres Food Mfrs Fedn 1980-; *Style* - James Cleminson Esq, MC; Loddon Hall, Hales, Norfolk

CLEMITSON, Rear-Adm Francis Edward; CB (1952); s of William Clemitson; *b* 9 Nov 1899; *Educ* Christ's Hosp; *m* 1933, Kathleen Farquhar Shand; 2 da; *Career* joined RN 1917, Rear-Adm (E) 1949, Dep Engr-in-Ch of the Fleet (Admin) Admiralty 1950-53, ret; *Style* - Rear-Admiral Francis Clemitson, CB;

Tanhurst, Bramley, Surrey (☎ Bramley 3148)

CLEPHANE, Kenneth George Thomas; s of late George Clephane; *b* 26 April 1917; *Educ* Bristol Cathedral Sch; *m* 1944, Edna Marjorie, nee Waite; 2 da; *Career* former md The International Twist Drill Co Ltd, md The Aldridge Tool & Engrg Co Ltd 1970-77, md The Sheffield Twist Drill & Steel Co Ltd 1977-; *Style* - Kenneth Clephane Esq; Sickleholme Cottage, Bamford, Sheffield (☎ 04334 384)

CLERK, Sir John Dutton; 10 Bt (NS 1679), of Penicuik, Edinburgh, CBE (1966), VRD, FRSE (1977), JP; s of Sir George Clerk, 9 Bt (d 1943); *b* 30 Jan 191; *Educ* Stowe; *m* 1944, Evelyn, nee Robertson; 2 s, 2 da; *Heir* s, Robert Clerk; *Career* Cdre RN ret, Brig Queen's Body Guard for Scotland Roy Co of Archers 1973, Ld-Lt Midlothian 1972- (formerly Vice-Lt); *Style* - Sir John Clerk, Bt, CBE, VRD, JP; Penicuik House, Penicuik, Midlothian, Scotland (☎ Penicuik 74318)

CLERK, Robert Maxwell; s and h of Sir John Clerk, 10 Bt; *b* 3 April 1945; *Educ* Winchester, London U (BSc Agric); *m* 1970, Felicity Faye, nee Collins; 1 s, 1 da; *Career* ARICS; *Style* - Robert Clerk Esq; Lachlanwells, Forres, Morayshire

CLERKE, Francis Ludlow Longueville; s and h of Sir John Clerke, 12 Bt; *b* 25 Jan 1953; *Style* - Francis Clerke Esq

CLERKE, Sir John Edward Longueville; 12 Bt (E 1660), of Hitcham, Buckinghamshire; s of late Francis Clerke, s of 11 Bt; suc gf 1930; *b* 29 Oct 1913; *Educ* Eton, Magdalene Cambridge; *m* 1948, Mary, da of Lt-Col I R Beviss Bond; 1 s, 2 da; *Heir* s, Francis Clerk; *Career* Capt Roy Wilts Yeo (TA); *Style* - Sir John Clerke, Bt; Westbrook House, Bromham, Chippenham, Wilts

CLEVERLEY FORD, Rev Preb Douglas William; s of late Arthur Ford; *b* 4 March 1914; *Educ* Great Yarmouth G S, London U; *m* 1939, Olga Mary, nee Gilbart-Smith; *Career* deacon 1937, RD of Westminster 1965-74, Prebendary of St Paul's Cathedral 1968-, Chaplain to HM the Queen 1973-, Sr Chaplain to the Archbp of Canterbury 1975-; *Style* - The Rev Prebendary Douglas Cleverley Ford; Lambeth Palace, SE1; Rostrevor, Lingfield, Surrey

CLIFDEN, Viscountess; Margaret; da of Ray Carter, of St Louis, US; *m* 1, John Thursky; m 2 John Monins (decd); m 3, 1948, as his 2 w, 8 Viscount Clifden (d 1974); *Style* - The Rt Hon the Viscountess Clifden; La Vieille Demure, Beaumont, Jersey

CLIFFORD OF CHUDLEIGH, 13 Baron (E 1672); (Lewis) Hugh Clifford; OBE (1962), DL (Devon 1964); s of 12 Baron (d 1964); *b* 13 April 1916; *Educ* Beaumont, Hertford Coll Oxford; *m* 1945, Hon Katharine, da of Baron Fisher; 2 s, 2 da; *Heir* s, Hon Thomas Clifford; *Career* 2 Lt Devonshire Regt 1935, Col 1961, Dep Hon Col The Wessex Yeomanry 1971-72, Hon Col D Sqdn 1972-, ADC to HM 1964-69, farmer; *Clubs* Roy Yacht Sqdn; *Style* - The Rt Hon the Lord Clifford of Chudleigh, OBE, DL; Ugbrooke Park, Chudleigh, S Devon; Morella, Montrose, Vic, Australia

CLIFFORD, Hon Lady - Alice Devin; da of John Murton Gundry; *m* 1925, Capt the Hon Sir Bede Edmund Hugh Clifford, GCMG, CB, MVO (d 1969); 3 da (*see* also Viscountess Norwich); *Style* - The Hon Lady Clifford; Jacob's Well, nr Guildford, Surrey

CLIFFORD, David; s of late Robert Clifford; *b* 20 July 1940; *Educ* Friends' Sch Great Ayton, N Yorks; Sunderland Tech Coll, Newcastle Coll of Further Education (MCIT); *m* 1963, Margaret; 2 s; *Career* gen man Econofreight Transport Ltd 1976-78, dir and gen man Seaham Harbour Dock Co 1978-; *Style* - David Clifford Esq; 7 East View, Seaham, Co Durham (☎ 0783 813641)

CLIFFORD OF CHUDLEIGH, Baroness; Hon Katharine; da of late 2 Baron Fisher; *b* 1919; *m* 1945, 13 Baron Clifford of Chudleigh, *qv*; *Style* - The Rt

Hon the Lady Clifford of Chudleigh; Ugbrooke Park, Chudleigh, S Devon

CLIFFORD, Sir (Geoffrey) Miles; KBE (1949, OBE 1939), CMG (1944); *b* 1897; *m* 1, 1920, Ivy Dorothy (decd), nee Eland; m 2, Mary, nee Turner; *Career* Colonial Admin Service (Nigeria) 1921, Gov and CIC Falkland Isles 1946-54, former dir Leverhulme Trust, chm Nigerian Electricity Supply Corpn 1957-77; *Style* - Sir Miles Clifford, KBE, CMG; Kingswood Lodge, Trinity Close, Tunbridge Wells, Kent

CLIFFORD OF CHUDLEIGH, Elizabeth, Baroness - Mary Elizabeth; da of late Rt Hon Sir Adrian Knox, KCMG, KC, former Chief Justice of Australia; *m* 1934, as his 2 w, 12 Baron Clifford of Chudleigh (d 1964); *Style* - The Rt Hon Elizabeth, Lady Clifford of Chudleigh; El Reposo, San Roque, Spain

CLIFFORD, Sir Roger Charles Joseph Gerrard; 6 Bt (UK 1887), of Flaxbourne, Marlborough, New Zealand; s of late Charles William Clifford (s of 1 Bt); suc bro 1970; *b* 28 May 1910; *Educ* Beaumont Coll Old Windsor, Harper Adams Agric Coll; *m* 1, 1934, Henrietta Millicent Kiver (d 1971); 2 s, 1 da; m 2, 1973, Gretchen Patrice Pollock; *Heir* s, Roger Joseph Clifford; *Career* former man Rod Weir & Co Ltd; *Style* - Sir Roger Clifford, Bt; 17 Kotare st, Waikanae, New Zealand

CLIFFORD, Hon Rollo Hugh; s of 13 Baron Clifford of Chudleigh; *b* 15 Mar 1954; *Educ* Downside; *m* 1977, Fiona Margaret, da of Richard Todd, actor; 1 da (Elizabeth Alice, b 4 Feb 1981); *Career* formerly on London Metal Exchange; ptnr Mgmnt Training Consultant, The MAST Organisation; *Style* - The Hon Rollo Clifford

CLIFFORD, Roger Joseph; s (twin, by 1 m) and h of Sir Roger Clifford, 6 Bt; *b* 5 June 1936; *m* 1968, Joanna Theresa, nee Ward; 1 da; *Style* - Roger Clifford Esq; 135 Totara st, Christchurch, New Zealand

CLIFFORD, Capt the Hon Thomas Hugh; s and h of 13 Baron Clifford of Chudleigh; *b* 17 March 1948; *Educ* Downside, Oxford U; *m* 1980, Suzanne, da of late Campbell Austin; *Career* late Capt Coldstream Gds; *Style* - Capt the Hon Thomas Clifford

CLIFFORD-JONES, Neville Leo; s of late William Clifford-Jones, MBE; *b* 18 Jan 1931; *Educ* Ampleforth; *m* 1958, Susan Patricia Lancaster, nee Titley; 4 da; *Career* chartered accountant; chm SGB Group Ltd, dir British American & General Trust Ltd; *Style* - Neville Clifford-Jones Esq; Shoes Farm, Ockley, Surrey (☎ Forest Green 264)

CLIFTON OF RATHMORE, Lord; Ivo Donald Stuart Bligh; s and h of 11 Earl of Darnley; *b* 1968; *Style* - Lord Clifton of Rathmore

CLIFTON, Lt-Col Peter Thomas; DSO (1945), JP (Notts 1952-59), DL (1954); s of Lt-Col Percy Clifton, CMG, DSO, TD; *b* 24 Jan 1911; *Educ* Eton, Sandhurst; *m* 1, 1934 (m dis 1936), Ursula, da of Sir Edward Packe; m 2, 1948, Patricia Mary Adela, nee Gibson-Watt, widow of Maj Robert Cobbold and sister of Baron Gibson-Watt, MC**, PC, DL; 2 da; *Career* 2 Lieutenant Grenadier Guards 1931, Lt-Col 1944, memb HM Body Guard of Hon Corps of Gentlemen at Arms from 1960, Standard Bearer 1979-81, ret; *Style* - Lt-Col Peter Clifton, DSO, JP, DL; Dummer House, Basingstoke, Hants (☎ Dummer (STD Code 025 675) 306)

CLINTON, 22 Baron (E 1299); Gerard Neville Mark Fane Trefusis, JP (Bideford 1963), DL (Devon 1977); s of Capt Charles Fane (ka 1940), s of Hon Harriet Trefusis, herself da of 21 Baron Clinton (d 1957); assumed additional surname Trefusis by Deed Poll 1958 and suc to Barony 1965 on termination of abeyance; *b* 7 Oct 1934; *Educ* Gordonstoun; *m* 1959, Nicola Harriette Purdon Coote (gggda of Robert, yr bro of Sir Charles Coote, 9 Bt); 1 s, 2 da; *Heir* s, Hon Charles Fane Trefusis; *Career* memb Prince of Wales's Councils 1968-79; landowner; *Style* - The Rt Hon the Lord Clinton, JP, DL; Heanton Satchville, nr Okehampton, N Devon (☎ Dolton 224)

CLITHEROE, 1 Baron (UK 1955); Sir Ralph Assheton; 2 Bt (UK 1945), KCVO (1977), PC (1944), FSA, JP (Lancs 1934), DL (1955); Lord of the Manor of Downham and other manors; s of Sir Ralph Clitheroe, 1 Bt (d 1955); *b* 24 Feb 1901; *Educ* Eton, Ch Ch Oxford; *m* 1924, Hon Sylvia , da of 6 Baron Hotham; 2 s, 1 da; *Heir* s, Hon Ralph Assheton; *Career* barr 1925, MP (Nat U) Rushcliffe Notts 1934-45, City of London 1945-50, Blackburn W 1950-55, former Ld-Lt of Lancs, late chm Borax Hldgs (dir 1947-), dir Mercantile Investment Tst; High Steward of Westminster 1962-, KStJ; *Style* - The Rt Hon the Lord Clitheroe, KCVO, PC, JP, DL; 17 Chelsea Park gdns, SW3 (☎ 01 352 4020); Downham Hall, Clitheroe, Lancs (☎ Chatburn 210)

CLITHEROE, Baroness; Hon Sylvia Benita Francis; da of 6 Baron Hotham (d 1923); *b* 1903; *m* 1924, 1 Baron Clitheroe, KCVO, PC; *Career* FRICS; a Gov of Westminster Hosp, and a memb of Council of Lancaster U, memb Lancs War Agricultural Exec Ctee 1941-48, and of Agricultural Exec Ctee 1948-59; *Style* - The Rt Hon the Lady Clitheroe; Downham Hall, Clitheroe, Lancs; 17 Chelsea Park gdns, SW3

CLIVE, Lady Mary Katharine; *née* Pakenham; da of late 5 Earl of Longford, KP, MVO; *b* 1907; *m* 1939, Major Meysey George Dallas Clive, Gren Gds (ka 1943); 1 s, 1 da; *Style* - Lady Mary Clive; Whitfield, Allensmore, Herefordshire

CLIVE-PONSONBY-FANE, Charles Edward Brabazon; JP (1979); s of late Nicholas Brabazon Clive-Ponsonby-Fane, 2 s of Edward Clive (1 cous four times removed of (Robert) Clive of India) by Edward's w Violet, ggda of 4 Earl of Bessborough by Lady Maria Fane (da of 10 Earl of Westmorland); Nicholas m, as her 2 husb, Petronilla Dunsterville, whose mother was Eveline, da of Sir Henry Goldney, 3 & penultimate Bt, JP; *b* 10 Aug 1941; *Educ* Harrow, L'Institut de Touraine France, RAC Cirencester; *m* 1974, Judy Barbara, nee Bushby; 2 da; *Career* viticulturalist, chm Historic Houses Assocn (Wessex) 1979; *Clubs* Somerset County Cricket, MCC, I Zingari; *Style* - Charles Clive-Ponsonby-Fane Esq, JP; Brympton d'Evercy, Yeovil, Somerset

CLOAKE, Graham Arthur; s of late Wilfred Cloake; *b* 1 Jan 1934; *Educ* Badingham Coll; *m* 1961, Jennifer Noel, nee Smith; 2 s, 1 da; *Career* sr ptnr Pidgeon De Smitt Stockbrokers 1979-, non exec dir St Swithins Hldgs, TIL Finance; *Style* - Graham Cloake Esq; 9 Preston rd, Wimbledon, SW20 (☎ 01 947 2962)

CLOAKE, John Cecil; CMG (1977); s of late Dr Cecil Cloake; *b* 2 Dec 1924; *Educ* KCS Wimbledon, Peterhouse Cambridge; *m* 1956, Margaret Thomure, nee Morris; 1 s; *Career* entd HM Foreign Service 1948, Counsellor (Commercial) Tehran 1968-72, head Trade Relations and Exports Dept FCO 1973-76, Ambass to Bulgaria 1976-80; *Style* - John Cloake Esq, CMG; 4 The Terrace, Richmond Hill, Richmond, Surrey

CLOGHER, 96 Bishop of, 1980-; Right Rev Gordon McMullan; *b* 1934; *Educ* Queen's University Belfast; *m* Kathleen; 2 s; *Career* deacon 1962, priest 1963; Archdeacon of Down 1979-80 and Rector St Columba, Knock, Belfast 1976-80; *Style* -The Rt Rev the Lord Bishop of Clogher; The See House, Thornfield, Fivemiletown, Co Tyrone, Northern Ireland (☎ Fivemiletown 265)

CLOSE, David John; s of John Edward Close (d 1969); *b* 10 May 1929; *Educ* Queen Elizabeth's G S Mansfield, King's Coll London; *m* 1971, Jan, nee Wileman; 2 da; *Career* FIPM, FBIM, FIIM, personnel dir Simon Engrg (contracting gp) 1974-, personnel offr NCB 1956-63, gp personnel man Sangamo Weston 1963-64, personnel man Pirelli 1965-69, personnel and admin dir Davy & United Eng 1969-71, personnel and admin dir Kearney & Trecker 1971-73, gen personnel man Reliant Motor Co 1973-74; *Recreations* walking, gardening, DIY, music, dog training; *Style* - David Close Esq; Glengarth, Diglee rd, Furness Vale, Stockport, Cheshire (☎ New Mills 42342)

CLOUGH, (John) Alan; CBE (1972), MC (1945); s of John Clough; *b* 20 March 1924; *Educ* Marlborough, Leeds U; *m* 1,

1949 (m dis 1961), Margaret Joy, nee Catton; 1 s, 2 da; m 2, 1961, Mary Cowan, nee Catherwood; 1 s, 1 da; *Career* ch exec and dep chm British Mohair Spinners Ltd, dir Christopher Waud Ltd, Robert Clough (Keighley) Hldgs Ltd, Stork Bros Ltd, Smith (Allerton) Ltd and others; *Style* - Alan Clough Esq, CBE, MC; Spitalcroft Green, Knaresborough, N Yorks (☎ Harrogate 863232)

CLOUTMAN, Air Vice-Marshal Geoffrey William; s of Rev Walter Evans Cloutman; *b* 1 April 1920; *Educ* Cheltenham G S, Queen Mary Coll, London U London Hosp; *m* 1949, Sylvia, nee Brown; 3 da; *Career* FDSRCS, QHDS 1976, joined RAFVR 1942, Princ Dental Offr Strike Command 1973, Dir of Dental Services RAF 1977-; *Style* - Air Vice-Marshal Geoffrey Cloutman; 56 Moor lane, Rickmansworth, Herts (☎ Rickmansworth 72697)

CLOVER, His Honour Judge - Robert Gordon; TD (1951), QC (1958), JP (Bucks 1969); s of late Henry Clover; *b* 14 Nov 1911; *Educ* Lancing, Exeter Coll Oxford (MA, BCL); *m* 1947, Elizabeth Suzanne, nee McCorquodale; 2 s; *Career* barr 1935, dep cmmr National Insurance 1961-65, Circuit Judge 1965-; *Style* - His Honour Judge Clover, TD, QC, JP; The Garth, Marlow, Bucks (☎ 4170)

CLOWES, Peter Josceline; TD; s of late Cdr William Clowes; *b* 12 May 1935; *Educ* Eton, Trin Cambridge (MA); *m* 1969, Monique Françoise Marie Antoinette, nee d'Arcier; 2 s; *Career* md Frowds Ltd, dir G & L Ralli Investment & Trustee Co Ltd, Ralli Bondite Ltd, Ralliseal Ltd; *Style* - Peter Clowes, Esq, TD; Closewood House, Newlands lane, Denmead, Hants

CLOWES, Richard Norris Thyne; s of Edward Norris Thyne Clowes (d 1976); *b* 18 May 1937; *Educ* Framlingham Coll; *m* 1960, Marion Joyce, 2 da; *Career* CA, ptnr Pannell Kerr Forster, co cnclr 1969-74; *Recreations* racing (owner); *Clubs* Ipswich and Suffolk, Newmarket Race; *Style* - Richard Clowes Esq; Herb Cottage, 9 Mill Lane, Gt Blakenham, Ipswich, Suffolk

CLUCAS, Sir Kenneth Henry; KCB (1976, CB 1969); s of late Rev J H Clucas; *b* 18 Nov 1921; *Educ* Kingswood Sch, Emmanuel Cambridge; *m* 1960, Barbara, da of Rear-Adm R P Hunter, USN (retd); 2 da; *Career* Perm Sec Dept of Prices and Consumer Protection 1974-79, Perm Sec Dept of Trade 1979-; *Style* - Sir Kenneth Clucas, KCB; Cariad, Knoll rd, Godalming, Surrey (☎ 6430)

CLUFF, Algy (John Gordon); s of Harold Cluff; *b* 19 April 1940; *Educ* Stowe; *Career* 2 Lt Grenadiers Gds 1959, Capt Gds Independent Parachute Co, founder, chm and ch exec Cluff Oil, contested (C) Ardwick Manchester 1966, md CCP North Seas Associates Ltd, dep chm Cluff Oil (Australia), proprietor The Spectator 1981-; *Style* - Algy Cluff Esq; 90 Eaton sq, SW1; Clova House, Lumsden, W Aberdeenshire (☎ Lumsden 336)

CLUSKEY, Frank; TD Dublin S Central 1965-; *b* 1930; *Educ* St Vincent's Sch Glasnevin, Harvard U; *m* Eileen Gillespie; 1 s, 2 da; *Career* Ldr Irish Lab Pty 1977-, former Lord Mayor of Dublin, Opposition Spokesman on Justice, Social Welfare and Labour; *Style* - Frank Cluskey Esq, TD; 1 Glasnevin Park, Dublin 11, Ireland

CLUTTERBUCK, Vice-Adm Sir David Granville; KBE (1968), CB (1965); s of late Charles Clutterbuck; *b* 25 Jan 1913; *Educ* HMS Conway; *m* 1937, Rose Mere, nee Vaile; 2 da; *Career* joined RN 1929, Rear-Adm 1963, Vice-Adm 1966, Dep Supreme Allied Cdr Atlantic 1966-68, ret; admin dir Business Graduates Assocn Ltd 1969-; *Style* - Vice-Admiral Sir David Clutterbuck, KBE, CB; 29 Elvaston pla, SW7

CLUTTERBUCK, Edmund Harry Michael; OBE (1957); s of Maj-Gen W E Clutterbuck; *b* 22 July 1920; *Educ* Winchester Coll, New Coll Oxford; *m* 1945, Anne Agatha Woodsend; 1 s, 3 da; *Career* dir Scottish and Newcastle Breweries Ltd 1960-, dir Scottish Brewers Ltd, Brewers' Food Supply Co Ltd, Wm Younger & Co Ltd and others; *Style* - Edmund Clutterbuck Esq, OBE; 4 Kinellan rd, Edinburgh 12 (☎ 337 6027)

CLUTTERBUCK, Jasper Meadows; s of late Hugh Clutterbuck; *b* 5 Feb 1935; *Educ* Eton; *m* 1958, Marguerite Susan, nee Birnie; 1 s, 1 da; *Career* dir Whitbread & Co; *Style* - Jasper Clutterbuck Esq; Mottisfont House, nr Romsey, Hants

CLUTTERBUCK, Maj-Gen Richard Lewis; CB (1971), OBE (1958); s of late Col L St J R Clutterbuck, OBE, late RA; *b* 22 Nov 1917; *Educ* Radley, Pembroke Coll Cambridge (MA, PhD); *m* 1948, Angela Muriel, nee Barford; 3 s; *Career* 2 Lt RE 1937, Maj-Gen 1968, Ch Army Instructor Roy Coll of Defence Studies 1971-72, Col Cmdt RE 1972-77, Politics lectr Exeter U 1972-, author; *Style* - Maj-Gen Richard Clutterbuck, CB, OBE; Dept of Politics, University of Exeter, Exeter, Devon

CLUTTON, Rafe Henry; s of late Robin Clutton; *b* 13 June 1929; *Educ* Tonbridge; *m* 1954, Jill Olwyn, Evans; 4 s, 1 da; *Career* chartered surveyor, ptnr Cluttons 1955-, dir Legal & General Gp Ltd 1972-, memb National Theatre Bd 1976-; *Style* - Rafe Clutton Esq; Fairfield, North Chailey, Sussex (☎ Newick 2431)

CLWYD, 2 Baron (UK 1919); Sir (John) Trevor Roberts; 2 Bt (UK 1908), JP (Co of London 1950); s of 1 Baron (d 1955); *b* 28 Nov 1900; *Educ* Gresham's Sch, Trin Cambridge; *m* 1932, Joan de Bois, nee Murray; 1 s, 1 da; *Heir* s, John Roberts; *Career* barr 1930, Assist Sec of Commissions Lord Chancellor's Dept House of Lords 1949-61; *Style* - The Rt Hon the Lord Clwyd, JP; 15 Aubrey rd, W8 (☎ 01 727 7911); Trimmings, Gracious st, Selborne, Hants

CLWYD, Ann (Ann Clwyd Roberts); MEP (L) Mid and W Wales 1979-; da of Gwilym Lewis; *b* 21 March 1937; *Educ* Holywell G S, The Queen's Sch Chester, Univ Coll Bangor; *m* 1963, Owen Dryhurst Roberts; *Career* contested Denbigh 1970, Gloucester Oct 1974, journalist The Guardian and The Observer, broadcaster, v-chm Welsh Arts Council 1975-; *Style* - Miss Ann Clwyd, MEP; 1 Lon Werdd, St Fagans, Cardiff (☎ 593492)

CLYDE, Lady Elizabeth; *née* Wellesley; da of 7 Duke of Wellington; *b* 26 Dec 1918; *m* 1939 (m dis 1959), Maj Thomas Clyde, RHG; 2 s (of which the er is Jeremy Clyde, the actor); *Style* - Lady Elizabeth Clyde; Oliver's Farm, Bramley, Hants

CLYDESMUIR, 2 Baron (UK 1948); Ronald John Bilsland Colville; KT (1972), CB (1965), MBE (1944), TD; s of 1 Baron (d 1954); *b* 21 May 1917; *Educ* Charterhouse, Trin Cambridge; *m* 1946, Joan Marguerita, da of Lt-Col Ernest Brabazon Booth, DSO, MD; 2 s, 2 da; *Heir* s, Hon David Colville; *Career* Ld-Lt Lanarkshire 1963 (formerly V-Lt, DL 1955), Lt Roy Co of Archers (Queen's Body Guard for Scotland), dir Bank of Scotland (Gov to 1980), dir Scottish Provident Instn, Scotbits Securities Ltd, Barclays Bank, chm North Sea Assets Ltd; *Style* - The Rt Hon Lord Clydesmuir KT CB MBE TD, HM Lord-Lieut for Lanarks; Langlees House, Biggar, Lanarkshire (☎ Biggar 20057)

COAKER, Maj-Gen Ronald Edward; CB (1972), CBE (1963), MC (1942), DL (Rutland 1973); s of late Lt-Col Vere Coaker, DSO; *b* 28 Nov 1917; *Educ* Wellington, Sandhurst; *m* 1946, Constance Aimee Johanna, nee Curzon; 1 s, 2 da; *Career* 2 Lt IA (Skinner's Horse) 1937, RAPC 1939-45, Maj-Gen 1966, Assist Ch of Staff (Intelligence) SHAPE 1967-70, Dir of Mil Operations MOD 1970-72, ret, Col 17/21 Lancers 1965-75; *Style* - Maj-Gen Ronald Coaker, CB, CBE, MC, DL; Seaton Old Rectory, Uppingham, Rutland (☎ Morcott 276); Hall Farm, Lockington, Derby (☎ Kegworth 2226)

COATE, Maj-Gen Sir Raymond Douglas; KBE (1967), CB (1966); s of Frederick Coate; *b* 8 May 1908; *Educ* King Edward's Sch Bath, Sandhurst; *m* 1939, Frances Margaret Varley; 2 s; *Career* Devonshire Regt 1928, Roy Army Pay Corps 1937, Col Cmdt 1970-74, chm Roy Homes for Officers' Widows and Daughters Wimbledon 1969-; *Style* - Maj-Gen Sir Raymond Coate, KBE, CB; 18 Roehampton Close, SW15

COATES, David Charlton Frederick; s and h of Brig Sir Frederick Coates, 2 Bt; *b* 16 Feb 1948; *Educ* Millfield; *m* 1973,

Christine Helen, nee Marshall; 1 s; *Style* - David Coates Esq; 30 Hauxton rd, Little Shelford, Cambridge

COATES, Sir Ernest William; CMG (1970); s of Thomas Coates; *b* 30 Nov 1916; *Educ* Ballarat H S, Melbourne U; *m* 1, 1943, Phyllis Morris (d 1971); 1 s, 3 da; m 2, 1974, Patricia Ann, nee Fisher; *Career* State Dir of Finance and Perm Head of Victoria Treasury Australia 1959-77, company director, kt 1973; *Style* - Sir Ernest Coates, CMG; 64 Molesworth st, Kew, Vic 3101, Australia (☎ 8618226)

COATES, Brig Sir Frederick Gregory Lindsay; 2 Bt (UK 1921), of Haypark, City of Belfast; s of Sir William Coates, 1 Bt (d 1932); *b* 19 May 1916; *Educ* Eton, Sandhurst; *m* 1940, Joan Nugent, da of Maj-Gen Sir Charlton Spinks, KBE, DSO; 1 s, 2 da; *Heir* s, David Coates; *Career* Roy Tank Regt 1936, Brig British Defence Staff Washington DC 1966-69, mil adviser Defence Sales MOD 1969-71, ret; *Style* - Brig Sir Frederick Coates, Bt; Launchfield, Briantspuddle, Dorchester, Dorset

COATES, William Muir Nelson; s of Victor Airth Coates; *b* 18 June 1934; *Educ* Fettes, Edinburgh U; *m* 1959, Christina, nee MacLeod; 1 s, 1 da; *Career* civil engineer, CEng, MICE; md Curral Lewis & Martin Ltd 1976 (formerly contracts dir); *Style* - William Coates Esq; Boxmoor, Meer End, Kenilworth, Warwicks (☎ 0676 32038)

COATS, Sir Alastair Francis Stuart; 4 Bt (UK 1905), of Auchendrane, Maybole, Co Ayr; s of Lt-Col Sir James Coats, 3 Bt, MC; *b* 18 Nov 1921; *Educ* Eton; *m* 1947, Lukyn, da of Capt Charles Gordon; 1 s, 1 da; *Heir* s, Alexander Coats; *Career* Capt Coldstream Guards 1939-45; *Style* - Sir Alastair Coats, Bt; Birchwood House, Durford Wood, Petersfield, Hants (☎ Liss 2254)

COATS, Alexander James; s and h of Sir Alastair Coats, Bt; *b* 6 July 1951; *Educ* Eton; *Style* - Alexander Coats Esq

COATS, Hon Mrs (Elizabeth Lilian Graham); *née* MacAndrew; da of 1 Baron MacAndrew, TD, PC (d 1979); *b* 1929; *m* 1950, William David Coats; 2 s, 1 da; *Style* - The Hon Mrs Coats; The Cottage, Symington, Ayrshire

COBB, Hon Mrs; Hon (Rosamond Stella) Frances; *née* Byng; da of 10 Viscount Torrington (d 1961); *b* 1937; *m* 1960, Antony B Cobb; 1 s, 1 da; *Style* - The Hon Mrs Cobb; Highbury, Lane End, Bembridge, Isle of Wight

COBBE, Hon Mrs (Isabelle Anne Marie Henrietta); da of late 20 Viscount Dillon; *b* 1942; *m* 1970, Richard Alexander Charles Cobbe; 2 s, 2 da (twins); *Style* - The Hon Mrs Cobbe; 16a Lyndewode rd, Cambridge

COBBOLD, 1 Baron (UK 1960); Cameron Fromanteel Cobbold; KG (1970), GCVO (1963), PC (1959), DL (Herts 1972); s of late Lt-Col Clement Cobbold; *b* 14 Sept 1904; *Educ* Eton, King's Cambridge; *m* 1930, Lady (Margaret) Hermione (Millicent), da of 2 Earl of Lytton, KG, GCSI, GCIE, PC; 2 s, 1 da; *Heir* s, Hon David Lytton Cobbold; *Career* Lord Chamberlain of HM Household 1963-71, a Perm Lord in Waiting to HM the Queen 1971-, former Gov of the Bank of England. one of HM Lts for the City of London, v-pres British Heart Foundation, Steward of the Courts of Eton 1975; *Style* - The Rt Hon the Lord Cobbold, KG, GCVO, PC, DL; Lake House, Knebworth, Herts (☎ Stevenage 812310)

COBBOLD, Lady Blanche Katharine; *née* Cavendish; da of late 9 Duke of Devonshire, KG, GCMG, GCVO, TD; *b* 1898; *m* 1919, Lt-Col John Murray Cobbold, Scots Gds (killed on active service 1944); 2 s, 2 da; *Career* DStJ, sometime Senior Commandant ATS JP Suffolk 1951-66; *Style* - Lady Blanche Cobbold; Glemham Hall, Woodbridge, Suffolk

COBBOLD, Baroness - Lady (Margaret) Hermione (Millicent); *née* Lytton; da of 2 Earl of Lytton, KG, GCSI, GCIE, PC (d 1947); *b* 1905; *m* 1930, 1 Baron Cobbold, KG, GCVO, PC; *Style* - The Rt Hon the Lady Cobbold; Lake House, Knebworth, Herts

COBBOLD, Hon Rowland John Fromanteel; s of 1 Baron Cobbold, KG, GCVO, PC; *b* 1944; *m* 1969, Sophia Augusta, nee White-Spunner; 1 s, 1 da; *Style* - The Hon Rowland Cobbold; 25 Fernshaw rd, SW10

COBHAM, 11 Viscount (GB 1718); Sir John William Leonard Lyttelton; 14 Bt (E 1618); also Baron Cobham (GB 1718), Lord Lyttelton, Baron of Frankley (1756, renewed 1794), and Baron Westcote of Ballymore (I 1776); s of 10 Viscount (d 1977); *b* 5 June 1943; *Educ* Eton, Christ's Coll New Zealand, RAC Cirencester; *m* 1974, Penelope Ann, nee Cooper; *Heir* bro, Hon Christopher Lyttelton; *Career* ptnr Hagley Hall Farms 1976-; *Style* - The Rt Hon the Viscount Cobham; Hagley Hall, Stourbridge, Worcs (☎ Hagley 885823); 20 Kylestrome House, Cundy st, Ebury st, SW1 (☎ 01 730 5756)

COBHAM, Baroness - Christina Jean; da of Albert Edward Honeybone; *m* 1923 (m dis 1934, remarried 1949), 13 Baron Cobham (d 1951, when title went into abeyance); *Style* - The Rt Hon the Lady Cobham; 510 Barren Joey rd, Avalon, NSW, Australia

COBHAM, Dowager Viscountess - Elizabeth Alison; da of late John Reeder Makeig-Jones, CBE, late ICS; *m* 1942, 10 Viscount Cobham (d 1977); 4 s (including 11 Viscount), 4 da (Hon Mrs Dugdale; Lady Forester, w of 8 Baron; Hon Mrs Kemp-Gee; Hon Mrs Bedford); *Career* CStJ; *Style* - The Rt Hon the Dowager Viscountess Cobham; 8 Marine Parade, Budleigh Salterton, Devon

COBURN, Alfred Henry; CBE (1979); s of late Alfred Coburn; *b* 12 Feb 1922; *m* 1944, Betty Winifred, nee Robinson; 2 da; *Career* dir The Nestle Co (UK) Ltd, md Findus Ltd, md Chambourcy Food Products Ltd, FRSA, FIGD; *Style* - Alfred Coburn Esq, CBE; Woodside, Icklingham rd, Cobham, Surrey

COCHRANE OF CULTS, 3 Baron (UK 1919); Thomas Charles Anthony Cochrane; s of 2 Baron (d 1968, gs of 11 Earl of Dundonald through his father and gs of 6 Earl of Glasgow through his mother) by his 1 w Hon Elin Douglas-Pennant (da of 2 Baron Penrhyn); *b* 31 Oct 1922; *Educ* privately; *Heir* bro, Hon Vere Cochrane; *Career* fndr/tstee Gardeners' Tst; *Style* - The Rt Hon the Lord Cochrane of Cults; Balgownie, 18 Cliff ter, Buckie, Banffshire

COCHRANE, Alexander Desmond; s and h of Sir Marc Cochrane, 4 Bt; *b* 7 May 1973; *Style* - Alexander Cochrane Esq

COCHRANE, Alexander John Cameron; s of Dr Alexander Cochrane; *b* 19 July 1933; *Educ* Edinburgh Acad, Univ Oxford; *m* 1958, Rosemary Aline, nee Ogg; 1 s, 2 da; *Career* former headmaster Arnold Sch Blackpool, headmaster Fettes Coll Edinburgh 1979-; *Style* - Alexander Cochrane Esq; The Lodge, Fettes College, Edinburgh

COCHRANE, Hon Lady - Hilda Frances Holme; da of late Francis Holme Wiggin; *m* 1930, Air Ch Marshal the Hon Sir Ralph Alexander Cochrane, GBE, KCB, AFC (d 1977); 2 s, 1 da; *Style* - The Hon Lady Cochrane; Grove Farmhouse, Shipton-under-Wychwood, Oxon

COCHRANE, Lord; Iain Alexander Douglas Blair Cochrane; s (by 1 m) and h of 14 Earl of Dundonald; *b* 17 Feb 1961; *Style* - Lord Cochrane

COCHRANE, Hon (John Douglas) Julian; s of late 2 Baron Cochrane of Cults; *b* 1929; *Educ* Eton; *m* 1955, Vaila Rose, da of Cdr Robert Falby, RN (ret); 1 s, 2 da; *Style* - The Hon Julian Cochrane; Townend House, Hopton, Derbys

COCHRANE, Sir (Henry) Marc (Sursock); 4 Bt (UK 1903); s of Sir Desmond Cochrane, 3 Bt (d 1979); *b* 23 Oct 1946; *Educ* Eton, Trin Coll Dublin (MA); *m* 1969, Hala, da of Fouad es-Said; 2 s, 1 da; *Heir* s, Alexander Cochrane; *Career* Hon Consul Gen of Ireland in Beirut, dir Hambros Bank; *Style* - Sir Marc Cochrane, Bt; Woodbrook, Bray, Co Wicklow (☎ 862008); Palais Sursock, PO Box 154, Beirut, Lebanon

COCHRANE, Lady Tanya Jean Farquhar; da (by 1 m) of 14 Earl of

Dundonald; *b* 1964; *Style* - Lady Tanya Cochrane

COCHRANE, Hon (Ralph Henry) Vere Cochrane; s of 2 Baron Cochrane of Cults; hp of bro, 3 Baron; *b* 1926; *Educ* Eton, King's Cambridge; *m* 1956, Janet Mary, nee Watson; 2 s; *Clubs* Caledonian, New (Edinburgh); *Style* - The Hon Vere Cochrane; Cults, Cupar, Fife

COCKAYNE, Dame Elizabeth; DBE (1955); da of late William Cockayne; *b* 29 Oct 1894; *Educ* Burton-on-Trent Secondary Sch; *Career* SRN, SCM, ch nursing offr Miny of Health 1948-58, ret, matron W London, St Charles and Roy Free Hosps, supervisor Training Schs LCC, princ matron TANS; *Style* - Dame Elizabeth Cockayne, DBE; Rushett Cottage, Little Heath lane, Cobham, Surrey

COCKBURN, Charles Christopher; s and h of Sir John Cockburn, 12 Bt; *b* 19 Nov 1950; *Style* - Charles Cockburn Esq

COCKBURN, Hon Mrs Emma Christina; *née* Tennant; da of 2 Baron Glenconner by his 2 w; *b* 20 Oct 1937; *m* 1, 1957 (m dis 1962), Sebastian, s of Henry Yorke and Hon Adelaide Biddulph, er da of 2 Baron Biddulph (Henry was 3 s of Vincent Wodehouse Yorke, JP, by Hon Maud Wyndham, da of 2 Baron Leconfield; Vincent was s of John Yorke, JP, DL, sometime MP Tewkesbury and E Glos, by his 2 w, Sophia, da of Baron Vincent van Tuyll van Serooskerken; John was ggs of Rt Rev Hon James Yorke, DD, sometime Bp of Ely and 5 s of 1 Earl of Hardwicke); 1 s; m 2, 1963 (m dis), Christopher Booker, the journalist and author (*qv*); m 3, 1968 (m dis 1973), Alexander, s of Claud Cockburn, the journalist (*qv*), by Patricia (da of John Arbuthnot, MVO, ggs of Sir William Arbuthnot, 1 Bt); *Style* - The Hon Mrs Emma Cockburn

COCKBURN OF THAT ILK, Sir John Elliot Cockburn; 12 Bt (NS 1671); s of Lt-Col Sir John Cockburn of that Ilk, 11 Bt, DSO (d 1949); *b* 7 Dec 1925; *Educ* RNC Dartmouth, RAC Cirencester; *m* 1949, Glory Patricia, nee Mullings; 3 s, 2 da; *Heir* s, Charles Cockburn; *Career* md Cellar Management Ltd; *Style* - Sir John Cockburn of that Ilk, Bt; 48 Frewin rd, SW18

COCKBURN, Sir Robert; KBE (1960, OBE 1946), CB (1953); s of late Rev R T Cockburn; *b* 31 March 1909; *Educ* Southern Secondary Sch, Municipal Coll Portsmouth, London U; *m* 1935, Phyllis Hoyland; 2 da; *Career* PhD, MSc, MA, ch scientist Miny of Aviation 1959-64, dir RAE Farnborough 1964-69, chm National Computing Centre 1970-77, sr res fell Churchill Cambridge 1970-77; *Style* - Sir Robert Cockburn, KBE, CB; 21 Fitzroy rd, Fleet, Hants (☎ Fleet 5518)

COCKBURN-CAMPBELL, Alexander Thomas; s and h of Sir Thomas Cockburn-Campbell, 6 Bt; *b* 16 March 1945; *m* 1969, Kerry Anne, da of Sgt K Johnson; 1 s; *Style* - Alexander Cockburn-Campbell Esq; Lot 7, Lewis rd, Forrestfield 6058, W Australia

COCKBURN-CAMPBELL, Sir Thomas; 6 Bt (UK 1821), of Gartsford, Ross-shire; s of Sir Alexander Thomas Cockburn-Campbell, 5 Bt (d 1935); *b* 8 Dec 1918; *Educ* Church of England G S Melbourne; *m* 1944, Josephine Zoi, da of Harold Forward, of Cunjardine, W Australia; 1 s; *Heir* s, Alexander Thomas Cockburn-Campbell; *Style* - Sir Thomas Cockburn-Campbell, Bt; Lot 194, Welshpool rd, Wattle Grove, WA 6107, Australia

COCKCROFT, Dr Wilfred Halliday; s of Wilfred Cockcroft; *b* 7 June 1923; *Educ* Keighley Boys' G S, Balliol Oxford; *m* 1949, Barbara Rhona Huggan; 2 s; *Career* MA, DPhil, FIMA, prof of Pure Mathematics Hull U 1961, chm University Grants Ctee 1973-76, Vice-Chancellor New University of Ulster 1976-; *Style* - Dr Wilfred Cockcroft; The New University of Ulster, Coleraine, N Ireland (☎ 4141)

COCKER, Sir William Wiggins; OBE (1946), JP; s of late Wiggins Cocker; *b* 17 Oct 1896; *m* 1, 1922, Mary Emma, nee Bowker (d 1965); 1 s, 1 da; m 2, 1970, Mrs Rhoda Slinger; *Career* dir Cocker Chemicals Co Ltd, Lloyd's underwriter, pres British Tar Products Ltd, kt 1955;

Style - Sir William Cocker, OBE, JP; 384 Clifton drive North, St Annes-on-Sea, Lancs

COCKERAM, Eric Paul; MP (C) Ludlow 1979-, JP (City of Liverpool 1960); s of J W Cockeram; *b* 4 July 1924; *Educ* The Leys Sch Cambridge; *m* 1949, Frances Irving; 2 s, 2 da; *Career* MP Bebington 1970-Feb 1974, former PPS to Mins for Industry, and Posts and Telecommunications, dir TSB (NW), Liverpool Bldg Soc, chm Watson Prickard Ltd, liveryman Worshipful Co of Glovers, Freeman of City of London; *Style* - Eric Cockeram Esq, MP, JP; House of Commons, SW1

COCKERELL, Sir Christopher Sydney; CBE (1966), FRS (1967); s of late Sir Sydney Cockerell; *b* 4 June 1910; *Educ* Gresham's, Peterhouse Cambridge; *m* 1937, Margaret Elinor Belsham; 2 da; *Career* inventor of the hovercraft, former dir and consultant Hovercraft Dvpt Ltd, chm Ripplecraft Co Ltd 1950-79, chm Wavepower Ltd; kt 1969; *Style* - Sir Christopher Cockerell, CBE, FRS; 16 Prospect pla, Hythe, Hants

COCKFIELD, Baron (Life Peer UK 1978); (Francis) Arthur Cockfield; s of late Lt C F Cockfield; *b* 28 Sept 1916; *Educ* Dover County, LSE; *m* Aileen Monica Mudie, choreographer; *Career* barr 1942, former fin dir Boots Pure Drug Co Ltd, chm Price Cmmn 1973-77, Min of State Treasury 1979-, kt 1973; *Style* - The Rt Hon the Lord Cockfield; Connaught House, Mount Row, Berkeley Square, W1

COCKRAM, Sir John; s of Alfred John Cockram; *b* 10 July 1908; *Educ* St Aloysius Coll Highgate; *m* 1937, Phyllis Eleanor, nee Henning; 1 s, 2 da; *Career* chartered accountant, former gen man and dir Colne Valley Water Co, dir and chm Rickmansworth and Uxbridge Valley Water Co, kt 1964; *Style* - Sir John Cockram; Rebels' Corner, The Common, Chorleywood, Herts

COCKS, Sir (Thomas George) Barnett; KCB (1963, CB 1961), OBE 1949; *b* 1907; *Educ* Blundells Sch, Worcester Coll Oxford; *m* 1952, Iris Mary Symon, nee Coltman; 1 s, 1 da (step); *Career* Clerk of the House of Commons 1962-73, Trustee of the History of Parliament; *Style* - Sir Barnett Cocks, KCB, OBE; 13 Langford Green, SE5 (☎ 01 274 5448)

COCKS, Michael Francis Lovell; PC (1976), MP (L) Bristol S 1970-; s of Dr H F Lovell Cocks; *b* 19 Aug 1929; *Educ* Bristol U; *m* 1954, Janet Macfarlane; 2 s, 2 da; *Career* former lectr, contested Bristol W 1959, S Glos 1964 and 1966, Govt Ch Whip and Parly Sec to Treasury 1976-79; *Style* - The Rt Hon Michael Cocks, PC, MP; House of Commons, SW1

COCKS, Philip Sebastian Somers; s of late John Sebastian Somers Cocks, CVO, CBE, gs of Hon John James Thomas Somers Cocks, bro of 5 Baron Somers; hp of kinsman, 8 Baron; *b* 4 Jan 1948; *Style* - Philip Cocks Esq

CODRINGTON, Christopher George Wayne; s (by 2 m) and h of Sir Simon Codrington, 3 Bt; *b* 1960; *Style* - Christopher Codrington Esq

CODRINGTON, Giles Peter; s of late Lt-Cdr Sir William Codrington, 7 Bt, and hp of bro, 8 Bt; *b* 28 Oct 1943; *Style* - Giles Codrington Esq

CODRINGTON, Sir Simon Francis Bethell; 3 Bt (UK 1876), of Dodington, Gloucestershire; s of Sir Christopher Codrington, 2 Bt (d 1979); *b* 14 Aug 1923; *Educ* Eton; *m* 1, 1947 (m dis 1959) Joanne, nee Molineaux; m 2, 1959 (m dis 1979), Pamela Joy Halliday, da of Maj George Wise; 3 s; m 3, 1980, Sarah, nee Pennell; *Heir* s, Christopher Codrington; *Career* formerly Maj Coldstream Gds; *Style* - Sir Simon Codrington, Bt; Dodington, Chipping Sodbury, Glos

CODRINGTON, Sir William Alexander; 8 Bt (GB 1721), of Dodington, Gloucestershire; s of Lt-Cdr Sir William Codrington, 5 Bt (d 1961); *b* 5 July 1934; *Educ* St Andrew Coll S Africa, S African Naval Coll; *Heir* bro, Giles Codrington; *Career* Merchant Navy 1952, Worldwide Shipping 1976, memb Hon Co of Master Mariners, FNI; *Style* - Sir William Codrington, Bt; 99 St James Drive,

Wandsworth Common, SW17

COGGAN, Hon Dorothy Ann; da of Rt Rev and Rt Hon Lord Coggan, PC, DD; *b* 1938; *Style* - The Hon Dorothy Coggan

COGGAN, Baron (Life Peer UK 1980); Rt Rev and Rt Hon (Frederick) Donald Coggan; PC (1961), DD (1957); s of late Cornish Coggan; *b* 9 Oct 1909; *Educ* Merchant Taylors' Sch, St John's Cambridge, Wycliffe Hall Oxford; *m* 1935, Jean Braithwaite, nee Strain; 2 da; *Career* prof of New Testament Wycliffe Coll Toronto 1937-44, princ London Coll of Divinity 1944-56, Bp of Bradford 1956-61, Archbp of York 1961-74, Archbp of Canterbury 1974-80; *Style* - The Rt Rev and Rt Hon Lord Coggan, PC, DD; Kingshead House, Sissinghurst, Kent (☎ 443)

COGGAN, Hon Ruth Evelyn; da of Rt Rev and Rt Hon Lord Coggan, PC, DD; *b* 1940; *Style* - The Hon Ruth Coggan

COGHILL, Egerton James Nevill Tobias; s (by 1 m) and h of Sir Joscelyn Coghill, 7 Bt; *b* 26 March 1930; *Educ* Gordonstoun, Pembroke Cambridge; *m* 1958, Gabriel Nancy, da of Maj Dudley Claud Douglas Ryder; 1 s, 1 da; *Career* Headmaster of Aberlour House; *Style* - Egerton Coghill Esq; Aberlour House, Aberlour, Banffshire

COGHILL, Sir Joscelyn Ambrose Cramer; 7 Bt (GB 1778), of Coghill, Yorkshire; s of late Sir Egerton Coghill, 5 Bt; suc bro, Col Sir (Marmaduke Nevill) Patrick Somerville Coghill, 6 Bt, TD, 1981; *b* 30 Sept 1902; *Educ* Haileybury; *m* 1, 1926 (m dis 1949), Elizabeth Gwendoline, nee Atkins (d 1980); 1 s, 1 da; m 2, 1949 (m dis 1971), Louise Fernande (d 1978), da of Col Gaston Berdonneau of Paris; 3 da; *Heir* s, Egerton Coghil; *Career* formerly Lt S Wales Borderers, Lt-Cdr RNVR 1939-45; *Style* - Sir Joscelyn Coghill, Bt; 2 Muirton Cottages, Craigellachier, Banffshire

COGILL, Hon Mrs (Patricia Mary); *née* St Clair; da of 16 Lord Sinclair, MVO (d 1957); *b* 1912; *m* 1940, Lt-Cl Charles Archibald Richard Cogill, OBE, Scots Gds (d 1975); 1 s, 2 da; *Style* - The Hon Mrs Cogill; The Pyghtle, Great Witchingham, Norwich

COHEN, His Honour Arthur - (Nathaniel) Arthur (Jim); JP (Surrey 1958); s of late Sir Benjamin Cohen, KC; *b* 19 Jan 1898; *Educ* Rugby, CCC Oxford; *m* 1, 1927 (m dis), Judith Luard; 2 s; m 2, 1936, Joyce, nee Collingridge; *Career* barr 1923, Circuit Judge 1956-70; *Style* - His Honour Arthur Cohen, JP; Bay Tree Cottage, Crockham Hill, Edenbridge, Kent

COHEN, Sir Edward; s of late Brig Hon Harold Cohen of Melbourne; *b* 1912; *Educ* Scotch Coll Melbourne, Ormond Coll Melbourne U; *m* 1939, Meryl D Fink; 1 s; *Career* slr, co dir, chm- Commercial Union Assurance Co of Australia Ltd, Derwent Metals Pty Ltd, E Z Industries Ltd, Carlton & United Breweries Ltd, Electrolytic Zinc Co of Australasia Ltd, Emu Bay Railway Co Ltd; consultant Paveys Melbourne; kt 1970; *Style* - Sir Edward Cohen; 390 Lonsdale st, Melbourne, Vic 3000, Australia; Orrong rd, Toorak, Vic 3142, Australia

COHEN, Edmund George; s of Henry Cohen; *b* 16 Sept 1926; *Educ* Harrow, Jesus Cambridge (MA); *m* 1951, Daphne, nee Froomberg; 2 s; *Career* chm Courts (Furnishers) Ltd 1976-; *Style* - Edmund Cohen Esq; 15 Somerset rd, Wimbledon, SW19 (☎ 01 947 0975)

COHEN, Hon Hugh Lionel; s of Baron Cohen (Life Peer, d 1973); *b* 1925; *Educ* Eton, New Coll Oxford; *m* 1953, Jane, da of Rt Hon Sir Seymour Edward Karminski; children; *Career* RNVR 1939-45; *Style* - The Hon Hugh Cohen; Ambarrow Wood, Sandhurst, Camberley, Surrey

COHEN, Sir Jack; OBE (1951), JP (Sunderland 1939); s of Samuel Cohen; *b* 2 Nov 1896; *m* 1921, Kitty, nee Sinclair; 1 s, 1 da; *Career* Mayor of Sunderland 1949-50, Ald 1939-74; kt 1965; *Style* - Sir Jack Cohen, OBE, JP; 16 Barnes Park rd, Sunderland, Tyne and Wear (☎ 226593)

COHEN, Hon John Christopher Coleman; s of Baron Cohen of Brighton (Life Peer, d 1966); *b* 1940; *Educ* Stowe, McGill U; *m* 1965, Anne-Marie, da of Eugene Krauss, of Paris; children; *Style* - The Hon John Cohen; 47 Quickswood, Chalcots pk, NW3

COHEN, Cdr Kenneth H S; CB (1954), CMG (1946), RN; s of late Herman Cohen; *b* 15 March 1900; *Educ* Elstree Sch, Eastbourne Coll; *m* 1932, Mary, nee Joseph; 1 s, 1 da; *Career* cadet RN 1918, Cdr 1940, European adviser to United Steel Companies 1953-66, chllr Royal Inst of International Affairs 1963-75, v-pres Franco-British Soc 1972- (chm 1967-72) and European League for Economic Co-operation 1972-; *Style* - Cdr Kenneth Cohen, CB, CMG, RN; 33 Bloomfield ter, SW1 (☎ 01 730 3228)

COHEN, (Lewis) Lennard; s of late Samuel Cohen; *b* 2 Dec 1925; *Educ* Clifton Coll, Peterhouse Cambridge; *m* 1953 (m dis 1973), Norma Beverley, nee Cash; 2 da; *Career* dir Baird Textile Hds Ltd 1978-; *Style* - Lennard Cohen Esq; Flat 12, 9 Beaufort gdns, SW3 (☎ 01 584 0040)

COHEN, Hon Leonard Harold Lionel; s of Baron Cohen (Life Peer, d 1973); *b* 1 Jan 1922; *Educ* Eton, New Coll Oxford; *m* 1949, Eleanor Lucy, da of late Philip Q Henriques; 2 s, 1 da; *Career* Rifle Bde 1939-45, barr 1948, md S Hoffnung & Co Ltd, Dir-Gen Accepting Houses Ctee 1976- *Style* - The Hon Leonard Cohen; 57 Bedford gdns, Campden Hill, W8

COHEN, Her Honour Judge Myrella; QC (1970); da of Samuel Cohen; *b* 16 Dec 1927; *Educ* Manchester H S for Girls, Colwyn Bay G S, Manchester U; *m* 1953, Lt-Col Mordaunt Cohen, TD; 1 s, 1 da; *Career* barr 1950, Circuit Judge 1972-; *Style* - Her Honour Judge Myrella Cohen, QC; c/o Crown Court, Moot Hall, Newcastle upon Tyne

COHEN, Nat(han); *Career* dir EMI Films Ltd (former chm and ch exec), EMI Film and Theatre Corpn Ltd, EMI Film Productions Ltd, producer of Carry On films; *Style* - Nat Cohen Esq; EMI Films Ltd, 142 Wardour st, W1 (☎ 01 437 0444)

COHEN OF BRIGHTON, Baroness - Renie; JP (Brighton); da of Simon Friezeimon Frieze *m* 1, Leonard Bodlender (decd); m 2, 1961, as his 2 w, Baron Cohen of Brighton (Life Peer, d 1966); *Style* - The Rt Hon the Lady Cohen of Brighton, JP; 11f Bedford Towers, Kings Road, Brighton, East Sussex (☎ Brighton (STD Code 0273) 24227)

COHEN, Sir Rex Arthur Louis; KBE (1964, OBE 1944); s of Rex Cohen; *b* 27 Nov 1906; *Educ* Rugby, Trin Cambridge; *m* 1932, Nina Alice, nee Castello; 1 da; *Career* chm Higgs & Hill Ltd 1966-72, dir Tribune Investment Trust; *Style* - Sir Rex Cohen, KBE; Ruckmans Farm, Oakwood Hill, nr Dorking, Surrey (☎ Oakwood Hill 255)

COHEN, Robert Neil; s of Herbert Edward Cohen; *b* 17 Nov 1904; *Educ* St Paul's Sch; *m* 1940, Ragnhild Vivan Margareta, nee Berg; 3 children; *Career* chm A Cohen & Co Ltd, Jacob Metals Ltd, dir Bengal Ingot Co Ltd; *Style* - Robert Cohen Esq; 25 Fort rd, Guildford, Surrey (☎ 73806)

COHEN, Stanley; MP (L) Leeds S East 1970-; s of Thomas Cohen; *b* 31 July 1927; *Educ* St Patrick's and St Charles' Schs Leeds; *m* 1954, Brenda Patricia, nee Rafferty; 3 s, 1 da; *Career* RN 1947-49, British Rail 1951-70, contested Barkston Ash 1966, PPS to Min of State DES 1976-79; *Style* - Stanley Cohen Esq, MP; 164 Ring rd, Halton, Leeds LS15 7AE (☎ Leeds 649568)

COKAYNE, Hon Dorothy Grace; da of late 1 Baron Ashbourne and Grace, da of the late Rev the Hon John Marsham (s of 3 Earl of Romney); *b* 1907; *Style* - The Hon Dorothy Cokayne; Windy Brae, Rectory Farm, Finchampstead, Berks

COKAYNE, Hon Edmund Willoughby Marsham; s of late 1 Baron Cullen of Ashbourne, KBE, by Grace, da of late Rev the Hon John Marsham (s of 3 Earl of Romney); hp of bro, 2 Baron; *b* 18 May 1916; *Educ* Eton; *m* 1943, Janet Manson, da of late William Douglas Watson of Canterbury; *Career* late Fl Lt RAF; *Style* - The Hon Edmund Cokayne; 305 Orange dve, Casa Grande, Arizona, USA 85222

COKAYNE, Hon John O'Brien Marsham; s of late 1 Baron Cullen of Ashbourne and Grace, da of the late Rev the Hon John Marsham (s of 3 Earl of Romney); *b* 1920; *Educ* Eton; *m* 1948, Anne Frances (d 1971), da of late Bertram Clayton of Wakefield, Yorks; 1 s; *Style* - The Hon John Cokayne; 14 St Omer rd, Cowley, Oxford

COKE, Viscount; Edward Douglas Coke; s and h of 6 Earl of Leicester; *b* 6 May 1936; *Educ* St Andrew's Coll Grahamstown S Africa; *m* 1962, Valeria, nee Potter; 2 s, 1 da; *Heir* s, Hon Thomas Coke; *Style* - Viscount Coke; Burnham Norton, King's Lynn, Norfolk (☎ Burnham Market 495)

COKE, Hon Laura-Jane Elizabeth; da of Viscount Coke; *b* 1968

COKE, Hon Mrs Richard - Elizabeth Vera Catherine; da of late Louis-Leopold M B de Beaumont; *m* 1932, as his 2 wife, Maj the Hon Richard Coke (d 1964); *Style* - The Hon Mrs Richard Coke; 10 Knight st, Walsingham, Norfolk

COKE, Hon Rupert Henry John ; s of Viscount Coke; *b* 1975

COKE, Hon Thomas Edward; s of Viscount Coke; *b* 6 July 1965

COKE, Hon Wenman John; s of 6 Earl of Leicester; *b* 1940; *m* 1969, Carolyn May, da of late D D Steuart Redler, of Cape Town , S Africa; 2 s, 1 da ; *Style* - The Hon Wenman Coke; 106 Park st, Vryheid, Natal

COKER, Bryan Sydney; s of Sydney Orlando Coker (d 1954); *b* 25 Dec 1924; *Educ* Palmer's Endowed Sch Essex; *m* 1949, Doreen Edith, nee Caton; 3 da; *Career* CA (FICA), sec Thurrock District of Industries 1966-, gen sec World Cncl of Young Men's Service Clubs 1973-79, Essex Co Cncl Educn Ctee 1970-77; *Recreations* association football, rotary, canasta; *Clubs* Grays Athletic Football, Rotary Club of Grays Thurrock, Grays 41; *Style* - Bryan Coker Esq; Alfriston, 14 College Avenue, Grays, Essex (☎ 0375 4949)

COKER, Dame Elizabeth; DBE (1979), DL (Essex 1974); da of William Lowe; *Educ* Grove Park Sch Wrexham, Queen Mary Coll London U; *m* 1947, Frank L Coker, LDS, RCS; 1 da; *Career* chm Essex Area Health Authority 1973-, former chm Harlow Dvpt Corpn, chm Basildon Dvpt Corpn 1980-; *Style* - Dame Elizabeth Coker, DBE, DL; Winnington House, Danbury, Chelmsford, Essex (☎ Danbury 2555)

COLAHAN, Air Vice-Marshal William Edward; CB (1978), CBE (1973), DFC (1945); s of Dr W E Colahan; *b* 7 Aug 1923; *Educ* Templeton H S South Africa, Cape Town U; *m* 1949, Kathleen Anne, nee Butler; 1 s, 2 da; *Career* S African Air Force 1941-46, RAF 1947, Air V-Marshal 1973, Assist Ch of Air Staff (Operations) 1973-75, Air Offr Comdg and Cmdt RAF Coll Cranwell 1975-78, ret, offr careers counsellor RAF 1978-; *Style* - Air Vice-Marshal William Colahan CB CBE DFC; RAF College, Cranwell, Sleaford, Lincs (☎ Sleaford 302489)

COLBECK-WELCH, Air Vice-Marshal Edward Lawrence; CB (1960), OBE (1948), DFC (1941); s of late Major G S M Colbeck-Welch; *b* 29 Jan 1914; *Educ* Leeds G S; *m* 1938, Doreen, nee Jenkin; 1 s, 2 da; *Career* RAF 1933, No 22 Sqdn 1934-37, SASO HQ No 13 (F) Gp 1959, Air Vice-Marshal 1961, SASO HQ Fighter Command 1960-63, ret; *Recreations* sailing; *Style* - Air Vice-Marshal Edward Colbeck-Welch CB, OBE, DFC; La Cote au Palier, St Martin, Jersey, CI

COLCHESTER, Suffragan Bishop of 1966-; Rt Rev Roderic Norman Coote; DD; s of late Cdr B T Coote; *b* 13 April 1915; *Educ* Woking Co Sch, Trin Coll Dublin; *m* 1964, Erica Lynette, da of late Rev E G Shrubbs, MBE; 1 s, 2 da; *Career* curate 1938-41, Suffragan Bp of Fulham 1957-66, Archdeacon of Colchester 1969-72; *Style* - The Rt Rev the Lord Bishop of Colchester; The Bishop's House, 32 Inglis rd, Colchester, Essex

COLDSTREAM, Sir George Phillips; KCB (1955, CB 1949), KCVO (1963), QC

(1960); s of late Francis Coldstream; *b* 20 Dec 1907; *Educ* Rugby, Oriel Oxford; *m* 1, 1934 (m dis 1948), Mary Morna, nee Carmichael; 1 da (and 1 decd); m 2, Sheila Hope, wid of Lt-Col J H H Whitty, DSO, MC; *Career* barr 1930, Dep Clerk of the Crown 1944-54, Clerk of the Crown in Chancery and Perm Sec to the Lord Chancellor 1954-68; *Style* - Sir George Coldstream, KCB, KCVO, QC; The Gate House, Seaford, E Sussex (☎ Seaford 892801)

COLDSTREAM, Sir William Menzies; CBE (1952); s of George Probyn Coldstream, MB, CM; *b* 28 Feb 1908; *Educ* Slade Sch, Univ Coll London; *m* 1, 1931 (m dis 1942), Nancy Culliford Sharp; 2 da; m 2, 1961, Monica Mary, nee Hoyer; 1 s, 2 da; *Career* painter, fell Univ Coll London, sr fell Royal Coll of Art, Slade Prof of Fine Art Univ Coll London U 1949-75, V-Chm Arts Council of Great Britain 1962-70, co-founder Sch of Drawing and Painting Euston Rd 1937, kt 1956; *Style* - Sir William Coldstream, CBE; University College London, Gower st, WC1 (☎ 01 387 7050)

COLE, Viscount; Andrew John Galbraith Cole; s and h of 6 Earl of Enniskillen; *b* 28 April 1942; *Educ* Eton; *m* 1964, Sarah, da of Maj-Gen J Keith-Edwards CBE DSO MC, of Nairobi; 3 da; *Career* late Capt Irish Gds, company dir, pilot; *Style* - Viscount Cole; Milima House, PO Box 44580, Nairobi, Kenya

COLE, Hon Amanda Mary; da of Viscount Cole; *b* 4 May 1966; *Style* - The Hon Amanda Cole

COLE, (Alexander) Colin; CVO (1979, MVO 1977), TD (1972); s of late Capt Edward Cole; *b* 16 May 1922; *Educ* Dulwich, Pembroke Coll Cambridge, BNC Oxford; *m* 1944, Valerie, da of late Capt Stanley Card; 4 s, 3 da; *Career* barr 1949, Windsor Herald of Arms 1966, Maj 6 (Volunteer) Bn Queen's Regt 1971-73, Lt-Col RARO, Sheriff City of London 1976-77, one of Court of Assistants of Hon Artillery Co, freeman and liveryman Basketmakers, Scriveners' and Painter Stainers Cos, Garter Principal King of Arms 1978- (registrar and librarian 1967-74), OStJ; *Style* - Colin Cole Esq, CVO, TD; College of Arms, Queen Victoria st, EC4 (☎ 01 248 1188); Holly House, Burstow, Surrey

COLE, Hon Mrs (Cecilia Anne); *née* Ridley; da of 4 Viscount Ridley, TD, JP, DL; *b* 1 Dec 1953; *m* 1978, Berkeley Arthur Cole, s of Arthur Cole, bro of 6 Earl of Enniskillen, MBE, JP, DL; *Style* - The Hon Mrs Cole

COLE, Claude Neville David; CBE (1977), JP; s of late W J Cole; *b* 4 June 1928; *Educ* Royal Masonic Sch, Harvard Business Sch; *m* 1951, Alma Gwlithyn Williams; 1 s (and 1 decd), 1 da; *Career* journalist, dir Thomson Org Ltd, jt dep md Thomson British Hldgs 1980-, dir Thomson Regional Newspapers Ltd, Reuters Ltd, chm Thomson Int Press Consultancy Ltd; *Style* - Claude Cole Esq, CBE, JP; 71 Ashley gdns, SW1 (☎ 01 828 1792)

COLE, Sir David Lee; KCMG (1975, CMG 1965), MC 1944; s of late Brig D H Cole, CBE; *b* 31 Aug 1920; *Educ* Cheltenham Coll, Sidney Sussex Cambridge; *m* 1945, Dorothy, nee Patton; 1 s; *Career* Dominions Office 1947, Private Sec to Rt Hon the Earl of Home 1957-60, Min New Delhi (Political) 1967-70, Assist Under-Sec of State FCO 1970-73, Ambass to Thailand 1973-78, ret; *Style* - Sir David Cole, KCMG, MC; 49 Drayton gdns, SW10

COLE, Hon Emma Frances; da of Viscount Cole; *b* 14 Feb 1969; *Style* - The Hon Emma Cole

COLE, Maj-Gen Eric Stuart; CB (1960), CBE (1945); s of John Cole; *b* 10 Feb 1906; *m* 1941, Doris Hartley; *Career* Maj-Gen 1958, Dir of Telecommunications War Office 1958-61, ret, consultant dir Granger Associates Ltd Weybridge (formerly md), former pres Radio Soc of Great Britain; *Style* - Maj-Gen Eric Cole, CB, CBE; 28 Royal av, SW3

COLE, Frank (George Francis); *b* 3 Nov 1918; *Educ* Manchester G S; *m* 1940, Gwendoline Mary Laver; 2 s, 1 da; *Career* chm James Cooke & Sons Ltd, Crane's

Screw (Hldgs) Ltd, Hillcrest Engineering Ltd, dir Armstrong Equipment Ltd, G Clancey Ltd, Clarkson Head Harris Ltd; *Style* - Frank Cole Esq; 27 Garnet ct, Chelmscote rd, Olton, Solihull, W Midlands (☎ 021 707 2749)

COLE, Frank Mortimore; s of Albert Percival Cole (d 1955); *b* 26 Aug 1904; *Educ* St Paul's, Sutton Valence Sch; *m* 1934, Susanna Evelyn Norah, nee Capron; 1 s, 1 da; *Career* Lt RNVR, chm & md Cole & Son (holder of The Royal Warrant to HM as suppliers of wallpaper); *Recreations* sailing, painting pictures; *Clubs* Cruising Assoc, Naval; *Style* - Frank Cole Esq; The Old Rectory, Erwarton, Ipswich, Suffolk (☎ Shotley 223)

COLE, Hon Juliet Anthea; da of Baron Cole (Life Peer, d 1978); *b* 1951; *Style* - The Hon Juliet Cole; 24 Drayson Mews, W8

COLE, Hon Jonathan Dare; s of Baron Cole (Life Peer, d 1978); *b* 1946; *Educ* Eton, Hertford Oxford; *Style* - The Hon Jonathan Cole

COLE, Hon Lucy Caroline; da of Viscount Cole; *b* 1970; *Style* - The Hon Lucy Cole

COLE, William Charles; MVO (1966); s of Frederick George Cole; *b* 9 Oct 1909; *Educ* St Olave's G S, RAM; *m* 1, Elizabeth Brown Caw (d 1942); 3 da; m 2, Winifred Mitchell; 1 s; *Career* former prof and lectr RAM and former lectr Roy Acad of Dancing, Master of the Music at HM the Queen's Chapel of the Savoy 1954-, Hon Sec Royal Philharmonic Soc 1969-, memb Cncl Roy Coll of Organists 1960; *Style* - William Cole Esq, MVO; Packways, Hindhead, Surrey (☎ 4917)

COLE, William Scott; CB (1949), CBE (1946); s of late William Scott Cole; *b* 29 March 1902; *Educ* Victoria Coll Jersey, RMA Woolwich; *m* 1, 1948 (m dis 1970), Kathleen Winifred Coleing; 1 da; m 2, 1971, Alice Rose Pitts, wid of Dr G T Pitts; *Career* Corps of Roy Engineers 1921, Dep Quartermaster-Gen War Office 1955, Maj-Gen 1956, ret 1958; *Clubs* Army & Navy; *Style* - Maj-Gen William Cole, CB, CBE

COLE-FONTAYN, Hon Mrs (Barbara Wendy Maia); *née* Latham; da of 1 Baron Latham (d 1970); *b* 1920; *m* 1, 1941 (m dis 1945), Capt Denis Wildish, RASC; m 2, 1946 (m dis 1951), Peter Bruckmann; 1 da; m 3, 1966, Malcolm Blundell Cole-Fontayn; *Career* 1942-44 as First Class Aircraft Woman WAAF *Style* - The Hon Mrs Cole-Fontayn

COLEBY, Anthony Laurie; s of Dr Leslie Coleby (d 1971); *b* 27 April 1935; *Educ* Winchester, CCC Cambridge; *m* 1966, Rosemary Melian Elisabeth, da of Sir (Isham) Peter Garran KCMG, *qv*; 1 s, 2 da; *Career* personal assist to md IMF 1964-67, assist dir Bank of England 1980- (dep ch cashier 1973-80); *Recreations* choral singing, railways, transport; *Clubs* Overseas Bankers; *Style* - Anthony Coleby Esq; Bank of England, EC2 (☎ 01 601 4444)

COLECLOUGH, Peter Cecil; s of late Thomas Coleclough; *b* 5 March 1917; *Educ* Bradfield; *m* 1944, Pamela Beresford, nee Rhodes; 2 s; *Career* chm Howard Machinery Ltd 1969-, dir National Westminster Bank Ltd (and chm SE Region) and NCR Ltd, former pres Royal Warrant Holders Assoc, chm SE Region CBI 1971-72; *Recreations* fishing; *Style* - Peter Coleclough Esq; Longlands Hall, Stonham Aspal, Stowmarket, Suffolk (☎ Stonham 242)

COLEMAN, Donald Richard; CBE (1979), MP (L) Neath 1964-; s of late Albert Coleman; *b* 19 Sept 1925; *Educ* Cadoxton Boys' Sch Barry, Cardiff Tech Coll; *m* 1, 1966, Phyllis Eileen, nee Williams (d 1963); 1 s; m 2, 1966, Margaret Elizabeth Morgan; 1 da; *Career* former metallurgist Steel Co of Wales Ltd, PPS to Min of State for Wales 1967-70, Opposition Whip 1970-74, a Lord Cmmr HM Treasury 1974-79, V-Chamberlain of the Household 1978-79; *Style* - Donald Coleman Esq, CBE, MP; Penderyn, 18 Penywern rd, Bryncoch, Neath, W Glamorgan (☎ Neath 4599)

COLERAINE, 2 Baron (UK 1954); James Martin Bonar Law; s of 1 Baron, PC (d 1980, himself s of Andrew Bonar Law, briefly (1922-23) PM); *b* 8 Aug 1931;

Educ Eton, Trin Oxford; *m* 1, 1958 (m dis 1966), Emma Elizabeth, nee Richards; 2 da; m 2, 1966, Anne Patricia, da of Maj-Gen Ralph Farrant, CB; 1 s, 2 da; *Heir* s, Hon James Law; *Style* - The Rt Hon the Lord Coleraine; 3/5 Kensington Pk gdns, W11 (☎ 01 221 4148)

COLERIDGE, 4 Baron (UK 1873); Richard Duke Coleridge; KBE (1971, CBE 1951, OBE 1944), DL (Devon 1973); s of 3 Baron (d 1955, gs of 1 Baron, who in his turn was gn to S T Coleridge, the poet); *b* 24 Sept 1905; *Educ* RNCs Osborne and Dartmouth; *m* 1936, Rosamund, da of late Adm Sir William Wordsworth Fisher, GCB, GCVO; 2 s; *Heir* s, Hon William Coleridge; *Career* Capt (ret) RN, ch staff offr to Marshal of the RAF Lord Tedder 1950-51, exec sec NATO 1952-70, chm Devon and Exeter Savings Bank 1971-75, chm SW Trustee Savings Bank 1975; *Style* - The Rt Hon the Lord Coleridge, KBE, DL; The Chanter's House, Ottery St Mary, S Devon (☎ 2417)

COLERIDGE, David Ean; s of late Guy Coleridge; *b* 7 June 1932; *Educ* Eton; *m* 1955, Susan, nee Senior; 2 c; *Career* Lloyds underwriter, chm A L Sturge Gp of Cos 1978-; *Recreations* shooting, golf and family; *Style* - David Coleridge Esq; 21 Margaretta ter, SW3; Spring Pond, Wispen, nr Midhurst, W Sussex

COLERIDGE, Lady (Marguerite) Georgina Christine; *née* Hay; da of 11 Marquess of Tweeddale (d 1967); *b* 1916; *m* 1941, Capt Arthur Coleridge, Irish Gds, s of John Coleridge, FRIBA (d 1934); 1 da; *Career* - journalist *Style* - Lady Georgina Coleridge; 33 Peel st, W8 (☎ 01 727 7732)

COLERIDGE, Hon John Seymour Duke; s of late 3 Baron Coleridge; *b* 1908; *m* 1934, Dora Lovelace, nee Carter; *Style* - The Hon John Coleridge; Paxtons, St John's Hill, Shaftesbury, Dorset

COLERIDGE, Hon Mrs Ronald - Ursula Mary; da of late Rev William Turner Long; *m* 1937, Hon Ronald Duke Coleridge (d 1972); 1 s, 1 da; *Style* - The Hon Mrs Ronald Coleridge; Blandford House, Chaffcombe, Chard, Somerset

COLERIDGE, Hon Samuel John Taylor; s of 4 Baron Coleridge, KBE; *b* 1942; *Educ* Winchester, Trin Oxford; *m* 1973, Patricia Susan, da of John Basil Edwards, CBE; 2 da; *Career* Maj Grenadier Gds, attached Army Air Corps 1964-68 and 22 Special Air Ser Regt 1968-71; *Style* - The Hon Samuel Coleridge; 30 St John's av, SW15

COLERIDGE, Hon William Duke; s and h of 4 Baron Coleridge, KBE; *b* 18 June 1937; *Educ* Eton; *m* 1962, Everild Tania, da of Lt-Col Beauchamp Hamborough; 1 s, 2 da; *Career* Maj Coldstream Gds (ret), commanded Gds Ind Parachute Co 1970-72; *Style* - The Hon William Coleridge; The Chanter's House, Ottery St Mary, S Devon

COLES, Sir Arthur William; s of George Coles; *b* 6 Aug 1892; *Educ* State Sch and Geelong Coll; *m* 1919, Lilian Florence, nee Knight; 2 s (and 1 decd), 3 da; *Career* Lord Mayor of Melbourne 1938-40, md G J Coles & Co 1931-44 (also founder ptnr, gen man and dir), memb House of Representatives 1940-46; kt 1960; *Style* - Sir Arthur Coles; 3 Majella ct, Kew, Victoria 3101, Australia

COLES, Hon Mrs; Hon Bridget; *née* Hope; da of 2 Baron Rankeillour, GCIE, MC, by Grizel, da of Brig-Gen Sir Robert Gilmour, 1 Bt, CB, CVO, DSO; *b* 17 Oct 1920; *m* 1942, Lt-Col George Coles; 3 da; *Style* - The Hon Mrs Coles; c/o Lloyds Bank, Spalding, Lincs

COLES, Sir Edgar Barton; s of George Coles; *b* 3 June 1899; *Educ* Scotch Coll Launceston Tasmania; *m* 1927, Dame Mabel Coles; 1 s, 2 da; *Career* joined G J Coles & Co Ltd 1919, dir 1930- (md 1944-67, chm 1963-68), kt 1959; *Style* - Sir Edgar Coles; 236 Bourke st, Melbourne, Vic 3000, Australia; Hendra, Mt Eliza, Vic 3930, Australia (☎ Mt Eliza 71291)

COLES, Sir Kenneth Frank; s of George Coles; *b* 19 April 1896; *m* 1925, Marjorie Evelyn Tolley; 1 s, 2 da; *Career* joined G J Coles & Co Ltd 1920, chm 1956-63, dir to 1976, former dir Australian Oil and Gas Corpn, kt 1957; *Style* - Sir Kenneth Coles; 83 Victoria rd, Bellevue Hill, Sydney,

Australia (☎ 36 4728)

COLES, Dame Mabel Irene; DBE (1971, CBE 1965); da of late E Johnston; *m* 1927, Sir Edgar Coles; 1 s, 2 da; *Career* pres Australian Women's Liberal Club 1965-, dir Asthma Foundation of Victoria 1965, pres Royal Women's Hosp Melbourne 1968-72; *Style* - Dame Mabel Coles, DBE; Hendra, Williams rd, Mount Eliza, Vic 3930, Australia

COLES, Sir Norman Cameron; s of George Coles; *b* 10 Sept 1907; *Educ* Launceston C of E G S Tasmania, Trinity G S Kew Victoria; *m* 1932, Dorothy Verna Deague; 1 s, 1 da; *Career* joined G J Coles & Co 1924, chm 1968-79 (md 1967-75), kt 1977; *Style* - Sir Norman Coles; 236 Bourke st, Melbourne, Vic 3000, Australia (☎ 66 6048); 28 Somers av, Malvern, Vic 3144, Australia

COLFOX, Sir (William) John; 2 Bt (UK 1939), of Symondsbury, Co Dorset, JP (Dorset 1962), DL (1977); s of Sir Philip Colfox, 1 Bt, MC (d 1966); *b* 25 April 1924; *Educ* Eton; *m* 1962, Frederica Loveday, da of Adm Sir Victor Crutchley; 2 s, 3 da; *Heir* s, Philip Colfox; *Career* Lt RNVR 1939-45, High Sheriff of Dorset 1969, land agent 1950; *Style* - Sir John Colfox, Bt, JP, DL; Symondsbury House, Bridport, Dorset (☎ Bridport 22956)

COLFOX, Philip John; s and h of Sir John Colfox, 2 Bt; *b* 27 Dec 1962; *Style* - Philip Colfox Esq

COLGRAIN, 3 Baron (UK 1946); David Colin Campbell; s of 2 Baron, MC (d 1973); *b* 24 April 1920; *Educ* Eton, Trin Cambridge; *m* 1, 1945 (m dis 1964), Veronica Margaret, da of late Lt-Col William Leckie Webster, RAMC; 1 s, 1 da; m 2, 1973, Mrs Sheila M Hudson; *Heir* s, Hon Alastair Campbell; *Career* late 9 Lancers, md Anthony Gibbs Hldgs Ltd 1954-; *Style* - The Rt Hon the Lord Colgrain; Flat 4, 51 Winchester st, SW1 (☎ 01 834 4822); Bushes Farm, Weald, Sevenoaks, Kent

COLGRAIN, Madge, Baroness - Margaret Emily; da of late Percy William Carver; *m* 1917, 2 Baron Colgrain, MC (d 1973); 3 s (3 Baron, Hon Robert & Hon Neil Campbell), 1 da (Hon Mrs Young); *Style* - The Rt Hon Madge, Lady Colgrain; Everlands, Sevenoaks, Kent

COLLETT, Christopher; s of Sir Henry Seymour Collett, 2 Bt (d 1971), and hp of nephew, 3 Bt; *b* 10 June 1931; *Educ* Harrow, Emmanuel Cambridge (MA); *m* 1959, Christine Anne, nee Griffiths; 2 s, 1 da; *Career* Capt RA (TA), FCA, freeman of City of London, liveryman of Glovers' Co, common councilman 1974-; *Style* - Christopher Collett Esq; 121 Home Park rd, Wimbledon, SW19

COLLETT, Rear-Adm George Kempthorne; CB (1957), DSC (1942); s of William George Collett; *b* 25 Jan 1907; *Educ* RNC Osborne and Dartmouth; *m* 1937, Rongnye, da of Sir Charles Bell, KCIE, CMG; 1 s, 1 da; *Career* joined RN 1920, naval liaison offr to Gen de Gaulle 1940, Rear-Adm 1955, Vice Naval Dep to SHAPE Paris 1955-57, ret 1958; *Style* - Rear-Adm George Collett, CB, DSC; Coombe Farm, Churt, Farnham, Surrey (☎ Headley Down 712533)

COLLETT, Sir Ian Seymour; 3 Bt (UK 1934), of Bridge Ward in the City of London; s of David Seymour Collett (d 1962); suc gf 1971; *b* 5 Oct 1953; *Educ* Lancing; *Heir* unc, Christopher Collett; *Style* - Sir Ian Collett, Bt; North View Cottage, 15 North View, Wimbledon Common, SW19 (☎ 01 947 8422)

COLLETT, Sir (Thomas) Kingsley; CBE (1956); s of late Sir Charles Collett, 1 Bt; *b* 7 March 1905; *Educ* Bishop's Stortford Coll; *m* 1930, Beatrice Olive, nee Brown; *Career* ch commoner City of London Common Council 1955, former dir Adams Bros & Shardlow Ltd (Creative Printers), freeman City of London, liveryman Distillers' Co, one of HM Lts for City of London 1958, kt 1968; *Style* - Sir Kingsley Collett, CBE; 5 Moorlands, Wilderness rd, Chislehurst, Kent

COLLETT, Lady; Ruth Mildred; da of late William Thomas Hatch, MICE, MIEE; *m* 1920, Sir Henry Seymour Collett, 2 Bt (d 1971); *Style* - Lady Collett;

Flat 1, Orchard Green, Homefield rd, Bromley, Kent

COLLIE, George Francis; CBE (1964, MBE 1943), JP (Aberdeen); s of late George Collie; *b* 1 April 1909; *Educ* Aberdeen G S, Aberdeen U (BL); *m* 1949, Margery Constance Fullarton, nee Wishart; 2 s; *Career* advocate Aberdeen, sr ptnr James & George Collie Slrs Aberdeen, pres Aberdeen University Press (chm 1959-1979); *Recreations* vintage cars; *Clubs* Army & Navy, Royal Northern (Aberdeen); *Style* - George Collie Esq, CBE, JP; Morkeu, Cults, Aberdeen (☎ 867636); A33 Le Surcouf, Cannes Marina, 06210 Mandelieu, France (☎ 93 495873)

COLLIER, Benjamino; s of William Collier, *qv*; *b* 2 Feb 1958; *Style* - Benjamino Collier Esq

COLLIER, Air Vice-Marshal Sir (Alfred) Conrad; KCB (1947, CB 1943), CBE (1941); *b* 16 Nov 1895; *Educ* Sherborne; *m* 1, 1920, G M C Luis (d 1961); 2 s, 1 da; m 2, 1963, Kathleen, nee Donaghy, JP; *Career* 2 Lt King's Own (RL) Regt 1914, Air V-Marshal 1946, controller Tech and Operational Servs Miny of Civil Aviation 1947-48, ch exec Guided Weapons Div English Electric Aviation Ltd to 1960, ret, gov Nat Hosp for Nervous Diseases 1961-64; *Style* - Air Vice-Marshal Sir Conrad Collier, KCB, CBE; c/o Lloyds Bank Ltd, Walton-on-Thames, Surrey

COLLIER, Hon Mrs Eric - Lena Victoria (Queenie); da of late James Kennedy, of Forfar; *m* 1953, as his 2 w, the Hon Eric (Cecil Frederick) Collier (d 1968); *Style* - The Hon Mrs Eric Collier; Corscombe, Dorchester, Dorset

COLLIER, Gerard; s of William Adrian Larry Collier, MB (disclaimed Barony of Monkswell for life 1964); *b* 28 Jan 1947; *Educ* George Heriot's Sch, Edinburgh and Portsmouth Polytechnic; *Style* - Gerard Collier Esq; Curator's House, Royal Botanic Gdns, Edinburgh

COLLIER, Hon Lorna Evelyn; da of 3 Baron Monkswell (d 1964); *b* 24 Jan 1915; *Style* - The Hon Lorna Collier; 23 Eastbury ave, Northwood, Middx

COLLIER, Hon Mrs Muriel Joan Lowry; *née* Lamb; da of 1 Baron Rochester, CMG; *b* 1921; *Educ* LMH Oxford; *m* 1947 (m dis 1957), William, s of Sir Laurence Collier, KCMG (sometime Ambass Oslo and s of Hon John Collier, OBE, 2 s of 1 Baron Monkswell, by John's 2 w Ethel, sis of his 1 w and 5 da of Rt Hon Thomas Huxley, PC, FRS), and 1 cous once removed of Aldous Huxley, the novelist, and Sir Julian Huxley, the biologist; 1 s, 1 da; *Career* Sr Lectr Educn Loughborough Coll Educn; late 3 Sec Br Embassy Oslo; *Style* - The Hon Mrs Muriel Collier; 26 George st, Cambridge

COLLIER, Neill Adrian Jose; s of William Adrian Larry Collier, (disclaimed Barony of Monkswell for life 1964); *b* 20 Aug 1948; *Educ* George Heriot's Sch, Edinburgh; *Style* - Neill Collier Esq; Curator's House, Royal Botanic Gdns, Edinburgh

COLLIER, Tiaré Penelope Katherine; da of William Adrian Larry Collier (disclaimed Barony of Monkswell for life 1964); *b* 5 Sept 1952; *Educ* Friends Sch, Saffron Walden; *Style* - Miss Tiaré Collier

COLLIER, William Adrian Larry; s of Hon Gerard Collier (himself 2 s of 2 Baron Monkswell); suc unc, 3 Baron, 1964, but disclaimed Barony for life 7 April 1964; *b* 25 Nov 1913; *Educ* Edinburgh U; *m* 1, 1939 (m dis 1945), Erika, da of Dr E Kellner; m 2, 1945 (m dis 1950), Helen, da of James Dunbar, of Edinburgh; 2 s; m 3, 1951, Nora Selby; 1 s, 1 da; *Heir* s, Gerard Collier; *Career* MB, BCh, DPH; adopted additional name Larry 1932; late memb Halstead UDC & Co Cllr Essex; GP ; compiled World Index of Imprints used on tablets & other solid dose forms 1964 (4 edn 1973); served WW II RAMC, NW Europe & M East; *Style* - Dr William Collier; 1 Brett Manor, Brett rd, E8 (☎ 01 986 8837)

COLLIN, Lady Clarissa; *née* Duncombe; da of late 3 Earl of Feversham (d 1963, when Earldom (only) became extinct); *b* 11 Oct 1938; *Educ* Heathfield Sch Ascot; *m* 1966, Nicholas Spencer

Collin; 1 s, 1 da; *Style* - Lady Clarissa Collin; Wytherstone House, Pockley, York

COLLIN, Maj-Gen Geoffrey de Egglesfield; CB (1975), MC (1944), DL (N Yorks 1977); s of late Charles de Egglesfield Collin; *b* 18 July 1921; *Educ* Wellington; *m* 1949, Angela Stella, nee Young; 1 s, 3 da; *Career* 2 Lt RA 1941, Maj-Gen RA HQ BAOR 1971-73, GOC NE District York 1973-76, ret, Col Cmdt RA 1976-; *Style* - Maj-Gen Geoffrey Collin, CB, MC, DL; Old Vicarage, Roecliffe, York

COLLINGS, Maj-Gen Wilfred d'Auvergne; CB (1946), CBE (1941); s of C d'Auvergne Collings, MD; *b* 8 Aug 1893; *Educ* Elizabeth Coll Guernsey, Sandhurst; *m* 1928, Nancy Draper Bishop; 2 s, 1 da; *Career* Admin Staff Coll Henley 1914, Maj-Gen 1944, 21 Army Gp 1944-45, ret 1948, Ch of Supply and Transport Div UN Relief and Works Agency in Nr East 1949-53; *Style* - Maj-Gen Wilfred Collings, CB, CBE; La Verdure, Clifton, St Peter Port, Guernsey, CI

COLLINGWOOD, Lt-Gen Sir (Richard) George; KBE (1959, CBE 1951), CB (1954), DSO (1944); s of Col C G Collingwood; *b* 7 Oct 1903; *Educ* RNC Osborne and Dartmouth; *Career* Cameronians 1923, GOCIC Scottish Command and Gov Edinburgh Castle (Lt-Gen) 1958-61, ret, Col Cameronians 1964-69; *Style* - Lt-Gen Sir George Collingwood, KBE, CB, DSO; Abbey Lands, Alnwick, Northumberland (☎ Alnwick 2220)

COLLINGWOOD, Brig Sydney; CMG (1957), CBE (1945), MC (1917); s of late Sir William Collingwood, KBE, MICE, JP; *b* 10 July 1892; *Educ* Liverpool Coll, RMA; *m* 1, 1915, Charlotte Annie (decd), da of Col James Oughterson, late 18 Roy Irish; 2 s, 1 da; m 2, 1940, Eileen Mary, nee Wilson (d 1977), wid of Maj W D G Batten, 3 Gurkha Rifles; *Career* 2 Lt RA, Brig 1940, dep dir Personal Services War Office 1942-46, ret 1946, regional dir Southern Region Imperial War Graves Cmmn (HQ Rome) 1946-57; *Style* - Brig Sydney Collingwood, CMG, CBE, MC; Cliffordine House, Rendcomb, Cirencester, Glos

COLLINS, Sir Arthur James Robert; KCVO (1980, CVO 1963); s of Col William Collins, DSO, JP, DL, of Cundall Manor, York, Lord of the Manor of Cundall and Patron of the Living of Farnham, by Lady Evelyn Innes-Ker, OBE (4 da of 7 Duke of Roxburghe); *b* 10 July 1911; *Educ* Eton, Ch Ch Oxford; *m* 1965, Elizabeth, da of Rear-Adm Sir Arthur Bromley, 8 Bt, KCMG, KCVO (a remote cous of Lord Carrington, the For Sec), and widow of 6 Baron Sudeley; *Career* served WW II Maj RHG, Adj 2 Household Cav Regt; slr, ptnr Withers & Co 1937, sr ptnr 1962; *Clubs* Turf, White's; *Style* - Sir Arthur Collins, KCVO; Kirkman Bank, Knaresborough, N Yorks (☎ 0423 863136); 38 Clarence ter, NW1 (☎ 01 723 4198)

COLLINS, Basil Eugene Sinclair; s of late Albert Collins; *b* 21 Dec 1923; *Educ* Great Yarmouth G S; *m* 1942, Doris, nee Slott; 2 da; *Career* md Cadbury Schweppes Ltd, chm Cadbury Schweppes Europe Ltd and Cadbury Schweppes Export Ltd, dir Cadbury Schweppes Gp of Cos, chm Chivers & Sons Ltd, dep chm Jeyes Gp Ltd, FZS, FBIM; *Style* - Basil Collins Esq; Wyddal Parva, Buntingford, Herts

COLLINS, Sir Charles Henry; CMG (1941); s of late C H Collins; *b* 10 Feb 1887; *Educ* King's Coll London U; *m* 1913, Florence E Campkin (d 1968); 1 s (decd), 1 da (and 1 decd); *Career* Ceylon Civil Service 1910, acting ch sec 1944, 1945 and 1947, adviser on changes for new constitution 1946, ret 1948, kt 1947; *Style* - Sir Charles Collins, CMG; Devoncroft, Clandon rd, West Clandon, Guildford, Surrey (☎ Guildford 222542)

COLLINS, Sir David Charles; CBE (1969); s of Richard Collins; *b* 23 Jan 1908; *Educ* GS and Tech Coll; *m* 1936, Dorothy Bootyman; *Career* chartered mechanical engr, joined Westland Aircraft Ltd 1951, now dir (chm 1970-77), dir Normalair-Garrett (Hldgs) Ltd, kt 1975, FIMechE, FIProdE, FRAeS; *Style* - Sir David Collins, CBE; Little Gables, Redwood rd, Sidmouth, Devon (☎ Sidmouth 6756)

COLLINS, Sir Geoffrey Abdy; s of Philip Collins; *b* 5 June 1888; *Educ* Rugby, Christ's Cambridge; *m* 1936, Joan Mary, nee Ratcliffe; 1 s, 4 da; *Career* solicitor 1913, pres Law Society 1951-52, kt 1952; *Style* - Sir Geoffrey Collins; Mullion, 20 Ballard Estate, Swanage, Dorset (☎ 2030)

COLLINS, Hon Ian Grenville Victor; s of Baron Stonham (Life Peer, d 1971); *b* 1941; *Educ* Queen's Coll Taunton, Kingston G S; *m* 1968, Sandra Felicity Bell; children; *Style* - The Hon Ian Collins; Park Farm, Mileham, Kings Lynn, Norfolk

COLLINS, Vice-Adm Sir John Augustine; KBE (1951), CB (1940); s of Michael Collins, MD; *b* 7 Jan 1899; *Educ* Roy Australian Naval Coll; *m* 1930, Phyllis Laishley, nee McLachlan; 1 da; *Career* Roy Australian Navy 1913, V-Adm 1950, Ch of Naval Staff and First Naval Memb Australian Commonwealth Naval Bd Melbourne 1948-55, ret, Australian High Cmmr New Zealand 1955-62; *Style* - Vice-Adm Sir John Collins, KBE, CB; 13 Dumaresq rd, Rose Bay, Sydney, NSW 2029, Australia

COLLINS, Maj-Gen Joseph Clinton; CB (1953), CBE (1951, OBE 1946); *b* 8 Jan 1895; *Educ* London Hosp; *m* 1925, Patricia Williams; 2 da; *Career* RNVR and RAMC 1914-18, Maj-Gen 1951, Dir Medical Services 1953-54, ret, CStJ (1948); *Style* - Maj-Gen Joseph Collins, CB, CBE; c/o Williams and Glyn's Bank Ltd, Whitehall, SW1

COLLINS, John Ernest Harley; MBE (1944), DSC (1945) and Bar (1945); s of late G W Collins; *b* 24 April 1923; *Educ* King Edward's Sch Birmingham, Birmingham U; *m* 1946, Hon Gillian, nee Smith, da of 2 Baron Bicester; 1 s, 1 da; *Career* chm Morgan Grenfell Hldgs Ltd 1974-79, chm Guardian Royal Exchange Assurance 1974-, dir Chartered Consolidated Ltd, Rank Hovis McDougall Ltd, High Sheriff of Oxon 1975-; *Style* - John Collins Esq, MBE, DSC*; Tusmore Park, Bicester, Oxon (☎ Fritwell 209)

COLLINS, Kenneth Darlington; MEP (L) E Strathclyde 1979-; s of late Nicholas Collins; *b* 12 Aug 1939; *Educ* St John's G S, Hamilton Acad, Glasgow U, Strathclyde U; *m* 1966, Georgina Frances, nee Pollard; 1 s, 1 da; *Career* social geographer, lectr Paisley Coll of Technology 1969-79, former Bd memb E Kilbride Dvpt Corpn; *Style* - Kenneth Collins Esq, MEP; 11 Stuarton pk, East Kilbride, Lanarkshire (☎ E Kilbride 37282)

COLLINS, Rear-Adm Kenneth St Barbe; CB (1959), OBE (1945), DSC (1942); s of late Charles Bury Collins, Col RE; *b* 9 June 1904; *Educ* Lydgate House Sch Hunstanton Norfolk; *m* 1932, Helen Mary Keen; 1 s, 1 da; *Career* joined RN 1918, Rear-Adm 1957, Hydrographer of the Navy 1955-60, ret, consultant to Survey and Mapping Branch of Dept of Mines and Tech Surveys Ottawa 1960-63; *Style* - Rear-Adm Kenneth Collins, CB, OBE, DSC; The Old Parsonage, Bentley, nr Farnham, Surrey (☎ Bentley 3227)

COLLINS, Norman Richard; s of late Oliver Norman Collins; *b* 3 Oct 1907; *Educ* William Ellis Sch Hampstead; *m* 1931, Sarah Helen, nee Martin; 1 s, 2 da; *Career* author, novels include *London Belongs to Me* 1945 (also TV series); former dir ITV News, ATV Network, dir Assoc Communications Corpn (formerly dep chm), chm Loch Ness Investigation Bureau, Central Sch of Speech and Drama; *Style* - Norman Collins Esq; Mulberry House, Curch Row, NW3

COLLINS, Lady Sara Elena; *née* Hely-Hutchinson; da of 7 Earl of Donoughmore; *b* 1930; *m* 1951, William Janson Collins; 1 s, 3 da; *Style* - Lady Sara Collins; House of Craigie, by Kilmarnock, Ayrshire

COLLINS, Terence Bernard; s of late George Bernard Collins; *b* 3 March 1927; *Educ* Marist Coll Hull, St Andrews U (MA); *m* 1956, Barbara, nee Lowday; 2 s, 2 da; *Career* v-chm and md Berger Jenson Nicholson 1975-, dir Hoechst UK 1979-, dir Hoechst Australia 1980-, dir A G Stanley 1979-, memb of Council of Cranfield Inst of Technol 1980-; *Recreations* music, sailing, golf; *Style* - Terence Collins Esq; 2 Astell st, SW3

COLLINSON, His Honour Judge - Richard Jeffreys Hampton; s of Kenneth Hampton Collinson; *b* 7 April 1924; *Educ* Heath G S Halifax, Wadham Oxford; *m* 1955, Gwendolen Hester Ward; 2 s, 2 da; *Career* barr 1950, a Circuit Judge 1975-; *Style* - His Honour Judge Collinson; Merehaven, 2 Mere lane, Wallasey, Merseyside (☎ 051 639 5818)

COLLIS, Herbert Charles Clive; OBE, MC; s of the late Frank Collis; *b* 13 Oct 1898; *Educ* Denstone Coll; *m* 1, 1926, Dorothy Elizabeth, nee Riley; 1 child; m 2, 1962, Doris; *Career* captain Special Reserve Royal Field Artillery, solicitor Notary Public, Clerk to the Justices Petty Sessional Div Cheadle Staffs 1945-68, assistant dep coroner for N W Staffs and City of Stoke on Trent 1936-66; *Recreations* shooting, fishing, formerly hunting; *Style* - Herbert Collis Esq, OBE, MC; Rosehill, Cheadle, Staffs (☎ 05384 3125)

COLLISON, Baron (Life Peer UK 1964); Harold Francis Collison; CBE (1961); *b* 10 May 1909; *Educ* The Hay Currie LCC Sch, Crypt Sch Gloucester; *m* 1946, Ivy Kate Hanks; *Career* farm worker 1934-53, Gen Sec Nat Union of Agricultural Workers 1944-46, Pres Int Fedn of Agric and Allied Workers 1960-76, chm Supplementary Benefits Cmmn 1969-75, chm Land Settlement Assoc 1977-; *Style* - The Rt Hon the Lord Collison, CBE; Honeywood, 163 Old Nazeing rd, Broxbourne, Herts (☎ Hoddesdon 63597)

COLLYEAR, John Gowen; s of late John Robert Collyear; *b* 19 Feb 1927; *Educ* Watford G S, Manchester and Leeds Us; *m* 1953, Catherine Barbara, nee Newman; 1 s, 2 da; *Career* Lt RE; engr, gp md Assoc Engrg Ltd 1975-; *Recreations* golf, bridge, music; *Clubs* Reform, Moor Park; *Style* - John Collyear Esq; Barfields, Stockton, Rugby, Warwicks (☎ 092681 3837)

COLMAN, Hon Mrs; Hon Cynthia; da (twin) of 1 Baron Sherfield, GCB, GCMG; *b* 1935; *m* 1967, Oliver James Colman, s of Sir Jeremiah Colman, 2 Bt (d 1961) and bro of 3 Bt; 1 s, 1 da; *Style* - The Hon Mrs Colman; 35 Greville rd, NW6

COLMAN, Jeremiah Michael Powlett; s and h of Sir Michael Colman, 3 Bt; *b* 23 Jan 1958; *Style* - Jeremiah Colman Esq

COLMAN, Lady Mary Cecilia; *née* Bowes-Lyon; da (twin) of late Hon Michael Claude Hamilton Bowes-Lyon, 5 s of 14 Earl; sis of 17 Earl; raised to the rank of an Earl's da 1974; *b* 1932; *m* 1951, Timothy James Alan Colman, late Lt RN; 2 s, 3 da; *Career* appointed an Extra Lady-in-Waiting to HRH Princess Alexandra, the Hon Mrs Angus Olgilvy 1970; *Style* - Lady Mary Colman; Bixley Manor, Norwich, Norfolk

COLMAN, Sir Michael Jeremiah; 3 Bt (UK 1907), of Gatton Park, Surrey; s of Sir Jeremiah Colman, 2 Bt (d 1961); *b* 7 July 1928; *Educ* Eton; *m* 1955, Judith Jean Wallop, da of Vice-Adm Sir Peveril William-Powlett; 2 s, 3 da; *Heir* s, Jeremiah Colman; *Career* dir Reckitt & Colman Ltd, Waterer's Sons & Crisp Ltd, memb Council Roy Warrant Holders 1977-; *Style* - Sir Michael Colman, Bt; Malshanger, Basingstoke, Hants (☎ 780241); Tarvie, Bridge of Cally, Blairgowrie, Perthshire (☎ Strathardle 264)

COLMAN, Lady; Nona Ann; da of late Edward H M Willian; *m* 1952, Sir Nigel Claudian Dalziel Colman, 1 Bt (d 1966, when title became extinct); *Style* - Lady Colman; Middleton Manor, Winterslow, Salisbury, Wilts

COLMAN, Hon Mrs (Victoria Helen); *née* Loder; da of 1 Baron Wakehurst; *b* 1899; *m* 1928, Maj Alan Coleman; 2 adopted s; *Style* - The Hon Mrs Colman; 66 Campbell Court, Queens' Gate gdns, SW7

COLONNA-CZOSNOWSKI, Karol Anthony; s of Eustace Colonna-Czosnowski (descended from Roscislaw, whose designation of Comes (which he appears to have born c 1250) was essentially a feudal one, in some ways comparable with W European seigneuries or lordships; the Colonna-Czosnowskis are said to be connected with the Colonna-Walewskis, ancestors of whom (the Colonnas) allegedly migrated from Italy to

North East Europe in the 10 century; a sr branch of the family was granted the title of Count by Pope Leo XIII and the King of Italy in the 1890s); *b* 24 Feb 1921; *Educ* St Joseph's Coll, Chyrow, Poland; *m* 1948, Maria, da of late Baron Stanislas Heydel of Guernica, Spain; *Career* Capt Italy 1944, chm Bishopsgate Steels Ltd and associated companies; *Recreations* foxhunting; *Clubs* Brooks's; *Style* - Karol Colonna-Czosnowski Esq; 4 Currie Hill close, SW19 (☎ 01 946 6798)

COLQUHOUN, Maj-Gen Sir Cyril Harry; KCVO (1968, CVO 1965), CB (1955), OBE (1945); s of late Capt Harry Colquhoun; *b* 1903; *m* 1930, Stella Irene, nee Rose; 1 s; *Career* 2 Lt RA 1923, GOC Malta 1956-59, ret 1960, Col Cmdt RA 1962-69, sec Central Chancery of the Orders of Knighthood 1960-68, Extra Gentleman Usher to HM the Queen 1968-; *Style* - Maj-Gen Sir Cyril Colquhoun KCVO CB OBE; Longwalls, Shenington, Banbury, Oxon (☎ Edgehill 246)

COLQUHOUN OF LUSS, Capt Sir Ivar Iain; 8 Bt (GB 1786), JP (Dunbartonshire 1951), DL (1952); s of Lt-Col Sir Iain Colquhoun of Luss, 7 Bt, KT DSO (d 1948); bro of Countess of Arran; *b* 4 Jan 1916; *Educ* Eton; *m* 1943, Kathleen, nee Duncan; 1 s (and 1 decd), 1 da (Duchess of Argyll); *Heir* s, Malcolm Colquhoun *Career* Capt Gren Gds, Ch of Clan Colquhoun, Hon Sheriff (formerly Hon Sheriff Substitute); *Clubs* White's, Puffin's, Roy Ocean Racing; *Style* - Capt Sir Ivar Colquhoun of Luss, Bt, JP DL; 37 Radnor walk, SW3 (☎ 01 352 9510); Eilean da Mheinn, Crinan, Argyllshire; Camstraddan, Luss, Dunbartonshire

COLQUHOUN, YR OF LUSS, Malcolm Rory; s and h of Capt Sir Ivar Colquhoun of Luss, 8 Bt; *b* 20 Dec 1947; *Educ* Eton; *m* 1978, Susan, da of Stewart Timmerman, of Harrisburg, Pa, USA *Style* - Malcolm Colquhoun, yr of Luss

COLSTON, Michael; s of late Sir Charles Colston, CBE, MC, DCM; *b* 24 July 1932; *Educ* Ridley Coll Canada, Stowe, Caius Cambridge; *m* 1977, Judith Angela, da of Gp-Capt Nelson Briggs, CBE, AFC; *Career* chm Charles Colston Gp, Tallent Engineering Ltd, ITS Rubber Ltd; *Style* - Michael Colston Esq; C6 Albany, Piccadilly, W1 (☎ 01 734 2452); Ewelme Park, Nettlebed, Oxon (☎ 0494 641279)

COLT, Sir Edward William Dutton; 10 Bt (E 1694), of St James's-in-the-Fields Liberty of Westminster, Middlesex; s of Major John Rochfort Colt, N Staffs Regt (half-bro of 9 Bt, d 1944); suc unc Sir Henry Archer Colt, 9 Bt, DSO, MC (d 1951); *b* 22 Sept 1936; *Educ* Stoke House Seaford, Douai Sch, Univ Coll London; *m* 1, 1966 (m dis 1972), Jane Caroline, nee Lewis; m 2, 1979, Suzanne Nelson, nee Knickerbocker; *Heir* none; *Career* MB, MRCP, FACP, Assist Attending Physician St Luke's Hosp New York, consultant in Endocrinology St Barnabas Hosp Bronx New York; *Style* - Sir Edward Colt, Bt; 12 East 88 st, New York, NY 10028, USA

COLTHURST, Charles St John; s and h of Sir Richard Colthurst, 9 Bt; *b* 21 May 1955; *Educ* Eton, Magdalene Cambridge, Univ Coll Dublin; *Career* Lloyd's underwriter; *Style* - Charles Colthurst Esq; Turret Farm, Blarney, Co Cork

COLTHURST, Sir Richard La Touche; 9 Bt (I 1744), of Ardrum, Cork; s of Sir Richard Colthurst, 8 Bt (d 1955); *b* 14 Aug 1928; *Educ* Harrow, Peterhouse Cambridge; *m* 1953, Janet Georgina, nee Wilson-Wright; 3 s, 1 da; *Heir* s, Charles Colthurst; *Career* Lloyd's underwriter, dir Rose Thomson Young (Underwriting) Ltd, liveryman Worshipful Co of Grocers; *Style* - Sir Richard Colthurst, Bt; Wheatlands, Crockham Hill, Kent (☎ Crockham Hill 260); Blarney Castle, Co Cork, Eire (☎ Cork 85252)

COLVILLE OF CULROSS, 4 Viscount (UK 1902); John Mark Alexander Colville; QC (1978); also 14 Lord Colville of Culross (S precedency 1609) and Baron Colville of Culross (UK 1885); s of 3 Viscount (killed on active serv 1945); 1 cous once removed of Sir John Colville, *qv*, and half 2 cous once removed of Lord Carrington the For Sec; *b* 19 July 1933; *Educ* Rugby, New Coll Oxford; *m* 1, 1958 (m dis 1973), Mary Elizabeth Webb-Bowen; 4 s; m 2, 1974, Margaret Birgitta, da of Maj-Gen Cyril Norton, CB, CBE, and former wife of 2 Visc Davidson; 1 s; *Heir* s, Master of Colville; *Career* UK Rep UN Human Rights Cmmn 1980-; exec dir Br Electric Traction Co 1981-, dir Wembley Stadium 1981-, Thames TV 1981-; Lt Gren Gds (Res), barr 1960, Min of State Home Office 1972-74, memb Roy Co of Archers (Queen's Body Gd for Scotland); *Style* - The Rt Hon the Viscount Colville of Culross, QC; 2 Mitre Court Bldgs, Temple, EC4 (☎ 01 353 4844)

COLVILLE, Hon (Charles) Anthony; s of late 3 Visc Colville of Culross; *b* 1935; *Educ* Rugby, Magdalen Oxford; *m* 1965, Katherine, nee Sankey; 2 s; *Career* BA, late Sub-Lt RNR, solicitor 1969, Overseas Civil Service Kenya 1958-64; *Style* - The Hon Anthony Colville; Lime Park, Herstmonceux, Sussex

COLVILLE, Hon Alexander Fergus Gale; s of 4 Visc Colville of Culross; *b* 1964; *Style* - The Hon Alexander Colville

COLVILLE, Hon Andrew John; s of 2 Baron Clydesmuir, KT, CB, MBE, TD; *b* 1953; *m* 1978, Elaine Genevieve, nee Davy; *Style* - The Hon Andrew Colville

COLVILLE, Hon Angus Richmond; s of late 3 Visc Colville of Culross; *b* 1939; *Educ* Rugby; *Career* Lt Grenadiers Gds (Res), FRICS; *Style* - The Hon Angus Colville

COLVILLE, Sir (Henry) Cecil; s of John William Colville; *b* 27 Aug 1891; *Educ* Melbourne C of E G S; *m* 1916, Harriet Elizabeth Tatchell; 2 da; *Career* MS (Melbourne), FRACS, pediatric surgn Alfred Hosp Melbourne 1924-51, pres BMA Federal Council 1955-62, kt 1962; *Style* - Sir Cecil Colville; 1045 Burke rd, Hawthorn, Vic 3123, Australia (☎ Melbourne 82 5252)

COLVILLE, Master of - Hon Charles Mark Townshend Colville; s and h of 4 Visc Colville of Culross; *b* 5 Sept 1959; *Educ* Rugby; *Style* - The Master of Colville

COLVILLE, Hon David Ronald; s and h of 2 Baron Clydesmuir, KT, CB, MBE, TD; *b* 8 April 1949; *m* 1978, Aline Frances, nee Merriam; 1 s; *Style* - The Hon David Colville

COLVILLE, Hon Elizabeth Anne; da of 2 Baron Clydesmuir, KT, CB, MBE, TD; *b* 1955; *Style* - The Hon Elizabeth Colville

COLVILLE, Hon Edmund Carleton; s (by 1 m) of 4 Visc Colville of Culross; *b* 1978; *Style* - The Hon Edmund Colville

COLVILLE, Maj-Gen Edward Charles; CB (1955), DSO (1944) and Bar (1945), JP (W Sussex 1960), DL (1962); s of late Adm the Hon Sir Stanley Colville, GCB, GCMG, GCVO; *b* 1 Sept 1905; *Educ* Marlborough, Sandhurst; *m* 1934, Barbara Joan Denny; 2 da; *Career* 2 Lt Gordon Highlanders 1925, Maj-Gen 1955, ch of Staff FARELF 1954-55, GOC 51 (Highland) Inf Div (TA) and Highland Dist 1956-59,
ret; *Style* - Maj-Gen Edward Colville, CB, DSO*, JP, DL; Old Bartons, Stoughton, nr Chichester, W Sussex (☎ Compton 278)

COLVILLE, Lady Joan; *née* Child-Villiers; da of 8 Earl of Jersey (d 1923); *b* 1911; *m* 1933, Lt David Richard Colville, RNVR, s of late Hon George Charles Colville, MBE (3 s of 1 Viscount Colville of Culross); 2 s; *Style* - Lady Joan Colville; Old Vicarage, Dorton, nr Aylesbury, Bucks; Ducie House, Bembridge, IOW

COLVILLE, Sir John Rupert; CB (1955), CVO (1949); s of late Hon George Colville, 3 s of 1 Viscount Colville of Culross by Hon Cecil Carington, da of 2 Baron Carrington; *b* 28 Jan 1915; *Educ* Harrow, Trin Cambridge; *m* 1948, Lady Margaret Egerton, da of 4 Earl of Ellesmere; 2 s, 1 da; *Career* Page of Honour to HM King George V 1927-31, HM Diplomatic Service 1937-55, private sec to Rt Hon Neville Chamberlain 1939-40, to Rt Hon Winston Churchill 1940-41 and 1943-45, to Rt Hon Clement Attlee 1945, to HRH Princess Elizabeth 1947-49, princ private sec to Rt Hon Sir Winston Churchill, KG 1951-55; dir Hill Samuel & Co, Grindlays Bank, Coutts & Co, Provident Life Assoc, chm Eucalyptus Pulp Mills Ltd, Thames Valley Broadcasting, kt 1974; *Style* - Sir John

Colville, CB, CVO; The Old Rectory, Stratfield Saye, Reading, Berks (☎ Turgis Green 203)

COLVILLE OF CULROSS, Dowager Viscountess - Kathleen Myrtle; OBE (1961); da of Brig-Gen Henry Richmond Gale, CMG; *m* 1931, 3 Viscount Colville of Culross (ka 1945); 3 s; *Career* late Chief Cmmr Scotland Girl Guides Assoc; *Style* - The Rt Hon the Dowager Viscountess Colville of Culross, OBE; Fawsyde, Kinneff, Montrose, Angus

COLVILLE, Lady Margaret; *née* Egerton; da of 4 Earl of Ellesmere; *b* 20 July 1918; *m* 1948, Sir John Colville; 2 s, 1 da; *Career* ATS (Jr Subaltern) 1939-45, Lady in Waiting to HRH Princess Elizabeth 1946-49; *Style* - Lady Margaret Colville; The Old Rectory, Stratfield Saye, Reading, Berks (☎ Turgis Green 203)

COLVILLE, Hon Rupert George Streatfield; s of 4 Visc Colville of Culross; *b* 1966; *Style* - The Hon Rupert Colville

COLVILLE, Hon Richard James Innys; s of 4 Visc Colville of Culross; *b* 1961; *Style* - The Hon Richard Colville

COLVIN, Michael Keith Beale; MP (C) Bristol N W 1979-; s of late Capt Ivan Colvin, RN; *b* 27 Sept 1932; *Educ* Eton, Sandhurst, RAC Cirencester; *m* Nichola, da of Sir Nicholas Cayzer, Bt; 1 s, 2 da; *Career* landowner, farmer, with J Walter Thompson & Co Ltd 1958-63, former part-time memb Cons Pty Res Dept; *Style* - Michael Colvin Esq MP; Tangley House, nr Andover, Hants (☎ Chute Standen 215)

COLVIN, Brig Dame Mary Katherine Rosamond; DBE (1959, OBE 1947); da of Lt-Col F F Colvin, CBE; *b* 25 Oct 1907; *Career* ATS 1939, Brig 1957, dep dir Eastern Command 1956-57, dir WRAC 1957-61, Hon ADC to the Queen 1957-61, a Lady in Waiting to HRH the late Princess Royal 1962-64, extra Lady in Waiting 1964-65; *Style* - Brig Dame Mary Colvin, DBE; Pasture House, North Luffenham, Oakham, Rutland

COLWYN, 3 Baron (UK 1917); Sir Ian Anthony Hamilton-Smith; 3 Bt (UK 1912); s of 2 Baron (d 1966); *b* 1 Jan 1942; *Educ* Cheltenham Coll, London U; *m* 1, 1964 (m dis 1977), Sonia Jane, nee Morgan; 1 s, 1 da; m 2, 1977, Nicola Jeanne, nee Tyers; *Heir* s, Hon Craig Hamilton-Smith; *Career* BDS, LDS, RCS, dental surgeon 1966-; *Style* - The Rt Hon the Lord Colwyn; 29 Oakley gdns, SW3 (☎ 01 352 2483); Painswick House, Cheltenham, Glos; 23 Wimpole st, W1 (☎ 01 637 8427)

COLWYN, Miriam, Baroness; da of late Victor Bruce Ferguson; *m* 1940 (m dis 1951), 2 Baron Colwyn who d 1966; *Style* - Miriam, Lady Colwyn; 32 Barford lane, Charlton Kings, Cheltenham, Glos

COLYER-FERGUSSON, Sir James Herbert Hamilton; 4 Bt (UK 1866), of Spitalhaugh, Peeblesshire; s of Max Colyer-Fergusson, Capt RASC, s of 3 Bt (killed on active serv 1940); suc gf 1951; *b* 10 Jan 1917; *Educ* Harrow, Balliol Oxford; *Heir* none; *Career* formerly Capt The Buffs, former offr BR, dep curator Historical Relics British Railways Bd 1968, ret; *Style* - Sir James Colyer-Fergusson, Bt; 61 Onslow sq, SW7

COLYTON, 1 Baron (UK 1956); Henry Lennox d'Aubigne Hopkinson; CMG (1944), PC (1952); s of late Sir Henry Hopkinson, KCVO; *b* 3 Jan 1902; *Educ* Eton, Trin Cambridge; *m* 1, 1927, Alice Labouisse (d 1953), da of Henry Eno, of Maine, USA; 1 s; m 2, 1956, Mrs Barbara Estella Addams, da of late Stephen Barb of New York; *Heir* s, Hon Nicholas Hopkinson; *Career* HM Diplomatic Service 1924-1946, Min Plenipotentiary Lisbon 1943, Dep British High Cmmr in Italy and V-Pres Political Sect Allied Control Cmmn 1944-46, MP (C) Taunton Somerset 1950-56, Min of State for Colonial Affairs 1952-55, delegate Gen Assembly UN 1952-55, OStJ 1959; *Style* - The Rt Hon the Lord Colyton, CMG, PC; Le Formentor, av Princesse Grace, Monte Carlo, Monaco (☎ 93 309296)

COMBE, Lady Mary Esther Constance; *née* Needham; da of late Maj the Hon Francis Edward Needham, MVO (2 s of 3 Earl of Kilmorey); *b* 1918; *m* 1949, Cdr

Anthony Boyce Combe, RN (ret); 3 s, 1 da; *Style* - Lady Mary Combe; Grove Cottage, South Creake, Fakenham, Norfolk

COMBE, Lady Silvia (Beatrice); *née* Coke; da of 4 Earl of Leicester (d 1949); *b* 1909; *m* 1932, Capt Simon Harvey Combe, MC (d 1965); 1 s, 1 da; *Career* JP; *Style* - Lady Silvia Combe, JP; The Manor House, Burnham Thorpe, Kings Lynn

COMBERMERE, 5 Viscount (UK 1826); Sir Michael Wellington Stapleton-Cotton; 10 Bt (E 1677); Baron Combermere (UK 1814); s of 4 Viscount Combermere (d 1969); *b* 8 Aug 1929; *Educ* Eton, King's Coll London U; *m* 1961, Pamela Elizabeth, da of Rev Robert Gustavus Coulson; 1 s, 2 da; *Heir* s, Hon Thomas Stapleton-Cotton; *Career* BD, MTh, lectr Biblical and Religious Studies Dept of Extra-Mural Studies London U 1972-; *Style* - The Rt Hon the Viscount Combermere; 46 Smith st, SW3 (☎ 01 352 1319)

COMBS, Sir Willis Ide; KCVO (1974), CMG (1962); s of Willis Ide Combs of Napier, NZ; *b* 6 May 1916; *Educ* Dannevirke H S, Victoria Coll NZ, St John's Cambridge; *m* 1942, Grace Willis; 2 da; *Career* Foreign Service 1956, Counsellor Rangoon 1965, Assist Under-Sec of State FCO 1968, Ambass to Indonesia 1970-75, ret; *Style* - Sir Willis Combs, KCVO, CMG; Sunset, Wadhurst Park, Wadhurst, E Sussex

COMINS, Peter Crawford Melhuish; s of late Capt Dennis Comins, MC; *b* 25 Nov 1930; *Educ* Ampleforth, Lincoln Coll Oxford; *m* 1963, Dinah, nee Collins; 3 s; *Career* dir Borax Consolidated Ltd, Borax Hldgs Ltd 1969-; *Recreations* shooting, skiing, swimming; *Style* - Peter Comins Esq; 15 Turners Reach House, 9 Chelsea Embankment, SW3 (☎ 01 352 2027); Tremara, Wiveton, Holt, Norfolk (☎ Cley 740 800)

COMPSTON, Vice-Adm Sir Peter Maxwell; KCB (1970, CB 1967); s of Dr G D Compston; *b* 12 Sept 1915; *Educ* Epsom Coll; *m* 1, 1939 (m dis), Valerie Bocquet; 1 s, 1 da; *Career* RN 1937, Rear-Adm 1965, Ch of British Naval Staff and Naval Attache Washington 1965-67, Flag Offr Flotillas Western Fleet 1967-68, Dep Supreme Allied Cdr Atlantic (V-Adm) 1968-70, ret; *Style* - Vice-Admiral Sir Peter Compston, KCB; Holmwood, Stroud, nr Petersfield, Hants

COMPTON, Lady Clare Victoria Frances; da of 7 Marquess of Northampton; *b* 1980

COMPTON, Earl; Daniel Bingham Compton; s and h of 7 Marq of Northampton; *b* 16 Jan 1973; *Style* - Earl Compton

COMPTON, Sir Edmund Gerald; GCB (1971, KCB 1965, CB 1948), KBE (1955); s of late Edmund Spencer Compton, MC; *b* 30 July 1906; *Educ* Rugby, New Coll Oxford; *m* 1934, Betty Tresyllian, nee Williams; 1 s, 4 da; *Career* Civil Service 1929, Colonial Office 1930, Treasury 1931, Comptroller and Auditor General Exchequer and Audit Dept 1958-66, Parly Cmmr for Admin 1967-71, and in Northern Ireland 1969-71; *Style* - Sir Edmund Compton, GCB, KBE; 1/80 Elm Park gdns, SW10 (☎ 01 351 3790)

COMPTON, Lady Lara Katrina; da of 7 Marquess of Northampton; *b* 1968

COMPTON, Robert Edward John; s of late Major Edward Compton, JP, DL (s of Lord Alwyne Compton, DSO, DL, sometime MP Bedford & Brentwood, 3 s of 4 Marquess of Northampton); *b* 11 July 1922; *Educ* Eton, Magdalen Oxford; *m* 1951, Ursula Jane, nee Kenyon-Slaney; 2 s; *Career* publisher, business consultant, landowner, farmer; European public affairs dir Time 1965-79, chm Time Life Int 1979, High Sheriff N Yorks 1978; dir Extel Corpn Chicago 1973, Transtel 1974; V-Chm Nat Tst Yorks 1970; *Recreations* gardening, golf, shooting; *Clubs* White's, Swinley Forest Golf; *Style* - Robert Compton Esq; 42 Ennismore gdns, SW7 (☎ 01 589 7643); Newby Hall, Ripon, N Yorks (☎ 09012 3315)

COMPTON, Lord William James Bingham; s of 6 Marquess of Northampton, DSO (d 1978); *b* 1947;

Educ Bryanston; *m* 1973, Marlene, da of late Francis Hosie; 1 s, 1 da; *Style* - Lord William Compton

COMPTON-MILLER, Sir John Francis; MBE (1945), TD; s of Frederic Miller, MD; *b* 11 May 1900; *Educ* St Paul's Sch, New Coll Oxford; *m* 1, 1925, Alice Irene Mary, nee Bakewell (d 1931); 1 s; m 2, 1936, Mary, da of Rev Alexander MacEwen Baird-Smith; 1 s, 1 da; *Career* barr 1923, kt 1969, Sr Registrar Family Div 1964-72 (formerly registrar); *Style* - Sir John Compton-Miller, MBE, TD; 2 Crown Office, Temple, EC4 (☎ 01 583 1352)

COMRIE, Rear-Adm Alexander Peter; s of late Robert Comrie; *b* 27 March 1924; *Educ* Sutton Valence, Roy Coll of Defence Studies; *m* 1945, Madeleine Irene, nee Bullock; 1 s, 1 da; *Career* RN 1945, Dep Controller Aircraft MOD 1978-81, Dir Gen Aircraft (Navy) 1981-, FIEE, FRAeS; *Style* - Rear-Adm Alexander Comrie; 12 Spindale close, Havant, Hants (☎ 483946)

COMYN, Hon Mr Justice; Hon Sir James Peter; s of late James Comyn, QC; *b* 8 March 1921; *Educ* Oratory Sch, New Coll Oxford; *m* 1967, Anne, nee Chaundler; 1 s, 1 da; *Career* former pres Oxford Union, barr (I) 1947, QC 1961, Recorder of the Crown Court 1972-77, Judge of the High Court Family Div 1978-79, Queen's Bench Div 1979-; *Style* - The Hon Mr Justice Comyn; Belvin, Tara, Co Meath, Ireland (☎ Navan 25111); Royal Courts of Justice, Strand, WC2

CONAN DOYLE, Air Cmdt Jean Lena Annette (Lady Bromet); DBE (1963, OBE 1948); da of late Sir Arthur Conan Doyle; *b* 21 Dec 1912; *m* 1965, Air V-Marshal Sir Geoffrey Bromet, *qv*; *Career* No 46 (Co of Sussex) ATS Raf Co 1938, Dep Dir WRAF 1952-54 and 1960-62, Air Cmdt 1963, Hon ADC to HM the Queen 1963-66, ret 1966; *Style* - Air Cmdt Dame Jean Conan Doyle, DBE; Flat 6, 72 Cadogan sq, SW1; Home Green, Littlestone-on-Sea, New Romney, Kent

CONANT, Sir John Ernest Michael Conant; 2 Bt (UK 1954) of Lyndon Co Rutland; s of Sir Roger Conant, 1 Bt, CVO (d 1973); *b* 24 April 1923; *Educ* Eton, CCC Cambridge; *m* 1950, Periwinkle Elizabeth, nee Thorp; 2 s (and 1 decd), 2 da; *Heir* s, Simon Conant; *Career* farmer, High Sheriff of Rutland 1960; *Style* - Sir John Conant, Bt; Lyndon Hall, Oakham, Rutland (☎ Manton 275)

CONANT, Mary, Lady; Mary; da of A H Worth; *m* 1972, as his 2 w, Sir Roger John Edward Conant, CVO, 1 Bt (d 1973); 3 s; *Style* - Mary, Lady Conant; 26 Lowndes Lodge, Cadogan pla, SW1

CONANT, Simon Edward Christopher; s and h of Sir John Conant, 2 Bt; *b* 13 Oct 1958; *Style* - Simon Conant Esq

CONCANNON, Don (John Dennis); PC (1978), MP (L) Mansfield 1966-; *b* 16 May 1930; *Educ* Rossington Secdy Sch; *m* 1953, Iris May Wilson; 2 s, 2 da; *Career* V-Chamberlain HM Household 1974, Parly Under-Sec of State N Ireland Office 1974-76, Min of State N Ireland Office 1976-79, Opposition Spokesman for Defence 1979-; *Style* - The Rt Hon Don Concannon, PC, MP; 69 Skegby lane, Mansfield, Notts (☎ Mansfield 27235)

CONDLIFFE, John Bell; KCMG (Hon 1978); s of late Alfred Bell Condliffe of Potter, Australia; *b* 23 Dec 1891; *Educ* Canterbury U Christchurch New Zealand; *m* 1916, Olive Grace, nee Mills; 2 s, 1 da; *Career* prof of Economics Berkeley U California 1940-58 (now Emeritus), consultant Stanford Res Inst 1959-74, staff scientist Stanford Res Inst 1966-76; *Style* - John Bell Esq, KCMG; 1641 Canyonwood Court No 1, Walnut Creek, Calif 94595, USA

CONESFORD, Baroness - Anne Sadelbia Mary; da of late John Bowyer Nichols, FSA; *m* 1927, 1 Baron Conesford (d 1974, when title became extinct); *Style* - The Rt Hon the Lady Conesford; 23 The Green, Wanborough, Oxon

CONGLETON, 8 Baron (UK 1841); Sir Christopher Patrick Parnell; 11 Bt (I 1766); s of 6 Baron Congleton (d 1932) and Hon Edith Howard, MBE, da of late Baroness Strathcona and Mount Royal (in own right) and R J B Howard; suc bro

1967; *b* 11 March 1930; *Educ* Eton, New Coll Oxford; *m* 1955, Anna Hedvig, da of G A Sommerfelt of Oslo, Norway; 2 s, 3 da; *Heir* s, Hon John Parnell; *Career* former memb Salisbury and Wilton RDC, chm Salisbury and S Wilts Museum 1972-77, pres National Ski Fedn of Great Britain 1976-; *Style* - The Rt Hon the Lord Congleton; Ebbesbourne Wake, Salisbury, Wilts

CONLAN, Bernard; MP (L) Gateshead E 1964-; *b* 24 Oct 1923; *Educ* Manchester Secdy Sch; *m* ; 1 da; *Career* contested High Peak 1959, v-chm Parly Lab Party Trade Union Gp 1979-, memb Select Ctee on Defence 1979-; *Style* - Bernard Conlan Esq, MP; House of Commons, SW1; 33 Beccles rd, Sale, Cheshire

CONNELL, Sir Charles Gibson; s of late Sir Isaac Connell, SSC; *b* 11 March 1899; *Educ* Melville Coll Edinburgh, Edinburgh U; *m* 1927, Constance Margaret Weir (d 1976); 1 s, 1 da; *Career* dir Edinburgh Bldg Soc 1937-79, pres Scottish Wildlife Trust, consultant Connell & Connell, WS, Edinburgh, kt 1952; *Style* - Sir Charles Connell; 12 Abbotsford pk, Edinburgh 10 (☎ 031 447 2026)

CONNELL, David Allan Maclean; s of late John Maclean Connell; *b* 18 Jan 1930; *Educ* Stowe, Ch Ch Oxford; *m* 1954, Bridget Willink, nee Fletcher; 3 children; *Career* md and v-chm John Walker & Sons Ltd, dir Distillers Co Ltd; *Clubs* Vincents Club Oxford, MCC; *Style* - David Connell Esq; Windy Ridge, Effingham Common rd, Effingham, Surrey

CONNELL, Lady Susan (Jean); *née* Carnegie; da of 12 Earl of Northesk (d 1975); *b* 1930; *m* 1955, David Blackall Connell, MB, BS; 2 s, 1 da; *Style* - Lady Susan Connell; Blackwick, Devenish rd, Ascot, Berks

CONNERY, Sean (Thomas); s of Joseph Connery; *b* 25 Aug 1930; *m* 1, 1962 (m dis 1974), Diane, da of Sir Raphael Cilento, *qv*; 1 s; m 2, 1975, Micheline Roquebrune; *Career* film actor in Murder on the Orient Express (1974), and formerly as James Bond; *Style* - Sean Connery Esq; Michael S Ovitz, Creative Artists Agency Inc, Suite 1400, 1888 Century pk E, Los Angeles, Calif 90067, USA

CONNOLLY, Sir Willis Henry; CBE (1962); s of Joseph Connolly; *b* 25 Nov 1901; *Educ* Benalla H S, Melbourne U; *m* 1927, Mary Milton Clark; 1 s, 1 da; *Career* chm State Electricity Cmmn of Victoria 1956-71 (joined 1921), kt 1971; *Style* - Sir Willis Connolly, CBE; 16 Monkstadt st, St Kilda, Victoria 3182, Australia (☎ 91 2670)

CONNOR, Bishop of, 1969-; Rt Rev Arthur Hamilton Butler; MBE (1944); s of George Booker; *b* 8 March 1912; *Educ* Friars Sch Bangor, Trin Coll Dublin; *m* 1, 1938, Betty (d 1976), nee Pringle; 1 s; m 2, 1979, Dr Elizabeth Mayne; *Career* ordained 1935, Bp of Tuam 1958-69; *Style* - The Rt Rev the Lord Bishop of Connor, MBE; Bishop's House, 22 Deramore pk, Belfast (☎ Belfast 669442)

CONOLLY-CAREW, Hon Diana Sylvia; da of 6 Baron Carew; *b* 1940; *Style* -The Hon Diana Conolly-Carew

CONOLLY-CAREW, Hon Patrick Thomas; s and h of 6 Baron Carew, CBE; *b* 6 March 1938; *Educ* Harrow; *m* 1962, Celia Mary, da of Col the Hon Charles Cubitt, CBE, DSO, TD; 1 s, 3 da; *Career* late Capt Roy Horse Gds; *Style* - The Hon Patrick Conolly-Carew; Donadea House, Naas, Co Kildare, Ireland

CONRAN, Shirley Ida; da of W Thirley Pearce; *b* 21 Sept 1932; *Educ* St Paul's Girls' Sch; *m* 1955, Terence Orby Conran; 2 s; *Career* designer, founded Conran Fabrics Ltd 1957, founded Textile Design Studio 1958, memb Selection Ctee Design Centre 1961; journalist, first woman editor Observer Colour Magazine 1964, with Observer 1969-70, Vanity Fair 1970-71, author of *Superwoman* books and *Futures* (1979); *Style* - Mrs Terence Conran; c/o Coutts Bank, 14 Lombard st, EC4

CONSTABLE-MAXWELL-STUART, Peter D'Arcy John Joseph; s of Capt Francis Constable-Maxwell-Stuart (s of Edmund Constable-Maxwell-Stuart, himself 4 s of Hon Henry Constable-Maxwell-Stuart, bro of 10 Lord Herries of Terregles; Edmund m his 1 cous, Hon

Mary Constable-Maxwell, da of 10 Lord); *b* 16 Nov 1922; *Educ* Downside; *m* 1956, Flora, da of Sir Alexander Carr-Saunders, FBA, of Brompton Sq, SW3; 1 da; *Career* owner of Traquair House, oldest inhabited house in Scotland; late Capt Indian Army; *Style* - Peter Constable-Maxwell-Stuart Esq; Traquair House, Innerleithen, Peebles-shire

CONSTANTINE OF STANMORE, Baron (Life Peer UK 1981); Theodore; CBE (1956), AE (1945), DL (Greater London 1967); s of Leonard Constantine; *b* 15 March 1910; *Educ* Acton Coll; *m* 1935, Sylvia Mary, nee Legge-Pointing; 1 s, 1 da; *Career* dir Anscon Ltd, Bassacre Dvpts Ltd, Area Properties Ltd, pres National Union Conservative and Unionist Assocs 1980-, master Worshipful Co of Coachmakers 1975, freeman of City of London, High Sheriff of Greater London 1967, kt 1964; *Style* - The Rt Hon Lord Constantine of Stanmore, CBE, AE, DL; Hunters Beck, Uxbridge rd, Stanmore, Middx

CONSTANTINE, Air Chief Marshal Sir Hugh Alex; KBE (1958, CBE 1944), CB (1946), DSO (1942); s of Cdr Henry Constantine, RN; *b* 23 May 1908; *Educ* Christ's Hosp, RAF Cranwell; *m* 1937, Helen, da of J W Bourne of Sydney, Australia; 1 da; *Career* commissioned RAF 1927, Air Marshal 1958, AOCIC Flying Training Command 1959-61, Cmdt Imperial Defence Coll 1961-64, Air Ch Marshal 1961, ret 1964, co-ordinator Anglo-American Community Relations MOD (Air) 1964-77; *Style* - Air Chief Marshal Sir Hugh Constantine, KBE, CB, DSO; 4 Chester Row, SW1 (☎ 01 730 0700)

CONSTANTINE, Joseph; s of late Maj R A Constantine, TD, J; *b* 12 Feb 1928; *Educ* Eton; *m* 1954, Mary Rose, nee Cotter; 2 da; *Career* FRICS, md Constantine Hldgs Ltd 1964-; *Style* - Joseph Constantine Esq; 3 Cottesmore gdns, W8 (☎ 01 937 5213); The Priory, Knipton, Grantham, Lincs (☎ 047 682 238)

CONYNGHAM, 7 Marquess (I 1816); Frederick William Henry Francis Conyngham; also (sits as) Baron Minster (UK 1821), Earl Conyngham (I 1781), Baron Conyngham (I 1781), Viscount Conyngham (I 1789), Viscount Mount Charles (I 1797), Earl of Mount Charles and Viscount Slane (I 1816); s of 6 Marquess Conyngham (d 1974) by his 2 w Antoinette; *b* 13 March 1924; *Educ* Eton; *m* 1, 1950 (m dis 1970), Eileen Wren, da of Capt C W Newsam; 3 s; m 2, 1971, Mrs Elizabeth Ann Rudd; *Heir* s, Earl of Mount Charles; *Career* late Capt Irish Gds, patron of one living; *Style* - The Most Hon the Marquess Conyngham; Bifrons, nr Canterbury, Kent; Cronk Ghennie House, Ramsay, Isle of Man

CONYNGHAM, Lord Frederick William Patrick; s (by 1 m) of 7 Marquess Conyngham; *b* 1959; *Style* - Lord Frederick Conyngham

CONYNGHAM, Lady Henrietta Tamara Juliet; da of Earl of Mount Charles, *qv*; *b* 1976; *Style* - Lady Henrietta Conyngham

CONYNGHAM, Dowager Marchioness - Stella; da of Francis Thompson, MRCS, LRCP; *m* 1, Robert Newton Tory, of Dorset (decd); m 2, 1966, as his 3 w, 6 Marquess Conyngham (d 1974); *Style* - The Most Hon the Dowager Marchioness Conyngham; Les Pres, St Lawrence, Jersey, CI

CONYNGHAM, Lord Simon Charles Eveleigh Wren; s (by 1 m) of 7 Marquess Conyngham; *b* 1953; *Educ* Harrow; *m* 1978, Eileen S, da of Wing Cdr F W Breeze; 1 da; *Style* - Lord Simon Conyngham

COOK, Sir Christopher Wymondham Rayner Herbert; 5 Bt (UK 1886) of Richmond, Surrey; s of Sir Francis Cook, 4 Bt (d 1978); *b* 24 March 1938; *Educ* King's Sch Canterbury; *m* 1, 1958 (m dis 1975), Mrs Malina Gunasekera; 1 s, 1 da; m 2, 1975, Mrs Margaret Miller, da of late John Murray; 1 da; *Heir* s, Richard Cook; *Career* dir Diamond Guarantees Ltd 1980- *Style* - Sir Christopher Cook, Bt; La Fontenelle, Ville au Roi, St Peter Port, Guernsey, CI

COOK, Air Vice-Marshal Eric; DFC (1945); s of late Thomas Cook; *b* 30 April 1920; *Educ* Sunderland Tech Coll; *m* 1953, Thelma, nee Withnell; 1 s; *Career* joined RAF 1940, dir of Flying Training 1971, Air V-Marshal 1972, Dir-Gen RAF Training 1972-75, bursar and fell Hughes Hall Cambridge 1975-; *Style* - Air Vice-Marshal Eric Cook, DFC; Hawkwood, Madeley Court, Hemingford Grey, Cambs (☎ St Ives 63647)

COOK, Sir (Philip) Halford; OBE (1965); s of Rev R Osborne Cook; *b* 10 Oct 1912; *Educ* Wesley Coll Melbourne, Queen's Coll Melbourne U, Univ Coll London U, Columbia and Kansas Us; *m* 1945, Myra , nee Dean; 1 s, 1 da; *Career* former industrial relations lectr, Australia Dept of Labour and National Service 1952-72, Ambass and Special Labour Adviser in Europe Australian Permanent Mission Geneva 1973-77, ret, kt 1976; *Style* - Sir Halford Cook, OBE; 11 Boisdale st, Surrey Hills, Vic 3127, Australia (☎ Melbourne 884793)

COOK, Rear-Adm James William Dunbar; CB (1975); s of George Home Cook; *b* 24 Jan 1918; *Educ* St Lawrence Coll Ramsgate, Pangbourne Coll; *m* 1943, Edith Williams; 1 s, 2 da; *Career* RN 1940, Rear-Adm 1972, Asst Ch of Naval Staff (Ops) 1973-75, ret, head of personnel and administration Ocean Inchcape Ltd 1975-; *Style* - Rear-Admiral James Cook, CB; Springways Cottage, Farnham lane, Haslemere, Surrey (☎ 3615)

COOK, Kenneth Clifford; OBE (1979); s of late George Kenneth Cook; *b* 4 Sept 1916; *Educ* The Leas Sch Hoylake, Oundle; *m* 1945, Barbara Isabel, da of late Rt Hon Lord Jamieson, PC, KC; 2 s, 2 da; *Career* chartered accountant (FCA), dir Thomas Bell & Co (Liverpool) Ltd, KStJ 1966; *Recreations* tennis, hockey; *Clubs* Athenaeum Liverpool, Reform; *Style* - Kenneth Cook Esq, OBE; 8 Hill rd, Birkenhead (☎ 051 652 1252)

COOK, Michael John; s of George Henry Cook (d 1947); *b* 20 June 1930; *Educ* Leeds Grammar Sch, Worksop Coll and Leeds U; *m* 1, 1958, Anne Margaret; 3 s, 1 da; m 2, 1974, Patricia Anne; 1 da; *Career* Lt RA (Nat Serv Canal Zone); slr; sr ptnr Ward Bowie; Crown Court Recorder 1980; author and broadcaster; past pres London Slrs Litigation Assoc; *Recreations* squash, gardening, reading and theatre; *Clubs* Athenaeum, United and Cecil and Law Soc; *Style* - Michael Cook Esq; Clement House, 99 Aldwych, Strand, London

COOK, Peter Charles Henry; s of Leslie Cook; *b* 13 June 1935; *Educ* Manchester G S; *m* 1957, Olive, nee Poulton; 2 s, 1 da; *Career* FICA, ACMA, former div fin dir Tube Investments Ltd, fin dir Simon Engineering Ltd; *Style* - Peter Cook Esq; Marlpool, Heybridge lane, Prestbury, Cheshire

COOK, Roy Edward; s of Herbert Edward Cook of Horsforth, W Yorks (d 1972); *b* 25 April 1927; *Educ* Dauntsey's Sch Devizes; *m* 1973, Shevaun Mary, da of John Knock of Howsham Hall, York; 2 s (and 1 s, 2 da by previous m); *Career* chm Derwent Valley Railway Co, memb Lloyds; *Recreations* sailing (yacht- Bonnie Blink, aux Sloop 6 tons), country life; *Clubs* Royal Cruising, Royal Yorkshire Yacht (Cdre 1979-80); *Style* - Roy Cook Esq; Kyreham House, Crambe, York (☎ Whitwell on the Hill 268)

COOK, Robin (Robert Finlayson); MP (L) Edinburgh Central 1974-; s of Peter Cook; *b* 28 Feb 1946; *Educ* Aberdeen G S, Edinburgh U; *m* 1969, Margaret Whitmore; 2 s; *Career* memb Tribune Gp; *Style* - Robin Cook Esq, MP; House of Commons, SW1

COOK, Richard Herbert Aster Maurice; s (by 1 m) and h of Sir Christopher Cook, 5 Bt; *b* 30 June 1959; *Style* - Richard Cook Esq

COOK, Sir William Richard Joseph; KCB (1970, CB 1951), FRS (1962); s of John Cook; *b* 10 April 1905; *Educ* Trowbridge H S, Bristol U; *m* 1929, Grace, nee Purnell; 1 da; *Career* Dep Ch Adviser MOD 1964-67, Ch Adviser (Projects and Res) 1968-70, former dir Rolls Royce Ltd, GEC-Marconi Electronics Ltd, chm Marconi Int Marine Co 1971-75, dir Buck & Hickman Ltd 1970-, kt 1958; *Style* - Sir

William Cook, KCB, FRS; Adbury Springs, Newbury, Berks (☎ Newbury 40409)

COOKE, Dr Arthur Hafford; MBE (1946); s of late Sydney Herbert Cooke; *b* 13 Dec 1912; *Educ* Wyggeston G S Leicester, Ch Ch Oxford; *m* 1939, Ilse (d 1973), da of late Prof Hans Sachs; 2 s; *Career* fell New Coll Oxford 1946-76, physics lectr 1944-71, Reader in Physics 1971-76, Warden of New Coll 1976-; *Style* - Dr Arthur Cooke, MBE; New College, Oxford (☎ 48451)

COOKE, Rear-Adm Anthony John; CB (1980); s of Rear-Adm John Ernest Cooke, CB; *b* 21 Sept 1927; *Educ* St Edward's Sch Oxford; *m* 1951, Margaret Anne, nee Hynard; 2 s, 3 da; *Career* RN 1945, Cdre in Command Clyde Submarine Base 1973-75, Rear-Adm 1976, Sr Naval Memb Directing Staff RCDS 1975-78, Adm Pres RNC Greenwich 1978-80; freeman City of London, liveryman Shipwrights' Co; *Style* - Rear-Admiral Anthony Cooke, CB; Chalkhurst, Eynsford, Kent (☎ Farningham 862789)

COOKE, Anthony Roderick Chichester Bancroft; s of late Maj-Gen Ronald Cooke, CB, CBE, DSO; *b* 24 July 1941; *Educ* Ampleforth, London Business Sch (MSc); *m* 1972, Daryll, nee Aird-Ross; 2 s, 1 da; *Career* FICA, dir Ellerman Lines Ltd 1976-, ch exec Ellerman City Liners 1979-; *Recreations* gardening, music, hunting, shooting; *Style* - Anthony Cooke Esq; Poland Court, Odiham, Hants (☎ 2060)

COOKE, Diana, Lady; Diana; da of Maj-Gen Sir Maxwell Perceval, KCB, DSO, JP; *m* 1932, Maj Sir Charles Arthur John Cooke, 11 Bt (d 1978); 1 s, 1 da; *Style* - Diana, Lady Cooke; 15 The Esplanade, Fowey, Cornwall

COOKE, Lt-Col Sir David William Perceval; 12 Bt (E 1661), of Wheatley Hall, Yorks; s of Sir Charles Cooke, 11 Bt (d 1978); *b* 28 April 1935; *Educ* Wellington, Sandhurst; *m* 1959, Margaret Frances, nee Skinner; 3 da; *Heir* kinsman, Edmund Cooke-Yarborough; *Career* 4/7 Royal Dragoon Gds 1955, Lt-Col 1977, Cmdg Offr 25 Transport and Movemts Regt Roy Corps of Transport 1977-; *Style* - Lt-Col Sir David Cooke, Bt; 20 Oriel grove, Moreton-in-Marsh, Glos (☎ 0608 50703)

COOKE, Gilbert Andrew; s of Gilbert Cooke; *b* 7 March 1923; *Educ* Bournemouth Sch; *m* 1949, Katherine McGovern; 1 s, 1 da; *Career* chartered accountant (FCA), md C T Bowring & Co Ltd 1976- (dir 1969-); *Style* - Gilbert Cooke Esq; Kilmarth, Onslow rd, Burwood Park, Walton-on-Thames, Surrey (☎ Walton 40451)

COOKE, Air Vice-Marshal John Nigel Carlyle; OBE (1954), QHP (1979); s of Air Marshal Sir Cyril Cooke, KCB, CBE; *b* 16 Jan 1922; *Educ* Felsted Sch, St Mary's Hosp Paddington; *m* 1958, Elizabeth Helena Murray Johnstone; 2 s, 1 da; *Career* prof of Aviation Medicine 1974-79, Dean of Air Force Medicine 1979-; *Style* - Air Vice-Marshal John Cooke, OBE, QHP; 4 Lincoln close, Stoke Mandeville, Bucks (☎ 3852)

COOKE, His Honour Judge; (Richard) Kenneth; OBE (1945); s of Richard Cooke; *b* 17 March 1917; *Educ* Sebright Sch Wolverley, Birmingham U; *m* 1945, Gwendoline Mary Black; *Career* slr 1939, practising 1945-52, Metropolitan Stipendiary Magistrate 1970, Recorder of the Crown Court 1972-1980, a Circuit Judge (SE) 1980-; *Style* - His Honour Judge Cooke, OBE; 8 St Paul's sq, Church rd, Bromley, Kent (☎ 01 464 6761)

COOKE, (William) Peter; s of late Douglas Edgar Cooke, MC; *b* 1 Feb 1932; *Educ* Kingswood Sch, Merton Oxford; *m* 1957, Maureen Elizabeth, nee Haslam-Fox; 2 s, 2 da; *Career* banker, joined Bank of England 1955, head of Banking Supervision 1976-; *Style* - William Cooke Esq; Heathside, Fulmer Way, Gerrards Cross, Bucks

COOKE, Rt Hon Mr Justice; Rt Hon Sir Robin Brunskill; PC (1977); s of Philip Brunskill Cooke; *b* 9 May 1926; *Educ* Wanganui Collegiate Sch, Victoria Univ Coll Wellington NZ, Gonville and Caius Cambridge; *m* 1952, Phyllis Annette

Miller; 3 s; *Career* barr 1954, practised NZ 1955-72, QC 1964, Judge of Court of Appeal of New Zealand 1976-, kt 1977; *Style* - The Rt Hon Mr Justice Cooke; 4 Homewood cresc, Karori, Wellington, New Zealand (☎ 768 059)

COOKE, Raymond Edgar; OBE; s of late Edgar Jonathan Cooke; *b* 14 Feb 1925; *Educ* London U; *m* 1948 (m dis 1968), Marjorie Evelyn; 1 s, 1 da; *Career* former designs engineer BBC, tech dir Wharfedale Wireless Works Ltd 1955-61, md KEF Electronics Ltd 1961-, FRSA, FBKSTS, FAES; *Style* - Raymond Cooke Esq, OBE; Kingswood Lodge, Nevill pk, Tunbridge Wells, Kent (☎ 31843)

COOKE, Sir Robert Gordon; s of late Robert V Cooke; *b* 29 May 1930; *Educ* Harrow, Ch Ch Oxford; *m* 1966, Jenifer Patricia Evelyn, nee King; 1 s, 1 da; *Career* MP (C) Bristol W 1957-1979, former Parly Priv Sec to Mins of State Home Office, of Health, of Works; dir Westward Television 1970-, memb Historic Bldgs Council for England, special adviser on Palace of Westminster to Sec of State for the Environment 1979-, kt 1979; *Style* - Sir Robert Cooke; Athelhampton, Dorchester, Dorset (☎ Puddletown 363)

COOKE, Hon Mrs (Sarah Myfida Mary); *née* Tyrell-Kenyon; MBE (1952); da of 4 Baron Kenyon (d 1927); *b* 1917; *m* 1966, Col Desmond Aubrey Robert Bancroft Cooke, late 13/18 Hussars; *Career* formerly in VAD; *Style* - The Hon Mrs Cooke; 10 Guthrie st, SW3

COOKE, Tom Harry; s of late Tom Cooke; *b* 26 March 1923; *Educ* Bacup and Rawtenstall G S; *m* 12, Jean Margaret, nee Taylor; 4 da; *Career* journalist 1939, ed-in-ch and dir St Regis (formerly Tillotsons) Newspapers 1965-, gp ed dir St Regis Newspapers Ltd 1979-, former pres Guild of British Newspaper Editors, memb Press Council; *Style* - Tom Cooke Esq; St Regis Newspapers Ltd, Mealhouse lane, Bolton, Lancs; 2 Hill Side, Bolton, Lancs (☎ 492170)

COOKE-YARBOROUGH, Edmund Harry; s of late George Cooke-Yarborough; kinsman and hp of Sir David Cooke, 12 Bt; *b* 25 Dec 1918; *Educ* Ch Ch Oxford; *m* 1952, Anthea Katharine, nee Dixon; 1 s, 1 da; *Career* Dep Ch Scientist UK Atomic Authority; *Style* - Edmund Cooke-Yarborough Esq; Lincoln Lodge, Longworth, nr Abingdon, Oxon

COOLEY, Sir Alan Sydenham; CBE (1972); s of Hector Cooley; *b* 17 Sept 1920; *Educ* Geelong G S, Melbourne U; *m* 1949, Nancie Chisholm Young; 4 da; *Career* kt 1976, chm Australian Public Service Bd 1971-77, sec Dept of Productivity 1977-; *Style* - Sir Alan Cooley, CBE; Dept of Productivity, Anzac Park W Building, Constitution av, Canberra, ACT 2600, Australia (☎ 48 2743)

COOLS-LARTIGUE, Sir Louis; OBE (1955); s of Theodore Cools-Lartigue; *b* 18 Jan 1905; *Educ* Convents of St Lucia and Dominica, Dominica G S; *m* 1932, Eugene, nee Royer; 2 s, 4 da; *Career* Dominica Civil Service 1924, Ch Sec Windward Islands 1951, ret 1960, Gov of Dominica 1967-78, KStJ 1975, kt 1968; *Style* - Sir Louis Cools-Lartigue, OBE; 7 Virgin lane, Roseau, Commonwealth of Dominica, West Indies

COOMBE, John David; s of Sidney Coombe; *b* 17 March 1945; *Educ* Haberdashers' Aske's, London U (BScEcon); *m* 1970, Gail Alicia, nee Brazier; 3 da; *Career* chartered accountant, gp tres The Charterhouse Gp Ltd 1976-; *Style* - John Coombe Esq; Up Yonder, 76 Valley rd, Chorleywood, Herts (☎ Rickmansworth 76817)

COOP, Sir Maurice Fletcher; s of George Harry Coop; *b* 11 Sept 1907; *Educ* Epworth Coll Rhyl, Emmanuel Cambridge; *m* 1948, Elsie Hilda Brazier; *Career* solicitor 1932, dir Dunlop Rubber Co Ltd 1966-70, kt 1973; *Style* - Sir Maurice Coop; 39 Hill st, Berkeley sq, W1 (☎ 01 491 4549)

COOPER OF STOCKTON HEATH, Baron (Life Peer UK 1966); John Cooper; s of late John Ainsworth Cooper; *b* 7 June 1908; *Educ* Stockton Heath Council Sch, Lymm G S; *m* 1, 1934 (m dis 1969), Nellie Spencer; 3 da; m 2, 1969, Mrs Joan Rogers; *Career* MP (L) Deptford

1950-51, pres TUC 1970-71, joined NUGMW 1928, gen sec and tres 1962-73, gen sec and tres National Water Council 1973-77; *Style* - The Rt Hon the Lord Cooper of Stockton Heath; 23 Kelvin grove, Chessington, Surrey (☎ 01 397 3908)

COOPER, Hon Alice Clare Antonia Opportune (Artemis); da of 2 Viscount Norwich; *b* 1953; *Style* - The Hon Artemis Cooper

COOPER, Alexander Paston Astley; s and h of Sir Patrick Cooper, 6 Bt; *b* 1 Feb 1943; *m* 1974, Minnie Margaret, nee Harrison; *Style* - Alexander Cooper Esq; 47 Denholme, Upholland, nr Skelmersdale, Lancs

COOPER, Beryl Phyllis; QC (1977); da of Charles Augustus Cooper; *b* 24 Nov 1927; *Educ* Surbiton H S, Birmingham U (BCom); *Career* Recorder of the Crown Court 1977-, Criminal Injuries Compensation Bd 1978; *Style* - Miss Beryl Cooper, QC; 42 Great Brownings, College rd, Dulwich, SE21

COOPER, Sir Charles Eric Daniel; 5 Bt (UK 1863) of Woollahra, New South Wales; s of Sir Daniel Cooper, 4 Bt (d 1954); *b* 5 Oct 106; *Educ* Harrow, Sandhurst; *m* 1, 1931, Alice Estelle, nee Winfold (d 1952); m 2, 1953, Mary Elisabeth, da of Capt J Graham Clarke; 2 s; *Heir* s, William Cooper; *Career* Major (ret) Royal Dragoons; *Style* - Sir Charles Cooper, Bt; Cranbourne Grange, Sutton Scotney, Winchester, Hants

COOPER, David Jackson; s of late Charles Cooper; *b* 3 Feb 1929; *Educ* Churchers Coll Petersfield, Univ Coll Southampton, Univ Coll N Wales; *m* 1954, Patricia Mary; 3 s, 2 da; *Career* md Forest Thinnings Ltd 1962-, dir Economic Forestry (Hldgs) Ltd 1977-, dir Furniture and Timber Industry Training Bd 1979-, sr v-pres British Timber Merchants Assoc 1980-; *Style* - David Cooper Esq; Candovers, Hartley Mauditt, Alton, Hants (☎ office Alton 83504, home Selborne 293)

COOPER, Lady Diana Olivia Winifred Maud (Diana, Viscountess Norwich); *née* Manners; da of 8 Duke of Rutland, KG, by Violet, da of Col Hon Charles Lindsay, CB (3 s of 24 Earl of Crawford and (7 Earl of) Balcarres); *b* 29 Aug 1892; *m* 1919, Rt Hon Sir (Alfred) Duff Cooper, GCMG, DSO, PC, cr 1 Viscount Norwich 1952 (d 1954); 1 s (present Viscount, the TV presenter John Julius Norwich, *qv*); *Career* actress, celebrated for her performance in Max Reinhardt's 'The Miracle'; authoress of a biographical trilogy 'The Rainbow Comes and Goes', 'The Light of Common Day', and 'Trumpets from the Steep'; perhaps the most celebrated English Beauty of her generation and allegedly the model for (among others) Evelyn Waugh's character Mrs Stitch; *Style* - Lady Diana Cooper; 10 Warwick av, W2

COOPER, Sir Frank; GCB (1979, KCB 1974, CB 1970), CMG (1961); s of late Valentine Cooper; *b* 2 Dec 1922; *Educ* Manchester G S, Pembroke Coll Oxford; *m* 1948, Peggie, nee Claxton; 2 s, 1 da; *Career* Civil Service 1948, dep sec CSD 1970-73, Perm Under-Sec of State N Ireland Office 1973-76, Perm Under-Sec of State MOD 1976-; *Style* - Sir Frank Cooper, GCB, CMG; Delafield, Camden Park rd, Chislehurst, Kent

COOPER, Sir Frank (Francis) Ashmole; 4 Bt (UK 1905) of Shenstone Court, Shenstone, Co Stafford; s of late Sir Richard Cooper, 2 Bt; suc bro 1970; *b* 9 Aug 1905; *Educ* Lancing, King's Cambridge, Univ Coll London (PhD); *m* 1933, Dorothy Frances Hendrika, da of late Emile Deen; 1 s, 2 da (and 1 decd); *Heir* s, Richard Cooper; *Career* former tech dir Cooper McDougall and Robertson Ltd, chm Ashmole Investment Trust Ltd 1969-74; *Style* - Sir Frank Cooper, Bt; La Bastide de la Maraouro, 06490 Tourrettes sur Loup, France

COOPER, Sir Gilbert Alexander; CBE (1964), ED (1943); s of Alexander Cooper; *b* 31 July 1903; *Educ* Saltus G S Bermuda, McGill U Canada; *Career* memb House of Assembly Bermuda 1948-68, memb Legislative Assembly 1968-72, kt 1972; *Style* - Sir Gilbert Cooper, CBE, ED; Shoreland, Pembroke, Bermuda (☎ 5 4189)

COOPER, Lt-Gen Sir George Leslie Conroy; KCB (1979), MC (1953); s of late Lt-Col G C Cooper; *b* 10 Aug 1925; *Educ* Downside, Trin Cambridge; *m* 1957, Cynthia Mary Hume; 1 s, 1 da; *Career* Lt-Col (Cmd Roy Engineers) 4 Div 1966-68, dir Army Staff Duties 1976-79, GOC S E District 1979-81, Adj-Gen MOD 1981-, Col Cmdt RPC 1981-; *Style* - Lt-Gen Sir George Cooper, KCB, MC; c/o Barclays Bank Ltd, 3-5 King st, Reading, Berks

COOPER, Hon Jason Charles Duff Bede; s and h of 2 Viscount Norwich; *b* 27 Oct 1959; *Style* - The Hon Jason Cooper

COOPER, Maj-Gen Kenneth Christie; CB (1955), DSO (1945), OBE (1943); s of E C Cooper; *b* 18 Oct 1905; *Educ* Berkhamsted Sch; *m* 1933, Barbara Harding-Newman; 1 s, 1 da; *Career* 2 Lt Roy Tank Corps 1927, Maj-Gen 1953, Cdr 7 Armoured Div 1953-56, Ch of Staff to CIC Allied Forces N Europe 1956-59, ret; *Style* - Maj-Gen Kenneth Cooper, CB, DSO, OBE; West End House, Donhead St Andrew, Shaftesbury, Dorset

COOPER, Lady Maureen Isabel; *née* Le Poer Trench; da of late 6 Earl of Clancarty; *b* 1923; *m* 1949, Christopher Colin Cooper; 1 s, 1 da; *Style* - Lady Maureen Cooper; El Madronal, San Pedro de Alcantara, Malaga, Spain

COOPER, Sir Patrick Graham Astley; 6 Bt (UK 1821) of Gadebridge, Hertfordshire; s of late Col Clifton Cooper, DSO, RA (gs of 2 Bt); suc kinsman Sir Henry Lovick Cooper, 5 Bt 1959; *b* 4 Aug 1918; *Educ* Marlborough; *m* 1942, Audrey Ann Jervoise, da of late Major D P J Collas, Military Knight of Windsor; 1 s, 2 da; *Heir* s, Alexander Cooper; *Career* former sr assist land cmmr Miny of Ag and Fish, dir Crendon Concrete Ltd Long Crendon 1973-; *Style* - Sir Patrick Cooper, Bt; Monkton Cottage, Monks Risborough, Aylesbury, Bucks (☎ Princes Risborough 4210)

COOPER, Robert Douglas; s of late Peter Cooper; *b* 16 March 1939; *Educ* Daniel Stewart's Coll Edinburgh, Heriot-Watt U; *Career* md Bass Bristol, dir Bass Wales & West Ltd; *Style* - Robert Cooper Esq; Stoneways, Rodmoor rd, Portishead, Bristol BS20 9HZ (☎ 842221)

COOPER, Richard John; s of William George Cooper (d 1979); *Educ* Slough G S; *m* 1950, Margaret Pauline, nee Gould, 1 s, 1 da; *Career* former regional pres (Berks Bucks and Oxon region) Construction Surveyors Inst, dir Farrow Construction Ltd; *Recreations* deep sea fishing, golf, youth work; *Clubs* Eccentric; *Style* - Richard Cooper Esq; Brantwood, 39 Littleton rd, Harrow, Middlesex

COOPER, Richard Powell; s and h of Sir Frank Cooper, 4 Bt; *b* 13 April 1934; *Educ* Marlborough; *m* 1957, Angela Marjorie, nee Wilson; 1 s, 2 da; *Style* - Richard Cooper Esq; Sedgehill Manor, Shaftesbury, Dorset

COOPER, William Daniel Charles; s (by 2 m) and h of Sir Charles Cooper, 5 Bt; *b* 5 March 1955; *Style* - William Cooper Esq

COOPER-HEYMAN, Hon Mrs - Hon Isobel; *née* Pargiter; da of Baron Pargiter, CBE (Life Peer); *b* 1931; *m* 1964, Ernest Cooper-Heyman; *Career* Pharmaceutical Chemist; *Style* - The Hon Mrs Cooper-Heyman; 34 Van Dyke Close, Redhill, Surrey RH1 2DS

COOPER-KEY, Hon Lady (Lorna Peggy Vyvyan); *née* Harmsworth; da of 2 Viscount Rothermere by his 1 w Margaret; *b* 24 Oct 1920; *m* 1941, Sir Neill Cooper-Key, *qv*; *Style* - The Hon Lady Cooper-Key; La Celinotte, Meribel les Allues, Savoie, France

COOPER-KEY, Sir Neill; s of late Capt E Cooper-Key, CB,MVO; *b* 26 April 1907; *Educ* RNC Dartmouth; *m* 1941, Hon Lorna Harmsworth, da of 2 Viscount Rothermere; 1 s, 1 da; *Career* Irish Gds 1939-45, MP (C) Hastings 1945-70, v-chm Associated Newspapers Gp 1971, kt 1960; *Style* - Sir Neill Cooper-Key; The Grange, Ramsden, Oxon; 24 Kensington Heights, Campden Hill rd, W8

COOTE, Sir Christopher John; 15 Bt (I 1621) of Castle Cuffe, Queen's County, Ireland; s of Rear-Adm Sir John Coote, 14

Bt, CB, CBE, DSC (d 1978); *b* 22 Sept 1928; *Educ* Winchester, Ch Ch Oxford; *m* 1952, Ann Georgiana, da of Lt-Col Donald James Handford, RA; 1 s, 1 da; *Heir* s, Nicholas Coote; *Career* late Lt 17/21 Lancers, coffeee and tea merchant; *Style* - Sir Christopher Coote, Bt; Russets, Blackpond lane, Farnham Royal, Bucks

COOTE, Nicholas Patrick; s and h of Sir Christopher Coote, 15 Bt; *b* 28 July 1953; *Educ* Winchester; *m* 1980, Mona, nee Bedelian; *Style* - Nicholas Coote Esq

COPE, Lady; Eveline; da of late Alfred Bishop; *m* 1936, as his 2 w, Sir Mordaunt Leckonby Cope, 16 Bt, MC, (d 1972, when title became extinct); *Style* - Lady Cope; 5 Headbourne Worthy House, Winchester, Hants

COPE, John Ambrose; MP (C) S Glos 1974-; s of George Cope, MC, FRIBA; *b* 13 May 1937; *Educ* Oakham Sch Rutland; *m* 1969, Djemila Lovell Payne, da of Col P V L Payne; 2 da; *Career* personal assist to Chm Cons Pty 1967-70, contested Woolwich E 1970, special assist to Sec of State for Trade and Industry 1972-74, assist Govt whip 1979-; *Style* - John Cope Esq, MP; Bluegates, Berkeley, Glos

COPE, Samantha Mary; da of John Cope and Davina Nutting (resumed maiden name since m dis 1969), da of Edward Nutting (er bro of Rt Hon Sir Anthony Nutting, 3 Bt, PC); Edward Nutting m, as her 2 husb, Lady Rosemary Eliot (da of 6 Earl of St Germans, MC, by his w Lady Blanche Somerset, da of 9 Duke of Beaufort); is a coheiress presumptive to Baronies of Botetourt and Herbert, at present held by 10 Duke of Beaufort, KG, GCVO, PC; *b* 23 Sept 1963; *Style* - Miss Samantha Cope

COPE-STRACHAN, Lady; Joan Penelope; *née* Cope; da of 14 Bt (Cope, of Hanwell, Oxfordshire); assumed surname Cope-Strachan by deed poll 1969; *m* 1949, Sir Duncan Alexander Grant, 13 Bt (d 1961); *Style* - Lady Cope-Strachan; 34 Morehampton rd, Ballsbridge, Dublin 4; Manzanares 22, Madrid 5, Spain

COPISAROW, Alcon Charles; s of late Maurice Copisarow; *b* 25 June 1920; *Educ* Manchester U, Imperial Coll London, Sorbonne (DSc); *m* 1953, Diana Elissa, da of Major Ellis Castello, MC, TD; 2 s, 2 da; *Career* Lt RN, sr ptnr McKinsey & Co Inc 1966-76, memb British National Oil Corpn, chm Gen Cmmrs for Income Tax, dep chm of govs English-Speaking Union, trustee Duke of Edinburgh's Award; *Clubs* Athenaeum; *Style* - Alcon Copisarow Esq; The White House, Denham Village, Bucks

COPLESTONE-BOUGHEY, His Honour Judge; John Fenton; s of late Cdr A F Coplestone-Boughey, RN; *b* 5 Feb 1912; *Educ* Shrewsbury, BNC Oxford; *m* 1944, Gilian Beatrice, nee Counsell; 1 s, 1 da; *Career* barr 1935, former dir Chester Chronicle and Associated Newspapers, a Circuit Judge 1969-; *Style* - His Honour Judge Coplestone-Boughey; 82 Oakley st, SW3 (☎ 01 352 6287)

COPPLESON, Sir Lionel Wolfe; s of Albert Coppleson; *b* New South Wales, 29 May 1901; *Educ* Sydney G S; *m* 1, 1929, Edith Maude, nee Bamford; 1 s, 1 da; m 2, 1972, Marjorie Florence, nee Simpson; *Career* kt 1969, company dir, former chm Custom Credit Corporation Gp; *Style* - Sir Lionel Coppleson; Addenbrooke, 21 Cranbrook rd, Bellevue Hill, NSW 2023, Australia (☎ 36 6475)

COPPLESTONE, Frank Henry; s of late Rev Frank T Copplestone; *b* 26 Feb 1925; *Educ* Truro Sch, Nottingham U; *m* 1, 1950, Margaret Mary, nee Walker (d 1973); 3 s; m 2, 1977, Penelope Labovitch, nee Perrick; 1 s, 1 da (both step); *Career* dir ITV News Ltd 1977-, ITV Publications Ltd 1976-; *Style* - Frank Copplestone Esq; ITV News Ltd, 48 Wells st, W1

CORBALLY STOURTON, Hon Mrs Edward P J - Beatrice Cicely; da of late H E Page, of Wragby, Lincs and Titchwell, Norfolk; *m* 1934, Hon Edward Plantagenet Joseph Corbally Stourton (d 1966, having assumed in 1927, the additional name of Corbally); 1 s, 1 da; *Style* - The Hon Mrs Edward P J Corbally Stourton; The Garden House, Hullavington, Chippenham, Wilts

CORBET, Lt-Col Sir John Vincent; 7 Bt (UK 1808), of Moreton Corbet, Shropshire, MBE (1946), JP (Salop 1957), DL (1961); s of late Archer Corbet (ggs of 1 Bt); suc kinsman Sir Gerald Vincent Corbet, 6 Bt, 1955; *b* 27 Feb 1911; *Educ* Shrewsbury, RMA Woolwich, Magdalene Cambridge; *m* 1, 1937, Elfrida Isobel Francis; m 2, 1948, Doreen Elizabeth Stewart, nee Ritchie (d 1964); m 3, 1965, Annie Elizabeth, MBE, da of James Lorimer, of Christchurch, New Zealand; *Career* RE (ret 1955), High Sheriff of Salop 1966, OStJ; *Style* - Lt-Col Sir John Corbet, Bt, MBE, JP, DL; Acton Reynald, nr Shrewsbury, Salop (☎ Clive 259)

CORBET, Air Vice-Marshal Lancelot Miller; CB (1958), CBE (1944); s of late John Miller Corbet; *b* Brunswick Australia, 19 April 1898; *Educ* Melbourne H S, Scotch Coll Melbourne, Melbourne U; *m* 1924, Gwenllian Elizabeth, nee Powell; 1 s; *Career* RAF 1933, Dep Dir-Gen of Medical Services Air Miny 1956-58, ret, KStJ; *Style* - Air Vice-Marshal Lancelot Corbet, CB, CBE; 24 Hensman st, South Perth 6151, Western Australia (☎ Perth 367 3025)

CORBETT, Hon Mrs; Hon Catherine; *née* Lyon-Dalberg-Acton; da of 3 Baron Acton, CMG, MBE, TD; *b* 30 Sept 1939; *m* 1960, Hon Joseph Corbett, 4 s (but 2 surviving) of 2 Baron Rowallan, KT, KBE, MC, TD; 1 s,1 da; *Style* - The Hon Mrs Corbett; Chittlegrove, Rendcomb, nr Cirencester, Glos

CORBETT, Hon Joseph Mervyn; 4 s but 2 surviving of 2 Baron Rowallan, KT, KBE, MC, TD, DL (d 1977); *b* 22 April 1929; *Educ* Eton, CCC Cambridge; *m* 1960, Hon Catherine Lyon-Dalberg-Acton, da of 3 Baron Acton, CMG, MBE, TD; 1 s, 1 da; *Career* Lt RSF; *Style* - The Hon Joseph Corbett; Chittlegrove, Rendcomb, nr Cirencester, Glos

CORBETT, Hon John Polson Cameron; s and h of 3 Baron Rowallan by his 1 w, Eleanor; *b* 8 March 1947; *Educ* Eton, RAC Cirencester; *m* 1971, (Susan) Jane Diane, da of James Green, of S Linden, Northumberland ; 1 s (Jason b 21 April 1972), 1 da (Joanna b 8 June 1974); *Career* estate agent & farmer; *Recreations* skiing, riding; *Style* - The Hon John Corbett; Rowallan, Kilmarnock, Ayrshire

CORBETT, Hon Robert Cameron; s of 2 Baron Rowallan, KT, KBE, MC, TD, DL; *b* 29 Nov 1940; *Educ* Eton, Ch Ch Oxford; *Style* - The Hon Robert Corbett

CORBETT, Richard Panton; s of Richard William Corbett; *b* 17 Feb 1938; *Educ* Eton; *m* 1, 1962 (m dis 1972), Leila Francis; 1 s; m 2, 1974, Antoinette Sibley; 1 s, 1 da; *Career* md Singer & Friedlander Ltd 1973-, dir Saxon Oil Ltd 1980-, dir First British American Corpn Ltd 1980, Interfinance & Investment Ltd 1974-; *Recreations* tennis, shooting, opera; *Clubs* Boodle's; *Style* - Richard Corbett Esq; 24 Chapel st, SW1 (☎ 01 235 4506)

CORCORAN, His Honour Judge; Percy John; s of late Michael Corcoran of Macclesfield, S Australia; *b* 26 Nov 1920; *Educ* Christian Brothers' Coll Adelaide; *m* 1949, Jean, JP, nee Fowler; 1 s, 1 da; *Career* Roy Australian Air Force 1941-47, barr 1948, former Assist Recorder Blackpool and Blackburn, a Circuit Judge 1970-; *Style* - His Honour Judge Corcoran; 18 Stanstead rd, Caterham, Surrey (☎ 42423)

CORDIAL, Ian Fergusson; s of late John Cordial; *b* 14 Nov 1926; *Educ* Kilmarnock Acad, Edinburgh U (MA); *m* 1953, Anna Hall Scobbie, nee Hood; 1 s, 2 da; *Career* dir Patons & Baldwins Ltd, chm British Hand Knitting Assoc; rugby internationalist; *Style* - Ian Cordial Esq; The Ashes, Barton, Richmond, N Yorks (☎ Barton 232)

CORDINGLEY, Hon Mrs (Emma Geraldine Anne); *née* Wallop; da of Viscount Lymington; *b* 1958; *m* 1981, Gerald, s of T Cordingley and Mrs Mabel Cordingley, of Bridlington, Yorks; *Style* - The Hon Mrs Cordingley; c/o The Old Rectory, Aldon Lane, Offham, Maidstone, Kent

COREN, Alan; s of Samuel Coren; *b* 27 June 1938; *Educ* East Barnet G S, Wadham Oxford, Yale, Berkeley U of California; *m* 1963, Anne Kasriel; 1 s, 1 da;

Career joined Punch 1963, editor 1978-, humourist; *Style* - Alan Coren Esq; 23 Tudor st, EC4

CORFIELD, Sir Frederick Vernon; PC (1970), QC (1972); s of late Brig F A Corfield, DSO, OBE, IA; *b* 1 June 1915; *Educ* Cheltenham Coll, RMA Woolwich; *m* 1945, Elizabeth Mary Ruth Taylor; *Career* barr 1945, MP (C) S Glos 1955-Feb 1974, Min for Aerospace Dept of Trade and Industry 1971-72, a Recorder of the Crown Court 1979-; *Style* - The Rt Hon Sir Frederick Corfield, PC QC; Wordings Orchard, Sheepscombe, nr Stroud, Glos; 2 Paper Buildings, Temple, EC4

CORFIELD, Sir Kenneth George; s of Stanley Corfield; *b* 27 Jan 1924; *Educ* S Staffs Coll of Advanced Technol; *m* 1960; 1 da; *Career* chm Standard Telephones and Cables (N Ireland) 1974-, chm Standard Telephones and Cables Ltd 1979- (dir 1969-), v-pres ITT Europe Inc 1967-, sr offr International Telephone and Telegraph Corpn (UK) 1974-, memb Advisory Council for Applied Res and Dvpt 1981-; *Style* - Sir Kenneth Corfield; 14 Elm Walk, Hampstead, NW3

CORISH, Brendan; TD Wexford 1945; *Educ* Christian Brothers' Sch Wexford; *m* ; 3 s; *Career* v-chm Republic of Ireland Labour Pty 1946-49, Pty Leader 1960-77, former Dep Prime Minister (Tanaiste) and Min for Health and Social Welfare 1973-77, memb Council of State 1964-; *Style* - Brendan Corish Esq, TD; Leinster House, Kildare st, Dublin 2, Ireland

CORK, CLOYNE AND ROSS, 76 (cr 630), 71 (cr 604), 56 Bishop of (cr 600) respectively 1978-; Rt Rev Samuel Greenfield Poyntz; s of James Poyntz; *b* 4 March 1926; *Educ* Portora Roy Sch Enniskillen, Dublin U; *m* 1952, Noreen Henrietta Armstrong; 1 s, 2 da; *Career* deacon 1950, priest 1951, Archdeacon of Dublin and Chaplain to Archbishop of Dublin 1974-78; *Style* - The Rt Rev the Lord Bishop of Cork, Cloyne and Ross; The Palace, Bishop's st, Cork, Eire (☎ Cork 21214)

CORK, Sir Kenneth Russell; GBE (1978); s of William Henry Cork; *b* 21 Aug 1913; *Educ* Berkhamsted; *m* 1937, Nina, nee Lippold; 1 s, 1 da; *Career* FCA, chm Griffin Publications, sr ptnr W H Cork Gully & Co (CA) 1946-, former dir Ladbroke Gp Ltd, Richard Costain Ltd, chm Plantation Hldgs Ltd 1977-78, Lord Mayor of London 1978-79, Alderman Sheriff of the City of London 1975-76, liveryman Worshipful Co of Horners and Worshipful Co of Chartered Accountants in England and Wales, KStJ 1979, one of HM Lts for City of London 1980; *Style* - Sir Kenneth Cork, GBE; Cherry Trees, Grimms lane, Great Missenden, Bucks (☎ Great Missenden 2628)

CORK AND ORRERY, 13 Earl of (I 1620); Patrick Reginald Boyle; sits as Baron Boyle of Marston (GB 1711); also Baron Boyle of Youghal (I 1616), Viscount Dungarvan (I 1620), Viscount Boyle of Kinalmeaky, Baron of Bandon Bridge and Baron Boyle of Broghill (I 1628), Earl of Orrery (I 1660); s of Major the Hon Reginald Courtenay Boyle, MBE, MC (d 1946); suc unc, 12 Earl 1967 (whose ancestor, 5 Earl, gave his name to the astronomical instrument known as an Orrery); *b* 7 Feb 1910; *Educ* Harrow, Sandhurst; *m* 1, 1952, Dorothy Kate, da of Robert Ramsden and formerly w of (1) Marchese Demetrio Imperiati di Francavilla (presumably the Marquessate conferred by King Victor Amadeus III of Piedmont 1779) and (2) G F Scelsi; m 2, 1978, Mary Gabrielle, da of late Louis Ginnett and widow of Kenneth McFarlane Walker; *Heir* bro, Hon John Boyle, DSC; *Career* S E Asia 1941-45 Burma Rifles and Maj Cameronians (Scottish Rifles) (severely wounded), Dep Speaker and Dep Chm of Ctees House of Lords 1973-78, memb of Grand Council Cancer Res Campaign, Hereditary Life Gov and Exec Chm Christian Faith Soc, FRSA 1947; *Clubs* Roy Thames Yacht; *Style* - The Rt Hon the Earl of Cork and Orrery; Flint House, Heyshott, Midhurst, W Sussex

CORKE, Hon Mrs (Shirley Frances); *née* Bridges; da of 1 Baron Bridges, KG, GCB, GCVO, MC, FRS (d 1969), and Hon Katharine, da of 2 Baron Farrer; *b* 1924; *m* 1957, Hilary Topham Corke; 1 s, 3 da; *Style* - The Hon Mrs Corke; Eversheds, Abinger Hammer, Surrey (☎

Dorking 730868)

CORLETT, Gerald Lingham; s of late Alfred Lingham Corlett; *b* 8 May 1925; *Educ* Rossall, Aberdeen U; *m* 1957, Helen, nee Williamson; 3 s, 1 da; *Career* Lt Roy Indian Artillery, md Higsons Brewery Ltd 1966-; *Style* - Gerald Corlett Esq; Hortiack, Kings drive, West Kirby, Merseyside

CORLEY, Sir Kenneth Sholl Ferrand; s of late S W Corley; *b* 3 Nov 1908; *Educ* St Bees Cumberland; *m* 1937, Olwen Mary Yeoman; 1 s, 1 da; *Career* chm and ch exec Joseph Lucas (Industries) Ltd 1969-73 (joined 1927), kt 1972; *Style* - Sir Kenneth Corley; 34 Dingle lane, Solihull, W Midlands (☎ 021 705 1597); Yewtree, Wasdale, Cumbria (☎ Wasdale 285)

CORLEY, His Honour Judge; Michael Early Ferrand; s of Ferrand Edward Corley; *b* 11 Oct 1909; *Educ* Marlborough, Oriel Oxford; *Career* barr 1934, a Circuit Judge 1967-; *Style* - His Honour Judge Corley; 3 Brockley Grove, Hutton, Brentwood, Essex

CORMACK, Hon Mrs (Gwendoline Rita) Jean; da of late 1 Baron Davies; *b* 1929; *m* 1950 (m dis), John McRae Cormack, AFC; 3 da; *Style* - The Hon Mrs Jean Cormack; Plas Dinam, Llandinam, Powys; 19a Clarendon gdns, W9 (☎ 01 289 1931)

CORMACK, Sir Magnus Cameron; KBE (1970); s of William Petrie Cormack; *b* 12 Feb 1906; *Educ* St Peter's Sch Adelaide S Australia; *m* 1935, Mary Gordon Macmeiken; 1 s, 3 da; *Career* farmer, pres Liberal Pty Organisation 1947-49, senator Victoria 1951-53 and 1962-78, Pres of Senate 1971-74; *Style* - Sir Magnus Cormack, KBE; 7 Market ct, Portland, Vict 3305, Australia

CORMACK, Lady Miranda Maxwell; *née* Needham; da of 1 Earl of Kilmuir (d 1967); *b* 1928; *m* 1960, Michael Ormiston Cormack; 2 s, 1 da; *Style* - Lady Miranda Cormack; 31 White Hart Wood, Sevenoaks, Kent

CORMACK, Patrick Thomas; MP (C) Staffs S W 1974-; s of Thomas Charles Cormack; *b* 18 May 1939; *Educ* St James' Choir Sch, Havelock Sch Grimsby; *m* 1967, Kathleen Mary McDonald; 2 s; *Career* former history teacher, MP Cannock 1970-74, memb Roy Cmmn on Historical Manuscripts 1981-, trustee Historic Churches Preservation Trust; *Style* - Patrick Cormack Esq, MP; House of Commons, SW1

CORMIE, John David; s of John George Cormie; *b* 8 Dec 1930; *Educ* City of London Sch, Cambridge U; *m* 1956, Margaret Killer; 2 s, 2 da; *Career* FCA, fin dir Reed International Ltd 1976-; *Style* - John Cormie Esq; 18 Marryat rd, Wimbledon, SW19 (☎ 01 946 0938)

CORNES, John Addis; s of John Frederick Cornes; *b* 16 Aug 1944; *Educ* Eton, Oxford U; *m* 1971, Veronica Mary Alicia; 2 c; *Career* investment dir M & G Dual Trust, M & G Investment Management; *Recreations* walking, watching sport; *Style* - John Cornes Esq; Woodgates Farm, East Bergholt, Colchester, Essex

CORNESS, Colin Ross; s of late Thomas Corness; *b* 9 Oct 1931; *Educ* Uppingham, Magdalene Cambridge, Harvard; *Career* Lt 3 Carabiniers (Prince of Wales) Dragoons Gds, barr 1956, chm and ch exec Redland Ltd 1977- (md 1967-), dir W H Smith & Son Ltd, Chubb & Son Ltd; *Recreations* squash rackets, music, travel; *Style* - Colin Corness Esq; 14 Alexander sq, SW3 (☎ 01 584 5986)

CORNFORD, Sir (Edward) Clifford; KCB (1977, CB 1966); s of John Herbert Cornford; *b* 6 Feb 1918; *Educ* Kimbolton Sch, Jesus Cambridge; *m* 1945, Catherine Muir; 3 s, 3 da; *Career* FRAeS, FEng, Royal Aircraft Establishment 1938, Ch Exec and Perm Under-Sec of State MOD (Procurement Exec) 1975-77, Ch of Defence Procurement 1977-80; *Style* - Sir Clifford Cornford, KCB; Beechurst, Shaftesbury rd, Woking, Surrey (☎ 68919)

CORNFORTH, Sir John Warcup; CBE (1972), FRS (1953); s of J W Cornforth of Sydney Australia; *b* 7 Sept 1917; *Educ*

Sydney H S, Sydney and Oxford Us (DPhil); *m* 1941, Rita, nee Harradence; 1 s, 2 da; *Career* former dir Shell Res Milstead Laboratory of Chemical Enzymology 1962-75, associate prof in Molecular Sciences Warwick U 1965-71, Royal Society Research Prof Sussex U 1975-, jt Nobel Prize winner for Chemistry 1975, kt 1977; *Style* - Sir John Cornforth, CBE, FRS; Saxon Down, Cuilfail, Lewes, E Sussex

CORNOCK, Maj-Gen Archibald Rae; CB (1975), OBE (1968); s of Matthew Cornock; *b* 4 May 1920; *Educ* Coatbridge; *m* 1951, Dorothy Margaret Cecilia Plant; 2 da; *Career* dir of Clothing Procurement 1972-73, dir of Army Quartering 1973-75, Col Cdt RAOC 1976-, chm London Electricity Consultative Council 1980-; *Style* - Maj-Gen Archibald Cornock, CB, OBE; 14 St Johns av, Putney Hill, SW15 (☎ 01 789 5892)

CORNWALL-LEGH, Charles Legh Shuldham; CBE (1977, OBE 1971), AEA (1946), DL (Cheshire 1940); s of Charles Henry George Cornwall-Legh (d 1934, sixth in descent from 16 and last Baron of Burford, so styled although the Barons were never summoned to Parliament; the 16 Baron was himself sixteenth in descent from Richard King of the Romans, Earl of Cornewall and Provence, and Count of Poitou, 2 s of King John; Richard, the f of the 1 Baron, was the Earl of Cornewall's bastard); *b* 10 Feb 1903; *Educ* King's Sch Bruton, Hertford Coll Oxford; *m* 1930, Dorothy Catherine Whitson, nee Scott; 1 s, 2 da; *Career* Flight Lt AAF & RAF 1939-45, High Sheriff Cheshire 1939, JP 1938-74, CC 1949-77, chm Cheshire Police Authority 1957-74; co-heir to Baronies of Grey of Codnor (*see also* 18 Baron Zouche) and Basset (of Sapcote, abeyant since 1378); *Clubs* Carlton, MCC; *Style* - Charles Cornwall-Legh Esq, CBE, AEA, DL; High Legh House, Knutsford, Cheshire (☎ Lymm 3168)

CORNWALLIS, 2 Baron (UK 1927); Wykeham Stanley Cornwallis; KCVO (1968), KBE (1945), MC, JP (Kent), DL; s of 1 Baron (d 1935, whose paternal grandmother was Lady Jemima Mann, da of 5 & last Earl Cornwallis); *b* 14 March 1892; *Educ* Eton, Sandhurst; *m* 1, 1917, Cecily Etha Mary (d 1943), da of Sir James Walker, 3 Bt; 1 s (and 1 da decd); m 2, 1948, Esmé Ethel Alice (d 1969), da of late Capt J Montmorency de Beaumont, 5 Roy Irish Lancers, and widow of Maj Sir Robert James Milo Walker, 4 Bt; *Heir* s, Hon Fiennes Cornwallis; *Career* pres Whitbread Fremlins Ltd, dir Whitbread Investment Co, pres Isherwood Foster & Stacey, former dir Barclays Bank, one of HM Lts for City of London (former HM Lt for City and Co of Canterbury and former Lord Lt of Kent and Custos Rotulorum), JP, DL Kent, KStJ; *Style* - The Rt Hon the Lord Cornwallis, KCVO, KBE, MC, JP, DL; Ashurst Park, Tunbridge Wells, Kent (☎ Fordcombe 212); Dundurn House, St Fillans, Perthshire

CORNWALLIS, Hon Fiennes Neil Wykeham; OBE (1963), DL (Kent 1976); s (by 1 m) and h of 2 Baron Cornwallis, KCVO, KBE, MC; *b* 26 June 1921; *Educ* Eton; *m* 1, 1942 (m dis 1948), da of Lt-Col Lacy Scott; 1 s; m 2, 1951, Agnes Jean, da of Capt H Russell Landale; 1 s, 3 da; *Career* formerly in Coldstream Gds, dir Checkers Ltd, County Quality (Promotion & Marketing Ltd), Northinvest Ltd, chm Town and Country Building Soc 1977-; *Style* - The Hon Fiennes Cornwallis, OBE, DL; Ruck Farm, Horsmonden, Tonbridge, Kent; 25b Queen's Gate Mews, SW7 (☎ 01 589 1167)

CORRIE, John Alexander; MP (C) Bute and N Ayr 1974-; s of John Corrie; *b* 29 July 1935; *Educ* Kirkcudbright Acad, George Watson's Coll, Lincoln Agric Coll NZ; *m* 1965, Jean Sandra Hardie; 1 s, 2 da; *Career* farmer Scotland (formerly New Zealand), contested N Lanark 1964, Central Ayr 1966, MEP 1975-76 and 1977-79, memb EEC Fisheries Ctee, PPS to Sec of State for Scotland 1979-; *Style* - John Corrie Esq, MP; 3d Morpeth ter, SW1; Park of Tongland, Kircudbright; Carlung Farm, W Kilbride, Ayrshire

CORRIGAN, Thomas Stephen; s of Thomas Corrigan; *b* 2 July 1932; *Educ* Beulah Hill; *m* 1963, Sally Margaret, nee Everitt; 2 da; *Career* chartered accountant; pres British Paper & Board Industry Fedn 1975-77, Master Worshipful Co of Makers of Playing Cards 1978-79, chm and md Inveresk Gp Ltd 1974- (md 1971-); *Recreations* tennis, golf; *Clubs* MCC; *Style* - Thomas Corrigan Esq; Inveresk Gp Ltd, Clan House, 19 Tudor st, EC4

CORRY, Sir James Perowne Ivo Myles; 3 Bt (UK 1885) of Dunraven, Co Antrim; s of Sir William Corry, 2 Bt (d 1926); *b* 10 June 1892; *Educ* Eton, Trin Cambridge; *m* 1, 1921 (m dis 1937), Molly Irene, da of late Maj O Bell; 1 s, 2 da; m 2, 1946, Cynthia, da of late Capt F H Mahony and wid of Capt David Polson; 1 da; *Heir* s, Lt-Cdr William Corry, RN; *Career* sometime Sub-Lt RNVR, v-pres Roy Merchant Navy Sch, Roy Alfred Merchant Seamen's Soc, King George's Fund for Sailors; *Style* - Sir James Corry, Bt; Dunraven, Fauvic, Jersey, CI

CORRY, Lt-Cdr William James; s (by 1 m) and h of Sir James Corry, 3 Bt; *b* 1 Aug 1924; *m* 1945, Diana, da of Lt-Col J B Lapsley, MC; 4 s, 2 da; *Career* Lt-Cdr RN (ret); *Style* - Lt-Cdr William Corry, RN; Farm Cottage, Adsdean, Funtington, W Sussex

CORTAZZI, Sir Henry Arthur Hugh; KCMG (1980, CMG 1969); *b* 2 May 1924; *Educ* Sedbergh Sch, St Andrews and London Us; *m* 1956, Elizabeth Esther Montagu; 1 s, 2 da; *Career* Foreign Office 1949, Dep Under-Sec of State FCO 1975-80, Ambass to Japan 1980-; *Style* - Sir Henry Cortazzi, KCMG; 8 Browning close, Randolph av, W9 (☎ 01 286 8904); Ballsocks, Ballsocks lane, Vines Cross, Heathfield, E Sussex

CORVEDALE, Viscount; Benedict Alexander Stanley Baldwin; s and h of 4 Earl Baldwin of Bewdley, *qv*; *b* 28 Dec 1973; *Style* - Viscount Corvedale

CORY, Clinton Charles Donald; s and h of Sir Clinton Cory, 4 Bt; *b* 13 Sept 1937; *Educ* Brighton Coll; *Style* - Clinton Cory Esq

CORY, Sir Clinton James Donald; 4 Bt (UK 1919) of Coryton, Whitchurch, Glamorgan; s of late Sir Donald Cory, 2 Bt; suc bro 1941; *b* 1 March 1909; *Educ* Brighton Coll; *m* 1935, Mary, da of Arthur Douglas Hunt, MD, ChB; 1 s; *Heir* s, Clinton Cory; *Career* Squadron Ldr RAF Vol Reserve; *Style* - Sir Clinton Cory, Bt; 18 Cloisters rd, Letchworth, Herts (☎ Letchworth 77206)

CORY, John; JP (Glam 1961), DL (Glam 1968); s of late John Cory; *b* 30 June 1928; *Educ* Eton, Trin Cambridge; *m* 1965, Sarah Christine, nee Meade; 2 da; *Career* dir John Cory & Sons Ltd, Cardiff Building Soc; former chm Cardiff RDC, Jt MFH Glamorgan 1962-67, KStJ; *Style* - John Cory Esq, JP, DL; The Grange, St Brides-super-Ely, Cardiff (☎ Peterston-super-Ely 760211)

CORY, (Charles) Raymond; s of Charles Cory; *b* 20 Oct 1922; *Educ* Harrow, Ch Ch Oxford; *m* 1946, Vivienne Mary Roberts; 3 da *Career* chm S Glam Health Authority, chm John Cory & Sons Ltd 1965-; *Style* - Raymond Cory Esq; The Coach House, Llanblethian, Cowbridge, S Glam (☎ Cowbridge 2251)

CORY-WRIGHT, Lady Jane Katherine; *née* Douglas; da of 11 Marquess of Queensberry (d 1954); *b* 1926; *m* 1949, David Arthur Cory-Wright, s of Maj Sir Geoffrey Cory-Wright, 3 Bt (d 1969); 3 s; *Style* - Lady Jane Cory-Wright; Jarmins Orchard, Barton St David, Somerton, Somerset

CORY-WRIGHT, Roland Anthony; s and h of Sir Richard Cory-Wright, 4 Bt, *b* 11 March 1979

CORY-WRIGHT, Sir Richard Michael; 4 Bt (UK 1903), of Caen Wood Towers, Highgate, St Pancras, Co London and Hornsey, Middx; s of Capt (Anthony John) Julian Cory-Wright (ka 1944) and gs of Capt Sir Geoffrey Cory-Wright, 3 Bt (d 1969); *b* 17 Jan 1944; *Educ* Eton, Birmingham U; *m* 1976, Veronica Mary, da of James Bolton; 2 s; *Heir* s, Roland Cory-Wright, b 11 March 1979; *Career* Patron of one living; *Style* - Sir Richard Cory-Wright, Bt; Cox's Farm, Winterbrook lane, Wallingford, Oxon

CORYTON, Air Chief Marshal Sir (William) Alec; KCB (1950, CB 1942), KBE (1945), MVO (1919), DFC (1922); s of late William Coryton; *b* 16 Feb 1895; *Educ* Eton, Cambridge; *m* 1925, Philippa Dorothea, nee Hanbury; 3 da (*see Sir Michael Nall, 2 Bt*); *Career* RAF 1917, Air Marshal 1946, Air Ch Marshal 1950, Controller of Supplies (Air) Miny of Supply 1946-50, Ch Exec Guided Weapons 1950-51, ret; dep chm Bristol Siddeley Engines Ltd 1959-64, md Bristol Aeroplane Co Ltd Engine Div 1951, chm and md Bristol Aero-Engines Ltd 1955; *Style* - Air Chief Marshal Sir Alec Coryton KCB, KBE, MVO, DFC; Two Leas, Langton-Matravers, Dorset (☎ Swanage 2009)

CORYTON, Maj Jeffery; MC (1944), JP; s of Capt John Tillie Coryton (d 1965); *b* 16 Aug 1922; *Educ* Eton; *m* 1954, Kathleen, nee Wedgwood; *Career* Maj Rifle Bde (1939-45 NW Europe, ret 1954), JP Cornwall, High Sheriff 1972; *Recreations* field sports; *Clubs* Army and Navy; *Style* - Maj Jeffery Coryton MC, JP; Pentillie Castle, Saltash, Cornwall

COSGRAVE, Lady Louisa; da of 6 Earl Cathcart; *b* 1948; *m* 1975, Norman Kirkpatrick Cosgrave *Style* - Lady Louisa Cosgrave

COSGRAVE, Liam; TD (ie MP) 1943-; s of late William Cosgrave; *b* 1920; *Educ* Synge St Christian Bros, Castlenock Coll Dublin, King's Inns; *m* 1952, Vera Osborne; 2 s, 1 da; *Career* barr 1943, leader Fine Gael Pty 1965-77, Min for Defence 1976, Head of Govt of Ireland (Taoiseach) 1973-77; *Style* - Liam Cosgrave Esq; Beechpark,Templeogue, Co Dublin

COSH, Nicholas John; s of John Henry Cosh; *b* 6 Aug 1946; *Educ* Dulwich, Queens' Cambridge; *m* 1973, Anne Rosemary, da of Lewis Nickolls, CBE (d 1970); 2 s; *Career* professional cricketer Surrey CCC 1968-70, chartered accountant (FCA) 1972, merchant banker, dir Charterhouse Japhet Ltd 1978 (joined 1972-); *Recreations* cricket (Blue 1966-68), golf, bridge, opera, rugby (Blue 1966); *Clubs* MCC (ctee memb), Hawks; *Style* - Nicholas Cosh Esq; 1 Paternoster Row, St Paul's, EC4 (☎ 01 248 3999)

COSLETT, Air Marshal Sir (Thomas) Norman; KCB (1963, CB 1960), OBE (1942); s of late Evan Coslett; *b* 8 Nov 1909; *Educ* Barry G S, RAF Halton and Cranwell; *m* 1938, Audrey Garrett; *Career* Air V-Marshal 1962, Air Marshal 1963, AOCIC Maintenance Command 1963-66, ret, dir Flight Refuelling (Hldgs) Ltd 1966-CEng, FIMechE; *Style* - Air Marshal Sir Norman Coslett, KCB, OBE; c/o Barclays Bank, Sandton City, Sandton, 2196, S Africa

COSTAIN, Sir Albert Percy; MP (C) Folkestone and Hythe 1959-; s of William Costain; *b* 5 July 1910; *Educ* King James G S Knaresborough, Coll of Estate Management London; *m* 1933, Joan Mary, da of John William Whiter; 1 s, 1 da; *Career* kt 1980, chm Richard Costain Ltd 1966-69, FIOB, PPS to Min of Technol 1970, to Chllr of Duchy of Lancaster 1970-72, to Sec of State for Environment 1972-74; *Clubs* Carlton, Walton Heath Golf; *Style* - Sir Albert Costain, MP; 2 Albion Villas, Folkestone, Kent; Inwarren, Kingswood, Surrey (☎ Mogador 2443)

COSTAR, Sir Norman Edgar; KCMG (1963, CMG 1953); *b* 18 May 1909; *Educ* Battersea G S; *Career* Colonial Office 1932, Dep UK High Cmmr Ceylon 1953-57, Australia 1960-62, British High Cmmr Trinidad and Tobago 1962-66, Cyprus 1967-69, Immigration Appeals Adjudicator 1970-; *Clubs* Oxford and Cambridge; *Style* - Sir Norman Costar, KCMG

COTTENHAM, 8 Earl of (UK 1850); Sir Kenelm Charles Everard Digby Pepys; Bt (GB 1784 and UK 1801); also Baron Cottenham (UK 1836) & Viscount Crowhurst (UK 1850); s of 7 Earl (d 1968, 2 cous seven times removed of Samuel Pepys the diarist) and Lady Angela Nevill (decd), da of late 4 Marquess of Abergavenny; *b* 27 Nov 1948; *Educ* Eton; *m* 1975, Sarah, da of Capt S Lombard-Hobson, CVO, OBE, RN; *Heir* kinsman, Charles Pepys, *qv*; *Style* - The Rt Hon The Earl of Cottenham; Lodge Farm, Ringmer, Sussex (☎ 813483/813530/ 813266)

COTTER, Sir Delaval James Alfred; 6

Bt (I 1763) of Rockforest, Cork, DSO (1944); s of Sir James Cotter, 5 Bt (d 1924); *b* 29 April 1911; *Educ* Malvern, RMC Sandhurst; *m* 1, 1943 (m dis 1949), Roma, da of Adrian Rome of Salisbury, S Rhodesia and wid of Sqdn Ldr K A K MacEwen; 2 da; m 2, 1952, Mrs Eveline Mary Paterson, da of late E J Mardon and wid of Lt-Col J F Paterson, OBE; *Heir* n, Patrick Cotter; *Career* late 13/18 Roy Hussars, NW Europe 1944-45, JP Wilts 1962-63; *Clubs* Cavalry and Guards'; *Style* - Sir Delaval Cotter, Bt, DSO; Green Lines, Iwerne Courtney, Blandford Forum, Dorset

COTTER, Patrick Laurence Delaval; s of Laurence Stopford Llewelyn Cotter (ka 1943), s of 5 Bt, and Grace, nee Downing (who m 2, Lt-Col Geoffrey Rittson-Thomas (decd) and m 3, C D Burnett-Hitchcock); hp of unc, Sir Delaval Cotter, 6 Bt; *b* 21 Nov 1941; *Educ* Blundell's and RAC Cirencester; *m* 1967, Janet, da of George Potter; 1 s, 2 da; *Style* - Patrick Cotter Esq; West Aish, Morchard Bishop, Crediton, Devon

COTTERELL, Christopher Sturge; s of Richard Archbold Cotterell; *b* 1 Oct 1932; *Educ* Beaumont Coll; *m* 1960, Angela Mary, da of late Jack Cheshire, OBE; 2 s; *Career* 2 Lt King's Shrophsire L I Korea, Capt 4 Bn (TA), company dir 1961-, jt md Machin & Kingsley Ltd 1979-, pres Timber Trades Fedn 1981, chm Fibre Building Board Fedn 1972-75, memb Inst of Directors; *Recreations* cricket, yeast (bread and beer making); *Style* - Christopher Cotterell Esq; Flat 2, 166 Cambridge st, SW1 (☎ 01 821 7828); Guernsey, 106 Westhall rd, Warlingham, Surrey (☎ Upper Warlingham 2439)

COTTERELL, Hon Mrs (Harriet Pauline Sophia); *née* Stonor; da of late 6 Baron Camoys; *b* 1943; *m* 1965, Jonathan Julian Cotterell; 2 s, 1 da; *Style* - The Hon Mrs Cotterell; 3 Clarendon close, W2

COTTERELL, Henry Richard Geers; s and h of Sir John Cotterell, 6 Bt; *b* 22 Aug 1961; *Style* - Henry Cotterell Esq

COTTERELL, Sir John Henry Geers; 6 Bt (UK 1805) of Garnons, Herefordshire; s of Lt-Col Sir Richard Cotterell, 5 Bt, CBE (d 1978) and 1 w, Lady Lettice, nee Lygon (d 1973, da of late 7 Earl Beauchamp, KG, KCMG, TD, PC and Lady Lettice Grosvenor, da of late Earl Grosvenor, s of 1 Duke of Westminster); *b* 8 May 1935; *Educ* Eton, Sandhurst; *m* 1959, Vanda Alexandra Clare, da of Maj Philip Alexander Clement Bridgewater; 3 s, 1 da; *Heir* s, Henry Cotterell; *Career* offr Roy Horse Gds 1955-61, former v-chm Hereford and Worcs CC; *Style* - Sir John Cotterell, Bt; Garnons, nr Hereford (☎ Bridge Sollars 232)

COTTERELL, Hon Lady - Hon Molly Patricia; *née* Berry; da of late 1 Visc Camrose; *b* 1915; *m* 1, 1936, Capt Roger Charles Chetwode (d 1940), s of 1 Baron Chetwode; 2 s; m 2, 1942 (m dis 1948), 1 Baron Sherwood; m 3, 1958, as his 2nd w, Sir Richard Charles Geers Cotterell, 5 Bt, CBE, TD (d 1978) ; *Style* - The Hon Lady Cotterell; Garnons, Hereford

COTTESLOE, 4 Baron (UK 1874); Sir John Walgrave Halford Fremantle, 4 Bt (UK 1821), GBE (1960), TD; Baron of the Austrian Empire (1816); s of 3 Baron Cottesloe, CB (d 1956); *b* 2 March 1900; *Educ* Eton, Trin Cambridge; *m* 1, 1926 (m dis 1945), Lady Elizabeth Harris, da of 5 Earl of Malmesbury and Hon Dorothy, CBE, da of 6 Baron Calthorpe; 1 s, 1 da; m 2, 1959, Gloria Jean Irene Dunn, da (adopted) of late W E Hill; 1 s, 2 da; *Heir* s, Hon John Fremantle; *Career* chm Battersea Dogs' Home, former DL Co London, chm Tate Gallery 1959-60, South Bank Theatre Bd 1962-77, Arts Council 1960-65, Heritage in Danger 1973-, Thomas Tapling & Co Ltd; *Clubs* Travellers'; *Style* - The Rt Hon The Lord Cottesloe, GBE, TD; 89 York Mansions, Prince of Wales dve, Battersea Park, SW11 (☎ 01 622 9349)

COTTON, Bernard Edward; CBE (1976); s of Hugh Harry Cotton; *b* 8 Oct 1920; *Educ* Sheffield City G S, Sheffield U; *m* 1944, Stephanie Anne, da of Rev A E Furnival; 3 s; *Career* dir Renold Ltd, Baker Perkins Ltd, pres Samuel Osborn & Co Ltd 1978- (chm and ch exec 1969-78); *Recreations* gardening; *Clubs* Cavalry and

Guards; *Style* - Bernard Cotton Esq, CBE; 2 Moorbank rd, Sheffield (☎ 303082)

COTTON, His Honour Judge; John Anthony; s of Frederick Thomas Hooley Cotton; *b* 6 March 1926; *Educ* Stonyhurst, Lincoln Oxford; *m* 1960, Johanna Aritia, da of Johan Adrian van Lookeren Campagne of Holland; 3 s, 2 da; *Career* barr 1949, dep chm W Riding of Yorks Quarter Sessions 1967-71, Recorder of Halifax 1971, of Crown Court 1972, Circuit Judge 1973-; *Style* - His Hon Judge Cotton; 81 Lyndhurst rd, Sheffield (☎ 585569)

COTTON, Sir John Richard; KCMG (1969, CMG 1959), OBE (1947, MBE 1944); s of late J J Cotton, ICS; *b* 22 Jan 1909; *Educ* Wellington, Sandhurst; *m* 1937, Mary Bridget Connors; 3 s; *Career* IPS 1934, HM For Service 1947, cnsllr Brussels 1957-62, consul-gen Sao Paulo 1962-65, Ambass Congo Republic and Barundi 1965-69, ret; adjudicator Immigration Appeals 1970; *Clubs* Army & Navy; *Style* - Sir John Cotton, KCMG, OBE; Lansing House, Hartley Wintney, Hants (☎ 2681)

COTTON, Hon Sir Robert Carrington; KCMG (1978); s of H L Carrington Cotton; *b* 29 Nov 1915; *Educ* St Peter's Coll Adelaide; *m* 1937, Eve Elizabeth MacDougall; 1 s, 2 da; *Career* former pres of Liberal Pty (NSW), memb Senate 1965, Min Industry and Commerce 1975-77, Consul-Gen New York 1978-; *Style* - Hon Sir Robert Cotton, KCMG; Australian Consulate-General, International Bldg, 636 5th av, New York, NY 10020, USA

COTTON, William Frederick; OBE (1976), JP (Richmond 1976); s of William Edward Cotton; *b* 1928; *Educ* Ardingly Coll; *m* 1, 1950, Bernadine, nee Sinclair; 3 da; m 2, 1965, Ann Corfield; *Career* dep md BBC TV 1981 (formerly controller BBC 1); *Style* - William Cotton Esq, OBE, JP; 19 Model Cottages, E Sheen, SW14 (☎ 01 878 2430)

COTTRELL, Sir Alan Howard; FRS (1955); s of Albert Cottrell; *b* 17 July 1919; *Educ* Moseley G S, Birmingham U; *m* 1944, Jean Elizabeth, da of Ernest Harber; 1 s; *Career* former lectr and prof of Physical Metallurgy Birmingham U, Chief Scientific Adviser HM Govt 1971-74 (formerly dep chief), former v-pres Royal Society, V-Chancellor Cambridge U 1977-79, Master Jesus Coll Cambridge 1974-, memb Security Cmmn 1981-, kt 1971; *Style* - Sir Alan Cottrell, FRS; Master's Lodge, Jesus College, Cambridge (☎ 353310)

COTTRELL, Hon Mrs (Fiona Caroline Mary); *née* Watson; da of 3 Baron Manton; *b* 1953; *m* 1978, Mark S Cottrell; *Style* - The Hon Mrs Cottrell

COTTRELL, Henry Claude; s of Henry Cottrell (d 1953); *b* 13 June 1921; *Educ* Lawrence Sheriff Sch Rugby; *m* 1949, Audrey, da of Thomas Hannah (d 1936); 1 s; *Career* Corporal RAF; actuary, former sr ptnr Phillips & Drew, Stockbrokers, chm Property Unit Trust, dir Associated Sprayers Ltd, Caffyns Ltd, French Kier Hldgs Ltd, Watts Blake Bearne & Co Ltd, OStJ 1979; *Recreations* fly fishing; *Clubs* City Livery, Fly Fishers; *Style* - Henry Cottrell Esq; Whitecraigs, Parkfield, Sevenoaks, Kent (☎ 0732 61228)

COTTRELL, James Swinfen; s of Cdr Vincent Swinfen Cottrell (d 1956); *b* 10 Sept 1932; *Educ* Pangbourne Coll; *Career* shipbroker, AICS, dir The Baltic Exchange, Eskglen Shipping Co Ltd, Howe Robinson & Co Ltd, Howe Matheson & Co Ltd, Howe Robinson (Hldgs) Ltd, Matheson Chartering Ltd; *Recreations* sailing; *Clubs* Roy Solent Yacht, Island Sailing, City of London; *Style* - James Cottrell Esq; 41 Queensdale rd, Holland Park, W11 (☎ 01 603 6380)

COTTRELL, Richard John; MEP (C) Bristol 1979-; s of John Charles Cottrell; *b* 11 July 1943; *Educ* Court Fields Sch Wellington Somerset; *m* 1965, Dinah Louise, da of Leonard David; 2 da; *Career* journalist, formerly with Bristol Evening Post and Harlech TV; *Recreations* travel; *Style* - Richard Cottrell Esq, MEP; Combeside, Back lane, Croscombe, Wells, Somerset

COTTS, Sir (Robert) Crichton Mitchell; 3 Bt (UK 1921) of Coldharbour Wood, Rogate, Sussex; s of Sir William Cotts, 1 Bt, KBE, MP (d 1932) and late Agnes, da of Robert Sloane; suc bro 1964; *b* 22 Oct 1903; *Educ* Harrow, Balliol Oxford; *m* 1942, Barbara, da of late Capt Herbert J A Throckmorton, RN (s of late Sir Richard Throckmorton, 10 Bt); 2 s, 3 da; *Heir* s, Richard Cotts; *Career* Maj (ret) Irish Gds; *Style* - Sir Crichton Cotts, Bt; Valley Farm, nr Woodbridge, Suffolk

COTTS, Richard Crichton Mitchell; s and h of Sir (Robert) Crichton Mitchell Cotts, 3 Bt; *b* 26 July 1946; *Educ* Oratory Sch; *Style* - Richard Cotts Esq

COUCHMAN, Dame Elizabeth May Ramsay; DBE (1961, OBE 1941), JP; da of late Archibald Tannock; *b* 1878; *Educ* Univ of Western Australia; *m* 1917, Claude Ernest Couchman (decd); *Career* pres Australian Women's Nat League 1927-45, sr v-pres Roy Commonwealth Soc 1950-61, memb Liberal Pty; *Style* - Dame Elizabeth Couchman, DBE, JP

COULSHED, Dame (Mary) Frances; DBE (1953, CBE 1949), TD (1951); da of Wilfred Coulshed; *b* 10 Nov 1904; *Educ* Parkfields Cedars Derby, Convent of the Sacred Heart Kensington; *Career* Dep Dir War Office 1950, Dir WRAC 1951-54, ADC to HM the King 1951, to HM the Queen 1952-54; *Style* - Dame Frances Coulshed, DBE, TD; 815 Endsleigh Court, Upper Woburn Place, WC1

COULSON, Hon Mrs (Elisabeth Anne); da of Baron Crowther-Hunt (Life Peer); *b* 1947; *m* 1976, Peter John Coulson; children; *Style* - The Hon Mrs Coulson; 37 Deodar rd, Putney, SW15

COULSON, Sir John Eltringham; KCMG (1957, CMG 1946); s of H J Coulson; *b* 13 Sept 1909; *Educ* Rugby, CCC Cambridge; *m* 1944, Mavis Ninette Beazley, da of late Edwin Beazley; 2 s; *Career* Diplomatic Service 1932, Ambass to Sweden 1960-63, Dep Under-Sec of State FO 163-65, Ch of Diplomatic Service Admin 1965, former Sec-Gen of EFTA, pres Hants British Red Cross Soc 1972-79, dir Atlas Copco (GB), Sheerness Steel Co; *Style* - Sir John Coulson, KCMG; The Old Mill, Selborne, Hants

COULTHARD, His Honour Judge; Alan George Weall Coulthard; s of George Coulthard and Cicely, nee Minns; *b* 20 Jan 1924; *Educ* Watford G S; *m* 1948, Jacqueline, da of Dr T James, of Fishguard; 2 s, 2 da; *Career* barr 1959, Crown Court Recorder 1972-81, Circuit Judge (SE) 1981-; contested (Lib) Pembrokes 1964; broadcaster; *Style* - His Hon Judge Coulthard; c/o SE Circuit Office, 4th Floor, Thanet House, 231/2 Strand, WC2 (☎ 01 353 8060)

COULTHARD, Air Vice-Marshal Colin Weall; CB (1975), AFC (1953) and Bar (1958); s of late Wing Cdr George Coulthard; *b* 27 Feb 1921; *Educ* Watford G S, De Havilland Aeronautical Tech Sch; *m* 1, 1941 (m dis), Nora Creighton; 1 s, 2 da; m 2, 1957, Eileen Pamela, da of Frederick Barber; 1 s; *Career* RAF 1941, dir Operational Requirements (1) (RAF) Miny of Defence 1967-68, Air Cdre 1967, Cdr RAF Staff and Air Attaché Washington 1970-72, Air V-Marshal 1972, Defence Sales MOD 1973-75, ret, FRAeS; *Style* - Air Vice-Marshal Colin Coulthard, CB, AFC*; Fiddlers, Old Truro rd, Goonhavern, Truro, Cornwall (☎ Zelah 312)

COUNSELL, Her Honour Judge Hazel; Hazel Counsell; da of Arthur Henry Counsell; *b* 7 Jan 1931; *Educ* Clifton H S, Bristol U; *Career* barr 1956, Recorder of the Crown Court 1976-77, Circuit Judge 1978-; *Style* - Her Hon Judge Hazel Counsell; The Penthouse, Wallcroft, Durdham Park, Bristol (☎ 22144)

COUNSELL, His Honour Judge; Paul Hayward; s of Frederick Counsell; *b* 13 Nov 1926; *Educ* Colston Sch Bristol, Queen's Oxford; *m* 1959, Joan Agnes Strachan; 1 s, 2 da; *Career* slr 1951, barr 1962, Slr-Gen Rhodesia 1963-64, Zambia 1964, a Circuit Judge 1973-; *Style* - His Hon Judge Counsell; c/o Hitchin County Court, Station House, Nightingale rd, Hitchin, Herts (☎ 50011)

COUPER, James George; s and h of Sir Nicholas Couper, 6 Bt; *b* 27 Oct 1977

COUPER, Margaret, Lady; Margaret Grace; da of late Robert Dashwood Thomas of Southwick, Kirkcudbrightshire; *m* 1941, Sir George Robert Cecil Couper, 5 Bt (d 1975); 1 s, 1 da (twins); *Style* - Margaret, Lady Couper; Annery Barton, Monkleigh, Bideford, N Devon

COUPER, Sir (Robert) Nicholas Oliver; 6 Bt (UK 1841); s of Maj Sir George Couper, 5 Bt (d 1975); *b* 9 Oct 1945; *Educ* Eton, RMA Sandhurst; *m* 1972, Curzon Henrietta, da of Maj George Burrell MacKean, JP, DL; 1 s, 1 da; *Heir* s, James Couper; *Career* Maj Blues and Royals (ret); estate agent; *Style* - Sir Nicholas Couper, Bt; 39 Cloncurry st, SW6

COURT, Hon Sir Charles Walter Michael; KCMG (1979), OBE (1946), MLA (Lib) Nedlands 1953-; s of late W J Court of Perth; *b* Crawley, England 29 Sept 1911; *Educ* Leederville State Sch, Rosalie State Sch, Perth Boys' Sch; *m* 1936, Rita, nee Steffanoni; 5 s; *Career* chartered accountant, practised to 1970, former Leader of Opposition W Australia, Premier of W Australia 1974-, Min co-ordinating Economic and Regional Dvpt and Treasurer 1974- kt 1972; *Style* - Hon Sir Charles Court, KCMG, OBE, MLA; 46 Waratah av, Nedlands, WA 6009, Australia

COURTENAY, Lady Camilla Gabrielle; da of late 16 Earl of Devon; *b* 1913; *Style* - Lady Camilla Courtenay; The Briary, Exton, Exeter, Devon

COURTENAY, Hon Camilla Mary; da of Lord Courtenay, *qv*; *b* 1974

COURTENAY, Hon Charles Peregrine; s of Lord Courtenay, *qv*; *b* 14 Aug 1975

COURTENAY, Hon Eleonora Venetia; da of Lord Courtenay, *qv*; *b* 1971

COURTENAY, Hon Sir (Woldrich) Harrison; KBE (1973, OBE 1950), LLD, QC (1974); s of William Courtenay; *b* 15 July 1904; *Educ* Belize H S British Honduras; *m* 1929, Josephine Robinson; 4 s, 1 da; *Career* barr 1936, slr Supreme Court Belize 1937, Speaker House of Reps Belize 1963-74 (formerly of Leg Assembly), Registrar Anglican Diocese 1946-, Chancellor 1956-; *Style* - Hon Sir Harrison Courtenay, KBE, LLD, QC; Cloverleaf Park, Northern Highway, Belize

COURTENAY, Lord; Hugh Rupert Courtenay; s and h of 17 Earl of Devon; *b* 5 May 1942; *Educ* Winchester, Magdalene Cambridge; *m* 1967, Dianna Frances, nee Watherston; 1 s, 3 da; *Career* chartered surveyor, Messrs Stratton & Holborow; *Style* - Lord Courtenay; The Stables House, Powderham, nr Exeter, Devon

COURTENAY, Lady Mary Elizabeth; da of late 16 Earl of Devon; *b* 1910; *Career* State Registered Nurse; *Style* - Lady Mary Courtenay; The Briary, Exton, Exeter, Devon

COURTENAY, Hon Rebecca Eildon; da of Lord Courtenay, *qv*; *b* 1969

COURTOWN, 9 Earl of (I 1762); James Patrick Montagu Burgoyne Winthrop Stopford; also (sits as) Baron Saltersford (GB 1796), Baron Courtown (I 1758), Viscount Stopford (I 1762); s of 8 Earl of Courtown, OBE, TD, DL (d 1975); *b* 19 March 1954; *Educ* Eton, Berkshire Ag Coll; *Heir* bro, Hon Jeremy Stopford; *Style* - The Rt Hon the Earl of Courtown; Beechshade, Cambridge rd, Beaconsfield, Bucks

COURTOWN, Countess of; Patricia; da of late Harry Stephen Winthrop of Auckland, New Zealand; *m* 1951, as his 2 w, 8 Earl of Courtown (d 1975); 2 s, 1 da; *Style* - The Rt Hon the Countess of Courtown; Beechshade, Cambridge rd, Beaconsfield, Bucks

COUSINS, Rt Hon Frank; PC (1965); *b* 8 Sept 1904; *Educ* King Edward Sch Doncaster; *m* 1930, Annie Elizabeth, da of Aldmn Judd; 2 s, 2 da; *Career* Gen Sec TGWU 1959-69, Min of Technol 1964-66, MP (L) Warwicks Nuneaton 1965-67, memb NEDC, chm Community Relations Cmmn 1968-70; *Style* - The Rt Hon Frank Cousins; Danby Ridge, Top st, North Wheatley, Retford, Notts

COUTANCHE, Jurat the Hon John Alexander Gore; s of Baron Coutanche (Life Peer, d 1973); *b* 1925; *m* 1, 1949, Jean Veronica (d 1977), da of late Alexander Thomson Dawson; children; m 2, 1978, Gillian Margaret, da of late Brig John Douglas Fellowes Fisher, CBE; *Career* Lt-Cdr RNR, Jurat of Roy Court of Jersey; *Style* - Jurat the Hon John Coutanche; Clos des Tours, St Aubin, Jersey, CI

COUTTS, Sir Walter Fleming; GCMG (1962, KCMG 1961, CMG 1953), MBE (1949); s of late Rev John William Coutts, MA, DD; *b* 30 Nov 1912; *Educ* Glasgow Acad, St Andrews U, St John's Cambridge; *m* 1942, Janet Elizabeth, CStJ, da of A C Jamieson; 1 s, 1 da; *Career* Colonial Service Kenya 1936, Gov Uganda 1961-62, Gov-Gen and CIC Uganda 1962-63, former Asst V-Chllr (Admin) Warwick U, chm Pergamon Press 1972-74, chm Grindlays (Commercial) Hldgs 1974-78, dir Inchcape (E Africa) Ltd 1970-78, Assam Investments 1964-78, dir Farmington Trust 1971-78, kt 1961; *Style* - Sir Walter Coutts, GCMG, MBE; 19 Malindi st, Willetton, WA 6155, Australia (☎ Perth 457 2995)

COUTTS DONALD, William Frederick James; s of late William Coutts Donald; *b* 27 Sept 1940; *Educ* Westminster Sch, Edinburgh U; *m* 1980, Priscilla Mary, nee Aldington; 1 da; *Career* chartered accountant, dir Horne Bros Ltd 1974-; *Style* - William Coutts Donald Esq; 47 Rosebank, 47 Holyport rd, SW6 (☎ 01 381 3616)

COUZENS, Sir Kenneth Edward,; KCB (1979, CB 1976); s of Albert Couzens; *b* 29 May 1925; *Educ* Portsmouth G S, Caius Cambridge; *m* 1947, Muriel Eileen Fey; 1 s, 1 da; *Career* dep sec HM Treasury (joined 1951) Incomes Policy and Public Finance 1973-77, Second Perm Sec Overseas Finance 1977-; *Style* - Sir Kenneth Couzens, KCB; Coverts Edge, Woodsway, Oxshott, Surrey (☎ Oxshott 3207)

COVACEVICH, Sir (Anthony) Thomas; DFC (1943); s of Prosper Covacevich; *b* 1 March 1915; *Educ* Townsville and Brisbane G Ss; *m* 1944, Gladys Rose, nee Bryant; 1 s, 1 da; *Career* slr Supreme Court of Queensland 1938, company dir, sr ptnr MacDonnells (Cairns, Queensland), kt 1978; *Style* - Sir Thomas Covacevich, DFC; 17 Temora close, Edge Hill, Cairns, Queensland, Australia (☎ 51 4000)

COVENTRY, 11 Earl of (E 1697); George William Coventry; Viscount Deerhurst (I 1697); s of 10 Earl (ka 1940) and Hon Nesta Philipps (whc m 2, 1953, Maj Terence Fisher-Hoch), da of 1 and last Baron Kylsant; *b* 25 Jan 1934; *Educ* Eton, RMA Sandhurst; *m* 1, 1955 (m dis 1963), Marie Farquhar-Médard; 1 s; m 2, 1969 (m dis 1975), Ann, da of Frederick William James Cripps; m 3, 1980, Valerie Birch; *Heir* s, Viscount Deerhurst, *qv*; *Career* late 2 Lt Gren Gds; *Style* - The Rt Hon The Earl of Coventry; Earls Croome Court, Earls Croome, Worcester

COVENTRY, Lady Anne Donne; da of late 10 Earl of Coventry and Hon Nesta Philipps, da of 1 Baron Kylsant; *b* 1922; *Style* - Lady Anne Coventry; Ayton House, Abernethy, Perthshire

COVENTRY, 6 Bishop of (cr 1918), 1976-; Rt Rev John Gibbs; s of late A E Gibbs of Bournemouth; *b* 15 March 1917; *Educ* Bristol U, Western Coll Bristol, Lincoln Theological Coll; *m* 1943, G Marion, da of late W J Bishop of Poole, Dorset; 1 s, 1 da; *Career* ordained 1955, examining chaplain to Bp of Norwich 1968-73, Bp Suffragan of Bradwell 1973-76; *Style* - The Rt Rev The Lord Bishop of Coventry; Bishop's House, 23 Davenport rd, Coventry, W Midlands

COVENTRY, Lady Maria Alice; da of late 10 Earl of Coventry and Hon Nesta Philipps, da of 1 Baron Kylsant; *b* 1931; *m* 1954 (m dis 1968), John Richard Lewes; *Career* resumed maiden name Coventry 1968; *Style* - Lady Maria Coventry; Levant Lodge, Earls Croome, Worcester

COWAN, Maj-Gen David Tennant; CB (1945), CBE (1945), DSO (1942) and Bar (1944), MC (1916); s of Charles Thomas Cowan of Reading; *b* 8 Oct 1896; *Educ* Reading, Glasgow U; *m* 1, 1920, Anne Elliot Dunlop (d 1973); 1 s (ka), 1 da; m 2,

1973, Frances Elisabeth Newall, wid of Lt-Col F H A Stables; *Career* 2 Lt 2 Bn Argyll and Sutherland Highlanders 1915, Cmmd 1/6 Gurkha Rifles 1939, Maj-Gen 1942, Cmmd British and Indian Div British Commonwealth Occupation Force Japan 1945-47, ret 1948, RARO 1948, Cmdt Devon ACF 1949-58, pt-time sec Assoc of Managers of Approved Schs; *Style* - Maj-Gen David Cowan, CB, CBE, DSO*, MC; Ridgecoombe, Penton Grafton, Andover, Hants

COWAN, Hon Mrs; Hon Sheila Mary; da of Baron Lowry, PC (Life Peer); *b* 1950; *m* 1974, Jonathan Austyn Cowan; *Style* - The Hon Mrs Cowan; 22 Westmorland rd, Harrow, Middx

COWANS, Harry Lowes; MP (L) Newcastle Central Nov 1976-; *b* 1932; *m* m; 1 s, 3 da; *Career* former BR Branch Sec, memb Tyne and Wear CC; *Style* - Harry Cowans Esq, MP; 4 Station Cottages, Elysium lane, Bensham, Gateshead

COWARD, Charles Richard; JP (S Westminster 1970); s of late Alfred Coward; *b* 13 Sept 1912; *Educ* Tech Coll; *m* 1938, Catherine Elizabeth, nee Summersby; 1 s; *Career* FCIS, chm S G Whitaker Ltd, Gayqueen Property Co Ltd, James Martin (Contractor) Ltd, Solex Heating Ltd, Master Worshipful Co of Fletchers 1979-80, former pres City Livery Club; *Recreations* tennis, the dog and the country, London City; *Clubs* City Livery, Guildhall; *Style* - Charles Coward Esq, JP; 18b Cadogan ct, Draycott av, SW3 (☎ 01 589 9467); Holbrooks, Ockley, Surrey (☎ Dorking 711132)

COWDEROY, Norman Derrick; s of late Frank Cowderoy; *b* 11 June 1928; *Educ* Kingston G S, Balliol Oxford; *m* 1955, Jennifer Margaret Veryan, nee Coulton; 3 s; *Career* BA; shipbroker; dir H Clarkson & Co Ltd 1966; viticulturalist, founder Rock Lodge Vineyard Sussex 1965, memb English Vineyards Assoc; *Style* - Norman Cowderoy Esq; Rock Lodge, Scaynes Hill, Sussex

COWDRAY, 3 Viscount (UK 1917); Sir Weetman John Churchill Pearson; 3 Bt (UK 1894), TD; also Baron Cowdray (UK 1910); s (twin) of 2 Viscount (d 1933) and late Agnes, da of Lord Edward Spencer-Churchill (5 s of 6 Duke of Marlborough); bro of late Hon Mrs Campbell-Preston, Lady Cranworth and Lady McCorquodale of Newton, also of Viscountess Blakenham; *b* 27 Feb 1910; *Educ* Eton, Ch Ch Oxford; *m* 1, 1939 (m dis 1950), Lady Anne Bridgeman, da of 5 Earl of Bradford; 1 s, 2 da; m 2, 1953, Elizabeth Georgiana Mather, da of Sir Anthony Mather-Jackson, Bt, *qv*; 1 s, 2 da; *Heir* s, Hon Michael Pearson; *Career* PPS to Under-Sec of State for Air 1941-42, chm S Pearson & Son Ltd 1954-77, Capt Sussex Yeomanry; *Clubs* White's, Cavalry and Guards; *Also see Viscountess Blakenham, Hon Mrs Campbell-Preston, Baron Cranworth*; *Style* - The Rt Hon The Viscount Cowdray, TD; Cowdray Park, Midhurst, W Sussex (☎ 2461); Dunecht, Skene, Aberdeenshire (☎ Lyne of Skene 244)

COWDRAY, Lady Anne Pamela; *née* Bridgeman; da of 5 Earl of Bradford (d 1957); *b* 12 June 1913; *m* 1939 (m dis 1950), 3 Viscount Cowdray, TD, DL; 1 s, 2 da; *Style* - Lady Anne Cowdray; 97b Drayton gdns, SW10; Broadleas, Devizes, Wilts (☎ 2035)

COWDREY, (Michael) Colin; CBE (1972); s of late Ernest Cowdrey of Bangalore, India; *b* 24 Dec 1932; *Educ* Tonbridge, BNC Oxford; *m* 1956, Penelope Susan, da of late Stuart Chiesman; 3 s, 1 da; *Career* cricketer, Capt Kent County 1957-71, 112 appearances for England, Capt 23 times, exec Barclays Bank International, local dir Barclays Bank, dir Whitbread Fremlins, liveryman Skinners' Co; *Recreations* golf, shooting; *Clubs* MCC; *Style* - Colin Cowdrey Esq, CBE; Barclays Bank International, 168 Fenchurch st, EC3

COWELL, Alan Christopher; MC (1944); s of Edmund Frederick Cowell (d 1928); *b* 4 Feb 1920; *Educ* St Christopher Sch Letchworth; *m* 1949, Muriel Dorothy, da of late Ben Marsden; 2 s, 1 da; *Career* Maj India Army, dir Electronic Rentals Gp and subsidiary cos 1947-; *Recreations* racing (horse- 'Super Bleuet'), rowing, rugby, wrestling; *Clubs* Army & Navy,

RAC; *Style* - Alan Cowell Esq, MC; Normans, Rusper, Horsham, Sussex (☎ Rusper 452)

COWELL, Roger Housden; s of Ernest Frederick Cowell; *b* 3 Sept 1939; *Educ* King's Sch Rochester; *m* 1963, Margaret Anne, nee Hillier; 1 s, 1 da; *Career* chartered engineer, dir Ozonair Engineering Co Ltd, Climavent SA, Paris; *Recreations* squash, gardening, horology; *Clubs* Rumford; *Style* - Roger Cowell Esq; Rooks Drift, Southfleet, Kent (☎ 047483 2660)

COWEN, John Rutland; s of late John William Cowen; *b* 18 Oct 1931; *Educ* Aldenham; *m* 1, 1955 (m dis 1979), Jennifer Alice; m 2, 1980, Marie Victoria Gwendolyn, da of Cdr Edric Knapton, DSO, DSC; 2 da; *Career* dir General Vacuum Services Ltd, Materic Investments Ltd, Apas Ltd, Cloudbourne Ltd; chm Materic Management Services Ltd 1978-, md Richard Hayes Investments Ltd 1979-, md Myddleton Publishing Co Ltd 1981-, FInstM, FBIM; *Style* - John Cowen Esq; 3 Westbourne Park rd, W2 (☎ 01 229 0676)

COWEN, Hon Mrs (Shelagh Mary); yr da of 1 and last Baron Rank, JP (d 1972), and Hon Laura Marshall (er da of 1 and last Baron Marshall of Chipstead); *b* 14 March 1923; *m* 1, 1945 (m dis 1955), Fred Packard, of Los Angeles; 1 s, 1 da; m 2, 1957, Maj Rosslyn Cowen, MBE; 2 s; *Style* - The Hon Mrs Cowen; Pipers Hill, Sutton Scotney, Winchester, Hants

COWEN, Sir Zelman; AK (1977), GCMG (1977), GCVO (1980), QC (1972); s of late Bernard Cowen; *b* 7 Oct 1919; *Educ* Scotch Coll Melbourne, Melbourne U, New and Oriel Colls Oxford (BCL, MA, DCL); *m* 1945, Anna, da of H J Wittner of Melbourne; 3 s, 1 da; *Career* barr Gray's Inn 1947, Vic 1951, Queensland (Aust) 1971; former Prof of Public Law and Dean of Faculty of Law Melbourne U, V-Chllr U of New England NSW 1967-70, of U of Queensland 1970-77, Chllr and Principal Kt Order of Australia 1977, kt 1976, KStJ (A) 1977, Gov-Gen of Australia 1977-; *Style* - His Excellency Sir Zelman Cowen, AK, GCMG, GCVO, QC; Government House, Canberra, ACT 2600, Australia

COWIE, Thomas; s of Thomas Stephenson Knowles Cowie (d 1960); *b* 9 Sept 1922; *Educ* Bede G S Sunderland; *m* 1, 1948 (m dis 1975), Lillas Roberts, nee Hunam; 1 s, 4 da; m 2, 1975, Mrs Diana Carole Wentworth Evans; 2 da (and 1 step s, 1 step da); *Career* chm and md T Cowie Ltd (Motor Distributor and Finance Co), chm Sunderland Cons Assoc, dir Civic Trust of North East; *Recreations* shooting, walking; *Clubs* Carlton; *Style* - Thomas Cowie Esq; Broadwood Hall, Lanchester, Co Durham

COWIE, Thomas Andrew; s of Thomas Cowie of Broadwood Hall, Lanchester, Co Durham; *b* 17 Feb 1950; *Educ* Rugby, Magdalene Cambridge; *Career* dir T Cowie Ltd; *Recreations* golf, squash; *Clubs* Hawks, Jesters; *Style* - Thomas Cowie Esq; Millfield House, Hylton rd, Sunderland, Tyne and Wear (☎ Sunderland 44122)

COWIE, Hon Lord; William Lorn Kerr Cowie; s of late Charles Renie Cowie, MBE; *b* 1 June 1926; *Educ* Fettes Coll, Clare Cambridge, Glasgow U; *m* 1958, Camilla Henrietta Grizel Hoyle; 2 s, 2 da; *Career* Sub Lt RNVR 1944-47, advocate Scotland 1952, QC (Scot 1967), appointed a Lord of Session with title of Lord Cowie 1977; *Style* - The Hon Lord Cowie; 20 Blacket pla, Edinburgh 9 (☎ 031 667 8238)

COWLEY, 7 Earl (UK 1857); Garrett Graham Wellesley; also Baron Cowley of Wellesley (UK 1828), Viscount Dangan (UK 1857); s of 4 Earl Cowley (d 1962) by his 2 w, Mary Elsie, nee Himes; suc half nephew, 6 Earl, 1975; *b* 30 July 1934; *Educ* S California U, Harvard U (MBA); *m* 1, 1961 (m dis 1966), Elizabeth Suzannne Lennon; 1 s, 1 da; m 2, 1968, Isabelle O'Bready of Quebec, Canada; *Heir* s, Viscount Dangan, *qv*; *Career* investment analyst, formerly with Wells Fargo Bank; dir Bank of America International Ltd (London) 1978- (v-pres and sr investment man Trust Dept San Francisco 1974-78); *Style* - The Rt Hon The Earl Cowley; 53 Holland Park Mews, W11 (☎ 01 727 9378)

COWLEY, Elsie, Countess; (Mary) Elsie; *née* Himes; *m* 1933, as his 2 w, 4 Earl Cowley (d 1962); 2 s (7 Earl & late Hon Brian Wellesley); *Style* - The Rt Hon Elsie, Countess Cowley; 4900 Plumas st, Reno, Nevada 89509, USA

COWLEY, Lt-Gen Sir John Guise; GC (AM 1935), KBE (1958, CBE 1946, OBE 1943), CB (1954); s of Rev Henry Guise Beatson Cowley of Dorchester, Dorset; *b* 20 Aug 1905; *Educ* Wellington, RMA Woolwich; *m* 1941, Irene Sybil, da of Percy Dreuille Millen of Berkhamsted; 1 s, 3 da; *Career* 2 Lt RE 1925, Lt-Gen 1957, Controller of Munitions Miny of Supply 1957-60, Master-Gen of the Ordnance (War Office) 1960-62, ret; chm Bowmaker Ltd 1962-71, Keith and Henderson Ltd 1973-76, former dir C T Bowring & Co Ltd, Alastair Watson Ltd, British Oxygen Ltd, FRSA; *Clubs* Army and Navy; *Style* - Lt-Gen Sir John Cowley, GC, KBE, CB; Whitemoor, Sandy Down, Boldre, Lymington, Hants (☎ Brockenhurst 3369)

COWPER, Sir Norman Lethbridge; CBE (1958); s of Cecil Spencer de Grey Cowper; *b* 15 Sept 1896; *Educ* Sydney G S, Sydney U; *m* 1925, Dorothea Huntly, nee McRae; 3 da; *Career* slr NSW 1923, ptnr Allen Allen & Hemsley 1924-70, former Dir Australian Inst of Political Science, kt 1967; *Style* - Sir Norman Cowper, CBE; Wivenhoe, Millewa av, Wahroonga, Sydney, Australia (☎ 48 2336)

COWPERTHWAITE, Sir John James; KBE (1968, OBE 1960), CMG (1964); s of late John James Cowperthwaite of Edinburgh; *b* 25 April 1915; *Educ* Merchiston Castle Sch, St Andrews U, Christ's Cambridge; *m* 1941, Sheila Mary, nee Thomson; 1 s; *Career* Colonial Admin Service Hong Kong 1941, Sierra Leone 1942-45, fin sec Hong Kong 1961-71, int advr Jardine Fleming & Co Ltd 1972-; *Clubs* Roy Hong Kong Jockey, Roy Hong Kong Golf, Roy and Ancient Golf *Style* - Sir John Cowperthwaite, KBE, CMG; 25 South st, St Andrews, Fife (☎ 74759)

COX, His Honour Judge Anthony; (James) Anthony; s of Herbert Sidney Cox (d 1972); *b* 21 April 1924; *Educ* Cotham Sch Bristol, Bristol U (LLB); *m* 1950, Doris Margaret, da of Vincent Percy Fretwell (d 1933); 3 s, 1 da; *Career* barr 1949, Recorder of the Crown Court 1972-76, Circuit Judge 1976-; *Recreations* golf, sailing, the arts; *Clubs* MCC, Clifton (Bristol), Roy Western Yacht; *Style* - His Hon Judge Anthony Cox; Haldonhay, Lower Court rd, Newton Ferrers, Plymouth, Devon

COX, Bradley Richard; s of Leslie Charles Cox (d 1978); *b* 12 Dec 1936; *Educ* Greenmore Coll; *m* , Patricia; 1 da; *Career* RAF National Service, dir Tavern Furnishings Ltd, Queen's Award for Export 1979; *Recreations* sailing, tennis; *Style* - Bradley Cox Esq; 47 Russell rd, Moor Park, Northwood, Middx

COX, Sir Christopher William Machell; GCMG (1970, KCMG 1950, CMG 1944); s of late A H Machell Cox; *b* 17 Nov 1899; *Educ* Clifton Coll Balliol Oxford; *Career* advr on Education to Sec of State for Colonies 1940-61, advr of Education to Sec for Tech Co-operation 1961-64, Hon Fellow New Coll Oxford 1970 (Fell 1926-70), advr on Education Miny of Overseas Dvpt 1964-70; *Style* - Sir Christopher Cox, GCMG; New College, Oxford

COX, His Honour Judge Edward; (Albert) Edward; s of Frederick Stringer Cox; *b* 26 Sept 1916; *m* 1962, Alwyn Winifred, JP; *Career* slr 1938, princ ptnr Claude Hornby & Cox 1946-76, Recorder of the Crown Court 1972-77, Circuit Judge 1977-; *Style* - His Hon Judge Edward Cox; 38 Carlton Hill, NW8

COX, Lady; Elizabeth Anne Priestley; *née* Marten; *m* 1948, Sir Robert Cox, KCB, sometime ch exec PSA (d 1981); 1 s, 1 da; *Style* - Lady Cox; 2 Marsham st, SW1

COX, Sir (Ernest) Gordon; KBE (1964), TD, FRS (1954); s of Ernest Henry Cox of Bath; *b* 24 April 1906; *Educ* City of Bath Boys' Sch, Bristol U; *m* 1, 192, Lucie Grace (d 1962), da of Charles Baker; 1 s, 1 da; m 2, 1968, Prof Mary Rosaleen Truter, DSc, da of Dr D N Jackman; *Career* reader in Chemical Crystallography Birmingham U 1940, Prof of Inorganic and Structural Chemistry Leeds U 1945-60, Sec Ag Res Council 1960-71, FRIC, FInstP; *Style* - Sir Gordon Cox, KBE, TD, FRS; 117 Hampstead Way, NW11 (☎ 01 455 2618)

COX, Sir Geoffrey Sandford; CBE (1959, MBE 1945); s of Sandford Cox of Wellington, NZ; *b* 7 April 1910; *Educ* Southland H S New Zealand, Otago U New Zealand, Oriel Oxford; *m* 1935, Cecily Barbara Talbot Turner; 2 s, 2 da; *Career* journalist; editor and ch exec ITN 1956-68, dep chm Yorkshire TV 1968-71, chm Tyne Tees TV 1972-74, chm Upitn Inc (USA) 1975-, London Broadcasting Co 1977-81, kt 1966; *Clubs* Garrick; *Style* - Sir Geoffrey Cox, CBE

COX, John; s of Frank Cox; *b* 26 Nov 1946; *Educ* Queen Mary's G S Walsall; *m* 1971, Rosemary Anne, nee Chisolm; 2 da; *Career* FICA, dir E Walters (Ludlow) Ltd 1979-, Heaps of Nantwich Ltd 1977-, Tillies-Paveley Ltd 1978-; *Style* - John Cox Esq; The Forge, Orleton, nr Ludlow, Salop

COX, Air Vice-Marshal Joseph; CB (1957), OBE (1950), DFC (1940); s of Frank Cox (d 1947); *b* 25 Oct 1904; *Educ* Peter Symond's Sch Winchester; *m* 1933, Dorothy, da of late William Thomas; 1 da; *Career* RAF 1928, Station Cdr RAF Finningley 1951-52, AOC RAF Ceylon 1952-55, Air V-Marshal 1955, Sr Air Staff Offr Flying Trng Cmmd 1955-58, ret; *Clubs* MCC, RAF and RAF Reserves and Adastrian Cricket; *Style* - Air Vice-Marshal Joseph Cox, CB, OBE, DFC; Pippins, 19 Highmoor rd, Caversham, Reading, Berks (☎ 472761)

COX, Vice-Adm John Michael Holland; s of late Thomas Cox, MBE; *b* 27 Oct 1928; *Educ* Hilton Hall Natal South Africa; *m* 1962, Anne Garden Farquharson Seth-Smith; 1 s, 1 da; *Career* Britannia Roy Naval Coll 1946, dir Naval Operations and Trade 1973-75, Cdr Standing Naval Force Atlantic 1976-77, Ch of Staff to CIC Naval Home Cmmd 1977-79, Cdr Anti-Submarine Gp 2 and Flag Offr 3 Flotilla 1979, V-Adm 1981-; *Style* - Vice-Adm John Cox

COX, John Stanley; s of Stanley William Cox, FCA,; *b* 21 May 1938; *Educ* St Dunstans College, Catford; *m* 1962, Irene; 1 s, 1 da (marr diss); *Career* Chartered Accountant; Senior partner in Edward Moore & Sons; C A since 1975; formerly in partnership with father (now retired); *Recreations* Rugby football, cricket, squash; *Clubs* Shirley Wanderers RFC, Purley Cricket; *Style* - John Cox Esq; 5 Brambledown rd, Wallington, Surrey

COX, Sir John William; CBE (1946); s of Henry James Cox; *b* 29 April 1900; *Educ* Saltus G S Bermuda; *m* 1926, Dorothy Carlyle, nee Darrell; 3 s; *Career* memb House of Assembly of Bermuda 1930-68, Speaker 1948-68, pres Pearman Waltington & Co Ltd, kt 1951; *Style* - Sir John Cox, CBE; The Grove, Devonshire Parish, Bermuda

COX, Sir Mencea Ethereal; s of James William Cox; *b* 28 Nov 1906; *Career* former Dep Premier and Leader of House of Assembly of Barbados, memb Senate of Barbados, kt 1980; *Style* - Sir Mencea Cox; Ambury, Clapham, St Michael, Barbados, W Indies (☎ 77766)

COX, Norman Ernest; CMG (1973); s of late Ernest William Cox; *b* 28 Aug 1921; *Educ* Lycée Français Madrid, King's Coll London; *m* 1945, Maruja Margarita, nee Cruz; 1 s, 1 da; *Career* HM Diplomatic Service 1945, counsellor (commercial) Br Embassy Moscow 1969-72, Inst of American Studies London U 1972-73, Dip Serv Inspector 1973-74, Ambass to Ecuador 1974-77, to Mexico 1977-; *Style* - Norman Cox Esq, CMG; c/o FCO, SW1

COX, Peter Donald; s of late Edward Donald Cox; *b* 19 Aug 1928; *Educ* RNC Dartmouth; *m* 1953, Philippa Belle, nee Brandon; 1 s, 2 da; *Career* Lt-Cdr RN, ret 1958, exec dir James Pearsall & Co Ltd 1961-78, exec dir Crewhorne Textiles Ltd 1976- (both subsids of Bridport-Gundry Hldgs Ltd); *Recreations* squash, tennis, bridge, philately; *Style* - Peter Cox Esq; Mayfield, West Monkton, Taunton, Somerset (☎ W Monckton 412382)

COX, Sir Trenchard; CBE (1954); s of late William Pallett Cox; *b* 31 July 1905;

Educ Eton, King's Cambridge; *m* 1935, Mary Désirée (d 1973), da of late Sir Hugh Anderson, Master of Gonville and Caius Coll Cambridge; *Career* FRSA, FSA, FMA, former V-Pres RSA and Dir Birmingham Museum and Art Gallery, Dir and Sec Victoria and Albert Museum 1956-66, kt 1961, author of gallery guides and books on art; *Style* - Sir Trenchard Cox, CBE; 33 Queen's Gate gdns, SW7 (☎ 01 584 0231)

COX, Thomas Michael; MP (L) Wandsworth Tooting 1974-; *b* 1930; *Educ* LSE; *Career* MP Wandsworth Central 1970-74, former Asst Gov Whip, Lord Cmmr of the Treasury 1977-79; *Style* - Thomas Cox Esq, MP; House of Commons, SW1

COXEN, Lady; Kathleen Alice; da of late Edward Doncaster of Snettisham, Norfolk; *m* 1912, Maj Sir William George Coxen, 1 Bt (Lord Mayor of London 1939-40, d 1946 when title became extinct); *Style* - Lady Coxen; 8a Wellswood Park, Torquay, Devon

COXWELL-ROGERS, Maj-Gen Norman Annesley; CB (1944), CBE (1943, OBE 1933), DSO (1940); s of late Henry Annesley Coxwell-Rogers; *b* 29 May 1896; *Educ* Cheltenham, RMA Woolwich; *m* 1928, Diana, da of John Coston; 1 s, 1 da; *Career* 2 Lt RE 1915, Maj-Gen 1943, served France, N Africa, Sicily, Italy 1939-45, ret 1946, Col Cmdt RE 1956-61; *Style* - Maj-Gen Norman Coxwell-Rogers, CB, CBE, DSO; Rossley Manor, nr Cheltenham, Glos (☎ Andoversford 233)

COZENS, Brig Dame (Florence) Barbara; DBE (1963), RRC (1958); da of late Capt A Cozens, S Staffs Regt; *b* 24 Dec 1906; *Educ* Seabury Sch Worthing, Nightingale Sch St Thomas Hosp (nurse training); *Career* QAIMNS 1933, Brig 1960, Matron-in-Ch and Dir of Army Nursing Servs 1960-64, ret, Ch Nursing Offr St John Amb Brigade 1965-72, Col Cmdt QARANC 1966-69, DStJ; *Style* - Brig Dame Barbara Cozens, DBE, RRC; 174 Old Dover rd, Canterbury, Kent

COZENS, Air Cdre Henry Iliffe; CB (1946), AFC (1939); s of Samuel George Cozens (d 1940); *b* 13 March 1904; *Educ* St Dunstans Coll, Downing Cambridge; *m* 1956, Gillian Mary, da of Owen Rupert Pigott (d 1965); 1 s, 2 da; *Career* Air Cdre RAF 1949, Dir of Plans Air Miny 1949-1951, SHAPE 1951-54, Air Offr Admin Home Cmmd 1954, ret 1956, bursar Ashorne Hill Coll Br Steel Fedn 1957-70; *Recreations* music, current affairs; *Clubs* RAF; *Style* - Air Cdre Henry Cozens, CB, AFC; Horley Manor, Banbury, Oxon (☎ Wroxton St Mary 256)

COZENS-HARDY, Hon Beryl Gladys; OBE (1971), JP (Norfolk); da of late 3 Baron Cozens-Hardy; *b* 1911; *Career* chm World Ctee, World Assoc of Girl Guides and Girl Scouts 1972-75; *Style* - The Hon Beryl Cozens-Hardy, OBE, JP; The Glebe, Letheringsett, Holt, Norfolk

CRABTREE, John Raymond; s of late Harold Crabtree; *b* 1 May 1925; *Educ* Emanuel Sch, Christ's Cambridge; *m* 1959, Evelyn Mary, da of Capt Charles Benstead, MC, MA, RN (ret); 3 s; *Career* chartered civil engr, dir PA Management Consultants Ltd 1973- (joined 1955); *Style* - John Crabtree Esq; Bank House, Tanworth-in-Arden, Solihull, W Midlands (☎ Tanworth-in-Arden 2291)

CRACROFT, Air Vice-Marshal Peter Dicken; CB (1954), AFC (1932); s of Lt-Col H Cracroft; *b* 29 Nov 1907; *Educ* Monkton Combe Sch Bath; *m* 1932, Margaret Eliza Sugden Patchett; 2 s; *Career* RAF 1927, Sr Air Staff Offr HQ Coastal Cmmd 1953-55, AOC Scotland and 18 Gp 1955-58, ret; *Style* - Air Vice-Marshal Peter Cracroft, CB, AFC; Alderney House, Burton Bradstock, Bridport, Dorset

CRADOCK, Sir Percy; KCMG (1980, CMG 1968); *b* 26 Oct 1923; *m* 1953, Birthe Marie Dyrlund; *Career* Foreign Office 1954, Ambass to German Democratic Republic 1976-78, Ambass to China 1978-; *Style* - Sir Percy Cradock, KCMG; c/o FCO, SW1

CRADOCK-HARTOPP, Sir John Edmund; 9 Bt (GB 1796), of Freathby, Leicestershire, TD; s of late Francis Gerald

Cradock-Hartopp (s of late Col Edmund Charles Cradock-Hartopp, 2 s of 3 Bt); suc Kinsman, Sir George Francis Fleetwood Cradock-Hartopp, 8 Bt, 1949; *b* 8 April 1912; *Educ* Uppingham; *m* 1953, Prudence, da of Sir Frederick Leith-Ross, GCMG, KCB; 3 da; *Heir* cous, Lt-Cdr Kenneth Alston Cradock-Hartopp, MBE, DSC, RN; *Career* 1939-45 War as Major RE (despatches twice), dir Firth Brown Tools Ltd 1961-76; *Recreations* golf (semi-finalist English Golf Champ 1935, first reserve Eng v France 1935), cricket, tennis, motoring; *Clubs* East India, Devonshire Sports and Public Schools, MCC, Royal and Ancient (St Andrews); *Style* - Sir John Cradock-Hartopp, Bt, TD; The Cottage, 27 Wool rd, Wimbledon Common, SW20

CRADOCK-HARTOPP, Lt-Cdr Kenneth Alston; MBE (1946), DSC (1952), FRGS (1949); s of Maj Louis Montague Cradock-Hartopp (d 1957); hp of cous, Sir John Edmund Cradock-Hartopp, 9 Bt; *b* 26 Feb 1918; *m* 1942, Gwendolyn Amy Lilian, da of late Capt Victor Crowther Upton; 1 da; *Career* Lt-Cdr (ret) RN; 1939-45 War and Korea (commanded HMNZ frigate *Taupo* 1951-52), US Leg Merit 1953; associate memb Inst of Management; *Style* - Lieutenant-Commander Kenneth Cradock-Hartopp, MBE, DSC; Old Barley Mow, Helidon, Daventry, Northants

CRAIB, Douglas Duncan Simpson; CBE (1974), DL (Moray 1974); s of Peter Barton Salsbury Simpson (d 1916); changed name by deed poll 1930; *b* 5 April 1914; *Educ* Aberdeen G S, Dundee H S; *m* 1939, Moyra Louise, da of late Alex Ewan Booth; 1 s, 1 da; *Career* Capt (Seaforth Highlanders); farmer; dir Cromar Nominees Ltd, D & M Craib Ltd; memb Potato Marketing Bd of GB 1968-, Bd of N Scotland Coll of Agric 1970-, Bd Rowett Res Inst 1970-; tstee The MacRobert Trusts Scotland 1970-, former chm of dirs Roy Highland & Agric Soc of Scotland; *Clubs* Farmers (London), Elgin (Moray), Roy Northern & Univ (Aberdeen); *Style* - Douglas Craib Esq, CBE, DL; Stynie House, Fochabers, Morayshire (☎ Fochabers 820 231)

CRAIG, Air Marshal Sir David Brownrigg; KCB (1980, CB 1978), OBE (1967); s of Maj Francis Brownrigg Craig; *b* 17 Sept 1929; *Educ* Radley, Lincoln Coll Oxford; *m* 1955, Elisabeth June Derenburg; 1 s, 1 da; *Career* Cmmd RAF 1951, AOC No 1 Gp RAF Strike Cmmd 1978-80, Vice-Ch of Air Staff 1980-; *Style* - Air Marshal Sir David Craig, KCB, OBE; Heathfield, Firbank lane, Woking, Surrey (☎ 72585)

CRAIG, (Albert) James (Macqueen); CMG (1975); s of James Craig; *b* 13 July 1924; *Educ* Liverpool Inst H S, Queen's Oxford; *m* 1952, Margaret Hutchinson; 3 s, 1 da; *Career* former lectr in Arabic Durham U, For Service 1956, fell St Anthony's Coll Oxford 1970-71, Ambass to Syria 1976-79, to Saudi Arabia 1979-; *Style* - James Craig Esq, CMG; FCO, SW1

CRAIG, Rt Hon William; PC (NI 1963); s of late John Craig; *b* 2 Dec 1924; *Educ* Dungannon Roy Sch, Larne G S, Queen's U Belfast; *m* 1960, Doris Hilgendorff; 2 s; *Career* slr 1952, MP (U) Larne Div Antrim NI Parlt 1960-73, MP (UU) Belfast E 1974-79, Min of Dvpt 1965-66, founder and former leader Ulster Vanguard and Vanguard Unionist Parties; *Style* - The Rt Hon William Craig; 23 Annadale av, Belfast, Northern Ireland (☎ 644096)

CRAIG MCFEELY, Cmdt Elizabeth Sarah Anne; da of late Lt-Col Cecil Michael Craig McFeely, DSO, OBE, MC; *b* 28 April 1927; *Educ* St Rose's Convent Stroud, Anstey Coll of PE; *Career* WRNS 1952, Naval Memb Bd of Management NAAFI 1977-79, Hon ADC to HM the Queen 1979-, Dir WRNS 1979-; *Style* - Cmdt Elizabeth Craig McFeely; Moonrakers, Mockbeggar lane, Biddenden, nr Cranbrook, Kent (☎ Biddenden 291325)

CRAIGAVON, 3 Viscount (UK 1927); Sir Janric Fraser Craig; 3 Bt (UK 1918); s of 2 Viscount (d 1974); *b* 9 June 1944; *Educ* Eton, London U (BA); *Heir* none; *Career* ACA; *Style* - The Rt Hon The Viscount Craigavon; Flat 13, 65 Courtfield gdns, SW5 (☎ 01 373 9834)

CRAIGAVON, Viscountess; (Angela) Fiona; da of late Percy Tatchell; *m* 1939, 2 Viscount Craigavon (d 1974); 1 s (3 Viscount), 2 da (Hon Mrs MacInnes, Hon Mrs MacDonald); *Style* - The Rt Hon the Viscountess Craigavon; 27 Launceston pla, W8

CRAIGEN, James Mark; MP (L and Co-op) Glasgow Maryhill 1974-; s of James Craigen; *b* 2 Aug 1938; *Educ* Shawlands Acad Glasgow, Strathclyde and Heriot-Watt Us; *m* 1971, Sheena Millar; *Career* compositor 1954-61, Asst Sec and Industrial Liaison Offr Scottish Busines Educn Cncl 1968-74, PPS to Sec of State for Scotland 1974-76; *Style* - James Craigen Esq, MP; 38 Downie Grove, Edinburgh 12

CRAIGMYLE, 3 Baron (UK 1929); Thomas Donald Mackay Shaw; s of 2 Baron (d 1944) and Lady Margaret Cargill Mackay (d 1958), da of 1 Earl of Inchcape; *b* 17 Nov 1923; *Educ* Eton, Trin Oxford; *m* 1955, Anthea Esther Christine, da of late E C Rich; 3 s, 3 da; *Heir* s, Hon Thomas Columba Shaw; *Career* FRSA, CStJ, chm Craigmyle & Co Ltd, Claridge Mills Ltd, dir Inchcape & Co Ltd; *Clubs* Roy Thames Yacht, Caledonian, Bengal (Calcutta); *Style* - The Rt Hon The Lord Craigmyle; 18 The Boltons, SW10 (☎ 01 373 3533/3515); Scottas, Knoydart, Inverness-shire

CRAIGTON, Baron (Life Peer UK 1959); Jack Nixon Browne; CBE (1944), PC (1961); s of Edwin Gilbert Izod of Rugby, and Johannesburg, S Africa; assumed surname Browne in lieu of patronymic 1920; *b* 3 Sept 1904; *Educ* Cheltenham Coll; *m* 1, 1936 (m dis 1949), Helen Anne, da of late G J Inglis of Glasgow; 1 s; m 2, 1950, Eileen Humphrey, da of Henry Whitford Nolan of London; *Career* contested (C) Govan Glasgow 1945, MP (C) Govan 1950-55, MP Craigton Glasgow 1955-Sept 1959, PPS to Sec of State for Scotland 1952-55, Parly Under-Sec Scottish Office 1955-59, Min of State SO 159-64, former Pres and Chm City of Westminster Chamber of Commerce, chm Fauna and Flora Preservation Soc; *Style* - The Rt Hon The Lord Craigton, CBE, PC; Friary House, Friary Island, Wraysbury, nr Staines, Middx (☎ Wraysbury 2213)

CRAIK, Lady; Mary Frances; da of late Rt Hon Alfred Lyttelton, KC, MP (s of late 4 Baron Lyttelton, KCMG, PC, FRS by 1 w, Mary, da of Sir Stephen Glynne, 8 Bt; bro of 5 Lord Lyttelton and 8 Visc Cobham) and 2 w, Dame Edith Sophy, GBE (d 1948), da of late Archibald Balfour; sis of late 1 Visc Chandos, KG, DSO, MC, PC; *b* 1895; *m* 1928, Sir George Lillie Craik, 2 Bt, MC (d 1929); *Style* - Lady Craik; 5a Dean's Yard, Westminster, SW1

CRAINER, George Scott; s of George Crainer; *b* 29 April 1936; *Educ* Greenock H S; *m* 1959, Isobel, nee Webster; 2 c; *Career* md Bury & Masco (Hds) Ltd 1975-dir Scapa Gp Ltd 1978-; CA, FCMA; *Style* - George Crainer Esq; 3 Parkstone rd, Barton, Preston, Lancs (☎ 0772 862922)

CRAMER, Hon Sir John Oscar; s of J N Cramer; *b* 18 Feb 1897; *Educ* State Public Schs; *m* 1921, Mary (*see Dame Mary Cramer*); 2 s, 2 da; *Career* md Higgins (Bldgs) Ltd, former Mayor of N Sydney, sr ptnr Cramer Bros Real Estate Auctioneers, MHR (Lib) Bennelong NSW 1949-74, kt 1964; *Style* - The Hon Sir John Cramer; Unit 7, 47a Shirley rd, Wollstonecraft, NSW 2065, Australia

CRAMER, Dame Mary Theresa; DBE (1971); da of William M Earls; *m* 1921, Hon Sir John Cramer, *qv*; *Career* Red Cross; former Pres Mater Hospital Auxiliary, Sydney, New South Wales; *Style* - Dame Mary Cramer, DBE

CRANBORNE, Viscount; Robert Michael James (Gascoyne) Cecil; MP (C) Dorset S 1979-; s and h of 6 Marq of Salisbury, *qv*; *b* 30 Sept 1946; *Educ* Eton, Oxford; *m* 1970, Hannah Ann, da of Lt-Col William Joseph Stirling of Keir, s of Brig-Gen Archibald Stirling of Keir (s of 9 Bt (Stirling-Maxwell, dormant)) and Hon Margaret, da of 13 Lord Lovat; 2 s, 3 da; *Heir* s, Hon Robert Cecil; *Style* - Viscount Cranborne, MP; The Lodge House, Hatfield Park, Herts; Tregonwell Lodge, Cranborne, Wimborne, Dorset

CRANBROOK, 5 Earl of (UK 1892); Gathorne Gathorne-Hardy; also Viscount Cranbrook (UK 1878), Baron Medway (UK 1892); s of 4 Earl, CBE (d 1978) by his 2 w, Dowager Countess of Cranbrook, OBE, JP, *qv*; *b* 20 June 1933; *Educ* Eton, CCC Cambridge, Birmingham U; *m* 1967, Caroline, da of Col Ralph George Edward Jarvis of Doddington Hall, Lincoln, and Antonia (ggda of 3 Earl of Clanwilliam); 2 s, 1 da; *Heir* s, Lord Medway; *Career* FRGS; former sr zoology lectr Malaya U 1961-70, ed Ibis 1973-80, Skinner and Freeman of City of London, OStJ, FLS, FZS; *Style* - The Rt Hon The Earl of Cranbrook; c/o National Westminster Bank, St James's sq, SW1

CRANBROOK, Dowager Countess of; Fidelity; OBE, JP; da of Hugh Exton Seebohm, JP of Hitchin; *m* 1932, as his 2 w, 4 Earl of Cranbrook, CBE (d 1978); 2 s, 3 da; *Style* - The Rt Hon The Dowager Countess of Cranbrook, OBE, JP; Red House Farm, Great Glemham, Saxmundham, Suffolk

CRANE, Sir Harry Walter Victor; OBE (1949), JP (1961); s of William Crane; *b* 12 Feb 1903; *m* 1930, Winefride Mary, nee Wing; 1 s; *Career* regional and national Trade Union official 1934-65, Industrial Relations Consultant 1965-, FREconS, kt 1966; *Style* - Sir Harry Crane, OBE, JP; Riverain, 22 Cliff dve, Radcliffe-on-Trent, Nottingham (☎ Radcliffe-on-Trent 2683)

CRANE, John Lawrence Beale; s of late Walter Fred Crane; *b* 15 April 1921; *Educ* Bedford Sch, St Catharine's Cambridge; *m* 1960, Dorothy Jean, nee Toney; 1 step da; *Career* chartered mechanical engineer, dir Crane Fruehauf Ltd 1960-, pres Commercial Trailer Assoc 1980-; *Style* - John Crane Esq; Topfields, Fakenham rd, Hoe, Dereham, Norfolk (☎ Gressenhall 283)

CRANE, Sir James William Donald; CBE (1977); s of William James Crane; *b* 1 Jan 1921; *m* 1942, Patricia Hodge; 1 s, 1 da; *Career* Met Police 1946, Ch Inspr of Constabulary 1979- (formerly Inspr), kt 1980 *Style* - Sir James Crane CBE; Home Off, 50 Queen Anne's Gate, SW1

CRANLEY, Viscount; Rupert Charles William Bullard Onslow; s and h of 7 Earl of Onslow; *b* 16 June 1967; *Style* - Viscount Cranley

CRANWORTH, 3 Baron (UK 1899); Philip Bertram Gurdon; s of Hon Robin Gurdon (ka 1942, s of late 2 Baron, KG, MC, who d 1964) & Hon Yoskyl Pearson, da of 2 Viscount Cowdray (who m 2, Lt-Col Alistair Gibb and m 3, 1 Baron McCorquodale of Newton, KCVO, PC); *b* 24 May 1940; *Educ* Eton, Magdalene Cambridge; *m* 1968, Frances Henrietta Montagu Douglas Scott, da of late Lord William Walter Montagu Douglas Scott, MC (s of 7 Duke of Buccleuch) and Lady Rachel Douglas-Home (da of 13 Earl of Home); 2 s, 1 da; *Heir* s, Hon Sacha Gurdon; *Career* late Lt Roy Wilts Yeo; *Style* - The Rt Hon The Lord Cranworth; Grundisburgh Hall, Woodbridge, Suffolk

CRATHORNE, 2 Baron (UK 1959); Sir Charles James Dugdale; 2 Bt (UK 1945); s of 1 Baron, TD, PC (d 1977) and Nancy, OBE (d 1969), da of Sir Charles Tennant, 1 Bt, whereby Lord Crathorne is nephew to Baroness Elliot of Harwood, Lady (w of 2 Baron) Wakehurst, also half-nephew to Margot Asquith, Lady (w of 4 Baron) Ribblesdale and Lord (1 Baron) Glenconner; *b* 12 Sept 1939; *Educ* Eton, Trin Cambridge; *m* 1970, Sylvia Mary, da of Brig Arthur Montgomery, OBE, TD; 1 s, 2 da; *Heir* s, Hon Thomas Dugdale; *Career* with Sotheby & Co 1963-66, assist to Pres Parke-Bernet NY 1966-69, James Dugdale & Assocs London (Indep Fine Art Consultancy Service) 1969-, fine art lectr, memb Yorks National Tst; dir Sloane Club Ltd, Radio Tees; FRSA, tstee Captain Cook Tst; *Style* - The Rt Hon The Lord Crathorne; 14 Bedford gdns, W8 (☎ 01 727 9833); Crathorne House, Yarm, Cleveland (☎ Hutton Rudby 700431)

CRAUFURD, Hon Mrs (Caroline Helen); *née* Berry; da of 2 Viscount Kemsley; *b* 1942; *m* 1965, John Peter Houison Craufurd of Craufurdland and Braehead; 2 s, 1 da; *Style* - The Hon Mrs Craufurd; Craufurdland Castle, Kilmarnock, Ayrshire

CRAUFURD, Sir Robert James; 9 Bt (GB 1781), of Kilbirney, North Britain; s of Sir James Craufurd, 8 Bt (d 1970); *b* 18 March 1937; *Educ* Harrow, Univ Coll Oxford; *m* 1964, Catherine Penelope, da of late Capt Horatio Westmacott, RN; 3 da; *Heir* none; *Career* memb London Stock Exchange 1969; *Style* - Sir Robert Craufurd, Bt; Brightwood, Aldbury, Tring, Herts

CRAUFURD, Ruth, Lady; Ruth Marjorie; da of Frederic Corder of Ipswich; *m* 1931, Sir James Gregan Craufurd, 8 Bt (d 1970); 1 s, 2 da; *Style* - Ruth, Lady Craufurd; Brightwood, Aldbury, Tring, Herts

CRAVEN, 7 Earl of (UK 1801); Thomas Robert Douglas Craven; also Baron Craven (E 1665), Viscount Uffington (GB 1801); s (by 2 m) of 6 Earl of Craven (d 1965); *b* 24 Aug 1957; *Educ* Downside; *Heir* bro, Hon Simon Craven; *Style* - The Rt Hon the Earl of Craven; Hamstead House, Hamstead Marshall, Newbury, Berks

CRAVEN, Lady; Marjorie Kathleen Wallis; da of late Alfred Henry Hopkins; *m* 1945, as his 2 w, Sir Derek Worthington Clunes Craven, 2 Bt (d 1946, when title became extinct); *Style* - Lady Craven; Aberfeldie, Peckon's Hill, Ludwell, Shaftesbury, Dorset

CRAVEN, Air Marshal Sir Robert Edward; KBE (1970, OBE 1954), CB (1966), DFC (1940); s of Gerald Craven of Port Elizabeth, S Africa; *b* 16 Jan 1916; *Educ* Scarborough Coll; *m* 1940, Joan Peters; 1 s, 1 da; *Career* RAF 1937, Air V-Marshal 1965, SASO Flying Training Cmmd 1967, SASO Training Cmmd 1968-69, Cdr Maritime Air Forces (AOC 18 Gp) 1969-72, Air-Marshal 1970, ret; *Clubs* RAF; *Style* - Air Marshal Sir Robert Craven, KBE, CB, DFC; Letcombe House, Letcombe Regis, Oxon

CRAVEN, Hon Simon George; s (by 2 m) of late 6 Earl of Craven and hp of bro, 7 Earl; *b* 16 Sept 1961; *Style* - The Hon Simon Craven

CRAWFORD, Sir (Archibald James) Dirom; s of Malcolm Crawford; *b* 24 Nov 1899; *Educ* Winchester, Sandhurst; *Career* Chm W Area Cons and Unionist Assoc 1951-56, Pres 1956-59, Hon Tres 1959-, kt 1957; *Style* - Sir Dirom Crawford; Park House, Over Stowey, Bridgwater, Somerset (☎ Nether Stowey 269)

CRAWFORD, David Gordon; *b* 10 June 1928; *Educ* Ashford G S, LSE; *m* 1953, Anne Sturgeon Burns; 1 s, 3 da; *Career* FO 1956-, Ambass Qatar 1974-78, Consul-Gen Atlanta 1978-81, Ambass to Bahrain (announced 1981); *Style* - David Crawford Esq; c/o FCO, SW1

CRAWFORD, Brig Sir Douglas Inglis; CB (1952), DSO (1945), TD (1942), DL (Merseyside 1979); s of Archibald Inglis; *b* 22 March 1904; *Educ* Uppingham, Magdalene Cambridge; *Career* former dir Roy Insurance Co Ltd, v-chm United Biscuits 1962-74, former chm William Crawford Ltd, chm D S Crawford Ltd, Lord-Lt Merseyside 1974-79, DL Lancs 1951, KStJ 1974, High Sheriff of Co Palatine of Lancs 1969-70, kt 1964; *Clubs* White's, Roy and Ancient Golf (St Andrews); *Style* - Brig Sir Douglas Crawford, CB, DSO, TD, DL; Fernlea, Mossley Hill, Liverpool L18 8BP (☎ Allerton 2013)

CRAWFORD, Eric Oliver; s of John Wilson Crawford of Dundee; *b* 18 May 1933; *Educ* Glasgow Acad; *m* 1963 (m dis 1978), Rosalind Jill, da of Reginald Herbert Diaper Ellwood; 3 da; *Career* chartered accountant; dir Garthmore Investment Ltd 1970-, dir London and Lomond Investment Tst Ltd 1980-, chm Anglo-Scottish Investment Tst Ltd 1968-, chm Scan Data Int Ltd 1971-; *Clubs* City of London, Caledonian; *Style* - Eric Crawford Esq; Sundial House, Maddox lane, Bookham, Surrey

CRAWFORD, Hon Sir George Hunter; s of Frederick Charles Crawford; *b* 12 Dec 1911; *Educ* E Launceston State Sch, Launceston Church G S, Tasmania U; *m* 1, 1936, Helen Zoë (d 1976), nee Henderson; 2 s, 1 da; m 2, 1979, Nancy Jean Garrott, nee Findlay; *Career* barr and slr; Judge of Supreme Court of Tasmania 1958-, kt 1972; *Style* - The Hon Sir George

Crawford; 10a Wentworth st, Launceston, Tasmania 7250, Australia

CRAWFORD, Maj-Gen George Oswald; CB (1956), CBE (1944); s of Cl Arthur Gosset Crawford of Nailsworth, Glos; *b* 1902; *Educ* Bradfield and RMC; *m* 1, Sophie Cecilia (d 1974), da of J C Yorke; 2 s, 1 da; m 2, 1974, Ella Brown of Shalford, Surrey; *Career* 2 Lt Glos Regt 1922, RAOC 1928, Maj-Gen 1955, ADC to HM the Queen 1954-55, Dir of Ordnance Services War Office 1958-61; *Style* - Maj-Gen George Crawford, CB, CBE; Gwyers, Dinton, Wilts

CRAWFORD, Sir John Grenfell; AC (1978), CBE (1954); s of Henry Crawford; *b* 4 April 1910; *Educ* Sydney U, Harvard U; *m* 1935, Jessie Anderson Morgan; 1 da; *Career* economic advr; Sec Aust Civil Service to 1960, Chllr U of Papua and New Guinea 1972-75, of Australian National University Canberra 1976- (Prof 1960-67), Sr Ag Advr World Bank Washington 1967-kt 1959; *Style* - Sir John Crawford, AC, CBE; 32 Melbourne av, Deakin, ACT 2000, Australia

CRAWFORD, Lady Susanna; *née* Montgomerie; da of late 17 Earl of Eglinton and Winton and Ursula, da of Hon Ronald Watson (s of late Baron Watson, Life Peer); *b* 1941; *m* 1963, Capt David Dundas Euing Crawford; 2 s (twins); 1 da; *Style* - Lady Susanna Crawford; Hazyhill, Humbie, E Lothian

CRAWFORD, Sir (Robert) Stewart; GCMG (1973, KCMG 1966, CMG 1951), CVO (1955); s of late Sir William Crawford, KBE; *b* 27 Aug 1913; *Educ* Gresham's Sch Holt, Oriel Oxford; *m* 1938, Mary Katharine, nee Corbett; 3 s (and 1 decd), 1 da; *Career* Foreign Office 1947, Political Resident Persian Gulf 1966-70, Dep Under-Sec FCO 1970-73, chm Ctee of Broadcasting Coverage 1973-74, BBC Gen Advsy Cncl 1975; *Clubs* Oxford and Cambridge; *Style* - Sir Stewart Crawford, GCMG, CVO; 5a Manchester st, W1; Ruperts Elm, Northfield End, Henley-on-Thames, Oxon (☎ 4702)

CRAWFORD, (Prof) Sir Theo(dore); s of late Theodore Crawford; *b* 23 Dec 1911; *Educ* St Peter's Sch York, Glasgow Acad, Glasgow U; *m* 1, 1938, Margaret Donald Green, MD (d 1973); 2 s, 3 da; m 2, 1974, Priscilla Leathley Chater; *Career* Dir of Pathological Services St George's Hosp and Medical Sch 1946-77, Prof of Pathology London U 1948-77, now Emeritus, FRCP, former Pres Roy Coll of Pathologists, kt 1973; *Style* - Sir Theo Crawford; St George's Hosp, SW1; 51 Whitelands House, Cheltenham ter, King's rd, SW3 (☎ 01 730 4428); Garrien, Strathlachlan, Strachur, Argyll (☎ Strachur 205)

CRAWFORD, Vice-Adm Sir William Godfrey; KBE (1961), CB (1958), DSC (1941); s of late H E V Crawford; *b* 14 Sept 1907; *Educ* RNC Dartmouth; *m* 1939, Mary Felicity Rosa, da of late Sir Philip Williams, 2 Bt; 3 s, 1 da; *Career* Lt RN 1929, Rear-Adm 1956, Imperial Defence Coll 1956-58, Flag Offr Sea Training 1958-60, V-Adm 1959, Cdr Br Navy Staff and Naval Attaché Washington 1960-62, ret 1963; Dir Overseas Offices BTA 1964-72; *Clubs* Naval and Military, Roy Cruising; *Style* - Vice-Admiral Sir William Crawford, KBE, CB, DSC; Abbotsford, Uplyme, Lyme Regis, Dorset (☎ Lyme Regis 2756)

CRAWFORD, William Hamilton Raymund; QC (1980); s of Col Mervyn Crawford, DSO, JP, DL (d 1977) of Dunscore, Dumfriesshire; *b* 10 Nov 1936; *Educ* Winchester, Emmanuel Cambridge; *m* 1965, Marilyn Jean, da of John Millar Colville; 1 s, 2 da; *Career* barr 1964, dep chm Ag Land Tribunal 1978, Recorder of the Crown Court 1979; *Recreations* fishing, shooting, hill farming, clocks; *Clubs* Naval and Military, Northern Counties; *Style* - William Crawford Esq, QC; Gilmerston, Dunscore, Dumfriesshire (☎ 285); Kitty Frisk, Hexham, Northumberland (☎ 603482)

CRAWFORD AND BALCARRES, 29 (S 1398) and 12 (S 1651) Earl of; Robert Alexander Lindsay; PC (1972), DL (Fife 1953); Lord Lindsay of Crawford (*ante* 1143), Lord Lindsay of Balcarres (S 1633), Lord Balniel (S 1651), Baron Wigan (UK 1826), Baron Wigan of Pitcorthie, Fife (UK 1974); Premier Earl on Union Roll of

Scotland; Chief of the Clan Lindsay; s of 28 Earl of Crawford and 11 of Balcarres, KT, GBE, FSA and Mary, da of late Col the Rt Hon Lord Richard Cavendish, CB, CMG, PC (gs of 7 Duke of Devonshire) and Lady Moyra de Vere Beauclerk (da of 10 Duke of St Albans); *b* 5 March 1927; *Educ* Eton, Trin Cambridge; *m* 1949, Ruth Beatrice, da of Leo Meyer-Bechtler of Zürich; 2 s, 2 da; *Heir* s, Lord Balniel, *qv*; *Career* former chm Lombard N Central Bank, dir Nat West Bank, v-chm Sun Alliance & London Insurance Gp, First Crown Estate Cmmr 1980-; MP (C) Hertford 1955-74, Welwyn and Hatfield 1974, Min of State for Defence 1970-72, Min of State for For and Commonwealth Affairs 1972-74, chm Historic Buildings Cncl for Scotland; *Style* - The Rt Hon The Earl of Crawford and Balcarres, PC, DL; 107 Frognal, NW3 (☎ 01 431 1584); Balcarres, Colinsburgh, Fife

CRAWFORD AND BALCARRES, Mary, Countess of; Mary Katharine; da of late Col the Rt Hon Lord Richard Cavendish, CB, CMG, PC (gs of 7 Duke of Devonshire) and Lady Moyra de Vere Beauclerk (da of 10 Duke of St Albans); *b* 20 July 1903; *m* 1925, 28 (and 11) Earl (d 1975); 3 s (29 Earl, Hon Patrick & Hon Thomas Lindsay); *Style* - The Rt Hon Mary, Countess of Crawford and Balcarres; Balcarres, Colinsburgh, Fife

CRAWFORD-COMPTON, Air Vice-Marshal William Vernon; CB (1965), CBE (1957), DSO (1943) and Bar (1945), DFC (1941) and Bar (1942); s of William Gilbert Crawford-Compton; *b* 2 March 1915; *Educ* New Plymouth H S New Zealand; *m* 1, 1949 (m dis 1978), Chloe Clifford Brown; 2 da; m 2, 1978, Dolores Perle Goodhew; *Career* RAF 1939, Air Offr in Charge of Admin Nr E Air Force 1962-63, SASO 1963-66, Air V-Marshal 1963, AOC 22 Gp Tech Training Cmmd 1966, ret 1969 *Style* - Air Vice-Marshal William Crawford-Compton CB CBE DSO* DFC*; Church House, Yapton, Arundel, W Sussex

CRAWLEY, Desmond John Chetwode; CMG (1964), CVO (1961); s of Col C G Chetwode Crawley, OBE of Harpenden, Herts (d 1963); *b* 2 June 1917; *Educ* The King's Sch Ely, Queen's Oxford; *m* 1945, Daphne Lesley, da of Sir Vere Mockett, MBE (d 1977); 2 s, 1 da; *Career* ICS 1938-46, IPS 1946-47, Commonwealth Service 1947-65, Diplomatic Service 1963-75, Ambass to Bulgaria 1966-70, Min to Holy See 1970-75, ret; *Clubs* Oxford and Cambridge; *Style* - Desmond Crawley Esq, CMG, CVO; 35 Chartfield av, SW15 (☎ 01 788 9529)

CRAWLEY-BOEVEY, Thomas Hyde Crawley-Boevey; s and h of Sir Thomas Crawley-Boevey, 8 Bt; *b* 26 June 1958; *Style* - Thomas Crawley-Boevey Esq

CRAWLEY-BOEVEY, Sir Thomas Michael Blake; 8 Bt (GB 1784) of Highgrove, Glos; s of Sir Launcelot Valentine Hyde Crawley-Boevey, 7 Bt (d 1928) and Elizabeth Goodeth, da of Herbert d'Auvergne Innes; *b* 29 Sept 1928; *Educ* Wellington, St John's Cambridge; *m* 1957, Laura, da of Jan Pouwels Coelingh of Wassenaar, Holland (d 1979); 2 s; *Heir* s, Thomas Crawley-Boevey; *Career* former shipping agent; ed Money Which? 1968-76, ed Which? 1976-80, Ed-in-Ch 1980-; *Style* - Sir Thomas Crawley-Boevey, Bt; 41 Thornhill rd, N1 (☎ 01 607 5575)

CRAWSHAW, 4 Baron (UK 1892); Sir William Michael Clifton Brooks; 4 Bt (UK 1891); s of 3 Baron (d 1946) and Sheila, da of late Lt-Col P R Clifton, CMG, DSO; *b* 25 March 1933; *Educ* Eton, Ch Ch Oxford; *Heir* bro, Hon David Brooks; *Career* Lord of the Manor of Long Whatton, Patron of the Living of Shepshed; Tres Loughborough Div Cons Assoc 1954-58, Co Cmmr Leics Boy Scouts 1958-; *Style* - The Rt Hon The Lord Crawshaw; Whatton, Loughborough, Leics (☎ Hathern 225)

CRAWSHAW, Sir (Edward) Daniel (Weston); QC (Aden 1949); s of Godfrey Edward Crawshaw of Yorks; *b* 10 Sept 1903; *Educ* St Bees Sch, Selwyn Cambridge; *m* 1942, Rosemary Treffry; 1 s (and 1 decd), 2 da; *Career* slr 1929, barr 1946, Puisne Judge Tanganyika 1952-60, Justice of Appeal Court of Appeal for Eastern Africa 1960-65, Cmmr Foreign Compensation Cmmn 1965-75, kt 1964; *Style* - Sir Daniel Crawshaw, QC; 1 Fort rd, Guildford, Surrey (☎ 76883)

CRAWSHAW, Lt-Col Richard; OBE (1958), TD (1958), DL (Merseyside 1970), MP (L) Toxteth Liverpool 1964-; s of Percy Crawshaw (d 1946); *b* 25 Sept 1917; *Educ* Pendleton G S, Tatterford Sch, Pembroke Cambridge, London U; *m* 1960, Audrey Frances Lima; *Career* barr 1948, 8 Army Cmd Yorks and Lancs Parachute Bn (TA) 1954-57, late Liverpool CCllr *Style* - Lt-Col Richard Crawshaw OBE TD DL MP; The Orchard, Aintree lane, Liverpool, Lancs (☎ 051 526 7886)

CRAWSHAY, Hon Mrs (Harriet Anne Mary Tyrrell); da of 1 Baron Tyrrell (d 1947); *b* 1904; *m* 1, 1930 (m dis 1932, he d 1974), Sir Adrian Holman, KBE, CMG, MC; m 2, 1934, Capt Jack William Leslie Crawshay, MC (d 1950); *Career* assumed by deed poll 1930, the additional Christian names of Mary Tyrrell; *Style* - The Hon Mrs Crawshay; 5 Surrey Cottage, Norfolk Place, Littlehampton, Sussex

CRAWSHAY, Col Sir William Robert; DSO (1945), ERD, TD; s of late Capt J W L Crawshay, MC and late Hon Mrs George Egerton; *b* 27 May 1920; *Educ* Eton; *m* 1950, Elisabeth Mary Boyd Reynolds, da of Lt-Col Guy Reynolds; *Career* V-Lord Lt of Gwent 1979- (DL Glam 1964, Monmouthshire 1970, Gwent 1974), Parachute Regt (TA) 1947-60, ADC to HM the Queen 1966-71, Hon Col 3 RRW (V) Bn 1970-, late chm Welsh Arts Cncl, Pres Welsh Cncl, KStJ 1969, kt 1972 *Style* - Col Sir William Crawshay DSO ERD TD, HM Vice Lord-Lieut for Gwent; Llanfair Court, Abergavenny, Gwent

CREASEY, Gen Sir Timothy May; KCB (1978, CB 1975), OBE (1966); s of late Lt-Col G M Creasey and late Phyllis, da of V-Adm F C B Robinson, RN; *b* 21 Sept 1923; *Educ* Clifton; *m* 1951, Ruth Annette, da of Maj J I H Friend, OBE, MC, DL, JP of Northdown, Kent; 1 s (and 1 decd), 1 da; *Career* Baluch Regt IA 1942, Roy Norfolk 1946, GOC N Ireland 1977-79, CIC UK Land Forces 1980-81, ret; *Clubs* Army and Navy, MCC; *Style* - Gen Sir Timothy May, KCB, OBE; c/o Williams & Glyns Bank Ltd, Holt's Branch, Whitehall, SW1

CREASY, Sir Gerald Hallen; KCMG (1946, CMG 1943), KCVO (1954), OBE (1937); s of Leonard Creasy; *b* 1 Nov 1897; *Educ* Rugby; *m* 125, Helen Duff, da of Reginald Jacomb; 1 s, 1 da; *Career* Colonial Office 1920, Gov and CIC Gold Coast 1947-49, Gov and CIC Malta 1949-54, ret, GCStJ 1970 (KStJ 1949); *Style* - Sir Gerald Creasy KCMG KCVO OBE; 2 Burlington ct, Eastbourne, E Sussex (☎ Eastbourne 27147)

CRESSMAN, Harry Gordon; s of Harry Edwin Cressman (d 1965); *b* 10 Jan 1927; *Educ* Eversfield Prep Sch, Black-Foxe Mil Inst Los Angeles California; *m* 1948, Barbara Ann, nee Brodine, 2 s, 1 da; *Career* tech Sgt US Army Coast Artillery, joined Bristol St Motors Ltd 1948 (dir 1949, md 1951),md chm and ch exec BSC Int 1967-80, dir Heron Motor Gp Ltd 1980 (md 1981), appointed Bd of Heron Corp Ltd 1981; *Recreations* travel, racing, football, boats; *Clubs* American, Carlton, Lyford Cay (Nassau), Port La Galère (France), Ends of the Earth Club; *Style* - Harry Cressman Esq; 34 Petersham pla, South Kensington, SW 7 (☎ 01 584 2731); Eastcote Paddocks, Hampton-in-Arden, Solihull, West Midlands (☎ 067 55 2168); 1 Ave de l'Astrolabe, Port La Galère, Theoule, Alpes Maritimes, France (☎ (93) 90 32 26)

CRESWELL, Sir Michael Justin; KCMG (1960, CMG 1952); s of late Col Edmund Creswell, RE; *b* 21 Sept 1909; *Educ* Rugby, New Coll Oxford; *m* 1, 1939, Elizabeth Colshorn; 1 s; m 2, 1950, Baroness C M thoe Schwartzenberg, da of Baron W H thoe Schwartzenberg en Hohenlansberg, of Santa Barbara, California; 1 s; *Career* Foreign Office 1933, Ambass to Finland 1954-58, Sr Civilian Instr Imperial Defence Coll 1958-60, Ambass to Yugoslavia 1960-64, Ambass to Argentine 1964-69, ret; *Style* - Sir Michael Creswell, KCMG; Copse Hill, Ewhurst, nr Cranleigh, Surrey (☎ Ewhurst 311)

CRESWICK, Sir Alec (Alexander Reid); s of late H F Creswick; *b* 1912; *Educ* Melbourne C of E G S, St John's Oxford; *m* 1, Claudia, nee Palmer; 2 da; m 2, Dinah, nee Hordern; 2 da; *Career* former dir Carlton and United Breweries Ltd, chm Victoria Racing Club Ctee 1969-

77; pastoralist; kt 1974; *Style* - Sir Alec Creswick; Allanvale, Avenel, Victoria 3664, Australia

CREW, Air Vice-Marshal Edward Dixon; CB (1973), DSO (1944) and Bar (1950), DFC (1941) and Bar (1942); s of F D Crew, MB, MRCS, LRCP; *b* 24 Dec 1917; *Educ* Felsted, Downing Coll Cambridge; *m* 1945, Virginia, da of Milton Martin; 1 s; *Career* RAFVR 1939, AOC Central Reconnaissance Establishment 1968-69, Dep Controller Nat Air Traffic Servs 1969-73, Air V-Marshal 1969, ret 1973; DOE Planning Inspectorate 1973-; *Style* - Air Vice-Marshal Edward Dixon, CB, DSO*, DFC*; National Westminster Bank Ltd, 10 Benet st, Cambridge

CREWE, Quentin Hugh; s of Maj Hugh Dodds Crewe, CMG, TD, of HM Consular Serv (né Dodds but changed name by deed poll 1945) and Lady Annabel, nee Milnes, da of 1 and last Marquess of Crewe, KG, PC, JP, by his 1 w, Sibyl (da of Sir Frederick Graham, 3 Bt, and Lady Hermione Seymour, da of 12 Duke of Somerset); the Marquess was rep through his mother of the ancient family of Hungerford; *b* 14 Nov 1926; *Educ* Eton, Trin Cambridge; *m* 1, 1956, Martha Sharp; 1 s (Sebastian b 1958), 1 da (Sabrina b 1959); m 2, 1961, Angela Huth; 1 da (Candida b 1964) (and 1 s decd); m 3, 1970, Susan, da of Capt Richard Cavendish, JP, DL (s of Col Rt Hon Lord Richard Cavendish, CB, CMG, yr bro of 9 Duke of Devonshire, by Lord Richard's w Lady Moyra Beauclerk, da of 10 Duke of St Albans); 1 s (Nathaniel b 1971), 1 da (Charity b 1972); *Career* writer (particularly on food), journalist and farmer; has written for Queen, Vogue, Daily Mail, Sunday Times, Sunday Mirror, Sunday Telegraph, Spectator; *Recreations* travel; *Clubs* Tarporley Hunt; *Style* - Quentin Crewe Esq; 1 Cottesmore Court, W8 (☎ 01 937 0365); Netherset Hey, Madeley, Crewe, Cheshire (☎ Stoke-on-Trent 750300)

CREWE-READ, Hon Mrs (Diana Mary Wroughton); *née* Robins; da of 1 and last Baron Robins, KBE, DSO, ED (d 1962); *b* 11 Nov 1920; *Educ* St Mary's Wantage; *m* 1940, Col John Crewe-Read, OBE; 2 s, 1 da; *Style* - The Hon Mrs Crewe-Read; Croft House, Aston Tirrold, Didcot, Oxon (☎ Blewbury 850318)

CRIBB, Evelyn Francis Theodore; s of Canon Charles Theodore Cribb (d 1976); *b* 24 June 1929; *Educ* Marlborough, Christ's Cambridge; *m* 1956, Jane Howard, da of Ronald Le Grice Eyre (d 1940); 1 s, 2 da; *Career* barrister 1954, various appointments General Motors, GEC, BOC, Co Sec 1971- and dir 1977- Freemans Ltd, Fulham Cncl (Con Leader) 1959-62; *Style* - Evelyn Cribb Esq; 4 Clare Lawn av, E Sheen, London, SW14 (☎ 01-876 7171)

CRICHTON, Lady Cleone Lucinda; da of 6 Earl of Erne; *b* 1959; *Style* - Lady Cleone Crichton

CRICHTON, Lady Davina Jane; da of 6 Earl of Erne; *b* 1961; *Style* - Lady Davina Crichton

CRICHTON, Viscount; John Henry Michael Ninian Crichton; s & h of 9 Earl of Erne; *b* 19 June 1971 *Style* - Viscount Crichton

CRICHTON, Lady Katherine Patricia; da of 6 Earl of Erne; *b* 1962; *Style* - Lady Katherine Crichton

CRICHTON, Maurice; s of Maurice Crichton of Glasgow (d 1957); *b* 4 June 1928; *Educ* Kelvinside Acad, Cargilfield, Sedbergh; *m* 1959, Diana Russell, da of John Russell Lang, CBE; 3 s, 1 da; *Career* chartered accountant; ptnr Touche Ross & Co, dir Woolwich Equitable Bldg Soc, memb E Kilbride Dvpt Corpn Bd; *Recreations* golf, shooting, music; *Clubs* Caledonian, Western Glasgow; *Style* - Maurice Crichton Esq; Hall of Caldwell, Uplawmoor, Glasgow (☎ 050 585 248)

CRICHTON, Sir (John) Robertson (Dunn); s of Alexander Cansh Crichton; *b* 2 Nov 1912; *Educ* Sedbergh, Balliol Oxford; *m* 1944, Margaret Vanderlip, da of Col Livingston Watrous of Washington DC and Nantucket, Mass, USA; 2 s, 1 da; *Career* barr 1936, bencher 1959, Recorder of Manchester (formerly Blackpool) and Judge of Crown Court at Manchester

1960-67, kt 1967, Judge of High Court Queen's Bench Div 1967-77; *Style* - Sir Robertson Crichton; Hempfield, Dunham Massey, Altrincham, Cheshire (☎ 061 928 6101)

CRICHTON, Lady Tara Guinevere; da of 6 Earl of Erne; *b* 1967

CRICHTON-BROWN, Sir Robert; KCMG (1980); s of late L Crichton-Brown of Sydney; *b* 23 Aug 1919; *m* 1941, Norah Isabelle, nee Turnbull; 1 s, 1 da; *Career* co-ordinator HRH the Duke of Edinburgh's Award Scheme (Australia); company chm and dir, v-chm Rothmans of Pall Mall Australia Ltd, chm and md Security and General Insurance Co Ltd, kt 1972; memb Lloyd's *Style* - Sir Robert Crichton-Brown, KCMG; 11 Castlereagh st, Sydney, NSW 2000, Australia

CRICHTON-STUART, Lady Janet Egidia; *née* Montgomerie; da of late 16 Earl of Eglinton and Winton by 1 w, Lady Beatrice Dalrymple, da of 11 Earl of Stair; *b* 1911; *m* 1934, Capt Lord Robert Crichton-Stuart, Scots Gds (s of 4 Marq of Bute and who d 1976); 2 s; *Style* - Lady Robert Crichton-Stuart; Holmhill, Thornhill, Dumfries-shire

CRIPPS, (Matthew) Anthony Leonard; CBE (1977), DSO (1943), TD (1947), QC (1958); s of Maj the Hon Leonard Harrison Cripps, CBE (d 1959 - 3 s of 1 Baron Parmoor); hp of 4 Baron; *b* 30 Dec 1913; *Educ* Eton, Ch Ch Oxford; *m* 1941, Margaret, da of late G Johnson-Scott, of Hill House, Ashby-de-la-Zouch; 3 s; *Career* 1939-45 War in Norway, N Africa and Italy; barr Middle Temple 1938, Inner Temple 1961, Bencher 1965, Recorder of Nottingham 1961-71, Recorder of Crown Court 1972-, memb Senate of four Inns of Court 1967-71, chm of Disciplinary Ctee of Milk Marketing Bd 1956-, and of Home Sec's Adv Ctee on Serv Candidates 1966- (dep chm 1965-66), memb Bar Council 1967-69 and 1970-74, and of Min of Agric's Ctee of Inquiry into Foot and Mouth Disease 1968-69, chm Reigate Cons Assocn 1961-64, of Research Ctee Soc of Cons Lawyers 1963-67 and of Cons Party Research Ctee of Inquiry into Discrimination against Women in Law and Admin 1968-69, memb Exec Ctee Nat Union of Cons Assocns 1964-72, Judge of Canterbury Court of Arches 1969-, Cmmr for Local Govt Election Petitions 1978-, dep Sr Judge of British Sovereign Bases Area Cyprus 1978-, chm RSPCA Legal Adv Ctee 1977-, chm Nat panel of Approved Coal Merchants Scheme 1972-; *Clubs* Brooks's, Lansdowne; *Style* - Anthony Cripps Esq, CBE, DSO, TD, QC; Alton House, Felbridge, East Grinstead, Sussex RH19 2PP (☎ 23238)

CRISP, Bernard David James; s of Bertie Bela Crisp (d 1968); *b* 11 June 1926; *Educ* Whitgift, Liverpool U; *m* 1947, Lorna Jean, da of Sydney James Clarke (d 1971); 1 s, 1 da; *Career* Order of St John; Lt RNVR; md Cunard Travel Ltd, sales and marketing dir Cunard Line Ltd, dir Cunard Hotels Ltd; *Style* - Bernard Crisp Esq; 2 Norfolk ave, Sanderstead, Surrey

CRISP, John Charles; s and h of Sir Peter Crisp, 4 Bt; *b* 10 Dec 1955; *Style* - John Crisp Esq

CRISP, Sir (John) Peter; 4 Bt (UK 1913) of Bungay, Suffolk; s of Sir John Wilson Crisp, 3 Bt (d 1950); *b* 19 May 1925; *Educ* Westminster; *m* 1954, Judith Mary, da of late H E Gillett; 3 s, 1 da; *Heir* s, John Crisp; *Style* - Sir Peter Crisp, Bt; Crabtree Cottage, Drungewick lane, Loxwood, W Sussex (☎ 752374)

CRITCHETT, Charles George Montague; s (by 2 m) and h of Sir Ian Critchett, 3 Bt; *b* 2 April 1965; *Style* - Charles Critchett Esq

CRITCHETT, Dowager Lady; Innes; da of late Col Francis George Archibald Wiehe; *m* 1914, Sir (George) Montague Critchett, 2 Bt, MVO (d 1941); *Style* - The Dowager Lady Critchett; 17 Master close, Oxted, Surrey

CRITCHETT, Sir Ian George Lorraine; 3 Bt (UK 1908) of Harley St, Boro' of St Marylebone; s of Sir Montague Critchett, 2 Bt (d 1941) and Innes, nee Wiehe; *b* 9 Dec 1920; *Educ* Harrow, Clare Cambridge; *m* 1, 1948, Paulette Mary Lorraine (d 1962) da of late Col H B Humfrey; m 2, 1964,

Jocelyn Daphne Margret, da of Cdr C M Hall; 1 s, 1 da; *Heir* s, Charles Critchett; *Career* FO 1948, 2 Sec Cairo 1956, 1 Sec FO 1962; *Style* - Sir Ian Critchett, Bt; Uplands Lodge, Pains Hill, Limpsfield, Surrey

CRITCHLEY, Julian Michael Gordon; MP (C) Aldershot 1974-; s of Dr Macdonald Critchley; *b* 8 Dec 1930; *Educ* Shrewsbury, Sorbonne, Pembroke Oxford; *m* 1965, Mrs Heather Goodrick; 1 s, 1 da; *Career* chm Bow Gp 1966-67, MP (C) Rochester and Chatham 1959-74; *Style* - Julian Critchley Esq, MP; The Brewer's House, 18 Bridge sq, Farnham, Surrey (☎ 722075)

CROCKFORD, Philip David Vyvyan; s of Philip Theodore Clive Crockford (d 1950); *b* 21 Nov 1930; *Educ* Merchant Taylors Sch, Sandhurst; *m* 1953, Margaret Kathleen, da of late Maj Charles Deane Cowper; 1 s, 2 da; *Career* Lt RA; dir Alexander Howden Underwriting Ltd, gov Forres Sch Tst Ltd; *Recreations* tennis, hunting; *Clubs* Gresham, Army and Navy; *Style* - Philip Crockford Esq; Little Ridge, Eastington, Northleach, Glos; 31 Wimpole st, W1

CROFT, 2 Baron (UK 1940); Sir Michael Henry Glendower Page Croft; 2 Bt (UK 1924); s of 1 Baron, CMG, TD, PC (d 1947) and Hon Nancy Beatrice Borwick, da of 1 Baron Borwick; *b* 20 Aug 1916; *Educ* Eton, Trin Hall Cambridge; *m* 1948, Lady Antoinette Conyngham (d 1959) da of 6 Marquess Conyngham; 1 s, 1 da; *Heir* s, Hon Bernard Croft; *Career* barr 1952, former dir Henry Page & Co and Ware Properties Ltd, FRSA, OStJ; *Style* - The Rt Hon The Lord Croft; Croft Castle, nr Leominster, Herefordshire

CROFT, Sir Bernard Hugh Denman; 13 Bt (E 1671) of Croft Castle, Herefordshire; s of Sir Hugh Matthew Fiennes Croft, 12 Bt (d 1954); *b* 24 Aug 1903; *Educ* Armidale Sch New South Wales; *m* 1931, Helen Margaret, da of H Weaver; 3 s; *Heir* s, Owen Croft; *Style* - Sir Bernard Croft, Bt; Salisbury Court, Uralla, NSW 2358, Australia (☎ Uralla 24)

CROFT, Hon Bernard William Henry Page; s and h of 2 Baron Croft by his w, Lady Antoinette Fredericka Hersey Cecilia Conyngham (d 1959), da of 6 Marquess Conyngham; *b* 28 Aug 1949; *Educ* Stowe, Wales U (BSc Econ); *Style* - The Hon Bernard Croft

CROFT, Major Sir John Archibald Radcliffe; 5 Bt (UK 1818) of Cowling Hall, Yorks; s of Tom Radcliffe Croft, OBE (d 1964, s of 2 Bt); suc cous 1979; *b* 27 March 1910; *Educ* King's Canterbury; *m* 1953, Lucy Elizabeth, da of late Maj William Dallas Loney Jupp, OBE; 1 s; *Heir* s, Thomas Croft; *Career* W Yorks Regt (ret); *Style* - Major Sir John Croft, Bt; Cornerways, Stodmarsh, Canterbury, Kent (☎ Littlebourne 256)

CROFT, Owen Glendower; s and h of Sir Bernard Croft, 13 Bt; *b* 26 April 1932; *m* 1959, Sally, da of Dr T M Mansfield of Brisbane, Queensland; 1 s, 2 da; *Style* - Owen Croft Esq

CROFT, Thomas Stephen Hutton; s and h of Maj Sir John Croft, 5 Bt; *b* 12 June 1959; *Educ* King's Sch Canterbury, Univ Coll London U; *Style* - Thomas Croft Esq

CROFTON, 6 Baron (I 1797); Sir Charles Edward Piers Crofton; 9 Bt (I 1758); s of 5 Baron (d 1974) and Ann, da of Gp Capt Charles Tighe; *b* 27 April 1949; *m* 1976, Maureen Jacqueline, da of S Bray of Taunton; *Heir* bro, Hon Guy Crofton; *Career* with Buries Markes (Ship Management) Ltd; *Style* - The Rt Hon The Lord Crofton; Longford House, Beltra, Co Sligo, Eire

CROFTON, Hon Arthur Blaise Adrian; s of late 5 Baron Crofton; *b* 1957; *Style* - The Hon Arthur Crofton

CROFTON, Derek Fergus Regan; s of late William Crofton; *b* 15 Feb 1934; *Educ* Rockwell Coll, Univ Coll Dublin; *m* 1959, Marian Emily, nee Lindsay; 2 s, 1 da; *Career* chartered accountant 1958, finance dir and co sec Shell Chemicals UK Ltd 1974-, chm Vencel Resil Ltd 1974-, dir Ward Blenkinsop Ltd; *Style* - Derek Crofton Esq; The Red Lodge, North rd,

Hale, Cheshire (☎ 061 980 8280)

CROFTON, Hon Guy Patrick Gilbert; s of 5 Baron Crofton (d 1974), and hp of bro, 6 Baron; *b* 17 June 1951; *Style* - The Hon Guy Crofton

CROFTON, Hugh Denis; s of Lt-Col Sir Morgan George Crofton, 6 Bt, DSO; unc and hp of Sir Patrick Crofton, 7 Bt; *b* 10 April 1937; *Educ* Eton, Worcester Coll Oxford, Bristol U; *Style* - Hugh Crofton Esq

CROFTON, Mary, Baroness; Mary; da of late Maj Irvine Hatfield Friend, OBE, MC, DL; *m* 1, Robert T Flach; m 2, 1964, as his 2 w, 5 Baron Crofton (d 1974); *Style* - The Rt Hon Mary, Lady Crofton; Flat 1, 123 Gloucester ter, W2 (☎ 01 402 5015)

CROFTON, (Henry Edward) Melville; MBE (1970); s of late Brig Roger Crofton, CIE, MC, by 2 w, Dorothy Frances, da of Col Henry Melville Hatchell, DSO; hp of kinsman, Sir Malby Crofton, 5 Bt; *b* 15 Aug 1931; *Educ* Hilton Coll Natal, Trin Cambridge; *m* 1955, Mary Brigid, twin da of late Gerald K Riddle; 2 s, 1 da; *Career* former Prin Admin Offr Overseas Civil Serv; *Style* - Melville Crofton Esq, MBE; Haldon, St Giles Hill, Winchester, Hants

CROFTON, Margaret, Lady; Margaret Amelia; da of late Judge Morris Dallett of Philadelphia, USA; *m* 1933, as his 3 w, Lt-Col Sir Morgan George Crofton, 6 Bt, DSO (d 1958); *Style* - Margaret, Lady Crofton; Woodbridge, Brockenhurst, Hants

CROFTON, Hon Mrs Marcus - Madeleine Barbara (Pratt); da of late William Heath; *m* 1951, as his 4 w, Hon (Arthur) Marcus Lowther Crofton, Maj Irish Gds (d 1962); *Style* - The Hon Mrs Marcus Crofton; 401, 1430 Newport av, Victoria BC, Canada

CROFTON, Sir Malby Sturges; 5 Bt (UK 1838) of Longford House, Sligo (but name does not, at time of going to press, appear on the Official Roll of Baronets); s of Sir Malby Richard Henry Crofton, 4 Bt, DSO and Bar (d 1962); *b* 11 Jan 1923; *Educ* Eton, Trin Cambridge; *m* 1961 (m dis 1966), Elizabeth Madeline Nina, da of late Maj Rhys Clavel Mansel; *Heir* kinsman, (Henry Edward) Melville Crofton; *Career* Mayor Kensington and Chelsea 1978- (Leader Kensington Boro Cncl 1968-77), ptnr Messrs Fenn & Crosthwaite, memb London Stock Exchange 1957-75, memb GLC 1970-73 and (N Ealing) 1977; *Style* - Sir Malby Crofton, Bt; Longford House, Co Sligo, Eire; 17 Launceston pla, W8

CROFTON, Sir (Hugh) Patrick Simon; 7 Bt (UK 1801), of Mohill, Leitrim; s of late Major Morgan George Crofton (s of 6 Bt); suc grandfather, Lt-Col Sir Morgan George Crofton, DSO 1958; *b* 2 Dec 1936; *Educ* Eton; *m* 1967, Mrs Lene Eddowes, da of Kai Augustinus, of Copenhagen; 1 da; *Heir* unc, Hugh Crofton; *Career* late 2 Lt Welsh Gds, md Sir Patrick Crofton Enterprises Ltd; *Style* - Sir Patrick Crofton, Bt; Mohill Castle, Co Leitrim

CROHAM, Baron (Life Peer UK 1977); Douglas Albert Vivian Allen; GCB (1973, KCB 1967, CB 1963); s of Albert John Allen of Croydon (ka 1918); *b* 15 Dec 1917; *Educ* Wallington G S, LSE; *m* 1941, Sybil Eileen, da of John Marco Allegro of Carshalton, Surrey; 2 s, 1 da; *Career* former civil servant, Perm Sec of Treasury 1968-74, of CSD 1974-77; dir Pilkington Bros Ltd 1978-, dep chm British Nat Oil Corpn 1978-, advr to Gov of Bank of England 1978-; *Recreations* tennis, woodwork; *Clubs* Reform, Civil Service; *Style* - The Rt Hon The Lord Croham, GCB; 9 Manor Way, South Croydon, Surrey (☎ 01 688 0496)

CROMARTIE, 4 Earl of (UK 1861); Roderick Grant Francis Mackenzie; MC (1945), TD (1964), JP (Ross and Cromarty 1937), DL (1976); also Viscount Tarbat (UK 1861), Baron Castlehaven (UK 1861), Baron MacLeod of Castle Leod (UK 1861); Chief of the Clan Mackenzie; s of Countess of Cromartie (d 1962; 3 in line, the first holder of the Earldom of this 2 cr - also a woman- being ggda of Isabella, herself da of 3 Earl of Cromarty (*sic*) of the 1 cr, whose honours were forfeit by attainder, resulting from his being 'out' in the '45) and Col Edward Walter Blunt (d 1949), who assumed additional surname Mackenzie 1905; present Peer discontinued the surname Blunt for himself and his son; *b* 24 Oct 1904; *Educ* Charterhouse, RMC Sandhurst; *m* 1, 1933 (m dis 1945), Dorothy, da of B G Downing of Kentucky, USA; 2 da; m 2, 1947 (m dis 1962), Olga, da of late Stuart Laurance of Paris; 1 s; m 3, 1962, Lilias Garvie, MB, ChB, da of Prof (James) Walter MacLeod, OBE, FRS, FRSE; *Heir* s, Viscount Tarbat, *qv*; *Career* FSAS, Maj Seaforth Highlanders (ret), CC Ross and Cromarty 1963-77, Convener Dist Cncl 1975-77, Freeman 1977, Hon Sheriff; *Clubs* Pratt's, Army and Navy; *Style* - The Rt Hon The Earl of Cromartie, MC, TD, JP, DL; Castle Leod, Strathpeffer, Ross and Cromarty

CROMER, 3 Earl of (UK 1901); George Rowland Stanley Baring; KG (1977), GCMG (1974, KCMG 1971), MBE (1945), PC (1966); also Baron Cromer (UK 1892), Viscount Cromer (UK 1899), Viscount Errington (UK 1901); s of 2 Earl, GCB, GCIE, GCVO, PC (d 1953) and Lady Ruby Elliot, da of 4 Earl of Minto; *b* 28 July 1918; *Educ* Eton, Trin Cambridge; *m* 1942, Hon Esmé Harmsworth, CVO, da of 2 Viscount Rothermere; 2 s, 1 da (decd); *Heir* s, Viscount Errington, *qv*; *Career* Page of Honour to HM King George V (who stood sponsor at his birth) 1933-35, Lt-Col Gren Gds, advr Baring Bros & Co Ltd 1974- (formerly dir and md), former chm IBM (UK) Ltd, dir Daily Mail & Gen Tst Ltd 1974- (and 1949-61, 1966-70), dir Imperial Gp Ltd 1974-80, P & O 1974-80, memb advsy cncl IBM Corpn New York 1967-, chm Int Advsy Cncl Morgan Guaranty Tst Co of New York 1977-, int advr Marsh & McLennan Cos New York, European advr Gov Res Corpn Washington 1974-; *Clubs* Brooks's, Beefsteak, White's, Roy Yacht Squadron; *Style* - The Rt Hon The Earl of Cromer, KG, GCMG, MBE, PC; Beaufield House, St Saviour, Jersey, CI (☎ Jersey 61671)

CROMPTON, Hon Mrs (Virginia Clementine); da of 2 Baron Keyes; *b* 1950; *m* 1972, Roger Martyn Crompton; *Style* - The Hon Mrs Crompton

CROMWELL, 6 Baron (E 1375); David Godfrey Bewicke-Copley; s of 5 Baron, DSO, MC (d 1966, in whose favour the Barony, abeyant since 1497, was called out 1923; he was fifteenth in descent from Sir John FitzWilliam, 1 cous of 3 Baron Cromwell (Ralph), Lord High Treasurer of England, an interesting parallel with the present Lord Cromwell's position as Government Broker; Ralph built Tattershall Castle in Lincs, part of which still stands, thanks to Lord Curzon buying it in 1912) and Freda, da of Sir Frederick Cripps, DSO; Freda was 3 cous of that other arbiter of the nation's financial destiny, Sir Stafford Cripps; *b* 29 May 1929; *Educ* Eton, Magdalene Cambridge; *m* 1954, Vivian, da of late Hugh de Lisle Penfold of Isle of Man; 2 s, 2 da; *Heir* s, Hon Godfrey Bewicke-Copley; *Career* barr 1954, memb London Stock Exchange, ptnr Mullens & Co 1960-, Govt Broker 1981- (Second Govt Broker 1973-81); *Recreations* hunting, tennis, gardening; *Style* - The Rt Hon The Lord Cromwell; The Manor House, Great Milton, Oxon (☎ Great Milton 230)

CRONIN, Gerald Francis; s of late William Francis Cronin; *b* 28 Jan 1927; *Educ* Highgate Sch, Oxford U; *m* 1952, Margaret Patricia, nee McNamara; 2 s, 1 da; *Career* chartered accountant, fin dir Wellco Hldgs Ltd 1968-; *Style* - Gerald Cronin Esq; 59 Park View rd, Ealing, W5 (☎ 01 997 2786)

CROOK, 1 Baron (UK 1947); Reginald Douglas; JP (Surrey 1948); s of late Percy Edwin Crook; *b* 2 March 1901; *Educ* Strand Sch; *m* 1922, Ida Gertrude, da of Joseph Haddon; 1 s; *Heir* s, Hon Douglas Crook; *Career* chm National Dock Labour Bd; gen sec of Min of Labour Staff Assoc and ed of Civil Service Argus 1925-51, Liveryman of City of London, Apothecary, Past Master of Spectacle Makers' Co, Life Memb of Court of Guild of Freemen (Master 1972-73), KStJ, V-Pres Roy Soc for Prevention of Accidents, Founder and Pres of Cystic Fibrosis Res Foundation, former delegate UN; *Style* - The Rt Hon The Lord Crook, JP; Breedene, Princes av, Carshalton, Surrey (☎ 01 643 2620)

CROOK, Colin; s of late Richard Crook; *b* 1 June 1942; *Educ* Harris Coll Preston,

Liverpool Polytechnic; *m* 1965, Dorothy Jean, nee Taylor; 2 s; *Career* md Rank Precision Industries 1978-80, dir Operations Microcomputers Motorola Austin Texas 1975-78, md Zynar Ltd, FEng, CEng, MIEE, MIERE, MIEEE, MACM; *Style* - Colin Crook Esq; The Old School House, Harvest Hill, Hedsor, Bourne End, Bucks (☎ Bourne End 27479)

CROOK, Hon Douglas Edwin; s of 1 Baron Crook, *qv*; *b* 19 Nov 1926; *Educ* Whitgift Sch Croydon, Imperial Coll of Science and Technol (BSc); *m* 1954, Ellenor, da of late Robert Rouse; 1 s, 1 da; *Career* MICE; *Style* - The Hon Douglas Crook

CROOKENDEN, Lt-Gen Sir Napier; KCB (1970, CB 1966), DSO (1945), OBE (1954), DL (Kent 1979); s of late Col Arthur Crookenden, CBE, DSO; *b* 31 Aug 1915; *Educ* Wellington, RMC Sandhurst; *m* 1948, Patricia Nassau, da of 2 Baron Kindersley, CBE, MC; 2 s, 2 da; *Career* Cheshire Regt 1935, GOCIC Western Cmmd 1969-72, Col Cheshire Regt 1969-71, Co Cmdt Prince of Wales Div 1971-74, tstee Imperial War Museum, dir Lloyds Bank Ltd SE Regnl Bd, Flextech Ltd; Lt HM Tower of London 1975-81, chm SSAFA 1974-; *Style* - Lt-Gen Sir Napier Crookenden, KCB, DSO, OBE, DL; Sissinghurst Place, Cranbrook, Kent (☎ 712863)

CROOKENDEN, Hon Lady; Hon Patricia Nassau; da of 2 Baron Kindersley, CBE, MC (d 1976); *b* 1922; *m* 1948, Lt-Gen Sir Napier Crookenden, KCB, DSO, OBE; 2 s, 2 da; *Style* - The Hon Lady Crookenden; Sissinghurst Place, Cranbrook, Kent

CROOKSHANK, John Kennedy; s of Lt-Col C K Crookshank; *b* 15 Aug 1932; *Educ* Repton, Sandhurst; *m* 1974, Diana Lesley, nee Brookes; 1 s, 1 da (and 4 step children); *Career* ADC to Govr of Gibraltar 1958-60, publishing dir IPC 1972-; *Style* - John Kennedy Esq; Ivy House, Westbourne, Emsworth, Hants

CROOM-JOHNSON, Hon Mr Justice; Hon Sir David Powell; DSC (1944), VRD (1953); s of late Hon Sir Reginald Powell Croom-Johnson; *b* 28 Nov 1914; *Educ* Stowe, Trin Hall Cambridge; *m* 1940, Barbara Douglas, da of Erskine Douglas Warren of Toronto; 1 da; *Career* barr 1938, Recorder of Winchester 1962-71, Judge of Courts of Appeal Jersey and Guernsey 1966-71, High Court Judge Queen's Bench Div 1971-, kt 1971; *Style* - The Hon Mr Justice Croom-Johnson, DSC, VRD; Roy Courts of Justice, WC2

CROPPER, James Anthony; s of late Anthony Cropper; *b* 22 Dec 1938; *Educ* Eton, Magdalene Cambridge (BA); *m* 1967, Susan Rosemary, nee Davis; 1 s (and 1 s decd), 1 da; *Career* chm James Cropper & Co Ltd (Papermakers), High Sheriff of Westmorland 1971; *Style* - James Cropper Esq; Tolson Hall, Kendal, Cumbria (☎ Kendal 22011)

CROPPER, Hon Mrs (Rosalind Evelyn); *née* Younger; da of 3 Viscount Younger of Leckie, OBE, TD; *b* 12 Oct 1937; *m* 1960, Thomas Ross Charles, s of Cecil Howe Cropper, DSO, MC, of Sydney; 2 s, 2 da; *Style* - The Hon Mrs Cropper; Greenhills, Willow Tree, NSW, Australia

CROSET, Paul John Francis; OBE (1967); s of Louis Croset; *b* 15 March 1919; *Educ* Rishworth and Stamford Schs; *m* 1944, Margaret Vivien, nee Suckling; 3 da; *Career* engineer; chm and founder Holset Engineering Co Ltd 1952-, chm Readicut Internat Ltd 1977- *Style* - Paul Croset Esq OBE; Fenay Wood, Fenay Bridge, Huddersfield (☎ 0484 30837)

CROSS, 3 Viscount (UK 1886); Assheton Henry Cross; s of 2 Viscount (d 1932) and Maud, da of late Maj-Gen Inigo Richmond Jones, CVO, CB (Maud's maternal grandfather being Hon Richard Charteris, 2 s of 9 Earl of Wemyss and March); *b* 7 May 1920; *Educ* Shrewsbury, Magdalene Cambridge; *m* 1, 1952 (m dis 1957), Patricia Mary, da of Edward Pearson Hewetson, of Windermere; 2 da; m 2, 1972 (m dis 1977), Mrs Victoria Webb *Heir* none; *Career* formerly Capt Scots Gds; *Style* - The Rt Hon The Viscount Cross; Delph Cottage, Itchenor, Sussex

CROSS OF CHELSEA, Baron (Life Peer UK 1971); (Arthur) Geoffrey (Neale) Cross; PC (1969); s of late Arthur George Cross; *b* 1 Dec 1904; *Educ* Westminster, Trin Cambridge; *m* 1952, Mildred Joan, da of late Lt-Col Theodore Eardley-Wilmot, DSO (gn of Sir John Eardley Wilmot, 2 Bt), and widow of Thomas Walton Davies; 1 da; *Career* barr 1930, KC 1949, Bencher 1959, Judge of the High Court Chancery Div 1960-69, Lord Justice of Appeal 1969-71, a Lord of Appeal in Ordinary 1971-75, Chllr of Co Palatine of Durham 1959, chm Takeover Panel Appeals Ctee 1976-, kt 1960; *Style* - The Rt Hon The Lord Cross of Chelsea, PC; The Bridge House, Leintwardine, Craven Arms, Shropshire (☎ Leintwardine 205)

CROSS, Denis Charles; s of late Lt Charles Cross, RN; *b* 13 May 1938; *Educ* Downside, Balliol Oxford; *m* 1963, Margaret McAdam, nee Black; 2 s, 3 da; *Career* dir Hambros Bank Ltd 1971-; *Style* - Denis Cross Esq; 18 Bolingbroke grove, SW11 (☎ 01 673 8187)

CROSS, Air Chief Marshal Sir Kenneth Bryan Boyd; KCB (1959, CB 1954), CBE (1945), DSO (1943) DFC (1940); s of Pembroke Cross; *b* 4 Oct 1911; *Educ* Kingswood Sch Bath; *m* 1945, Brenda Megan, da of Wing-Cdr F J B Powell; 2 s, 1 da; *Career* RAF 1930, AOCIC Bomber Cmmd 1959-63, Air Ch Marshal 1965, AOCIC T'Port Cmmd 1963-66, ret 1967, dir Red Cross; *Style* - Air Chief Marshal Sir Kenneth Cross, KCB, CBE, DSO, DFC; 12 Callow st, SW3

CROSS, Hon Mrs (Laura Georgina Kiloran); *née* Grosvenor; da (twin) of late 5 Baron Ebury, DSO by 2 w, Hon Denise Yard-Buller (da of 3 Baron Churston); *b* 1946; *m* 1969, G R Mark Cross; *Style* - The Hon Mrs Cross; Bartons Lodge, Eversholt, Bletchley, Bucks (☎ Ridgmont 333)

CROSS, Hon Nicola; da (by 1 m) of 3 Viscount Cross; *b* 1954; *Style* - The Hon Nicola Cross

Cross; *b* 19 Aug 1942; *Educ* Bradford G S; *m* 1967, Angela Mary, nee Seymour; 2 da; *Career* FCA, dir/sec Heydemann Shaw Ltd (subsid of Coats Patons Ltd) 1974-; *Style* - Robert Cross Esq; Little Oaks, Ridgeway, Tranmere Park, Guiseley, W Yorks

CROSS, Lady; Sheila; da of late Gilbert Moffit of Gwalia, W Australia; *m* 1939, Sir William Coats Cross, 2 Bt (d 1947, Btcy became extinct 1962); *Style* - Lady Cross; 16a Richardson av, Claremont, Perth, W Australia

CROSS, Hon Venetia Clare; da (by 1 m) of 3 Viscount Cross; *b* 1953; *Style* - The Hon Venetia Cross

CROSSE, John Ernest; s of Ernest Crosse (d 1972); *b* 11 Jan 1926; *Educ* Sebright Sch nr Kidderminster; *m* 1, 1952, Evelyn; m 2, 1980, Janet; 1 s, 2 da; *Career* SEAC 1945-47, md Solartron Engineering Ltd 1952-58, Solartron (Farnborough) Ltd 1958-63, chm Plasmec Ltd 1963-, CBIM; *Style* - John Crosse Esq; Holt Pound House, Holt Pound, Farnham, Surrey (☎ 0424 3186); Plasmec Ltd, Weydon lane, Farnham, Surrey (☎ 0252 721236)

CROSSLEY, Hon Alicia Phyllis Belinda; da of 3 Baron Somerleyton; *b* 1969

CROSSLEY, Sir Christopher John; 3 Bt (UK 1909) of Glenfield, Dunham Massey, Co Chester; s of late Lt-Cdr Nigel Crossley, RN, s of late Eric Crossley, OBE (s of 1 Bt); suc great-unc, Sir Kenneth Irwin Crossley, 2 Bt, 1957; *b* 25 Sept 1931; *Educ* Canford; *m* 1, 1959 (m dis 1969), Carolyne Louise, nee Sykes; 2 s; m 2, 1977, Lesley A, da of late Dr K A J Chamberlain; *Heir* s, Nicholas Crossley; *Career* Lt-Cdr RN (ret); *Style* - Sir Christopher Crossley, Bt; PO Box 100, Heliopolis, Egypt

CROSSLEY, Hon Camilla Mary Laura; da of 3 Baron Somerleyton; *b* 1967

CROSSLEY, Elizabeth, Lady; Elizabeth Joyce; da of late E Shenton of Boxmoor, Herts; *m* 1954, as his 2 w, Sir Kenneth Irwin Crossley, 2 Bt (d 1957); *Style* -

House, Devizes, Wilts

CROSSLEY, Hon Hugh Francis Savile; s and h of 3 Baron Somerleyton; *b* 27 Sept 1971; *Style* - The Hon Hugh Crossley

CROSSLEY, Hon Isabel Alicia Claire; da of 3 Baron Somerleyton; *b* 1964

CROSSLEY, Hon Louisa Bridget Vivien; da of 3 Baron Somerleyton; *b* 1974

CROSSLEY, Nicholas John; s (by 1 m) and h of Sir Christopher Crossley, 3 Bt; *b* 10 Dec 1962; *Style* - Nicholas Crossley Esq

CROSSLEY, Robert Alan; MC (1945), TD (1946); s of Lt Alan Hastings Crossley of Letton Ct, Hereford; *b* 27 March 1912; *Educ* Hellington Coll, Clare Coll Camb; *m* 1938, Gabrielle Mary, da of Sir Robert A Burrows; 3 da; *Career* Maj RA, France 1940, Middle East, Italy; MI Med E, dep and later md Piller-Wedge 1971-75, dir British Moulded Fibre 1958-80; *Style* - Robert Crossley Esq, MC, TD; c/o National Westminster Bank Ltd, 187 High st, Boston Spa, Wetherby, W Yorkshire

CROSSLEY, Hon Richard Nicholas; TD (1974); s of late 2 Baron Somerleyton, MC; *b* 1932; *Educ* Eton, Sandhurst; *m* 1958, Alexandra Ann Maitland, da of Wing Cdr G D Welch; 1 s, 2 da; *Career* Brevet-Col 1977, Col TA NE Dist 1978-81; farmer 1963-81, MFH 1969; Capt 9 Queen's Roy Lancers (ret), Maj Queen's Own Yeo (TA), Cmdg Offr Queen's Own Yeo 1973-76, Col Gen Staff (TA) 1978, appointed ADC TAVR to HM The Queen 1980; *Recreations* hunting, shooting, stalking, sailing; *Clubs* Cavalry & Guards, Yorkshire; *Style* - The Hon Richard Crossley, TD; Westfield Farm, Settrington, Malton, York

CROSTHWAITE, Sir (Ponsonby) Moore; KCMG (1960, CMG 1951); s of late P M Crosthwaite, MICE; *b* 13 Aug 1907; *Educ* Rugby, CCC Oxford; *Career* Diplomatic Serv 1932, Ambass to Sweden 1963-66, to the Lebanon 1958-63; *Clubs* Athenaeum; *Style* - Sir Moore Crosthwaite, KCMG; 17 Crescent Grove, SW4

CROUCH, David (Lance); MP (C) Canterbury 1966-; s of late Stanley Crouch; *b* 23 June 1919; *Educ* Univ Coll Sch; *m* 1947, Margaret, da of Maj Sydney Maplesden Noakes, DSO; 1 s, 1 da; *Career* company dir (own company); contested W Leeds 1959; *Style* - David Crouch Esq, MP; The Oast House, Fisher st, Badlesmere, Faversham, Kent; 3 Tufton ct, Tufton st, SW1

CROWDER, John Fairfax; Knight's Cross of Austria (1975); s of Charles Fairfax Crowder (d 1951); *b* 7 July 1902; *Educ* Lancing, King's Coll Cambridge; *m* 1931, Ursula Reynolds, da of Benjamin John Fletcher OBE (d 1951); 2 da; *Career* slr, Hon-Consul of Austria (Midlands) 1961; dep div food officer Midlands 1942-45; Pres Birmingham Law Society 1948-49; board of Governors United Birmingham Hosps 1947-57; gov City of Birmingham Coll of Commerce 1962-65, and Sch of Music 1968-70 and the Queen's Coll 1951-78; *Recreations* singing, travelling; *Clubs* United Oxford & Cambridge; *Style* - John Crowder Esq; 11/77 Warwick sq, SW1; 46 Westfield rd, Birmingham 15 (☎ 021 454 5131)

CROWDER, Hon Mrs (Patricia Winifred Mary); *née* Stourton; da of 25 Baron Mowbray, 26 Segrave and 22 Stourton, MC (d 1965); *b* 1924; *m* 1948, Frederick Petre Crowder, QC, MP; *Career* sometime in Foreign Office; *Style* - The Hon Mrs Crowder; Charlestown, St Austell, Cornwall

CROWDY, Edmund Porter; VRD; s of Lt-Col C Crowdy (d 1938); *b* 13 March 1925; *Educ* Greshams, Sidney Sussex Coll Cambridge; *m* 1958, Sheila Mary, nee Davison; 2 s (Nicholas John, Charles Richard), 2 da (Sarah Jane b 1962, Philippa Kate b 1967); *Career* Cmdr RNVR, engineer, md Hawthorne Leslie (Engineers) Ltd 1972-78, Clark-Hawthorne Ltd 1978-80, Doxford Engines Ltd 1980-, British Shipbuilders Engineering Technical Services Ltd 1981-; *Recreations* campanology, golf; *Style* - Edmund Crowdy Esq, VRD; 18 Manor rd, Benton, Newcastle-on-Tyne (☎ Newcastle 666 418)

CROWLEY-MILLING, Air Marshal Sir Denis; KCB (1973), CBE (1963), DSO (1943) and Bar (1942); s of T W Crowley-Milling; *b* 22 March 1919; *Educ* Malvern; *m* 1943, Lorna Jean Jeboult, nee Stuttard; 1 s decd, 2 da; *Career* RAFVR 1937-39, AOC No 38 Gp RAF Odiham 1970-72, AOC 46 Gp RAF Upavon 1973, controller RAF Benevolent Fund 1975-81, Gentleman Usher of the Scarlet Rod to the Order of the Bath 1979-; *Style* - Air Marshal Sir Denis Crowley-Milling KCB CBE DSO*; c/o Barclays Bank Ltd, 46 Park Lane, W1

CROWTHER, Hon Charles Worth; s of Baron Crowther (Life Peer, d 1972); *b* 1939; *m* 1963, Barbara, da of Prof Norman Merrett Hancox, MD; c; *Style* - The Hon Charles Crowther; Bourne Bank, Bourne End, Bucks

CROWTHER, Hon David Richard Geoffrey; s of Baron Crowther (Life Peer, d 1972); *b* 1943; *m* 1974, Martina, nee Menn-Fink; *Style* - The Hon David Crowther

CROWTHER, Hon Felicity Margaret; da of Baron Crowther (Life Peer, d 1972); *b* 1947; *Style* - The Hon Felicity Crowther

CROWTHER, Hon Mrs (Moyra Christine); *née* Wilson; da of Baron Wilson of Radcliffe; *b* 5 Feb 1943; *Educ* Stand G S Whitefield, Birmingham U; *m* 1964, Dr Arthur Crowther (d 1979); 2 da (Katherine, Caroline); *Recreations* badminton, tennis, bridge; *Style* - The Hon Mrs Crowther; 8 Delfur rd, Bramhall, Stockport, Cheshire

CROWTHER, Hon Nicola Mary; da of Baron Crowther (Life Peer, d 1972); *b* 1950; *Style* - The Hon Nicola Crowther

CROWTHER, Ronald David; s of Harry Crowther; *b* 30 Oct 1928; *Educ* Cockburn H S Leeds; *m* 1961, Audrey, nee Ramsden; *Career* chartered accountant (FCA), fin dir Barr & Wallace Arnold Trust Ltd 1973-; *Recreations* golf, gardening; *Style* - Ronald Crowther Esq; 104 Main st, Shadwell, Leeds 17 (☎ office Leeds 36041, home Leeds 662143)

CROWTHER, (Joseph) Stanley; MP (L) Rotherham 1976-; s of Cyril Crowther; *b* 30 May 1925; *Educ* Rotherham G S, Rotherham Coll of Technol; *m* 1948, Margaret Royston; 2 s; *Career* journalist formerly with Yorkshire Evening Post; Mayor of Rotherham 1971-72 & 1975-76; *Style* - Stanley Crowther Esq, MP; 15 Clifton cres South, Rotherham (☎ 64559)

CROWTHER-HUNT, Baron (Life Peer UK 1973); Norman Crowther Crowther-Hunt; s of late Ernest Angus Hunt of Bradford; assumed by deed poll 1973 surname Crowther-Hunt; *b* 13 March 1920; *Educ* Sidney Sussex Coll Cambridge (MA, PhD); *m* 1944, Joyce, da of late Rev Joseph Stackhouse, of Walsall Wood, Staffs; 3 da; *Career* politics lectr and fellow Exeter Coll Oxford 1952- (and former domestic bursar); *Style* - The Rt Hon The Lord Crowther-Hunt; Exeter College, Oxford (☎ 44681); 14 Apsley rd, Oxford (☎ 58342)

CROWTHER-HUNT, Hon Penelope Carol; da of Baron Crowther-Hunt (Life Peer); *b* 1955; *Style* - The Hon Penelope Crowther-Hunt

CROWTHER-HUNT, Hon Rosamund Shirley; da of Baron Crowther-Hunt (Life Peer); *b* 1950; *Style* - The Hon Rosamund Crowther-Hunt

CROWTON, Frederick Edward; JP (Birmingham); s of Frederick Joseph Crowton (d 1951); *b* 10 Sept 1921; *Educ* Holy Family Sch Birmingham, Sparkhill Commercial Sch; *m* 1947, Vera, nee Judd; 1 s, 1 da; *Career* FInstM, md Mitchells & Butlers Central 1976-, md Bass Mitchells & Butlers 1968-, London sales man 1964; *Recreations* walking, reading, charity work; *Clubs* Priory (Birmingham), Variety Club of GB, Catenian Assoc, Birmingham Chamber of Commerce; *Style* - Frederick Crowton Esq, JP; Squirrels Leap, Featherbed Lane, Pathlow, Wilmcote, nr Stratford-on-Avon (☎ 0789 67198)

CROXTON, Derrick Gwynn; s of Charles William Croxton of Maidstone, Kent (d 1968); *b* 10 Jan 1923; *Educ* King's Sch Rochester, U Coll London; *m* 1947, Rachel Ann, da of late William Griffith

Thomas; 2 da; *Career* Capt RE, Major RASC Italy, chemical engineer/gen management trainee Reed International 1949, works dir Kimberly-Clark Ltd 1954, md Kimberly-Clark Ltd 1961-; *Recreations* tennis, sailing, beekeeping; *Clubs* Medway Yacht; *Style* - Derrick Croxton Esq; Somerfield rd, Maidstone, Kent (☎ 0622 58161)

CRUICKSHANK, George; s of George Cruickshank; *b* 13 July 1936; *Educ* Melville Coll and Heriot Watt U Edinburgh; *m* Catherine, nee Macdonald; 1 s, 1 da; *Career* dir Scottish Discount Co Ltd, Lloyds & Scottish Gp of Cos, Carvan Credit Ltd; *Style* - George Cruicksank Esq; 28 Inveralmond drive, Edinburgh 4

CRUICKSHANK, Flight-Lt John Alexander; VC (1944); s of James Cruickshank; *b* 20 May 1920; *Educ* Aberdeen G S, Daniel Stewart's Coll Edinburgh; *m* 1955, Marian R Beverley of Toronto; *Career* RA 1939, RAFVR (Coastal Cmmd) 1941; ADC to Lord High Cmmr to Gen Assembly of Church of Scotland 1946-48, formerly with Commercial Bank of Scotland Ltd Edinburgh, with Grindlays Bank Ltd 1952-76; *Style* - Flight-Lt John Cruickshank, VC; 34 Frogston rd West, Edinburgh 10 (☎ 031 445 1215)

CRUTCHLEY, Adm Sir Victor Alexander Charles; VC (1918), KCB (1946, CB 1945), DSC (1918), DL (Dorset 1957); s of late Percy Edward Crutchley and late Hon Frederica Louisa, da of 3 Baron Southampton and Ismania, nee Nugent, gda of Sir Charles Jenkinson, 10 Bt; *b* 2 Nov 1893; *Educ* Osborne and Dartmouth RNCs; *m* 1930, Joan Elizabeth Loveday (d 1980), da of late William Coryton; 1 s, 1 da (m Sir John Colfox, Bt, *qv*); *Career* HMS Brilliant and HMS Vindictive WW1, HMS Warspite 1937-40, Cmmd Australian Naval Sqdn 1942-44, Flag Offr Gibraltar 1945-47, ret 1947, Adm 1947, High Sheriff of Dorset 1955; *Style* - Adm Sir Victor Crutchley, VC, KCB, DSC, DL; Mappercombe Manor, Nettlecombe, Bridport

CRYER, (George) Robert; MP (L) Keighley Feb 1974-; *b* 1934; *Educ* Salt H S Shipley, Hull U; *m* 1963, Ann, nee Place; 1 s, 1 da; *Career* contested Darwen Lancs 1964, memb Keighley Boro Cncl 1971-74, parly Under-Sec of State Dept of Industry 1976-78; *Style* - Robert Cryer Esq, MP; Holyoake, Providence lane, Oakworth, Keighley, W Yorks (☎ Haworth 42595)

CUBBON, Sir Brian Crossland; KCB (1977, CB 1974); *b* 1928; *Educ* Bury G S, Trin Cambridge; *m* 1956, Elizabeth Lorin Richardson; 3 s, 1 da; *Career* Home Office 1951; Perm Under-Sec of State N Ireland Office 1976-79, Perm Under-Sec of State HO 1979-; *Style* - Sir Brian Cubbon, KCB; Home Office, SW1

CUBITT, Alick John Archibald; s of late Hon Jeremy John Cubitt (yr s of 3 Baron Ashcombe) and hp of kinsman, 4 Baron; *b* 10 Aug 1927; *m* 1, 1956, Priscilla Rosemary (d 1957), da of Thomas Cecil Gouldsmith; m 2, 1961, Jennifer Faith, da of late Lt-Gen William Henry Ewart Gott, CB, CBE, DSO, MC; 1 da; *Career* late Capt Roy Dragoons; *Style* - Alick Cubitt Esq; Chetwode Manor, Buckingham

CUBITT, Hon Mrs Charles - Rosamond Mary Edith; da of late Capt Sir Montague Cholmeley, 4 Bt; *b* 1904; *m* 1927, Col the Hon Charles Guy Cubitt, CBE, DSO, TD, DL, RA (TA) (d 1979); 1 s, 2 da; *Style* - The Hon Mrs Charles Cubitt; Dormers, Tetbury, Glos

CUBITT, Hon Mrs Roland; Sonia Rosemary; *née* Keppel; OBE (1959); da of Lt-Col Hon George Keppel, MVO (3 s of 7 Earl of Albemarle, KCMG, PC), and Alice (da of Adm Sir William Edmonstone, 4 Bt, CB, DL); *b* 24 May 1900; *m* 1920 (m dis 1947), Hon Roland Cubitt (later 3 Baron Ashcombe); 2 s (4 Baron Ashcombe and late Hon Jeremy Cubitt), 1 da (Hon Mrs Shand, *qv*); *Career* DStJ; *Style* - The Hon Mrs Roland Cubitt, OBE; Hall Place, W Meon, Hants

CUDLIPP, Baron (Life Peer UK 1974); Hugh Kinsman Cudlipp; OBE (1945); s of William Cudlipp, of Cardiff; *b* 28 Aug 1913; *Educ* Howard Gdns Sch Cardiff; *m* 1; m 2, 1945, Eileen Ascroft (d 1962); m 3, 1963, Jodi, da of late John L Hyland, of Palm Beach, Fla, USA; *Career* journalist;

chm IPC Ltd 1968-73 (formerly dep chm), dep chm Reed International Bd 1970-73, former dir Associated Television Ltd, chm IPC Newspaper Div 1970-73, chm Mirror Newspapers Ltd 1963-68, advr to PM on counter-inflation policies 1976; author of *Publish and be Damned* (1955) and *At Your Peril* (1962), *Walking on the Water* (1976), kt 1973; *Style* - The Rt Hon The Lord Cudlipp, OBE; The Dene, Hook Lane, Aldingbourne, W Sussex

CULHANE, Rosalind (Lady Padmore); MVO (1938), OBE (1949); da of late F W S Culhane; *m* 1964, Sir Thomas Padmore, *qv*; *Career* former Assist Priv Sec to Mr Chamberlain, Treasury Welfare Advr 1943-64; *Style* - Lady Padmore, MVO, OBE; 39 Cholmeley cres, N6 (☎ 01 340 6587)

CULLEN OF ASHBOURNE, 2 Baron (UK 1920); Charles Borlase Marsham Cokayne; MBE (1945); s of 1 Baron, KBE (d 1932) and Grace (d 1971), da of late Rev the Hon John Marsham (s of 3 Earl of Romney); *b* 6 Oct 1912; *Educ* Eton; *m* 1, 1942, Valerie Catharine Mary, nee Collbran; 1 da; m 3, 1948, Patricia Mary, da of Col S Clulow-Gray; *Heir* bro, Hon Edmund Cokayne; *Career* one of HM Lts City of London 1976, a Lord in Waiting to HM (Govt Whip) 1979-, Maj Roy Corps of Signals (TA); *Clubs* MCC; *Style* - The Rt Hon Lord Cullen of Ashbourne MBE; 75 Cadogan gdns, SW3 (☎ 01 589 1981)

CULLEN, Hon Mrs (Harriet Mary Margaret); *née* Berry; da of Baron Hartwell, MBE, TD (Life Peer); *b* 8 Nov 1944; *m* 1981, Don Martin Cullen, er s of Don Martin and Doña Mercedes Cullen, of Buenos Aires; *Style* - The Hon Mrs Cullen

CULLEN, Peter; DSC (1944); s of late Walter Cullen; *b* 22 Aug 1920; *Educ* Rugby and Oxford U; *m* 1941, Jane Primrose, nee Greener; 4 s, 2 da; *Career* Lt RN, chm Cullens Stores Ltd 1980-, md 1978-; *Recreations* hunting, stalking, walking; *Style* - Peter Cullen Esq, DSC; The Old Rectory, Winkfield, Windsor, Berks (☎ 03447 2623)

CULLIMORE, Colin Stuart; CBE (1978); s of late Reginald Cullimore; *b* 13 July 1931; *Educ* Westminster Sch, National Coll of Food Technology; *m* 1952, Kathleen Anyta, nee Lamming; 1 s; *Career* Maj Parachute Regt 1956, md J H Dewhurst Ltd, dir Albion Insurance Co Ltd, British & Argentine Meat Co Ltd, Dewfreeze Ltd, Eastmans Ltd and others; *Style* - Colin Cullimore Esq, CBE; Barons, Chobham, Woking, Surrey (☎ Chobham 8645)

CULLIMORE, William Rae; s of late William Cullimore; *b* 28 Nov 1918; *Educ* Shrewsbury, Gonville and Caius Cambridge; *m* 1948, Stella, nee Russell; 1 s, 1 da; *Career* slr; Clerk to Dean and Chapter Chester Cathedral, chm Chester Waterworks co, dep chm Wrexham and E Denbighshire Water Co; *Style* - William Cullimore Esq; Faulkners Lodge, Christleton, Chester; Manor Farm, Morton, Thornbury, Avon

CULLINAN, Hon Mrs (Dorothea Joy); da of 1 Baron Horder, GCVO, MD (d 1955); *b* 1905; *m* 1930, Edward Revill Cullinan, CBE, MD, FRCP (d 1965); 3 s, 1 da; *Style* - The Hon Mrs Cullinan; 10 Camden Mews, NW1

CULME-SEYMOUR, Lady (Mary) Faith; *née* Montagu; da (by 1 m) of late 9 Earl of Sandwich; *b* 1911; *m* 1, 1938 (m dis 1941), Philip Booth Nesbitt; 1 da; m 2, 1948, Cdr Sir Michael Culme-Seymour, 5 Bt, RN (ret), *qv*; *Style* - Lady Faith Culme-Seymour; Wytherston, Powerstock, Bridport, Dorset

CULME-SEYMOUR, John Dennis; s of late John Wentworth Culme-Seymour, s of 3 Bt and Evelyn, da of late C A Smith-Ryland; hp of cousin, Sir Michael Culme-Seymour, 5 Bt; *b* 3 Dec 1923; *Educ* Winchester; *m* 1957, (Elizabeth) Jane, da of Lt-Col Kenneth Mackessack of Ardgye, Elgin; 1 da; *Career* Capt Rifle Brig European War and Far East 1942-45; *Style* - John Culme-Seymour Esq; Ty Gwyn, Crickhowell, Breconshire

CULME-SEYMOUR, Cdr Sir Michael; 5 Bt (UK 1809), RN; s of Vice-Adm Sir Michael Culme-Seymour, 4 Bt, KCB, MVO (d 1925); *b* 26 April 1909; *m* 1948,

Lady (Mary) Faith Nesbitt, da of 9 Earl of Sandwich; 2 s (decd), 1 step da; *Heir* cous, John Culme-Seymour; *Career* farmer and landowner, ADC to Gov-Gen of Canada 1933-35, former CC Northants, RN ret 1947, DL Northants 1958-71, High Sheriff Northants 1966; *Style* - Cdr Sir Michael Culme-Seymour, Bt, RN; Wytherston, Powerstock, Bridport, Dorset (☎ Powerstock 211)

CULME-SEYMOUR, Maj Mark Charles; s of Capt George Culme-Seymour (*see* John Churchill, whose (former) 2 w is Capt C-S's sis); *b* 20 Dec 1910; *Educ* Wellington, New Coll Oxford; *m* 1, 1935 (m dis 1938), Babette, da of David Patric-Jones; m 2, 1941 (m dis 1949), Princesse Hélène Marie de la Trémoïlle, 3 da of Prince Louis Charles Marie, 12 Duc de Thouars, Prince & 11 Duc de la Trémoïlle, Premier Duc de France, 12 Prince de Tarante and 16 Prince de Talmond, and formerly w of Sir Campbell Mitchell-Cotts, 2 Bt; m 3, 1956 (m dis 1967), Patricia, da of late Charles Reid-Graham and widow of Geoffrey Ansell; 1 s, 2 da; m 4, 1973, Mary Darrall, da of Leander Armistead Riely, of Oklahoma City, and widow of Philip Kidd; *Career* served WW II Maj Rifle Bde M East & Italy; *Style* - Maj Mark Culme-Seymour; Vinas Viejas, Rancho Domingo, Benalmadena, Malaga, Spain

CUMING, Hon Mrs (Christine Veronica Helen); *née* Robertson; da of 1 Baron Robertson of Oakridge, GCB, GBE, KCMG, KCVO, DSO, MC; *b* 3 Aug 1927; *m* 1949, Lt-Col Robert Cuming, MBE, JP; 2 s, 1 da; *Style* - The Hon Mrs Cuming; Hill Farm, Bragenham, Beds

CUMING, Col Robert Hugh; MBE (1960), JP (1972), DL (Bucks 1976); s of Hugh Philip Cuming (d 1959); *b* 10 Sept 1920; *Educ* The Oratory Sch *m* 1949, Hon Christine Veronica Helen, da of 1 Baron Robertson of Oakridge; 2 s, 1 da; *Career* Col Reg Army, ret 1962; chm Quarantine Kennels Assoc 1969, Bucks Cncl of Voluntary Youth Serv 1975-78, memb exec cncl ACFA 1976-, memb of Thames Valley Police Authority 1979-; *Recreations* shooting, fishing; *Clubs* Cavalry and Guards, Kennel Club; *Style* - Col Robert Cuming MBE JP DL; Hill Farm, Bragenham, Bucks (☎ Soulbury 257)

CUMINGS, Sir Charles (Cecil George); KBE (1951); s of late Capt C E G Cumings; *b* 30 March 1904; *Educ* St Andrew's Coll, Rhodes Univ Coll Grahamstown S Africa, New Coll Oxford; *m* 1942, Enid Gethen; 1 s, 1 da; *Career* barr 1927, law lectr Rhodes U 1953-55, U of Rhodesia 1960-77; *Style* - Sir Charles Cumings, KBE (1951); 17 Elkedra close, Hawker, ACT 2614, Australia

CUMMING, John Alan; s of John Cumming; *b* 6 March 1932; *Educ* George Watson's Coll Edinburgh; *m* 1958, Isobel Beaumont, nee Sked; 3 s; *Career* chartered accountant; dir Woolwich Equitable Building Society 1978- (gen man 1969, ch gen man 1976); *Style* - John Cumming Esq; 8 Prince Consort drive, Chislehurst, Kent (☎ 01 467 8382)

CUMMING, John Stuart; s of Stuart F M Cumming, MC (d 1961); *b* 18 March 1928; *Educ* CCC Cambridge; *m* 1956, Iseult Margaret, da of late Carl W Mercer; 1 s, 3 da; *Career* Lt RAOC; Memb Inst of Chartered Accountants of Scotland, admitted 1955, investment dir Hambros Bank Ltd 1977-; *Recreations* travel, gardening; *Style* - John Cumming Esq; Cheyne House, Langton Green, Tunbridge Wells, Kent (☎ Langton 2066)

CUMMING, Lt-Col Sir Ronald Stuart; TD; s of John F Cumming, OBE, DL, JP; *b* 1900; *Educ* Uppingham, Aberdeen U; *m* 1925, Mary, OBE, da of Wm Hendrie, of Hamilton, Ontario; 2 da; *Career* joined John Walker & Sons 1920, dir 1931, chm 1957-63, chm Distillers Co Ltd 1963-67 (formerly dir), kt 1965; *Clubs* Boodle's, New (Edinburgh); *Style* - Lt-Col Sir Ronald Cumming, TD; Sourden, Rothes, Morayshire

CUMMING-BRUCE, Rt Hon Lord Justice; Rt Hon Sir (James) Roualeyn Hovell-Thurlow-Cumming-Bruce; PC (1977); s (twin) of late 6 Baron Thurlow; *b* 9 March 1912; *Educ* Shrewsbury, Magdalene Cambridge; *m* 1955, Lady (Anne) Sarah Alethea Marjorie Savile, da of 6 Earl of Mexborough and Hon Margaret Eva de Burgh Knatchbull-Hugessen, da of 2 Baron Brabourne; 2 s, 1 da; *Career* barr 1937, Judge of High Court Family Div 1964-77, Presiding Judge NE Circuit 1971-74, a Lord Justice of Appeal 1977-, kt 1964; *Style* - Rt Hon Lord Justice Cumming-Bruce PC; 1 Mulberry Walk, SW3 (☎ 01 352 5754)

CUMMING-BRUCE, Lady (Anne) Sarah Alethea Marjorie; *née* Savile; da of 6 Earl of Mexborough (d 1945); *b* 1919; *m* 1955, the Rt Hon Lord Justice Cumming-Bruce (Hon Sir James Roualeyn Hovell-Thurlow-Cumming-Bruce) *qv*; *Style* - Lady Sarah Cumming-Bruce; 1 Mulberry Walk, SW3

CUNARD, Sir Guy Alick; 7 Bt (UK 1859) of Bush Hill, Middx; s of late Capt Alick Cunard (ggs of 1 Bt, who established Cunard Line of mail steamers); suc bro, Sir Henry Palmes Cunard, 6 Bt 1973; *b* 2 Sept 1911; *Educ* Eton, RMC Sandhurst; *Heir* none; *Career* 16/5 Lancers 1931, 4/7 Roy Dragoon Gds 1933, Maj (ret); *Style* - Sir Guy Cunard, Bt; The Garden House, Wintringham, Malton, N Yorks (☎ Rillington 286)

CUNLIFFE, 3 Baron (UK 1914); Roger Cunliffe; s of 2 Baron Cunliffe (d 1963) by his 1 w, Joan, da of Cecil Lubbock (n of 1 Baron Avebury); *b* 12 Jan 1932; *Educ* Eton, Trin Cambridge; *m* 1957, Clemency Ann, da of Maj Benyon Hoare, of Aldeburgh, Suffolk; 2 s, 1 da; *Heir* s, Hon Henry Cunliffe; *Career* architect, RIBA, AA Dipl, princ Cunliffe/SCP 1977-; *Style* - The Rt Hon The Lord Cunliffe; 1 Hurst av, N6 (☎ 01 348 0386)

CUNLIFFE, Andrew Mark; s of late Sir Cyril Cunliffe, 8 Bt, and hp of bro, Sir David Cunliffe, 9 Bt; *b* 17 April 1959; *Style* - Andrew Cunliffe Esq

CUNLIFFE, Sir David Ellis; 9 Bt (GB 1759), of Liverpool, Lancashire; s of Sir Cyril Henry Cunliffe, 8 Bt (d 1969); *b* 29 Oct 1957; *Heir* bro, Andrew Cunliffe; *Style* - Sir David Cunliffe, Bt; 17 Gurney Court rd, St Albans, Herts

CUNLIFFE, Hon Geoffrey; s of late 1 Baron Cunliffe, GBE; *b* 1903; *Educ* Eton, Trin Cambridge; *m* 1, 1922, Patrick Sidney (d 1940), da of late Robert B Frend of Ardsallagh, Co Tipperary; 1 s; m 2, 1941 (m dis 1947), Gavrelle, wid of Christopher Hobhouse; 1 s, 1 da; m 3, 1947, Barbara Waring, da of late Dr J A Gibb of Maidstone; *Career* controller of aluminium Miny of Supply and Miny of Aircraft Prodn 1939-41, former memb of Industrial and Export Cncl BOT; *Style* - The Hon Geoffrey Cunliffe; Poyntzfield House, Conon Bridge, Ross-Shire

CUNLIFFE, Hon Henry; s and h of 3 Baron Cunliffe; *b* 9 March 1962; *Style* - The Hon Henry Cunliffe

CUNLIFFE, Kathleen, Baroness; Kathleen Elsie; da of Ernest Brownfield Pope, of Wargrave, Berks; *m* 1, Capt Philip Robinson, RAMC (decd); m 2, 1952, as his 2 w, 2 Baron Cunliffe (d 1963); *Style* - The Rt Hon Kathleen, Lady Cunliffe; The Old Rectory, Waterperry, Oxford

CUNLIFFE, Hon Luke; s of 3 Baron Cunliffe; *b* 1965; *Style* - The Hon Luke Cunliffe

CUNLIFFE, Lawrence Francis; MP (L) Leigh 1979-; *Style* - Lawrence Cunliffe Esq, MP; House of Commons, SW1

CUNLIFFE, Hon Merlin; s of late 2 Baron Cunliffe; *b* 1935; *Educ* Eton; *m* 1, 1960 (m dis), Deborah Rutherford Grimwade; 2 da; m 2, 1978, Mrs Amanda June Foster, nee Rogers; *Style* - The Hon Merlin Cunliffe; Wills rd, Dixon's Creek, Vic 3775, Australia

CUNLIFFE, Hon Rachel Henrietta; da of 3 Baron Cunliffe; *b* 1960; *Style* - The Hon Rachel Cunliffe

CUNLIFFE-LISTER, Hon Nicholas John; s of late Maj the Hon John Yarburgh Cunliffe-Lister, eld s of 1 Earl of Swinton, GBE, CH, MC, MP; raised to the rank of an Earl's son 1974; hp of bro, 2 Earl; *b* 4 Sept 1939; *Educ* Winchester, Worcester Coll Oxford; *m* 1966, (Elizabeth) Susan, da of Rt Hon William Whitelaw CH MC PC MP and Cecilia, gda of Sir John Hay, 9 Bt; 2 s, 1 da *Career* late 2 Lt WG, slr 1966; *Style* - The Hon Nicholas Cunliffe-Lister; Glebe House, Masham, Ripon, Yorks

CUNLIFFE-OWEN, Sir Dudley Herbert; 2 Bt (UK 1920) of Bray, Berks; s of Sir Hugo Cunliffe-Owen, 1 Bt (d 1947); *b* 27 March 1923; *Educ* RNC Dartmouth; *m* 1, 1947, Mary Maud, nee Redgrave (d 1956); m 2, 1956 (m dis 1962), Hon Juliana Eveline Nettlefold, nee Curzon, da of 2 Viscount Scarsdale, TD; 1 da; m 3, 1964, Jean, da of late Surg Cdr A N Forsyth, RN; 1 s, 1 da; *Heir* s, Hugo Cunliffe-Owen; *Career* md Palace Entertainments Ltd 1965-; *Style* - Sir Dudley Cunliffe-Owen, Bt; Eyreton House, Quarterbridge, Douglas, IoM (☎ Douglas 4545)

CUNLIFFE-OWEN, Hugo Dudley; s and h of Sir Dudley Herbert Cunliffe-Owen, RN, 2 Bt; *b* 16 May 1966; *Style* - Hugo Cunliffe-Owen Esq

CUNLIFFE-OWEN, Mauricia, Lady - Mauricia Martha; da of late Herbert Shaw, of San Francisco, Calif, USA; *m* 1935, as his 3 w, Sir Hugo Cunliffe-Owen, 1 Bt (d 1947); *Style* - Mauricia, Lady Cunliffe-Owen

CUNNACK, Hon Mrs (Alice Elizabeth Millicent); *née* Wemyss; da of 1 Baron Wester Wemyss (extinct 1933); *b* 1906; *m* 1953, Maj Francis Cunnack, RA (ret, d 1974); *Style* - The Hon Mrs Cunnack

CUNNINGHAM, Gen Sir Alan Gordon; GCMG (1948), KCB (1941), DSO (1918), MC (1915); s of Prof D J Cunningham, FRS; *b* 1 May 1887; *Educ* Cheltenham, RMA Woolwich; *m* 1951, Margery, da of Samuel Slater, CMG, CIE, ICS and wid of Sir Harold Snagge, KBE; *Career* RA 1906, Cmdt Staff Coll 1942-43, GOC Eastern Cmmd 1944-45, Gen 1945, ret 1946; Col Cmdt RA 1944-54, High Cmmr Palestine 1945-48, former Pres Cncl of Cheltenham Coll, DL Hants 1950; *Style* - Gen Sir Alan Cunningham GCMG KCB DSO MC DL; c/o Lloyds Bank Ltd, 6 Pall Mall, SW1

CUNNINGHAM, Lady; Dorothy Enid; da of late Edwin Riley of Bilston, Staffs; *m* 1935, Sir (Samuel) Knox Cunningham, 1 Bt, QC (d 1976, when title became extinct); *Style* - Lady Cunningham; Derhams House, Minchinhampton, Stroud, Glos

CUNNINGHAM, Hon Mrs (Edith Louise); *née* MacDermott; da of Baron MacDermott, MC, PC, (Life Peer) (d 1979); *b* 1930; *Educ* MB and BCh 1954; *m* 1955, Samuel Barbour Cunningham; *Style* - The Hon Mrs Cunningham; Woodville, Malone Park (Central), Belfast 9

CUNNINGHAM, George; MP (L) Islington S and Finsbury 1974-; s of Harry Jackson Cunningham; *b* 10 June 1931; *Educ* Dunfermline H S, Blackpool G S, Manchester and London Us; *m* 1957, Mavis, nee Walton; 1 s, 1 da; *Career* formerly with C'wlth Relations Office, contested Henley 1966, MP SW Islington 1970-74, MEP 1978-79; *Style* - George Cunningham Esq, MP; 28 Manor gdns, Hampton, Middx (☎ 01 979 6221)

CUNNINGHAM, Lt-Gen Sir Hugh Patrick; KBE (1975, OBE 1966); s of late Sir Charles Banks Cunningham, CSI; *b* 4 Nov 1921; *Educ* Charterhouse; *m* 1955, Jill, da of J S Jeffrey; 2 s, 2 da; *Career* 2 Lt RE 1942, GOC SW District 1971-74, ACGS (OR) MOD 1974-75, Lt-Gen 1975, Dep Ch of Defence Staff (OR) 1976-78, ret; Col Cmdt RE 1976-, Col Queen's Gurkha Engineers; *Clubs* Army & Navy, MCC, Athenaeum; *Style* - Lt-Gen Sir Hugh Cunningham, KBE; Little Leigh, East Knoyle, Salisbury, Wilts

CUNNINGHAM, Dr John Anderson; MP (L) Whitehaven, Cumberland; s of Andrew Cunningham; *b* 4 Aug 1939 *Educ* Jarrow G S, Bede Sch, Durham U; *m* 1964, Maureen; 1 s, 2 da; *Career* chemist; PPS to PM 1976, Parly Under-Sec of State Dept of Energy 1976-79; *Style* - Dr John Cunningham, MP; House of Commons, SW1

CUNYNGHAME, Sir Andrew David Francis; 12 Bt (NS 1702) of Milncraig, Ayrshire; s of Sir (Henry) David St Leger Brooke Selwyn, 11 Bt (d 1978) and Hon Lady (Pamela) Cunynghame, da of late 5 Baron Stanley of Alderley; *b* 25 Dec 1942; *Educ* Eton; *m* 1972, Harriet Ann, da of

Charles Thomas Dupont, of Montreal, Canada; *Heir* bro, John Cunynghame; *Career* FCA; *Clubs* Brooks's; *Style* - Sir Andrew Cunynghame, Bt; 69 Hillgate pla, W8; The School House, Williamscote, Banbury, Oxon

CUNYNGHAME, John Philip Henry Michael Selwyn; s of late Sir (Henry) David St Leger Brooke Selwyn Cunynghame, 11 Bt; hp of bro, Sir Andrew Cunynghame, 12 Bt; *b* 9 Sept 1944; *Educ* Eton; *Style* - John Cunynghame Esq

CUNYNGHAME, Hon Lady; Hon Pamela Margaret; da of late 5 Baron Stanley of Alderley, KCMG; *b* 1909; *m* 1941, Sqdn Ldr Sir (Henry) David St Leger Brooke Selwyn Cunynghame, 11 Bt, RAFVR (d 1978); 3 s; *Career* actress; *Style* - The Hon Lady Cunynghame; 15 Madeline rd, SE20

CURLING, David Richard Michael; s of Lt-Col Richard Robinson Curling, DSO (d 1953); *b* 9 May 1923; *Educ* Gordonstoun; *m* 1954, Olive Marigold, MB, BS, da of Douglas Cory-Wright, CBE; 1 s, 2 da; *Career* Midshipman RNR Atlantic, Indian Ocean; advertiser, dir J Walter Thompson Co Ltd, High Sheriff of Bucks 1980-81; *Recreations* sailing, shooting; *Clubs* Roy Yacht Squadron, Boodle's, Roy Ocean Racing; *Style* - David Curling Esq; The Rosary, Coleshill, nr Amersham, Bucks (☎ Amersham 6431)

CURLING, Hon Mrs - Hon Melissa; da of Baron Llewelyn-Davies; *b* 1945; *m* 1974, Christopher Curling *Style* - The Hon Mrs Curling

CURRER-BRIGGS, (Arthur) Noel; s of the late R M Currer-Briggs; *b* 21 Nov 1919; *Educ* Bryanston Sch, St Catherine's Cambridge; *m* 1948, Barbara, da of Col R W Hey (m dis 1980); *Career* major Mediterranean, Foreign Service (Intelligence Coordination Staff) 1948-49, farmer 1950-62, genealogist and author 1960-; *Recreations* motor-cycle riding; *Style* - Noel Currer-Briggs Esq; c/o Barclays Bank, 28/30 Park Row, Leeds

CURREY, Hon Mrs (Heather Mary); *née* Drummond of Megginch; da and co-heiress presumptive of 15 Baron Strange; *b* 9 Nov 1931; *m* 1954, Lt-Cdr Andrew Christian Currey, RN, s of Rear-Adm Philip Currey, CB, OBE; 2 s, 1 da; *Style* - The Hon Mrs Currey; Tholt E Will, Sulby, Isle of Man

CURRIE, Sir Alick Bradley; 6 Bt (UK 1847); s of late George Hugh Currie, gs of 1 Bt; suc kinsman Sir Walter Mordaunt Currie, 5 Bt, 1978; *b* 8 June 1904; *Heir* n, Donald Currie; *Career* US Dept of Commerce, ret; *Style* - Sir Alick Currie, Bt; 13467 County rd, 501 Bayfield, Colorado 81122, USA

CURRIE, Donald Scott; s of George Currie (d 1980) and Janet, nee Scott; hp of unc, Sir Alick Currie, 6 Bt; *b* 1930; *m* 1, 1948 (m dis 1951), Charlotte, nee Johnstone, of Arizona, USA; 1 s, 2 da (twins); m 2, 1952, Barbara Lee, da of A P Garnier of California; 1 s, 2 da; *Style* - Donald Currie Esq

CURRILL, George Frederick; JP; *b* 22 Sept 1912; *m* 1938, Muriel Emily; 1 s; *Career* jt md Hunts Office Equipment Gp 1955-73, chm Omal Group Ltd 1974-, former pres Office Machines Fedn; *Style* - George Currill Esq, JP; 51 Kennett rd, Oxford (☎ 61745); 26 Drummond rd, Bournemouth (☎ 33319)

CURRY, David Maurice; MEP (C) NE Essex 1979-; s of Thomas Curry; *b* 13 June 1944; *Educ* Ripon G S, CCC Oxford; *m* 1971, Anne Roullett; 1 s, 2 da; *Career* reporter Newcastle Journal 1967-70, ed Financial Times (trade, intern Co News, Brussels corr, Paris corr) 1970-79; *Recreations* digging, exercising dog on bicycle, romanesque architecture; *Style* - David Curry Esq, MEP; The Old Maltings, Arkesden, Essex (☎ 079 985 368)

CURRY, John Arthur Hugh; s of Col Alfred Curry (d 1975); *b* 7 June 1938; *Educ* King's Coll Sch Wimbledon, St Edmund Hall Oxford, Harvard Grad Sch of Business Admin; *m* 1962, Anne Rosemary, nee Lewis; 3 s, 1 da; *Career* FICA, jt ch exec Unitech Ltd, dir Data Recognition Ltd, H & T Components Ltd, Solid State Controls Ltd, UIC Ltd, ACL Ltd, APT

Electronics Ltd amongst others; *Recreations* tennis, rugby, travel; *Clubs* All England Lawn Tennis and Croquet; *Style* - John Curry Esq; New Place, The Ridges, Finchampstead, Berks

CURRY-TOWNELEY-O'HAGAN, Hon Mrs (Helen Frances Alice Towneley); *née* O'Hagan; da of 3 Baron O'Hagan (d 1961); *b* 1912; *m* 1940, Capt Ian Desmond Curry, RA, who assumed by deed poll 1942 the surname of Curry-Towneley-O'Hagan (d 1969); 1 s; *Style* - The Hon Mrs Curry-Towneley-O'Hagan; 24 Burgh st, Islington, N1

CURTIS, Maj Edward Philip; s of late Gerald Edward Curtis; hp of kinsman, Sir William Curtis, 7 Bt; *b* 25 June 1940; *Educ* Bradfield, RMA Sandhurst; *m* 1978, Catherine, nee Armstrong, of Christchurch New Zealand; 1 da; *Career* Maj 16/5 Lancers; *Style* - Maj Edward Curtis; Cwm Bach Lodge, Glasbury-on-Wye, via Hereford

CURTIS, John Gilbert; s of late Col A G Curtis; *b* 2 Oct 1932; *Educ* Charterhouse, Worcester Coll Oxford; *m* 1963, Susan Judith, nee Whitefield; 2 s; *Career* Lt Royal Green Jackets; dir Matheson & Co Ltd 1967-, UKPI 1979-, Jamesons Chocolates 1980-; *Style* - John Curtis Esq; Clayhurst, Odiham, Hants

CURTIS, Lady; Joan Margaret; da of late Reginald Nicholson; *m* 1934, Sir Peter Curtis, 6 Bt (d 1976); 1 s, 2 da; *Style* - Lady Curtis; Little Manor, Bishop's Waltham, Hants

CURTIS, Rowland William; JP (1974); s of late Harold Curtis; *b* 1 March 1921; *Educ* Thorne G S; *m* 1941, Edith Eleanor, nee Harrison; 2 c; *Career* dir Royal Hotel (Scarborough) Ltd 1974-, md Futurist Enterprises Ltd 1967-, dir Futurist Theatrical Hire Ltd 1974-; *Style* - Rowland Curtis Esq JP; The Low Hall, West Ayton, Scarborough, Yorks (☎ 0723 862267)

CURTIS, Sir William Peter; 7 Bt (UK 1802), of Cullands Grove, Middlesex; s of Sir Peter Curtis, 6 Bt (d 1976); *b* 9 April 1935; *Educ* Winchester, Trin Oxford, RAC Cirencester; *Heir* kinsman, Maj Edward Curtis; *Career* late 16/5 Lancers; *Clubs* Cavalry; *Style* - Sir William Curtis, Bt; Oak Lodge, Bank st, Bishop's Waltham, Hants

CURTISS, Air Marshal Sir John Bagot; KCB (1980, CB 1979); s of Major E F B Curtiss; *b* 6 Dec 1924; *Educ* Radley, Wanganui Collegiate Sch New Zealand, Worcester Coll Oxford; *m* 1946, Peggy Drughorn, da of Edward Bowie; 3 s, 1 da; *Career* Dir-Gen Organisation RAF 1975-77, Cmdt Staff Coll 1977-80, Air Offr Cmdg No 18 Gp 1980-; *Clubs* RAF, MCC; *Style* - Air Marshal Sir John Curtiss, KCB; c/o Coutts & Co, 1 Old Park lane, W1

CURZON, Lady Charlotte Elizabeth Anne; da of 6 Earl Howe, CBE; *b* 1948; *Style* - Lady Charlotte Curzon

CURZON, Sir Clifford Michael; CBE (1958); s of Michael Curzon; *b* 18 May 1907; *Educ* Roy Acad of Music; *m* 1931, Lucille (d 1977), da of Edward Wallace; 2 s (adopted); *Career* concert pianist, kt 1977; *Style* - Sir Clifford Curzon, CBE; The Close, Glenridding, Cumbria; The White House, Millfield Place, N6

CURZON, Hon Diana Geraline; da of late 2 Viscount Scarsdale; *b* 1934; *Style* - The Hon Diana Curzon; Cruz 47, Atico, Barcelona, Spain

CURZON, Hon David James Nathaniel; s (by 1 m) of 3 Viscount Scarsdale; *b* 1958; *Educ* Stowe; *m* 1981, Ruth Linton; *Style* - The Hon David Curzon

CURZON, Frederick Richard Penn; s of late Cdr (Chambré) George (William Penn) Curzon (d 1976), and hp of cous, 6 Earl Howe, CBE; *b* 29 Jan 1951; *Educ* Rugby, Ch Ch Oxford; *Style* - Frederick Curzon Esq; Windsor Croft, Windsor Lane, Great Missenden, Bucks

CURZON, Hon James Fergus Nathaniel; s (by 2 m) of 3 Viscount Scarsdale; *b* 1970

CURZON, Hon Peter Ghislain Nathaniel; s (by 1 m) and h of 3 Viscount Scarsdale; *b* 6 March 1949; *Educ*

Ampleforth; *Style* - The Hon Peter Curzon; 106 Long Drive, W3

CURZON, Hon Richard Francis Nathaniel; s (by 2 m) of 3 Viscount Scarsdale; *b* 1969

CUSSINS, Manny; Officer OStJ, 1977; s of Israel Cussins (d 1939); *b* 26 Oct 1905; *Educ* Hull Tech Coll; *m* 1, 1939, Muriel Field, da of Maurice Field (d 1946); 3 s, 2 da; m 2, 1952, Muriel Benjamin, da of Philip Benjamin (d 1969); *Career* chm Waring & Gillow Hldgs Ltd; chm Arncliffe Hldgs Ltd, Leeds United Assoc Football Club Ltd; pres Donisthorpe Hall for Aged Jews, Leeds; *Recreations* old people's welfare, watching football; *Style* - Manny Cussins Esq; 19 Sandmoor Court, Harrogate Road, Leeds 17, Yorks (☎ 0532 38151)

CUST, Hon Peregrine Edward Quintin; s and h of 7 Baron Brownlow; *b* 9 July 1974; *Style* - The Hon Peregrine Cust

CUTHBERT, Vice-Adm Sir John Wilson; KBE (1957, CBE 1945), CB (1953), DL (Hants 1977); s of William Cuthbert of Glasgow; *b* 9 April 1902; *Educ* Kelvinside Acad, RN Coll; *m* 1928, Betty Wake (CBE, former Ch Woman Fire Offr NFS); *Career* RN 1916, V-Adm 1954, Adm Cmdg Reserves 1955-56, Flag Offr Scotland 1956-58, ret; memb Roy Co of Archers (Queen's Bodyguard for Scotland); *Style* - Vice-Adm Sir John Cuthbert, KBE, CB, DL; Ibthorpe Manor Farm, Hurstbourne Tarrant, nr Andover, Hants (☎ Hurstbourne Tarrant 237)

CUTHBERT, Lady Victoria (Lucy Diana); *née* Percy; da of 10 Duke of Northumberland, KG, TD, PC; *b* 1949; *m* 1975, John Aidan Cuthbert; 1 da; *Style* - Lady Victoria Cuthbert; Beaufront Castle, Hexham, Northumberland

CUTHBERTSON, Sir David Paton; CBE (1957); s of John Cuthbertson, MBE; *b* 9 May 1900; *Educ* Glasgow U; *m* 1928, Jean Prentice, da of late Rev Alexander Telfer; 2 s, 1 da; *Career* former lectr in Pathological Biochemistry and Clinical Biochemist Roy Infirmary and Glasgow U, former consultant dir C'wlth Bureau of Animal Nutrition and Hon Consultant in Physiology and Nutrition to Army 1946-65, Hon Sr Res Fell Pathological Biochemistry Glasgow U, dir Rowett Res Inst 1945-65, Hon Consultant Biochemical Dept Roy Infirmary Glasgow, kt 1965; *Style* - Sir David Cuthbertson, CBE; 11 Willockston rd, Troon, Ayrshire (☎ 312028)

CUTLER, Sir Horace Walter; OBE (1963); s of Albert Benjamin Cutler; *b* 28 July 1912; *Educ* Harrow G S; *m* 1957, Christiane, da of Dr Klaus Muthesius; 1 s, 3 da; *Career* former Mayor of Harrow, Dep Leader (1964-67 and 1973-74) and Leader (1974-77) of Opposition Gtr London Cncl, memb for Harrow W 1964-, Leader Gtr London Cncl 1977-81, Leader Oppn 1981-, contested (C) Willesden East 1970, kt 1979; *Style* - Sir Horace Cutler, OBE; Hawkswood, Hawkswood lane, Gerrards Cross, Bucks (☎ Fulmer 3182)

CZERNIN, Hon Mrs; Hon (Mary) Hazel Caridwen; *née* Scott-Ellis; da of 9 Baron Howard de Walden and 5 Baron Seaford; *b* 12 Aug 1935; *m* 1957, Joseph Czernin, s of late Count Franz Josef Czernin (of the family granted title of Count or *Reichsgraf* of the Holy Roman Empire by the Emperor Ferdinand III 1652 with the *prädikats 'Hoch und Wohlgeboren'*); 1 s, 5 da; *Career* co-heiress to Barony of Howard de Walden; *Style* - The Hon Mrs Czernin; 2 The Boltons, SW10; White Oak House, Highclere, Newbury, Berks RG15 9RJ

CZERNIN, Countess Maud Sarah; da of Ronald Hamilton, OBE (d 1958; s of Rt Hon Lord George Hamilton, GCSI, JP, 3 s of 1 Duke of Abercorn, KG, PC; Lord George Hamilton m Lady Maud Lascelles, CI, da of 3 Earl of Harewood), and Florence (the actress 'Sarah Brooke'), da of Maj Hanna; *b* 4 April 1917; *m* 1939 (m dis 1947; he d 1962), Count Manfred Czernin, DSO, MC, DFC, s of Count Otto Czernin; 1 s, 1 da; *Style* - Countess Maud Czernin; 1 Egerton gdns, SW3

D

D'ABO, Lady Ursula; *née* Manners; da of late 9 Duke of Rutland; *b* 1916; *m* 1, 1943 (m dis 1948), Anthony Freire Marreco, late Lt RNVR; m 2, 1951, Robert Erland Nicolai d'Abo (d 1970); 2 s, 1 da; *Career* was a Train Bearer to HM the Queen at the Coronation of HM King George VI; *Style* - Lady Ursula d'Abo; 29 Kensington sq, W8; West Wratting Park, Cambs

D'AETH, Prof Richard; s of Walter D'Aeth and Marion Turnbull; *b* 3 June 1912; *Educ* Bedford Sch, Emmanuel Coll Cambridge, Harvard U; *m* 1943, Pamela Straker; 2 da; *Career* PhD, Prof of Educn Univ Coll of West Indies 1952-58, U of Exeter 1958-77, pres Hughes Hall Cambridge 1978-; *Style* - Prof Richard D'Aeth; Hughes Hall, Cambridge

D'AMBRUMENIL, Christopher Hugh; s of Lewis d'Ambrumenil (d 1968); *b* 17 Jan 1926; *Educ* Wellington; *m* 1962, Cathleen Marion, nee Speight; *Career* Capt Coldstream Gds WW II; chm Pyman Bell & Co Ltd 1980-; chm Annual Proposers Ctee Northumberland Co Cncl 1971-81, memb Hexham Rural District Cncl 1964-74; *Clubs* Cavalry and Guards, Northern Counties (Newcastle); *Style* - Christopher d'Ambrumenil Esq; West House, Horsley, Northumberland

D'AMBRUMENIL, David Philip; s of late Sir Philip d'Ambrumenil; *b* 1 Aug 1930; *Educ* Rugby; New Coll Oxford; *Career* dir Gardner Mountain & d'Ambrumenil 1960-, man and sec Pyman Bell & Co Ltd, Timber Research & Dvpt Assoc; *Style* - David d'Ambrumenil Esq; 71 Eaton Terrace, SWI (☎ 01 730 2929)

D'ANGERVILLE, Count (Comte, *see below*); Howard; Kt Grand Cross- Sacred Mil Order of Constantine of St George of Naples, Roy Order of Crown of Yugoslavia, Roy Order of St Sava, Roy Order of White Eagle; Roy Yugoslavian War Cross & Sword of Honour; s of Henry, Comte & Seigneur d'Angerville (himself s of Henri-Georges-Charles, Comte & Seigneur d'Angerville, descended from the 11 century Norman family of d'Angerville, specifically Guillaume d'Angerville, Marshal of Normandy 1205; the title of Marquis was conferred by Napoleon III for the sr line of d'Angerville d'Auvrecher 1864, and the title of Comte confirmed by Roy Decree for the cadet line represented by the subject of this article); *m* 1, Audrey Lindsay-Vail (d 1978); m 2, 1981, Hisako, da of Prof Ishiguro, of Japan; *Career* late Chllr to HM late King of Yugoslavia (Personal Envoy to Madrid Embassy and to Lisbon & Rome); Privy Counsellor & Envoy of HRH Infante Don Jaime of Spain (eldest surviving s of Alfonso XIII); late Envoy of late Head of Roy House of Bourbon-Sicily (HRH Prince Ferdinand); consultant- Chancery & Consul-Gen of San Marino in London, USA authorities European immigration research; ed Annuaire de la Noblesse de France 1950-; author, ed and publisher of various works on Royalties and Nobilities of the World; FRSA, V-Pres Cancer Res Soc in Kensington; *Recreations* fencing, esoteric studies; *Style* - Count d'Angerville; 2 Rue Bellanger, 92200 Neuilly, France; Observatory House, Observatory gdns, W8

D'AVIGDOR-GOLDSMID, Maj-Gen Sir James Arthur; 3 Bt (UK 1934), of Somerhill, Co Kent, CB (1965), OBE (1955), MC (1944); 2 s of Sir Osmond d'Avigdor-Goldsmid, 1 Bt, JP, DL (d 1940, né d'Avigdor, gs of Count Solomon d'Avigdor by Rachel Goldsmid, da of Sir Isaac Goldsmid, 1 Bt (of the cr of 1841), JP, DL, who was also Baron de Goldsmid and de Palmeira in the Peerage of Portugal; Rachel's sis Augusta m Elias Mocatta and her niece Mary m Frederick Mocatta, alliances which led to the eminence of the bullion broking house of Mocatta & Goldsmid; another sis of Rachel's m Nathaniel Montefiore (a Rothschild on his mother Henrietta's side), n of Sir Moses Montefiore, 1 & last Bt and a celebrated philanthropist); Sir Osmond added the 'Goldsmid' on succeeding to the estates of his 1 cous once removed Sir

Julian Goldsmid, 3 & last Bt; Sir James suc his bro, Sir Harry d'Avigdor-Goldsmid, 2 Bt, DSO, MC, JP, DL, for many years MP for Walsall and former chm Pergamon Press, in 1976; *b* 19 Dec 1912; *Educ* Harrow, Sandhurst; *Heir* none; *Career* Maj-Gen; served Roy Dragoon Gds 1932-53 (Cmmd 1950-53), WW II France & Germany; Dir RAC 1962-65, Pres Reg Commission Bd 1965, Dir TA & Cadets 1966-68; Col 4/7 Roy Dragoon Gds 1963-73, Hon Col Queen's Own Mercian Yeo 1972-77; MP (C) Lichfield & Tamworth 1970-74; memb Horserace Betting Levy Bd 1974-77, chm- Racecourse Security Servs 1977-80, SE TAVR Assoc 1974-78, Tattersall's Cttee 1980, Exec Cttee Govs Corps Commissionaires 1980; *Clubs* Cavalry & Guards, Turf, Jockey; race horses- 'Skylander', 'Sardine', 'Norman Emperor'; *Style* - Maj-Gen Sir James d'Avigdor-Goldsmid Bt CB OBE MC; 101 Mount st, W1 (☎ 01 499 1989)

D'AVIGDOR-GOLDSMID, Lady - Rosemary Margaret; da of Lt-Col Charles Nicholl; *b* 22 July 1910; *m* 1, 1931 (m dis 1934), Sir Peter Horlick, 3 Bt; m 2, 1940, Maj Sir Henry Joseph d'Avigdor-Goldsmid, 2 Bt, MC, TD, MP (C) Walsall S 1955-74 (d 1976); 2 da (1 decd); *Recreations* racing (race horses- 'Hoodwink', 'Repoussé'); *Style* - Lady d'Avigdor-Goldsmid; Somerhill, Tonbridge, Kent (☎ 0732 352314); 10 Eaton Mansions, Cliveden Place, SW1 (☎ 01 730 3034)

D'ERLANGER, Hon Mrs - Hon Mary Elizabeth Josephine; *née* Pellew; da of 9 Viscount Exmouth; *b* 1947; *m* 1969, Robin Gerard d'Erlanger; 2 s, 2 da; *Style* - The Hon Mrs d'Erlanger; Craddock House, Craddock, Cullompton, Devon

D'OYLY, Sir John Rochfort; 13 Bt (E 1663) of Shottisham, Norfolk; s of Sir Hastings Hadley D'Oyly, 11 Bt (d 1948) and bro of 12 Bt (d 1962); *b* 19 April 1900; *Educ* HMS 'Conway' and Gonville and Caius Coll Cambridge; *m* 1930 (m dis 1944), Kathleen, da of Robert Brown Gillespie, of Yatiyantota, Ceylon; 2 da; *Heir* half-bro Nigel Hadley Miller D'Oyly; *Career* served as mid-shipman in Grand Fleet 1916-18, Baltic operations 1919, specialized in Physical and Recreational Training 1921, served in 1939-45 War (Cdr RN Coll Greenwich, S Atlantic, Atlantic, E Indies and Pacific); *Style* - Sir John D'Oyly, Bt; c/o Lloyds Bank Ltd, 39 Piccadilly, W1

D'OYLY, Nigel Hadley Miller; s of Sir Hastings D'Oyly, 11 Bt, by his 2 w Evelyn; half bro and hp of Sir John Rochfort D'Oyly, 13 Bt; *b* 6 July 1914; *Educ* Radley, Sandhurst; *m* 1940, Dolores, da of Robert Gregory, of New Lodge, Crowhurst, Sussex; 1 s (Hadley, b 1956, m Emma Dent), 2 da (Mrs Charles (Carol) Pearce, Sherry b 1946); *Career* civil engrg, md OPS (London) & Co; formerly Maj Royal Scots Gds; *Recreations* rugger, tennis, swimming, photography; *Clubs* SCGB, Knights'; *Style* - Nigel D'Oyly Esq; 16 Barkston gdns, SW5 (☎ 01 373 2928)

DA SILVA, John Burke; CMG (1969); s of John Christian da Silva (d 1965); *b* 30 Aug 1918; *Educ* Stowe Sch, Trin Cambridge; *m* 1, 1940, Janice Margaret, nee Mayor (d 1963); 1 da; m 2, 1963, Jennifer Jane, da of Capt The Hon Trevor Tempest Parker RN (d 1973); 1 s, 2 da; *Career* Maj Intelligence Corps 1940-46 (dispatches), Control Cmmn Germany 1946-49, HM Diplomatic Service (Germany, Rome, Hamburg, Bahrein, Aden, Washington) 1950-73; consultant Commercial Union Assur Co Ltd 1973-; *Recreations* oriental art; *Clubs* Bath; *Style* - John da Silva Esq, CMG; Copse Close, Virginia Water, Surrey (☎ Wentworth 2342)

DABORN, Alan Francis; OBE (1966), TD (1963), JP (1970), DL (1971); s of Alwyn Victor Daborn (d 1969); *b* 20 Feb 1923; *Educ* Kings Coll Sch Wimbledon; *m* 1949, Thelma Elizabeth; 2 s; *Career* served in HM Forces 1942-46, chartered surveyor, ptnr Alwyn Daborn and Son (now amalgamated with John German Ralph Day); *Clubs* Naval and Military; *Style* - Alan Daborn Esq, OBE, TD, JP, DL; 1 Dogpole ct, Shrewsbury, Shropshire (☎ Shrewsbury 56176)

DACIE, Sir John Vivian, MD; s of John Charles Dacie; *b* 20 July 1912; *Educ* King's Coll London, King's Coll Hosp; *m*

1938, Margaret Kathleen Victoria, nee Thynne; 3 s, 2 da; *Career* sr lectr British Postgraduate Medical Sch 1946-57; Prof of Haematology, London U, 1957-; author; kt 1976; *Style* - Sir John Dacie, MD; 10 Alan rd, Wimbledon, SW19 (☎ 01 946 6086)

DACRE OF GLANTON, Baron (Life Peer UK 1979); Hugh Redwald Trevor-Roper; s of Dr Bertie William Edward Trevor-Roper (s of Richard Trevor-Roper, whose widow Grace m her 1 husb's 1 cous Hugh Trevor-Roper; Richard's ggf was Rev Hon Richard Roper, 4 s of 8 Baron Teynham by his 2 w, Baroness Dacre; when Lady Dacre's grandson's widow d she left her property of Plas-Teg in Wales to her late husb (18 Baron Dacre)'s 1 cous Cadwallader, who added Trevor to his name of Roper; hence both the surname and choice of title of Cadwallader's gggs, the present Life Peer - the current Lady Dacre is his 5 cous twice removed); *b* 15 Jan 1914; *Educ* Charterhouse, Ch Ch Oxford; *m* 1954, Lady Alexandra Haig, da of Field-Marshal 1 Earl Haig, the WW I General; *Career* Master Peterhouse 1980-, formerly Student & Tutor Ch Ch & Regius Prof Modern History Oxford 1957-80; Nat Dir Times Newspapers 1974; *Clubs* Athenaeum, Beefsteak, Savile; *Style* - Rt Hon Lord Dacre of Glanton; Chiefswood, Melrose, Roxburghshire; Peterhouse, Cambridge

DACRE, Baroness (E 1321); Hon Rachel Leila ; *née* Brand; da of 4 Viscount Hampden, who was also 26 Baron Dacre, following whose death (1965) the Viscountcy passed to his bro while the Barony of Dacre fell into abeyance between the two survivng da, till terminated in favour of Rachel, the er, 1970; Lady Dacre's mother was Leila, gda of Sir Charles Seely, 1 Bt; the story that the Dacres were so named for their prowess at the siege of Acre during the Third Crusade appears less plausible than romantic, when the prior existence of the place name (a variant of which is mentioned by Bede) in Cumbria is born in mind; *b* 24 Oct 1929; *m* 1951, Hon William Douglas-Home, *qv*; 1 s, 3 da; *Heir* s, Hon James Thomas Archibald Douglas-Home, b 16 May 1952; *Style* - The Rt Hon The Lady Dacre; Drayton House, East Meon, Hants (☎ 250)

DACRE OF GLANTON, Baroness - Lady Alexandra Henrietta Louise; *née* Haig; *b* 1907; *m* 1, 1941 (m diss 1954), Rear-Adm Clarence Dinsmore Howard-Johnston, CB, DSO, DSC; 2 s, 1 da; m 2, 1954, Hugh Trevor-Roper, *see Dacre of Glanton, Baron*; *Career* chm Music Therapy Charity, Edinburgh Festival Guild, Border Regn; Organiser Oxford Subscription Concerts 1962-80; *Recreations* music, painting, interior decoration, gardening; *Style* - The Rt Hon The Lady Dacre of Glanton; The Master's Lodge, Peterhouse, Cambridge; Chiefswood, Melrose, Roxburghshire

DACRE LACY, Alastair de Saumarez; s of Edward Dacre Lacy; *b* 29 Nov 1928; *Educ* Bradfield Coll; *m* 1960, Avril, nee Ranger; 2 da; *Career* chm and md Technicare Int 1972-; Queens's Award for Export Achievement 1979; *Style* - Alastair Dacre Lacy Esq; Earls Grove, Peasemore, Nr Newbury, Berks

DAFFERN, Antony Richard; s of late Edward William Daffern; *b* 14 May 1934; *Educ* King Edward VI Sch Nuneaton, Manchester U; *m* 1959, Freda, nee Appleby; 2 da; *Career* co dir, asst md Telefusion Ltd 1978-; memb NTRA Cncl 1978-; *Style* - Antony Daffern Esq; 27 Rowland lane, Cleveleys, Blackpool (☎ 854562)

DAHL, Roald; s of Harald Dahl (d 1920); *b* 13 Sept 1916; *Educ* Repton; *m* 1953, Patricia, nee Neal; 1 s, 3 da (1 c decd); *Career* Wing Cdr RAF 1939-42 (Western Desert, Greece, Syria), writer; *Recreations* gaming, cultivating orchids (phalaenopsis only), drinking fine wine, collecting paintings, furniture and antiques; *Clubs* Ritz Casino; *Style* - Roald Dahl Esq; Gipsy House, Great Missenden, Bucks (☎ Great Missenden 2757)

DAINTON, Prof Sir Frederick Sydney; s of George Whalley Dainton; *b* 11 Nov 1914; *Educ* Central Sch Sheffield, St John's Oxford; *m* 1942, Barbara Hazlitt, JP (1971) Oxford, nee Wright; 1 s, 2 da; *Career* former fell St Catherine's Cambridge; V-Chllr Nottingham U, 1965-

70; chm Cncl for Scientific Policy, 1970-; former chm Univ Grants Ctee, Chllr Sheffield U 1978-; kt 1971; *Style* - Professor Sir Frederick Dainton; Fieldside, Water Eaton la, Oxford (☎ Kidlington 5132)

DAINTY, Hon Mrs; Hon Priscilla; *née* Wolfenden; da of Baron Wolfenden, CBE; *b* 1937; *m* 1959, Col F L Dainty; *Style* - The Hon Mrs Dainty; Garderhouse, Whalsay, Shetland Isles

DAKIN, Dorothy Danvers; da of Edwin Lionel Dakin and Mary Danvers Dakin (nee Walker); *b* 22 Oct 1919; *Educ* Sherborne Sch for Girls, Newnham Coll Cambridge; *Career* Headmistress The Red Maids' Sch Bristol 1961-, chm Jt Cncl ISIS 1977-; *Style* - Miss Dorothy Dakin; The Red Maids' Sch, Westbury-on-Trym, Bristol (☎ 626131)

DALDRY, Sir Leonard Charles; KBE (1963, CBE 1960); s of Charles Henry Daldry (d 1965); *b* 6 Oct 1908; *m* 1, 1938, Joan Mary (d 1976), nee Crisp; m 2, 1976, Monica Mary, nee Benson; 1 s, 1 da; *Career* former Special Memb of Nigerian House of Reps 1955-60, sen Fed Legislature Nigeria 1960-61, chm Nigerian Bd Barclays Bank DCO 1961-63, ret, chm St Loye's Coll for Disabled Exeter 1969-; *Clubs* Athenaeum; *Style* - Sir Leonard Daldry, KBE; Prospect House, Up West Terrace, Budleigh Salterton, Devon (☎ 3205)

DALE, David Kenneth Hay; CBE; *Career* Gov Monserrat 1980-; *Style* - David Dale Esq CBE; c/o Foreign and Commonwealth Office, London SW1

DALE, Jim; *b* 15 Aug 1935; *Educ* Kettering G S; *m* 1957, Patricia Joan Gardiner; 3 s, 1 da; *Career* actor, singer, composer, lyricist; films include Lock Up Your Daughters, The Winter's Tale, National Health, Adolf Hitler-My Part in His Downfall; composed film music for The Winter's Tale, Georgy Girl (amongst others); *Style* - Jim Dale Esq; 26 Pembridge Villas, London W11 (☎ 01 229 3678)

DALE, Robert Alan; *Career* gen man Lucas Batteries Ltd, dir Lucas World Serv Ltd, exec chm Lucas Chloride EV Systems (electric vehicle components); *Style* - Robert Dale Esq; c/o Lucas Batteries Ltd, Formans rd, Birmingham B11

DALE, Sir William Leonard; KCMG(1965); s of late Rev William Dale; *b* 1906; *Educ* Hymers Coll Hull; *m* 1966, Mrs Gloria Spellman Finn, nee Spellman; 1 da; *Career* barr 1931; entered Colonial Office, 1935; legal adviser Govt of Libya, 1951-53, to Min of Education, 1954, to Sec of State for Commonwealth Relations, 1961-66; international legal consultant; *Style* - Sir William Dale, KCMG; 20 De Beauvoir sq, N1 (☎ 01 249 3760); Lamb Building, Temple, EC4

DALGARNO, Frederick George Scott; s of Frederick Dalgarno; *b* 17 June 1943; *Educ* Robert Gordon's Coll Aberdeen, Aberdeen U, Strathclyde U; *m* 1969, Moyra, da of William Ellis; 1 s, 2 da; *Career* ptnr Paull & Williamsons advocates (Aberdeen), chm Amsteel Gp, dir Melville Street Investments Edinburgh, Future Technology Systems; *Recreations* golf, soccer, swimming; *Style* - Frederick Dalgarno Esq; 14 Westfield ter, Aberdeen (☎ 0224 22470)

DALGETY, Hugh Barkly Gonnerman; s of late Arthur William Hugh Dalgety; *b* 16 Aug 1943; *Educ* Milton Abbey; RAC Circencester; *m* 1976, Margaret Anne, nee Baring; 1 s, 1 da; *Career* Lord of the Manor and Patron of the Livings of Lockerley and East Tytherley; MFH Tedworth 1964-65, Hursley 1975-78; Portman from 1978; *Style* - Hugh Dalgety Esq; Lockerley Hall, Romsey, Hants (☎ 40253)

DALGETY, Hon Mrs (Hilda Louise Lauchlan); *née* Urquhart; da of Baron Tayside (Life Peer, d 1975); *b* 1950; *Educ* St Leonards Sch St Andrews, Bedford Coll of Physical Education; *m* 1978, John Alexander Dalgety; *Style* - The Hon Mrs Dalgety; 1 Marchmont st, Edinburgh

DALGLISH, Capt James Stephen; CVO (1955), CBE (1963); s of Rear Adm Robin Campsie Dalglish CB (d 1934); *b* 1 Oct 1913; *Educ* RNC Dartmouth; *m* 1939, Evelyn Mary da of Rev Arthur Llewellyn Meyricke (d 1950); 1 s, 1 da; *Career* Capt

RN (ret 1963) served Atlantic, Mediterranean, Pacific, Welfare Offr Metropolitan Police 1963-73; *Recreations* gardening, painting; *Style* - Capt James Dalglish RN; Park Hall, Aislaby, Whitby, N Yorks (☎ Whitby 810213)

DALHOUSIE, 16 Earl of (S 1633); Simon Ramsay; KT (1971), GCVO (1979), GBE (1957), MC (1944),; also Lord Ramsay of Dalhousie (S precedence of 1618), Lord Ramsay and Carrington (S 1633) and Baron Ramsay (UK 1875); s of 14 Earl (d 1928) and Lady Mary Heathcote-Drummond-Willoughby (da of 1 Earl of Ancaster); suc bro, 15 Earl, 1950; 1 cous twice removed of the 1 and last Marquess of Dalhousie, the celebrated Gov-Gen of India during the Mutiny and a period of great expansion of Br possessions in the sub-continent; *b* 17 Oct 1914; *Educ* Eton, Ch Ch Oxford; *m* 1940, Margaret, CStJ, da of Brig-Gen Archibald Stirling of Keir, JP, DL, MP (d 1931); 3 s, 2 da; *Heir* s, Lord Ramsay *qv*; *Career* 4/5 bn Black Watch, Maj 1942; memb Roy Co of Archers (Queen's Bodyguard for Scotland) 1956; MP (C) Forfarshire 1945-50, Con Whip 1946-48, DL (1951), JP (1967) Angus, Ld-Lt 1967-; Gov-Gen Fedn of Rhodesia and Nyasaland 1957-63; Lord Chamberlain to HM Queen Elizabeth the Queen Mother from 1965; Chllr Dundee University 1977-; *Recreations* gardening, shooting, fishing; *Clubs* White's; *Style* - Rt Hon Earl of Dalhousie KT GCVO GBE MC JP, HM Lord-Lieut for Angus; 5 Margaretta terr, SW3 (☎ 01-352 6477); Brechin Castle, Brechin, Angus (☎ 2176)

DALKEITH, Earl of; Richard Walter John Montagu Douglas Scott; s and h of 9 & 11 Duke of Buccleuch & Queensberry, KT, VRD, JP; *b* 14 Feb 1954; *Educ* Eton; *Heir* bro, Lord William Montagu Douglas Scott; *Career* with BBC External Servs, Page of Honour to HM Queen Elizabeth The Queen Mother 1967-69; *Style* - Earl of Dalkeith; 46 Bedford gdns, W8

DALLMEYER, Hon Mrs (Ursula Nina); *née* Balfour; da of 3 Baron Kinross; *b* 1914; *m* 1939, Col Christopher James York Dallmeyer, DSO, Writer to the Signet; 3 s, 1 da; *Style* - The Hon Mrs Dallmeyer; Green Corner, Tyninghame, Dunbar, E Lothian

DALMENY, Lord; Harry Ronald Neil Primrose; s and h of 7 Earl of Rosebery; *b* 20 Nov 1967; *Style* - Lord Dalmeny

DALRYMPLE, Hon David Hew; s of 13 Earl of Stair; *b* 1963 *Style* - The Hon David Dalrymple

DALRYMPLE, Viscount; John David James Dalrymple; s and h of 13 Earl of Stair, KCVO, MBE; *b* 4 Sept 1961; *Style* - Viscount Dalrymple

DALRYMPLE, Hon Michael Colin; s of 13 Earl of Stair; *b* 1965; *Style* - The Hon Michael Dalrymple

DALRYMPLE-CHAMPNEYS, Lady - Norma Hull; da of late Col Richard Hull Lewis; *m* 1, A S Russell, DSc; m 2, 1974, as his 2 w, Sir Weldon Dalrymple-Champneys, 2 and last Bt (d 1980); *Style* - Lady Dalrymple-Champneys

DALRYMPLE-HAMILTON, Hon Mrs - Hon Mary Helen; *née* Colville; da of 1 Baron Clydesmuir; *b* 1927; *m* 1949, Capt North Edward Frederick Dalrymple-Hamilton, CVO, MBE, DSC, RN; 2 s; *Style* - The Hon Mrs Dalrymple-Hamilton; Lovestone House, Bargany, Girvan, Ayrshire

DALRYMPLE-HAMILTON OF BARGANY, Capt North Edward Frederick; CVO (1961, MVO 1954), MBE (1953), DSC (1943), JP (1980), DL (Ayrshire 1973); s of Admiral Sir Frederick Hew George Dalrymple Hamilton of Bargany, KCB (d 1974, gs of 10 Earl of Stair, KT, JP, DL) by his w Gwendolen, 3 da of Sir Cuthbert Peek, 2 Bt; *b* 17 Feb 1922; *Educ* Eton; *m* 1949, Mary Helen, da of Rt Hon David John Colville GCIE TD PC, 1 Baron Clydesmuir (d 1954); 2 s (North John Frederick b 1950, James Hew Ronald b 1955); *Career* entered RN 1940, European and Korean wars, Cmdr 1954, cmdng HMS Scarborough 1958, Exec Offr HM Yacht Britannia 1959-60, Capt 1960, Capt (F) 17th Frigate Sqdn 1963, Dir of Naval Signals MOD 1965, Capt Admiralty Surface Weapons Establishment 1967, ret

1970, Brig Royal Co of Archers (Queen's Bodyguard for Scotland); *Clubs* New (Edinburgh), Pratt's; *Style* - Capt North Dalrymple-Hamilton of Bargany, CVO, MBE, DSC, JP, DL, RN; Lovestone House, Bargany, Girvan, Ayrshire (☎ Old Dailly 227)

DALRYMPLE-HAY, Sir James Brian; 6 Bt (GB 1798) of Park Place, Wigtownshire; s of Lt-Col Brian George Rowland Dalrymple-Hay (d 1943); cous of 5 Bt (d 1952); *b* 1928; *Educ* Blundells; *m* 1958, Helen Sylvia, da of late Stephen Herbert Card; 3 da; *Heir* bro, John Hugh Dalrymple-Hay; *Career* Lt RM 1948; ptnr in firm of Estate Agents; *Style* - Sir James Dalrymple-Hay, Bt; The Red House, Church st, Warnham, nr Horsham, W Sussex

DALRYMPLE-HAY, John Hugh; s of late Lt-Col Brian Dalrymple-Hay and hp of bro Sir James Dalrymple-Hay, 6 Bt, *qv*; *b* 16 Dec 1929; *Educ* Blundell's Sch; *m* 1962, Jennifer Phyllis Roberta, nee Johnston; 1 s; *Career* late Capt Royal Scots Fusiliers; *Style* - John Dalrymple-Hay Esq; Penn View, 52 Burkes rd, Beaconsfield, Bucks

DALRYMPLE-WHITE, Sir Henry Arthur Dalrymple; 2 Bt (UK 1926) of High Mark, Co Wigtown; DFC and Bar; s of Lt-Col Sir Godfrey Dalrymple Dalrymple-White, 1 Bt (d 1954, himself s of Gen Sir Henry Dalrymple White, KCB, who commanded the 6 Inniskilling Dragoons throughout the Crimean War and was in his turn maternal gs of Sir Hew Dalrymple, 1 Bt); *b* 5 Nov 1917; *Educ* Eton, Magdalene Cambridge, London U; *m* 1948 (m dis 1956), Mary, da of Capt Robert H C Thomas; 1 s; *Heir* s, Jan Hew Dalrymple-White, b 26 Nov 1950, educ Stowe; *Career* formerly wing-cdr RAF Vol Reserve; European War 1939-45; *Style* - Sir Henry Dalrymple-White, Bt, DFC*; c/o Brown Shipley Ltd, Founders ct, Lothbury, EC2

DALRYMPLE-WHITE, Jan Hew; s of and h of Sir Henry Arthur Dalrymple Dalrymple-White, qv, 2 Bt; *b* 26 Nov 1950; *Educ* Stowe; *Style* - Jan Dalrymple-White Esq

DALTON, Sir Alan (Nugent Goring); CBE (1969); s of Harold Goring Dalton and Phyllis Marguerite (nee Ash); *b* 26 Nov 1923; *Educ* King Edward VI Sch Southampton; *Career* man dir English Clays, Lovering and Pochin and Co Ltd 1961-, dep chm English China Clays Ltd 1968-, memb Sun Alliance and London Assurance Gp Bd 1976-, SW Reg Bd Nat Westminster Bank Ltd 1977-, chm British Railways (Western) Bd 1978-; fell Inst of Dirs, FBIM, FRSA; kt 1977; *Style* - Sir Alan Dalton, CBE; John Keay House, St Austell, Cornwall

DALTON, Maj-Gen John Cecil D'Arcy; CB (1954), CBE (1948, OBE 1943), DL (N Riding and N Yorks); s of Maj-Gen James Cecil Dalton (d 1931); *b* 2 Mar 1907; *Educ* Cheltenham, RMA Woolwich; *m* 1942, Pamela Frances, da of late Brig-Gen Eric Segrave, DSO; 2 s; *Career* Maj-Gen NW Europe 1940 and 1944, N Africa 1942-43, Korea 1952-54; Ch of Staff British Commonwealth Forces Korea 1952-54, V-Quarter Master Gen War Office 1960-62, V-Ld Lt N Yorks 1977-; High Sheriff Yorks 1970; *Recreations* shooting; *Clubs* Army and Navy; *Style* - Maj-Gen John Dalton CB CBE DL, HM Vice Lord-Lieut for N Yorks; Hauxwell Hall, Leyburn, N Yorks (☎ Bedale 50286)

DALY, Michael Francis; s of late William Thomas Daly and of Hilda Frances Daly; *b* 7 Apr 1931; *Educ* Downside, Gonville and Caius Cambridge; *m* 1, 1963, Sally Malcolm Angwin (d 1966); 1 da; m 2, 1971, Juliet Mary Siragusa (nee Arning); 1 step da; *Career* Transreef Industrial & Investment Co 1955-66, General Electric Co London 1966; HM Diplomatic Service- 1 sec FCO 1967, 1 sec (Commercial) Rio de Janeira 1969, 1 sec (Inf) and Head of Chancery Dublin 1973, assist Cultural Relations Dept FCO 1976, Counsellor Consul-Gen and Head of Chancery Brasilia 1977-78, Ambass to Ivory Coast Upper Volta and Niger 1978-; *Style* - Michael Daly Esq; Foreign and Commonwealth Office, SW1

DALYELL, Gordon Wheatley; s and h of (Sir) Tam Dalyell (of The Binns, Bt), MP, *qv*; *b* 26 Sept 1965; *Style* - Gordon

Dalyell Esq

DALYELL, Hon Mrs (Kathleen Mary Agnes); da of Baron Wheatley; *b* 1937; *m* 1963, Tam Dalyell, MP, *qv*; 1 s, 1 da; *Style* - The Hon Mrs Dalyell

DALYELL (OF THE BINNS), (Sir) Tam (Thomas); (11 Bt, NS 1685), MP (L) W Lothian 1962-; s of late Lt-Col Gordon Loch, CIE, JP, DL and (Dame) Eleanor Isabel (de jure Baronetess) who d 1972 (da of Sir James Bruce Wilkie-Dalyell, 9 Bt) and who with her husband assumed the surname and arms of Dalyell of The Binns; established his claim 1973 but does not use title; *b* 9 Aug 1932; *Educ* Eton, King's Cambridge; *m* 1963, Hon Kathleen, *qv*, da of Baron Wheatley; 1 s, 1 da; *Heir* s, Gordon Wheatley Dalyell; *Career* former teacher; PPS to Min of Housing and Local Govt 1964-66, PPS to Leader of House of Commons 1967-68, and to Sec of State for Social Security 1968-70, v-chm Parly Lab Pty 1974, MEP 1975-79; political columnist of New Scientist 1968-, author of *Devolution- the End of Britain?*; *Style* - Tam Dalyell Esq, MP; The Binns, Linlithgow, Scotland (☎ Philipstoun 255)

DALZELL, Lady Muriel Marjorie; *née* Dalzell; da of late 13 Earl of Carnwath; *b* 1903; *m* 1927, Lt-Col John Norton Taylor, who assumed surname Dalzell on marrying; 1 s; *Style* - Lady Muriel Dalzell; Sand House, Wedmore, Somerset

DALZIEL, Ian Martin; MEP (C) Lothians 1979-; s of John Calvin Dalziel and Elizabeth Roy Dalziel; *b* 21 June 1947; *Educ* Daniel Stewart's Coll Edinburgh, St John's Cambridge, Université Libre de Bruxelles (Weiner Anspach Foundation Scholarship 1970); *m* 1972, Nadia Maria Iacouazzi; 2 s; *Career* Mullens & Co 1970-72, exec in Corporate Fin Dept Mfrs Hanover Ltd 1972-; memb Richmond upon Thames Cncl 1978-79; *Style* - Ian Dalziel Esq, MEP; 21 Greenhill gdns, Edinburgh (☎ 031 447 3441)

DAMANT, David Cyril; s of William Alexander Arthur Damant; *b* 15 Mar 1937; *Educ* Queens' Cambridge; *Career* chm Soc of Investment Analysts 1980-, former ptnr Investment Research Cambridge, dir Clive Investments Ltd 1977-; *Style* - David Damant Esq; Agar House, Agar Street, London WC2; 16 Orchard Street, Cambridge (☎ 0223 357768)

DAMERELL, Derek Vivian; s of William James Damerell (Lt-Col) and Zoe Damerell; *b* 4 Aug 1921; *Educ* Imperial Service Coll, Edinburgh U, Harvard Business Sch; *Career* parent bd BPB Industries 1953-64, regional dir Int Wool Secretariat 1965-73, dir The Medical Centre, chm and founder Independent Hospital Gp Council, gov and ch exec BUPA 1974-; *Style* - Derek Damerell Esq; Stodham Park, Liss, Hampshire (☎ 073 082 2316)

DAMERELL, Lady Mary Barbara; *née* Carnegie; da of 13 Earl of Northesk; *b* 10 Feb 1953; *m* 1977, William Patrick Damerell; *Style* - Lady Mary Damerell, Springwaters, Ballamodha, Ballasalla, Isle of Man (☎ Castletown (STD Code 0624) 823291)

DANCKWERTS, Lady (Ella Hamilton); *née* Marshall; *m* 1969, as his 2 wife, Rt Hon Sir Harold Otto Danckwerts, PC (d 1978); 1 s, 1 da *Style* - Lady Danckwerts

DANGAN, Elizabeth, Viscountess; Elizabeth Anne; da of late Pelham Rawstorn Papillon, DSO; *m* 1 Flight-Lieutenant Stephen Alers Hankey, RA (decd); m 2, 1944 (m dis 1950), Denis Arthur, Viscount Dangan (later 5 Earl Cowley); *Style* - Elizabeth, Viscountess Dangan; PO Box 285, Paget, Bermuda

DANGAN, Viscount; Garrett Graham Wellesley; s (by 1 m) and h of 7 Earl Cowley; *b* 30 March 1965; *Style* - Viscount Dangan; c/o The Rt Hon The Earl Cowley; 53 Holland Park Mews, London W11 (☎ 01 727 9378)

DANIEL, Gerald Ernest; s of Ernest and Beata May Daniel; *b* 7 dec 1919; *Educ* Huish's Grammar Sch Taunton; *m* 1942, Ecila Roslyn Dillow; 1 s, 1 da; *Career* FCA, IPFA, FRVA, various appointments in Borough Treasurers' Depts 1935-74, dir Horizon Midlands Ltd 1975-; *Style* - Gerald Daniel Esq; County Hall, W Bridgford, Nottingham (☎ 863366); 242 Melton rd, Edwalton, Nottingham (☎ 231025

DANIEL, Norman Alexander; CBE (1974, OBE 1968); s of George Frederick Daniel (d 1945); *b* 8 May 1919; *Educ* Frensham Heights Sch, Queen's Coll Oxford, Edinburgh U; *m* 1941, Marion Ruth, nee Pethybridge; (1 s decd); *Career* dir Visitors Dept Br Cncl London 1970, Cultural Attaché Cairo 1971, Br Cncl rep and Cultural Cnsllr Br Embassy Cairo 1973-79 (ret), gen sec Coptic Archaeological Soc 1979-; *Style* - Norman Daniel Esq, CBE; 1 rue Masna al-Tarabich, Abbasiah, Cairo, Egypt; Landmark, Flimwell, Wadhurst, Sussex (☎ Flimwell 325)

DANIEL, Reginald Jack; OBE (1958); s of Reginald Daniel Daniel and Florence Emily, nee Woods; *b* 27 Feb 1920; *Educ* Roy Naval Engrg Coll Keyham, Roy Naval Coll Greenwich; *Career* submarine designer; dep dir Submarine Design and Production 1970-74, dir-gen Ships and head of RCNC and MOD 1974-79, bd memb British Shipbuilders 1979-; F Eng, FRINA, FIMarE, RCNC; *Style* - Reginald Daniel Esq OBE; Meadowland, Cleveland Walk, Bath

DANIEL, Lady Valerie Davidia; *née* Lloyd George; da of 2 Earl Lloyd-George of Dwyfor; *b* 1918; *m* 1940, Sir Goronwy Hopkin Daniel, KCVO, CB; 1 s, 2 da; *Style* - Lady Valerie Daniel; Plas Penglais, Aberystwyth, Dyfed

DANIELL, Brig Kenneth Francis; CBE (1963, OBE 1955); s of F E Daniell, DSO (ka 1916); *b* 22 Oct 1910; *Educ* Malvern, RMA Woolwich, Cambridge U; *m* 1935, Doreen Norah, da of Canon A French (d 1943); 3 s, 1 da; *Career* Brig (Malta, India, Burma, Middle East, BAOR) ret as Ch Engr Western Command 1963; dir of works C'wlth War Graves Cmmn 1963-71; *Style* - Brig Kenneth Daniell CBE; Higher Chalk, Iwerne Minster, Blandford, Dorset (☎ Fontmell Magna 811787)

DANIELL, Sir Peter Averell; TD (1950), DL (Surrey 1976); s of late Roger Henry Averell Daniell; *b* 8 Dec 1909; *Educ* Eton, Trinity Oxford; *m* 1935, Leonie Mayne, da of late Henry B Harrison; 2 s, 1 da; *Career* served 1939-45 with KRRC; sr ptnr Mullens and Co, Govt Broker 1963-73, kt 1971; *Clubs* Brooks's, Alpine; *Style* - Sir Peter Daniell, TD, DL; Glebe House, Buckland, Surrey (☎ 939 2320)

DANIELS, George; s of George Daniels; *b* 19 Aug 1926; *m* 1964, Juliet Anne, nee Marryat; 1 da; *Career* author, watchmaker, horological consultant; FBHI 1951, FSA 1976; Master of Worshipful Co of Clockmakers 1980; Victor Kullberg Medal, Stockholm Watch Guild 1977; *Style* - George Daniels Esq; 34 New Bond st, W1

DANIELS, Jeffery; s of John Henry and Edith Mary Daniels; *b* 13 July 1932; *Educ* Milford Haven Grammar Sch; Balliol Oxford; *Career* Teacher (ILEA) 1956-69; dir Geffrye Museum London 1969-; Hon Sec London Fedn of Museums and Art Galleries; contrib to the Times and various art magazines; *Style* - Jeffery Daniels Esq; 5 Edith Grove, SW10 (☎ 01 352 7692)

DANIELS, Karl; s of Harold George Daniels of Ipswich (d 1965); *b* 1 Dec 1935; *Educ* Ipswich Sch; *m* 1960, Janice Margaret, da of Vernon Billing; 2 s; *Career* pension scheme consultant; md Noble Lowndes Pensions Ltd 1979-, dir Lowndes Associated Pensions Ltd, English Pension Trustees Ltd, Lowndes Management Incentives Ltd, Scottish Pension Trustees Ltd 1976-; *Clubs* RAC; *Style* - Karl Daniels Esq; Church Cottage, Church rd, Lingfield, Surrey (☎ 832023)

DANIELS, Laurence John; CB (1979), OBE (1970); s of Leslie Daniels and Margaret, nee Bradley; *b* 11 August 1916; *Educ* Rostrevor Coll S Australia, Sydney Univ; *m* 1943, Joyce Carey; 2 s, 8 da; *Career* AASA 1939, C'wlth (Australian) Taxation Office 1934-53, C'wlth Dept of Health 1953-72; dir-Gen Dept of Social Security 1973-77, sec Dept of Capital Territory (Australia) 1977-; *Style* - Laurence Daniels Esq, CB, OBE; 5 Nares Crest, Forrest, ACT 2603, Australia (☎ 062 95 1896)

DANIELS, Raymond Alfred; MC (1946); s of late Alfred Daniels; *b* 15 July 1923; *Educ* Bedford Modern Sch; *m* 1954, Helen, nee Clark; 3 s; *Career* md William Press & Son 1975-; *Style* - Raymond Daniels Esq, MC; Greystock, 64 Merrybent, Darlington, Co Durham (☎ 0325 74 238)

DANKS, Arthur Reginald; MBE (1976), TD (1945); s of Arthur Benjamin Danks (d 1925); *b* 12 April 1906; *Educ* Malvern; *m* 1951, Hon Serena Mary, *qv*, da of late 4 Baron Gifford; 1 s, 1 da; *Career* Hon Artillery Co (RHA) 1926-40, 2 Regt RHA 1940, Bank of England to 1945, gen cmmr for Income Tax Gloucester Area; *Style* - Arthur Danks Esq, MBE, TD; Lealands Cottage, Box, Stroud, Glos

DANKS, Hon Mrs; Hon Serena Mary; *née* Gifford; da of 4 Baron Gifford; *b* 1919; *m* 1, 1940 Patrick de Gruchy Vignoles Crawshay Warren; 1 s; m 2, 1951, Arthur Reginald Danks, MBE, TD; 1 s, 1 da; *Style* - The Hon Mrs Danks; Lealands Cottage, Box, Stroud, Glos

DANN, Howard Ernest; CBE (1965); *b* 27 April 1914; *Educ* Brighton Grammar Sch (Dux); Univ of Melbourne; *m* 1946, Marjorie Bush; 2 s; *Career* cmmr Snowy Mountains Hydro-Electric Authority 1967-74 (ch engr investigations and assoc cmmr 1959-67), dir Snowy Mountains Engrg Corpn 1970-74; FIE Aust, MASCE; *Style* - Howard Dann Esq, CBE; 18 Rookwood st, North Balwyn, Victoria 3104, Australia (☎ 859 4428)

DANNATT, Professor (James) Trevor; s of George Herbert and Jane Ellen Dannatt; *b* 15 Jan 1920; *Educ* Colfes Sch, Sch of Architecture Regent Polytechnic; *m* 1953, Joan Howell Davies; 1 s, da; *Career* commencd private practice 1952, sr ptnr Trevor Dannatt & Partners (Architects); Prof of Architecture Manchester Univ 1975-; ARA 1977, FRIBA; ed Architects' Year Book 1945-62; *Style* - Prof Trevor Dannatt; 115 Crawford st, WI (☎ 01 486 6844)

DANSON, Hon Barnett Jerome; PC (Canada); s of Joseph B Danson and Saidie W Danson; *b* 8 Feb 1921; *Educ* Toronto public and high schs; *m* 1943, Isobel, nee Bull; *Career* principal (pres) Danson Corp Ltd (Scarborough) 1953-74; MP (L) York North 1968-79, Parly Sec Prime Minister Trudeau 1970-72, Min of State Urban Affairs 1974-76, of Nat Defence 1976-79; *Style* - The Hon Barnett Danson PC

DARBOURNE, John William Charles; CBE (1977); s of late William Leslie Darbourne and Violet Yorke; *b* 11 Jan 1935; *Educ* Battersea G S, UCL, Harvard; *Career* ptnr Darbourne & Darke (Architects and Landscape planners) 1961-; RIBA, AILA; *Style* - John Darbourne Esq, CBE; 10 Dynevor rd, Richmond, Surrey (☎ 01 940 2241)

DARBY, Dr Francis John; TD (1964); s of late Col John Francis Darby, CBE, and Georgina Alice; *b* 24 Feb 1920; *Educ* Nottingham H S, Edinburgh Acad, Edinburgh U; *Career* medical offr Miny of Pensions and Nat Insurance 1964-70, dep ch medical advisor Dept of Health & Socl Security 1978- (sr medical offr 1970-74, princ offr 1974-78) Hon Physician to HM 1980-; memb Worshipful Soc of Apothecaries of London 1978, Freeman City of London 1979; FRSM; *Style* - Dr Francis Darby, TD; 4 Berystede, Kingston Hill, Kingston-upon-Thames, Surrey (☎ 01 549 5773)

DARBY, Prof Henry Clifford; CBE (1978, OBE 1946); s of Evan Darby; *b* 7 Feb 1909; *Educ* Neath County Sch, St Catharine's Cambridge; *Career* prof of Geography UCL 1949-66, Cambridge 1966-76, now Emeritus; Fell King's Cambridge; author geographical and historical publications; *Style* - Prof Henry Darby, CBE; 60 Storey's Way, Camridge (☎ 54745)

DARBY, Hon Mrs; Hon Meriel Kathleen; *née* Douglas-Home; da of Baron Home of the Hirsel; *b* 1939; *m* 1964, Adrian Marten George Darby; 1 s, 1 da; *Style* - The Hon Mrs Darby; 12 Park Town, Oxford

DARBY, Peter Howard; CBE (1973), QFSM (1970); s of William Cyril Darby and Beatrice Colin; *b* 8 July 1924; *Educ* Coll of Advanced Technol, Birmingham;

m 1948, Ellen Josephine Glynn; 1 s, 1 da; *Career* Chief officer of the London Fire Brigade 1977-; freeman City of London; liveryman Worshipful Co of Basketmakers; *Style* - Peter Darby Esq, CBE, QFSM; London Fire Brigade Headquarters, 8 Albert Embankment, SE1 (☎ 01 582 3811)

DARCY DE KNAYTH, Baroness (18 in line, E 1332); Davina Marcia Ingrams; *née* Herbert; da of 17 Baron Darcy de Knayth (né Hon Mervyn Herbert, 2 s of 4 Earl of Powis by his w (Violet) Countess of Powis, in whose favour the abeyance existing in the Barony of Darcy de Knayth was terminated in 1903) and Vida, da of late Capt James Harold Cuthbert, DSO; *b* 10 July 1938; *m* 1960, Rupert George Ingrams (yr bro of Richard, ed of Private Eye; he (Rupert) was k in car crash 1964; his maternal gf was Sir James Reid, 1 Bt); 1 s, 2 da; *Heir* s, Hon Caspar Ingrams; *Style* - The Rt Hon The Lady Darcy de Knayth; Camley Corner, Stubbings, Maidenhead, Berks (☎ Littlewick Green 2935)

DARE, Hon Mrs (Phyllida Anne); da of Baron Benson (Life Peer), GBE; *b* 1943; *m* 1967, Simon Dare; *Style* - The Hon Mrs Dare; 10 Bowerdean st, SW6

DARELL, Guy Jeffrey Adair; s and h of Sir Jeffrey Lionel Darell, 8 Bt, MC, *qv*; *b* 8 June 1961; *Style* - Guy Darell Esq

DARELL, Sir Jeffrey Lionel; 8 Bt (GB 1795), of Richmond Hill, Surrey, MC (1945); s of Col Guy Marsland Darell, MC (d 1947), 3 s of 5 Bt; suc cous, Sir William Darell, 7 Bt (d 1959); *b* 2 Oct 1919; *Educ* Eton, RMC Sandhurst; *m* 1953, Bridget Mary, da of Maj-Gen Sir Allan Adair, 6 Bt, GCVO, CB, DSO, MC; 1 s, 2 da; *Heir* s, Guy Jeffrey Adair Darell; *Career* Brig (ret) Coldstream Guards, served in 1939-45 War, Lt-Col 1957, cmd 1 Batn Coldstream Guards 1957-59, AAG War Office 1959-61, Cdr RMA Sandhurst 1961-64, regimental Lt-Col cmdg Coldstream Guards 1964, v-pres Regular Commissions Bd 1968, Cmdt Mons Officer Cadet Sch 1970-72; *Style* - Brigadier Sir Jeffrey Darell, Bt, MC; Denton Lodge, Harleston, Norfolk (☎ Homersfield 206); 55 Green st, W1 (☎ 01 629 3860)

DARELL-BROWN, Hon Mrs - Hon Christina Louise; *née* Vanneck; da of 6 Baron Huntingfield; *b* 1946; *m* 1967, Anthony Darell-Brown; 2 s, 1 da; *Style* - The Hon Mrs Darell-Brown; 29 Underhill rd, Dulwich, SE22

DARESBURY, 2 Baron (UK 1927); Sir Edward Greenall; 3 Bt (UK 1876), JP (Cheshire 1945); s of 1 Baron, CVO (d 1938); *b* 12 Oct 1902; *Educ* Eton; *m* 1, 1925, Joan (d 1926), da of Capt R T O Sheriffe; m 2, 1927, Josephine (d 1958), da of Brig-Gen Sir Joseph Laycock, KCMG, DSO, TD; 1 s; m 3, 1966, Lady Helena Albreda Marie Gabriella (d 1970), da of late 7 Earl Fitzwilliam and formely w of Maj Chetwode C H Hilton-Green; *Heir* s, Hon Edward Greenall; *Career* late 2 Lt 1 Life Gds, jt master Belvoir Foxhounds 1934-77, MFH Co Limerick 1947; *Style* - The Rt Hon The Lord Daresbury, JP; Altavilla, Askeaton, Co Limerick, Eire (☎ Rathkeale 138)

DARLING OF HILLSBOROUGH, Baron (UK Life Peer 1974); George Darling; PC (1966); s of Frederick William Darling; *b* 20 July 1905; *Educ* Elementary Sch, Liverpool and Cambridge Us; *m* 1932, Dorothy, da of Thomas Hodge; 1 s, 1 da; *Career* Min of State Bd of Trade 1964-68; V-Pres Cncl of Europe 1970-74; MP for Hillsborough div of Sheffield (L & Co-op) 1950-74; *Style* - Rt Hon Lord Darling of Hillsborough PC; 17 Amersham Road, Beaconsfield, Buckinghamshire (☎ 049 46 3352)

DARLING, 2 Baron (UK 1924); Robert Charles Henry Darling; DL (Avon 1972); s of Maj Hon John Darling, DSO (s of 1 Baron); suc gf 1936; *b* 15 May 1919; *Educ* Wellington, Sandhurst; *m* 1942, Bridget, da of Rev Francis Dickson; 1 s, 2 da; *Heir* s, Hon Robert Darling; *Career* Maj Italy WW II; ch exec Roy Bath & SW Counties Soc 1961-79; dir Bristol Waterways 1978-, Regnl Dir Lloyds Bank 1979-; *Recreations* fishing, gardening; *Style* - The Rt Hon Lord Darling, DL; Puckpits, Limpley Stoke, Bath, Avon (☎ 2146)

DARLING, Prof Arthur Ivan; CBE (1971); s of John and Henrietta Darling; *b* 21 Nov 1916; *Educ* Whitley Bay G S, King's Coll Durham U; *m* 1948, Kathleen Pollard; 1 s, 3 da; *Career* Prof Dental Medicine Bristol U 1959-; *Style* - Prof Arthur Darling CBE, 7 Rylestone Grove, Bristol BS9 3UT, Avon

DARLING, Hon Sir Clifford; MP (Bahamas); s of Charles and Aremelia Darling; *b* 6 Feb 1922; *Educ* Acklins Public Sch; several public schools in Nassau; *Career* senator 1964-67; dep speaker House of Assembly 1967-69; Min of State 1969; Min of Labour and Welfare 1971; now Min of Labour and National Insurance; kt 1977; *Style* - The Hon Sir Clifford Darling, MP; House of Assembly, Nassau, Bahamas; C H Bain Building, PO Box 1525, Nassau

DARLING, Lt-Cdr Gerald Ralph Auchinleck; RD (1968), QC (1968); s of Lt-Col Ralph Reginald Auchinleck Darling of N Ireland; *b* 8 Dec 1921; *Educ* Harrow, Hertford Oxford; *m* 1954, Susan Ann, da of Brig Mervyn Hobbs, OBE, MC of W Australia; 1 s, 1 da; *Career* Lt-Cdr, fleet fighter Pilot, test pilot, Mediterranean Indian Ocean Pacific 1940-46, RNR to 1968; barr 1950, bencher of Middle Temple 1970, Lloyd's Appeal Arbitrator 1978, Judge of Admiralty Ct of Cinque Ports 1978; *Recreations* fly fishing, shooting; *Style* - Lt-Cdr Gerald Darling, RD, QC; 1 Essex Ct, Temple, EC4 (☎ 01 353 1377); Crevenagh House, Omagh, Co Tryone (☎ 0662 2138)

DARLING, Henry Shillington; CBE (1967); s of late J S Darling, MD, FRCS and Marjorie Shillington Darling; *b* 22 June 1914; *Educ* Watts' Endowed Sch, Greenmount Agric Coll N Ireland, Queen's U Belfast, Imperial Coll Tropical Agriculture Trinidad; *m* 1940, Vera Thompson Chapman, LDS, Belfast; 1 s, 2 da; *Career* AICTA, PhD, Head of Hop Research Dept London U 1954-62, prof of Ag and dir of Inst for Ag Res Ahmadu Bello U Nigeria 1967-68, dir gen Int Centre for Ag Res in Dry Areas 1977-; AICTA, PhD; *Style* - Henry Darling Esq, CBE; 2 Tudor End, Kennington, Ashford, Kent

DARLING, Hon Isabel; da of Baron Darling of Hillsborough (Life Peer); *b* 1948; *Style* - The Hon Isabel Darling

DARLING, Hon Lucinda Mary Joan; da of 2 Baron Darling; *b* 1958; *Style* - The Hon Lucinda Darling

DARLING, Hon Peter George; s of Baron Darling of Hillsborough (Life Peer); *b* 1950; *Style* - The Hon Peter Darling

DARLING, Hon Robert Julian Henry; s of 2 Baron Darling; *b* 29 Apr 1944; *Educ* Wellington; *m* 1970, Janet, nee Mallinson; 2 s, 1 da; *Style* - The Hon Robert Darling; The White House, Intwood, Norwich

DARLINGTON, Col (Henry) John; OBE (1945), DL (1967); s of Col Sir Henry Clayton Darlington, KCB, CMG, TD (d 1959); *b* 18 April 1912; *Educ* Shrewsbury, Ch Ch Oxford; *m* 1938, Nancy Baldwin, da of Baldwin Harry Bent, JP; *Career* regular offr King's Own Roy Regt 1935, Lt-Col AA and QMG 3 Inf div 1953-55 Malaya, Cdr 6 Bn Roy Malay Regt 1955-58 (despatches 1957), Col QMG Co-ord War Office 1958-60, Bde Col Lancaster Bde 1961-63, ret 1963; Regtl Sec King's Own Roy Regt 1963-75, Hon Col 4 King's Own Border (T and AVR) 1975-78, chm House of Laity, Blackburn Dioc Synod 1973, chm St John Cncl Lancs 1975-80; Hon Col Lancs County Cadet Force 1980-; *Clubs* Army and Navy; *Style* - Col John Darlington, OBE, DL; Whitehorn House, Melling, nr Carnforth, Lancashire LA6 2RB

DARNLEY, 11 Earl of (I 1725); Adam Ivo Stuart Bligh; sits as Baron Clifton of Leighton (E 1608); also Baron Clifton of Rathmore (I 1721), Viscount Darnley (I 1723); s of 9 Earl (d 1955), by his 3 w, Rosemary, da of late Edmund Potter; suc half-bro, 10 Earl 1980; *b* 8 Nov 1941; *Educ* Harrow, Ch Ch Oxford; *m* 1965, Susan Elaine, JP, da of late Sir Donald Forsyth Anderson and Margaret (Lady Anderson), sis of Sir Harry Llewellyn, 3 Bt, CBE (father of Roddy Llewellyn); 1 s, 1 da; *Heir* s, Lord Clifton of Rathmore; *Style* - The Rt Hon The Earl of Darnley; Hambledon

House, nr Portsmouth, Hants (☎ 070 132 380)

DARTMOUTH, 9 Earl of (GB 1711); Gerald Humphry Legge; also Baron Dartmouth (E 1682) and Viscount Lewisham (GB 1711); s of 8 Earl, CVO, DSO, RN (ret) (d 1962) and Roma, Countess of Dartmouth, *qv*; *b* 26 April 1924; *Educ* Eton; *m* 1, 1948 (m dis 1976), Raine, da of late Alexander George McCorquodale and who m 2, 8 Earl Spencer, MVO, *qv*; 3 s, 1 da; m 2, 1980, Mrs Gwendoline May Seguin, da of late Charles René Seguin; *Heir* s, Viscount Lewisham; *Career* FCA, Capt Coldstream Gds (despatches) WW II, former md Rea Bros Ltd, chm Long & Hambly, Ocean Wilsons Holdings Ltd, Scottish Investment Tst Ltd; *Clubs* Buck's, Bath; *Style* - The Rt Hon The Earl of Dartmouth; The Manor House, Chipperfield, King's Langley, Herts (☎ 64498)

DARTMOUTH, Roma, Countess of - Roma Ernestine; da of Sir Ernest Burford Horlick, 2 Bt; *b* 1903; *m* 1923, 8 Earl of Dartmouth (d 1962); 1 s (9 Earl), 1 da (Lady Herschell, w of 3 Baron); *Style* - The Rt Hon Roma, Countess of Dartmouth; 15b Bedford Towers, Brighton, Sussex

DARVALL, Frank; CBE (1954); s of late RT Darvall and Annie E Johnson; *b* 16 Apr 1906; *Educ* Dover Coll, U of Reading, London U, Columbia; *m* 1931, Dorothy, nee Edmonds; (1 s, decd); *Career* 1 Sec HM Embassy Washington 1946-49, v-chm Kinsman Trust 1949-56, dir gen English Speaking Union of C'wlth 1949-57, ed (European) World Review 1958-59, dir British Information Services Eastern Caribbean 1961-66, Consul Boston 1966-68, Foreign & C'wlth Off 1968-70; gov Sulgrave Manor, memb Cncl of Haileybury and Imperial Service Coll; *Style* - Frank Darvall Esq CBE; c/o Lloyds Bank Ltd, 1 Butler pla, SW1

DARWEN, 2 Baron (UK 1946); Cedric Percival Davies; s of 1 Baron Darwen (d 1950); *b* 18 Feb 1915; *Educ* Sidcot Sch, Manchester U (BA Hons); *m* 1934, Kathleen Dora, da of the late George Sharples Walker; 3 s, 1 da; *Heir* s, Hon Roger Michael Davies; *Career* chm and md Darwen Finlayson Ltd 1954-73, pres Independent Publishers' Guild 1973-; *Style* - The Rt Hon the Lord Darwen; White Lodge, Sandelswood End, Beaconsfield, Bucks (☎ 3355)

DARWIN, George Erasmus; s of William Robert Darwin (gs of Charles Darwin and who d 1970); *b* 11 Feb 1927; *Educ* Winchester, Trin Cambridge; *m* 1956, Shuna Mary, da of George Ronald Service (d 1961); 2 s, 1 da; *Career* with Bacock & Wilcox Ltd 1957-78, ch exec Richardsons (West Garth Gp) 1978-, chm Home Grown Products (Hldgs) 1979-; *Recreations* sailing, bridge; *Clubs* Savile; *Style* - George Darwin Esq; 7 Tor gdns, W8 (☎ 01 937 9410)

DARYNGTON, 2 Baron (UK 1923); Jocelyn Arthur Pike Pease; s of 1 Baron Daryngton, PC (d 1949); *b* 30 May 1908; *Educ* Eton, Trinity Cambridge; *Heir* none; *Career* memb Inner Temple 1932, assist master Doone Hse and Stone Hse prep schs Thanet; *Style* - The Rt Hon the Lord Daryngton; 7 Stocks Mead, Washington, Pulborough, W Sussex

DAS NEVES, Hon Mrs; Hon Amanda Mary Alnwick; *née* Grey; da of Baron Grey of Naunton; *b* 1951; *Educ* St Mary's Sch Calne, Bedford Coll, U of London; *m* 1975, Jose das Neves; *Style* - The Hon Mrs das Neves

DASHWOOD, Edward John Francis; s (by 1 m) and h of Sir Francis John Vernon Hereward Dashwood, 11 Bt, *qv*; *b* 25 Sept 1964; *Style* - Edward Dashwood Esq

DASHWOOD, Sir Francis John Vernon Hereward; 11 Bt (Premier Bt of GB, cr 1707), of West Wycombe, Buckinghamshire; s of Sir John Dashwood, 10 Bt, CVO (d 1966, sixth in descent from Sir Francis Dashwood, 2 Bt, who was also Baron Le Despencer from 1762 to his death, which moralists maintained was an unconscionable long time a-coming inasmuch as Sir Francis was founder of the eponymous club the 'Franciscans', more notorious as the 'Hell-Fire Club' (motto 'fay ce que voudras', from Rabelais' abbey of Thelema in 'Gargantua'); he was also

Chllr of the Exchequer, arch-master of the Dilettanti Soc and joint Postmaster-General); *b* 7 Aug 1925; *Educ* Eton, Ch Ch Oxford, Harvard Business Sch; *m* 1, 1957, Victoria (d 1976), da of Maj John Foley, Baron de Rutzen (whose ancestor Augustus, Col in the Army of the Grand Duchy of Lithuania, obtained an acknowledgement of nobility from King Wladislaw IV of Poland *ante* 1677), of Slebech Park, Pembrokeshire, by his w Eleanor, da of Capt Pelham Thursby Pelham; 1 s, 3 da (Emily b 1958, Georgina b 1960, Caroline b 1962); m 2, 1977, Marcella, wid of Jack Frye, OBE; *Heir* s, Edward John Francis; *Career* landowner, Lloyd's Underwriter and Memb; farmer; High Sheriff Bucks 1976; chm Bucks Branch CLA 1980; contested (C) W Bromwich 1955 and Gloucester 1957; *Recreations* shooting, tennis; *Clubs* Brooks's, White's; *Style* - Sir Francis Dashwood, Bt; West Wycombe Park, High Wycombe, Buckinghamshire (☎ 0494 23720)

DASHWOOD, Dowager Lady - Helen Moira; da of late Lt-Col Eaton; *m* 1922, Sir John Lindsay Dashwood, CVO, 10 Bt (d 1966); *Style* - Dowager Lady Dashwood; 10 Cumberland House, Kensington High Street, London W8 (☎ 01 937 7314)

DASHWOOD, John Arthur; 2 s of Sir Robert Henry Seymour Dashwood, 7 Bt, DL; hp of n Sir Richard Dashwood, 9 Bt; *b* 17 July 1910; *m* Patricia Maud, only da of Frederick Burrows *Style* - John Dashwood Esq; Mombasa, Kenya

DASHWOOD, Sir Richard James; 9 Bt (E 1684), of Kirtlington Park, Oxfordshire; s of Sir Henry Dashwood, 8 Bt (d 1972); *b* 14 Feb 1950; *Educ* Eton; *Heir* unc, John Arthur Dashwood; *Career* Lt 14/20 King's Hussars; T&AVR 1973; *Clubs* Cavalry and Guards'; *Style* - Sir Richard Dashwood, Bt; Ledwell House, Sandford St Martin, Oxfordshire (☎ Great Tew (060 883) 267)

DAUBENY DE MOLEYNS, Andrew Wesley; s of late Hon Francis Alexander Innys Eveleigh-Ross-de-Moleyns (s of 6 Baron Ventry), by his 2 w Joan; hp of uncle, 7 Baron; *b* 28 May 1943; *m* 1963, Nelly Edouard Renée, da of Abel Chaumillon, of Loma de los Riseos, Villa Angel, Torremolinos, Malaga, Spain; 1 s, 2 da; *Career* assumed by deed poll 1966 the surname of Daubeny de Moleyns; *Style* - Andrew Daubeny de Moleyns Esq; Clay of Allan Farm, Fearn, Ross-shire

DAUNT, Maj-Gen Brian; CB (1956), CBE (1953), DSO (1943); s of Dr Wiliam Daunt (d 1920); *b* 16 March 1900; *Educ* Tonbridge, RMA Woolwich; *m* 1938, Millicent Margaret, da of late Capt Alfred Balfour RIN; 2 da (1 s decd); *Career* RA 1920-65 (ret); Brig 1944, Maj-Gen 1954, Col-Cmdt RA 1960-65, controller Home Dept BRCS 1957-66, CStJ; *Recreations* the arts, gardening; *Clubs* Army and Navy; *Style* - Maj-Gen Brian Daunt, CB, CBE, DSO; Blackstone House, Brightwell-cum-Sotwell, Wallingford, Oxon (☎ Wallingford 37060)

DAVENPORT, Brian John; QC (1980); s of Robert Cecil Davenport; *b* 17 Mar 1936; *Educ* Bryanston Sch, Worcester Oxford; *m* 1969, Erica Tickell, nee Willmer; 2 s, 1 da; *Career* junior counsel to Dept of Employment 1972-74; to Board of Inland Revenue 1974-80; *Style* - Brian Davenport Esq, QC; 43 Downshire Hill, NW3 (☎ 01 435 3332)

DAVENPORT, Montague; CBE (1972, OBE 1959); s of Hayward Montague Davenport (d 1959); *b* 26 May 1916; *Educ* Sherborne and Pharmaceutics Soc Coll; *m* 1952, Olive Margaret, da of Donald Frank Brabner; 2 s; *Career* served 1939-45 war as Lt-Cdr RNVR; assist sec FCO 1971-78 (entered 1946); *Clubs* Army and Navy; *Style* - Montague Davenport Esq, CBE; Chalcots, Orchard way, Esher, Surrey (☎ 62384)

DAVENPORT, (Arthur) Nigel; s of Maj Arthur Davenport, MC, of Sidney Sussex Coll Cambridge; *b* 23 May 1928; *Educ* Cheltenham, Trin Oxford; *m* 1, Helena (m dis, she d); m 2, 1972 (m dis 1980; she m 1, 1968, Mark Durden-Smith), Maria Penelope Katharine (b 12 Sept 1945), da of

Sir William Aitken, KBE, MP (d 1964, n of 1 Baron Beaverbrook) and sis of Jonathan Aitken, MP; 1 s, 1 da; *Career* late memb OUDS, served WW II RASC; actor 1951-, writer, co dir; V-Pres Equity 1978-81; *Recreations* gardening, travel; *Clubs* Garrick; *Style* - Nigel Davenport Esq; 5 Anns Close, Kinnerton st, SW1

DAVENPORT, Robert Simpson; s of Richard Simpson Davenport; *b* 7 Jan 1941; *Educ* Canford Sch; *m* 1970, Patricia, nee Temple; 2 s; *Career* formerly with Singleton Fabian & Co, then Peat Marwick Mitchell & Co; exec dir S G Warburg & Co Ltd 1975- (joined 1968); *Style* - Robert Davenport Esq; 1 Genoa av, SW15 (☎ 01 788 1236)

DAVENTRY, 2 Viscount (UK 1943); (Robert) Oliver FitzRoy; s of Capt Rt Hon Edward Algernon FitzRoy, PC, MP (d 1943) and 1 Viscountess Daventry (d 1962); *b* 10 Jan 1893; *Educ* RN Colls Osborne and Dartmouth; *m* 1916, Grace Zöe (d 1978), da of Claude Guinness; 4 da (1 da decd); *Heir* n, Francis Humphrey Maurice FitzRoy Newdegate, *qv*; *Career* served in Gt War 1914-19, Capt 1936, cmding HMS 'Rodney' (despatches), ret; High Sheriff 1956; *Style* - The Rt Hon the Viscount Daventry; 82 Swan Court, SW3 (☎ 01-352 7200)

DAVEY, Francis; s of Wilfred Henry Davey; *b* 23 Mar 1932; *Educ* Plymouth Coll, New Coll Oxford, CCC Cambridge; *m* 1960, Margaret Filby Lake; *Career* head classics dept, Warwick Sch 1960-66, headmaster Dr Morgan's G S Bridgwater 1966-73, headmaster of Merchant Taylors' Sch 1974-; *Style* - Francis Davey Esq; Merchant Taylors' School, Sandy Lodge, Northwood, Middx (☎ Northwood 21850)

DAVEY, Hon Mrs (Heather Mary); *née* Grasmere; da of Baron Morris of Grasmere; *b* 1925; *m* 1, 1946, Tom Berry Caldwell (m dis); m 2, 1972, Alfred G Davey; *Style* - The Hon Mrs Davey; Coach House, Kirk Hammerton, York

DAVEY, Hon Mrs; Hon Mary; *née* Bowden; da of Baron Bowden; *b* 1940; *m* 1964, Dr Roger George Davey; ch; *Career* teacher of deaf children; *Style* - The Hon Mrs Davey; Box 582, 95 Oakland av, Hudson Heights, JOP 1JO, Quebec, Canada

DAVEY, William; CBE (1978); *b* 15 June 1917; *Educ* Univ Coll Nottingham, Technical Coll Huddersfield; *m* 1941, Eunice Battye; 2 s; *Career* head of dept of Chemistry and Biology The Polytechnic of London 1953-59, principal Coll of Technology Portsmouth 1960-69; FRSA, FRIC, FBIM; pres Portsmouth Polytechnic 1969-; *Style* - William Davey Esq, CBE; 67 Ferndale, Waterlooville, Portsmouth, Hants (☎ 3014)

DAVID, Baroness (Life Peer UK 1978); Nora Ratcliff David; JP (Cambridge City 1965); da of George Blockley Blakesley; *b* 1913; *Educ* Ashby-de-la-Zouch Girls' G S, St Felix Southwold, Newnham Cambridge; *m* 1935, Richard William David; 2 s, 2 da; *Career* former Cambridge City Cllr, Cambs Co Cllr 1974-, memb Bd Peterborough Dvpt Corpn 1976-78, Baroness-in-Waiting to HM 1978-79; *Style* - The Rt Hon the Lady David, JP; 50 Highsett, Cambridge (☎ 50376); Cove, New Polzeath, Cornwall

DAVID, Mrs Elizabeth; OBE (1976); da of Rupert Sackville Gwynne, MP, and Hon Stella Ridley; *m* 1944, Lt-Col Ivor Anthony David (m dis 1960); *Career* author of numerous cookery books; Chevalier du Mérite Agricole (France) 1977; *Style* - Mrs Elizabeth David, OBE; c/o Penguin Books, 536 King's Road, SW10

DAVID, Hon Nicholas Christopher; s of Richard William and Baroness David; *b* 1937; *m* 1, 1962, Hilke Hennig (m dis); m 2, 1977, Iva Williams; *Style* - The Hon Nicholas David; Dept of Archaeology, Univ of Ibadan, Nigeria

DAVID, Richard (William); CBE (1967); s of Rev F P and Mary W David; *Educ* Winchester Coll, CCC Cambridge; *m* 1935, Nora (Baroness David, *qv*); 2 s, 2 da; *Career* publisher, formerly publisher to the U, Cambridge U Press, pres Botanical Soc of the British Isles 1979-; *Style* - Richard David Esq, CBE; 50 Highsett,

Cambridge; Cove, New Polzeath, Wadebridge, Cornwall

DAVID, Hon Richard Sebastian David; s of Richard William David, CBE, and Baroness David, *qqv*; *b* 1940; *m* 1963, Eva Ross; *Career* MB, BChir, MA, FRCS; surgn, gen practitioner Fort Macleod Alberta 1975-; *Style* - The Hon Richard David; Box 820, Fort Macleod, Alberta, Canada

DAVIDGE, (Cecil) Vere; s of Cecil William Davidge (d 1936); *b* 14 Feb 1901; *Educ* Abingdon Sch, Pembroke Coll Oxford; *m* 1, 1928, Catherine (d 1948); 1 s, 1 da; m 2, 1961, Philippa, da of Peter Lester; 1 s, 1 da; *Career* served 1940-44 as temp princ HM Treasury and Cabinet Office; barr Inner Temple; High Sheriff Northants 1950; chm Northamptonshire Record Soc 1967-, chm Oakley Hunt 1967- *Style* - Vere Davidge Esq; Little Houghton, Northampton (☎ Northampton 890234)

DAVIDSON, 2 Viscount (UK 1937); John Andrew Davidson; s of 1 Viscount, GCVO, CH, CB, PC (d 1970) and Hon Dame Frances, DBE (*see* Dowager Viscountess Davidson); *b* 22 Dec 1928; *Educ* Westminster, Pembroke Coll Cambridge; *m* 1, 1956 (m dis 1974), Margaret Birgitta, da of Maj-Gen Cyril Henry Norton, CB, CBE, DSO; 4 da; m 2, 1975, Mrs Pamela Joy Dobb, da of John Vergette; *Heir* bro, Hon Malcolm Davidson; *Career* served with Black Watch and 5 Bn King's African Rifles 1947-49, dir Strutt & Parker (Farms) Ltd 1960-75, memb Cncl CLA 1965-75; RASE 1973; *Style* - The Rt Hon The Viscount Davidson; 63 Chester Row, SW1; The Old Rectory, Stonham Aspal, Stowmarket, Suffolk

DAVIDSON, Andrew Page; s of George Smith Davidson of Tuross, ACT, Australia; *b* 30 Jan 1941; *Educ* Prince of Wales Sch Nairobi, Liverpool U; *m* 1964, Angela Mary, nee Davies; 3 s, 1 da; *Career* Veterinary surgeon 1966-; dir Veterinary Pharmaceuticals Ltd, Consolidated Agricultural Suppliers Ltd and others; *Style* - Andrew Davidson Esq; 34 Almoners av, Cambridge

DAVIDSON, Brian; CBE (1966); s of Edward Fitzwilliam Davidson (d 1953); *b* 14 Sept 1909; *Educ* Winchester and New Coll Oxford; *m* 1935, Priscilla Margaret, da of late Arthur Farquhar Chilver; 2 s (1 d 1970), 1 da; *Career* barr 1933, slr 1939; Air Miny & Miny Aircraft Production 1940-43, dir 1951-68; assist legal adviser of the British Gas Corp 1969-75; *Style* - Brian Davidson Esq, CBE; Sands Court, Dodington, Avon, BS17 6SE (☎ Chipping Sodbury 313077)

DAVIDSON, Hon (Georgina) Caroline; da of 2 Viscount Davidson; *b* 1958; *Style* - The Hon Caroline Davidson

DAVIDSON, Hon Camilla Birgitta; da (twin) of 2 Viscount Davidson; *b* 1963; *Style* - The Hon Camilla Davidson

DAVIDSON, Hon Mrs (Elizabeth Mand); *née* Younger; da of 2 Viscount Younger of Leckie; *b* 1913; *m* 1937, Lt-Col Kenneth Bulstrode Lloyd Davidson; 4 s, 1 da; *Style* - The Hon Mrs Davidson; The Manor House, Eglinton, Co Londonderry, N Ireland (☎ 222)

DAVIDSON, Dowager Viscountess; Hon Dame Frances Joan Davidson; *née* Dickinson; DBE (1952, OBE 1920); cr Baroness Northchurch (Life Peeress UK 1963); da of late 1 Baron Dickinson, KBE and Minnie, da of late Gen Sir Richard John Meade, KCSI, CIE; *b* 1894; *m* 1919, 1 Viscount Davidson, GCVO, CH, CB, PC (d 1970); 2 s, 2 da; *Career* MP (U) Hemel Hempstead 1937-59; *Style* - The Rt Hon The Dowager Viscountess Davidson, DBE; 16 Lord North st, London SW1 (☎ 01 222 2167)

DAVIDSON, Howard William; CMG (1961), MBE (1942); s of late Joseph Christopher Davidson, of Johannesburg S Africa; *b* 30 July 1911; *Educ* King Edward VII Sch Johannesburg, Witwatersrand U, Oriel Coll Oxford; *m* 1, 1941 (m dis 1955), Anne Elizabeth, da of late R C Power; 1 da; m 2, 1956 (m dis 1972), Dorothy Janet, da of late Sir William Polson, KCMG, of Wanganui, NZ; *Career* Colonial Admin Serv 1935-63, Sierra Leone, Fiji, N Borneo; Min of Fin Sabah Malaysia 1963-4, Fin

Advr 1964-65; *Recreations* cricket, gardening; *Clubs* E India Sports & Public Schs, Cowdray Park Polo; *Style* - Howard Davidson Esq, CMG, MBE; Glebe Cottage, Tillington, Petworth, Sussex (☎ Petworth 42548)

DAVIDSON, Ian Douglas; CBE (1957); s of Rev John Davidson, JP, and Elizabeth Helen, nee Whyte; *b* 27 Oct 1901; *Educ* King William's Coll; *m* 1, 1936, Claire Louise, nee Gempp (d 1937); 1 da; m 2, 1938, Eugenia, da of Marqués de Mohernando (presumably the Sp cr of 1906 by Alfonso XIII); 1 da *Career* pres Mexican Eagle Oil Co 1936-47, Cia Shell de Venezuela 1953-57, Canadian Shell Ltd 1957-61; *Style* - Ian Davidson Esq CBE; 494 Avenue rd, Toronto, Canada

DAVIDSON, Hon Kristina Louise; da (twin) of 2 Viscount Davidson; *b* 1963; *Style* - The Hon Kristina Davidson

DAVIDSON, Hon Malcolm William Mackenzie; s of 1 Viscount Davidson; *b* 28 Aug 1934; *Educ* Westminster, Pembroke Cambridge; *m* 1970, Mrs Evelyn Ann Carew Perfect, nee Storey; 1 s, 1 da; *Style* - The Hon Malcolm Davidson; Widden Hill House, Horton, Chipping Sodbury, Bristol

DAVIDSON, Maj Philip Lowthian; JP (1950), DL (Cumbria 1972); s of William Davidson (d 1937); *b* 4 June 1902; *Educ* Queen Elizabeth G S Penrith; *m* 1949, Barbara Margery, nee Keay (d 1976); *Career* Maj RE (UK, India), chartered architect in private practice (ret 1977); *Recreations* foxhunting - MFH Blencathra Hunt, watching Rugby Union and cricket; *Clubs* English Speaking Union; *Style* - Maj Philip Davidson JP DL; 38 St John st, Keswick, Cumbria (☎ Keswick 72922)

DAVIDSON, Air V-Marshal Sinclair Melville; CBE (1968); s of James Stewart Davidson (d 1961); *b* 1 Nov 1922; *Educ* Bousfield Sch Kensington, RAF Cranwell, RAF Tech Coll; *m* 1944, Jean Irene, nee Flay; 1 s (and 1 decd); *Career* Air V-marshal RAF; 1941-45 despatches, air staff Air Miny 1957-60, Assist Cmdt RAF Locking 1963-64, Chm Jt Signal Bd (Middle East) 1965, Dir of Signals (Air) MOD 1969-71, Air Offr Wales and Station Cdr RAF St Athan 1972-74, Assist Ch of Defence Staff (signals) 1974-75, Sec Inst of Electronic and Radio Engineers 1977-; *Recreations* theology, parish affairs, maintenance of home and garden; *Clubs* RAF; *Style* - Air V-Marshal Sinclair Davidson, CBE; 38 River ct, Inverness ter, W2 (☎ 01 229 7106); Moy Cottage, Fielden Lane, Crowborough, E Sussex (☎ 4724)

DAVIDSON-HOUSTON, Major Aubrey Claud; s of late Lt-Col Wilfred Bennett Davidson-Houston, CMG, and Annie Henrietta Hunt; *b* 2 Feb 1906; *Educ* St Edward's Sch Oxford, RMC Sandhurst, Slade Sch of Fine Art; *Career* portrait painter 1952-; portraits of the Royal Family, for regts, City Livery Cos, Oxford, and Cambridge; *Style* - Major Aubrey Davidson-Houston; Hillview, West End Lane, Esher, Surrey, (☎ 64749); 4 Chelsea Studios, 412 Fulham rd, SW6 (☎ 01-385 2569)

DAVIE, Alan; CBE (1972); *b* 1920; *Educ* Edinburgh Coll of Art; *Career* painter-exhibitions include Hayward Gall 1974, 25 Years of British Art RA 1977, works in public collections worldwide; poet; jazz musician; jewellry designer; Saltire Award RSA 1977; *Style* - Alan Davie Esq, CBE; Gamels Studio, Rush Green, Hertford

DAVIE, Sir Paul Christopher; s of Charles Christopher Davie (d 1939); *b* 30 Sept 1901; *Educ* Winchester, New Coll Oxford; *m* 1938, Betty Muriel, da of Capt Robert Ronald Henderson, MP (d 1932); 1 s, 1 da; *Career* barr Lincoln's Inn 1925; assist legal advr Home Office 1947-53, City Remembrancer 1953-67, chm National Deaf Children's Soc; kt 1967; *Style* - Sir Paul Davie; The Old Rectory, Bentley, nr Farnham, Surrey GU10 5HU

DAVIE-THORNHILL, Capt Humphrey Bache Christopher; JP (1954), DL (Derbys); s of Lt-Col Bertie George Davie (d 1917); *b* 5 Feb 1905; *Educ* Eton, Trin Hall Cambridge; *m* 1930, Anna Elizabeth (d 1976), da of Sir John Barlow, 1 Bt, JP (d 1932); 2 s, 1 da; *Career* served 1939-45 RA Armaments Inspection Dept (Capt 1942); High Sheriff (Derbys 1955), freeman of Barnstaple; *Clubs* Naval and Military; *Style* - Capt Humphrey Davie-Thornhill, JP, DL; Stanton Hall, Matlock, Derbys (☎ Youlgrave 216)

DAVIES, 3 Baron (UK 1932); David Davies; s of 2 Baron Davies (ka 1944); *b* 2 Oct 1940; *Educ* Eton, King's Coll Cambridge; *m* 1972, Beryl, da of W J Oliver; 1 s, 2 da; *Heir* s, David Daniel Davies; *Career* chm Welsh National Opera Co 1975-; *Style* - The Rt Hon the Lord Davies; Plas Dinam, Llandinam, Powys (Montgomeryshire)

DAVIES OF PENRHYS, Baron (Life Peer UK 1974); Gwilym Elfed Davies; s of David Davies (d 1942); *b* 9 Oct 1913; *m* 1940, Gwyneth, da of Daniel Rees; 2 s, 1 da; *Career* memb St John Ambulance Bde 1926-46; CC (1954) Glamorgan, MP (L) Rhondda (E) 1959-74, PPS to Min of Labour 1964-68, PPS to Min of Power 1968; *Style* - The Rt Hon the Lord Davies of Penrhys; Maes-y-Ffrwd, Ferndale rd, Tylorstown, Ferndale, Rhondda, Glamorgan (☎ Ferndale 730 254)

DAVIES OF LEEK, Baron (Life Peer UK 1970); Harold Davies; PC (1969); *b* 1904; *Educ* Lewis' G S; *m* Jessie Bateman (d 1979); 1 da; *Career* Pres N Staffs Tutors' Assoc 1951-; MP (L) Staffs 1945-70, Parly Sec Miny Pensions & Nat Insur 1964-66, Peace Mission Hanoi 1965, Parly Sec to Miny Soc Security 1966-67, PPS to PM 1967-70; *Style* - The Rt Hon Lord Davies of Leek PC; 77 Montpelier Rise, NW1 (☎ 01 455 8015); 81 Trentham Road, Longton, Stoke on Trent, Staffordshire (☎ Stoke on Trent (STD Code 0782) 39976)

DAVIES, Air Marshal Sir Alan Cyril; KCB (1979, CB 1974), CBE (1967); s of Richard Davies, of Maidstone; *b* 31 March 1924; *m* Julia Elizabeth Ghislaine, nee Russell; 2 s (and 1 decd); *Career* RAF 1941, cmmn 1943; cmd Jt Anti-Submarine Sch Flight 1952-54, cmd Air Sea WarfareDvpt Unit 1958-59, Air Warfare Coll 1962; Dep Dir Operational Requirements MOD 1964-66, cmd RAF Stradishall Suffolk 1967-68, Dir of Air Plans MOD 1969-72, Assist Ch of Air Staff MOD 1972-74, Dep Ch of Staff HQ Allied Air Forces Central Europe 1974-77, Dep CIC RAF Strike Command 1977; *Clubs* RAF; *Style* - Air Marshal Sir Alan Davies, KCB, CBE; c/o Lloyds Bank Ltd, 6 Pall Mall, SW1

DAVIES, Albert John; s of David Daniel and Annie Hilda Davies; *b* 21 Jan 1919; *Educ* Amman Valley G S, University College of Wales Aberystwyth; *m* 1944, Winnifred Ivy, nee Emberton; 1 s, 1 da *Career* Ch Ag Offr, Ag Devpt & Advsy Serv, Miny Ag Fish & Food 1971-79; dep dir Nat Ag Advsy Service 1968-71 *Style* - Albert Davies Esq; 38a Ewell Downs rd, Ewell, Surrey

DAVIES, Very Rev Alun Radcliffe; s of Rev Rhys Davies and Jane Davies; *b* 6 May 1923; *Educ* Cowbridge G S, Univ Coll Cardiff, Keble Coll Oxford, St Michael's Coll Llandaff; *m* 1952, Winifred Margaret Pullen; 2 s, 1 da; *Career* Archdeacon of Llandaff 1971-77, Residentiary Canon of Llandaff Cathedral 1975-77, Dean 1977-; *Style* - The Very Rev Alun Davies; The Deanery, The Cathedral Green, Llandaff, Cardiff (☎ Cardiff 561545)

DAVIES, (James) Brian Meredith; s of late Dr G Meredith Davies and Caroline Meredith Davies; *b* 27 Jan 1920; *Educ* Bedford Sch, Med Sch St Mary's Hosp, London U; *m* 1944, Charlotte, nee Pillar; 3 s; *Career* dir Socl Servs City of Liverpool 1971-; Hon lectr in (Preventive) Paediatrics U of Liverpool 1964-; MD, DPH, MFCM, FFCM; *Style* - Brian Davies Esq MD; Tree Tops, Church rd, Thornton Hough, Wirral, Merseyside (☎ 051-336 3435, office 051-227 3911)

DAVIES, Donald; CBE (1978, OBE 1973); s of late Wilfred Lawson Davies and Alwyne Davies; *b* 13 Feb 1924; *Educ* Ebbw Vale Grammar Sch, Univ Coll Cardiff; *m* 1948, Mabel, nee Hellyar, 2 da; *Career* civil engrg; bd memb National Coal Bd 1973-; FIMinE; *Style* - Donald Davies Esq, CBE; Wendy Cottage, Dukes Wood av, Gerrard's Cross, Bucks (☎ 85083)

DAVIES, David Cyril; s of D T Davies and Mrs G Davies, JP; *b* 7 Oct 1925; *Educ* Lewis Sch Pengam, Univ Coll Wales Aberystwyth; *Career* Headmaster Crown

Woods Sch 1971-; LLB; *Style* - David Davies Esq; 9 Plaxtol Close, Bromley, Kent (☎ 01-464 4187)

DAVIES, Hon David Daniel; s of 3 Baron Davies; *b* 23 Oct 1975; *Style* - The Hon David Davies

DAVIES, Hon David Daniel; s of Baron Davies of Penrhys; *b* 1944; *m* 1969, Cheryl, nee Herbert; *Style* - The Hon David Davies

DAVIES, Hon Eldrydd; da of 3 Baron Davies; *b* 1973; *Style* - The Hon Eldrydd Davies

DAVIES, Elidir (Leslie Wish); s of late Rev Thomas John Landy Davies and Hetty Boucher, nee Wish; *b* 3 Jan 1907; *Educ* Colchester Sch, Bartlett Sch of Architecture, London U; *m* 1, Vera, nee Goodwin (d 1974); m 2, 1976, Kathleen Burke-Collis; *Career* chartered architect Elidir L W Davies and Partners, FRIBA, FRSA; *Style* - Elidir Davies Esq; Hesmonds Oast, East Hoathly, Sussex (☎ Halland 337)

DAVIES, Hon Edward David Grant; s of 1 Baron Davies; *b* 1925; *Educ* Gordonstoun, King's Cambridge; *m* 1, 1949, Patricia Musto; 1 s, 3 da; m 2, 1975, Shirley, nee Harrison; *Career* chm London Tst *Style* - The Hon Edward Davies; Cefngwyfed, Tregynon, Newton, Powys

DAVIES, Edward Gwynfryn; CBE (1970), JP (Port Talbot 1948), DL (Glam 1972); s of Edward Davies; *b* 28 Nov 1904; *Educ* Port Talbot; *m* 1932, Sarah Annie Adams; 2 s; *Career* Mining Indust 1918-21, Steel Indust 1921-69; memb Forestry Cmmn 1959-73, chm National Ctee for Wales 1963-73; *Style* - Edward Davies Esq, CBE, JP, DL; Min-y-Gors, Heol-y-Graig, Cwmavon, Port Talbot, W Glam (☎ Cwmavon 342)

DAVIES, Eric Lawrence; s of late William Davies; *b* 20 Sept 1921; *m* 1948, Francis, nee Evans; 2 s, 1 da; *Career* md Davies Pritchard & Richmond Ltd; dir-Lecontrol Ltd, Summit Link Ltd, Millers (Widnes) Ltd, A T Hillman Ltd, Widnes Installation Ltd, DPR (Automation) Ltd; *Style* - Eric Davies Esq; Hillcrest, Manley rd, Frodsham, Warrington, Merseyside

DAVIES, Ellis Roger; JP, DL (1972); s of Evan Llewelyn Davies (d 1948); *b* 30 Oct 1905; *Educ* Univ Coll Swansea; *m* 1952, Gwendoline Mary, da of late John Owen Roberts; 1 s; *Career* assist slr Manchester Corpn 1929-35, dep clerk of the Cncl and of the Peace Berks 1935-51, clerk to Lieutenancy and of the Cncl Roy Co of Berkshire 1951-71; Gen Commr of Income Tax (Berks) 1974-80; *Style* - Ellis Davies Esq, JP, DL; Field house, Swallowfield, Berks (☎ Reading 883351)

DAVIES, Hon Gwynfor; s of Baron Davies of Penrhys; *b* 1942; *m* 1969, Linda, nee Henry; *Style* - The Hon Gwynfor Davies

DAVIES, Graham Penry; s of Alcwyn Penry Davies (d 1958); *b* 16 Sept 1925; *Educ* City of London Sch, Peterhouse Coll Cambridge; *m* 1953, Rosemary Graham, nee Down; 1 s, 2 da; *Career* Sub-Lt (A) (AE) RNVR; dep chm and md Erith & Co Ltd 1972-; pres Soc of Builders Merchants 1978-80, cncl RNVR Offrs Assoc 1976-; memb Inst of Management Consultants; *Recreations* golf, yacht racing (yacht 'Fleur Vigeur'); *Clubs* Naval Club, Parkstone Yacht Club, Parkstone Gold Club; *Style* - Graham Davies Esq; 66 Anthonys av, Poole, Dorset (☎ Canford Cliffs 707 298)

DAVIES, Gwilym Prys; s of William and Mary Matilda Davies; *b* 8 Dec 1923; *Educ* Towyn Sch, Univ Coll Wales Aberystwyth; *m* 1951, Llinos Evans; 3 da; *Career* ptnr Morgan Bruce and Nicholas slrs, Cardiff, Pontypridd and Porth 1957-; *Style* - Gwilym Davies Esq; Lluest, 78 Church rd, Tonteg, Pontypridd, Mid Glam (☎ Newton Llantwit 2462)

DAVIES, George Raymond; OBE (1977); s of George John Davies (d 1935); *b* 3 Oct 1916; *Educ* E Ham Grammar Sch; *m* 1945, Sylvia nee Newling; 1 s, 1 da; *Career* md Bowker Publishing Co Ltd 1966-69; Pres Int Booksellers Fedn 1978-; chm BA Service House Ltd 1977-; Book Trade Benevolent Soc 1974-; dir The Booksellers Assoc of Great Britain and

Ireland 1964-66 and 1970-; *Style* - George Davies Esq, OBE; Crotchets, Mayfield, East Sussex (☎ Mayfield (STD Code 043 55) 2356)

DAVIES, (Edward) Hunter; s of late John Hunter Davies and Marion; *b* 7 Jan 1936; *Educ* Creighton Sch Carlisle, Carlisle G S, U Coll Durham; *m* 1960, Margaret Forster, qv; 1 s, 2 da; *Career* author; journalist Sunday Times 1960-; ed Sunday Times Magazine 1975-77; *Style* Hunter Davies Esq; 11 Boscastle Road, NW5 (☎ 01-485 3785)

DAVIES, Handel; CB (1962); *s* of late Henry John Davies; *b* 1912; *Educ* Aberdare Grammar School, University of Wales; *m* 1942, Mary Graham, da of R G Harris, of Farnborough; *Career* joined Roy Aircraft Establishment and Miny Aircraft Production 1936, Ch Suptdt Aeroplane and Armament Experimental Establishment Boscombe Down 1952-55; Sci Advsr Air Miny 1955-56, dir-gen Miny of Supply 1957-59, dep dir Roy Aircraft Establishment Farnborough 1959-63; tech dir BAC 1969-77; FRAeS *Style* - Handel Davies Esq, CB; Keel Cottage, Woodham Road, Horsell, Surrey (☎ Woking 4192)

DAVIES, Hubert Gordon; CBE (1965), AE (1946); s of Hubert Offen Davies (d 1948); *b* 25 July 1919; *Educ* Purley G S, Regent St Polytechnic; *m* 1941, Alice Rhoda, da of late Philip Lawrence; 1 s, 1 da *Career* assist Air Force advisor UK High Commr Ottawa 1954-56, dir Management and Staff Training MOD 1965-67, Commanding Offr RAF Tern Hill Shropshire 1967-70, dep dir Warr Coll Greenwich 1972-74, sr Management Dvlt Advr HCITB Wembley 1974-77, Regional Man South and East HCITB 1977-; *Style* - Hubert Davies Esq, CBE, AE; Pantiles, 18 Garnet drive, Ratton, Eastbourne, E Sussex (☎ Eastbourne 57207); Apt 201 Gommar, Puerto Pollensa, Mallorca

DAVIES, Harold Haydn; CB (1956), MC (1917); s of late John Davies; *b* 27 Dec 1897; *Educ* London, Pembroke Coll Cambridge; *m* 1926, Cecilia, da of Morgan Michael; 1 s, 1 da; *Career* served 1914-1918 War with Civil Serv Rifles, served Min of Health 1921-51, dep Establishment Offr Min of Housing and Local Govt 1951-52, chm Welsh Bd of Health 1952-57, O St J (1957); *Style* - Harold Davies Esq, CB, MC; 'Woodlands', Coombe Park, Kingston Upon Thames, Surrey (☎ 01-546 2030)

DAVIES, Hon Islwyn Edmund Evan; JP (Montgomeryshire); s of 1 Baron Davies; *b* 1926; *Educ* Gordonstoun; *m* 1959, Camilla Anne, nee Coulden; 3 s; *Style* - The Hon Islwyn Davies, JP; Berthddu, Llandinam, Powys

DAVIES, Rev Jacob Arthur Christian; s of Jacob S Davies and Christiana; *b* 24 May 1925; *Educ* U of Reading (BSc), Selwyn Coll Cambridge, Imperial Coll of Tropical Agriculture; *m* Sylvia Onikeh Cole; 2 s, 2 da; *Career* High Cmmr for Sierra Leone in London 1972-74; Non-resident Ambass to Denmark, Sweden and Norway 1972-74; dir Personnel Div FAO 1976- (formerly dep dir Agricultural Operations Div); *Style* - The Rev Jacob Davies; Agricultural Operations Division, FAO, Viale Delle Terme di Caracalla, Rome, Italy

DAVIES, Prof John Duncan; s of Ioan and Gertrude Davies; *b* 19 Mar 1929; *Educ* Pontardawe Sch, Treforest Sch of Mines, London U; *m* 1949, Barbara, nee Morgan; 3 da; *Career* formerly Prof of Civil Engrg and Dean of U Coll Swansea, princ West Glam Inst of Higher Educn 1976-77, dir Polytechnic of Wales 1978-; memb Open U Delegacy 1978-79-; PhD, DSc; *Style* - Prof John Davies; Polytechnic of Wales, Treforest, Pontypridd, Mid Glam, Wales (☎ 405133)

DAVIES, Jack Gale Wilmot; OBE (1946); s of Langford George Davies, MD, BCh, MRCS, LRCP and Lily Barnes Davies; *b* 10 Sept 1911; *Educ* Tonbridge Sch, St John's Coll Cambridge; *m* 1949, Georgette O'Dell, nee Vanson; 1 s; *Career* formerly exec dir Bank of England; dir Portals Hldgs Ltd 1976-; *Style* - Jack Davies Esq OBE; 31 Wingate way, Cambridge (☎ 841284)

DAVIES, Hon Jonathan Hugh; s of 2 Baron Davies; *b* 1944; *Educ* Eton, Univ Coll Oxford; *m* 1966, Mary Veronica, da of Sir (William) Godfrey Agnew, KCVO; 2s, 3 da; *Style* - The Hon Jonathan Davies; Stonehill House, Abingdon, Berks

DAVIES, John Howard Gay; s of late E E Davies; *b* 17 Jan 1923; *Educ* Bromsgrove Sch; Wadham Oxford; *m* 1, 1948, Eira Morgan (m dis 1953); m 2, 1955, Betty Walmsley; 1 s; *Career* formerly assist ed Sunday Times; exec assist to editorial dir Thomson Newspapers Ltd; ed Western Mail; editorial dir Thomson Regional Newspapers Ltd 1972-; *Style* - John Davies Esq; 41 Chartfield ave, SW15 (☎ 01-788 8685)

DAVIES, Hon Lucy; da of 3 Baron Davies; *b* 1978; *Style* - The Hon Lucy Davies

DAVIES, V-Adm Sir Lancelot (Richard) Bell; KBE (1977); s of V-Adm Richard Bell Davies, VC, CB, DSO, AFC; *b* 18 Feb 1926; *Educ* Boxgrove Sch Guildford, RN Coll Dartmouth; *m* 1949, Emmeline Joan, nee Molengraaf; 1 s, 2 da; *Career* supreme allied Cdr Atlantic's Rep in Europe 1975-78; FBIM; Cmdt Nato Def Coll Rome 1978-; *Style* - Vice-Adm Sir Lancelot Bell Davies KBE; Holly Lodge, Barnes Lane, Sarisbury, Southampton (☎ Locks Heath 3131)

DAVIES, Lucy Myfanwy; *née* Anwyl-Passingham; CBE (1968, OBE, 1962); da of late Col A M O Anwyl-Passingham, CBE, JP, DL, and late Margaret Anwyl-Passingham; *b* 8 April 1913; *Educ* Francis Holland Graham St Sch; *m* 1955, Major D. W. Davies, TD, RAMC (d 1959); *Career* Dep Dir WRAC, 1964-68; Dep Controller Commandant WRAC, 1967-77; ret, 1968; underwriting memb of Lloyds from 1971; OStJ 1938; *Style* - Col Lucy Davies, CBE; 6 Elm Place, SW7 (☎ 01 373 5731)

DAVIES, L T; *Career* md Clifford Motor Components Ltd; *Style* - L T Davies Esq; Woden rd West, Wednesbury, W Midlands

DAVIES, Lyn Theodore; *Career* chm, Royal Worcester Spode Ltd; Hammersley China Ltd; Palissy Pottery Ltd; W.T. Copeland & Sons Ltd; *Style* - Lyn Davies Esq

DAVIES, (Albert) Meredith; s of Rev E.A. Davies; *b* 30 July 1922; *Educ* Roy Coll of Music, Stationers' Company's Sch, Keble Oxford, Accademia di Santa Cecilia Rome; *m* 1949, Betty Hazel, nee Bates; 3 s, 1 da; *Career* Principal Trinity Coll of Music 1979-, conductor Roy Choral Soc 1972- and Leeds Philharmonic Soc 1975-; *Style* - Meredith Davies Esq; c/o Trinity Coll of Music, Mandeville Place, W1

DAVIES, Doctor Michael; s of William James Davis; *b* 9 June 1923; *Educ* UC Exeter, Bristol Univ; *m* 1951, Helena Hobbs, nee Campbell; *Career* dir of Nuclear Energy, other primary sources and electricity; Cmmn of European Communities from 1973; *Style* - Dr Michael Davies; 1049 Brussels, Belgium (☎ 735 00 40)

DAVIES, Lady (Mary Bailey); *née* Liptrot; *m* 1933, Rt Hon Sir (William) Arthian Davies, PC (d 1979); 1 da; *Style* - Lady Davies; Ballinger Lodge, Great Missenden, Bucks

DAVIES, Hon Mrs (Mary Beatrix); *née* James; da of 3 Baron Northbourne; *b* 1902; *m* 1926, Nicholas Llewelyn Davies; 1 da; *Style* - The Hon Mrs Davies; Eythorne House, Eythorne, Dover, Kent

DAVIES, Hon Philip Cedric Mark; s of 2 Baron Darwen; *b* 1951; *Style* - The Hon Philip Davies

DAVIES, Peter Maxwell; *b* 8 Sept 1934; *Educ* Leigh Grammar Sch; Manchester Univ; Royal Manchester Coll of Music, *Career* composer; Dir of Music, Dartington Hall Summer Sch Music 1979- *Style* - Peter Maxwell Davies Esq; c/o Boosey & Hawkes, PO Box IBR, London WI

DAVIES, Patrick Taylor; CMG (1978), OBE (1967); s of Andrew Taylor Davies and Olive Kathleen Mary Davies; *b* 10 Aug 1927; *Educ* Shrewsbury Sch; St John's Coll. Camb, BA; Trin Coll Oxford; *m* 1959,Marjorie Eileen, nee Wilkinson; 2 da;

Career entered H M Colonial Admin Service, Nigeria 1952; Perm Sec Kano State, 1970-79 and Chief Inspector Area Courts 1972-79; *Style* - Patrick Taylor Esq, CMG, OBE; Rose Cottage, Childs Ercall, Salop (☎ 255)

DAVIES, Ryland; s of Gethin and Joan Davies; *b* 9 Feb 1943; *Educ* Roy Manchester Coll of Music (Fellow 1971); *m* 1966, Anne Elizabeth Howells; *Career* opera singer (tenor); Welsh Nat Opera, Glyndebourne Festival Chorus, Royal Opera, Sadler's Wells Opera, Salzburg, New York Met; also many recordings; *Style* - Ryland Davies Esq; Milestone, Broom Close, Esher, Surrey

DAVIES, Hon (Francis) Ronald; s of 1 Baron Darwen; *b* 1920; *Educ* Bootham Sch; *m* 1942, Margaret Phyllis, nee Cocksworth; 2 s, 1 da; *Career* barr Gray's Inn 1948; *Style* - The Hon Ronald Davies; 39 Parkside, Mill Hill, NW7

DAVIES, Hon Roger Michael; s & h of 2 Baron Darwen; *b* 28 June 1938; *Educ* Bootham Sch York; *m* 1961, Gillian Irene, nee Hardy; 2 s, 3 da; *Style* - The Hon Roger Davies; Labourer's Rest, Green st, Pleshey, Chelmsford, Essex

DAVIES, Stuart Duncan; CBE (1968); s of William Lewis Davies and Alice Dryden Duncan; *b* 5 Dec 1906; *Educ* Westminster City Sch, London U; *m* 1935, Ethel Rosalie Ann Radcliffe, 1 da; *Career* FEng, Hon FRAeS; formerly tech dir Hawker Siddeley Aviation Ltd, Dawty Rotol Ltd; formerly Roy Aeronautical Soc; *Style* - Stuart Davies Esq CBE; Sheridans, Arun Way, Aldwick Bay, Bognor Regis, W Sussex

DAVIES, Hon Stephen Humphrey; s of 2 Baron Darwen; *b* 1945; *m* 1968, Kathleen Prestwood; 1 s, 1 da; *Style* - The Hon Stephen Davies

DAVIES, Stuart Harold; *Career* dir Stanley Tools Ltd; *Style* - Stuart Davies Esq; Stanley Tools, Woodside, Sheffield

DAVIES, Stanley Mason (Sam); CMG (1971); s of Charles Davies (d 1948); *b* 7 Feb 1919; *Educ* Bootle G S, Sch of Mil Engrg; *m* 1943, Diana Joan; 3 da; *Career* Capt RE Europe WW II, Civil Servant 1936-76, Und-Sec Dept of Health and Social Security 1975-76 (Assist Sec 1969-75), dir Vickers Ltd (Medical) 1977-, dir Simonsen & Weels Ltd (Denmark) 1978-, consultant Sterling Winthrop Gp Ltd 1977-, Croix de Guerre (Fr) 1944; *Recreations* philately, ornithology, archaeology (Fellow Society of Antiquaries Edin); *Clubs* Savile; *Style* - Stanley Davies Esq, CMG; 31 Leverstock Green rd, Hemel Hempstead (☎ 0442 54312)

DAVIES, Hon Thomas Barratt; s of 1 Baron Darwen; *b* 1916; *Educ* Bootham Sch, Coll of Art Liverpool; *m* 1941, Doreen, nee Allen; 1 s, 3 da; *Style* - The Hon Thomas Davies; 18 St Winifreds rd, Bournemouth

DAVIES, Thomas Idwal; CBE (1975); s of John Ffôs Davies (d 1931); *b* 15 Jan 1913; *Educ* St Davids Coll Sch Lampeter Cards, U Coll of Wales Aberystwyth; *m* 1, 1940, Bessie Olwen (d 1969), nee Rotheroe; 1 s, 1 da, m 2, 1973, Ronwen, nee Jones; *Career* HM Staff Insp of Schs 1952-75, hon professorial fell U Coll of N Wales Bangor 1970-80, author of *School Organisation* 1969; *Recreations* delving into Cardiganshire history; *Clubs* Roy Overseas League; *Style* - Thomas Davies Esq, CBE; 99 Chester rd, Wrexham, Clwyd (☎ 266196)

DAVIES, Hon Mrs - Hon Teresa Katherine; *née* David; da of Richard William and Baroness David; *b* 1944; *m* 1967, Llewlyn Anthony Davies; *Style* - The Hon Mrs Davies; 50 Clarence rd, Birmingham 13

DAVIES, Lady Venetia Constance Kathleen Luz; *née* Hay; da of 14 Earl of Kinnoull; *b* 1929; *m* 1953, Maj Joseph Trevor Davies; 2 da; *Style* - Lady Venetia Davies; 48 George st, Helensburgh, Dunbartonshire

DAVIES, W A; *Career* chm Holco Trading Co Ltd; *Style* - W A Davies Esq; Holco Trading Co Ltd, 8 Lloyds ave, EC3

DAVIS, Lady Alison Elizabeth; da of 1 Earl Attlee; *b* 1930; *m* 1952, Richard Lionel Lance Davis; 3 da; *Style* - Lady

Alison Davis; Westcott, Beacon Rise, Sevenoaks, Kent

DAVIS, Arthur John; RD (1967); s of Alan Wilfrid Davis; *Educ* G Schs; *m* 1950, Jean Elizabeth Edna Hobbs; 1 s, 1 da (and 1 da decd); *Career* served war, RN 1942-46; entered Lloyds Bank 1941; chief gen man 1978-; FIB (1969); *Style* - Arthur Davis Esq RD; Church Farm House, Aldbury, Tring, Herts (☎ Aldbury Common 321)

DAVIS, Hon Mrs; Hon Beatrice Margaret; da of 1 Viscount Mills; *b* 1916; *m* 1941, Walter Goodwin Davis; *Style* - The Hon Mrs Davis; 3 The Dale, Wootton Wawen, Solihull, Warwicks

DAVIS, Sir Colin (Rex); CBE (1965); s of Reginald Davis; *b* 25 Sept 1927; *Educ* Christ's Hospital, Royal College of Music; *m* 1, 1949, April Cantelo (m dis 1964); 1 s, 1 da; m 2, 1964, Ashraf Naini; 3 s, 1 da; *Career* formerly conductor BBC Scottish Orchestra; Sadler's Wells (musical dir 1961-65); ch conductor BBC Symphony Orchestra 1967-71; conducted at Bayreuth 1977; musical dir Royal Opera House, Covent Garden 1971-; principal guest conductor Boston Symphony Orchestra 1972-; London Symphony Orchestra 1974-kt 1980; *Style* - Sir Colin Davis CBE; Royal Opera House, Covent Garden, WC2

DAVIS, Sir Charles (Sigmund); CB (1960); s of Maurice Davis (d 1943); *b* 22 Jan 1909; *Educ* Trin Coll Cambridge; *m* 1940, Pamela Mary, da of Kenneth Dawson OBE (d 1957); 2 da (Caroline Mary m 1964, Elizabeth Ann m 1967); *Career* kt 1965, 1940-45 Home Guard, barrister (Inner Temple 1930), 2 Counsel to the Speaker House of Commons since 1974, legal adviser to Min of Agriculture Fisheries and Food and The Forestry Cmmn 1957-74; *Recreations* music (LRAM, ARCM); *Style* - Sir Charles Davis, CB; The Little House, 43 Wolsey Road, East Molesey, Surrey (☎ 01 979 6617)

DAVIS, Mrs (Chloë Marion); OBE (1975); da of Richard Henry Pound; *b* 15 Feb 1909; *m* 1928, Edward Thomas Davis; 1 s; *Career* Consumer Consultative Ctee, EEC 1973-76; memb Council on Tribunals, 1970-79; Consumer Standards Advisory Ctee of British Standards Institution, 1965-78 (chm 1970-73); chm Consumer Affairs Gp of National Organisations 1973-; *Style* - Mrs Edward Davis OBE; Auberville Cottage, 246 Dover rd, Walmer, Kent

DAVIS, Sir Dermot Renn; Knighted 1980; *Career* Chief Justice, Gibraltar; *Style* - Sir Dermot Davis

DAVIS, Lady (Gertrude) Elizabeth; *née* Phipps; da of 3 Marquess of Normanby; *b* 1908; *m* 1934, Adm Sir William Wellclose Davis, GCB, DSO; 2 s, 2 da; *Style* - Lady Elizabeth Davis; Coglan House, Longhope, Glos

DAVIS, Sir (Ernest) Howard; CMG (1969), OBE (1960); *b* 22 Apr 1918; *Educ* Christian Bros Sch Gibraltar, Coll of St Joseph Blackpool, London U; *m* 1948, Marie, nee Bellott; 2 s; *Career* dep gov Gibraltar 1971-78, kt 1978; *Style* - Sir Howard Davis, CMG, OBE; 36 South Barrack rd, Gibraltar (☎ A 70358)

DAVIS, John Burton; s of Percy Oliver Davis (d 1980); *b* 20 Oct 1922; *Educ* Trin Sch of John Whitgift, Croydon; Queen Mary Coll London U (BSc); *m* 1944, Irene Margaret, da of late William Victor Reid; 1 s, 1 da; *Career* Lt REME, sr exec Lead Industries Gp Ltd, dir Associated Lead Mfrs Ltd, Associated Lead Mfrs (Pty) Ltd S Africa, Frys Metals (Pty) Ltd S Africa, Waldies Ltd Calcutta India, dir Tewin Wood Roads Ltd; *Style* - John Davies Esq; 5 Bishops rd, Tewin Wood, Welwyn, Herts (☎ Bulls Green 597)

DAVIS, James Gresham; s of late Col Robert Davis, OBE, JP; *b* 20 July 1928; *Educ* Bradfield Coll, Clare Cambridge; *m* 1973, Johanna Adrianna, nee Verhoef; 3 da; *Career* FCIT, dir Kleinwort Benson Ltd, dir DFDS Ltd, v-chm Harley Mullion & Co, dir K B Shipbrokers (HK) Ltd; *Style* - James Davis Esq; Summer Lawn, Dovercourt, Harwich, Essex (☎ 02555 2981); 115 Woodsford sq, Addison rd, W14 (☎ 01 602 0675)

DAVIS, Sir John Gilbert; 3 Bt (UK

1946); s of Sir Gilbert Davis, 2 Bt (d 1973); *b* 17 Aug 1936; *Educ* Oundle, RNC Dartmouth; *m* 1960, Elizabeth Margaret, da of Robert Smith Turnbull, of Falkirk; 1 s, 2 da; *Heir* s, Richard Charles Davis; *Career* v-pres Abtibi Paper Co Ltd (Toronto) and other paper cos; *Style* - Sir John Davis, Bt; 70 York Mills rd, Toronto, Ont M2P IB7, Canada

DAVIS, Dr Michael; s of William James Davis (d 1955); *b* 9 June 1923; *Educ* Us of Exeter, Bristol, Toronto, London; *m* 1951, Helena Hobbs, nee Campbell; *Career* Lieutenant RNVR 4th Cruiser Sqdn Br Pacific Fleet 1943-46 (dispatch 1944), 1956-73 UK Atomic Energy Authority (inc commercial dir, technical advisor), 1973- dir of Nuclear Energy Commission of the EEC, FIMM, FInstP; *Recreations* sculpture; *Clubs* United Oxford and Cambridge; *Style* - Dr Michael Davis; 200 rue de la Loi, 1049 Brussels, Belgium (☎ 736-6000)

DAVIS, Richard Charles; s and h of Sir John Gilbert Davis, 3 Bt, *qv*; *b* 11 April 1970; *Style* - Richard Davis Esq

DAVIS, Air Vice-Marshal Robert Leslie; s of Sidney Davis; *b* 22 March 1930; *Educ* Woolsingham Grammer Sch and Bede Sch Collegiate, Sunderland, Co Durham; *m* 1956, Diana, nee Bryant; 1 s, 1 da; *Career* Comdr RAF Staff and Air Attache, British Defence Staff, Washington, DC from 1977-80; Comdr British Forces and Air Officer Commanding, Cyprus 1980; *Style* - Air Vice-Marshal Robert Davis; The Elms, High st, Witton-le-Wear, Co Durham

DAVIS, Sidney; CBE (1970); s of Septimus David (d 1965); *b* 4 Jan 1909; *Educ* St John's S Shields; *m* 1957, Vera, da of Peter Sladek (d 1961); 2 s; *Career* served 1939-45 War; ch transportation offr UNRRA mission to Central Europe 1945-46, ch supt (Traffic) Nigerian Railways 1953-60 (former dep ch); chm and md Makeri (Tin) Smelting Co Ltd, Nigeria 1960-73; ret 1977; *Style* - Sidney Davis Esq, CBE; Claremont, Yatesbury Close, Farnham, Surrey (☎ Farnham 713932)

DAVIS, Sir Thomas Robert Alexander Harries; KBE (1980); s of Sidney Thomas Davis; *b* 11 June 1917; *Educ* King's Coll Auckland, NZ; Otago Univ Med Sch; Sch of Tropical Medicine, Sydney Univ; Harvard Sch of Public Health; FRSTM & H; *Career* Private Medical Practice 1974-78; Pa Tu Te Rangi Ariki 1979; Premier, Cook Islands 1978-; *Style* - The Hon Sir Thomas Davis KBE; Premier's Dept, Rarotonga, Cook Islands

DAVIS, Sir William (Wellclose); GCB (1959, KCB 1956, CB 1952), DSO and bar, DL (Glos, 1963); s of Walter Stewart Davis, JP (d 1946); *b* 11 Oct 1901; *Educ* Summerfields Oxford. RN Colls Osborne and Dartmouth; *m* 1934 Lady Elizabeth Phipps, da of Rev 3 Marq of Normanby (d 1932); 2 s, 2 da; *Career* joined RN 1917, served in 1914-18 and 1939-45 Wars; ch of staff to c-in-c Home Fleet (Cdre 1 class) 1948-50, naval sec to First Lord of the Admiralty 1950-52, V-Adm 1953, Adm 1956, c-in-c Home Fleet and Nato c-in-c Eastern Atlantic 1958-60, ret 1960; first and principal naval ADC to HM the Queen 1959-60; v-pres of European Atlantic Gp; *Clubs* Naval and Military; *Style* - Sir William Davis, GCB, DSO*, DL; Coglan House, Longhope, Gloucestershire (☎ 830282)

DAVIS, W A; *Career* chm Lancia (England) Ltd; *Style* - W A Davis Esq; Lancia England Ltd, 372 Ealing rd, Alperton, Wembley, Middx

DAVIS, William Allan; s of Wilfred Egwin Davis (d 1953); *b* 19 June 1921; *Educ* Cardinal Vaughan Sch Kensington; *m* 1944, Audrey Pamela, da of late Lionel Arthur Lough; 2 s, 1 da; *Career* CA; sr ptnr Armitage and Norton London; Alderman, Cripplegate Ward City of London 1976; *Clubs* City Livery and Oriental; *Style* - William Davis Esq; 37 Braybank, Bray, Maidenhead, Berks; Willoughby House, Barbican, London, EC2Y 8BN (☎ 01-638 5354)

DAVIS, Hon William Grenville; QC (Can); s of Albert Grenville; *b* 30 July 1929; *Educ* Brampton High Sch, Univ Coll, U of Toronto, Osgoode Hall Law Sch; *m* 1, 1953, Helen, nee Macphee (d 1962); m 2, 1963, Kathleen Louise, nee

Mackay; 2 s, 3 da; *Career* called to Bar of Ontario 1955; former Memb (C) Provincial Parliament; Minister of Education 1962-71 and Minister of U Affairs 1964-71; premier of Ontario and pres of the Council, Ontario 1971-; leader Progressive Conservative Party; *Style* - The Hon William Davis QC; Office of the Premier of Ontario, Parliament Buildings, Toronto, Ontario, Canada; 61 Main Street South, Brampton, Ontario

DAVIS, William Herbert; TD; s of William Davis; *b* 27 July 1919; *Educ* Waverley G S, U of Aston (BSc); *m* 1945, Barbara Mary Joan, nee Summerfield; 1 da; *Career* CEng; FIMechE; FiProdE; MIPlantE; FBIM; FIWM; SME(USA); formerly chm and ch exec Triumph Motor Co Ltd; md Rover Triumph BLUK Ltd; dir British Leyland Motor Corpn; dir Military Contracts and Govt Affairs 1976-; *Style* - William Davis Esq TD; Arosa, The Holloway, Alvechurch, Worcs (☎ Redditch 66187)

DAVIS-GOFF, Sir Robert William ; 4 Bt (UK 1905); s of Sir Ernest Davis-Goff, 3 Bt (d 1980); *b* 12 Sept 1955; *Educ* Cheltenham; *m* 1978, Nathalie Sheelagh, da of Terence Chadwick, of Lissen Hall, Swords, Co Dublin; 1 s; *Heir* s, William Nathaniel Davis-Goff (b 20 April 1980); *Career* picture dealer; *Recreations* shooting; *Clubs* Kildare Street & University; *Style* - Sir Robert Davis-Goff, Bt; 199 Strand rd, Dublin 4

DAVIS-GOFF, William Nathaniel; s and h of Sir Robert Davis-Goff, 4 Bt; *b* 20 April 1980

DAVISON, Hon Alexander; s and h of 2 Baron Broughshane; *b* 1936; *Educ* Eton; *m* 1, 1961, Teresa Clare (m dis 1966), da of James Bramwell; 2 da; m 2, Cecilia Ann, da of J W Ingrams (m dis 1977, she d 1977); 1 s; *Style* - The Hon Alexander Davison

DAVISON, Barry George; s of William Davison; *b* 12 Dec 1935; *m* 1960, Jean Doreen; 3 da (Tracy b 1962, Katharine b 1964, Joanne b 1970); *Career* 2nd Lt RA, FCA 1967, chm and md Foster Bros Clothing Co Ltd 1978-, chm Non Foods Policy Ctee Retail Consortium 1981-, dir-Foster Gp of Cos, Adams Gp of Cos, Stone Gp of Cos, and others; *Recreations* golf; *Clubs* Olton Golf Club; *Style* - Barry Davison Esq; The Firs, Lovelace av, Solihull, West Midlands (☎ 021 705 2850); 7 Links Court, Thurlestone, Devon (☎ Thurlestone 770)

DAVISON, Hon Mrs; Hon Elizabeth Slater; da of Baron Slater, BEM (Life Peer); *b* 1934; *m* 1955, Frank Davison; *Style* - The Hon Mrs Davison; 1 Seymour grove, Eaglescliffe, Co Durham

DAVISON, Ian Frederic Hay; s of Eric Hay Davison; *b* 30 June 1931; *Educ* Dulwich Coll, LSE (BSc Econ), U of Michigan; *m* 1955, Maureen Patricia Blacker; 1 s, 2 da; *Career* ACA; FCA; man ptnr Arthur Andersen & Co, Chartered Accountants; memb Institute of Chartered Accountants; Inflation Accounting Steering Gp 1975-; price Commission 1975-; *Style* - Ian Davison Esq; 53 Lee rd, Blackheath, SE3 (☎ 01 852 8506)

DAVISON, Hon (William) Kensington; DSO, DFC; s of 1 Baron Broughshane, KBE (d 1953); *b* 1914; *Educ* Shrewsbury and Magdalen Oxford; *Career* barr Inner Temple; *Style* - The Hon Kensington Davison DSO DFC; 3 Godfrey st, SW3 (☎ 01 352 7826)

DAVISON, Rt Hon Sir Ronald (Keith); GBE (1978), CMG (1975), PC (1978), QC (NZ) 1965; s of Joseph James Davison; *b* 16 Nov 1920; *Educ* Auckland U (LLB); *Career* admitted as barr and slr 1948; chm Montana Wines Ltd 1971-78; dir NZ Insurance Co Ltd 1975-78); Chief Justice of New Zealand 1978; *Style* - The Rt Hon Sir Ronald Davison GBE CMG, Chief Justice of New Zealand; Chief Justice's Chambers, Supreme Court, Wellington, New Zealand

DAVSON; *see* Glyn, Bt, Sir Anthony

DAVSON, Christopher Michael Edward; s of Sir Edward Davson, KCMG, 1 Bt (d 1937); hp to bro Sir Anthony Glyn, 2 Bt, *qv*; *b* 26 May 1927; *m* 1, 1962, Evelyn, nee Wardrop (m dis 1972); 1 s; m 2, 1975, Kate, da of Ludo Foster, of

Greatham Manor, Pulborough, Sussex; *Style* - Christopher Davson Esq; 5 Market rd, Rye, Sussex

DAVY, Brig George Mark Oswald; CB (1945), CBE (1943), DSO (1941); s of Capt George Charles Hague Davy (d 1934); *b* 22 Sept 1898; *Educ* Charterhouse, RMC; *m* 1932, Isabel Gwendolen (d 1970), da of late E Alan Hay; 1 s; *Career* Served 1914-1918 War (gassed and captured), Capt 3 Hussars 1931, Cdr 3 and 7 Armoured Bdes and Dir Mil Ops, Cdr Land Forces Adriatic, ret 1948; painter (horses in oils, landscapes and seascapes in water cols) and sculptor, assoc memb Nat Soc of Painters, Sculptors and Printmakers, life v-pres Chelsea Art Soc; *Clubs* Cavalry; *Style* - Brig George Davy, CB, CBE, DSO; Jordanstone House, Alyth, Blairgowrie, Perthshire (☎ Alyth 2350)

DAWES, Professor Geoffrey Sharman; CBE (1980); s of Rev W. Dawes; *b* 21 Jan 1918; *Educ* Repton Sch; New Coll Oxford (BA, BSc); *m* 1941, Margaret Monk; 2 s, 2 da; *Career* dir, Nuffield Inst for Medical Research, Oxford, from 1948; memb, Medical Research Council, from 1978; BM, BCh, DM; *Style* - Prof Geoffrey Dawes; 8 Belbroughton rd, Oxford (☎ 58131)

DAWES, Jack; *Career* chm Allied Colloids; Signo Ltd; dir James Capel & Co; Supra Gp Ltd; *Style* - Jack Dawes Esq; James Capel & Co, Winchester House, 100 Old Broad st, EC2

DAWICK, Viscount; Alexander Douglas Derrick Haig; s and h of 2 Earl Haig, OBE; *b* 30 June 1961; *Educ* Stowe; *Style* - Viscount Dawick

DAWKINS, Thomas William; *Career* FIStructE; dir Frankipile Australia Pty Ltd, Australia; MacDonald, Gibbs & Co; md Frankipile Ltd; *Style* - Thomas Dawkins Esq; Frankipile Ltd, Davis House, High st, Croydon

DAWNAY, Lady Angela Christine Rose; *née* Montagu Douglas Scott; da of 7 Duke of Buccleuch and Queensberry; *b* 1906; *m* 1936, V-Adm Sir Peter Dawnay, KCVO, CB, DSC; *Style* - Lady Angela Dawnay; The Old Post Cottage, Wield, Alresford, Hants

DAWNAY, Hon Mrs (Iris Irene Adele); *née* Peake; MVO (1957); da of 1 Viscount Ingleby; *b* 23 July 1923; *m* 1963, Oliver, s of Maj-Gen Guy Dawnay, CB, CMG, DSO, MVO, of Longparish House, Hants; 1 da (Emma Jane Clarissa b 1964); *Career* Lady-in-Waiting to HRH The Princess Margaret 1952-62; *Style* - The Hon Mrs Dawnay, MVO; Wexcombe House, Marlborough, Wilts (☎ Oxenwood 229); Flat 5, 32 Onslow sq, SW7 (☎ 01 584 3963)

DAWNAY, Hon James Richard; s of 10 Viscount Downe; *b* 1937; *m* 1976, Gillian, nee Dance, former w of Capt Simon George Melville Portal; 1 s; *Style* - The Hon James Dawnay; 8 Scarsdale Villas, W8

DAWNAY, Hon Richard Henry; s and h of 11 Viscount Downe; *b* 9 April 1967

DAWNAY, Hon Sarah Frances; da of 11 Visc Downe; *b* 2 April 1970

DAWNAY, Lady Katharine Nora de la Poer; *née* Beresford; da of 6 Marquess of Waterford; *b* 1899; *m* 1926, Maj-Gen Sir David Dawnay, KCVO, CB, DSO (d 1971); 2 s, 2 da; *Style* - Lady Katharine Dawnay; Whitfield Court, Waterford, Eire

DAWOOD, Nessim Joseph; s of late Yousef Dawood; *b* 27 Aug 1927; *Educ* Exeter and London Us; *m* 1949, Juliet, nee Abraham; 3 s; *Career* md The Arabic Advertising and Publishing Co Ltd, London, 1958; dir Contemporary Translations Ltd, London, 1962-, Bradbury Wilkinson (Graphics) Ltd, 1975; Middle East Consultant; Arabist; *Style* - Nessim Dawood Esq; Berkeley Square House, Berkeley sq, W1 (01 409 0953)

DAWSON, David John; CBE (1971); s of Rev John Thomas Dawson (d 1933); *b* 15 April 1909; *Educ* King Edward's Sch Birmingham and St Bartholomew's Hosp Medical Coll; *m* 1940, Violet Winifred, da of Dr C W Gilbert (d 1942); 2 s, 1 da; *Career* served in 1939-45 War as specialist in Aviation Medicine, sr specialist in neuropsychiatry RAF 1948-71; CStJ; *Clubs* Royal Air Force; *Style* - David Dawson Esq, CBE; Singletons, High st, Avening, Tetbury, Glos (☎ Nailsworth 2611)

DAWSON, Maj Sir (Hugh Halliday) Trevor; 3 Bt (UK 1920), of Edgwarebury, co Middlesex; s of Cdr Sir Hugh Trevor, 5 Bt, CBE, RN (d 1976); *b* 6 June 1931; *Educ* Harrow, RMA Sandhurst; *m* 1955, Caroline Jane, da of William Acton; 2 s; *Heir* s, Hugh Michael Trevor; *Career* late Maj Scots Gds; chm Arbuthnot Securities Ltd 1976-81, Dawson and Forbes Ltd, Investment Bankers; dir Arbuthnot Latham and Co Ltd Merchant Bankers 1965-1980, Arbuthnot Latham Hldgs Ltd 1969; *Clubs* White's, Turf, Buck's, Pratt's, City of London; *Style* - Maj Sir Trevor Dawson, Bt; China Cottage, E Stowell, Marlborough, Wilts; 31 Eaton Sq, London, SW1 (☎ 01 235 1493)

DAWSON, Hugh Michael Trevor; s and h of Sir (Hugh Halliday) Trevor Dawson, 3 Bt, *qv*; *b* 28 March 1956; *Style* - Hugh Dawson Esq

DAWSON, Hon Mrs (Ivy Maude); *née* Eden; da of late Hon George Eden (3 s of 4 Baron Auckland) and aunt of 9 Baron; *b* 1899; *m* 1927, John Dawson; *Style* - The Hon Mrs Dawson; 1 Wickfield close, Woolmer Green, Knebworth, Herts

DAWSON, James Gordon; CBE (1980); s of late James Dawson; *b* 3 Feb 1916; *Educ* Aberdeen G S, Aberdeen U; *m* 1941, Doris Irene, nee Rowe; 1 s, 1 da; *Career* chartered engineer Perkins Engines 1955-66, tech dir Dowty Gp Ltd 1966-69, md Zenith Carburettor Co Ltd 1977-81 (formerly dir), chm pres Instn of Mechanical Engineers 1979-80; *Style* - James Dawson Esq, CBE; Mildmay House, Manor Farm, Apethorpe, Peterborough (☎ Kings Cliffe 348)

DAWSON, James Lawrence; s of Albert Lawrence Dawson; *b* 1 April 1924; *Educ* Sale H S, Royal Engineering Coll, City U; *m* 1947, Olive Joan, nee Turner; 3 s; *Career* civil engineer; dir Civil Engineering Services, Property Services Agency, 1979-; *Style* - James Dawson Esq; The Maltings, Oxted, Surrey (5495)

DAWSON, Mark Patrick; s of Douglas Dawson; *b* 19 Oct 1941; *Educ* Wellington; *m* 1940, Carol Anne, nee Groves; 2 s; *Career* former chm and md Pickford Dawson & Holland Ltd, md Jardine Matheson Insurance Brokers UK Ltd 1978-79, also md Jardine Matheson Underwriting Agencies Ltd 1979-; *Clubs* Boodle's, City of London; *Style* - Mark Dawson Esq; Leaden Hall, Leavenham, Colchester, Essex (☎ Colchester (STD Code 0787) 210480)

DAWSON, Ven Peter; s of Leonard Smith and Cicely Alice Dawson; *b* 31 Mar 1929; *Educ* Manchester G S, Keble Oxford, Ridley Hall Cambridge; *m* 1955, Kathleen Mary Sansome; 1 s, 3 da; *Career* rector of Morden, Diocese Southwark 1968-77; rural dean of Merton 1975-77; archdeacon of Norfolk 1977-; *Style* - The Ven the Archdeacon of Norfolk; Intwood Rectory, Norwich, Norfolk (☎ Norwich (STD Code 0603) 51946)

DAWSON, Vera, Lady (Vera Anne Loch); da of late Maj Sir Frederick Loch Halliday, CIE, MVO; *m* 1918, Cdr Sir Hugh Trevor Dawson, 2 Bt, DSO, MC, TD (d 1976); *Style* - Vera, Lady Dawson; Casina Lodge, 8 Park Village West, London NW1

DAWSON-DAMER, Hon Edward Lionel Seymour; s of 7 Earl of Portarlington; *b* 1967; *Style* - The Hon Edward Dawson-Damer; c/o The Rt Hon Earl of Portarlington, 19 Coolong Road Vaucluse, NSW 2030, Australia

DAWSON-DAMER, Hon Henry Lionel Seymour; s of 7 Earl of Portarlington; *b* 1971; *Style* - The Hon Henry Dawson-Damer; c/o The Rt Hon Earl of Portarlington, 19 Coolong Road, Vaucluse, NSW 2030, Australia

DAWSON-DAMER, Hon Lionel John Charles Seymour; s of late 6 Earl of Portarlington; *b* 1940; *Educ* Eton; *m* 1965 (m dis 1975) Rosemary Ashley Morrett, nee Hancock; *Style* - The Hon Lionel Dawson-Damer; Oran Park, Narella, NSW 2567, Australia

DAWSON-DAMER, Lady Marina Davina; da of 7 Earl of Portarlington; *b* 1969; *Style* - Lady Marina Dawson-Damer

DAY, Sir Robin; s of late William Day; *b* 24 Oct 1923; *Educ* Bembridge Sch, St Edmund Hall Oxford; *m* 1965, Katherine Mary, nee Ainslie; 2 s; *Career* called to the Bar 1951; television broadcaster and journalist; presenter Panorama BBC 1967-72; presenter World at One BBC Radio 4; chm Hansard Society for Parliamentary Government 1981, kt 1980; *Style* - Sir Robin Day; c/o BBC TV Studios, Lime grove, London W12

DAY, Stephen Peter; s of Frank Day; *b* 19 Jan 1938; *Educ* Bancroft's Sch, CCC Cambridge; *m* 1965, Angela, nee Waudby; 1 s, 2 da; *Career* Ambass to Qatar 1981-; HMOCS 1961-65, FO 1965-, Consul-Gen Edmonton 1979-81; has also served Singapore, Beirut; *Style* - Stephen Day Esq; c/o FCO, SW1; 92 West End Lane, Esher, Surrey (☎ 64138)

DAYSH, Prof George Henry John; CBE (1973); s of Alfred John Daysh; *b* 1901; *Educ* Eggars G S Alton, Univ Coll Reading, Wadham Oxford; *m* 1927, Sheila Guthrie (d 1971), da of Alexander Ferrier Angus Fairweather; 1 s, 1 da; *Career* MLitt, Prof of Geography Armstrong Coll 1943-66, later King's Coll Durham U and Newcastle U, dep v-chllr Newcastle U 1963-66, Emeritus Prof 1966-, former co dir, chm Tyne Tees TV Ltd Newcastle 1968-72; *Style* - Prof George Daysh, CBE; 2 Dunkirk ter, Corbridge, Northumberland (☎ 2154)

DE BARTOLOME, Stephen Martin; CBE; *Career* chm Bank of Europe Ltd, Union Transport Finance Ltd, Wagon Finance Ltd; dep chm Pegler-Hattersley Ltd; dir Spear & Jackson Int Ltd, Bramber Engineering Co Ltd and others; *Style* - Stephen de Bartolome Esq, CBE; Wagon Finance Corpation, 3 Endcliffe cres, Sheffield

DE BATHE, Lady; Deborah; *née* Warschowsky, formerly wife of Dr Poul Henius; *m* 1931, as his 2 wife, Sir Hugo Gerald de Bathe, 5 Bt (d 1940); *Style* - Lady de Bathe

DE BATHE, Lady; Edna; *née* Terrell; *m* 1932, Sir Christopher Albert de Bathe, 6 and last Bt (k 1941); *Style* - Lady de Bathe

DE BELLAIGUE, Hon Mrs - Hon Sylvia Corisande; da of late 8 Baron Rodney; *b* 1930; *Educ* McGill U Canada; *m* 1962, Eric de Bellaigue; 2 s; *Style* - The Hon Mrs de Bellaigue; 7 Blomfield Road, W9 (☎ 01 286 5549)

DE BOER, Anthony Peter; s of Goffe de Boer and Irene Kathleen, nee Grist; *b* 22 June 1918; *Educ* Westminster Sch; *m* 1942, Pamela, nee Bullock; 1 s; *Career* chm-Steel Bros from 1980, Attock Petroleum from 1974, Tomatin Distillers from 1978, British Road Federation from 1972; dir Tarmac Ltd from 1971, Burmah Oil Co Ltd from 1978, Chloride Group from 1976, National Bus Co from 1969; *Style* - Anthony de Boer Esq; Halletts Barn, Ditchling Common, Hassocks, Sussex (☎ Hassocks 2442)

DE BONA, G; *Career* chm Alfa Romeo (GB) Ltd; *Style* - G De Bona Esq; Alfa Romeo (GB) Ltd, Edgware rd, NW2

DE BONO, Edward Francis Charles Publins; s of late Prof Joseph de Bono; *b* 19 May 1933; *Educ* St Edward's Coll, Malta; Royal Univ of Malta; Christ Church Oxford (Rhodes Scholar); BSc, MD Malta; D Phil Oxon; PhD Cantab; *Career* Asst Dir of Research, dept of Investigative Medicine, Cambridge Univ, 1963-76; dir of the Cognitive Research Trust, Camb from 1971; Lecturer in Medicine, dept of investigative medicine, Camb Univ from 1976; Books *The Use of Lateral Thinking* (1967) and *Lateral Thinking, a Text Book of Creativity* (1970) *Style* - Dr Edward de Bono; Cranmer Hall, Fakenham, Norfolk

DE BOURBON DE PARME, HRH Princess (Jeanne de) Chantal Marie Hélène Antoinette Charlotte; only da of Prince Luigi de Bourbon de Parme (10 s, by his 2 w Maria Antonia, da of Miguel 1

of Portugal, of Duke Roberto I of Parma); *b* 24 Nov 1946, Cannes; *m* Panayotis Skinas; at least 1 s (Alexandre Dmitri); *Style* - HRH Princess Chantal de Bourbon de Parme

DE BUNSEN, Hon Mrs - Hon Alexandra; *née* Carington; da of 6 Baron Carrington; *b* 1943; *m* 1965, Maj Peter N de Bunsen, Coldstream Guards (ret); 2 s, 1 da; *Style* - The Hon Mrs de Bunsen; Park House, Newbold Pacey, Warwick

DE CABARRUS, Lady Caroline Mary; *née* Percy; da of 10 Duke of Northumberland; *b* 1947; *m* 1973, Count Pierre de Cabarrus; 1 da; *Style* - Lady Caroline de Cabarrus

DE CAICEDO, Marquesa - Hon Camilla Edith Mairi Elizabeth; *née* Jessel; da of 2 Baron Jessel (by 1 m); *b* 1940; *m* 1960, Don Juan Carlos del Prado y Ruspoli, 11 Marques de Caicedo (cr of Philip V of Spain 1712; b 30 June 1934, succession recognised 28 Sept 1966); 2 s; *Style* - Marquesa de Caicedo; C Alonso Cano 43, Madrid, Spain

DE CASA MAURY, Winifred Marquesa; Winifred May; da of Charles Birkin, CMG, TD, JP, DL (4 s of Sir Thomas Birkin, 1 Bt, JP, DL) and 1 cous once removed of Jane Birkin, *qv*, the actress; *m* 1, 1913 (m dis 1931), Rt Hon William Dudley Ward, PC, er s of Capt William Humble Dudley Ward (by Hon Eugénie, da of 1 Viscount Esher) and gn of 1 Earl of Dudley; 2 da (Ladies Reed and Laycock, *qqv*); m 2, 1937 (m dis 1954), Peter (Pedro Jose Isidro Manuel Ricardo Mone Maury, Marqués) de Casa Maury (cr 1897 by Pope Leo XIII and authorised in Spain by Queen Regent Christina 1897); *Style* - Winifred, Marquesa de Casa Maury; 36 Old Church st, SW3

DE CHAIR, Lady (Anne) Juliet Dorothea Maud; *née* Wentworth-Fitzwilliam; da of 8 Earl Fitzwilliam; *b* 1935; *Educ* St Hilda's Oxford; *m* 1, 1960, as his 2 w, 6 Marquess of Bristol (m dis 1972); m 2, 1974, Capt Somerset Struben de Chair; 1 da; *Style* - Lady Juliet de Chair; St Osyth's Priory, St Osyth, Essex

DE CHAZAL, Paul André; s of Claude de Chazal; *b* 25 Sept 1942; *Educ* Downside, Sydney Sussex Coll Cambridge; *m* 1978, Donatienne, da of Jean Louis Dierckx de Casterle; 1 da; *Career* solictor, ptnr Messrs Simmons and Simmons, dir British American Insurance Co Ltd and Windsor Life Assurance Co Ltd; *Style* - Paul de Chazal Esq; 15 Patten rd, SW1 (☎ 01 874 5003)

DE CHIMAY, Princess Alphonse; Mary Brenda; da of Capt Lord Ernest Hamilton, 7 s of 1 Duke of Abercorn, KG, PC, and Pamela (da of Capt Frederic Campbell, 4 s of Sir Guy Campbell, 1 Bt, CB, by Sir Guy's 2 w, Pamela, da of Lord Edward FitzGerald, 5 s of 1 Duke of Leinster); *b* 28 March 1897; *m* 1922, Lt-Col Prince Alphonse de Chimay, TD, Scots Gds, s of Prince Alphonse de Chimay, Comte de Caraman; 1 da (Marchioness of Hertford) *Style* - Princess Alphonse de Chimay; The Garden House, Arrow, Alcester, Warwicks (☎ 2513)

DE CLIFFORD, 26 Baron (E 1299); Edward Southwell Russell; OBE (1955), TD (1944); s of 25 Baron (d 1909); *b* 31 Jan 1907; *Educ* Eton; *m* 1, 1926 (m dis 1973), Dorothy Evelyn Meyrick; 2 s; m 2, 1973, Mina Margaret, da of G E Sands; *Heir* s, Hon John Edward Southwell Russell; *Career* Col (ret) REME, late R Gloucestershire Hussars (TA); *Style* - The Rt Hon The Lord de Clifford, OBE, TD; The Birches, Silvington, Cleobury Mortimer, Kidderminster, Worcs

DE COSTECAUDE DE SAINT VICTOR, Alain; *Career* md Renault Ltd; *Style* - Alain de Costecaude de Saint Victor Esq; Renault Ltd, Western ave, W3 (☎ 01 992 3481)

DE COURCY, Hon Diana Ruth; da of late 29 Baron Kingsale; *b* 1951; *Style* - The Hon Diana de Courcy

DE COURCY, Kenneth Hugh; s of late Stephen de Courcy (eighth in descent from 10 Baron Kingsale); *b* 6 Nov 1909; *Educ* King's Coll Sch; *m* 1950, Rosemary Katherine, nee Baker (m dis 1973); 2 s, 2 da; *Career* served Coldstream Gds Lt supp reserve; ed Special Office Brief 1969-; *Recreations* travel; *Style* - Kenneth de

Courcy Esq; Yeomans Cottage, Longborough, Moreton-in-Marsh, Glos (☎ 30803)

DE COURCY, Nevinson Russell; s of Nevinson William de Courcy (ggs of Adm Hon Michael de Courcy, 3 s of 20 Baron Kingsale); hp to kinsman, 30 Baron; *b* 21 July 1920 (posthumously); *m* 1954, Nora Lydia, da of James Plint, of Lancs; 1 s (Nevinson Mark, b 11 May 1958), 1 da (Katherine Grace, b 26 April 1955); *Career* MA, MICE, MNZIE; *Style* - Nevinson de Courcy Esq; 15 Market rd, Remuera, Auckland 5, New Zealand

DE COURCY LING, John; MEP (C) Midland Central 1979-; s of late Arthur Norman Ling and Veronica de Courcy; *b* 14 Oct 1933; *Educ* King Edward's Sch Edgbaston, Clare Cambridge; *m* 1959, Jennifer, nee Haynes; 1 s, 3 da; *Career* FO 1959-78; underwriting memb of Lloyds 1969-; *Style* - John de Courcy Ling Esq MEP; 31 Chapel st, SW1 (☎ 01 235 5655); Bellehatch Park, Henley-on-Thames, Oxon

DE DEO, J E; *Career* chm Young & Rubican Hldgs Ltd; *Style* - J E De Deo Esq; Young & Rubican Hldgs Ltd, Great London House, Hampstead rd, NW1

DE FERRANTI, Sebastian Basil Joseph Ziani; s of late Sir Vincent de Ferranti; *b* 5 Oct 1927; *Educ* Ampleforth; *m* 1953, Mona Helen, nee Cunningham; 1 s, 2 da; *Career* chm Ferranti Ltd 1963-; chm Civic Trust for North-West 1978-; *Style* - Sebastian de Ferranti Esq; Henbury Hall, Macclesfield, Cheshire (☎ 2477)

DE FRESNES, Christopher Ian; s of 12 Baron de Fresnes (Fr); *b* 1942; *Educ* Ampleforth, Glasgow Sch of Art; *Style* - Christopher de Fresnes Esq; Flat 3, Arden House, 107 Earl's Court rd, SW5

DE FRESNES, Lady Fiona Huddleston; *née* Abney-Hastings; da of 13 Countess of Loudoun; *b* 1923; *m* 1940, Capt Robert Conray-Robertson, now Baron de Fresnes; 3 s, 2 da; *Style* - Lady Fiona de Fresnes; Cessnock Castle, Galston, Ayrshire, Scotland

DE FRESNES, Iona Mary Nicole; da of 12 Baron de Fresnes (Fr); *b* 30 June 1957; *Style* - Miss Iona de Fresnes

DE FRESNES, Nigel Diarmid; s of 12 Baron de Fresnes (Fr); *b* 1944; *Educ* Ampleforth; *m* 1965, Dolores, da of Isidore Grinder, of Clinton BC, Canada; 1 s, 2 da; *Style* - Nigel de Fresnes Esq; Bellavista Farm, Box 71, Milner, nr Langley, BC Canada

DE FRESNES, Paulyn Armand; s of 12 Baron de Fresnes (Fr); *b* 1949; *Educ* Ampleforth; *Style* - Paulyn de Fresnes Esq; Cessnock Castle, Galston, Ayrshire (☎ Galston 314)

DE FRESNES, Vivian Robert James George; s of 12 Baron de Fresnes (Fr); *b* 30 June 1960; *Style* - Vivian de Fresnes Esq

DE FREYNE, 7 Baron (UK 1851); Francis Arthur John French; s of 6 Baron, JP, DL (d 1935), by Victoria, da of Sir John Arnott, 2 Bt; *b* 3 Sept 1927; *m* 1, 1954 (m dis 1978), Shirley Ann, da of late D R Pobjoy; 2 s, 1 da; m 2, 1978, Sheelin Deirdre, da of Col Henry O'Kelly, DSO, and widow of William Walker Stevenson; *Style* - The Rt Hon The Lord De Freyne; Craigewilliam, Maynooth, Co Kildare

DE GERLACHE DE GOMERY, Baron (Belgian 1924, by King Albert I); Philippe; MVO (1963); s of Baron de Gerlache de Goméry (cr Baron 1924, Polar explorer, the first to winter in the Antarctic, d 1934), himself gn of Baron (Etienne Constantin) de Gerlache de Goméry (cr 1844), who was Pres of the Belgian Congress and led the Delegation that offered the crown to Prince Leopold of Saxe-Saalfeld-Coburg (son-in-law of George IV) after the secession of what is now Belgium from Holland in 1830; a second Barony (cr 1885, the first having become extinct 1883) is held by a senior branch of the family; a common ancestor of both lines was Jean Louis de Gerlache, Seigneur de Goméry, who received a confirmation of nobility from the Empress Maria-Teresa 1751; *b* 12 Nov 1906; *Educ* Bedales, Decroly (Brussels), Antwerp U; *m* 1937, Yvonne, da of Maurice Verhoustraeten; 1 s; *Heir* s, Baron Jean de

Gerlache de Goméry, b 20 Dec 1952; *Career* Capt Cdr Belgian Artillery 1940; Head Belgian Ec Mission London 1946-47, Special Counsellor Belgian Embassy London 1948-73, Administrator-Gen Anglo-Belgian Club 1974; *Recreations* painting, walking, reading; *Clubs* Anglo-Belgian; *Style* - Baron de Gerlache de Goméry MVO; 3 Upper Cheyne Row, SW3 (☎ 01 352 3343)

DE GREY, Hon Mrs - Hon Amanda Lucy; *née* Annan; da of Baron Annan (Life Peer); *b* 1952; *m* 1977, Spencer Thomas de Grey; *Style* - The Hon Mrs de Grey; 56 Clapham Manor st, SW4

DE GREY, Hon Elizabeth Anne; da of 9 Baron Walsingham, MC; *b* 24 July 1966; *Style* - The Hon Elizabeth de Grey

DE GREY, Hon Robert; s and h of 9 Baron Walsingham, MC; *b* 21 June 1969; *Style* - The Hon Robert de Grey

DE GREY, Capt Hon Richard Patrick; TD (1951); s of 7 Baron Walsingham (d 1929); *b* 17 March 1900; *Educ* Eton and Trin Cambridge; *m* 1, 1925, Cynthia (d 1967), da of late Thomas Hewitt Myring; m 2, 1969, Dorothy, da of late Thomas Knight; *Career* land agent ret; 2 Lt Cambridgeshire Regt 1939, served 1939-45 (Norway and Malaya); Capt 1941, POW; *Recreations* formerly cricket & shooting, now chiefly reminiscence; *Clubs* Naval & Military, Norfolk (Norwich); *Style* - The Hon Richard de Grey TD; Hassocks, Merton, Thetford, Norfolk; Fredmoen, Aa-i-Fosna, Norway

DE GREY, Hon Sarah Jane; da of 9 Baron Walsingham, MC; *b* 24 Sept 1964; *Style* - The Hon Sarah de Grey

DE HAVILLAND, John Anthony; s of Maj-Gen Peter Hugh de Havilland, CBE, DL of Horkesley Hall, Colchester; *b* 14 April 1938; *Educ* Eton, Trin Cambridge; *m* 1964, Hilary Anne, da of Robert Ewen MacKenzie of Brigby, nr Brigg, Lincs; 1 s, 2 da; *Career* joined J Henry Schroder Wagg & Co Ltd 1959, md 1971-; *Recreations* shooting (for England 1961-, Capt English VIII 1979-); *Clubs* Army and Navy; *Style* - John de Havilland Esq; Shimpling Hall, Bury St Edmunds, Suffolk

DE HAVILLAND, Peter Hugh; CBE (1945, OBE 1940), DL (Essex 1962); s of Hugh de Beauvoir de Havilland, JP (d 1952); *b* 29 July 1904; *Educ* Eton, RMC Woolwich; *m* 1930, Helen Elizabeth Wrey (d 1976), da of W W Otter-Barry (d 1973); 2 s; *Career* 2 Lt RA 1925, Col 1949, Maj-Gen 1954, served 1939-45 War, UK Mil Rep to Supreme HQ Europe 1951-53, ch of staff Northern Command 1953-55, ret *Style* - Maj-Gen Peter de Havilland CBE, DL; Horkesley Hall, Colchester, Essex (☎ Colchester 271 259)

DE HOGHTON, Sir (Richard) Bernard Cuthbert; 14 Bt (E 1611); s of late Sir Cuthbert de Hoghton, 12 Bt, and half-brother of Sir (Henry Philip) Anthony Mary de Hoghton, 13 Bt (d 1978); *b* 26 Jan 1945; *Educ* Ampleforth, McGill U Montreal, Birmingham U; *m* 1974, Rosanna Stella Virginia, da of Terzo Buratti, of Florence; 1 s, 1 da; *Heir* s, Thomas de Hoghton (b 1980); *Career* stockbroker, with de Zoete & Bevan & Co from 1977; landowner; *Recreations* shooting, tennis, skiing; *Style* - Sir Bernard de Hoghton, Bt; Hoghton Tower, Hoghton, Preston, Lancs (Hoghton 2986)

DE JONG, Maj Nicholas Charles Callard; s of David de Jong; *b* 15 Oct 1911; *Educ* Queen Elizabeth's Crediton, Technological Coll Cardiff, U of S Wales; *m* 1937, Olwen May East; 1 da; *Career* dir Pitney Bowes Ltd 1973-; *Style* - Maj Nicholas de Jong; 33 Mount ave, Westcliff-on-Sea, Essex (☎ Southend 75824)

DE KERMAINGANT, Hon Mrs - Hon Fanny; *née* Venables-Vernon; da of late 8 Baron Vernon; *b* 1886; *m* 1, 1910, Maurice Raoul-Duval (d 1916); m 2, 1918, Lieut Jean de Kermaingant; 1 s; 2 da; *Style* - The Hon Mrs de Kermaingant

DE KOENIGSWARTER, Baroness Kathleen; Hon Kathleen Annie Pannonica; *née* Rothschild; da of Hon Nathaniel Rothschild (2 s of 1 Baron Rothschild) and Rozsika (da of Capt Alfred von Wertheimstein, of Nagyvarad, Hungary); *b* 10 Dec 1913; *m* 1935 (m dis 1956), Baron Jules de Koenigswarter, Fr

Ambass Extraordinary at New York, s of Baron Louis de Koenigswarter, of Paris (Barony cr by Napoleon III 1870); 2 s (Barons Patrick b 1936, and Shaun b 1948), 3 da (Baronesses Janka b 1938, Berit b 1946, and Kari b 1950); *Career* late membs' rep American Fedn Musicians; *Recreations* raising cats, listening to jazz; *Style* - The Hon Kathleen Koenigswarter,; 63 Kingswood rd, Weehawken, NJ, USA (☎ 201 863 2358)

DE L'ISLE, 1 Viscount (UK 1956); Sir William Philip Sidney; 9 Bt (UK 1806 & 1818), of Castle Goring, Sussex, and of Penshurst Place, Kent, respectively, VC (1944), KG (1968), GCMG (1961), GCVO (1963), PC (1951); also Baron De L'Isle and Dudley (UK 1835); s of 5 Baron De L'Isle and Dudley, JP (d 1945), and Winifred (da of Roland Bevan and Hon Agneta, da of 10 Lord Kinnaird and great niece of Douglas James Kinnaird, the friend of both Byron (he visited him during the Venetian phase) and Sheridan); the 5 Baron was 2 cous (strictly 2 half-cous, because of Sir Bysshe Shelley's 2 m) twice removed of the poet Shelley, while also tenth in descent from Robert, 1 Earl of Leicester, bro of Sir Philip Sidney, the altruistic courtier poet, and nephew of Elizabeth I's favourite, Leicester; *b* 23 May 1909; *Educ* Eton, Magdalene Cambridge; *m* 1, 1940, Hon Jacqueline Vereker (d 1962), da of Field-Marshal 6 Viscount Gort, VC, GCB, CBE, DSO, MVO, MC; 1 s, 4 da; m 2, 1966, Margaret, widow of 3 Baron Glanusk, da of Maj-Gen Thomas Shoubridge, CB, CMG, DSO, and sis of Lt-Col Patrick Lort Phillips, of Lawrenny; *Heir* s, Hon Philip Sidney; *Career* chm Property Growth Assur 1977-; Chllr Order of St Michael & St George 1968-; Gov-Gen Australia 1961-65; KStJ; served Gren Gds Res 1929 & WW II; MP (C) Chelsea 1944-45, Sec State Air 1951-55; Pres Br Heart Fndn, Chm Freedom Assoc 1975-, Tstees Churchill Memorial Tst; FCA; *Style* - Rt Hon Viscount De L'Isle VC KG GCMG GCVO PC; Glanusk Park, Crickhowell, Brecon; Penshurst Place, Tonbridge, Kent (☎ Penshurst 870223)

DE LA BEDOYERE, Comtesse Michael; Charlotte; *née* Halbik; *b* 24 Nov 1931; *Educ* The Old Palace, Mayfield, Sussex; *m* 1961, as his 2 w, Comte Michael de la Bédoyère, sometime ed Catholic Herald and gs through his f of Alexis Huchet, Marquis de la Bédoyère (who m 1869 Hon Mildred Greville-Nugent, da of 1 Baron Greville); Charles Huchet de la Bédoyère was cr Comte 1710 and was Procureur-Général of the Bretagne Parlement, while another Huchet was cr Comte 1815 by Napoleon; Bertrand Huchet, Seigneur de la Huchetais and Sec of State to Jean V, Duke of Brittany, m c 1420 Jeanne de la Bédoyère, Dame de la Bédoyère; Comte Michael was gs through his mother of Dr A Thorold, sometime Bp of Winchester; 2 children; *Career* md Search Press Ltd, Burns & Oates Ltd (publishers to the Holy See 1842-), Search for Leisure Ltd; *Recreations* gardening, swimming, photography; *Clubs* Hurlingham; *Style* - Comtesse Michael de la Bédoyère; Elylands, Edenbridge, Kent

DE LA BERE, Adrian; s of late Sir Rupert De la Bère, 1 Bt; hp of bro, Sir Cameron De la Bère, 2 Bt; *b* 17 Sept 1939; *Style* - Adrian De la Bère Esq

DE LA BERE, Sir Cameron; 2 Bt (UK 1953); s of Sir Rupert De la Bère, 1 Bt, KCVO (d 1978); *b* 12 Feb 1933; *Educ* Tonbridge and abroad; *m* 1964, Clairemonde, da of Casimir Kaufmann, of Geneva; 1 da; *Heir* bro, Adrian De la Bère; *Career* Liveryman, Skinner's Co; *Style* - Sir Cameron De la Bère Bt; 1 Avenue Theodore Flournoy, 1207 Geneva, Switzerland (☎ 31 26 86)

DE LA MARE, Richard Herbert Ingpen; s of late Walter John de la Mare; *b* 4 June 1901; *Educ* Whitgift Sch Croydon, Keble Oxford; *m* 1930, Amy Catherine, nee Donaldson (d 1968); 3 s, 1 da; *Career* pres Faber & Faber (Publishers) Ltd 1971-; *Style* - Richard de la Mare Esq; Much Hadham Hall, Herts (☎ 2663)

DE LA RUE, Andrew George Ilay; s and h of Sir Eric de la Rue, 3 Bt; *b* 3 Feb 1946; *Style* - Andrew de la Rue Esq

DE LA RUE, Sir Eric Vincent; 3 Bt (UK 1898); s of Sir Evelyn Andros de la

Rue, 2 Bt, JP (d 1950); *b* 5 Aug 1906; *Educ* Oundle; *m* 1, 1945, Cecilia (d 1963), da of late Maj Walter Waring, DL, MP (d 1930); 2 s; m 2, 1964, Christine, da of Kurt Schellin, MD, of Connecticut, USA; 1 s; *Heir* s, Andrew George Ilay de la Rue; *Career* Capt Nottinghamshire Yeo 1942-45; *Style* - Sir Eric de la Rue, Bt; Caldra, Duns, Berwickshire (☎ 3294)

DE LA WARR, 10 Earl (GB 1761); William Herbrand Sackville; DL (1975 E Sussex); also Baron De La Warr (E 1299 & 1570), Viscount Cantelupe (GB 1761), and Baron Buckhurst (UK 1864); s of 9 Earl De La Warr, GBE, PC (d 1976, 10 in descent from 3 Baron De La Warr, Gov & Capt-Gen of Virginia 1610-11, after whom the State of Delaware is named), by his 1 w Diana, da of Capt Henry Gerard Leigh (who owned Luton Hoo prior to the Wernhers); *b* 16 Oct 1921; *Educ* Eton; *m* 1948, Anne Rachel, da of Geoffrey Charles Devas, MC (whose mother was paternal gda of 1 Earl Cawdor), and Joan (great niece of Sir Henry Campbell-Bannerman, Lib PM 1906-08); 2 s, 1 da; *Heir* s, Lord Buckhurst *qv*; *Career* Lt R Sussex Regt 1941, Hon Col Sussex Army Cadet Force; pres London Young Conservatives 1947-49, md Rediffusion Ltd 1978-, dir British Electric Traction Co Ltd, Portals Holdings Ltd and Wembley Stadium Ltd; *Clubs* White's; *Style* - The Rt Hon The Earl De La Warr, DL; 93 Eaton Place, SW1 (☎ 01 235 7990); (office) 2 Dean Trench st, SW1 (☎ 01 222 9809); Buckhurst Park, Withyam, E Sussex (☎ Hartfield 346)

DE LA WARR, Sylvia, Countess; Sylvia Margaret; DBE (1957); da of William Reginald Harrison; *m* 1, 1 and last Earl of Kilmuir, GCVO, PC (d 1967); 2 da (Lady Pamela Blackmore, Lady Miranda Cormack; also 1 da decd); m 2, 1968 as his 2 w, 9 Earl De La Warr, GBE, PC (d 1976); *Style* - The Rt Hon Sylvia, Countess De La Warr, DBE; 23 The Priory, Prior pk, Blackheath, SE3 (☎ 01 318 0840)

DE LALANNE MIRRLEES, Count (Fr, Italy, San Marino); Robin Ian Evelyn Stuart; suc 1962; gs of Ambassador La Lanne & godson of 11 Duke of Argyll; *b* 13 Jan 1925; *Educ* Merton Coll Oxford; *Career* Richmond Herald of Arms 1962-67 (Rouge Dragon Pursuivant 1952-62); Freeman City of London, Laird of Island of Bernera, Patrician of San Marino; served India 1942-46, ADC to HM the King of Yugoslavia 1963-70, co-editor Annuaire de France 1966-; *Recreations* hunting, piloting, travelling, painting, sculpture; *Clubs* Buck's, Turf, Puffin's (Edinburgh), Travellers' (Paris); *Style* - Count de Lalanne Mirrlees; Inchdrewer Castle, Banff; Villa Lambins-Lalanne, Le Touquet, France; Schloss Ratzenegg, Carinthia, Austria; 25 Holland Park Avenue, W11 (☎ 01 727 2525); 115 Rue de la Pompe, Paris XVI

DE LASZLO, Damon Patrick; s of Patrick David de Laszlo (d 1980); *b* 8 Oct 1942; *Educ* Gordonstoun; *m* 1972, Hon Sandra Daphne, da of late 2 Baron Hacking; 2 s, 1 da; *Career* memb Lloyd's, company director; *Recreations* shooting, scuba diving; *Clubs* Boodle's, Special Forces, City of London; *Style* - Damon de Laszlo Esq; 24 Durand gdns, SW9 (☎ 01 735 1036); Southfield Farm, Chawton, nr Alton, Hants (☎ 0420 83318)

DE LASZLO, Hon Mrs (Sandra Daphne); *née* Hacking; da of 2 Baron Hacking (d 1971); *b* 10 June 1950; *Educ* Lady Eden and Benenden Schs and Madrid Univ; *m* 1972, Damon Patrick de Laszlo; *Style* - The Hon Mrs de Laszlo; 24 Durand gdns, SW9

DE LIGNE LA TREMOILLE, HH Princess Charles - Lady Moira Forbes; da of 9 Earl of Granard; *b* 1951; *m* 1971, HH Prince Charles Antoine Louis Lamora de Ligne La Tremoille; *Style* - HH Princess Charles de Ligne La Tremoille; Chateau d'Antoin, 7640 Hainault, Belgium

DE LISLE, Hon Mrs - Hon Mary Rose; *née* Peake; da of late 1 Viscount Ingleby; *b* 1940; *m* 1959, Maj Everard John Robert March Phillips de Lisle, *qv*; 2 s, 1 da; *Style* - The Hon Mrs de Lisle; 4 Hereford Mansions, Hereford rd, W2; Stockerston Hall, Uppingham, Leics (☎ 2404)

DE LOGERES, Joseph Léon Paul Regis Marc de Fontaines;

Career chm Michelin Tyre Co Ltd; *Style* - Joseph De Logeres Esq; Michelin Tyre Co Ltd, Campbell rd, Stoke-on-Trent, Staffs

DE LONGUËIL, 11 Baron (sole title in Peerage of Canada, cr 1700); Raymond David Grant; s of 10 Baron (d 1959, whose half unc, 7 Baron, received recognition of cr of Louis XIV by Queen Victoria in 1880 under terms of Treaty of Quebec which ceded sovereignty of Canada from Fr to GB; through the 6 Baron's 2 w, the present Baron is 4 cous once removed of the editor of this book) and Ernestine (da of Hon Ernest Bowes-Lyon, himself 3 s of 13 Earl of Strathmore), whereby the Baron is 2 cous to HM The Queen; *b* 3 Sept 1921; *m* 1946, Anne, da of Patrick Maltby; 1 s; *Heir* s, Michael Charles, b 1947; *Style* - Baron de Longuëil; Navarreux, Basses Pyrénées, France

DE LOTBINIERE, Seymour Joly; CVO (1956), OBE (1953); s of late Brig-Gen H G Joly de Lotbinière, DSO; *b* 21 Oct 1905; *Educ* Eton; Trinity Coll Camb; *m* 1944, Mona Lewis; 1 s; *Career* BBC 1932-67; Govr Bristol Old Vic Trust 1963-67; CC W Suffolk 1970-74; *Style* - Seymour de Lotbinière Esq CVO OBE; Brandon Hall, Brandon, Suffolk (☎ Thetford 810227)

DE MARFFY VON VERSEGH, Hon Mrs; Pelline Margot; *née* Lyon-Dalberg-Acton; da of 3 Baron Acton; *b* 1932; *m* 1953, Lazlo de Marffy von Versegh; 6 s, 1 da; *Style* - Hon Mrs de Marffy von Versegh; Ealing Farm, PO Box 29, Umvukwes, Rhodesia

DE MAULEY, 6 Baron (UK 1838); Gerald John Ponsonby; s of 5 Baron de Mauley (d 1962); *b* 19 Dec 1921; *Educ* Eton, Ch Ch Oxford (BA, MA); *m* 1954, Helen, widow of Lt-Col Brian Abdy Collins, OBE, MC, and da of Hon Charles Sholto Douglas (d 1960, 2 s of 19 Earl of Morton); *Heir* bro, Hon Thomas Maurice Ponsonby, *qv*; *Career* Lt Leics Yeo, Capt RA, served 1939-45 (France), barr Middle Temple; *Style* - The Rt Hon The Lord de Mauley; Langford House, Little Faringdon, Lechlade, Glos

DE MAULEY, Dowager Baroness - Elgiva Margaret; da of late Hon Cospatrick Thomas Dundas, JP, DL (himself younger brother of 3 Earl, later 1 Marquess, of Zetland), by his w Maud (yr da of Hon George Fitzwilliam, who in his turn was 3 s of 5 Earl Fitzwilliam); *m* 1920, 5 Baron de Mauley (Hubert William Ponsonby) (d 1962); 2 s (6 Baron & Hon Thomas Ponsonby), 2 da (Hon Mrs Grimston, Hon Mrs Holman); *Style* - The Rt Hon Dowager Lady de Mauley; The New House, Little Faringdon, Lechlade, Glos

DE MEYER, Lady Susan Ankaret, *née* Howard; da of late 11 Earl of Carlisle; *b* 1948; *m* 1, 1967 (m dis 1978), Charles James Buchanan-Jardine; 1 da; m 2, 1978, Hugh Stephens (which name he renounced by Deed Poll 1979, & assumed name of Count Hubert Charles de Meyer); 1 s; *Style* - Lady Susan de Meyer; 37 Lennox gdns, SW1; Lower Heyford Mill, Oxford

DE MONTMORENCY, Sir Arnold Geoffroy; 19 Bt (I 1631), of Knockagh, Co Tipperary; s of James Edward Geoffroy de Montmorency (d 1934); suc cous Sir Reginald d'Alton Lodge de Montmorency, 18 Bt, 1979; *b* 27 July 1908; *Educ* Westminster, Peterhouse Cambridge; *m* 1949 (m annulled 1953) and remarried, 1972, Nettie Hay, da of William Anderson; *Heir* none; *Career* chm (part-time) Industl Tbnls 1975-, chm Contemporay Review Co 1962-; barr, Middle Temple, 1932; served war, Maj RASC 1939-45; *Clubs* Nat Liberal; *Style* - Sir Arnold de Montmorency Bt; 2 Garden ct, Temple, EC4

DE PEYER, Gervase; *b* 11 Apr 1926; *Educ* King Alfred's London, Bedales, Royal College of Music; *m* 1, 1950, Sylvia Southcombe (m dis 1971); 1 s, 2 da; m 2, 1971, Susan Rosalind Daniel; *Career* ARCM; Hon ARAM; dir London Symphony Wind Ensemble; founder and conductor, The Melos Sinfonia; founder memb The Melos Ensemble of London; solo clarinettist Chamber Music Soc of Lincoln Center, New York 1969; Gold Medal Worshipful Co of Musicians 1948; *Style* - Gervase de Peyer Esq; 16 Langford pla, St John's Wood, NW8 (☎ 01 624 4098)

DE RAMSEY, 3 Baron (UK 1887); Ailwyn Edward Fellowes; KBE (1974), DL (1973 Huntingdon and Peterborough, 1974 Cambs); s of Capt Hon Coulson Churchill Fellowes (d 1915, s of 2 Baron and Lady Rosamond Spencer-Churchill, sis of 8 Duke of Marlborough and Lord Randolph S-C, making present Lord De Ramsey 1 cous once removed to late Sir Winston Churchill); suc gf, 2 Baron, 1925; *b* 16 March 1910; *Educ* Oundle; *m* 1937, Lilah, da of Frank Labouchere; 2 s, 2 da; *Heir* s, Hon John Ailwyn Fellowes; *Career* Capt (135 Fd Regt) Herts Yeo RA (TA) 1939; patron of four livings; Ld-Lt of Huntingdonshire 1947-65, of Huntingdon and Peterborough 1965-68; pres Country Landowners' Assoc 1963-65; *Style* - The Rt Hon The Lord De Ramsey, KBE, DL; Abbots Ripton Hall, Huntingdon (☎ Abbots Ripton 234)

DE ROS, Baroness (E 1264); Georgiana Angela; *née* Ross; holder of Premier Barony of England; da of Hon Angela Dixon (da of 1 Baron Glentoran) by her husb Lt-Cdr Peter Ross (ka 1940), er s of Baroness (Una) de Ros (26 holder, d 1956 but abeyance not ended till 1958, and 24 in descent from the union of William de Ros and Isabella, illegitimate da of William The Lion, King of Scotland; also 14 in descent from the m of 12 Baron with Ann, whose mother was Ann Plantagenet, sis of Edward IV); *b* 2 May 1933; *Educ* Wycombe Abbey and Studley Agricultural Coll; *m* 1954, Cdr John David Maxwell RN (ret); 1 s, 1 da; *Heir* s, Hon Peter Trevor Maxwell; *Career* National Diploma in Dairying; *Style* - The Rt Hon The Lady de Ros; Old Court, Strangford, Co Down, N Ireland (☎ Strangford 205)

DE SALIS, 9 Count (Holy Roman Empire 1748, cr by Francis I); John Bernard Philip Humbert de Salis; also Hereditary Knight of the Golden Spur (1571); s of 8 Count de Salis (Lt-Col Irish Gds), of Lough Gur, Co Limerick (d 1949, descended from the Envoy of the Grisons to Queen Anne at the time of the Treaty of Utrecht; an earlier member of the family was cr a Baron of the HRE by the Emperor Rudolf II in 1582 for gallantry against the Turks); the 8 Count's mother was Princess Hélène de Riquet, da of Prince Eugène de Caraman-Chimay (Belgian cr 1889 by Leopold II); *b* 16 Nov 1947; *Educ* Downside, CCC Cambridge; *m* 1973, Contessa Samaritana, da of Conte di Serego della Scala, of Verona; *Heir* cous, Maj Charles John de Salis (s of Anthony, yr bro of 8 Count, by Françoise, da of Gen Vicomte de la Panouse), b 25 Jan 1930; *Career* Kt of Honour & Devotion Sov Mil Order Malta 1974; late Capt 9/12 Roy Lancers (Prince of Wales's); barr; delegate Internat Cttee Red Cross; memb Cncl Br Assoc Order of Malta; *Recreations* melancholia; *Clubs* Cavalry & Guards, Travellers', Beefsteak; *Style* - Count de Salis; Mezzane di Sotto, Verona, Italy (☎ 045 89237); 28 Upper Cheyne Row, SW3 (☎ 01 352 7799)

DE SAUMAREZ, 6 Baron (UK 1831); James Victor Broke Saumarez; s of 5 Baron de Saumarez (d 1969); *b* 28 April 1924; *Educ* Eton, Millfield, Magdalene Coll Cambridge; *m* 1953, Joan, da of Douglas Raymond Charlton; 2 s (twin), 1 da; *Heir* s, Hon Eric Douglas Saumarez; *Career* served with Life Gds BAOR; farmer; dir Shrubland Health Clinic Ltd; *Style* - The Rt Hon the Lord de Saumarez; Shrubland Vista, Coddenham, Ipswich, Suffolk (☎ 830220)

DE SAUMAREZ, Gunhild, Baroness; Gunhild; da of late Maj-Gen Viktor Gustaf Balck, KCMG, of Stockholm; *m* 1914, 5 Baron de Saumarez (d 1969); 1 s (6 Baron; also 1 s decd), 2 da (Hon Mrs Palmer; Hon Lady Llewellyn, w of Lt-Col Sir Harry, 7 Bt, CBE, DL); *Style* - The Rt Hon Gunhild, Lady de Saumarez; Ratel River Estate, Bredasdorp, Cape Prov, South Africa

DE SPON, Baron (HRE 1742); John Seymour; also Noble of the HRE (1612), Baron of France (Louis XV 1743), and of Bavaria (1742); s of John Baron de Spon (d 1966, himself ggs of François Nicolas Baron de Spon, Premier Président du Conseil Souverain d'Alsace 1776-90, and s in his turn of Jean François Baron de Spon, Imperial & Bavarian Ambassador to Frederick the Great of Prussia 1743-47), of Colmar House, Northwood, and Torquay; *b* 28 Dec 1913; *Educ* King's Coll London; *m* 1948 (m dis 1953), Florence, da of

William John Shaw, of Nuneaton; *Career* ret journalist, formerly with Western Morning News, Rand Daily Mail, Daily Mirror, News of the World, Sunday Times, Daily Telegraph; ed Burke's Peerage, Burke's Landed Gentry 1941-46; FRGS 1963; Freeman City of London; contested N Kensington in Lib interest 1935; *Recreations* shooting; *Style* - Baron de Spon; 17 Goodwood Court, Devonshire st, W1 (☎ 01 636 2649)

DE TRAFFORD, Hon Mrs - Hon Cecilia; *née* Strickland; da of late 1 Baron Strickland; *b* 1897; *m* 1927, Capt Hubert Edmund Francis de Trafford, formerly 1 Dragoons (d 1974); *Career* MLA Malta 1950-53; *Style* - The Hon Mrs de Trafford; Xlendi, Gozo, Malta

DE TRAFFORD, Dermot Humphrey; VRD; s (by 1 m) and h of Sir Rudolph de Trafford, 5 Bt, OBE; *b* 9 Jan 1925; *m* 1, 1948 (m dis 1973), Patricia Mary, nee Beeley; 3 s, 6 da; m 2, 1974, Xandra Carandini, da of late Lt-Col Geoffrey Trollope Lee and former w of Roderick Walter; *Career* Lt Cdr RNR E Mediterranean, md GHP Group Ltd 1961, chm GHP 1966-77, dep chm Imperial Continental Gas Association 1972- (dir 1963-), dep chm The Low and Bonar Group Ltd 1980-, dir Petrofina SA and UNERG SA Brussels; *Recreations* gardening, golf; *Clubs* White's, Roy Ocean Racing; *Style* - Dermot de Trafford Esq, VRD; 59 Onslow sq, SW7; The Old Vicarage, Appleshaw, nr Andover, Hants

DE TRAFFORD, Sir Rudolph Edgar Francis; 5 Bt (UK 1841), of Trafford Park, Lancashire, OBE (1919); s of Sir Humphrey de Trafford, 3 Bt (d 1929), and bro of Sir Humphrey Edmund de Trafford, 4 Bt (d 1971); *b* 31 Aug 1894; *Educ* Downside Sch, Trinity Coll Cambridge; *m* 1, 1924 (m dis 1938), June Isabel, MBE; 1 s; m 2, 1939, Katherine, da of W W Blake; *Heir* s, Dermot Humphrey de Trafford; *Career* served 1914-1918 War; Intelligence Corps and Gen Staff GHQ; former chm Atlas Assurance, Philip Hill Higginson & Elliott-Automation; *Style* - Sir Rudolph de Trafford, Bt, OBE; 70 Eaton sq, SW1 (☎ 01 235 1823)

DE VESCI, 6 Viscount (I 1776); Sir John Eustace Vesey; 8 Bt (I 1689); also Baron Knapton (I 1750); s of Col Hon Thomas Eustace Vesey (d 1946, yr bro of 5 Viscount) and Lady Cecily Vesey, nee Browne (d 1976, da of 5 Earl of Kenmare); suc unc, 5 Viscount, 1958; *b* 25 Feb 1919; *Educ* Eton and Trinity Coll Cambridge; *m* 1950, Susan Anne, da of Ronald Owen Lloyd Armstrong-Jones, MBE, QC (d 1966), and sis of 1 Earl of Snowdon; 1 s, 2 da (and 1 decd); *Heir* s, Hon Thomas Eustace Vesey; *Career* former land agent; served 1939-45 with Irish Gds (Norway, N Africa and Italy), FRICS; *Clubs* Turf and White's; *Style* - The Rt Hon The Viscount de Vesci; Abbeyleix, Co Leix, Ireland (☎ 31162)

DE VESCI, Lois, Viscountess; Frances Lois; da of Sir Cecil Lister-Kaye, 4 Bt, JP, DL, by Lady Beatrice Pelham-Clinton-Hope (da of 6 Duke of Newcastle); *b* 28 Oct 1882; *m* 1, 1905, 5 Earl of Rosse (d of war wounds 1918); 2 s (6 Earl & Hon Desmond Parsons, both now decd; Lady de V's 2 gs are 7 Earl & (another) Hon Desmond Parsons), 1 da (late Lady Bridget Parsons); m 2, 1920, as his 2 w, 5 Viscount de Vesci, JP, DL (d 1958); *Style* - Rt Hon Lois, Viscountess de Vesci; Womersley Park, Doncaster

DE VIBRAYE, Comtesse Honor Cecilia; *née* Paget; da of Adm Sir Alfred Paget, KCB, KCMG, DSO (2 s of Gen Lord Alfred Paget, CB, MP, 5 s of 1 Marquess of Anglesey by his 2 w Lady Charlotte, da of 1 Earl Cadogan), and Viti, da of Rt Hon Sir William Macgregor, GCMG, CB, PC; *b* 18 June 1907; *m* 1, 1928 (m dis 1930), Lt-Cdr Vivian Bowlby, RN (ret), s of Col Robert Bowlby; m 2, 1936 (m dis 1946), Ralph Gledhill, of Portland Oregon; m 3, 1952 (m dis 1957), Comte François Hurault de Vibraye (presumably a collateral of the Huraults, anciently (c 1479) Seigneurs of, among other fiefs, Cheverny (Loir-et-Cher), la Grange, and Vibraye, and descended from a Seigneur of St Denis-sur-Loire c 1340, a member of this family being cr Marquis by Louis XIII 1625, while the 6 Marquis had conferred on him again the title of Marquis (having already been cr a *Pair de France*

(Peer) 1815) by Louis XVIII 1817); *Style* - Comtesse Honor de Vibraye

DE VIGIER, William Alphonse; Hon CBE (1978); s of late Dr Wilhelm Von Vigier; *b* 22 Jan 1912; *Educ* La Châtaigneraie, Coppet, Switz; *m* 1939, Betty Agnes; 2 da; *Career* chm and md and founder Acrow Ltd; chm Acrow Corpn of America, Acrow Zimbabwe, Acrow Iberica; dir Acrow Argentina, Acrow Australia, Acrow Richmond, Acrow India, Acrow Engineers (Pty) Johannesburg and Vigier Cement Switz; *Style* - William de Vigier Esq CBE (Hon); Tinkers Lodge, Marsh lane, Mill Hill, NW7; Sommerhaus, Soleure, Switzerland

DE VILALLONGA, Hon Mrs - Hon Essylt Priscilla; da of 8 Baron Howard de Walden (d 1946); *b* 1916; *m* 1945, Don Jose Luis Vilallonga (m dis 1972); 1 s, 1 da; *Style* - The Hon Mrs de Vilallonga; 1253 N Havenhurst dve, W Hollywood, Ca 90046, USA

DE VILLIERS, 3 Baron (UK 1910); Arthur Percy de Villiers; s of 2 Baron de Villiers (d 1934); *b* 17 Dec 1911; *Educ* Diocesan Coll S Africa and Magdalen Coll Oxford; *m* 1939 (m dis 1958), Edna Alexis Lovett, da of Dr A D MacKinnon; 1 s, 2 da; *Heir* s, Hon Alexander Charles de Villiers; *Career* barrister Inner Temple 1938; Auckland Supreme Court 1949; farmer; *Style* - The Rt Hon the Lord de Villiers; PO Box 66, Kumeu, Auckland, New Zealand

DE VILLIERS, Hon Alexander Charles; s and h of 3 Baron de Villiers; *b* 29 Dec 1940; *m* 1966; *Style* - The Hon Alexander de Villiers; 6 Phyllis rd, Claremont, Cape, S Africa

DE VILLIERS, Hon John Maurice; s of 2 Baron de Villiers (d 1934); *b* 1915; *Educ* Wadham Oxford; U of Cape Town; *m* 1946, Christine Mary, da of A C Buller; 2 da; *Career* consultant to the legal firm Cloete and Partners; *Style* - The Hon John de Villiers; 117 St George's Dwarsriviershoek, Stellenbosch, S Africa

DE VINK, Peter Henry John; s of Dr Louis Peter Henry John de Vink of Amsterdam; *b* 9 Oct 1940; *Educ* St Martins Coll Groningen and Montessori Lyceum Amsterdam, Edinburgh U; *m* 1967, Jenipher Jean, nee Murray-Lyon; 1 s, 1 da; *Career* fin engineer, chm and md Edinburgh Financial & General Holdings Ltd 1978-, dir of Scotbit Securities Ltd 1970-, North Sea Assets Ltd 1973-, Ben Line Offshore Contractors Ltd 1974-, Redpath de Groot Caledonian Ltd 1978-, Edinburgh Chamber of Commerce & Manufactures 1978-, memb of exec of Scottish Cncl (Dvpt & Indust) 1981-; *Recreations* shooting, fishing, golf; *Clubs* New Club (Edinburgh); *Style* - Peter de Vink Esq; Cotswold, Barnton av, Edinburgh (☎ 336 2004); Timber Cottage, Arniston, Gorebridge, Midlothian (☎ Temple 343)

DE WAAL, Constant Hendrick; CB (1977); s of late Hendrick de Waal; *b* 1 May 1931; *Educ* Tonbridge Sch; Pembroke Coll; Cambridge; *m* 1964, Julia Jessel; 2 s; *Career* called to the Bar, Lincoln's Inn, 1953; Law Commn, 1969-71; Parliamentary Counsel from 1971; *Style* - Constant de Waal Esq CBE; 62 Sussex st, SW10

DE WICHFIELD, Lady Maryel - Lady Angela Alice Maryel; *née* Drummond; da of late 16 Earl of Perth; *b* 1912; *m* 1, 1937, Count Alessandro Augusto Giovanni Giacinto Barnaba Manassei di Collestatte (m dis 1959 and he d 1962); 2 s, 1 da; m 2, 1960, Viggo de Wichfield; *Style* - Lady Maryel de Wichfield; 41 Lennox Gdns, SW3

DE WINTER, Edward John; *Career* jt md Combined English Stores Gp; dir B Maggs and Co Ltd; Gordon Fabrics Ltd; Kendal and Sons Ltd; Salisbury Handbags Ltd and others; *Style* - Edward de Winter Esq; Combined English Stores Gp, Lamerton Bldg, 23-34 High st, Ealing, W5

DE WOLF, V-Adm Harry George; CBE (1946), DSO (1944), DSC (1944); s of late Harry George De Wolf; *b* 1903; *m* 1931, Gwendolen Fowle; 1 s, 1 da; *Career* served War 1939-45; v-ch of Naval Staff 1950-52; chm Canadian Jt Staff Washington 1953-55; ch of Naval Staff Canada 1956-60, ret; *Style* - Vice-Admiral Harry De Wolf CBE DSO DSC; 119 Minto pla, Rockcliffe

Park, Ottawa, Ontario, Canada; Old Post Office, Somerset, Bermuda

DE YARBURGH-BATESON, Hon Ann Katharine; da of 6 Baron Deramore; *b* 1950; *Style* - The Hon Ann de Yarburgh-Bateson

DE YARBURGH-BATESON, Hon Mrs Eustace - Elsie Florence; da of late H Jones; *m* 1, Capt Charles Cottam, MC (decd); m 2, 1927, Hon Eustace de Yarburgh-Bateson (d 1958); *Style* - The Hon Mrs Eustace de Yarburgh-Bateson; Blackborough Lodge, Lincoln sq, Hunstanton, Norfolk

DE YARBURGH-BATESON, Hon Judith Katharine; da of 4 Baron Deramore; *b* 1909; *Style* - The Hon Judith de Yarburgh-Bateson

DE ZULUETA, Hon Lady - Hon Marie-Louise; *née* Hennessy; da of late 2 Baron Windlesham; *b* 1930; *m* 1955, Sir Philip Francis de Zulueta; 1 s, 1 da; *Style* - The Hon Lady de Zulueta; 11 Vicarage gdns, W8; Eastergate House, Eastergate, nr Chichester, Sussex

DE ZULUETA, Sir Philip Francis; s of Prof Francis de Zulueta (d 1958, gs of Pedro Jose de Zulueta, 2 Conde de Torre Diaz, confirmation and grant of arms Spain 1774); 2 cous of late Rev Canon Alfonso de Zulueta, 5 Conde de Torre Diaz; *b* 2 Jan 1925; *Educ* Beaumont and New Coll Oxford (MA); *m* 1955, Hon Marie-Louise, da of 2 Baron Windlesham (d 1962); 1 s, 1 da; *Career* chm Antony Gibbs Hldgs to 1981; special advsr to Bd Hongkong & Shanghai Banking Corpn 1981-; served in Welsh Gds 1943-47 (NW Europe), Capt 1945, HM Foreign Serv 1949-64, private sec to the Prime Minister 1955-64, assist sec HM Treasury 1962, dir Hill Samuel and Co Ltd 1965-72, kt 1963; *Clubs* Beefsteak, Pratt's, White's and Jockey (Paris); *Style* - Sir Philip de Zulueta; Eastergate House, Eastergate, W Sussex (☎ 2108); 11 Vicarage gdns, London, W8 (☎ 229 1177)

DEACON ELLIOTT, Robert; CB (1967), OBE (1954), DFC (1941) (two mentions); s of Frank Deacon Elliott (d 1966); *b* 20 Nov 1914; *Educ* Northampton; *m* 1948, Grace Joan, da of late William Wiles; 2 s, 1 da; *Career* joined RAF 1937, served in Second World War, Gp Capt 1956, Air Cdre 1962, AOC RAF Malta 1966-68 and dep CIC (Air) Allied Forces Mediterranean 1966-67, ret 1968; Bursar Civil Service Coll Sunningdale 1969-79; *Clubs* RAF; *Style* - Robert Deacon Elliott Esq, CB, OBE, DFC; Wild Rose Cottage, Little London, Andover, Hants (☎ 64563)

DEADMAN, Henry; CBE; s of late James Deadman; *b* 5 Aug 1908; *Educ* N W London Polytechnic; *m* 1936, Winifred Margery, nee Elmer; 2 da; *Career* former regional dir N Midland Region of Miny of Fuel and Power, head of Branch Gas Div Miny of Power 1959-61, Asst Sec and Sr Officer for Wales 1961-69; *Style* - Henry Deadman Esq, CBE; Meadowcroft, Whitegate rd, Minehead, Somerset

DEAKIN, Maj-Gen Cecil Martin Fothergill; CB (1961), CBE (1956); s of William R Deakin; *b* 20 June 1910; *Educ* Winchester; *m* 1934, Evelyn Mary Frances, da of Sir Arthur Grant, 10 Bt, CBE, DSO (d 1931); 1 s, 1 da; *Career* served 1939-45 War, Cdr 2 Bn Grenadier Gds 1945-46, Cdr 1 Bn 1947-50, Cdr 32 Guards Bde, served in Near East 1956 (despatches), BGS 1957-59, dir of Military Training 1959, GOC 56 London div (TA) 1960, dir TA 1960-62, Cmdt Jt Services Staff Coll 1962-65, ret 1965, dir Mental Health Foundation 1966-, pres Grenadier Gds' Assoc 1966-, Royal Yacht Squadron; *Style* - Major-General Cecil Deakin, CB, CBE; Stocks Farm House, Beenham, Berkshire

DEAKIN, Hon Mrs - Hon Rose Albinia; *née* Donaldson; da of Baron Donaldson of Kingsbridge (Life Peer); *b* 1937; *m* 1961, Nicholas Deakin; children; *Style* - The Hon Mrs Deakin

DEAL, John Leonard; s of late Isaac Deal; *b* 30 March 1922; *Educ* Devonport H S, Exeter Coll Oxford; *m* 1946, Brenda Frances, nee Joiner; 2 s, 1 da; *Career* oil company exec, dir Irish Refining Co 1968-79, dir The Associated Octel Co Ltd 1974-Mainline Pipeline Ltd 1978-, dir United

Kingdom Oil Pipeline 1979; *Style* - John Deal Esq; 16 Huntersfield close, Reigate, Surrey (☎ 48185)

DEALTRY, Thomas Richard; s of George Raymond Dealtry and Edith, nee Gardner; *b* 24 Nov 1936; *Educ* Cranfield Inst of Advanced Technol; *m* 1962, Pauline, nee Sedgwick; 1 s, 1 da; *Career* dir Gulf Region Planning, Gulf Organisation for Industrial Consulting 1978-; MIMechE, MInstM; *Style* - Thomas Dealtry Esq; PO Box 5114, Doha, Qatar, Arabian Gulf; Fruinfield, Lomond st, Helensburgh (☎el 4622)

DEAN, Lady Anne; *née* Gibson; *m* 1943, Sir Maurice Joseph Dean, KCB (d 1978); 1 s, 1 da; *Style* - Lady Dean; 27, Bathgate rd, SW19

DEAN, Barbara Florence; da of Albert Sidney and Helen Catherine Dean; *b* 1 Sept 1924; *Educ* N London Collegiate Sch, Girton Coll Cambridge, London Inst of Educn; *Career* Headmistress Godolphin and Latymer School Hammersmith 1974- (formerly Dep); *Style* - Miss Barbara Dean 9 Stuart av, Ealing, W5 (☎ 01 992 8324)

DEAN, Ian Hall; *Career* dep chm Excess Insurance Gp; dir Excess Underwriting Management Ltd; The Policy Signing and Accounting Centre Ltd; *Style* - Ian Dean Esq; Excess Insurance Gp, Excess House, 13 Fenchurch ave, EC3

DEAN, Hon Mrs - Hon Jenefer; *née* Mills; da of 5 Baron Hillingdon (by 1 m); *b* 1935; *m* 1962, His Honour Judge Joseph Dean; 1 s, 2 da; *Style* - The Hon Mrs Dean; The Hall, West Brabourne, Kent

DEAN, Sir John (Norman); s of George Dean (d 1928); *b* 13 Dec 1899; *Educ* Felsted and King's Coll London; *m* 1, 1935, Charlotte Helen Audrey (d 1973); 1 s (d); m 2, 1974, Isabel Bothwell-Thomson; *Career* Flying Offr RAF 1916-1919; former assist to pres of General Cable Corp of New York, former chm Submarine Cables Ltd, former chm and md The Telegraph Construction and Maintenance Co Ltd, former chm Telcon Enterprises Overseas Ltd, former chm and md The Selborne Plantation Co Ltd, former dir Philips Electrical Co Ltd, Telcon Australia Pty Ltd and Industria Venezolana De Cables Electicos; kt 1957; *Clubs* Army and Navy; *Style* - Sir John Dean; Kiln Ridge, Ide Hill, Sevenoaks, Kent (☎ Ide Hill 245)

DEAN, Sir Patrick (Henry); GCMG (1963); s of Prof Henry Roy Dean (d 1961); *b* 16 Mar 1909; *Educ* Rugby, Gonville and Caius Cambridge; *m* 1947, Patricia Wallace, nee Jackson; 2 s; *Career* chm Cambridge Petroleum Royalties 1975-, dir Taylor Woodrow 1969-, Amex Bank 1976-, Int Adviser American Express 1969-, dir Ingersoll-Rand Holdings 1971-81, chm Governing Body Rugby Sch 1972-, chm English-Speaking Union 1973-; *Recreations* walking, shooting; *Clubs* Brooks's; *Style* - Sir Patrick Dean GCMG; 5 Bentinck st, W1 (☎ 01 935 0881)

DEAN, Hon Mrs - Hon Thalia Mary; *née* Shaw; da of late 2 Baron Craigmyle; *b* 1918; *m* 1939, Winton Basil Dean; 1 s; *Style* - The Hon Mrs Dean; Hambledon Hurst, Godalming, Surrey

DEANE, Hon Betty Charlotte; da of 8 Baron Muskerry; *b* 1951; *Style* - The Hon Betty Deane

DEANE, Hon Robert Fitzmaurice; s and h of 8 Baron Muskerry; *b* 26 March 1948; *Educ* Sandford Park Sch Dublin, Trin Coll Dublin; *Style* - The Hon Robert Deane

DEANS, Rodger William; CB (1977); s of Andrew and Elizabeth Deans; *b* 21 Dec 1917; *Educ* Perth Academy, Edinburgh U; *m* 1943, Joan Radley; 1 s, 1 da; *Career* slr, Scottish Office 1947-; assist slr 1962-71; slr to Sec of State for Scotland and to HM Treasury 1971-; *Style* - Rodger Deans Esq CB; 25 Grange rd, Edinburgh 9 (☎ 031 667 1893)

DEARE, Ronald Frank Robert; s of late Albert Victor Deare and of Lilian Deare; *b* 9 Oct 1927; *Educ* Wellington Sch; *m* 1952, Iris Mann; 1 s; *Career* private sec to Minister of Overseas Development 1971; assist sec 1973; Counsellor (Overseas Development) British Embassy, Washington; alternate exec dir of the World Bank 1976-; *Style* - Ronald Deare

Esq; c/o British Embassy, 3100 Massachusetts ave, Washington, DC 20008, USA; 10 Fairford Close, Haywards Heath, W Sussex (☎ 50590)

DEARING, Ronald Ernest; CB (1979); s of E H A Dearing and M T Dearing; *b* 27 July 1930; *Educ* Doncaster G S, Hull U (BSc Econ), London Business Sch; *m* 1954, Margaret Patricia Riley; 2 da; *Career* regional dir, North Region, DTI, 1972-74, and under-sec, DTI, later Dept of Industry, 1972-76; MBIM; dep sec, Dept of Industry 1976-; chm Posts and Giro, GPO; *Style* - Ronald Dearing Esq CB; 33 Claremont rd, Surbiton, Surrey

DEARNLEY, Christopher Hugh; s of Rev Charles Dearnley; *b* 11 Feb 1930; *Educ* Cranleigh Sch, Worcester Coll Oxford (organ scholar); *m* 1957, Bridget, nee Wateridge; 3 s, 1 da; *Career* FRCO; organist of St Paul's Cathedral 1968-; chm Friends of Cathedral Music 1971-; *Style* - Christopher Dearnley Esq; 8b Amen ct, EC4

DEAVIN, Stanley Gwynne; CBE (1971, OBE 1958); s of Percy John and Annie Deavin; *b* 8 Aug 1905; *Educ* Hymer's Coll Hull; *m* 1934, Louise Faviell; 1 s, 1 da; *Career* chartered accountant; former chm North Eastern Gas Bd; ret; FCA, OStJ; *Style* - Stanley Deavin Esq CBE; 50 Hookstone Drive, Harrogate, N Yorks (☎ 884301)

DEBARGE, Hon Mrs (Robina Jane); *née* Cayzer; da of 2 Baron Rotherwick; *b* 24 Jan 1953; *m* 1981, Dr Olivier Debarge, of Paris; *Style* - The Hon Mrs Debarge

DEBENHAM, Hon Mrs - Hon Daphne Joan; *née* Rodney; da of 1 and last Baron Godber; *b* 1923; *m* 1942, Archibald Ian Scott Debenham, DFC; 2 s, 2 da; *Style* - The Hon Mrs Debenham; Pollard Hill, Limpsfield, Surrey

DEBENHAM, George Andrew; s and h of Sir Gilbert Ridley Debenham, 3 Bt; *b* 10 April 1938; *Educ* Bryanston, Trin Camb; *m* 1969, Penelope Jane, da of John David Armishaw Carter; 1 s, 1 da; *Style* - George Debenham Esq

DEBENHAM, Sir Gilbert Ridley; 3 Bt (UK 1931), of Bladen, co Dorset; s of Sir Ernest Ridley Debenham, 1 Bt, JP (d 1952); suc bro, Sir Piers Kenrick Debenham, 2 Bt, 1964; *b* 28 June 1906; *Educ* Eton, Trinity Coll Cambridge; *m* 1935, Violet Mary, da of His Honour Judge (George Herbert) Higgins (d 1937); 3 s, 1 da; *Heir* s, George Andrew Debenham; *Career* consultant psychiatrist NHS 1949-; farmer; *Style* - Sir Gilbert Debenham, Bt; Tonerspuddle Farm, Dorchester, Dorset (☎ Bere Regis 245)

DEBY, John Bedford; QC (1980); s of late Reginald Bedford Deby; *b* 19 Dec 1931; *Educ* Winchester Coll; Trin Coll Camb (MA); *Career* called to the Bar, Inner Temple, 1954; a Recorder of the Crown Court from 1977; *Style* - John Bedford Esq, QC; 11 Britannia rd, SW6 (☎ 01 736 4976)

DECIES, 6 Baron (I 1812); Arthur George Marcus Douglas de la Poer Beresford; s of 5 Baron Decies, DSO, PC, (d 1944, ggs of 1 Baron, who was bro of 1 Marquess of Waterford), by his 1 w Vivien, da of George Jay Gould and gda of the legendary Jay Gould, whose business methods were considered a mite unsavoury even in an age that contained such examples of manipulative ruthlessness as J P Morgan and 'Commodore' Vanderbilt; *b* 24 April 1915; *Educ* Bryanston, Bonn U; *m* 1, 1937, Ann Trevor (d 1945); m 2, 1945, Diana, da of Wing Cdr G Turner-Cain; 1 s, 2 da; *Heir* s, Hon Marcus Hugh Tristan de la Poer Beresford; *Career* served 1939-45 as Flying Offr RAF Vol Res; DFC (USA); *Style* - The Rt Hon The Lord Decies; c/o Coutts and Co, 1 Park Lane, W1

DEE, Prof Philip Ivor; CBE (1946, OBE 1943); s of Albert John Dee; *b* 8 Apr 1904; *Educ* Marling Sch Stroud, Sidney Sussex Cambridge; *m* 1929, Phyllis Elsie Tyle; 2 da; *Career* prof of Natural Philosophy at U of Glasgow 1943-72 now Emeritus; *Style* - Prof Philip Dee, CBE; Speedwell, Buchanan Castle Estate, Drymen, Stirlingshire (☎ 283)

DEEN, Hon Mrs - Hon Lilian Anne Grenville; da of Rev Hon Louis Chandos Francis Temple Morgan-Grenville (d

1944); *b* 1924; *m* 1, 1951, Ernest F Harris, CBE (d 1965); m 2, 1965, Maurice Emile Deen (d 1971); granted title, rank and precedence of a Baron's da 1947; *Style* - The Hon Mrs Deen; 144B, Château Périgord, Monte-Carlo, Monaco

DEERHURST, Viscount; Edward George William Omar Coventry; s (by 1 m) and h of 11 Earl of Coventry; *b* 24 Sept 1957; *Style* - Viscount Deerhurst

DEKKER, Wisse; CBE (Hon 1978); *b* 26 Apr 1924; *Educ* Holland; *m* 1946, Helena Brouwer; 1 s, 1 da; *Career* v-pres Philips' Lamps, Holland 1979-; chm 1973-76 and md 1972-76 Philips Electronic & Assoc Industries Ltd; FBIM; *Style* - Wisse Dekker Esq CBE; Pieter Zeemansstraat 6, Eindhoven, Holland (☎ 040 7 56702)

DEL STROTHER, A J; *Career* sec Nationwide Building Soc; *Style* - A del Strother Esq; Nationwide Building Soc, New Oxford House, High Holborn, WC1

DELACOURT-SMITH OF ALTERYN, Baroness (Life Peeress UK 1974); Margaret Rosalind; da of F J Hando; *b* 5 April 1916; *Educ* Newport High Sch, St Anne's Coll Oxford; *m* 1939, Baron Delacourt-Smith, PC (Life Peer) (d 1972); 1 s, 2 da; m 2, 1978, Prof Charles Blackton; *Career* Cncllr of Roy Borough of New Windsor 1962-65, JP 1962-67; *Style* - The Rt Hon The Lady Delacourt-Smith of Alteryn; 56 Aberdare gdns, NW6 (☎ 01 624 1728)

DELACOURT-SMITH, Hon Lesley Clare; da of Baron Delacourt-Smith (Life Peer) (d 1972); *b* 28 Sept 1948; *Educ* Frensham Heights, Sussex U; *Style* - The Hon Lesley Delacourt-Smith; 13 Thornfield rd, W 12

DELACOURT-SMITH, Hon Stephen; s of Baron Delacourt-Smith (Life Peer) (d 1972); *b* 16 July 1946; *Educ* Windsor G S, West London Coll; *Style* - The Hon Stephen Delacourt-Smith; 4 Weech Hall, Fortune Green rd, NW6 (☎ 01 794 6111)

DELAMERE, 5 Baron (UK 1821); Hugh George Cholmondeley; s of 4 Baron Delamere (d 1978, whose gf 2 Baron was fifth cous of 1 Marquess Cholmondeley) by his 1 w, Phyllis, da of Lord George Montagu Douglas Scott (3 s of 6 Duke of Buccleuch); *b* 18 Jan 1934; *Educ* Eton, Magdalene Coll Camb; *m* 1964, Ann Willoughby, da of Sir Patrick Renison, GCMG, and formerly w of Michael Tinné; 1 s; *Heir* s Hon Thomas Patrick Gilbert Cholmondeley, b 19 June 1968; *Style* - Lord Delamere; Sugonoi Farm, Soysambu, Elmenteita, Kenya

DELAMERE, Diana, Baroness; Diana; da of late Seymour Caldwell; *m* 1 (m dis), Vernon Motion; m 2, 1940, as his 2 w, Sir (Henry John) Delves Broughton, 11 Bt (d 1942); m 3, 1943 (m dis 1955), Gilbert de Préville Colville; m 4, as his 3 w, 4 Baron Delamere (d 1979); *Style* - The Rt Hon Diana, Lady Delamere; Soysambu, Elmenteita, Kenya

DELAMERE, Mary, Baroness - Hon (Ruth) Mary Clarisse; *née* Ashley; da of 1 Baron Mount Temple (d 1939); *b* 1906; *m* 1, 1927 (m dis 1940, he d 1977), Capt Alec Cunningham-Reid, DFC; 1 s, 1 da; resumed by deed poll 1938, her maiden name of Ashley; m 2, 1940 (m dis 1943), Capt Ernest Laurie Gardner, s of late Sir Ernest Gardner; 2 s; m 3, 1944 (m dis 1955, he d 1979), 4 Baron Delamere; *Style* - Mary, Lady Delamere; The Hall, Six Mile Bottom, nr Newmarket, Suffolk

DELAP, Hon Mrs - Hon Anastasia Diana; *née* Noble; da of Baron Glenkinglas (Life Peer); *b* 1948; *m* 1967, Jonathan Sinclair Delap; 2 s; *Style* - The Hon Mrs Delap; Little Armsworth, Alresford, Hants

DELEVINGNE, Hon Mrs (Angela Margo Hamar); *née* Greenwood; da of late 1 Viscount Greenwood, PC, KC, and late Dame Margery, DBE, da of late Rev Walter Spencer; *b* 1912; *m* 1937, Edward Dudley Delevingne (d 1974); 2 s, 1 da; *Style* - The Hon Mrs Delevingne; 52 Sheffield Terrace, W8

DELEVINGNE, Charles Hamar; s of Hon Mrs Delevingne, *qv*; *b* 25 June 1949; *Educ* Embley Park; *Career* estate agent; partner John German Ralph Pay; *Style* - Charles Delevingne Esq

DELFONT, Baron (Life Peer UK 1976); Bernard Delfont; s of Isaac Winogradsky (d 1936), of Odessa, Russia; *b* 5 Sept 1909; *Educ* Rochelle St Sch; *m* 1946, Helen Violet Carolyn Lynne; 1 s, 2 da; *Career* chm and ch exec EMI Film and Theatre Corpn, dir Trust Houses Forte Leisure Ltd and other cos, pres Entertainment Artists Benevolent Fund, past ch Barker Variety Club of Gt Britain, kt 1974; *Style* - The Rt Hon The Lord Delfont; 30-31 Golden sq, W1A 4QX, (☎ 01 437 9234)

DELFONT, Hon David; s of Baron Delfont (Life Peer); *b* 1953; *Style* - The Hon David Delfont

DELFONT, Hon Susan; da of Baron Delfont (Life Peer); *b* 1947; *Style* - The Hon Susan Delfont

DELL, Ven Robert Sydney; s of Sydney Edward Dell (d 1967); *b* 20 May 1922; *Educ* Harrow County Sch, Emmanuel Coll Cambridge, Ridley Hall; *m* 1953, Doreen Molly, da of William Layton (d 1957); 1 s, 1 da; *Career* ordained 1948, Archdeacon of Derby 1973-, Hon Canon of Derby Cathedral and Examining Chaplain to the Bishop of Derby; memb of the Gen Synod of the Church of England; v-princ of Ridley Hall Cambridge 1957-65, Vicar of Chesterton Cambridge 1966-73; *Style* - The Ven the Archdeacon of Derby; 72 Pastures Hill, Littleover, Derby, DE3 7BB (☎ Derby 512700)

DELVIN, Lord; Sean Charles Weston Nugent; s and h of 13 Earl of Westmeath; *b* 16 Feb 1965; *Educ* Ampleforth; *Style* - Lord Delvin

DEMPSTER, Lady Camilla Dorothy Godolphin; *née* Osborne; da of late 11 Duke of Leeds; *b* 1950; *m* 1, 1971 (m dis 1976), Robert Julian Brownlow Harris; m 2, 1977, Nigel R P Dempster; *Style* - Lady Camilla Dempster; 11 Neville ter, SW7

DEMPSTER, Nigel R P; *m* 1977, Lady Camilla Dorothy Godolphin, nee Osborne, da of 11 Duke of Leeds; *Career* journalist, Daily Mail; *Style* - Nigel Dempster Esq; 11 Neville ter, SW7

DEN BRINKER, Carl Siegmund; s of late Hermanus den Brinker; *b* 29 March 1930; *Educ* St Franciscus Coll Rotterdam, Bath U (MSc); *m* 1965, Margaret, nee Todd; 1 s, 3 da; *Career* CEng, FIERE, SenMIEEE, physicist, Texas Instruments Ltd 1961-75, Mackintosh Consultants 1976-78, tech dir Redifon Telecomm Ltd 1978-; *Style* - Carl den Brinker Esq; 55 Underhill rd, SE22 (☎ 01 693 5970)

DENBIGH AND DESMOND, 11 & 10 Earl of (E 1622 & I 1622); William Rudolph Michael Feilding; also Baron Feilding, Viscount Feilding (both E 1620), Baron Feilding, Viscount Callan (both I 1622), and Baron St Liz (E 1663); s of 10 (& 9) Earl of Denbigh and Desmond (d 1966, 2 cous seven times removed of Henry Fielding the novelist and magistrate); *b* 2 Aug 1943; *Educ* Eton; *m* 1965, Caroline Judith Vivienne, da of Lt-Col Geoffrey Cooke; 1 s, 2 da; *Heir* s, Viscount Feilding *qv*; *Style* - The Rt Hon The Earl of Denbigh and Desmond; 21 Moore Park rd, SW6 (☎ 01 736 0460); Pailton House, Newnham Paddox, Rugby, Warwicks (☎ 832726)

DENBIGH AND DESMOND, Betty, Countess of; Verena Barbara; da of William Price; *m* 1, Lt-Col Thomas Paget Feilding Johnson (decd); m 2, 1940, 10 Earl of Denbigh and Desmond (d 1966); 1 s (11 Earl), 1 da (Lady Clare Doig); *Style* - The Rt Hon Betty, Countess of Denbigh and Desmond; Pailton House, Rugby, Warwicks

DENBY, Sir Richard Kenneth; s of late John Henry Denby; *b* 20 March 1915; *Educ* Ackworth Sch, nr Pontefract; Leeds University (LLB); *m* 1939, Mildred Eileen, nee Pickles (d 1974); 1 s, 2 da; *Career* pres Law Society 1977-78; kt 1978; slr, senior partner A V Hammond & Co; chm Parkland Textile (Holdings) Ltd, from 1979 (dir from 1975); vice-chm Bradford & Bingley Building Soc from 1979, chm and founder memb Pennine Radio; *Style* - Sir Richard Denby; Chilliswood, South Parade, Ilkley - W Yorks (☎ home 609076, office Bradford 34700)

DENCER, Geoffrey Hargreaves; s of late Charles Dencer; *b* 20 Sept 1928; *Educ* Stockport G S, Manchester U (BSc); *m*

1981, Patricia, nee Crocome; children by previous m; *Career* chartered civil engineer, construction dir IDC Construction Ltd Stratford 1970- (formerly with Charles Tennet & Son Stockton on Tees); *Style* - Geoffrey Dencer Esq; Sparrow Cottage, 33 Coughton Lane, Coughton, Alcester, Warwicks

DENCH, Judi(th) Olivia (Mrs Michael Williams); *née* Dench; OBE (1970); da of Reginald Arthur and Eleanora Olave Dench; *b* 9 Dec 1934; *Educ* The Mount Sch, York; Central Sch of Speech and Drama; *m* 1971, Michael Williams; 1 da; *Career* actress, associate memb, Royal Shakespeare Co 1969-; numerous performances in Shakespeare, RSC, at Aldwych, The Old Vic, also films and TV; *Style* - Miss Judi Dench, OBE

DENHAM, 2 Baron (UK 1937), Sir; Bertram Stanley Mitford Bowyer; 10 Bt (E 1660), of Denham, 2 Bt (UK 1933), of Weston Underwood, PC (1980); s of 1 Baron Denham (d 1948), and Hon Daphne Freeman-Mitford, da of 1 Baron Redesdale and aunt of Nancy, Jessica, Debo and Unity Mitford (*see* Hon Mrs Treuhaft); suc to Btcy of Denham on death of kinsman 1950; *b* 3 Oct 1927; *Educ* Eton, King's Coll Cambridge; *m* 1956, Jean, da of Kenneth McCorquodale, MC, TD, and 1 cous of Ian McCorquodale, *qv*, also aunt of Neil McCorquodale; 3 s, 1 da; *Heir* s, Hon Richard Grenville George Bowyer; *Career* late Lt Oxford and Bucks LI, a Lord in Waiting to HM the Queen 1961-64 and 1970-71, Capt of Yeomen of the Gd and dep ch whip House of Lords 1974-78, ch whip 1978-, Capt of the Hon Corps of Gentlemen at Arms 1979-; *Clubs* White's, Pratt's; *Style* - The Rt Hon The Lord Denham, PC; The Laundry Cottage, Weston Underwood, Olney, Bucks (☎ Bedford 711535)

DENHAM, Dowager Baroness - Hon Daphne ; *née* Freeman-Mitford; da of late 1 Baron Redesdale, GCVO, KCB; *b* 1895; *m* 1919, 1 Baron Denham, MC (d 1948); 2s (1 ka), 1 da; *Style* - The Rt Hon Dowager Lady Denham; 10 West st, Olney, Bucks (☎ Bedford 711427)

DENHAM, John Hartley; *Career* dir and jt man Bradford Property Trust Ltd, dir Cliffe Hill Second Investments Ltd and Halifax Building Soc; *Style* - John Denham Esq

DENHAM, Lady Mary Ane; *née* Stuart; da of late 18 Earl of Moray; *b* 1926; *m* 1, 1945 (m dis 1960), Leonard Byng, late Lt, Grenadier Gds (d 1974); 2 s, 3 da; m 2, 1961, Col John Bovill Denham, OBE, late Scots Gds; 1 s, 1 da; *Style* - Lady Mary Denham; 1 Terrace Villas, Hammersmith ter, W6

DENINGTON, Baroness (Life Peer UK 1978); Dame Evelyn Joyce; DBE (1974, CBE 1966); da of Philip Bursill, of Woolwich; *b* 9 Aug 1907; *Educ* Blackheath H S, Bedford Coll London U; *m* 1935, Cecil Dallas Denington, s of Richard Denington, of Wanstead; *Career* former teacher, chm GLC 1975-76, dep leader (L) Oppn GLC 1967-73, memb Stevenage Dvpt Corpn 1950-80 (chm 1966-80), memb Gtr London Secondary Housing Assoc 1978-, and other housing assocs; *Style* - The Rt Hon The Lady Denington, DBE; Weale House, 29 Crescent Grove, SW4

DENISON, John Law; CBE (1960, MBE 1945); s of Rev Herbert Bouchier Wiggins Denison (d 1968); *b* 21 Jan 1911; *Educ* Brighton Coll, Roy Coll of Music (FRCM, Hon RAM, Hon GSM); *m* 1, 1936 (m dis 1946), Annie Brown; m 2, 1947, Evelyn Donald (nee Moir) (d 1958); m 3, 1960 Audrey Burnaby (d 1970); m 4, 1972, Françoise Henriette, nee Garrigues; *Career* served 1939-45 War; music dir Arts Cncl of GB 1948-65, chm Cultural Programme, London Celebrations, Queen's Silver Jubilee, hon tres Roy Philharmonic Soc, dir South Bank concert Halls 1965-76, Cdr Order of Lion Finland; *Clubs* Army and Navy; *Style* - John Denison Esq, CBE; Lion Lodge, Yatton Keynell, Chippenham, Wilts; 12 Ennismore Gdns, London, SW7 1AA

DENISON, William N; QC (1980); *Career* called to the Bar 1952, South Eastern Circuit; *Style* - William Denison Esq QC; 6 King's Bench Walk, Temple, EC4

DENISON-PENDER, Hon Emma Charlotte; da of 3 Baron Pender; *b* 1964

DENISON-PENDER, Hon Henry John Richard; s and h of 3 Baron Pender; *b* 1968; *Style* - The Hon Henry Denison-Pender

DENISON-PENDER, Hon Mary Anne Louise; da of 3 Baron Pender; *b* 1965; *Style* - The Hon Mary Denison-Pender

DENISON-PENDER, Hon Robin Charles; s of 2 Baron Pender, CBE (d 1965) and bro of 3 Baron; *b* 7 Sept 1935; *Educ* Eton; *m* 1966, Clare Nell, da of Lt-Col James C Thomson, MBE, TD, JP, DL, of Stable Court, Walkern, Herts; 2 s, 1 da; *Career* late 2 Lt 11 Hussars 1954-56, memb of London Stock Exchange, a Vice-Pres, Royal Albert Hall 1970; *Recreations* golf, gardening, films; *Clubs* White's; *Style* - The Hon Robin Denison-Pender; Jessups, Mark Beech, Edenbridge, Kent (☎ Cowden 684)

DENISON-PENDER, Hon Richard Ernest; TD (1945); s of 1 Baron Pender (d 1949); *b* 1914; *Educ* Eton; *m* 1939, Louise (d 1973), only da of late Henry Gilbey Riviere; 2 s, 1 da; *Career* Pres Sandwich & Dist Branch Roy Br Legion 1974-, Hon Visitor Archives Cable & Wireless Ltd 1980; Roy Signals (TA) 1934-53, capt 1939, served 1939-45 (despatches), Maj 1941; ADC to Gen Sir Walter Kirke, GCB, 1939, memb London Stock Exchange 1948-72; Bronze Star Medal (USA); *Recreations* cruising, writing; *Clubs* Army & Navy; *Style* - The Hon Richard Denison-Pender TD; Great Eastern, North rd, Sandwich Bay, Kent (☎ 0304 613087)

DENMAN, 5 Baron (UK 1834); Sir Charles Spencer Denman; 2 Bt (UK 1945), of Staffield, Co Cumberland; s of 1 Bt (d 1957); suc cous 4 Baron 1971; *b* 7 July 1916; *Educ* Shrewsbury; *m* 1943, Sheila Anne, da of Lt-Col A B Stewart, DSO; 3 s, 1 da; *Heir* s, Hon Richard Thomas Stewart Denman; *Career* served 1939-45 War with DCLI (TA), Maj 1943; contested Leeds central in Con interest 1945; chm Tennant Guaranty Ltd, Marine and Gen Life Assurance Soc; dep chm British Bank of Middle East; dir Consolidated Gold Fields Ltd and others; *Clubs* Brooks's; *Style* - The Rt Hon The Lord Denman; Highden House, Washington, Pulborough, W Sussex (☎ Findon 2102)

John is writing to this man

DENMAN, Hon Christopher John; s of 5 Baron Denman, MC; *b* 5 Sept 1955; *Style* -The Hon Christopher Denman

DENMAN, Lady Frances Esmé; *née* Curzon; da of late 5 Earl Howe; *b* 1939; *m* 1, 1962, Derek Alan Whiting; 2 s; m 2, 1976, Harold Denman; 1 s; *Style* - Lady Frances Denman; Wybarnes, Ticehurst, E Sussex

DENMAN, Harold; s of late Hon Sir Richard Denman, Bt; *b* 26 Jan 1922; *Educ* Repton, Balliol Oxford; *m* 1976, Lady Frances Esmé Curzon, da of 5 Earl Howe; 1 s; *Career* Capt RA 1939-45, dir Tennant Budd Ltd 1959; *Style* - Harold Denman Esq; Wybarnes, Ticehurst, E Sussex (☎ 200332)

DENMAN, Hon James Stewart; s of 5 Baron Denman, MC; *b* 7 Aug 1954; *Educ* Stowe, The Mill Littlehampton; *Style* - The Hon James Denman

DENMAN, Hon Richard Thomas Stewart; s and h of 5 Baron Denman, MC; *b* 4 Oct 1946; *Educ* Milton Abbey; *Career* articled to Deloitte, 1966; *Clubs* Brooks's; *Style* - The Hon Richard Denman

DENNING, Baron (Life Peer UK 1957); Alfred Thompson Denning; PC (1948), DL (Hants 1978); s of late Charles Denning; *b* 23 Jan 1899; *Educ* Andover Grammar Sch, Magdalen Coll Oxford; *m* 1, 1932, Mary (d 1941), da of late Rev F N Harvey; 1 s; m 2, 1945, Joan Daria Stuart, da of John Taylor and widow of J M B Stuart, CIE; *Career* barr Lincoln's Inn 1923, KC 1938, and a Bencher 1944, Chllr of Diocese of Southwark 1937-44, and of London 1942-44, Recorder of Plymouth 1944, a Judge of the High Court of Justice 1944-48, a Lord Justice of Appeal 1948-57, a Lord of Appeal in Ordinary 1957-62, Master of the Rolls 1962-; tres Lincoln's Inn 1964; kt 1944; *Clubs* Athenaeum; *Style* -The Rt Hon The Lord Denning PC DL;

11 Old Square, Lincoln's Inn, WC2 (☎ 01 405 5896); The Lawn, Whitchurch, Hants (☎ 2144)

DENNING, Sir Reginald Francis Stewart; KCVO (1975), KBE (1946), CB (1944); s of Charles Denning (d 1941); *b* 12 June 1894; *Educ* privately, Staff Coll Camberley; *m* 1927, Eileen Violet (OBE 1969), da of late H W Currie; 2 s, 1 da; *Career* served WW 1; Col 1939, Brig 1941, Subst Col 1942, Princ Administrative Offr to The Supreme Allied Cdr SE Asia 1944-46, Ch of Staff Eastern Commd 1947-49, Col Bedfordshire and Hertfordshire Regts 1948-58, Col E Anglian Regt 16/44 Foot 1958-64, Col Roy Anglian Regt 1964-66, GOC N Ireland 1949-52, Chm SSAFA 1953-74; *Clubs* Army and Navy, MCC; *Style* - Sir Reginald Denning, KCVO, KBE, CB; Delmonden Grange, Hawkhurst, Kent (☎ 2286)

DENNING, Hon Robert Gordon; s of Baron Denning, PC, DL; *b* 3 Aug 1938; *Educ* Winchester and Magdalen Coll Oxford; *m* 1967, Elizabeth Carlyle Margaret, da of E R Chilton of Oxford; children; *Career* MA, PhD; 2 Lt KRRC 1957-58; *Style* - The Hon Robert Denning; The Lawn, Whithurch, Hants

DENNINGTON, Dudley; s of John Dennington and Beryl Dennington; *b* 21 Apr 1927; *Educ* Clifton Coll Bristol, Imperial Coll London U (BSc); *m* 1951, Margaret Patricia Stewart; 2 da; *Career* ACGI; FICE; FIStructE; partner Bullen & Partners 1972-; visiting prof King's Coll London U 1978-; *Style* - Dudley Dennington Esq; Corkran rd, Surbiton, Surrey

DENNIS, John Michael; s of late Leslie Ray Dennis; *b* 11 June 1935; *Educ* Stanley Tech Sch; *m* 1958, Pamela Margaret, nee Saunders; 1 s, 2 da; *Career* dir Henlys (West) Ltd 1971-, Henlys Ltd 1979-, R E Hailton Ltd 1980-, Longs Newcastle Ltd 1981-; former Hereford City Councillor; *Style* - John Dennis Esq; The Garstons, Rosemary Lane, Stroat, nr Chepstow, Gwent

DENNIS, Raymond Andrew; s of Sir Raymond Dennis, KBE (d 1939); *Educ* Down House; *m* 1968, Penelope, da of Col John Luggard (d 1969); 1 s, 1 da; *Career* underwriting agent and farmer, dir R L Glover and Co (Underwriting Agents) Ltd, memb Lloyd's; *Recreations* fishing, painting; *Clubs* City of London, Bath; *Style* - Raymond Dennis Esq; 8 Kanning pla, W8; Berry House, Shillingford, Tiverton, Devon

DENNISON, Mervyn William; CBE (1967), MC (1944), DL (1972); s of Rev W Telford Dennison (d 1959); *b* 13 July 1914; *Educ* Methodist Coll Belfast, Queen's Univ of Belfast (BA); *m* 1944, Helen Maud, da of Claud George Spiller (d 1958); 1 s, 1 da; *Career* called to the Bar of N Ireland 1945, Middle Temple 1964; served 1939-45 War; Crown Counsel N Rhodesia 1947, sr Crown Counsel and Parliamentary Draftsman, Fed Govt of Rhodesia and Nyasaland 1953; QC N Rhodesia 1960, High Ct Judge N Rhodesia/Zambia 1961-66, sec Fermanagh County Cncl 1966-73; ch cmmr Planning and Water Appeals Cmmns for N Ireland 1973-80; KStJ 1978 (CStJ 1964); *Style* - Mervyn Dennison Esq, CBE, MC, DL; Creevyloughgare, Saintfield, Co Down, N Ireland (☎ Saintfield 510397)

DENNISON, Stanley Raymond; CBE (1946); s of late Stanley and Florence Ann Dennison; *b* 15 June 1912; *Educ* U of Durham, Trin Cambridge; *Career* former prof of Economics, Univ Coll of Swansea; Queen's U of Belfast; U of Newcastle and Chief Economic Assist, War Cabinet Secretariat; Vice-Chancellor, U of Hull 1972-79 and Hon Prof 1974-79; vice-chm, Ctee of Vice-Chancellors and Principals of the UK 1977-79; *Style* - Stanley Dennison Esq CBE; 17 Preston ave, North Shields, Tyne and Wear

DENNISS, Gordon Kenneth; CBE (1979); s of Harold Denniss; *b* 29 Apr 1915; *Educ* Dulwich Coll, Coll of Estate Mgmnt; *m* 1939, Violet Fiedler; 1 s, 2 da; *Career* sr ptnr Eastmann & Denniss Chartered Surveyors London 1945-; governing dir London Consultants (Mid E) 1977-; *Style* - Gordon Denniss Esq CBE; 6 Belgrave pla, SW1 (☎ 01 235 4858); Lodgefield Farm, Blackham, E Sussex (☎ Fordcombe 276)

DENNISTON, Robin Alastair; s of late Alexander Guthrie Denniston, CMG, CBE; *b* 25 Dec 1926; *Educ* Westminster Sch, Ch Ch Oxford; *m* 1950, Anne Alice Kyffin Evans; 1 s, 2 da; *Career* former md Hodder & Stoughton, former dep chm George Weidenfeld & Nicholson; former chm Sphere Books, Thomas Nelson & Sons, Michael Joseph, George Rainbird; dir Thomson Publications & Hamish Hamilton, academic publisher OUP; ordained Deacon 1978; non-exec chm A R Mowbray & Co 1974-; *Style* - Robin Denniston Esq; The Hope Farm, Clifton-on-Teme, Worcs (☎ Upper Sapey 248); St Thomas House, Becket st, Oxford (☎ 44192)

DENNY, Sir Anthony Coningham de Waltham; 8 Bt (I 1782), of Castle Moyle, Kerry; s of Rev Sir Henry Lyttelton Lyster Denny, 7 Bt (d 1953); *b* 22 April 1925; *Educ* Clayesmore Sch, Anglo-French Art Centre and Regent St Polytech Sch of Architecture; *m* 1949, Anne Catherine, da of late Samuel Beverley; 2 s, 1 da adopted; *Heir* s, Piers Anthony de Waltham Denny; *Career* served with RAF (air crew) 1943-47; designer; ptnr in Verity and Beverley, Architects and Design Consultants; Hereditary Freeman of Cork; *Style* - Sir Anthony Denny, Bt; Daneway House, Sapperton, Glos (☎ Frampton Mansell 232); 11 Chalcot sq, NW1 (☎ 01 722 3047)

DENNY, Capt Anthony Miles; *Career* HM Lt for City of London 1980-; *Style* - Anthony Denny Esq

DENNY, Sir Alistair Maurice Archibald; 3 Bt (UK 1913), of Dumbarton, Co Dunbarton; s of Sir Maurice Edward Denny, 2 Bt, KBE (d 1955); *b* 11 Sept 1922; *Educ* Marlborough; *m* 1949, Elizabeth, da of Maj Sir (Ernest) Guy Richard Lloyd, 1 Bt, DSO of Lochgoilhead, Argyll; 2 s (and 1 s d); *Heir* s, Charles Alistair Maurice Denny; *Career* served with Fleet Air Arm 1944-46; *Clubs* Naval; *Style* - Sir Alistair Denny, Bt; Damside of Strathairly, Upper Largo, Fife (☎ 214)

DENNY, Charles Alistair Maurice; s and h of Sir Alistair Denny, 3 Bt; *b* 7 Oct 1950; *Style* - Charles Denny Esq

DENNY, James Frederick Lowndes; *Career* chm E M Denny (Hldgs) Ltd; Denny Meat Trading Ltd and E M Denny & Co Ltd; dir Coey Ltd and the Ulster Farmers' Ltd; *Style* - James Denny Esq; E M Denny Holdings Ltd, Battlebridge House, Tooley st, SE1

DENNY, Jon Patrick Maynard; *Career* chm Plasticisers Ltd and Plasticisers Engineering Ltd; dir Readicut International Ltd; Firth Gp of Cos; Shaw Gp of Cos and others; *Style* - Jon Denny Esq; Readicut International Ltd, Terry Mills, Norbury, W Yorks

DENNY, Marjorie, Lady - Marjorie; da of late William Lysaght, CBE; *m* 1916, Sir Maurice Edward Denny, KBE, 2 Bt (d 1955); *Style* - Marjorie, Lady Denny; Gateside House, Drymen, Glasgow

DENNY, Piers Anthony de Waltham; s and h of Sir Anthony Denny, 8 Bt; *b* 14 March 1954; *Educ* King Alfred Sch, Westfield Coll London U; *Style* - Piers Denny Esq

DENNYS, Hon Mrs - Hon Lavinia Mary Yolande; *née* Lyttelton; da of late 9 Viscount Cobham; *b* 21 Aug 1921; *m* 1, 1945, Capt Cecil Francis Burney Rolt, 23 Hussars (d 1945); m 2, 1949, Maj John Edward Dennys, MC (d 1973); 1 s; *Career* Subaltern ATS 1941-45; *Style* - The Hon Mrs Dennys; Cannon Cottage, Fore st, Budleigh Salterton, Devon

DENT, Hon Mrs - Hon Ann Camilla; *née* Denison-Pender; da of 3 Baron Pender, CBE (d 1965); *b* 18 June 1931; *m* 1952, Robin, s of Rear-Adm John Dent, CB, OBE (d 1973); 2 da (Annabel Jane, Jennifer Ann); *Style* - The Hon Mrs Dent; 44 Smith st, SW3 (☎ 01 352 1234)

DENT, Lady Elizabeth - Lady Elizabeth Blanche Mary; *née* Hay; da of late 13 Earl of Kinnoull; *b* 1903; *m* 1, 1925, Peter Stanley Chappell (m dis 1935); 1 s; m 2, 1935, Douglas William Ernest Gordon (d 1951, m dis 1945); m 3, 1945, William H S Dent, MC; *Style* - Lady Elizabeth Dent; Fig Tree Cottage, Northiam, Sussex

DENT, John; CBE (1976, OBE 1968); s of Harry F Dent; *b* 5 Oct 1923; *Educ* King's Coll, London U (BSc); *m* 1954, Pamela Ann, nee Bailey; 1 s; *Career* CEng; FRAeS; FIMechE; FIEE; dir Engineering Gp, Dunlop Ltd, Coventry, 1968-76; dir Dunlop Holdings Ltd 1970-; md Dunlop 1978-; dir Industrie Perella SpA 1978-; Dunlop AG 1979-; *Style* - John Dent Esq CBE; Dunlop Holdings Ltd, Dunlop House, 25 Ryder st, SW1 (☎ 01 930 6700); Hellidon Grange, Hellidon, Daventry, Northants (☎ Byfield 60589)

DENT, Sir Robert Annesley Wilkinson; CB (1951); s of Robert Wilkinson Dent (d 1940); *b* 27 Jan 1895; *Educ* Eton, Trinity Coll Cambridge; *m* 1927, Elspeth Muriel, da of Sir Alfred Tritton, 2 Bt; 1 s, 3 da; *Career* Served WW 1914-18 with King's Rifle Corps (Lt), rejoined 1940 and served 1939-45 with GHQ Home Forces and at War Office AQMG (temp Lt-Col) 1943-45, Assist Clerk House of Commons 1920, Clerk of Public Bills 1948-59, High Sheriff Westmorland 1960; kt 1960; *Recreations* gardening; *Style* - Sir Robert Dent, CB; Lyvennet Bank, Maulds Meaburn, Penrith, Cumbria CA10 3HN (☎ Penrith 225)

DENT, Ronald Henry; s of late Henry Francis Dent; *b* 9 Feb 1913; *Educ* Portsmouth G S; *m* 1939, Olive May, nee Wilby; 1 s, 1 da; *Career* dir Cape Industries Ltd, (chm 1962-79); English China Clays Ltd; Powell Duffryn Ltd; FBIM; dir International Cancer Foundation 1978-; *Style* - Ronald Dent Esq; Badgers Copse, Birtley Green, Bramley, Surrey (☎ Bramley 3649)

DENT, Hon Rosamond Mary (Sister Ancilla, OSB); da of W H S Dent, MC, and 19 Baroness Furnivall (d 1969, when the Barony became abeyant between Sister Ancilla and Hon Mrs Bence, *qv*); *b* 3 June 1933; *Educ* Holy Child Convent, Mayfield; co-heiress to Barony of mother; renounced right in favour of sis; *Style* - Sister Ancilla OSB; Minster Abbey, Minster, nr Ramsgate, Kent

DENT, Hon Mrs - Hon Sarah; *née* Douglas-Home; da of Baroness Dacre and Hon William Douglas-Home; *b* 1954; *m* 1977, Nicholas Charles Dent; *Style* - The Hon Mrs Dent

DENTON, Charles Henry; s of Alan Denton; *b* 20 Dec 1937; *Educ* Reading Sch, Bristol U; *m* 1961, Eleanor Mary, nee Player; 1 s, 2 da; *Career* BA; Director of Programmes ATV, md Black Lion Films; *Style* - Charles Denton Esq; 16 Holland Park av, W11; Manor Farm, Wolverton, Stratford on Avon, Warwicks

DENTON, Prof Eric James; CBE (1974); s of George Denton; *b* 30 Sept 1923; *Educ* Doncaster G S, St John's Cambridge, Univ Coll London; *m* 1946 Nancy Emily, nee Wright; 2 s, 1 da; *Career* FRS (1964); Royal Soc Res Prof U of Bristol 1964-74; dir Laboratory of Marine Biological Assoc, Plymouth 1974-; *Style* - Prof Eric Denton CBE; St Germans, Saltash, Cornwall (☎ St Germans 204); The Laboratory, Citadel Hill, Plymouth, Devon (☎ 2176)

DERAMORE, 6 Baron (UK 1885); Sir Richard Arthur de Yarburgh-Bateson; 7 Bt (UK 1818); s of 4 Baron Deramore (d 1943) and bro of 5 Baron (d 1964); *b* 9 April 1911; *Educ* Harrow and St John's Coll Cambridge; *m* 1948, Janet Mary, da of John Ware; 1 da; *Heir* none; *Career* served 1940-45 in RAFVR; chartered architect; memb Cncl Architectural Assoc 1951-54; ARIBA; ptnr Cherry and Deramore 1965-70; dir and design consultant MI Advertising Ltd; practising as Arthur Deramore in Bucks, then Yorks 1970-; *Clubs* RAF; *Style* - The Rt Hon The Lord Deramore; Heslington House, Aislaby, Pickering, N Yorks (☎ 73195)

DERBY, 18 Earl of (E 1485); Sir Edward John Stanley; 12 Bt (E 1627), MC (1944), DL (Lancs 1946); also Baron Stanley of Bickerstaffe (UK 1832) and Baron Stanley of Preston (UK 1886); s of Col Rt Hon Lord Stanley (as he was styled), MC, PC (d 1938) and gs of 17 Earl, KG, GCB, GCVO, PC (d 1948, himself gs of 14 Earl, the Conservative PM and one of that distinguished body of men (thought to constitute a foursome, the others being the 3 Marquess of Lansdowne, Disraeli and Sir Winston

Churchill) who have refused a Dukedom; the 13 Earl (his father), on the other hand, belonged to that rather more numerous group of people who have solicited the supreme accolade of the Strawberry Leaf, if Queen Victoria's diary is to be trusted); Lord Derby is fifteenth in descent from the 1 Earl who placed the humpback Richard's crown on Henry Tudor's brow after Bosworth; through the 1 Earl's w, Lord Derby is twentieth in descent from Princess Elizabeth Plantagenet, da of Edward I; *b* 21 April 1918; *Educ* Eton, Magdalen Oxford; *m* 1948, Lady Isabel, JP, da of Hon Henry Augustus Milles-Lade, JP (d 1937) and sis of 4 Earl Sondes; *Heir* bro, Capt Hon Richard Oliver Stanley, *qv*; *Career* Chm NW Area TA Assoc 1979-, Pres Rugby Football League 1948-, Professional Golfers' Assoc 1964-; late Maj Gren Gds (Res); Hon Col 5/8 Bn, King's Regt (Cmding) 5 Bn 1947-51, Hon Col 1951-67, Queen's Lancashire Regt, TAVR Hon Col 1 and 2 Bns Lancastrian Vols 1967-75; Hon Capt Mersey Div RNR; Hon LLD Liverpool and Lancaster, pres of Merseyside Chamber of Commerce 1972; Ld-Lt of Co Lancaster 1951-68; Pro-Chllr of Univ of Lancaster 1964-71; Constable of Lancaster Castle 1972-; *Clubs* White's and Jockey; *Style* - The Rt Hon The Earl of Derby, MC, DL; Stanley House, Newmarket, Suffolk (☎ 3011); Knowsley, Prescot, Lancs (☎ 051 489 6147)

DERBY, 4 Bishop of (cr 1927) 1969-; Rt Rev Cyril William Johnston Bowles; s of late William C A Bowles, of Scotstoun, Glasgow; *b* 9 May 1916; *Educ* Brentwood Sch, Emmanuel and Jesus Colls Cambridge, Ridley Hall Cambridge; *m* 1965, Florence Joan, da of late John Eastaugh, of Windlesham, Surrey; *Career* ordained 1939, archdeacon of Swindon (dioc of Bristol) 1963-69, hon canon of Ely Cathedral 1963-69; *Style* - The Rt Rev The Lord Bishop of Derby; The Bishop's House, 6 King st, Duffield, Derby (☎ 46744)

DERBY, Countess of; Lady Isabel; da of late Henry Augustus Milles-Lade, s of 1 Earl Sondes, DL; raised to the rank of an Earl's da 1942; *b* 1920; *m* 1948, 18 Earl of Derby, *qv*; *Style* - The Rt Hon The Countess of Derby; Stanley House, Newmarket; Knowsley Hall, Prescot, Lancs

DERBYSHIRE, Andrew George; s of late Samuel Reginald Derbyshire; *b* 7 Oct 9; *Educ* Chesterfield G S, Queens' Coll Cambridge; *m* Lily Rhodes, nee Binns; 3 s, 1 da; *Career* FRIBA; FSIA; architect; partner, Robert Matthew, Johnson-Marshall & Partners; *Style* - Andrew Derbyshire Esq; 42 Weymouth st, W1 (☎ 01 486 4222); 4 Sunnyfield, Hatfield, Herts (☎ 65903)

DERRINGTON, John Anthony; s of late John Derrington; *b* 24 Dec 1921; *Educ* Battersea Polytechnic (BSc), Imperial Coll London DIC; *m* 1971, Beryl June, nee Kimber; 1 s, 3 da; *Career* chartered civil engineer, dir Sir Robert McAlpine & Sons, chm National Maritime Inst; *Recreations* gardening, travel, reading; *Style* - John Derrington Esq; 47 Melbury rd, Kensington W14 (☎ 01 602 3196); 3 Gorham av, Rottingdean, Sussex

DERRY, Air Cdre Arthur Llewellyn; CBE (1955, OBE 1946); s of Llewellyn Derry (d 1944); *b* 29 Aug 1902; *Educ* Midland Coll Leicester; *m* 1925, Gwladys, da of Daniel Edwards (d 1950); 1 s; *Career* cmmnd RAF 1925, served 1939-45 (N W Europe and W Africa), Gp-Capt 1947, dir of Personnel Air Ministry 1955, Air Cdre 1956, AOC RAF Record Office Gloucester 1958, ret 1960; *Clubs* RAF; *Style* - Air Cdre Arthur Derry, CBE; East Approach Drive, Cheltenham, Glos (☎ Cheltenham 26489)

DERWENT, 4 Baron (UK 1881); Sir Patrick Robin Gilbert Vanden-Bempde-Johnstone; 6 Bt (GB 1795), CBE (1974); s of Hon Edward Henry Vanden-Bempde-Johnstone (d 1903) and bro of 3 Baron Derwent (d 1949); *b* 26 Oct 1901; *Educ* Charterhouse and RMC; *m* 1929, Marie Louise, da of late M Albert Picard; 1 s; *Heir* s, Hon Robin Evelyn Leo Johnstone, MVO, *qv*; *Career* Maj KRRC; opposition whip House of Lords 1950-51; min of State, Bd of Trade 1962-63, min of State, Home Office 1963-64; chm British Road Fedn 1954-62, dep speaker House of Lords 1970; *Style* - The Rt Hon The Lord

Derwent, CBE; Hackness Hall, Scarborough, N Yorks (☎ 82205); 48 Cadogan Place, SW1 (☎ 01 235 5870)

DESCH, Stephen Conway; QC (1980); s of Harold Ernest Desch; *b* 17 Nov 1939; *Educ* Dauntsey's Sch, Magdalen Oxford, Northwestern U Chicago; *m* 1973, Julia Beatrice, nee Little; 2 da; *Career* called to the Bar, Gray's Inn 1962; Midland Circuit 1964; Recorder of the Crown Court 1979-; *Style* - Stephen Desch Esq QC; 113 Knatchbull rd, SE5 (☎ 01 274 9639)

DESHMUKH, Sir Chintaman Dwarkanath; CIE (1937); s of D G Deshmukh; *b* 14 Jan 1896; *Educ* Elphinstone High Sch, Elphinstone Coll Bombay, Jesus Cambridge; *m* 1, 1920, Rosina, nee Silcox; 1 da; m 2, 1953, Srimathi Durgabai; *Career* called to Bar 1963; late Min of Finance India; pres India International Centre, New Delhi 1959-; Council of Social Development 1969-, kt 1944; *Style* - Sir Chintaman Deshmukh, CIE; India International Centre, 40 Lodi Estate, New Delhi, India

DEUTSCH, André; s of late Bruno Deutsch; *b* 15 Nov 1917; *Career* set up André Deutsch Ltd 1951, since when chm and md; founder African Universities Press, Lagos and E Africa Publishing House, Kenya; *Style* - André Deutsch Esq; 5 Selwood ter, SW7

DEVAS, Michael Campbell; MC (1945); s of late Geoffrey Charles Devas, MC; *b* 6 June 1924; *Educ* Eton; *m* 1, 1952 (m dis 1952), Patience Merryday, da of late Sir Albert Stern, KBE, CMG; 1 s, 1 da; m 2, 1967, Gillian Barbara, da of late Col H Hewett; 2 s, 1 da; *Career* banker; joined M Samuel & Co Ltd 1947, dir 1960, dir Kleinwort Benson Ltd 1965-, chm Charter Trust and Agency Ltd 1972-; *Recreations* sailing, skiing; *Clubs* White's, Roy Yacht Squadron; *Style* - Michael Devas Esq, MC; Hunton Court, Maidstone, Kent (☎ Hunton 307)

DEVAS, Hon Mrs - Hon Penelope Anne; *née* O'Neill; da of Baron O'Neill of the Maine (Life Peer); *b* 1947; *m* 1970, Christopher William Kerr Devas, whose mother, Monica, was ggda of Rev Lord Henry Kerr (3 s of 6 Marquess of Lothian) and Louisa (da of Gen Hon Sir Alexander Hope, GCB, 4 s of 2 Earl of Hopetoun); *Style* - The Hon Mrs Devas; Oxley Green Farm, Tolleshunt D'Arcy, Maldon, Essex

DEVAS, William George; CBE (1959), DFC (1944), AFC (1943); s of late Ambrose Joseph Devas; *b* 17 Dec 1912; *Educ* Beaumont Coll; *m* 1939, Monica Mary Cecil, da of late Henry Francis Hobart Kerr; 2 s; *Career* Gp Capt RAF, served India 1935-37, S Africa 1941-43, Bomber Command 1944, RAF Staff Coll 1948-50, Hong Kong 1950-52, Cyprus 1956-58, Thorney Island 1958-60, Norway 1960-62, ADC to HM the Queen 1965-68, ret 1968; *Style* - William Devas Esq, CBE, DFC, AFC; Brick Kiln Farmhouse, Chilgrove, Chichester, W Sussex PO18 9HS (☎ E Marden 240)

DEVEREUX, Hon Charles Robin de Bohun; s and h of 18 Viscount Hereford; *b* 1975; *Style* - The Hon Charles Devereux

DEVEREUX, Hon Edward Mark de Breteuil; s of 18 Viscount Hereford; *b* 1977; *Style* - The Hon Edward Devereux

DEVESI, Sir Baddeley; GCMG (1980); s of Mostyn Tagabasoe Norua; *b* 16 Oct 1941; *Educ* St Stephen's Sch Auckland, Ardmore Teachers' Coll Auckland; *Career* gov-gen Solomon Islands 1978-; *Style* - Sir Baddeley Devesi, GCMG; Government House, Honiara, Solomon Islands

DEVESON, G R; *Career* md Senior Engineering Gp Ltd; *Style* - G R Deveson Esq; Senior Engineering Gp Ltd, Senior House, 21 Derby rd, Watford, Herts

DEVILLE, Harold Godfrey (Oscar); CBE (1979); s of Harold DeVille (d 1980); *b* 11 April 1925; *Educ* Burton-on-Trent Grammar Sch and Trinity Coll Cambridge; *m* 1947, Pamela Fay, da of Capt Rowland Ellis (decd); 1 s; *Career* Lt RN 1943-46; personnel man Ford Motor Co 1949-65; dir and exec dep chm BICC Ltd 1980- (former v-chm); memb, Cmmn on Industrial Relations 1971-74, Central Arbitration Ctee 1976-77, Cncl Advisory Conciliation and Arbitration Serv 1976-,

Cncl Confederation of British Industry 1977-, Cncl Industrial Soc 1977-; *Style* - Harold DeVille Esq, CBE; 146 Whitehall Ct, London SW1A 2FL; Bexton Mews, Bexton Lane, Knutsford, Cheshire (☎ Knutsford 2270)

DEVITT, James Hugh Thomas; s (by 3 m) and h of Lt-Col Sir Thomas Devitt, 2 Bt; *b* 18 Sept 1956; *Style* - James Devitt Esq

DEVITT, Peter Kenneth; DL (1959); s of Howson Foulger Devitt (d 1949); *b* 4 June 1911; *Educ* Sherborne; *m* 1935, Eunice Stephanie, da of late Sir Charles Sheriton Swan; 1 s, 3 da; *Career* served 1939-45 War with RAUXAF (Battle of Britain and despatches), Wing Cdr 1944; memb of Lloyd's; Gov Roy Merchant Navy Sch; dir Devitt Langton and Dawnay Day and Howson Devitt (Agencies) Ltd; memb Ct of Worshipful Co of Skinners; *Style* - Wing Cdr Peter Devitt, DL; Westfield Lodge, Budleigh Salterton, Devon (☎ 039-54-3113)

DEVITT, Lt-Col Sir Thomas Gordon; 2 Bt (UK 1916), of Chelsea, co London; s of late Arthur Devitt, s of 1 Bt; suc gf, Sir Thomas Lane Devitt, 1 Bt, 1923; *b* 27 Dec 1902; *Educ* Sherborne, CCC Cambridge; *m* 1, 1930 (m dis 1936), Joan Mary, da of late Charles Freemantle; m 2, 1937 (m dis 1953), Lydia Mary, da of late Edward Beloe; 2 da; m 3, 1953, Janet Lilian, da of late Col H S Ellis, CBE, MC; 1 s, 1 da; *Heir* s, James Hunt Thomas Devitt; *Career* Regular Army 1926-30; ptnr Devitt and Moore; former chm Sharmans Garages Ltd and Macers Ltd; former chm govrs Nautical Coll Pangbourne and a govr of Sherborne Sch; chm Nat Serv for Seafarers; *Clubs* MCC; *Style* - Lt-Col Sir Thomas Devitt, Bt; 5 Rembrandt close, Holbein Place, SW1; 49 Lexden rd, Colchester, Essex (☎ Colchester 77958)

DEVLIN, Baron (Life Peer UK 1961); Patrick Arthur Devlin; PC (1960); s of William J Devlin; *b* 25 Nov 1905; *Educ* Stonyhurst and Christ's Coll Cambridge; *m* 1932, Madeleine, da of Sir Bernard Oppenheimer, 1 Bt; 4 s, 2 da; *Career* barr Gray's Inn 1929, bencher 1947, tres 1963; KC 1945; a Justice of the High Court (Queen's Bench Divn) 1948-60, a Lord Justice of Appeal 1960-61, a Lord of Appeal in Ordinary 1961-64; chm Bedford Coll for Women 1953-59; chm Ctee of Inquiry into Dock Labour Scheme 1955-56; chm Nyasaland Cmmn of Inquiry 1959; chm Press Cncl 1964-69; High Steward of Cambridge U 1966-, kt 1948; *Style* - The Rt Hon the Lord Devlin, PC; West Wick House, Pewsey, Wilts (☎ 3458)

DEVLIN, Hon Dominick; s of Baron Devlin PC (Life Peer); *b* 2 Dec 1942; *Educ* Winchester, Univ Coll London; *m* 1967, Carla, da of Lamberto Fulloni; 1 s; *Style* - The Hon Dominick Devlin; 4 Chemin de Chaumont, 1232 Confignon, Switzerland

DEVLIN, Hon Gilpatrick; s of Baron Devlin PC (Life Peer); *b* 26 Dec 1938; *Educ* Winchester; *m* 1967, Glenna, da of J Parry-Evans; c; *Style* - The Hon Gilpatrick Devlin; 19, 1 ave East, Johannesburg, S Africa

DEVLIN, Hon Matthew; s of Baron Devlin PC (Life Peer); *b* 8 June 1946; *Educ* Winchester and New Coll Oxford; *m* 1969, Rosemary Joan, da Lt Co E C Van der Kiste; c; *Style* - The Hon Matthew Devlin; West Wick House, Pewsey, Wilts (☎ 3458)

DEVLIN, Stuart Leslie; *b* 9 Oct 1931; *Educ* Gordon Inst of Technol Geelong, Roy Melbourne Inst of Technol and RCA; *m* 1962, Kim Hose; *Career* DesRCA (Silversmith, & Industrial Design/Engrg); goldsmith, silversmith, designer; Freeman City of London; Liveryman, Goldsmiths' Co; *Style* - Stuart Devlin Esq; 25 Conduit st, W1 (☎ 01 408 0044)

DEVLIN, Hon Timothy; s of Baron Devlin PC (Life Peer); *b* 28 July 1944; *Educ* Winchester, Univ Coll Oxford; *m* 1967, Angela, da of A J G Laramy; 2 s, 2 da; *Career* journalist, former news ed TLS, reporter The Times 1971-73, educ correspondent 1973-77, nat dir ISIS 1977-; *Style* - The Hon Timothy Devlin; Jeakes House, Mermaid st, Rye, E Sussex

DEVON, 17 Earl of (E 1553); Sir Charles Christopher Courtenay; 13 Bt (I 1644); s of Rev the 16 Earl, MA (d 1935, 2 cous thrice removed of the 9 Earl (William Beckford's 'Kitty'), the 'astonishing' revival of the Earldom in whose favour in 1831 excited Vicary Gibbs's implicit disapprobation (tho' to be fair the prime mover seems to have been the Earl's 3 cous & eventual heir, at the time Clerk Assistant of Parliament); contemporary coy references to the Earl skulking in foreign climes instead of facing the music like a Courtenay (motto *Ubi lapsus? Quid feci?*) imply that he was thought to share the taste for which supposedly Lord Hungerford (of Heytesbury) paid with his head in 1541 and Lords Byron and Beauchamp (equally supposedly, but some centuries later) with exile); *b* 13 July 1916; *Educ* Winchester, RMC; *m* 1939, Sybil Venetia, da of Capt John Vickris Taylor, JP (d 1956), and formerly w of 6 Earl of Cottenham; 1 s, 1 da; *Heir* s, (styled) Lord Courtenay, *qv*; *Career* Capt Coldstream Gds (RARO), WW II (wounded, despatches), actg Maj 1942; patron of four livings; JP (1950) Devon; *Style* - The Rt Hon Earl of Devon JP; Powderham Castle, Exeter (☎ 0626 253)

DEVONALD, Hon Mrs (Charlotte Elizabeth Ann); da of 2 Baron Croft, *qv*; *b* 1952; *Educ* Benenden; *m* 1975, Emrys Thomas Devonald; 1 da; *Style* - The Hon Mrs Devonald; 2 Cherry Tree Dell, Chorleywood Common, Herts

DEVONPORT, 3 Viscount (UK 1917); Sir Terence Kearley; 3 Bt (UK 1908); also Baron Devonport (UK 1910); s of 2 Viscount Devonport (d 1973); *b* 29 Aug 1944; *Educ* Aiglon Coll (Chesières-Villars) Switzerland and Selwyn Coll Cambridge; *m* 1968 (m dis 1979), Elizabeth Rosemary, nee Hopton; 2 da; *Heir* kinsman, Chester Dagley Hugh Kearley; *Career* Dip Arch RIBA, BPhil (Newcastle), landscape architect and rural consultant; *Style* - The Rt Hon the Viscount Devonport; Linnheads House, W Woodburn, nr Hexham, Northumberland

DEVONPORT, Sheila, Viscountess - Sheila Isabel; *née* Murray; *m* 1938, 2 Viscount Devonport (d 1973); 1 s (present peer), 1 da; *Style* - The Rt Hon Sheila, Viscountess Devonport; Peasmarsh Place, Sussex

DEVONSHIRE, 11 Duke of (E 1694); Andrew Robert Buxton Cavendish; MC (1944), PC (1964); also Baron Cavendish of Hardwicke (E 1605; the 1 Baron's mother was the celebrated 'Bess of Hardwick' and his niece Lady Arabella Stuart, centre of various intrigues against Elizabeth I and James I; it is through Arabella that the 1 Baron is said to have got his Peerage), Earl of Devonshire (E 1618), Marquess of Hartington (E 1694), and Earl of Burlington and Baron Cavendish of Keighley (both UK 1831); s of 10 Duke of Devonshire, KG, MBE, TD (d 1950), and Lady Mary Gascoyne-Cecil, CBE, da of 4 Marquess of Salisbury; His Grace is ggs of one Conservative PM (Lord Salisbury) and nephew by marriage of another (Harold Macmillan); 1 cous of Maurice Macmillan and Lord Stuart of Findhorn; *b* 2 Jan 1920; *Educ* Eton and Trinity Coll Cambridge; *m* 1941, Hon Deborah Vivien (a non-exec dir of the housing div of Tarmac Ltd 1981-), 6 da of 2 Baron Redesdale (d 1958) and sis of Nancy, Unity and Jessica Mitford (*see* Hon Mrs Treuhaft) also of Hon Lady Mosley, *qv*; 1 s, 2 da; *Heir* s, Marquess of Hartington, *qv*; *Career* stood for Chesterfield in Con interest 1945 & 1950; memb Horserace Totalisator Bd 1977-; Pres Derbyshire Boy Scouts Assoc, V-Lt for Derbyshire and a KStJ; Parliamentary Under-Sec of State for Commonwealth Relations 1960-62, and Min of State Commonwealth Relations Office 1962-64; Chllr of Manchester U 1965-; 1939-45 War as Capt Coldstream Gds; *Clubs* Brooks's, White's and Pratt's; *Style* - His Grace the Duke of Devonshire MC PC, HM Vice-Lieut for Derbyshire; Chatsworth, Bakewell, Derbys; Bolton Abbey, Yorks; Lismore Castle, Co Waterford; 4 Chesterfield st, W1 (☎ 01-499 5803)

DEVONSHIRE, Dowager Duchess of; Lady Mary Alice; *née* Gascoyne-Cecil; GCVO (1955), CBE (1946); da of 4 Marquess of Salisbury, KG, PC (d 1947); *b* 29 July 1895; *m* 1917, 10 Duke of Devonshire, KG, MBE (d 1950); 2 s (elder ka 1944, yr- 11 Duke); 2 da (Lady Elizabeth Cavendish, Lady Anne Tree); *Career* Mistress of the Robes to HM the Queen 1953-66; chllr Exeter U 1956-71; *Style* - Her Grace the Dowager Duchess of

Devonshire, GCVO, CBE; 107 Eaton Square, SW1 (☎ 01 235 8798)

DEWAR, Lady Elisabeth Jeronima; *née* Waldegrave; da of 12 Earl Waldegrave; *b* 1936; *m* 1963, Hon John Dewar, s of 3 Baron Forteviot; *Style* - Lady Elisabeth Dewar; Aberdalgie House, nr Perth

DEWAR, George Duncan Hamilton; s of George Readman Dewar; *b* 11 Sept 1916; *Educ* High Sch of Glasgow; *m* 1940, Elizabeth Lawson Potts Lowrie; 1 s, 1 da; *Career* chartered accountant; partner Peat, Marwick, Mitchell & Co, Glasgow from 1949; *Style* - George Dewar Esq; (office) 135 Buchanan st, Glasgow (☎ 204 1481); 82 Langside dve, Glasgow (☎ 637 1734)

DEWAR, Col Gordon John Alistair; CBE (1967, MBE 1949); s of Gordon Duncan Dewar (d 1975); *b* 8 Nov 1915; *Educ* Cheltenham and RMC Sandhurst; *m* 1940, Rachel Louisa, da of late Lt-Col Edmund Gray Stuart Truell; 1 s, 3 da; *Career* Col late R Hampshire Regt, Palestine 1936-38, NW Europe 1944-45, Egypt 1946-49, Malaya 1953-56 (despatches), cmd British Forces British Guyana 1965-66, UK nat mil rep SHAPE 1967-68, Col A/Q E Midlands 1968-70, ret 1970; sec Army and Combined Servs Cricket and Hockey Assocs 1972-80; *Clubs* Army and Navy, MCC; *Style* - Col Gordon Dewar, CBE; Queen Anne Cottage, Millbridge, Frensham, Farnham, Surrey (☎ Frensham 2527)

DEWAR, Ian Stewart; s of late William Stewart Dewar; *Educ* Penarth County Sch; UC Cardiff; Jesus Coll; *m* 1968, Nora Stephanie House; 1 s, 1 da; *Career* under-sec, Welsh Office from 1973; *Style* - Ian Dewar Esq; Stanwell rd, Penarth, South Glamorgan (☎ Cardiff 703244)

DEWAR, Hon John James Evelyn; s and h of 3 Baron Forteviot, MBE; *b* 5 Apr 1938; *Educ* Eton; *m* 1963, Lady Elisabeth Jeronima, da of 12 Earl Waldergrave, KG; 1 s, 3 da; *Style* - The Hon John Dewar; Aberdalgie House, Perth

DEWAR, Brig Michael Preston Douglas; CB (1958), CBE (1956); s of V-Adm Robert Gordon Douglas Dewar, CBE (d 1948); *b* 1 Oct 1906; *Educ* Winchester and RMC Sandhurst; *m* 1934, Winifred Elizabeth (d 1971), da of late Charles Murphy, FRCS; 1 s, 1 da; *Career* 2 Lt The Buffs 1926, Lt-Col 1948, Brig 1955, UK nat mil rep SHAPE 1955-58, memb of Pension Appeals Tribunal 1969-80 dep dir Manpower Planning (War Office) 1952-55, ret 1959; *Clubs* Army and Navy; *Style* - Brig Michael Dewar, CB, CBE; Gt Maytham Hall, Rolvenden, nr Cranbrook, Kent, TN17 4NE (☎ Rolvenden 375)

DEWAR, Robert James; CMG (1969), CBE (1964); s of late Dr Robert Scott Dewar; *b* 1923; *Educ* Glasgow H S, Edinburgh U, Wadham Oxford; *m* 1947, Christina Marianne, da of late Olaf August Ljungberger of Stockholm; 2 s, 1 da; *Career* ch conservator of Forests 1960-64, perm sec Natural Resources Malawi 1964-69; staff memb World Bank 1969-, ch of Ag Div Regional Mission for Eastern Africa 1974-; *Clubs* Roy Commonwealth Soc; *Style* - Robert Dewar Esq, CMG, CBE; c/o World Bank, PO Box 30577, Nairobi, Kenya

DEWAR, Hon Simon Thomas; s of 3 Baron Forteviot, MBE; *b* 1941; *Educ* Bradfield; *m* 1970, Helen Elizabeth, nee Bassett (m dis 1973); *Style* - The Hon Simon Dewar; Terling Park, Moree, NSW 2400, Australia

DEWEY, Sir Anthony Hugh; 3 Bt (UK 1917) of South Hill Wood, Bromley, Kent, JP (1961); s of Maj Hugh Grahame Dewey, MC (d 1936) and gs of 2 Bt (d 1948); *b* 31 July 1921; *Educ* Wellington and Roy Agric Coll Cirencester; *m* 1949, Sylvia, da of late Dr Ross MacMahon; 2 s, 3 da; *Heir* s Rupert Grahame Dewey; *Career* served 1940-46 (NW Europe) as Capt RA; *Style* - Sir Anthony Dewey, Bt, JP; Silton Lodge, Gillingham, Dorset (☎ Bourton 324)

DEWEY, Rupert Grahame; s and h of Sir Anthony Dewey, 3 Bt; *b* 29 March 1953; *m* 1978, Suzanne Rosemary, da of Andrew Lusk; *Style* - Rupert Dewey Esq

DEWHURST, Hon Mrs - Hon Irene Margareta; *née* Dewar; da of late 2 Baron

Forteviot; *b* 1908; *m* 1934, Lt-Col Hugh Littleton Dewhurst, RA; 1 s, 2 da; *Style* - The Hon Mrs Dewhurst; Dungarthill, Dunkeld, Perthshire

DEWHURST, Prof Sir (Christopher) John; s of late John Dewhurst; *b* 2 July 1920; *Educ* St Josephs Coll Dumfries, Victoria U Manchester; *m* 1952, Hazel Mary Atkin; 2 s, 1 da; *Career* FRCOG; FRCSE; Hon FACOG; Hon FRCSI; Hon FCOG (SA); prof Obstetrics and Gynaecology, London U at Queen Charlotte's Hospital for Women 1967- kt 1977; *Style* - Prof Sir John Dewhurst; 39 Old Slade Lane, Iver, Bucks (☎ 653 395)

DEWHURST, William; s of late William Dewhurst; *b* 12 Jan 1921; *Educ* Bolton Polytechnic; *m* 1940, Emily, nee Horridge; 2 s; *Career* CEng, MIMechE, engineer, works director British Reinforced Concrete Engrg Co Stafford 1949-; *Style* - William Dewhurst Esq; Evesham, Old Coach Lane, Brocton, Stafford (☎ Stafford 57777)

DEXTER, John; *Career* former actor; dir; plays include St Joan, Equus, As You Like It for the National Theatre; also opera; Assoc dir National Theatre 1963; dir of production Metropolitan Opera New York 1974-; *Style* - John Dexter Esq; c/o Metropolitan Opera, Lincoln Centre, New York, NY10023, USA

DEXTER, Keith; CB (1978); s of Arthur William Dexter; *b* 3 April 1928; *Educ* Dixie Grammar Sch Market Bosworth; Nottingham and Illinois Us; *m* 1954, Marjorie Billbrough; *Career* under-sec MAFF (Meat and Fatstock) 1971-75; dir gen Agricultural Dvpt and Advisory Serv (dep sec), MAFF 1975-; *Style* - Keith Dexter Esq CB; 7 The Uplands, Harpenden, Herts (☎ 3955)

DHERSE, Jean-Loup Marie; s of Louis Charles Dherse of Paris; *b* 17 Jan 1933; *Educ* William Penn Charter Sch Philadelphia, Ecole Polytechnique, Ecole des Mines de Paris; *m* 1958, Melia Marie Hedwige, da of Rene de Cassin de Kainlis; 2 da; *Career* with Ciments Lafarge 1964-68, Pechiney Ugine Kuhlmann 1968-74, dir The Rio Tinto Zinc Corpn Ltd 1974-; *Recreations* skiing; *Style* - Jean-Loup Dherse Esq; 18 Chester st, SW1 (☎ 01 235 0476); Trianel, Perriers/Andelle, Eure, France (3332 490713); La Campagne, Maleribes, Gassin, Var, France (3394 970396)

DI MANDRIOLE, Marchese (San Marino 1963 AD & in year 1663 of the Republic); Olimpio Forte; DSC IMOS 1 Class, Commemorative War Cross 1941-45 of Roy Yugoslav Army, memb Sov Mil Order Malta, Kt Cdr of Italian Republic, Kt Cdr Holy Sepulchre, Kt Order St Gregory the Great, Kt Cdr Roy Order St Sava, Grand Offr Order Roy Crown Yugoslavia, Grand Cross Order Merit MESICO Legion de Honor de la Republica de Cuba (pre-Castro), Palmes de Grand Croix de l'Ordre de l'Encouragement Public Français; s of Francesco Forte (d 1940, of the same family as Sir Charles Forte; other prominent members include Angelo Forte di Lecce, granted title of Baron by Charles VIII of France 1495 in Naples, and Giovanni Forte, who was made a Kt of Justice in the Order of Constantine and St George) and Maria, nee Ciaraldi; *b* 8 March 1918, in Casalattico, Frosinone; *Educ* in Casalattico; *m* 1948, Iolanda Dese, born in Scotland to Silviano Forte (d 1955); 1 s (Francesco Pietro b 25 Jan 1952), 1 da (Sandra Francesca Maria b 9 July 1949); *Heir* s, *see* above; *Career* served with Italian Army 1936-40 Abyssinia, 1940-46 Italian Army and Allied Resistance Force Underground Movement (captured thrice by German Army and escaped), Lt 1945, Hon Lt-Col Allied Resistance Force IMOS 1947; industl & property developer 1947-, mktg consultant; now in import/export, owner of catering establishments, co dir & chm; *Recreations* sailing; *Style* - Marchese di Mandriole; 7 Station rd, Bexhill-on-Sea, Sussex (☎ 216737)

DI PALMA, Mrs Ernest Jones (Vera June); da of late William Di Palma; *b* 14 July 1931; *Educ* Haverstock Central Sch London; *m* 1972, Ernest Jones; *Career* FCCA; FTII; dir Mobile Training & Exhibitions Ltd 1977-; taxation specialist; *Style* - Mrs Ernest Jones; 538 Willoughby House, Barbican, EC2 (☎ 01 628 6846); Temple Close, Sigford Gower, Banbury,

Oxon

DIAMAND, Peter; Hon CBE (1972); *b* 1913; *Educ* Schiller-Realgymnasium Berlin, Berlin U; *m* 1, 1948, Maria Curcio (m dis 1971); m 2, Sylvia Rosenberg (m dis 1979); 1 s; *Career* dir Edinburgh Int Festival 1965-78, consultant Orchestre de Paris 1976-, dir and gen man Roy Philharmonic Orchestra 1978-; *Style* - Peter Diamand Esq Hon CBE; 97 New Bond st, W1 (☎ 01 629 4078)

DIAMOND, Baron (Life Peer UK 1970); John Diamond; PC (1965); s of late Rev S Diamond, of Leeds; *b* 30 April 1907; *Educ* Leeds Grammar Sch; *m* 1, 1932 (m dis 1947); 2 s, 1 da; m 2, 1948, Julie; 1 da; *Career* former dir Sadlers Wells Trust Ltd and London Opera Centre; MP (Lab) Manchester 1945-51, Gloucester 1957-70; ch sec to the Treasury 1964-70 (memb of Cabinet 1968-70); dep chm of ctees House of Lords 1974; chm Roy Cmmn on the Distribution of Income and Wealth 1974-79; chm Industry and Parliament Trust 1976-; trustee Cncl for Social Democracy 1981-; hon tres Fabian Soc; *Style* - The Rt Hon The Lord Diamond, PC; Aynhoe, Doggetts Wood Lane, Chalfont St Giles, Bucks

DIAMOND, Hon Derek; s of Baron Diamond PC (Life Peer); *b* 1933; *Style* - The Hon Derek Diamond; c/o 44 Chenies, Bucks

DIAMOND, Hon Joan; da of Baron Diamond PC (Life Peer); *b* 1949; *Style* - The Hon Joan Diamond; c/o 44 Chenies, Bucks

DIAMOND, Hon Martin; s of Baron Diamond PC (Life Peer); *b* 1935; *Style* - The Hon Martin Diamond; c/o 44 Chenies, Bucks

DIAMOND, Hon Ruth; da of Baron Diamond PC (Life Peer); *b* 1937; *Style* - The Hon Ruth Diamond; 100 Preston rd, Wembley, Middx

DIBBEN, Kenneth Francis; s of Stanley Cyril Dibben; *b* 13 Feb 1929; *Educ* King Edward VI Sch Southampton, Worcester Roy G S, Southampton U; *m* 1962, Dora Mary Bower, nee Tunbridge; 1 s; *Career* chartered accountant; dir Kalamazoo, Clark Son & Morland; chm Tesel Services, Victoria Babyfoods; former dir Hambros Bank Ltd, Conservative Party candidate; *Style* - Kenneth Dibben Esq; 4 Smith sq, SW1 (☎ 01 222 3269); Water House, Berwick St John, Shaftesbury, Dorset (☎ 0747 88 275)

DICK-LAUDER, Sir George Andrew; 12 Bt (NS 1690) of Fountainhall, Haddingtonshire; s of Lt-Col Sir John North Dalrymple Dick-Lauder, 11 Bt; *b* 17 Nov 1917; *Educ* Stowe and RMC; *m* 1945, Hester Marguerite, da of late Lt-Col G C Sorell-Cameron, CBE; 2 s, 2 da; *Heir* s Piers Robert Dick-Lauder; *Career* Maj Black Watch, served in Palestine, Somaliland, 52 ME Commandos, Sudan, Crete (POW); ret 1960; chllr Commandery of Lochore 1974; novelist and au of several books; *Clubs* Puffin's (Edinburgh); *Style* - Sir George Dick-Lauder, Bt; Firth Mill House, nr Auchendinny, Roslin, Midlothian

DICK-LAUDER, Piers Robert; s and h of Sir George Dick-Lauder, 12 Bt; *b* 3 Oct 1947; *Style* - Piers Dick-Lauder Esq

DICKENS, Prof Arthur Geoffrey; CMG (1974), FBA (1966); s of Arthur James Dickens (d 1957); *b* 6 July 1910; *Educ* Hymer's Coll Hull and Magdalen Coll Oxford; *m* 1936, Molly (d 1978), da of Walter Bygott; 2 s; *Career* Fell Keble Coll Oxford 1933-49, Prof of History, Univ of Hull 1949-62 (Pro-Vice Chllr 1959-62) and King's Coll London 1962-67, dir Inst of Historical Research Univ of London 1967-77, Fell British Acad 1966-; Foreign Sec of the British Acad 1969-79, hon v-pres of Historical Assoc and Royal Historical Soc; au of several books; *Recreations* studying modern British Art; *Clubs* Athenaeum; *Style* - Prof Arthur Dickens, CMG, FBA; Institute of Historical Research, Senate House, WC1E 7HU

DICKENS, Geoffrey Kenneth; JP, MP (C) Huddersfield West 1979-; s of John Wilfred Dickens; *b* 26 Aug 1931; *Educ* E Lane Sch Wembley; Harrow and Acton Tech Colls; *m* 1956, Norma Evelyn Boothby; 2 s; *Career* Herts CC 1970-75; JP

St Albans later Barnsley 1968; *Style* - Geoffrey Dickens Esq JP MP; Water Hall, Water Hall Lane, Peninstone, Sheffield, S Yorks

DICKENS, Monica Enid (Mrs R O Stratton); da of late Henry Charles Dickens; *b* 10 May 1915; *Educ* St Paul's Girls' Sch Hammersmith; *m* 1951, Cdr Roy Olin Stratton, US Navy; 2 da; *Career* writer; founder of US Samaritans; published autobiography, *An Open Book*, 1978; *Style* - Mrs R O Stratton; North Falmouth, Mass 02556, USA

DICKENSON, Lt-Col Charles Royal; CMG(1965); s of Charles Roland; *b* 17 June 1907; *Educ* Shaftesbury G S, Dorset; *m* 1960, Hendrika Jacoba Margaretta Schippers; 2 da; *Career* Postmaster-General of Rhodesia, 1964-68; ret; *Style* - Lt-Col Charles Dickenson, CMG; Koekoekstraat 50, Maassluis, Holland (☎ 21658)

DICKER, Col Geoffrey Seymour Hamilton; CBE (1965), TD (1953), DL (1963); s of A S H Dicker, MBE, FCA (d 1974); *b* 20 July 1920; *Educ* Haileybury, King's Coll Cambridge; *m* 1942, Josephine Helen, da of F G Penman, MA; 1 s, 2 da (1 decd); *Career* Roy Signals 1940, Adj 6 Armoured Divisional Signals 1943-45, GSO (2) AFHQ Casserta 1945-46 (MBE despatches), cmmned TA 1948, Hon Col 54 (E Anglian) Signal Regt (TA) 1960-67, Hon Col 36 (E) Signal Regt (V) 1979-, ADC (TA) to HM the Queen 1965-70, v-chm Cncl of TA and VR Assocs 1975-80, Hon Col Cmdt Roy Corps of Signals 1970-80, chm Reserve Forces Assoc 1976-, v-pres (UK) Inter-Allied Confederation of Reserve Offrs 1976-; CA 1950, ptnr Lovewell Blake and Co, Gt Yarmouth, Lowestoft, Norwich and Thetford; *Clubs* Norfolk, Army and Navy, Royal Norfolk and Suffolk Yacht (Cdre 1978-80), Norfolk Broads Yacht (1959-62); *Style* - Col Geoffrey Dicker, CBE, TD, DL; Springfield, Brundall, Norfolk, NR13 5PH (☎ Norwich 712357)

DICKIE, Rev Prof Edgar Primrose; MC; s of William Dickie; *b* 12 Aug 1897; *Educ* Dumfries Acad, Edinburgh U, Ch Ch Oxford, New Coll Edinburgh, Marburgh Tubingen; *m* 1927, Ishbel Graham Holmes; *Career* Emeritus Professor of Divinity, St Mary's Coll, St Andrews U, 1967- (Prof 1935-67); Extra Chaplain to HM the Queen in Scotland 1967- (Chaplain 1956-67); *Style* - The Rev Prof Edgar Dickie, MC; Surma, Hepburn gdns, St Andrews, Fife (☎ 73617)

DICKINS, Basil Gordon; CBE (1952, OBE 1945); s of late Basil Dickins; *b* 1 July 1908; *Educ* Private schs and Imperial Coll of Science and Technol; *m* 1, 1935, Molly Aileen (d 1969), da of late Horace Walters Reburn; m 2, 1971, Edith, wid of Warren Parkinson; *Career* HQ Bomber Command RAF 1941-45; assist scientific adviser Air Miny 1945, dir Technical Personnel Admin 1948, dep scientific adviser to Air Miny 1952, dir of Guided Weapons Research and Dvpt Miny of Supply 1956, dir gen Atomic Weapons Miny of Supply 1959, dir gen Guided Weapons Miny of Technol 1962, dep controller Guided Weapons Miny of Aviation 1966-68; *Style* - Basil Dickins Esq, CBE; Villa Caprice, La Folie, Millbrook, Jersey, Channel Islands (☎ Jersey 30819)

DICKINSON, 2 Baron (UK 1930); Richard Clavering Hyett Dickinson; s of Hon Richard Sebastian Willoughby Dickinson, DSO (d 1935) and gs of 1 Baron (d 1943); *b* 2 March 1926; *Educ* Eton, Trinity Coll Oxford; *m* 1957, (Margaret) Ann, da of Brig-Gen G R McMeekan, CBE, DSO; 2 s; *Heir* s Hon Martin Hyett Dickinson; *Career* late Capt Coldstream Gds; *Style* - The Rt Hon the Lord Dickinson; Painswick House, Painswick, Glos (☎ Painswick 3204)

DICKINSON, Hon Andrew; yr s of 2 Baron Dickinson; *b* 15 Feb 1963; *Style* - The Hon Andrew Dickinson

DICKINSON, Hon David Christopher; 4 s of the Hon Richard Sebastian Willoughby Dickinson, DSO (d 1935), of Washwell House, Painswick, Gloucs; *b* 1935; *Educ* Eton and Trin Coll Oxford; *m* 1970, Caroline Mary, nee Toosey; granted 1944 title, rank and precedence of a Baron's son, which would have been his had his father survived to succeed to the title; *Style* - The Hon David Dickinson;

The Hollins, Utkinton, Tarporley, Cheshire

DICKINSON, Rev Hon Hugh Geoffrey; s of The Hon Richard Sebastian Willoughby Dickinson, DSO (d 1935), of Washwell House, Painswick, Gloucs; *b* 1929; *Educ* Westminster; Trin Coll Oxford; Cuddesdon Theological Coll; *m* 1963, Jean Marjorie, da of Arthur Storey, of 25 Woodbourne ave, Leeds; 1 s, 1 da; *Career* granted 1944, title, rank and precedence as the son of a Baron, which would have been his had his father survived to succeed to the title; ordained 1956, chaplain Trin Coll Camb 1958-63; chaplain Winchester Coll 1963-69; bishop's adviser for Adult Education, Coventry Diocese, 1969-77; vicar of St Michael's, St Albans, from; 1977; *Style* - The Rev the Hon Hugh Dickinson; St Michael's Vicarage, St Albans, Herts

DICKINSON, Hon Martin Hyett; elder s and h of 2 Baron Dickinson; *b* 30 Jan 1961; *Style* - The Hon Martin Dickinson

DICKINSON, Hon Mrs - May Southey; *née* Lovemore; *m* 1924, Hon Richard Sebastian Willoughby Dickinson, DSO (d 1935), only s of 1 Baron Dickinson; 1 s (present peer); *Career* JP; *Style* - The Hon Mrs Dickinson, JP; The Poultry Court, Painswick, Glos

DICKINSON, Hon Peter Malcolm de Brissac; s of Hon Richard Sebastian Dickinson (s of 1 Baron Dickinson; died before succeeding); *b* 16 Dec 1927; *Educ* Eton, King's Cambridge; *m* 1953, Mary Rose Barnard; 2 s, 2 da; *Career* author; asst ed Punch, 1952-69; chm Management Ctee, Society of Authors, 1978-80; raised to the rank of a Baron's son, 1944; *Style* - The Hon Peter Dickinson; 33 Queensdale rd, W11

DICKSON, Alec (Alexander) Graeme; CBE (1967, MBE 1945); s of late Norman Dickson; *b* 23 May 1914; *Educ* Rugby, New Coll Oxford; *m* 1951, Mora Hope Robertson; *Career* founder and first dir VSO 1958-62; founder Community Service Volunteers 1962, hon dir 1962-, hon pres 1981-; consultant to Commonwealth Secretariat 1974-77; *Style* - Alec Dickson Esq CBE; Blenheim rd, W4 (01 994 7437)

DICKSON, Bt-Col David Eric Livingstone; TD (1951), DL (Staffs 1959); s of Frederic Livingstone Dickson (d 1960); *b* 25 June 1916; *Educ* Shrewsbury; *m* 1944, Ruth Marjorie, da of Col Randolf Nelson Greenwood, MC, JP (d 1977); 2 s; *Career* served with 41 S/L Regt RA (Great Britain, France, Belgium, Holland, Germany, despatches 1946), Cdr 576 LAA/SL Regt RA (TA) 1948-53 & 14 Bn Mobile Defence Corps 1956-59, Bt-Col 1959, slr 1947, partner firm of Challinors & Dickson 1949-; *Style* - Bt-Col David Dickson TD, DL; The Hill, Barlaston, Stoke-on-Trent, Staffs (☎ Barlaston 2434)

DICKSON, Ian Anderson; WS; s of Robert Anderson Dickson, DDS; *b* 1905; *Educ* Edinburgh Acad, Harrow, U of Edinburgh; *m* 1943, Margaret Forbes, nee Ross; 4 s; *Career* Sheriff of S Strathclyde, Dumfries & Galloway at Hamilton 1951-77; *Style* - Ian Dickson Esq, WS; 9 Cleveden gdns, Glasgow (☎ 339 7731); Rockview, Elie, Fife (☎ 30324)

DICKSON, Jennifer; RA (1976); da of late John Liston Dickson; *b* 17 Sept 1936; *Educ* Goldsmith's Coll Sch for Art London U, S W Hayter's Atelier 17 Paris; *m* 1961, Ronald Andrew Sweetman; *Career* artist and feminist; *Recreations* collecting antique clothing; *Style* - Mrs Sweetman; 227 Bank st, 9 Ottawa, Ontario K2P 1W9, Canada (☎ 236 5602); 508 Gilmour st, Ottawa, Ontario K1R 5L4, Canada (☎ 236 5602)

DICKSON, John Abernethy; CB (1970); s of John Dickson (d 1918); *b* 19 Sept 1915; *Educ* Robert Gordon's Coll Aberdeen, Aberdeen U; *m* 1942, Helen Drummond, da of Peter Drummond Jardine (d 1974); 2 da; *Career* joined Forestry Cmmn 1938, head of Harvesting and Marketing 1965-68, dir gen and dep chm 1968-76, chm Commonwealth Forestry Assoc 1972-75, dir Economic Forestry (Scotland) Ltd 1977-, dir Forest Thinnings Ltd 1978-; *Clubs* Caledonian; *Style* - John Dickson Esq, CB; 56 Oxgangs rd, Edinburgh (☎ 031 445 1067)

DICKSON, John Granville; FCIS, AIB; *Career* jt md Hanger Investments Ltd; dir Hanger Group of Cos, Interleasing Truck Rental Ltd, Interleasing (UK) Ltd; *Style* - John Dickson Esq; Hanger Investments Ltd, Dilworth House, 190 Broad st, Birmingham B15 lEA

DICKSON, Lt-Col Leonard Elliot; CBE (1972), MC (1944), TD (1950), DL (Glasgow 1963); s of Rev R Marcus Dickson, DD, of Hope Bank, Lanark (d 1967); *b* 17 March 1915; *Educ* Uppingham and Magdalene Coll Cambridge; *m* 1950, Mary Elisabeth, da of late Lt-Col L A Cuthbertson; 1 s, 1 da; *Career* served 1939-45 War with 1 Glasgow Highlanders in NW Europe, Lt-Col 1952; slr of Dickson, Haddon and Co of Glasgow; *Clubs* Royal Scottish Automobile (Glasgow); *Style* - Lt-Col Leonard Dickson, CBE, MC, TD, DL; Bridge End, Gartmore, by Stirling (☎ Aberfoyle 220)

DICKSON, Hon Mrs (Lynda Mary Kathleen); da (by 2 m) of Sir Max Aitken, 2 Bt (2 Baron Beaverbrook, who disclaimed his peerage 1964); *b* 1948; *m* 1, 1969, Nicolas Saxton; m 2, 1977, Jonathan James Dickson; *Style* - The Hon Mrs Dickson; 76 Hurlingham rd, SW6

DICKSON, Dame Violet Penelope; DBE (1976, MBE 1942); *b* 3 Sept 1896; *Educ* St Edwards Sch Oxford, Woodhall Spa High Sch, Les Charmettes Vevey Switz, Wadham Oxford; *m* 1920, Harold Richard Patrick Dickson, CIE (d 1959), s of John Dickson (d 1908); 1 s, 1 da; *Career* FRZS and memb Roy Central Asian Soc; au of 'Wildflowers of Kuwait and Bahrain' and 'Forty Years in Kuwait'; Lawrence of Arabia Medal; *Style* - Dame Violet Dickson, DBE; Seef, Kuwait, Arabia

DIEHL, Hon Mrs; Hon Sybil Diana; da of late 3 Baron Tollemache; *b* 1930; *m* 1966, Harold Diehl; *Style* - The Hon Mrs Diehl

DIGBY, 12 Baron (I 1620 and GB 1765); Edward Henry Kenelm Digby; JP (Dorset 1959), DL (1957); s of 11 Baron, KG, DSO, MC (d 1964), and Hon Pamela Bruce, da of 2 Baron Aberdare; bro-in-law of Averell Harriman; *b* 24 July 1924; *Educ* Eton, Trinity Coll Oxford and RMC; *m*1952, Dione Marian, da of Rear-Adm Robert Sherbrooke VC CB DSO; 2 s, 1 da; *Heir* s Hon Henry Digby; *Career* Capt Coldstream Gds 1947, ADC to CIC FARELF 1950-51, BAOR 1951-52; V-Lt Dorset 1965, now Ld-Lt; memb Dorchester RDC 1962, dep chm SW Econ Planning Cncl, dir Brooklyns Westbrick Ltd, pres Roy Bath and West Soc 1976, chm Roy Ag Soc of the C'wlth; *Clubs* Turf and Pratt's; *Style* - The Rt Hon the Lord Digby, JP, HM Vice Lord-Lieut for Dorset; Minterne, Dorchester, Dorset (☎ Cerne Abbas 370)

DIGBY, Hon (Albert) Elmar; 3 s of 10 Baron Digby (d 1920); *b* 1911; *Style* - The Hon Elmar Digby

DIGBY, Hon Henry Noel Kenelm; s and h of 12 Baron Digby; *b* 6 Jan 1954; *Educ* Eton; *m* 1980, Susan E, nee Watts; *Style* - The Hon Henry Digby

DIGBY, Hon Rupert Simon; yr s of 12 Baron Digby; *b* 21 Aug 1956; *Educ* Eton; Southampton Univ; *Style* - The Hon Rupert Digby

DIGBY, Hon Zara Jane; da of 12 Baron Digby; *b* 1958; *Style* - The Hon Zara Digby

DIGBY-BESTE, Lady (Amy Mary Taylor); *m* 1958, as his 2 wife, Capt Sir Henry Aloysius Bruno Digby-Beste, CIE, OBE (d 1964); *Style* - Lady Digby-Beste; 12 First av, Hove , Sussex

DIGGENS, Ronald William; OBE (1945); s of Frederick Diggens; *b* 26 Nov 1911; *Educ* Haberdashers' Aske's; *Career* chm Allnatt London Properties 1962-78, Guildhall Property Co 1963-78, dir Slough Estates 1956-; owner of yacht 'Lankelly', aeroplane 'Piper Aztec'*Style* - Ronald Diggens Esq, OBE; Sedgley, 14 Russell rd, Moor Park, Northwood, Middx; Polridmouth Cottage, Menabilly, Cornwall

DIGNAN, Maj-Gen Albert Patrick; CB (1978), MBE (1952); s of Joseph William Dignan (d 1964); *b* 25 July 1920; *Educ* Christian Brothers Sch Dublin, Trinity Coll Dublin; *m* 1952, Eileen, da of James John White (d 1956); 2 s, 1 da; *Career* Brig

Cmmdg Consultant Surgeon Far E Land Forces 1969-71, sr consultant surgeon and assist prof of Military Surgery Queen Alexandra Military Hosp Millbank 1972-73, QHS 1974-78, hon consultant surgeon Roy Hospital Chelsea, hon consultant Oncology and Radiotherapy Westminster Hosp 1975-78, consultant in Accident and Emergency Medicine Ealing Hosp 1978-79; *Recreations* gardening and golf; *Style* - Maj-Gen Albert Dignan CB MBE QHS; 37 Queens rd, Beckenham, Kent (☎658 7690)

DILHORNE, 2 Viscount (UK 1964); Sir John Mervyn Manningham-Buller, 5 Bt (UK 1866); also Baron Dilhorne (UK 1962); s of 1 Viscount Dilhorne, sometime Lord High Chllr & Ld of Appeal in Ordinary (d 1980, ggs of Sir Edward M-B, 1 Bt, who was bro of 1 Baron Churston) by his w Lady Mary Lindsay (4 da of 27 Earl of Crawford and Balcarres); *b* 28 Feb 1932; *Educ* Eton; *m* 1955 (m dis 1973) Gillian Evelyn, nee Stockwell, JP; 2 s, 1 da; *Heir* s, Hon James Edward Manningham-Buller, b 1956; *Career* barr 1979, Fellow Inst of Taxation; formerly Coldstream Gds; md Stewart Smith (LP&M) Ltd 1970-74; *Style* - The Rt Hon the Viscount Dilhorne; 58 Jubilee Place, SW3 (☎ 01 352 2997); Horninghold Manor, Market Harborough, Leics (☎ Hallaton 641)

DILHORNE, Mary, Viscountess - Lady Mary Lilian ; *née* Lindsay; da of late 27 Earl of Crawford and Balcarres; *b* 1910; *m* 1930, 1 Viscount Dilhorne (d 1980); 1 s (present peer); 3 da; *Style* - The Rt Hon Mary, Viscountess Dilhorne; Horninghold Manor, Market Harborough, Leics

DILKE, Charles John Wentworth; s (by 1 m) and h of Sir John Fisher Wentworth Dilke, 5 Bt; *b* 21 Feb 1937; *Educ* Winchester, King's Cambridge (BA); *Style* - Charles Dilke Esq

DILKE, Sir John Fisher Wentworth; 5 Bt (UK 1862), of Sloane Street, Chelsea; s of Sir Fisher W Dilke, 4 Bt (d 1944); *b* 8 May 1906; *Educ* Winchester and New Coll Oxford; *m* 1, 1934 (m dis 1949), Sheila, da of Sir William Seeds, KCMG; 2 s; m 2, 1951, Iris Evelyn, da of late Ernest Clark; *Heir* s, Charles John Wentworth Dilke; *Career* HM's Foreign Serv 1929-32, late staff of 'The Times', British Official Wireless 1941, BBC External Dept 1950; *Style* - Sir John Dilke, Bt; Ludpits, Etchingham, E Sussex

DILKES, Frank Pool; s of late Frank Pool Dilkes; *b* 30 April 1918; *Educ* High Pavement Nottingham, London U (external); *m* 1955, Audrey Helen, nee Tyler; 3 s, 1 da; *Career* RAOC, REME India and Burma; 1 year attached to Indian Army (mentioned in despatches); dep chm and md West Bromwich Building Soc 1961-; *Style* - Frank Dilkes Esq; 282 Broadway N, Walsall, W Midlands

DILL, Sir (Nicolas) Bayard; CBE(1951); s of Thomas Melville Dill; *b* 28 Dec 1905; *Educ* Saltus G S Bermuda, Trinity Hall Cambridge; *m* 1930, Lucy Clare Dill; 2 s; *Career* sr ptnr Conyers Dill & Pearman, Barristers-at-Law, 1948-; knighted 1955; *Style* - Sir Bayard Dill, CBE; Newbold Place, Devonshire, Bermuda (2-4463)

DILLON, 21 Viscount (I 1622); Charles Henry Robert Dillon; also Count Dillon (Fr cr of Louis XIV 1711 for Hon Arthur Dillon, 3 s of 7 Visc & f of 10 & 11 Viscs, who was Col Proprietor of the Dillon Regt, promoted to Lt-Gen in the Fr service, Gov of Toulon, and cr titular Earl Dillon 1721/22 by the Chevalier de St Georges, otherwise known as the Old Pretender or, to his supporters, James III); s of 20 Viscount Dillon (d 1979); *b* 18 Jan 1945; *Educ* Downside, Sandhurst, RCA; *m* 1972, Mary Jane, nee Young; 1s, 1 da; *Heir* s, Hon Henry Benedict Dillon; *Career* designer; *Style* - The Rt Hon The Viscount Dillon; 83 Talfourd rd, SE15 (☎ 01 701 5931); Rath House, Termonfecklin, Drogheda, Co Louth

DILLON, Hon Mr Justice; Hon Sir (George) Brian (Hugh) Dillon; s of Capt George Crozier Dillon, RN (d 1946); *b* 2 Oct 1925; *Educ* Winchester Coll and New Coll Oxford; *m* 1954, Alison Janetta Drummond, da of Hubert Samuel Lane MC (d 1962); 2 s, 2 da; *Career* barr Lincoln's Inn 1948, QC 1965, Bencher Lincoln's Inn 1973, judge of the High Court of Justice, Chancery Div 1969-; *Style* - The Hon Mr Justice Dillon; Bridge Farm

House, Grundisburgh, Woodbridge; Royal Courts of Justice, WC2

DILLON, Hon Beatrice Inès Renée; da of 21 Viscount Dillon; *b* 1978

DILLON, Hon Mrs (Erica Helen Susan) da of 13 Baron Rollo; *b* 12 Dec 1939; *m* 1970, Valentine Dillon; *Career* antique dealer; *Style* - Hon Mrs Dillon; 45 Sandford rd, Ranelagh, Dublin

DILLON, Hon Henry Benedict; s and h of 21 Viscount Dillon; *b* 6 Jan 1973

DILLON, Irène, Viscountess; Irène Marie France; s of René Merandon du Plessis, of Whitehall, Mauritius; *m* 1939, 20 Viscount Dillon (d 1979); 4 s (including 21 Viscount), 3 da (including Hon Mrs Cobbe); *Style* - The Rt Hon Irène, Viscountess Dillon; Rath House, Termonfeckin, Drogheda, Eire

DILLON, Hon Inès Marie Jeanne; 2 da of 20 Viscount Dillon; *b* 1952; *Style* - The Hon Inès Dillon

DILLON, Sir John Vincent; CMG(1974); s of Roger Dillon; *b* 6 Aug 1908; *Educ* Christian Brothers Coll Melbourne; *m* 1935, Sheila Lorraine D'Arcy; 3 s, 1 da; *Career* Ombudsman for Victoria (Cmmr for Administrative Investigations) 1973-; knighted 1980; *Style* - Sir John Dillon, CMG; 25 Kelvin Grove, Armadale, Vic 3143, Australia

DILLON, Sir Max; s of Cyril Dillon; *b* 30 June 1913; *Educ* Wesley Coll Melbourne, Melbourne U; *m* 1940, Estelle Mary Jones; 1 s, 1 da; *Career* gen man Cable Makers Australia Pty Ltd, 1957-70; dep md Metal Manufacturers Ltd Group, 1970-75; pres Confedn of Aust Industry, 1977; knighted 1979; *Style* - Sir Max Dillon; 33 Church st, Pymble, NSW 2073, Australia (44 3160)

DILLON, Hon Michael Edmond; 4 s (twin) of 20 Viscount Dillon; *b* 29 Oct 1957; *Educ* Glenstal Abbey Sch Co Limerick; *Style* - The Hon Michael Dillon

DILLON, Hon Madeleine Mary; 4 but 3 survg da (twin) of 20 Viscount Dillon (d 1979); *b* 29 Oct 1957; *Educ* Loreto Convent, Balbriggan, Co Dublin; St Mary's Convent, Ascot; Université Catholique, Angers; *Recreations* riding, travel, racing, stamp collecting; *Style* - The Hon Madeleine Dillon; 38 St James's Place, SW1 (☎ 01 493 1938); Rath House, Termonfeckin, Drogheda, Co Louth, Eire (☎ 041 22110)

DILLON, Hon Patrick Dominic; s of 20 Viscount Dillon; *b* 9 March 1956; *Educ* St Gerards Sch, Bray, Co Wicklow, and Downside; *Style* - The Hon Patrick Dillon

DILLON, Hon Mrs; Hon Priscilla Frances; da of 2 Baron Hazlerigg; *b* 1952; *m* 1975, Hon Richard Dillon, s of 20 Viscount Dillon; *Style* - The Hon Mrs Dillon; 5 Edith grove, London SW10

DILLON, Hon Richard Arthur Louis; s of 20 Viscount Dillon; *b* 1948; *Educ* Downside; *m* 1975, Hon Priscilla Frances, nee Hazlerigg; *Career* served RHG 1966-69 (Corporal); *Style* - The Hon Richard Dillon; 5 Edith Grove, London, SW10

DILLON, Sir Robert William Charlier; 8 Bt (UK 1801) of Lismullen, Meath; also a Baron of the Holy Roman Empire; s of Robert Arthur Dillon (d 1925), gggs of 1 Bt; suc kinsman, Sir John Fox Dillon, 7 Bt, 1925; *b* 17 Jan 1914; *Educ* Lancing and Trinity Coll Dublin; *m* 1947, Synolda, da of late Cholmondeley Clarke; *Heir* none; *Style* - Sir Robert Dillon, Bt; Overdene, Wentworth pla, Wicklow, Ireland

DILLWYN-VENABLES-LLEWELYN, Lady Delia Mary; da of late Capt Michael Hugh Hicks-Beach, MP (Viscount Quenington, s of 1 Earl St Aldwyn, and who died before succeeding) ; *m* 1934, Brig Sir (Charles) Michael Dillwyn-Venables-Llewelyn, MVO, 3 Bt (d 1976); 1 s, 1 da; *Career* raised to the rank of an Earl's daughter, 1920; *Style* - Lady Delia Dillwyn-Venables-Llewelyn; Llysdinam, Newbridge-on-Wye, Powys

DILLWYN-VENABLES-LLEWELYN, Sir John Michael; 4 Bt (UK 1890) of Penllergaer, Llangyfelach and Ynis-y-gerwn, Cadoxton juxta Neath, of Glamorganshire; s of Brig Sir (Charles) Michael Dillwyn-Venables-Llewelyn, 3 Bt,

MVO (d 1976); *b* 12 Aug 1938; *Educ* Eton and Magdalene Coll Cambridge; *m* 1, 1963 (m dis 1972), Nina, da of late J S Hallan; 2 da; m 2, 1975, Nina Gay Richardson Oliver; *Heir* none; *Career* farmer *Style* - Sir John Dillwyn-Venables-Llewelyn, Bt; Talwen Uchaf Farm, Garth Brengy, Brecon, Powys (☎ Brecon 4263)

DILNOT, Mary (Mrs Thomas Ruffle); da of George Dilnot; *b* 23 Jan 1921; *Educ* St Mary's Coll Hampton; *m* 1974, Thomas Ruffle; *Career* ed Woman's Weekly 1971-; dir IPC Women's Magazines Gp 1976-; *Style* - Mrs Thomas Ruffle; 28 Manor rd S, Hinchley Wood, Surrey

DIMBLEBY, David; s of late Richard Dimbleby; *b* 28 Oct 1938; *Educ* Charterhouse, Ch Ch Oxford, Paris U, Perugia U; *m* 1967, Josceline Rose, nee Gaskell; 1 s, 2 da; *Career* television broadcaster; presenter Panorama BBC 1; md Dimbleby Newspaper Gp 1966-; *Style* - David Dimbleby Esq; 14 King st, Richmond, Surrey

DIMBLEBY, Jonathan; s of late Richard Dimbleby; *b* 31 July 1944; *Educ* U Coll London; *m* 1968, Bel Mooney; 1 s; *Career* broadcaster; Yorkshire TV 1979-; journalist; contributor to New Statesman; *Style* - Jonathan Dimbleby Esq; c/o David Higham Associates Ltd, 5 Lower John st, W1

DIMSON, Mrs S B - Gladys Felicia; CBE (1976); da of late I Sieve; *b* Laurel Bank Sch Glasgow, Glasgow U, London Sch of Economics; *m* 1936, Dr S B Dimson; 1 da; *Career* memb GLC for Battersea North 1973-; memb Inner London Education Authority 1970-; *Style* - Mrs S B Dimson, CBE; 34 Sheldon ave, Highgate, N6 (☎ 01 340 5133)

DINWIDDY, Hon Mrs; Hon Caroline Lesley; *née* Franks; da of Baron Franks (Life Peer); *b* 1939; *m* 1962, John Rowland Dinwiddy; children; *Style* - The Hon Mrs Dinwiddy; Little St Anne's Coach House, Bakeham Lane, Englefield Green, Surrey

DIPLOCK, Baron (Life Peer UK 1968); Rt Hon Sir (William John) Kenneth Diplock; PC (1961); s of W J Hubert Diplock, of Croydon; *b* 8 Dec 1907; *Educ* Whitgift, Univ Coll Oxford (Hon Fell 1958); *m* 1938, Margaret Sarah, da of George Atcheson, of Londonderry; *Career* barr 1932, KC 1948, bencher 1956, Judge of the High Court of Justice (Queen's Bench Div) 1956-61, a Lord Justice of Appeal 1961-68, a Lord of Appeal in Ordinary 1968-, Judge of Restrictive Practices Court 1960-, pres 1961-, kt 1956; *Style* - The Rt Hon The Lord Diplock, PC; 1 Crown Office Row, Temple, EC4 (☎ 01 353 4536); Wansford in England, Peterborough, Northants

DIPPLE, Hon Mrs (Susan Margaret Nevill); da of 7 Baron Money-Coutts; *b* 1933; *m* 1, 1956 (m dis 1965), Michael John Turner, QC; 1 s, 1 da; m 2, 1965, Ian A K Dipple; 2 da; *Style* - The Hon Mrs Dipple; Nether Walstead, Lindfield, Sussex

DIRAC, Prof Paul Adrien Maurice; OM (1973); s of 8 Aug 1902; *m* 1937, Margit Wigner; *Career* FRS; BSc; PhD; Lucasian Prof of Mathematics, Cambridge 1932-69, now Emeritus; fellow of St John's Cambridge; prof of Physics Florida State U 1971-; Nobel Prize in Physics 1933; *Style* - Prof Paul Dirac Esq, OM; Dept of Physics, Florida State U, Tallahassee, Florida 32306, USA; St John's Coll, Cambridge

DISLEY, John Ivor; CBE (1979); s of Harold Disley; *b* 20 Nov 1928; *Educ* Oswestry High Sch, Loughborough Coll (Hon DCL); *m* 1958, Sylvia Cheeseman; 2 da; *Career* v-chm Sports Council 1974-; chm Silva Compasses Ltd; *Style* - John Disley Esq, CBE; Hampton House, Upper Sunbury rd, Hampton, Middlesex (☎ 01 979 1707)

DIVINE, Arthur Durham (David Divine); CBE (1976, OBE 1946), DSM (1940); s of Arthur Henry Divine; *b* 27 July 1904; *Educ* Rondebosch High Sch Cape Town, Kingswood Coll Grahamstown S Africa; *m* 1931, Elizabeth Ann, nee MacAlister; 2 da; *Career* journalist; former War Correspondent and Defence Correspondent Sunday Times; au - David Divine and under pseudonym David Raine; *Style* - Arthur Divine Esq, CBE

DSM; 24 Keats Grove, Hampstead, NW3 (☎ 01-435 6928)

DIX, Alan Michael; s of late Capt Charles Dix; *b* 29 June 1922; *Educ* Stenhus Kostskole; *m* 1955, Helen Catherine, nee McLaren; 1 s; *Career* md Volkswagen (GB) Ltd 1968-72, pres Mid-Atlantic Toyota Inc USA 1972-73, dir-gen The Motor Agents Assoc Ltd London; *Style* - Alan Dix Esq; 112 Speed House, Barbican, London (☎ 01 638 657); Edifici Hort del Sola 1.1, La Massana, Andorra (☎ 010 33 07835352)

DIX, Derek John; s of late John Thomas Dix, of Richmond, Surrey; *b* 27 July 1933 *Educ* Gainsboro' Richmond; *m* 1981, Patricia; *Career* area sales man Associated Biscuits 1966, regional sales man 1969, gen sales man 1975, sales/marketing dir MoDo Consumer Products Ltd (part of Mo Och Domsjo AB) 1978-; *Recreations* charity work, Lions International; *Style* - Derek Dix Esq; 62 Mount Way, Waverton, Chester

DIXIE, Lady (Dorothy Penelope); *née* King-Kirkman; *m* 1950, as his 2nd wife, Sir (Alexander Archibald Douglas) Wolstan Dixie, 13 Bt (d 1975, when title became extinct); 1 da; *Style* - Lady Dixie; Bosworth Park, Leics

DIXON, Dr Bernard; s of late Ronald Dixon; *b* 17 July 1938; *Educ* Queen Elizabeth Grammar Sch Darlington, King's Coll, U of Durham, U of Newcastle upon Tyne; *m* 1963, Margaret Helen Charlton; 2 s, 1 da; *Career* BSc, PhD, MIBiol; ed New Scientist 1969- (dep ed 1968-69); European ed Omni 1978-; *Style* - Dr Bernard Dixon; 81 Falmouth rd, Chelmsford, Essex (☎ 58421)

DIXON, Donald; MP (L) 1979-; s of Christopher Albert Dixon; *b* 6 March 1929; *Career* shipyard worker 1947-74; Branch sec GMWU 1974-79; councillor Sth Tyneside MDC 1963-; *Style* - Donald Dixon Esq MP; 1 Hillcrest, Jarrow (☎ 897635)

DIXON, Hon Mrs (Daphne Cecil Rosemary); da of late 1 Baron Harmsworth; *b* 1901; *m* 1, 1928 (m dis 1937), Capt Colin David Brodie; m 2, 1938, Lt-Col Harold Macneile Dixon, RASC; 2 da; *Style* - The Hon Mrs Dixon; Lagham Manor, South Godstone, Surrey

DIXON, Ian Leonard; s of Leonard Frank Dixon; *b* 3 Nov 1938; *Educ* S W Essex County Tech Sch, Harvard Business Sch; *m* 1961, Valerie Diana, da of late Alexander Barclay; 2 s, 1 da; *Career* chartered builder; gp md The John Wilmott Gp 1971-, CC Beds 1977-, tstee The Bedford Charity 1977-; *Recreations* shooting, philately; *Clubs* Carlton; *Style* - Ian Dixon Esq; Holwell Bay House, Hitchin, Herts (☎ 0462 813704)

DIXON, Capt Sir John George; 3 Bt (UK 1919) of Astle, Chelford, co Palatine of Chester; s of Sir John Dixon, 2 Bt (d 1976); *b* 17 Sept 1911; *Educ* Cranleigh; *m* 1947, Caroline, da of Charles T Hilterman; 1 da; *Heir* bro, Nigel Dixon; *Clubs* Cavalry; *Style* - Capt Sir John Dixon, Bt; Ave des Mousquetaires 19, 1814 La Tour de Peilz, Vaud, Switzerland

DIXON, Kenneth Herbert Morley; s of Arnold Morley Dixon (d 1975); *b* 19 Aug 1929; *Educ* Cranbrook Sch Sydney Australia; Manchester U; *m* 1955, Patricia Oldbury, nee Whalley; 2 s (Michael, Giles b 1969); *Career* Lt Roy signals, BAOR, Cyprus; chm Rowntree Mackintosh Ltd 1981- (dep chm 1978-81), dir Rowntree and Co Ltd, Rowntree Mackintosh (Ingredients) Ltd, chm Fox's Glacier Mints Ltd, dir Fox's Hldgs (Leicester) Ltd, and others; *Recreations* reading, music, fell walking; *Style* - Kenneth Dixon Esq; Rowntree Mackintosh Ltd, Wigginton rd, York (☎ (0904) 53071)

DIXON, Nigel; s of Sir George Dixon, 1 Bt (d 1976) and hp of bro, Sir John George Dixon, 3 Bt; *b* 28 Feb 1920; *m* 1948, Margaret Josephine, nee Collett; 1 s; *Career* Capt RN (ret); *Style* - Nigel Dixon Esq; Little Woolgarston House, Corfe Castle, Dorset

DIXON, Hon Peter Herbert; s of 2 Baron Glentoran; *b* 15 May 1948; *Educ* Eton, Grenoble U; *m* 1975, Jane Blanch, da of Eric Cutler; 2 da (Louise Vyvyan Mary b 1977, Rose Clare b 1980); *Career* CA;

Recreations tennis, shooting; *Clubs* Boodle's; *Style* - The Hon Peter Dixon; The Old Rectory, Yattendon, Newbury, Berks

DIXON, Peter John Bellett; *Career* chm Byrena Products Ltd, Metrep Industrial Products Ltd, Resora Ltd, chm and man dir Lirna Ltd, co dir Turner Curzon Ltd; *Style* - Peter Dixon Esq; Wood-Bridge rd, Guildford, Surrey

DIXON, Maj-Gen Roy Laurence Cayley; CB (1976), MC (1944); s of Lt-Col Sidney Frank Dixon, MC (d 1972); *b* 19 Sept 1924; *Educ* Haileybury and Edinburgh U; *Career* served WW II with 5 RTR in NW Europe, instructor Staff Coll 1961-64, Cdr 5 RTR 1966-67, Brig 1968, Roy Coll of Defence Studies 1971, Cdr Roy Armoured Corps Germany 1968-70, Maj-Gen 1974, dir Army Aviation Forces 1974-76, ch of staff Allied Forces N Europe 1977-80, ret 1980; *Recreations* skiing, sailing, theatre and music; *Clubs* Army and Navy; *Style* - Maj-Gen Roy Dixon, CB, MC; Jolyon, Mattingley, Basingstoke, Hants RG27 8JY (☎ Heckfield 443)

DIXON, Hon Thomas Robin Valerian; MBE (1969); s and h of 2 Baron Glentoran; *b* 21 April 1935; *Educ* Eton; *m* 1959, Rona, da of Capt G Colville, of Hill House, Bishop's Waltham, Hants; 3 s; *Career* 2 Lt Grenadier Gds 1954; Capt 1958; Maj 1966; *Style* - The Hon Thomas Dixon, MBE; Drumadarragh House, Doagh, Co Antrim (☎ Doagh 222)

DIXON, Gp Capt William Michael; CBE (1972), DSO (1943), DFC (1941), AFC (1958); s of late William Michael Dixon; *b* 29 July 1920; *Educ* Hartlepool; *m* 1944, Mary Margaret, nee Spence (d 1957); 3 s; *Career* former ADC to the Queen; dir Aircraft Projects (RAF), MOD 1972-75; Bursar Summer Fields Sch Oxford; *Style* - Group Captain William Dixon CBE DSO DFC AFC; Lower Farm, Sutton, Oxford (☎ 881 553)

DJANOGHY, H A S; *Career* chm Nottingham Mfrg Co Ltd, dir Mansfield Gp of cos, Stevensons Gp of cos and others; *Style* - H A S Djanoghy Esq; Nottingham Manufacturing Co Ltd, Botany Avenue, Mansfield, Notts

DOBB, Erlam Stanley; CB (1963), TD; s of Arthur Erlam Dobb (d 1957); *b* 16 Aug 1910; *Educ* Ruthin and Univ Coll of N Wales; *m* 1937, Margaret, da of Percy Williams (d 1955); *Career* assist and Land Cmmr Min of Agriculture Fisheries and Food 1935-47, Agricultural Land Serv 1947-71, dir 1959-70, dir-gen ADAS 1973-75, gov Roy Agricultural Coll 1960-75, chm of trustees of Thomas Phillips Price Trust 1971-, memb Agricultural Research Cncl 1973-75; *Clubs* Farmers'; *Style* - Erlam Dobb Esq, CB, TD; Churchgate, Westerham, Kent (☎ 62294)

DOBB, Sidney; s of John Dobb (d 1953); *b* 5 Dec 1919; *Educ* The Brunts Sch Mansfield Notts; *m* 1947, Margaret, da of Arthur McIntosh; 2 s, 1 da; *Career* FICA, assist md The Marconi Co Ltd, assist md GEC-Marconi Electronics Ltd; *Recreations* walking, visiting family; *Style* - Sidney Dobb Esq; The Red House, 83 Galleywood rd, Great Baddow, Chelmsford, Essex (☎ Chelmsford (0245) 72205)

DOBIE, Brig Joseph Leo; CBE (1969); s of David Walter Dobie (d 1943); *b* 26 Sept 1914; *Educ* Tynemouth High Sch, Durham U and Military Coll of Science; *m* 1940, Joan Clare, da of Frank Watson; 1 s, 3 da; *Career* served WW II; Cmdt Army Apprentices' Sch Aborfield 1962-65, Insp of REME MOD 1966-69, External Relations Electrical Research Assoc and Marketing Exec Ltd 1970-74, dir External Activities IEE London 1974-79, exec Special Projects 1979-; *Style* - Brig Joseph Dobie, CBE; Findings, Tower rd, Hindhead, Surrey GU26 6ST (☎ Hindhead 5469)

DOBSON, Maj-Gen Anthony Henry George; CB (1967), OBE (1953), MC (1942); s of Col Arthur Curtis Dobson, DSO (d 1954); *b* 15 Dec 1911; *Educ* Cheltenham Coll, RMA Woolwich, Clare Coll Cambridge; *m* 1945, Nellie, nee Homberger; 2 s, 2 da; *Career* RE, commissioned 1931 (Maj-Gen 1964), Mid East 1940-42, POW 1942-44, NW Europe 1945, DQMG Br Army of the Rhine 1962-64, Ch Engr BAOR/Northern Army Gp 1964-67, ret 1967, Inspector Dept of Environment 1969-78; *Recreations* skiing, travel; *Clubs* Army & Navy, Ski Club of GB, Kandahar Ski, Lions Int; *Style* - Maj-Gen Anthony Dobson CB OBE MC; Ramillies, Compton Way, Farnham, Surrey (☎ Runfold 2350)

DOBSON, Hon Mrs (Anne Mary); *née* Hope; da of late 3 Baron Rankeillour; *b* 1936; *m* 1958, John Stephen Dobson; 1 s, 2 da; *Style* - The Hon Mrs Dobson; Papplewick Lodge, Notts

DOBSON, Christopher Selby Austin; CBE (1976); s of Alban Tabor Austin Dobson, CB, CVO, CBE (d 1962); *b* 25 Aug 1916; *Educ* Clifton Coll and Emmanuel Coll Cambridge; *m* 1941, Helen Broughton, da of Capt E Turner; 1 s, 1 da; *Career* assist Nat Cncl of Socl Serv 1938-39, Lt Middx regt 1940-46, temp princ Min of Educn 1946-47, assist librarian House of Lords 1947-56, librarian 1956-77, ret 1977; *Style* - Christopher Dobson Esq, CBE; Loxbeech, Mount st, Battle, E Sussex (☎ 4409)

DOBSON, Frank Gordon; MP (L) Holborn and St Pancras South, 1979-; s of James William Dobson; *b* 15 March 1940; *Educ* Archbishop Holgate's G S York, LSE; *m* 1967, Janet Mary Alker; 3 c; *Career* former administrator Central Electricity Council; asst sec Commn for Local Administration, 1975-79; *Style* - Frank Dobson Esq, MP; 2 Museum Chambers, Bury pla, WC1, (☎ 01 242 5760)

DOBSON, Cdre John Petter; CBE(1961), DSC(1940), RD(1940), RNR (ret); s of Lt-Cdr John Dobson, RNR; *b* 2 Sept 1901; *Educ* Middlesbrough H S, Liverpool Coll; *m* 1942, Edith Agnes Ferguson (d 1979); 1 da; *Career* RNR from 1917; Admiralty Berthing Officer, Sydney, Australia, 1944-45; in command CPS, 1946-61; Master, Empress of Canada (Canadian Pacific Steamships Ltd Flagship), 1961-62; ret; memb Hon Company of Master Mariners, Freeman and Liveryman of City of London ; *Style* - Commodore John Dobson, CBE, DSC, RD; Sea View Cottage, Sandsend, Whitby, N Yorks (☎ 222)

DOBSON, John Stephen; s of late John Dobson; *b* 19 July 1932; *Educ* Ampleforth; *m* 1958, Hon Anne Mary, nee Hope, da of late 3 Baron Rankeillour; 1 s, 2 da; *Career* High Sheriff of Notts 1975-76, textile mfr and co chm 1964-, Dist Councillor 1974-, JP 1962 *Style* - John Dobson Esq JP; Papplewick Lodge, Notts (☎ 0602 632975); 14 Fawcett rd, Aldeburgh, Suffolk; 209 Lillie rd, SW6 (☎ 01 385 4872)

DOBSON, Sir Richard (Portway); s of Prof John Frederic Dobson (d 1948); *b* 11 Feb 1914; *Educ* Clifton Coll and King's Coll Cambridge; *m* 1946, Emily Margaret, da of J R Herridge; 1 step da; *Career* served in China 1936-40, Fl-Lt RAF 1941-45 (pilot); with British-American Tobacco Co Ltd in China, Rhodesia and London 1946, dir 1955, chm 1970-76, pres 1976-79; dir Exxon Corpn, Davy Int 1975, Lloyds Bank Int 1976, non-exec chm British Leyland 1976-77; kt 1976; *Clubs* United Oxford and Cambridge University; *Style* - Sir Richard Dobson; 16 Marchmont rd, Richmond upon Thames, Surrey (☎ 01 940 1504)

DOCKER, Lady - Norah; *née* Collins; *m* 1949, as her 2 husband, Sir Bernard Dudley Frank Docker, KBE (d 1978); *Style* - Lady Docker; Rozel Bay, St Helier, Jersey, CI

DODD, Denis Featherstone; TD and Bar (1946); s of late Ralph Dodd; *b* 27 July 1914; *Educ* St Peters Sch York; *m* 1943, Emily Lavington, nee Lindsay; 1 s, 2 da; *Career* chartered accountant, former chm Concentric Ltd, British Rollmakers Corpn, Samuel Groves & Co Ltd; dir Johnson & Firth Brown Ltd, Leys Foundries & Engineering Ltd, chm Thomas Walker & Son Ltd; *Style* - Denis Dodd Esq, TD*; 2 Morningside, Sutton Coldfield, W Midlands; Braeside, Elgol, Broadford, Isle of Skye

DODD, Air V-Marshal Frank Leslie; CBE (1968), DSO (1944), DFC (1944), AFC (1943) and 2 bars (1955 and 1959); s of Frank Herbert Dodd (d 1944); *b* 5 March 1919; *Educ* King Edward VI Sch Stafford and Reading U; *m* 1942, Joyce Lilian, da of George Francis Banyard (d 1960); 1 s, 3 da; *Career* joined RAF 1938,

Photo-Recce Mosquitos 1944-45, station Cdr RAF Coningsby 1961-63, Cmdt Central Flying Sch 1965-68, Air Cdre 1966, dir RAF Establishments 1968-70, dir-gen Special Air Defence Project 1970-74, Air V-Marshal 1970, ret 1974; administrator MacRobert Trusts 1974-; *Clubs* Roy Northern, RAF *Style* - Air Vice-Marshal Frank Dodd CBE DSO DFC AFC**; The Lodge, Tarland, Aberdeen

DODD, Kenneth Arthur (Ken Dodd); s of Arthur Dodd; *b* 1931; *Educ* Holf H S Liverpool; *Career* singer, comedian, actor, entertainer; *Style* - Ken Dodd Esq; 76 Thomas Lane, Knotty Ash, Liverpool

DODD-NOBLE, Lady Elizabeth Theresa ; da of Hon Reginald Courtenay Boyle MBE MC (d 1946 before he could succeed to the Earldom of Cork and Orrery); *b* 1920; *m* 1947, Adrian Dodd-Noble; 4 s, 1 da; *Career* granted rank of an Earl's daughter 1967; *Style* - Lady Elizabeth Dodd-Noble; Rands, High Roding, Dunmow, Essex

DODDS, Sir Ralph Jordan; 2 Bt (UK 1964) of W Chiltington, co Sussex; s of Sir (Edward) Charles Dodds, 1 Bt, MVO, (d 1973); *b* 25 March 1928; *Educ* Winchester and RMA Sandhurst; *m* 1954, Marion, da of Sir Daniel Thomas Davies, KCVO (d 1966); 2 da; *Career* dir Stewart Wrightson (UK) Ltd 1973-, underwriting memb of Lloyd's 1964-; *Clubs* Cavalry; *Style* - Sir Ralph Dodds, Bt; Picton House, Thames Ditton, Surrey

DODSON, Hon Christopher Mark; s and h of 3 Baron Monk Bretton; *b* 2 Aug 1958; *Style* - The Hon Christopher Dodson

DODSON, Sir Derek Sherborne Lindsell; KCMG (1975, CMG 1953), MC (1945); s of Charles Sherborne Dodson, MD (d 1957); *b* 20 Jan 1920; *Educ* Stowe Sch, RMC Sandhurst; *m* 1952, Julie Maynard, da of Hon Maynard Bertram Barnes (d 1970); 1 s, 1 da; *Career* served 1939-48 in Roy Scots Fus, mil assist to British Cmmr Allied Control Cmmn for Bulgaria 1945-46, private sec to Min of State, Foreign Office 1955-58, consul at Elisabethville 1962-63, counsellor and consul-gen British Embassy Athens 1966-69, ambassador to Hungary 1970-73, to Brazil 1973-77, to Turkey 1977-80; *Clubs* Boodle's and Travellers'; *Style* - Sir Derek Dodson, KCMG, MC; Gable House, Leadenham, Lincoln (☎ Loveden 72212)

DODSON, Ernest; *Career* chm Readson Ltd, Hall & Earl Ltd, William Yates & Son Ltd, Wood Bros (Glossop) Hldgs Ltd, company director; *Style* - Ernest Dodson Esq; Readson Ltd, Orient House, Granby Row, Manchester M1 7AJ

DODSON, Hon Henry George Murray; s of 3 Baron Monk Bretton; *b* 11 Feb 1960 *Style* - The Hon Henry Dodson

DODSWORTH, Robert Leslie; s of Harold Dodsworth; *b* 7 Sept 1936; *Educ* Barnard Castle Sch, Durham U; *m* 1964, Hazel Joan, nee Moyse; 2 s; *Career* chartered accountant; md Ransomes, Sims & Jeffries Ltd, Ipswich 1977-; *Style* - Robert Dodsworth Esq; 223 Rushmere rd, Ipswich, Suffolk (☎ 74974)

DOIG, Lady (Imelda) Clare; *née* Feilding; da of late 10 Earl of Denbigh and Desmond; *b* 1941; *m* 1966, David Rodney Doig; 1 s, 2 da; *Style* - Lady Clare Doig; PO Box 441, Kiambu, Kenya

DOLIN, Sir Anton (Patrick Healey-Kay); s of H G Kay and Helen Maud Kay (nee Healey); *b* 27 July 1904; *Career* ballet dancer, choreographer; artistic dir Les Grands Ballets Canadiens Montreal, co-chm Ballet Dept Indiana U; kt 1980 *Style* - Sir Anton Dolin; 99 Madison st, New Bedford, Mass 02740 USA

DOLLEY, Christopher; s of of late Dr Leslie George Francis Dolley; *b* 11 Oct 1931; *Educ* Bancrofts Sch, CCC Cambridge; *m* 1966, Christine Elizabeth Cooper, 3 s; *Career* chm Penguin Books 1971-73 (formerly export man, dir, man dir), dir Book Dvpt IPC 1973-77, chm Damis Group Ltd 1974; *Style* - Christopher Dolley Esq,; Fulwood House, Bolton Avenue, Windsor, Berks (☎ 66961)

DOLLIMORE, Geoffrey Percival; CBE (1972); s of Herbert Noah Dollimore (d 1969); *b* 20 Sept 1924; *Educ* De Havilland Aeronautical Tech Sch; *m* 1948, Barbara Jessica, da of Francis Stephen Taylor (d

1968); 1 s, 1 da; *Career* ch engr Weapons, Hunting Percival Aircraft Ltd, tech dir Hunting Engrg Ltd 1962, md 1966, chm 1975-; dir Hunting Associated Industries Ltd 1970, chm Hunting Oilfield Servs Ltd 1970, dir Hunter Petroleum Servs Ltd; Liveryman Ironmongers Co; *Clubs* Athenaeum; *Style* - Geoffrey Dollimore Esq, CBE; 18 Box lane, Boxmoor, Hemel Hempstead, Herts (☎ 56256)

DOLLOND, Steven; s of Charles Dollond; *b* 28 Nov 1943; *Educ* Quintin Sch, Lincoln Coll Oxford, Harvard Business Sch (MBA); *Career* investment analyst; private office of Leader of the Opposition 1968-70, contested (C) Eton and Slough Feb and Oct 1974, management consultant Arthur D Little 1972-77, bd memb and marketing dir Nat Res Dvpt Corpn 1977-; *Recreations* politics; *Clubs* Carlton; *Style* - Steven Dollond Esq; 804 Grenville House, Dolphin sq, SW1 (☎ 01 834 3800)

DOMINGO, Rashid; s of late Achmat Domingo and Princess Vlei, of Cape Town *b* 24 June 1937; *Educ* Trafalgar H S Cape Town, Cape Town U; *m* 1962, Moreeda, nee Maureen Virginia Sheffers; 1 s, 1 da; *Career* production man Seravac Laboratories 1961-67, Miles Seravac Laboratories 1967-71, md Biozyme Laboratories Ltd 1971; *Style* - Rashid Domingo Esq; The Beeches, Pen-y-Pound, Abergavenny, Gwent (☎ 4652)

DOMVILLE, Sir (Gerald) Guy; 7 Bt (UK 1814) of St Albans, Hertfordshire; s of Rear-Adm Sir William Cecil Henry Domville 4 Bt, CB (d 1904) and bro of 5 Bt (d 1919) and 6 Bt (d 1930); *b* 3 March 1896; *Educ* Wellington Coll; *m* 1920 (m dis 1930), Beatrice Mary, da of Brig-Gen Robert Seymour Vandeleur, CB, CMG; *Heir* none; *Career* served in Gt War 1914-1919 as Lt RNVR, re-employed 1939-45; *Clubs* Roy Thames Yacht and Portland; *Style* - Sir Guy Domville, Bt; 60 Knightsbridge, SW1 (☎ 235 2121)

DON, Laurence; *Career* dep chm and jt md Bejam Gp, dir Bejam Gp of Cos, Chandos Press Ltd and others; *Style* - Laurence Don Esq; Bejam Group Ltd, 1 Garland rd, Honeypot Lane, Stanmore, Middx

DON, Stuart Warren; s of Stuart M Don (d 1931); *b* 14 Sept 1914; *Educ* Hotchkiss Sch, Princeton U; *m* 1938, Elsie Burke, da of Herbert Foster (d 1962); 3 da; *Career* Lt-Col US Army; exec recruitment John Courtis and Ptnrs 1976-, v-pres Chemical Bank NY Trust 1959-69, Chase Manhattan Bank 1954-59, dir American Chamber of Commerce (UK) 1958- (pres 1967-69), US/UK Educational Cmmn 1968-, trustee American Sch in London 1969-; *Reçreations* foxhunting; *Clubs* Boodle's, City of London, Bucks, American; *Style* - Stuart Don Esq; The Green, Kingham, Oxon; Orchard ct, Portman sq, London, W1 (☎ 935 6704)

DON-WAUCHOPE, Sir Patrick George; 10 Bt (NS 1667), of Newton; s of Patrick Hamilton Don-Wauchope, WS (d 1939), 3 s of 8 Bt; suc unc, Sir John Douglas Don-Wauchope, 9 Bt, 1951; *b* 7 May 1898; *Educ* Edinburgh Acad; *m* 1936 (m dis 1947), Ismay Lilian Ursula, da of S Hodges; 2 s; *Heir* s, Roger Hamilton Don-Wauchope; *Career* horticulturist (ret); served 1914-18 with RAF (France and Belgium, wounded, two medals), 1939-46 (Egypt and Italy); *Style* - Sir Patrick Don-Wauchope, Bt; Private Bag 729, Margate, Natal, S Africa

DON-WAUCHOPE, Roger Hamilton; s and h of Sir Patrick Don-Wauchope, 10 Bt; *b* 16 Oct 1938; *Educ* Hilton Coll Natal; *m* 1963, Sallee, da of Lt-Col Harold Mill-Colman, OBE, AMICE, of Durban; 2 s, 1 da; *Career* chartered accountant S Africa; *Style* - Roger Don-Wauchope Esq; Festival, 54 Haygarth rd, K100f 3600 Natal, S Africa

DONALD, Hon Mrs (Angela Caroline); da of Baron McFadzean (Life Peer); *b* 1942; *m* 1963, Robin Vyvyan Carter Donald; c; *Style* - The Hon Mrs Donald; Osborne House, Bathampton, Bath

DONALD, David Mitchell Cooke; *Career* chm Britannic Syndicate Ltd, Claverhouse Investment Trust Ltd, London and Holyrood Trust Ltd, Mercantile & General Reinsurance Co Ltd, dir Robert Fleming Hldgs Ltd and others; *Style* - David Donald Esq; Robert Fleming Holdings Ltd, 8 Crosby sq, EC3

DONALD, William; *Career* md William Donald Ltd; *Style* - William Donald Esq; William Donald Ltd, The Meat Factory, Portlethen, Aberdeen

DONALDSON OF KINGSBRIDGE, Baron (Life Peer UK 1967); John George Stuart Donaldson; OBE (1944); s of late Rev S A Donaldson, Master of Magdalene Coll Cambridge; *b* 9 Oct 1907; *Educ* Eton and Trinity Coll Cambridge; *m* 1935, Frances Annesley, da of Frederick Lonsdale; 1 s, 2 da; *Career* chm Nat Cncl for the Care and Resettlement of Offenders 1965-74, dir Roy Opera House, Covent Gdn 1958, dir Sadler's Wells Opera 1962, chm Fedn of Zoos 1971, Parly Under Sec State for N Ireland 1974-76, Min of State Dept of Educn and Science 1976-, chm Hotels Catering NEDO 1972; *Clubs* Brooks's; *Style* - The Rt Hon the Lord Donaldson of Kingsbridge, OBE; 1 Chalcot cres, NW1 (☎ 722 4695)

DONALDSON, Lady; Dorothy Mary; JP (Inner London 1960); da of Reginald George Gale Warwick; *b* 29 Aug 1921; *Educ* Portsmouth H S for Girls, Middx Hosp; *m* 1945, Rt Hon Lord Justice Donaldson; 1 s, 2 da; *Career* SRN, memb NE Thames RHA 1976-; Alderman City of London (Coleman Street Ward) 1975-, Sheriff 1981- (first woman Sheriff in the City's history); *Style* - Lady Donaldson JP

DONALDSON, Hamish; s of James Donaldson of Ferring, Sussex; *b* 13 June 1936; *Educ* Oundle, Christ's Cambridge; *m* 1965, Linda, da of Dr Leslie Challis Bousfield (d 1980); 3 da; *Career* Nat Service Cmmn Seaforth Highlanders Gibraltar 1955-57, Scottish area man De La Rue Bill Machines Ltd 1964-1966, management consultant and sr ptnr Urwick Dynamics Ltd 1966-73, dir/head of banking services Hill Samuel & Co Ltd 1978-81; author of *A Guide To The Successful Management of Computer Projects* (1978), *Designing A Distributed Processing System* (1979); *Recreations* amateur operatics, golf; *Style* - Hamish Donaldson Esq; Edgecombe Hill rd, Haslemere, Surrey (☎ 0428 4473)

DONALDSON, Rt Hon Lord Justice; Rt Hon Sir John Francis Donaldson; PC (1979); s of Malcolm Donaldson, FRCS, FRCOG, and Evelyn Maunsell; *b* 6 Oct 1920; *Educ* Charterhouse, Trin Cambridge; *m* 1945, Dorothy (*see* Lady Donaldson); 1 s, 2 da; *Career* served WW II Roy Signals; barr 1946, QC 1961, High Court Judge (Queen's Bench) 1966-79, Ld Justice of Appeal 1979-; *Style* - The Rt Hon Lord Justice Donaldson PC; Roy Courts of Justice, Strand, WC2 (☎ 01 450 7641/ (home) 637 9658)

DONALDSON, Hon Thomas Hay; s of Baron Donaldson of Kingsbridge, OBE (Life Peer); *b* 1 June 1936; *Educ* Eton, Cincinnati Ohio USA, Trinity Cambridge; *m* 1962, Natalie, nee Wadowsky; 1 s, 3 da; *Career* with Empire Trust Co, New York, 1958-62, W E Hutton and Co, New York, 1962-63, Morgan Guaranty Trust Co of New York, London Office, 1963-; *Style* - The Hon Thomas Donaldson; Cinderella Cottage, Village way, Little Chalfont, Bucks (02 404 2282)

DONALDSON, William J; *Career* chm Micrographix Pty Ltd South Africa, gen man Bell & Howell (European region), dir Bell & Howell Gp of Cos; *Style* - William Donaldson Esq; Bell & Howell Ltd, Alperton House, Bridgewater rd, Wembley, Middx

DONEGALL, 7 Marquess of (I 1791); Dermot Richard Claud Chichester; sits as Baron Fisherwick (GB 1790); also Viscount Chichester of Carrickfergus and Baron Chichester of Belfast (I 1625), Earl of Donegall (I 1647), Earl of Belfast (I 1791), Baron Templemore (UK 1831); Hereditary Lord High Admiral of Lough Neagh and Gov of Carrickfergus Castle; s of 4 Baron Templemore, PC, KCVO, DSO, OBE, DL, JP (d 1953) and Hon Clare, nee Wingfield, da of 7 Viscount Powerscourt; suc kinsman 6 Marq of Donegall 1975, having suc as 5 Baron Templemore 1953; *b* 18 April 1916; *Educ* Harrow, RMC; *m* 1946, Lady Josceline Legge, da of 7 Earl of Dartmouth, GCVO, TD (d 1958), and Lady Ruperta Wynn-Carrington (da of 1 & last Marquess of Lincolnshire), whereby Lady Donegall is 1 cous once removed to Lord Carrington, the

For Sec; 1 s, 2 da; *Heir* s, Earl of Belfast; *Career* 2 Lt 7 Hussars 1936, Maj 1944, one of HM Bodyguard, Hon Corps of Gentlemen at Arms 1966; *Clubs* Cavalry & Guards; *Style* - The Most Hon The Marquess of Donegall; Dunbrody Park, Arthurstown, Co Wexford, Eire (☎ Waterford 89104)

DONEGALL, Marchioness of; Lady Josceline Gabrielle; *née* Legge; da of late 7 Earl of Dartmouth; *b* 1918; *m* 1946, 7 Marquess of Donegall; *Career* First Aid Nursing Yeo; *Style* - The Most Hon the Marchioness of Donegall; Dunbrody Park, Arthurstown, Co Wexford, Eire

DONEGALL, Maureen, Marchioness of - Maureen; da of Maj Geoffrey Scholfield, MC; *m* 1, Douglas McKenzie; m 2, 1968, as his 2 wife, 6 Marquess of Donegall (d 1975); *Style* - The Most Hon Maureen, Marchioness of Donegall; 39 Clabon Mews, SW1

DONERAILE, 9 Viscount (I 1785); Richard St John St Leger; also Baron Doneraile (I 1776); s of 8 Viscount (d 1957); *b* 29 Oct 1923; *Educ* George Washington Sch; *m* 1945, Melva Jean Clifton; 3 s, 2 da *Heir* s, Hon Richard Allen St Leger; *Style* - The Rt Hon the Viscount Doneraile; 4002 West Flight st, Santa Ana, Calif, USA, 92744

DONNE, David Lucas; s of late Dr Cecil Lucas Donne; *b* 17 Aug 1925; *Educ* Stowe; *m* 1, 1957, Jennifer Margaret Duncan (d 1975); 2 s, 1 da; m 2, 1978, Claire, nee Yates; *Career* called to the Bar Middle Temple 1949, chm Dalgety 1977- (dep chm 1975-77), chm Crest Nicholson 1973-, William Lea 1972, dir M L Holdings, Royal Trust of Canada, Steetley (dep chm 1979-); *Style* - David Donne Esq; 99 Abbotsbury rd, Holland Park, W14

DONNE, Hon Sir Gaven John; KBE (1979); s of Jack Alfred Donne; *b* 8 May 1914; *Educ* Palmerston North Boys' H S, Hastings H S, Victoria U Wellington, Auckland U New Zealand; *m* 1946, Isabel Fenwick, nee Hall; 2 s, 2 da; *Career* called to the Bar and admitted slr 1938, Stipendiary Magistrate 1958-75, Puisne Judge Supreme Court of Western Samoa 1970-71, Ch Justice Western Samoa 1972-75, memb Court of Appeal of Western Samoa 1975, Ch Justice and Representative of the Queen in the Cook Islands 1975, Chief Justice of Niue 1974-; *Style* - The Hon Sir Gaven Donne, KBE; Otaramarae, Lake Rotoiti Rotorua, New Zealand; Govt House, Rarotonga, Cook Islands

DONNELLY, Maurice John; s of late Col James Donnelly; *b* 31 May 1933; *Educ* Stonyhurst, Durham U (BSc); *m* 1980, June, nee Donohue; 3 da; *Career* ch exec Lunesdale Farmers Ltd 1966-74, joined Tube Investments Subsidiary 1975, sales dir TI New World Ltd 1980; *Recreations* golf, squash; *Style* - Maurice Donnelly Esq; Eden Vale, Marine rd, Morecambe, Lancs (☎ 0524 415544)

DONNER, John Melville; s of Gerald Melville Donner and Pearl, da of late Sir Frank Sanderson, 1 Bt; *b* 18 July 1930; *Educ* Stowe, RMA Sandhurst; *m* 1952, Patricia Mary, nee Jenkins; 1 s, 1 da; *Career* Coldstream Gds 1948-53, entered Lloyd's 1955 (Arbon Langrish), elected memb 1964, dir Fenchurch Insurance Holding 1969, md 1969-74, chm Donner Underwriting Agencies Ltd 1977, J D Underwriting Ltd 1979 and R D Underwriting Agencies at Lloyd's 1980, Freeman of City of London 1977; *Recreations* old vehicles, gardening, walking, travel, food and wine; *Clubs* Carlton, Boodle's, Bentley Drivers; *Style* - John Donner Esq; 39 Bramerton st, SW3 (☎ 01 352 9964); Quarkhill, Crowcombe, Taunton

DONNET OF BALGAY, Baron (Life Peer UK 1978); Alexander Mitchell Donnet; CBE (1975); s of Alexander Mitchell Donnet; *b* 1916; *Educ* Harris Academy Dundee; *m* 1945, Mary, née Black; 2 s; *Career* Scottish sec National Union of General and Municipal Workers 1959-78, Nat chm of Union 1964-76, pres Scottish TUC 1977, chm Scottish Transport Gp 1978-; *Style* - The Rt Hon Lord Donnet of Balgay CBE; 8 Jordanhill dve, Glasgow G13

DONNET, Hon Stephen Christopher; s of Baron Donnet of Balgay (Life Peer); *b*

1960 *Style* - The Hon Stephen Donnet

DONNETT, Hon Gavin Alexander; s of Baron Donnet of Balgay (Life Peer); *b* 1950; *m* 1976, Margaret Louise Scott; *Style* - The Hon Gavin Donnett; 9 Scotscraig, Broughty Ferry, Dundee

DONOUGHMORE, 7 Earl of (I 1800); Col John Michael Henry Hely-Hutchinson; sits as Viscount Hutchinson of Knocklofty (UK 1821); also Baron Donoughmore of Knocklofty (I 1783) and Viscount Donoughmore of Knocklofty (I 1797, which Peerage has been confused with the style 'Viscount Suirdale', the eldest s & h of the Earls of Donoughmore being so designated since 1832); s of 6 Earl, KP, PC (d 1948); *b* 12 Nov 1902; *Educ* Winchester, Magdalen Oxford; *m* 1925, Dorothy Jean, MBE, da of late John Beaumont Hotham, gggs of Gen George Hotham, bro of 1 and 2 Barons Hotham; 2 s, 1 da; *Heir* s, Viscount Suirdale (*see* above); *Career* Col late Roy Armoured Corps (TA), former chm and dir Peruvian Corpn, MP (C) Peterborough Northants 1943-45, Grand Master Freemasons' Grand Lodge of Ireland 1964; *Style* - The Rt Hon Earl of Donoughmore; Knocklofty Grange, Clonmel, Co Tipperary, Eire

DONOUGHUE, Bernard; s of Thomas Donoughue and Maud Andrews; *b* 1934; *Educ* Northampton G S, Lincoln & Nuffield Colls Oxford; *m* 1959, Carol Goodman; 2 s, 2 da; *Career* journalist, formerly with The Economist, Sunday Times, Sunday Telegraph, now (1981-) Assist Ed (Policies) The Times; former Sr Lecturer & Reader LSE; Sr Policy Advsr to PM (Sir Harold Wilson, then James Callaghan) 1974-79; memb CS Coll Advsy Cncl, Advsy Bd Wissenschaftzentrum Berlin 1978; *Style* - Bernard Donoughue Esq; 7 Brookfield Park, NW5 (☎ 01 485 5427)

DONOVAN, Baroness Marjorie; *née* Murray; *m* 1925, Baron Donovan (Life Peer, d 1971); 2 s, 1 da; *Style* - The Rt Hon the Lady Donovan; Lamb Building, Temple, EC4

DONOVAN, Hon Hugh Desmond; s of Baron Donovan, PC (Life Peer, d 1971); *b* 23 Feb 1934; *Educ* Harrow, New Coll Oxford; *m* 1968, Margaret, da of Hugh Forbes Arbuthnott (ggs of 8 Viscount of Arbuthnott); 1 s; *Career* served RN as midshipman; barr; *Recreations* golf; *Clubs* Roy Wimbledon Golf; *Style* - The Hon Hugh Donovan; 40 Felden st, SW6 (☎ 01 731 4001)

DONOVAN, Hon John; s of Baron Donovan, PC (Life Peer, d 1971); *b* 3 July 1938; *Educ* Harrow, Univ Oxford; *m* 1973, Pauline Nicole Christine, nee Klene; *Style* - The Hon John Donovan; 23 Brook's Mews, W1

DONOVAN, John Edward; s of late Leslie Donovan, Maj RE; *b* 24 Sept 1930; *Educ* Wimbledon Coll; *m* 1957, Margaret Bridget, nee O'Brien; 1 s (twin); 2 da; *Career* Flying Offr RAF Nat Service, FCA, ATII, gp ch accountant London Weekend Television Ltd; *Recreations* badminton, music, reading; *Style* - John Donovan Esq; St Josephs, 56 Molesey Park rd, East Molesey, Surrey

DOOLITLE, Lieutenant General James Harold; Hon KCB (1945); s of Frank H Doolittle; *b* 14 Dec 1896; *Educ* Univ of California (AB); MIT (MS, ScD); *m* 1917, Josepine E Daniels; 2 s; *Career* former trustee, Aerospace Corpn (chm of Exec Comtee and vice-chm, Board of Trustees 1965-69); chm of board, Space Technology laboratories Inc 1959-62; dir Mutual of Omaha Insurance Co; United Benefit Life Insurance Co; *Style* - Lt-Gen James Doolittle, KCB; 1015 Cass, Suite 3, Monterey, California 93940, USA (☎ 408 373 3292)

DORCHESTER, Bishop Suffragan of 1979-; Rt Rev Conrad John Eustace Meyer; s of late William Eustace Meyer; *b* 2 July 1922; *Educ* Clifton Coll, Pembroke Coll Cambridge, Westcott House; *m* 1960, Mary, da of late Alec John Wiltshire; *Career* Lt (S) RNVR and later Chaplain RNVR; vicar of Devoran Truro 1954-64, Diocesan Youth Chaplain 1956-60, Diocesan Sec for Education 1960-69, Hon Canon of Truro 1960-69, Archdeacon of Bodmin 1969-79, Examining Chaplain to Bp of Truro 1973-79, Provost of Western Div of the Woodard Schs 1970-, chm Ctee for Mission SPCK; *Recreations* civil defence (memb Inst of Civil Defence), archaeology, swimming, walking; *Clubs* Roy C'wlth Soc; *Style* - The Rt Rev The Bishop of Dorchester; c/o Nat West Bank, Truro, Cornwall; Diocesan Church House, North Hinksey, Oxford

DORCHESTER, Baroness - Hon Kathleen; da of 6 and last Baron de Blaquiere (d 1920); *b* 17 Feb 1891; *m* 1911, 2 and last Baron Dorchester, OBE (d 1963); 2 da; *Style* - The Rt Hon Lady Dorchester; The Dower House, Greywell, Basingstoke, Hants (☎ Odiham 2184)

DORMAN, Lt-Col Sir Charles Geoffrey; 3 Bt (UK 1923), of Nunthorpe, York, MC (1942); s of Sir Bedford Lockwood Dorman, 2 Bt, CBE (d 1956); *b* 18 Sept 1920; *Educ* Rugby, BNC Oxford; *m* 1954 (m dis 1972), Elizabeth Ann (CStJ), da of late George Gilmour Gilmour-White, OBE, JP; 1 da; *Heir* kinsman, Philip Dorman; *Career* Capt 13/18 Roy Hussars 1947, Maj 1954, Lt-Col 1961, GSO (1) (ADSR) AORE 1961-64, GSOI (W), IFVME 1964, ret 1970; *Style* - Lt-Col Sir Charles Dorman, Bt, MC; Hutton Grange, Gt Rollright, Chipping Norton, Oxon (☎ Hook Norton 737535)

DORMAN , Philip Henry Keppel; s of late Richard Dorman, gs of 1 Bt; hp of kinsman, Sir Charles Dorman, 3 Bt, MC; *b* 19 May 1954; *Educ* Marlborough; *Style* - Philip Dorman Esq

DORMER, 16 Baron (E 1615); Sir Joseph Spencer Philip Dormer; 16 Bt (E 1615); s of 14 Baron Dormer, CBE (d 1922) and bro of 15 Baron Dormer (d 1975); *b* 4 Sept 1914; *Educ* Ampleforth and Ch Ch Oxford; *Heir* cous, Robert Francis Edward Baptist Dormer; *Career* late Capt Scots Gds; *Style* - The Rt Hon the Lord Dormer; Grove Park, Warwick, Orchard Hill, Pershore, Worcs

DORMER, Baroness - Lady Maureen Thérèse Josephine; *née* Noel; da of 4 Earl of Gainsborough; *b* 1917; *m* 1944, 15 Baron Dormer (d 1975); 2 da (Hon Mrs Meek, Hon Catherine Dormer); *Style* - The Rt Hon Lady Dormer; 12 Campden House Court, Gloucester Walk, W8 (☎ 01 937 0310); Grove Park, Warwick

DORMER, Hon Rosamund Jane; da of 14 Baron Dormer, CBE (d 1922); *b* 1911; *Career* Jr Cdr ATS 1942; JP(1948) Warwicks; *Style* - The Hon Rosamund Dormer, JP; Ridgeacre Farm, Broad Green, Worcs

DORNHORST, Antony Clifford; CBE (1977) MD; s of Ernst Dornhurst; *b* 2 April 1915; *Educ* St Clement Danes Sch; St Thomas's Hospital Medical Sch; MB, BS, MD, FRCP; *m* 1946, Helen Mary Innes; 3 da; *Career* Prof of Medicine, St George's Hospital Medical Sch from 1959; civilian consultant in Aviation Medicine to RAF from 1973; *Style* - Prof Antony Dornhorst CBE; 8 Albert Place, W8 (☎ 01 937 8782)

DORRELL, Stephen James; MP (C) Loughborough 1979-; *Educ* Uppingham, Brasenose Oxford; *Career* personal asst to Rt Hon Peter Walker MP 1974; export dir family clothing firm; fought (C) Kingston-upon-Hull East 1974 *Style* - Stephen Dorrell Esq MP; House of Commons, SWI

DOTRICE, Roy; *b* 26 May 1925; *Educ* Dayton Sch and Intermediate Sch, Guernsey; *m* 1946, Kay Newman; 3 da; *Career* actor, Royal Shakespeare Co; performances at Aldwych, Chichester Festival Shakespeare Theatre, Criterion (Brief Lives, 1969), Broadway, amongst others; *Style* - Roy Dotrice Esq; Talbot House, St Martin's Lane, WC2

DOUBLEDAY, Lt-Col Garth Leslie; TD (1950), JP (Kent 1956), DL (1965); s of Sir Leslie Doubleday (d 1975); *b* 13 July 1913; *Educ* Charterhouse and Clare Coll Cambridge; *m* 1946, May Alison, da of Frank Hann; 3 s, 3 da; *Career* served 1939-45 War with RA (Middle E), Cdr 516 LAA regt (TA) 1949-52, High Sheriff 1976-77, master of Fruiterers Co 1968, gen cmmr of Income Tax 1970; *Clubs* Farmers' and MCC; *Style* - Lt-Col Garth Doubleday, TD, JP, DL; Rodmersham House, Rodmersham, Sittingbourne, Kent (☎ Sittingbourne 23545)

DOUBLEDAY, John Gordon; OBE (1975); s of late Douglas Collins

Doubleday; *b* 27 Nov 1920; *Educ* Bedford Sch; St John's Coll Camb; *m* 1961, Ruth Helen, nee Walls; 1 s, 2 da; *Career* entered HM Diplomatic Service, 1965; dep British High Commr Bahamas, 1973-76; dep British High Commr, Sri Lanka, 1976-78; HM Ambassador to Liberia from 1978; *Style* - John Doubleday Esq, OBE; Foreign and Commonwealth Office, SW1

DOUGHERTY, Maj-Gen Sir Ivan Noel; CBE (1946), DSO (1941) and Bar (1943), ED; *b* 6 April 1907; *Educ* Mudgee HS, Sydney Teachers' Coll, Univ of Sydney; *m* 1936, Emily Phyllis nee Lofts; 2 s 2 da (and 1 c decd); *Career* Maj-Gen AIF 1939-45 (North Africa, Greece, Crete, Southwest Pacific), educationist with New South Wales Dept of Education 1928-55 (inc headmaster 1946-47, insp of schools 1948-53, staff insp 1953-55), dir of Civil Defence for NSW 1955-73, kt 1968; *Clubs* Imperial Service Club (Sydney, Australia); *Style* - Major-General Sir Ivan Dougherty CBE DSO* ED; 4 Leumeah Street, Cronulla, New South Wales 2230, Australia (☎ 523-5465)

DOUGHTY, Peter Harford; *Career* dir Magnet & Southerns Ltd, Southern Evans gp of cos, Andersons (Denton Holme) Ltd and others; *Style* - Peter Doughty Esq; Magnet & Southerns Ltd, 128 Queen Victoria st, EC4

DOUGHTY, Roy Leslie; *Career* chm Marshall's Universal Ltd, chm and md London Wall Gp of Unit Trust Ltd, md Ridgefield Management Ltd, Highclere Investments Ltd; *Style* - Roy Doughty Esq; Universal Ltd, 468/472 Purley Way, Croydon, Surrey

DOUGHTY, William Roland; *Career* chm Cape Building and Insulation Services Ltd, Cape Insulation Ltd, md Cape Industries Ltd, dir Cape Gp of Cos; *Style* - William Doughty Esq; Cape Industries Ltd, 114 Park st, London, W1

DOUGLAS, Lady Alice; da (by 1 m) of 12 Marquess of Queensberry; *b* 23 July 1965 *Style* - Lady Alice Douglas

DOUGLAS, Mrs Kingman; Adèle; da of Frederic E Astaire and sis of Fred, the dancer, singer and actor; she too was a celebrated dancer; *m* 1, 1932, Lord Charles Cavendish (d 1944), 2 s of 9 Duke of Devonshire, KG, GCMG, GCVO, PC, JP, DL, by Lady Evelyn Fitzmaurice, GCVO, JP, er da of 5 Marquess of Lansdowne, KG; 1 da decd; m 2, 1947, Kingman Douglas, investment banker, of New York (d 1971); *Style* - Mrs Kingman Douglas; 41 Biltmore Estates, Phoenix, Arizona 85016, USA

DOUGLAS OF BARLOCH, Baroness; Adela Elizabeth; da of George Derbridge, DD; *m* 1, Capt George La Croix Baudains, DSO, MC; *m* 2, 1971, as his 2nd wife, 1 Baron Douglas of Barloch (d 1980, when title became extinct); 1 da (Hon Mrs Ulyatt); *Style* - The Rt Hon The Lady Douglas of Barloch; 73 Cambridge Mansions, SW11; Mayfield Manor, Three Oaks, Hastings, Sussex

DOUGLAS, Hon Mrs Charles (Florence); *née* Timson; *m* 1926, as his 2nd wife, Hon Charles William Sholto Douglas (d 1960); 1 s (present Earl of Morton); *Style* - The Hon Mrs Charles Douglas; Backbridge, Malmesbury, Wilts

DOUGLAS, Lady Emma; da (by 1 m) of 12 Marquess of Queensberry; *b* 1956; *Style* - Lady Emma Douglas

DOUGLAS, Hon Mrs (Ethel Georgiana Frances); *née* Somerset; da of 3 Baron Raglan, GBE, CB, and Lady Ethel Ponsonby (da of 7 Earl of Bessborough); *b* 4 June 1889; *m* 1914, Hon William Sholto Douglas (d 1932), s of 19 Earl of Morton; 3 s, 1 da; *Style* - The Hon Mrs Douglas; Carlton Old Hall, Lincoln

DOUGLAS, Lord Gawain Archibald; s of 11 Marquess of Queensberry (d 1954); *b* 1948; *Educ* Downside, Royal Acad of Music; *m* 1971, Nicolette Eustace; 2 s, 3 da; *Style* - Lord Gawain Douglas; 10 Archery sq, Walmer, Deal, Kent

DOUGLAS, Gavin Stuart; RD (1970), QC (Scot 1971); s of late Gilbert Georgeson Douglas; *b* 12 June 1932; *Educ* South Morningside Sch, George Heriot's

Sch, Edinburgh U (MA, LLB); *Career* Hon Sheriff, 1965-71; chm of Industrial Tribunals, 1966-78; Counsel to Sec of Scotland under Private Legislation Procedure (Scotland) Act, 1936, 1969-75; Senior Counsel, 1975-; ed, Session Cases, 1977-; *Style* - Gavin Douglas Esq RD QC; Parliament House, Parliament sq, Edinburgh 1

DOUGLAS OF KIRTLESIDE, Baroness; Hazel; da of late George Eric Maas Walker and widow of Capt W E R Walker; *m* 2, 1955, as his 3 wife, 1 Baron Douglas of Kirtleside (d 1969, when title became extinct); 1 da (Hon Katharine Douglas); *Style* - The Rt Hon the Lady Douglas of Kirtleside,; Misbourne Cottage, Denham Village, Bucks

DOUGLAS, John Robert Tomkys; s of Sir Robert McCallum Douglas, OBE, Hon DSc; *b* 24 July 1930; *Educ* Oundle Sch, Birmingham U; *m* 1957, Sheila Margaret, nee Varey; 2 s, 1 da; *Career* civil engineer; chm Robert M Douglas Hldgs Ltd 1977 (md 1976), chm R M Douglas Construction Ltd 1977 (md 1975), dir Douglas Gp of Cos, dep chm Rapid Metal Developments Ltd; *Recreations* sailing, skiing, music; *Clubs* Caledonian, Roy Engineer Yacht, The Birmingham; *Style* - John Douglas Esq; Criffel, 12 Digby rd, Sutton Coldfield, W Midlands (☎ 021 355 1515)

DOUGLAS, Kenneth; *b* 28 Oct 1920; *Educ* Sunderland Technical Coll; *m* 1942, Doris Lewer; 1 s, 2 da; *Career* dep chm Govan Shipbuilders 1971-73; chm Douglas (Kilbride) Ltd 1972-77; chm and md Steel Structures Ltd 1974-76; ship repair marketing dir British Shipbuilders 1978-79; md Austin and Pickersgill Ld 1979-; chm Kenton Shipping Services, Darlington 1968-; *Style* - Kenneth Douglas Esq; 20 Thornholme rd, Sunderland, Tyne & Wear

DOUGLAS, Hon Katharine Ann; da of 1 and last Baron Douglas of Kirtleside; *b* 1957; *Style* - The Hon Katharine Douglas

DOUGLAS, Lady Kate Cordelia Sasha; da (by 2 m) of 12 Marq of Queensberry; *b* 1969 *Style* - Lady Kate Douglas

DOUGLAS, Lord Milo Luke Dickon; s (by 2 m) of 12 Marquess of Queensberry; *b* 1978; *Style* - Lord Milo Douglas

DOUGLAS, Sir Robert (McCallum); s of John Douglas; *b* 2 Feb 1899; *Educ* Terregles Sch, Dumfries Acad; *m* 1927, Millicent Irene Tomkeys Morgan (d 1980); 1 s, 2 da; *Career* dir Robert M Douglas Hldgs 1930-; kt 1976; *Style* - Sir Robert Douglas; Dunstall Hall, Barton-under-Needwood, Burton-on-Trent, Staffs (☎ Barton-under-Needwood 2471)

DOUGLAS, Sir (Edward) Sholto; s of Hon Mr Justice E A Douglas; *b* 23 Dec 1909; *Educ* St Ignatius Coll Sydney; *m* 1939, Mary Constance Curr; *Career* Solicitor of the Supreme Court of Queensland 1934-, kt 1977; *Style* - Sir Sholto Douglas; 81 Markwell st, Hamilton, Brisbane, Queensland 4007, Australia (☎ 268.2759)

DOUGLAS, Sir Sholto Courtenay Mackenzie; 5 Bt (UK 1831), of Glenbervie, Kincardine, MC; s of late Donald Sholto Mackenzie Douglas, s of late Capt Donald Douglas, 6 s of 1 Bt; suc kinsman, Sir Kenneth Douglas, 4 Bt, 1954; *b* 27 June 1890; *m* 1929 (m dis 1959), Lorna Tichborne, da of Capt Hugh Nangle; 2 da; *Heir* none; *Career* Capt Seaforth Highlanders WW I (MC), re-employed 1939-45; *Style* - Sir Sholto Douglas, Bt, MC; 192 Cooden dve, Cooden, Sussex (☎ 2389)

DOUGLAS AND CLYDESDALE, Marquess of; Alexander Douglas Douglas-Hamilton; s and h of 15 Duke of Hamilton; *b* 31 March 1978; *Style* - Marquess of Douglas and Clydesale

DOUGLAS-HAMILTON, Lady Anne; da of 15 Duke of Hamilton; *b* 1976

DOUGLAS-HAMILTON, Lord David Stephen; s of late 14 Duke of Hamilton; *b* 1952; *Educ* Eton; *Style* - Lord David Douglas-Hamilton

DOUGLAS-HAMILTON, Lady Eleanor; da of 15 Duke of Hamilton; *b* 1973

DOUGLAS-HAMILTON, Lord Hugh

Malcolm; s of 14 Duke of Hamilton; *b* 1946; *Educ* Eton; *m* 1971, June Mary Curtis; 1 s, 1 da; *Style* - Lord Hugh Douglas-Hamilton; Begbie Farmhouse, Haddington, E Lothian

DOUGLAS-HAMILTON, Lady James A; Hon Priscilla Susan; *née* Buchan; da of 2 Baron Tweedsmuir, CBE, CD; *b* 1949; *m* 1974, Lord James Alexander Douglas-Hamilton, MP; 1 s; *Style* - Lady James A Douglas-Hamilton; 3 Blackie House, Lady Stair's Close, Edinburgh (☎ 031 225 1482)

DOUGLAS-HAMILTON, Lord Patrick George; s of 14 Duke of Hamilton; *b* 1950; *Style* - Lord Patrick Douglas-Hamilton; 107 Eaton sq, SW1; Lennoxlove, Haddington, E Lothian (☎ 2156)

DOUGLAS-HOME, Hon (Lavinia) Caroline; da of Lord Home of the Hirsel, KT, PC; *b* 11 Oct 1937; *Career* a woman of the bedchamber (temp) to HM Queen Elizabeth, the Queen Mother 1963-65, a lady-in-waiting (temp) to HRH the Duchess of Kent 1966-67, since when extra lady-in-waiting; *Style* - The Hon Caroline Douglas-Home; Castlemains, Douglas, Lanarkshire; The Hirsel, Coldstream, Berwickshire (☎ 2345)

DOUGLAS-HOME, Charles Cospatrick; s of late Hon Henry Douglas-Home (s of late 13 Earl of Home and Lady Lilian, nee Lambton, da of 4 Earl of Durham) by 1 w, Lady Margaret Spencer, da of 6 Earl Spencer; *b* 1 Sept 1937; *Educ* Eton; *m* 1966, Jessica Violet Gwynne; 2 s; *Career* military correspondent, then political and diplomatic correspondent, Daily Express, 1961-64; foreign ed, The Times, 1978-81, dep ed 1981- (formerly defence correspondent, features ed, home ed); *Style* - Charles Douglas-Home Esq; 18 Mortimer cresc, NW6 (☎ 01 624 6424)

DOUGLAS-HOME, Hon David Alexander Cospatrick; s of Baron Home of the Hirsel and h to Earldom of Home (disclaimed by his father, 1963); *b* 20 Nov 1943; *Educ* Eton, Ch Ch Oxford; *m* 1972, Jane Margaret, nee Williams-Wynne; 1 da; *Career* dir Morgan Grenfell & Co Ltd, 1974-, Morgan Grenfell (Asia) Ltd (deputy chairman, 1979-), Morgan Grenfell (Scotland), 1978-; *Style* - The Hon David Douglas-Home; 11 Moore Street, Chelsea, London SW3

DOUGLAS-HOME, Hon Dinah Lilian; da of Baroness Dacre and Hon William Douglas-Home; *b* 22 Jan 1964; *Style* - The Hon Dinah Douglas-Home; c/o The Rt Hon Lady Dacre, Drayton House, East Meon, Hants

DOUGLAS-HOME, Hon Edward Charles; s of 14 Earl of Home, KT, TD (d 1951); *b* 1920; *Educ* Eton; *m* 1946, Nancy Rose, da of Sir Thomas D Straker-Smith; 3 s; *Career* 2 Lt 155 Field Regt RA; *Style* - The Hon Edward Douglas-Home; Westnewton, Kirknewton, Wooler, Northumberland

DOUGLAS-HOME, Hon Gian Leila; da of Baroness Dacre and Hon William Douglas-Home; *b* 23 June 1958; *Style* - The Hon Gian Douglas-Home; c/o The Rt Hon Lady Dacre, Drayton House, East Meon, Hants

DOUGLAS-HOME, Hon James Thomas Archibald; s of Hon William Douglas-Home and Baroness Dacre and h to the Barony of Dacre; *b* 16 May 1952; *Style* - The Hon James Douglas-Home; Drayton House, East Meon, Hants

DOUGLAS-HOME, Lady (Alexandra) Margaret Elizabeth; da of late 6 Earl Spencer; *b* 1906; *m* 1931 (m dis 1947), Maj Hon Henry Montagu Douglas-Home (d 1980); 2 s (1 decd), 1 da; *Style* - Lady Margaret Douglas-Home; Trimmers, Burnham Market, King's Lynn, Norfolk (☎ Burnham Market 243)

DOUGLAS-HOME, Hon William; s of 13 Earl of Home, KT, TD (d 1951); *b* 3 June 1912; *Educ* Eton and New Coll Oxford; *m* 1951, Baroness Dacre, *qv*; 1 s, 3 da; *Career* 2 Lt The Buffs 1941, Capt 1943; author and playwright; *Style* - The Hon William Douglas-Home; Drayton House, East Meon, Hampshire (☎ East Meon (STD Code 073 087) 250)

DOUGLAS-PENNANT, Hon Eileen Maud; da of 5 Baron Penrhyn; *b* 1901 *Style* - The Hon Eileen Douglas-Pennant

DOUGLAS-PENNANT, Hon Gillian Francis; da of 6 Baron Penrhyn; *b* 1955 *Style* - The Hon Gillian Douglas-Pennant

DOUGLAS-PENNANT, Lady Janet Marcia Rose; da of 6 Earl of Yarborough; *b* 1923; *m* 1948, John Charles, s of Sir Charles Harper KBE CMG; John changed his surname to Douglas-Pennant by Roy Licence 1950; 2 s *Style* - Lady Janet Douglas-Pennant; Penrhyn, Bangor, N Wales

DOUGLAS-PENNANT, Hon Nigel; s of 5 Baron Penrhyn (d 1967), and hp of bro, 6 Baron Penrhyn, DSO, MBE; *b* 22 Dec 1901; *Educ* Eton, Clare Cambridge; *m* 1, 1935, Margaret Kirkham (d 1938); 1 s; m 2, 1940, Eleanor Craig; 1 s, 1 da; *Career* late Maj RM; *Style* - The Hon Nigel Douglas-Pennant; Brook House, Glensford, Sudbury, Suffolk

DOUGLAS-PENNANT, Hon Rosemary; da of 6 Baron Penrhyn; *b* 1957 *Style* - Hon Rosemary Douglas-Pennant

DOUGLAS-PENNANT, Lady; Sheila; *née* Brotherhood; *m* 1, 1937, as his 2 w, Adm Hon Sir Cyril Douglas-Pennant KCB CBE DSO DSC (d 1961, s of 5 Baron Penrhyn); m 2, 1972 (m dis 1977), as his 3 w, Sir Marshall Warmington, 3 Bt *Career* resumed name Douglas-Pennant 1977; OStJ 1980 *Style* - Lady Douglas-Pennant; Itchen Abbas Lodge, Winchester, Hants

DOUGLAS-PENNANT, Hon Susan Victoria; da of 5 Baron Penrhyn; *b* 1918 *Style* - The Hon Susan Douglas-Pennant

DOUGLAS-SCOTT-MONTAGU, Hon Jonathan Deane; s of 3 Baron Montagu of Beaulieu by his 2 w Fiona; *b* 1975; *Style* - Hon Jonathan Douglas-Scott-Montagu

DOUGLAS-SCOTT-MONTAGU, Hon Mary Rachel; da of 3 Baron Montagu of Beaulieu; *b* 1964 *Style* - The Hon Mary Douglas-Scott-Montagu

DOUGLAS-SCOTT-MONTAGU, Hon Ralph; s (by 1 m) and h of 3 Baron Montagu of Beaulieu; *b* 13 March 1961; *Style* - The Hon Ralph Douglas-Scott-Montagu

DOUGLASS OF CLEVELAND, Baroness; Edith; da of Charles Amer; *m* 1926, Baron Douglass of Cleveland (Life Peer, d 1978); 1 da (Hon Mrs Long); *Style* - The Rt Hon Lady Douglass of Cleveland; 5 The Chase, Stanmore, Middx

DOUNE, Lord; John Douglas Stuart; s and h of 20 Earl of Moray; *b* 29 Aug 1966; *Style* - Lord Doune

DOURO, Marquess of; Arthur Charles Valerian Wellesley; MEP (C) Surrey 1979-; s and h of 8 Duke of Wellington; *b* 19 Aug 1945; *Educ* Eton, Ch Ch Oxford; *m* 1977, HRH Princess Antonia, da of HRH Prince Frederick von Preussen (d 1966, s of HIH Crown Prince Wilhelm, himself s and h of Kaiser Wilhelm II and technically Kaiser for three days 28 Nov to 1 Dec 1918, known more familiarly in the UK as Crown Prince Willi, the celebrated Col in Chief of the Death's Head Hussars) by Lady Brigid Ness, *qv*, and 3 cous once removed to HM The Queen; 1 s, 1 da; *Heir* s, Earl of Mornington; *Career* dep chm Thames Valley B'dcasting, dir Eucalyptus Pulp Mills; contested (C) Islington N 1974; *Style* - Marquess of Douro, MEP; The Rectory, Stratfield Saye, Reading; Apsley House, Piccadilly, W1

DOVE, Maj-Gen Arthur Julian Hadfield; CB (1948), CBE (1946, MBE 1937); s of Rev Julian Llewellyn Dove (d 1948); *b* 25 Aug 1902; *Educ* Haileybury Coll, RMA Woolwich; *m* 1948, Betty Eyre Godson, da of Roderick George Bartholomew (d 1969); 1 da; *Career* 2 Lt RE 1922, served Palestine 1936-38, France 1940; Col 1946, ch engr Combined Operations 1943-44, dep dir Mil Operations 1944-48, mil rep Peace Conference Paris 1946, dir of Quartering 1954-57, Maj-Gen 1955, ret 1957; tech dir FBI 1957-61; *Clubs* Roy Commonwealth Soc; *Style* - Maj-Gen Arthur Dove, CB, CBE; Moors Farm, Flanchford rd, Reigate, Surrey (☎ Reigate 45436)

DOVE, Hon Mrs - Hon Elizabeth; *née*

Carington; da of late 5 Baron Carrington; *b* 1917; *m* 1943, William Lionel Dove; 2 s; *Style* - The Hon Mrs Dove; Elm House, Childwall, Liverpool 16, Lancs

DOVE, Ernest Baker; s of Ernest Jasper Dove (d 1960); *b* 1 March 1917; *Educ* Wandsworth Tech Coll, Battersea Polytechnic; *m* 1940, Margaret Yvonne, nee Baxter; 1 s (Peter Ernest m 1965), 1 da (Janet Lillian Rosemary m 1970); *Career* design engineer, tech dir Teleflex and Teleflex Morse (ch designer 1956-62, ch engineer 1962-64); *Recreations* art, yachting; *Style* - Ernest Dove Esq; 6 Thorney rd, Capel St Mary, Ipswich, Suffolk (☎ 310 890)

DOVE, Leonard Ernest; CBE (1969); s of Alfred Dove (d 1955); *b* 10 Feb 1913; *Educ* Wilson's Grammar Sch Camberwell; *m* 1938, Florence May, da of William Humphrey Shipley (d 1942); 1 s (& 1 decd), 2 da *Career* accountant & comptroller Gen Bd Customs & Excise 1963-73, hon tres Methodist Church Overseas Div 1972- *Style* - Leonard Dove Esq CBE; 23 Stambourne Way, W Wickham, Kent (☎ 777 5213)

DOVENER, John Montague; QC (1972); s of John Reginald Dovener (d 1942); *b* 7 Dec 1923; *Educ* Shrewsbury; *m* 1973, Shirley, da of Phillip Don (d 1975); *Career* barr Middle Temple 1953; au under pseudonym Montague Jon; *Style* - John Dovener Esq, QC; 2 Pump ct, Temple, EC4Y 7AH (☎ 353 3106)

DOVER, Den (Denshore); MP(C) Chorley, 1979-; *b* 4 April 1938; *Educ* Manchester G S, Manchester U; *m* 1959, Anne Marina Wright; 1 s, 1 da; *Career* contracts man Wimpey Laing Iran, 1975-77; dir of Housing Construction GLC, 1977-79; *Style* - Den Dover Esq, MP; 30 Countess way, Euxton , Chorley, Lancs

DOVER, Sir Kenneth James; s of P H J Dover; *b* 11 Mar 1920; *Educ* St Paul's Sch, Balliol Oxford (MA, DLitt); *m* 1947, Audrey Ruth Latimer; 1 s, 1 da; *Career* former Dean of the Faculty of Arts and Professor of Greek, St Andrews U; Pres CCC Oxford 1976-, kt 1977; Pres British Academy, 1978-; *Style* - Sir Kenneth Dover; Corpus Christi College, Oxford (☎ 42950)

DOW, Hon Mrs (Jessica Catherine); da of late 2 Baron Stamp; *b* 1936; *Educ* London U (BA); *m* 1961, John Edward Chalmers Dow; 2 da; *Style* - The Hon Mrs Dow; 21 Chemin de la Fontanettaz, 1012 Pully/Lausanne, Switzerland

DOWDESWELL, Lt-Col John Windsor; MC (1943), TD (1947), DL (Tyne & Wear 1976); s of Maj Thomas Dowdeswell (d 1967); *b* 11 June 1920; *Educ* Malvern Coll; *m* 1948, Phyllis Audrey, da of Donald Gomersal Horsfield (d 1972); 1 s, 1 da; *Career* War serv with RA, 50 Div; chm Engineering Co 1979- (md 1960-63); magistrate Gateshead 1955-; *Style* - Lt-Col John Dowdeswell, MC, TD, DL; 40 Oakfield rd, Gosforth, Newcastle, NE3 4HS (☎ 852196)

DOWDING, Baron (Life Peer UK 1943); Wing Cdr Derek Hugh Tremenheere Dowding; s of Air Chief Marshal 1 Baron Dowding, GCB, GCVO, CMG (d 1970); *b* 9 Jan 1919; *Educ* Winchester, Cranwell; *m* 1, 1940 (m dis 1946), Joan Myrle, da of Donald Stuart, of Nairn; m 2, 1947 (m dis 1960), Alison, da of Dr James Bannerman, of Norwich; 2 s; m 3, 1961, Mrs Odette Hughes, da of Louis Houles; *Heir* s, Hon Piers Dowding; *Career* Pilot Offr 1939 74 (F) Sqdn; UK, M East WW II; CO No 49 Sqdn 1950, Wing Cdr 1951; *Style* - Wing Commander The Rt Hon The Lord Dowding; 501 Gilbert House, Barbican, London EC2 (☎ 01 628 8547)

DOWDING, Muriel, Baroness; Muriel; da of late John Albino; *Educ* Walthamstow Hall Sevenoaks and Convent of the Holy Child Sussex, *m* 1, 1935, Maxwell Whiting (ka 1944); 1 s; m 2, 1951, as his 2 w, Air Ch Marshal 1 Baron Dowding, GCB, GCVO (d 1970); *Career* pres Nat Anti-Vivisection Soc, trustee of Ferne Animal Sanctuary, pres Nat Animal Rescue Kennels, hon tres Int Assoc Against Painful Experiments on Animals, founder and chm Beauty Without Cruelty; *Style* - The Rt Hon Muriel, Lady

Dowding; 1 Calverley Park, Tunbridge Wells, Kent (☎ 28812)

DOWDING, Hon Mark Denis James; s of 2 Baron Dowding; *b* 1949 *Style* - The Hon Mark Dowding

DOWDING, Michael Frederick; CBE (1973); s of Guy Francis Dowding (d 1947); *b* 19 Nov 1918; *Educ* Westminster, Magdalene Cambridge; *m* 1947, Rosemary, da of Somerville Hastings; 1 s, 2 da; *Career* served WW II as Maj RA in NW Europe (despatches); engrg and sales dir Davy United Eng Co Ltd 1951-59 and md 1961-64; independent consulting engr and dir Davy Loewy Ltd 1972-, chm Michael Dowding Assocs Ltd, consulting engineers, dir Ashmore Benson Pease Ltd, James Armstrong and Co Ltd,Rolair (UK) Ltd, NM Rothschild and Sons Int Ltd 1979-; *Style* - Michael Dowding Esq, CBE; Bod Isaf Farm, Aberdaron, Gwynnedd; 55 Drayton gdns, SW10 (☎ 01 373 0380)

DOWDING, Hon Piers Hugh Tremenheere; s & h of 2 Baron Dowding; *b* 18 Feb 1948; *Educ* Fettes; *Style* - The Hon Piers Dowding

DOWLEN, A D; *Career* md C T Bowring (Insurance) Hldgs Ltd; Queen's Award Export 1977; *Style* - A Dowlen Esq

DOWLEY, Laurence Edward; *Career* CA; md USMC Int Ltd, dir and pres-USM Int Finance Corpn Delaware, USA and USM Overseas Capital Corpn NV, Netherlands Antilles; dir Mobbs Miller Ltd; *Style* - Laurence Dowley Esq; USMC Int Ltd, PO Box 88, British United House, Belgrave rd, Leicester

DOWLING, Sir Hallam (Walter); KBE (1978, CBE 1968); s of Walter Dowling; *b* 18 Aug 1909; *Educ* Wellington Coll, Victoria U of Wellington NZ; *m* 1936 Dorothea Agnes, nee Nolan; 2 s, 2 da; *Career* barr and slr 1933-; sr ptnr Dowling, Wacher & Co, Barristers and Solicitors, Napier NZ; pres and chm Hawke's Bay Med Research Foundation Inc; v-pres & councillor Hospital Boards Assoc of NZ; dir AA Mutual Insurance Gp; NZ Motor World; *Style* - Sir Hallam Dowling KBE; 48 Avondale rd, Taradale, Napier, New Zealand (☎ Napier 442 040)

DOWN, Sir Alastair (Frederick); OBE (1944, MBE 1942), MC (1940), TD (1951); s of Capt Frederick Edward Down (d 1959); *b* 23 July 1914; *Educ* Marlborough Coll; *m* 1947, 'Bunny' (Maysie Hilda), da of Capt Vernon Mellon; 2 s, 2 da; *Career* served in 1939-45 War (despatches 2), with 8 Army and 1 Canadian Army as Lt-Col and Col; CA 1938, dep chm and md British Petroleum Co Ltd 1962-75, pres BP Gp in Canada 1957-62, chm and ch exec Burma Oil Co Ltd 1975- (dep chm 1969-75); kt 1978; *Recreations* shooting, golf and fishing; *Style* - Sir Alastair Down, OBE, MC, TD; The Hold, Manningford Bruce, Pewsey, Wilts

DOWNE, 11 Viscount (I 1681); John Christian George Dawnay; sits as Baron Dawnay of Danby (UK 1897); s of 10 Viscount Downe (d 1965); *b* 18 Jan 1935; *Educ* Eton, Ch Ch Oxford; *m* 1965, Alison Diana, da of I F H Sconce, MBE; 1 s, 1 da; *Heir* s, Hon Richard Dawnay; *Career* Lt Gren Gds 1954, industrial man electronics industry; *Recreations* analogue circuit design railways (selectively); *Clubs* Pratt's, Guards and Cavalry; *Style* - The Rt Hon The Viscount Downe; Wykeham Abbey, Scarborough, N Yorks (☎ 862404); 5 Douro Place, W8 (☎ 01 937 9449)

DOWNES, George Stretton; CBE (1976); s of late George Downes; *b* 2 Mar 1914; *Educ* Cardinal Vaughan Sch Kensington; *m* 1939, Sheila Gavigan; 2 s, 2 da; *Career* sec Metropolitan Police Office 1969; deputy receiver Metropolitan Police District 1973-76; ret; *Style* - George Downes Esq CBE; 45 Westbury rd, New Malden, Surrey

DOWNES, Ralph (William); CBE (1969); s of late James William Downes; *b* 16 Aug 1904; *Educ* Derby Secdy Sch, RCM London, Keble Oxford; *m* 1929, Agnes Mary, nee Rix (d 1980); 1 s (Prof Kerry Downes); *Career* organist, writer, conductor, consultant, Prof of Organ RCM 1954-75, Organist Emeritus London Oratory, organ designer Royal Festival Hall, Gloucester Cathedral, The Oratory, S Giovanni Cathedral and others; KSG

(Papal) 1970; *Style* - Ralph Downes Esq, CBE; c/o The Oratory, SW7

DOWNEY, Gordon Stanley; CB (1980); s of Stanley Downey; *b* 26 April 1928; *Educ* Tiffin's Sch, LSE; *m* 1952, Jacqueline Goldsmith; 2 da; *Career* Comptroller & Auditor Gen 1981-, Dep Sec Domestic Econ Sector HM Treasury 1981; Dep Sec CPRS Cabinet Off 1978-81; Min Works 1951, Treasury 1952- (Min Health 1961-62), Dep Sec 1976; *Style* - Gordon Downey Esq CB; 52 Sandy Lane, Petersham, Richmond, Surrey (☎ 01 940 3557)

DOWNEY, Maurice Edmund; s of late Edmund Downey, author; *b* 2 April 1930; *Educ* Waterpark Coll Waterford Ireland; *m* 1956, Marie, da of late Timothy Flynn; 5 children; *Career* chartered accountant; ptnr Reynolds Cooper McCarron (CA) 1973-, dir Irish Lee Assurance Co 1978-, chm Waterford Harbour Commissioners 1976-, Mayor of Waterford 1970-71, former cncl memb Inst of Chartered Accountants in Ireland; *Recreations* rugby, walking, travel; *Style* - Maurice Downey Esq; Milltown Grove, Milltown, Dublin (☎ 01 697236); Fairview, Newtown, Waterford, Eire (☎ 051 74191)

DOWNING, Dr Anthony Leighton; s of Sydney Downing; *b* 27 Mar 1926; *Educ* Arnold Sch Blackpool, Cambridge and London Us; *m* 1952, Kathleen Margaret Frost; 1 da; *Career* dir Water Pollution Research Laboratory 1966-73; ptnr Binnie & Partners, Consulting Engineers 1973-; FIChemE; FIBiol, Hon FIPHE, FIWES, FRSA; *Style* - Dr Anthony Downing; 2 Tewin close, Tewin Wood, Welwyn, Herts (☎ Bulls Green 474)

DOWNS, Diarmuid; CBE (1979); s of John Downs; *b* 23 Apr 1922; *Educ* Gunnersbury Catholic G S, City Univ London; *m* 1951, Mary Carmel Chillman; 1 s, 3 da; *Career* chm and md, Riccardo Consulting Engineers Ltd 1976-; *Style* - Diarmuid Downs Esq CBE; The Downs, 143 New Church rd, Hove, E Sussex (☎ Brighton 419357)

DOWNS, Richard Hudson; s of Arthur Stanley Downs (d 1931); *b* 19 July 1920; *Educ* West Leeds H S, London Poly, Bradford Tech; *m* 1942, Mary; 1 s; *Career* Fl-Lt UK and India; chm Cindex Ltd; *Recreations* aviation; *Style* - Richard Downs Esq; Coin de Haut, Coin Colin, St Martin's, Guernsey, CI (☎ 0481 37430)

DOWNSHIRE, 7 Marquess of (I 1789); Arthur Wills Percy Wellington Blundell Trumbull Sandys Hill; sits as Earl of Hillsborough (GB 1772); also Viscount Hillsborough and Baron Hill (I 1717), Earl of Hillsborough and Viscount Kilwarlin (I 1751), Baron Harwich (GB 1756), Viscount Fairford (GB 1772); Hereditary Constable of Hillsborough Fort; patron of one living; s of 6 Marquess (d 1918) by 1 w, Katherine, da of Hon (Hugh) Henry Hare, s of 2 Earl of Listowel, KP; *b* 7 April 1894; *Educ* Abbotsholme Sch Derbyshire, Christ's Cambridge; *m* 1953, Mrs Noreen Gray-Miller, da of late William Barraclough; *Heir* n, (Arthur) Robin Hill; *Career* 2 Lt Berks Yeo 1914-16; *Style* - The Most Hon The Marquess of Downshire; Flat 5, 81 Onslow sq, SW7 (☎ 01 584 9799)

DOWNWARD, Maj-Gen Peter Aldcroft; CB (1979), DSO (1967), DFC (1952); s of late Aldcroft Leonard Downward; *b* 10 Apr 1924; *Educ* King William's Coll, Isle of Man; *m* 1953 Hilda Hinckley Wood (d 1976); 2 s; *Career* enlisted 1942; Cdr Berlin Infantry Brigade 1971-74; Col The Queen's Lancashire Regiment 1978-; Lt-Gov and Sec The Royal Hospital Chelsea 1979-; *Style* - Maj-Gen Peter Downward CB DSO DFC; Lieutenant-Governor's House, Royal Hospital, London SW3

DOWNWARD, Sir William Atkinson; DL (Lancs 1971); s of George Thomas Downward (d 1915); *b* 5 Dec 1912; *Educ* Manchester High Sch, Manchester Coll of Technol; *m* 1946, Enid da of late Alderman Charles Wood; *Career* memb Manchester City Cncl 1946. Court of Govs Manchester U 1969, Lord Mayor of Manchester 1970-71, kt 1977; Alderman Manchester 1971-74, Ld-Lt Greater Manchester 1974-, dir Manchester Roy Exchange Theatre Co 1976-, chm Manchester Overseas Students Welfare Conf 1972-; *Style* - Sir William Downward,

HM Lord-Lieut for Gter Manchester; 23 Kenmore rd, Northenden, Manchester, M22 4AE (☎ 998 4742)

DOWSON, Graham Randall; s of late Cyril James Dowson; *b* 13 Jan 1923; *Educ* Alleyn Court Sch, City of London Sch, Ecole Alpina Switzerland; *m* 1, 1954, Fay Weston (m dis 1974); 2 da; m 2, 1975, Denise Shurman; *Career* chm Erskine House Investments 1975-, dir Erskine Gp of Cos, Carron Co (Hldgs) Ltd, Carron Investments Ltd, Marinex Petroleum Ltd, Cambridge Communications Ltd and others, dep chm Nimslo Ltd and Nimslo European Hldgs, chm Pincus Vidler Arthur Fitzgerald; *Style* - Graham Dowson Esq; 193 Cromwell Tower, Barbican, London EC2 (☎ 01 588 0396)

DOYLE, Bernard; *aet* 40 in June 1981, b Manchester; *Educ* Manchester U (civil engrg), Harvard Business Sch; *Career* late with BR; former management consultant in London, Brussels, US; with Booker McConnell 1973-81 (dir 1979), chm Booker McConnell Engrg to 1981; ch exec SPD 1981 (salary as of June 1981 £25,000 pa); *Style* - Bernard Doyle Esq; c/o Council for Social Democracy, 29 Queen Anne's Gate, SW1 (☎ 01 222 4141)

DOYLE, Sir John Francis Reginald William Hastings; 5 Bt (UK 1828); s of Sir Arthur Doyle 4 Bt (d 1948); *b* 3 Jan 1912; *Educ* Eton, RMC; *m* 1947, Carmen Diana (d 1980), da of Col C Steel; 1 da; *Heir* none; *Career* Maj Cameronian Scottish Rifles, with R Irish Fus 1932-41 and 1945-46, Palestine 1938 (medal with clasp), France 1940, Italy 1943 *Style* - Sir John Doyle, Bt; Glebe House, Camolin, co Wexford, Eire

DOYLE, Hon Mrs (Katharine Alexandra); *née* McClintock-Bunbury; da of 4 Baron Rathdonnell; *b* 1940; *m* 1960, James Joseph Doyle; *Style* - The Hon Mrs Doyle; Tobinstown, Tullow, Co Carlow

DRABBLE, (Mrs) Margaret (Swift); *da* of His Honour J Drabble; *b* 5 June 1939; *Educ* The Mount Sch York, Newnham Cambridge; *m* 1960, Clive Walter Swift (m dis 1975); 2 s, 1 da; *Career* author; dep chm National Book League; Hon DLitt, Sheffield; *Books* The Millstone, The Needle's Eye, The Realms of Gold, The Ice Age; *Style* - Miss Margaret Drabble

DRACUP, Michael Henry Empsall; *Career* ch exec and jt md Lister & Co Ltd; *Style* - Michael Dracup Esq; Lister & Co Ltd, Manningham Mills, Bradford, Yorks

DRAKE, Sir (Arthur) Eric (Courtney); CBE (1952); s of Dr Arthur William Courtney Drake (d 1964); *b* 29 Nov 1910; *Educ* Shrewsbury Sch, Pembroke Coll Cambridge; *m* 1, 1935, Rosemary, da of P L Moore; 2 da; m 2, 1950, Margaret Elizabeth, da of late Ralph Goodbarne Wilson; 2 s; *Career* md British Petroleum Co Ltd 1958, chm 1969-75; dep chm Peninsular and Oriental Steam Navigation Co 1976-, dir Kleinwort Benson Lonsdale Ltd, Toronto-Dominion Bank Canada, Société Francaise des Petroles, BP, Hudsons's Bay Co and other cos; dep chm P & O 1976-; pres Cncl Chamber of Shipping in UK 1964, life memb of court of City U 1969, hon Petroleum advisor British Army 1971-, chm Mary Rose Trust 1979-; kt 1970; *Recreations* sailing and shooting; *Clubs* Roy Yacht Sqdn, Leander; *Also* owns 14 ton ketch 'Shimran'; *Style* - Sir Eric Drake, CBE; The Old Rectory, Cheriton, nr Alresford, Hants (☎ Brandean 334)

DRAKE, Hon Mrs - Hon Rosemary Etheldreda Adderley; da of 6 Baron Norton; *b* 17 Oct 1913; *m* 1949, Rev John Paul Drake, s of Canon Frederick Drake; 1 s, 1 da; *Career* memb Chartered Soc Physiotherapy, in charge of Physiotherapy Dept Westminster Hosp 1947-50; *Style* - The Hon Mrs Drake; Stewkley Vicarage, Leighton Buzzard, Beds (☎ 287)

DRAKE-BROCKMAN, Hon Sir Thomas Charles; DFC (1944); s of R J Drake-Brockman; *b* 15 May 1919; *Educ* Guildford G S; *m* 1, 1942, Edith Sykes (m dis); 1 s, 4 da; m 2, 1972, Mary McGinnity; *Career* former Min for Air, Min for Administrative Services and Min for Aboriginal Affairs; former dep pres of Senate; Senator (Country Party) for W Australia 1958-78, kt 1979 *Style* - The Hon Sir Thomas Drake-Brockman DFC; c/o Commonwealth Parliament Offices, 191 St

George's ter, Perth, WA 6000, Australia

DRAPER, Donald Alfred James; DFC (1944), AE; s of the late Alfred Burns Draper; *b* 10 April 1919; *Educ* Uppingham; *m* 1939, Eglantine Mary, da of J D Walker, OBE; 2 s, 2 da; *Career* JP 1953, DL 1967, chartered accountant, ptnr Kidsons, pres Lewisham Branch of RAFA, Mayor of Lewisham 1953-54, Court of Common Council City of London 1955-58; *Clubs* City Livery, RAF; *Style* - Donald Draper Esq, DFC, AE, JP, DL; 52 Belmont Hill, London SE13 (☎ 01 852 4160)

DRAPER, Gerald Carter; OBE (1974); s of Alfred Henderson Draper (d 1962); *b* 24 Nov 1926; *Educ* Avoca Sch, Trin Coll Dublin; *m* 1951, Winifred Lilian, nee Howe; 1 s, 3 da; *Career* dir Commercial Operations British Airways 1978; dir British Airways Associated Cos 1972- and British Intercontinental Hotels Ltd 1976-; chm British Airtours Ltd 1978-; Silver Wing Surface Arrangements Ltd 1971-; dep chm Trust Houses Forte Travel Ltd 1974-; ALTA Ltd 1977-; *Recreations* shooting, yachting, tennis; *Clubs* N Surrey Gun, St George's Lawn Tennis; *Style* - Gerald Draper Esq, OBE; Old Chestnut, Onslow rd, Barwood Pk, Walton-on-Thames, Surrey

DRAPER, Prof Col Gerald Irving Anthony Dare; OBE (1965); s of Harold Irvine Draper (d 1930); *b* 30 May 1914; *Educ* privately, King's Coll London; *m* 1951, Julia Jean, nee Bald; *Career* barr 1945, Ir Gds 1941-44; Mil Prosecutor, War Crimes Trials Germany, 1945-49; ret as Col, 1956; former lectr and reader in Int Law London U; Prof of Law, Sussex U, 1976-79 (formerly reader); a chm of Industrial Tribunals 1966-; *Recreations* contemplating the follies of mankind, drinking champagne in the sun; *Clubs* Cavalry and Guards, Beefsteak; *Style* - Prof Col Gerald Draper, OBE; 2 Hare Court, Temple, EC4; 16 Southover High st, Lewes, Sussex (☎ 2387)

DRAYSON, Brig Harold Percy; CBE (1958); s of Col Alfred Percy Drayson (d 1953); *b* 19 March 1905; *Educ* Wellington Coll, RMA Woolwich, St John's Cambridge; *m* 1945, René Lucie Jeanne, da of Capitaine de Vaisseau Robert Lecoq; 1 s (step); *Career* 2 Lt RE 1925, served 1939-45 War (NW Europe), Lt-Col 1949, Brig 1956; dir RE Equipment Miny of Supply 1953-56, dir of Engrg Stores War Off 1956-58, ret 1958; *Clubs* Army and Navy; *Style* - Brig Harold Drayson, CBE; 7 Wellswood park, Torquay, Devon, TQ1 2QB (☎ 22116)

DRAYSON, Hon Mrs - Hon Shirley Joan Bailey; da of Hon Herbert Crawshay Bailey, JP (d 1936); *b* 1912; *m* 1946, George Dupin Drayson (d 1969); 1 s; *Career* granted title, rank and precedence of a Baron's da which would have been hers had her father survived to succeed to Barony of Glanusk; *Style* - The Hon Mrs Drayson; Rectory Cottage, Rectory lane, Ashington, Sussex

DREW, Cdre Harold; CBE (1945), DSC (1916); s of Charles Drew (d 1917); *b* 15 March 1895; *Educ* Oswestry Grammar, HMS 'Conway', RNC Greenwich; *m* 1921, Isabel Kate, da of Edward Donald Nicholson (d 1936); 1 da; *Career* joined RN 1913, served 1914-19 and 1939-45 in Atlantic, Mediterranean and SE Asia, Capt 1939, dep C-in-C and Ch of Staff, Indian Navy 1948-51, ADC to the King 1948; *Clubs* Roy Naval and Gymkhana (Delhi); *Style* - Cdre Harold Drew, CBE, DSC, RN; Red Hall, Parkhouse rd, Barrhead, Glasgow

DREW, Jane Beverly; *b* 24 Mar 1911; *Educ* Croydon; *m* 1, 2 da; m 2, 1942, Edwin Maxwell Fry; *Career* FRIBA; architect; ptnr, Fry Drew and ptnrs, 1946-; author; *Style* - Miss Jane Drew; 63 Gloucester pla, W1 (☎ 01-486 2972)

DREW, Norman Vincent; *Career* BSc; md The Ryvita Co Ltd; CChem; FRIC; FIFST; FRSH; *Style* - Norman Drew Esq; The Ryvita Co Ltd, Old Wareham rd, Poole, Dorset

DREW, Peter Leonard; s of Leonard George Drew (d 1942); *b* 28 Feb 1943; *Educ* King's Coll Wimbledon; *m* 1972, Angela Margaret, nee Naylor; 2 da (Anneli b 1976, Tamsin b 1979); *Career* chm

TKM Travel Division, chm and md-Wings Ltd, Owners Services Ltd (OSC); *Recreations* golf, squash; *Style* - Peter Drew Esq; Barwick House, Barwick, nr Ware, Herts

DREW, Lt-Gen Sir (William) Robert (Macfarlane); KCB (1965, CB 1962), CBE (1952, OBE 1940); s of William Hughes Drew of NSW Australia (d 1936); *b* 4 Oct 1907; *Educ* Sydney G S, Sydney U; *m* 1934, Dorothy Merle, da of Alfred Edwin Dakingsmith of NSW Australia; 1 s, 1 da; *Career* KStJ (1978, CStJ 1965), Lt-Gen, Medical Offr 1931-69, Cmdt Roy Army Medical Coll 1960-63, dir Medical Servs BOAR 1963-65, dir-gen Medical Servs 1965-69, dep dir British Postgraduate Medical Fedn London U 1970-78; co dir; *Recreations* swimming, travel; *Clubs* Army and Navy, Australian (Sydney), Roy Sydney G C; *Style* - Lt-Gen Sir Robert Drew KCB CBE; c/o Williams & Glyn's Bank, 22 Whitehall, SW1

DREWITT, Geoffrey Bernard; TD (1952), DL (Cornwall 1969); s of Frederick George Drewitt (d 1962); *b* 5 Nov 1912; *Educ* Blundells Sch, Architectural Assoc Sch of Architecture; *m* 1938, Elma Alberta Joan, da of Albert John Thomas; 1 s, 2 da; *Career* Lt-Col DCLI, NW Europe; architect, FRIBA, Croix de Guerre (1945); *Style* - Lt-Col Geoffrey Drewitt, TD, DL; 5 Clarence pla, Penzance, Cornwall (☎ 2922)

DREXEL, Hon Mrs - Hon (Mildred Sophia) Noreen Stonor; da of 5 Baron Camoys; *b* 1917; *m* 1941, John R Drexel; 1 s, 1 da; *Style* - The Hon Mrs Drexel; Stonor Lodge, Bellevue ave, Newport, Rhode Island, USA

DREXLER, George; *Career* chm Ofrex Gp Ltd; dir Ofrex Gp of Cos, Fordigraph Gp of Cos Rexel Gp of Cos; *Style* - George Drexler Esq; Ofrex Gp Ltd, Ofrex House, Stephen st, London W1

DREYFUS, John Gustave; s of Edmond Dreyfus (d 1947); *b* 15 April 1918; *Educ* Oundle Sch, Trin Cambridge; *m* 1948, Irène, da of late Charles Thurnauer; 1 s, 2 da; *Career* typographical adviser to Cambridge University Press (formerly assist printer) and Monotype Corpn 1955-, dir Curwen Press 1970-; typographical historian and lecturer; *Recreations* theatre, travel; *Clubs* Garrick; *Style* - John Dreyfus Esq; 38 Lennox gdns, SW1 (☎ 01 584 3510)

DRIBBEL, Jack Lodewyk Charles; s of late Alexander Dribbell; *b* 30 July 1922; *Educ* Westminster; *m* 1945, Rinalda, da of late Vittorio Duranti, of Ravenna; 2 s *Career* wine merchant, md Findlater, Mackie Todd & Co Ltd 1970-1981, Mayor of Westminster 1961-62, OStJ; *Recreations* painting, golf; *Style* - Jack Dribbel Esq; Dalkeith, Chester av, Richmond, Surrey (☎ 01 940 2732)

DRING, Lt-Col Sir (Arthur) John; KBE (1952), CIE (1943), DL (1972); s of Sir William Dring, KCIE, VD (d 1912); *b* 4 Nov 1902; *Educ* Winchester and RMC Sandhurst; *m* 1 1934, Marjorie Wadham (d 1943), da of late J C Wadham; 2 da; m 2, 1946, Alice Deborah, widow of Maj-Gen J Marshall CB DSO OBE and da of late Maj-Gen Gerald Cree CB CMG; *Career* joined Guides Cavalry IA 1923, Maj 1939, transferred political serv 1927, dep sec Viceroy's exec cncl 1936, sec to gov NWFP 1937-40, political agent S Waziristan 1940 (despatches), dir of Civil supplies NWFP 1943-47, ch sec 1947, prime minister to Nawab of Bahawalpur 1948-52; *Recreations* gardening and riding; *Style* - Lt-Col Sir John Dring, KBE, CIE, DL; Ava Cottage, Purbrook, Hants (☎ Waterlooville 3000)

DRISCOLL, James Patrick; s of Henry James Driscoll (d 1965); *b* 24 Apr 1925; *Educ* Coleg Sant Illtyd Cardiff, U Coll Cardiff; *m* 1955, Jeanne Lawrence, nee Williams; 1 s, 1 da; *Career* assist lectr U Coll Cardiff 1951-53, British Iron & Steel Fedn 1953-67, ec dir 1967-80, md Corporate Strategy British Steel Corpn 1975-, dir Nationalised Industries Chairmen's Gp 1980-, chm and md Woodcote Consultants Ltd 1980-; *Recreations* travel, reading; *Style* - James Driscoll Esq; 78 Burton Ct, Franklin's Row, SW3 (☎ 01 730 6681); Foxley Hatch, Birch lane, Purley, Surrey (☎ 01 668 4081)

DRIVER, Sir Arthur John; s of Percy John Driver (d 1924); *b* 20 March 1900; *m* 1937, Margaret Jessie Isobel, da of Hugh McMeekin (d 1941); 1 s, 2 da; *Career* served in RAF 1918, pres of Law Soc 1961-62, JP SW London, memb Cncl and hon registrar Imperial Soc of Knights Bachelor 1978-, memb of Cncl of the Independent Univ Coll at Buckingham; kt 1962; *Recreations* local affairs and gardening; *Club* Reform *Style* - Sir Arthur Driver JP; Frogmore Cottage, E Clandon, Guildford, Surrey (☎ 0483 222 355)

DRIVER, His Honour Maj Arthur Robert; s of late Henry Driver; *b* 25 Nov 1909; *Educ* Hale Sch, Perth; U of W Australia; *m* 1, 1936; 1 s, 1 da; 2, 1949, Marjorie Campbell, nee Leighton; *Career* administrator of the Northern Territory and Pres of Legislative Council of Northern Territory, Australia, 1946-51; former chief migration officer and chief of operations, Inter-Governmental Committee for European migration, Geneva; company dir AMIEA 1960-72, ret; *Style* - His Honour Major Arthur Driver; 35 Amaroo Drive, Buderim, Qld 4556, Australia

DRIVER, Christopher Prout; s of Dr Arthur Driver (decd); *b* 1 Dec 1932; *Educ* Rugby Sch, Ch Ch Oxford; *m* 1958, Margaret Elizabeth, nee Perfect; 3 da; *Career* writer and ed; features ed The Guardian 1964-8, ed The Good Food Guide 1969-; *Style* - Christopher Driver Esq; 6 Church rd, Highgate, London, N6; The Book In Hand, Bell st, Shaftesbury, Dorset

DRIVER, Sir Eric; s of William Driver; *b* 19 Jan 1911; *Educ* Strand Sch London, King's Coll, London U; *m* 1, 1938, Winifred Bane; 2 da; m 2, 1972, Sheila Mary Johnson; *Career* civil engr ICI Ltd 1938-; ch civil engr Mond Div to 1973, chm Mersey Regional Health Authority 1973-, kt 1979; *Style* - Sir Eric Driver; Chapel House, Crowley, Northwich, Cheshire

DROGHEDA, 11 Earl of (I 1661); Charles Garrett Ponsonby Moore; KG (1972), KBE (1964, OBE 1964); also Baron Moore (I 1616 & UK 1954, the latter of which Lord Drogheda sits as) and Viscount Moore (I 1621); s of 10 Earl of Drogheda, KCMG, PC (d 1957), by his 1 w, Kathleen, CBE, da of Charles Pelham Burn; *b* 23 April 1910; *Educ* Eton, Trin Cambridge; *m* 1935, Joan, da of William Carr; 1 s; *Heir* s, Viscount Moore; *Career* late Capt TA; chm Roy Ballet Sch 1978-, Henry Sotheran 1977-, Clifton Nurseries 1979-, P & D Colnaghi 1980-; dir Times Newspapers Hldgs 1981-, Pearson Longman Ltd, Economist Newspaper Ltd, Industrial & Trade Fairs Hldgs, Earls Court & Olympia Ltd; late Chm Financial Times (md 1945-70), Roy Opera House Covent Gdn, London Celebrations Cttee Queen's Silver Jubilee; late Tstee Br Museum, late Jt-Chm (with Sir Robert Mayer) Youth & Music; *Clubs* White's; *Style* - The Rt Hon Earl of Drogheda KG KBE; Parkside House, Wick Lane, Englefield Green, Surrey (☎ Egham 2800)

DROMGOOLE, Patrick Shirley Brooks Fleming; s of Nicholas Arthur Humphrey Dromgoole; *b* 30 Aug 1930; *Educ* Dulwich Coll, U Coll Oxford; *m* 1960, Jennifer Veronica Jill, da of S O Davis of Weymouth; 3 children; *Career* assist md HTV Ltd, member of Lloyd's, Fellow of the Roy Television Soc; *Recreations* farming, numismatism; *Clubs* Savile, Clifton (Bristol); *Style* - Patrick Dromgoole Esq; 28 Holland rd, W14; Barrows Farm, Theale, Wedmore, Somerset

DRUMALBYN, 1 Baron (UK 1963); Niall Malcolm Stewart Macpherson; KBE (1974), PC (1962); s of Sir (Thomas) Stewart Macpherson, CIE, LLD, MA, JP (d 1949); *b* 3 Aug 1908; *Educ* Edinburgh Acad, Fettes, Trin Oxford; *m* 1937, Margaret Phyllis (d 1979), da of late J J Runge and Mrs T A Ross, OBE; 2 da (and 1 decd) *Heir* none *Career* MP (Nat Lib) Dumfriesshire 1945-50, (Nat Lib & U) 1950-63, Nat Lib Scottish Whip 1945-50, Lib Unionist Scottish Whip 1950-55, chm Br C'wlth Producers' Org 1952-55, pres 1967-70, chm Advertising Standards Authority 1965-70, and 1974-77, Jt Parly Under-Sec of State for Scotland 1955-60, Parly Sec to Bd of Trade 1960-62, Min of Pensions and Nat Insurance 1962-63, Min of State Bd of Trade 1963-64, Min without Portfolio; *Style* - The Rt Hon The Lord

Drumalbyn KBE PC; Claytons, Beeches Hill, Bishop's Waltham, Southampton

DRUMLANRIG, Viscount; Sholto Francis Guy Douglas; s and h of 12 Marquess of Queensberry; *b* 1 June 1967; *Style* - Viscount Drumlanrig

DRUMMOND OF MEGGINCH, Hon Mrs - Hon (Jean) Cherry; da and co-heiress of 15 Baron Strange; *b* 17 Dec 1928; *Educ* Oxenfoord Caitle Sch, St Andrews U, Cambridge U; *m* 1952, Capt Humphrey ap Evans, MC, who assumed name Drummond of Megginch by decree of Lyon Court, 1966; 3 s (Capt Adam Drummond, Gren Gds, b 1953; Humphrey Drummond b 1963; John Drummond b 1966) 3 da (Charlotte b 1955, Amélie b 1963, Catherine b 1967); *Style* - The Hon Mrs Drummond of Megginch; Megginch Castle, Errol, Perthshire (☎ Errol 222); Tresco, 160 Kennington rd, SE11 (☎ 01 735 3681)

DRUMMOND, Lady Elizabeth Helen; *née* Kennedy; da of 7 Marquess of Ailsa; *b* 23 Feb 1955; *m* 1976, Rev Norman Walker Drummond, MA, BD; 1 s (Andrew b 1977), 1 da (Margaret b 1980); *Style* - Lady Elizabeth Drummond; Manse of the Black Watch, 1 BW, BFFO 106; Farend, Tantallon ter, N Berwick, E Lothian

DRUMMOND OF MEGGINCH, Capt Humphrey; MC (1945); s of Maj James John Pugh Evans, MBE, MC (d 1945); *b* 18 Sept 1922; *Educ* Eton and Trinity Coll Cambridge; *m* 1952, Hon Cherry, da of 15 Baron Strange; 3 s, 3 da; *Career* changed name by decree of Court of Lord Lyon 1966; served 1940-45 with 1 Mountain Regt; Indian political serv; gen sec Cncl for Preservation of Rural Wales 1947-51, Welsh rep of Nat Trust 1949-54, Gold Staff offr coronation of HM Queen Elizabeth II; author and farmer, chm Soc of Authors (Sco); *Clubs* Garrrick; *Style* - Capt Humphrey Drummond of Megginch, MC; Tresco, 160 Kennington rd, London SE11 (☎ 01 735 3681); Megginch Castle, Errol, Perths

DRUMMOND, Hon James David; s and h of Viscount Strathallan; *b* 24 Oct 1965; *Style* - The Hon James Drummond

DRUMMOND, Hon James Reginald; s of 17 Earl of Perth, PC; *b* 1933; *Educ* Downside and Trin Cambridge; *m* 1961, Marybelle, da of Capt Charles Gordon; *Style* - The Hon James Drummond; Lotus House, Beeswing, Dumfries; 1 Clarendon mews, London W2

DRUMMOND, John Richard Gray; s of late Capt A R G Drummond; *b* 25 Nov 1934; *Educ* Canford; Trin, Cambridge; *Career* joined BBC 1958; former asst head Music and Arts; dir Edinburgh International Festival 1978-; *Style* - John Drummond Esq; c/o Edinburgh Festival Society, 21 Market st, Edinburgh (☎ 031-226 4001)

DRUMMOND, Patrick Thomas; s of Thomas John Drummond, MM; *b* 11 May 1937; *m* 1961 (m dis); 2 children; *Career* dir Associated Asphalt Co Ltd, London Roadstone Ltd; *Recreations* golf; *Style* - Patrick Drummond Esq; 19 Josephine ct, Southcote rd, Reading, Berks (☎ 599403)

DRUMMOND, Hon Robert Eric; s of Viscount Strathallan; *b* 7 May 1967; *Style* - The Hon Robert Drummond

DRUMMOND, Hon Mrs - Hon Theodosia Beatrix Catherine Mary Meade; da of Lord Gillford (Richard Charles Meade, d 1905), s of 4 Earl of Clanwilliam; *b* 1898; *m* 1961, Angus Julian Drummond; *Style* - The Hon Mrs Drummond; 62 Ashley gdns, London SW1

DRUMMOND-HAY, Lady Bettina Mary; *née* Lindsay; da of 29 Earl of Crawford and (12 of) Balcarres; *b* 26 June 1950; *Educ* Camden Sch for Girls, Goldsmith's Coll; *m* 1975, Peter Charles, s of John Hay-Drummond-Hay, himself gs of Sir Robert Drummond-Hay, who added the first 'Hay' to his name; Sir Robert was in turn gs of Edward Drummond-Hay, whose f had been The Very Rev Edward Hay-Drummond, yr bro of 10 Earl of Kinnoull and Dean of Bocking; the Dean's (first) w (and mother of Edward) was Elizabeth, da of William, Count de Vismes (conceivably a connection of Philippe de Vismes, descended from the Sovereign Counts de Vismes & Ponthieu, who was a Huguenot immigrant to

England after the Revocation of the Edict of Nantes 1685; the title was recognised by the Orleanist regime of Louis-Philippe 1838); 2 da (Tamsin Rachel b 1977, Alice Ruth b 1980); *Career* school teacher; *Style* - Lady Bettina Drummond-Hay; 107 Frognal, NW3 (☎ 01 435 3342); Le Pestou, 82400 Castelsagrat, France (☎ 63 - 94 21 91)

DRUMMOND-HAY, Lady Margaret; *née* Douglas-Hamilton; da of late 13 Duke of Hamilton and (19) Brandon; *b* 1907; *m* 1930, Maj James Drummond-Hay; 2 s, 4 da; *Style* - Lady Margaret Drummond-Hay; Elvita, Hythe rd, Ramsgate, Kent

DRUMMOND-MURRAY, Hon Mrs Barbara Mary; *née* Hope; da of 2 Baron Rankeillour; *b* 1930; *m* 1954, Peter Drummond-Murray of Mastrick; 4 s, 1 da; *Style* - The Hon Mrs Drummond-Murray; Old Hadlow House, Hadlow Down, Uckfield, Sussex

DRUMMOND-MURRAY OF MASTRICK, (William Edward) Peter Louis; s of Edward John Drummond-Murray of Mastrick; *b* 24 Nov 1929; *Educ* Beaumont; *m* 1954, Hon Barbara Mary, nee Hope, da and co-heir of late 2 Baron Rankeillour, GCIE, MC; 4 s, 1 da; *Career* empld N M Rothschild & Co, dir New Court Fund Managers Ltd and other cos, ch exec Hosp of St John and St Elizabeth London 1978-, Chllr British Assoc Sovereign Military Order of Malta 1977-, Kt of Honour and Devotion Sovereign Military Order of Malta 1971; *Recreations* archaeology, genealogy, heraldry; *Clubs* New Club (Edinburgh), Puffin's (Edinburgh); *Style* - Peter Drummond-Murray of Mastrick; 74 Grove End rd, NW8 (☎ 01 586 3179); Old Hadlow House, Hadlow Down, Uckfield, Sussex (☎ 082 585 225)

DRURY, Charles Mills; CBE (1946, MBE 1942), DSO (1944), ED (1956); s of Victor Drury; *b* 17 May 1912; *Educ* Bishops Coll Sch Lennoxville; RMC Canada Kingston; McGill U; Paris U; *m* 1939, Jane Ferrier Counsell (decd); 2 s, 2 da; *Career* former Min Public Works; former Min of State for Science and Technology; chm Nat Capital Cmmn, Canada 1978-; *Style* - Charles Drury Esq, CBE, DSO, ED; 48 Rideau st, Ottawa, Ontario K1N 8KS, Canada

DRURY, Rev Canon John Henry; s of Henry Drury; *b* 23 May 1936; *Educ* Bradfield; Trinity Hall and Westcott House, Cambridge (MA); *m* 1972, (Frances) Clare Nineham; 2 da; *Career* resident canon of Norwich Cathedral and examining chaplain to Bp of Norwich, 1973; vice-dean of Norwich, 1978; lecturer in religious studies, U of Sussex 1979-; *Style* - The Rev Canon John Drury; Sussex University, Brighton (☎ 607755)

DRYDEN, John Frederick Simon; s & h of Sir John Dryden, 11 Bt; *b* 26 May 1976 *Style* - John Dryden

DRYDEN, Sir John Stephen Gyles; 11 Bt (GB 1733) of Ambrosden, Oxfordshire and 8 Bt (GB 1795) of Canons-Ashby, Northamptonshire; s of Sir Noel Percy Hugh Dryden, 10 Bt (d 1970, sixth in descent from Sir Erasmus Dryden, 6 Bt, the bro of the poet John Dryden); *b* 26 Sept 1943; *Educ* Oratory Sch; *m* 1970, Diana Constance, da of Cyril Tomlinson, of New Zealand; 1 s *Heir* s, John Frederick Simon Dryden; *Style* - Sir John Dryden, Bt; c/o Midland Bank Ltd, Redhill, Surrey

DRYDEN, Rosamund, Lady; Rosamund Mary; *née* Scrope; *m* 1941, Sir Noel Percy Hugh Dryden, 10 Bt (d 1970); *Style* - Rosamund, Lady Dryden; c/o Williams & Glyn's Bank, Old Brompton rd, London SW7

DRYSDALE, Lady; Maisie Joyce; formerly Purves-Smith; *m* 1965, as his 2 w, Sir Russell Drysdale, AC, the Australian artist (d 1981); *Style* - Lady Drysdale; Bouddi Farm, Kilcare Heights, Hardy's Bay, NSW 2256, Australia

DU BUISSON, Hon Mrs - Hon Sylvia Grace Portman; da of 4 Viscount Portman; *b* 1900; *m* 1932, Maj Thomas Gerard du Buisson, MBE, MC, late RA; *Style* - The Hon Mrs du Buisson; Reydon Lodge, Bury rd, Newmarket, Suffolk

DU CANE, John Peter; OBE (1964); s of Charles Du Cane; *b* 16 Apr 1921; *Educ*

Canford Sch Wimborne; *m* 1945, Patricia Wallace, nee Desmond; 2 s; *Career* chm, Selection Trust Ltd 1978- (dir 1966-, md 1975-), dir Amax Inc; chm Seltrust Hldgs Ltd, Australia; *Style* - John Du Cane Esq OBE; 20 Jameson st, London W8 (☎ 01 727 1974)

DU CANE, Cdr Peter; CBE (1964, OBE 1942); s of C H C Du Cane; *b* 18 Mar 1901; *Educ* Royal Navy Coll; *Career* designer of high speed craft; consultant Vosper Ltd, Shipbuilders, Portsmouth (md 1931-63; dep chm 1963-73); C Eng, FIMechE, FRINA, AFRAeS, FRSA; *Style* - Cdr Peter Du Cane CBE RN; Seamark, Glandore, Co Cork, Ireland (☎ Leap 95)

DU CROS, Sir Claude Philip Arthur Mallet; 3 Bt (UK 1916) of Canons, Middx; s of Sir Philip Harvey du Cros, 2 Bt (d 1975); *b* 22 Dec 1922; *m* 1, 1953 (m dis 1974), Mrs Christine Nancy Tordoff, da of late F E Bennett; 1 s; m 2, 1974, Margaret Roy, da of late Roland Frater; *Heir* s, Julian Claude Arthur Mallet du Cros; *Career* farmer; *Style* - Sir Claude du Cros, Bt; Longmeadow, Ballaugh, Glen, Ramsey, Isle of Man

DU CROS, Julian Claude Arthur Mallet; s & h of Sir Claude Du Cros, 3 Bt; *b* 23 Apr 1955; *Educ* Eton; *Style* - Julian du Cros Esq

DU CROS, Rosemary, Lady - Rosemary; da of Sir John David Rees, 1 Bt, KCIE, CVO, MP; *m* 1950, as his 2 w, Capt Sir Philip Harvey du Cros, 2 Bt (d 1975); *Style* - Rosemary, Lady du Cros; Little Bocombe, Parkham, Bideford, N Devon

DU HEAUME, Sir (Francis) Herbert; CIE (1943), OBE (1932), KPM (1924); s of George du Heaume, OBE (d 1949); *b* 27 May 1897; *Educ* St George's Coll London; *m* 1923, Blanche Helen Learmonth, da of James Tainsh, of Hamilton Scotland; 2 s; *Career* served in Gt War 1914-18 as Capt with Civil Serv Rifles; joined Indian Police 1920, dep dir Civil Defence 1943, dep insp-gen of Police Punjab 1945, ret 1947; Indian Police Medal; kt 1948; *Style* - Sir Herbert du Heaume, CIE, OBE, KPM; Hoarthorns Cottage, Malvern way, Edge End, Coleford, Glos

DU MAURIER, Dame Daphne; DBE; also Lady Browning; da of Sir Gerald du Maurier, the actor-manager and himself s of George, the author (notably of 'Trilby') and artist ('Punch' for the last two or three decades of the 19 century was full of his illustrations); *b* 13 May 1907; *Educ* privately and in Paris; *m* 1932, Lt-Gen Sir Frederick Browning, KCVO, DSO (decd); 1 s, 2 da (one of whom, Tessa, m (1) Capt (now Maj) Peter de Zulueta, 6 Conde de Torre Diaz (since the death of Canon de Zulueta in 1980) & 1 cous of Sir Philip de Zulueta; m (2), 1970, 2 Viscount Montgomery of Alamein, s of the WW II hero); *Career* writer, notably of 'Jamaica Inn' & 'Rebecca'; *Recreations* walking, swimming; *Style* - Dame Daphne du Maurier, DBE; Kilmarth, Par, Cornwall

DU PARCQ, Hon John Renouf; s of Baron du Parcq (Life Peer, d 1949); *b* 9 June 1917; *Educ* Rugby, Exeter Coll Oxford; *m* 1940, Elizabeth, da of Evan Skull Poole; 1 s, 1 da; *Career* chartered electrical engr ret 1972; *Recreations* joinery; *Style* - The Hon John du Parcq; Smithy Paddock, Fulmodestone, Fakenham, Norfolk (☎ Thursford 542)

DU PREEZ, Hon Mrs (Carina Gillian); *née* Hacking; da of 2 Baron Hacking (d 1971); *b* 28 May 1956; *Educ* Benenden; *m* 1981, Jac Jacobus du Preez; *Recreations* swimming, tennis, walking; *Style* - The Hon Mrs du Preez; 8 Winters Wynd, Newlands 7700, Cape Province, S Africa (☎ Cape Town 619324)

DU SAUTOY, Peter Francis; CBE (1971); s of Col E F du Sautoy, OBE, TD, DL (d 1964); *b* 19 Feb 1912; *Educ* Uppingham, Wadham Oxford; *m* 1937, Phyllis Mary (Mollie), da of Sir Francis Floud, KCB, KCSI, KCMG (d 1965); 2 s; *Career* assist educn offr City of Oxford 1937-40, served with RAF 1940-45, pres Publishers Assoc 1967-69, dir Faber and Faber Ltd 1946-77 (chm 1971-77), v-chm Faber Music Ltd 1977- (chm 1971-76); *Clubs* Garrick; *Style* - Peter du Sautoy Esq, CBE; 31 Lee rd, Aldeburgh, Suffolk, IP15 5EY

DU VIVIER, Richard Adolphe Charles; CBE (1973, MBE 1945); s of James du Vivier, of Belgium; *b* 27 Dec 1911; *Educ* Malvern, King's Cambridge; *m* 1936, Margaret, da of Sir Robert Aske, 1 Bt; 2 s, 2 da; *Career* Maj WW II (served N Africa, Italy, NW Europe); ret schoolmaster, Br Cncl Rep Uruguay & Mexico 1951-55 & 1970-73; *Recreations* tennis, golf; *Clubs* Hurlingham, Sudbury Golf; *Style* - Richard du Vivier Esq, CBE; 45 Chatsworth rd, W5

DUBLIN, 61 Archbishop of (1042); Most Rev Henry Robert McAdoo; 65 Bp of Glendalough (612); s of James McAdoo; *b* 1916; *Educ* Cork G S, Mountjoy Sch Dublin, Trinity Coll Dublin; *m* 1940, Lesley Dalziel Weir; 1 s, 2 da; *Career* Bp of Ossory, Ferne and Leighlin 1967-77; Archbishop of Dublin 1977-; *Style* - The Most Rev the Lord Archbishop of Dublin; The See House, 17 Temple rd, Milltown, Dublin 6

DUBS, Alfred; MP (L) Wandsworth, Battersea South 1979-; *b* Dec 1932; *Style* - Alfred Dubs Esq, MP; House of Commons, London, SW1

DUCAT-AMOS, Air Cmdt Barbara Mary; CB (1974), RRC (1 Class) (1971); da of Capt George William Ducat-Amos (d 1942); *b* 9 Feb 1921; *Educ* The Abbey Sch Reading, Nightingale Training Sch, St Thomas's; *Career* trained SRN and CMB (pt 1), St Thomas's, sr matron RAF hosp Changi Singapore 1968-70, dep matron RAF hosp Nocton Hall 1967-68, matron in ch Princess Mary's RAF Nursing Serv and dir RAF Nursing Servs 1972-78, Queen's hon nursing sis 1972-78; *Recreations* music, theatre and travel; *Clubs* RAF; *Style* - Air Cmdt Barbara Ducat-Amos, CB, RRC; c/o Barclays Bank, King st, Reading

DUCHENE, Louis-Francois; s of Louis and Marguerite Duchêne; *b* 17 Feb 1927; *Educ* St Paul's, LSE; *m* 1952, Anne Purves *Career* Director Sussex European Res Centre Sussex University 1974-; former leader writer Manchester Guardian; *Style* - Louis-Francois Duchêne Esq; 3 Powis Villas, Brighton, East Sussex (☎ Brighton 29258)

DUCIE, 6 Earl of (UK 1837); Basil Howard Moreton; also Baron Ducie (GB 1763) and Baron Moreton (UK 1837); s of Hon Algernon Howard Moreton, 2 s of 4 Earl of Ducie and who d 1951; suc unc 1952; *b* 15 Nov 1917; *Educ* C of E Grammar Sch Brisbane Queensland; *m* 1950, Alison May, da of Leslie Atkins Bates, of Brisbane, Queensland; 3 s, 1 da; *Heir* s, Lord Moreton; *Career* patron of 2 livings; served 1941-45 with 62 A I Bn and 2/3 A I Bn New Guinea and Islands; *Style* - The Rt Hon The Earl of Ducie; Tortworth House, Tortworth, Wotton-under-Edge, Glos

DUCKWORTH, Anthony John Stanhope; s of late Sir George Duckworth, CB; *b* 2 Oct 1913; *Educ* Eton, Trin Cambridge; *m* 1941, Audrey Diana, nee Tollenaar; 2 s, 1 da; *Career* sr ptnr Fielding Newson-Smith Stockbrokers 1970-77, dir Eagle Star Trust Co Ltd (former chm), Moet & Chandon (London) Ltd, Parfums Christian Dior (UK) Ltd; *Recreations* shooting, golf; *Clubs* Bucks; *Style* - Anthony Duckworth Esq; 2 Eaton pla, SW1 (☎ 01 235 4776); Southacre House, Southacre, nr Kings Lynn, Norfolk (☎ Castleacre 272)

DUCKWORTH, Edward Richard Dyce; s and h of Sir Richard Duckworth, 3 Bt; *b* 13 July 1943; *Educ* Marlborough; *m* 1976, Patricia, da of Thomas Cahill, of Eton, Berks; *Style* - Edward Duckworth Esq

DUCKWORTH, John Clifford; s of Harold Duckworth; *b* 27 Dec 1916; *Educ* KCS Wimbledon, Oxford U; *m* 1942, Dorothy, nee Wills; 3 s; *Career* md Nat Res Dvpt Corp, 1959-1970; chm- IDJ Investment Servs Ltd, Lintott Engrg Ltd; dir Erinream Securities Ltd, Spear & Jackson Int Ltd and Bridon Ltd; *Style* - John Duckworth Esq; Wells House, nr Pangbourne, Berks

DUCKWORTH, Hon Mrs - Hon (Mary) Katharine Medina Chatfield; OBE (1946); *da* of Adm of the Fleet 1 Baron Chatfield GCB OM KCMG CVO PC; *b* 1911; *m* 1947, Henry George Austen de L'Etang Herbert Duckworth, RA; 2 da; *Career* WVS 1939-

46; *Style* - The Hon Mrs Duckworth OBE; Dalingridge Place, Sharpthorne, Sussex

DUCKWORTH, Sir Richard Dyce; 3 Bt (UK 1909), of Grosvenor Place, City of Westminster; s of Sir Edward Dyce Duckworth, 2 Bt (d 1945); *b* 30 Sept 1918; *Educ* Marlborough; *m* 1942, Violet Alison, da of Lt-Col George Boothby Wauchope, DSO, of Highclere, Newbury; 2 s; *Heir* s, Edward Duckworth; *Career* formerly Maj RA; *Style* - Sir Richard Duckworth, Bt; Dunwood Cottage, Shootash, Romsey, Hants (☎ 513228)

DUCKWORTH-KING, Lady; Alice Patricia; da of Thomas Rutledge, of Fugar House, Ravensworth, co Durham; *m* 1943, as his 2 wife, Sir John Richard Duckworth-King, 7 Bt (d 1972, when the title became ext); *Style* - Lady Duckworth-King; 47 Avenue de Hassan, 11 Tangier, Morocco

DUDDERIDGE, P; *Career* md Soundcraft Electronics Ltd; Winner of Queen's Award for Export Achievement 1979; *Style* - P Dudderidge Esq; Soundcraft Electronics Ltd, 5 Great Sutton st, London, EC1

DUDLEY, Baroness (14 in line, E 1439); Barbara Amy Felicity Wallace; *née* Lea-Smith; da of 12 Baron Dudley (d 1936); suc bro 1972; *b* 23 April 1907; *m* 1929, Guy Raymond Hill Wallace (d 1967); 3 s, 1 da; *Heir* s, Hon Jim Wallace; *Style* - The Rt Hon The Lady Dudley; Hill House, Kempsey, Worcs (☎ 820253)

DUDLEY, 4 Earl of (UK 1860); William Humble David Ward; also Baron Ward of Birmingham (E 1664) and Viscount Ednam (UK 1860); s of 3 Earl of Dudley, MC (d 1969) by his 1 w, Lady Rosemary, nee Sutherland-Leveson-Gower, RRC (d 1930), da of 4 Duke of Sutherland; *b* 5 Jan 1920; *Educ* Eton, Ch Ch Oxford; *m* 1, 1946 (m dis 1961), Stella, da of Miguel Carcano, KCMG, KBE, sometime Argentinian Ambass to UK; 1 s, 2 da (twins); m 2, 1961, Maureen Swanson; 1 s, 5 da; *Heir* s, Viscount Ednam; *Career* 2 Lt 10 Hussars 1941, Capt 1945; chm Integrated Building Products Ltd, Grecon Systems Ltd, Noise Control Products Ltd and DAW Tools & Manufacturing Ltd, dir Baggeridge Brick Co Ltd and Tribune Investment Trust Ltd; *Clubs* White's, Pratt's, Roy Yacht Sqdn; *Style* - The Rt Hon The Earl of Dudley; Vention House, Putsborough, N Devon; 6 Cottesmore gdns, W8 (☎ 01 937 5671)

DUDLEY, Hon Mrs - Hon Betty Montague; da of 1 Baron Amulree; *b* 1920; *m* 1941, John Forbes Dudley; 1 da; *Style* - The Hon Mrs Dudley; 76 Eastcourt rd, Burbage, Wilts

DUDLEY, Grace, Countess of; Grace Maria Kolin; *m* 1, Prince Stanislas Radziwill; m 2, 1961, as his 3 w, 3 Earl of Dudley (d 1969); *Style* - The Rt Hon Grace, Countess of Dudley; Greycliff, Nassau, Bahamas

DUDLEY, Prof Norman Alfred; CBE (1977); s of Alfred Dudley; *b* 29 Feb 1916; *Educ* Kings Norton G S, U of London, Birmingham Coll of Technology; *m* 1940, Hilda Florence nee Miles; 1 s, 2 da; *Career* Lucas Prof of engrg prodn U of Birmingham, 1959-80, head of dept of engrg prodn and dir U Institute for Engineering Production 1956-80, emeritus prof 1981, ed of Int Journal of Prodn Res 1961-80, FEng, FIProdE, MBIM; *Recreations* gardening, genealogy; *Clubs* Athenaeum *Style* - Prof Norman Dudley CBE; 37 Abbots Close, Knowle, Solihull, W Midlands (☎ Knowle 5976)

DUDLEY-WILLIAMS, Sir Rolf Dudley; 1 Bt (UK 1964) of City and Co of the City of Exeter; s of Arthur Williams of Plymouth; *b* 17 June 1908; *Educ* Plymouth Coll and RAF Coll Cranwell; *m* 1940, Margaret Helen, da of F E Robinson, OBE; 2 s; *Heir* s Alastair Edgcumbe James Dudley-Williams; *Career* assumed surname of Dudley-Williams by deed poll 1964; pilot offr RAF 1928, founded Power Jets Ltd 1936, md 1941; MP (C) Exeter 1951-66 , PPS to Christopher Soames (now Lord Soames) 1958-60, chm W Area of Nat Union of Con Assocs 1961-64; *Clubs* RAF; *Style* - Sir Rolf Dudley-Williams, Bt; The Old Manse, S Petherton, Somerset

DUDMAN, George Edward; CB (1973);

s of William James Dudman (d 1940); *b* 2 Dec 1916; *Educ* Merchant Taylors' Sch London and St John's Coll Oxford; *m* 1955, Joan Doris, da of Frederick John Eaton (d 1956); 1 s, 1 da; *Career* HM Forces 1940-46, FO (German sec) 1946-49, called to the bar 1950, Law Offrs' Dept 1951-65 (legal sec 1958-65), legal adviser Dept of Educn and Science 1965-77, ed Statues in Force 1977-; *Recreations* chess, painting, cooking, gardening and studying philosophy; *Style* - George Dudman Esq, CB; 10 Viga Road, Grange Park, London, N21 (☎ 01 360 5129)

DUFF-ASSHETON-SMITH, Hon Lady - Hon (Millicent) Joan, *née* Marjoribanks; da of 3 and last Baron Tweedmouth (d 1935); *b* 1906; *m* 1935 (m annulled) Sir (Charles) Michael Robert Vivian Duff-Assheton-Smith, Bt (d 1980, having dropped the 'Assheton-Smith' (1945) and resumed original surname of Duff); *Style* - The Hon Lady Duff-Assheton-Smith; 45 Westminster Gardens, London, SW1

DUFF-GORDON, Sir Andrew Cosmo Lewis; 8 Bt (UK 1813), of Halkin, Ayrshire; s of Sir Douglas Frederick Duff-Gordon, 7 Bt (d 1964); *b* 17 Oct 1933; *Educ* Repton; *m* 1, 1967 (m dis 1975), Grania Mary, da of Fitzgerald Villiers-Stuart, of Dromana, Villierstown, Co Waterford; 1 s; m 2, 1975, Eveline (Evie) Virginia, da of Samuel Soames, of Boxford House, Newbury; 2 s; *Heir* s, Cosmo Duff-Gordon; *Career* late Worcs and Cheshire Regt; underwriting memb Lloyd's, dir Christand Underwriting Agencies Ltd; *Style* - Sir Andrew Duff-Gordon, Bt; 27 Cathcart rd, SW10; Downton House, Walton,Presteigne, Powys (☎ New Radnor 223)

DUFF-GORDON, Cosmo Henry Villiers; s and h of Sir Andrew Duff-Gordon, 8 Bt; *b* 18 June 1968; *Style* - Cosmo Duff-Gordon Esq

DUFFELL, Michael Royson; s of Roy John Duffell (d 1979); *b* 19 June 1939; *Educ* Dulwich Coll; *m* 1964, Gisela, nee Rothkehl; 1 s, 1 da; *Career* reception man, Hyde Park Hotel 1966-69, gen man Grosvenor Hotel Chester 1969-76, controller of the Household to HM King Hussein of Jordan 1976-80, gen man The Ritz 1980-; *Recreations* sports; *Style* - Michael Duffell Esq; 26 Brechin pl, SW7 (☎ 01 373 2213)

DUFFERIN AND AVA, 5 Marquess of (UK 1888); Sir Sheridan Frederick Terence Hamilton-Temple-Blackwood; 10 Bt (I 1763); also Baron Dufferin and Clandeboye (I 1800), Baron Clandeboye (UK 1850), Earl of Dufferin, Viscount Clandeboye (both UK 1871), and Earl of Ava (UK 1888); s of 4 Marquess of Dufferin and Ava (ka 1945, gs of 1 Marquess, whose mother's paternal gf was Richard Brinsley Sheridan, the playwright and friend of 'Prinny'; the 1 Marquess's aunt was Caroline, The Hon Mrs George Norton, whose friendship with Lord Melbourne, the PM, resulted in a charge of criminal conversation being brought by her husb; Caroline was allegedly the model for the eponymous heroine of Meredith's 'Diana of the Crossways', which book drew from Lord Dufferin refutation of the rumour that Caroline told The Times of Peel's conversion to Free Trade; the 1 Marquess's mother and 2 aunts were known as the 'Three Graces' and are possibly the inspiration for an anecdote in Aldous Huxley's 'Crome Yellow') and Maureen, Marchioness of Dufferin and Ava, *qv*; *b* 9 July 1938; *Educ* Eton; *m* 1964, his 6 cous, Lindy, da of Gp Capt Loel Guinness, *qv*, by his 2 w, Lady Isabel Manners (yr da of 9 Duke of Rutland); *Heir* to Barony of Dufferin and Clandeboye and Btcy- Sir Francis Temple, 6 Bt; to Marquessate, Earldoms, Viscountcy and Barony of Clandeboye- none; *Career* late 2 Lt RHG; Tstee Wallace Collection 1973-; *Style* - The Most Hon The Marquess of Dufferin and Ava; Clandeboye, Co Down, N Ireland; 4 Holland Villas rd, W14 (☎ 01 937 3163)

DUFFERIN AND AVA, Marchioness of; Lindy (Serena Belinda Rosemary); *née* Guinness; da of Gp Capt Loel Guinness, OBE, by his 2 w, Lady Isabel Manners (yr da of 9 Duke of Rutland and niece of Lady Diana Cooper, *qv*); *b* 25 March 1941; *m* 1964, 5 Marquess of Dufferin and Ava; *Career* writer and artist; *Style* - The Most Hon The Marchioness of

Dufferin and Ava; 4 Holland Villas rd, W14

DUFFERIN AND AVA, Maureen, Marchioness of (Mrs John Maude); Maureen Constance; *née* Guinness; da of Hon Arthur Guinness, 2 s of 1 Earl of Iveagh; sis of Oonagh Guinness (Mrs Miguel Ferreras); 1 cous once removed of the MPs Paul Channon and Hon Mark Lennox-Boyd, also of Marchioness of Douro (HRH Princess Antonia von Preussen); *b* 31 Jan 1907; *m* 1, 1930, 4 Marquess of Dufferin and Ava (ka 1945); 1 s (5 Marquess), 2 da (Lady Caroline Lowell, Lady Perdita Hamilton-Temple-Blackwood); m 2, 1948 (m dis 1954), Maj Harry Buchanan, MC; m 3, 1955, His Hon Judge (John) Maude, QC, s of the actor-manager Cyril Maude (himself gs of Capt Hon Francis Maude, RN, 6 s of 1 Viscount Hawarden; Cyril's mother was Hon Georgiana Hanbury-Tracy, da of 2 Baron Sudeley); *Career* allegedly the original of Sir Osbert Lancaster's 'Maudie Littlehampton' in his pocket cartoons; *Style*- Maureen, Marchioness of Dufferin and Ava; 4 Hans Crescent, SW1 (☎ 01 235 1432); The Owl House, Lamberhurst, Kent

DUFFUS OF DALCLAVERHOUSE, James Coutts; s of James Montague Coutts Duffus of Dalclaverhouse and of the Mansion of Claverhouse, by Dundee, Angus (d 1947); *b* 3 June 1919; *Educ* Arnhall Coll Sch Dundee; *Career* Corps of RE (TA) (despatches) WW II; holder in life-rent of the superiority of the lands, estate and feudal fief of Dalclaverhouse, Co Angus; recognised in present name and style by Lord Lyon King of Arms 1955; archivist; FRSA, FSA Scot; *Style* - James Duffus of Dalclaverhouse; 68 New Cavendish st, W1 (☎ 01 580 5152)

DUFFUS, Hon Sir William (Algernon Holwell); s of late William Alexander Duffus, JP; *b* 13 Aug 1911; *Educ* Cornwall Coll Jamaica and Titchfield Sch; *m* 1938, Helen, da of late Richard Hollinsed, JP, of Jamaica; 2 s, 1 da; *Career* slr Supreme Court, Jamaica 1933, magistrate and ch magistrate Jamaica 1943, Nigeria 1955, judge of High Court W Nigeria 1957, justice of appeal for E Africa 1964, pres Court of Appeal for E Africa 1970-75, justice of the Courts of Appeal for Bahamas, Bermuda, Belize and the Turks and Caicos Islands 1975-; kt 1971; *Style* - The Hon Sir William Duffus; Cudworth Cottage, Great Wilbraham, Cambridge (☎ 880530)

DUFFY, Bryan S A; *Career* jt chm Brown & Jackson Ltd; *Style* - Bryan Duffy Esq; Brown & Jackson Ltd, Battle Bridge House, 300 Gray's Inn rd, London WC1

DUFFY, Maureen Patricia; da of Grace Wright; *b* 1933; *Educ* Trowbridge High Sch; Sarah Bonnell High Sch for Girls; King's Coll London U (BA); *Career* author, playwright and poet; co-fndr Writers' Action Gp; jt chm Writers' Guild of Great Britain 1977-78; v-pres Beauty Without Cruelty; *Style* - Miss Maureen Duffy; 8 Roland gdns, London SW7

DUFFY, Terence; s of John Duffy; *b* 3 May 1922; *Educ* St Joseph's RC Sch Wolverhampton; *m* 1957, Joyce Sturgess; 1 s, 1 da; *Career* pres, Amlgamated Union of Engineering Workers 1978- (memb Exec Council 1976); memb, TUC General Council 1978-; *Style* - Terence Duffy Esq; 9 Ashfield grove, Wolverhampton, W Midlands (☎ 783528)

DUFTY, Arthur Richard; CBE (1971); s of Thomas Ernest Dufty (d 1915); *b* 25 June 1911; *Educ* Rugby, Liverpool Sch of Architecture; *m* 1937, Kate Brazley, da of Charles Ainsworth (d 1928); 3 children; *Career* served in 1939-45 War as Lt RNVR in N Sea; sec and gen ed to Roy Cmmn on Historical Monuments (E) 1962-72, master of the Armouries in HM Tower of London 1963-76, pres Soc of Antiquaries 1978-; *Recreations* appreciation of architecture, gardens and music; *Clubs* Athenaeum, Arts and Naval; *Style* - Arthur Dufty Esq, CBE; Kelmscott Manor, Oxfordshire; 46 Trafalgar ct, Farnham, Surrey

DUGAN OF VICTORIA, Baroness; Ruby Lilian; da of late Charles Abbott, of Abbott Abbey, Co Cork; *m* 1912, Maj Gen 1 Baron Dugan of Victoria, GCMG, CB, DSO (d 1951, when title became extinct); *Career* DStJ; *Style* - The Rt Hon The Lady

Dugan of Victoria

DUGAN-CHAPMAN, Charles; s of the late Jakob Czajka of Poland; *b* 18 Jan 1918; *Educ* Cieszanow Poland; *m* 1944, Mary Elizabeth, nee Chapman; 2 da; *Career* flying officer Polish Squadron RAF Europe, chm and md Stewart Plastics Ltd 1947; *Recreations* golf, bridge, skiing; *Clubs* The Portland, Sunningdale Golf; *Style* - Charles Dugan-Chapman, Esq; 4 Wilton Crescent, W1 (☎ 01 235 3157); Broomhall, Broomhall Lane, Sunningdale, Berks (☎ Ascot 20947)

DUGDALE, Hon Charlotte; da of 2 Baron Crathorne; *b* 1972; *Style* - The Hon Charlotte Dugdale

DUGDALE, Hon David John; s of late 1 Baron Crathorne, PC, TD; *b* 4 May 1942; *Educ* Eton, Trin Cambridge; *m* 1972, Susan Louise, da of late Maj L A Powell (d 1972); 1 s, 1 da; *Career* farmer and engineer; dir Westair Ltd and Westair Dynamics Ltd; *Recreations* building, photography, shooting; *Style* - The Hon David Dugdale; Park House, Crathorne, Yarm, Cleveland (☎ Stokesley 700225)

DUGDALE, Hon Mrs - Hon Juliet Meriel Lyttelton; JP; da of 10 Viscount Cobham; *b* 1944; *m* 1967, John Michael Dugdale; 1 s, 3 da; *Style* - The Hon Mrs Dugdale JP; Birch Farm, Kinlet, Bewdley, Worcs

DUGDALE, John Robert Stratford; s of Sir William Dugdale, 1 Bt (d 1965); *b* 10 May 1923; *Educ* Eton, Ch Ch Oxford; *m* 1956, Kathryn CVO JP, da of Col Rt Hon Oliver Frederick George Stanley, MC, MP (d 1950, himself 2 s of 17 Earl of Derby); 2 s, 2 da; *Career* CCllr (1969) Salop, Ld-Lt 1975-; chm Telford Dvpt Corp 1971-75, KStJ; *Clubs* Brooks's, White's and MCC; *Style* - John Dugdale Esq, HM Lord-Lieut for Shropshire; Tickwood Hall, Much Wenlock, Salop (☎ Telford 882644)

DUGDALE, Katherine Edith Helen; CVO (1973), JP; *da* of Rt Hon Oliver Stanley (2 s of 17 Earl of Derby by Hon Sibyl, gda of 5 Earl Cadogan); *b* 4 Nov 1923; *m* 1956, John Dugdale; 2 s, 2 da; *Career* JP Salop 1964; Woman of the Bedchamber to the Queen 1955- (Temporary Extra, 1961-71); *Style* - Mrs John Dugdale CVO JP; Tickwood Hall, Much Wenlock, Salop (☎ Telford 882644)

DUGDALE, Peter Robin; s of Dr James Dugdale; *b* 12 Feb 1928; *Educ* Canford, Magdalen Oxford; *m* 1957, Esme Cyraine Brown; 3 da; *Career* md Guardian Royal Exchange Assurance 1978-, chm Trade Indemnity Insurance Co Ltd 1980-; dep chm British Insurance Assoc 1979; *Style* - Peter Dugdale Esq; Trentham House, Emsworth, Hants (☎ 024 34 2934)

DUGDALE, Hon Thomas Arthur John; s and h of 2 Baron Crathorne; *b* 30 Sept 1977; *Style* - The Hon Thomas Dugdale

DUGDALE, William Matthew Stratford; s and h of Sir William Stratford Dugdale, 2 Bt; *b* 22 Feb 1959; *Style* - William Dugdale Esq

DUGDALE, Sir William Stratford; 2 Bt (UK 1936) of Merevale and Blyth, co Warwick; MC (1943), JP (Warwicks 1951), DL (1955); s of Sir William Francis Stratford Dugdale, 1 Bt (d 1965); *b* 29 March 1922; *Educ* Eton and Balliol Coll Oxford; *m* 1, 1952, Lady Belinda Pleydell-Bouverie (d 1961), da of 7 Earl of Radnor; 1 s, 3 da; m 2, 1967, Cecilia Mary, da of Lt-Col Sir William Mount, 2 Bt; 1 s, 1 da; *Heir* s William Matthew Stratford Dugdale; *Career* Capt Grenadier Gds 1944, served in Africa and Italy (despatches); slr 1949, High Sheriff Warwicks 1971-72; chm Trent River Authority 1965-73, Severn Trent Water Authority 1974-; High Steward of Stratford upon Avon 1976-; dir Phoenix Assurance and other cos; *Clubs* Brooks's, White's and MCC; *Style* - Sir William Dugdale, Bt, MC, JP, DL; Blyth Hall, Coleshill, Birmingham; Merevale Hall, Atherstone, Warwickshire; 24 Bryanston Mews West, W1 (☎ 01 262 2510)

DUGMORE, Rev Prof Clifford William; s of Rev Canon William Ernest Dugmore, MA, RD; *b* 9 May 1909; *Educ* King Edward VI Sch Birmingham, Exeter Coll Oxford, Queens' Cambridge; *Career* prof of Ecclesiastical History, King's Coll U of London 1958-76, emeritus prof 1976-;

memb Advisory Editorial Board, The Journal of Ecclesiastical History 1979- (ed 1950-78); British memb, Editorial Board, Novum Testamentum, 1956; author; *Style* - Rev Prof Clifford Dugmore; 77 The Street, Puttenham, Surrey (☎ Guildford 810460)

DUKE, Hon Derek John Philip; s and h of 3 Baron Merrivale; *b* 16 Mar 1948; *Educ* Arcachon France, Lycée Francais London, Lycée Janson de Sailly Paris; *Style* - The Hon Derek Duke; 15 Rue Raynouard, Paris XVI, France (☎ Auteuil 75 99)

DUKE, Neville Frederick; DSO (1943), OBE (1953), DFC and 2 Bars (1942, 1943, 1944), AFC (1948), MC (Czech 1946); s of Frederick Duke; *b* 11 Jan 1922; *Educ* Convent of St Mary and Judds Sch Tonbridge; *m* 1947, Gwendoline Dorothy Fellows; *Career* ret from RAF (Squadron Leader) 1948; test pilot; md Duke Aviation; man Dowty Gp Aircraft Operating Unit; Technical Adviser, consultant and ch test pilot Miles Aviation Ltd; *Style* - Neville Duke Esq DSO OBE DFC** AFC MC; Bywater House, Pierside, Lymington, Hants

DUKE-WOOLLEY, Hon Mrs Elizabeth Alice Cecilia; *née* Jolliffe; da of 3 Baron Hylton (d 1945); *b* 1906; *m* 1, 1928 (m dis 1937), Lt-Col Edmond Joly de Lotbinière (kt 1964); 2 s; m 2, 1938 (m dis 1946), Hilary Beecham Duke-Woolley, DFC, RAF; *Style* - The Hon Mrs Elizabeth Duke-Woolley

DULVERTON, 2 Baron (UK 1929); Sir Frederick Anthony Hamilton Wills; 3 Bt (UK 1897), CBE (1974), TD, DL (Glos 1979); s of 1 Baron Dulverton, OBE (d 1956) and Victoria, OBE, da of Rear-Adm Sir Edward Chichester, 9 Bt, CB, CMG; *b* 19 Dec 1915; *Educ* Eton, Magdalen Oxford; *m* 1, 1939 (m dis 1960), Judith Betty, da of Lt-Col Hon Ian Leslie-Melville, TD, s of 11 Earl of Leven and 10 of Melville; 2 s, 2 da; m 2, 1962, Ruth Violet Mary, da of Sir Walter Randolph Fitzroy Farquhar, 5 Bt, and formerly w of Maj R G Fanshawe; *Heir* s, Hon Gilbert Wills; *Career* Jt MFH N Cotswold 1950-56, Heythrop 1967-70; 2 Lt Lovat Scouts 1936, Maj 1944, pres Timber Growers' Orgn Ltd, Bath and Wells and Southern Counties Ag Soc 1973, Three Counties Ag Soc 1975, British Deer Soc, memb Home Grown Timber Advsy Ctee, Red Deer Cmmn, Scottish Advsy Ctee to Nature Conservancy Cncl, chm Dulverton Tst, tstee World Wildlife Fund; *Style* - The Rt Hon The Lord Dulverton, CBE, TD, DL; Batsford Park, Moreton-in-Marsh, Glos (☎ 50303); Fassfern, Kinlocheil, Fort William, Inverness-shire (☎ Kinlocheil 232)

DUMAS, Henry; CBE (1974), MC (1945); s of Henry Raymond McLeod Dumas (d 1971); *b* 31 May 1915; *Educ* Radley and New Coll Oxford; *m* 1945, Hester Hermoine, da of Brig Henry John Lenton of Capetown SA (d 1953); 1 s, 2 da; *Career* served in WW II with RAC and RTR; dep chm Willis Faber and Dumas 1969-71 (former dir), chm Lloyd's Insurance Brokers Assoc 1960-61, memb Ctee of Lloyd's 1962-66, hon marine insurance adviser to Dept of Trade 1962-79; high sheriff Surrey 1966-67; *Recreations* natural history, golf, shooting and philately; *Clubs* Farmers'; *Style* - Maj Henry Dumas, CBE, MC; Iken Hall, Woodbridge, Suffolk (☎ Snape 440)

DUMFRIES, Earl of; John Colum Crichton-Stuart; s and h of 6 Marquess of Bute; *b* 26 April 1958; *Style* - Earl of Dumfries; Mount Stuart, Rothesay, Isle of Bute

DUMMETT, Prof Michael Anthony Eardley; s of George Herbert Dummett; *b* 27 Jun 1925; *Educ* Sandroyd Sch, Winchester Coll, Ch Ch Oxford; *m* 1951, Ann Chesney; 3 s, 2 da (1 s, 1 da, decd); *Career* reader Philosophy of Mathematics Oxford U 1962-74, fell All Souls Coll Oxford 1950-79 (sr research fell 1974-79), Wykeham Prof of Logic Oxford U, fell New Coll Oxford 1979-, author of books on philosophy and Tarot, FBA (1968); *Style* - Prof Michael Dummett; 54 Park Town, Oxford (☎ 58698)

DUNALLEY, 6 Baron (I 1800); Henry Desmond Graham Prittie; s of 5 Baron (d 1948); *b* 14 Oct 1912; *Educ* Stowe and RMC; *m* 1947, Philippa, da of Maj Hon

Philip Plantagenet Cary, s of 12 Viscount Falkland, JP, DL; 2 s, 1 da; *Heir* s, Hon Henry Prittie; *Career* Rifle Bde 1933, served E Africa, Mid East, Italy and SEAC 1939-46, Lt-Col, ret 1953; *Recreations* fishing; *Clubs* Kildare Street & University (Dublin); *Style* - The Rt Hon The Lord Dunalley; Glendalough Lodge, Recess, Co Galway, Eire (☎ Recess 2)

DUNBAR, Sir Archibald Ranulph; 11 Bt (NS 1700), of Northfield, Moray; s of Maj Sir (Archibald) Edward Dunbar, 10 Bt, MC (d 1969); *b* 8 Aug 1927; *Educ* Wellington, Pembroke Coll Cambridge, Imperial Coll of Tropical Ag Trinidad; *m* 1974, Amelia Millar Sommerville, da of H C Davidson, of Currie, Midlothian; 1 s, 2 da; *Heir* s, Edward Horace Dunbar; *Career* entered Colonial Service 1953, Ag Offr Uganda, ret 1970 *Style* - Sir Archibald Dunbar, Bt; The Old Manse, Duffus, Elgin (☎ Hopeman 270)

DUNBAR, Sir Drummond Cospatrick Ninian; 9 Bt (NS 1698), of Durn, Banffshire, MC (1943); s of Sir George Alexander Drummond, 8 Bt (d 1949); *b* 9 May 1917; *Educ* Radley and Worcester Coll Oxford; *m* 1957, Sheila Barbara Mary, da of John B de Fonblanque; 1 s; *Heir* s, Robert Drummond Cospatrick Dunbar; *Career* served 1939-45 (Middle E 1942-43, Sicily 1943, Normandy 1944), Maj Black Watch, ret 1958; *Clubs* Naval and Military; *Style* - Sir Drummond Dunbar, Bt, MC; Beaufield House, St Saviour, Jersey, CI

DUNBAR, Edward Horace; s and h of Sir Archibald Dunbar, 11 Bt; *b* 18 Mar 1977; *Style* - Edward Dunbar Esq

DUNBAR, Esther, Lady - Esther Naomi; da of William Henry Robinson; *m* 1930, as his 2 w, Sir Adrian Ivor Dunbar, 12 Bt (d 1977); *Style* - Esther, Lady Dunbar

DUNBAR, John Greenwell; s of John Dunbar; *b* 1 Mar 1930; *Educ* UCS London; Balliol Oxford; *m* 1974, Elizabeth Mill Blyth; *Career* sec Royal Commission on the Ancient and Historical Monuments of Scotland 1978-; memb Ancient Monuments Board for Scotland 1978; FSA, FSA Scot, MA; *Style* - John Dunbar Esq; Patie's Mill, Carlops, by Penicuik, Midlothian (☎ West Linton 250)

DUNBAR, Sir Jean Ivor; 13 Bt (NS 1694), of Mochrum, Wigtownshire; s of Sir Adrian Ivor Dunbar, 12 Bt (d 1977); *b* 4 Apr 1918; *m* 1944, Rose Jeanne Hertsch; 2 s, 1 da; *Career* late Sgt Mountain Engineers, USA Army; *Style* - Sir Jean Dunbar, Bt; 44/55 39th st, Long Island City, New York, USA

DUNBAR, James Michael; s and h of Sir Jean Dunbar, 13 Bt; *b* 17 Jan 1950; *Career* Capt USAF; *Style* - James Dunbar Esq

DUNBAR OF HEMPRIGGS, Dame Maureen Daisy Helen; Btss (NS 1706), of Hempriggs, Caithness-shire; da of late Courtenay Edward Moore, s of late Jessie Mona Duff (who m Rev Canon Courtenay Moore), da of de jure 5 Bt; suc kinsman, Sir George Cospatrick Duff-Sutherland-Dunbar, 7 Bt, 1963; assumed name of Dunbar 1963, and recognised in the name of Dunbar of Hempriggs by Lyon Court 1965; *b* 19 Aug 1906; *Educ* Headington Sch Oxford, RCM; *m* 1940, Leonard James Blake, former dir of music Malvern Coll; 1 s, 1 da; *Heir* s, Richard Dunbar of Hempriggs, yr; *Career* music teacher; *Style* - Lady Dunbar of Hempriggs, Btss; 51 Gloucester st, Winchcombe, Cheltenham, Glos; Ackergill Tower, Wick, Caithness

DUNBAR, Robert Drummond Cospatrick; s and h of Sir Drummond Dunbar, 9 Bt; *b* 17 June 1958; *Educ* Harrow, Ch Ch Oxford; *Style* - Robert Dunbar Esq

DUNBAR OF HEMPRIGGS, YOUNGER, Richard Francis; s and h of Lady Maureen Dunbar of Hempriggs, Btss; *b* 8 Jan 1945; *m* 1969, (Elizabeth Margaret) Jane, da of George Lister, of Gloucester; 1 da; *Style* - Richard Dunbar of Hempriggs, yr; 712 Crossway rd, Burlingame, Cal 94010, USA

DUNBOYNE, 28 Baron (18 by Patent) (I 1324 and 1541); His Hon Judge Patrick Theobald Tower Butler; s of 27 Baron (d 1945) and Dora, da of late Tom Tower, OBE, late RNVR; *b* 27 Jan 1917;

Educ Winchester, Trin Cambridge; *m* 1950, Anne Marie, da of Sir Victor Alexander Louis Mallet, GCMG, CVO; 1 s, 3 da; *Heir* s, Hon John Fitzwalter Butler; *Career* barr Mid Temple 1949, Inner Temple 1962, King's Inns Dublin 1966, FO 1945-46, recorder of Hastings 1961-71, a dep chm Kent Quarter Sessions 1963-71, of Middx Quarter Sessions 1962-65, of Inner London Quarter Sessions 1971, a Circuit Judge 1972-; *Style* - His Hon Judge The Lord Dunboyne; 36 Ormonde Gate, SW3 (☎ 01 352 1837); Wittersham House, nr Tenterden, Kent (☎ 079 77 365)

DUNCAN, Lady - Beatrice Mary Moore; da of Thomas O'Carroll and widow of Maj Philip Blair-Oliphant; *m* 1960, as his 2 w, Sir James Alexander Lawson Duncan, 1 Bt (d 1974); *Style* - Lady Duncan; Jordanston, by Alyth, Perthshire

DUNCAN, Hon Mrs - Hon Clare Veronica James; da of Baron Saint Brides (Life Peer 1977); *b* 1950; *m* 1970, Patrick Duncan; c; *Style* - The Hon Mrs Duncan; Station Biologique Le Sambuc, La Tour du Valat, Bouches du Rhône, France

DUNCAN, Lady - Etelka de Vangel; *m* 1958, Sir (Charles Edgar) Oliver Duncan, 3 and last Bt (d 1964); *Style* - Lady Duncan; Horsforth Hall, Guiseley, W Yorks

DUNCAN, George; s of William Duncan (d 1966); *b* 9 Nov 1933; *Educ* London Sch of Ec, Wharton Sch of Finance, Pennsylvania U; *m* 1965, Frauke Ulricke; 1 da; *Career* ch exec Truman Hanbury Buxton Ltd 1971-72, v-chm Int Distillers and Vintners Ltd 1972, chm Lloyds and Scottish Ltd 1976-, ch exec Yule Catto and Co Ltd 1973-75; FCA, FBIM; *Recreations* tennis, riding and opera; *Style* - George Duncan Esq; Fisher's Gate, Withyham, Hartfield, E Sussex (☎ Hartfield 246)

DUNCAN, Ian McIntosh; s of late James Duncan; *b* 25 Nov 1931; *Educ* Royal H S Edinburgh; *m* 1958, Marjorie Anne, nee Brown; 3 s; *Career* chartered accountant, dir Cavenham Ltd, chm Anglo-Continental Finance & Investment, dir Grand Union (USA); *Recreations* tennis, squash, badminton, golf; *Style* - Ian Duncan Esq; Flat 14, Keythorpes, Manor rd, Eastcliff, Bournemouth, Dorset; 14 Wrensfield, Hemel Hempstead, Herts (☎ 0442 51980)

DUNCAN, Sir James Blair; s of John Duncan; *b* 24 Aug 1927; *Educ* Whitehall Sch Glasgow; *m* 1974, Betty Psaltis; *Career* chm and ch exec Transport Dvpt Gp Ltd 1975-; MICA (Scot); kt 1981 *Style* - Sir James Duncan; 17 Kingston House South, Ennismore Gdns, London, SW7

DUNCAN, John M; *Career* jt md J & W Henderson (Hldgs) Ltd; *Style* - John Duncan Esq; Henderson House, 111 Gallowgate, Aberdeen

DUNCAN, Stanley Frederick St Clare; s of Stanley Duncan; *b* 13 Nov 1927; *Educ* Latymer Upper; *m* 1967, Jennifer Bennett; 2 da; *Career* For Serv 1967- (India Off 1946, CRO 1947-67); Head Consular Dept FCO 1977-80, Canadian Nat Def Coll Kingston Ontario 1980-81; Br Ambass Bolivia 1981-; *Style* - Stanley Duncan Esq; 91 Gloucester st, SW1

DUNCAN, Hon Mrs - Hon (Doreen) Synolda Tower Butler; da of late 27 Baron Dunboyne; *b* 1918; *m* 1945, Maj Atholl Duncan, MC, RA; 2 s, 2 da; *Style* - The Hon Mrs Duncan; Flat 62/63, 15 Portman sq, London W1

DUNCAN-MILLAR, Ian Alastair; CBE (1978), MC; s of Sir James Duncan Millar; *b* 22 Nov 1914; *Educ* Gresham's Sch, Trinity Coll Cambridge; *m* 1945, Louise Reid McCosh; 2 s, 2 da; *Career* dir Macdonald Fraser and Co Ltd, Perth 1961-, chm Tayside Sound Ltd 1979, memb Roy Co of Archers (Queen's Body Guard for Scotland) 1956-, DL (1963), JP (1952) Perthshire; *Style* - Ian Duncan-Millar Esq CBE MC JP DL; Remony, Aberfeldy, Perthshire (☎ Kenmore 209)

DUNCAN-SANDYS, Baron (Life Peer UK 1974); Duncan Edwin Duncan-Sandys; CH (1973), PC (1944); s of Capt George John Sandys, formerly MP for Wells (d 1937); changed surname to Duncan-Sandys by Deed Poll 1974; *b* 24 Jan 1908; *Educ* Eton, Magdalen Oxford; *m*

1, 1935 (m dis 1960), Diana (d 1963), da of Rt Hon Sir Winston Churchill, KG, MP (d 1965); 1 s, 2 da; m 2, 1962, Marie-Claire, da of Adrien Schmitt of Paris, and formerly Viscountess Hudson; 1 da; *Career* Diplomatic Serv 1930, MP (C) Lambeth Norwood 1935-45, Wandsworth Streatham 1950-74, Min of Defence 1957-59, Min of Aviation 1959-60, Sec of State for C'wlth Relations 1960-64, Sec of State for Colonies 1962-64, Min in Charge of Central African Office 1963-64, chm Lonrho 1972- (consultant at £50,000 pa to 1973, when received £130,000 in compensation to become chm; the payment of the latter sum (perfectly legally) into a Cayman Islands account prompted Edward Heath's celebrated remark about the 'unacceptable face of capitalism' and in turn the rather less celebrated riposte (from a contributor to the Spectator) that the phrase said more about Heath than it did about capitalism), dir House of Fraser; founded European Movement 1947, memb European Consultative Assembly 1950-51, pres and founder Civic Trust, pres Europa Nostra 1969-; *Style* - The Rt Hon The Lord Duncan-Sandys CH PC; 86 Vincent sq, SW1 (☎ 01 834 5886)

DUNCOMBE, Hon Jake Barnaby; s of 6 Baron Feversham; *b* 17 Mar 1972; *Style* - The Hon Jake Duncombe

DUNCOMBE, Hon Jasper Orlando Slingsby; s and h of 6 Baron Feversham; *b* 14 Mar 1968; *Style* - The Hon Jasper Duncombe

DUNCOMBE, Hon Melissa Rose; da of 6 Baron Feversham; *b* 1973; *Style* - The Hon Melissa Duncombe

DUNCUMB, Dr Peter; s of William Duncumb; *b* 26 Jan 1931; *Educ* Oundle Sch, Clare Cambridge; *m* 1955, Anne Leslie Taylor; 2 s, 1 da; *Career* dir and gen man Tube Investments Research Laboratories 1979- (assist dir 1972-79); *Style* - Dr Peter Duncumb; 5 Woolards Lane, Great Shelford, Cambridge (☎ Cambridge 843 064)

DUNDAS, Lord (Richard) Bruce; s of 3 Marquess of Zetland; *b* 16 Jan 1951; *Educ* Harrow; *m* 1974, Jane, da of E Wright; 1 s, 1 da; *Style* - Lord Bruce Dundas; 18 Wetherby gdns, London SW5

DUNDAS, Lord David Paul Nicholas; s of 3 Marquess of Zetland; *b* 2 June 1945; *Educ* Harrow and Central Sch of Speech and Drama; *m* 1971, Corinna, da of Denys Scott, of Chelsea; 1 s, 1 da; *Career* actor; *Style* - Lord David Dundas; 4 Bolingbroke Grove, SW11

DUNDAS, Lady Henrietta Kate; da of Earl of Ronaldshay; *b* 9 Feb 1970; *Style* - Lady Henrietta Dundas

DUNDAS, Hugh McKenzie; s of late Hon Richard Serle Dundas (3 s of 6 Viscount Melville); hp to Viscountcy of Melville; *b* 3 June 1910; *Educ* Sask U; *m* 1939, Catherine Sanderson, da of late John Wallace, of Edinburgh; 1 s, 1 da; *Clubs* Toronto Royal Canadian Military Inst, and Pembroke Golf and Country; *Style* - Hugh Dundas Esq; 298 Alfred st, Pembroke, Ontario, Canada

DUNDAS, Gp Capt Hugh Spencer Lisle; CBE (1977), DSO & Bar (1944, 1945), DFC (1941), DL (Surrey 1969); 2 s of Frederick Dundas (s of Lord John Dundas, sometime MP Richmond and yr bro of 3 Earl & 1 Marquess of Zetland; Lord John m Hon Alice Wood, 2 da of 1 Viscount Halifax and hence great aunt of the pre-war For Sec, the 1 Earl of H) and Sylvia, da of Hugh Phillipps (whose f was 1 cous of Ambrose Phillipps de Lisle, the Catholic writer, ecumenicist and founder of the first Cistercian Abbey in England since the Reformation); *b* 22 July 1920; *Educ* Stowe; *m* 1950, Hon Enid Lawrence, 2 da of 1 Baron Oaksey & (3) Trevethin and sis of Hon John Geoffrey Lawrence, the gentleman rider and racing correspondent; 1 s, 2 da; *Career* served RAF WW II Mediterranean, ret 1947; md Br Electric Traction 1973-81, dep chm 1981-; chm Thames TV 1981-, Rediffusion 1978-, Rediffusion TV 1978-, BET Omnibus Servs 1978-, BET Invests 1978-; dir Bdcast Relay Serv (Overseas) Ltd, Rediffusion Hldgs, Wembley Stadium Ltd; formerly with Beaverbrook Newspapers Ltd; memb Cncl, & Fin & Gen Purposes Ctee RAF Benevolent Fund 1976-, Cncl Nat Soc Cancer Relief 1976-; *Clubs*

White's, RAF; *Style* - Gp Capt Hugh Dundas, CBE, DSO*, DFC, DL; The Schoolroom, Dockenfield, Farnham, Surrey (☎ Frensham 2331); 55 Iverna Court, W8 (☎ 01 937 0773)

DUNDAS, Lady; Isabel; da of Charles Goring; *m* 1933, Maj Sir Thomas Calderwood Dundas, 7 and last Bt, MBE (d 1970); *Style* - Lady Dundas; 6 The Green, Slaugham, Handcross, Sussex

DUNDAS, Hon James Edward; s of Lord Dundas (Robin Lawrence Dundas, s of Earl Ronaldshay); *b* 2 May 1967; *Style* - The Hon James Dundas

DUNDAS, Robert Giffen; CBE (1961); s of James Dundas; *b* 4 March 1909; *Educ* Edinburgh U; *m* 1938, Pauleen Gosling; 3 s, 1 da; *Career* former consul HM Diplomatic Serv, consul-gen Amsterdam 1966-69; ret; *Style* - Robert Dundas Esq, CBE; 43 Imber Close, Ember Lane, Esher, Surrey (☎ 01 398 7040)

DUNDAS, Hon Mrs - Hon (Enid) Rosamund Lawrence; da of late 1 Baron Oaksey and 3 Baron Trevethin; *b* 1924; *m* 1950, Gp Capt Hugh Spencer Lisle Dundas, CBE, DSO, DFC, RAF (ret); *Style* - The Hon Mrs Dundas; The Schoolroom, Dockenfield, Farnham, Surrey; 55 Iverna ct, London W8 (☎ 01 937 0773)

DUNDAS, Lord; Robin Lawrence Dundas; s and h of Earl of Ronaldshay and gs of 3 Marquess of Zetland, ED, DL; *b* 5 March 1965; *Style* - Lord Dundas

DUNDAS, Hon Mrs Richard - Mathilde Mary; *née* Saxon; *m* 1926, as his 2 w, Hon Richard Serle Dundas (d 1968), s of late 6 Viscount Melville; 2 da; *Style* - The Hon Mrs Richard Dundas; 786 Island Road, Victoria, BC, Canada

DUNDAS, Sir Robert Whyte Melville; 6 Bt (UK 1821); s of Sir George Whyte Melville Dundas, 5 Bt (d 1934); *b* 31 Oct 1881; *m* 1926, Dorothea Emilie Victoria (d 1963), da of late A W Wiseman, MusB, of Monmouth; *Heir* none; *Career* admin offr Nigeria 1911-30; *Style* - Sir Robert Dundas, Bt; Comrie House, Comrie, Perthshire (☎ 330)

DUNDAS, Lady Victoria Clare; da of Earl of Ronaldshay; *b* 2 Jan 1973; *Style* - Lady Victoria Dundas

DUNDAS, Lady Viola Mary; da of 2 Marquess of Zetland, GCSI, GCIE, PC (d 1961); *b* 4 Jan 1910; *Style* - Lady Viola Dundas; Flat 11, Sloane Ave Mansions, Chelsea, SW3 (☎ 01 584 9427); Cromwell House, Speen, nr Newbury, Berks (☎ Newbury 44386)

DUNDEE, 11 Earl of (S 1660); Henry James Scrymgeour of Dundee; PC (1959), JP (Fife 1927), DL (1933); Viscount Dudhope and Lord Scrymgeour (S 1641), Lord Inverkeithing (S 1660), Lord Glassary (UK 1954); Hereditary Roy Standard Bearer for Scotland; s of Col Henry Scrymgeour-Wedderburn, de jure 10 Earl (d 1924); claim to Viscountcy of Dudhope admitted by Ctee for Privileges of House of Lords 1952, and to Earldom of Dundee 1953; *b* 3 May 1902; *Educ* Winchester, Balliol Oxford; *m* 1946, his former sis-in-law Patricia Katherine, da of late Col Lord Herbert Montagu Douglas Scott, s of 6 Duke of Buccleuch and 8 of Queensberry, KG, KT, PC, and widow of (1) Lt-Col Walter Douglas Faulkner, MC, Irish Gds and (2) Lt-Col the Hon David Scrymgeour-Wedderburn, DSO, Scots Gds, s of de jure 10 Earl of Dundee; 1 s; *Heir* s, Lord Scrymgeour; *Career* MP (C) Renfrewshire W 1931-45, PPS to Sec of Bd of Education 1933-35, to Parly Sec to Min of Agric 1935-36, to Sec of State for Scotland 1936, Parly Under-Sec of State for Scotland 1936-39, Jt Under-Sec 1941-42, served with Black Watch 1939-41, Min without Portfolio 1958-61, Min of State FO 1961-64, Dep Leader of House of Lords 1962-64; *Style* - The Rt Hon The Earl of Dundee, PC, JP, DL; Birkhill, Cupar, Fife (☎ Gauldry 209)

DUNDERDALE, Cdr Wilfred Albert; CMG (1942), MBE (1920); s of Richard Albert Dunderdale (d 1945); *b* 24 Dec 1899; *Educ* Russia; *m* 1, 1952, Mrs Dorothy Mabel Brayshaw Hyde (d 1978), da of James Murray Crofts, DSC, CBE; m 2, 1980, Deborah Jackson McLeod, da of Eugene Bailey Jackson, of USA (d 1935);

Career trained as naval architect 1914-17, RNVR end of WW I, with Mediterranean Fleet 1918-22 (despatches), transferred to British Embassy Constantinople 1922-26, Paris Embassy 1926-40, Cdre 1939, attached Foreign Serv London 1946-67; ret 1967; *Recreations* yachting; *Clubs* Boodle's; *Style* - Cdr Wilfred Dunderdale, CMG, MBE, RNVR; Castlefield, Bletchingley, Surrey, RH1 4LB

DUNDONALD, 14 Earl of (S 1669); Maj Ian Douglas Leonard Cochrane; also Lord Cochrane of Dundonald (S 1647), Lord Cochrane of Paisley and Ochiltree (S 1669), and Marquez de Maranham (Empire of Brazil 1823 by Dom Pedro for 10 Earl, *see* below); s of late Hon Douglas Roger Cochrane, 2 s of 12 Earl, (whereby Lord Dundonald is gggs of 10 Earl, better known as Lord Cochrane, the brilliant but quarrelsome naval commander who destroyed Napoleon's last hopes of naval success at the Basque Roads in 1809; also a radical MP, a speculator on the stock exchange (and a convicted fraud, tho' he always protested his innocence), the friend of various S American nations in shaking off Iberian hegemony (he commanded the Chilean navy under Chile and served the Peruvians and Brazilians), not to mention the Greeks (he commanded their navy too), and lastly an inventor (he was an early supporter of steam and the screw propeller for warships), in which latter capacity he offered (during the Crimean War) to put into practice a scheme for destroying the enemy fleet that he had been maturing since 1811; the committee that judged the plan intriguingly pronounced it practical but inhumane); suc unc (13 Earl) 1958; *b* 6 Dec 1918; *Educ* Wellington, RMC Sandhurst; *m* 1, 1960, Aphra Farquhar (d 1972), da of late Cdr George Fetherstonhaugh, of The Beacon, Benenden, Kent; 1 s, 1 da; m 2, 1978, Ann Margaret, da of late Sir Joseph Harkness, CMG, OBE; *Heir* s, Lord Cochrane; *Career* joined 1 Bn Black Watch 1938, GSO 2 War Office and GSO 2 Army Council Secretariat 1952-53, ret; a Scottish Rep Peer 1959-63, chm de Jersey & Co (Finland) Ltd Gp of Cos, chm Secure Holdings Ltd, chm Anglo-Chilean Soc 1958-65, pres of Ayr and Bute Assoc of Youth Clubs; *Style* - Maj The Rt Hon The Earl of Dundonald; Lochnell Castle, Ledaig, Argyll; Beacon Hall, Benenden, Cranbrook, Kent

DUNHAM, Cyril John; s of late Frederick Arthur Dunham; *b* 22 April 1908; *Educ* Watford G S, Coll of Estate Management; *m* 1937, Vera Georgia, nee Ellwood; 1 s, 2 da; *Career* FRICS, tech adviser to War Damage Cmmn, dir Nationwide Building Soc 1944- (past chm), dep chm Peterborough Dvpt Corpn, past chm Building Socs Assoc; *Style* - Cyril Dunham Esq; 15 Turner close, Hampstead, NW11 (☎ 01 455 8348)

DUNICAN, Peter Thomas; CBE (1977); s of Peter Dunican; *b* 15 March 1918; *Educ* Central Sch Clapham, Battersea Polytechnic; *m* 1942, Irene May Jordan; 2 s, 1 da (and 1 da decd); *Career* chm Ove Arup Partnership 1977- (formerly structural engr, sr ptnr), chm National Building Agency 1978-; *Style* - Peter Dunican Esq, CBE; 60 Ryecroft rd, London, SW16 (☎ 01 670 7056)

DUNKERLEY, Harvey John; CBE (1953); s of Joseph Braithwaite Dunkerley; *b* 10 Oct 1902; *Educ* Owen's Sch London, Magdalen Coll Oxford; *m* 1, 1928, Kay Hargreaves (d 1958); m 2, 1961, Thelma Couch; 1 s, 3 da; *Career* former controller Midland Region BBC 1948-64; ret; *Style* - Harvey Dunkerley Esq, CBE; Gallipot Farm, Broadway, Worcs (☎ Evesham 830 395)

DUNKLEY, Capt James Lewis; CBE (1970, OBE 1946), RD (1943); s of William Edward Dunkley (d 1911); *b* 13 Sept 1908; *Educ* Lawrence Sheriff, Rugby, Thames Nautical Training Coll HMS 'Worcester'; *m* 1937, Phyllis Mary (d 1970), da of William John Cale; 1 da; *Career* served in 1939-45 War in armed merchant cruisers; cadet Peninsular and Oriental Steam Navigation Co 1925, Cdre 1964-67, marine man P & O Passenger Div 1971-72, Master of the Hon Co of Master Mariners 1970; *Clubs* City Livery; *Style* - Capt James Dunkley, CBE, RD; 1 Collindale gdns, Clacton on Sea, Essex (☎ Clacton 813950)

DUNKLEY, Philip Parker; MC; *Career* exec chm Mitchell Gp Ltd and subsidiary cos, dep chm Bestobell Ltd, chm Mitchell Cotts Ltd, dir Consolidated Gold Fields Ltd; *Style* - Philip Dunkley Esq, MC; Mitchell Cotts Gp Ltd, Cotts House, Camomile st, London, EC3

DUNLEATH, 4 Baron (UK 1892); Charles Edward Henry John Mulholland; TD, DL (Co Down 1964); s of 3 Baron Dunleath, CBE, DSO (d 1956) and Henrietta, da of late Most Rev C F D'Arcy, Archbishop of Armagh; *b* 23 June 1933; *Educ* Eton, Cambridge U; *m* 1959, Dorinda Margery, da of late Lt-Gen Arthur Percival, CB, DSO and Bar, OBE, MC; *Heir* cous, Maj Sir Michael Mulholland, 2 Bt; *Career* 11 Hussars, cmd N Irish Horse, actg Lt-Col 1967-69; nat gov BBC for N Ireland 1967-73, memb N Ireland Legislative Assembly and Dep. Speaker 1973-75, memb N Ireland Constitutional Convention 1975-76, chm Carreras of N Ireland 1974-, N Ireland Independent TV Ltd, Dunleath Estates Ltd, Ulster & General Hldgs Ltd; *Style* - The Rt Hon The Lord Dunleath, TD, DL; Ballywater Park, Newtownards, Co Down, N Ireland (☎ Ballywater 203)

DUNLOP, Sir (Ernest) Edward; CMG (1965), OBE (1947); s of James Henry Dunlop, of Benalla, Australia (d 1947); *b* 12 July 1907; *Educ* Benalla High Sch, Melbourne U, Ormond Coll and British Postgrad Med Sch Hammersmith; *m* 1945, Helen Leigh Raeburn, da of Mephan John Ferguson (d 1949); 2 s; *Career* surgeon specialist EMS St Mary's Hosp Paddington 1939, Capt RAAMC 1935, medical liaison offr British Troops Greece and Crete 1941, CO 1 Allied Gen Hosp Java 1942, Cdr various prison camps and hospitals in Java, Malaya and Siam 1942-45, ADMS 'Blackforce' 1946 (despatches), Col RAAMC (ret); consultant surgn Roy Melbourne Hosp 1967-, hon surgn Roy Victorian Eye and Ear Hosp 1949-67, consultant surgn Peter Macallum Clinic for Cancer 1955-67, Colombo Plan adviser Thailand and Ceylon 1956, India 1960, Gordon Taylor Oration Malaysia 1978, pres Anti Cancer Cncl of Victoria 1980-; 'Australian of the Year' award 1977; kt 1969; *Recreations* golf, travelling and farming; *Clubs* Melbourne Naval and Military, Melbourne Cricket and British Barbarian; *Style* - Sir Edward Dunlop, CMG, OBE; 605 Toorak rd, Toorak, Australia, 3142; 4 Parliament pla, Melbourne, Australia, 3002

DUNLOP, Frank; CBE (1977); s of Charles Norman Dunlop; *b* 15 Feb 1927; *Educ* Kibworth Beauchamp G S, Univ Coll London; *Career* theatre dir (Old Vic, Nat Theatre, RSC, Roy Ct, amongst others), former assoc dir and admin dir Nat Theatre, dir The Young Vic 1969-77, consultant 1977-; *Style* - Frank Dunlop Esq, CBE; The Young Vic, The Cut, London, SE1

DUNLOP, Norman Gordon Edward; s of Ross Munn Dunlop; *b* 16 April 1928; *Educ* Trinity Coll Glenalmond; *m* 1952, Jean Taylor; 1 s, 1 da; *Career* former ch exec Commercial Union Assurance Co Ltd, dir Inchcape Berhad, Singapore 1979-*Style* - Norman Dunlop Esq; 6 Cluny Hill, Singapore 10 (☎ 669 279)

DUNLOP, Robert Fergus; AE (1956); s of Maj A Fergus Dunlop TD, OBE (d 1980); *b* 22 June 1929; *Educ* Marlborough, Cambridge U, MIT; *m* 1966, Jane Clare, da of Lt-Col George Hervey McManus (d 1959); 1 s, 2 da; *Career* dir Lonrho Ltd and subsids 1972-, with Westland Aircraft Ltd 1967-70, Br Aircraft Corpn and Bristol Aeroplane Co Ltd 1952-80; *Recreations* sailing, skiing; *Style* - Robert Dunlop Esq, AE; 42 Woodford Square, W14 (☎ 01 602 2579)

DUNLOP, Roy Leslie; CMG (1965); s of late E J D Dunlop, of Sydney; *b* 14 April 1899; *Educ* Rockhampton; *m* 1925, Olive M F Black; 1 s; *Career* clerk of Parliament, Queensland 1954-68; *Style* - Roy Dunlop Esq, CMG; 30 Ralston st, Wilston, Queensland, Australia

DUNLOP, Thomas; s and h of Sir Thomas Dunlop, 3 Bt; *b* 22 April 1951; *Style* - Thomas Dunlop Esq

DUNLOP, Sir Thomas; 3 Bt (UK 1916) of Woodbourne, Co Renfrew; s of Sir Thomas Dunlop, 2 Bt (d 1963); *b* 11 April 1912; *Educ* Shrewsbury and St John's Coll

Cambridge; *m* 1947, Adda Mary Alison, da of Thomas Arthur Smith (d 1952); 1 s, 2 da; *Heir* s, Thomas Dunlop; *Career* CA; ptnr Thomas Dunlop and Sons, late chm of Savings Bank of Glasgow, gov Hutcheson's Sch 1957-80; OStJ 1965; *Recreations* fishing, shooting and golf; *Clubs* Western Glasgow; *Style* - Sir Thomas Dunlop, Bt; The Corrie, Kilmacolm, Renfrewshire (☎ 0505 87 3239)

DUNLOP, Sir William (Norman Gough); s of Norman Matthew Dunlop; *b* 9 April 1914; *Educ* Waitiki Boys' H S; *m* 1940, Ruby Jean Archie; 3 s, 3 da; *Career* farmer; md Dunlop Farms Ltd, kt 1975; *Style* - Sir William Dunlop; 242 Main rd, Monks Bay, Christchurch 8, New Zealand (☎ Christchurch 849056)

DUNLUCE, Viscount; title normally born by eldest s and h of Earl of Antrim, *qv*, but which present Earl continues to be known by

DUNMORE, 11 Earl of (S 1686); Kenneth Randolph Murray; also Viscount Fincastle, Lord Murray of Blair, Moulin and Tillemot (both S 1686), and Baron Dunmore (UK 1831); 2 s of Arthur Charles Murray (d 1964); suc er bro 1981; the Earls of Dunmore descend from the 2 s of 1 Marquess of Athole; *b* 6 June 1913; *m* 1938, Margaret Joy, da of late P D Cousins, of Burnie Tasmania; 2 s; *Heir* s, Viscount Fincastle; *Career* late Sgt 12/50 Bn Australian Infantry; *Style* - The Rt Hon the Earl of Dunmore; Gravelly Beach, 7251 W Tamar, Tasmania, Australia

DUNMORE, Anne, Countess of; Anne Augusta; da of Thomas Clouston Wallace, of Holodyke, Dounby, Orkney; *b* 3 April 1939; *m* 1967, 9 Earl of Dunmore (d 1980); 2 da; *Style* - The Rt Hon Anne, Countess of Dunmore; 14 Regent ter, Edinburgh 7

DUNMORE, Patricia, Countess of; Patricia Mary; da of Frank Coles, of W Tamar Tasmania; *m* 1948, Reginald Murray, later 10 Earl of Dunmore (d 1981); 2 da (Lady Susan Price, Lady Elizabeth Parkinson); *Style* - Rt Hon Patricia, Countess of Dunmore; Gravelly Beach, 7251 W Tamar, Tasmania

DUNN, Angus Henry; s of late Col H G M Dunn; *b* 30 Dec 1944; *Educ* Marlborough, King's Cambridge, Pennsylvania U; *m* 1973, Carolyn Jane, nee Bartlett; 2 s; *Career* HM Diplomatic Service 1968-72 (Kuala Lumpur, Bonn), joined Morgan Grenfell & Co Ltd 1972, dir 1978-; *Style* - Angus Dunn Esq; Dower House, Oxon Hoath, Tonbridge, Kent

DUNN, Air V-Marshal Eric Clive; CB (1980), BEM (1951); s of W E Dunn; *b* 27 Nov 1927; *Educ* Bridlington Sch; *m* 1951, Margaret Gray; 3 da; *Career* AOM, RAF Support Command 1977-, C Eng, MRAeS, MBIM; *Style* - Air Vice-Marshal Eric Dunn, CB, BEM; 37 Park Lane, Brampton, Huntingdon, Cambs (☎ Huntingdon 52121)

DUNN, Brig Keith Frederick William; CBE (1941), DL (1960); s of late Brig-Gen R H W Dunn, DL, of Althrey, Wrexham; *b* 31 July 1891; *Educ* Wellington Coll and RMA Woolwich; *m* 1, 1915, Ava (d 1938), da of Brig-Gen H F Kays, CB; 1 s, 1 da; m 2, 1946, Joan, wid of Maj Claude de Lisle Bush and da of Col Sir Frank Beauchamp, 1 Bt; *Career* 2 Lt RA 1911, served 1914-19, Equitation Sch Weedon 1922-25, Adj RMA 1926-29, Lt-Col 1938, Brig 1939, cmmd 5 Cavalry Bde Middle East Forces 1940-41, ret 1942, cmmd Glos Sub-District 1942-45, ch training offr Min of Ag and Fisheries 1946-47; *Recreations* hunting, fishing and golf; *Clubs* Army and Navy; *Style* - Brig Keith Dunn, CBE, DL; Bencombe House, Uley, Dursley, Glos (☎ Dursley 860 255)

DUNN, Lydia; *Educ* U of Cal Berkeley; *Career* export man Swire & Maclaine 1970 (now md), cncllr Trade Policy Res Centre 1980-, memb finance ctee Hong Kong Legislative Cncl, dir Swire Gp 1981-, John Swire & Co; *Style* - Miss Lydia Dunn

DUNN, Lady Mary Helen Alma Graham; da of 6 Duke of Montrose; *b* 1909; *m* 1, 1931, Maj John Percival Townshend Boscawen, MBE, Gren Gds (d 1972); m 2, 1975, Brig Leslie Dunn, TD, DL; *Style* - Lady Mary Dunn; 8 Wheatfield rd, Ayr

DUNN, Lady Mary Sybil; da of 5 Earl of Rosslyn; *b* 1912; *m* 1, 1933 (m dis 1944), Philip Gordon Dunn (afterwards 2 Bt); 2 da; m 2, 1946 (m dis 1959) as his 2 w, Robin Francis Campbell, DSO; m 3, 1962 (m dis 1969), Charles R McCabe; re-m 4, 1969, Sir Philip Gordon Dunn, 2 and last Bt (d 1976); *Style* - Lady Mary Dunn; Draycot Fitzpayne Manor, Marlborough, Wilts

DUNN, Robert John; MP (C) Dartford 1979-; s of Robert Dunn; *b* 14 July 1946; *Educ* state schs, Univ of Salford; *m* 1976, Janet Elizabeth, da of Denis Wall RM; *Career* contested (C) Eccles 1974; *Clubs* Carlton; *Style* - Robert Dunn Esq, MP; House of Commons, SW1 (☎ 01 219 5209)

DUNN, Lt-Col Sir (Francis) Vivian; KCVO (1969), OBE (1960), RM; s of Capt W J Dunn, MVO, RHG; *b* 24 Dec 1908; *Educ* Winchester, Konservatorium der Musik Cologne, Roy Acad of Music; *m* 1938, Margery Kathleen Halliday; 1 s, 2 da; *Career* dir of music Roy Marines, ret 1968; Liveryman Worshipful Co of Musicans; ARAM, FRAM; *Style* - Lt-Col Sir Vivian Dunn, KCVO, OBE, RM; 16 W Common, Haywards Heath, Sussex (☎ 412987)

DUNN-MEYNELL, Hugo Arthur; s of Arthur James Dunn of London (d 1959); *b* 4 April 1926; *Educ* John Fisher Sch Purley; *m* 1, 1952 (m dis 1980), Nadine Madeleine, da of late Percy Denson; 3 s, 1 da; m 2, 1980, Alice Wooledge, da of Dr Pierre Joseph Salmon, of Hillsborough, California; *Career* wine and food writer and consultant; pres Lonsdale Advertising Int 1978-, chm International Wine and Food Soc 1978-80; *Recreations* wine and travel; *Clubs* Athenaeum; *Style* - Hugo Dunn-Meynell Esq

DUNNE, Hon Mrs - Hon Cecily Marion Violet Joan Fiennes; da of late 18 Baron Saye and Sele; *b* 1900; *m* 1928, John William Dunne (d 1949); 1 s, 2 da; *Style* - The Hon Mrs Dunne; Green End, Chadlington, Oxon

DUNNE, Lady Miranda; *née* Lowther; da of 7 Earl of Lonsdale; *b* 1955; *m* 1978, Patrick Dunne *Style* - Lady Miranda Dunne

DUNNE, Hon Mrs - Hon Mary Elizabeth Jill Rodd; da of late 2 Baron Rennell; *b* 1932; *m* 1954, Michael Langan Dunne; 2 s, 3 da; *Style* - The Hon Mrs Dunne; 7 Elvaston Mews, London SW7; Ashley Farm, Stansbatch, Pembridge, Herefordshire

DUNNETT, Dorothy; da of late Alexander Halliday; *b* 25 Aug 1923; *Educ* James Gillespie's H S for Girls Edinburgh; *m* 1946, Alastair Mactavish Dunnett (LLD); 2 s; *Career* novelist and portrait painter, civil servant 1940-55, on Literature Bursary Panel Scottish Arts Council 1975-79, dir Scottish Investments Ltd 1979-, trustee Scottish National War Memorial 1962-; *Style* - Mrs Alastair Dunnett; 87 Colinton rd, Edinburgh 10 (☎ 031 337 2107)

DUNNING, Kathleen, Lady; Kathleen Lawrie Cuthbert; da of J Patrick Cuthbert, MC; *m* 1936, Sir William Leonard Dunning, 2 Bt (d 1961); *Style* - Kathleen, Lady Dunning; Barclayhills, Guildtown, Perth

DUNNING, Sir Simon William Patrick; 3 Bt (UK 1930) of Beedinglee, Lower Beeding, Sussex; s of Sir William Leonard Dunning, 2 Bt (d 1961); *b* 14 Dec 1939; *Educ* Eton; *m* 1975, Frances Deirdre Morton, da of Maj Patrick William Morton Lancaster; 1 da; *Heir* none; *Career* insurance broker and underwriting memb of Lloyd's; *Clubs* Turf and Western (Glasgow); *Style* - Sir Simon Dunning, Bt; Low Auchengillan, Blanefield, by Glasgow, G63 9AU (☎ Blanefield 70323)

DUNNINGTON-JEFFERSON, Isobel, Lady; Frances Isobel; da of Col Herbert Anderson Cape, DSO, of Thorganby, York; *m* 1938, Lt-Col Sir John Alexander Dunnington-Jefferson, 1 Bt (d 1979); *Style* - Isobel, Lady Dunnington-Jefferson; Deighton House, Escrick, York

DUNNINGTON-JEFFERSON, John Alexander; s and h of Sir Mervyn Dunnington-Jefferson, 2 Bt; *b* 23 March 1980; *Style* - John Dunnington-Jefferson Esq

DUNNINGTON-JEFFERSON, Sir Mervyn Stewart; 2 Bt (UK 1958); s of Lt-Col Sir John Alexander Dunnington-Jefferson, 1 Bt, DSO (d 1979); *b* 5 Aug 1943; *Educ* Eton; *m* 1971, Caroline Anna, da of John Bayley, of Hillam Hall, Monk Fryston, Yorks; 1 s, 2 da; *Heir* s, John Dunnington-Jefferson; *Career* jt founder and dir Hatton Builders Ltd 1968-; *Style* - Sir Mervyn Dunnington-Jefferson, Bt; 7 Bolingbroke Gr, SW11 (☎ 01 675 3395)

DUNRAVEN AND MOUNT-EARL, 7 Earl of (I 1822); Sir Thady Windham Thomas Wyndham-Quin; 7 Bt (GB 1781); also Baron Adare (I 1800), Viscount Mount-Earl (I 1816), Viscount Adare (I 1822); s of 6 Earl, CB, CBE, MC (d 1965); *b* 27 Oct 1939; *Educ* Ludgrove and Le Rosey Switzerland; *m* 1969, Geraldine, da of Air Cdre Gerard W McAleer, CBE; 1 da; *Heir* unc, Capt Hon Valentine Wyndham-Quin, RN; *Style* - The Rt Hon The Earl of Dunraven and Mount-Earl; Adare Manor, Adare, Co Limerick, Ireland (☎ 061 91201)

DUNRAVEN AND MOUNT-EARL, Nancy, Countess of; da of Thomas Burks Yuille, of Virginia; *m* 1934, as his 2 w, 6 Earl of Dunraven and Mount-Earl, CB, CBE, MC (d 1965); 1 s (7 Earl), 2 da (Lady Melissa Brooke, w of Maj Sir George B, 3 Bt, MBE; Marchioness of Waterford, w of 8 Marquess); *Style* - The Rt Hon Nancy, Countess of Dunraven and Mount-Earl; Kilgobbin, Adare, Limerick

DUNROSSIL, 2 Viscount (UK 1959); John William Morrison; s of 1 Viscount, GCMG, MC, PC, QC (d 1961); *b* 22 May 1926; *Educ* Fettes, Oriel Oxford; *m* 1, 1951 (m dis 1969), Mavis, da of A L Spencer-Payne, LRCP, MRCS, LDS; 3 s, 1 da; m 2, 1969, Diana Mary Cunliffe, da of C M Vise; 2 da; *Heir* s, Hon Andrew William Reginald Morrison; *Career* RAF 1945-48, C'wlth Rels Office 1951, Private Sec to Sec of State 1952-54, 2 Sec Canberra Australia 1954-56, First Sec and Dep Actg High Cmmr E Pakistan 1958-60, First Sec Pretoria Capetown 1961-64 (seconded to For Serv 1961), Dip Serv Admin Off 1965, High Cmmr Fiji and High Cmmr Republic of Nauru, and Tuvalu 1978-; *Style* - The Rt Hon The Viscount Dunrossil; FCO, SW1

DUNROSSIL, Allison, Viscountess; (Catherine) Allison; da of Rev William Swan, DD, of S Leith; *Educ* MA, Edinburgh; *m* 1924, 1 Viscount Dunrossil, GCMG, MC, PC, QC (d 1961); 4 s (including 2 Viscount); *Career* barr Inner Temple 1926, dep pres Victoria League for Commonwealth Friendship, CStJ; *Style* - The Rt Hon Allison, Viscountess Dunrossil; Yew Tree Cottage, Withington, Glos; 1 Temple gdns, EC4

DUNSANY, 19 Baron (I 1439); Lt-Col Randal Arthur Henry Plunkett; s of 18 Baron Dunsany, DL, LittD, the author (d 1957) and Lady Beatrice (d 1970), nee Child-Villiers, da of 7 Earl of Jersey; hp to Barony of Killeen (*see* 12 Earl of Fingall); *b* 25 Aug 1906; *Educ* Eton; *m* 1, 1938 (m dis 1947), Mrs Vera Bryce, da of Senhor G De Sà Sottomaior, of São Paulo, Brazil; 1 s; m 2, 1947, Sheila Victoria Katrin, da of Sir Henry Philipps, 2 Bt, and widow of Maj John Frederick Foley, Baron de Rutzen, Welsh Gds; 1 da; *Heir* s, Hon Edward Plunkett; *Career* joined 16/5 Lancers (SR) 1926, transfd IA 1928, Guides Cavalry Indian Armoured Corps, ret 1947; *Style* - Lt-Col The Rt Hon The Lord Dunsany; Dunsany Castle, Co Meath, Ireland (☎ 046 25198)

DUNSTAN, Hon Donald Allan; QC; *b* 21 Sept 1926; *Educ* St Peter's Coll and Adelaide U; *m* 1, 1949 (m dis), Gretel Ellis; 2 s, 1 da; m 2, 1976, Adele Koh (d 1978); *Career* former Premier of S Australia and MP (Lab); *Style* - The Hon Donald Dunstan, QC; 242 Parade, Norwood 5067, S Australia (☎ 332 4949)

DUNSTAN, Lt-Gen Donald Beaumont; CB (1972), CBE (1969, MBE 1954); s of Oscar Reginald Dunstan; *Educ* Prince Alfred Coll S Australia, RMC Duntroon; *m* 1947, Beryl June Dunningham; 2 s; *Career* ch of the General Stafff Australia 1977; *Style* - Lt-Gen Donald Dunstan, CB, CBE; 57 National Circuit, Forrest, ACT 2603, Australia

DUNSTER, (Herbert) John; CB (1978); s of Herbert Dunster (d 1930); *b* 27 July 1922; *Educ* UCS, Imperial Coll of Science and Technol; *m* 1945, Rosemary Elizabeth, nee Gallagher; 1 s, 3 da; *Career* ARCS, scientist (radiology), Roy Naval Scientific Serv 1942, scientist UK Atomic Energy Authority 1946-71, assist dir Nat Radiological Protection Bd 1971-76, dep dir-gen Health and Safety Exec 1976-; *Recreations* music, photography, work; *Style* - John Dunster Esq, CB; Hill Cottage, 65 Castlebar rd, W5 (☎ 01 997 0439)

DUNTZE, Sir George Edwin Douglas; 6 Bt (GB 1774), CMG (1960); s of Sir George Puxley Duntze, 5 Bt (d 1974); *b* 1 June 1913; *Educ* Shrewsbury, Trinity Coll Oxford; *m* 1, 1941 (m dis 1966), Joan (d 1972), da of late Maj F E Bradstock DSO MC; 1 da; m 2, 1966, Mrs Nesta Evill, da of late T R P Herbert; *Heir* kinsman, John Alexander Duntze; *Career* HM Overseas Serv Uganda, provincial cmmr W Province 1952; *Style* - Sir George Duntze, Bt, CMG; 25 Ennismore gdns, SW7

DUNTZE, John Alexander; s (by 1 m) of late John Alexander Ralph Duntze, gggs of 1 Bt; hp of kinsman, Sir George Duntze, 6 Bt, CMG; *b* 13 Nov 1909; *m* 1935, Emily Ellsworth, nee Harlow; *Career* mechanical engr; *Style* - John Duntze Esq; St John's pla, Westport, Connecticut, USA

DUNWOODY, Hon Mrs Gwyneth Patricia; MP (L) Cheshire (Crewe) 1974-; da of Baroness Phillips (Life Peeress); *b* 12 Dec 1930; *Educ* Fulham County Secondary Sch, Convent of Notre Dame; *m* 1954 (m dis 1975), Dr John Elliott Orr Dunwoody; 2 s, 1 da; *Career* MP (L) Exeter 1966-70, parly sec Bd of Trade 1967-70, UK memb of European Parl 1975-79, dir Film Production Assoc of GB 1970-74; *Style* - The Hon Mrs Gwyneth, Dunwoody, MP; 113 Cromwell Tower, Beech st, EC2Y 6DD (☎ 01 588 2615)

DUPPLIN, Viscount; Charles William Harley Hay; s and h of 15 Earl of Kinnoull; *b* 20 Dec 1962; *Educ* Eton; *Style* - Viscount Dupplin

DUPREE, Sir Peter; 5 Bt (UK 1921); s of Sir Victor Dupree, 4 Bt (d 1976); *b* 20 Feb 1924; *m* 1947, Joan, da of late Capt James Desborough Hunt; *Heir* kinsman, Thomas William James David Dupree, b 5 Feb 1930; *Style* - Sir Peter Dupree, Bt; Great Seabrights, Galley Wood, nr Chelmsford, Essex

DURACK, Dame Mary (Mrs Horrie Miller); DBE, (1978, OBE 1966); da of Michael Patrick Durack; *b* 20 Feb 1913; *Educ* Loreto Convent Perth; *m* 1938, Capt HC Miller; 2 s, 2 da (and 2 da decd); *Career* novelist, playwright, and historian; *Style* - Dame Mary Durack, DBE; 12 Bellevue ave, Nedlands 6009, W Australia (☎ 386 1117)

DURAND, Rev Sir (Henry Mortimer) Dickon Marion St George; 4 Bt (UK 1892); s of late Lt-Cdr Mortimer Henry Marion Durand, RN, s of 1 Bt; suc unc, Brig Sir Alan Algernon Marion Durand, 3 Bt, MC, 1971; *b* 19 June 1934; *Educ* Wellington, Sydney U; *m* 1971, Stella Evelyn, da of Capt Christopher L'Estrange, of Lisnalurg, Sligo; 2 s, 2 da; *Heir* s, Edward Durand; *Career* ordained 1969, formerly priest-in-charge St Benedict's Ashford Common, Bp's Curate in charge Kilbixy Union of Parishes, Ballinacargy, Mullingar 1979-; *Style* - Rev Sir Dickon Durand, Bt; c/o Barclays Bank, Cobham, Surrey

DURAND, Edward Alan Christopher Percy; s and h of Rev Sir Dickon Durand, 4 Bt; *b* 21 Feb 1974; *Style* - Edward Durand Esq

DURAND, Lady; Evelyn Sherbrooke; CBE (1955); da of Charles Crane, of The Reddings, nr Cheltenham; *m* 1, 1921, as his 2 w, Sir Stanley Tubbs, 1 & last Bt (d 1941); m 2, 1944, Brig Sir Alan Durand, 3 Bt, MC (d 1971); *Career* JP; V-Pres Stroud Con Assoc; memb Nat Exec Con Pty; *Style* - Lady Durand, CBE, JP; Ellerncroft, Wotton-under-Edge, Glos

DURBIN, Leslie; CBE (1976), MVO (1943); s of Harry Durbin; *b* 21 Feb 1913; *Educ* Central Sch of Arts and Crafts; *m* 1940, Phyllis Ethel Durbin; 1 s, 1 da; *Career* silversmith, designed Silver Jubilee Hallmark; *Style* - Leslie Durbin Esq, CBE, MVO; 298a Kew rd, Richmond, Surrey

DURBRIDGE, Francis (Henry); s of

Francis Durbridge; *b* 25 Nov 1912; *Educ* Bradford G S, Wylde Green Coll, Birmingham U; *m* 1940, Norah Elizabeth Lawley; 2 s; *Career* playwright, short-story writer, producer (TV and radio); *Style* - Francis Durbridge Esq; 4 Fairacres, Roehampton lane, London, SW15

DURHAM, Earldom of (UK 1833); *see* Lambton, Antony Claud Frederick

DURHAM, Countess of; Hermione; da of Sir George Bullough, 1 and last Bt; *m* 1931, as his 2 w, 5 Earl of Durham (d 1970); 1 s (Hon John Lambton); *Style* - The Rt Hon the Countess of Durham; West Marden Hall, Chichester, Sussex

DURHAM, 91 Bishop of (cr 635) 1973- Rt Rev John Stapylton Habgood; s of Arthur Henry Habgood, DSO, MB, BCh and Vera, da of late Richard Chetwynd-Stapylton, ggggs of 4 Viscount Chetwynd; *b* 23 June 1927; *Educ* Eton, King's Cambridge, Cuddesdon Oxford; *m* 1961, Rosalie Mary Anne, da of Edward Lansdown Boston; 2 s, 2 da; *Career* former demonstrator in Pharmacology Cambridge; ordained 1954, rector St John's Jedburgh 1962-67, Principal of Queen's Coll Birmingham 1967-73, Hon Canon of Birmingham Cathedral 1971-73; patron of 101 livings, the Archdeaconries of Durham and Auckland, and all the Canonries in his Cathedral (the see was first established at Holy Island 635, but on the invasion of the Danes removed to Chester-le-Street and finally to Durham); *Clubs* Athenaeum; DIY; *Style* - The Rt Rev The Lord Bishop of Durham; Auckland Castle, Bishop Auckland, Co Durham (☎ 2576)

DURHAM, Kenneth; s of late George Durham; *b* 28 July 1924; *Educ* Queen Elizabeth GS Blackburn, Manchester U (BSc); *m* 1946, Irene Markham; 1 s, 1 da; *Career* v-chm Unilever Ltd 1978- (dir 1974-); *Style* - Kenneth Durham Esq; Burfield, Pangbourne Hill, Pangbourne, Berks (☎ 2265)

DURIE, Sir Alexander Charles; CBE (1973); s of Charles Durie (d 1948); *b* 15 July 1915; *Educ* Queen's Coll Taunton; *m* 1941, Joyce May, da of late Lionel Richard Hargreaves; 1 s, 1 da; *Career* dir Shell Co of Australia Ltd 1954-56, md Shell-Mexico and BP Ltd 1963-64, v-pres AA 1977- (dir gen 1964-77), cncl Alliance Internationale de Tourisme/FIA Jt Ctee 1974, pres 1971-77; kt 1977; *Clubs* Junior Carlton, Royal and Ancient; *Style* - Sir Alexander Durie, CBE; Redwood House, Windlesham, Surrey (☎ 72035)

DURKIN, Air Marshal Sir Herbert; KBE (1976), CB (1973); s of Herbert Durkin (d 1968); *b* 31 March 1922; *Educ* Burnley G S, Emmanuel Cambridge; *m* 1951, Dorothy Hope, da of Walter Taylor Johnson; 1 s, 2 da; *Career* joined RAF 1941, served WW II in Europe and India, Gp Capt 1962, Air Cdre 1968, dir of Engrg Policy (RAF) MOD 1967, Air V-Marshal 1971, Air Marshal 1976, ret 1978; chm and dir of several cos, pres Instn of Electrical Engrs 1980-81; *Recreations* golf; *Clubs* RAF; *Style* - Air Marshal Sir Herbert Durkin, KBE, CB; Willowbank, Drakes Drive, Northwood, Middx (☎ Northwood 23167)

DURLACHER, Nicholas John; s of John Sydney Durlacher MC; *b* 20 March 1946; *Educ* Stowe, Magdalene Cambridge; *m* 1971, Mary Caroline, da of Maj G McLaren (d 1978); 1 s; *Career* memb London Stock Exchange, ptnr Wedd Durlacher Mordaunt & Co 1971-; *Recreations* skiing, tennis, golf, shooting; *Clubs* City of London, Bath; *Style* - Nicholas Durlacher Esq; Archendines Fordham, nr Colchester, Essex (☎ Colchester 240 627)

DURLACHER, Lady Sheila Mary; da of 7 Earl of Clonmell (d 1928); *b* 1906; *m* 1, 1926, Lt-Col Mansel Halkett Jackson, DSC, MC (m dis 1930); 1 s; m 2, 1930, Esmond Otho Durlacher (m dis 1947); 2 s, 1 da; *Style* - Lady Sheila Durlacher; 162 Rivermead Court, Ranelagh gdns, London SW6

DURRAN, Percy; CBE (1966); s of late Dr John George Durran; *b* 26 Sept 1911; *Educ* Daniel Stewart's Coll Edinburgh, Edinburgh U; *m* 1969, Joanna Brenda, da of late C W Nash; *Career* Sudan Vet Serv 1935-55, FAO of UN Ethiopa 1955-56,

HM Overseas Serv Nigeria 1956-57, vet and animal husbandry adviser Middle East Development Div Beirut 1957-71; *Style* - Percy Durran Esq, CBE; Caledon, Gatehouse of Fleet, Kirkcudbrightshire (☎ Gatehouse 521)

DURRANT, Albert Arthur Molteno; CBE (1954); s of late Sir Arthur Isaac Durrant, CBE, MVO; *b* 11 Sept 1898; *Educ* Alleyn's Sch Dulwich; *m* 1922, Kathleen, da of late A J Wright; *Career* ch engr (buses and coaches) London Passenger Transport Bd 1935, ch mechanical engr (road services) 1945-65; *Style* - Albert Durrant Esq, CBE; 108 Chiltern ct, Baker st, NW1

DURRANT, William Alexander Estridge; JP; s and h of Sir William Durrant, 7 Bt; *b* 26 Nov 1929; *m* 1953, Dorothy Croker, BA; 1 s, 1 da; *Career* Capt 12/16 Hunter River Lancers; *Style* - William Durrant Esq, JP; Spring pk, Gaspard via Quirindi, NSW, Australia

DURRANT, Sir William Henry Estridge; 7 Bt (GB 1784), JP (NSW 1940); s of Sir William Henry Estridge Durrant, 6 Bt (d 1953); *b* 1 April 1901; *m* 1927, Georgina Beryl Gwendoline (d 1968), da of Alexander Purse; 1 s, 1 da; *Heir* s, William Alexander Estridge; *Career* served 1939-45; *Style* - Sir William Durrant, Bt, JP; Woodside Gardens, Yardley ave, Waitara, NSW 2077, Australia

DURRELL, Lawrence George; s of Lawrence Samuel Durrell; *b* 27 Feb 1912; *Educ* Coll of St Joseph Darjeeling India, St Edmund's Sch Canterbury; *m* 1, 1937; m 2 1947; m 3, 1960; 2 da; *Career* novelist, playwright, poet; works include Bitter Lemons (1957), The Alexandria Quartet; *Style* - Lawrence Durrell Esq; c/o Grindlay's Bank, 13 St James's sq, SW1

DURY, Mrs Guy - (Rose Mary) Dorothy; da of Leveson William Vernon-Harcourt (d 1909) and gggda of 1 Baron Vernon; *b* 1900; *m* 1, 1922, Hon Frederick Somerset Gough-Calthorpe (d 1935); 1 s (10 Baron Calthorpe, *qv*); m 2, 1949, Lt-Col Guy Alexander Ingram Dury, MC (d 1976); *Style* - Mrs Guy Dury; Loxwood, Firegrove rd, Cross-in-Hand, Heathfield, E Sussex

DUTHIE, Robert Grieve; CBE (1978); s of late George Duthie; *b* 2 Oct 1928; *Educ* Greenock Acad; *m* 1955, Violetta Noel, da of late Harold MacLean; 2 s, 1 da; *Career* chartered accountant, former chm Greenock Provident Bank and Made-up-Textiles Assoc, chm Black & Edgington Ltd 1967-, Scottish Dvpt Agency 1980-, dir Royal Bank of Scotland Ltd 1978-, Clyde Port Authority 1971- (chm 1977-79), British Assets Trust Ltd 1977-, Edinburgh American Assets Trust 1977-; *Recreations* curling, golf; *Style* - Robert Duthie Esq, CBE; Port Glasgow, Renfrews (☎ 0475 22642)

DUTTON, Francis Moore; s of Thomas Moore Dutton (d 1939); *b* 21 Dec 1899; *Educ* St Bees Sch Cumberland; *m* 1, 1932, Amy Louisa Huntly (d 1946); m 2, 1948, Margaret Marian Worthington (d 1980); 1 s, 1 da; *Career* served First and Second World Wars, High Sheriff Cheshire 1968, land owner; *Style* - Francis Dutton Esq; Tushingham Hall, Whitchurch, Shropshire (☎ Whitchurch 2225)

DUTTON, Hon Juliet Elizabeth; da of 6 Baron Sherborne, DSO (d 1949); *b* 1915; *Style* - The Hon Juliet Dutton; Windrush Manor, Windrush, Burford, Oxfordborne (☎ Glos 206)

DUTTON, Hon Mrs George; Pauline Stewart Shephard; s of Maj Stewart Robinson; *m* 1959, as his 2 w, Hon George Dutton (d 1981), yr s of 6 Baron Sherborne; *Style* - The Hon Mrs George Dutton; Westerly, Kingsthorne, Herefordshire (☎ Golden Valley 540 309)

DUTTON, Ralph Stawell; s of Henry Dutton (himself gs of 2 Baron Sherborne); hp of 2 cous once removed, 7 Baron Sherborne; *b* 1898; *Educ* Eton, Ch Ch Oxford; *Career* FSA; High Sheriff Hants 1944; author; *Style* - Ralph Dutton Esq; Hinton Ampner House, Alresford, Hants

DUVOLLET, Hon Mrs (Sheila Helen Parnell); da of late 6 Baron Congleton; *b* 1923; *m* 1959, Roger Henry Duvollet; 1 da; *Style* - The Hon Mrs Duvollet; Burton Lodge, Burton Bradstock, Bridport, Dorset

DUXBURY, Philip Thomas; *Career* md Magnet Joinery Ltd, jt md Magnet & Southerns Ltd, dir Magnet Jt Gp of Cos; *Style* - Philip Duxbury Esq; Magnet and Southerns Ltd, 128 Queen Victoria st, London, EC4

DWEK, Joseph Claude; *Career* chm and md Bodycote International Ltd, dir Bodycote Gp of Cos, Taylor and Hartley Gp of Cos, Urania Gp of Cos; BSc, BA, ATI; *Style* - Joseph Dwek Esq; Bodycote International Ltd, 104 Stanford st, Manchester

DWORKIN, Prof Ronald Myles; s of David Dworkin; *b* 11 Dec 1931; *Educ* Harvard Coll, Oxford U, Harvard Law Sch; *m* 1958, Betsy Celia Ross; 1 s, 1 da; *Career* Professor of Jurisprudence Oxford U 1969, Fell Univ Coll 1969-; FBA; *Style* - Prof Ronald Dworkin; University Coll, Oxford

DYER, Lady; Barbara; JP; da of Irenius Brackenbury, CBE; *m* 1925, Sir Leonard Schroeder Swinnerton Dyer, 15 Bt (d 1975); *Career* chm National Fedn of Women's Insts 1957-61; *Style* - Lady Dyer, JP; Westhorpe Cottage, Craven Arms, Salop

DYER-BENNET, Maj Richard Stewart; s of Frederick Dyer-Bennet (assumed additional surname Bennet 1894), gs of Sir Thomas Swinnerton Dyer, 9 Bt, JP; hp to 2 cous once removed, Prof Sir Peter Swinnerton-Dyer, 16 Bt; *b* 6 Oct 1886; *m* 1912, Miriam (d 1973), da of Prof Edward Clapp, of Calif U ; 4 s, 1 da; *Career* ret Maj Leics Regt; served WW I; *Style* - Maj Richard Dyer-Bennet; 98 Mayplace rd E, Barnehurst, Kent

DYKE, David William; s and h of Sir Derek Dyke, 9 Bt; *b* 5 Jan 1955; *Style* - David Dyke Esq

DYKE, Sir Derek William Hart; 9 Bt (1676); s of Sir Oliver Hamilton Augustus Hart Dyke, 8 Bt (d 1969); *b* 4 Dec 1924; *m* 1, 1953 (m dis 1963), Dorothy Moses, of Hamilton, Ontario; 1 s, 1 da; m 2, 1964 (m dis 1972), Margaret Dickson Elder; *Heir* s David William Dyke; *Style* - Sir Derek Dyke, Bt; 80 Erie ave, Hamilton, Ontario L8N 2W6, Canada

DYKE, Mildred, Lady; Mildred Turnover; da of James Blackwood and wid of Cecil Berens JP; *m* 1945, as his 2 w, Sir Oliver Hamilton Augustus Hart Dyke, 8 Bt (d 1969); *Style* - Mildred, Lady Dyke; The Homestead, Fordown, Nottingham rd, Natal, S Africa

DYKE, Trevor Hart; DSO, DL (1981) Derbys; s of Col Percyvall Hart Dyke, DSO; *b* 1905; *Educ* Marlborough; *m* 1, 1933 (m dis 1965), Eileen Joyce, nee Niblock-Stuart; m 2, 1965, Mary Eliot; 1 s, 1 da; *Career* Brig late Queen's R Regt; *Style* - Trevor Dyke Esq, DSO, DL; Clough House, Bamford, Derbys

DYKES, Hon Mrs - Hon Jean Helen Latham; da of late 1 Baron Latham; *b* 1921; *m* 1, 1945, Sqdn Ldr W Ronald Gellatly, AFC (m annulled 1960); 1 s; m 2, 1970, James Oswald Dykes; *Style* - The Hon Mrs Dykes; 78 Sackville rd, Hove, Sussex

DYMOND, Charles Edward; CBE (1976); s of Charles George Dymond; *b* 15 Oct 1916; *Educ* Tiverton G S, Exeter U (BSc); *m* 1945, Dorothy Jean Peaker; 2 s, 2 da; *Career* Consul-Gen Perth 1973-76, ret; *Style* - Charles Dymond Esq, CBE; PO Box 15, Sawyers Valley, 6074, W Australia

DYNES, John Brian; s of John Dynes; *b* 17 Oct 1933; *Educ* Portadown Tech Coll, Queen's U Belfast; *m* 1961, Alice Mary, nee Graham; 1 s, 1 da; *Career* md Henry Denny & Sons (Ulster) Ltd 1977-, Ulster Farmers' Bacon (Newry) Ltd 1973-, dir Henry Denny & Sons Ltd 1978-, ACMA; *Recreations* golf, bridge, amateur radio; *Style* - John Dynes Esq; 30 Breagh rd, Portadown, Clogher, Narin, Co Donegal (☎ 0762 38360)

DYNEVOR, 9 Baron (GB 1780); Richard Charles Uryan Rhys; s of 8 Baron Dynevor, CBE, MC (d 1962, fifth in descent from Baroness Dynevor, herself da of 1 & last Earl Talbot, of the same family as the Earls of Shrewsbury); *b* 19 June 1935; *Educ* Eton, Magdalene Coll Cambridge; *m* 1959 (m dis 1978), Lucy Catherine King, da of Sir John

Rothenstein, CBE; 1 s, 3 da; *Heir* s Hon Hugo Griffith Uryan Rhys; *Style* - The Rt Hon the Lord Dynevor; Flat 2, 17 Sheffield ter, W8 (☎ 01 727 7439)

DYSART, Countess of (eleventh holder of title, S 1643); Rosamund Agnes; *née* Greaves; also Lady Huntingtower (S 1643); da of Maj Owain Edward Whitehead Greaves, JP, DL (d 1941) and Countess of Dysart (tenth holder, d 1975); *b* 15 Feb 1914; *Heir* sis Lady Katherine Grant *qv*; *Style* - The Rt Hon the Countess of Dysart; Bryn Garth, Grosmont, Abergavenny, Gwent

DYSON, Richard George; s of Eric Dyson; *b* 9 Feb 1929; *Educ* Bradfield Coll, CCC Oxford; *Career* slr 1956, ptnr Field Fisher and Co, Field Fisher and Martineau (formerly Field Roscoe and Co) 1957, master of the Supreme Court of Judicature (Chancery Div) 1973-; *Style* - Richard Dyson Esq; 10 Barnsbury sq, N1 (☎ 01 607 4360)

E

EADIE, Alastair Gordon; s of Col James Alister Eadie, DSO, TD, DL (d 1961); *b* 25 June 1940; *Educ* Eton *m* 1966, Jacqueline Noel Trench, da of Lt-Col 5 Baron Ashtown, OBE (d 1979); 3 s; *Career* dir Int Distillers and Vintners (Home Trade), Gilbey Vintners Ltd and Morgan Furze Ltd; *Recreations* shooting and stalking; *Style* - Alastair Eadie Esq; Bourne Orchard, Brickendon, Hertford, SG13 8NU

EADIE, John Harold Ward; s of Harold George Eadie, CBE; *b* 29 May 1909; *Educ* Cheltenham Coll; *m* 1946, Ellice Aylmer, CBE, da of Rt Rev R T Hearn, LLD, sometime Bp of Cork, Cloyne and Ross; *Career* Maj RASC and Combined Operations, chm Gilbertson & Page Ltd and Gilbertson & Page (Can) Inc; *Recreations* cricket, golf; *Clubs* Royal and Ancient, MCC, Kennel Club; *Style* - John Eadie Esq; 74 Roebuck House, Palace st, SW1 (☎ 01 828 6158)

EADIE, Hon Mrs (Jacqueline Noel); da of (by 1 m) 5 Baron Ashtown; *b* 1940; *m* 1966, Alastair Gordon Eadie; 3 s; *Style* - The Hon Mrs Eadie; Bourne Orchard, Brickendon, Herts

EADIE, Sam; s of late George Eadie; *b* 12 March 1935; *Educ* Trin Coll Glenalmond, Exeter Coll Oxford; *m* 1958, Fiona Stewart; 1 s, 2 da; *Career* RNVR 1953-57, dir Lewis & Peat (Overseas) Ltd 1977-, dir AGB Market Research SA Geneva 1980-, research consultant 1978-; *Recreations* squash, skiing, music, travel, languages; *Style* - Sam Eadie Esq; 4 Wotton Way, Cheam, Surrey (☎ 01 393 4230)

EADY, Hon Arabella Victoria Eleanor Swinfen; da of 3 Baron Swinfen; *b* 1969; *Style* - The Hon Arabella Eady

EADY, Hon Charles Roger Peregrine Swinfen; s and h of 3 Baron Swinfen; *b* 8 Mar 1971; *Style* - The Hon Charles Eady

EADY, Hon Georgina Mary Rose Swinfen; da of 3 Baron Swinfen; *b* 1964; *Style* - The Hon Georgina Eady

EADY, Hon Katherine Anne Dorothy Swinfen; da of 3 Baron Swinfen; *b* 1966; *Style* - The Hon Katherine Eady

EADY, Hon (Hugh) Toby Swinfen; s of 2 Baron Swinfen; *b* 1941; *Educ* Bryanston; Wadham Oxford; *Style* - The Hon Toby Eady; 12 High st, SW1

EARDLEY-WILMOT, Sir John Assheton; 5 Bt (UK 1821) of Berkswell Hall, Warwickshire, MVO (1956), DSC (1943); s of Cdr Frederick Neville Eardley-Wilmot (d 1956) and n of Maj Sir John Eardley-Wilmot, 4 Bt (d 1970); *b* 2 Jan 1917; *Educ* Stubbington and RNC Dartmouth; *m* 1939, Diana Elizabeth, da of late Cdr Aubrey Moore; 1 s, 1 da; *Heir* s, Michael John Assheton Eardley-Wilmot; *Career* Cdr (RN) ret 1967; on staff Monopolies Cmmn 1967-, Liveryman of Paviours' Co; *Recreations* fishing; *Clubs* Wig and Pen; *Style* - Sir John Eardley-Wilmot, Bt, MVO, DSC; 41 Margravine gdns, W6 8RN (☎ 01 748 3723)

EARDLEY-WILMOT, Michael John Assheton; s and h of Sir John Eardley-Wilmot, 5 Bt, MVO, DSC; *b* 13 Jan 1941; *Educ* Clifton; *m* 1971, Wendy, da of A J Wolstenholme; 2 s, 1 da; *Career* md Famous Names Hldgs; *Style* - Michael Eardley-Wilmot Esq; c/o Famous Names Hldgs, Bristol, BS5 6HR; Sixpenny, Aldbourne, Wilts

EARL, Hon Mrs - Hon Honor; *née* Maugham; da of 1 Viscount Maugham; *m* 1925, Sebastian Earl; 2 s; *Style* - The Hon Mrs Earl; 14 South Terrace, SW7; Chilland Ford, Martyr Worthy, nr Winchester, Hants

EARLAM, Peter Francis; s of late Dr F Earlam; *b* 16 Dec 1931; *Educ* Uppingham, St John's Cambridge (MA); *m* 1957, Amanda Mary, nee Hornsby; 2 s, 1 da; *Career* dir Elder Dempster Lines Liverpool 1970-, ch exec UK West Africa Lines Liverpool 1974-; *Style* - Peter Earlam Esq; 29 Croome Drive, West Kirby, Wirral, Merseyside (☎ 051 6257717); Lamare, Ravenspoint, Trearddur Bay, Anglesey (☎ 0407 860451)

EARLE, Sir (Hardman) George (Algernon); 6 Bt (UK 1869) of Allerton Tower, Woolton, Lancashire; s of Sir Hardman Alexander Mort Earle, 5 Bt (d 1979); *b* 4 Feb 1932; *Educ* Eton; *m* 1967, Diana Gillian Bligh, da of Col Frederick Ferris Bligh St George, CVO (d 1970), ggs of Sir Richard Bligh St George, 2 Bt; 1 s, 1 da; *Heir* s, Robert George Bligh Earle; *Career* Ensign in Grenadier Gds (Nat Serv), memb of London Metal Exchange 1962-73; *Recreations* fox hunting; *Clubs* Roy Yacht Sqdn, Kildare St and U Dublin; *Style* - Sir George Earle, Bt; Abington, Murroe, Co Limerick, Eire (☎ Limerick 81108)

EARLE, Michael George; s of Henry George Earle; *b* 30 July 1944; *Educ* Sir William Borlase's Sch; *Career* dir British General Tube Co Ltd Slough 1977-, dir Keene Game Products (UK) Ltd 1978-, dir Keene Game Products (Overseas) Ltd 1978-; *Recreations* shooting; *Clubs* National Rifle Association; *Style* - Michael Earle Esq; 227 Marlow Bottom, Marlow, Bucks (☎ Marlow 71618)

EARLE, Col Peter Beaumont; MC (1945), DL (1967); s of Loftus Earle (d 1949); *b* 9 April 1917; *Educ* Eton and RMC Sandhurst; *m* 1, 1940, Ursula, da of late Maj F W Warre, OBE, MC; 1 s, 1 da; m 2, 1971, Judith, da of Dr G T MacKinnell Childs (d 1980); *Career* King's Roy Rifle Corps 1937-58, Col 1958, MA to CIGS War Office 1943-45; dir Henry Kendall and Sons Ltd 1959-, warden St George's Hanover Sq W1 1962-; Croix de Guerre (France) 1945, Cdr Order of Merit (Peru) 1964; *Clubs* Brooks's; *Style* - Col Peter Earle, MC, DL; 22 Harcourt ter, SW10 9JR; King's Farm, Noar Hill, Selborne, Hants, GU34 3LW (☎ 042 050 393)

EARLE, Robert George Bligh; s and h of Sir George Earle, 6 Bt; *b* 24 Jan 1970

EASON, His Honour Robert Kinley; s of Henry Alexander Eason (d 1926); *b* 12 April 1908; *Educ* Douglas High Sch, King Williams Coll and Univ Coll London; *m* 1937, Nora Muriel, da of Robert Coffey; *Career* called to the Bar Gray's Inn 1929, adv Manx Bar 1930, High Bailiff and Ch Magistrate IOM 1961-69, a High Court Judge (Deemster) IOM 1969; First Deemster, Clerk of the Rolls and Dep Gov IOM to 1980; chm IOM Income Tax Appeal Cmmrs 1974-80 & Tourist Appeal Trib 1969-74; pres Ellynyn Ny Gael 1974, Anti-Cancer Assoc 1969-, Wireless Telegraphy Appeal Bd for IOM 1971-; Queen's Silver Jubilee Medal 1977; *Style* - His Honour Robert Eason; Greenacres, Highfield Drive, Baldrine, Lonan, IOM

EASTAUGH, Lady Laura Mary; da of 3 Earl of Selborne; *b* 1915; *m* 1948, Rt Rev Cyril Eastaugh, MC, 34 Bp of Peterborough; 1 s, 2 da; *Career* Lambeth Dip in Theology, 1944; Chaplain's Asst, ATS, 1942-46; sec to Women's Land Army (Hants) 1940-42; *Style* - Lady Laura Eastaugh; Blackmoor, Hants

EASTMAN, Rev Canon Derek Ian Tennent; MC (1945); s of late Archibald Tennent Eastman; *b* 22 Jan 1919; *Educ* Winchester, Ch Ch Oxford, Cuddesdon

Theol Coll Oxford; *m* 1949, Judith Mary, da of Canon Philip David Bevington Miller; 3 s, 1 da; *Career* clerk in Holy Orders, assist curate Brighouse 1948-51, priest-in-charge St Andrew's Caversham 1951-56, vicar of Headington Oxford 1956-64, vicar of Banbury 1964-70, archdeacon of Buckingham and vicar of Chilton and Dorton 1970-77, proctor in convocation for Dioc of Oxford 1964-70, memb Gen Synod 1975-77, canon of St George's Chapel Windsor 1977-; *Recreations* gardening, painting; *Style* - The Rev Canon Derek Eastman, MC; 4 The Cloisters; Windsor Castle, Berks (☎ 64142)

EASTMAN, Lady Mary Agatha; da of late 4 Earl Cawdor; *b* 1905; *m* 1931, Brig Henry Claud Warrington Eastman, DSO, MVO, late RA; 1 s, 1 da; *Style* - Lady Mary Eastman; Leigh House, Newtown, Newbury, Berks

EASTON, Hon Mrs (Caroline Ina Mande); da of 9 Baron Hawke; *b* 13 Feb 1937; *Educ* Hatherop Castle Glos; *m* 1960, John Francis Easton; 1 s, 1 da; *Career* barr Middle Temple 1959 (not practising now); *Recreations* music, sport; *Style* - The Hon Mrs Easton; The Old Hall, Barley, nr Royston, Herts (☎ Barkway 368)

EASTWOOD, Herbert David; CBE (1973), MC (1944); s of Rev Canon John Eastwood (d 1968); *b* 27 Jan 1919; *Educ* All Saints Sch Bloxham and St Edmund Hall Oxford; *m* 1948, Betty Ann Margaret, da of Walter Vivian Douglas Skrine (d 1964); 1 s; *Career* served 1939-45 War in Oxford and Bucks LI and Parachute Regt in Sicily, Italy and NW Europe, War Office 1957-79, ret; *Recreations* enjoying retirement in the countryside; *Clubs* Army and Navy; *Style* - Herbert Eastwood Esq, CBE, MC; Sandpits, Gastard, Corsham, Wilts, SN13 9QW (☎ Lacock 240)

EASTWOOD, Wilfred; s of Wilfred Andrew Eastwood (d 1977); *b* 15 Aug 1923; *Educ* Hemsworth Grammar; *m* 1947, Dorothy Jean, da of Charles St George Gover; 1 s, 1 da; *Career* consulting engr; snr ptnr Eastwood and Ptnrs, prof of Civil Engrg Univ of Sheffield 1964-70, pres Instn of Structural Engrs 1976-77; *Recreations* watching cricket and gardening; *Clubs* Yorkshire County Cricket; *Style* - Wilfred Eastwood Esq; 242 Abbeydale Road South, Dore, Sheffield, S17 3LL (☎ 0742 364645)

EATES, Edward Caston; CMG (1968), MVO (1961), QPM (1961, CPM 1955); s of Edward Eates (d 1953); *b* 8 April 1916; *Educ* Highgate Sch and King's Coll London; *m* 1942, Maureen Teresa, da of Daniel McGee (d 1968); *Career* served in WW II with 22 (Cheshire) Regt and 2 Derby Yeo, Maj 1944; entered Colonial Police Serv 1946, Nigeria 1946-54, Sierra Leone 1954-57, The Gambia (Cmmr) 1957-63, Hong Kong 1963-69 (Cmmr 1967-69); FCO 1971-76; *Recreations* watching cricket and football, travel; *Clubs* Roy Commonwealth Soc, E India Sports and Public Schs and Surrey CCC; *Style* - Edward Eates Esq, CMG, MVO, QPM; Banjul, Toadpit Lane, Ottery St Mary, Devon, EX11 1LQ (☎ 040 481 2838)

EATON, Maj Thomas Christopher; OBE (1962), TD (1946), DL (1971); s of Frederic Ray Eaton (d 1962), of Norwich; *b* 13 Oct 1918; *Educ* Stowe; *m* 1958, Robin Elizabeth, da of Alexander Berry Austin (ka 1944); 1 s, 2 da; *Career* slr and notary public 1947, served 4 Bn Roy Norfolk Regt (TA) 1936-50, served in WW II (wounded, despatches, POW Singapore 1942-45), memb Norwich City Cncl 1949-74 (leader 1969-70), Lord Mayor of Norwich 1957-58, trustee E Anglian Trustee Savings Bank; *Recreations* theatre and travel; *Clubs* Norfolk; *Style* - Maj Thomas Eaton, OBE, TD, DL; 3 Albemarle rd, Norwich (☎ Norwich 53962)

EAYRS, Gp Capt Douglas Joyce; CB (1955), CBE (1946), DFC (1944); s of William Henry Eayrs (d 1944); *b* 13 July 1944; *Educ* Oakham Sch, RAF Coll Cranwell; *m* 1949, Doreen Arthy, nee Scriven; 2 s, 1 da; *Career* gp capt RAF 1944, Australia, Europe, Kenya, cmding offr Central Flying Sch Australia 1941-3, sr RAF offr Kenya 1952-54; *Clubs* RAF; *Style* - Gp Capt Douglas Eayrs, CB, CBE, DFC; North Farmcote, Winchcombe, Glos

EBBISHAM, 2 Baron (UK 1928); Sir Rowland Roberts Blades; 2 Bt (UK 1922), TD; s of 1 Baron, GBE (d 1953); *b* 3

Sept 1912; *Educ* Winchester, Ch Ch Oxford; *m* 1949, Flavia Mary, da of Charles F Meade (gs of 3 Earl of Clanwilliam) and Lady Aileen, nee Brodrick, da of 1 Earl of Midleton; 3 da; *Heir* none; *Career* common councilman City of London Candlewick Ward 1948-, pres London Chamber of Commerce 1958-61, pres Assoc of British Chambers of Commerce 1968-70, Master Mercers' Co 1963-64, one of HM Lieuts for City of London; *Style* - The Rt Hon The Lord Ebbisham, TD; The Old Rectory, Bletchingley, Surrey (☎ Godstone 843388)

EBERSTEIN, Robert David; s of late Douglas Eberstein; *b* 12 Feb 1941; *Educ* Wellington; *m* 1968, Rosemary Margaret, nee Hemming; 1 s, 2 da; *Career* FCA, fin dir Smith Kline & French Laboratories Ltd, regional dir Smith Kline & French International Co 1979-; *Style* - Robert Eberstein Esq; Church House, Codicote, Herts (☎ 0438 820618)

EBERT, Peter; s of late Prof Carl Elbert, CBE, of Calif USA; *b* 6 April 1918; *Educ* Salem Sch Germany and Gordonstoun Sch Scotland; *m* 1, 1944, Kathleen Havinden; 2 da; m 2, Silvia Ashmole; 5 s, 3 da; *Career* theatre dir; dir of Productions Scottish Opera 1964-76, Opera Sch Toronto U 1967-68; intendant theatres in Augsburg 1968-73, Bielefeld 1973-75, Wiesbaden 1975-77; gen admin Scottish Opera 1977-80; Hon Doctor of Music St Andrew's U 1979; *Clubs* Caledonian; *Style* - Peter Ebert Esq; Ades House, Chailey, E Sussex, BN8 4HP (☎ Newick 2441)

EBRAHIM, Sir (Mahomed) Currimbhoy; 4 Bt (UK 1910), of Bombay; s of Sir (Huseinali) Currimbhoy Ebrahim, 3 Bt (d 1952); *b* 24 June 1935; *m* 1958, Dur-e-Mariam, da of Minuchehir Ahmud Nurudin Ahmed Ghulam Ally Nana, of Karachi; 3 s, 1 da; *Heir* s, Zulfiqar Ali Currimbhoy Ebrahim; *Career* memb Standing Council of Baronetage; *Style* - Sir Currimbhoy Ebrahim, Bt; Baitullah 33, Bait-ul-Aman Mirza Kalig Beg rd, Jameshed Quarters, Karachi, Pakistan

EBRAHIM, Zulfiqar Ali Currimbhoy; s and h of Sir Currimbhoy Ebrahim, 4 Bt; *b* 5 Aug 1960; *Style* - Zulfiqar Currimbhoy Ebrahim Esq

EBRINGTON, Viscount; Charles Hugh Richard Fortescue; s (by 1 m) and h of 7 Earl Fortescue; *b* 10 May 1951; *Educ* Eton; *m* 1974, Julia, da of Air Cdre J A Sowrey; 1 da; *Style* - Viscount Ebrington; Ebrington Manor, Chipping Campden, Glos

EBURY, 6 Baron (UK 1857); Francis Egerton Grosvenor; s of 5 Baron Ebury, DSO (d 1957, whose ggf, 1 Baron, was yr bro of 2 Marquess of Westminster and 2 Earl of Wilton; thus Lord Ebury is hp to 7 Earl of Wilton and ultimately, since Lord Wilton is himself hp to all the 6 Duke of Westminster's titles except the Dukedom, might inherit those honours too), by his 1 w, Anne, da of Herbert Acland-Troyte, MC (gn of Sir Thomas Acland, 10 Bt); *b* 8 Feb 1934; *Educ* Eton; *m* 1, 1957 (m dis 1962), Gillian, da of Martin Soames and Myra Drummond, niece of 16 Earl of Perth; 1 s; m 2, 1963 (m dis 1973), Kyra, da of L Aslin; m 3, 1974, Suzanne, da of Graham Suckling, of NZ; 1 da; *Heir* s, Hon Julian Grosvenor; *Recreations* golf; *Style* - The Rt Hon Lord Ebury; 5 Landale rd, Toorak 3142, Melbourne, Australia

EBURY, Denise, Baroness - Hon Denise Margaret; *née* Yarde-Buller; da of late 3 Baron Churston; *b* 1916; *m* 1941 (m dis 1954), as his 2 w, 5 Baron Ebury (d 1957); *Style* - Denise, Lady Ebury; Barton's Lodge, Eversholt, Bucks

EBURY, Dowager Baroness; Sheila Winifred; da of Arthur Edward Dashfield; *b* 28 April 1925; *m* 1954, as his 3 w, 5 Baron Ebury (d 1957); *Style* - Rt Hon Dowager Lady Ebury; 37 Linkside av, Five Mile dve, Wolvercote, Oxford; 5 Landale rd, Toorak, Melbourne, Australia

ECCLES, 1 Viscount (UK 1964); David McAdam Eccles; KCVO (1953), PC (1951); also 1 Baron Eccles (UK 1962); s of W McAdam Eccles, FRCS; *b* 18 Sept 1904; *Educ* Winchester, New Coll Oxford; *m* 1928, Hon Sybil (d 1977), da of Viscount Dawson of Penn, GCVO, KCB, KCMG, PC; 2 s, 1 da; *Heir* s, Hon John Dawson Eccles; *Career* MP (C) Chippenham Wilts 1943-62, Min of Works

1951-54, of Education 1954-57, pres Bd of Trade 1957-59, Paymaster Gen 1970-73, chm Br Library Bd 1973-78, pres World Crafts Cncl 1974-78; *Style* - The Rt Hon The Viscount Eccles, KCVO PC; Dean Farm, Chute, nr Andover, Hants (☎ Chute Standen 210); 6 Barton st, SW1 (☎ 01 222 1387)

ECCLES, Hon Mrs (Milba Hartley); da of Baron Williamson (Life Peer); *b* 1926; *m* 1952, Jack Fleming Eccles; children; *Style* - The Hon Mrs Eccles; 11 Sutton rd, Alderley Edge, Cheshire

ECCLES, Hon Simon Dawson; s of 1 Viscount Eccles; *b* 11 Sept 1934; *Educ* Repton; *m* 1961, Sheelin, da of Henry Edmund Ryan, of Long Meadow, Goring, Oxon; 1 s, 1 da; *Career* Capt Roy Fusiliers, ptnr Grieveson Grant & Co Stockbrokers (London); *Recreations* tobogganing, music; *Style* - The Hon Simon Eccles; 5 Little Boltons, SW10

ECHLIN, Sir Norman David Fenton; 10 Bt (I 1721); s of Sir John Frederick, 9 Bt (d 1932); *b* 1 Dec 1925; *Educ* Masonic Boys' Sch Clonskeagh Co Dublin; *m* 1953, Mary Christine, da of John Arthur, of Oswestry, Salop; *Style* - Sir Norman Echlin, Bt; Nartopa, Marina av, Appley, Ryde, Isle of Wight

ECKERSLEY, Sir Donald Payze; OBE (1976); s of late W R Eckersley; *b* 1 Nov 1922; *Educ* Muresk Agricultural Coll WA; *m* 1949, Marjorie, da of R Clarke; 1 s, 2 da; *Career* formerly pres Australian Farmers Federation; Man of the Year in Agriculture 1979; pres Nat Farmers Federation; kt 1981; *Style* - Sir Donald Eckersley, OBE; Korijedale, Harvey, WA 6220, Australia

ECKERSLEY-MASLIN, Rear-Adm David Michael; s of Cdr C Eckersley-Maslin RN OBE, of Tasmania; *b* 27 Sept 1929; *Educ* RN Coll Dartmouth; *m* 1955, Shirley Ann, da of late Capt H Martin, RN, DSC; 1 s, 1 da; *Career* Rear-Adm; Capt HMS Eastbourne 1966-68, HMS Euryalus 1971-72, HMS Fife 1975, HMS Blake 1976, Roy Coll of Defence Studies 1977, dir Naval Op Requirements 1978-80, Flag Offr Sea Training 1980-; *Recreations* cricket, tennis, squash; *Clubs* MCC, Roy Commonwealth; *Style* - Rear-Adm David Eckersley-Maslin; Dunningwell Hall Court, Shedfield, Southampton, Hants (☎ Wickham 832350)

EDDEN, Alan John; CMG (1957); s of Thomas Frederick Edden (d 1953); *b* 2 Dec 1912; *Educ* Latymer Sch Edmonton and Gonville and Caius Coll Cambridge; *m* 1939, Pauline Johanna Agnes, da of Lt-Col J W Klay (d 1942); 1 s; *Career* entered HM Consular Serv 1935; Counsellor Foreign Office 1954-58, Beirut 1958-62; HM Consul-Gen Durban 1962-66; HM Ambassador to Cameroon, Central African Republic, Gabon and Chad 1966-70, Equatorial Guinea 1969-70, Lebanon 1970-71; *Recreations* music; *Clubs* Victoria (Pietermaritzburg SA); *Style* - Alan Edden Esq, CMG; 77 Hosking rd, Pietermaritzburg, S Africa

EDEN, Hon Andrew Francis; s of 7 Baron Henley; *b* 4 Sept 1955; *Educ* Dragon Sch Oxford, Clifton Coll Bristol; *Style* - The Hon Andrew Eden; Scaleby Castle, Carlisle, Cumberland

EDEN, Hon Ingaret Barbara; da of late 7 Baron Henley; *b* 1951; *Style* - The Hon Ingaret Eden

EDEN, Rt Hon Sir John Benedict; 9 Bt (E 1672), of West Auckland, Durham, and 7 Bt (GB 1776), of Maryland, America, PC (1972), MP (C) W Bournemouth Feb 1954-; s of Sir Timothy Calvert Eden, 8 and 6 Bt (d 1963); *b* 15 Sept 1925; *Educ* Eton, St Paul's Sch USA; *m* 1, 1958 (m dis 1974), Belinda Jane, da of late Sir (Frederick) John Pascoe; 2 s, 2 da; m 2, 1977, Margaret Ann, da of late Robin Gordon, and formerly w of Viscount Strathallan, *qv*; *Heir* s, Robert Frederick Calvert Eden; *Career* Oppn Front Bench Spokesman for Power 1968-70, Min of State Miny of Technology June-Oct 1970, Min for Industry 1970-72, Min of Post and Telecommunications 1972-74, pres Independent Schs Assoc 1969-71, memb Trade and Industry Sub-Ctee of House of Commons Expenditure Ctee 1974-76, pres Wessex Area of Nat Union of Con and Unionist Assocs 1974-77; dir Central & Sheerwood Ltd and other cos; *Style* - Rt Hon Sir John Eden, Bt, PC, MP; 41

Victoria rd, W8; Knoyle Place, East Knoyle, Salisbury, Wilts

EDEN, Robert Frederick Calvert; s (by 1 m) and h of Rt Hon Sir John Eden, 9 Bt, PC, MP; *b* 30 April 1964; *Style* - Robert Eden Esq

EDEN, Hon Robert Ian Burnard; s and h of 9 Baron Auckland; *b* 25 July 1962; *Style* - The Hon Robert Eden

EDEN, Hon Ronald John; s of 8 Baron Auckland, MC (d 1957); *b* 5 March 1931; *Educ* Glenalmond, Ch Ch Oxford; *m* 1957, Rosemary Dorothy Marion, da of Sir John Crowder (d 1961), of 116 Ashley Gdns SW1; 2 s; *Career* former stockbroker; *Style* - The Hon Ronald Eden; Cromlix, Dunblane, Perthshire

EDEN, Dr Richard John; OBE (1978); s of James Arthur Eden; *b* 2 July 1922; *Educ* Hertford Grammar Sch and Cambridge U; *m* 1949, Elsie Jane, da of late Herbert Edwards; 1 s, 1 da and 1 step da; *Career* Capt REME Airborne Forces Europe and India; reader in Theoretical Physics 1964-, head of Energy Research Group, Cavendish Lab Cambridge U; visiting prof or scientist at various Us in USA and Europe 1954-73; *Recreations* reading and painting; *Clubs* Army and Navy; *Style* - Dr Richard Eden, OBE; 6 Wootton way, Cambridge, CB3 9LX

EDEN, Hon Roger Quentin Eden; s of 6 Baron Henley (d 1962); *b* 1922; *Educ* Rugby; *m* 1946, Carys Wynne, da of I H D Davies, of Camwy, Penrhyndeudraeth, Merionethshire; 2 s, 2 da; *Career* flying officer RAF 1944; *Style* - The Hon Roger Eden; 29A Hamilton ter, NW8 (☎ 01 286 1645); Askerton Castle, Brampton, Cumberland

EDGCUMBE, Robert Charles; s of late George Aubrey Valletort Edgcumbe (bro of 7 Earl of Mount Edgcumbe); hp to Earldom of Mount Edgcumbe; *b* 1 June 1939; *m* 1960, Joan; 5 da; *Style* - Robert Edgcumbe Esq; PO Box 153, Kawerau, New Zealand

EDGE, Sir Knowles; 2 Bt (UK 1937) of Ribble Lodge, Lytham St Annes, Co Lancaster, JP (1955); s of Sir William Knowles, 1 Bt (d 1948); *b* 31 Dec 1905; *Educ* Bolton and Trinity Hall Cambridge; *m* 1932, Dorothea Eunice (d 1976), da of Robert Walker; 2 s; *Heir* s, William Edge; *Clubs* Athenaeum; *Style* - Sir Knowles Edge, Bt, JP; Fair Lawn, Fairlawn rd, Lytham, Lancs

EDGE, Maj-Gen Raymond Cyril Alexander; CB (1968), MBE (1945); s of Raymond Clive Edge (d 1951), of Cheltenham; *b* 21 July 1912; *Educ* Cheltenham Coll, RMA Woolwich and Caius Coll Cambridge; *m* 1939, Margaret Patricia, da of William Wallace McKee (d 1921) of Tyrone, N Ireland; 1 s, 1 da; *Career* 2 Lt RE 1932, served in 1939-45 War (India, Burma (despatches) and Malaya), Col 1954, Brig 1961, dep dir of Survey MELF 1958, dir Ordnance Survey 1961-65, Maj-Gen 1965, ret 1969; memb Sec of State for the Environment's Panel of Ind Insprs 1970-, v-pres & chm Geodesy Sub Ctee, Roy Soc 1968-74; *Recreations* music; *Clubs* Army and Navy; *Style* - Maj-Gen Raymond Edge, CB, MBE; Greenway House, N Curry, Taunton, Som (☎ N Curry 490358)

EDGE, William; s and h of Sir Knowles Edge, 2 Bt; *b* 5 Oct 1936; *m* 1959, Avril Elizabeth Denson; 2 s, 2 da; *Style* - William Edge Esq; 66 Harrow rd, Maidenhead, Berks

EDMONDS, Dr Herbert; s of Dr Arthur Edmonds; *b* 24 July 1930; *Educ* Mountain Ash County G S, Wales (Cardiff) and Leeds U; *m* 1960, Hannah, nee Oppenheimer; 3 s, 1 da; *Career* Chemistry; FRSC; md Coutinho Caro & Co Ltd, past chm Int Steel Trade Assoc; *Style* - Dr Herbert Edmonds

EDMONDS, Cdr John Christopher; CMG (1978), CVO (1971); s of Capt Archibald Charles Mackay Edmonds, OBE (d 1961); *b* 23 June 1921; *Educ* Kelly Coll; *m* 1, 1948 (m dis 1965), Elena Tornow; 2 s; m 2, 1966, Armine, da of Clement Hilton Williams, MBE (d 1963); *Career* served RN 1939-59; Cdr 1957, staff NATO Defence Coll 1953-55, C-in-C Home Fleet 1955-57, Ch of Defence Staff 1958-59; entered Diplomatic Serv 1959,

Counsellor British Embassy Ankara 1968-71, Paris 1972-74, head of Arms Control and Disarmament Dept Foreign and Commonwealth Office 1974-77; leader United Kingdom Delegation to Comprehensive Test Ban Treaty negotiations Geneva, with personal rank of Ambassador; *Recreations* gardening, golf and travel; *Clubs* Army and Navy; *Style* - Cdr John Edmonds, CMG, CVO, RN; North Lodge, Sonning, Berkshire (☎ 0734 690017)

EDMONDS, Richard Edward Howard; JP; s of late Eric Edmonds; *b* 7 July 1925; *Educ* Wellington, Oriel Oxford; *m* 1958, Sarah Anne, da of Hugh Merriman, DSO, MC, TD, DL; 1 s, 1 da; *Career* chairman Clements (Watford) Ltd, chairman Coln Gravel Ltd, Evening Post and Echo, company dir, farmer; *Recreations* shooting, fishing, skiing; *Style* - Richard Edmonds Esq, JP; Micklefield Hall, Rickmansworth, Herts (☎ Rickmansworth 74747)

EDMONDS, Hon Mrs (Thelma Margaret Leighton); *née* Seager; da of late 1 Baron Leighton of St Mellons, CBE; *b* 6 Nov 1923; *Educ* Queenswood Sch, London U (Social Science); *m* 1951, Michael Leighton Edmonds; 1 s, 2 da; *Career* magistrate 1962-68, medical social worker; *Recreations* talking with friends; *Style* - Hon Mrs Edmonds; Topsham, Devon

EDMONDSON, Hon Anthony James Kinghorn; s of 1 Baron Sandford; *b* 1924; *Educ* Eton, Harvard University USA; *m* 1, 1947 (m dis 1969), Olivia Charlotte, nee Hunt; 3 s, 1 da; m 2, 1969, Hilary Pauline, nee Trusler; 1 s; *Career* Capt (ret) Grenadier Guards; *Style* - The Hon Anthony Edmondson; Upton Manor, East Knoyle, Salisbury, Wiltshire

EDMONDSON, Hon James John Mowbray; s and h of 2 Baron Sandford, DSC; *b* 1 July, 1949; *Educ* Westbourne House Preparatory Sch Chichester Sussex, Eton, York U; *m* 1973, Ellen Sarah, nee Shapiro, 1 da; *Career* school teacher; *Style* - The Hon James Edmondson; 103 North Warwick ave, Burnaby, BC, Canada

EDMONDSON, Hon Margaret Catharine (Peggy); da of 2 Baron Sandford, DSC; *b* 7 Nov 1947; *Educ* Downe House Newbury, St Albans Coll of Further Education, La Korrigane St Servan France, Trinity Coll Dublin; *Career* social worker; *Style* - The Hon Margaret Edmondson; 6 Smith sq, SW1 (☎ 01 222 5715)

EDMONSTONE, Sir Archibald Bruce Charles; 7 Bt (GB 1774) of Duntreath, Stirlingshire; s of Sir Archibald Charles Edmonstone, 6 Bt (d 1954); *b* 3 Aug 1934 *Educ* Stowe; *m* 1, 1957 (m dis 1967), Jane (who m 2, HSH Prince Martin Lubomirski), da of Maj-Gen Edward Charles Colville, CB, DSO (s of Adm the Hon Sir Stanley Colville, GCB, GCMG, GCVO (2 s of 1 Viscount Colville of Culross) by his w Lady Adelaide Meade, da of 4 Earl of Clanwilliam); 2 s, 1 da; m 2, 1969, Juliet Elizabeth, da of Maj-Gen C M F Deakin, CB, CBE; 1 s, 1 da; *Heir* s, Archibald Edward Charles Edmonstone; *Style* - Sir Archibald Edmonstone, Bt; Duntreath Castle, Blanefield, Stirlingshire (☎ 215)

EDMONSTONE, Hon Mrs (Alicia Evelyn); *née* Browne; da of late 5 Baron Kilmaine; *b* 1909; *m* 1939, Cdr Edward St John Edmonstone, RN (ret); *Style* - The Hon Mrs Edmonstone; Barcombe Old Rectory, nr Lewes, Sussex

EDMONSTONE, Archibald Edward Charles; s (by 1 m) and h of Sir Archibald Edmonstone, 7 Bt; *b* 4 Feb 1961; *Style* - Archibald Edmonstone Esq

EDMONSTONE, Dowager Lady; Gwendolyn Mary; da of late Marshall Field; *m* 1923, Sir Archibald Charles Edmonstone, 6 Bt (d 1954); *Style* - Dowager Lady Edmonstone; Lettre Cottage, Killearn, Glasgow

EDMUND-DAVIES, Baron (Life Peer UK 1974); Herbert Edmund Edmund-Davies; PC (1966); s of Morgan John Davies, of Mountain Ash, Glam; *b* 15 July

1906; *Educ* Mountain Ash, King's Coll London, Exeter Coll Oxford; *m* 1935, Eurwen, da of late John Williams, JP, of Barry; 3 da; *Career* barr 1929, bencher 1948, tres 1965 and 1966, former recorder of Merthyr Tydfil, Swansea, Cardiff, a judge of the High Court of Justice Queen's Bench Div 1958-66, a Lord Justice of Appeal 1966-74, a Lord of Appeal in Ordinary 1974-, Life Gov and Fell King's Coll London, Pro-Chllr U of Wales 1974-, chm Aberfan Inquiry Tribunal 1966, kt 1958; added 'Edmund-' to original surname 1974; *Style* - The Rt Hon The Lord Edmund-Davies, PC; 5 Gray's Inn sq, WC1

EDNAM, Viscount; William Humble David Jeremy Ward; s and h of Earl of Dudley; *b* 27 March 1947; *Educ* Eton, Ch Ch Oxford; *m* 1, 1972 (m dis 1976), Sarah, da of Sir Alastair Coats, 4 Bt; m 2, 1976 (m dis 1980), da of George Robert Pinney; 1 da; *Style* - Viscount Ednam; Rowlandson Ground, nr Coniston, Cumbria (☎ Coniston 397)

EDWARD, David Alexander Ogilvy; QC (Sco 1974); s of John Ogilvy Christie Edward (d 1960); *b* 14 Nov 1934; *Educ* Sedbergh Sch, Univ Coll Oxford and Edinburgh U; *m* 1962, Elizabeth Young, da of Terence McSherry, of Edinburgh; 2 s, 2 da; *Career* Lt RNVR (nat serv) 1955-57; Adv 1962, Clerk of the Faculty of Advs 1967-70, tres 1970-77, pres Consultative Ctee of the Bars and Law Socs of the European Community 1978-80, trustee Nat Library of Scotland 1966-, memb Law Advisory Panel British Cncl, Panel of Arbitrators Int Centre for Settlement of Investment Disputes 1979-; *Clubs* New (Edinburgh) and Scottish Arts; *Style* - David Edward Esq, QC; 32 Heriot Row, Edinburgh (☎ 031 225 7153)

EDWARD, Hon Mrs (Gillian Margaret); *née* Hunter; da of Baron Hunter of Newington, MBE (Life Peer); *m* 1973, Malcolm Greig Edward; *Style* - The Hon Mrs Edward; 111 Chichester dve, Quinton, Birmingham 32

EDWARDES, Hon David; DSC (1944); 3 s of late 6 Baron Kensington, CMG, DSO, TD, JP, DL; *b* 19 July 1907; *Educ* Eton; *m* 1939, Elizabeth, da of Robert Broadley; 3 da; *Career* Cdr RN (ret); served war 1939-44 (DSC); *Recreations* shooting, fishing; *Style* - The Hon David Edwardes DSC; The Old Stables, Woolston, N Cadbury, Yeovil, Somerset (☎ N Cadbury 40458)

EDWARDES, Hugh Ivor; s of Capt Hon Owen Edwardes (2 s of 6 Baron Kensington, CMG, DSO, TD, JP, DL); hp to unc, 7 Baron; *b* 24 Nov 1933; *Educ* Eton; *m* 1961, Juliet, da of Alexander Massy Anderson; 2 s (William Owen Alexander, b 21 July 1964; Hugh Rupert, b 25 Jan 1967), 1 da (Amanda Louise Massy, b 22 May 1962); *Style* - Hugh Edwardes Esq; Ringwood Farm, Kassier rd, Assagay, PO Hillcrest, Natal, South Africa

EDWARDES, Hon Michael George; MBE (1944); 3 s of 6 Baron Kensington, CMG, DSO, TD; *b* 29 July 1910; *Educ* Eton, Sandhurst; *m* 1946, Sylvia Inez Pakenham, da of Col Hope Johnston, CB, and former w of Lt-Col Alfred McGaw; *Career* Lt-Col regular 1930-57, served M East, Italy, NW Europe; memb Hon Corps Gentlemen-at-Arms 1959-80; *Recreations* fishing; *Clubs* Army & Navy; *Style* - Lt-Col The Hon Michael Edwardes MBE; The Stables, The Green, Tetbury, Glos (☎ 53030)

EDWARDES, Sir Michael Owen; s of Denys Edwardes; *b* 11 Oct 1930; *Educ* St Andrew's Coll Grahamstown S Africa, Rhodes U; *m* 1958, Mary Margaret, nee Finlay; 3 da; *Career* chm BL Ltd 1977- (salary raised to £100,000 pa as of June 1981), dep chm Chloride Gp Ltd 1977-, memb CBI Cncl, FBIM, kt 1979; *Style* - Sir Michael Edwardes; Nuffield House, 41-46 Piccadilly, W1 (☎ 01 439 8281)

EDWARDES JONES, Air Marshal Sir (John) Humphrey; KCB (1957, CB 1954), CBE (1943), DFC (1940), AFC (1941); s of George Morgan Edwardes

Jones, KC (d 1935); *b* 15 Aug 1905; *Educ* Brighton Coll and Pembroke Coll Cambridge; *m* 1935, Margaret Lucy Rose, da of Donald Hatt Noble Graham (ka 1915); 1 s, 1 da; *Career* RAF 1926-61; Wing Cdr 1940, served 1939-45 (Fighter Cmmd and Med), Air Cdre 1950, SASO Second Tactical Air Force 1952-55, Air V-Marshal 1953, Cmdt Sch of Land/Air Warfare 1955-57, C-in-C 2 TAF 1957-61, Air Marshal 1958, ret 1961; *Recreations* golf; *Clubs* RAF; *Style* - Air Marshal Sir Humphrey Edwardes Jones, KCB, CBE, DFC, AFC; Old Marks, Holtye, Sussex (☎ Cowden 317)

EDWARDS, Hon Mrs (Ann Cecily Mary); da of 8 Baron Talbot of Malahide, MC (d 1975); *b* 1931; *m* 1955, Col Edward Reginald Edwards; 3 s; *Style* - The Hon Mrs Edwards; Malahide Cottage, West End, Hornton, Banbury, Oxon

EDWARDS, Brig Arthur Bertie Duncan; CBE (1944), MC (1920); s of Joseph Edwards; *b* 1898; *Educ* RMA; *m* 1925, Clara, nee Barkworth, JP; 3 s; *Career* RE WW I, Brig 1943; dep dir of Works BAOR 1946-48, CE Eastern Command 1948, ret 1951; *Style* - Brig Arthur Edwards, CBE, MC

EDWARDS, Alan Kenneth Warneford; s of late Trevor James Edwards; *b* 6 June 1927; *Educ* Birkenhead Sch; *m* 1952, Valerie Frances, nee Burbridge; 3 s, 1 da; *Career* chartered accountant, in practice 1954-1961, fin dir Lonsdale Universal Ltd 1962, md and dep chm 1969-; *Recreations* cricket, motor racing, rugby; *Clubs* MCC; *Style* - Alan Edwards Esq; Hill Close, Sandy Lane, Cobham, Surrey (☎ Cobham 2068)

EDWARDS, Hon Mrs (Catherine Gerran); *née* Lloyd; da of Baron Lloyd of Kilgerran, CBE, QC (Life Peer); *b* 1 March 1947; *Educ* Roedean; *m* 1972, Philip Gwynfryn Edwards; 3 c; *Recreations* tennis; *Clubs* Roy Commonwealth Society; *Style* - The Hon Mrs Edwards; 13 Lancaster av, Hadley Wood, Herts (☎ 01 440 9503)

EDWARDS, Sir Christopher John Churchill; 5 Bt (1866) of Pye Nest, Yorkshire; s of Sir Charles Edwards, 4 Bt (d 1963); *b* 16 Aug 1941; *Educ* Frensham Heights Sch and Loughborough Coll; *m* 1972, Gladys Irene Vogelgesang; 1 s; *Heir* s, David Charles Priestley Edwards; *Style* - Sir Christopher Edwards, Bt; 6133 Laurelgrove ave, N Hollywood, Calif 91606, USA

EDWARDS, Sir (John) Clive Leighton; 2 Bt (UK 1921) of Treforia, Co Glamorgan; s of Sir John Bryn Edwards, 1 Bt (d 1922); *b* 11 Oct 1916; *Educ* Winchester; *Heir* none; *Career* European War 1940-45 with RASC and as Capt Roy Pioneer Corps; *Style* - Sir Clive Edwards, Bt; Milntown, Lezayre, nr Ramsey, IOM

EDWARDS, David Charles Priestley; s and h of Sir Christopher Edwards, 5 Bt; *b* 22 Feb 1974; *Style* - David Edwards Esq

EDWARDS, David St John; s of Capt Herbert Edwards (ka 1917); *b* 16 April 1917; *Educ* Wellington, St John's Cambridge; *m* 1947, Kathleen Mary, da of Surgn Rear-Adm Gilbert Syms; 1 s, 2 da; *Career* freight forwarder, dir LEP Transport & Associated Cos 1960-, chm Express Container Transport 1972-; *Recreations* sailing, bridge; *Style* - David Edwards Esq; Shenley, The Drive, Woking, Surrey (☎ 61535)

EDWARDS, Geoffrey Francis; CBE (1975, OBE 1968, MBE 1956), TD (1949); s of Oliver Edwards (d 1938); *b* 28 Sept 1917; *Educ* Brighton Coll; *m* 1961, Johanna Elisabeth Franziska, da of Dr Werner Heinen (d 1976); 1 da; *Career* Maj NW Europe 1939-45; former memb HM Diplomatic Serv, Finance Div Control Cmmn for Germany 1945-49, British Mil Govt Berlin 1949-66, HM Consul-Gen Berlin 1966-75, ret 1975; *Recreations* gardening, fishing and golf; *Style* - Geoffrey Edwards Esq, CBE, TD; Whitegates, Mathon rd, Colwall, nr Malvern

EDWARDS, Sir George Robert; OM (1971), CBE (1952, MBE 1945), DL (Surrey 1981); *b* 9 July 1908; *Educ* SW Essex Tech, London U; *m* 1935, Marjorie, nee Thurgood; 1 da; *Career* kt 1957, FRS 1968, chm BAC 1963-75, Pro-Chllr Emeritus Surrey U 1979-, aeronautical engr, formerly with Vickers and Vickers-Armstrong; *Style* - Sir George Edwards

OM CBE DL; Albury Heights, White Lane, Guildford, Surrey (☎ 504488)

EDWARDS, John; s of late Arthur Leonard Edwards; *b* 2 Jan 1932; *Educ* Wolverhampton Municipal GS; *m* 1954, Nancy Woodcock; 1 s, 1 da; *Career* Journalist; ed Yorkshire Post 1969-; *Style* - John Edwards Esq; 1 Egerton rd, West Pk, Leeds

EDWARDS, John Coates; s of Herbert John Edwards; *b* 25 Nov 1934; *Educ* Skinners' Sch Tunbridge Wells, Brasenose Oxford; *m* 1959, Mary, nee Harris; 1 s, 1 da; *Career* civil servant; head of British Dvpt Div in the Caribbean 1978-, UK dir Caribbean Devpt Bank; *Style* - John Edwards Esq; PO Box 167, Bridgetown, Barbados (☎ 62190); Fairways, Ightham, Sevenoaks, Kent (☎ Borough Green 885455)

EDWARDS, Prof James Griffith; s of Dr J T Edwards; *b* 3 Oct 1928; *Educ* Andover G S, Balliol Oxford, St Bartholomew's Hosp Med Sch; *m* 1969, Evelyn Humphries, da of Robert Morrison; 1 s, 1 da (1 da decd); *Career* Prof of Addiction Behaviour, Inst of Psychiatry 1979-; dir Addiction Research Unit, Inst of Psychiatry 1970-; Hon Consultant Psychiatrist, Bethlem Roy and Mandsley Hosps 1967-; med dir Alcohol Educn Centre 1980-; ed British Journal of Addiction 1978-; *Style* - Prof James Edwards; 42 Crooms Hill, London, SE10

EDWARDS, John Revill; s of Revill Edwards; *b* 18 July 1947; *Educ* Oundle, Aston U, Wharton Graduate Sch of Finance Pennsylvania U; *m* 1970, Vienneta Diane, nee Oxford; 2 s; *Career* dep md Edgar Vaughan & Co Ltd, dir Evco Seals Ltd, Kevco Chemicals Ltd; *Style* - John Edwards Esq; Old Birchwood Farm, Hoar Cross, Burton-on-Trent, Staffs (☎ Hoar Cross 381)

EDWARDS, Joseph Robert; CBE (1963), JP; s of Walter Smith Edwards; *b* 5 July 1908; *Educ* High Sch Gt Yarmouth; *m* 1, 1936, Frances Mabel Haddon Bourne (d 1975); 3 s, 1 da; m 2, 1976, Joan Constance Mary Tattersall; *Career* chm Penta Motors Ltd Reading 1978-, dir British Printing Corpn; *Style* - Joseph Edwards Esq, CBE, JP; Flat 16, Shoreacres, Banks rd, Sandbanks, nr Bournemouth, Dorset (☎ Canford Cliffs 709315)

EDWARDS, James Valentine; CVO (1977); s of Capt Alfred Edwards, OBE (d 1964); *b* 4 Feb 1925; *Educ* Radley and Magdalen Oxford; *m* 1965, Barbara, da of Sir John Colbrook Hanbury-Williams, CVO (d 1965); 2 da (and 1 step s and 1 step da); *Career* able seaman (served Atlantic 1943 and Pacific 1944-45); headmaster Heatherdown Sch 1959-; *Recreations* skiing, mountain walking and golf; *Clubs* MCC, Free Foresters and Vincent's (Oxford); *Style* - James Edwards Esq CVO; Heatherdown, Ascot, Berks (☎ Winkfield Row 2770)

EDWARDS, (John) Michael; QC (1981); s of late Dr James Thomas Edwards; *b* 16 Oct 1925; *Educ* Andover G S, Univ Coll Oxford; *m* 1, 1952, Morna Joyce, nee Piper; 1 s, 1 da; m 2, 1964, Rosemary Ann, nee Moore; 2 s; *Career* barr Middle Temple 1949; joined British Steel Corp 1967, chm and md (Overseas Serv) 1975-81; Provost, City of London Polytechnic 1981-; Freeman, City of London; Yeoman, Ironmongers Co; *Clubs* Garrick; *Style* - Michael Edwards Esq, QC; City of London Polytechnic, 117-119 Houndsditch, EC3 (☎ 01 283 1030)

EDWARDS, Peter Guy; s of Brig Claud Taylor Edwards, CBE (d 1979); *b* 9 Feb 1924; *Educ* Clifton Coll, Durham U (BSc); *m* 1959, Jill Mary, da of William Devas Everington; 1 s, 2 da; *Career* Capt Roy Engineers Europe and SEAC, High Sheriff Co Durham 1968-69, pres BISPA 1975-77, chm Brown Bayley Steels Ltd and Dunford Hadfields 1970-77, dir Hunting Petroleum Services 1978, chm Lake & Elliot Ltd 1979-; *Recreations* field sports; *Clubs* Northern Counties; *Style* - Peter Edwards Esq; Low Walworth Hall, Darlington, Co Durham (☎ 68004)

EDWARDS, Robert John; s of William Gordon Edwards (d 1938); *b* 26 Oct 1925; *Educ* Ranelagh Sch Bracknell; *m* 1, 1952 (m dis 1972), Laura Ellwood; 4 c; m 2, 1977, Brigid O'Neil, da of late Edmond

Segrave; *Career* ed Tribune 1951-54, dep ed Sunday Express 1957-59, ed Daily Express 1960 (man ed 1959-61), ed Evening Citizen Glasgow 1962-63, ed Daily Express 1963-65, ed Sunday People 1966-72, ed Sunday Mirror 1972-; *Recreations* sailing; *Clubs* Kennel, Reform, Roy Southern Yacht, Variety Club of GB; *Style* - Robert Edwards Esq; 74 Duns Tew, Oxon

EDWARDS, Sydney Clive; s of late Edward George Edwards; *b* 29 Oct 1935; *Educ* Newton-Le-Willows G S; *m* 1960, Marjorie Eleanor, nee Fowler; 1 s, 1 da; *Career* chartered accountant, fin dir Mojo Carryway Ltd 1975-77, fin dir Lo-Cost Stores Ltd 1977-; *Style* - Sydney Edwards Esq; 22 Woodlands rd, Parkgate, South Wirral, Cheshire

EDWARDS, William Philip Neville; CBE (1949); s of Neville Perrin Edwards (d 1965); *b* 5 Aug 1904; *Educ* Rugby Sch, Corpus Christi Coll Cambridge and Princeton U USA; *m* 1, 1932, Hon Sheila (d 1976), da of 13 Viscount Falkland, OBE (d 1961); 2 s; m 2, 1976, Joan Mullins, da of Reginald Graham Barker; *Career* cnsllr British Embassy Washington, in charge of British Information Serv in USA 1946-49; dir Confedn of British Industry 1949-66; md British Overseas Fairs Ltd 1960-66, chm 1966-68; head of Industrial Information Div, Miny of Supply 1941-42; *Recreations* golf and gardening; *Style* - William Edwards Esq, CBE; Four Winds, Kithurst lane, Storrington, W Sussex

EDWARDS-MOSS, David John; s and h of Sir John Edwards-Moss, 4 Bt; *b* 2 Feb 1955; *Style* - David Edwards-Moss Esq

EDWARDS-MOSS, Sir John Herbert Theodore; 4 Bt (UK 1868) of Roby Hall, Lancashire; s of late Maj John Edwards-Moss, 2 s of 2 Bt; suc unc, Sir Thomas Edwards-Moss, 3 Bt, 1960; *b* 24 June 1913; *m* 1951, Jane Rebie, da of Carteret John Kempson; 5 s, 1 da; *Heir* s, David John Edwards-Moss; *Style* - Sir John Edwards-Moss, Bt; Ruffold Farm, Cranleigh, Surrey

EELLS, Hon Mrs (Harriet Elizabeth); *née* Bridges; da of 2 Baron Bridges, CMG; *b* 1958; *m* 1981, John C Eells; *Style* - The Hon Mrs Eells

EFFINGHAM, 6 Earl of (UK 1837); Mowbray Henry Gordon Howard; also Baron Howard of Effingham (E 1554); s of 5 Earl (d 1946, tenth in descent from 1 Baron Howard of Effingham, who was eldest s of 2 Duke of Norfolk by his 2 w; the Lord Howard of Effingham who commmanded the fleet that destroyed the Armada, was the 2 Baron; the present Lord descends from his yr bro); *b* 29 Nov 1905; *Educ* Lancing; *m* 1, 1938 (m dis 1946), Maria Melvin Gertler; m 2, 1952 (m dis 1971), Mrs Gladys Irene, da of late Capt William Freeman, Merchant Navy, and formerly w of Frederick Charles Kerry; m 3, 1972, (Mabel) Suzanne Mingay, da of late Maurice Jules-Marie Le Pen, of Paris, and widow of Wing Cdr Francis Talbot Cragg; *Heir* n, Lt-Cdr David Peter Mowbray Algernon Howard; *Career* RA and 3 Maritime Regt WW II; *Style* - The Rt Hon The Earl of Effingham; House of Lords, SW1

EGAN, John; *aet* 41 in June 1981; *Career* chm Jaguar Cars (BL) 1980-, with Massey Ferguson to 1980; *Style* - John Egan Esq; c/o Jaguar Rover Triumph Ltd, Browns Lane, Coventry, Leics (☎ 402121/402141)

EGAN, Patrick Valentine Martin; s of Eric Egan; *b* 17 July 1930; *Educ* Downside; *m* 1953, Mary Theresa, nee Coleman; 3 da; *Career* 2 Lt Roy Artillery Far East 1949-50, exec dir Unilever Ltd and Unilever NV; *Recreations* riding, hunting, gardening; *Style* - Patrick Egan Esq; Whiteways, Sissinghurst, Cranbrook, Kent (☎ Cranbrook 713201)

EGAN, Trevor A; *Career* dir Carborundum gp of Cos; *Style* - Trevor Egan Esq; Carborundum Data Systems Ltd, Risley, Warrington, Lancs

EGERTON, Brian Balguy Le Belward; s of 14 Bt; hp of bro, Sir Philip Grey Egerton, 15 Bt, *qv*; *b* 5 Feb 1925; *Educ* Repton; *Style* -Brian Egerton Esq; Rhue 58, by Ullapool, Ross

EGERTON, Cyril Reginald; s of late

Hon Francis William George Egerton (2 s of 3 Earl of Ellesmere); hp of 1 cous, 6 Duke of Sutherland; *b* 7 Sept 1905; *Educ* Lancing, Trin Cambridge; *m* 1, 1934, Mary (d 1949), da of Rt Hon Sir Ronald Hugh Campbell, GCMG; 1 s (Francis), 3 da (Mrs Michael (Lucy) Pelham, Katharine, Mrs Thomas (Alice) Fremantle); m 2, 1954, Mary Truda, da of Late Sir (Thomas) Sydney Lea, 2 Bt; *Career* 1939-45 War as Capt Hampshire Regt, was Prime Warden of Dyers' Co 1954; *Style* - Cyril Egerton Esq; Hall Farm, Newmarket, Suffolk

EGERTON, Francis Louis; MC; s of Louis Edwin Egerton (s of Sir Alfred Egerton, KCVO, CB, by his w Hon Mary Ormsby-Gore, er da of 2 Baron Harlech) and bro of Sir Alfred Egerton, who adopted Francis after his f's death in action 1917; Louis's w was Jane, da of Rev Lord Victor Seymour, 4 s of 5 Marquess of Hertford; *b* 14 Feb 1918; *Educ* Eton, Ch Ch Oxford; *Career* Capt Welsh Guards, private sec to Sir Alexander Cadogan at Sec Cncl New York 1946-47, chm Mallett & Son 1950-; *Recreations* travelling, gardening; *Clubs* White's; *Style* - Francis Egerton Esq, MC; 12 Alexander sq, SW3 (☎ 01 589 5098)

EGERTON, Maj George Josslyn Barrington; JP (Herefordshire 1962), DL (Breconshire 1962); s of Maj Josslyn Seymour Egerton (d 1946); *b* 21 Aug 1915; *Educ* Radley Coll; *m* 1946, Flora, nee Watson; 2 da (twins Susan, Shan b 1948); *Career* South Wales Borderers 1936-60, Libya 1941-42, POW 1942-45, Malaya 1951-53, Regimental Sec 1960-69, A/Regt Sec Roy Regt of Wales and Curator 24 Regt Museum 1969-80, chm Dore & Bredwardine Bench 1974-; *Recreations* shooting, fishing, gardening; *Clubs* Army & Navy, Pall Mall, Free Foresters, MCC; *Style* - Maj George Egerton JP, DL; Penymacs House, Hay-on-Wye, via Hereford (☎ (0497) 820423)

EGERTON, Sir Seymour John Louis; GCVO (1977, KCVO 1970); s of Capt Louis Egerton (2 s of Sir Alfred Egerton, KCVO, CB, himself sixth in descent from Hon Thomas Egerton, 3 s of 2 Earl of Bridgwater, of an illegitimate line from the ancestors of the Grey-Egerton Bts) and Jane, da of Rev Lord Victor Seymour (4 s of 5 Marquess of Hertford); *b* 24 Sept 1915; *Educ* Eton; *Career* served WW II Capt Gren Gds; banker, chm Coutts & Co 1951-76; Sheriff Gter London 1968; *Clubs* Boodle's, Beefsteak, Pratt's; *Style* - Sir Seymour Egerton, GCVO; Flat A, 51 Eaton sq, SW1 (☎ 01 235 2164)

EGERTON, Stephen Loftus; CMG (1978); s of William le Belward Egerton (ggs of William Egerton, yr bro of Sir John and Rev Sir Philip Grey-Egerton, 8 & 9 Bts respectively); *b* 21 July 1932; *Educ* Eton, Trin Cambridge; *m* 1958, Caroline, da of Maj Thomas Cary-Elwes, TD, of Thurton Hall, Norwich; 1 s, 1 da; *Career* Ambass to Baghdad (to Iran during 1980); For Serv 1956-, Consul-Gen Rio de Janeiro 1977-80; *Style* - Stephen Egerton Esq, CMG; 31 Crescent Wood rd, Dulwich SE 26

EGERTON-WARBURTON, Hon Mrs - Hon Marya Anne; *née* Noble; da of Baron Glenkinglas (Life Peer); *b* 1944; *m* 1969, Peter Egerton-Warburton; *Style* - The Hon Mrs Egerton-Warburton; Mulberry House, Bentworth, Hants

EGERTON-WARBURTON, Peter; s of late Col Geoffrey Egerton-Warburton, DSO, TD, JP, DL (ggs of Rowland Egerton, bro of Sir John Grey-Egerton, 8 Bt, and Rev Sir Philip Grey-Egerton, 9 Bt), by Hon Georgiana Dormer, da of 14 Baron Dormer, CBE, DL; *b* 17 Jan 1933; *Educ* Eton; *m* 1969, Marya Anne, da of Baron Glenkinglas, PC; 3 s, 1 da (twin); *Career* Major Cheshire Yeo, Lord of the Manor of Grafton, Patron of the Livings of Plemstall and Guilden Sutton, ptnr John D Wood Estate Agents, landowner; *Clubs* White's, Pratt's; *Style* - Peter Egerton-Warburton Esq; 54 Princes Gate Mews, SW7 (☎ 01 589 9254); Mulberry House, Bentworth, Alton, Hants (☎ Alton 62360)

EGGLESTON, Prof Samuel John; s of Edmund Eggleston (d 1959); *b* 11 Nov 1926; *Educ* Chippenham Grammar Sch and London U; *m* 1957, Greta Margaret, da of James Patrick (d 1967); 2 s, 2 da; *Career* prof of Educn Keele U 1967-, chm Bd of Social Sciences 1976-, dir of Research Multi Cultural Educn 1978-, memb Consultative Ctee Assessment of

Performance Unit and Research Advisory Gp DES 1980-, academic adviser Routledge and Kegan Paul 1977-; lecturer and examiner many home and overseas Us; *Recreations* work in design and craft, skiing, riding, travel and gardening; *Style* - Prof Samuel Eggleston; Whitmore House, Newcastle-under-Lyme, Staffordshire (☎ Whitmore 680483)

EGLESTON, Lady Clarissa; *née* Windsor-Clive; da of 2 Earl of Plymouth; *b* 1931; *m* 1953, Maj Keith Maclean Forbes Egleston, late Rifle Bde; 1 s, 2 da; *Style* - Lady Clarissa Egleston; 7 Ernest gdns, W4

EGLINTON AND WINTON, 18 Earl of (S 1507 and UK 1859); Archibald George Montgomerie; Lord Montgomerie (S 1449), Baron Seton and Tranent (UK 1859), Baron Ardrossan (UK 1806); Hereditary Sheriff of Renfrewshire; s of 17 Earl of Eglinton and Winton (d 1966) and Ursula, da of Hon Ronald Bannatyne Watson, s of Baron Watson (Life Peer, d 1899); *b* 27 Aug 1939; *Educ* Eton; *m* 1964, Marion Carolina, da of John Henry Dunn-Yarker, of Le Château, La Tour de Peilz, Vaud, Switzerland; 4 s; *Heir* s, Lord Montgomerie; *Style* - The Rt Hon The Earl of Eglinton and Winton; The Dutch House, West Green, Hartley Wintney, Hants (☎ 3160)

EGLINTON AND WINTON, Ursula, Countess of; Ursula Joan; da of Hon Ronald Watson (2 s of Baron Watson, Life Peer cr 1880, extinct 1899); *m* 1938, 17 Earl of Eglinton and Winton (d 1966); 1 s (18 Earl), 2 da (Lady Susanna Crawford, Lady Elizabeth Barne, & 1 other da decd); *Style* - The Rt Hon Ursula, Countess of Eglinton and Winton; Slaphouse, Monument rd, Ayr

EGMONT, 11 Earl of (I 1733); Sir Frederick George Moore Perceval; 15 Bt (I 1661); also Baron Perceval (I 1715), Viscount Perceval (I 1722), Baron Lovell and Holland (GB 1762), Baron Arden (I 1770), Baron Arden (UK 1802); s of Frederick Joseph Trevelyan Perceval (d 1932 before establishing claim to Earldom but counts as 10 Earl for numerical purposes), ggs of Spencer Perceval, the PM whose thanks for going off the gold standard was assassination at the hands of Bellingham, a resentful bankrupt; *b* 14 April 1914; *m* 1932, Ann Geraldine, da of D G Moodie; 1 s (and 2 decd), 1 da; *Heir* s, Viscount Perceval; *Style* - The Rt Hon The Earl of Egmont; Two-dot Ranch, Nanton, Alberta, Canada

EGNER, William Edward; CBE (1974), JP (1968); s of George August Egner (d 1943); *b* 20 Feb 1911; *Educ* Jarrow Secondary Sch and Durham U; *m* 1939, Anne Muriel, da of John Davison Young (d 1968); 1 s, 2 da; *Career* sr Scientific Offr Fighter Cmmd RAF, Scientific Adviser C-in-C Flying Training Cmmd RAF and OIC of the Operational Research Section 1943-45; headmaster Heanor Grammar Sch Derbyshire 1946-50, Ormskirk Grammar Sch Lancs 1950-55, Grammar Tech Sch for Boys S Shields 1955-74, Harton Comprehensive Sch S Shields 1974-76, ret 1976; *Recreations* travel, painting in oils and music; *Clubs* Victory (London); *Style* - William Egner Esq, CBE, JP; 43 Sunderland rd, S Shields, Tyne and Wear (☎ S Shields 562821)

EGREMONT, 2 Baron (UK 1963) and 7 Baron Leconfield (UK 1859); (John) Max Henry Scawen Wyndham; s of 6 Baron Leconfield and 1 Baron Egremont, MBE (d 1972; as John Wyndham was Priv Sec to Harold Macmillan when PM; was also 1 cous of Mrs John Peyton, 2 w of the sometime Con Min of T'port); Lord Egremont is 1 cous thrice removed of Wilfrid Scawen Blunt, the poet, Eastern traveller, Islamophile and self-publicist; *b* 21 April 1948; *Educ* Eton, Ch Ch Oxford; *m* 1978, Caroline, da of Alexander Nelson and Hon Audrey Paget (da of 1 and last Baron Queenborough, s of Lord Alfred Paget, the 5 s of 1 Marquess of Anglesey); 2 da; *Heir* bro, Hon Harry Wyndham; *Career* farmer & writer ('The Cousins' dealt partly with Blunt); *Style* - The Rt Hon Lord Egremont; Petworth House, Petworth, Sussex (☎ 42447)

EGREMONT, Dowager Baroness, and Leconfield; Pamela; da of Capt Hon Valentine Wyndham Quin (2 s of 5 Earl of Dunraven and Mount-Earl) and sis of Lady Roderic Pratt and Marchioness of

Salisbury (w of 6 Marquess); *b* 29 April 1925; *m* 1947, 1 Baron Egremont (and 6 Baron Leconfield), MBE; 2 s (2 Baron Egremont (and 7 Baron Leconfield), Hon Harry Wyndham), 1 da (Hon Mrs Chisholm); *Style* - The Rt Hon The Dowager Lady Egremont; Cockermouth Castle, Cockermouth, Cumbria; 62 Chester sq, SW1 (☎ 01 730 2003)

EHRMANN, Ralph Rudolph Matthias; s of Robert Ehrmann (d 1947); *b* 8 March 1925; *Educ* St Paul's Sch, Reading U; *m* 1955, Inge Miriam, da of late Hans Landecker; 1 s, 2 da; *Career* chm Airfix Industries 1977-81, chm Clabir Corpn USA 1977-, dir General Defense Corpn USA 1980-; *Recreations* reading, theatre, riding, skiing, swimming, sailing; *Clubs* Hurlingham; *Style* - Ralph Ehrmann Esq; 41 Hornton st, W8 (☎ 01 937 7590)

EIGNER, Omar El Said; *Career* MechE; dir Capper-Neill Gp of Cos, Applied Res and Engrg Ltd; md Capper-Neill Int Ltd; *Style* - Omar Eigner Esq; PO Box 75, Bold, St Helens, Merseyside

EILBECK, Roger Antony; s of William Arthur Eilbeck (d 1958); *b* 20 Nov 1924; *Educ* Wallasey G S, Liverpool Univ; barr, Middle Temple; *m* 1948, Beryl; *Career* Sub-Lt RNVR, France & Germany, South East Asia; HM Consul at Florence and concurrently HM Consul-Gen for San Marino 1980; Home Office 1947-66; Consul Amsterdam 1967; First Secretary Rabat 1971; FCO 1973; Head of Chancery Damascus 1976; Consul Palermo 1978; Consul Venice 1980; *Recreations* the English countryside; *Clubs* Carlton, Naval; *Style* - Roger Eilbeck Esq; c/o FCO, King Charles St, London SWI

EISLER, Hon Mrs (Jean Mary); da of 1 Baron Layton, CH, CBE (d 1966); *b* 1916; *m* 1944, Paul Eisler (d 1966); 2 s; *Career* music therapist at Goldie Leigh Hosp SE2; *Style* - The Hon Mrs Eisler; Kozi 15, Prague 1, Czechoslovakia; Syskon Cottage, 2 Millfield Lane, N6

ELDER-JONES, His Honour Thomas; s of David Jones, JP (d 1952); *b* 4 Oct 1904; *Educ* Shrewsbury and Trinity Coll Oxford; *m* 1948, Hon Diana Katherine (d 1978), da of John Southwell Russell, 25 Baron de Clifford, of Dalgan Park, Co Mayo (d 1909); 1 da; *Career* barr Inner Temple 1927, served 1939-43 with 2 Roy Gloucestershire Huss, ret with Hon rank of Maj; County Court Judge 1953, circuit 34, 1957, circuit 52, ret 1976; sec Coal Mines Conciliation Bd 1943-53; *Recreations* foxhunting; *Clubs* United Oxford and Cambridge Us; *Style* - His Honour Thomas Elder-Jones; The Dower House, Somerford Keynes, Cirencester, Glos

ELDON, 5 Earl of (UK 1821); John Joseph Nicholas Scott; Baron Eldon (GB 1799), Viscount Encombe (UK 1821); s of 4 Earl of Eldon, GCVO (d 1976, fifth in descent from the 1 Earl, as High a Tory as he was a Lord Chllr) and Hon Margaret Fraser, OBE (d 1969), da of 16 Lord Lovat; *b* 24 April 1937; *Educ* Ampleforth, Trin Oxford; *m* 1961, Countess Claudine, da of Count Franz von Montjoye-Vaufrey and de la Roche (originally a cr of Louis XV of France 1736, confirmed 1743 (also by Louis) and later by Emperor Franz Josef of Austria-Hungary 1888), of Vienna; 1 s, 2 da; *Heir* s, Viscount Encombe; *Career* 2 Lt Scots Gds, Lt Army Emergency Reserve; *Style* - The Rt Hon The Earl of Eldon; 2 Coach House Lane, Wimbledon, SW19

ELDRIDGE, Eric William, CB (1965), OBE (1948); s of late William Eldridge; *b* 15 April 1906; *Educ* Millfields Central Sch and City of London Coll; *m* 1936, Doris Margaret, da of Peter Kerr (d 1964); 1 s, 1 da; *Career* slr 1934, consultant with Lee and Pembertons Slrs 1971-, ch administrative offr Public Trustee Office 1955-60, assist Public Trustee 1960-63, Public Trustee 1963-71; *Recreations* foreign travel and gardening; *Style* - Eric Eldridge Esq, CB, OBE; Gull Cottage, 249 High st, Aldeburgh, Suffolk; Old Stocks, Gorelands Lane, Chalfont St Giles, Bucks

ELFORD, Hon Mrs Rowena (Frances); da of (by 1 m) 2 Viscount St Davids; *b* 1940; *m* 1959, (m dis 1977), David Elford; 1 s, 3 da; *Style* - The Hon Mrs Rowena Elford; 4 Holland Court, Oakleigh, 3166 Victoria, Australia

ELGIN AND KINCARDINE, 11 & 15 Earl of (S 1633 & 1647); Andrew Douglas Alexander Thomas Bruce; JP (Fife 1951), DL (1955); also Lord Bruce of Kinloss (S 1604), Lord Bruce of Torry (S 1647), Baron Elgin (UK 1849); 37 Chief of the Name of Bruce; s of 10 Earl of Elgin KT CMG TD (ggs of the (7) Earl whose removing from Athens of the marbles that bear his name aroused an outcry even then, Byron and Hobhouse being the most articulate in condemning what he had done- 'Some retribution still might Pallas claim When Venus half avenged Minerva's shame' (Lord B, presumably referring to Elgin's divorce in 1808) 'Quod non fecerunt Goti Hoc fecerunt Scoti' (Hobhouse, ignorant of the damage - vastly greater than either Goth or Pict accomplished - that a Turkish shell was to do the Parthenon some dozen years later) and Hon Dame Katherine Elizabeth Cochrane, DBE, da of 1 Baron Cochrane of Cults; *b* 17 Feb 1924; *Educ* Eton, Balliol Oxford; *m* 1959, Victoria Mary, da of Dudley Usher, of Larach Bhan, Kilchrennan, Argyll; 3 s, 2 da; *Heir* s, Lord Bruce; *Career* pres Roy Scottish Automobile Club, Brig Roy Co of Archers (HM Body Guard for Scotland), chm Nat Savings Ctee Scotland, Grand Master Mason of Scotland 1961-65, Lord High Cmmr to Gen Assembly of Church of Scotland 1980-; dir Dominion Insurance Co, Gurr Johns & Co, Scottish Amicable Life Assurance Soc (and pres), Roy Highland and Ag Soc 1973-76; *Style* - The Rt Hon The Earl of Elgin and Kincardine, JP, DL; Broomhall, Dunfermline (☎ 0383 87 222)

ELGIN AND KINCARDINE, Dowager Countess of; Hon Dame Katherine Elizabeth; *née* Cochrane; DBE (1938, MBE 1919); da of 1 Baron Cochrane of Cults (Hon Thomas Cochrane, yr s of 11 Earl of Dundonald), sometime MP Ayrshire N & Under Sec Home Off, by his w Lady Gertrude Boyle, OBE (da of 6 Earl of Glasgow); *b* 1890; *m* 1921, 10 Earl of Elgin and Kincardine (d 1968); 3 s (including 11 Earl), 3 da (Lady Martha Bruce, Lady Jean Wemyss, Lady Alison Stewart-Patterson); *Style* - The Rt Hon Dowager Countess of Elgin and Kincardine DBE; Culross Abbey House, Culross, Dunfermline, Fife

ELIBANK, 14 Lord (S 1643); Sir Alan D'Ardis Erskine-Murray; 14 Bt (NS 1628); s of Maj Robert Alan Erskine-Murray, OBE, unc of 13 Lord, and who d 1939; suc cous 1973; *b* Wynberg S Africa 31 Dec 1923; *Educ* Bedford, Peterhouse Cambridge; *m* 1962, Valerie Sylvia, da of late Herbert William Dennis; 2 s; *Heir* s, Master of Elibank; *Career* barr 1949-55, personnel man Shell International Petroleum Co 1955-77, gen man and rep in Qatar 1977-; *Style* - The Rt Hon The Lord Elibank; The Coach House, Charters rd, Sunningdale, Ascot, Berks (☎ Ascot 22099)

ELIBANK, Master of; Hon Robert Francis Alan Erskine-Murray; s and h of 14 Lord Elibank; *b* 10 Oct 1964; *Style* - The Master of Elibank

ELIOT, Lady Alethea Constance Dorothy Sydney; da of late 1 Earl of Buxton; *b* 1910; *m* 1934, Ven Peter Charles Eliot, MBE, TD, late Lt-Col RA (TA); *Style* - Lady Alethea Eliot; The Old House, Kingsland, Leominster, Herefordshire

ELIOT, Hon Francis Michael; s of Lord Eliot; *b* 16 Nov 1971; *Style* - The Hon Francis Eliot

ELIOT, Lady; Hon Jacquetta Jean Frederica; *née* Lampson; da of late 1 Baron Killearn, GCMG, CB, MVO by 2 w, Jacqueline, da of late Marchese Senator Aldo Castellan, KCMG, FRCP, FACP; half-sis of 2 Baron; *b* 1943; *m* 1964, Lord Eliot, *qv*; *Style* - Lady Eliot; Port Eliot, St Germans, Cornwall

ELIOT, Hon Jago Nicholas Aldo; s of Lord Eliot; *b* 24 Mar 1966; *Style* - The Hon Jago Eliot

ELIOT, Hon Louis Robert Aldo; s of Lord Eliot; *b* 11 Apr 1968; *Style* - The Hon Louis Eliot

ELIOT, Peter Charles; MBE (1945), TD (1945); s of Hon Edward Granville Eliot, bro of 7 & 8 Earls of St Germans, by his w Clare (da of William Phelips, JP, DL, by his 2 w Constance, da of Hon Sir Spencer Ponsonby-Fane, GCB, PC, 6 s of 4 Earl of

Bessborough), sis of Edward & Gerald Phelips, the last of their family to possess Montacute, the exquisite Somersetshire mansion in Ham stone which was leased by Curzon and whither he retired for the fatal Saturday to Monday at Bonar Law's death, thinking, in his hubris, that, despite lack of telephonic communication with the outside world, he would still be sent for to kiss hands as PM; *b* 30 Oct 1910; *Educ* Wellington, Magdalene Cambridge; *m* 1934, Lady Alethea Sydney, da of 1 and last Earl Buxton, GCMG, PC, sometime Gov-Gen & CIC S Africa and gs of Sir Thomas Buxton, 1 Bt, by his (the Earl's) 2 w, Dame Mildred Smith, GBE, JP (of the Abel Smiths of Midhurst), sis of 1 Baron Bicester; *Career* Lt-Col Cmmdg Kent Yeo RA (TA), served WW II BEF, M East & Italy; slr 1934-53; ordained 1954, Rural Dean 1960-61, Archdeacon Worcester 1961-75, Resident Canon Worcester 1965-75; *Recreations* sightseeing, sketching, gardening; *Clubs* Travellers'; *Style* - The Rev Peter Eliot, MBE, TD; The Old House, Kingsland, Leominster, Herefordshire

ELIOT, Lord; Peregrine Nicholas Eliot; s (by 1 m) and h of 9 Earl of St Germans; *b* 2 Jan 1941; *Educ* Eton; *m* 1964, Hon Jacquetta (*see* Lady Eliot); 3 s; *Heir* s, Hon Jago Eliot; *Career* landowner; *Recreations* mucking about (owner of yacht 'Tender to Jacquetta'); *Clubs* Pratt's; *Style* - Lord Eliot; Port Enid, St Germans, Cornwall

ELIOT, Hon (Montagu) Robert (Vere); s of 8 Earl of St Germans, KCVO, OBE (d 1960); *b* 28 Oct 1923; *Educ* Eton and Ch Ch Oxford; *Career* Gren Gds 1943-52, Capt (ret), N W Europe (wounded) 1944, Palestine (medal) 1945-48; retired company dir, memb Westminster City Cncl 1952-61, Cornwall City Cncl 1977-, contested (C) Mansfield Notts 1959; a Page of Honour to HM 1937-40, a Train Bearer at Coronation of King George VI; has Coronation Medal (1937); *Recreations* bridge, reading; *Clubs* Carlton, Bath; *Style* - The Hon Robert Eliot; Lux Cross House, Pengover rd, Liskeard, Cornwall (☎ 0579 42755)

ELIOTT OF STOBS, Sir Arthur Francis Augustus Boswell; 11 Bt (NS 1666) of Stobs, Roxburghshire; s of Sir Gilbert Alexander Boswell Eliott, 10 Bt (d 1958); *b* 2 Jan 1915; *Educ* Harrow and King's Coll Cambridge; *m* 1947, Frances Aileen, da of Sir Francis Kennedy McClean, AFC, (d 1955); 1 da; *Heir* kinsman, Charles Joseph Alexander Eliott; *Career* Chief of the Clan Eliott or Elliot; Maj King's Own Scottish Borderers 1939-45, served in E Africa and Burma 1941-45 with King's African Rifles, memb of Roy Co of Archers (Queen's Bodyguard for Scotland); sr ptnr of Gilbert Eliott and Co Stockbrokers 1958-68; memb Stock Exchange Cncl 1965-68; *Clubs* New (Edinburgh) and Leander; *Style* - Sir Arthur Eliott of Stobs, Bt; Redheugh, Newcastleton, Roxburghshire (☎ Liddesdale 213)

ELIOTT, Charles Joseph Alexander; s of late Charles Rawdon Heathfield Eliott, s of half-bro of 9 Bt; kinsman and hp of Sir Arthur Eliott of Stobs, 11 Bt; *b* 9 Jan 1937; *m* 1959, Wendy, nee Bailey; 1 s, 3 da; *Style* - Charles Eliott Esq; Cohoe st, Toowoomba, Qld 4350, Australia

ELIOTT, Hon Mrs; Hon Rosemary Aletta de Villers; da of 3 Baron de Villiers; *b* 1946; *Educ* Rhodes U; *m* 1967, Robin Anderson Eliott TD; 2 s; *Style* - The Hon Mrs Eliott; 52 St John rd, Houghton, Johannesburg; Sangar Hill Farm, Magaliesburg, Transvaal

ELKINGTON, Robert John; s of John Elkington, OBE; *b* 7 Oct 1949; *Educ* Eton, Exeter U; *m* 1974, Penelope Josephine, da of Lt-Col Richard Taylor, DSO; 1 s; *Career* banker, md Gerrard and National Discount Co Ltd; *Recreations* tennis, shooting, golf; *Clubs* Boodle's, Pratt's, Hurlingham, Sunningdale G C; *Style* - Robert Elkington Esq; 4 Manresa rd, SW3 (☎ 01 352 7427)

ELLDRED, David William; s of late William Elldred; *b* 20 Feb 1920; *Educ* Dorchester G S; *m* 1944, Margaret, nee Russell; 1 s, 1 da; *Career* dir Glanfield Lawrence Ltd, md Glanfield Lawrence (Wakefield) Ltd, dir Glanfield Lawrence (Horbury) Ltd; *Style* - David Elldred Esq;

25 Park Lane, Bretton, Wakefield, W Yorks (☎ 0924 85592)

ELLENBOROUGH, 8 Baron (UK 1802); Richard Edward Cecil Law; s of 7 Baron (d 1945); *b* 14 Jan 1926; *Educ* Eton, Magdalene Cambridge; *m* 1953, Rachel Mary, da of late Maj Ivor Mathews Hedley, 17 Lancers; 3 s; *Heir* s, Hon Rupert Law; *Career* stockbroker; dir Towry Law & Co; *Style* - The Rt Hon The Lord Ellenborough; Springhill House, Groombridge, E Sussex (☎ 456)

ELLENBOROUGH, Dorothy, Baroness; (Helen) Dorothy; da of H W Lovatt, late of Co Down; *m* 1923, 7 Baron Ellenborough (d 1945); 2 s (8 Baron, Hon Cecil Law); *Style* - The Rt Hon Dorothy, Lady Ellenborough; 119 Ashley gdns, SW1 (☎ 01 828 8188)

ELLERTON, Geoffrey James; CMG (1963), MBE (1956); s of Sir (Frederick) Cecil Ellerton (d 1962); *b* 25 April 1920; *Educ* Highgate Sch and Hertford Coll Oxford; *m* 1946, Peggy Eleanor, da of Frederick George Watson (d 1954); 3 s; *Career* Colonial Administrative Serv Kenya 1945-63; sec to Cmmns on Management and Staffing in Local Govt 1964; chm Elder Dempster Lines 1972-74, exec dir Ocean Transport and Trading Ltd 1972-80, chm Electra Gp Serv 1980-; *Recreations* reading and music; *Clubs* MCC and Reform; *Style* - Geoffrey Ellerton Esq, CMG, MBE; Greygarth, Wood Lane, Parkgate, S Wirral (☎ 051 336 3692)

ELLES, Baroness (Life Peeress UK 1972); Diana Louie Elles; MEP (C) Thames Valley 1979-; da of late Col Stewart Francis Newcombe; *b* 19 July 1921; *Educ* London U; *m* 1945, Neil Patrick Moncrieff Elles; 1 s, 1 da; *Career* Fl Offr WAAF 1942-45; barr 1956, MEP 1973-75, Oppn Front Bench Spokesman on Foreign and European Affairs 1975-79, dep chm European Democratic Gp European Parlt 1979-, chm Cons Pty Int Office 1973-78, memb Women's Nat Advisory Ctee; *Style* - The Rt Hon The Lady Elles, MEP; 75 Ashley gdns, SW1 (☎ 01 828 0175); Villa Fontana, Lucca, Italy

ELLES, Hon James Edmund Moncrieff; s of Baroness Elles, MEP (Life Peeress); *b* 3 Sept 1949; *Educ* Eton, Edinburgh U; *m* 1977, Françoise, da of François Le Bail; 1 da; *Career* Admin External Rels EEC 1977-80; Assist to Dep Dir-Gen Ag EEC 1980-; *Recreations* skiing, golf, tennis; *Clubs* Roy & Ancient Golf; *Style* - The Hon James Elles

ELLETSON, Roger Chandos; s of Harry Chandos Elletson of Parrox Hall, Preesall, Lancs; *b* 4 June 1911; *Educ* Harrow; *m* 1958, Pamela Mary, nee Brown; 3 s, 2 da; *Career* md Smith & Philips Witney 1937-39, founder R C Elletson & Co Ltd 1947, dir Humphrey Lloyd & Sons Ltd, Parrox Investments Ltd and others, Lloyds underwriter, part-time journalist; *Recreations* bridge, golf, ski-ing; *Clubs* Brooks's, Royal Lytham Golf; *Style* - Roger Elletson Esq; Grey House, Forton, Preston, Lancs (☎ 0524 791225)

ELLIOT OF HARWOOD, Baroness (Life Peeress UK 1958); Katharine; DBE (1958, CBE 1946), JP (Roxburghshire 1967); da of late Sir Charles Tennant, 1 Bt; *b* 15 Jan 1903; *Educ* Abbot's Hill; *m* 1934, Rt Hon Walter Elliot, CH, MC, PC, FRS, MP (d 1958); *Career* contested (C) Kelvingrove Glasgow 1958, CC 1946-75, chm Consumer Cncl 1963-68, chm Carnegie UK Trust 1965-69, UK delegate to UN Gen Assembly New York 1954-56 and 1957, chm Nat Union of Cons and Unionist Assocs 1957-58; *Style* - The Rt Hon The Lady Elliot of Harwood DBE JP; 17 Lord North st, SW1 (☎ 01 222 3230); Harwood, Bonchester Bridge, Hawick, Roxburghshire

ELLIOT, Lady Anne; *née* Child-Villiers; da of late 9 Earl of Jersey; *b* 1916; *m* 1937, Maj Alexander Henry Elliot, late RA; *Style* - Lady Anne Elliot; Broadford, Chobham, Surrey

ELLIOT, Gerald Henry; MA; *Career* chm Salvesen Offshore Holdings Ltd; dir Scottish Provident Instn, Christian Salvesen Ltd; *Style* - Gerald Elliot Esq; 50 East Fetters ave, Edinburgh 4

ELLIOT-MURRAY-KYNYNMOUND,

Hon (George Esmond) Dominic; s of 5 Earl of Minto (d 1975), and hp of bro, 6 Earl of Minto, MBE; *b* 13 Jan 1931; *Educ* Eton and Madrid U; *m* 1962, Countess Bunny Esterhazy, da of Count Thomas Esterhazy, of Geneva, Switzerland; 2 s (Alexander b 1963, Esmond b 1965); *Career* formerly Lt, Scots Gds, served Malaya, London; co dir; *Clubs* White's, New (Edinburgh); *Style* - The Hon Dominic Elliot-Murray-Kynynmound; 37 Lowndes sq, SW1 (☎ 01 235 9926/9979); **Butterha', Minto, Hawick, Scotland**

ELLIOT-MURRAY-KYNYNMOUND, Lady Laura; da of 6 Earl of Minto, MBE; *b* 1956; *Style* - Lady Laura Elliot-Murray-Kynynmound

ELLIOTT, Clive Christopher Hugh; s and h of Sir Hugh Elliott, 3 Bt; *b* 12 Aug 1945; *Educ* Bryanston and Univ Coll Oxford; *m* 1975, Marie Thérèse, da of Moritz Ruttimann, of Switzerland; 2 s (Ivo Antony Moritz, Nicolas Clive Johan); *Career* research offr Cape Town U 1968-75; FAO Project Supervisor Tchad 1975-78; Offr in charge FAO Regnl Quelea Project, Arusha, Tanzania 1978-; *Recreations* tennis, skiing; *Style* - Clive Elliott Esq; PO Box 364, Arusha, Tanzania

ELLIOTT, Hon Mrs - Hon Elinor; *née* Spring Rice; da of 6 Baron Monteagle of Brandon; *b* 1950; *m* 1974, Myles Clare Elliott; 1 s, 1 da; *Style* - The Hon Mrs Elliott

ELLIOTT, Grahame Nicholas; s of Charles Morris William Elliott (d 1966); *b* 23 Dec 1938; *Educ* Mill Hill Sch; *m* 1968, Zita Catherine, nee Jones; 3 c; *Career* CA, sen ptnr Elliott Templeton Sankey & Co; *Clubs* Turf, St James's (Manchester), Raquets (Manchester), Manchester; *Style* Grahame Elliott Esq; Highbury, Harrop rd, Hale, Ches (☎ 061 980 4857)

ELLIOTT, Sir Hugh Francis Ivo; 3 Bt (UK 1905) of Limpsfield, Surrey, OBE (1953); s of Sir Ivo D'Oyly Elliott, 2 Bt (d 1961); *b* 10 March 1913; *Educ* Dragon Sch Oxford, Eastbourne Coll and Univ Coll Oxford; *m* 1939, Elizabeth Margaret, da of Adolphus G Phillipson (d 1948); 1 s, 2 da; *Heir* s, Clive Christopher Hugh Elliott; *Career* HM Overseas Civil Serv (Tanganyika Administration 1937-61, seconded as Administrator Tristan da Cunha 1950-52, perm sec Min of Natural Resources 1958-61); Int Union for Conservation of Nature and Natural Resources 1961-80 (Sec-Gen 1964-66); *Recreations* travel and natural history; *Style* - Sir Hugh Elliott, Bt, OBE; 173 Woodstock rd, Oxford

ELLIOTT, Sir Randal Forbes; KBE (1977, OBE 1975); s of late Sir James Sands Elliott; *b* 12 Oct 1922; *Educ* Wanganui Coll Sch, Otago U New Zealand; *m* 1949, Pauline June nee Young; 1 s, 6 da; *Career* KStJ 1978, Gp Capt RNZAF, Ophthalmic Surgeon Wellington Hosp 1953-, Ophthalmic Consultant N Z Armed Forces 1960-, chancellor of St John (NZ); *Recreations* skiing, mountaineering, sailing; *Clubs* Wellington; *Style* - Sir Randal Elliott KBE; 22 Marine dve, Lowry Bay, Wellington, New Zealand (☎ Wellington 684 823)

ELLIOTT, Hon Lord; Walter Archibald; MC (1943), QC (1960); s of late Prof T R Elliott, CBE, DSO, FRS; *b* 6 Sept 1922; *Educ* Eton, Edinburgh U; *m* 1954, Susan Isobel, da of late Phillip Mackenzie Ross; 2 s; *Career* Capt Scots Gds Italy, N W Europe WW II, barr and advocate 1950, pres Land's Tribunal for Scotland 1971-, chm of Scottish Land Court with title Lord Elliott 1978-, memb Queen's Body Guard for Scotland (Roy Co of Archers); *Recreations* gardening, travel, shooting; *Clubs* New, Scottish Arts (both Edinburgh); *Style* - The Hon Lord Elliott, MC, QC; Morton House, Fairmilehead, Edinburgh 10 (☎ 031 445 2548)

ELLIOTT, Maj William Richmond Cameron; MC (1944) and Bar (1945), DL (1963); s of William Elliott, MC (d 1971); *b* 31 July 1921; *Educ* Edinburgh Acad; *m* 1947, Shelagh Waugh, da of Robert Simmons, CMG, CBE; 1 s; *Career* memb Roy Co of Archers (Queen's Bodyguard Scotland); farmer; chm Tennent Caledonian Breweries Ltd, dir Bass Ltd 1977-; *Recreations* shooting; *Clubs* New (Edinburgh); *Style* - Maj William Elliott,

MC*, DL; Newbyth, E Linton, E Lothian (☎ 062 087 241)

ELLIS, Arthur John; *Career* FCCA, FCMA, FCIS, MBCS; dir Lincoln Investments Ltd, Kent Storage and Distribution Servs Ltd; md and ch exec Fyffes Gp Ltd; *Style* - Arthur Ellis Esq; 15 Stratton st, W1

ELLIS, Lady Angela Mary; *née* Shirley; er da of 13 Earl Ferrers; *b* 16 June 1954; *m* 1975, Jonathan Ellis, ACA; 2 da (Louise Mary b 1977, Georgina b 17 June 1981); *Style* - Lady Angela Ellis; 9 Culmstock rd, SW11 (☎ 01 228 0736)

ELLIS, B J; *Career* sec Abbey National Building Society; *Style* - B J Ellis Esq; Abbey National Building Society, Abbey House, Baker st, London NWI

ELLIS, Humphry Francis; MBE (1945); s of Dr John Constable Ellis (d 1928); *b* 17 July 1907; *Educ* Tonbridge Sch and Magdalen Coll Oxford; *m* 1933, Barbara Pauline, da of late Wilfrid Hasseldine; 1 s, 1 da; *Career* writer and editor; former ed Punch; contributor New Yorker 1954-; *Recreations* fishing, gardening, birds and watching rugby and cricket; *Clubs* Garrick and MCC; *Style* - Humphry Ellis Esq, MBE; Hill Croft, Kingston St Mary, Taunton, Somerset (☎ Kingston St Mary 264)

ELLIS, Roger Henry; s of Francis Henry Ellis (d 1953); *b* 9 June 1910; *Educ* Sedbergh Sch and King's Coll Cambridge; *m* 1939, (Audrey) Honor, da of (Herbert) Arthur Baker, DL; 2 da; *Career* Maj 5 Fus (Africa, Italy and Germany); assist keeper Public Record Office 1934, princ assist keeper 1954, consultant ed 1972-; sec Roy Cmmn on Historical Manuscripts 1957-72; *Clubs* Athenaeum; *Style* - Roger Ellis Esq; Cloth Hill, 6 The Mount, Hampstead (☎ 01 435 4254)

ELLIS, Col Wilfred Desmond; OBE (1952), TD (1944) and 3 Bars, DL (1962); s of Bertram Wyburne Ellis (d 1944); *b* 7 Nov 1914; *Educ* Temple Grove and Canford Sch; *m* 1947, Effie Douglas, JP, da of Dr Alex Barr (d 1976); 1 s, 2 da; *Career* cmmd Middx regt (TA) 1937, Dep Cdr 47 (London) Inf Bde 1957-62, Col Middx Army Cadet Force 1958-62; ADC to HM The Queen 1966-69; man Conversion Exec and Customer Serv, The Gas Cncl 1966; ret 1972; lay memb Press Cncl 1969-75; *Recreations* shooting and local affairs; *Style* - Col Wilfred Ellis, OBE, TD***, DL; Lea Barn, Winter Hill, Cookham Dean, Berks (☎ Marlow 4230)

ELLIS, Dr William Herbert Baxter; AFC (1954); s of William Baxter Ellis; *b* 2 July 1921; *Educ* Oundle Sch, Durham U; *m* 1 1947, Margaret Mary (m dis); 1 s, 1 da; m 2, 1977, Mollie Marguerite Clarke, nee Weller; 1 da (step); *Career* Royal Navy 1945-59, Surgeon Cmdr Fleet Air Arm Pilot, motor industry 1960-71, dir gen Dr Barnardo's 1971-73, Employment Med Advisory Service 1973-81, consultant Dept of Health and Social Security 1973-; *Recreations* study of humanity; *Clubs* Army & Navy, Naval & Military; *Style* - Dr Herbert Ellis, AFC; The Manor House, Compton Abdale, Nr Cheltenham, Glos

ELLISON, Prof Arthur James; s of Lawrence Joseph Ellison (d 1978); *b* 10 Jan 1920; *Educ* Solihull Sch and London U; *m* 1963, Marian Elizabeth, da of John Gordon Gumbrell (d 1976); 1 s, 1 da; *Career* Prof of Electrical and Electronic Engrg and head of dept City U London 1972-; lecturer and sr lecturer Queen Mary Coll London 1958-72; design engr British Thomson-Houston Co Ltd 1947-58; *Recreations* reading, meditation, psychical research and travel; *Style* - Prof Arthur Ellison; 10 Foxgrove ave, Beckenham, Kent (☎ 01 650 3801)

ELLS, Eric John; s of Eric Edwin (d 1975); *b* 6 April 1929; *Educ* Blackfen Centl Sch; *m* 1952, Amelia Florence Baulch; 1 s, 2 da; *Career* dir Jitra Rubber Plantations Ltd, Rubber Estates of Ceylon Ltd and others; assist md M P Evans & Co Ltd; *Recreations* ballroom dancing, swimming; *Style* - Eric Ells Esq; 10 Hurstwood dve, Bickley, Bromley, Kent (☎ 01 467 6456)

ELMHIRST, Robert; MC (1943); s of the late William Elmhirst; *b* 21 July 1909; *Educ* Wantage Sch Berks; *m* 1938, Kirsteen Simpson, nee Beveridge; 1 s, 1 da;

Career Lt Col France, Africa, Greece, Italy, now solicitor; *Recreations* formerly boxing, golf; *Style* - Robert Elmhirst, Esq; 5 Castle Green, Laughton-en-le-Morthen, Nr Sheffield (☎ Dinnington 2364)

ELMI, His Excellency Mr Mohamed Jama; *Career* Somali Ambass to UK; *Style* - HE Mr Mohamed Jama Elmi; Somali Embassy, 60 Portland Place, W1 (☎ 01 580 7148)

ELPHINSTON, Alexander; s and h of Sir John Elphinston, 11 Bt; *b* 6 June 1955; *Educ* Repton and St John's Coll Durham; *Style* - Alexander Elphinston Esq

ELPHINSTON OF GLACK, Sir John; 11 Bt (NS 1701) of Logie, Co Aberdeen; s of Thomas George Elphinston (d 1967), s of de jure 9 Bt; suc unc, Sir Alexander Logie Elphinstone of Glack, 10 Bt (d 1970); *b* 12 Aug 1924; *Educ* Repton Sch and Cambridge U; *m* 1953, Margaret Doreen, da of Edric Tasker (d 1970); 4 s; *Heir* s Alexander Elphinston; *Career* chm Lancs, Cheshire, IOM branch of Roy Instn of Chartered Surveyors, Agric Div 1975; sch govr; estates man ICI, Mond Div; *Recreations* shooting and ornithology; *Style* - Sir John Elphinston of Glack, Bt; Pilgrims, Churchfields, Northwich, Cheshire (☎ Sandiway 883327)

ELPHINSTONE, 18 Lord (S 1509); James Alexander Elphinstone; also Baron Elphinstone (UK 1859); s of Rev Hon Andrew Elphinstone (2 s of 16 Lord by Lady Mary Bowes-Lyon, da of 14 Earl of Strathmore and sis of HM Queen Elizabeth the Queen Mother); 2 cous of HRH The Prince of Wales; *b* 22 April 1953; *Educ* Eton, RAC Cirencester; *m* 1978, Willa, yr da of Maj David Chetwode, MBE, Coldstream Gds, nephew of 1 Baron Chetwode and 1 cous of Lady Betjeman; 1 s; *Heir* s, Master of Elphinstone (b 15 April 1980); *Career* farmer; ARICS; *Clubs* Turf; *Style* - The Rt Hon Lord Elphinstone; Drumkilbo, Meigle, Blairgowrie, Perths (☎ Meigle 216)

ELPHINSTONE, Master of; Hon Alexander Mountstuart Elphinstone; s and h of 18 Lord Elphinstone; 3 cous of Master Peter Phillips; *b* 15 April 1980; *Style* - The Master of Elphinstone

ELPHINSTONE, Sir (Maurice) Douglas Warburton; 5 Bt (UK 1816) of Sowerby, Cumberland, TD; s of Rev Canon Maurice Curteis Elphinstone (d 1969), 4 s of 3 Bt; suc cous, Sir Howard Graham Elphinstone, 4 Bt, 1975; *b* 13 April 1909; *Educ* Loretto and Jesus Coll Cambridge; *m* 1943, Barbara, da of late George Ramsay Main; 1 s, 1 da; *Heir* s John Howard Main Elphinstone; *Career* served 1939-45 War as Maj London Scottish; FFA, FRSE; *Style* - Sir Douglas Elphinstone, Bt, TD; Wetheral Crook, Scotby, Carlisle, Cumbria

ELPHINSTONE, John Howard Main; s and h of Sir Douglas Elphinstone, 5 Bt, TD; *b* 25 Feb 1949; *Educ* Loretto; *Style* - John Elphinstone Esq

ELPHINSTONE, Keith; MBE (1945); s of late Sydney Elphinstone; *b* 6 April 1919; *Educ* Surbiton Co Sch, London Poly; *m* 1948, Frances Naomi, nee Mills; 3 da; *Career* dep chm Sale Tilney & Co, chm Badalex Ltd, chm Peabody Industrial Ltd, chm Sintered Glass Products Ltd, chm Sale Tilney Int Ltd, chm Peabody Woma Ltd; *Recreations* gardening; *Style* - Keith Elphinstone Esq; Killaspy, North rd, Chesham Bois, Amersham, Bucks (☎ Amersham 3780)

ELSTOB, Peter Frederick Egerton; s of Frederick Charles Elstob (d 1974); *b* 22 Dec 1915; *Educ* Michigan U; *m* 1, 1937 (m dis 1953), Medora Leigh-Smith; 3 s, 2 da; m 2, 1953, Barbara Zacheisz; 1 s, 1 da; *Career* author, novelist, mil historian; Sec-Gen Int PEN 1974-; md of cosmetic manufacturing business, Archie Press Ltd and other cos; *Recreations* travel and playing the stock exchange; *Clubs* Garrick and Savage; *Style* - Peter Elstob Esq; Coolderry, Massey's Lane, E Boldre, Hants; 22 Belsize Park gdns, NW3 4LH

ELTON, 2 Baron (UK 1934); Rodney Elton; TD (1970); s of 1 Baron Elton (d 1973); *b* 2 March 1930; *Educ* Eton, New Coll Oxford; *m* 1, 1958 (m dis 1979), Anne Frances, da of Brig R A G Tilney; 1 s, 3 da; m 2, 1979, (Susan) Richenda, da of late Sir

Hugh Gurney, KCMG, MVO; *Heir* s, Hon Edward Paget Elton; *Career* former teacher and lectr; Oppn Spokesman on Education and Welsh Affairs 1974-79, Dep Sec Int Affairs Ctee of Gen Synod of C of E 1976-78, v-chm Andry Montgomery Ltd 1977-79, Parly Under-Sec of State N Ireland Office 1979- (Education 1980-, Agriculture 1981-), contested (C) Loughborough Leics 1966 and 1970; *Clubs* Athenaeum, Cavalry and Guards, Beefsteak; *Style* - The Rt Hon The Lord Elton, TD; House of Lords, SW1

ELTON, Hon Annabel; da of 2 Baron Elton; *b* 1960; *Style* - The Hon Annabel Elton

ELTON, Sir Charles Abraham Grierson; 11 Bt (GB 1717) of Bristol; s of Sir Arthur Hallam Rice Elton, 10 Bt (d 1973); *b* 23 May 1953; *Educ* Eton; *Heir* kinsman, Charles Tierney Hallam Elton; *Career* dir S Avon Mercury; *Style* - Sir Charles Elton, Bt; Clevedon Court, Clevedon, Somerset

ELTON, Charles Tierney Hallam; s of late Charles Henry Elton (gs of 6 Bt), by 1 w, Edith, da of J F Ward; hp of kinsman, Sir Charles Elton, 11 Bt; *b* 1898; *m* 1924, Helen (d 1963), da of late Capt Frederick Waud; 1 da; *Style* - Charles Elton Esq

ELTON, Hon Edward Paget; s and h of 2 Baron Elton; *b* 28 May 1966

ELTON, George Alfred Hugh; s of Horace William Elton (d 1980); *b* 27 Feb 1925; *Educ* Sutton County Sch and London U; *m* 1951, Theodora Rose Edith, da of George Henry Theodore Kingham (d 1965); 2 da; *Career* ch scientist (Fisheries and Food) Min of Ag, Fish and Food (formerly chf scientific adviser Food); und-sec MAFF 1974-; *Recreations* golf; *Clubs* Athenaeum, Savage and MCC; *Style* - George Elton Esq; Green Nook, Bridle Lane, Loudwater, Rickmansworth, Herts

ELTON, Hon Jane; da of 2 Baron Elton; *b* 1962; *Style* - The Hon Jane Elton

ELTON, Hon Lucy; da of 2 Baron Elton; *b* 1963; *Style* - The Hon Lucy Elton

ELTON, Lady; Margaret Ann; *née* Bjornson; *m* 1948, Sir Arthur Hallam Rice Elton, 10 Bt (d 1973); *Style* - Lady Elton; Clevedon Court, Clevedon, Somerset

ELVEDEN, Viscount; Arthur Edward Rory Guinness; s and h of 3 Earl of Iveagh; *b* 10 Aug 1969; *Style* - Viscount Elveden

ELWES, Henry William George; s of Maj John Elwes, Scots Gds (ka N Africa 1943); a distant cous of Capt Jeremy Elwes, *qv*; *b* 24 Oct 1935; *Educ* Eton, RAC Cirencester; *m* 1962, Carolyn, da of Joseph Cripps (3 cous of the draconian post war Chllr Sir Stafford Cripps) and 1 cous of 6 Baron Cromwell, also 4 cous of 4 Baron Parmoor; 3 s; *Career* late Lt Scots Gds; farmer & forestry; High Sheriff Glos 1979-80; V-Chm Glos CC 1975-; chm Western Woodland Owners Ltd 1971-; *Clubs* Gloucester; *Style* - Henry Elwes Esq; Colesbourne Park, Cheltenham, Glos (☎ Coberley 262)

ELWES, Jeremy Gervase Geoffrey Philip; DL (Lincs 1969, Humberside 1974); s of Lt-Col Rudolph Elwes, OBE, MC (whose mother was Lady Winefride Feilding, da of 8 Earl of Denbigh, while his f, Gervase, was Privy Chamberlain to the Pope); *b* 1 Sept 1921; *Educ* Ampleforth; *m* 1955, Clare, da of Maj Gen Arthur Beveridge, CB, OBE, MC; 4 s; *Career* served WW II Capt M East; farms 6,000 acres in Lincs from 1949; chm Cncl Preservation Rural England (Lincs) 1957-; High Sheriff Lincs 1969; V-Chm Radio Humberside 1970-73, fndr Shrievalty Assoc 1971, fndr chm Euro-Latin Commercial Co, Linvend, Elwes Enterprises; *Recreations* Natural History; *Clubs* Green Jackets; *Style* - Capt Jeremy Elwes, DL; 29 Halsey st, SW3 (☎ 01 581 3683); Elsham Hall, Brigg, S Humberside (☎ Barnetby 738)

ELWES, Hon Mrs (Rosalie Ann); *née* Hennessy; da of 2 Baron Windlesham; *b* 1934; *m* 1960, Peter John Gervase Elwes; 3 s, 1 da; *Style* - The Hon Mrs Elwes; 75 Murray rd, Wimbledon, SW19

ELWORTHY, Baron (Life Peer UK 1972); Marshal of the RAF (Samuel)

Charles Elworthy; KG (1977), GCB (1962), CBE (1946), DSO, MVO (4 Class 1953), DFC, AFC; s of late Capt Percy Ashton Elworthy, late 1 Life Gds, of Gordon's Valley, Timaru, New Zealand; *b* 23 March 1911; *Educ* Marlborough, Trin Cambridge; *m* 1936, Audrey, da of late Arthur Joseph Hutchinson, OBE, of Auckland, New Zealand; 3 s, 1 da; *Career* RAF 1935, barr 1935, Ch of Air Staff 1963-67, Ch of Defence Staff 1967-71, Marshal of RAF 1967, Constable and Gov of Windsor Castle 1971-78, Lord Lt Gtr London 1973-78, KStJ; dir Nat Bank of NZ, BP (NZ) and others; *Style* - Marshal of The RAF The Rt Hon The Lord Elworthy KG GCB CBE DSO MVO; Gordon's Valley, RD2, Timaru, New Zealand

ELWORTHY, Hon Anthony Arthur; s of Baron Elworthy, GCB, CBE, DSO, MVO, DFC, AFC (Life Peer); *b* 1940; *m* 1967, Penelope Hendry; *Style* - The Hon Anthony Elworthy; c/o Lipton Ltd, Box 2080, Johannesburg 2000, S Africa

ELWORTHY, Hon Christopher Ashton; s of Baron Elworthy, GCB, CBE, DSO, MVO, DFC, AFC (Life Peer); *b* 1946; *m* 1968, Anne, da of late Harry Bell Lewis Johnstone; *Style* - The Hon Christopher Elworthy; Gordon's Valley, Station, RD2, Timaru, New Zealand

ELWORTHY, Hon Timothy Charles; s of Baron Elworthy, GCB, CBE, DSO, MVO, DFC, AFC (Life Peer); *b* 27 Jan 1938; *Educ* Radley and RAF Coll Cranwell; *m* 1, 1961 (m dis), Victoria Ann, da of Lt-Col H C W Bowring; m 2, 1971, Anabel, da of late Reginald Ernest Harding, OBE; children; *Career* RAF, Wing Cdr; *Style* - The Hon Timothy Elworthy; c/o Australia & New Zealand Banking Gp Ltd, 18/24 Maltravers st, WC2

ELWYN-JONES, Baron (Life Peer UK 1974); (Frederick) Elwyn-Jones; CH (1976), PC (1964); s of Frederick Jones, of Llanelli, Carmarthenshire; *b* 24 Oct 1909; *Educ* Llanelli G S, Univ Coll of Wales Aberystwyth, Caius Cambridge (pres Union 1931); *m* 1937, Pearl Binder; 1 s, 2 da; *Career* barr Gray's Inn 1935, QC 1953, QC N Ireland 1958, bencher 1960, tres 1980, recorder 1949-74, MP (L) Plaistow W Ham 1945-50, W Ham South 1950-74, Newham S 1974, PPS to Attorney-Gen 1946-51, Attorney-Gen 1964-70, Lord Chllr 1974-79, a Lord of Appeal 1979-, Pres Univ Coll Cardiff 1971-, kt 1964; *Style* - The Rt Hon The Lord Elwyn-Jones CH PC; House of Lords, SW1

ELY, 8 Marquess of (I 1801); Sir Charles John Tottenham; 9 Bt (I 1780); sits as Baron Loftus (UK 1801); also Baron Loftus (I 1785), Viscount Loftus (I 1789); s of George Leonard Tottenham (d 1928) and gggs of Rt Rev Lord Robert Ponsonby Tottenham, Bp of Clogher, 2 s of 1 Marquess; suc kinsman 1969; *b* 30 May 1913; *Educ* Queen's U Kingston Ontario; *m* 1, 1938, Katherine Elizabeth (d 1975), da of Lt-Col W H Craig, of Kingston, Ontario; 3 s, 1 da; m 2, 1978, Elspeth Ann, da of late P T Hay, of Highgate; *Heir* s, Viscount Loftus; *Career* headmaster Boulden House, Trin Coll Sch, Port Hope, Ontario; *Style* - The Most Hon The Marquess of Ely; 20 Arundel Court, Jubilee Place, SW3 (☎ 01 352 9172); Trinity Coll Sch, Port Hope, Ontario, Canada

ELY, 66 Bishop of (cr 1109) 1977-; Rt Rev Peter Knight Walker; s of late George Walker; *b* 6 Dec 1919; *Educ* Leeds G S, Queen's Oxford; *m* 1973, Mary Jean, JP, da of Lt-Col J A Ferguson, OBE; *Career* former dean and lectr CCC Cambridge, Princ Westcott House Cambridge 1962-72, Hon Canon of Ely Cathedral 1966-72, Bp of Dorchester (Suffragan for Diocese of Oxford) 1972, Canon of Christ Church Oxford 1972-77; patron of 92 livings (11 alternately), 3 Canonries, 20 Hon Canonries, and the Archdeaconries of Ely, Huntingdon, and Wisbech; *Clubs* Cambridge County, Naval; *Style* - The Rt Rev the Lord Bishop of Ely; The Bishop's House, Ely, Cambs (2749)

ELY, Thea, Marchioness of; Thea Margaret Gordon; da of late Lars G Gronvold; *m* 1928, 7 Marquess of Ely (d 1969); *Style* - The Most Hon Thea, Marchioness of Ely; 23 The Avenue, Chichester, W Sussex

ELY, Vernon Newbury; CBE (1972); s of Bernard Ely (d 1947); *b* 14 Jan 1907; *Educ* King's Coll Sch Wimbledon and Berkhamsted Sch; *m* 1947, late Florence Maud, da of Walter Armstrong Higgins (d 1917); 1 s; *Career* Wing Cdr RAF 1941-45; pres S London Amateur Athletic Assoc 1947-55; chm Elys Ltd 1947-; cncl memb Wimbledon Chamber of Commerce 1947-65 (v-pres 1954-); pres Exec Ctee Drapers Chamber of Trade 1976-; pres Surbiton Lawn Tennis and Squash Club 1968-; memb Home Office Ctee on Crime Prevention 1971-72; memb of Unit Retail Planning Information Working Party and Cncl 1973-75; pres Assoc of Retail Distributors 1978; *Recreations* real tennis; *Clubs* Surrey CCC, MCC and Roy Tennis Court; *Also* yacht, Fleur Elyse; *Style* - Vernon Ely Esq, CBE; Elys, Wimbledon, SW19 (☎ 01 946 9191); 42 West Farm ave, Ashtead, Surrey

ELYSTAN-MORGAN, Baron (Life Peer UK 1981); (Dafydd) Elystan; s of Dewi Morgan (d 1971), of Llandre, Aberystwyth, Cardiganshire; *b* 7 Dec 1932; *Educ* Ardwyn G S Aberystwyth, Univ Coll of Wales Aberystwyth; *m* 1959, Alwen, da of William E Roberts, of Carrog, Merioneth; 1 s, 1 da; *Career* MP (L) Cardiganshire 1966-74; parly under-sec of State Home Office 1968-70; pres Welsh Local Authorities Assoc 1967-73; chm Welsh Parly Party 1967-68; barr Gray's Inn 1971 (formerly a slr); *Style* - The Rt Hon the Lord Elystan-Morgan; Carreg-Afon, Dolau, Bow Street, Dyfed (☎ Bow Street 408)

EMERSON, Michael Ronald; s of James Emerson, of Wilmslow, Cheshire; *b* 12 May 1940; *Educ* Hurstpierpoint Coll and Balliol Coll Oxford; *m* 1966, Barbara Christine, da of late Harold Brierley; 1 s, 3 da; *Career* dir Macroeconomic Analyses and Policy, Directorate-Gen for Economic and Financial Affairs EEC, Brussels, 1980- (late Nat Ec Advsr to Pres Commission) *Style* - Michael Emerson Esq; 50 Rue Clement Delpierre, 1310 La Hulpe, Belgium (☎ 02 354 3730)

EMERY, Anthony Hayward; s of Thomas Frederick Emery; *b* 10 July 1930; *Educ* Bablake Sch Coventry, Bristol U (BA), U Coll London; *Career* dir IPC Business Press Ltd (London), chm Industry Services International (Nuneaton), IPC Video (London); *Recreations* architectural historian (author of *Dartington Hall*); *Style* - Anthony Emery Esq; 105 Clapham Common Northside, SW4; Willow House, Biddestone, Wilts

EMERY, George Edward; CB (1980); s of Frederick Arthur Emery (d 1930); *b* 2 March 1920; *Educ* Bemrose Sch Derby; *m* 1946, Margaret; 2 da *Career* Under-Sec MOD 1973; dir-gen Defence Accounts MOD 1973-80; ret; *Recreations* gardening and amateur dramatics; *Style* - George Emery Esq, CB; 3 The Orchard, Freshford, Bath (☎ Limpley Stoke 3561)

EMLYN, Viscount; Colin Robert Vaughan Campbell; s (by 1 m) and h of 6 Earl Cawdor; *b* 30 June 1962; *Style* - Viscount Emlyn

EMMANUEL, Ronald Mark; *aet* 42 as of June 1981; *m* 1965, Carole, da of late Bernard Walsh, chm Wheeler's Restaurants; *Career* served in Boy Scouts; street trader to 1964; joined Wheeler's 1964, subsequently jt md then dep chm, chm 1981- (annual turnover as of mid summer 1981 £6,000,000; staff turnover 5 per cent pa); dir Wheeler's (Fishmongers) Ltd; *Style* - Ronald Emmanuel Esq; c/o Wheeler's Restaurants Ltd, Wheeler House, 25a Lisle st, WC2 (☎ 01 437 8968)

EMMET, Hon Christopher Anthony Robert; JP (W Sussex); s of Baroness Emmet of Amberley (Life Peeress, d 1980) and late Thomas Addis Emmet; *b* 21 Nov 1925; *Educ* Ampleforth, Balliol Oxford; *m* 1947, Lady Miranda, *qv*; 1 s, 3 da; *Career* W Sussex Co Cllr (Pulborough) 1952-62; Cdre Arun Yacht Club Littlehampton 1972-73, pres Pulborough and Dist Photographic Soc 1964, pres Houghton Bridge and Dist Angling Soc 1960; *Recreations* owner of 36 ft Halberdier Ketch 'Sarua of Beaulieu'; *Style* - The Hon Christopher Emmet, JP; Sorrels House, Fittleworth, Petworth, Sussex

EMMET, Hon David Alastair Rennell; s of Baroness Emmet of Amberley (Life

Peeress, d 1980) and late Thomas Addis Emmet; *b* 1928; *Educ* Ampleforth, Worcester Coll Oxford; *m* 1967, Sylvia Delia, da of late Willis Knowles, of Buenos Aires; 1 s, 1 da; *Career* memb British Community Cncl Argentina 1964-68; *Style* - The Hon David Emmet; 2 Edificio Las Docas, Calle 12, Purta del Este, Maldonado, Uruguay

EMMET, Hon Mrs; (Jocelyn); *née* Portman; da of late 4 Viscount Portman; *b* 1903; *m* 1923, Capt James Albert Garland Emmet, LG (ret); 2 s, 1 da *Style* - The Hon Mrs Emmet; Allée des Amazones, Le Touquet, France; Le Sommet, Route de Valtonne, 06, Le Cannet, France, AM

EMMET, Lady Miranda Mary; *née* Fitzalan Howard; da of 3 Baron Howard of Glossop and sis of 17 Duke of Norfolk (raised to the rank of a Duke's da, 1975); *m* 1947, Hon Christopher Anthony Robert Emmet, JP, *qv*; *Style* - Lady Miranda Emmet; Field House, Newland, Selby, N Yorks

EMMS, David Acfield; s of the late Archibald George Emms; *b* 16 Feb 1925; *Educ* Tonbridge Sch, Brasenose Oxford; *m* 1950, Pamela Baker, nee Speed; 3 s, 1 da; *Career* Captain Royal Indian Airborne Artillery, assistant master Uppingham Sch 1951-60, headmaster Cranleigh Sch 1960-70, headmaster Sherborne Sch 1970-74, master Dulwich Coll 1975-; *Recreations* sailing, gardening, watching rugger; *Clubs* East India, Devonshire, Sports & Public Schools; *Style* - David Emms Esq; Elm Lawn, Dulwich Common, SE21; Seaforth, Spinney Lane, Itchenor, Nr Chichester, West Sussex (☎ Birdham 512585)

EMPSON, Sir Charles; KCMG (1956); s of late Arthur Reginald Empson; *b* 24 April 1898; *Educ* Harrow and Magdalene Coll Cambridge; *m* 1931, Monica Rosemary, da of late Rev Canon J W S Tomlin; 1 s 1 da; *Career* served 1917-19 with RFA in Mesopotamia; HM Foreign Serv (Baghdad, Palestine, Rome, Cairo and S E Asia); Min (Commercial) HM Embassy Washington 1950-55, Chile 1955-58; Rural District Cllr Bridge-Blean 1960-74; *Clubs* English Speaking Union; *Style* - Sir Charles Empson, KCMG; Seatonden, Ickham, Canterbury, Kent

EMSLIE, Baron (Life Peer UK 1979); George Carlyle Emslie; MBE (1946), PC (1972), QC (S 1957); s of Alexander Emslie; *b* 6 Dec 1919; *Educ* The High Sch of Glasgow, Glasgow U (MA, LLB, Hon LLD); *m* 1942, Lilias Ann Mailer, nee Hannington; 3 s; *Career* advocate Scotland 1948, Sheriff of Perth and Angus 1963-66, Senator of the Coll of Justice, a Lord of Session with title Lord Emslie 1970, Lord Justice Gen of Scotland and Lord Pres of the Court of Sessions 1972; *Recreations* golf; *Clubs* New (Edinburgh), Caledonian (London); *Style* - The Rt Hon the Lord Emslie, MBE, PC, QC; 47 Heriot Row, Edinburgh (☎ 031 225 3657)

EMSLIE, Hon Derek Robert Alexander; s of Baron Emslie, MBE, PC, QC (Life Peer); *b* 1949; *Educ* Cambridge U and Edinburgh (LLB); *m* 1974, Elizabeth Jane Cameron, da of Andrew MacLaren Carstairs; children; *Style* - The Hon Derek Emslie

EMSLIE, Hon George Nigel Hannington; s of Baron Emslie, MBE, PC, QC (Life Peer); *b* 1947; *Educ* Cambridge U and Edinburgh (LLB); *m* 1973, Heather Ann, nee Davis; children; *Style* - The Hon George Emslie

EMSLIE, Hon Richard Hannington; s of Baron Emslie, MBE, PC, QC (Life Peer); *b* 28 July 1957; *Educ* Edinburgh Acad, Trin Coll Glenalmond, Gonville & Caius Cambridge; *Career* biologist, researching for PhD Witwatersrand U Jo'burg; white rhino management & conservation; *Recreations* football, golf, skiing; *Clubs* Scottish Ski; *Style* - The Hon Richard Emslie; Umfolozi Game Reserve, PO Box 99, 3935 Mtubatuba, Rep of S Africa; 47 Heriot Row, Edinburgh EH3 6EX (☎ 031 225 3657)

ENCOMBE, Viscount; John Francis Thomas Marie Joseph Columba Fidelis Scott; s and h of 5 Earl of Eldon; *b* 9 July 1962; *Style* - Viscount Encombe

ENERGLYN, Baron (Life Peer UK 1968); William David Evans; DL (Notts 1974); s of David George Evans, of

Caerphilly; *b* 25 Dec 1912; *Educ* Caerphilly G S, Univ Coll Cardiff (MSc, DSc, PhD); *m* 1941, Jean Thompson, da of John Miller, of Cardiff; *Career* Prof of Geology Nottingham U 1949-78; FRGS, FLS, MIME, MIMM, FGS; *Style* - The Rt Hon The Lord Energlyn, DL; 7 The Dentons, Denton rd, Eastbourne, Sussex

ENFIELD, Viscount; Thomas Edmund Byng; s (by 1 m) and h of 7 Earl of Strafford; *b* 26 Sept 1936; *Educ* Eton, Clare Cambridge; *m* 1, 1963, Jennifer Mary Denise, da of late Rt Hon William Morrison May, MP; 2 s, 2 da; m 2, 1981, Mrs Judy Howard; *Heir* s, Hon William Byng; *Style* - Viscount Enfield; 23 Lamont rd, SW10; Abbots Worthy House, Abbots Worthy, Winchester

ENGLAND, Glyn; *b* 19 April 1921; *Educ* Penarth County Sch, Queen Mary Coll London U, LSE; *m* 1942, Tania, nee Reichenbach; 2 da; *Career* CEng, FIEE, FIMechE, FBIM; WW II 1942-47, Electricity Supply Industry 1974-, Ch Operations Engr CEBG 1966-71, dir-gen SW Region 1971-73, chm SW Electricity Bd 1973-77, chm Central Electricity Generating Bd 1977- (part-time memb 1975-77, salary as chm £42,000 pa as of June 1981); *Recreations* actively enjoying the countryside; *Style* - Glyn England Esq; Woodbridge Farm, Ubley, Bristol (☎ Blagdon 62479)

ENGLAND, John Howard Leslie; *Career* dir Mosspak (Potatoes) Ltd, Andrew Allan (Produce) Ltd, James Gardiner (Perth) Ltd, jt md J E England & Sons (Wellington) Ltd; *Style* - J H L England Esq; Mansell rd, Wellington, Telford, Shropshire

ENGLAND, John Ronald; *Career* dir Andrew Allan (Produce) Ltd, Cambridge Potato Co Ltd, chm Mosspak (Potatoes) Ltd, chm and jt md J E England & Sons (Wellington) Ltd; *Style* - J R England Esq; Mansell Road, Wellington, Telford, Shrops

ENGLISH, Cyril; *Career* dep chm Nationwide Building Society; *Style* - Cyril English Esq; Nationwide Building Society, New Oxford House, High Holborn, London WCI

ENGLISH, John; *Career* asst gen man Northern Rock Building Society; *Style* - John English Esq; Northern Rock Building Society, Gosforth, Newcastle-upon-Tyne

ENNISKILLEN, 6 Earl of (I 1789); David Lowry Cole; MBE (1954), JP (Co Fermanagh 1972); also Baron Mountflorence (I 1760), Viscount Enniskillen (I 1776) and Baron Grinstead (UK 1815); s of Hon Galbraith Cole (3 s of 4 Earl of Enniskillen) and Lady Eleanor Balfour (da of 2 Earl of Balfour); suc unc (5 Earl) 1963; *b* 10 Sept 1918; *Educ* Eton, Trin Cambridge; *m* 1, 1940 (m dis 1955), Sonia, da of late Maj Thomas Syers by his w Mary (who, after the Maj's death, m, as his 2 w, her son-in-law to be's unc, the 5 Earl); 1 s, 1 da; m 2, 1955, Nancy, da of late Dr John MacLennan, of Bridgeport, Conn; *Heir* s, Viscount Cole; *Career* served WW II Capt Irish Gds; Cmmdt Kenya Police Reserve 1950-55; agriculturist; memb Kenya Legve Cncl 1961-63, Fermanagh CC 1968-69, DL Fermanagh 1964-78; *Recreations* forestry, fishing, shooting, golf; *Clubs* Carlton, Turf, Muthaiga Country (Nairobi); *Style* - The Rt Hon Earl of Enniskillen MBE JP; PO Kiltarlity, by Beauly, Inverness; (Seat) Florence Court, Enniskillen, N Ireland; PO Box 30100 Nairobi, Kenya

ENNISMORE, Viscount; Francis Michael Hare; s (by 3 m) and h of 5 Earl of Listowel, GCMG, PC; *b* 28 June 1964; *Style* - Viscount Ennismore

ENSOR, David (Alick Charles Davidson); s of Charles William Ensor (d 1946); *b* 27 Nov 1906; *Educ* Westminster Sch; *m* 1, 1932, Norah Russell; 1 s, 2 da; m 2 1944, Frances Vivienne, da of F W Mason; 1 s, 2 da; *Career* slr 1928; prosecuting slr Newcastle-upon-Tyne 1932, Metropolitan Police 1935-37; Clerk of Peace London 1937-40; served 1939-44 (France, Africa, India, Far East); ret from law 1948; regular broadcaster for radio and television 1957-; author of several books and contributor to several journals; ret 1970; *Recreations* reading; *Style* - David Ensor Esq; L'Etoile d'Or, 66701 Argelès-sur-Mer, France

ENSOR, David; *Career* md Croydon Advertiser, chm Methodist Newspaper Co, V-Pres Methodist Conference 1981-; *Style* - David Ensor Esq; c/o Croydon Advertiser, Advertiser House, Brighton rd, S Croydon, Surrey (☎ 01 668 4111)

EPSTEIN, Hon Mrs (Edwina Maureen); *née* Stanley; da of 6 Baron Stanley of Alderley; *b* 1933; *m* 1, 1953 (m dis 1966), John Dawnay Innes (d 1966); 2 s, 1 da; m 2, 1968, J Philip, s of Dr Samuel Hyman Epstein, of Boston Mass; *Style* - The Hon Mrs Epstein; 22 Stevenage rd, SW6 (☎ 01 736 5034)

ERNE, 6 Earl of (I 1798); Henry George Victor John Crichton; JP, DL (Co Fermanagh); sits as Baron Fermanagh (UK 1876); also Baron Erne (I 1768) and Viscount Erne (I 1781); s of 5 Earl (ka 1940) and Lady Davidema, da of 2 Earl of Lytton, KG, GCSI, GCIE, PC; *b* 9 July 1937; *Educ* Eton; *m* 1958 (m dis 1980), Camilla Marguerite, da of late Wing Cdr Owen G E Roberts; 1 s, 4 da; *Heir* s, Viscount Crichton; *Career* Page of Honour to HM King George VI 1952, to HM The Queen 1952-54, RNVR 1954-57, Able Seaman RN 1957, Lt North Irish Horse 1960-68; *Style* - The Rt Hon The Earl of Erne, JP, DL; 10 Kylestrome House, Cundy Street Flats, Ebury st, SW1 (☎ 01 730 1700); Crom Castle, Newtown Butler, Co Fermanagh (☎ Newtownbutler 208)

ERNEST, Robert Charles; *Career* chm Kimberly-Clark Ltd; *Style* - Robert Ernest Esq; Larkfield, Maidstone, Kent

ERRINGTON, Viscount; Evelyn Rowland Esmond Baring; s and h of 3 Earl of Cromer, KG, GCMG, MBE, PC; *b* 3 June 1946; *Educ* Eton; *m* 1971, Plern, da of Dr Charanphat Isarangkun Na Ayudhya (d 1978), of Thailand; *Career* man China Div Inchcape Far East Ltd 1977-; *Recreations* boating (yacht- 'M V Parika'), climbing; *Clubs* Turf, Oriental, Hong Kong, Roy Hong Kong Yacht; *Style* - Viscount Errington; 7B Bowen rd, Hong Kong BCC (☎ 5-236426 and 5-262448)

ERRINGTON, Col Sir Geoffrey Frederick; 2 Bt (UK 1963) of Ness, in Co Palatine of Chester; s of Sir Eric Errington, 1 Bt (d 1973); *b* 15 Feb 1926; *Educ* Rugby Sch and New Coll Oxford; *m* 1955, Diana Kathleen Forbes, da of late Edward Barry Davenport; 3 s; *Heir* s Robin Davenport Errington; *Career* GSO 3 (Int) HQ 11 Armd Div 1950-52, GSO 3 MI 3 (b) War Office 1955-57, Bde Maj 146 Inf Bde 1959-61, Co Cdr RMA Sandhurst 1963-65, Mil Assist to Adj-Gen 1965-67, CO 1 Bn King's Regt 1967-69, GSO 1 HQ 1 BR Corps 1969-71, Col GS HQ N W District 1971, Col King's Regt 1975-; ret; dir Exec Appointments Ltd 1979-, Guy Redmayne and Ptnrs Ltd 1980-; *Recreations* sailing and skiing; *Clubs* Army and Navy; *Style* - Col Sir Geoffrey Errington, Bt; 203a Gloucester pla, London, NW1; Stone Hill Farm, Sellindge, Ashford, Kent (☎ 3191)

ERRINGTON, Robin Davenport; s and h of Col Sir Geoffrey Errington, 2 Bt; *b* 1 July 1957; *Educ* Eton; *Style* - Robin Errington Esq

ERROLL OF HALE, 1 Baron (UK 1964); Frederick James Erroll; PC (1960); s of George Murison Erroll, *b* 27 May 1914; *Educ* Oundle, Trin Cambridge; *m* 1950, Elizabeth, da of R Sowton Barrow; *Career* MP (C) Altrincham and Sale 1945-64, Parly Sec Miny of Supply 1955-56, Bd of Trade 1956-58, Economic Sec to Treasury 1958-59, Min of State Bd of Trade 1959-61, Pres Bd of Trade 1961-63, Min of Power 1963-64, memb NEDC 1962-63, chm Bowater Corpn 1973-, chm Consolidated Gold Fields 1976-, and others; *Style* - The Rt Hon The Lord Erroll of Hale PC; 1/6 Hyde Pk Gdns, W2 (☎ 01 402 7188); House of Lords, SW1

ERROLL, 24 Earl of (S 1452); Merlin Sereld Victor Gilbert Hay; also 28 Hereditary Lord High Constable of Scotland (conferred as Great Constable of Scotland *ante* 1309 and made hereditary by charter of Robert I 1314), Lord Hay (S 1449) and Lord Slains (S 1452); s of Countess of Erroll (d 1978) by her 1 husb, Sir Iain Moncreiffe of that Ilk, 11 Bt, to whose Btcy Lord Erroll is h; through his gggggf (the 18 Earl)'s w, Elizabeth FitzClarence (who, through marrying into higher rank, was not granted precedence of a Marquess's s or da like most of her siblings) Lord Erroll is sixth cous once removed to HRH The Prince of Wales (*see* Munster, Earl of); *b* 20 April 1948; *Educ* Eton, Trin Cambridge; *Heir* bro, Hon Peregrine Moncreiffe; *Career* computer consultant, OStJ, memb Roy Co of Archers (Queen's Bodyguard for Scotland) & Lt Atholl Highlanders; Ch of the Hays; as Lord High Constable, has precedence in Scotland before all other hereditary honours except the Blood Royal; also maintains private officer-of-arms (Slains Pursuivant) and is charged with jurisdiction in all matters of affray within a radius of four miles of the Monarch's person in Scotland; *Recreations* skiing, climbing, parachuting, territorials; *Clubs* Turf, White's, Pratt's, Puffin's *Style* - The Rt Hon The Earl of Erroll; Houghton Down, Stockbridge, Hants (☎ 026481 824/766); Old Slains, Collieston, Ellon, Aberdeenshire

ERSKINE OF RERRICK, 2 Baron (UK 1964); Maj Sir Iain Maxwell Erskine; 2 Bt (UK 1961); s of 1 Baron (d 1980); *b* 22 Jan 1926; *Educ* Harrow; *m* 1, 1955 (m dis 1964), Marie Elisabeth (now Countess of Caledon), da of late Maj Richard Burton Allen, 3 Dragoon Gds; m 2, 1974, Marie Josephine, da of Dr Josef Klupt; 3 da; *Heir* none; *Career* Maj (ret) Gren Gds, served Europe, M & Far East, NZ, Africa; pilot; Comptroller to Gov-Gen of New Zealand 1960-61, PRO Household Div London Dist HQ 1964-66; professional photographer, promotion consultant, co dir; OStJ, Chevalier of Legion of Honour; *Recreations* fishing, flying, photography, food; *Clubs* Caledonian, Guards, Special Forces; *Style* - Maj The Rt Hon The Lord Erskine of Rerrick; 52 Rawlings st, SW3; Barclays Bank, E Sheen Branch, 256 Upper Richmond rd, SW14

ERSKINE, Hon (Richard) Alastair; s of late 6 Baron Erskine and bro of 16 Earl of Buchan; *b* 1901; *Educ* Charterhouse; *m* 1933, Patricia, da of late Major Paul Fitzgerald Norbury, DSO; 1 s; *Style* - The Hon Alastair Erskine; Cheesecombe Farm, Hawkley, Liss, Hants

ERSKINE, Hon Alexander David; 2 s of 13 Earl of Mar and 15 of Kellie; *b* 26 Oct 1952; *Educ* Eton and Pembroke Coll Cambridge; *m* 1977, Katherine Shawford, da of T C Capel, of Narrabri, NSW; 1 s; *Career* economist Dept of PM and Cabinet Canberra Australia 1979-; *Recreations* hillwalking, outdoor sports; *Style* - The Hon Alexander Erskine; 8 Robson st, Garran, ACT 2605, Australia (010 61 61 824121)

ERSKINE, Hon Arabella Fleur; da of Lord Cardross (s and h of 16 Earl of Buchan); *b* 1969; *Style* - The Hon Arabella Erskine

ERSKINE, Hon Cora McLeave; da of 2 Baron Erskine of Rerrick; *b* 1981

ERSKINE, Sir (Thomas) David; 5 Bt (UK 1821), of Cambo, Fife; JP (Fife 1951), DL (1955); s of Lt-Col Sir Thomas Erskine, 4 Bt, DSO, DL (d 1944, third in descent from Sir David Erskine, 1 Bt, natural gs of 9 Earl of Kellie), and Magdalen, da of Sir Ralph Anstruther, 6 Bt; *b* 31 July 1912; *Educ* Eton, Magdalene Cambridge; *m* 1947, Ann, da of Lt-Col Neil Fraser-Tytler, DSO*, MC, TD, DL, of Aldourie Castle, Inverness; 2 s, 1 da; *Heir* s, Thomas Erskine; *Career* V-Lt Fife 1981-; served M East, India, Malaya as Maj Indian Corps Engrs; with Butterfield & Swire Honkong & China 1935-41; landed proprietor & farmer 1946-; *Recreations* gardening, shooting, travel; *Club* New *Style* - Sir David Erskine, Bt, JP, HM Vice-Lieut for Fife; Westnewhall, Kingsbarns, St Andrews, Fife (☎ Crail 228)

ERSKINE, Hon David Hervey; s of late John Francis Ashley, Lord Erskine, GCSI, GCIE; *b* 1924; *Educ* Eton and Trinity, Cambridge; *m* 1953, Jean Violet, da of Lt-Col Archibald Vivian Campbell Douglas; 3 da; *Career* Italy and Palestine 1943-45 (Italy Star); barr, Inner Temple, 1950; late Capt Scots Gds; CC and JP for Suffolk; *Clubs* Guards; *Style* - The Hon David Erskine JP; Felsham House, Felsham, Bury St Edmunds, Suffolk

ERSKINE, Donald Seymour; DL (1969); s of Col Sir Arthur Edward Erskine, GCVO, DSO (d 1963); *b* 28 May 1925; *Educ* Wellington Coll; *m* 1963, Catharine Annandale, da of late Kenneth T McLelland; 1 s, 4 da; *Career* served

1943-47 as Capt RA (Europe and Palestine); chartered surveyor; factor for Country Gentlemen's Assoc 1950-55, ALPF Wallace of Candacraig 1955-61; factor and dep dir Nat Trust for Scotland 1961-; *Recreations* shooting and singing; *Clubs* New (Edinburgh); *Style* - Donald Erskine Esq, DL; Cleish House, Cleish, Kinross (☎ Cleish Hills 232)

ERSKINE, Sir (Robert) George; CBE (1945); s of late John Erskine; *b* 5 Nov 1896; *Educ* Kirkcudbright Acad and Edinburgh U (BL); *Career* served 1914-19; on staff Nat Bank of Scotland 1913-29 then joined Morgan Grenfell and Co Ltd now memb of Dirs Advisory Ctee; former dir London and Provincial Trust Ltd and Alan Paine Ltd; memb London Advisory Ctee Scottish Cncl (Development and Industry); High Sheriff Surrey 1963-64; freeman of City of London; kt 1948; *Clubs* Caledonian and City of London; *Style* - Sir George Erskine, CBE; Busbridge Wood, nr Godalming, Surrey (☎ Hascombe 378)

ERSKINE, Hon Griselda Maxwell; da (by 2 m) of 2 Baron Erskine of Rerrick; *b* 1979

ERSKINE OF RERRICK, Henrietta, Baroness; Henrietta; da of late William Dunnett, of Caithness; *m* 1922, 1 Baron Erskine of Rerrick, GBE (d 1980); 1 s (2 Baron), 1 da (Hon Mrs Butler); *Career* CStJ; *Style* - The Rt Hon Henrietta, Lady Erskine of Rerrick; The Croft, Westside, 8 Churchfields av, Weybridge, Surrey

ERSKINE, Hon Henrietta Cora; da of 2 Baron Erskine of Rerrick; *b* 1975; *Style* - The Hon Henrietta Erskine

ERSKINE, Hon Henry Thomas Alexander; s of Lord Cardross (s and h of 16 Earl of Buchan); *b* 31 May 1960; *Style* - The Hon Henry Erskine

ERSKINE, Lord; James Thorne Erskine; s and h of 13 Earl of Mar & (15 of) Kellie, JP; *b* 10 March 1949; *Educ* Eton, Moray House Coll of Educn Edinburgh; *m* 1974, Mary Irene, da of Dougal Kirk and formerly w of Roderick Mooney; *Heir* bro, Hon Alexander Erskine; *Career* Page of Honour to HM 1972 & 1973; Social Worker Inverness Prison 1979-; Pilot Offr RAuxAF (2622 Highland Sqdn); former social worker Sheffield, York, Edinburgh, Elgin, Forres; *Recreations* Roy Aux Airforce Regt, cycling, camping, Elder of Church of Scotland; *Style* - Lord Erskine; Birchfield, Nethybridge, Inverness-shire (☎ 047 982 613)

ERSKINE, Hon Michael John; s of 13 Earl of Mar and 15 of Kellie; *b* 1956; *Educ* Eton and Edinburgh U; *Recreations* hillwalking, travel, outdoor sports; *Clubs* New (Edinburgh); *Style* - The Hon Michael Erskine; c/o Claremont House, Alloa, Clackmannanshire (☎ 0259 212020)

ERSKINE, Hon Montagu John; s of Lord Cardross (s and h of 16 Earl of Buchan); *b* 1966; *Style* - The Hon Montagu Erskine

ERSKINE, Hon Robert William Hervey; s of late John Francis Ashley, Lord Erskine, GCSI, GCIE; *b* 13 Oct 1930; *Educ* Eton and King's, Cambridge; *m* 1, 1955 (m dis 1964), Jennifer Shirley, da of L J Cardew Wood, of Farnham Royal Bucks; m 2, 1969 (m dis 1975), Annemarie Alvarez de Toledo, da of Jean Lattes, of Paris; 1 s; m 3, 1977, Belinda, da of Raymond Blackburn, of London; 1 s; *Career* late 2 Lt, Scots Gds; *Clubs* Savile; *Style* - The Hon Robert Erskine; 100 Elgin Cres, W11 (☎ 01 221 6229)

ERSKINE, Thomas Peter Neil; s and h of Sir David Erskine, 5 Bt, JP, DL; *b* 28 March 1950; *m* 1972, Catherine, da of Col G Hewlett; (Struan Thomas b 1977, James Dunbar b 1979); *Style* - Thomas Erskine Esq

ERSKINE-HILL, Alexander Roger; s and h of Sir Robert Erskine-Hill, 2 Bt; *b* 15 Aug 1949; *Educ* Eton, Aberdeen U (LLB); *Career* company director; *Style* - Alexander Erskine-Hill Esq; Quothquhan Lodge, Biggar, Lanarkshire

ERSKINE-HILL, Sir Robert; 2 Bt (UK 1945) of Quothquhan, Co Lanark; s of Sir Alexander Galloway Erskine-Hill, 1 Bt, KC, DL (d 1947); *b* 6 Feb 1917; *Educ* Eton and Trinity Coll Cambridge; *m* 1942, Christine Alison, da of late Capt Henry James Johnstone; 2 s, 2 da; *Heir* s Alexander Roger Erskine-Hill; *Career* served RNVR 1936-42; memb Roy Co of Archers (Queen's Bodygd for Scotland); CA; ptnr Chiene and Tait; chm Life Assoc of Scotland; *Style* - Sir Robert Erskine-Hill, Bt; Quothquhan Lodge, Biggar, Lanarks (☎ Tinto 332)

ERSKINE-MURRAY, Arthur Sydney Elibank; s of late Lt-Col Arthur Erskine-Murray CBE DSO (gs of 7 Lord Elibank) *b* 29 March 1909; *Educ* Bedford Sch, Birmingham U (BSc); *m* 1940, Florence Duncan, nee Robertson; 2 da; *Career* MICE, MBIM, memb Inst of Dirs, management consultant then v-chm Inbucon Ltd 1944-69, md Thomas Poole & Gladstone 1973-78, chm Churchill Guns Ltd 1974-76, dir Grindley of Stoke Ltd 1974-78, Bentley Pianos Ltd 1974-78, S Newman Ltd 1973-78; *Style* - Sydney Erskine-Murray Esq; Myrtle Bank, Great Amwell, Ware, Herts (☎ Ware 870146)

ERSKINE-MURRAY, Hon Timothy Alexander Elibank; s of 14 Lord Elibank; *b* 1967; *Style* - The Hon Timothy Erskine-Murray

ESCRITT, (Charles) Ewart; OBE (1970); s of Rev Charles Escritt (d 1949); *b* 26 Aug 1905; *Educ* Christ's Hosp and Keble Coll Oxford; *m* 1939, Ruth Mary, da of Thomas Chapman Metcalf (d 1962); 2 s, 1 da; *Career* assist master Bromsgrove Sch 1928-29, staff of Tootal Broadhurst Lee Co Ltd 1933-47; served 1939-45, Div RASC Capt 1940, POW Singapore and Thailand 1942-45; gp training offr Oxford U Appointments Ctee Sec 1947-70, Prof Fell Keble Coll 1965-70; *Recreations* Japanese studies; *Clubs* Oxford Union; *Style* - Ewart Escritt Esq, OBE; 32 Portland rd, Summertown, Oxford (☎ 57072)

ESHER, 4 Viscount (UK 1897); Maj Lionel Gordon Baliol Brett; CBE (1970); also Baron Esher (UK 1885); s of 3 Viscount, GBE (d 1963); *b* 18 July 1913; *Educ* Eton, New Coll Oxford; *m* 1935, (Helena) Christina Olive, da of Ebenezer John Lecky Pike, CBE, MC, DL, of Ditcham Park, Petersfield, Hants; 5 s, 1 da; *Heir* s, Hon Christopher Brett; *Career* Rector and Vice-Provost Roy Coll of Art 1971-78, pres Royal Inst of British Architects 1965-67, memb Roy Fine Art Cmmn 1951-69, tstee London Museum, chm Northern Home Counties Nat Tst 1979-, former chm Art Panel Arts Cncl of GB; *Style* - Maj The Rt Hon The Viscount Esher CBE; Christmas Common Tower, Watlington, Oxford

ESMONDE, Eithne, Lady - Eithne Moira Grattan; da of late Sir Thomas Henry Grattan Esmonde, 11 Bt; *b* 1902; *m* 1927, Sir Anthony Charles Esmonde, 15 Bt (d 1981); 3 s, 3 da; *Style* - Eithne, Lady Esmonde; Ballynastragh, Gorey, Co Wexford

ESMONDE, His Honour Judge Sir John Henry Grattan; 16 Bt (I 1629); s of Sir Anthony Esmonde, 15 Bt (d 1981); *b* 27 June 1928; *Educ* National U of Ireland; *m* 1957, Pamela Mary, nee Bourke; 3 s, 2 da; *Heir* s, Thomas Esmonde; *Career* barr Dublin 1950, Circuit Judge W Circuit Co Galway and Co Mayo 1977-; *Style* - His Honour Judge Sir John Esmonde, Bt; 6 Nutley av, Donnybrook, Dublin 4 (☎ 693040)

ESMONDE, Thomas Francis Grattan; s and h of His Honour Judge Sir John Esmonde, 16 Bt; *b* 1960; *Style* - Thomas Esmonde Esq

ESPLEN, John Graham; s and h of Sir William Esplen, 2 Bt; *b* 4 Aug 1932; *m* 1956, Valerie Joan, da of Maj-Gen Albert Lambooy, CB, OBE; 1 s, 3 da; *Style* - John Esplen Esq; Orchards, W Clandon, Surrey

ESPLEN, Sir William Graham; 2 Bt (UK 1921) of Hardres Court, Canterbury; s of Sir John Esplen, 1 Bt, KBE (d 1930); *b* 29 Dec 1899; *Educ* Harrow; *m* 1928 (m dis 1951), Aline Octavia, da of A Octavius Hedley (d 1926); 1 s; *Heir* s John Graham Esplen; *Style* - Sir William Esplen, Bt; Heron Bridge, Newsham, nr Richmond, N Yorks (☎ Barningham 233)

ESPLIN, Air Vice-Marshal Ian George; CB (1963), OBE (1946), DFC (1943); s of Donald Thomas Esplin (d 1962); *b* 26 Feb

1914; *Educ* Sydney U, Oxford U; *m* 1944, Patricia Kaleen, nee Barlow; 1 s, 1 da; *Career* Air V-Marshal RAF, UK, Germany, India, USA; *Recreations* golf, tennis, swimming, photography *Clubs* Vincent's, Leander; *Style* - Air Vice-Marshal Ian Esplin CB OBE DFC; c/o Nat West Bank Ltd, St James's Sq, SW1

ESSEX, 10 Earl of (E 1661); Robert Edward de Vere Capell; also Baron Capell of Hadham (E 1641) and Viscount Malden (E 1661); s of Arthur Capell (gs of Capt Hon Algernon Capell, RN, bro of 6 Earl of Essex, by the Capt's w Caroline, da of Vice-Adm Hon Sir Charles Paget, KCB, 5 s of 1 Earl of Uxbridge and yr bro of 1 Marquess of Anglesey); suc 9 Earl (his 3 cous once removed) 1981; eighth in descent from 1 Earl, not to be confused with the Earl of Essex, no relation, who was the incompetent Parliamentarian CIC during the Great Rebellion; in fact the f of the 1 (Capell) Earl of the 2 creation was beheaded for loyalty to his king, while the last (Devereux) Earl of Essex of the 1 cr was actually voted a Dukedom by the insurgent Parliament; *b* 13 Jan 1920; *m* 1942, Doris, da of George Tomlinson; 1 s; *Heir* s, Viscount Malden; *Career* served WW II , Fl Sgt RAF; clerical offr Civ Serv for 25 years, now ptnr in small grocery business; *Style* - The Rt Hon The Earl of Essex; 2 Novak Place, Torrisholme, Morecambe, Lancs

ESSEX, Arthur Christian; *Career* FCA; chm Aberdare Cables Ltd, Pirelli Enfield Supertension Cables Ltd (and md), Pirelli Enfield Supertension Cables (SA) (Pty) Ltd, Pirelli General Cables (SA) (Pty) Ltd, md Pirelli General Cable Works Ltd; *Style* - Arthur Essex Esq; Pirelli General Cable Works Ltd, Thavies Inn House, 3-4 Holborn Circus, EC1

ESSEX, Christine, Countess of; Christine Mary; da of late George Frederick Davis; *m* 1957, as his 4 w, 8 Earl of Essex (d 1966); *Style* - The Rt Hon Christine, Countess of Essex; 16 Ocean dve, Merimbula, NSW 2548, Australia

ESSEX, Nona, Countess of; Nona Isobel; da of David Wilson Miller, of Christchurch, NZ; *m* 1, Francis Smythe, of Sussex (decd); m 2, 1957, as his 2 w, 9 Earl of Essex, TD (d 1981); *Style* - Rt Hon Nona, Countess of Essex; Floyds Farm, Wingrave, Aylesbury, Bucks

ESSINGTON-BOULTON, Hon Mrs; Hon Crystal; *née* Russell; da of 2 Baron Russell of Liverpool, CBE, MC, by his 2 w, Betty, nee Ewart; *b* 4 Jan 1936; *m* 1955, John Essington-Boulton; 1 s, 1 da; *Style* - The Hon Mrs Essington-Boulton; 3 Belgrave cres, Bath, Avon

ESSON-SCOTT, Hon Mrs - Hon Rosemary Sylvia; da of 13 Viscount Falkland & sis of present peer; *b* 1910; *m* 1, 1928, John de Perigault Gurney Mayhew (m dis 1936); 2, 1937, Aubrey Esson-Scott; *Style* - The Hon Mrs Esson-Scott; 122 Marine Gate, Brighton, Sussex

ETHERTON, Ralph Humphrey; s of Louis John Walpole Etherton (d 1943); *b* 11 Feb 1904; *Educ* Charterhouse and Trinity Hall Cambridge; *m* 1944, Johanne Patricia, da of late Gerald Cloherty; 1 s, 1 da; *Career* barr Inner Temple 1926; chm Coningsby Club 1933-34; MP (Nat C) Stretford Div of Lancs 1939-45; served in RAFVR as Fl Lt 1940-42; memb Parliamentary Delegation to Aust and NZ 1944; *Recreations* riding and travel; *Clubs* Carlton and Pratt's; *Style* - Ralph Etherton Esq; Greentree Hall, Balcombe, Sussex (☎ Balcombe 319)

EUGSTER, Gen Sir Basil Oscar Paul; KCB (1970), KCVO (1968), CBE (1962), DSO (1945), MC (1938) and Bar (1940), DL (1977); s of Col Oscar Louis Eugster, DSO (d 1930); *b* 15 Aug 1914; *Educ* Beaumont and Ch Ch Oxford (MA); *m* 1939, Marcia Elaine, da of Air-Cdre Sir Percy Smyth-Osbourne, CMG, CBE (d 1969); 2 s; *Career* 2 Lt Irish Gds 1935, served 1939-45 War (Narvik, Italy and NW Europe), Bde Maj HQ 140 Inf Bde 1943-44, Jt Servs Staff Coll 1950, AAG War Office 1954-56, Cmdt Eaton Hall Offr Cadet Sch 1956-58, Cmdt Sch of Infantry Warminster 1962, Brig 1962, GOC 4 Div BAOR 1963-65, GOC London District and Maj-Gen cmding Household Bde 1965-68, Cdr British Forces Hong Kong 1968-70, GOC-in-C Southern Command 1971-72, C-in-C UK Land Forces 1972-74, ADC

(Gen) to HM The Queen 1973; ret 1974; *Clubs* White's and Pratt's; *Style* - Gen Sir Basil Eugster KCB KCVO CBE DSO MC* DL; Holmedown, Exbourne, N Devon (☎ Exbourne 241)

EUSTACE, Hon Mrs (Dorothy Anne); da of 1 Baron Percy of Newcastle; *b* 1926; *Educ* Durham U (MB, BS); *m* 1957, Maj Thomas Robert Hales Eustace, Royal Irish Fusiliers; 1 s, 2 da; *Style* - The Hon Mrs Eustace; Glebe House, Boughton Aluph, Ashford, Kent

EUSTON, Earl of; James Oliver Charles FitzRoy; s and h of 11 Duke of Grafton, KG; *b* 13 Dec 1947; *Educ* Eton, Magdalene Cambridge; *m* 1972, Lady Clare, nee Kerr, da of 12 Marquess of Lothian; 1 s, 2 da; *Heir* s, Viscount Ipswich; *Career* a Page of Honour to HM The Queen 1962-63, dir Smith St Aubyn & Co (Hldgs); *Style* - Earl of Euston; 6 Vicarage gdns, W8

EVANS OF CLAUGHTON, Baron (Life Peer UK 1978); David Thomas Gruffyd; s of Maj John Cynlais Evans; *b* 9 Feb 1928; *Educ* Birkenhead Sch, Friars Sch Bangor, Liverpool U (LLB); *m* 1956, Moira Elizabeth, da of late James Rankin; 1 s, 3 da; *Career* slr 1952, pres Lib Pty 1977-78 (chm 1965-68), Lib Pty Spokesman on Local Govt in House of Lords; *Recreations* golf, watching Welsh rugby and Liverpool Football Club; *Clubs* Nat Lib, Wirral Golf, Oxton CC, Birkenhead Squash Racquets; *Style* - The Rt Hon The Lord Evans of Claughton; Sunridge, 69 Bidston rd, Claughton, Birkenhead, Merseyside (☎ 051 652 3425)

EVANS OF HUNGERSHALL, Baron (Life Peer UK 1967); (Benjamin) Ifor Evans; s of Benjamin Evans, of London; *b* 19 Aug 1899; *Educ* Stationers' Co's Sch, Univ Coll London; *m* 1923, Marjorie Ruth, da of John Measures, of Ifield, Sussex; 1 da; *Career* Prof of English Lang and Lit Univ Coll Southampton 1925-26, Sheffield U 1926-33, Queen Mary Coll London U 1933-44 (Princ 1944-51), Provost Univ Coll London 1951-66; chm Roy Soc of Literature 1974 (FRSL), former v-chm Arts Cncl, kt 1955; *Style* - The Rt Hon The Lord Evans of Hungershall; 317 Minster House, St James Court, Buckingham Gate, SW1 (☎ 01 834 8783)

EVANS, Sir Anthony Adney; 2 Bt (UK 1920); s of Sir Walter Harry Evans, 1 Bt (d 1954); *b* 5 Aug 1922; *Educ* Shrewsbury, Oxford U; *m* 1, 1948 (m dis 1957), Rita Beatrice, da of late Alfred David Kettle, of Souldern, Oxon; 2 s, 1 da; m 2, 1958, Sylvia Jean; *Style* - Sir Anthony Evans, Bt; Almer Manor, Blandford, Dorset

EVANS, Hon Mrs (Audrey Mary); da of 1 Visc Leathers, CH, PC (d 1965); *b* 21 Dec 1915; *Educ* Benenden, St Andrews U; *m* 1938, Edward Noel Evans (d 1964); 2 s, 1 da; *Career* publisher; *Recreations* travel; *Style* - The Hon Mrs Evans; 28 Hyde Park gdns, W2 (☎ 01 723 2909); 6 Cunliffe Close, West Wittering, Sussex (☎ 0243 663201)

EVANS, Collis William; CB (1958), CBE (1949); s of Walter James Evans (d 1954); *b* 27 May 1895; *m* 1, 1938, Annie Urquhart (d 1957); m 2, 1970, Hilda Stewart; *Career* served 1914-18 with Yeomanry and RFA Middle E, Macedonia and France, financial adviser RAF Middle E 1939-44, assist sec Dept of Civil Aviation 1944, Under-Sec 1948-59, ret *Style* Collis Evans Esq, CB, CBE; Ringle Crouch, Nash, Bucks (☎ Whaddon 285)

EVANS, Hon David Robert Cynlais; s of Baron Evans of Claughton (Life Peer); *b* 1964; *Style* - The Hon David Evans

EVANS, Prof (David) Ellis; s of David Evans (d 1948); *b* 23 Sept 1930; *Educ* Llandeilo Grammar Sch, Univ Coll of Wales Aberystwyth, Univ Coll of Swansea and Jesus Coll Oxford; *m* 1957, Sheila Mary, da of David Thomas Jeremy, of Swansea, Wales; 2 da; *Career* former Lectr, Reader and Prof of Welsh Language and Literature, Univ Coll Swansea; Jesus Prof of Celtic Oxford and Fell of Jesus Coll 1978-; *Recreations* music and walking; *Style* - Prof Ellis Evans; Jesus Coll, Oxford; 23 Kings ave, Marcham, Abingdon, Oxon (☎ Frilford Heath 391306)

EVANS, Hon Elizabeth Ann Cynlais; da of Baron Evans of Claughton (Life Peer); *b* 1957; *Style* - The Hon Elizabeth

Evans

EVANS, Hon Edward Broke; VRD; s of late 1 Baron Mountevans; *b* 1924; *Educ* Wellington; *m* 1947, Elaine Elisabeth, nee Cove; 2 s, 1 da; *Career* Cdr (E) RNR (ret), employed ICI Ltd; *Style* - The Hon Edward Evans, VRD; 15 York Mansions, Prince of Wales Drive, SW11

EVANS, Evelyn Jane Alice; CBE (1960, MBE 1955); da of Charles Evans (d 1971); *b* 22 March 1910; *Educ* Barr's Hill Grammar Sch Coventry; *Career* chartered librarian; dir of Library Servs Ghana Library Bd 1945-65, UNESCO library consultant Sri Lanka 1967-70; *Recreations* reading, walking and dogs; *Style* - Miss Evelyn Evans, CBE; 8 Park Close, Beadon, Oxford (☎ 811359)

EVANS, Edward Somers Fleming; s of the late Capt E F H Evans, JP; *b* 26 April 1910; *Educ* Whitbourne Hall Worcester, Cheltenham Coll, CCC Oxford; *m* 1947, Erica Grace, da of the late Col W D Conner; 2 s; *Career* served with 1 Bn Worc Regt Middle East 1940-41, Staff Captain HQ Western Command 1942-45, farmer, High Sheriff Herefordshire 1964, chm Herefordshire Country Landowners Assoc 1971-74, chm Western Region Timber Growers Organisation 1975-78; *Recreations* shooting, fishing; *Clubs* Royal Commonwealth Society; *Style* - Edward Evans Esq; Dial House, Whitbourne, Nr Worcester (☎ Knightwick 223)

EVANS, Sir (Sidney) Harold; 1 Bt (UK 1963) of Rottingdean, Co Sussex; CMG (1957), OBE (1945); s of Sidney Evans (d 1956); *b* 29 April 1911; *Educ* King Edward VI Sch Stourbridge; *m* 1945, Elizabeth, da of late William Jaffray; 1 s (decd), 1 da; *Heir* none; *Career* with British Legation Helsinki 1940-41; Min of Information rep in W Africa (staff of resident minister) 1942-46; chf information offr Colonial Office 1953-57; head of information and research Independent Television Authority 1964-66; adviser on Public Relations to Bd of Vickers Ltd 1966-76; chm of Health Educn Cncl 1973-76; *Recreations* reading, walking, gardening, travel, photography *Style* - Sir Harold Evans, Bt, CMG OBE; 3 Challoners Close, Rottingdean, Brighton (☎ 33397)

EVANS, Hon Mrs (Isla Elizabeth Ritchie); *née* Calder; da of Baron Ritchie-Calder (Life Peer), CBE; *b* 7 Sept 1947; *Educ* Nonsuch Co Sch Cheam, St George's Edinburgh, Froebel Inst of Education; *m* 1971, Alan Evans; *Style* - The Hon Mrs Evans; 56 Bedford Court Mansions, Bedford av, WC1

EVANS, James; *Career* jt dep md Thomson British Holdings Ltd; dir Thomson Organisation Ltd, Thomson Newspapers Ltd, Thomson North Sea Ltd and subsidiaries, Thomson Withy Grove Ltd, The Solicitors' Law Stationery Soc Ltd; *Style* - James Evans Esq; 4 Stratford Place, London W1

EVANS, James Donald; s of Arthur Evans; *b* 12 Nov 1926; *Educ* Roy G S High Wycombe; *m* 1946, Freda, nee Bristow; 5 children; *Career* ed The Northern Echo 1966-; dir North of England Newspapers 1973, ed-in-ch 1966-; *Recreations* reading, driving and travel; *Clubs* Nat Liberal; *Style* - James Evans Esq; 4 Harewood Hill, Darlington, Co Durham

EVANS, Col James Ellis; CBE (1975, OBE 1952), TD (1947); s of James Evans (d 1970); *b* 6 Aug 1910; *Educ* Epworth Coll Rhyl; *Career* served 1939-45 with RA (France, N Africa and Italy), Lt-Col 1944, Cdr 384 Light Regt RA (RWF) TA 1947-52, Col 1955; chm Denbighshire and Flintshire T and AF Assoc 1961-68 and N Wales Sub-Assoc of Wales and Monmouthshire TA and VR Assoc 1968-71; CA; memb Prestatyn UDC 1939-74, chm 1947; chm N Wales Police Authority 1976; DL (1953), JP (1951) Flintshire, V-Lt 1970-74, Vice Ld-Lt 1977-79 Clwyd, HM Ld-Lt 1979-; *Clubs* E India, Devonshire, Sports and Public Schs; City; *Style* - Col James Evans CBE TD JP, HM Lord-Lieut for Clwyd; Trafford Mount, Gronant rd, Prestatyn, Clwyd (☎ Prestatyn 4119)

EVANS, Hon Jane Lucy Cynlais; da of Baron Evans of Claughton (Life Peer); *b* 1968; *Style* - The Hon Jane Evans

EVANS, Jean-Paul Robert Marix; *Career* LLB; CBIM; chm Moore Business

Forms Ltd; dir Lamson Gp of Cos, Moore Business Forms Gp of Cos; *Style* - Jean-Paul Evans Esq; Moore Business Forms Ltd, Moore House, 75-79 Southwark st, London SE1

EVANS, John Russell; s of Henry Claude Evans; *b* 2 Aug 1945; *Educ* King James I G S Bishop Auckland, City U London; *m* (m dis); 1 s, 1 da; *Career* 1980- md Bonser Engineering, 1979- manufacturing dir Lansing Henley, 1978-79 md Park Bros, 1977-78 gen man Butec Electrics (British Leyland); *Recreations* reading, rugby, squash; *Style* - John Evans Esq; Fox's Leap, Redbrook rd, Monmouth, Gwent (☎ Monmouth 6162)

EVANS, Lt-Col John Roberts; TD (1954), DL (1973); s of David James Haydn Evans (d 1961); *b* 16 Jan 1917; *Educ* Llandovery Coll and Exeter U; *m* 1945, Sheila Rita, da of Richard Ball (d 1940); 1 s, 1 da; *Career* served in WW II with HAC and RA (India and Far E), with Welch Regt (TA) 1947-66, Lt-Col 6 (Glam) Bn Welch Regt 1963-66; admitted a slr 1952; pres Cardiff and District Law Soc 1981- (former v-pres); Hon slr Welsh Rugby Union; trustee Llandovery Coll; Memb of Court of Govs Univ Coll Cardiff; *Recreations* rugby, football, music and fishing; *Clubs* Army and Navy, Cardiff and County; *Style* - Lt-Col John Evans, TD, DL; Greenbanks, Highfields, Llandaff, Cardiff, S Glam (☎ 562480)

EVANS, Hon Jeffrey Richard de Corban; s of 2 Baron Mountevans (d 1974), and hp of bro, 3 Baron; *b* 13 May 1948; *Educ* Nautical Coll Pangbourne, Pembroke Coll Cambridge; *m* 1972, Hon Juliet Wilson, da of 2 Baron Moran, KCMG; 2 s (Alexander b 1975, Julian b 1977); *Career* Liveryman of Worshipful Co of Shipwrights; shipbroker, with H Clarkson & Co; *Recreations* cross-country skiing, fishing, reading, walking the dog; *Style* - The Hon Jeffrey Evans; 14 Quick st, N1 (☎ 01 837 0913)

EVANS, Hon Mrs Lelgarde de Clare Elizabeth; *née* Philipps; da of 1 Visc St Davids; *b* 1918; *m* 1950 (m dis), Colin Evans; 2 s, 1 da *Style* - Hon Mrs Lelgarde Evans; Ballinter Bridge, Navan, Co Meath

EVANS, Col Lionel Vincent; TD (1942), JP (1961), DL (1954); s of Alderman George Frederick Evans, JP (Lord Mayor Cardiff 1935-36) (d 1953); *b* 8 March 1904; *Educ* Taunton Sch; *m* 1936, Catherine Elizabeth, da of Nelson Simmons Merrett (d 1950); 1 da; *Career* 2 Lt Welch Regt (TA) 1924, Maj 1934, served 1939-45 (UK), Lt-Col Home Gd 1952, Col Cmdt Glam Army Cadet Force 1954-56; sales man Nat Coal Bd (former Powell Duffryn Collieries) 1921-66; gov Taunton Sch 1921, chm of Sch of Govs 1965-71; Governing Body Church in Wales 1954-74; chm Welch Regt Benevolent Fund 1978-; *Clubs* Cardiff and County, Cardiff Exchange and Naval and Military; *Style* - Col Lionel Evans, TD, JP, DL; 49 Tydraw rd, Roath Park, Cardiff (☎ Cardiff 486571)

EVANS, Lady; Madge (Margaret); da of J B & S J Gribbin, of Heaton Moor, Cheshire; *m* 1930, Sir Trevor Evans, CBE (d 1981), late dir Beaverbrook Newspapers; 1 s (Richard), 1 da (Marilyn); *Style* - Lady Evans; 17 Wolsey Close, Kingston Hill, Surrey (☎ 01 940 6016)

EVANS, Dr Philip Rainsford; CBE (1967); s of Charles Irwin Evans (d 1941); *b* 14 April 1910; *Educ* Sidcot Sch Winscombe, Leighton Park Sch Reading, Manchester U (MSc, MD), Columbia U New York; *m* 1935, Barbara Dorothy Fordyce, da of Bernard Hay-Cooper (d 1931); 3 s, 1 da; *Career* served 1939-45 War as Lt-Col RAMC (N Africa and Italy) (despatches), adviser in Medicine CMF 1946; dir Paediatric Dept Guy's Hosp Medical Sch 1946-71, physician Hosp for Sick Children 1946-75, physician-paediatrician to HM The Queen 1971-76; *Style* - Dr Philip Evans, CBE; 24 Abbey rd, London, NW8 (☎ 01 624 1668)

EVANS, Robert; s of Gwilym Evans; *b* 28 May 1927; *Educ* Old Swan Coll Liverpool, City Tech Liverpool, Blackburn Tech and Liverpool U; *m* 1950, Lilian May, nee Ward; 1 s, 1 da; *Career* dep chm N Thames Gas 1975-77, chm E Midlands Gas Regn 1977- *Recreations* reading, DIY, golf *Style* - Robert Evans Esq; Hunters Lodge, 22 George Fox Lane, Fenny

Drayton, Nuneaton, Warwickshire (☎ Atherstone 5518)

EVANS, Russell Wilmot; MC (1945); s of late William Henry Evans; *b* 4 Nov 1922; *Educ* King Edward's Sch Birmingham, Birmingham U (LLB); *m* 1956, Pamela Muriel, nee Hayward; 2 s, 1 da; *Career* dep chm The Rank Organisation 1981-, gp md 1975-, dir Rank Xerox Ltd 1973-, Southern Television 1974, Fuji Xerox Ltd 1976-, chm Butlin's Ltd, Rank City Wall Ltd; *Recreations* tennis, squash, photography; *Clubs* English Speaking Union, Roehampton Club; *Style* - Russell Evans Esq, MC; Walnut Tree, Roehampton Gate, SW15 (☎ 01 876 2433)

EVANS, Hon Sarah Louise Cynlais; da of Baron Evans of Claughton (Life Peer); *b* 1966; *Style* - The Hon Sarah Evans

EVANS, Ven Thomas Eric; s of Eric John Rhys Evans; *b* 1 Feb 1928; *Educ* St David's Coll, St Cat's Oxford; *m* 1957, Linda Kathleen, nee Budge; 2 da; *Career* Archdeacon of Cheltenham 1975-, chm Cncl for Care of Churches 1981-, memb of Standing Cttee of Gen Synod 1981-, dir Ecclesiastical Insurance Office 1978-, canon missioner Gloucester Cathedral 1969-75; *Recreations* travel (especially Middle East); *Clubs* Carlton, The Downhill Only (Wengen, Switzerland); *Style* - The Ven The Archdeacon of Cheltenham; 9 College Green, Gloucester (☎ Glos 20620)

EVANS, William; s of late Eben Evans; *b* 24 Nov 1895; *Educ* Univ Coll of Wales, Aberystwyth and London Hosp Medical Coll; *m* 1936, Christine (d 1964), da of late J Lessels Downie; *Career* offr 19 Lancashire Fus 1917-19; High Sheriff Cardiganshire 1959; consulting cardiologist to London Hosp, Nat Heart Hosp, Inst of Cardiology, Roy Soc of Musicans; RN (1946-67); author of several text books of diseases of the heart and contributor to various scientific journals; Hon Memb of Order of Druids 1960; *Recreations* writing, farming and fishing; *Clubs* Athenaeum; *Style* - William Evans Esq; Bryndomen, Tregaron, Dyfed (☎ 097 44 404)

EVANS-BEVAN, David Gawain; s and h of Sir Martyn Evans-Bevan, 2 Bt; *b* 16 Sept 1961; *Style* - David Evans-Bevan Esq

EVANS-BEVAN, Sir Martyn Evan; 2 Bt (UK 1958); s of Sir David Martyn Evans-Bevan, 1 Bt (d 1973); *b* 1 April 1932; *Educ* Uppingham; *m* 1957, Jennifer Jane Marion, da of Robert Hugh Stevens, of Eardisley, Herefords; 4 s; *Heir* s, David Evans-Bevan; *Career* High Sheriff of Breconshire 1967-68, Freeman of City of London, Liveryman Worshipful Co of Farmers; company dir; *Style* - Sir Martyn Evans-Bevan, Bt; Felin-Newydd, Llande Falle, Brecon, Powys

EVANS-FREKE, (Hon Mrs Ralfe); Dorothy May; *da* of H G Surrey; *m* 1941, as his 3 w, Maj Hon Ralfe Evans-Freke, MBE (d 1969, s of 9 Baron Carbery); *Style* - The Hon Mrs Ralfe Evans-Freke; 15 Queen Elizabeth Close, Palace Plain, Norwich

EVANS-FREKE, Hon John Anthony; s of 11 Baron Carbery; *b* 1949; *Educ* Downside; Royal Agricultural Coll Cirencester (ARICS); *m* 1972, Veronica Jane, nee Williams; 1 s; *Style* - The Hon John Evans-Freke; Hazelby Farm House, Twyford, Winchester, Hants

EVANS-FREKE, Hon Michael Peter; s and h of 11 Baron Carbery; *b* 11 Oct 1942; *Educ* Downside, Ch Ch Oxford (MA), Strathclyde U (MBA); *m* 1967, Claudia Janet Elizabeth, nee Gurney; 1 s, 2 da; *Style* - The Hon Michael Evans-Freke; Westfield House, Goudhurst rd, Marden, Tonbridge, Kent

EVANS-FREKE, Hon Stephan Ralfe; s of 11 Baron Carbery; *b* 1952; *Educ* Downside, Trinity Cambridge; *Style* - The Hon Stephan Evans-Freke

EVE, Hon Amy Janet; da of 2 Baron Silsoe; *b* 1964; *Style* - The Hon Amy Eve

EVE, Robin Anthony; s of late Frederick Latymer Eve; *b* 20 April 1934; *Educ* City of London Freemen's Sch; *m* 1953, Anne Augusta, nee Mead; 2 s, 2 da; *Career* FCIS, FCCA, ATII, MIMC, dir Midland Bank Industrial Finances Ltd, common councilman Corpn of London Ward of

Cheap 1980; *Recreations* sailing (yacht Contessa 32 'Picardy II'), music, fishing; *Clubs* City Livery, City Livery Yacht Club; *Style* - Robin Eve Esq; 36 Poultry, EC2 (☎ 01 638 8861); Aldersmead, Shepherds Hill, Merstham, Surrey (☎ Merstham 2540)

EVE, Hon Simon Rupert; s and h of 2 Baron Silsoe; *b* 17 April 1966; *Style* - The Hon Simon Eve

EVELEIGH-ROSS-DE-MOLEYNS, Hon Mrs Francis; Olivia Phoebe; da of Capt Percy Leathers; *m* 1, 1950, Lord John Conyngham (d 1963, s of 6 Marquess Conyngham); *m* 2, 1963, as his 4 w, Hon Francis Eveleigh-Ross-de-Moleyns (d 1964, s of 6 Baron Ventry); *Style* - The Hon Mrs Francis Eveleigh-Ross-de-Moleyns; 317 The Water gdns, Hyde Park, W2 .

EVELING, Walter Raphael Taylor; CBE (1960); s of Raphael Eveling (d 1943); *b* 8 March 1908; *Educ* Paradise House Sch London; *m* 1935, Annie Ferguson, da of W Newman (d 1951); 1 s; *Career* chartered surveyor; assist chf valuer Bd of Inland Revenue 1951-65 and dep chf valuer 1965-68; ret 1968; British memb of Expert Ctee in Berlin on Valuation of Reparations 1945; *Style* - Walter Eveling Esq, CBE; 11 Thornhill close, Ramsey, Isle of Man (☎ 0624 813855)

EVELYN, John Patrick Michael Hugh; s of Maj Peter Evelyn, Gren Gds (presumed d of wounds 1943, ggs through his paternal grandmother of Rev George Chichester, bro of 1 Baron O'Neill and hence of the oldest traceable family in Europe, the O'Neills, of the Irish Roy House of Tara; Peter was also tenth in line from George Evelyn, of Wotton, MP for Surrey and bro of John, the diarist and gardener whose misfortune it was to have Peter the Great as subtenant at his house of Sayes Court); *b* 16 Oct 1939; *Educ* Eton; *m* 1, 1965 (m dis 1974), Jennifer Browne; 1 s; m 2, 1974, Anne, da of Richard Lindsell, DFC, of Northwood House, Sharpthorne, Sussex; 2 s; *Career* farmer, CCllr Surrey; *Recreations* winter & field sports; *Clubs* Boodle's; *Style* - John Evelyn Esq; The Estate Office, Wotton, Dorking, Surrey

EVERALL, John Harold; s of William Everall (d 1946); *b* 12 Oct 1908; *Educ* Malvern Coll; *m* 1935, Breda, da of late Gerald Sherlock, of Dublin; 1 s, 1 da; *Career* FRICS, Hon FRASC, breeder of pedigree Hereford cattle, Int judge at Palermo, Buenos Aires, Sydney Australia, Nairobi Kenya, also Roy Highland, Roy Dublin, Roy Welsh shows; dir QMP Ltd 1958-65, liveryman City of London, chm Meon Valley Beagles Hunt Ctee 1972-79; *Recreations* beagling, fishing; *Clubs* Travellers'; *Style* - John Everall Esq; Courtyards, Crawley, Winchester, Hants (☎ Sparsholt 273)

EVERARD, Lt-Col Sir Nugent Henry; 3 Bt (UK 1911); s of Maj Sir Richard William Everard, 2 Bt (d 1929); *b* 28 Feb 1905; *Educ* Harrow; *m* 1933, Frances Audrey (d 1975), da of John C Jesson; 1 s, 1 da; *Heir* s, Robin Charles Everard; *Career* Lt 1 Bn Duke of Wellington's Regt 1925-29, Capt 1937, Lt-Col 1941-48, ret 1958; *Style* - Lt-Col Sir Nugent Everard, Bt

EVERARD, Robin Charles; s and h of Lt-Col Sir Nugent Everard, 3 Bt; *b* 5 Oct 1939; *m* 1963, Ariel Ingrid, da of Col Peter Cleasby-Thompson, MBE, MC; 1 s, 2 da; *Style* - Robin Everard Esq; Great House, Layer de la Haye, Colchester, Essex

EVERETT, Edwin Arthur; CBE (1975); s of Ernest George Everett (d 1964); *b* 20 May 1917; *Educ* Hampton Sch; *m* 1944, Joan Margaret, da of Capt Arnold George Stanford (d 1916); 2 s; *Career* The Queen's Westminsters (KRRC) 1935-39, Roy W African Frontier Force 1940-43, RAOC 1943-49 (Capt TA), Middle East 1943, Normandy, Holland and Germany 1944-46 (war crimes trials); slr of Supreme Court 1939-47, District Registrar of High Court 1979-; memb of County Court Rule Ctee 1968-79, pres Assoc of County Court and District Registrars 1975; *Recreations* photography, gardening and travel; *Clubs* Roy Overseas League; *Style* - Edwin Everett Esq, CBE; 37 West ave, Worthing, W Sussex (☎ 48025)

EVERITT, William Howard; s of Howard George Everitt (d 1978); *b* 27 Feb 1940; *Educ* Brentwood Sch, Leeds U

(BSc); *m* 1963, Anthea Cecilia, da of late William Nield; 2 children; *Career* dir Associated Engineering Group Ltd 1978-; *Recreations* golf, squash; *Style* - William Everitt Esq; Horley House, Hornton Lane, Horley, nr Banbury, Oxon (☎ Wroxton St Mary (029 573) 603)

EVERSHED, Baroness; Cicely Elizabeth Joan; OBE (1977), JP (Norfolk); da of Hon Mr Justice (Hon Sir Charles) Bennett; *b* 19 Oct 1908; *m* 1929, 1 & last Baron Evershed (d 1966); *Career* FSA; Red Cross ret; *Recreations* gardening; *Clubs* VAD Ladies; *Style* - The Rt Hon Lady Evershed OBE JP; Tudor Lodgings, Castle Acre, King's Lynn, Norfolk

EVERY, Cecil Tom; CBE (1946); s of E J T E Every (d 1924), of Plymouth; *b* 12 March 1902; *Educ* Univ Coll Sch; *m* 1, 1927 (m dis 1952), Marjorie Hope, da of Charles Henry Bishop; 1 s, 2 da; m 2, 1952, Mary, da of Joseph Foxton; 1 da; *Career* ptnr Langdon and Every; *Style* - Cecil Every Esq, CBE; Furlong, Chagford, Newton Abbot, Devon (☎ 064 73 2402)

EVERY, Henry John Michael; s (by 2 m) and h of Sir John Every, 12 Bt; *b* 6 April 1947; *Educ* Malvern; *m* 1974, Susan, da of Kenneth Beaton, JP; 2 s; *Style* - Henry Every Esq; 4 Oaklands rd, E Sheen, London SW14

EVERY, Sir John Simon; 12 Bt (E 1641); s of Sir Edward Oswald Every, 11 Bt (d 1959); *b* 24 April 1914; *Educ* Harrow; *m* 1, 1938 (m dis 1942), Annette Constance, da of late Maj Francis William Massy Drew, DSO, Prince of Wales's Vols (S Lancs Regt), of Drewscourt, Cork; m 2, 1943, Janet Marion, da of John Page, of Blakeney, Norfolk; 1 s, 2 da; *Heir* s, Henry Every; *Career* Capt The Foresters; company dir; Patron of one living; *Style* - Sir John Every, Bt; Egginton, Derby (☎ Etwall 2245)

EVETTS, Hon Mrs (Susan Katharine); da of late 1 Baron Ismay; *b* 1922; *m* 1 (m dis 1946), Maj Neville Ewart Hyde Chance; 1 da; m 2, Lt-Col Michael John Evetts, MC, RHF; 2 s; *Style* - The Hon Mrs Evetts; Wormington Grange, Broadway, Worcs

EVISON, Lady Beatrix Dora; *née* Alexander; da of 1 & last Earl Alexander of Hillsborough; *b* 1909; *Educ* London U; *m* 1936, William Bernard Evison; 1 s, 1 da; *Style* - Lady Beatrix Evison; Cranleigh, 101 Old Park Ave, Enfield, Middx

EWART, Sir (William) Ivan Cecil; 6 Bt (UK 1887) of Glenmachan, Strandtown, Co Down and of Glenbank, Belfast, Co Antrim; DSC (1945), JP; s of late Maj William Basil Ewart, gs of 1 Bt; suc kinsman, Sir Talbot Ewart, 5 Bt, 1959; *b* 18 July 1919; *Educ* Radley; *m* 1948, Pauline Chevallier (d 1964), da of late Wing Cdr R Chevallier Preston, OBE, AFC, JP; 1 s, 2 da; *Heir* s William Michael Ewart; *Career* chm William Ewart and Son Ltd 1968-73, Ewart New Northern Ltd 1973-77; pres NI Chamber of Commerce and Industry 1974-; High Sheriff Co Antrim 1976; 1939-45 War as Lt RNVR (POW Germany); *Clubs* Naval; *Style* - Sir Ivan Ewart, Bt, DSC, JP; PO Box 46656, Nairobi, Kenya; Hill House, Hillsborough (☎ Hillsborough 683000)

EWART, John Walter Douglas; s of Maxwell Douglas Ewart; *b* 27 Jan 1924; *Educ* Beaumont, Old Windsor, Berks; *m* 1946, Joan Valerie, nee Hoghton; 1 da; *Career* Lt Roy Horse Gds 1942-46, High Sheriff 1977-78, md Paterson Ewart Gp Ltd 1958-70, md Carclo Engineering Gp Ltd 1973-, memb Northants County Council 1970-, memb Oxford Regional Health Authority; *Recreations* hunting and sailing; *Clubs* Cavalry and Guards, Royal London Yacht Club; *Style* - John Ewart Esq; Astrop, Banbury, Oxfordshire (☎ Banbury 811210)

EWART, William Michael; s and h of Sir Ivan Ewart, 6 Bt; *b* 10 June 1953; *Style* - William Ewart Esq

EWART-BIGGS, Baroness (Life Peeress UK 1981); Felicity Jane; *m* Christopher Thomas Ewart-Biggs, CMG, OBE (assassinated 1976), formerly in PUSD FCO and Ambass to Dublin; *aet* 51 in April 1981; *Career* sometime L candidate for GLC, memb Chelsea Labour Pty, sought selection as MEP candidate;

Pres Peace People's Movement in Britain 1977; *Style* - Rt Hon Lady Ewart-Biggs

EWEN, Peter; s of late Alexander Ewen; *b* 4 June 1903; *Educ* Merchant Taylors' Crosby; *m* 1932, Janet Howat, nee Allan; 2 da; *Career* chartered accountant 1927, chm Scruttons Ltd, dir Michelin Tyre Co Ltd; *Style* - Peter Ewen Esq; Kestor, Howton rd, Moretonhampstead, Devon (☎ 06474 307)

EWING, Vice-Adm Sir (Robert) Alastair; KBE (1962), CB (1959), DSC (1943); s of Ian Ewing (d 1971); *b* 10 April 1909; *Educ* Fernden (Haslemere), RNC Dartmouth; *m* 1940, Diana (d 1980), da of late Harry Archer; 1 s; *Career* joined RN 1923, served 1939-45; Capt 1947, Rear-Adm 1957, Capt HMS 'Vanguard' 1953-54, Naval Sec to First Lord of the Admiralty 1956-58, Flag Offr Flotillas (Mediterranean) 1958-60, Adm Cmmding Reserves and Dir of Recruiting 1960-62, ret *Clubs* Roy Yacht Sqdn; *Style* - Vice-Adm Sir Alastair Ewing, KBE, CB, DSC; PH-5, 1200 Marine Way, N Palm Beach, Florida (☎ 33408)

EWING, James Henry; CBE (1949); s of late George Brown Ewing; *b* 8 Mar 1899; *Educ* Felsted and Exeter Coll Oxford; *m* 1, 1927, Winifred Marian (d 1960), da of late Joseph Thomas Kirkby; m 2, 1961, Erika Tenzer, da of late Dr F Gossen; m 3, 1963, Marjorie Colborne, da of late Henry Robson; *Career* served 1914-18 War with Middx Regt and 1939-45 War as Lt-Col RE and assist dir of Transportation, War Office (OBE); Min of Transport rep in Japan 1946, head of Bd of Trade Supply Mission in Tokyo 1947-49; Order of Rising Sun (Japan) (3 class); *Style* - James Ewing Esq, CBE; 23 George's Wood rd, Brookman's Park, Hatfield, Herts (☎ Potter's Bar 54432)

EXETER, 6 Marquess of (UK 1801); David George Brownlow Cecil; KCMG (1943), DL (Huntingdon and Peterborough 1965); also Baron Burghley (E 1571), Earl of Exeter (E 1605); Hereditary Grand Almoner; Lord Paramount of the Soke of Peterborough; s of 5 Marquess, KG, CMG (d 1956) and Hon Myra, nee Orde-Powlett (d 1973), da of 4 Baron Bolton; *b* 9 Feb 1905; *Educ* Eton, Magdalene Cambridge; *m* 1, 1929 (m dis 1946), Lady Mary Theresa, nee Montagu Douglas Scott, da of 7 Duke of Buccleuch, KT, GCVO; 3 da; m 2, 1946, Diana Mary, da of late Hon Arnold Henderson, OBE, s of 1 Baron Faringdon, and widow of Col David Forbes; 1 da; *Heir* bro, Lord (William) Martin Alleyne Cecil; *Career* PPS to Parly Sec Miny of Supply 1939-40, Lt-Col Assist Dir Tank Supply Dept Miny of Supply 1941-42, Controller of Aircraft Repairs and Overseas Supplies Miny of Aircraft Production 1942-43, MP (C) Peterborough Northants 1931-43; Gov and CIC Bermuda 1943-45; former co dir, chm Birmid Qualcast 1946-76; former chm Br Olympic Assoc, pres Internat Olympic Assoc 1946-75, Doyen Internat Olympic Cteë (formerly v-pres), Olympic medal winner; MFH own pack 1935-39, E Sussex 1939-53, Jt Master Old Berks Hunt 1957-66; patron of 17 livings; KStJ; Rector of St Andrews U 1949-52, Mayor of Stamford 1961; *Style* - The Most Hon The Marquess of Exeter KCMG DL; 5 Empire House, Thurloe Place, SW7 (☎ 01 584 6704); Burghley House, Stamford, Lincs (☎ 3131)

EXETER, 68 Bishop of (cr 1050) 1973-; Rt Rev Eric Arthur John Mercer; s of Ambrose John Mercer, of Kent; *b* 6 Dec 1917; *Educ* Dover G S, Kelham Theol Coll; *m* 1951, Rosemary Wilma, da of John William Denby, of Barrow on Humber; 1 s, 1 da; *Career* ordained 1947, Bishop Suffragan of Birkenhead (Dioc of Chester) 1965-73; patron of 121 livings and of two alternately with the Crown, the Precentorship, Chancellorship, Treasureship, Subdeanery, 4 Canonries, and 29 Prebends in his Cathedral, and the Archdeaconries of Exeter, Totnes, Barnstaple, and Plymouth; *Style* - The Rt Rev The Lord Bishop of Exeter; The Palace, Exeter

EXMOUTH, 10 Viscount (UK 1816); Sir Paul Edward Pellew; 10 Bt (GB 1796); also Baron Exmouth (UK 1814); s of 9 Viscount (d 1970) and Maria Luisa, Marquesa de Olias (Sp cr of 1625), da of late Luis de Urquijo, Marqués de Amurrio, of Madrid; *b* 8 Oct 1940; *Educ* Downside; *m* 1, 1964 (m dis 1974), Maria

Krystina de Garay, da of late D Recaredo de Garay y Garay, of Madrid; 1 da; m 2, 1975, Rosemary Frances, da of Francis Harold Scoones MRCS LRCP JP and formerly w of Earl of Burford, *qv*; 2 s (twins); *Heir* s, Hon Edward Pellew; *Career* memb IOD, Lords Cross-Bencher; patron of one living; *Style* - The Rt Hon The Viscount Exmouth; Canonteign, nr Exeter, Devon (☎ Christow 52666)

EXMOUTH, Maria Luisa, Viscountess; Maria Luisa; also Marquesa de Olias (Sp cr 1652 of Philip IV); da of Luis de Urquijo, Marqués de Amurrio, of Madrid, by his w Marquesa de Zarreal; *m* 1, Gonzalo Alvarez-Builla (decd); m 2, 1938, 9 Viscount Exmouth (d 1970); 2 s (10 Viscount, Hon Peter Pellew), 2 da (Hon Mrs/Señora Llanso, Hon Mrs d'Erlanger); *Style* - The Rt Hon Maria Luisa, Viscountess Exmouth; Canonteign Manor, Lower Ashton, Exeter

EXTON, Rodney Noel; JP (Surrey 1968); s of Maj Noel Exton (d 1969); *b* 28 Dec 1927; *Educ* Clifton Coll, Lincoln Coll Oxford, CCC Cambridge; *m* 1961, Pamela Beresford, da of Alan Hardie, of Melbourne, Victoria, and wid of Ian Menzies Sinclair, of Glen Innes, NSW; 2 s, 2 da (all step); *Career* master Eton 1951, assist master, later housemaster Mill Hill Sch 1952-63, in Australia with NSW State Education Dept 1959-60, headmaster of Reed's Sch Cobham 1964-77, tres Soc of Head Masters of Independent Schs 1966, memb LEA Ctee 1970, ESU/HMC Page Scholar to USA 1971, memb Nat Working Pty on Disadvantaged Children 1972, HMC Rep on Br Atlantic Ctee 1974, dir ISCO 1978-; *Style* - Rodney Exton Esq, JP; Williams & Glyn's Bank (Holt's), Farnborough, Hants (☎ Camberley 21188)

EYKYN, Hon Mrs (Kathleen Sarah); *née* Vestey; da of late 2 Baron Vestey; *b* 1909; *m* 1, 1928, Maj Philip Wilfrid Cripps KRRC (m dis 1936, he d 1965); 1 s; m 2, 1936, Capt Maurice John Kingscote (m dis 1942, he d 1959); m 3, 1942, Maj Geoffrey Harbord MC (d 1953); m 4, 1955, Cdr William Canning Eykyn, RN (d 1972) *Style* - The Hon Mrs Eykyn; The Long Cottage, Sandwich, Kent; 8 Ennismore Gdns, London SW7

EYRE, Hon Mrs (Dorothy Elizabeth Anne); *née* Lyon-Dalberg-Acton; da of late 2 Baron Acton; *b* 1906; *m* 1928, Edward Eyre (d 1962); 5 s, 2 da; *Style* - The Hon Mrs Eyre; 33 Bury Walk, SW3

EYRE, Hon Mrs (Edith Joy Marion); *née* Best; da of 7 Baron Wynford; *b* 1915; *m* 1937, Cdr Walpole John Eyre, RN (ret); 1 s, 1 da; *Style* - The Hon Mrs Eyre; Sadborow, Myll, Thorncombe, Chard, Somerset

EYSTON, Lady Agnes (Marjorie Alice Mary); *née* Savile; da of late 6 Earl of Mexborough; *b* 1907; *m* 1930, Capt Thomas More Eyston, Roy Berks Regt (ka 1940); 2 s, 2 da; *Style* - Lady Agnes Eyston; Hendred House, Wantage, Oxon

EYSTON, Lady Anne Priscilla; *née* Maitland; da of late Viscount Maitland (s of 15 Earl of Lauderdale); *b* 1940; *m* 1968, John Joseph Eyston, s of Capt Thomas More Eyston (d 1940); 1 s, 2 da; *Style* - Lady Anne Eyston; Mapledurham House, Reading, Berks (☎ Kidmore End 3350)

EYSTON, John Joseph; s of Capt Thomas More Eyston (d 1940 of wounds received in action in Belgium; ggs of Charles Eyston, whose w, Agnes, was of the Blount family, long proprietors of Mapledurham House; the latter is generally conceded to have been the model for Toad Hall in 'The Wind in the Willows') and Lady Agnes Savile, da of 6 Earl of Mexborough; bro of Thomas Eyston, of East Hendred; *b* 27 April 1934; *Educ* Ampleforth, Trin Cambridge; *m* 1968, Hon (now Lady) Anne Maitland, da of Viscount Maitland (s and sometime h of 15 Earl of Lauderdale, who, however, he predeceased) and 2 cous once removed of Lady Olga Maitland, the gossip columnist; 1 s, 2 da; *Style* - John Eyston Esq; Mapledurham House, Reading (☎ 073 525 3350)

EYSTON, Thomas More; s of Thomas More Eyston, JP, and Lady Agnes Savile, da of 6 Earl of Mexborough; bro of John Eyston, of Mapledurham, *qv*; *b* 24 Dec 1931; *Educ* Ampleforth, Trin Cambridge;

Career Lord of the Manor of Arches, Abbey Manor and Catmore; *Style* - Thomas Eyston Esq; Hendred House, Wantage, Berks (☎ E Hendred 203)

EZRA, Sir Derek; MBE (1945); s of late David Ezra; *b* 23 Feb 1919; *Educ* Monmouth Sch, Magdalene Cambridge; *m* 1950, Julia Elizabeth Wilkins; *Career* memb UK Delegation to European Coal and Steel Community 1952-56, regional sales man NCB 1958-60, dir-gen marketing 1960-65, bd memb 1965-67, dep chm 1967-71, chm 1971- (salary as of June 1981 £48,000 pa); dir Sankey Building Supplies, Associated Heat Services Ltd, British Fuel Co, chm Br Inst of Management 1976-78, pres Coal Industry Soc 1981-, kt 1974; *Style* - Sir Derek Ezra, MBE; Nat Coal Bd, Hobart House, Grosvenor pla, SW1 (☎ 01 235 2020)

F

FABER, Hon Mrs (Diana Catriona); *née* Howard; da of late 3 Baron Strathcona and Mount Royal by Hon Diana, nee Loder, da of 1 Baron Wakehurst; *b* 1935; *m* 1956, Michael Leslie Ogilvy Faber; 2 s, 2 da (twins); *Style* - The Hon Mrs Faber; The Mill, Bawburgh, Norwich, Norfolk

FABER, Richard Stanley; CMG (1977); s of Sir Geoffrey Faber (d 1961); *b* 6 Dec 1924; *Educ* Westminster Sch, Ch Ch Oxford; *Career* HM Ambassador at Algiers 1977-, HM Foreign Diplomatic Serv 1950- (Baghdad, Paris, Abidjan, Washington, The Hague, Cairo); *Clubs* Travellers'; *Style* - Richard Faber Esq, CMG; c/o FCO, King Charles st, SW1

FABER, Thomas Erle; s of Sir Geoffrey Cust Faber (d 1961); *b* 25 April 1927; *Educ* Oundle Sch, Trin Coll Cambridge; *m* 1959, Penelope Marie, nee Morton; 2 s, 2 da; *Career* chm Faber & Faber (Publishers) Ltd 1976-79, lecturer in physics Cambridge U and Fellow Corpus Christi Coll Cambridge 1953-; *Recreations* shooting, fishing, walking; *Style* - Thomas Faber Esq; The Old Vicarage, Thompson's Lane, Cambridge (☎ 0223 356685)

FACEY, Mathew George Charles; s of William Facey; *b* 11 Dec 1937; *Educ* Cardiff H S for Boys; *m* 1967, Judith Ann, nee Davies; 1 s, 1 da; *Career* md SNW Ltd, Everbright Fasteners Ltd, Metric Fasteners Ltd; *Recreations* music, literature; *Club* London Welsh; *Style* - Mathew Facey Esq; The Beeches, 19 Park Road, Hampton Hill, Middlesex

FACK, Robbert; s of F W Fack (d 1963), of Amsterdam; *b* 1 Jan 1917; *Educ* Univ of Amsterdam; *m* 1943, Patricia Henshaw, da of C L Hawkins; 4 s; *Career* Netherlands Ambass to the Court of St James's and to Iceland 1976-; Min of Foreign Affairs The Hague 1945-46; New York (UN) 1946-48; various posts for Miny of Foreign Affairs (Rome, Canberra, Bonn) *Recreations* music, reading, walking; *Clubs* Dutch (London), Special Forces, Beefsteak; *Style* - HE Monsieur Robbert Fack; The Royal Netherlands Embassy, 38 Hyde Park Gate, London SW7 (☎ 01 584 5040); 8 Palace Green, Kensington, London W8 (☎ 01 937 6437)

FAGE, Prof John Donnelly; s of late Arthur Fage, CBE; *b* 3 June 1921; *Educ* Tonbridge Sch, Magdalene Cambridge; *m* 1949, Jean, nee Banister; 1 s, 1 da; *Career* sr lectr Univ Coll of the Gold Coast 1949-55, prof of History 1955-59, Dep Principal 1957-59, lectr African History London U 1959-63, dean Faculty of Arts Birmingham U 1975-78, pres African Studies Assoc of the UK 1968-69, chm Culture Advisory Ctee of UK Nat Cmmn for UNESCO 1978-, jt ed The Journal of African History 1960-73, gen ed The Cambridge History of Africa 1975-, dir Centre of W African Studies and prof of African History U of Birmingham 1963- *Clubs* Athenaeum; *Style* - Prof John Fage; 17 Antringham gdns, Birmingham, B15 3QL (☎ 021 455 0020)

FAGG, William Buller; CMG (1967); s of William Percy Fagg (d 1934); *b* 28 Apr 1914; *Educ* Dulwich Coll, Magdalene Cambridge; *Career* ethnologist, tribal art historian and consultant, writer; keeper Dept of Ethnography, British Museum 1969- (assist keeper 1938-55, dep keeper 1955-69), consultant on tribal art to Christie's 1974- hon sec Royal Anthropological Inst 1939-56, v pres 1969-72, hon ed Man 1947-65; *Recreations* photography, music, cycling, travel; *Style* - William Fagg Esq, CMG; 6 Galata Road, Barnes, SW13 9NQ (☎ 01 748 6620)

FAGGE, John Christopher; s and h of Sir John Fagge, 11 Bt; *b* 30 April 1942; *Style* - John Fagge Esq

FAGGE, Sir John William Frederick; 11 Bt (E 1660); s of late Archibald Theodore Fagge, 4 s of 8 Bt; suc unc, Sir John Harry Lee Fagge, 10 Bt, 1940; *b* 25 Sept 1910; *m* 1940, Ivy Gertrude, da of William Edward Frier, of Newington, Kent; 1 s, 1 da; *Heir* s, John Christopher Fagge; *Career* farmer; *Style* - Sir John Fagge, Bt; 26 The Mall, Faversham, Kent

FAIRBAIRN, Sir (James) Brooke; 6 Bt (UK 1869), of Ardwick, Lancashire; s of Sir William Fairbairn, 5 Bt (d 1972); *b* 10 Dec 1930; *Educ* Stowe; *m* 1960, Mary, da of Dr William Russell Scott, MB, ChB, FFARCS; 2 s, 1 da; *Heir* s, Robert Fairbairn; *Career* proprietor of J Brooke Fairbairn & Co, of Newmarket (furnishers & fabric converters) *Club* City Livery *Style* - Sir Brooke Fairbairn, Bt; (business) The Railway Station, Newmarket, Suffolk (☎ 0638 5766); Barkway House, Bury rd, Newmarket, Suffolk (☎ 0638 2733)

FAIRBAIRN, Hon Sir David Eric; KBE (1977), DFC (1944); s of Clive Prell Fairbairn of NSW Australia (d 1961); *b* 3 Mar 1917; *Educ* Geelong G S Corio Victoria, Jesus Cambridge; *m* 1945, Ruth Antill, da of late Dr Robert Affleck Robertson, of NSW; 3 da *Career* farmer, politician, diplomat, memb House of Reps 1949-75, minister for Air 1962-64, minster for Nat Dvpt 1964-69, minister for Education and Science 1971, minister for Defence 1971-72, Australian Ambassador to the Netherlands 1977-80; *Recreations* golf; *Clubs* Melbourne, Commonwealth (Canberra), Hawks (Cambridge), Leander; *Style* - Hon Sir David Fairbairn, KBE, DFC; 2/3 Tasmania Circle, Forrest, ACT Canberra, Australia (☎ Canberra 951229); Dunraven, Thurgoona, via Albury, NSW (☎ Table Top 262254)

FAIRBAIRN, Hon Mrs Elizabeth Mary; *née* Mackay; da of 13 Lord Reay; *b* 21 June 1938; *m* 1962, Nicholas Fairbairn, QC, MP (m dis 1979); 3 da; *Style* - The Hon Mrs Elizabeth Fairbairn

FAIRBAIRN, Nicholas Hardwick; QC (Scotland 1972), MP (C) Kinross & Perths W Oct 1974-; s of William Fairbairn and Mary More-Gordon; *b* 24 Dec 1933; *Educ* Loretto, Edinburgh U; *m* 1962, Hon Elizabeth Mackay (m dis 1979), da of 13 Lord Reay; 3 s (and 1 s & 1 da decd); *Career* Capt RA (TA); Commissioner N Lighthouses 1979-; Slr-Gen (Scot) 1979-; holder of territorial Barony of Fordell; Hon Pres Soc Preservation Duddington Village; chm Traverse Theatre Edinburgh 1964-72; *Recreations* excellence; *Clubs* Beefsteak, Buck's, Puffin's, New (both Edinburgh); *Style* - Nicholas Fairbairn Esq, QC, MP; 21 Roupell st, SE1; Fordell Castle, By Dunfermline, Fife (☎ 0383 828311)

FAIRBAIRN, Sir Robert Duncan; JP (Glasgow 1962); s of late Robert Fairbairn; *b* 25 Sept 1910; *Educ* Perth Acad; *m* 1939, Sylvia Lucinda, da of late Rev Henry Coulter; 2 s, 1 da; *Career* chm Clydesdale Bank Ltd 1975-, dir Scottish Amicable Life Assurance Soc (formerly chm), Midland Bank Ltd, former dir British National Oil Corpn, pres Inst of Bankers in Scotland 1961-63, kt 1975; *Recreations* golf, fishing; *Clubs* Caledonian, MCC, Western (Glasgow), Corinthian Casuals, Roy and Ancient (St Andrews); *Style* - Sir Robert Fairbairn, JP; The Grange, Hazelwood, Bridge of Weir, Renfrewshire (☎ Bridge of Weir 612102)

FAIRBAIRN, Robert William; s and h of Sir Brooke Fairbairn, 6 Bt; *b* 10 April 1965; *Educ* King's Sch Ely; *Style* - Robert Fairbairn Esq

FAIRBAIRN, Hon Mrs; Hon Susan; *née* Hill; da of Baron Hill of Luton, PC (Life Peer); *b* 1936; *m* 1958, David Ritchie Fairbairn; *Style* - The Hon Mrs Fairbairn; 7 Marlow Mills, Mill Lane, Marlow, Bucks

FAIRBANKS, Douglas (Elton) (Jr); Hon KBE (1949), DSC (1944); s of Douglas Fairbanks (Sr); *b* 9 Dec 1909; *Educ* Bovée Sch, Knickerbocker Greys Mil Sch, Harvard Military, Polytechnic (New York and Los Angeles); *m* 1939, Mary Lee Epling; 3 da; *Career* theatre, cinema and television actor; producer; writer, sculptor and painter; former v-pres Franco-British War Relief and nat v-pres Ctee 'Defend America by Aiding the Allies' 1939-40, former Presidential Envoy; Capt USNR, ret; chm Douglas Fairbanks Ltd, Fairtel Inc (US), Boltons Trading Co, Inc and dir other cos; KStJ 1950; has received a great number of foreign decorations; *Style* - Douglas Fairbanks Esq, KBE, DSC; The Vicarage, 448 North Lake Way, Palm Beach, Florida 33480, USA; 575 Park av, New York, NY 10021, USA; c/o Miss E Noll, 32 South Eaton pla, London SW1

FAIRCHILD, Roy Dormer; s of Percy Wilfred Fairchild; *b* 23 April 1933; *Educ* Spring Grove G S; *m* 1956, Gilda Mary, nee Rook; 1 s, 3 da; *Career* accountant (FCCA, FCMA, FCT), gp fin dir Colt Int & Assoc Cos Ltd 1972-, dir High Speed Tool Co Ltd 1978-; *Recreations* cycle racing (memb Veterans Time Trials Assoc); *Style* - Roy Fairchild Esq; Pennyfarthing, Kingsway, Craigweil-on-Sea, W Sussex PO21 4DQ (☎ Pagham 3023)

FAIRFAX OF CAMERON, 14 Lord (S 1627); Nicholas John Albert Fairfax; s of 13 Lord (d 1964, ninth in descent from the bro of the 2 Lord, who defeated Rupert at Marston Moor, and unc of the 3 Lord, who as CIC of the Parliamentarians was the victor of Naseby); *b* 4 Jan 1956; *Educ* Eton, Downing Cambridge; *Heir* bro, Hon Hugh Fairfax; *Career* barr; *Clubs* Queen's; *Style* - The Rt Hon The Lord Fairfax of Cameron; 159 Ebury st, SW1 (☎ 01 730 2955)

FAIRFAX, Hon Rupert Alexander James; s of 13 Lord Fairfax of Cameron (d 1964) and bro of 14 Lord; *b* 21 Jan 1961; *Style* - The Hon Rupert Fairfax

FAIRFAX OF CAMERON, Lady; Sonia Helen; JP (Berks 1957); da of Capt Cecil Gunston, MC (er bro of Sir Derrick Gunston, 1 Bt), by his w Lady Doris Hamilton-Temple-Blackwood (herself da of 2 Marquess of Dufferin and Ava); Lady Fairfax of Cameron is sis of Mrs Geoffrey Luttrell, formerly châtelaine of Dunster Castle; *m* 1951, 13 Lord Fairfax of Cameron (d 1964); 3 s (including 14 Lord), 1 da (Hon Mrs Bell); *Career* temp Lady of the Bedchamber to HM 1967-71; *Style* - The Rt Hon Lady Fairfax of Cameron JP; Gay's House, Holyport, Maidenhead, Berks

FAIRFAX-LUCY, Duncan Cameron Ramsay-; s of late Capt Ewen Aymer Robert Ramsay-Fairfax-Lucy; hp of kinsman, Sir Edmund Ramsay-Fairfax-Lucy, 6 Bt; *b* 18 Sept 1932; *m* 1964, Janet Barclay, da of P A B Niven; 1 s, 1 da; *Career* FCA; *Style* - Duncan Ramsay-Fairfax-Lucy Esq; Cage Green Farm, Shipburne rd, Tonbridge, Kent

FAIRFAX-LUCY, Sir Edmund John William Hugh Ramsay-; 6 Bt (UK 1836); s of Maj Sir Brian Fulke Ramsay-Fairfax-Lucy, 5 Bt (d 1974) and Hon Alice, nee Buchan, da of 1 Baron Tweedsmuir GCMG GCVO CH PC; *b* 4 May 1945; *Educ* Eton; *m* 1974, Sylvia, da of Graeme Ogden, of The Old Manor, Rudge, Somerset; *Heir* kinsman, Duncan Cameron Ramsay-Fairfax-Lucy; *Style* - Sir Edmund Ramsay-Fairfax-Lucy, Bt; Charlecote Park, Warwick

FAIRHAVEN, 3 Baron (UK 1961); Ailwyn Henry George Broughton; JP (Bottisham 1975), DL (Cambridgeshire and Isle of Ely); s of 2 Baron (d 1973) and Hon Diana, da of Capt Hon Coulson Fellowes (s of 2 Baron De Ramsey, JP, DL, and Lady Rosamond, nee Spencer-Churchill, da of 7 Duke of Marlborough, KG); *b* 16 Nov 1936; *Educ* Eton, RMA Sandhurst; *m* 1960, Kathleen Patricia, da of Col James Henry Magill, OBE; 4 s; 2 da; *Heir* s, Hon James Broughton; *Career* Vice Lord-Lt Cambridgeshire 1977-; *Style*

- The Rt Hon The Lord Fairhaven, JP, HM Vice Lord-Lieut for Cambridgeshire; Anglesey Abbey, Cambridge (☎ 811746)

FAIRHAVEN, Joyce, Baroness; Joyce Irene; da of Edward Miller; *m* 1, Lt Gerald Dickens, RN (decd); m 2, 1952, as his 2 w, 2 Baron Fairhaven (d 1973); *Style* - The Rt Hon Joyce, Lady Fairhaven; S Walsham, Norwich

FAIRLIE OF MYRES, Capt David Ogilvy; JP (Fife 1981), DL (1975); s of James Ogilvy Fairlie of Myres (d 1960); *b* 1 Oct 1923; *Educ* Ampleforth Coll, Oriel Oxford; *m* 1969, Ann Constance, da of late Dermot Francis Bolger, of Madeira *Career* Capt Roy Signals, army offr 1943-59, Cupar district commr for Scouts 1960-66, Co Cmmr for Scouts 1966-; *Recreations* hill walking, photography, beekeeping, shooting, sailing; *Clubs* Army & Navy, Roy Overseas, Roy & Ancient; *Style* - Capt David Fairlie of Myres, JP, DL; Quinta Da Alegria, São Rogud, Funchal, Madeira; Myres Castle, Auchtermuchty, Cupar, Fife (☎ 033 72 350)

FAIRLIE-CUNINGHAME, Sir William Alan; 15 Bt (NS 1630), of Robertland, Ayrshire, MC; s of late Sir William Edward Fairlie-Cuninghame (who assumed surname of Fairlie-Cuninghame in lieu of his patronymic Cuningham); suc bro, Sir Hussey Burgh Fairlie-Cuninghame, 14 Bt, 1939; *b* 31 Jan 1893; *Educ* Sydney U; *m* 1929, Irene Alice (d 1970), da of late Henry Margrave Terry; 1 s; *Heir* s, William Henry Fairlie-Cuninghame; *Career* served WW I (MC); former Lt Australian Forces (Res); former master St John's Sch Vaucluse Sydney, research offr C'wlth Scientific and Industrial Research Org (Metrology Div) 1943-58; *Style* - Sir William Fairlie-Cuninghame Bt MC; 62 Farrer Brown ct, Nuffield Village, Castle Hill, NSW 2154, Australia

FAIRLIE-CUNINGHAME, William Henry; s and h of Sir William Fairlie-Cuninghame, 15 Bt, MC; *b* 1 Oct 1930; *m* 1972, Janet Menzies, da of late Roy Menzies Saddington; 1 s; *Style* - William Fairlie-Cuninghame Esq; 29A Orinoco rd, Pymble, New South Wales, Australia

FAIRN, Duncan; s of Percy Frederick Fairn (decd 1941); *b* 1 June 1906; *Educ* Battersea County Sch, LSE; *m* 1930, Marion Cristina, nee Sturrock; 1 s (decd); *Career* teacher and prison official, warden York Educnl Settlement 1930-38, Prison Gov 1938-48, prison cmmr 1955-63, Assist Under-Sec of State in Charge of Prisons 1964-67, Lord Chancellor's Training Offr 1967-72 UK delegate to UN Socl Dvpt Cmmn 1967-71; *Recreations* reading, walking, music and people; *Clubs* Authors'; *Style* - Duncan Fairn Esq; Lavender Cottage, 82 Paines Lane, Pinner, Middlesex (☎ 01 866 9650)

FAIRTLOUGH, Gerard Howard; s of late Maj-Gen Eric Fairtlough, DSO, MC; *b* 5 Sept 1930; *Educ* Marlborough, King's Cambridge; *m* 1954, Elizabeth Ann, nee Betambeau; 2 s, 2 da; *Career* Lt RA, md Shell UK Ltd 1974-78, div dir NEB 1978-80, ch exec Celltech Ltd 1980-; *Recreations* walking, theatre, yoga; *Style* - Gerard Fairtlough Esq; 5 Belmont Grove, SE13 (☎ 01 852 4904)

FAIRWEATHER, Brig Claude Cyril; CB (1967), CBE (1965, OBE 1944), TD (1944), JP (N Yorks 1963), DL (1949); s of late Nicholas Fairweather; *b* 17 March 1906; *Educ* St Peter's Sch York; *m* 1930, Alice Mary, da of late Sir William Crosthwaite, JP; 1 s, 1 da; *Career* 2 Lt Roy Corps of Signals 1928, Lt-Col 1941, Col 1943, Brig 1945, CSO Wingate Exp 1943-44, CSO 34 Ind Corps 1944-45, Hon Col 34 (N) Signal Regt (V) 1967-75, former chm N Riding T&AFA and memb TA Ctees, chm N of England TAVRA 1968-71, Cdr N Yorks St John Ambulance Bde 1972-77 (formerly Co Cmmr N Riding), chm Order of St John Cncl 1977-, KStJ 1978 (OStJ 1967, CStJ 1974), chm Cleveland Area Health Authority 1973-76, chm St Luke's Hosp Management Ctee 1959-74; *Recreations* golf, cricket, rugby football; *Clubs* Army and Navy, Cleveland (Middlesbrough), Roy and Ancient (St Andrews); *Style* - Brig Claude Fairweather CB CBE TD JP DL; The White Lodge, Hutton Rudby, Yarm, Cleveland

FAITH, (Irene) Sheila, JP (Inner London 1978), LDS, MP (C) Belper 1979-; da of late Isaac Book; *b* 3 June 1928; *Educ*

Central H S Newcastle, Durham U (LDS); *m* 1950, Dennis Faith; *Career* dental surgeon; memb Northumberland CC 1970-74, contested Newcastle Central Oct 1974, memb Newcastle City Council 1975-77, JP Northumberland 1972-74, Newcastle 1974-78, memb Select Ctee on Health and Soc Services 1979, on Unopposed Bills 1980-; *Clubs* United and Cecil; *Style* - Mrs Dennis Faith, JP, MP; 2 North Wood Lodge, Oak Hill pk, NW3 (☎ 01 435 3365)

FAITHFULL, Baroness (Life Peeress UK 1975); Lucy Faithfull; OBE (1972); da of late Sydney Leigh Faithfull; *b* 26 Dec 1910; *Educ* Bournemouth H S, Birmingham U; *Career* memb LCC 1935-40, Min of Health 1940-48, inspr Home Office (Children's Branch) 1948-58, children's offr Oxford City 1958-70, dir of Social Services Oxford 1970-74, memb Cncl and Exec Fin Ctee Dr Barnardo's; *Style* - The Rt Hon The Lady Faithfull, OBE; 303 Woodstock rd, Oxford (☎ 55389)

FALCON, Michael Gascoigne; CBE (1979), JP (Norfolk 1967); s of Michael Falcon (d 1976); *b* 28 Jan 1928; *Educ* Stowe, Heriot Watt Coll; *m* 1954, April Daphne Claire, nee Lambert; 2 s, 1 da; *Career* former head brewer and jt md E Lacon & Co Gt Yarmouth, exec dir Edgar Watts (Bungay Suffolk) 1968-73, dir Securicor East Ltd 1969-72, tstee E Anglian Tstee Savings Bank 1963-75, chm Norwich Union Insurance Gp 1981- (dir 1963, v-chm 1979), chm Lloyds Bank Eastern Counties Regional Bd 1979- (dir 1972-), dir Lloyds Bank UK Management Ltd 1979-, chm Nat Seed Dvpt Org Ltd 1972-, chm Pauls & Whites Ltd 1976- (dir 1973-), High Sheriff of Norfolk 1979-80, OStJ 1968; *Recreations* country pursuits; *Clubs* Norfolk County, MCC, Roy Norfolk and Suffolk Yacht, Farmers; *Style* - Michael Gascoigne Esq, CBE, JP; Keswick Old Hall, Norwich, Norfolk (☎ 54348); Kirkgate, Loweswater, Cockermouth, Cumbria (☎ Lorton 271); Lloyds Bank Ltd, 16 Gentleman's Walk, Norwich

FALCONER OF HALKERTON, Lordship (S 1646); *see* Falconer, Peter Serrell

FALCONER, Hon Mr Justice; Hon Sir Douglas William Falconer; MBE (1946); s of late William Falconer; *b* 20 Sept 1914; *Educ* Westoe S Shields, King's Coll Durham U; *m* 1941, Joan Beryl Argent, da of late Archibald Samuel Bishop; 1 s, 1 da; *Career* barr 1950, QC 1967, bencher Middle Temple 1972, appointed to exercise appellate jurisdiction of BOT under Trade Marks Act 1970, member Standing Advsy Ctee on Patents 1975-79, on Trade Marks 1975-79, chm Patent Bar Assoc 1971-80, memb Senate of Four Inns of Court 1973-74, of Four Inns of Court and Bar 1974-77, a Judge of High Court of Justice 1981-; *Recreations* music, theatre; *Style* - The Hon Mr Justice Falconer, MBE; Ridgewell House, West Street, Reigate, Sussex (☎ 44374); 6 Pump ct, Temple, EC4 (☎ 01 353 8588)

FALCONER, Peter Serrell; s of Thomas Falconer, FRIBA (eighth in descent from Patrick Falconer of Newton, unc of 1 Lord Falconer of Halkerton, S Lordship cr 1646, which was subsequently held by the Earls of Kintore, with the death of the tenth of whom in 1966 the Lordship became dormant; Peter is the presumed heir); *b* 7 March 1916; *Educ* Bloxham; *m* 1941, Mary, da of Rev C Hodson; 3 s (Thomas b 1946, Richard b 1949, William b 1952), 1 da (Caroline b 1942 m Maj Paul Weller); *Career* FRIBA; *Style* - Peter Falconer Esq; St Francis, Minchinhampton, Glos

FALKENDER, Baroness (Life Peeress UK 1974); Marcia Matilda Falkender; CBE (1970); da of Harry Field; assumed by deed poll 1974 surname Falkender in lieu of Williams; *b* 1932; *Educ* Queen Mary Coll London U; *m* 1955 (m dis 1960), George Edmund Charles Williams; *Career* sec to Morgan Phillips (Gen Sec of Labour Pty) 1955-56, Private Sec to Rt Hon Sir Harold Wilson, KG, OBE, MP 1956-; *Style* - The Rt Hon The Lady Falkender, CBE; 3 Wyndham Mews, Upper Montagu st, W1

FALKINER, Edmond Charles; s and h of Sir Terence Falkiner, 8 Bt; *b* 24 June 1938; *m* 1960, Janet Iris, da of Arthur Edward Bruce Darby, of The Park, Stoke Lacey, Bromyard, Herefords; 2 s; *Style* - Edmond Falkiner Esq; 37 Salisbury rd,

Barnet, Herts

FALKINER, Lt-Col Sir Terence Edmond Patrick; 8 Bt (I 1778), DL (Herefords); s of Sir Leslie Falkiner, 7 Bt (d 1917) by Kathleen (gda of 3 Baron Bolton) *b* 17 March 1903 *Educ* Oratory Sch Birmingham; *m* 1925, Mildrede, da of Sir John Cotterell, 4 Bt; 2 s, 3 da; *Heir* s, Edmond Falkiner; *Career* Captain Coldstream Gds 1934, Maj 1940, Lt-Col 1942, asst mil sec Eastern Command 1948-51, Southern Command 1951-55, ret; KStJ; *Style* - Lt-Col Sir Terence Falkiner, Bt, DL; Kingsthorne House, Hereford (☎ Wormelow 343)

FALKLAND, 14 Viscount (S 1620); Lucius Henry Charles Plantagenet Cary; also 14 Lord Carye (S 1620); s of 13 Viscount (d 1961); *b* 25 Jan 1905; *Educ* Eton; *m* 1, 1926 (m dis 1933), Joan Sylvia, da of Capt Charles Bonham Southey, of Frinton-on-Sea; 2 da; m 2, 1933 (m dis 1958), Constance Mary, da of late Capt Edward Berry; 1 s; m 3, 1958 (m dis 1974), Charlotte Anne, da of late Bevil Granville, of Chadley, Wellesbourne, Warwick; *Heir* s, Master of Falkland; *Career* Flying Offr RAFVR 1941-45 (invalided); *Style* - The Rt Hon The Viscount Falkland; 18 Tower Park, Fowey, Cornwall (☎ 3211)

FALKLAND, Master of; Hon Lucius Edward William Plantagenet Cary; s (by 2 m) and h of 14 Viscount Falkland; *b* 8 May 1935; *Educ* Wellington; *m* 1962, Caroline Anne, da of late Lt-Cdr Gerald Butler, DSC, RN; 1 s, 2 da (and 1 da decd); *Career* ch exec C T Bowring Trading (Hldgs) Ltd; *Style* - The Master of Falkland; Court House, Winchfield, nr Basingstoke, Hants (☎ Hartley Wintney 3273)

FALKNER, Sir (Donald) Keith; s of late John Charles Falkner; *b* 1 March 1900; *Educ* New Coll Sch, Perse Sch, RCM, private study Berlin, Vienna, Paris; *m* 1930, Christabel Margaret, da of Thomas Fletcher Fullard; 2 da; *Career* assist lay vicar St Paul's Cathedral 1922-26, singer 1923-40, music offr British Cncl Italy 1946-50, Prof of Music Cornell U, NY, USA 1950-60, dir RCM 1960-74; kt 1967; *Recreations* past- all ball games; present- golf, gardening; *Clubs* Athenaeum, MCC, Free Foresters, RAC; *Style* - Sir Keith Falkner; Low Cottages, Ilketshall St Margaret, Bungay, Suffolk (☎ 0986 2573)

FALLA, Paul Stephen; s of late Brig Norris Stephen Falla, CMG, DSO, of Wellington, New Zealand; *b* 25 Oct 1913; *Educ* Wellington and Christ's Coll New Zealand, Balliol Oxford; *m* 1958, Elizabeth Mary, nee Herzfeld; 1 da; *Career* HM Foreign Service 1936-67, counsellor (FO, FCO) 1950-, Dep Dir of Research 1958-67, ed Oxford English-Russian Dictionary 1967-; translator of about 40 books on politics, history, art, etc; *Recreations* reading (history, politics, philosophy, belles-lettres), studying languages; *Clubs* Travellers'; *Style* - Paul Falla Esq; 63 Freelands rd, Bromley, Kent (☎ 01 460 4995)

FALLER, John Benson; s of Albert Faller (d 1967); *b* 26 Sept 1921; *Educ* Downside Sch, Jesus Coll Cambridge; *m* 1947, Mary, nee Sheridan; 1 s (decd), 2 da; *Career* chm Henry W Peabody Grain Ltd and its subsidiaries; *Recreations* shooting; *Clubs* Boodle's, City Univ, MCC; *Style* - John Faller Esq; Benton House, Worplesdon Hill, Surrey

FALMOUTH, 9 Viscount (GB 1720); George Hugh Boscawen; also 26 Baron Le Despencer (E 1264) and Baron Boscawen-Rose (GB 1720); s of 8 Viscount (d 1962); *b* 31 Oct 1919; *Educ* Eton, Trin Cambridge; *m* 1953, Elizabeth, da of A H Browne, of W Peckham; 4 s; *Heir* s, Hon Evelyn Boscawen; *Career* Patron of 5 livings; Capt Coldstream Gds; Ld-Lt for Cornwall 1977- (DL 1968); *Style* - The Rt Hon The Viscount Falmouth, HM Lord-Lieut for Cornwall; Tregothnan, Truro, Cornwall; Buston, Hunton, Kent

FALMOUTH, Dowager Viscountess; Mary Margaret Désirée; *née* Meynell; CBE (1946); da of Hon Frederick Meynell (né Wood but took name Meynell instead 1905), 4 s of 1 Viscount Halifax; *b* 25 Oct 1894; *Educ* privately; *m* 1915, 8 Viscount Falmouth (d 1962); 3 s (9 Viscount, Hon Henry & Robert Boscawen) and 1 s decd, 1 da (Hon Mrs Verney); *Career* memb Br Red Cross Soc & VAD 1914-19 also Red

Cross 1939-52, chm Centl Hosp Supply Serv & Overseas Relief Serv; late V-Chm Con Pty Orgn 1929-38, Cncl Overseas Br Voluntary Servs; *Style* - Rt Hon Dowager Viscountess Falmouth CBE; 28 Chelsea sq, SW3 (☎ 01 352 4272)

FANE, Hon Mrs Mountjoy; Agatha Isabel; da of Lt-Col Arthur Acland-Hood-Reynardson, OBE (2 s of Sir Alexander Fuller-Acland-Hood, 3 Bt); *b* 3 Oct 1903; *m* 1926, Lt-Col Hon Mountjoy Fane, TD (d 1963, s of 14 Earl of Westmorland); 1 s, 1 da; *Style* - The Hon Mrs Mountjoy Fane; The Thatched House, Teigh, Oakham, Leics

FANE, Lady Camilla Diana; da of 15 Earl of Westmorland; *b* 26 Dec 1957; *Style* - Lady Camilla Fane

FANE, Lady Gloria Sybil; da of 13 Earl of Westmorland, CBE, JP, by his 1 w, Lady Sybil St Clair-Erskine, da of 4 Earl of Rosslyn; *b* 11 April 1902; *Style* - Lady Gloria Fane

FANE, Hon Harry St Clair; 2 s of 15 Earl of Westmorland; *b* 19 March 1953; *Educ* Harrow; *Career* Page of Honour to HM 1966-68, hp to bro Lord Burghersh; *Style* - The Hon Harry Fane

FANE, Hon Julian Charles; s of 14 Earl of Westmorland; *b* 25 May 1927; *Educ* Harrow; *m* 1976, Gillian, yr da of John Kidston Swire and sis of John and Adrian Swire of the Far East trading empire; *Style* - The Hon Julian Fane; 32 Blenheim ter, NW8

FANE, Julian Francis; s of Lt Francis Fane, RN (4 in descent from Hon Henry Fane, MP, 2 s of 8 Earl of Westmorland); *b* 2 Oct 1938; *Educ* Marlborough, Emmanuel Cambridge; *m* 1965, Julia, da of Michael Allday; 1 s, 1 da; *Career* High Sheriff Lincs 1981; *Style* - Julian Fane Esq; Fulbeck Manor, Grantham, Lincs

FANE, Col Julian Patrick; MC (1940) and Bar (1945); s of Col Cecil Fane, CMG, DSO (d 1960); *b* 17 Feb 1921; *Educ* Stowe, RMA Sandhurst; *m* 1, 1949, Lady Ann Mary Lowther, (d 1956), da of Anthony Edward, Viscount Lowther, s of 6 Earl of Lonsdale; 1 s, 1 da; m 2, 1959, Diane Ewart, da of Ivan Hill; 1 s, 1 da; *Career* 2 Lt Gloucestershire Regt 1939, 2 Bn GHQ Liaison Regt and Staff (despatches) WW II, 12 Roy Lancers 1946, Life Gds 1960, ret 1969; former dir Samuel Montagu & Co Ltd, currently dir Orion Bank Ltd; *Recreations* shooting, riding, art collecting; *Style* - Col Julian Fane, MC*; Ives Farm, Stratfield Saye, Reading, Berks (☎ Turgis Green 241)

FANE, Vere John Alexander; s of late John Fane; *b* 21 April 1935; *Educ* Eton, Trin Cambridge; *m* 1964, Tessa Helen Murray, nee Prain; 1 s, 1 da; *Career* Lt Coldstream Gds, chm Wallace Bros & Co (Hldgs); *Recreations* shooting; *Clubs* White's, Pratt's, City of London; *Style* - Vere Fane Esq; 14 Craven Hill Mews, W2

FANE DE SALIS, Gp Capt Arthur Regester; OBE (1944), DL (Worcs 1963); s of Sir Cecil Fane De Salis KCB (d 1948, gs of Peter John, 5 Count De Salis, by Peter's 3 wife Henrietta, da of Rt Rev William Foster, sometime Bp of Kilmore); *b* 18 Nov 1911; *Educ* Stowe, Trin Coll Cambridge; *m* 1937, Nancy Mary, da of Cdr Gerald Hubbard Welch, RN (d 1928); 1 s, 1 da; *Career* joined RAF 1935, served 1939-45 S Rhodesia 1940, W Desert AF 1942, 2 TAF 1944, Gp Capt 1945 (ret 1957), County Cmmr Worcs Scouts 1963-75; *Style* - Gp Capt Arthur Fane De Salis OBE DL; Turret House, Hampton Lovett, Droitwich, Worcs (☎ Droitwich 3261)

FANE TREFUSIS, Hon Caroline Harriet; da of 22 Baron Clinton; *b* 1960; *Style* - The Hon Caroline Fane Trefusis

FANE TREFUSIS, Hon Charles Patrick Rolle; s and h of 22 Baron Clinton; *b* 21 March 1962; *Style* - The Hon Charles Fane Trefusis

FANE TREFUSIS, Hon Henrietta Jane; da of 22 Baron Clinton; *b* 1964; *Style* - The Hon Henrietta Fane Trefusis

FANE-SAUNDERS, Bernard; CBE (1954); s of William Henry Fane-Saunders (d 1916); *b* 24 Jan 1906; *Educ*

Cheltenham, Trin Hall Cambridge; *m* 1930, Ellis Mary, nee Chevers; 2 s; *Career* chm Pakistan Tobacco Co 1949-56, pres UK Assoc of Pakistan 1953-56, pres Assoc Chambers of Commerce of Pakistan, chm Karachi Chamber of Commerce 1954-55; *Style* - Bernard Fane-Saunders Esq, CBE; 17 Carlyle Mansions, Cheyne Walk, SW3 (☎ 01 352 9998)

FANSHAWE, Hon Mrs (Maura Clare); *née* Evans-Freke; da of 11 Baron Carbery; *b* 13 Sept 1946; *m* 1966, Richard Henry William Fanshawe; *Style* - The Hon Mrs Fanshawe; 30 Bark pla, W2

FANSHAWE, Capt Peter Evelyn; CBE (1966, OBE 1946), DSC (1952); s of Capt Guy Dalrymple Fanshawe, RN (d 1962); *b* 13 Sept 1911; *Educ* Twyford Sch nr Winchester, RN Coll Dartmouth; *m* 1936, Helen Mary, da of Maj S W Trafford (d 1953); 1 s (Richard Henry William b 1939, m 1966 The Hon Maura Claire Evans-Freke, da of 11 Baron Carbery), 1 da (Veronica Evelyn b 1947, m 1977 Maj Charles Napier St Pierre Bunbury); *Career* POW Germany 1940-45, cmd HMS Amethyst 1950-52, cmd Royal Australian Naval Air Station Nowra NSW 1955-57, Naval Staff Admiralty 1959-61, Naval Assist to Naval Sec MOD 1962-66, currently Sec of Royal Naval Club of 1765-1785 (United 1889); *Recreations* gardening, yachting (Freeward 25 'Elf'); *Clubs* Army and Navy, Royal Yacht Squadron (Naval Member); *Style* - Capt Peter Fanshawe, CBE, DSC, RN; 12 Lincoln av, Wimbledon, SW19 (☎ 01 947 1323)

FARAM, Hon Mrs (Felicity Lila); *née* Wallace; da of Baroness Dudley and late Guy Wallace; *b* 1944; *m* 1967, Philip Neil Faram; 3 s; *Style* - The Hon Mrs Faram; Heath Hill, Queen Hill, Upton-on-Severn, Worcs

FARINGDON, 3 Baron (UK 1916); Sir Charles Michael Henderson; 3 Bt (UK 1902); s of late Lt-Col the Hon Michael Thomas Henderson, 16/5 Lancers, 2 s of 1 Baron; suc unc 1977; *b* 3 July 1937; *Educ* Eton, Trin Cambridge; *m* 1959, Sarah, da of Maj John Marjoribanks Askew and Lady Susan Askew, *qv*; 3 s, 1 da; *Heir* s, Hon James Henderson; *Style* - The Rt Hon The Lord Faringdon; Barnsley Park, Cirencester, Glos; Buscot Park, Faringdon, Oxon

FARMBROUGH, Ven David John; s of late Charles Septimus Farmbrough; *b* 4 May 1929; *Educ* Bedford, Lincoln Coll Oxford; *m* 1955, Angela Priscilla, da of Walter Adam Hill; 1 s, 3 da; *Career* deacon 1953, priest 1954, priest-in-charge St John's Hatfield 1957-63, vicar of Bishop's Stortford 1963-74, archdeacon of St Albans 1974-; *Recreations* sailing, gardening; *Style* - The Ven The Archdeacon of St Albans; 6 Sopwell lane, St Albans, Herts (☎ 57973)

FARMER, Hugh Robert Macdonald; CB (1967); s of Charles Edward Farmer (d 1935); *b* 3 Dec 1907; *Educ* Cheam, Eton, New Coll Oxford; *m* 1, 1934, Penelope Frances, nee Boothby, (d 1963); 1 s, 3 da; m 2, 1966, Jean, widow of Peter Bluett Winch; *Career* assist clerk House of Commons 1931, sr clerk 1943; clerk of Private Bills 1958-60, clerk of ctees 1960-65, clerk/administrator 1965-72; *Recreations* golf and gardening; *Clubs* MCC; *Style* - Hugh Farmer Esq, CB; Grayswood Cottage, Haslemere, Surrey

FARNDALE, Maj-Gen Martin Baker; CB (1980); s of Alfred Farndale, of Leyburn, N Yorks; *b* 6 Jan 1929; *Educ* Yorebridge Sch Yorks, RMA Sandhurst; *m* 1955, Margaret Anne, da of late Percy Robert Buckingham; 1 s; *Career* RA 1948, command First Regt RHA 1969-71, Sec Defence Policy Staff 1971-73, Cdr 7 Armoured Bde 1973-75, Dir Public Relations (Army) 1975-78, Dir Military Operations 1978-80, GOC 2 Armoured Div British Army of the Rhine 1980-; *Recreations* gardening, military history; *Clubs* E India, Sports, Public Schs and Devonshire; *Style* - Maj-Gen Martin Farndale, CB; c/o Lloyds Bank, 6 Pall Mall, SW1

FARNELL, Alan Chaffer; s of late William Sugden Farnell, of Birkenshaw, Bradford; *b* 9 March 1904; *Educ* Giggleswick Sch; *m* 1933, Pamela, da of late Ernest Bridge; 3 s; *Career* Flying Offr RAF, chm Farnell Electronics Ltd group of cos 1966-76, Life President 1976-; *Recreations* foreign travel; *Style* - Alan Farnell Esq; Apartado 101, A Vista de Pájaro, (Urb) La Noria, Mijas (Malaga), Spain (☎ Malaga 48 53 56)

FARNHAM, 12 Baron (I 1756); Sir Barry Owen Somerset Maxwell; 14 Bt (NS 1627); s of Hon Somerset Arthur Maxwell, MP (died of wounds received in action 1942); suc gf 1957; *b* 7 July 1931; *Educ* Eton, Harvard U; *m* 1, 1959, Diana Marion, da of Nigel Gunnis; 2 da (adopted); *Heir* bro, Hon Simon Kenlis Maxwell; *Career* dir Brown Shipley & Co Merchant Bankers 1959-, chm Avon Rubber Co and Brown Shipley Hldgs; *Style* - The Rt Hon The Lord Farnham; 11 Earl's Court gdns, SW5 (☎ 01 373 8367); Farnham, Co Cavan

FARNHILL, Rear-Adm Kenneth Haydn; CB (1968), OBE (1945); s of Herbert Haydn Farnhill (d 1953); *b* 1938, Helen May, nee Houghton; 1 s, 1 da; *Educ* Bedford; *m* 1938, Helen May, nee Houghton; 1 s, 1 da; *Career* joined RN 1930, served 1939-45 Home Fleet Admiralty, Sec to Controller of Navy 1953-56, Capt Roy Naval Supply Sch 1958-59, Dir of Management and Support Intelligence 1966-69; *Clubs* Royal Commonwealth Society; *Style* - Rear-Adm Kenneth Farnhill, CB, OBE; 1 Christchurch Gardens, Widley, Portsmouth, Hants (☎ Cosham 77187)

FARQUHAR, Michael Fitzroy Henry; s and h of Lt-Col Sir Peter Farquhar, 6 Bt, DSO*; *b* 29 June 1938; *m* 1963, Veronica Geraldine, da of Patrick Hornidge, of Newton Ferrers, S Devon; 2 s; *Style* - Michael Farquhar Esq; Home Close Farm, Burford, Oxon

FARQUHAR, Lt-Col Sir Peter Walter; 6 Bt (GB 1796), DSO (1943) and Bar (1944), JP (Dorset 1955); s of Capt Sir Walter Randolph Fitzroy Farquhar, 5 Bt (d 1918); *b* 8 Oct 1904; *Educ* Eton; *m* 1937, Elizabeth Evelyn (Mrs Andrew Knowles), da of late Francis Cecil Albert Hurt, of Alderwasley, nr Derby; 3 s; *Heir* s, Michael Fitzroy Henry Farquhar; *Career* Lt The Greys 1926, 16/5 Lancers 1927-29, Maj 9 Lancers 1941, Lt-Col commanding 3 Hussars 1942-44; jt master Tedworth Foxhounds 1927-31, Meynell Foxhounds 1931-34, Whaddon Chase Foxhounds 1934-38, Portman Foxhounds 1947-59; chm Dorset Assoc of Boys' Clubs 1947-62, of Nat Assoc of Boys' Clubs Dvpt Ctee 1964-73; *Style* - Lt-Col Sir Peter Farquhar Bt DSO* JP; West Kington House, West Kington, Chippenham, Wilts (☎ Castle Combe 782331)

FARQUHARSON, Capt Colin Andrew; JP (Aberdeenshire 1969), DL (1966); s of late Norman Donald Farquharson, of Whitehouse, Alford, Aberdeenshire; *b* 9 Aug 1923; *Educ* Rugby; *m* 1948, Jean Sybil Mary, da of late Brig-Gen John Harry Hamilton, DSO, JP, DL, of Skene House, Aberdeenshire; 2 da (and 1 decd) (*see* Master of Arbuthnott); *Career* Capt Gren Gds 1942-48; chartered surveyor (land agent), FRICS; memb Roy Co of Archers (Queen's Bodyguard for Scotland); *Recreations* shooting, fishing; *Clubs* Roy Northern, University (both Aberdeen); MCC; *Style* - Capt Colin Farquharson, JP, DL; Whitehouse, Alford, Aberdeenshire (☎ Whitehouse 203)

FARQUHARSON, Hon Mr Justice; Hon Sir Donald Henry; s of Charles Anderson Farquharson (d 1929); *b* 26 Feb 1929; *Educ* Roy Commercial Travellers Schs, Keble Coll Oxford; *m* 1960, Helen Mary, nee Simpson; 3 s (and 1 decd); *Career* kt 1981; High Court Judge (Queen's Bench) 1981-; barr 1952, dep chm Essex Quarter Sessions 1970-2, QC 1972, Recorder of Crown Courts 1972-81,legal assessor Gen Medical Council and Gen Dental Council 1978, Bencher Inner Temple 1979; *Recreations* opera going; *Style* - The Hon Mr Justice Farquharson; 2 Harcourt Bldgs, Temple, EC4 (☎ 01 353 2622); Kumra Lodge, Kelvedon Hatch, Brentwood, Essex (☎ 0277 72213)

FARR, Dennis Larry Ashwell; s of Arthur William Farr (d 1961); *b* 3 Apr 1929; *Educ* Luton Grammar Sch, London U, Courtauld Inst of Art; *m* 1959, Diana, nee Pullein-Thompson (author); 1 s, 1 da; *Career* assist keeper Tate Gallery 1954-64, curator Paul Mellon Collection, Washington DC 1965-66, sr lectr and dep keeper University Art Collections Glasgow U 1967-69, dir Birmingham City Museums Art Gallery 1969-80, dir Courtauld Inst Galleries London U 1980-; *Recreations* reading, riding, music, and foreign travel; *Clubs* Athenaeum, Inst of Contemporary Arts; *Style* - Dennis Farr Esq JP; The Cottage, School Square, Longborough, Moreton-in-Marsh, Glos

FARRAR, Rex Gordon; MVO (1975); *b* 22 Aug 1925; *m* 1, 1955, Mary Katharine Shutts (d 1977); 1 s; m 2, 1978, Masako Ikeda; *Career* served RN 1944-47; FO 1947-, V-Consul New Orleans 1953, 2 Sec Jakarta 1960, 1 Sec 1963, 1 Sec Commercial Caracas 1964; 1 Sec, Head of Chancery and Consul San Salvador 1968; 1 Sec Commercial Tokyo 1971; 1 Sec, Head Chancery and Consul Rangoon 1978-80; Consul-Gen at Osaka Nov 1980-; *Style* - Rex Farrar Esq, MVO; c/o FCO, SW1

FARRELL, Charles; MC; s of Gerald William Farrell (d 1919); *b* 10 Feb 1919; *Educ* Ampleforth, Ch Ch Oxford; *m* 1949, Lady Katherine Paget, *qv*, da of 6 Marquess of Anglesey GCVO by Lady Victoria Manners, da of 8 Duke of Rutland; 1 s, 3 da; *Career* Maj Scots Gds NW Europe 1944-45 (despatches), HM Foreign Service 1947-57, md British Sidac Ltd 1960-71, chm Sidex Ltd (jt co with ICI Ltd) 1966-71, memb CBI Trade and Policy Ctee 1970-74, chm Montagu Fine Art Ltd 1972-80; *Recreations* skiing, shooting, tennis; *Clubs* White's, Buck's, Beefsteak; *Style* - Charles Farrell Esq, MC; Pyrton Manor, Watlington, Oxon (☎ 2327)

FARRELL, Hon Mrs (Clodagh Mary); *née* Morris; da of 2 Baron Morris (d 1975); *b* 1936; *m* 1964, Lt-Col Thomas Hugh Francis Farrell, DL, TD; 1 s, 1 da; *Style* - The Hon Mrs Farrell; 20 New Walk, Beverley, Yorks

FARRELL, Lady Katherine Mary Veronica; *née* Paget; da of 6 Marquess of Anglesey, GCVO, and twin sis of 7 Marquess; *b* 8 Oct 1922; *m* 1, 1941, Lt-Col Jocelyn Gurney, DSO, MC (m dis 1948, he d 1973), Welsh Gds, 2 s of Sir Eustace Gurney, of Walsingham Abbey, Norfolk; 1 da; m 2, 1949, Charles Farrell, MC, Foreign Serv, *qv*; 1 s, 3 da; *Style* - Lady Katherine Farrell; Pyrton Manor, Watlington, Oxon (☎ 327)

FARRELL, Thomas Hugh Francis; TD (1969), DL (Yorks 1971, Humberside 1974); s of Hugh Farrell (d 1959); *b* 3 Feb 1930 *Educ* Ampleforth, U Coll Hull *m* 1964 Hon Clodagh, da of 2 Baron Morris; 1 s, 1 da *Career* slr 1952, Sheriff of Hull 1960-61, chm Hull Con Fedn 1963-68, chm Beverley Civic Soc 1970-74, tres Hull U 1976-1980, cncl chm Hull U 1980-; *Clubs* Cavalry and Guards; *Style* - Thomas Farrell Esq, TD, DL; 20 New Walk, Beverley, North Humberside (☎ Hum 885207)

FARRER, Brian Ainsworth; QC (1978); s of Albert Ainsworth Farrer (d 1966); *b* 7 Apr 1930; *Educ* King's Coll Taunton, Univ Coll London; *m* 1960, Gwendoline Valerie, nee Wadd; 2 s, 1 da; *Career* barr Grays Inn 1957, Recorder of the Crown Court, Midland/Oxford Circuit 1974-; *Recreations* golf, bridge, chess; *Clubs* Aberdovey G C, Druids Heath G C; *Style* - Brian Farrer Esq, QC; Shutt Cross House, Aldridge, Staffordshire (☎ 53602)

FARRER, Charles Matthew; CVO (1973); s of Sir (Walter) Leslie Farrer, KCVO, *qv*, and Hon Lady (Marjorie Laura) Farrer (d 1981), da of 1 Viscount Hanworth, KBE, PC; *b* 3 Dec 1929; *Educ* Bryanston, Balliol Oxford; *m* 1962, Johanna Creszentia Maria Dorothea, da of Prof Hans-Herman Bennhold, of Tubingen, Germany; 1 s, 1 da; *Career* slr 1956, private slr to HM The Queen 1965-, ptnr Messrs Farrer & Co 1959-; *Style* - Charles Farrer Esq, CVO; 6 Priory av, Bedford pk, W4

FARRER, Sir (Walter) Leslie; KCVO (1948); s of late Bryan Farrer, JP, of Binnegar Hall, Dorset; *b* 30 Jan 1900; *Educ* Rugby, Balliol Oxford; *m* 1926, Hon Marjorie Laura, nee Pollock (d 1981), da of 1 Viscount Hanworth, KBE, PC; 1 s (*see* Charles Matthew Farrer), 1 da; *Career* ptnr Messrs Farrer & Co (slrs) 1927-64, private slr to HM King George VI and to HM The Queen 1937-64, dir London Life

Assoc Ltd, former Prime Warden Fishmongers' Co; *Style* - Sir Leslie Farrer, KCVO; Charlwood Place Farm, Charlwood, Surrey

FARRER, Margaret Irene; OBE (1970); da of Alfred (d 1954) and Emblyn Farrer; *b* 23 Feb 1914; *Educ* Poltimore Coll Exeter, London U; *Career* nurse and midwife, chm Central Midwives Bd 1973-79, ch nursing offr Thames Group 1971-74, v-pres Royal Coll of Midwives 1977-; *Style* - Miss Margaret Farrer OBE; Coombe Brook, Dawlish, S Devon (☎ 0626 863323)

FARRER, William Oliver; s of John Oliver Farrer, MC (d 1942); *b* 23 June 1926; *Educ* Eton, Balliol Oxford; *m* 1, 1955, Margery Hope (d 1976), da of William Yates (d 1931); 2 s, 1 da; m 2, 1979, Hazel Mary, da of Robert Clark Taylor (d 1963); *Career* Lieut Coldstream Guards; solicitor, ptnr Farrer & Co 1955, sr ptnr 1976; *Recreations* golf, music; *Clubs* Brooks's, MCC, R & A; *Style* - William Farrer Esq; Popmoor, Fernhurst, Haslemere, Surrey (☎ Haslemere 2564)

FARRIMOND, Herbert Leonard; CBE (1977); s of late George Farrimond; *b* 4 Oct 1924; *Educ* St Cuthbert's G S Newcastle, Durham U; *m* 1951, Patricia Sara, da of Col James Craig McGrath, MC; 1 s; *Career* Lt HM Royal Marines; former personnel dir ICI (IMI) and Dunlop Ltd, full-time memb British Railways Bd 1971-77, chm British Transport Hotels Ltd 1976-78, memb of ACAS 1974-78, dir Portsmouth & Sunderland Newspapers Ltd 1978-80, chm H L Farrimond and Associates (advisers to industrial/commercial organisations) 1978-, pt-time memb British Waterways Bd 1980-; *Style* - Herbert Farrimond Esq, CBE; Crinan, 26 Box Lane, Boxmoor, Hemel Hempstead, Herts (☎ 0442 52348); 9 Ardgare, Shandon, Helensburgh, Dunbartonshire (☎ 0436 820803)

FARRINGTON, Maj Sir Henry Francis Colden; 7 Bt (UK 1818); s of Sir Henry Anthony Farrington, 6 Bt (d 1944); *b* 25 April 1914; *Educ* Haileybury; *m* 1947, Anne, da of late Maj William Albert Gillam, DSO, Border Regt; 1 s, 1 da; *Heir* s, Henry William Farrington; *Career* 2 Lt RA 1939, Maj 1949, ret 1960; *Style* - Maj Sir Henry Farrington, Bt; Higher Ford Farm, Wiveliscombe, Taunton, Somerset (☎ Wiveliscombe 23219)

FARRINGTON, Henry William; s and h of Maj Sir Henry Farrington, 7 Bt; *b* 27 March 1951; *Educ* Haileybury; *m* 1979, Diana Donne, da of George Albert Broughton, of N Pemberton, Somerset; *Career* ARICS; *Style* - Henry Farrington Esq

FARTHING, Thomas William; s of late Thomas Farthing; *b* 19 Dec 1927; *Educ* Middlesbrough H S, Jesus Cambridge (MA, PhD); *m* 1955; 1 s, 1 da; *Career* metallurgist; IMI Research 1951-58, Beryllium Project man IMI 1958-62, res man Traditional Metals IMI 1962-64, European research dir International Copper Res Assoc 1964-66, md Wolverhampton Metal Ltd 1966-74, md IMI Titanium 1974-; *Style* - Thomas Farthing Esq; c/o IMI Titanium, PO Box 216, Birmingham B6 7BA (☎ 021 356 4848)

FAUCONBERG AND CONYERS, Baronies of (E 1283 & 1509); *see* Miller, Lady Diana and Lycett, Lady Wendy

FAULKNER, Hon Brian David Alexander; s of Baron Faulkner of Downpatrick (Life Peer, d 1977); *b* 1951; *Style* - The Hon Brian Faulkner

FAULKNER, Hon Mrs (Deborah Jane); da of 2 Baron MacAndrew; *b* 1956; *m* 1979, Capt Mark William Bingham Faulkner, 5 Royal Inniskilling Dragoon Gds; *Style* - The Hon Mrs Faulkner

FAULKNER, Sir Eric Odin; MBE (1945); s of Sir Alfred Edward Faulkner CB CBE (d 1963); *b* 21 April 1914; *Educ* Bradfield Coll, CCC Cambridge; *m* 1939, Joan Mary, da of Lt-Col F A M Webster; 1 s, 1 da; *Career* Lt-Col RA WW II; banker; chm Glyn Mills & Co 1963-68, dir Vickers Ltd 1957-79, Hudsons Bay Co 1950-70, Union Discount Co 1949-70 (chm 1959-70), chm Lloyds Bank Ltd 1968-77, pres British Bankers Assoc 1979-, chm

Industrial Soc 1973-76, Warden Bradfield Coll 1965-, kt 1974; *Recreations* fishing (formerly cricket and associaton football (CUAFC XI 1935); *Style* - Sir Eric Faulkner, MBE; Chart Cottage, Seal Chart, Sevenoaks, Kent

FAULKNER, Hugh; OBE (1980); s of Frank Faulkner (d 1964); *b* 8 June 1916; *Educ* Lutterworth Grammar School; *m* 1954, Anne Carlton, nee Milner; 1 s, 1 da; *Career* dir Help the Aged 1962-, trustee Voluntary and Christian Service, Phyllis Trust, Lester Trust; *Recreations* music, gardening; *Clubs* Nat Lib; *Style* - Hugh Faulkner Esq, OBE; Longfield, 4 One Tree Lane, Beaconsfield, Bucks (☎ 04946 4769)

FAULKNER, Hon James Michael Sewell; s of Baron Faulkner of Downpatrick (Life Peer, d 1977); *b* 1956; *Style* - The Hon James Faulkner

FAULKNER OF DOWNPATRICK, Baroness; Lucy Barbara Ethel; da of William John Harkness Forsythe, of Bangor (d 1960); *b* 1 July 1925; *Educ* Trin Coll Dublin; *m* 1951, Baron Faulkner of Downpatrick (Life Peer d 1977); 2 s, 1 da; *Career* Nat Govr (NI) BBC 1978-; co dir; genealogist; *Recreations* hunting, dressage, painting; *Clubs* Roy Overseas League; *Style* - The Rt Hon the Lady Faulkner of Downpatrick; Highlands, Farranfad, Downpatrick, Co Down (☎ 039687 663)

FAULKNER, Hon Lucy Claire; da of Baron Faulkner of Downpatrick (Life Peer, d 1977); *b* 1954; *Style* - The Hon Lucy Faulkner

FAULKNER, Sir Percy; KBE (1964), CB (1950); s of late Thomas Faulkner; *b* 11 May 1907; *Educ* Roy Academical Institution Belfast, Trin Coll Dublin; *m* 1933, Joyce Rosemary Lois, da of late Albert MacDonagh; 1 s, 1 da; *Career* Civil Service- dep sec Miny of Transport and Civil Aviation 1957-61, controller HM Stationery Office and Queen's Printer of Acts 1961-67; *Clubs* Athenaeum; *Style* - Sir Percy Faulkner, KBE, CB; Armathwaite, Motherby, Penrith, Cumbria (☎ Greystoke 438)

FAULKS, His Hon Judge; Peter Ronald Faulks; MC (1943); s of late Maj James Faulks, of Reigate Heath, Surrey; *b* 24 Dec 1917; *Educ* Tonbridge, Sidney Sussex Coll Cambridge; *m* 1949, Pamela Brenda, da of late Philip Henry (Peter) Lawless; 2 s; *Career* slr 1949-80, recorder of the Crown Court 1972-80, dep chm Agricultural Land Tribunal (S E England) 1972-80, a circuit judge 1980-; *Recreations* country life; *Clubs* MCC, Farmers'; *Style* - His Honour Judge Faulks, MC; Downs Cottage, Boxford, Newbury, Berks (☎ Boxford 382)

FAURE WALKER, Hon Mrs Angela Mary; *née* Chaloner; da of 2 Baron Gisborough, TD, JP; *b* 5 April 1925; *m* 1946 (m dis 1973), Roderick, late Maj Coldstream Gds and 2 s of Henry Faure Walker, of Highley Manor, Balcombe, Sussex; 2 s, 1 da; *Style* - The Hon Mrs Angela Faure Walker; Geranium Cottage, Ditchling, Sussex

FAURE WALKER, Roderick Edward; s of late Henry Faure Walker of Highley Manor, Balcombe, Sussex (and bro of Lt-Col Henry Faure Walker of Sandon Bury, Herts); *b* 26 Jan 1914; *Educ* Eton, CCC Oxford; *m* 1946 (m dis 1973), Hon Angela Mary Chaloner, *qv*, da of 3 Baron Gisborough and Shane, nee Newton, gda of 1 Bt; 2 s, 1 da (and 1 decd); *Career* slr 1947, ptnr Allen & Overy (Slrs) 1950-56, dir Hall Bros Steamship Co Ltd 1955-80, memb Lloyd's, late CCllr E Sussex, memb Cncl Roy Coll of Music 1979-, churchwarden St George's Hanover Sq 1949-; *Clubs* Boodle's; *Style* - Roderick Faure Walker Esq; 86 Sydney st, SW3 (☎ 01 351 0557)

FAWCETT, Robert; MBE (1945), TD (1946); s of late Percival Charles Fawcett; *b* 16 June 1917; *Educ* Rugby, Trin Oxford; *m* 1939, Esmé Boileau, da of Lt-Col George Boileau Henderson, DSO; 1 s, 1 da (1 c decd); *Career* chartered accountant, ptnr Messrs Jackson Taylor Abernethy & Co 1948-1976, company dir, directorships include Andrew Weir & Co Ltd, United Baltic Corpn Ltd, Spink & Son Ltd; *Recreations* reading, travelling; *Clubs* MCC; *Style* - Robert Fawcett Esq, MBE, TD; Sempstead, Ewhurst Green, nr

Robertsbridge, Sussex (☎ Staplecross 058083 609)

FAWCUS, Sir (Robert) Peter; KBE (1964), CMG (1960); s of late Arthur Francis Fawcus, OBE; *b* 13 Sept 1915; *Educ* Charterhouse, Clare Cambridge; *m* 1943, Isabel Constance, da of late Simon Ethelston; 1 s, 1 da; *Career* barr 1941; Colonial Administrative Serv- Admin Basutoland 1946-54, Government Sec Bechuanaland Protectorate 1954-59, resident cmmr 1959-63, Queen's cmmr 1963-65, ret; *Recreations* gardening; *Clubs* Roy C'wlth Soc; *Style* - Sir Peter Fawcus, KBE, CMG; Dochart House, Killin, Perthshire (☎ Killin 225)

FAYRER, Colin Robert; s of late Lt-Col James Outram Spens Fayrer, 4 s of 1 Bt; hp of kinsman, Sir John Fayrer, 4 Bt; *b* 28 Feb 1907; *m* 1946, Evelyn Elinor May, da of late Thomas A Carey; 2 da; *Style* - Colin Fayrer Esq; Forest House, 99 Blean Common, Blean, Canterbury, Kent

FAYRER, Sir John Lang Macpherson; 4 Bt (UK 1896); s of Lt-Cdr Sir Joseph Herbert Fayrer, 3 Bt, DSC, RNVR (d 1976); *b* 18 Oct 1944; *Educ* Edinburgh Acad; *Heir* kinsman, Colin Robert Fayrer; *Career* assoc memb of Roy Soc for Promotion of Health; memb Hotel, Catering and Institutional Management Assoc; *Style* - Sir John Fayrer, Bt; Overhailes, Haddington, E Lothian

FEATHER, Baroness - Alice Helena; da of John Fernyhough; *m* 1930, Baron Feather (Life Peer, d 1976); *Style* - The Rt Hon Lady Feather; 43 Shelley Crescent, Heston, Hounslow, Middx

FEATHER, Hon Harry Alexander; s of Baron Feather (Life Peer, d 1976); *b* 1938; *m* 1972, Patricia Lesley, nee Green; *Style* - The Hon Harry Feather

FEATHERSTONE, Col (William) Patrick Davies; MC (1944), TD (1960), JP (Staffs 1967), DL (1963); s of late Lt-Col Henry Walter Featherstone, OBE, TD, MD; *b* 17 Sept 1919; *Educ* Rugby, Trin Cambridge; *m* 1949, Olive Joan Llewellyn, da of late Lt-Col Richard Henry Waddy, DSO; 2 s, 1 da; *Career* Col (Hon Col 1972) Staffs Yeo, Lt-Col commanding (UK) 1959-62, Capt (RA) France and Germany WW II; farmer; High Sheriff of Staffs 1969-70, Vice Ld-Lt of Staffs 1976-; *Recreations* shooting; *Style* - Col Patrick Featherstone MC TD JP, HM Vice Lord-Lieut for Staffordshire; Yoxall Lodge, Newchurch, nr Burton-on-Trent, Staffs (☎ Hoar Cross 237)

FEBEN, Eric Graham; s of late Stanley Oswald Feben; *b* 4 July 1916; *Educ* Cncl Educn (Matriculation); *m* 1939, Ernestine Paula, da of late Ernest Alfred White; 2 da (1 decd); *Career* road transport operator (ret); High Sheriff Co of Isle of Wight 1979-80, Mayor South Wight Borough Cncl 1974-75, chm IOW Rural Dist Cncl 1968-71, sec/man Shanklin & Sandown Golf Club; *Recreations* golf; *Style* - Eric Feben Esq; Pound Cottage, Calbourne, Newport, IOW (☎ Calbourne 276)

FEENY, Peter Joseph; DL (W Midlands 1975); s of Gerard Feeny (d 1966); *b* 19 March 1916; *Educ* Stonyhurst; *m* 1948, Anne, nee Best; 4 children; *Career* Maj WW II, memb of Stock Exchange 1952, pres Birmingham Consular Assoc 1969-70, hon Consul for Thailand 1960; *Recreations* travel, squash rackets, lawn tennis; *Clubs* All England Lawn Tennis; *Style* - Peter Feeny Esq, DL; 2 Greening dve, Edgbaston, Birmingham, B15 2XA (☎ 454 4002)

FEILDEN, Henry Rudyard; s and h of Sir Henry Feilden, 6 Bt; *b* 26 Sept 1951; *Educ* Kent Coll Canterbury, Bristol U; *Career* MRCVS; *Style* - Henry Feilden Esq

FEILDEN, Sir Henry Wemyss; 6 Bt (UK 1846), of Feniscowles, Lancashire; da of Col Wemyss Feilden, CMG (3 s of Sir William Feilden, 3 Bt, JP); suc 1 cous, Sir William Feilden, 5 Bt, MC, 1976; *b* 1 Dec 1916; *Educ* Canford Sch, King's Coll London; *m* 1943, Ethel, da of late John Atkinson; 1 s, 1 da; *Heir* s, Henry Feilden; *Career* RE WW II; Civ Serv ret; *Recreations* gardening, watching cricket; *Clubs* MCC; *Style* - Sir Henry Feilden, Bt; Little Dene, Heathfield rd, Burwash, Etchingham, E Sussex (☎ Burwash 882205)

FEILDING, Viscount; Alexander Stephen Rudolph Feilding; s and h of 11 Earl of Denbigh and Desmond; *b* 4 Nov 1970

FEILDING, Hon Henry Anthony; MC; s of late Lt-Col Rudolph Edmund Aloysius, Viscount Feilding (eld s of late 9 Earl of Denbigh); *b* 1924; *Educ* Ampleforth, King's Cambridge; *m* 1950, Dunia Maureen, nee Spencer; 1 s, 1 da; *Career* late Capt Coldstream Gds, High Sheriff of Warwicks 1978; *Style* - The Hon Henry Feilding, MC; The Manor House, Pailton, nr Rugby

FEILDING, Hon Hugh Richard; s of late Lt-Col Rudolph Edmund Aloysius, Viscount Feilding, CMG, DSO (eld s of late 9 Earl of Denbigh); *b* 1920; *Educ* Ampleforth; *m* 1944, Sheila Katharine, da of Brig Charles Arthur Bolton, CBE; 1 s; *Career* FCA; late Sqdn Ldr RAFVR; *Style* - The Hon Hugh Feilding; Home Farm, Bainton, Driffield, E Yorks

FEILDING, Lady Louisa Helen; da of 11 Earl of Denbigh and Desmond; *b* 1969; *Style* - Lady Louisa Feilding

FEILDING, Hon Mrs Basil; Rosemary; da of late Cdr (Frederick) Neville Eardley-Wilmot, RN (ret); *m* 1939, Capt the Hon Basil Egerton Feilding (d 1970); 3 s, 2 da; *Style* - The Hon Mrs Basil Feilding; The Park Cottage, Newnham Paddox, Rugby, Warwicks

FEILDING, Lady Samantha Clare Barbara; da of 11 Earl of Denbigh and Desmond; *b* 1966; *Style* - Lady Samantha Feilding

FELLOWES, Hon Andrew Edward; s of 3 Baron De Ramsey, KBE; *b* 1950; *m* 1974, Anne Mary, nee Tweedy; 1 da; *Style* - The Hon Andrew Fellowes; Bodsey House, Ramsey, Huntingdon, Cambridgeshire

FELLOWES, Hon (John) David Coulson; s of late Capt the Hon Coulson Churchill Fellowes (eld s of 2 Baron De Ramsey) and half-bro of 3 Baron; *b* 1915; *Educ* Eton, Univ Coll Oxford; *m* 1, 1946 (m dis 1962), Louise (d 1975), da of Lt Sir James Henry Domville, 5 Bt, RN; 1 s, 1 da; m 2, 1963, Joan Lynette, nee Rees (d 1965); m 3, 1977, Mervyn, da of late Reinold De Tole and former w of Peter Sherwood; *Style* - The Hon David Fellowes; Flat 3, 17 Elgin cres, W11

FELLOWES, Lady (Cynthia) Jane; da (by 1 m) of 8 Earl Spencer, MVO, JP, DL, *qv*; sis of HRH The Princess of Wales (*see* Royal Family); *b* 11 Feb 1957; *Educ* West Heath; *m* 1978, Robert Fellowes, s of Lady Fellowes (Jane, gda of 2 Viscount Hampden, GCMG) and Capt Sir William Albemarle Fellowes, KCVO; 1 da (Laura Jane b 1980); *Style* - Lady Jane Fellowes; 5 Warwick sq, SW1

FELLOWES, Hon John Ailwyn; s and h of 3 Baron De Ramsey, KBE; *b* 27 Feb 1942; *Educ* Winchester; *m* 1973, Phyllida Mary, nee Forsyth; 1 s; *Style* - The Hon John Fellowes; Abbey House, Ramsey, Huntingdon, Cambridgeshire

FELLOWES, Robert; s of Sir William Albemarle Fellowes, KCVO, Agent to HM at Sandringham 1936-64, and Jane, nee Ferguson (whose m, Hon Margaret Brand, was da of 2 Viscount Hampden & 24 Baron Dacre); *b* 11 Dec 1941; *Educ* Eton; *m* 1978, Lady (Cynthia) Jane Spencer (*see* Lady Jane Fellowes); 1 da; *Career* Lt Scots Gds 1960-63; dir Allen Harvey & Ross (discount brokers & bankers) 1968-77; Assist Priv Sec to HM The Queen 1977-; *Recreations* cricket, shooting, golf; *Clubs* White's, Pratt's, MCC; *Style* - Robert Fellowes Esq; 5a The Old Barracks, Kensington Palace, W8 (☎ 01 937 2979)

FELLOWES, Brig Reginald William Lyon; CBE (1943), MC (1916) and Bar (1918); s of late Frederick William Fellowes; *b* 6 Aug 1895; *Educ* Wellington, RMA; *m* 1, 1921 (m dis 1946), Dulcie Margaret Hunt, da of Edmund Peel; 1 s (and 1 decd); m 2, 1947, Marion Grace Joan, da of late Percy Beard, of Bitterne, Southampton; *Career* commissioned RFA 1914, served WW I, ret 1938; re-employed 1939, served France, Iraq, Persia, Italy (despatches, Legion of Honour), demobilised 1945; farmer; *Clubs* New (Edinburgh); *Style* - Brig Reginald

Fellowes, CBE, MC*; Cladich, Dalmally, Argyll (☎ Dalmally 246)

FELLOWES, Sir William Albemarle; KCVO (1964, CVO 1962); s of late Charles Arthur Fellowes, of Shotesham Park, Norfolk; *b* 10 Sept 1899; *Educ* Oriel Oxford; *m* 1934, Jane Charlotte, da of Brig-Gen Algernon Francis Halford Ferguson; 2 s, 2 da; *Career* FRICS, FLAS; DL Norfolk 1965-81; Capt Scots Gd, Agent to HM King George VI (Sandringham) 1936-52, Agent to HM The Queen (Sandringham) 1952-64; *Recreations* shooting, fishing; *Style* - Sir William Fellowes, KCVO; Flitcham House, Flitcham, King's Lynn, Norfolk

FENDER, Percy George Herbert; s of late Percy Robert Fender; *b* 22 Aug 1892; *Educ* St George's Coll Weybridge, St Paul's Sch; *m* 1, 1924, late Ruth Marian Clapham; 1 s, 1 da; m 2, 1962, late Susan Victoria Gordon, nee Kyffin; *Career* capt Surrey CC 1921-35, MCC 1920-21 Australia, S Africa 1922-23, First Special Cricket Correspondent 1928-29, world record for fastest hundred ever made (35 mins) 1920, world record fastest five wickets at Lords 1927, wrote articles for sporting magazines The Field etc, Crescens Robinson Co Ltd 1912-70 (chm 1943-68), chm and md Herbert Fender & Co to 1976, WW II Wing Cdr 1945, freeman City of London 1960, Grant of Arms 1966, currently chm and md London Wine Exchange; *Books* Defending the Ashes, Turn of the Wheel, The Tests of 1930, Kissing the Rod 1934, Lonsdale Library on Cricket, ABC of Cricket; *Recreations* real tennis, billiards, golf, bridge; *Clubs* RAF, Surrey Co Cricket; *Style* - Percy Fender Esq; Old Strood, Nowhurst Lane, Broadbridge Heath, Horsham, Sussex

FENNELL, John Desmond Augustine; QC (1974); s of Dr Augustine Joseph Fennell (d 1980); *b* 17 Sept 1933; *Educ* Ampleforth, CCC Cambridge; *m* 1966, Susan Primrose, nee Trusted; 1 s, 2 da; *Career* Lt Grenadier Guards 1956-58, barr Inner Temple 1959, dep chm Bedfordshire Quarter Sessions 1971-72, Crown Court Recorder 1972-, chm Buckingham Div Conservative Assoc 1976-79, chm WARA (formed to oppose the siting of 3rd London Airport in Bucks) 1968-70 and 1979-; *Recreations* politics, the environment; *Clubs* Cavalry and Guards; *Style* - John Fennell Esq, QC; Lawn House, Winslow, Buckingham (☎ Winslow (029 671) 2464); 2 Crown Office Row, Temple, EC4 (☎ 01 353 1365)

FENNESSY, Sir Edward; CBE (1957, OBE Mil 1944); s of Edward Patrick Fennessy (d 1955); *b* 17 Jan 1912; *Educ* West Ham G S, Queen Mary Coll London U; *m* 1937, Marion, da of late Albert Edwin Banks; 1 s, 1 da; *Career* md Decca Radar 1950-65, md Plessey Electronics 1965-69, managing director Post Office Telecommunications 1969-77, dep chm Post Office 1975-77, chm LKB Biochrom 1978-, dep chm Muirhead and LKB Instruments Ltd; kt 1975; *Recreations* gardening, sailing, golf; *Clubs* RAF, Island Sailing; *Style* - Sir Edward Fennessy, CBE; Northbrook, Littleford Lane, Shamley Green, Surrey (☎ Guildford 892444)

FENNEY, Roger Johnson; CBE (1973, MBE Mil 1945); s of James Henry Fenney, of St Helens (d 1952); *b* 11 Sept 1916; *Educ* Cowley G S, Manchester U; *m* 1942, Dorothy Porteus; 2 da; *Career* sec Statutory Bd 1947-80, chm Special Tstees Charing Cross Hosp 1980-; *Style* - Roger Fenney Esq, CBE; 11 Gilray House, Gloucester ter, W2 (☎ 01 262 8313); Chiltern Cottage, Lower Assendon, Henley-on-Thames, Oxon

FENTON, Alexander; s of Alexander Fenton (decd); *b* 26 June 1929; *Educ* Turriff Academy, Aberdeen U, Cambridge U; *m* 1956, Evelyn Elizabeth, nee Hunter; 2 da; *Career* dir Nat Museum of Antiquities of Scotland; author; *Recreations* languages; *Clubs* New Club (Edinburgh); *Style* - Alexander Fenton Esq; 132 Blackford av, Edinburgh EH9, Scotland (☎ 667 5456)

FENTON, Charles Miller; *Career* FTI, FBIM, chm BBA Automotive Ltd, BBA Properties Ltd, Fenton Hldgs Ltd, md BBA Group Ltd; *Style* - Charles Fenton Esq; PO Box 20, Cleckheaton, Yorks

FENTON, Derek Risian; MVO (1977), MBE (1973); s of Arthur Fenton (d 1954); *b* 20 July 1921; *Educ* Clark's Coll; *m* 1943, Iris Mary, nee Diamond; 1 s, 1 da; *Career* KStJ 1975, freeman City of London, md Heston Codan Rubber Ltd, cmmr London District (Prince of Wales) St John Ambulance Brigade; *Recreations* St John Ambulance Brigade; *Clubs* Directors; *Style* - Derek Fenton Esq, MVO, MBE; 54 Hillside rd, Southall, Middlesex

FENTON, Hon Mrs (Geraldine Jane); *née* Milner; da of 2 Baron Milner of Leeds; *b* 1954; *m* 1978, Mark Anthony Fenton; *Style* - The Hon Mrs Fenton

FENTON, Wilfrid David Drysdale; CBE (1962); s of late David Fenton, slr; *b* 27 March 1908; *Educ* George Watson's Coll Edinburgh, Edinburgh U; *m* 1, 1955 (m dis 1974), Isobel Stewart; m 2, 1974, Elaine Herman, nee Surut; 1 s, 1 da (both step); *Career* sec and commercial engr N of Scotland Hydro Electric Bd 1944-55, chm Uganda Electricity Bd Kampala 1955-62, chm S Wales Electricity Bd St Mellons Cardiff 1962-68, chm London Electricity Bd 1968-72, dep chm Central Electricity Generating Bd 1972-75, md Br Electricity International 1975-77, dir Project Dvpt Gp (Europe) 1978-; *Recreations* golf; *Clubs* Caledonian, Roy C'wlth Soc, English Speaking Union; *Style* - Wilfrid Fenton Esq, CBE; 31 Cadogan Lane, SW1 (☎ 01 235 7278)

FENWICK, Charles Sebastian; MVO (1977); s of David Fenwick; *b* 7 Apr 1946; *Educ* Ampleforth; *Career* Maj, regt offr Grenadier Guards 1965-78, Equerry to HRH The Duke of Edinburgh 1975-77, dir- By Pass Nurseries Ltd 1978-, By Pass Nurseries (Seeds) Ltd 1978-; *Clubs* Turf; *Style* - Charles Fenwick Esq, MVO; Presbytery House, Withermarsh Green, nr Stoke-by-Mayland, Suffolk

FERENS, Sir Thomas Robinson; CBE (1952); s of J J T Ferens, of Hull (d 1957); *b* 4 Jan 1903; *Educ* Rydal, Leeds U; *m* 1934, Jessie, da of late P G Sanderson, of Scarborough; 1 da; *Career* engineer, md Shipham & Co Ltd, George Clark & Son (Hull) Ltd, dir Newman Hender Ltd, ret 1970; kt 1957; *Recreations* fly fishing; *Style* - Sir Thomas Ferens, CBE; Sunderlandwick House, Driffield, Humberside (☎ Driffield 42323)

FERGUSON, Andrew John Duncan; *Career* FCA; dir Johnston gp of cos, JB Hldgs Ltd; *Style* - Andrew Ferguson Esq; Johnston House, Hatchlands rd, Redhill, Surrey

FERGUSON, Charles Logan; *Career* dir Vendops Ltd, gp md Blackwood Hodge Ltd; *Style* - Charles Ferguson Esq; 25 Berkeley sq, London, W1

FERGUSON, John Napier; *Career* B Com, CA, FMCA, JDipMa; chm and md BSR Ltd, chm Associated Engineering Ltd, dir EPS Moulders Ltd, McDonald Electric (Scotland) Ltd; *Style* - John Ferguson Esq; BSR Ltd, Monarch Works, Cradley Heath, Warley, W Midlands

FERGUSON DAVIE, Antony Francis; s and h of Rev Sir (Arthur) Patrick Ferguson Davie, 5 Bt, TD; *b* 23 March 1952; *Style* - Antony Ferguson Davie Esq

FERGUSON DAVIE, Rev Sir (Arthur) Patrick; 5 Bt (E 1641, revived UK 1847 in favour of Gen Henry Ferguson, who m Frances, sis of Sir John Davie, 9 Bt, and who assumed by Roy licence additional surname and arms of Davie), TD; s of late Lt-Col Arthur Francis Ferguson Davie, CIE, DSO, 3 s of 3 Bt; suc unc, Sir William Ferguson Davie, 4 Bt, 1947; *b* 17 March 1909; *Educ* Wellington, Lincoln Oxford; *m* 1949, Iris Dawn Cable-Buller, da of Capt Michael Francis Buller; 1 s; *Heir* s, Antony Ferguson Davie; *Career* ordained 1934, RD of Cadbury 1966-68, Hon Chaplain to Bp of Exeter 1949-73; *Style* - Rev Sir Patrick Ferguson Davie Bt TD; Skalatos House, Girne, Mersin 10, Turkey

FERGUSSON, Adam; s and h of Sir Charles Fergusson, 9 Bt; *b* 29 Dec 1962; *Style* - Adam Fergusson Esq

FERGUSSON, Hon Lady (Amanda Mary); *née* Noel-Paton; da of Baron Ferrier (Life Peer); *b* 17 March 1933; *m* 1961, Sir Charles Fergusson, 9 Bt, *qv*; *Recreations* equitation; *Style* - The Hon

Lady Fergusson; Kilkerran, Maybole, Ayrshire (☎ 06554 207)

FERGUSSON, Sir Charles; 9 Bt (NS 1703); s of Sir James Fergusson, 8 Bt, LLD (d 1973); *b* 10 May 1931; *Educ* Eton, Edinburgh Ag Coll; *m* 1961, Hon Amanda Mary Noel-Paton, da of Baron Ferrier (Life Peer); 2 s; *Heir* s, Adam Fergusson; *Style* - Sir Charles Fergusson, Bt; Kilkerran, Maybole, Ayrshire (☎ Crosshill 207)

FERGUSSON HANNAY, Lady; Doris; *née* Leslie; *Educ* London, Brussels, Florence; *m* 1936, Sir Walter Fergusson (Leisrinck) Hannay (d 1961); *Career* served in Civil Defence 1941-45; novelist, historian (as Doris Leslie); *Style* - Lady Fergusson Hannay; c/o A P Watt & Son, 26/28 Bedford Row, WC1

FERMOR, Hon Mrs (Joan Elizabeth); *née* Eyres Monsell; da of 1 Viscount Monsell, GBE (d 1969); *b* 1912; *m* 1, 1939 (m dis 1947), William John Rayner, CBE; m 2, 1968, Patrick Michael Leigh Fermor, DSO, OBE; *Style* - The Hon Mrs Fermor; Kardamyli, Messenia, Greece

FERMOR-HESKETH, Hon John; s of 2 Baron Hesketh (d 1955); *b* 15 March 1953; *Educ* Ampleforth; *m* 1980, Anna, da of Hamish Wallace; *Style* - The Hon John Fermor-Hesketh

FERMOR-HESKETH, Hon Robert; s of 2 Baron Hesketh (d 1955); hp of bro, 3 Baron Hesketh; *b* 1 Nov 1951; *Educ* Ampleforth; *m* 1979, Jeanne, da of Patrick McDowell, of Co Clare; *Style* - The Hon Robert Hesketh

FERMOY, 5 Baron (I 1856); Edmund James Burke Roche; s of 4 Baron (d 1955) and Ruth, Lady Fermoy, DCVO, OBE, JP; unc to HRH The Princess of Wales; *b* 20 March 1939; *Educ* Eton, RMA Sandhurst, RAC Cirencester; *m* 1964, Lavinia Frances Elizabeth, da of late Capt John Pitman, of Malmesbury, Wilts; 2 s, 1 da; *Heir* s, Hon Patrick Roche; *Career* tstee Pheasant Tst; late Capt Roy Horse Gds; chm Eddington Bindery Ltd, dist cllr (Hungerford) Newbury 1976-79; *Clubs* White's, Turf; *Style* - The Rt Hon The Lord Fermoy; Eddington House, Hungerford, Berks (☎ 2540)

FERMOY, Ruth, Baroness; Ruth Sylvia; DCVO (1979, CVO 1966), OBE (1952), JP (Norfolk 1944); da of William Smith Gill, CB, VD, of Aberdeenshire; *b* 2 Oct 1908; *m* 1931, 4 Baron Fermoy (d 1955); 1 s (6 Baron Fermoy), 2 da (Hon Mrs Gunningham, Hon Mrs Shand Kydd, through whom Ruth is grandmother of HRH The Princess of Wales); *Career* Hon MusDE Anglia U 1975; Extra Woman of the Bedchamber to HM Queen Elizabeth The Queen Mother 1959-60, since when a Woman of the Bedchamber; Freedom of King's Lynn 1963; Hon RAM 1968; *Style* - Rt Hon Ruth, Lady Fermoy DCVO OBE JP; 36 Eaton sq, SW1 (☎ 01 235 1514)

FERRERS, 13 Earl (GB 1711); Sir Robert Washington Shirley; 19 Bt (E 1611); also Viscount Tamworth (GB 1711); s of 12 Earl Ferrers (d 1954, 17 in descent from Sir Hugh Shirley, Grand Falconer to Henry IV and victim of mistaken identity at the Battle of Shrewsbury through being accoutred as the King; 16 in descent from Sir Ralph Shirley, one of the principal commanders at Agincourt; ninth in descent from Dorothy, da of Elizabeth I's spoilt and ultimately traitorous favourite Essex (his soured feelings for HM curdled to insurrection when the renewal of his patent for sweet wines was refused), through whom Lord Ferrers descends from Edward III, hence the quartering of the arms of Fr & Eng on the Shirley escutcheon; and fifth in descent from Hon Walter Shirley, yr bro of 4 Earl, the last Lord to be tried for homicide by his Peers (which did not save him from swinging at Tyburn for murdering his steward in a fit of rage), and unc of the Countess of Huntingdon who was a friend to Methodism); bro-in-law to John Luttrell, *qv*; *b* 8 June 1929; *Educ* Winchester, Magdalene Cambridge; *m* 1951, Annabel, da of Brig William Carr, CVO, DSO, JP, DL, *qv*; 2 s, 3 da; *Heir* s, Viscount Tamworth; *Career* late Lt Coldstream Gds, served Malaya; Lord-in-Waiting & Govt Whip 1962-64 & 1971-74, Jt-Dep Ldr Oppn Ho Lds 1976-79, Parly Sec Ag Fish & Food 1974, Min State Ag Fish & Food 1979-; memb Armitage Cttee

Political Activity Civ Servants 1976; High Steward Norwich Cathedral 1979-; Dep Ldr Lords 1979-; Tstee E Anglian TSB 1957-75 (V-Chm 1971-75), TSB of E England 1975-79 (Chm 1977-79), memb Centl Bd TSB 1977-79, dir Centl TSB Ltd 1978-79, TSB Trustcard 1978-79; dir (1975-79)- Norwich Union Life Insur Soc, N U Fire Insur Soc, Scottish Union & Nat Insur Co, Maritime Insur Co; *Recreations* shooting, music, travel; *Clubs* Beefsteak; *Style* - The Rt Hon Earl Ferrers; Hedenham Hall, Bungay, Suffolk (☎ Woodton 250)

FERRIER, Baron (Life Peer UK 1958); Victor Ferrier Noel-Paton; ED, DL (Lanarks 1960); s of late Frederick Waller Ferrier Noel-Paton, of Edinburgh; *b* 29 Jan 1900; *Educ* Edinburgh Acad; *m* 1932, Joane Mary, da of late Sir Gilbert Wiles, KCIE, CSI; 1 s, 3 da; *Career* memb Queen's Body Guard for Scotland (Roy Co of Archers), formerly MLC Bombay, former dir Imperial Bank of India, pres Bombay Chamber of Commerce, Maj (ret) Bombay Light Horse Aux Force India and Army in India (Res), Hon ADC to Gov of Bombay; *Style* - The Rt Hon The Lord Ferrier, ED, DL; Kilkerran, Maybole, Ayrshire (☎ Crosshill 515)

FETHERSTONHAUGH FRAMPTON Roger Henry Charles; s of Henry Rupert Fetherstonhaugh Frampton (d 1955); *b* 5 Feb 1899; *Educ* RN Colleges Osborne and Dartmouth; *m* 1927, Bridget Sybil, da of Sir Mansfeldt De Cardonnel Findlay (d 1932); 4 da; *Career* Commander Jutland 1916, Irish Sea Convoys, Sicily and Normandy landings, Pacific 1939-45, district fishery Officer Miny of Agriculture and Fisheries 1927-39 and 1945-56; *Recreations* fishing, shooting; *Style* - Roger Fetherstonhaugh Frampton Esq; Moreton House, Dorchester, Dorset (☎ Bindon Abbey 462493)

FEVERSHAM, 6 Baron (UK 1826); Charles Antony Peter Duncombe; s of Col Antony John Duncombe-Anderson, TD, gggs of 1 Baron; suc to Barony of kinsman, 3 Earl of Feversham, 1963, the Earldom becoming extinct; *b* 3 Jan 1945; *Educ* Eton; *m* 1, 1966, Shannon (d 1976), da of late Sir Thomas Foy, CSI, CIE; 2 s, 1 da; m 2, 1979, Pauline, da of John Aldridge, of Newark, Notts; *Heir* s, Hon Jasper Duncombe; *Career* Pres Yorks Parish Cncls Assoc 1977-; journalist, author of *A Wolf in Tooth* 1967, *Great Yachts* 1970; chm Yorks Arts Assoc 1969, chm Standing Ctee of Regional Arts Assocs 1969-76, co-pres Arvon Foundation 1976-; *Style* - The Rt Hon The Lord Feversham; Beckdale House, Helmsley, York

FEVERSHAM, Countess of; Lady Anne Dorothy; *née* Wood; MBE (1950); twin da (her sis died after 4 days) of 1 Earl of Halifax; *b* 31 July 1910; *m* 1936, 3 and last Earl of Feversham (d 1963); 1 da (Lady Clarissa Collin); *Style* - Rt Hon Countess of Feversham, MBE; Pennyholme, Fadmoor, Yorks

FEY, Hon Mrs (Sybilla Laura Russell); da (by 1 m) of late 18 Baron St John of Bletso; *b* 1915; *m* 1943, Howard Ernest Churchill Fey; 2 da; *Style* - The Hon Mrs Fey; Delfryn, Old rd, Minera, nr Wrexham, North Wales

FFOLKES, Sir Robert Francis Alexander; 7 Bt (GB 1774); s of Sir (Edward John) Patrick Boschetti ffolkes, 6 Bt (d 1960); *b* 2 Dec 1943; *Educ* Stowe, Ch Ch Oxford; *Style* - Sir Robert ffolkes, Bt; 18 Chiddingstone st, SW6

FFORDE, Lady Jean (Sybil Violet); *née* Graham; DL (Ayr and Arran); da of 6 Duke of Montrose, KT, CB, CVO, VD, LLD (d 1954); *b* 1920; *m* 1947 (m dis 1957), Col John Patrick Ilbert Fforde; 1 s; *Career* 7; *Style* - Lady Jean Fforde, DL; Strabane, Brodick, Isle of Arran

FFOWCS WILLIAMS, Prof John Eirwyn; s of Rev Abel Ffowcs Williams, of Swansea Hall, Swansea, Tasmania; *b* 25 May 1935; *Educ* Friends Sch Great Ayton, Derby Tech Coll, Southampton U; *m* 1959, Anne Beatrice, da of Percy Mason; 2 s, 1 da; *Career* Rolls Royce Prof of Applied Mathematics at Imperial Coll London 1969-72 (formerly Reader), Rank Prof of Engineering Cambridge U 1977-; *Recreations* friends and cigars; *Clubs* Athenaeum, Danish; *Style* - Prof John Ffowcs Williams; Emmanuel College, Cambridge (☎ 0223 48275)

FFRENCH, 7 Baron (I 1798); Sir Peter Martin Joseph Charles John ffrench; 8 Bt (I 1779); s of Capt Hon John Martin Valentine ffrench (d 1946), s of 5 Baron, and Sophia, da of late Giovanni Brambilla, of Como, Italy; suc unc 1955; *b* 2 May 1926; *m* 1954, Sonia Katherine, da of late Maj Digby Coddington Cayley, ggs of 7 Bt; 1 s, 2 da; *Heir* s, Hon Robuck ffrench; *Style* - The Rt Hon The Lord ffrench; Castle ffrench, Ballinasloe, Co Galway

FFRENCH BLAKE, Lady Caroline Anne de Vere; *née* Beauclerk; da (by 2 m) of 13 Duke of St Albans, OBE; *b* 1951; *Educ* Fritham House, Queen's Gate Sch; *m* 1970, Neil St John ffrench Blake; 2 da; *Style* - Lady Caroline ffrench Blake; Barn House, Midgham, Woolhampton, Reading, Berks

FFRENCH BLAKE, Neil St John; s of Lt-Col Robert Lifford Valentine, DSO, of Midgham Park Farm, Woolhampton, Berks; *b* 4 Nov 1940; *Educ* Eton; *m* 1970, Lady Caroline de Vere Beauclerk, da of 13 Duke of St Albans by his 2 w; 2 da; *Career* BBC producer 1963-69, md Network Broadcasting Ltd 1969-73, Programme Controller Thames Valley B'dcasting Ltd 1975-80; md CTV Productions Ltd; author and songwriter; *Recreations* skiing, golf; *Style* - Neil ffrench Blake Esq; Barn House, Midgham, Berks (☎ Woolhampton 3535)

FICKLING, Benjamin William; CBE (1973); s of late Robert Marshall Fickling; *b* 14 July 1909; *Educ* Framlingham Coll, St George's Hosp, Roy Dental Hosp; *m* 1942, Shirley Dona, da of late Albert Latimer Walker, FRCS; 2 s, 1 da; *Career* dental surgn St George's Hosp 1936-74, to Roy Dental Hosp of London 1935-74, oral surgn to Dept of Dental and Oral Surgery Roy Coll of Surgeons of England 1968-71, dir Medical Sickness Annuity & Life Assurance Soc 1967-, dir Perm Insurance Soc and Medical Sickness Fin Corpn; FRCS, FDS, MGDS RCS; *Recreations* travel, gardening; *Clubs* Ski Club of GB; *Style* - Benjamin Fickling Esq, CBE; Linksview, Linksway, Northwood, Middx (☎ Northwood 22035)

FIDLER, Michael M; JP (Lancs 1958); s of late Louis Fidler; *b* 10 Feb 1916; *Educ* Salford G S, Salford Roy Tech Coll; *m* 1939, Maidie, da of Jack Davis; 1 s, 1 da; *Career* business consultant in clothing industry; md H & L Fidler Ltd 1941-70, Michael Lewis Ltd 1942-70, Wibye Ltd 1968-, pres Gen Zionist Org of GB 1973-, chm Internat Org Cmmn World Jewish Congress 1975-, founder and nat dir Conservative Friends of Israel 1974-, MP (C) Bury and Radcliffe 1970-74; former cllr & alderman Borough of Prestwich, dir Friendship with Israel Gp (All Party) European Parlt 1979-; *Style* - Michael Fidler Esq, JP; 51 Tavistock ct, Tavistock sq, WC1; 1 Woodcliffe Lodge, Sedgley Park rd, Prestwich, Manchester M25 8JX; 94 Jermyn st, St James's, SW1

FIELD, Arnold; OBE (1965); s of late Wilfred Field; *b* 19 May 1917; *Educ* Sutton Coldfield Roy Sch, Erdington C of E, Birmingham Tech Coll; *m* 1943, Kathleen Dulcie, da of late Albert Bennett; 1 s, 1 da; *Career* centre superintendent London Air Traffic Control Centre 1968-71, dir Civil Air Traffic Operations 1971-74, jt field cdr UK Nat Air Traffic Serv 1974-77; aviation consultant; *Recreations* vintage motor cars, flying; *Clubs* Bentley Drivers; *Style* - Arnold Field Esq, OBE; Footprints, Stoke Wood, Stoke Poges, Bucks (☎ Farnham Common 270)

FIELD, Hon Mrs (Honora Elizabeth Dundas); *née* Chaloner; JP (Salop 1951); da of 1 Baron Gisborough, JP, DL, sometime MP W Wilts and Liverpool Abercromby; *m* 1929, Col Frank Drummond Shuttleworth Field, OBE, MC (d 1958); *Career* has Kaisar-i-Hind Silver Medal; *Style* - The Hon Mrs Field, JP; Stocking Cottage, Balsham, Cambs

FIELD, Sir John Osbaldiston; KBE (1967), CMG (1959); s of late Frank Osbaldiston Field; *b* 30 Oct 1913; *Educ* Boys' H S Stellenbosch S Africa, Magdalene Cambridge; *m* 1951, Irene Margaret, da of late Harold Godfrey Judd, CBE; *Career* Col Administrative Serv (Nigeria) 1936, Cmmr Cameroons and UK Special Rep for Br Cameroons at UN Tsteeship Cncl 1956-61, Gov and CIC St Helena 1962-68, Staff Liaison Offr HM Overseas Civil Serv 1968, Acting Administrator Montserrat 1969, Resident

Cmmr (1970-72) and Gov Gilbert & Ellice Islands Colony 1972-73; *Recreations* fishing; *Clubs* Oxford and Cambridge, Victoria (Pietermaritzburg); *Style* - Sir John Field, KBE, CMG; Little Park, Himeville, Natal, S Africa 4585 (☎ Himeville 21)

FIELDEN, Noel Lindsay; CBE (1953, MBE 1942); da of late William Swire, of Longden Manor, Shrewsbury; *b* 15 Jan 1895; *m* 1921, Arthur Fielden, OBE (d 1975), s of Edward Fielden, of Court of Hill, Ludlow; 1 da (and 1 s ka 1944); *Career* former JP Salop, Cdr ATS; *Recreations* gardening, fox-hunting; *Style* - Mrs Arthur Fielden, CBE; Longden Manor, Shrewsbury (☎ Pontesbury 368)

FIELDHOUSE, Sir Harold; KBE (1949, OBE 1934), CB (1947); s of late Frank Fieldhouse; *b* 18 Aug 1892; *Educ* Armley Higher Grade Sch Leeds; *m* 1922, Mabel Elaine, da of George Henry Elliott (d 1914); 2 s (*see* Vice-Adm Sir John (David Elliott) Fieldhouse, KCB); *Career* local govt offr 1909-34, civil servant 1934-59, sec Nat Assistance Bd 1946-59; *Recreations* golf, bridge, music, reading; *Clubs* City Livery, West Hill Golf, Grim's Dyke Golf; *Style* - Sir Harold Fieldhouse, KBE, CB; 5 Gayton ct, Harrow, Middx (☎ 01 427 0918); c/o Midland Bank, Station rd, Harrow, Middx

FIELDHOUSE, Adm Sir John David Elliott; KCB (1981); s of Sir Harold Fieldhouse, KBE, CB, *qv*; *b* 12 Feb 1928; *Educ* RNC Dartmouth; *m* 1953, Margaret Cull; 1 s, 2 da; *Career* dir Naval Warfare MOD 1973-74, Flag Offr Second Flotilla 1974-76, Flag Offr Submarines 1976-78, Controller of Navy 1979-81, CIC Fleet, Allied CIC Channel and CIC Eastern Atlantic Area with Actg Rank of Admiral 1981-, Adm July 1981-; *Style* - Adm Sir John Fieldhouse, KCB; Pippins, 16 Ryde pla, Lee-on-Solent, Hants (☎ Lee-on-Solent 550892)

FIELDING, Hon Mrs (Daphne Winifred Louise); da of 4 Baron Vivian, DSO (d 1940); *b* 1904; *m* 1, 1926 (m dis 1953), 6 Marquess of Bath; m 2, 1953 (m dis 1978), Major Alexander Wallace Fielding, DSO; *Style* - The Hon Mrs Daphne Fielding; 4 Rue du 4 Septembre, Uzès, 30700, France

FIELDING, Leslie; s of Percy Archer Fielding (d 1963); *b* 29 July 1932; *Educ* Queen Elizabeth's Sch Barnet, Emmanuel Cambridge, Sch of Oriental and African Studies London, St Antony's Coll Oxford; *m* 1978, Dr Sally Patricia Joyce (FRHistS), da of late Robert Stanley Thomas Stibbs; 1 da; *Career* diplomat; For Serv 1956, Tehran 1957-60, FO 1960-64, Phnom Penh (chargé d'affaires) 1964-66, Paris 1966-70, FCO 1970-73, transferred to European Cmmn in Brussels 1973-78, head of Delegation of Cmmn of European Communities in Japan 1978-; *Recreations* living in the country; *Clubs* Travellers'; *Style* - Leslie Fielding Esq; EC Delegation, Kowa 25, 8-7 Sanbancho, Chiyoda-Ku, Japan (☎ (03) 239 0441)

FIENNES, *see also* **Twisleton-Wykeham-Fiennes**

FIENNES, David Eustace Martindale Twisleton-Wykeham-; CBE (1964); s of Gerard Yorke Twisleton-Wykeham-Fiennes, CBE (d 1926, s of Rev Hon Wingfield Twisleton-Wykeham-Fiennes, 4 s of 16 Baron Saye and Sele); *b* 7 March 1916; *Educ* Winchester Coll, New Coll Oxford; *Career* dir Booker Agriculture International Ltd, C'wlth Dvpt Corpn Regional Controller E Asia and Pacific 1955-64 (Controller of Operations 1965-67); *Recreations* travelling; *Style* - David Twisleton-Wykeham-Fiennes Esq CBE; Woadmill Farm, Broughton, Banbury, Oxon (☎ Banbury 58898)

FIENNES, Hon Martin Guy; s (twin) of 21 Baron Saye and Sele; *b* 27 Feb 1961; *Educ* Eton, in 2 year (as of Oct 1981) at BNC Oxford; *Style* - The Hon Martin Fiennes; Broughton Castle, Banbury, Oxon (☎ 62624); 44 Cathcart rd, SW10 (☎ 01 352 8606)

FIENNES, Very Rev Hon Oliver William Twisleton-Wykeham-; s of late 20 Baron Saye and Sele OBE MC, and Hersey, da of late Capt Sir Thomas Dacres Butler, KCVO; *b* 1926; *Educ* Eton, New Coll Oxford; *m* 1956, Juliet, da of Dr Trevor Heaton; 2 s, 2 da; *Career* late Lt

Rifle Bde, ChapStJ, Dean of Lincoln 1968-; *Style* - The Very Rev the Hon Oliver Twisleton-Wykeham-Fiennes; The Deanery, Lincoln

FIENNES, Hon Richard Ingel; s and h of 21 Baron Saye and Sele; *b* 19 Aug 1959; *Style* - The Hon Richard Fiennes

FIENNES, Hon Susannah Hersey; da (twin) of 21 Baron Saye and Sele; *b* 1961; *Style* - The Hon Susannah Fiennes

FIENNES, Hon William John; s of 21 Baron Saye and Sele; *b* 1970; *Style* - The Hon William Fiennes

FIFE, 3 Duke of (UK 1900); James George Alexander Bannerman Carnegie; also Earl of Macduff (UK 1900); s of 11 Earl of Southesk (whose h His Grace is) and HRH Princess Maud Alexandra Victoria Georgina Bertha, 2 da of 1 Duke of Fife by HRH The Princess Royal (eldest da of King Edward VII), through whom His Grace is 2 cous of HM The Queen; *b* 23 Sept 1929; *Educ* Gordonstoun, RAC Cirencester; *m* 1956 (m dis 1966), Hon Caroline Dewar, da of 3 Baron Forteviot (she m 2 Gen Sir Richard Worsley); 1 s, 1 da; *Heir* s, Earl of Macduff; *Career* Freeman City of London; served Malaya 1948-50 Scots Gds; landowner, farmer; *Clubs* Turf; *Style* - His Grace The Duke of Fife; Elsick House, Stonehaven, Kincardineshire

FIGG, Sir Leonard Clifford William; KCMG (1981, CMG 1974); s of late Sir Clifford Figg; *b* 17 Aug 1923; *Educ* Charterhouse, Trin Oxford; *m* 1955, Jane Brown; 3 s; *Career* assist under sec of State 1977-80, ambass to Eire 1980-; *Style* - Sir Leonard Figg, KCMG; c/o Foreign and Commonwealth Office, SW1

FIMISTER, John Malcolm; s of George Cadenhead Fimister (d 1962); *b* 10 May 1926; *Educ* Stowe; *m* 1965, Mary Forsyth, da of Wilfrid Bowring Stoddart, JP (d 1973); 1 s, 2 da; *Career* Capt King's Roy Rifle Corps 1943-48, md H E Moss & Co Ltd 1964-70, md Cunard-Brocklebank Bulkers Ltd 1970-73, dir Cunard SS Co Ltd 1971-73, exec dir Common Bros Ltd 1973-, chm Horncastle Crawford & West Ltd 1979-, memb Baltic Exchange; *Recreations* tennis, sailing; *Style* - John Fimister Esq; Blake Hall, Kensworth, Dunstable, Beds

FINCASTLE, Viscount; Malcolm Kenneth Murray; er s and h of 11 Earl of Dunmore; *b* 1946; *m* 1970, Joy Anne, da of A Partridge, of Launceston, Tasmania; *Style* - Viscount Fincastle; PO Box 100, East Devonport, Tasmania

FINCH HATTON, Lady Alice Nan Christiane; da of 16 (& 11) Earl of Winchilsea and Nottingham; *b* 2 May 1970; *Style* - Lady Alice Finch Hatton

FINCH HATTON, Hon Robin Heneage; 2 s of 15 (& 10) Earl of Winchilsea & Nottingham; *b* 1 Nov 1939; *Educ* Gordonstoun; *m* 1962, Molly, da of Col Palgrave Powell, MBE, TD; 2 s, 1 da; *Style* - The Hon Robin Finch Hatton; Town House Farmhouse, Clemsfold, Horsham, Sussex

FINDLAY, Ian Herbert Fyfe; s of late Prof Alexander Findlay, CBE; *b* 5 Feb 1918; *Educ* Fettes Coll Edinburgh; *m* 1950, Alison Mary, da of late Bernard George Ashby; 2 s, 1 da; *Career* chm Price Forbes (Hldgs) Ltd 1967-72, dep chm Sedgwick Forbes (Hldgs) Ltd 1972-74 (chm 1974-77), chm Lloyd's Insurance Brokers Assoc 1969-70, chm Lloyd's 1978-79 (dep chm 1977), chm British Insurance Brokers Assoc 1980-, memb Cncl Guide Dogs for the Blind Assoc 1980-; *Recreations* golf; *Clubs* City of London, Roy Ancient Golf, Addington Golf; *Style* - Ian Findlay Esq; 24 Forest Ridge, Keston Park, Kent (☎ Farnborough (Kent) 52993)

FINDLAY, Cdr James Buchanan; CBE (1957), DL (Ayrshire 1945), RN; s of Maj Robert Elmsall Findlay (d 1928), of Boturich Castle, Dunbartonshire; *b* 7 Jan 1895; *Educ* RNCs Osborne and Dartmouth; *m* 1923, Mary Sancroft Findlay-Hamilton, of Carnell, Ayrshire; 3 s, 1 da; *Career* Cdr RN WW I, ret; dir T D Findlay and Sons Ltd 1926-52, dir Scottish Amicable Life Assur Soc 1933-72, dir Union Bank of Scotland 1933-71, V-Lt of Ayrshire 1966-69; *Recreations* formerly all games, shooting and fishing; *Clubs*

Lansdowne; *Style* - Cdr James Findlay, CBE, DL, RN; The Garden House, Carnell, Kilmarnock, Ayrshire (☎ Fiveways 209)

FINDLAY, Lady Mary Cecilia; *née* Legge; da of late 7 Earl of Dartmouth; *b* 1906; *m* 1929, Cdr Noel Charles Mansfeldt Findlay, RN (ret), s of Sir Mansfeldt de Cardonnel Findlay, GBE, KCMG, CB; 2 s, 1 da; *Style* - Lady Mary Findlay; Court Lodge, Hastingleigh, Ashford, Kent

FINGALL, 12 Earl of (I 1628); Oliver James Horace Plunkett; MC; sits as Baron Fingall (UK 1831); also Baron Killeen (I 1449); s of 11 Earl (d 1929); *b* 17 June 1896; *Educ* Downside; *m* 1926, Jessica (d 1965), da of Allan Hughes, of Lynch, Allerford, Somerset; m 2, 1966, Clair, da of Henry Salmon, of Ballarat, and widow of Frank Richardson, of Geelong, Australia; *Heir* (to Barony of Killeen only) kinsman, Baron Dunsany; *Career* Maj (ret) 17/21 Lancers; *Style* - The Rt Hon The Earl of Fingall, MC; The Commons, Dunsany, Co Meath (☎ Navan 25193)

FINGERHUT, John Hyman; s of late Abraham Fingerhut, of Manchester; *b* 2 Nov 1910; *Educ* Manchester G S, Manchester U; *m* 1950, Beatrice (FCA), da of late Michael Leigh; 2 s, 2 da; *Career* md Merck Sharp & Dohme Ltd 1963-67, chm Merck Sharp & Dohme Ltd 1967-72, regional dir Merck Sharp & Dohme Internat (consultant 1975-77), chm Thomas Morson & Son Ltd 1967-72, consultant to pharmaceutical industry; *Recreations* music, reading, gardening, washing-up; *Style* - John Fingerhut Esq; 76 Green Lane, Edgware, Middx (☎ 01 958 6163)

FINGLAND, Sir Stanley James Gunn; KCMG (1979, CMG 1966); s of late Samuel Gunn Fingland; *b* 19 Dec 1919; *Educ* Royal H S Edinburgh; *m* 1946, Nell, da of late Charles Lister; 1 s, 1 da; *Career* Maj Roy Signals (despatches Italy) 1939-47; HM Diplomatic Serv- Br Dep High Cmmr Port of Spain 1962, Salisbury Rhodesia 1964, Br High Cmmr Freetown 1966-69, Assist Under-Sec of State FO 1969-71, Br Ambass Havana 1972-75, Br High Cmmr Nairobi 1975-79 (concurrently Br Rep to the UN Environmental Programme and to UN Habitat HQ in Nairobi); *Recreations* fishing; *Clubs* Roy Overseas League; *Style* - Sir Stanley Fingland, KCMG; 34 Ashdown, Eaton rd, Hove, Sussex (☎ Brighton 723324)

FINLAISON, Brig Alexander Montagu; CBE (1957), DSO (1944); s of late Maj-Gen J B Finlaison, late RM; *b* 14 March 1904; *Educ* RNCs Osborne and Dartmouth, RMC Sandhurst; *m* 1935, Monica Mary Louise, da of T W Donald, of Grendon, Stirling; 2 da; *Career* Cameronians (Scottish Rifles) 1924, served Sudan Defence Force 1932-38, BGS Scottish Command 1954-57, ADC to HM THe Queen 1955-57, ret 1957; Commandant Queen Victoria Sch Dunblane 1957-64; *Clubs* Naval and Military; *Style* - Brig Alexander Finlaison, CBE, DSO; Gledenholm, Ae, Dumfries (☎ Parkgate 242)

FINLAY, Air Cdre Denis; CBE (1950); s of James Finlay (d 1921); *b* 4 Jan 1912; *Educ* King Edward VI G S Southampton, RAF Coll Cranwell; *m* 1939, Pamela Mary (d 1969), nee Barrett; 1 child; *Career* Air Cdre RAF, Europe NW Africa Italy, dir of Personal Serv (A), Cmdt Aircrew Selection Centre; *Style* - Air Cdre Denis Finlay, CBE; Casa Pamela, Benisa, Alicante, Spain

FINLAY, David Ronald James Bell; s and h of Sir Graeme Finlay, 1 Bt, ERD; *b* 16 Nov 1963; *Educ* Marlborough; *Recreations* shooting, skiing, chess, photography; *Style* - David Finlay Esq; c/o La Campagne, Rozel, Jersey, CI (☎ 0534 51194)

FINLAY, Sir Graeme Bell; 1 Bt (UK 1964), of Epping, Co Essex, ERD; s of James Finlay; *b* 29 Oct 1917; *Educ* Marlborough, UCL; *m* 1953, June, da of Francis Drake, OBE, MC, DL, of the 10 Roy Hussars; 1 s, 2 da; *Heir* s, David Finlay; *Career* MP (C) Epping 1951-64; Dep County Court Judge & Dep Circuit Judge 1967-72 (barr 1946), Assist Juge d'Instruction & Judge of Petty Debts Court Jersey 1972-77; Assist Govt Whip 1957-59, Ld Commissioner Treasury 1959-

60, V-Chamberlain HM Household 1960-64; served WW II Maj S Wales Borderers; *Style* - Sir Graeme Finlay, Bt, ERD; La Campagne, Rozel, St Martin, Jersey, CI (☎ 0534 51194)

FINLAY, (William) Ian (Robertson); CBE (1965); s of William Robertson Finlay (d 1961); *b* 2 Dec 1906; *Educ* Edinburgh Acad, Edinburgh U; *m* 1933, Mary Scott, da of William Henderson Pringle (d 1967); 2 s, 1 da; *Career* art historian and author; dir Roy Scottish Museum 1961-71, keeper of Dept of Art and Archaeology in Royal Scottish Museum 1956-61, Hon Prof of Antiquities to Roy Scottish Acad 1966- and Hon Academician (HRSA); memb Livery of Worshipful Co of Goldsmiths and Freeman of City of London; *Style* - Ian Finlay Esq, CBE; Currie Riggs, Balerno, Midlothian (☎ 031 449 4249); High Corrie, Isle of Arran

FINLAY, Jane Little; da of James Whyte Hepburn (d 1978); *b* 29 Sept 1917; *Educ* Hutcheson's Girls' G S, Glasgow U, Jordanhill Coll Glasgow; *m* 1941, John Alexander Finlay, s of The Rev John Adamson Finlay (d 1978); 1 s, 2 da (1 da decd); *Career* dep chm Equal Opportunities Cmmn 1980; part time memb VAT Tribunals 1974; memb Bromley Community Health Cncl 1974-80; pres British Federation of Univ Womem 1975-78; co chm Women's Nat Commission 1975-77; *Clubs* University Women's; *Style* - Mrs John Finlay; 16 Old Buildings, Lincoln's Inn, WC2 (☎ 01 405 1325); Golf Road, Bickley, Bromley, Kent

FINLAY, Robert Derek; s of William Templeton Finlay (d 1972); *b* 16 May 1932; *Educ* Kingston G S, Emmanuel Cambridge; *m* 1956, Una Ann, da of late David Smith Grant; 2 s, 1 da; *Career* Capt Gordon Highlanders, sr v-pres H J Heinz Co 1981- (md H J Heinz 1971-81); *Recreations* music, tennis; *Clubs* Highland Brigade, Leander, Duquesne; *Style* - Robert Finlay Esq; Back Bone rd, Sewickley Heights, Pennsylvania 15143, USA

FINLEY, Sir Peter Hamilton; OBE, DFC; s of late C A Finley; *b* 6 Dec 1919; *Educ* The King's Sch Paramatta; *m* 1947, Berenice, da of W V Armstrong; 1 s, 1 da; *Career* kt 1981; chm Custom Credit Corpn Ltd 1973-; dir Nat Bank of Asia Ltd 1970-; *Style* - Sir Peter Finley, OBE, DFC; 50 Treatts rd, Lindfield, NSW 2070, Australia

FINN, Hugh Roderick; CBE (1974), DL (Kent 1979); s of George William Finn; *b* 12 April 1911; *Educ* Haileybury; *m* 1954, Mel; 2 s; *Career* farmer and co dir, chm Stonefarms Ltd; dir and chm of a number of Ag Marketing Cos, fell of Roy Ag Soc 1970, gov Wye Coll and chm Estates Panel 1952-, memb Lord Chllr's Advsy Ctee (Kent), chm Kent Ag Exec Ctee 1954-68; *Clubs* Athenaeum; *Style* - Hugh Finn Esq, CBE, DL; Nackington Farmhouse, Canterbury, Kent

FINSBERG, Geoffrey; MBE (1959), JP (Inner London 1962), MP Hampstead 1970-; s of Monte Finsberg, MC (d 1972); *b* 13 June 1926; *Educ* City of London Sch; *m* 1969, Pamela Benbow, da of Roland Benbow Hill; *Career* parly under-sec of State Dept of Environment 1979-, memb Hampstead Boro Cncl 149-65, memb Camden Boro Cncl 1964-74, v-chm Cons Pty 1975-79; *Recreations* bridge; *Clubs* St Stephen's Constitutional; *Style* - Geoffrey Finsberg Esq, MBE, JP, MP; 80 Westbere rd, NW2 (☎ 01 435 5320); Rosewell, White rd, Methwold, Norfolk

FINTRIE, Lord; James Alexander Norman Graham; s and h of Marquess of Graham; *b* 16 Aug 1973; *Heir* bro, Lord Ronald Graham; *Style* - Lord Fintrie

FIRBANK, Maj-Gen Cecil Llewellyn; CB (1953), CBE (1951), DSO (1944), and Bar (1945), DL (Somerset 1959); s of Godfrey Firbank (d 1925); *b* 18 March 1903; *Educ* Cheltenham Coll, RMC Sandhurst; *m* 1, 1934, Audrey, nee Hobhouse (m dis 1952); 1 s; m 2, 1952, Mary Brenda, nee Fleetwood-Wilson; *Career* Maj-Gen, 1 Somerset LI 1924, GOC SW Dist and 43 Wessex Div (TA) 1951-54, Dir of Infantry War Office 1955-58, Hon Col 4/5 Somerset LI (TA) 1955-60, dir Civil Defence for Wales 1960-65; *Recreations* field sports; *Clubs* Army and Navy; *Style* - Maj-Gen Cecil Firbank CB, CBE, DSO*, DL; The Owls, Charlton Horethorne, nr Sherborne, Dorset (☎

Corton Denham 279)

FIREMAN, Bruce Anthony; s of Michael Fireman; *b* 14 Feb 1944; *Educ* Kilburn G S, Jesus Cambridge; *m* 1968, Barbara, nee Mollett; *Career* slr 1970; merchant banker, acting head fin Charterhouse Japhet 1981, dir strategic planning 1981-; dir- Blousit Ltd, Charterhouse Japhet, Japhet Investment Tst, Kildsmemo Ltd, Kinsbourne Investments, New Issue Permanent Investments, New Issue Unit Tst Managers, Phaldine Ltd, Southern Cross TV, Southwood Hall Management, Watbaine Ltd; *Style* - Bruce Fireman Esq; c/o Charterhouse Japhet Ltd, 1 Paternoster Row, St Paul's, EC4 (☎ 01 248 3999); 19 Southwood Hall, N6 (☎ 01 444 7125)

FIRMSTON-WILLIAMS, Peter; OBE (1979); s of Geoffrey Firmston-Williams (d 1964); *b* 30 Aug 1918; *Educ* Harrow; *m* 1945, Margaret, da of Wilfred Butters Beaulah (d 1967); 1 s, 1 da; *Career* Capt (mil) N Africa, Low Countries and Germany, md Cooper & Co's Stores Ltd 1958-62, md Key Markets Ltd 1962-71, dir Associated Dairies Ltd 1973-, md Asda Stores Ltd 1971-; *Recreations* golf, water skiing; *Style* - Peter Firmston-Williams Esq, OBE; 30 Rowland pla, Northwood, Middx (☎ 092 74 24530); Almsford House, 4 Fulwith Mill Lane, Harrogate, N Yorks (☎ 879430)

FIRNBERG, David; s of Leopold Bernard Firnberg; *b* 1 May 1930; *Educ* Merchant Taylors'; *m* 1957, Sylvia Elizabeth, nee du Cros; 1 s, 3 da; *Career* dir Nat Computing Centre 1975-80, pres Assoc of Project Managers 1977-, md Urwick Nexos Ltd 1980-; *Recreations* writing; *Clubs* English Speaking Union, Wig and Pen; *Style* - David Firnberg Esq; The Great House, Buckland Common, Tring, Herts

FIRTH, Maurice Murrowood; CBE (1959); s of Harry Firth (d 1942); *b* 28 Jan 1911; *Educ* Malvern, Jena U Germany; *m* 1, 1938 (m dis 1951), Joan, da of late Dr Gerald Rickett; 1 s, 2 da; m 2, 1952, Isobel Alwynne, da of late Wilfred Ash; *Career* Cdr RNVR; slr 1933; entered Foreign Office 1946, 1st Sec Staff of Cmmr Gen Singapore 1948-51, 1st Sec Vienna 1953-57, Ankara 1958-62; *Recreations* golf, yachting; *Clubs* New Zealand Golf; *Style* - Maurice Firth Esq CBE; 14 Priory Mansions, Drayton gdns, SW10

FIRTH, Prof Sir Raymond William; s of Wesley Hugh Bourne Firth (d 1977); *b* 25 March 1901; *Educ* Auckland G S (NZ), Auckland University College, LSE; *m* 1936, Rosemary, da of Sir Gilbert Upcott, KCB (d 1967); 1 s; *Career* Prof of Anthropology U of London 1944-68 (now Emeritus); kt 1973; *Recreations* Romanesque architecture, early music; *Clubs* Athenaeum; *Style* - Prof Sir Raymond Firth; 33 Southwood av, N6 (☎ 01 348 0768)

FISCHEL, John Roy; s of late Roy Fischel, MC; *b* 2 Sept 1924; *Educ* Cheltenham and Royal Navy; *m* 1952, Anita, da of late Capt Maximilian Despard, DSC, RN; 2 s, 3 da; *Career* commodity merchant, chm L M Fischel & Co Ltd 1966- (dir 1960-), chm L M Fischel (Sugar) Ltd 1965-, dir Corrie MacColl & Sons Ltd 1967-, dir Baltic Mercantile & Shipping Exchange 1975-80; *Recreations* shooting, sailing (yacht- 'Matawa'); *Clubs* Castaways, RCC, RNSA, MCC, KCCC; *Style* - John Fischel Esq; The Mount, Shoreham, nr Sevenoaks, Kent

FISHBOURNE, Joseph Russell; CBE (1957), DL (Essex 1962); s of Lt-Col C E Fishbourne (late 5 Fusiliers, ka 1916), of Ashfield Hall, Queen's Co, Eire; *b* 18 Nov 1909; *Educ* Harrow, RMC Sandhurst, Army Staff Coll; *m* 1937, Jean Caroline, da of Col L G Harrison, of Morant Bay, Jamaica (d 1950); 1 s, 1 da; *Career* Brig; commissioned 5 Fusiliers 1929, transferred to 3 Carabiniers 1937, Commanding Officer 1950-53, Colonel of Regiment 1957-66, Regional Sec Country Landowners Assoc 1963-78; *Recreations* shooting, fishing and countryside; *Clubs* Cavalry, Essex Club; *Style* - Brig Joseph Fishbourne, CBE, DL; Lime House, Earls Colne, nr Colchester, Essex (☎ Earls Colne 2493)

FISHBURN, J Dudley; s of late Eskdale Fishburn and Mrs Peter Murray-Lee, & step s of Peter Murray-Lee, of Eaton sq

(Mr Fishburn's family were formerly the proprietors of the fine Tudor mansion Bramfield House, now the Police College, near Basingstoke); *b* 8 June 1946; *Educ* Eton, Harvard; *m* 1981, Victoria, da of Jack Boles and step da of Lady Anne Boles, nee Waldegrave (da of Earl Waldegrave); *Career* exec ed The Economist; Cons candidate IOW 1979; *Clubs* Harvard Club of New York; *Style* - Dudley Fishburn Esq; 16 West Halkin st, SW1 (☎ 01 235 1184)

FISHER OF REDNAL, Baroness (Life Peeress UK 1974); Doris Mary Gertrude Fisher; JP (Birmingham 1961); da of late Frederick James Satchwell, BEM; *b* 13 Sept 1919; *Educ* Tinker's Farm Girls' Sch, Fircroft Coll, Bournville Day Continuation Coll; *m* 1939, Joseph Fisher (decd); 2 da; *Career* joined Lab Pty 1945, memb Birmingham City Cncl 1952-74, MP (L) Birmingham (Ladywood) 1970-74, MEP 1975-79, hon alderman Birmingham 1974, memb Warrington New Town Dvpt Corpn 1974-, memb Gen Medical Cncl 1974-79, v-pres Assoc of Municipal Authorities; *Style* - The Rt Hon The Lady Fisher of Rednal JP; 36 Irwin av, Rednal, Birmingham (☎ 021 453 3365)

FISHER, 3 Baron (UK 1909); John Vavasseur Fisher; DSC (1944), JP (Norfolk 1970), DL (1968); s of 2 Baron (d 1955, himself s of Adm of the Fleet 1 Baron (Sir John) Fisher, GCB, OM, GCVO, better known as Jacky Fisher, whose feud with Lord Charles Beresford so galvanised naval circles prior to WW I); *b* 24 July 1921; *Educ* Stowe, Trin Cambridge; *m* 1, 1949 (m dis 1969), Elizabeth Ann Penelope, da of late Maj Herbert Holt, MC; 2 s, 2 da; m 2, 1970, Hon Rosamund Ann, nee Clifford, da of 12 Baron Clifford of Chudleigh and formerly w of Geoffrey Forrester Fairbairn; *Heir* s, Hon Patrick Vavasseur Fisher; *Career* sometime Lt RNVR WW II; dir Kilverstone Latin American Zoo 1973, memb Eastern Gas Bd 1961-70, memb E Anglian Economic Planning Cncl 1972; *Style* - The Rt Hon The Lord Fisher, DSC, JP, DL; Kilverstone Hall, Thetford, Norfolk (☎ 2222)

FISHER, Hon Bridget Ann; da (by 1 m) of 3 Baron Fisher; *b* 1956; *Style* - The Hon Bridget Fisher

FISHER, Hon Benjamin Vavasseur; s (by 1 m) of 3 Baron Fisher; *b* 1958; *Style* - The Hon Benjamin Fisher

FISHER, Charles Murray; s of Hon Alderman K J Fisher of Cheltenham; *b* 24 Dec 1949; *Educ* Cheltenham Coll, Oxford U; *Career* dir Sharpe & Fisher Ltd 1980-, Sharpe & Fisher (Wales) Ltd 1979-, md Sandford Ltd 1979-, Bayshill Estate Ltd 1979-; *Recreations* travel, sport; *Clubs* MCC, Annabel's; *Style* - Charles Fisher Esq; Rossetti Gd Mansions, Flood st, SW3 (☎ 01 352 7548); Hampnett Lodge, Hampnett, Glos (☎ Northleach 596)

FISHER, Hon Francis Forman; MC (1944); s of late Most Rev Baron Fisher of Lambeth; *b* 25 Sept 1919; *Educ* Repton, Clare Cambridge (BA, MA), Oxford (MA); *Career* late Maj Sherwood Foresters TA (Res), housemaster of Repton Sch 1954-66, former warden St Edward's Sch Oxford, master Wellington Coll 1966-, chm Headmasters' Conference 1973; memb Archbishop of Canterbury's Commission on Christian Initiation; a gov of several schs; *Recreations* cricket, golf; *Style* - The Hon Francis Fisher, MC; The Master's Lodge, Wellington College, Crowthorne, Berks

FISHER, Francis George Robson; s of John Henry Fisher (d 1941); *b* 9 April 1921; *Educ* Liverpool College, Oxford U; *m* 1965, Sheila Vernon, da of late David Dunsire; 1 s; *Career* schoolmaster, housemaster and head of English Kingswood Sch Bath 1950-59, headmaster Bryanston Sch Blandford 1959-74, ch master of King Edward's Sch Birmingham and head master of the Schs of King Edward VI in Birmingham 1974-; *Recreations* music, sailing, reading; *Style* - Francis Fisher Esq; Vince House, 341 Bristol rd, Birmingham, B5 7SW

FISHER, Hon Mrs (Gwen Elfrida Penelope); *née* Abbott; da of 4 Baron Tenterden (d 1939, when the Barony became extinct); *b* 1908; *m* 1941, William Fisher; 2 s; *Style* - The Hon Mrs Fisher

FISHER, Hon Geoffrey Robert Chevallier; s of late Baron Fisher of Lambeth (Life Peer); *b* 1926; *Educ* Repton, Emmanuel Cambridge (BA, MB, BChir); *m* 1961, Jill Audrey, nee Cooper; children; *Career* D (Obst) RCOG 1952, Surg Lt RN (Emergency Res); *Style* - The Hon Geoffrey Fisher; 3 Wendover Drive, New Malden, Surrey

FISHER, Hon Humphrey Richmond; s of late Baron Fisher of Lambeth (Life Peer); *b* 1923; *Educ* Repton; *m* 1959, Diana Beresford, da of C Beresford Davis; *Career* Lt RA, film technician and producer 1946-54, exec producer BBC TV 1954-64, rep Australia and NZ 1964-67 and Head of Science and Features BBC TV 1967-69, Dir of Television Features Australian Broadcasting Cmmn 1969-; *Style* - The Hon Humphrey Fisher; 32 South st, Edgecliff, NSW 2027, Australia

FISHER, Col Jocelyn; CBE (1967); *b* 10 April 1913; *Career* Col WRAC; *Clubs* Naval and Military; *Style* - Col Jocelyn Fisher CBE; 21 Victoria rd, Topsham, Exeter (☎ Topsham 3061)

FISHER, Lady Jane Angela; da of George Paulet and sis of 18 Marquess of Winchester; *b* 15 Nov 1939; *m* 1972, Christopher John Fisher; *Career* raised to rank of Marquess's da 1970; *Style* - Lady Jane Fisher

FISHER, Lady Karen (Jean); *née* Carnegie; da of 13 Earl of Northesk; *b* 1951; *m* 1977, Hon Patrick Vavasseur Fisher, s of 3 Baron Fisher, DSC; 1 da; *Style* - Lady Karen Fisher; 217 New King's rd, SW6

FISHER OF CAMDEN, Baroness; Millie; da of Isaac Gluckstein; *m* 1930, Baron Fisher of Camden (Life Peer, d 1979); 1 da; *Style* - The Rt Hon the Lady Fisher of Camden; 48 Viceroy ct, Prince Albert rd, NW8

FISHER, Hon Patrick Vavasseur; s (by 1 m) and h of 3 Baron Fisher; *b* 14 June 1953; *m* 1977, Lady Karen Jean Carnegie, da of 13 Earl of Northesk; 1 s, 1 da; *Style* - The Hon Patrick Fisher; 217 New King's rd, SW6 (☎ 01 731 3079)

FISHER, Baroness - Hon Rosamund Ann; *née* Clifford; da of late 12 Baron Clifford of Chudleigh; *b* 22 May 1924; *Educ* St Mary's Convent Ascot; *m* 1, 1946 (m dis 1965), Geoffrey Forester Fairbairn (decd); 2 s, 1 da; m 2, 1970, 3 Baron Fisher; *Career* zoo director and author; *Style* - The Rt Hon the Lady Fisher; Kilverstone Hall, Thetford; Marklye, Rushlake Green, Heathfield, Sussex

FISHER OF LAMBETH, Baroness; Rosamond Chevallier; da of late Rev Arthur Francis Emilius Forman; *m* 1917, Most Rev and Rt Hon Baron Fisher of Lambeth (Life Peer, d 1972); *Style* - The Rt Hon the Lady Fisher of Lambeth; Trent Rectory, Sherborne, Dorset

FISHER, Rear-Adm Ralph Lindsay; CB (1957), DSO (1940), OBE (1941), DSC (1943); s of Frank Lindsay Fisher CBE (d 1947); *b* 18 June 1903; *Educ* RNCs Osborne and Dartmouth; *m* 1934, Ursula Mary, da of Dr Edmund Arthur Carver (d 1946); 5 da; *Career* Rear-Adm RN; 1929-31 officer training, 1937-39 training cruiser; WW II - cmd destroyers Atlantic Arctic and Mediterranean, on staff Med, and with Eighth Army; acting Commandant Joint Services Staff Coll 1948-50, Ch of Staff Far East 1950-52, 'Indefatigable' 1952-54, Flag Officerr Ground Training 1955-57, ret; *Recreations* cruising under sail (owner of yacht 'Yeong'); *Clubs* Naval and Military, Royal Cruising; *Style* - Rear-Adm Ralph Fisher CB DSO OBE DSC; Crossaig, Tarbert, Argyll, Scotland (☎ Skipness 234)

FISHER, Capt Roger Roland Sutton; CBE (1973), DSC (1944); s of Surgn-Capt Arthur Roland Fisher (d 1973); *b* 3 Aug 1919; *Educ* Clifton Coll; *m* 1949, June Audrey, da of Neville Foster, OBE, MC (d 1978); 1 s, 1 da; *Career* Capt RN- 1937 Cadetship, 1957-59 Cdr HM Naval Base Bahrain, 1964-66 Dep Sec to Chs of Staff, 1967-70 Ch Naval Judge Advocate, 1971-73 cmd HMS Pembroke, 1973 ret; called to the Bar Gray's Inn 1950, dep Circuit Judge SE Circuit 1973-, Legal Chm Indust Tribunals 1976-; marine artist, FRSA 1978; *Recreations* painting, sailing; *Style* - Capt Roger Fisher CBE DSC RN; 34 Kidbrooke Grove, Blackheath, SE3

FISHER, Hon Richard Temple; s of late Baron Fisher of Lambeth (Life Peer); *b* 1930; *Educ* St Edward's Sch Oxford, King's Cambridge; *m* 1969, Clare Margaret, da of J Lewen Le Fanu; children; *Career* Hon Maj TA Gen List late 16/5 Queen's Roy Lancers, assist master and housemaster Repton 1953-69, Headmaster of Bilton Grange Prep Sch 1969-; *Style* - The Hon Richard Fisher; Bilton Grange, Dunchurch, Rugby

FISHER-HOCH, Hon Mrs (Nesta Donne); *née* Philipps; DL (Carmarthenshire); da of late 1 Baron Kylsant; *b* 1903; *m* 1, 1921, 10 Earl of Coventry (ka 1940); 1 s, 2 da; m 2, 1953, Maj Terrance Vincent Fisher-Hoch, RA; *Career* Ch Cdr ATS 1939-45; *Style* - The Hon Mrs Fisher-Hoch, DL; Plâs Llanstephan, Carmarthen, Dyfed, Wales

FISKE, Hon Giles Geoffrey; s (by 1 m) of late Baron Fiske (Life Peer); *b* 1935; *Style* - The Hon Giles Fiske; 23 Blenheim rd, NW8

FISKE, Baroness; Josephine; da of Alan Coppin, JP, of Hong Kong; *m* 1955, as his 2 w, Baron Fiske (Life Peer, d 1975); *Style* - The Rt Hon the Lady Fiske; 23 Blenheim rd, St John's Wood, NW8

FISON, Charles William; s and h of Sir Richard Fison, 4 Bt, DSC; *b* 6 Feb 1954; *Style* - Charles Fison Esq

FISON, Sir Richard Guy; 4 Bt (UK 1905), DSC (1944); s of Capt Sir (William) Guy Fison, 3 Bt, MC (d 1964); *b* 9 Jan 1917; *Educ* Eton, New Coll Oxford; *m* 1952, Elyn, da of Mogens Hartmann, of Bordeaux; 1 s, 1 da; *Heir* s, Charles William Fison; *Career* vintner; *Style* - Sir Richard Fison, Bt, DSC; Wingate, Long Sutton, Basingstoke, Hants (☎ Long Sutton 576)

FITCH, Brian Hill; s of late Stanley Fitch; *b* 19 May 1930; *Educ* Haileybury; *m* 1955, Susan Margaret, nee Edwards; 1 s, 1 da; *Career* money broker, property investment specialist, chm and md London Financial Agency Ltd 1972-, md The London & Westminster Property Co Ltd 1962-; *Recreations* curio and antique collector; *Clubs* Rolls Royce Enthusiasts Club; *Style* - Brian Fitch Esq; Grayleigh, Gerrards Cross, Bucks (☎ Gerrards Cross 84702)

FITTON, Lady Eileen Cecil Theo; *née* Paulet; da of Capt Charles Paulet, MVO; sis of 17 Marquess of Winchester (d 1968); *b* 1916; *m* Joseph Fitton; *Career* raised to rank of Marquess's da 1970; *Style* - Lady Eileen Fitton; 1610E 11th Av, Vancouver 12, BC, Canada

FITZ-CLARENCE, Viscount; Anthony Charles Fitz-Clarence; s (by 1 m) and h of 6 Earl of Munster; *b* 21 March 1926; *Educ* St Edward's Sch Oxford; *m* 1, 1949 (m dis 1966), Louise Marguerite Diana Delvigne; 2 da; m 2, 1966 (m dis 1979), Mrs Pamela Margaret Hyde, nee Spooner; 1 da; m 3, 1979, Alexa, da of late Lt-Col E B Maxwell; *Career* RN 1942-46; graphic designer (stained glass) 1950-79, conservator for the Burrell Collection 1979-; *Clubs* Chelsea Arts; *Style* - Viscount Fitz-Clarence; 17 Lowndes st, Barrhead, Glasgow (☎ 041 881 1595)

FITZ-CLARENCE, Hon Georgina; da of Viscount Fitz-Clarence by his 2 w; *b* 1966; *Style* - The Hon Georgina Fitz-Clarence

FITZALAN HOWARD, Lady Carina Mary Gabriel; da of 17 Duke of Norfolk, CB, CBE, MC; *b* 20 Feb 1952; *Style* - Lady Carina Fitzalan Howard

FITZALAN HOWARD, Lord Gerald Bernard; s of 17 Duke of Norfolk, CB, CBE, MC; *b* 13 June 1962; *Style* - Lord Gerald Fitzalan Howard

FITZALAN-HOWARD, Lord Martin; JP (N R Yorks 1966); s of 3 Baron Howard of Glossop, MBE, and Baroness Beaumont, OBE, and bro of 17 Duke of Norkfolk, CB, CBE, MC; *b* 22 Oct 1922; *Educ* Ampleforth and Trin Cambridge; *m* 1948, Bridget Anne, da of late Lt-Col Arnold Ramsay Keppel (fourth in descent from Hon Frederick Keppel, sometime Bp of Exeter and 4 s of 2 Earl of Albemarle, KG, KB); 1 s, 4 da; *Career* late Capt Grenadier Guards; High Sheriff 1979-80; 1939-45 War (wounded), Palestine 1945-46; *Style* -

Lord Martin Fitzalan-Howard, JP; Brockfield Hall, York

FITZALAN-HOWARD, Lord Mark; s of 3 Baron Howard of Glossop, MBE, and Baroness Beaumont, OBE; bro of 17 Duke of Norfolk, CB, CBE, MC; *b* 28 March 1934; *Educ* Ampleforth; *m* 1961, Jacynth Rosemary, da of Sir Martin Alexander Lindsay of Dowhill, 1 Bt, CBE, DSO; 2 da; *Career* late Coldstream Gds; *Style* - Lord Mark Fitzalan-Howard; 13 Campden Hill Sq, W8

FITZALAN-HOWARD, Lady Mary (Katharine); MVO (1974); da of 16 Duke of Norfolk, KG, GCVO, GBE, TD, PC (d 1975); *b* 14 Aug 1940; *Career* hp to Lordship of Herries of Terregles; Lady-in-Waiting to HRH Princess Alexandra, the Hon Mrs Angus Ogilvy, 1964-; *Style* - Lady Mary Fitzalan-Howard, MVO

FITZALAN-HOWARD, Lord Michael; KCVO (1971, MVO 4 Class 1952), CB (1968), CBE (1962, MBE 1949), MC (1944), DL (Wilts 1974); 2 s of 3 Baron Howard of Glossop, MBE, and Baroness Beaumont, OBE (Barony called out of abeyance in her favour 1896); bro of 17 Duke of Norfolk; *b* 22 Oct 1916; *Educ* Ampleforth, Trin Cambridge; *m* 1, 1946, Jean (d 1947), da of Sir Hew Hamilton-Dalrymple, 9 Bt; 1 da ; m 2, 1950, Jane, da of Capt W Meade Newman; 4 s, 1 da; *Career* Maj-Gen, late Scots Gds; Kt Sov Order Malta; GOC London Dist & Maj-Gen Cmmdg Household Div 1968-71; Marshal Diplomatic Corps 1972-81; served WW II NW Europe & Palestine & Malaya subsequently; granted rank of Duke's s 1975; Col Life Gds 1979-, Gold Stick to HM 1979-; chm Cncl TAVR Assocs 1973-; *Clubs* Turf, Buck's; *Style* - Maj-Gen Lord Michael Fitzalan-Howard KCVO CB CBE MC DL; St James's Palace, SW1; Fovant House, Fovant, Wilts (☎ 617)

FITZALAN-HOWARD, Lady Sarah Margaret; da of 16 Duke of Norfolk, KG, GCVO, GBE, TD, PC (d 1975); *b* 28 Sept 1941; *Style* - Lady Sarah Fitzalan-Howard

FITZGEORGE-BALFOUR, Sir (Robert George) Victor; KCB (1968, CB 1965), CBE (1945), DSO (1950), MC (1939), DL (W Sussex 1977); s of Robert Balfour, of Stirling, and Iris FitzGeorge, who m subsequently (as his 2 w) Prince Vladimir Emmanuelovitch Galitzine (*see* Prince George Galitzine); Iris was da of Col George FitzGeorge, Roy Welch Fusiliers, who was in his turn s of HRH Prince George, 2 Duke of Cambridge (whose f was 7 s of George III), by HRH's w Louisa, nee Fairbrother (their nuptials not only took place contrary to the Royal Marriage Act but three and a half years after the Col's birth); the General is hence 4 cous once removed to HM The Queen; *b* 15 Sept 1913; *Educ* Eton, King's Cambridge; *m* 1938, Mary, da of Adm Arthur Christian, CB, MVO, and descended from an ancient family of Manx landowners, one of whom was involved in a dispute with the then sovereign of the IOM, the Earl of Derby; 1 s (Robin, b 1951, educ Eton), 1 da (Diana, b 1946); *Career* chm Nat Fund for Research into Crippling Diseases 1975-, chm Gen Action Research for the Crippled Child; served Coldstream Gds 1934-73 in M East, NW Europe (WW II), later Dir Mil Ops MOD, Sr Army Instructor IDC, V-Ch Gen Staff 1968-70, UK Mil Rep NATO 1971-73; Col Cmdt HAC 1976-; *Clubs* Army & Navy; *Style* - Gen Sir Victor FitzGeorge-Balfour KCB CBE DSO MC DL; The Old Rectory, W Chiltington, W Sussex (☎ 2255)

FITZGERALD, Adrian James Andrew Denis; s and h of Sir George FitzGerald, 5 Bt, MC; *b* 24 June 1940; *Educ* Harrow; *Career* Cllr Roy Boro of Kensington and Chelsea; *Style* - Adrian FitzGerald Esq; 16 Clareville st, SW7; Lackaneask, Valentia Island, Co Kerry

FITZGERALD, Rev Daniel Patrick; s of late Sir John Fitzgerald, 2 Bt and hp of bro, Rev (Sir) Edward Fitzgerald (3 Bt); *b* 28 June 1916; *Style* - The Rev Daniel Fitzgerald

FITZGERALD, Hon Mrs Eustace - Dorothy Anderson; da of late George Walter Constable; *m* 1936, as his 2 w, Hon Eustace Robert FitzGerald (s of late Baron FitzGerald, Life Peer) who d 1944; *Style* - The Hon Mrs Eustace FitzGerald; 1 Harbour Close, Haven rd, Canford Cliffs, Poole, Dorset

FITZGERALD, Rev (Sir) Edward Thomas; (3 Bt, UK 1903); s of Sir John Joseph Fitzgerald, 2 Bt (d 1957); suc his father but does not use title; *b* 7 March 1912; *Heir* bro, Rev Daniel Patrick Fitzgerald; *Career* Roman Catholic priest; *Style* - The Rev Edward Fitzgerald; Mayfield, Cork

FITZGERALD, Lady Francesca Emily Purcell; da of Marquess of Kildare; *b* 6 July 1976; *Style* - Lady Francesca FitzGerald

FITZGERALD, Garret; s of Desmond FitzGerald (Min External Affrs Irish Free State 1922-27, Min Def 1927-32); *b* 9 Feb 1926; *Educ* St Brigid's Sch Bray, Coláiste na Rinne Waterford, Belvedere Coll Dublin, U Coll Dublin & King's Inns Dublin; *m* 1947, Joan, da of Charles O'Farrell; 2 s, 1 da; *Career* Taoiseach (literally chieftain; practically, PM) of Eire July 1981-; Ldr Fine Gael, V-Pres European People's Pty (Christian Democratic Gp European Parl) and Electoral Reform Soc London; statistician and political economist; formerly with Aer Lingus, currently on secondment from post as lecturer in Dept Political Economy U Coll Dublin; memb Irish Senate 1965-69, Minister for Foreign Affairs 1973-77, President Council of Ministers EEC January-June 1975; md EIU Ireland; Irish correspondent BBC, Financial Times, Economist, etc, economic correspondent Irish Times; barrister; member of Dáil (TD) Dublin South East; *Style* - Garret FitzGerald Esq, TD

FITZGERALD, Maj Sir George Peter Maurice; 5 Bt (UK 1880), MC (1944); 23 Knight of Kerry; s of Capt Sir Arthur Henry Brinsley FitzGerald, 4 Bt (d 1967); *b* 27 Feb 1917; *Educ* Harrow, RMC; *m* 1939, Angela Dora, da of late Capt James Rankin Mitchell; 1 s, 1 da; *Heir* s, Adrian James Andrew FitzGerald; *Career* 2 Lt Irish Gds 137, served Palestine 1938 (despatches), and Norway, N Africa, Italy 1939-45, Maj 1943, ret 1948; *Style* - Maj Sir George FitzGerald, Bt, MC; Cedar Court, Alderton, nr Woodbridge, Suffolk (☎ Shottisham 331)

FITZGERALD, Lord John; 2 s of 8 Duke of Leinster by his 2 w Anne; *b* 3 March 1952; *Career* Capt 5 Inniskilling Dragoon Gds; *Style* - Lord John FitzGerald

FITZGERALD, Sir William James; MC (1918), QC (1936); s of Joseph Fitzgerald MB (d 1926); *b* 19 May 1894; *Educ* Blackrock Coll Dublin, Trin Coll Dublin; *m* m 1, 1933, Erica, nee Clarke (m dis 1946); 1 s; m 2, 1956, Cynthia Mary, nee Foster; *Career* kt 1944, barr 1922, Crown Counsel Nigeria 1924, Attorney-Gen N Rhodesia 1932-36 (Palestine 1937-44), Ch Justice Palestine 1944-48, pres Lands Tribunal England 1950-65; *Clubs* Athenaeum; *Style* - Sir William Fitzgerald, MC, QC; 47 Sussex sq, Brighton (☎ 688059)

FITZHARRIS, Viscount; James Carleton Harris; s and h of 6 Earl of Malmesbury; *b* 19 June 1946; *Educ* Eton, Queen's Coll St Andrews U (MA); *m* 1969, Sally Ann, da of Sir Richard Newton Rycroft, 7 Bt; 3 s, 1 da; *Heir* s, Hon James Harris; *Style* - Viscount FitzHarris; Heather Row Farm House, Nately Scures, Basingstoke, Hants (☎ Hook 3138)

FITZHERBERT, Hon Aileen Mary; da of 14 Baron Stafford; *b* 1953; *Style* - The Hon Aileen Fitzherbert

FITZHERBERT, Hon Francis Melfort William; s and h of 14 Baron Stafford; *b* 13 March 1954; *Educ* Ampleforth, Reading U, RAC Cirencester; *m* 1980, Katharine Mary, da of John Codrington, of Barnes, SW; *Career* farmer; *Recreations* country sports, cricket, golf; *Clubs* Army & Navy, Free Foresters, I Zingari, Trentham Golf; *Style* - The Hon Francis Fitzherbert; Gorsty Hill Farm, Yarnfield, Stone, Staffs

FITZHERBERT, Sir John Richard Frederick; 6 Bt (GB 1784), TD; s of Ven Henry Edward FitzHerbert, (Archdeacon of Derby 1942-52, s of 5 Bt) (d 1958); suc unc, Sir William FitzHerbert, 7 Bt, 1963; *b* 15 Sept 1913; *Educ* Charterhouse, RAC Cirencester; *m* 1957, Kathleen Anne, da of late H Johnson Rees and formerly w of Henry Astell; *Heir* nephew, Richard

Ranulph FitzHerbert; *Career* formerly Capt Sherwood Foresters (TA); chartered surveyor; *Recreations* fishing; *Style* - Sir John FitzHerbert, Bt, TD; Tissington Hall, Ashbourne, Derbyshire (☎ Parwich 246)

FITZHERBERT, Hon Philip Basil; s of 14 Baron Stafford; *b* 1962; *Style* - The Hon Philip Fitzherbert

FITZHERBERT, Richard Ranulph; s of late Rev David FitzHerbert, MC, bro of 8 Bt; hp of unc, Sir John FitzHerbert, 8 Bt; *b* 2 Nov 1963; *Style* - Richard FitzHerbert Esq

FITZHERBERT, Hon Thomas Alastair; s of 14 Baron Stafford; *b* 1955; *Career* Lt Guards' Div; *Style* - The Hon Thomas Fitzherbert

FITZHERBERT, Hon Wendy Helen; da of 14 Baron Fitzherbert; *b* 1961; *Style* - The Hon Wendy Fitzherbert

FITZHERBERT-BROCKHOLES, Michael John; JP (1960 Lancashire), DL (1975); s of John William Fitzherbert-Brockholes, CBE, MC, JP, DL (d 1963), and Hon Eileen French, da of 4 Baron de Freyne; *b* 12 June 1920; *Educ* Oratory Sch, New Coll Oxford; *m* 1950, Mary Edith, da of Capt Charles Moore, CVO, MC (d 1965), sometime extra equerry to HM, by his w, Lady Dorothie Feilding, da of 9 Earl of Denbigh, GCVO; 4 s; *Career* Maj Scots Gds (Italy North West Europe) 1940-46; memb Lancashire C C 1967-, chm Education Ctee 1977-; OStJ; *Recreations* gardening; *Style* - Michael Fitzherbert-Brockholes Esq JP, DL; Claughton Hall, Garstang, nr Preston, Lancashire (☎ Brock 40286)

FITZMAURICE, Lt-Col Sir Desmond FitzJohn; CIE (1941); s of John Day Stokes Fitzmaurice ICS (d 1897); *b* 17 Aug 1893; *Educ* Bradfield Coll, RMA, Cambridge; *m* 1926, Nancy, da of Rev John Sherlock Leake (d 1934); 1 s, 2 da; *Career* 1914-1930 RE (France, Belgium, Italy, India) Lt-Col, 1928-29 Ch Engr Callender Cable & Construction Co, 1929-33 Dep Master of the Mint Bombay & Calcutta, 1934-46 Master Security Printing India and Controller of Stamps India & Burma, kt 1946; *Recreations* genealogy, wine-making, travel, languages; *Style* - Lt-Col Sir Desmond Fitzmaurice CIE; 10B South Park rd, Wimbledon, SW19 (☎ 01 543 1843)

FITZMAURICE, Sir Gerald Gray; GCMG (1960, KCMG 1954, CMG 1946), QC (1957); s of Vice-Adm Sir Maurice Fitzmaurice, KCVO, CB, CMG, (d 1923 in Simonstown, when CIC S African States); *b* 24 Oct 1901; *Educ* Malvern, Gonville and Caius Cambridge; *m* 1933, Alice Evelina Alexandra, da of C P Sandberg, CBE; 2 s (eld s d 1979); *Career* barr 1925, Foreign Serv legal advr 1929, ch legal advr to FO 1953-60, bencher Gray's Inn 1961, judge of Internat Court of Justice 1960-73, judge of European Court of Human Rights Strasbourg 1974-80; *Clubs* Athenaeum, United Oxford & Cambridge; *Style* - Sir Gerald Fitzmaurice, GCMG, QC; 3 Gray's Inn Square, Holborn, WCI (☎ 01 242 4339); 2 Hare ct, Temple, EC4 (☎ 01 353 0076/583 2574); Oldenhove, 52 Laan Van Meerdervoort (5A), The Hague 2012 (☎ 60 41 73)

FITZROY, Charles; s of 4 Baron (cr of GB 1780) Southampton (d 1958; descended from the 1 Baron, who was yr bro of 3 Duke of Grafton) and late Lady Hilda Mary Dundas, da of 1 Marquess of Zetland; disclaimed his peerage for life 1964; *b* 3 Jan 1904; *Educ* Harrow; *m* 1, 1927, Margaret (d 1931), da of Rev Prebendary Herbert Mackworth Drake, Vicar of Pomeroy, Devon; 1 s; m 2, 1940 (m dis 1944), Mrs Phyllis Joan Leslie; m 3, 1951, Rachel Christine, da of Charles Zaman, of Lille, France; *Heir* (to disclaimed Barony) s, Hon Charles FitzRoy; *Career* late Lt Roy Horse Guards; *Style* - Charles FitzRoy Esq; Preluna Hotel, Sliema, Malta

FITZROY, Hon Charles James; s (by 1 m) and h of Charles FitzRoy, 5 Baron Southampton who disclaimed his peerage for life; *b* 12 Aug 1928; *m* 1951, Pamela Anne, da of Edward Percy Henniker; 1 s, 1 da; *Style* - The Hon Charles FitzRoy

FITZROY, Lord Edward Anthony Charles; s of 10 Duke of Grafton (d 1970);

b 1928; *Educ* Eton, RMA; *m* 1956, Veronica Mary, da of Maj R F Ruttledge, of Moorefield, Ballybrack, Co Dublin, Eire; 1 s, 2 da; *Career* joined Coldstream Gds 1948, Capt 1954, ret 1955; chm and md Imperial Foods Int Technical Services Ltd; dir Imperial Foods Ltd and Ross Poultry (New Zealand) Ltd; memb Lloyd's; *Recreations* shooting, stalking, gardening; *Clubs* Pratt's; *Style* - Lord Edward FitzRoy; 18p Warwick sq, SW1; Norton House, Norwich, Norfolk (☎ Raveningham 303)

FITZROY, Hon Nancy Jean; BEM; da of late Viscountess Daventry and late Capt the Rt Hon Edward Algernon FitzRoy, MP; *b* 1894; *Career* Sergeant Dispenser VAD 1939-46; *Style* - The Hon Nancy FitzRoy, BEM; Mayfield Convent, London rd, Hook, Hants

FITZROY NEWDEGATE, Francis Humphrey Maurice; JP (Warwickshire 1960), DL (1970); s of late Cdr the Hon John Maurice FitzRoy Newdegate, RN (s of 1 Viscountess Daventry, assumed by Roy Licence additional surname Newdegate, d 1976); hp of unc, 2 Viscount Daventry; *b* 17 Dec 1921; *Educ* Eton; *m* 1959, Rosemary, da of Lt-Gen 1 Baron Norrie, GCMG, GCVO, CB, DSO, MC (d 1977); 2 s, 1 da; *Career* Capt Coldstream Gds 1943; ADC to Viceroy of India 1946-48; High Sheriff Warwicks 1970, Vice Ld-Lt 1974; *Clubs* Boodle's; *Style* - Francis FitzRoy Newdegate Esq, JP, DL; Temple House, Arbury, Nuneaton, Warwickshire (☎ Nuneaton 383514)

FITZROY NEWDEGATE, Hon Mrs John - Lucia Charlotte Susan; OBE, JP; da of late Sir Francis Newdigate-Newdegate, GCMG; *m* 191, Cdr the Hon John Maurice FitzRoy Newdegate, RN (s of late Viscountess Daventry; assumed by Roy licence 1936 additional surname and arms of Newdegate, d 1976); 1 s, 2 da; *Career* DStJ; *Style* - The Hon Mrs John FitzRoy Newdegate, OBE, JP; Arbury Hall, Nuneaton, Warwicks

FITZWALTER, 21 Baron (E 1295); Fitzwalter Brooke Plumptre; JP (Kent 1949); s of George Beresford Plumptre, yr bro of 20 Baron (d 1932, but the present Lord FitzWalter was not summoned to Parl till 1952); Lord FitzWalter is eleventh in descent from Frances, w of Sir Thomas Mildmay and half sis of 3 Earl of Sussex (whose 2 w Frances, da of Sir William Sydney, of Penshurst, left £5,000 to establish a Cambridge Coll to be called 'Sydney-Sussex'); Frances was twelfth in descent from Robert FitzWalter, the leading enforcer among the Barons of Magna Carta; *b* 15 Jan 1914; *Educ* Diocesan Coll Cape Town, Jesus Cambridge; *m* 1951, Margaret, da of Herbert William Deedes, JP, and sis of William Deedes, the ed of the Daily Telegraph, also 3 cous of late Anthony Chenevix Trench, sometime Headmaster of Eton; 5 s; *Heir* s, Hon Julian Plumptre; *Career* served WW II Capt; landowner & farmer; *Recreations* shooting, gardening; *Style* - The Rt Hon Lord FitzWalter JP; Goodnestone Park, Canterbury, Kent (☎ 0304 840218)

FITZWILLIAM, Countess; Joyce Elizabeth; da of Lt-Col Philip Langdale, OBE, TD, JP, DL (ggs of 17 Baron Stourton); *b* 25 April 1898; *m* 1, 1922 (m dis 1956), 2 & last Viscount FitzAlan of Derwent (d 1962); 2 da (Hon Mrs Ward, Hon Mrs Hastings); m 2, 1956, 10 & last Earl Fitzwilliam; *Style* - The Rt Hon Countess Fitzwilliam; Wentworth Woodhouse, Rotherham, Yorks; Milton, Peterborough

FITZWILLIAMS, Maj Reginald Clixby Lloyd; JP (1958), DL (1970); s of Maj C C L Fitzwilliams (d 1960); *b* 2 Dec 1916; *Educ* Eton, Magdalene Coll Cambridge; *m* 1943, Pauline Agatha, nee Cave; 2 da; *Career* chartered accountant, chm Humberside CC 1980-81; *Style* - Maj Reginald Fitzwilliams, JP, DL; Hazeldene, The Avenue, Healing, Grimsby

FLANDERS, Dennis; s of Bernard Charles Flanders (d 1964); *b* 2 July 1915; *Educ* Merchant Taylors' Sch (various art schools); *m* 1952, Dalma Joan Darnley; 1 s, 1 da; *Career* Staff Sergeant RE 1942-46; artist (drawings of Britain, particularly elaborate architectural compositions - townscapes and landscapes); RBA 1970, ARWS 1970, RWS 1976; *Recreations* travel; *Clubs* Art Workers Guild (Master

1975); *Style* - Dennis Flanders Esq; 51 Gt Ormond st, WCI (☎ 01 405 9317); Baker's Cross House, Cranbrook, Kent (☎ 0580 712018)

FLAVELL, Geoffrey; s of William Alfred Flavell, JP, of Dunedin, New Zealand (d 1953); *b* 23 Feb 1913; *Educ* Waitaki and Otago H S, U of Otago, St Bartholomew's Hosp London; *m* 1943, Joan Margaret, da of late Sydney Ewart Adams, of Hawkwell, Essex; *Career* ret rank of Wing Cdr RAF 1958 (former advr in surgery RAF); former consultant thoracic surgn to Hosps of N E Thames Regional Health Authority and to Roy Masonic Hosp; Hon Consultant Thoracic Surg to The London Hosp (and former head of Dept of Cardio-Vascular and Thoracic Surgery), to Chelmsford Gp Hosps, to Harlow and Epping Gp and to Whipps Cross Hosp 1978-; FRCS, FRCP; *Recreations* architecture, art, history, wine & food; *Clubs* RAF; *Style* - Geoffrey Flavell Esq; Belfield House, Weymouth, Dorset (☎ 784 013)

FLAVELLE, Sir (Joseph) David Ellsworth; 3 Bt (UK 1917); s of Sir (Joseph) Ellsworth Flavelle, 2 Bt (d 1977); *b* 9 Nov 1921; *m* 1942, Muriel Barbara, da of David Reginald Morton; 3 da; *Heir* bro, William Ellsworth Flavelle; *Style* - Sir David Flavelle, Bt; 1420 Watersedge rd, Clarkson, Ontario, Canada L5J IA4

FLAVELLE, William Ellsworth; s of late Sir (Joseph) Ellsworth Flavelle, 2 Bt; hp of bro, Sir (Joseph) David Flavelle, 3 Bt; *b* 26 Feb 1926; *Style* - William Flavelle Esq

FLEMING, Sir Charles (Alexander); KBE (1977, OBE 1964), FRS (1967); s of George Herbert Fleming, of Auckland, New Zealand (d 1942); *b* 9 Sept 1916; *Educ* King's College Auckland, U of New Zealand; *m* 1941, Margaret Alison, da of Stanley George Chambers, of Auckland, NZ; 3 da; *Career* asst geologist 1949, paleontologist, then ch paleontologist 1952 NZ Geological Survey Dept of Scientific & Indust Research, NZ; tstee National Art Gallery and Dominion Museum Board, memb Environmental Council NZ, National Parks Authority; *Recreations* gramaphone, natural history, fishing for NZ Whitebait; *Clubs* Explorers' New York, Wellington (NZ), The University Club (Wellington); *Style* - Sir Charles Fleming, KBE, FRS; 42 Wadestown Rd, Wellington, New Zealand (☎ Wellington 737 288)

FLEMING, Christopher Michael; s of late Capt Michael Valentine Fleming; *b* 8 May 1937; *Educ* Eton; *m* 1974, Judith Marion, da of Col Godfrey Jeans; 2 da; *Career* dir Thomas Borthwick & Sons Ltd; *Recreations* shooting, fishing, racing; *Clubs* Turf; *Style* - Christopher Fleming Esq; Temple Guiting House, nr Cheltenham, Glos

FLEMING, Hon Mrs (Dorothy Charmian); *née* Hermon-Hodge; da of 2 Baron Wyfold, DSO, MVO, by Dorothy, nee Fleming, aunt of Peter and Ian, the writers; *b* 4 Jan 1913; *m* 1938, her 1 cous Richard, yr bro of Peter and Ian; 4 s (two of whom m sisters, daughters of Sir Hereward Wake, 14 Bt), 3 da; *Style* - The Hon Mrs Fleming; Leygore Manor, Northleach, Glos (☎ 234); 12 Hyde Park sq, W2 (☎ 01 262 3395)

FLEMING, Hon Mrs (Gloria Lavinia Eileen); da of Baroness Emmet of Amberley (Life Peeress, d 1980, da of 1 Baron Rennell, GCB, GCMG, GCVO) and late Thomas Emmet; *b* 1924; *m* 1950, Maj Mark Winton Slane Fleming, 10 Roy Hussars (PWO), ret; 1 s, 3 da; *Style* - The Hon Mrs Fleming; Ardath, Shamley Green, nr Guildford, Surrey

FLEMING, Patrick Lyons; s of Col Frank Fleming, DSO, TD (d 1964); *b* 3 Apr 1905; *Educ* Shrewsbury, Lincoln Oxford; *m* 1929, Eleanor Mignon (d 1970), nee Tapper; 1 da (and 1 decd); *Career* retired company dir, formerly dir Drayton Gp, amongst others; former memb IOD (tres 1974); *Style* - Patrick Fleming Esq; Baltic House, The Common, Cranleigh, Surrey

FLEMING, Roger John Cary; OBE (1957), TD, JP (Aberdeenshire 1959), DL (1966); s of Col Frank Fleming, DSO, TD, DL, (d 1964); *b* 18 March 1918; *Educ* Shrewsbury School and abroad; *m* 1946, Judith Ann Quentin, da of late James

Wotherspoon Clarke Jackson; 1 s, 2 da; *Career* Col (TA) 1957, RA WW II, ADC (TA) to HM The Queen 1963-68; chm John Fleming & Co Ltd Timber Importers Aberdeen, dir of other cos; chm City of Aberdeen Territorial and Aux Forces Assoc 1962-65, chm Aberdeen Harbour Bd 1966-78, memb Court of U of Aberdeen 1978-; *Recreations* hill walking; *Clubs* Bath, Royal Northern (Aberdeen); *Style* - Roger Fleming Esq, OBE, TD, JP, DL; Bogarn House, Banchory, Kincardineshire (☎ 03302 2173)

FLEMING, Thomas Kelman; OBE (1980); s of Rev Peter Fleming (d 1939); *b* 29 Jun 1927; *Educ* Daniel Stewart's Coll Edinburgh; *Career* actor, writer, producer, broadcaster, co-founder and dir Edinburgh Gateway Co 1953-65, dir Edinburgh Civic Theatre Trust 1965-66, RSC 1962-64, gov Scottish Theatre Trust 1980-, BBC radio commentator Coronation 1953, Silver Wedding 1972, Princess Anne's Wedding 1973, State visits USA and Japan, Silver Jubilee 1977, HM Queen Elizabeth the Queen Mother's Installation Lord Warden, Cinque Ports 1979, Queen Mother's 80th Birthday 1980, The Royal Wedding 1981, The Cenotaph Services of Remembrance 1962, 1965-, funeral of Lord Mountbatten of Burma; *Recreations* hill walking; *Style* - Tom Fleming Esq, OBE; 56 Murrayfield Gardens, Edinburgh; Tomfarclas, Ballindalloch, Banffshire

FLETCHER, Baron (Life Peer UK 1970); Eric George Molyneux Fletcher; PC (1967); s of late Clarence George Eugene Fletcher, Town Clerk of Islington; *b* 26 March 1903; *Educ* Radley, London U; *m* 1929, Bessie Winifred, da of late James Butt, of Enfield; 2 s, 1 da; *Career* FSA; slr 1924, former sr ptnr Denton Hall & Burgin, now consultant; former dir Assoc Br Picture Corpn Ltd and other cos; memb LCC 1934-39 (chm Fin Ctee), Min Without Portfolio 1964-66, Dep Speaker and chm Ways and Means House of Commons 1966-68, pres Br Archaeological Assoc 1960-63, tstee Br Museum 1968-77, MP (L) Islington 1945-70, kt 1964; *Style* - The Rt Hon The Lord Fletcher, PC; 3 Gray's Inn pla, WC1 (☎ 01 405 5345); The Barn, The Green, Sarratt, Rickmansworth, Herts (☎ King's Langley 65385)

FLETCHER, Archibald Peter; s of Walter Archibald Fletcher (d 1970); *b* 24 Dec 1930; *Educ* Kingswood Sch Bath; London Hosp Medical College; St Mary's Hosp Medical School; *m* 1972, Patricia Elizabeth Samson; 3 s, 2 da; *Career* sr lectr Chemical Pathology St Mary's Hosp London 1967-70, head of Biochemistry American Nat Red Cross 1970-73, princ med offr, medical assessor to Ctee on Safety of Medicines 1977-, ch scientific offr, sr med offr DHSS 1978, res physicican Upjohn Internat 1978-80, currently sr med offr DHSS; *Recreations* gardening, cooking; *Clubs* Wig and Pen, Royal Society of Medicine; *Style* - Archibald Fletcher Esq; Hall Corner Cottage, Little Maplestead, Halstead, Essex (☎ Halstead 475465)

FLETCHER, Rev the Hon David Clare Molyneux; s of Baron Fletcher, PC (Life Peer); *b* 1932; *Educ* Repton, Worcester Coll Oxford; *m* 1970, Susan Charlotte Langford; *Career* ordained 1958, curate of St Mary's Islington 1958, Scripture Union staff worker 1962; *Style* - The Rev the Hon David Fletcher; 4 Burfield rd, Chorleywood, Herts

FLETCHER, Edward Joseph; MP (L) Darlington 1964-; *b* 25 Feb 1911; *Educ* St Mary's Sch Handsworth, Fircroft Coll Birmingham; *m*; 2 da; *Style* - Edward Fletcher Esq, MP; House of Commons, London SW1

FLETCHER, Geoffrey; MBE (1944), TD (1947), JP (Kent 1965), DL (1979); s of Brigadier Harold Fletcher, OBE, TD, JP (d 1964); *b* 27 April 1920; *Educ* Repton; *m* 1947, Cynthia Diana Howard, da of late David Howard Lloyd; 2 s, 2 da; *Career* Major BEF 1940 and 1944; engineer, FIAgrE; chm and md Drake & Fletcher Ltd; *Recreations* golf, bridge, gardening; *Clubs* Farmers', Roy St Georges Golf; *Style* - Geoffrey Fletcher Esq MBE TD JP DL; Thornham Friars, Pilgrims Way, Thurnham, Kent

FLETCHER, Geoffrey Bernard Abbott; s of James Alexander Fletcher, of Burgess Hill, Sussex; *b* 28 Nov 1903; *Educ* Rugby Sch, King's Camb; *Career* assist lectr in Classic U of Leeds 1927-28, lectr in Greek U of Liverpool 1928-36, Prof of Classics U of Durham King's Coll Newcastle-upon-Tyne 1937-46, Prof of Latin 1946-63, Prof of Latin U of Newcastle-upon-Tyne 1963-69, now Emeritus Prof; *Recreations* music, reading, art galleries, travel; *Clubs* Athenaeum; *Style* - Geoffrey Fletcher Esq; Thirlmere Lodge, Elmfield rd, Gosforth, Newcastle-upon-Tyne (☎ Gosforth 852873)

FLETCHER, Rev the Hon Jonathan James Molyneux; s of Baron Fletcher, PC (Life Peer); *b* 1942; *Educ* Repton, Hertford Coll Oxford; *Career* deacon 1968, ordained priest 1969, curate Christ Church Cockfosters 1968-72, curate Holy Sepulchre Church Cambridge 1972; *Style* - The Rev the Hon Jonathan Fletcher; 33 Ellington st, N7

FLETCHER, Hon Mrs (Louisa Mary Sylvia); *née* Seely; da of 1 Baron Mottistone, CB, CMG, DSO, TD (d 1947); *b* 1913; *m* 1941, Charles Montagu Fletcher, CBE, MD, FRCP, s of late Sir Walter Morley Fletcher, KBE, CB, MD, ScD, FRS; 1 s, 2 da; *Style* - The Hon Mrs Fletcher; 20 Drayton gdns, SW10

FLETCHER, Lady Victoria Mary Dolores; *née* Feilding; da of late 9 Earl of Denbigh; *b* 1901; *m* 1933, Walter Miles Fletcher; 2 s; *Style* - Lady Victoria Fletcher; 107 Forbes st, Grenfell, NSW, Australia

FLETCHER-COOKE, Sir John; CMG (1952); s of Capt Charles Arthur Fletcher-Cooke (d 1924); *b* 8 Aug 1911; *Educ* Malvern, Université de Paris, St Edmund Hall Oxford; *m* 1, 1949 (m dis 1971), Alice, nee Egner; 2 s, 1 da; m 2, 1977, Marie-Louise Fourier de la Barre, wid of Louis Vicomte de la Barre and da of Roger Joachim Ducassou, of French Colonial Service (d 1947); *Career* kt 1962, Colonial Office 1936-42 and 1946, POW Japan 1942-45, Under-Sec Govt of Palestine 1946-48, Colonial Sec and occasional Actg Gov Cyprus 1951-55, occasional Actg Gov Tanganyika 1959-61, stood for (C) Luton 1963, MP (C) Southampton Test 1964-66, author; *Recreations* writing, building dry Cotswold stone walls; *Clubs* Travellers', Royal Commonwealth Society; *Style* - Sir John Fletcher-Cooke CMG; c/o Lloyds Bank Ltd, Finsbury Circus Branch, 3 Broad St pla, EC2

FLETCHER-VANE, Hon Christopher John; s of 1 Baron Inglewood, TD; *b* 1953; *Educ* Eton, Trin Cambridge; *Career* barr Inner Temple 1976; *Style* - The Hon Christopher Fletcher-Vane

FLETCHER-VANE, Hon William Richard; s and h of 1 Baron Inglewood, TD; *b* 31 July 1951; *Educ* Eton, Trin Cambridge; *Career* barr, Lincoln's Inn 1975; *Style* - The Hon William Fletcher-Vane

FLETT, Sir Martin Teall; KCB (1965); s of Sir John Smith Flett, KBE (d 1947); *b* 30 July 1911; *Educ* George Watson's Coll, St Paul's Sch, St John's Oxford; *m* 1936, Mary, da of late Sir Alec Martin, KBE; 2 s, 1 da; *Career* civil serv, permanent under-sec Air Ministry 1963-64, RAF (MOD) 1964-68, Equipment (MOD) 1968-71, ret 1971; *Clubs* Athenaeum, RAF, Roy Wimbledon Golf; *Style* - Sir Martin Flett, KCB; 45 Campden Hill rd, W8 (☎ 01 937 9498)

FLEW, Prof Antony Garrard Newton; s of Rev Dr R Newton Flew (d 1962); *b* 11 Feb 1923; *Educ* Kingswood Sch Bath, St John's Oxford; *m* 1952, Annis Ruth Harty, da of Col Frank Siegfried Vernon Donnison; 2 da; *Career* prof of Philosophy at Keele U 1954-71, Calgary U 1972-73, Reading U 1973-; *Recreations* walking, house maintenance; *Style* - Prof Antony Flew; 26 Alexandra rd, Reading, Berks (☎ 61848)

FLINN, Donal Patrick; s of Hugo Victor Flinn (Parly Sec Dept of Finance, Coleen, Co Cork); *b* 8 Nov 1923; *Educ* Christian Brothers Coll Cork, Univ Coll Cork (BComm); *m* 1954, Heather Mary, nee Cole; 2 s, 1 da; *Career* FICA (pres 1976-77), chm Barclays Bank Int (Irish Branch), chm De La Rue Smurfit Ltd, dir Aer Lingus, council memb Irish Management Inst, bd memb US Chamber of Commerce; *Recreations* golf, tennis, fishing; *Style* - Donal Flinn Esq; Carragoona, 41 Cowper rd, Rathmines, Dublin 6 (☎ 977965); Hurrican Lodge, Glenbeigh, Co Kerry (☎ Glenbeigh 55)

FLINT, David; TD (1950); s of David Flint, JP (d 1940); *b* 24 Feb 1919; *Educ* H S Glasgow, Glasgow U; *m* 1953, Dorothy Mary Maclachlan, nee Jardine; 2 s, 1 da; *Career* Maj WW II, CA, ptnr Mann Judd Gordon & Co 1950-71, prof of Accountancy Glasgow U 1964-, pres Inst of CAs of Scotland 1975-76, dean of Faculty of Law Glasgow U 1971-73; *Recreations* golf; *Style* - David Flint Esq, TD; 3 Merrylee rd, Newlands, Glasgow (☎ 637 30600)

FLOOD, Brig George Robert; MC (1945); s of Rev J C Flood (d 1963); *b* 26 Nov 1919; *Educ* Lancing Coll, Reading U; *m* 1945, Jeanette Mary Lapage, da of late Col John Sydney Lapage Norris; 1 s, 1 da; *Career* Roy Berks Regt 1939, BEF 1939-40 Parachute Regt 1958; Cdr 44 Para Brigade 1965-68, Assist Cdr Sandhurst 1968-71, V-Pres Regular Cmmn Bd 1971-74, Cmdt JATE 1972, ADC 1972-74; *Recreations* cricket, gardening, sailing, golf; *Clubs* MCC, Free Foresters, Army and Navy; *Style* - Brig George Flood, MC; Cheverell Mill, Little Cheverell, Devizes, Wilts (☎ Lavington 2481)

FLOREY, Hon Charles du Vé; s of late Baron Florey, OM, PRS, MD (Life Peer); *b* 11 Sept 1934; *Educ* Rugby; Cambridge and Yale Us; *m* 1966, Susan Jill, nee Hopkins; 1 s, 1 da; *Career* MB, MPH (Yale), sr lectr Dept of Clinical Epidemiology and Social Med St Thomas's Hosp Med Sch; *Style* - The Hon Charles Florey; St Thomas's Hospital Medical School, SE1

FLOREY, Baroness - Hon Margaret Augusta; *née* Fremantle; da of late 3 Baron Cottesloe; *b* 1904; *Educ* Oxford U; *m* 1, 1930 (m dis 1946), Denys Arthur Jennings, BM, BCh; m 2, 1967, Baron Florey, OM, FRS (d 1968); *Career* lecturer Oxford U (Pathology) 1945-72, Fellow of LMH Oxford 1952-72; *Style* - The Rt Hon the Lady Florey; 4 Elsfield rd, Old Marston, Oxford

FLOWER, Dennis L(owndes); s of Spenser (Aldborough) Flower; *b* 30 May 1915; *Educ* Stowe, Cambridge U; *Career* High Sheriff of Warwicks 1981, chm Exec Cncl Shakespeare Birthplace Trust 1966-, v-chm Exec Cncl Roy Shakespeare Theatre, with Flower & Sons (Brewers, Stratford-on-Avon, later Whitbread Flowers) 1939-77; *Recreations* fishing; *Clubs* Boodle's; *Style* - Dennis Flower Esq; Umington Manor, Shipston-on-Stour, Warwicks

FLOWER, Lady Gloria Regina Malet; *née* Vaughan; da of 7 Earl of Lisburne (d 1965); *b* 1916; *m* 1, 1935 (m dis 1952), Maj Nigel Thomas Loveridge Fisher, MC, MP, s of late Cdr Sir Thomas Fisher, KBE, RN; 1 s, 1 da; m 2, 1952, Ronald Philip Flower, OBE; 1 s; *Style* - Lady Gloria Flower; Manor Farm Cottage, Weston Patrick, Nr Basingstoke

FLOWER, Hon Michael Llowarch Warburton; s and h of 10 Viscount Ashbrook, KCVO, MBE; *b* 9 Dec 1935; *Educ* Eton, Worcester Coll Oxford; *m* 1971, Zoë Mary, da of late Francis H A Engleheart, of The Priory, Stoke-by-Nayland, Suffolk; 2 s, 1 da; *Career* 2 Lt Gren Gds 1955, slr 1963; *Style* - The Hon Michael Flower; The Old Parsonage, Arely Green, Northwich, Cheshire

FLOWERS, Baron (Life Peer UK 1979); Brian Hilton Flowers; FRS (1961); s of late Rev Harold J Flowers, of Swansea; *b* 13 Sept 1924; *Educ* Bishop Gore G S Swansea, Gonville and Caius Cambridge, Birmingham U; *m* 1951, Mary Frances, da of late Sir Leonard Behrens, CBE; *Career* physicist; Head of Theoretical Physics Div at Atomic Energy Research Establishment Harwell 1952-58, Prof of Theoretical Physics Manchester U 1958-61, Langworthy Prof of Physics Manchester U 1961-72, chm Science Research Cncl 1967-73, chm Roy Cmmn on Evironmental Pollution 1973-76, chm Standing Cmmn on Energy and Environment 1978, Rector Imperial Coll of Science and Technol 1973-; kt 1969; *Style* - The Rt Hon The Lord Flowers, FRS; Imperial Coll, SW7 (☎ 01 589 5111)

FLOYD, David Henry Cecil; s and h of

Sir Giles Floyd, 7 Bt; *b* 2 April 1956; *Educ* Eton; *m* 1981, Caroline, da of John Beckley, of Manor Farm, Bowerchalke, Wilts; *Style* - David Floyd Esq

FLOYD, Sir Giles Henry Charles; 7 Bt (UK 1816); s of Lt-Col Sir John Duckett Floyd, 6 Bt, TD (d 1975); *b* 27 Feb 1932; *Educ* Eton; *m* 1954, Lady Gillian Moyra Katherine Cecil (m dis 1978) da 6 Marquess of Exeter, KCMG; 2 s; *Heir* s David Henry Cecil Floyd; *Career* farms dir Burghley Estate Farms 1958-, High Sheriff of Rutland 1968; *Recreations* field sports; *Clubs* Turf, Farmers'; *Style* - Sir Giles Floyd, Bt; Tinwell Manor, Stamford, Lincs (☎ Stamford 2676)

FLOYD, John Anthony; s of Lt-Col Arthur Bowen Floyd, DSO, OBE (d 1974); *b* 12 May 1923; *Educ* Eton; *m* 1948, Margaret, da of late Maj Hugo Rosselli-Worlington; 2 da; *Career* chm Christie Manson & Woods Ltd 1974-, chm Christies Int Ltd 1976-; *Clubs* Boodle's, White's, MCC; *Style* - John Floyd Esq; 26 Park Village East, NW1 (☎ 387 6311); Ecchinswell House, Newbury, Berks (☎ Kingsclear 298237)

FLOYDE, Marilyn Ysanne; da of Kenneth Arthur Floyde (d 1970); *b* 7 Oct 1950; *Educ* Roy Tunbridge Wells G S, Dartington Hall Devon; *m* 1979, John Franklin Pierce; 1 s; *Career* teacher, lecturer Dovecot Arts Centre 1976-78, theatre and dance officer South West Arts 1978-81, memb IBA Gen Adv Cncl, acting chm Dance Tales; *Recreations* walking, choreography, piano; *Style* - Miss Marilyn Floyde; Northridge, Newton St Cyres, Exeter, Devon (☎ 039 285 311)

FLOYER-ACLAND, Stafford Nugent; CBE (1967), DL (Dorset 1975); s of Lt-Gen Arthur Nugent Floyer-Acland, CB, DSO, MC, DL (d 1980); *b* 23 Dec 1916; *Educ* Marlborough Coll, RMC Sandhurst; *m* 1950, Patricia Egidia Hastings, da of Lt-Col Richard St Barbe Emmott (d 1949); 2 s, 1 da; *Career* formerly CIC Administration and Dep Cdr Land Forces Borneo, Cdr Force Troops Sabah 1965-66; Brig Northern Command 1966-67; Cdr West Country Bde 1963-65; High Sheriff Dorset 1974-75; farmer; *Recreations* shooting, fishing; *Style* - Brig Stafford Floyer-Acland, CBE, DL; The Manor House, West Stafford, Dorchester, Dorset (☎ Dorchester 4005)

FLYNN, Prof Frederick Valentine; s of Fredrick Walter Flynn (d 1957); *b* 6 Oct 1924; *Educ* U Coll London, U Coll Hospital Medical Sch London; *m* 1955, Catherine Ann, nee Warrick; 1 s, 1 da; *Career* prof of Chemical Pathology in London U at U Coll Sch of Medicine 1970-consultant chemical pathologist to U Coll Hospital London 1960-, civil consultant in chemical Pathology to RN 1978-; *Recreations* photography, gardening; *Style* - Prof Frederick Flynn; 20 Oakleigh av, Whetstone, N20 (☎ 01 445 0882)

FOCKE, Lady Tana Marie; *née* Alexander; da of 6 Earl of Caledon (d 1980) by 2 w, Baroness Anne (d 1963), da of Baron Nicolai de Graevenitz; *b* 1945; *m* 1973, Paul Everard Justice Focke; 2 da; *Style* - Lady Tana Focke; 7 Cheyne Walk, SW3

FODEN, Edwin Peter; s of Edwin Richard Foden (d 1950); *b* 24 Feb 1930; *Educ* Rossall Sch, N Staffs Tech Coll; *m* 1957, Judith, da of James Harding Baxter of Nantwich, Cheshire; 3 s; *Career* Lt REME (UK and Germany), fndr ERF Ltd, chm and md ERF (Hldgs) Ltd, chm and dir ERF Ltd, ERF S Africa (Pty) Ltd, Cheshire Fire Engineering Ltd, ERF Plastics Ltd, memb Nat Cncl of CBI (chm Regnl CBI), V-Pres SMMT 1981; *Recreations* golfing, shooting, yachting (Motor Yacht 'Dolores IV'); *Clubs* REME Officers', Clyde Cruising, Annabel's *Style* - Edwin Foden Esq; Oak Farm, The Heath, Sandbach, Cheshire (☎ 2732)

FODEN, William Bertram; CB (1945); s of William Genders Foden; *b* 19 Sept 1892; *Educ* H S Newcastle Staffs, St John's Cambridge; *m* 1920, Zelie, nee Kingsford; 1 s, 1 da; *Career* research chemist, Research Dept Woolwich Arsenal 1918, Air Ministry 1919, Princ 1925, Assist Sec 1937, Dir of Accounts 1942, Assist Under-Sec of State 1943, ret 1953; *Recreations* tennis, badminton; *Clubs* Oxford and Cambridge; *Style* - William Foden Esq,

CB; 43 Westwood Close, Crediton, Exeter, Devon (☎ Crediton 2709)

FOGG, Cyril Percival; CB (1973); s of Henry Fogg (d 1961); *b* 28 Nov 1914; *Educ* Cambridge U; *m* 1939, Margaret Amie, nee Belper; 2 da; *Career* defence scientist MOD, dir gen of Electronics Research & Developement 1964-67, dep controller of Electronics 1967-73, director Admiralty Surface Weapons Establishment 1973-75, ret 1975; *Recreations* bird watching, continental caravan touring; *Style* - Cyril Fogg Esq, CB; 1 Fairfield Close, Old Bosham, Chichester, W Sussex (☎ Bosham 572609)

FOLEY, 8 Baron (GB 1776); Adrian Gerald Foley; s of 7 Baron (d 1927); *b* 9 Aug 1923; *m* 1, 1958 (m dis 1971), Patricia, da of Joseph Zoellner III, of Pasadena, California; 1 s, 1 da; m 2, 1972, Ghislaine, da of Cornelius Dresselhuys, of Long Island, USA and formerly w of (1) Maj Denis James Alexander, later 6 Earl of Caledon, and (2) 4 Baron Ashcombe, *qv*; *Heir* s, Hon Thomas Foley; *Career* composer and pianist; *Style* - The Rt Hon The Lord Foley; c/o Marbella Club, Marbella, Malaga, Spain

FOLEY, Hon Alexandra Mary; da (by 1 m) of 8 Baron Foley; *b* 3 April 1960; *Style* - The Hon Alexandra Foley

FOLEY, Hon Thomas Henry; s (by 1 m) and h of 8 Baron Foley; *b* 1 April 1961; *Style* - The Hon Thomas Foley

FOLJAMBE, Lady Jane Rosamond Mary; da of late Capt Peter Foljambe and sis of 5 Earl of Liverpool; raised to the rank of an Earl's da 1970; *b* 1943; *Style* - Lady Jane Foljambe

FOLJAMBE, Hon Ralph Edward Anthony Savile; s of 5 Earl of Liverpool; *b* 1974; *Style* - The Hon Ralph Foljambe

FOLKARD, Brig Gilbert John; CBE (1959); s of William Nisbet Folkard (d 1934); *b* 10 Feb 1905; *Educ* Bradfield Coll, RMC Sandhurst; *Career* RAEC (formerly 2 Lt DLI then transferred AEC 1937) India, Burma, Palestine, Far East, Germany WW II; temp Brig 1956, ch education offr Western Command 1959, education offr Eastern Command 1962, ret 1965; princ Finchale Training Coll for Disabled People Durham 1966-76; *Recreations* physical education, boxing, fencing; *Clubs* Victory Services; *Style* - Brig Gilbert Folkard, CBE; 5 Merewood ct, Carew rd, Eastbourne, Sussex (☎ 23142)

FOLKESTONE, Viscount; William Pleydell-Bouverie; s (by 1 m) and h of 8 Earl of Radnor; *b* 5 Jan 1955; *Educ* Harrow, RAC Cirencester; *Style* - Viscount Folkestone; Longford Castle, Salisbury, Wilts (☎ Salisbury 29732)

FOLLOWS, Sir Denis; CBE (1967, MBE 1951); s of Amos Follows (d 1963); *b* 13 April 1908; *Educ* City Sch Lincoln, Nottingham U; *m* 1938, Mary Elizabeth, nee Milner; 2 da; *Career* kt 1978, Fl Lt RAF 1940-46, school master Chiswick G S 1932-40, sec Br Air Line Pilots Assoc 1946-62, sec The Football Assoc 1962-73, chm Br Olympic Assoc 1977-; *Style* - Sir Denis Follows CBE; 70 Barrowgate rd, Chiswick, W4 (☎ 994 5782)

FONTEYN, Dame Margot; DBE (1956, CBE 1951); Dame Margot Fonteyn de Arias; *b* 18 May 1919; *m* 1955, Roberto Arias,*qv*; *Career* Prima Ballerina, Pres Roy Acad of Dancing 1954- Chllr Durham U 1982-; *Style* - Dame Margot Fonteyn, DBE; c/o Royal Opera House, Covent Garden, WC2

FOOKS, John Anthony; s of William John Fooks; *b* 24 Aug 1933; *Educ* Shrewsbury, Trin Cambridge; *m* 1959, Maureen Heather, da of Percival Charles Jones, former High Sheriff of Gwent; 3 s, 1 da; *Career* CA, dep chm Garnar Scotblair Ltd 1980 (dir 1971), chm Cardiff & Provincal Properties Ltd 1980, gen cmmr Inland Revenue; *Recreations* golf, shooting, tennis, music, bridge; *Clubs* Oxford and Cambridge, Rye G C, Golf Match; *Style* - John Fooks Esq; 13 Merrick sq, SE1; Dale Hill Farm House, Ticehurst, Sussex

FOOT, Baron (Life Peer UK 1967); John Mackintosh Foot; s of late Rt Hon Isaac Foot, PC, and bro of Lord Caradon and Michael Foot, Leader of the Oppn; *b* 17 Feb 1909; *Educ* Bembridge Sch, Balliol Oxford; *m* 1936, Anne Bailey, da of Clifford Bailey Farr, MD, of Bryn Mawr, Pa, USA; 1 s, 1 da; *Career* slr 1934, sr ptnr Foot & Bowden of Plymouth, chm UK Immigrants Advsy Serv 1970-78; stood for Parl as Lib candidate Basingstoke 1934 & 1935, Bodmin 1945 & 1950; Pres Dartmoor Preservn Assoc 1976-, Commons, Open Spaces & Footpaths Preservn Soc, UK Immigrants Advsy Serv; Maj RASC WW II; *Style* - The Rt Hon The Lord Foot; Yew Tree, Crapstone, Yelverton, Devon (☎ Yelverton 3417)

FOOT, Hon Benjamin Arthur; s of Baron Caradon (Life Peer); *b* 1949; *m* 1981, Sally, da of late Maj M F S Rudkin, of Shoreham-by-Sea, Sussex; *Style* - The Hon Benjamin Foot

FOOT, Hon John Winslow; s of Baron Foot (Life Peer); *b* 23 Oct 1939; *Educ* Sidcot Sch, Philadelphia Coll of Art USA; *Style* - The Hon John Foot; Yew Tree, Crapstone, Yelverton, Devon

FOOT, Rt Hon Michael; PC (1974), MP (L) Ebbw Vale 1960-; s of Rt Hon Isaac Foot, PC, and bro of Lords Caradon and Foot; *b* 23 July 1913; *Educ* Forres Sch, Leighton Park, Wadham Oxford; *m* 1949, Jill Craigie; *Career* stood as L candidate for Mon 1935, MP (L) Devonport (now David Owen's constituency) 1945-55, ed Tribune 1948-52 & 1955-60 & md 1945-74 (actg ed Evening Standard 1942, later book critic; wrote column for Daily Herald 1944-64); Sec State Employment 1974-76, Leader House Commons 1976-79; *Style* - The Rt Hon Michael Foot PC MP; House of Commons, SW1

FOOT, Hon Oliver Isaac; s of Baron Caradon (Life Peer); *b* 1947; *Educ* Leighton Park Sch, RAC Cirencester, Goddard Coll Vermont USA; *Style* - The Hon Oliver Foot

FOOT, Hon Paul Mackintosh; s of Baron Caradon (Life Peer); *b* 1937; *Educ* Univ Coll Oxford; *m* 1962 (m dis 1970), Monica, nee Beckinsale; c; *Career* journalist; *Style* - The Hon Paul Foot; 14 Canfield gdns, NW6

FOOTE, Maj-Gen Henry Robert Bowreman; VC (1944), CB (1952), DSO (1942); s of Lt-Col Henry Bruce Foote (d 1932); *b* 5 Dec 1904; *Educ* St Cyprians Eastbourne, Bedford, Sandhurst; *m* 1944, Anita Flint (d 1970); *Career* Capt Roy Tank Regt 1936; dir-gen Fighting Vehicles Min of Supply 1953-55, Maj-Gen 1951, dir RAC War Office 1955-58, ret 1958; Col Cmdt Roy Tank Regt 1957-64; *Recreations* golf; *Clubs* Army and Navy; *Style* - Maj-Gen Henry Foote, VC, CB, DSO; Furzefield, W Chiltington, Pulborough, Sussex (☎ W Chiltington 2130)

FORBES, 23 Lord (Premier S Lordship 1445); Nigel Ivan Forbes; KBE (1960), JP (Aberdeenshire 1955), DL (1958); s of 22 Lord Forbes (d 1953) and Lady Mabel Anson, da of 3 Earl of Lichfield; Lord Forbes is 1 cous once removed of Patrick (Lord) Lichfield, the photographer; *b* 18 Feb 1918; *Educ* Harrow, Sandhurst; *m* 1943, Hon Rosemary Hamilton-Russell, da of 9 Viscount Boyne; 2 s, 1 da; *Heir* s, Master of Forbes; *Career* served WW II Maj Gren Gds; chm Rolawn Turf Growers Ltd; dir Grampian TV; farmer & landowner; Min State Scottish Off 1959-60; *Recreations* wildlife, sport, travel; *Clubs* Army & Navy; *Style* - The Rt Hon Lord Forbes KBE JP DL; Balforbes, Alford, Aberdeenshire (☎ 033 63 216)

FORBES, Alastair (Cameron); 3 s of James Grant Forbes (d 1955); *b* 2 May 1918; *Educ* Winchester, King's Coll Cambridge; *m* m 1, Charlotte, nee Bergsoe (m dis 1960); 1 s; m 2, 1966, Hon Georgina Ward, da of 1 Viscount Ward of Witley (m dis 1970); *Career* journalist, contributor Times Literary Supplement, Listener, Spectator, American Scholar, etc, advr Brainstormcentre Europe 1969-79, unuccessfully contested S Hendon as Liberal in Gen Election 1945, diplomatic and war correspondent Observer, Sunday Times, France Libre, Daily Mail 1941-45; *Recreations* reading, conversation, walking, cross-country skiing; *Clubs* White's, Beefsteak; *Style* - Alastair Forbes Esq; 1837 Château D'Oex, Switzerland (☎ 29 4 76 50); Les Essarts, St Briac, I & V France (☎ 99 88 32 66)

FORBES, Hon Sir Alastair Granville; s of Granville Forbes (d 1943); *b* 3 Jan 1908; *Educ* Blundell's Sch, Clare Cambridge; *m* 1936, Constance Irene Mary, da of late Capt Everard Hughes White, DSO, DSC; 2 da; *Career* barr, HM Colonial Serv 1936, HM Overseas Judiciary 1956, puisne judge Kenya 1956, justice of Appeal, Ct of Appeal for Eastern Africa 1957, v-pres of the Ct 1958, federal justice Federal Supreme Ct of Rhodesia and Nyasaland 1963, pres Cts of Appeal for Seychelles, St Helena, Falkland Is and British Antarctic Territories 1965 and Gibraltar 1970, pres Pensions Appeal Tribunals for England and Wales 1973-80; kt 1960; *Recreations* gardening, fishing, shooting; *Clubs* Roy Commonwealth Soc; *Style* - Hon Sir Alastair Forbes; Beeches, Marnhull, Sturminster Newton, Dorset (☎ Marnhull 820458)

FORBES, Donald Logan; JP (Essex 1954); s of Charles Bracey Forbes (d 1934); *b* 9 Dec 1908; *m* 1, 1935, Dorothy Ellen (d 1949), nee King; 1 s, 2 da; m 2, 1950, Valda Paula Collier, nee Tribe; *Career* Defence Medal, Coronation Medal, FCA, memb Wanstead and Woodford Borough Cncl 1938-64 (alderman 1952, mayor 1953-54), pres Woodford Con Assoc 1978; dir of Lonach Property Trust Ltd, Incorporated Mansfield House U Settlement, Manor House (Wanstead) Ltd; *Clubs* Naval and Military; *Style* - Donald Forbes Esq, JP; Lonach, Woodland Close, Woodford Green, Essex (☎ 01 504 2670)

FORBES OF BRUX, Hon Sir Ewan; 11 Bt (NS 1630), of Craigievar, Aberdeenshire, JP (Aberdeenshire 1969); s of late 18 Lord Sempill; suc to Btcy only of bro, 19 Lord Sempill, AFC, 1965; *b* 6 Sept 1912; *Educ* Munich, Aberdeen U (MB and ChB); *m* 1953, Isabella, da of late Alexander Mitchell, of Glenrinnes; *Heir* kinsman, John Alexander Cumnock Forbes-Sempill; *Style* - Hon Sir Ewan Forbes of Brux, Bt, JP; Brux Lodge, Alford, Aberdeenshire (☎ Kildrummy 223)

FORBES, Maj Hamish Stewart; MBE (Mil 1945), MC; s of late Lt-Col James Stewart Forbes, gs of 3 Bt; hp of kinsman, Col Sir John Stewart Forbes, 6 Bt, DSO, JP, DL; *b* 15 Feb 1916; *Educ* Eton; *m* 1945, Jacynthe Elizabeth Mary, da of late Eric Gordon Underwood; 1 s, 3 da; *Career* Maj (ret) Welsh Gds; *Style* - Maj Hamish Forbes, MBE, MC; Hambledon Cottage, Henley-on-Thames, Oxon; 23 Tryon st, SW3

FORBES, Hon Jonathan Andrew; s of 23 Lord Forbes, KBE; *b* 20 Aug 1947; *Educ* Eton; *m* 1981, Nichola Frances, da of Hon Julian Hawke (bro and h of 9 Baron Hawke); *Career* Capt Grenadier Gds; *Style* - The Hon Jonathan Forbes

FORBES, James Duncan Mallen; VRD; s of James Alexander Forbes; *b* 19 Dec 1926; *Educ* City of London Sch; *m* 1960, June, da of Harry De Behr Acheson-Gray; 1 s, 1 da; *Career* chm Liverpool Steamship Owners Assoc 1971-72, md Booker Line Ltd, chm Such & Schooley Ltd, dir Liverpool Maritime Terminals Ltd, dir London Steamship Owners Mutual Insurance Assocs Ltd; *Style* - James Forbes Esq, VRD; 30 Boundary rd, West Kirby, Wirral, Merseyside (☎ 051 625 5598)

FORBES, V-Adm Sir John Morrison; KCB (1978); s of Lt-Col Robert Hogg Forbes, OBE (d 1976); *b* 16 Aug 1925; *Educ* RN Coll Dartmouth; *m* 1950, Joyce Newenham, da of late Addison Perrit Hadden of Ireland; 2 s, 2 da; *Career* Kesatria Manku Negara 1968, 2 in command and operational Cdr Roy Malaysian Navy 1966-68, directorate of Naval Plans 1969-71, Capt HMS Triumph 1971-72, Capt RN Coll Dartmouth 1972-74, Naval Sec 1974-76, V-Adm 1977, Flag Offr Plymouth 1977-79; *Recreations* country pursuits; *Clubs* Army & Navy, RCC, RNSA; *Style* - V-Adm Sir John Forbes, KCB; c/o Coutts and Co, 440 Strand, WC2

FORBES, Col Sir John Stewart; 6 Bt (UK 1823), DSO, JP (Aberdeenshire 1955), DL (1953); s of Sir Charles Stewart Forbes, 5 Bt (d 1927); *b* 8 Jan 1901; *Educ* Wellington; *m* 1933, Agnes Jessie, da of Lt-Col David Lorraine Wilson-Farquharson, DSO, of Allargue, Corgarff, Aberdeenshire; 5 da; *Heir* kinsman, Maj

Hamish Stewart Forbes, MBE, MC; *Career* Col (ret) late RE, Hon Col 51 (Highland) Div Engineers 1960-67; Vice-Lt for Aberdeenshire 1973-; *Style* - Col Sir John Forbes Bt DSO JP HM Vice-Lieut for Aberdeenshire; Allargue, Corgarff, Aberdeenshire

FORBES, Master of; Hon Malcolm Nigel Forbes; s and h of 23 Lord Forbes; *b* 6 May 1946; *Educ* Eton, Aberdeen U; *m* 1970, Carole, da of N Whitehead, of Aberdeen; 1 s, 1 da; *Heir* s, Neil Malcolm Ross Forbes (b 1970); *Career* fin dir Instock Disposables Ltd; *Recreations* cricket, shooting, skiing; *Clubs* Roy Northern & University (Aberdeen); *Style* - The Master of Forbes; Finzeauch, Whitehouse, Alford, Aberdeenshire (☎ Whitehouse 209)

FORBES, Hon Mrs (Pamela Susan); *née* McCorquodale; da of 1 and last Baron McCorquodale (d 1971); *b* 1934; *m* 1956, William Frederick Eustace Forbes; *Style* - The Hon Mrs Forbes; Dinning House, Gargunnock, by Stirling

FORBES ADAM, Hon Mrs (Irene Constance); *née* Lawley; da of 3 Baron Wenlock; *b* 1889; *m* 1920, Colin Forbes Adam, CSI, JP, DL, 3 s of Sir Frank Forbes Adam, 1 Bt, CB, CIE, JP, DL; 2 s, 1 da (and 1 s decd); *Career* DStJ; *Style* - The Hon Mrs Forbes Adam; The Grange, Elvington, York

FORBES ADAM, Nigel Colin; JP (1960); s of Colin Forbes Adam, CSI, DL (3 s of Sir Frank Forbes Adam, 1 Bt); *b* 7 Dec 1930; *Educ* Eton, King's Cambridge; *m* 1954, Teresa, da of Cdr David Robertson, RN; 4 s (Charles, Titus, Julian, Harry); *Career* late Army Capt; landowner & farmer; High Sheriff Yorks 1976; *Recreations* tennis, shooting; *Clubs* Yorkshire, Travellers'; *Style* - Nigel Forbes Adam Esq, JP; Skipwith Hall, Selby, Yorks

FORBES ADAM, Hon Mrs (Vivien Elisabeth); *née* Mosley; da of Sir Oswald Mosley, 6 Bt, by his 1 w, Lady Cynthia Curzon (da of 1 and last Marquess Curzon of Kedleston); sis of 3 Baron Ravensdale; *b* 25 Feb 1921; *m* 1949, Desmond Forbes Adam (d 1958), 2 s of Colin Forbes Adam, CSI, JP, DL (3 s of Sir Frank Forbes Adam, 1 Bt, CB, CIE, JP, DL) of Skipworth Hall, Yorks, by his w, Hon Irene Lawley (da of 3 Baron Wenlock, GCSI, GCIE, KCB, PC); 1 s, 2 da; *Career* raised to rank of da of a Baroness 1967; *Style* - The Hon Mrs Forbes Adam; Forebrae, Dunkeld, Perths (☎ 035 04 232); 11 Mulberry Walk, SW3 (☎ 01 352 3107)

FORBES-CABLE, Hon Mrs (Kirstine Elizabeth); *née* Forbes-Sempill; da of late Lord Sempill (19 in line) by 2 w, Cecilia, nee Dunbar-Kilburn; half-sis of Lady Sempill, *qv*; *b* 9 Aug 1944; *m* 1968, John Michael Forbes-Cable (who assumed by deed poll 1968 the additional name of Forbes); 2 s (William Richard Craigievar b 1970, Malcolm Dunbar Craigievar b 1972); *Style* - The Hon Mrs Forbes-Cable; Flat 8, 17-20 Embankment gdns, SW3 (☎ 01 351 2125); Upper Craigievar, Alford, Aberdeenshire (☎ Muir of Fowlis 368)

FORBES-LEITH OF FYVIE, Sir Andrew George; 3 Bt (UK 1923); s of Sir (Robert) Ian (Algernon) Forbes-Leith of Fyvie, 2 Bt, KT, MBE (d 1973); *b* 20 Oct 1929; *Educ* Eton; *m* 1962, Jane Kate (d 1969), da of late David McCall-McCowan, of Dalwhat, Moniaive, Dumfries; 2 s, 2 da; *Heir* s, George Forbes-Leith; *Style* - Sir Andrew Forbes-Leith of Fyvie, Bt; Fyvie Castle, Aberdeenshire (☎ Fyvie 208); Dunachton, Kingussie, Inverness-shire (☎ Kincraig 226)

FORBES-LEITH, George Ian David; s and h of Sir Andrew George Forbes-Leith of Fyvie, 3 Bt; *b* 26 May 1967; *Style* - George Forbes-Leith Esq

FORBES-SEMPILL, Hon Brigid Gabriel; da of late Lord Sempill (19 in line) by 2 w, Cecilia, nee Dunbar-Kilburn; half-sis of Lady Sempill, *qv*; *b* 1945; *Style* - The Hon Brigid Forbes-Sempill

FORBES-SEMPILL, John Alexander Cumnock; s (by 3 m) of late Rear-Adm the Hon Arthur Lionel Ochoncar Forbes-Sempill, s of 17 Lord Sempill; hp of kinsman, Hon Sir Ewan Forbes of Brux, 11 Bt, JP; *b* 29 Aug 1927; *m* 1, 1958 (m dis 1964), Penelope, da of Arthur Grey-

Pennington; m 2, 1966, Jane Carolyn, da of C Gordon Evans, of Chelsfield, Kent; *Career* late Capt Seaforth Highlanders; actor-manager; *Style* - John Forbes-Sempill Esq; 3 Mallord st, SW3

FORBES-SEMPILL, Hon Janet Cecilia; da of 19 Lord Sempill by his 2 w, Cecilia (*see* Cecilia, Lady Sempill); half-sis of Lady Sempill, *qv*; *b* 4 May 1942; *Educ* Colchester Coll of Art *Style* - The Hon Janet Forbes- Sempill

FORD, Andrew Russell; s and h of Sir Henry Ford, Bt, TD, JP; *b* 29 June 1943; *Educ* Winchester, New Coll Oxford; *m* 1968, Penelope Anne, da of Harry Relph, of Rotherby, Leics; 1 s, 1 da; *Style* - Andrew Ford Esq; 30 Boundary rd, Chippenham, Wilts

FORD, Hon Mrs (Caroline Jane); *née* Nelson; da of 2 Baron Nelson of Stafford; *b* 1942; *m* 1964, Michael John Henry Ford; 2 s, 1 da; *Style* - The Hon Mrs Ford; The Old Rectory, Buckerell, Honiton, Devon

FORD, Sir Edward William Spencer; KCB (1967, CB 1952), KCVO (1957, MVO 1949); s of the Very Rev Lionel Ford, Dean of York (d 1932); *b* 24 July, 1910; *Educ* Eton, New Coll Oxford; *m* 1949, Hon Virginia, da of 1 and last Baron Brand; 2 s; *Career* OStJ 1976, Lt-Col, WW II, barr-at-law 1937, practised 1937-39, assist private sec to HM King George VI 1946-52, assist private sec HM the Queen 1952-67, sec Pilgrim Trust 1967-75; *Clubs* White's, MCC, Beefsteak; *Style* - Sir Edward Ford, KCB, KCVO; Eydon Hall, Eydon, Daventry, Northants (☎ Byfield 60282); 18 Hale House, 34 de Vere gdns, W8 (☎ 01 937 2818)

FORD, Air Marshal Sir Geoffrey (Harold); KBE (1979), CB (1975); s of Harold Alfred Ford (d 1961); *b* 6 Aug 1923; *Educ* Lewes G S, Bristol U; *m* 1951, Valerie, nee Finn; 2 s; *Career* RAF Air-Marshal, WW II, technical branch 1942, air offr engineering Strike Command 1973-76, dir gen engineering and supply 1976-78, ch engineer 1978-; *Clubs* RAF; *Style* - Air Marshal Sir Geoffrey Ford KBE CB; c/o Barclays Bank Ltd, The Old Bank, Lewes, E Sussex

FORD, Sir Hugh; FRS (1967); s of Arthur Ford (d 1969); *b* 16 July 1913; *Educ* Northampton Sch, Imperial Coll London U; *m* 1942, Wynyard, nee Scholfield; 2 da; *Career* kt 1975; research engineer ICI 1939-42, ch engineer British Iron & Steel Fedn 1942-48, reader then prof of Applied Mechanics Imperial Coll 1948-65, prof of Mechanical Engineering and head of Dept 1965-78, Pro Rector Imperial Coll 1978-80, pres Inst of Mechanical Engineers 1976-77, chm Ford & Dain Ptnrs 1971-, dir Prutec 1981-; *Recreations* gardening, music; *Clubs* Athenaeum; *Style* - Sir Hugh Ford; 18 Shrewsbury House, Cheyne Walk, SW3; Shamley Cottage, Shamley Green, Surrey

FORD, Harold Frank; s of Sir Patrick Johnson Ford, 1 Bt (d 1945); *b* 17 May 1915; *Educ* Winchester, Univ Oxford, Edinburgh U; *m* 1948, Lucy Mary, da of late Sheriff John Rudolph Burnet; 1 s, 3 da; *Career* Capt WW II, Maj Home Guard, advocate 1945, sheriff substitute Forfar 1951-71, sheriff Perth 1971-80; *Recreations* gardening, golf, shooting; *Clubs* New, Edinburgh, Hon Co Edinburgh Golfers, Roy Perth Golfing Soc; *Style* - Harold Ford Esq; Broomhill, by Stanley, Perthshire

FORD, Sir Henry Russell; 2 Bt (UK 1929), TD (1954), JP (E Lothian 1951); s of Sir Patrick Johnston Ford, 1 Bt (d 1945); *b* 30 April 1911; *Educ* Winchester, New Coll Oxford; *m* 1936, Mary Elizabeth, da of late Godfrey F Wright, of Whiddon, Bovey Tracey; 1 s, 3 da; *Heir* s, Andrew Russell Ford; *Career* 2 Lt 1939, RA, Lt-Col 1945 (despatches); *Style* - Sir Henry Ford, Bt, TD, JP; Seaforth, Gullane, E Lothian (☎ Gullane 842214)

FORD, Sir John Archibald; KCMG (1977, CMG 1967), MC (1945); s of Ronald Mylne Ford (d 1963); *b* 19 Feb 1922; *Educ* Sedbergh Sch, Oriel Oxford; *m* 1956, Emaline, da of late Mahlon Burnette of USA; 2 da; *Career* Maj RA Field, HM Diplomatic Serv, Cconsul Ggen New York, Dir Gen British Trade Dvpt USA 1971-75, Br Ambass Jakarta 1975-78, British High Cmmr Ottowa 1978-; *Recreations* walking, writing, sailing; *Clubs* Farmers,

Yvonne Arnaud Theatre, Roy Commonwealth Soc, RHS; *Style* - Sir John Ford, KCMG, MC; 153 Whitehall ct, SW1; Earnscliffe, Ottawa, Canada

FORD, James Allan; CB (1978), MC (1946); s of Douglas Ford (d 1948); *b* 10 Jun 1920; *Educ* Roy High Sch Edinburgh, Edinburgh U; *m* 1948, Isobel, nee Dunnett; 1 s, 1 da; *Career* Civil Serv, Registrar Gen Scotland 1966-69, Princ Establishment Offr Scottish Off 1969-79, ret 1979, novelist; *Recreations* trout fishing; *Clubs* Scottish Arts, Roy Scots, Roy Commonwealth Soc; *Style* - James Ford Esq, CB, MC; 29 Lady Road, Edinburgh, EH16 5PA (☎ 667 4489)

FORD, Lady; Katherine Olive; da of James Charles Yorke, JP (ggs of 1 Earl of Hardwicke); *m* 1918, Sir (Francis Charles) Rupert Ford, 5 Bt (d 1948); *Style* - Lady Ford; Treown, Wilfred rd, Boscombe, Bournemouth

FORD, Sir Leslie (Ewart); OBE (1945); s of Elias Ford, OBE (d 1935); *b* 27 July 1897; *Educ* Cardiff H S, LSE; *m* 1925, Mary Mabel, nee Powles; 1 da; *Career* kt 1956; CStJ; Col Engr & Railway Staff Corps (TA) WW I, European War Welch Regt and Monmouthshire Regt 1957, Maj Home Gd WW II; Great Western Railway 1912, ch docks man 1944, gen man Port of London Authority 1948-64, freeman City of London 1963, freeman Watermen and Lightermen River Thames 1963; *Recreations* golf; *Clubs* MCC; *Style* - Sir Leslie Ford, OBE; 26 Bedford gdns, Campden Hill, W8 (☎ 01 727 5595)

FORD, Michael John Henry; s of Lt-Col Mortimer Noel Ford, TD, DL; *b* 23 May 1936; *Educ* Harrow; *m* 1964, Hon Caroline Jane, *qv*, da of 2 Baron Nelson of Stafford; 3 c; *Career* dir estate agents firm, cncl of Sail T'ning Assoc, govr West of England Sch; *Recreations* sailing, shooting, fishing; *Clubs* Roy Ocean Racing; *Style* - Michael Ford Esq; The Old Rectory, Buckerell, Honiton, Devon (☎ 850332)

FORD, (John) Peter; CBE (1969); s of late E Ford; *b* 20 Feb 1912; *Educ* Wrekin Coll, Gonville & Caius Cambridge; *m* 1939, Phoebe Seys, nee Wood; 1 s, 2 da; *Career* chm and md International Joint Ventures Ltd 1974-, md- Brush Export Ltd, Assoctd Br Oil Engines Export Ltd 1949-58, Coventry Climax International Ltd 1958-63, dir Plessey Overseas Ltd 1963-70, chm Inst of Export 1954-56 and 1965-67, v-pres London Chamber of Commerce 1972-, chm British Shippers Council 1972-75, Master Worshipful Company of Ironmongers 1981; *Recreations* Athletics (Cambridge Univ and International teams); *Clubs* United Oxford & Cambridge Univ, City Livery, MCC, Hawks (Cambridge), Royal Wimbledon Golf; *Style* - Peter Ford Esq CBE; 40 Fairacres, Roehampton Lane, SW15 (☎ 01 870 2146)

FORD, Roger Henry; s of Herbert Stanley Ford (d 1937); *b* 9 Jan 1919; *Educ* West Ham Sch; *m* 1941, Eileen Margaret, nee Searle; 1 s, 1 da; *Career* Capt WW II Europe, chartered accountant, sr ptnr McCabe & Ford; *Recreations* horticulture; *Clubs* The Maidstone (Kent); *Style* - Roger Ford Esq; Wildacres, Holtwood Avenue, Aylesford, Maidstone

FORD, Gp Capt Walter Ronald CBE (1960); s of Henry William Ford (d 1952); *b* 19 Oct 1913; *Educ* Hampton; *m* 1940, Pamela Hope, da of late Fl Lt Robert Cecil Clayton; 3 s, 4 da; *Career* Gp Capt, ret RAF 1963, assist sec MCC 1970-79; *Recreations* cricket, golf; *Clubs* RAF, MCC; *Style* - Gp Capt Walter Ford, CBE; Moss, Byworth, Petworth, W Sussex

FORDE, Lady Anthea Geraldine; *née* Lowry-Corry; da of 7 Earl Belmore, JP, DL (d 1960); *b* 16 Feb 1942; *m* 1965, Patrick Mathew Forde, of Co Down; 2 s, 1 da; *Style* - Lady Anthea Forde; Seaforde, Co Down, N Ireland (☎ 225)

FORDHAM, Hon Mrs (June Jane Coupar); *née* Barrie; da of 1 and last Baron Abertay, KBE (d 1940); *b* 1928; *m* 1, 1952, Brig Alan Breitmeyer; 1 s, 1 da; m 2, 1977, Christopher Fordham, FRICS; *Style* - The Hon Mrs Fordham; Bartlow Park, Cambs; Odsey Park, Ashwell, Herts; 20 Chancellor House, Hyde Park Gate, SW7

FORDYCE, Lt-Col Alexander (Alastair); MBE (1944 Mil), JP (1959), DL (Lancs 1975); s of Alexander Fordyce (d 1926); *b* 30 Sep 1916; *Educ* Perth Acad; *m* 1942, Christian Margaret, nee Smith; 2 s; *Career* Lt-Col WW II, co dir (ret), jt man dir Perrite Ltd 1957-80, jt man dir Manchester Rubber Co Ltd 1966-80, dir Perrite (Ireland) Ltd 1977-80, dir Harvey & Sons Ltd 1959-69; *Recreations* travel; *Clubs* Army & Navy; *Style* - Lt-Col Alexander Fordyce, MBE, JP, DL; Whitelands, 24 Livesey Branch rd, Feniscowles, Blackburn, Lancs

FORDYCE, Capt Charles Elphinstone; s of Boston Elphinstone Fordyce (d 1932) of Ashogle; *b* 1897; *Educ* Shrewsbury, RMC; *m* 1935, Hon Violet Ethel Mary Hennessy, da of 1 Baron Windlesham, OBE, JP; 1 s, 1 da; *Career* served WW I Seaforth Highlanders, Capt 1927, NW Frontier 1930-31; *Clubs* Army & Navy, Boodle's; *Style* - Charles Fordyce Esq; Bracken Lodge, Churt, Farnham, Surrey (☎ Hindhead 5122)

FORESTER, 8 Baron (UK 1821); (George Cecil) Brooke Weld-Forester; s of 7 Baron (d 1977) and Marie, da of Col Sir Herbert Perrott, 6 Bt, CH, CB; *b* 20 Feb 1938; *Educ* Eton, RAC Cirencester; *m* 1967, Hon (Elizabeth) Catherine Lyttelton, da of late 10 Viscount Cobham, KG, GCMG, GCVO, TD, PC; 1 s, 3 da; *Heir* s, Hon Charles Forester; *Career* Patron of 3 livings; this nobleman has in his possession a licence of the time of Henry VIII, giving to John Forester of Watling st, Co Salop, the privilege of wearing his hat in the Royal presence; *Style* - The Rt Hon The Lord Forester; Willey Park, Broseley, Salop (☎ Telford 882146)

FORESTER, Baroness - Hon (Elizabeth) Catherine; *née* Lyttelton; da of 10 Viscount Cobham, KG, GCMG, GCVO, TD, PC (d 1977); *b* 1946; *m* 1967, 8 Baron Forester, *qv*; *Style* - The Rt Hon the Lady Forester; Willey Park, Broseley, Salop

FORESTER, Dowager Baroness; Marie Louise Priscilla; da of late Col Sir Herbert Charles Perrott, 6 Bt, CH, CB; *b* 1909; *m* 1931, 7 Baron Forester (d 1977); 1 s, 4 da; *Career* DStJ, pres St John's Ambulance Nursing Divs 1928-31, pres of Shropshire Nursing Divs 1931-75, Patron Shropshire Assoc of Youth Clubs 1965- (first pres 1946); *Style* - The Rt Hon the Dowager Lady Forester; Willey Old Hall, Broseley, Salop; Marasha, Box 6, Raffin, Rhodesia

FORESTIER-WALKER, Sir Clive Radzivill; 5 Bt (UK 1835); s of Radzivill Frederick Forestier-Walker, & gs of 2 Bt; suc 1 cous once removed, Sir George Ferdinand Forestier-Walker, 4 Bt (d 1976); *b* 30 April 1922; *m* 1948, Pamela Mercy (m dis 1976), da of Clifford Leach, of Chiswick, W4; 3 da; *Heir* kinsman, Michael Leolin Forestier-Walker, b 24 April 1949; *Style* - Sir Clive Forestier-Walker, Bt; 42 Old Vicarage Park, Narborough, King's Lynn, Norfolk (☎ Narborough 516)

FORESTIER-WALKER, George Clive; s of Edmund Annesley Forestier-Walker, of Broombank, Aldeburgh, Suffolk (gggs of Sir George Walker, 1 Bt, GCB), by his w Bridget, da of Cdr Sir Geoffrey Hughes-Onslow, KBE, DSC, JP, DL, RN (kin to the Earls of Onslow) and Hon Eileen, da of 4 Baron Crofton; *b* 17 April 1946; *Educ* Wellington; *m* 1970, Christian, da of John Gurney, *qv*, of Walsingham Abbey, Norfolk; 3 da (Camilla b 1973, Susanna b 1976, Liza b 1980); *Career* Major; *Recreations* shooting, skiing, sailing (yacht- 'Casala'); *Clubs* Cavalry & Guards; *Style* - Maj George Forestier-Walker; Mulberry Hse, Heather Drive, Sunningdale, Berks SLS OHP (☎ Ascot 20566)

FORMAN, John Denis; OBE (1956); s of Adam Forman, Dumcrieff, Moffatt, Scotland; *b* 13 October 1917; *Educ* Loretto, Musselburgh; Pembroke Coll Camb; *m* 1948, Helen Blondel; 2 s; *Career* kt 1976; Lt-Col (OSDEF Battle Sch, North Africa, Italy); chm (1974) and joint managing dir (1965) Granada TV Ltd; Chief Production Office, Central Office of Information Films 1947; dir British Film Institute 1948-55; chm Board of Governors, British Film Institute 1971-73; dir of Royal Opera House 1980; Council memb Royal Northern Coll of Music 1977; *Recreations* music; *Clubs* Savile; *Style* - John Forman Esq, OBE; The Mill House, Howe St, Great Waltham, Essex

FORMAN HARDY, Col Thomas Eben; CBE (1966), MC (1943), TD (1945), DL (Notts 1963); s of William Eben Hardy; *b* 30 Aug 1919; *Educ* Harrow, Trin Cambridge; *m* 1946, Marjorie Senior, nee Edgar; 1 s (and 1 decd), 1 da; *Career* col WW II, jt acting Master S Notts Hunt 1957-65, High Sheriff (Notts 1960), ADC (TA) HM the Queen 1966-71, chm T Bailey Forman Ltd, proprietors of Nottingham Evening Post, chm Hardys & Hansons Ltd, Forman Hardy Farms, chm E Midlands TAVR 1980-; *Recreations* shooting, flying, sailing; *Clubs* Cavalry & Guards, Roy Cornwall Yacht; *Style* - Col Thomas Forman Hardy, CBE, MC, TD, DL; Car Colston Hall, Bingham, Notts (☎ East Bridgford 20254)

FORRES, 4 Baron (UK 1922); Sir Alastair Stephen Grant Williamson; 4 Bt (UK 1909); s of 3 Baron (d 1978) by his 1 w, Gillian; *b* 16 May 1946; *Educ* Eton; *m* 1969, Margaret, da of George Mallam, of Mullumbimby, NSW; 2 s; *Heir* s, Hon George Williamson; *Career* chm Agriscot Pty Ltd; dir Jaga Trading Pty Ltd; Australian rep Tattersalls; *Clubs* Australian Jockey, Tattersalls (Sydney), Sydney Turf; *Style* - The Rt Hon Lord Forres; c/o Messrs Clark, Oliver, Dewar & Webster, Brothockbank House, Arbroath, Angus; 31 Tite st, SW3 (☎ 01 352 1333)

FORRES, Cecily, Baroness; Cecily Josephine; da of Maj Sir Alexander Gordon-Cumming, 5 Bt, MC, by Elizabeth, nee Richardson, who later m 5 Earl Cawdor; *b* 11 Dec 1925; *m* 1, 1957, as his 2 w, 2 Earl of Woolton (d 1969); m 2, 1969, 3 Baron Forres (m dis 1974, he d 1978); *Style* - Cecily, Lady Forres; Glenogil, by Forfar, Angus; 31 Tite st, SW3 (☎ 01 352 1333)

FORREST, Andrew Patrick McEwen; s of Rev Andrew James Forrest, BD (d 1960); *b* 25 March 1923 *Educ* Dundee H S, St Andrew's U, U of Wales; *m* 1, 1955, Margaret Beryl (decd 1961), da of Capt Frederick Hall, MBE; 1 s, 1 da; m 2, 1964, Margaret Anne, nee Stewart; 1 da; *Career* lectr and sr lectr surgery Glasgow U and Western Infirmary 1954-62, prof of surgery Welsh National Sch of Medicine 1962-71, Regius Prof Clinical Surgery Edinburgh 1971, memb Medical Research Cncl 1976-80; *Style* - Andrew Forrest Esq; 8 Gordon ter, Edinburgh, EH16 5QL (☎ 667 3203)

FORREST, John Orchover; *b* 4 May 1918; *Educ* Central Foundation Sch, Univ of London, Guy's Hospital Dental Sch; *m* 1944, Irene, nee Leanse; 2 s; *Career* senior Hosp Dental Officer Guy's Hospital Sch of Hygiene 1961-68, Hon Lecturer Guy's Dental 1969-71, Gibbs Prize Scholar 1968, pres British Periodontal Soc 1964, pres British Endodontic Soc 1966, pres British Dental Assoc Metropolitan branch 1977, UK Regent Int College Dentists 1980-; *Recreations* serious photography, picture framing, 2 out of the 3 R's, travel; *Clubs* RAF; *Style* - John Forrest Esq; c/o Coutts & Co, 16 Cavendish square, W1

FORRESTER, Lady Caroline *née* Lowther; da of 7 Earl of Lonsdale; *b* 1959; *m* 1978, Guy Forrester; *Style* - Lady Caroline Forrester

FORRESTER, Maj-Gen Michael; CB (1969), CBE (1963), DSO (1943) and Bar (1944), MC (1939) and Bar (1941); s of James Forrester (d 1962); *b* 31 Aug 1917; *Educ* Haileybury; *m* 1947 (m dis); 2 s; *Career* Maj-Gen, Cdr 16 Parachute Brigade Gp 1961-63, Cdr 4 Div 1965-67, dir of Infantry 1968-70, ret 1970; *Recreations* countryside, gardening; *Style* - Maj-Gen Michael Forrester, CB, CBE, DSO*, MC*; Pullens, West Worldham, Alton, Hants

FORRESTER-PATON, His Hon Judge; Douglas Shaw Forrester-Paton; QC (1965); s of Alexander Forrester-Paton, JP (d 1954); *b* 22 Jun 1921; *Educ* Gresham's, Oxford U; *m* 1948, Agnete, da of late Holger Tuxen, of Hellerup, Denmark; 1 s, 2 da; *Career* Sqdn Ldr RAFVR, barr 1947, Recorder of Middlesbrough 1963-68, Recorder of Teesside 1968-70, Co Court Judge 1970-71, Circuit Judge 1972-; *Recreations* walking *Style* - His Hon Judge Forrester-Paton, QC; 24 Kirkby Lane, Gt

Broughton, Middlesbrough (☎ Stokesley 712301)

FORSBERG, Cdr (Charles) Gerald; OBE (1955); s of Charles Forsberg, of Vancouver (d 1913); *b* 18 Jun 1912; *Educ* Polytechnic Sch, training ship Mercury, Sir John Cass Coll; *m* 1952, Joyce Whewell, nee Hogarth; 1 s, 1 da; *Career* Cdr RN, cmd HM ships Vega, Mameluke, Chaplet, Thames, Isis in Norway, Malta convoys, Greece, Crete, North Sea convoys, master mariner 1938, mentioned in despatches, dep dir Marine Services (naval) 1958-75; author/journalist; *Recreations* marathon swimming (England to France record 1957-59); *Clubs* Otter Swimming; *Style* - Commander Gerald Forsberg OBE; c/o Barclays Bank International, 1 Cockspur st, SW1

FORSTER, Charles Ian Kennerley; CBE (1964); s of Douglas Wakefield Forster, Bishop of Middleham (d 1963); *b* 18 July 1911; *Educ* Rossall Sch; *m* 1, 1942 (m dis 1974), Thelma Primrose, nee Horton; 1 s, 1 da; m 2, 1975, Violet Loraine, nee Sperling; *Career* fell of Inst of Actuaries 1936, Sun Life Assurance Soc 1928-46, Admiralty Statistics Branch 1946-54, Miny of Power, Mintech DTI Economics and Statistics (under sec 1972), energy consultant Nat Coal Bd 1972-; *Recreations* stamp collecting; *Style* - Charles Forster, Esq, CBE; 140 Watchfield Court, Sutton Court Road, Chiswick, London W4 (☎ 01 994 3128)

FORSTER, Eric Brown; MBE (1952); s of Frank Forster (d 1951); *b* 19 May 1917; *Educ* Queen Elizabeth G S Hexham Northumberland; *m* 1943, Margaret Bessie Letitia, da of late Lt-Col Arthur Wood, MBE; 1 s, 2 da; *Career* Brig, command paymaster Hong Kong 1962-64, dir of Cost and Management Accounting (Army Dept) 1966-68, ret 1968, gen man Potato Marketing Bd 1970-; *Recreations* gardening, golf; *Clubs* MCC, Worplesdon Golf *Style* - Eric Foster Esq MBE; Littledene, Guildown av, Guildford, Surrey (☎ 62313)

FORSTER OF HARRABY, Baroness; Muriel; da of late Samuel Vosper; *m* 1917, 1 Baron Forster of Harraby (d 1972, when title became extinct); 1 da; *Style* - The Rt Hon the Lady Forster of Harraby; 84 Albemarle rd, Beckenham, Kent; Brick ct, Temple, EC4

FORSYTH, Cyril Theodore; CBE (1969); s of Edwin Forsyth (d 1979); *b* 9 Sept 1899; *Educ* People's Coll Nottingham, Nottingham U; *m* 1921, Mary Agnes, nee Kerr; 2 da; *Career* accountant, ch exec offr Nottingham Co-op Soc Ltd 1943-65; *Recreations* golf, cricket; *Clubs* Victory Services; *Style* - Cyril Forsyth Esq, CBE; Redlands, 45 Loughborough rd, Ruddington, Nottingham (☎ 211454)

FORTER, Alexis; OBE (1963); s of Sqdn Ldr Michael Forter, OBE (d 1971); *b* 6 Sept 1925; *Educ* St Paul's Sch, Magdalen Oxford; *m* 1971, Elizabeth Barbara Jane, da of Joseph Neville Wood, CBE; *Career* HM Foreign Serv 1950, first sec Baghdad 1957-58, Tehran 1959-64, Saigon 1966-69, Nairobi 1971-73, counsellor Paris 1977-; *Recreations* beagling, music, shooting; *Clubs* Travellers' *Style* - Alexis Forter Esq, OBE; c/o FCO, SW1

FORTESCUE, 7 Earl (GB 1789); Richard Archibald Fortescue; JP (Oxon 1964); also Baron Fortescue (GB 1746), Viscount Ebrington (GB 1789); s of 6 Earl, MC, TD (d 1977), by his 1 w Marjorie, OBE; *b* 14 April 1922; *Educ* Eton, Ch Ch Oxford; *m* 1, 1949, Penelope Jane (d 1959), da of late Robert Evelyn Henderson by his w Beatrice (da of Sir William Clerke, 11 Bt); 1 s, 1 da; m 2, 1961, Margaret Anne, da of Michael Stratton; 2 da; *Heir* s, Viscount Ebrington; *Career* late Capt Coldstream Gds; *Style* - The Rt Hon The Earl Fortescue, JP; The Old Farm, Swinbrook, Burford, Oxon (☎ Burford 3135)

FORTESCUE, Lady Celia Anne; da (by 1 m) of 7 Earl Fortescue; *b* 1957; *Style* - Lady Celia Fortescue

FORTESCUE, Lady Laura Margaret; da (by 2 m) of 7 Earl Fortescue; *b* 1962; *Style* - Lady Laura Fortescue

FORTESCUE, Lady Margaret; da of

late 5 Earl Fortescue; *b* 1923; *m* 1948 (m dis 1968), Bernard van Cutsem (d 1975); 2 da (*see* Viscountess Sudley); *Career* resumed surname Fortescue 1966; *Style* - Lady Margaret Fortescue; Castle Hill, Barnstaple, N Devon

FORTESCUE, Hon Martin Denzil; s of late 6 Earl Fortescue, MC, TD; *b* 1924; *Educ* Eton; *m* 1954, Prudence Louisa, da of Sir Charles Samuel Rowley, 6 Bt, TD; 2 s, 2 da; *Career* Lt RN (Emergency List); *Style* - The Hon Martin Fortescue; Wincombe Park, Shaftesbury, Dorset

FORTESCUE, Hon Seymour Henry; s (by 2 m) of late 6 Earl Fortescue, MC, TD; *b* 1942; *Educ* Eton, Trin Cambridge, London Graduate Sch of Business Studies; *m* 1966, Julia, da of Sir John Arthur Pilcher, GCMG; 1 s, 1 da; *Style* - The Hon Seymour Fortescue; 7 The Terrace, Barnes, SW13

FORTESCUE, Lady Sarah Jane; da (by 2 m) of 7 Earl Fortescue; *b* 1963; *Style* - Lady Sarah Fortescue

FORTESCUE, Sybil, Countess - Hon Sybil Mary; da of 3 Viscount Hardinge, CB (d 1924) and Mary Frances (who m 2, 1928, as his 3 w, 3 Marquess of Abergavenny, and who d 1954), da of late Hon Ralph Pelham Nevill, bro of 1 Marquess of Abergavenny; *b* 4 Dec 1898; *m* 1, 1922, 4 Baron Penrhyn (m dis 1941, he d 1949); m 2, 1941, 6 Earl Fortescue, MC, TD, (d 1977); 1 s (Hon Seymour Fortescue); *Career* OstJ; *Style* - The Rt Hon Sybil, Countess Fortescue; The Three Gables, Chipping Campden, Glos

FORTEVIOT, 3 Baron (UK 1917); Sir Henry Evelyn Alexander Dewar; 3 Bt (UK 1907), MBE (Mil 1943), DL (Perth 1961); s (by 2 m) of 1 Baron (d 1929, who came to London with his way to make in the world vowing to change the then popular belief in the superiority of Irish whiskey over Scotch; the rest is drinking history and the name Dewar now a household one); suc half-bro 1947; former f-in-law to the Duke of Fife; *b* 23 Feb 1906; *Educ* Eton, St John's Oxford; *m* 1933, Cynthia Monica, da of late Piers Cecil Le Gendre Starkie (whose w Cicely was 2 da of Sir James de Hoghton, 11 Bt), of the family of Starkie of Huntroyde (itself a branch of the Starkeys (or Starkies) of Stretton, one of whom was Sir Oliver Starkey, Latin Secretary to de la Vallette during the siege of Malta in 1565 and his successor as Grand Master); 2 s, 2 da (the er of whom, Hon Caroline, m (1) 3 Duke of Fife, *qv* (m dis) and (2) Gen Sir Richard Worsley, *qv*); *Heir* s, Hon John James Evelyn Dewar; *Career* chm John Dewar & Sons Ltd 1954-76, late dir Buchanan-Dewar Ltd and Distillers Co; *Style* - The Rt Hon The Lord Forteviot MBE DL; Dupplin Castle, Perth, Perthshire

FORWELL, Dr George Dick; QHP (1980); s of Harold Cecil Forwell (d 1955); *b* 6 July 1928; *Educ* George Watson's Coll, Edinburgh U (MB, ChB, PhD); *m* 1957, Catherine Forsyth Campbell, nee Cousland; 2 da; *Career* lectr Dept of Public Health & Social Medicine, assist dean Faculty of Medicine Edinburgh U 1959-63, sr adminve Medical offr Eastern Regional Hospital Bd 1963-67, princ Medical offr Scottish Home & Health Dept 1967-73, ch adminve Medical offr Greater Glasgow Health Bd 1973-; *Recreations* running, golf, travel; *Clubs* Roy Coll of Physicians (Edinburgh and Glasgow); *Style* - Dr George Forwell, QHP; 60 Whittingehame dr, Glasgow (☎ 334 7122)

FORWOOD, Sir Dudley Richard; 3 Bt (UK 1895), of The Priory, Gateacre, Childwall, co Palatine of Lancaster; s of Lt-Col Sir Dudley Baines Forwood, 2 Bt, CMG (d 1961); *b* 6 June 1912; *Educ* Stowe; *m* 1952, Mary Gwendolene Cullingford, nee Foster; *Heir* cousin, Peter Noel Forwood; *Career* Hon Attaché Br Legation 1934-37, Equerry to HRH the Duke of Windsor 1937-39, underwriting memb of Lloyd's, Hon Dir Roy Agric Soc of England, Official Verderer of New Forest 1974-, chm Crufts 1973-, chm New Forest Consultative Panel 1970, trustee The Kennel Club, Master of New Forest Buckhounds; *Recreations* hunting, wildlife conservation, gardening; *Style* - Sir Dudley Forwood Bt; The Old House Burley, nr Ringwood, Hants (☎ 04253 2345); 43 Addison rd, W14 (☎ 603 3620)

FORWOOD, Peter Noel; s (by 2 m) of late Arthur Noel Forwood, 3 s of 1 Bt; hp of cousin, Sir Dudley Richard Forwood, 3 Bt; *b* 15 Oct 1925; *Educ* Radley; *m* 1950, Roy, da of James Murphy, MBE, FRCS, LRCP, of Horsham, Sussex; 6 da; *Career* Welsh Gds WW II; *Style* - Peter Forwood Esq; Newhouse Farm, Shillinglee, Chiddingfold, Surrey

FOSKETT, Douglas John; OBE (1978); s of John Henry Foskett (d 1959); *b* 27 June 1918; *Educ* Bancroft's 1929-36, Queen Mary Coll, London U 1939, Birkbeck Coll London U 1955; *m* 1948, Joy, nee McCann; 1 s, 2 da; *Career* librarian, Metal Box Co Ltd 1948-57, London U Inst of Educn 1957-78, dir and Goldsmiths' librarian London U 1978-; *Recreations* travel, reading, writing, cricket; *Clubs* MCC, Sussex CC; *Style* - Douglas Foskett Esq, OBE; 1 Daleside, Gerrards Cross, Bucks (☎ 82835)

FOSTER, Lady Caroline Ann; da (by 1 m) of 7 Earl Cadogan; *b* 1946; *m* 1965, Euan Woodroffe Foster; 2 s; *Style* - Lady Caroline Foster ; 57 Cadogan sq, SW1

FOSTER, David Kenneth Dudley; s of Kenneth Dudley Foster, MBE (d 1972); *b* 20 Apr 1931; *Educ* Charterhouse, Pembroke Cambridge; *m* 1962, Hon Susan Elizabeth, da of Viscount Bridgeman, KBE, CB, DSO, MC; 3 s; *Career* dep chm and md Foster Bros Ltd; *Recreations* skiing, chess; *Style* - David Foster Esq; Beech House, Shifnal, Salop (☎ 0952 460261)

FOSTER, Francis Harold; DSO (1945), OBE (1944), TD and 3 Bars, DL (Sussex 1968); s of Capt William Thomas Benjamin Foster (1945); *b* 6 Feb 1904; *Educ* St Leonards Sch Seaford, Uckfield G S; *m* 1, 1930, Dorothy Christian (decd 1962), nee Brooke, 2 da; m 2, 1963, (Gwendolene) Rebecca, nee Funnell; *Career* cmmnd RE (TA) 1924, maj 1936, BEF 1940 (despatches), 1942-45 (despatches), substive Col 1950, Hon Col 1950-67, cmdt Sussex ACF 1960-69; RIBA chartered architect, private practice at Seaford 1933-73; *Clubs* Sussex; *Style* - Col Francis Foster, DSO, OBE, TD***, DL; Little Wildbees, Arlington, Polegate, E Sussex (☎ 1027)

FOSTER, Hon Mrs (Gillian Rosemary); da of 23 Lord Forbes, KBE; *b* 1949; *Educ* St Mary's Sch Wantage; *m* 1969, Alexander Neil Foster; 1 s, 1 da; *Style* - The Hon Mrs Foster; Church Farm House, Blakesley, Towcester, Northants

FOSTER, Sir John Gregory; 3 Bt (UK 1930); s of Sir Thomas Saxby Gregory, 2 Bt (d 1957); *b* 26 Feb 1927; *Educ* Michaelhouse Coll Natal, Witwatersrand U (MB and BCh); *m* 1956, Jean Millicent, da of late Elwin Watts, FRCSE, of Germiston, S Africa; 1 s, 3 da; *Heir* s, Saxby Foster; *Career* MRCP Edinburgh 1955, medical registrar 1955-56, medical offr 1957, physician 1961; *Style* - Sir John Foster, Bt; 122 York st, PO Box 325, George Cape Province, S Africa (☎ George 3251)

FOSTER, Maj-Gen Norman Leslie; CB (1961), DSO (1945); s of Col Arthur Leslie Foster (d 1956); *b* 26 Aug 1909; *Educ* Westminster, Roy Mil Acad Woolwich; *m* 1937, Joan Constance, da of late Canon Thomas Drury of Dublin; 2 s; *Career* WW II, CRA 11 Armoured Div 1955-56, dep mil sec (War Office) 1958-59, maj-gen 1959, GDC Roy Nigerian Army 1959-62, pres Regular Cmmns Bd 1962-65, ret 1965, dir Security (Army) MOD 1965-73, security adviser Civil Serv Dept 1974-79, col cmdt Roy Regiment of Artillery 1966-74; chm Truman & Knightley Educational Trust 1977-; *Recreations* golf, fishing, shooting; *Clubs* Army & Navy; *Style* - Maj-Gen Norman Foster, CB, DSO; Besborough, Heath End, Farnham, Surrey (☎ Aldershot 23540)

FOSTER, Peter Martin; CMG (1975); s of Capt F A P Foster (d 1948); *b* 25 May 1924; *Educ* Sherborne, CCC Cambridge; *m* 1947, Angela Hope, nee Cross; 1 s, 1 da; *Career* Maj Roy Horse Gds WW II, HM Diplomatic Serv 1948, HM Embassy Vienna 1948-52, FO 1952-54, Warsaw 1954-56, FO 1956-59, S Africa 1959-61, FO 1961-64, Bonn 1964-66, Kampala (dep high Cmmn) 1966-68, Imperial Defence Coll 1969, Tel Aviv (counsellor) 1970-72, FCO (head of Central and S Africa Dept)

1972-74, Strasbourg (Ambass and UK Perm Rep Cncl of Europe) 1974-78, Ambass German Democratic Repub 1978-81, ret 1981; *Clubs* Roy Commonwealth Soc; *Style* - Peter Martin Esq, CMG; Rew Cottage, Abinger Common, Dorking, Surrey; (☎ 730114) c/o Midland Bank Ltd, 455 Strand, WC2

FOSTER, Saxby Gregory; s and h of Sir John Gregory Foster, 3 Bt; *b* 3 Sept 1957; *Style* - Saxby Gregory Esq

FOSTER, Hon Mrs; Hon Sarah Rachel Jane; *née* Kay-Shuttleworth; da of late 4 Baron Shuttleworth; *b* 18 July 1950; *Educ* Southover Manor, City and Guilds Art Sch; *m* 1970, Richard Francis Foster; 1 s, 2 da; *Style* - The Hon Mrs Foster; Manor House Farm, Colkirk, Fakenham, Norfolk; 29 Bedford gdns, W8

FOSTER, William Robert Brudenell; s of Col Herbert Anderton Foster (d 1930); *b* 14 Apr 1911; *Educ* Wellington, CCC Oxford; *m* 1942, Jean Leslie, nee Urquhart; 3 s, 1 da; *Career* liveryman Clothworkers' Co 1932, master 1976-77, dir and chm John Foster & Son Ltd 1939-76, dir and v-chm Enfield Rolling Mills Ltd 1941-1976, dir MJM Holdings, Mount Isa Mines Ltd 1955-78, dir and chm St Piran Mining Ltd 1943-76, dir and v-chm London Brick 1970-81, High Sheriff Norfolk 1970, High Steward's ctee Norwich Cathedral 1970-80, FRSA; *Recreations* field sports, architecture, art, travel; *Clubs* Carlton, Pratt's, Norfolk; *Style* - William Foster Esq; Cranmer ct, Sloane av, SW3 (☎ 01 589 6724); Lexham Hall, King's Lynn, Norfolk (☎ Litcham 239); Gannochy Lodge, Edzell, Angus (☎ 322)

FOSTER SUTTON, Sir Stafford William Powell; KBE (1957, OBE Mil 1945), CMG (1948), QC (Jamaica 1938, Malaya 1948); s of G Foster Sutton (d 1948); *b* 24 Dec 1898; *Educ* St Mary Magdalen Sch, private tutor; *m* 1919, Linda Dorothy, da of late John Humber Allwood, OBE of Jamaica; 1 s (decd), 1 da; *Career* kt 1951, Barr 1926, slr gen Jamaica 1936, attorney gen Cyprus 1940, attorney gen Kenya 1944, acting gov Aug and Sept 1947, attorney gen Malaya 1948, ch justice Malaya 1950, Actg High Cmmr Sept-Dec 1950, Pres W African Appeal Court 1951, Ch Justice Nigeria 1955-58, Actg Govr Gen Nigeria 1957, pres Pension Appeal Tribunals for England and Wales 1958-73, memb of Ct Worshipful Tallow Chandlers Co; *Clubs* Roy Overseas League; *Style* - Sir Stafford Foster Sutton, KBE CMG QC; 7 London rd, Saffron Walden, Essex, (☎ 22246)

FOULKES, George; MP (L) S Ayrshire, JP; s of George Foulkes (decd); *b* 21 Jan 1942; *Educ* Keith G S, Haberdashers' Aske's Sch, Edinburgh U; *m* 1970, Elizabeth Anna, nee Hope; 2 s, 1 da; *Career* pres Edinburgh U Science Research Cncl 1963-64, Scottish Union of Students 1965-67, rector's assessor at Edinburgh U, dir Enterprise Youth 1968-73, dir Age Concern Scotland 1973-79, councillor Edinburgh City Council 1970-75, councillor Lothian regional cncl 1975-79, chm Lothian Region Education Ctee; *Recreations* boating, fishing; *Style* - George Foulkes Esq, JP, MP; 31 Monument rd, Ayr, Scotland (☎ 65776)

FOULKES, Thomas Herbert Fisher; CB (1962), OBE (1945); s of Maj-Gen Charles Howard Foulkes, CB, CMG, DSO (d 1969); *b* 28 May 1908; *Educ* Clifton Coll, St Cat's Cambridge; *m* 1947, Delphine Elizabeth, nee Smith; 2 s; *Career* Lt Col (Burma), Brig BAOR, MELF and 2 in command UK, Maj Gen UK, GSO I, 14th 1942-44, Cdr RE 17 Indian Div (Burma), Cdr 35 Engr Regt (canal zone) 1951-53, Cdr RE 1st British Corps (BAOR) 1956-57, CE Southern Command (UK) 1957-58, Engr in Ch Army 1960-63, ret 1963; Col Cmdt Roy Engrs 1963-73; *Recreations* shooting, gardening, photography; *Clubs* Army & Navy; *Style* - Maj-Gen Thomas Foulkes, CB, OBE; The Warren, Fitzroy Road, Fleet, Hampshire (☎ 6650)

FOUNTAIN, Hon Mrs (Wendy Shona Coulter); *née* Macpherson; da of 2 Baron Macpherson of Drumochter; *b* 1950; *m* 1972, Brian Anthony Fountain; 1 s; *Style* - The Hon Mrs Fountain; 40 Station ave, Wickford, Essex

FOWKE, David Frederick Gustavus; s of late Lt-Col Gerrard Fowke, 2 s of 3 Bt; hp of unc, Sir Frederick Fowke, 4 Bt; *b* 28 Aug 1950; *Style* - David Fowke Esq; c/o Mrs Gerrard Fowke, 4 Queen's Park Road, Bondi Junction, New South Wales 2022, Australia

FOWKE, Sir Frederick Woollaston Rawdon; 4 Bt (UK 1814), of Lowesby, Leicestershire; s of Sir Frederick Ferrers Conant Fowke 3 Bt (d 1948); *b* 14 Dec 1910; *Educ* Uppingham Sch; *m* 1948, Barbara Ethel, nee Townsend; 2 da; *Heir* n David Frederick Gustavus Fowke; *Career* sometime Capt Derbyshire Yeo 1939-43 (wounded), farmer (ret); *Style* - Sir Frederick Fowke Bt; Lower Woolstone, Bishops Tawton, Barnstaple (☎ Swimbridge 323)

FOWLER, Lady Jennifer Evelyn; *née* Chichester; da of 7 Marquess of Donegall; *b* 1949; *m* 1971, John Robert Henry Fowler; *Style* - Lady Jennifer Fowler; Clegarrow, Enfield, Co Meath, Republic of Ireland (☎ Enfield 130)

FOWLER, Keith Harrison; s of late Lancelot Harrison Fowler; *b* 20 May 1934; *Educ* Aldenham Sch; *m* 1961, Nicki Belinda, nee Pertwee; 3 c; *Career* Lt (Army) Suez Canal, ACIS, AMInstM, exec chm Edman Group 1977-, dir British Chess Magazine 1980-, memb Cncl National Advertising Benevolent Soc 1978-, govr Winchester House Sch 1968-; *Recreations* sailing, gardening, walking, crested china; *Clubs* Arts, Pathfinder, Solus; *Style* - Keith Fowler Esq; Herberts Hole Cottage, Ballinger, Great Missenden, Buckinghamshire (☎ 024 06 2034)

FOWLER, Peter Jon; s of William Joseph Fowler (d 1978); *b* 14 Jun 1936; *Educ* King Edward VI G S Morpeth Northumberland, Lincoln Coll Oxford, Bristol U; *m* 1959, Elizabeth, nee Burley; 3 da; *Career* reader in Archaeology Bristol U 1972-79, sec Roy Cmmn on Historical Monuments 1979-; *Recreations* writing, reading, sport; *Style* - Peter Fowler Esq; 1a Althrop rd, St Albans, Herts (☎ 61715)

FOWLER, Sir Robert Doughty; KCMG (1966, CMG 1967); s of William Fowler (d 1944); *b* 6 March 1914 *Educ* Queen Elizabeth's G S Mansfield, Emmanuel Coll Cambridge; *m* 1939, Margaret, da of Dr John MacFarquhar MacLeod (d 1957); 1 s, 1 da; *Career* Lt Col South East Asia, Burma Civil Service 1937-48, Home Civil Service/Diplomatic Service 1948-70, Additional Secretary to Governer of Burma 1947-8, High Commissioner Tanzania 1964-65, Ambassador Khartoum 1966-70, Gibraltar Referendum Administrator 1967; *Recreations* painting, photography; *Clubs* Royal Commonwealth Society, Leander; *Style* - Sir Robert Fowler KCMG; 7 Leicester Close, Henley on Thames, Oxon (☎ Henley 2404)

FOX, Levi; OBE (1964), DL (1967 Warwickshire); s of John William Fox (d 1952); *b* 28 Aug 1914; *Educ* Ashby De La Zouch Boys' G S, Oxford U; *m* 1938, Jane, nee Richards; 1 s, 1 da; *Career* dir and secretary- Incorporated Trust, Shakespeare Birthplace Trust 1945-; *Recreations* gardening; *Style* - Levi Fox Esq, OBE, DL; Silver Birches, 27 Welcombe rd, Stratford upon Avon, Warwickshire

FOX, Hon Mrs (Margaret Joan); da of late 1 Visc Davidson; *b* 1922; *m* 1943, the Ven Benjamin George Burton Fox, MC, TD, Archdeacon of Wisbech; 1 s, 4 da (inc twins); *Style* - The Hon Mrs Fox; The Vicarage, Haddenham, Ely, Cambridgeshire

FOX, Philip Hamilton; DL (1977); s of Cuthbert Lloyd Fox (d 1972); *b* 11 March 1922 *Educ* Harrow, Magdalene Cambridge; *m* 1948, Rona, nee Briggs; 3 s; *Career* Lt Northern Europe 1944-45, ship and travel agent, High Sheriff of Cornwall 1973-74, Fellow of Institute of Chartered Shipbrokers 1966, chm Falmouth Harbour Commissioners; *Recreations* sailing, gardening; *Clubs* Royal Cruising, Royal Ocean Racing, Royal Cornwall Yacht; *Style* - Philip Hamilton Fox Esq, DL; Stable Court, Mawnan Smith, Falmouth, Cornwall

FOX, Robert Trench; s of late Waldo

Trench Fox; *b* 1 Jan 1937; *Educ* Winchester, Univ Oxford; *m* 1962, Lindsay Garrett, da of late Sir Donald Forsyth Anderson; 2 s, 2 da; *Career* dir Kleinwort Benson Ltd 1972-, Barclays Bank Int Ltd 1978-, London dir Bank of New South Wales 1974-; *Recreations* shooting, walking, sailing; *Clubs* Brooks's; *Style* - Robert Fox Esq; Cheriton House, Cheriton, Alresford, Hants (☎ Bramdean 230)

FOX, Sir Theodore (Fortescue); s of Robert Fortescue Fox, MD, FRCP (d 1940); *b* 26 Nov 1899; *Educ* Leighton Park, Pembroke Coll Cambridge; *m* 1930, Margaret Evelyn, nee McDougall; 4 s (1 decd); *Career* kt 1962, Major RAMC, dir Family Planning Association 1964-67, editor The Lancet 1944-64; *Recreations* gardening, family history; *Clubs* Athenaeum; *Style* - Sir Theodore Fox; Green House, Rotherfield, East Sussex (☎ Rotherfield 2870)

FOX, Winifred Marjorie (Mrs Eustace Gray Debros); *née* Fox; da of Frederick Charles Fox (d 1968); *b* 31 March 1915; *Educ* Streatham County Sch, St Hugh's Oxford; *m* 1953, Eustace Gray Debros, formerly Eustacius Debroswki (d 1954); 1 da; *Career* entered Home Civil Service, assistant Principal Unemployment Assistance Board 1937, War Cabinet Office 1942, Principal 1943, Minister of Town & Country Planning 1944, Assistant Secretary 1948, Minister of Housing & Local Government 1952, Under-Secretary Local Government 1963, resident chm Civil Service Selection Board 1971-72, Under-Secretary Dept of Environmont (Planning) 1972-77; *Recreations* reading, listening to music; *Style* - Miss Winifred Fox; (☎ Brackley 702100)

FOX-PITT-RIVERS, Hon Mrs Emily Rachel; da of late 1 Baron Forster; *b* 1896; *m* 1915 (m dis 1930), Capt George Henry Lane Fox-Pitt-Rivers, Royal Dragoons (d 1966); 2 s; *Style* - The Hon Mrs Emily Fox-Pitt-Rivers; Lepe, Fawley, Southampton

FOX-STRANGWAYS, Hon Raymond George; s of 8 Earl of Ilchester (d 1970), and hp of bro, 9 Earl; *b* 11 Nov 1921; *Educ* Exeter Sch, and Seale Hayne Agric Coll; *m* 1941, Margaret Vera, da of late James Force, of North Surrey, BC; 2 s; *Career* Civil Service 1949-76, WW II in RAF; *Style* - The Hon Raymond Fox-Strangways; Downes, Cherry Orchard, Trull, Taunton

FOXELL, Rev Maurice Frederic; KCVO (1965); s of The Rev William James Foxell; *b* 15 Aug 1888; *Educ* Christ's Hospital, Queen's Oxford; *m* 1914, Mariana Helen Emily, nee Fountain; 2 s, 2 da; *Career* minor canon of St George's Chapel Windsor Castle 1917-20, minor canon of St Paul's Cathedral 1921-39, Priest in Ordinary Chapel Royal 1931-48, rector of St James Garlickhythe EC 1939-64, sub-dean of HM Chapel Royal 1948-65; *Recreations* watercolour painting, piano; *Style* - The Rev Maurice Foxell, KCVO; The College of St Barnabas, Lingfield, Surrey (☎ Dormansland 508)

FOXLEY-NORRIS, Air Chief Marshal Sir Christopher Neil; GCB (1973, KCB 1968, CB 1966), DSO (1945), OBE (1956); s of Major J P Foxley-Norris (d 1923); *b* 16 March 1917; *Educ* Winchester, Trin Oxford, Middle Temple; *m* 1948, Joan Lovell, da of Major P H Hughes (d 1953); *Career* Air Chief Marshal 1970, Ch of Personnel and Logistics MOD 1971-74, ret; chm Battle of Britain Fighter Assoc 1978-, Leonard Cheshire Fndn 1974-, chm General Portfolio Life Insurance Co, dir Brookdale Hutton & Assocs 1974-; V-Pres Royal United Services Institute; *Recreations* sailing, golf, cricket, writing, bridge; *Clubs* RAF, Huntercombe Golf, Lucifers; *Style* - Air Chief Marshal Sir Christopher Foxley-Norris, GCB, DSO, OBE; Tumble Wood, Northend Common, Henley on Thames (☎ Turville Heath 457)

FOXON, Harold Peter; OBE (1976); s of William Henry Foxon (d 1967); *b* 7 April 1919; *Educ* Bancrofts; *m* 1948, Elizabeth Mary, da of Capt Harold Butterfield (d 1974); 1 s, 3 da; *Career* Capt Royal Signals East Africa and Middle East, dep ch exec and md Inchcape & Co Ltd 1979-; *Recreations* golf; *Clubs* Oriental, City; *Style* - Harold Foxon Esq, OBE; 48 Abingdon Court, W8 (☎ 01 937 8113); Thurso, Ashlyns rd, Frinton on Sea, Essex

FOXWELL, Lady Edith Sybil; *da* of Capt Hon Lionel Lambart DSO (s of 9 Earl of Cavan); *b* 1918; *m* 1940, Ivan Foxwell, Maj Roy Norfolk Regt; 2 da; *Career* raised to rank of Earl's daughter 1947; *Style* - Lady Edith Foxwell; 45 Chester sq, SW1; Home Farm, Sherston, Wilts

FOXWELL, Ivan Cottam; s of Lt Col Herbert Somerton Foxwell (ka 1943); *b* 22 Feb 1914; *Educ* Stubbington House, Wellington, RMC Sandhurst; *m* 1940, Lady Edith Sybil, qv, da of Capt The Hon Lionel Lambart, DSO, RN, s of late 9 Earl of Cavan, KP, PC; 2 da; *Career* substantive Major Royal Norfolk Regiment, served BEF France 1940, France and Germany 1944-45, film producer and screenwriter 1947-; *Recreations* reading, writing, swimming; *Clubs* Buck's, Pratt's; *Style* - Ivan Foxwell Esq; Paradis Roc, Chemin De Saint Christophe, 06130 Grasse, France

FOZARD, John William; s of John Fozard (d 1958); *b* 16 Jan 1928; *Educ* London U, Coll of Aeronautics; *m* 1951, Mary, da of Charles Burley Ward, VC; 2 s; *Career* chartered engineer, FRAeS, FJMechE, FAIAA, Marketing dir Kingston-Brough Div, British Aerospace 1978-, chief designer Harrier 1963-78, V-pres Royal Aeronautical Socity 1980-; *Recreations* music, engineering history; *Style* - John Fozard Esq; Wychbury Cottage, Warreners lane, St George's Hill, Weybridge (☎ 97 45204)

FRAME, Sir Alistair Gilchrist; s of Alexander Frame; *b* 3 April 1929; *Educ* Glasgow, Cambridge U; *m* 1953, Sheila Mathieson; 1 da; *Career* chm and ch exec Rio Tinto Zinc Corpn (Export Services) 1978-; dir Plessey Co Ltd 1978-; kt 1981; *Style* - Sir Alistair Frame; 13 Montpelier pla, SW7

FRANCE, Sir Arnold William; GCB (1972, KCB 1965, CB 1957); s of William France; *b* 20 April 1911 *Educ* Bishop's Stortford Coll; *m* 1940, Frances Margaret Linton, da of Dr Charles John Linton Palmer (d 1926); 4 da; *Career* Captain Middle East, retd civil servant, HM Treasury 1945-63, Ministry of Health 1963-68, permanent secretary 1964-68, chm Board Inland Revenue 1968-73; *Recreations* walking; *Clubs* Reform; *Style* - Sir Arnold France, GCB; Thornton Cottage, Lingfield, Surrey (☎ 0364 832278)

FRANCIS, Sir Frank Chalton; KCB (1960, CB 1958); s of the late F W Francis; *b* 5 Oct 1901; *Educ* Liverpool Institute, Liverpool U, Emmanuel Coll Cambridge; *m* 1927, Katrina Florence, nee McClennon; 2 s, 1 da; *Career* formerly dir and Principal Librarian of British Museum 1959-68; *Clubs* Athenaeum, Royal Commonwealth Society, Grolier (New York); *Style* - Sir Frank Francis, KCB; The Vine, Nether Winchendon, Aylesbury, Bucks (☎ Haddenham 290184)

FRANCIS, George Carwardine; s of Guy Lancelot Brereton Francis (d 1962); *b* 15 April 1929; *Educ* Malvern; *m* 1960, Barbara Peggy, da of John Francis Brooke, of W Chiltington; 2 da; *Career* slr; md Chepstow Racecourse Co Ltd 1963-; *Recreations* cricket, racquets, real tennis, squash; *Clubs* MCC, Free Foresters, I Zingari; *Style* - George Francis Esq; East Cliff, Chepstow, Gwent (☎ 02912 2072)

FRANCIS, John Lionel; DL (Dyfed 1971); s of Major John Francis, DSO, TD, DL, (d 1960); *b* 4 July 1921; *Educ* Cheltenham, RAC Cirencester; *m* 1947, Susan Mary, nee Macleod; 2 da (Mrs (Sophie Patricia Marguerite) Boggis-Rolfe, Mrs (Judith Joanna Mary) Bromley-Davenport); *Career* OstJ 1977, FRICS, High Sheriff of Carmarthenshire 1969-, chm 1973-77, now pres Carmarthen Conservative Assoc, chm 1957-60, now V-pres Carmarthen & Cardigan Country Landowners Association; *Clubs* Cavalry & Guards; *Style* - John Francis Esq, DL; Llwynhelig, Llandilo, Dyfed (☎ Llandilo 2302)

FRANCIS, His Honour Judge; (William) Norman; s of late Llewellyn Francis (d 1953); *b* 19 Mar 1921; *Educ* Bradfield, Lincoln Coll Oxford; *m* 1951, Anthea Constance, nee Kerry; 1 s, 1 da; *Career* Lt RA, barrister Grays Inn 1946-69, County Court Judge 1969-71, Circuit Judge 1972-, dep chm Brecknock Quarter Sessions 1963-71, chancellor diocese of Llandaff 1979-, memb Criminal Law Revision Ctee 1977-; *Recreations* hockey, walking; *Clubs* Cardiff Athletic (trustee); *Style* - His Hon Judge Francis; 2 The Woodlands, Lisvane, Cardiff (☎ 0222 753070)

FRANCKLIN, (Mavourn Baldwin) Philip; DSC (1940); s of Capt Philip Francklin MVO, RN (ka 1914); *b* 15 Jan 1913; *Educ* Royal Naval College Dartmouth; *m* 1949, Xenia Alexandra Riddel, nee Davidson; 2 s (1 decd), 1 da; *Career* KStJ 1972, Commander RN Norway, N Atlantic 1939-44, Korea 1950-51, Naval-Air assistant to 5 Sea Lord 1947-49, assistant Naval Attaché Paris 1952-53, DL Notts 1963, V-Lt 1968, Lord Lt 1972-; *Recreations* shooting, golf; *Clubs* Boodle's; *Style* - Commmander Philip Francklin DSC, HM Lord-Lieut for Notts; Gonalston Hall, Nottingham

FRANK, Sir Frederick Charles; OBE (1946); s of Frederick Frank (d 1971); *b* 6 Mar 1911; *Educ* Thetford G S, Ipswich Sch, Lincoln Coll Oxford; *m* 1940, Maia Maita, da of Prof Boris Michaelovich Asche (d 1943); 1 c (d at birth); *Career* kt 1977, scientist, Air Scientific Intelligence 1940-46, Bristol U Dept of Physics 1946-76, Professor 1954, Head of Dept 1969-76, FRS 1954, V-pres Royal Society 1967-69, Royal Medallist 1979; *Recreations* gardening; *Clubs* Athenaeum; *Style* - Sir Frederick Frank, OBE; Orchard Cottage, Grove rd, Coombe Dingle, Bristol (☎ 0272 681708)

FRANK, Robert Andrew; s (by 2 m) and h of Sir Robert Frank, 3 Bt; *b* 16 May 1964; *Style* - Robert Frank Esq

FRANK, Sir Robert John Frank; 3 Bt (UK 1920); s of late Sir Howard Frank, 1 Bt, GBE, KCB; suc bro, Sir Howard Frederick Frank, 2 Bt, 1944; *b* 16 March 1925; *Educ* Harrow; *m* 1, 1950 (m dis 1959), Angela Elizabeth, da of Sir Kenelm Henry Ernest Cayley, 10 Bt; 2 da; m 2, 1960, Margaret Joyce, da of Herbert Victor Truesdale, of Heswall, Cheshire; 1 s; *Heir* s, Robert Andrew Frank; *Career* chartered surveyor, auctioneer, estate agent; dir Ashdale Land & Property Co Ltd; *Style* - Sir Robert Frank, Bt; Ruscombe End, Waltham St Lawrence, nr Reading, Berks (☎ Shurlock Row 417)

FRANKLAND, Hon Mrs Barbara Mary; *née* Frankland; da of Baroness Zouche (17 holder of the title) and Sir Frederick Frankland, 10 Bt; aunt of 18 Baron Zouche; *b* 1906; *m* 1, 1926 (m dis 1937), Brig (now Sir) Otho Prior-Palmer, DSO; 1 da; m 2, 1937 (m dis 1943), 5 Earl of Normanton (d 1967); m 3, 1943 (m dis 1962), Peter Lucas; resumed name of Frankland by deed poll 1958; *Style* - The Hon Mrs Barbara Frankland; Ridge House, Stockland, Honiton, Devon (☎ Wilmington 325)

FRANKLAND, Hon Roger Nathaniel; s of Baroness Zouche (17 holder of the title) and Sir Frederick Frankland, 10 Bt; hp to nephew, 18 Baron Zouche; *b* 11 April 1909; *Educ* Charterhouse, Pembroke Cambridge; *m* 1, 1931, Elizabeth (m dis 1947), da of Arthur Sanday; 2 s; m 2, 1947, Olivia, da of Hon Nigel Campbell (2 s of 3 Earl Cawdor) and former w of (1) Arthur, s of Adm Sir Arthur Leveson, GCB, and (2) Maj Samuel Bucknill; *Career* late Wing Cdr RAuxAF; *Style* - The Hon Roger Frankland; 39 Cadogan sq, SW1 (☎ 01 235 8322)

FRANKLAND-PAYNE-GALLWEY, Sir Philip; 6 Bt (UK 1812); s of Lt-Col Lowry Philip Payne-Gallwey, OBE, MC, ggs of 1 Bt; suc kinsman, Sir Reginald Frankland-Payne-Gallwey, 5 Bt, 1964; assumed by Roy Licence 1966 the additional surname of Frankland before that of Payne and Gallwey; *b* 15 March 1935; *Educ* Eton; *Heir* none; *Career* late Lt 11 Hussars; *Style* - Sir Philip Frankland-Payne-Gallwey Bt; The Little House, Boxford, Newbury, Berks (☎ Boxford 315)

FRANKLIN, Sir Eric Alexander; CBE (1952), Star of Jordan (1963); s of William John Franklin, of Burma (d 1942) *b* 3 July 1910; *Educ* English H S Burma, Univ Coll Rangoon, Emmanuel Coll Cambridge; *m* 1936,, Joyce Stella, nee Lucas; *Career* kt 1954, Indian Civil Service 1935, district and sessions Judge Arakon 1941-42, dep secretary to Government Burma 1942-45, Registrar High Court Rangoon 1946-49, dep secretary to Gov Pakistan 1949-52, establishment officer 1953-55, establishment secretary, cabinet sec Karachi 1956-57, chm Sudan Government 1958-59, United Nations Administrative Advisor to Jordan Government 1960-63, sr Admin Advisor to Nepal Government 1964-67, chm Cambridgeshire Society for the Blind 1969-74, V-pres 1974-; *Recreations* walking in alpine valleys, gardening, caring for dogs; *Style* - Sir Eric Franklin, CBE; The Birches, 16 Cavendish avenue, Cambridge (☎ 48661)

FRANKLIN, George Henry; s of George Edward Franklin RN (d 1975); *b* 15 June 1923; *Educ* Hastings G S, Hastings Sch of Art, Architectural Assoc Sch of Architecture; *m* 1950, Sylvia Daisy, nee Allen; 3 s, 1 da; *Career* Capt Parachute Squadron Royal Engineers, SE Asia Bengal Sappers and Miners Indian Engineers, architect Finchley Borough Council 1952-54, Christian Medical College Punjab India 1954-57, Physical Planning Adviser Republic of Indonesia 1958-62, Government of Malaysia 1963-64, Commonwealth Assoc of Planners, Ex Co memb Europe 1970-80, Pres 1980-; *Recreations* third world interests and activities, fly fishing; *Clubs* Royal Commonwealth Society; *Style* - George Franklin Esq; 24 Oakleigh Park North, N20 (☎ 01 445 0336)

FRANKLIN, John Andrew; s of Bernard Franklin (d 1979); *b* 21 Nov 1943; *Educ* Rugby, Pembroke Cambridge (MA Law and Economics); *m* 1976, Elizabeth Anthea, da of Samuel John Noel Bartley of Constantine Bay, Cornwall; 1 s; *Career* solicitor Slaughter and May 1968-72, dir Morgan Grenfell & Co Ltd 1979- (joined 1972), dep chm Morgan Grenfell Inc 1981- *Recreations* skiing, sailing, golf; *Clubs* Bath, Roy Harwich Yacht, Hurlingham, HAC; The Leash, Raquet and Tennis Club, New York; *Style* - John Franklin Esq; c/o Morgan Grenfell & Co Ltd, 23 Great Winchester st, EC2 (☎ 01 588 4545)

FRANKLIN, Norman Jessel; s of Cecil Franklin (d 1961); *b* 21 Jan 1928; *Educ* Charterhouse, Balliol Oxford; *m* 1953, Jill, nee Leslie; 4 c; *Career* publisher, chm Routledge & Kegan Paul Ltd 1966; *Recreations* cycling, gardening, reading; *Style* - Norman Franklin Esq; 78 Lawn rd, NW3

FRANKLIN, Peter Howard Arthur Louis; s of Howard William Franklin (d 1961); *b* 11 Feb 1915; *Educ* Felsted, Sandhurst; *m* 1967, Vera Mary, nee Stubbs; 1 s (step); *Career* DL Essex 1963-67 and 1977-, commandant Essex ACF, Hon Col Essex ACF 1960, dir J G Franklin & Sons 1960-70, dep dir Essex Red Cross 1971-80, pres Essex Regimental Assoc 1962, chm Essex Ctee East Anglian TA VR 1969-80; *Recreations* sailing, golf; *Clubs* Army & Navy; *Style* - Peter Franklin Esq, DL; 79 Lexden rd, Colchester, Essex (☎ Colchester 76728)

FRANKLIN, Raoul Norman; s of Norman George Franklin of Auckland, NZ (d 1977); *b* 3 June 1935; *Educ* Howick DH Sch, Auckland G S, Auckland U Coll, Oxford U; *m* 1961, Faith, da of Lt Col Harold Thomson Carew Ivens (d 1950); 2 s; *Career* Capt Defence Scientific Corps, university lecturer in Engineering Science Oxford U 1966-78, V-Chllr The City U 1978-; *Recreations* walking; *Style* - Raoul Franklin Esq; The City University, Northampton Square, EC1 (☎ 01 253 4399)

FRANKLIN, Rt Rev William Alfred; OBE (1965); s of George Amos Franklin (d 1956); *b* 16 July 1916; *Educ* Church Sch in London, Kelham Theological Coll Nottingham; *m* 1945, Winifred Agnes, nee Jarvis; 1 s, 1 da; *Career* ordained deacon and priest 1940, curate St John's Bethnal Green 1940-43, St John's Palmers Green 1943-45, asst chaplain St Saviour's Buenos Aires 1945-48, rector Holy Trinity Lomas De Zamora BA 1948-58, rector canon and sub dean St Andrew's Santiago Chile 1958-65, archdeacon Diocese Colombia South America 1965-71, Assistant Bishop of Peterborough 1978-; *Recreations* fishing, writing, studies in growth of church; *Clubs* Royal Commonwealth Society; *Style* - The Rt Rev William Franklin, OBE; 4 Penfold drive, Great Billing, Northampton (☎ Northampton 407839)

FRANKS, Baron (Life Peer UK 1962); Oliver Shewell Franks; OM (1977),

GCMG (1952), KCB (1946), CBE (1942), PC (1949), FBA (1960), DL (Oxon 1978); s of Rev Robert Sleightholme Franks, of Leppington, Winscombe, Somerset; *b* 16 Feb 1905; *Educ* Bristol G S, Queen's Oxford; *m* 1931, Barbara Mary, da of H G Tanner; 2 da; *Career* Prof of Moral Phil Glasgow U 1937-45, Provost of Queen's Coll Oxford 1946-48, Ambass to USA 1948-52, chm Lloyds Bank 1954-62, Provost of Worcester Coll Oxford 1962-76, memb Cncl Duchy of Cornwall 1966-, Chllr U of E Anglia 1965-; chm Cttees on Official Secrets Act, Section 2 (1971-72), Cttee on Ministerial Memoirs 1976, Political Honours Scrutiny Cttee 1976-; *Style* - The Rt Hon The Lord Franks, OM, GCMG, KCB, CBE, PC, DL; Blackall Farm, Charlbury Road, Oxford (☎ (STD Code 0865) 511286)

FRANKS, Anthony Kenric Stapleton; s of Maurice Kenric Franks (d 1955); *b* 13 June 1928; *Educ* Nautical Coll Pangbourne; *m* 1960, Sarah Georgina Cochrane, nee Watson; 3 s; *Career* md Phicom Ltd 1971 (prev Plantation Hldgs Ltd), dir Rank Phicom Video Group Ltd; *Recreations* shooting, sailing (owner of yacht 'Quatorze Encore', Flying Fifteen Class); *Clubs* Roy Yacht Squad, City of London; *Style* - Anthony Franks Esq; Becketts, Matfield, Tonbridge, Kent (☎ 089 272 2175)

FRANKS, His Hon Judge; Desmond Gerald Fergus Franks; s of the late Frederick Franks, MC; *b* 24 Jan 1928; *Educ* Cathedral Choir Sch Canterbury, Manchester G S, Univ Coll London; *m* 1952, Margaret Leigh, da of the late Clarence Daniel; 1 da; *Career* barr 1952, North Circuit, asst Recorder Salford 1966, dep Recorder Salford 1971, Recorder of Crown Court 1972; Circuit Judge 1972-; *Recreations* music, photography; *Style* - His Hon Judge Franks; 4 Beathwaite drive, Bramhall, Cheshire (☎ 061 485 065)

FRASER OF ALLANDER, Barony of (UK 1964); *see* Fraser, 2 Bt, Sir Hugh

FRASER OF KILMORACK, Baron (Life Peer UK 1974); (Richard) Michael Fraser; CBE (1955, MBE Mil 1945); s of late Col Thomas Fraser, CBE, DSO, TD, LLD, DL; *b* 28 Oct 1915; *Educ* Fettes Coll, King's Cambridge; *m* 1944, Elizabeth Chloë, da of Brig Cyril Alexander Fraser Drummond, OBE; 1 s (and 1 s decd); *Career* entered Cons Research Dept 1946 (head of Home Affairs Section 1950-51, dir 1951-64, chm 1970-74), sec to Cons Pty Advsy Ctee on Policy 1951-64, dep chm 1970-75, sec to Cons Leader's Consultative Ctee 1964-70 and 1974-75, dep chm Cons Pty Org 1964-75, dir Glaxo Hldgs Ltd; *Style* - The Rt Hon The Lord Fraser of Kilmorack, CBE; 18 Drayton ct, Drayton gdns, SW10 (☎ 01 370 1543)

FRASER OF TULLYBELTON, Baron (Life Peer UK 1978); Walter Ian Reid Fraser; PC (1974); s of Alexander Fraser; *b* 3 Feb 1911; *Educ* Repton, Balliol Oxford, Glasgow U; *m* 1943, Mary, da of Lt-Col Ian Macdonell; 1 s; *Career* Maj RA UK & Burma; advocate 1936, QC 1954, Ld of Session (as Lord Fraser) 1964-75 & Ld of Appeal in Ordinary 1975-; memb Roy Co of Archers (Queen's Bodyguard for Scotland); *Recreations* shooting, walking; *Clubs* New (Edinburgh), Garrick; *Style* - Rt Hon Lord Fraser of Tullybelton PC; Tullybelton House, Bankfoot, Perths (☎ 312); 35 Cleaver sq, SE11 (☎ 01 735 3663)

FRASER, Lady Antonia (Lady Antonia Pinter); *née* Pakenham; da of 7 Earl of Longford, PC, and Lady Longford, the biographer of Queen Victoria and the Duke of Wellington; *b* 27 Aug 1932; *Educ* Dragon Sch Oxford, St Mary's Convent Ascot, LMH Oxford; *m* 1, 1956 (m dis 1977), Rt Hon Sir Hugh Fraser, MBE, PC, MP (s of 16 Lord Lovat); 3 s (Benjamin, b 1961; Damian, b 1964; Orlando, b 1967), 3 da (Rebecca, b 1957; Flora, b 1958, now Mrs Robert Powell-Jones; Natasha, b 1964); m 2, 1980, Harold Pinter, CBE, the playwright and s of Hyman Pinter; *Career* writer; chm Soc of Authors 1974-75; *Recreations* life in the garden; *Style* - Lady Antonia Fraser; c/o Curtis Brown, 1 Craven Hill, W2

FRASER, Hon Alexander Andrew Macdonell; s of Baron Fraser of

Tullybelton (Life Peer); *b* 1946; *Style* - The Hon Alexander Fraser

FRASER, Hon Ann Lewis; da of late 1 Baron Fraser of Allander; *b* 1932; *Style* - The Hon Ann Fraser

FRASER, Angus McKay; CB (1981), TD (1965); s of Thomas Fraser; *b* 10 March 1928; *Educ* Falkirk H S, Glasgow & Bordeaux Us; *m* 1955 (m dis 1968), Margaret Neilson; 1 s, 1 da; *Career* served 44 Para Bde (TA) 1953-66, Customs & Excise 1952-61, Treasury 1961-64, Customs & Excise again 1965-80; Dep Sec CSD 1980- & 1 Civ Serv Commissioner 1981-; *Style* - Angus Fraser Esq, CB, TD; 84 Ennerdale rd, Kew, Surrey (☎ 01 940 9913)

FRASER, Hon Andrew Roy Matthew; s of 17 Lord Lovat, DSO, MC, TD; *b* 1952; *Educ* Ampleforth and Magdalen Coll, Oxford; *m* 1979, Hon Charlotte Anne Greville, da of David Robin Francis Guy, Lord Brook; *Style* - The Hon Andrew Fraser; 20 Argyle rd, W8 (☎ 01 937 0607)

FRASER, Hon Angus Simon James; s of Baron Fraser of Kilmorack (Life Peer); *b* 1945; *m* 1970, Jennifer Anne, nee Craig; children; *Style* - The Hon Angus Fraser; 4 Ivy House, Five Oak Green, Tonbridge, Kent

FRASER, Hon Belinda Ann; da (by 1 m) of Sir Hugh Fraser, 2 Bt (2 Baron Fraser of Allander, who disclaimed his peerage for life 1966); *b* 1964; *Style* - The Hon Belinda Fraser

FRASER, Sir Bruce Donald; KCB (1961, CB 1956); s of Maj Gen Sir Theodore Fraser KCB CSI CMG (d 1953); *b* 18 Nov 1910; *Educ* Bedford Sch, Trinity Coll Cambridge; *m* 1939, Audrey, da of Lt Col E L Croslegh (d 1942); 1 s (decd), 1 da; *Career* civil servant ret, permanent secretary Ministry of Health 1960-64, comptroller and auditor general 1966-71; *Clubs* Athenaeum; *Style* - Sir Bruce Fraser, KCB; Jonathan, St Dogmael's, Cardigan, Dyfed (☎ Cardigan (0239) 2387)

FRASER, Sir Basil Malcolm; 2 Bt (UK 1921); s of Sir (John) Malcolm Fraser, 1 Bt, GBE (d 1949); *b* 2 Jan 1920; *Educ* Eton, Cambridge U; *Heir* none; *Career* Capt RE WW II, Madras Sappers and Miners (despatches); *Style* - Sir Basil Fraser, Bt; 175 Beach st, Deal, Kent

FRASER, Hon Cordelia; da of late 2 Baron Strathalmond, CMG, OBE, TD; *b* 1949; *Style* - The Hon Cordelia Fraser

FRASER, Hon Mrs (Charlotte Anne); *née* Greville; da of Lord Brooke (s and h of 7 Earl of Warwick) by Sarah, da of (Alfred) Chester Beatty, the financier; *b* 6 June 1958; *m* 1979, Hon Andrew (Roy Matthew) Fraser, *qv*, 4 s of 15 Lord Lovat; *Style* - The Hon Mrs Fraser; 20 Argyle rd, W8 (☎ 01 937 0607)

FRASER, Charles Annand; MVO (1968); s of Very Rev John Annand Fraser; *b* 16 Oct 1928; *Educ* Hamilton Academy, Edinburgh U; *m* 1957, Ann, da of William Francis Scott-Kerr (d 1976); 4 s; *Career* writer to the Signet, ptnr W & J Burness Edinburgh, purse bearer to Lord High Commisioner to General Assembly of Church of Scotland 1969-, dir United Biscuits (Holdings) Ltd 1978-, Scottish Widows Fund 1978-, British Assets Trust Ltd 1969-, Scottish Television Ltd 1979-, Trustee Scottish Trust 1978-, memb of Council of Law Society of Scotland 1966-72, chm of Scottish Division of Institute of Directors 1978-80; *Recreations* gardening, skiing, squash, piping; *Clubs* New (Edinburgh), Caledonian (London), Hon Co of Edinburgh Golfers, R & A St Andrews; *Style* - Charles Fraser Esq, MVO; Shepherd House, Inveresk, Midlothian (☎ 031 665 2570); Wester Dalvoult, by Boat of Garten, Inverness-shire

FRASER, Hon Caroline Emily; da (by 1 m) of Sir Hugh Fraser, 2 Bt (2 Baron Fraser of Allander, who disclaimed his peerage for life 1966); *b* 1966; *Style* - The Hon Caroline Fraser

FRASER, Gen Sir David William; GCB (1980, KCB 1973), OBE (1962); s of the late Brig The Hon William Fraser, DSO, MC; *b* 30 Dec 1920; *Educ* Eton, Ch Ch Oxford; *m* 1 1947, Anne, da of the late Brig

E W S Balfour; 1 da; m 2, 1957, Julia, nee De La Hey; 2 s, 2 da; *Career* service- UK and North West Europe 1939-45, Malaya 1948, Egypt 1952-54, Cyprus 1958, British Cameroons 1961, Borneo 1965, Germany 1969-71, NATO Brussels 1975-77, GOC 4 Division 1969-71, assistant chief of Defence Staff 1971-73, V-chief of General Staff 1973-75, British Military Representative to NATO 1975-77, Commandant Royal Coll of Defence Studies 1977-80; *Recreations* shooting; *Clubs* Turf, Pratt's; *Style* - Gen Sir David Fraser, GCB, OBE; Valenders, Isington, Alton, Hants (☎ Bentley 3166)

FRASER, Hon Mrs (Elizabeth Penelope); *née* Methuen; da of 5 Baron Methuen (d 1975); *b* 1928; *m* 1956, Malcolm Henry Alastair Fraser; 2 da; *Style* - The Hon Mrs Fraser; Grey Gables, Pilton, Shepton Mallet, Som

FRASER, Hon Fiona Mary; da of 17 Lord Lovat, DSO, MC, TD; *b* 1941; *Style* - The Hon Fiona Fraser

FRASER, Hon George Edward; s of 3 Baron Strathalmond; *b* 1979

FRASER, Hon Mrs George - Margaret Elizabeth; da of Reginald Barnes, of St Ermin's, Westminster; *m* 1934, as his 2 w, Rear-Adm Hon George Fraser DSO RN, s of 18 Lord Saltoun (d 1970); 2 s; *Style* - The Hon Mrs George Fraser; Languedoc, Firgrove, Cape Province, S Africa

FRASER, Sir Hugh; 2 Bt (UK 1961); s of 1 Baron Fraser of Allander (UK cr 1964), LLD, JP, DL and Kate, da of late Sir Andrew Lewis, JP; suc to Btcy and Barony 1966, but disclaimed latter for life; *b* 18 Dec 1936; *Educ* St Mary's Melrose, Kelvinside Acad; *m* 1, 1962 (m dis 1971), Patricia Mary, da of John Bowie; 3 da; m 2, 1973, Aileen Margaret, da of George Paterson Ross; *Heir* none; *Career* dir House of Fraser (chm 1966-80), dir Harrods 1966-(chm 1966-76, md 1970-76), dir Binns Ltd (formerly chm and md), dir John Barker & Co Ltd and other cos; *Style* - Sir Hugh Fraser, Bt; Cattermuir Lodge, Croftamie, Glasgow G63 OHG (☎ Drymen 421)

FRASER, Hon Hugh Alastair Joseph; s of 17 Lord Lovat, DSO, MC, TD; *b* 1947; *Educ* Ampleforth and Christ Church, Oxford; *m* 1976, Drusilla Jane, da of J Alastair Montgomerie, of Auchenbothie Mains, Kilmalcolm, Renfrewshire; 1 s, 1 da; *Style* - The Hon Hugh Fraser

FRASER, Lt-Cdr Ian Edward; VC (1945), DSC (1943), RD and Bar (1948), JP (Wirral 1957); s of Sydney Fraser (d 1976); *b* 18 Dec 1920; *Educ* Royal G S High Wycombe; *m* 1943, Melba Estelle, da of late Stanley Hughes; 4 s, 2 da; *Career* HMS Conway 1936-38, Lt-Cdr RN Atlantic, Pacific, N Africa, N Sea; dir Star Offshore Services Ltd 1975-, chm Nordive (W Africa Ltd), md North Sea Diving Services Ltd 1965-75, md Universal Divers Ltd 1946-81; *Recreations* sailing, golf, photography; *Clubs* Naval, Hoylake Sailing Club, W Cheshire S C; *Style* - Lt-Cdr Ian Fraser, VC, DSC, RD*, JP; Innisfallen, 47 Warren dve, Wallasey, Merseyside (☎ 051 639 3355)

FRASER, Ian Montagu; MC (1945); s of Col Herbert Cecil Fraser, DSO OBE TD (d 1943); *b* 14 Oct 1916; *Educ* Shrewsbury Sch, Christ Church Oxford; *m* 1 1945, Mary (d 1964), nee Stanley; 1 s, 1 da; m 2, 1967, Angela Mary, nee Meston; 2 s; *Career* served War 1939-45, NW Frontier, Iraq, Syria, Persia, Western Desert; secretary to Trustees The Buttle Trust 1978, dep secretary 1971-; dir GUS Export Corporation 1967-70, MP (C) Sutton Plymouth 1959-66, PPS to Sec of State for the Colonies 1962, assistant Govt Whip 1962-64, Opposition Whip 1964-66, Gen Sec The John Lewis Partnership 1956-59; *Recreations* flyfishing, sailing; *Clubs* Carlton, Royal Western Yacht (Plymouth); *Style* - Ian Montagu Fraser Esq, MC; How Hatch, How Lane, Chipstead, Surrey (☎ Downland 51944)

FRASER, Iain Michael; s and h of Prof Sir James Fraser, 2 Bt; *b* 27 June 1951; *Style* - Iain Fraser Esq

FRASER, Very Rev John Annand; MBE (1940), TD (1945), DD; s of Rev Charles Fraser BD, (d 1944); *b* 21 June 1894; *Educ* Robert Gordon's Coll Aberdeen, Aberdeen U; *m* 1925, Leila, da of the late Col Ewan Campbell; 1 s, 1 da; *Career* WW 1914-18 and WW 1939-45;

Minister Church of Scotland ord 1923, Moderator of General Assembly 1958-59, Convener of Business Ctee, General Assembly and other major Ctees 1962-67, memb Broadcasting Council for Scotland 1963-67; *Recreations* fishing, gardening; *Clubs* Caledonian (Edinburgh); *Style* - The Very Rev John Fraser MBE TD; 133 Glasgow rd, Perth (☎ Perth 21462)

FRASER, Prof Sir James David; 2 Bt (UK 1943), of Tain, Co Ross; s of Sir John Fraser, 1 Bt, KCVO, MC (d 1947); *b* 19 July 1924; *Educ* Edinburgh Acad, Magdalen Oxford, Edinburgh U; *m* 1950, Edith Maureen, da of Rev John Reay, MC; 2 s; *Heir* s, Iain Fraser; *Career* late Maj RAMC, served Far East 1949-51; Postgrad Dean Edinburgh U Med Sch 1981-, late Prof Clinical Science in Surgery Southampton U; *Recreations* golf, gardening; *Style* - Prof Sir James Fraser, Bt; 2 Lennox st, Edinburgh (☎ 031 332 3205)

FRASER OF ALLANDER, Baroness; Katie Hutcheon; da of late Sir Andrew Jopp Williams Lewis, LLD; *m* 1931, 1 Baron Fraser of Allander (d 1966); 1 s (Sir Hugh Fraser, 2 Bt - he disclaimed his Peerage), 1 da (Hon Ann Fraser); *Style* - The Rt Hon the Lady Fraser of Allander; Allander Lodge, Milngavie, Dunbartonshire

FRASER, Hon Kim Maurice; s of 17 Lord Lovat, DSO, MC, TD; *b* 1946; *Educ* Ampleforth; *m* 1975, Joanna Katherine, da of Maj Geoffrey Edward Ford North, MC; 1 s; *Career* Lt Scots Gds; *Style* - The Hon Kim Fraser; c/o Beaufort Castle, Beauly, Inverness-shire

FRASER, Rt Hon (John) Malcolm; CH (1977), PC (1976); s of the late J Neville Fraser of Victoria; *b* 21 May 1930; *Educ* Tudor House, Melbourne C of E Grammar Sch, Magdalen Coll Oxford; *m* 1956, Tamara Sandford, nee Beggs; 2 s, 2 da; *Career* memb Federal Parliament (Liberal) Australia from 1955, minister for Army 1966-68, minister for Education and Science 1968-69 and 1971-72, leader of the Opposition 1975, prime minister Australia 1975-; *Recreations* fishing, photography, vintage cars, motorcycles; *Clubs* Melbourne Scots, Melbourne, Commonwealth (Canberra); *Style* - Rt Hon Malcolm Fraser, CH, PC; Parliament House, Canberra, Australia (☎ 062/733200)

FRASER, Hon Patricia Lydia; da (by 1 m) of Sir Hugh Fraser, 2 Bt (2 Baron Fraser of Allander, who disclaimed his peerage for life 1966); *b* 1963; *Style* - The Hon Patricia Fraser

FRASER, Ronald Petrie; CB (1972); s of the late Thomas Petrie Fraser; *b* 2 June 1917; *Educ* Daniel Stewart's Coll Edinburgh, Edinburgh U, The Queen's Coll Oxford; *m* 1962, Ruth Wright, nee Anderson; 1 da *Career* entered HM Civil Service 1940, under-secretary Scottish Education Dept 1963-67, under-secretary Ministry of Agriculture, Fisheries and Food 1968-70, dep sec Scottish Home and Health Dept 1971, secretary 1972-77; ch counting officer for Referendum under Scotland Act 1978; *Recreations* music, walking; *Clubs* New (Edinburgh); *Style* - Ronald Fraser Esq, CB; 40A Lygon rd, Edinburgh

FRASER, Thomas Cameron; CB (1966), MBE (1945), TD (1951); s of Dr Thomas Fraser, CBE, DSO, DL (d 1952); *b* 21 Jan 1909; *Educ* Fettes Coll, Univ Coll Oxford; *m* 1934, Dorothy Graham, nee Partridge; 2 s, 2 da; *Career* Lt-Col RA ADGB; dir and sec Wool Textile Delegation, (Wool and Allied Textile Employers Cncl) 1947-62, formerly indust dir Nat Exec Dvpt Ctee (temp dir gen 1973), chm Wool Textile Exec Dvpt Ctee 1970-77, dir Cmmn of Inquiry into Indust & Commercial Representation 1970-72, princ Advice Centre on Organization of Indust & Commercial Representation 1974-,sec Engrg Indust Cncl 1976-; *Recreations* walking, travel; *Clubs* United Oxford and Cambridge University, RAC; *Style* - Thomas Fraser Esq, CB, MBE, TD; 25 Bedford gdns, W8 (☎ 01 727 0674)

FRASER, Hon William Gordon; s and h of 3 Baron Strathalmond; *b* 24 Sept 1976; *Style* - The Hon William Fraser

FRASER, Sir William Kerr; KCB (1979); s of the late Alexander Macmillan

Fraser; *b* 18 Mar 1929; *Educ* Eastwood Sch, Glasgow U; *m* 1956, Marion Anne, nee Forbes; 3 s, 1 da; *Career* Permanent Under-Secretary of State, Scottish Office 1978-; *Clubs* New (Edinburgh); *Style* - Sir William Fraser, KCB; 14 Braid Avenue, Edinburgh (☎ 031 447 3751)

FRASER-TYTLER, Christian Helen; *née* Shairp; CBE (1940), TD, JP (Inverness-shire 1958); da of the late John Campbell Shairp; *b* 23 Aug 1897; *m* 1919, Col Neil Fraser-Tytler; 2 da; *Career* Foreign Office 1917-19, War Office 1939-43, AA Command until 1945; *Recreations* fishing, reading; *Style* - Mrs Neil Fraser-Tytler, CBE, TD, JP; Old Clune House, Aldourie, Inverness (☎ Dores (STD Code 046 375) 216)

FRAZER, Hon Mrs (Una Mary); da of late 1 Viscount Slim, KG, GCB, GCMG, GCVO, GBE, DSO, MC; *b* 1930; *m* 1953, Maj Peter Nigel Stewart Frazer, Gren Gds; 3 da; *Style* - The Hon Mrs Frazer; Puddington Lodge, Tiverton, Devon

FREAN, Denis Edward; CBE (1973, OBE 1964); s of Charles Frean, of Bournemouth (d 1921); *b* 23 Sept 1913; *Educ* Stowe; *m* 1943, Margareta, da of the late Leonard Bucknall Eyre, MBE, of Sweden; 3 s; *Career* solicitor until 1939, Helsingfors U 1940-41, British Council Service- Turin 1947-51, London 1951-52, Melbourne 1952, British Guiana 1952-54, Warsaw 1954-56, Dublin 1956-59, Baghdad 1959-64, Lisbon 1964-66, British Council Representive and Cultural Attache British Embassy, Pretoria 1968-75; *Recreations* enamelling, photography; *Style* - Denis Frean Esq, CBE; 1 St Martins Row, Upton Grey, Basingstoke, Hants (☎ Upton Grey 416)

FREDERICK, Sir Charles Boscawen; 10 Bt (GB 1723), of Burwood House, Surrey, JP (Bucks); s of Lt-Col Sir Edward Boscawen Frederick, 9 Bt, CVO (d 1956); *b* 11 April 1919; *Educ* Eton; *m* 1949, Rosemary, da of Lt-Col Robert John Halkett Baddeley MC; 2 s, 2 da; *Heir* s Christopher St John Frederick; *Career* Maj (ret) Grenadier Guards; memb Gen Cmmn Income Tax 1966-, memb Stock Exhcange Cncl 1973-75, chm Provincial Unit of Stock Exchange 1973-75, memb London Stock Exchange 1954-62; *Recreations* sailing, fishing; *Style* - Sir Charles Frederick, Bt, JP; The Granary, Lerryn, Lostwithiel, Cornwall

FREDERICK, Christopher St John; s and h of Sir Charles Frederick, 10 Bt; *b* 28 June 1950; *Style* - Christopher Frederick Esq

FREDJOHN, Dennis; s of the late Maurice Fredjohn; *b* 22 Feb 1925; *Educ* Westminster City Sch, St John's Cambridge; *m* 1947, Pamela Jill, nee Samms; 1 s, 2 da; *Career* Flight Officer RAF, Lt RN 1939-45 War; exec dir Rio Tinto Zinc 1970-73, dir Arbuthnot Latham Holdings 1973-, md Alusuisse (UK) Ltd 1976-; *Recreations* squash, farming, bridge; *Style* - Dennis Fredjohn Esq; Fairfields, Redmarley, Glos (☎ 053 181 477)

FREEMAN, Dowager Lady; Elizabeth; MBE (1945); da of late Ernest Tatham Richmond, FRIBA, s of Sir William Richmond, KCB, by Ernest's w Margaret (3 da of Henry Lubbock, JP, DL, 2 s of Sir John Lubbock, 3 Bt, and yr bro of 1 Baron Avebury); *m* 1935, as his 2 w, Air Ch Marshal Sir Wilfrid Freeman, 1 Bt, GCB, DSO, MC (d 1953); 2 da (Joan, b 1936, m 1955 John Morgan-Grenville, gs of Lady Kinloss in her own right; Susan, b 1939, m 1962 Robin Malcolm); *Style* - Dowager Lady Freeman; Loch Caol Cottage, by Bunessan, Isle of Mull

FREEMAN, Ifan Charles Harold; CMG (1964), TD (1960); s of the late C E D W Freeman; *b* 11 Sept 1910; *Educ* Friars Sch Bangor, Univ of Wales; *m* 1937, Enid Marguerite, nee Hallum; 2 da; *Career* served with Royal Artillery 1939-45, Colonial Service- Kenya 1946-58, Nyasaland 1958-71, dir of Education 1958-61, Permanent Secretary 1961-65, Registrar University of Malawi 1965-71; *Recreations* gardening,; *Clubs* Royal Commonwealth; *Style* - Ifan Freeman Esq, CMG, TD; Swy Y Wylan, Marianglas, Gwynedd (☎ Moelfre (024 888) 515)

FREEMAN, Sir James Robin; 3 Bt (UK 1945), of Murtle, Co Aberdeen; s of Sir

Keith Freeman, 2 Bt (d 1981), and Patricia, Lady Freeman, *qv*; *b* 21 July 1955; *Heir* none; *Style* - Sir James Freeman, Bt; c/o Midland Bank, 151 Hoe st, Walthamstow, E17

FREEMAN, Nicholas Hall; s of William Freeman; *b* 25 July 1939; *Educ* Stoneygate Sch, King's Sch Canterbury; *Career* barrister, called to Bar 1968, memb Kensington and Chelsea Council 1968, chm Town Planning Ctee 1975, Leader of the Council 1977, contested (C) Hartlepool Feb and Oct 1974, V-chm General Purposes Ctee London Boroughs' Assoc 1978, chancellor of Diocese Leicester 1979- *Recreations* reading particularly biography, holidays in France, theatre; *Clubs* Carlton; *Style* - Nicholas Freeman Esq; 51 Harrington Gardens, SW7 (☎ 01 370 3197)

FREEMAN, Patricia, Lady; Patricia Denison; da of late Charles W Thomas, of Sandown, IOW; *m* 1946, Sir Keith Freeman, 2 Bt (d 1981); 1 s (Sir James, 3 Bt), 1 da (and 1 s decd); *Style* - Patricia, Lady Freeman

FREEMAN, Sir Ralph; CVO (1964), CBE (1952, MBE 1945); s of the late Sir Ralph Freeman; *b* 3 Feb 1911; *Educ* Uppingham, Worcester Coll Oxford; *m* 1939, Joan Elizabeth, da of the late Col J G Rose of South Africa; 2 s, 1 da; *Career* kt 1970, Temp Major 1939-45 War, Colonel, Engr and Railway Staff Corps, RE (TAVR), Col Comdg 1969-74, ret 1976; chartered engineer, consulting engineer, ptnr Freeman, Fox & Ptnrs 1947-79, sr ptnr 1963-79, consultant to Freeman, Fox & Ptnrs 1979-, past Pres Institute Civil Engineers 1966-67, Assoc of Consultant Engineers 1974-75, Welding Institute 1974-76; *Recreations* sailing, golf, DIY; *Clubs* Army & Navy, Leander; *Style* - Sir Ralph Freeman, CVO, CBE; Ballards Shaw, Ballards Lane, Limpsfield, Oxted (☎ Limpsfield Chart (088388) 3284)

FREEMAN, Capt Spencer; CBE (1942); s of the late A Freeman; *b* 10 Dec 1892; *Educ* Johannesburg Coll South Africa, Technical Institute York USA; *m* 1924, Hilda Kathleen (d 1978), nee Toler; 1 s; *Career* organised entire Mechanical Transport Salvage in France 1914-18, dir-Min of Aircraft Production, Min of Supply and Admiralty 1940-41, Prin dir Regional and Emergency Services Organisation 1941-44, memb Industrial and Export Council, Board of Trade 1944-45, memb Radio Board, Radio Planning and Production Ctee 1944-45, served In European War 1914-19, dir Hospitals Trust 1940; *Books* Production under Fire (1967), You Can Get to the Top (1972), Take Your Measure (1972); *Recreations* all sports; *Clubs* Naval and Military, University (Dublin); *Style* - Capt Spencer Freeman, CBE; Knocklyon House, Templeogue, Dublin, Eire (☎ Dublin 900234)

FREEMAN, Lady Winefride (Alice); *née* Fitzalan-Howard; da of 15 Duke of Norfolk, KG, CVO, PC (d 1917); *b* 1914; *m* 1943, Lt-Col John Edward Broke Freeman, s of late Sir Philip Horace Freeman, KCVO, KBE; 1 s, 2 da; *Career* JP Suffolk; *Style* - Lady Winefride Freeman, JP; Buxhall Vale, Stowmarket, Suffolk

FREEMAN-GRENVILLE, Hon Hester Josephine Anne; yr da of Lady Kinloss; *b* 9 May 1960; *Style* - The Hon Hester Freeman-Grenville

FREEMAN-GRENVILLE, Hon Teresa Mary Nugent; er da of Lady Kinloss; *b* 20 July 1957; *Style* - The Hon Teresa Freeman-Grenville

FREEMAN-THOMAS, Hon Mrs; Hon Moyra; *née* Marjoribanks; da of 3 Baron Tweedmouth (d 1935); *b* 1902; *m* 1, 1923, Lt-Col Reginald Francis Heyworth (ka 1941); 1 s, 1 da; m 2, 1943, Maj Reginald Brodrick Freeman-Thomas; *Style* - The Hon Mrs Freeman-Thomas; Kingswall House, nr Malmesbury, Wilts

FREER, Charles Edward Jesse; DL; s of the late Canon S Thorold Winckley; *b* 4 Mar 1901; *Educ* Radley; *m* 1 1927, Violet Muriel (d 1944), nee Gee; 2 s, 2 da; 2 m, 1945, Cynthia Lilian, nee Braithwaite; 2 da; *Career* Lt Col 1943-44, served in France and Iceland; solicitor, chm Leicestershire Quarter Session 1949-72, chm Mental Health Tribunal-Sheffield

Regional Board 1960-72, a chm of Industrial Tribunals 1966-72; *Recreations* reading, walking, travel; *Clubs* East India, Sports and Public Schools; *Style* - Charles Freer Esq, DL; Shoal House, Pearce avenue, Parkstone, Poole (☎ 0202 748393)

FREER, Air Chief Marshal Sir Robert (William George); GBE (1981, CBE 1966), KCB (1977); s of the late William Freer; *b* 1 Sept 1923; *Educ* Gosport G S; *m* 1950, Margaret Tinkler, da of the late J W Elkington; 1 s, 1 da; *Career* Queens Commendation 1955, Air Chief Marshal, currently Commandant Royal Coll of Defence Studies Jan 1980-, commanded 92 Fighter Sqdn 1955-57, station commander RAF Seletar 1963-66, Air ADC to HM Queen 1969-71, dep cmmdt RAF Staff College 1969-71, SASO HQ Near East Air Force 1971-72, AOC 11 Group 1972-75, Dir-Gen Organisation MOD Air 1975, AOC 18 Group 1975-78, dep C-in-C RAF Strike Command 1979-; *Recreations* tennis, golf; *Clubs* RAF, N Hants Golf *Style* - Air Chief Marshal Sir Robert Freer GBE, KCB; c/o Lloyds Bank, 6 Pall Mall, SW1

FREESTON, Hon Mrs (Anne Boswall); *née* Jackson; da of Baron Jackson of Burnley (Life Peer, d 1970); *b* 1939; *m* 1967, David Garner Freeston; *Style* - The Hon Mrs Freeston; Hazel Cottage, North Heath, Chieveley, Newbury, Berks

FREETH, Denzil Kingson; s of the late Walter Freeth; *b* 10 July 1924; *Educ* Sherborne Sch, Trinity Hall Cambridge; *Career* Flying Officer RAF, pres Union Society Cambridge 1949, chm Cambridge Univ Conservative Assoc 1949, memb Parliament (C) for Basingstoke 1955-64, Parliamentary secretary to Minister for Science 1961-63, memb London Stock Exchange 1964-, Churchwarden All Saints Church Margaret Street W1 1977-; *Recreations* good food, wine, conversation; *Clubs* Carlton, Pitt (Cambridge); *Style* - Denzil Freeth Esq; 3 Brasenose House, 35 Kensington High st, W8 (☎ 01 937 8685)

FREMANTLE, Hon Christopher Evelyn; s of late 3 Baron Cottesloe; *b* 1906; *Educ* Eton, Balliol Oxford; *m* 1930, Anne Marie Huth, da of late Rt Hon Frederick Huth Jackson; 3 s; *Style* - The Hon Christopher Fremantle; 252 East 78th st, New York, NY 10021, USA

FREMANTLE, Hon Cecilia Jane; da of 4 Baron Cottlesloe; *b* 1962; *Style* - The Hon Cecilia Fremantle

FREMANTLE, Hon Edward Walgrave; s (by 2 m) of 4 Baron Cottesloe; *b* 1961; *Style* - The Hon Edward Fremantle

FREMANTLE, Hon Flora Catherine; da of 4 Baron Cottlesloe; *b* 1967; *Style* - The Hon Flora Fremantle

FREMANTLE, Hon John Tapling; DL (Bucks 1978); s and h of Baron Cottesloe, GBE; *b* 22 Jan 1927; *Educ* Eton; *m* 1958, Elizabeth Ann, da of Lt Col Henry Shelley Barker, DSO (d 1970); 1 s, 2 da; *Career* RN 1945, Lt 1949, Lt-Cdr 1957, Cdr 1962, ret 1966; High Sheriff Bucks 1969-70, gen cmmr of taxes (Aylesbury) 1979, pres Buckingham & Winslow District Scout Assoc, v-pres WAGBI Hosp Savings Assoc, chm Bucks Co Agricultural Assoc, past chm Bucks Banch CLA 1976-79; *Recreations* shooting, stalking, crosswords; *Clubs* Travellers'; *Style* - The Hon John Fremantle, DL; The Old House, Swanbourne, Milton Keynes, Bucks (☎ Mursley 263)

FREMANTLE, Hon Katharine Dorothy Honor; da of late 3 Baron Cottesloe; *b* 1919 *Educ* Girton Cambridge; *Career* PhD London 1956; *Style* - The Hon Katharine Fremantle; Dennenlaan 48, Hollandsche Rading, Netherlands

FRENCH, Cecil Charles John; s of late Ernest French; *b* 16 April 1926; *Educ* Newport Essex Sch, King's Coll London U (MSc), Columbia U New York; *m* 1, 1956, Olive Joyce (d 1969); 2 da; m 2, 1971, Shirley Frances; 1 s, 1 da; *Career* chartered engineer, tech dir Ricardo Consulting Engineers Ltd, md G Cussons Ltd; *Recreations* folk dancing, photography; *Style* - Cecil French Esq; 303 Upper Shoreham rd, Shoreham-by-Sea, Sussex (☎ 07917 2050); Flat J, Fairway House, Leegate rd, Heaton Moor, Stockport

FRENCH, Lady Essex Eleonora; OBE (1918); da of 1 Earl of Ypres, KP, GCB, OM, GCVO, KCMG, PC, and Eleonora, da of Richard Selby-Lowndes (3 s of William Selby-Lowndes, of Whaddon Hall, Bucks, MP Bucks 1807-20, whose paternal grandmother was ninth in descent from George Duke of Clarence, the bro of Edward IV drowned in a butt of Malmsey); *b* 1886; *Career* DGStJ; *Style* - Lady Essex French, OBE; The Lodge, 32 Sheldon av, N6

FRENCH, Hon Fulke Charles Arthur John; s (by 1 m) of 7 Baron De Freyne; *b* 21 April 1957; *Style* - The Hon Fulke French

FRENCH, Capt Godfrey Alexander; CBE (1954), RN; s of Alexander Weatherhead French (d 1958); *b* 1 July 1900; *Educ* RN Colls Osborne and Dartmouth, Selwyn Cambridge; *m* 1, 1927, Mary Neville, da of Capt John William Edward Gilhespy, OBE, RN; 1 s; m 2, 1941, Margaret Annis, da of late Adm Hon Sir Matthew Best, KCB, DSO, MVO, widow of Cdr Alexander Pollock Gibson, RN; 1 s, 1 da; *Career* served in 1914-18 War and 1939-45 War; jt planning staff, ch of Staff's Ctee 1940-42; dir of training RIN 1943-44; dep dir Plans Div Admiralty 1944-46; cmd HMS 'Norfolk' 1947-49; ch of staff and dep C-in-C Indian Navy 1951-54; Admiralty Regional offr SW Region 1954-62; Hydrographic Dept, MOD (N) 1962-78, ret; *Recreations* formerly shooting, walking, travel, squash, rowing, rugby; *Clubs* Army & Navy, Himalayan; *Style* - Capt Godfrey French, CBE, RN; The Old Rectory, Stoke Abbott, Beaminster, Dorset

FRENCH, Hon Mrs Hubert - Mary Frances; da of Charles Hasslacher; *m* 1937, Hon Hubert John French (d 1961); 2 s, 2 da; *Style* - The Hon Mrs Hubert French; Stychfield, Stychens lane, Bletchingley, Redhill, Surrey

FRENCH, Lady Iona Mary; *née* Huddleston; da of Countess of Loudoun (d 1960) and Capt Reginald Mowbray Chichester Huddleston; *b* 17 March 1922; *m* 1951, Robert French, TD (d 1970); *Career* served in WAAF WW II; *Style* - Lady Iona French; The Beeches, Skelmorlie, Ayrshire (☎ Wemyss Bay 2287)

FRENCH, Lady Lucy Kathleen; 4 da of 3 Earl of Ypres (by his 2 w Deborah); *b* 1975; *Style* - Lady Lucy French

FRENCH, Hon Patrick Dominick Fitzstephen Jude; s (by 1 m) of 7 Baron De Freyne; *b* 1969; *Style* - The Hon Patrick French

FRENCH, Lady Rosemary; *née* Mackay; da of 2 Earl of Inchape (d 1939); *b* 1936; *m* 1957, Francis Martin French; 1 s, 3 da; *Style* - Lady Rosemary French; Little Offley, Hitchin, Herts

FRENCH, Lady Sarah Mary Essex; 2 da of 3 Earl of Ypres by his 1 w Maureen; *b* 22 May 1953; *Style* - Lady Sarah French

FRENCH, Hon Vanessa Rose Bradbury; da (by 1 m) of 7 Baron De Freyne; *b* 1958; *Style* - The Hon Vanessa French

FRENCH, Hon Mrs William - Victoria Louise; da of late William Dalglish Bellasis, JP; *m* 1920, Capt the Hon William Joseph French (d 1974); 2 da; *Style* - The Hon Mrs William French; Beech House, Sturminster Newton, Dorset

FREUD, Anna; CBE (1967); da of Prof Sigmund Freud (d 1939); *b* 3 Dec 1895; *Educ* Cottage Lyceum Vienna; *Career* psychoanalyst; dir Hampstead Child Therapy Course & Clinic 1952- *Style* - Miss Anna Freud CBE; 20 Maresfield gdns, NW3 (☎ 01 435 2002); Far End, Walberswick, Southwold, Suffolk (☎ 050 272 2033)

FREYBERG, 2 Baron (UK 1951); Col Paul Richard Freyberg; OBE (Mil 1965), MC (1945); s of 1 Baron Freyberg, VC, GCMG, KCB, KBE, DSO and 3 Bars and Dame Barbara, GBE (d 1973), da of Sir Herbert Jekyll, KCMG, and widow of Hon Francis Walter Stafford McLaren, MP, s of 1 Baron Aberconway, KC; *b* 27 May 1923; *Educ* Eton; *m* 1960, Ivry Perronelle Katharine, da of late Cyril Harrower Guild, of Aspall Hall, nr Debenham, Suffolk; 1 s, 3 da; *Heir* s, Hon

Valerian Freyberg; *Career* Col late Gren Gds; with New Zealand Expeditionary Force 1940-42, with Gren Gds 1942-45, AAG HQ London Dist 1962-65, cmd HAC Inf Bn 1965-68, on Defence Policy Staff MOD 1968-71, Dir Volunteers Territorials and Cadets 1971-75, Col Gen Staff 1975-78; *Style* - Col The Rt Hon The Lord Freyberg OBE MC; Munstead House, Godalming, Surrey (☎ 6004)

FREYBERG, Hon Annabel Pauline; da of 2 Baron Freyberg, OBE, MC; *b* 1961; *Style* - The Hon Annabel Freyberg

FREYBERG, Hon Christina Marie Gabriel; da of 2 Baron Freyberg, OBE, MC; *b* 1967; *Style* - The Hon Christina Freyberg

FREYBERG, Hon Valerian Bernard; s and h of 2 Baron Freyberg, OBE, MC; *b* 15 Dec 1970; *Style* - The Hon Valerian Freyberg

FREYBERG, Hon Venetia Rose; da of 2 Baron Freyberg, OBE, MC; *b* 1963; *Style* - The Hon Venetia Freyberg

FRICKER, Alan Derek; s of late Norman Fricker, OBE; *b* 20 June 1924; *Educ* Charterhouse, Trin Oxford; *m* 1950, Margaret Mary, nee Snelgrove; 2 s, 4 da; *Career* barr 1949, dir Cawood Solid Fuels Ltd; *Recreations* sailing, fishing, walking; *Clubs* Naval Club, New Club Cheltenham; *Style* - Alan Fricker Esq; The Cottage, Mill st, Prestbury, Cheltenham, Glos (☎ 0242 44555)

FRICKER, (Anthony) Nigel; s of the late Dr William Shapland Fricker; *b* 7 July 1937; *Educ* King's Sch Chester, Liverpool U; *m* 1960, Marilyn Ann, nee Martin; 1 s, 1 da; *Career* barrister, Prosecuting Counsel to DHSS, Wales and Chester Circuit (North) 1975-77, a Recorder of the Crown Court 1975-, QC 1977; *Clubs* Bristol Channel Yacht (yacht- 'Mumbles'); *Style* - Nigel Fricker Esq, QC; Farrar's Building, Temple, EC4 (☎ 01 583 9241)

FRIEBE, John Percy; s of Charles Friebe (d 1962); *b* 9 May 1931; *Educ* Glasgow H S, Glasgow U; *m* 1966, Laura Mary, da of Archibald Fleming (d 1961); *Career* memb Inst of Chartered Accountants of Scotland, memb Inst of Cost and Management Accountants, gp md Stoddard Hldgs Ltd, dir Millard Bros and Smith & McLaurin Ltd; *Recreations* golf, gardening; *Clubs* High Sch Club Ltd; *Style* - John Friebe Esq; Greystones, Montrose ter, Bridge of Weir, Renfrewshire

FRITH, Donald Alfred; OBE (1980); s of the late Charles Henry Frith; *b* 13 May 1918; *Educ* Whitgift, Christ's Coll Cambridge; *m* 1941, Mary Webster, nee Tyler; 4 s, 1 da; *Career* teacher and Deme Warden Univ Coll Sch 1946-52, headmaster Richmond Sch Yorkshire 1953-59, headmaster Archbishop Holgate's Sch York 1959-78, secretary Headmasters' Conference and Secondary Heads Assoc 1979-; *Recreations* music, reading, walking, gardening; *Clubs* Athenaeum, Yorkshire (York); *Style* - Donald Frith Esq, OBE; 4D Hungershall Park, Tunbridge Wells, Kent (☎ Tunbridge Wells 27409)

FRIZZELL, Colin Frazer; s of Thomas Norman Frizzell (d 1976); *b* 8 April 1939; *Educ* Oundle; *m* 1962, Anna Georgina, da of Thomas Stewart-Johnstone; 2 da; *Career* Lt Roy Fusiliers, chm The Frizzell Group Ltd, Lloyds Insurance Brokers and Underwriters; *Recreations* golf, tennis, fly fishing; *Clubs* Naval and Military; *Style* - Colin Frizzell Esq; Chuffs House, Holyport, nr Maidenhead, Berks (☎ Maidenhead 20827)

FROGGATT, Sir Leslie Trevor; s of late L Froggatt; *b* 8 Apr 1920; *Educ* Birkenhead Park Cheshire; *m* 1945, Jessie, da of P M Grant; 3 s; *Career* chm and ch exec offr Shell Gp of Cos Australia 1969-; kt 1981; *Style* - Sir Leslie Froggatt; 20 Albany rd, Toorak, Vic 3142, Australia

FROHLICH, Herbert; FRS (1951); s of the late Julius Jakob Frohlich of Munich; *b* 9 Dec 1905; *Educ* Univ of Munich; *m* 1950, Audrey Fanchon, nee Aungst; *Career* physicist, Professor and Head of Dept of Theoretical Physics, Univ of Liverpool 1948-73; *Clubs* The Royal Society; *Style* - Herbert Frohlich Esq, FRS; The University, Oxford st, Liverpool (☎ 051 709 6022)

FROST, Albert Edward; s of Charles Albert Frost (d 1953); *b* 7 Mar 1914; *Educ* Oulton Sch Liverpool, London U; *m* 1942, Eugenie Maud; *Career* barrister-at-law Middle Temple, HM Inspector of Taxes 1937-49, dep head taxation ICI Ltd 1949-57, dep treasurer 1957-60, treasurer 1960-68, finance dir 1968-76, dir- Marks & Spencer 1976-, S.S.Warburg 1976-, BL Ltd 1977-80, British Airways 1976-80, British Steel Corpn 1980-, memb council St.Thomas's Medical Sch, memb Council and fin Ctee Morley Coll London, dir Youth Music Ltd; *Recreations* violin, swimming, athletics, walking, arts generally; *Clubs* RAC; *Style* - Albert Frost Esq; Michael House, Baker st, W1 (☎ 01 935 4422)

FROST, Hon Mrs (Joyce Ida Jessie); *née* Montagu; JP (Wilts); da of late 2 Baron Swaythling; *b* 1909; *m* 1941, as his 2 w, Capt Oliver Harry Frost, MBE, MC, former Middx Regt and RAF (d 1977); 1 s; *Style* - The Hon Mrs Frost, JP; The Orchard House, Ogbourne St George, Wilts

FROST, Air Commodore John William; CBE (1966), DFC (1945); s of John Frost (d 1974); *b* 30 July 1921; *Educ* Longton H S Stoke-on-Trent; *m* 1950, Shelagh, nee Baldock; 1 s, 2 da; *Career* Air Commodore 1968, fighter command 1949-53, dep dir RAF projects Mini of Defence 1967-68, dir personnel services RAF MOD 1968-70, chief of staff, UK Mil Representative HQ NATO 1972-76, retd 1976, head of protocol MOD 1977-; *Recreations* reading, rough shooting, caravanning, photography, country interests; *Clubs* RAF; *Style* - Air Commodore J W Frost, CBE, DFC; 20 Wise's Firs, Sulhamstead, Reading, Berks (☎ Burghfield Common (073 529) 2372)

FROST, Hon Mrs; Hon Marygold; *née* Mills; da of 3 Baron Hillingdon (d 1952); *b* 1924; *m* 1948, Kenneth Frost; 2 s, 4 da; *Style* - The Hon Mrs Frost; 2 Eaton Cottages, Dolman's Hill, Lytchett Matravers, Dorset

FROST, Norman; CBE (1959), KPM (1950); s of the late William Frost; *b* 18 March 1899; *Educ* March; *m* 1927, Ivy Edna, nee Bush; 2 s; *Career* OStJ 1958, Royal Engineers (Signals), Belgium, France, Germany; Police Service, Ch Constable- Peterborough 1926-43, Boston 1944-47, Eastbourne 1947-54, Bristol 1954-64, Cmmdt Police T'ning Sch 1945-47 *Recreations* charity voluntary work, gardening; *Clubs* St John House; *Style* - Norman Frost Esq, CBE, KPM; Westovers, Wedmore, Somerset (☎ Wedmore 712568)

FROST, Hon Raymond; s of Baroness Gaitskell by her 1 husb, David Frost; *b* 6 May 1924; *Educ* Oundle, Worcester Coll Oxford; *m* 1958, June, da of Eduardo Rodriquez del Rey; 1 s, 1 da; *Career* Dir, Econ Devpt Inst at World Bank, Washington, DC; *Style* - The Hon Raymond Frost; 2917 Q st NW, Washington DC, 20007 USA

FRY, Francis Wilfrid; OBE (1967); s of late Sir John Pease Fry, 2 Bt; hp of bro, Sr John Nicholas Pease Fry, 4 Bt; *b* 2 May 1904; *Educ* Clifton, Trin Cambridge; *m* 1954, Anne Pease, JP, da of late Kenneth Henry Wilson, OBE, JP, of Park Hall, Kidderminster; *Career* MIMinE; *Style* - Francis Fry Esq, OBE; Cleveland Lodge, Gt Ayton, Middlesbrough, Cleveland

FRY, Sir John Nicholas Pease; 4 Bt (UK 1894), of Woodburn, Blackwell, co Durham; s of Sir John Pease Fry, 2 Bt (d 1957) of the Quaker cocoa manufacturing family; suc bro, Sir Theodore Penrose Fry, 3 Bt, 1971; *b* 23 Oct 1897; *Educ* Clifton Coll Bristol, Trin Coll Cambridge; *m* 1927, Helen Murray, nee Bott (d 1981); 1 da (1 c decd); *Heir* bro Francis Wilfred Fry; *Recreations* sleeping, reading; *Style* - Sir John Fry, Bt; c/o Nat West Bank, Chalfont StGiles, Bucks

FRYE, Eric; s of William Barnard Frye (d 1949); *b* 15 March 1923; *Educ* Tom Hood Coll, S E Essex Tech Coll; *m* 1947, Doreen Joan, da of Edward Thomas Day (d 1958); 2 c; *Career* warrant offr, air observer Europe, POW Japan 1941-45; chartered accountant 1952, sr exec Ford Motor Co 1964, dir Staveley Industries 1964-67, The Plessey Co Ltd 1969-78 (dep ch exec 1976-78), company dir and consultant;

Recreations golf, travel, carpentry; *Style* - Eric Frye Esq; Inglewood, Thoby lane, Mountnessing, Brentwood, Essex (☎ Ingatestone 2505); Casa Doric, Quinta do Paraiso, Praia do Carvoeiro, Algarve, Portugal

FRYER, John Albert; CBE (1970); s of George Albert Fryer; *b* 17 Jan 1925; *Educ* Portsmouth N Secdy Sch, Southern Coll Art Winchester, Univ Coll London, Southampton U; *m* 1960, Brenda Sheila, nee Baugh; 1 s; *Career* Lt Royal Engineers, Far East Land Forces, Colonial Survey Service N Borneo 1948, ARICS 1960, dir Lands & Surveys, Sabah, Malaysia 1966-70, Transportation Research Officer GLC 1970; *Recreations* genealogy; *Clubs* Royal Commonwealth Society, Mensa; *Style* - John Fryer Esq, CBE; New Orchard, 6 Meadowlands, Havant, Hants

FRYER, Maj-Gen Wilfred George; CB (1956), CBE (1951, OBE 1941); s of the late James Fryer; *b* 1 May 1900; *Educ* Christ Coll Brecon, RMA Woolwich; *m* 1931, Jean Eleanore, nee Graham; 3 s (1 decd); *Career* WW II 1944-45- Western Desert, France and Germany, Suez Canal, chief engineer British Army Staff, Washington DC 1945, Singapore District 1948-51, Southern Command UK 1951-53, Middle East Land Forces 1954-57; *Recreations* skiing, sailing; *Clubs* Hurlingham, Royal Ocean Racing (Transatlantic Race 1931), Army & Navy, Royal Lymington Yacht; *Style* - Maj Gen Wilfred Fryer, CB, CBE; Critchells Green Farmhouse, Lockerley, Romsey, Hants (☎ Lockerley 40312)

FUCHS, Sir Vivian (Ernest); s of the late E Fuchs; *b* 11 Feb 1908; *Educ* Brighton Coll, St John's Coll Cambridge; *m* 1933, Joyce, nee Connell; 1 s, 1 da (1 da decd); *Career* kt 1958; Major West Africa, NW Europe, geologist, various expeditions- Greenland 1929, East Africa 1930-31, 1934, 1937-38, field cmdr Falkland Islands Dependencies Survey 1947-50, dir FIDS Scientific Bureau 1950-55, dir British Antarctic Survey 1958-73, leader Commonwealth Trans-Antarctic Expedition 1955-58; *Recreations* squash rackets, sailing; *Clubs* Athenaeum, Naval & Military; *Style* - Sir Vivian Fuchs; 78 Barton rd, Cambridge (☎ 0223 59238)

FULFORD, Francis Christopher; s of the late Lt Col Francis Edgar Anthony Fulford; *b* 31 Aug 1952; *Educ* Milton Abbey; *Career* memb Lloyd's, Lloyd's broker; *Recreations* shooting, territorial army, books; *Clubs* Turf; *Style* - Francis Fulford Esq; Great Fulford, Dunsford, Nr Exeter, Devon (☎ Cheriton Bishop 205)

FULLARD, Hon Mrs - Hon Glenys; *née* Macdonald; da of 1 Baron Macdonald of Gwaenysgor, KCMG, PC (d 1966); *b* 1923; *m* 1949, Robert Fullard, BSc; 2 da; *Career* JP Lancs; *Style* - The Hon Mrs Fullard JP; 2 Thornley Lane, Grotton, Oldham, Lancs

FULLER, Anthony Gerard Fleetwood; s of Maj Sir J G H F Fuller, Bt; *b* 4 June 1940; *Educ* Eton; *m* 1964, Julia Mary, da of Lt-Col E A Cooper-Key, MBE, MC; 1 s, 1 da; *Career* Lloyd's underwriter, dir Fuller Smith & Turner Ltd 1967-, md 1978-, Freeman & Livery of Brewers' Co; *Style* - Anthony Fuller Esq; 1 Bellvue Cottages, Chiswick Mall, W4 (☎ 01 994 2162); Little Chalfield Manor, Melksham, Wilts (☎ 022 16 5934)

FULLER, Edward; s of the late John Wesley Fuller; *b* 28 July 1920; *Educ* Verden Tech Coll Northwich; *m* 1947, Joan, nee O'Kane; 3 s, 3 da; *Career* Lt RNVR, dir- Edgley & Lumley Ltd, W J Furse & Co Ltd, John Faulkner & Sons Ltd, M Macdonald & Co, Padfield & Howes Ltd, SGB Ltd, Storm Ltd; *Style* - Edward Fuller Esq; Risley Lodge, Risley, Derby (☎ 0602 397524)

FULLER, Sir (John) Gerard Henry Fleetwood; 2 Bt (UK 1910); s of Sir John Michael Fleetwood Fuller, 1 Bt, KCMG (d 1915); *b* 8 July 1906; *Educ* Uppingham; *m* 1, 1931 (m dis 1944), Lady Fiona Pratt, da of 4 Marquess Camden; 2 s; m 2, 1945, Kathleen Elizabeth, MBE (DStJ, d 1964), da of Sir George Herbert Farrar, 1 Bt (ext), DSO; m 3, 1966, Mrs Mary Leventon, da of Dr D Leigh Spence, of Melksham, Wilts; *Heir* s, John William Fleetwood Fuller; *Career* Maj (ret) Life Gds, Co Cllr of Wilts 1947, Co Alderman 1961, Master of Avon Vale Foxhounds 1947-61 and 1962-64, JP

Wilts 1946; *Style* - Sir Gerard Fuller, Bt, JP; Neston Park, Corsham, Wilts (☎ Hawthorn 810211); Balmore, Cannich, Inverness-shire (☎ Cannich 262)

FULLER, John William Fleetwood; s (by 1 m) of Sir (John) Gerard Fuller, 2 Bt; *b* 18 Dec 1936; *m* 1968, Lorna Marion, da of F R Kemp-Potter, of Findon, Sussex; 3 s; *Career* Maj (ret) Life Gds; *Style* - John Fuller Esq; Ganbrook Farm, Broughton Gifford, Melksham, Wilts

FULLER, Paul Malcolm; s of John Taylor Fuller of Billericay, Essex; *b* 4 Nov 1946; *Educ* Southend H S for Boys; *m* 1969, Jenifer Mary Elizabeth, da of Percy Beere (d 1955); 1 s, 2 da; *Career* accountant; memb Inst of Dirs, fin dir Lacrinoid Products Ltd 1973-78, fin dir TKM Foods Ltd 1978-; *Recreations* walking; *Style* - Paul Fuller Esq; Pen-Y-Bryn House, 1 Buckingham rd, Hockley, Essex

FULLER-ACLAND-HOOD, Dr the Hon Mrs John; Phyllis Lily Frances; da of Dr Denys Bouhier Inbert Hallett (d 1969); *b* 14 Oct 1915; *Educ* Cheltenham Ladies' Coll, Univ Coll London, Univ Coll Hosp London; *m* 1939, Hon (Arthur) John Palmer Fuller-Acland-Hood (d 1964), s of 1 Baron St Audries (d 1917) and Hon Mildred Rose Eveleigh de Moleyns, da of 4 Baron Ventry; 3 da; *Career* Flight Lt RAF Medical Service 1942-43; registered medical practitioner House Surgeon U Coll Hosp 1940-41, Govt Health Service Singapore 1952-53, psychiatrist Mendip Hosp Wells 1964-79; *Recreations* gardening, bridge, archaeology, local history, music *Clubs* VAD Ladies *Style* - Dr The Hon Mrs John Acland-Hood; Wootton House, nr Glastonbury, Somerset

FULLER-ACLAND-HOOD, Sir (Alexander) William; 8 Bt (UK 1806), of Hartington, co Derby, and 6 Bt (UK 1809), of St Audries, co Somerset; s of late William Fuller-Acland-Hood, 5 s of 3 Bt (cr 1809); suc cous, 2 Baron St Audries (also 7 and 5 Bt) 1971; *b* 5 March 1901; *Educ* Wellington, RMA Woolwich, U of California; *m* 1925, Mary V, da of late Augustus Edward Jessup, of Philadelphia, USA; 1 da (1 s decd); *Heir* none; *Career* formerly Lt RE, ret as Prof Los Angeles City Coll, naturalised an American citizen 1926; in remainder to Irish Barony of Bridport; *Style* - Sir William Fuller-Acland-Hood, Bt; SR2 Box 577, 29 Palms, Calif 92277, USA (☎ 714 3679345)

FULLERTON, John Charles Mark; s of Capt John Robert Rankin Fullerton (d 1966); *b* 21 Dec 1924; *Educ* Eton; *m* 1955, Pamela Blanche, da of Robert Crespigny Gwynedd Vivian, of Jersey; 2 s, 1 da *Career* Staff Capt 60th Rifles KRRC, advertising MIPA, man dir Ogilvy & Mather Ltd 1978-79 Hong Kong (dir 1967), chm Assoc of Accredited Advertising Agents (Hong Kong) 1979; *Recreations* writing novels, sailing; *Clubs* Roy Lymington Yacht, Hong Kong; *Style* - John Fullerton Esq; Shepherd's Green, Mt Pleasant, Lymington, Hants (☎ 682291)

FULLWOOD, Keith Saxon; s of Percy Fullwood; *b* 9 May 1928; *Educ* High Sch Sheffield; *m* 1962, Rosemary Anne, nee Law; 2 s; *Career* chartered secretary, FCIS, FBIM, accountant John Brown Gp 1954-60, gp ch accountant Bestwood Gp 1960-62, gp sec Sprite Gp 1962-67, dir Autopack Ltd, Scientific & Educational Aids Ltd 1967-, liveryman Scriveners Co and Chartered Secretaries Co; *Style* - Keith Fullwood Esq; Shazam, Defford, Worcs (☎ 995 750241)

FULLWOOD, Neville; CBE (1974); s of John William Fullwood (d 1968); *b* 5 Sept 1914; *Educ* Priory Sch Shrewsbury, Trin Oxford; *m* 1946, Daphne Fay, nee Bush; 1 da; *Career* HM Inspector of Schs (Scotland) 1951, HM ch insp 1966; HM depute sr ch insp 1973-74, ret *Recreations* reading, music; *Style* - Neville Fullwood Esq, CBE; Roskeen, 17 Glenbrook, Balerno, Edinburgh (☎ 449 3925)

FULTON, Baron (Life Peer UK 1966); John Scott Fulton; s of Angus Robertson Fulton, LLD, DSc, of Dundee (d 1958); *b* 27 May 1902; *Educ* Dundee H S, St Andrews U, Balliol Oxford; *m* 1939, Jacqueline, da of Kenneth Edward Towler Wilkinson; 3 s, 1 da; *Career* fell and tutor in Philosophy then Politics Balliol Coll

Oxford 1928-47, Prin Univ Coll Swansea 1947-59, Vice-Chancellor U of Wales 1952-54 and 58-59, U of Sussex 1959-67; v-chm & govr BBC 1965-70; kt 1964; *Recreations* golf, mountaineering, gardening; *Clubs* Athenaeum; *Style* - The Rt Hon the Lord Fulton; Brook House, Thornton Dale, Pickering, N Yorks (☎ Pickering 74221)

FULTON, Hon Alan Scott; s of Baron Fulton (Life Peer); *b* 1946; *Educ* Eton, Balliol Oxford; *Style* - The Hon Alan Fulton

FULTON, Hon Charity Marion Anne; da of Baron Fulton (Life Peer); *b* 1951 *Style* - The Hon Charity Fulton

FULTON, Hon Duncan John Rowntree; s of Baron Fulton (Life Peer); *b* 1949; *Educ* Eton, Balliol Oxford; *Style* - The Hon Duncan Fulton

FULTON, Hon (Kenneth Angus) Oliver; s of Baron Fulton (Life Peer); *b* 1941; *Educ* Eton, Balliol Oxford, California U; *m* 1970, Lynee, nee Alexander; *Style* - The Hon Oliver Fulton; Brook House, Thornton Dale, Yorks (☎ 221)

FULTON, Sidney James; CMG (1952); s of Lt Col Henry Fulton, DSO, Seychelles (d 1944); *b* 29 Feb 1912; *Educ* St.Paul's Sch, Ch Ch Oxford; *m* 1946, Cynthia Mary, da of Capt J L M Shaw (d 1921); 1 s, 2 da; *Career* Control Commission for Germany 1946, Office of the Commissioner General for the UK in SF Asia 1952-57, Foreign Office 1958-66; *Recreations* gardening; *Clubs* Travellers'; *Style* - Sidney Fulton Esq CMG; The Old Farmhouse, Tainfield, Kingston St Mary, Somerset

FUMMI, Lady (Cynthia) Anne; *née* Lindsay; da of late 27 Earl of Crawford and 10 of Balcarres, KT, PC, by Constance, da of Sir Henry Carstairs Pelly, MP, 3 Bt; *b* 1904; *m* 1, 1931, Per Erik Folke Arnander (d 1933), First Sec Swedish Legation Rome; 1 s; m 2, 1934, Giovanni Fummi (d 1970); 1 da; *Style* - Lady Anne Fummi; 10 Lochmore House, Cundy st Flats, Ebury st, SW18

FUNSHINE, Geoffrey Nicholas Christopher Peter; s of Leonard Funshine (d 1976); *b* 16 Nov 1936; *Educ* Shrewsbury; *m* 1962, Barbara Joan, nee Foxcroft; 1 s, 2 da; *Career* chm The Grand Theatre Trust Ltd 1981-, md BPB Corpn 1976, dir The 525 Co and subsidiaries 1959; *Recreations* pleasure, ice skating, squash, travel; *Clubs* Cambridge Union, Primrose, Fylde Conservative, Travellers and Explorers; owner of yacht 'Spirit of Funshine'; *Style* - Geoffrey Funshine Esq; Grosvenor House, Grosvenor rd, Poulton-le-Fylde

FURNER, Air Vice-Marshal Derek; CBE (1973, OBE 1963), DFC (1943), AFC (1954); s of Vivian J Furner (d 1933); *b* 14 Nov 1933; *Educ* Westcliff H S Essex; *m* 1948, Patricia, nee Donnelly; 3 s; *Career* AOC Central Reconnaissance Establishment 1969-70, sec NATO Mil Ctee Brussels 1970-73, assist Air sec MOD 1973-76, dir gen man Harlequin Wallcoverings Ltd 1976-; *Clubs* RAF; *Style* - Air Vice-Marshal Derek Furner CBE DFC AFC; 2 High Trees, Stock, Essex (☎ 840753)

FURNESS, 2 Viscount (UK 1918); William Anthony Furness; also Baron Furness (UK 1910); s of 1 Viscount (d 1940) and the celebrated Thelma, Lady Furness (twin da of Harry Hays Morgan, sometime US Consul at Buenos Aires); *b* 31 March 1929; *Educ* Downside, USA; *Career* formerly Gdsm Welsh Gds (invalided); Kt of Justice and Grand Offr of Merit Sov Mil Order of Malta (memb of Bd of Auditors 1979-), KStJ, delegate to 42, 43, 44, 48, 50 and 52 Inter-Parly Union of Conferences, founder chm Anglo-Mongolian Soc 1963-67, memb Cncl of Hansard Soc for Parly Govt 1955-67; *Style* - The Rt Hon The Viscount Furness; Palazzo Malta, Via Condotti 68, 00187 Rome, Italy; c/o Midland Bank Ltd, 69 Pall Mall, SW1

FURNESS, Michael Fitzroy Roberts; s and h of Sir Stephen Furness, 3 Bt; *b* 12 Oct 1962; *Style* - Michael Furness Esq

FURNESS, Sir Stephen Roberts; 3 Bt (UK 1913), of Tunstall Grange, W Hartlepool; s of Sir Christopher Furness, 2 Bt (d 1974, 2 cous of 2 Viscount Furness);

b 10 Oct 1933; *Educ* Charterhouse; *m* 1961, Mary, da of Jack Fitzroy Cann, of Devon; 1 s, 1 da; *Heir* s, Michael Fitzroy Roberts Furness; *Career* late Lt RN, ret 1962; farmer & sporting artist (as Robin Furness); jt MFH Bedale Foxhounds 1979; *Recreations* hunting, racing, looking at paintings; *Style* - Sir Stephen Furness, Bt; Stanhow Farm, Gt Langton, Northallerton, Yorks (☎ Kirkby Fleetham 614)

FURNESS, Flower, Lady; (Violet) Flower Chipchase; OBE (1970); da of Lt-Col Gerard Chipchase Roberts, of Hollingside, Durham; *m* 1930, Sir Christopher Furness, 2 Bt (d 1974); 2 s (Sir Stephen, 3 Bt; Simon), 1 da (Mrs Paul Payne); *Style* - Flower, Lady Furness OBE; Netherbyres, Eyemouth, Berwicks

FURNISS, Air Vice-Marshal Peter; DFC (1944), TD (1964); s of John Furniss *b* 16 July 1919; *Educ* Sedbergh Sch; *m* 1954, Denise Andrée Gisèle, da of Charles Cotet, of France; 1 s, 2 da; *Career* cmmd Liverpool Scottish TA, Queen's Own Cameron Highlanders 1939, seconded to RAF 1942, cmmd fighter sqdn, demobilised 1946; solicitor 1948, Legal Branch RAF 1950, Dir of Legal Servs, HQ Air Forces Middle East, Aden 1961-63, HQ Far East Air Force Singapore 1969-71, HQ RAF Germany 1973-74, Dep Dir Legal Servs RAF 1975-78, Dir Legal Servs 1978-; *Recreations* country pursuits *Clubs* RAF *Style* - Air Vice-Marshal Peter Furniss, DFC, TD; 18 Sevington Park, Loose, Maidstone, Kent (☎ 44620)

FURNIVALL, Barony of (E 1295); *see* Hon Rosamond Dent, Hon Mrs Bence

FYFE, James Gordon; TD (1956), WS, DL (Peebleshire 1966); s of Alexander Fyfe (d 1978); *b* 5 May 1918; *Educ* George Watson's Coll, Edinburgh U; *m* 1, 1942, Phyllis Una (decd 1956), nee Goodford; 1 s; m 2, 1958, Katherine Jean Wolfe, nee Murray; *Career* Maj WW II; *Recreations* fishing, curling; *Clubs* Caledonian (Edinburgh); *Style* - James Fyfe Esq, TD, WS, DL; Meldonfoot, Peebles, Peeblesshire, Scotland (☎ Kirkton Manor 252)

G

GADSBY, Gordon Neville; CB (1972); s of William Gadsby (d 1978); *b* 29 Jan 1914; *Educ* King Edward VI Sch Stratford, Birmingham U; *m* 1938, Jeanne, nee Harris; 2 s, 1 da; *Career* FRSC, consultant NUS Corpn USA 1980-, gp ldr The Mitre Corpn USA 1976-80, min Defence Research & Dvpt Br Embassy Washington 1972-75, dir Chemical Defence Establisment 1968-72, dep ch scientist (Army) MOD 1967-68, dir Biological & Chemical Def MOD 1965-67, dir Army Operational Res Establishment 1961-64 *Recreations* oil painting *Style* - Gordon Gadsby Esq CB; Beech Gate, Compton Down, Winchester (☎ 0962 712231); 1453 Laburnum st, McLean, Virginia, USA (☎ (703) 536-3737)

GADSDON, Lady; Hilda Mary; da of John Hedges; *m* 1929, late Sir Lawrence Gadsdon; *Style* - Lady Gadsdon; 14 Dean st, Cottesloe, W Australia

GAGE, 6 Viscount (I 1720); Sir Henry Rainald Gage; 13 Bt (E 1622), KCVO (1939); also Baron Gage of Castlebar (I 1720) and Baron Gage of High Meadow (GB 1790); sits in House of Lords as latter; s of 5 Viscount Gage, DL (strictly speaking the title is 'Gage of Castle Island' ; 5 Viscount d 1912, being gggs of Hon Thomas Gage, Gov & CIC in N America at the start of the War of Independence), by Leila, da of Rev Frederick Peel (n of Rt Hon Sir Robert Peel, 2 Bt, the statesman and PM) by his w, Hon Adelaide Hanbury-Tracy, da of 2 Baron Sudeley; *b* 30 Dec 1895; *Educ* Eton; *m* 1, 1931, Hon Alexandra Grenfell (d 1969, da of 1 Baron Desborough, KG, GCVO, JP, DL, and Ethel Fane, coheir to the Barony of Butler), sis of the poet (Hon) Julian Grenfell, k in WW I; 2 s, 1 da; m 2, 1971, Diana, da of Col The Rt Hon Lord Richard Cavendish, CB, CMG (bro of 9 Duke of Devonshire, KG, GCMG, GCVO, PC), by Lady

Moyra Beauclerk, da of 10 Duke of St Albans (*see* Gage, Viscountess); *Heir* s, Hon George Gage; *Career* former V-Lt Sussex, former chm E Sussex CC; Patron Nat Fedn Housing Socs; served WW I & II; Lord-in-Waiting to HM 1924-29 & 1931-39; DL 1927; *Clubs* White's, Brooks's; *Style* - The Rt Hon The Viscount Gage, KCVO, DL; Firle Place, Lewes (☎ Glynde 256)

GAGE, Viscountess; Diana; 4 da of Col Rt Hon Lord Richard Cavendish, CB, CMG (bro of 9 Duke of Devonshire, KG, GCMG, GCVO, PC, JP, DL), and Lady Moyra Beauclerk, da of 10 Duke of St Albans; *b* 15 Sept 1909; *m* 1, 1935 (m dis 1937), as his 1 w, Robert (Bob) Boothby, MP (now Baron Boothby, KBE); m 2, 1942, Lt-Col Hon Ian Campbell-Gray (d 1946), 3 s of Henry Craig-Campbell and Lady Gray (holder of the Scottish Lordship in her own right and gm of 22 Lord Gray); m 3, 1971, as his 2 w, 6 Viscount Gage, KCVO; *Style* - The Rt Hon The Viscountess Gage; Firle Place, Lewes, Sussex

GAGE, Hon George John St Clere; s of 6 Visc Gage; *b* 8 July 1932; *Educ* Ludgrove and Eton; *m* 1971, Valerie Ann, yr da of J E Dutch, of Horam, Sussex ; *Style* - The Hon George Gage; White Friars, Alciston, Polegate, Sussex

GAGE, Hon Henry Nicolas; 2 s of 6 Visc Gage; *b* 1934; *Educ* Eton and Ch Ch Oxford; *Career* 2 Lt Coldstream Gds 1953; *Style* - The Hon Henry Gage; The Cottage, Charwelton, Rugby, Warwickshire (☎ Byfield 205)

GAGGERO, John George; JP (1972); s of Sir George Gaggero, OBE, JP, of Gibraltar; *b* 3 March 1934; *Educ* Downside; *m* 1961, Valerie, da of John Malin, OBE, JP, of Gibraltar; 2 s, 2 da; *Career* formerly Lt 12 Roy Lancers Malaya; dep chm Bland Gp including Gibraltar Airways, Rock Hotel, Cadogan Travel 1970- memb Roy Inst Naval Architects; *Recreations* boating (motor yacht- 'Queva'); *Clubs* Roy Gibraltar Yacht, Cavalry & Guards; *Style* - John Gaggero Esq, JP; 15 Bayside rd, Gibraltar (☎ 2274)

GAINFORD, 3 Baron (UK 1917); Joseph Edward Pease; s of 2 Baron Gainford, TD (d 1971), by Veronica, Baroness Gainford, *qv*; *b* 25 Dec 1921; *Educ* Eton, Gordonstoun; *m* 1953, Theophila, da of late Henry Tyndale and Ruth (da of Alexander Radcliffe, of Bag Park, S Devon); 2 da; *Heir* bro, Hon George Pease; *Career* FRGS, MSST, served WW II as Sgt RAF; UK Del to UN 1973; memb Coll of Guardians Nat Shrine of Our Lady of Walsingham 1979-, Plaisterers' Co 1976 *Style* - The Rt Hon The Lord Gainford; 60 Lansdowne rd, W11 (☎ 01 229 6279)

GAINFORD, Veronica, Baroness - Veronica Margaret; da of Sir George J W Noble, 2 Bt (d 1937); *b* 1900; *m* 1921, 2 Baron Gainford (d 1971); 3 s; *Style* - The Rt Hon Veronica, Lady Gainford; Duntaynish, Tavyallich, Argyll (☎ 275)

GAINSBOROUGH, 5 Earl of (UK 1841); Sir Anthony Gerard Edward Noel; 7 Bt (GB 1781), JP (Leics 1974, formerly Rutland 1957); also Baron Barham (UK 1805), Viscount Campden and Baron Noel (both UK 1841); s of 4 Earl of Gainsborough, OBE, TD, JP (d 1927), sometime Private Chamberlain to Popes Benedict XV & Pius XI; *b* 24 Oct 1923; *Educ* Worth Sussex, Georgetown Maryland; *m* 1947, Mary, da of Hon John Stourton, TD, of Miniature Hall, Wadhurst, 2 s of (24) Baron Mowbray, (25 Baron) Segrave, and (21 Baron) Stourton, by John's 2 w, Caroline, nee O'Dwyer; 4 s, 3 da (and 1 da decd); *Heir* s, Viscount Campden; *Career* patron of two livings (but being a Roman Catholic cannot present), Bailiff Grand Cross Sov Mil Order of Malta (Pres Br Assoc 1968-74); KStJ; chm Rutland CC 1970-73; *Clubs* Boodle's, Brooks's, Roy Yacht Sqdn, Bembridge Sailing; *Style* - The Rt Hon Earl of Gainsborough JP; Exton Park, Oakham, Leics (☎ 812209)

GAIRDNER, Hon Lady - Hon Evelyn Constance; *née* Handcock; da of late 5 Baron Castlemaine; *b* 1897; *m* 1925, Lt-Gen Sir Charles Henry Gairdner, GBE, KCMG, KCVO, CB, late 10 Hussars; *Career* CStJ; *Style* - Hon Lady Gairdner; 24 The Esplanade, Peppermint Grove W, Australia

GAITSKELL, Baroness (Life Peeress UK 1963); Anna Dora; da of Leon Creditor, immigrant from Lithuania 1903 & fndr *Jewish Voice*; *m* 1, 1921 (m dis 1937), David, s of Louis Frost; 1 s; m 2, 1937, Rt Hon Hugh Gaitskell, CBE, MP (d 1963); 2 da; *Career* Tstee Anglo-German Fndn 1974-, memb House of Lords All Pty Cttee on Human Rights 1977-; *Style* - The Rt Hon The Lady Gaitskell; 18 Frognal gdns, NW3

GALBRAITH, Hon David Muir Galloway; s of Cdr 1 Baron Strathclyde, PC, JP; *b* 8 March 1928; *Educ* Wellington, RAC Cirencester; *m* 1967, Marion, da of Maj Bruce Bingham Kennedy; 1 s, 3 da; *Career* chartered land agent, chartered surveyor; *Recreations* country pursuits; *Style* - The Hon David Galbraith; Burnbrae Lodge, Mauchline, Ayrshire (☎ 50210)

GALBRAITH, Hon James Muir Galloway; s of 1 Baron Strathclyde, PC, JP; *b* 27 Sept 1920; *Educ* RNC Dartmouth, Ch Ch Oxford, RAC Cirencester; *m* 1945, Anne, da of Maj Kenneth Paget, of Itchen Abbas; 3 s, 1 da; *Career* served with RN WW II; chartered surveyor; chm Edinburgh Bd Sun Alliance Insur Gp, Timber Growers Gt Britain; dir Buccleuch Estates Ltd; JP Inverness-shire 1953-54; *Clubs* Army & Navy, New (Edinburgh); *Style* - The Hon James Galbraith; Rawflat, Ancrum, Roxburghshire (☎ 302)

GALBRAITH, Hon Thomas Galloway Dunlop; MP (U) Glasgow Hillhead 1948-; s and h of 1 Baron Strathclyde, PC, JP; *b* 10 March 1917; *Educ* Wellington, Ch Ch Oxford, Glasgow U; *m* 1956, Simone, da of Jean du Roy de Blicquy, of Bois d'Hautmont, Wauthier Braine, Brabant; 2 s, 1 da; *Career* Scottish Unionist Whip 1950; Ld Commissioner of Treasury 1951, Comptroller of HM Household 1954, Treasurer of HM Household 1956; Civil Ld of Admlty 1957, Under-Sec of State Scottish Off 1959, Parly Sec Min of T'port 1963-64; Pres Scottish Georgian Soc 1970-80; *Clubs* Carlton, RAC, New (Edinburgh); *Style* - The Hon Thomas Galbraith, MP; Old Barskimming, Mauchline, Ayrshire (☎ 0290 50334); 2 Cowley st, SW1 (☎ 01 222 2966)

GALBRAITH, William Campbell; QC (1977); s of William Galbraith; *b* 25 Feb 1935; *Educ* Merchiston, Pembroke Cambridge, Edinburgh Univ; *m* 1959, Mary Waller; 3 s; *Career* barrister; *Style* - William Galbraith Esq, QC

GALE, Hon George Alexander; CC (1977); s of late Robert Gale; *b* 24 June 1906; *Educ* Toronto U; Osgoode Hall Law Sch Toronto; *m* 1934, Hilda Daly; 3 s; *Career* Ch Justice of Ontario 1967-76; vice-chm Ontario Law Reform Cmmn from 1977; *Style* - The Hon George Gale CC; 2 Brookfield rd, Willowdale, Ontario, Canada

GALE, George Edwin; CBE (1973); s of James Edmund Gale (d 1951); *b* 11 Dec 1910; *Educ* Royal G S High Wycombe, Selhurst G S Croydon, London U; *m* 1935, Carole Fisher, nee Waldron; 1 s, 2 da; *Career* FRSC, scientist (chemist) with Admiralty (later RN Scientific Serv) 1939-64, Lt RNVR scientific intelligence 1944-45, seconded to Indian Navy as scientific adviser 1951-54, dir Scientific & Technical Services Branch DHSS; *Recreations* writing, philately; *Clubs* Royal Naval and Royal Albert Yacht Club (Portsmouth); *Style* - George Gale Esq, CBE; 23 St Helen's ct, St Helen's Parade, Southsea, Hants (☎ 0705 818095)

GALE, Michael; QC (1977); s of Joseph Gale; *b* 12 Aug 1932; *Educ* Cheltenham G S, King's Coll Cambridge; *m* 1963, Joanna Bloom; 1 s, 2 da *Career* Recorder of Crown Court 1977-; *Style* - Michael Gale Esq, QC; 6 Pump Court, Temple EC4 (☎ 01 353 7242)

GALITZINE, Prince (Russian kniaz, cr 1408 confirmed 1798) George; name also spelt Golitsyn or Golitzine; s of Prince Vladimir Emanuelovitch Galitzine (d 1954) by his 1 w Countess Catherine von Carlow (product of the morganatic m between Natalia, nee Wonlarsky, cr Countess von Carlow, and HH Duke Georg of Mecklenburg-Strelitz; the latter's maternal gf was yst s of Tsar Paul I of Russia, while through his mother's mother Georg was fifth in descent from HRH Princess Augusta, sis of George III; hence Prince George Galitzine is sixth cous once removed of HM The Queen); *b* 3 May 1916; *Educ* Lancing, St Paul's, BNC Oxford; *m* 1, 1943 (m dis 1954), Baroness Anne-Marie von Slatin, da of Maj-Gen (Baron) Sir Rudolf von Slatin Pasha (d 1928); 2 s, 1 da; m 2, 1963, Jean, da of Frederick Dawnay; 1 da; *Heir* s, Prince Alexander Galitzine; *Career* formerly Maj Welsh Gds Gen Staff Europe; co dir Roy Humane Soc Medal 1936; *Recreations* travel, photography, skiing; *Style* - Prince George Galitzine; Mulberry Cottage, Brown Candover, Alresford, Hants; 113 Eaton sq, SW1 (☎ 01 235 3113)

GALLAGHER, Hon Mrs; Hon Kristin; da of Baron Wynne-Jones (Life Peer); *b* 1931; *m* 1956, Dr Charles Joseph Gallagher (d 1964); *Style* - The Hon Mrs Gallagher

GALLAGHER, Michael; MEP (L) Nottingham 1979-; s of Michael Gallagher; *b* 1 July 1934; *Educ* Us of Nottingham and Wales; *m* 1959, Kathleen Gallagher; 2 s, 3 da; *Style* - Michael Gallagher Esq, MEP; The Cliff, 31 Woodhouse rd, Mansfield, Notts (☎ 31659)

GALLAGHER, Patrick Joseph; DFC (1943); s of Patrick Gallagher; *b* 15 Apr 1921; *Educ* Prior Park, Bath; *m* 1950, Veronica Bateman; 1 s; *Career* md Patrick Gallagher Associates 1979-; *Style* - Patrick Gallagher Esq, DFC; Flat 5, 30 Hans rd, SW3 (☎ 01 584 3865)

GALLAGHER, Patrick Joseph David; s of Matthew Gallagher, of Cashel, Co Sligo; *b* 28 Feb 1909; *Educ* Trin Coll Dublin; *m* 1944, Mary Gleason, da of Joseph Gleason, of Philadelphia; 3 s, 2 da; *Career* dep chm Abbey Ltd Dublin 1977-, dir Abbey Homesteads Ltd London; *Recreations* golf, football; *Clubs* Kildare Street University; *Style* - Patrick Gallagher Esq; Liskilleen, Shankhill, Dublin, Eire (☎ 01 852426)

GALLICHAN, Richard Raymond Grandin; DSC (1944); s of Cdr Sydney Gallichan RNR (d 1975); *b* 16 July 1918; *Educ* Portsmouth G S; *m* 1948, Barbara Jean, nee Robshaw; 2 children; *Career* Lt RNVR WW II; slr, sr ptnr Cameron Kemm 1964-80, joint sr ptnr Cameron Markby; underwriting memb of Lloyd's 1977; *Recreations* golf, swimming, snooker, bridge; *Style* - Richard Gallichan Esq, DSC; c/o Lloyds Bank Ltd, Broad st, St Helier, Jersey, CI

GALLIERS-PRATT, Anthony Malcolm; CBE (1977); s of George Galliers-Pratt; *b* 31 Jan 1926; *Educ* Eton; *m* 1950, Angela, da of Sir Charles Cayzer, 3 Bt; 3 s ; *Career* chm F Pratt Engineering Corpn Ltd 1974-; *Style* - Anthony Galliers-Pratt Esq, CBE; Mawley Hall, Cleobury Mortimer, Worcs (☎ 436)

GALLIFORD, Peter; *Career* chm Galliford Brindley Ltd; *Style* - Peter Galliford Esq; Galliford Brindley Ltd, Leicester rd, Wolvey, Hinckley, Leics

GALLINER, Peter; s of Dr Maritz Galliner; *b* 19 Sept 1920; *Educ* Berlin and London; *m* 1948, Edith Goldschmidt; 1 da; *Career* chm Peter Galliner Associates 1970-; dir International Press Inst from 1975; *Style* - Peter Galliner Esq; 27 Queen's Grove, NW8 (☎ 01 722 0361)

GALLOWAY, 13 Earl of (S 1623); Sir Randolph Keith Reginald Stewart; 12 Bt (of Corsewell S 1627 and 10 Bt of Burray S 1687); also Lord Garlies (S 1607) and Baron Stewart of Garlies (GB 1796); s of 12 Earl of Galloway, JP (d 1978); *b* 14 Oct 1928; *Educ* Harrow; *m* 1975, Mrs Lily Budge, da of late Andrew Miller; *Heir* cous, Alexander Stewart, MBE, TD; *Style* - The Rt Hon the Earl of Galloway; 4 Bernard ter, Edinburgh 8

GALLOWAY, Lady - Dorothy; da of late Frank H White; *m* 1920, Lt-Gen Sir Alexander Galloway, KBE, CB, DSO, MC (d 1977); *Style* - Lady Galloway; Norham, Northumberland (☎ 304)

GALPERN, Baron (Life Peer UK 1979); Myer Galpern; JP (City of Glasgow), DL (Co of City of Glasgow 1962); s of Maurice Galpern; *b* 1903; *Educ* Hutcheson's Boys' G S, Glasgow U; *m* 1940, Alice Campbell, JP, da of late Thomas Stewart; 1 s, 1 da; *Career* Ld-Lt Co of City of Glasgow 1958-59, Ld Provost Glasgow 1958-60; MP (L) Glasgow Shettlestone 1959-79, 2 Dep Chm Ways &

Means 1974-76, First Dep Chm 1976-79; kt 1960; *Style* - Rt Hon Lord Galpern JP DL; 42 Kelvin Court, Glasgow

GALPERN, Hon Maurice Lionel; s of Baron Galpern, JP, DL; *b* 1945; *m* 1971, Karen Ellen, da of Jay Honickman; *Style* - The Hon Maurice Galpern; Red Gorton, Springkell ave, Glasgow

GALTON, Raymond; s of Herbert Galton; *b* 17 July 1930; *Educ* Garth Sch, Morden; *m* 1956, Tonia Phillips; 1 s, 2 da; *Career* scriptwriter and author; *Style* - Raymond Galton Esq; The Ivy House, Hampton Court, Middx (☎ 01 977 1236)

GALWAY, 12 Viscount (I 1727); George Rupert Monckton-Arundell; CD; also Baron Killard (I 1727); s of Philip Marmaduke Monckton (d 1965); suc 1 cous once removed, 11 Viscount, 1980; *b* 13 Oct 1922; *m* 1944, Fiona, nee Taylor; 1 s, 3 da; *Heir* s, John Philip Monckton-Arundell; *Career* Lt-Cdr RCN ret; *Style* - The Rt Hon the Viscount Galway, CD; 583 Berkshire Drive, London, Ontario, Canada

GALWAY, James; OBE (1977); s of James Galway; *b* 8 Dec 1939; *Educ* St Paul's, RCM, Guildhall Sch of Music, Conservatoire National Supérieur de Musique (Paris); *m* 1972, Anna Renggli; 1 s, 2 (twin) da; 1 s by former marriage; *Career* flautist; *Style* - James Galway Esq, OBE; c/o London Artists, 73 Baker st, W1

GALWAY, Dowager Viscountess - Hon Lucia Margaret; da of 3 Baron Annaly (d 1922); *b* 1891; *m* 1922, 8 Viscount Galway, GCMG, DSO, OBE, PC (d 1943); 1 s, 3 da; *Career* served World War I 1914-18 (overseas); a maid of honour to Queen Alexandra 1919-22; JP (1944) Notts; *Style* - The Rt Hon the Dowager Viscountess Galway, JP; Serlby Hall, Bawtry, Doncaster, Yorks

GAMBLE, David; s and h of Sir David Gamble, 4 Bt ; *b* 5 June 1933; *Educ* Shrewsbury; *m* 1956, Dawn Adrienne, nee Gittins; 1 s, 2 da; *Style* - David Gamble Esq; Scotland House, South st, Castle Cary, Somerset

GAMBLE, Sir David Arthur Josias; 4 Bt (UK 1897); s of Sir David Gamble, 3 Bt (d 1943); *b* 9 Dec 1907; *Educ* Shrewsbury, Wadham Oxford; *m* 1, 1932, Elinor Mary (d 1961), da of Henry E Cole; 1 s; m 2, 1965, Evelyn Gamble; *Heir* s, David Gamble; *Career* chm Cirencester RDC 1958-59; *Style* - Sir David Gamble, Bt; Wood End, Tregony, Truro, Cornwall

GAMBLE, Sir (Frederick) Herbert; KBE (1964), CMG (1955); s of Frederick West Gamble (d 1951); *b* 21 May 1907; *Educ* Portora Royal Sch Enniskillen, Trin Coll Dublin; *m* 1942, Janine, da of Marc Corbisier de Cobreville; 2 da; *Career* HM Diplomatic Serv (ret), entered Levant Consular Serv 1930, HM Consul Suez 1945-46; commercial counsellor- Bagdad 1948-52, Athens 1952-55, HM Ambass Ecuador 1955-59; HM Consul-Gen Los Angeles 1959-64, HM Ambass Bolivia 1964-67; *Recreations* golf, gardening; *Style* - Sir Herbert Gamble, KBE, CMG; Santana, Delgany, Co Wicklow, Ireland (☎ 01 874189)

GAMMELL, James Gilbert Sydney; MBE (1944); s of Lt-Gen Sir James Gammell, KCB, DSO, MC; *b* 4 Mar 1920; *Educ* Winchester; *m* 1944, Susan Bowring Toms; 5 s, 1 da; *Career* chartered accountant 1949; chm Ivory and Sime Ltd 1975-; dir Bank of Scotland 1969-; Standard Life Assurance Co 1954-; *Style* - James Gammell Esq, MBE; Foxhall, Kirkliston, W Lothian, 3275

GANDAR, Hon Leslie Walter; JP; s of Max Gandar; *b* 26 Jan 1919; *Educ* Wellington Coll; Victoria U, Wellington; *m* 1945, Justine, nee Smith; *Career* New Zealand High Commissioner in UK 1979-; *Style* - The Hon Leslie Gandar, JP; 43 Chelsea sq, SW1 (☎ 01 352 9346)

GANDELL, Sir Alan Thomas; CBE (1959); s of William Gandell; *b* 8 Oct 1904; *Educ* Greymouth Dist High Sch; *m* 1933, Edna, nee Wallis; 1 s; *Career* FCIT; kt 1978; chllr Order of St John NZ 1972-; memb NZ National Ports Authority 1969-; *Style* - Sir Alan Gandell, CBE; 43 Donald st, Karori, Wellington 5, New Zealand (☎ 767 313)

GANE, Michael; s of Rudolf Gane; *b* 29 July 1927; *Educ* Us of Edinburgh, London and Oxford; *m* 1954, Madge Taylor; 1 da; *Career* dir England Nature Conservancy Council 1974-; *Style* - Michael Gane Esq; 12 Cartwright gdns, Aynho, nr Banbury, Oxon (☎ Croughton 810 694)

GANE, Richard Howard; s of Richard Gane; *b* 5 Nov 1912; *Educ* Kingston G S; *m* 1, 1939, Betty Franklin (d 1976); 2 s, 1 da; m 2, 1977, Elizabeth Gaymer; *Career* chm George Wimpey & Co Ltd 1973-76; *Style* - Richard Gane Esq; Woodlands, Cranley rd, Burwood pk, Walton-on-Thames, Surrey

GANILAU, Ratu Sir Penaia Kanatabatu; KBE (1974, OBE 1960), CMG (1968), CVO (1970), DSO (1956), ED (1974); *b* 28 July 1918; *Educ* in Fiji; *m* 1, 1949, Adi Laisa Dlaisomosomo Yavaca (decd); 5 s, 2 da; m 2, 1975, Adi Davila *Career* dep PM Fiji 1973-; min for Home Affairs 1975-; min for Fijian Affairs and Rural Development 1977-; *Style* - Ratu Sir Penaia Ganilau, KBE, CMG, CVO, DSO, ED; Ministry for Fijian Affairs, Sura, Fiji

GAON, Dr Solomon; s of Isaac Gaon; *b* 15 Dec 1912; *Educ* Jesuit Secondary Sch, Travnik, Yugoslavia; Jewish Teachers' Seminary, Sarajevo; Jews Coll, London U; *m* 1944, Regina Hassan; 1 s, 1 da; *Career* Haham (Chief Rabbi) Association of Sephardi Congregations 1977-; Haham of Communities affiliated to World Sephardi Federation in the Diaspora 1978-; *Style* - Dr Solomon Gaon; 25 Ashworth rd, W9 (☎ 01 289 1575)

GARDINER, Baron (Life Peer UK 1963); Gerald Austin Gardiner; CH (1975), PC (1964); s of Sir Robert Gardiner and Baroness Alice Marie, da of Baron Hermann Ludwig Wilhelm Karl Georg von Ziegesar; *b* 30 May 1900; *Educ* Harrow, Magdalen Oxford; *m* 1, 1925, Lesly (d 1966), da of Alderman Edwin Trouson, JP, of Penzance; 1 da; m 2, 1970, Muriel, da of Charles Baker, and formerly w of Sydney Box; *Career* barr 1925, KC 1948, Chm Gen Cncl Bar 1958 & 1959; LCC Alderman 1961-63; Lord High Chllr 1964-70; elected to Internat Commission of Jurists 1971; Chllr OU 1973-; served WW I 2 Lt Coldstream Gds; *Style* - Rt Hon Lord Gardiner CH PC; Mote End, Nan Clark's Lane, Mill Hill, NW7

GARDINER, Hon Carol; da of Baron Gardiner, CH, PC, QC, (Life Peer); *b* 1929; *Style* - The Hon Carol Gardiner; 109 East 89th st, New York 10028, USA

GARDINER, David Alfred William; s of Neil Gardiner, of Burghfield Common, Berks; *b* 11 April 1935; *Educ* Winchester, Imperial Coll London, Harvard Business Sch; *m* 1963, Carolyn, da of Thomas Naylor, of The Grange, Ashton, Chester; 2 s, 1 da; *Career* co dir Huntley & Palmers Assoc Biscuits (Europe) and A B Truck Servs; *Recreations* field sports; *Style* - David Gardiner Esq; The Old Rectory, Lilley, nr Newbury, Berks (☎ 04882 227)

GARDINER, (John) Duncan (Broderick); s of Frederick Gardiner; *b* 12 Jan 1937; *Educ* St Edward's Sch, Oxford; *m* 1965, Geraldine Mallen; 1 s, 1 da; *Career* newspaper ed; ed Western Mail; *Style* - Duncan Gardiner Esq;

GARDINER, Brig Richard; CB (1954), CBE (1946, OBE 1944); s of Maj Alec Gardiner (ka 1914); *b* 28 Oct 1900; *Educ* Uppingham, RMA Woolwich; *m* 1924, Catherine, da of Capt Victor Oliver, RN; 2 s; *Career* served 1920-53, India, M East BAOR; Dir Engr Stores War Off 1950-53, md Peruvian Corpn Peru 1954-63; *Style* - Brig Richard Gardiner, CB, CBE; Bridgham Farmhouse, Shamley Green, Guildford, Surrey (☎ Cranleigh 4546)

GARDINER, Hon Mrs (Susanna Catherine Crawshay); da of Baron Greenwood of Rossendale, PC (Life Peer); *b* 1943; *m* 1970, Christopher Gardiner; *Style* - The Hon Mrs Gardiner; 1 Oak Tree House, Redington gdns, NW3

GARDINER, Victor Alec; OBE (1977); *b* 9 Aug 1929; *Educ* Whitgift and City and Guilds Schs; *m* ; 1s, 2 da; *Career* dir and gen man London Weekend TV 1971-; dir London Weekend TV (Holdings) Ltd and London Weekend Services Ltd 1976-; chm Dynamic Technology Ltd and Standard Music Ltd 1972- ; *Style* - Victor Gardiner

Esq, OBE; The Gables, Sulhamstead, Reading, Berks

GARDNER, Barony of (I 1800, UK 1806); *see* Gardner, Alan Legge

GARDNER OF PARKES, Baroness (Life Peeress UK 1981); (Rachel) Trixie Anne; JP (N Westminster Inner London 1971); da of Hon Gregory McGirr (d 1949); *b* 17 July 1927; *Educ* Monte Sant Angelo Coll N Sydney, Sydney U; *m* 1956, Kevin, s of George Gardner; 3 da (Hon Sarah Gardner, Hon Rachel Gardner b 1961, Hon Joanna Gardner b 1964); *Career* dentist; memb Westminster City Cncl and GLC (Havering 1970-73, Enfield-Southgate 1977-), Con candidate Blackburn 1970 and N Cornwall 1974 Gen Elections; Br Chm European Union of Women 1978-; Gov Nat Heart Hosp 1974-; *Recreations* gardening, cooking, travel, historic buildings, family life; *Style* - Rt Hon Lady Gardner of Parkes JP; 10 Loudoun rd, NW8

GARDNER, Alan Legge; s of Alan Hyde Gardner (who claimed the Barony of Gardner, dormant from 1883, and who d 1891) and Jane, da of Unjem Shiko, of the Royal House of Delhi; *b* 25 Oct 1881; *Educ* Allahabad Govt Sch; *m* 1, 1908, Christiana (d 1918), da of D Wilson Gardner; 1 s; m 2, 1918, Ellen Orde; claims the dormant Barony of Gardner; *Style* - Alan Gardner Esq; Village Bhnowta, Dadri, Dist Bulandshahr, Uttar Pradesh, India

GARDNER, Cecil John; *Career* md Gardner's Transformers Ltd, winner of a Queen's Award for Export 1980; *Style* - Cecil Gardner Esq; Somerford, Christchurch, Dorset

GARDNER, John Linton; CBE (1976); s of Capt Alfred Linton Gardner RAMC (ka 1918); *b* 2 March 1917; *Educ* Wellington Coll, Exeter Coll Oxford; *m* 1955, Jane Margaret Mary, nee Abercrombie; 1 s, 2 da; *Career* ch music master Repton 1939-40, music staff Royal Opera House 1946-52, Prof Harmony and Composition RAM 1956-, dir of music Morley Coll 1965-69, dir of music St Paul's Girls' Sch 1962-75; *Recreations* tesseraphily, egrephily; *Style* - John Gardner Esq, CBE; 10 Lynton rd, New Malden, Surrey; c/o National Wesminster Bank, 1 Wimbledon Bridge, SW19

GARDNER, Trevelyan Codrington; CBE (1960); s of Lt-Cdr Thomas Gardner, DSC, RN (d 1928); *b* 3 Aug 1917; *Educ* Taunton's Sch, Queen's Coll Oxford; *m* 1944, Briege Theresa, nee Feehan; 2 s, 3 da; *Career* Maj Roy Hampshire Regt 1939-45, 1946-64 Colonial Service (incl Sec for Fin N Rhodesia 1958-60, Min of Fin N Rhodesia 1960-64), tres Cambridge U, fellow Wolfson Coll Cambridge; *Recreations* golf, gardening; *Clubs* Gog Magog Golf; *Style* - Trevelyan Gardner Esq, CBE; Hill Court, Whittlesford, Cambridge (☎ Cambridge 832483/358933)

GARDNER-THORPE, Col Sir Ronald Laurence; GBE (1980), TD (1950); s of the late J A Gardner-Thorpe; *b* 13 May 1917; *Educ* De La Salle Coll Southsea Hants, Univ of Padua; *m* 1938, Hazel Mary St George, nee Dees; 1 s; *Career* served in Europe, Central Mediterranean, USA, underwriting memb Lloyd's, Governor St John's Coll Hants 1963, JP Inner London 1965, and City of London 1969 (dep chm City of London 1970), v-pres British Red Cross City 1978, Hon Treasurer Inner London Magistrates, memb of Council of Magistrates Assoc; company director; *Clubs* Bishopsgate Ward, City Livery, United Wards, Royal Society of St George, The Belfry; *Style* -Col Sir Ronald Gardner-Thorpe, GBE,TD,JP; 8 Cadogan Square, London SW1 (☎ 01 235 0413)

GAREL-JONES, (William Armand Thomas) Tristan; MP (C) Watford 1979-; s of Bernard Garel-Jones; *b* 28 Feb 1941; *Educ* King's Sch, Canterbury; *m* 1966, Catalina, nee Garrigues; 4 s, 1 da; *Career* PPS to Barney Hayhoe *qv* 1981-; *Style* - Tristan Garel-Jones Esq, MP; 12 Catherine pla, SW1 (☎ 01 828 3348)

GARFITT, His Honour Judge; Alan; s of Rush Garfitt; *b* 20 Dec 1920; *Educ* King Edward VII G S, King's Lynn; Metropolitan Coll and Inns of Court Sch of Law; *m* 1, 1941, Muriel Jaggers; 1 s, 1 da;

m 2, 1973, Ivie Hudson; m 3, 1978, Rosemary Lazell; 1 s; *Career* barrister 1948; circuit judge 1977; *Style* - His Honour Judge Garfitt; Leap House, Barcham rd, Soham, Ely, Cambs

GARLAND, Douglas Walter; s of Frank Garland, of Sutton; *b* 5 May 1931; *Educ* Sutton County Sch; *m* 1953, Audrey, da of Cyril Plenty; 1 s, 2 da; *Career* FCA; commercial & fin dir Ross Nitrovit 1980-; chm Dalton Parish Cncl 1976-; *Recreations* squash; *Style* - Douglas Garland Esq; Pond House, Dalton, nr Thirsk, N Yorks (☎ 0845 577418)

GARLAND, Patrick Neville; QC (1972); s of Frank Neville Garland; *b* 22 July 1929; *Educ* Uppingham Sch, Sidney Sussex Coll Cambridge; *m* 1955, Jane Elizabeth, nee Bird; 2 s, 1 da; *Career* barr Middle Temple 1953, assist recorder Norwich 1971, Crown Court recorder 1972, bencher Middle Temple 1979; *Recreations* gardening, shooting, sailing, industrial archaeology; *Clubs* Cumberland Lawn Tennis, Grafham Sailing, Norfolk; *Style* - Patrick Garland Esq, QC; 9 Ranulf rd, NW2 (☎ 01 435 5877); 11 King's Bench Walk, Temple, EC4 (☎ 01 353 9281); 23 Grove rd, Norwich (☎ 0603 21820)

GARLAND, His Excellency Hon (Ransley) Victor; s of I V Garland; *b* 5 May 1934; *Educ* Hale Sch, W Australia U; *m* 1960, Lynette Jamieson; 2 s, 1 da; *Career* FCA, ACIS; memb House Reps (Lib) for Curtin, W Australia 1969-, Min Business & Consumer Affrs & Min Assisting Min for Indust & Commerce 1979-81; Australian High Commissioner London 1981-; *Style* - His Excellency The Hon Victor Garland; Australia House, Strand, WC2 (☎ 01 438 8000)

GARMOYLE, Viscount; Simon Dallas Cairns; s and h of 5 Earl Cairns; *b* 27 May 1939; *Educ* Eton, Cambridge U; *m* 1964, Amanda Mary, da of late Maj Edgar Fitzgerald Heathcoat-Amory; 3 s; *Heir* s, Hon Hugh Sebastian Cairns; *Career* dir Mercury Securities 1981-; *Style* - Viscount Garmoyle; Queen Hoo Hall, Tewin, Herts

GARNER, Baron (Life Peer UK 1969); Joseph John Saville Garner; GCMG (1965, KCMG 1954, CMG 1948); s of Joseph Garner, of Highgate; *b* 14 Feb 1908; *Educ* Highgate Sch, Jesus Cambridge; *m* 1938, Margaret, da of Herman Beckman, of Indiana; 2 s, 1 da; *Career* Head Diplomatic Serv 1965-68, Perm Under-Sec State C'wlth Off 1962-68; chm Inst C'wlth Studies & C'wlth Scholarship Commission, London Bd Bank of Adelaide; *Style* - Rt Hon Lord Garner GCMG; 1 Courtenay sq, SE11; Highdown Farm House, Horam, Sussex (☎ Chiddingly 432)

GARNER, Hon Christopher John Saville; s of Baron Garner, GCMG (Life Peer); *b* 28 Feb 1939; *Educ* Highgate, Jesus Cambridge; *m* 1962, Janet Mary, da of Maj Harold Vaughan Rees; 1 s; *Career* British Council officer 1963-71; assistant representative Freetown, Sierra Leone 1964-67; Staff Recruitment Dept, British Council London 1967-70, assistant representative, Athens, Greece 1970-71; lectr College of Technology, Bournemouth from 1971; *Style* - The Hon Christopher Garner; 11 Stokewood rd, Bournemouth, Hants

GARNER, Frederic Francis; CMG (1959); s of Frank Hastings Garner (d 1920); *b* 9 July 1910; *Educ* Rugby, Worcester Coll Oxford; *m* 1946, Muriel, nee Merrick; *Career* entered Br Consular Service in China 1932, served in various consular posts China and elsewhere. HM Ambass, Phnom Penh 1958-61, San Jose Costa Rica 1961-68, ret 1968; *Style* - Frederic Garner Esq, CMG; 44 Belgrave Mews, SW1 (☎ 01 235 7507)

GARNER, Frederick Leonard; s of Leonard Garner; *b* 7 Apr 1920; *Educ* Sutton County Sch; *m* 1953, Giovanna Anzani; *Career* chm Pearl Assurance Co from 1977; *Style* - Frederick Garner Esq; 98 Tudor ave, Worcester Park, Surrey (☎ 01 337 3313)

GARNER, Lady - Hilda Annie; da of John E Green, of Redhill; *m* 1921, Sir Harry Garner, KBE, CB, (d 1977); 1 s, 1 da ; *Style* - Lady Garner; 3 Grange rd, Camberley, Surrey (☎ 22736)

GARNER, Hon Joseph Jonathan; s of Baron Garner, GCMG (Life Peer); *b* 29 Dec 1940; *Educ* Highgate Sch, Jesus Cambridge; *m* 1969, Brigitte, da of Louis Pittet; 1 s ; *Style* - The Hon Joseph Garner; 44 Holmewood rd, SW2

GARNER , Anthony Stuart; s of Edward Garner; *b* 28 Jan 1927; *Educ* Liverpool Coll; *m* 1967, Shirley Taylor; *Career* dir of Organisation Conservative Central Office from 1976; *Style* - Anthony Garner Esq; 1 Blomfield rd, W9

GARNETT, (William) John (Poulton Maxwell); CBE (1970); s of Dr Maxwell Garnett, CBE; *b* 6 Aug 1921; *Educ* Rugby, Kent Sch (USA), Trinity Cambridge; *m* 1943, Barbara Rutherford-Smith; 2 s, 2 da; *Career* chm Spencer Stuart and Associates, management consultants 1979- *Style* - John Garnett Esq CBE; 31 Charlwood rd, SW15 (☎ 01 788 5248)

GARNETT, Hon Mrs; Hon Sylvia; da of Baron Swann (Life Peer); *m*, Christopher Garnett; *Style* - The Hon Mrs Garnett

GARNETT-ORME, Ian; s of George Garnett-Orme; *b* 23 Jan 1910; *Educ* Eton, Magdalene Cambridge; *m* 1946, Katharine Clifton Brown; *Career* dir Brown Shipley Holdings Ltd (chm 1963-75); dir United States Debenture Corpn Ltd 1951- (chm 1958-78); *Style* - Ian Garnett-Orme Esq; Founders Court, Lothbury, EC2

GARNIER, Thomas Stenhouse; s of Rev Thomas Garnier, OBE; *b* 26 Oct 1932; *Educ* Berkhamsted, Trin Oxford; *m* 1961, Heather, da of James Grant; 2 s, 2 da; *Career* md Kalamazoo Gp 1977-; *Recreations* riding, swimming, languages, bridge; *Style* - Thomas Garnier Esq; Manor Farm House, Alderton, nr Tewkesbury, Glos (☎ 024262 419)

GARNOCK, Viscount; David Bethune Lindesay-Bethune; s and h of 14 Earl of Lindsay; *b* 9 Feb 1926; *Educ* Eton, Magdalene Cambridge; *m* 1, 1953 (m dis 1968), the Hon Mary Clare Douglas Scott Montagu, da of 2 Baron Montagu of Beaulieu (d 1929); 1 s, 1 da; m 2, 1969, Penelope Georgina, da of late Anthony Crommelin Crossley, MP (himself only s of Sir Kenneth Crossley, 2 Bt), and formerly wife of Maj Henry Ronald Burn-Callander, MC; *Heir* s, Hon James Lindesay-Bethune (Master of Garnock); *Career* Scots Gds 1943-45, US & Canadian Railroads 1948-50, dir Carpets Internat Gp Services Ltd, Crossley-Karastan Carpet Mills Ltd, Crossley-Karastan Carpet Mills Ltd Canada, Festiniog Railway Co Ltd, patron Servern Valley Railway (Hldgs) Ltd, chm Romney Hythe and Dymchurch Light Rly Co 1976-, Sallingbury Ltd 1977-, dir Abbey Life Insur Co of Canada 1964-, Bain Dawes Ltd (Northern) 1978-, Bain Dawes (Canada) 1978-, Jubilee Park (Leisure Projects) Ltd 1979-, v-chm N American Adv Gp BOTB 1973-, v-pres Transport Trust 1973-, chm British Carpets Maufacturers Assoc Export Council 1976-, memb Roy Co Archers (Queen's Body Guard for Scotland) 1960-; *Clubs* Bath; *Style* - Viscount Garnock; Combermere Abbey, Whitchurch, Salop (☎ Burleydam 287); Coates House, Upper Largo, Fife

GARNOCK, Master of; Hon James Randolph Lindesay-Bethune; s (by 1 m) and h of Viscount Garnock; *b* 19 Nov 1955; *Style* - The Master of Garnock

GARNSWORTHY, Hon Charles Edyvean; s of Baron Garnsworthy, OBE (Life Peer, d 1974); *b* 1974; *Style* - The Hon Charles Garnsworthy

GARNSWORTHY, Baroness - Sue; da of Harold Taylor; *m* 1, Michael Farley; m 2, 1973, as his 2 w, Baron Garnsworthy, OBE (d 1974); 1 s; *Style* - The Rt Hon the Lady Garnsworthy; Little Dormers, Smithy Lane, Lower Kingswood, Tadworth, Surrey

GARRETT, Lady - Frances Margaret; *m* 1, -- Lipson-Ward; m 2, 1967, Sir Hugh Garrett, KCIE, CSI, (d 1978); *Style* - Lady Garrett; Hesketh Cottage, Hesketh rd, Torquay, Devon (☎ 23549)

GARRETT, Nicholas Young; s of Geoffrey Elmer Garrett, 73 The Strand, Walmer, Kent; *b* 5 June 1936; *Educ* Sherborne Sch, Worcester Oxford; *Career*

National Service 1954-6; 2 Lieut, Royal Artillery; slr, admitted 1962; *Clubs* Garrick; *Style* - Nicholas Garrett Esq; 6 Drayton Gdns, London, SW10 (☎ 370 2976)

GARRETT, Richard Anthony; s of Charles Garrett; *b* 4 July 1918; *Educ* King's Sch Worcester; *m* 1946, Marie, da of Rear-Adm Robin Dalglish; 1 s, 2 da (and 1 da decd); *Career* chm T J & J Smith Ltd 1978-, Frederick Muller Ltd, Nat Assoc Boys' Clubs 1980-; dir HTV 1978-; memb Heritage in Danger, Nat Cttee Electoral Reform, Glyndebourne Arts Tst; *Recreations* golf, gardening, music, opera, reading; *Clubs* Naval & Military, MCC, Bristol & Clifton Golf, Clifton Rugby, Clifton Cricket; *Style* - Richard Garrett Esq; Marlwood Grange, Thornbury, Bristol BS12 2JB (☎ Thornbury 412630)

GARRETT, Hon Sir Raymond William; AFC (1943), AEA (1945), JP; s of James John Percival Garrett (d 1914); *b* 19 Oct 1900; *Educ* Roy Melbourne Tech Coll, Melbourne U; *m* 1934, Vera Halliday, nee Lugton; 1 s, 2 da; *Career* kt 1973, pres Legislative Cncl Victoria 1968-76, chm Parliamentary Library Cttee and v-chm House Cttee 1968-76, chm of dirs Ilford (Aust) Pty Ltd 1969-75, dir Cine Serv Pty Ltd 1940-73, Life Gov Lady Nell Seeing Eye Dog Sch; *Recreations* photography, motoring; *Clubs* Air Force, Roy Auto of Victoria; *Style* - Hon Sir Raymond Garrett AFC AEA JP; Flat 4, 24 Tintern ave, Toorak, Victoria 3142, Australia

GARRETT, Lady - Shirley Lorraine; da of Stanley Hunter, of Melbourne, Victoria; *m* 1925, late Lt-Gen Sir Ragnar Garrett, KBE, CB; 1 s, 1 da; *Style* - Lady Garrett; 16 Blake ct, Mount Eliza, Victoria 3930, Australia

GARRETT, Terence; CBE (1967); s of Percy Herbert Garrett (d 1972); *b* 27 Sept 1929; *Educ* Alleyn's Sch, Caius Cambridge; *m* 1960, Grace Elizabeth Bridgeman, da of Rev Basil Braund; 2 s, 3 da; *Career* Instructor Lt Roy Navy, counsellor (science & tech) Br Embassy Bonn 1978-, sec to Bd Gov & Gen Conf Int Nat Atomic Energy Agency Vienna 1976-78, Int Tech Collaboration Unit Dept of Trade 1974-76, counsellor (scientific) Br Embassy Moscow 1962-66 & 1970-74; *Recreations* squash, travel; *Clubs* Roy Commonwealth Soc; *Style* - Terence Garrett Esq, CBE; Lime Tree Farmhouse, Chilton, Didcot, Oxon (☎ Abingdon 834521)

GARRETT, Hon Mrs (Valda Jean); *née* Vernon; da of 5 Baron Lyveden (d 1973); *b* 1918; *m* 1937, Basil George Garrett; 1 s, 3 da; *Style* - The Hon Mrs Garrett; 18 Tarikaka st, Ngaio, New Zealand

GARRIOCH, Sir (William) Henry; s of Alfred Garrioch and Jeanne Marie Madeleine Colin; *b* 4 May 1916; *Educ* Royal Coll, Mauritius; *m* 1964, Jeanne Louise Marie Thérèse Desvaux de Marigny; *Career* barrister 1952, ch justice Mauritius 1977-78; kt 1978; *Style* - Sir Henry Garrioch; Lees st, Curepipe, Mauritius (☎ 862708)

GARROD, Norman John; s of Frank Albert Garrod (d 1965); *b* 10 July 1924; *Educ* Alleyn's Sch Dulwich; *m* 1945, Beryl Portia, nee Bastow; 2 children; *Career* master printer, chm and md Garrod and Lofthouse Ltd; *Recreations* fishing; *Clubs* Garrick, RAC, No 10; *Style* - Norman Garrod Esq; 'Great Common', Big Common Lane, Bletchingley, Surrey (☎ Godstone 843375)

GARTHWAITE, (William) Mark Charles; s and h of Sir William Garthwaite, 2 Bt, DSC; *b* 4 Nov 1946; *Educ* Gordonstoun, Pennsylvania U; *m* 1979, Victoria, da of Gen Sir Henry Tuzo and formerly Mrs Hohler; 1 da; *Style* - Mark Garthwaite Esq

GARTHWAITE, Sir William Francis Cuthbert; 2 Bt (UK 1919), DSC (1941) and Bar (1942); s of Sir William Garthwaite, 1 Bt (d 1956); *b* 3 Jan 1906; *Educ* Bradfield Coll, Hertford Coll Oxford; *m* 1, 1931 (m dis 1937), Hon Dorothy, da of 1 Baron Duveen; m 2, 1945 (m dis 1952), Patricia Beatrice Eden, da of late Cdr Charles Eden Neate, RN, and wid of Cdr Barry Leonard, RN; 1 s; m 1957, Patricia Merriel, da of Sir Philip d'Ambrumenil; 3 s (inc twins); *Heir* s, (William) Mark

Garthwaite; *Career* Lt-Cdr (A) RNR, RN pilot and with RAF WW II; *Style* - Sir William Garthwaite, Bt, DSC*; Matfield House, Matfield, Kent (☎ Brenchley 2454)

GARTHWAITE, Hon Mrs (Waveney Mancroft); *née* Samuel; da of 1 Baron Mancroft (d 1942); *b* 1916; *m* 1950, Anthony William Garthwaite (d 1972), s of Sir William Garthwaite, 1 Bt (d 1956); 1 s; *Style* - The Hon Mrs Garthwaite; 98 Bickenhall Mansions, W1

GARTON, Hon Mrs (Annabel Jocelyne); da of 2 Viscount Hudson (d 1963, when the Viscountcy became ext); *b* 1952; *m* 1970, Anthony Juan Garton; 1 s, 1 da; *Style* - The Hon Mrs Garton; 8 Moncorvo Close, SW7

GARTON, John Leslie; CBE (1974, MBE 1946); s of Charles Leslie Garton (d 1940); *b* 1 April 1916; *Educ* Eton, Magdalen Coll Oxford; *m* 1939, Elizabeth Frances, da of Sir Walter Erskine Crum, OBE (d 1923); 2 s (and 1 s decd); *Career* Maj TA 1938-51, chm Coca-Cola Bottling Co (Oxford) Ltd 1951-65, chm Coca-Cola Western Bottlers Ltd 1966-71, High Sheriff Bucks 1977, Thames Conservator 1970-74, chm Henley Royal Regatta 1966-77, pres 1978-, pres Amateur Rowing Assoc 1969-77 (hon life v-pres 1978-), Capt of Leander 1946 (chm 1958-59, pres 1980) chm World Rowing Championships 1975, British Olympic Assoc Finance and Gen Purposes Ctee 1969-77; *Recreations* shooting, fishing, supporting the sport of rowing; *Clubs* Leander; *Style* - John Garton Esq, CBE; Fingest Manor, Henley-on-Thames, Oxfordshire (☎ Turville Heath 332)

GARTON, Lady Lucy Catherine Mary; *née* Primrose; da of 7 Earl of Rosebery, DL; *b* 29 Dec 1955; *Educ* Benenden; *m* 1976, (Anthony Gavin) Charles, s of Anthony Garton, of Hyde Pk Gdns; 1 child decd; *Style* - Lady Lucy Garton; 1/37 Wilton cres, SW1 (☎ 01 235 5747)

GARVAGH, 5 Baron (UK 1818); (Alexander Leopold Ivor) George Canning; s of 4 Baron (d 1956, himself s of 3 Baron by Florence, MBE, da of Baron Joseph de Bretton (of a Danish cr, either that of Christian VII of 1767 or the one of Frederick V of 1763), of Copenhagen; the 3 Baron was in his turn 1 cous once removed of George Canning, briefly PM in 1827, and Stratford Canning, cr Viscount Stratford de Redcliffe, & Ambass to the Sublime Porte 1841-58; the latter's naturally hasty temper, not wholly stifled by a lifetime in diplomatic braid (for he sparred with John Quincey Adams when *en poste* at Washington 1819-23), was allowed full vent in retirement - on an outing in Italy in 1858 he ordered a miller to divert a stream that crossed a road awkwardly and, returning later that day, was enraged to find his wishes not observed; he also wrote poetry (and was praised by Byron in youth) and was one of the last MPs to sit for that most notorious of rotten boroughs, Old Sarum, which he did briefly in 1829); *b* 6 Oct 1920; *Educ* Eton, Ch Ch Oxford; *m* 1, 1947 (m dis 1973), Edith, da of Jack Cooper, of Worplesdon; 1 s, 2 da; m 2, 1974, Cynthia, da of Eric Pretty, CMG; *Heir* s, Hon Spencer George Stratford de Redcliffe Canning; *Career* Pres Disaster Relief Assoc; served Indian Army WW II in Burma; chm Lord Garvagh & Ptnrs, Stonehaven Tankers, Independent Chartering, Gow Wilson Ltd; dir AODC (UK), Craftroad Ltd; consultant ptnr Stummel Towning Co; memb Baltic Exchange; MBIM, Fellow IOD; *Style* - The Rt Hon Lord Garvagh; Lyzzick Gate, Millbeck, Keswick, Cumbria; 12 South End Row, W8

GARVAGH, Dora, Baroness; Gladys Dora May; da of Bayley Parker, of Edgbaston; *m* 1, Lt-Col D M Dimmer, VC; m 2, 1919, as his 2 w, 4 Baron Garvagh (d 1956); 2 s (5 Baron, 1 s ka 1944), 2 da (Hon Mrs Sutcliffe, Hon Mrs Svenningson); *Style* - The Rt Hon Dora, Lady Garvagh; Lyzzick Gate, Millbeck, Keswick, Cumbria

GARVEY, Sir Ronald Herbert; KCMG (1950), KCVO (1953), MBE (1940); s of Rev Herbert Richard Garvey (d 1955); *b* 4 July 1903; *Educ* Trent Coll, Emmanuel Coll Cambridge; *m* 1934, Patricia Dorothy Edge, da of Dr V W T McGusty CMG OBE; 1 s (Richard), 3 da (Grania, Lavinia, Julia); *Career* KStJ 1954, entered Colonial

Service 1926 W Pacific High Cmmn, Acting Gov Windward Is BWI 1946 1948, Gov and C-in-C Br Honduras 1948-52, Gov and C-in-C Fiji and Gov Pitcairn Is, Consul-Gen Western Pacific, Sr Cmmr for UK in S Pacific Cmmn 1952-58, Lt-Gov Isle of Man 1959-66; dir Garveys (London) SA; memb East Anglian Tourist Bd; *Recreations* golf, gardening, eating and drinking Garvey sherry, writing; *Clubs* Royal Commonwealth Soc; *Style* - Sir Ronald Garvey, KCMG, KCVO, MBE; The Priory, Wrentham, Beccles, Suffolk (☎ 050 275 274), Hambleton House, 17 B Curzon st, W1

GASCOIGNE, Hon Mrs; Hon (Elizabeth) Ann; *née* Harcourt; da of 2 & last Viscount Harcourt by his 1 w Hon Maud Grosvenor (da of 4 Baron Ebury); *b* 1932; *m* 1954, Crispin Gascoigne, s of Maj-Gen Sir Julian Gascoigne, KCMG, KCVO, CB, DSO; *Style* - The Hon Mrs Gascoigne; Ronans, Winkfield Row, Bracknell, Berks

GASCOIGNE, (Arthur) Bamber; s of Derrick (Ernest Frederick) Gascoigne (of the old Yorks family dating back to the 14 century, and gggs of Gen Isaac Gascoigne, whose er bro's da Frances was the Gascoigne heiress who m 2 Marquess of Salisbury, whence also the Salisbury family name of Gascoyne-Cecil) and Hon Mary (Midi), sis of 3 Baron O'Neill (through which connection Mr Gascoigne belongs to the oldest traceable family in Europe, the O'Neills of the Irish Royal House of Tara, records of which date from AD 360); also half-cous once removed to Quentin Crewe, *qv*; *b* 24 Jan 1935; *Educ* Eton, Magdalene Cambridge; *m* 1965, Christina Ditchburn; *Career* author and TV presenter, notably of 'University Challenge' and 'The Christians'; *Style* - Bamber Gascoigne Esq; 1 St Helena ter, Richmond, Surrey; c/o Jonathan Cape, 30 Bedford sq, WC1

GASCOIGNE, Hon Mrs (Mary Louisa Hermione); *née* O'Neill; da of late Capt the Hon Arthur Edward Bruce O'Neill, MP (ka 1914) and sis of 3 Baron O'Neill (d 1944); *b* 1905; *m* 1934, Lt-Col (Derick) Ernest Frederick Orby Gascoigne, (d 1972) s of Brig-Gen Sir (Ernest) Frederick (Orby) Gascoigne, KCVO, CMG, DSO; 2 s (Bamber Gascoigne, *qv*, Brian), 1 da (Hon Mrs William Plowden); *Style* - The Hon Mrs Gascoigne; 162 Cranmer Court, Whiteheads Grove, SW3 (☎ 01 581 1903)

GASCOYNE-CECIL, *see* Cecil

GASELEE, Nick (Nicholas Auriol Digby Charles); s of Lt-Col Auriol Stephen Gaselee, OBE, of Tonbridge; *b* 30 Jan 1939; *Educ* Charterhouse; *m* 1966, Judith Mary, da of Dr Gilmer; 1 s (James Dominic, b 31 May 1968), 1 da (Sarah Jane, *qv*); *Career* Life Gds 1958-63; racing trainer to HRH The Prince of Wales; *Recreations* coursing; *Clubs* Turf; *Style* - Nicholas Gaselee Esq; Saxon Cottage, Upper Lambourn, Berks (☎ Lambourn 71503)

GASELEE, Sarah Jane; da of Nick Gaselee, *qv*; *b* 2 June 1970; *Educ* Southover Manor, Lewes; *Career* bridesmaid to Lady Diana Spencer at her marriage to HRH The Prince of Wales 1981; *Style* - Miss Sarah Jane Gaselee; Saxon Cottage, Upper Lambourn, Berks (☎ Lambourn 71503)

GASKELL, William Peter; CBE (1964, MBE 1953); s of William Gaskell, late Headmaster Lawrence Roy Mil Sch Sanawar India; *b* 9 June 1914; *Educ* Dragon Sch Oxford, Blundell's, Sch of Metalliferous Mining Camborne; *Career* Capt Roy W Africa Frontier Force, mining engr Colonial Service 1937-64 (incl Ch Insp of Mines Nigeria 1952-64); lectr Sch of Management & Business Studies Brooklands Coll Weybridge 1965-74; *Recreations* badminton, singing, motoring; *Clubs* Royal Commonwealth Soc; *Style* - William Gaskell Esq, CBE; 3 Cove Row, Weymouth, Dorset (☎ Weymouth 74067)

GASS, Sir Michael (David Irving); KCMG (1969, CMG 1960); s of George Irving Gass (d 1947); *b* 24 April 1916; *Educ* King's Sch Bruton, Ch Ch Oxford, Queens' Coll Cambridge; *m* 1975, Elizabeth Periam, da of late Hon John Palmer Fuller-Acland-Hood (d 1964, 2 s of 1 Baron St Audries); *Career* Maj The Gold Coast Regt, HM Overseas Civil Serv (ret), Assist Dist Cmmr Gold Coast 1939 (Dist

Cmmr 1945), Assist Regional Offr Ashanti 1953, Permanent Sec Min of the Interior Ghana 1957, Ch Sec to Western Pacific Cmmn 1958, Colonial Sec Hong Kong 1965, High Cmmr for Western Pacific and Br High Cmmr for New Hebrides 1969, ret 1973, elected memb Somerset CC 1977; *Recreations* ornithology; *Clubs* East India, Devonshire, Sports and Public Schools (London), Hong Kong (Hong Kong); *Style* - Sir Michael Gass, KCMG; Fairfield, Stogursey, Bridgwater, Somerset (☎ Nether Stowey 732251)

GASTAMBIDE, Philippe; QC (1979); s of Maurice Gastambide and Marthe, nee Kullman; *b* 30 Sept 1905; *Educ* Sorbonne, Ch Ch Oxford; *m* 1, 1931, Pascale Miraband (decd); 1 s, 2 da; m 2, 1970, Nicole Vingtain; *Career* barr 1934; avocat honoraire a la Cour de Paris 1979; *Style* - Philippe Gastambide Esq, QC; 4 Rue d'Anjou, 75008 Paris (☎ 266 13 44)

GATES, Malcolm Gilbert; s of the late Douglas Gilbert Gates; *b* 6 March 1940; *Educ* Wallington Sch Surrey, Southampton U; *m* 1963, Valerie Diane, nee Hudson; 3 c; *Career* md Royal Trust Bank (Jersey) Ltd, dir- The Royal Trust Company of Canada (CI) Ltd, Quest Fund Management (Jersey) Ltd, International Investment Trust Co Ltd; *Recreations* golf, sailing; *Clubs* Victoria, Royal Commonwealth; *Style* - Malcolm Gates Esq; Les Arbres, Grouville, Jersey, CI

GATHORNE-HARDY, Hon Argus Edward; s of 5 Earl of Cranbrook, *qv*; *b* 1973

GATHORNE-HARDY, Hon Mrs Antony - Mary Catherine; da of late Bernard Joseph Smartt; *m* 1974, as his 2 w, Cdr the Hon Antony Gathorne Gathorne-Hardy, MB, ChB (s of late 3 Earl of Cranbrook and Lady Dorothy Montagu Boyle, da of 7 Earl of Glasgow, and who d 1976); *Style* - The Hon Mrs Antony Gathorne-Hardy; 21 Cranebrook, Manor rd, Twickenham, Middx

GATHORNE-HARDY, Lady Flora; da of 5 Earl of Cranbrook, *qv*; *b* 1971

GATHORNE-HARDY, Hon Hugh; s of late 4 Earl of Cranbrook by 2 w, Fidelity (*see* Dowager Countess of Cranbrook); *b* 1941; *Educ* Eton, CCC Cambridge; *m* 1971, Caroline Elisabeth, da of William Nigel Ritchie (gs of 1 Baron Ritchie of Dundee) and Baroness Sibylla (da of late Baron van Hirschberg, of Murnau, Bavaria); 1 s; *Style* - The Hon Hugh Gathorne-Hardy; Great Glemham House, Saxmundham, Suffolk (☎ Rendham 543)

GAU, John Glen Mackay; s of Cullis Gau and Nan Munro; *b* 25 March 1940; *Educ* Haileybury, Trinity Hall Cambridge, Wisconsin U; *m* 1966, Susan Tebbs; 2 s; *Career* head of Current Affairs Programmes BBC TV 1978-; *Style* - John Gau Esq; 82 Home Park rd, SW19 (☎ 01 946 4686)

GAUDRY, Roger; CC (1968); *b* 15 Dec 1913; *Educ* Laval and Oxford U; *m* 1941, Madeleine Vallée; 2 s, 3 da; *Career* FRSC; pres International Assoc of Universities 1975-; *Style* - Roger Gaudry Esq, CC; 445 Beverley ave, Mount Royal, Montreal

GAULT, David Hamilton; s of Leslie Gault; *b* 9 Apr 1928; *Educ* Fettes; *m* 1950, Felicity Gribble; 3 s, 2 da; *Career* exec chm Gallic Management; *Style* - David Gault Esq; Telegraph House, N Marden, Chichester, W Sussex (☎ Harting 206)

GAUNT, David; s of Edgar Gaunt, of Hawksworth Hall, Guiseley, Yorks; *b* 29 June 1920; *Educ* Winchester, Magdalene Cambridge; *m* 1965, Elizabeth, da of William Robertson, of Helensburgh; *Career* former Capt served N Africa, Italy, Balkans; chm Reuben Gaunt & Sons, dir Robertson Res Hldgs; Pres Bradford Chamber of Commerce 1961, High Sheriff W Yorks 1977-78; *Recreations* fishing, shooting, gardening; *Clubs* Special Forces, Shrievalty Assoc; *Style* - David Gaunt Esq; The Nunnery, Arthington, Otley, W Yorks (☎ 0532 886236)

GAUNT, James Harold; s of James Gaunt (d 1965); *b* 22 April 1910; *Educ* in Edinburgh; *m* 1943, Flora, nee Copland; 1 da; *Career* chm Steel Bros Hldgs Ltd 1970- *Style* - James Gaunt Esq; Palfreys, Park Lane, Ashtead, Surrey (☎ 72675)

GAUSSEN, Hon Mrs (Diana Bridget); da of late Hon Robert Godfrey de Bohun Devereux (only s of 17 Viscount Hereford); *b* 1931; *m* 1967, Major Samuel Charles Casamaijor Gaussen, Welsh Gds; 1 s, 1 da; raised to the rank of a Viscount's da 1953; *Style* - The Hon Mrs Gaussen; 22 St Mary Abbot's ter, W14; Nutbeam, Duntisbourne Leer, Cirencester, Glos

GAUTREY, H; *Career* sec Halifax Bldg Soc; *Style* - H Gautrey Esq; c/o Halifax Bldg Soc, Trinity rd, Halifax, Yorks

GAVINS, A S; *Career* assist gen man Leeds Permanent Bldg Soc; *Style* - A S Gavins Esq; c/o Leeds Permanent Building Soc, Permanent House, The Headrow, Leeds LS1 1NS

GAZARETH, Prosper George; *Career* md Michelin Tyre Co; *Style* - Prosper Gazareth Esq; c/o Michelin Tyre Co, Campbell rd, Stoke-on-Trent, Staffs

GAZE, Michael Anthony; *Career* chm Nat Carbonising Co Ltd; *Style* - Michael Gaze Esq; c/o National Carbonising Ltd, Thorney House, 34 Smith sq, SW1

GEDDES OF EPSOM, Baron (Life Peer UK 1958); Charles John Geddes; CBE (1950); s of Thomas Varney Geddes; *b* 1 March 1897; *Educ* Blackheath Central Sch; *m* 1920, Julia, da of Cornelius Burke; 1 da; *Career* kt 1957; chm Polyglass Ltd; served WW II Lt RFC; late Gen Sec PO Workers Union, Pres TUC 1954-55; *Style* - Rt Hon Lord Geddes of Epsom CBE; 5 Cleeve Close, Framfield, Sussex (☎ 562)

GEDDES, 3 Baron (UK 1942); Euan Michael Ross Geddes; s of 2 Baron, KBE (d 1975); *b* 3 Sept 1937; *Educ* Rugby, Gonville & Caius Cambridge, Harvard Business Sch; *m* 1966, Gillian, da of William Butler, of Henley; 1 s, 1 da; *Heir* s, Hon James George Neil Geddes *Career* dir Hare Court Investment Co, Geddes & Co; *Clubs* Brooks's; *Style* - The Rt Hon Lord Geddes; 83 Kingsway, WC2 (☎ 01 405 8621)

GEDDES, Hon David Campbell; TD; s of 1 Baron Geddes, GCMG, KCB, PC (d 1954); *b* 11 March 1917; *Educ* Stowe, Gonville and Caius Cambridge; *m* 1948, Gerda, da of State Cllr Gerdt Meyer Brunn, of Bergen, Norway; 2 da; *Career* dir Jardine Matheson Hongkong 1953-58 & assoc cos; joined RA 1938, served 1939-45 on staff, Maj 1943; civil servant Foreign & Commonwealth Office, Overseas Dvpt Administration (Princ 1969-77); FRGS; *Style* - The Hon David Geddes TD; Oldhouse Farm, Hildenborough, Tonbridge, Kent

GEDDES, Enid, Baroness; Enid Mary; da of Clarence Howell Butler, of Tenterden, Kent; *m* 1931, 2 Baron Geddes (d 1975); 2 s (3 Baron & 1 s decd), 1 da (Hon Mrs van Koetsveld); *Style* - The Rt Hon Enid, Lady Geddes; 12 Courtenay pla, Lymington, Hants

GEDDES, Ford Irvine; MBE (Mil 1943); s of Irvine Campbell Geddes, whereby he is 1 cous of Sir Reay Geddes and 1 cous once removed of 3 Baron Geddes; *b* 17 Jan 1913; *Educ* Loretto, Caius Cambridge; *m* 1945, Barbara, da of Charles Parry Okeden; 1 s (David b 1959), 4 da (Jennian b 1947; Mrs Michael (Merryn) Lloyd; Fiona b 1950; Ailie b 1956); *Career* late chm P&O Steam Navigation Co (dir 1960-72); memb London Advsy Bd Bank of NSW 1950-; *Clubs* City of London, Union (Sydney); *Style* - Ford Geddes Esq, MBE; The Manor, Berwick St John, Shaftesbury, Dorset (☎ Donhead 363)

GEDDES, Guy Turner; s of Col Guy Westland Geddes, DSO, OBE, DL, of Guildford (d 1955); *b* 15 June 1930; *Educ* Charterhouse; *m* 1; 1 s, 2 da; m 2, 1976, Marcela, da of Adm Julio Giannotti Landa, CIC Peruvian Navy; 1 s (1 step s); *Career* dir Hogg Robinson Gp 1975, md Hogg Robinson Int & Reinsurance 1980; *Recreations* painting, fishing; *Clubs* Carlton; *Style* - Guy Geddes Esq; 28 Sussex st, SW1 (☎ 01 834 1609)

GEDDES, Hon James George Neil; s and h of 3 Baron Geddes; *b* 10 Sept 1969; *Style* - The Hon James Geddes

GEDDES, Hon John Reay Campbell; TD; s of 1 Baron Geddes GCMG KCB PC (d 1954); *b* 1915; *Educ* Stowe, Edinburgh U and London U; *m* 1944,

Diana Elizabeth, JP, da of Brig Charles Copley Swift, OBE, MC, and late Mrs W M Henning, of Frome House, Dorset; 1 s; *Career* Maj Roy Tank Regt (TA) 1938-46 (wounded), Lt Roy Gloucester Hussars 1947, Capt 1949; advr on public relations to chm of Pearson Longman Ltd and The Financial Times; *Clubs* Brooks's; *Style* - The Hon John Geddes TD; 15 Merrick sq, Southwark, SE1 (☎ 01 407 7569); Ballynew, Moyard, Co Galway

GEDDES, Hon Mrs Alexander; HSH Altgräfin Marie-Anne Helena Emmanuela; da of HSH 6 Prince (Franz Joseph) of Salm-Reiffersheidt, Krautheim und Dyck; *m* 1964, as his 2 w, Col Hon Alexander Campbell Geddes, OBE, MC, TD, (d 1972, s of 1 Baron Geddes); 1 s, 1 da; *Style* - The Hon Mrs Alexander Geddes; Petersham Lodge, Richmond, Surrey; 12 Courtenay pla, Lymington, Hants

GEDDES, Hon Margaret Clair; da of 3 Baron Geddes; *b* 1967; *Style* - The Hon Margaret Geddes

GEDDES, Sir (Anthony) Reay Mackay; KBE (1968, OBE 1943); s of Rt Hon Sir Eric Geddes, GCB, GBE, PC, and 1 cous once removed of 3 Baron Geddes; *b* 7 May 1912; *Educ* Rugby, Magdalene Cambridge; *m* 1938, Imogen, da of Capt Hay Matthey; 2 s (Duncan, b 1942, educ Eton & Magdalene Cambridge, m 1968 Contessa Donatella, da of Conte Nardi dei Flaccomio, of Florence; Piers b 1950, educ Eton), 3 da (Alison m Capt Martin Dean Coldstream Gds, Lindsay b 1946, Candida b 1948); *Career* Hon Pres Dunlop Hldgs 1978- (chm 1968-78); dep chm Midland Bank 1978- (dir 1967-), dir Shell T'port & Trading 1968-, Rank Org 1975-; served RAFVR WW II; *Style* - Sir Reay Geddes, KBE; 13 Wilton Crescent, SW1 (☎ 01 235 5179)

GEE, Geoffrey; CBE (1958); s of Thomas Gee (d 1962); *b* 6 June 1910; *Educ* New Mills Sch, Manchester U, Cambridge U; *m* 1934, Marion, nee Bowden; 1 s, 2 da; *Career* FRS 1951, dir of research, Br Rubber Producers Research Assoc 1947-53, Prof of Chemistry Manchester U 1953-77 (with periods of appointment as Pro-V-Chllr); *Recreations* gardening; *Clubs* Royal Society; *Style* - Geoffrey Gee Esq, CBE; 8 Holmfield Drive, Cheadle Hume, Cheshire (☎ 061 485 3713)

GEE, Hon Mrs (Joan Mary); da of 1 Baron Hives, MBE, PC (d 1965); *b* 1917; *m* 1939, Adrian Gee; 2 da; *Style* - The Hon Mrs Gee; The Knoll House, Duffield Bank, Duffield, Derbys

GELBER, Lady Henrietta (Mary); *née* Spencer-Churchill; da of 11 Duke of Marlborough; *b* 1958; *m* 1980, Nathan Gelber; *Style* - Lady Henrietta Gelber

GELL, Peter Donald Marriott; s of Harold Gell, MC, of Chipping Campden, Glos; *b* 17 March 1929; *Educ* Sherborne, Worcester Coll Oxford; *m* 1960, Jean, da of Lt-Col David Livingstone Graham, of Crowborough; 1 s, 3 da; *Career* FCA, FCIS; dir Bunzl Pulp & Paper; *Recreations* music, field sports; *Style* - Peter Gell Esq; Shearings, Witheridge Lane, Penn, Bucks (☎ 3243)

GELLHORN, Hon Mrs (Olive Shirley); da of 1 Baron Layton (d 1966); *b* 1918; *m* 1943, Peter Gellhorn, the conductor; 2 s, 2 da; *Career* music teacher; *Recreations* concerts and plays; *Style* - The Hon Mrs Gellhorn; 33 Leinster ave, SW14 7JW

GENT, Marcus James; OBE (1974); s of of Sir Edward Gent, KCMG, DSO, OBE, MC (d 1948); *b* 5 Feb 1925; *Educ* Malvern; Trinity Coll, Oxford; *m* 1952, Marian Elizabeth, da of Lancelot Newling Rawes (d 1976); 4 da; *Career* barrister 1950, chm The Guthrie Corp Ltd 1979; *Style* - Marcus Gent Esq OBE; 15 South Terrace, SW7 (☎ 01 581 2443)

GEOFFREY-LLOYD, Baron (Life Peer UK 1974); Geoffrey William Lloyd; PC (1943); s of G Lloyd, of Newbury; *b* 17 Jan 1902; *Educ* Harrow, Trin Cambridge; *Career* MP (C) Birmingham Ladywood 1931-45, King's Norton 1950-55, Sutton Coldfield 1955-74; PPS to Stanley Baldwin as PM 1935, Sec Petroleum 1940-42, Parly Sec Min Fuel & Power 1942-45, Gov BBC 1946-49, Min Fuel & Power 1951-55, Educn 1957-59; chm Leeds Castle Fndn 1974-; *Clubs* Carlton, Pratt's, Roy Yacht

Sqdn; *Style* - Rt Hon Lord Geoffrey-Lloyd PC; 77 Chester sq, SW1 (☎ 01 730 0014)

GEORGE, John Charles Grossmith; s of Col Edward Harry George, OBE (d 1957); *b* 15 Dec 1930; *Educ* Ampleforth; *m* 1972, Margaret Mary Maria Mercedes, da of Maj Edric Humphrey Weld, TD, JP (d 1969); *Career* Lt (Nat Serv), College of Arms 1963-72, Garioch Pursuivant of Arms 1976-, cncl memb The Heraldry Soc 1976-, dir of ceremonies The British Assoc Sov Mil Order Malta 1976-80, FSA (Scot) 1975-, Kt of Obedience Sov Mil Order of Malta 1975, Kt of Grace & Devotion 1971, Offr of the Ord Pro Merito Melitensi 1980; author; *Books* The Puffin Book of Flags; *Recreations* 19th century English operetta, hagiography, astronomy; *Style* - John George Esq; 15 Kennington Palace Court, Sancroft st, SE11 (☎ 01 735 6712)

GEORGE, Miss Mary; CBE (1974, MBE 1953); da of Percy John George (d 1959); *b* 18 Oct 1912; *Educ* Roy Holloway Coll, London U; *Career* HM Privy Purse Office 1934-37, Amalgamated Press Ltd 1937-42, assist princ Dominions Office 1942-45, info offr Miny of Food 1954-52, princ info offr Miny of Ag Fish & Food 1952-56, dir Electrical Assoc for Women 1956-75, chm Consumer Standards Advisory Ctee of Br Standards Inst and Over Forty Assoc for Women Workers; past chm Nat Soc for Clean Air; *Recreations* reading, gardening, painting; *Style* - Miss Mary George, CBE; Rabs Cottage, Cousley Wood, Wadhurst, E Sussex

GEORGE, W A ; *Career* md Weetabix Ltd; *Style* - W A George Esq; Weetabix Mills, Burton Latimer, Kettering, Northants

GEORGE-BROWN, Baron (Life Peer UK 1970); George Alfred George-Brown; PC (1951); s of George Brown; *b* 2 Sept 1914; *m* 1937, Sophie, da of Solomon Levene, JP; 2 da; *Career* changed name to George-Brown 1970; MP (L) Belper 1945-70, Dep Ldr Labour Pty 1960-70, Pres SDA 1981; Min of Works 1951, Ec Affrs Sec & chm NEDC 1964-66, For Sec 1966-68; industl cllr Courtaulds 1968-73; dir Br Northrop, GT Japan Investment Tst, Commercial Credit Servs Hldgs; chm G C Turner Gp, J Compton Sons & Webb 1980-; *Style* - Rt Hon Lord George-Brown PC; Sharon, Jevington, Sussex

GERAGHTY, Lady - Lilian Irene; da of Frederick Glover Travis, of New Malden, Surrey; *m* 1946, Sir William Geraghty, KCB, (d 1977); *Style* - Lady Geraghty; 11 Kelvin Grove, Chessington, Surrey (☎ Lower Hook 3721)

GERAHTY, Lady - Violet; *m* 1, Watson; 2, as his 3 w, Sir Charles Gerahty, JP, (d 1978); *Style* - Lady Gerahty

GERARD, 4 Baron (UK 1876): Sir Robert William Alwyn Frederick Gerard; 16 Bt (E 1611); s of 3 Baron, MC (d 1953) by his cous Mary, da of Sir Martin Gosselin, GCVO, KCMG, CB, and Hon Katharine Gerard (2 da of 1 Baron); *b* 23 May 1918; *Educ* Ampleforth; *Heir* 2 cous once removed, Anthony Gerard; *Style* - Rt Hon Lord Gerard; Blakesware, Ware, Herts (☎ 3665)

GERARD, Anthony Robert Hugo; s of Maj Rupert Gerard, MBE (d 1978, great nephew of 2 Baron); hp to 2 cous once removed, 4 Baron Gerard; *b* 3 Dec 1949; *Style* - Anthony Gerard Esq

GERARD, Hon Heloise Katherine; da of of 3 Baron Gerard (d 1953); *b* 1911; *Style* - The Hon Heloise Gerard; Blakesware, Ware, Herts (☎ 3665)

GERBER, F; *Career* chm Roche Products Ltd; *Style* - F Gerber Esq; 40 Broadwater rd, Welwyn Garden City, Herts

GERKEN, Rear-Adm Robert William Frank; CBE; *aet* 48 in June 1981; *Career* Capt Fleet (CIC Fleet's Staff at Northwood Middx) to 1981, Rear-Adm July 1981-, Flag Offr 2 Flotilla, Capt 1972-81; sometime Directing Staff RN Staff Coll; *Style* - Rear-Adm Robert Gerken, CBE; c/o MOD Main Building, Whitehall, SW1 (☎ 01 218 9000)

GERMAINE, E S; *Career* gen man Leeds Permanent Building Society; *Style* - E S Germaine Esq; Permanent House, The Headrow, Leeds LS1 INS

GERRARD, R E; *Career* chm Walkers Crisps Ltd; *Style* - R E Gerrard Esq; Feature rd, Thurmaston, Leics

GERRARD, Ronald Tillbrook; s of Henry Gerrard; *b* 23 April 1918; *Educ* Imperial Coll of Science and Technology, London U; *m* 1950, Cecilia Brenner; 3 s, 1 da; *Career* sr ptnr Binnie and Partners consulting engrs 1974-; *Style* - Ronald Gerrard Esq; 6 Ashdown rd, Epsom, Surrey (☎ 24834)

GERRARD-WRIGHT, Maj-Gen Richard Eustace John; CBE (1977, OBE 1971, MBE 1965); s of of Rev R L Gerrard-Wright; *b* 9 May 1930; *Educ* Christ's Hospital; Sandhurst; *m* 1960, Susan Young; 2 s, 2 da; *Career* G O C Eastern dist from 1980; *Style* - Maj-Gen Richard Gerrard-Wright CBE; c/o Lloyds Bank Ltd, Cox's and Kings Branch, 6 Pall Mall, SW1

GESTETNER, David; *Career* jt chm Gestetner Holdings Ltd; *Style* - David Gestetner Esq; 41 Fawley rd, Tottenham , N17

GETHIN, Richard Joseph St Lawrence; s and h of Sir Richard Gethin, 9 Bt; *b* 29 Sept 1949; *m* 1974, Jacqueline, da of Cdr David Cox; 2 da; *Style* - Richard Gethin Esq; Greystones, Faringdon, Oxon

GETHIN, Lt-Col Sir Richard Patrick St Lawrence; 9 Bt (I 1665), of Gethinsgrott, Cork; s of Col Sir Richard Walter St Lawrence Gethin, 8 Bt, CMG, DSO (d 1946); *b* 15 May 1911; *Educ* Oundle; *m* 1946, Fara (2 Offr WRNS), da of late J H Bartlett; 1 s, 4 da; *Heir* s, Richard Joseph St Lawrence Gethin; *Career* Lt-Col REME, ret 1957; author of *Restoring Antique Furniture* 1974; *Style* - Lt-Col Sir Richard Gethin, Bt; Easter Cottage, Bredon, nr Tewkesbury, Glos (☎ Bredon 72354)

GETHING, Air Cdre Richard Templeton; CB (1960), OBE (1945), AFC (1939); s of George Gething; *b* 11 Aug 1911; *Educ* Malvern, Sydney Sussex Cambridge; *m* 1940, Margaret, da of late Sir Herbert Gepp; 1 s, 1 da; *Style* - Air Cdre Richard Gething, CB, OBE, AFC; Garden Hill, Kangaroo Ground, Victoria 3097, Australia

GIBB, Hon Mrs (Annabel Martha); *née* Howie; da of Baron Howie of Troon; *b* 1956; *m* 1979, -- Gibb; *Style* - The Hon Mrs Gibb

GIBB, Bill (William Elphinstone); s of George Gibb, of New Pitsligo, Aberdeenshire; *b* 23 Jan 1943; *Educ* Fraserburgh Acad, St Martin's Sch of Art, RCA; *Career* couturier; Vogue Designer of the Year 1970; *Recreations* costume research, travel; *Clubs* The Gardens, The Embassy, Legends; *Style* - Bill Gibb Esq; c/o Barclays Bank, Edgware rd, W2; 38 Drayton Court, Drayton gdns, SW10

GIBB, Frank; *Career* dep chm Nat Nuclear Corpn to 1981, chm 1981-; *Style* - Frank Gibb Esq; c/o National Nuclear Corpn, 22 Buckingham Gate, SW1 (☎ 01 828 2714)

GIBB, George Dutton; CB (1979); s of William Forsyth Gibb (d 1947); *b* 9 March 1920; *Educ* St Helen's Coll Southsea, Guy's Hosp, London U; *m* 1948, Mary, da of Sir Victor Dupree, 4 Bt (d 1976); 2 da; *Career* Lt RNVR, dental surgeon (LDS, RCS 1950, FDS, RCS 1979), general practitioner 1950-71, ch dental offr, Dept of Health & Social Security 1971-; *Recreations* home and garden; *Style* - George Gibb Esq, CB; Yenda, 10 Haw Lane, Bledlow Ridge, High Wycombe, Bucks (☎ Bledlow Ridge (024 027) 300)

GIBB, Walter Frame; DSO (1945), DFC (1943); *b* 26 Mar 1919; *Educ* Clifton; *m* 1944, Pauline Reed; 3 da; *Career* JP (1974) Bristol; MRAeS; md British Aerospace Australia Ltd 1978-; *Style* - Walter Gibb Esq DSO DFC JP; ICI House, 61-69 Marcquarrie st, Sydney, NSW 2000, Aust

GIBB , Frank Ross; *Career* chm Taylor Woodrow Construction Ltd; FICE; *Style* - Frank Gibb Esq; 345 Ruislip rd, Southall, Middx

GIBBINGS, Hon Mrs (Louise Barbara); *née* Lambert; da of 2 Viscount Lambert, TD; *b* 1944; *m* 1975,

Peter Walter Gibbings; 1 s; *Style* - The Hon Mrs Gibbings; 10 The Vale, Chelsea, SW3

GIBBONS, Hon John David; s of of late Edmund Gibbons, CBE, and Winifred Gibbon, MBE ; *b* 15 June 1927; *Educ* in Bermuda and Connecticut, Harvard; *m* 1958, Lully Lorentzen; 3 s (and 1 da by former marriage); *Career* JP (1974) Bermuda, MP Bermuda 1974-77, premier of Bermuda 1977-; *Style* - The Hon John Gibbons, JP; Leeward, Point Shares, Pembroke, Bermuda (☎ 809 29 52396)

GIBBONS, Sir John Edward; 8 Bt (GB 1752); s of Maj Sir Alexander Doran Gibbons, 7 Bt, 1956; *b* 14 Nov 1914; *Educ* Charterhouse, Peterhouse Cambridge; *m* 1937 (m dis 1951), Mersa Wentworth, da of late Maj Edward Baynton Grove Foster, of Warmwell, Dorset; 1 s, 2 da; *Heir* s, William Gibbons; *Career* Capt Dorset Regt; regional dir (Nottingham) Arts Council of Great Britain 1946-50; *Style* - Sir John Gibbons, Bt; 2 Malt Cottages, Preston, Weymouth, Dorset

GIBBONS, Stella Dorothea; da of of C P J T Gibbons; *b* 5 Jan 1902; *Educ* N London Collegiate Sch, U Coll London; *m* 1933, Allan Bourne Webb (d 1959); 1 da; *Career* poet and novelist; FRSL; *Books* Cold Comfort Farm; *Style* - Miss Stella Gibbons; 19 Oakeshott ave, Highgate, N6 (☎ 01 340 2566)

GIBBONS, William Edward Doran; s and h of Sir John Gibbons, 8 Bt, *qv*; *b* 13 Jan 1948; *Educ* Pangbourne, RNC Dartmouth, Bristol U; *m* 1972, Patricia, da of Roland Archer Howse; 1 da; *Style* - William Gibbons Esq; 8 Lombard st, Old Portsmouth, Hants

GIBBS, Andrew Antony; MBE (1945), TD (1945); s of The Ven Archdeacon, The Hon Kenneth Francis Gibbs DD (d 1935, 5 s of 1 Baron Aldenham); *b* 31 March 1914; *Educ* Winchester, Ch Ch Oxford; *m* 1947, Elizabeth Joan, wid of Capt Peter Foljambe (ka 1944) and da of Maj Eric Montagu Flint DSO (d 1962); 2 s; *Career* Maj Herts Regt WW II; dir- Barclays Bank 1962-, Barclays UK Management Ltd 1971-79, Barclays Insurance Services Co Ltd 1970-75, and York Waterworks Co 1969-; memb York Diocesan Bd of Fin 1964-, chm Dean & Chapter of York Finance Ctee 1969-; hon life memb BRCS; *Recreations* shooting; *Clubs* Travellers', Pratt's, MCC; *Style* - Andrew Gibbs Esq, MBE, TD; Kilrington Hall, Thirsk, N Yorkshire (☎ Upsall 213)

GIBBS, Hon Antonia Mary; da of 5 Baron Aldenham and 3 Baron Hunsdon of Hunsdon; *b* 1958; *Style* - The Hon Antonia Gibbs

GIBBS, Christopher Henry; 5 s of late Hon Sir Geoffrey Gibbs, KCMG (2 s of 1 Baron Hunsdon of Hunsdon, JP, himself 4 s of 1 Baron Aldenham, JP), and Hon Lady Gibbs, CBE, JP; *b* 29 July 1938; *Educ* Eton, Stanbridge; *Career* dir Christopher Gibbs Ltd (antique dealers); *Style* - Christopher Gibbs Esq; c/o Christopher Gibbs Ltd, 118 New Bond st, W1

GIBBS, David Charles Leslie; eldest s of late Hon Sir Geoffrey Gibbs, KCMG (2 s of 1 Baron Hunsdon of Hunsdon, JP, himself 4 s of 1 Baron Aldenham, JP), and Hon Lady Gibbs, CBE, JP; *b* 15 Aug 1927; *Educ* Eton, Ch Ch Oxford; *m* 1965, Charmian, da of Dalzell Mein, of Toolong Australia; 2 s, 2 da; *Career* dir Antony Gibbs & Sons, Australian Pastoral Co, London County Freehold & Leasehold Properties; *Style* - David Gibbs Esq; 21 William st, S Yarra, Melbourne, Vict, Australia

GIBBS, David Phillip; s of Wiliam Charles Gibbs; *b* 6 May 1941; *Educ* Cranleigh Sch; *m* 1964, Gillian (m dis 1981); 2 s, 1 da; *Career* dir Hambros Bank Ltd; *Recreations* golf, tennis, jogging; *Style* - David Gibbs Esq; c/o Hambros Bank, 41 Bishopsgate, EC2 (☎ 01 588 2851)

GIBBS, Hon Mrs (Elizabeth Beatrice); *née* Baring; da of 1 Baron Howick of Glendale, KG, GCMG, KCVO (d 1973); *b* 1940; *m* 1962, Capt Nicholas Albany Gibbs; 1 s, 2 da; *Style* - The Hon Mrs Gibbs; 1628 32nd st, NW Washington DC 20007, USA

GIBBS, Hon Eustace Hubert Beilby; s of 1 Baron Wraxall; hp to bro, 2 Baron; *b* 3 July 1929; *Educ* Eton, Ch Ch Oxford; *m* 1957, Evelyn, da of Sydney Scott, of Southwold; 3 s (Anthony Hubert b 19 Aug 1958, Andrew Christopher b 17 May 1965, Jonathan Charles William b 27 April 1969), 2 da (Miranda Caroline b 26 Jan 1961, Alexandra Mary Henrietta b 28 May 1971); *Career* entered Foreign Serv 1954; *Recreations* music, golf; *Clubs* Brooks's, Pratt's, Beefsteak; *Style* - The Hon Eustace Gibbs; Coddenham House, Coddenham, Ipswich, Suffolk (☎ Coddenham 332)

GIBBS, Hon George Henry Paul; s of 5 Baron Aldenham, and 3 Baron Hunsdon of Hunsdon; *b* 1950; *m* 1973, Janet Elizabeth, da of Harold Leonard Scott; 2 s; *Style* - The Hon George Gibbs; Essex Cottage, Anstey, Buntingford, Herts

GIBBS, Rt Hon Mr Justice; Rt Hon Sir Harry; GCMG (1981), KBE (1970), PC (1972); s of Harry Victor Gibbs, of Ipswich Qld; *b* 7 Feb 1917; *Educ* Ipswich G S, Qld U; *m* 1944, Muriel, da of Hugh Dunn, of Maryborough Qld; 1 s, 3 da; *Career* QC 1957; barr Qld 1939; Justice High Court Australia 1970; *Recreations* tennis, theatre; *Clubs* Australian (Sydney); *Style* - The Rt Hon Mr Justice Gibbs, GCMG, KBE, PC; 27 Stanhope rd, Killara 2071, Australia (☎ 498 6924)

GIBBS, Lady Hilaria Agnes; *née* Edgcumbe; da of 6 Earl of Mount Edgcumbe, TD, DL (d 1965); *b* 16 Jan 1908; *m* 1933, Lt-Col Denis Lucius Alban Gibbs, DSO* (gs of Rev Hon John Gibbs, yr bro of 1 Baron Aldenham); 4 da; *Career* former Pres Tavistock Branch Red Cross, Pres Plymouth League of Pity for fifteen years; *Style* - Lady Hilaria Gibbs; Aldenham, Deer Park Lane, Tavistock, Devon (☎ 2731)

GIBBS, Rt Hon Sir Humphrey Vicary; GCVO (1969, KCVO 1965), KCMG (1960), OBE (1959), PC (1969); s of 1 Baron Hunsdon of Hunsdon (d 1935); *b* 22 Nov 1902; *Educ* Eton, Trin Cambridge; *m* 1934, Molly Peel, DBE, CStJ, da of late J Peel Nelson, of Bulawayo; 5 s; *Career* Governor of Rhodesia 1959-69; Hon LLD Birmingham 1969, Hon DCL East Anglia 1969; *Clubs* Athenaeum, Bulawayo (Bulawayo, Zimbabwe), Salisbury (Salisbury, Zimbabwe); *Style* - The Rt Hon Sir Humphrey Gibbs, GCVO, KCMG, OBE, PC; Bonisa Farm, Private Bag 5583W, Bulawayo, Zimbabwe

GIBBS, Jeremy Herbert; s of Rt Hon Sir Humphrey Gibbs, GCVO, KCMG, OBE (3 s of 1 Baron Hunsdon of Hunsdon), and Dame Molly Gibbs, DBE; *b* 26 May 1935; *Educ* Bishops Sch Cape Town, Ch Ch Oxford; *m* 1958, Alison, da of Col Douglas Martin; 4 da; *Career* insur broker; Gov St Mary's Sch Wantage, London House for Overseas Students; *Recreations* fishing; *Clubs* Bulawayo (Zimbabwe); *Style* - Jeremy Gibbs Esq; 10 Bassett rd, W10 (☎ 01 969 5872)

GIBBS, Julian Herbert; 3 s of Hon Sir Geoffrey Gibbs, KCMG (2 s of 1 Baron Hunsdon of Hunsdon, JP, himself 4 s of 1 Baron Aldenham, JP); *b* 26 Nov 1932; *Educ* Eton; *Career* 2 Lt KRRC 1951-53, Lt Queen's Westminster (TA) 1953-55; dir Antony Gibbs Life & Pensions Ltd; *Style* - Julian Gibbs Esq

GIBBS, Dame Molly (Peel); DBE (1969); da of of John Peel Nelson; *b* 13 July 1912; *Educ* Girls' High Sch, Barnato Park, Johannesburg; *m* 1934, Rt Hon Sir Humphrey Gibbs,*qv*; 5 s; *Style* - Dame Molly Gibbs, DBE; Bonisa, Private Bag 5583W, Bulawayo, Zimbabwe (☎ 69002)

GIBBS, Maj Martin Antony; JP (Wilts 1966), DL (1977); s of Col William Otter Gibbs, JP, DL, 10 Roy Hussars, of Barrow Court, Barrow Gurney, Somerset, who m Janet Gibbs, his cous and sis of 1 Baron Wraxall; *b* 12 March 1916; *Educ* Eton, Sandhurst; *m* 1947, Elsie, da of Sir Hew Hamilton-Dalrymple, 9 Bt; 2 s, 4 da - of whom Antony, the elder s, m 1974 Virginia, yst da of Hon Keith Rous (2 s of 3 Earl of Stradbroke, KCMG, CB, CVO, CBE, VD, TD, JP) by his 2 w, April, da of late Brig-Gen Hon Arthur Asquith, DSO (3 s of 1 Earl of Oxford and Asquith, KG, PC, Liberal PM 1908-16, by his 1 w Helen), and Hon Betty Manners, da of 3 Baron Manners; Anstice (the 2 da, b 1951) m 1978 Anthony, yst s of Hon Edmund

Howard, CMG, MVO (4 s of 1 Baron Howard of Penrith, GCB, GCMG, CVO, PC, by Lady Isabella Giustiniani Bandini, 5 da of 8 Earl of Newburgh); *Career* Maj Coldstream Gds (ret 1952); *Recreations* horticulture, dendrology; *Clubs* Cavalry & Guards, Pratt's; *Style* - Maj Martin Gibbs, JP, DL; Sheldon Manor, Chippenham, Wilts (☎ 3120)

GIBBS, Brevet-Col Martin St John Valentine; CB (1958), DSO (1942), TD, JP (Glos 1965); s of Maj Guy Melvil Gibbs, TD, of Cirencester (yr bro of William Otter Gibbs, *see* Gibbs, Maj M A), and Margaret, da of Henry St John (gs of Hon Ferdinand St John, 2 s of 3 Viscount Bolingbroke and 4 Viscount St John by his 2 w Isabella Baroness Hompesch) by his w Maud (da of Hon Pascoe Glyn, sometime MP E Dorset and 5 s of 1 Baron Wolverton); *b* 14 Feb 1917; *Educ* Eton; *m* 1947, Mary, da of Lt-Col Philip Mitford and widow of Capt Michael Wills, MC; 2 da, 3 step s; *Career* 2 Lt Roy Wiltshire Yeo 1937, Maj 1942, Lt-Col 1951, Bt-Col 1955, Col 1958; Ld-Lt Glos 1978; Hon Col Roy Wilts Yeomanry Sqdn TAVR 1972, Col Cmmdt Yeomanry RAC 1975; High Sheriff Glos 1958; *Recreations* country pursuits; *Clubs* Cavalry & Guards, MCC; *Style* - Brevet-Col Martin Gibbs CB DSO TD JP, HM Ld-Lt for Gloucestershire; Ewen Manor, Ewen, Cirencester, Glos (☎ Kemble 206)

GIBBS, Field Marshal Sir Roland Christopher; GCB (1976, KCB 1972), CBE (1968), DSO (1945), MC (1943), DL (Wilts 1980); s of Maj Guy Melvil Gibbs, TD, by his w Margaret, nee St John; bro of Martin Gibbs, CB, DSO, TD, JP, *qv*; *b* 22 June 1921; *Educ* Eton, Sandhurst; *m* 1955, Davina, da of Lt-Col Eion Merry, MC, of Lucknam Park, Chippenham, and Jean (da of Hon Arthur Crichton, 3 s of 4 Earl of Erne, KP, PC, sometime MP Enniskillen; Hon Arthur Crichton m Katherine, da of Col Hon Walter Trefusis, CB, 3 s of 19 Baron Clinton, by the Col's w, Lady Mary Montagu Douglas Scott, yst da of 5 Duke of Buccleuch); 2 s, 1 da; *Career* CIC UKLF 1974-76, CGS 1976-79, served WW II M East, Italy, NW Europe; Cdr 16 Para Bde 1963-66; *Recreations* out of door recreations, painting; *Clubs* Turf; *Style* - Field Marshal Sir Roland Gibbs GCB CBE DSO MC DL; Patney Rectory, Devizes, Wilts (☎ Chirton 733)

GIBBS, Roger Geoffrey; s of of Hon Sir Geoffrey Gibbs, KCMG (2 s of 1 Baron Hunsdon of Hunsdon, JP, who himself was 4 s of 1 Baron Aldenham) and Hon Lady Gibbs, CBE, JP; *b* 13 Oct 1934; *Educ* Eton; Millfield; *Career* dir Arsenal Football Club 1980-, Roy Nat Pension Fund for Nurses; chm Gerrard and National Discount Co Ltd 1975-; *Recreations* sport; *Clubs* Pratt's, Swinley; *Style* - Roger Gibbs Esq; 23 Tregunter rd, SW10 (☎ 01 370 3465)

GIBBS, Hon Rosalind Mary; da of 1 Baron Hunsdon of Hunsdon (d 1935); *b* 1898; *Style* - The Hon Rosalind Gibbs

GIBBS, Lady Sarah; *née* Bingham; da of 6 Earl of Lucan, MC (d 1964); *b* 1936; *Educ* Badminton Sch, Bristol; *m* 1958, the Rev William Gilbert Gibbs; 1 s, 3 da; *Career* Magistrate for mid-Northants, 1980; *Style* - Lady Sarah Gibbs; The Vicarage, Guilsborough, Northampton

GIBBS, Somerset Bryan; s of Maj Bryan Northam Gibbs, MBE; *b* 16 Jan 1926; *Educ* Eton; *m* 1950, Elspeth, da of Maj F Russi, MC; 3 s, 1 da; *Career* memb Stock Exchange 1952-77, chm Capel-Cure Myers 1975-77; dir Concorde Rotaflex, Moray Firth Maltings, Equity Consort Investment Tst, Equity Income Tst; *Recreations* golf, sailing, photography; *Clubs* Boodle's, City of London; *Style* - Somerset Gibbs Esq; 62 Oakwood Court, W 14 (☎ 01 602 2633); Mead Lodge, Stanstead Abbotts, Ware, Herts (☎ Roydon 3142)

GIBBS, Stephen Cokayne; 2 s of late Hon Sir Geoffrey Gibbs, KCMG (2 s of 1 Baron Hunsdon of Hunsdon, JP, himself 4 s of 1 Baron Aldenham, JP), and Hon Lady Gibbs, CBE, JP; *b* 18 July 1929; *Educ* Eton; *m* 1972, Lavinia, da of Sir Edmund Bacon, 13 Bt, KG, KBE, TD; 2 s, 1 da; *Career* late 2 Lt KRRC, Maj QVR (TA) 1960-63 & Roy Greenjackets; dir Charles Barker Gp 1962-, Vaux Breweries Ltd 1971-; *Recreations* shooting, gardening; *Clubs* White's, Pratt's; *Style* -

Stephen Gibbs Esq; Dougarie, Isle of Arran, KA27 8EB (☎ 077084 229)

GIBBS, Hon Vicary Tyser; s and h of 5 Baron Aldenham and 3 Baron Hunsdon of Hunsdon; *b* 9 June 1948; *Educ* Eton; *m* 1980, Josephine Nicola, da of John Fell, of Lower Bourne, Farnham, Surrey; *Style* - The Hon Vicary Gibbs

GIBRALTAR, Suffragan Bishop of; Rt Rev Ambrose Walter Marcus Weekes; CB (Mil) 1971; s of Lt-Cdr William Charles Tinnoth Weekes (d 1958); *b* 25 April 1919; *Educ* Rochester Cathedral Choir Sch, Sir Joseph Williamson's Rochester, King's Coll London, Scholae Cancelarli Lincoln; *Career* Deacon 1942, Priest 1943, Chaplain RN 1944-72, Dean of Gibraltar 1973-78, Assist Bishop of Gibraltar 1978, Suffragan Bishop in Europe 1980; *Recreations* music, yachting; *Clubs* Athenaeum, Naval & Mil; *Style* - The Rt Rev the Suffragan Bishop of Gibraltar, CB; Fig Tree House Queenborough, Kent; 11 Lanark rd, Maida Vale, W9

GIBSON, Baron (Life Peer UK 1975); Richard Patrick Tallentyre Gibson; s of Thornely Carbutt Gibson; *b* 5 Feb 1916; *Educ* Eton, Magdalen Oxford; *m* 1945, Elizabeth, da of Hon Clive Pearson (2 s of 1 Viscount Cowdray) and Hon Alicia Knatchbull-Hugessen (da of 1 Baron Brabourne); 4 s; *Career* served WW II Maj Middx Yeo; chm S Pearson & Son 1978-, Nat Tst 1977-, late chm Financial Times, Economist Newspaper, Pearson Longman; dir Westminster Press, Whitehall Securities; memb Bd Roy Opera House, Tstee Glyndebourne Festival Opera; *Clubs* Brooks's; *Style* - The Rt Hon Lord Gibson; 4 Swan Walk, SW3 (☎ 01 351 0344/352 3650); Penn's Rocks, Groombridge, Sussex (☎ 244)

GIBSON, Sir Alexander Drummond; CBE (1967); s of James McClure Gibson (d 1946); *b* 11 Feb 1926; *Educ* Dalziel H S Motherwell, Glasgow U, RCM, Mozarteum (Salzburg), Accademia Chigiano (Siena); *m* 1959, Anne Veronica, nee Waggett; 3 s (James b 1959, Philip b 1962, John b 1965), 1 da (Claire b 1958); *Career* kt 1977, orchestral conductor, 1959- principal conductor and musical dir Scottish Nat Orch, 1962- founder and artistic dir Scottish Opera, 1980-82 principal guest conductor Houston Symphony Orch, OStJ 1975, FRSE 1978, FRSA 1980, Arnold Bax Medal for Conducting 1959, Sibelius Medal 1978, Br Music Year Book Musician of the Year 1980; *Recreations* music, reading; *Clubs* Garrick, Oriental; *Style* - Sir Alexander Gibson, CBE; 15 Cleveden gdns, Glasgow G12 (☎ 041 339 6668)

GIBSON, Hon (Edward) Barry Greynville; s and h of Vice-Adm 3 Baron Ashbourne, CB, DSO, JP; *b* 28 Jan 1933; *Educ* Rugby; *m* 1967, Yvonne, da of Maj Gordon Ham; 3 s; *Career* Lt-Cdr RN, M East 1967-69; now stockbroker; *Style* - The Hon Barry Gibson; 107 Sussex rd, Petersfield, Hants

GIBSON, Rev Christopher Herbert; CP; s and h of Sir Christopher Gibson, 3 Bt,*qv*; *b* 17 July 1948; *Career* ordained priest 1975; *Style* - Rev Christopher Gibson, CP; Holy Cross, Buenos Aires, Argentina

GIBSON, Sir Christopher Herbert; 3 Bt (UK 1931); s of Sir Christopher Herbert Gibson, 2 Bt (d 1962); *b* 2 Feb 1921; *Educ* St George's Coll Argentina; *m* 1941, Lilian Lake, da of late Dr George Byron Young, of Colchester, Essex; 1 s, 3 da; *Heir* s, Rev Christopher Gibson, CP; *Career* man of Leach's Argentine Estates 1946-51, of Encyclopaedia Britannica 1952-55, design draughtsman Babcox & Wilcox USA 1956-57, tea plantation man then ranch man Liebig's Extract of Meat Co 1958-64, bldg inspector Industries Kaiser Argentina 1964-68, man and part owner Lakanto Poultry Farms 1969-76; *Style* - Sir Christopher Gibson, Bt; Suite 107, 6660 Buswell st, Richmond, BC V6Y 2G8, Canada

GIBSON, Hon Clive Patrick; s of Baron Gibson (Life Peer) and Elizabeth, da of late Hon Clive Pearson (2 s of 1 Viscount Cowdray, GCVO, PC, DL) and Hon Alicia Knatchbull-Hugessen (da of 1 Baron Brabourne); *b* 24 Jan 1948; *Educ* Eton, Oxford; *m* 1974, Anne, da of late Comte Jacques de Chauvigny de Blot; 1 s,

1 da; *Career* chm Château Latour; dir Financial Times, Penguin Books, Economist; *Recreations* music, shooting, skiing; *Clubs* Brooks's; *Style* - The Hon Clive Gibson; Parham Park, Pulborough, Sussex; 29a Monmouth House, Hyde Park Gate, SW7

GIBSON, Rev (Sir) David; (4 Bt, UK 1926); s of Sir Ackroyd Herbert Gibson; suc father 1975, but does not use title; *b* 18 July 1922; *Style* - The Rev David Gibson; Our Lady and St Neot, West st, Liskeard, Cornwall

GIBSON, Lt-Col Edgar Matheson; TD (1975), DL (1976); s of James Edgar Gibson (d 1976); *b* 1 Nov 1934; *Educ* Kirkwall G S, Gray's Coll of Art; *m* 1960, Jean, nee McCarrick; 2 s, 2 da; *Career* Lt-Col, Nat Serv 1958-60, TA & TAVR 1961-, Cadet Cmdt Orkney 1979, JSLO Orkney 1980; school master, Head of Art Kirkwall G S; *Recreations* painting, sculpture, whisky tasting; *Clubs* Highland Brigade Club; *Style* - Lt-Col Edgar Matheson, TD, DL; Transcona, New Scapa rd, Kirkwall, Orkney (☎ 0856 2849)

GIBSON, Hon Mrs (Frances Towneley); *née* Strachey; da of late Hon (Thomas) Anthony Edward Towneley Strachey and sis of 4 Baron O'Hagan; *b* 1948; *m* 1967, Hon Hugh Marcus Thornely Gibson, s of Baron Gibson (Life Peer); 1 s, 2 da; *Style* - The Hon Mrs Gibson; The Fold, Parwich, Ashbourne, Derbys

GIBSON, Hon Hugh Marcus Thornely; da of Baron Gibson, *qv*; *b* 1946; *m* 1967, Hon Frances, da of late Hon Anthony Strachey; 1s, 2 da; *Style* - The Hon Hugh Gibson; The Fold, Parwich, Ashbourne, Derbys

GIBSON, Joseph David; CBE (1979); s of late Charles Gibson and Mamao Lavenia Gibson; *b* 26 Jan 1928; *Educ* Auckland U, NZ; *m* Emily Bentley; 3 s, 2 da; *Career* High Commissioner for Fiji from 1976; *Style* - Joseph Gibson Esq CBE; 97 Platts Lane, NW3 (☎ 01 794 1806)

GIBSON, Col Leonard Young; CBE (1961, MBE 1940), TD (1947), DL (Northumberland 1971); s of William McLure Gibson (d 1959); *b* 4 Dec 1911; *Educ* Royal G S Newcastle on Tyne, Paris; *m* 1949, Pauline Mary, nee Anthony; 1 s, 1 da; *Career* TA 1932-61, GSO1 Mil Govt Germany 1945, Dep Cdr RA 50 Div TA 1959-61, Col, ret; Croix de Guerre 1944, memb T&AFA Northumberland 1958-68, pres Master of Harriers & Beagles Assoc, & of Newcastle & Dist Beagles 1946-*Recreations* beagling, breeding hounds & horses (Committee stallion 'Leander'); *Clubs* Army & Navy, Northern Counties; *Style* - Col Leonard Gibson CBE TD DL; Simonburn Cottage, Humshaugh, Hexham, Northumb (☎ 043 481 402)

GIBSON, Capt Michael Bradford; s of Lt-Col B T Gibson; *b* 20 March 1929; *Educ* Taunton Sch, Sandhurst, Sidney Sussex Cambridge; *m* 1953, Mary Legg; 2 s; *Career* md Racquet Sports International Ltd from 1976; *Style* - Capt Michael Gibson; Olde Deane, Warnham, Horsham, Sussex (☎ 65589)

GIBSON, Rt Hon Lord Justice; Rt Hon Sir Maurice White; PC (1975); s of late William James Gibson, of Belfast; *b* 1 May 1913; *Educ* Roy Belfast Academical Institution, Queen's U of Belfast; *m* 1945, Cecily, da of Dudley Roy Johnson; 1 s, 1 da; *Career* barr 1937, 1938 (NI) and (Inner Bar) 1956, formerly Puisne Judge, Lord Justice of Appeal in N Ireland 1975-; kt 1975; *Style* - The Rt Hon Lord Justice Gibson, PC; 13 Bromhill pk, Belfast, N Ireland; Doonin, Kilcar, Co Donegal, Eire

GIBSON, Hon Mr Justice; Hon Sir Peter Leslie Gibson; s of Harold Gibson and Martha, nee Diercking; *b* 10 June 1934; *Educ* Malvern, Worcester Oxford; *m* 1968, Katharine Hadow; 2 s, 1 da; *Career* High Court Judge (Chancery) 1981-, kt 1981; barr 1960, 2 Jr Counsel Inland Revenue 1970-72; *Style* - The Hon Mr Justice Gibson; 114 Elgin Crescent, W11 (☎ 01 229 6741)

GIBSON, Hon Piers Nathaniel; s of Baron Gibson, *qv*; *b* 15 March 1956; *Educ* Eton, Magdalen Oxford; *Career* independent film producer; *Clubs*

Annabel's; *Style* - The Hon Piers Gibson; 41 Ovington st, SW3 (☎ 01 589 2830)

GIBSON, Maj William David; s of of G C Gibson, OBE, of Landwade Hall, Exning, Suffolk; *b* 26 Feb 1925; *Educ* Harrow, Trinity Coll Cambridge; *m* 1, 1959, Charlotte (d 1973), da of N S Pryor, JP, DL; 3 s, 1 da; m 2, 1975, Jane, da of late Col L L Hassell, DSO, MC,; *Career* chm W J Tatem Ltd 1974-; *Style* - Maj William Gibson; Edradynate, Aberfeldy, Perthshire (☎ Strathtay 215)

GIBSON, Hon William David; OBE (1944), TD; s of Hon Edward Gibson (d 1928) and gs of 1 Baron Ashbourne; bro of 3 Baron Ashbourne, CB, DSO, JP; raised to rank of Baron's s 1943; *b* 22 March 1914; *Educ* Sherborne, Trin Cambridge; *m* 1947, Sabina, da of Dr Ernst Landsberg, of Cape Town; 3 da; *Career* Second Master Clifton 1966-74 (Housemaster 1948-65); formerly Col (WW II) served France, N Africa, Italy; *Recreations* sailing, skiing, bridge; *Style* - The Hon William Gibson, OBE, TD; Buckley Cottage, Batson, Salcombe, Devon (☎ 3143)

GIBSON, Hon William Knatchbull; s of Baron Gibson, *qv*; *b* 1951; *Style* - The Hon William Gibson; 11 Paultons sq, SW3

GIBSON, Air Vice-Marshal William Norman; CBE (1956), DFC; s of late Hamilton Gibson; *b* 28 April 1915; *Educ* in New Zealand; *m* 1938, Grace, nee Downton; 1 da; *Career* RAAF ret; *Style* - Air Vice-Marshal William Gibson CBE DFC; 26 Hillcrest ave, Mona Vale, NSW 2103, Australia

GIBSON FLEMING, Maj William Harry; JP (Dorset 1963), DL (1974); s of Harry Gibson Fleming, of Ascot; *b* 4 Aug 1918; *Educ* Eton, Magdalene Cambridge; *m* 1955, Selina, da of Lt-Col Sir Randolf Baker, 4 and last Bt, DSO, DL (d 1959); 1 s, 1 da; *Career* served WW II Malta, N Africa, Italy; Staff Coll Camberley, ret 1956; landowner & farmer; chm Blandford Magistrates 1972-; memb Exec Cttee CLA 1978-; Gen Commissioner Income Tax; *Recreations* shooting, fishing, golf; *Clubs* Cavalry & Guards, MCC; *Style* - Maj William Gibson Fleming, JP, DL; Ranston, Blandford, Dorset (☎ Childe Okeford 860271)

GIBSON-CRAIG-CARMICHAEL, Sir David Peter William; 15 Bt of Keirhill (NS 1702) and 8 Bt of Riccarton (UK 1831); s of late 14 and 7 Bt (d 1969); *b* 21 July 1946; *Educ* Queen's U Kingston Canada (BSc Geology); *m* 1973, Patricia, nee Skarnic; 1 s, 1 da; *Heir* s, Peter Gibson-Craig-Carmichael; *Style* - Sir David Gibson-Craig-Carmichael, Bt; Casilla 2461, Santiago, Chile

GIBSON-CRAIG-CARMICHAEL, Emily, Lady - Emily Ellen; da of Henry Rummell, of Falkland Islands; *m* 1914, Sir Eardley Gibson-Craig-Carmichael, 13 Bt (d 1939); *Style* - Emily, Lady Gibson-Craig-Carmichael; Casilla 2461, Santiago, Chile

GIBSON-CRAIG-CARMICHAEL, Peter William; s and h of Sir David Gibson-Craig-Carmichael, 15 and 8 Bt, *qv*; *b* 29 Dec 1975

GIBSON-WATT, Baron (Life Peer UK 1979); (James) David Gibson-Watt; MC (1943) & 2 Bars, PC (1974), DL (Radnorshire 1968, now Powys); s of Maj James Gibson-Watt, JP, DL (ggs of James Watt the engineer and father of the steam engine) and Marjorie, nee Ricardo (gggda of David Ricardo, the political economist and first of that originally Sephardic family to reside at Gatcombe Park, now the property of Capt and HRH The Princess Anne, Mrs Mark Phillips); *b* 11 Sept 1918; *Educ* Eton, Trin Cambridge; *m* 1942, Diana, 2 da of Sir Charles Hambro (Lord Gibson-Watt's yr bro m her yr sis); 2 s (and 1 s decd), 2 da; *Career* Forestry Commissioner 1976-, served WW II Welsh Gds; MP (C) Hereford 1956-74, Ld Commissioner Treasury 1959-61, Min State Welsh Off 1970-74; FRAgS; chm Cncl on Tbnls 1980-; memb Historic Bldgs Cncl Wales 1975-; *Clubs* Boodle's; *Style* - Rt Hon Lord Gibson-Watt MC** PC DL; Doldowlod, Llandrindod Wells, Powys (☎ Newbridge-on-Wye 208)

GIBSON-WATT, Hon Julian David; s of of Baron Gibson-Watt, MC**, PC, JP, DL,*qv*; *b* 1946; *Educ* Eton, Trinity Coll

Cambridge; *m* 1970, Patricia (m dis), da of Lennox Hewitt, CBE, of Canberra; *Style* - The Hon Julian Gibson-Watt

GIBSON-WATT, Hon Robin; s of Baron Gibson-Watt, MC**, PC, JP, DL,*qv*; *b* 1949; *Educ* Eton; *m* 1971, Marcia, da of Sir Roger Cary, 2 Bt; 2 s, 1 da; *Career* High Sheriff Powys 1981; *Style* - The Hon Robin Gibson-Watt; Gelli Garn, Llanyre, Llandrindod Wells, Powys

GIBSON-WATT, Hon Sian; da of Baron Gibson-Watt, MC**, PC, JP, DL, *qv*; *b* 1962; *Style* - The Hon Sian Gibson-Watt

GIDDINGS, Air Marshal Sir (Kenneth Charles) Michael; KCB (1975), OBE (1953), DFC (1945), AFC and Bar (1950, 1955); s of Charles Giddings; *b* 27 Aug 1920; *Educ* Ealing County Sch, UCL; *m* 1946, Elizabeth, da of Joseph McConnell; 2 s, 2 da; *Career* former test pilot; Dep Ch Def Staff Op Requirements 1973-76; Ind Panel Inspector DOE 1978-; *Recreations* golf, gardening, music; *Clubs* RAF; *Style* - Air Marshal Sir Michael Giddings, KCB, OBE, DFC, AFC*; 159 Long Lane, Tilehurst, Reading, Berks (☎ 23012)

GIELGUD, Maina; da of Lewis Gielgud and Elisabeth Grussner; *b* 14 Jan 1945; *Career* freelance ballerina; formerly with Royal Ballet; *Style* - Miss Maina Gielgud; Stirling Court, 3 Marshall st, W1 (☎ 01 734 6612)

GIFFARD, Adam Edward; s and h of 3 Earl of Halsbury (but does not use courtesy title Viscount Tiverton); *b* 3 June 1934; *Educ* Stowe, Jesus Cambridge; *m* 1, 1963, Mrs Ellen Huxley, da of late Brynjolf Hovde; m 2, 1976, Joanna Elizabeth, da of Frederick Harry Cole; 2 da; *Career* late 2 Lt Seaforth Highlanders; *Style* - Adam Giffard Esq; P O Box 13, North Branch, NY 12766, USA

GIFFARD, Peter Richard de Longueville; s of Thomas Giffard, MBE, JP, DL (d 1971), and Angela, da of Sir William Trollope, 10 Bt; is senior male representative of the Giffards of Chillington, one of the few English families to be able to trace their ancestry from pre-Conquest times, who flourished in Normandy in the tenth century, came over with William The Conqueror are mentioned in Domesday and have held Chillington since 1178; bro of Baroness Airey of Abingdon; *b* 20 May 1921; *Educ* Eton and Christ Church, Oxford; *m* 1949, Mary, da of Ronald Gandar Dower, (d 1963), of Old Park, Warninglid, Sussex; 1 s, 1 da; *Career* barrister 1947; dir S Staffs Waterworks Co 1974; member exec committee CLA 1979; chm W Midlands Branch Nat Trust; Pres Staffordshire Soc 1979; *Recreations* shooting, tree planting; *Clubs* Army & Navy; *Style* - Peter Giffard Esq; Chillington Hall, Codsall Wood, Wolverhampton (☎ Brewood 850236)

GIFFIN, Michael; s of John Metcalfe Giffin; *b* 2 May 1935; *Educ* Sevenoaks Sch; *m* 1963, Jane Agnes, nee Wright; 2 s, 1 da; *Career* chartered accountant, md St Olaf Bonding Co Ltd 1973-81, dep chm & ch exec Hays Business Serv Ltd 1981-; *Recreations* sailing; *Clubs* RAC; *Style* - Michael Giffin Esq; Tussocks, 19 Burntwood rd, Sevenoaks, Kent (☎ 0732 51536)

GIFFORD, 6 Baron (UK 1824); Anthony Maurice Gifford; s of 5 Baron (d 1961); *b* 1 May 1940; *Educ* Winchester, King's Cambridge; *m* 1965, Katherine, da of Dr Max Mundy, of Kensington; 1 s, 1 da; *Heir* s, Hon Thomas Gifford; *Career* barr 1962, chm Cttee for Freedom Mozambique, Angola & Guiné 1968-75, N Kensington Law Centre 1974-77, Legal Action Gp 1978-; *Style* - The Rt Hon Lord Gifford; 35 Wellington st, WC2 (☎ 01 836 5917)

GIFFORD, Hon Polly Anna; da of of Baron Gifford, *qv*; *b* 1969; *Style* - The Hon Polly Gifford

GIFFORD, Hon Thomas Adam; s and h of Baron Gifford, *qv*; *b* 1 Dec 1967; *Style* - The Hon Thomas Gifford

GIFFORD , Margaret, Baroness; Ellice Margaret; da of late Arthur Wigram Allen, of Merioola, Woollahra, NSW; *m* 1939, 5 Baron Gifford (d 1961); 1 s (6 Baron); *Style* - The Rt Hon Margaret, Lady Gifford; Merioola, Highclere, Newbury

GIGNOUX, Peter Alan; s of Evelyn Gignoux Jr (d 1968); *b* 17 June 1945; *Educ* St Albans Sch; *Career* commodity broker, v-pres E F Hutton Gp; *Recreations* shooting, travelling, arbitage; *Clubs* Buck's, Mark's, St Anthony (New York); *Style* - Peter Gignoux Esq; 22 Woodfall st, Chelsea

GILBERT, Brian Geoffrey; s of Donald William Gilbert (d 1968); *b* 18 July 1927; *Educ* Bishopshalt Sch Hillingdon, Middx; *m* 1978, Maxine, da of George Haley (d 1971); 2 da; *Career* md & gp ch exec Low & Bonar PLC 1973-; *Recreations* golf, fishing; *Clubs* Roy & Ancient; *Style* - Brian Gilbert Esq; Braetrees, Hepburn gdns, St Andrews, Fife (☎ 75595)

GILBERT, Duncan Maurice; s of Maurice Frank Gilbert (d 1951); *b* 14 May 1934; *Educ* Solihull Sch; *m* 1958, Josephine Anne, nee Wilcox; 2 s; *Career* FCIS, FCMA, Capital and County Laundries Ltd Cowley 1961 (dir 1965-79, md 1979-); *Recreations* sailing, cycling, music; *Clubs* Exeter Golf & Country, Starcross Fishing & Cruising, Exeter Wheelers; *Style* - Duncan Gilbert Esq; 22 Rosebarn ave, Exeter, Devon (☎ Exeter 59777)

GILBERT, Lt-Col Ernle Reginald Forester; s of Capt Humphrey Gilbert, of Bishopstone House, Bishopstone, Hereford; *b* 1 June 1921; *Educ* Marlborough; *m* 1946, Helene, da of Prof Dr Hans Reiter, of Graz; 1 da; *Career* reg army offr 1940-61, served N Africa, Italy, Greece, Palestine, Malaya; consultant Keyser Ullman 1971-75, and Save & Prosper 1966-70; *Recreations* cricket, natural history, shooting, fishing; *Clubs* Army & Navy; *Style* - Lt-Col Ernle Gilbert; Bishopstone House, Bishopstone, Hereford

GILBERT, Ian Herbert Gillet; *Career* chartered accountant, dir Baker Perkins Holdings Ltd; *Style* - Ian Gilbert Esq; Westwood Works, Westfield rd, Peterborough

GILBERT, John Charles Rudyard; *Career* md The Morgan Crucible Co Ltd; *Style* - John Gilbert Esq; 98 Petty France, SW1

GILBERT, Brig Sir William Herbert Ellery; KBE (1976, OBE 1945), DSO (1944); s of Ellery George Gilbert; *b* 20 July 1916; *Educ* Wanganui Collegiate Sch, NZ; RMC, Duntroon, Australia; *m* 1944, Patricia Farrer; 2 s, 1 da; *Career* dir NZ Security Intelligence Service 1956-76; *Style* - Brig Sir William Gilbert, KBE, DSO; 38 Chatsworth rd, Silverstream, New Zealand (☎ Wellington 286570)

GILBERT, Cdr Walter Raleigh; DL (1962); s of late Walter Raleigh Gilbert, JP; *b* 1889; *Educ* HMS Britannia; *m* 1, 1917 (m dis 1926), late Lady Beryl, da of 5 Earl of Clancarty; 1 s (k in flying accident 1942), 1 da; m 2, 1934, Joan Mary Boileau, nee Willock; 4 s, 1 da; *Career* Lt RN 1909, ret 1920, High Sheriff Devon 1957, civil Defence Area Controller S Devon 1960; *Style* - Cdr Walter Gilbert, DL, RN; Compton, Marldon, S Devon

GILBERTSON, Arthur Geoffrey; s of Charles Geoffrey Gilbertson (d 1963); *b* 18 May 1913; *Educ* Shrewsbury; *m* 1937, Hilarie Annette, nee Williams-Thomas; 3 da; *Career* High Sheriff Glamorgan 1970, magistrate 1959-, chm Vale of Glamorgan Magistrates 1981, memb Western Railway Board 1963-77, dir Roy Briersley Crystal 1965-, pres S Glamorgan British Red Cross Soc 1974-80; *Recreations* cricket, fishing, shooting, gardening; *Clubs* MCC; *Style* - Arthur Gilbertson Esq; Castle Cottage, Llanblethian, Cowbridge, S Glamorgan (☎ 2809)

GILBEY, Hon Anthony William; s and h of 10 Baron Vaux of Harrowden by his w (and 1 cous) Maureen Gilbey; *b* 25 May 1940; *Educ* Ampleforth; *m* 1964, Beverley, da of Charles Walton, of Cooden, Sussex; 2 s, 1 da; *Career* FICA, farmer; *Recreations* fishing, shooting; *Style* - The Hon Anthony Gilbey; Rusko, Gatehouse of Fleet, Kirkcudbrightshire

GILBEY, Sir (Walter) Derek; 3 Bt (UK 1893); s of late Walter Ewart Gilbey, s of 2 Bt; suc gf, Sir (Henry) Walter Gilbey, 2 Bt, 1945; *b* 11 March 1913; *Educ* Eton; *m* 1948, Elizabeth Mary, da of Col K G Campbell, of Standen House, Newport, Isle of Wight; 1 s, 1 da; *Heir* s, (Walter)

Gavin Gilbey; *Career* Lt Black Watch 1940-45; *Style* - Sir Derek Gilbey, Bt; Grovelands, Wineham, nr Henfield, Sussex

GILBEY, (Walter) Gavin; s and h of Sir Derek Gilbey, 3 Bt; *b* 14 April 1949; *Educ* Eton; *m* 1980, Mary Pacetti; *Style* - Gavin Gilbey Esq; 9615 SW 118th st, S Miami, Fla, USA

GILBEY, Hon Mary Agnes Margaret; da of Baroness Vaux of Harrowden (d 1958); *b* 1928; *Style* - The Hon Mary Gilbey; Dolphins, Gt Harrowden, Wellingborough

GILBEY, Hon Michael Christopher; 3 s of 10 Baron Vaux of Harrowden and Maureen, nee Gilbey (a 1 cous, da of Hugh Gilbey, himself yr bro of William Gilbey who m Baroness Vaux of Harrowden, mother of 9 and 10 Barons); *b* 29 Dec 1949; *Educ* Ampleforth, St Andrews U; *m* 1971, Linda, da of Arthur Gilbey (ggs of Sir Walter Gilbey, 1 Bt) and his 3 cous once removed; 3 s; *Career* chartered surveyor (ARICS) 1974-; md M & W Gilbey (Wine Merchants), of Eton; *Recreations* golf, sailing; *Style* - The Hon Michael Gilbey; Red Hatch, Harpsden Woods, Henley-on-Thames, Oxon (☎ 3202)

GILBEY, Mark Newman; s of Henry Newman Gilbey (s of Newman Gilbey, JP, who was both n of Sir Walter Gilbey, 1 Bt, and great unc of 9 and 10 Barons Vaux of Harrowden); *b* 21 Nov 1923; *Educ* Beaumont, Trin Cambridge; *Career* served Italy 1944-45 as Capt Gren Gds; fndr & chm Duncan Gilbey & Matheson Gp of Cos; *Recreations* travel, reading, antique and picture collecting; *Clubs* Boodle's, Buck's; *Style* - Mark Gilbey Esq; Ile de Gorée, Dakar, Senegal (216966); Dar el Bab, Casbah, Tangier, Morocco (☎ 32942)

GILBEY, Walter Anthony; s of Sir Walter Gilbey, 2 Bt, JP, by his 2 w Marion; uncle of Sir Derek Gilbey, 3 Bt; *b* 25 Feb 1935 (as Anthony Walter, but assumed present order of names by Deed Poll 1958); *Educ* Eton; *m* 1964, Jennifer, da of Capt James Price, of Ramsey, IOM (whose mother Mariquita was sis of Sir Robert O'Brien, 4 Bt), by his w, Hon Anne Younger (yr da of 2 Viscount Younger of Leckie); 1 s, 1 da (and 1 other child); *Career* fin dir IDV 1962-72; chm Fin Cttee Berks CC 1973, Mannin Tst Bank 1972-; dir IOM Steam Packet Co 1976-; *Recreations* riding, driving horses; *Clubs* Union League (Philadelphia); *Style* - Walter Gilbey Esq; Ballacallin Mooar, Crosby, Marown, IOM (☎ 0624 851450)

GILBEY, Hon William John; s of 10 Baron Vaux of Harrowden (*see* Anthony and Michael Gilbey); *b* 1944; *Educ* Ampleforth; *m* 1971, Caroline, da of Alan Ball, of Ramsbury, Wilts; 2 s, 1 da; *Style* - The Hon William Gilbey; The Grange, Waltham St Lawrence, Twyford, Berks

GILCHRIST, Archibald; *b* 17 Dec 1929; *Educ* Loretto; *m* 1958, Elizabeth Greenlees; 2 s, 1 da; *Career* chm and md Govan Shipbuilders Ltd; *Style* - Archibald Gilchrist Esq; Inchmaholm, Barnton ave, Edinburgh (☎ 031 336 4288)

GILCHRIST, Sir (James) Finlay (Elder); OBE (1946); s of late Thomas Gilchrist; *b* 13 Aug 1903; *Educ* Glasgow Acad; *m* 1933, Dorothy Narizzano; 2 s, 1 da; *Career* life pres and dir Harrisons and Crosfield Ltd; *Style* - Sir Finlay Gilchrist OBE; South Cottage, Hapstead Farm, Ardingly, Sussex (☎ 892 368)

GILCHRIST, Richard Ian; MBE, VRD and Bar; s of John Gilchrist (d 1980); *b* 6 Oct 1922; *Educ* Pangbourne; *m* 1949, Alice, da of Dr Thomas Somerville Reeves (d 1960); 1 s, 1 da; *Career* chm Burtonwood Brewery Co, Hook Norton Brewerey Co; member of Tarporley and Cheshire hunts ; *Style* - Richard Gilchrist Esq MBE, VRD*; Manley Cottage, Manley, Cheshire (☎ 203)

GILKISON, Sir Alan Fleming, of New Zealand; kt 1980 for services to export, aviation and the community; *Style* - Sir Alan Gilkison

GILL, Anthony Keith; C Eng, ACGI, BSc; FIMechE, FIProdE; *Career* md Lucas Industries; *Style* - Anthony Gill Esq; Gt King st, Birmingham B19 2XF

GILL, Hon Mrs - Hon Charlotte Mary Magdalen; *née* Hunt; da of Baron Hunt of Tamworth, GCB, and Hon Magdalen, da of 1 Baron Robinson; *b* 1947; *m* 1976, Dr Herbert Gill; *Style* - The Hon Mrs Gill

GILL, Donald Phillott Chapple; s of Robert Carey Chapple Gill (d 1960); *b* 16 May 1918; *Educ* Shrewsbury; *m* 1, 1944, Anne Irvine (d 1961) whose 1 husband was Hon John Yarburgh Cunliffe-Lister (d on active serv 1943 and who was 2 s of 1 Earl of Swinton); m 2, 1965, Angela Faith, nee Barker; *Career* Lt 17/21 Lancers 1941 Tunisia; cotton broker, dir R & C Gill Ltd; *Recreations* shooting, fishing; *Style* - Donald Gill Esq; Greenage, Llanfyllin, Powys (☎ 069 184 305)

GILL, Frank Maxey; s of Frederick Gill, DSO; *b* 25 Sept 1919; *Educ* Marlborough; De Havilland Aeronautical Technical Sch; *m* 1, 1942, Sheila Gordon (decd); 3 da; m 2, 1952, Erica Fulcher; 1 s; *Career* dir Gill and Duffus Group Ltd 1957-; *Style* - Frank Gill Esq; Tile House, Reigate Heath, Reigate, Surrey

GILL, Air Vice-Marshal Harry; CB (1979), OBE (1968); s of John Gill; *b* 30 Oct 1922; *Educ* Barnby rd Sch; Newark Technical Coll; *m* 1951, Diana, nee Wood; 1 da; *Career* dir gen supply, RAF, 1976-79; *Style* - Air Vice-Marshal Harry Gill CB OBE; Briar Cottage, Hawley, Surrey (☎ Camberley 31587)

GILL, James Kenneth; FIPA; *Career* chm Saatchi and Saatchi Ltd; *Style* - James Gill Esq; 80-84 Charlotte st, W1

GILL, Hon Mrs (Rosemary Eva Gorell); *née* Barnes; da of 3 Baron Gorell, CBE, MC; *b* 9 July 1925; *Educ* Priors Field, Masters Sch Dobbs Ferry New York, NFF Roehampton, Bedford Coll London; *m* 1960, Peter, s of Charles Gill, CBE; 1 s, 2 da; *Career* teacher; chm Yorks Regnl European Mvmnt 1970-74, Fawcett Soc 1976-80; Ripon Diocesan Synod 1979-; *Recreations* reading, gardening, observing; *Style* - The Hon Mrs Gill; St Annes House, Nun Monkton, York (☎ 0901 30256)

GILL, His Honour Judge (Stanley Sanderson); s of Sanderson Gill, OBE, of Snow Hill Grange, Wakefield; *b* 3 Dec 1923; *Educ* Queen Elizabeth's Sch Wakefield, Magdalene Cambridge; *m* 1954, Margaret, da of James Grady, of Coventry; 1 s, 2 da; *Career* formerly Fl Lt Bomber Cmmd Europe; barr 1950-71; County Court Judge 1971, Circuit Judge 1972-; *Style* - His Hon Judge Gill; Downe, Baldersby, Thirsk, N Yorks (☎ Melmerby 283)

GILLAM, Gp Capt Denys Edgar; DSO and 2 Bars, DFC and bar, AFC, DL (W Riding Yorks 1959); s of Thomas Henry Gillam (d 1947); *b* 18 Nov 1915; *Educ* Wreakin Coll; *m* 1945, Nancye Joan, da of late Godfrey Short of S Africa; 1 s, 2 da; *Career* RAF 1935, gp capt 1944, ret 1946; md British Furtex Ltd, chm Homfray & Co Ltd 1971; *Clubs* RAF; *Style* - Gp Capt Denys Gillam, DSO**, DFC*,AFC, DL; The Glebe, Brawby, Malton, N Yorks (☎ Kirbymoorside 31530)

GILLAN, Sir (James) Angus; KBE (1939), CMG (1935); s of Rev James Gillan (d 1932); *b* 11 Oct 1885; *Educ* Edinburgh Academy, Magdalen Coll Oxford; *m* 1917, Margaret Douglas (d 1973), nee Ord-Mackenzie; 1 s, (and 1 da decd); *Career* entered Sudan Political Serv 1909, Assist Political and Intelligence Offr Western Frontier Force 1916, Gov Kordofan Prov 1928, Assist Civil Sec 1929, Civil Sec 1934, ret 1939, controller Empire Div Br Cncl 1942-51, Br Cncl Rep in Australia 1949-51, Order of the Nile 1935; *Recreations* rowing (pre-WW I), shooting, tennis, unskilled gardening and carpentry; *Clubs* Athenaeum, Leander, Royal Over-Seas League; *Style* - Sir Angus Gillan, KBE, CMG; Sheep Cote Cottage, Leigh, Reigate, Surrey (☎ Norwood Hill 862432)

GILLESPIE, D W; *Career* chm N G Bailey and Co Ltd; *Style* - D W Gillespie Esq; Heathcote, Ilkley, W Yorks

GILLETT, Eric Robert; s of Robert Gillett; *b* 14 Jan 1928; *Educ* St Bede's G S; Bradford U; *Career* dir Bowmaker Ltd 1972- (branch man 1958-61, personal assist to gen man 1961-66, regional man 1966-70, assist gen man 1970-72); pres

United Assoc for the Protection of Trade 1977- (hon tres 1974); *Recreations* tennis; *Clubs* West Hants Lawn Tennis Club; *Style* - Eric Gillett Esq; 24a East av, Bournemouth (☎ 0202 296253)

GILLETT, Nicholas Danvers Penrose; s and h of Sir Robin Gillett, 2 Bt, GBE, RD; *b* 24 Sept 1955; *Educ* Pangbourne and Imperial Coll London; *Career* trials engr with Br Aerospace 1977-; *Recreations* photography, sub-aqua, computing, reading; *Style* - Nicholas Gillett Esq

GILLETT, Sir Robin Danvers Penrose; 2 Bt (UK 1959), of Bassishaw Ward, City of London, GBE (1976), RD (1965); s of Sir Harold Gillett, 1 Bt, MC, FCA (d 1976); *b* 9 Nov 1925; *Educ* Pangbourne NC; *m* 1950, Elizabeth, da of John Findlay, JP, of Busby House, Lanarks; 2 s; *Heir* s, Nicholas Gillett; *Career* Lloyd's Underwriter; dir Wigham Poland Home Ltd; Ld Mayor London 1976-77 (Alderman 1969-, Sheriff 1973-74); V-Chm PLA; Pres Inst of Adminve Management 1980-; UK Pres RLSS 1978-; Elder Bro Trinity House 1978; *Recreations* sailing, photography (yacht- 'Lady Libby'); *Clubs* Roy Yacht Sqdn, Roy London Yacht (Rear Cdre), City Livery Yacht (Adm); *Style* - Sir Robin Gillett, Bt, GBE, RD; Elm Cottage, Biddestone, Wilts; 4 Fairholt st, SW7 (☎ 01 589 9860)

GILLHAM, Anthony John; s of Leslie James Gillham; *b* 17 May 1939; *Educ* Whitgift Sch, Imperial Coll London U; *m* 1969, Sheila Marion, nee Adnitt; 2 s; *Career* commissioned Cheshire Yeomanry 1968; chemical engr, md Carless Chemicals Ltd 1977-; *Recreations* fishing; *Clubs* Inst of Directors; *Style* - Anthony Gillham Esq; The Grange, Chop Gate, Middlesbrough, Cleveland (☎ Bilsdale 351)

GILLITT, Barry; s of Charles Leslie Gillitt; *b* 25 March 1932; *Educ* Shrewsbury, Cambridge; *m* 1957, Audrey, da of Edward Player, CBE; 2 s, 1 da; *Career* FCA, FTII; High Sheriff Warwicks 1974-75; Chm Coventry Diocesan Bd of Finance; *Recreations* sailing (yacht- 'Voodoo'), skiing, walking; *Clubs* RAC; *Style* - Barry Gillitt Esq; The Stone House, Leek Wootton, Warwicks (☎ Kenilworth 54673)

GILLOT, Nicholas Richard; TD (1948); s of Capt Bernard Henry Gillot (d 1954); *b* 21 Aug 1917; *Educ* Oundle; *m* 1966, Isobel Barrett; *Career* Capt, Royal Signals UK, Middle East, British Columbia, Germany; man dir Joseph Gillott & Sons Ltd 1948-72; chm Best & Lloyd Ltd 1972-74; man dir British Castors Ltd 1974-79; chm 1979-80; Hon Treasurer, Birmingham Chamber of Industry and Commerce 1979-; *Recreations* gardening, property maintenance; *Style* - Nicholas Gillot Esq, TD; Lawn Cottage, Bromsgrove rd, Clent, Stourbridge, West Midlands

GILLOW, Joseph Michael; s of Henry Paulyn Gillow (d 1966); *b* 24 June 1921; *Educ* Ampleforth; *m* 1949, Maivis Raymonde; 1 da; *Career* Hon Capt Army, Burma; chm & man dir Aynsley China Ltd; dir Waterford Glass Ltd; bloodstock breeder and farmer; *Recreations* hunting, fishing, shooting; *Clubs* Sportsman's, British pottery; *Style* - Joseph Gillow Esq; Heath Farm, Peover Heath, Nr Knutsford, Cheshire (☎ 0625 861340)

GILMORE, J F; *Career* md Catalytic International Inc, Winner of Queen's Award for Export Achievement 1979; *Style* - J F Gilmore Esq; 48 Leicester Square, WC2

GILMOUR, Andrew; CMG (1949); s of late James Gilmour; *b* 18 July 1898; *Educ* Edinburgh High Sch; *m* Nelle Twigg; 2 s, 3 da (and 1 s k in action); *Career* Malayan Civil Servant; *Style* - Andrew Gilmour Esq, CMG; Garden Cottage, Gifford, E Lothian (☎ 305)

GILMOUR, Alexander Clement; s of Sir John Gilmour, 2 Bt, (d 1977) and Lady Mary Gilmour, da of 3 Duke of Abercorn; 2 s, 1 da; *b* 23 Aug 1931; *Educ* Eton; *m* 1954, Barbara, da of the Hon Denis Berry, *qv*; *Career* dir Carr Sebag and Co 1972-; *Style* - Alexander Gilmour Esq; Denchworth Manor, Wantage, Oxon

GILMOUR, Col Allan Macdonald; OBE (1961), MC and Bar (1942, 1943),

DSC (US 1945); s of Capt Allan Gilmour, of Rosehall, Sutherland (ka Salonica 1916); *b* 23 Nov 1916; *Educ* Winchester; *m* 1941, Jean, da of Capt E Wood, of Gollanfield, Inverness-shire; 3 s, 1 da; *Career* Col Seaforth Highlanders, served WW II M East, Sicily, Italy, NW Europe, ret from army 1966; memb Sutherland DC, Highland Regnl Cncl and Health Bd; HM Ld-Lt Sutherland 1972-; *Recreations* fishing; *Style* - Col Allan Gilmour, OBE, MC*, DSC; HM Lord-Lieut for Sutherland, Invernauld, Rosehall, Sutherland (☎ 204)

GILMOUR, David Robert; s and h of Rt Hon Sir Ian Gilmour, MP, 3 Bt, *qv*; *b* 14 Nov 1952; *Educ* Eton and Balliol Coll Oxford; *m* 1975, Sarah Anne, da of Michael Bradstock, of Donnington Castle House, Newbury; 1 s, 1 da; *Style* - David Gilmour Esq; Farthingworth House, Montpelier Row, Twickenham, Middx

GILMOUR, Rt Hon Sir Ian Hedworth John Little; 3 Bt (UK 1926), PC (1973), MP (C) Chesham and Amersham 1974-; s of Sir John Little Gilmour, 2 Bt (d 1977); *b* 8 July 1926; *Educ* Eton, Balliol Oxford; *m* 1951, Lady Caroline Margaret Montagu Douglas Scott, da of 8 Duke of Buccleuch and Queensberry; 4 s, 1 da; *Heir* s, David Robert Gilmour; *Career* late Gren Gds, barr 1952, ed The Spectator 1954-59, under-sec MOD 1970-71, Min of State for Defence Procurement MOD 1971-72, for Defence 1972-74, Sec of State for Defence 1974, chm Con Research Dept 1974-75, MP Norfolk Central 1962-74, Lord Privy Seal 1979-; *Style* - The Rt Hon Sir Ian Gilmour Bt PC MP; The Ferry House, Old Isleworth, Middx (☎ 01 560 6769)

GILMOUR, John; s and h of Sir John Gilmour, 3 Bt, DSO, TD, JP, DL; *b* 15 July 1944; *Educ* Eton, Aberdeen U; *m* 1967, Valerie Jardine, da of G W Russell; 2 s, 2 da; *Career* farmer, memb Roy Co of Archers (Queen's Bodyguard for Scotland); Capt Fife and Forfar Yeo/Scottish Horse (TA); MFH 1972-; co dir; *Recreations* riding, fishing, reading; *Style* - John Gilmour Esq; Balcormo Mains, Leven, Fife

GILMOUR, Col Sir John Edward; 3 Bt (UK 1897), of Lundin and Montrave, Parishes of Largo and Scoonie, Co Fife, and South Walton, Mearns, Co Renfrew, DSO (1945), TD, JP (Fife 1957); s of Col Rt Hon Sir John Gilmour, 2 Bt, GCVO, DSO*, PC, sometime MP E Renfrewshire and Glasgow Pollok (d 1940), by his 1 w, Mary, da of Edward Lambert, of Telham Court, Sussex; *b* 24 Oct 1912; *Educ* Eton, Trin Hall Cambridge, Dundee Sch of Economics; *m* 1941, Ursula, da of Frank Oliver Wills, of Cote Lodge, Westbury-on-Trym; 2 s (of whom the yr, Andrew, m 1971 Mary, twin da of Sir Henry de la Poer Beresford-Peirse, 4 Bt, DSO, JP, by his w, Lady Mabel Campbell, JP, 2 da of 3 Earl Cawdor); *Heir* s, John Gilmour; *Career* MP (C) E Fife 1961-79, chm Con & Unionist Pty Scotland 1965-67; DL Fife 1953-, HM Ld-Lt 1980- (Vice Ld-Lt 1979-80); Bt Col 1950; Ensign Roy Co of Archers (Queen's Bodyguard for Scotland); *Recreations* hunting, gardening, shooting; *Clubs* Roy & Ancient St Andrews; *Style* - Col Sir John Gilmour Bt DSO TD JP, HM Lord-Lieut for Fife; Montrave, Leven, Fife (☎ 0333 26159)

GILMOUR, Lady Mary Cecilia Rhodesia; *née* Hamilton; da of 3 Duke of Abercorn; *b* 1896; *m* 1, 1917, Capt Robert Kenyon-Slaney, Gren Gds (m dis 1930; he d 1965); m 2, 1930, Sir John Gilmour, 2 Bt, (d 1977); *Style* - Lady Mary Gilmour; 5 Lynedoch Place, Edinburgh

GILMOUR, Hon Mrs Victoria Laura; OBE, TD; da of late Henry Arthur Cadogan (Viscount Chelsea, s of 5 Earl Cadogan) and Hon Mildred, nee Sturt; *b* 1901; *m* 1922 (m dis 1929), John Little Gilmour (afterwards 2 Bt, d 1977); *Career* formerly Controller ATS; acted as Lady-in-Waiting to HM Queen Elizabeth the Queen Mother when Duchess of York; *Style* - The Hon Mrs Victoria Gilmour, OBE, TD; Dacres, Bentworth, Hants

GILPIN, John; twin s of J Gilpin; *b* 10 Feb 1930; *Educ* Cone-Ripman Coll; *m* 1960, Sally Judd; *Career* ballet dancer, artistic dir Pittsburgh Ballet Company, Penn, USA; *Style* - John Gilpin Esq; 3 Orme Court, W2

GIMENA, Lady Anne-Marie Ines; *née*

Ward; da (twin, by 1 m) of 4 Earl of Dudley; *b* 1955; *m* 1978, Laureano Perez-Andujar Gimena, of Madrid *Style* - Lady Anne-Marie Gimena

GINTELL, Burton; *b* 11 May 1935; *Educ* City U NYC; *Career* md J G Turney & Son Ltd (Queen's Award for Export 1980, William Whiteley & Co, Glenforres Glenlivet Distillery Co Ltd 1978- *Style* - Burton Gintell Esq; Atlas House, 57a Catherine Place, SW1 (☎ 01 834 3771)

GIORDANO, Richard Vincent; *Educ* Harvard (BA), LLB, PhD; *Career* md BOC International Ltd; *Style* - Richard Giordano Esq; Group Head Office, Hammersmith House, Hammersmith Bridge rd, W6

GIRDLESTONE, G; *Career* md Camvac Holdings Ltd, winner of a Queen's Award for Export 1980 ; *Style* - G Girdlestone Esq; Thetford, Norfolk

GIRLING, Col Donald Barry, MC,TD; *Career* HM Lieut for City of London 1980; *Style* - Colonel Donald Girling, MC,TD

GIRLING, Hon Mrs (Eleanor Brigit); er da of 3 Viscount Addison; *b* 1938; *m* 1972, Michael Girling; *Style* - The Hon Mrs Girling; 9 Levana Close, SW19

GIROLAMI, Paul; s of Peter Girolami (d 1956); *b* 25 Jan 1926; *Educ* LSE; *m* 1952, Christabel, nee Lewis; 3 c; *Career* chartered accountant; *Style* - Paul Girolami Esq; Burghley rd, SW19 (☎ 01 946 0608)

GIROUARD, Mark; s of Richard Désiré Girouard (s of Col Sir Percy Girouard, KCMG, DSO, sometime CIC N Nigeria & Br E Africa Protectorates, by his w Mary, da of Hon Sir Richard Solomon, KCB, KCMG, KCVO; Sir Percy was s of Hon Désiré Girouard, sometime Puisne Judge Supreme Court Dominion of Canada) and Lady Blanche de la Poer Beresford (da of 6 Marquess of Waterford, KP, and Lady Beatrix Fitzmaurice, da of 5 Marquess of Lansdowne); *b* 7 Oct 1931; *Educ* Ampleforth, Ch Ch Oxford, Courtauld Inst of Art, Bartlett Sch, UCL; *m* 1970, Dorothy Dorf; 1 da; *Career* writer and architectural historian, PhD, Slade Prof of Fine Art Oxford 1975-76; memb Roy Fine Art Commission, Roy Commission Hist Monuments, Hist Bldgs Cncl, Cncl Victorian Soc; Hon FRIBA; *Style* - Mark Girouard Esq; 35 Colville rd, W11

GISBOROUGH, 3 Baron (UK 1917); Thomas Richard John Long Chaloner; s of 2 Baron Gisborough, TD, JP (d 1951); *b* 1 July 1927; *Educ* Eton, RAC Cirencester; *m* 1960, Shane, da of Sidney Newton, of Hyde Park Gate (2 s of Sir Louis Newton, 1 Bt); 2 s; *Heir* s, Hon Thomas Chaloner; *Career* CCllr N R Yorks & Cleveland 1964-77; Ld-Lt Cleveland 1981- (DL N Riding Yorks & Cleveland 1973-); farmer & landowner; formerly Lt-Col Green Howards (TA); *Recreations* gliding, bridge, hunting, piano, cricket, tennis; *Clubs* Northern Counties (Newcastle); *Style* - The Rt Hon Lord Gisborough, HM Lord-Lieut for Cleveland; 37 Bury Walk, SW3 (☎ 01 581 0260); Gisborough House, Guisborough, Cleveland (☎ 0287 32002)

GITLINS, R; *Career* md Analytical Instruments Ltd; winner of a Queen's Award for Technological Achievement 1980; *Style* - R Gitlins Esq; Pampisford, Cambridge

GLADSTONE, Charles Angus; s and h of Sir William Gladstone, 7 Bt, DL; *b* 11 April 1964; *Style* - Charles Gladstone Esq

GLADSTONE, Lady - Dora; *m* 1, Capt W D Brown, DSC, RN, (decd); m 2, 1966, Adm Sir Gerald Gladstone, GBE, KCB, (d 1978) ; *Style* - Lady Gladstone; Forsters, Bradpole, Bridport, Dorset

GLADSTONE, Isla Margaret; da of late Sir Walter Erskine Crum; *m* 1925, (Sir) Charles Andrew Gladstone, 6 Bt, but did not use title, (d 1968); *Style* - Mrs Charles Gladstone; North Park, Hawarden, Deeside, Clwyd

GLADSTONE, Hon Mrs; Hon Josephine; da of Baron Elwyn-Jones, CH, PC (Life Peer); *m* 1972, as his 2 w, James Francis Gladstone, s of 6 Bt (gs of Rt Hon William Gladstone, PM); 1 s; *Style* - The Hon Mrs Gladstone; 180 Bonad rd,

Chestnut Hill, S Brookline, MA 02167, USA

GLADSTONE, Sir (Erskine) William; 7 Bt (UK 1846), of Fasque and Balfour, Kincardineshire, DL (Flintshire 1969, Clwyd 1974); s of (Sir) Charles Andrew Gladstone (6 Bt) (d 1968); ggs of Rt Hon William Gladstone, PM; *b* 29 Oct 1925; *Educ* Eton, Ch Ch Oxford; *m* 1962, Rosamund Anne, da of late Maj Robert Alexander Hambro; 2 s, 1 da; *Heir* s, Charles Angus Gladstone; *Career* assist master Eton 1951-61, headmaster Lancing 1961-69, Chief Scout of the UK and Overseas Branches 1972-, chm World Scout Ctee; *Style* - Sir William Gladstone, Bt, DL; Hawarden Castle, Deeside, Clwyd (☎ Hawarden 532210); Fasque, Laurencekirk, Kincardineshire

GLADWYN, 1 Baron (UK 1960); (Hubert Miles) Gladwyn Jebb; GCMG (1954, KCMG 191949, CMG 1942), GCVO (1957), CB (1947); s of Sydney Jebb, JP (whose mother was Hon Alice Dundas, sis of 5 & 6 Viscounts Melville), by his 1 w, Rose, nee Chichester (of a Devon landed family distantly related to the Chichester Marquesses of Donegall, Chichester Barons Donoughmore, Chichester Barons O'Neill, the extinct Chichester Baronets of Arlington, and the extant landed Chichesters of Calverleigh); *b* 25 April 1900; *Educ* Eton, Magdalen Oxford; *m* 1929, Cynthia, da of Sir Saxton Noble, 3 Bt; 1 s, 2 da; *Heir* s, Hon Miles Jebb; *Career* Dep Lib Ldr Ho of Lds & Lib Spokesman For Affrs & Def 1965-, FO 1924-60 (Ambass France 1954-60, Perm UK Rep UNO 1950-54); stood as Lib MEP candidate Suffolk 1979; v-chm European Movement, Campaign for European Political Community; author of books on De Gaulle; *Style* - Rt Hon Lord Gladwyn GCMG GCVO CB; 62 Whitehall Court, SW1 (☎ 01 930 3160); Bramfield Hall, Halesworth, Suffolk (☎ Bramfield 241)

GLAMIS, Lord; Michael Fergus Bowes Lyon; s and h of 17 Earl of Strathmore and Kinghorne; *b* 7 June 1957; *Career* a Page of Honour to HM Queen Elizabeth The Queen Mother (his great aunt) 1971-73; probationary 2 Lt Short Serv Cmmn 1980-; *Style* - Lord Glamis

GLANDINE, Viscount; Richard James; s and h of 6 Earl of Norbury; *b* 5 March 1967; *Style* - Viscount Glandine

GLANUSK, 4 Baron (UK 1899); Sir David Russell Bailey; 5 Bt (UK 1852); s of Hon Herbert Bailey (4 s of 1 Baron) & Kathleen, da of Sir Shirley Salt, 3 Bt; suc 1 cous, 3 Baron, 1948; *b* 19 Nov 1917; *Educ* Eton; *m* 1941, Lorna, da of Capt Ernest Andrews, MBE, RA; 1 s, 1 da; *Heir* s, Hon Christopher Bailey; *Career* Lt-Cdr RN ret; md Wandel & Goltermann (UK) Ltd 1966-; chm Hatfield Instruments Ltd; *Style* - The Rt Hon Lord Glanusk; Sawmill House, Park Farm rd, High Wycombe, Bucks (☎ 24159)

GLANVILLE, Lt-Col Robert Cardew; OBE (Mil 1954), MC (1941), DL (Derbys 1967); s of Gerald Glanville, of St Germans Cornwall; *b* 29 Feb 1912; *Educ* Blundells, Sandhurst; *m* 1947, Alice, da of John Allen, of Ilford; *Career* formerly reg army offr, served WW II E Africa & Abyssinia, Ceylon & Burma, NW Europe, also 1932-58 ending as Cdr Support Bn Supreme HQ Allied Powers Europe 1956-58, TA Sec Derbys 1958-6; *Recreations* gardening; *Clubs* Army & Navy, County (Derby); *Style* - Lt-Col Robert Glanville, OBE, MC, DL; Catchfrench, Bridge Hill, Belper, Derbys (☎ 3255)

GLASGOW, 9 Earl of (S 1703); David William Maurice Boyle; CB (1962), DSC (1941); also Lord Boyle (S 1699), Lord Boyle and Viscount of Kelburn (S 1703), Baron Fairlie (UK 1897); s of 8 Earl of Glasgow, DSO (d 1963); *b* 24 July 1910; *Educ* Eton; *m* 1937, Dorothea (m dis 1942), da of Col Sir Archibald Lyle, 2 Bt, MC, TD, JP, DL, by his w, Dorothy, da of Sir James de Hoghton, 11 Bt, CBE; 1 s, 2 da; m 2, 1962, Hon Ursula, da of 4 Baron Vivian, DSO (by his 2 w, Nancy, MBE, da of Sir Edward Lycett Green, 2 Bt), and former w of Maj Philip Bridgewater and Sir William Wrixon-Becher, 5 Bt; *Heir* s, Viscount of Kelburn; *Career* Rear-Adm (1961), Flag Offr Malta 1961-63; memb Roy Co of Archers (Queen's Bodyguard for Scotland); *Recreations* shooting, travel; *Clubs* New (Edinburgh); *Style* - The Rt

Hon The Earl of Glasgow, CB, DSC; Kelburn, Fairlie, Ayrshire (☎ 204)

GLASGOW, Archbishop of (RC) 1974- Thomas Joseph Winning; s of Thomas Winning (d 1959); *b* 3 June 1925; *Educ* Our Lady's H S Motherwell, Blairs Coll Aberdeen, St Peter's Coll Bearsden, Pontifical Scots Coll and Pontifical Gregorian U Rome; *Career* Spiritual Dir Pontifical Scots Coll Rome 1961-66, Pres Scottish Catholic Tbnl 1970-71, Aux Bp Glasgow 1971-74; *Recreations* golf; *Style* - His Grace the Archbishop of Glasgow; The Oaks, 40 Newlands rd, Glasgow G43 2JD

GLASGOW, Countess of; Hon Ursula Vanda Maud; da of 4 Baron Vivian, DSO (d 1940); *b* 1912; *m* 1, 1935 (m dis 1946), Maj Philip Alexander Clement Bridgewater; 1 s, 1 da; m 2, 1946 (m dis 1960), Maj Sir William Fane Wrixon-Becher, MC, 5 Bt; 1 s, 1 da; m 3, 1962, 9 Earl of Glasgow; *Style* - The Rt Hon the Countess of Glasgow; Kelburn Fairlie, Ayrshire; 110 Cheyne Walk, SW10

GLASSON, Christopher Paul; s of Donald Trelawney Glasson; *b* 4 Jan 1941; *Educ* Latymer Upper Sch, Emmanuel Cambridge; *m* 1964, Julie, nee Gill; 2 children; *Career* dir of Antocks Lairn Gp and UK subsidiaries 1976, Leabank Office Furniture Ltd, pres Vinco MT SA (France) 1980; *Recreations* golf, squash, music, philately; *Clubs* Inst of Dirs, Cambridge Union; *Style* - Christopher Glasson Esq; Woodfields, Chipstead, Sevenoaks, Kent (☎ 56358)

GLASSPOLE, Sir Florizel Augustus; GCMG (1981), CD; s of late Rev Theophilus Glasspole; *b* 25 Sept 1909; *Educ* Wolmer's Boys' Sch, Ruskin Coll Oxford; *m* 1934, Ina Josephine Kinlocke; 1 da; *Career* Gov-Gen Jamaica 1974-, accountant 1932-44, dir City Printery Ltd 1944-50, Gen Sec Jamaica TUC 1939-52, memb House of Reps 1944-73, Min Educn 1957-62 and 1972-73, Leader of House 1955-62 and 1972-73, Min of Labour 1955-57; *Recreations* sports, gardening; *Style* - H E Sir Florizel Glasspole GCMG CD; King's House, Kingston, Jamaica

GLAZEBROOK , William Francis; *b* 29 March 1929; *Educ* Wharton Graduate Sch; *m* 1955, Cecily McClatchy; 3 s, 4 da ; *Career* md 1974-, ch exec 1977-, Rank Xerox Ltd; *Style* - William Francis Glazebrook Esq; 56 Cumberland ter, NW1

GLEESON, John Patrick; *Career* chm and md M J Gleeson (Contractors) Ltd; *Style* - John Gleeson Esq; Haredon House, North Cheam, Surrey

GLENAMARA, Baron (Life Peer UK 1977); Edward Watson Short; CH (1976), PC (1964); s of Charles Short, of Westmorland; *b* 17 Dec 1912; *Educ* Bede Coll Durham U; *m* 1941, Jennie, da of Thomas Sewell, of Newcastle; 1 s, 1 da; *Career* served WW II Capt DLI; MP (L) Newcastle-upon-Tyne Centl 1951-76, Oppn Whip (N) 1955-62, Dep Ch Oppn Whip 1962-64, Govt Ch Whip (& Parly Sec Treasury) 1964-66, Postmaster Gen 1966-68, Sec State Educn & Sci 1968-70, Ld Pres Cncl & Ldr Commons 1974-76, Dep Ldr Lab Pty 1972-76; *Style* - Rt Hon Lord Glenamara CH PC; Glenridding, Cumbria (273); 4 Patterdale gdns, Newcastle upon Tyne 7 (☎ 651991)

GLENAPP, Viscount; Kenneth Peter Lyle Mackay; s and h of 3 Earl of Inchcape; *b* 23 Jan 1943; *Educ* Eton; *m* 1966, Georgina, da of S C Nisbet; 1 s, 2 da; *Heir* s, Hon Fergus Mackay; *Career* late 2 Lt 9/12 Roy Lancers, regional dir Gray Mackenzie & Co Ltd Bahrain 1978-; *Style* - Viscount Glenapp; P O Box 210, Bahrain

GLENARTHUR, 4 Baron (UK 1918); Sir Simon Mark Arthur; 4 Bt (UK 1903); s of 3 Baron Glenarthur, OBE, DL (d 1976), by his 2 w (*see* Glenarthur, Margaret, Baroness); *b* 7 Oct 1944; *Educ* Eton; *m* 1969, Susan, da of Cdr Hubert Barry, RN (ret), and Violet, da of Col Sir Edward Ruggles-Brise, 1 Bt (Cdr Barry was 2 s of William Barry, JP (himself 4 s of Sir Francis Barry, 1 Bt, DL, Baron de Barry in Portugal and sometime MP Windsor), by his w, Lady Grace Murray, MBE, da of 7 Earl of Dunmore); 1 s, 1 da; *Heir* s, Hon Edward Arthur; *Career* Maj (ret) Roy Hussars (TA) 1975-80; Capt Br Airways Helicopters Ltd 1976-; dir Aberdeen & Texas Corporate Finance Ltd

1977-; *Recreations* shooting, flying; *Clubs* Cavalry & Guards; *Style* - The Rt Hon The Lord Glenarthur; Birch Hill, Torphins, Banchory, Kincardineshire (☎ 033982 287)

GLENARTHUR, Margaret, Baroness; Margaret Risk; da of late Capt Henry Howie; *m* 1939, as his 2 w, 3 Baron Glenarthur (d 1976); 2 s (4 Baron, Hon Matthew Arthur), 1 da (Hon Mrs Vernon); *Style* - The Rt Hon Margaret, Lady Glenarthur; Stairaird, Mauchline, Ayrshire

GLENAVY, 4 Baron (UK 1921); Sir Michael Mussen Campbell; 4 Bt (UK 1916); s of 2 Baron (d 1963) and bro of 3 Baron (Patrick Campbell, the columnist, author, broadcaster and wit, who d 1980); *b* 25 Oct 1924; *Educ* St Columba's Coll; Trinity Coll, Dublin; *Heir* none; *Career* barrister; *Style* - The Rt Hon The Lord Glenavy; 39 Kendal st, W2 (☎ 01 262 6040)

GLENAVY, Baroness; Vivienne; da of of Charles Knight, MC; *m* 1, Eric Drake (decd); m 2, Hartley Sharpe; m 3, Charles Orme; m 4, 1966, as his 3 w, 3 Baron Glenavy (Patrick Campbell, the author, who d 1980); *Style* - The Rt Hon The Lady Glenavy; La Tranche, Le Rouret 06, France

GLENCAIRN, Earldom of (S 1488, dormant since 1796); the sr male rep of the descendants of Andrew Cuninghame 1 of Corsehill, 2 s of 4 Earl (among whose descendants through female lines is the editor of this book) is Sir John Cuninghame, 12 Bt; Sir Walter Montgomery-Cuninghame, 4 Bt, claimed the Earldom July 1797, as did Sir Adam Fergusson, 3 Bt (gggs of the 10 Earl through the female line); the question of whether the heir-of-line or heir general had the right to the dignity (given that an heir male's succession was not challenged prior to the Union of Scotland & England) was not cleared up

GLENCONNER, 2 Baron (UK 1911); Sir Christopher Grey Tennant; 3 Bt (UK 1885); s of 1 Baron Glenconner (d 1920; as Sir Edward Tennant, 2 Bt, sat as Lib MP Salisbury 1906-10; bro of Margot Asquith - Emma, his 5 sis, who m 1 Earl of Oxford and Asquith, KG, PM 1908-16) by Pamela, yst da of Hon Percy Scawen Wyndham, JP, DL, sometime MP W Cumberland (2 s of 1 Baron Leconfield); *b* 14 June 1899; *m* 1, 1925 (m dis 1935), Pamela, da of Sir Richard Paget, 2 Bt, and Lady Muriel Finch-Hatton, CBE (da of 12 Earl of Winchilsea and Nottingham); 2 s; m 2, 1935, Elizabeth, da of Lt-Col Evelyn Harcourt Powell, Gren Gds, of Kensington; 1 s, 2 da; *Heir* s, Hon Colin Tennant; *Career* sometime chm Tharsis Sulphur & Copper Co; *Clubs* White's; *Style* - The Rt Hon The Lord Glenconner; Rovinia, Liapades, Corfu, Greece

GLENDEVON, 1 Baron (UK 1964); Lord John Adrian Hope; PC (1959); s of 2 (twin) s of 2 Marquess of Linlithgow; *b* 7 April 1912; *Educ* Eton, Ch Ch Oxford; *m* 1948, Elizabeth, da of Somerset Maugham, CH, FRSL, the author (and yr bro of 1 Viscount Maugham), by his w Syrie (the fashionable pre-war interior decorator), former w of Henry (later Sir Henry) Wellcome and da of Dr Thomas Barnardo, the philanthropist (Elizabeth's 1 husb was Vincent, s of Charles Paravicini, sometime Swiss Min to the UK); 2 s; *Heir* s, Hon Julian Hope; *Career* temp Maj Scots Gds reserve; MP (C) Midlothian N & Peebles 1945-50, Edinburgh Pentlands 1950-64, Min Works 1959-62 (Jt Parly Under Sec Scotland 1957-59, Parly Under Sec State C'wlth Rels 1956-57 & For Affrs 1954-56); FRSA, chm Roy C'wlth Soc 1963-66, Hist Bldgs Cncl England 1973-75; dir & dep chm Ciba-Geigy (UK) Ltd 1971-78; dir ITT (UK), Colonial Mutual Life Assur Soc, Br Electric Traction Omnibus Servs; *Style* - The Rt Hon Lord Glendevon PC; Durham House, Durham Place, SW3 (☎ 01 352 6478)

GLENDINING, Rev Canon Alan; MVO (1979); s of Vincent Glendining, MS, FRCS, of King's Langley, Herts; *b* 17 March 1924; *Educ* Radley; *m* 1948, Margaret, da of Lt-Col Claud Hawes, DSO, of St Andrews; 1 s, 2 da; *Career* Hon Chaplain to HM The Queen 1979, Hon Canon Norwich 1977; Rector Sandringham Gp of Parishes 1970-79 & Domestic Chaplain to HM The Queen;

Recreations shooting, books; *Style* - The Rev Canon Alan Glendining MVO; St Margaret's Rectory, 16 Corton rd, Lowestoft, Suffolk (☎ 3046)

GLENDINNING, Hon Mrs Victoria; *née* Seebohm; da of Baron Seebohm, TD (Life Peer), and Evangeline (da of His Hon Sir Gerald Hurst, QC); *b* 23 April 1937; *Educ* St Mary's Wantage, Millfield, Somerville Oxford; *m* 1958 (m dis 1981), Prof Oliver Glendinning; 4 s; *Career* authoress and journalist; works include books on Edith Sitwell and Elizabeth Bowen; *Recreations* gardening; *Style* - The Hon Mrs Victoria Glendinning; c/o Barclays Bank, High st, Hitchin, Herts

GLENDYNE, 3 Baron (UK 1922); Sir Robert Nivison; 3 Bt (UK 1914); s of 2 Baron (d 1967); *b* 27 Oct 1926; *Educ* Harrow; *m* 1953, Elizabeth, yr da of Sir Stephen Cecil Armitage, CBE, JP, DL, of Hawksworth Manor, Notts; 1 s, 2 da; *Heir* s, Hon John Nivison; *Career* served Gren Gds WW II as Lt; sr ptnr R Nivison & Co (stockbrokers); *Clubs* City of London; *Style* - The Rt Hon Lord Glendyne; Hurdcott, Barford St Martin, Salisbury, Wilts (☎ Wilton 2221)

GLENKINGLAS, Baron (Life Peer UK 1974); Michael Antony Cristobal Noble; PC (1962); s of 3 & yst s of Sir John Noble, 1 Bt, of the 1923 cr (who was himself 3 s of Sir Andrew Noble, 1 Bt, KCB, of the 1902 cr); *b* 19 March 1913; *Educ* Eton, Magdalen Oxford; *m* 1940, Anne, da of Sir Neville Pearson, 2 Bt, by his 1 w, Hon Mary Mond (da of 1 Baron Melchett); 4 da; *Career* served WW II Sqdn Ldr RAFVR; MP (C) Argyll 1958-74, Govt Scottish Whip 1960-62, Sec State Scotland 1962-64, Pres BOT 1970 (June-Oct), Min Tde 1970-72; chm Br Ag Export Cncl 1973-77; dir Monteith Hldgs 1974-; *Clubs* Boodle's, New (Edinburgh); *Style* - The Rt Hon Lord Glenkinglas PC; Strone, Cairndow, Argyll (☎ Cairndow 284)

GLENNY, Reginald Thomas; CBE (1964); s of Walter Glenny; *b* 10 July 1914; *Educ* Alleyn's Sch Dulwich; *m* 1, 1939, Edith, nee Stevenson (d 1957); m 2, 1960, Florence, da of Joseph Wilson; *Career* Capt (TA), served WW II France, S Asia; memb Stock Exchange 1948-; chm Finance Ctee London Diocese 1977-, Gter London Con Assoc 1969-72; *Recreations* watching cricket, playing politics; *Clubs* MCC; *Style* - Reginald Glenny, Esq, CBE; 22 Clarewood rd, Seymour Place, W1 (☎ 01 262 8217)

GLENTORAN, 2 Baron (UK 1939); Sir Daniel Stewart Thomas Bingham Dixon; 4 Bt (UK 1903), KBE (1973), PC (NI 1953); s of 1 Baron, OBE, PC, JP, DL (d 1950) and Hon Emily Bingham (da of 5 Baron Clanmorris); *b* 19 Jan 1912; *Educ* Eton, Sandhurst; *m* 1933, Lady Diana Wellesley, da of 3 Earl Cowley; 2 s, 1 da; *Heir* s, Hon Thomas Dixon; *Career* served WW II and as regular Gren Gds, Lt-Col ret, Hon Col 6 Bn RUR (TA); MP (U) NI Parl Belfast Bloomfield 1950-61, Min Commerce 1953-61; Min NI Senate 1961-72, Speaker 1964-72; HM Lt Belfast 1950-76, Lord-Lieut 1976-; *Style* - The Rt Hon Lord Glentoran KBE PC, HM Lord-Lieut for Belfast; Drumadarragh House, Doagh, Co Antrim, N Ireland (☎ 222)

GLENTORAN, Baroness - Lady Diana Mary; *née* Wellesley; da of late 3 Earl Cowley; *b* 1914; *m* 1933, 2 Baron Glentoran; 2 s, 1 da; *Style* - The Rt Hon the Lady Glentoran; Drumdarragh House, Doagh, Co Antrim

GLENTWORTH, Viscount; Edmund Christopher Pery; s and h of 6 Earl of Limerick; *b* 10 Feb 1963; *Style* - Viscount Glentworth

GLIN, 29 Knight of (The Black Knight, I hereditary knighthood c 1300-30); Desmond John Villiers FitzGerald; s of 28 Knight of Glin (Desmond Windham Otho FitzGerald, d 1949, descended from John Fitz-Thomas FitzGerald, f of three bros- The White Knight, The Knight of Glin and The Knight of Kerry; John was himself n of 1 Baron Offaly, from whom the Dukes of Leinster descend) by his w Veronica, yr da of Ernest Villiers, MP, and Hon Elaine Guest, 3 da of 1 Baron Wimborne; *b* 13 July 1937; *Educ* Stowe, U of BC, Harvard; *m* 1, 1966 (m dis 1970), Lulu (Louise) Vava Lucia Henriette, da of Marquis de la Falaise de la Condraye, of

Paris; m 2, 1979, Olda Anne, da of Thomas Willes, of Brompton sq, SW; 3 da; *Heir* kinsman, Gerald FitzGerald; *Career* Assist Dep Keeper, Dept Furniture & Woodwork, V & A 1965-75; Irish Agent Christie's 1975-; V-Pres Irish Georgian Soc; author of books on Irish art, architecture and history; *Recreations* art history; *Clubs* White's, Beefsteak, Kildare & University (Dublin); *Style* - The Knight of Glin; 52 Waterloo rd, Dublin 4 (☎ 0001 680585); Glin Castle, Co Limerick, Eire (☎ 068 34173 & 34112)

GLOSSOP, Peter; s of of Cyril Glossop; *b* 6 July 1928; *Educ* High Storrs GS, Sheffield; *m* 1, 1955, Joyce Blackham (m dis 1977); m 2, 1977, Michelle Amos; *Career* singer (baritone) guest artist, Royal Opera House, Covent Garden; *Style* - Peter Glossop Esq; Elmcroft, 91 Cambridge rd, Teddington, Middx

GLOVER, Anthony Richard Hayson; s of of Arthur Glover (d 1941); *b* 29 May 1934; *Educ* Emmanuel Cambridge; *m* 1960, Ann, da of John Scupham, OBE; 2 s, 1 da; *Career* dep controller, HMSO from 1976; *Style* - Anthony Glover Esq; 7 Hillside rd, Thorpe St Andrew, Norwich (☎ 33508)

GLOVER, Lt-Gen Sir James Malcolm; KCB (1981), MBE (1964); s of of Maj-Gen Malcolm Glover, CB, OBE; *b* 25 March 1929; *Educ* Wellington; Sandhurst; *m* 1958, Janet Diones De Pree; 1 s, 1 da ; *Career* formerly Roy Green Jackets and Cdr Land Forces N Ireland; dep ch Defence Staff (Intelligence) MOD from 1980; *Style* - Lt-Gen Sir James Glover, KCB, MBE; West End Farmhouse, Medstead, Alton, Hants (☎ 62150)

GLOVER, John Neville; CMG (1963); s of John Glover; *b* 12 July 1913; *Educ* Tonbridge; *m* 1, 1940, Margaret, da of Stanley Burdick, MBE; 1 s; m 2, 1956, June, da of Wing Cdr Arthur Gaskell, DSC; *Career* served RAF WW II and after in RAFVR; barr 1949; Law Revision Commissioner & Legal Draftsman for various overseas territories 1967-; *Recreations* fly fishing; *Clubs* RAF; *Style* - John Glover Esq, CMG; Clam End, Trebullett, Launceston, Cornwall (☎ Coads Green 347)

GLYN, Dr Alan; ERD, MP (C) Windsor & Maidenhead 1974-; s of John Glyn, late RHG (Blues) and barr (d 1938); *b* 26 Sept 1918; *Educ* Westminster, Gonville & Caius Cambridge, Bart's & St George's Hosps; *m* 1962, Lady Rosula Windsor-Clive (b 30 April 1935), 3 da of 2 Earl of Plymouth, PC, by Lady Irene Charteris (da of 11 & 7 Earl of Wemyss and March); 2 da; *Career* Dr 1948; served WW II Far East and again as Capt (Hon Maj) RHG to 1967; barr 1955; MP Wandsworth Clapham 1959-64, Windsor 1970-74; memb Inner London Med Cttee 1967-, GLC Valuation Panel 1967-; Freeman City of London 1961; *Clubs* Carlton; *Style* - Dr Alan Glyn, ERD, MP; 17 Cadogan Place, SW1 (☎ 01 235 2957)

GLYN, Sir Anthony Geoffrey Leo Simon; 2 Bt (UK 1927); s of Sir Edward Rae Davson, 1 Bt, KCMG (d 1937), and Margot Elinor, OBE, da of Clayton Louis Glyn and his wife Elinor Sutherland (the novelist Elinor Glyn); assumed by deed poll 1957 the surname of Glyn in lieu of his patronymic and the additional forename of Anthony; *b* 13 March 1922; *Educ* Eton; *m* 1946, Susan Eleanor (barr), da of Lt-Col Sir Rhys Rhys Williams, 1 Bt, DSO, QC; 1 da (and 1 da decd); *Heir* bro, Christopher Michael Edward Davson; *Career* Welsh Gds (Capt) 1941-46; author; *Style* - Sir Anthony Glyn, Bt; 13 rue le Regrattier, Ile Saint-Louis, Paris 75004

GLYN, Barbara, Lady; da of William Ritchie Jardine; *m* 1, Gp Capt F Henwood; m 2, 1970, as his 2 w, Sir Richard Glyn, Bt, OBE, TD, (d 1980) ; *Style* - Barbara, Lady Glyn; 53 Belgravia Court, Ebury st, SW1

GLYN, Hilary Beaujolais; s of Maurice Glyn, of Albury Hall, Ware, and Hon Maud, nee Grosvenor, da of 2 Baron Ebury, DL, by his w, Hon Emilie White (yr da of 1 Baron Annaly); *b* 12 Jan 1916; *Educ* Eton; New Coll, Oxford; *m* 1938, Caroline, da of W P Bull, KC, (d 1948); 1 s, 2 da ; *Career* md Gallaher Ltd 1975-76; ret; *Recreations* gardening, shooting; *Style* - Hilary Glyn Esq; Oakum House, Albury, Ware, Herts (☎ Albury 328)

GLYN, Jeremy Christopher; s of Sir Francis Glyn, KCMG, JP (gs of Hon Pascoe Glyn, 5 s of 1 Baron Wolverton) by his 1 w, Jane; hp to 2 cous once removed, 5 Baron Wolverton; *b* 1 Oct 1930; *Educ* Eton, Worcester Coll Oxford; *m* 1956, Robina, da of Sir George Harford, 2 Bt; 1 da; *Career* farmer; *Recreations* shooting, fishing, country pursuits; *Clubs* Boodle's; *Style* - Jeremy Glyn Esq; The Bury, Little Hadham, Ware, Herts (☎ 0279 53092)

GLYN, Maj John Patrick Riversdale; CBE (1974); s of Maurice Glyn (gs of 1 Baron Wolverton) by Hon Maud Grosvenor, JP, da of 2 Baron Ebury; *b* 17 April 1913; *Educ* Eton, New Coll Oxford; *m* 1937, Audrey Stubbs; 2 s, 2 da; *Career* md Glyn Mills & Co 1950-70, chm Ag Mortgage Co 1964-, Alexanders Discount Co 1961-, Yorkshire Bank 1970-, Extel Ad & PR Servs 1972-, First Nat Fin Corpn 1975-; FIB 1978; *Style* - Maj John Glyn, CBE; The Dower House, Chute Standen, Andover, Hants (☎ Chute Standen 228)

GLYN, Lady Rosula Caroline; *née* Windsor-Clive; da of 2 Earl of Plymouth, PC (d 1943); *b* 1935; *m* 1962, Dr Alan Glyn, ERD, MP; 2 da; *Style* - Lady Rosula Glyn; 17 Cadogan Place, SW1

GLYN, Sir Richard Lindsay; 6 Bt (1800) of Gaunt's House, Dorset, and 10 Bt (1759); s of of Sir Richard Hamilton Glyn, OBE, TD, 5 and 9 Bt, (d 1980); *b* 3 Aug 1943; *Educ* Eton; *m* 1970 (m dis 1979), Carolyn, da of Roy Frank Williams, of Pasadena, Calif, USA (1979); 1 s, 1 da; *Heir* s Richard Glyn, *qv*; *Career* Lloyd's Underwriter from 1977; *Style* - Sir Richard Glyn Bt; Ashton Farmhouse, Stanbridge, Wimborne, Dorset (☎ Witchampton 840585)

GLYN, Richard Rufus Francis; s and h of Sir Richard Glyn, Bt,*qv*; *b* 8 Jan 1971; *Style* - Richard Glyn Esq

GLYN-JONES, Lady - Kathleen; da of Thomas Melville; *m* 1921, Sir Hildreth Glyn-Jones, TD, (d 1980); 2 da, (and 1 da decd); *Style* - Lady Glyn-Jones; 33 The Strand, Topsham, Exeter (☎ Topsham 5483)

GLYNN, Maurice; *Career* md Reads Ltd; *Style* - Maurice Glynn Esq; Orrell Lane, Liverpool L9 8BW

GLYNN, Prudence Loveday; also Lady Windlesham; da of Lt-Col Rupert Trevor Wallace Glynn, MC, of Harlesford House, Tetsworth, Oxon; *b* 22 Jan 1935; *m* 1965, 3 Baron Windlesham, *qv*; 1 s, 1 da; *Career* columnist The Times (fashion ed 1966-80); memb CNAA 1977-, CNAA Cttee Art & Design 1972-, Crafts Cncl 1977-, late memb Design Cncl; *Style* - Rt Hon Lady Windlesham; The Manor House, Westhall Hill, Burford, Oxon (☎ 01 637 7301)

GLYNN, Stanley Frederick Henry; *b* 5 Aug 1918; *Educ* Mercers'; *m* 1943, Mary Keith, nee Dewdney; 2 da; *Career* Maj N Africa, Italy, Greece; auctioneer, estate agent, Knight Frank and Rutley 1935-79, govr BUPA 1970, chm BUPA Medical Foundation 1979, dir Sussex Mutual Building Soc 1970-, memb of Lloyd's; *Recreations* tennis, walking, gardening, watching cricket; *Clubs* Carlton, MCC, Farmer's, Inst of Dirs; *Style* - Stanley Glynn Esq; Rosemount, Cricket Ground rd, Chislehurst, Kent; (☎ 01 467 5197); 21 Cliffe House, Radnor Cliff, Folkestone, Kent (☎ 38008)

GLYNNE-WALTON, Hon Mrs (Caroline Jane Grenville); *née* Freeman-Grenville; da of late Rev the Hon Luis Chandos Francis Temple Morgan-Grenville, Master of Kinloss; sis of Lady Kinloss; *b* 1931; *m* 1958, Gordon Glynne-Walton, FRGS, FRMetSoc, FRAS, FGS; 2 da; *Career* raised to the rank of a Baron's da 1947; *Style* - The Hon Mrs Glynne-Walton; White Lea Grange, Batley, Yorks

GODBER, Hon Andrew Robin; s of of Baron Godber of Willington PC DL of Willington Manor, Bedford (Life Peer, d 1980); *b* 7 Sept 1943; *Educ* Bedford Sch; *m* 1969 Genevieve, da of late Kenneth Parrish, of Higham Gobion, Herts; 2 s; *Career* author; *Recreations* sailing; *Clubs* Roy Cinque Ports Yacht, Sandwich Bay Sailing; *Style* - The Hon Andrew Godber; Weddington Farm House, Ash, nr Canterbury, Kent (☎ Ash 812041)

GODBER, Geoffrey Chapman; CBE (1961), DL (W Sussex 1975); s of Isaac Godber, of Willington Manor, Beds; er bro of Baron Godber of Willington, PC, DL (Joseph Godber, sometime Min of Ag, Fish & Food; d 1980); *b* 22 Sept 1912; *Educ* Bedford Sch; *m* 1937, Norah, da of Reginald Finney, of Willington; 3 s; *Career* slr 1936; Clerk of CC & Lieutenancy W Sussex 1966-75; memb Br Waterways Bd 1975-, dep chm Shoreham Port Authority 1976-; *Recreations* sailing (ketch 'Geno'), shooting; *Clubs* Naval & Military, Sussex; *Style* - Geoffrey Godber Esq, CBE, DL; Pricklows, Singleton, Chichester, W Sussex (☎ Singleton 238)

GODBER OF WILLINGTON, Baroness; Miriam; da of Haydon Sanders, of Lowestoft; *m* 1936, Baron Godber of Willington, PC (Life Peer, d 1980); 2 s; *Style* - The Rt Hon the Lady Godber of Willington; Willington Manor, nr Bedford

GODBER, Robert Christopher; s of Geoffrey Chapman Godber, CBE; *b* 3 Nov 1938; *Educ* Bedford, Merton Oxford; *m* 1962, Frances Merryn Candy, nee Bretherton; 3 s, 1 da; *Career* dir Travis & Arnold Ltd, responsible for Group Policy on Timber and Forest Products 1973-, branch man Travis & Arnold (Rugby) 1969-73, (Cambridge) 1967-69; *Recreations* sailing (yacht 'Minnow'), shooting, badminton; *Clubs* Banbury Sailing, Leander, Roy Ag Soc of England; *Style* - Robert Godber Esq; Greys Orchard, Barby, Rugby (☎ 890257)

GODBER, Hon Richard Thomas; s of Baron Godber of Willington, PC (Life Peer, d 1980); *b* 1938; *m* 1962, Candida, da of late Albert Parrish; *Style* - The Hon Richard Godber; Hall Farm, Little Linford, nr Milton Keynes

GODBER, Baroness; Violet Ethel Beatrice; JP; da of George Lovesy, of Cheltenham; *m* 1914, 1 and last Baron Godber (d 1976); 2 da; *Style* - The Rt Hon the Lady Godber, JP; Cranesden, Mayfield, Sussex (3271)

GODDARD, Harold Keith; QC (1979); s of Harold Goddard; *b* 9 July 1936; *Educ* Manchester G S; Corpus Christi Coll, Cambridge; *m* 1963, Susan, nee Stansfield; 2 s; *Career* barrister 1959; recorder of the Crown Court from 1978; *Style* - Harold Goddard Esq, QC; 77 Manchester rd, Wilmslow, Cheshire (☎ 26409)

GODFREY, Hon Mrs - Hon (Sonja) Lois; *née* Mitchison; da of Baron Mitchison, CBE, QC (Life Peer) (d 1970); *m* 1959, John Godfrey; *Style* - The Hon Mrs Godfrey

GODLEY, Hon Christopher John; s and h of 3 Baron Kilbracken, DSC; *b* 1 Jan 1945; *Educ* Rugby, Reading U; *m* 1969, Gillian, da of Lt-Cdr Stuart Birse, OBE, DSC, RN (ret), of Alverstoke, Hants; 1 s, 1 da; *Career* agriculturist; *Style* - The Hon Christopher Godley; 23 The Avenue, Andover, Hants

GODLEY, Hon Wynne Alexander Hugh; s of 2 Baron Kilbracken, CB, KC (d 1950); *b* 2 Sept 1926; *Educ* Rugby; New Coll, Oxford; *m* 1955, Kathleen, da of Sir Jacob Epstein, KBE; 1 da; *Career* formerly professional oboist; served Treasury 1957-70; dir Investing in Success Equities Ltd 1970-, Roy Opera House Covent Garden 1976-; dir of Dept Applied Economics, Cambridge U and fellow King's Coll, Cambridge 1970-; *Style* - The Hon Wynne Godley; Eversden House, Great Eversden, Cambs

GODMAN, Desmond Frederick Shirley; JP (Glos 1962); s of Lt-Col E Godman, OBE; *b* 31 Jan 1927; *Educ* Winchester, Cambridge; *m* 1954, Angela, da of Rev J Rowson; 2 s, 2 da; *Career* High Sheriff Glos 1976; *Clubs* Farmers; *Style* - Desmond Godman Esq, JP; Great Rissington Manor, Cheltenham, Glos (☎ 0451 20312)

GODWIN, Dame (Beatrice) Anne; DBE (1962); da of William Godwin (d 1932); *b* 6 July 1897; *Career* formerly gen sec Clerical & Administrative Workers' Union; gov BBC 1962-68; memb Industrial Court 1963-69; *Style* - Dame Anne Godwin, DBE; 25 Fulbrooks av, Worcester Park, Surrey

GODWIN, George; *Career* chm and joint md Martonair International Ltd ; *Style* - George Godwin Esq; 128 St Margaret's rd,

Twickenham, Middx

GOEHR, Prof Alexander; s of Walter Goehr; *b* 10 Aug 1932; *Educ* Berkhamstead; Royal Manchester Coll of Music; Paris Conservatoire; *m* 1, 1954, Audrey Baker (m dis 1971); 3 da; m 2, 1972, Anthea Staunton; 1 s; *Career* composer; Prof of Music and fellow of Trinity Hall Cambridge from 1976; *Style* - Prof Alexander Goehr; Trinity Hall, Cambridge

GOFF, Hon Mrs (Angela Estelle); *née* Kitson; da of 2 Baron Airedale; *b* 1905; *m* 1927, George Goff (d 1957); 1 s, 1 da; *Style* - The Hon Mrs Goff; 20 Field Way, Broad Oak, Brede, E Sussex

GOFF, Martyn; OBE (1977); s of Jacob Goff; *b* 7 June 1923; *Educ* Clifton; *Career* dir National Book League 1970-; reviewer and author; *Style* - Martyn Goff Esq, OBE; Tedworth House, Tedworth sq, SW3 (☎ 01 352 3164)

GOFF, Lady - Marjorie Morwenna; da of late Rev A Garfield Curnow, of Wallington; *m* 1944, late Rt Hon Lord Justice Goff; 2 da; *Style* - Lady Goff; Kingsley Croft, Downs Way, Tadworth, Surrey (☎ 3636)

GOLD, Joseph; *Career* chm and joint man dir Centrovincial Estates Ltd; *Style* - Joseph Gold, Esq; 4-6 Savile Row, W1

GOLD, Sir Joseph; kt 1980; *Career* formerly General Counsel to IMF; *Style* - Sir Joseph Gold

GOLD, Hon Mrs (Jocelyne Mary); *née* Boot; da of 2 and last Baron Trent (d 1956); *b* 1917; *m* 1947, Maj Harcourt Michael Scudamore Gold, MC; 1 s, 1 da; *Style* - The Hon Mrs Gold; West Stratton House, nr Winchester, Hants

GOLD, Jack; *b* 28 June 1930; *Educ* London U; *m* 1957, Denyse, nee Macpherson; 2 s, 1 da; *Career* film director; *Style* - Jack Gold, Esq; 18 Avenue rd, N6

GOLDBERG, Mark; *Career* man dir A Goldberg and Sons Ltd; *Style* - Mark Goldberg, Esq; 21 Candleiggs, Glasgow G1 1LD

GOLDBY, Hon Mrs (Helen Rosa); da of Baron Tomlin (Life Peer d 1935); *b* 1906; *m* 1932, Prof Frank Goldby, MD, FRCP; *Style* - The Hon Mrs Goldby; 1 St Mark's Court, Barton rd, Cambridge

GOLDINER, Hon Mrs; Hon Sigrid; da of Baron Wynne-Jones (Life Peer); *b* 1935; *m* 1962, Dr Marvin Goldiner, of Oakland, Cal, USA; *Style* - The Hon Mrs Goldiner

GOLDING, William Gerald; CBE (1966); s of Alec Golding; *b* 19 Sept 1911; *Educ* Marlborough G S; Brasenose Coll, Oxford; *Career* author; ; *Books* Lord of the Flies (1954) (filmed 1963); *Also* winner of Booker prize 1980 with *Rites of Passage*; *Style* - William Golding, Esq, CBE; Ebble Thatch, Bowerchalke, Wilts (☎ Broad Chalke 275)

GOLDING, Terence Edward; s of Sydney Golding; *b* 7 April 1932; *Educ* Harrow County G S; *m* 1955, Sheila, nee Francis; 1 s 1 da; *Career* ch exec National Exhibition Centre, Birmingham, from 1978, FCA 1967 *Style* - Terence Golding, Esq; Pinn Cottage, Pinner Hill, Pinner, Middx (☎ 01 866 2610)

GOLDMAN, Peter; CBE (1959); s of Capt Samuel Goldman (d 1959); *b* 4 Jan 1925; *Educ* London U, Cambridge U; *m* 1970, Stella Maris, da of Col Garrett Joyce (d 1964); *Career* dir Consumers' Assoc 1964-, dir Conservative Political Centre 1955-64; *Clubs* Carlton; *Style* - Peter Goldman Esq, CBE; 34 Campbell Court, Queen's Gate gdns, SW7 (☎ 01 589 9464)

GOLDSMITH, Lady Annabel; *née* Vane-Tempest-Stewart; da of 8 Marquess of Londonderry (d 1955); *b* 11 June 1934; *Educ* Southover Manor Lewes; *m* 1, 1954 (m diss 1975), Marcus Oswald Hornby Lecky Birley, s of late Sir Oswald Hornby Lecky Birley, MC; 2 s (Rupert, b 1955; Robin, b 1958), 1 da (Jane India, b 1961, m 1981 Julian Halsey Luke Colchester); m 2, 1978, Sir James Michael Goldsmith; 2 s (Zacharias, b 1975; Benjamin, b 1980), 1 da (Jemima Marcelle, b 1974); *Style* - Lady Annabel Goldsmith; Ormeley Lodge, Ham Common, Surrey (☎ 01 940 5677/8)

GOLDSMITH, Edward Rene David; s of of late Frank Goldsmith, OBE, TD, MP (C) Stowmarket 1910-18; and Marcelle, nee Mouillier; *b* 8 Nov 1928; *Educ* Magdalen Coll, Oxford; *m* 1953, Gillian Pretty; 1 s, 1 da; *Career* editor *The Ecologist* from 1969; *Style* - Edward Goldsmith Esq; Whitehay, Withiel, Bodmin, Cornwall (☎ Lanivet 237)

GOLDSMITH, Sir James Michael; s of Frank Goldsmith, OBE, TD, MP (C) Stowmarket 1910-18; *b* 26 Feb 1933; *Educ* Eton; *m* 1, Maria Patino (d 1954); 1 da; m 2, Ginette Lery; 1 s, 1 da; m 3, 1978, as her 2 husband, Lady Annabel Birley, nee Vane-Tempest-Stewart, da of 8 Marquess of Londonderry; 1 s, 1 da; *Career* chm Cavenham Ltd, Generale Occidentale SA Paris; Groupe Express; General Oriental, Hong Kong; publisher of *Now* magazine; kt 1976; *Style* - Sir James Goldsmith; Ormeley Lodge, Ham Common, Surrey

GOLDSMITH, Walter Kenneth; s of Lionel Goldsmith; *b* 19 Jan 1938; *Educ* Merchant Taylors' Sch; *m* 1961, Rosemary, nee Salter; 2 s, 2 da; *Career* FCA; dir gen IOD from 1979; pres Pacific International Operations, Black and Decker USA, 1976; *Style* - Walter Goldsmith Esq; 58 Wolsey rd, Moor Park, Northwood, Middx (☎ 25500)

GOLDSTEIN, Ralph; *Career* chm Superdrug Stores Ltd; *Style* - Ralph Goldstein Esq; Felnex Trading Estate, 190 London rd, Hackbridge, Surrey

GOLDSTEIN, Ron; *Career* man dir Superdrug Stores Ltd; *Style* - Ron Goldstein Esq; Felnex Trading Estate, 190 London rd, Hackbridge, Surrey

GOLLANCZ, Livia Ruth; da of Victor Gollancz; *b* 25 May 1920; *Educ* St Paul's Girls' Sch; *Career* hornplayer 1940-53; governing dir and joint man dir Victor Gollancz Ltd from 1965; *Style* - Miss Livia Gollancz; 14 Henrietta st, WC2

GOLODETZ, Alexander; s of Benjamin Golodetz; *b* 1909; *Educ* Chillon Coll, Switzerland; LSE; Trinity Coll, Cambridge; *m* 1964, Anne, nee Wood; *Career* chm Lonconex Ltd from 1971; ptnr M Golodetz, commodity merchants, from 1953; *Style* - Alexander Golodetz Esq; Summerhouse, Birdham, Sussex

GOMEZ, Jill; *Educ* RAM and Guildhall Sch of Music; *Career* singer; *Style* - Miss Jill Gomez; c/o Lies Askonas, 19a Air, st, Regent st, W1

GONZI, Most Rev Michael; KBE (1946); s of of Joseph Gonzi; *b* 13 May 1885; *Educ* Malta Seminary; Malta U; Beda Coll, Rome; *Career* Priest 1908; Archbishop of Malta 1943-76; Archbishop Emeritus of Malta DD, ICD, BLit; *Style* - The Most Rev Michael Gonzi, KBE; Archbishop's Palace, Valletta, Malta GC

GOOCH, Charles Albert; s of Ernest Edward Gooch; *b* 15 Sept 1938; *Educ* Coleman St Ward Sch London; *m* 1974, June Margaret, nee Reardon; 2 da (Charlotte Louise b 1976, Jessica Helen b 1978); *Career* chm Shaw & Marvin Ltd (public co), chm and md Buckland Securities Ltd group of companies; *Recreations* squash, football; *Style* - Charles Gooch Esq; 5-25 Scrutton st, EC2 (☎ 01 739 3604)

GOOCH, Sir (Richard) John (Sherlock); 12 Bt (GB 1746), JP (Suffolk 1970); s of Sir Robert Eric Sherlock Gooch, 11 Bt, KCVO, DSO, JP, DL (d 1978), and Katharine (d 1974), da of late Maj-Gen Sir Edward Walter Clervaux Chaytor, KCMG, KCVO, CB; *b* 22 March 1930; *Educ* Eton; *Heir* bro, Maj Timothy Gooch, MBE, *qv Career* Capt Life Gds; *Style* - Sir John Gooch, Bt JP; Benacre Hall, Beccles, Suffolk (☎ Lowestoft 740333)

GOOCH, Sir Robert Douglas; 4 Bt (UK 1866); s of Sir Daniel Fulthorpe Gooch, 3 Bt (d 1926); *b* 19 Sept 1905; *Educ* Brighton Coll; *m* 1, 1928 (m dis 1930), Moyra Katharine, da of Charles Howard Sanders, MB; m 2, 1930, Mary Eileen (d 1979), da of late Colin George Barrett, and wid of Maj H L Gifford; 1 da; *Heir* kinsman, Trevor Sherlock Gooch, VRD; *Style* - Sir Robert Gooch, Bt

GOOCH, Maj Timothy Robert Sherlock; MBE (1970); s of late Sir Robert

Eric Sherlock Gooch, KCVO, DSO, JP, DL, 11 Bt (d 1978) and Katharine (d 1974), da of late Maj-Gen Sir Edward Walter Clervaux Chaytor, KCMG, KCVO, CB; hp of bro, Sir (Richard) John (Sherlock) Gooch, 12 Bt; *b* 1934; *Educ* Eton; *m* 1963, Susan, da of Maj-Gen Kenneth Christie Cooper, CB, DSO, OBE; 2 da; *Career* Maj Life Gds; *Style* - Maj Timothy Gooch, MBE; The Cedars, Covehithe, Beccles, Suffolk

GOOCH, Trevor Sherlock; VRD; s of Charles Trevor Gooch, (d 1963); hp to Btcy of kinsman, Sir Robert Gooch, 4 Bt; *b* 15 June 1915; *m* 1, 1956, Denys Anne (d 1976); 1 s, 4 da; m 2, 1978, Jean, nee Wright; *Career* Fl-Lt RAFVR; *Style* - Trevor Gooch Esq, VRD; Jardin de la Roque, Mont de la Roque, St Aubin, Jersey, CI

GOOD, Anthony Richard; s of Richard George Good; *b* 20 Apr 1930; *Educ* Reading U; *m* 1956, Sallie Lorraine, da of Archibald Wilson; 2 s, 2 da; *Career* current appointments- dir Grand Metropolitan Ltd, chief exec Milk and Foods Div, chm of Express Dairy Co Ltd; *Recreations* shooting and fishing; *Style* - Anthony Good Esq; Warborough Farm, Letcombe Regis, Nr Wantage, Oxfordshire (☎ Wantage 3244)

GOODALE, Hon Mrs (Pamela Muriel Dorine); da of Harold Hirst (d 1919, s of 1 Baron Hirst); *b* 16 April 1918; *Educ* Luckley, Wokingham; *m* 1, 1940 (m dis 1947), Capt Arthur Colyer, RA; m 2, 1949, Roy Goodale (d 1969); 1 s; *Career* WW II, Staff Capt ATS; chm Lingfield Parish Cncl 1957-69 (memb 1955-69); chm Godstone RDC 1969-72 (memb 1955-76); raised to rank of Baron's da 1943 *Recreations* political work *Style* - The Hon Mrs Goodale; Peartrees, Dormansland, Surrey (☎ Lingfield 832368)

GOODALL, Arthur David Saunders; CMG (1979); s of late Arthur Goodall; *b* 9 Oct 1931; *Educ* Ampleforth and Trinity Coll, Oxford; *m* 1962, Morwenna, nee Peecock; 2 s, 1 da; *Career* HM Diplomatic Service; Minister, Bonn 1979-; *Style* - Arthur Goodall Esq, CMG; c/o Foreign and Commonwealth Office, SW1

GOODALL, Christopher James Cruice *Career* md Gordon and Gotch Hldgs Ltd; *Style* - Christopher Goodall Esq; Gotch House, 30 St Bride st, EC4

GOODALL, Peter; TD (1946); s of Maj Tom Goodall, DSO, MC (d 1977); *b* 14 July 1920; *Educ* Ashville Coll Harrogate; *m* 1948, Sonja Jeanne, nee Burt; 1 s, 1 da; *Career* Capt Duke of Wellington's Regt & Parachute Regt, chm and ch exec Hepworth Ceramic Holdings; *Recreations* shooting, fishing; *Style* - Peter Goodall Esq, TD; Mill Bank House, High Flatts, nr Huddersfield, W Yorks (☎ High Flatts 227)

GOODALL, Ralph William, *Career* MA, BSc, ATI; md Scapa Gp Ltd; *Style* - Ralph Goodall Esq; Cartmell rd, Blackburn, Lancs

GOODE, George Henry; *Career* FCCA; md Twinlock Ltd; *Style* - George Goode Esq; Twinlock Ltd, 346 Croydon rd, Beckenham, Kent

GOODEN, Benjamin Bernard Woulfe; s of C Gooden (d 1969); *b* 16 July 1925; *Educ* Harrow, Trin Oxford; *m* 1, 1952 (dis 1966), Elizabeth Sara, nee Woodham-Smith; 1 s, 2 da; m 2, 1973, Rose Emma Margaret, da of late Hon Douglas Vivian (2 s of 4 Baron Vivian); 1 s; *Career* barr 1951, ptnr James Capel & Co 1957-71, dir M & G Securities Ltd 1974-, hon tres the Bach Choir 1972-, underwriting memb of Lloyd's 1972-; *Recreations* cricket, choral music, railways; *Clubs* MCC; *Style* - Benjamin Gooden Esq; Ferryside, Riverside, Twickenham, Middlesex (☎ 01 892 1448)

GOODENOUGH, Dorothea, Lady - Dorothea Louisa; da of late Ven Hon Kenneth Gibbs, DD, s of 1 Baron Aldenham; *b* 1897; *m* 1924, Sir William Goodenough, 1 Bt (d 1951); *Style* - Dorothea, Lady Goodenough; Filkins Hall, Lechlade, Glos

GOODENOUGH, Frederick Roger; s of Sir William Macnamara Goodenough 1 Bt (d 1951), bro of Sir Richard Goodenough, 2 Bt; *b* 21 Dec 1927; *Educ* Eton, Magdalene Cambridge; *m* 1954,

Marguerite June, nee Mackintosh; 2 s, 2 da; *Career* dir Barclays Bank Ltd 1979-, Barclays Bank UK Ltd 1971-, Barclays Bank Int Ltd 1977-, local dir Barclays Bank Ltd Birmingham 1958-60, Reading 1960-69, Oxford 1969-, curator Oxford U Chest 1974-, chm Nuffield Orthopaedic Trust 1981-, chm Shiplake Coll 1966-74, sr ptnr Broadwell Manor Farm 1968-; *Recreations* shooting, fishing, photography, ornithology; *Clubs* Brooks's *Style* - Frederick Goodenough Esq; Broadwell Manor, Lechlade, Glos

GOODENOUGH, Sir Richard Edmund; 2 Bt (UK 1943); s of Sir William Macnamara Goodenough, 1 Bt (d 1951); *b* 9 June 1925; *Educ* Eton, Ch Ch Oxford; *m* 1951, Jane Isobel, da of late H S P McLernon, of New Zealand; 1 s, 2 da; *Heir* s, William Goodenough; *Career* Coldstream Gds WW II; *Style* - Sir Richard Goodenough, Bt

GOODENOUGH, Samuel Kenneth Henry; s of late Sir William Goodenough, 1 Bt; *b* 3 April 1930; *Educ* Eton and Christ Church, Oxford; *m* 1979, Patricia, nee Barnett; 1 step s, 1 step da; *Career* sr partner Knight Frank and Rutley 1978- (joined 1952, ptnr 1961), ptnr in overseas ptnrships of Knight Frank and Rutley, ptnr in family farming enterprise 1965-; liveryman Goldsmiths' Co; *Recreations* shooting, painting, organ playing, gardening; *Clubs* Brooks's, Pratt's, New (Edinburgh); *Style* - Samuel Goodenough Esq; 4 Stanhope gdns, SW7 (☎ 01 370 6674); Filkins Hall, Filkins, Lechlade, Glos (☎ Filkins 413)

GOODENOUGH, William McLernon; s and h of Sir Richard Goodenough, 2 Bt; *b* 5 Aug 1954; *Style* - William Goodenough Esq

GOODEVE, Lady - Janet; PhD; *m* 1932, Sir Charles Frederick Goodeve, OBE (d 1980); 2 s; *Style* - Lady Goodeve; 38 Middleway, NW11 (☎ 01 455 7308)

GOODHART, Hon Mrs (Celia McClare); *née* Herbert; da of 2 Baron Hemingford; *b* 1939; *Educ* Oxford U (MA); *m* 1966, William Howard Goodhart; 1 s, 2 da; *Style* - The Hon Mrs Goodhart; 43 Campden Hill sq, W8

GOODHART, Martin Andrew; s and h of Sir Robert Goodhart, 4 Bt; *b* 9 Sept 1974

GOODHART, Margaret, Lady - Margaret Mary Eileen; da of late Morgan Morgan, of Cray, Powys; *m* 1944, Sir John Goodhart, 3 Bt (d 1979); 1 s, 1 da; *Style* - Margaret, Lady Goodhart; Holtye, 17 Mavelstone Close, Bromley, Kent

GOODHART, Philip Carter; MP (C) Bromley Beckenham 1957-; s of Prof Arthur Goodhart, Hon KBE, QC, FBA; *b* 3 Nov 1925; *Educ* Hotchkiss Sch USA, Trin Cambridge; *m* 1950, Valerie Winant; 3 s, 4 da; *Career* Parly-Under Sec Def (Admin Matters) 1981-, Parly Under-Sec NI Off 1979-81; served KRRC & Para Regt 1943-47; on Daily Telegraph 1950-55, Sunday Times 1955-57; stood for Consett Co Durham (Cons) 1950; memb Con Advsy Cttee Policy 1973-; *Clubs* Athenaeum; *Style* - Philip Goodhart Esq MP; Whitebarn, Boars Hill, Oxford (☎ 735294); 27 Phillimore gdns, W8 (☎ 01 937 0822)

GOODHART, Sir Robert Anthony Gordon; 4 Bt (UK 1911); s of Sir John Goodhart, 3 Bt (d 1979); *b* 15 Dec 1948; *Educ* Rugby; Guy's Hosp Med Sch; *m* 1972, Kathleen, nee MacRae; 1 s, 1 da; *Heir* s Martin Goodhart; *Career* GP 1976-; *Recreations* cricket, sailing, music; *Style* - Sir Robert Goodhart, Bt; c/o Lloyds Bank, Beaminster, Dorset

GOODHART, William Howard; QC; s of Prof A L Goodhart, Hon KBE, QC (d 1978); *b* 18 Jan 1933; *Educ* Eton; Trinity Coll, Cambridge and Harvard Law Sch; *m* 1966, Hon Celia Herbert, da of 2 Baron Hemingford, qv; 1 s, 2 da; *Career* barr, 1957; QC 1979; *Style* - William Goodhart Esq, QC; 43 Campden Hill sq, W8 (☎ 01 21 4830); Youlbury House, Boars Hill, Oxford (☎ 735477)

GOODING, Air Vice-Marshal Keith Horace; CB (1966), OBE (1951); s of Horace Milford Gooding (d 1953); *b* 2 Sept 1913; *Educ* King Edward VI Southampton; *m* 1, 1943, Peggy Eileen (d 1962), nee Gatfield; 1 s; 2 m, 1968, Jean, nee Underwood; 2 s, 1 da; *Career* RAF 1938, Air Vice-Marshal 1965, air offr Administration HQ Maintenance Command 1965-68, dir-gen Supply (RAF) MOD 1968-71, ret 1971; *Recreations* tennis, bridge; *Clubs* RAF; *Style* - Air Vice-Marshal Keith Gooding, CB, OBE; c/o Lloyds Bank Ltd, Surbiton, Surrey

GOODLIFE, D H; *Career* man dir OCS Gp Ltd; *Style* - D H Goodlife Esq; Eagle st, WC1

GOODLIFE, W G; *Career* chm OCS Gp Ltd; *Style* - W G Goodlife Esq; Eagle st, WC1

GOODMAN, Baron (Life Peer UK 1965); Arnold Abraham Goodman; CH (1972); s of Joseph and Bertha Goodman; *b* 21 Aug 1913; *Educ* UCL, Downing Cambridge; *Career* slr 1936, sr ptnr Messrs Goodman Derrick & Co; served WW II RA TA as Maj; memb Roy Commission Working of Tbnls of Enquiry Act 1921; chm Theatres' Tst 1976-, Theatre Investment Fund 1976-, Motability 1977-, Jewish Chronicle Tst; dir Roy Opera House Covent Gdn & ENO; chm Charter Film Productions; Pres Nat Book League, Inst Jewish Affrs; dep chm Br Cncl 1974-; Master Univ Oxford 1976-; dir Davis-Poynter Ltd, Epsom Grand Stand Assoc, Hazlitt Hldgs, Jack Hylton Ltd, J M L Stone & Co, P L Travers Ltd, Racecourse Hldgs Tst, Sandown Park Ltd, Treborsnave Tst Co, Utd Racecourses Ltd; *Style* - The Rt Hon Lord Goodman CH; University College, Oxford (☎ 41661)

GOODMAN, B J; *Career* man dir Preece Cardew and Rider (Queen's Award for Export Achievement 1979); *Style* - B J Goodman, Esq; Brighton, E Sussex

GOODMAN, Frederick; s of Hyman Goodman (d 1924); *b* 4 Nov 1910; *Educ* London Univ, Chelsea Poly and sundry Business Schs; *m* 1974, Iris Gene; *Career* conslt accountant & dir Brilaw Properties Ltd, Keystone Credits Ltd, RS Holdings Ltd, Headtown Ltd, Powerlistic Ltd, Upton Heath Properties Ltd, St James Court Estate (1977) Ltd; underwriter of Lloyd's; *Recreations* charity work *Style* - Frederick Goodman Esq; 11 Warwick pl, London W9 (☎ 01 286 0970); 29/30 Fitzroy sq, London WI (☎ 01 388 2444)

GOODMAN, Hon Mrs (Janet Teresa); *née* Addington; da of 7 Viscount Sidmouth; *b* 1949; *m* 1972, Anthony Goodman; 2 da; *Style* - The Hon Mrs Goodman; 68 Wierda rd, East Wierda Valley, Sandton 2196, S Africa

GOODRICH, Hon Mrs; Hon Audrey; da of late 1 Baron Elton; *b* 1922; *m* 1948, Rev Brian William Frere Goodrich (d 1977), former Assist Cmmr Singapore Police; 5 s, 1 da; *Style* - The Hon Mrs Goodrich; Hill House, Enford, Pewsey, Wilts

GOODSON, Lt-Col Sir Alfred Lassam; 2 Bt (UK 1922); s of Sir Alfred Lassam Goodson, 1 Bt (d 1940); *b* 26 Aug 1893; *Educ* Radley; *m* 1, 1920, Joan (d 1939), da of Christopher Leyland; m 2, 1941, Enid Clayton Leyland, da of late Col Robert Clayton Swan; *Heir* n, Mark Weston Lassam Goodson; *Career* Capt City of London Yeo (despatches) WW I; MFH College Valley 1924; *Style* - Lt-Col Sir Alfred Goodson, Bt; Corbet Tower, Kelso, Roxburghshire (☎ Morebattle 203)

GOODSON, Hugh Lassam; OBE (1973); 3 s of Sir Alfred Goodson, 1 Bt (d 1940); *b* 9 July 1905; *Educ* privately; *m* 1945, June Patricia, da of Maj Joseph Hunter, CBE, MC, DL; 2 s, 2 da; *Career* chm Liberal Nat Organisation SW area 1940-43, JP 1938-52 Devon, High Sheriff 1954, chm Cncl of St John (Devon) 1959-64; formerly chm Roy Yacht Sqdn Syndicate taking Yacht Sceptre to USA 1958 to challenge for America's Cup, Rear-Cdre Roy London Yacht Club; gov dir Devonshire Investment Estates; Fell Inst of Directors; CStJ; *Recreations* sailing, shooting; *Clubs* Royal Yacht Squadron; *Style* - Hugh Goodson Esq, OBE; Waddeton ct, Brixham, Devon (☎ Churston 842120)

GOODSON, Mark Weston Lassam; s of late Maj Alan Goodson; n and hp of Sir Alfred Goodson, 2 Bt; *b* 12 Dec 1925; *m*

1949, Barbara, nee Andrews; 1 s, 3 da; *Style* - Mark Goodson Esq

GOODWIN, John Macleod; *Career* md Highland Distilleries Ltd; CA ; *Style* - John Goodwin Esq; 106 West Nile st, Glasgow G1 2QY

GOODWIN, Matthew Dean; CBE (1980); s of Matthew Goodwin; *b* 12 Dec 1929; *Educ* Glasgow Acad; *m* 1955, Margaret Eileen; 2 da; *Career* memb Inst Chartered Accountants of Scotland 1952, ptnr Davidson Down McGown 1958-68, chm Hewden Stuart Plant Ltd 1979- (fin dir 1965-79), memb Irvine Devpt Corpn 1980-; *Recreations* bridge, shooting, fishing, farming; *Clubs* Western (Glasgow); *Style* - Matthew Goodwin Esq, CBE; 32 Kelvin Court, Glasgow (☎ 041 357 0275); Shuttlefield, Lamington, Biggar, Lanarks (☎ 08995676)

GOODWIN, Timothy John Medlicott; s of Lt-Col Edward Guy Medlicott Goodwin, MC, RA; *b* 27 March 1935; *Educ* Stonyhurst and Lanchester College; *m* 1961, Elizabeth Joan; 1 s, 1 da; *Career* Lt Royal Artillery, BAOR, thereafter QOWWY (TA); man dir The Charles Rickards Group Ltd since 1979; formerly dir Giltspur Precision Industries Ltd from 1977; *Recreations* ornithology, forestry; *Style* - Timothy Goodwin Esq; Duncote Hall, Duncote, nr Towcester, Northants (☎ Towcester 50934)

GOOLD, Sir George Leonard; 7 Bt (UK 1801), of Old Court, Co Cork; s of Sir George Goold, 6 Bt (d 1967, descended from a Mayor of Cork *temp* Henry VII); *b* 26 Aug 1923; *Educ* St Mark's Sch, St John's Coll; *m* 1945, Joy, da of William Cutler; 1 s, 4 da; *Heir* s, George Goold; *Recreations* fishing, bowls, shooting; *Style* - Sir George Goold, Bt; 5 Afford rd, Port Pirie, S Australia (☎ 086 323617)

GOOLD, George William; s and heir of Sir George Goold, 7 Bt; *b* 25 March 1950; *m* 1973, Julie, nee Crack; 2 s; *Style* - George Goold Esq; 25 Penglase st, Whyalla Playford, S Australia 5600

GOOLD-ADAMS, Richard John Moreton; CBE (1974); s of Sir Hamilton Goold-Adams, GCMG (d 1920); *b* 24 Jan 1916; *Educ* Winchester, New Coll Oxford; *m* 1939, Diana Mary Ponsonby, nee Blennerhassett; *Career* Maj Italy 1945, economist and co dir; editorial staff The Economist 1947-55, dir within Guthrie Gp of Companies 1954-69, broadcaster, journalist, lecturer, author, chm SS Great Britain Project 1968-, chm Int Inst for Strategic Studies 1963-73; *Recreations* photography; *Clubs* Travellers'; *Style* - Richard Goold-Adams Esq, CBE; 11 Richmond rd, Lansdown, Bath, Avon

GOONETILLEKE, Lady - Phillis Mary; *m* 1968, as his 2 w, Sir Oliver Goonetilleke, GCMG KCVO, KBE (d 1978); *Style* - Lady Goonetilleke; 14 Albion Gate, Hyde Park pla, W2

GOOSSENS, Leon Jean; CBE (1950); s of late Eugene Goossens; *b* 12 June 1897; *Educ* Liverpool Coll of Music; *m* 1, 1926; 1 da; 2, 1933, Leslie, nee Burrowes; 2 da; *Career* solo oboist FRCM, Hon RAM; *Style* - Leon Goossens Esq, CBE; Park Cottage, 7a Ravenscourt sq, W6

GORARD, Anthony John; s of William Gorard; *b* 15 July 1927; *Educ* Ealing G S; *m* 1954, Barbara Hampton; 1 s, 3 da; *Career* ch exec, Cardiff Independent Radio Station 1979; *Style* - A J Gorard, Esq; Chew Hill House, Chew Magna, Somerset

GORDON, A G; *Career* md William Grant and Sons Ltd; *Style* - A G Gordon, Esq; Glenfiddich Distillery, Dufftown, Banffshire

GORDON, Lord Adam Granville; KCVO (1970, CVO 1960), MBE (1945); s of late Lt-Col (Granville Cecil) Douglas Gordon, CVO, DSO (s of late Lord Granville Armyne Gordon, 6 s of 10 Marquess of Huntly) and bro of 12 Marquess; *b* 1909; *Educ* Eton; *m* 1947, Pamela, da of Alexander Herriot Bowhill, CBE, of Inchmarlo, Banchory, Kincardineshire; 2 s; *Career* Maj RA (TA), and a memb of Queen's Body Guard for Scotland (Roy Co of Archers), Comptroller of the Household to HM Queen Elizabeth the Queen Mother 1953-74, an Extra Equerry to HM Queen

Elizabeth the Queen Mother 1974-, 1939-45 War in N Africa and Italy (despatches, MBE); *Style*[1] - Lord Adam Gordon, KCVO, MBE; Hethersett, Littleworth Cross, Seale, Farnham, Surrey

GORDON, Lady Amy Jane; da of Earl of Aboyne and gda of 12 Marquess of Huntly; *b* 1975; *Style* - Lady Amy Gordon

GORDON, Lord Alastair Ninian John; s of 3 Marquess of Aberdeen and Temair, DSO (d 1972), by his 1 w, Cecile, da of George Drummond (ggggs of Andrew Drummond, yr bro of 4 Viscount Strathallan and founder of Messrs Drummond, the bankers) by Elizabeth (da of Rev Frederick Norman and Lady Adeliza Manners, da of 5 Duke of Rutland); hp of bro, 5 Marquess; *b* 20 July 1920; *Educ* Harrow; *m* 1950, Anne, da of Lt-Col Gerald Barry, MC (s of William Barry, JP, 4 s of Sir Francis Barry, 1 Bt, by William's w Lady Grace Murray, MBE, da of 7 Earl of Dunmore); 1 s, 2 da; *Career* served WW II Capt Scots Gds; memb Roy Co of Archers (Queen's Bodyguard for Scotland); painter and memb Internat Assoc Art Critics; *Recreations* music, people; *Clubs* Arts, MCC, Puffin's *Style* - Lord Alastair Gordon; Quicks Green, Pangbourne, Berks (☎ Upper Basildon 331)

GORDON, Sir Charles Addison Somerville Snowden; KCB (1981, CB 1970); s of Charles Gordon Snowden Gordon, TD (d 1961); *b* 25 July 1918; *Educ* Winchester, Balliol Oxford; *m* 1943, Janet Margaret, da of late Douglas Porteous Beattie, of Dewsbury, Yorks; 1 s, 1 da; *Career* served 1939-45 in Fleet Air Arm (Lt (A) RNVR); assist clerk House of Commons 1946, sr clerk 1947, clerk of the House of Commons 1979-; *Style* - Sir Charles Gordon, KCB; 279 Lonsdale rd, Barnes, SW13 (☎ 01 748 6735)

GORDON, Lord Douglas Claude Alexander; DSO (1945); s of late Lt-Col (Granville Cecil) Douglas Gordon, CVO, DSO (s of late Lord Granville Armyne Gordon, 6 s of 10 Marquess of Huntly), and bro of 12 Marquess; *b* 1916; *Educ* Eton; *m* 1, 1940 (m dis 1961), Suzanne, da of late Lt-Col Arthur Houssemayne du Boulay, DSO; 2 s, 1 da; m 2, 1962, Mrs Bridget Hutchison, da of late Gerald Bryan Ingram; 1 da; *Career* Italy 1943-45 (DSO), Page of Honour to HM 1930-33, Lt-Col Black Watch, memb Queen's Body Guard for Scotland (Roy Co of Archers); *Clubs* Army and Navy; *Style* - Lord Douglas Gordon, DSO

GORDON, Maj-Gen Desmond Spencer; CB (1961), CBE (1952), DSO (1943), JP (Hants 1968), DL (Hants 1980); s of Harold Easty Gordon (ka 1917); *b* 25 Dec 1911; *Educ* Haileybury Coll, RMC Sandhurst; *m* 1940, Sybil Mary, nee Thompson; 1 s, 1 da; *Career* KStJ 1973, Green Howards Regt 1932, Lt-Col WW II, assist Ch of Defence Staff MOD 1964-66, ret 1968; cmmr in ch St John Ambulance 1973-78; *Clubs* Army and Navy; *Style* - Maj-Gen Desmond Gordon, CB, CBE, DSO, JP, DL; Southfields, Greywell, Basingstoke, Hants (☎ Odiham 2088)

GORDON, Rt Hon John Bowie Peter; PC (1978); s of Dr W Gordon, CBE, and Dr Doris Gordon, OBE; *b* 24 July 1921; *Educ* St Andrew's Coll Christ Church, Lincoln Coll Canterbury; *m* 1943, Dorothy, nee Morton; 2 s, 1 da ; *Career* MP (Clutha) 1960-78; former Min of Transport, of Marine & Fisheries, and of Labour & State Servs (1975-78); ret 1978; co dir; *Style* - The Rt Hon John Gordon, PC; Tapanui, Otago, New Zealand

GORDON, Sir John Charles; 9 Bt (NS 1706); s of Sir Robert Charles Gordon, 8 Bt (d 1939); probably next in remainder to Viscountcy of Kenmure and Lordship of Lochinvar; *b* 4 Jan 1901; *m* 1928, Marion, da of late James B Wright, of Neutral Bay, N Sydney, N S Wales; 1 s, 1 da; *Heir* s, Robert James Gordon; *Style* - Sir John Gordon, Bt; 61 Farrer-Brown ct, Huffield Village, Castle Hill, NSW 2154

GORDON, John Edwin; s of Dennis Lionel Shute Gordon (d 1940); *b* 14 Dec 1939; *Educ* Tonbridge, Queens' Cambridge; *m* 1968, Monica Anne, nee Law; 1 s, 2 da; *Career* CA, memb of Stock Exchange, dir Robert Fleming & Co 1974-77; dir Laing & Cruickshank, United Wire Gp Ltd, American Oil Field Systems Ltd;

Recreations fishing; *Clubs* Boodle's; Leander; *Style* - John Gordon Esq; 50 Castelnau, SW13 (☎ 01 748 1906)

GORDON, Lady; Katharine; da of late J Hornsby, of Manor House, Letcombe Regis; *m* 1953, as his 2 w, Sir Home Seton Charles Montagu Gordon, 12 Bt (d 1956); *Style* - Lady Gordon; St Edmunds, Rottingdean, Sussex

GORDON, Sir Keith Lyndell; CMG (1966); s of late George Gordon; *b* 1906; *Educ* St Mary's Coll St Lucia; *Career* barr Middle Temple 1935, a justice of appeal West Indies Associated States Supreme Court 1967-71; kt 1979; chm Public Service Bd of Appeal; *Style* - Sir Keith Gordon, CMG; Vigie, Castries, St Lucia, Windward Islands

GORDON, Murray Graham; s of Solomon Gordon; *b* 13 May 1922; *Educ* Collegiate Liverpool, Univ of Liverpool Sch of Art; *m* 1950, Vera, nee Denby; 2 s; *Career*Lt-Col (acting) India & Burma (Substantive Major); chm & md Combined English Stores Gp 1970-; *Recreations* golf, tennis, squash; *Clubs* Carlton, RAC; *Style* - Murray Gordon Esq; Chelsea House, 3 The Vale, SW3 (☎ 352 9311); Blackhouse Farm Cottage, Sandy Lane, Henfield, Sussex (☎ Henfield 3125)

GORDON, M J; *Career* md Badger Ltd; *Style* - M J Gordon Esq; Turiff Bldg, Gt West rd, Brentford, Middx

GORDON, Lord Roderic Armyne; MBE (1943), TD; s of late Lt-Col (Granville Cecil) Douglas Gordon, CVO, DSO (s of late Lord Granville Armyne Gordon, 6 s of 10 Marquess of Huntly); bro of 12 Marquess; *b* 1914; *Educ* Stowe; *m* 1, 1937 (m dis 1949), Anne, da of late Lt-Col the Hon Sir Osbert Eustace Vesey, KCVO,CMG, CBE; 2 s; m 2, 1949, Baroness Joana Alexandra de Stuers; *Career* N Africa 1943; is Major 72 (Hampshire) Anti-Aircraft Brig RA (TA); *Style* - Lord Roderic Gordon, MBE, TD; Shady Springs Farm, Bentley, Alberta, Canada

GORDON, Robert James; s and h of Sir John Gordon, 9 Bt; *b* 17 Aug 1932; *m* 1976, Helen Perry, of Sydney; *Style* - Robert Gordon Esq; 61 Farrer-Brown Court, Nuffield Village, Castle Hill NSW 2154, Australia

GORDON, Robert Wilson; MC (1944); s of late Malcolm Gordon; *b* 3 March 1915; *Educ* Harrow; *m* 1, 1946, Joan (d 1965), da of late Brig A G Kenchington, CBE, MC; 1 da; m 2, 1967, Mrs Diana Ansell, nee Tyrwhitt-Drake; *Career* dep chm Stock Exchange 1965-68, ptnr Pidgeon de Smitt (stockbrokers); *Style* - Robert Gordon Esq, MC; 41 Cadogan sq, SW1 (☎ 01 235 4496)

GORDON CUMMING, Alexander Penrose; s and h of Sir William Gordon Cumming, 6 Bt; *b* 15 April 1954; *Style* - Alexander Gordon Cumming Esq

GORDON CUMMING, Sir William Gordon; 6 Bt (UK 1804), of Altyre, Forres; s of Maj Sir Alexander Penrose Gordon-Cumming, 5 Bt (d 1939); *b* 19 June 1928; *Educ* Eton; *m* 1953 (m dis 1972), Elisabeth, da of Maj-Gen Sir William Robert Norris Hinde, KBE, CB, DSO; 1 s, 3 da; *Heir* s, Alexander Gordon Cumming; *Career* late Lt Roy Scots Greys; *Style* - Sir William Gordon Cumming, Bt; Altyre, Forres, Morayshire

GORDON LENNOX, Rear-Adm Sir Alexander Henry Charles; KCVO (1972), CB (1962), DSO (1942); s of Lord Bernard Gordon Lennox (ka 1914, 3 s of 7 Duke of Richmond & Gordon), by Hon Evelyn (d as result of enemy action 1944), da of 1 Baron Loch; *b* 9 April 1911; *Educ* RNC Dartmouth; *m* 1936, Barbara, da of Maj-Gen Julian Steele; 2 s (Michael, m 1974 Jennifer, da of Capt Hon Vicary Gibbs, er s of 4 Baron Aldenham; Andrew); *Career* RN 1924-62, Serjeant at Arms House of Commons 1962-77; *Recreations* field sports; *Style* - Rear-Adm Sir Alexander Gordon Lennox, KCVO, CB, DSO; Quags Corner, Minstead, Midhurst, W Sussex (☎ 3623)

GORDON LENNOX, Lt-Gen Sir George Charles; KBE (1964), CB (1959), CVO (1952), DSO (1943); er s of Lord Bernard Gordon Lennox (ka 1914, *see* Rear-Adm Sir Alexander H C Gordon Lennox); *b* 29 May 1908; *Educ* Eton, Sandhurst; *m* 1931, Nancy, da of Maj Sir

Lionel Darell, 6 Bt, DSO, by his w Eleanor (great aunt of Lord Ravensdale and Simon Mosley, *qqv*) and herself aunt of Bruno Schroder, *qv*; 2 s (Bernard, David); *Career* King of Arms Order Br Empire 1968-; served Gren Gds 1928-52 (Staff & Regt WW II), Cmmdt Sandhurst 1960-63, GOC-in-C Scottish Cmmd & Gov Edinburgh Castle 1964-66; *Clubs* Cavalry & Guards; *Style* - Lt-Gen Sir George Gordon Lennox KBE; Gordon Castle, Fochabers, Morayshire (☎ 820275)

GORDON LENNOX, Lord Nicholas Charles; CMG (1978), MVO (4 Cl 1957); s of 9 Duke of Richmond and Gordon; *b* 1931; *Educ* Eton, Worcester Coll Oxford; *m* 1958, Mary, da of Brig Hudleston Noel Hedworth Williamson, DSO, MC, of South Nore, W Wittering, Sussex; 1 s, 3 da; *Career* 2 Lt KRRC, entered Foreign Service 1954; first sec and head of Chancery Br Embassy Madrid 1966-71, counsellor 1971, seconded to Cabinet Office 1971, head of Foreign Office News Dept 1973-74, head of N America Dept 1974-75, head of Chancery Br Embassy Paris 1975-79, Assist Under-Sec of State FCO 1979-; *Style* - Lord Nicholas Gordon Lennox, CMG, MVO; c/o FCO, SW1

GORDON-DUFF, Maj John Beauchamp; MBE (1942), DL (1942-64); s of Archibald Hay Gordon-Duff (d 1938); *b* 15 Feb 1899; *Educ* Winchester, RMC Sandhurst; *m* 1937, Ellen Susan, da of late Hon Charles Platt Williams of NY USA; 1 s (decd), 1 da; *Career* maj, Rifle Brigade WW I wounded, WW II Malta Palestine, ADC to Viceroy of India (Lord Irwin), mil sec to Field Marshal Viscount Gort, VC; *Style* - Maj John Gordon-Duff, MBE, DL; Tanzie, Craigellachie, Banffshire (☎ 214); Lindridge Priory, Tenbury Wells, Worcs (☎ Eardiston 274)

GORDON-DUFF, Lt-Col Thomas Robert; MC (1945), JP (Banffshire 1959); s of Capt Lachlan Gordon-Duff, DL (ka 1914), himself s of Thomas Gordon-Duff, CBE, JP, and Thomas's w Pauline, sis of 1 Baron Glenconner, Lady Ribblesdale and Margot Asquith and half-sis of Ladies Wakehurst, Elliot of Harwood and Crathorne (ie the children of Sir Charles Tennant, 1 Bt); *b* 5 Oct 1911; *Educ* Eton, Sandhurst; *m* 1946, Jean, da of Leslie Moir, of Bicester; 1 s; *Career* Brevet Col TA Gordon Highlanders, CO 5/6 Bn 1947-51; POW Calais 1940; DL Banffshire 1948, V-Ld Lt 1961, Ld-Lt 1964; CCllr 1949-75, Coroner 1962-71; landed proprietor; *Recreations* fishing, shooting; *Clubs* Army & Navy; *Style* - Col Thomas Gordon-Duff MC JP, HM Lord-Lieut for Banffshire; Drummuir, Keith, Banffshire

GORDON-FINLAYSON, Maj-Gen Robert; OBE (1957, MBE 1945), JP (1972), DL (Notts 1974); s of Gen Sir Robert Gordon-Finlayson, KCB, CMG, DSO, DL (d 1956); *b* 28 Oct 1916; *Educ* Winchester, RMA Woolwich; *m* 1945, Alexandra, nee Bartholomew; 2 s; *Career* Maj-Gen ret 1970, Honorary Col Worcs & Sherwood Foresters Regt TAVR 1971-78, chm Notts Co Army Benevolent Fund 1970-, pres Notts Co Roy British Legion 1971-79, v-pres Notts Co SSAFA 1970-, v-pres Notts Co Scouts 1971, high sheriff 1974; *Recreations* shooting, fishing, gardening, skiing, walking; *Style* - Maj-Gen Robert Gordon-Finlayson, OBE, JP, DL; South Collingham Manor, Newark, Notts (☎ 892204)

GORDON-IVES, Hon Mrs (Gwladys Marjorie); *née* Ridley; da of 2 Viscount Ridley, JP, DL, by Hon Rosamond Guest, DBE, 4 da of 1 Baron Wimborne; *b* 17 Sept 1900; *m* 1920, Capt Cecil Gordon-Ives, Scots Gds (d 1928); *Style* - The Hon Mrs Gordon-Ives; Rock House, Annestown, Waterford, Eire

GORDON-SMITH, Ralph; s of late Sir Allan Gordon-Smith, KBE, DL; *b* 22 May 1905; *Educ* Bradfield; *m* 1932, Beryl Cundy; *Career* Pres Smiths Industs Ltd 1973-; *Style* - Ralph Gordon-Smith Esq; 23 Kingston House East, Princes Gate, SW7 (☎ 01 584 9428); Brook House, Bosham, W Sussex (☎ 573475)

GORDON-WALKER, Hon Alan Rudolf; twin s of Baron Gordon-Walker, CH, PC, (Life Peer, d 1980); ; *b* 1946; *Educ* Wellington and Ch Ch Oxford; *m* 1976, Louise, d of Gen Sir Charles Henry Pepys Harington, GCB, CBE, DSO, MC; *Career* dir Hodder and Stoughton Ltd; *Style* - The Hon Alan Gordon-Walker; 22 Eddiscombe rd, SW6

GORDON-WALKER, Hon Robin Chrestien; twin s of Baron Gordon-Walker, CH, PC (Life Peer, d 1980); *b* 15 May 1946; *Educ* Wellington, E Anglia U; *m* 1974, June, da of Patrick Barr, of Eversholt, Bucks; 1 s, 1 da; *Career* political correspondent of COI; *Recreations* squash, cricket, swimming, racing; *Clubs* Dulwich Squash; *Style* - The Hon Robin Gordon-Walker; 10 Eastmearn rd, SE21 (☎ 01 670 9203)

GORDON-WALKER, Baroness; Audrey Muriel; da of Norman Rudolf, of Jamaica; *m* 1935, Baron Gordon-Walker, CH, PC (Life Peer, d 1980); 2 s, 3 da; *Style* - The Rt Hon The Lady Gordon-Walker; 105/106 Frobisher House, Dolphin sq, SW1

GORDON-WATSON, Brig Michael; OBE (1949), MC and 2 Bars (1938, 1940, 1944); s of Sir Charles Gordon-Watson, KBE, CMG, FRCS; *b* 23 Feb 1913; *Educ* Downside, Ch Ch Oxford; *m* 1942, Thalia, da of Charles Gordon; 3 s, 2 da; *Career* Gen Staff HQ BAOR, served Palestine, Norway, N Africa, Italy, NW Europe; farmer & bloodstock breeder; memb Cncl Sov Mil Order Malta, St John's & St Elizabeth's Hosp Management Bd, Tattersall's Cttee, Cncl Thoroughbred Breeders Assoc; JP; *Recreations* shooting, stalking, fishing, racing; *Clubs* White's; *Style* - Brig Michael Gordon-Watson OBE MC** JP; East Blagdon Farm, Cranborne, Dorset (☎ 304)

GORE, Francis St John Corbet; s of Francis Gore (gs of Rev William Gore, unc of Sir St George Ralph Gore, 9 Bt, and gn of Sir Ralph Gore, 6 Bt, 1 and last Earl of Ross); hp to Btcy of kinsman, Sir Richard Gore, 13 Bt; *b* 8 April 1921; *Educ* Wellington; *m* 1951, Priscilla Margaret (m dis 1976), da of Cecil King, *qv*; 2 s, 1 da; *Career* late Capt Roy Northumberland Fusiliers, served WW II; *Style* - Francis Gore Esq; 25 Elvaston Place, SW7

GORE, Michael B G; s of Dr Victor Gore; *b* 25 Oct 1937; *Educ* Felsted, Peterhouse Cambridge; *m* 1972, Mozella, nee Ransom; 2 s, 1 da; *Career* chartered accountant/merchant banker, sr dir S G Warburg & Co Ltd Merchant Bankers (joined 1964), Kemp Chatteris & Co Chartered Accountants 1959-64; *Style* - Michael Gore Esq; c/o S G Warburg & Co Ltd, 30 Gresham st, EC2

GORE, Nigel Hugh St George; s of late Sir St George Richard Gore, 12 Bt; hp of n, Sir Richard Gore, 13 Bt; *b* 23 Dec 1922; *m* 1952, Beth, nee Hooper; 1 da; *Style* - Nigel Gore Esq; Eurone, Goondiwindi, Queensland, Australia

GORE, Paul Annesley; CMG (1964), CVO (1961), JP (Suffolk 1976); s of Charles Henry Gore OBE (d 1941) s of Sir Francis Gore KCB, whose f (yr bro of 4 Earl of Arran) m Lady Augusta Ponsonby, 2 da of 4 Earl of Bessborough; *b* 28 Feb 1921; *Educ* Winchester, Ch Ch Oxford; *m* 1946, Gillian Mary, nee Allen-Stevens; 3 s; *Career* Capt 16/5 Lancers (N Africa, Italy) 1941-46, Colonial Adminstrative Serv 1948-65, dep gov Gambia 1962-65, JP Oxford 1972-74; *Recreations* sailing; *Clubs* Cruising Assoc; owner of yacht 'Sula Sula'; *Style* - Paul Gore Esq CMG CVO JP; 1 Burkitt rd, Woodbridge, Suffolk (☎ Woodbridge 5748)

GORE, Sir Richard Ralph St George; 13 Bt (I 1622); s of Sir St George Ralph Gore, 12 Bt (gn of 9 Bt, d 1973); *b* 19 Nov 1954; *Educ* The King's Sch Parramatta, New England U; *Heir* unc, Nigel Gore; *Recreations* tennis, golf, handcrafts; *Style* - Sir Richard Gore, Bt; Wycanna, Talwood, Qld, 4322 Australia

GORE, Lady - Shirley; da of C Tabor, of Wauchope, NSW; *m* 1950, Sir St George Ralph Gore, 12 Bt (d 1973); 1 s, 3 da; *Style* - Lady Gore; Wycanna, Talwood, Queensland 4322, Australia

GORE BROWNE, Sir Thomas Anthony; s of Sir Eric Gore Browne; *b* 20 June 1918; *Educ* Eton, Trin Cambridge; *m* 1946, Lavinia, da of Gen Sir Charles Loyd, GCVO, KCB, DSO, MC; 3 s, 1 da; *Career* offr Gren Gds 1938-48; ptnr Mullens & Co 1949, sr Govt broker 1973-; kt 1980; *Clubs* Brooks's, White's; *Style* - Sir Thomas Gore Browne; 15 Moorgate, EC2; The Old Rectory, Lydlinch, Sturminster Newton, Dorset (☎ 0258 72074); Flat 4, 17 Sloane Court West, SW3

(☎ 01 730 5947)

GORE-BOOTH, Baron (Life Peer UK 1969); Paul Henry Gore-Booth; GCMG (1965, KCMG 1957, CMG 1949), KCVO (1961); s of Mordaunt Gore-Booth (yr bro of Sir Josslyn Gore-Booth, 6 Bt, and great nephew through his mother Georgina of 9 Earl of Scarbrough; also seventh in descent from Sir Francis Gore, whose bro Sir Arthur was ancestor of the Earls of Arran); *b* 3 Feb 1909; *Educ* Eton, Balliol Oxford; *m* 1940, Patricia, da of Montague Ellerton, of Adelaide & Yokohama; 2 s, 2 da; *Career* Registrar Order of St Michael & St George 1966-79; For Serv (ret) 1933-69 (Head Diplomatic Serv 1968-69, PUS FO 1965-69, High Commissioner India 1960-65, Ambass Burma 1953-56); Pres Sherlock Holmes Soc of London 1967-79; *Books* Satow's Guide to Diplomatic Practice (ed of 5 edn, 1978); *Clubs* Athenaeum, Baker Street Irregulars; *Style* - Rt Hon Lord Gore-Booth GCMG KCVO; 70 Ashley gdns, SW1 (☎ 01 828 8280)

GORE-BOOTH, Angus Josslyn; s of Sir Josslyn Augustus Richard Gore-Booth, 6 Bt, JP, DL (d 1944); bro and hp of Sir Michael Savile Gore-Booth, 7 Bt; *b* 25 June 1920; *m* 1948 (m dis 1954), Hon Rosemary Myra Vane, da of 10 Baron Barnard, CMG, MC; 1 s, 1 da; *Career* 1939-45, Capt Irish Gds; *Style* - Angus Gore-Booth Esq; Lissadell, Sligo, Ireland

GORE-BOOTH, Hon Christopher Hugh; yr s (twin) of Baron Gore-Booth, GCMG, KCVO (Life Peer); *b* 1943; *Educ* Eton, Durham U; *m* 1979, Mrs Jolanta Nicholls, da of late Dr L S Bernacinski; 1 s; *Style* - The Hon Christopher Gore-Booth; 42 Ringford rd, SW18

GORE-BOOTH, Hon Celia Mary; da of Baron Gore-Booth, GCMG, KCVO (Life Peer); *b* 6 Jan 1946; *Educ* Downe House Sch, London Acad for Music and Dramatic Art, York Repertory Theatre 1967, Jacques Lecoq Sch Paris 1968-69; *Style* - The Hon Celia Gore-Booth; 29 The Vale, SW3

GORE-BOOTH, Hon David Alwyn; er s (twin) of Baron Gore-Booth, GCMG, KCVO (Life Peer); *b* 1943; *Educ* Eton, Ch Ch Oxford; *m* 1964, Jillian Sarah (m dis 1970), da of James Wyatt Valpy, of Somerset West, S Africa; 2 s; m 2, 1977, Mary, da of Sir David Muirhead, KCMG, CVO; *Career* memb HM Diplomatic Service from 1964, third sec Baghdad 1966-67, third then second sec Lusaka 1967-69, second then first sec Tripoli 1969-71, FCO 1971-74, first sec Office of UK Perm Rep to European Communities Brussels 1974; counsellor (commercial) Jeddah 1980-; *Style* - The Hon David Gore-Booth; c/o Foreign and Commonwealth Office, King Charles st, SW1; 31 Lorn rd, London SW9 (☎ 01 733 3229)

GORE-BOOTH, Sir Michael Savile; 7 Bt (I 1760), of Artarman, Sligo; s of Sir Josslyn Gore-Booth, 6 Bt, JP, DL (d 1944, he was descended from a cadet branch of the Gore Baronets and Gores who became Earls of Arran); *b* 24 July 1908; *Educ* Rugby, Trinity Coll Cambridge; *Heir* bro, Angus Gore-Booth; *Style* - Sir Michael Gore-Booth, Bt; Lissadel, Sligo, Eire

GORE-BOOTH, Hon Mrs (Rosemary Myra); *née* Vane; da of 10 Baron Barnard, CMG, OBE, MC (d 1946) and Sylvia, da of Herbert Straker; *b* 1921; *m* 1948 (m dis 1954), Angus Josslyn Gore-Booth; 1 s, 1 da; *Career* chm Barnard Castle Rural District Council 1972-73; *Style* - The Hon Mrs Gore-Booth; The White House, Gainford, Darlington, Co Durham (☎ 386)

GORE-LANGTON, Lady Joan (Isabella); *née* Hope; da of 2 Marquess of Linlithgow, KG, KT, GCSI, GCIE, OBE, TD (d 1952), and Doreen, CI (d 1965), da of Rt Hon Sir Frederick Milner; *b* 1915; *m* 1952, Col Ian William Gore-Langton, MBE; 1 da; *Style* - Lady Joan Gore-Langton; Southpark, Robertsbridge, Sussex

GORELL, 4 Baron (UK 1909); Timothy John Radcliffe Barnes; s of 3 Baron Gorell, CBE, MC, sometime ed 'Cornhill Magazine' and Under-Sec State for Air (d 1963), and Maud (da of Alexander Radcliffe, of Bag Park, S Devon); through her Lord Gorell is 1 cous of Sir William van Straubenzee, MBE, MP (C) for Wokingham; *b* 2 Aug 1927; *Educ* Eton, New Coll Oxford; *m* 1954, Joan, da of John Collins, MC; 2 adopted da; *Heir* bro, Hon Ronald Barnes; *Career* late Lt Rifle Bde; barr 1951; sr exec Roy Dutch Shell Gp; *Recreations* golf, tennis, gardening; *Clubs* Roehampton Golf; *Style* - The Rt Hon Lord Gorell; 4 Roehampton Gate, SW15 (☎ 01 876 6042)

GORELL BARNES, Henry Gorell; s of Sir William Gorell Barnes, KCMG, CB, Mattishall Hall, Mattishall, Norfolk; *b* 10 Feb 1939; *Educ* Westminster School; Pembroke College, Cambridge; *m* 1965, Gillian Mary; 2 c; *Career* dir Morgan Grenfell & Co Ltd since 1971; chm The Athlone Trust since 1980; *Recreations* real tennis, fishing, gardening *Clubs* Brooks's, City of London, Racquet & Tennis NY *Style* - Henry Gorell Barnes Esq; 89 Randolph ave, London W9 (☎ 01 286 1079)

GORING, Edward Yelverton Combe; s of late Maj Frederick Yelverton Goring and bro and hp of Sir William Goring, 13 Bt; *b* 20 June 1936; *Educ* Wellington; *m* 1969, Daphne Seller; 2 da; *Career* Lt-Cdr RN; *Style* - Edward Goring Esq; Lee Farm Cottage, Free st, Bishop's Waltham, Hants

GORING, Lady Hersey Margaret; *née* Boyle; 2 da of 8 Earl of Glasgow, DSO, DL; *b* 11 July 1914; *m* 1, 1940, Cdr Hon John Waldegrave (k on active serv 1944), s of 5 and last Baron Radstock (*see* Baroness Fritz von Bültzingslöwen); 2 da; m 2, 1947, John Goring, CBE, TD, DL, s of Charles Goring, JP, DL (ggs of Sir Charles Goring, 5 Bt); 2 s, 2 da; *Style* - Lady Hersey Goring; Findon Park House, Findon, Sussex

GORING, Marius; s of Dr Charles Goring; *b* 23 May 1912; *Educ* Perse Sch Cambridge; Frankfurt U, Vienna U, Munich U and Paris U; *m* 1, 1931, Mary Steel (m dis); 1 da; m 2, 1941, Lucie Mannheim (d 1976); m 3, 1977, Prudence FitzGerald; *Career* actor, V-Pres Equity 1975-; *Style* - Marius Goring, Esq; Middle Court, The Green, Hampton Court, Surrey (☎ 01 977 4030)

GORING, Sir William Burton Nigel; 13 Bt (E 1678, with precedency of 1627); s of late Maj Frederick Yelverton Goring, 6 s of 11 Bt; suc unc, Sir Forster Gurney Goring, 12 Bt, 1956; *b* 21 June 1933; *Educ* Wellington; *m* 1960, Hon Caroline Thellusson, da of 8 Baron Rendlesham; *Heir* bro, Edward Goring; *Career* late Lt 1 Roy Sussex Regt; *Style* - Sir William Goring, Bt; 89 Cornwall gdns, SW7

GORMAN, John Reginald; CVO (1961), CBE (1974), MC (1944); s of Maj J Gorman, MC (d 1980); *b* 1 Feb 1923; *Educ* Rockport, Haileybury, ISC, Harvard Business Sch; *m* 1948, Norah Heather, nee Caruth; 2 s, 2 da; *Career* Capt Irish Guards WW II; v-chm and ch exec N Ireland Housing Executive 1979-, formerly personnel dir BOAC; *Clubs* Guards and Cavalry, Ulster; *Style* - John Gorman Esq, CVO, CBE, MC; The Red House, Rademon, Crossgar, Co Down, Ireland

GORMANSTON, 17 Viscount (I 1478, Premier Viscount of Ireland); Jenico Nicholas Dudley Preston; also Baron Gormanston (I 1365-70 and UK 1868, which latter sits as); s of 16 Viscount (ka 1940) and Pamela, nee Hanly (whose mother was Lady Marjorie, nee Feilding, da of 9 Earl of Denbigh); *b* 19 Nov 1939; *Educ* Downside; *m* 1974, Eva Landzianowska; 2 s; *Heir* s, Hon Jenico Preston; *Style* - The Rt Hon Viscount Gormanston; 16 Parkside, SW1 (☎ 01 235 6552/6689)

GORONWY-ROBERTS, Hon Ann Elisabeth; da of Baron Goronwy-Roberts, PC (Life Peer, d 1981); *b* 1947; *Style* - The Hon Ann Goronwy-Roberts

GORONWY-ROBERTS, Baroness; Marian; s of David Evans, of Aberdare; *m* 1942, Baron Goronwy-Roberts, PC, Min State FCO & Dep Ldr Ho Lds 1975-79 (Life Peer, d 1981); 1 s, 1 da; *Style* - Rt Hon Lady Goronwy-Roberts; Plas Newydd, Pwllheli, Gwynedd

GORONWY-ROBERTS, Hon Owen Dafydd; s of Baron Goronwy-Roberts, PC (Life Peer, d 1981); *b* 1946; *m* 1979; *Style* - The

Hon Owen Goronwy-Roberts

GORT, 8 Viscount (I 1816); Colin Leopold Prendergast Vereker; JP (Castletown IOM 1962); also Baron Kiltarton (I 1810); s of Cdr Leopold Vereker, JP, RNVR (gs of 4 Viscount, himself ggs of Juliana, sis of 1 Viscount and through whom the Viscountcy was heritable by special remainder; her f, Charles Smyth, descended from a da of Sir Thomas Cusack, Ld Chllr of Ireland in Edward VI's time; Cusack's other da m ArchBp Ussher of Armagh, whose computing of the date of creation at 4,000 BC long remained an article of dogma with certain fundamentalists); suc 1 cous once removed, 7 Viscount, 1975; *b* 21 June 1916; *Educ* Sevenoaks; *m* 1946, Bettine, da of Godfrey Green, of Douglas IOM, and formerly w of Arthur Jarand; 2 s, 1 da; *Heir* s, Hon Foley Vereker; *Career* Lt-Cdr RNVR, served WW II Mediterranean, Africa, Indian Ocean, Home Fleet, Atlantic, Russian Convoy; dir Williams Glyn's Bank IOM; memb House of Keys 1966-71; *Recreations* golf, gardening, antique restoration; *Clubs* Carlton; *Style* - The Rt Hon Viscount Gort JP; Westwood, The Crofts, Castletown, IOM (☎ 2545)

GOSCHEN, 4 Viscount (UK 1900); Giles John Harry Goschen; s of 3 Viscount Goschen, KBE (d 1977), by his 2 w Alvin; *b* 16 Nov 1965; *Heir* none; *Style* - The Rt Hon The Viscount Goschen; Hilton House, Crowthorne, Berks

GOSCHEN, Viscountess - Alvin; da of late H England, of Durban, Natal; *m* 1955, as his 2 w, 3 Viscount Goschen, KBE (d 1977); 1 s (4 Viscount); *Style* - The Rt Hon The Viscountess Goschen; Hilton House, Crowthorne, Berks

GOSCHEN, Hon Caroline Elizabeth; da of 3 Visc Goschen, KBE (d 1977); *b* 1963; *Style* - The Hon Caroline Goschen

GOSCHEN, Edward Alexander; s and h of Sir Edward Christian Goschen, 3 Bt, DSO; *b* 13 March 1949; *Educ* Eton; *m* 1976, Louise, da of Lt-Col Ronald Chance, MC; *Style* - Edward Goschen Esq

GOSCHEN, Sir Edward Christian; 3 Bt (UK 1916), DSO (1944); s of Sir Edward Goschen, 2 Bt (d 1933, himself nephew of 1 Viscount Goschen), and Countess Mary Danneskiold-Samsoe (d 1964), 7 da of 5 Count (Christian) Danneskiold-Samsoe (descended from Countess of Samsoe, nee Sophie Moth, so cr by Christian V of Denmark 1677, by whom she had a natural s Christian, cr Count Danneskiold-Samsoe 1695) and Countess Henriette (da of Count Krag-Juel-Vind-Frijs, of a Danish cr of 1867); *b* 2 Sept 1913; *Educ* Eton, Trin Oxford; *m* 1946, Cynthia, da of Rt Hon Sir Alexander Cadogan, OM, GCMG, KCB, PC, sometime PUS at the FO (7 s of 5 Earl Cadogan), by his w Lady Theodosia Acheson, da of 4 Earl of Gosford; 1 s, 1 da; *Heir* s, Edward Goschen; *Career* memb Stock Exchange Cncl, dep chm 1968-71; C'wlth War Graves Commissioner 1977-; *Style* - Sir Edward Goschen, Bt, DSO; Lower Farm House, Hampstead Norreys, Newbury, Berks (☎ Hermitage 201270)

GOSDEN, Norman Frank; *Career* dep chm Abbey National Bldg Soc; FCIS, FCCA, FBS; *Style* - Norman Gosden Esq; Abbey House, Baker st, NW1

GOSFORD, 7 Earl of (I 1806); Sir Charles David Alexander John Sparrow Acheson; 13 Bt (NS 1628); also Baron Gosford (I 1776), Viscount Gosford (I 1785), Baron Worlingham (UK 1835, which sits as), and Baron Acheson of Clancairny (UK 1847); s of 6 Earl of Gosford, OBE (d 1966), by his 1 w, Francesca, er da of Francesco Cagiati, of Rome; *b* 13 July 1942; *Educ* Harrow, Byam Shaw Sch of Drawing & Painting, Roy Acad Schs; *Heir* unc, Hon Patrick Acheson; *Style* - The Rt Hon The Earl of Gosford; House of Lords, SW1

GOSFORD, Countess of - Cynthia Margaret; da of late Capt Henry Cave West RHA; *m* 1, Maj James Pringle Delius (d 1944); m 2, 1960, as his 2 w, 6 Earl of Gosford, OBE (d 1966); *Style* - The Rt Hon The Countess of Gosford; Heath Cottage, Camberley, Surrey

GOSLING, Peter Alfred; s of William Thomas Gosling (decd); *b* 29 Apr 1924; *Educ* Clacton on Sea Co H S; *m* 1947, Doris Eva Emily, nee Smith; 1 s David, 1

da Susan; *Career* WW II Roy Engineers Burma, md Radio Rentals Ltd; *Recreations* hunting, gardening; *Style* - Peter Gosling Esq; Pinfarthings, Gt Somerford, Chippenham, Wilts (☎ Seagry 720374)

GOSLING, William Douglas; MBE (1949), TD, DL (Essex 1952); s of William Sullivan Gosling (d 1952) and Lady Victoria Kerr, 5 da of 9 Marquess of Lothian; *b* 11 Sept 1904; *Educ* Eton, Cambridge; *m* 1935, Rosemary, da of Hon Victor A F Russell, CBE (3 s of 1 Baron Ampthill); *Career* Lt-Col Commanding Essex Yeo 1951, Maj RA (TA) Middle East WW II, farmer, local dir Barclays Bank, High Sheriff Essex 1958, patron of living of Farnham, Herts; *Style* - William Gosling Esq, MBE, TD, DL; Thrimley House, Farnham, Bishop's Stortford

GOSNAY, His Hon Judge; Maxwell Gosney; s of William Gosnay (d 1958); *b* 31 July 1923; *Educ* Leeds G S, Ch Ch Oxford; *m* 1959, Constance Ann, nee Hardy; 1 s, 1 da; *Career* HM circuit judge 1973-, barr 1945, assist recorder Leeds 1965-72, dep cmmr Yorks Traffic Authority 1965-71, dep chm W Riding Quarter Sessions 1967-72, recorder Crown Ct 1972-73; *Recreations* golf, reading; *Clubs* Leeds; *Style* - His Hon Judge Gosnay; 25 Park Lane, Leeds 8, Yorks (☎ 663066)

GOSWELL, Brian Laurence; s of Albert George Goswell (d 1971); *b* 26 Nov 1935; *Educ* St David's Sch High Wycombe, Durham U; *m* 1961, Deirdre Gillian, nee Stones; 2 s; *Career* man ptnr Healey and Baker, Fellow Incorporated Soc of Valuers and Auctioneers and Hon Tres of Soc, Associate Chartered Inst of Arbitrators; *Recreations* shooting, horse racing, cricket; *Clubs* Turf, Carlton, City Livery; *Style* - Brian Goswell Esq; 118 Old Broad st, EC2 (☎ 628 4361); Pipers, Camley Park, Pinkneys Green, Berks (☎ 0628 30768)

GOTHARD, Lady - Margaret Vera; da of John Fitchett Hall (d 1952); *m* 1961, Sir Clifford Gothard, OBE, JP (d 1979); *Style* - Lady Gothard; Bearwood House, Burton-on-Trent, Staffs (☎ 3112)

GOTTLIEB, Stephen Louis Gerald; *Career* chm Polygram Leisure Ltd; *Style* - Stephen Gottlieb Esq; Abacus House, Gutter Lane, Cheapside, EC2

GOTTO, Capt Renfrew; CBE (1950), DSO (1940) and Bar; s of Sidney Gotto (d 1961); *b* 1 Dec 1900; *Educ* RN Colls Osborne and Dartmouth, Caius Cambridge; *m* 1931, Lorna Anne Florence, nee McEachran; 2 s, 1 da; *Career* Capt RN, WW I, WW II, cmd HMS Queen Elizabeth and HMS Vengeance, Naval Assault Gp Cdr Normandy Invasion; *Recreations* gardening, bird watching; *Style* - Capt Renfrew Gotto, CBE, DSO*, RN; Sparrow's House, Cockfield, Bury St Edmunds, Suffolk (☎ Cockfield Green 828334)

GOTZ, Lady (Mary Spencer); da of Hector Ranson, of New Zealand; *m* 1962, as his 2 w, late Sir Frank Gotz, KCVO; *Style* - Lady Gotz; 327 Fenton st, Rotorua, New Zealand

GOUDIE, Hon William Henry; MC (1944); s of Henry Goudie; *b* 21 Aug 1916; *Educ* Bristol G S; *m* 1948, Mourilyan Munro; 2 s; *Career* exec dir and dep chm Tasmania Law Reform Cmmn 1974- *Style* -Hon William Goudie MC; 24 Nimala st, Rosny, Hobart, Tasmania 7018, Aust

GOUGH, 5 Viscount (UK 1849); Sir Shane Hugh Maryon Gough; 5 Bt (UK 1842); also Baron Gough of Chinkangfoo and of Maharajpore and the Sutlej (UK 1842); s of 4 Viscount Gough, MC, JP, DL (d 1951, ggs of Field Marshal 1 Viscount, KP, GCB, GCSI, PC, whose full title was Viscount Gough of Goojerat (the shortened form 'Viscount Gough' appears to be the moden usage) and whose brilliant exploits in the two Sikh Wars resulted in the annexation of the Punjab to British India), by his w Margaretta (da of Sir Spencer Maryon-Wilson, 11 Bt); *b* 26 Aug 1941; *Educ* Winchester; *Heir* none; *Career* late Lt Irish Gds; memb Roy Co of Archers (Queen's Bodyguard for Scotland); *Clubs* White's, Pratt's, MCC; *Style* - The Rt Hon Viscount Gough; Keppoch Estate Office, Strathpeffer, Ross-shire (☎ 224); 17 Stanhope gdns, SW7 (☎ 01 370 3569)

GOUGH, Cecil Ernest Freeman; CMG (1956); s of Ernest Gough, of Hockley, Essex; *b* 29 Oct 1911; *Educ* Southend H S, LSE; *m* 1938, Gwendolen, da of Martin Longman, of Hockley; 1 s, 1 da; *Career* assist dir gen Br Property Fedn 1978-80; formerly civil servant, Inland Revenue, MOD, FO, Admlty; md Airwork Overseas Ltd 1968-71; *Recreations* cookery, gardening, reading; *Clubs* Naval & Military; *Style* - Cecil Gough Esq, CMG; 13 Canonbury Park South, N1 (☎ 01 226 6378)

GOUGH, Lady Hyacinth Kathleen Anne; *née* Needham; da of 4 Earl of Kilmorey, OBE, VRD, PC (d 1961); *b* 1923; *m* 1953, John Hubert Gough; 3 da; *Style* - Lady Hyacinth Gough

GOUGH, Rt Rev Hugh Rowlands; CMG (1965), OBE (Mil 1945), TD (1945); s of Rev Charles Gough; *b* 19 Sept 1905; *Educ* Weymouth Coll, Trin Cambridge, London Coll of Divinity; *m* 1929, Hon Madeline, da of 12 Baron Kinnaird, KT, KBE, JP, DL, by his wife Frances, JP, da of Thomas Clifton, of Lytham Hall, Lancs; 1 da; *Career* DAC(haplain)G 10 Corps Italy 1943-45; Bp of Barking 1948-59, ArchBp Sydney & Primate Australia 1959-66; OStJ 1959; *Recreations* bird watching; *Clubs* National; *See also* The Hon Mrs Gough *Style* - The Rt Rev Hugh Gough, CMG, OBE, TD; Forge House, Over Wallop, Stockbridge, Hants (☎ Wallop 315)

GOUGH, John Osborne; s of Reginald Gough (d 1972); *b* 26 March 1932; *Educ* Tonbridge, Bristol U; *m* 1958, Patricia Annette, da of Kenneth Blandford Lalonde; 2 children; *Career* ch exec Kleen-e-ze Hldgs 1972-; *Recreations* rackets, fishing; *Clubs* Bath; *Style* - John Gough Esq; 14 Richmond Hill, Bristol BS8 1AT (☎ 0272 37700)

GOUGH, Hon Mrs (Madeline Elisabeth); da of 12 Lord Kinnaird, KT, KBE (d 1972); *b* 1908; *m* 1929, Rt Rev Hugh Rowlands Gough, CMG, OBE, TD, *qv*; 1 da; *Style* - The Hon Mrs Gough; 12 St James's sq, Bath

GOULD, Kenneth; CBE (1973), TD; s of Capt William Gould; *b* 5 Feb 1919; *Educ* Manchester G S, Victoria U Manchester; *m* 1946, Kathleen, da of Dr Thomas O'Connell; 1 s, 1 da; *Career* Lt-Col RA (TA), served Pacific, Burma; slr 1947; chm Singapore Internat Chamber of Commerce 1971-73; gov London Sch Oriental & African Studies; dir Inchcape & Co 1971-; dep chm London Advsy Bd of Norwich Union Insur Gp; *Recreations* shooting, golf, cricket; *Clubs* Oriental, City of London, Singapore Cricket, Roy Island Country, Tanglin (last three Singapore); *Style* - Kenneth Gould Esq, CBE, TD; Tithe Barn, Courts Mount rd, Haslemere, Surrey (☎ 0428 2879)

GOULDING, Senator Hon Lady - Hon Valerie Hamilton; *née* Monckton; da of 1 Viscount Monckton of Brenchley, GCVO, KCMG, MC, PC, QC (d 1965); *b* 1918; *Educ* Hon LLD, Nat U of Ireland; *m* 1939, Wing Cdr Sir William Basil Goulding, 3 Bt; *Career* late Subaltern WRAC (Reserve); Senator of Republic of Ireland; chm and md Central Remedial Clinic, Dublin; Dame of Honour and Devotion, Sovereign Mil Order of Malta; *Style* - Senator the Hon Lady Goulding; Ballyrusheen, Co Cork; Dargle Cottage, Enniskerry, Co Wicklow

GOULDING, Sir William Basil; 3 Bt (UK 1904); s of Sir (William) Lingard Amphlett Goulding, 2 Bt (d 1935); *b* 4 Nov 1909; *Educ* Winchester, Oxford U; *m* 1939, Hon Valerie Hamilton Monckton, da of 1 Viscount Monckton of Brenchley; 3 s; *Heir* s, William Lingard Walter Goulding; *Career* dir Fitzwilton Ltd (former chm), former dir Bank of Ireland and Rio Tinto Zinc Corpn; *Style* - Sir William Goulding, Bt; Dargle Cottage, Enniskerry, Co Wicklow, Eire; Ballyrusheen, Co Cork

GOULDING, William Lingard Walter; s and h of Sir William Goulding, 3 Bt; *b* 11 July 1940; *Educ* Winchester, Trin Coll Dublin; *Style* - William Goulding Esq

GOURLAY, Hon Mrs (Patricia Drake); *née* Normand; da of Baron Normand (Life Peer) (d 1962); *b* 1917; *m* 1948, Douglas William Gourlay; *Style* - The Hon Mrs

Gourlay; Craigmuir, Moniaive, Thornhill, Dumfriesshire

GOVETT, Peter John; s of the late Francis Govett; *b* 3 Sept 1935; *Educ* Harrow, Oriel Oxford; *m* 1, 1964, Janet Adorian; 1 s, 1 da; m 2, 1978, Carolyn Odhams; *Career* commodity broker, dir Shearson Loeb Rhoades Ltd; *Recreations* theatre; *Style* - Peter Govett Esq; 404 Fulham rd, London SW6 (☎ 01 385 2294); The Old Chapel, Ashampstead Green, Newbury, Berks (☎ Compton 512)

GOWRIE, 2 Earl of (UK 1945); Alexander Patrick Greysteil Ruthven; also Baron Ruthven of Gowrie (UK 1919), Baron Gowrie (UK 1935), and Viscount Ruthven of Canberra (UK 1945); s of Maj Hon Patrick Hore Ruthven (s of 1 Earl of Gowrie, himself 2 s of 9 Lord Ruthven of Freeland); *b* 26 Nov 1939; *Educ* Eton, Balliol Oxford, Harvard; *m* 1, 1962 (m dis 1974), Xandra, yr da of Col Robert Bingley, CVO, DSO, OBE; 1 s; m 2, 1974, Countess Adelheid, yst da of Count Fritz-Dietlof von der Schulenburg (himself 4 s of 6 Count von der Schulenburg, of a cr of the Holy Roman Empire of 1728 by Charles VI, recognised by King Frederick William I of Prussia 1729, Elector Frederick Augustus II of Saxony 1740 and the Elector George II (aka George II of Great Britain) of Hanover 1747) and London ed of Quick magazine till 1981; *Heir* s, Viscount Ruthven of Canberra; *Career* officially recognised in the name of Ruthven by Warrant of Lord Lyon King of Arms 1957; former lecturer/tutor State U of New York, UCL and Harvard; Con Whip 1971-72, Lord In Waiting 1972-74, Oppn Spokesman Ec Affrs 1974-79, Min of State Dept Employment 1979-; *Style* - The Rt Hon Earl of Gowrie; House of Lords, SW1; 34 King st, Covent Garden, WC2

GRAAFF, David de Villiers; s and h of Sir de Villiers Graaff, 2 Bt, MBE; *b* 3 May 1940; *Educ* Diocesan Coll S Africa, Stellenbosch U, Grenoble U, Magdalen Oxford; *Style* - David Graaff Esq

GRAAFF, Sir de Villiers; 2 Bt (UK 1911), MBE (1947); s of Sir David Pieter de Villiers Graaff, 1 Bt, sometime High Commissioner for Union of S Africa in London (d 1931); *b* 8 Dec 1913; *Educ* Cape Town U, Magdalen Oxford; *m* 1939, Ena, da of Frederick Voigt; 2 s, 1 da; *Heir* s, David de Villiers Graaff; *Career* advocate S Africa Supreme Court 1938-, Ldr Oppn in SA 1957-77 (MP 1948-77); dir Graaffs Tst, Southern Life, Milnerton Estates; *Recreations* fishing, riding, cricket; *Clubs* Civil Service, Kelvin Grove, Western Province Cricket; *Style* - Sir de Villiers Graaff, Bt, MBE; De Grendel, Private Bag, GPO, Cape Town 8000, S Africa (☎ 582068 & 430143, home & office)

GRADE, Baron (Life Peer UK 1976); Lew Grade; s of Isaac and Olga Winogradsky; bro of Lord Delfont; *b* 25 Dec 1906; *Educ* Rochelle st Sch EC2; *m* 1942, Kathleen, da of John Moody; 1 s; *Career* chm and ch exec Assoc Communications Corpn Ltd; Pres ATV Network; chm and md ITC Entertainment, chm Bentray Investments, ACC Enterprises, Stoll Moss Theatres; OStJ; kt 1969; *Style* - The Rt Hon Lord Grade; c/o ATV House, 17 Gt Cumberland Place, W1 (☎ 01 262 8040)

GRADON, Air Cdre Oswald; CBE (1970, OBE 1951); s of James Gradon; *b* 8 Nov 1915; *Educ* Houghton Sch; *m* 1955, Judith, da of Wilfrid Foster; 2 s; *Career* FCA; bursar Oundle 1971-78; dir RAF Manning 1967-71; *Recreations* tennis; *Clubs* RAF; *Style* - Air Cdre Oswald Gradon, CBE; 34 Thornton Court, Thornton rd, Girton, Cambridge (☎ 0223 277201)

GRAESSER, Sir Alastair Stewart Durward; DSO (1960), MC (1944), TD (1950), JP (Flintshire 1956), DL (1960); s of Norman Hugo Graesser, JP (d 1970); *b* 17 Nov 1915; *Educ* Oundle, Gonville and Caius Cambridge; *m* 1939, Diana Aline, nee Neale; 1 s, 3 da; *Career* Commander OstJ 1980, Col WW II, Hon Col Roy Welch Fusiliers 1973-80, Cheshire Yeomanry 1949-54, memb Wales and Marches Postal Bd, trustee Wales and Border Cos TSB, md Trustee Municipal Mutual Insurance Ltd, dir Dvpt Corpn for Wales, dir Grosvenor Hotel Co Ltd Chester, chm Nat Union and Unionist Assoc 1974-75, High Sheriff Flintshire 1963, Vice-Ld Lt Clwyd 1980; kt 1973;

Recreations boxing (Half Blue), rugby football, rowing, shooting, gardening; *Clubs* Bath, Grosvenor (Chester), Leander, Hawk's (Cambridge); *Style* - Sir Alastair Graesser DSO MC TD JP, HM Vice Lord-Lieut for Clwyd;Sweet Briar, Berghill Lane, Babbinswood, Oswestry, Salop (☎ 62395)

GRAFTON, 11 Duke of (E 1675); Hugh Denis Charles FitzRoy; KG (1976), DL (Suffolk 1973); also Earl of Euston, Viscount Ipswich and Baron Sudbury (E 1672); s of 10 Duke of Grafton (d 1970, eighth in descent from the 1 Duke, natural s of Charles II (who long refused to acknowledge him) and (Barbara) Duchess of Cleveland; among the devices for His Grace's support (mostly redeemed about the mid-nineteenth century) were the prisage and butlerage of imported wine, the Receiver Generalship of profits of Seals in the Courts of King's Bench and levies on the excise and Post Office) and Lady Doreen Buxton, 2 da of 1 Earl Buxton, GCMG; *b* 3 April 1919; *Educ* Eton, Magdalene Cambridge; *m* 1946, Fortune, GCVO, JP, Mistress of the Robes to HM 1967- and da of late Capt Eric Smith (whereby Her Grace is 4 cous once removed to Lord Carrington, and 5 cous of Lord Ravensdale); 2 s, 3 da; *Heir* s, Earl of Euston; *Career* Hon FRIBA, late Capt Gren Gds; patron of four livings & Hereditary Ranger Whittlebury Forest; chm Soc for Preservn of Ancient Bldgs, Nat Tst E Anglian Regnl Cttee, Exec Cttee Historic Churches Preservn Tst; memb Historic Bldgs Cncl for England & Cathedrals Advsy Cttee; chm Sir John Soane's Museum; V-Chm Tstees Nat Portrait Gallery; memb Roy Fine Art Commission; *Clubs* Boodle's; *Style* - His Grace The Duke of Grafton KG DL; Euston Hall, Thetford, Norfolk (☎ 3282)

GRAFTON, Peter Witheridge; CBE (1972); s of the late J H Grafton; *b* 19 May 1916; *Educ* Westminster Sch, Sutton Valence Sch, London Poly, London U; *m* 1, 1939, Joan, nee Bleackley (d 1969); 3 da (1 decd); m 2, 1971, Margaret Ruth, nee Ward; 2 s; *Career* chartered quantity surveyor, pres Royal Inst Chartered Surveyors 1978-79, chm National Joint Consultation Ctee for Constructive Industry 1974, chm governing body Sutton Valence Sch, memb United Westminster Schools Trust; *Recreations* golf, some writing; *Clubs* Reform, East India; *Style* - Peter Grafton Esq, CBE; Corner Cottage, 10 Stanhopes, Limpsfield, Surrey (☎ Oxted 6685)

GRAHAM, Lady Alastair (Sheelah Violet Edgeworth); da of Essex Edgeworth Reade (d 1908) and Sheelah Lady Ruggles Brise; *m* 1944, as his 2 w, Capt Lord Alastair Graham, RN (d 1976, s of late 5 Duke of Montrose); *Style* - Lady Alastair Graham; Apple Tree Cottage, Campsea Ash, Woodbridge, Suffolk

GRAHAM, Capt Andrew John Noble; s and h of Sir John Noble Graham, 4 Bt, KCMG; *b* 21 Oct 1956; *Educ* Eton, Trin Cambridge; *Career* Capt Argyll and Sutherland Highlanders; *Recreations* fishing, shooting, stalking, piping; *Style* - Capt Andrew Graham; c/o 8 St Maur rd, SW6 (☎ 01 731 4884)

GRAHAM, Alexander Michael; s of Dr Walter Graham; *b* 27 Sept 1938; *Educ* St Paul's Sch; *m* 1964, Carolyn, da of Lt-Col Alan Stansfeld; 3 da; *Career* TA with Gordon Highlanders, insurance broker, md Frizzell Group Ltd; *Recreations* shooting, golf, wine; *Clubs* Bath, City Livery, Highland Brigade; *Style* - Alexander Graham Esq; Walden Abbotts, High st, Whitwell, Herts (☎ Whitwell 223)

GRAHAM, Lady Cairistiona Anne; da of 7 Duke of Montrose; *b* 1955; *Style* - Lady Cairistiona Graham

GRAHAM, Brig Cyril Carew; CBE (1958), DSO (1950); s of the late Capt C E Graham; *b* 26 Oct 1907; *Educ* Imperial Service Coll Sandhurst; *m* 1959, Kathleen Margaret, nee Colley; *Career* Brig HQ MEF 1942-43, Italy 1943-48, Malaya 1948-, DAA & QMG HQ Army Troops Aden 1941, DAAG MEF Cairo 1942-43, cmd 43 Gurkha Lorried Bde 1943-44, and 1 Bn 10 Princess Mary's Own Gurkha Rifles 1948-50, North Malaya District 1953, HQ British Gurkhas India 1954-58; *Recreations* golf; *Clubs* Army & Navy; *Style* - Brig Cyril Graham, CBE, DSO; Broadmead, Ludham, Norfolk

GRAHAM, Lord Calum Ian; s of 7 Duke of Montrose; *b* 1958; *Educ* St Andrew's Coll, Grahamstown; *Style* - Lord Calum Graham

GRAHAM, Maj Sir Charles Spencer Richard; 6 Bt (GB 1783), DL (Cumberland 1970); s of Lt-Col Sir (Frederick) Fergus Graham, 5 Bt, KBE, TD (d 1978); *b* 16 July 1919; *Educ* Eton; *m* 1944, Susan, OBE, da of Maj Robert Lambton Surtees, OBE, of Littlestone, Kent; 2 s, 1 da; *Heir* s, James Fergus Surtees Graham; *Career* Maj Scots Gds, ret 1950; High Sheriff of Cumberland 1955-56, pres Country Landowners Assoc 1971-73, memb Nat Water Cncl 1973; *Style* - Maj Sir Charles Graham Bt DL; Crofthead, Longtown, Cumbria (☎ Longtown 231)

GRAHAM, Hon Mrs (Daphne); *née* Bootle-Wilbraham; da of late 6 Baron Skelmersdale and Ann, da of Percy Quilter (s of 1 Bt); *b* 1946; *m* 1980, Jocelyn Peter Gore Graham; *Style* - The Hon Mrs Graham

GRAHAM, Lord Donald Alasdair; s of 7 Duke of Montrose; *b* 28 Oct 1956; *Educ* St Andrew's Coll Grahamstown; *Style* - Lord Donald Graham

GRAHAM, Rev Douglas Leslie; s of Very Rev George Frederick Graham, Dean of Kildare (d 1962); *b* 4 Oct 1909; *Educ* Portora Royal Sch, Trin Coll Dublin; *m* 1935, Gladys Winifred Ann, nee Brittain; 3 s; *Career* Chaplain RNVR (home & N Atlantic), assist master Eton 1934-41, head Portora Royal then Dean Close Schs, assist master Williston Acad Massachusetts 1968-72; *Recreations* the three R's, birds; *Clubs* Friendly Brothers of St Patrick (Dublin); *Style* - Rev Douglas Graham; Forest Cottage, West Woods, Lockeridge, Marlborough, Wiltshire (☎ Lockeridge 432)

GRAHAM, Lady Hermione Elizabeth; da of Marquess of Graham; *b* 1971; *Style* - Lady Hermione Graham

GRAHAM, Brig Herbert Leslie; CBE (1947), MC (1917), DL (Hants 1955); s of C B Graham (d 1907); *b* 22 Sept 1893; *Educ* Eton, Magdalen Coll Oxford; *m* 1937, Nan (d 1974), nee Macintyre; *Career* 1914-18 France & Belgium (wounded 1915), served 1939-45 in Norway & UK with 1 Bn Scots Guards, Lt-Col 1940, Brig 1948, ret 1948; *Recreations* shooting, golf, gardening; *Clubs* Cavalry and Guards, MCC, Swinley Forest Golf; *Style* - Brig Herbert Graham, CBE, MC, DL; Pond Farm, Darby Green, Blackwater, Hants (☎ Yateley 2149)

GRAHAM, Marquess of; James; s and h of 7 Duke of Montrose; *b* 6 April 1935; *Educ* Loretto; *m* 1970, Catherine Elizabeth MacDonnell, da of late Capt N A T Young, Queen's Own Cameron Highlanders, of Canada; 2 s, 1 da; *Heir* s, Lord Fintrie; *Style* - Marquess of Graham; Auchmar, Drymen, Glasgow

GRAHAM, Sir John Alexander Noble; 4 Bt (UK 1906), KCMG (1979, CMG 1972); s of Sir Reginald Graham, 3 Bt, VC, OBE (d 1980), and Rachel, Lady Graham, *qv*; *b* 15 July 1926; *Educ* Eton, Trin Cambridge; *m* 1956, Marygold Elinor Gabrielle, da of Lt-Col Clive Austin, JP, DL (d 1974), and Lady Lilian , nee Lumley, sis of 11 Earl of Scarbrough, KG, GCSI, GCVO, TD, PC; 2 s, 1 da; *Heir* s, Capt Andrew Graham; *Career* HM Diplomatic Serv, Ambass to Iran 1979-80, FCO Dep Under-Sec 1977-79 & 1980-; *Recreations* outdoor activities; *Clubs* Army & Navy; *Style* - Sir John Graham, Bt, KCMG; 8 St Maur rd, SW6

GRAHAM, James Bellingham; s and h of Sir Richard Graham, 10 Bt, OBE, JP, DL; *b* 8 Oct 1940; *Style* - James Graham Esq

GRAHAM, James Fergus Surtees; s and h of Maj Sir Charles Graham, 6 Bt; *b* 29 July 1946; *Educ* Milton Abbey; *m* 1973, Serena Jane, da of Ronald Frank Kershaw; 1 da; *Style* - James Graham Esq

GRAHAM, Sir John Moodie; 2 Bt (UK 1964); s of Sir Clarence Johnston Graham, 1 Bt (d 1966); *b* 3 April 1938; *Educ* Trin Coll Glenalmond, Queen's U Belfast; *m* 1970, Valerie Rosemary, da of late Frank Gill, of Belfast; 3 da; *Heir* none; *Career* pres N Ireland Leukaemia Research Fund, dir John Graham (Dromore) Ltd,

Electrical Supplies Ltd, Concrete (NI) Ltd, Ulster Quarries Ltd, G H Fieldhouse Plant (NI) Ltd; *Style* - Sir John Graham, Bt; Sketrick Island, Killinchy, Co Down, N Ireland (☎ 541449)

GRAHAM, Lady Lilias Catriona Maighearad; da of 7 Duke of Montrose; *b* 16 Feb 1960; *Style* - Lady Lilias Graham

GRAHAM, Hon Mrs - Hon Margaret Beatrice ; *née* Lopes; da of 1 Baron Roborough (d 1938); *b* 1898; *m* 1927, Maj Henry Archibald Roger Graham (d 1970); 1 s, 4 da; *Style* - The Hon Mrs Graham; 12 Hans Crescent, SW1; Mill Cottage, Micheldever, Hants

GRAHAM, Marigold Evelyn; da of Sir J Crosland Graham (d 1946); *b* 17 Feb 1931; *Educ* St Leonard's Sch, St Andrews U; *Career* High Sheriff Clwyd 1981; farmer; N Wales regnl rep Riding for Disabled Assoc 1970-77; V-Pres BRCS Denbighshire, V-Chm Br Horse Soc NE Wales; *Recreations* hunting, travel; *Style* - Miss Marigold Graham; Plas-yn-Rhos, Ruthin, Clwyd (☎ 08242 2048/2875)

GRAHAM, Malcolm Gray Douglas; s of Malcolm Graham; *b* 18 Feb 1930; *Educ* Shrewsbury; *m* 1980, Sara Anne, nee Anderson; 2 step s; *Career* dep chm The Midland News Assoc Ltd 1978-, chm - Express & Star Ltd, Shropshire Star Ltd, Shropshire Weekly Newspapers Ltd 1980-, pres Young Newspapermen's Assoc 1969, West Midlands Newspaper Soc 1973-74, chm Evening Newspaper Advertising Bureau 1978-79; *Recreations* shooting; *Style* - Macolm Graham Esq; Roughton Manor, Worfield, nr Bridgnorth, Shropshire

GRAHAM, Lady Ronald (Nancy Edith); da of late Edgar Baker; *m* 1, 1927 (m diss 1938), Maj Dudley Ryder; m 2, 1938, Lt-Cdr Lord Ronald Malise Hamilton Graham, JP (d 1978), s of 6 Duke of Montrose; *Style* - Lady Ronald Graham; Achavoulin, Blackwaterfoot, Isle of Arran

GRAHAM, Sir Richard Bellingham; 10 Bt (E 1662), of Norton Conyers, Yorks, OBE (1946), JP (N Riding Yorks 1953), DL (1961); s of Sir Reginald Graham, 9 Bt, DSO, JP, DL (d 1940), by his w Katherine, JP, da of Frank Stobart, JP, DL, of Marske Hall, Richmond, N Yorks; *b* 17 May 1912; *Educ* Eton, Magdalene Cambridge; *m* 1939, Beatrice, da of Lt-Col Michael Seymour Spencer-Smith, DSO, MC, of Stansted (gn of Sir Charles Smith, 2 Bt, and s of Rev Spencer Hamilton-Spencer-Smith by his w, Mary, da of Adm Cospatric Baillie-Hamilton, gn of 7 Earl of Haddington); 3 s; *Heir* s, James Graham; *Career* landowner & co dir; chm Yorkshire TV, Yorkshire Insur Co; Pro-Chllr Leeds U; High Sheriff Yorks 1961; Wing Cdr RAFVR; *Recreations* travel, fishing; *Clubs* Yorkshire, Brooks's; *Style* - Sir Richard Graham, Bt, OBE, JP, DL; Norton Conyers, Ripon, N Yorks (☎ Melmerby 33)

GRAHAM, Lord Ronald John Christopher; s of Marquess of Graham; *b* 1975

GRAHAM, Robin Ogilvie; s of Col Ogilvie Blair Graham, DSO, OBE, TD, DL; *b* 15 July 1929; *Educ* Eton, Trin Coll Oxford; *m* 1953, Judith Marian, da of Col Arthur Norris Swan Corbett, OBE, of Ireland; 2 s, 2 da; *Career* barr 1954, md Allsopps Brewery Nairobi Kenya 1960-64, dir E African Breweries Ltd 1962-64, dir Ansells Brewery Ltd Birmingham 1964-68, dir HP Bulmer Ltd Hereford 1968-75, dir Courage Central Ltd 1975-; *Recreations* shooting, travel, photography; *Clubs* Guards and Cavalry; *Style* - Robin Graham Esq; The Old Rectory, Stretton on Fosse, Moreton in Marsh, Glos (☎ Shipston on Stour 61261)

GRAHAM, Rachel, Lady - Rachel Septima; da of Col Sir Alexander Sprot, 1 and last Bt, CMG, DL, MP (d 1929); *m* 1920, Sir (John) Reginald Noble Graham, 3 Bt,VC, OBE (d 1980); 1 s, 1 da; *Style* - Rachel, Lady Graham; The Mailens, Gullane, E Lothian

GRAHAM, Ralph Stuart; s (by 2 m) and h of Sir Ralph Graham, 13 Bt; *b* 5 Nov 1950; *m* 1972, Roxanne (d 1975), da of Mrs Lovette Gurzan, of Elmont, Long Island, New York; m 2, 19--, Deena Louise Vandergrift; *Style* - Ralph Graham Esq

GRAHAM, Sir Ralph Wolfe; 13 Bt (E 1629); s of late Percival Harris Graham, 2 s of 10 Bt; suc cous, Sir Montrose Stuart Graham, 12 Bt, 1975; *b* 14 July 1908; *m* 1, 1939 (m dis 1949), Gertrude, da of Charles Kaminski, of Brooklyn, New York; m 2, 1949, Geraldine, da of Austin Velour, of Brooklyn, New York; 2 s; *Heir* s, Ralph Stuart Graham; *Style* - Sir Ralph Graham, Bt; 134 Leisureville Blvd, Boynton Beach, Fla 33435, USA

GRAHAM, Stuart Twentyman; CBE (1981), DFC (1943); s of Twentyman Graham (d 1923); *b* 26 Aug 1921; *Educ* Kilburn Grammar; *m* 1948, Betty June, nee Cox; 1 s (Neil); *Career* Sqd Ldr RAF 1940-46, joined Midland Bank Ltd 1938, jt gen man 1966-70, assist ch gen man 1970-74, dir and ch gen man 1974-81, gp ch exec 1981-; *Recreations* music, reading, photography; *Clubs* Overseas Bankers, St James'; *Style* - Stuart Graham Esq, CBE, DFC; Midland Bank Ltd, Head Office, Poultry, EC2 (☎ 01 606 9911)

GRAHAM-CLARKE, Philip Audley; s of Gerald Graham-Clarke (d 1961); *b* 6 Oct 1924; *Educ* Eton, Edinburgh U; *m* 1960 (m dis 1974), Nora Margaret, nee Keep; 1 da (Emma b 1962); *Career* Maj RA (BAOR, India, W Africa, USA), chartered accountant 1966, DL Monmouthshire 1963-73, Co Cmmr for Scouts Monmouthshire 1962-69; *Style* - Philip Graham-Clarke Esq; Hortons, The Street, Broughton Gifford, Melksham, Wiltshire (☎ North Trowbridge 782586)

GRAHAM-MOON, Sir Peter Wilfred Giles; 5 Bt (UK 1855), of Portman Square, Middx; s of Sir Wilfred Graham Moon, 4 Bt (d 1954), by his 2 w, Doris, nee Jobson; *b* 24 Oct 1942; *Educ* Lancing; *m* 1967, Sarah, da of Lt-Col Michael Smith, MC, MB, BS, MRCS, LRCPM, IMS, of The Grange, Headley, Hants (gs of Sir Thomas Smith, 1 Bt, KCVO, Hon Serjeant-Surgeon to King Edward VII); 2 s; *Heir* s, Rupert Graham-Moon; *Career* chm & md Joblux Ltd; *Recreations* golf, shooting, motor rallying; *Clubs* Roy Cork Yacht; *Style* - Sir Peter Graham-Moon, Bt; Cromwell House, Shipton-under-Wychwood, Oxon (☎ 0993 831020)

GRAHAM-MOON, Rupert Francis Wilfred; s and h of Sir Peter Wilfred Giles Graham-Moon, 5 Bt; *b* 29 Apr 1968; *Style* - Rupert Graham-Moon Esq

GRAHAM-TOLER, Lady Patricia Margaret; da of 6 Earl of Norbury; *b* 1970; *Style* - Lady Patricia Graham-Toler

GRAHAM-VIVIAN, Henry Richard; TD (1955), JP (1970); s of Richard Preston Graham-Vivian, MVO, MC (d 1979); *b* 13 April 1923; *Educ* Eton, Oxford; *m* 1955, Rosemary, da of Lt-Col Giffard Loftus Tyringham (d 1976); 1 s, 1 da; *Career* Capt Coldstream Guards Normandy, territorial service with Duke of Cornwall's Light Infantry 1946-60, High Sheriff Cornwall 1965; *Recreations* shooting, fishing; *Clubs* Army and Navy; *Style* - Henry Graham-Vivian Esq, TD, JP; Bosahan, Manaccan, nr Helston, Cornwall (☎ Manaccan 330)

GRAINGER, Keith Elphinston; CBE (1958); s of William Granger (d 1959), of Sydney, Australia; *b* 22 March 1903; *Educ* Sydney H S and Sydney U; *m* 1930, Ina Ruth, nee Forsyth; 1 s; *Career* cmmr Australian Pub Serv Bd 1953-68, chm Canberra Tech Coll Advisory Council 1969-75, chm Canberra Commercial Property Management Ltd 1969-, dist gov Rotary Internat 1970-71 (Paul Harris fell 1975), tres and tstee RAAF Women's Patriotic Educn Fund 1974; *Style* - Keith Grainger Esq, CBE; 3 Cain pla, Torrens, Canberra, ACT, Australia

GRANARD, 9 Earl of (I 1684); Sir Arthur Patrick Hastings Forbes; 10 Bt (S 1628), AFC (1941); also Viscount Granard, Baron Clanehugh (both I 1675) and Baron Granard (UK 1806, which sits as); s of 8 Earl of Granard (d 1948, eighth in descent from 1 Earl, who was himself ggs of Hon Patrick Forbes, 3 s of 2 Lord Forbes); *b* 10 April 1915; *Educ* Eton, Trin Cambridge; *m* 1949, Marie, da of Jean Maurel, of Millau, Aveyron, and formerly w of Prince Humbert de Faucigny Lucinge (cr of Charles X of France 1828); 2 da (HH Princesse Charles (Lady Moira) de Ligne de La Tremoille, of the family of mediatised Princes of the Holy Roman Empire; Lady Georgina Forbes); *Heir* bro, Hon John Forbes; *Career* Air Cdre RAFVR, served WW II; *Clubs* White's; *Style* - The Rt Hon Earl of Granard AFC; Castle Forbes, Newtown Forbes, Co Longford, Eire; 11 Rue Louis de Savoie, Morges, Switzerland

GRANBY, Marquess of; David Charles Robert Manners; s and h of 10 Duke of Rutland, CBE, by his 2 w, Frances; *b* 8 May 1959; *Style* - Marquess of Granby

GRANT, Sir Archibald; 13 Bt (NS 1705); s of Capt Sir Francis Cullen Grant, 12 Bt (d 1966); *b* 2 Sept 1954; *Heir* bro, Francis Tollemache Grant; *Style* - Sir Archibald Grant, Bt; House of Monymusk, Monymusk, Aberdeenshire

GRANT OF GRANT, Hon Amanda Caroline; da of 5 Baron Strathspey and 32 Chief of the Clan Grant, by his 2 w, Olive; *b* 16 Feb 1955; *Educ* St Margaret's Sch Bushey, Central Sch of Art & Design; *Career* graphic designer; *Style* - The Hon Amanda Grant of Grant; Williams & Glyn's Bank, Holts Branch, 22 Whitehall, SW1

GRANT, Andrew Francis Joseph; CB (1971); s of Francis Herbert Grant (d 1976); *b* 25 Feb 1911; *Educ* St Joseph's Coll SE19, King's Coll London U; *m* 1934, Mary, nee Harrison; 2 s (Peter m 1961, Jeremy m 1964), 2 da (Clare m 1956, Susan m 1978) *Career* civil engr, entered civil engr-in-ch's dept Admiralty 1937, Fleet Civil Engr Med 1960-63, dir for Wales Min of Public Building & Works 1963-66, dir Far East Region 1966-68, dir Home Regional Serv Dept of Environment 1968-71, Civil Serv Appeal Bd 1972; *Recreations* painting, golf, travel; *Clubs* Civil Service; *Style* - Andrew Grant Esq, CB; The Lodge, Herington Grove, Hutton Mount, Brentwood, Essex (☎ Brentwood 216486)

GRANT, Alexander Ludovic; TD (1940), JP (Cheshire 1951), DL (1963); s of John Peter Grant (d 1927); *b* 26 March 1901; *Educ* Winchester Coll, New Coll Oxford; *m* 1946, Elizabeth Langley, nee Barbour; 2 da; *Career* served Lovat Scouts 1920-40 (Maj 1935); dir Barclays Bank Ltd 1945-73; High Sheriff of Cheshire 1956; *Recreations* formerly shooting, hunting; now gardening, birdwatching; *Clubs* Pratt's, MCC; *Style* - Alexander Grant Esq, TD, JP, DL; Marbury Hall, Whitchurch, Shropshire (☎ Whitchurch 3731)

GRANT, Denzil Mohun Bede; s of late Sir Duncan Grant, 13 Bt; hp of bro, Sir Patrick Grant, 14 Bt; *b* 19 April 1955; *m* 1977, Nicola, da of A T Savill, of Godalming; *Style* - Denzil Grant Esq; Upper Street, Standsfield, nr Clare, Suffolk

GRANT, Brig Eneas Henry George; CBE (1951), DSO (1944) and Bar (1945), MC (1936), JP (1957), DL (Inverness-shire 1958); s of Col Hugh Gough Grant, CB (d 1922); *b* 14 Aug 1901; *Educ* Wellington Coll Berks, RMC Sandhurst; *m* 1926, Lilian Marion (d 1978), nee O'Neill; 1 s (and 1 s decd); *Career* Regular Army Seaforth Highlanders 1920-48 (Adjutant 1928-33, Brigade Commander 1944-49), Cdr Gold Coast District and Colonel Commandant Gold Coast Regiment 1949-52, Brig 1952 (acting 1944, temporary 1945-52), retired 1955; chairman TA & AF Assoc Inverness-shire 1961-65; *Recreations* country pursuits; *Clubs* Highland; *Style* - Brig Eneas Grant, CBE, DSO*, MC, JP, DL; Inverbrough Lodge, Tomatin, Inverness-shire, Scotland (☎ Tomatin 216)

GRANT, Francis Tollemache; s of late Capt Sir Francis Grant, 12 Bt; hp of bro, Sir Archibald Grant, 13 Bt; *b* 18 Dec 1955; *Style* - Francis Grant Esq

GRANT, Rear-Adm John; CB (1960), DSO (1942); s of Maj-Gen Sir Philip Grant, KCB, CMG (d 1943); *b* 13 Oct 1908; *Educ* RNC Dartmouth and Greenwich, Joint Serv Staff Coll, Imperial Defence Coll; *m* 1935, Ruth Hayward, nee Slade; 2 s (Duncan, Andrew m), 2 da (Tessa m, Grizel m); *Career* RN, cmding offr, HM Ships Beverley, Philante (1940-43), Opportune, Crispin, Cleopatra, Vernon (1943-56), Rear-Adm; flag offr cmding The Reserve Fleet 1959-61, ret 1961, Rank Organisation 1961-65, dir Conference of the Electronics Indust 1965-71; *Recreations* gardening, shooting, fishing; *Clubs* Senior United Service; *Style* - Rear-Adm John Grant, CB, DSO; 4 Priors Barton, Kingsgate rd, Winchester, Hampshire

GRANT OF GRANT, Hon Mrs (Geraldine) Janet; da of 5 Baron Strathspey; *b* 10 June 1940; *m* 1963 (m dis 1972), Neil Hamish Cantlie, s of late Adm Sir Colin Cantlie, KBE, CB, DSC; resumed maiden name of Grant of Grant; *Style* - The Hon Mrs Janet Grant of Grant; 24 Denbigh rd, W11

GRANT, Sir James Monteith; KCVO (1969), WS; s of James Ricketts Grant (d 1943), of Edinburgh; *b* 19 Oct 1903; *Educ* Edinburgh Acad and Edinburgh U; *m* 1, 1935, Agnes Winifried Comrie (d 1955), da of Stuart Lorimer, of Edinburgh; m 2, 1958, Yvonne Margaret, da of Geoffrey Legh Wilkinson, of Leeds; 1 da; *Career* Carrick Pursuivant 1946, Marchmont Herald 1957-69, Lord Lyon King of Arms 1969-, sec of Order of Thistle 1971-81; OStJ (1967), KStJ (1970); *Clubs* New (Edinburgh), Scottish Arts; *Style* - Sir James Grant, KCVO, WS; 40 Corstorphine rd, Edinburgh 12 (☎ 031 337 1209)

GRANT OF ROTHIEMURCHUS, Lt-Col John Peter; MBE (Mil 1945); s of Bt-Col John Grant of Rothiemurchus, CB, MC, TD, JP, DL (d 1963); *b* 13 Jan 1915; *Educ* Winchester and Grenoble University; *m* 1941 (separated 1975), Lady Katherine Greaves (*see* Grant of Rothiemurchus, Lady Katherine); 1 s, 1 da (*see* Buxton, Andrew); *Heir* s, John Grant of Rothiemurchus, yr; *Career* served WW I; landowner and farmer; memb Advisory Ctee for Protection of Birds in Scotland 1954-, V-Pres Royal Society for the Protection of Birds, memb Council Fauna and Flora Preservation Society; FRSA 1971; *Recreations* nature conservation, ornithology; *Clubs* Naval & Military, Puffin's (Edinburgh); *Style* - Lt-Col John Grant of Rothiemurchus MBE; Drumintoul Lodge, Rothiemurchus, Aviemore, Inverness-shire (☎ 0479 810298); 30 Buckingham ter, Edinburgh 4 (☎ 031 332 7151)

GRANT OF ROTHIEMURCHUS, YR., John Peter; s of Lt-Col John Grant of Rothiemurchus, MBE, and Lady Katherine Grant of Rothiemurchus, *qqv*; *b* 22 Oct 1946; *Educ* Gordonstoun; *m* 1973, Philippa, da of John Chance, of Widmer Lodge, nr Princes Risborough; *Style* - John Grant of Rothiemurchus, yr

GRANT OF GRANT, Hon James Patrick Trevor; s and h of 5 Baron Strathspey; *b* 9 Sept 1943; *Educ* abroad; *m* 1966, Linda, nee Piggott; 1 da; *Style* - The Hon James Grant of Grant; Flichity Farm, Strathnairn, Inverness-shire

GRANT OF ROTHIEMURCHUS, Lady Katherine; *née* Greaves; 2 da of Countess of Dysart (d 1975, the 10 holder of the title) and Maj Owain Greaves, DL, RHG (d 1941); hp to sis, Countess of Dysart (11 holder of the title); *b* 1 June 1918; *m* 1941 (separated 1975), Lt-Col John Grant of Rothiemurchus, MBE, Lovat Scouts, s of Col John Grant of Rothiemurchus, CB, MC, TD, JP, DL; 1 s, 1 da (Jane, m 1965, Andrew Buxton, *qv*); *Style* - Lady Katherine Grant of Rothiemurchus; Rothiemurchus, Aviemore, Inverness-shire

GRANT OF GRANT, Hon Michael Patrick Francis; s of 5 Baron Strathspey; *b* 22 April 1953; *Educ* Harrow and Oriel Coll, Oxford; *Career* Estate Agent and Property Investment Fund Manager; *Recreations* sailing (yacht- 'Solan'); *Style* - The Hon Michael Grant of Grant; Elms Ride, W Wittering, W Sussex (☎ 3246)

GRANT, Sir Patrick Alexander Benedict; 14 Bt (NS 1688); s of Sir Duncan Alexander Grant, 13 Bt (d 1961); *b* 5 Feb 1953; *Educ* Abbey Sch Fort Augustus; *Heir* bro, Denzil Grant; *Career* Chieftain of Clan Donnachy; *Style* - Sir Patrick Grant, Bt; 34 Morehampton rd, Donnybrook, Dublin 4; Doire-nan-Guibhais, Duncaston, Conon Bridge, Ross-shire

GRANT, Air Vice-Marshal Stanley Bernard; CB (1969), DFC (1942) & Bar (1943); s of Harry Alexander Gwatkin Grant (d 1934); *b* 31 May 1919; *Educ* Charterhouse, RAF Coll Cranwell; *m* 1, 1948, Barbara Jean (d 1963), nee Watts; 1 s (David), 1 da (Julia); m 2, 1965, Mme Christiane Py, nee Bech; 1 step s, 2 step da; *Career* joined RAF 1937, WW II (UK, Malta, Egypt, Italy), Gp Capt 1957, Air Cdre 1962, HQ AAFCE 1963-65, sr RAF instr IDC 1965-68, Cdr Br Forces Gulf 1968-69. ret 1970; *Recreations* bricolage; *Clubs* Royal Air Force; *Style* - Air Vice-Marshal Stanley Grant, CB, DFC*; 14 rue des Cordeliers, 83170 - Brignoles, France (☎ 69-18-90)

GRANT, William Laurence; s of Arthur John Grant (d 1949); *b* 26 July 1904; *Educ* The Stationers' Company's School; *m* 1931, Ruby Gwyneth, da of The Rev William James Clay, Vicar & Rural Dean of Risley, Glos; 3 children (1 decd); *Career* gen man Pearl Assurance Co Ltd 1949-67; pres The Insurance Inst of London 1953-54; pres The Chartered Insurance Inst 1964-65; pres The Insurance Benevolent Assoc 1955-56; *Recreations* walking, reading, theatre, ballet, foreign travel; *Clubs* RAC, English Speaking Union, Royal Overseas League; *Style* - William Grant Esq; Motts Hill, Walton-on-the-Hill, Surrey (☎ Tadworth 2516); Beach Gate, Feldway Beach, W Sussex; (☎ Bognor Regis 23515)

GRANT-FERRIS, Hon (Henry Michael) Piers; OSB (1959); s of Baron Harvington, PC (Life Peer); *b* 9 April 1933; *Educ* Ampleforth, Strawberry Hill Teaching Coll; *Career* Lt Irish Gds, served Germany 1953 & Egypt 1954; monk of St Benedict, priest 1964-, teacher Ampleforth Prep Sch 1965-75, assist priest Workington 1977-; Sov Mil Order of Malta 1980; *Recreations* mountaineering, swimming, skiing, riding; *Clubs* Br Ski, Kandahar Ski, Swiss Alpine; *Style* - Rev The Hon Piers Grant-Ferris, OSB; The Priory, Workington, Cumbria (☎ 0900 2114)

GRANT-SUTTIE, James Edward; s and h of Sir (George) Philip Grant-Suttie, 8 Bt; *b* 29 March 1965; *Style* - James Grant-Suttie Esq

GRANT-SUTTIE, Sir (George) Philip; 8 Bt (NS 1702); s of late Maj George Grant-Suttie, gs of 2 Bt; suc kinsman, Sir George Grant-Suttie, 7 Bt, 1947; *b* 20 Dec 1938; *Educ* Sussex Composite H S New Brunswick, McGill U; *m* 1962 (m dis 1969), Elspeth Mary, da of Maj-Gen Robert Elliott Urquhart, CB, DSO; *Heir* s, James Grant-Suttie; *Career* farmer, writer, pilot; *Recreations* flying, fishing, forestry (owner- Entstrom Helicopter and Cessna 206); *Style* - Sir Philip Grant-Suttie, Bt; 1 Great Stuart st, Edinburgh 3 (☎ 031 225 6813); Sheriff Hall, North Berwick (☎ 0620 3750); Balgone, North Berwick (☎ 0620 3750)

GRANTCHESTER, 2 Baron (UK 1953); Kenneth Bent Suenson-Taylor; QC (1971); s of 1 Baron Grantchester, OBE (d 1976), and Mamie, da of Albert Suenson, of Copenhagen; *b* 18 Aug 1921; *Educ* Westminster, Christ's Cambridge; *m* 1947, Betty, da of John Moores, CBE; 3 s, 3 da; *Heir* s, Hon Christopher Suenson-Taylor; *Career* former Capt RA; Pres VAT Tbnls 1972, Recorder 1974, chm Licensed Dealers' Tbnl 1975, Pres Aircraft & Shipping Industs Arbitration Tbnl 1980; *Clubs* Buck's; *Style* - The Rt Hon The Lord Grantchester QC; The Gate House, Coombe Wood rd, Kingston Hill, Surrey (☎ 01 546 9088)

GRANTLEY, 7 Baron (GB 1782); John Richard Brinsley Norton; MC (1944); s of 6 Baron Grantley (d 1954, ggs of George Norton by his w Caroline, herself gda of the playwright Sheridan and centre of the scandal involving Melbourne, *see* Marquess of Dufferin and Ava; the strict title of the Barony is 'Lord Grantley, Baron of Markenfield') and Jean, da of Brig-Gen Sir David Kinloch, 11 Bt, CB, MVO; *b* 30 July 1923; *Educ* Eton, New Coll Oxford; *m* 1955, Lady Deirdre Hare, da of 5 Earl of Listowel; 2 s; *Heir* s, Hon Richard Norton; *Career* memb Lloyd's, dir Leslie & Godwin Ltd; served WW II Capt Gren Gds; *Clubs* White's, Pratt's; *Style* - The Rt Hon Lord Grantley MC; Markenfield Hall, Ripon, N Yorks; 53 Lower Belgrave st, SW1 (☎ 01 730 1746)

GRANTLEY, Baroness - Lady Deirdre Freda Mary; *née* Hare; da of 5 Earl of

Listowel, GCMG, PC; *b* 1935; *Educ* Lady Margaret Hall, Oxford; *m* 1955, 7 Baron Grantley, qv; *Style* - The Rt Hon the Lady Grantley; Markenfield Hall, Ripon; 53 Lower Belgrave st, SW1

GRANVILLE OF EYE, Baron (Life Peer UK 1967); Edgar Louis Granville; s of Reginald Granville; *b* 12 Feb 1899; *Educ* High Wycombe, Melbourne; *m* 1943, Elizabeth, da of Rev William Cecil Hunter; 1 da; *Career* former md E L Granville & Co; MP (Lib) Suffolk Eye 1929-51, PPS to Sir Herbert Samuel 1931 & Sir John Simon Nat Govt 1931-36, joined Lab Pty 1951; served WW I &II; *Style* - Rt Hon Lord Granville of Eye; 112 Charlton Lane, Cheltenham, Glos

GRANVILLE, 5 Earl (UK 1833); Granville James Leveson-Gower; MC (1945), DL (Inverness-shire 1974); also Viscount Granville of Stone Park (UK 1815) and Baron Leveson of Stone (UK 1833, eldest s & h usually styled simply Lord Leveson); s of 4 Earl Granville (d 1953, gs of 1 Earl, who was himself yr bro of 1 Duke of Sutherland) and Lady Rose Bowes-Lyon, da of 14 Earl of Strathmore and sis of HM Queen Elizabeth The Queen Mother; through his mother Lord Granville is therefore 1 cous of HM The Queen; *b* 6 Dec 1918; *Educ* Eton; *m* 1958, Doon, da of Fl Lt Hon Brinsley Sheridan Plunket (2 s of 5 Baron Plunket, gs of 1 Marquess of Dufferin and Ava, and gggs of the playwright Sheridan); 2 s, 1 da; *Heir* s, Lord Leveson; *Career* Maj Coldstream Gds, supp reserve; Pres Navy League 1953-66; served WW II N Africa & Italy; V-Ld-Lt Western Isles (Islands Area) 1976-; *Style* - The Rt Hon Earl Granville, MC, DL, HM Vice Lord-Lieut for the Western Isles; Callernish, Sollas, N Uist, Outer Hebrides, Inverness-shire; 49 Lyall Mews, SW1 (☎ 01 235 1026)

GRANVILLE-WEST, Baron (Life Peer UK 1958); Daniel Granville West; s of John West, of Monmouthshire; *b* 17 March 1904; *m* 1937, Vera, JP, da of J Hopkins, of Pontypool; 1 s, 1 da; *Career* slr 1929, sr ptnr D Granville West, Chivers & Morgan, of Newbridge & Pontypool; PPS to Home Sec 1950-51 and MP (L) Pontypool 1946-58; served WW II RAFVR Fl Lt; *Style* - Rt Hon Lord Granville-West; Brynderwen, Abersychan, Pontypool, Gwent (☎ Talywain 236)

GRATTAN-BELLEW, Sir Henry Charles; 5 Bt (UK 1838); s of Lt-Col Sir Charles Christopher Grattan-Bellew, 4 Bt, MC (d 1948); *b* 12 May 1933; *Educ* Ampleforth; *m* 1, 1956 (m dis 1966), Naomi, da of late Dr Charles Cyril Morgan, of Chester, and formerly w of Herbert Ellis; m 2, 1967 (m dis 1974), Gillian Hilley; 1 s, 1 da; m 3, 1978, Elzabé Amy, da of Henry Gilbert Body, of Utrecht, Natal, and wid of J B Westerveld, of Pretoria; *Heir* s, Patrick Grattan-Bellew; *Career* assist dist cmmr Kenya Police Reserve 1953-54, dist offr Kenya Administration 1954-55; journalist, radio, TV broadcaster, publisher; *Style* - Sir Henry Grattan-Bellew, Bt; Sandford Park, Bergville, Natal 3350, S Africa; Walton Heath, Illovo, Johannesburg, Transvaal 2196, S Africa

GRATTAN-BELLEW, Patrick Charles; s (by 2 m) of Sir Henry Grattan-Bellew, 5 Bt; *b* 1970

GRAUBARD, Lady Mary Jane; *née* Cavendish-Bentinck; da of 9 Duke of Portland, CMG; *b* 1919; *m* 1 1963 (m dis 1978), Alexander Georgiades; 2s; m 2 1978, Prof Stephen Graubard; *Style* - Lady Mary Graubard; 91 Garden st, Cambridge, Mass 02138, USA

GRAVELL, David William; s of Canon William James Gravell (d 1968); *b* 9 June 1925; *Educ* Marlborough, Trin Cambridge; *m* 1955, Cecil Katherine, nee Eastwood; 3 s, 1 da; *Career* shipbroker, chm British Philippine Soc Exec Ctee 1966-67, chm Killick Martin & Co (dir 1954) 1975, memb British Waterways Bd 1980-, chm St Olave's Hart St Patronage Trust 1980, memb Cncl of Malaysia-Singapore Commercial Assoc 1975-; *Recreations* watching cricket, listening to music, seeing the world; *Clubs* MCC, Inst of Dirs, City of London; *Style* - David Gravell Esq; Eastgate, 73 Leman st, E1 (☎ 01 488 1488)

GRAVES, 8 Baron (I 1794); Peter George Wellesley Graves; s of 7 Baron (d

1963); *b* 21 Oct 1911; *Educ* Harrow; *m* 1960, Winifred (the actress Vanessa Lee), da of Alfred Moule and widow of Warde Morgan; *Heir* 2 cous once removed, Maj Evelyn Graves; *Career* actor; *Style* - The Rt Hon Lord Graves; c/o Coutts & Co, 440 Strand, WC2

GRAVES, Hon Cerise Evelyn Georgina; da of 6 Baron Graves (d 1937); *b* 18 July 1906; *Style* - The Hon Cerise Graves; Halsted, Tilford, Farnham, Surrey

GRAY, 22 Lord (S 1445); Angus Diarmid Ian Campbell-Gray; s of Master of Gray (Maj Hon Lindsay Campbell-Gray, MC, s of Lady Gray, 21 holder of the title, and Henry Campbell, whose mother was Lady Anne, da of 9 Earl of Lindsay); suc grandmother 1946; *b* 3 July 1931; *Educ* Eton; *m* 1959, Patricia, da of Capt Philip Alexander (gs of 3 Earl of Caledon); 4 s; *Heir* s, Master of Gray; *Style* - The Rt Hon Lord Gray; Airds Bay House, Taynuilt, Argyll

GRAY, Charles Reginald; MBE (1945), TD (1950); s of Charles Wilson Gray (d 1969); *b* 3 July 1920; *Educ* Moseley Coll; *m* 1941, Anne, nee Bradshaw; 2 s; *Career* Lt-Col WW II, chm The Dutton-Forshaw Gp Ltd, chm- Sterling Foods Ltd, Grayfriars Estates Ltd, Williams & Gray Ltd, William Clarke (Bradford) Ltd, Cabana Soft Drinks Ltd, dir of 62 companies; *Recreations* shooting; *Clubs* Cavalry and Guards; *Style* - Charles Gray Esq, MBE, TD; Wennington Old Farm, Wennington, nr Lancaster (☎ Hornby 21330)

GRAY, Maj-Gen (Reginald) John; CB (1973); s of the late Dr Cyril Gray; *b* 26 Nov 1916; *Educ* Ascham House, Gosforth and Russell Sch, Durham U; *m* 1943, Esme, da of the late Maj G R G Ship; 1 s, 1 da; *Career* CStJ 1971, OStJ 1957, served 1939-45 in India, Burma, NW Europe, Egypt, Malta, BAOR, chief Medical Officer British Red Cross Society 1974-, dir International Generics Ltd 1974-, Col Cmdt RAMC 1977-, chm RAMC Assoc 1980-, dep dir Gen AMS 1967-69, dir UK Land Forces 1972-73, QHS 1970-73; fellow of Royal Society of Medicine memb BMA and Casualty Surgeons Assoc; *Recreations*growing some things, repairing others, fermenting grape juice; *Style* - Maj-Gen John Gray, CB; 11 Hampton Close, Wimbledon, SW20 (☎ 01 946 7429)

GRAY, John Magnus; CBE (1971, MBE 1945), ERD (1946); s of the late Lewis Campbell Gray, CA; *b* 15 Oct 1915; *Educ* Horris Hill, Winchester; *m* 1947, Patricia Mary, nee Eggar; 1 da; *Career* md William Ewart & Son Ltd, linen manufacturers, (Belfast) 1958-72, chm Irish Linen Guild 1958-64, and Central Council of Irish Linen Industry 1968-74, chm Northern Ireland Electricity Serv 1974-80 & Belfast Branch RNLI 1970-76, memb Councils of FBI and CBI 1956-74 and 1979-80; *Recreations* golf, gardening; *Clubs* Army & Navy, Ulster (Belfast); *Style* - John Gray Esq CBE ERD; Blairlodge, Dundrum,Newcastle, Co Down (☎ Dundrum 271)

GRAY, Maj-Gen Michael Stuart; OBE (1971); s of Lt-Cdr Frank Gray, RNVR (ka 1940); *b* 3 May 1932; *Educ* Christ's Hosp Horsham, RMA Sandhurst; *m* 1958, Juliette Antonia; 3 children; *Career* reg offr Br Army, memb Royal Coll Defence Studies 1976, Cdr 16 Parachute Bde 1977, Cdr 6 Field Force and COMUKMF 1977-79, Cdr Br Army Staff and Mil Attaché 1979-81 with additional responsibilities of Head Br Defence Staff and Defence Attaché Washington 1981; *Recreations* recovery and restoration of weapons and armoured vehicles from Normandy, gardening and house maintenance, drawing, painting, photography; *Style* - Maj-Gen Michael Gray, OBE; c/o National Westminster Bank Ltd, 60 Market pl, Beverley, North Humberside; British Defence Staff, British Forces Post Office 2

GRAY, Nicholas Anthony; s of late Sir William Gray, 2 Bt; hp of n, Sir William Hume Gray, 3 Bt; *b* 1934; *m* 1956, Amanda, da of H W Edwards, of Newbury; 1 da; *Style* - Nicholas Gray Esq; 43 Markham sq, SW3; Skutterskelfe House, Hutton Rudby, Yarm, Yorks

GRAY, Simon James Holliday; s of Dr James Gray; *b* 21 Oct 1936; *Educ* Westminster, Dalhousie U, Trin

Cambridge; *m* 1965, Beryl Mary Kevern; 1 s, 1 da; *Career* lecturer in English Queen Mary Coll London 1965-, novelist, playwright (works include *Otherwise Engaged*, voted Best Play 1976-77 by NY Drama Critics Circle); *Recreations* squash, watching cricket and soccer, tennis, swimming; *Clubs* MCC; *Style* - Simon Gray Esq; c/o Judy Daish Assocs, Globe Theatre, Shaftesbury av, W1 (☎ 01 734 9261)

GRAY, Sir William Hume; 3 Bt (UK 1917); s of late William Talbot Gray, s of 2 Bt; suc gf, Sir William Gray, 2 Bt, 1978; *b* 26 July 1955; *Educ* Eton; *Heir* unc, Nicholas Anthony Gray; *Style* - Sir William Gray, Bt; Eggleston Hall, Eggleston, Barnard Castle, Co Durham

GRAYSON, Sir Ronald Henry Rudyard; 3 Bt (UK 1922); s of Sir Denys Henry Harrington, 2 Bt (d 1955); *b* 15 Nov 1916; *Educ* Harrow; *m* 1, 1936 (m dis 1944), Babette Vivienne, da of late Count Vivien Hollender; m 2, 1946, Dorothy Vera Hoare, da of Charles Serrell; *Heir* unc, Rupert Grayson; *Career* RAF WW II; *Style* - Sir Ronald Grayson, Bt; PO Box 24, Brooklyn, NSW 2253, Australia

GRAYSON, Rupert Stanley Harrington; s of late Sir Henry Grayson, 1 Bt, KBE; hp of n, Sir Ronald Grayson, 3 Bt; *b* 22 July 1897; *Educ* Harrow; *m* 1, 1919, Ruby, nee Banks; m 2, 1950, Vari Colette, da of Maj Henry O'Shea, of Cork; *Career* writer; Kt of Order of Holy Sepulchre; King's For Serv Messenger 1939-45; *Style* - Rupert Grayson Esq; c/o Midland Bank, Hythe, Kent

GREAVES, John Frederick; CBE (1966, OBE 1960); s of Alfred Greaves (d 1949); *b* 6 July 1905; *m* 1, 1929, Anne-Marie, nee Van de Weil; 2 s; m 2, 1952, Jean Mary, nee Daly; 2 s; *Career* chartered accountant ret 1974, European ptnr Coopers & Lybrand 1949-74, pres Br Chamber of Commerce in Belgium 1958-60, Chevalier de l'Ordre de Leopold (Belgium) 1949, Officier de l'Ordre de la Couronne (Belgium) 1969; *Recreations* golf, gardening; *Clubs* Cercle Royal Gaulois (Brussels); *Style* - John Greaves Esq, CBE; Double Houses, Charing Heath, Kent (☎ Charing 2139); 36 Buckingham Gate, SW1 (☎ 01 834 5710)

GREEN, Hon Mrs - Hon Claerwen; da of Baron Gibson-Watt, MC, PC; *b* 1952; *m* 1, 1970 (m dis); m 2 -- Green; *Style* - Hon Mrs Green

GREEN, Maj George Hugh; MBE (1958), MC (1946), TD (1947), DL (Caithness 1965); s of George Green; *b* 21 Oct 1911; *Educ* Wick H S, Edinburgh U; *m* 1936, Isobel, da of Peter Myron; 2 s; *Career* served WW II N Africa, NW Europe; headmaster to 1977; V-Lt Caithness 1973-; *Recreations* gardening, beekeeping; *Clubs* Highland Brigade; *Style* - Maj George Green, MBE, MC, TD, DL, HM Vice-Lieut for Caithness; Tjaldur, Gerston, Halkirk, Caithness (☎ 639)

GREEN, John Richard Daniel; s of John Everard Green (d 1966); *b* 8 Oct 1926; *Educ* Harrow, Ch Ch Oxford; *m* 1949, The Hon Jane Smith, da of 2 Baron Bicester (d 1968); 1 s, 2 da; *Career* Sub-Lt RNVR Home Fleet, Insurance Broker at Lloyd's; *Recreations* yacht racing, salmon fishing, shooting; *Clubs* Royal Yacht Squadron, City of London Club; *Style* - John Green Esq; 38 Chelsea Park gdns, SW3 (☎ 01 352 6126)

GREEN, Lewis Homer; s of Ernest Sydney Green (d 1980); *b* 14 Nov 1935; *Educ* Sherrardswood Sch, College of Printing; *m* 1961, Mary Valentine; 3 children; *Career* director & publisher; Sales dir, 1963-73; man dir Unwin Brothers Ltd 1973-79; dir Staples Printers Ltd 1975; dir Europa Publications Ltd 1979; dir Crosham Books Ltd 1979; Chief Exec Maltins Publishing Group 1979; *Recreations* the wood engravings of George Mackly & Gertrude Homes, sport, homemaking; *Style* - Lewis Green Esq; The Knoll, Shiplake, Henley-on-Thames, Oxon RG9 3JT

GREEN, Martin; s of Samuel Green (d 1967); *b* 7 Oct 1933; *Educ* Whittinghame Coll Brighton, Manchester U; *m* 1960, (m dis 1980), Gillian Susan; 3 s, 1 da; *Career* md Adsega Ltd 1960-65, md of Wrensons Stores Ltd, David Greig Ltd, Lampa Ltd 1971-74, dir Scottish Heritable Trust Ltd

1976-, dir Associated Tooling Industries Ltd 1978-, dir The Jessel Trust Ltd 1981-; *Style* - Martin Green Esq; 101 Dovehouse st, SW3 (☎ 01 352 2783)

GREEN, Dame Mary Georgina; DBE (1968); da of Edwin Green, of Wellingborough; *b* 27 July 1913; *Educ* Wellingborough H S, Westfield Coll London; *Career* Govr BBC 1968-73; chm Gen Optical Cncl 1979-; former Headmistress Kidbrooke Sch London; *Recreations* gardening; *Clubs* English Speaking Union; *Style* - Dame Mary Green, DBE; 45 Winn rd, SE12

GREEN, Peter Frederick; s of Frederick Arthur Green (d 1964); *b* 5 Sept 1922; *Educ* Berkhamstead; *m* 1949, Ruth Joy Griggs; 1 s, 1 da; *Career* dir LCP Holdings Ltd 1975-; chm Evans Halshaw Holdings Ltd 1975-; *Recreations* Golf; *Style* - Peter Green Esq; Windrush, Wawensmere rd, Wootton Wawen, Warwickshire (☎ 056 42 2395)

GREEN, Richard Chevallier; s of Lionel Green, MBE, JP, DL, of Kington, Herefs; *b* 22 May 1924; *Educ* Wellington, RAC Cirencester; *m* 1959, Julia, da of Roger de Wesselow; 1 s, 3 da; *Career* farmer; High Sheriff Herefs & Worcs 1981-82; *Recreations* shooting, fishing, travel, boating (yacht- 'Whittern'); *Clubs* Roy Yacht Sqdn, Farmers'; *Style* - Richard Green Esq; The Whittern, Lyonshall, Kington, Herefs (☎ 05448 241/205)

GREEN, Sir (Edward) Stephen Lycett; 4 Bt (UK 1886), CBE (1964), JP (Norfolk 1946, supp list 1980), DL (1961); s of Sir Edward Arthur Lycett Green, 3 Bt (d 1941); *b* 18 April 1910; *Educ* Eton, Magdalene Cambridge; *m* 1935, Constance Mary, da of late Ven Harry Sydney Radcliffe, Archdeacon of Lincoln; 1 da; *Heir* bro, Simon Lycett Green; *Career* barr 1933, Co Cllr Norfolk 1946-49, dep chm Norfolk Quarter Sessions 1948-71, chm E Anglian Regional Hosp Bd 1959-74, High Sheriff Norfolk 1973-74; *Style* - Sir Stephen Green, Bt, CBE, JP, DL; Ken Hill, Snettisham, King's Lynn, Norfolk (☎ Snettisham 202); Flat D, 60 Pont st, SW1 (☎ 01 589 5958)

GREEN, Lt-Col Simon Lycett; TD, JP (Wakefield), DL (W Riding Yorks); s of late Sir Edward Green, 3 Bt; hp of bro, Sir (Edward) Stephen Green, 4 Bt, CBE; *b* 11 July 1912; *Educ* Eton, Magdalene Cambridge; *m* 1, 1935 (m dis 1971), Gladys, da of late A Ranicar, JP; 1 da; m 2, 1971, Mary, da of late George Ramsden, of Wakefield; *Career* Lt-Col Cmdg Yorks Dragoons Yeo 1947-51; chm Green's Economiser Gp Ltd 1956-; *Recreations* shooting and racing (owner racehorses- 'Even Melody', 'Canton', 'Cliff Bank'; *Clubs* White's; *Style* - Lt-Col Simon Green, TD, JP, DL; Cliff Bank, N Rigton, Leeds (☎ Harrogate 74582)

GREEN-PRICE, John Chase; s of late Lt-Col Francis Chase Green-Price (d 1975) and hp to baronetcy of Green-Price; *b* 27 June 1947; *Style* - John Green-Price Esq

GREEN-PRICE, Lady; Jean Chalmers Scott; da of David Low Stark, of Arbroath; *m* 1956, as his 2 w, Capt Sir John Green-Price, 4 Bt (d 1964); *Style* - Lady Green-Price; Gwernaffel, Knighton, Powys

GREEN-PRICE, Sir Robert John; 5 Bt (UK 1874); s of Capt Sir John Green-Price, 4 Bt (d 1964); *b* 22 Oct 1940; *Educ* Shrewsbury; *Heir* kinsman, John Chase Green-Price; *Career* Capt (ret) RCT; ADC to Gov of Bermuda 1969-72; *Style* - Sir Robert Green-Price, Bt; Gwernaffel, Knighton, Powys (☎ Knighton 528580)

GREENACRE, Andrew John; s of the late John Edwin Greenacre; *b* 5 May 1931; *Educ* East Ham G S, Trinity Coll Oxford; *Career* 2 Lt Royal Artillery Germany, finance dir Glaxo Laboratories Ltd 1975-78, and Glaxo Operations UK Ltd 1978-; *Clubs* Oxford and Cambridge University; *Style* - Andrew Greenacre Esq; 10 Hayes Court, Sunnyside, Wimbledon, London SW19 (☎ 01 946 9413)

GREENACRE, Lady Elizabeth Marjory; *née* Lindesay-Bethune; da of 14 Earl of Lindesay, DL; *b* 31 May 1932; *m* 1960 (m dis 1970), Maj David Greenacre, late Welsh Gds, s of Brig W Greenacre, CB, DSO, MVO; 2 s, 1 da; *Style* - Lady Elizabeth Greenacre; Selby House, Ham Common, Richmond, Surrey

GREENALL, Hon Edward Gilbert; s and h of 2 Baron Daresbury by his 2 w, Josephine (d 1958, da of Brig-Gen Sir Frederick Laycock, KCMG, DSO, whose w Katherine was 3 da of Hon Hugh Hare, 4 s of 2 Earl of Listowel, KP); *b* 27 Nov 1928; *Educ* Eton; *m* 1952, Margaret Ada, da of Charles John Crawford (d 1940) by his w Ella, sis of Sir Denis Anson, 4 Bt; 3 s, 1 da; *Career* chm Randall & Vautier Ltd, Grunhalle Lager Internat; dir Hill Samuel & Co; *Recreations* power boating, skiing; *Style* - The Hon Edward Greenall; Crossbow House, Trinity, Jersey, CI (0534 63316)

GREENAWAY, Sir Derek Burdick; 2 Bt (UK 1933), CBE (1974), TD, JP (Kent 1962), DL (1973); s of Sir Percy Walter Greenaway, 1 Bt (d 1956); *b* 27 May 1910; *Educ* Marlborough; *m* 1937, Sheila Beatrice, da of late Richard Cyril Lockett; 1 s, 1 da; *Heir* s, John Greenaway; *Career* High Sheriff Kent 1971-72, chm and md Daniel Greenaway & Son Ltd, printers; jt master Old Surrey and Burstow Fox Hounds 1958-66, pres Sevenoaks Div Conservative Assoc 1963-66 (and former chm), chm SE Area Con and Unionist Assoc 1975, Master Stationers' & Newspaper Makers' Co 1974-75; Hon Col 44 (HC) Signal Regt, (Cinque Ports) (TA) 1966-67, Hon Col 36 (Eastern) Signal Regt (V) 1967-74; *Recreations* hunting, shooting, fishing; *Clubs* Carlton, City of London, MCC; *Style* - Sir Derek Greenaway, Bt, CBE, TD, JP, DL; Dunmore, Four Elms, Edenbridge, Kent (☎ 073 270 275)

GREENAWAY, John Michael Burdick; s and h of Sir Derek Greenaway, 2 Bt, CBE, TD, JP, DL; *b* 9 Aug 1944; *Educ* Harrow; *Career* Lt Life Gds (ret); dir Daniel Greenaway & Sons Ltd; *Style* - John Greenaway Esq

GREENE OF HARROW WEALD, Baron (Life Peer UK 1974); Sidney Francis Greene; CBE (1966); s of Frank Greene; *b* 12 Feb 1910; *m* 1936, Masel Carter; 3 da; *Career* kt 1970; Gen Sec NUR 1957-74, chm TUC 1969-70; dir Bank of England 1970-78; dir Trades Union Unit Tst 1970-, RTZ 1975-80, Times Newspaper Hldgs 1980; FCIT, JP London 1941-65; *Style* - Rt Hon Lord Greene of Harrow Weald CBE; 26 Kynaston Wood, Boxtree rd, Harrow Weald, Middx

GREENE, Edward Reginald; CMG (1952); s of Edward Greene (d 1938); *b* 26 Nov 1904; *Educ* Bedales Sch, St John's Coll Cambridge; *m* 1964, Irmingard, nee Spitza; *Career* joined E Johnston & Co Ltd (coffee merchants) 1927, Min of Food 1943-52 (dir of Coffee, dir of Raw Cocoa), Hon v-pres Brazilian Chamber of Commerce 1968-, FRSA 1971; *Recreations* painting; *Clubs* Garrick, City of London; *Style* - Edward Greene Esq CMG; Orbell House, Castle Hedingham, Essex (☎ Hedingham 60298)

GREENHALF, William Douglas George; s of John William Greenhalf (decd); *b* 8 May 1918; *m* 1966, Phyliss Doreen; 1 s; *Career* md and jt owner Shipton Communications Ltd; *Recreations* golf, work, swimming; *Style* - William Greenhalf Esq; En-Joie, Henton, Oxford (☎ Kingston Blount 52922)

GREENHILL OF HARROW, Baron (Life Peer UK 1974); Denis Arthur Greenhill; GCMG (1972, KCMG 1967, CMG 1960), OBE (1941); s of James Greenhill; *b* 7 Nov 1913; *Educ* Bishop's Stortford Coll, Ch Ch Oxford; *m* 1941, Angela, da of William McCulloch; 2 s; *Career* FO 1946-73, PUS FCO & Head Dip Serv 1969-73; served WW II Col RE Tstee Rayne Fndn, Pres Roy Soc Asian Affrs, Gov BUPA 1978-; memb Security Commission 1973-, dir S G Warburg, Clerical Medical & Gen Assur, Wellcome Fndn, BAT Industs, Hawker Siddeley Gp, Leyland Internat 1977-; *Clubs* Travellers'; *Style* - Rt Hon Lord Greenhill of Harrow GCMG, OBE; 25 Hamilton House, Vicarage Gate, W8 (☎ 01 937 8362)

GREENHILL, 2 Baron (UK 1950); Stanley Ernest Greenhill; s of 1 Baron, OBE (d 1967); *b* 17 July 1917; *Educ* Kelvinside Acad Glasgow, Glasgow Toronto & California Us; *m* 1946, Margaret, da of Thomas Newlands, of Ontario; 2 da; *Heir* bro, Hon Malcolm Greenhill; *Career* FRSM, FRCP, MD, DPH; served WW II RAF; former WHO consultant; Prof & Chm Dept Community Medicine, Alberta U 1959-; *Style* - Rt Hon Lord Greenhill; c/o 28 Gorselands, Newbury, Berks; 10223, 137th st, Edmonton, Alberta, Canada (☎ 403 452 4650)

GREENHILL, Ida, Baroness; Ida; da of Mark Goodman; *m* 1914, 1 Baron Greenhill, OBE (d 1967); 2 s (2 Baron, Hon Malcolm Greenhill), 1 da (decd); *Style* - The Rt Hon Ida, Lady Greenhill; 28 Gorselands, Newbury, Berks (☎ 45651)

GREENOCK, Lord; Charles Alan Andrew Cathcart; s and h of 6 Earl Cathcart, CB, DSO, MC; *b* 30 Nov 1952; *Educ* Eton; *Career* late Scots Gds, Res of Officers to 1980; *Style* - Lord Greenock

GREENWAY, 4 Baron (UK 1927); Sir Ambrose Charles Drexel Greenway; 4 Bt (UK 1919); s of 3 Baron (d 1975); *b* 21 May 1941; *Educ* Winchester; *Heir* bro, Hon Mervyn Greenway; *Career* marine photographer; *Clubs* Roy London Yacht, House of Lords Yacht; *Style* - The Rt Hon Lord Greenway; c/o House of Lords, SW1

GREENWAY, Baroness; Cordelia Mary; da of Maj Humphrey Campbell Stephen, JP, of Dormansland, Surrey; *m* 1939, 3 Baron Greenway (d 1975); 3 s (including 4 Baron); *Style* - The Rt Hon The Lady Greenway; 703 Collingwood House, Dolphin sq, SW1

GREENWAY, Harry; MP (C) N Ealing 1979-; s of John Greenway; *b* 4 Oct 1934; *Educ* Warwick Sch, Coll of St Mark & St John London, Caen U; *m* 1969, Carol, da of Maj John Hooper; 1 s, 2 da; *Career* former schoolmaster; chm All Pty Adult Educn Ctee 1979-; memb Parly Select Ctee on Educn, Science & Arts 1979-; *Recreations*riding, hockey, tennis, music, cricket; *Clubs* SCGB, St Stephen's Constitutional; *Style* - Harry Greenway Esq, MP; House of Commons, SW1

GREENWAY, Hon Mervyn Stephen Kelvynge; s of 3 Baron Greenway; bro and hp of 4 Baron Greenway; *b* 19 Aug 1942; *Educ* Winchester; *Career* FCA, stockbroker with Capel Cure Myers Freeman City of London, Liveryman Vintners Co; *Recreations* racing, bridge, golf, cricket, tennis; *Clubs* Turf, MCC; *Style* - The Hon Mervyn Greenway; 504 Frobisher House, Dolphin sq, SW1 (☎ 01 821 1893)

GREENWAY, Lady Sheelah Florence Lisette; *née* King-Tenison; da of 9 Earl of Kingston (d 1946); *b* 1900; *m* 1923, Cdr Thomas Cleveland Greenway, RN (d 1959); 1 s; *Style* - Lady Sheelah Greenway; W Somerset Home, Blenheim Lodge, Minehead, Somerset

GREENWELL, Sir Edward Bernard; 4 Bt (UK 1906), of Marden Park, Godstone, Co Surrey and Greenwell, Wolsingham, Co Durham; s of Sir Peter Greenwell, 3 Bt, TD (d 1978), and Jean, Lady Greenwell, *qv*; *b* 10 June 1948; *Educ* Eton, Nottingham U, Cranfield Inst of Technology (MBA); *m* 1974, Sarah, da of Lt-Col Philip Gore-Anley, of Sculthorpe House, Fakenham; 2 da; *Heir* bro, Maj James Greenwell; *Career* farmer; *Clubs* Turf; *Style* - Sir Edward Greenwell, Bt; Gedgrave Hall, Woodbridge, Suffolk (☎ Orford 440)

GREENWELL, Jean, Lady; Jean Henrietta Rose; 2 da of Peter Haig Thomas and Lady Alexandra Agar (2 da of 4 Earl of Normanton, DL, by Lady Amy Byng, da of 4 Earl of Strafford, CB); *b* 1920; *m* 1940, Sir Peter Greenwell, 3 Bt, TD, DL (d 1978); 2 s, 1 da; *Style* - Jean, Lady Greenwell; Butley Abbey Farm, Woodbridge, Suffolk

GREENWELL, Maj James Peter; 2 s of Sir Peter Greenwell, 3 Bt, TD, DL (d 1978); hp of bro, Sir Edward Greenwell, 4 Bt; *b* 27 May 1950; *Educ* Eton; *m* 1979, Serena, da of Hon Colin Dalrymple, DL (4 s of 12 Earl of Stair, KT, DSO, JP, DL), by his 2 w, Fiona (da of Adm Sir Ralph Edwards, KCB, KBE); *Career* Blues & Royals; *Style* - Maj James Greenwell

GREENWOOD OF ROSSENDALE, Baron (Life Peer UK 1970); (Arthur William James) Anthony Greenwood; PC (1964); s of Rt Hon Arthur Greenwood, CH, MP; *b* 14 Sept 1911; *Educ* Kingston GS, Merchant Taylors', Balliol Oxford; *m*

1940, Gillian, da of Leslie Crawshay-Williams, of Bridgend, and Joyce (gda through her f of 1 Baron Monkswell and through her mother of Rt Hon Thomas Huxley); 2 da; *Career* MP (L) Heywood & Radcliffe Lancs 1946-50, Rossendale Lancs 1950-70; chm Ho Lds Select Cttee Europe, Dep Speaker 1977-; Min Overseas Devpt 1965-66, Housing & Local Govt 1966-70, memb NEC Lab Pty 1954-70; chm Local Govt T'ning Bd 1975-; Pro-Chllr Lancaster U 1972-; *Style* - Rt Hon Lord Greenwood of Rossendale PC; 38 Downshire Hill, NW3

GREENWOOD, 2 Viscount (UK 1937); Sir David Henry Hamar Greenwood; 2 Bt (UK 1915); also Baron Greenwood (UK 1929); s of 1 Viscount Greenwood, PC, KC (d 1948), and Dame Margery Spencer, DBE, da of late Rev Walter Spencer, of Fownhope Court, Herefs; *b* 30 Oct 1914; *Educ* privately and Bowers Gifford; *Heir* bro, Hon Michael Greenwood; *Career* farmer FRGS; *Recreations* reading, walking, shooting; *Clubs* Roy Geographical Soc; *Style* - The Rt Hon The Viscount Greenwood; c/o Maj A A Greenwood, 6 Picaterre, Alderney, CI; c/o Maj A A Greenwood, 11 Surfside dve, Qualicum Beach, Vancouver Island, BC, Canada

GREENWOOD, Allen Harold Claude; CBE (1974), JP (Surrey and Hampshire 1962); s of Lt-Col Thomas Claude Greenwood (d 1958); *b* 4 June 1917; *Educ* Cheltenham Coll, Coll of Aeronautical Engrg London; *Career* Lt-Cdr (A) RNVR 1942-52, dep chm Br Aerospace 1977-, chm Br Aircraft Corpn 1975-77, chm Remploy Ltd 1976-79, chm Br Aerospace Inc (USA) 1977-, pres Cheltenham Coll Cncl, chm cncl St John's Sch Leatherhead; *Recreations* sailing, motoring, travel; *Clubs* White's, RAC, Royal Lymington Yacht; *Style* - Allen Greenwood Esq, CBE, JP; 2 Rookcliff, Milford-on-Sea, Hampshire (☎ 2893)

GREENWOOD, John Richard; s of the late John Eric Greenwood; *b* 18 March 1926; *Educ* Eton; *m* 1953, Penelope Anne, da of Lt Col Sir Walter Raymond Burrell, 8 Bt, CBE, TD, DL; 2 s, 2 da; *Career* late Captain Grenadier Guards, JP 1966-74, County Council East Sussex 1966, and West Sussex 1974, High Sheriff Sussex 1971-; *Recreations* shooting, more shooting, fishing; *Clubs* White's; *Style* - John Greenwood Esq; Stone Hall, Balcombe, West Sussex (☎ Balcombe 371); Lairg Lodge, Sutherland (☎ Lairg 2004)

GREGG, Dr Thomas James Myles; OBE (1945); s of the late Dr Thomas Alexander Gregg; *b* 10 Jan 1911; *Educ* Clifton Coll, Trinity Coll Dublin; *m* 1938, Mary Charlotte, nee Williams; 1 s, 2 da; *Career* KStJ 1969, Wing Cdr 2 Tactical Air Force, Europe, general practitioner 1946-55, regional Medical Officer Welsh Board of Health 1955-61, divisional Medical Officer Welsh Office 1961-71, chief surgeon for Wales St John Ambulance Brigade 1962-71, JP County Monmouth 1950-55; *Recreations* rugby, football, squash; *Clubs* Civil Service; *Style* - Dr Thomas Gregg, OBE; Shearwater, Amroth, Nr Marberth, Dyfed (☎ Saundersfoot 812349)

GREGSON, Baron (Life Peer UK 1975); John Gregson; DL (Gter Manchester 1979); s of John Gregson; *b* 29 Jan 1924; *Career* exec dir Fairey Hldgs; dir Fairey Engrg, Fairey Hydraulics, Fairey Nuclear Ltd, pt-time memb BSC 1976-; AMCT, MBIM; *Style* - The Rt Hon Lord Gregson DL; c/o Fairey Holdings Ltd, Cranford Lane, Heston, Middx; The Hollow, Offerton rd, Stockport, Cheshire

GREGSON, Peter Lewis; s of Walter Gregson; *b* 28 June 1936; *Educ* Nottingham H S, Balliol Oxford; *Career* Head Executive Secretariat Cabinet Off Aug 1981-, Dep Sec Dept Trade 1980-81, formerly with BOT 1961-66; Sec NEB 1975-77, Under-Sec Dept Trade 1977-80; *Style* - Peter Gregson Esq; Dept of Trade, 1 Victoria St, SW1

GREGSON, William Derek Hadfield; CBE (1970); s of W Gregson (d 1929); *b* 27 Jan 1920; *Educ* Alpine Coll Villars Switz, Faraday House Engrg Coll; *m* 1944, Rosalind Helen, nee Reeves; 3 s, 1 da; *Career* RAF NW Europe Sqdn Ldr 1939-45, dir Ferranti EI 1969-, assist gen man Ferranti (Scotland) Ltd 1959-, dep chm

BAA 1975-; dir Anderson Strathclyde Ltd, Scottish National Orchestra, Scottish Telecommunications Bd 1977-, East of Scotland Industl Devpts Ltd, Scottish Cncl (Devpt & Indust); memb Soc of Br Aerospace Cos (chm equip gp ctee 1967), FIIM; *Recreations* reading, collecting old silver, cabinet-making, automation in the home; *Clubs* RAF; *Style* - William Gregson Esq, CBE; 15 Barnton av, Edinburgh EH4 6AJ (☎ 031 336 3896)

GREIG, Henry Louis Carron; CVO (1972); s of Gp Capt Sir Louis Greig, KBE, CVO, DL, of Thatched House Lodge, Richmond Park; *b* 21 Feb 1925; *Educ* Eton; *m* 1955, Monica, da of Hon John Stourton, TD, *qv*; 2 s and twin s & da; *Career* Capt Scots Gds NW Europe 1945; Gentleman Usher to HM The Queen 1962-; chm H Clarkson & Co 1973- (md 1962-, dir 1954-); dir James Purdy & Sons 1972-, Baltic Mercantile & Shipping Exchange 1978-; *Clubs* White's; *Style* - Henry Greig Esq, CVO; Binsness, Forres, Moray; Brook House, Fleet, Hants

GREIG, James Dennis; CMG (1967); s of Dennis Greig, of Eccles (d 1971); *b* 14 July 1926; *Educ* Winchester, Clare Cambridge, LSE; *m* 1, 1952 (m dis 1960), Pamela Stock; 1 s, 1 da; m 2, 1960 (m dis 1967), Mrs Elizabeth Brown, da of Horace Starke, of N Carolina; 1 da; m 3, 1968, Paula, da of Percival Cook, of Gillingham Kent; *Career* Lt The Black Watch RHR & Nigeria Regt 1944-47 (Burma); Dir Population Bureau Min Overseas Devpt 1976-80; freelance population consultant; *Recreations* shooting, gardening, bowls; *Clubs* Hurlingham; *Style* - James Greig Esq, CMG; The Braw Bothy, Eccles, Kelso, Roxburghshire; Beverley Close, SW13 (☎ 01 876 5354)

GRENFELL, 3 Baron (UK 1902); Julian Pascoe Francis St Leger Grenfell; s of 2 Baron Grenfell, CBE, TD (d 1976), by his 1 w, Elizabeth (gda of 1 Baron Shaughnessy); *b* 23 May 1935; *Educ* Eton, King's Cambridge; *m* 1, 1961, Loretta, da of Alfredo Reali, of Florence; 1 da; m 2, 1970, Gabrielle, da of Dr Ernst Raab; 2 da; *Heir* 1 cous, Francis Grenfell; *Career* Capt Queen's Westminsters (TA) KRRC; Ch Info & Pub Affrs World Bank Europe 1970, Dep Dir European Off World Bank 1973, Special Rep World Bank to UNO 1974; broadcaster (current affrs & religious) ATV etc; *Style* - The Rt Hon Lord Grenfell; Room 2435, United Nations, New York City, New York 10017, USA (☎ 212 754 6008)

GRENFELL, Francis Pascoe John; s of Maj Hon Arthur Grenfell (2 s of 1 Baron Grenfell) and Eleanor, da of Hon (Mr Justice) Sir John James, of Saltash; hp to 1 cous, 3 Baron Grenfell; *b* 28 Feb 1938; *Educ* Eton, Ch Ch Oxford; *m* 1977, Elizabeth, da of Hugh Kenyon and Mary (da of Sir Peile Thompson, 4 Bt); *Style* - Francis Grenfell Esq; Lenten House, Lenten, Grantham, Lincs

GRENFELL, Irene, Baroness; Irene Lilian; da of Harry Cartwright, of Buenos Aires; *m* 1946, as his 2 w, 2 Baron Grenfell (d 1976); 1 da (Hon Aline Grenfell); *Style* - The Rt Hon Irene, Lady Grenfell; 13 Liphook Crescent, Honor Oak, Forest Hill, SE 23 (☎ 01 699 8528)

GRENFELL, (Sybil) Vera; CBE (1961), MVO (1945); da of Col Arthur Grenfell, DSO, TD (d 1958, n of 1 Baron Grenfell), by his 1 w, Lady Victoria Grey, da of 4 Earl Grey; *b* 21 July 1902; *Career* Lady-in-Waiting to late HRH Princess Alice of Athlone 1943-45; former chm Highway Clubs Incorporated, Florence Nightingale Aid in Sickness Tst (1975-80); *Style* - Miss Vera Grenfell, CBE, MVO; Paddock Cottage, Newlands dve, Maidenhead, Bucks (☎ 26521)

GRENSIDE, John Peter; CBE (1974); s of the late Harold Cutcliffe Grenside; *b* 23 Jan 1921; *Educ* Rugby; *m* 1946, Yvonne Thérèse, nee Grau; 1 s, 1 da; *Career* Captain RA, UK, Europe, India, chartered acccountant, ACA 1948, FCA 1960, pres Inst of Chartered Accountants in England and Wales 1975-76, partner Peat, Marwick, Mitchell & Co 1960-, chm Peat Marwick International 1980-; *Recreations* tennis, bridge; *Clubs* Athenaeum, MCC, Queens, Hurlingham, Pilgrims; *Style* - John Grenside Esq, CBE; 51 Cadogan Lane, SW1 (☎ 01 235 3372)

GRESWELL, Air Cdre Jeaffreson Herbert; CB (1967), CBE (1962, OBE 1945), DSO (1944), DFC (1942); s of the late William Territt Greswell; *b* 28 July 1916; *Educ* Repton; *m* 1939, Gwyneth Alice, nee Hayes; 1 s, 3 da; *Career* commissioned RAF 1935, WW II served in coastal command, OC 179 Sqdn Gibraltar 1943-44, HQ 18 Group 1944-45, Air Liaison Offr British Pacific Fleet 1946-47, HQ Far East Air Force Admin Plans 1947-49, dep dir JASS Londonderry 1949-52, OC RAF Kinloss 1957-59, HQ Coastal CD Air Plans 1959-61, dep standing group rep NATO HQ Paris 1961-64, Commandant Royal Observer Corps 1964-68; *Recreations* croquet; *Style* - Air Cdre Jeaffresson Greswell CB CBE DSO DFC; Picket Lodge, Ringwood, Hants (☎ Ringwood 3853)

GRETTON, 2 Baron (UK 1944); John Frederic Gretton; OBE (1950); s of 1 Baron, CBE, VD, TD, PC (d 1947), and Hon Maud Eveleigh-de-Moleyns (4 da of 4 Baron Ventry); *b* 15 Aug 1902; *Educ* Eton; *m* 1930, Margaret, da of Capt Henrik Loeffler; 2 s, 2 da; *Heir* s, Hon John Gretton; *Career* Pres Inst of Brewing 1960; MP (C) Burton Staffs 1943-45; *Clubs* Carlton; *Style* - The Rt Hon Lord Gretton, OBE; 77 Sussex sq, W2; Stapleford Park, Melton Mowbray, Leics (☎ Wymondham 229)

GREVILLE, 4 Baron (UK 1869); Ronald Charles Fulke Greville; s of 3 Baron, OBE, JP, DL (d 1952, sixth in descent from Hon Algernon Greville, 2 s of 5 Baron Brooke and unc of 1 Earl of Warwick; also bro-in-law of Hon Mrs Ronnie Greville, the brewer's daughter (her f was Rt Hon William M'Ewan PC) and inter-war years society hostess, who was also owner of the exquisite Polesden Lacey (where HM Queen Elizabeth the Queen Mother, then the Duchess of York, honeymooned) and which became one of the first properties of the fledgling National Trust on her death in 1942); *b* 11 April 1912; *Educ* Eton, Magdalen Oxford; *Heir* none; *Clubs* Hurlingham; *Style* - The Rt Hon Lord Greville; Cubberley, Ross-on-Wye, Herefs (☎ 3522); 75 Swan Court, Chelsea Manor st, SW3 (☎ 01 352 3444)

GREVILLE, Hon Guy David; s and h of Lord Brooke, JP; gs of 7 Earl of Warwick; *b* 30 Jan 1957; *Educ* Eton, Ecole des Roches; *Style* - The Hon Guy Greville; 17 Mayfair st, Mount Claremont, Perth, WA 6010, Australia (☎ 61 9(2) 384 9940)

GREW, James; JP (1974); s of late James Grew; *b* 25 Oct 1929; *Educ* Downside Sch; *m* 1955, Pauline Peta, da of Prof John Cunningham; 2 s (Jonatham James b 1958, Christopher Nicholas b 1969), 2 da (Michaela Maria b 1962, Philippa Peta b 1967); *Career* N Ireland Economic Cncl 1970-74, N Ireland Community Relations Cmmn 1971-74, Craigavon Dvpt Cmmn 1971-73, Crawford Ctee on Broadcasting Coverage 1973-74, BBC Advisory Ctee N Ireland 1976-80, BBC Gen Advisory Cncl London 1976-80, chm Post Office Users Cncl N Ireland 1976-81, memb Post Office Users Nat Cncl London 1976-81, Standing Advisory Cmmn on Human Rights 1980-82, Ind Broadcasting Authority N Ireland Advisory Ctee 1981-83; *Recreations* sailing (8 metre Trimaran 'His Mistress'); *Clubs* Challoner Pont Street; *Style* - James Grew Esq, JP; Peacefield, Ballinacorr, Portadown, Co Armagh, N Ireland

GREY OF NAUNTON, Baron (Life Peer UK 1968); Ralph Francis Alnwick Grey; GCMG (1964, KCMG 1959, CMG 1955), GCVO (1973, KCVO 1956), OBE (1951); s of Francis Grey, an accountant in NZ (whose f, Robert, was sometime headmaster Rochdale G S); *b* 15 April 1910; *Educ* Wellington Coll NZ, Auckland U Coll, Pembroke Cambridge; *m* 1944, Esma, da of Albert Burcher, of NZ, and widow of Pilot Offr Kenneth Kirkcaldie, RAFVR; 2 s, 1 da; *Career* barr & slr NZ; Govr & CIC Br Guiana, Bahamas, Turks & Caicos Is, N Ireland (1957-73 altogether); chm Cwlth Devpt Corpn 1979-80; chm Centl Cncl Roy Overseas League 1976-81; Freeman City of London; Pres Chartered Inst of Secs NI 1970-; Bailiff of Egle Order of St John 1975-, GCStJ 1976; *Recreations* golf; *Clubs* Travellers', Ulster; *Style* - Rt Hon Lord Grey of Naunton GCMG GCVO OBE; Overbrook, Naunton, Glos (☎ Guiting Power 263)

GREY, 6 Earl (UK 1806); Sir Richard Fleming George Charles Grey; 7 Bt (GB

1746); also Baron Grey of Howick (UK 1801) and Viscount Howick (UK 1806); s of Albert Grey (ggs of Adm Hon George Grey, himself 4 s of 2 Earl Grey, the PM (1830-34) at the passing of the Reform Bill and, according to his traducers (of whom Hobhouse, in a radical mood, was one) a prodigious amalgam of arrogance, avarice and nepotism; Creevy was complimentary about him, while Greville balanced an appreciation of his oratorical skills by a critical sketch of his character); suc 2 cous twice removed 1963; *b* 5 March 1939; *Educ* Hounslow Coll, Hammersmith Coll of Bldg; *m* 1, 1966 (m dis 1974), Margaret, da of Henry Bradford, of Ashburton; m 2, 1974, Stephanie, da of Donald Gaskell-Brown, of Newton Ferrers, Plymouth, and formerly w of Surgn-Cdr Neil Denham, RN; *Heir* bro, Philip Grey; *Career* Pres Cost & Exec Accountants Assoc 1978; memb Lib Pty; *Style* - The Rt Hon The Earl Grey; Rainbow House, Pennally Terrace, Boscastle, Cornwall; 40 Compton av, Mannamead, Plymouth, Devon

GREY, Sir Anthony Dysart; 7 Bt (UK 1814); suc gf, Sir Robin Edward Dysart Grey, 6 Bt, 1974; *b* 19 Oct 1949; *m* 1970, Donna (museum curator), da of Donald Daniels, of Park Lane, W1; *Heir* none; *Career* man Fibre Glass Div Bel Art Corpn; *Style* - Sir Anthony Grey, Bt; Van Riper Hopper House, 533 Berdan av, Wayne, NJ 07470, USA

GREY, Lt-Col James Michael Harling; CBE (1973), TD (1949), JP (1968), DL (Lancs 1975); s of Sir John Grey, of Burnley; *b* 5 Feb 1916; *Educ* Wrekin; *m* 1967, Ruth (d 1978), da of Arthur Haighton, of Yorks; 1 step da; *Career* formerly RA (TA); chm Cotton & Allied Textiles Indust Training Bd 1967-, Indust Ctee Br Textile Employment Assoc 1969-; *Recreations* sailing, walking, reading; *Clubs* Nat Liberal, Roy Windermere Yacht; *Style* - Lt-Col James Grey, CBE, TD, JP, DL; Shay Cross, Wiswell, Blackburn, Lancs

GREY, Sir Paul Francis; KCMG (1963, CMG 1951); s of Col Arthur Grey, CIE; *b* 2 Dec 1908; *Educ* Charterhouse, Ch Ch Oxford; *m* 1936, Agnes, da of Richard Weld-Blundell, of Ince-Blundell, Lancs; 3 s; *Career* Foreign Serv 1933-; Ambass Prague 1957-60, Berne 1960-64; *Style* - Sir Paul Grey KCMG; c/o Messrs Child & Co, 1 Fleet st, EC4

GREY, Philip Kent; s of Albert Grey; hp to bro, 6 Earl Grey; *b* 11 May 1940; *m* 1968, Ann, da of Cecil Applegate, of Kingsbridge, Devon; 1 s (Alexander Edward b 20 Dec 1968), 1 da (Vanessa Catherine b 1975); *Career* Master Mariner, licensed Trin House Sea Pilot (Corpn of Hull, Trin House); Offr RFA Serv; *Style* - Philip Grey Esq; Westcroft, Rock, Wadebridge, N Cornwall

GREY DE RUTHYN, Barony of (E 1324); *see* Lubienski Bodenham, Count Charles

GREY EGERTON, Sir Philip John Caledon; 15 Bt (E 1617), of Egerton and Oulton, Cheshire; s of Sir Philip Reginald Le Belward Grey Egerton, 14 Bt (d 1962); *b* 19 Oct 1920; *Educ* Eton; *m* 1951, Margaret Voase (d 1971), da of late Rowland Rank, of Aldwick Place, Aldwick, W Sussex, and wid of Sqdn Ldr Robert Ullman, RAF; *Heir* bro, Brian Balguy Le Belward Egerton; *Career* late Capt Welsh Gds; *Style* - Sir Philip Grey Egerton, Bt; Little Oulton, Tarporley, Ches

GREY-TURNER, Dr Elston; CBE (1979), MC (1944), TD (1955); s of Prof George Grey Turner, of Huntercombe Manor, Taplow; *b* 16 Aug 1916; *Educ* Winchester, Trin Cambridge, Bart's Hosp; *m* 1952, Lilias, da of Col Sterling Charles Tomlinson, of Walney House, Hereford; 2 s, 1 da; *Career* WW II N Africa, Italy, Germany; Hon Physician to HM The Queen 1960-62; Sec BMA 1976-79, Sec-Gen Standing Ctee Drs of EEC 1976; OStJ, Queen's Silver Jubilee Medal 1977; *Recreations* gardening, handyman, travel; *Clubs* Carlton; *Style* - Dr Elston Grey-Turner, CBE, MC, TD; The Manor House, Petersham, Surrey (☎ 01 940 6788)

GRIBBON, Maj-Gen Nigel St George; OBE (1960); s of the late Brig W H Gribbon, CMG, CBE; *b* 6 Feb 1917; *Educ* Rugby, Sandhurst, RAF Staff Coll, Canadian National Defence Coll; *m* 1943,

Rowan Mary, nee MacLeish; 2 s, 1 da; *Career* Maj-Gen Iraq 1941, Western Desert 1942, Palestine 1946, Trieste 1947-48, Malaysia 1948-50, Hong Kong 1953-54, BAOR 1967-69, SHAPE 1970-72, AMS War Office 1960-62, DMC Ministry of Defence 1966-67, ACOS NORTHAG 1967-69, ACOS (Intelligence) SHAPE 1970-72; chm Partnerplan Public Affairs Ltd 1973-74, man dir Sallingbury Ltd 1975-, dir Gatewood Engineers 1976-; pres Canada-UK Chamber of Commerce 1981-*Recreations* sailing (Sloop 'Dendre'); *Clubs* Army & Navy, Little Ship; *Style* - Maj-Gen Nigel Gribbon, OBE; 99 Pump street, Orford, Woodbridge, Suffolk (☎ Orford 413)

GRIDLEY, 2 Baron (UK 1955); Arnold Hudson Gridley; s of 1 Baron, KBE (d 1965); *b* 26 May 1906; *Educ* Oundle; *m* 1948, Edna Lesley, da of Richard Wheen, of Shanghai; 1 s, 3 da; *Heir* s, Hon Richard Gridley; *Career* entered Colonial Serv Malaya 1928, interned by Japanese WW II, Actg Dep Comptroller Fedn Malaya 1956, ret 1957; memb Cncl Overseas Serv Pensions Assoc 1966-; chm Centralised Audio Systems 1968-; Govt Tstee Far East Fund 1973- (for POWs and Internees); kt 1957; dir Lawdon Ltd; *Clubs* Roy Overseas League; *Style* - The Rt Hon Lord Gridley; Coneygore, Stoke Trister, Wincanton, Somerset (☎ 32209)

GRIER, Anthony MacGregor; CMG (1963); s of Very Rev Roy MacGregor Grier; *b* 12 April 1911; *Educ* St Edward's Sch Oxford, Exeter Coll Oxford; *m* 1946, Hon Patricia, da of 1 Baron Spens, KBE, PC, by his 1 w, Hilda; 2 s, 1 da; *Career* memb (C) Hereford & Worcester CC 1977-; Gen Man Redditch Dvpt Corpn 1964-76; formerly with Colonial Office; *Recreations* tennis, shooting, golf; *Clubs* E India & Sports, Roy C'wlth Soc; *Style* - Anthony Grier Esq, CMG; Mulberry House, Abbots Morton, Worcester (☎ Inkberrow 792422)

GRIER, Hon Mrs (Patricia Mary); *née* Spens; da of 1 Baron Spens, KBE, PC; *b* 15 July 1919; *Educ* Heathfield; *m* 1946, Anthony, s of Very Rev Roy Grier; 2 s, 1 da; *Career* served WW II as Capt FANY SOE in Europe and Far East; Dep-Pres Hereford & Worcester Red Cross; *Recreations* golf, tennis; *Clubs* Special Forces; *Style* - The Hon Mrs Grier; Mulberry House, Abbots Morton, Worcester (☎ 0386 792422)

GRIERSON, Lady Daphne Olive; *née* Lambart; da of 11 Earl of Cavan; *b* 22 Dec 1909; *m* 1944, Kenneth (d 1976), s of Douglas Grierson, barr, of Shirley, Warwicks; 1 s; *Style* - Lady Daphne Grierson; Flat 9, 32 Onslow sq, SW7

GRIERSON, Michael John Bewes; s of late Lt-Col Alexander Grierson, RM (ret), 2 s of 9 Bt; hp of kinsman, Sir Richard Grierson, 11 Bt; *b* 24 July 1921; *m* 1971, Valerie Anne, da of Russell Wright, of Gidea Park, Essex; *Style* - Michael Grierson Esq; 71 Wyatt Park rd, Streatham Hill, SW2

GRIERSON, Sir Richard Douglas; 11 Bt (NS 1685); s of Maj Sir Robert Gilbert White Grierson, 10 Bt (d 1957); *b* 25 June 1912; *Educ* Imperial Serv Coll Windsor; *Heir* kinsman, Michael John Bewes Grierson; *Style* - Sir Richard Grierson, Bt; 4 Modena rd, Hove, Sussex

GRIEVE, Alan Thomas; s of Lewis Miller Grieve (d 1963); *b* 22 Jan 1928; *Educ* Aldenham Sch, Trin Hall Cambridge; *m* 1, 1957, Anne, nee Dulake; 2 s (Charles b 1960, Ivan b 1962), 1 da (Amanda b 1958); m 2, 1971, Karen Louise, nee Dunn; 1 s (Thomas b 1973), 1 da (Lara b 1974); *Career* Capt City of London Yeomanry TA; slr, sr ptnr Taylor & Humbert; dir- Baggeridge Brick Co Ltd, Colibri Lighters Ltd, Huntsmoor Nominees Ltd, Irvine Sellars Int Ltd, Irvine Sellars Ltd, John Graham & Co Ltd, Reliance Properties Ltd, Reliance Nursing & Social Care Services Ltd, Silva & Cosens Ltd, Stenham Ltd, Tetra Molectric Ltd, Vigers Stevens & Adams Ltd, Irvine Sellars Gp (Holdings) Ltd, Nellauda Ltd, Medical Insurance Agency Ltd, Oakham School Enterprises Ltd, Stenham Investments Ltd, Lowesby Estate Co Ltd, Tavistock Computer Services Ltd, St George's Hosp Ltd, Wintmace Ltd; tstee Oakham Sch & Jerwood Oakham Foundation; *Recreations* skiing, sailing, racing; *Clubs* Boodle's, Aula, Asparagus;

Style - Alan Grieve Esq; Brimpton House, Brimpton, Berks (☎ Woolhampton 2100)

GRIEVE, William Percival; QC (1962), MP (C) Warwicks Solihull 1964-; s of 2 Lt William Grieve (ka Ypres 1915), of Kirkcudbrightshire and Argentina; *b* 25 March 1915; *Educ* privately and Trin Hall Cambridge; *m* 1949, Evelyn, da of Commandant Edouard Mijouain, of Paris; 1 s, 1 da (and 1 s decd); *Career* late Maj Middx Regt; barr 1938; Recorder N'hampton 1965-71, Crown Court 1971; *Recreations* swimming, travel, theatre; *Clubs* Carlton, Hurlingham; *Style* - William Grieve Esq QC MP; 1 King's Bench Walk, Temple, EC4 (☎ 01 353 8436); 32 Gunterstone rd, W14 (☎ 01 603 0376)

GRIEVE, Hon Lord; William Robertson Grieve; VRD (1958); s of William Grieve (ka 1917), of Glasgow; *b* 21 Oct 1917; *Educ* Glasgow Acad, Sedbergh, Glasgow U; *m* 1947, Lorna, da of Rear-Adm Edward Benn, CB; 1 s, 1 da; *Career* late Lt-Cdr RNVR; Sen Coll of Justice Scotland (Lord of Session) 1972-; advocate 1947, QC 1957, Sheriff Renfrew & Argyll 1964-72, Judge of Appeal Jersey & Guernsey 1971-72; chm Governors Fettes Tst 1978; *Recreations* golf, painting; *Clubs* New (Edinburgh), Hon Co of Edinburgh Golfers; *Style* - The Hon Lord Grieve VRD; 20 Belgrave Cres, Edinburgh 4 (☎ 031 332 7500)

GRIFFIN, Adm Sir Anthony Templer Frederick Griffith; GCB (1975, KCB 1971, CB 1967); s of the late Col F M G Griffin, MC; *b* 24 Nov 1920; *Educ* Royal Naval Coll Dartmouth; *m* 1943, Rosemary Ann, da of the late Vice-Adm Hickling, DSO of New Zealand; 2 s, 1 da; *Career* Captain Ark Royal 1964-65, Controller of Navy 1971-75, chm British Shipbuilders 1975-80; *Recreations* sailing; *Clubs* Army & Navy; *Style* - Adm Sir Anthony Griffin, GCB; Moat Cottage, The Drive, Bosham, Chichester, W Sussex (☎ Bosham 573373)

GRIFFIN, Sir David; CBE (1972); s of the late Eric Furnival Griffin; *b* 8 July 1915; *Educ* Cranbrook Sch Sydney, Univ of Sydney; *m* 1941, Jean Falconer, nee Blackstock-White; 2 s; *Career* kt 1974, exec chm Nabalco Pty Ltd 1965-80, hon chm 1980-, chm- Barclays Bank Group in Australia 1975-, Vanguard Insurance Co Ltd 1974-, Aetna Life of Australia & New Zealand 1974-, Robert Bosch Australia Ltd 1976-, dep chm Oil Search Ltd 1950-, dir- John Fairfax Ltd 1977-, Davis Consolidated Ltd 1978-, Australian Elizabethan Theatre Trust 1974-, Atlas Copco Pty Ltd 1974-, commissioner Tertiary Education Commission 1977-, councillor Royal Agriculture Society 1975-; *Recreations* golf, trout fishing; *Clubs* Union (Sydney), Royal Sydney Golf, Pine Valley Golf (New Jersey-USA), Elanora Country (Sydney); *Style* - Sir David Griffin, CBE; 10 Churchill rd, Rose Bay, New South Wales 2029 (☎ 371 0073)

GRIFFIN, Lady Jane; *née* Bingham; da of 6 Earl of Lucan, MC (d 1964); *b* 1932; *Educ* Badminton Sch, Bristol; MB and BS London, 1957; *m* 1960, James D Griffin; 3 s, 1 da; *Style* - Lady Jane Griffin; 444 East 66th st, New York, NY 10021, USA

GRIFFITH, David Humphrey; s of Maj HW Griffith, MBE; *b* 17 Feb 1936; *Educ* Eton; *m* 1966, Philippa Claire, nee Roberts; 1 s, 3 da; *Career* dir Greenall Whitley & Co Ltd 1964-, dir Dennis Ruabon Ltd 1973-; *Recreations* gardening, fishing, shooting, racing; *Clubs* Boodle's; *Style* - David Griffith Esq; Garthmeilio, Llangwm, Corwen, Clwyd, N Wales (☎ 049 082 269)

GRIFFITHS, Rt Rev (Michael) Ambrose; s of the late Henry Griffiths; *b* 4 Dec 1928; *Educ* Ampleforth, Balliol Oxford; *Career* senior science master Ampleforth Coll 1965-70, Procurator (Bursar) Ampleforth 1972-76, Abbot of Ampleforth 1976-; *Recreations* walking, scouting; *Style* - Rt Rev Ambrose Griffiths; Ampleforth Abbey, York (☎ Ampleforth 421)

GRIFFITHS, Air Vice-Marshal Arthur; CB (1972), AFC (1964); s of Edward Griffiths (d 1960); *b* 22 Aug 1922; *Educ* Hawarden G S; *m* 1950, Nancy, nee Sumpter; 1 da; *Career* RAF 1940-77 (served in UK, Germany, Canada, Far East, Australia), chm Cititel Consultancy Ltd 1978-, dir-

Consolidated Safeguards Ltd, Secureguard Ltd 1980-; *Clubs* Royal Air Force; *Style* - Air Vice-Marshal Arthur Griffiths, CB AFC; 47 Murray rd, Northwood, Middx (☎ Northwood 27973)

GRIFFITHS, Rev David Nigel; FSA; s of the late William Cross Griffiths, LDS; *b* 29 Oct 1927; *Educ* Cranbrook Sch, Worcester Coll Oxford, Lincoln Theological Coll; *m* 1953, Joan, nee Fillingham; 2 s, 1 da; *Career* chaplain RNR, clerk in Holy Orders, ordained 1958, v-chancellor and librarian of Lincoln Cathedral 1967-73, Rector of Windsor 1973-, Chaplain to HM The Queen 1977-, Rural Dean of Maidenhead 1977-; *Recreations* serendipity; *Style* - Rev David Griffiths, FSA; The Rectory, Park street, Windsor, Berks (☎ 075 35 64572)

GRIGG, Hon Anthony Ulick David Dundas; s of 1 Baron Altrincham, KCMG, KCVO, DSO, MC, PC (d 1955), and hp of bro, John Edward Poynder Grigg (2 Baron, who disclaimed his Peerage for life 1963); *b* 12 Jan 1934; *Educ* Eton, New Coll Oxford; *m* 1965, Eliane de Cassagnes de Beaufort, da of the Marquis de Miramon, of 4 Hanover Ter, NW1; 2 s, 1 da; *Career* late 2 Lt Gren Gds; *Style* - The Hon Anthony Grigg; 31 Ladbroke Grove, W11

GRIGG, John Edward Poynder; s of 1 Baron Altrincham, KCMG, KCVO, DSO, MC, PC (d 1955), and Hon Joan Dickson-Poynder, da of 1 Baron Islington; disclaimed Barony for life 1963; *b* 15 April 1924; *Educ* Eton, New Coll Oxford; *m* 1958, Patricia, da of Harold Campbell, of Co Down; *Heir* bro, Hon Anthony Grigg; *Career* journalist; served WW II Lt Gren Gds; ed National and English Review 1954-60; *Style* - John Grigg Esq; 32 Dartmouth Row, SE10 (☎ 01 692 4973)

GRIMOND, Hon Mrs (Laura Miranda); da of Sir Maurice Bonham Carter, KCB, KCVO, by his w, Baroness Asquith of Yarnbury, DBE (d 1969; Lady Violet Bonham Carter, da of 1 Earl of Oxford and Asquith, KG, PC - H H Asquith, Lib PM 1908-16 - by his 1 w); *b* 13 Oct 1918; *m* 1938, Rt Hon Jo Grimond, MP; 2 s, 1 da (and 1 s decd); *Style* - The Hon Mrs Grimond; The Old Manse of Firth, Kirkwall, Orkney (☎ Finstown 393)

GRIMSHAW, Peter Bernard; s of Bernard George Grimshaw (d 1972); *b* 13 Sept 1923; *Educ* Purley Sch; *m* 1947, Barbara, da of Capt H Saunders, MC (d 1962); 1 s, 1 da; *Career* md Crusader Insurance Co 1980- (gen man investments 1976-80) FCIS 1963; *Recreations* golf, outdoor activities; *Style* - Peter Grimshaw Esq; Scammells Lodge, Red Lane, Blackbrook, nr Dorking, Surrey (☎ Dorking 6423)

GRIMSHAW, Hon Mrs (Shelagh Mary Margaret); *née* Milner; da of 1 Baron Milner of Leeds, MC, TD, PC (d 1967); *b* 1925; *m* 1948 (m dis 1965), Harry Barker Grimshaw; 1 s, 1 da; *Style* - The Hon Mrs Grimshaw; High Barn, Thorner, Yorks

GRIMSTON OF WESTBURY, 2 Baron (UK 1964); Sir Robert Walter Sigismund Grimston; 2 Bt (UK 1952); s of 1 Baron Grimston of Westbury, briefly (1945) Parly Sec to Min of Supply (d 1979, himself er s of Canon Hon Robert Grimston, who was in his turn 3 s of 2 Earl of Verulam), by his w Sybil (d 1977), da of Sir Sigmund Neumann, 1 Bt (later anglicised to Newman); *b* 14 June 1925; *Educ* Eton; *m* 1949, Hon June Ponsonby, da of 5 Baron de Mauley; 2 s, 1 da; *Heir* s, Hon Robert Grimston; *Career* late Lt Scots Gds, served NW Europe WW II; Liveryman Gold and Silver Wyre Drawers' Co; formerly in oil and publishing; chm Gray's Inn Ltd (Underwriter Agency) 1970-; dir Hinton Hill & Coles 1962-; *Clubs* Boodle's, City of London; *Style* - Rt Hon Lord Grimston of Westbury; The Old Rectory, Westwell, Burford, Oxon (☎ 2251)

GRIMSTON, Hon Cecil Anthony Sylvester; s of 1 Baron Grimston of Westbury (d 1979) and Sybil (d 1977), da of Sir Sigmund Neumann, 1 Bt; *b* 28 Feb 1927; *Educ* Eton, Magdalene Cambridge; *m* 1958, Dawn, da of Guy Janson, of Fair Hall, Southover, Lewes; 2 s; *Career* late Coldstream Gds; chartered surveyor, ptnr Strutt & Parker FRICS, FRSA;

Recreations shooting, all sport, gardening; *Clubs* Bath, MCC; *Style* - The Hon Cecil Grimston; Wellington Vane, nr Lewes, E Sussex (☎ Ringmer 812241)

GRIMSTON, Hon Gerald Charles Walter; 2 s of 2 Baron Grimston of Westbury by his w Hon June Ponsonby (da of 5 Baron de Mauley, JP, and Elgiva, herself da of Hon Cospatrick Dundas, JP, DL, bro of 3 Earl and 1 Marquess of Zetland); *b* 4 Sept 1953; *Educ* Eton, Exeter U; *m* 1980, Katherine, da of Maj Rupert Berkeley Kettle, DL, of Leamington Spa; *Career* Capt Scots Gds; *Recreations* cricket, skiing, real tennis, shooting; *Clubs* Cavalry & Guards; *Style* - Capt The Hon Gerald Grimston; c/o Midland Bank, 69 Pall Mall, SW1

GRIMSTON, Hon Hugo Guy Sylvester; s of 7 Earl of Verulam; *b* 1979; *Style* - The Hon Hugo Grimston

GRIMSTON, Lady Iona Charlotte; da of 6 Earl of Verulam (d 1973); *b* 1953; *Style* - Lady Iona Grimston

GRIMSTON, Viscount; James Walter Grimston; s and h of 7 Earl of Verulam; *b* 6 Jan 1978; *Style* - Viscount Grimston

GRIMSTONE, Hon (Janet Elizabeth Gudrun); *née* Suenson-Taylor; da of 2 Baron Grantchester, QC; *b* 26 June 1949; *Educ* Cheltenham Ladies Coll, St Hilda's Oxford; *m* 1973, Gerald, s of Edgar Grimstone, of Sanderstead; 1 s, 1 da; *Career* conservator of paintings; *Style* - The Hon Mrs Grimstone; 103 Home Park rd, SW19 (☎ 01 946 9402)

GRIMTHORPE, 4 Baron (UK 1886); Sir Christopher John Beckett; 8 Bt (UK 1813), OBE (1958), DL (N Yorks, formerly E Riding, 1969); s of 3 Baron, TD (d 1963) by his 1 w Mary; through his gf's sis, Maud, Lord Grimthorpe is 2 cous of 22 Baron Hastings; *b* 16 Sept 1915; *Educ* Eton; *m* 1954, Lady Elizabeth Lumley, da of 11 Earl of Scarbrough; 2 s, 1 da; *Heir* s, Hon Edward Beckett; *Career* patron of 2 livings; Brig (ret) 9 Queen's Roy Lancers (Col Cmmdg 1955-58), Col 9/12 Lancers 1973-; Brig RAC HQ W Cmmd 1961-64, Dep Cdr Malta & Libya 1964-67; ADC to HM 1964-68; dir Standard B'dcasting Corpn Canada (UK) Ltd 1972-, Thirsk Racecourse Ltd 1972-, Yorkshire Post Newspapers 1973-; *Clubs* Cavalry & Guards; *Style* - The Rt Hon Lord Grimthorpe OBE DL; Westow Hall, York (☎ Whitwell-on-the-Hill 225); 87 Dorset House, Gloucester Place, NW1 (☎ 01 486 4374)

GRIMTHORPE, Dowager Baroness; Angela; da of Edward Courage; *b* 6 Oct 1901; *m* 1945, as his 2 w, 3 Baron Grimthorpe, TD (d 1963); 1 s (Hon William Beckett, *qv*); *Style* - The Rt Hon Dowager Lady Grimthorpe; Cross House, Ampleforth, N Yorks

GRIMTHORPE, Baroness; Lady Elizabeth; *née* Lumley; da of late 11 Earl of Scarbrough, KG, GCSI, GCIE, GCVO, TD, PC and Katharine, nee McEwen, DCVO; *b* 1925; *m* 1954, 4 Baron Grimthorpe, *qv*; *Career* appointed a Lady of the Bedchamber to HM Queen Elizabeth, The Queen Mother 1973; *Style* - The Rt Hon The Lady Grimthorpe; Westow Hall, York

GRIMWOOD-TAYLOR, Col James Richard Sancroft; TD (1950), DL (Derbys 1961); s of Sancroft Grimwood Taylor; *b* 8 Sept 1916; *Educ* Rugby, CCC Cambridge; *m* 1949, Anne Isobel, da of Henry Freeman; 2 s; *Career* served WW II Roy Signals, HQ 2 & 11 Corps, War Office; slr, memb Cncl Law Soc 1969-; Under-Sheriff Derbys; Diocesan Registrar Derby 1961-; *Clubs* County (Derby); *Style* - Col James Grimwood-Taylor TD DL; The Highfield House, Hulland Ward, Derby (☎ 0335 70278)

GRINDON, John Evelyn; CVO (1957), DSO (1945), AFC (1948); s of Thomas Edward Grindon (ka 1917); *b* 30 Sept 1917; *Educ* Dulwich Coll, RAF Coll Cranwell; *Career* Advanced Air Striking Force BEF 1939-40, Bomber Command (Fl and Sqdn Cdr) No 5 Gp 1940-45, cmd The Queen's Flight 1953-56, Gp Capt 1956, ret 1959; dir/gen man in publishing/printing 1961-71; Metropolitan Police New Scotland Yard (B13) 1976-; *Recreations* sailing, music, racing; *Clubs*

Royal Air Force; *Style* - John Grindon Esq, CVO, DSO, AFC; 1 Ovington gdns, SW3

GRINLING, Jasper Gibbons; CBE (1978); s of Anthony Grinling; *b* 29 Jan 1924; *Educ* Harrow, King's Cambridge; *m* 1950, Gertrude; 1 s, 2 da; *Career* Capt 12 Lancers 1942-46; md Gilbeys Ltd 1964, IDV 1967; dir N British Distillery Co 1968-, dir Corporate Affairs Grand Met; memb Cncl Scotch Whisky Assoc 1968; *Recreations* gardening, jazz drumming; *Clubs* Oriental; *Style* - Jasper Grinling Esq, CBE; The Old Vicarage, Helions Bumpstead, Suffolk (☎ 044 084 316)

GRINSTED, William Angus; CBE (1960); s of John Grinsted; *b* 29 Aug 1904; *Educ* Annan Acad, Imperial Coll London; *m* 1942, Kathleen, da of Capt Alexander Mackenzie; *Career* Sqdn Ldr RAFVR E Africa 1943-46; meteorologist; consultant Plessey Co 1961-79; *Clubs* Roy Overseas League; *Style* - William Grinsted Esq, CBE; 92b High st, Lindfield, W Sussex (☎ 4313)

GRISEWOOD, W Kenneth; s of Col A E Grisewood (d 1968); *b* 28 Oct 1911; *Educ* Warriston, Cranleigh, Univ d'Aix-en-Provence; *m* 1938, Ursula Girdlestone, da of Maj A G Hills (d 1943); 1 s, 2 da; *Career* md Caltex E Africa 1958-60; chm Conoco UK 1968-73 (md 1961-68); cncl memb Inst of Petroleum, pres Oil Industries Club 1967-68, memb British Ctee of World Petroleum Congresses 1973-77; FRSA; *Clubs* East India, Devonshire Sports & Public Schools; *Style* - Kenneth Grisewood Esq; 7 Withycombe Close, Constantia 7800, Cape Town, South Africa (☎ Cape Town 74 4420)

GROCOTT, Bruce Joseph; s of Reginald Grocott; *b* 1 Nov 1940; *Educ* Leicester U, Manchester U; *m* 1965, Sally Barbara, nee Ridgway; 2 s; *Career* television political journalist, MP (Lab) for Lichfield & Tamworth 1974-79 (PPS to Min for Local Govt Planning 1975-76, Min of Agriculture 1976-78), lecturer in politics 1965-74; *Clubs* Chasetown Working Men's; *Style* - Bruce Grocott Esq; 1 Brookside House, Uttoxeter, Staffs (☎ 088 93 4029)

GROOM, Air Marshal Sir Victor Emmanuel; KCVO (1953), KBE (1952, CBE 1945, OBE 1940), CB (1944), DFC and Bar (1918 and 1921); s of William Groom; *b* 4 Aug 1898; *Educ* Alleyn's Sch *m* 1, 1924, Maisie (d 1961), da of Athelstan Maule; 1 s (and 1 s decd); m 2, 1969, Muriel, da of Joseph Windsor and widow of Capt G Brown; *Career* Head RAF Staff planning invasion 1942-43; CIC MEAF 1952; AOCIC Tech Training Cmmd 1952-55; *Recreations* RAF; *Style* - Air Marshal Sir Victor Groom, KCVO, KBE, CB, DFC*; 8 Somerville House, Manor Fields, Putney Hill SW 15 (☎ 01 788 1290)

GROSSART, Angus McFarlane McLeod; s of William Grossart; *b* 6 April 1937; *Educ* Glasgow Acad and U; *m* 1978, Marion Gay Kerr; *Career* md Noble Grossart (merchant bank) 1969-; chm Scottish Investment Tst; *Recreations* golf, castle restoration; *Clubs* New (Edinburgh), Roy & Ancient St Andrews; *Style* - Angus Grossart Esq; 48 Queen st, Edinburgh EH2 3VR (☎ 031 226 7011)

GROSVENOR, Hon Richard Alexander; s of 5 Baron Ebury, DSO, by his 2 w, Hon Denise Yarde-Buller (da of 3 Baron Churston); *b* 5 July 1946; *Educ* Milton Abbey; Perugia, Montpelier, Lyons, Tours and Munich Us; *m* 1970, Gabriella, da of Dr Xavier Speckert; 1 s; *Career* self-employed; *Style* - The Hon Richard Grosvenor; c/o Barclays Bank, 23 St James's st, SW1

GROSVENOR, Lady Tamara Katherine; da of 6 Duke of Westminster; *b* 1979; *Style* - Lady Tamara Grosvenor

GROSVENOR, Hon William Wellesley; s of 5 Baron Ebury, DSO, by his 2 w, Hon Denise Yarde-Buller (da of 3 Baron Churston); *b* 12 Sept 1942; *Educ* Eton, Perugia U, Trin Oxford; *m* 1966, Ellen, da of Dr Günter Seeliger (decd), sometime Fedl German Ambass to Mexico; 1 s, 1 da; *Career* publicist; *Recreations* shooting, fishing, bridge; *Clubs* Portland, St James's; *Style* - The Hon William Grosvenor; 41-43 Portman sq, W1 (☎ 01 487 4900)

GROTRIAN, Sir John Appelbe Brent;

2 Bt (UK 1934), of Leighton Buzzard, Co Bedford; s of Sir Herbert Grotrian, 1 Bt, KC (d 1951); *b* 16 Feb 1904; *Educ* Eton, Trin Oxford; *Heir* n, Philip Grotrian; *Style* - Sir John Grotrian, Bt; Raughmere House, Lavant, Chichester, W Sussex (☎ 527120)

GROTRIAN, Philip Christian Brent; s of late Sqdn Ldr Robert Grotrian, s of 1 Bt, by 1 w, Elizabeth, da of late Maj Herbert Hardy-Wrigley; hp of unc, Sir John Grotrian, 2 Bt; *b* 26 March 1935; *Educ* Eton, Trin Coll Toronto; *m* 1960, Anne Isabel, da of Robert Sieger Whyte, of Toronto; 1 s; *Style* - Philip Grotrian Esq; 295 Glen rd, Toronto 5, Canada

GROUSE, Leonard David; s of Isaac Michael Grouse (d 1960); *Educ* Bishopshalt Sch, London Sch of Ecs; *m* 1957, Jeanette Pauline, nee Thurgood; 1 s, 1 da; *Career* ATII, HM Insp of Taxes 1952-56, dir Noble Lowndes & Ptnrs Ltd 1964-65, md Gp Assurance Consultants 1965-71, dir Stewart Wrightson Ltd 1971-77, dir Wigham Poland Holdings 1977-81; *Recreations* squash, chess, backgammon, reading, horses (Run Deep, Master Sport), racing; *Clubs* Savile, RAC; *Style* - Leonard Grouse Esq; Highfield, Golfside, Cheam, Surrey (☎ 01 642 1935)

GROVE, Sir Charles Gerald; 5 Bt (UK 1874); s of late Walter Peel Grove; suc bro, Sir Walter Grove, 4 Bt, 1974; *b* 10 Dec 1929; *Style* - Sir Charles Grove, Bt; USA

GROVE, Edmund Frank; CVO (1974, MVO 4 Class 1963, MVO 5 Class 1953); s of Edmond Grove; *b* 20 July 1920; *m* 1945, Grete Elisabet, da of Martinus Skou, of Denmark; 2 da; *Career* served WW II M East RASC; memb Roy Household 1946-; Ch Accountant Privy Purse 1963-, Serjeant-at-Arms to HM The Queen 1975- *Recreations* gardening, fishing; *Style* - Edmund Grove Esq, CVO; Chapel Cottage, W Newton, Norfolk; 5 Lower Ward, Windsor Castle (☎ 68286)

GROVE, Harold Thomas; s of late Walter Peel Grove; hp of bro, Sir Charles Grove, 5 Bt; *b* 6 Dec 1930; *Style* - Harold Grove Esq

GROVE, William Dennis; s of William Grove (d 1968); *b* 23 July 1927; *Educ* Gowerton Sch, King's Coll London; *m* 1953, Audrey Irma, nee Saxel; 1 s, 1 da; *Career* Lt SWB, overseas gen man Dunlop Ltd 1968-70, chm and ch exec T P T Ltd 1970-; *Recreations* rugby, golf; *Clubs* Saracens R F C, Bramall Park G C; *Style* - William Grove Esq; Woodstock, 36 Manor rd, Bramhall, Cheshire (☎ 061 485 5965)

GRUBB, Lt-Col Alexander James Watkins; JP (Cheshire 1956), DL (1972); s of Col Alexander Grubb, CMG, DSO, JP; *b* 25 July 1909; *Educ* Wellington, RMA Woolwich; *m* 1, 1936, Margaret (d 1972), da of Richard Dale, of Malpas; 2 s; m 2, 1973, Lois, widow of Maj R David; *Career* served RA 1929-50 (GSO 1 AA Gp Warrington 1949-50); chm Malpas Area Con Assoc 1956-59; High Sheriff Cheshire 1972; chm Cheshire Police Authority 1978-79, Runcorn Dvpt Corpn Licensed Premises Ctee 1972; *Recreations* hunting, shooting, cricket; *Clubs* Army & Navy; *Style* - Lt-Col Alexander Grubb, JP, DL; c/o Nat West Bank, Chester

GRUBB, Ralph Ernest Watkins; DL (E Sussex); s of Rev Ernest Grubb; *b* 12 April 1911; *Educ* Wellington, Trin Cambridge; *m* 1944, Caroline, da of William Arbuthnot; 1 s, 2 da (and 1 decd); *Career* Maj Palestine 1945-6; barr; chartered land agent, FRICS; High Sheriff Sussex 1972-73; chm Sussex County Playing Fields Assoc 1974-; Nat Tst Regnl Commissioner 1974-; *Recreations* cricket, shooting; *Clubs* Farmers, Roy C'wlth Soc; *Style* - Maj Ralph Grubb DL; Otters Hatch, Beach st, Deal, Kent (☎ 5533); Mayes House, E Grinstead, Sussex (☎ Sharpthorne 810597)

GRUGEON, Sir John Drury; s of Drury Grugeon, of Westfield Lodge, Broadstairs; *b* 20 Sept 1928; *Educ* Epsom G S, Sandhurst; *m* 1955, Mary, da of Walter Rickards, of Hoath Farm, Canterbury; 1 s, 1 da; *Career* late Actg Maj Europe, M & Far East; Ldr Kent CC 1973- (chm Policy Ctee Assoc CCs 1978-); memb Medway Ports Authority 1977-, Consultative Cncl Local Govt Finance; exec man Unit Tst; kt 1980; *Recreations* shooting, cricket; *Clubs* MCC, Kent County Cricket; *Style* - Sir

John Grugeon; Sand Pett, Charing, Kent (☎ 2322)

GRUNDY, Vincent Arthur; s of Cecil Frederick Grundy (decd); *b* 6 Dec 1931; *Educ* Worksop Coll; *m* 1957, Moira Patricia, nee Barbour; 1 da; *Career* dir Trafalgar House Ltd, md Cementation Specialist Holdings Ltd; *Clubs* Carlton; *Style* - Vincent Grundy Esq; Morvin, Manor Close, Penn, High Wycombe (☎ Penn 4366)

GRYLLS, (William) Michael John; MP (C) NW Surrey 1974; s of Brig W Grylls, OBE, of Blandford; *b* 21 Feb 1934; *Educ* RNC Dartmouth, Paris & Madrid Us; *m* 1965, Sarah, da of Neville Montague Ford; 1 s, 1 da; *Career* contested Fulham 1964 & 1966; V-Chm Con Indust Ctee 1975-, Chm Small Business Bureau 1979-, Parly Spokesman IOD 1979- MP Chertsey 1970-74; *Recreations* gardening, shooting, sailing, skiing; *Style* - Michael Grylls Esq, MP; Walcot House, 139 Kennington rd, SE11 (☎ 01 735 6297)

GRYLLS, Shadwell Harry; CBE (1970); s of Horace Grylls; *b* 19 July 1909; *Educ* Rugby, Trin Cambridge; *m* 1936, Joyce, da of Edward Hancock; 1 s, 2 da; *Career* FIMechE; ch engr Rolls-Royce Car Div 1951-69; *Style* - Shadwell Grylls Esq, CBE; Bute House, Elmley Castle, Worcs (☎ 315)

GUERITZ, Rear-Adm Edward Findlay; CB (1971), OBE (1957), DSC (1942) and Bar (1944); s of the late Elton L Gueritz; *b* 8 Sept 1919; *Educ* Cheltenham Coll; *m* 1947, Pamela Amanda Bernhardina, nee Jeans; 1 s, 1 da; *Career* Rear-Adm 1939-45 War, Mediterranean and Eastern Waters, Adm-Pres RN Coll Greenwich 1968-70, cmd Joint Welfare Establishment 1970-72, chief hon steward Westminster Abbey 1975-, pres Society for Nautical Research 1975-, dir Royal United Services Inst for Defence Station 1979-; *Clubs* Army & Navy; *Style* - Rear-Adm Edward Gueritz CB OBE DSC*; 56B The Close, Salisbury, Wilts (☎ Salisbury 3649)

GUERNSEY, Lord; Charles Heneage Finch-Knightley; s and h of 11 Earl of Aylesford; *b* 27 March 1947; *Educ* Oundle, Trin Cambridge; *m* 1971, Penelope Anstice, da of Kenneth A G Crawley, of London; 3 da; *Style* - Lord Guernsey; Rookwood, Packington Park, Meriden, Coventry CV7 7HF

GUEST, Baron (Life Peer UK 1961); Christopher William Graham Guest; PC (1961); s of Edward Guest, JP, FRSE, sometime Treasurer City of Edinburgh (himself s of Rev Charles Guest, Vicar of Christ Church, Burton-on-Trent); *b* 7 Nov 1901; *Educ* Merchiston, Clare Cambridge; *m* 1, 1928 (m dis 1940), Constance, da of Finlay Ramage; 1 s; m 2, 1941, Catharine, da of John Hotham (himself s of Adm of the Fleet Sir Charles Hotham, GCB, GCVO, who was in turn ggs of Gen George Hotham, bro of the 8, 9, 11, and 12 Hotham Bts, the latter two being also the 1 & 2 Barons Hotham); 3 s, 1 da; *Career* Scottish advocate 1925, barr (Inner Temple) 1929, KC 1945; Sheriff Ayr & Bute 1952-54, Perth & Angus 1954-55; Dean Faculty of Advocates 1955-57, Lord of Session (title Lord Guest) 1957-61, Lord of Appeal in Ordinary 1961-71; served WW II 2 Lt RA (TA) & as Maj Judge Advocate Gen's Branch War Off; stood as U candidate Kirkcaldy Burghs 1945; *Clubs* Buck's, New (Edinburgh); *Style* - The Rt Hon Lord Guest PC; 22 Lennox st, Edinburgh EH4 1QA (☎ 031 332 4833)

GUEST, Albert Sidney; *b* 17 Nov 1934; *Educ* Sladen Kidderminster, Birmingham U; *m* 1962, Maureen, nee Corker; 1 s, 1 da; *Career* sales dir Heckmondwike Carpets 1978-, memb Inst of Marketing; *Recreations* golf, walking; *Clubs* Woodsome Hall (Huddersfield), Adega (Huddersfield), Dubai Country; *Style* - Albert Guest Esq; 11 Fenay Crescent, Almondbury, Huddersfield, West Yorks

GUEST, Hon Charles James; s of Maj 2 Viscount Wimborne, OBE, by his w, Lady Mabel Fox-Strangways (da of 6 Earl of Ilchester); *b* 10 July 1950; *Educ* Harrow, Sandhurst; *m* 1976, Simone, da of Patrick Whinney, of Guernsey; 2 s; *Career* served 9/12 Roy Lancers 1973, Lt RARO 1976 then RW Yeomanry, full Lt 1981 (seniority 1979); *Recreations* shooting, fishing;

Clubs Turf, Flyfishers'; *Style* - Lieut The Hon Charles Guest; Truckwell Manor Farm, Lydeard St Lawrence, Taunton, Somerset (☎ Stogumber 327)

GUEST, Ivor Forbes; s of Cecil Marmaduke Guest (d 1954); *b* 14 April 1920; *Educ* Lancing Coll, Trin Cambridge; *m* 1962, Ann; *Career* solicitor, dance historian; sec Radcliffe Trust 1966-; chm Roy Academy of Dancing from 1969; *Clubs* Garrick, MCC; *Style* - Ivor Forbes Esq; 17 Holland Park, London WII (☎ 229 3780)

GUEST, Hon Ivor Mervyn Vigors; s and h of 3 Viscount Wimborne; *b* 19 Sept 1968; *Style* - The Hon Ivor Guest

GUEST, Hon Simon Edward Graham; WS; s of Baron Guest, PC (Life Peer), by his 2 w, Catherine Hotham (gda of Adm of the Fleet Sir Charles Hotham, GCB, GCVO, and cous of Lord Hotham); *b* 22 April 1949; *Educ* Charterhouse, Dundee U; *m* 1977, Fiona, da of Robert Wilson Taylor Lamont; 1 s, 1 da; *Career* slr; *Recreations* shooting, golf, hockey; *Clubs* New (Edinburgh); *Style* - The Hon Simon Guest, WS; 40 Hope ter, Edinburgh 9

GUETERBOCK, Hon Mrs (Cynthia Ella); da of Eva Mary Fitzhardinge, Baroness Berkeley (16 in line, d 1964) and late Col Frank Wigram Foley, CBE, DSO; heiress presumptive of sis, Baroness Berkeley (17 in line); *b* 31 Jan 1909; *m* 1937, Brig Ernest Adolphus Leopold Gueterbock, late RE; 1 s (Anthony Fitzhardinge b 1939); *Recreations* golf, bridge; *Clubs* Naval & Military; *Style* - The Hon Mrs Gueterbock; The Plough, Terrick, Aylesbury, Bucks

GUILD, Ivor Reginald; s of the late Col A M Guild, DSO, TD, DL; *b* 2 April 1924; *Educ* Cargilfield, Rugby, New Coll Oxford, Edinburgh U; *Career* Writer to the Signet, procurator fiscal of Lyon Court 1961-, clerk to Abbey Court of Holyroodhouse 1970-79, bailie of Abbey Court 1979-, chm National Museum of Antiquities Scotland 1981-, editor Scottish Genealogist 1959-; *Recreations* golf, genealogy; *Clubs* New (Edinburgh); *Style* - Ivor Guild Esq WS; New Club, 86 Princes st, Edinburgh

GUILDFORD, 6 Bishop of (1927) 1973-; Rt Rev David Alan Brown; s of Russell Brown; *b* 11 July 1922; *Educ* London Coll of Divinity, Sch Oriental & African Studies London U; *m* 1954, Elizabeth, da of Dr John Warwick Hele; 2 s, 1 da; *Career* chm Cttee Rels with People Other Faiths 1978-, C of E Bd Mission & Unity 1977-; Rural Dean Reculver 1972-73; *Clubs* Roy C'wlth Soc; *Style* - The Rt Rev The Bishop of Guildford; Willow Grange, Woking rd, Guildford, Surrey (☎ 73922)

GUILFORD, 9 Earl of (GB 1752); Edward Francis North; JP (Dover & E Kent), DL (Kent 1976); also Baron Guilford (E 1683); s of Lord North (k accidentally 1940, predeceasing his f, the 8 Earl, who d 1949); Lord Guilford is sixth in descent from Brownlow North, Bp of Winchester and half-bro of Lord North (later 2 Earl of Guilford), the able and genial (according to Gibbon he was virtually without a personal enemy, tho' his political foes were legion) but indolent (Horace Walpole's epithet) and 'gluttonously buffoonish' PM during the American War of Independence; Lord Guilford is also thirteenth in descent from the union of 2 Baron North and Winifred, da of Richard (1 Baron) Rich, that dexterous Tudor statesman at whose door may be laid the judicial murders of Saint (and Sir) Thomas More and Fisher; of him it was said 'though officially Lord Chancellor and practically spoliator in chief of the monasteries, his most appropriate post, in a career beside which the Vicar of Bray's seems obstinately consistent, was the Commissionership of Sewers for Middlesex' (held 1528-29); *b* 22 Sept 1933; *Educ* Eton; *m* 1956, Osyth Vere Napier, da of Cyril Leeston; 1 s; *Heir* s, Lord North; the eldest s & h of the Earls of Guilford appears to have been so designated since 1829, though the actual Barony of North remained in a senior but female line of the family; *Career* patron of 3 livings; *see* Lady Barbara Bossom; *Style* - The Rt Hon Earl of Guilford JP DL; Waldershare Park, Dover, Kent (☎ 820244)

GUILLAUME, John; s of Reginald Guillaume (d 1953); *b* 9 May 1925; *Educ*

Cheltenham Coll; *m* 1975, Angela Rae, da of Norman Moffett; 1 s, 2 da; *Career* slr, sr ptnr Guillaume & Sons Slrs; Master Worshipful Co of Slrs of the City of London 1980-81; *Recreations* cruising, skiing, tennis, gardening, choral music; *Clubs* City Livery, Roy Cruising, St George's Hill Lawn Tennis; owner of yacht- 'New Melody'; *Style* - John Guillaume Esq; Camelot, Burwood Park, Walton-on-Thames, Surrey

GUINNESS, Alexandra; da of late Patrick Guinness (*see* Guinness, Loel); *b* 24 Aug 1956; *Style* - Miss Alexandra Guinness

GUINNESS, Hon Catriona Rose; da of 2 Baron Moyne; *b* 1950; *Educ* Cranborne Chase and Winchester Co HS; LMH Oxford; *Career* botanist; *Style* - The Hon Catriona Guinness

GUINNESS, Hon Mrs Diarmid - Felicity; da of Sir Andrew Hunter Carnwath, KCVO, of The Old Vicarage, Ugley, Bishop's Stortford, Herts; *m* 1962, Hon Diarmid Edward Guinness (d 1977); 1 s, 3 da; *Style* - The Hon Mrs Diarmid Guinness; 9 St Albans Grove, W8; Crawlboys Farm, Ludgershall, Andover, Hants

GUINNESS, Brig Dennis Robert; CBE (1956); s of Ernest Guinness, of Kenya and Clandon, Surrey; *b* 24 Nov 1903; *Educ* RNCs Dartmouth & Osborne, Haileybury; *m* 1931, Elizabeth, da of F Howland, of USA; 1 s, 1 da; *Career* Brig 1943, CE Cyprus, ret 1956; *Style* - Brig Dennis Guinness, CBE; Yew Tree Cottage, Hazeley Bottom, Hartley Wintney, Hants (☎ 2600)

GUINNESS, Hon Desmond Walter; s of 2 Baron Moyne; *b* 1931; *Educ* Gordonstoun and Ch Ch Oxford; *m* 1954, HSH Princess Marie-Gabrielle Sophie Joti Elisabeth Albertine Almeria, da of HSH Prince Albrecht Eberhard Karl Gero-Maria von Urach, Count of Württemberg; 1 s, 1 da; *Style* - The Hon Desmond Guinness; Leixlip Castle, Co Kildare

GUINNESS, Edward Douglas; CBE (1946); 2 s of Howard Guinness and bro of late Sir Arthur Guinness, KCMG (hence great unc to Sabrina Guinness, *qv*); *b* 19 April 1893; *Educ* Rugby; *m* 1, 1931 (m dis 1970), Martha, da of John Sheldon and former w of Richard Goss, Gren Gds; 2 s (Howard and John Ralph Sidney, *qqv*); m 2, 1970, Mrs Jeanne Amy Thompson; *Career* sometime Capt RNR (served WW I & II), ptnr Guinness Mahon, dir & chm Sheldon Gp; *Style* - Edward Guinness Esq, CBE; Palazzo Polignac, Venice, Italy

GUINNESS, Lady Emma Lavinia; da of 3 Earl of Iveagh; *b* 1963; *Style* - Lady Emma Guinness

GUINNESS, Hon Erskine Stuart Richard; s of 2 Baron Moyne; *b* 1953; *Educ* Winchester, Edinburgh U; *Style* - The Hon Erskine Guinness

GUINNESS, Hon Finn Benjamin; s of 2 Baron Moyne; *b* 1945; *Educ* Winchester, Ch Ch Oxford and Inst of Animal Genetics, Edinburgh U; *Career* biologist; *Style* - The Hon Finn Guinness

GUINNESS, Hon Fiona Evelyn; da of 2 Baron Moyne; *b* 1940; *Educ* Cranborne Chase and Magill U, Canada; *Career* Zoologist; *Style* - The Hon Fiona Guinness

GUINNESS, Lt-Cdr Sir Howard Christian Sheldon; er s of Edward Guinness, CBE, *qv*, by his 1 w; *b* 3 June 1932; *Educ* Eton; *m* 1958, Evadne, da of Capt Evan Gibbs, Coldstream Gds (n of 1 Baron Wraxall); 2 s (Christopher Edward Howard, b 9 Jan 1963; Dominic Evan Mark, b 20 June 1966), 1 da (Annabel Evadne, b 20 Sept 1959); *Career* kt 1981; late RNR, dir S G Warburg & Co, Harris & Sheldon Gp, Youghal Carpets Hldgs; *Clubs* White's; *Style* - Lt-Cdr Sir Howard Guinness; Knowl Hill House, Kingsclere, Newbury, Berks (☎ Kingsclere 298357)

GUINNESS, Hon Jonathan Bryan; s and h of 2 Baron Moyne by his 1 w, Hon Diana, nee Freeman-Mitford (da of 2 Baron Redesdale and who subsequently m Sir Oswald Mosley, 6 Bt, *see* Mosley, Hon Lady); *b* 16 March 1930; *Educ* Eton and Trinity Coll Oxford; *m* 1, 1951 (m dis 1963), Ingrid, da of Maj Guy Wyndham, MC (ggs of 1 Baron Leconfield), by his 2 w, Grethe; 2 s, 1 da; m 2, 1964, Mrs Suzanne Phillips, da of H Lisney, of Gerona, Spain; 1 s, 1 da; *Career* dir A Guinness Son & Co, Leopold Joseph & Sons; former Reuters journalist, chm Monday Club 1972-7; *Clubs* Carlton, Beefsteak, Ibstock Working Men's; *Style* - The Hon Jonathan Guinness; 17 Kensington sq, W8; Osbaston Hall, Market Bosworth, Nuneaton; Ermita de San Sebastian, Cadaques, Gerona, Spain

GUINNESS, James Edward Alexander Rundell; s of Sir Arthur Guinness, KCMG, of Hawley Place, Hants; *b* 23 Sept 1924; *Educ* Eton, Oxford; *m* 1953, Pauline, da of Vivien Mander; 1 s (Hugo), 4 da (Miranda, Sabrina, Anita, Julia who m 1980 Michael Samuel, 2 s of Hon Peter Samuel, 2 s of 2 Viscount Bearsted, MC); *Career* late Sub-Lt RNVR; dep chm Guinness Peat Gp; chm Public Works Loan Bd; dir Guinness Mahon; *Recreations* hunting, shooting, fishing; *Clubs* Brooks's, Pratt's, Roy Yacht Sqdn; *Also* distant cous of Lords Moyne and Iveagh and Loel Guinness; *Style* - James Guinness Esq; 36 Phillimore gdns, W8 (☎ 01 937 8877)

GUINNESS, John Ralph Sidney; s of Edward Guinness, CBE, *qv*, by his 1 w; *b* 23 Dec 1935; *Educ* Rugby, Trin Hall Cambridge; *m* 1967, Valerie, da of Roger North, JP (7 in descent from Roger North, KC, MP Dunwich, memoirist and yr bro of 1 Baron Guilford, whose descendants became Earls of Guilford), whose mother was Grace, da of Gen Hon Sir Percy Feilding, KCB, 2 s of 7 Earl of Denbigh, PC (the General's w being Lady Thynne, da of 3 Marquess of Bath); 1 s, 1 da (and 1 s decd); *Career* FCO; seconded Centl Policy Review Staff (Cabinet Off) 1977-; Counsellor 1974; *Recreations* iconography; *Clubs* Brooks's; *Style* - John Guinness Esq; 9 Hereford sq, SW7 (☎ 01 373 8648)

GUINNESS, Hon Kieran Arthur; s of 2 Baron Moyne; *b* 1949; *Educ* Winchester and Ch Ch Oxford; *Career* botanist; *Style* - The Hon Kieran Guinness

GUINNESS, Sir Kenelm Ernest Lee; 4 Bt (UK 1867); s of late Kenelm Edward Lee Guinness, MBE, RNVR, gs of 1 Bt; suc unc, Sir Algernon Guinness, 3 Bt, 1954; *b* 13 Dec 1928; *Educ* Eton, MIT; *m* 1961, Mrs Jane Nevin Dickson; 2 s; *Heir* s, Kenelm Edward Lee Guinness; *Career* late 2 Lt Roy Horse Gds; *Style* - Sir Kenelm Guinness, Bt; 2184, 35th st NW, Washington DC, USA

GUINNESS, Kenelm Edward Lee; s and h of Sir Kenelm Guinness, 4 Bt; *b* 30 Jan 1962; *Style* - Kenelm Guinness Esq

GUINNESS, Loel; s of late Lt Patrick Guinness (who m Countess Dolores von Fürstenberg, his f's 3 w's da by her former husb, Count Franz Egon von Fürstenberg) and gs of Gp Capt Loel Guinness, OBE (by his 1 w, Hon Joan Yarde-Buller, now Princess Joan Aly Khan, *qv*); *b* 22 Oct 1957; *Style* - Loel Guinness Esq

GUINNESS, Gp Capt (Thomas) Loel Evelyn Bulkeley; OBE (1942); s of Benjamin Guinness (4 s of Richard Guinness) by his 1 w, Bridget, da of Sir Richard Williams-Bulkeley, 11 Bt, and Mary, nee Baring (da of Henry Baring, sometime MP Marlborough and n of 1 Baron Ashburton and Sir Thomas Baring, 2 Bt; Henry m as his 1 w Lady Augusta Brudenell, da of 6 Earl of Cardigan); *b* 9 June 1906; *Educ* Sandhurst; *m* 1, 1927 (m dis 1936), Hon Joan Yarde-Buller (da of 3 Baron Churston, MVO, OBE; *see* Aly Khan, Princess Joan); 1 s (Patrick Guinness, k in motor accident 1965, having m Countess Dolores von Fürstenberg and leaving 1 s, 2 da; *see* Guinness, Loel, Alexandra, Victoria separately); m 2, 1936 (m dis 1951), Lady Isabel Manners, yr da of 9 Duke of Rutland; 1 s (William), 1 da (Marchioness of Dufferin and Ava); m 3, Gloria (d 1980, da of Raphael Rubio, of Mexico, and former w of (1) Count Franz Egon von Fürstenberg and (2) Ahmed Fakhry); *Career* late Lt Irish Gds, served WW II, MP Bath 1931-45; *Clubs* White's; *Style* - Gp Capt Loel Guinness, OBE; Villa Zanroe, Epaliages 1066, Vaud, Switzerland; 20 Place de la Madeleine, Paris 8, France

GUINNESS, Lady Louisa Jane; da of 3 Earl of Iveagh; *b* 1967; *Style* - Lady Louisa Guinness

GUINNESS, Hon Murtogh David; s of 1 Baron Moyne DSO TD PC (assas 1944); *b* 1913; *m* 1949, Nancy Vivian Laura, da of late Cyril Edward Tarbolton; *Style* - The Hon Murtogh Guinness; 117 E 80th st, New York, USA

GUINNESS, Hon Mirabel Jane; da of 2 Baron Moyne; *b* 1956; *Educ* Cranborne Chase and E Anglia U; *Style* - The Hon Mirabel Guinness

GUINNESS, Hon Rory Michael Benjamin; s of 3 Earl of Iveagh; *b* 1974; *Style* - The Hon Rory Guinness

GUINNESS, Sabrina; da of James Guinness, *qv*; *Style* - Miss Sabrina Guinness

GUINNESS, Hon Thomasin Margaret; da of 2 Baron Moyne; *b* 1947; *Educ* Cranborne Chase and Farnham Coll of Art; *Career* potter and painter; *Style* - The Hon Thomasin Guinness

GUINNESS, Victoria; da of late Patrick Guinness (*see* Guinness, Loel); *b* 30 Jan 1960; *Style* - Miss Victoria Guinness

GUINNESS, William Loel Seymour; s of Gp Capt Loel Guinness, OBE, by his 2 w, Lady Isabel Manners (yr da of 9 Duke of Rutland and niece of Lady Diana Cooper, *qv*); is bro of Marchioness of Dufferin and Ava, *qv*; *b* 28 Dec 1939; *Educ* Eton; *m* 1971, (Agnes Elizabeth) Lynn, da of Ian Day, of Natal; 2 s; *Career* served Irish Gds 1959-61; *Clubs* White's; *Style* - William Guinness Esq; 10 Bourne st, W1

GUISE, Christopher James; s of late Sir Anselm Guise, 6 Bt; hp of bro, Sir John Guise, 7 Bt; *b* 10 July 1930; *Educ* Stowe; *m* 1969, Mrs Carole Hoskins Benson, da of Jack Master, of The Dower House, Crawley, Winchester; 1 s, 1 da; *Style* - Christopher Guise Esq; 97 Hurlingham rd, SW6

GUISE, George Robert John; s of George Wilfred Guise; *b* 17 June 1943; *Educ* Ratcliffe Coll, Ch Ch Oxford, Hatfield Coll Dunelm; *m* 1972, Hilary Hope, nee Hastings; 2 s; *Career* exec dir Consolidated Gold Fields 1981, dir Renison Goldfields Consolidated (Australia) 1981-; *Recreations* shooting, music, physics; *Clubs* Moorgate Well; *Style* - George Guise Esq; 6 Shouldham st, W1 (☎ 01 606 1020)

GUISE, Sir John Grant; 7 Bt (GB 1783), of Highnam Court, Glos; s of Sir Anselm Guise, 6 Bt, JP (d 1970), by his w Margaret, da of Sir James Grant, 1 and last Bt (*see* Guise, Lady); *b* 15 Dec 1927; *Educ* Winchester, Sandhurst; *Heir* bro, Christopher Guise; *Career* Capt 3 Hussars (ret 1959); Jockey Club Official 1968-; Patron of one living; *Clubs* Turf; *Style* - Sir John Guise, Bt; Elmore Court, Gloucester (☎ 0452 720293)

GUJADHUR, Hon Sir Radhamohun; CMG (1973); *b* 1909; *Educ* in Curepipe Mauritius and St Xavier Coll Calcutta; *m* ; 8 children; *Career* slr; memb Legislative Assembly Mauritius, dep Speaker MLA 1974-, chairman of Consortium Cinématographique Maurice Ltée, dir Trianon Estates Ltd; kt 1976; *Style* - Hon Sir Radhamohun Gujadhur, CMG; Port Louis, Mauritius

GULL, Sir Michael Swinnerton Cameron; 4 Bt (UK 1872); s of Capt Sir Richard Cameron Gull, 3 Bt (d 1960); *b* 24 Jan 1919; *Educ* Eton; *m* 1950, Mrs Yvonne Bawtree, da of late Albert Oliver Macarius Heslop, of Cape Town, S Africa; 1 s, 1 da; *Heir* s, Rupert Gull; *Career* formerly 2 Lt Scots Gds (Supp Reserve); *Style* - Sir Michael Gull, Bt; 2 Harcourt rd, Claremont, Cape Town, S Africa

GULL, Rupert William Cameron; s and h of Sir Michael Gull, 4 Bt; *b* 14 July 1954; *Educ* Diocesan Coll Cape Town, Cape Town U; *m* 1980, Gillian Lee, da of Robert MacFarlaine; *Style* - Rupert Gull Esq; 2 Harcourt rd, Claremont 7700, Cape Town, S Africa

GULLIVER, James Gerald; s of William Gulliver; *b* 17 Aug 1930; *Educ* Campbeltown G S, Glasgow U, Harvard; *m* 1, 1958, Margaret, nee Cormack; 3 s, 2 da; m 2, 1977, Joanne, nee Sims; *Career* chm James Gulliver Assocs Ltd 1977-, Alpine Hldgs Ltd 1977-, Gulliver Foods Ltd 1978-, Gulliver Hotels Ltd 1978-; FBIM, FRSA; *Style* - James Gulliver Esq; Delamere House, Gt Wymondley, Herts (☎ Stevenage 68583)

GULLY, Hon Edward Thomas William; s and h of 4 Viscount Selby; *b*

21 Sept 1967; *Style* - The Hon Edward Gully

GUMBEL, Henry Edward; s of Gustav Ludwig Gumbel (d 1942); *b* 31 Aug 1913; *Educ* Univs of Zurich, Geneva, Heidelberg, Berlin, London Sch of Ecs; *m* 1946, Ellen, nee Frank; 3 s, 2 da; *Career* Doctor of Laws 1935, barr Middle Temple, dir Willis Faber Ltd and assoc cos 1956, chm Sovereign Insurance Co 1977, chm Allianz Int Insurance Co 1980, dir Storebrand (UK) 1972, Tokio (UK) 1972, chm British Insurance Law Assoc 1979, v-pres Chartered Insurance Inst; *Recreations* tennis, skiing, walking, music, reading; *Style* - Henry Gumbel Esq; Windybrae, The Highlands, E Horsley, Surrey

GUMLEY, Kenneth Louis; s of Lindsay Douglas Gumley, JP (d 1973); *b* 7 Oct 1932; *Educ* Fettes Coll; *m* 1959, Anne Hogg, da of Lt-Col Robert Hogg Forbes OBE (d 1978); 1 s (John Lindsay Robert b 1967), 1 da (Sally Catherine b 1961); *Career* chartered surveyor, sr ptnr Gumley's Estate Agents Edinburgh, md-Cramond Inn Ltd, The Joint Properties Ltd, Edgar Park Curling Club Ltd, dir-Lennox Property Co Ltd, Scottish Provident Property Co Ltd; *Recreations* curling, sailing (yachts owned- 'Mistress' - Int Etchells Class, 'Sardelle' - Sovereign 32); *Clubs* New Club (Edinburgh), Royal Forth Yacht Club, Royal Caledonian Curling Club; *Style* - Kenneth Gumley Esq; Almondfield, 18 Whitehouse rd, Edinburgh EH4 (☎ 031 336 4839)

GUMMER, John Selwyn; MP (C) Eye Suffolk 1979-; s of Canon Selwyn Gummer; *b* 26 Nov 1939; *Educ* King's Sch Rochester, Selwyn Cambridge; *m* 1977, Penelope, da of John Gardner; 2 s; *Career* assist Govt Whip 1981-, chm Siemssen Hunter to 1980; dir Shandwick Publishing Co 1966-, Siemssen Hunter Ltd 1973-, md EP Gp of Cos 1975-, chm Selwyn Shandwick Int 1976-81; memb Gen Synod C of E 1978-; MP (C) Lewisham W 1970-74, PPS to Min of Ag 1972; *Recreations* reading, writing, Victorian buildings; *Style* - John Gummer Esq, MP; 25 Creffield rd, W5; Clarence House, Fressingfield, Suffolk, via Diss, Norfolk (☎ 347)

GUN-MUNRO, Sir Sydney Douglas; MBE (1957); s of Barclay and Marie Josephine Gun-Munro; *b* 29 Nov 1916; *Educ* Grenada Boys' Secondary Sch, King's Coll Hosp London; *m* 1943, Joan Benjamin; 2 s, 1 da; *Career* kt 1977, Gov-Gen St Vincent WI 1979-, Dist Mo Bequia St Vincent 1972-76 ; *Style* - Sir Sydney Gun-Munro, MBE; Government House, St Vincent, West Indies (☎ 71917)

GUNN, Thom (Thomson William); s of Herbert Smith Gunn; *b* 29 Aug 1929; *Educ* U C Sch Hampstead, Trin Cambridge; *Career* poet; *Style* - Thom Gunn Esq; 1216 Cole st, San Francisco, Calif 94117, USA

GUNN, Sir William Archer; KBE (1961), CMG (1955), JP; s of late Walter Gunn; *b* 1 Feb 1914; *Educ* King's Sch Parramatta NSW; *m* 1939, Mary, nee Haydon; 1 s, 2 da; *Career* grazier and co dir; chm Int Wool Secretariat 1961-73, dir Rothmans of Pall Mall (Australia) Ltd, Grazcos Co-op Ltd, Clausen Steamship Co (Australia) Pty Ltd, Walter Reid & Co Ltd, Gunn Rural Management Pty Ltd; chm and md Moline Pastoral Co Pty Ltd, Roper Valley Pty Ltd, Coolibah Pty Ltd, Mataranba Pty Ltd, Unibeef Australia Pty Ltd, Gunn Dvpt Pty Ltd; *Style* - Sir William Gunn, KBE, CMG, JP; 98 Windermere rd, Ascot, Qld 4007, Australia (☎ Brisbane 268 2688); Wool Exchange, 69 Eagle st, Brisbane, Qld 4000 (☎ Brisbane 21 4044)

GUNNING, Lt-Cdr Charles Theodore; RCN; s and h of Sir Robert Gunning, 8 Bt; *b* 19 June 1935; *Educ* Canadian Mil Coll Roy Roads, RN Engrg Coll, Nova Scotia Tech Coll; *m* 1969, Sarah, da of Col Patrick Easton, of Tonbridge; 1 da; *Career* engrg consultant; *Recreations* squash, rugby (refereeing), skiing; *Clubs* RMC of Canada, Ottawa Athletic, Roy C'wlth Soc (Pres Ottawa Branch 1975-78 and 1980); *Style* - Lt-Cdr Charles Gunning, RCN; 2940 McCarthy rd, Ottawa, Canada (☎ 613 731 0493)

GUNNING, Sir Robert Charles; 8 Bt (GB 1778); s of late Charles Archibald John Gunning (ggs of 6 Bt); suc kinsman, Brig-Gen Sir Charles Vere Gunning, 7 Bt, CB, CMG, 1950; *b* 2 Dec 1901; *Educ* St

Paul's Sch, Leeds U; *m* 1934, Helen Nancy, da of late Vice-Adm Sir Theodore John Hallett, KBE, CB; 8 s, 2 da (and 1 da decd); *Heir* s, Lt-Cdr Charles Gunning, RCN; *Career* Lt RA (TA) Anti-Aircraft Command, Capt 1940; *Style* - Sir Robert Gunning, Bt; Peace River, Alberta, Canada

GUNNINGHAM, Hon Mrs (Mary Cynthia Burke); *née* Roche; da of 4 Baron Fermoy; aunt of HRH The Princess of Wales; *b* 1934; *m* 1, 1954 (m dis 1966), Hon Anthony Berry, MP (6 s of 1 Viscount Kemsley); m 2, 1973 (m dis 1980), Dennis Geoghegan; m 3, 1981, Michael Gunningham; *Style* - The Hon Mrs Gunningham; 40 Chester Terrace, Regent's Park, NW1

GUNSTON, Maj Sir Derrick Wellesley; 1 Bt (UK 1938), MC; s of late Capt Bernard H Gunston; *b* 26 Feb 1891; *Educ* Harrow, Trin Cambridge; *m* 1917, Evelyn Bligh, OBE, da of late Howard Bligh St George; 1 s; *Heir* s, Richard Gunston; *Career* Maj 7 Bn Glos Regt (TA) & Capt Irish Gds (Res); memb Parly Mission to Newfoundland 1943, PPS (unpaid) to Min of Health 1926, to Chllr of Exchequer 1931 (resigned 1936), to Under-Sec of State for War 1940; MP (C) Thornbury Div of Glos 1924-1945; *Style* - Maj Sir Derrick Gunston, Bt, MC; 14 Pelham cres, SW7; Fram Cottage, Bembridge, Isle of Wight

GUNSTON, Richard Wellesley; s and h of Sir Derrick Gunston, 1 Bt, MC; *b* 15 March 1924; *Educ* Harrow, Clare Cambridge; *m* 1, 1947 (m dis 1956), da of Sir Arthur Colegate, MP; 1 da; m 2, 1959 (m dis), Joan, da of Mrs Marie Walker, of Somerset West, Cape Province, S Africa; 1 s; m 3, 1962, Veronica Elizabeth Loyd, da of Maj Haines, and widow of Capt Vivian Loyd; *Career* Colonial Serv Nigeria, Nyasaland, Bechuanaland 1948-60; *Style* - Richard Gunston Esq

GUNTHER, Sir John Thomson; CMG (1965), OBE (1954); s of C M Gunther; *b* 2 Oct 1910; *Educ* Sydney U; *m* 1938; 1 s, 3 da; *Career* kt 1975, MB, DTM&H Sydney, Vice-Chllr U of Papua and New Guinea 1966-72, expert on tropical medicine; *Style* - Sir John Gunther, CMG, OBE; Onkara st, Buderim, Qld 4556 Australia

GUPWELL, Reginald John; s of Alfred John Gupwell (d 1936); *b* 21 Jan 1908; *Educ* King Edward's Birmingham; *m* 1, 1938, Betty (d 1965), nee Fraley; 1 s (Peter Hugh b 1946); m 2, 1969, Gene Gladys, nee Hurford; *Career* Maj (England, Egypt, Iraq); chm A J Gupwell Ltd Shopfitters 1975-81 (dir 1936, md 1962-75); pres Nat Assoc of Shopfitters 1963-64; *Recreations* golf, bridge, walking; *Clubs* Harbourne Golf Club, Edgbaston Proiry Club, St Pauls Club; *Style* - Reginald Gupwell Esq; 2 Lloyd sq, Niell Close, Edgbaston, Birmingham (☎ 021 455 7323)

GURDON, Hon Sacha William Robin; s and h of 3 Baron Cranworth; *b* 12 Aug 1970; *Style* - The Hon Sacha Gurdon

GURNEY, David Quintin; s of Richard Quintin Gurney (d 1980); *b* 6 Feb 1941; *Educ* Harrow, Cambridge, Grenoble U; *m* 1965, Jacqueline McLeod, nee Rawle; 1 s, 2 da; *Career* banker, local dir Barclays Bank Ltd Darlington 1978, farmer, chm/dir Bawdeswell Farms Ltd; *Recreations* field sports; *Clubs* Farmers', MCC; *Style* - David Gurney Esq; The East House, Great Smeaton, Northallerton, N Yorks (☎ St Smeaton 211); Bawkeswell Hall, Norfolk (☎ 036 288 307)

GURNEY, John; s of Sir Eustace Gurney, JP (d 1927); *b* 3 July 1905; *Educ* Eton, New Coll Oxford; *m* 1932, Ann, da of Capt Frederick Ogilvy, RN (3 s of Sir Reginald Ogilvy, 10 Bt, JP, DL, by his w Hon Olivia, da of 9 Lord Kinnaird, KT, PC); 5 da (Priscilla, m Gregory Meath-Baker; Jean, m Patrick Mayhew, QC, MP, *qv*; Elizabeth Olivia, m Timothy Bristol; Elizabeth; Ruth, m Maj Clive Forestier, *qv*, 5 in descent from Sir George Townshend Walker, 1 Bt, GCB); *Career* JP Norfolk 1930-75; md Medici Soc 1935-, chm & md Walsingham Estate Co 1928-; served with Roy Norfolk Regt & W Africa Frontier Force 1939-43; *Recreations* photography; *Clubs* Norfolk (Norwich); *Style* - John Gurney Esq; The Abbey, Walsingham, Norfolk (☎ 032 872 219)

GURNEY, Hon Mrs; Hon (Diana) Miranda; *née* Hovell-Thurlow-Cumming-Bruce; da of 8 Baron Thurlow, KCMG; *b* 1954; *m* 1981, Michael J Gurney, s of J C Gurney; *Style* - The Hon Mrs Gurney

GUTCH, Sir John; KCMG (1957, CMG 1952), OBE (1947); s of Clement Gutch; *b* 12 July 1905; *Educ* Aldenham, Gonville & Caius Cambridge; *m* 1938, Diana, da of Evelyn Worsley; 3 s; *Career* Colonial Admin Serv 1928-60, High Commissioner W Pacific 1955-60; *Recreations* gardening, painting, travel; *Style* - Sir John Gutch, KCMG, OBE; Littleworth Cross, Seale, Farnham, Surrey (☎ Runfold 2081)

GUTHRIE, Giles Malcolm Welcome; s and h of Sir Malcolm Guthrie, 3 Bt; *b* 16 Oct 1972

GUTHRIE, Sir Malcolm Connop; 3 Bt (UK 1936), of Brent Eleigh Hall, Co Suffolk; s of Sir Giles Guthrie, 2 Bt, OBE, DSC (d 1979), and Rhona, Lady Guthrie; *b* 16 Dec 1942; *Educ* Millfield; *m* 1967, Victoria, da of Douglas Willcock; 1 s, 1 da; *Heir* s, Giles Guthrie; *Recreations* competitive shooting, water skiing; *Style* - Sir Malcolm Guthrie, Bt; Belbroughton, nr Stourbridge, Worcs

GUTHRIE, Rhona, Lady; Rhona Leslie; da of Frederic Stileman, of Plaistow, Sussex; *m* 1939, Sir Giles Guthrie, 2 Bt, OBE, DSC (d 1979); 2 s (Sir Malcolm Guthrie, 3 Bt, *qv*, and Alastair Guthrie); *Style* - Rhona, Lady Guthrie; Rozel, St Martin, Jersey, CI

GUY, Lt-Gen Sir Roland Kelvin; KCB (1980), CBE (1978, MBE 1955), DSO (1972); s of Lt-Col Norman Guy; *b* 25 June 1928; *Educ* Wellington, Sandhurst; *m* 1957, Dierdre, da of Brig P Graves-Morris, DSO, MC; 2 da; *Career* Col Cmmdt Small Arms Sch Corps 1981-, Ch of Staff HQ BAOR 1978-80, Mil Sec 1980-, Col Cmmdt 1 Bn Roy Green Jackets July 1981-*Style* - Lt-Gen Sir Roland Guy, KCB, CBE, DSO; c/o MOD, Whitehall, SW1

GWILLIAM, Freda Howitt; CBE (1966); da of Frederick Gwilliam (d 1966); *b* 29 July 1907; *Educ* Nottingham H S, Girton Cambridge; *Career* educn advr Colonial Off later Min Overseas Dvpt 1947-70, chm Exec Ctee VOS 1970-77; *Clubs* Roy C'wlth Soc; *Style* - Miss Freda Gwilliam, CBE; One Ash, Frant, E Sussex (☎ 295)

GWILT, George David; s of the late Richard Lloyd Gwilt; *b* 11 Nov 1927; *Educ* Sedbergh Sch, St John's Coll Cambridge; *m* 1956, Ann Dalton, da of Arthur J Sylvester of Conn USA; 3 s; *Career* actuary, joined Standard Life Co 1949, assistant official 1956, assistant actuary 1957, statistician 1962, mechanisation man 1964, systems man 1969, dep pensions man 1972, pensions actuary 173, assistant gen man and pensions man 1977, assist gen man (fin) 1978, gen man and actuary 1979; trustee TSB of South of Scotland 1966; pres Faculty of Actuaries 1981; *Recreations* flute playing; *Clubs* RAF, New (Edinburgh); *Style* - George Gwilt Esq; 39 Oxgangs rd, Edinburgh (☎ 031 445 1266)

GWINNETT, Lady Doreen Stella; *née* Lowry-Corry; sis of 7 Earl Belmore, JP, DL; *b* 29 July 1916; *m* 1948, Rev John Gwinnett, MC; 1 s; raised to the rank of Earl's da 1951; served WW II 2 Offr WRNS; *Style* - Lady Doreen Gwinnett; Flat 1, 18 Flaghead rd, Canford Cliffs, Poole, Dorset

GWYDYR-JONES, Brig Llewellyn; DSO, OBE, DL (Denbighshire 1969); s of Evelyn Gwydyr-Jones, of Richmond, Surrey; *b* 28 Nov 1900; *Educ* Marlborough, Sandhurst; *m* 1939, Valentine, da of Richard Oswald Mills, of Oxted; *Career* High Sheriff Denbighs 1966; memb Denbighs CC; ret as Brig 1952; *Recreations* hunting and other country sports; *Style* - Brig Llewellyn Gwydyr-Jones, DSO, OBE DL; River House, Erbistock, nr Wrexham, N Wales (☎ Overton-on-Dee 269)

GWYNEDD, Viscount; David Richard Owen; s and h of 3 Earl Lloyd-George of Dwyfor; *b* 22 June 1951; *Educ* Eton; *Style* - Viscount Gwynedd

GWYNNE-EVANS, Francis Loring; s of late Sir Evan Gwynne-Evans, 2 Bt; hp of bro, Sir Ian Gwynne-Evans, 3 Bt; *b* 2 Feb

1914; *m* 1, 1937 (m dis 1958), Elisabeth Fforde, da of J Fforde-Tipping, of Bellurgan Park, Dundalk, Eire; 2 s, 1 da; m 2, 1958, Gloria Marie Reynolds; 2 s, 3 da; *Style* - Francis Gwynne-Evans Esq; Maywood, Wadhurst Park, Wadhurst, Sussex

GWYNNE-EVANS, Sir Ian William; 3 Bt (UK 1913); s of Sir Evan Gwynne-Evans, 2 Bt (d 1959); *b* 21 Feb 1909; *m* 1, 1935, Elspeth, da of Rt Hon Sir Godfrey Pattison Collins, KBE, CMG, MP; 2 da; m 2, 1946, Monica Dalrymple, da of Douglas Clinch, of Durban; *Heir* bro, Francis Gwynne-Evans; *Style* - Sir Ian Gwynne-Evans, Bt; 57 Eastwood rd, Dunkeld, Johannesburg, S Africa

H

HACKING, 3 Baron (UK 1945); Sir Douglas David Hacking; 3 Bt (UK 1938); s of 2 Baron (d 1971); *b* 17 April 1938; *Educ* Charterhouse, Clare Cambridge; *m* 1965, Rosemary, da of Frank Forrest, of Dorset; 2 s, 1 da; *Heir* s, Hon Douglas Hacking; *Career* barr 1963-76, attorney New York State 1975, served RN 1956-58, slr Supreme Court Eng & Wales 1977; Freeman Merchant Taylors' Co & City of London; *Style* - The Rt Hon Lord Hacking; Lane & Ptnrs, 46/47 Bloomsbury sq, WC1; 252 Clapham rd, SW9

HACKING, Hon Belinda Anne; da of 3 Baron Hacking; *b* 1966; *Style* - The Hon Belinda Hacking

HACKING, C G; *Career* md C G Hacking & Sons Ltd; *Style* - C G Hacking Esq; C G Hacking & Sons Ltd, Calverts Bldgs, 50-52 Borough High st, SE1

HACKING, Hon Douglas Francis; s and h of 3 Baron Hacking; *b* 8 Aug 1968

HACKING, Hon Daniel Robert; s of 3 Baron Hacking; *b* 27 May 1972

HACKING, Daphne, Baroness - Daphne Violet; *née* Finnis; *Educ* Priors Field and Paris; *m* 1936, 2 Baron Hacking (d 1971); 2s (3 Baron, Hon Leslie Hacking), 2 da (Hon Mrs de Laszlo, Hon Mrs du Preez); *Style* - The Rt Hon Daphne, Lady Hacking; 45 Cadogan Sq, SW1 (☎ 01 235 7798)

HACKING, Hon Edgar Bolton; MBE (1942), TD (1950); s of 1 Baron Hacking OBE PC (d 1950); *b* 1912; *Educ* Charterhouse, Clare Coll Cambridge, and London Hosp; *m* 1 1943, (m dis 1950), Winifred Mary, da of John Christie Kelly; 2 da; m 2 1950, Evangeline Grace, da of late Percy Burstal Shearing; 2 s, 1 da; *Career* MRCS, LRCP, FFARCS, BCh, DA; fell Assoc of Anaesthetists; sr resident anaesthetist London Hosp 1939; MO to Queen's Westminsters (TA) 1938-40; served with RAMC as anaesthetic specialist; Maj 1940-45; sr assist anaesthetist Groote Schuur Hosp; anaesthetist instr Cape Town U 1946-51 and Stellenbosch U 1958; *Clubs* MCC and Western Province Sports; *Style* - The Hon Edgar Hacking, MBE, TD; Leeming, Alice rd, Claremont, Cape Town (☎ 77-4544)

HACKING, Hon Mrs (Fiona Margaret); *née* Noel-Paton; da of Baron Ferrier (Life Peer); *b* 1943; *m* 1967, Hon Leslie Bruce Hacking; *Style* - The Hon Mrs Hacking; Burchett's, Lower Moushill Lane, Milford, Surrey

HACKING, Hon Leslie Bruce; s of 2 Baron Hacking (d 1971); *b* 16 June 1940; *Educ* Hawtreys and Eton Coll; *m* 1967, Hon Fiona Margaret Noel-Paton, da of Baron Ferrier (Life Peer); 1 s, 1 da ; *Career* apprenticed to Haberdashers' Co 1955, liveryman 1962; freedom of City of London 1962; stockbroker; *Clubs* MCC; *Style* - The Hon Leslie Hacking; Burchetts, Lower Mousehill Lane, Milford, Surrey

HACKING, Dowager Baroness - Margery Allen; *née* Bolton; OBE (1956); *m* 1909, 1 Baron Hacking, PC, OBE (d 1950); 2 s (2 Baron, who d 1971, leaving 2 s, 2 da, including 3 Baron; Hon Edgar Hacking, MBE), 1 da (Hon Lady Waller); *Style* - The Rt Hon Dowager Lady Hacking OBE; 8 Dorchester Court, Sloane st, SW1

HADDINGTON, 12 Earl of (S 1619); George Baillie-Hamilton; KT (1951), MC, TD; also Lord Binning (S 1613) and Lord Byres and Binning (S 1619); s of Lord Binning, CB, MVO (eldest s of 11 Earl); suc gf 1917; *b* 18 Sept 1894; *Educ* Eton; *m* 1923, Sarah, da of late G Cook, of Montreal; 1 s, 1 da; *Heir* s, Lord Binning; *Career* FRSE; Pres Soc of Antiquaries Scotland, Scottish Georgian Soc, chm Tstees Nat Museum Antiquities Scotland, Tstee Nat Library Scotland; Rep Peer Scotland 1922-63, Lt Roy Co Archers (Queen's Bodyguard for Scotland); Maj late Tank Corps (TA); Ld-Lt Berwicks 1952-69; served WW I & II; sometime on staff Gov-Gen Canada; bore ivory rod of Queen at Coronation of George VI 1937; *Clubs* New (Edinburgh); *Style* - Rt Hon Earl of Haddington KT MC TD; Mellerstain, Gordon, Scotland

HADDON, Brig Thomas; CBE (1961); s of Maj J T Haddon, DCM (d 1937); *b* 19 Feb 1913; *Educ* Hamilton Acad Lanarkshire, RMC Sandhurst; *m* 1939, Clodagh, da of late Lt-Col Hon Bertrand Russell, DSO; 3 s; *Career* 1 Bn Border Regt WW II (staff Europe, Middle East), UK Cabinet Offices, Lt-Col 1955, Brig 1961, ret 1968, ADC to HM the Queen 1964-68; *Style* - Brig Thomas Haddon, CBE; Combe End, Hindhead, Surrey (☎ 4931)

HADDON, Hon Mrs (Teresa Mary); da of 1 Viscount Head, GCMG, CBE, MC, PC; *b* 1938; *m* 1972, Richard Deacon Haddon; 2 s, 1 da; *Style* - The Hon Mrs Haddon; Farrrer House, Eton College, Windsor, Bucks

HADEN-GUEST, 3 Baron (UK 1950); Richard Haden Haden-Guest; s of 1 Baron, MC, by his 1 w Edith; suc 2 Baron (er bro) 1974; *b* 20 July 1904; *Educ* Bembridge; *m* 1, 1926 (m dis 1934), Hilda, da of Thomas Russell-Cruise; 1 da; m 2, 1934, Olive, da of Anders Nilsson; m 3, 1951, Marjorie, da of Dr Douglas Kennard; *Heir* s, half-bro, Hon Peter Haden-Guest; *Style* - The Rt Hon Lord Haden-Guest; 3 Chemin des Cret de Champel, 1206 Geneva, Switzerland (☎ 476940)

HADEN-GUEST, Dorothy, Baroness; Dorothy; da of Thomas Roseberry Good, late of Princeton, NJ; *m* 1968, as his 2 wife, 2 Baron Haden-Guest (d 1974); *Style* - The Rt Hon Dorothy, Lady Haden-Guest; 105 Bayard Lane, Princeton, New Jersey 08540, USA

HADEN-GUEST, Hon Hadley; da of 2 Baron Haden-Guest (d 1974); *b* 1949; *Style* - The Hon Hadley Haden-Guest; 1148 Fifth av, New York City, NY, USA

HADEN-GUEST, Hon Peter Haden; s of 2 Baron Haden-Guest (d 1974), and hp of half-bro, 3 Baron; *b* 1913; *Educ* City of London Sch, New Coll Oxford; *m* 1945, Jean, da of late Dr Albert George Hindes, of New York; 2 s, 1 da; *Career* United Nations Official 1946-72 (Ch of Editorial Control UN HQ, Ch Editor UN Office Geneva, and Ch of Repertory Editing Gp UN HQ New York); 1939-45 War as Lt RCNVR; *Style* - The Hon Peter Haden-Guest; 198 Old Stone Highway, East Hampton, New York 11937, USA

HADFIELD, (Ellis) Charles Raymond; CMG (1959); s of Alexander Hadfield (d 1926); *b* 5 Aug 1909; *Educ* Blundell's, St Edmund Hall Oxford; *m* 1945, Alice, da of Lt-Col Henry Smyth, DSO (d 1941); 1 s, 1 da (and 1 da decd); *Career* dir pubns COI 1946-48, dir David & Charles 1960-64, author; *Recreations* writing, exploring canals; *Style* - Charles Hadfield Esq, CMG; 13 Meadow Way, S Cerney, Cirencester, Glos (☎ 860422)

HADFIELD, Hon Mrs; Hon Maureen; da of Baron Segal (Life Peer); *b* 1935; *m* 1956, Jeremy Hadfield; children; *Style* - The Hon Mrs Hadfield; 19 Christchurch Hill, NW3

HADLEY, Lady Paulina Mary Louise; *née* Pepys; da of late 6 Earl of Cottenham; *b* 1930; *m* 1973, Denis Bernard Hadley; *Style* - Lady Paulina Hadley; White Hill House, Odiham, Hants

HADWEN, Lady Sibell Anne Julia; *née* Blunt-Mackenzie; da (by 1 m) of Earl of Cromartie (4 in line), *qv*; *b* 1934; *m* 1953

(m dis 1961), Francis Edward Lascelles-Hadwen; 1 s, 1 da; *Style* - Lady Sibell Hadwen

HAGART-ALEXANDER, Claud; s and h of Sir Claud Hagart-Alexander, 3 Bt; *b* 5 Nov 1963; *Style* - Claud Hagart-Alexander Esq

HAGART-ALEXANDER, Sir Claud; 3 Bt (UK 1886), of Ballochmyle, Co Ayr; s of late Wilfred Archibald Alexander, 2 s of 2 Bt; suc gf 1945; additional surname Hagart recognised by decree of Lord Lyon 1948; *b* 6 Jan 1927; *Educ* Sherborne, CCC Cambridge; *m* 1959, Hilda Etain, da of Miles Malcolm Acheson; 2 s, 2 da; *Heir* s, Claud Hagart-Alexander; *Style* - Sir Claud Hagart-Alexander, Bt, DL; Kingencleugh House, Mauchline, Ayrshire (☎ Mauchline 50217)

HAGDRUP, Alan; s of Sofus Vilhelm Hagdrup, of Cheam; *b* 19 May 1932; *Educ* Epsom Coll, UCL; *m* 1958, Elizabeth, da of Lt-Col Harold Mason, OBE, MC, TD; 1 s, 2 da; *Career* dir Hanson T'port Gp 1969-, Hanson Tst 1974-; ptnr Goulden's (slrs) 1962-69; *Recreations* golf, skiing, bridge, music; *Clubs* Walton Heath Golf, Kingswood Golf; *Style* - Alan Hagdrup Esq; Thornfield, Axes Lane, Salfords, Redhill, Surrey (☎ 61205)

HAGGERSTON, see (Constable) Maxwell-Scott, Sir Michael, Bt

HAHN, Oscar Rudolph Eric Max; CBE (1972); *b* 27 July 1923; *Educ* Gordonstoun, Trin Cambridge; *m* 1958, Margaret, da of James Walker, WS, of Edinburgh; 1 s, 3 da; *Career* FIME; dir GKN 1974-81, BKL Alloys 1968-71; Pres Birmingham Chamber of Commerce 1966; *Recreations* sailing, shooting, fishing; *Style* - Oscar Hahn Esq, CBE; Burnside House, Duffus, Elgin, Moray (☎ 034 383 227); Bunkers Hill, Welford on Avon, Warwicks (☎ 0789 750282)

HAIG, 2 Earl (UK 1919); George Alexander Eugene Douglas Haig; OBE (1965), DL (Roxburghshire 1953); also Viscount Dawick, Baron Haig (both UK 1919) and 30 Laird of Bemersyde; s of Field Marshal 1 Earl Haig, KT, GCB, OM, GCVO, KCIE (d 1928), by his w, Hon Dorothy, GCStJ, 2 da of 3 Baron Vivian; *b* 15 March 1918; *Educ* Stowe, Ch Ch Oxford; *m* 1, 1956 (m dis 1981), Adrienne, da of Derrick Morley; 1 s, 2 da; m 2, 1981, Doña Geroloma Lopez y Royo; *Heir* s, Viscount Dawick; *Career* Capt Roy Scots Greys M East Force 1939-42; POW 1942-45, Maj on disbandment of Home Gd; artist (studied at Camberwell Sch Arts & Crafts); memb Roy Co of Archers (Queen's Bodyguard for Scotland); FRSA, KStJ; Train Bearer at Coronation of King George VI; Vice-Lt Berwicks 1967-70; memb Cncl Earl Haig Fund, Pres & Chm Offrs' Assoc (Scottish Cttee) 1977-; Tstee Scottish Nat War Memorial; *Recreations* fishing, shooting; *Clubs* New (Edinburgh), Cavalry & Guards, Beefsteak; *Style* - The Rt Hon The Earl Haig OBE DL; Bemersyde, Melrose, Roxburghshire (☎ St Boswells 2762)

HAIG, Lady Elizabeth Vivienne Thérèse; da of 2 Earl Haig, OBE, DL; *b* 1 March 1959; *Educ* St George's Edinburgh, Bedales Sch Hampshire, St Martin's Sch of Art; *Career* glass engraver; *Style* - Lady Elizabeth Haig

HAIG, Lady (Adrienne) Raina; da of 2 Earl Haig, OBE, DL; *b* 19 Feb 1958; *Educ* Bedales, BNC Oxford; *Career* studying for BA in Sanskrit; *Style* - Lady Raina Haig

HAIGH, (Austin) Anthony Francis; CMG (1954); s of Percy Haigh, ICS; *b* 29 Aug 1907; *Educ* Eton, King's Cambridge; *m* 1, 1935, Gertrude (m dis 1971), da of Frank Dodd; 2 s, 2 da; m 2, 1971, Eleanore, da of Tom Bullimore and widow of J Herbert; *Career* For Serv ret; Dir Educn & Cultural & Scientific Affrs Cncl Europe 1962-6; *Clubs* Leander; *Style* - Anthony Haigh Esq, CMG; The Furnace, Crowhurst, nr Battle, E Sussex (☎ Crowhurst 279)

HAIGH, John Randal; s of Fred Haigh, of Huddersfield; *b* 12 Dec 1919; *Educ* King James's Sch Almondbury, St Cat's Cambridge; *m* 1952, Zara, da of William Martin, of Coulsdon; 1 s, 1 da; *Career* FIA 1951; dir (1972-) & investment advsr (1974-) Imperial Gp; *Recreations* golf, walking, music, watching cricket and rugby football; *Clubs* MCC, HAC; *Style* - John Haigh Esq; Broad Beech, Valley Way, Gerrards Cross, Bucks (☎ 85634)

HAILSHAM, Viscountcy of (UK 1929); *see* Hailsham of St Marylebone, Baron

HAILSHAM OF ST MARYLEBONE, Baron (Life Peer UK 1970); Quintin McGarel Hogg; CH (1974), PC (1956); s of 1 Viscount Hailsham (d 1950) by his 1 w Elizabeth, da of Judge James Brown, of Nashville, Tennessee, and widow of Hon Archibald Marjoribanks (s of Lord Tweedmouth); disclaimed Peerage for life 1963; *b* 9 Oct 1907; *Educ* Eton, Ch Ch Oxford; *m* 1, 1931, Natalie (m dis 1943), da of Alan Sullivan, of Sheerland House, Pluckley, Kent; m 2, 1944, Mary (d 1978), da of Richard Martin, of Kensington; 2 s, 3 da; *Heir* (to Viscountcy and Barony of Hailsham, UK cr respectively 1928 & 1929, only) s, Hon Douglas Hogg, MP; *Career* Fellow All Souls 1931-38 & 1962-; barr 1932, QC 1953, Ld Chllr 1970-74 & 1979-; MP (C) Oxford City 1938-58, St Marylebone 1963-70, 1 Ld Admlty 1956-57, Min Educn 1957, Dep Ldr House of Lords 1957-60, Ld Pres Cncl 1957-59 & 1960-64, Ld Privy Seal 1959-60, Ldr House of Lords 1960-63, Min Science & Technology 1959-64; Rector Glasgow U 1959; ed Halsbury's Laws of England (4 edn) 1972-; served WW II Rifle Bde; chm Con Pty Orgn 1957-59 FRS; *Style* - Rt Hon Lord Hailsham of St Marylebone CH PC; Corner House, Heathview gdns, SW15 (☎ 01 789 3954/788 2256)

HAINES, Sir Cyril Henry; KBE (1962, CBE 1953, MBE 1930); s of late W J Haines, OBE; *b* 2 March 1895; *Educ* Hele's Sch Exeter; *m* 1934, Mary Theodora, da of the late Rev J W P Silvester, BD, Hon CF; 2 da; *Career* active service 1915-19, called to Bar 1926, appointed assist British Agent to Anglo-Mexican Claims Commission, served in Mexico City 1929-30, appt Registrar HMB Supreme Court for China 1930, assist Judge HBM Consular Court for Egypt 1943, Judge of HBM Consular Court for Egypt 1946, assist Judge of HBM Chief Court for Persian Gulf 1949-59, head of Claims Dept in Foreign Office 1949-54, Judge of HBM Chief Court for Persian Gulf 1959-61, chm SW London Rent Tribunal 1962-66, and of Abbeyfield Orpington Society 1961-75, ret, appointed president of the same 1975; *Recreations* gardening, walking; *Style* - Sir Cyril Haines, KBE; Wood Lea, 5 The Glen, Farnborough Park, Orpington (☎ Farnborough 54507)

HAINING, Thomas Nivison; s of William Haining, of Ayrshire; *b* 15 March 1927; *Educ* Edinburgh and Göttingen Us; *m* 1955, Dorothy, nee Robson; 1 s; *Career* HM For Serv 1952-, UK Ambass to Mongolian People's Republic 1979- FRGS; *Clubs* RAC; *Style* - Thomas Haining Esq; c/o FCO, SW1

HAIRE, Hon Christopher Peter; s of Baron Haire of Whiteabbey (Life Peer, d 1966); *b* 6 Feb 1951; *Educ* Michael Hall Sch Forest Row Sussex, Holland Pk Sch W8; *Style* - The Hon Christopher Haire; 34 Elm Pk gdns, SW10 (☎ 01 352 6846)

HAIRE, Hon Michael John Kemeny; s of Baron Haire of Whiteabbey (Life Peer, d 1966); *b* 19 Dec 1945; *Educ* St Paul's, UCL, Pennsylvania U ; *Style* - The Hon Michael Haire; 34 Elm Pk gdns, SW10 (☎ 01 352 6846)

HAIRE OF WHITEABBEY, Baroness - Suzanne Elizabeth; da of Dr Eugene Kemeny, of London; *m* 1939, Baron Haire of Whiteabbey (Life Peer, d 1966); 2 s; *Style* - The Rt Hon Lady Haire of Whiteabbey; Lynford Hall, Mundford, Norfolk; Whiteabbey House, Belfast

HALDANE, James; s of Herbert Haldane; *b* 14 May 1903; *Educ* Winchester, Magdalen Oxford; *m* 1939, Joanna, da of Col William Thorburn; 2 s, 1 da (and 1 da decd); *Career* CA 1929, ptnr Lindsay Jamieson & Haldane 1930-70; co dir; *Recreations* golf; *Clubs* Bath New (Edinburgh), Hon Co of Edinburgh Golfers; *Style* - James Haldane Esq; The Old Schoolhouse, Gleneagles, Auchterarder, Perthshire (☎ Blackford 427); 11 Grosvenor Cres, Edinburgh (☎ 031 337 5544)

HALDANE, James Martin; s of James Haldane, of Edinburgh; *b* 18 Sept 1941; *Educ* Winchester, Magdalen Oxford; *m* 1968, Petronella, da of Sir Peter Scarlett, KCMG, KCVO, of Cheltenham; 1 s, 2 da; *Career* CA, ptnr Arthur Young McClelland Moores & Co 1970; chm Scottish Philharmonic Soc 1978-; *Recreations* music, golf; *Clubs* Brooks's, New (Edinburgh); *Style* - James Haldane Esq; Gleneagles, Auchterarder, Perthshire (☎ Blackford 388); 19 Buckingham Ter, Edinburgh (☎ 031 332 5554)

HALE, Baron (Life Peer UK 1972); (Charles) Leslie Hale; s of Benjamin Hale; *b* 13 July 1902; *Educ* Ashby de la Zouch Boys' G S; *m* 1926, Dorothy (d 1971), da of Joseph Latham; 1 s, 1 da; *Career* MP (L) Oldham 1945-50, Oldham W 1950-68, Freeman Oldham 1969, memb Leics CC 1925-50; served WW II RA; slr 1923; dir Stableford & Co, Lab candidate Nottingham S 1929; *Style* - The Rt Hon Lord Hale; 92 College rd, SE21

HALE, Hon Dorothy Lesley; da of Baron Hale (Life Peer); *b* 1927; *Style* - The Hon Dorothy Hale; 92 College rd, SE21

HALE, Hon Ian Wiliam Percy; s of Baron Hale (Life Peer); *b* 1930; *Style* - The Hon Ian Hale; 92 College rd, SE21

HALEY, Sir William John; KCMG (1946); s of Frank Haley; *b* 24 May 1901; *Educ* Victoria Coll Jersey; *m* 1921, Susan, da of John Gibbons; 2 s, 2 da; *Career* md Manchester Guardian & Evening News 1939-43, dir Reuters 1939-43; dir-gen BBC 1944-52, ed The Times 1952-66, chm Times Newspapers 1967, ed-in-chief Encyclopaedia Britannica 1968-69; *Recreations* reading; *Style* - Sir William Haley, KCMG; Beau Site, Gorey Hill, Jersey, CI (☎ 51068)

HALIFAX, 3 Earl of (UK 1944); Sir Charles Edward Peter Neil Wood; 7 Bt (GB 1784); also Viscount Halifax (UK 1866), Baron Irwin (UK 1925); s of 2 Earl of Halifax (d 1980); *b* 14 March 1944; *Educ* Eton, Ch Ch Oxford; *m* 1976, as her 2 husb, Camilla, da of Charles Younger, who m 1, 1973 (m dis 1976), Richard Parker-Bowles (gs of Sir Humphrey de Trafford, 4 Bt, MC, through his m and gggs of 6 Earl of Macclesfield through his f); 1 s, 1 da; *Heir* s, Lord Irwin; *Career* dir Hambro's Bank; co-owner with late f of 'Shirley Heights' (1978 Derby winner); OStJ; *Style* - The Rt Hon The Earl of Halifax; Great Givendale, Pocklington, York

HALIFAX, Ruth, Countess of - Ruth Alice Hannah Mary; da of late Rt Hon Neil James Archibald Primrose, MC, MP (ka 1917), 2 s of 5 Earl of Rosebery, and Lady Victoria Alice Louise Stanley (d 1927), da of 17 Earl of Derby; *b* 18 April 1916; *m* 1936, 2 Earl of Halifax (d 1980); 1 s (3 Earl), 2 da (Lady Caroline Gosling, Lady Susan Watson); *Style* - The Rt Hon Ruth, Countess of Halifax; Low House, Kirby Underdale, York

HALL, 2 Viscount (UK 1946); (William George) Leonard Hall; s of 1 Viscount (d 1965), by his 1 w Margaret; *b* 9 March 1913; *Educ* Christ Coll Brecon, UCH; *m* 1, 1935, Joan (d 1962), da of William Griffiths, of Glam; 2 da; m 2, 1963, Constance (d 1972), da of Rupert Gathorne Hardy; m 3, 1974, Marie-Colette, da of Col Henri Bach; *Heir* none; *Career* MRCS, LRCP; served RNVR WW II, late assist MOH Merthyr Tydfil; investment dir; chm PO 1969-70; *Style* - The Rt Hon Viscount Hall; Belgrave Cottage, Upper Belgrave st, SW1 (☎ 01 235 9279); Solvain, 41210 St Viatre, Loir et Cher, France (☎ 54 83 63 67)

HALL, Alfred Charles; CBE (1977, OBE 1966); s of Alfred Hall (d 1951); *b* 2 Aug 1917; *Educ* Oratory Sch; *m* 1946, Clara Georgievna, nee Strunin; 5 s, 1 da; *Career* WW II Intelligence Corps, HM Diplomatic Serv; Br dep high cmmr in S India 1975-77, counsellor (ec and dvpt) Br High Cmmn Nigeria 1972-75, attached to Dept of Trade 1969-71, counsellor Canberra, counsellor (info) Nigeria, 1 Sec India Pakistan and Canada, attached to HM Embassies Cairo Tehran Moscow, grants offr Save the Children Fund 1979-; *Recreations* gardening, journalism; *Clubs* Royal Commonwealth, Royal Horticultural; *Style* - Alfred Hall Esq, CBE; White Cliff, St Margarets Bay, Kent (☎ Dover 852230)

HALL, Alice, Viscountess; Alice Martha; OBE (1962); da of Ben Walker, of Rugby; *m* 1964, as his 2 w, 1 Viscount Hall (d 1965); *Style* - The Rt Hon Alice, Viscountess Hall OBE; Stanton Lodge, 82 Woodmarket, Lutterworth, Leics

HALL, Austin Patrick; TD (1970); s of Austin Percy Hall, of Harrogate; *b* 13 March 1932; *Educ* King James G S Knaresborough, Bradford Coll of Advanced Technology; *m* 1957, Dorothy, da of George Whitfield, of Harrogate; 1 s, 2 da; *Career* chartered engr, builder & FCIA; ch exec Bovis Civil Engrg 1974-, dir Bovis Ltd 1977-; *Recreations* boating, golf; *Clubs* RAC, IOD; *Style* - Austin Hall Esq, TD; Albury, Vicarage Lane, Steeple Ashton, Trowbridge, Wilts

HALL, Dr Cecil Charles; CB (1968); s of Frederick Hall, of Croydon; *b* 10 May 1907; *Educ* Beckenham G S; *m* 1950, Margaret, da of James Nicoll, of Sanderstead; *Career* Dir Warren Spring Lab, Dept of Indust 1964-68; *Recreations* gardening, plant breeding; *Style* - Dr Cecil Hall, CB; 17 Sollershott West, Letchworth, Herts (☎ 4339)

HALL, David Bernard; s and h of Sir John Bernard Hall, 3 Bt, by his w Delia Mary, da of Lt-Col James Innes, DSO, by his 3 w, Evelyn (*see* Joly de Lotbinière, Lady) gda of Hon William Dawnay, JP, DL, 6 s of 7 Viscount Downe; *b* 12 May 1961; *Educ* Eton, York U; *Career* clerk Bank of America (Hamburg) 1980, student 1980-81; *Recreations* water skiing, marathon running, tennis; *Clubs* Lansdowne; *Style* - David Hall Esq; Inver House, Lochinver, Sutherland

HALL, Sir Douglas Basil; 14 Bt (NS 1687), of Dunglass, Haddingtonshire, KCMG (1959, CMG 1958); s of late Capt Lionel Erskine Hall; suc bro Sir Neville Hall, 13 Bt 1978; *b* 1 Feb 1909; *Educ* Radley, Keble Coll Oxford; *m* 1933, Rachel Marion Gartside-Tippinge; 1 s, 2 da (and 1 s decd); *Heir* s, John Douglas Hoste Hall; *Career* JP Devon 1964, and memb Police Authority for Devon and Cornwall 1971-79; entered Overseas Civil Serv as a Cadet N Rhodesia 1930, Dist Officer 1932-50, Sr Dist Officer 1950-53, Provincial Cmmr 1953, Admin Sec 1955-56, Sec for Native Affairs 1956, and Gov and C-in-C of Somaliland Protectorate 1959-60; *Style* - Sir Douglas Hall, Bt, KCMG, DL, JP; Barnford, Ringmore, nr Kingsbridge, Devon (☎ Bigbury-on-Sea 401)

HALL, David Christopher; s of Sir Frederick Hall, 2 Bt (d 1949), and bro and h of Sir (Frederick) John (Frank) Hall, 3 Bt; *b* 30 Dec 1937; *m* 1962, Irene, nee Duncan; 1 s, 1 da; *Career* joiner/cabinet maker 1962-79; woodwork teacher 1980-; *Style* - David Hall Esq; Inverene, 368 Queens rd, Aberdeen (☎ 0224 29766)

HALL, David John Lees; s of Herbert Hall; *b* 19 Feb 1946; *Educ* Felsted, Nottingham U; *m* 1972, Yvonne Pepita, da of Douglas Acock, of Essex; 1 s; *Career* engr; dir; chm- Monometer Manufacturing Ltd 1974-, R M Catterson Smith Ltd 1979-; associate memb Inst Br Foundrymen 1970-; *Recreations* yachting, skiing, squash; *Clubs* Roy Ocean Racing, Roy Corinthian Yacht, Roy Burnham Yacht, Courtland Park Country; *Style* - David Hall Esq; 1 Thorpe Bay gdns, Thorpe Bay, Essex; Clopton Manor, nr Kettering, Northants

HALL, Dorothy, Lady - Dorothy Maud; da of late William Lawrence Jones; *m* 1957, Sir Neville Reynolds Hall, 13 Bt (d 1978); *Style* - Dorothy, Lady Hall; Ash Cottage, Ash, Dartmouth, S Devon

HALL, Maj-Gen Edward Michael; CB (1970), MBE (1944), DL (Cornwall 1972); s of Brig Edward George Hall, CB, CBE (d 1968); *b* 16 July 1915; *Educ* Sherborne Sch, Peterhouse Coll Cambridge; *m* 1948, Nina Diana, da of Maj Valentine Goold McArthur, MC (d 1966); 3 s; *Career* commissioned RE 1935, ch of staff Northern Command 1965-66, mil dep to Head of Defence Sales 1966-70, Cmmr St John Ambulance Cornwall 1971-; *Recreations* country pursuits; *Style* - Maj-Gen Edward Hall, CB, MBE, DL; Treworgey Manor, Liskeard, Cornwall (☎ Liskeard 42568)

HALL, Harold Percival; CMG (1963), MBE (1947); s of Maj George Hall; *b* 9

Sept 1913; *Educ* Portsmouth G S, Sandhurst; *m* 1939, Margery, da of Joseph Dickson, MIEE; 3 s; *Career* late Maj NWFP; Colonial Off 1947-66; MOD Assist Under-Sec 1966-73; Indian Army 1933-37 & 1940-43, Indian Political Serv 1937-40; *Recreations* gardening; *Style* - Harold Hall Esq, CMG, MBE; 77 Moss Lane, Pinner, Middx (☎ 01 866 1162)

HALL, Sir John Bernard; 3 Bt (UK 1919), of Burton Park, Sussex; s of Lt-Col Sir Douglas Hall, 2 Bt, DSO (d 1962), by his 2 w, Nancie (da of Col John Mellor, CB, JP, DL); *b* 20 March 1932; *Educ* Eton, Trin Oxford; *m* 1957, Delia, da of Lt-Col James Innes, DSO (d 1949), by Evelyn (*see* Joly de Lotbinière, Lt-Col Sir Edmond); 1 s, 2 da; *Heir* s, David Hall; *Career* late Lt Roy Fusiliers RARO; dir Bank of America Internat 1974-, European Brazilian Bank 1976-, dir J Henry Schroder Wagg 1967-73; *Recreations* travel, fishing; *Clubs* Boodle's, Lansdowne, Overseas Bankers; *Style* - Sir John Hall, Bt; Inver House, Lochinver, Lairg, Sutherland; Penrose House, Patmore Heath, Albury, Ware, Herts (☎ Albury 255)

HALL, John Douglas Hoste; s and h of Sir Douglas Hall, 14 Bt, KCMG; *b* 7 Jan 1945; *Educ* Dover Coll, Gonville and Caius Cambridge, Southampton U; *m* 1972, Angela, nee Keys; 1 s; *Career* lectr Dartington Coll of Art; *Style* - John Hall Esq; Jepthahs, Staverton, Totnes, Devon

HALL, Sir (Frederick) John (Frank); 3 Bt (UK 1923), of Grafham, Co Surrey; s of Sir Frederick Henry Hall, 2 Bt (d 1949); *b* 14 Aug 1931; *Educ* Bryanston; *m* 1, 1956 (m dis 1960), Felicity Anne, da of late Edward Rivers-Fletcher, of Norwich; m 2, 1961 (m dis 1967), Patricia Ann, da of Douglas Atkinson, of Greystead, Longlands Rd, Carlisle; 2 da; re-m 1967 his 1 w, Felicity Anne; 2 da; *Heir* bro, David Christopher Hall; *Style* - Sir John Hall, Bt; Carradale, 29 Embercourt rd, Thames Ditton, Surrey KT7 OLH (☎ 01 398 2801)

HALL, Maj-Gen Kenneth; CB (1976), OBE (1962, MBE 1958); s of Frank Hall; *b* 29 July 1916; *Educ* Worksop Coll, St John's Cambridge; *m* 1945, Celia, da of Henry Francis; 2 s; *Career* Col Cmmdt Roy Army Educnl Corps 1978-, Dir Army Educn 1972-76 (Commissioned Roy Tank Regt 1940-49); *Recreations* golf, reading, boxing (Cambridge Blue 1937, -38, -39); *Clubs* Army & Navy, Roehampton, Hawks; *Style* - Maj-Gen Kenneth Hall, CB, OBE; 42 Exeter House, Putney Heath, SW15 (☎ 01 788 4794)

HALL, Peter Dudley; OBE (1980); s of Leonard Hall, of Sidmouth; *b* 13 Nov 1919; *Educ* Tiffins Sch, London U; *m* 1945, Eldwyth Gladys, da of John Marsden, of Malvern; 1 s, 1 da; *Career* ret chartered engr; Pres Br Computer Soc 1981-82; *Recreations* tennis, golf, music; *Clubs* Athenaeum; *Style* - Peter Hall Esq, OBE; Brendon Cottage, Henshaw Lane, Siddington, nr Macclesfield, Cheshire (☎ Marton Heath 363)

HALL, Richard Nicholas Congreve; *Career* chm and md Hall Engineering (Holdings) Ltd; dir BRC Steel Ltd, James Jackson & Co Ltd, Press Steel Industs Ltd, Stingray Investments (Pty) Ltd, Shrewsbury Tool & Die Co Ltd, Wm Deakin & Co Ltd; *Style* - Richard Hall Esq; c/o Hall Engineering Ltd, 2 Lygon Place, SW1

HALL, Col Thomas Armitage; OBE (1966); s of Athelstan Argyle Hall; *b* 13 April 1928; *Educ* Eton; *m* 1954, Mariette, da of Sir Antony Hornby; 2 s, 4 da; *Career* Hon Col Roy Hussars (Cmdg Offr 11 Hussars 1965-66) 1974-; memb HM Bodyguard 1980-; High Sheriff Oxon 1981; *Recreations* skiing, shooting, travel; *Clubs* Guards & Cavalry; *Style* - Col Thomas Hall, OBE; Chiselhampton House, Stadhampton, Oxford (☎ 0865 890350)

HALL, Dr Trevor Henry; JP (Leeds 1959); s of H Roxby Hall, of Wakefield; *b* 28 May 1910; *Educ* Wakefield Sch, Trin Cambridge, Leeds U; *m* 1, 1937, Dorothy (d 1973), da of A Keningley, of Nostell; 1 s, 1 da; m 2, 1977, Marguerite, widow of Dr R McMorris; 1 step s, 1 step da; *Career* FSA, ptnr V Stanley Walker & Son Chartered Surveyors 1945-; FRICS, PhD; dir Huddersfield Bldg Soc 1958- (Huddersfield & Bradford BS since merger

1974); chm Legal & General Assurance Soc (N Regnl & Scottish Bds) 1978-; Pres Leeds Library 1969-; author of various books on the supernatural and Sherlock Holmes; *Style* - Dr Trevor Hall, JP; The Lodge, Selby, N Yorks (☎ 3372)

HALL-THOMPSON, Maj (Robert) Lloyd; ERD (1953), TD (1956), JP (1959); s of Col The Rt Hon S H Hall-Thompson PC, JP, DL, MP (d 1954); *b* 9 April 1920; *Educ* Campbell Coll Prep Sch, Campbell Coll Roy Sch; *m* 1948, Alison (Freda), nee Leitch; 1 s, 1 da; *Career* Maj RA 1939-46, joined Unionist Party 1938, v-pres Clifton Unionist Assoc (chm 1954-57), MP (U) Clifton 1969-73, memb (U) N Belfast NI Constitutional Convention 1975-76, dir of several companies; *Recreations* horse riding, hunting, racing, eventing, show jumping, breeding, golf, reading; *Clubs* Ulster; *Style* - Maj Lloyd Hall-Thompson ERD, TD, JP; Maymount, Ballylesson, Co Down, N Ireland

HALLAM, 1 Bishop of (RC diocese est 1980) 1980-; Rt Rev Gerald Moverley; s of William Moverley and Irene, nee Dewhirst; *b* 9 April 1922; *Educ* St Bede's G S Bradford, Ushaw Coll Durham, Angelicum U Rome; *Career* priest 1946, Aux Bp Leeds 1968-80, Domestic Prelate to HH Pope Paul VI 1965-77; JCD; *Style* - The Rt Rev Bishop Moverley; Quarters, Carsick Hill Way, Sheffield (☎ 301596)

HALLETT, Len C; *Career* md Crown House Ltd; *Style* - Len Hallett Esq; 2 Lygon Place, SW1

HALLIDAY, Ian; *Career* ch exec NEB 1980-; *Style* - Ian Halliday Esq; c/o National Enterprise Board, 12 Grosvenor gdns, SW1 (☎ 01 730 9600)

HALLIFAX, Rear-Adm David John; s of Vice-Adm Ronald Hallifax, of Shedfield Hants; *b* 3 Sept 1927; *Educ* Winchester; *m* 1962, Anne, da of Lt-Col J Blakiston Houston, of Beltrim Castle, Gortin, Co Tyrone; 2 s, 1 da; *Career* Ch Staff to CIC Fleet 1980- (RN 1945-); *Recreations* sailing, gardening; *Clubs* Roy Yacht Sqdn, Farmers, Pratt's; *Style* - Rear-Adm David Hallifax; c/o Lloyds Bank, Winchester, Hants

HALLINAN, Sir Eric; s of Edward Hallinan, of Co Cork; *b* 28 Oct 1900; *Educ* Downside, Trin Coll Dublin; *m* 1936, Monica, da of George Gallwey Waters, of Midleton House, Midleton, Co Cork; 1 s, 1 da; *Career* barr 1923; Justice of Appeal Bahamas 1966-68, Ch Justice WI 1958-61 kt 1955; *Clubs* Roy C'wlth Soc, Kildare Street & University (Dublin); *Style* - Sir Eric Hallinan; Calle Margarita Blanca 5, Pueblo Lopez, Fuen Girola, Malaga, Spain (☎ 47 19 27)

HALLINAN, Sir (Adrian) Lincoln; DL (Glam 1969); s of Sir Charles Hallinan, CBE, of Cardiff; *b* 13 Nov 1922; *Educ* Downside; *m* 1955, Mary, da of Dr Evan Parry-Evans, JP; 2 s, 2 da; *Career* barr 1950, Recorder 1972, Stipendiary Magistrate S Glam 1976; Ld Mayor Cardiff 1969-70; kt 1971; *Recreations* collecting; *Clubs* Cardiff & County; *Style* - Sir Lincoln Hallinan, DL; 63 Cathedral rd, Cardiff

HALLOWES, Odette Marie-Céline; GC (1946), MBE (1945); da of Sergeant Gaston Eugène Brailly, of Villers sous Ailly, Somme (k 1918); *b* 28 April 1912; *Educ* Convent of Ste Thérèse Amiens, and privately; *m* 1, 1931, Roy Samson; 3 da; m 2, 1947, Capt Peter Churchill, DSO; m 3, 1956, Geoffrey, s of Edward Hallowes, of Monte Carlo; *Career* late Cdr FANY; V-Pres Mil Medallists League, Women of the Year Luncheon; Pres 282 (E Ham) Air Cadet Sqdn; memb Ctee VC & GC Assoc; *Recreations* reading, conversation; *Clubs* Naval & Military, Special Forces; *Style* - Mrs Geoffrey Hallowes, GC, MBE; 8 Eriswell rd, Burwood Pk, Walton-on-Thames, Surrey

HALLSWORTH, Norris Edward; s of Norris Carl Hallsworth; *b* 9 March 1941; *Educ* Long Eaton G S; *m* 1964, Sylvia Christine, da of Leonard Smith; 2 s; *Career* CA; md Slack & Parr; various other gp dirships; *Clubs* Longcliffe Golf; *Style* - Norris Hallsworth Esq; 28 Shepshed rd, Hathern, Loughborough, Leics

HALPERN, Ralph Mark; *aet* 42 in July 1981; *Career* joined Peter Robinson

Menswear 1961, co-founder Top Shop chain (& first ch exec), ch exec Peter Robinson 1976, also Jackson the Tailor, Burton Retail and Top Man; ch exec Burton Menswear 1977, chm August 1981- memb IOD; *Style* - Ralph Halpern Esq; c/o The Burton Group Ltd, 214 Oxford st, W1 (☎ 01 636 8040)

HALPIN, William Richard Crozier; s of William Halpin, of Ford Lodge, Cavan, Eire; *b* 28 June 1912; *Educ* Rugby, CCC Cambridge; *m* 1939, Hilary, da of Col Gilbert Keighley-Bell; 1 s, 2 da; *Career* FCA; chm Albion Bottle 1975-80; *Recreations* beagling; *Clubs* Carlton; *Style* - William Halpin Esq; 11 Provost rd, NW3 (☎ 01 722 4637)

HALSBURY, 3 Earl of (UK 1898); John Anthony Hardinge Giffard; also Baron Halsbury (UK 1885) and Viscount Tiverton (UK 1898); s of 2 Earl (d 1943, s of 1 Earl, Lord Chllr in three Conservative administrations (though no great lawyer if the story of his drawing up his own will less than perfectly is true; his obituary's account of him sometimes being seen strolling to the Temple around midday carrying a novel rather than his brief is not entirely to be explained by his inhabiting a more leisured age; his tardiness in arriving at court may owe something to his descent from Robert Giffard, who c 1130 paid a warhorse to the Exchequer rather than answer a plea by a claimant, but between whom and the Giffard descendants of Osbern de Bolbec (who lived about the final quarter of the tenth century) by his marriage to Weva or Avelina (sis of Gunora, Duchess of Normandy), no definite link has been shown); *b* 4 June 1908; *Educ* Eton; *m* 1, 1930, Ismay (m dis 1936), da of Lt-Col Lord Ninian Crichton-Stuart (himself 2 s of 3 Marquess of Bute) by his w Hon Gwendolen Preston (da of 14 Viscount Gormanston); 1 s; m 2, 1936, Elizabeth, da of Maj Harry Godley, DSO, and his w Elizabeth (great niece of 3 Earl Annesley); 2 da; *Heir* s, Adam Giffard (Viscount Tiverton, but does not use title); *Career* FRS, FEng, 1 Chllr Brunel U 1966, chm Meteorological Cttee 1970-; late md NRDC & Gov BBC; Gov LSE 1959-, UMIST 1966-; *Style* - The Rt Hon Earl of Halsbury; 4 Campden House, 29 Sheffield Terrace, W8 (☎ 01 727 3035)

HALSEY, Rev Sir John Walter Brooke; 4 Bt (UK 1920); s of Sir Thomas Edgar Halsey, 3 Bt, DSO (d 1970); *b* 26 Dec 1933; *Educ* Eton, Magdalene Cambridge; *Heir* unc, William Edmund Halsey; *Career* Deacon 1961, Priest 1962, Diocese of York, Curate of Stocksbridge 1961-65, Brother in Community of the Transfiguration 1965-; *Style* - The Reverend Brother John Halsey; Community of the Transfiguration, Manse rd, Roslin, Midlothian

HALSEY, William Edmund; s of Sir Walter Johnston Halsey, 2 Bt, OBE (d 1950), and unc and hp of Rev Bro John Halsey, 4 Bt; *b* 8 Jan 1903; *m* 1931, Barbara Dorothea, da of Charles Lindsay Orr Ewing, MP (s of Sir Archibald Orr Ewing, 1 Bt, and who d 1903) and Lady Augusta Helen Elizabeth Boyle (da of 7 Earl of Glasgow and who d 1967); 1 da; *Style* - William Halsey Esq; The Knowe, Skelmorlie, Ayrshire

HALSTEAD, Ronald; CBE (1976); s of Richard Halstead, of Lancs; *b* 17 May 1927; *Educ* Lancaster Roy G S, Queens' Cambridge; *m* 1968, Yvonne (d 1978), da of Emile de Monchaux, of Australia; 2 s; *Career* chm Beecham Products 1967- (md Consumer Products 1973-); FRSC, FBIM, FInstM, FIGD; memb Cncl CBI, Ag Res Cncl; dir Otis Elevator Co (UK) 1978-, BSC 1979-; *Recreations* squash, skiing; *Clubs* Carlton, Hurlingham, Lansdowne, Roy Thames Yacht; *Style* - Ronald Halstead Esq, CBE; 37 Edwardes sq, W8 (☎ 01 603 9010)

HAMBLEDEN, 4 Viscount (UK 1891); William Herbert Smith; s of 3 Viscount (d 1948) and Lady Patricia Herbert (*see* Dowager Viscountess Hambleden); *b* 2 April 1930; *Educ* Eton; *m* 1955, Contessa Maria Carmela Attolico di Adelfia, da of Conte Bernardo Attolico, of Rome; 5 s; *Heir* s, Hon William Smith; *Style* - The Rt Hon Viscount Hambleden; The Manor House, Hambleden, Henley-on-Thames, Oxon (☎ Hambleden 335)

HAMBLEDEN, Dowager Viscountess; Lady Patricia; *née* Herbert; DCVO

(1953), JP (1961); da of 15 Earl of Pembroke and (12 Earl of) Montgomery, JP, DL (d 1960), by his w, Lady Beatrice Paget, CBE (yr da of Lord Alexander Paget and sis of 6 Marquess of Anglesey, GCVO); *b* 12 Nov 1904; *m* 1928, 3 Viscount Hambleden (d 1948, s of 2 Viscount by Lady Esther Gore, 3 da of 5 Earl of Arran); 3 s (4 Viscount, Hon Richard and Hon Philip Smith, *qqv*), 2 da (Hon Mrs Brand, Hon Mrs Townend, *qqv*); *Career* Lady-in-Waiting to HM The Queen (now HM Queen Elizabeth The Queen Mother) 1937-; *Style* - Rt Hon Dowager Viscountess Hambleden, DCVO, JP; Hill House, Ewelme, Oxon (☎ 0491 39242)

HAMBLIN, Frederick Thomas; CBE (1966); s of John Hamblin, of Kingswood, Bristol; *b* 14 Oct 1914; *Educ* Kingswood G S, Bristol U; *m* 1, Audrey, da of John Lawrence, of Chedworth Glos; 2 s, 1 da; m 2, Christa, da of Judge Ernst Schmidt, of Schloss Hilbringen, W Germany; 2 da; *Career* Co Sec Kearney & Trecker Marwin, chm ICI Switzerland 1968-70 FCIS, Freeman City of London; *Recreations* sailing, archaeology; *Clubs* Athenaeum; *Style* - Frederick Hamblin Esq, CBE; Hilbringen, Roedean Way, Brighton, Sussex (☎ 603719)

HAMBLING, Sir Herbert Hugh; 3 Bt (UK 1924); s of Sir (Herbert) Guy (Musgrave), 2 Bt (d 1966); *b* 3 Aug 1919; *Educ* Eton; *m* 1950, Ann Page, da of late Judge Hugo Edmund Oswald, of Seattle, USA; 1 s; *Heir* s, Herbert Peter Hugh; *Career* British Airways Ltd 1937-39, RAF Training and Atlantic Ferry Command 1939-46, BOAC Montreal 1948, Seattle 1950, Manager Sir Guy Hambling & Son 1956; *Style* - Sir Herbert Hambling, Bt; Rookery Park, Yoxford, Suffolk (☎ Yoxford 310); 1219 Evergreen Point rd, Bellevue, Washington 98004, USA

HAMBLING, Herbert Peter Hugh; s and h of Sir Herbert Hugh Hambling, 3 Bt; *b* 6 Sept 1953; *Style* - Herbert Hambling Esq

HAMBRO, Hon Mrs (Charlotte Clementine); *née* Soames; da of Baron Soames, GCMG, GCVO, CH, CBE, PC (Life Peer), and Hon Mary, DBE, da of late Rt Hon Sir Winston Spencer-Churchill, KG, OM, CH, TD, FRS (d 1965, s of Rt Hon Lord Randolph Spencer-Churchill, PC, JP, DL, MP, 3 s of 7 Duke of Marlborough, KG, PC; the 7 Duke's w was Lady Frances Vane, da of 3 Marquess of Londonderry, KG), by his w, Baroness Spencer-Churchill, GBE (da of Sir Henry Hozier, KCB, and Lady Henrietta Ogilvy, da of 5 Earl of Airlie, KT); *b* 17 July 1954; *m* 1973, (Alexander) Richard Hambro, 1 da - Clementine Silvia, *qv*; *Style* - The Hon Mrs Hambro; 49 Egerton Cres, SW3

HAMBRO, Clementine Silvia; da of Richard Hambro and Hon Mrs Hambro, *qqv*; *b* 1976; *Educ* Young England Kindergarten, St George's Square, Pimlico; *Career* bridesmaid to Lady Diana Spencer at her marriage to HRH The Prince of Wales 1981; *Style* - Miss Clementine Hambro; 49 Egerton Cres, SW3

HAMBRO, Jocelyn Olaf; MC (1944); s of Ronald Hambro, JP, and Winifred, 5 da of Martin Ridley-Smith (ggs of Abel Smith, MP for Nottingham, consequently cousin to Lords Bicester and Carrington) by his 2 w (also his 1 w's sis), Cecilia (da of Henry Stuart, gs of 1 Marquess of Bute); *b* 7 March 1919; *Educ* Eton, Trin Cambridge; *m* 1, 1942, Ann (d 1972), da of Rowland Muir, of Binfield; 3 s (Rupert, Richard, James m 1981 Diana Cherry, *qqv* for other details of the Hambros); m 2, 1976, Duchess of Roxburghe (Margaret, da of late Frederick McConnel; m 1, Lt-Col James Church, MC; m 2, 1954, as his 3 w, 9 Duke, who d 1974); *Career* chm Hambros Ltd 1970-, Phoenix Assur Co 1978-, The Hambros Tst, Hambros Investment Tst, HIT Securities, Hambros Diamond Investment Corpn, Hereditaments Ltd, Berkeley Hambro Property Co, Newmarket Estates & Property Co, Rosedimond Investment Tst, Waverton Property Co, Wiltons (St James's) Ltd; served Coldstream Gds WW II; *Clubs* Jockey, White's, Pratt's; *Style* - Jocelyn Hambro Esq, MC; Waverton House, Moreton-in-Marsh, Glos; 16 Victoria rd, W8 (☎ 01 937 4550/7573)

HAMBRO, Peter Charles Percival; s of Lt-Col Everard Bingham Hambro, MBE (d 1971, ggs of Baron Hambro (cr a Danish Baron 1851, and founder of the Hambros as Br bankers) by his 1 w), of Durrington House, Old Harlow, Essex; *b* 18 Jan 1945; *Educ* Eton; *m* 1968, Karen Guinevere Gould, da of Capt George Brodrick, of Dunley Manor, Whitchurch, Hants; 3 s; *Career* md Smith St Aubyn & Co Hldgs; dir City of Oxford Investment Tst; *Recreations* shooting, fishing, golf; *Clubs* Pratt's, White's, Deepdale Golf (New York); *Style* - Peter Hambro Esq; Durrington House, Old Harlow, Essex (☎ 0279 29930); 38 Sussex st, SW1 (☎ 01 828 0473)

HAMBRO, (Alexander) Richard; s of Jocelyn Hambro, MC, *qv*; *b* 1 Oct 1946; *Educ* Eton; *m* 1973, Hon Charlotte, da of Baron Soames, GCMG, GCVO, CH, CBE, PC, *qqv*; 1 da (*see* Hambro, Clementine); *Style* - Richard Hambro Esq; 49 Egerton Cres, SW3

HAMBRO, Rupert Nicholas; s of Jocelyn Hambro, MC, of Waverton House, Stow on Wold, Glos; *b* 27 June 1943; *Educ* Eton, Aix-en-Provence; *m* 1970, Mary, da of Francis Boyer; 1 s, 1 da; *Career* exec dir Hambros Bank 1974- (dir 1969-); chm Assoc of Internat Bond Dealers 1979-; *Recreations* racing, shooting; *Clubs* White's; *Style* - Rupert Hambro Esq; 5 The Boltons, SW10 (☎ 01 373 1441)

HAMBURGER, Sir Sidney Cyril; CBE (1966), JP; s of Isidore Hamburger; *b* 14 July 1914; *Educ* Salford G S; *m* 1940; 3 s; *Career* chm North Western Regional Health Authority 1973-; kt 1981 *Style* - Sir Sidney Hamburger, CBE, JP; 26 New Hall rd, Salford

HAMILL, Patrick; QPM (1979); s of late Hugh Hamill; *b* 29 April 1930; *Educ* St Patrick's H S Dumbarton; *m* 1954, Nellie; 4 s, 1 da; *Career* OStJ 1977, chief constable Strathclyde Police; *Style* - Patrick Hamill Esq, QPM; Chief Constable, Strathclyde Police, Police Headquarters, 173 Pitt st, Glasgow (☎ 041 204 2626)

HAMILTON OF DALZELL, 3 Baron (UK 1886); John d'Henin Hamilton; KCVO (1981), MC (1945), JP (Guildford 1957-); s of Maj Hon Leslie Hamilton, MVO, Coldstream Gds (ka 1914, bro of 2 Baron, KT, CVO, MC, who d 1952), by Amy, da of Col Horace Ricardo, CVO, Gren Gds, of Bramley Park, Surrey; *b* 1 May 1911; *Educ* Eton, Sandhurst; *m* 1935, Rosemary Olive, da of Hon Sir John Coke, KCVO (5 s of 2 Earl of Leicester, KG, JP, DL, by his 2 w, Hon Georgina Cavendish, da of 2 Baron Chesham), by Hon Dorothy Levy-Lawson, only child of 1 and last Viscount (and 2 Baron) Burnham, GCMG, CH; 2 s, 1 da; *Heir* s, Hon James Hamilton; *Career* Maj Coldstream Gds, served 1931-37 & 1939-45; farmer; Ld-Lt Surrey 1973- (DL 1957, V-Lt to 1973); chm Ld Chllr's Cttee Legal Aid 1972-79, Ld-in-Waiting to HM The Queen 1968-81; *Style* - Rt Hon Lord Hamilton of Dalzell KCVO MC JP, HM Lord-Lieut for Surrey; Snowdenham House, Guildford, Surrey (☎ 892002)

HAMILTON, Lord (Claud) Anthony; s of 4 Duke of Abercorn (d 1979) and Dowager Duchess of Hamilton, DCVO, *qv*; *b* 8 July 1939; *Educ* Eton; *Career* 2 Lt Irish Gds; *Style* - Lord Anthony Hamilton; Barons Court, Omagh, Co Tyrone

HAMILTON, Andrew Caradoc; s and h of Sir (Robert Charles) Richard Caradoc Hamilton, 9 Bt; *b* 23 Sept 1953; *Style* - Andrew Hamilton Esq

HAMILTON, Hon Archibald Gavin; MP (C) Epsom & Ewell 1978-; 2 s of 3 Baron Hamilton of Dalzell, MC, JP, by his w Rosemary (da of Hon Sir John Spencer Coke, KCVO, 5 s of 2 Earl of Leicester, KG, JP, DL, by His Lordship's 2 w Hon Georgina Cavendish, da of 2 Baron Chesham; Sir John's w was Hon Dorothy Levy-Lawson, only child of 1 and last Viscount (and 2 Baron) Burnham, GCMG, CH); *b* 30 Dec 1941; *Educ* Eton; *m* 1968, Anne, da of late Cdr Trevelyan Napier, DSC, RN; 3 da; *Career* md Br Quadruplex Ltd 1975-, Cncllr Kensington & Chelsea 1968-71; PPS to Sec of State Energy 1979-; *Style* - The Hon Archibald Hamilton MP; Daneshole, Bramley, Surrey; 7 Portland rd, W11

HAMILTON, Adrian Walter; QC (1973); s of Walter George Norrell Hamilton (d 1957); *b* 11 March 1923; *Educ* Highgate Sch and Balliol Coll Oxford (MA); *m* 1966, Jill Margaret Beverlie, da of Stanley Richard Brimblecombe, of Eastbourne; 2 da; *Career* Lt RNVR (Atlantic, Mediterranean, English Channel); barrister 1949, Lincoln's Inn and Middle Temple, recorder of the Crown Court 1974, memb Senate of Inns of Court and the Bar 1976-, tres 1979-, memb cncl of Legal Educn 1977-, Inspr Peek Foods Ltd 1977-, bencher of Lincoln's Inn 1979; *Recreations* golf, sailing and family; *Clubs* Garrick *Style* - Adrian Hamilton Esq QC; 7 King's Bench Walk, Temple, EC4 (☎ 01 353 3684)

HAMILTON, Lady Claud David; Genesta Mary; da of Cuthbert Heath, of Anstie Grange, Holmwood, Surrey; *m* 1, Arthur McNeill Farquhar; m 2, Capt Edward Caswell Long; m 3, 1946, Lord Claud David Hamilton (d 1968), 2 s of 3 Duke of Abercorn, KG, KP, PC; *Style* - Lady Claud Hamilton; c/o Lloyds Bank, 39 Old Bond st, W1

HAMILTON, Lady Claud Nigel; Violet Ruby; da of James Ashton, of London; *m* 1, Lt-Cdr Keith Newall, RN (ret); m 2, 1933, Lord Claud Nigel Hamilton, GCVO, CMG, DSO (d 1975), 7 s of 2 Duke of Abercorn, KG, CB, PC, and Lady Mary Curzon (4 da of 1 Earl Howe); *Style* - Lady Claud Hamilton; 8 Russell Court, St James's, SW1 (☎ Whitehall 1152)

HAMILTON, Sir (Charles) Denis; DSO (1944), TD (1976); s of Charles Henry Hamilton; *b* 6 Dec 1918; *Educ* Middlesbrough H S; *m* 1939, Olive, da of Thomas Hedley Wanless; 4 s (Michael Denis m 1, 1963, Jacqueline Sprot, m 2, 1980, Leonor Holazo; Charles Nigel m 1, 1966, Hannah Pfeifer (d 1972), m 2, 1975, Outi Palovesi; Adrian Donald m 1969 Sandra Boler; John Andrew m 1979 Linda Seaward); *Career* kt 1976; chm Br Museum Publications Ltd, Nat Cncl T'ning Journalists 1957, Pres C'wlth Press Union 1981, 1 Pres Internat Press Inst 1978-, Governor Br Inst of Florence 1974-; ed Sunday Times 1961-67, ed-in-chief Times Newspapers 1967-81; chm Times Newspapers Hldgs 1981-, Reuters 1979-; dir- Thomson Br Hldgs, Thomson Orgn, Evening Gazette Ltd, Newcastle Chronicle & Journal Ltd; Tstee Br Museum; memb Br Library Bd; *Recreations* fruit farming; *Clubs* Garrick, RAC; *Style* - Sir Denis Hamilton DSO TD; Weston House, Nutbourne, Chichester, W Sussex (☎ 02434 3351); 25 Roebuck House, Stag Place, Palace st, SW1 (☎ 01 828 0410)

HAMILTON, Sir Edward Sydney; 7 Bt (GB 1776), of Marlborough House, Hampshire, and 5 Bt (UK 1819), of Trebinshun House, Brecknockshire; s of Sir (Thomas) Sydney (Percival) Hamilton, 6 and 4 Bt (d 1966); *b* 14 April 1925 *Educ* Canford Sch; *Heir* none; *Career* RE 1943-47, 1 Royal Sussex Home Guard 1953-56; *Style* - Sir Edward Hamilton, Bt; The Cottage, East Lavant, nr Chichester, West Sussex (☎ Chichester 527414)

HAMILTON, Hon Evelyn William James; s of 3 Baron Holm Patrick; *b* 1961; *Style* - The Hon Evelyn Hamilton

HAMILTON, Brig Hugh Gray Wybrants; CBE (1964, MBE 1945), DL (Northants 1977); s of Lt-Col Henry Wybrants Hamilton (d 1946); *b* 16 May 1918; *Educ* Wellington, RMA Woolwich, Peterhouse Cambridge; *m* 1944, Claire, da of Henry Buxton (d 1965); 2 da; *Career* served with RE 1938-68, gen man Corby Devpt Corpn 1968-80; *Recreations* riding, sailing, DIY; *Style* - Brig Hugh Hamilton, CBE, DL; Covert House, E Haddon, Northants (☎ 488)

HAMILTON, Hon Hans James David; s and h of 3 Baron Holm Patrick; *b* 15 March 1955; *Style* - The Hon Hans Hamilton

HAMILTON, Hon Ion Henry James; s of 3 Baron Holm Patrick; *b* 1956; *Style* - The Hon Ion Hamilton

HAMILTON, Adm Sir John (Graham); GBE (1966, KBE 1963, CBE 1958), CB (1960); s of Col Ernest Graham Hamilton, CMG, DSO, MC (d 1950); *b* 12 July 1910; *Educ* R N Coll Dartmouth; *m* 1938, Dorothy Nina, da of Col John Emer

Turner, CMG, DSO (d 1955), of Sandhurst, Berks; *Career* joined RN 1924, served 1939-45 War, Capt 1949; dep dir Radio Equipment 1950-51, cmd 5 Destroyer Sqdn 1952-53, dir of Naval Ordnance 1954-56, cmd HMS 'Newfoundland' 1956-58, Rear-Adm 1958, Naval Sec to 1 Lord of the Admiralty 1958-60, Vice-Adm 1961, flag offr Air (Home) 1962-63, flag offr Naval Air Command 1963-64, Adm 1964, C-in-C Mediterranean and Allied Forces 1964-67, ret 1967; nat pres Inst of Marketing 1972-75; *Style* - Adm Sir John Hamilton, GBE, CB; Chapel Barn, Abbotsbury, Dorset (☎ Abbotsbury 507)

HAMILTON, Marquess of; James Harold Charles Hamilton; s and h of 5 Duke of Abercorn; *b* 19 Aug 1969; *Heir* bro, Lord Nicholas Hamilton; *Style* - Marquess of Hamilton

HAMILTON, Hon James Leslie; s and h of 3 Baron Hamilton of Dalzell, MC, JP; *b* 11 Feb 1938; *Educ* Eton; *m* 1967, Corinna, da of Sir Pierson John Dixon, GCMG, CB (d 1965), and sis of Piers Dixon, *qv*; 4 s (inc twins); *Career* 2 Lt Coldstream Gds 1957-58; *Style* - The Hon James Hamilton; 19 St Petersburgh Place, W2 (☎ 01 229 6033)

HAMILTON, Lord Nicholas Edward Claud; s of 5 Duke of Abercorn; hp to bro, Marquess of Hamilton; *b* 1979; *Style* - Lord Nicholas Hamilton

HAMILTON, Peter B; father d 1944; *b* 17 Oct 1928; *Educ* Bedford Sch, St Andrews U, Harvard (MBA); *m* 1953, Gwendolen Clark; 1 s, 1 da; *Career* gp ch exec APV Hldgs 1980-, chm & ch exec GKN Engrg & Construction Servs 1978-79, Firth Cleveland 1977-79; *Recreations* sailing (sloop- 'Moorea II'); *Clubs* Roy Southampton Yacht; *Style* - Peter Hamilton Esq; 31 Chantrey View rd, Guildford, Surrey (☎ 0483 65318)

HAMILTON, Sir Patrick George; 2 Bt (UK 1937), of Ilford, Co Essex; s of Maj Sir (Collingwood) George Clements Hamilton, 1 Bt (d 1947); *b* 17 Nov 1908; *Educ* Eton, Trin Oxford; *m* 1941, Winifred Mary (Pix) Stone, CBE, da of late Hammond B Jenkins, of Maddings, Hadstock; *Heir* none; *Career* md and later chm Tyresoles Ltd 1934-53, dir Simon Engineering Ltd 1937-78, Renold Ltd 1952-78, Lloyds Bank Ltd 1953-79, chm Expanded Metal Co Ltd 1955-78, Possum Controls Ltd, Norbruy Ltd; *Clubs* Carlton; *Style* - Sir Patrick Hamilton, Bt; Maddings, Hadstock, nr Linton, Cambs; 39 Hyde Park Gate, SW7 (☎ 01 581 3990)

HAMILTON, Robert Abraham; CBE (1971); s of late I Hamilton; *b* 5 Feb 1909; *Educ* Royal Belfast Academical Inst, Queen's Univ Belfast, Fitzwilliam Hall Cambridge; *m* 1935, Caroline Dorothea, nee Adams; 2 s; *Career* pro chancellor Queen's U 1980-, dir- Central Agric Control Board ICI Ltd 1944-58, Billingham Div ICI Ltd 1958-64, W & HM Goulding Ltd 1964-71, Pharmaceutical Div ICI Ltd 1955-60, Scottish Agric Industries Ltd 1959-64, dep chm Agric Div ICI Ltd 1964-71, chm- Plant Protection Ltd, Richardsons Fertilisers Ltd, Ulster Fertilisers Ltd 1964-71, Northern Ireland Agric Trust 1967-74, NI Tourist Board 1970-75, Pigs Marketing Board Investment Company 1971-77, Unipork Ltd 1976-78, pres Société Pour La Protection de L'Agriculture (Paris) 1967-71; *Recreations* gardening, travelling; *Clubs* Ulster, Farmers'; *Style* - Robert Hamilton Esq, CBE; Glebe Way, 112 Gateside rd, Ballywillan, Co Antrim (☎ Portrush 823639)

HAMILTON, Sir (Robert Charles) Richard Caradoc; 9 Bt (NS 1646), of Silvertonhill, Lanarkshire; s of Sir Robert Hamilton, 8 Bt (d 1959), by Irene, 2 da of Sir Charles Mordaunt, 10 Bt; *b* 8 Sept 1911; *Educ* Charterhouse, St Peter's Coll Oxford; *m* 1952, Elizabeth Vidal, da of Sir William Pell Barton, KCIE, CSI, formerly of Lower Lodge, Ardingly; 1 s, 3 da; *Heir* s, Andrew Hamilton; *Career* schoolmaster Ardingly Coll 1946-1960; estate owner; chm Warwicks Branch CLA; memb Gen Cncl Tennis & Rackets Assoc; *Recreations* real tennis; *Style* - Sir Richard Hamilton, Bt; The Old Rectory, Walton, Warwick (☎ Stratford-on-Avon 840460)

HAMILTON AND BRANDON, 15 and 12 Duke of (S 1643, GB 1711); Angus Alan Douglas Douglas-Hamilton; also Earl of Arran (S 1389), Marquess of Douglas, Lord Abernethy and Jedburgh Forest (both S 1633), Marquess of Clydesdale, Earl of Arran and Cambridge, Lord Aven and Innerdale (all S 1643), Earl of Lanark, Lord Machansire and Polmont (both S 1661), Baron Dutton (GB 1711), Premier Duke in the Peerage of Scotland, hereditary Keeper of Holyrood House; s of 14 & 11 Duke of Hamilton and Brandon, KT, GCVO, AFC, PC (d 1973), and Elizabeth, Duchess of Hamilton and Brandon, *qv*; *b* 13 Sept 1938; *Educ* Eton, Balliol Oxford; *m* 1972, Sarah, da of Sir Walter Scott, 4 Bt; 1 s, 2 da; *Heir* s, Marquess of Douglas and Clydesdale; *Career* Fl Lt RAF to 1967, has sr commercial pilot's license, test pilot Scottish Aviation 1971-72; KStJ & Prior Order of St John in Scotland 1975-, memb Roy Co Archers (Queen's Bodyguard for Scotland); *Style* - His Grace The Duke of Hamilton and Brandon; Lennoxlove, Haddington, E Lothian; 8 Eccleston Mews, SW1 (☎ 01 235 7213)

HAMILTON AND BRANDON, Elizabeth, Duchess of; Lady Elizabeth Ivy; *née* Percy; da of 8 Duke of Northumberland, KG, CBE, MVO; *b* 25 May 1916; *m* 1937, 14 Duke of Hamilton and (11 of) Brandon, KT, GCVO, AFC, PC (d 1973); 5 s (including 15 Duke); *Style* - Her Grace Elizabeth, Duchess of Hamilton and Brandon; North Port, Lennoxlove, Haddington, E Lothian (☎ 2478)

HAMILTON STUBBER, Lt-Col John Henry; DL (1971); s of Maj Robert Hamilton Stubber, DSO, of Beechill, Co Armagh (d 1963); *b* 5 Sept 1921; *Educ* Eton and Trinity Coll Cambridge; *m* 1953, Fiona Patricia, da of Capt Geoffrey W Breitmeyer, of Didmarton Glos (d 1952); 4 s; *Career* Coldstream Gds 1941, served 1941-45 (France and Germany, despatches 1945), Capt 1944, ret 1948; Maj Ulster Defence Regt 1970, ret Hon Brevet Lt-Col 1978; former JP Glos, High Sherriff Co Tyrone 1972, chm Dungannon District Cncl 1973-79, Ld-Lt Co Tyrone 1979-; *Clubs* Turf, Ulster & MCC; *Style* - Lt-Col John Hamilton Stubber, HM Lord-Lieut for Co Tyrone; Aughentaine, Fivemiletown, Co Tyrone, N Ireland (☎ 036 552 271)

HAMILTON-DALRYMPLE, Dowager Lady; Ann Dorothea; da of late Augustus Thorne, JP, DL; *m* 1919, Sir Hew Clifford Hamilton-Dalrymple, 9 Bt (d 1959); *Style* - Dowager Lady Hamilton-Dalrymple; Blackdykes, N Berwick, E Lothian

HAMILTON-DALRYMPLE, Lady Anne-Louise Mary; *née* Keppel; da of 9 Earl of Albemarle, MC, by his 2 w, Dame Diana Grove, DBE (*see* Countess of Albemarle); *b* 17 March 1932; *m* 1954, Maj Sir Hew Fleetwood Hamilton-Dalrymple, 10 Bt, CVO; 4 s; *Style* - Lady Anne - Louise Hamilton - Dalrymple; Leuchie, N Berwick, E Lothian (☎ 2903)

HAMILTON-DALRYMPLE, Sir Hew Fleetwood; 10 Bt (NS 1698), of North Berwick, Haddingtonshire, CVO (1974), DL (E Lothian 1964); s of Sir Hew Clifford Hamilton-Dalrymple, 9 Bt (d 1959); *b* 9 April 1926; *Educ* Ampleforth; *m* 1954, Lady Anne-Louise Mary, *qv*, nee Keppel, da of 9 Earl of Albemarle; 4 s; *Heir* s, Hew Richard Hamilton-Dalrymple; *Career* Maj (ret) Gren Gds, Ensign and Adjt of Queen's Body Guard for Scotland (Roy Co of Archers), dir Scottish & Newcastle Breweries, Scottish American Investment Co, Stewart Unit Trust Managers, Vice-Lt E Lothian 1973; *Clubs* Cavalry and Guards; *Style* - Sir Hew Hamilton-Dalrymple Bt CVO, HM Vice-Lt for E Lothian; Leuchie, N Berwick, E Lothian (☎ N Berwick 2903)

HAMILTON-DALRYMPLE, Hew Richard; s and h of Sir Hew Hamilton-Dalrymple, 10 Bt, CVO; *b* 3 Sept 1955; *Educ* Ampleforth, CCC Oxford; *Style* - Hew Hamilton-Dalrymple Esq

HAMILTON-MEIKLE, Capt Evelyn Francis; CBE (1969, MBE 1942); s of Col James Hamilton-Meikle, DSO, JP, (d 1941); *b* 18 July 1917; *Educ* Hurst Grange, Stirling and RNC Dartmouth; *m* 1940, Patricia Mary, da of Lt-Cdr John Abney Hall, RN, of Headley, Hants; 1 s, 1 da; *Career* entered RN 1931; cmd coastal craft 1939-44, Channel and N Sea 1939-42, Far East 1943-44, N Sea 1944-45; HM Ships 'Melbreak' 1945, 'Whirlwind' 1950, 'Largo

Bay' 1951, 'Pomona' 1954, 'Albert' 1956-57, 'Decoy' 1960-62, 'Terror' 1962-64, 'Lion' 1964-66; NA to Sec 1966-70; ret as Capt 1970; memb of Queen's Bodyguard for Scotland (Roy Co of Archers); *Recreations* shooting, stalking and sailing; *Style* - Capt Evelyn Hamilton-Meikle CBE RN; Nether Kinellan, Strathpeffer, Ross (☎ 384)

HAMILTON-RUSSELL, Hon Gustavus Michael Stucley; s and h of 10 Viscount Boyne, JP, DL; *b* 27 May 1965; *Style* - The Hon Gustavus Hamilton-Russell

HAMILTON-RUSSELL, Hon Lucy Jane; da of 10 Viscount Boyne, JP, DL; *b* 13 Sept 1961; *Style* - The Hon Lucy Hamilton-Russell

HAMILTON-RUSSELL, Hon Mrs (Pamela Penelope); *née* Cayzer; da of 1 Baron Rotherwick, JP, DL; *b* 1912; *m* 1939, Brig Hon Richard Hamilton-Russell, DSO, MVO, DL, *qv*; *Style* - The Hon Mrs Hamilton-Russell; Normanby House, Sinnington, York

HAMILTON-RUSSELL, Hon Richard Gustavus; DSO (1943) and Bar (1944), MVO (4 Class 1977), DL (N Yorks 1973); 2 s of 9 Viscount Boyne, JP, DL; *b* 4 Feb 1909; *Educ* Eton, Sandhurst; *m* 1939, Hon Pamela Cayzer, da of 1 Baron Rotherwick; 2 s (Brian, b 1940, m 1967 Lea Wild, m dis 1981; Richard, b 1943, m 1965 Prudence Pockney), 1 da (Veronica, b 1949, m 1971 Nicholas Jones); *Career* served WW II N Africa & Italy; Brig late 17/21 Lancers (Col 1957-65); memb HM's Body Guard of Hon Corps of Gentlemen at Arms 1956- (Standard Bearer 1977); High Sheriff Yorks 1968; *Clubs* Cavalry & Guards; *Style* - Brig Hon Richard Hamilton-Russell, DSO*, MVO, DL; Normanby House, Sinnington, York (☎ Kirby Moorside 31483)

HAMILTON-RUSSELL, Hon Sara Emma; da of 10 Viscount Boyne, JP, DL; *b* 15 July 1959; *Style* - The Hon Sara Hamilton-Russell

HAMILTON-SMITH, Hon Timothy; s of late 2 Baron Colwyn; *b* 1944; *Educ* Cheltenham, Oxford U (MA); *m* 1967, Carolyn, nee Hodge; 2 da; *Style* - The Hon Timothy Hamilton-Smith; 45 Third av, Claremont 7700, S Africa

HAMILTON-TEMPLE-BLACKWOOD, Lady Perdita - see Blackwood

HAMLYN, Paul Bertrand Wolfgang; s of Prof Richard Hamburger; *b* 12 Feb 1926; *Educ* St Christopher's Sch Letchworth; *m* 1, 1952, Eileen (m dis 1969), da of Col Richard Watson; 1 s, 1 da; m 2, 1970, Mrs Helen Guest; *Career* publisher; fndr Hamlyn Publishing Gp, fndr & chm Octopus Publishing Gp 1971; Mandarin Publishers (Hong Kong) 1971; dir News International 1970-, TV-AM Ltd 1981-; memb cncl ICA 1977-; *Style* - Paul Hamlyn Esq; Edgeworth Manor, Edgeworth, nr Stroud, Glos (☎ 028 582 494); 64 Old Church st, SW3 (☎ 01 352 8369)

HAMMICK, Dowager Lady; Mary Adeliza; da of late Lt-Col Henry Welch-Thornton; *m* 1925, as his 2 wife, Sir George Frederick Hammick, 4 Bt (d 1964); *Style* - Dowager Lady Hammick

HAMMICK, Paul St Vincent; s and h of Sir Stephen George Hammick, 5 Bt; *b* 1 Jan 1955; *Style* - Paul Hammick Esq

HAMMICK, Sir Stephen George; 5 Bt (UK 1834); s of Sir George Frederick Hammick, 4 Bt (d 1964); *b* 27 Dec 1926; *Educ* Stowe; *m* 1953, Gillian Elizabeth, da of late Maj Pierre Elliot Inchbald, MC; 2 s, 1 da; *Heir* s, Paul St Vincent Hammick; *Career* RN as Rating (hostilities only) 1944-48, RAC Cirencester 1949-50, MFH Cattistock Hunt 1961 and 1962, CC Dorset 1958; farmer with 450 acres; High Sheriff Dorset 1981; *Style* - Sir Stephen Hammick, Bt; Badgers, Wraxall, Dorchester, Dorset (☎ Evershot 343)

HAMMOND, Catherine Elizabeth; CBE (1950); da of Frank Ernest Rauleigh Eddolls; *b* 22 Dec 1909; *Educ* Lassington House Highworth, Chesterville Sch Cirencester; *m* 1, 1930, Albert Edward Haynes (decd); 1 s, 1 da; m 2, 1949,

Aldwyn Hammond (d 1958); *Career* Col WRAC, dep dir HQ Eastern Command 1947-50, Hon Col 54 (E Anglian) Div/Dist WRAC (TA) 1964-68, Town Mayor Highworth 1979-81, chm Highworth Branch RNLI 1971-, chm WRAC Assoc Cncl 1966-70; *Recreations* racing, hockey; *Style* - Mrs Aldwyn Hammond CBE; Red Down, Highworth, Wilts (☎ 0793 762331)

HAMMOND-MAUDE, Hon Mrs (Sonia Mary); *née* Peake; da of 1 Viscount Ingleby (d 1966); *b* 1924; *m* 1, 1946 (m dis 1958), 12 Marquess of Tweeddale, GC (d 1979); m 2, 1966, Maj Michael William Vernon Hammond-Maude, JP, 5 Roy Inniskilling Dragoon Gds (ret); *Style* - The Hon Mrs Hammond-Maude; Mitton Cottage, Arncliffe, Skipton, N Yorks

HAMPDEN, 6 Viscount (UK 1884); Anthony David Brand; s of 5 Viscount Hampden (d 1975) and Hon Imogen Rhys, da of 7 Baron Dynevor; *b* 7 May 1937; *Educ* Eton; *m* 1969, Cara Fiona, da of Capt Claud Proby, 2 s of Sir Richard Proby, 1 Bt, MC, JP, DL; 2 s, 1 da; *Heir* s, Hon Francis Brand; *Clubs* White's; *Style* - The Rt Hon The Viscount Hampden; Glynde Place, Glynde, Lewes, Sussex (☎ 079 159 337)

HAMPDEN, Imogen, Viscountess; Hon Imogen Alice; *née* Rhys; da of late 7 Baron Dynevor and Lady Margaret Child-Villiers, da of 7 Earl of Jersey; *b* 1903; *m* 1936, 5 Viscount Hampden (d 1975); 1 s (6 Viscount), 2 da (Hon Mrs Hodgson, Hon Mrs Chetwode); *Style* - The Rt Hon Imogen, Viscountess Hampden; Trevor House, Glynde, Lewes, Sussex

HAMPDEN, Leila Viscountess - Leila Emily; da of Lt-Col Frank Seely, JP, DL (d 1928, 3 s of Sir Charles Seely, 1 Bt), of Ramsdale Park, Notts; *b* 1900; *m* 1923, 4 Viscount Hampden, CMG (d 1965); 4 da (Lady Dacre, w of Hon William Douglas-Home; Hon Mrs Ogilvie Thompson; other 2 decd); *Style* - The Rt Hon Leila, Viscountess Hampden; Mill Court, Alton, Hants (☎ Bentley 3125)

HAMPSHIRE, Lady; Eve; *née* Rowell; *m* 1956, Sir Peter Hampshire, KCMG, sometime High Commissioner to Trinidad & Tobago (d 1981); *Style* - Lady Hampshire; Old School House, Risby, Bury St Edmunds, Suffolk (☎ 810245)

HAMPSHIRE, Susan; da of late G K Hampshire; *b* 12 May 1942; *Educ* Hampshire Sch Knightsbridge London; *m* 1967 (m dis 1974), Pierre Julian Granier-Deferre; 1 s (1 da decd); *Career* actress; The Forsyte Saga - Emmy Award for Best Actress 1970; The First Churchills - Emmy Award for Best Actress 1971; Vanity Fair - Emmy Award Best Actress 1973; *Recreations* writing, history, gardening, walking; *Style* - Miss Susan Hampshire

HAMPTON, 6 Baron (UK 1874); Sir Richard Humphrey Russell Pakington; 6 Bt (UK 1846); s of 5 Baron Hampton, OBE, FRIBA (d 1974), by his w Grace, da of Rt Hon Sir Albert Spicer, 1 Bt; *b* 25 May 1925; *Educ* Eton, Balliol Oxford; *m* 1958, Jane, da of Thomas Arnott, OBE, TD, MB, ChB; 1 s, 2 da; *Heir* s, Hon John Pakington; *Career* served RNVR WW II Sub-Lt; in advertising to 1958, CPRE Worcs 1958-71, CA with Tansley Witt & Co 1971-73; *Style* - The Rt Hon Lord Hampton; Palace Farmhouse, Upton-on-Severn, Worcs (☎ 2512)

HAMPTON, Kenneth Brian; s of Eric James Hampton (d 1931); *b* 13 Mar 1926; *Educ* St Christopher Sch Letchworth, St Catharine's Coll Cambridge; *m* 1951, Kathleen Ann Graham, nee Murray; *Career* Capt Oxf & Bucks Lt Infty (BAOR), chm PA International Management Consultants Ltd 1981- (joined 1958, dir personnel services gp 1976-79, md and int ch exec 1979-); *Recreations* sailing, opera; *Clubs* Royal Thames YC, Itchenor SC; *Style* - Kenneth Hampton Esq; Fairway, Itchenor Green, Chichester, West Sussex (☎ 0243 512 410); 34 Sloane Court West, SW3 (☎ 01 730 1815)

HAMYLTON JONES, Keith; CMG (1979); s of G Jones, of Fairholm, Sussex; *b* 12 Oct 1924; *Educ* St Paul's, Balliol Coll Oxford; *m* 1953, Eira, da of B Morgan; 1 da; *Career* Capt HM Welsh Gds (Italy, Germany and S France), HM Foreign Serv 1949, Warsaw, Lisbon, Manila, Montevideo, Rangoon; HM Consul-Gen to

Katanga 1970-72, Ambassador to Costa Rica 1974-79, Honduras 1975-78, Nicaragua 1976-79; *Recreations* reading and writing (pen-name Peter Myllent); *Clubs* Chelsea Arts; *Style* - Keith Hamylton Jones Esq, CMG; Morval House, Morval, nr Looe, Cornwall (☎ Looe 2342)

HANBURY, Lt-Col Christopher Lionel; MBE (1946), TD (1943), DL (1956); s of Col Lionel Henry Hanbury, CMG, VD (d 1954); *b* 6 March 1905; *Educ* Eton and Ch Ch Oxford; *m* 1932, Lettice Mary (d 1980), da of Arthur Finch Charrington (d 1922); 2 s, 1 da; *Career* served 1939-45 with Roy Bucks Yeo (France, India and Burma), GSO (1) GHQ India, Maj 1940, JP (1956) Bucks, High Sherrif 1954; *Recreations* field sports and bird watching; *Style* - Lt-Col Christopher Hanbury, MBE, TD, JP, DL; Juniper Hill, Burnham, Bucks (☎ Burnham 3652)

HANBURY-TRACY-DOMVILE, Claud Edward Frederick; TD; s of late Maj Eric Thomas Henry Hanbury-Tracy, OBE (gs of 2 Baron Sudeley); assumed by deed poll 1961 additional surname of Domvile; hp of kinsman, 7 Baron; *b* 11 Jan 1904; *Educ* Eton, Trin Cambridge; *m* 1, 1927 (m dis 1948), Veronica Mary, da of late Cyril Grant Cunard (gs of 1 Bt); 2 s, 1 da; m 2, 1954, Marcella Elizabeth, da of late Canon J Willis-Price; *Career* ARICS; Maj RA (TA); *Style* - Claud Hanbury-Tracy-Domvile Esq, TD; c/o Barclays Bank, 16 Whitehall, SW1

HANCOCK, John Stuart; s of W J S Hancock; *b* 8 June 1941; *Educ* Dynevor Sch Swansea, Birmingham U; *m* 1977, Marjorie Elizabeth; *Career* chartered accountant, fin dir T T Pascoe Ltd; *Recreations* travel, walking, gardening; *Style* - John Hancock Esq; Somercombe House, Higher Lane, Langland, Swansea

HANCOCK, Maj-Gen Michael Stephen; CB (1972), MBE (1953); s of Rev William Hancock (d 1926); *b* 19 July 1917; *Educ* Marlborough, RMA Woolwich; *m* 1941, Constance, da of Brig-Gen Robert Ovens, CMG, of Aughnagaddy House, Ramelton, Co Donegal; 1 s, 1 da; *Career* 1970-72 Vice QMG, Col Cmdt Roy Signals 1970-77, chm Combined Cadet Force Assoc 1972-, Planning Inspector DOE 1972-; *Style* - Maj-Gen Michael Hancock, CB, MBE; Brakey Hill, Godstone, Surrey (☎ 842273)

HANCOCK, Ronald Philip; s of Philip Henry Hancock (d 1953); *b* 9 Aug 1921; *Educ* Shrewsbury House, Epsom Coll; *m* 1958, Stella Florence, da of Arthur Howard Mathias, CBE (d 1970); 2 s, 1 da; *Career* Lt RNVR, memb Lloyd's, International Insurance Consultant, farmer, Freeman of the City of London, memb of Worshipful Co of Carmen, dir De Falbe Halsey & Co (Holdings) Ltd 1972-74, chm European Risk Management Ltd 1972-77, chm A R M International Ltd 1972-, dir- International Risk Management Ltd 1972-77, American Risk Management Inc (USA) 1972-77, Common Bros Insurance Services Ltd 1973-, Medical Insurance Agency Ltd 1974-; *Recreations* ocean racing and cruising, hunting, horse driving trials; *Clubs* Royal Thames, Lloyd's Yacht; *Style* - Ronald Hancock Esq; Hillside Farm, Shere rd, West Horsley, Surrey (☎ 04865 2098)

HANDCOCK, Clifford Frederick; s of late Henry Handcock and hp of cous, 8 Baron Castlemaine; *b* 3 Oct 1896; *m* 1928, Margaret, nee Nicholls (d 1954); 3 s; *Style* - Clifford Handcock Esq

HANDCOCK, John Eric; s of late Eric George Handcock; *b* 7 Oct 1930; *Educ* Aldenham Sch, King's Coll London U; *m* 1956, Joan Margaret, da of Wilfred Joseph Bigg, CMG; 2 s, 2 da; *Career* solicitor, senior ptnr Lovegrove & Durant 1966-, pres Berks, Bucks & Oxon Incorporated Law Society 1979-80, dep captain lay stewards St George's Chapel Windsor Castle 1977-81; *Recreations* history, travel, wine, books; *Clubs* Law Society; *Style* - John Handcock Esq; Red Deer House, Kingswood Rise, Englefield Green, Surrey (☎ Egham 34289)

HANDFORD, John; s of John Handford; *b* 8 May 1905; *m* 1929, Gladys; *Career* chm J Handford & Son (Manchester),

Milford Mutual Facilities 1949-; *Recreations* bowls; *Style* - John Handford Esq; 303 Stockport rd, Rose Hill, Marple, Cheshire (☎ 061 427 2734)

HANEBECK, F G; *Career* md of Agemaspark Ltd, Winner of Queen's Award for Export Achievement 1979; *Style* -F G Hanebeck Esq; Agesmaspark Ltd, Lincoln rd, Cressex Industrial Estate, High Wycombe, Bucks

HANHAM, Sir Michael William; 12 Bt (E 1667), of Wimborne, Dorsetshire, DFC (1944); s of Patrick Hanham (3 s of Col Phelips Hanham, bro of Sir John Hanham, 9 Bt, by his w Gertrude, da of Lt-Col Patrick Paget, 3 s of Hon Sir Edward Paget, GCB, bro of 1 Marquess of Anglesey, by Sir Edward's 2 w Lady Harriet Legge, da of 3 Earl of Dartmouth); suc kinsman, Sir Henry Hanham, 11 Bt, 1973; *b* 31 Oct 1922; *Educ* Winchester; *m* 1945, Margaret, da of Wing Cdr Harold Thomas; 1 s, 1 da; *Heir* s, William Hanham; *Career* Flying Offr RAF Pathfinder Force 1944-45, Actg Fl Lt India 1946; with BOAC 1947-61; own garden furniture workshop 1963-74; running family estate at Wimborne 1974-; *Clubs* Pathfinder; *Style* - Sir Michael Hanham, Bt, DFC; Deans Court, Wimborne, Dorset

HANHAM, William John Edward; s and h of Sir Michael Hanham, 12 Bt, DFC; *b* 4 Sept 1957; *Educ* Winchester; *Style* - William Hanham Esq,

HANKEY, 2 Baron (UK 1939); Robert Maurice Alers Hankey; KCMG (1955, CMG 1947), KCVO (1956); s of 1 Baron Hankey, GCB, GCMG, GCVO, PC (d 1963); *b* 4 July 1905; *Educ* Rugby, New Coll Oxford; *m* 1, 1930, Frances (d 1957), da of Walter Stuart-Menteth (4 s of Sir James Stuart-Menteth, 4 Bt, by Sir James's 1 w, Frances, da of Gen Sir James Sleigh, KCB); 2 s, 2 da; m 2, 1962, Joanna, da of Rev James Johnston Wright; *Heir* s, Hon Donald Hankey; *Career* FO 1927-65, ending as UK Rep OECD 1962-65; Pres Anglo Swedish Soc; V-Pres European Inst Business Admin Fontainebleau 1962-; dir Alliance Bldg Soc; *Recreations* reading, skiing, tennis, golf; *Clubs* Roy C'wlth Soc; *Style* - The Rt Hon Lord Hankey KCMG KCVO; Hethe House, Cowden, Edenbridge, Kent (☎ 034286 538)

HANKEY, Hon Alexander Maurice Alers; s of 2 Baron Hankey, KCMG, KCVO; *b* 18 Aug 1947; *Educ* Rugy, Trin Cambridge, MIT; *m* 1970, Deborah, nee Benson; *Style* - The Hon Alexander Hankey; Hethe House, Cowden, Kent

HANKEY, Hon Christopher Alers; OBE (1958); s of 1 Baron Hankey, GCB, GCMG, GCVO, PC (d 1963); *b* 1911; *Educ* Rugby, Oxford U and London U; *m* 1, 1945, Prudence May (m dis 1957), da of Keith Brodribb; 1 da; m 2, 1958, Helen Christine, da of late Alexander John Cassavetti; 1 s; *Career* late Maj RM; Principal Minister of Overseas Development 1964-72; *Style* - The Hon Christopher Hankey OBE; New Cottage, French st, nr Westerham, Kent

HANKEY, Hon Donald Robin Alers; s of 2 Baron Hankey, KCMG, KCVO; *b* 12 June 1938; *Educ* Rugby, UCL; *m* 1963, Margaretha Thorndahl (m dis 1974); m 2, 1974, Eileen Désirée, da of Maj-Gen Stuart Hedley Molesworth Battye, CB; 2 da; *Style* - The Hon Donald Hankey; 41 Grandison rd, SW11

HANKINSON, Cyril Francis James; s of Charles Hankinson, MBE, JP (d 1959); *b* 4 Nov 1895; *Educ* Queen Elizabeth's G S, Wimborne; *m* 1942, Lillian (d 1974), da of Walter Read, FSI (d 1937); 1 s; *Career* ed Debrett's Peerage 1935-62; *Recreations* reading, watching cricket; *Clubs* MCC; *Style* - Cyril Hankinson Esq; 13 Welsby Court, Eaton Rise, W5 (☎ 01 997 5018)

HANLEY, Hon Lady; Hon Lorna Margaret Dorothy; da of Hon Claude Hope-Morley (d 1968), and sis of 3 Baron Hollenden; *b* 1929; *m* 1957, Sir Michael Bowen Hanley, KCB; *Career* JP High Wycombe; raised to the rank of a Baron's da; *Style* - The Hon Lady Hanley, JP

HANLON, Lady Colleen; *née* Wellesley; da of late 4 Earl Cowley; *b* 1925; *m* 1945, Paul A Hanlon, MD, late Capt US Army; 5 s, 2 da; *Style* - Lady Colleen Hanlon; 543 Westmoreland av, Kingston, Pennsylvania, USA

HANMER, Lady Frances Jane; *née* Cole; da of late 5 Earl of Enniskillen, KP and Charlotte, nee Baird; *b* 1914; *m* 1954, as his 2 w, Gp Capt Henry Ivan Hanmer, DFC, RAF, gggs of 2 Bt; 1 s; *Style* - Lady Frances Hanmer; Westhorpe Hall, Southwell, Notts

HANMER, Sir John Wyndham Edward; 8 Bt (GB 1774), of Hanmer, Flintshire, JP (Clwyd 1971), DL (1978); s of Lt-Col Sir Edward Hanmer, 7 Bt (d 1977), by his 1 w, Aileen; *b* 27 Sept 1928; *Educ* Eton; *m* 1954, Audrey, da of Maj Arthur Congreve, of the same family (which held land in Staffs from *temp* Edward II) as William Congreve, the Restoration playwright; 2 s; *Heir* s, Wyndham Hanmer; *Career* landowner & farmer; dir Chester Race Co 1978, Ludlow Race Club Ltd 1980 High Sheriff Clwyd 1977; *Recreations* shooting, racing; *Clubs* Army & Navy; *Style* - Sir John Hanmer, Bt, JP, DL; The Mere House, Hanmer, Whitchurch, Salop (☎ Hanmer 383)

HANMER, Wyndham Richard Guy; s and h of Sir John Wyndham Edward Hanmer, 8 Bt; *b* 27 Nov 1955; *Educ* Wellington; *Career* Kent Blues and Royals; *Style* - Wyndham Hanmer Esq

HANNAH, John James Miller; CBE (1960); s of John Miller Hannah, OBE, JP (d 1942); *b* 24 Feb 1903; *Educ* Merchiston Castle Edinburgh, West of Scotland Agricultural Coll; *m* 1938, Mary Motion, nee Crawford; 3 da; *Career* farmer, gov West of Scotland Agricultural Coll 1937-80 (chm 1971-75), memb South Western Agricultural Exec Ctee 1948-72, memb Cncl of Hannah Research Inst 1945-80 (v-chm 1972-80, hon fell 1980), memb Scottish Agric Consultative Panel 1965-; *Style* - John Hannah Esq, CBE; 3 Baird rd, Alloway, Ayr, Scotland (☎ Ayr 41937)

HANNAM, John Gordon; MP (C) Exeter 1970-; s of Thomas Hannam (d 1955); *b* 2 Aug 1929; *Educ* Yeovil G S; *m* 1956, Wendy, nee Macartney; 2 da; *Career* chm Con Energy Cttee 1979, -80, -81, memb Bd Nat Theatre, PPS Min of Industry 1972-73, PPS to Ch Sec Treasury 1973-74, chm West Country Gp Con MPs 1979-, Pres Br Motels Fedn 1974-; *Style* - John Hannam Esq, MP; 35 Tufton Court, SW1 (☎ 01 224 4736); Woodslea House, Brampford Speke, Exeter (☎ 039 284 209)

HANNON, Lady Fiona (Mary); *née* Graham; da of 7 Duke of Montrose; *b* 1932; *m* 1966, Peter Alexander O'Brien Hannon; 2 da; *Style* - Lady Fiona Hannon; PO Box 10144, Johannesburg, S Africa

HANSCOMB, Hon Mrs (Elinor Ruth); *née* McNair; da of 1 Baron McNair, CBE, QC, LLD (d 1975); *b* 1924; *m* 1955, Raymond Hanscomb; 2 s, 1 da; *Style* - The Hon Mrs Hanscomb; Powells End, Kempley, Dymock, Glos

HANSON, Sir Anthony Leslie Oswald; 4 Bt (UK 1887), of Bryanston Sq, Co Middlesex; s of Sir Gerald Stanhope Hanson, 2 Bt; suc half-bro Sir Richard Leslie Reginald Hanson, 1 Bt, 1951; *b* 27 Nov 1934; *Educ* Gordonstoun; *m* 1964, Denise Jane, da of R S Rolph, of Stoke-sub-Hamdon; *Career* late RNVR; *Style* - Sir Anthony Hanson, Bt

HANSON, Charles Rupert Patrick; s and h of Sir (Charles) John Hanson, 3 Bt; *b* 25 June 1945; *Educ* Eton, Centl London Poly; *m* 1977, Wanda, da of Don Arturo Larrain, of Santiago, Chile; 1 s; *Career* tech, legal and commercial translator 1977-; *Recreations* classical music, writing poetry, tennis; *Style* - Charles Hanson Esq; 125 Ditchling rd, Brighton, E Sussex (☎ 0273 697882)

HANSON, Derrick George; s of late John Henry Hanson; *b* 9 Feb 1927; *Educ* Waterloo G S, London U, Liverpool U; *m* 1 1951, Daphne Elizabeth (decd); 1 s, 2 da; m 2, 1974, Hazel Mary; *Career* dir & gen man Martins Bank Trust Co 1968, Barclays Bank Trust Co 1969-76, chm Barclays Unicorn 1972-76, senior adviser (UK) Manufacturers Hanover Trust Co 1977-79, pres City Univ Business Sch 1977-, pres Assoc of Banking Teachers 1977-, dir Liverpool Building Society, chm Tring Hall Securities Ltd, chm City of London & European Property Co Ltd, dir Phillips Fine Art Auctioneers, chm Moneyguide Ltd, dir Toye & Co Ltd, chm Christian Arts Trust, dir Albany Investment Trust Ltd, memb of Council

Liverpool Univ; *Recreations* golf, gardening, music, hill-walking; *Style* - Derrick Hanson Esq; 21 Old Buildngs, Lincoln's Inn, WC2 (☎ 01 242 9365); Tower Grange, Grange Lane, Formby, Liverpool (☎ Formby 74040)

HANSON, Sir James (Edward); s of Robert Hanson, CBE (d 1973); *b* 20 Jan 1922; *m* 1959, Geraldine; 2 s, 1 step da; *Career* industrialist, chm Hanson Trust Ltd 1965-, dir (former chm) Trident Television 1970-, chm Hanson Transport Gp Ltd 1965-; kt 1976; *Recreations* hunting (former MFH Grove and Rufford) and photography; *Clubs* Brooks's, Huddersfield Borough and Roy Thames Yacht; *Style* - Sir James Hanson; 180 Brompton rd, London, SW3 1HF

HANSON, Sir (Charles) John; 3 Bt (UK 1918), of Fowey, Cornwall; s of Sir Charles Edwin Bourne Hanson, 2 Bt (d 1958); *b* 28 Feb 1919; *Educ* Eton, Clare Cambridge; *m* 1, 1944 (m dis 1968), Patricia Helen, da of late Adm Sir (Eric James) Patrick Brind, GBE, KCB; 1 s, 1 da; m 2, 1968, Violet Helen, da of late Charles Ormonde Trew, and formerly wife of late Capt Philip Cecil Langdon Yorke, OBE, RN; *Heir* s, Charles Rupert Patrick Hanson; *Career* late Capt, The Duke of Cornwall's Light Infantry; served War of 1939-45; memb London Stock Exchange; *Clubs* MCC; *Style* - Sir John Hanson, Bt; Gunn House, Shelfanger, nr Diss, Norfolk; 4 Holland Park rd, W14

HANSON, John Leslie; *Career* chm Parklands Textile (Holdings) Ltd; v-chm Halifax Bldg Soc; dir Park Lane Hotel Ltd; memb IOD; *Style* - John Hanson Esq; c/o Parkland Textiles; Albion Mills, Greengates, Bradford, Yorks

HANSON, Richard William Durrant; TD; s of William George Hanson; *b* 11 Aug 1935; *Educ* Eton; *m* 1961, Elizabeth Deirdre Dewar, da of the late Dr A D Frazer; 1 s, 2 da; *Career* v-chm and md Hardys & Hansons Ltd, Kimberley Brewery Nottingham, High Sheriff of Nottinghamshire 1980-81; *Recreations* shooting, tennis; *Clubs* MCC; *Style* - Richard Hanson Esq, TD; Budby Castle, Newark, Notts (☎ Mansfield 822293)

HANWORTH, 2 Viscount (UK 1936); Sir David Bertram Pollock; 2 Bt (UK 1922); also Baron Hanworth (UK 1926); s of Charles Pollock (s of 1 Viscount Hanworth, KBE, PC, JP, who d 1936 and was 4 s of George Pollock, himself the 3 s of Rt Hon Sir Frederick Pollock, 1 Bt, PC; His Lordship m Laura, da of Sir Thomas Salt, 1 Bt, sometime MP Stafford, JP, DL, whose w, Emma, was great niece of Cardinal Manning); *b* 1 Aug 1916; *Educ* Wellington, Trin Cambridge; *m* 1940, Isolda, da of Geoffrey Parker (3 s of Hon Cecil Parker, JP, by his w Rosamond, da of Most Rev Charles Longley, DD, sometime Archbishop of Canterbury; Cecil was 2 s of 6 Earl of Macclesfield, DL, by his 2 w, Lady Mary Grosvenor, da of 2 Marquess of Westminster, KG); 2 s, 1 da; by this marriage the gggg nephew of a Cardinal was joined in holy matrimony with the ggda of an Archbishop of Canterbury, moreover the archiepiscopate of the one (Manning's at Westminster) commenced half way (1865) through that of the other (1862-68); another interesting feature is the commingling of the blood lines of an Archbishop of Westminster with that of the Marquesses and Dukes of the same designation; *Heir* s, Hon David Pollock; *Career* barr 1958; late Lt-Col RE; CEng, MIMechE, FIEE, FIQA, FRPS; author of books on colour photography; *Style* - The Rt Hon The Viscount Hanworth; Quoin Cottage, Shamley Green, Guildford, Surrey (☎ 893018)

HARBERTON, 10 Viscount (I 1791); Thomas de Vautort Pomeroy; also Baron Harberton (I 1783); s of 8 Viscount Harberton, OBE (d 1956); suc bro, 9 Viscount, 1980; *b* 19 Oct 1910; *Educ* Eton; *m* 1, 1939 (m dis 1946), Nancy, da of C Penoyer, of San Francisco; m 2, 1950, Pauline (d 1971), da of Wilfred Baker, of Plymouth; m 3, 1978, Vilma (Wilhelmine), da of Heinrich Wahl and widow of Sir Arthur Butt, 1 Bt; *Heir* bro, Hon Robert Pomeroy; *Career* Lt-Col Welsh Gds (1931-41) and RAOC from 1941; *Clubs* Cavalry & Guards, Roy Overseas League; *Style* - The Rt Hon The Viscount Harberton; Le Formentor, 27 Av Princesse Grace, Monte Carlo, Monaco (☎ 509629)

HARBISON, Air Vice-Marshal William; CB (1977), CBE (1965), AFC (1956); s of William Harbison, of Garvagh NI; *b* 11 April 1922; *Educ* Ballymena Acad; *m* 1950, Helen, da of William Blaine Geneva, of Bloomington, Illinois; 2 s; *Career* V-Pres Br Aerospace Washington DC 1979-; AOC HQ 11 Gp RAF 1975-77; Cdr RAF Staff and Air Attaché Washington 1972-75; *Recreations* motoring; *Clubs* RAF, Army & Navy (Washington); *Style* - Air Vice-Marshal William Harbison, CB, CBE, AFC; c/o Cox's & King's Branch of Lloyds Bank, 6 Pall Mall, SW1

HARBORD, Hon Lettice Evelyn; da of late 6 Baron Suffield, CB, MVO; *b* 1904; *Style* - The Hon Lettice Harbord; Harbord House, 131 Overstrand rd, Cromer, Norfolk

HARBORD-HAMOND, Hon Charles Anthony Assheton; s and h of 11 Baron Suffield, MC; *b* 3 Dec 1953; *Educ* Eton; *Career* Capt Coldstream Gds, temp Equerry to HM 1977-; *Style* - The Hon Charles Harbord-Hamond

HARBORD-HAMOND, Hon Caroline Mary Elaine; da of 11 Baron Suffield, MC; *b* 1960; *Style* - The Hon Caroline Harbord-Hamond

HARBORD-HAMOND, Hon Charity Patricia; da of late 10 Baron Suffield; *b* 1917; *Style* - The Hon Charity Harbord-Hamond; The Willows, Dedham, Colchester, Suffolk

HARBORD-HAMOND, Hon John Edward Richard; s of 11 Baron Suffield, MC; *b* 1956; *Style* - The Hon John Harbord-Hamond

HARBORD-HAMOND, Hon Penelope Mary; da of late 10 Baron Suffield; *b* 1915; *Style* - The Hon Penelope Harbord-Hamond; Walton House, Walton st, SW3

HARBORD-HAMOND, Hon Robert Philip Morden; s of 11 Baron Suffield, MC; *b* 1964; *Style* - The Hon Robert Harbord-Hamond

HARCOURT-MUNNING, Frank Wilfred; CBE (1968); s of Capt Charles Harcourt-Munning (last Adm Short Blue Fleet); *b* 28 Sept 1905; *Educ* Milford Haven G S; *m* 1932, Elizabeth (d 1943), nee Semple; *Career* opera tenor till age 27, Parl Candidate (L) Tavistock 1950/51, fndr War on Want 1956, fndr chm Marr-Munning Tst, Life Govr Nat Children's Homes; *Style* - Frank Harcourt-Munning Esq, CBE; Harcourt Lodge, 9 Madeley rd, W5 (☎ 01 998 9593)

HARCUS, Rear-Adm Ronald Albert; CB (1976); s of Henry Harcus (d 1966); *b* 25 Oct 1921; *Educ* St Olave's G S, RNC Greenwich, Roy Coll of Defence Studies; *m* 1946, Jean, nee Heckman; 2 s, 2 da; *Career* RN ret, Assist Ch Fleet Support MOD 1974-76, md RWO (Marine Equipment) 1976-; *Recreations* sailing, fishing, gardening; *Style* - Rear-Adm Ronald Harcus, CB; Higher Leigh, Kingsbridge, Devon (☎ 2436)

HARDEN, Donald Benjamin; CBE (1969, OBE 1956); s of John Mason Harden, Bp of Tuam, Killala and Achonry 1927-31 (d 1931); *b* 8 July 1901; *Educ* Westminster, Trin Cambridge; *m* 1, 1934, Cecil Ursula (d 1963), da of Rev James Adolphus Harriss; 1 da; m 2, 1965, Dorothy, nee McDonald, of Vict Australia; *Career* FSA, dir London Museum 1956-70; *Recreations* archaeology, history, antiquarianism; *Clubs* Athenaeum; *Style* - Donald Harden Esq, CBE; 12 St Andrew's Mans, Dorset st, W1 (☎ 01 935 5121)

HARDEN, Maj James Richard Edwards; DSO (1945), MC (1944), JP (Armagh 1956, Caernarvonshire 1971), DL (Armagh 1946, Caernarvonshire 1968); s of James Harden (d 1945); *b* 12 Dec 1916; *Educ* Bedford Sch, Sandhurst; *m* 1948, Ursula, da of Gerald Strutt (d 1956); 1 s, 2 da; *Career* High Sheriff Caernarvonshire 1971-72, Ulster Unionist MP 1948-54, chm Regnl Land Drainage Cttee Welsh Water Authority 1973-; *Recreations* shooting; *Style* - Maj James Harden, DSO, MC, JP, DL; Nanhoran, Pwllheli, Gwynedd (☎ 0758 83610)

HARDING OF PETHERTON, 1 Baron (UK 1958); Allan Francis John

Harding; GCB (1951, KCB 1944), CBE (1941), DSO and Two Bars (1941, 1942, 1943), MC (1917); s of Francis Harding; *b* 10 Feb 1896; *Educ* Ilminster G S; *m* 1927, Mary, CStJ, da of Joseph Rooke, JP, of Knutsford; 1 s; *Heir* s, Hon John Harding; *Career* Field Marshal 1953, late Somerset LI; ADC Gen to George VI 1950, HM The Queen 1952-53; chm Horserace Betting Levy Bd 1961-67; Col Life Gds & Gold Stick to HM 1957-64; KStJ; Gov & CIC Cyprus 1955-57, CIGS 1952-55, CIC BAOR 1951-52, CIC FELF 1949-51; *Style* - Field Marshal Rt Hon Lord Harding of Petherton GCB CBE DSO** MC; Lower Farm, Nether Compton, Sherborne, Dorset

HARDING, Christopher George Francis; s of Frank Harding, of Amersham; *b* 17 Oct 1939; *Educ* Merchant Taylors', CCC Oxford; *m* 1, 1963, Susan Lilian; 1 s, 1 da; m 2, 1978, Françoise Marie, da of Christian Grouillé; 3 step children; *Career* md Hanson T'port Gp 1974, dir Hanson Tst 1979; *Recreations* tennis, squash, travel, music; *Style* - Christopher Harding Esq; Field House, Netherton, Huddersfield (☎ 0484 661128)

HARDING, Derek William; s of William Arthur Harding (d 1972); *b* 16 Dec 1930; *Educ* Glendale G S London, Bristol Univ; *Career* engineer Pye Ltd 1954-56, sr Physics Master Thornbury G S Bristol 1956-60, sr lecturer Physical Science St Paul's Coll Cheltenham 1960-64, registrar sec Inst Metallurgists 1969-76, sec gen Br Computer Soc 1976-; *Recreations* music, sailing; *Clubs* Athenaeum; *Style* - Derek Harding Esq; 16 Exeter rd, N14 (☎ 01 368 1463)

HARDING, Gp Capt Eric Cranston; CBE (1958); s of late Albert William Harding, of Plymouth, Devon; *b*1913; *Educ* Plymouth Coll and RAF Coll Cranwell; *m* 1937, Brenda Florence, da of late Bertram Joseph Chubb, MBE, of Portsmouth; 1 s;*Career* Group Capt RAF (ret); *Style* - Gp Capt Eric Harding, CBE; Apartado 169 de Correos, Mahon, Minorca, Spain

HARDING, George William; CMG (1977), CVO (1972); s of Lt-Col George Richardson Harding, DSO, MBE; *b* 18 Jan 1927; *Educ* Aldenham Sch and St John's Coll Cambridge; *m* 1955, Sheila Margaret Ormond, da of Maj John Ormond Riddel, of Trinidad; 4 s; *Career* Lt Roy Marines 1945-48, entered Diplomatic Serv 1950, HM Ambassador to Peru 1977-79, Assist Under-Sec of State FCO 1979-81, Ambass Brazil 1981-; *Clubs* Garrick and Leander; *Style* - George Harding Esq, CMG, CVO; c/o Foreign and Commonwealth Office, King Charles st, SW1

HARDING, George William Cecil; s of Col George Harding, DSO, of Co Laois, Eire; *b* 12 July 1916; *Educ* Wellington, RMA; *m* 1947, Beatrice, da of Col Geoffrey Youl, MC, of Tasmania; 3 da; *Career* late Maj (RA, ret 1958), served Europe, M East, Pacific; chm Ewart New Northern Ltd 1977-, Capital Gearing Tst 1963-; landowner (inherited from f) 1957-; *Recreations* travel; *Clubs* Naval & Military, Ulster (Belfast); *Style* - Maj George Harding; Tulachnore, Pike of Rushall, Portlaoise, Ireland (☎ 0502 35113)

HARDING, Maj Hon John Charles; s and h of Field Marshal 1 Baron Harding of Petherton, GCB, CBE, DSO, MC; *b* 12 Feb 1928; *Educ* Marlborough, Worcester Oxford; *m* 1966, Harriet, da of Maj-Gen James Hare, CB, DSO (d 1970); 2 s, 1 da; *Career* Maj 11 Hussars, ret 1968; *Style* - Maj The Hon John Harding; The Vine House, Nether Compton, Sherborne, Dorset (☎ 3140)

HARDING, Katharine Mary; *née* Phipps; da of 3 Marquess of Normanby (d 1932), but she does not use courtesy title; *b* 1905; *m* 1949, Roy Amon Harding (d 1960); *Style* - Mrs Roy Harding; c/o Lloyds Bank, 16 St James's st, SW1

HARDING, His Honour Rowe; DL (W Glam 1970); s of Albert Harding (d 1940), of Swansea; *b* 10 Sept 1901; *Educ* Gowerton County Sch, Pembroke Cambridge; *m* 1933, Elizabeth, da of John George (d 1963), of Hirwaun; 1 s, 1 da (and 1 da decd); *Career* Circuit Judge 1953-76, chm Swansea Porcelain Ltd 1976- *Recreations* gardening, watching rugby and cricket; *Clubs* Cardiff and County,

Swansea City and County; *Style* - His Hon Rowe Harding, DL; The Old Rectory, Ilston, Gower, Swansea, W Glam (☎ Penmaen 243)

HARDING-DAVIES, Hon Francis William; s of Rt Hon John Harding-Davies, PC (d 1979) and Baroness Harding-Davies, *qv*; *b* 1943; *m* 1971, Lynda Squires; c; *Style* - The Hon Francis Harding-Davies

HARDING-DAVIES, Baroness, Vera Georgina; da of George Bates; *m* 1943, Rt Hon John Harding-Davies, PC, nominated Life Peer (Baron) 1979 but who d before Peerage was cr; 1 s, 1 da; raised to rank of Baron's widow 1980; *Style* - The Rt Hon The Lady Harding-Davies; 79 Rivermead Court, SW6

HARDINGE OF PENSHURST, 3 Baron (UK 1910); George Edward Charles Hardinge; s of 2 Baron, GCB, GCVO, MC, PC (d 1960) and Helen, Baroness Hardinge of Penshurst, *qv*; *b* 31 Oct 1921; *Educ* Eton; *m* 1, 1944 (m dis 1962), Janet (d 1970), da of Lt-Col Francis Balfour, CIE, CVO, CBE, MC (n of 1 & 2 Earls of Balfour); 3 s; m 2, 1966, Mrs Margaret Trezise, da of William Jerrum; 1 s; *Heir* s, Hon Julian Hardinge; *Career* Lt Cdr RN ret; Page of Honour to HM 1933-38, Train Bearer at Coronation of George VI; *Clubs* Brooks's; *Style* - The Rt Hon Lord Hardinge of Penshurst; Chalkfield, Friston, E Sussex (☎ E Dean 3155)

HARDINGE, 5 Viscount (UK 1846); Nicholas Henry Paul Hardinge; s of 4 Viscount (d 1979); *b* 15 Aug 1929; *Educ* Harrow; *m* 1955, Zoe Anne, da of Senator Hartland de Montarville Molson, OBE, of Montreal; 3 s; *Heir* s Hon Charles Hardinge; *Career* md Roy Bank of Canada 1979-; *Recreations* shooting, fishing, tennis; *Clubs* Cavalry and Guards, Mount Royal (Montreal), Mount Bruno Country (Montreal); *Style* - The Rt Hon The Viscount Hardinge; Flat 2, 2 Hyde Pk gdns, W2 (☎ 01 262 8694)

HARDINGE, Hon Andrew Hartland; s of 5 Viscount Hardinge; *b* 1960; *Style* - The Hon Andrew Hardinge

HARDINGE, Hon Charles Alexander; s of 3 Baron Hardinge of Penshurst; *b* 17 May 1967

HARDINGE, Hon Charles Henry Nicholas; s and h of 5 Viscount Hardinge; *b* 25 Aug 1956; *Style* - The Hon Charles Hardinge

HARDINGE, Hon Edward Frederick; s of 3 Baron Hardinge of Penshurst; *b* 25 Oct 1958; *Educ* Gordonstoun; *Style* - The Hon Edward Hardinge

HARDINGE, Hon Hugh Francis; s of 3 Baron Hardinge of Penshurst; *b* 9 April 1948; *Educ* Eton; *Style* - The Hon Hugh Hardinge; Hunts Barn, Mayfield, Sussex (☎ 2151)

HARDINGE OF PENSHURST, Helen, Baroness - Helen Mary; da of Lord Edward H Gascoyne-Cecil KCMG DSO (d 1918, 4 s of 3 Marq of Salisbury) and Violet Georgina (d 1958), da of late Adm Frederick Maxse and ggda of 5 Earl of Berkeley, and who m 2, 1921, 1 Visc Milner; *b* 11 May 1901; *m* 1921, 2 Baron Hardinge of Penshurst, GCB, GCVO, MC, PC (d 1960); 1 s, 2 da ; *Style* - The Rt Hon Helen, Lady Hardinge of Penshurst; South Park, Penshurst, Tonbridge, Kent (☎ Penshurst 215)

HARDINGE, Hon Julian Alexander; s of 3 Baron Hardinge of Penshurst; *b* 23 Aug 1945; *Educ* Eton, Trinity Cambridge; *Career* Page of Honour to HM the Queen 1959-62; *Style* - The Hon Julian Hardinge; Hunts Barn, Mayfield, Sussex (☎ 2151); South Park, Penshurst, Kent; (☎ 215); Higham Lodge, Salehurst, Robertsbridge, Sussex (☎ Robertsbridge 351)

HARDINGE, Margaret, Viscountess - Margaret (Elizabeth Arnot); da of late Hugh Fleming, of Wynyards, Rockcliffe, Ottawa; *m* 1928, 4 Viscount Hardinge, MBE (d 1979); 1 s (5 Viscount), 2 da (Hon Mrs Worsley, Hon Mrs Raymond); *Style* - The Rt Hon Margaret, Viscountess Hardinge; 1523 Summerhill ave, Montreal

HARDINGE, Hon Maximillian Evelyn; s of 5 Viscount Hardinge; *b* 19 Jan 1969

HARDINGE, Sir Robert Arnold; 7 Bt (UK 1801), of Lurran, Fermanagh; s of Sir Robert Hardinge, 6 Bt (d 1973); *b* 19 Dec 1914; *Heir* kinsman, 5 Viscount Hardinge; *Style* - Sir Robert Hardinge, Bt

HARDWICK, Dr Donald; CBE; *Career* chm Firth Brown Ltd, River Don Stampings Ltd; dir Glossup Super Alloys, Mitchell Somers Ltd; BMet, PhD, FIM, memb IOD; *Style* - Dr Donald Hardwick, CBE; PO Box 114, Atlas Works, Sheffield S4 7US

HARDWICKE, 10 Earl of (GB 1754); Joseph Philip Sebastian Yorke; also Baron Hardwicke (GB 1733) and Viscount Royston (GB 1754); s of Viscount Royston (d 1973, s & h of 9 Earl, who d 1974); *b* 3 Feb 1971; *Heir* kinsman, Richard Yorke; *Style* - The Rt Hon Earl of Hardwicke; 9 Fernshaw rd, SW10

HARDWICKE, Countess of - Enid Munnick; *m* 1, Roy Boulting, the film producer & one half of the Boulting Bros; m 2, 1970, as his 2 w, 9 Earl of Hardwicke (d 1974); *Style* - The Rt Hon The Countess of Hardwicke

HARDY, Hon Lady; Hon Diana Joan; *née* Allsopp; da of 3 Baron Hindlip (d 1931); *b* 1908; *m* 1930, Lt-Col Sir Rupert John Hardy, 4 Bt; 1 s, 1 da; *Style* - The Hon Lady Hardy; Barleythorpe House, Oakham, Rutland

HARDY, Sir Harry; JP (Morley 1948); s of Friend Hardy; *b* 10 Sept 1896; *Educ* Leeds U; *m* 1, 1922, Remie (d 1955), nee Siddle; m 2, 1957, Mollie, nee Dixon; *Career* chartered textile technologist; ATI; kt 1956; ; *Style* - Sir Harry Hardy, JP; 45 The Roundway, Dartmouth Park, Morley, nr Leeds (☎ 535150)

HARDY, Herbert Charles; s of Charles Hardy; *b* 13 Dec 1928; *Educ* Sandhurst; *m* 1960, Irene Burrows; 1 da; *Career* dir News International Ltd 1972- (man dir and ch exec 1978-), News Gp Newspapers Ltd 1969-; *Style* - Herbert Hardy Esq; 30 Bouverie st, EC4 (☎ 01 353 3030)

HARDY, Sir James Gilbert; OBE (1975); s of late T M Hardy; *b* 20 Nov 1932; *Educ* St Peter's SA Inst of Tech; *m* 1956, Anne, da of R A Jackson; 2 s; *Career* dir Thomas Hardy & Sons Pty Ltd Sydney 1962-; kt 1981; *Style* - Sir James Hardy OBE; 7/10 Marine Parade, Manly East, NSW 2095, Australia

HARDY, Hon Mrs (Joanna Mary); da of Baron Porritt, GCMG, GCVO, CBE (Life Peer and 1 Bt); *b* 1948; *m* 1969, Simon Patrick Meredith Hardy; 2 s; *Style* - The Hon Mrs Hardy; 23 Baronsmead rd, SW13

HARDY, Laurence Carey; s of Herbert Ronald Hardy (d 1954); *b* 17 Nov 1929; *Educ* Royal Naval Coll, Dartmouth; *m* 1953, Rebeka Ann; 1 s, 3 da; *Career* Lieutenant RN, Korea, Malaya; dir Allied Leather Industries Ltd (1967); dir Freshfield Lane Brickworks Ltd (1980); High Sheriff East Sussex 1976; Conservator Ashdown Forest 1977; *Recreations* shooting, fishing, conservation, gardening; *Style* - Laurence Hardy Esq; Latchetts Dane Hill, Haywards Heath, W Sussex, RH17 7HQ (☎ 0825 790237)

HARDY, Peter; *Career* jt md Illingworth Morris & Co Ltd; chm Brook Walker & Co Ltd, Hawick Hosiery, J & J Crombie, Reid Welsh, Samuel Salter & Co, Strachan & Co, Weensland Spinning Co, William Playne & Co; chm and md Winterbottom Strachan & Playne Ltd; dir Joshuah Hoyle & Co Ltd, Troydale Industs Ltd; BA, FCIS; *Style* - Peter Hardy Esq; c/o Illingworth Morris, Victoria rd, Saltaire, Shipley, Yorks

HARDY, Peter; MP (L) Rother Valley 1970-; s of Lawrence Hardy; *b* 17 July 1931; *Educ* Wath upon Dearne G S, Westminster Coll London, Sheffield U; *m* 1954, Margaret Brookes; 2 s (and 1 decd); *Career* PPS to Foreign Sec 1976-79; *Style* - Peter Hardy Esq, MP; 52 Sandygate, Wath upon Dearne, Rotherham, S Yorks (☎ 874590)

HARDY, Richard Charles Chandos; s and h of Lt-Col Sir Rupert Hardy, 4 Bt, and Hon Diana Allsopp, da of 3 Baron Hindlip; *b* 6 Feb 1945; *m* 1972, Venetia, da of Simon Wingfield Digby, TD, DL; 2 da; *Style* - Richard Hardy Esq; Springfield House, Gillingham, Dorset

HARDY, His Hon Judge; Robert James; s of James Hardy; *b* 12 July 1924; *Educ* Wrekin, UCL; *m* 1951, Maureen Scott; 1 s, 1 da; *Career* barr 1950, Circuit Judge 1979-; *Style* - His Hon Judge Hardy; Fallow Green, Overhill Lane, Wilmslow Pk, Wilmslow, Cheshire (☎ 528031); Betlem, Mallorca

HARDY, Sir Rupert John; 4 Bt (UK 1876), of Dunstall Hall, Co Stafford; s of Sir Bertram Hardy, 3 Bt (d 1953), by his w, Violet, da of Hon Sir Edward Chandos Leigh, KCB, KC, JP (2 s of 1 Baron Leigh); *b* 24 Oct 1902; *Educ* Eton, Trin Hall Cambridge; *m* 1930, Hon Diana Allsopp, da of 3 Baron Hindlip, OBE, JP, DL, by his w, Agatha (da of John Thynne, DL, 5 s of Rev Lord John Thynne, 3 s of 2 Marquess of Bath, KG); 1 s, 1 da; *Heir* s, Richard Hardy; *Career* Lt-Col Life Gds, served WW II 8 Army in W Desert, Palestine, Syria, France; ret from army 1948, rejoined as RARO 1952; Lt-Col Cmmdg Household Cavalry 1952-56; *Recreations* hunting, shooting; *Clubs* Turf; *Style* - Sir Rupert Hardy, Bt; Barleythorpe House, Oakham, Rutland (☎ 2794)

HARDY, Richard Somers Angus; DL (Staffs 1971); s of Richard T A Hardy (d 1947); *b* 9 May 1905; *Educ* Stonyhurst, New Coll Oxford; *m* 1934, Evelyn Margaret Mary, nee Mostyn (d 1978); 1 s, 1 da; *Career* Maj Middle East and NW Europe, solicitor (ret), Under Sheriff of Staffs 1947-69, High Sheriff Staffs 1971-72; *Recreations* shooting, fishing, watching cricket; *Clubs* Buck's, Boodle's, Pratt's; *Style* - Richard Hardy Esq, DL; Haselour Cottage, Hárlaston, nr Tamworth, Staffs (☎ Harlaston 579)

HARDY , Sir James Douglas; CBE (1955, OBE 1953); s of James Hardy; *b* 8 June 1915; *Educ* Gonville and Caius Cambridge; *m* 1937, Robina, nee Bookless; 2 s; *Career* kt 1962, ch project manager and UN advsr adminve reform Govt of Morocco 1975-76; *Style* - Sir James Hardy, CBE; c/o Midland Bank, Poultry and Princes st, EC2

HARÈ, Hon Alan Victor; MC (1942); s of 4 Earl of Listowel and Hon Freda, da of 2 Baron Derwent; *b* 14 March 1919; *Educ* Eton, New Coll Oxford; *m* 1945, Jill, nee North; 1 s, 1 da; *Career* FCO 1947-61, dir Pearson Longman 1975-, dep chm Industrial & Trade Fairs Hldgs 1977-, chm (1978-) and ch exec (1975-) Financial Times Ltd; *Style* - The Hon Alan Hare, MC; Flat 12, 53 Rutland Gate, SW7 (☎ 01 581 2184)

HARE, Ann, Lady - Barbara Mary Theodora (Ann); da of late Joseph Walton; *m* 1960, as his 3 w, Maj Sir Ralph Hare, 4 Bt (d 1976); *Style* - Ann, Lady Hare; Stow Bardolph, King's Lynn, Norfolk

HARE, David; s of Clifford Hare; *b* 5 June 1947; *Educ* Lancing, Jesus Cambridge; *m* 1970, Margaret Matheson; 2 s, 1 da; *Career* playwright; *Style* - David Hare Esq; 39 Richborne ter, SW8

HARE, Lady Diana; da of 5 Earl of Listowel, GCMG, PC; *b* 1965

HARE, Doreen, Lady; Doreen Pleasance Anna; da of late Maj Sir Richard Ludwigg Bagge, DSO, of Gaywood Hall, King's Lynn; *m* 1928 (m dis 1944), Maj Sir Ralph Leigh Hare, 4 Bt (d 1976); *Style* - Doreen, Lady Hare; 14 Empire House, Thurloe Place, SW7 (☎ 01 589 6191)

HARE, Lady Fiona Eve Akua; da of 5 Earl of Listowel, GCMG, PC; *b* 1960; *Style* - Lady Fiona Hare

HARE, Prof Frederick Kenneth; OC (1978); s of Frederick Hare; *b* 5 Feb 1919; *Educ* Windsor G S, King's Coll London; *m* 1, 1941, Suzanne Bates (m dis 1952); 1 s; m 2, 1952, Helen Morrill; 1 s, 1 da; *Career* PhD, FRSC, geographer, Provost Trin Coll U, Toronto, 1979-; *Style* - Prof Frederick Hare, OC; Trinity College, 6 Hoskin av, Toronto, Canada

HARE, Hon Michael John; s and h of 1 Visc Blakenham, OBE, PC, and Hon Beryl Pearson (da of 2 Visc Cowdray); gs of 4 Earl of Listowel; *b* 25 Jan 1928; *Educ* Eton, Harvard; *m* 1965, Marcia (his 1 cous), da of Maj Hon Alan Hare; 1 s, 2 da; *Career* ch exec S Pearson & Son 1978-, chm Pearson Longman 1979-, Treas RSPB

1977-; *Style* - The Hon Michael Hare; 30 St Leonards Terrace, SW3 (☎ 01 828 9020)

HARE, Philip Leigh; s of Edward Philip Leigh Hare (d 1954) and his 3 w, Lady Kathleen (d 1971), nee Stanhope, da of 9 Earl of Harrington, and widow of Edward Morant, JP, of Brockenhurst Park, Hants; hp of cous, Sir Thomas Hare, 5 Bt; *b* 13 Oct 1922; *m* 1950, Anne, da of Maj Geoffrey Nicholson, CBE, MC; 1 s, 1 da (twins); *Style* - Philip Hare Esq; Darlingscott Farm, Darlingscott, Shipston-on-Stour, Worcs

HARE, Lady Rose Amanda; *née* Bligh; da (by 2 m) of 9 Earl of Darnley; *b* 1935; *m* 1961, Sir Thomas Hare, 5 Bt; 2 da; *Style* - Lady Rose Hare; Stow Bardolph, King's Lynn, Norfolk

HARE, Hon Mrs Richard - Dora; da of late Mark Gordine, of St Petersburg, Russia; *m* 1936, Hon Richard Gilbert Hare (d 1966); *Style* - The Hon Mrs Richard Hare; Dorich House, Kingston Vale, SW15

HARE, Sir Thomas; 5 Bt (UK 1818), of Stow Hall, Norfolk; s of Maj Sir Ralph Leigh Hare, 4 Bt (d 1976, an earlier Btcy in the family, dating from 1641, died out in 1764), by his 1 w, Doreen, da of Maj Sir Richard Bagge, DSO; *b* 27 July 1930; *Educ* Eton, Magdalene Cambridge; *m* 1961, Lady Rose Amanda Bligh, da of 9 Earl of Darnley; 2 da; *Heir* cous, Philip Leigh Hare; *Career* Lt RARO Coldstream Gds; chartered surveyor (ARICS), landowner and farmer; *Recreations* gardening, walking, cricket, forestry; *Clubs* RAC; *Style* - Sir Thomas Hare, Bt; Stow Bardolph, King's Lynn, Norfolk PE34 3HU

HARE, Hon Timothy Patrick; s of 5 Earl of Listowel, GCMG, PC; *b* 1966

HARE, William Rowan; CBE (1968), JP (Norwich 1961); s of Warren Hare; *b* 9 April 1905; *Educ* Stamford Sch, CCC Oxford; *m* 1932, Dorothea, da of W La Fontaine, of Istanbul; 2 s; *Career* Sheriff Norwich 1979-80, chm J & J Colman Ltd 1960-70; *Recreations* cricket, music; *Clubs* Reform, MCC, Norfolk (Norwich); *Style* - William Hare Esq, CBE, JP; 9 Grove av, Norwich

HAREWOOD, 7 Earl of (UK 1812); George Henry Hubert Lascelles; also Baron Harewood (GB 1796) and Viscount Lascelles (UK 1812); s of 6 Earl of Harewood, KG, GCVO, DSO, TD (d 1947), and HRH Princess Mary (The Princess Royal), CI, GCVO, GBE, RRC, TD, CD (d 1965), only da of HM King George V; *b* 7 Feb 1923; *Educ* Eton, King's Cambridge; *m* 1, 1949 (m dis 1967; she m 2, 1973, as his 2 w, Rt Hon Jeremy Thorpe), Maria Donata Nanetta Paulina Gustava Erwina Wilhelmina (Marion), da of late Erwin Stein; 3 s; m 2, 1967, Patricia Elizabeth, da of Charles Tuckwell, of Sydney; 1 s; *Heir* s, Viscount Lascelles; *Career* md ENO 1972-, ENO North 1978-; ADC to Earl of Athlone 1945-46; ed magazine 'Opera' 1950-53; memb Gen Advsy Cncl BBC 1969-; Pres Leeds Utd Football Club; *Recreations* shooting, watching football, films; *Style* - The Rt Hon The Earl of Harewood; Harewood House, Leeds, LS17 9LG (☎ 0532 886333)

HARFORD, Anstice, Lady; Anstice Marion; da of late Sir Alfred Tritton, 2 Bt; *m* 1931, Lt-Col Sir George Arthur Harford, 2 Bt, OBE (d 1967); *Style* - Anstice, Lady Harford; The Old Rectory, Great Somerford, Chippenham, Wilts

HARFORD, Sir James Dundas; KBE (1956), CMG (1943); s of late Rev Dundas Harford; *b* 7 Jan 1899; *Educ* Repton, Balliol Oxford; *m* 1, 1932, Countess Thelma, da of Count Albert Metaxa; 1 s; m 2, 1937, Lilias, da of Maj Archibald Campbell; 2 da; *Career* Gov and CIC St Helena 1954-58; *Style* - Sir James Harford, KBE, CMG; Links Cottage, Rother rd, Seaford, E Sussex (☎ 0923 892115)

HARFORD, Mark John; s and h of Sir Timothy Harford, 3 Bt; *b* 6 Aug 1964; *Style* - Mark Harford Esq

HARFORD, Sir (John) Timothy Harford; 3 Bt (UK 1934), of Falcondale, Co Cardigan; s of Lt-Col Sir George Arthur Harford, 2 Bt, OBE (d 1967); *b* 6 July 1932; *Educ* Harrow, Worcester Coll

Oxford, Harvard Business Sch; *m* 1962, Carolyn, da of Brig Guy John de Wette Mullens, OBE, of North House, Weyhill, Andover; 2 s, 1 da; *Heir* s, Mark John Harford; *Career* dir Singer & Friedlander Ltd 1970-; *Style* - Sir Timothy Harford, Bt; South House, South Littleton, Evesham, Worcs (☎ Evesham 830478)

HARGREAVES, Brig Kenneth; CBE (1956, MBE 1939), TD (1942), DL (W Yorks 1978); s of late Henry Hargreaves; *b* 23 Feb 1903; *Educ* Haileybury; *m* 1, 1958, Else Allen (d 1968); 1 s, 1 da (both adopted) m 2, 1969, Hon Mrs Packe (Hon Margaret, nee Lane Fox, da of 1 Baron Bingley); 2 step da; *Career* Ld-Lt W Yorks 1974-78, Hon Pres Hargreaves Gp 1974-, dir Sadler's Wells Tst 1969, ENO 1975- (& pres Friends ENO North 1978), High Steward Selby Abbey 1974, KStJ 1970; *Style* - Brig Kenneth Hargreaves, CBE, TD, DL; Easby House, Gt Ouseburn, N Yorks (☎ Boroughbridge 30548)

HARGROVES, Col Robert Louis; CBE (1965), DL (Staffs 1974); s of William Robert Hargroves (d 1946); *b* 10 Dec 1917; *Educ* St John's Coll Southsea; *m* 1940, Eileen Elizabeth, da of Lt-Col W Anderson CIE (d 1947); 4 da; *Career* served WW II (Sicily and Italy), Brig 1964, Col The Staffordshire Regt (The Prince of Wales) 1971-77; *Recreations* field sports; *Style* - Col Robert Hargroves CBE, DL; Foxhill, Naunton, Cheltenham, Glos (☎ Guiting Power 416)

HARINGTON, Gen Sir Charles Henry Pepys; GCB (1969, KCB 1964, CB 1961), CBE (1957, OBE 1953), DSO (1944), MC (1940); s of Lt-Col H Harington and Dorothy Pepys; *b* 5 May 1910; *Educ* Malvern, Sandhurst; *m* 1942, Victoire Williams-Freeman; 1 s, 2 da; *Career* DCGS 1966, Ch of Personnel & Logistics to the 3 Servs 1968-71, ADC (Gen) to HM The Queen 1969-71, chm Govrs Star & Garter Home, memb London Bd Northern Rock Bldg Soc; *Style* - Gen Sir Charles Harington, GCB, CBE, DSO, MC; 19 Rivermead Court, SW6

HARINGTON, Maj-Gen John; CB (Mil 1967), OBE (Mil 1958); s of Col Henry Harington; *b* 7 Nov 1912; *Educ* Aldenham, RMA Woolwich; *m* 1943, Nancy, da of Maj S Allen, of Canterbury; 1 s; *Career* Brig RA Far East Land Forces 1962; DMS (2) War Off and MOD 1962-64; Ch of Staff to CIC Far East Cmmd 1964-67; *Recreations* skiing, golf, shooting; *Clubs* Army & Navy, SCGB; *Style* - Maj-Gen John Harington, CB, OBE; Harkaway, Goodworth Clatford, Andover, Hants (☎ 0264 61764)

HARINGTON, Kenneth Douglas Evelyn Herbert; s of His Hon Edward Harington, JP, 3 s of Sir Richard Harington, 11 Bt, JP, DL, and descendant of the regicide 3 Bt; *b* 30 Sept 1911; *Educ* Stowe; *m* 1, 1939, Lady Cecilia Bowes-Lyon (d 1947), er da of 15 Earl of Strathmore and Kinghorne, JP, DL, bro of HM Queen Elizabeth The Queen Mother, by his w, Lady Dorothy Osborne, 3 da of 10 Duke of Leeds; m 2, 1950, Maureen, da of Brig-Gen Sir Robert McCalmont, KCVO, CBE, DSO; 2 s; *Career* barr 1952; Metropolitan Stipendiary Magistrate 1967-; Hon Attaché Br Legation Stockholm 1930-32; *Recreations* shooting, fishing, gardening; *Style* - Kenneth Harington Esq; Sotchers, Bury Gate, Pulborough, Sussex (☎ Fittleworth 227); 36 Lennox gdns, SW1 (☎ 01 589 8951)

HARINGTON, Nicholas John; s of His Honour the late John Charles Dundas, QC (s of Sir Richard Harington, 12 Bt); hp to Baronetcy of unc, Sir Richard Dundas Harington, 13 Bt; *b* 14 May 1942; *Educ* Eton, Ch Ch Oxford; *Style* - Nicholas Harington Esq

HARINGTON, Sir Richard Dundas; 13 Bt (E 1611), of Ridlington, Rutland; s of Sir Richard Harington, 12 Bt (d 1931, (1?) cous ten times removed of Sir John Harington the Elizabethan (he was the Queen's godson) courtier-wit, translator of 'Orlando Furioso', and apostle of modern plumbing; also twentieth in descent (through the 1 Bt's mother Lucy, nee Sidney) from Edward I) and Hon Selina, nee Dundas, da of 6 Visc Melville; *b* 16 Oct 1900; *Educ* Eton; *Heir* n Nicholas John Harington; *Style* - Sir Richard Harington, Bt; c/o Coutts & Co, 440 The Strand, WC2

HARINGTON, (Edward Henry) Vernon; s of late His Hon Edward Harington (3 s of Sir Richard Harington, 11 Bt, JP, DL); *b* 13 Sept 1907; *Educ* Eton; *m* 1, 1937, Mary (m dis 1949), da of Louis Egerton (ka 1917, s of Sir Alfred Egerton, KCVO, CB, by his w, Hon Mary, nee Ormsby-Gore, er da of 2 Baron Harlech) and Jane, er surviving da of Rev Lord Victor Seymour (s of 5 Marquess of Hertford, GCB, PC, DL); 1 da (and 1 da decd); m 2, 1950, Mary, JP, da of late Lt-Col R Cox, MC; 2 da; *Career* Recorder of Crown Court 1972-74, barr 1930, Priv Sec to Lord Chancellor and Dep Serjeant-at-Arms House of Lords 1934-40; chm Hereford, Worcester, Warwicks and W Midlands Regnl Agric Wages Cttee; *Recreations* shooting, fishing; *Style* - Vernon Harington Esq; Woodlands House, Whitbourne, Worcester (☎ Knightwick 437)

HARKNESS, Lt-Col Hon Douglas Scott; GM (1943), ED (1944), PC (Can 1957); *b* 29 March 1903; *Educ* Alberta U; *m* 1932, Frances, nee McMillan; 1 s; *Career* MP 1945-72, Min of Nat Defence Canada 1960-63; *Style* - Lt-Col Hon Douglas Harkness, GM, ED, PC; 716 Imperial Way SW, Calgary, Alberta, Canada (☎ 403 243 0825)

HARKNESS, John Leigh; s of Verney Harknes, OBE (d 1980); *b* 29 June 1918; *Educ* Whitgift; *m* 1947, Betty, nee Moore; 2 s, 1 da; *Career* rose breeder, md R Harkness & Co 1960-77, sec Br Assoc Rose Breeders 1973-, v-pres 1969- Roy Nat Rose Soc; *Style* - John Harkness Esq; 1 Bank Alley, Southwold, Suffolk (☎ 722030)

HARKNESS, Rear-Adm James Percy Knowles; CB (1971); s of Capt P Harkness, W Yorks Regt; *b* 28 Nov 1916; *m* 1949, Joan, da of late Vice-Adm N Sulivan, CVO; 2 da; *Career* Dir-Gen Naval Manpower 1970-72; *Style* - Rear-Adm James Harkness, CB

HARKNESS, Capt Kenneth Lanyon; CBE (1963), DSC (1940); s of late Maj T Harkness and late Mrs G de Burgh; *b* 24 Aug 1900; *Educ* RNCs Osborne and Dartmouth, Cambridge; *m* 1, 1932, Joan (d 1979), da of Maj Arthur Lovell; 1 da; m 2, 1979, Mrs Powell (Mary, nee Stroud); *Career* Ch of Staff CIC Portsmouth 1947, Regnl Dir CD London 1954-65; *Style* - Capt Kenneth Harkness, CBE, DSC; Far Rockaway, Durford Wood, Petersfield, Hants (☎ Liss 3173)

HARLAND, David Henry Cave, s of Percy Harland, of Rotherfield Sussex (d 1948); *b* 17 Jan 1916; *Educ* Roborough Sch Eastbourne, Bart's Hosp London; *m* 1956, Norah, nee Burke; 1 da; *Career* High Sheriff Beds 1976-77, consultant surgn Luton and Dunstable Hosp 1956-78, FRCS; *Style* - David Harland Esq; St Johns, Woburn Sands, Milton Keynes (☎ 0908 583229)

HARLAND, Air Marshal Sir Reginald Edward Wynyard; KBE (1974), CB (1972); s of Charles Harland; *b* 30 May 1920; *Educ* Stowe, Trinity Cambridge; *m* 1942, Doreen Romanis; 3 s (1 decd), 2 da; *Career* AOC-in-C RAF Support Cmmd 1973-77, with W S Atkins & Ptnrs Epsom 1977-; *Style* - Air Marshal Sir Reginald Harland, KBE CB; Battlecrease Hall, Russell rd, Shepperton, Middx (☎ Walton-on-Thames 26060)

HARLECH, 5 Baron (GB 1876); William David Ormsby-Gore; KCMG (1961), PC (1957); s of 4 Baron Harlech, KG, GCMG, PC (d 1964), and Lady Beatrice Gascoyne-Cecil, da of 4 Marq of Salisbury; *b* 20 May 1918; *Educ* Eton, New Coll Oxford; *m* 1, 1940, Sylvia (d 1967), da of late Hugh Lloyd Thomas, CMG, CVO; 1 s (and 1 s decd), 3 da; m 2, 1969, Pamela, nee Colin, of New York; 1 da; *Heir* s Hon Francis Ormsby-Gore; *Career* MP (C) Oswestry 1950-61, Min State For Affrs 1957-61; Dep Ldr Oppn Ho Lds 1966-67; Tstee Pilgrim Tst; Br Ambass to Washington 1961-65, Pres Br Bd Film Censors 1965-, chm Harlech TV, Kennedy Meml Trust; dir Morgan Crucible, Commercial Bank of Wales, chm Nat Ctee for Electoral Reform; *Clubs* Pratt's; *Style* - The Rt Hon The Lord Harlech, KCMG, PC; 14a Ladbroke rd, W11 (☎ 01 229 6701); Glyn, Talsarnau, Gwynedd (Harlech 338)

HARLEY, Christopher Charles; JP (1960); s of Maj John Harley, of Brampton Bryan (d 1960); *b* 31 Dec 1926; *Educ* Eton, Magdalene Cambridge; *m* 1959, Susan, da of Sir Roderick Barclay, GCVO, KCMG; 4 s; *Career* landowner, farmer, forester, FLS, MIMechE; *Recreations* rare trees and books, shooting; *Clubs* Overseas League; *Style* - Christopher Harley Esq, JP; Brampton Bryan Hall, Bucknell, Salop (☎ 241)

HARLEY, Sir Thomas Winlack; MBE (1944), MC (1918) DL (Cheshire 1962); s of George Harley; *b* 27 June 1895; *Educ* Birkenhead Sch, Eton; *m* 1924, Margaret Hilda (d 1981), da of late Canon Bardsley; 3 s; *Career* consultant lawyer; kt 1960; *Style* - Sir Thomas Harley, MBE, MC, DL; Hesketh Hey, Thornton Hough, Wirral, Merseyside (☎ 051 336 3439)

HARLOCK, Maj-Gen Hugh George Frederick; CBE (1953); s of James Harlock; *b* 20 Aug 1900; *Educ* Wesley Coll Melbourne, RMC Duntroon; *m* 1935, Florence, nee Ewing; 1 s, 1 da; *Career* GOC N Cmmd, Australian Mil Fces 1954-57; *Style* - Maj-Gen Hugh Harlock, CBE; 2 Holmes st, Toowong, Qld 4066, Australia

HARMAN, Jeremiah LeRoy; QC (1968); s of late Rt Hon Sir Charles Harman; *b* 13 April 1930; *Educ* Eton; *m* 1960, Erica, da of Hon Sir Maurice Bridgeman; 2 s, 1 da; *Career* barr 1954; *Style* - Jeremiah Harman Esq, QC; Gt Shefford House, Newbury, Berks (☎ Gt Shefford 212); Sra-na-Cloya, nr Louisburgh, Co Mayo; 9 Old Sq, Lincoln's Inn, WC2 (☎ 01 405 0846)

HARMAN, Gen Sir Jack Wentworth; GCB (1978, KCB 1974), OBE (1962), MC (1943); s of late Lt-Gen Sir Wentworth Harman, KCB, DSO; *b* 20 July 1920; *Educ* Wellington, Sandhurst; *m* 1947, Gwladys, widow of Lt-Col R Murphy and da of Sir Idwal Lloyd; 1 da and 2 step da; *Career* Dep Supreme Allied Cdr Europe 1978-81; *Style* - Gen Sir Jack Harman, GCB, OBE, MC; Dinton, nr Salisbury, Wilts (☎ Teffont 288)

HARMAN, Robert Donald; QC (1974); s of late Herbert Harman, MC; *b* 26 Sept 1928; *Educ* St Paul's, Magdalen Oxford; *m* 1, 1960, Sarah (d 1965), nee Cleverly; 2 s; m 2, 1968, Rosamond, JP, da of late Cdr G Scott, RN; 2 da; *Career* barr 1954, recorder of Crown Court 1972-; *Style* - Robert Harman, Esq, QC; 17 Pelham Cres, SW7 (☎ 01 584 4304); 2 Harcourt Bldgs, Temple EC4 (☎ 01 353 2112); Waldershare Cottage, Sandwich Bay, Kent (☎ Sandwich 2760)

HARMAR-NICHOLLS, Baron (Life Peer 1974), of Peterborough, Cambs; Sir Harmar Harmar-Nicholls; 1 Bt (1960), JP, MEP (C) Gtr Manchester S 1979-; s of Charles Nicholls; *b* 1 Nov 1912; *Educ* Q Mary's G S Walsall; *m* 1940, Dorothy, nee Edwards; 2 da; *Heir* none; *Career* MP (C) Peterborough 1950-74, chm Nicholls & Hennessy (Hotels) Ltd, Malvern Festival Theatre Trust Ltd, Pleasurama 1970-; dir J & H Nicholls & Co , Radio Luxemburg (London) Ltd; Lloyd's Underwriter; *Style* - The Rt Hon The Lord Harmar-Nicholls JP, MEP; Abbeylands, Weston, Stafford (☎ 252)

HARMAR-NICHOLLS, Hon Susan Frances Nicholls; da of Baron Harmar-Nicholls (Life Peer and 1 Bt); *b* 1943; *Style* - The Hon Susan Harmar-Nicholls

HARMER, Sir (John) Dudley; OBE (1963), JP (Kent 1962); s of Ernest Harmer; *b* 27 July 1913; *Educ* Merchant Taylors', Wye Coll; *m* 1947, Erika Minder-Lanz, of Switzerland; 2 s; *Career* chm 1966-71 SE Area Conservative Provincial Cncl, dep chm Kent Agric Exec Cttee 1964-72; *Style* - Sir Dudley Harmer, OBE, JP; Stone Hill, Egerton, Ashford, Kent (☎ Egerton 241)

HARMER , Sir Frederic Evelyn; CMG (1945); s of late Sir Sidney Harmer, KBE; *b* 3 Nov 1905; *Educ* Eton, King's Cambridge; *m* 1, 1931, Barbara (d 1972), da of late Maj J Hamilton, JP, of Fyne Court, Bridgwater; 1 s, 3 da; m 2, 1973, Daphne Shelton Agar; *Career* with Treasury 1939-45, dep chm P&OSN Co 1957-70, govt dir BP 1953-70; kt 1968 *Style* - Sir Frederic Harmer, CMG; Tiggins Field, Kelsale, Saxmundham, Suffolk (☎ 3156)

HARMOOD-BANNER, Sir George Knowles; 3 Bt (UK 1924); s of Sir Harmood Harmood-Banner, 2 Bt (d 1950); *b* 9 Nov 1918; *Educ* Eton, Cambridge U; *m* 1947, Rosemary Jane, da of Col Maurice Lawrence Treston, CBE, FRCS, FRCOG, late IMS; 2 da; *Heir* none; *Career* 1939-45 War, 2 Lt Roy Welch Fus 1942, attached to East African Engineers (SEAC), transferred RASC 1945; *Style* - Sir George Harmood-Banner, Bt; c/o The Bank of Nova Scotia, 62-63 Threadneedle st, EC2P 2LS

HARMSWORTH, 2 Baron (UK 1939); Cecil Desmond Bernard Harmsworth; s of 1 Baron (d 1948); *b* 19 Aug 1903; *Educ* Eton, Ch Ch Oxford; *m* 1926, Dorothy, da of Hon J Heinlein, sometime State Senator, of Ohio; 1 da; *Heir* bro, Hon Eric Harmsworth; *Career* formerly publisher; painter, particularly portraits; *Style* - Rt Hon Lord Harmsworth; Lime Lodge, Egham, Surrey (☎ 2379)

HARMSWORTH, Hon Camilla Patricia Caroline; da of 3 Viscount Rothermere; *b* 28 July 1964; *Style* - The Hon Camilla Harmsworth

HARMSWORTH, Elen, Lady; Elen; da of Nicolaj Billenstein, of Randers, Denmark; *m* 1925, Sir Hildebrand Alfred Beresford Harmsworth, 2 Bt (d 1977); *Style* - Elen, Lady Harmsworth; Deepdene, Shottermill, Haslemere, Surrey

HARMSWORTH, Hon Eric Beauchamp Northcliffe; s of 1 Baron Harmsworth (d 1948), and hp of bro, 2 Baron; *b* 28 Aug 1905; *Educ* Eton, Ch Ch Oxford; *m* 1, 1935, Hélène (d 1962), da of Col Jules-Raymond Dehove, of Paris; 1 s, 1 da; m 2, 1964, Helen Gordon (Hudson), da of late Maj-Gen Granville George Loch, CB, CMG, CBE, DSO; *Style* - The Hon Eric Harmsworth; 27 Hartington rd, Chiswick, W4

HARMSWORTH, Hon Esmond Vyvyan; s of 2 Viscount Rothermere by his 3 w Mary, Viscountess Rothermere, *qv*; *b* 18 June 1967; *Style* - The Hon Esmond Harmsworth

HARMSWORTH, Hildebrand Esmund Miles; s and h of Sir Hildebrand Harold Harmsworth, 3 Bt; *b* 1 Sept 1964; *Style* - Hildebrand Harmsworth Esq

HARMSWORTH, Sir Hildebrand Harold; 3 Bt (UK 1922), of Freshwater Grove, Parish of Shipley, Co Sussex; s of Sir Hildebrand Alfred Beresford, 2 Bt (d 1977); *b* 5 June 1931; *Educ* Harrow, Trin Coll Dublin; *m* 1960, Gillian Andrea, da of William John Lewis, of Tetbury, Glos; 1 s, 2 da; *Heir* s, Hildebrand Esmund Miles; *Style* - Sir Hildebrand Harmsworth, Bt; Ewlyn Villa, 42 Leckhampton rd, Cheltenham, Glos

HARMSWORTH, Lady Jessamine Cecile Marjorie; *née* Gordon; da of 3 Marquess of Aberdeen & Temair; *b* 14 Aug 1910; *m* 1937, Michael St John Harmsworth, DL, nephew of Lords Northcliffe, Rothermere and Harmsworth; 2 s, 4 da; *Career* chm Caithness County Music Cttee, Pres County Save the Children Fund; *Style* - Lady Jessamine Harmsworth; Thrumster House, Caithness

HARMSWORTH, Hon (Harold) Jonathan Esmond Vere; s and h of 3 Viscount Rothermere; *b* 3 Dec 1967; *Style* - The Hon Jonathan Harmsworth

HARMSWORTH, Stanley George Michael St John; DL (Caithness); s of Vyvyan Harmsworth; *b* 13 Oct 1916; *Educ* Harrow; *m* 1937, Lady Jessamine Gordon, da of 3 Marquess of Aberdeen and Temair, DSO, by his 1 w, Cecile, nee Drummond; 2 s, 4 da; *Career* Capt WW II Seaforth Highlanders; co dir; *Style* - Stanley Harmsworth Esq, DL; Thrumster House, Caithness

HARMSWORTH, St John Bernard Vyvyan; s of Vyvyan Harmsworth and Constance Catt; *b* 28 Nov 1912; *Educ* Harrow, New Coll Oxford; *m* 1937, Jane, da of Basil Boothby; 3 da; *Career* barr 1937, metropolitan magistrate 1961-; *Style* - St John Harmsworth Esq; 25 Whitelands, SW3

HARMSWORTH BLUNT, Margaret, Lady; Margaret Hunam; da of William Redhead, of Carville Hall, Brentford, *m* 1, 1920 (m dis 1938), 2 Viscount Rothermere (d 1978); 1 s (3 Viscount), 2 da (Hon Lady Cooper-Key, Countess of Cromer, *qqv*); m 2, Capt Thomas Hussey, RN (ret); m 3, 1947, as his 2 w, Sir John Blunt, 10 Bt (d 1969); *Style* - Margaret, Lady Harmsworth Blunt; The Old Mill, Mayfield, Sussex

HARN, Hon Mrs (Mary Clare); *née* Douglas-Scott-Montagu; da of 2 Baron Montagu of Beaulieu, KCIE, CSI (d 1929); *b* 1909; *m* 1, 1953 (m dis 1968), Viscount Garnock, s of 14 Earl of Lindsay; m 2, 1979, Timothy Charles Austin Harn; *Style* - The Hon Mrs Harn

HARNDEN, Arthur Baker; CB (1969), TD (1950); s of Cecil Henry Harnden (d 1962); *b* 6 Jan 1909; *Educ* various state schools, London U; *m* 1, 1935, Maisie Elizabeth Annie (d 1970), nee Winterburn; 1 s; m 2, 1971, Jean Kathleen, nee Wheeler; *Career* Lt-Col (GSO1) War Office, civil servant (GPO), chartered engineer, 1962-67 dir London Telecommunications Region, 1967-79 sr dir Operations, 1969 chm Supplementary Benefits Appeal Tribunal, ret 1969; *Recreations* painting, pottery; *Style* - Arthur Harnden Esq, CB, TD; Comrie, Dipley, Hartley Wintney, Hants (☎ 025 126 3265)

HARPER, Sir Arthur Grant; KCVO (1959, CVO 1954), CBE (1954), JP (1949); s of William Harper; *b* 16 July 1898; *Educ* Hastings High Sch; *m* 1925, Hilda Evans; 2 s, 1 da; *Career* former dir of Royal Tours of NZ and former Clerk of the Writs NZ; ret chm Williams Hldgs Ltd, Wareham Assocs, Woolshed Restaurant Ltd; *Style* - Sir Arthur Harper, KCVO, CBE, JP; Flat 1, 50 Devonshire rd, Miramar, Wellington, New Zealand (☎ 886 425)

HARPER, Charles Anthony des Noettes; CBE (1969, OBE 1964); s of Dr Charles Harper, of Finchley; *b* 17 July 1916; *Educ* St Edward's Oxford; *m* 1947, Francesca, da of Col F Beecham, of Cape Town; 1 da; *Career* Brig, served WW II NW Europe, later India, Malaya, Singapore; MOD HQ Intelligence Centre 1974-81; *Clubs* Army & Navy; *Style* - Brig Charles Harper, CBE; Venus House, The Street, Appledore, Ashford, Kent (☎ Appledore 375)

HARPER, Frank Appleby; CB (1979), MBE (1954); s of Frank Harper (d 1928); *b* 11 April 1920; *Educ* Centl G S Birmingham; *m* 1, 1943, Daphne, nee Short (d 1965); 1 da; m 2, 1968 (as her 2 husband), Jillian, da of Col G Brooks, of Farnham; *Career* RE to 1964; Home Civil Service 1964, dir Dept of Ed and Science (Establishments and Organistaion) 1974-80; *Style* - Frank Harper Esq, CB, MBE; Lochnell, 1 Searle rd, Farnham, Surrey (☎ 714127)

HARPER, Hon Mrs (Hazel Eleanor); da of Baron Woolley, CBE, DL (Life Peer); *b* 11 Dec 1938; *Educ* Malvern Girls Coll; *m* 1961, William David Harper; 2 s, 1 da; *Career* SRN, Magistrate 1980, part time night nursing superintendent; JP duties; *Recreations* golf, archery, swimming; *Clubs* Royal Liverpool Golf, Calday Bowmen; *Style* - The Hon Mrs Harper; Felsberg, Gerard rd, West Kirby, Wirral (☎ 051 625 9840)

HARPER, James Norman; s of His Honour Judge Norman Harper (d 1967); *b* 30 Dec 1932; *Educ* Marlborough, Magdalen Oxford; *m* 1956, Blanka Miroslava Eva, da of Miroslav Sigmund of Henley on Thames; 1 s, 1 da; *Career* Lt RA (Nat Serv and TA for 3 years); called to the Bar Gray's Inn 1957, appointed a Recorder 1980; *Recreations* cricket and hockey; *Clubs* MCC; *Style* - James Harper Esq; 59 Kenton rd, Gosforth, Newcastle upon Tyne, NE3 4NJ (☎ 857611)

HARPER, Martin John; s of Frank Harper, of Welford-on-Avon; *b* 26 March 1925; *Educ* King Edward's G S Birmingham, LSE; *m* 1949, Stella, da of Frank Ainsdale, of Southport; 1 s, 2 da; *Career* merchant banker; dir Keyser Ullmann 1971, London Interstate Bank 1980, Charterhouse Japhet 1980 (Head Banking Div); *Recreations* reading, music, walking; *Clubs* Carlton, Overseas Bankers; *Style* - Martin Harper Esq; 1 Paternoster Row, EC4 (☎ 01 248 3999); 46a Priestlands Park rd, Sidcup, Kent (☎ 01 300 1264)

HARPHAM, Sir William; KBE (1966, OBE 1948), CMG (1953); s of William Harpham, of Grimsby (d 1932); *b* 3 Dec 1906; *Educ* Wintringham Secdy Sch Grimsby, Christ's Cambridge; *m* 1945, Isabelle, da of Maurice Droz; 1 s, 1 da; *Career* HM For Serv to 1967, Ambass to Bulgaria 1964-66, Dir Gt Britain-East Europe Centre 1967-80; *Clubs* Travellers', RAC; *Style* - Sir William Harpham, KBE, CMG; 9 Kings Keep, Putney Hill, SW15 (☎ 01 788 1383)

HARRIES, Hon Mrs (Anne Marjorie); *née* Sidney; da (by 1 m) of 1 Visc De L'Isle, VC, KG, GCMG, GCVO, PC; *b* 1947; *m* 1967, David Alexander Harries, s of Rear-Adm David Hugh Harries, CB, CBE; 2 s, 1 da; *Style* - The Hon Mrs Harries; Hayselden Manor, Sissinghurst, Kent

HARRIMAN, Hon Mrs (Pamela Beryl); da of late 11 Baron Digby, KG, DSO, MC, TD; *b* 1920; *m* 1, 1939 (m dis 1946), Maj the Hon Randolph Frederick Edward Spencer-Churchill, MBE (d 1968); m 2, 1960, Leland Hayward (d 1971); m 3, 1971, (William) Averell Harriman; *Style* - The Hon Mrs Harriman; 3038 N Street NW, Washington DC, 20007, USA

HARRINGTON, 11 Earl of (GB 1742); William Henry Leicester Stanhope; also Viscount Stanhope of Mahon, Baron Stanhope of Elvaston (both GB 1717), Baron Harrington (GB 1730), and Viscount Petersham (GB 1742); s of 10 Earl of Harrington, MC (d 1929, whose great great unc, the 4 Earl (the original of Lord Fitzbooby in Disraeli's 'Coningsby'), was the inventor of the blend of snuff known as Petersham mixture; snuff was the colour he used for his livery and equipage; he never went out of doors before six in the evening); suc kinsman, 7 & last Earl Stanhope, in the Viscountcy of Stanhope of Mahon and the Barony of Stanhope of Elvaston 1967; *b* 24 Aug 1922; *Educ* Eton; *m* 1, 1942, Eileen (m dis 1946), da of Sir John Foley Grey, 8 Bt; 1 s, 1 da; m 2, 1947, Anne (m dis 1962), da of Maj Richard Chute, of Co Limerick; 1 s, 2 da; m 3, 1964, Priscilla, da of Hon Archibald Cubitt (5 s of 2 Baron Ashcombe) by his 2 w Sibell; 1 s, 1 da; *Heir* s, Viscount Petersham; *Career* late Capt RAC, served WW II; landowner (c 700 acres), adopted Irish citizenship 1965; *Style* - The Rt Hon Earl of Harrington; Greenmount Stud, Patrickswell, Co Limerick, Eire (☎ (061) 9 61 18/47/29)

HARRIS, 5 Baron (UK 1815); George St Vincent Harris; CBE (1972), MC, JP (Kent 1919), DL (1936); s of 4 Baron Harris, GCSI, GCIE, CB, sometime ADC to Edward VII (d 1932, presumably the Lord Harris of whom, when attired in a bowler hat, Edward VII is alleged to have enquired 'Goin' rattin' Harris?') by his w Hon Lucy Jervis, CI (da of 3 Viscount St Vincent); *b* 3 Sept 1889; *Educ* Eton, Ch Ch Oxford; *m* 1918, Dorothy, da of Rev John Crookes; 1 s; *Heir* s, Hon George Harris; *Career* chm Kent Police Authority 1945-64, Capt Yeo ret; V-Lt Kent 1944-72; KStJ, Co Commissioner St John Ambulance Bde 1940-45, served WW I; *Clubs* MCC, Carlton, Beefsteak; *Style* - The Rt Hon Lord Harris CBE MC JP DL; Belmont Park, Faversham, Kent

HARRIS OF GREENWICH, Baron (Life Peer UK 1974); John Henry Harris; s of Alfred Harris; *b* 5 April 1930; *Educ* Pinner G S; *m* 1952, Patricia, da of George Alstrom; 1 s, 1 da; *Career* chm Parole Bd England & Wales 1979-, Westward TV 1980-; PA to Ldr Oppn 1959, Dir Publicity L Pty 1962-64; Special Assist- For Sec 1964-66, Home Sec 1966-67, Chllr Exchequer 1967-70; Min State Home Off 1974-79; politial correspondent Economist 1970-74; *Style* - Rt Hon Lord Harris of Greenwich; House of Lords, SW1

HARRIS OF HIGH CROSS, Baron (Life Peer UK 1979); Ralph Harris; s of William Henry Harris (d 1954); *b* 10 Dec 1924; *Educ* Tottenham G S, Queens' Cambridge; *m* 1949, Jose Pauline, da of Roger Fredrick Jeffery (d 1975); 1 s, 1 da (and 1 da decd); *Career* contested (C) Kirkcaldy 1951, ldr writer Glasgow Herald 1955, lecturer St Andrews U 1949-56 (in political economy), gen dir Inst of Ec Affairs 1957-, memb Cncl U Coll at Buckingham, dir Churchill Press; *Style* - The Rt Hon The Lord Harris of High Cross; 4 Walmar Close, Beech Hill,

Hadley Wood, Barnet, Herts (☎ 01 449 6212)

HARRIS, Anthony Kyrle Travers; s and h of Marshal of the RAF Sir Arthur Harris, 1 Bt, GCB, OBE, AFC; *b* 18 March 1918; *Educ* Oundle; *Career* 1939-45 War with Queen Victoria's Rifles and Wiltshire Regt; *Style* - Anthony Harris Esq; c/o Barclays Bank, Queen's Gate, SW7

HARRIS, Marshal of the RAF Sir Arthur Travers; 1 Bt (UK 1953), of Chepping Wycombe, Bucks, GCB (1945, KCB 1942, CB 1940), OBE (1927), AFC (1918); s of George S T Harris, of PWD India; *b* 13 April 1892; *m* 1, 1916, Barbara, da of Lt-Col E W K Money; 1 s, 2 da; m 2, 1938, Thérèse, da of Maj E P Hearne; 1 da; *Heir* s, Anthony Kyrle Travers; *Career* Hon LLD Liverpool, is Marshal of the RAF, 1914-18 War with 1 Rhodesian Regt RFC and RAF in SW Africa, France, India, Mesopotamia and Middle East (despatches), 1939-45 War, was Air Officer Cmdg RAF Palestine and Transjordan 1938-39, and No 5 Gp 1939-40, Dep Ch of Air Staff 1940-41, Head of RAF Delegation to USA 1941, and Air Officer Cmdng-in-Ch Bomber Command 1942-45, received Freedom of Honiton 1945, of Chepping Wycombe 1946, and City of London 1978; *Clubs* Army and Navy, Pathfinders, Royal and Ancient (St Andrews), Bankers (New York), Nederlands (Cape Town); *Style* - Marshal of the RAF Sir Arthur Harris, Bt, GCB, OBE, AFC; The Ferry House, Goring-on-Thames, Oxfordshire RG8 9DX

HARRIS, Hon Charles Edward; s of Viscount FitzHarris; *b* 1972; *Style* - The Hon Charles Harris

HARRIS, Christopher John Ashford; s and h of Sir Jack (Wolfred) Ashford Harris, 2 Bt; *b* 26 Aug 1934; *m* 1957, Anna, da of F de Malmanche, of Auckland, NZ; 1 s, 2 da; *Style* - Christopher Harris Esq; 21 Anne st, Wadestown, Wellington, New Zealand

HARRIS, Cecil Rhodes; s of Frederick Harris; *b* 4 May 1923; *Educ* Kingston G S; *m* 1946, Gwenyth, da of Hugh Evans; 1 s, 2 da; *Career* dep ch gen man Commercial Union Assur 1980- (exec dir 1976, dir 1975-, Co Sec 1974-78); *Recreations* bible study; *Style* - Cecil Harris Esq; 35a Plough Lane, Purley, Surrey (☎ 01 668 2820)

HARRIS, Hon Deborah Jane Alstrom; da of Baron Harris of Greenwich (Life Peer); *b* 1958; *Style* - The Hon Deborah Harris

HARRIS, Hon Francis Oliver Alstrom; s of Baron Harris of Greenwich (Life Peer); *b* 1961; *Style* - The Hon Francis Harris

HARRIS, Hon Guy Richard; s of Viscount FitzHarris; *b* 1975; *Style* - The Hon Guy Harris

HARRIS, Geoffrey Ronald; s of Clarence Edgar Harris; *b* 10 Sept 1926; *Educ* Whitgift; *m* 1953, Joan, da of George Jarvis; 2 s, 1 da; *Career* formerly Lt, served Germany, India; insur broker; dir Stewart Wrightson (Marine) 1965, Codresa, Madrid 1973, Stewart Wrightson Chile Ltd 1978 and assoc cos; *Recreations* sport, travel; *Style* - Geoffrey Harris Esq; Rookwood, Lower Park rd, Chipstead, Surrey (☎ Downland 53768)

HARRIS, Hon George Robert John; s and h of 5 Baron Harris, CBE, MC; *b* 17 April 1920; *Educ* Eton, Ch Ch Oxford; *Career* Capt RA; *Clubs* Lansdowne; *Style* - The Hon George Harris; Huntingfield, Faversham, Kent (☎ Eastling 282)

HARRIS, Hugh Martin West; JP (Surrey 1961, Sussex 1971); s of Sir Sidney Harris, CB, CVO, of Wimbledon; *b* 12 May 1919; *Educ* Marlborough, Queen's Oxford; *m* 1, 1947, Ann (d 1967); m 2, 1967, Isobel (m dis), da of Alexander Macdonald, of Larkhall, Lanarks; m 3, 1971, Jean Chisholm-Batten; *Career* chm Broad & Co 1974 (md 1965); *Recreations* local affairs, family; *Clubs* Naval & Military, HAC; *Style* - Lt-Col Hugh Harris, JP; 17 Oathill rd, Haywards Heath, Sussex (☎ 56205)

HARRIS, Joseph Hugh; JP (Penrith 1971); s of John Frederick Harris; *b* 3 June 1932; *Educ* Harrow and RAC Cirencester;

m 1957, Anne, da of Brig L H McRobert (d 1981); 3 s; *Career* Lt 11 Hussars PAO; farmer/landowner, sr steward Roy Ag Soc of England 1960-77, hon dir Roy Show 1978, chm dirs Grasmere Sports 1977, chm govs Aysgarth Sch 1975, high sheriff Cumbria 1976-77, dir Cumbrian Newspaper Ltd; *Recreations* shooting and field sports; *Style* - Joseph Harris Esq, JP; Brackenburgh, Calthwaite, Penrith, Cumbria, CA11 9PW (☎ Calthwaite 253)

HARRIS, Hon James Hugh Carleton; s and h of Viscount FitzHarris; *b* 29 April 1970; *Style* - The Hon James Harris

HARRIS, Hon Julian Paul; s of Baron Harris of High Cross (Life Peer); *Style* - The Hon Julian Harris; 4 Walmar Close, Beech Hill, Hadley Wood, Barnet, Herts (☎ 01 449 6212)

HARRIS, John Percival; His Honour Judge Harris; DSC (1945), QC (1974); s of Thomas Percival Harris, of Ebbor Hall, Somerset; *b* 16 Feb 1925; *Educ* Wells Cathedral Sch and Pembroke Coll Cambridge; *m* 1959, Janet Valerie, da of Archibald William Douglas, of Jersey, Channel Islands; 1 s, 2 da; *Career* Sub-Lt RNVR 1943-46; barr Middle Temple 1949-74, recorder of Crown Court 1972-, Circuit Judge 1980-; *Recreations* golf, reading and Victorian paintings; *Style* - His Honour Judge Harris, DSC, QC; Tudor ct, Fairmile Park rd, Cobham, Surrey, KT11 2PP (☎ Cobham 4756)

HARRIS, Sir Jack Wolfred Ashford; 2 Bt (UK 1932), of Bethnal Green, Co London; s of Rt Hon Sir Percy Harris, 1 Bt, PC, DL (1952); *b* 23 July 1906; *Educ* Shrewsbury, Trin Hall Cambridge; *m* 1933, Patricia, da of Arthur Penman, of NSW; 2 s, 1 da; *Heir* s, Christopher John Ashford Harris; *Career* chm Bing Harris & Co NZ 1935-, past pres Wellington Chamber of Commerce; *Recreations* reading, gardening, swimming, writing; *Clubs* Wellington, Northern; *Style* - Sir Jack Harris, Bt; Flat 12, Quarterdeck, Carabella st, Kirribilli, NSW, Australia; Te Rama, Waikanae, New Zealand (☎ 5001)

HARRIS, Hon Mrs (Linda Carol); *née* Bellow; da of Baron Bellwin, JP (Life Peer); *m* 1976, Leslie Harris; *Style* - The Hon Mrs Harris; 33 High Ash av, Leeds 17

HARRIS, Paul Ratliff; OBE (1980); s of Maurice Harris, of Bexhill; *b* 31 Aug 1913; *Educ* Gresham's; *m* 1946, Barbara, da of Lyn Albrecht, of Melbourne; 3 s, 1 da; *Career* formerly Lt-Col SE Asia Cmmd, HQ Supreme Allied Cmmd; dep chm & jt md M P Harris Hldgs; *Recreations* golf, sailing, vintage cars; *Clubs* Naval, Rolls Royce Enthusiasts, Bentley Drivers; *Style* - Paul Harris Esq, OBE; Wannock Place, Jevington rd, Polegate, E Sussex (☎ 4160)

HARRIS, Rosina Mary; da of Alfred Harris, DSO, CBE (d 1976); *b* 30 May 1921; *Educ* Oxford (BCL, MA); *Career* served with American Ambulance Corps in the UK during War; solictor; appointed senior ptnr of Joynson-Hicks & Co 1977; appointed deputy chm of Blundell-Permoglaze Holdings 1981; Queen's Silver Jubilee Medal; *Recreations* riding; *Clubs* Naval & Military; *Style* - Miss Rosina Harris; 23 Devonshire Place, London WI (☎ 01 935 6041)

HARRIS, Richard Travis; s of Douglas Harris (d 1964); *b* 15 Apr 1919; *Educ* Charterhouse, RMA Woolwich; *m* 1, 1941, June Constance; 1 s, 2 da; m 2, 1953, Margaret Sophia, nee Aron; *Career* Lt-Col, Roy Signals 1939, France 1940, W Desert 1941-43, Italy 1943, Staff Coll 1944, Instructor Sch of Infantry 1944-45, Sudan Defence Force 1947-50, ret 1950; md Rediffusion (Nigeria) Ltd 1951-54, dep gen man Associated Rediffusion Ltd 1954-57, md Dolland & Aitchison Ltd 1970-78, chm and md Dolland & Aitchison Gp Ltd 1970, dir Gallaher Ltd 1978-, dep chm Gallaher Ltd; *Recreations* flyfishing; *Clubs* Roy Western Yacht Club of England; *Style* - Richard Harris Esq; 21 Lucy's Mill, Mill Lane, Stratford upon Avon, Warwicks (☎ 6616)

HARRIS, Hon Mrs (Thelma Eirene); *née* Kitson; da of 2 Baron Airedale, JP; *b* 1902; *m* 1923, Noel Gordon Harris, MD, MRCS, FRCP, DPM (d 1963; s of Sir Alexander Harris, KCMG, CB, CVO); 1 s (James Mallet-Harris, who m Primrose, da of late Sir Philip du Cros, 2 Bt, and lives at Mallet Court, Curry Mallet, Somerset), 3 da; *Style* - The Hon Mrs Harris; The Cottage, Ford, Wiveliscombe, Taunton, Somerset (☎ Wiveliscombe 244)

HARRIS, William Barclay; QC (1961); s of William Cecil Harris, of the landed gentry family formerly of Westcotes; *b* 25 Nov 1911; *Educ* Harrow, Trin Cambridge; *m* 1937, Elizabeth, da of Capt Sir Clive Milnes-Coates, 2 Bt, OBE, JP, and Lady Celia, nee Crewe-Milnes, JP, da of 1 and last Marquess of Crewe, KG; 1 s, 2 da; *Career* served 1940-45 Maj Coldstream Gds, N Africa, Italy, Germany; barr 1937; chm Rowton Hotels 1965-, Church Commissioner 1966-, chm Redundant Churches Cttee 1972-; *Recreations* shooting; *Clubs* Brooks's, Athenaeum, MCC; *Style* - William Harris Esq, QC; Moatlands, E Grinstead, W Sussex (☎ Sharpthorne 810228); 29 Barkston gdns, SW5 (☎ 01 373 8793)

HARRIS, William Cecil; s of Richard Cecil Harris (d 1928); *b* 3 Dec 1913; *Educ* William Hulmes Sch Manchester; *m* 1940, Florence Annie, da of James Henry Tidswell (d 1942); 1 s; *Career* Fl Lt, Burma (BAFSEA); insurance exec, ch gen man Phoenix Gp 1969-78, dep chm 1979-, pres Chartered Insurance Inst 1972-73, chm British Insurance Assoc 1976, master Worshipful Co of Insurers 1979-; *Recreations* golf and forestry; *Clubs* City Livery; *Style* - William Harris Esq; Hardbarrow Copse, Threals Lane, W Chiltington, Pulborough (☎ 079 832300)

HARRIS, Sir William Woolf; OBE (1961), JP (Bow St 1952); s of Simon Harris; *b* 19 Aug 1910; *Educ* Princeton; *m* 1952, Beverly, da of Howard Bowden, of Minneapolis; 1 s, 2 da; *Career* chm of many construction cos; chm Nat Union Con Assocs 1971-73, memb Con Pty Advsy Cttee on Policy 1965-75, Cncl Imperial Soc of Kts Batchelor 1978-, High Sheriff Gtr London 1971-77; kt 1974; *Style* - Sir William Harris, OBE, JP; 165 Bickenhall Mans, Gloucester pla, W1 (☎ 01 935 3752)

HARRIS-BURLAND, William; CBE (1953), TD; s of William Malcolm Harris-Burland (d 1956), of Seaton, S Devon; *b* 10 July 1902; *Educ* Whitgift Sch Croydon; *m* 1931, Stella Mary, da of Lt-Cdr William Webb (d 1950); *Career* served 1939-45 as Lt-Col with Special Operations Exec (Poland, Romania, Yugoslavia and Turkey), Allied Control Cmmn in Romania 1944-46; CA 1946-53 with Control Cmmn for Germany in charge of re-organisation of German Steel Industry also UK chm of Combined Steel Gp, Finance Dept of British Transport Cmmn 1954-67, dir of Accounts and Statistics British Railways 1961-, financial adviser to Hotels and Catering and Inland Waterways Sub-Cmmns, dir of several provincial bus cos; *Recreations* gardening and walking; *Clubs* Special Forces; *Style* - William Harris-Burland Esq, CBE, TD; 27 Chenies av, Little Chalfont, Amersham, Bucks (☎ 2093)

HARRISON, Alexander; CBE (1955); s of late John Harrison, CBE, DL, of Edinburgh; *b* 26 Feb 1890; *Educ* Merchiston Castle Sch and Edinburgh U; *m* 1931, Jean Muriel, da of John Small (d 1931); 1 s, 3 da; *Career* served 1914-18 War as temp Maj Roy Scots, Machine Gun Corps; CA; dep chm Trustee Savings Bank Assoc 1947-59, chm Edinburgh Savings Bank 1945-54, British Linen Bank 1945-68, Edinburgh Investment Trust 1945-60, Standard Life Assurance Co 1955-57, memb Edinburgh Town Cncl 1946-48; *Recreations* mountaineering; *Clubs* New (Edinburgh) and Alpine; *Style* - Alexander Harrison Esq, CBE; 3a Tipperlinn rd, EH10 5ET (☎ 031 447 7434)

HARRISON, Antony Roy; TD (1946), DL (1947); s of Ernest Charlton Harrison; *b* 17 June 1905; *Educ* King's Sch Worcester; *m* 1932, Margaret Lovell, da of Sidney Charles Harrison, of Birmingham; 3 s, 1 da; *Career* Lt-Col 1943, cmd 61 Inf divn Battle Sch 1943, cmd 1 Worcs Regt 1944, cmd 8 Worcs Regt 1945, served N W Europe (despatches); admitted a slr 1928; *Recreations* fishing, shooting and golf; *Clubs* Army and Navy, Union and County (Worcester); *Style* - Antony Harrison Esq, TD, DL; Lobden, Upper Colwall, nr Malvern, Worcs (☎ Colwall 40348)

HARRISON, (Alastair) Brian (Clarke); s of late Brig E Harrison, of Melbourne; *b*

3 Oct 1921; *Educ* Geelong G S, Trin Cambridge; *m* 1952, Elizabeth Hood Hardie, of NSW; 1 s, 1 da; *Career* dir Grindlay (Australia) Ltd, Agricultural Investments Australia Ltd, Commercial Bank of Australia Ltd, MP (C) Maldon 1955-74, Min of Ag Fish & Food 1958-60, High Sheriff Essex 1979 *Clubs* Carlton, Pratt's, Melbourne; *Style* - Brian Harrison Esq; Green Farm House, Copford, Colchester, Essex

HARRISON, Brian Fraser; s of James Fraser Harrison, County Court Judge (d 1974); *b* 6 Sept 1918; *Educ* St Christopher's Sch, Liverpool Coll; *m* 1939, Constance Kathleen Fraser, nee Bennion; 1 s; *Career* slr; ptnr Mace & Jones 1948-81, consultant 1981, memb Lord Chancellor's Liverpool Circuit Advisory Ctee 1972-; professional artist, author; *Books* Advocacy at Pelly Sessions, Work of a Magistrate, A Business of Your Own, A Business of Your Own Today; *Clubs* Law Soc, Jubilee, British Legal Assoc, Soc of Authors, Guild of Mastercraftmen; *Style* - Brian Harrison Esq; Mouldsworth House, Mouldsworth, Chester (☎ Manley 316)

HARRISON, Sir (Robert) Colin; 4 Bt (UK 1922), of Eaglescliffe, Co Durham; s of late Sir John Fowler Harrison, 2 Bt; suc bro, Sir (John) Wyndham Harrison, 3 Bt, 1955; *b* 25 May 1938; *Educ* Radley, St John's Cambridge; *m* 1963, Maureen Marie, da of E Leonard Chiverton, of Garth Corner, Vivers Place, Kirkbymoorside, Yorks; 1 s, 2 da; *Heir* s, John Wyndham Fowler Harrison; *Career* Cmmnd 5 Roy Northumberland Fus (Nat Ser) 1957-59, chm Young Master Printers Nat Ctee 1972-73; *Style* - Sir Colin Harrison, Bt; Keld Close, Hutton-le-Hole, York (☎ Lastingham 329)

HARRISON, Sir Cyril Ernest; s of Alfred Harrison; *b* 14 Dec 1901; *Educ* Burnley G S; *m* 1927, Ethel (d 1971), da of Edward Wood, FCA, JP, of Burnley; 2 s; *Career* kt 1963, chm English Sewing Cotton Co 1963-68, FBIM, FCIS; *Style* - Sir Cyril Harrison; 8 Harefield Drive, Holly rd South, Wilmslow, Cheshire (☎ 522186)

HARRISON, Maj-Gen Desmond; CB (1946), DSO (1940); s of R J Harrison, JP; *b* 11 Nov 1896; *Educ* Kilkenny Coll, Trinity Coll Dublin and RMA Woolwich; *m*; 2 s (1 decd), 2 da; *Career* served 1914-19 with RE and 1939-45 in 2 Div, CRE 3 Div, engr-in-ch SEAC 1943, dir Fortifications and Works War Office 1946, Col 1944, temp Maj-Gen 1944, ret 1947; dir Overseas Food Corpn 1947-49; *Recreations* golf, shooting and fishing; *Clubs* Anglo Belgian; *Style* - Maj-Gen Desmond Harrison, CB, DSO; 55 Hans rd, London, SW3 1RN (☎ 01 584 4867)

HARRISON, Hon Mrs - Hon (Joan) Elizabeth; *née* Rees-Williams; da of 1 Baron Ogmore, TD, PC (d 1976); *b* 1936; *Educ* Croham Hurst Sch and at Mont Olivet, Lausanne; *m* 1, 1957 (m dis 1969), Richard St John Harris, actor; 3 s; m 2, 1971 (m dis 1975), Rex Carey Harrison, actor; *Style* - The Hon Mrs Harrison; 71 Cadogan sq, SW1

HARRISON, Sir Ernest Thomas; OBE (1972); s of Ernest Horace Harrison; *b* 11 May 1926; *Educ* Trinity G S London; *m* 1960, Phyllis Brenda Knight; 3 s, 2 da; *Career* chm and md Racal Electronics Ltd 1966-; kt 1981; *Style* - Sir Ernest Harrison, OBE; Mackenzies, Tilford, nr Farnham, Surrey

HARRISON, Lady Isabella Bianca Rosa; *née* Child-Villiers; da of 9 Earl of Jersey; *b* 1950; *m* 1974, Peter Edward Harrison; 1 s, 1 da; *Style* - Lady Isabella Harrison; 13 Paradise Walk, SW3

HARRISON, Col John George; OBE (1975), TD (1960), DL (1973); s of James Harrison (d 1960); *b* 15 March 1920; *Educ* Bridgend Grammar Sch, St Luke's and Loughborough Colls; *m* 1946, Mona Patricia, da of Onslow Francis Froud (d 1950); 1 s, 2 da; *Career* served in WW II with Indian Inf, cmd Devon (1 RV) (TA) 1961-64, Dep Cdr 130 Inf Bde (TA) 1965-67, Territorial Col SW District 1967-68, Cmdt Devon ACF 1970-75; sch master; *Clubs* Exeter Golf and Country; *Style* - Col John Harrison, OBE, TD, DL; Ivy Cottage, 36 Buckerell ave, Exeter, Devon (☎ 0392 74959)

HARRISON, John Wyndham Fowler; s and h of Sir Colin Harrison, 4 Bt; *b* 14 Dec 1972; *Style* - John Harrison Esq

HARRISON, Kathleen Lady; Kathleen; da of Robert Livingston, of The Gables, Eaglescliffe, Co Durham; *m* 1930, Sir (John) Fowler Harrison, 2 Bt (d 1947); *Style* - Kathleen, Lady Harrison; Bonnie Banks, Sproxton, Helmsley, York YO6 5BJ

HARRISON, Kenneth Arthur; TD; *Career* chm Bostwick Doors (UK) Ltd, winner of Queen's Award for Export Achievement 1980; *Style* - Kenneth Harrison Esq, TD; c/o Bostwick Doors (UK) Ltd, Stockport, Cheshire

HARRISON, Hon Mrs Leila Cecilia; *née* Littleton; da of 4 Baron Hatherton (d 1944); *b* 1902; *m* 1922, (m dis 1949), Stuart Sandbach Harrison, MC, late Lt Irish Gds; 2 s, 1 da; *Style* - The Hon Mrs Leila Harrison; La Brétche, Roquebrune, Cap Martin, France AM

HARRISON, Sir Michael James Harwood; 2 Bt (UK 1961); s of Col Sir Harwood Harrison, 1 Bt, TD (d 1980), MP (C) Eye 1951-79, of Little Manor, Woodbridge, Suffolk; *b* 28 March 1936; *Educ* Rugby; *m* 1967, Louise, da of Edward Buxton Clive, of Swanmore Lodge, Swanmore, Hants; 1 s, 2 da; *Heir* s, Edwin Michael Harwood Harrison, b 29 May 1981; *Career* Lloyd's Insurance Broker, with Antony Gibbs Sage (aviation dir) 1978-, Freeman City of London, Liveryman Mercers' Co 1967-, memb Council Sail Training Assoc 1968-, dir of priv cos 1980-; *Style* - Sir Michael Harrison, Bt; 35 Paulton's sq, SW3 (☎ 01 352 1760)

HARRISON, (Desmond) Roger (Wingate); s of Maj-Gen Desmond Harrison, CB, DSO; *b* 9 Apr 1933; *Educ* Rugby, Worcester Coll Oxford; *m* 1965, Victoria, MVO, da of Rear-Adm J Lee Barber; 4 da; *Career* jt md The Observer 1977, dir Capital Radio, Weekend TV, Duke of York's Theatre; *Recreations* fishing, shooting; *Clubs* Cavalry; *Style* - Roger Harrison Esq; 35 Argyll rd, W8 (☎ 01 937 2770)

HARRISON, Seymour Warwick; JP; s of Alfred Harry Harrison (d 1978); *b* 10 March 1927; *Educ* Clifton Coll; *m* 1952, Marian, da of J Stuart Golfar (d 1966); 1 s, 3 da; *Career* industrialist; md-Saul D Harrison and Sons Ltd, Fraise Property Co Ltd, Dispofab Ltd, European Disposables BV (Holland), Kings Laundry (Gt Yarmouth) Ltd; *Recreations* gliding, riding, rugby football; *Style* - Seymour Harrison Esq, JP; 66B St James Beach Club, St James, Barbados

HARRISON-SMITH, Capt Sydney Alick; CBE (1959); s of Paymaster Rear-Adm Sir Francis Harrison Smith, KCB; *b* 29 Aug 1905; *Educ* St Peter's Seaford, RNCs Osborne & Dartmouth, RN Engrg Coll Keyham; *m* 1, 1933, Diana Mary Wyndham, da of Lt-Col Wyndham Philip Bannerman (d 1930); 1 s, 2 da; m 2, 1959, Margery, nee Hickes, wid of Sir Philip Whitehead, 4 Bt; *Career* Capt RN (China 1930-31, 1933-35 & 1947, Mediterranean 1938-40, Admiralty 1935-37, 1940-45, 1950-54, AERE Harwell 1954-58, ret 1958); 1958-64 Swan Hunter as nuclear advsr head of Engrg Dept, Neptune Yard; 1965-71 Vickers Shipbuilding as liaison offr with Cammell Laird in building of nuclear submarines; *Recreations* gardening, motoring; *Style* - Capt Sydney Harrison-Smith CBE RN; Cedarwood Cottage, S Moreton, Didcot, Oxon (☎ Didcot 813356)

HARROD, Lady Lucinda; *née* Lambton; da of Antony Lambton (6 Earl of Durham who disclaimed peerage 1970); *b* 1943; *m* 1965, Henry Mark Harrod, s of Sir (Henry) Roy Forbes Harrod; 2 s; *Style* - Lady Lucinda Harrod

HARROWBY, 6 Earl of (UK 1809); Dudley Ryder; JP (Staffs 1929), DL (1925); also Baron Harrowby (GB 1776) and Viscount Sandon (UK 1809); s of 5 Earl (d 1956) and Hon Dame Mabel Smith, DBE, da of Emily, Viscountess Hambleden; *b* 11 Oct 1892; *Educ* Eton, Ch Ch Oxford; *m* 1922, Lady Helena Coventry (d 1974), sis of 10 Earl of Coventry; 2 s, 1 da; *Heir* s, Viscount Sandon; *Career* patron of five livings; served WW I (Maj RA) & II; late Alderman & memb LCC; Assist Priv Sec to Sec State Colonies 1919-20, PPS Sec State Air 1922-23; Col Cmmdt Staffs Army Cadet Force 1946-50; memb Commission on Hist MSS 1935-66; MP (C) Shrewsbury 1922-23 & 1924-29; *Clubs* Travellers'; *Style* - The Rt Hon Earl of Harrowby JP DL; Burnt Norton, Chipping Campden, Glos; Sandon Hall, Stafford (☎ Sandon 392)

HARRY, Ralph Gordon; s of late Jenkin Campbell Harry; *b* 25 June 1908; *Educ* Moncton House Sch, Univ Coll Cardiff; *m* 1938, Dorothy Mary, nee Crafter; 2 da; *Career* assistant to Public Analyst Cardiff (Inst of Prev Med) 1934-37, head Cosmetic Preparations Research Dept, Beecham Research 1947-49, chief Experimental Chemist Maclean Group of Companies 1949-53, fellow Royal Soc Medicine, founder v-chm 1948-50, hon memb 1973; *Recreations* photography, music; *Clubs* Royal Society of Medicine; *Style* - Ralph Harry Esq; 61 Kimberley rd, Penylan, Cardiff (☎ Cardiff 495075)

HART, Christopher Charles Dudley; s of the late Rev Canon Charles Dudley Hart; *b* 15 Dec 1913; *Educ* St Edward's Oxford; *m* 1946, Meryl Pera, nee Wardle; 2 da; *Career* solicitor (senior partner), pres Nottinghamshire Law Soc 1964, former chm of Governors Lilley and Stone Sch Newark until 1980, pres Mental Health Tribunals; *Recreations* tennis, ornithology, photography; *Style* - Christopher Hart Esq; The Burnt House, South Collingham, Newark, Notts (☎ Newark 892238)

HARTE, Geoffrey Charles; s of Charles Fredrick Harte; *b* 16 Sept 1923; *Educ* Plympton G S; *m* 1950, Moira, nee Kennedy; 1 s; *Career* chm and md J & S Marine Ltd, exec dir Cray Electronics Gp; *Recreations* music, reading, sailing; *Clubs* Roy Cornwall Yacht, Inst of Dirs; *Style* - Geoffrey Harte Esq; Combers Week, Harracott, Barnstaple, N Devon (☎ 85448)

HARTFORD, Norman; s of William Lovelock Hartford; *b* 6 Jan 1920; *Educ* various state schools; *m* 1943, Doreen Lilian, nee Hildred; 1 s (Colin Anthony b 1948); *Career* W/Sgt NW Europe 1944, glider pilot at Arnhem; property manager, dir- Allnatt London Properties Ltd 1962-, Guildhall Property Holdings Co Ltd 1962-; *Recreations* walking, sailing (yacht- 'Scendor'); *Clubs* Royal Thames Yacht; *Style* - Norman Hartford Esq; 9 West Hayes, Lymington, Hampshire (☎ office- 01 965 6711)

HARTINGTON, Marquess of; Peregrine Andrew Morny Cavendish; s and h of 11 Duke of Devonshire, MC, PC, by Hon Deborah (Debo) Freeman-Mitford, sis of Nancy, Jessica and Unity Mitford (*see* Treuhaft, Hon Mrs) and Hon Lady Mosley, *qv*; *b* 27 April 1944; *Educ* Eton, Exeter Coll Oxford; *m* 1967, Amanda Carmen, da of late Cdr Edward Gavin Heywood-Lonsdale, RN; 1 s, 2 da; *Heir* Earl of Burlington; *Career* V-Chm Br Field Sports Soc 1981-; *Style* - Marquess of Hartington; 15 Christ Church rd, SW14 (☎ 01 878 2272); Chatsworth, Bakewell, Derbys

HARTLEY, Hon Mrs Angela Hermione; *née* Marshall; da of Baron Marshall of Leeds; *b* 1944; *m* 1966 (m dis 1980), Myles Spencer Harrison Hartley; *Style* - The Hon Mrs Angela Hartley; The Old Rectory, Brandsby, N Yorks

HARTWELL, Baron (Life Peer UK 1968); Hon (William) Michael Berry; MBE (1945), TD; 2 s of 1 Viscount Camrose; hp to bro, 2 Viscount; *b* 18 May 1911; *Educ* Eton, Ch Ch Oxford; *m* 1936, Lady Pamela Smith, yr da of 1 Earl of Birkenhead (F E Smith); 2 s, 2 da; *Career* chm & ed-in-chief Daily & Sunday Telegraph; served WW II, Lt-Col 1944; formerly ed Glasgow Sunday Mail, man ed Sunday Times, chm Amalgamated Press; *Clubs* White's, Roy Yacht Sqdn, Beefsteak; *Style* - The Rt Hon Lord Hartwell MBE TD; Oving House, Whitchurch, Aylesbury, Bucks (☎ Whitchurch 307); 18 Cowley st, SW1 (☎ 01 222 4673)

HARTWELL, Sir Brodrick William Charles Elwin; 5 Bt (UK 1805), of Dale Hall, Essex; s of Sir Brodrick Hartwell, 4 Bt (d 1948), by his 2 w, Joan; *b* 7 Aug 1909; *Educ* Bedford Sch; *m* 1, 1937, Marie, da of Simon Mullins (m dis 1950); 1 s; m 2, 1951, Mary, MBE, da of J Church; (1 s,

1 da both decd); *Heir* s, Francis Antony Charles Peter Hartwell; *Career* served RAF 1928-29, Army 1931-48 (Capt Leics Regt); *Style* - Sir Brodrick Hartwell, Bt; 50 High Street, Lavendon, nr Olney, Bucks (☎ Bedford 712619)

HARTWELL, Eric; s of Alfred Hartwell (d 1931); *b* 10 Aug 1915; *Educ* Mall Sch Twickenham, Worthing H S; *m* 1, 1937, Gladys Bennett (m dis); 1 s, 1 da; m 2, 1952, Dorothy, da of Harold Mowbray (decd), of Middx; 1 s, 1 da; *Career* ch exec and v-chm (1972-) Trusthouse Forte 1978- *Recreations* yachting (owns yacht- 'Kandora'), painting, photography; *Clubs* Nat Sporting, River Emergency Serv, Magic Circle, Thames Motor Yacht; *Style* - Eric Hartwell Esq; Tall Trees, 129 Totteridge Lane, N20 (☎ 01 455 2321)

HARTWELL, Edward George; s of late Edward Hartwell; *b* 29 April 1922; *Educ* Poole G S, Reading Sch; *m* 1938, Kathleen Joan, nee Montague; 1 c; *Career* engine room artificer RN, served 1942-46; dir- Hunt & Co Ltd (Holdings Co), Hunts Auto & Marine Ltd, Hunts Engineering (Bournemouth) Ltd; *Recreations* walking, swimming; *Style* - Edward Hartwell Esq; 12 Herm rd, Parkstone, Poole, Dorset

HARTWELL, Francis Antony Charles Peter; s and h of Sir Brodrick William Charles Elwin Hartwell, 5 Bt; *b* 1 June 1940; *Educ* Thames Nautical Training Coll, HMS Worcester, Cadet RNR; *m* 1968, Barbara Phyllis Rae, da of H Rae Green, of Sydney, Aust; 1 s; *Style* - Francis Hartwell Esq; c/o Barclays Bank, 11 High st, Olney, Bucks

HARVEY OF PRESTBURY, Baron (Life Peer UK 1971); Arthur Vere Harvey; CBE (1942); s of Arthur Harvey; *b* 31 Jan 1906; *Educ* Framlingham Coll; *m* 1, 1940 (m dis 1954), Jacqueline, da of W Dunnett; 2 s; m 2, 1955 (m dis 1977), Hilary (d 1978), da of David Charles and formerly w of Lt-Col Brian Robertson Williams; m 3, 1978, Carol, da of late Austin Cassar-Torreggiani; *Career* Air Cdre RAuxAF; FRAeS, kt 1957; served RAF 1925-30, flying instructor; dir Far East Aviation Co & Far East Flying T'ning Sch 1930-35; advsr to S Chinese AF & Sqdn Ldr AAF; MP (C) Macclesfield 1945-71, chm 1922 Cttee 1966-70; dir Film Corpn of America (UK), Tradewinds Airways; *Clubs* Roy Yacht Sqdn, Buck's, RAF; *Style* - Rt Hon Lord Harvey of Prestbury CBE; Villa Wardija, Malta

HARVEY OF TASBURGH, 2 Baron (UK 1954); Sir Peter Charles Oliver Harvey; 5 Bt (UK 1868); s of 1 Baron, GCMG, GCVO, CB, Ambass France 1948-54 (d 1968), and Maud, da of Arthur Williams-Wynn (gn of Sir Watkin Williams-Wynn, 4 Bt; Maud's maternal great grandfather was 5 Earl Fitzwilliam); *b* 28 Jan 1921; *Educ* Eton, Trin Cambridge; *m* 1957, Penelope, yr da of Lt-Col Sir William Makins, 3 Bt; 2 da; *Heir* bro, Hon John Harvey; *Career* served WW II RA N Africa & Italy; CA; investment consultant Brown Shipley & Co 1978-; formerly with Bank of England, Lloyds Bank, English Transcontinental Ltd; *Style* - Rt Hon Lord Harvey of Tasburgh; Crownick Woods, Restronguet, Mylor, Cornwall; 36 Lennox gdns, SW1 (☎ 01 589 5765)

HARVEY, (Sir) Charles Richard Musgrave; 3 Bt (UK 1933), of Threadneedle St, City of London (but does not use title); s of Sir Richard Musgrave Harvey, 2 Bt (d 1978); *b* 7 April 1937; *Educ* Marlborough, Pembroke Cambridge; *m* 1967, Celia Vivien, da of George Henry Hodson; 1 s, 1 da; *Heir* s, Paul Richard Harvey; *Career* Fell Inst of Development Studies, Sussex U; *Style* - Charles Harvey Esq

HARVEY, Frances, Lady; Frances Estelle; da of late Lindsay Crompton Lawford, of Montreal; *m* 1930, Lt-Cdr Sir Richard Musgrave Harvey, 2 Bt, RN (d 1978); *Style* - Frances, Lady Harvey; Chisenbury Priory, Pewsey, Wilts

HARVEY, Hon Guy Alan Vere; s of Baron Harvey of Prestbury; *b* 1947; *m* 1977, Margaret C B, da of Lewis Robertson, of The Blair, Blairlogie, Stirling; *Style* - The Hon Guy Harvey

HARVEY, Ian Douglas; TD (1945); s of Maj Douglas Harvey, DSO (ka 1917); *b* 25 Jan 1914; *Educ* Fettes, Ch Ch Oxford; *m*

1949, Clare, da of Sir Basil Mayhew, KBE; 2 da; *Career* author and journalist, MP (C) Harrow E 1950-58, Parly Sec Min of Supply 1956-57, Parly-Under Sec FO 1957-58, chm Paddington Con Assoc 1980- *Recreations* swimming, squash, bicycling; *Style* - Ian Harvey Esq, TD; 62D St Michael's st, W2

HARVEY, Hon Juliet Annora Christine; da of 2 Baron Harvey of Tasburgh; *b* 1958; *Style* - The Hon Juliet Harvey

HARVEY, Hon John Wynn; s of 1 Baron Harvey of Tasburgh, GCMG, GCVO, CB (d 1968), and hp of bro, 2 Baron; *b* 4 Nov 1923; *Educ* Eton, Westminster, Cambridge U; *m* 1950, Elena Maria-Teresa, da of late Giambattista, Marchese Curtopassi; 2 s, 1 da; *Career* 1941-45 War with King's Roy Rifle Corps and Essex Regt; *Style* - The Hon John Harvey; Coed-y-Maen, Meifod, Powys; 55 Addison rd, W14 (☎ 01 602 1639)

HARVEY, Lady; Lydia; da of Alexis Konshine, of Petrograd, Russia; *m* 1921, as his 2 wife, Sir Charles Robert Lambart Edward Harvey, 3 Bt (d 1954); *Style* - Lady Harvey

HARVEY, Hon Miranda Jean; da of 2 Baron Harvey of Tasburgh; *b* 1960; *Style* - The Hon Miranda Harvey

HARVEY, Lady Mary Katherine; *née* Coke; da of 4 Earl of Leicester (d 1949) and Marion, da of Col Hon Walter Trefusis, CB (s of 19 Baron Clinton by his w, Lady Elizabeth Kerr, da of 6 Marquess of Lothian); *b* 7 March 1920; *m* 1940, Maj Thomas Harvey, CVO, DSO; 1 s, 2 da; *Career* Woman of the Bedchamber to HM Queen Elizabeth the Queen Mother 1961-63; *Style* - Lady Mary Harvey; Warham House, Warham, Wells-next-the-Sea, Norfolk (☎ Fakenham 710457)

HARVEY, Peter Martin Seaver; s of George Edward Harvey (d 1960); *b* 16 July 1927; *Educ* St John's Coll, Hurstpierpoint Coll of Estate Management; *m* 1962, Maureen Richardson, da of Dr Arthur Gray (d 1979); 1 s, 1 da; *Career* Capt India & Malaya; md Herring Son & Daw Chartered Surveyors 1976-79 (ptnr/dir 1964-75); FRICS; *Recreations* shooting, fly-fishing, squash; *Clubs* Army & Navy; *Style* - Peter Harvey Esq; Flat 5, 26/28 Sackville St, W1 (☎ 01 439 4581); Kempson House, Whitchurch, Bucks

HARVEY, Paul Richard; s and h of (Sir) Charles Richard Musgrave Harvey, 3 Bt (but does not use title); *b* 2 June 1971; *Style* - Paul Harvey Esq

HARVEY, Hon Philip William Vere; s of Baron Harvey of Prestbury (Life Peer); *b* 1942; *Style* - The Hon Philip Harvey

HARVEY, Richard Jon Stanley; QC (1970); s of Nehemiah Harvey, of Co Westmeath (d 1952); *b* 30 Aug 1917; *Educ* Newtown Sch Waterford, Mountjoy Sch Dublin, Trin Coll Dublin; *m* 1942, Yvonne, da of Joseph D'Abreu, FRCS (d 1973); *Career* barr 1947, Crown Court Recorder 1972, Parly Candidate (C) Woolwich E 1951 and 1952, Romford 1955 and 1959, received into Catholic Ch 1952; *Books* Harvey on Industrial Relations; *Recreations* walking, swimming, reading, writing pseudonymous poetry and novels; *Clubs* Carlton, Norfolk, Roy West Norfolk Golf; *Style* - Richard Harvey Esq, QC; 3 Raymond Bldgs, Gray's Inn, WC1 (☎ 01 405 9420); The Barge, Gt Walsingham, Norfolk (☎ Walsingham 330)

HARVEY, Maj Thomas Cockayne; CVO (1951), DSO (1944); s of Col John Harvey, DSO, whose mother, Rosa, was 6 da of Adm Hon Keith Stewart, CB (2 s of 8 Earl of Galloway) by Mary Fitzroy (paternally ggda of 3 Duke of Grafton and maternally gda of 4 Duke of Richmond); *b* 22 Aug 1918; *Educ* Radley, Balliol Oxford; *m* 1940, Lady Mary, nee Coke, da of 4 Earl of Leicester and Marion (da of late Col Hon Walter Trefusis, CB, 3 s of 19 Baron Clinton); 1 s, 2 da; *Career* chm White's; 1946-51 Priv Sec to HM The Queen 1946-51, 1951-52 Extra Gentleman Usher to HM King George VI, to HM The Queen 1952-; regnl dir Lloyds Bank 1980-; *Recreations* golf, shooting; *Clubs* White's, Beefsteak; *Style* - Maj Thomas Harvey, CVO, DSO; 2 Catherine Wheel

Yard, Little St James's st, SW1 (☎ 01 499 6692); Warham House, Warham, Wells-next-the-Sea, Norfolk (☎ Fakenham 710457)

HARVEY-JAMIESON, Lt-Col Harvey Morro; OBE (1969); s of Maj Alexander Harvey Morro Jamieson, OBE (d 1945); *b* 9 Dec 1908; *Educ* Edinburgh Acad, RMC Sandhurst and Edinburgh U; *m* 1933, Frances, da of Col Julian Yorke Hayter Ridout, DSO (d 1951); 3 s; *Career* assumed name of Harvey-Jamieson by authority of Lord Lyon; commanded 1 Bn KOSB 1928, Maj RA (TA) 1939, Lt-Col 1943, memb Queen's Bodyguard for Scotland (Roy Co of Archers) 1934-; clerk and sec of The Co of Merchants of the City of Edinburgh 1946-71; *Clubs* Roy Forth Yacht; *Style* - Lt-Col Harvey Harvey-Jamieson, OBE, DL; Walhampton Cottage, Walhampton, Lymington, Hants, SO4 8SA (☎ Lymington 74589)

HARVIE-WATT, Sir George Steven; 1 Bt (UK 1945), of Bathgate, Co Linlithgow, TD and Three Bars (1942), QC (KC 1945); s of James McDougal Watt, of Woodlands House, Armadale, W Lothian, and Jessie Harvie; *b* 23 Aug 1903; *Educ* George Watson's Coll Edinburgh; Glasgow & Edinburgh Us; *m* 1932, Jane, da of Paymaster-Capt Archibald Taylor, OBE, RN; 2 s, 1 da; *Heir* s, James Harvie-Watt; *Career* barr Inner Temple 1930, memb Roy Co of Archers (Queen's Bodyguard for Scotland); DL Surrey 1942, Greater London 1966-78; JP London 1944-56; pres Consolidated Gold Fields Ltd 1973- (chm 1960-69), dir Clydesdale Bank Ltd and other cos, MP (U) Keighley 1931-35, Richmond (Surrey) 1937-59; Parly Sec to Rt Hon Winston Churchill when PM 1941-45; commissioned RE TA 1924, Bt-Maj 1935, Lt-Col 1938, Brig 1941, Hon Col 566 LAA Regt 1949-62, ADC to King George VI 1948-52, ADC to the Queen 1952-58, Hon Freeman City of London; FRSA; *Clubs* Caledonian; *Style* - Sir George Harvie-Watt Bt TD*** QC; Sea Tangle, Earlsferry, Fife (☎ 0333 330506)

HARVIE-WATT, James; s and h of Sir George Harvie-Watt, 1 Bt, TD***, QC; *b* 25 Aug 1964; *Educ* Eton, Ch Ch Oxford; *m* 1966, Roseline, da of Baron Louis de Chollet, of Fribourg, Switz (d 1972); 1 s, 1 da; *Career* Lt London Scottish (TA) 1959-67; CA 1965 (with Coopers & Lybrand 1962-70), exec The British Electric Traction Co Ltd, and dir of subsid cos 1970-78, md Wembley Stadium Ltd 1973-78; exec ctee London Tourist Bd 1977-80, Sports Cncl 1980-, OStJ 1964, dir private cos; *Recreations* shooting, tennis, reading; *Clubs* White's, Pratt's, Sunningdale Golf; *Style* - James Harvie-Watt Esq; 15 Somerset sq, W14 (☎ 01 602 6944)

HARVINGTON, Baron (Life Peer UK 1974); Robert Grant Grant-Ferris; AE (1942), PC (1971); s of Dr Robert Grant-Ferris; *b* 30 Dec 1907; *Educ* Douai; *m* 1930, Florence, da of Maj William De Vine, MC; 1 s, 1 da; *Career* barr 1937; kt 1969; late Wing Cdr Auxiliary (now Roy) AF WW II Europe, Malta, Egypt, India; MP (C) N St Pancras 1937-45 & Nantwich 1955-74; Dep Speaker Ho of Commons 1970-74; KStJ; *Recreations* golf, motor yachting; *Clubs* Carlton, Roy Thames Yacht, RAF, Roy & Ancient, MCC, Roy Yacht Sqdn; *Style* - The Rt Hon Lord Harvington, AE, PC; La Vieille Maison, The Bulwarks, St Aubin, Jersey, CI

HARWOOD, Hon Mrs (Elizabeth Margaret); *née* Leonard; da of Baron Leonard, OBE (Life Peer); *b* 1946; *Educ* U of Wales (LLB); *m* 1963, Michael Harwood, of The Hague, Netherlands; *Style* - The Hon Mrs Harwood

HARWOOD, John Keith; s of Col George Harwood, of Putney; *b* 30 Sept 1926; *Educ* Canford Sch Dorset; *m* 1, 1948, Nicolette (m dis 1954, she d 1962), da of Frank Popplewell, OBE, of Wonersh; 1 da; m 2, 1955, Lady Felicity, da of 1 Earl Attlee, KG, OM, CH, PC, FRS (d 1967); 1 s, 3 da; *Career* md UK & Ireland Buying Off R H Macy & Co Inc (NY); FBIM, memb Inst of Export; chm Export Buying Offs Assoc; *Recreations* shooting, gardening, cricket; *Clubs* Knotty Green Cricket, Beaconsfield Rugby, IOD; *Style* - John Harwood Esq; 6 Hogback Wood rd, Beaconsfield, Bucks (☎ 04946 3248)

HASELGROVE, Dennis Cliff; CB (1963); s of Harry Haselgrove (d 1956), of

Chingford; *b* 18 Aug 1914; *Educ* Uppingham, King's Cambridge; *m* 1941, Evelyn, nee Johnston; 1 s; *Career* Under-Sec Min of T'port 1957-71, Dept of Environment 1971-75, ret; *Recreations* archaeology, local history, philately, travel; *Style* - Dennis Haselgrove Esq, CB; 10 Church Gate, SW6 (☎ 01 736 5213)

HASELHURST, Alan Gordon Barraclough; MP (C) Saffron Walden 1977-; s of John Haselhurst and Alyse, nee Barraclough; *b* 23 June 1937; *Educ* Cheltenham, Oriel Oxford; *m* 1977, Angela, da of John Bailey; 2 s; *Career* MP Middleton and Prestwich 1970-74, PPS to Sec of State Educn 1979-; *Recreations* squash, music; *Style* - Alan Haselhurst Esq, MP; House of Commons, SW1

HASLAM, Christopher Nigel Culloden; s of Maj William Leslie Culloden Haslam (d 1943); *b* 18 May 1929; *Educ* Pembroke Cambridge; *m* 1956, Daphne Margaret, da of Sir Francis Low (d 1972); 3 c; *Career* chartered accountant ACA 1956, FCA 1966; fin dir Shell Oil New Zealand 1962-63, Brunei Shell Petroleum 1963-67; ch fin exec Shell Int Chemical Co Ltd 1967-81; fin dir Shell Co Ltd 1981-; *Recreations* sports, racing; *Style* - Christopher Haslam Esq; Rusland, Walker's Ridge, Camberley (☎ Camberley 26889)

HASLAM, Hon Mrs - Hon Judith; *née* Browne; da of 4 Baron Oranmore and Browne; *b* 1934; *m* 1958, (Ralph) Michael Haslam; 2 s, 1 da; *Style* - The Hon Mrs Haslam; Cairngill, Dalbeattie, Kirkudbrightshire

HASLAM, John; s of William Haslam; *b* 17 June 1931; *Educ* King George V G S, Southport & Liverpool U; *m* 1953, Jean Annie, nee Capstick; 2 s; *Career* joined BBC 1955, man BBC Radio Broadcasts 1974-81, assist press sec to HM Queen 1981-; *Recreations* fell-walking, reading, music, Times Crossword; *Style* - John Haslam Esq; 78 Parkway, SW20 (☎ 01 542 3328)

HASLAM, William Geoffrey; DFC (1944); s of William Haslam (d 1938); *b* 11 Oct 1914; *Educ* New Coll and Ashville Coll Harrogate; *m* 1940, Valda, da of Norman Adamson (d 1956); 2 s, 1 da; *Career* dep chm Prudential Assur Co 1980-*Recreations* golf, reading; *Style* - William Haslam Esq, DFC; 6 Ashbourne rd, W5 (☎ 01 997 8164)

HASLUCK, Rt Hon Sir Paul Meernaa Caedwalla; KG (1979), GCMG (1969), GCVO (1970), PC (1966); s of the late E M C Hasluck, of Perth, Aust; *b* 1 April 1905; *Educ* Perth Modern Sch, U of Western Australia; *m* 1932, Alexandra Margaret Martin, nee Darker; 2 s; *Career* KStJ 1969, Australian Foreign Service 1941-47, official war historian, memb Australian Parliament 1949-69, Cabinet Minister 1951-69, Min for Territories 1951-63, Defence 1963-64, Foreign Affairs 1964-69, Governer-General Australia 1969-74; *Recreations* book collecting, recorded music, the Australian Bush; *Clubs* Weld (Perth), Claremont Football; *Style* - Rt Hon Sir Paul Hasluck, KG, GCMG, GCVO; 2 Adams rd, Dalkeith, Western Australia 6009

HASTILOW, Michael Alexander; s of Cyril A F Hastilow CBE (d 1975); *b* 21 Sept 1923; *Educ* Mill Hill Sch, Birmingham U; *m* 1953, Sheila Mary, da of Maj J J Barker, RCS (d 1947); 1 s, 2 da; *Career* dir Glynwed Ltd 1969-81, pres Br Non-Ferrous Metals Federation 1979-80, chm Nat Home Improvement Cncl 1980-81, memb Construction Exports Advsy Bd 1975-78, memb Cmmn for New Towns 1978-, memb EDC for Bldg 1980-; *Recreations* railways, cricket; *Clubs* Old Mill Hillians, RAC; *Style* - Michael Hastilow Esq; The Mount, 3 Kendal End rd, Rednal, Birmingham

HASTINGS, 22 Baron (E 1290); Sir Edward Delaval Henry Astley; 12 Bt (E 1660); s of 21 Baron (d 1956) and Lady Marguerite Nevill, da of 3 Marquess of Abergavenny; *b* 14 April 1912; *Educ* Eton; *m* 1954, Catherine (Cecilia), yr da of Capt Harold Virgo Hinton and formerly w of Vernon Coats; 2 s, 1 da; *Heir* s, Hon Delaval Astley; *Career* proprietor of Seaton Delaval (completed c 1728 - another of Vanbrugh's masterpieces (*see* George Howard), where mediaeval banquets, more suited to the antiquity of the owner's Barony than that of his seat, are held, and which has been badly damaged by fire at various times, particularly in the 19 century); Maj Coldstream Gds ret; patron seven livings; Ld in Waiting to HM 1961-62, Jt Parly Sec Min Housing & Local Govt 1962-64; former farmer S Rhodesia (now Zimbabwe); Pres Br Italian Soc 1972-, Br Epilepsy Assoc; Gov Br Inst Florence, Roy Ballet; chm Roy Ballet Benevolent Fund; *Style* - The Rt Hon Lord Hastings; Seaton Delaval Hall, Northumberland; Fulmodeston Hall, Fakenham, Norfolk (☎ Thursford 231)

HASTINGS, Hon Mrs (Elizabeth Anne Marie Gabrielle); *née* Fitzalan-Howard; da of late 2 Viscount Fitzalan of Derwent; *b* 1934; *m* 1, 1952 (m dis 1960), Sir Vivyan Naylor-Leyland, 3 Bt; m 2, 1975, Stephen Lewis Edmonstone Hastings, MC, MP; *Style* - The Hon Mrs Hastings; 12a Ennismore gdns, SW7 (☎ 01 589 6494)

HASTINGS, Hon Mrs (Eileen Ellen); *née* Wise; da of 1 Baron Wise, DL; *b* 28 Sept 1916; *m* 1940, Sqdn Ldr Gerald Hastings; 3 da; *Style* - The Hon Mrs Hastings

HASTINGS, Hon Mrs (Grisell Annabella Gem); *née* Cochrane-Baillie; da of 2 Baron Lamington (d 1951); *b* 1898; *m* 1922, Capt Edward George Godolphin Hastings, CBE, RN (d 1973, ggs of 11 Earl of Huntingdon); 3 da; *Style* - The Hon Mrs Hastings; Baldy's Gardens, Cuilfail, Lewes, Sussex

HASTINGS, Lt-Col Robin Hood William Stewart; DSO & Bar (1944, 1945), OBE (1946), MC; s of Hon Osmond Hastings, 2 s of 13 Earl of Huntingdon by Mary, da of Col Hon John Westenra (3 s of 2 Baron Rossmore); hp to cous, 15 Earl of Huntingdon; *b* 16 Jan 1917; *Educ* Stowe, Ch Ch Oxford; *m* 1950, Jean, da of Henry Palethorpe, of Stone Manor, Chaddesley Corbett, Worcs, and formerly w of John Holbech; 1 da; *Career* served WW II Rifle Bde; *Style* - Lt-Col Robin Hastings DSO* OBE MC; 2 Billing rd, SW10 (☎ 01 352 9834)

HASTINGS, Lady Selina Shirley; da of 15 Earl of Huntingdon by his 2 w, Margaret; *b* 5 March 1945; *Career* journalist with Daily Telegraph (book page); *Style* - Lady Selina Hastings; 9 Rothwell st, NW1 (☎ 01 586 2101)

HASTINGS-BASS, William Edward Robin Hood; s of Capt Peter Hastings-Bass (assumed additional name Bass 1954, d 1964) and Priscilla (b 1920, m 1947, dir Newbury Race Course, memb Jockey Club), da of Capt Sir Malcolm Bullock, 1 Bt, MBE, and Lady Victoria Stanley (da of 17 Earl of Derby); through paternal gf (Hon Aubrey Hastings, 3 s of 13 Earl of Huntingdon) he is next in line to that Earldom after Lt-Col Robin Hastings, *qv*; *b* 30 Jan 1948; *Educ* Winchester, Trin Cambridge; *Style* - William Hastings-Bass Esq; Wells Head House, Kingsclere, Newbury, Berks

HATCH OF LUSBY, Baron (Life Peer UK 1978); John Charles Hatch; s of John James Hatch; *b* 1 Nov 1917; *Educ* Keighley Boys' G S, Sidney Sussex Cambridge; *Career* journalist, broadcaster, author, lecturer; Head C'wlth Dept Lab Pty HQ 1954-61; Nat Organiser ILP 1944-48; specialist in African studies; *Style* - Rt Hon Lord Hatch of Lusby; End Cottage, Lusby, Spilsby, Lincs (☎ Winceby 630)

HATHERTON, 7 Baron (UK 1835); Thomas Charles Tasman Littleton; TD (1953); s of 4 Baron, JP, DL (fourteenth in descent from Richard Littleton or Lyttelton, yr bro of Sir William Lyttelton, ancestor of the Viscounts Cobham; also eleventh in descent from the union of Sir Edward Littleton with Margaret, gda of 1 Viscount Hereford, whereby Lord Hatherton has the right to quarter the Royal Arms of Plantagenet, inasmuch as the 1 Viscount's mother was ggda of Thomas of Woodstock, Duke of Gloucester and 5 s of Edward III); suc bro, 6 Baron, 1973; *b* 6 Oct 1907; *Educ* St Edward's Sch; *m* 1933, Ann, da of Lt-Cdr Thomas MacLeod, RN; 1 da; *Heir* 1 cous once removed, Edward Littleton; *Career* Capt RA (TA) ret, served WW II; *Style* - The Rt Hon Lord Hatherton TD; Walhouse, Hutton Henry, Castle Eden, Co Durham

HATHERTON, Kathleen, Baroness; Kathleen May; da of late Clarence Ernest Orlando Whitchurch; *m* m 1, Maj Oscar Westendarp; m 2, 1952, as his 2 w, 5 Baron Hatherton (d 1969); *Style* - The Rt Hon Kathleen, Lady Hatherton; Hatherton Hall, Cannock, Staffs (☎ 3127)

HATHERTON, Mary, Baroness; Mary; da of John Roberts, of Ruthin Denbighshire; *m* 1955, as his 2 w, 6 Baron Hatherton (d 1973); 1 da (Hon Moonyeen Littleton); *Career* Capt (ret) QAIMNS; *Style* - The Rt Hon Mary Lady Hatherton; Swiss Cottage, Acton Scott, Church Stretton, Salop

HATHORN, Eric Anthony; s of James Hathorn, of Edinburgh; *b* 18 June 1929; *Educ* Wellington, Merton Oxford; *m* 1966, Hon Jean, *qv*, da of 1 & last Baron Evans, GCVO, FRCP (d 1963); 2 s, 1 da; *Career* formerly 2 Lt Gren Gds; with ICI 1952-68; joined L Messel & Co (Stockbrokers) 1968, ptnr in Beardsley Bishop Escombe 1973-; *Recreations* travel, theatre, opera, gardening; *Clubs* City University; *Style* - Eric Hathorn Esq; 51 Netherall gdns, NW3 (☎ 01 794 6892)

HATHORN, Hon Mrs (Jean Rosemary); *née* Evans; da of 1 and last Baron Evans (d 1963); *b* 1934; *m* 1966, Eric Hathorn, *qv*; 2 s, 1 da; *Style* - The Hon Mrs Hathorn; 51 Netherhall gdns, NW3

HAVARD, Dr John David Jayne; s of Dr Arthur Havard; *b* 5 May 1924; *Educ* Malvern, Jesus Cambridge, Middx Hosp Med Sch; *m* 1950, Margaret, da of Albert Collis, OBE; 2 s, 1 da; *Career* barr, GP Lowestoft 1952-58, with BMA 1958-, Sec 1980-; dep chm Staff Side Gen Whitley Cncl (Health Servs); chm Sci Cttee Internat Driver Behaviour Res Assoc; *Recreations* Bach Choir, Br countryside, history; *Clubs* Oxford & Cambridge; *Style* -Dr John Havard; 1 Wilton sq, N1 (☎ 01 359 2802)

HAVARD-EVANS, Samuel James; OBE (1971), JP; s of David Lewis Evans (d 1961); *b* 10 April 1904; *Educ* Emlyn Grammar Sch, St John's Coll Florida, Gray's Inn; *Career* Sqdn Ldr RAF, legal adviser Records Office RAF Gloucester, barrister-at-law 1931, dep chm Carmarthenshire Quarter Sessions 1955-71, chm Ag Land Trib (Wales), Medical Appeal Trib (Wales), acted as Dep County Court Judge 1952-, Dep Circuit Judge 1971-79, pres Carmarthen Rotary Club 1955, v-pres Carmarthenshire Antiquarian Soc; *Style* - Samuel Havard-Evans, OBE, JP; 29 Bronwydd rd, Carmarthen, Dyfed, SA31 2AJ (☎ 6331)

HAVELOCK-ALLAN, Sir Anthony James Allan; 4 Bt (UK 1858), of Lucknow; s of Allan (2 s of Sir Henry Havelock-Allan, 1 Bt, VC, GCB, MP), and Annie Julia, da of Sir William Chaytor, 3 Bt; suc bro, Sir Henry Ralph Moreton Havelock-Allan, 3 Bt, 1975; *b* 28 Feb 1905; *Educ* Charterhouse, and Switzerland; *m* 1, 1939 (m dis 1952), Valerie Louise Hobson, da of late Cdr Robert Gordon Hobson, RN; 2 s; m 2, 1979, Maria Theresa Consuela (Sara) Ruiz de Villafranca, da of late Don Carlos Ruiz de Villafranca (formerly Ambass to Chile and to Brazil); *Heir* s, Simon Havelock-Allan; *Career* film producer; formerly produced quota films for Paramount, produced for Pinebrook Ltd and Two Cities Films 1938-40, Assoc Producer to Noel Coward 1941, with David Lean and Ronald Neame formed Cineguild 1942; Producer, Assoc Producer or in charge of production for Cineguild 1942-47, formed Constellation Films 1949; chm British Film Academy 1952, chm Council of Soc of Film and Television Arts (now BAFTA) 1962, 1963, a Gov British Film Inst and memb Institute's Production Ctee 1958-65; *Style* - Sir Anthony Havelock-Allan, Bt; c/o Messrs Gorrie Whitson & Sons, 9 Cavendish sq, W1

HAVELOCK-ALLAN, Doris, Lady; Doris Pamela; da of Sir Maurice Levy, JP, DL, 1 Bt (d 1933); *m* 1937, as his 3 w, Sir Henry Spencer Moreton Havelock-Allan, 2 Bt (d 1953); *Career* Organiser of WVS Darlington 1938-44, Co Pres Durham Co (Women's Section), and Nat Vice-Pres British Legion; SStJ; *Style* - Doris, Lady Havelock-Allan; Whorlton House, Barnard Castle, co Durham

HAVELOCK-ALLAN, Simon Anthony Henry; s and h of Sir Anthony Havelock-Allan, 4 Bt; *b* 6 May 1944; *Style* - Simon Havelock-Allan Esq

HAVILAND, Julian; *aet* 50 in May 1981; *Educ* Eton, Magdalene Cambridge; *Career* Political Ed The Times June 1981- (suc Fred Emery, who became Home Ed); Political Ed ITN to 1981; has worked for Surrey Advertiser, Evening Standard, Daily Telegraph; *Style* - Julian Haviland Esq; c/o The Times, New Printing House sq, Gray's Inn rd, WC1 (☎ 01 837 1234)

HAW, Hon Mrs - Hon Helen Elizabeth Delaval; *née* Astley; da of 21 Baron Hastings (d 1956); *b* 1907; *m* 1, 1930, Ian Bulloch (m dis 1940); 3 s; m 2, 1941, George Field (d 1941); m 3, 1948, John David Haw, s of late George Haw; *Style* - The Hon Mrs Haw

HAWARDEN, 8 Viscount (I 1793); Sir Robert Leslie Eustace Maude; 10 Bt (I 1705); also Baron de Montalt (I 1785); s of 7 Viscount (d 1958) by his w Marion (da of Albert Wright, whose w Margaretta was sis of 20 Baron FitzWalter); *b* 26 March 1926; *Educ* Winchester, Ch Ch Oxford; *m* 1957, Susannah, da of Maj Charles Gardner (gggs of 1 Baron Gardner); 2 s, 1 da; *Heir* s, Hon Connan Maude; *Career* served Coldstream Gds 1945-46; landowner & farmer; *Style* - The Rt Hon Viscount Hawarden; Wingham Court, Canterbury, Kent (☎ Wingham 222)

HAWKE, 9 Baron (GB 1776); Bladen Wilmer Hawke; s of 8 Baron Hawke (d 1939); *b* 31 Dec 1901; *Educ* Winchester, King's Cambridge; *m* 1934, Ina, da of Henry Faure Walker (d 1940), of Highley Manor, Balcombe, Sussex; 7 da (who include the w of Nicholas Scott, MP); *Heir* bro, Hon Julian Hawke; *Career* Lord in Waiting 1953-57, Church Commissioner 1958-73, chm Chichester Diocesan Bd of Finance 1962-72; *Recreations* golf, gardening; *Clubs* Carlton; *Style* - The Rt Hon The Lord Hawke; Faygate Place, Horsham, W Sussex (☎ Faygate 252); c/o Barclays Bank, Tadcaster, Yorks

HAWKE, Hon Julian Stanhope Theodore; s of 8 Baron Hawke (d 1939); bro and hp of 9 Baron Hawke; *b* 19 Oct 1904; *Educ* Eton, King's Cambridge; *m* 1, 1933, Angela Margaret Griselda, da of late Capt Edmund Bury; 2 da; m 2, 1947, Georgette Margaret, da of George Davidson, of Eaton sq; 1 s, 3 da; *Career* Wing Cdr 1945; ret textile converter, dir Glazebrook Steel Co 1933-69; *Recreations* shooting, golf; *Clubs* Roy Liverpool Golf; *Style* - The Hon Julian Hawke; Old Mill House, Cuddington, Cheshire (☎ Sandiway 882248)

HAWKE, Hon Olivia Mary; da of 9 Baron Hawke; *b* 1955; *Educ* Heathfield Sch; *Style* - The Hon Olivia Hawke; Faygate Place, Faygate, Sussex

HAWKES, Michael John; s of Wilfred Arthur Hawkes (d 1968); *b* 7 May 1929; *Educ* Bedford Sch, New Coll Oxford; *m* 1957; 4 children; *Career* banker, v-chm Kleinwort Benson Ltd, chm Sharps Pixley Ltd; *Style* - Michael Hawkes Esq; c/o 20 Fenchurch st, EC3 (☎ 01 623 8000)

HAWKES, Hon Mrs (Shelah St George); *née* Caulfeild; da of late 9 Visc Charlemont; *b* 1914; *m* 1946, John Arnold Hawkes, B Com, ACA, late Prof Natal U, S Africa; 1 s; *Style* - The Hon Mrs Hawkes; 18 St Aubins ct, Ferring, Sussex

HAWKESBURY, Viscount; Luke Marmaduke Peter Savile Foljambe; s and h of 5 Earl of Liverpool; *b* 26 March 1972; *Style* - Viscount Hawkesbury

HAWKEY, Lady; Mabel Dorothy McMullan; da of late Sir Thomas Edward McConnell, CBE, MP, of Belfast; *m* 1947, as his 2 w, Sir Roger Pryce Hawkey, 2 and last Bt (d 1975); *Style* - Lady Hawkey

HAWKINS, Sir Arthur Ernest; s of Rev Harry Hawkins; *b* 10 June 1913; *Educ* The Blue Sch Wells, Gt Yarmouth G S, London U; *m* 1939, Laura, da of Albert Draper; 1 s, 2 da; *Career* kt 1976; memb CEGB 1970- (chm 1972-77); memb Nuclear Power Advsy Bd 1973-; *Recreations* fell walking, swimming, motoring; *Clubs* RAC; *Style* - Sir Arthur Hawkins; 61 Rowan rd, Brook Green, W6 (☎ 01 603 2849)

HAWKINS, Blanche, Lady; (Marjorie) Blanche; da of A E Hampden-Smithers, of Springs, Transvaal; *m* 1920, Sir Villiers Geoffrey Caesar Hawkins, 6 Bt (d 1955); *Style* - Blanche, Lady Hawkins; 187 Lynnwood rd, Brooklyn, Pretoria, Transvaal, S Africa

HAWKINS, Air Vice-Marshal Desmond Ernest; CB (1971), CBE (1967), DFC and Bar (1942); s of Ernest Hawkins; *b* 27 Dec 1919; *Educ* Bancroft Sch Essex; *m* 1947, Joan, da of James Munro; 1 s; *Career* RAF 1938; Dir Gen Personal Servs (RAF) MOD 1971-74; md Services Kinema Corporation 1974-80; *Recreations* sailing (yacht- 'Barada'); *Clubs* Roy Lymington Yacht, Cruising Assoc, RAF Sailing; *Style* - Air Vice-Marshal Desmond Hawkins, CB, CBE, DFC*; c/o Barclays Bank, 10 Cornhill, Bridgwater, Somerset

HAWKINS, Howard Caesar; s and h of Sir Humphry Villiers Caesar Hawkins, 7 Bt; *b* 17 Nov 1956; *Style* - Howard Hawkins Esq

HAWKINS, Sir Humphry Villiers Caesar; 7 Bt (GB 1778); s of Sir Villiers Geoffrey Caesar Hawkins, 6 Bt (d 1955); *b* 10 Aug 1923; *Educ* Hilton Coll, Witwatersrand U; *m* 1952, Anita, da of Charles H Funkey; 2 s, 3 da; *Heir* s, Howard Hawkins; *Career* European War 1942-45 with 6 S African Armoured Div; medical practitioner; MB, ChB; *Clubs* Johannesburg County; *Style* - Sir Humphry Hawkins, Bt; 41 Hume rd, Dunkeld, Johannesburg, S Africa

HAWKINS, Lady (Virginia Anne Noel); da of Gp Capt Noel Heath; *b* 31 Dec 1925; *Educ* Ascham Sch Sydney, Frensham Mittagong Australia; *m* 1947, Maj Sir Michael Hawkins, KCVO, MBE (Priv Sec to HRH The Duke of Gloucester and who d 1977), s of Lancelot Hawkins, of Bilney Hall, Norfolk; 1 da; *Recreations* gardening, buying pictures; *Style* - Lady Hawkins; 37 Rumbold rd, SW6 (☎ 01 736 3701)

HAWKS, Lady Kara Virginia Louisa; *née* King-Tenison; da of 10 Earl of Kingston (d 1948); *b* 1938; *m* 1964 (m dis 1974), Anthony John Conroy Hawks, MB, BS, DCH; 1 da; *Style* - Lady Kara Hawks; White Gates, Old Romsey rd, Cadnam, Southampton

HAWLEY, Sir Donald Frederick; KCMG (1978, CMG 1970), MBE (1955); s of late Frederick George Hawley, of Little Gadsden, Herts; *b* 22 May 1921; *Educ* Radley, New Coll Oxford; *m* 1964, Ruth, da of Rev Percy Howes (d 1964), of Charmouth, Somerset; 1 s, 3 da; *Career* barr 1951, Diplomatic Serv 1955-81, Br High Commissioner Malaysia 1977-81; *Recreations* tennis, golf, squash, sailing; *Clubs* Athenaeum; *Style* - Sir Donald Hawley, KCMG, MBE; Little Cheverell House, nr Devizes, Wilts (☎ Lavington 3322)

HAWLEY, Sir David Henry; 7 Bt (GB 1795), DL (Lincs 1952); s of Capt Cyril Hawley, KRRC (ka 1914) and Ursula, da of Henry St John (gs of Hon Ferdinand St John and ggs of 3 Visc Bolingbroke and (4 Visc) St John); suc unc, Capt Sir Henry Hawley, 4 Bt, 1923; *b* 13 May 1913; *Educ* Eton, Magdalene Cambridge; *m* 1938, Hermione, da of Col Lancelot Gregson, OBE, Gren Gds (d 1935), and Violet, nee Woodhouse (whose mother, Lady Felicity, nee Anson, was da of 3 Earl of Lichfield, JP, DL); 1 s, 2 da; *Heir* s, Henry Hawley; *Career* FRICS, ptnr Jas Martin & Co 1950-80; High Sheriff Lincs 1962-63, chm Lincoln Diocesan Advsy Cttee 1978-; *Recreations* shooting, travel, history; *Style* - Sir David Hawley, Bt, DL; Tumby Lawn, Boston, Lincs (☎ Coningsby 42337)

HAWLEY, Henry Nicholas; s and h of Sir David Hawley, Bt, DL; *b* 26 Nov 1939; *Educ* Stowe; *Style* - Henry Hawley Esq; Tumby Lawn, Boston, Lincs

HAWORTH, Sir (Arthur) Geoffrey; 2 Bt (UK 1911); s of Sir Arthur Adlington Haworth, 1 Bt (d 1944); *b* 5 April 1896; *Educ* Rugby, New Coll Oxford; *m* 1926, Emily Dorothea (d 1980), da of H E Gaddum, of The Priory, Bowdon, Cheshire; 2 s, 2 da; *Heir* s, Philip Haworth; *Career* 1914-19 War as Lt Queen's Own Roy W Kent Regt and Machine Gun Corps (despatches), chm Hallé Concert Soc 1965-77, Manchester Palace Theatre

Trust Ltd 1978-; FRSA 1969, JP Chester 1937-70, Hon MA Manchester 1972; *Clubs* Farmers'; *Style* - Sir Geoffrey Haworth, Bt; The Red Brook, Lower Peover, Cheshire

HAWORTH, Philip; s and h of Sir Geoffrey Haworth, 2 Bt; *b* 17 Jan 1927; *Educ* Reading U (BSc); *m* 1951, Joan Helen, da of late Stanley Percival Clark, of Ipswich; 4 s, 1 da; *Style* - Philip Haworth Esq; Free Green Farm, Over Peover, Knutsford, Cheshire

HAWSER, His Honour Judge; Cyril Lewis Hawser; QC (1959); s of Abraham Hawser, MBE (d 1966); *b* 5 Oct 1916; *Educ* Cardiff H S, Balliol Oxford; *m* 1940, Phyllis, da of Herbert Greatrex (d 1965); 1 s, 1 da; *Career* barr 1938, Circuit Judge 1978-; *Recreations* tennis, chess, reading; *Style* - His Hon Judge Hawser, QC; 39 Eaton sq, SW1 (☎ 01 235 6566)

HAWTHORNE LEWIS, Lady; *m* Sir William Hawthorne Lewis, KCSI, KCIE, Gov Orissa 1941-46 (d 1970), s of Thomas Lewis, Dir Pub Instruction UP India; *Style* - Lady Hawthorne Lewis; The Bridge House, Wilton, Salisbury, Wilts (☎ Wilton 2233)

HAWTREY, Stephen Charles; CB (1966); s of Edmond Hawtrey (d 1942); *b* 8 July 1907; *Educ* Eton, Trin Cambridge; *m* 1934, Leila, da of Lt-Col Wilmot Blomefield (d 1926); 2 s, 1 da; *Career* Clerk of the Journals House of Commons 1958-72; *Style* - Stephen Hawtrey Esq, CB; 52 New st, Henley-on-Thames, Oxon (☎ 4521)

HAY, Lord Andrew Arthur George; s of 12 Marquess of Tweeddale, GC (d 1979); *b* 1959; *Educ* Fettes; *Style* - Lord Andrew Hay

HAY, Lord Alistair James Montagu; s of 12 Marquess of Tweeddale, GC (d 1979); *b* 1955; *Educ* Eton, Univ Coll Oxford; *Style* - Lord Alistair Hay

HAY, Lady Atalanta Rose; da of 15 Earl of Kinnoull; *b* 1974; *Style* - Lady Atalanta Hay

HAY, Sir Arthur Thomas Erroll; 10 Bt (NS 1663), of Park, Wigtownshire; s of Sir Lewis John Erroll Hay, 9 Bt (d 1923); *b* 13 April 1909; *Educ* Fettes Coll Edinburgh, Liverpool U; ISO 1974, DiplArch, ARIBA 1935; *m* 1, 1935 (m dis 1942), Hertha Hedwig Paula Louise, da of late Ludwig Stölzle, of Nagelberg, Austria, and widow of Walter Biheller; 1 s; m 2, 1943, Mrs Rosemary Anne Weymouth, da of late Vice-Adm Aubrey Lambert; *Heir* s, John Hay; *Career* 1939-45 War RE, 2 Lt 1943, Lt 1944; retired civil servant; *Style* - Sir Arthur Hay, Bt; c/o Lloyds Bank, Castle st, Farnham, Surrey

HAY, Lady Alexandra Victoria Caroline Anne; da of Countess of Erroll (who retained her maiden name Hay under Scots Law and d 1978) and 1 husband, Sir (Rupert) Iain Kay Moncreiffe of that Ilk, 11 Bt, *qv*; *b* 1955; *Style* - Lady Alexandra Hay

HAY, Lord Charles David Montagu; s of 12 Marquess of Tweeddale, GC (d 1979), and hp of twin bro, 13 Marquess; *b* 6 Aug 1947; *Educ* Milton Abbey Sch, Trin Oxford; *Style* - Lord Charles Hay

HAY, Sir Frederick Baden-Powell; 10 Bt (NS 1703), of Alderston; s of late Frederick Howard Hay (next bro of 9 Bt); suc unc, Sir Edward Hamilton Hay, 11 Bt, 1936; *b* 24 June 1900; *m* 1935, Henrietta Margaret, da of Herbert William Reid; *Heir* bro, Ronald Hay; *Career* is an agent, formerly a grocer; *Clubs* Royal Caledonian (Melbourne); *Style* - Sir Frederick Hay, Bt; Unit 14, 32 Mentone Parade, Mentone, Vic 3194, Australia (☎ 550 3726)

HAY, Lord Hamish David Montagu; s of 12 Marquess of Tweeddale, GC (d 1979); *b* 1959 (twin); *Educ* Fettes; *Style* - Lord Hamish Hay

HAY, Lady Iona Charlotte; da of 15 Earl of Kinnoull; *b* 1967; *Style* - Lady Iona Hay

HAY, Lady; Isobel Rose; da of late Sir Alexander Walker, KBE; *m* 1958, as his 2 w, Sir Duncan Edwyn Hay, 10 Bt (d 1965); *Style* - Lady Hay; Haystoun, Peebles, Scotland

HAY, John Erroll Audley; s and h of Sir Arthur Hay, 10 Bt; *b* 3 Dec 1935; *Educ* Gordonstoun, St Andrews U; *Style* - John Hay Esq; c/o National Westminster Bank, Fitzroy sq, W1

HAY, Lady Melissa Ann; da of 15 Earl of Kinnoull; *b* 1964; *Style* - Lady Melissa Hay

HAY, Lady Marioth Christina; da of Lt-Col Lord Edward Hay, DL, (3 s of 10 Marquess of Tweeddale, KT, DL) by his 1 w, Violet, da of Maj Cameron Barclay; *b* 1 Sept 1918; *m* 1, 1940 (m dis 1954), Lt-Col George Trotter (2 s of Col Algernon Trotter, DSO, MVO, JP, DL, by Lady Edith Montgomerie, yr da of 15 Earl of Eglinton and Winton); 2 s, 1 da; m 2, 1954, as his 2 w, Sqdn Ldr Sir Gifford Fox, 2 and last Bt (d 1959); m 3, 1963 (m dis 1971), Sir John James, KCVO, CB; raised to the rank of a Marquess's da 1970; resumed surname Hay 1971; *Style* - Lady Marioth Hay; Forbes Lodge, Gifford, E Lothian (☎ 212)

HAY, Lady (Helen) Olga; *née* Maitland; da of 17 Earl of Lauderdale; *b* 1944; *m* 1969, Robin William Patrick Hamilton Hay; 2 s (Alastair b 1972, Fergus b 1981), 1 da (Camilla b 1975); *Career* journalist (the gossip columnist Lady Olga Maitland); *Style* - Lady Olga Hay; 21 Cloudesley st, N1 (☎ 01 837 9212)

HAY, Sir (Alan) Philip; KCVO (1960, CVO 1953), TD; s of Edward Alan Hay; *b* 27 Feb 1918; *Educ* Harrow, Trin Cambridge; *m* 1948, Lady Margaret, DCVO (d 1975), da of Brig Lord Henry Seymour, DSO*, and Lady Helen Grosvenor (da of 1 Duke of Westminster), and sis of 8 Marquess of Hertford, DL; 3 s; *Career* Priv Sec to HRH Princess Marina Duchess of Kent 1948-68, Tres to HRH The Duke of Kent, dir Sotheby & Co 1969-, Nat Mutual Life Assoc of Australasia 1967-; *Clubs* Boodle's, Buck's, Pratt's; *Style* - Sir Philip Hay, KCVO, TD; Nottingham Cottage, Kensington Palace, W8 (☎ 01 937 5514)

HAY, Peter Laurence; s of Norman Leslie Stephen Hay (d 1979); *b* 7 March 1950; *Educ* St Paul's Sch London and Brunel U; *Career* dir Norman Hay Ltd and Borough Plating Ltd; *Recreations* flying helicopters; *Style* - Peter Hay Esq; 40 Strand-on-the-Green, W4 (☎ 01 995 4111)

HAY, Ronald Nelson; s of late Frederick Howard Hay (bro of 9 Bt); hp of bro, Sir Frederick Hay, 10 Bt; *b* 9 July 1910; *m* 1940, Rita, da of John Munyard; 1 s, 1 da; *Style* - Ronald Hay Esq; Murrumbeena, Melbourne, Australia

HAY-DRUMMOND, Lady Betty Mary Seton; *née* Montgomerie; da of late 16 Earl of Eglinton and Winton by 1 w, Lady Beatrice Dalrymple, da of 11 Earl of Stair; *b* 1912; *m* 1933, Capt George Vane Hay-Drummond, ggs of Lt-Col the Hon Charles Hay-Drummond (s of 11 Earl of Kinnoull); 1 s, 1 da; *Style* - Lady Betty Hay-Drummond; Dornoch Mill, Crieff, Perthshire

HAYDON, Hon Mrs (Kathleen Mary); *née* Seely; da of 1 Baron Mottistone, CB, CMG, DSO, TD (d 1947); *b* 1907; *m* 1946, (Clement) Maxwell Winton Haydon; *Style* - The Hon Mrs Haydon; Paddock Hill, Lymington, Hants

HAYDON, Sir Robin (Walter Robert); KCMG (1980, CMG 1970); s of Walter Haydon (d 1946); *b* 29 May 1920; *Educ* Dover G S; *m* 1941, Joan, da of Col Reginald Tewson (d 1948); 1 s, 1 da (and 1 da decd); *Career* dir Imperial Gp 1980-, Ambass to Eire 1976-80 (High Cmmr Malta 1974-76), Ch Press Sec 10 Downing Street 1973-74; *Recreations* tennis, walking, swimming; *Clubs* Travellers', Roy C'wlth Soc; *Style* - Sir Robin Haydon, KCMG; c/o Lloyds Bank, Cox's & King's Branch, 6 Pall Mall, SW1

HAYEK, Maj Anthony George; DL (Staffs 1971); s of Gustav Hayek (d 1924); *b* 6 Aug 1920; *Educ* AKAD Gymnasium Vienna, Ecole Sup de Commerce Lausanne, Keele U; *m* 1972, Nicola Jane, da of late Prof Walter Simon; 3 s; *Career* maj RAOC and Indian Army, chartered engineer, companion British Inst of Management, co adviser, chm Alexander & Duncan Ltd 1978, dir Mangocd Ltd 1973, dir Railweight Ltd 197, senior ptnr Board Power 1979-; *Recreations* shooting, beagling, travel; *Style* - Maj Anthony Hayek, DL; The Spinney, Butterton, Newcastle, Staffs (☎ 619001)

HAYES, Sir Claude James; KCMG (1974, CMG 1969); s of James Benjamin Fidge Hayes (d 1951); *b* 23 March 1912; *Educ* Ardingly, St Edmund Hall Oxford, Sorbonne U Paris, New Coll Oxford; *m* 1940, Joan, nee McCarthy; 2 s, 1 da; *Career* BEF 1939 - Lt-Col; Combined Operations N W Europe; civil serv cmmr 1949, HM Treasury 1957-64, princ fin offr Ministry of Overseas Dvpt 1965-68, chm Crown Agents 1968-74, v-chm E D Sassoon, interim cmmr for W Indies 1968-; *Recreations* garden maintenance and betterment, old oak furniture, Georgian domestic chattels, Wealden timber houses; *Clubs* United Oxford and Cambridge; *Style* - Sir Claude Hayes, KCMG; Prinkham, Chiddingstone Hoath, Kent (☎ Cowden 335)

HAYES, Vice-Adm Sir John Osler Chattock; KCB (1967, CB 1964), OBE (1945); s of Maj Lionel Chattock Hayes (d 1962); *b* 9 May 1913; *Educ* RN Coll Dartmouth; *m* 1939, Hon Rosalind Mary, da of 2 and last Viscount Finlay; 2 s, 1 da; *Career* v-adm Flag Offr Scotland and N Ireland 1966-68, flag offr 2 in command Western Fleet 1964-66, naval sec to First Lord of Admiralty 1962-64, HM Ld-Lt of Ross and Cromarty, Skye and Lochalsh 1977-, memb Queen's Bodyguard for Scotland 1969-, pres King George's Fund for Sailors (Scotland) 1968-79; *Recreations* walking, music, writing; *Clubs* Roy Overseas League; *Style* - V-Adm Sir John Hayes, KCB, OBE; Arabella House, by Tain, Ross & Cromarty (☎ Nigg Station 293)

HAYES, Michael Richard Lloyd; DL (Pembs 1963); s of late R S Hayes, JP; *b* 26 March 1921; *Educ* Cheltenham Coll, RN Colls Pangbourne and Dartmouth, Keyham and Manadon Colleges; *m* 1943, Cynthia Kathleen, nee Shelley; 3 da; *Career* CStJ 1970, High Sheriff Pembrokeshire 1963-64, acting Lt-Cdr RN HMS Jamaica Arctic Convoys, HMS Mauritius; liveryman Worshipful Company Shipwrights 1956; dir Hayes Industries (Wales) Ltd 1958-, commissioner St John Ambulance Brigade and Inspectorate Chief Commissioner for Wales 1980-, founder chm Richard Hayes Investments Ltd 1965-, and of Haven Automation International Ltd 1970-, Haven Automation (Singapore) Ltd 1973-, Haven Auto Ltd (Hong Kong) Ltd 1975-, APAP Ltd 1978-, Cosheston Fish Farms Ltd 1978-, chm Ashmead Securities Ltd 1973-, dir Body Matter Ltd 1980-, Galley Slaves (Studio) Ltd 1980-; *Recreations* shooting, fishing, tennis, sailing; *Clubs* Royal Yacht Squadron, Royal Thames Yacht, East India & Devonshire Sports & Public Schools; *Style* - Michael Hayes Esq, DL; Four Ashes, Cosheston, Pembroke Dock, Dyfed (☎ Pembroke 2670); 4 Iverna Gardens, London W8 (☎ 01 937 3322)

HAYES, Hon Lady (Rosalind Mary); da of late 2 Visc Finlay; *b* 1914; *m* 1939, Vice-Adm Sir John Osler Chattock Hayes, KCB, OBE; 2 s, 1 da; *Style* - The Hon Lady Hayes; Arabella House, by Tain, Ross-shire

HAYES, Hon Mrs - Hon Sarah; da of 2 Baron Maclay, KBE (d 1969); *b* 1937; *m* 1968, David Richard Hayes, s of Eric Gerald Hayes (d 1958) ; *Style* - The Hon Mrs Hayes; Factors House, Pityulish, Aviemore, Inverness-shire

HAYNES, Hon Mrs (Penelope Margaret); *née* Gilbey; da of 10 Baron Vaux of Harrowden; *b* 1942; *m* 1965, John Charles Haynes; 2 s, 2 da; *Style* - The Hon Mrs Haynes; Evelith Mill, Shifnal, Salop

HAYTER, 3 Baron (UK 1927); Sir George Charles Hayter Chubb; 3 Bt (UK 1909), KCVO (1977), CBE (1976); s of 2 Baron (d 1967) by his 1 w Mary; *b* 25 April 1911; *Educ* Leys Sch, Trin Cambridge; *m* 1940, Elizabeth, MBE, da of Thomas Rumbold (ggs of Sir Thomas Rumbold, 1 Bt); 3 s, 1 da; *Heir* s, Hon George Chubb; *Career* chm Chubb & Son's Lock & Safe Co 1957- (md 1941-); dir Charles Early & Marriott (Witney) Ltd 1952-; Pres Roy Warrant Holders Assoc 1967; *Style* - The Rt Hon Lord Hayter KCVO CBE; Ashtead House, Ashtead, Surrey (☎ 73476)

HAYTER, Alison, Baroness; Margaret Alison; da of J G Pickard, of Leicester; *m* 1949, as his 2 w, 2 Baron Hayter (d 1967); *Style* - The Rt Hon Alison, Lady Hayter; 31 Iverna gdns, Kensington, W8 (☎ 01 937 6860)

HAYWARD, Sir Edward Waterfield; s of Arthur Dudley Hayward (d 1954); *b* 10 Nov 1903; *Educ* Collegiate Sch of St Peter, Adelaide; *m* 1972, Jean Katherine; *Career* kt 1961, KStJ, Lt-Col 2 AIF 1939-45 (Middle East, New Guinea, Borneo), Patron Rats of Tobruk Assoc, chm Coca-Cola Bottlers (Adelaide) Ltd, dir Bennett & Fisher Ltd, owner Silverton Park Hereford Stud & Hillbilly Poll Hereford Stud, racehorse owner and breeder; *Recreations* polo, golf; *Clubs* Melbourne, Adelaide, Australian (Sydney) Naval and Military, Royal Adelaide Golf Club, Royal Sydney Golf Club; *Style* - Sir Edward Hayward; Carrick Hill, Springfield, Adelaide, South Australia (☎ 79-3886)

HAYWARD, John Edward James; s of late Edward John Hayward, CBE; *b* 17 Nov 1917; *Educ* Westminster Sch, Balliol Coll Oxford; *m* 1950, Ruth, nee Holden; 1 s, 1 da; *Career* solicitor, senior partner Messrs Wilde Safte 1977-; *Clubs* Lansdowne; *Style* - John Hayward Esq; Ockham Cottage, Ockham, Surrey (☎ 048643 2230) and (☎ 01 236 3050)

HAYWARD, Lady Patricia Mary; *née* Stopford; da of late 7 Earl of Courtown; *b* 1906; *m* 1934, Maurice John Hayward, Malayan Civil Service (ret), s of Sir Maurice Henry Weston Hayward, KCSI; 1 s, 3 da; *Style* - Lady Patricia Hayward; White Hart House, Haddenham, Aylesbury, Bucks

HAYWOOD, Bryan; s of Arthur Haywood; *b* 1 May 1939; *Educ* King Edward VII, Leics; *m* ; 1 s (Timothy); *Career* dir Balfour Kilpatrick Ltd 1975-, dir Balfour Kilpatrick Int Ltd UK, dir Kilpatrick Gp of Cos; *Recreations* country life; *Clubs* St James, Inst of Dirs; *Style* - Bryan Haywood Esq; Flat A, 13 Upper Belgrave st, SW1 (☎ 01 235 8514); 35 Kent rd, E Molesey, Surrey (☎ 01 979 9714)

HAZLERIGG, 2 Baron (UK 1945); Sir Arthur Grey Hazlerigg; 14 Bt (E 1622), MC (1945), JP (Leics 1946), DL (1946); s of 1 Baron (d 1949, eighth in descent from Sir Arthur Hesilrige, 2 Bt, the 'fidus Achates' to the Parliamentarian Sir William Waller in the Civil War and Col of a regiment of cuirassiers known as 'The Lobsters'; he refused the invitation from Cromwell to a Peerage that his descendant accepted at the hands of Sir Winston Churchill); *b* 24 Feb 1910; *Educ* Eton, Trin Cambridge; *m* 1945, Patricia (d 1972), da of John Pullar, of Natal S Africa; 1 s, 2 da; *Heir* s, Hon Arthur Hazlerigg; *Career* served WW II Maj RA (TA) & Leics Yeo; *Style* - The Rt Hon Lord Hazlerigg MC JP DL; Noseley Hall, Leicester (☎ Billesdon 322)

HAZLERIGG, Hon Arthur Grey; s and h of 2 Baron Hazlerigg, MC; *b* 5 May 1951; *Style* - The Hon Arthur Hazlerigg

HAZLERIGG, Hon Edith Bridget; da of 1 Baron Hazlerigg (d 1949); *b* 1908; *Career* JP Leics; European War 1939-45 as Sr Cdr ATS; *Style* - The Hon Edith Hazlerigg, JP; Church Cottage, Carlton Curlieu, Leicester

HAZLERIGG, Hon Robert Maynard; s of 1 Baron Hazlerigg (d 1949); *b* 1916; *Educ* Eton, Trin Cambridge (BA); *m* 1942, Rose, da of Charles Cox; 2 da; *Career* Major RA (TA); *Style* - The Hon Robert Hazlerigg; Cottonsfield Farm, Three Gates, Billesdon, Leicester

HAZLERIGG, Hon Thomas Heron; s of 1 Baron Hazlerigg (d 1949); *b* 1914; *Educ* Eton, Trin Cambridge (BA); *m* 1, 1942 (m dis 1956), Audrey Cecil, da of late Maj Cecil Robert Bates, DSO, MC; 2 s; m 2, 1957 (m dis 1974), Doussa (Cayzer), da of Fahmy Bey Wissa, of Ramelh, Egypt; *Career* late Maj Leics Yeo, formerly Flying Officer RAF Reserve; *Style* - The Hon Thomas Hazlerigg; Caflida, Klosters, Switzerland

HEAD, 1 Viscount (UK 1960); Anthony Henry Head; GCMG (1963, KCMG 1961), CBE (1946), MC (1940), PC (1951); s of Geoffrey Head, of Mayfair; *b* 19 Dec 1906; *Educ* Eton; *m* 1935, Lady

Dorothea Ashley-Cooper, da of 9 Earl of Shaftesbury; 2 s, 1 da; *Heir* s, Hon Richard Head; *Career* Brig Life Gds ret; ch mil planner Combined Ops 1942-43; Sec State War 1951-56, Min Def 1956-57, MP (C) Carshalton 1945-60; High Commissioner Nigeria 1960-63, Malaysia 1963-66; Pres RNIB 1975-; Col Cmmdt SAS 1968-76; chm Wessex Nat Tst 1970-76; *Style* - The Rt Hon Viscount Head GCMG CBE MC PC; Throope Manor, Bishopstone, Salisbury (☎ Coombe Bissett 318)

HEAD, Viscountess; Lady Dorothea Louise; *née* Ashley-Cooper; da of late 9 Earl of Shaftesbury and aunt of 10 Earl, *qv*; *b* 1907; *m* 1935, 1 Viscount Head, *qv*; *Career* OStJ; *Style* - The Rt Hon The Viscountess Head; Throope Manor, Bishopstone, Salisbury, Wilts

HEAD, Major Sir Francis David Somerville; 5 Bt (UK 1838); s of Sir Robert Pollock Somerville Head, 4 Bt (d 1924); *b* 17 Oct 1916; *Educ* Eton, Peterhouse Cambridge; *m* 1, 1950 (m dis 1965), Susan Patricia, da of late Arthur Douglas Ramsay, OBE; 1 s, 1 da; m 2, 1967, Penelope Marion Acheson, da of late Wilfrid Archibald Alexander; *Heir* s, Richard Head; *Career* Maj (ret) Queen's Own Cameron Highlanders; 1939-45 War (wounded, prisoner); *Clubs* Naval and Military; *Style* - Major Sir Francis Head, Bt; 10 Fairway, Merrow, Guildford, Surrey

HEAD, Hon Richard Antony; s and h of 1 Viscount Head, GCMG, CBE, MC, PC; *b* 27 Feb 1937; *Educ* Eton and RMA Sandhurst; *m* 1974, Alicia Brigid, da of Julian Salmond, of Maidford, Norton, Malmesbury, Wilts; *Career* late Capt Life Guards; *Style* - The Hon Richard Head; Rhonehurst, Lambourn, Newbury

HEAD, Richard Douglas Somerville; s and h of Sir Francis David Somerville Head, 5 Bt; *b* 16 Jan 1951; *Educ* Eton, Magdalene Cambridge; *Style* - Richard Head Esq

HEAD, Hon Simon Andrew; s of 1 Viscount Head, GCMG, CBE, MC, PC; *b* 1944; *Educ* Eton, Ch Ch Oxford and Berkeley U Calif; *Style* - The Hon Simon Head

HEADFORT, 6 Marquess of (I 1800); Sir Thomas Geoffrey Charles Michael Taylour; 9 Bt (I 1704); also Baron Headfort (I 1760), Viscount Headfort (I 1762), Earl of Bective (I 1766) and Baron Kenlis (UK 1831, which sits as); s of 5 Marquess, TD (d 1960), by his w Elsie, widow of Sir Rupert Clarke, 2 Bt, and da of James Tucker; *b* 20 Jan 1932; *Educ* Stowe, Christ's Cambridge; *m* 1, 1958 (m dis 1969), Hon Elizabeth Nall-Cain, da of 2 Baron Brocket; 1 s, 2 da; m 2, 1972, Virginia, da of Mr Justice Nable, of Manila; *Heir* s, Earl of Bective; *Career* FRICS, FIArb; holds Commercial Pilot's Licence; Freeman Guild of Air Pilots & Air Navigators; late 2 Lt Life Gds, actg PO RAFVR; dir Bective Electrical Co 1953, sales man & ch pilot Lancashire Aircraft Co 1959; Lloyd's underwriter; inspector Roy Hongkong Aux Police; *Style* - The Most Hon The Marquess of Headfort; 1425 Figueroa st, Paco, Manila, Philippines; Affix Ltd, 302, Hang Chong Bldg, 5 Queen's rd Central, Hong Kong (☎ 235166); Ellerslie, Crosby, IOM (☎ Marown 851521)

HEADLEY, 7 Baron (I 1797); Sir Charles Rowland Allanson-Winn; 7 & 13 Bt (GB 1776, of Warley; E 1660, of Nostell); s of 5 Baron by his 1 w Teresa, nee Johnson; suc bro, 6 Baron, 1969; *b* 19 May 1902; *Educ* Bedford Sch; *m* 1927, Hilda, da of Thomas Thorpe; 1 s, 3 da; *Heir* s, Hon John Allanson-Winn; *Style* - The Rt Hon Lord Headley; Torton Top, Torton Hill rd, Arundel, W Sussex (☎ 882569)

HEADLEY, Edith, Baroness; Edith Jane; da of late Rev George Dods, DD, minister of the parish of Barr, Ayrshire; *m* 1936, 6 Baron Headley (d 1969); *Style* - The Rt Hon Edith, Lady Headley; Haworth House, Turnberry, Ayrshire

HEALEY, Rt Hon Denis Winston; CH (1979), MBE (1945), PC (1964), MP (L) E Leeds 1955-; s of William Healey, of Keighley, Yorks; *b* 30 Aug 1917; *Educ* Bradford G S, Balliol Oxford; *m* 1945, Edna May, da of Edward Edmunds, of Coleford, Glos; 1 s, 2 da; *Career* Int Sec Lab Party 1946-52, memb Parly Ctee Lab Party 1959, MP (L) Leeds S E 1952-55,

Sec of State for Defence 1964-70, Oppn Spokesman on Foreign and Commonwealth Affairs 1971, Shadow Chllr 1972-74, Chllr of the Exchequer 1974-79; former exec memb Fabian Soc; *Style* - The Rt Hon Denis Healey, CH, MBE, MP; House of Commons, SW1

HEALING, Hon Mrs (Elisabeth Mary Lionel Margaret); da of 16 Baron Petre (d 1915); *b* (posthumous) 1915; *m* 1935, Robert Peter Healing; 1 s, 2 da; *Style* - The Hon Mrs Healing; The Priory, Kemerton, Glos; 9 Yeomans Row, SW3

HEARLEY, Timothy Michael; s of Maurice James Goodwin Hearley, CBE (d 1975); *b* 10 March 1942; *Educ* Malvern, Oxford; *m* 1966, Pauline Muriel, nee Dunn; 3 s (Philip Michael b 1967, James Paul b 1970, Richard Matthew b 1973); *Career* memb of Stock Exchange; chm- The Beaver Gp Ltd, CH Industrials Ltd, Garden Wines Ltd; dir- Chackmore Management Services Ltd, McAnally Co Services Ltd, MCS Amalgamations Ltd, Medfurn Ltd, Oceanic Commercial Holdings Ltd, Protea Properties Ltd, Quantum Investments Ltd, R Grenville Financial Management Ltd, Richard Grenville Ltd, Securitex Investments Ltd, Telephone Consultancy Ltd; co-chm Aston Martin 1981-; *Recreations* tennis, piano, ballet, theatre; *Clubs* City University Club; *Style* - Timothy Hearley Esq; Rush Leys, 4 Birds Hill Rise, Oxshott, Surrey (☎ Oxshott 2506)

HEARNE, Graham James; s of Frank Hearne; *b* 23 Nov 1937; *Educ* George Dixon G S Birmingham; *m* 1961, Carol Jean, nee Brown; 1 s, 2 da; *Career* admitted solicitor 1959, practised law in UK and USA 1959-67, exec Industrial Reorganisation Corpn 1967-70, exec dir N M Rothschild & Sons Ltd 1970-77, fin dir Courtaulds Ltd 1977-81, chief exec Tricentrol Ltd 1981-; *Clubs* Reform; *Style* - Graham Hearne Esq; 1 East Heath rd, NW3 (☎ 01 794 4987); Redhill House, Lydney, Glos (☎ 0594 42600)

HEATH, Samuel Bonython; s of Denis William Heath; *b* 11 Feb 1938; *Educ* Rugby; *m*; 3 children; *Career* chm and md Samuel Heath and Sons Ltd 1970- (jt md 1963-70); *Recreations* travel and languages; *Clubs* Eccentric Club London; *Style* - Samuel Heath Esq; Churchill Glebe, Churchill, Spetchley, nr Worcester (☎ Spetchley 640)

HEATHCOAT-AMORY, Ian; JP, DL (Devon 1981); s and h of Sir William Heathcoat-Amory, 5 Bt, DSO, by his w Margaret, da of Col Sir Arthur Doyle, 4 Bt, JP (d 1948, whose own w, Joyce, was da of Hon Greville Howard and gda of 17 Earl of Suffolk and (10 Earl of) Berkshire, and in addition maternal gda of 4 Marquess Townshend); *b* 3 Feb 1942; *Educ* Eton; *m* 1972, Frances, da of Jocelyn Pomeroy (gggs of 4 Viscount Harberton); 3 s; *Style* - Ian Heathcoat-Amory Esq, JP, DL; Hayne House, Tiverton, Devon

HEATHCOAT-AMORY, Hon Mrs; Hon Margaret Irène Gaenor; JP (1968); da of 8 Baron Howard de Walden (d 1945); *b* 2 June 1919; *Educ* Benenden; *m* 1938, Richard Frank, s of Lt-Col Harry William Ludovic Heathcoat-Amory (d 1945); 1 s, 2 da; *Career* organiser Acton Soc Trust; *Style* - The Hon Mrs Heathcoat-Amory, JP; 88 Cadogan pla, London SW1 (☎ 235 7834)

HEATHCOAT-AMORY, Brig Roderick; MC; s of Sir Ian Murray Heathcoat-Amory; *b* 30 Jan 1907; *Educ* Eton; *m* 1947, Sonia Myrtle, da of late Cdre E C Denison; 1 s, 1 da (and 2 step); *Career* Brig, Palestine, Syria, N Africa, Italy, NW Europe; High Sheriff Yorks 1971; *Recreations* outdoor sports; *Clubs* Cavalry and Guards; *Style* - Brig Roderick Heathcoat-Amory, MC; Oswaldkirk Hall, York (☎ Ampleforth 248)

HEATHCOAT-AMORY, Sir William; 5 Bt (UK 1874), of Knightshayes Court, Tiverton, Devon, DSO (1943); s of late Sir Ian Murray Heathcoat Heathcoat-Amory, 2 Bt, CBE; suc bro, Sir Derick, KG, GCMG, TD, PC (who was cr Viscount Amory 1960) in his Baronetcy 1981; *b* 19 Aug 1901; *Educ* Eton; *m* 1933, Margaret Isabella Dorothy Evelyn, da of Col Sir Arthur Havelock James Doyle, 4 Bt; 2 s, 2 da (twins); *Heir* s, Ian Heathcoat-Amory; *Career* Lt-Col KRRC; memb HM Bodyguard of Hon Corps of Gentlemen-at-

Arms 1950-66; *Style* - Sir William Heathcoat-Amory, Bt, DSO; Calverleigh Court, Tiverton, Devon

HEATHCOTE, Sir Michael Perryman; 11 Bt (GB 1733); s of Sir Leonard Vyvyan Heathcote, 10 Bt (d 1963); *b* 7 Aug 1927; *Educ* Winchester, Clare Cambridge; *m* 1956, Victoria, da of Cdr J E R Wilford, RD, RNR, of Ackland Cottage, Shirley Holms, Lymington, Hants; 2 s, 1 da; *Heir* s, Timothy Heathcote; *Career* late 2 Lt 9 Lancers; in remainder to the Earldom of Macclesfield; farmer; *Style* - Sir Michael Heathcote, Bt; Warborne Farm, Boldre, Lymington, Hants (☎ Lymington 73478); Carie and Carwhin, Lawers, by Aberfeldy, Perthshire

HEATHCOTE, (Gilbert) Simon; CBE (Mil 1964, MBE 1945); s of Lt-Col Robert Heathcote, DSO (gggs of Sir Gilbert Heathcote, 3 Bt, MP, by Sir Gilbert's 2 w); hp to Baronetcy of kinsman, 3 Earl of Ancaster, KCVO, TD; *b* 21 Sept 1913; *Educ* Eton; *m* 1939, Patricia, da of Brig James Leslie, MC; 1 s, 1 da; *Career* Brig (ret) RA, served WW II NW Europe; *Clubs* Army & Navy; *Style* - Brig Simon Heathcote, CBE; Autumn Cottage, Chiddingfold, Surrey; Manton Hall, Oakham, Rutland

HEATHCOTE, Timothy Gilbert; s and h of Sir Michael Perryman Heathcote, 11 Bt; *b* 25 May 1927; *Style* - Timothy Heathcote Esq

HEATHCOTE-DRUMMOND-WILLOUGHBY, Lady (Nancy) Jane Marie; da (and hp to father's Barony of Willoughby de Eresby) of 3 Earl of Ancaster, KCVO, TD, JP, DL, by his w, Hon Nancy, nee Astor; *b* 1 Dec 1934; *Career* a Train Bearer to HM The Queen at the Coronation 1953; *Style* - Lady Jane Heathcote-Drummond-Willoughby; Grimsthorpe Castle, Bourne, Lincs; 5 Wilton Row, SW1 (☎ 01 235 1345)

HEATON, Lady Jane; *née* Butler; da of 6 Marquess of Ormonde, CVO, MC (d 1971); *b* 1925; *m* 1945 (m dis 1952), Lt Peter Heaton, RNVR; 1 s; *Style* - Lady Jane Heaton; La Chapelle St Jean, La Garde Freinet, Var, France

HEATON, Noel Thomas; *Educ* Manchester Coll of Technology; *m* 1946, Sheila Mary, nee McAndry; 1 da; *Career* mktg dir Wickman Machine Tools Ltd, UK 1970-79, USA 1976-, France 1976-, John Brown Machine Tool Div 1980-; *Recreations* special constabulary (Div Cmdt Warwicks); *Style* - Noel Heaton Esq; 21 Covent Close, Kenilworth, Warwicks (☎ 53598)

HEATON, Stuart Michael; s of Arthur Heaton (d 1965); *b* 29 May 1924; *Educ* Ledbury G S, Herefordshire; *Career* dir Alfred Herbert (India) Ltd 1947-1958, chm and md Ciro Holdings Ltd (employed 1964-); *Recreations* having nothing to do; *Clubs* Oriental; *Style* - Stuart Heaton Esq; Ciro Pearls Ltd, 178 Regent St, W1 (☎ 01 734 7631)

HEBER-PERCY, Hon Mrs (Margaret Jane); *née* Lever; da of 3 Viscount Leverhulme, TD; *b* 1947; *m* 1966, Algernon Eustace Hugh Heber-Percy; *Style* - The Hon Mrs Heber-Percy; Hodnet Hall, Market Drayton, Salop

HEDDLE, (Bentley) John; MP (C) Lichfield and Tamsworth 1979-; s of Oliver Heddle; *b* 15 Sept 1943; *Educ* Bishop's Stortford Coll, Coll of Estate Management (London U); *m* 1964, Judith, da of Dr Richard Robinson; 2 s, 2 da; *Career* consultant ptnr Elliott, Son & Boyton (Chartered Surveyors), dir of companies including Giffard Securities Ltd and Cornhill Investments Ltd; *Recreations* politics, reading music, cricket, relaxing with family; *Clubs* Carlton; *Style* - John Heddle Esq, MP; The Manor, Barham, Canterbury, Kent (☎ Barham 205)

HEENAN, Maurice; CMG (1966), QC (Hong Kong 1962); s of David Donnoghue Heenan of New Zealand (d 1942); *b* 8 Oct 1912; *Educ* Ashburton Coll, Canterbury Coll, New Zealand U; *m* 1951, Claire Gabriela Stephanie, nee Ciho; 2 da (Ingrid Anne m 1973, Karen Maria); *Career* barr and slr of Supreme Ct of New Zealand 1937-40, Maj 2 NZEF active serv 1940-45, Crown Counsel Palestine 1946-48, Slr-Gen Hong Kong 1961, HM's Attorney Gen Hong Kong (ex-officio memb of Exec Cncl & memb of Legislative Cncl Hong

Kong) 1961-66, Dep-Dir Gen Legal Div (Office of Legal Affairs) Offices of Sec-Gen UN New York 1966-73, Gen-Counsel UN Relief & Works Agency for Palestine Refugees in the Near East 1973-77; *Recreations* rugby, squash, tennis, skiing, fishing, golf; *Clubs* The Country Club of New Canaan, The Hong Kong Club; *Style* - Maurice Heenan Esq, CMG, QC; Plane Trees, West rd, New Canaan, Connecticut, USA

HEFFER, John N M; s of Sidney Heffer (decd); *b* 8 Jan 1919; *Educ* Leys Cambridge; *m* 1944, Margaret, nee Moore; 3 s; *Career* bookseller and stationer, chm of W Heffer & Sons Ltd and subsidiary co Heffers Printers Ltd; *Recreations* sailing, gardening, shooting; *Style* - John Heffer Esq; Solway, Drayton, Cambridge (Crafts Hill 80628)

HEFFLER, Hon Mrs; Hon Tara Francesca; 2 da (by 1 m) of Viscount Fitz-Clarence (s and h of 6 Earl of Munster); *b* 6 Aug 1952; *m* 1979, Ross Jean Heffler; *Style* - The Hon Mrs Heffler

HEIMANN, Hon Mrs (Diana Hester); *née* Macleod; da of Baroness Macleod of Borve (Life Baroness); *b* 1944; *m* 1968, David Heimann; *Style* - The Hon Mrs Heimann; Hertfordshire House, Coleshill, Bucks

HELPMANN, Sir Robert Murray; CBE (1964); s of James Murray Helpmann (d 1928); *b* 9 April 1909; *Educ* Prince Alfred's Coll Adelaide; *Career* actor, dancer, producer, choreographer, director; former premier danseur Sadler's Wells Ballet, dir Australian Ballet 1965-76; kt 1968; *Style* - Sir Robert Helpmann, CBE

HELSBY, George; s of George Isaac Helsby (d 1948); *b* 9 Dec 1941; *Educ* Ellergreen H S; *m* 1967, Joyce; 2 da; *Career* chm and ch exec Burnett & Hallamshire Holdings Ltd; *Recreations* music, philosophy; *Style* - George Helsby Esq; Ashleigh House, Cavendish rd, Sheffield

HELSBY, Hon Nigel Charles; s of Baron Helsby (Life Peer d 1978); *b* 1941; *m* 1941, Sylvia Rosena, da of Ronald Brown, of Burnham-on-Crouch; children; *Style* - The Hon Nigel Helsby; Abbots Wood, The Street, Salcott-cum-Virley, Maldon, Essex

HELSBY, Baroness; Wilmett Mary; da of late W G Maddison, of Durham; *m* 1938, Baron Helsby, GCB, KBE (Life Peer d 1978); 1 s (Hon Nigel Helsby), 1 da (Hon Mrs St Pier); *Style* - The Rt Hon the Lady Helsby; Logmore Farm, Dorking, Surrey

HELY, Brig Alfred Francis; CB (1951), CBE (1945), DSO (1941), TD, DL (Lancs 1951); s of Alfred Francis Hely; *b* 1902; *Educ* St Edward's Coll & Liverpool U; *Career* 2 Lt RA (TA) 1926, Brig 1942, CRA Ind Div 1942-45, CRA 42 Lancs Div 1947-50, ret 1961; *Style* - Brig Alfred Hely CB CBE DSO TD DL; Flat 2, Inchbroom, 21 Bidston rd, Birkenhead, Merseyside

HELY-HUTCHINSON, Hon David Edward; s of late 6 Earl of Donoughmore, KP, PC; *b* 1911; *Educ* Winchester, New Coll Oxford; *m* 1934, Barbara Mary, nee Wyld; 5 da; *Career* formerly Lt-Col RA (TA); *Clubs* Flyfishers', White's, Kildare Street (Dublin); *Style* - The Hon David Hely-Hutchinson; Cranston, North Berwick, East Lothian; Middlewick, Corsham, Wilts

HELY-HUTCHINSON, Hon John Michael James; s of Viscount Suirdale; *b* 7 Aug 1952; *m* 1977, Marie-Claire, da of Gerard Van den Reiss; 1 s, 1 da; *Style* - The Hon John Hely-Hutchinson

HELY-HUTCHINSON, Hon Mark; s of 7 Earl of Donoughmore; *b* 1934; *Educ* Eton, Magdalen Oxford, MIT USA (SM); *m* 1962, Margaret, da of late Dr Robert Rowan Woods; 2 s, 1 da; *Career* late 2 Irish Gds; *Style* - The Hon Mark Hely-Hutchinson; Larch Hill, Santry, Co Dublin

HELY-HUTCHINSON, Hon Nicholas David; s of Viscount Suirdale; *b* 1955; *Style* - The Hon Nicholas Hely-Hutchinson

HELY-HUTCHINSON, Hon Ralph Charles; s of Viscount Suirdale; *b* 1961; *Style* - The Hon Ralph Hely-Hutchinson

HELY-HUTCHINSON, Hon Timothy Mark; s of Viscount Suirdale; *b* 1953; *Style* - The Hon Timothy Hely-Hutchinson

HEMINGFORD, 2 Baron (UK 1943); Dennis George Ruddock Herbert; JP (Cambs 1974, Hunts 1960-65, Huntingdon & Peterborough 1965-74); s of Rt Hon 1 Baron Hemingford, KBE, PC, sometime Dep Spkr Ho Commons (d 1947); *b* 25 March 1904; *Educ* Oundle, Brasenose Oxford; *m* 1932, Elizabeth McClare (d 1979), da of Col John Clark, TD; 1 s, 2 da; *Heir* s, Hon Dennis Herbert; *Career* Ld-Lt Huntingdon & Peterborough 1968-74, Lt Cambs 1974-75; former chm African Bureau (now V-Pres), Hunts CC, Huntingdon & Peterborough CC; formerly in teaching & teacher t'ning in Africa; *Style* - The Rt Hon Lord Hemingford JP; The Coach House, Hemingford Abbots, Huntingdon (☎ St Ives 62375)

HEMMING, John Henry; s of H Harold Hemming, OBE, MC (d 1976); *b* 5 Jan 1935; *Educ* Eton, Oxford U; *m* 1979, Sukie Mary, da of Michael J Babington-Smith, CBE; 1 s; *Career* publisher, chm Municipal Publications Ltd (dep chm 1967) 1976-, dir and sec Roy Geographical Soc 1975-, author, six books published 1970-; *Recreations* writing, travel, exploration; *Clubs* Travellers', Beefsteak, Geographical, Annabel's; *Style* - John Hemming Esq; 10 Edwardes sq, W8 (☎ 01 602 6697)

HEMPHILL, 5 Baron (UK 1906); Peter Patrick Fitzroy Martyn Martyn-Hemphill; s of 4 Baron (d 1957); *b* 5 Sept 1928; *Educ* Downside, BNC Oxford; *m* 1952, Olivia, da of Maj Robert Ruttledge, MC, of Co Mayo, and sis of Lady Edward FitzRoy (herself da-in-law of 10 Duke of Grafton); 1 s, 2 da; *Heir* s, Hon Charles Martyn-Hemphill; *Career* assumed additional surname Martyn by deed poll 1959; *Clubs* RAC, White's, Kildare Street & University (Dublin), County (Galway); *Style* - The Rt Hon Lord Hemphill; Tulira, Ardrahan, Co Galway, Eire (☎ 4)

HEMPHILL, Hon Mrs; Pamela; *née* Rhodes; da of Baron Rhodes, KG, DFC*, PC, DL; *b* 1 May 1927; *m* 1953, Walter, s of Wesley Hemphill; 2 s, 2 da; *Style* - The Hon Mrs Hemphill; 4237 Osage av, Philadelphia 4, Pa, USA

HEMSLEY, Hon Mrs (Gwenllian Ellen); *née* James; da of 4 Baron Northbourne; *b* 1929; *m* 1, 1952 (m annulled 1960), Michael Hugh Rose; m 2, 1960, Thomas Jeffrey Hemsley, the singer; 3 s; *Style* -The Hon Mrs Hemsley; 10 Denewood rd, Highgate, N6

HENDERSON, 1 Baron (UK 1945); William Watson Henderson; PC (1950); 2 s of Rt Hon Arthur Henderson; *b* 8 Aug 1891; *Educ* Queen Elizabeth G S Darlington; *Heir* none; *Career* late Head Press & Publicity Lab Pty; PPS Sec State India 1929-31, PA to Min Without Portfolio 1940-42, Ld in Waiting & Additional Memb Air Cncl 1945-47, Jt Under-Sec State Foreign Affrs 1948-51; late chm Alliance Bldg Soc; Pres UN Parly Gp & UN Assoc Westminster; MP Enfield 1923-24 & 1929-31; journalist; *Style* - The Rt Hon Lord Henderson PC; 707 Collingwood House, Dolphin sq, SW1 (☎ 01 834 3800)

HENDERSON, Hon Angus George; s of 3 Baron Faringdon; *b* 1969; *Style* - The Hon Angus Henderson

HENDERSON, (George) Clifford (McLaren); s of Robert McLaren Henderson (d 1962); *b* 7 Feb 1938; *Educ* Bembridge Sch IOW; *Career* dir Frank Partridge 1973-77, dir Stair & Co (New York) 1977-79, antiques consultant 1979-; *Recreations* music, swimming, theatre; *Style* - Clifford Henderson Esq; 23 Lochmore House, Ebury st, SW1 (☎ 01 730 2725)

HENDERSON, Hon Mrs (Elizabeth Frances); da of 1 Baron May, KBE (d 1946); *b* 1907; *m* 1955, George Leonard Brunton Henderson, MRCVS; 2 s; *Style* - The Hon Mrs Henderson; Oak Lodge, Oak Hill Grove, Surbiton, Surrey KT6 6DS

HENDERSON, Hon Mrs Flora Elizabeth; *née* Hewitt; da of 8 Viscount Lifford; *b* 1947; *m* 1965 (m dis 1975), Edward Bell Henderson; 2 da; *Style* - The Hon Mrs Flora Henderson

HENDERSON, Ian Thomson; CBE (1978), TD; s of Thomson Henderson, MD (d 1959); *b* 12 July 1908; *Educ* Uppingham, Magdalen Coll Oxford; *m* 1, 1932, Monica Wingfield (d 1962), da of Sir Edward Verner, 5 Bt (d 1935) of Seale, Surrey; 1 s, 2 da; m 2, 1963, Imelda, da of Thomas Davey, of Belfast; 1 s; *Career* Lt-Col; slr; memb of London Stock Exchange 1936-51; fin consultant, chm & dir of public cos; *Books* author of books on ceramics & golf; *Recreations* tennis, golf; *Clubs* City U, MCC; *Style* - Ian Henderson Esq CBE TD; Pond House, Crawley, Winchester, Hants SO21 2PR (☎ Sparsholt 415)

HENDERSON, John Crombie; s of Maj Morrice Pitcairn Henderson, TD; *b* 8 April 1939; *Educ* Uppingham; *m* 1968, Marylou Susan, da of Maj-Gen Sir Francis de Guingand, KBE, CB, DSO (d 1979); 2 da; *Career* memb Stock Exchange 1969, ptnr Capel-Cure Myers 1970- (joined co 1964), Lt The Black Watch 1959-63; *Recreations* shooting, fishing, golf; *Clubs* Turf, Berkshire Golf; *Style* - John Henderson Esq; 56 Abingdon rd, W8 (☎ 937 0628)

HENDERSON, Hon James Harold; s and h of 3 Baron Faringdon; *b* 14 July 1961; *Style* - The Hon James Henderson

HENDERSON, John Ronald; MBE (1944), DL (Berks); s of late Major R H W Henderson; *b* 6 May 1920; *Educ* Eton, Cambridge; *m* 1, 1949, Katherine Sarah (d 1972), da of the late Maj-Gen Beckwith-Smith; 2 s, 1 da; m 2, 1976, Catherine Christien; 1 step s, 2 step da; *Career* ptnr Cazenove & Co, dir Barclays Bank, Witan Investment Tst, Howard De Walden Estates, Whitbread Investment Tst; *Recreations* racing, shooting, hunting; *Clubs* White's, Pratt's; *Style* - John Henderson Esq, MBE, DL; West Woodhay House, Newbury, Berks (☎ Inkpen 271); 3/4 Balfour Place, W1

HENDERSON, Kenneth David Druitt; CMG (1951); s of George Henderson; *b* 4 Sept 1903; *Educ* Trin Coll Glenalmond, Univ Coll Oxford; *m* 1935, Margery, nee Atkinson; 1 s, 2 da; *Career* Sudan Political Serv 1926 (govr Darfur 1949-53); sec Spalding Tsts 1953-; *Style* - Kenneth Henderson Esq, CMG; Orchard House, Steeple Langford, Wilts

HENDERSON, Hon Mrs Michael - Esther Isabelle; da of late Alfred Edward Coleman; step mother of 3 Baron Faringdon; *m* 1948, as his 2 w, Lt-Col the Hon Michael Thomas Henderson, 16/5 Lancers, s of 1 Baron Henderson, CH, and who d 1953; *Style* - The Hon Mrs Michael Henderson; Flat 13, 30 Bramham gdns, Kensington, SW5

HENDERSON, Michael John Glidden; s of William Glidden Henderson (d 1946); *b* 19 Aug 1938; *Educ* St Benedict's Sch Ealing; *m* 1965, Stephanie Maria, nee Dyer; 4 s; *Career* FCA, md Lead Industries Gp Ltd (dir 1975) 1979-; *Recreations* tennis, cricket, golf; *Style* - Michael Henderson Esq; Langdale, Woodland Drive, E Horsley, Sussex (☎ 3844)

HENDERSON, Capt Oscar William James; DL (Belfast 1979); s of Cdr Oscar Henderson, CVO, CBE, DSO, RN; *b* 17 Aug 1924; *Educ* Brackenber House Belfast, Bradfield Coll; *m* 1949, Rachel Primrose, da of Col J Forrest, CMG; 3 da; *Career* Capt Irish Gds 1942-47; chairman Century Newspapers Ltd, dir Ulster TV Ltd, Ulster Sheltered Employment Ltd and others; *Recreations* gardening, fishing; *Clubs* Ulster (Belfast); *Style* - Capt Oscar Henderson, DL; Glenalmond, Quarry rd, Belfast (☎ 63145)

HENDERSON, Robert Brumwell; CBE (1979); s of late Cdr Oscar Henderson, CVO, CBE, DSO, RN; *b* 28 July 1929; *Educ* Brackenber House Sch Belfast, Bradfield, Trin Coll Dublin; *m* 1970, Patricia Ann, nee Davison; 2 da; *Career* journalist; 1951-59, dir- ITN 1964-68, ITV Publications 1968-, deputy chm North West Oil and Gas, dir North-South Trading Ltd, chm Cinema and Television Benevolent Fund, NI; *Books* Midnight Oil (1961), A Television First (1977); *Recreations* reading, theatre and cinema, golf; *Clubs* Bath, Royal County Down Golf, Moyola Country, Malone Golf; *Style* - Robert Henderson Esq, CBE; Ulster Television, Havelock House, Ormeau rd, Belfast; 5 Dorchester Park, Belfast BT9 6RH

HENDERSON, Roy Galbraith; CBE (1970); s of late Rev Dr Alexander Roy Henderson; *b* 4 July 1899; *Educ* Nottingham H S, Royal Academy Music; *m* 1926, Bertha Collin, nee Smyth; 3 c; *Career* baritone singer, Glyndebourne & Covent Garden, conductor Choral Societies in Huddersfield 1932, Nottingham 1936, Bournemouth 1942, Professor of Singing RA 1940-75; *Recreations* cricket, trout fishing, gardening, DIY; *Clubs* MCC; *Style* - Roy Henderson Esq, CBE; The Cottage, 3 Eton Avenue, Hampstead, NW3 (☎ 01 722 3144)

HENDERSON, Hon Roderic Harold Dalzell; s of Lt-Col Hon Harold Greenwood Henderson, CVO, MP (d 1922) and Lady Violet Dalzell, da of 14 Earl of Carnwath (d 1956); bro of 2 Baron Faringdon; *b* 3 March 1909; *Educ* Eton, Pembroke Coll Cambridge; *Heir* hon attaché British Legation Stockholm 1932-33, and to HM Embassy Uruguay, civil attaché and private sec HM Embassy Buenos Aires 1943-46, Rome 1946, dir Ellis Memorial Boston Mass; granted title rank and precedence of a Baron's s 1935; *Recreations* swimming; *Style* - The Hon Roderic Henderson; 565 Tuckerman av, Middleton, RI 02846, USA (☎ 401 846 9358); 100 Alhambra pl, W Palm Beach, Florida, USA 33405

HENDERSON, Hon Susannah Jane; da of 3 Baron Faringdon; *b* 1963; *Style* - The Hon Susannah Henderson

HENDERSON, Hon Thomas Alexander Gavin; s of 3 Baron Faringdon; *b* 1966; *Style* - The Hon Thomas Henderson

HENDERSON-STEWART, David; s and h of Sir David James Henderson-Stewart, 2 Bt; *b* 2 Feb 1973; *Style* - David Henderson-Stewart Esq

HENDERSON-STEWART, Sir David James; 2 Bt (UK 1957), of Callumshill, Co Perth; s of Sir James Henderson-Stewart, 1 Bt, MP (d 1961); *b* 3 July 1941; *Educ* Eton, Trin Oxford; *m* 1972, Anne, da of Count Serge de Pahlen; 3 s; *Heir* s, David Henderson-Stewart; *Clubs* Travellers'; *Style* - Sir David Henderson-Stewart, Bt; 3 Chepstow Crescent, W11 (☎ 01 221 6255)

HENDRY, Hon Mrs (Elspeth Mariot); da of 1 Baron Ironside, GCB, CMG, DSO (d 1959); *b* 1917; *m* 1941, Capt Andrew Gilbert Hendry, Black Watch (Roy Highland Regt); 3 s; *Style* - The Hon Mrs Hendry; Kerbet House, Kinnettles, Forfar, Angus

HENDRY, (Alexander) Forbes; OBE (1957), MC (1940), TD (1950), JP (1975), DL (1965); s of late Alexander Hendry; *b* 24 Oct 1908; *Educ* Stirling H S, Glasgow U; *m* 1938, Margaret, nee Whitehead; 1 s, 2 da; *Career* solicitor and dir, MP West Aberdeenshire 1959-66, provost Burgh of Denny & Dunipace 1971-74, Honorary Sheriff 1976, pres Scottish Conservative & Unionist Assoc 1974-75, chm Aberlour Child Care Trust 1979, chm- Cannerton Brick Co Ltd, Cruikshank & Co Ltd; *Recreations* solving crossword puzzles; *Clubs* Caledonian (Edinburgh), County (Stirling); *Style* - Forbes Hendry Esq, OBE, MC, TD, JP DL; Braes, Dunipace, Stirlingshire (☎ 0324 822345)

HENDY, Hon Mrs (Mary Jemima); *née* Best; da of 6 Baron Wynford, DSO (d 1940), and Hon Eva Napier, da of 2 Baron Napier of Magdala; *b* 1912; *m* 1944, John Hendy; 2 s; *Style* - The Hon Mrs Hendy; 15 Ranelagh rd, W5

HENLEY, 8 Baron (I 1799); Oliver Michael Robert Eden; also (and sits as) Baron Northington (UK 1885); s of 7 Baron (d 1977, 4 cous of Sir Anthony Eden, cr Earl of Avon) by his 2 w Nancy; *b* 22 Nov 1953; *Educ* Clifton, Durham U; *Heir* bro, Hon Andrew Eden; *Career* barr Middle Temple 1977; *Style* - The Rt Hon Lord Henley; Scaleby Castle, Carlisle, Cumbria

HENLEY, Nancy, Baroness; Nancy Mary; da of Stanley Walton, of The Hill, Gisland, Carlisle; *m* 1949 (m dis 1975), as his 2 w, 7 Baron Henley (d 1977); *Style* - Nancy, Lady Henley; 29 Somerset st, Kingsdown, Bristol 2

HENN, Alan Wesley; s of Thomas Wesley Henn; *b* 24 Sept 1930; *Educ*

Uppingham Sch; *m* 1956, Anne Whishaw, nee Webb; 1 s, 2 da; *Career* Lt RA; past-chm Nat Assoc of Goldsmiths, chm- TA Henn & Son Ltd and assoc cos, Beacon Broadcasting Co Ltd (W Midland ILR Station), Jewellery Advisory Centre, v-chm Midshires Building Soc; *Recreations* shooting, fishing; *Style* - Alan Henn Esq; Rudge Hall, Pattingham, nr Wolverhampton (☎ 0902 700 667); 28 Devonshire Close, W1 (☎ 01 637 1609)

HENNESSY, Hon James Rupert; s and h of 3 Baron Windlesham, CVO, PC, by his w Prudence Glynn, *qv*; *b* 9 Nov 1968; *Style* - The Hon James Hennessy

HENNESSY, Hon Victoria Jane; da of 3 Baron Windlesham, CVO, PC; *b* 17 July 1966; *Style* - The Hon Victoria Hennessy

HENNIKER, 8 Baron (I 1800); Sir John Patrick Edward Chandos Henniker-Major; 9 Bt (GB 1765), KCMG (1965, CMG 1956), CVO (1960), MC (1945); also Baron Hartismere (UK 1866, which sits as); s of 7 Baron (d 1980), and Molly, da of Sir Robert Burnet, KCVO, MD; *b* 19 Feb 1916; *Educ* Stowe, Trin Cambridge; *m* 1, 1946, Margaret (d 1974), da of James Benning, of Montreal; 2 s, 1 da; m 2, 1976, Mrs Julia Poland, da of George Mason, of Kew; *Heir* s, Hon Mark Henniker-Major; *Career* For Serv 1938-68, served WW II Maj Rifle Bde; Ambass Jordan 1960-62, Denmark 1962-66, Assist Under-Sec FO 1967-68, Dir-Gen Br Cncl 1968-72; memb Parole Bd 1979, dir Wates Fndn 1972-78; *Clubs* Boodle's; *Style* - The Rt Hon Lord Henniker KCMG CVO MC; The Red House, Thornham Magna, Eye, Suffolk (☎ Mellis 336)

HENNIKER, Adrian Chandos; s and h of Sir Mark Chandos Auberon Henniker, 8 Bt, CBE, DSO, MC; *b* 18 Oct 1946; *Educ* Marlborough; *m* 1971, Ann, da of Stuart Britton, of Malvern House, Fairwater rd, Llandaff, Cardiff; 2 da (twins); *Style* - Adrian Henniker Esq; Cerrig Mawrian, Llanover, Abergavenny, Gwent

HENNIKER, Brig Sir Mark Chandos Auberon; 8 Bt (UK 1813), CBE (1953, OBE 1944), DSO (1944), MC (1933), DL (Gwent 1963); s of late Frederick Chandos Henniker (ggs of 1 Bt); suc cous, Lt-Col Sir Robert Henniker, 7 Bt, MC, 1958; *b* 23 Jan 1906; *Educ* Marlborough, RMA, King's Cambridge; *m* 1945, Kathleen Denys, da of late John Anderson, of Pilgrim's Way, Farnham, Surrey; 1 s, 1 da; *Heir* s, Adrian Chandos Henniker; *Career* Brig (ret) late RE, Hon Col REME 1964-68, Mohmand Operations 1933 (MC), 1939-45 War in France, N Africa, Sicily, Italy and NW Europe (wounded, OBE, DSO), Malaya 1952-54 (despatches, CBE), Suez 1956 (despatches); *Clubs* Athenaeum; *Style* - Brigadier Sir Mark Henniker, Bt, CBE, DSO, MC, DL; Pistyll, Began rd, St Mellons, Cardiff

HENNIKER HEATON, Clement Algernon Charles; CBE (1965); s of late Sir John Henniker Heaton, 2 Bt, and hp of n, Sir Yvo Henniker Heaton, 4 Bt; *b* 11 Dec 1909; *Educ* Wellington Coll; *m* 1940, Marjorie, da of W E Speight, of Bournemouth; 2 s, 1 da; *Career* late Maj TA (Reserve), FIL, dir of Cotton Spinners Fedn, UK Employers' Delegate to ILO 1969, and a companion of Textile Inst 1970 (pres 1973); 1939-45 War with 14/20 Hussars; *Style* - Clement Henniker Heaton Esq CBE; Southdene, Goring-on-Thames, Reading, Berks

HENNIKER HEATON, Lady; Margaret Patricia; da of late Lt Percy Wright, Canadian Mounted Rifles; *m* 1948, as his 2 w, Wing Cdr Sir (John Victor) Peregrine Henniker Heaton, 3 Bt (d 1971); *Style* - Lady Henniker Heaton; 14 Woodville rd, Ealing, W5

HENNIKER HEATON, Sir Yvo Robert; 4 Bt (UK 1912); s of Wing Cdr Sir (John Victor) Peregrine Henniker Heaton, 3 Bt (d 1971); *b* 24 April 1954; *m* 1978, Freda, da of B Jones; *Heir* unc, Clement Henniker Heaton; *Style* - Sir Yvo Henniker-Heaton, Bt; 6 Lord Nelson st, Sneinton, Nottingham

HENNIKER-MAJOR, Hon Charles John Giles; s of 8 Baron Henniker, KCMG, CVO, MC; *b* 1949; *Educ* Stowe; *m* 1980, Mrs Sally D M Kemp, da of Donald Newby, of Halesworth, Suffolk; 1 da; *Style* - The Hon Charles Henniker-Major

HENNIKER-MAJOR, Hon Mark Ian Philip Chandos; s and h of 8 Baron Henniker, KCMG, CVO, MC; *b* 29 Sept 1947; *Educ* Eton, Trin Cambridge (MA); AMRAeS; *m* 1973, Mrs Lesley Antoinette Masterton-Smith, da of Wing Cdr G W Foskett, of Fernvale, Qld, Aust; 3 da (Jessica b 1977, Josephine b 1979, Harriet Laura b 29 June 1981); *Career* solicitor; *Style* - The Hon Mark Henniker-Major; Thornham Hall, Thornham Magna, Eye, Suffolk

HENNIKER-MAJOR, Hon Richard Arthur Otway; s of 7 Baron Henniker (d 1980); *b* 1917; *Educ* Stowe, and Magdalene Cambridge (BA); *m* 1946, Nancy Pauline, da of late Sir John Armitage Stainton, KCB, KBE, QC; 2 s; *Career* solicitor 1948; Lt (ret) RA, 1939-45 War (prisoner); *Style* - The Hon Richard Henniker-Major; 6 Berkeley gdns, W8

HENRIQUES, Sir Cyril George Xavier; QC; s of Cyril Charles Henriques; *b* 5 July 1908; *Educ* Xavieran Coll London, Univ Coll London; *m* 1938, Marjory Brunhilde, nee Burrowes; 2 da; *Career* kt 1963, barrister at law 1936, Crown prosecutor Jamaica 1939, resident magistrate Jamaica 1944, Attorney-General Belize 1951, chief justice Windward & Leeward Islands, judge of appeal Jamaica 1963, pres of Court of Appeal of Jamaica 1969; *Recreations* reading, writing, theatre; *Style* - Sir Cyril Henriques, QC; Caribocho Rios Aptmts Ltd, Apt 111 Ocho Rios, St Ann, Jamaica (☎ 0974 5003)

HENRY, Hon Mrs (Christian Alison); da of Baron Hughes, CBE, PC (Life Peer); *b* 1952; *Educ* Strathclyde U (BSc); *m* 1973, Alan Cameron Cassels Henry; *Style* - The Hon Mrs Henry; Casselmuir, Auchterarder, Perthshire

HENRY, Denis Valentine; s of Rt Hon Sir Denis Stanislaus Henry, 1 Bt (d 1925), and hp of bro, Sir James Holmes Henry, 2 Bt, CMG, MC, TD; *b* 29 June 1917; *Educ* Shrewsbury, Clare Cambridge; *m* 1956, Elizabeth, da of Rowland Walker; 1 s, 2 da; *Career* formerly Lt Roy Ulster Rifles; *Style* - Denis Henry Esq; 9 White rd, Blackburn, Lancs

HENRY, Hon Mrs (Helen Judith); *née* Cocks; da of late 7 Baron Somers; *b* 1901; *m* 1, 1949, T Everett Malen (d 1961); m 2, 1965, Earl G Henry; *Style* - The Hon Mrs Henry; 270 Hames rd, SP66 Watsonville, Cal 95076, USA

HENRY, Sir James Holmes; 2 Bt (UK 1923), CMG (1960), MC (1944), TD (1950), QC (Tanganyika 1953, Cyprus 1957); s of Rt Hon Sir Denis Stanislaus Henry, 1 Bt (d 1925); *b* 22 Sept 1911; *Educ* Mount St Mary's Coll Chesterfield, Downside, Univ Coll London; *m* 1, 1941 (m dis 1948), Susan Mary, da of Arthur G Blackwell; m 2, 1949, Christina Hilary, da of Sir Hugh Oliver Holmes, KBE, CMG, MC, QC, and widow of Lt-Cdr Christopher Hayward Wells, RN; 3 da; *Heir* bro, Denis Henry; *Career* barr Inner Temple 1934, Crown Counsel Tanganyika 1946, Legal Draftsman 1949, Slr-Gen 1952, Attorney-Gen Cyprus 1956, memb Foreign Compensation Cmmn 1960-, chm 1977-; 1939-45 War in Middle East and Italy as Capt London Irish Rifles (R Ulster Rifles), (wounded, MC); *Clubs* Travellers', Royal Commonwealth Soc; *Style* - Sir James Henry, Bt, CMG, MC, TD, QC; Kandy Lodge, 18 Ormond av, Hampton-on-Thames, Middx

HENSMAN, Hon Mrs (Mary Sheila); *née* Wakefield; da of 1 Baron Wakefield of Kendal; *b* 1922; *m* 1945, Brig Richard Hensman, CBE; 1 s, 1 da; *Style* - The Hon Mrs Hensman; 4 St James's Terrace Mews, NW8

HEPBURN, Bryan Audley St John; CMG (1962); s of late A F St John Hepburn; *b* 24 Feb 1911; *Educ* Cornwall Coll Jamaica; *m* 1940, Sybil Isabel, nee Myers; 2 da; *Career* fin secretary Sarawak 1958-63, assistant secretary Colonial Service 1944, Ministry of Overseas Development 1966-73, principal assistant secretary Colonial Service 1947, dvpt secretary Sarawak 1951, dir Malayan and Borneo Airways 1958-63, chm Sarawak Electricity Supply Corpn; *Recreations* golf; *Clubs* Royal Overseas League, Haywards Heath Golf; *Style* - Bryan Hepburn Esq, CMG; 7 Weald Rise, Haywards Heath, Sussex

HEPBURN, James Michael Harley; s of

John Harley Hepburn (d 1966); *b* 7 July 1934; *Educ* Loretto Sch; *m* 1963, Ethne Margaret Forbes, nee Binnington; 3 da; *Career* dir Fife Forge Co Ltd and The Girls Sch Co 1970-, md William Paton Ltd 1980- (sales dir 1964-1980); *Recreations* squash, skiing, hill walking, gardening; *Style* - James Hepburn Esq; Craigend, Bridge of Weir, Renfrewshire (☎ 0505 612093)

HEPBURNE-SCOTT, Hon Francis Michael; MC; s of late Capt the Hon Walter Thomas Hepburne-Scott and bro of 10 Lord Polwarth, TD; *b* 1920; *Educ* Eton, King's Cambridge; *m* 1946, Marjorie Hamilton, da of Horatio John Ross; 2 s, 1 da; *Career* sometime Maj, Lothians and Border Horse; consultant Smiths Gore, Chartered Surveyors; FRICS; *Style* - The Hon Francis Hepburne-Scott MC; Newhouse, Lilliesleaf, Melrose, Roxburghshire

HEPBURNE-SCOTT, Hon Patrick John; s of 9 Lord Polwarth (d 1944); *b* 1899; *Educ* Trin, Cambridge; *m* 1, 1925, Cona (d 1961), da of late C Fielding Smith, of Dublin; 2 da; m 2, 1963, Margaret Mary, da of late A G Riddle, of Harrow, Middx; *Career* formerly Lt 8 Bn Roy Scots, sometime Rector of Kirkley; *Style* - The Hon Patrick Hepburne-Scott; 13 Castle Rise, Belmesthorpe, Stamford, Lincs

HEPPEL, Richard Purdon; CMG (1959); s of late Rear-Adm Walter George Heppel; *b* 27 Oct 1913; *Educ* Rugby, Balliol Coll Oxford; *m* 1949, Ruth Theodora, nee Matthews; 2 s, 1 da; *Career* entered HM Diplomatic Service 1936, secretary at Rome, Tehran and Athens 1939-46, private secretary to Minister of State for Foreign Affairs 1946, under-sec of State 1946-47, Head of Chancery Karachi 1948-49 and Madrid 1950-53, counsellor Saigon 1953-54, HM Ambassador Phnom Penh 1954-56, minister counsellor Vienna 1956-58, head of SE Asia Dept Foreign Office 1959, and Consular Dept 1961-63, Imperial Defence Coll 1960, HM Consul General Stuttgart 1963-69; *Recreations* dramatics, gardening; *Style* - Richard Heppel Esq, CMG; Barns Piece, Nether Winchendon, Aylesbury, Bucks (☎ Haddenham 290285)

HERBERT, Hon Carolyn Penelope; da of Lord Porchester (s and h of 6 Earl of Carnarvon); *b* 1962; *Style* - The Hon Carolyn Herbert

HERBERT, Hon David Alexander Reginald; s of 15 Earl of Pembroke and Montgomery, MVO (d 1960); *b* 1908; *Educ* Eton; *Career* 1939-45 War as Lt RNVR; *Style* - The Hon David Herbert; Box 2304, Tangier (Socco)

HERBERT, Lady Diana Mary; da of 16 Earl of Pembroke and Montgomery, CVO (d 1969) and Lady Mary Dorothea Hope, da of 1 Marquess of Linlithgow; *b* 1937; *Style* - Lady Diana Herbert

HERBERT, David Passmore; s of late A H Herbert; *b* 11 Jan 1935; *Educ* The Leys Sch, Queens' Cambridge; *m* 1966, Rosemary Elaine, nee Bawtree; 2 s; *Career* solicitor and partner Messrs Triggs Turner & Co 1962-71, group secretary and solicitor of the Davies & Newman Group of Companies 1971-78, dir Davies & Newman Hldgs Ltd 1978-, dir Dan-Smedvig Ltd 1979-; *Recreations* sailing, gardening, reading; *Clubs* Oxford & Cambridge U; *Style* - David Herbert Esq; Meadowfold, South rd, Liphook, Hants (☎ Liphook 722029)

HERBERT, Lady Emma Louise; da of 17 Earl of Pembroke and Montgomery; *b* 1969; *Style* - Lady Emma Herbert

HERBERT, Lady Flora Katinka; da of 17 Earl of Pembroke and Montgomery; *b* 1970; *Style* - Lady Flora Herbert

HERBERT, Hon George Reginald Oliver Molyneux; s and h of Lord Porchester (s and h of 6 Earl of Carnarvon); *b* 10 Nov 1956; *Career* a Page of Honour to HM the Queen 1969-73; *Style* - The Hon George Herbert

HERBERT, George William; s of late Rt Rev Percy Mark Herbert, KCVO, DD, by his w, Hon Elaine Letitia Algitha Orde-Powlett, da of 5 Baron Bolton; hp of cous, 6 Earl of Powis; *b* 4 June 1925; *Educ* Eton, Trin Cambridge; *m* 1949, the Hon Katherne Odeyne de Grey, da of 8 Baron Walsingham; 4 s, 2 adopted da; *Career*

FRICS; *Style* - George Herbert Esq; Marrington Hall, Chirbury, Powys

HERBERT, Hon Henry Malcolm; s of Lord Porchester (s and h of 6 Earl of Carnarvon); *b* 1959; *Style* - The Hon Henry Herbert

HERBERT, Hon Mrs (Isabella Russell); da of 1 Baron Rea; *b* 22 Aug 1897; *Educ* Newnham Cambridge; *m* 1922, His Hon Jesse Herbert, MC, QC (d 1972), 2 s of Sir Jesse Herbert; 2 da; *Style* - The Hon Mrs Herbert; Swallowfield Park, Reading, Berks

HERBERT, Hon Mrs (Katharine Odeyne); *née* de Grey; da of 8 Baron Walsingham; *b* 1928; *m* 1949, George Herbert (ggs of 2 Earl of Powis); 4 s, 2 adopted da; *Style* - The Hon Mrs Herbert; Marrington Hall, Chirbury, Powys

HERBERT, Hon Mrs Mervyn - Mary Elizabeth; da of J E Willard (former US Ambassador to Madrid); *m* 1921, Hon Mervyn Robert Howard Molyneux Herbert (3 s of 4 Earl of Carnarvon and who died 1929); 1 s, 2 da; *Style* - The Hon Mrs Mervyn Herbert; 25 Eaton sq, SW1

HERBERT, Hon (Dennis) Nicholas; s and h of 2 Baron Hemingford; *b* 25 July 1934; *Educ* Oundle, Clare Cambridge (MA); *m* 1958, Jennifer Mary Toresen, da of Frederick William Bailey, of Harrogate; 1 s, 3 da; *Career* journalist Reuters London and Washington DC 1956-61; with The Times as - assistant Washington correspondent 1961-65, Middle East correspondent 1965-68, dep features ed 1968-70; ed Cambridge Evening News 1970-74, editorial dir Westminster Press 1974-, v-pres Guild of British Newspaper Editors 1979-80; *Recreations* destructive gardening, Victorian military history, genealogy; *Clubs* City Livery, Royal Commonwealth Soc; *Style* - The Hon Nicholas Herbert; The Old Rectory, Hemingford Abbots, Huntingdon, Cambs

HERBERT, Vice-Adm Peter Geoffrey Marshall; OBE (1969); s of A G Herbert; *b* 28 Feb 1929; *Educ* Dunchurch Hall, RN Coll Dartmouth; *m* 1953, Ann Maureen, nee McKeown; 1 s, 1 da; *Career* served in subs 1949-56; Cdr Nuclear sub HMS Valiant 1963-68, dep dir Naval Equipment 1969, Cdr 10 Submarine Squadron 1970-71, dep ch Polaris Exec 1976-78 and Flag Offr Carriers and Amphibious Ships 1978-79; dir gen Naval Manpower and Training 1980-81, Flag Offr subs and Cdr subs E Atlantic 1981-; FBIM, MINucE; *Recreations* golf, swimming, woodwork, gardening; *Clubs* Roy C'wlth Soc; *Style* - Vice-Adm Peter Herbert, OBE; Clare Cottage, East Cholderton, Andover, Hants (☎ Weyhill 2489)

HERBERT, Lady Sophia Elizabeth; da of 17 Earl of Pembroke and Montgomery; *b* 1966; *Style* - Lady Sophia Herbert

HERBERT, Lord; William Alexander Sidney; s and h of 17 Earl of Pembroke and Montgomery; *b* 18 May 1978; *Style* - Lord Herbert

HERD, Lt-Col Foster Bradford; TD, DL (Surrey 1981); *Style* - Lt-Col Foster Herd TD DL; The Cottage, Guildford rd, Woking, Surrey (☎ 65025)

HEREFORD, 18 Viscount (E 1550); Sir Robert Milo Leicester Devereux; 15 Bt (E 1611); premier Viscount in the Peerage of England (and only the thirteenth created, it being a late dignity in England; the first (Beaumont) only antedated Hereford by 90 years); s of Hon Robert Godfrey de Bohun Devereux (d 1934, s of 17 Viscount, himself 10 in descent from the union of Sir Edward Devereux, 1 Bt (who was the first of the last batch of Bts cr in 1611) and Catherine, nee Arden (*see* George Arden); Sir Edward was half great-uncle to Robert Devereux, 2 Earl of Essex (*see* Earl Ferrers); Sir Edward's f was, through his mother, fifth in descent from Thomas of Woodstock, Duke of Gloucester and 5 s of Edward III) and Audrey, who m, as her 2 husb, 7 Earl of Lisburne; suc gf 1952; *b* 4 Nov 1932; *Educ* Eton; *m* 1969, Susan, da of Maj Maurice Godley, of Sevenoaks (Lady Hereford is thereby 3 cous of Lord Kilbracken); 2 s; *Heir* s, Hon Charles Devereux; *Career* OStJ; memb Roy Philharmonic Soc, Roy Philharmonic Assoc; *Clubs* Boodle's, House of Lords Yacht, Lloyd's Yacht; *Style* - The Rt Hon

Viscount Hereford; Haseley Court, Little Haseley, Oxon (☎ Gt Milton 500)

HEREFORD, 102 Bishop (cr 676) 1974-; Rt Rev John Richard Gordon Eastaugh; s of Gordon Eastaugh; *b* 11 March 1920; *Educ* Leeds U; *m* 1963, Bridget, da of Sir Hugh Chance, CBE (bro of Sir Robert Chance, 3 Bt); 2 s, 1 da; *Career* curate 1944, vicar St Peter Eaton Sq 1967-74, archdeacon Middx 1966-74, Sub-Prelate Order St John 1978-; patron 64 livings, the 3 Canonries, the Archdeaconries of Hereford and Ludlow, and the Prebends of his Cathedral; *Style* - The Rt Rev The Bishop of Hereford; The Bishop's House, The Palace, Hereford

HERMON-HODGE, Hon Mrs Robert; Sybil Rika; da of Capt Percy Hare (3 s of Hon Hugh Hare, 4 s of 2 Earl of Listowel, KP) and Matilda, da of Henry Tiarks, through whom she is 1 cous once removed of the Marchioness of Tavistock and 2 cous twice removed of Capt Mark Phillips; *b* 7 Oct 1907; *m* 1934, Maj Hon Robert Hermon-Hodge, DSO (d 1937), 2 s of 1 Baron Wyfold, TD, JP, DL; *Style* - The Hon Mrs Robert Hermon-Hodge; Eastridge, Ramsbury, Marlborough, Wilts

HERMON-HODGE, Hon Valentine Kathleen; da of 2 Baron Wyfold, DSO, MVO, JP, DL, and Dorothy, nee Fleming, aunt of the writers Ian and Peter Fleming; *b* 2 Feb 1918; *Style* - The Hon Valentine Hermon-Hodge; Sarsden House, Churchill, Oxon (☎ Chipping Norton 2551)

HERMON-WORSLEY, Hon Mrs (Nona Carol); *née* Hermon-Hodge; da of 1 Baron Wyfold, TD, JP, DL, and Frances, da of Edward Hermon, of Wyfold Court, Oxon (whose name the 1 Baron added to his original name of Hodge), sometime MP Preston; *b* 20 Nov 1897; *m* 1924, Harold Worsley, MC (d 1956, having added the name Hermon 1924), s of Canon Edward Worsley, of Brackley, Northants; *Style* - The Hon Mrs Hermon-Worsley; Bensgrove Farm, Goring Heath, Oxon (☎ Checkendon 313)

HERON, John Brian; s of John Heron, of Littleborough Lancs; *b* 22 Jan 1933; *Educ* Manchester G S, St Cat's Cambridge; *m* 1968, Margaret, da of Harvey Jessop, of Heywood; 1 s, 1 da; *Career* ch exec & dep chm TBA Industl Products, chm TBA-Bishop, Telford Rubber Processors; dir TBA Iberica (all 1979-); *Recreations* sailing (yacht- 'Mahogany'); *Clubs* Cambridge U Cruising, Oxford & Cambridge Sailing Soc, Hollingworth Lake Sailing; *Style* - John Heron Esq; 15 Lowerfold Way, Rochdale, Lancs (☎ 0706 40660)

HERON-MAXWELL, Nigel Mellor; s and h of Sir Patrick Ivor Heron-Maxwell, 9 Bt; *b* 30 Jan 1944; *Educ* Milton Abbey; *m* 1972, May Elizabeth Angela, da of W Ewing; 1 s, 1 da; *Style* - Nigel Heron-Maxwell Esq; 105 Codicote re, Welwyn, Herts

HERON-MAXWELL, Sir Patrick Ivor; 9 Bt (NS 1683); s of Sir Ivor Walter Heron-Maxwell, 8 Bt (d 1928); *b* 26 July 1916; *Educ* Stowe; *m* 1942, D Geraldine E, da of late Claud Paget Mellor; 3 s; *Heir* s, Nigel Heron-Maxwell; *Style* - Sir Patrick Heron-Maxwell, Bt; 9 Cowslip Hill, Letchworth, Herts

HEROYS, Peter; s of Vladimir B Heroys (d 1977); *b* 12 Aug 1939; *Educ* Tonbridge Sch; *m* 1965, Kirsten, da of late Otto Niewen, of Denmark; 2 da; *Career* sr aircraftsman RAF Cyprus 1960-61, dir Grindlay Brandts & subsid, dir Grindlay Brandts Export Finance Ltd; *Clubs* Travellers'; *Style* - Peter Heroys Esq; Oakgates, 6 Semley rd, Hassocks, Sussex (☎ 3202)

HERRIES OF TERREGLES, Lady (14 holder Sco Lordship 1490); Lady Anne Elizabeth; *née* Fitzalan-Howard; eldest da of 16 Duke of Norfolk, KG, GCVO, GBE, TD, PC (d 1975, when the Dukedom and all other honours save the Lordship passed to his kinsman, 17 Duke, *qv*; His late Grace's mother was Lady Herries of Terregles *suo jure* following the death of her f, the 11 Lord) and Lavinia, Duchess of Norfolk, *qv*; Lady Herries of Terregles is also 3 cous once removed to Peter Maxwell-Stuart, *qv*, the proprietor of Traquair; *b* 12 June 1938; *Heiress* sis, Lady Mary Fitzalan-Howard; *Career* racehorse trainer; *Style* - The Rt Hon Lady Herries of Terregles; The Dover House, Poling, Arundel, Sussex (☎ Patching 200)

HERSCHELL, 3 Baron (UK 1886); Rognvald Richard Farrer Herschell; s of 2 Baron, GCVO (d 1929), by his w Annie, herself da of Sir Arthur Nicolson, 10 Bt; *b* 13 Sept 1923; *Educ* Eton; *m* 1948, Lady Heather Legge, da of 8 Earl of Dartmouth; 1 da; *Heir* none; *Career* Page of Honour at Coronation of George VI; late Capt Coldstream Gds; *Style* - The Rt Hon Lord Herschell; Westfield House, Ardington, Wantage, Berks (☎ E Hendred 224)

HERSCHELL, Hon Arabella Jane; da of 3 Baron Herschell; *b* 1955; *Style* - The Hon Arabella Herschell

HERSCHELL, Baroness; Lady Heather Margaret Mary; *née* Legge; da of late 8 Earl of Dartmouth; *b* 1925; *m* 1948, 3 Baron Herschell, *qv*; *Style* - The Rt Hon the Lady Herschell; Westfield House, Ardington, Wantage, Berks

HERSEY, Hon Mrs (Katherine Viola); *née* James; da of 4 Baron Northbourne; *b* 1940; *m* 1963, John Wharton Hersey; 3 s; *Style* - The Hon Mrs Hersey

HERTFORD, 8 Marquess of (GB 1793); Hugh Edward Conway Seymour; DL (Warwicks 1959); also Lord Conway, Baron Conway of Ragley (E 1703), Baron Conway of Killultagh (I 1712), Viscount Beauchamp, Earl of Hertford (both GB 1750), and Earl of Yarmouth (GB 1793); s of Brig-Gen Lord Henry Seymour, DSO (2 s of 6 Marquess, himself 1 cous twice removed of the legendary 3 Marquess, whose portrayal as Lords Monmouth and Steyne by Disraeli and Thackeray (not to mention other, less accomplished pictures by such as Bulwer) expressed all the awe mixed with disapproval that the middle class felt for the last grand seigneur of the eighteenth century; Lord Hertford's son, the 4 Marquess, amassed much of what is now the Wallace Collection), and Lady Helen Grosvenor (da of 1 Duke of Westminster); *b* 29 March 1930; *Educ* Eton; *m* 1956, Comtesse Pamela Thérèse Louise de Caraman-Chimay, da of Lt-Col Prince Alphonse de Chimay, TD (of the jr line of the Princely family originally cr of that rank by Emperor Maximilian 1486; this jr line (though in the last generation c 1800 through the female) was itself cr Princes by William I of The Netherlands (as then constituted) 1834, and later recognised (1865) by Leopold I of Belgium); Prince Alphonse's w was Mary, da of Lord Ernest Hamilton (7 s of 1 Duke of Abercorn); 1 s, 3 da; *Heir* s, Earl of Yarmouth; *Career* late Lt Gren Gds & Hertford Public Relations Ltd; estate manager and proprietor of Ragley Hall (palladian in style, designed 1680 by Robert Hooke, a runner up to Wren in the competition to redesign London after the Great Fire, but better known as the testy physicist who in some respects led where Newton followed); patron of 3 livings; *Clubs* White's, Pratt's, Turf; *Style* - The Most Hon The Marquess of Hertford DL; Ragley Hall, Alcester, Warwicks (☎ 762455)

HERVEY, Lord Frederick William Augustus; s of 6 Marquess of Bristol; *b* 19 Oct 1979; *Style* - Lord Frederick Hervey

HERVEY, Lord (Frederick William Charles) Nicholas Wentworth; s of 6 Marquess of Bristol and Lady Anne Fitzwilliam (da of 8 Earl Fitzwilliam); hp of half-bro, Earl Jermyn; *b* 26 Nov 1961; *Educ* Yale (student as of June 1981); *Career* Pres Internat Youth Assoc Monarchist League; *Recreations* skiing, swimming, golf; *Clubs* Hurlingham, CLA; *Style* - Lord Nicholas Hervey; The Dutch House, 167 Pavilion rd, SW1 (☎ 01 235 4080); PO Box 5714, Yale University, Yale Station, New Haven, Conn CT 06520, USA

HERVEY, Lady Victoria Frederica Isabella; da of 6 Marquess of Bristol; *b* 6 Oct 1976; *Style* - Lady Victoria Hervey

HERVEY-BATHURST, Hon Mrs; Hon (Violet) Elizabeth Virginia; *née* Cocks; da of late 6 Baron Somers, KCMG, DSO, MC; *b* 1922; *m* 1947, Maj Benjamin Alexander Frederick Hervey-Bathurst, Gren Gds, half-bro of Sir Frederick Hervey-Bathurst, 6 Bt; 2 s; *Career* formerly 3 Offr WRNS; *Style* - The Hon

Mrs Hervey-Bathurst; Eastnor Castle, Ledbury, Herefordshire

HERVEY-BATHURST, Frederick John Charles Gordon; s and h of Sir Frederick Peter Methuen Hervey-Bathurst, 6 Bt; *b* 23 April 1934; *Educ* Eton, Trin Cambridge; *m* 1957, Caroline Myrtle, da of Sir William Randle Starkey, 2 Bt; 1 s, 2 da; *Career* Lt Gren Gds (Reserve); *Style* - Frederick Hervey-Bathurst Esq; Somborne Park, King's Somborne, Hants; 450 Kings rd, SW10

HERVEY-BATHURST, Sir Frederick Peter Methuen; 6 Bt (UK 1818); s of Maj Sir Frederick Edward William Hervey-Bathurst, 5 Bt, DSO (d 1956), and Hon Moira O'Brien, da of 14 Baron Inchiquin; *b* 26 Jan 1903; *Educ* Eton; *m* 1, 1933 (m dis 1956), Maureen Gladys Diana, da of Charles Gordon, of Boveridge Park, Salisbury; 1 s, 1 da; m 2, 1958, Cornelia, da of late Frederic White Shepard, of New York, USA, and widow of Dr John Lawrence Riker, of Rumson, NJ, USA; *Heir* s, Frederick Hervey-Bathurst; *Career* Capt late Gren Gds; *Clubs* Cavalry and Guards, Royal Ocean Racing; *Style* - Sir Frederick Hervey-Bathurst, Bt; Bellevue av, Rumson, New Jersey 07760, USA (☎ 842 0791); Somborne Park, King's Somborne, Hants

HESELTINE, William Frederick Payne; CB (1977), CVO (1969, MVO 1961); s of Henry William Heseltine, of W Australia; *b* 17 July 1930; *Educ* Christ Church G S Claremont, U of Western Australia; *m* 1959, Audrey Margaret, da of late Stanley Nolan, of Sydney; 1 s, 1 da; *Career* Australian (Commonwealth) Civil Serv 1951-62, private sec to PM of Australia (R G Menzies) 1955-59, courtier 1960-61 and 1965-, press sec to HM the Queen 1968-72, dep private sec 1977-; *Clubs* Press, Bafta; *Style* - William Heseltine Esq, CB, CVO; St James's Palace, SW1

HESKETH, 3 Baron (UK 1935); Sir Thomas Alexander Fermor-Hesketh; 10 Bt (GB 1761); s of 2 Baron Hesketh (d 1955) and Dowager Lady Hesketh, *qv*; *b* 28 Oct 1950; *Educ* Ampleforth; *m* 1977, Hon Claire, nee Watson, da of 3 Baron Manton; *Heir* bro, Hon Robert Fermor-Hesketh; *Clubs* Turf; *Style* - The Rt Hon The Lord Hesketh; Easton Neston, Towcester, Northants (☎ 50445)

HESKETH, Baroness - Hon Claire Georgina; *née* Watson; da of 3 Baron Manton; *b* 1952; *see* Hesketh, Baron; *Style* - The Rt Hon The Lady Hesketh

HESKETH, Dowager Baroness; Christian Mary; da of Sir John McEwen, 1 Bt, JP, DL, and Bridget, da of Rt Hon Sir Francis Lindley, GCMG, CB, CBE, by his w, Hon Etheldreda Fraser (3 da of 13 Lord Lovat); *b* 17 July 1929; *Educ* John Watson's Sch, St Mary's Convent Ascot; *m* 1949, 2 Baron Hesketh, DL (d 1955); 3 s (including 3 Baron); *Career* High Sheriff Northants 1981, chm Daventry Con Assoc 1964-74, county organiser WRVS; *Style* - The Rt Hon The Dowager Lady Hesketh; 20a Tregunter rd, SW10 (☎ 01 373 9321); Pomfret Lodge, Towcester, Northants (☎ 50526)

HESKETH, Lady Mary Constance; *née* Lumley; OBE (1974); da of late 11 Earl of Scarbrough, KG, GCSI, GCIE, GCVO, TD, PC, and Dame Katharine, nee McEwen, DCVO; *b* 1923; *m* 1952, Col Roger Fleetwood Hesketh, OBE, TD, DL; 1 s, 2 da; *Career* DStJ; *Style* - Lady Mary Hesketh, OBE; Meols Hall, Southport, Lancs

HESSAYON, David Gerald; s of Jack Hessayon (d 1958); *b* 13 Feb 1928; *Educ* Leeds U, Manchester U; *m* 1951, Joan Parker, da of Weeden T Gray of USA; 2 da; *Career* chm Pan Britannia Industries 1972-, chm British Agrochemicals Assoc 1980-81; *Books* The House Plant Expert, The Rose Expert; *Recreations* Times crossword, American folk music; *Clubs* London Press; *Style* - David Hessayon Esq; c/o PBI, Waltham Cross, Herts (☎ 23691)

HESSE AND BY RHINE, HRH The Princess of; Hon Margaret Campbell; *née* Geddes; da of 1 Baron Geddes; *b* 1913; *m* 1937, (the day after the death of his er bro in an air crash, whereby he succeeded), HRH Prince Louis (Ludwig) Hermann Alexander Chlodwig, of Hesse and by

Rhine (reigned 1937-68, when d, as Ludwig V), whose aunt on his f's side m Tsar Nicholas II and was murdered at Ekaterinburg 1918, while his paternal grandmother was Princess Alice, 2 da of Queen Victoria; also, through his paternal gf's bro, 2 cous of late Earl Mountbatten of Burma ; 1 adopted s (Moritz, Prince of Hesse); *Style* - HRH The Princess of Hesse and by Rhine; Schloss Wolfsgarten, 607 Langen, Hessen, W Germany

HEWART, Viscountess; Jean; da of late James Reid Stewart, of Wanganui, NZ; *m* 1934, as his 2 w, 1 and last Viscount Hewart (d 1964); *Style* - The Rt Hon the Viscountess Hewart; 197 Queen's Gate, SW7 (☎ 01 589 9708)

HEWETT, Sir John George; 5 Bt (UK 1813), of Nether Seale, Leics, MC (1919); s of Sir Harald George Hewett, 4 Bt (d 1949); *b* 23 Oct 1895; *Educ* Cheltenham; *m* 1926, Yuilleen Maude (d 1980), da of late Samuel Frederick Smithson, of Lauriston, Camberley, Surrey; 2 s; *Heir* s, Peter Hewett; *Career* British East Africa during European War 1914-18 as Capt King's African Rifles; *Style* - Sir John Hewett, Bt, MC; Ol'Morogi, Naivasha, Kenya

HEWETT, Kenneth Arthur John; s of Arthur Charles Frederick Hewett (d 1961); *b* 17 Apr 1921; *Educ* Westminster City Sch; *m* 1945, Jean Rosaline, nee Nye; 1 s, 1 da; *Career* co dir shipping, jt md and v-chm Davies Turner & Co Ltd, dir Davies Turner Motors Ltd, dir Manchester Int Terminal Ltd, cncl memb Inst of Freight Forwarders Ltd; *Recreations* golf, music, swimming; *Clubs* E India, Devonshire (Eastbourne); *Style* - Kenneth Hewett Esq; Kenleigh, Meads Brow, Beachy Head rd, Eastbourne, Sussex (☎ 36294); 41 St James rd, Mitcham, Surrey (☎ 01 640 7268)

HEWETT, Peter John Smithson; MM; s and h of Sir John George Hewett, 5 Bt, MC; *b* 27 June 1931; *Educ* Bradfield Coll, Jesus Cambridge; *m* 1958, Jennifer Ann Cooper, da of E T Jones, of Nairobi, Kenya; 2 s, 1 da; *Career* barr Gray's Inn 1954, attached Special Branch Kenya Police 1957; practising advocate Kenya; *Style* - Peter Hewett Esq, MM; P O Box 40763, Nairobi, Kenya

HEWITT, Charles Edward James; s and h of Sir Nicholas Charles Joseph Hewitt, 3 Bt; *b* 15 Nov 1970; *Style* - Charles Hewitt Esq

HEWITT, Hon Mrs (Diana Marie Faith); da of late Hon Edward Crofton (s of late 5 Baron Crofton); *b* 1927; *m* 1, 1949, Cdr Hugh May, RN; 1 s, 1 da; m 2, 1963, Cdr Edward Michael George Hewitt, RN; 1 s, 1 da; raised to the rank of a Baron's daughter 1948; *Style* - The Hon Mrs Hewitt; Flat H, 63 Drayton gdns, SW10

HEWITT, Edwin John; s of Sydney Hewitt (d 1968); *b* 14 April 1934; *Educ* Berkhamsted; *m* 1957, Jennefer Judy, nee Oakley; 3 c; *Career* chartered accountant (FCA) 1975-; dir & jt gen man Co-operative Bank Ltd; *Recreations* riding, music, chess; *Style* - Edwin Hewitt Esq; Tudor Lodge, Lyme Green, nr Macclesfield, Cheshire (☎ Sutton 2209)

HEWITT, Harry Ronald; s of Charles William Hewitt (d 1951); *b* 12 Apr 1920; *Educ* City of Leeds H S, Leeds Coll of Technology, London U; *m* 1954, Rosemary Olive, nee Hiscock; 2 s, 1 da; *Career* chemist, chemical engineer, gp md and ch exec offr Johnson Matthey & Co Ltd 1976-; *Recreations* golf, tennis, flying, skiing; *Style* - Harry Hewitt Esq; 6 Loom Lane, Radlett, Herts (☎ 5243)

HEWITT, Hon (Edward) James Wingfield; s and h of 8 Visc Lifford; *b* 27 Jan 1949; *Educ* Aiglon Coll Switzerland; *m* 1976, Alison, da of Robert Law, of Turnpike House, Withersfield, Suffolk; 1 s, 1 da; *Career* stockbroker, ptnr A H Cobbold of Winchester; *Recreations* shooting and stalking; *Clubs* Turf; *Style* - The Hon James Hewitt; Little Bullington House, Sutton Scotney, nr Winchester, Hants

HEWITT, Marguerite, Lady; Marguerite; da of Charles Burgess, of Deepdene, Filey; *m* 1940, Maj Sir Joseph Hewitt, 2 Bt (d 1973); *Style* - Marguerite, Lady Hewitt; Lebberston Hall, nr

Scarborough

HEWITT, Sir Nicholas Charles Joseph; 3 Bt (UK 1921); s of Maj Sir Joseph Hewitt, 2 Bt (d 1973); *b* 12 Nov 1947; *m* 1969, Pamela Margaret, da of Geoffrey J M Hunt, TD, of Broadacres, Scalby, Scarborough; 2 s, 1 da; *Heir* s, Charles Hewitt; *Style* - Sir Nicholas Hewitt, Bt; The Forge, Hutton Buscel, Scarborough, N Yorks (☎ Scarborough 862307)

HEWLETT, Hon (Thomas) Anthony; s of Baron Hewlett (Life Peer d 1979); *b* 1952; *Educ* Oundle, Magdalene Cambridge; *m* 1980, Jane Elizabeth, da of B Dawson, of Aldeburgh, Suffolk; *Style* - The Hon Anthony Hewlett

HEWLETT, Baroness; Millicent; da of Sir John Taylor, KBE, CMG; *m* 1949, Baron Hewlett (Life Peer d 1979); 2 s; *Style* - The Rt Hon the Lady Hewlett; Dane Edge, Swettenham, Congleton, Cheshire

HEWLETT, Hon (John) Richard; s of Baron Hewlett (Life Peer d 1979); *b* 1955; *Educ* Oundle, Bath Acad of Art; *Style* - The Hon Richard Hewlett

HEYCOCK, Baron (Life Peer UK 1967); Llewellyn Heycock; CBE (1959), JP (Glam 1949, Port Talbot), DL (Glam 1963); s of William Heycock, of Port Talbot; *b* 12 Aug 1905; *Educ* Port Talbot Eastern Sch; *m* 1930, Elizabeth Olive, da of Emmanuel Rees; 1 s; *Career* former engine driver, chm W Glam CC; memb exec cttee Roy Nat Eisteddfod of Wales; CStJ; *Style* - Rt Hon Lord Heycock CBE JP DL; 1 Llewellyn Close, Taibach, Port Talbot, W Glam (☎ 2565)

HEYCOCK, Hon Clayton Rees; s of Baron Heycock (Life Peer); *b* 1941; *Style* - The Hon Clayton Heycock; 6 Tanygroes Place, Tailbach, Port Talbot, W Glam

HEYDON, Wilfred Howard; s of William Archibald Heydon (d 1941); *b* 10 Aug 1913; *Educ* County G S Crewe, London U; *m* 1941, Phyllis May, nee Finill; 3 s (Raymond John, Gordon Howard, Douglas William); *Career* civil engineer, MICE, dir William Press & Son Ltd 1959-; *Recreations* gardening, walking; *Clubs* St Stephens Constitutional; *Style* - Wilfred Heydon Esq; 37 The Ridgeway, Cuffley, Potters Bar, Herts (☎ Cuffley 2546)

HEYGATE, Sir George Lloyd; 5 Bt (UK 1831); s of Sir John Edward Nourse Heygate, 4 Bt (d 1976); *b* 28 Oct 1936; *Educ* Repton, Trin Cambridge; *m* 1960, Hildegard Mathilde, da of August Anton Kleinjohann, of Wildstrasse 69, Duisburg, Germany; *Heir* bro, Richard Heygate; *Career* slr 1965; *Style* - Sir George Heygate, Bt; Willow Grange, Wissett, Halesworth, Suffolk

HEYGATE, Richard Gage; s of Sir John Edward Nourse Heygate, 4 Bt (d 1976), and hp of bro, Sir George Lloyd Heygate, 5 Bt; *b* 30 Jan 1940; *Educ* Repton, Balliol Oxford; *m* 1968 (m dis 1972), Carol Rosemary, da of late Cdr Richard Michell, RN, of Leith House, Amberley, Sussex; *Style* - Richard Heygate Esq

HEYMANN, Louis; s of Josef Heymann (d 1954); *b* 14 Sept 1929; *Educ* Bradford G S, LSE; *m* 1976, Marion Elizabeth, nee Stephens; 2 s, 1 da; *Career* banker, ch exec Leopold Joseph & Sons Ltd; *Recreations* opera, ballet; *Style* - Louis Heymann Esq; 7 Frognal Way, NW3 (☎ 01 435 7891)

HEYNES, David Gordon; s of Gordon Albert Arthur Heynes; *b* 17 Apr 1945; *Educ* Charterhouse; *m* 1968, Jennifer Jane, nee Dreyer; 2 s, 1 da; *Career* CA, Hill Samuel & Co Ltd 1969-71, ch exec Park Place Investments Ltd 1981 (dir 1972-); *Recreations* shooting and motor racing; *Style* - David Heynes Esq; Newton Lodge, Buckland, Faringdon, Oxfordshire 036787 225

HEYS, Derek Isaac; CBE (1971), TD (1945); s of late Isaac Heys; *b* 6 Aug 1911; *Educ* Birkenhead Sch; *m* 1936, Margaret Helena, nee Ashcroft; 1 s, 1 da (1 s decd); *Career* senior ptnr Messrs Heys, Wall & Co 1945-72, national chm Inst of Shipping & Forwarding Agents 1962-63, chm Merseyside Chamber of Commerce & Industry 1970 & 1971, consul for Belgium in Liverpool (Honorary) 1964-76, v-pres

Inst Freight Forwarders Ltd, chm International Relations Ctee, v-pres Assoc of British Chambers of Commerce, governor of Birkenhead Sch 1976; *Style* - Derek Heys Esq, CBE, TD; Fairway Cottage, Pinfold Lane, West Kirby, Wirral (☎ 051 632 4242)

HEYTESBURY, 6 Baron (UK 1828); Sir Francis William Holmes à Court; 7 Bt (GB 1795); s of 5 Baron (d 1971); *b* 8 Nov 1931; *Educ* Bryanston, Pembroke Cambridge; *m* 1962, Alison, da of Michael Balfour, CBE, of Hampstead; 1 s, 1 da; *Heir* s, Hon James Holmes à Court; *Style* - The Rt Hon Lord Heytesbury; 1 Ashfield Close, Petersham

HEYWOOD, Sir Oliver Kerr; 5 Bt (UK 1838); s of late Maj-Gen Cecil Percival Heywood, CB, CMG, DSO (2 s of 3 Bt); suc unc, Lt-Col Sir (Graham) Percival, CB, DSO, TD, 1946; *b* 30 June 1920; *Educ* Eton, Trin Cambridge; *m* 1947, Denise (Kenworthy), da of late Jocelyn William Godefroi, MVO; 3 s; *Heir* s, Peter Heywood; *Career* European War 1940-45 as Capt Coldstream Gds (despatches); artist; *Style* - Sir Oliver Heywood, Bt; Viner's Wood, Wickstreet, Stroud, Glos

HEYWOOD, Peter; s and h of Sir Oliver Kerr Heywood, 5 Bt; *b* 10 Dec 1947; *m* 1970, Jacqueline Anne, da of Robert Frederick Hunt, CBE, of Greenacre, Charlton Park Gate, Cheltenham; 2 da; *Style* - Peter Heywood Esq; 65 Rue de la Grande Bruyère, Rixensart, Belgium

HEYWOOD, Hon Mrs (Rosalind Louise Balfour); *née* Bruce; da of 3 Baron Aberdare, GBE; *b* 11 Nov 1923; *m* 1956, Benjamin Heywood, s of Col Henry Heywood, MC, of Wimbledon; 2 da; *Career* served 1943-46 WRNS; *Style* - The Hon Mrs Heywood; 1 Elm Park rd, SW3 (☎ 01 352 0429)

HEYWOOD-LONSDALE, Hon Mrs (Jean Helen); *née* Rollo; da of 12 Lord Rollo; *b* 2 Dec 1926; *m* 1952, Lt-Col Robert Heywood-Lonsdale, MBE, MC, Gren Gds (s of John H-L, DSO, OBE, TD, JP, sometime MFH The Bicester, and Hon Helen Annesley, 3 da of 11 Viscount Valentia); 1 s, 3 da; *Style* - The Hon Mrs Heywood-Lonsdale; Mount Farm, Churchill, Oxon

HEYWORTH, Baroness; Lois; da of Stevenson Dunlop, of Woodstock, Ont, Canada; *m* 1924, 1 and last Baron Heyworth (d 1974); *Style* - The Rt Hon The Lady Heyworth; 20 Sussex sq, W2

HIBBERT-HINGSTON, Andrew Donovan Huntly; s of Col Alan T Hingston (d 1973); *b* 9 Sept 1926; *Educ* Clifton, Queens' Cambridge; *m* 1952, Evelyn Valery, da of Maj-Gen Hugh Hibbert, DSO; 2 s, 1 da; *Career* engineer, dir The Rom River Co Ltd 1963-; *Recreations* country pursuits; *Style* - Andrew Hibbert-Hingston Esq; Kilsall Hall, Shifnal, Salop

HICHENS, Antony Peverell; s of Lt-Cdr Robert Peverell Hichens; *b* 10 Sept 1936; *Educ* Stowe, Magdalen Oxford, U of Pennsylvania; *m* 1963, Sczerina Neomi, da of Dr F Hobday; 1 da; *Career* dep md Redland Ltd 1979 (fin dir 1972), fin md Consolidated Gold Fields Ltd; *Recreations* travel, boats, wine; *Clubs* Naval and Military; *Style* - Antony Hichens Esq; Parkhurst, Abinger Common, Surrey

HICKMAN, Sir (Richard) Glenn; 4 Bt (UK 1903); s of Sir (Alfred) Howard Whitby Hickman, 3 Bt (d 1979); *b* 12 April 1949; *Educ* Eton; *Heir* unc, Patrick Nelson Hickman; *Clubs* Turf; *Style* - Sir Glenn Hickman, Bt; Twin Cottage, Batlers Green, Radlett, Herts

HICKMAN, John Alfred; s of Joseph Hickman (d 1950); *b* 26 Sept 1908; *Educ* St George's Sch Eastbourne; *m* 1931, Muriel Parker Hunt, da of Edward Parker Hunt (d 1942); 4 c; *Career* surveyor & property developer; chm Chalford Property Co Ltd, dir Kingston gp of cos; *Recreations* golf, tennis, swimming; *Clubs* Coombe Hill GC, Mill Reef (Antigua); *Style* - John Hickman Esq; St Aubyns, Kingston Hill, Surrey (☎ 01 546 8722); Flagstones, Gorse Ave, Kingston Gorse, East Preston, Sussex (☎ Rustington 5606)

HICKMAN, Lady; Margaret D (Thatcher); da of Leonard Kempson, of

Potters Bar, Middx; *m* 1948, Sir (Alfred) Howard Whitby Hickman, 3 Bt (d 1979); *Style* - Lady Hickman; Twin Cottage, Batlers Green, Radlett, Herts

HICKMAN, Beryl, Lady; Nancy Beryl; da of Capt Trevor George Morse-Evans; *m* 1940, as his 2 wife, Sir Alfred Edward Hickman, 2 Bt (d 1947); *Style* - Beryl, Lady Hickman; Charringworth Court, Winchcombe, Glos

HICKMAN, Patrick Nelson; s of Maj Sir Alfred Edward Hickman, 2 Bt (d 1947), and hp of n, Sir Richard Hickman, 4 Bt; *b* 13 March 1921; *m* 1, 1944 (m dis 1950), Mary Lena, da of Capt J A D Perrins; 1 s, 1 da; m 2, 1953 (Margaret) Gail, da of Col C R St Aubyn, of Paris, France; 1 s, 1 da; *Career* Fl Lt RAFVR, ret; Freeman of City of London, Liveryman of Fishmongers' Co; *Clubs* Brooks's; *Style* - Patrick Hickman Esq; 5 The Vale, Chelsea, SW3; Hale Park, Fordingbridge, Hants

HICKS, David; s of the late Herbert Hicks; *b* 25 March 1929; *Educ* Charterhouse, Central Sch of Art & Design; *m* 1960, Lady Pamela Carmen Louise, da of late Earl Mountbatten of Burma, KG, OM, DSO; 1 s, 2 da; *Career* interior and product designer; *Recreations* gardening, riding, shooting; *Style* - David Hicks Esq; The Grove, Brightwell Baldwin, Oxon; Albany, Piccadilly, W1 (☎ 01 930 1991)

HICKS, Howard Arthur; CBE (1981); s of the late I L Hicks; *b* 3 May 1914; *Educ* Pontypridd, The Polytechnic of Wales; *m* 1940, Anne Maureen, nee Lang; 1 s, 1 da; *Career* Major Royal Engineers France, Belgium, Holland and Germany; chm IDC Group Ltd 1957-, chm Aston Technical Management & Planning Services Ltd, dir- Prudential Pensions Ltd, Candover Ltd, Heritage Theatre Series Ltd, chm Cold Rolled Sections Group Ltd, pres Inst Production Engineers 1980-81, and Inst Materials Handling 1977-80; *Recreations* Pontypridd Rugby Football, theatre; *Clubs* Athenaeum, Carlton, Cardiff & County, Phoenix (Lima, Peru); *Style* - Howard Hicks Esq, CBE; Avonfield, Stratford Upon Avon (☎ 0789 293594)

HICKS, India Amanda Caroline; da of David Hicks and Lady Pamela, da of 1 Earl Mountbatten of Burma, KG, GCB, OM, GCSI, GCIE, GCVO, DSO, PC, FRS (assassinated 1979); *b* 1967; *Career* bridesmaid to Lady Diana Spencer at her marriage to HRH The Prince of Wales 1981; *Style* - Miss India Hicks; The Grove, Brightwell Baldwin, Berks (☎ Wallingford 35353)

HICKS, Lady Pamela (Carmen Louise); *née* Mountbatten; da of 1 Earl Mountbatten of Burma, KG, GCB, OM, GCSI, GCIE, GCVO, DSO, PC, FRS (assas 1979); *b* 1929; *m* 1960, David N Hicks, *qv*; 1 s, 2 da; *Career* Lady-in-Waiting to HM the Queen on her tour to Australia and New Zealand 1953-54; *Style* - Lady Pamela Hicks; Albany, Piccadilly, W1; The Grove, Brightwell Baldwin, Watlington, Oxon; Classiebawn Castle, Cliffoney, Co Sligo, Eire

HICKS BEACH, Hon David Seymour; s of 2 Earl St Aldwyn; *b* 1955; *Career* a Page of Honour to HM 1969-71; *Style* - The Hon David Hicks Beach

HICKS BEACH, Hon Peter Hugh; s of 2 Earl St Aldwyn, KBE, TD, PC; *b* 1952; *Style* - The Hon Peter Hicks Beach

HIGGS, John Walter Yeoman; s of Walter Frank Higgs (d 1961); *b* 1 Sept 1923; *Educ* Oundle School; Emmanuel College Cambridge; *m* 1948, Elizabeth Patricia; 2 da; *Career* University of Reading 1948-57; University of Oxford 1958-73; fellow of Exeter College, Oxford 1963-73; Food & Agriculture Organisation of the United Nations 1970-74; memb of the Prince of Wales's Council 1979-; Secretary & Keeper of the Records, Duchy of Cornwall 1981; *Recreations* fishing and shooting; *Clubs* Farmer's, Leander *Style* - John Higgs Esq; Arkleton, Langholm, Dumfriesshire (☎ Ewes 247); 10 Buckingham Gate, London, SW1 (☎ 01 828 3550)

HIGHAM, Hon Mrs - Hon Barbara Constance; da of 3 Viscount Hampden, GCVO, KCB, CMG (d 1958); *b* 1907; *m* 1934, Ronald Harry Higham (d 1966); 1 s, 1 da, (Hon Mrs Victor Grosvenor); *Style*

- The Hon Mrs Higham; 47 Wynnstay gdns, W8

HIGHAM, William Michael; s of Thomas Ashworth Higham (d 1959); *b* 21 Nov 1928; *Educ* Stowe; *m* 1953, Gillian Mary, nee Higham; 3 s, 2 da; *Career* chm and md Highams Ltd 1975-; *Recreations* tennis, swimming, squash; *Style* - William Higham Esq; Norcliffe Lodge, Styal, Wilmslow, Cheshire (☎ 525149)

HIGHETT, Hon Mrs (Jean Mary); *née* Montagu; da (by 1 m) of 3 Baron Swaythling, OBE; *b* 1927; *m* 1951, Lintorn Trevor Highett, MC; 1 s, 2 da; *Style* - The Hon Mrs Highett; 2A Gore st, SW7

HIGNETT, John Mulock; s of Reginald Hignett, sculptor; *aet* 47 in June 1981; *Career* head corporate fin Lazard Bros in 1981 (joined 1963, manager issues dept 1971, dir 1972), non-exec dir DER Printing Machines (1980 turnover £2,000,000, pre-tax profit £320,000), non-exec dir Carless Capel & Leonard; dir-gen Panel on Takeovers & Mergers Aug 1981-; CA; *Recreations* growing orchids; *Clubs* IOD; *Style* - John Hignett Esq; c/o Panel on Takeovers & Mergers, Stock Exchange Building, EC2 (☎ 01 601 4444/4848 and 01 628 2318)

HILDYARD, Angus Jeremy Christopher; DL (1977); s of Maj Donald Maxwell Dunlop (d 1963); changed name by Deed Poll from Dunlop to Hildyard 1945; *b* 15 Feb 1928; *Educ* Charterhouse, RMA Sandhurst; *m* 1954, Hon Aislinn (*see* Hon Mrs (A M K) Hildyard); 1 s, 1 da; *Career* adj Regt Staff Capt RA, ret 1960, High Sheriff Humberside 1978-79, hon sec Georgian Soc for E Yorks, gen cmmr Income Tax, memb Regional Ctee (Yorks) Nat Trust, memb Regional Ctee (Yorks) Historic Houses Assoc, memb Exec Ctee Yorks Tourist Bd; *Recreations* gardening, classical architecture; *Clubs* Army and Navy; *Style* - Angus Hildyard Esq, DL; The White Hall, Winestead in Holderness, Hull, N Humberside (☎ 0964 30242)

HILDYARD, Hon Mrs (Aislinn Mary Katharine); *née* Morris; da of 2 Baron Morris (d 1975); *b* 1934; *m* 1954, Capt Angus Jeremy Christopher Hildyard, DL, RA (ret); 1 s, 1 da; *Style* - The Hon Mrs Hildyard; The White Hall, Winestead in Holderness, N Humberside

HILDYARD, Sir David Henry Thoroton; KCMG (1975, CMG 1966), DFC (1943); s of His Hon Gerard Hildyard, QC, DL; *b* 4 May 1916; *Educ* Eton, Ch Ch Oxford; *m* 1947, Millicent, da of Sir Edward Baron, and wid of Wing Cdr R Longmore; 1 s, 1 da; *Career* Foreign Service 1948, Foreign Off 1965, Ambass to Chile 1970-73, Br Perm Rep to UN 1973-76, ret; *Style* - Sir David Hildyard, KCMG, DFC; 10 The Little Boltons, SW10

HILL, 8 Viscount (UK 1842); Sir Antony Rowland Clegg-Hill; 10 Bt (GB 1727); also Baron Hill of Almaraz and of Hardwicke (UK 1816); strictly speaking the full title of the Viscountcy is: Viscount Hill of Hawkestone and of Hardwicke; s of 7 Viscount Hill (d 1974, fourth in descent from John, er bro of 1 Viscount, who commanded Adam's Brigade in the Battle of Waterloo, was second in command of the Army of Occupation (of France) 1815-18 and was CIC 1828-42, but whose hardest task may well have been curbing the intemperate activities of Lord Cardigan while in the last named office) by his 1 w Elisabeth, nee Smyth-Osbourne; *b* 19 March 1931; *Educ* Kelly Coll, Sandhurst; *m* 1963, Juanita, da of John Pertwee, of Surrey; *Heir* cous, Peter Clegg-Hill; *Career* late Capt RA; has freedom of Shrewsbury; *Style* - The Rt Hon Viscount Hill; c/o House of Lords, SW1

HILL OF LUTON, Baron (Life Peer UK 1963); Charles Hill; PC (1955); s of Charles Hill and Florence Cook, of London; *b* 15 Jan 1904; *Educ* St Olave's Sch, Trin Cambridge; *m* 1931, Marion Spencer, da of M Wallace, of Halifax; 2 s, 3 da; *Career* MD, DPH, LLD; formerly doctor London Hosp, Dep MOH Oxford; MP (Lib & C) Luton 1950-63, Postmaster-Gen 1955-57, Chllr Duchy Lancaster 1957-61, Min Housing & Local Govt & Welsh Affrs 1961-62; chm: ITA 1963-67, Govrs BBC 1967-72, Abbey Nat Bldg Soc 1976-78; former Pres World Medical Assoc; chm Chest, Heart & Stroke Assoc 1974-; *Clubs* Reform; *Style* - Rt Hon Lord Hill of Luton PC; 5 Bamville Wood, E Common, Harpenden, Herts

HILL, Lady Anne Catherine Dorothy; *née* Gathorne-Hardy; da of late 3 Earl of Cranbrook and Lady Dorothy Montagu Boyle, da of 7 Earl of Glasgow; *b* 1911; *m* 1938, George Heywood Hill; 2 da; *Style* - Lady Anne Hill; Snape Priory, Saxmundham, Suffolk

HILL, Brian John; *aet* 48; *Career* jt md Higgs & Hill, Pres London Regn Nat Fedn Bldg Trades Employers 1981-, MA, FRICS, FIOB, dir- AMO Construction, Banstead Heights Ltd, Carlow Investments, City and Municipal Properties, Clement Av Properties, Contact Supplies, Diespeker Concrete Co, Formcrete Ltd, Gazeway Plant Hire, Iverna Shop Dvpts, Kleine Reinforced Concrete, Moduluxe Homes Ltd, Muncip Dvpts, Universal Estates Ltd; *Style* - Brian Hill Esq; c/o Higgs & Hill Ltd, Crown House, Kingston rd, New Malden, Surrey

HILL, Brian Lionel; s of Lionel Hill (d 1965); *b* 21 Dec 1935; *Educ* Hornchurch G S; *m* 1960, Julia Mary, nee Woolford; 1 s (Simon Charles b 1967), 1 da (Penelope Jane b 1965); *Career* FCA, engaged in fin and industl management, gp fin controller Bestobell Ltd, dir Columbia Controls Inc USA, General Connectors Corp USA, Room Ready Ltd; *Recreations* sailing, hunting; *Style* - Brian Hill Esq; Bestobell House, 16 Bath rd, Slough (☎ 33477); Old Orchard, Redlynch, Salisbury, Wilts (☎ Downton 21177)

HILL, Molly, Viscountess; Catherine Mary (Molly); da of Dr Rowland Venables Lloyd-Williams, of Maiford, Denbigh; *m* 1942, as his 2 w, 7 Viscount Hill (d 1974); *Style* - The Rt Hon Molly, Viscountess Hill

HILL, Edith, Lady; Edith Muriel; da of W O Thomas, of Oakhurst, Liverpool, and Bryn Glas, Mold, N Wales; *m* 1919, Sir (George) Cyril Rowley Hill, 8 Bt (d 1980); *Style* - Edith, Lady Hill; 100a Leighton av, Leigh-on-Sea

HILL, Sir George Alfred Rowley; 9 Bt (I 1779), of Brook Hall, Londonderry; s of Alfred Rowley Hill (d 1946, bro of 7 Bt); suc cous, Sir (George) Cyril Rowley Hill 1980; *b* 11 Oct 1899; *Educ* Melville Coll Edinburgh; *m* 1, 1924 (m dis 1938), Rose Ethel Kathleen, MBE, da of late William Spratt; 1 s; m 2, 1938, Jessie Anne Roberts, of Leics; 1 s, 1 da; *Heir* s, Richard Hill; *Career* formerly Lt Bengal Nagpur Railway Bn Aux Force (India), N Russia 1919, 1939-44 War as Lt RNVR; *Style* - Sir George Hill, Bt; c/o Barclays Bank, Berwick-upon-Tweed, TD15 1AF

HILL OF WIVENHOE, Baroness; Hannah; da of Usher Rosen, of Newcastle upon Tyne, and formerly wife of Colin Crowther; *m* 1960, as his 2 wife, Baron Hill of Wivenhoe (Life Peer d 1969); *Style* - The Rt Hon the Lady Hill of Wivenhoe; 3 Eskdale av, Kings rd Estate, Wallsend, Northumberland

HILL, Harold James; s of Arthur Frederick Hill (d 1952); *b* 18 May 1920; *Educ* Wolverhampton G S; *m* 1949, Sheila Gwendolen, da of Hughes Alfred Thomas (d 1966); 2 children; *Career* chm George Hill Industs Ltd, dir Beacon Broadcasting Ltd; *Style* - Harold Hill Esq; Cosford Grange, Shifnal, Shropshire (☎ Albrighton 2501)

HILL, Hon John; s of Baron Hill of Luton, PC (Life Peer); *b* 1945; *Educ* Epsom, and Cambridge U; *Style* - The Hon John Hill; 1 Oatley Park av, Oatley, New South Wales, Australia

HILL, Jeremy Adrian; s of Lt-Col Cecil Vivian Hill (d 1978); *b* 16 Jan 1940; *Educ* Eton, Ch Ch Oxford; *m* 1965, Virginia Ann, da of Maj Gordon Darwin Wilmot; 3 s; *Career* dir J Henry Schroder Wagg & Co; *Recreations* tennis, shooting; *Style* - Jeremy Hill Esq; Peyton Hall, Bures, Suffolk

HILL, Sir James Frederick; 4 Bt (UK 1916), of Bradford; s of Sir James Hill, 3 Bt (d 1976); *b* 5 Dec 1943; *Educ* Wrekin Coll; *m* 1966, Sandra Elizabeth, da of J C Ingram, of Lenner House, Beamsley, Bolton Abbey, Yorks; 1 s, 3 da; *Heir* s, James Laurence Ingram Hill; *Career* chm Sir James Hill & Sons Ltd, dir Huddersfield & Bradford Building Soc, Intasun (North) Ltd, Air Europe Ltd; *Style* - Sir James Hill, Bt; Moorlands,

Moor Lane, Menston, Ilkley, W Yorks LS29 6AS (☎ Ilkley 74360)

HILL, James Laurence Ingram; s and h of Sir James Frederick Hill, 4 Bt; *b* 22 Sept 1973; *Style* - James Hill Esq

HILL, Hon Mrs (Juliet Mary); *née* Weld-Forester; da of late 7 Baron Forester; *b* 1934; *m* 1957, (Arthur) Robin Iain Hill (n and h of 7 Marq of Downshire); 2 s, 1 da; *Style* - The Hon Mrs Hill; 13 Lowndes Close, SW1; Clifton Castle, Ripon, N Yorks

HILL, Sir John McGregor; s of John Campbell Hill; *b* 21 Feb 1921; *Educ* King's Coll London, St John's Coll Cambridge; *m* 1947, Nora Eileen, nee Hellett; 2 s, 1 da; *Career* kt 1969, Fl Lt RAF 1941, FInstP, FIChemE, FInstE, joined UKAEA 1950 (memb for Prodn 1964-67); memb: Advisory Cncl on Technol 1968-70, Nuclear Power Advisory Bd 1973-, Energy Cmmn 1977-79; chm: Br Nuclear Fuels Ltd 1971-, Radiochemical Centre Ltd 1975-, UK Atomic Energy Authority 1967- (salary £42,000 pa as of June 1981); *Recreations* golf; *Clubs* East India, Devonshire, Sports and Public Schools; *Style* - Sir John Hill; Dominic House, Sudbrook Lane, Petersham, Surrey (☎ 01 940 7221)

HILL, Marjory, Lady; Marjory; JP; da of late Frank Croft, of Brocka, Lindale, Grange-over-Sands; *m* 1930, Sir James Hill, 3 Bt (d 1976); *Style* - Marjory, Lady Hill; Brea House, Trebetherick, Wadebridge, Cornwall

HILL, Marcus Tufton; s of late Lt-Col the Hon George Chenevix Hill (bro of 6 Baron Sandys) and Hon Patricia, nee Tufton, da of 2 Baron Hothfield by his 1 w, Lady Ierne Hastings (da of 13 Earl of Huntingdon); hp of cous, 7 Baron Sandys; *b* 15 March 1931; *Educ* Eton, St John's Cambridge; *Career* late RAF; *Style* - Marcus Hill Esq; Flat 13, Regina ct, Molyneux Park rd, Tunbridge Wells, Kent

HILL, Hon Robert; s of Baron Hill of Luton, PC (Life Peer); *b* 1938; *Educ* Epsom, and Harpur Adams Agricultural Coll; *m* 1960, Ann, da of E Williamson, of Southampton; *Style* - The Hon Robert Hill; Model Farm, Crewe Green, Cheshire

HILL, Richard George Rowley; MBE; s and h of Sir George Alfred Rowley Hill, 9 Bt; *b* 18 Dec 1925; *Educ* Clayesmore Sch, Glasgow U; *m* 1, 1954, Angela Mary (d 1974), da of Lt-Col Stanley Herbert Gallon, of Berwick-on-Tweed; m 2, 1975, Zoreen Joy MacPherson, da of late Norman Warburton Tippett, of Kirkland, Berwick-on-Tweed, and widow of Andrew David Wilson Marshall, KOSB; 2 da; *Career* Maj KOSB (ret); *Style* - Richard Hill Esq, MBE

HILL, (Arthur) Robin Ian; s of late Capt Lord (Arthur) Francis Hill, The Greys Reserve (yr s of late 6 Marq of Downshire) and hp of unc, 7 Marquess; *b* 10 May 1929; *Educ* Eton; *m* 1957, Hon Juliet Mary Weld-Forester, da of 7 Baron Forester; 2 s (Nicholas, Anthony b 1961), 1 da (Georgina b 1964); *Career* 2 Lt BAOR; FCA; *Recreations* tennis, golf, shooting; *Clubs* White's; *Style* - Robin Hill Esq; Clifton Castle, Ripon, N Yorks (☎ Masham 326); 60 Cheniston gdns, W8 (☎ 01 937 5978)

HILL, Hon Mrs (Yvonne Aletta); da of late 2 Baron de Villiers; *b* 1913; *Educ* LMH Oxford; *m* 1939, James Kenneth Hill; 3 s, 1 da; *Style* - The Hon Mrs Hill; Edgehill, 22 Wynhdorn av, Buderim, Queensland, Australia

HILL-NORTON, Baron (Life Peer UK 1978); Peter John Hill-Norton; GCB (1970, KCB 1967, CB 1964); s of Capt Martin John Norton; *b* 8 Feb 1915; *Educ* RNCs Dartmouth & Greenwich; *m* 1936, Margaret, da of Carl Adolph Linstow; 1 s, 1 da; *Career* Adm of the Fleet, CIC UK Forces Far East 1969-70, 1 Sea Lord 1970-71, Ch Def Staff 1971-74, chm NATO Mil Cttee 1974-77; joined RN 1932, served WW II Arctic Convoys & NW Approaches; *Style* - Adm of the Fleet The Rt Hon The Lord Hill-Norton, GCB; King's Mill House, S Nutfield, Surrey (☎ Nutfield Ridge 3309)

HILL-NORTON, Hon Nicholas John; s of Baron Hill-Norton, GCB (Life Peer); *b* 1939; *m* 1966, Jennifer Ann, da of Vice-Adm Dènis Mason, CB, CVO; *Career*

Capt RN; *Style* - The Hon Nicholas Hill-Norton; Ivy Cottage, Newton Valence, Alton, Hants

HILL-TREVOR, Hon Iain Robert; s of 4 Baron Trevor; *b* 1971; *Style* - The Hon Iain Hill-Trevor

HILL-TREVOR, Hon Marke Charles; s and h of 4 Baron Trevor; *b* 8 Jan 1970; *Style* - The Hon Marke Hill-Trevor

HILL-TREVOR, Hon Nevill Edward; s of 3 Baron Trevor (d 1950); *b* 1931; *m* 1963, Deborah, da of late W T B Jowitt, of Killinghall, Harrogate; 2 da; *Career* Flying Officer RAF (ret), ADC to C-in-C Fighter Command 1958-59, ADC to Ch of Air Staff 1960-61, High Sheriff Denbighshire 1965-66, DL Denbighshire (now Clwyd); *Style* - The Hon Nevill Hill-Trevor, DL; Plas Lledrod, Llansilin, Clwyd

HILL-WOOD, Sir David Basil; 3 Bt (UK 1921); s of Sir Basil Samuel Hill Hill-Wood, 2 Bt (d 1954), and Hon Joan Louisa Brand, da of 3 Viscount Hampden; *b* 12 Nov 1926; *Educ* Eton; *m* 1970, Jennifer Anne McKenzie Stratmann (assumed that surname by deed poll 1960), da of late Peter McKenzie Strang; 2 s, 1 da; *Heir* s, Samuel Hill-Wood *Career* Grenadier Gds 1945-48, partner Myers & Co and Capel-Cure Myers Ltd 1958-77, dir Guinness Mahon & Co 1977-; *Clubs* White's, Melbourne (Australia); *Style* - Sir David Hill-Wood, Bt; Dacre Farm, Farley Hill, Reading, Berks (☎ Eversley 733185); 58 Cathcart rd, SW10 (☎ 01 352 0389)

HILL-WOOD, Hon Lady - Hon Joan Louisa; *née* Brand; da of 3 Viscount Hampden, GCVO, KCB, CMG (d 1958); *b* 1904; *m* 1925, Capt Sir Basil Samuel Hill Hill-Wood, 2 Bt (d 1954); 1 s, 1 da; *Style* - The Hon Lady Hill-Wood; Knipton Lodge, Grantham, Lincs (☎ Knipton 226)

HILL-WOOD, Samuel Thomas; s and h of Sir David Basil Hill-Wood, 3 Bt; *b* 24 Aug 1971; *Style* - Samuel Hill-Wood Esq

HILLEARY, Hon Mrs (Grace Janet Mary); *née* Best; da of 6 Baron Wynford, DSO (d 1940), and Hon Eva Napier, da of 2 Baron Napier of Magdala; *b* 1907; *m* 1930, Edward Hilleary, MVO; 3 da; *Style* - The Hon Mrs Hilleary; Nettlebed House, Droxford, Hants

HILLGARTH, Hon Mrs Mary Sidney Katherine Almina; *née* Gardner; da of 1 and last Baron Burghclere, PC (d 1921, when Barony became extinct) by Lady Winifred Herbert, da of 4 Earl of Carnarvon; *b* 1896; *m* 1, 1914, Hon Geoffrey Hope-Morley (m dis 1928; he suc his father as 2 Baron Hollenden 1929 and d 1977); 2 da; m 2, 1929 (m dis 1946), Capt Alan Hugh Hillgarth, CMG, OBE, RN (ret); 1 s; *Style* - The Hon Mrs Mary Hillgarth; Son Torrella de Santa Maria, Isla de Mallorca, Spain

HILLINGDON, 5 Baron (UK 1886); Sir Patrick Charles Mills; 6 Bt (UK 1868), MC (1945), TD; 3 s of Cdr Hon Geoffrey Mills (himself 6 s of 1 Baron Hillingdon, JP, DL, sometime MP W Kent) by his 1 w Grace, da of Hungerford Boddam, sometime Judge of the Madras High Court; suc 4 Baron (1 cous once removed) 1978; *b* 4 Nov 1906; *Educ* Lancing, St Cat's Cambridge; *m* 1, 1931 (m dis 1939), Nancy, da of Brinsley Nixon, of Westward Ho; 2 da; m 2, 1945, Mary (d 1976), da of W Hoare-Ward, of Brighton; *Heir* none; *Career* Lt-Col & Bt Col Kent Yeo WW II, served France, M East, Italy; memb London Stock Exchange 1934-76 (ptnr Marks Bulteel Mills & Co 1937-63, Greener Dreyfus & Co 1963-68, Cohen De Smitt Greener Dreyfus 1968-76); *Style* - The Rt Hon Lord Hillingdon MC TD; The Tod House, Seal, Kent (☎ Sevenoaks 61819)

HILLINGDON, Baroness; Phoebe Maxwell; da of late Capt Mervyn James Hamilton, of Cornacassa, Monaghan, by his w, Hildred (herself da of Hon Bernard Ward, CB, who in his turn was 4 s of 3 Viscount Bangor); *m* 1, Lt-Cdr John Sholto Fitzpatrick Cooke, CBE, RNVR; m 2, John Cooper; m 3, as his 2 wife, 4 Baron Hillingdon (d 1978); *Style* - The Rt Hon The Lady Hillingdon; Messing Park, Kelvedon, Essex

HILLMAN, Arthur Joseph; TD (1946), JP (1961); s of Arthur Lionel Hillman, JP (d 1958); *b* 21 Feb 1917; *Educ* Stonyhurst; *m* 1943, Marjorie Pamela, nee Smith; 3 da; *Career* maj WW II, France 1939-40, Middle East 1941-42, dir and md Hillman Douglas Ltd 1934-69, chm and dir Hillman Newby Ltd 1969-78, gov BUPA Ltd 1981-; *Recreations* golf; *Clubs* Blackwell GC; *Style* - Arthur Hillman Esq, TD, JP; Keys Cottage, Lower Bentley, Bromsgrove, Worcs

HILLS, Air Cdre D G M; OBE; *Career* MB, BS, MFCM, DPH; Dep Dir-Gen RAF Med Servs 1978-, Hon Surgn to HM 1981-; *Style* - Air Commodore D Hills, OBE; c/o MOD, SW1

HILLS, Lady Rosemary Ethel; *née* Baring; da of 2 Earl of Cromer, GCB, GCIE, GCVO, PC (d 1953) and Lady Ruby, da of 4 Earl of Minto; *b* 1908; *m* 1932, Lt-Col John David Hills, MC, former headmaster of Bradfield Coll; 1 s, 2 da (*see* Hon (H E) Christopher Willoughby); *Style* - Lady Rosemary Hills; House by the Dyke, Chirk, Wrexham, Denbighshire

HILTON, Bernard Carter; s of Clifford Hilton (d 1921); *b* 24 Aug 1921; *Educ* Rugby Coll of Engineering Technology; *m* 1, 1949, Betty Doreen; 1 da; m 2, 1976, Margaret Cynthia, nee Edwards; *Career* chm Apex Fireplaces (Staffs) Ltd 1976-, v-chm & ch exec A I Welders Ltd 1979-, former chm Constructional & Special Products Div Aurora Holdings Ltd 1979-, chm Engineering Div Firth Cleveland Ltd; *Recreations* lecturing, travel, reading; *Clubs* Reform; *Style* - Bernard Hilton Esq; 46 Thames st, Hampton, Middlesex (☎ 01 979 9627); The Glen, Sheffield S10 3FN (☎ 663188); Allesgo, Burn rd, Inverness (☎ 35752)

HINCHINGBROOKE, Viscount; courtesy title of eldest s & h of Earl of Sandwich; has not been used by John Edward Hollister Montagu, *qv*, since 1970

HINCHLIFF, Stephen; CBE (1976); s of Gordon Henry Hinchliff (d 1976); *b* 11 July 1926; *Educ* Almondbury G S, Huddersfield, Boulevard Nautical Coll, Huddersfield Coll of Tech, Cranfield Inst of Tech; *m* 1951, Margaret Arrundale, nee Crossland; 2 c; *Career* FIMechE, FIProdE, CBIM, FRSA, dep chm Dowty Gp Ltd 1973-76, md Dowty Gp Industrial Div 1973-76, dir Renwick Gp 1977-81, md Dexion-Comino Int Ltd 1976-, chm Dexion Gp of companies 1976-; *Recreations* squash, badminton, tennis; *Style* - Stephen Hinchliff Esq, CBE; 18 Newcourt Park, Charlton Kings, Cheltenham, Glos (☎ Cheltenham 517541)

HINDE, Lady; Evelyn Muriel; da of Capt H FitzHerbert Wright, of Yeldersley Hall, Derby; *m* 1926, Maj-Gen Sir Robert Hinde, KBE, CB, DSO & 2 Bars (d 1981); 1 s, 3 da (including Countess Cawdor and Lady Gordon Cumming); *Style* - Lady Hinde; Shrewton House, Shrewton, Salisbury, Wilts (☎ 233)

HINDLEY, Hon Elizabeth Cairns; da of 1 and last Viscount Hyndley (d 1963); *b* 1912; *Style* - The Hon Elizabeth Hindley; Meads Cottage, Rondle Wood, nr Liphook, Hants

HINDLEY, Hon Millicent Joyce; da of 1 and last Viscount Hyndley (d 1963); *b* 1914; *Style* - The Hon Millicent Hindley

HINDLIP, 5 Baron (UK 1886); Sir Henry Richard Allsopp; 5 Bt (UK 1880), JP (Wilts 1957), DL (1956); s of 3 Baron Hindlip, OBE, JP, DL, by his w Agatha (herself da of John Thynne, who was in his turn 6 s of Rev Lord John Thynne, 3 s of 2 Marquess of Bath); suc er bro (4 Baron) 1966; *b* 1 July 1912; *Educ* Eton, Sandhurst; *m* 1939, Cecily, da of Lt-Col Malcolm Borwick, DSO (nephew of 1 Baron Borwick and sometime Joint Master of The Pytchley); 2 s, 1 da; *Heir* s, Hon Charles Allsopp; *Career* 2 Lt Coldstream Gds 1932, Maj 1941, ret 1948, served WW II NW Europe; *Clubs* White's, Pratt's, Turf; *Style* - The Rt Hon Lord Hindlip JP DL; Vern Leaze, Calne, Wilts (☎ Calne 3229)

HINDLIP, Tulla, Baroness; Hansina Cecilia Elfrida; da of late Frederick William Harris; *m* 1939, as his 2 wife, 4 Baron Hindlip (d 1966); 2 da (Hon Mrs Velissaropoulos, Hon Elizabeth Allsopp); *Style* - The Rt Hon Tulla, Lady Hindlip;

Botches, Wivelsfield Green, Haywards Heath, Sussex

HINDS, William James; MBE (1969), JP; s of Ben Hinds; *b* 9 Sept 1910; *Educ* Queen Elizabeth's G S Carmarthen, Pibwrlwyd Farm Inst, U Coll of Wales; *m* 1938, Gwendolen, da of Thomas Harries; *Career* High Sheriff Dyfed 1981-82; memb S Wales Milk Mkting Bd 1952-, SW Wales River Authority; *Recreations* fishing, rugby; *Style* - William Hinds Esq, MBE, JP; Danyrallt, Abergorlech rd, Carmarthen, Dyfed (☎ 0267 88233)

HINES, His Honour (Vivian) Gerald Hines; QC (1964); s of the late John Hines; *b* 24 Dec 1912; *Educ* Earls Colne G S; *m* 1, 1950, Janet (d 1957), nee Graham; m 2, 1960, Barbara, nee Gunton; *Career* slr 1935-42, barr 1943, deputy chairman Quarter Sessions Essex 1955-67, County of London 1965; chm- Quarter Sessions NE London 1965-68, Middlesex 1969, Inner London 1969-70; additional judge Central Criminal Court 1968-69, Circuit Judge 1971-79; *Recreations* reading, writing; *Clubs* Essex; *Style* - His Honour Gerald Hines, QC; Littlefield, Great Bentley, Colchester, Essex (☎ Great Bentley 250555)

HINTON OF BANKSIDE, Baron (Life Peer UK 1965); Christopher Hinton; OM (1976), KBE (1957); s of Frederick Hinton, of Laycock, Wilts; *b* 12 May 1901; *Educ* Chippenham G S, Trin Cambridge; *m* 1931, Lillian (d 1973), da of Thomas Boyer; 1 da; *Career* FRS, FRSA, FIChemE, FIMechE, FIEE of Inst of Metals; engr; kt 1951; dir UKAEA 1954-57, late chm CEGB, dep chm Electricity Supply Res Cncl 1965-; Pres Cncl of Engineering Instns 1976- *Style* - Rt Hon Lord Hinton of Bankside OM KBE; Tiverton Lodge, Dulwich Common, SE21 (☎ 01 693 6447)

HIRSHFIELD, Baron (Life Peer UK 1967); Desmond Barel Hirshfield; s of Leopold Hirshfield; *b* 17 May 1913; *Educ* City of London Sch, Birkbeck Coll London; *m* 1951, Bronia, da of Joseph Eisen, of Tel Aviv; *Career* FCA, jt sr ptnr Stoy Horwath & Co (CA), Pres Horwath & Horwath Internat, chm Horwath & Horwath (UK), fndr chm Trades Union Unit Tst Managers Ltd 1961; memb Top Salaries Review Body 1975-; dep chm MLH Consultants, chm TUUT Charitable Tst, Norwood Fndn, Norwood Charitable Tst, Woodmond Securities, Ralmond Securities, Ralwood Securities, Fieldwood Securities; Gov LSE; Pres Br Assoc Hotel Accountants; Tres UK Cttee UNICEF; *Style* - The Rt Hon Lord Hirshfield; 54 Baker st, W1 (☎ 01 486 5888)

HIRST, Alan Frank; s of Frank Leonard Hirst CBE, (d 1961); *b* 9 Dec 1922; *Educ* Epsom College; *m* 1944, Jenny Clarissa; 4 c; *Career* md RHM Gen Products Ltd 1976-; *Recreations* gardening; *Clubs* RNVR; *Style* - Alan Hirst Esq; Quenington, Hawks Hill, Guildford rd, Leatherhead, Surrey (☎ 72242)

HITCHCOCK, Geoffrey Lionel Henry; CBE (1975, OBE 1957); s of the late Major Frank Bridge Hitchcock, MC; *b* 10 Sept 1915; *Educ* The Oratory Sch, Hertford Coll Oxford; *m* 1950, Rosemary Eva, nee de Las Casas; 2 s, 1 da; *Career* joined British Council 1939, representative Germany, Austria 1954-59, Yugoslavia 1962-67, controller Home Division 1970-73, cultural counsellor British Embassy Paris 1973-76; *Recreations* race-going, gardening; *Clubs* Travellers'; *Style* - Geoffrey Hitchcock Esq, CBE; 1 Storey's Way, Cambridge (☎ Cambridge 350112)

HIVES, 2 Baron (UK 1950); John Warwick Hives; s of 1 Baron Hives, CH, MBE, sometime chm & md Rolls-Royce (d 1965); *b* 26 Nov 1913; *Educ* Derby Sch; *m* 1, 1937, Olwen Protheroe Llewellin (d 1972); m 2, 1972, Gladys, da of Alfred Seals; *Heir* n, Matthew Hives; *Career* farmer; *Clubs* Farmers'; *Style* - The Rt Hon Lord Hives; Bendalls, Milton, Derby (☎ Burton on Trent 703319)

HIVES, Hon David Benjamin; s of 1 Baron Hives, CH, MBE (d 1965); *b* 1931; *Educ* Repton; *m* 1954, Shirley, da of late Harold Walker, of Cumberland House, Duffield, Derby; 1 s, 2 da; *Career* Gp Capt RAF; *Style* - The Hon David Hives; Halfacre, 28 St Peter's Way, Chorley Wood, Herts

HIVES, Hon Michael Bruce; s of 1 Baron Hives, CH, MBE (d 1965); *b* 1926; *Educ* Repton; *m* 1951, Janet Rosemary, da of late W E Gee, of Lynngarth, Duffield, Derby; 2 s, 1 da; *Style* - The Hon Michael Hives; Fairfield, The Pastures, Duffield, Derbys

HIVES, Matthew Peter; s of Lt Hon Peter Anthony Hives, RNVR (d 1974, 3 s of 1 Baron Hives, CH, MBE, who d 1965); hp of unc, 2 Baron Hives; *b* 25 May 1971; *Style* - Matthew Hives Esq; Harmer Garry, Harmer Green Lane, Welwyn, Herts (☎ 4353)

HIVES, Hon Mrs Peter - Dinah; da of F Wilson-North, of Walcott, Norfolk; *m* 1956, the Hon Peter Anthony Hives (d 1974); 1 s, 3 da; *Style* - The Hon Mrs Peter Hives;Harmer Garry, Harmer Green Lane, Welwyn, Herts

HOARE, Lady Alma; *née* Stopford; da of late 6 Earl of Courtown; *b* 1889; *m* 1922, Lt-Col Geoffrey Lennard Hoare, CBE (d 1960); 1 s, 2 da; *Style* - Lady Alma Hoare; Little Barn, Benenden, Cranbrook, Kent

HOARE, Lady Christina Alice; da of late 8 Earl of Antrim, KBE; *b* 1938; *m* 1963, Joseph Andrew Christopher Hoare, s of late Sir Reginald Hervey Hoare, KCMG; 1 s, 2 da; *Style* - Lady Christina Hoare; 34 Seymour Walk, SW10

HOARE, Charles James; s and h of Sir Timothy Edward Charles Hoare, 8 Bt; *b* 15 March 1971; *Style* - Charles Hoare Esq

HOARE, David John; s of Sir Peter William Hoare, 7 Bt (d 1973), and hp of bro, Sir Peter Richard David Hoare, 8 Bt; *b* 8 Oct 1935; *Educ* Eton; *m* 1965, Mary Vanessa, da of Peter Cardew, of Westhanger, Cleeve, Bristol; 1 s; *Career* banker & farmer; *Recreations* fishing, shooting, skiing; *Style* - David Hoare Esq; 40 Cadogan sq, SW1 (☎ 01 584 2384); Luscombe Castle, Dawlish, Devon

HOARE, Ernest George; *b* 9 June 1927; *Educ* Saltash G S; *m* 1950, Nancy Beatrice; 3 s; *Career* CA; md J & F Pool Hldgs 1970-; dir Western Motor Hldgs 1980-; memb Industl Tbnls Panel; *Recreations* gardening, committee work; *Clubs* Roy Thames Yacht; *Style* - Ernest Hoare Esq; 51 Pendarves rd, Camborne, Cornwall (☎ 0209 714332)

HOARE, Sir Frederick Alfred; 1 Bt (UK 1962), of Fleet Street, City of London; s of late Frederick Henry Hoare; *b* 11 Feb 1913; *Educ* Wellington; *m* 1, 1939, Norah Mary (d 1973), da of Addison James Wheeler; 2 da; m 2, 1974, Oonah Alice (d 1980), da of late Brig-Gen David Ramsay Sladen, CMG, DSO, of Rhydoldog, Rhayader, Powys, and formerly wife of (1) Maj Keith Hathorn Johnston Stewart, KOSB, and (2) Lt-Col Norman Peter Dew, OBE; *Heir* none; *Career* managing partner C Hoare & Co Bankers 1947-; dir Messrs Hoare Trustees, Mitre Court Securities Ltd, Mitre Court Cranes Ltd, Mitre Court Property Holding Co, The Trust Union Ltd, Grimersta Estate Ltd, Tuscan Development Co, Hoare's Bank Nominees Ltd, Trust Union Finance Ltd; chm General Practice Finance Corpn 1966-73, Lord Mayor of London 1961-62, formerly one of HM Lts for City of London; chm Anglers' Co-operative Assoc, John Eastwood Water Protection Trust Ltd; memb Court of Assistants and Prime Warden of Goldsmiths' Co 1966-67; kt 1958, KStJ; *Clubs* Garrick, City Livery, Flyfishers'; *Style* - Sir Frederick Hoare, Bt; 34 Cadogan sq, SW1

HOARE, Hon Mrs - Hon Frances Evelyn; *née* Hogg; da of Baron Hailsham of St Marylebone (Life Peer); *b* 1949; *Educ* St Paul's Girls' Sch , Homerton Teacher Training Coll Cambridge; *m* 1970, Richard Quintin Hoare; 2 s, 1 da; *Style* - The Hon Mrs Hoare; 1 Logan pla, W8

HOARE, Henry Peregrine Rennie; s of Henry Hoare, JP (d 1965); *b* 24 Sept 1901; *Educ* Wellington, Cambridge; *m* 1, Lady Beatrix Lilian Ethel Cadogan, da of 16 Earl Cadogan, CBE (m dis 1941); 1 s, 1 da; m 2, 1941, Anne (m dis 1946) formerly w of 5 Baron Ebury and da of Maj Herbert Walter Acland Troyte, MC (d 1943); m 3, 1947, (Dorothy) Margaret, da of John Duncan Hairs (d 1925), of Montego Bay, Jamaica; 2 s, 2 da; *Career* ptnr C Hoare & Co (bankers) 1928-; *Recreations* forestry;

Clubs Garrick; *Style* - Henry Hoare Esq; Gasper House, Stourton, Warminster, Wilts (☎ Bourton 214)

HOARE, Henry Richard; s of Charles Richard Hoare (d 1933) and Hon Mrs Hoare (d 1949), da of 1 Visc Chaplin; *b* 26 Oct 1922; *Educ* Eton; *Career* High Sheriff Rutland 1961; *Style* - Henry Hoare Esq; Wardley House, Wardley, Uppingham, Leics (☎ Belton 249)

HOARE, Joseph Andrew Christopher; s of Sir Reginald Hoare, KCMG (d 1954) and Lucy (d 1971), da of William Cavendish-Bentinck JP; *b* 23 March 1925; *Educ* Eton, Balliol Oxford; *m* 1963, Lady Christina, *qv*, da of 13 Earl of Antrim, KBE; 1 s, 2 da; *Career* stockbroker, dir Canadian Overseas Packaging Industs; *Clubs* Brooks's; *Style* - Joseph Hoare Esq; 34 Seymour Walk, SW10; Amberdown and Hartridge Farms,Sissinghurst, Kent

HOARE, Laura, Lady; Laura Ray; da of Sir John Esplen, 1 Bt, KBE (d 1930); *m* 1929, Sir Peter William Hoare, 7 Bt (d 1973); *Style* - Laura, Lady Hoare; Luscombe Castle, Dawlish, Devon

HOARE, Nina, Lady; Nina Mary; da of late Charles Nugent Hope-Wallace, MBE; *m* 1932, Maj Sir Edward O'Bryen Hoare, 7 Bt (d 1969); *Style* - Nina, Lady Hoare; 61 Flask Walk, NW3

HOARE, Sir Peter Richard David; 8 Bt (GB 1786); s of Sir Peter Hoare, 7 Bt (d 1973), of Luscombe Castle, Dawlish; *b* 22 March 1932; *Educ* Eton; *m* 1961 (m dis 1967), Jane, da of Daniel Orme, of Bulleigh Barton, Ipplepen, S Devon; m 2, 1978, Katrin Alexa, da of late Erwin Bernstiel, and formerly wife of Sir Michael Robin Adderley Hodson, 6 Bt; *Heir* bro, David John Hoare; *Career* dir N Bentley Securities A G Zurich; *Style* - Sir Peter Hoare, Bt; Avda Meritdell 114, Andorra La Vella, Principality of Andorra

HOARE, Quintin Vincent; OBE (1945); s of Maj Vincent Hoare (ka 1915); *b* 21 June 1907; *Educ* Eton, Oriel Oxford; *m* 1, 1936 (m dis 1952), Lucy, da of Very Rev Edward Selwyn, dean of Winchester (d 1959); 3 s; m 2, 1952, Mia, da of Lt-Col Charles Hezlet, DSO (d 1965); 2 s, 1 da; *Career* ptnr C Hoare & Co, bankers; *Clubs* Portland, St James and White's; *Style* - Quintin Hoare Esq, OBE; Monks, Oakwood Hill, Dorking, Surrey (☎ Oakwood Hill 349); 37 Fleet st, EC4

HOARE, Maj Robert; MC, DL (Rutland 1965); s of Christopher Hoare, of Gateley Hall, Norfolk; *b* 1 Dec 1909; *Educ* Harrow, Cambridge; *m* 1, 1933, Oriel Susannah, da of Col Hon Guy Wilson, CMG, DSO, TD (d 1943); 2 da; m 2, 1939, Betty McCall; 1 s, 2 da; *Career* Nat Hunt Cttee 1956, High Sheriff Rutland 1963; *Clubs* Turf and Jockey; *Style* - Maj Robert Hoare, MC, DL; The Hall, Hambleton, Oakham, Leics (☎ 2250)

HOARE, Col Ronald John; CBE (1947); *b* 31 Aug 1913; *Educ* St Paul's; *m* 1948, Anne Louise, da of late Ronald Deterding, of Kelling Hall, Holt, Norfolk; 1 s, 2 da; *Career* Col RA ret, chm R J Hoare Gp; *Recreations* shooting; *Clubs* Boodle's, Cavalry & Guards; *Style* - Col Ronald Hoare, CBE; Chute Forest House, Andover, Hants (☎ Chute Standen 203)

HOARE, Sir Timothy Edward Charles; 8 Bt (I 1784); s of Sir Edward O'Bryen Hoare, 7 Bt (d 1969); *b* 11 Nov 1934; *Educ* Radley, Worcester Coll Oxford; *m* 1969, Felicity Anne, da of Peter Boddington; 1 s, 2 da; *Heir* s Charles Hoare; *Career* dir Career Plan Ltd, New Metals and Chemicals Ltd, memb Gen Synod of Church of England 1970-; *Style* - Sir Timothy Hoare, Bt; 10 Belitha Villas, N1

HOBART, John Vere; s and h of Sir Robert Hobart, 3 Bt; *b* 9 April 1945; *Style* - John Hobart Esq

HOBART, Lt-Cdr Sir Robert Hampden; 3 Bt (UK 1914); s of Lt-Col Sir (Claud) Vere Cavendish Hobart, 2 Bt, DSO, OBE (d 1949); *b* 7 May 1915; *Educ* Wixenford, RNC Dartmouth; *m* 1, 1942, Sylvia (d 1965), da of Henry A Argo, of Durban, Natal; 3 s, 1 da; m 2, 1975, Caroline Fleur, da of late Col Henry Monckton Vatcher, MC, of Valeran, St Brelade's Jersey, widow of the 11 Duke of Leeds, and formerly wife of Peter Hendrik

Peregrine Hoos; *Heir* s, John Hobart; *Career* Sub-Lt RN 1935, Lt-Cdr 1945, 1939-45 War (wounded, two medals, four stars), ret 1950; contested (Nat Lib) Hillsborough Div of Sheffield 1945, (C and Lib) Itchen Div of Southampton 1950; *Clubs* Travellers', Royal London Yacht, Roy Yacht Sqdn, Roy Southern Yacht, Bembridge Sailing; *Style* - Lt-Cdr Sir Robert Hobart, Bt, RN; Gatcombe Park, Newport, Isle of Wight

HOBART-HAMPDEN, (George) Miles; s of late Cyril Langel Hobart-Hampden, ggs of 6 Earl of Buckinghamshire; hp of kinsman, 9 Earl; *b* 15 Dec 1944; *Educ* Clifton Coll, Exeter U, London U (MA); *m* 1, 1968, Susan Jennifer, only da of R W Adams; m 2, 1975, Alison Wightman, da of late W Forrest, of Edinburgh; *Style* - Miles Hobart-Hampden Esq; c/o Roy Bank of Scotland, Charing Cross West Branch, 9 Clifton pla, Glasgow C3 7LD

HOBBS, Hon Mrs (Julia Elizabeth Heather); *née* Hamilton; da of 13 Lord Belhaven and Stenton; *b* 1956; *m* 1, 1975, Richard Newbury; m 2, 1979, Stephen Hobbs; *Style* - The Hon Mrs Hobbs

HOBDAY, Sir Gordon Ivan; s of Alexander Hobday (d 1971); *b* 1 Feb 1916; *Educ* Long Eaton G S, U Coll Nottingham; *m* 1940, Margaret Joule; 1 da; *Career* chm Boots Co Ltd 1972-81, chm ATV Midlands April 1981-; kt 1979; BSc, PhD, FRIC; *Clubs* Athenaeum *Style* - Sir Gordon Hobday; c/o The Boots Co, Nottingham (☎ 56111)

HOBHOUSE, Sir Charles Chisholm; 6 Bt (UK 1812), TD; s of Sir Reginald Hobhouse, 5 Bt, JP (d 1947, gs of Sir Charles Hobhouse, 3 Bt, who was himself nephew of Sir John Cam Hobhouse, 2 Bt, in youth the friend of, and fellow debauchee with, Lord Byron (who apostrophised the equal facility with which Hobhouse spewed forth breakfast and verses on the Lisbon packet); in maturity an MP, Sec for War, Ch Sec for Ireland and Pres of the Bd of Control; elevated to the Peerage as Baron Broughton, he was allegedly the first to use the phrase 'His Majesty's Opposition'); bro of Hon Mrs Alexander Money-Coutts; *b* 7 Dec 1906; *Educ* Eton; *m* 1, 1946, Mary (d 1955), da of John Park, of Northumberland; m 2, 1959, Jo (Elspeth Jean), da of Thomas Spinney, of Morocco; 1 s; *Heir* s, Charles Hobhouse; *Career* late Maj N Somerset Yeo; *Recreations* hunting, shooting; *Style* - Sir Charles Hobhouse, Bt, TD; The Manor, Monkton Farleigh, Bradford-on-Avon, Wilts (☎ Bath 858558)

HOBHOUSE, Charles John Spinney; s and h of Sir Charles Hobhouse, 6 Bt, by his 2 w; *b* 27 Oct 1962; *Style* - Charles Hobhouse Esq

HOBHOUSE, Henry; s of late Sir Arthur Hobhouse, JP, sometime MP Wells, and Konradin, da of Rt Hon Frederick Huth Jackson, PC (gs of Sir William Jackson, 1 Bt); through his paternal grandmother Hermine, Henry is 2 cous once removed of Daniel and Luke Meinertzhagen and 3 cous of Nicholas, *qqv*; he is also ggs of Henry Hobhouse, JP, DL, and Hon Charlotte Talbot, yst da of 3 Baron Talbot of Malahide (of Henry the JP's 3 bros, one was a Bishop, one an Archdeacon and the yst, Arthur, was 1 & last Baron Hobhouse); the family is descended from a yr bro of John Hobhouse, f of the 1 Bt (*see* Sir Charles Hobhouse, 6 Bt, TD); *b* 26 Dec 1924; *Educ* Eton; *m* 1, 1947 (m dis 1954); 1 da; m 2, 1954, Pamela, JP (d 1981), yst da of Charles Hill, JP; 4 s; *Career* served WW II RNVR; CCllr Somerset 1981; *Style* - Henry Hobhouse Esq; Halfway House, Hadspen Village, Castle Cary, Somerset (☎ 50115)

HOBSON, Baroness; Doris Mary; da of Fred Spink, of Kensington; *m* 1933, Baron Hobson (Life Peer d 1966); 1 da (Hon Mrs Jeanneret); *Style* - The Rt Hon the Lady Hobson; 115 Dewsbury rd, NW10 (☎ 01 452 4740)

HOBSON, Lady (Irene) June Beatrice; *née* Butler; MBE (1943); da of late 7 Earl of Carrick; *b* 1901; *m* 1, 1923 (m dis), John Sills Charlton; 1 s; m 2, Col Anthony Gordon Hobson, IA (ret); *Career* Supt St John Ambulance Bde Overseas, Burma; OStJ; *Style* - Lady June Hobson, MBE; Quinta de Sao Bento, Sintra, Portugal

HODDER, James Gordon; s of Arthur Sylvester Hodder (d 1974); *b* 14 Jan 1920; *Educ* Hardyes Sch Dorchester, London U; *m* 1950, Eileen Margaret, da of Thomas John Scott; 2 s; *Career* slr 1948; Gibson & Weldon 1948-50, Powers Samas Accounting Machines Ltd 1950-52, Marsh & Baxter Ltd 1952-57; v-chm Metal Box Ltd 1979- (entered 1957, assist sec 1964, sec 1970, dir 1972); *Recreations* music, reading, cricket, swimming, walking, theatre; *Clubs* MCC, Wig and Pen; *Style* - James Hodder Esq; 7 South dve, Wokingham, Berks (☎ (0734) 780246)

HODGE, Andrew; s and h of Sir John Rowland Hodge, 2 Bt, MBE; *b* 3 Dec 1968; *Style* - Andrew Hodge Esq

HODGE, Sir John Rowland; 2 Bt (UK 1921), MBE (1940); s of Sir Rowland Hodge, 1 Bt (d 1950); *b* 1 May 1913; *Educ* Wrekin Coll, and Switzerland; *m* 1, 1936 (m dis 1939), Peggy Ann, da of Sydney Raymond Kent; m 2, 1939 (m dis 1961), da of late Sydney Foster Wilson; 3 da; m 3, 1962 (m dis 1967), Jeanne Wood Anderson, da of late Cdr W E Buchanan, of Edinburgh; m 4, 1967, Vivien, da of Alfred Knightley, of Norwood; 1 s, 1 da; *Heir* s, Andrew Hodge; *Career* formerly Lt-Cdr RNVR, formerly Lt Oxfordshire and Bucks LI, European War 1939-40; *Clubs* British Racing Drivers, Naval, Royal Malta Yacht, Royal Yachting Assoc, Cruising Assoc; *Style* - Sir John Hodge, Bt, MBE; Casa Toro, St Andrews, Malta (☎ 37583)

HODGE, Ronald Jacob; s of Jacob Hodge (d 1964); *b* 16 May 1926; *Educ* Wycliffe Coll Stonehouse, New Coll Oxford; *m* 1956, Pauline Phyllis, nee Beale; 3 da (Nicola, Alison, Virginia); *Career* Lt Mddx Regt, chm USMC Int Ltd Leicester and dir of other cos in same gp in UK, USA, France, Germany, Japan, Sweden, Denmark, Finland, Australia, Spain; *Recreations* golf, music, horticulture; *Clubs* Edgbaston Golf Club; *Style* - Ronald Hodge Esq; Park Mount, 259 Bristol rd, Birmingham B5 (☎ 021 472 0683)

HODGE, Dowager Lady - Vera Estelle; da of late John Fraser; *m* 1, Capt de Grey Warter, 4 Dragoon Gds (decd); m 2, 1919, 5 Earl Cathcart (d 1927 having obtained a divorce); 1 s (6 Earl); m 3, 1930, as his 2 w, Sir Rowland Frederic William Hodge, 1 Bt (d 1950); *Style* - Dowager Lady Hodge; 50 Lennox gdns, SW1

HODGES, Hon Mrs (Naomi Katharine); *née* Lloyd; da of Baron Lloyd of Hampstead (Life Peer); *b* 1946; *m* 1967, Peter Campbell Hodges; *Style* - The Hon Mrs Hodges; 3 Cleveland rd, Barnes, SW13

HODGKIN, Hon Mrs (Katharine Mary); da of 1 and last Viscount Hewart (d 1964); *b* 1907; *m* 1929, Eliot Hodgkin; 1 s, 1 da; *Style* - The Hon Mrs Hodgkin; Shelley's Hare Hatch, Twyford, Berks

HODGKINSON, Hon Mrs (Virginia Yvonne Lloyd); *née* Lloyd Mostyn; da of 5 Baron Mostyn, MC; *b* 1946; *m* 1973, John Robert Hodgkinson; 2 s; *Style* - The Hon Mrs Hodgkinson; 28 Hereford sq, SW7

HODSON, Baron (Life Peer UK 1960); (Francis Lord) Charlton Hodson; MC, PC (1951); s of Rev Thomas Hodson, R of Oddington, Glos; *b* 17 Sept 1895; *Educ* Cheltenham Coll, Wadham Oxford (Hon Fell 1939); *m* 1918, Susan Mary (d 1965), da of Maj William Greaves Blake, DL, Scots Greys, and 9 Lancers; 1 s, 1 da (and 1 s ka 1942); *Career* barr Inner Temple 1921, KC 1937, memb Permanent Court of Arbitration at The Hague 1949-73, Jr Counsel to Treasury (Probate) 1935-37, a Judge of High Court of Justice (Probate, Divorce and Admiralty Div) 1937-51, a Lord Justice of Appeal 1951-60, and a Lord of Appeal in Ordinary 1960-71, 1914-19 War in Gallipoli and Mesopotamia as Capt Gloucestershire Regt (wounded, MC, Cavalier of Order of Crown of Italy, 1914-15 star, two medals); kt 1937; *Style* - The Rt Hon Lord Hodson MC PC; Fishers, Rotherfield Greys, Oxon (☎ 303)

HODSON, Anne, Lady; Anne Elizabeth Adderley; da of Lt-Col Adderley Cradock, formerly of Hill House, Sherborne St John, Basingstoke; *m* 1928, Maj Sir Edmond Adair Hodson, DSO, 5 Bt (d 1972); *Style* - Anne, Lady Hodson;

The White House, Awbridge, Romsey, Hants

HODSON, Hon Charles Christopher Philip; s of Baron Hodson, MC (Life Peer); *b* 1922; *m* 1953, Rose, da of Sir Charles Markham, 2 Bt; 1 s, 3 da; *Style* - The Hon Charles Hodson; Stoney Hall, Hannington, Hants

HODSON, Sir Michael Robin Adderley; 6 Bt (I 1787), of Holybrooke House, Wicklow; s of Maj Sir Edmond Adair Hodson, 5 Bt, DSO (d 1972); *b* 5 March 1932; *Educ* Eton; *m* 1963 (m dis 1978), Katrin Alexa, da of late Erwin Bernstiel, of St Andrew's House, St Andrew's Major, Dinas Powis, Glam; 3 da; m 2, 1978, Catherine, da of John Henry Seymour; *Heir* bro, Patrick Hodson; *Career* Capt (ret) Scots Gds; *Style* - Sir Michael Hodson, Bt; Bellehatch, Henley-on-Thames, Oxon

HODSON, Patrick Richard; s of Maj Sir Edmond Adair Hodson, 5 Bt, DSO (d 1972), and hp of bro, Sir Michael Robin Adderley Hodson, 6 Bt; *b* 27 Nov 1934; *Educ* Eton; *m* 1961, June, da of H M Shepherd-Cross, of The Old Rectory, Brandsby, Yorks; 3 s; *Career* Capt (ret) Rifle Bde; *Style* - Patrick Hodson Esq; Shipton Slade Farm, Woodstock, Oxford

HODSON, William Francis; s of William H Hodson (d 1961); *b* 9 July 1921; *Educ* King George V Sch Southport; *m* Nancy, nee Partington; 1 s, 1 da; *Career* maj Roy Glos Hussars (TA) 1939-40, adj Manchester Regt 1941-45, gen Staff Offr 1945-46, Kent Yeomanry (TA) 1947-58, dir Smith, Kline & French Laboratories Ltd 1957-, memb Bd of Welwyn Garden City Dvpt Corp and memb of Cmmn for New Towns 1963-77, memb NW Thames Regional Health Authority 1973-; *Recreations* golf; *Clubs* Army and Navy; *Style* - William Hodson Esq; The Old Chequers, Church st, Welwyn, Herts (☎ 5451); 5 The Whinlands, Thorpeness, Leiston, Suffolk

HOGAN, Thomas Patrick; s of Daniel Hogan (d 1920); *b* 4 Aug 1908; *Educ* Mount St Joseph Coll, Univ Coll Dublin; *m* 1949, Mary Joan, nee Bourke; 5 c; *Career* FIEE, chm- National Transport Co, Pye Ireland, Blackwood Hodge, hon Consul-Gen Iceland, Order of Falcon (Iceland); *Recreations* golf, sailing; *Clubs* Royal Irish Yacht, Portmarnock Golf; *Style* - Thomas Hogan Esq; Monkstown Castle, Co Dublin, Ireland (☎ Dublin 808103)

HOGG, Hon Lady; Hon Aline Emily; *née* Partington; da of 2 and last Baron Doverdale; *b* 1907; *m* 1936, Lt-Col Sir Kenneth Weir Hogg, 6 Bt, OBE; *Style* - The Hon Lady Hogg

HOGG, Arthur Ramsay; MBE (1945); s of late Ernest Charles Hogg (d 1907), and hp of cous, Sir Kenneth Weir Hogg, OBE, 6 Bt; *b* 24 Oct 1896; *Educ* Sherborne, Ch Ch Oxford; *m* 1924, Mary Aileen Hester Lee (d 1980), da of late P H Lee Evans; 3 s, 1 da; *Career* European War 1914-18 as Capt Roy W Kent Regt (twice wounded), European War 1940-45 as Major Gen List; *Style* - Arthur Hogg Esq MBE; 27 Elgin rd, Bournemouth

HOGG, Lady; Barbara Elisabeth; da of late Capt Arden Franklyn; *m* 1, 1936, Brig Viscount Garmoyle, DSO, late Rifle Bde (ka 1942); m 2, Sir John Nicholson Hogg, TD; 1 s, 1 da *Style* - Lady Hogg; The Red House, Shedfield, Southampton, Hants

HOGG, Hon Douglas Martin; MP (C) Grantham 1979-; s of Baron Hailsham of Marylebone (Life Peer 1970; suc as 2 Visc Hailsham 1950, disclaimed Viscountcy 1963); *b* 5 Feb 1945; *Educ* Eton, Ch Ch Oxford; *m* 1968, Sarah Elizabeth Mary, da of Lord Boyd-Carpenter, PC (Life Peer); 1 s, 1 da; *Career* Pres Oxford Union 1965, barr Lincoln's Inn 1968; *Also* ha to Viscountcy of Hailsham; *Style* - The Hon Douglas Hogg, MP; 11 Mallord st, SW3

HOGG, John Goldsborough; s of F G Hogg (d 1969); *b* 21 Jan 1925; *Educ* Harrow, Trin Cambridge; *m* 1955, Sarah Edith, da of late 1 Baron Noel-Buxton, PC; 2 da; *Career* Lloyd's Insurance Broker 1947-81, dep chm Hogg Robinson Gp; *Recreations* golf, shooting, fishing, skiing, flying; *Clubs* Bath; *Style* - John Hogg Esq; Old Broad Oak, Brenchley, Kent, (☎ 2318)

HOGG, Hon James Richard Martin; s of Baron Hailsham of St Marylebone (Life Peer; disclaimed Viscountcy of Hailsham 1963); *b* 1951; *Educ* Eton; *Style* - The Hon James Hogg; The Corner House, Heathview gdns, Putney Heath, SW15

HOGG, Hon Katharine Amelia; da of Baron Hailsham of St Marylebone (Life Peer; disclaimed Viscountcy of Hailsham 1963); *b* 18 Oct 1962; *Educ* Roedean, St Peter's Coll Oxford (studying theology); *Style* - The Hon Katharine Hogg

HOGG, Sir Kenneth Weir; 6 Bt (UK 1846), OBE (1946); s of Guy Weir Hogg, JP (gs of 1 Bt and who d 1943); suc kinsman, Sir Ronald Tracy McGarel-Hogg, 4 Baron Magheramorne, 1957; *b* 13 Sept 1894; *Educ* Haileybury, Ch Ch Oxford; *m* 1936, the Hon Aline Emily Partington, da of 2 Baron Doverdale (d 1949); *Heir* cous, Maj Arthur Ramsay Hogg, MBE; *Career* European War 1914-18 (wounded), and 1939-45 War, Lt-Col Irish Guards 1915-33; *Clubs* White's, Portland; *Style* - Sir Kenneth Hogg, Bt, OBE; 2 Curzon Place, Park Lane, W1

HOGG, Hon Mary Claire; da of Baron Hailsham of St Marylebone, CH (Life Peer; disclaimed Viscountcy of Hailsham 1963); *b* 15 Jan 1947; *Educ* St Paul's Girls' Sch; *Career* barr 1968; *Recreations* riding, walking, sailing, reading; *Style* - The Hon Mary Hogg; 51 Campana rd, SW6 (☎ 01 736 7937)

HOGG, Hon Mrs (Sarah Elizabeth Mary); da of Baron Boyd-Carpenter, PC, DL (Life Peer); *b* 1946; *m* 1969, Hon Douglas Hogg, MP, *qv*; *Style* - The Hon Mrs Hogg

HOGG, Hon Mrs (Sarah Edith Noel); *née* Noel-Buxton; da of 1 Baron Noel-Buxton, PC (d 1948); *b* 1928; *m* 1955, John Goldsborough Hogg; 2 da; *Style* - The Hon Mrs Hogg; Old Broad Oak, Brenchley, Kent

HOGG, Hon William Neil McGarel; s of 1 Visc Hailsham, PC (d 1950); *b* 1910; *Educ* Eton; *Career* 3 Sec Diplomatic Serv 1933, 2 Sec 1938, 1 Sec 1944, ret 1948; *Clubs* Athenaeum and Alpine; *Style* - The Hon William Hogg; Hotel Seeburg, 6008 Lucerne, Switzerland

HOLBECH, Geoffrey Victor Leigh; s of late Ronald Herbert Acland Holbech; *b* 12 Nov 1918; *Educ* Stowe; *m* 1950, Elizabeth, nee Harrisson; 2 s, 2 da; *Style* - Geoffrey Holbech Esq; Farnborough Hall, Banbury, Oxfordshire (☎ Farnborough 202)

HOLBOROW, Lady Mary Christina; *née* Stopford; da (by 1 m) of late 8 Earl of Courtown; *b* 1936; *m* 1959, Geoffrey Jermyn Holborow; 1 s, 1 da; *Style* - Lady Mary Holborow; Ladock House, Ladock, Truro, Cornwall

HOLBROW, Hon Mrs; Hon Rosemary; da (by 1 m) of late Baron Fiske (Life Peer); *b* 1931; *m* A Holbrow, of Worcester; *Style* - The Hon Mrs Holbrow

HOLCROFT, Charles Anthony Culcheth; s and h of Sir Peter George Culcheth Holcroft, 3 Bt; *b* 9 Jan 1954; *Style* - Charles Holcroft Esq

HOLCROFT, Elizabeth, Lady; (Maybel) Elizabeth; da of Raymond Playfair, of Nairobi, and formerly wife of 5 Earl of Bandon, GBE, CB, CVO, DSO (d 1979); *m* 1965, as his 2 wife, Sir Reginald Culcheth Holcroft, TD, 2 Bt (d 1978); *Style* - Elizabeth, Lady Holcroft; Wrentnall House, Pulverbatch, Salop

HOLCROFT, Sir Peter George Culcheth; 3 Bt (UK 1921), JP (Shropshire 1976); s of Sir Reginald Culcheth Holcroft, 2 Bt, TD (d 1978); *b* 29 April 1931; *Educ* Eton; *m* 1956, Rosemary Rachel, da of late Capt George Nevill Deas, 8 Hussars; 3 s, 1 da; *Heir* s, Charles Holcroft; *Career* High Sheriff of Shropshire 1969; *Style* - Sir Peter Holcroft, Bt, JP; Eaton Mascott Hall, Cross Houses, Shrewsbury

HOLDEN, Lady; Betty; da of late William Shaw, of Portland Place, W1; *m* 1937, Sir George Holden, 3 Bt (d 1976); *Style* - Lady Holden; Second House, Orchard rd, Dorking, Surrey

HOLDEN, Brian Peter John; s of Sir George Holden, 3 Bt (d 1976), and hp of n, Sir John Holden, 4 Bt; *b* 12 April 1944; *Style* - Brian Holden Esq

HOLDEN, Hon Donna Diana; da of 2 and last Baron Holden (d 1951); *b* 1916; *Style* - The Hon Donna Holden; 4 Georgian Court, Babbacombe rd, Torquay

HOLDEN, Sir Edward; 6 Bt (UK 1893), of Oakworth House, Keighley, Yorks; s of Sir Isaac Holden, 5 Bt (d 1962); *b* 8 Oct 1916; *Educ* Leys Sch and Christ's Coll Cambridge, St Thomas's Hosp; MRCS, LRCP (1942); *m* 1942, Frances Joan, da of John Spark, JP, of Ludlow, Stockton-on-Tees; 2 adopted s; *Heir* bro, Paul Holden; *Career* consultant anaesthetist Darlington and Northallerton Group Hospitals 1957-74; Fell of Faculty of Anaesthetists 1958; *Clubs* Farmers'; *Style* - Sir Edward Holden, Bt; Brigante, Stanwick-St-John, Richmond, N Yorks DL11 7RT (☎ Piercebridge 474)

HOLDEN, Sir John David; 4 Bt (UK 1919), of The Firs, Leigh, Co Lancaster; s of late David George Holden (er s of Sir George Holden, 3 Bt); suc gf 1976; *b* 16 Dec 1968; *Heir* unc, Brian Holden; *Style* - Sir John Holden, Bt; Woodhouse Farm, Sutton-on-Derwent, York

HOLDEN, Paul; s of Sir Isaac Holden, 5 Bt (d 1962), and hp of bro, Sir Edward Holden, 6 Bt; *b* 1923; *m* 1950, Vivien Mary, da of late Hedley Broxholme Oldham, of Allesley, Coventry; 1 s, 2 da; *Style* - Paul Holden Esq; Glenside, Rowhills, Heath End, Farnham, Surrey

HOLDER, Sir John Eric Duncan; 3 Bt (UK 1898), of Pitmaston, Moseley, Worcs; s of Sir Henry Charles Holder, 2 Bt (d 1945), and Evelyn (d 1956), da of Sir Robert Ropner, 1 Bt; *b* 2 Aug 1899; *Educ* Uppingham and BNC Oxford; *m* 1927 (m dis 1971), Evelyn Josephine, da of late William J F Blain; 1 s, 2 da; m 2, 1971, Marjorie Emily, da of late Frank R Markham; *Heir* s, John Holder; *Style* - Sir John Holder, Bt; Mulberry House, 17 Johnsons dve, Hampton, Middx TW12 2EQ

HOLDER, John Henry; s and h of Sir John Eric Duncan Holder, 3 Bt; *b* 12 March 1928; *m* 1960, Catharine Harrison, da of late Leonard Baker; 2 s (twins), 1 da; *Career* RAC; *Style* - John Holder Esq; 18 Clarkson av, Wisbech, Cambs

HOLDERNESS, Baron (Life Peer UK 1979); Hon Richard Frederick Wood; PC (1959), DL (Yorks E Riding 1967); 3 s of 1 Earl of Halifax, KG, OM, GCSI, GCMG, GCIE, TD, PC, sometime Viceroy of India & For Sec (d 1959), by his w Lady Dorothy Onslow, CI, DCVO, JP, DGStJ (yr da of 4 Earl of Onslow); unc of present (3) Earl of Halifax, 1 cous of 6 Earl of Onslow, 1 cous once removed of Lady Teresa (w of Auberon) Waugh, and distant cousin of Cranley Onslow, MP (C) for Woking; *b* 5 Oct 1920; *Educ* Eton, New Coll Oxford; *m* 1947, Diana, da of late Col Edward Orlando Kellett, DSO, MP, (whose widow, Myrtle, m as her 2 husb Hon William McGowan, 2 s of 1 Baron McGowan); 1 s, 1 da (Hon Mrs (Edward) Brooksbank, whose husb is s & h to Sir William Brooksbank, 2 Bt); *Career* late Lt KRRC, Hon Col 4 Bn Roy Green Jackets TAVR; MP (C) Bridlington 1950-79, Parly Sec Min Pensions & NI 1955-58 & 1963-64, Min Labour 1958-59; Min Overseas Dvpt 1970-74; served WW II M East; dir Hargreaves Gp 1974-; *Style* - The Rt Hon Lord Holderness PC DL; 49 Cadogan Place, SW1 (☎ 01 235 1597); Flat Top House, Bishop Wilton, York (☎ Bishop Wilton 266)

HOLDERNESS, Martin William; s and h of Sir Richard William Holderness, 3 Bt; *b* 24 May 1957; *Style* - Martin Holderness Esq

HOLDERNESS, Sir Richard William; 3 Bt (UK 1920), of Tadworth, Co Surrey; s of Sir Ernest Holderness, 2 Bt, CBE (d 1968); *b* 30 Nov 1927; *Educ* Corpus Christi Oxford; *m* 1953, Pamela, da of Eric Chapman, CBE, of 34 Upper Mall, W6; 2 s, 1 da; *Heir* s, Martin Holderness; *Career* partner, Whiteheads, Estate Agents and Surveyors 1967-; FRICS 1976; *Style* - Sir Richard Holderness, Bt; Rosetree House, Boxgrove, Chichester, Sussex; 12 Chapel rd, Worthing, W Sussex

HOLDERNESS-RODDAM, Hon Mrs - Hon (Erin) Moira; *née* Massey; da of late 6 Baron Clarina; *b* 1909; *m* 1939, Maj Peter Roddam Holderness-Roddam (d 1970); 1 s; *Style* - The Hon Mrs Holderness-Roddam; PO Box 10944, GPO Hobart, Tasmania 7002

HOLLAND, Anthony Delano Rokeby; s of the late H D Holland; *b* 20 Feb 1929; *Educ* Harrow; *m* 1973, Anne Patricia Russell, da of Russell Lang, CBE; 1 da; *Career* Lt Coldstream Guards Palestine, exec chm The Lincroft Kilgour Group Ltd and Holland & Lewis (Holdings) Ltd; *Recreations* hunting, tennis, golf; *Clubs* MCC, Sunningdale Golf; *Style* - Anthony Holland Esq; Windlesham Manor, Windlesham, Surrey

HOLLAND, Frank Robert Dacre; s of Ernest Holland (d 1975); *b* 24 March 1924; *Educ* Whitgift; *m* 1948, Margaret Lindsay, da of John Aird (d 1920); 1 da; *Career* Capt 4 Hussars Italy 1944-47; chm C E Heath Co Ltd, Lloyd's Insurance Broker and Underwriters 1973-; dir British Aviation Insurance Co 1973, Trade Indemnity Co 1973, Greyhound Corpn USA 1974; *Recreations* travel, gardening; *Style* - Frank Holland Esq; Moatside, 68 Ashley rd, Walton-on-Thames

HOLLAND, Guy Hope; s of Sir (Alfred Reginald) Sothern Holland, 1 Bt (d 1948), and hp of bro, Sir Jim Holland, 2 Bt, TD; *b* 19 July 1918; *Educ* Ch Ch Oxford; *m* 1945, Joan Marianne, da of late Capt Herbert Edmund Street, 20 Hussars; 2 da; *Career* late Capt Roy Scots Greys; *Clubs* Boodle's, Pratt's; *Style* - Guy Holland Esq; Sheepbridge Hill Barn, nr Eastleach, Cirencester, Glos

HOLLAND, Sir Jim Sothern; 2 Bt (UK 1917), of Westwell Manor, Co Oxford, TD (1950); s of Sir (Alfred Reginald) Sothern, 1 Bt (d 1948); *b* 31 March 1911; *Educ* Marlborough, Trin Oxford; *m* 1937, Elisabeth Hilda Margaret, da of Thomas Francis Vaughan Prickard, CVO, CA, FRICS, of Dderw, Rhayader, Powys; 2 da; *Heir* bro, Guy Holland; *Career* formerly a manager and alternate dir of Charter Consolidated Ltd, dir Central Mining & Investment Corpn Ltd, Rand Mines Ltd, Price & Pierce Ltd, ADC to Govr and C-in-C Malta 1942-44, 1939-45 War (1939-45 Star, Africa Star, Defence and War Medals); *Clubs* Bath; *Style* - Sir Jim Holland, Bt, TD; Dderw, Rhayader, Powys (☎ Rhayader 810226)

HOLLAND, Paul Reginald; s of Redvers Albert Holland (d 1971); *b* 22 June 1937; *Educ* Rotherham Coll of Technology; *m* 1979, Jean Whittaker, nee Whipp; *Career* FCMA, MBIM; gp fin dir and co sec Fletcher Sutcliffe Wild Ltd, Universal Works; dir Aqua Hydraulics Ltd, fin dir Richard Sutcliffe Ltd; *Recreations* sport, travel, gardening; *Clubs* Yorkshire County Cricket; *Style* - Paul Holland Esq; Casa-Mia, 45A Munsbrough Lane, Greasbrough, Rotherham, South Yorkshire

HOLLAND-HIBBERT, Hon Diana; MBE (1946); da of 4 Viscount Knutsford (d 1976); *b* 1914; *Career* late Senior Cdr ATS, 1939-45 War; *Style* - The Hon Diana Holland-Hibbert, MBE; Munden, Watford, Herts

HOLLAND-HIBBERT, Michael; s of Hon Wilfrid Holland-Hibbert (d 1961 - yr s of late 3 Viscount Knutsford); hp of cous, 5 Viscount Knutsford, CBE; *b* 27 Dec 1926; *Educ* Eton, Trin Cambridge; *m* 1951, Hon Sheila C Portman, *qv*, da of late 5 Viscount Portman; 2 s, 1 da; *Career* late Capt Welsh Gds, local dir Barclays Bank Exeter, DL Devon 1977, High Sheriff 1977-78; *Style* - Michael Holland-Hibbert Esq DL; Broadclyst House, Exeter

HOLLAND-HIBBERT, Hon Mrs (Sheila Constance); *née* Portman; da of 5 Viscount Portman (d 1942); *b* 1927; *m* 1951, Michael Holland-Hibbert, *qv*, s of Hon Wilfrid Holland-Hibbert, (yr s of 3 Visc Knutsford); 2 s, 1 da; *Style* - The Hon Mrs Holland-Hibbert; Broadclyst House, Exeter

HOLLAND-HIBBERT, Hon Mrs Wilfrid - Isabel Audrey; da of late Mark Fenwick; *m* 1918, Hon Wilfrid Holland-Hibbert (d 1961), s of 3 Viscount Knutsford (d 1935); *Style* - The Hon Mrs

Wilfrid Holland-Hibbert; Grove House, Beckley, Oxford

HOLLENDEN, 3 Baron (UK 1912); Gordon Hope Hope-Morley; s of Hon Claude Hope-Morley (d 1968, yr s of 1 Baron), and Lady Dorothy Edith Isabel Hobart-Hampden-Mercer-Henderson (d 1972), da of 7 Earl of Buckinghamshire; suc unc 1977; *b* 8 Jan 1914; *Educ* Eton; *m* 1945, Sonja, da of late Thorolf Sundt, of Bergen, Norway; 3 s; *Heir* s, Hon Ian Hampden Hope-Morley; *Career* Maj (ret) Black Watch, 1939-45 War, Alderman City of London 1954-58, ret as chm I & R Morley Ltd; *Clubs* Brooks's; *Style* - The Rt Hon the Lord Hollenden; Hall Place, Leigh, Tonbridge, Kent (☎ Hildenborough 832255)

HOLLENDEN, Anne, Baroness; Violet Norris; da of Alfred Leverton, of Peterborough; *m* 1, Dr Frank Howitt, CVO, MD, FRCP (decd); m 2, 1963, as his 3 wife, 2 Baron Hollenden (d 1977); *Style* - The Rt Hon Anne, Lady Hollenden; Valley Farm, Duntisbourne Hill, nr Cirencester

HOLLIDAY, Hon Mrs; Hon (Celia) Mary; *née* Bethell; da of 5 Baron Westbury, MC; *b* 5 March 1955; *m* 1980, L Brook Holliday; *Style* - The Hon Mrs Holliday

HOLLIS, Richard George; s of George Edward Hollis (d 1981); *b* 19 Nov 1934; *Educ* Bancrofts Sch Essex; *m* 1967, Belinda Jacqueline, nee Rose; 2 da; *Career* Capt Nat Serv; FCA, fin dir HP Bulmer Holdings Ltd 1967-, non exec dir Chloride Alcad Ltd (Chloride Gp) 1977-, memb Consumers Ctees for GB, and England and Wales 1979-; *Recreations* fishing, music; *Clubs* Flyfishers; *Style* - Richard Hollis Esq; Fairfield, Kingsland, Leominster, Herefords (☎ 056 881 248)

HOLLOWAY, Frank; s of the late Frank Holloway; *b* 20 Oct 1924; *Educ* Burnage H S Manchester; *m* 1949, Elizabeth, nee Beattie; 3 da; *Career* md and board memb British Steel Corp 1978-, various senior financial appointments in The United Steel Companies and later British Steel Corp 1949-72, md supplies and production control BSC 1973-76, md finance and supplies BSC 1976-80; *Recreations* cricket, collecting books; *Style* - Frank Holloway Esq; 11 Copperfield Way, Chislehurst, Kent (☎ 01 467 9559)

HOLLOWAY, Michael George; TD; s of George Henry Holloway; *b* 6 Sept 1930; *Educ* The King's Sch Chester, Liverpool U; *m* 1962, Jennifer Jean, da of Charles Palmer (d 1942); 2 s, 1 da; *Career* Major, (T A); solicitor and commissioner for oaths (ptnr, David Hughes & co Chester); HM Coroner City of Chester 1969-74; HM Coroner for Cheshire (West Dist) appointed 1974; HM Coroner for Clwyd (S Dist) appointed 1977; *Recreations* shooting, golf, rowing; *Clubs* City Club, Chester; *Style* - Michael Holloway Esq; Wyngate, Bridge Drive, Christleton, Chester CH3 6AW (☎ 0244 36665)

HOLM, Hon Mrs (Rosetta Mancroft); *née* Samuel; da of 1 Baron Mancroft (d 1942); *b* 1918; *m* 1, 1947, Alfred John Bostock Hill, late Puisne Judge, Malaya (d 1959); m 2, 1966, Dr Cai Christian Holm; *Style* - The Hon Mrs Holm; 12 Eaton Place, SW1

HOLMAN, Lady (Adeline Betty); da of Sir Gilbert Fox, 1 Bt (d 1925); *b* 18 July 1906; *Educ* Heathfield Ascot; *m* 1, 1929, Capt Basil Allfrey (m dis 1939); 2 s; m 2, 1940, as his 2 w, Sir Adrian Holman, KBE, CMG, MC (d 1947); *Recreations* waterfowl collecting, gardening; *Clubs* Bath; *Style* - Lady Holman; Bohunt Manor, Liphook, Hants

HOLMAN, Lady Diana Elizabeth Virginia Sydney; *née* Baird; da of 12 Earl of Kintore; *b* 1937; *m* 1957, John Francis Holman, OBE; 2 s, 2 da; *Style* - Lady Diana Holman; Rickarton House, Stonehaven, Kincardineshire; 24 Wellington sq, SW3

HOLMAN, Hon Mrs (Elizabeth Winifred); *née* Ponsonby; da of late 5 Baron de Mauley; *b* 1928; *m* 1950, Christopher Boot Holman; *Style* - The Hon Mrs Holman; Sheilbridge, Acharacle, Argyllshire; Foxcote, Shipston-on-Stour, Warwicks

HOLMAN, Hon Mrs (Margaret Amy); *née* Boot; da of late 1 Baron Trent; *b* 1892; *m* 1921, Alexander McArthur Holman; 3 s; *Style* - The Hon Mrs Holman; Springland, Millbrook, Jersey

HOLMES, Alan Wilson Jackson; s of Luke Jackson Holmes (d 1979); *b* 13 Sept 1945; *Educ* Portora Roy Sch Enniskillen, Cambridge U; *m* 1970, Frances-Maria, nee Kadwell; 2 s, 1 da; *Career* dir Courage (Central) Ltd 1973-, chm Courage (Scotland) Ltd 1979-; *Recreations* golf, theatre; *Clubs* Roy and Ancient GC; *Style* - Alan Holmes Esq; Woodcote House, Clayfield rd, Kennington, Oxon (☎ Oxford 739666)

HOLMES À COURT, Hon James William; s and h of 6 Baron Heytesbury; *b* 30 July 1967; *Style* - The Hon James Holmes à Court

HOLMES À COURT, Hon Sarah Camilla; da of 6 Baron Heytesbury; *b* 1965; *Style* - The Hon Sarah Holmes à Court

HOLM PATRICK, 3 Baron (UK 1897); James Hans Hamilton; s of 2 Baron Holm Patrick, DSO, MC (d 1942), by his w Lady Edina Hope (formerly w of Sir Thomas Ainsworth, 2 Bt, and da of 4 Marquess Conyngham); through his grandmother, Lady Victoria Wellesley, Lord Holm Patrick is 2 cous of the (8) Duke of Wellington while through his paternal aunt he is 1 cous of Lord (4 Baron) Swansea; *b* 29 Nov 1928; *Educ* Eton; *m* 1954, Anne, da of Cdr Ernest Brass, RN (ret), of Haverfordwest; 3 s; *Heir* s, Hon Hans Hamilton; *Career* late Lt 16/5 Lancers; *Style* - The Rt Hon Lord Holm Patrick; Tara Beg, Dunsany, Co Meath, Eire (☎ (046) 2 51 38)

HOLROYD, Lady Sheila Mary; da of late 4 Earl Cairns; *b* 1905; *m* 1930, Maj Charles Ivor Patrick Holroyd, late Rifle Bde; 2 s, 3 da; *Style* - Lady Sheila Holroyd; Providence Cottage, Chute Cadley, Andover, Hants

HOLT, Rear-Adm John Bayley; CB (1969), DL (Surrey 1981); s of Arthur Holt and Gertrude, nee Bayley; *b* 1 June 1912; *Educ* William Hulme G S Manchester, Manchester U; *m* 1940, Olga Creake; 3 da; *Career* RN; dir-gen Aircraft (Naval) 1967-70; dir Premmit Assocs, Premmit Engrg Servs, Elint Engrg; FIEE; *Style* - Rear-Adm John Holt CB DL; Rowley Cottage, Thursley, Godalming, Surrey (☎ 702140)

HOLT, Lady; Margaret; da of T S Lupton, formerly of Runswick, Cheadle Hulme, Ches; *m* 1931, Sir Edward Holt, 2 Bt (d 1968, when the title became ext); *Style* - Lady Holt

HOLT, Vesey Martin Edward; s of late M D V Holt; *b* 28 March 1927; *Educ* Radley, Cirencester; *m* 1955, Elizabeth Jane, nee Sanger; 1 s, 1 da; *Career* farmer, High Sheriff Shropshire 1981, County Council 1968-74, pres Shropshire County Cricket Club 1973-; *Recreations* shooting, cricket; *Clubs* Brooks's, MCC; *Style* - Vesey Holt Esq; Orleton Hall, Wellington, Telford, Salop (☎ Telford 42780); 42 Stanford rd, London, W8 (☎ 01 937 4970)

HOMAN, Hon Mrs (Mary Graham); *née* Buckley; da of 2 Baron Wrenbury; *b* 30 May 1929; *m* 1961, John, yr s of Capt Charles Homan, Elder Bro of Trin House; 1 s, 2 da; *Style* - The Hon Mrs Homan; 30 High st, Ticehurst, Sussex

HOME, Earldom of (S 1605); *see* Home of the Hirsel, Baron

HOME OF THE HIRSEL, Baron (Life Peer UK 1974); Alexander Frederick Douglas-Home; KT (1962), PC (1951), DL (Lanarks 1960); s of 13 Earl of Home, KT, TD, JP, DL (S cr of 1605, d 1951, when Lord Home of the Hirsel, then Lord Dunglass, became Earl of Home, also Lord Home (S 1473), Lord Dunglass (in earnest as opposed to merely enjoying the courtesy title, S 1605) and Baron Douglas (UK 1875); Lord Home disclaimed his Peerages for life on becoming PM in 1963, a seat in the Commons being thought necessary), by his w, Lady Lilian Lambton (da of 4 Earl of Durham, whereby Lord Home of the Hirsel is 1 cous of Antony Lambton (who also disclaimed his titles of (6) Earl of Durham etc for life), a fellow memb of Mr Heath's govt of 1970-74 and fellow descendant of 'Radical Jack' (1 Earl of) Durham, whom an extraordinary coalition of The Times, Guizot, Sir Spencer Walpole, and Lord Brougham united in abusing); bro of (Hon) William Douglas-Home, the playwright, husb of Lady Dacre and *quondam* aspiring politician; unc of Robin D-H, the writer, and Charles D-H, foreign ed The Times; *b* 2 July 1903; *Educ* Eton (where Cyril Connolly remarked of him that in the eighteenth century he would have become PM), Ch Ch Oxford; *m* 1936, Elizabeth, da of Very Rev Cyril Alington, DD (sometime Dean of Durham and Lord Home of the Hirsel's old headmaster at Eton), by his w Hon Hester Lyttelton (da of 4 Baron Lyttelton and 3 cous once removed of HRH The Princess of Wales); 1 s, 3 da; *Heir* s (to all titles except Life Barony), Hon David Douglas-Home (styled Lord Dunglass 1951-63); *Career* Maj Lanark Yeo (TA Reserve), Brig Roy Co Archers (Queen's Bodyguard for Scotland); MP (C) Lanark 1931-45 & 1950-51, Kinross & W Perth 1963-74, PPS to Chllr Exchequer 1936-37, to PM (Neville Chamberlain) 1937-40; Jt Under Sec State Foreign Affrs May-July 1945, Min State Scottish Off 1951-55, Sec State C'wlth Rels 1955-60 (Ld Pres Cncl Jan-Sept 1957 & Oct 1959-July 1960), Ldr Ho Lds 1957-60, For Sec 1960-63, PM 1963-64, Ldr Oppn 1964-65, For Sec 1970-74; Chllr Order of Thistle 1973-, 1 Chllr Heriot-Watt U 1966-77, Hon Pres NATO Cncl 1973, Grand Master Primrose League 1966, Pres MCC 1966-67; Freedom of Edinburgh 1969, memb NFU 1964; *Clubs* Travellers', Carlton, Buck's; *Style* - The Rt Hon Lord Home of the Hirsel KT PC DL; The Hirsel, Coldstream, Berwicks (☎ 2345); Castlemains, Douglas, Lanarks (☎ 241); 26 Laxford House, Cundy st, SW1 (☎ 01 730 1443); c/o House of Lords, SW1

HOME, Sir David George; 13 Bt (NS 1671), of Blackadder, Co Berwick; s of Sir John Home, 12 Bt (d 1938), and Hon Gwendolina H R Mostyn (d 1960), sis of 7 Baron Vaux of Harrowden (d 1935); *b* 21 Jan 1904; *Educ* Harrow, Jesus Cambridge; *m* 1933, Sheila, da of late Mervyn Campbell Stephen; 2 s, 2 da; *Heir* s, John Home; *Career* Major late Argyll and Sutherland Highlanders, memb Queen's Body Guard for Scotland (Roy Co of Archers); claims dormant Scottish Earldom of Dunbar (cr 1607); *Clubs* Brooks's, New (Edinburgh), Royal and Ancient (St Andrews); *Style* - Sir David Home, Bt; Winterfield, North Berwick, East Lothian

HOME, John; s and h of Sir David George Home, 13 Bt; *b* 1 June 1936; *Educ* Harrow, Jesus Cambridge; *m* 1966, Nancy Helen, da of H G Elliott, of Perth, W Aust, and widow of Cdr Ian Macgregor, RAN; 1 s, 1 da; *Clubs* New (Edinburgh), Union (Sydney); *Style* - John Home Esq; 31 Parsley rd, Vaucluse, NSW 2030, Australia

HONAN, John Patric; s of Patrick William Honan (d 1971); *b* 26 July 1923; *Educ* Xaverian Coll London, Emmanuel Cambridge; *m* 1, (m dis); 2 da; m 2, 1977, Margaret Stella, nee Cracknell; *Career* md Southon-Horton Laboratories Ltd (dep md 1974) 1976-, marketing dir Horton Cleaning Products 1966-, marketing man Izal Overseas Ltd 1960; *Recreations* horticulture, music; *Clubs* Inst of Dirs; *Style* - John Honan Esq; The Chestnuts, Towpath, Shepperton, Surrey (☎ Walton on Thames 41850); c/o Southon-Horton Laboratories Ltd, Bourne rd, Bexley, Kent (☎ Crayford 529114)

HONEY, Bill (William Andrew); *b* 19 Dec 1938; *Educ* Eastbourne G S; *m* 1963, Maureen, nee McGrane; 2 s, 1 da; *Career* FCA, FCIS, ATII, FCIArb, FBIM, sr ptnr Honey Barrett & Co (and assoc cos), W A Honey & Co, Cornfield Secretarial, dir Capital Matters Ltd, Cornfield Fin and Management Ltd, Data Matters Ltd, Eastbourne & Dist Chamber of Commerce Ltd, Export Matters Ltd, Honbar 2 Ltd, Honey Barrett & Co, Income Matters Ltd, Investment Matters Ltd, Management Matters Ltd, Mistywell Ltd, Money Matters Ltd, Mortgage Matters Ltd, Ocklynge Laundry Ltd, Patricia (Eastbourne) Ltd, Property Matters Ltd, Security Matters Ltd, White Chalk Investments Ltd, Ultramark Ltd, Freeman of City of London; *Recreations* family, home life; *Clubs* City Livery; *Style* - Bill Honey Esq; Appledown, Old Willingdon rd, Friston, E Dean, Eastbourne, E Sussex (☎ 03215 2022); Honeysuckle Cottage,

Hill Bottom, Worth Matravers, Swanage, Dorset

HONYWOOD, Filmer Courtenay William; s and h of Sir William Wynne Honywood, 10 Bt, MC; *b* 20 May 1930; *Educ* Downside, RMA Sandhurst, RAC Cirencester; ARICS; *m* 1956, Elizabeth Margaret Mary Cynthia, da of late Sir Alastair George Lionel Joseph Miller, 6 Bt; 2 s, 2 da; *Career* late 3 Carabiniers (Prince of Wales' Dragoon Gds), assist surveyor Miny of Agric Fisheries and Food Maidstone 1966-73, surveyor Cockermouth Cumbria 1973-74, since when sr lands officer SE Region Central Electricity Generating Bd; *Style* - Filmer Honywood Esq; Greenway Forstal Farmhouse, Hollingbourne, Maidstone, Kent

HONYWOOD, Sir William Wynne; 10 Bt (E 1660), of Evington, Kent, MC; s of late Sir John William Honywood, 8 Bt; suc bro, Sir Courtenay John Honywood, 7 Bt, 1944; *b* 7 April 1891; *Educ* Downside; *m* 1923, Maud Naylor (d 1953), da of late William Hodgson Wilson, of Hexgreave Park, Southwell, Notts; 1 s, 2 da; *Heir* s, Filmer Honywood; *Career* Col (ret), Maj late 17/21 Lancers, and Lt-Col late KSLI, 1914-18 War in France, Belgium and German E Africa (despatches thrice, MC), 1939-45 War in France and Cyrenaica, Adj Ceylon Mounted Rifles and Ceylon Planters' Rifle Corps 1928-31, was Dep Dir of Pioneers and Labour, Cyrenaica Dist 1945-46, and Cmdt Roy Pioneer Corps Depot, Middle East, and Officer Cmdg Troops, Qassasin 1946-48; *Style* - Sir William Honywood, Bt, MC; c/o Lloyds Bank Ltd, 6 Pall Mall, SW1

HOOD, 6 Viscount (GB 1796); Sir Samuel Hood; 6 Bt (GB 1778), GCMG (1969, KCMG 1960, CMG 1953); also Baron Hood (I 1782 & GB 1795); s of Rear-Adm Hon Horace Hood, KCB (never invested due to death at Jutland 1916), MVO, DSO; suc unc, 5 Viscount (d 1933, fifth in descent from 1 Viscount, the naval hero who captured Corsica 1793); *b* 15 Oct 1910; *Educ* Eton, Trin Cambridge; *Heir* bro, Hon Alexander Hood; *Career* Assist Priv Sec to Sec State India 1936-39, Priv Sec to Min of Inf 1939-41; Dep Under Sec FCO 1962-69 (served FO 1942-69); Dep Spkr & Dep Chm Cttees House of Lds 1971-; *Clubs* Brooks's, Travellers', Swinley Forest Golf; *Style* - The Rt Hon Viscount Hood, GCMG; 5/30 Eaton sq, SW1 (☎ 01 235 1360)

HOOD, Hon Mrs Alexander - Diana Maud; CVO (1957, MVO 4 Class 1952); da of Hon George Lyttelton (2 s of 8 Viscount Cobham) and Pamela (da of Charles Adeane, CB, by Madeline Wyndham, niece of 2 Baron Leconfield); sis of Humphrey Lyttelton, *qv*; *b* 1920; *m* 1957, Hon Alexander Hood, *qv*; *Career* Assist Press Sec HM King George VI 1947-52 & HM The Queen 1952-57; *Style* - The Hon Mrs Alexander Hood, CVO; 67 Chelsea sq, SW3

HOOD, Hon Alexander Lambert; s of Rear-Adm Hon Horace Hood, KCB (never invested due to death in action at Jutland 1916), MVO, DSO, 3 s of 4 Viscount Hood; hp to bro, 6 Viscount Hood; *b* 11 March 1914; *Educ* RNC Dartmouth, Trin Cambridge, Harvard Business Sch (MBA); *m* 1957, Diana Maud, CVO, da of Hon George Lyttelton, sometime assist master at Eton (2 s of 8 Viscount Cobham), and sis of Humphrey Lyttelton, the jazz musician and writer; 3 s; *Career* late Lt Cdr RNVR; chm Tanks Consolidated Investment Ltd 1972-; dir J Henry Schroder Wagg to 1975; dir- Elbar Industl, Abbott Labs, George Wimpey, Hermitage Investments, Petrofina (UK) Ltd, Union Minière SA Belgium; *Clubs* Brooks's; *Style* - The Hon Alexander Hood; Luders Court, Bridport, Dorset (☎ 0308 22983); 67 Chelsea sq, SW3 (☎ 01 352 4952)

HOOD, Hon Lady; Hon Ferelith Rosemary Florence; *née* Kenworthy; da of late 10 Baron Strabolgi by 1 w, Doris, Baroness Strabolgi, *qv*; *b* 1918; *m* 1946, Sir Harold Joseph Hood, 2 Bt, TD, *qv*; *Style* - The Hon Lady Hood; 31 Avenue rd, St John's Wood, NW8

HOOD, Sir Harold Joseph; 2 Bt (UK 1922), of Wimbledon, Co Surrey, TD; s of Sir Joseph Hood, 1 Bt (d 1931); *b* 23 Jan 1916; *Educ* Downside; *m* 1946, the Hon Ferelith Rosemary Florence Kenworthy, da of 10 Baron Strabolgi; 2 s, 2 da (and 1 s decd); *Heir* s, John Hood; *Career* 2 Lt 58 Middx Bn RE (AA) (TA) 1939, Lt RA 1941; managing ed The Catholic Directory 1959-60, ed The Catholic Who's Who 1952 edn, circulation dir Universe 1953-60, circulation dir Catholic Herald 1961-; kt of St Gregory the Great, and of Sovereign Mil Order of Malta; *Clubs* Royal Automobile, MCC, Challoner; *Style* - Sir Harold Hood, Bt, TD; 31 Avenue rd, NW8 6BS (☎ 01 722 9088)

HOOD, John Joseph Harold; s and h of Sir Harold Joseph Hood, TD, 2 Bt; *b* 27 Aug 1952; *Style* - John Hood Esq

HOOD, Hon Peregrine Alexander Nelson; s and h of 4 Viscount Bridport; *b* 30 Aug 1974; *Style* - The Hon Peregrine Hood

HOOK, Hon Mrs (Edith Deirdre); *née* Handcock; da of late 7 Baron Castlemaine; *b* 1936; *m* 1, 1957 (m dis 1974), Keith Moss, BEM; 1 s; m 2, 1975, Terence Hook; *Style* - The Hon Mrs Hook

HOOLE-LOWSLEY-WILLIAMS, Hon Mrs; Olivia; *née* Bootle-Wilbraham; da of late 6 Baron Skelmersdale and Ann, da of Percy Quilter (s of 1 Bt); *b* 1938; *m* 1961, Anthony John Hoole-Lowsley-Williams; 2 s; *Style* - The Hon Mrs Hoole-Lowsley-Williams; The Square House, Harrow Barrow, nr Callington, Cornwall

HOOPER, Sir Anthony Robin Maurice; 2 Bt (UK 1962), of Tenterden, Co Kent; s of Sir Frederic Collins, 1 Bt (d 1963); *b* 26 Oct 1918; *Educ* Radley, New Coll Oxford; *m* 1970 (m dis 1973), Cynthia Theresa Mary, da of late Lt-Col William James Holdsworth Howard, DSO; *Heir* none; *Career* RA 1939-41, News Chronicle 1941-42, Political Research Centre 1942-44, actor 1944-50, temp civil servant Cabinet Office 1950-52, assist design manager Schweppes Ltd 1952-64, dir Couper Gallery 1964-68; *Clubs* Savile; *Style* - Sir Anthony Hooper, Bt; 3 St George's Court, Gloucester rd, SW7

HOOPER, Hon Mrs (Lucinda Mary Deirdre); *née* Evans; da of 2 Baron Mountevans (d 1974); *b* 1951; *m* 1980, John E Hooper; *Style* - The Hon Mrs Hooper

HOOPER, Prudence, Lady; Prudence Avery (Neill); da of late Basil Wenham, of Armscote, Warwicks; *m* 1945, as his 2 wife, Sir Frederic Collins Hooper, 1 Bt (d 1963); *Style* - Prudence, Lady Hooper; 40 Pont st, SW1

HOOSON, Baron (Life Peer UK 1979); (Hugh) Emlyn Hooson; QC (1960); s of Hugh Hooson, of Denbigh; *b* 26 March 1925; *Educ* Denbigh G S, U Coll of Wales; *m* 1950, Shirley Wynne, da of Sir George Hamer, CBE, of Powys; 2 da; *Career* barr 1949, dep chm Merioneth QS 1960-67, chm 1967-71, Recorder Merthyr Tydfil 1971 & Swansea 1971, Recorder Crown Court 1972-; MP (Lib) Montgomeryshire 1962-79, Ldr Welsh Lib Pty 1966-79; farmer; *Style* - The Rt Hon Lord Hooson QC; Summerfield, Llanidloes, Powys (☎ 2298); 1 Dr Johnson's Bldgs, Temple, EC4 (☎ 01 353 7972)

HOPE, Hon Alexander John Adrian; s of Earl of Hopetoun; *b* 1971; *Style* - The Hon Alexander Hope

HOPE, Sir Archibald Philip; 17 Bt (NS 1628), of Craighall, Co Fife, OBE (1945), DFC (1940), AE (1943); s of Sir John Augustus Hope, OBE, 16 Bt (d 1924), and Hon Mary Bruce, OBE, JP Midlothian, da of 10 Lord Balfour of Burleigh; *b* 27 March 1912; *Educ* Eton, Balliol Oxford; *m* 1938, Ruth, da of Carl R Davis, of Fryern, Storrington, Sussex; 2 s; *Heir* s, John Hope; *Career* RAFO 1930-35, 601 (County of London) Sqdn AAF 1935-39, 1939-45 (despatches twice, DFC, OBE), Wing Cdr (acting Gp Capt), AAF, Airwork 1945-56, dir D Napier & Son Ltd 1956-61, dir Napier Aero Engines Ltd 1961-68, ch exec 1962-68, English Electric Co 1968-70, chm Air Transport Users Ctee CAA 1977-79, The Air League 1965-68, memb of Queen's Bodyguard for Scotland (Roy Co of Archers); *Clubs* RAF, New (Edinburgh), Nairobi (Nairobi); *Style* - Sir Archibald Hope, Bt, OBE, DFC, AE; The Manor House, Somerford Keynes, nr Cirencester, Glos GL7 6DL (☎ Ashton Keynes 250)

HOPE, Bryan; s of Edward Sydney Hope (d 1959); *b* 27 July 1930; *m* 1964, Julia, da of Aubrey Tearle; 2 da; *Career* dir- Int Publishing Corpn, IPC Business Press Ltd, Butterworth & Co (Publishers) Ltd; chm- IPC Business Press (Sales & Distribution) Ltd, IPC Exhibitions Ltd, IPC Conferences Ltd; dir Periodical Publishers Assoc Ltd and Int Wine & Spirit Competition Ltd; *Recreations* fly fishing, vegetable gardening; *Clubs* RAC; *Style* - Bryan Hope Esq; Wynchmoor, Pursers Lane, Peaslake, nr Guildford (☎ 730523)

HOPE, Hon Mrs (Diana Lyall); *née* Mackie; da of Baron Mackie of Benshie (Life Peer); *b* 1946; *m* 1968, John Carlyle Hope; *Style* - The Hon Mrs Hope; 3 St Bernard Crescent, Edinburgh

HOPE, John Carl Alexander; s and h of Sir Archibald Philip Hope, 17 Bt, OBE, DFC, AE; *b* 10 June 1939; *Educ* Eton; *m* 1968, Merle Pringle, da of Robert Douglas, of Southside, Holbrook, Ipswich; 1 s, 1 da; *Style* - John Hope Esq; 10 Furlong rd, N7

HOPE, Michael Richard; s of Hon Richard Hope, OBE (yst s of 1 Baron Rankeillour), and Helen (da of Alfred Charlemagne Lambart, gs of 7 Earl of Cavan); hp of cous, 4 Baron Rankeillour; *b* 21 Oct 1940; *Educ* Downside; *m* 1964, Elizabeth, da of Col Francis Fuller, of the Rajputana Rifles; 1 s, 2 da; *Style* - Michael Hope Esq; Barningham Hall, Bury St Edmunds, Suffolk

HOPE, Sir Robert Holms-Kerr; 3 Bt (UK 1932), of Kinnettles, Co Angus; s of Sir Harry Hope, 1 Bt (d 1959); suc bro, Sir James Hope, 2 Bt, MM, 1979; *b* 12 April 1900; *m* 1928, Margaret Eleanor, da of the Very Rev Marshall Lang, DD, of The Manse, Whittingehame, East Lothian; *Heir* none; *Style* - Sir Robert Hope, Bt; Barneyhill, Dunbar, East Lothian

HOPE-DUNBAR, Charles; s and h of Sir David Hope-Dunbar, 8 Bt; *b* 5 March 1975; *Style* - Charles Hope-Dunbar Esq

HOPE-DUNBAR, Sir David; 8 Bt (NS 1664), of Baldoon; s of Major Sir Basil Douglas Hope-Dunbar, 7 Bt (d 1961); *b* 13 July 1941; *Educ* Eton, RAC Cirencester; ARICS 1966; *m* 1971, Kathleen Ruth, da of late J Timothy Kenrick; 1 s, 2 da; *Heir* s, Charles Hope-Dunbar; *Style* - Sir David Hope-Dunbar, Bt; Banks Farm, Kirkcudbright (☎ Kirkcudbright 30424)

HOPE-DUNBAR, Edith, Lady; Edith Maude Maclaren; da of late Malcolm Cross; *m* 1940, as his 2 wife, Maj Sir Basil Douglas Hope-Dunbar, 7 Bt (d 1961); *Style* - Edith, Lady Hope-Dunbar; Crofthead Cottage, by Kirkcudbright

HOPE-MORLEY, Hon Andrew James Sundt; s of 3 Baron Hollenden; *b* 1952; *Educ* Eton; *Style* - The Hon Andrew Hope-Morley

HOPE-MORLEY, Hon Ian Hampden; s and h of 3 Baron Hollenden; *b* 23 Oct 1946; *Educ* Eton; *m* 1972, Béatrice Saulnier, da of Baron Pierre d'Anchald, of Paris (presumably of the Auvergne family, a member of whom was ennobled as Baron by Louis XVIII 1816, while the rank of Vicomte was conferred on an unspecified member of the family by Charles X 1828); 1 s (Edward b 9 April 1981), 1 da (Juliette b 1974); *Style* - The Hon Ian Hope-Morley

HOPE-MORLEY, Hon Robin Gordon; s of 3 Baron Hollenden; *b* 1949; *Educ* Brickwall, Northiam; *Style* - The Hon Robin Hope-Morley

HOPE-NICHOLSON, (Charles) Felix Otho Victor Gabriel John Adrian; s of William Hedley Kenelm Hope-Nicholson by Jaqueline, da of Adrian Hope (s of Col William Hope, VC, and Margaret, nee Cunninghame-Graham, through the latter of whom Mr Hope-Nicholson is 10 cous twice removed - through common descent from 7 Earl of Glencairn - of the editor of this book; the Col was gggs of Hon Charles Hope-Vere, 2 s of 1 Earl of Hopetoun, KT, *see* Marquess of Linlithgow) and Laura (2 da of Sir Thomas Troubridge, 3 Bt, CB, and Louisa, nee Gurney, of the extensive Norfolk family); bro of Marie-Jacqueline Lancaster, the biographer of Brian Howard, and Mme Jean Hugo (whose husb is descended from the poet and novelist Victor); *b* 21 July 1921; *Educ* Eton, Ch Ch Oxford; *Recreations* opera, genealogy; *Style* - Felix Hope-Nicholson Esq; More House, 52 Tite st, SW3

HOPE-WALLACE, (Dorothy) Jaqueline; CBE (1958); da of Charles Nugent Hope-Wallace (d 1953); *b* 29 May 1909; *Educ* Lady Margaret Hall Oxford; *Career* civil servant; under-sec 1959-69, Corby Development Corpn 1970-80, chm Nat Corpn Care of Old People 1978-80, chm British Institute for Recorded Sound 1974-45, chm Friends Univ Coll Hospital 1973-; *Recreations* arts, travel, gardening; *Style* - Miss Jaqueline Hope-Wallace CBE; 17 Ashley ct, Morpeth ter, London SW1

HOPETOUN, Earl of; Adrian John Charles Hope; s and h of 3 Marquess of Linlithgow, MC; *b* 1 July 1946; *m* 1, 1968 (m dis), Anne, da of Arthur Leveson, of Hall Place, Ropley, Hants; 2 s; m 2, 1980, Peta C Binding; 1 da; *Heir* s, Viscount Aithrie; *Style* - Earl of Hopetoun; 36 Edwardes sq, W8 (☎ 01 603 9971)

HOPKINSON, Hon Nicholas Henry Eno; s (by 1 m) and h of 1 Baron Colyton, CMG, PC; *b* 18 Jan 1932; *Educ* Eton, Trin Cambridge; *m* 1957, Fiona Margaret, da of Sir (Thomas) Torquil Alphonso Munro, 5 Bt; 2 s; *Style* - The Hon Nicholas Hopkinson; Ascreave House, Kingoldrum, Angus

HOPLEY, Ven Arthur; s of Ernest Charles (d 1943); *b* 17 Oct 1906; *Educ* Sir George Monoux Sch, Wells Theological Coll; *m* 1934, Marjorie Carswell, da of John Niven (d 1938); 2 s; *Career* Archdeacon of Bath 1962-71, Archdeacon of Taunton 1971-77, Archdeacon Emeritus of Bath and Wells 1977; *Style* - The Ven Arthur Hopley; The Old Parsonage, Angersleigh, Taunton, Somerset

HOPPER, Brian Barnes; *b* 10 Jan 1926; *Educ* King George V Sch Southport, Liverpool U; *m* 1952, Mavis Priscilla; 1 s, 2 da; *Career* gen man Chester Waterworks Co, projects man Unilever Ltd 1965-80, formerly civil engineer Shell-Mex & BP Ltd, CEGB, and consulting civil engrs; *Recreations* golf, tennis, badminton; *Clubs* Eaton GC, Chester Lawn Tennis; *Style* - Brian Hopper Esq; Dunvegan House, Curzon Park N, Chester (☎ 675186)

HOPPER, William Joseph; MEP (C) Greater Manchester W 1979-; s of the late I Vance Hopper; *b* 9 Aug 1929; *Educ* Queen's Park Sec Sch, Glasgow U; *m* 1959, Melissa Carmen; 1 da; *Career* financial analyst W R Grace & Co New York 1956-59, London office manager H Hentz & Co (memb NY Stock Exchange) 1960-66, gen man S G Warburg & Co Ltd 1966-69, dir Hill Samuel & Co Ltd 1969-74, and Morgan Grenfell & Co Ltd 1975-79, consultant Morgan Grenfell 1979-; *Recreations* listening to music (records), geriatric squash, gardening; *Clubs* St James (Manchester); *Style* - William Hopper Esq, MEP; 23 Great Winchester st, London EC2

HOPWOOD, Hon (Francis) Michael; s and h of 3 Baron Southborough; *b* 3 May 1922; *Educ* Wellington Coll, Ch Ch Oxford; *m* 1945, Moyna Kemp, da of Robert John Kemp Chattey; 1 da (adopted); *Career* underwriting member of Lloyd's 1949, dir Glanvill Enthoven & Co Ltd 1954, deputy chairman 1977-80, dir Robert Woodson Ltd 1950 and chm 1970-72; *Clubs* Brooks's, City of London; *Style* - The Hon Michael Hopwood; 50A Eaton Square, SW1 (☎ 01 235 3181)

HORD, Brian Howard; MEP (C) London W 1979-; s of late Charles Hord; *b* 20 June 1934; *Educ* Reedham Sch, Purley G S; *m* 1960, Christine Marian, da of Reginald Lucas; 2 children; *Career* FRICS; ptnr in firm of chartered surveyors London; *Recreations* squash, bee-keeping; *Clubs* Carlton; *Style* - Brian Hord Esq, MEP; Whitesides, Pilgrims Way East, Otford, Sevenoaks, Kent (☎ 3743)

HORDER, 2 Baron (UK 1933); Sir Thomas Mervyn Horder; 2 Bt (UK 1923); s of 1 Baron Horder, GCVO, DL, MD, whose position as physician (whether in Ordinary or Extra) to no fewer than four monarchs (Edward VII, George V, George VI and HM The Queen) may constitute a record (d 1955); *b* 8 Dec 1910; *Educ* Winchester, Trin Cambridge; *m* 1946 (m dis 1957), Mary Ross, da of Dr William Scott McDougall, of Wallington, Surrey; *Heir* none; *Career* Wing Cdr RAFVR, served WW II India & SE Asia; chm Gerald Duckworth & Co 1948-70; *Style* - The Rt Hon Lord Horder; c/o Gerald Duckworth & Co, 43 Gloucester

Crescent, NW1 (☎ 01 485 3484); Ashford Chase, Petersfield, Hants

HORLICK, Beryta, Lady; Beryta (Murray); da of Roland Allport, of Sydney, NSW; *m* 1934 (m dis 1948), as his 2 wife (re-m 1957, as his 4 wife), Sir Peter James Cunliffe Horlick, 3 Bt (d 1958); *Style* - Beryta, Lady Horlick

HORLICK, Vice-Adm Sir Edwin John; KBE (1981); *b* 1925; *Educ* Bedford Modern Sch; *m* ; 4 s; *Career* Chief Naval Engineer Offr, Dir Gen Ships Miny of Defence 1979-; *Style* - Vice-Adm Sir Edwin Horlick, KBE; Director General Ships, Miny of Defence (Navy), Foxhill, Bath

HORLICK, James Cunliffe William; s and h of Sir John James Macdonald Horlick, 5 Bt; *b* 19 Nov 1956; *Educ* Eton; *Career* 2 Lt Coldstream Gds; *Style* - James Horlick Esq

HORLICK, Sir John James Macdonald; 5 Bt (UK 1914), of Cowley Manor, Co Gloucester; s of Lt-Col Sir James Nockells Horlick, 4 Bt, OBE, MC (d 1972); *b* 9 April 1922; *Educ* Eton, Babson Inst of Business Admin, Wellesley Hills, Mass, USA; *m* 1948, June, da of Douglas Cory-Wright, CBE; 1 s, 2 da; *Heir* s, James Horlick; *Career* served War as Capt Coldstream Gds, dep chm Horlicks Ltd 1968-72, partner Tournaig Farming Co 1973-, chm Highland Fish Farmers 1978-; *Clubs* Beefsteak, Bath; *Style* - Sir John Horlick, Bt; Tournaig, Poolewe, Achnasheen, Ross-shire (☎ Poolewe 250); Howberry Lane Cottage, Nuffield, nr Nettlebed, Oxon (☎ Nettlebed 641454)

HORLICK, Dowager Lady; Sophie Sonia Theolesco; *m* 1931, as his 2 wife, Sir Ernest Burford Horlick, 2 Bt (d 1934); *Style* - Dowager Lady Horlick

HORN, Hon Mrs (Angela Ierne Evelyn Dixon); *née* Dixon; da of late 1 Baron Glentoran; *b* 1907; *m* 1, 1929, Lt-Cdr Peter Ross, RN (eld s of Una Mary, Baroness de Ros and ka 1940); 2 da (*see Baroness de Ros*); m 2, 1943 Lt-Col Trevor Langdale Horn, MC, 16/5 Lancers (d 1966); 1 da; *Style* - The Hon Mrs Horn; Luckington ct, Chippenham, Wilts

HORN, Hon Mrs (Ann Loveday Dean); da of Baron Soper (Life Peer); *b* 1931; *m* 1952, Gabriel Horn, MD; *Style* - The Hon Mrs Horn; King's College, Cambridge

HORNAK, Lady Patricia Sybil; *née* Douglas; da of 11 Marquess of Queensberry (d 1954); *b* 1918; *m* 1, 1938 (m dis 1950), Capt Count John Gerard de Bendern; 1 s, 2 da; m 2, 1954 (m dis 1960), Herman Hornak; 2 s; *Style* - Lady Patricia Hornak; 36 St James's rd, Tunbridge Wells, Kent

HORNBY, Derrick Richard; s of Richard Wittingham Hornby (d 1964); *b* 11 Jan 1926; *Educ* Southampton; *m* 1948, June, da of Nathaniel Steele (d 1963); *Career* chm Carrington Viyella 1980, Spillers Foods Ltd 1973; md Edenvale (Express Dairy) 1968; *Recreations* golf, salmon fishing; *Clubs* Wentworth, Nat Sporting Club; *Style* - Derrick Hornby Esq; 26a Shawfield st, Chelsea, London SW3 (☎ 01 352 6862)

HORNBY, Simon Michael; s of Michael Hornby, of Pusey House, Faringdon, Oxon, and Nicolette, da of Capt Hon Cyril Ward, MVO, RN (5 s of 1 Earl of Dudley) by Baroness Irene de Brienen (da of late Baron de Brienen); Simon's mother's sisters were (1) late Countess Paul Munster (da-in-law of Prince Alexander Munster von Derneburg) (2) late Countess of Ilchester; *b* 29 Dec 1934; *Educ* Eton, New College Oxford; *m* 1968, Sheran Cazalet; *Career* ch exec W H Smith & Son Ltd 1978-, dir S Pearson & Son Ltd 1978-, tstee British Museum 1975-, memb cncl National Trust 1976- (memb exec ctee 1966-), chm National Book League 1978-80; *Recreations* gardening, looking at things; *Clubs* Garrick; *Style* - Simon Hornby Esq; 8 Ennismore gdns, SW7 (☎ 01 584 1597); Lake House, Pusey, Faringdon, Oxon (☎ 036787 659)

HORNE, Sir Alan Edgar; 2 Bt (UK 1929), of Shackleford, Surrey, MC; s of Sir (William) Edgar Horne, 1 Bt (d 1941); *b* 19 Sept 1889; *Educ* Eton, Univ Coll Oxford; *m* 1, 1915, Henriette (d 1918), da of Arthur W Kelly; 1 da; m 2, 1923 (m dis 1931), Roslyn (d 1961), da of John Brian Robinson; (1 s decd); *Heir* gs, Gray Horne; *Career* European War 1914-19 in France and Balkans as Capt Surrey Yeo and on Staff (despatches four times, MC, French Croix de Guerre), European War 1939-45 in Middle East as Lt-Col Roy Pioneer Corps; *Clubs* Cavalry and Guards, MCC; *Style* - Sir Alan Horne, Bt, MC; Flat 4 1 The Paragon, Blackheath SE3

HORNE, (Alan) Gray (Antony); s of late Antony Edgar Alan Horne (only s of 2 Bt), and hp of gf, Sir Alan Edgar Horne, MC, 2 Bt; *b* 11 July 1948; *Style* - Gray Horne Esq

HORNE, Lady Ursula Florence; *née* Hamilton-Temple-Blackwood; da of late 2 Marq of Dufferin and Ava; *b* 1899; *m* 1926, Arthur Swithin Newton Horne, former Gov Sec Federated Malay States (d 1954); *Style* - Lady Ursula Horne; 51 Ovington st, SW3

HORNER, Stephen John; s of Harold Wallington Horner (d 1966); *b* 11 May 1944; *Educ* Radley Coll; *m* 1968, Susan Helen, nee Hancock; 2 s (Simon Wallington b 1971, Edward John b 1975); *Career* FCA, fin dir Agar Cross & Co Ltd 1977-80, fin dir Westland Technologies Division, Westland Aircraft Ltd 1980-; *Recreations* spectator of rugby football; rowing, fishing, gardening; *Clubs* Thames Rowing Club; *Style* - Stephen Horner Esq; The Old Vicarage, Bishopwood, nr Chard, Somerset (☎ Buckland St Mary (046 034) 232)

HORNSBY, Lady Elizabeth Anne Mary (Rufus); *née* Isaacs; da of 2 Marquess of Reading, GCMG, CBE, MC, TD, PC, QC, and Hon Eva Mond, CBE, JP (da of 1 Baron Melchett); *b* 11 Oct 1921; *m* 1945, Maj Derek Hornsby (d 1971), s of Maj Frank Hornsby (d 1935) and Hon Muriel Strutt (yst da of 2 Baron Belper, JP, DL), hence 1 cous of Lavinia, Duchess of Norfolk, and 1 cous once removed of Lady Herries of Terregles, *qqv*; 2 s (Richard Gerald m 1980 Maria Lara, David Julian m 1975 Julie Ann Witford); *Career* Jr Cdr ATS WW II; *Style* - Lady Elizabeth Hornsby; Flat K, 19 Warwick sq, SW1 (☎ 01 821 7051)

HORNSBY-SMITH, Baroness (Life Peeress UK 1974); (Margaret) Patricia Hornsby-Smith; DBE (1961), PC (1959); s of Frederick Hornsby-Smith, of E Sheen; *b* 17 March 1914; *Career* Miny Ec Warfare WW II, Barnes Borough Cncl 1945-49; MP (C) Chislehurst 1950-66 & 1970-Feb 1974; Jt Parly Sec Min Pensions & NI 1959-61; UK Del to UN Assembly 1958; Pres Electrical Assoc for Women 1975-, V-Chm Arthritis & Rheumatism Cncl for Res 1974-; FRSA; *Style* - Rt Hon Lady Hornsby-Smith DBE PC; 31 Stafford Mansions, Stafford Place, SW1

HORNYOLD, Antony Frederick; Marchese (presumably fifteenth of the Habsburg cr, second of the Papal cr) di Gandolfi (Emperor Charles V 1529, Pope Leo XIII 1895), Duca di Gandolfi (Pope Leo XIII 1899); s of Ralph Gandolfi-Hornyold (d 1938), s of Thomas G-H, cr *Marchese* Gandolfi by Pope Leo XIII 1895 and *Duca* 1899, Thomas being in his turn s of John Vincent Gandolfi-Hornyold (12 *Marchese* di Gandolfi, of the cr of Emperor Charles V of 1529, according to Ruvigny), whose mother Teresa was sis of Thomas Hornyold, then sr male rep of the old Hornyold recusant family (Teresa and Thomas's aunt by marriage was Mrs Fitzherbert, who George IV, when Prince of Wales, m in contravention of the Royal Marriages Act); John Vincent's f was gs of *Count* (according to one source) Pietro Gandolfi, of Genoa, Leghorn and London; John Vincent m Charlotte Langdale (gda of 17 Baron Stourton); *b* 20 June 1931; *Educ* Ampleforth, Trin Cambridge; *Heir* bro, Simon Hornyold (b 11 Feb 1933, educ Ampleforth, residence - 11 Calle de Obispo Torres, Ibiza); *Career* FO 1957-67 (1 Sec Rawalpindi 1966-67) MOD 1967-; Kt of Order of St Benedict, Kt of Sov Mil Order of Malta; *Style* - Antony Hornyold Esq; Flat 5, 51 Cadogan sq, SW1 (☎ 01 235 9581)

HORNYOLD-STRICKLAND, Thomas Henry; DSC (1946); also 7 Count della Catena (Malta 1745 by Grand Master Pinto); s of Henry Hornyold-Strickland, JP, sometime Ld-Lt Westmorland, and Hon Mary Strickland, CBE (da of 1 & last Baron Strickland, GCMG, and 6 Count della Catena, by his w Lady Edeline

Sackville, da of 7 Earl de la Warr); *b* 20 Jan 1951; *Educ* Ampleforth; *m* 1951, Angela, da of Francis Engleheart, JP, of The Priory, Stoke Nayland, Suffolk (of a family of 14 century Silesian origins); 4 s, 2 da; *Heir* s, Henry Hornyold-Strickland (b 15 Dec 1951, educ Ampleforth & Exeter Coll Oxford); *Career* resident of Sizergh Castle (Nat Tst now owns), a fortified mansion with one of the best preseved Peel Towers in the country; Lt-Cdr RN (ret); served WW II ; Kt Sov Mil Order Malta; *Style* - Thomas Hornyold-Strickland Esq, Count della Catena, DSC; N Wing, Sizergh Castle, Kendal, Cumbria (☎ Sedgwick 60285)

HORRELL, John R; *aet* 52 in July 1981; *Career* chm Assoc of County Councils 1981-, v-chm to 1981; dairy farmer in Cambs; memb Peterborough CC 1963, later chm Cambs CC; *Style* - John Horrell Esq; c/o Association of County Councils, 66a Eaton sq, SW1 (☎ 01 235 1200)

HORROCKS, Raymond; s of Cecil Horrocks (d 1933); *b* 9 Jan 1930; *Educ* Bolton County Grammar Sch; *m* 1953, Pamela Florence, nee Mottistone; 3 da (Susan m 1976, Lynn m 1979, Raina b 1962); *Career* Sgt BAOR; exec dir BL Ltd 1981-, chm BL Cars Ltd 1979-, dir BLMC Ltd 1981-, md Austin Motors 1978-79, dep md Leyland 1977, regional dir Materials Handling Gp Eaton Corp 1972-77, Ford Motor Co 1963-72; *Recreations* fly fishing, motoring, gardening, walking; *Style* - Raymond Horrocks Esq; Far End, River View rd, Pangbourne, nr Reading, Berks

HORSBRUGH-PORTER, Sir Andrew Marshall Horsbrugh; 3 Bt (UK 1902), of Merrion Sq, City and Co of Dublin, DSO (1940) & Bar (1945); s of Sir John Horsbrugh-Porter, 2 Bt (d 1953); *b* 1 June 1907; *Educ* Winchester, RMC Sandhurst; *m* 1933, Annette Mary, da of Brig-Gen Robert Clayton Browne-Clayton, DSO; 1 s, 2 da; *Heir* s, John Horsbrugh-Porter; *Career* Col (ret) 12 Lancers, WW II France, Belgium, Italy (wounded, despatches, DSO*), Mil Advr UK High Cmmr New Delhi 1952; *Clubs* Cavalry and Guards; *Style* - Sir Andrew Horsbrugh-Porter Bt DSO*; Manor Farm House, Salford, Chipping Norton, Oxon

HORSBRUGH-PORTER, John Simon; s and h of Sir Andrew Marshall Horsbrugh Horsbrugh-Porter 3 Bt DSO*; *b* 18 Dec 1938; *Educ* Winchester and Trin Cambridge; *m* 1964, Lavinia Rose, da of Ralph Meredyth Turton, of Kildale Hall, Whitby; 1 s, 2 da; *Style* - John Horsbrugh-Porter Esq; Bowers Croft, Magpie Lane, Coleshill, Bucks

HORSFALL, Edward John Wright; s and h of Sir John Musgrave Horsfall 3 Bt MC TD JP; *b* 17 Dec 1940; *Educ* Uppingham; *m* 1965, Rosemary, da of Frank N King, of East Morton, Keighley; 3 s; *Style* - Edward Horsfall Esq; Shoebridge, Eastburn, Keighley, Yorks

HORSFALL, Sir John Musgrave; 3 Bt (UK 1909), MC (1946), TD (1949) and Clasp (1951), JP (N Yorks 1959); s of Sir (John) Donald Horsfall, 2 Bt (d 1975); *b* 26 Aug 1915; *Educ* Uppingham; *m* 1940, Cassandra Nora Bernardine, da of late George Wright, of Brinkworth Hall, Elvington, York; 2 s, 1 da; *Heir* s, Edward Horsfall; *Career* late Maj Duke of Wellington's (W Riding) Regt, Lloyd's Underwriter, dir Hayfield Textiles Ltd, Worsted Spinner Fedn Ltd (pres 1962-64), Skipton Building Soc, pres Skipton Divnl Con Assoc 1966-79; Burma 1939-45 (MC); *Clubs* Union (Bradford); *Style* - Sir John Horsfall, Bt, MC, TD and Clasp, JP; Greenfield House, Embsay, Skipton, N Yorks (☎ Skipton 4560)

HORSFIELD, Thomas Norman Roger; TD (1970) & Bar (1976); s of Norman Horsfield (d 1968); *b* 21 Feb 1936; *Educ* Barrow G S, Manchester U; *m* 1962, Ann, da of James William Evans, Wolverhampton; 1 s, 1 da; *Career* md Ayrion Saunders (Midland) Ltd; *Recreations* shooting; *Clubs* Roy Automobile, English XX Bisley; *Style* - Thomas Horsfield Esq, TD*

HORSLEY, Lady Angela Leslie; *née* Courtenay; da of late 16 Earl of Devon; *b* 1918; *m* 1947, Harold Cecil Horsley, MBE, Malayan Civil Service (ret) (d 1969); 2 s; *Style* - Lady Angela Horsley; Marwood House, Offwell, Honiton, Devon

HORSLEY-BERESFORD, Hon Mrs William - Ida Kaye; *m* 1941, as his 4 w, Hon William Arthur de la Poer Horsley-Beresford (s of late 3 Baron Decies and who d 1949); 1 s, 1 da; *Style* - The Hon Mrs William Horsley-Beresford; 53 Overstrand Mansions, Prince of Wales Drive, SW11

HORT, Andrew Edwin Fenton; s and h of Sir James Fenton Hort, 8 Bt; *b* 15 Nov 1954; *Style* - Andrew Hort Esq

HORT, Gwendolene, Lady; Gwendolene; da of late Sir Walter Galpin Alcock, MVO, MusD, of The Close, Salisbury; *m* 1922, Sir Fenton George Hort, 7 Bt (d 1960); *Style* - Gwendolene, Lady Hort; Mountjoy Cottage, Omagh, Co Tyrone

HORT, Sir James Fenton; 8 Bt (GB 1767), of Castle Strange, Middx; s of Sir Fenton George Hort, 7 Bt (d 1960), and Gwendolene, da of late Sir Walter Alcock, MVO; *b* 6 Sept 1926; *Educ* Marlborough, Trin Cambridge (BA, MB, BChir); *m* 1951, Joan, da of late Edward Peat, of Swallownest, Sheffield; 2 s, 2 da; *Heir* s, Andrew Hort; *Style* - Sir James Hort, Bt; Poundgate Lodge, Uckfield rd, Crowborough, Sussex

HORTON, Clive Fielding; s of Frank Fielding Horton (d 1970); *b* 3 July 1931; *Educ* Dover Coll; *m* 1959, Wendy Bradley, da of Henry Bert Jordan; 3 da; *Career* CA, sr ptnr Day, Smith and Hunter, pres S Eastern Soc of CAs 1972-73, memb of cncl Inst of CAs in England and Wales 1973-77; *Clubs* Bearsted G C (Capt 1974); *Style* - Clive Horton Esq; 14 Conway Rd, Maidstone, Kent (☎ Maidstone 53695)

HORTON, Hon Mrs (Fiona Catherine); Peake; s of 2 Viscount Ingleby; *b* 1955; *m* 1977, (Gavin) Tobias Alexander Winterbottom Horton (formerly Winterbottom); 2 da; *Style* - The Hon Mrs Horton; 38 Faroe rd, W14

HORTON, Robert Baynes; s of the late W Horton; *b* 18 Aug 1939; *Educ* King's Sch Canterbury, St Andrews University, Massachusetts Inst of Tech; *m* 1962, Sally Doreen, nee Wells; 2 c; *Career* British Petroleum Co Ltd 1960-, gen man BP Tankers 1975-76, and Corporate Planning 1976-78, dep md BP Chemicals 1978-80, md BP Chemicals 1980-, dir BP International 1980-; *Recreations* shooting, political biography, opera; *Style* - Robert Horton Esq; Stoke Abbas, South Stoke, Oxon (☎ Goring 873366)

HORTON, Hon Mrs (Susan Elizabeth); da of Baron Donovan (Life Peer, d 1971); *b* 1936; *m* 1960, Gerard Francis Horton; c; *Style* - The Hon Mrs Horton; 27 Weemala rd, Northbridge, NSW, Australia

HOSEASON-BROWN, Theodore; s of James Hoseason-Brown (d 1947); *b* 6 Apr 1908; *Educ* Clifton, Emmanuel Cambridge; *Career* Bahia-Sol Investments Ltd, Talk Publications Ltd, Templegate Industrial Securities Ltd, Wessex Dvpts Ltd; dir HTV Ltd & HTV Gp Ltd 1967-78, and Radio Avonside Ltd 1979-81; *Recreations* golf, swimming, walking; *Clubs* Brooks's, Clifton Club, Constitutional Club (Bristol); *Style* - Theodore Hoseason-Brown Esq; 6 Norland rd, Clifton, Bristol, BS8 3LP (☎ Bristol 34179)

HOSKINS, Arthur Henry James; s of Alfred George Hoskins; *b* 14 Jan 1923; *m* 1949, Margaret Lilian Rose, da of Albert Davis (d 1959); 1 child; *Career* certified accountant, chartered sec; gp md Matthew Hall and Co Ltd; *Recreations* reading, walking; *Style* - Arthur Hoskins Esq; 2 Acorn Close, Chislehurst, Kent (☎ 01 467 0755)

HOSKYNS, Sir Benedict Leigh; 16 Bt (E 1676), of Harewood, Herefordshire; s of Rev Sir Edwyn Clement Hoskyns, 13 Bt, MC, DD (d 1937); suc bro, Sir John Chevallier Hoskyns, 15 Bt, 1956; *b* 27 May 1928; *Educ* Haileybury, Corpus Christi Cambridge (MB and BChir 1952), London Hospital; *m* 1953, Ann, da of Harry Wilkinson; 2 s, 2 da; *Heir* s, Edwyn Hoskyns; *Career* Capt RAMC (ret), in general practice 1958-; DObstRCOG; *Style* - Sir Benedict Hoskyns, Bt; Harewood, Great Oakley, nr Harwich, Essex (☎ Ramsay 880341)

HOSKYNS, Edwyn Wren; s and h of Sir

Benedict Leigh Hoskyns, 16 Bt; *b* 4 Feb 1956; *Educ* Nottingham U Medical School (BM, BS 1979); *Career* senior chorister King's Coll Cambridge 1969; *Style* - Edwyn Hoskyns Esq

HOSKYNS, Hon Mrs (Katharine Margaret); da of Baron Kaldor (Life Peer); *b* 1937; *m* 1958, Anthony Hungerford Hoskyns, s of Sir Chandos Wren Hoskyns, 14 Bt (ka 1945); 1 s, 2 da; *Style* - The Hon Mrs Hoskyns; 25 Hamilton gdns, NW8

HOSKYNS, Mary, Lady; Mary Trym; da of late Edwin Budden, of Macclesfield; *m* 1922, the Rev Sir Edwyn Clement Hoskyns, MC, 13 Bt (d 1937); *Career* MA 1922, late Research Fell of Newnham Coll Cambridge; *Style* - Mary, Lady Hoskyns; 25 Hamilton gdns, NW8

HOTHAM, 8 Baron (I 1797); Sir Henry Durand Hotham; 18 Bt (E 1662), DL (Humberside 1981); 3 s of 7 Baron Hotham, CBE (d 1967), and Lady Letitia Cecil, da of 5 Marquess of Exeter; *b* 3 May 1940; *Educ* Eton; *m* 1972, Alexandra, 2 da of Maj Andrew Charles Stirling Home Drummond Moray; 2 s, 1 da; *Heir* s, Hon William Hotham; *Career* late Lt Gren Gds; patron of 1 living; ADC to Govr Tasmania 1963-66; *Style* - The Rt Hon Lord Hotham DL; Scorborough Hall, Driffield, Yorks; Dalton Hall, Dalton Holme, Beverley, Yorks

HOTHAM, Hon Elizabeth Henrietta Alexandra; da of 8 Baron Hotham; *b* 1976; *Style* - The Hon Elizabeth Hotham

HOTHAM, Hon George Andrew; s of 8 Baron Hotham; *b* 1974; *Style* - The Hon George Hotham

HOTHAM, Hon Jocelyne Mary Emma; da of 6 Baron Hotham (d 1923); *b* 1908; *Style* - The Hon Jocelyne Hotham; Ridout Cottage, Tarrant Gunville, Blandford, Dorset

HOTHAM, Dowager Baroness; Lady Letitia Sibell Winifred; *née* Cecil; da of late 5 Marquess of Exeter, KG, CMG, TD, and Hon Myra, nee Orde-Powlett, da of 4 Baron Bolton and Lady Algitha Lumley, da of 9 Earl of Scarbrough; *b* 1903; *m* 1937, 7 Baron Hotham (d 1967); 6 s (including 8 Baron; 3 are decd); *Career* Lady-in-Waiting to HRH the Duchess of Gloucester 1935-37; *Style* - The Rt Hon The Dowager Lady Hotham; The School House, Dalton Holme, Beverley, Yorks

HOTHAM, Hon Nicholas Charles Frederick; s of 7 Baron Hotham, CBE (d 1967); *b* 1947; *Educ* Eton; *m* 1974, Jane Brydon, of Thurley Beck Farm, Harwood Dale, Scarborough, Yorks; *Style* - The Hon Nicholas Hotham

HOTHAM, Maj Hon Peter; s of Capt Henry Edward Hotham (d 1912), and bro of 7 Baron (d 1967); *b* 1904; *Educ* Winchester and RMC; *m* 1934, Margaret, da of Col Sir Robert Williams-Wynn, 9 Bt, KCB, DSO, TD (d 1951); 1 s, 2 da; *Career* Capt KOYLI 1936, Maj 1941, ret 1947; raised to the rank of a Baron's son 1924; *Clubs* Buck's; *Style* - Major the Hon Peter Hotham; Plas Newydd, Glascoed, Abergele, N Wales

HOTHAM, Hon Peter William; s of 7 Baron Hotham, CBE (d 1967); *b* 1944; *Educ* Eton, Ch Ch Oxford; *m* 1978, Deborah S, da of late G Macdonald-Brown, of Rose Cottage, Campsall, Doncaster; 1 da; *Style* - The Hon Peter Hotham

HOTHAM, Hon William Beaumont; s and h of 8 Baron Hotham; *b* 13 Oct 1972; *Style* - The Hon William Hotham

HOTHFIELD, 4 Baron (UK 1881); Sir Thomas Sackville Tufton; 5 Bt (UK 1851); s of Hon Sackville Tufton (himself 2 s of 1 Baron, whose own f, Sir Richard Tufton, 1 Bt, was thought to be the love child of the 11 & last Earl of Thanet - he was certainly his heir; the Earl's f, gf, and ggf all had the forename Sackville in commemoration of the marriage of 2 Earl of Thanet with Lady Margaret Sackville, da of 3 Earl of Dorset); suc 3 Baron (1 cous) 1961; *b* 20 July 1916; *Educ* Eton, Cambridge; *Heir* 1 cous, George Tufton; *Style* - The Rt Hon Lord Hothfield; c/o House of Lords, SW1; Broome Park Hotel, Barham, Canterbury, Kent

HOTHFIELD, Baroness; Dorothy; da of late William George Raphael, of 9 Connaught Place, W2; *m* 1918, 3 Baron Hothfield (d 1961); *Style* - The Rt Hon the Lady Hothfield; Castle Hill, Englefield Green, Surrey

HOUGH, George Hubert; CBE (1965); *b* 21 Oct 1921; *Educ* Winsford Verdin G S Cheshire; King's Coll London U; *m* 1943, Hazel Ayrton; 1 s, 2 da; *Career* chm Forthstar Ltd 1980; dir Programmed Neuro Cybernetics Ltd 1979; chm & ch exec British Smelter Constructions Ltd 1978-80; memb of British Aerospace Board and appointed to Board of BAC Guided Weapons Div 1977; managing dir Hawker Siddeley Dynamics Ltd 1977-78; *Recreations* shooting, golf, dinghy sailing; *Clubs* St James's; *Style* - George Hough Esq, CBE; Trelyon, Rock, Nr Wadebridge, Cornwall (☎ 3454)

HOUGHTON OF SOWERBY, Baron (Life Peer UK 1974); Arthur Leslie Noel Douglas Houghton; CH (1967), PC (1964); s of John Houghton, of Long Eaton, Derbys; *b* 11 Aug 1898; *m* 1939, Vera, da of John Travis, of Southall; *Career* Sec Inland Revenue Staff Fedn 1922-60, MP (L) Sowerby 1949-74, Chllr Duchy of Lancaster 1964-66, Min Without Portfolio 1966-67, Chm PLP 1967-74; broadcaster BBC 1941-64, LCC Alderman 1947-49, memb Gen Cncl TUC 1952-60; V-Pres RSPCA 1978; memb Roy Commission on Standards of Conduct in Public Life; *Style* - Rt Hon Lord Houghton of Sowerby CH PC; Becks Cottage, Whitehill Lane, Bletchingley, Surrey (☎ Godstone 3340); 110 Marsham Court, SW1 (☎ 01 834 0602)

HOUGHTON, Herbert; s of Herbert Edward Houghton (d 1961); *b* 4 Oct 1920; *Educ* William Hulmes' G S Manchester; *m* 1939, Dorothy, da of Stuart Ballantyne; 1 s, 1 da; *Career* dir British Vita Co Ltd 1971-, Reed Stenhouse Cos Ltd (Canada) 1976-; chm: Reed Stenhouse & Partners Ltd 1977-80, Continental Reed Stenhouse Management (USA) 1979-, Stenhouse Hldgs Ltd 1979-; *Recreations* golf, reading, gardening, foreign travel; *Style* - Herbert Houghton Esq; Hazleford Hall, Lead Mill, Hathersage, Derbyshire (☎ Hope Valley 50297)

HOULDSWORTH, Sir (Harold) Basil; 2 Bt (UK 1956), of Heckmondwike, West Riding of Yorkshire; s of Sir Hubert Stanley, 1 Bt, QC (d Feb 1956); *b* 21 July 1922; *Educ* Heckmondwike G S, Leeds Sch of Medicine; MRCS, LRCP 1946, FFARCS 1954, DA Eng 1951; *m* 1946, Norah C, da of Arthur Halmshaw; 1 da; *Heir* none; *Career* consultant anaesthetist Barnsley and District Hospitals 1954-; *Style* - Sir Basil Houldsworth, Bt; Shadwell House, Lundhill rd, Wombwell, nr Barnsley, Yorks (☎ Wombwell 3191)

HOULDSWORTH, Sir Reginald Douglas Henry; 4 Bt (UK 1887), of Reddish, Manchester, Co Lancaster, and Coodham, Symington, Ayrshire, OBE (1945), TD (1944), DL (Ayrshire 1970); s of Col Sir William Thomas Reginald Houldsworth, CBE, TD (d 1960); *b* 9 July 1903; *Educ* Shrewsbury, Cambridge U; *m* 1934, Margaret May, da of late Cecil Emilius Laurie; 1 s, 2 da; *Heir* s, Richard Houldsworth; *Career* landowner; Hon Col Ayrshire Yeo (TA), (Lt Col cmdg 1940); *Clubs* Cavalry and Guards, Western Meeting (Ayr), Prestwick (Prestwick); *Style* - Sir Reginald Houldsworth, Bt, OBE, TD, DL; Kirkbride, Maybole, Ayrshire (☎ Crosshill 202)

HOULDSWORTH, Richard Thomas Reginald; s and h of Sir Reginald Douglas Henry Houldsworth, 4 Bt, OBE, TD; *b* 2 Aug 1947; *m* 1970, Jane, da of Alistair Orr, of Sydehead, Beith; 2 s; *Style* - Richard Houldsworth Esq; Parkfairn, Crosshill, Ayrshire

HOUNSFIELD, Sir Godfrey Newbold; CBE (1976); s of Thomas Hounsfield; *b* 28 Aug 1919; *Educ* Magnus G S Newark, City Coll London; *Career* sr staff scientist Central Research Laboratories of Thorn EMI Hayes Middx; kt 1981; *Style* - Sir Godfrey Hounsfield, CBE; South Airfield Farm, Winthorpe, nr Newark, Notts

HOUSDEN, Norman Charles Nelson; s of Charles Frederick Webb Housden (d 1950); *b* 1 Jan 1919; *Educ* Loughton; *m* 1940, Marjorie Violet, nee Meeson; 1 da; *Career* CA, chm Arlington Motor

Holdings 1955-; *Recreations* boating (MY 'Bluefinch'), aircraft ('Partenavia Victor'); *Style* - Norman Housden Esq; White Heron, Fort George, St Peter Port, Guernsey, Channel Islands

HOUSEMAN, Alexander Randolph; s of Capt Alexander William Houseman (d 1962); *b* 9 May 1920; *Educ* Stockport G S, Stockport Coll; *m* 1942, Betty Edith, da of Alfred G Norrington (d 1976); 1 da; *Career* engr, man consultant; dir, md, then dep chm P E Consulting Gp 1968-, dir Record Ridgway Ltd 1978- and British Rail Engrg Ltd 1979-, chm W Canning Ltd 1975-80; *Recreations* walking, swimming, sailing, photography, motoring; *Clubs* Caledonian, RAYC; *Style* - Alexander Houseman Esq; 11 Kings Av, Ealing, W5 2SJ (☎ 01 997 3936)

HOUSTON, Hon Mrs; Hon Averil; *née* Vivian; JP (Herts); da of late 3 Baron Swansea, DSO, MVO, and Hon Winifred, nee Hamilton, da of 1 Baron Holm Patrick, PC, and Lady Victoria, nee Wellesley, sis of 3 and 4 Dukes of Wellington; *b* 1930; *m* 1953, Alexander William Houston; 2 s, 1 da; *Style* - The Hon Mrs Houston, JP; The Little House, Datchworth, Knebworth, Herts

HOUSTOUN-BOSWALL, Sir Thomas; 7 Bt (UK 1836); s of Maj Sir Gordon Houstoun-Boswall, 6 Bt (d 1961); *b* 13 Feb 1919; *m* 1, 1945 (m dis 1970), Margaret, da of George Bullen-Smith; 1 s, 1 da; m 2, 1971, Anne-Lucie, da of Pierre Naquet; *Heir* s, Thomas Alford Houstoun-Boswall; *Career* Pilot Offr RAF Vol Reserve WW II; *Style* - Sir Thomas Houstoun-Boswall, Bt; Heath Grange, Lingfield, Surrey (☎ Lingfield 833809)

HOUSTOUN-BOSWALL, Thomas Alford; s and h of Sir Thomas Houstoun-Boswall, 7 Bt; *b* 23 May 1947; *m* 1971, Eliana Michele, da of Dr John Pearse, of New York; 1 s; *Style* - Thomas Houstoun-Boswall Esq; 26 Montpelier st, SW3

HOVELL-THURLOW-CUMMING-BRUCE, Hon Aubyn Cecilia; da of 8 Baron Thurlow, KCMG; *b* 1958; *Style* - The Hon Aubyn Hovell-Thurlow-Cumming-Bruce

HOVELL-THURLOW-CUMMING-BRUCE, Hon Alexander Pascoe; OBE (1960); s of 7 Baron Thurlow, CB, CBE, DSO (d 1971); *b* 1917; *Educ* Shrewsbury, Trin Cambridge; *m* 1942, Catherine Agnes, da of the Rev Hamilton Blackwood, of Scalby, Yorks; 2 s, 1 da; *Career* Colonial Admin Serv 1941-60, Home Civil Serv 1961-78; *Style* - The Hon Alexander Hovell-Thurlow-Cumming-Bruce OBE; Little House, Dedham, Colchester, Essex

HOVELL-THURLOW-CUMMING-BRUCE, Hon Peter Torquil Francis; 2 s of 8 Baron Thurlow, KCMG; *b* 21 April 1962; *Educ* Shrewsbury; *Style* - The Hon Peter Hovell-Thurlow-Cumming-Bruce

HOVELL-THURLOW-CUMMING-BRUCE, Hon Roualeyn Robert; s and h of 8 Baron Thurlow, KCMG; *b* 13 April 1952; *Educ* Milton Abbey; *m* 1980, Bridget Anne Julia, da of (Hugh) Bruce Ismay Cheape, TD, of Fossoway Lodge, Kinross; *Style* - The Hon Roualeyn Hovell-Thurlow-Cumming-Bruce

HOVELL-THURLOW-CUMMING-BRUCE, see also Cumming-Bruce

HOW, Denzil Robert Onslow; s of Robert Boothby How, of St Andrews (through whose paternal grandmother, Madeline, Denzil is 1 cous twice removed of Lord ('Bob') Boothby), and Virginia, da of Capt Oliver Hughes-Onslow, JP; through his mother Denzil is kin to James Hughes-Onslow, paperback reviewer The Spectator, and seventh cous once removed to Lady Teresa, w of that other contributor to The Spectator, Auberon Waugh; *b* 3 Aug 1944; *Educ* Eton, Trin Cambridge; *m* 1968, Sarah, da of John Collins, of Tusmore Park, Bicester; 4 da (Nicola b 1970, Antonia b 1975, Francesca b 1978, Georgina b 1981); *Career* chm Rediweld Hldgs 1972-, md Vistaplan 1977-, dir Roden Plastics; *Recreations* stalking, shooting, skiing, golf, tennis, cricket, racing; *Clubs* MCC, Pitt (Cambridge); *Style* - Denzil How Esq; The Old House, Guilsborough, Northants (☎ 0604 740066)

HOW, Peter Cecil; s of Cecil How; *b* 27 June 1931; *Educ* Oundle Sch, Open U; *m* 1951, Jane, nee Erickson; 2 s; *Career* dir

Frogatt & Prior Ltd 1955, chm How Gp Ltd and Assoc Cos (dir 1963) 1974-; *Recreations* travel, theatre, music; *Clubs* East India; City Livery; *Style* - Peter How Esq; 3109 Heatherwood Lane, Sarasota, Florida USA

HOWARD OF PENRITH, 2 Baron (UK 1930); Francis Philip Howard; DL (Glos 1960); 2 s of 1 Baron Howard of Penrith, GCB, GCMG, CVO (d 1939, himself 4 s of Henry Howard, n of 12 Duke of Norfolk; hence Lord Howard of Penrith is 1 cous twice removed of Auberon Waugh), by his w Lady Isabella Giustiniani-Bandini, herself da of 8 Earl of Newburgh, Duca di Mondragone and Prince Giustiniani Bandini; *b* 5 Oct 1905; *Educ* Downside, Trin Cambridge; *m* 1944, Anne, da of John Hotham (fifth in descent from Sir Beaumont Hotham, 7 Bt and f of 8, 9, 11 & 12 Bts, the last two being also 1 & 2 Barons Hotham) and sis of Lady Guest and Countess of Donoughmore (w of 7 Earl); 4 s; *Heir* s, Hon Philip Howard; *Career* barr 1931; Capt RA, served WW II; *Style* - The Rt Hon Lord Howard of Penrith DL; Dean Farm, Coln St Aldwyns, Glos

HOWARD, Hon Andrew Barnaby; s (twin, by 1 m) of 4 Baron Strathcona and Mount Royal; *b* 1963; *Style* - The Hon Andrew Howard

HOWARD, Hon Barnaby John; s of late 3 Baron Strathcona and Mount Royal, and Hon Diana, nee Loder, da of 1 Baron Wakehurst; *b* 1925; *Educ* Eton, Trin Cambridge; *m* 1, 1952 (m dis 1967), Elizabeth, da of Frank M Mayfield, of St Louis, Missouri, USA; 1 s, 2 da; m 2, 1970, Mrs F N H Bishop, da of late Ambrose Chambers; *Career* Cmmmr S Rhodesian Forestry Cmmn 1957, Sub-Lt RNVR (Air Branch) WW II; *Style* - The Hon Barnaby Howard; RR3 Pinebrook rd, Bedford, New York, USA 1056; Beaverdam Farm, PO Box 238, Umtali, Rhodesia; St Ann's Bay, Englishtown, Nova Scotia, Canada

HOWARD, Hon Caroline Anne; da (by 1 m) of 4 Baron Strathcona and Mount Royal; *b* 1959; *Style* - The Hon Caroline Howard

HOWARD, Lady Carolyn Bridget Dacre; da of late 11 Earl of Carlisle; *b* 1919; *Career* Subaltern ATS, transfd to FANY Ambulance Corps 1939-45; *Style* - Lady Carolyn Howard; The Old Tannery, Temple Sowerby, Penrith

HOWARD, Hon Donald Alexander Smith; s (by 1 m) and h of 4 Baron Strathcona and Mount Royal; *b* 24 June 1961; *Style* - The Hon Donald Howard

HOWARD, Hon David Francis; s of 2 Baron Howard of Penrith; *b* 1949; *Style* - The Hon David Howard

HOWARD, David Howarth Seymour; s and h of Sir (Hamilton) Edward de Coucey Howard, 2 Bt, GBE; *b* 29 Dec 1945; *Educ* Radley, Worcester Coll Oxford; *m* 1968, Valerie Picton, da of late Derek W Crosse, of Chase House, Callis Court Rd, Broadstairs; 1 s, 2 da; *Career* Common Councilman City of London, Councillor of London Borough of Sutton, memb of Stock Exchange; *Style* - David Howard Esq; 18 Finsbury Circus, EC2

HOWARD, Cdr David (Peter) Mowbray Algernon; s of Hon John Anthony Frederick Charles Howard (d 1971, s of 5 Earl of Effingham); hp of 6 Earl; *b* 29 April 1939; *Educ* Fettes; *m* 1964, Anne Mary (m dis 1975), da of Harrison Sayer, of Saffron Walden; 1 s; *Career* Cdr RN at MOD; *Recreations* squash; *Style* - Cdr David Howard, RN; 134 High st, Old Portsmouth, Hants; 69 Vandon Court, Petty France, SW1

HOWARD, David Sanctuary; s of H Howard (d 1979); *b* 22 Jan 1928; *Educ* Stowe; *m* 1, 1952, Elizabeth, da of late Adm Sir Dudley North, GCVO; 1 s, 2 da; m 2, 1974, Anna-Maria, da of late Dante Bocci; *Career* co dir 1960-73, author of *Chinese Armorial Porcelain* 1974, *China for the West* 1978, and others, lectr, dir Heirloom & Howard Ltd 1973-; *Clubs* Oriental; *Style* - David Howard Esq; 1 Hay Hill, W1 (☎ 01 493 5868)

HOWARD, Hon Edmund Bernard Carlo; CMG (1969), MVO (1961); s of 1 Baron Howard of Penrith GCB GCMG CVO PC (d 1939); *b* 1909; *Educ* Downside, New Coll Oxford; *m* 1936, Cécile, da of Charles Geoffroy-Dechaume, of Valmondois, France; 3 s, 1 da; *Career* barr Middle Temple 1934, 2 Sec (Information) Rome 1947-51, and in Foreign Office 1951-53, 1 Sec Madrid 1953-57, Head of Chancery Bogota 1957-59, Consul-Gen San Marino and Florence 1960-61, Counsellor Rome 1961-65, Consul-Gen Genoa 1965-69; *Style* - The Hon Edmund Howard, CMG, MVO; Jerome Cottage, Marlow Common, Bucks SL7 2QR

HOWARD, Sir (Hamilton) Edward (de Coucey); 2 Bt (UK 1955), of Great Rissington, Co Gloucester, GBE (1972); s of Sir (Harold Walter) Seymour Howard, 1 Bt (d 1956); *b* 29 Oct 1915; *Educ* Radley, Worcester Coll Oxford; Hon DSc London; *m* 1943, Elizabeth Howarth, da of Maj P H Ludlow; 2 s; *Heir* s, David Howard; *Career* sr partner of the firm of Charles Stanley & Co, Stockbrokers, chm LRC Int Ltd, memb of the Stock Exchange London 1946, Sheriff of the City of London 1966, Lord Mayor of London 1971-72, HM Lt City of London 1976, Master of the Gardeners' Co 1961; Flying Offr RAF WW II (despatches); *Clubs* City of London, City Livery, United Wards; *Style* - Sir Edward Howard, Bt, GBE; Courtlands, Bishops Walk, Shirley Hills, Surrey (☎ 01 656 4444)

HOWARD, Hon Emma Laura Louise; da (twin, by 1 m) of 4 Baron Strathcona and Mount Royal; *b* 1963; *Style* - The Hon Emma Howard

HOWARD, Francis John Adrian; s of Ewen Storrs Howard, Capetown (d 1979); *b* 11 July 1935; *Educ* Michaelhouse, Natal SA; U of Natal, SA; *m* 1961, Lynette; 2 s; *Career* dir Charter Consolidated Ltd 1978, Cape Industs Ltd 1977, Benalt Tin & Wolfram Ltd 1977, Anderson Strathclyde Ltd 1980, The Diamond Trading Co 1973-75; *Recreations* tennis, shooting, skiing; *Clubs* Rand (Jo'burg), Hurlingham; *Style* - Francis Howard Esq; 2 Inkerman ter, Allen St, London W8 6QX

HOWARD, George Anthony Geoffrey; DL (N R Yorks 1971); 2 s of Hon Geoffrey Howard, JP (5 s of 9 Earl of Carlisle by Hon Rosalind Stanley, da of 2 Baron Stanley of Alderley, through whom George is 2 cous once removed to Nancy and the other Mitford sisters), and Hon Ethel Methuen, da of Field-Marshal 3 Baron Methuen, GCB; *b* 22 May 1920; *Educ* Eton, Balliol Oxford; *m* 1949, Lady Cecilia FitzRoy, da of 8 Duke of Grafton; 4 s; *Career* proprietor of Castle Howard, with Blenheim and Seaton Delaval one of the triumphs of Sir John Vanbrugh's genius and the setting for the film of 'Brideshead Revisited'; chm BBC 1980- (Gov 1972-), Pres HHA 1978-; served WW II Green Howards; Pres Yorks Philosophical Soc; *Clubs* White's, Brooks's, Pratt's; *Style* - George Howard Esq, DL; 18 Ennismore Mews, SW7; Castle Howard, York

HOWARD, Hon Mrs Henry; Adèle le Bourgeois; da of late Reese Denny Alsop, of New York City, USA; *m* 1937, Lt-Col the Hon Henry Anthony Camillo Howard, CMG, Coldstream Gds (d 1977), s of 1 Baron Howard of Penrith GCB GCMG CVO (d 1939); 4 da; *Style* - The Hon Mrs Henry Howard; Bushby House, Greystoke, Penrith, Cumberland

HOWARD, Hon Hubert John Edward Dominic; s of 1 Baron Howard of Penrith GCB GCMG CVO (d 1939); *b* 1907; *Educ* Downside, Trin Cambridge; *m* 1951, Donna Lelia Calista Ada Caetani (d 1977), da of 18 Duke of Sermoneta; *Style* - The Hon Hubert Howard; Palazzo Caetani, Rome, Italy; Lyulph's Tower, Ullswater, Cumberland

HOWARD, Hon Jonathan Alan; s of late 3 Earl of Strathcona and Mount Royal and Hon Diana, nee Loder, da of 1 Baron Wakehurst; *b* 1933; *Educ* Eton, Trin Cambridge, Roy Inst of Tech Stockholm; *m* 1, 1956 (m dis 1969), Hon Brigid Mary, nee Westenra, da of 6 Baron Rossmore; 2 da; m 2, 1970, Cecilia Philipson; 1 s; *Career* late 2 Lt Coldstream Gds, and Argyll & Sutherland Highlanders (TA); *Style* - The Hon Jonathan Howard; Sporrvaegen, 8 Jakobsberg, Sweden

HOWARD, Hon Jane Elisabeth Stirling; da (by 1 m) of 4 Baron Strathcona and Mount Royal; *b* 1955; *Style* - The Hon Jane Howard

HOWARD, Hon Mrs (Jean Margaret); *née* Parnell; da of late 6 Baron Congleton; *b* 1922; *m* 1952, as his 2 w, Lt-Col Frederick Henry Howard, DSO, MC, late 3 Hussars; *Style* - The Hon Mrs Howard; Isle of Gometra, by Mull, Argyll

HOWARD, Lady Jane Mary; *née* Waldegrave; da of 12 Earl Waldegrave; *b* 1934; *m* 1, 1954 (m dis 1977), 4 Baron Strathcona and Mount Royal; m 2, 1977, Capt Duncan McIntosh, but announced intention of being known as Lady Jane Howard 1979; *Style* - Lady Jane Howard

HOWARD, John Philip; s and h of Sir William Howard Lawson, 5 Bt; assumed by Roy Licence surname and arms of Howard 1962; *b* 6 June 1934; *m* 1960, Jean Veronica, da of late Col John Evelyn Marsh, DSO, OBE; 2 s, 1 da; *Style* - John Howard Esq; Corby Castle, Carlisle

HOWARD, Lady Katharine Emma Frances Anita Robsham; da (by 2 m) of 21 Earl of Suffolk and (14 of) Berkshire; *b* 1976

HOWARD, Lady Leonora Stanley; *née* Baldwin; da of late 1 Earl Baldwin of Bewdley (Rt Hon Sir Stanley Baldwin, KG, MP, Prime Minister) and Dame Lucy, GBE, nee Ridsdale; *b* 1896; *m* 1922, Capt the Hon Sir Arthur Jared Palmer Howard, KBE, CVO (d 1971), s of Margaret Charlotte, Baroness Strathcona and Mount Royal (2 in line); 2 s, 2 da (*see* Hon Mrs Langley G H Russell); *Style* - Lady Leonora Howard; 8 Sandwich st, St Pancras, WC1

HOWARD, Hon Michael Edmund; s of 2 Baron Howard of Penrith; *b* 1947; *Style* - The Hon Michael Howard

HOWARD, Michael Jonathan; s of Alec Howard (d 1972); *b* 20 March 1927; *Educ* Bradfield Coll, Queen's Oxford; *m* 1953, Susan Mai, da of George Francis Pitt-Lewis; 2 s; *Career* chm and md Thames Case Ltd; FCA, Fell Institute of Cost & Management Accountants; *Recreations* riding (principally hunting), squash, music; *Clubs* Naval; *Style* - Michael Howard, Esq; Purleigh Lodge, Purleigh, Essex

HOWARD, Hon Philip Charles Wentworth; s of 12 Earl of Carlisle; *b* 1963; *Style* - The Hon Philip Howard

HOWARD, Hon Philip Esme; s and h of 2 Baron Howard of Penrith; *b* 1 May 1945; *m* 1969, Sarah, da of late Barclay Walker; 1 s, 2 da; *Style* - The Hon Philip Howard; 45 Erpingham rd, SW15

HOWARD, Philip Nicholas Howard; s of Peter Dunsmore Howard (d 1965); *b* 2 Nov 1933; *Educ* Eton, Trin Oxford; *m* 1959, Myrtle Janet Mary, da of Sir Reginald Houldsworth, 4 Bt, *qv*; 2 s, 1 da; *Career* Lt (Nat Service) Black Watch; literary editor The Times; author; *Recreations* reading, walking, talking; *Style* - Philip Howard Esq; 47 Ladbroke Grove, W11 (☎ 01 727 1077)

HOWARD, Peter Reuben; s of Edward Reuben Howard (d 1966); *b* 18 Feb 1922; *Educ* Sir Walter St Johns Sch, Battersea Polytechnic; *m* 1945, Betty, nee Morris; 1 da (Suzanne Barrell); *Career* dir-gen CEGB Transmission and Technical Services Division 1977-; *Recreations* general engineering, photography, gardening; *Style* - Peter Howard Esq; The Old Thatch, Blackmoor, Liss, Hampshire (☎ Bordon (04203) 3642)

HOWARD DE WALDEN, 9 Baron (E 1597); TD; John Osmael Scott-Ellis; also Baron Seaford (UK 1826); s of 8 Baron Howard de Walden (d 1946, gs of 1 Baron Seaford, whose w Elizabeth was gda of 4 Earl of Bristol (Lord Bristol's f's mother was maternal gda of 3 Earl of Suffolk, who also held the Barony of H de W; Lord Suffolk's gf, the first holder of the Earldom and the Barony, was otherwise Lord Thomas Howard, s of 4 Duke of Norfolk by his 2 w) and Margherita, CBE, DStJ, FRGS, da of Charles van Raalte, JP; *b* 27 Nov 1912; *Educ* Eton, Magdalene Cambridge; *m* 1, 1934, Countess Irene Harrach (d 1975), yst da of Count Hans Albrecht Harrach, of Munich (of a Mediatised Sovereign House of the Holy Roman Empire; the title *Reichsfreiherr von* or Baron of Harrach was conferred by Ferdinand I 1552 and under the Hungarian Crown 1563; the title of *Reichsgraf von* or Count of Harrach was cr by Emperor Ferdinand II 1627; one line of the family, now extinct, was even advanced to the dignity of *Reichsfürst* or Prince of the Empire); 4 da; m 2, 1978, Gillian, da of Cyril Buckley and formerly w of 17 Viscount Mountgarret; *Heiresses* all 4 da as coheiresses: Hon Mrs Czernin, Hon Mrs Buchan of Auchmacoy, Hon Mrs White, Hon Mrs Acloque; *Career* Maj Westminster Dragoons (TA); dir Howard de Walden Estates Ltd; *Clubs* Jockey (Sr Steward 1957, 1964, 1976), Turf; *Style* - The Rt Hon Lord Howard de Walden TD; Avington Manor, Hungerford, Berks (☎ Kintbury 229); Flat K, 90 Eaton sq, SW1 (☎ 01 235 7127)

HOWARD-SMITH, Hon Mrs (Patricia Ann); da of 1 Baron Lambury (d 1967); *b* 1929; *m* 1951 (m dis 1968) Capt Morfryn James Howard-Smith, RN; 1 s, 1 da; *Style* - The Hon Mrs Howard-Smith; c/o José Villalonga 52 Bis, El Terreno, Palma de Mallorca

HOWARTH, Lady Meriel (Aileen); *née* Brabazon; da of 13 Earl of Meath, CB, CBE (d 1949); *b* 1913; *m* 1947, Maj Ernest Gerald Howarth, MBE (d 1967); 4 da; *Style* - Lady Meriel Howarth; Congham Hall, King's Lynn, Norfolk

HOWE, 6 Earl (UK 1821); Edward Richard Assheton Penn Curzon; CBE (1961), JP (Bucks 1946), DL (1960); also Baron Howe of Langar (GB 1788), Baron Curzon of Penn (GB 1794) and Viscount Curzon of Penn (UK 1802); s of 5 Earl Howe, CBE, VD, PC (d 1964, ggs of 1 Earl, whose mother's f was the famous Admiral, cr Earl Howe, who won the action of the Glorious First of June in 1794, put down the mutiny at Spithead in 1797, and ran a superb (albeit doomed) defensive campaign during the close of the American War of Independence; known as 'Black Dick' by his men because of his swarthy complexion, he was popularly supposed to descend from George I through his mother, Mary Sophia (she - allegedly HM's da - being born of the Countess of Darlington in her own right; Lady Darlington's husb was Baron von Kielmansegge), though at least two dissenting opinions have been published) by his 1 w (and cous) Mary (da of Col Hon Montagu Curzon, himself s of 1 Earl Howe); *b* 7 Aug 1908; *Educ* Eton, CCC Cambridge; *m* 1, 1935 (m dis 1943), da of Sir Archibald Weigall, 1 Bt, KCMG; 2 da; m 2, 1946, Grace, OStJ, da of Stephen Wakeling, of Durban, and formerly w of Capt A Barker, also of Durban; 2 da; *Heir* 2 cous, Frederick Penn; *Career* Lt-Cdr RNVR, served WW II Atlantic & Pacific; Pres Chesham & Amersham Con Assoc 1972-; Pres St John Ambulance Bucks, King William IV Naval Asylum; Alderman Bucks, CCllr 1973-, V-Chm Bucks CC 1976-; CStJ; RAC Steward; *Also* godson of Edward VII; *Style* - The Rt Hon Earl Howe CBE JP DL; 20 Pitts Head Mews, W1 (☎ 01 499 4706); Penn House, Amersham, Bucks (☎ High Wycombe 713366)

HOWE, Charles Keith; s of Henry Beauclerk Howe (d 1948); *b* 11 March 1935; *Educ* Lancing, Trin Hall Cambridge; *m* 1960, Carole, da of Alma Thomas Absalom, of Copthorne, Sussex; 1 s, 2 da; *Career* jt md Crystalate Hldgs 1978- (dir 1971-); *Recreations* cricket; *Clubs* MCC; *Style* - Charles Howe Esq; Billhurst, Lingfield Common, Lingfield, Surrey (☎ 0342 832848)

HOWELL, Michael William Davis; s of Air Vice-Marshal E M T Howell, CBE, of Bank Farm, Lorton, Cumbria; *b* 11 June 1947; *Educ* Charterhouse, Trin Cambridge, Harvard Business Sch (MBA 1976); *m* 1975, Susan Wanda, da of Andrew Adie, of New Abbey, Scotland; *Career* Vice-Pres (European Businesses) Cummins Engine Co Ltd; *Recreations* tennis, squash, motorcycling; *Clubs* RAC; *Style* - Michael Howell Esq; c/o Nat West Bank, 21 Lombard st, EC3

HOWELL, Tudor Morgan; s of David John Howell; *b* 24 May 1924; *Educ* West Monmouth Sch, Cambridge U; *m* 1953, Sara Margaret Janey, da of Rev Geoffrey Earle Raven; 2 s, 1 da; *Career* Temp Sub Lt RNVR; medical practitioner, High Sheriff of Powys 1980; *Recreations* gardening; *Style* - Tudor Howell Esq; Ynyswen, Trefeglwys, Newtown, Powys (☎Trefeglwys 633)

HOWICK OF GLENDALE, 2 Baron (UK 1960); Charles Evelyn Baring; s of

1 Baron Howick of Glendale, KG, GCMG, KCVO (d 1973; otherwise Hon Sir Evelyn Baring, sometime Govr Kenya & yst s of 1 Earl of Cromer), by his w Lady Mary Grey (da of 5 Earl Grey); *b* 30 Dec 1937; *Educ* Eton, New Coll Oxford; *m* 1964, Clare, yr da of Col Cyril Darby, MC, of Kemerton Court, Tewkesbury; 1 s, 3 da; *Heir* s, Hon David Baring; *Career* md Baring Bros & Co 1969-; dir London Life Assoc 1972-; memb Exec Cttee Nat Art Collections Fund 1973-; *Clubs* Brooks's; *Style* - The Rt Hon Lord Howick of Glendale; Howick, Alnwick, Northumberland (☎ Longhoughton 624); 52 Chepstow Villas, W11 (☎ 01 229 2640)

HOWICK, Lady Mary Cecil Grey; da of 5 Earl Grey (d 1963); *b* 1907; *m* 1935, 1 Baron Howick of Glendale, KG, GCMG, KCVO (d 1973); 1 s (2 Baron), 2 da (Hon Lady Wakefield, Hon Mrs Gibbs); *Style* - Lady Mary Howick; Howick, Alnwick, Northumberland

HOWIE OF TROON, Baron (Life Peer UK 1978); William Howie; s of Peter Howie of Troon; *b* 2 March 1924; *Educ* Marr Coll Troon, Roy Tech Coll Glasgow; *m* 1951, Mairi, da of John Sanderson; 2 s, 2 da; *Career* civ engr & journalist; MP (L) Luton 1963-70, Assist Whip 1964-66, Ld Commissioner Treasury 1966-67, Comptroller HM Household 1967-68, V-Chm PLP 1968-70; gen man Thos Telford Ltd; MICE, memb Cncl City U 1968-; *Style* - Rt Hon Lord Howie of Troon; 34 Temple Fortune Lane, NW11 (☎ 01 455 0492)

HOWIE, Hon Angus; s of Baron Howie of Troon; *b* 20 May 1963; *Style* - The Hon Angus Howie

HOWIE, Hon Annabel Martha; da of Baron Howie of Troon (Life Peer); *b* 1956; *Style* - The Hon Annabel Howie

HOWIE, Hon Alisoun Mary Kyle; da of Baron Howie of Troon; *b* 1959; *Style* - The Hon Alisoun Howie

HOWIE, Hon Alexander Robin; s of Baron Howie of Troon; *b* 29 Oct 1965; *Style* - The Hon Alexander Howie

HOWIE, Hon Mrs (Kathleen Whalley); *née* Smith; MBE (1946); da of late 1 Baron Colwyn; *m* 1945, Robert Cullen Howie; *Style* - The Hon Mrs Howie MBE; Butts, Cottage, Rhinefield Road, Brockenhurst, Hants

HOWLAND, Lord; Andrew Ian Henry Russell; s and h of Marquess of Tavistock; *b* 30 March 1962; *Style* - Lord Howland

HOY, Hon Ian Richard; s of Baron Hoy (Life Peer d 1976); *b* 1945; *Style* - The Hon Ian Hoy

HOY, Baroness; Nancy Hamlyn Rae; da of John McArthur; *m* 1942, Baron Hoy, PC (Life Peer d 1976); 1 s (Hon Ian Hoy); *Style* - The Rt Hon the Lady Hoy; 77 Orchard rd, Edinburgh EH4 2EX

HOYER MILLAR, Hon Robert Charles Reneke; s of Baron Inchyra; *b* 4 Apr 1935; *Educ* Eton, New Coll Oxford; *m* 1961, Fiona Mary, E C R Sheffield (d 1977); 1 s, 2 da; *Career* regional gen man Barclays Bank Ltd 1976-; *Style* - The Hon Robert Hoyer Millar; Rookley Manor, Up Somborne, Stockbridge, Hampshire (☎ Kings Somborne 319)

HUBBARD, Hon Dominic Bryce; s and h of 5 Baron Addington; *b* 24 Aug 1963; *Style* - The Hon Dominic Hubbard

HUBBARD, Hon Frances Linden; da of 5 Baron Addington; *b* 26 July 1962; *Style* - The Hon Frances Hubbard

HUBBARD, Lady Miriam; *née* Fitzalan-Howard; da of 3 Baron Howard of Glossop, MBE, and Baroness Beaumont, OBE; sis of 17 Duke of Norfolk, CB, CBE, MC; *b* 1924; *m* 1952, Lt-Cdr Theodore Bernard Peregrine Hubbard, RN; 2 s, 3 da; *Style* - Lady Miriam Hubbard; Morton Hall, Bury St Edmunds, Suffolk

HUBBARD, Hon Michael Walter Leslie; s of 5 Baron Addington; *b* 6 July 1965; *Style* - The Hon Michael Hubbard

HUBBARD, Hon Sally Anne; da of 5 Baron Addington; *b* 19 Oct 1966; *Style* - The Hon Sally Hubbard

HUBBLE, Lady Jean; *née* Huddleston; da of Countess of Loudoun (d 1960) and Capt Reginald Mowbray Chichester Huddleston; *b* 3 Oct 1920; *m* 1, 1940 (m diss 1949), Edgar Wright Wakefield; 1 da; m 2, 1954, Capt Arthur Alexander Hubble; 1 da; became Lady Jean Campbell of Loudoun on succeeding to estate of Loudoun by deed of gift from her mother; coheiress to Baronies of Botreaux, Stanley (1456) and Hastings (1461); *Style* - Lady Jean Hubble; Loudoun Castle, Galston, Ayrshire

HUDSON, Hon Mrs; Hon Carola; *née* Browne; da of 6 Baron Kilmaine, CBE (d 1978); *b* 1932; *m* 1960, John Michael Carlyon Lowry Hudson; 2 s, 1 da; *Style* - The Hon Mrs Hudson; Gwavas Station, Tikokino, Hawkes Bay, NZ

HUDSON, Lady Cathleen Blanche Lily; *née* Eliot; da of 6 Earl of St Germans, MC, and Lady Blanche Somerset, da of 8 Duke of Beaufort; through Lady Blanche she is coheiress presumptive to the Baronies of Botetourt and Herbert, at present held by 10 Duke of Beaufort, KG, GCVO, PC; *b* 29 July 1921; *m* 1, 1946 (m dis 1956), John Seyfried, of Kensington, RHG; 1 s, 1 da; m 2, 1957, Sir Havelock Hudson; 1 s, 1 da; *Career* antique dealer, memb BADA; *Recreations* bridge; *Style* - Lady Cathleen Hudson; The Old Rectory, Stanford Dingley, Berks (☎ 0734 744346)

HUDSON, David Norman; s of the late Sir Edmund Peder Hudson; *b* 29 May 1945; *Educ* Marlborough Coll, Balliol Coll Oxford; *m* 1967, Rosemary McMahon, nee Turner; 1 s, 2 da; *Career* merchant banker, dir Samuel Montagu & Co Ltd 1974-; *Recreations* natural history, bridge, opera; *Style* - David Hudson Esq; Hare Hatch House, Hare Hatch, Reading, Berks (☎ Wargrave 2360)

HUDSON, Francis Edward; TD; s of Edward Hudson, of Bridge House, Harewood; *b* 10 June 1912; *Educ* Rugby; *m* 1944, Masha Violet, da of Col Murray Muirhead-Murray, DSO; 1 s, 1 da; *Career* former Maj Mid East; dep chm Yorkshire Post Newspapers 1958, chm Doncaster Newspapers, dir United Newspapers; *Recreations* fishing, shooting; *Style* - Francis Hudson Esq, TD; Winterfield House, Hornby, Bedale, Yorks (☎ Richmond 811619)

HUDSON, Lady Jane (Catherine); *née* Leslie-Melville; da of 14 Earl of Leven and Melville; *b* 1956; *m* 1977, Philip Mark Gurney Hudson; *Style* - The Hon Mrs Hudson; 71 Horder rd, SW6

HUDSON, Mrs Jonathan - Princess Anna; *née* Obolensky; *Style* - Mrs Jonathan Hudson

HUGGINS, Hon Haoli Elizabeth Jane; da of 2 Viscount Malvern (d 1978); *b* 1953; *Style* - The Hon Haoli Huggins

HUGGINS, Hon (Martin) James; s of 1 Viscount Malvern, CH, KCMG, FRCS (d 1971); *b* 13 Jan 1928; *Educ* Hilton Coll, Natal; *Career* farmer; heir to Viscountcy of nephew, Ashley Kevin Godfrey Huggins, 3 Viscount Malvern; *Style* - The Hon James Huggins; The Craig, PO Highlands, Salisbury, Zimbabwe

HUGGINS, Hon Mrs (Jean Audrey); *née* Wigg; da of Baron Wigg, PC; *b* 1932; *m* 1955, Andrew Huggins; *Style* - The Hon Mrs Huggins; Bryn-y-Mot, Nant-y-Camar rd, Craig-y-Don, Llandudno

HUGGINS, Hon Michael Patrick John; s of 2 Viscount Malvern (d 1978); *b* 1946; *Style* - The Hon Michael Huggins; c/o PO Box AP 50, Salisbury Airport, Zimbabwe

HUGH SMITH, Andrew Colin; s of Lt-Cdr Colin Hugh Smith RN (ret) (d 1975); *b* 6 Sept 1931; *Educ* Ampleforth, Trin Cambridge; *m* 1964, Venetia, da Lt-Col P H Flower; 2 s; *Career* barr 1957, memb Stock Exchange 1970, sr ptnr Capel-Cure 1979; *Recreations* reading, shooting, fishing, gardening; *Clubs* Brooks's; *Style* - Andrew Hugh Smith Esq; The Old Rectory, Grendon Underwood, Aylesbury, Bucks (☎ Grendon Underwood 200)

HUGHES, Baron (Life Peer UK 1961); William Hughes; CBE (1965, OBE 1942), PC (1970), DL (Dundee 1960); s of Joseph Hughes; *b* 22 Jan 1911; *Educ* Balfour Street Public Sch Dundee, Dundee

Tech; *m* 1951, Christian Clacher, da of James Gordon; 2 da; *Career* chm E Kilbride Devpt Corpn 1975-; Pres Scottish Fedn Housing Assocs 1975-, Scottish Assoc Mental Health 1975-; memb Cncl Europe & W European Union 1976-; HM Lt Co of Dundee 1954-60, JP Dundee 1943-76; stood for Parl (L) E Perths 1945 & 1950; Jt-Parly Under-Sec State Scotland 1964-69, Min State Scotland 1969-70 & 1974-75; *Style* - The Rt Hon Lord Hughes CBE PC DL; Muircroft, Auchterarder, Perths (☎ 2646)

HUGHES, Brian Thomas; s of late Thomas Hughes; *b* 3 May 1937; *Educ* St Joseph's Coll, Glasgow U; *m* 1962, Maureen Duignan, nee Smyth; 3 s; *Career* dir and md Ranco Motors Ltd 1969-73, dir Star Hotels Ltd 1973-, Tedvox Ltd 1978-, Crusoe Hotels Ltd 1979-; *Recreations* golf, skiing; *Clubs* New Golf, St Andrews; *Style* - Brian Hughes Esq; 91 Market st; St Andrews (☎ 0334 74509)

HUGHES, Sir David Collingwood; 14 Bt (GB 1773), of East Bergholt, Suffolk; s of Sir Richard Edgar Hughes, 13 Bt (d 1970); *b* 29 Dec 1936; *Educ* Oundle, Magdalene Cambridge; *m* 1964, Rosemary Ann, MA, LLB, da of Rev John Pain, of Framfield Vicarage, Uckfield, Sussex; 4 s; *Heir* s, Thomas Hughes; *Career* heraldic sculptor, md Louis Lejeune Ltd 1978-; *Style* - Sir David Hughes, Bt; The Berristead, Wilburton, Ely, Cambs (☎ Ely 740770)

HUGHES, George; s of Peter Hughes; *b* 4 May 1937; *Educ* Liverpool Coll, Gonville & Caius Cambridge, Harvard Business Sch; *m* 1963, Janet; 2 s; *Career* banker Paris 1960; IBM London 1960-69 (strategy development man 1968-69), merchant banking London 1969-70; chm and ch exec Hughes Int Ltd 1970-, Willowbrook Worldwide Ltd 1971-, Castle Hughes Gp Ltd 1975-; *Recreations* cattle farming, historic buildings, shooting soccer, tennis, squash, racehorses (owner of 'Willowbrook World'), owner of BAC 1-11; *Clubs* Carlton; *Style* - George Hughes Esq; Château Beauchamps, Sarthe, France; Hampton Court Castle, Herefordshire

HUGHES, Hon Harri Cledwyn; s of Baron Cledwyn of Penrhos (Life Peer); *b* 16 March 1955; *Educ* Holyhead Comprehensive, Davies's Tutorial London, Hammersmith & W London Coll; *Career* surveyor; *Recreations* squash, sailing, golf, photography; *Clubs* London Welsh Assoc; *Style* - The Hon Harri Hughes; 15 Tamar House, Kennington Lane, SE11 (☎ 01 735 9300); Swynol Le, Ravenspoint rd, Trearddur, Holyhead, Gwynedd (☎ 0407 860 544)

HUGHES, Jessica, Lady; Jessica; da of late B C Broomhall, FRCS, BA; *m* 1967, as his 2 wife, Sir Richard Edgar Hughes, 13 Bt (d 1970); *Style* - Jessica, Lady Hughes; 233 Kennington Lane, SE11 5DF

HUGHES, Hon Janet Margaret; da of Baron Hughes, CBE, PC (Life Peer); *b* 1956; *Educ* Edinburgh U (BSc); *Style* - The Hon Janet Hughes

HUGHES, Hon Mrs (Rosemary Catherine); *née* Merriman; da of 1 Baron Merriman (d 1962); *b* 1908; *m* 1934, Humphrey Morgan Hughes (d 1965); 1 da; *Style* - The Hon Mrs Hughes; Lovers' Cottage, Chalvington, Hailsham, E Sussex

HUGHES, Thomas Collingwood; s and h of Sir David Collingwood Hughes, 14 Bt; *b* 16 Feb 1966; *Style* - Thomas Hughes Esq

HUGHES-MORGAN, Maj-Gen Sir David John; 3 Bt (UK 1925), of Penally, Pembroke; CBE (Mil 1973, MBE Mil 1959); s of Sir John Vernon Hughes-Morgan, 2 Bt (d 1969); *b* 11 Oct 1925; *Educ* RNC Dartmouth; *m* 1959, Isabel Jean Blacklock Gellatly Milne, da of John Milne Lindsay, of Annan, Dumfriesshire; 3 s; *Heir* s, Ian Hughes-Morgan; *Career* Lt RN (ret); Col Army Legal Servs, formerly Brig HQ UKLF, dir Army Legal Servs 1980- (formerly of BAOR Legal Servs); *Style* - Maj-Gen Sir David Hughes-Morgan, Bt, CBE; c/o Nat West Bank Ltd, Brecon

HUGHES-MORGAN, Ian Parry David; s and h of Maj-Gen Sir David Hughes-Morgan, 3 Bt, CBE; *b* 22 Feb 1960; *Style* - Ian Hughes-Morgan Esq

HUGHES-WAKE-WALKER, Lady

Anne; da of late 7 Earl Spencer, TD, and Lady Cynthia, nee Hamilton, DCVO, OBE, da of 3 Duke of Abercorn; *b* 1920; *m* 1944, Capt Christopher Baldwin Hughes-Wake-Walker, RN, s of late Adm Sir (William) Frederic Wake-Walker, KCB, CBE, gs of 1 Bt (cr 1856); has assumed additional surname of Hughes; *Career* sometime 3 Offr WRNS; *Style* - Lady Anne Hughes-Wake-Walker; East Bergholt Lodge, Suffolk

HUGHESDON, Charles Frederick; *b* 10 Dec 1909; *Educ* Raines G S; *m* 1937, Florence Elizabeth (known as Florence Desmond); 1 c; *Career* chm Stewart Smith Group of Companies and of Stewart Wrightson Group of Companies until retirement 1976, chm Tradewinds Helicopters Ltd, dir Tradewinds Airways Ltd, chm Charles Street Company, hon treasurer Royal Aeronautical Society; *Recreations* horse riding, shooting, water skiing, yachting; *Clubs* RAF, Royal Thames Yacht; *Style* - Charles Hughesdon Esq; Dunsborough Park, Ripley, Surrey (☎ Ripley 3366)

HUIZINGA, Mrs Jacob; Mary; da of Kenneth Cookson, OBE, and Vivienne (da of Lt-Col Walter Butler, 3 s of Sir Richard Butler, 9 Bt); *b* 10 May 1916; *m* 1, 1941 (m dis 1953), as his 2 w, John G S Churchill, *qv*; m 2, 1954, Jacob Herman Huizinga, s of late Prof Johan Huizinga, author of 'The Waning of the Middle Ages'; *Style* - Mrs Jacob Huizinga; 8 Lennox Gdns Mews, SW1 (☎ 01 589 3973)

HULBERT-POWELL, Hon Mrs (Philippa Catherine); *née* St Aubyn; da of late 3 Baron St Levan and Hon Clementina, nee Nicolson, da of 1 Baron Carnock, making Mrs Hulbert-Powell niece of late Harold Nicolson, the writer, and 1 cous of Nigel Nicolson the biographer; *b* 1922; *m* 1948, Evelyn Charles Lacy Hulbert-Powell, late Lt Queen's Roy Regt; 2 s, 3 da; *Style* - The Hon Mrs Hulbert-Powell; Old Place Farm, Mayfield, Sussex

HULL, Hon Mrs (Patricia Ann); da of Baron Carron (Life Peer, d 1969); *b* 1945; *m* 1970, Victor Albert Hull; children; *Style* - The Hon Mrs Hull; 16-18 Hatton Garden, EC1

HULSE, Edward Jeremy Westrow; s and h of Sir (Hamilton) Westrow Hulse, 9 Bt; *b* 22 Nov 1932; *Educ* Eton; *m* 1957, Verity Ann, da of William Pilkington, of Ivywell, Routes des Issues, St John, Jersey; 1 s, 1 da; *Career* late Capt Scots Gds, High Sheriff of Hants 1978; *Style* - Edward Hulse Esq; Flat 4, 30 Queens Gate gdns, SW7

HULSE, Richard Arthur Samuel; 2 s of Sir Westrow Hulse, 9 Bt; *b* 22 March 1936; *Educ* Eton; *m* 1963, Caroline Susan Joan, da of Sir George Tapps-Gervis Meyrick, 6 Bt, MC; 1 s (George Richard b 1967), 1 da (Frances Jacintha Caroline b 1968); *Career* 2 Lt Scots Guards Nat Serv in Germany, exec dir Robert Barrow Ltd 1980, dir Bain Dawes (Int) Ltd 1973-80, chm Willmead Ltd; *Recreations* gardening, backgammon, racing; *Clubs* White's; *Style* - Richard Hulse Esq; Sherfield Mill, Sherfield English, nr Romsey, Hampshire (☎ 0794 22536)

HULSE, Sir (Hamilton) Westrow; 9 Bt (GB 1739), of Lincoln's Inn Fields; s of Sir Hamilton John Hulse, 8 Bt (d 1931); *b* 20 June 1909; *Educ* Eton, Ch Ch Oxford; *m* 1, 1932 (m dis 1937), Philippa Mabel, da of late A J Taylor, of Strensham Court, Worcs; 2 s; m 2, 1938, Ambrosine Nellie Orr (d 1940), da of late Capt H S Orr Wilson, RHA, of Dunardagh, Blackrock, Co Dublin; m 3, 1945 (m dis 1954), Dorothy, da of late William Durrant, and widow of James A M Hamilton; m 4, 1954, Lucy Elizabeth Smitheyt, da of Col George Redesdale Brooker Spain, CMG, TD, FSA; *Heir* s, Edward Hulse; *Career* barr Inner Temple 1932, formerly Wing Cdr RAF Vol Reserve, served 1939-45 War (despatches); *Clubs* Carlton, Bath, Leander; *Style* - Sir Westrow Hulse, Bt; Breamore, Hants (☎ Breamore 270)

HULTON, Sir Geoffrey Alan; 4 Bt (UK 1905), JP (Lancs 1955), DL (Greater Manchester 1974); s of Sir Roger Braddyll Hulton, 3 Bt (d 1956), and Hon Marjorie Evelyn Louise (d 1970), da of late 6 Viscount Mountmorres; *b* 21 Jan 1920; *Educ* Marlborough; *m* 1945, Mary Patricia, da of P A de Vere Reynolds, of

Farnborough, Hants; *Heir* none; *Career* Capt RM (ret), Far East 1941-45 (prisoner), owner of Hulton Park Estate, JP Lancs, Ch Scouts Cmmr, Pres of Westhoughton Constituency Conservative Assocn, V-Pres Country Landowners' Assocn (Lancs), and Lancs Co Cricket Club; Kt Cdr of Order of St Gregory The Great, Kt of Order of Holy Sepulchre; *Clubs* Lansdowne, Royal Overseas League, Spanish, Victory; *Style* - Sir Geoffrey Hulton, Bt, JP, DL; The Cottage, Hulton Park, Over Hulton, Bolton BL5 1BH (☎ Bolton 651324)

HUME, Lady Catherine Mary Clementina; *née* Heathcote-Drummond-Willoughby; da of 2 Earl of Ancaster, GCVO, TD; *b* 25 Sept 1906; *m* 1, 1935 (m dis 1947), John St Maur Ramsden (assassinated in Malaya 1948), s of Sir John Ramsden, 6 Bt; 1 da; m 2, 1948, Charles Wedderburn Hume (d 1974); *Style* - Lady Catherine Hume; Hunting Ridge Farm, Charlottesville, Va 22901, USA

HUME-WILLIAMS, Lady; Frances Mary; da of Edmond Groom, OBE, of Norfolk; *m* 1949, as his 2 w, Sir Roy Hume-Williams, 2 & last Bt (d 1980); *Style* - Lady Hume-Williams; Ardlui, The Highlands, East Horsley, Surrey

HUMFREY, Lady Emma Mary Helener; *née* French; 3 da of 3 Earl of Ypres by his 1 w Maureen; *b* 8 Dec 1958; *Educ* private tutor; *m* 1980, Charles Geoffrey, da of Charles Michael Humfrey, of Alderney; *Recreations* racing, shooting; *Style* - Lady Emma Humfrey; 30 Prince of Wales Mansions, Prince of Wales Drive, SW11 (☎ 01 720 9083)

HUMPHERY-SMITH, Cecil Raymond Julian; s of Frederick Humphery-Smith, MBE (d 1979); *b* 29 Oct 1928; *Educ* St John's Hurstpierpoint, London U, Sch of Hygiene & Tropical Medicine Parma; *m* 1951, Alice Elizabeth Gwendoline, da of late Charles Thomas Cogle, formerly Ch Inspr of Mines Keyna Colony; 1 s, 4 da; *Career* Kt of Obedience, Sov Mil Order Malta 1968, man Consumer Serv Dept HJ Heinz Co 1955-60, consultant De Rica SpA 1961-72, md Achievements Ltd 1961-81, dir and trustee Inst of Heraldic and Genealogical Studies, ed 'Family History' 1961-; *Recreations* writing sonnets, walking, listening to good music; *Clubs* Challoner; *Style* - Cecil Humphery-Smith Esq; Alcroft Grange, Hackington, Canterbury, Kent (☎ 62038); Fazarga, Moita-Fatima, 2495 Portugal

HUMPHREYS, Hon Mrs Honor; *née* Byng; da of 10 Viscount Torrington (d 1961); *b* 1912; *m* 1937 (m dis 1951), Lisle Marles Humphreys; *Style* - The Hon Mrs Honor Humphreys; 26 Swan Court, SW7

HUMPHREYS, Lt-Col Robert Benjamin; DL (Co Durham 1969); s of John Humphreys, of Castle House, Usk; *b* 14 Nov 1914; *Educ* Aldenham, Sandhurst; *m* 1942, Lorna Egremont, da of Douglas Hann, of Cascade House, Penpedair; 1 s, 1 da; *Career* Lt-Col 1956, ret 1961; Regimental Sec Durham LI 1968-79; *Recreations* hunting, gardening, entomology; *Clubs* Army & Navy; *Style* - Lt-Col Robert Humphreys, DL; Peppermires Cottage, Brancepeth, Co Durham (☎ Durham 780389)

HUMPHRYS, Arthur Francis Walter; OBE (1959, MBE 1945); s of Lt-Col Sir Francis Henry Humphrys, GCMG, GCVO, KBE, CIE (d 1971); *b* 20 Oct 1909; *Educ* Winchester, Ch Ch Oxford; *m* 1942, Lady Eugénie Pamela, da of Field Marshal the Rt Hon the Earl Wavell, GCB, GCSI, GCIE, CMG, MC (d 1950); 2 s, 1 da; *Career* Maj The Central India Horse, Egypt, Lybia, Abyssinia, Italy, Macedonia; Lt-Col, mil sec to Viceroy of India; served Roy Dutch Shell Gp of Cos in London, India and Pakistan; *Clubs* Army and Navy; *Style* - Arthur Humphrys Esq, OBE; Marston Meysey Grange, nr Cricklade, Wilts (☎ Kempsford 239)

HUMPHRYS, Lady Eugénie Pamela; *née* Wavell; da of 1 Earl Wavell (d 1950); *b* 1918; *m* 1942, Arthur Humphrys, OBE, s of Lt-Col Sir Francis Humphrys, GCMG, GCVO, KBE, CIE; 2 s, 1 da; *Style* - Lady Eugénie Humphrys; Marston Meysey Grange, Cricklade, Wilts

HUNLOKE, Lady Katharine Victoria; *née* Montagu; da (by 1 m) of Alexander

Montagu (10 Earl of Sandwich, who disclaimed peerages for life 1964); *b* 1945; *Educ* Cranborne Chase Sch, London U (BA); *m* 1965, Nicholas Victor Hunloke, s of Lt-Col Henry Hunloke, KCVO, by 1 w, Lady Anne, MBE, nee Cavendish (da of 9 Duke of Devonshire, KG, GCMG, GCVO, TD, PC, and Lady Evelyn Fitzmaurice, GCVO, da of 5 Marquess of Lansdowne), who m as her 3 husband (m annulled 1965) Alexander Montagu (ante); 1 s, 2 da; *Style* - Lady Katharine Hunloke; 52 Walham grove, SW6

HUNT, Baron (Life Peer UK 1966); (Henry Cecil) John Hunt; KG (1979), CBE (1945), DSO (1944); s of Capt C Hunt, MC; *b* 22 June 1910; *Educ* Marlborough, Sandhurst; *m* 1936, Joy, da of Dr Mowbray-Green; 4 da (Sally, Susan, Prudence, Jennifer); *Career* kt 1953, Leader Br Expedition to Mt Everest 1952-53; served WW II KRRC in Asia, post-war as GSO, ALF Centl Europe, Planning Staff MELF, HQ (1) Br Corps, Staff Coll, Cdr 168 Inf Bde TA 1955-56; Rector Aberdeen U 1963-66; Pres RGS 1977-80; Pres Cncl Nat Parks 1980-; *Style* - The Rt Hon Lord Hunt KG CBE DSO; Highway Cottage, Aston, Henley-on-Thames, Oxon

HUNT OF FAWLEY, Baron (Life Peer UK 1973); John Henderson Hunt; CBE (1970); s of Edmund Hunt, MCh, FRCS; *b* 3 July 1905; *Educ* Charterhouse, Balliol Oxford; *m* 1941, Elisabeth, da of Norman Evill, FRIBA; 2 s, 2 da; *Career* FRCP, FRCS, FRCGP, Pres RCGP 1967-70; Princ MO Provident Mutual Life Assur Assoc 1947-; memb Cncl St Dunstan's; *Style* - The Rt Hon Lord Hunt of Fawley CBE; 26 Cadogan Place, SW1 (☎ 01 235 5566); 82 Sloane st, SW1 (☎ 01 245 9333)

HUNT OF TANWORTH, Baron (Life Peer UK 1980); John Joseph Benedict; GCB (1977, KCB 1973, CB 1968); s of Maj A L Hunt (d 1959); *b* 23 Oct 1919; *Educ* Downside, Magdalene Cambridge; *m* 1, 1941, Hon Magdalen Mary (d 1971), da of 1 Baron Robinson (d 1952); 2 s, 1 da; m 2, 1973, Madeleine Frances, da of Sir William Hume, CMG, FRCP, and widow of Sir John Charles, KCB, FRCP; *Career* Sec of the Cabinet 1973-79, chm Banque Nationale de Paris 1980-, Disaster Emergency Ctee 1981-, dir Prudential Corp 1980-, IBM UK 1980-, advsy dir Unilever 1980-; *Style* - The Rt Hon The Lord Hunt of Tanworth GCB; 8 Wool rd, Wimbledon, SW20 (☎ 01 947 7640)

HUNT, Hon Christopher Godfrey Evill; s of Baron Hunt of Fawley, CBE (Life Peer); *b* 1947; *Educ* London U (MA, MB, BS, MRCS Eng, LRCP, DObst, RCOG); *Style* - The Hon Christopher Hunt

HUNT, (Henry) Holman; s of Henry Hunt (d 1951); *b* 13 May 1924; *Educ* Queen's Park Sch Glasgow, Glasgow U; *m* 1954, Sonja, nee Blom; 1 s, 2 da; *Career* management consultant, md PA Computers and Telecommunications 1976-, bd dir PA Management Consultants 1970-, memb Monopolies and Mergers Cmmn 1980-, pres Inst of Management Consultants 1974-75; *Recreations* music, reading, walking, travel, photography, gardening; *Clubs* Caledonian; *Style* - Holman Hunt Esq; 28 The Ridings, Epsom, Surrey (☎ Epsom 20974)

HUNT, John Marshall; JP (1967); s of Frederick Hunt; *b* 11 Aug 1931; *Educ* Lincoln Sch; *m* 1957, Charmian Elizabeth, nee Corthorn; 2 s, 2 da; *Career* FICA 1953, sr ptnr in practice Lincoln, joined J Nicholson & Co 1947 and admitted as ptnr 1958; *Recreations* antiques collecting, walking, music; *Clubs* Rotary Club of Lincoln; *Style* - John Hunt Esq, JP; Narrawood House, 28 Sewell rd, Lincoln (☎ Lincoln 28909)

HUNT, Hon Jonathan Philip Henderson; s of Baron Hunt of Fawley, CBE, (Life Peer); *b* 1947; *Educ* Oxford (BM, BCh); *m* 1977, Monika, da of Dr Herbert Kuhlmann, of Schloss Urstein, Salzburg, Austria; *Style* - The Hon Jonathan Hunt

HUNT, Hon Michael Anthony; s of Baron Hunt of Tamworth, GCB, and Hon Magdalen, da of 1 Baron Robinson; *b* 1942; *m* 1963, Rosemary Ann, da of late Col Theodore Ernle Longridge, OBE; children; *Style* - The Hon Michael Hunt; 45 Haslemere av, W13

HUNT, Hon Martin John; s of Baron Hunt of Tamworth, GCB, and Hon Magdalen, da of 1 Baron Robinson; *b* 1962; *Style* - The Hon Martin Hunt

HUNT, Rear-Adm Nicholas John Streynsham; MVO (1961); s of Brig J M Hunt; *b* 7 Nov 1930; *Educ* RNC Dartmouth; *m* 1966, Meriel Givan; 2 s, 1 da; *Career* flag offr 2 Flotilla 1980-81, dir-gen Naval Manpower & T'ning 1981-; assist priv sec to late Princess Marina, Duchess of Kent; exec offr HMS Ark Royal 1969-71; *Clubs* Boodle's; *Style* - Rear-Adm Nicholas Hunt, MVO; c/o MOD, SW1

HUNT, Roger Baldwyn; s of Brig John Montgomerie Hunt (d 1980); *b* 4 April 1928; *Educ* Charterhouse, Lincoln Coll Oxford; *m* 1957, Harriet Jessie Minette, da of Lt Graham Shepard RNVR (ka 1943); 1 s, 1 da; *Career* 2 Lt The Rifle Bde (Palestine) 1947-48, Lloyd's underwriting agent, memb of Lloyd's 1955, dir Laurence Philipps & Co (Insurance) Ltd 1966, md Laurence Philipps Ltd 1969, chm Laurence Philipps (Agencies) Ltd 1969; *Recreations* gardening, photography; *Clubs* Boodle's, MCC; *Style* - Roger Hunt Esq; 4 Winchester Close, Kingston-upon-Thames, Surrey (☎ 01 546 4000)

HUNT, Richard Bruce; s of late Percy Thompson Hunt; *b* 15 Dec 1927; *Educ* Christ's Hospital; *m* 1972, Ulrike Dorothea, nee Schmidt; 2 da; *Career* shipbroker, fellow Inst of Chartered Shipbrokers 1955, md R B Hunt & Ptnrs Ltd 1966-, dir Baltic Exchange 1977-80, governor Christ's Hospital 1980-, liveryman Worshipful Co of Shipwrights 1980; *Recreations* golf, skiing; *Clubs* MCC, Royal Lymington Yacht, RAC, Royal Wimbledon Golf; *Style* - Richard Hunt Esq; Cotts House, Camomile Street, London EC3 (☎ 01 283 6911/1234)

HUNTER OF NEWINGTON, Baron (Life Peer UK 1978); Robert Brockie Hunter; MBE (1945); s of Robert Marshall Hunter, actuary, of Edinburgh; *b* 14 July 1915; *Educ* George Watson's Coll, Edinburgh U; *m* 1940, Kathleen, da of James Wilkie Douglas, Master Painter, of Perth; 3 s, 1 da; *Career* former Chm Govt Ind Sci Cttee on Smoking & Health, advsr to Imperial Tobacco 1981-; served WW II as Lt-Col RAMC NW Europe & Egypt; Prof Materia Medica, Pharmacology & Therapeutics St Andrews U 1948-67, Dundee U 1967-68; V-Chllr & Pncpl Birmingham U 1968-; kt 1977; *Recreations* fishing; *Clubs* Oriental; *Style* - Rt Hon Lord Hunter of Newington MBE; 3 Oakdene dve, Fiery Hill rd, Barnt Green, Birmingham

HUNTER, Alexander Dudgeon; s of Ellis Dudgeon Hunter, Monkscroft Dunbar (d 1964); *b* 5 Sept 1920; *Educ* Merchiston Castle Edinburgh, Heriot-Watt Edinburgh; *m* 1944, Iris Patricia, da of William G R Findlay, of Felbrigg Dunbar (d 1963); *Career* chm Incorporated Brewers Guild (Scottish Section) 1962-64; chm, md & Head Brewer Dudgeon & Co Ltd Dunbar 1964-72, Belhaven Brewery co Ltd 1972-; dir Belhaven Brewery Gp Ltd London-; *Recreations* swimming, gardening; *Clubs* Merchistonian, Scottish Wayfarars, Dunbar S & RFC; *Style* - Alexander Hunter Esq; Monkscroft, Dunbar, East Lothian

HUNTER, Hon Alan Marshall; s of Baron Hunter of Newington, MBE; *b* 1946; *m* 1971, Elizabeth Goodall; *Style* - The Hon Alan Hunter; 199 Baberton Mains Drive, Edinburgh 14

HUNTER, Hon Mrs (Gemma Louise); da of 2 Viscount Simon, CMG; *b* 1934; *m* 1956, Brian Hunter; 2 s; *Style* - The Hon Mrs Hunter; 66 Westfields av, SW13

HUNTER, Hon Ian Thorburn; s of Baron Hunter of Newington, MBE; *b* 1951; *m* 1974, Angela Hill; *Style* - The Hon Ian Hunter; 27 Affleck gdns, Monikie, by Dundee

HUNTER, Hon Lady - Hon Joan; *née* Adderley; da of 5 Baron Norton (d 1945); *b* 1889; *m* 1913, Maj-Gen Sir Alan John Hunter, KCVO, CB, CMG, DSO, MC (d 1942); 2 s, 2 da; *Style* - The Hon Lady Hunter; The Bell House, Little Tew, Oxon

HUNTER, Dame Pamela; DBE (1981); honoured for political and public service in Northern area; *Style* - Dame Pamela Hunter, DBE

HUNTER, Hon Robert Douglas; s of Baron Hunter of Newington MBE; *b* 1945; *m* 1969, Marion Mckenzie; *Style* - The Hon Robert Hunter; 43 Edgbaston Pk rd, Edgbaston, Birmingham B15 2RS

HUNTER BLAIR, Edward Thomas; s and h of Sir James Hunter Blair, 7 Bt; *b* 15 Dec 1920; *Educ* Eton, Balliol Oxford; *m* 1956, Norma (d 1972), da of W S Harris; *Career* 1939-45 War with KOYLI, memb Kirkcudbright Co Council 1970-; *Style* - Edward Hunter Blair Esq; Parton House, Castle Douglas, Kirkcudbrightshire

HUNTER BLAIR, Sir James; 7 Bt (GB 1786), of Dunskey; s of Capt Sir Edward Hunter Blair, 6 Bt, RN (d 1945); *b* 7 May 1889; *Educ* Wellington, Balliol Oxford, Christ's Coll Cambridge; *m* 1, 1917, Jean Galloway (d 1953), da of Thomas Walker McIntyre, Sorn Castle, Ayrshire; 3 s (1 ka); m 2, 1954, Mrs Ethel Norah Collins (d 1966); *Heir* s, Edward Thomas Hunter Blair; *Career* served with Seaforth Highlanders WW I; district officer Forestry Commission 1920-28, forestry and farming Blairquhan 1928-; *Recreations* collecting pictures, bridge; *Clubs* Oxford & Cambridge, New (Edinburgh); *Style* - Sir James Hunter Blair, Bt; Milton, Maybole, Ayrshire (☎ Straiton 207)

HUNTER GORDON, John Hugh; s of late Major P Hunter Gordon, MC, DL; *b* 7 June 1942; *Educ* Cargilfield Sch, Eton, St Andrews U, U of Geneva; *m* 1966, Jillian Margaret, nee Fox-Carlyon; 3 children; *Career* md Ferranti Offshore Systems Ltd 1974, TRW-Ferranti Subsea Ltd 1977, dir Cairngorm Chairlift Co Ltd 1966; *Clubs* Highland; *Style* - John Hunter Gordon Esq; Highfield House, Kirknewton, Midlothian (☎ Mid-Calder 881489)

HUNTING, (Lindsay) Clive; s of Wing Commander Gerald Lindsay Hunting (d 1966); *b* 22 Dec 1925; *Educ* Loretto; Trin Hall Cambridge; *m* 1952, Shelagh nee Hill-Lowe; 1 s, 1 da; *Career* RN 1944-47; chm Air League 1968-71; pres Air Educ'n and Recreation Organisation 1970-; chm Hunting Gp 1975- (inc Hunting Gibson, Hunting Assoc Industs, Hunting Petroleum Servs & subsids) *Recreations* yachting (owner 'Fulmer Swift III'); *Clubs* Roy Yacht Sqdn; Roy London Yacht; City Livery; *Style* - Clive Hunting Esq; 14 Conduit Mews, W2 (☎ 01 402 7914);

HUNTINGDON, 15 Earl of (E 1529); Francis John Clarence Westenra Plantagenet Hastings; s of 14 Earl of Huntingdon (d 1939, ggs of 11 Earl, who in 1819 succeeded in establishing his right to the Earldom, after thirty years of dormancy from the 10 Earl's death; the 10 Earl, whose mother, Selina Countess of Huntingdon, helped found the Methodists, was sixth cous of 11 Earl; the Baronies of Botreaux, Hungerford, Moleyns, Hastings (of Hastings), and Hastings (of Hungerford) devolved on the 10 Earl's sis; both 10 & 11 Earls were seventh in descent from Katherine Pole, ggda of Edward IV's bro George Duke of Clarence, drowned in a butt of Malmsey); *b* 30 Jan 1901; *Educ* Eton, Ch Ch Oxford; *m* 1, 1925 (m dis 1943), as her 1 husb (*see* Lord Milford), Cristina (d 1953), da of Marchese Casati by his 1 w, the celebrated Marchesa of Augustus John's portrait; 1 da (Lady Moorea Black); m 2, 1944, Margaret, JP, da of Harry Lane, of Vernham Dean, Andover, and formerly w of Bryan Wallace; 2 da (Lady Selina Hastings and Lady Caroline Shackleton, *qqv*); *Heir* 1 cous, Lt-Col Robin Hastings, DSO*, OBE, MC; *Career* artist (studied under the Mexican social realist painter Diego Rivera); Prof Camberwell Sch Arts & Crafts 1938, Central 1950; served WW II ARP; Jt Parly Sec Min Ag & Fish 1945-50; *Style* - The Rt Hon Earl of Huntingdon; Blackbridge House, Beaulieu, Hants (☎ 612305)

HUNTINGDON, Countess of; Margaret; da of late H G Lane; *b* 23 June 1907; *Educ* St Stephen's Folkstone, St Hugh's Coll Oxford; *m* 1, 1934, Bryan, s of Edgar Wallace (m dis 1939); m 2, 1944, 15 Earl of Huntingdon; 2 da; *Career* novelist, biographer, journalist; *Style* - The Rt Hon the Countess of Huntingdon; Blackbridge House, Beaulieu, Hants

HUNTINGFIELD, 6 Baron (I 1796); Sir Gerard Charles Arcedeckne Vanneck; 7 Bt (GB 1751); s of 5 Baron (d 1969) by his 1 w Margaret; bro of Hon Sir Peter Vanneck (Ld Mayor of London 1978-79); *b* 29 May 1915; *Educ* Stowe, Trin Cambridge; *m* 1941, Janetta, da of Capt Reginald Errington, RN (ret), and Cecilia (gda of 4 Earl of Dartmouth); 1 s, 2 da (and 1 da decd); *Heir* s, Hon Joshua Vanneck; *Career* served WW II Fl Sgt RAFVR; UN Secretariat 1946-75; *Style* - The Rt Hon Lord Huntingfield; 34 Rue Gambetta, 1815 Clarens, Switzerland

HUNTINGFORD, Donald Roy; s of Roy Huntingford (d 1951); *b* 3 June 1920; *m* 1945, Joan, da of Frederick George Wingrove; 3 children; *Career* chartered accountant with Clark Pixley; *Style* - Donald Huntingford Esq; c/o Barclays Bank Ltd, Chingford, E 4

HUNTINGTON-WHITELEY, Sir Hugo Baldwin; 3 Bt (UK 1918), of Grimley, Worcester, DL (Worcs 1972); s of Capt Sir Maurice Huntington-Whiteley, 2 Bt, RN (d 1975), and Lady (Pamela) Margaret (d 1976), da of 1 Earl Baldwin of Bewdley, KG, PC; through his paternal gf (the 1 Bt) Sir Hugo is 2 cous of Lord (3 Baron) Marchamley; *b* 31 March 1924; *Educ* Eton; *m* 1959, Jean Marie Ramsay (JP 1973); 2 da; *Heir* bro, (John) Miles Huntington-Whiteley; *Career* partner Price Waterhouse & Co, Chartered Accountants, RN 1942-47, High Sheriff Worcs 1971; FCA; *Clubs* Brooks's; *Style* - Sir Hugo Huntington-Whiteley, Bt, DL; Ripple Hall, Tewkesbury, Glos (☎ Upton-on-Severn 2431)

HUNTINGTON-WHITELEY, (John) Miles; VRD and Clasp; s of Capt Sir Maurice Huntington-Whiteley, 2 Bt, RN, and hp of bro, Sir Hugo Huntington-Whiteley, 3 Bt; *b* 18 July 1929; *Educ* Eton, Trin Cambridge; *m* 1960, HIllH Countess Victoria Adelheid Clementine Louise, da of late HIllH Count Friedrich Wolfgang zu Castell-Rüdenhausen (ka 1940), himself n of HSH Casimir, 2 Prince of Castell-Rüdenhausen (cr of Prince Regent Luitpold of Bavaria 1901) & Count of Castell (HRE cr of 1205, the independent County being absorbed by Bavaria 1810, though sovereign rank of Counts recognised by German Diet 1829); Mrs Miles H-W's mother was HH Princess Caroline Mathilde, herself da of 2 Duke of Albany (as he was until his Br titles were removed 1919), whose f was Queen Victoria's 4 s; Mrs H-W is therefore 3 cous of HM The Queen; 1 s (Leopold Maurice b 1965), 2 da (Alice Louise Esther Margot b 1961, Beatrice Irene Helen Victoria b 1962); all three children are 4 cous of HRH The Prince of Wales & his siblings; *Career* Lt-Cdr RNR; *Style* - Miles Huntington-Whiteley Esq, VRD and Clasp; Farnborough Grange, Farnborough, Banbury, Oxon

HUNTLY, 12 Marquess of (S 1599); Douglas Charles Lindsey Gordon; Premier Marquess of Scotland; also Earl of Aboyne, Lord Gordon of Strathavon and Glenlivet (both S 1660), and Baron Meldrum of Morven (UK 1815); s of Lt-Col Douglas Gordon, CVO, DSO (himself s of Lord Granville Gordon , and gs of the 10 Marquess (whose own f, the 9 Marquess, died a nonagerian, having - during a long life in the ball room - danced with Marie Antoinette (who particularly admired his Highland Fling), Princess Charlotte and Queen Victoria; Sir William Fraser imputed to him as acute an interest in the suppers as in the dancing, since he was very poor); suc great unc, 11 Marquess, 1937; *b* 3 Feb 1908; *m* 1, 1941 (m dis 1965), Hon Pamela Berry, da of 1 Viscount Kemsley; 1 s, 1 da; m 2, 1977, Elizabeth, da of Lt-Cdr F Leigh, RD, RNR; *Heir* s, Earl of Aboyne; *Career* late Lt Gordon Highlanders (TA); *Style* - The Most Hon The Marquess of Huntly; Aboyne Castle, Aberdeenshire; Hollybrook, Ewhurst rd, Cranleigh, Surrey (☎ 71500)

HUNTLY, Pamela, Marchioness of; Hon (Mary) Pamela; *née* Berry; da of 1 Viscount Kemsley, GBE (d 1968); *b* 1918; *m* 1941 (m dis 1965), 12 Marquess of Huntly; 1 s (Earl of Aboyne), 1 da (Lady Lemina Lawson-Johnston); *Style* - Pamela, Marchioness of Huntly; 34 Groom Place, SW1 (☎ 01 235 5952)

HURD, Hon Douglas Richard; CBE (1974), MP (C) Mid Oxon 1974-; s of Baron Hurd (Life Peer d 1966); *b* 1930;

Educ Eton, Trin Cambridge; *m* 1960, Tatiana Elizabeth Michelle, da of A C Benedict Eyre, of West Burton House, Bury, Sussex; 3 s; *Career* Diplomatic Serv 1952-66, Priv Sec to Leader of Opposition 1968-70, Political Sec to PM 1970-74, Min of State FCO 1979-; *Clubs* Travellers'; *Style* - The Hon Douglas Hurd, CBE, MP; 2 Mitford Cottages, Westwell, Burford, Oxon

HURD, Hon Stephen Anthony; s of Baron Hurd (Life Peer d 1966); *b* 1933; *Educ* Winchester, Magdalene Cambridge; *m* 1973, Pepita, da of Lt-Col Walter Hingston, of The Old Vicarage, Ramsbury, Marlborough; *Style* - The Hon Stephen Hurd; Browns Farm, Marlborough, Wilts

HURD, Baroness; Stephanie Frances; da of Edred M Corner, FRCS; *m* 1928, Baron Hurd (Life Peer d 1966); 2 s (Hon Douglas Hurd, MP, Min State FCO; Hon Stephen Hurd); *Style* - The Rt Hon the Lady Hurd; The Old Oxyard, Oare, Marlborough, Wilts

HURST, Lady Barbara; *née* Lindsay; da of late 27 Earl of Crawford and 10 of Balcarres, KT, PC and Constance, da of Sir Henry Carstairs Pelly, 3 Bt, MP; *b* 1915; *m* 1939, Col Richard Lumley Hurst, Roy Sussex Regt TA, barr (d 1962), s of Sir Cecil James Barrington Hurst, GCMG, KCB; 1 s, 3 da; *Style* - Lady Barbara Hurst; Porters Farm, Rusper, Horsham, Sussex

HURST, John George; s of John G Hurst (d 1972); *b* 15 Mar 1926; *Educ* Steyning G S, Steyning Sussex; *m* 1954, Angela Mary Ellen, da of Claude James Marshall; 4 s; *Career* dir Spencer Gears Hldgs Ltd, md Southern Industries Coolers Ltd, chm Spencer Gears Ltd; *Recreations* golf, tennis, equestrian activity, swimming; *Clubs* Cavalry Guards, Institute of Dirs; *Style* - John Hurst Esq; Bullseye Cottage, Heathfield, E Sussex (☎ 04352 3541; 01 686 4651)

HUSKINSON, (George) Nicholas (Nevil); s of Thomas Leonard Bousfield Huskinson (d 1974) of Triscombe House, Taunton, Somerset; *b* 7 Dec 1948; *Educ* Eton, King's Cambridge; *m* 1972, Pennant Elfrida Lascelles, da of Thomas Lascelles Isa Shandon Valiant Iremonger of Cheyne Row, Chelsea; 1 s; *Career* barr Gray's Inn; *Recreations* wine and food, antique collecting, cooking; *Style* - Nicholas Huskinson Esq; The Giant's House, Newbourn, Woodbridge, Suffolk (☎ Waldringfield 641); 314 South Lambeth rd, Stockwell, London SW8 (☎ 01 622 6006)

HUSS, Lawrence John; s of Laurence Leslie Huss; *b* 16 March 1926; *Educ* H S Stirling; U of Glasgow; *m* 1952, Rita, nee Chaplin; 2 children *Career* Flying Offr RAF UK and Germany; dir and gen man Appleby Slag Co Ltd, Appleby Calumite Ltd, Frodingham Cement Co Ltd, dir Calumite SA, Luxembourg, 1968-; *Recreations* golf, fishing; *Style* - Lawrence Huss Esq; Dunluce, 26 Town Hill Broughton, Brigg, S Humberside DN20 OHO (☎ Brigg 53424)

HUSSEY, Marmaduke James; s of E R J Hussey, CMG (d 1958); *b* 29 Aug 1923; *Educ* Rugby Sch, Trin Oxford; *m* 1959, Lady Susan Katharine, da of Earl Waldegrave, KG, GCVO; *Career* Lt Gren Gds 1939-45; joined Associated Newspapers 1949, director 1964; md Harmsworth Pulications 1967-70; md and ch exec Times Newspapers Ltd 1970, joined Thomson Organisation Exec Bd 1971; a Rhodes Trustee 1972-; *Clubs* Brooks's; *Style* - Marmaduke Hussey Esq; Waldegrave House, Chewton Mendip, nr Bath, Somerset; 86 Chelsea Park gdns, London SW3 (☎ 01 352 1042)

HUSSEY, Lady Susan Katharine; *née* Waldegrave; CVO (1971); da of 12 Earl Waldegrave and sis of Hon William Waldegrave, MP; *b* 1 May 1939; *m* 1959, 'Duke' (Marmaduke) Hussey (V-Chm Times Newspapers Hldgs); 1 s (James Arthur, Page of Honour to HM The Queen 1975-76), 1 da; *Career* Woman of the Bedchamber to HM 1960-80 and Lady in Waiting to HM 1980- (Lady Susan's aunt by marriage 9 generations back being Sarah Churchill, Lady of the Bedchamber to Princess, later Queen, Anne); *Style* - Lady Susan Hussey; 86 Chelsea Park gdns, SW3 (☎ 01 352 1042)

HUSTON, Hon Mrs (Margot Lavinia); da of 6 Marq of Cholmondeley, GCVO, MC; *b* 1950; *m* 1978, (Walter) Anthony Huston (s of John Huston, film dir); 1 s; *Style* - The Hon Mrs Huston; Las Caletas, Puerto, Vallarta, Mexico

HUTCHINSON OF LULLINGTON, Baron (Life Peer UK 1978); Jeremy Nicholas Hutchinson; QC (1961); s of St John Hutchinson, QC; *b* 28 March 1915; *Educ* Stowe, Magdalen Oxford; *m* 1, 1940, Dame Peggy Ashcroft, DBE, the actress (m dis 1966); 1 s, 1 da; m 2, 1966, June Osborn; *Career* barr 1939, Recorder Bath 1962-72, Crown Court 1972-76; V-Chm Arts Cncl 1977-79, Chm Tstees Tate Gallery 1980- (Tstee 1977-); served WW II RNVR; *Style* - The Rt Hon Lord Hutchinson of Lullington, QC; 10 Blenheim rd, NW8 (☎ 01 624 4363); Queen Elizabeth Bldg, Temple, EC4 (☎ 01 583 9744)

HUTCHINSON, Hon Mrs Georgiana Ann; da of late 5 Baron Crofton; *b* 1955; *m* Brent Hutchinson; 1 da; *Style* - The Hon Mrs Hutchinson

HUTCHINSON, Hon Nicholas St John; s of Baron Hutchinson of Lullington, QC (Life Peer); *b* 1946; *Style* - The Hon Nicholas Hutchinson

HUTCHISON, James Colville; s and h of Sir Peter Craft Hutchison, 2 Bt; *b* 7 Oct 1967; *Style* - James Hutchison Esq

HUTCHISON, Sir Peter; 2 Bt (UK 1939), of Thurle, Streatley, Co Berks; s of Sir Robert Hutchison, MD (d 1960); *b* 27 Sept 1907; *Educ* Marlborough, Lincoln Coll Oxford; *m* 1949, Mary-Grace, da of the late Very Rev Algernon Giles Seymour; 2 s, 2 da; *Heir* s, Robert Hutchison; *Career* slr 1933, dep-clerk of the Peace and CC E Suffolk 1947-71, clerk of the Peace 1971; *Style* - Sir Peter Hutchison, Bt; Melton Mead, nr Woodbridge, Suffolk (☎ Woodbridge 2746)

HUTCHISON, Sir Peter Craft; 2 Bt (UK 1956), of Rossie, Co Perth; s of Sir James Riley Holt Hutchison, 1 Bt, DSO, TD (d 1979); *b* 5 June 1935; *Educ* Eton, Magdalene Cambridge; *m* 1966, Virginia, da of John Miller Colville, of Gribloch, Kippen, Stirlingshire; 1 s; *Heir* s, James Hutchison; *Career* Lt late Roy Scots Greys, dir Hutchsion & Craft Ltd, Insurance Brokers, Glasgow; *Style* - Sir Peter Hutchison, Bt; Milton House, Milton, by Dumbarton

HUTCHISON, Robert; s and h of Sir Peter Hutchsion, 2 Bt, of Thurle, Streatley, Co Berks; *b* 25 May 1954; *Style* - Robert Hutchison Esq

HUTCHISON, Winefryde, Lady; Winefryde Eleanor Mary; da of late Rev R H Craft; *m* 1928, Sir James Riley Holt Hutchison, 1 Bt, DSO, TD (d 1979); *Style* - Winefryde, Lady Hutchison; Rossie, Forgandenny, Perthshire; 32 Moore st, SW3

HUTTON, Hon Mrs (Jacqueline Patricia); *née* Grant of Grant; da (by 1 m) of 5 Baron Strathspey; *b* 1942; *m* 1966, Malcolm Usheen Lingen Hutton; *Style* - The Hon Mrs Hutton; Kinsley, Banchory, Kincardineshire

HYDE, Lord; George Edward Laurence Villiers; s and h of 7 Earl of Clarendon; *b* 12 Feb 1976; *Style* - Lord Hyde

HYDE-THOMSON, Paul Cater; s of Robert Hyde Hyde-Thomson (d 1970); *b* 17 Mar 1927; *Educ* Harrow, Ch Ch Oxford; *m* 1950, Zoë Caroline Georgia, da of Robin Regis d'Erlanger, MC (d 1934); 1 s, 4 da; *Career* Capt Roy Green Jackets; chm Ibstock Johnson Ltd; dir McKechnie Bros Ltd, William Mass Gp Ltd, Eucalyptus Pulp Mills Ltd, Cedar Investment Trust Ltd, FCA; High Sheriff Leics 1965, Leics County Council 1961-70; *Recreations* music, travel; *Clubs* Bath; *Style* - Paul Hyde-Thomson Esq; 46 Belgrave Mews North, SW1 (☎ 01 235 3144); The Stable House, North Kilworth, Lutterworth, Leics (☎ Market Harborough 880581)

HYLAND, James Bernard; s of David Bernard Hyland (d 1958); *b* 12 July 1935; *Educ* Presentation College Cork; National U of Ireland; U of Chicago; Inst of Chartered Accountants; *m* 1962, Eileen

Kiernan; 3 s, 2 da; *Career* gp man dir Youghal Carpets (Holdings) Ltd 1978-; dep gp ch exec Golden Vale Gp, Ireland; *Recreations* golf, reading, swimming, walking; *Clubs* United Services, Dublin, Fitzwilliam Ltd, Dublin, Cork County; *Style* - James Hyland Esq; Redclyffe, St Francis av, College rd, Cork, Ireland (☎ 021 45474)

HYLTON, 5 Baron (UK 1866); Sir Raymond Hervey Jolliffe; 5 Bt (UK 1821), DL (Somerset 1975); s of Lt-Col 4 Baron Hylton (d 1967, whose mother was Lady Alice Hervey, da of 3 Marquess of Bristol) and Lady Perdita Asquith (sis of 2 Earl of Oxford and Asquith and gda of 1 Earl, better known as HH Asquith, the Lib PM, by his 1 w Helen); *b* 13 June 1932; *Educ* Eton, Trin Oxford; *m* 1966, Joanna, da of Andrew de Bertodano, himself eldest s of 8 Marquès de Moral (cr by King Charles III of Spain 1765), by Andrew's w Lady Sylvia Savile (3 da of 6 Earl of Mexborough, JP, DL, and sis of Lady Agnes Eyston and Lady Beatrice Scrope); 4 s, 1 da; *Heir* s, Hon William Jolliffe; *Career* Lt Coldstream Gds Reserve; ARICS; Assist Priv Sec to Gov-Gen Canada 1960-62; chm Housing Assoc Charitable Tst, Help the Aged Housing Tst; Pres SW Regn Nat Soc Mentally Handicapped Children; *Style* - The Rt Hon Lord Hylton DL; Ammerdown, Radstock, Bath

HYLTON, Dowager Baroness; Lady Perdita Rose Mary; *née* Asquith; da of late Raymond Asquith (s of 1 Earl of Oxford and Asquith) and sis of 2 Earl; *b* 1910; *m* 1931, 4 Baron Hylton (d 1967); 2 s (5 Baron, Hon John Jolliffe), 1 da (Hon Mrs Windsor-Clive); *Style* - The Rt Hon Dowager Lady Hylton; Ammerdown, Radstock, Bath

HYLTON-FOSTER, Baroness (Life Peeress UK 1965); Hon Audrey Pellew; *née* Brown; da of 1 and last Viscount Ruffside, PC, DL (d 1958); *b* 19 May 1908; *Educ* St George's Ascot; *m* 1931, Rt Hon Sir Harry Hylton-Foster, QC, MP, Speaker House of Commons 1959-65 (d 1965); *Career* Pres & Chm London Red Cross 1960-; Convenor Cross Bench Peers 1974-; *Recreations* trout fishing, gardening; *Style* - The Rt Hon Lady Hylton-Foster; 54 Cranmer Court, Whitehead Grove, SW3 (☎ 01 584 2389); The Coach House, Tanhurst, Leith Hill, Holmbury St Mary, Dorking, Surrey (☎ 711975)

HYMAN, Hon Mrs (Laura Alice); *née* Boyd; da of 6 Baron Kilmarnock, MBE (d 1975); *b* 1934; *m* 1962, Anthony Hyman; *Style* - The Hon Mrs Hyman; 38a Downshire Hill, Hampstead, NW3

I

IDDESLEIGH, 4 Earl of (UK 1885); Sir Stafford Henry Northcote; 11 Bt (E 1641), DL (Devon 1979); also Viscount St Cyres (UK 1885); s of 3 Earl of Iddesleigh (d 1970, gs of 1 Earl, better known as Sir Stafford Northcote, who managed the remarkable feat of being a confidant of Gladstone in his youth and of Disraeli in maturity; described by Lord Dufferin in 1883 as a 'mixture of the Treasury Clerk, Sir Roger de Coverley, and the pantaloon on the pantomime stage', while Lord Wolseley said (1890) 'He would have made an admirable chief clerk in a bank'; portrayed by Trollope in 'The Three Clerks' as Sir Warwick Westend); bro of late Lady Lunn (w of Sir Arnold Lunn, the skier); *b* 14 July 1932; *Educ* Downside; *m* 1955, Mima (Maria Luisa) Alvarez-Builla y Urquijo, Condesa del Real Agrado (Sp 1771), da of Don Gonzalo Alvarez-Builla y Alvera and Maria Luisa, Viscountess Exmouth; 1 s, 1 da; *Heir* s, Viscount St Cyres; *Career* late 2 Lt Irish Gds; Kt Honour & Devotion Sov Mil Order Malta; *Clubs* Army & Navy; *Style* - The Rt Hon Earl of Iddesleigh, DL; Shillands House, Upton Pyne, Exeter, Devon (☎ 58916)

IDDESLEIGH, Dowager Countess of; Elizabeth; da of late Frederic Sawrey Archibald Lowndes, of 9 Barton st, Westminster, SW1; *m* 1930, 3 Earl of Iddesleigh (d 1970); 2 s (4 Earl, Hon

Edward Northcote), 2 da (Lady Catherine Northcote; Lady Hilda Swan, w of York Herald); *Style* - The Rt Hon the Dowager Countess of Iddesleigh; Pynes, Exeter EX5 5EF

IKERRIN, Viscount; David James Theobald Somerset Butler; s and h of 9 Earl of Carrick; *b* 9 Jan 1953; *Educ* Downside; *m* 1975, Philippa, da of Wing Cdr L V Craxton, RAF (ret); 3 s; *Style* - Viscount Ikerrin

ILCHESTER, 9 Earl of (GB 1756); Maurice Vivian de Touffreville Fox-Strangways; also Lord Ilchester, Baron of Woodford Strangways (GB 1741), Lord Ilchester and Stavordale, Baron of Redlynch (GB 1747); s of 8 Earl of Ilchester (d 1970, s of the noted music critic Arthur Fox-Strangways, translator of the songs of Brahms, Liszt, Wolf and Richard Strauss; Arthur was ggs of Rev Hon Charles Fox-Strangways, 3 s of 1 Earl, whose f, according to Lord Egmont in his Diary for 1742, had been a footman, valet to the Earl of Northumberland to be precise; Lord Egmont said that Lord Ilchester purchased his Barony of the Countess of Yarmouth, who combined towards George II the roles *vis à vis* Lloyd George of Frances Stevenson and Maundy Gregory; the 1 Earl was unc of Charles James Fox and great unc of the Lord Holland whose homonymous House gave its name to the 'set' of which Byron was for a while the darling; from 1889 Holland House reverted to the Earls of Ilchester before being bombed in WW II; it is now a Youth Hostel); *b* 1 April 1920; *Educ* Kingsbridge Sch; *m* 1941, Diana, da of George Simpson; *Heir* bro, Hon Raymond Fox-Strangways; *Career* served RAF 1936-76; chartered engr; *Recreations* outdoor activities, the arts; *Clubs* Brooks's, RAF; *Style* - The Rt Hon Earl of Ilchester; Farley Mill, Westerham, Kent

ILIFFE, 2 Baron (UK 1933); Edward Langton Iliffe; s of 1 Baron Iliffe, GBE (d 1960); *b* 25 Jan 1908; *Educ* Sherborne, Clare Coll Cambridge; *m* 1938, Renée, da of R Merandon du Plessis, of Mauritius; *Heir* n, Robert Iliffe; *Career* 1939-45 War with RAFVR (despatches), Vice-Chm Birmingham Post and Mail Ltd 1957-74, dir Coventry Evening Telegraph and of the Cambridge News, Trustee Shakespeare's Birthplace, High Sheriff Berks 1957, Hon Freeman City of Coventry; *Clubs* Brooks's, Carlton, Royal Yacht Squadron; *Style* - The Rt Hon the Lord Iliffe; 38 St James's Place, SW1 (☎ 01 493 1938); The Manor House, Yattendon, nr Newbury, Berks (☎ Hermitage 201579)

ILIFFE, Robert Peter Richard; s of Hon William Henry Richard Iliffe (d 1959 - yr s of late 1 Baron Iliffe, GBE, & hp of unc, 2 Baron; *b* 22 Nov 1944; *Educ* Eton, Ch Ch Oxford; *m* 1966, Rosemary Anne, da of Cdr Arthur Grey Skipwith, RN; 3 s, 1 da; *Career* chm The Birmingham Post & Mail Ltd 1978-, West Midlands Press Ltd, Coventry Newspapers Ltd, British Transfer Printing Co Ltd, Cambridge Newspapers Ltd, dir T Dillon & Co Ltd, Birmingham Boat Shows Ltd, memb Council Roy Agric Soc of England; *Style* - Robert Iliffe Esq; The Old Rectory, Ashow, Kenilworth, Warwickshire CV8 2LE

ILIFFE, Hon Mrs William - Christine Marie; da of Alfred Baton Baker, MD, of Hastings, Sussex; *m* 1940, the Hon William Henry Richard Iliffe (d 1959); 2 s; *Style* - The Hon Mrs William Iliffe; Croftdown, Aldworth, Reading, Berks

ILLINGWORTH, Hon Mrs (Katherine Elliott); da of Baron Foot (Life Peer); *b* 1937; *m* 1, 1955 David Stavely Gordon; children; m 2, David Illingworth (d 1976); children; *Style* - The Hon Mrs Illingworth

ILLINGWORTH, Lady Margaret Cynthia; *née* Lindsay; ARRC; da of late 27 Earl of Crawford and 10 of Balcarres, KT, PC and Constance, da of Sir Henry Carstairs Pelly, MP, 3 Bt; *b* 1902; *m* 1928, Lt-Col Henry Cyril Harker Illingworth, MC, JP, King's Roy Rifle Corps (Offr of Order of Crown of Roumania), (d 1979); *Style* - Lady Margaret Illingworth; Headon Lodge, Brompton-by-Sawdon, Scarborough, Yorks

ILLINGWORTH, Baroness; Margaret Mary Clare; ARRC; da of late William Basil Wilberforce, of Markington Hall, nr Harrogate, Yorks; *m* 1931, as his 2 wife, 1

and last Baron Illingworth (d 1942); *Career* Cmdt VAD; *Style* - The Rt Hon the Lady Illingworth; c/o National Provincial Bank, 12 Mount st, W1

IMBERT-TERRY, Sir Andrew Henry Bouhier; 4 Bt (UK 1917); s of Major Sir Edward Henry Bouhier Imbert-Terry, 3 Bt, MC (d 1978); *b* 5 Oct 1945; *Educ* Eton; *m* 1, 1972 (m dis 1974), Sarah Margaret, da of William Elwyn Francis Evans, MRCS, LRCP; m 2, 1979, Georgina Anne, da of Major Gerald Massie-Taylor, of Limassol, Cyprus; *Heir* bro, Michael Edward Stanley Imbert-Terry; *Career* formerly Capt Life Guards; *Style* - Sir Andrew Imbert-Terry, Bt; Mead Meadow House, nr Chobham, Surrey

IMBERT-TERRY, Dowager Lady; Jean; JP (1973); da of late Arthur Stanley Garton, of Danesfield, Marlow, Bucks; *m* 1944, Major Sir Edward Henry Bouhier Imbert-Terry, 3 Bt, MC (d 1978); *Style* - Dowager Lady Imbert-Terry, JP; Mead Meadow House, Chobham, Surrey

IMBERT-TERRY, Michael Edward Stanley; s of Major Sir Edward Henry Bouhier Imbert-Terry, MC, 3 Bt, and hp of bro, Sir Andrew Imbert-Terry, 4 Bt; *b* 18 April 1950; *Educ* Cranleigh; *m* 1975, Frances Dorothy, da of Peter Scott, of Ealing, W5; *Style* - Michael Imbert-Terry Esq; Little Henowe, St Ewe, Mevagissey, Cornwall

IMPEY, John Edward; s of Capt L A Impey; *b* 4 March 1931; *Educ* Eton; *m* 1959, Patricia, nee Creery; 1 s, 2 da; *Career* Coldstream Guards (Nat Serv Cmmn), memb Inst of Chartered Accountants of Scotland, dir County Bank Ltd (Merchant Bankers) 1967-79, v-chm Capper Neill Ltd (Engrg Group) 1979-; *Recreations* winter sports, country pursuits; *Style* - John Impey Esq; 16 Porchester Terrace, W2

IMRIE, Lady; Mary Isobel Rae Rowan; *m* 1953, Sir John Imrie, CBE, JP (d 1981); *Style* - Lady Imrie; Invervar Lodge, Glenlyon, Aberfeldy, Perthshire (☎ Glenlyon 203)

INCE, David Henry Gason; s of Maj Douglas Edward Ince (d 1966); *b* 23 Mar 1921; *Educ* Cheltenham Coll, Glasgow U; *m* 1954, Anne, da of Archer Robert Burton; 2 children; *Career* div man Guided Weapons Div Elliott Bros (London) Ltd 1958-60, assist gen man Elliott Flight Automation 1960-65, md Bryans Aeroequipment Ltd (former sales man) 1965-70, md LSM Controls, Seltronic Gp 1968-70, gp dir Gascoigne Gp Ltd 1971-, chm and dir- Gascoigne (R and D) Ltd, Gascoigne Sudstall GmbH, Samas SA, Boythorpe Ltd; *Recreations* gliding, woodworking, gardening; *Style* - David Ince Esq; Deanlands Farm, Newnham Lane, Hook, Basingstoke Hants (☎ Hook 2577)

INCHBALD, Denis John Elliot; s of Rev Christopher Chantrey Elliot Inchbald CF (d 1976); *b* 9 May 1923; *Educ* Oswestry Sch, Jesus Cambridge; *m* 1955, Jacqueline Hazel, nee Jones; *Career* Lt RNVR; Public Relations; hd of publicity British Industries Fair 1954-56, dir of PR Foote Cone & Belding Ltd 1959-68, chm & md Welbeck Public Relations Ltd 1968-, Pres Inst PR 1968-70, chm PRCA 1975; *Recreations* reading, gardening, photography, sailing, travel; *Clubs* Reform, Naval; *Style* - Denis Inchbald Esq; The Warren, 42 Dukes Wood dve Gerrards Cross, Bucks (☎ Gerrards Cross 84582)

INCHCAPE, 3 Earl of (UK 1929); Kenneth James William Mackay; also Baron Inchcape (UK 1911), Viscount Inchcape (UK 1924), and Viscount Glenapp (UK 1929); s of 2 Earl of Inchcape (d 1939, bro of late Lady Craigmyle and Lady Effie Millington-Drake) by his 1 w, Joan, da of Rt Hon John Moriarty, Ld Justice of Appeal in Ireland; *b* 27 Dec 1917; *Educ* Eton, Trin Cambridge; *m* 1, 1941 (m dis 1954), as her 2 husb, Aline, da of Sir Richard Pease, 2 Bt; 2 s, 1 da; m 2, 1965, Caroline, da of Cholmeley Harrison, of Emo Court, Co Leix; 2 s; *Heir* s, Viscount Glenapp; *Career* served WW II Maj 12 Roy Lancers, 27 Lancers Europe; exec chm Inchcape & Co 1958-, chm P & O SN Co 1973- (exec chm 1978-); dir BP, Guardian Roy Exchange Assur, Standard Chartered Bank; Freeman City of London; *Recreations* field sports, farming; *Clubs* Brooks's, Buck's, Turf,

Oriental, City; *Style* - The Rt Hon Earl of Inchcape; Addington Manor, Addington, Bucks (☎ Winslow 4545); Pearsie House, Kirriemuir, Angus

INCHIQUIN, 17 Baron (I 1543); Sir Phaedrig Lucius Ambrose O'Brien; 9 Bt (I 1686); s of 15 Baron, JP, DL (descended from Brian Boroimhe, Prince of Thomond, High King of Ireland in 1002 but who was k at the moment of victory against the Danes in the Battle of Clontarf 1014); suc bro (16 Baron) 1968 and is head of one of the small number of Irish families that still enjoy a Peerage; *b* 4 April 1900; *Educ* Eton, Magdalen Oxford, Imperial Coll London; *m* 1945, Vera, da of Rev Clifton Winter; *Heir* n, Conor O'Brien; *Career* Maj (ret) Rifle Bde; late Colonial Serv Overseas Geological Survey; served WW II E African Intelligence Corps (Abyssinia, Somalia, Madagascar); late coffee farmer in Kenya, geologist with Anglo-American Corpn, and consultant geologist; *Clubs* RAC; *Style* - The Rt Hon The Lord Inchiquin; Thomond House, Co Clare, Eire; Hanway Lodge, Richard's Castle, Ludlow, Salop (☎ Richard's Castle 210)

INCHYRA, 1 Baron (UK 1961); Frederick Robert Hoyer Millar; GCMG (1956, KCMG 1949, CMG 1939), CVO 1938; s of late Robert Hoyer Millar; *b* 6 June 1900; *Educ* Wellington, New Coll Oxford; *m* 1931, Elizabeth, da of late Jonkheer Reneke de Marees van Swinderen, formerly Netherlands Min in London; 2 s, 2 da; *Heir* s, Hon Robert Millar; *Career* Hon Attaché Brussels 1922, Dip Serv 1923, 3 Sec Berlin 1923, Paris 1924, 2 Sec FO 1928, Cairo 1930, 1 Sec FO 1935, Asst Priv Sec to Sec of State for Foreign Affairs 1934-38, 1 Sec at Washington 1939, acting Cllr 1941, Sec British Civil Secretariat Washington 1943, Cllr FO 1944, Min Washington 1948, UK Dep NATO Council 1950, UK Rep thereon 1952, High Cmmr German Federal Republic 1953-55, Ambass 1955-56 and Perm Under-Sec of State for Foreign Affairs 1957-61; King of Arms of Order of St Michael and St George 1961-75; *Clubs* Boodle's, Turf, New (Edinburgh), Metropolitan (Washington); *Style* - The Rt Hon Lord Inchyra, GCMG, CVO; Inchyra House, Glencarse, Perthshire

ING, Simon Burton; JP (1979); s of Cyril Henry Ing (d 1977); *b* 23 May 1938; *Educ* St Edward's Sch, London U; *m* 1962, Hazel Diana, da of Leonard Clare; 1 s, 1 da; *Career* CA; v chm Beeston Hall Sch 1978- (gov 1976), dir and v chm King's Lynn Festival 1979; FCA; *Recreations* golf, swimming, gardening; *Style* - Simon Ing Esq, JP; 15 King Street, King's Lynn, Norfolk (☎ 0553-4810)

INGE-INNES-LILLINGSTON, George David; DL (Staffs 1969); s of Cdr Hugh William Innes-Lillingston RN (d 1953); *b* 13 Nov 1923; *Educ* Stowe, Merton Coll Oxford; *m* 1, 1946, Alison Mary (d 1947), da of late Rev Frederick Green; 1 da; m 2, 1955, Elizabeth Violet Grizel, da of Lt-Gen Sir W M Thomson KCMG, CB, MC (d 1963); 2 s, 1 da; *Career* memb Agric Land Trib 1962-72, chm N Birmingham & Dist Hosps 1968-72, JP 1967-74, High Sheriff Staffs 1966, Staffs Br Country Landowners Assoc 1968 (pres 1979-), chm Agric & Horticulture Ctee British Standards Inst 1980-; *Recreations* growing trees, yachting; *Clubs* Boodle's, Farmers', Turf, Roy Highland Yacht (Oban); *Style* - George Inge-Innes-Lillingston Esq, DL; Thorpe Hall, Tamworth, Staffs (☎ Newton Regis 224)

INGESTRE, Viscount; James Richard Charles John Chetwynd-Talbot; s and h of 22 Earl of Shrewsbury and Waterford; *b* 11 Jan 1978; *Style* - Viscount Ingestre

INGILBY, Lady; Diana; da of late Brig-Gen Sir George Lethbridge Colvin, CB, CMG, DSO; *m* 1948, Maj Sir Joslan William Vivian Ingilby, 5 Bt (d 1974); *Style* - Lady Ingilby; Ripley Castle, Harrogate, Yorks

INGILBY, Sir Thomas Colvin William; 6 Bt (UK 1866), of Ripley Castle, Yorkshire; s of Maj Sir Joslan William Vivian Ingilby 5 Bt JP DL (d 1974); *b* 17 July 1955; *Educ* Eton Coll, Roy Agricultural Coll Cirencester; *Career* land agent Stephenson & Son York 1978-, lecture tours America 1978-79, teacher

Springvale Sch Rhodesia 1973-74; *Recreations* cricket, historic houses, travel, photography; *Style* - Sir Thomas Ingilby Bt; Ripley Castle, nr Harrogate, N Yorks (☎ Harrogate 770186)

INGLEBY, 2 Viscount (UK 1956); Martin Raymond Peake; s of 1 Viscount Ingleby (d 1966) and Joan Viscountess Ingleby, *qv*; *b* 31 May 1926; *Educ* Eton, Trin Oxford; *m* 1952, Susan, da of Capt Henderson Landale, of Ewell Manor, W Farleigh, Kent; 4 da; *Heir* none; *Career* barr Inner Temple 1956, dir Hargreaves Gp Ltd 1960, Northern Forestry Products Ltd; CC N Riding Yorks 1964-67; landowner; late Lt Coldstream Gds; *Recreations* forestry; *Style* - The Rt Hon Viscount Ingleby; Snilesworth, Northallerton, N Yorks (☎ Osmotherley 214); Flat 1, 61 Onslow sq, SW7 (☎ 01 589 0609)

INGLEFIELD-WATSON, Sir Derrick William; 4 Bt (UK 1895), TD (1945); s of late Sir John Watson, 2 Bt; suc bro, Sir John Watson, 3 Bt, 1918; *b* 7 Oct 1901; *Educ* Eton, Ch Ch Oxford; *m* 1, 1925 (m dis 1939), Margrett Georgina, da of Col Thomas Stokes George Hugh Robertson-Aikman, CB, of The Ross, Hamilton, Lanarkshire; 1 s, 1 da; m 2, 1946, Thérese (Terry), da of late Prof Charles Bodon, of Budapest; *Heir* s, John Inglefield-Watson; *Career* Capt (ret) Roy W Kent Regt (TA), CC Kent 1931-37, assumed by deed poll 1946 his christian name of Inglefield as an additional surname; *Style* - Sir Derrick Inglefield-Watson, Bt, TD; Ringshill House, Wouldham, nr Rochester, Kent (☎ Medway 61514)

INGLEFIELD-WATSON, Lt-Col John Forbes; s (by 1 m) and h of Sir Derrick Inglefield-Watson, 4 Bt, TD; *b* 16 May 1926; *Educ* Eton; *Career* Lt-Col RE; *Style* - Lt-Col John Inglefield-Watson

INGLEWOOD, 1 Baron (UK 1964); William Morgan (Fletcher-)Vane; TD, DL (Westmorland 1946, Cumbria 1974); s of Col Hon William Vane, JP, DL, yst bro of 9 Baron Barnard, and Lady Katharine Pakenham, da of 4 Earl of Longford; Lord Inglewood is hence 1 cous once removed of Lady Antonia Fraser (Pinter); *b* 12 April 1909; *Educ* Charterhouse, Trin Oxford; *m* 1949, Mary, da of Maj Sir Richard Proby, 1 Bt, MC; 2 s; *Heir* s, Hon William (Fletcher-)Vane; *Career* served WW II Europe & M East Lt-Col Durham LI; MP (C) Westmorland 1945-64; dir Spooner Industs 1963-80, chm 1966-68; assumed name Fletcher-Vane 1931; Jt Parly Sec Min Pensions & Nat Insur 1958-60, Min Ag 1960-62; *Clubs* Travellers'; *Style* - The Rt Hon Lord Inglewood TD DL; Hutton-in-the-Forest, Penrith, Cumbria (☎ Skelton 207); 9 Stack House, Cundy st, Ebury st, SW1 (☎ 01 730 1559)

INGLIS, Alastair Mackenzie; s and h of Sir Roderick Inglis of Glencorse, 10 Bt; *b* 28 July 1961; *Style* - Alastair Inglis of Glencorse, yr

INGLIS, James Craufuird Roger; s of Lt-Col John Inglis (d 1967); *b* 21 June 1925; *Educ* Winchester Coll, Cambridge, Edinburgh U; *m* 1952, Phoebe Aeonie, da of Edward Mackenzie Murray-Buchanan; 2 s, 4 da; *Career* Writer to the Signet; ptnr Shepherd & Wedderburn W S 1976-, chm British Assets Trust PLC 1978-(dir 1957-78), dir- Edinburgh American Assets Trust PLC and Atlantic Assets Trust PLC 1957-, Roy Bank of Scotland Ltd 1967-, Scottish Provident Instn for Mutual Life Assurance 1962-; *Recreations* golf; *Clubs* Roy & Ancient G C of St Andrews, Army & Navy, New Club (Edinburgh); *Style* - James Inglis Esq, WS; Inglisfield, Gifford, E Lothian (☎ Gifford 339)

INGLIS OF GLENCORSE, Sir Roderick John; 10 Bt (NS 1703), of Glencorse, Midlothian (formerly Mackenzie of Gairloch, Ross-shire); s of Sir Maxwell Ian Hector Inglis, 9 Bt (d 1974); *b* 25 Jan 1936; *Educ* Winchester, Edinburgh U (MB, ChB); *m* 1, 1960 (m dis 1975), Rachel Evelyn, da of Lt-Col N M Morris, of Dowdstown, Ardee, Co Louth; 3 s, 1 da; m 2, 1975, Geraldine, da of R H Kirk, of Thaxted, Essex; 1 da; *Heir* s, Alastair Inglis of Glencorse, yr; *Clubs* New (Edinburgh); *Style* - Sir Roderick Inglis of Glencorse, Bt; 35 Villiers Drive, Pietersmaritzburg, Natal, S Africa; Glencorse House, Penicuik, Midlothian

INGRAM, Sir James Herbert Charles; 4 Bt (UK 1893), of Swineshead Abbey, Lincolnshire; s of (Herbert) Robin Ingram (d 1979), and of Shiela (now Countess von der Schulenburg), da of late Charles Peczenik; suc gf, Sir Herbert Ingram, 3 Bt, 1980; *b* 6 May 1966; *Educ* Eton; *Heir* half bro, Nicholas Ingram; *Style* - Sir James Ingram, Bt; 8 Pitt st, W8 (☎ 01 937 0727)

INGRAM, Michael Warren; JP (1949), DL (Glos 1978); 2 s of Sir Herbert Ingram 2 Bt (d 1957); *b* 20 June 1917; *Educ* Winchester Coll, Balliol Oxford; *m* 1944, Auriol Blanche, da of Lt-Gen Sir Arthur Francis Smith, KCB, KBE, DSO, MC (d 1978, whose mother was Lady Blanche Keith Falconer, herself 2 da of 8 Earl of Kintore) and Hon Lady Smith (da of 1 Baron Somerleyton); 1 s, 3 da; *Career* chm: The Mycalex Co Ltd, Mycalex (Motors) Ltd, Ashcroft Electronics Ltd; dir: Mycalex Engrg Ltd, Nexus (Data Serv) Ltd, Power-lectric Ltd; *Recreations* tennis, golf, shooting, collecting English watercolours; *Clubs* Lansdowne; *Style* - Michael Ingram Esq, JP, DL; Driffield Manor, Cirencester, Glos (☎ Poulton (028585) 205)

INGRAM, Nicholas David; s of (Herbert) Robin Ingram (d 1979 - s of Sir Herbert Ingram, 3 Bt, who d 1980); hp of half-bro, Sir James Ingram, 4 Bt; *b* 12 June 1975; *Style* - Nicholas Ingram Esq

INGRAMS, Hon Catriona; da of Baroness Darcy de Knayth; *b* 1963; *Style* - The Hon Catriona Ingrams

INGRAMS, Hon Caspar David; s and h of Baroness Darcy de Knayth; *b* 5 Jan 1962; *Style* - The Hon Caspar Ingrams

INGRAMS, Hon Miranda; da of Baroness Darcy de Knayth; *b* 1960; *Style* - The Hon Miranda Ingrams

INMAN, Baroness; May Amelie; da of Edward Dew, of Harrow; *m* 1919, 1 and last Baron Inman, PC (d 1979); 1 da (Hon Mrs Kollitsis); *Style* - The Rt Hon the Lady Inman; Knaresborough House, Warninglid, Haywards Heath, Sussex

INMAN, Rex Nicholas; s of Joseph Edward Inman (d 1970); *b* 19 Feb 1925; *Educ* King Edward VII Sch Sheffield; *m* 1951, Margaret, nee Bradwell; 2 s, 1 da; *Career* FCA, fin dir Pegler-Hattersley Ltd; *Style* - Rex Inman Esq; Austfield House, Hillam, Leeds

INNES, Lt-Col Sir (Ronald Gordon) Berowald; 16 Bt (NS 1628), of Balvenie, Banffshire, OBE (1943); s of Capt James William Guy Innes CBE RN (d 1939); suc kinsman Sir Walter James Innes, 15 Bt 1978; *b* 14 July 1907; *Educ* Harrow, RMC Camberley, Staff Coll Camberley; *m* 1, 1933, Elizabeth Haughton (d 1958), da of late Alfred Fayle; 2 s, 1 da; m 2, 1961, Elizabeth Christian, da of late Lt-Col Charles Henry Watson; *Heir* s Peter Alexander Berowald Innes; *Career* Lt-Col Northumberland Div GSO 1939-45 (ret 1949), farmed in Kenya 1949-63; *Recreations* embroidery (needlepoint), continental touring by caravan; *Clubs* Naval & Military; *Style* - Lt-Col Sir Berowald Innes, Bt, OBE; The Loom House, Aultgowrie, By Muir of Ord, Ross and Cromarty

INNES OF COXTON, Sir Charles Kenneth Gordon; 11 Bt (NS 1686), of Coxton, Co Moray; s of Maj (Sir) Charles Gordon Deverell Innes, *de jure* 10 Bt (d 1953); *b* 28 Jan 1910; *Educ* Haileybury; *m* 1936, Margaret Colquhoun Lockhart, da of Frederick Charles Lockhart Robertson, and gda of late Sir James Colquhoun of Luss, 5 Bt; 1 s, 1 da; *Heir* s, David Innes; *Career* 1939-45 War RA, Capt Ayrshire Yeo; placed on Official Roll of Baronets 1973; *Style* - Sir Charles Innes of Coxton, Bt; October Cottage, Haslemere, Surrey GU27 2LF

INNES, David Charles Kenneth Gordon; s and h of Sir Charles Innes of Coxton, 11 Bt; *b* 17 April 1940; *Educ* Haileybury, London U; *m* 1969, Marjorie Alison, da of Ernest W Parker; 1 s, 1 da; *Career* ACGI; *Style* - David Innes Esq; 28 Wadham Close, Shepperton, Middx

INNES, Lady Lucy Buchan; *née* Sinclair; da of late 18 Earl of Caithness; *b* 1902; *m* 1928, Sir Thomas Innes of Learney, GCVO, LLD (d 1971); 2 s, 1 da; *Style* - Lady Lucy Innes; The Laigh Riggs,

Torphins, Aberdeenshire

INNES OF EDINGIGHT, Malcolm Rognvald; CVO (1981); s of late Sir Thomas Innes of Learney, GCVO and Lady Lucy Buchan, da of 18 Earl of Caithness; *b* 25 May 1938; *Educ* Edinburgh Academy, Edinburgh U; *m* 1963, Joan, da of Thomas D Hay, of Edinburgh; 3 s; *Career* Baron of Crommey (territorial); Marchmont Herald 1971-; memb Roy Co of Archers; *Style* - Malcolm Innes of Edingight CVO; 35 Inverleith Row, Edinburgh EH3 5QH

INNES, Peter Alexander Berowald; s and h of Lt-Col Sir Berowald Innes, 16 Bt, OBE; *b* 6 Jan 1937; *Educ* Bristol U; *m* 1959, Julia Mary, da of A S Levesley, of Burlington rd, Bristol; 2 s, 1 da; *Career* MICE; *Clubs* Naval and Military; *Style* - Peter Innes Esq; 25 Aster rd, Kempshott Hill, Basingstoke, Hants

INNES, Hon Mrs (Veronica Wenefryde Nefertari); *née* Bethell; da of Hon Richard Bethell; sis of 4 & 5 Barons Westbury; *b* 15 July 1917; *m* 1941, Lt-Col James Innes, Coldstream Gds, s of Lt-Col James Innes, DSO, by Lady Barbara Lowther, da of 6 Earl of Lonsdale, OBE, JP, DL; 2 s, 1 da; *Style* - The Hon Mrs Innes; Bransdale Lodge, Fadmoor, Yorks; 55 Cadogan Lane, SW 1

INNES-KER, Lord Robert Anthony; 2 s of 9 Duke of Roxburghe (d 1974); *b* 28 May 1959; *Career* 2 Lt Blues & Royals; *Style* - Lord Robert Innes-Ker

INNES-KER, Lady Rosanagh Viola Alexandra; da of 10 Duke of Roxburghe and Lady Jane Grosvenor, da of 5 Duke of Westminster; *b* 1979; *Style* - Lady Rosanagh Innes-Ker

INSCH, Gordon McConochie; s of James Gordon Insch (d 1977); *b* 18 June 1927; *Educ* Morrison's Academy Crieff, St Andrew's U, Glasgow U; *m* 1954, Audrey Keith, nee Drew; 1 s (Keith Gordon), 1 da (Lindsay Jane); *Career* gen man Special Projects Nat Nuclear Corp Ltd 1980-, dir Atomic Power Constructions Ltd 1971-, dir British Nuclear Design & Construction Ltd 1969-75; *Recreations* golf; *Clubs* Centro Espanol de Londres; *Style* - Gordon Insch Esq; 449 London rd, Leicester (☎ 704 720)

INSKIP, Hon Mrs (Clare Elizabeth Anne); *née* Buxton; da of 2 Baron Noel-Buxton (d 1980); *b* 1954; *m* 1977, Owen Hampden Inskip; *Style* - Hon Mrs Inskip

INSKIP, Hon Piers James Hampden; s and h of 2 Viscount Caldecote; *b* 20 May 1947; *Educ* Eton; *m* 1970, Susan Bridget, nee Mellen; *Style* - The Hon Piers Inskip

INVERFORTH, 3 Baron (UK 1919); (Andrew Charles) Roy Weir; s of 2 Baron Inverforth (d 1975); *b* 6 June 1932; *Educ* Malvern; *m* 1966, Jill Elizabeth, da of John Ward Thornycroft, CBE, of Steyne, Bembridge, IOW; 1 s, 1 da; *Heir* s, Hon Andrew Weir; *Career* chm and governing dir Andrew Weir & Co Ltd 1971-, chm The Bank Line Ltd 1971-, United Baltic Corpn Ltd 1974-, dir Gen Council of British Shipping Ltd 1975-, Baltic Mercantile & Shipping Exchange 1976-, London Advsy Bd Commercial Bank of Australia 1976-, Anglo-American Securities Corpn Ltd 1976-, North Atlantic Securities Corpn Ltd 1976-, The Baltic & Int Maritime Conf 1977-, Spink & Son Ltd 1978-, Aldeburgh Festival-Snape Maltings Foundn Ltd 1980-; *Clubs* Bath, Royal Automobile; *Style* - The Rt Hon the Lord Inverforth; 27 Hyde Park st, W2 2JS (☎ 01 283 1266); Walber House, Walberswick, Southwold, Suffolk IP18 6TS (Southwold 723110)

INVERFORTH, Iris, Baroness; Iris Beryl; da of late Charles Vincent, 4 Bn The Buffs; *m* 1929, 2 Baron Inverforth (d 1975); 2 s (3 Baron, Hon John Weir); *Style* - The Rt Hon Iris, Lady Inverforth; 24 Clarence Ter, Regents Park, NW1 4RD

INVERURIE, Master of; Hon James William Falconer Keith; s and h of Lord Inverurie; *b* 15 April 1976; *Style* - The Master of Inverurie

INVERURIE, Lord; Michael Canning William John Keith; Master of Kintore; s and h of 12 Earl of Kintore; *b* 22 Feb 1939; *Educ* Eton, RMA Sandhurst; *m* 1972,

Mary Plum, da of late Sqdn Leader E G Plum, of Rumson, NJ; 1 s, 1 da; *Heir* s, Master of Inverurie; *Career* late Lt Coldstream Gds; assumed surname of Keith in lieu of Baird; *Style* - Lord Inverurie; The Stables, Keith Hall, Inverurie, Aberdeenshire (☎ Inverurie 21755)

IPSWICH, Viscount; Henry Oliver Charles FitzRoy; s and h of Earl of Euston; *b* 6 April 1978; *Style* - Viscount Ipswich

IRBY, Hon George William Eustace Boteler; s and h of 10 Baron Boston; *b* 1 Aug 1971; *Style* - The Hon George Irby

IREMONGER, Lucille d'Oyen; da of Basil Oscar Parks JP (d 1947); *Educ* St Hugh's Oxford; *m* 1937, Thomas Lascelles Iremonger; 1 da; *Career* author, broadcaster, memb London Cncl 1961-65, has written many publications including 'Lord Aberdeen' (a biography of the 4 Earl of Aberdeen KG, KT, Prime Minister 1852-55); Lady Violet Astor Award and Lady Britten (Soc of Women Journalists) 1948, and Silver Musgrave Medal of the Inst of Jamaica for contribution to literature 1962-; *Recreations* riding; *Style* - Mrs Thomas Iremonger; 34 Cheyne Row, Chelsea, SW3; The Giant's House, Newbourn, nr Woodbridge, Suffolk

IREMONGER, Thomas Lascelles; s of Lt-Col H Iremonger, DSO, RMA (d 1937); *b* 14 March 1916; *Educ* Oriel Coll Oxford; *m* 1937, Lucille D'Oyen, nee Parks; 1 da; *Career* underwriting memb Lloyd's, MP (C) Ilford North 1954-74, district Offr Colonial Admin Serv (W Pacific), editor of 'Overseas', author of works on penal system and economics; *Recreations* small boat sailing; *Style* - Thomas Iremonger Esq; 34 Cheyne Row, Chelsea, SW3; The Giant's House, Newbourn, nr Woodbridge, Suffolk

IRONSIDE, 2 Baron (UK 1941); Edmund Oslac Ironside; s of 1 Baron Ironside, Field Marshal, GCB, CMG, DSO (d 1959); *b* 21 Sept 1924; *Educ* Tonbridge Sch; *m* 1950, Audrey Marigold, da of late Col the Hon Thomas George Breadalbane Morgan-Grenville, DSO, OBE, MC (3 s of Lady Kinloss in her own right); 1 s, 1 da; *Heir* s, Hon Charles Ironside; *Career* RN 1943-52 (Lt); dir Gemini Computer Systems Ltd 1973, dep chm Parly and Scientific Ctee 1974, pres Electric Vehicle Assoc 1976, European Electric Road Vehicle Assoc 1980, vice-pres Inst of Patentees and Inventors 1977, chm Advsy Cttee Science Reference Lib 1976-, Int Research and Development Co 1968-; *Clubs* Royal Ocean Racing; *Style* - The Rt Hon the Lord Ironside; Broomwood Manor, Chignal St James, Chelmsford, Essex (☎ Chelmsford 440231)

IRONSIDE, Hon Charles Edmund Grenville; s and h of 2 Baron Ironside; *b* 1 July 1956; *Style* - The Hon Charles Ironside

IRONSIDE, Mariot, Baroness; Mariot Ysabel; da of late Lt Charles Cheyne, ISC; *m* 1915, 1 Baron Ironside, GCB, CMG, DSO (d 1959); 1 s (2 Baron), 1 da (Hon Mrs Hendry); *Style* - The Rt Hon Mariot, Lady Ironside; Hampton Court Palace, East Molesey, Surrey

IRVINE ROBERTSON, Alexander; TD (1945), DL (1961 Stirlingshire); s of Duncan Irvine Robertson (d 1953); *b* 12 Nov 1912; *Educ* Fettes Coll Edinburgh, Edinburgh U; *m* 1939, Jean Margaret, da of Rev Alexander Gardon Fraser CBE, MC; 3 s (Alistair, James, John) 1 da (Penelope); *Career* 2 Lt TA 1931, WW II BEF, Lt-Col 1950, Bt-Col 1953; slr 1937, Mathie Macluckie & Lupton Slrs, councillor Royal Burgh of Stirling 1946-50, chm Stirlingshire T & AF Assoc 1965-68, dir of various companies; *Recreations* golf; *Style* - Alexander Irvine Robertson Esq, TD, DL; The Old Manse, Park Av, Stirling, Scotland (☎ Stirling 4526)

IRVING OF DARTFORD, Baron (Life Peer UK 1979); Sydney Irving; PC (1969), DL (Kent 1976); s of Sydney Irving, of Newcastle upon Tyne; *b* 1 July 1918; *Educ* Pendower Sch Newcastle upon Tyne, LSE; *m* 1942, Mildred, da of Charlton Weedy, of Morpeth; 1 s, 1 da (and 1 s decd); *Career* chm S Regional Council of Labour Party 1965-67, Alderman Dartford Borough Council, memb NW Kent Divnl Exec Kent Education Ctee 1952-74, MP (L and Co-op) Dartford 1955-70 and Feb 1974-79, Opposition Whip (S and S Western) 1959-64, Treasurer of the Household and Dep Ch Govt Whip 1964-66, chm of Ways and Means and Dep Speaker 1968-70, formerly chm of Select Ctees; *Style* - Rt Hon Lord Irving of Dartford PC DL; 10 Tynedale Close, Dartford, Kent (☎ 25105)

IRWIN, Basil William Seymour; MC, TD, DL (1967); s of Major William James Irwin (d 1960); *b* 27 May 1919; *Educ* Tonbridge; *m* 1949, Eleanor Ruth; *Career* Col, Europe, Middle East; ADC (TAVR) 1968-73; merchant banker (ret); formerly chm Leda Investment Trust Ltd & Archimedes Invest Trust Ltd; formerly v-chm Ionian Bank Ltd (relinquished 1978); *Clubs* Special Forces; *Style* - Basil Irwin Esq, MC, TD, DL; Stansted, Essex (☎ Bishops Stortford 812207)

IRWIN, Lord; James Charles Wood; s and h of 3 Earl of Halifax; *b* 24 Aug 1977; *Style* - Lord Irwin

IRWIN, Hon Mrs; Hon Mikaela; *née* Rawlinson; da of Baron Rawlinson of Ewell, PC, QC, by his 1 w, Haidee; *b* 1941; *m* 1964, Jonathan, s of John Irwin, of Chiswick; 3 s; *Style* - The Hon Mrs Irwin; Moyglare House, Maynooth, Co Kildare, Eire

ISAACS, Lord Alexander Gerald Rufus; s of 3 Marquess of Reading, MBE, MC (d 1980); *b* 25 April 1957; *Educ* St Paul's, Oriel Oxford; *Style* - Lord Alexander Isaacs

ISAACS, Lord Anthony Michael Rufus; s of 3 Marquess of Reading, MBE, MC (d 1980); hp of bro, 4 Marquess; *b* 22 Sept 1943; *Educ* Gordonstoun; *m* 1972 (m dis 1976), Anne Pugsley; *Style* - Lord Anthony Isaacs; 20 Oakley gdns, SW3

ISAACS, Lady Sybilla Alice; da of 4 Marquess of Reading; *b* 1980; *Style* - Lady Sybilla Isaacs

ISHAM, Sir Ian Vere Gyles; 13 Bt (E 1627), of Lamport, Northamptonshire; s of Lt-Col Vere Arthur Richard Isham MC (d 1968) and suc to kinsman Sir Gyles Isham, 12 Bt (d 1976); *b* 17 July 1923; *Educ* Eton, Worcester Coll Oxford; *Heir* bro, Norman Isham; *Career* marketing analyst and cartographer; *Clubs* Overseas; *Style* - Sir Ian Isham, Bt; 40 Turnpike Link, Croydon, Surrey (☎ 686 1256)

ISHAM, Norman Murray Crawford; s of late Lt-Col Vere Arthur Richard Isham, MC and hp of bro, Sir Ian Isham, 13 Bt; *b* 28 Jan 1930; *m* 1956, Joan, da of late Leonard James Genet, of Umtali, Rhodesia; 2 s, 1 da; *Style* - Norman Isham Esq; 5 Langton Way, Park Hill, Croydon

ISLES, Maj-Gen Donald Edward; CB (1978), OBE (1968); s of Harold Isles (d 1956); *b* 19 July 1924; *Educ* Roundhay Sch Leeds, Leeds U, RMCS, Jt Serv Staff Coll; *m* 1948, Sheila Mary, nee Thorpe; 3 s, 1 da; *Career* Maj-Gen RA 1944-78m (ret), Dir-Gen of Weapons MOD, Hon Col 3 Bn Yorks Volunteers 1977; dir and dep man British Manufacture & Research Co Ltd Grantham 1979-; *Recreations* squash, tennis, shooting; *Clubs* Army & Navy; *Style* - Maj-Gen Donald Isles CB, OBE; The Laurels, Denton, Grantham, Lincs (☎ Knipton 588)

IUUL, Michael Christian Stig; s of Stig Asgersson Iuul (d 1969); *b* 26 Jan 1943; *Educ* Herlufsholm Denmark, U of Copenhagen, DP Paris, U of Rome; *m* 1968, Annie Ingeborg, da of Hans Roger Bronnum Scavenius, Gentofte, Denmark; 2 s; *Career* md Carlsberg Brewery 1977-; dir Carlsberg Distributors, Sales and Scottish Importers 1977; dir Tuborg Lager Ltd 1981-; Hon Danish Consul 1981; *Recreations* yachting (yacht: 'Special Brew II'), skiing, tennis; *Club* RAC *Style* - Michael Iuul Esq; The Old House, Harlestone, Northants; Chesham st, SWI

IVANOVIC, Vane (Ivan) Stevan; s of Dr Ivan Ivanovič, of Zagreb; *b* 9 June 1913; *Educ* Westminster, Peterhouse; *m* 1939, June Veronica, da of Rev John Fisher, Canon of Colchester; 1 s, 2 da; *Career* served WW II Maj PWE M East & Italy; chm Yugoslav Shipping Ctee 1941, Ivanovič & Co 1949-67; Consul-Gen Monaco in London 1967- (Offr Order of

Grimaldi 1975); *Recreations* diving & spear fishing, athletics (track & field), jogging; *Clubs* White's, MCC, Brooks's; owner of motor yacht:'Taro'; *Style* - Vane Ivanovič Esq, Consulate General of Monaco; 1 Ruelle Ste Barbe, Monaco (☎ 300996); 4 Audley sq, W1 (☎ 01 629 0734)

IVE, John Patrick Francis; s of Frank George Ive (d 1973); *b* 20 April 1933; *Educ* Downside Sch; *m* 1956, Elizabeth Ann, nee Holmes; 2 children; *Career* md North American Reinsurance Div J H Minet & Co Ltd, chm Hartley Cooper Hldgs Ltd 1977-79 (dir 1965-79) and Hartley Cooper & Co Ltd 1975-79; *Recreations* golf, bird watching, stamp collecting; *Clubs* Annabel's; *Style* - John Ive Esq; Fidler's Hall, Shackleford, Godalming, Surrey (☎ Guildford 810737)

IVEAGH, 3 Earl of (UK 1919); Sir Arthur Francis Benjamin Guinness; 3 Bt (UK 1885); also Baron Iveagh (UK 1891), Viscount Iveagh (UK 1905), Viscount Elveden (UK 1919); s of Maj Arthur Onslow Edward Guinness, Viscount Elveden (ka 1945 - 2 s of 2 Earl), and Lady Elizabeth Hare, da of 4 Earl of Listowel (d 1931); suc gf, 2 Earl of Iveagh, KG, CB, CMG 1967; is 1 cous of Paul Channon, MP & Min for the Arts, also (HRH Princess Antonia, nee von Preussen) Marchioness of Douro, and Hon Mark Lennox-Boyd, MP; Lord Iveagh is, in addition, 1 cous once removed of (1) Maureen, Marchioness of Dufferin and Ava and (2) Jonathan Guinness, and, finally, great nephew of Lord (1 Baron) Moyne; *b* 20 May 1937; *Educ* Eton, Trin Cambridge; *m* 1963, Miranda Daphne Jane, da of Maj Charles Michael Smiley, of Castle Fraser, Aberdeenshire; 2 s, 2 da; *Heir* s, Viscount Elveden; *Career* memb Irish Senate 1973-77; chm Guinness Group 1975-; *Clubs* White's, Royal Yacht Sqdn (Cowes), Kildare st and University (Dublin); *Style* - The Rt Hon the Earl of Iveagh; Farmleigh, Castleknock, Co Dublin (☎ 21 30 16/21 36 63)

IVENS-FERRAZ, Lady Almary (Bridget); *née* Coke; da of 6 Earl of Leicester; *b* 1938; *m* 1963, Peter Ivens-Ferraz; 4 da; *Style* - Lady Almary Ivens-Ferraz; 19 Lady Smith st, Dan Pienaat, Bloemfontein, Orange Free State, S Africa; 33 Sixth ave, Parktown N, Johannesburg, S Africa

J

JACK, Hon Mrs (Fiona Georgina); *née* Ironside; da of 2 Baron Ironside; *b* 1954; *m* 1978, Roland Maclean Jack; *Style* - The Hon Mrs Jack; Barnston Old Rectory, Dunmow, Essex

JACKMAN, Bernard George Lovell; s of Leonard Jackman (d 1962); *b* 29 Oct 1914; *Educ* Bablake Sch Coventry, London U; *m* 1940, Joyce Alfreda, nee Litchfield; 1 s, 1 da; *Career* chartered engineer (electrical and automotive); industrial consultant Bernard Jackman Ltd 1975-, md Rover Co Ltd and Rover-Triumph (BL) 1972-75, dir and gen man Lockheed Hydraulic Brake Co Ltd 1956-64, chm Stonefield Vehicles Ltd 1977-80; Freeman of City of London, Liveryman Worshipful Co of Clockmakers (Jr Warden 1981); *Recreations* shooting, fishing, veteran cars; *Clubs* Bath, Flyfishers, Eccentric; *Style* - Bernard Jackman Esq; Plestowes House, Barford, Warwicks; Baldwins Corner, Upper Tysoe, Warwicks

JACKSON, Andrew Graham; s of Thomas Armitage Geoffrey Jackson; *b* 5 May 1937; *Educ* Denstone Coll, Jesus Coll Cambridge; *m* 1964, Christine Margaret, nee Chapman; 1 s (Matthew b 1971), 2 da (Sarah b 1967, Claire b 1969); *Career* Lt (Nat Service) Suez 1956; Stewarts & Lloyds Corby 1960-67, Denco Holdings Ltd 1967- (sales man 1967-69, sales dir 1969-72, dep md 1972-77, gp md 1977-); *Recreations* squash, scuba diving; *Style* - Andrew Jackson Esq; The Orchard, Lyde, Hereford (☎ (0432) 2830)

JACKSON, Maj-Gen Arthur James; s of Cdr A Jackson, RD, RNR (d 1978); *b* 31 March 1923; *Educ* Barton Sch, London U; *m* 1948, Joan Marguerite, da of Trevor Lyons Relton MBE (d 1946); 2 s, 2 da;

Career joined Royal Signals 1944, cmd 1946, BAOR 1948-64, MOD 1965-66, Cdr (Brig) 12 Signal Gp 1969-71, dir Telecommunications (Army), 1972-73, dep head Defence Sales MOD 1975-78 (ret); independent consultant 1978-; *Recreations* golf, shooting, gardening, organ music; *Clubs* Army & Navy; *Style* - Maj-Gen Arthur Jackson; Roughwood House, Fleet, Hampshire (☎ Fleet 7576); Tower Lodge, Brampford Speke, Devon (☎ Stoke Canon 233)

JACKSON, Enid, Lady; Enid; da of Stanley Hugh Groome, and formerly wife of Alfred Chester Beatty; *m* 1953, Sir John Montrésor Jackson, 6 Bt (d 1980); *Style* - Enid, Lady Jackson; Rose Cottage, Charing, Kent

JACKSON, Hon Edward Lawies; s and h of 3 Baron Allerton; *b* 23 March 1928; *Educ* Eton; *m* 1, 1953 (m dis 1971), Sally Moore, da of late Ian M Hezlett, of Cranbourne Corner, Ascot, Berks; 2 da; m 2, 1971, Susannah Albinia, da of (Alfred) Drewett Chaytor; 2 da; *Career* Capt (ret) Roy Horse Guards; *Style* - The Hon Edward Jackson; Dunesslin, by Dunscore, Dumfriesshire

JACKSON, Sir Geoffrey Holt Seymour; KCMG (1971); s of Samuel Seymour Jackson (d 1938); *b* 4 March 1915; *Educ* Bolton Sch, Emmanuel Cambridge; *m* 1939, Patricia Mary Evelyn, nee Delany; 1 s; *Career* HM Diplomatic Serv 1937-73 (ret); Sr Trade Cmmr Toronto 1965-69, Ambassador to Uruguay 1969-72, Dep Under-Sec of State 1973; *Recreations* writing, broadcasting; *Clubs* Canning; *Style* - Sir Geoffrey Jackson, KCMG; 63B Cadogan sq, SW1 (☎ 235 6870)

JACKSON, John Michael; s of John Cunliffe Jackson (d 1965); *b* 22 May 1932; *Educ* Shrewsbury & Trin Hall Cambridge; *m* 1957, Susan Mary, da of Jack Walmsley (d 1980); 1 s, 2 da; *Career* dir: Hillards Ltd (1978), James Neill Holdings Ltd (1979), John Foster & Son Ltd (1979), Sanderson, Murray & Elder (Holdings) Ltd (1980); chm Lambert Howarth Gp Ltd (1980); *Style* - John Jackson Esq; Noggarth Rise, Carr Hall rd, Barrowford, Nelson, Lancs (☎ 0282 65137)

JACKSON, Keith Arnold; s of late John Keith Jackson and hp of kinsman, Sir Robert Jackson, Bt; *b* 1921; *m* Pauline Mona, da of B P Climo, of Wellington, NZ; 4 s, 1 da; *Style* - Keith Jackson Esq; Coast rd, Wainuiomata, New Zealand

JACKSON OF BURNLEY, Baroness; Mary Elizabeth; da of Dr Robert Oliphant Boswall; *m* 1938, Baron Jackson of Burnley (Life Peer, d 1970); 2 da (Hon Mrs Freeston, Hon Mrs Moffatt); *Style* - The Rt Hon the Lady Jackson of Burnley; Burnley, 33 Park Close, Templar rd, Oxford

JACKSON, Sir Michael Roland, 5 Bt (UK 1902), of Stansted House, Stansted, Essex; s of Sir (Walter David) Russell Jackson, 4 Bt (d 1956); *b* 20 April 1919; *Educ* Stowe, Clare Cambridge; *m* 1, 1942 (m dis 1969), (Hilda) Margaret, da of Cecil George Herbert Richardson, CBE; 1 s, 1 da; m 2, 1969, Hazel Mary, da of Ernest Harold Edwards; *Heir* s, Thomas Jackson; *Career* served 1939-45 War; Fl Lt RAFVR; *Style* - Sir Michael Jackson, Bt; Dragon Cottage, Dragon's Green, Horsham, W Sussex

JACKSON, Sir Nicholas Fane St George; 3 Bt (UK 1913), of Eagle House, Wimbledon, Surrey; s of Sir Hugh Nicholas Jackson, 2 Bt (d 1979); *b* 4 Sept 1934; *Educ* Radley Coll, Wadham Coll Oxford; RAM, LRAM, ARCM; *m* 1, 1961 (m dis 1968), Jennifer Ann, da of F A Squire, of 8 Marylebone st, W1; m 2, 1972, Nadia Françoise Genevieve, da of Georges Michard; 1 s; *Heir* s, Thomas Jackson; *Career* organist, harpsichordist and composer; Organist St Anne's Soho 1963-68, St James's Piccadilly 1971-74, St Lawrence Jewry 1974-77, Organist and Master of the Choristers St David's Cathedral 1977-, Musical Dir St David's Cathedral Bach Festival 1979; memb The London Virtuosi; *Clubs* Bath; *Style* - Sir Nicholas Jackson, Bt; Organist's Lodgings, St Davids, Pembrokeshire (☎ St Davids 364)

JACKSON, Hon Mrs Pamela; *née* Freeman-Mitford; 2 da of 2 Baron

Redesdale, JP, and sis of Nancy, Jessica, and Unity Mitford, Hon Lady Mosley, and (Debo) Duchess of Devonshire; *b* 25 Nov 1907; *m* 1936 (m dis 1951), Wing Cdr Derek Ainslie Jackson, OBE, DFC, AFC, DSc, FRS, RAFVR, s of Sir Charles Jackson; *Style* - The Hon Mrs Pamela Jackson; Woodfield House, Caudle Green, Cheltenham, Glos (☎ Miserden 300)

JACKSON, Sir Robert; 7 Bt (UK 1815), of Arlsey, Bedfordshire; s of Maj Francis Gorham Jackson (d 1942 - 2 s of 4 Bt); suc kinsman, Sir John Montrésor Jackson, 6 Bt 1980; *b* 16 March 1910; *Educ* St George's Coll; *m* 1943, Maria E Casamayou, of Montevideo, Uruguay; 2 da; *Heir* kinsman, Keith Jackson; *Clubs* English (Montevideo); *Style* - Sir Robert Jackson, Bt; Santiago de Chile 1243, Montevideo, Uruguay (☎ 905487)

JACKSON, Hon Robert Ward; s of Baroness Jackson of Lodsworth, DBE (Life Peeress, d 1981), and of Cdr Sir Robert Gillman Allen Jackson, KCVO, CMG, OBE, RN; *b* 1956; *m* 1978, Caroline B, da of Richardson Peele, of Grey House, Stow-on-the-Wold, Glos; *Style* - The Hon Robert Jackson

JACKSON, Thomas Graham St George; s and h of Sir Nicholas Jackson, 3 Bt; *b* 5 Oct 1980; *Style* - Thomas Jackson Esq

JACKSON, Thomas St Felix; s and h of Sir Michael Jackson, 5 Bt; *b* 27 Sept 1946; *m* 1980, Victoria, da of George Scatliff, of Wineham, Sussex; *Style* - Thomas Jackson Esq

JACKSON, Violet, Lady; Violet Marguerite Loftus; da of late Loftus St George; *m* 1931, Sir Hugh Nicholas Jackson, 2 Bt (d 1979); *Style* - Violet, Lady Jackson; 38 Oakley st, SW3

JACKSON, William; s of late William Jackson and hp of cous, Sir Anthony Mather-Jackson, 6 Bt; *b* 18 Sept 1902; *Educ* Harrow, Balliol Oxford; *m* 1, 1927, Lady Ankaret Cecilia Caroline Howard (d 1945), da of late 10 Earl of Carlisle; 1 s, 1 da; m 2, 1966, Ina, da of late L J Joyce, FRCS, of Reading; *Clubs* VAD, English Speaking Union; *Style* - William Jackson Esq; Parkside, Neston, Cheshire

JACOB, Cdr John C; RN (ret); s of Ian Jacob, late Dir-Gen BBC; *Career* farmer; chm Radio Orwell, joined with Saxon Radio (founded 1981) as wholly owned subsid of Suffolk Gp Radio 1981-; *Style* - Cdr John Jacob, RN; c/o Radio Orwell, Electric House, Lloyds ave, Ipswich, Suffolk (☎ 216971); Abbey Farm, Snape, Suffolk (☎ 348)

JACOBSON, Baron (Life Peer UK 1975); Sydney Jacobson; MC (1944); s of Samuel Jacobson; *b* 26 Oct 1908; *Educ* Strand Sch London, King's Coll London; *m* 1938, Phyllis June, da of late Frank S Buck; 2 s, 1 da; *Career* special correspondent Picture Post 1945-48, editor Leader Magazine 1948-50, political ed Daily Mirror 1952-62, ed Daily Herald 1962-64, ed Sun 1964-65, chm Odhams Newspapers 1968, editorial dir IPC Newspapers 1968-74 (dep chm 1973-74); *Style* - The Rt Hon the Lord Jacobson, MC; 6 Avenue rd, St Albans, Herts (☎ St Albans 53873)

JACOBSON, Hon Colin; s of Baron Jacobson (Life Peer); *b* 1941; *m* 1972, Josephine, da of John William Gates; *Style* - The Hon Colin Jacobson; 48 Parkway, NW1

JACOBSON, Hon Philip; s of Baron Jacobson (Life Peer); *b* 1938; *m* 1967, Ann, da of late Gilbert Mathison; *Style* - The Hon Philip Jacobson; 29 Carmalt gdns, SW15

JACOBSON, Hon Pamela; da of Baron Jacobson (Life Peer); *b* 1944; *Style* - The Hon Pamela Jacobson; Witteys Lane, Thorncombe, nr Chard, Som

JACOBY, Hans Gert; *b* 7 July 1926; *Educ* Taplow G S, Westminster Tech Coll, Imperial Coll London, City and Guilds (BSC Eng); *m* 1955, Patricia Rose; 1 s; *Career* chm British Mantle Mfrs Assoc 1973-77 (memb exec bd), fndr memb and current chm (1977-) Clothing Export Cncl, md Jacoby & Bratt and Assoc Cos, chm Export Advsy Gp for Clothing (Economic Dvpt Ctee of Clothing Indust); *Style* - Hans

Jacoby Esq; 7 Kingwood Pk, Hendon av, Finchley, N3 (☎ 01 346 3763)

JACQUES, Baron (Life Peer UK 1968); John Henry Jacques; JP (Portsmouth); s of Thomas Dobson Jacques; *b* 11 Jan 1905; *Educ* Victoria U Manchester, Co-op Coll Manchester; *m* 1929, Constance, da of Harry White, of Bournville, Birmingham; 2 s, 1 da; *Career* ch exec Portsea Island Co-op Soc Ltd Portsmouth 1945-65, pres Co-op Congress 1961, chm Co-op Union 1964-70, pres Retail Trades Educn Council 1971-75, A Lord in Waiting (Govt Whip) 1974-77 and 1979, a dep chm of Ctees 1977-; *Clubs* Co-operative (Portsmouth); *Style* - The Rt Hon the Lord Jacques, JP; 23 Hilltop Crescent, Cosham, Portsmouth, Hants PO6 1BB (☎ Cosham 375511)

JACQUES, Hon Ann; da of Baron Jacques (Life Peer); *b* 1941; *Style* - The Hon Ann Jacques

JACQUES, Hon Cecil Philip; s of Baron Jacques (Life Peer); *b* 1930; *Educ* London U; *m* 1960, Rita Ann Florence Hurford; *Style* - The Hon Cecil Jacques

JACQUES, Hon Paul; s of Baron Jacques (Life Peer); *b* 1932; *m* 1958, Nina Mollie MacKenzie; *Career* MB, ChBEd; *Style* - The Hon Paul Jacques; 4 Potters Lane, East Leake, Loughborough, Leics

JAFFRAY, Anne, Lady; Anne; da of Capt J Otho Paget MC (d 1934); *m* 1, Sir John Godfrey Worsley-Taylor, 3 Bt (decd); m 2, 1950, Col Sir William Edmund Jaffray Bt, TD (d 1953); 1 s; *Career* former Hampshire CC and District Councillor; *Style* - Anne, Lady Jaffray; Haydown House, Weston Patrick, Basingstoke, Hants (☎ Long Sutton 310)

JAFFRAY, Sir William Otho Jaffray; 5 Bt (UK 1892), of Skilts, Studley, Warwickshire; s of Col Sir William Edmund Jaffray, 4 Bt, TD (d 1953); *b* 1 Nov 1951; *Educ* Eton; *m* 1981, Cynthia Ross Corrington, da of Mrs William M Geering, of Montreal, Quebec, Canada; *Style* - Sir William Jaffray, Bt; 87 Cadogan place, SW1; The Manor House, Priors Dean, Petersfield, Hants

JAKES, Clifford Duncan; s of Ernest Thomas James, of Leigh on Sea, Essex (d 1963); *b* 29 Dec 1942; *Educ* Westcliff H S Southend-on-Sea Essex, Aston U Birmingham; *Career* fell of Inst of CA in England and Wales; articled Wilkins Kennedy & Co London 1960-65; man trainee Tube Investments Ltd 1966-67; finance dir Raleigh Cycles (Malaysia) 1971-73; financial controller (overseas div) Raleigh Industries Ltd Nottingham; md Warren Plantation Holdings Ltd London 1977-; *Recreations* theatre, sport, preservation of wild life; *Clubs* Selangor, Malaysia and Bengal, Calcutta, India; *Style* - Clifford Jakes Esq; Ardley House, Woodlands park, Leigh on Sea, Essex (☎ Southend 557959)

JAKOBOVITS, Rabbi Dr Sir Immanuel; s of Rabbi Dr Julius Jakobovits; *b* 8 Feb 1921; *Educ* London U, Jews' Coll London, Yeshivah Etz Chaim London; *m* 1949, Amelie Munk; 2 s, 4 da; *Career* Ch Rabbi, The United Hebrew Congregations of the British C'wlth of Nations 1967-; kt 1981; *Style* - Rabbi Dr Sir Immanuel Jakobovits; Adler House, Tavistock sq, WC1 (☎ 01 387 1066)

JAMES OF RUSHOLME, Baron (Life Peer UK 1959); Eric John Francis James; s of late Francis William James, of Parkstone, Dorset; *b* 13 April 1909; *Educ* Taunton's Sch Southampton, Queen's Coll Oxford (Hon Fell 1959); *m* 1939, Cordelia Mary, sis of the former ed of the Evening Standard Charles Wintour and da of Maj-Gen FitzGerald Wintour, CB, CBE, and his w Alice (who was sis of Sir Augustus Foster, 4 & last Bt); 1 s; *Career* High Master Manchester G S 1945-62, Vice-Chllr York U 1962-72, chm Headmasters' Conference 1953-54, of Communications Research Ctee in Building Industry 1963, of Inquiry into Teacher Training 1971, and of Personal Social Services Cncl 1973-76, chm Roy Fine Art Cmmn 1976-79; Hon LLD McGill, York (Toronto), Hon DLitt New Brunswick, D Univ York, Hon FRIBA 1979 kt 1956; *Clubs* Athenaeum; *Style* - The Rt Hon the Lord James of Rusholme; Penhill Cottage, West Witton, Leyburn, N Yorks

JAMES, Hon Mrs Belinda Jane; *née* Siddeley; da of 3 Baron Kenilworth; *b* 1950; *m* 1971 (m dis 1974), Christopher Aston James; *Style* - The Hon Mrs Belinda James; 5 Manson Place, SW7

JAMES, Hon Christopher George Walter; s and h of 4 Baron Northbourne; *b* 18 Feb 1926; *Educ* Eton and Magdalen, Oxford; *m* 1959, Marie Sygne, da of Henri Claudel; 3 s, 2 da; *Career* FRICS; *Clubs* Brooks's; *Style* - The Hon Christopher James; Coldharbour, Northbourne, Kent; 11 Eaton Place, SW1; Evistones, Otterburn, Northumberland

JAMES, Cynlais Morgan; CMG (1976); s of Thomas James; *b* 29 April 1926; *Educ* Trin Cambridge; *m* 1953, Mary, da of Richard Désriré Girouard by his w Lady Blanche Maud de la Poer Beresford (da of 6 Marquess of Waterford, KP, and Lady Beatrix Fitzmaurice, da of 5 Marquess of Lansdowne), also sis of the architectural historian Mark Girouard, *qv*; 2 da; *Career* FO (now FCO) 1951-; Ambass to Poland 1981-, previously 1 Sec Moscow, Head W European Dept FCO & Min Paris; served RAF 1944-47; *Clubs* Brooks's, Travellers' (Paris); *Style* - Cynlais James Esq, CMG; c/o FCO, SW1

JAMES, Edward Frank Willis; s of William Dodge James, CVO, JP, DL, by Evelyn, CBE (da of Sir Charles Forbes of Newe, 4 Bt, DL, by Helen, 2 da of Sir Thomas Moncreiffe of Moncreiffe, 7 Bt); Edward is hence 2 cous once removed of Sir Iain Moncreiffe of that Ilk, 11 Bt, and 3 cous of 24 Earl of Erroll; *b* 16 Aug 1907 (HM King Edward VII stood sponsor); *Educ* Eton, Ch Ch Oxford; *m* 1931 (m dis 1934), Tillie (Ottilie Ethel) Losch, the actress and da of Eugene Losch, of Vienna; *Career* lord of the manors of West Dean and Binderton, patron of the living of West Dean; late Hon Attaché Rome; novelist, collector of paintings, particularly surrealist ones; *Style* - Edward James Esq; 3 Culross st, W1

JAMES, Jeremy Edward; s of Herbert Edward James; *b* 6 June 1941; *Educ* Dulwich Coll; *m* 1980, Jacqueline, da of Thomas Walter Latter (d 1975); 5 children; *Career* FCA England and Wales, fin dir Williams Hudson Ltd; *Recreations* golf; *Clubs* Langley Park G C, Rugby, Cricketers, Wellington; yacht: 'Andromeda'; *Style* - Jeremy James Esq; 29 Weymouth St, W1 (☎ 01 637 8354)

JAMES, Hon Mrs (Jaquetta Mary Theresa); da of late 11 Baron Digby, KG, DSO, MC, TD; *b* 1928; *m* 1950, David Pelham James, MBE, DSC, MP, s of Wing-Cdr Sir Archibald James, KBE, MC; 4 s, 2 da; *Career* former memb Mid-Sussex Hosp Ctee, memb Dorset Area Health Authority 1974-, chm Hamilton Lodge Sch for Deaf Children Brighton 1962-; *Style* - The Hon Mrs James; Viking House, Child Okeford, Blandford, Dorset; Torosay Castle, Isle of Mull

JAMES, Hon Oliver Francis Wintour; s of Baron James of Rusholme (Life Peer); *b* 1943; *Educ* Winchester, Balliol Oxford; *m* 1965, Rosanna, da of Maj Gordon Bentley Foster, of Sleightholme Dale, Fadmoor, York; *Style* - The Hon Oliver James; Beda Lodge, Rowlands Gill, Tyne and Wear

JAMES, Hon Roderick Morrice; s (by 1 m) of Baron Saint Brides (Life Peer); *b* 1956; *Style* - The Hon Roderick James; 14 Belgrave gdns, NW8

JAMES, Stephen Lawrence; s of Walter James, of Bristol; *b* 19 Oct 1930; *Educ* Clifton, St Cat's Cambridge; *m* 1955, Eleanor, da of Reginald Cave, of Bristol; 2 s, 2 da; *Career* slr, sr ptnr Simmons & Simmons, of Dominion st, London E; dir H Clarkson Hldgs, Silver Navigation Ltd, Tradinvest Bank & Tst Co of Nassau Ltd; *Recreations* yachting (yachts- 'Jacobus', 'Morning Tide'); *Clubs* Roy Yacht Sqdn, Roy Thames Yacht, Roy Lymington Yacht, Law Soc; *Style* - Stephen James Esq; Widden, Shirley Holms, Lymington, Hants (☎ 682226); 1 Pembroke gdns, W8 (☎ 01 602 5757)

JAMES, Lady Serena Mary Barbara; *née* Lumley; JP (Richmond); da of late 10 Earl of Scarbrough, KG, GBE, KCB, TD; *b* 1901; *m* 1923, as his 2 w (he m 1 Lady Evelyn Wellesley, da of 4 Duke of Wellington; 1 s), Hon Robert James, s of late 2 Baron Northbourne; 2 da (*see* Baron Westbury); *Career* DStJ; *Style* - Lady

Serena James, JP; St Nicholas, Richmond, Yorks

JAMES, Thomas Freedom; s of William Ewart James (d 1948); *b* 4 April 1919; *Educ* Hitchin G S, Herne Bay Coll; *m* 1948, June Elizabeth, nee Moss; 3 s, 1 da; *Career* building & civil engrg, chm The William Moss Gp Ltd 1977-; *Recreations* gardening, bee-keeping, DIY; *Style* - Thomas James Esq; Broadgates, Potkiln Lane, Jordans, Beaconsfield, Bucks (☎ 0207 4277)

JAMESON, Hon Mrs (Margaret Miranda); *née* Lampson; da of 1 Baron Killearn, GCMG, CB, MVO, PC (d 1964); *b* 1923; *m* 1946, Geoffrey John Eustace Jameson; 1 s; *Style* - The Hon Mrs Jameson; 64 Limerston st, SW10

JAMIESON, Lady Mariegold (Magdalene); da of 3 Baron Howard of Glossop, MBE, and Baroness Beaumont, OBE; sis of 17 Duke of Norfolk, CB, CBE, MC; *b* 1919; *m* 1957, Gerald James Auldjo Jamieson, s of Sir Archibald Auldjo Jamieson, KBE, MC; 2 s; *Style* - Lady Mariegold Jamieson; 17 Elvaston Place, SW7; Yarrow House, Elmham, Norfolk

JANES, (John) Douglas (Webster); CB (1975); s of John Arnold Janes (d 1949); *b* 17 Aug 1918; *Educ* Trin Acad Edinburgh, Southgate County Sch Mddx, City & Guilds Coll, London U; *m* 1943, Margaret Isabel, nee Smith; 1 s, 2 da; *Career* memb Home Grown Timber Advsy Ctee 1979-, princ fin offr Miny of Housing and Local Government, then DOE 1968-73 (dep sec 1973), ch exec Maplin Dvpt Authority 1973-74 (N Ireland Office 1974-79), various management organisation reviews 1979-80, sec The Bach Choir 1981-; *Recreations* singing in choirs, using my hands; *Style* - Douglas Janes Esq, CB; 136 Waterfall rd, Southgate, N14 (☎ 886 2133)

JANION, Rear-Adm Sir Hugh Penderel; KCVO (1981); s of Capt Ralph Penderel Janion RN (d 1963); *b* 28 Sept 1923; *Educ* Malvern Link Prep, RNC Dartmouth; *m* 1956, Elizabeth Monica, da of Col Cecil Ferard (d 1970); 1 s, 1 da; *Career* ADC to HM 1975, Extra Equerry 1975-; Flag Offr Roy Yachts 1975-81, Capt RN 1966-75, Cdr RN 1958-66, War Service Russian Convoys Combined Operations Korea; Younger Brother of Trinity House *Recreations* golf, sailing, gardening; *Clubs* Roy Naval, Roy Albert Yacht, Sherborne Golf; *Style* - Rear-Adm Sir Hugh Janion, KCVO; National Westminster Bank Ltd, 41 Lothbury, London EC2

JANNER, Baron (Life Peer UK 1970); Barnett Janner; s of Joseph Janner, of Barry, Glam; *b* 20 June 1892; *Educ* Barry Co Sch, U of Wales; *m* 1927, Elsie Sybil, CBE, JP, da of late Joseph Cohen; 1 s, 1 da; *Career* kt 1960; MP (Lib) Whitechapel & Stepney St George's 1931-35, MP (L) W Leicester 1945-50, Leicester NW 1950-70, memb exec ctee (formerly pres) Bd of Deputies of British Jews 1955-64, former pres Zionist Fedn of Gt Britain and Ireland, pres Assoc of Jewish Friendly Socs, v-pres Parly Anglo-Benelux Gp, past chm Inter-Parly Union, chm Anglo-Israel Parly Gp, chm Lords and Commons Slrs Gp; *Style* - The Rt Hon the Lord Janner; 45 Morpeth Mans, Morpeth ter, SW1 (☎ 01 828 8700); 22 Upper Brook st, W1 (☎ 01 629 3981); The Jungle, Stone rd, Broadstairs, Kent (☎ Thanet 61642)

JANNER, Hon Greville Ewan; QC (1971), MP (L) Leicester West 1974-; s of Baron Janner (Life Peer); *b* 11 July 1928; *Educ* Bishop's Coll Sch Canada, St Paul's Sch, Trin Hall Cambridge; *m* 1955, Myra Louise, nee Sheink; 1 s, 2 da; *Career* barr 1955, author, journalist, broadcaster; pres Bd Deputies British Jews 1979-, contested (L) Wimbledon 1955, MP (L) Leicester North West 1970-74, v-chm All-Party Parly Ctee for Release of Soviet Jewry, fndr memb Int Ctee for Human Rights in USSR, dir Jewish Chronicle Newspaper Ltd, FIPM 1976; *Recreations* Magic Circle; *Style* - The Hon Greville Janner, QC, MP; 2 Linnell dve, NW11 (☎ 455-5157)

JARDINE, Andrew Colin Douglas; s and h of Brig Sir Ian Jardine, 4 Bt, OBE, MC; *b* 30 Nov 1955; *Style* - Andrew Jardine Esq

JARDINE, Alexander Maule; s and h of Sir William Jardine, 11 Bt, OBE, TD, JP,

DL; *b* 24 Aug 1947; *Educ* Gordonstoun; *Style* - Alexander Jardine Esq

JARDINE, Brig Sir Ian Liddell; 4 Bt (UK 1916), of Godalming, Co Surrey, OBE (1966), MC (1945); s of Maj-Gen Sir Colin Arthur Jardine, 3 Bt, CB, DSO, MC (d 1957); *b* 13 Oct 1923; *Educ* Charterhouse; *m* 1948, Priscilla Daphne, da of Douglas Middleton Parnham Scott-Phillips, of Halkshill, Largs, Ayrshire; 2 s, 2 da; *Heir* s, Andrew Jardine; *Career* served War 1942-45, Coldstream Gds; 2 Lt 1943, Maj 1950, Lt-Col 1964, Col 1968, Brig 1969, Brig GS 1973-75, Brig Inf 1975-78, UKLF, ret; ADC to HM The Queen 1976-78; *Clubs* Brooks's; *Style* - Brigadier Sir Ian Jardine, Bt, OBE, MC; Coombe Place, Meonstoke, Southampton (☎ Droxford 569)

JARDINE, Jean, Lady; Jean Evelyn Livesey; da of late Maj-Gen Sir William Andrew Liddell, KCMG, CB; *m* 1919, Maj-Gen Sir Colin Arthur Jardine, 3 Bt, CB, DSO, MC, (d 1957); *Style* - Jean, Lady Jardine; 46 Abingdon Court, Abingdon Villa, W8

JARDINE, Col Sir William Edward; 11 Bt (NS 1672) of Applegirth, OBE (1966), JP (Dumfries 1963), DL (1967); s of Sir Alexander Jardine, 10 Bt (d 1942); *b* 15 April 1917; *m* 1944, Ann Graham, da of Lt-Col Claud Maitland (d 1943); 2 s; *Heir* s, Alexander Maule Jardine; *Career* farmer 1967-, 22 Chief of Clan Jardine, Maj (ret) KOSB, memb Roy Co Archers (Queen's Bodyguard for Scotland), Dumfries CC 1963-75, chm Roads Ctee 1970-75, memb Annadale & Eckdale DC 1975-, chm Gen Purposes Ctee, chm Solway River Purification Bd 1976-; *Recreations* shooting, fishing; *Clubs* Army & Navy; *Style* - Col Sir William Jardine, Bt, OBE, JP, DL; Denbie, Lockerbie, Dumfriesshire (☎ Carrutherstown 631)

JARMAN, Michael Charles; JP (1978); s of Charles Bertram Jarman; *b* 12 June 1936; *Educ* Rossall; *m* 1965, Helen Barbara, da of Cecil Charles Robinson; 1 s, 3 da; *Career* chm and md WIPAC Gp of Cos 1978- (dir 1964); fell Inst of Dirs 1966, memb Marketing Soc 1979, gov Roy Agricultural Soc 1979, memb Inst of Marketing 1981; *Recreations* salmon fishing, equestrian sports, farming; *Clubs* Farmers' Club; *Style* - Michael Jarman Esq, JP; Castle Fields, Buckingham (☎ 02802 2127)

JARMAN, Robert George Kerr; s of Maj Alfred Reginald Jarman (ret); *b* 10 May 1950; *Educ* The Leys Sch Cambridge; *Career* jt-md Debrett's Peerage Ltd; *Recreations* tennis, cricket, shooting, skiing, sailing; *Style* - Robert Jarman Esq; 32 Primrose Mansions, Prince of Wales dve, SW11 (☎ 01 720 1135)

JAUNCEY, Hon Lord; Charles Eliot Jauncey; s of Capt John Henry Jauncey, DSO, RN (d 1958); *b* 8 May 1925; *Educ* Radley, Ch Ch Oxford, Glasgow U; *m* 1, 1948, Jean (m dis 1969), da of Sir Angus Cunninghame Graham; 2 s, 1 da; m 2, 1973, Elizabeth (m dis 1977), widow of Maj John Ballingal MC; m 3, 1977, Camilla, da of late Lt-Col Charles Cathcart DSO (ggs of 2 Earl Cathcart); *Career* Senator Coll of Justice Scotland 1979-, advocate 1949, Kintyre Pursuivant of Arms 1955-71, Sheriff Principal Fife and Kinross 1971-74, Judge Courts of Appeal Jersey & Guernsey 1972-; memb Roy Co Archers (Queen's Bodyguard for Scotland); *Recreations* shooting, fishing, genealogy, bicycling; *Clubs* New (Edinburgh); *Style* - The Hon Lord Jauncey; Tullichettle, Comrie, Perths (☎ Comrie 349); 12 Moray place, Edinburgh (☎ 031 225 4612)

JAYNE, Oliver; *Career* barr, dep dir-gen Nat Fedn Bldg Trades Employers, chm CBI Industl Relations and Wages & Conditions Ctee 1981-; *Style* - Oliver Jayne Esq; c/o CBI, 21 Tothill st, SW1 (☎ 01 930 6711)

JEANNERET, Hon Mrs (Marian Elizabeth); da of Baron Hobson (Life Peer d 1966); *b* 1942; *Educ* Newnham Cambridge (MA, PhD); *m* 1968, Michel Jeanneret; *Style* - The Hon Mrs Jeanneret; 115 Dewsbury rd, NW10

JEFFERSON, Lady Caragh Seymour; *née* Le Poer Trench; da of late 6 Earl of Clancarty; *b* 1933; *m* 1, 1953 (m dis 1961), Lt-Cdr John Anthony Lake, RN; 1 s, 2 da;

m 2, 1961, Capt Arthur Jay Oken, USAF; m 3, 1966, Capt Donald Van Horn Lee, USAF; m 4; m 5, Mr Jefferson; *Style* - Lady Caragh Jefferson; 6019 Castle Queen, San Antonio, Texas, 78218 USA

JEFFREY, Brian Maurice; s of Maurice Frank Jeffery (d 1968); *b* 24 June 1941; *Educ* Northampton G S, Birmingham U; *m* 1963, Susan, nee Fearn; 1 s, 1 da; *Career* chm and md Swift and Co Ltd 1978-; *Recreations* sport, music; *Clubs* RAC, Durrant's; *Style* - Brian Jeffrey Esq; 11 Shootersway pk, Berkhamsted, Herts (☎ 251 3069)

JEFFREYS, 2 Baron (UK 1952); Mark George Christopher Jeffreys; s of late Christopher John Darell Jeffreys (ka 1940; only s of 1 Baron), and of Lady Rosemary Beatrice Agar, da of 4 Earl of Normanton; suc gf 1960; *b* 2 Feb 1932; *Educ* Eton, RMA Sandhurst; *m* 1, 1956 (m dis 1967), Sarah Annabella, da of Maj Henry Garnett, of Somerton House, Winkfield, Berks; 2 s, 2 da; m 2, 1967, Anne Louise, da of His Honour Judge Sir (William) Shirley Worthington-Evans, 2 Bt (Btcy now extinct); 1 da; *Heir* s, Hon Christopher Jeffreys; *Career* Maj late Gren Gds and Lord of Manor of Burkham; *Clubs* White's; *Style* - The Rt Hon the Lord Jeffreys; Saddlewood Manor, Leighterton, Tetbury, Glos

JEFFREYS, Hon Alexander Charles Darell; s of 2 Baron Jeffreys; *b* 1959; *Style* - The Hon Alexander Jeffreys

JEFFREYS, Hon Christopher Henry Mark; s and h of 2 Baron Jeffreys; *b* 22 May 1957; *Style* - The Hon Christopher Jeffreys

JEFFREYS, Hon George Christian Darell; s of late Capt Christopher John Darell Jeffreys, MVO (only s of 1 Baron Jeffreys); *b* 1939; *Educ* Eton; *m* 1967, Karen Elizabeth Mary, da of late Col Hugo Meynell, MC, of Hollybush Park, Burton-on-Trent; 2 da; *Career* Capt Gren Gds (ret); raised to the rank of a Baron's son 1961; *Clubs* Guards', Boodle's; *Style* - The Hon George Jeffreys; Willoughby House, Rugby, Warwicks

JEFFREYS, Hon Laura; da of 2 Baron Jeffreys; *b* 1961; *Style* - The Hon Laura Jeffreys

JEFFREYS, Hon Rose Amanda; da of 2 Baron Jeffreys; *b* 1962; *Style* - The Hon Rose Jeffreys

JEFFREYS, Lady Rosemary Beatrice; *née* Agar; da of 4 Earl of Normanton (d 1933); *b* 1908; *m* 1931, Capt Christopher John Darell Jeffreys, MVO, Gren Gds (ka 1940), s of 1 Baron Jeffreys; *Style* - Lady Rosemary Jeffreys; Chapel Cottage, Bentworth, Alton, Hants

JEFFREYS, Hon Sophie Louise; da of 2 Baron Jeffreys; *b* 1972; *Style* - The Hon Sophie Jeffreys

JEFFS, Julian; QC (1975); s of Alfred Wright Jeffs (d 1974); *b* 5 April 1931; *Educ* Mostyn House Sch, Wrekin Coll, Downing Cambridge; *m* 1966, Deborah, nee Bevan; 3 s; *Career* barr, author; Recorder 1975, memb Ctee of Management, Int Wine & Food Soc 1965-67 & 1971-, v-pres Circle of Wine Writers (chm 1970-72), gen ed Faber's Wine Series; *Recreations* wine, walking, old cars, Iberian things; *Clubs* Beefsteak, Garrick, Reform, Saintsbury; *Style* - Julian Jeffs Esq, QC; Francis Taylor Bldg, Temple, EC4 (☎ 353 5657); Church Farm House, East Ilsley, Newbury, Berks (☎ East Ilsley 216)

JEGER, Baroness (Life Peeress UK 1979); Lena May Jeger; da of Charles Chivers and Alice Chivers, of Yorkley, Gloucestershire; *b* 19 Nov 1915; *Educ* Southgate County Sch Middx, Birkbeck Coll London U; *m* 1948, Dr Santo Wayburn Jeger, MP (d 1953); *Career* Manchester Guardian London Staff 1951-54 and 1961-; memb Nat Exec Ctee Labour Party 1968-80 (vice-chm 1978-79, chm 1979-80), MP (L) Holborn and St Pancras South Nov 1953-1959 and 1964-74, Camden, Holborn and St Pancras South 1974-79; *Style* - The Rt Hon the Lady Jeger; 9 Cumberland Terrace, Regent's Park, London NW1

JEHANGIR, Sir Hirji; 3 Bt (UK 1908), of Bombay; s of Sir Cowasjee Jehangir, 2 Bt, GBE, KCIE (d 1962); *b* 1 Nov 1915; *Educ* St Xavier's Sch Bombay, Magdalene Cambridge; *m* 1952, Jinoo, da of K H Cama; 2 s; *Heir* s, Jehangir Hirji Jehangir; *Career* chm Jehangir Art Gallery Bombay, United Asia Publications, dir Coorla Spinning and Weaving Mill; *Clubs* Crockford's, Willingdon (Bombay); *Style* - Sir Hirji Jehangir, Bt; Readymoney House, Nepeansea rd, Bombay 400 006, India; 24 Kensington Court Gardens, Kensington, London W8

JEHANGIR, Jehangir Hirji; s and h of Sir Hirji Jehangir, 3 Bt; *b* 23 Nov 1953; *Style* - Jehangir Jehangir Esq; c/o Sir Hirji Jehangir, Bt, Readymoney House, Nepeansea Road, Bombay 400 006, India; 24 Kensington Court Gardens, London W8

JEJEEBHOY, Sir Jamsetjee; 7 Bt (UK 1857), of Bombay; s of late Rustamjee Jamsetjee Jejeebhoy (eldest s of late Rustamjee Jamsetjee Jejeebhoy, himself n of 4 Bt); suc kinsman Sir Jamsetjee Jejeebhoy, 6 Bt, 1968, when he assumed the name of Jamsetjee Jejeebhoy, in lieu of Maneckjee Rustamjee Jejeebhoy; *b* 19 April 1913; *Educ* Bombay University; *m* 1943, Shirin Jehengr H Cama; 1 s, 1 da; *Heir* s Rustomjee Jeejeebhoy; *Career* chm Sir Jamsetjee Jejeebhoy Charity Trust, Sir J J Parsee Benevolent Inst, Seth Rustomjee Jamsetjee Jejeebhoy Gujrat Sch Fund, memb exec ctee Bomanjee Dinshaw Petit Parsee Gen Hosp, created Special Exec Magistrate 1977; *Clubs* Willingdon Sports, WIAA, Western India Turf, Poona; *Style* - Sir Jamsetjee Jejeebhoy, Bt; Beaulieu, 95 Worli Seaface, Bombay 25; Maneckji Wadia Building, Mahatma Ghandi Road, Fort, Bombay 1, India

JEJEEBHOY, Rustomjee; s and h of Sir Jamsetjee Jejeebhoy, 7 Bt; *b* 16 Nov 1957; *Style* - Rustomjee Jejeebhoy Esq; Beaulieu, 95 Worli Seaface, Bombay 25; Maneckji Wadia Building, Mahatma Gandhi Road, Fort, Bombay 1, India

JEJEEBHOY, Soonoo, Lady; Soonoo; da of late Hormusji F Commissariat, of Bombay; *m* 1951, Sir Jamsetjee Jejeebhoy, 6 Bt (d 1968); *Style* - Soonoo, Lady Jejeebhoy; Sett Minar, Pedder rd, Bombay 26, India; Fountain Hall, 372 Koregaon Park, Poona

JELLEY, Bt-Col Marcus; OBE (1944), TD, DL (1950); s of Harry George Jelley (d 1937); *b* 18 Oct 1908; *Educ* Berkhamsted Sch; *m* 1945, Elizabeth Gwendolen, nee Noll; 2 s, 2 da; *Career* Bt-Col (RA), NW Europe; chm & dir A Bell & Co Ltd Northampton and A Bell & Co (Eire) Ltd Dublin, JP (Northants 1946-76); *Style* - Bt-Col Marcus Jelley OBE, TD, DL; Southlands, 5 The Avenue, Dallington, Northampton (☎ 0604 51704)

JELLICOE, 2 Earl (UK 1925); George Patrick John Rushworth Jellicoe; DSO (1942), MC (1944), PC (1963); also Viscount Jellicoe (UK 1917) and Viscount Brocas (UK 1925); s of Admiral of the Fleet, 1 Earl Jellicoe, GCB, OM, GCVO (d 1935, of whom, when his zeal for prosecuting the Battle of Jutland was impugned, Sir Winston Churchill remarked that he was the only man on either side who could have lost the war in an afternoon; his paternal grandmother was descended from the originally Norman family of Brocas, of Beaurepaire, Bramley, nr Basingstoke), and of late Florence Gwendoline, da of Sir Charles Cayzer, 1 Bt; godson of King George V; *b* 4 April 1918; *Educ* Winchester, Trin Cambridge; *m* 1, 1944 (m dis 1966), Patricia Christine, da of Jeremiah O'Kane, of Vancouver, Canada; 2 s, 2 da; m 2, 1966, Philippa, da of late Philip Dunne (of the same family as the poet John Donne), of Gatley Park, Leominster; 1 s, 1 da; *Heir* s, Viscount Brocas; *Career* Page of Hon to King George VI, 1939-45 War in Middle East as Lt-Col Coldstream Gds (wounded, despatches thrice, DSO, MC, Leg of Hon, French Croix de Guerre, Greek Mil Cross), a Lord-in-Waiting to HM Feb-June 1961, Jt Parly Sec Min of Housing and Local Govt 1961-62, Min of State Home Office 1962-63, First Lord of Admiralty 1963-64, Min of Defence for RN April-Oct 1964, Dep Leader of Opposition House of Lords 1967, Lord Privy Seal, and Leader of House of Lords 1970-73, chm Tate & Lyle

Ltd 1978-, dir S G Warburg & Co 1973-, Sotheby Holdings 1973-, Smiths Industries 1973-, Morgan Crucible 1974-; *Clubs* Brooks's; *Style* - The Rt Hon the Earl Jellicoe, DSO, MC, PC; Tidcombe Manor, Tidcombe, nr Marlborough, Wilts (☎ Oxenwood 225); 97 Onslow sq, SW7 (☎ 01 584 1551)

JELLICOE, Lady Daisy; da of 2 Earl Jellicoe, DSO, MC, PC; *b* 1970; *Style* - Lady Daisy Jellicoe

JELLICOE, Lady Emma Rose; da of 2 Earl Jellicoe, DSO, MC, PC; *b* 1967; *Style* - Lady Emma Jellicoe

JELLICOE, Hon Justin Amadeus; s and h of Viscount Brocas; *b* 1970; *Style* - The Hon Justin Jellicoe

JELLICOE, Hon John Philip; s of 2 Earl Jellicoe, DSO, MC, PC; *b* 1966; *Style* - The Hon John Jellicoe

JELLICOE, Hon Nicholas Charles; s of 2 Earl Jellicoe, DSO, MC, PC; *b* 1953; *Educ* Eton; *Style* - The Hon Nicholas Jellicoe

JELLICOE, Lady Zara Lison Josephine; da of 2 Earl Jellicoe, DSO, MC, PC; *b* 1948; *Style* - Lady Zara Jellicoe

JENKINS OF PUTNEY, Baron (UK 1981); Hugh Gater Jenkins; s of Joseph Jenkins and Florence, nee Gater; *b* 27 July 1908; *Educ* Enfield G S; *m* 1936, Marie, nee Crosbie; *Career* MP (L) Wandsworth 1964-79, Min Arts 1974-76; memb Nat Theatre Bd 1976-, late Assur Co and bank employee; chm CND 1979-, Theatres Advsy Cncnl 1980-, Battersea Arts Centre 1980-; dir Theatres Tst 1978-; *Style* - Rt Hon Lord Jenkins of Putney; 75 Kenilworth Court, Lower Richmond rd, SW15 (☎ 01 788 0371)

JENKINS, Hon Mrs (Judith Catharine Dean); da of Baron Soper (Life Peer); *b* 1942; *m* 1970, Alan Jenkins; *Style* - The Hon Mrs Jenkins; 33 Midholm, NW11

JENKINS, Maurice; s of David Jenkins (d 1978); *b* 9 July 1925; *Educ* Acklam Sch Middlesbrough, Manchester U, London U; *m* 1951, Dorothy, nee Tait; 1 s, 2 da; *Career* admin offr HM Overseas Civil Serv Nigeria 1951-62, dep chm Rugby Portland Cement Co Ltd 1976 (md 1968) and chm & dir of assoc cos; chm Cockburn Cement Ltd W Australia 1974-, memb London Bd Norwich Union Insurance Gp 1974-80, dir AP Bank Ltd 1981-, v-pres Nat Cncl of Building Material Producers 1976-, memb Nat Ec Dvpt Ctee for Civil Engineering 1972-; *Recreations* business, family; *Style* - Maurice Jenkins Esq; 5 Bilton rd, Rugby, Warwicks (☎ 65547)

JENKINSON, Sir Anthony Banks; 13 Bt (E 1661); s of late Capt John Banks Jenkinson (er s of 12 Bt); suc gf Sir George Banks Jenkinson, 12 Bt, 1915; *b* 3 July 1912; *Educ* Eton, Balliol Oxford; *m* 1943, Frances, da of Harry Stremmel, of New York, USA; 1 s, 2 da; *Heir* s, John Jenkinson; *Career* foreign correspondent 1935-40, editor Allied Labour News Service, London and New York 1940-46, md Cayman Boats Ltd Cayman Is 1947-52, Morgan's Harbour Ltd Port Royal Jamaica 1953-73, dir Port Royal Co of Merchants Ltd 1965-, Spanish Main Investments Ltd Grand Cayman 1962-, Caribbean Bank (Cayman) Ltd 1973-, Cayman Free Press Ltd 1974-; *Clubs* United Oxford & Cambridge University, MCC, Bembridge Sailing, Cayman Islands Yacht; *Style* - Sir Anthony Jenkinson, Bt; 491 South Church st, Grand Cayman, West Indies; Hawkesbury, Chippenham, Wilts

JENKINSON, John Banks; s and h of Sir Anthony Jenkinson, 13 Bt; *b* 16 Feb 1945; *Educ* Eton; *Style* - John Jenkinson Esq

JENKS, Constance, Lady; Constance Edith; da of W R Currie, of Beckenham, Kent; *m* 1939, as his 2 wife, Sir Maurice Jenks, 1 Bt (d 1946); *Style* - Constance, Lady Jenks; c/o 71 Midhurst Hill, Bexleyheath, Kent

JENKS, Maurice Arthur Brian; s and h of Sir Richard Atherley Jenks, 2 Bt; *b* 28 Oct 1933; *Educ* Charterhouse; *m* 1962, Susan L, da of Leslie Allen, of Glenside, Star Lane, Hooley, Surrey; 1 da; *Style* -

Maurice Jenks Esq; Milley Farm, Waltham St Lawrence, Reading

JENKS, Sir Richard Atherley; 2 Bt (UK 1932); s of Sir Maurice Jenks (d 1946); *b* 26 July 1906; *Educ* Charterhouse; *m* 1932, Marjorie Suzanne Arlette, da of late Sir Arthur Philip du Cros, 1 Bt; 2 s; *Heir* s, Maurice Jenks; *Career* chartered accountant, ret; *Style* - Sir Richard Jenks, Bt; 42 Sussex sq, W2 2SP (☎ 01 262 8356)

JENKYNS, Richard Henry Austen; s of Henry Leigh Jenkyns (whose mother Winifred was gda of the Rev James Austen-Leigh, himself n of Jane Austen), of Aldeburgh; *b* 18 March 1949; *Educ* Eton, Balliol Oxford; *Career* writer and classicist; winner of the Arts Cncl Nat Book Award of 1981 (£7,500) with 'The Victorians and Ancient Greece' (also Yorkshire Post Book Award 1981); Fellow All Souls 1972-81; lecturer in Classics Bristol U 1978-81, Fellow LMH Oxford 1981-; *Recreations* playing the piano, looking at buildings; *Style* - Richard Jenkyns Esq; Lady Margaret Hall, Oxford (☎ 0865 54353)

JENNINGS, Hon Mrs (Catherine Frances); *née* Donaldson; da of Baron Donaldson of Kingsbridge (Life Peer); *b* 1945; *m* 1973, G Mark Jennings; children; *Style* - The Hon Mrs Jennings; 57 Winsham Grove, SW11

JENNINGS, Hon Mrs (Deanna Christine); *née* Layton; da of 2 Baron Layton; *b* 1938; *m* 1964, Melvin Calverley Jennings, MB, FRCS; *Career* MB, BS, MRCS, LRCP; *Style* - The Hon Mrs Jennings; 66 Blackborough rd, Reigate, Surrey

JENNINGS, Col Michael Turberville Nevill; CBE (1968); s of Frank Nevill Jennings CBE DL JP (d 1957); *b* 23 Feb 1916; *Educ* Uppingham Sch, Clare Cambridge; *m* 1944, Jessie Jane, nee MacLeod; 2 s (1 s decd); *Career* cmd Queen's Roy Regt 1937-, Instructor Staff Coll Quetta 1944-47, cmd 6 Bn Queen's Roy Regt 1955-58, Dep Cmdt Roy Hong Kong Defence Force 1958-61; *Clubs* Army & Navy, Roy Solent Yacht; *Style* - Col Michael Jennings CBE; Mariners Cottage, Longs Wharf, Yarmouth, Isle of Wight (☎ Yarmouth 760364)

JENRICK, William John; s of Sidney Thomas Jenrick; *b* 23 Nov 1940; *Educ* Ducie H S; *m* 1975, Jennifer Ann, nee Robertson; 1 da (Jane Robertson b 1979); *Career* AICM, md: Cannon (Holdings) Ltd, Cannon Industries Ltd, Oakley Technical Developments Ltd, Gwyn J Evans Ltd; *Recreations* chess; *Style* - William Jenrick Esq; 2 The Paddock, Shifnal, Shropshire

JENSEN, Michael Harold; s of Eric Axel Jensen (d 1964); *b* 24 Oct 1942; *Educ* St Lawrence Coll; *m* 1969, Linda Jeniffer, nee Edwards; 2 da; *Career* md HL Thomson Ltd 1975-, md H L Thomson (E Anglia) Ltd, exec dir Hogg Robinson & Gardner, dir Mountain (Marine) Ltd, md Eden Court Property Co Ltd 1968-, memb Lloyd's 1980; *Recreations* shooting, sailing (motor yacht 'Choey Lin'); *Clubs* Les Ambassadeurs, Lloyd's Yacht, Haven Ports Yacht; *Style* - Michael Jensen Esq; Oaken, Falconers Park, Sawbridgeworth, Herts

JEPHCOTT, Sir (John) Anthony; 2 Bt (UK 1962); s of Sir Harry Jephcott, 1 Bt (d 1978); *b* 21 May 1924; *Educ* Aldenham, St John's Coll Oxford, LSE; *m* 1, 1949 (m dis 1978), Sylvia Mary, da of Thorsten F Relling, of Wellington, NZ; 2 da; m 2, 1978, Josephine Agnes, da of Philip Sheridan, of Perth, WA; *Heir* bro, Neil Jephcott; *Career* 1939-45 War with REME, later RAEC, formerly manufacturer of anaesthesia equipment, md Penlon Ltd 1952-73, Pen Medic Ltd, NZ 1973-78; orchardist; *Style* - Sir Anthony Jephcott, Bt; 144 Puriri Park rd, Whangarei, New Zealand

JEPHCOTT, Doris, Lady; Doris; da of Henry Gregory; *m* 1919, Sir Harry Jephcott, 1 Bt (d 1978); *Style* - Doris, Lady Jephcott; Weetwood, 1 Cheney st, Pinner, Middx

JEPHCOTT, Neil Welbourn; s of Sir Harry Jephcott, 1 Bt (d 1978), and hp of bro, Sir Anthony Jephcott, 2 Bt; *b* 3 June 1929; *Educ* Aldenham, and Emmanuel Cambridge; *m* 1951, Mary Denise (d 1977), da of Arthur Muddiman, of Abbots

Mead, W Clandon, Surrey; *Style* - Neil Jephcott Esq; Penvrane, Carnon Downs, Truro, Cornwall

JERMAN, Herbert Noel; CBE (1967); s of John Maurice Jerman (d 1960); *b* 11 Dec 1909; *Educ* Newtown County Boys' Sch, Univ Coll Wales Aberystwyth; *m* 1939, Blodwen Elizabeth, nee Jenkins; *Career* chm Clwyd/Powys Archaeological Trust 1974-, Small Business Consultant Welsh Dvpt Agency 1977-80, ch offr Wales Cncl for Small Industries in Rural Areas 1970-77, Assist Sec Welsh Office 1957-70; *Recreations* gardening; *Clubs* RAC; *Style* - Herbert Jerman Esq, CBE; Dolforgan Gardens, Kerry, Newtown, Powys (☎ 0686 88 204)

JERMYN, Earl; (Frederick William) John Augustus Hervey; s and h of 6 Marquess of Bristol; *b* 15 Sept 1954; *Educ* Harrow, Neufchâtel U; *Heir* half-bro, Lord Nicholas Hervey; *Career* governing ptnr Jermyn Shipping; dir Estate Associates Ltd; MInstD; *Clubs* Roy Thames Yacht, House of Lords Yacht; *Style* - Earl Jermyn; 45 Av Grande Bretagne, Monte Carlo

JERRAM, Maj-Gen Richard M; MBE; *aet* 52 as of June 1981; *Career* Dir RAC MOD 1981; Roy Tank Regt, Maj-Gen 1981- (Brig 30 June 1977-81), completed Overseas Def Coll Course and Army Staff Course; Logistics Section Equipment Management QMG 1979-81; *Style* - Maj-Gen Richard Jerram, MBE; c/o RAC, MOD, SW1 (☎ 01 218 9000)

JERSEY, 9 Earl of (E 1697); George Francis Child-Villiers; also Viscount Grandison (I 1620), Viscount Villiers (E 1691), Baron Villiers of Hoo (E 1691); s of 8 Earl of Jersey (d 1923; himself s of 7 Earl, who numbered 10 books produced by Caxton in his library until 1885, when he sold it; the 7 Earl's gf (the 5 Earl) won the Derby three times (in 1825, 1827 & 1836) and was m to Lady Sarah Fane (da of 10 Earl of Westmorland); the latter, generally dubbed 'Queen Sarah', was featured as Lady St Julians in Disraeli's 'Coningsby' and Zenobia in the same author's 'Endymion'; her mother-in-law and predecessor as Lady Jersey was for a while George IV's mistress, while her daughter-in-law and successor was da of Sir Robert Peel) and of Lady Cynthia Almina Constance Mary Needham, da of 3 Earl of Kilmorey (she m 2, 1925, W R Slessor (d 1945) and d 1947); *b* 15 Feb 1910; *Educ* Eton, Ch Ch Oxford; *m* 1, 1932 (m dis 1937), Patricia Kenneth, da of Kenneth Richards, of Cootamundra, NSW; 1 da; m 2, 1937 (m dis 1946), Virginia, da of James Cherrill, of Hollywood, USA; m 3, 1947, Bianca Maria Adriana Luciana, da of late Enrico Mottironi, of Via Goffredo Casalis, Turin, Italy; 2 s, 1 da; *Heir* s, Viscount Villiers; *Career* formerly Maj RA (TA), chm Jersey Island Semen Exports Ltd, Associated Hotels Ltd, Hotel Horizon Ltd, dir Jersey Gen Investment Trust Ltd, Jersey Gen Executor and Trustee Co Ltd; *Style* - The Rt Hon the Earl of Jersey; Radier Manor, Longueville, Jersey, CI (☎ (Jersey) Central 53102)

JERVIS, Hon Cassandra Phillida Anne; da of 7 Viscount St Vincent; *b* 1949; *Style* - The Hon Cassandra Jervis

JERVIS, Hon Edward Robert James; s and h of 7 Viscount St Vincent; *b* 12 May 1951; *Educ* Radley; *m* 1977, Victoria Margaret, da of Wilton Joseph Oldham, of Jersey; 1 da (Emma Margaret Anne b 1980); *Career* co dir; *Recreations* skiing, water sports, chess, backgammon; *Style* - The Hon Edward Jervis; Colinas Verdes 26, Bensafrim, Lagos 8600, Algarve, Portugal

JERVIS, Hon Ronald Nigel John; s of 7 Viscount St Vincent; *b* 1954; *Style* - The Hon Ronald Jervis

JESSEL, 2 Baron (UK 1924); Sir Edward Herbert Jessel; 2 Bt (UK 1917), CBE (1963); s of 1 Baron Jessel, CB, CMG (d 1950), and Maud (d 1965), 5 da of late Rt Hon Sir Julian Goldsmid, 3 Bt, MP; bro-in-law of Sir Geoffrey Agnew; *b* 25 March 1904; *Educ* Eton, Ch Ch Oxford; *m* 1, 1935 (m dis 1960), Lady Helen Maglona Vane-Tempest-Stewart, 3 da of 7 Marquess of Londonderry, KG, MVO, TD, PC (d 1949); 2 da (1 s decd); m 2, 1960, Jessica, da of late William de Wet; *Heir* none; *Career* barr Inner Temple 1926, dep speaker House of Lords 1963-77, chm Associated Leisure Ltd; *Clubs*

Garrick, White's; *Style* - The Rt Hon the Lord Jessel, CBE; 4 Sloane Terrace Mansions, SW1 (☎ 01 730 7843)

JESSEL, Hon Mrs (Amelia Grace); *née* FitzRoy; da of 2 Viscount Daventry; *b* 1930; *m* 1950, Capt David Charles George Jessel, Coldstream Gds (s of Sir Richard Jessel); 1 s, 1 da; *Style* - The Hon Mrs Jessel; The Grove House, Droxford, Hants

JESSEL, Sir Charles John; 3 Bt (UK 1883), of Ladham House, Goudhurst, Co Kent; s of Sir George Jessel, MC, 2 Bt (d 1977); *b* 29 Dec 1924; *Educ* Eton, Balliol Oxford; *m* 1, 1956, Shirley Cornelia (d 1977), da of John Waters, of Northampton; 2 s, 1 da; m 2, 1979, Gwendolyn Mary, da of late Laurance Devereux, OBE, and widow of Charles Langer; *Heir* s, George Jessel; *Career* Lt 15/19 Hussars (despatches) WW II, Hon Fell Psionic Med Soc 1977, former JP Kent; *Clubs* Cavalry and Guards; *Style* - Sir Charles Jessel, Bt; South Hill Farm, Hastingleigh, nr Ashford, Kent (☎ Elmsted 325)

JESSEL, David Charles George; s of Sir Richard Hugh Jessel (d 1979, bro of Sir George Jessel, 2 Bt); *b* 20 June 1924; *Educ* Eton; *m* 1, 1950, Hon Amelia FitzRoy (m dis 1978), da of Viscount Daventry *qv*; 1 s, 1 da; m 2, 1980, Matilda McCormick; *Career* chm Intervention Bd for Agricultural Produce 1980-, dep chm Eagle Star Hldgs 1980-, dep chm & md Eagle Star Properties 1980-, Jessel Toynbee & Co Ltd 1948 (md 1963-77), chm & dep chm London Discount Market Assoc 1967-71, chm Bernard Sunley Investment Trust 1977-80; *Recreations* fishing, shooting, sailing; *Clubs* Cavalry and Guards; *Style* - David Jessel Esq; 22 Cambridge rd, SW11 (☎ 01 228 8445)

JESSEL, George Elphinstone; s and h of Sir Charles Jessel, 3 Bt; *b* 15 Dec 1957; *Style* - George Jessel Esq

JESSEL, Joan Lady; Joan Betty; da of late Dr David Ewart, OBE, MD, FRCS, of Chichester, and formerly wife of late 2 Baron Russell of Liverpool; *m* 2, 1948, as his 2 wife, Sir George Jessel, MC, 2 Bt (d 1977); *Style* - Joan, Lady Jessel; Ladham House, Goudhurst, Kent

JESSON, Hon Mrs (Jean Davina); *née* Stuart; da of late 1 Viscount Stuart of Findhorn, CH, MVO, MC; *b* 1932; *m* 1, 1951, John Reedham Erksine Berney, Lt Roy Norfolk Regt (ka Korea 1952), s of late Maj Sir Thomas Reedham Berney, 10 Bt, MC; 1 s; m 2, 1954, Percy William Jesson, s of Lt-Col Harold Jesson; 2 s, 1 da; *Style* - The Hon Mrs Jesson; Finchingfield, Braintree, Essex

JEWITT, Anthony John; s of John Jewitt; *b* 7 Oct 1935; *Educ* Chingford G S, Harvard U; *m* 1958, Janet Julia; 3 children; *Career* gp chm ICC Information Gp 1969-; *Recreations* skiing, tennis, horse racing; owner of racehorse 'Marcom Boy'; *Style* - Anthony Jewitt Esq; Majenca, Pelling Hill, Old Windsor, Berks

JOBERNS, Geoffrey Lewis; s of William Lewis Joberns; *b* 6 Nov 1929; *Educ* Solihull Public Sch; *m* 1955, Barbara Anne, nee Hemming; 1 s (Stephen Lewis b 1969), 2 da (Karen Elizabeth Gaymond, Louise Anne b 1960); *Career* slr 1956 Price Atkins slrs Birmingham, memb Lloyd's Underwriters 1979, public company chm 1966, dir: Blendage Ltd, Blythe Investments Ltd, Cresswellshawe Properties Ltd, First City Properties Ltd, Joberns Securities Ltd, MLD (Solihull) Ltd, Miria Investments Ltd, Second City Dvpts Ltd, Tranleigh Properties Ltd, WPW Holdings Ltd; *Recreations* golf; *Clubs* Shirley Golf, Midlands Sporting Club; *Style* - Geoffrey Joberns Esq; Packwood Towers, Windmill Lane, Packwood, Solihull, West Midlands (☎ Knowle 2267)

JOBSON, Lady Lavinia (Anne); *née* Brabazon; da of 14 Earl of Meath; *b* 1945; *m* 1969, John Ernest Baron Jobson; 1 s, 3 da; *Style* - Lady Lavinia Jobson; Barnacullia, Kilmacanoge, Co Wicklow

JOCELYN, Hon Cecilia Rose; da of Viscount Jocelyn and gda of 9 Earl of Roden; *b* 1976; *Style* - The Hon Cecilia Jocelyn

JOCELYN, Hon James Michael; 3 s of 9 Earl of Roden; *b* 12 April 1943; *Educ* Stowe, Trin Coll Dublin; *Style* - The Hon James Jocelyn

JOCELYN, Viscount; Robert John Jocelyn; s and h of 9 Earl of Roden; *b* 25 Aug 1938; *Educ* Stowe; *m* 1970, Sara Cecilia, da of Brig Andrew Dunlop, of Que Que, Zimbabwe; 1 da; *Heir* bro, Hon Thomas Jocelyn; *Career* late Lt Irish Gds; *Style* - Viscount Jocelyn; The White House, Chaddleworth, Newbury, Berks

JOCELYN, Hon Thomas Alan; 2 s of 9 Earl of Roden; *b* 4 Oct 1941; *Educ* Stowe, RNC Dartmouth; *m* 1966, Fiona, da of Capt Rudland Dallas Cairns, DSC, RN, of Co Wexford; 2 da; *Career* hp of bro, Viscount Jocelyn; Lt-Cdr RN (ret); *Style* - Lt Cdr Hon Thomas Jocelyn, RN

JOFFRE RUSSELL, Hon Mrs (Easter Donatella); *née* Young; da of 2 Baron Kennet; *b* 1949; *m* 1981, Frank Joffre Russell; *Style* - The Hon Mrs Joffre Russell

JOHANSEN, Hon Mrs; Hon Jane; *née* Blyton; da of Baron Blyton (Life Peer); *b* 1920; *m* 1943, John Johansen (d 1955); children; *Style* - The Hon Mrs Johansen; 84 Nevison av, S Shields, Tyne & Wear

JOHN, Hon Mrs; Hon (Mary) Joan Fenella Hope; *née* Hope-Morley; da of 2 Baron Hollenden, JP (d 1977); *b* 1915; *m* 1, 1941 (m dis 1965), David Babington Smith, s of late Sir Henry Babington Smith, GBE, CH, KCB, CSI; 1 da; m 2, 1966, Geoffrey John; *Style* - The Hon Mrs John; Lime House, Kintbury, Newbury, Berks

JOHN, Richard; CBE (1969), JP (Glam 1969); s of Edward John (d 1947); *b* 5 June 1904; *Educ* Barry Sec Sch, Cardiff Tech Coll, Univ Coll Cardiff; *m* 1932, Bessie Louise, nee Dunn; 1 s; *Career* slr 1938, County Slr 1943-69, Hon Sec Lord Chllr's Adv Cttee Glam 1953-69, chm Cncl Welsh Nat Sch of Medicine and Fin Cttee, memb Mgmnt Cttee Tenovus Cancer (chm of Trustees), memb Ct Govs Wales U & Cardif U, memb Bd Civic Trust for Wales; *Recreations* gardening, shooting; *Clubs* Cardiff & County; *Style* - Richard John Esq, CBE, JP; 22 Fairwater rd, Llandaff, Cardiff (☎ 562891)

JOHN-MACKIE, Baron (Life Peer UK 1981); John Mackie; s of Maitland Mackie, OBE, farmer, and Mary, nee Yull; er bro of Baron Mackie of Benshie and Maitland Mackie, the Ld-Lieut of Aberdeenshire; *b* 24 Nov 1909; *Educ* Aberdeen G S, N of Scotland Coll of Ag; *m* 1934, Jeannie Inglis Milne; 3 s, 2 da; *Career* farmer in Essex and Middx, MP (L) Enfield E 1959-74, Jt Parly Sec Min Ag 1964-70; chm Forestry Commission 1976-79; *Style* - Rt Hon Lord John-Mackie; Harold's Park, Nazeing, Waltham Abbey, Essex (☎ Nazeing 2202)

JOHNS, Brooke Elliot Mackelcan; s of Jack Elliot Mackelcan Johns (d 1969); *b* 20 Sept 1939; *Educ* Marlborough Coll; *m* 1965, Angela Christine, da of Sir William Albert Fairbairn 5 Bt (d 1972); 2 s (Jeremy b 1967, Anthony b 1971); *Career* Chartered Accountant, md Moy Holdings Ltd (Dublin), dir Tace Ltd (London); *Recreations* outdoor activities; *Style* - Brooke Johns Esq; The Old Glebe House, Shankill, Co Dublin, Ireland (☎ Dublin 822425)

JOHNSON, Hon Mrs; Hon Anne; *née* Robbins; da of Baron Robbins, CH, CB; *b* 10 Oct 1925; *m* 1958, Christopher Johnson; has issue; *Style* - The Hon Mrs Johnson; 39 Wood Lane, N6

JOHNSON, Adrian Mackey; CBE (1968); s of Dr A M Johnson (d 1922); *b* 19 Jan 1916; *Educ* St Ignatius' Coll Riverview, Sydney U; *m* 1942, Margaret Flood, nee Nagle; 2 s, 3 da (1 s decd); *Career* consultant dermatologist, univ lecturer in Dermatology Sydney U 1966-76, Hon Physician and Head Dept of Dermatology Roy Prince Alfred Hospital 1954-81; *Recreations* racing, golf; *Clubs* University, Royal Sydney Golf; *Also* owner of racehorse Homme de Fer; *Style* - Adrian Johnson Esq, CBE; 1 Kirkoswald ave, Mosman, NSW 2088 (☎ 969 9657)

JOHNSON, Dame Celia; DBE (1981, CBE 1958); da of John Robert Johnson; *b* 18 Dec 1908; *Educ* St Paul's Girls' Sch, RADA; *m* 1935, Peter Fleming (d 1971); 1 s, 2 da; *Career* stage and film actress; plays include The Cherry Orchard (Chichester Festival Theatre), The Master Builder (Nat Theatre), Hamlet (Cambridge Theatre) and others; films include Brief

Encounter, A Kid for Two Farthings, The Prime of Miss Jean Brodie, and others; *Style* - Dame Celia Johnson, DBE; Merrimoles House, Nettlebed, Oxon

JOHNSON, Colpoys Guy; s and h of Sir Peter Johnson, 7 Bt; *b* 13 Nov 1965; *Style* - Colpoys Johnson Esq

JOHNSON, Christopher Louis McIntosh; s of Donald McIntosh Johnson, MP for Carlisle 1955-64 (d 1978); *b* 12 June 1931; *Educ* Winchester, Magdalen Oxford; *m* 1958, Anne; 1 s, 3 da; *Career* Capt Roy Army Educational Corps London; ec advr Lloyds Bank Ltd 1976, dir Financial Times 1972-76 (foreign ed 1965-67, md 1967-70, dir Business Enterprises Div 1971-72); *Recreations* sailing, music; *Clubs* Overseas Bankers; *Style* - Christopher Johnson Esq; 39 Wood Lane, London N6 (☎ 01 340 4970)

JOHNSON, Hon Mrs (Diana Margaret); da of Adm of the Fleet 1 Baron Keyes, GCB, KCVO, CMG, DSO (d 1945); *b* 1910; *m* 1936, Col James Robert Johnson, DSO, OBE, MC, Roy Welch Fus; 2 s, 1 da; *Style* - The Hon Mrs Johnson; Tingewick House, Buckingham

JOHNSON, Hon Mrs (Frances Ann); *née* Guest; da of 2 Viscount Wimborne, OBE, JP, DL; *b* 18 Nov 1942; *m* 1971, Ernest Johnson; *Style* - The Hon Mrs Johnson; 420 E 86th st, NYC, New York, USA

JOHNSON, Lady Ida Mary; *née* Ramsay; da of late 14 Earl of Dalhousie; *b* 1906; *m* 1938, Maj-Gen Sir George Frederick Johnson KCVO CB CBE DSO Scots Gds (d 1980); 2 s, 1 da; *Style* - Lady Ida Johnson; Castlesteads, Brampton, Cumberland

JOHNSON, Sir Peter Colpoys Paley; 7 Bt (GB 1755), of New York, North America; s of Lt-Col Sir John Johnson, 6 Bt, MBE (d 1975); *b* 26 March 1930; *Educ* Wellington Coll, RMC of Science Shrivenham; *m* 1, 1956, (m dis 1972), Clare, da of Dr Nigel Bruce; 1 s, 2 da; m 2, 1973, Caroline Elisabeth, da of Wing Cdr Sir John Hodsoll, CB (d 1971); 1 s; *Heir* s Colpoys Guy Johnson; *Career* RA 1949-61 (Capt); publisher; dir Nautical Publishing Co Ltd 1971-, Ocean Racing Correspondent Yachting World 1971-; *Recreations* sailing (yacht: 'Innovation'); *Clubs* Royal Yacht Squadron, Royal Ocean Racing, Royal Southern Yacht; *Style* - Sir Peter Johnson, Bt; Dene End, Buckland Dene, Lymington, Hampshire (☎ Lymington 75921)

JOHNSON, Hon Mrs (Patricia Mary); *née* French; da of 6 Baron De Freyne; *b* 1917; *m* 1941, Reginald Johnson (d 1958); 1 s, 1 da; *Style* - The Hon Mrs Johnson; 181 Rosendale rd, W Dulwich, SE21

JOHNSON, Robin Eliot; s of Maj Percy Eliot Johnson (d 1962), and hp of kinsman, Sir Victor Johnson, 6 Bt; *b* 1929; *Educ* St John's Coll Johannesburg; *m* 1954, Barbara Alfreda, da of late Alfred T Brown, of Germiston, Transvaal; 1 s, 2 da; *Style* - Robin Johnson Esq

JOHNSON, Victor Horace (Johnnie); s of the late Herbert Johnson; *b* 14 May 1920; *Educ* Handsworth G S, Birmingham Sch Architecture; *m* 1972, Gillian Margaret, nee Longmore; 2 s, 1 da, (also 2 step s, 1 step da); *Career* chartered builder, md Herbert Johnson 1946-61, chm Page-Johnson Builders 1961-72, chm West European Building Corpn 1969-78, dir Bovis 1972-74, chm Escadale Properties 1972, founder The Johnnie Johnson Trust 1961, and The Johnnie Johnson Adventure Trust/Youth Afloat 1972; *Recreations* flying, sailing, forestry, farming (yachts: 'Bucks Fizz' and 'British Maid'; aeroplane: Cessna Skylane Registered GILLI); *Clubs* RAF, Lloyd's Yacht, Roy Dart Yacht, Roy Perth Yacht (W Australia); *Style* - Victor Johnson Esq; Elmdon House, Elmdon Park, Solihull, West Midlands (☎ 021 742 3157); Farthings, Beacon rd, Kingswear, Dartmouth, Devon (☎ 080 425 577); Goodwell Farm, Gingin, Western Australia (☎ Gingin 6503)

JOHNSON, Sir Victor Philipse Hill; 6 Bt (UK 1818), of Bath; s of Capt Hugh Walter Beaumont Johnson (2 s of Capt William Victor Johnson, 2 s of 2 Bt); suc kinsman, Lt-Col Sir Henry Allen

Beaumont Johnson, 5 Bt, 1965; *b* 7 May 1905; *Educ* Cheltenham; *Heir* kinsman, Robin Johnson; *Career* 1939-45 War as Flying Officer RAFVR; *Style* - Sir Victor Johnson, Bt; Beach House, 64 Sea Lane, Goring-by-Sea, Worthing, Sussex (☎ Worthing 43630)

JOHNSON-FERGUSON, Ian Edward; s and h of Sir Neil Johnson-Ferguson, 3 Bt, TD, JP, DL; *b* 1 Feb 1932; *Educ* Ampleforth, Trin Cambridge; *m* 1964, Rosemary Teresa, da of C J Whitehead, of The Old House, Crockham Hill, Edenbridge; 3 s; *Style* - Ian Johnson-Ferguson Esq

JOHNSON-FERGUSON, Sir Neil Edward; 3 Bt (UK 1906), TD, JP (Dumfriesshire 1954), DL (Dumfriesshire 1957); s of Col Sir Edward Alexander James Johnson-Ferguson, 2 Bt (d 1953), and of Hon Elsie Dorothea McLaren (d 1973), da of late 1 Baron Aberconway; *b* 2 May 1905; *Educ* Winchester, Trin Cambridge; *m* 1931, Sheila Marian, da of late Col Herbert Swynfen Jervis, MC, Roy Munster Fus, of Tilford, Surrey; 4 s; *Heir* s, Ian Johnson-Ferguson; *Career* Lt-Col Royal Corps of Signals, Vice-Lt Dumfriesshire 1965-; American Legion of Merit; *Style* - Sir Neil Johnson-Ferguson, Bt TD JP, HM Vice-Lieut for Dumfriesshire; Fairyknowe, Eaglesfield, Dumfriesshire

JOHNSTON, Sir Alexander; GCB (1953), KBE (1962); s of Alexander Simpson Johnston (d 1960); *b* 27 Aug 1905; *Educ* George Heriot's Sch, Edinburgh U, London U; *m* 1947, Betty Joan, nee Harris; 1 s, 1 da; *Career* chm Bd of Inland Revenue 1958-68, dep chm Monopolies Cmmn 1969-76, dep chm Take-Over Panel 1970-, dep chm Cncl for the Securities Industry 1978-; *Recreations* gardening; *Clubs* Reform; *Style* - Sir Alexander Johnston, GCB KBE; 18 Mallord st, SW3 (☎ 352 6840)

JOHNSTON, Barrie Colin; s of Alfred John Johnston, OBE (d 1964); *b* 7 Aug 1925; *Educ* Epsom Coll; *m* 1952, Cynthia Anne, nee Clark; 1 s (Alastair John), 1 da (Nicola Mary); *Career* Lt RM Far East; merchant banker, dir Charterhouse Japhet Ltd 1973-, memb management ctee The Pension Fund Property Unit Trust 1966-, memb cncl Dr Barnardos 1980-, fin adviser Charities Aid Foundation 1976-; *Recreations* sport, travel; *Style* - Barrie Johnston Esq; Yew Cottage, 8 The Green, Ewell, Surrey (☎ 01 393 2920)

JOHNSTON, Sir Charles Hepburn; GCMG (1971, KCMG 1959, CMG 1953); s of Ernest Johnston; *b* 11 March 1912; *Educ* Winchester, Balliol Oxford; *m* 1944, Princess Natasha Bagration, da of Prince Constantine Bagration of Mukhrani; *Career* HM Diplomatic Serv 1936, Ambass Jordan 1956, Govr & CIC Aden 1960, Dep Under-Sec of State FO 1963, High Cmmr Australia 1965-71; *Clubs* White's; *Style* - Sir Charles Johnston, GCMG; 32 Kingston House S, Ennismore gdns, SW7

JOHNSTON, Edward Ingram; s of Samuel William Johnston (d 1954); *b* 27 May 1930; *Educ* Portora Roy Sch; *Career* CA; dir N Ireland Airports Ltd, Securicor (Ulster) Ltd, Citron Estates Ltd; chm United Dominions Trust (Car Plant) Ltd; *Recreations* reading, music and sport; *Style* - Edward Johnston Esq; 21 Torgrange, Cultra, Co Down (☎ Holywood 2974)

JOHNSTON, Hon Mrs (Elizabeth Rosemary); da of 2 Baron Hardinge of Penshurst, GCB, GCVO, MC, PC (d 1960) and Helen, Lady Hardinge of Penshurst, *qv*; *b* 1927; *Career* JP Berks; late WRNS; *see* Johnston, Lt-Col John Frederick Dame, CVO, MC; *Style* - The Hon Mrs Johnston, JP

JOHNSTON, Lt-Col John Frederick Dame; CVO (1977, MVO 1971), MC (1945); s of Frederick Johnston; *b* 24 Aug 1922; *Educ* Ampleforth; *m* 1949, Hon Elizabeth, da of 2 Baron Hardinge of Penshurst, GCB, GCVO, MC, PC (d 1960); 1 s, 1 da; *Career* Lt-Col Grenadier Guards 1941-64; Comptroller HM Household (Lord Chamberlain's Off) 1981- (Assist Comptroller 1964-81); *Recreations* golf, dog-handling; *Clubs* Pratt's, Swinley Forest Golf; *Style* - Lt-Col John Johnston CVO MC; Adelaide Cottage, Windsor Home Park, Berks (☎ Windsor 68286); Stone Hill, Newport, Dyfed (☎ 820722)

JOHNSTON, Richard Graves; JP (1962), DL (1963); s of George Paul Graves Johnston JP (d 1955); *b* 4 July 1914; *Educ* Canford Dorset, Trin Coll Dublin; *m* 1945, Lydia Constance, da of Lt-Col Michael John Furnell; 3 children; *Career* landowner, company director, High Sheriff Co Armagh 1959; *Recreations* hunting, water skiing; *Clubs* Kildare St Dublin; *Style* - Richard Johnston Esq, JP, DL; Kilmore House, Kilmore, Armagh, N Ireland (☎ Richhill 871234)

JOHNSTON, Robert William Fairfield; CMG (1960), CBE (1954), MC (1917), TD (1947) and 3 Bars; s of Capt Robert Johnston (d 1949); *b* 1 May 1895; *m* 1922, Agnes Scott, nee Justice; 1 s; *Career* Civil Serv 1910; Roy Scots WW I, Lt-Col RA WW II; assist sec MOD 1946-62, seconded as cnsllr FO UK Delegations to NATO and OEEC 1953-61; *Style* - Robert Johnston Esq CMG CBE MC TD***; 8 Broad ave, Queen's pk, Bournemouth, Dorset

JOHNSTON, Sir Thomas Alexander; 13 Bt (NS 1626), of Caskieben, Aberdeenshire; s of Sir Thomas Alexander Johnston, 12 Bt (d 1959); *b* 7 Sept 1916; *Educ* Alabama U; *m* 1941, Helen Torrey, da of Benjamin Franklin Du Bois; 1 s, 2 da; *Heir* s, Thomas Johnston; *Career* attorney-at-law, partner in legal firm of Howell, Johnston, Langford, Finkbohner and Lawler, Alabama, USA, memb Alabama House of Representatives 1941-49, memb Alabama State Senate 1949-54, pres Mobile Co Bar Assoc 1963, memb Alabama Constitution Revision Ctee 1970-76, Alabama Judicial Compensation Cmmn 1976-; *Clubs* Athelstan, Country (Mobile); *Style* - Sir Thomas Johnston, Bt; 350 W Delwood Drive, Mobile, Alabama, 36606, USA

JOHNSTON, Thomas Alexander; s and h of Sir Thomas Johnston, 13 Bt; *b* 1 Feb 1956; *Style* - Thomas Johnston Esq

JOHNSTONE, Air Vice-Marshal Alexander Vallance Riddell; CB (1966), DFC (1940), AE; s of Alexander Lang Johnstone (d 1950); *b* 2 June 1916; *Educ* Kelvinside Acad; *m* 1940, Margaret, nee Croll; 1 s, 2 da; *Career* Air Vice-Marshal RAF 1939-, Air Offr Scotland 1965-68, Cdr Air N Atlantic 1965-68, Air Cdr Borneo 1964-65, 1 Ch Air Staff Roy Malayan AF 1957-58; *Recreations* golf; *Clubs* RAF; *Style* - Air Vice-Marshal Alexander Johnstone CB DFC AE; 36 Greystoke Lodge, Hanger Lane, W5

JOHNSTONE, Sir Frederic Allan George; 10 Bt (NS 1700), of Westerhall, Dumfriesshire; s of Sir George Frederic Thomas Tankerville Johnstone, 9 Bt (d 1952); *b* 23 Feb 1906; *Educ* Imperial Service Coll; *m* 1, 1933 (m dis 1941), Gladys Hands; m 2, 1946, Doris, da of late W L Shortridge, of Blackheath, SE; 2 s; *Heir* s, George Johnstone; *Style* - Sir Frederic Johnstone, Bt; Urry's Cottage, Freshwater, Isle of Wight

JOHNSTONE, George Richard Douglas; s and h of Sir Frederic Johnstone, 10 Bt; *b* 21 Aug 1948; *Style* - George Johnstone Esq

JOHNSTONE, Hon Robin Evelyn Leo (Vanden-Bempde); MVO (1957); s and h of 4 Baron Derwent CBE; *b* 30 Oct 1930; *Educ* Winchester Coll; *m* 1957, Sybille Marie Louise, da of Vicomte de Simard de Pitray (d 1979); 1 s, 3 da; *Career* merchant banker, dir N M Rothschild & Sons Ltd, HM Diplomatic Serv FO 1954-69 (ret); *Recreations* fishing, shooting; *Style* - The Hon Robin Vanden-Bempde-Johnstone MVO; 27 The Crescent, SW13 (☎ 876 2528); Low Hall, Hackness, Scarborough, N Yorks

JOICEY, 4 Baron (UK 1906); Sir Michael Edward Joicey; 4 Bt (UK 1893); s of 3 Baron Joicey (d 1966) and Lady Joan Lambton, da of 4 Earl of Durham; through his mother Lord Joicey is 1 cous to Lord Home of the Hirsel and (6) Duke of Sutherland; *b* 28 Feb 1925; *Educ* Eton, Ch Ch Oxford; *m* 1952, Elisabeth, da of Lt-Col Hon Ian Melville, TD, yst s of 11 Earl of Leven and Melville; 2 s, 1 da; *Heir* s, Hon James Joicey; *Career* served WW II Capt Coldstream Gds; MFH The N Northumberland 1954-74; *Recreations* shooting, stalking, fishing; *Clubs* Bath, Kennel, Lansdowne, N Counties (Newcastle); *Style* - The Rt Hon Lord Joicey; Loch Choire Lodge, Kinbrace,

Sutherland (☎ 043 13 222); Etal Manor, Berwick on Tweed (☎ Crookham 205)

JOICEY, Hon Andrew Hugh; s of 4 Baron Joicey; *b* 1955; *Educ* Eton; *Style* - The Hon Andrew Joicey

JOICEY, Hon James Michael; s and h of 4 Baron Joicey; *b* 28 June 1953; *Educ* Eton; *Style* - The Hon James Joicey

JOICEY, Hon Katherine Jane; da of 4 Baron Joicey; *b* 1959; *Style* - The Hon Katherine Joicey

JOICEY-CECIL, James David Edward; s of Edward Wilfrid George Joicey-Cecil; *b* 24 Sept 1946; *Educ* Eton; *m* 1975, Jane Susanna Brydon, nee Adeley; 1 da; *Career* chartered accountant 1969, memb Stock Exchange 1978-, ptnr James Capel & Co 1978-; *Clubs* Carlton; *Style* - James Joicey-Cecil Esq; 49 Clapham Common South Side, SW4 (☎ 622 0576)

JOLLIFFE, Hon Alexander John Charles Martin; s of 5 Baron Hylton; *b* 1973; *Style* - The Hon Alexander Jolliffe

JOLLIFFE, Anthony Stuart; s of Robert Jolliffe; *b* 12 Aug 1938; *Educ* Porchester Sch Bournemouth; *m* 1962, Anne Elizabeth, nee Phillips; 1 s, 2 da; *Career* chartered accountant, senior ptnr Jolliffe Cork & Co, int chm Jolliffe Cork Ingram, dir Parent Board E. Fogarty & Co Ltd, dir Nikko Trading UK Ltd, dir Erskine House Inv Ltd, dir Marlborough Prop Hldgs Ltd, Sheriff City of London 1980-81; *Recreations* classic cars, boating, theatre; *Clubs* City Livery, Roy London Yacht, Thames Motor Yacht, Variety of Gt Br; *Also* owner of yacht Broom 37 'Kleen Sweep'; *Style* - Anthony Jolliffe Esq; Oakwood, 2 Park Close, Batchworth Heath, Rickmansworth, Herts (☎ North Wood 29877)

JOLLIFFE, Hon Andrew Thomas Peter; s of 5 Baron Hylton; *b* 1969; *Style* - The Hon Andrew Jolliffe

JOLLIFFE, Hon Emily Sylvia Rose Elizabeth; da of 5 Baron Hylton; *b* 1975; *Style* - The Hon Emily Jolliffe

JOLLIFFE, Hon Mrs (Victoria Catherine Elizabeth); *nee* Eden; da of 7 Baron Henley (d 1977); *b* 1944; *m* 1965, Hon John Hedworth Jolliffe, *qv*, s of 4 Baron Hylton (d 1967); 3 s; *Style* - The Hon Mrs Jolliffe; Potticks House, Bradford-on-Avon

JOLLIFFE, Hon John-Edward Arthur Raymond; s of 5 Baron Hylton; *b* 1977; *Style* - The Hon John-Edward Jolliffe

JOLLIFFE, Hon John Hedworth; s of 4 Baron Hylton (d 1967); *b* 1935; *Educ* Eton (King's Scholar), Ch Ch Oxford; *m* 1965, the Hon Victoria Catherine Elizabeth Eden, da of 7 Baron Henley; 3 s; *Career* co dir in Bristol; *Style* - The Hon John Jolliffe; Potticks House, Bradford-on-Avon

JOLLIFFE, Hon William Henry Martin; s and h of 5 Baron Hylton; *b* 1 April 1967; *Style* - The Hon William Jolliffe

JOLLY, Air Cdre Robert Malcolm; CBE (1969); s of Robert Imrie Jolly (d 1940); *b* 4 Aug 1920; *Educ* Skerry's Coll Newcastle; *m* 1946, Josette Jacqueline, nee Baindeky; *Career* Air Cdre 1940-75 RAF, dir of Personal Servs RAF 1970-75, ret; md Leonard Griffiths and Associates 1975-77, v-pres M W S Consultants Inc 1978-80; *Recreations* boating; *Clubs* RAF Arts; *Also* owner of motor cruiser 'Garbee'; *Style* - Air Cdre Robert Jolly, CBE; 1 Felbridge Close, Streatham, SW16 (☎ 769 4038)

JOLY, Hon Mrs Diana Olive; *née* Newall; da of 1 Baron Newall, GCB, OM, GCMG, CBE, AM (d 1963); *b* 1927; *m* 1956 (m dis 1967), John Leonard Joly; 1 da (Harriet Diana b 1960); *Style* - The Hon Mrs Diana Joly; Tower House, Reybridge, Chippenham, Wilts

JOLY DE LOTBINIÈRE, Lt-Col Sir Edmond; s of Brig-Gen Henri Gustave de Lotbinière, DSO, JP (descended from Michel, Marquis de Lotbinière, the sole Fr subject of Canadian birth to be created a Marquis, who was so honoured by Louis XVI in 1784), by his w Mildred, da of Charles Seymour Grenfell (1 cous of 1 Baron Grenfell, GCB, GCMG, PC); *b* 17 March 1903; *Educ* Eton, RMA Woolwich;

m 1, 1928 (m dis 1937), Hon Elizabeth Joliffe (da of 3 Baron Hylton); 2 s (Thomas and Michael, *qqv*); m 2, 1937, Helen (d 1953), da of Dr Hartley Ferrar, of NZ; m 3, 1954, as her 2 husb, Evelyn Adelaide (b 6 July 1904, er da of Nigel Dawnay, s of Hon William Dawnay, JP, DL, 6 s of 7 Viscount Downe, the Hon William having m Lady Adelaide Parker, 2 da of 6 Earl of Macclesfield), widow of Lt-Col James Innes, DSO (*see* Hall, Sir John Bernard, 3 Bt); *Career* served RE & RARO 1928-45; Pres Bury St Edmunds Construction Assoc 1972-79 (chm 1953-72), chm & md several cos making building materials; chm Eastern Provincial Area Con Assoc 1961-65; kt 1964; *Recreations* shooting, gardening, bridge; *Clubs* Naval and Military; *Style* - Lt-Col Sir Edmond Joly de Lotbinière; Horringer Manor, Bury St Edmunds, Suffolk (☎ Horringer 208)

JOLY DE LOTBINIÈRE, Michael Edmond; 2 s of Lt-Col Sir Edmond Joly de Lotbinière, *qv*, by his 1 w, Hon Elizabeth Joliffe (da of 3 Baron Hylton); *b* 3 Feb 1932; *Educ* Eton, Downing Cambridge; *m* 1956, Angela, yr da of Col Eugene St John Birnie, of Belgravia, by Lady Kathleen Courtenay, 3 da of 16 Earl of Devon; 2 s, 1 da; *Career* former tobacco farmer (Rhodesia, now Zimbabwe); dir building materials-manufacturing cos; *Style* - Michael Joly de Lotbinière Esq; Rougham House, Bury St Edmunds, Suffolk

JOLY DE LOTBINIÈRE, Thomas Henry; s of Lt-Col Sir Edmond Joly de Lotbinière, *qv*, by his 1 w, Hon Elizabeth Joliffe (da of 3 Baron Hylton); *b* 18 July 1929; *Educ* Eton, Trin Cambridge; *m* 1953, Prudence, da of Thomas Bevan, of Hadlow Down; 1 s, 2 da; *Career* ptnr Grenfell & Colegrave Stockbrokers 1978-; dir Cardinal Investment Tst, Gen Investors & Tstees, Gold Estates of Australia (1903) Ltd, Lignacite (Brandon) Ltd, Lothbury Assets, Spanish American Financial Tst; *Recreations* sailing, shooting; *Clubs* City University; *Style* - Thomas Joly de Lotbinière Esq; Barmoor House, Bletchingley, Surrey

JONES, Edward Appleby; s of Wilfred Jones (d 1977); *b* 21 April 1926; *Educ* Bede Collegiate Boys Sch Sunderland; *m* 1949, Jessie Isabell, nee Green; 1 s (Antony David); *Career* Sgt (Air Gunner) RAF; cost accountant Garricks (Caterers) Ltd 1951-63, regional accountant Cooperative Wholesale Soc 1963-69, fin dir and co sec-RB Bolton (Mining Engrg) Ltd 1969-, RB Bolton (Hydraulics) Ltd 1969-, RB Bolton (Engrs) Ltd 1969-, General Mining & Engrg Services Ltd 1977-; *Recreations* gardening, travel, reading; *Clubs* Inst of Directors; *Style* - Edward Jones Esq; Hartside, 177 Newcastle rd, Sunderland (☎ 78107)

JONES, Gerard; PC (1952); s of Timothy Jones (d 1959); *b* 15 June 1919; *Educ* Rockwell Coll, Presentation Coll Cork; *m* 1956, Breda Brooder; 4 children; *Career* dir Irish Shipping Ltd to 1970, Securicor to 1978, dir Jones Gp Ltd 1973-, Belgian Consul 1968; *Recreations* sailing, gardening; *Clubs* United Services, Real Club Nautico Palma, Roy Yacht Club Cork; *Style* - Gerard Jones Esq, PC, Belgian Consul; Lisheens, Rathfarnham, Dublin (☎ 909609); 3 Roebuck House, Stag Place, London (☎ 01 828 0537)

JONES, Geraint Stanley; s of Rev David Stanley Jones (d 1974); *b* 26 April 1936; *Educ* Pontypridd G S, U Coll N Wales Bangor; *m* 1961, Rhiannon, da of Emrys Williams (d 1971); 2 da (Sioned b 1965, Siwan b 1966); *Career* BBC studio man 1960-62, TV Producer 1965-73, Assist Head Programmes 1973-74, Head Progs Wales 1974-81, later Actg Controller, Controller Wales 1981-; *Recreations* music, painting; *Clubs* Cardiff & County (Cardiff); *Style* - Geraint Jones Esq; Y Goedlan, 8 Nant Fawr rd, Cyncoed, Cardiff, S Glam (0222 751038)

JONES, Ian Quayle; s of Arnold Bates Jones (d 1977); *b* 14 July 1941; *Educ* Strathallan Sch Forgandenny, Edinburgh U; *m* 1968, Christine Ann, da of Kenneth Macrae; 3 s; *Career* slr (Scotland), Writer to the Signet, ptnr Cowan and Stewart 1968-72; dir The British Linen Bank Ltd 1979-; *Recreations* golf, fishing, family; *Style* - Ian Jones Esq, WS; The Stone House, 1 Pentland Rd, Edinburgh

JONES, James; s of late James B Jones; *b* 1 March 1925; *Educ*

Kelvinside, Royal Tech Coll, West of Scotland Commercial Coll; *m* 1953, Janet Young Mitchell, nee Lockhart; 1 s, 1 da; *Career* md David Scott & Co Ltd 1960-68, L Sterne & Co Ltd 1968-71, J Jones (Glasgow) Ltd 1971-, Blairs Ltd 1974-; *Recreations* golf; *Clubs* Reform, Naval and Military, Royal Aero, Pathfinder, Royal Scottish Automobile; *Style* - James Jones Esq; 97 Kelvin court, Glasgow (☎ 041 221 1715)

JONES, Lady; Jean; *m* 1922, Sir Tom Barry Jones, 2 Bt (d 1952, when the title became ext); *Style* - Lady Jones

JONES, Hon Mrs Joanna Catherine; da of Maj Sir Arthur Lindsay Grant, 11 Bt (ka 1944), and Baroness Tweedsmuir of Belhelvie (Life Peeress, d 1978); *b* 1935; *m* 1954 (m dis 1966), Dominick Jones, s of Sir (George) Roderick Jones, KBE; 1 s; *Style* - The Hon Mrs Joanna Jones

JONES, John Clement; CBE (1972); s of Clement Jones (d 1916); *b* 22 June 1915; *Educ* Ardwyn Aberystwyth; *m* 1938, Marjorie, nee Gibson; 3 s; *Career* journalist and broadcaster; ed & dir Express & Star Wolverhampton 1960-75, C'wlth and UNESCO Media Consultant 1975-, exec dir Beacon Radio (programming) 1974-; pres Guild British Newspaper Eds, gov British Inst of Human Rights 1971-; *Recreations* gardening, beekeeping, writing, broadcasting; *Clubs* Athenaeum, Press; *Style* - John Jones Esq, CBE; 17 Swallowdale, Wightwick, Wolverhampton (☎ 0902 763253); 19 Crescent rd, Walton-on-Naze, Essex

JONES, Hon James Glynmore; s of Baron Maelor (Life Peer); *Style* - The Hon James Jones; Police Station, Llanddewi Velfrey, Pembs

JONES, John Hugh; s of the late Thomas Hugh Jones; *b* 6 Aug 1916; *Educ* Gowerton G S; *m* 1 1948, Ilby (decd), nee Rowland; 1 s, 2 da; 2 m, 1967, Joan, nee Freeston; *Career* Lloyds Bank Ltd 1934-77 (ch registrar 1964); dir and chief exec Joint Credit Card Ltd 1974, dir: Beaumont Properties Ltd, London Shop Property Trust Ltd, M F North Ltd, Guernsey Savings & Loan Corpn Ltd, and Jersey Savings & Loan Corp 1977-; chm: Beaumont Properties, London Shop Property Tst 1980- *Recreations* music, literature, country activities (local village affairs), gardening, rugby, charitable work; *Clubs* Carlton; *Style* - John Jones Esq; Severalls, East End Lane, Ditchling, Sussex (☎ 07918 2330)

JONES, Hon Mrs (Jennifer Margaret); da of Baron Pilkington (Life Peer); *b* 1933; *m* 1958, Dennis Jones; *Style* - The Hon Mrs Jones; Swallow Cottage, Burbage, Leics

JONES, James Peter Martin Benton; s and h of Sir Simon Warley Frederick Benton Jones, 4 Bt; *b* 1 Jan 1973; *Style* - James Jones Esq

JONES, Mrs Michael; Norvela F; *née* Forster; MEP (C) Birmingham S; da of late N B Forster; *b* 1931; *Educ* S Wilts G S Salisbury, Bedford Coll London; *m* 1981, D Michael J, s of Norman Jones and Mrs Margaret Jones; *Career* fndr chm & md consultancy in mktng, management, packaging, plastics; memb Cncl Bow Gp, London Chamber Commerce W European Cttee; *Style* - Mrs Michael Jones, MEP; 6 Regency House, Regency st, SW1 (☎ 01 821 5749); c/o Conservative Association, Britannia House, 50 Gt Charles st, Queensway, Birmingham B3 2NJ (☎ 021 236 7671); c/o IAL Industrial Aids Ltd, 14 Buckingham Palace rd, SW1 (☎ 01 828 5036)

JONES, Brig Percival de Courcy; OBE (1953); s of Percy de Courcy Jones (d 1922); *b* 9 Oct 1913; *Educ* Oundle Sch, Sandhurst; *m* 1947, Anne, nee Hollins (m dis 1951); 1 s; *Career* 2 Lt KSLI 1933-62 (ret), WW II (France, Burma), Lt-Col 1952, cmd KSLI 1953-55, Col Q War Office 1955-58, Brig 1961; ch sec Roy Life Saving Soc 1965-75 (dir 1969-75), cncllr AVDC 1976-79; *Recreations* skiing, gardening; *Clubs* Light Infantry; *Style* - Brig Percival Jones, OBE; Berry Cottage, Townsend Green, Haddenham, Bucks

JONES, Sir Simon Warley Frederick Benton; 4 Bt (UK 1919), of Treeton, West Riding of Yorkshire, JP (Lincs 1971); s of Lt-Col Sir Peter Fawcett Benton Jones 3

Bt, OBE (d 1972); *b* 11 Sept 1941; *Educ* Eton, Trin Coll Cambridge; *m* 1966, Margaret Fiona, da of David Rutherford Dickson; 2 s, 2 da; *Heir* s, James Peter Martin Benton Jones; *Career* farmer, High Sheriff Lincs 1977-78; *Recreations* shooting, fishing; *Style* - Sir Simon Jones Bt, JP; Irnham Hall, Grantham, Lincs (☎ Corby Glen 212); Sopley, Christchurch, Dorset

JOSEPH, Ernest Alex; s of Felix Joseph (d 1941); *b* 3 Jan 1923; *Educ* Townley Castle Sch London, Philanthropin Frankfurt; *m* 1950, Sylvia Ray, nee Findon; 1 s, 1 da; *Career* exec dir Lanca Gp of Cos; *Recreations* music, swimming, gardening; *Clubs* Marco Polo (Hong Kong); *Style* - Ernest Joseph Esq; 10 Monkville Av, NW11 (☎ 01 455 7682)

JOSEPH, James Samuel; s and h of Sir Keith Joseph, 2 Bt, PC, MP; *b* 27 Jan 1955; *Style* - James Joseph Esq

JOSEPH, Rt Hon Sir Keith Sinjohn; 2 Bt (UK 1943), PC (1962), MP (C) Leeds North-East 1956-; s of Sir Samuel George Joseph, 1 Bt (d 1944), and Edna, Lady Joseph (d 1981, leaving Sir Keith most of her £458,403 estate); *b* 17 Jan 1918; *Educ* Harrow, Magdalen Oxford; *m* 1951, Hellen Louise (separated 1978), da of Sigmar Guggenheimer, of NY; 1 s, 3 da; *Heir* s, James Joseph; *Career* 1939-45 War in Italy as Capt RA (wounded, despatches), barr Middle Temple 1946, Fell All Souls Oxford 1946-60, 1972-, contested (C) Baron's Court 1955, PPS to Parly Under-Sec of State CRO 1957-59, Parly Sec Min of Housing and Local Govt 1959-61, Min of State BOT 1961-62, Min of Housing and Local Govt and Min for Welsh Affairs 1962-64, Sec of State for Social Services DHSS 1970-74, Sec of State for Industry 1979-, co-founder and first chm Foundn for Management Educn 1959, founder and first chm Mulberry Housing Trust 1965-69, founder and chm Management Ctee Centre for Policy Studies Ltd 1974-79; FIOB, Common Councilman City of London for Ward of Portsoken 1946, Alderman 1946-49, Liveryman Vintners' Co; *Clubs* Carlton; *Style* - The Rt Hon Sir Keith Joseph Bt PC MP; 63 Limerston st, Chelsea, SW10 OBL

JOST, Dr H Peter; CBE (1969); s of Leo Jost (d 1941); *b* 25 Jan 1921; *Educ* City of Liverpool Tech Coll, Tech Coll Manchester; *m* 1948, Margaret Josephine, nee Kadesh; 2 da; *Career* Lord President's nominee on the Ct of Salford U, 1 Pres International Tribology Cncl 1973-, chm Manchester Tech Assoc London 1976-, memb Parliamentary & Scientific Cttee 1976-, memb Cncl Engrg Institutions 1977- (chm Home Affairs Cttee 1980-); *Recreations* music, gardening; *Clubs* Athenaeum; *Style* - Dr Peter Jost, CBE; Hill House, Wills Grove, Mill Hill, NW7

JOST, Hon Mrs (Marylyn Jane); *née* Macdonald; da of 2 Baron Macdonald of Gwaenysgor; *b* 1951; *m* 1977, Peter Jost; *Style* - The Hon Mrs Jost

JOURDAIN, James William; s of Henry James Jourdain (d 1966); *b* 28 Feb 1928; *Educ* Radley Coll; *m* 1953, Molly Elizabeth, da of Paul Gustavus Arthur Anthony OBE; 2 s (Richard, Michael), 2 da (Diana, Nicola); *Career* RNVR 1948-50; dir: Blyth Greene Jourdain & Co Ltd 1969-, Ireland Blyth & Co Ltd (Mauritius) 1972-, Bank of Mauritius 1967-69; chm Blyth Bros & Co Ltd Mauritius 1964-69, md Swire Blyth & Co Ltd London 1980-; *Recreations* sport, music, travel; *Clubs* City of London, MCC; *Style* - James Jourdain Esq; Tazar, Whiteman's Green, Cuckfield, Sussex (☎ Haywards Heath (0444) 54723)

JOURDAN, Martin Hubert Thomas; s of Charles Henry Hans Jourdan; *b* 22 Nov 1940; *Educ* Mill Hill Sch, Harvard Business Sch; *m* 1963, Enid Valerie; *Career* chairmaker, chm Parker Knoll Ltd 1977-; *Recreations* walking; *Clubs* Old Millhillians; *Style* - Martin Jourdan Esq; The Courtyard, Frogmoor, High Wycombe, Bucks (☎ 21144)

JOWITT, Juliet Diana Margaret; da of Lt-Col Robert Henry Langton Brackenbury, OBE, Yerdley Hse, Long Compton, Warwickshire (d 1978); *b* 24 August 1940; *Educ* Hatherop Castle; Switzerland and Spain; *m* 1963, Thomas Benson Jowitt; 1 s, 1 da; *Career* Associate Shopping Editor House & Garden and Vogue 1966-69; Colour Go

Round (Interior Design) from 1971 (Proprietor); JP (Hallikeld) 1973; Juvenile Panel (Thirsk) 1976; Independent Broadcasting Authority 1981; *Recreations* Foxhunting, Skiing, Travel, Fine Arts; *Style* - Mrs Thomas Jowitt, JP

JOYNSON-HICKS, Hon Crispin William; s and h of 3 Viscount Brentford, DL; *b* 7 April 1933; *Educ* Eton, New Coll Oxford; *m* 1964, Gillian Evelyn, da of Gerald Edward Schluter, OBE, of Nairobi, Kenya; 1 s, 2 da; *Career* slr 1960, ptnr legal firm of Joynson-Hicks & Co, late Lt 9 Lancers; *Style* - The Hon Crispin Joynson-Hicks; Shenstone, Gravel Path, Berkhamsted, Herts

JUDD, Bt-Col George Richard; TD, DL (Essex 1948); s of Edward Thomas Judd JP (d 1963); *b* 24 April 1914; *Educ* Gresham's Sch Norfolk; *m* 1956, Mary Stuart, nee Paton; 3 s; *Career* Lt-Col 1943 304 Field Regt RA (TA), Essex Yeo 1947-51, Bt-Col 1951, Hon-Col 1965-69, High Sheriff Essex 1974, chartered surveyor; *Clubs* Boodle's, City of London; *Style* - Col George Judd TD DL; Ardleigh Park, Colchester, Essex (☎ 230 246)

JURKIEWICZ, Hon Mrs (Enid Aughard); *née* Jones; da of Baron Maelor (Life Peer); *m*, E Jurkiewicz; *Style* - The Hon Mrs Jurkiewicz; 16 Snowdon Drive, Wrexham, Denbighshire

JURY, Peter Charles Cotton; s of Col Edward Cotton Jury; *b* 30 Aug 1919; *Educ* Rugby, King's Cambridge; *m* 1953, Ursula Joan, nee Abraham; 2 da; *Career* Capt 13/18 Roy Hussars (QNO) 1938-47; chm Trust Houses 1972-80 (md 1960-72) pres Int Hotel Assoc 1977-78; *Clubs* Pony Club Parent; *Style* - Peter Jury Esq; Struan Hill, Delgany, Co Wicklow, Eire (☎ Dublin 874785)

K

KABERRY, Christopher Donald; s and h of Sir Donald Kaberry, 1 Bt, TD DL MP; *b* 14 March 1943; *m* 1967, Gaenor Elizabeth Vowe, da of C Peake, of Durkar House, Durkar, Wakefield; 2 s, 1 da; *Style* - Christopher Kaberry Esq; Adel Willows South, Otley rd, Leeds 16

KABERRY, Sir Donald; 1 Bt (UK 1960), of Adel cum Eccup, City of Leeds, TD (1947), DL (W Yorks 1976), MP (C) Leeds NW 1950-; s of Abraham Kaberry; *b* 18 Aug 1907; *Educ* Leeds G S & U; *m* 1940, Lily, da of Edmund Scott, of Morley, W Yorks; 3 s; *Heir* s, Christopher Kaberry; *Career* formerly Actg Col RA, Parly Sec BOT 1955, formerly memb Leeds City Council, now Hon Alderman, chm W H Baxter Ltd, E Walker & Co Ltd, chm Assoc of Con Clubs 1961-, v-chm Con Party 1955-61, memb Speaker's Panel of Chairmen 1974-, pres Yorks Area Cncl of Con Party 1966-, Leeds Teaching Hosps Special Trustee 1974-; *Clubs* Carlton, St Stephen's Constitutional (Leeds); *Style* - Sir Donald Kaberry, Bt, TD, DL, MP; Beckfield, E Keswick, Leeds LS17 9DB (☎ Collingham Bridge 73257)

KADOORIE, Baron (Life Peer UK 1981); Lawrence; CBE, JP (1936); s of Sir Elly Kadoorie (d 1944); *b* 2 June 1899; *Educ* Cathedral Sch Shanghai, St Vincent's Eastbourne, Clifton Coll Bristol; *m* 1938, Muriel, nee Gubbay; 1 s, 1 da; *Career* kt 1974, ptnr Sir Elly Kadoorie & Sons, chm Sir Elly Kadoorie Successors Ltd, dir Sir Elly Kadoorie Continuation Ltd, chm Alaska Enterprises Ltd, chm Kadoorie Estates Ltd, chm and dir of various companies; *Recreations* sports cars, photography, Chinese works of art; *Style* - The Rt Hon the Lord Kadoorie, CBE, JP; 24 Kadoorie ave, Kowloon, Hong Kong (☎ 3 7116129)

KAGAN, Baron (Life Peer UK 1976); Joseph Kagan; s of Benjamin Kagan; *b* 6

June 1915; *Educ* High Sch Kaunas Lithuania, Leeds U; *m* 1943, Margaret Stromas; 2 s, 1 da; *Career* dir Kagan Textiles, chm Gannex Gp of Cos (founded 1951); kt 1970 (annulled 1981); *Style* - The Rt Hon the Lord Kagan; 15 Fixby rd, Huddersfield, Yorks (☎ 25202); Barkisland Hall, Barkisland, Halifax, W Yorks (☎ Elland 74121)

KAGAN, Hon Anne Eugenia; da of Baron Kagan (Life Peer); *b* 1965; *Style* - The Hon Anne Kagan

KAGAN, Hon Daniel; s of Baron Kagan (Life Peer); *b* 1953; *Style* - The Hon Daniel Kagan

KAGAN, Hon Michael George; s of Baron Kagan (Life Peer); *b* 1950; *Style* - The Hon Michael Kagan

KAHN, Baron (Life Peer UK 1965); Richard Ferdinand Kahn; CBE (1946); s of late Augustus Kahn, of London; *b* 10 Aug 1905; *Educ* St Paul's Sch, King's Coll Cambridge; *Career* temp Civil Servant in various Govt Depts 1939-46, Prof of Economics Cambridge U 1951-72, Fell King's Coll Cambridge; FBA 1960; *Clubs* Royal Automobile; *Style* - The Rt Hon the Lord Kahn, CBE; King's College, Cambridge CB2 1ST (☎ Cambridge 350411)

KALDOR, Baron (Life Peer UK 1974); Nicholas Kaldor; s of late Dr Julius Kaldor, of Budapest; *b* 12 May 1908; *Educ* Model Gymnasium Budapest, LSE (Hon Fell 1970), MA Camb, Hon Dr Dijon; *m* 1934, Clarissa Elisabeth, da of Henry Frederick Goldschmidt; 4 da; *Career* Fell King's Coll Camb 1949-, Asst Lecturer and Lecturer and Reader in Economics LSE 1932-47, dir of Research and Planning Div Economic Cmmn for Europe Geneva 1947-49, Reader in Economics Cambridge 1952-65, Prof of Economics 1966-75, now Emeritus, Advisor on Tax Reform Govt of India 1956, Econ Advisor Econ Cmmn for Latin America, Santiago, Chile 1956, and Govt of Ghana 1961, Fiscal Advisor Govt of Ceylon 1958, of Mexico 1960, of British Guiana 1961, of Turkey 1962, of Iran 1966, Special Advsr to Chllr of Exchequer 1964-68; FBA 1963; *Clubs* Reform; *Style* - The Rt Hon the Lord Kaldor; 27 Egerton gdns, SW3 (☎ 01 589 6903); King's College, Cambridge CB2 1ST; 2 Adams rd, Cambridge CB3 9AD (☎ Cambridge 59282)

KALDOR, Hon Mary Henrietta; da of Baron Kaldor (Life Peer); *b* 1946; *Style* - The Hon Mary Kaldor

KARA, Peter Bhupatsingh; s of Bhimsingh Kara of S Africa (d 1968); *b* 5 July 1944; *Educ* Damelin Coll S Africa; *m* 1969, Gita, da of Gulasingh Parmar of India; 1 s, 1 da; *Career* memb Assoc of Certified Accountants, fin dir Arthur Woollacott Ltd, Lowfield Ltd, dir Frith Foils (Sales) Ltd, sec Charles Pretzlik & Son Ltd, dir Wrappings & Packings (Engineering) Ltd, R Peters (London) Ltd; *Recreations* skiing, water skiing, cricket, squash, fencing; *Style* - Peter Kara Esq; 11 Fitzroy sq, W1 (☎ 01 388 9593); 73 Windmill Hill dve, Bletchley, Bucks

KAY-SHUTTLEWORTH, Hon --; s of 5 Baron Shuttleworth; *b* 1979

KAY-SHUTTLEWORTH, Hon David Charles; s of 5 Baron Shuttleworth; *b* 1978

KAY-SHUTTLEWORTH, Hon Edward Roger Noël; s of late 4 Baron Shuttleworth; *b* 1962; *Style* - The Hon Edward Kay-Shuttleworth

KAY-SHUTTLEWORTH, Hon Rosemary Florence Angela; da of late Capt the Hon Lawrence Ughtred Kay-Shuttleworth (s of 1 Baron Suttleworth); sis of 2 and 3 Barons; raised to the rank of a Baron's daughter 1940; *b* 1915; *Style* - The Hon Rosemary Kay-Shuttleworth; Fir Tree Cottage, Stedham, nr Midhurst, Sussex

KAY-SHUTTLEWORTH, Hon Robert James; s of late 4 Baron Shuttleworth, MC; *b* 1954; *Educ* Eton; *Style* - The Hon Robert Kay-Shuttleworth

KAY-SHUTTLEWORTH, Hon Thomas Edward; s and h of 5 Baron Shuttleworth; *b* 29 Sept 1976; *Style* - The Hon Thomas Kay-Shuttleworth

KAYE, David Alexander Gordon; s of Sir (Henry) Gordon Kaye, 2 Bt (d 1956), and hp of bro, Sir Stephen Kaye, 3 Bt; *b* 26 July 1919; *Educ* Cambridge U (BA); MRCS Eng and LRCP London 1943; *m* 1, 1942 (m dis 1950), Elizabeth, da of Capt Malcolm Hurtley, of Baynards Manor, Horsham, Sussex; m 2, 1955, Adelle, da of Denis Thomas, of Brisbane, Qld; 2 s, 4 da; *Style* - David Kaye Esq; Yerinandah, Moggill rd, The Gap, Brisbane, Queensland, Australia

KAYE, Sir Stephen Henry Gordon; 3 Bt (UK 1923), of Huddersfield, co York; s of Sir (Henry) Gordon Kaye, 2 Bt (d 1956); *b* 24 March 1917; *Educ* Stowe, Trin Cambridge; *Heir* bro, David Kaye; *Style* - Sir Stephen Kaye, Bt; Mortimore's, New Buildings, Sandford, nr Crediton, Devon EX17 4PP

KAYLL, Wing-Cdr Joseph Robert; DSO, OBE (1945), DFC (1940), JP (Sunderland), DL (Tyne & Wear); s of Maj Joseph Pelham Kayll, MBE (d 1971); *b* 12 Apr 1914; *Educ* Stowe; *m* 1940, Annette Lindsey, nee Nisbet; 2 s; *Career* Wing-Cdr, timber importer; *Recreations* sailing, shooting; *Clubs* Roy Ocean Racing, RNYC, SYC, WBA; *Style* - Wing-Cdr Joseph Kayll Esq, DSO, OBE, DFC, JP, DL; Hillside House, Hillside, Sunderland (☎ 283282)

KAZANTZIS, Judith Elizabeth; *née* Pakenham; da of 7 Earl of Longford, KG, PC (but does not use style of Lady); *b* 1940; *Educ* Oxford U; *m* 1963, Alexander John Kazantzis; 1 s, 1 da ; *Style* - Mrs Alexander Kazantzis; 7a Clarendon rd, W11; The Foreman's, nr Glynde, Sussex

KEANE, John Charles; s and h of Sir Richard Keane, 6 Bt; *b* 16 Sept 1941; *Educ* Eton, Ch Ch Oxford; *Style* - John Keane Esq

KEANE, Sir Richard Michael; 6 Bt (UK 1801), of Cappoquin, co Waterford; s of Lt-Col Sir John Keane 5 Bt, DSO (d 1956), and of Lady Eleanor Hicks-Beach (d 1960), da of late 1 Earl of St Aldwyn; *b* 29 Jan 1909; *Educ* Sherborne, Ch Ch Oxford; *m* 1939, Olivia Dorothy, da of Oliver Hawkshaw, TD; 2 s, 1 da; *Heir* s John Charles Keane; *Career* dip correspondent to Reuters 1935-37, dip corresp and asst to ed Sunday Times 1937-39, served with Co of London Yeo and 10 Roy Hussars 1939-44, liaison officer (Maj) with HQ Vojvodina Yugoslav partisans 1944, attached British Military Mission Belgrade 1944-45, publicity consultant to ICI Ltd 1950-62; farmer; *Recreations* fishing; *Style* - Sir Richard Keane Bt; Cappoquin House, Cappoquin, Co Waterford, Ireland (☎ 058 54004)

KEARLEY, Chester Dagley Hugh; s of late Hon Mark Hudson Kearley (s of 1 Viscount Devonport); kinsman and hp of 3 Viscount; *b* 29 April 1932; *m* 1974, Josefa Mesquida; *Style* - Chester Kearley Esq

KEARLEY, Hon Idonia Clare; da of 3 Viscount Devonport; *b* 1977

KEARLEY, Hon Marilyn Whitson; da of late 2 Viscount Devonport; *b* 1939 *Style* - The Hon Marilyn Kearley

KEARLEY, Hon Velvet Jane; da of 3 Viscount Devonport; *b* 1975

KEARTON, Baron (Life Peer UK 1970); Christopher Frank Kearton; OBE (1945); s of Christopher John Kearton; *b* 17 Feb 1911; *Educ* Hanley H S, St John's Coll Oxford; *m* 1936, Agnes Kathleen, da of Samuel Pratt Brander; 2 s, 2 da; *Career* part-time memb UKAEA 1955-, dir Hill Samuel Gp 1970-, Chllr Bath U 1980-; chm BPC 1981-, Courtaulds 1964-75, chm & ch exec BNOC 1976-79, pt-time memb CEGB 1974-80, pres Aslib 1980-, fell Imperial Coll London; FRS 1961; kt 1966; *Club* Athenaeum *Style* - Rt Hon Lord Kearton OBE; The Old House, Whitchurch, Bucks (☎ 232)

KEATLEY, John Rankin Macdonald; s of James Keatley; *b* 20 Aug 1933; *Educ* Aldenham, RAC Circencester; *m* 1964, Carolyn Margaret, da of Rodney Morell, of Melbourne Australia; 1 s (Robert b 1965), 1 da Arabella b 1967); *Career* chm Crosby House Gp; leader Cambridge City Cncl 1967-69; company director; *Club* Lansdowne *Style* - John Keatley Esq; Melbourn Lodge, Royston, Herts (☎ 60680)

KEEGAN, Thomas Denis; s of Thomas Keegan (d 1960); *b* 6 Sept 1925; *Educ* St Francis Xavier Liverpool; *m* 1960, Wendela, nee Oriel (m dis); 3 s; *Career* chm and ch exec British Air Ferries (1971), BAF Engrg; *Recreations* sailing; *Clubs* none; *Style* - Thomas Keegan Esq; Down House, Hatfield Heath, Herts (☎ 027982 370)

KEELING, Christopher Anthony Gedge; s of Sir Edward Keeling MC, MP, DL (d 1954); *b* 15 June 1930; *Educ* Eton, Royal Military Adademy, Sandhurst; *m* 1974, Rachael; 2 s, 1 da; *Career* Capt Grenadier Guards; md Fenchurch Underwriting Agencies Ltd since 1972; *Recreations* cricket, shooting; *Clubs* White's, MCC; *Style* - Christopher Keeling Esq; 18 Onslow sq, London SW7 (☎ 01 589 3727); Hodges Farm, Shipton Moyne, Tetbury, Glos

KEELING, John Arthur Bernard; DFC (1943); s of Sir John Henry Keeling (d 1978); *b* 31 Oct 1922; *Educ* Eton, Ch Ch Oxford; *m* 1961, Mary Jocelyn, nee Wenham; 2 s; *Career* CA 1949, chm London & Yorks Trust Ltd 1965- (dir 1952), chm W Riding Worsted & Woollen Mills Ltd 1968-75 (dir 1959), chm Safeguard Industrial Investments Ltd 1975- (dir 1959), dir Bowater Corp Ltd 1968-, dir Great Northern Investment Trust 1968, adviser British Airways Pension Fund 1959-, farmer 1967-; *Recreations* travel, gardening; *Clubs* White's; *Style* - John Keeling Esq, DFC; 48 Melton ct, Old Brompton rd, SW7 (☎ 01 584 0333); Hurst House, Sedlescombe, Sussex (☎ 340)

KEEN, Charles William Lyle; s of late Harold Hugh Keen; *b* 4 July 1936; *Educ* Winchester Coll, New Coll Oxford; *m* 1962, Lady Priscilla Mary Rose Curzon, da of 6 Earl Howe; 1 s (William b 1970), 3 da (Laura b 1963, Eleanor b 1965, Alice b 1966); *Career* Lt BAOR, local dir-Barclays Bank Reading 1967-71, Nottingham 1971-74, sr local dir Reading 1974-, dir Barclays Unicorn Group Ltd 1978-; *Style* - Charles Keen Esq; St Mary's Farm House, Beenham, Reading, Berks (☎ Woolhampton 3705)

KEEN, Lady Priscilla Mary Rose; *née* Curzon; da of 6 Earl Howe, CBE; *b* 1940; *m* 1962, Charles William Lyle Keen, *qv*; 1 s, 3 da; *Style* - Lady Priscilla Keen; St Mary's Farm, Beenham, Reading, Berks (☎ Woolhampton 3705)

KEEP, Hugh Charles John Martin; s of John Frederick Charles Keep; *b* 21 Nov 1945; *Educ* Bradfield Coll; *m* 1970, Rosemary Isabel, da of James Stuart Smith; 3 s; *Career* co dir Keep Brothers Ltd 1973; *Recreations* flyfishing, gardening, reading; *Clubs* Flyfishers; *Style* - Hugh Keep Esq; Hopkins, Long Marston, nr Stratford-on-Avon, Warks (☎ 0789 720 286)

KEIR WATSON, Robin; s of Robert Keir Watson (d 1929); *b* 12 Sept 1915; *Educ* Hillhead H S Glasgow, Glasgow U; *m* 1950, Veronica Josephine Yolande (d 1976); *Career* chartered engineer and accountant, chm Associated British Engineering Ltd 1970-80 (non exec dir 1980-); *Recreations* educational research in energy subjects, walking, country pursuits; *Clubs* Caledonian, RAC; *Style* - Robin Keir Watson Esq; 18 Kelvin ct, Glasgow, G12 0AB (☎ 041 334 8763)

KEITH OF KINKEL, Baron (Life Peer UK 1976); Hon Henry Shanks Keith; PC (1976); s of Baron Keith of Avonholm (Life Peer, d 1964); *b* 7 Feb 1922; *Educ* Edinburgh Acad, Magdalen Oxford (Hon Fell 1977), Edinburgh U; *m* 1955, Alison Hope Alan, da of Alan Brown; 4 s (incl twin s); 1 da; *Career* Scots Gds 1941-1945, advocate Scottish Bar 1950, barr Gray's Inn 1951, QC (Scot) 1962, Sheriff of Roxburgh, Berwick and Selkirk 1970-71, dep chm Parly Boundary Cmmn for Scotland 1976, Senator of College of Justice in Scotland with judicial title of Lord Keith 1971-77, Lord of Appeal in Ordinary 1977-, chm jt ctee on Consolidation Bills 1978; *Style* - Rt Hon the Lord Keith of Kinkel, PC; Woodend, Strathtummel, by Pitlochry, Perthshire (☎ Tummel Bridge 255)

KEITH OF CASTLEACRE, Baron (Life Peer UK 1980); Kenneth Alexander Keith; s of Edward Charles Keith (d 1972), of Dereham, Norfolk; *b* 30

Aug 1916; *Educ* Rugby; *m* 1, 1946 (m dis 1958), Lady Ariel Olivia Winifred Baird, 2 da of 1 Viscount Stonehaven, PC, GCMG, DSO and (Ethel) Sydney, Countess of Kintore; 1 s, 1 da; m 2, 1962 (m dis 1972), Mrs Nancy Hayward; m 3, 1973, Marie-Luz, da of Capt Robert Peel Dennistoun-Webster, and formerly wife of (1) Adrian Donald Henderson and (2) James Robert Hanbury; *Career* 2 Lt Welsh Gds 1939, Lt-Col 1945, served in N Africa, Italy, France and Germany (despatches, Croix de Guerre with Silver Star), asst to dir gen Political Intelligence Dept FO 1945-46, merchant banker and industrialist; vice-chm BEA 1964-71, chm Hill Samuel Gp Ltd 1970-80, dir British Airways 1971-72, chm and ch exec Rolls-Royce Ltd 1972-80, vice-chm Beecham Gp Ltd 1974- (dir 1949-), dir Eagle Star Insur Co 1955-75, Nat Provincial Bank 1967-69, Times Newspapers Ltd, Standard Telephones and Cables Ltd, IT&T (UK) Ltd, Bank of Nova Scotia Ltd; FBIM, kt 1969 *Recreations* farming, shooting, golf; *Clubs* White's, Pratt's, Racquet and Tennis (NY); *Style* - The Rt Hon the Lord Keith of Castleacre; 80 Eaton Square, SW1W 9AP (☎ 01 730 4000); The Wicken House, Castle Acre, Norfolk (Castle Acre 225)

KEITH, Hon Alastair James; s of Baron Keith of Castleacre (Life Peer); *b* 1947; *Educ* Eton; *Style* - The Hon Alastair Keith

KEITH, Hon Alexander Lindsay; s of Baron Keith of Kinkel (Life Peer); *b* 1967 (twin); *Style* - The Hon Alexander Keith

KEITH, Lady Ariel Olivia Winifred; *née* Baird; da of 1 Viscount Stonehaven, GCMG DSO PC (d 1941) and Countess of Kintore (d 1974); *b* 1916; *m* 1946 (m dis 1958), Sir Kenneth Alexander Keith; 1 s, 1 da; *Career* Lady-in-Waiting to HRH Princess Alice, Countess of Athlone 1940; *Style* - Lady Ariel Keith; Flat B, 9 Cadogan sq, SW1

KEITH, Hon Deborah Jane; da of Baron Keith of Kinkel (Life Peer); *b* 1957; *Style* - The Hon Deborah Keith

KEITH, Hon Hugo George; s of Baron Keith of Kinkel (Life Peer); *b* 1967; *Style* - The Hon Hugo Keith

KEITH, Hon Iona Delia Mary Gaddis; da of Lord Inverurie; *b* 1978; *Style* - The Hon Iona Keith

KEITH, Hon James Alan; s of Baron Keith of Kinkel (Life Peer); *b* 1959; *Style* - The Hon James Keith

KEITH OF AVONHOLM, Baroness; Jean Maitland; da of late Andrew Bennet, slr, of Arbroath; *m* 1915, 1 Baron Keith of Avonholm (Life Peer, d 1964); *Style* - The Rt Hon the Lady Keith of Avonholm; c/o Alex Morison & Co, WS, 33 Queen st, Edinburgh 2

KEITH, Robert Farquharson; CB (1973), OBE (1948); s of Dr Robert Donald Keith (d 1916); *b* 22 June 1912; *Educ* Fettes, Caius Coll Cambridge; *m* 1958, Jean Abernethy, nee Fisher; 1 s (Alexander b 1963); *Career* India Civil Service (deputy Cmmr Upper Sind Frontier) 1945-47, Home Civil Service Dept Employment (Under-Sec) 1965-71, chief registrar of trade unions 1971-74; *Clubs* Caledonian; *Style* - Robert Keith Esq, CB, OBE; Parkhead, Auchattie, near Banchory, Kincardineshire (☎ Banchory 2166)

KEITH, Hon Thomas Hamilton; s of Baron Keith of Kinkel (Life Peer); *b* 1961; *Style* - The Hon Thomas Keith

KEITH-MURRAY, Maj Peter; s of late David Keith-Murray, and hp of kinsman, Sir Patrick Murray of Ochtertyre, 12 Bt; *b* July 1935; *m* 1960, Judith Anne, da of late Andrew Tinsley; 1 s, 1 da; *Style* - Major Peter Keith-Murray

KELBURN, Viscount of; Patrick Robin Archibald Boyle; s and h of 9 Earl of Glasgow, CB, DSC; *b* 30 July 1939; *Educ* Eton; *m* 1975, Isobel, da of late George James; 1 s, 1 da; *Heir* s, Hon David Boyle; *Career* Sub-Lt RNR; *Style* - Viscount of Kelburn; Kelburn Estate, Fairlie, Ayrshire

KELLER, Hon Mrs (Susan Henriette); da of Baron Schon (Life Peer); *b* 23 Oct 1941; *Educ* Badminton Sch Bristol, Ecole

Hotelière Switzerland; *m* 1964, Richard Henry, s of Arthur Henshall Keller; 2 s (Philip Henry b 1964, Nicholas Frank b 1970), 1 da (Annabel Jane b 1967); *Recreations* antiques, tennis, golf; *Style* - The Hon Mrs Keller; Hillmorton, Wills Grove, Mill Hill Village, NW7 (☎ 01 959 4442)

KELLETT, Ida, Lady; Ida Mary Grace Weaver; *m* 1952, Sir Henry de Castres Kellett, 5 Bt (d 1966); *Style* - Ida, Lady Kellett

KELLETT, Stanley Charles; s and h of Sir Stanley Kellett, 6 Bt; *b* 5 March 1940; *m* 1, 1962 (m dis 1968), Lorraine May, da of F Winspear; m 2, 1968, Margaret Ann, da of J Bofinger; *Style* - Stanley Kellett Esq; 47 May rd, Dee Why, Sydney, NSW, Australia

KELLETT, Sir Stanley Everard; 6 Bt (UK 1801), of Lota, Cork; s of late Francis Stanley Kellett (2 s of 3 Bt); suc kinsman, Sir Henry de Castres Kellett, 5 Bt 1966; *b* 1911; *m* 1938, Audrey Margaret Phillips; 1 s, 1 da; *Heir* s, Stanley Kellett; *Style* - Sir Stanley Kellett, Bt; 33 Caroma av, Kyeemagh, NSW 2216, Australia

KELLY, Christopher Aliaga; s of Ambrose Aliaga Kelly (d 1953); *b* 28 Sept 1920; *Educ* St Mary's Coll Dublin; *m* 1948, Cynthia, da of Lt-Col Hon Thomas Morgan-Grenville (d 1965, 3 s of Lady Kinloss, 11 holder of Scottish Lordship); 1 s, 1 da; *Career* jt md Lead Industries Gp; dir: Allied Irish Banks Ltd, Irish Dunlop Co; chm: Goodlass Wall Ltd, Alexander Fergusson Ltd; dir: Fergusson Paints South Africa, Fry's Diecastings, Goodlass Nerlac Paints India, Valentine Varnish & Lacquer; past pres Confedn of Irish Indust *Club* Stephen's Green, Dublin; *Style* - Christopher Kelly Esq; 10 Rawlings st, SW3 (☎ 01-584-1155)

KELLY, Charles Henry; QPM (1978), DL (Staffs 1979); s of Charles Kelly; *b* 15 July 1930; *Educ* Douglas HS for Boys (IOM), London U; *m* 1952, Doris Kewley; 1 s, 1 da; *Career* 1972-76 Asst Ch Constable Essex, 1976-77 Dep Ch Constable Staffs, 1977 Ch Constable Staffs; OStJ 1979 *Recreations* music, cricket, reading *Clubs* Special Forces; *Style* - Charles Kelly Esq, QPM, DL; Baswich House, Cannock Road, Stafford (☎ 57717)

KELLY, Laurence Charles Kevin; s of Sir David Kelly, GCMG, MC (d 1959); *b* 11 Apr 1933; *Educ* Downside, New Coll Oxford; *m* 1963, Linda, nee McNair Scott; 1 s, 2 da; *Career* writer, *Lermontov-Tragedy in the Caucasus*, *St Petersburg*, fell Roy Geographical Soc, v-chm British Steel Consumers' Cncl 1974-, dep chm Helical Bar Ltd 1981-, bd memb N Ireland Dvpt Agency 1972-78; *Recreations* tennis, swimming, shooting *Clubs* Brooks's, Turf, Beefsteak; *Style* - Laurence Kelly Esq; 44 Ladbroke Grove, W11 (☎ 01 727 4663)

KELLY, Lady Mirabel (Magdalene); *née* Fitzalan-Howard; da of 3 Baron Howard of Glossop MBE by Baroness Beaumont, OBE, and sis of 17 Duke of Norfolk, CB, CBE, MC; *b* 1931; *m* 1952, Bernard Kelly, s of late Sir David Victor Kelly, GCMG, MC; 7 s, 1 da; *Style* - Lady Mirabel Kelly; 28 Carlyle sq, SW3; Yonder Tara, Inch, Co Wexford; Romden Castle, Smarden, Kent

KELSEY, Michael Edward; TD (1969); s of Wing Cdr George Kelsey, OBE, RAFVR (d 1980); *b* 16 April 1935; *Educ* Berkhamsted Sch, King's Coll London; *m* 1961, Anthea Mabel, da of Dr Arthur Sproul McFarlane (d 1978); 2 s, 1 da; *Career* Maj TA, chartered engineer, chm and ch exec: Crouse Hinds (UK) Ltd, Arrow-Hart (Europe) Ltd, Cablok Co Ltd; md Sealed Motor Construction Co 1976-79, earlier mgmnt apptmnts: Marconi Instruments, Cossor Electronics, Solartron Electronic Group; *Recreations* skiing, sailing, gardening; *Clubs* Royal Dart Yacht Club; *Style* - Michael Kelsey Esq, TD; The Manor House, Catcott, Near Bridgwater, Somerset (☎ Chilton Polden 722393)

KEMMIS, Hon Mrs (Bridget Mary Dean); da of Baron Soper (Life Peer); *b* 1933; *m* 1956, Owen H Kemmis, MA; *Style* - The Hon Mrs Kemmis; 92 Wildwood rd, NW11

KEMP, Roy; s of Robert Godfrey Kemp (d 1926); *b* 15 May 1911; *Educ*

Uppingham; *m* 1935, Elisabeth Marie Lynn, nee Aspinall; 2 s, 1 da; *Career* div offr Nat Fire Serv (GB and N Ireland), co dir, dep chm Leicester Building Soc 1955-, chm Allen Bastick & Billson Ltd 1946-, pres Leicester & District Hosiery Mfr's Assoc Ltd 1971-72; *Recreations* rugby football refereeing, squash racquets; *Clubs* Leicestershire, Leicestershire GC; *Style* - Roy Kemp Esq; Remlak, 28 The Oval, Oadby, Leicester (☎ 712081)

KEMP, Hon St John Durival; s and h of 1 Viscount Rochdale, OBE, TD, DL; *b* 15 Jan 1938; *Educ* Eton; *m* 1, 1960 (m dis 1974), Serena, da of Michael Clark-Hall; 2 s, 2 da; m 2, 1976, Elizabeth Anderton; *Style* - The Hon St John Kemp; Farmers Green, Mottram St Andrew, Prestbury, Cheshire

KEMSLEY, Viscount (UK 1945); Sir (Geoffrey) Lionel Berry; 2 Bt (UK 1928), DL (Leics 1972); Baron Kemsley (UK 1936); s of 1 Viscount Kemsley, GBE (d 1968); *b* 29 June 1909; *Educ* Marlborough, Magdalen Oxford; *m* 1933, Lady Hélène Hay, DStJ, da of 11 Marquess of Tweeddale (d 1967); 4 da; *Heir* bro, Hon Denis Berry; *Career* 1939-45 War as Capt Gren Gds (invalided out 1942), MP (C) Buckingham Div of Bucks 1943-45, dep chm Kemsley Newspapers Ltd 1938-59, master of Spectacle Makers' Co 1949-51 and 1959-61, pres Assoc of Independent Hospitals, chm St Andrew's Hosp Northampton, memb of Chapter Gen of OStJ, CC Northants 1964-70, High Sheriff Leics 1967; Vice-Chamberlain of HM Household 1979-; FRSA, KStJ; *Clubs* Bath, Turf, Pratt's; *Style* - The Rt Hon the Viscount Kemsley, DL; Thorpe Lubenham, Market Harborough, Leics (☎ Market Harborough 62816)

KEMSLEY, Viscountess; Lady Hélène Candida; *née* Hay; da of 11 Marquess of Tweeddale (d 1967); *b* 1913; *m* 1933, 2 Viscount Kemsley; *Career* DStJ; *Style* - The Rt Hon the Viscountess Kemsley; Thorpe Lubenham Hall, Market Harborough, Leics

KENILWORTH, 3 Baron (UK 1937); John Davenport Siddeley; s of 2 Baron Kenilworth, CBE, TD (d 1971); *b* 24 Jan 1924; *Educ* Marlborough, Magdalene Cambridge; *m* 1948, Jacqueline Palette, da of late Robert Gelpi; 1 s, 1 da; *Heir* s, Hon John Siddeley; *Career* chm, John Siddeley Internat Ltd, John Siddeley (Jewels) Ltd, dir Siddeley and Hammond, antiquarian booksellers, consultant designer to Max Murphy Designs Ltd, food editor Paris Vogue; Master Coachmakers' and Coach Harness Makers' Co 1969-70; FRSA; *Style* - The Rt Hon the Lord Kenilworth; (business) 4 Bourne House, Harriet st, SW1 (☎ 01 235 8757/7632); (home) 2 Lexham Walk, W8 (☎ 01 370 6805); 9 East 68th st, New York, NY 10021, USA

KENNARD, Sir George Arnold Ford; 3 Bt (UK 1891), of Fernhill, co Southampton; s of late Sir Coleridge Kennard, 1 Bt; suc bro, Sir Laurence Ury Charles Kennard, 2 Bt 1967; *b* 27 April 1915; *Educ* Eton; *m* 1, 1940 (m dis 1958), Cecilia Violet Cokayne, da of Maj Cecil John Cokayne Maunsell, JP; 1 da; m 2, 1958 (m dis 1974), Mrs Molly Jesse Rudd Miskin, da of late Hugh Wyllie, of Fishbourne, Sussex; *Heir* none; *Career* 1939-45 War (despatches twice, prisoner); Lt-Col (ret) late Comdg 4 Queen's Own Hussars, Midland rep for Cement Marketing Co; *Clubs* Cavalry and Guards; *Style* - Sir George Kennard, Bt; Cogwell, Tiverton, Devon (☎ Tiverton 2154)

KENNAWAY, Sir John Lawrence; 5 Bt (GB 1791), of Hyderabad, East Indies; s of Sir John Kennaway, 4 Bt (d 1956); *b* 7 Sept 1933; *Educ* Harrow, Trin Cambridge; *m* 1961, Christina Urszenyi, MB, ChB; 1 s, 2 da; *Heir* s, John Michael Kennaway; *Career* patron of one living; *Style* - Sir John Kennaway, Bt; Escot, Ottery St Mary, Devon EX11 1LU

KENNAWAY, John Michael; s and h of Sir John Kennaway, 5 Bt; *b* 17 Feb 1962; *Style* - John Kennaway Esq

KENNAWAY, Mary, Lady; Mary Félicité; da of late Rev Stewart Gordon Ponsonby; *m* 1931, Sir John Kennaway, 4 Bt (d 1956); *Style* - Mary, Lady Kennaway; Leat Cottage, Plymtree, Cullompton, Devon

KENNEDY, Lord David Thomas; s of 7 Marquess of Ailsa, OBE, DL; *b* 3 July 1958; *Educ* Strathallan Sch, Berks Coll of Ag; *Career* farmer; *Recreations* shooting, fishing, vintage car restoration, travel; *Clubs* New (Edinburgh); *Style* - Lord David Kennedy; Morriston Farm, Maidens, Maybole, Ayrshire

KENNEDY, Francis; CBE (1977, MBE 1958); s of James Kennedy; *b* 9 May 1926; *Educ* Manchester & London Us; *m* 1957, Anne O'Malley; 2 s, 2 da; *Career* Colonial Serv Nigeria 1953-63, For Serv 1964- (Atlanta, Lagos); Ambass to Angola & Ambass non-resident to São Tomé & Principe 1981-; *Clubs* Brooks's; *Style* - Francis Kennedy Esq, CBE; c/o FCO, SW1

KENNEDY, Lady Hugh; Katharine Louisa Clare; da of Francis Atherton, of Shalford, Surrey; *m* 1925, Lord Hugh Kennedy, MC (d 1970, s of 3 Marquess of Ailsa); 1 s; *Style* - Lady Hugh Kennedy; 27 The Abbey, Romsey, Hants

KENNEDY, Ludovic Henry Coverley; s of Capt Edward Kennedy, RN (d on active serv 1939; ggs of Hon Robert Kennedy, bro of 1 Marquess of Ailsa and 3 s of 11 Earl of Cassillis), and Rosalind, da of Sir Ludovic Grant, 11 Bt; *b* 3 Nov 1919; *Educ* Eton, Ch Ch Oxford; *m* 1950, Moira Shearer, the ballerina (*qv*); 1 s, 3 da; *Career* writer and broadcaster, formerly Sub-Lt RNVR; contested Rochdale in Lib interest 1958 and 1959; *Clubs* Brooks's, Army & Navy, MCC; *Style* - Ludovic Kennedy Esq; The Old Manse, Makerstoun, by Kelso, Roxburghshire

KENNEDY, Michael Edward; s and h of Lt-Col Sir (George) Ronald Derrick Kennedy, OBE, 7 Bt; *b* 12 April 1956; *Style* - Michael Kennedy Esq

KENNEDY, Lt-Col Sir (George) Ronald Derrick; 7 Bt (UK 1836), of Johnstown Kennedy, co Dublin, OBE (1975); s of Sir Derrick Edward de Vere Kennedy, 6 Bt (d 1976); *b* 19 Nov 1927; *Educ* Clifton Coll; *m* 1949, Noelle Mona, da of Charles Henry Green; 1 s, 1 da; *Heir* s, Michael Kennedy; *Career* Lt-Col RA, Defence Attaché Mexico City, Havana and El Salvador 1971-74, GSO 1 UK Delegn to Live Oak SHAPE 1974-77, Admin Commandant Dhekelia Garrison Cyprus 1977, ret 1979; Administrator World Pheasant Assoc; *Recreations* military history, foreign travel, sports; *Style* - Lt-Col Sir Ronald Kennedy, Bt, OBE; Harraton sq, Church Lane, Exning, nr Newmarket, Suffolk (☎ Exning 282)

KENNEDY, Lady Rosemary Margaret; da of Earl of Cassillis; *b* 1980; *Style* - Lady Rosemary Kennedy

KENNEDY, Hon Mrs; Hon Virginia; da (twin) of Baron Devlin (Life Peer); *b* 1940; *m* 1965, Paul Kennedy, QC; children; *Style* - The Hon Mrs Kennedy; Rydal, 11a Kent rd, Harrogate, Yorks

KENNET, 2 Baron (UK 1935); Wayland Hilton Young; s of 1 Baron Kennet, GBE, DSO, DSC, PC (d 1960), by his w Kathleen, da of Rev Canon Lloyd Stewart Bruce (himself 3 s of Sir James Bruce, 2 Bt) and widow of Capt Robert Scott, CVO, RN, the famous Antarctic explorer; Lady Kennet was a sculptress who executed several statues of her first husband, including the one erected in Waterloo Place; *b* 2 Aug 1923; *Educ* Stowe, Trin Cambridge, Perugia, Harvard; *m* 1948, Elizabeth Ann, da of Capt Bryan Fullerton Adams, DSO, RN, of Cherry Tree, Hacheston, Suffolk; 1 s, 5 da; *Heir* s, Hon Thoby Young; *Career* RN 1942-45, FO 1946-47 and 1949-51, deleg parly assemblies WEU and Council of Europe 1962-65, parly sec Min of Housing and Local Govt 1966-70, opposition spokesman on Foreign Affairs and Science Policy 1971-74, chm Adv Ctee on Oil Pollution of the Sea 1970-74, CPRE 1971-72, Internat Parly Conferences on the environment 1972-78, MEP 1978-79, SDP Whip House of Lords 1981-; Hon FRIBA 1970; author; *Style* - The Rt Hon the Lord Kennet; 100 Bayswater rd, W2 (☎ 01 723 2020)

KENNON, Vice-Adm James Edward Campbell; CBE (1974, OBE 1962); s of Robert Kennon, MC, FRCS; *b* 26 Nov 1925; *Educ* Stowe; *m* 1950, Anne, da of Capt Sir Stuart Paton, KCVO, CBE, RN (ret); 2 s, 1 da; *Career* Vice-Adm April

1981- (Rear-Adm to 1981); Ch of Fleet Support Oct 1981- (Port Adm Rosyth 1980); Ch Naval Supply & Secretariat Offr 1979-81; RN 1943-; Assist Ch Naval Staff Policy 1978-79, Sec to CIC Fleet 1968-70 & 1 Sea Lord 1971-74; *Style* - Vice-Adm James Kennon CBE; c/o MOD, SW1; Castlandhill House, Ferry Toll rd, Rosyth, Fife

KENSINGTON, 7 Baron (I 1776 & UK 1886); William Edwardes; s of 6 Baron Kensington, CMG, DSO, TD, JP, DL (d 1938), and Mabel, yr da of George Pilkington, JP (of a yr branch of the St Helens glass dynasty); *b* 15 May 1904; *Educ* Eton; *Heir* n, Hugh Edwardes; *Career* Lt-Col Indian Army ret; ADC to Gov Punjab 1932-35; served WW II India, Burma, Malaya; *Clubs* Cavalry and Guards; *Style* - The Rt Hon Lord Kensington; Mardan, PO Bromley, Zimbabwe

KENSWOOD, 2 Baron (UK 1951); John Michael Howard Whitfield; s of 1 Baron Kenswood (d 1963); *b* 6 April 1930; *Educ* Trin Sch Ontario, Harrow, Grenoble U, Emmanuel Cambridge; *m* 1951, Deirdre Anna Louise, da of Colin Malcolm Methven, of Errol, Perthshire; 4 s, 1 da; *Heir* s, Hon Michael Whitfield; *Style* - The Rt Hon the Lord Kenswood; Manor Farm, Roch, Haverfordwest, Dyfed (☎ Camrose 359)

KENSWOOD, Catherine, Baroness; Catherine (Chilver-Stainer); da of Frank Luxton; *m* 1962, as his 2 wife, 1 Baron Kenswood (d 1963); *Style* - The Rt Hon Catherine, Lady Kenswood; 84a Carlton Hill, NW8 (☎ 01 624 2613)

KENT, Roderick David; s of Dr B S Kent; *b* 14 Aug 1947; *Educ* King's Sch Canterbury, CCC Oxford; *m* 1972, Belinda Jane, nee Mitchell; 3 children; *Career* MBA 1972, md Close Bros Ltd 1975-; *Recreations* sports, gardening; *Style* - Roderick Kent Esq; Wolverton Cottage, Wolverton, nr Basingstoke, Hants (☎ Kingsclere 298 276)

KENWARD, Elizabeth; da of Brian Kemp-Welch, of Kineton, Warwicks (through whom Mrs Kenward is 2 cous once removed to Sir Simon Jones, 4 Bt, while her late bro, George, m, as her 2 husb, Lady Diana, Stanley (1 Earl) Baldwin's (of Bewdley) da); *b* 14 July 1906; *Educ* privately, Les Tournelles Brussels; *m* 1932 (m dis 1942), Peter Kenwood (d c 1977); 1 s; *Career* social ed; 'Jennifer' of Jennifer's Diary (Tatler 1944-59, Queen Magazine 1959-70) Harpers & Queen 1970-; *Recreations* flat racing, theatre; *Style* - Mrs Elizabeth Kenward; 39 Hill st, W1

KENWORTHY, Hon Basil Frederick de la Pole; TD; s of late 10 Baron Strabolgi by 1 w, Doris, da of Sir Frederick Whitley Whitley-Thomson, JP, MP; *b* 1920; *Educ* Oundle, Lincoln Coll Oxford; *m* 1948 (m dis 1965), Chloë, da of late Henry Gerard Walter Sandeman and Hon Phyllis, nee Legh, da of 2 Baron Newton, PC; 3 da; *Career* FInstPet, MInstT; Capt RA (TA Reserve); *Style* - The Hon Basil Kenworthy, TD; 149 Gloucester rd, SW7

KENWORTHY, Hon Mrs Cuthbert - Amy Catherine; da of late Frederick Evitt, of Rook Hall, Maldon, Essex; *m* 1913, Rev the Hon Cuthbert Reginald Leatham Kenworthy (d 1963), 2 s of 9 Baron Strabolgi; 1 s; *Style* - The Hon Mrs Cuthbert Kenworthy

KENWORTHY, Rev the Hon Jonathan Malcolm Atholl; s of late 10 Baron Strabolgi by 1 w, Doris, da of Sir Frederick Whitley Whitley-Thomson, JP, MP; hp of bro, 11 Baron; *b* 16 Sept 1916; *Educ* Oundle, Pembroke Coll and Ridley Hall Cambridge; *m* 1, 1943, Joan Marion (d 1963), da of late Claude Gilbert Gaster, of Tunbridge Wells; 2 da; m 2, 1963, Victoria Hewitt; 2 s, 1 da; *Career* Chap of St John's Bangalore and Vicar of Christ Church Penge 1966-75, Rector of Yelvertoft 1975-; *Style* - The Rev the Hon Jonathan Kenworthy; The Rectory, Yelvertoft, Northants

KENYON, 5 Baron (GB 1788); Sir Lloyd Tyrell-Kenyon; 5 Bt (GB 1784), CBE (1972); s of 4 Baron Kenyon (d 1927); *b* 13 Sept 1917; *Educ* Eton, Magdalene Cambridge; *m* 1946, Leila Mary, da of Cdr John Wyndham Cookson, RN (ret), by the Cdr's w Mary (da of Sir Alan Colquhoun,

6 Bt, KCB, JP, DL, and aunt of Countess of Arran); Leila was widow of Hugh William Jardine Ethelston Peel; 3 s, 1 da; *Heir* s, Hon Lloyd Tyrell-Kenyon; *Career* 2 Lt Shropshire Yeo 1937, Lt RA (TA), ret 1943 with hon rank of Capt; dir Lloyds Bank Ltd 1962- (chm N W Bd), pres U Coll of N Wales Bangor 1947-, trustee Nat Portrait Gallery 1953-, chm 1966-, memb Roy Cmmn on Historical MSS 1966-, Ancient Monuments Bd for Wales 1979-, DL (Flint 1948), CC Flint 1946 (chm 1954-55); Hon LLD Wales 1958; *Clubs* Brooks's, Cavalry and Guards, Beefsteak; *Style* - The Rt Hon the Lord Kenyon, CBE, DL; Cumbers House, Gredington, Whitchurch, Salop SY13 3DH (☎ Hanmer 330)

KEOWN-BOYD, Lt-Col William Dalison; CVO (1978), OBE (1948); s of Sir A W Keown-Boyd KBE, CMG (d 1955); *b* 13 June 1912; *Educ* Charterhouse, Sandhurst; *m* 1939, Anne Frances, nee Macpherson-Grant; 1 s, 1 da; *Career* Lt-Col Army 1931-58 (ret), jt serv mission Washington 1954-56, War Office 1956-58, sec Roy Warrant Holders Assoc 1966-79; *Recreations* fishing, travel; *Clubs* Army and Navy, MCC; *Style* - Lt-Col William Keown-Boyd CVO OBE; Planta No 4, Casa Gené El Arans, Ordino, Principat d'Andorra via Spain (☎ Andorra 35 439)

KEPPEL, Hon Mrs Arnold; Mildred; da of William Stanley Rodber, of Richmond Yorks; *m* 1, Flying Offr Allan Carter, RAF (decd); m 2, 1952, as his 3 w, Hon Arnold Keppel (d 1964), 2 s of 8 Earl of Albemarle, GCVO, CB, JP, and Lady Gertrude, only child of 1 and last Earl Egerton of Tatton; *Style* - The Hon Mrs Arnold Keppel; 1a Swan Court, Southsea rd, Datchet, Bucks

KEPPEL, Hon Walter Arnold Crispian; DSC (1942); 2 s of 9 Earl of Albemarle, MC (d 1979), by his 1 w, Lady Judith Carington (da of 1 and last Marquess of Lincolnshire and 3 Baron Carrington, KG, GCMG, PC, JP, DL, by Hon Cecilia Harbord, da of 5 Baron Suffield, KCB); hp of n, 10 Earl of Albemarle; *b* 6 Dec 1914; *Educ* RNC Dartmouth; *m* 1941, Aline, da of Brig-Gen John Harington, CB, CMG, DSO, JP (5 s of Sir Richard Harington, 11 Bt), by his w, Lady Frances Temple Gore Langton (4 da of 4 Earl Temple of Stowe); 2 s, 1 da; *Career* served with Fleet Air Arm as Lt-Cdr WW II; *Style* - The Hon Walter Keppel; Barton House, Meonstoke, Hants (☎ Droxford 318)

KERR, Hon Catherine Harriet; da of 2 Baron Teviot; *b* 1976; *Style* - The Hon Catherine Kerr

KERR, Hon Charles Robert; s and h of 2 Baron Teviot; *b* 19 Sept 1971; *Style* - The Hon Charles Kerr

KERR, Lady Clare Therese; da of Earl of Ancram; *b* 1979; *Style* - Lady Clare Kerr

KERR, Lady Elizabeth (Marian Frances); da of 12 Marquess of Lothian; *b* 1954; *Style* - Lady Elizabeth Kerr

KERR, Lord John Andrew Christopher; s of late Capt Andrew William Kerr, RN (gs of 7 Marq of Lothian) and bro of 12 Marquess of Lothian; *b* 1927; *Educ* Ampleforth and Christ Church, Oxford; *m* 1949, Isabel Marion, da of Sir Hugh Gurney, KCMG, MVO; 3 s, 2 da; *Career* late Capt Scots Guards; raised to the rank of a Marquess's son 1941; *Clubs* Beefsteak; *Style* - Lord John Kerr; Holly Bank, Wootton, Woodstock, Oxford

KERR, Lady Mary; da of Earl of Ancram (s & h of 12 Marquess of Lothian) and Lady Jane, nee Fitzalan Howard (da of 15 Duke of Norfolk); *b* 28 May 1981; *Style* - Lady Mary Kerr

KERR, Lord Ralph William Francis Joseph; s of 12 Marquess of Lothian; *b* 1957; *Educ* Ampleforth; *Style* - Lord Ralph Kerr; Monteviot, Jedburgh, Roxburghshire

KERRY, Francis Robert; s of Francis Kerry (d 1935); *b* 24 Oct 1914; *Educ* Burton-on-Trent G S; *m* 1965, Zena Pamela, da of Ewart Illsley (d 1972); 6 c; *Career* chm, Fine Art Developments Ltd & assoc cos; dir Drycon Bldrs Ltd; *Recreations* yachting; *Style* - Francis

Kerry Esq; Drakelow House, Burton-on-Trent, Staffs (☎ 286 68106); Casa Drakelow, 60 Urbanizaciones, Playa Fotges, Muro, Mallorca

KERSHAW, 4 Baron (UK 1947); Edward John Kershaw; s of 3 Baron Kershaw (d 1962); *b* 12 May 1936; *Educ* Selhurst G S Croydon; *m* 1963, Rosalind, da of Ian Strachan Rutherford, of 16 Castlegate, Richmond; 1 s, 2 da; *Heir* s, Hon John Kershaw; *Career* RAF 1955-57, Chartered Accountant 1964, partner in Kidsons, Chartered Accountants, Gloucester; *Style* - The Rt Hon the Lord Kershaw; c/o Kidsons, Chartered Accountants, 3 Beaufort Buildings, Spa rd, Gloucester

KERSHAW, Cissie, Baroness; Cissie Burness; da of Charles E Smyth, of Friern Barnet; *m* 1933, 2 Baron Kershaw (d July 1961); *Style* - The Rt Hon Cissie, Lady Kershaw; 29 St Ann's rd, Newquay, Cornwall

KERSHAW, Hon Donald Arthur; s of 1 Baron Kershaw, OBE (d 1961); *b* 1915; *m* 1942, Barbara Edith, da of Lt-Col Cecil Graham Ford, of Richmond; 2 s; *Career* slr 1939, JP SW London; *Style* - The Hon Donald Kershaw JP; 32 Hans rd, SW3 (☎ 01 581 2627)

KERSHAW, Hon Isobel Mary; da of 4 Baron Kershaw; *b* 1967; *Style* - The Hon Isobel Kershaw

KERSHAW, Joseph Anthony; s of Joseph Henry Kershaw; *b* 26 Nov 1935; *Educ* Ushaw Coll Durham, Preston Catholic Coll; *m* 1959, Ann, nee Whittle; 3 s, 2 da; *Career* ind management consultant 1975-, associate dir Foote Cone & Belding Ltd 1979-, Unilever Ltd 1958-67, gp marketing man Co-operative Wholesale Soc 1967-69, head of marketing (non-foods) CWS 1973-75, man dir Underline Ltd 1969-71, man dir Merchant Div Reed Int Ltd 1971-73, first dir Nat Consumer Cncl 1975; *Recreations* fishing, shooting, cooking, CPRE; *Clubs* Wellington; *Style* - Joseph Kershaw Esq; Westmead, Meins rd, Blackburn, Lancs (☎ 55915)

KERSHAW, Hon John Charles Edward; s and h of 4 Baron Kershaw; *b* 23 Dec 1971; *Style* - The Hon John Kershaw

KERSHAW, Katharine, Baroness; Katharine Dorothea; da of Charles H Staines, of Clapham, SW; *m* 1935, 3 Baron Kershaw (d 1962); *Style* - The Rt Hon Katharine, Lady Kershaw; 78 Sherwood av, Streatham Vale, SW16

KERSHAW, Hon Peter John; s of 1 Baron Kershaw, OBE (d 1961); *b* 1924; *Educ* Queen Elizabeth's Sch Barnet, King's Coll London; *m* 1948, Brenda Margaret, da of James Austin Smith, of Brighton; 1 s; *Career* Sub-Lt RNVR 1944-45; FICE; *Style* - The Hon Peter Kershaw; 22 Orchard Rise, Richmond, Surrey TW10 5BX

KERSHAW, Hon Victoria Anne; da of 4 Baron Kershaw; *b* 1964; *Style* - The Hon Victoria Kershaw

KERTESZ, Lady Gillian Moyra Katherine; *née* Cecil; da of 6 Marquess of Exeter, KCMG, and his 1 w, Lady Mary Montagu Douglas Scott, da of 7 Duke of Buccleuch; *b* 1935; *m* 1, 1954, (m dis 1979), Sir Giles Henry Charles Floyd, 7 Bt; 2 s; m 2, 1979, George Michael Kertesz; *Style* - Lady Gillian Kertesz; 57 Peel st, W8 (☎ 01 727 5898)

KESWICK, Henry Neville Lindley; s of Sir William Johnson Keswick; *b* 29 Sept 1938; *Educ* Eton, Trin Coll Cambridge; *Career* merchant, chm Matheson & Co Ltd 1975-, chm Jardine Matheson & Co Ltd 1972-75 (dir 1967-), dir Sun Alliance & London Insurance 1975-, Robert Fleming Holdings Ltd 1975-, United Racecourses Ltd 1977-, proprietor the Spectator 1975-81; *Recreations* country pursuits; *Clubs* White's, Turf; *Style* - Henry Keswick Esq; 10 Egerton pl, SW3 (☎ 01 589 1716); Oare House, Oare, Wilts (☎ Pewsey 2428)

KESWICK, Lady Sarah; *née* Ramsay; da of 16 Earl of Dalhousie, KT, GCVO, GBE, MC; *b* 1945; *m* 1966, Christopher Keswick; *Style* - Lady Sarah Keswick; 1a Ilchester pla, W14

KESWICK, Sir William Johnston; s of Maj Henry Keswick (d 1926); *b* 6 Dec 1903; *Educ* Winchester Coll, Trin Coll Cambridge; *m* 1937, Mary, da of Rt Hon Sir Francis Lindley; 3 s, 1 da *Career* kt 1972, Brig 21 Army Gp Europe & Egypt, dir Matheson & Co 1943-75 (chm 1949-66), dir Hudson's Bay Co 1943-72, dir Bank of England 1955-73, dir BP Co Ltd 1950-73, dir Jardine Matheson & Co Ltd (Hong Kong & Far East), memb Roy Co of Archers, memb National Gallery; *Recreations* shooting, gardening; *Clubs* White's; *Style* - Sir William Keswick; Theydon Priory, Theydon Bois, Essex (☎ Theydon Bois 2256); Glenkiln, Shawhead, Dumfries, Scotland

KETTELEY, John Henry Beevor; *Career* FCA; md Rea Bros; exec dir S G Warburg & Sons, Dufay Bitumastic 1981-; dir Br Tar Products; *Style* - John Ketteley Esq; c/o S G Warburg & Co, 30 Gresham st, EC2 (☎ 01 600 4555)

KETTLEWELL, Capt Nigel Ion Charles; s of Cdr Charles Robert Kettlewell (d 1963); *b* 19 Mar 1934; *Educ* Allhallows Sch, RN Coll Dartmouth; *m* 1964, Lady Serena Jane, nee Dundas, da of 3 Marquess of Zetland; 1 s, 2 da; *Career* qualified in Signals 1960, Staff College 1965, served HM Yacht Britannia 1957-58 and 1963-64, in command HM ships RNYL 1974-75, Brighton 1975-76, MOD 1976-, capt RN 1979, younger brother of Trinity House 1978; *Recreations* gardening, sheep rearing; *Clubs* Naval and Military; *Style* - Capt Nigel Kettlewell, RN; The Old Rectory, Newton Towey, Salisbury, Wilts (☎ Cholderton 311)

KETTLEWELL, Lady Serena Jane; *née* Dundas; da of 3 Marquess of Zetland, ED, DL; *b* 10 Sept 1940; *m* 1964, Cdr Nigel Ion Charles Kettlewell, RN; 1 s, 2 da; *Style* - Lady Serena Kettlewell; The Old Rectory, Newton Toney, Salisbury, Wilts

KEYDEN, James Aitken; s of John Keyden (d 1969); *b* 15 May 1909; *Educ* Glasgow H S; *m* 1940, Doris Margaret, nee Crawford; 2 s (and 1 decd), 3 da (and 1 decd); *Career* CA, dir Scottish United Investors Ltd 1961-80, chm Rowan & Boden Ltd 1968-71, dir Pressed Steel Co Ltd 1953-63, dir Scottish Gas Bd 1964-73, dir Brown Shipley & Co Ltd, dir Volvo Trucks (GB) Ltd; *Recreations* golf, fishing; *Clubs* Roy Scottish Automobile; *Style* - James Keyden Esq; St Malo, Kilmacolm, Renfrewshire (☎ 2478)

KEYES, 2 Baron (UK 1943); Sir Roger George Bowlby Keyes; 2 Bt (UK 1919); s of Admiral of the Fleet 1 Baron Keyes, GCB, KCVO, CMG, DSO, DCL (d 1945); *b* 14 March 1919; *Educ* King's Mead Sch Seaford, RNC Dartmouth; *m* 1947, Grizelda Mary, da of late Lt-Col William Packe, DSO; 3 s, 2 da; *Heir* s, Hon Charles Keyes; *Career* Lt RN (ret); European War 1939-45 in N Sea and Mediterranean; co dir, author; *Style* - The Rt Hon the Lord Keyes; Elmscroft, Charlton Lane, West Farleigh, nr Maidstone, Kent (☎ Maidstone 812477)

KEYES, Hon Adrian Christopher Noel; s of 2 Baron Keyes; *b* 1962; *Educ* Lancing Coll; *Style* - The Hon Adrian Keyes

KEYES, Hon Charles William Packe; s and h of 2 Baron Keyes; *b* 8 Dec 1951; *m* 1978, Sadiye Yasmin, da of Mahir Coskun, of Istanbul; *Style* - The Hon Charles Keyes

KEYES, Hon Elizabeth Mary; da of Adm of the Fleet 1 Baron Keyes, GCB, KCVO, CMG, DSO (d 1945); *b* 1915; *Career* European War 1939-45 with VAD (RN); *Style* - The Hon Elizabeth Keyes; Wood Lane Cottage, Tingewick, Buckingham MK18 4QS

KEYES, Hon (Leopold Roger) John; s of 2 Baron Keyes; *b* 1956; *Style* - The Hon John Keyes

KEYES, Hon Josephine Mary; da of 2 Baron Keyes; *b* 1958; *Style* - The Hon Josephine Keyes

KEYNES, Hon Mrs (Anne Pinsent); da of 1 Baron Adrian, OM; *b* 27 May 1924; *m* 1945, Richard, FRS, s of Sir Geoffrey Keynes and Margaret (da of Sir George Darwin, KCB, FRS, of Newnham Grange, Cambridge); 3 s; *Style* - The Hon Mrs Keynes; 3 Herschel rd, Cambridge (☎

53107)

KHAN, Prince Amyn; s of late Prince Aly Khan and Hon Joan, nee Yarde-Buller, da of 3 Baron Churston, MVO, OBE; *b* 1937; *Style* - Prince Amyn Khan

KHAN, Prince Rahim; s of HH The Aga Khan and Sally, da of Lt-Col A Croker Poole; *b* 1971; *Style* - Prince Rahim Khan

KHAN, Princess Zahra; da of HH The Aga Khan and Sally, da of Lt-Col A Croker Poole; *b* 1970; *Style* - Princess Zahra Khan

KIDD, Sir Robert Hill; KBE (1979), CB (1975); s of Andrew Kidd (1947); *b* 3 Feb 1918; *Educ* Roy Belfast Academical Instn, Dublin U; *m* 1942, Harriet Moore, nee Williamson; 3 s, 2 da; *Career* Northern Ireland Civil Serv 1947-79 (head of NICS 1976-79), dir Allied Irish Banks Ltd, chm Allied Irish Banks Ltd (N Ireland local bd), pro chancellor elect of New U of Ulster, trustee Scotch Irish Trust; *Recreations* golf, gardening, photography; *Clubs* Civil Service, Knock GC; *Style* - Sir Robert Kidd, KBE, CB; 24 Massey ct, Belfast, BT4 3GJ (☎ 768693)

KIDMAN, Thomas Walter; ERD (1954); s of Walter James Kidman (d 1980); *b* 28 Aug 1915; *Educ* Cambridge Central Sch, Cambridgeshire Tech Coll; *m* 1939, Lilian Rose, nee Souton; 1 s, 2 da; *Career* Maj Suffolk Regt WW II, served TA 1939-67, local govt offr 1930-48, sec E Anglian Regional Hospital Bd 1972 (admin offr 1948, assist sec 1952, dep sec 1957), regional administrator E Anglian Regnl Health Authority 1973-75, ret 1975, memb NHS Health Advsy Serv 1976-; *Recreations* photography, walking, gardening, golf; *Style* - Thomas Kidman Esq, ERD; Alwoodley, 225 Arbury rd, Cambridge (☎ 357384)

KIDSTON, Hon Mrs (Patricia Anne); *née* Manners; da of 4 Baron Manners, MC (d 1972); *b* 1927; *m* 1946, John Bonham Kidston (d 1968); 2 s, 1 da; *Style* - The Hon Mrs Kidston; Breach Farm, Dummer, Basingstoke

KILBRACKEN, 3 Baron (UK 1909); John Raymond Godley; DSC (1945); s of 2 Baron Kilbracken, CB, KC (d 1950), by his 1 w, Elizabeth; bro of Wynne Godley, the economist; *b* 17 Oct 1920; *Educ* Eton, Balliol Oxford; *m* 1943 (m dis 1949), Penelope, da of Rear-Adm Sir Cecil Reyne, KBE; 1 s (and 1 s decd); *Heir* s, Hon Christopher Godley; *Career* author, photographer, journalist; served WW II Lt-Cdr RNVR; *Recreations* bird watching; *Style* - The Rt Hon Lord Kilbracken DSC; Killegar, Cavan, Eire (☎ 34309)

KILBRANDON, Baron (Life Peer UK 1971); Charles James Dalrymple Shaw; PC (1971); s of James Edward Shaw, DL, of High Greenan, Ayr; *b* 15 Aug 1906; *Educ* Charterhouse, Balliol Oxford; *m* 1937, Ruth Caroline, da of Frank Morrison Seafield Grant, of Knockie, Inverness; 2 s, 3 da; *Career* Advocate Scotland 1932, KC 1949, Sheriff of Ayr and Bute 1954-57, of Perth and Angus 1957-58, Dean of Faculty of Advocates 1957-59, a Lord of Session with title of Lord Kilbrandon 1959-71, a Lord of Appeal in Ordinary 1971-76, chm Scottish Law Cmmn 1965-71; *Clubs* New, Royal Highland Yacht (Oban); *Style* - The Rt Hon the Lord Kilbrandon, PC; Kilbrandon House, Balvicar, by Oban, Argyll PA34 4RA (☎ Balvicar 239)

KILDARE, Marquess of; Maurice FitzGerald; s and h of 8 Duke of Leinster by his 2 w, Anne; *b* 7 April 1948; *Educ* Millfield; *m* 1972, Fiona, da of Harry Hollick, of Abingdon; 1 s, 1 da; *Heir* s, Earl of Offaly; *Career* landscape gardener & designer (has own business); Pres Oxfordshire Dyslexia Assoc 1978-; *Recreations* shooting, fishing, riding, squash; *Style* - Marquess of Kildare; 7 Littleworth Hill, Wantage, Oxon (☎ 67285)

KILGOUR, Victor Ernest; s of Henry Samuel Kilgour (d 1940); *b* 31 Oct 1915; *Educ* Haberdashers' Aske's; *m* 1945, Georgina Margaret, nee Eade; 2 da; *Career* Maj QO Cameron Highlanders, chartered surveyor, formerly sr ptnr Matthews & Goodman, dir Abbey Nat Building Soc 1970-80, dir Cornhill Insurance Co Ltd 1965-80; *Recreations* gardening; *Clubs* Carlton; *Style* - Victor Kilgour Esq; Brimley House, Stoke

Abbott, Beaminster, Dorset (☎ Broadwindsor 68774)

KILLANIN, 3 Baron (UK 1900); Sir Michael Morris; 3 Bt (UK 1885), MBE (1945), TD (1945); s of Lt-Col Hon George Morris (ka 1914, yr bro of 2 Baron & 2 s of 1 Baron); suc unc 1927; *b* 30 July 1914; *Educ* Eton, Sorbonne, Magdalene Cambridge; *m* 1945, Mary, MBE, da of Rev Canon Douglas Dunlop, of Co Galway; 3 s, 1 da; *Heir* s, Hon George Morris; *Career* author, film producer, former journalist, businessman; served with KRRC WW II Bde Maj, made 'The Quiet Man' with John Ford 1952; books include 'The Shell Guide to Ireland' (with Prof Michael Duignan) and 'The Olympic Games' (with John Rodda); dir Beamish & Crawford, Fitzwilton Ltd, Irish Shell Ltd, Northern Telecom Ltd, Ulster Bank Ltd; chm: Bovril (Ireland) Ltd, Chubb Alarms (Ireland) Ltd, Ulster Investment Bank, Lombard & Ulster Banking (Ireland), Gallaher's (Dublin) Ltd; memb Lloyd's; Pres Internat Olympic Cttee 1972-; memb Irish Turf Club & Irish Nat Hunt Steeplechase Cttee; *Clubs* Garrick, Beefsteak, County (Galway), Stephen's Green (Dublin); *Style* - The Rt Hon Lord Killanin MBE TD; St Annins, Spiddal, Co Galway (☎ 83103); 30 Lansdowne rd, Dublin 4, Eire (☎ 76 33 62)

KILLEARN, 2 Baron (UK 1943); Sir Graham Curtis Lampson; 4 Bt (UK 1866); s of 1 Baron Killearn, GCMG, CB, MVO, PC (d 1964, sometime Envoy to China and Egypt and gs of Sir Curtis Lampson, 1 Bt, a naturalised American (Vermont) who helped lay the Atlantic Telegraph), by his 1 w, Rachel, da of William Wilton Phipps and Dame Jessie Butler, DBE, JP; suc 1 cous once removed, Sir Curtis Lampson, 3 Bt, 1971; *b* 28 Oct 1919; *Educ* Eton, Magdalen Oxford; *m* 1946, Nadine, da of Vice-Adm Cecil Pilcher, DSO; 2 da (Hon Lady Bonsor, Hon Mrs Meynell, *qqv*); *Heir* half-bro, Hon Victor Lampson; *Career* Late Maj Scots Gds, served M East, Italy; *Style* - The Rt Hon Lord Killearn; 6 Trevor st, SW7 (☎ 01 584 7700)

KILLEARN, Dowager Baroness; Jacqueline Aldine Leslie; da of Marchese Senator Aldo Castellani, KCNG, FRCP, FACP; *m* 1934, as his 2 w, 1 Baron Killearn, GCMG, CB, MVO, PC (d 1964); *Style* - The Rt Hon the Dowager Lady Killearn; 35 Montpelier sq, SW7; Haremere Hall, Etchingham, Sussex

KILMAINE, 7 Baron (I 1789); Sir John David Henry Browne; 13 Bt (NS 1636); s of 6 Baron Kilmaine, CBE (d 1978); *b* 2 April 1948; *Educ* Eton; *Heir* kinsman, Peter Kilmaine Browne; *Career* dir Fusion (Bickenhill) Ltd 1969-, dir Whale Tankers Ltd 1974-; *Style* - The Rt Hon the Lord Kilmaine; Ravenshaw Hall, Ravenshaw Lane, Solihull, W Midlands

KILMAINE, Baroness; Wilhelmina Phyllis; da of late Scott Arnott, of Tanners, Brasted, Kent; *m* 1930, Lt-Col 6 Baron Kilmaine, CBE (d 1978); *Style* - The Rt Hon the Lady Kilmaine; The Mount House, Brasted, Kent

KILMANY, Baron (Life Peer UK 1966); Sir William John St Clair Anstruther-Gray; 1 Bt (UK 1956), MC (1943), PC (1962); s of late Lt-Col William Anstruther-Gray, JP, DL, MP (himself gs of John Anstruther-Thomson, whose w was gda through her mother of 10 Lord Elphinstone, while her mother's mother was Lady Clementina Fleming (heir of line of the Earls of Wigton, Marischal and Perth); John Anstruther-Thomson was in his turn gs of Sir Philip Anstruther, 2 Bt, by his w Catharine, paternal gda of 1 Marquess of Tweeddale and maternal gda of 1 Earl of Buccleuch); bro of late Lady Stratheden and Campbell (decd w of 4 Baron); *b* 5 March 1905; *Educ* Eton, Ch Ch Oxford; *m* 1934, Monica Helen, OBE, da of late Hon Geoffrey Lambton (2 s of 4 Earl of Durham) and hence 1 cous of Lord Home of the Hirsel, 4 Baron Joicey and 6 Duke of Sutherland; 2 da; *Career* Maj (ret) Coldstream Gds, 1939-45 War in N Africa and NW Europe, PPS to Sec of Dept of Overseas Trade 1935, to Sec of State for Scotland 1938, Asst Postmaster Gen May-July 1945, dep chm of Ways and Means House of Commons 1959-62 and chm and dep speaker 1962-64, chm 1922 Conservative Private Members Ctee 1964-66, MP (C) N Lanarkshire 1931-45, Berwick and E Lothian 1951-66, Ld Lt Fife

1974-80, memb Nat Hunt Ctee 1948-, Crown Nominee for Scotland on Gen Med Council 1952-64, memb Horserace Betting Levy Bd 1966-74; DL Fife 1953; *Clubs* Pratt's, Brooks's, Cavalry and Guards, Turf, Jockey, New (Edinburgh), Royal and Ancient (St Andrews); *Style* - The Rt Hon Lord Kilmany MC DL PC; Kilmany, Cupar, Fife (☎ Gauldry 247)

KILMARNOCK, 7 Baron (UK 1831); Alastair Ivor Gilbert Boyd; s of 6 Baron Kilmarnock, MBE, TD (d 1975), and of Hon Rosemary Guest (d 1971), da of late 1 Viscount Wimborne; *b* 11 May 1927; *Educ* Bradfield, King's Cambridge; *m* 1, 1954 (m dis 1969, she d 1975) Diana Mary, da of D Grant Gibson; m 2, 1977, Hilary Ann, da of Leonard Sidney Bardwell; *Heir* bro, Hon Robin Jordan Boyd; *Career* V-Pres Inst Sales & Mktng Management 1981-; Late Lt Irish Gds, Palestine 1947-48, Chief of Clan Boyd, Page to Lord High Constable of Scotland at Coronation of HM King George VI; Books: *Sabbatical Year* 1958, *The Road from Ronda* 1969 and *The Companion Guide to Madrid and Central Spain* 1974; *Clubs* Pratt's; *Style* - The Rt Hon the Lord Kilmarnock; Apartado 12, Ronda, Malaga, Spain

KILMARNOCK, Denise, Baroness; Denise Aubrey Doreen; da of late Maj Lewis Coker; *m* 1955, as his 2 wife, 6 Baron Kilmarnock, MBE (d 1975); *Style* - The Rt Hon Denise, Lady Kilmarnock; 28 Eaton Terrace, SW1

KILMOREY, Earl of, *see* Needham, R F

KILMOREY, Norah, Countess of; Lady Norah Frances; *née* Hastings; da of 14 Earl of Huntingdon; *b* 12 Sept 1894; *m* 1920, 4 Earl of Kilmorey (d 1961); 1 da (Lady Hyacinth Gough), and 1 da decd; *Style* - Rt Hon Norah, Countess of Kilmorey; Mourne Park, Newry, Co Down, N Ireland

KILROY, Patrick Canice; s of Thomas Kilroy (d 1977); *b* 12 October 1929; *Educ* St Kieran's Coll Kilkenny, Univ Coll Dublin; *m* 1958, Dorothy, da of Michael Donnelly, of Dublin (d 1958); 5 c; *Career* slr; chm Gowan Gp Ltd; dir Waterford Glass Ltd, Banque Nationale de Paris (Ireland) Ltd, Silvermines Ltd; *Recreations* golf *Clubs* Stephen's Green, Wilton CC; *Style* - Patrick Kilroy Esq; Anerley, 45 Cowper rd, Dublin 6 (☎ 766184)

KIMBALL, Sir Marcus Richard; MP (C) Lincolnshire 1956-; s of late Maj Lawrence Kimball; *b* 18 Oct 1928; *Educ* Eton, Trin Cambridge; *m* 1956, June Mary Fenwick, da of Montagu John Fenwick, of Great Stukeley Hall, Huntingdon; 2 da; *Career* Lt Leics PAO Yeo (TA) 1949, Capt 1952; CC (1955-64) Rutland; chm British Field Sports Soc 1966-; kt 1981; *Clubs* White's, Pratt's; *Style* - Sir Marcus Kimball, MP; Great Easton Manor, Market Harborough, Leics; 70 Cranmer ct, SW3

KIMBER, Sir Charles Dixon; 3 Bt (UK 1904); s of Sir Henry Dixon Kimber, 2 Bt (d 1950); *b* 7 Jan 1912; *Educ* Eton, Balliol Oxford; *m* 1, 1933 (m dis 1950), Ursula, da of late Ernest Roy Bird, MP; 3 s; m 2, 1959 (m dis 1965), Margaret, da of Francis John Bonham; 1 da; *Heir* s, Timothy Kimber; *Style* - Sir Charles Kimber, Bt; No 2 Duxford, Hinton Waldrist, nr Faringdon, Oxon (☎ Longworth 820004)

KIMBER, Timothy Roy Henry; s and h of Sir Charles Dixon Kimber, 3 Bt; *b* 3 June 1936; *Educ* Eton; *m* 1, 1960 (m dis 1974), Antonia Kathleen Brenda, da of Sir Francis John Watkin Williams, 8 Bt, QC; 2 s; m 2, 1979, Susan Hare, da of J K Brooks, of Hill Crest, Silverdale, Carnforth, Lancs, and widow of Richard Coulthurst North; *Style* - Timothy Kimber Esq; 7 Chelsea Lodge, 58 Tite st, SW3

KIMBERLEY, 4 Earl of (UK 1866); Sir John Wodehouse; 11 Bt (E 1611); also Baron Wodehouse (GB 1797); s of 3 Earl of Kimberley, CBE, MC (d 1941); 3 cous thrice removed of late P G Wodehouse; *b* 12 May 1924; *Educ* Eton, Magdalene Cambridge; *m* 1, 1945 (m dis 1948), Diana Evelyn, da of late Lt-Col the Hon Sir Piers Walter Legh, GCVO, KCB, CMG, CIE, OBE (yr s of 2 Baron Newton); m 2, 1949 (m dis 1952), Carmel June (Dunnett), da of late Michael Maguire, of Melbourne, Aust; 1 s; m 3, 1953 (m dis 1960) Mrs

Cynthia Abdy Westendarp, da of E Abdy Collins, FRCS, MRCP, of The Chantrey, Saxmundham, Suffolk; 2 s; m 4, 1961 (m dis 1965), Margaret, da of Alby Simons; 1 s; m 5, 1970, Gillian, da of Col Norman Ireland-Smith, and formerly wife of John Raw; *Heir* s, Lord Wodehouse; *Career* Lt Gren Gds 1942-45, memb House of Lords All Party Defence Study Gp 1976-, Sec 1978-, House of Lords All Party UFO Study Gp 1979-, former Liberal Spokesman on aviation and aerospace, defence, vol community services; left Lib Party May 1979, joined Cons Party; memb Electoral Reform Soc 1978, Cons Action for Electoral Reform 1979, vice-pres World Council on Alchoholism; ARAeS 1977; *Clubs* Cavalry and Guards, Bath, MCC, House of Lord's Yacht, Roy Cornwall Yacht, Falmouth Shark Angling (pres), Shark Angling of Gt Britain; *Style* - The Rt Hon the Earl of Kimberley; Hailstone House, Cricklade, Swindon, Wilts (☎ Swindon 750344)

KIMMINS, Malcolm Brian Johnston; s of Lt-Gen Sir Brian Kimmins, KBE, CB, DL (d 1979); *b* 12 Feb 1937; *Educ* Harrow, Grenoble U; *m* 1968, Jane Douglas, da of Thomas Douglas Pilkington; 1 s, 2 da; *Career* v-chm & md William Sanderson & Son Ltd, J & W Hardie Ltd; *Recreations* horse racing, golf, shooting; *Clubs* White's; race horses: Glen Berg and Rust Hall; *Style* - Malcolm Kimmins Esq; 5 Elm Park rd, SW3 (☎ 01 352 9657)

KIMPTON, Hon Mrs (Rachel Elizabeth); da of 1 Baron Hazlerigg (d 1949); *b* 1904; *m* 1928, Col Anthony Charles Ward Kimpton, Herts Yeo; 1 s, 2 da; *Style* - The Hon Mrs Kimpton; Sarunds House, Farnham, Blandford, Dorset

KINAHAN, Sir Robert George Caldwell (Robin); ERD (1946), JP (1950), DL (1962); s of Henry Kinahan (d 1958); *b* 24 Sept 1916; *Educ* Stowe; *m* 1950, Coralie Isabel, da of Capt Charles de Burgh RN (d 1968); 2 s, 3 da; *Career* kt 1961, dir Nat West Bank Ltd 1973-, dir Gallaher Ltd, dir Eagle Star Insur Co (Local), dir STC (NI) Ltd, chm Ulster Bank Ltd 1970 (dep chm 1964-70), chm E T Green Ltd 1964-, chm Inglis & Co Ltd 1962-, chm Bass Ireland Ltd 1958-78, High Sheriff Belfast 1955 and Co Antrim 1969, Lord Mayor of Belfast 1959-61, MP (N Ireland) Clifton 1958-59, cncllr and alderman Belfast Corpn 1949-64; *Recreations* gardening, farming; *Clubs* Ulster (Belfast), Kildare St, University (Dublin); *Style* - Sir Robin Kinahan ERD, JP, DL; Castle Upton, Templepatrick, Co Antrim, N Ireland (☎ Templepatrick 32466)

KINCRAIG, Hon Lord; Robert Smith Johnston; QC (1955); s of William Turner Johnston, iron merchant, of Glasgow; *b* 10 Oct 1918; *Educ* Strathallan, St John's Cambridge, Glasgow U; *m* 1943, Margaret Joan, da of Col A Graham, of Glasgow; 1 s, 1 da; *Career* advocate 1942, Sheriff Roxburgh & Berwick 1964-70, Sen Coll of Justice (S Ld of Session) 1972-; *Recreations* golf, gardening; *Clubs* Hon Co Edinburgh Golfers; *Style* - The Hon Lord Kincraig, QC; Westwood, Longniddry, E Lothian (☎ 52197)

KINDERSLEY, 3 Baron (UK 1941); Robert Hugh Molesworth Kindersley; s of 2 Baron Kindersley, CBE, MC (d 1976); *b* 18 Aug 1929; *Educ* Eton, Trin Oxford, Harvard Business Sch; *m* 1954, Venice Marigold (Rosie), da of Lord (Arthur) Francis Henry Hill (yr s of 6 Marquess of Downshire, who d 1953); 3 s, 1 da; *Heir* s, Hon Rupert Kindersley; *Career* Lt Scots Gds, Malaya 1948-49, dir London Assurance 1957-, Witan Investment Co Ltd 1958-, Lazard Bros & Co Ltd 1960-, Sun Alliance & London Insurance Gp 1965-, Swedish Match Co 1973-, Financial Adviser to Export Gp for the Constructional Industries 1961-, chm Commonwealth Devpt Corpn 1980-, pres Anglo-Taiwan Trade Ctee 1976-; memb Institut Int d'Etudes Bancaires 1971-, Ct Fishmongers' Co 1973; *Recreations* all sports, incl farming and gardening; *Clubs* All England Lawn Tennis and Croquet, Queen's; *Style* - The Rt Hon the Lord Kindersley; Ramhurst Manor, nr Tonbridge, Kent (☎ Hildenborough 832174); 18 Cheyne gdns, SW3 5QT (☎ 01 352 8738)

KINDERSLEY, Hon Anna Lucy; da of 3 Baron Kindersley; *b* 1965; *Style* - The

Hon Anna Kindersley

KINDERSLEY, David Guy Barnabas; MBE (1979); s of Guy Kindersley, OBE, JP, variously barrister, stockbroker, MP, publisher and brewer (bro of 1 Baron Kindersley, GBE), by his w Kathleen, da of Sir Edmund Elton, 8 Bt; *b* 11 June 1915; *Educ* Marlborough; *m* 1957, Barbara, nee Spells, widow of Martin Petrie; 2 s, 1 da; *Career* stone carver and alphabet designer, former pupil of the sculptor Eric Gill; late advsr to MOT for street name signs and Shell Film Unit for titles; consultant Letraset 1964-; chm Wynkyn de Worde Soc 1976; *Style* - David Kindersley Esq, MBE; 45 Highworth av, Cambridge (☎ 57349)

KINDERSLEY, Hon Dickon Michael; s of 3 Baron Kindersley; *b* 1962; *Style* - The Hon Dickon Kindersley

KINDERSLEY, Hon Mrs (Emily Grace); *née* Seely; da of 1 Baron Mottistone, PC, CB, CMG, DSO, TD (d 1947); *b* 1898; *m* 1937, as his 2 w, Lt-Col Archibald Ogilvie Lyttelton Kindersley, CMG, DL (d 1955); *Career* CCllr 1956-67 Isle of Wight; *Style* - The Hon Mrs Kindersley; Rose cottage, Mottistone, IOW

KINDERSLEY, Gay; s of Hon Philip Kindersley (4 s of 1 Baron Kindersley, GBE) by his 1 w, Oonagh, yst da of Hon Arthur Guinness (2 s of 1 Earl of Iveagh), who m (2) 4 Baron Oranmore and Browne and (3) Miguel Ferreras; Gay is consequently nephew to Maureen, Marchioness of Dufferin and Ava; he is also 2 cous of (1) Paul Channon, MP, Min for the Arts, (2) Mark Lennox-Boyd, MP, and (3) HRH Princess Antonia von Preussen, Marchioness of Douro; *b* 2 June 1930; *Educ* Eton; *m* 1, 1956 (m dis 1976), Margaret, da of Hugh Wakefield, of Mount St, Mayfair; 2 s, 2 da; m 2, 1976, Philippa Harper; 1 s; *Career* gentleman rider; *Clubs* Jockey; *Style* - Gay Kindersley Esq; Parsonage Farm, E Garston, Newbury, Berks (☎ Great Shefford 301/526/330)

KINDERSLEY, Hon Hugh Francis; s of 3 Baron Kindersley; *b* 1956; *Educ* Eton; *Style* - The Hon Hugh Kindersley

KINDERSLEY, Hon Philip Leyland; s of 1 Baron Kindersley, GBE (d 1954); *b* 1907; *Educ* Eton, Oxford U; *m* 1, 1929 (m dis 1936), Oonagh, da of Hon (Arthur) Ernest Guinness (d 1949, 2 s of late 1 Earl of Iveagh); 1 s, 1 da (decd); m 2, 1936, Valerie Violet (formerly w of late 4 Baron Brougham), da of Hon Gerald French, DSO (2 s of late 1 Earl of Ypres, KP, GCB, OM, GCVO, KCMG, PC) 1 s, 2 da; *Career* European War 1939-43 in N Africa (wounded, prisoner); Capt Coldstream Gds; *Clubs* White's; *Style* - The Hon Philip Kindersley; High Paddocks, Lye Green, Crowborough, Sussex

KINDERSLEY, Hon Rupert John Molesworth; s and h of 3 Baron Kindersley; *b* 11 March 1955; *Educ* Eton; *m* 1975, Sarah Anne, da of late John D Warde; *Style* - The Hon Rupert Kindersley; 209 Borden st, Toronto, Ont, Canada

KINDERSLEY, Hon Mrs Philip (Violet Valerie); *née* French, da of Lt-Col Hon Gerald French, DSO (2 s of 1 Earl of Ypres and an author); *b* 1909; *m* 1, 1931 (m dis 1934), 4 Baron Brougham and Vaux (d 1967); 1 s decd ; m 2, 1936, as his 2 w, Hon Philip Kindersley, 4 s of 1 Baron Kindersley, GBE; 1 s, 2 da (Mrs Robert Philipson-Stow and Hon Mrs Peregrine Fairfax); *Style* - The Hon Mrs Kindersley; High Paddocks, Lye Green, Crowborough, Sussex (☎ 3127)

KING, Cecil Harmsworth; s of Sir Lucas White King, CSI, JP, of Roebuck Hall, Dundrum, Co Dublin, by his w, Geraldine, da of Alfred Harmsworth and sis of 1 and last Viscount Northcliffe, JP, also sis of 1 Viscount Rothermere, also sis of 1 Baron Harmsworth; *b* 20 Feb 1901; *Educ* Winchester, Ch Ch Oxford; *m* 1, 1923, Agnes, da of Rev Canon George Cooke, Regius Prof of Hebrew Oxford; 2 s (and 1 s decd), 1 da; m 2, 1962, Dame Ruth Railton, DBE; *Career* dir Daily Mirror 1929, dep chm Sunday Pictorial 1942, Reuters 1953-59, Bank of England 1965-68; chm Daily Mirror Newspapers Ltd & Sunday Pictorial Newspapers Ltd 1951-63, IPC 1963-68, Reed Paper Gp 1963-68,

BFI 1948-52; *Recreations* reading; *Style* - Cecil King Esq; 23 Greenfield Park, Dublin 4, Eire (☎ 695870)

KING, Hon Mrs (Elizabeth Patricia); *née* White; da of 4 Baron Annaly, MC, and Lady Lavinia Spencer, da of 6 Earl Spencer, KG, GCVO, VD, PC; is 1 cous once removed of HRH Princess of Wales; *b* 5 Nov 1923; *m* 1945, Lt-Cdr James King, DSC, DL, RNVR, *qv*; 1 s, 2 da; *Style* - The Hon Mrs King; Rademon, Crossgar, Co Down, N Ireland (☎ 830214)

KING, Hon Mrs (Heather Grace); da of 1 Baron Baden-Powell, OM, GCMG, GCVO, KCB (d 1941); *b* 1915; *m* 1940, Wing Cdr John Hall King; 1 s (and 1 s presumed decd); *Style* - The Hon Mrs King; Swerbrook Farm, Wigginton, Banbury, Oxon (☎ Bloxham 353)

KING, John Christopher; s and h of Sir James King, 3 Bt, TD; *b* 31 March 1933; *Educ* Eton; *m* 1958 (m dis 1972), Patricia Monica, da of late Lt-Col Kingsley Osbern Nugent Foster, DSO, OBE; 1 s, 1 da; *Style* - John King Esq; Mühlweg, 8021 Deining, W Germany

KING, Sir James Granville Le Neve; 3 Bt (UK 1888), of Campsie, Stirlingshire, TD (1944); s of Sir John Westall King, 2 Bt (d 1940); *b* 17 Sept 1898; *Educ* Eton, King's Coll Cambridge; *m* 1928, Penelope Charlotte, da of Capt E M C Cooper-Key CB, MVO, RN; 1 s, 2 da; *Heir* s John Christopher King; *Career* formerly Major 99 Field Brig RA (TA), Jt Master South Berks Foxhounds 1935-39; *Clubs* Brooks's; *Style* - Sir James King, Bt, TD; Church Farm House, Chilbolton, Hampshire

KING, James Osborne; DSC (1945); s of James King (d 1943); *b* 8 Oct 1914; *Educ* Campbell Coll; *m* 1945, Hon Elizabeth Patricia White, da of 4 Baron Annaly (d 1970); 1 s, 2 da; *Career* Lt-Cdr W W II, estate agent, chm Osborne King and Megran (ret 1974), ptnr Fletcher King, dir C T Bowring (underwriting agencies) Ltd, dir Rediffusion (NW) Ltd (ret 1981), dir/sec Rademon Dvpts Ltd, chm Stubber Securities Ltd, dir Gwydir Valley Agricultural Investments Pty Ltd (Australia); *Recreations* shooting, sailing; *Clubs* Buck's, Kildare St (Dublin); *Style* - James King Esq, DSC; Rademon, Crossgar, Co Down, N Ireland (☎ Crossgar 830214)

KING, Hon Mrs (Madeleine Coleman); da of Baron Cohen of Brighton (Life Peer, d 1966); *b* 1946; *m* 1978, Ross King; *Style* - The Hon Mrs King; 10 Farmer st, W8

KING, Robert Charles Moss; CB (1955), DSO (1944), OBE (1944); s of Robert Charles Henry Moss King (d 1929); *b* 6 June 1904; *Educ* Clifton Coll, RMA Sandhurst; *m* 1939, Grizel Elizabeth Stuart Mackay; 2 da; *Career* Maj-Gen, Brig Burma Malaya Indonesia, Bde Cdr 1944-47, dep dir military operations 1953, cdr Home Cos District 1954-56, dir quartering War Office 1957-58, Dep Constable of Dover Castle; *Recreations* shooting, fishing; *Style* - Maj-Gen Robert King, CB, DSO, OBE; Church Place, Eversley Cross, Hants (☎ 732171)

KING, Sir Wayne Alexander; 8 Bt (UK 1815), of Charlestown, Roscommon; s of Sir Peter Alexander King, 7 Bt (d 1973); *b* 2 Feb 1962; *Style* - Sir Wayne King, Bt; Charlestown, 365 London rd, Upper Deal, Deal, Kent; Church View, Herne st, Herne, Herne Bay, Kent

KING-HALL, Hon Ann; da of Baron King-Hall (Life Peer, d 1966); *b* 1920; *Style* - The Hon Ann King-Hall; 11 North Side, Clapham Common, SW4

KING-HALL, Hon Susan; da of Baron King-Hall (Life Peer, d 1966); *b* 1927; *Style* - The Hon Susan King-Hall; Old Barn, Woldingham, Surrey

KING-TENISON, Lady Maria Lisette; da of 11 Earl of Kingston (by his 1 w); *b* 1970; *Style* - Lady Maria King-Tenison

KINGDOM, Thomas Doyle; CB (1959); s of Thomas Kingdom (d 1957); *b* 30 Oct 1910; *Educ* Rugby, King's Cambridge; *m* 1937, Elsie Margaret, da of Leslie Caie Scott, MBE; 2 da; *Career* assist princ Home Civil Serv (Inland Revenue) 1933, controller Gov Social Survey Dept 1967-70, chm W London Supplementary Benefit Appeal Tribunal 1971-, charities'

VAT adviser Nat Cncl of Soc Serv 1972-; *Clubs* United Oxford and Cambridge U; *Style* - Thomas Kingdom Esq, CB; 2 Grosvenor rd, Northwood, Middlesex, HA6 3HJ (☎ 22006)

KINGMAN, Prof John Frank Charles; s of Frank Kingman; *b* 28 Aug 1939; *Educ* Christ's Coll Finchley, Pembroke Cambridge; *m* 1964, Valerie Cromwell; 1 s, 1 da; *Career* FRS 1971; chm Sci & Engrg Res Cncl 1981- (5-year contract, £175,000,000 budget, £25,000 pa salary); Prof Maths Oxford 1969-81, Fellow St Anne's 1978, chm Sci Bd SRC 1979-81, Prof Maths Sussex U 1966-69; *Style* - Prof John Kingman; c/o Mathematical Institute, 24/28 St Giles, Oxford (☎ 54295/54141); 8 Montpelier Villas, Brighton, E Sussex (☎ 26981)

KINGS NORTON, Baron (Life Peer UK 1965); Harold Roxbee Cox; s of William Roxbee Cox (d 1931) of Birmingham; *b* 6 June 1902; *Educ* Kings Norton G S, Imperial Coll London (Fell); *m* 1927, Marjorie (d 1980), da of Ernest Withers (d 1939), of Northwood; 2 s; *Career* chm Landspeed Ltd 1975-, Applied Photophysics 1974-, Withers Estates 1976-, Submarine Prods 1978-, Berger Jenson & Nicholson Ltd 1967-75, Metal Box Co 1961-67, dir Dowty Rotol 1968-75, Ricardo & Co (Engineers) 1927 Ltd 1965-77, British Printing Corpn 1968-77, Hoechst UK 1970-75, pres Royal Institution 1969-76, Chllr Cranfield Inst of Technology 1969-; FIMechE, Hon FRAeS, Hon DSc, Hon DTech, Hon LLD; kt 1953; *Recreations* aeronautical antiques; *Clubs* Athenaeum; *Style* - The Rt Hon Lord Kings Norton; Westcote House, Chipping Campden, Glos (☎ Evesham 840440)

KINGSALE, 30 Baron (I c 1340, precedence 1397); John de Courcy; s of Lt-Cdr Hon Michael de Courcy, RN, s of 29 Baron Kingsale (fifth in descent from the Lord Kingsale who successfully claimed of George III the hereditary privilege of keeping his hat on in front of the king; his cous & predecessor had also successfully claimed this privilege under William III, tho' the legend that King John granted the permission first is apocryphal); *b* 27 Jan 1941; *Educ* Stowe, Sorbonne, Salzburg U; *Heir* 3 cous twice removed, Nevinson Russell de Courcy; *Career* journalist; chm Strand Publications 1970, Nat Assoc Serv to Realm 1979; dir D'Olier Grantmesnil & Courcy Acquisitions 1970; Premier Baron of Ireland; *Recreations* shooting, palaeontology, mulierosity; *Clubs* Guards & Cavalry; *Style* - The Rt Hon Lord Kingsale; Orchard Cottage, Upton Noble, Somerset

KINGSBOROUGH, Viscount; Robert Charles Henry King-Tenison; s and h of 11 Earl of Kingston; *b* 20 March 1969; *Style* - Viscount Kingsborough

KINGSBURY, Lady Patricia Mary Charlemont; *née* French; da of 2 Earl of Ypres by his 1 w Olivia, nee Lambart; *b* 6 July 1919; *m* 1942, Henry Kingsbury (d 1980), yst s of Gerald Kingsbury, JP (ggs through his mother of 1 Earl of Bradford); 2 s; *Style* - Lady Patricia Kingsbury; Skiathos, Greece; Wentworth Lodge, Iver Heath, Bucks (☎ Iver 653084)

KINGSTON, 11 Earl of (I 1768); Sir Barclay Robert Edwin King-Tenison; 15 Bt (I 1682); Baron Kingston of Rockingham (I 1764), Viscount Kingston of Kingsborough (I 1766), Baron Erris (I 1800), Viscount Lorton (I 1806); s of 10 Earl of Kingston (d 1948); *b* 23 Sept 1943; *Educ* Winchester; *m* 1, 1965 (m dis 1974), Patricia Mary, da of E C Killip, of Beoley Lodge, Uttoxeter, Staffs; 1 s, 1 da; m 2, 1974 (m dis 1979), Victoria, da of D C Edmonds, of Northwood, Middx; *Heir* s, Viscount Kingsborough; *Career* late Lt Royal Scots Greys; *Clubs* Cavalry and Guards; *Style* - The Rt Hon the Earl of Kingston; c/o Midland Bank Ltd, 47 Ludgate Hill, EC4

KININMONTH, Peter Wyatt; s of Alec Marshall Kininmonth, MBE (d 1968); *b* 23 June 1924; *Educ* Sedbergh Sch Yorks, BNC Oxford; *m* 1951, Priscilla Margaret, nee Sturge; 3 s, 1 da; *Career* chm PW Kininmonth (Holdings) Ltd, dir Fred S James & Co Inc Chicago Illinois USA, dir Harbridge House Inc Boston Mass USA; *Recreations* golf *Clubs* Vincent's, City of London, Swinley Forest GC, Rye GC;

Style - Peter Kininmonth Esq; Tappington Grange, Wadhurst, Sussex (☎ 2186)

KINLOCH, Sir Alexander Davenport; 12 Bt (NS 1686), of Gilmerton, East Lothian; s of Brig-Gen Sir David Alexander Kinloch, 11 Bt, CB, MVO (d 1944); *b* 17 Sept 1902; *Educ* Eton; *m* 1, 1929 (m dis 1945), Alexandra, da of Frederick Y Dalziel, of New York, USA; 2 da; m 2, 1946 (m dis 1965), Hilda Anna, da of late Thomas Walker, of Edinburgh; 1 s, 3 da; m 3, 1965, Ann, da of Group-Capt F L White; 1 s; *Heir* s, David Kinloch; *Career* Maj Special Reserve Gren Gds, ret 1952, memb Roy Co of Archers (Queen's Bodyguard Scotland); *Clubs* White's, New (Edinburgh); *Style* - Sir Alexander Kinloch, Bt; Gilmerton House, North Berwick, East Lothian

KINLOCH, David; s and h of Sir Alexander Davenport Kinloch, 12 Bt; *b* 5 Aug 1951; *Educ* Gordonstoun; *Style* - David Kinloch Esq

KINLOCH, David Oliphant; s and h of Sir John Kinloch, 4 Bt; *b* 15 Jan 1942; *Educ* Charterhouse; CA; *m* 1968 (m dis 1979), Susan Minette, da of Maj-Gen Robert Elliott Urquhart, CB, DSO; 3 da; *Style* - David Kinloch Esq; House of Aldie, Fossoway, Kinross-shire

KINLOCH, Sir John; 4 Bt (UK 1873), of Kinloch, co Perth; s of Sir George Kinloch, 3 Bt, OBE (d 1948); *b* 1 Nov 1907; *Educ* Charterhouse, Magdalene Cambridge; *m* 1934, Doris Ellaline, da of late Charles Joseph Head, of Imber Close, Esher, Surrey; 1 s, 2 da; *Heir* s, David Oliphant Kinloch; *Career* employed by Butterfield & Swire in China and Hong Kong 1931-63, by John Swire & Sons Ltd London 1964-73; *Clubs* New (Edinburgh); *Style* - Sir John Kinloch, Bt; Aldie Cottage, Kinross, Kinross-shire KY13 7QH (☎ Fossoway 305)

KINLOSS, Lady (S Lordship 1602); Beatrice Mary Grenville; *née* Morgan-Grenville; da of Rev the Master of Kinloss (2 s, but suc er bro as 'Master', of Lady Kinloss, 11 holder of the title & herself eldest da of 3 & last Duke of Buckingham and Chandos; the latter's f, the 2 Duke, was (1) ggs of George Grenville, PM 1763-65; (2) a prodigious spendthrift (he got through his - not inconsiderable - inheritance in 8 years and left under £200 in his will); (3) the original of the Duke of Agincourt in Disraeli's 'Coningsby'); suc grandmother as 12 holder of title 1944; *b* 18 Aug 1922; *Educ* Ravenscroft Sch Eastbourne; *m* 1950, Greville Stewart Parker, s of Rev Ernest Freeman (changed name with husb to Freeman-Grenville, recognised by Lord Lyon King of Arms 1950); 1 s, 2 da; *Heir* s, Master of Kinloss; *Career* Lady Kinloss's husb, Mr Freeman-Grenville, was with Overseas Civ Serv 1951-64, History Prof State U of New York 1969-74, and is an author, chiefly of books on African and Islamic history; *Style* - The Rt Hon Lady Kinloss; North View House, Sheriff Hutton, York (☎ 03477 447)

KINLOSS, Master of; Hon Bevil David Stewart Chandos Freeman-Grenville; s and h of Lady Kinloss; *b* 20 June 1953; *Style* - The Master of Kinloss

KINNAIRD, 13 Lord (S 1682); Graham Charles Kinnaird; Baron Kinnaird (UK 1860); s of 12 Lord Kinnaird, KT, KBE (d 1972); *b* 15 Sept 1912; *Educ* Eton; *m* 1, 1938 (m dis 1940), Nadia, da of Harold Augustus Fortington, OBE; m 2, 1940, Diana Margaret Elizabeth, da of late Robert Shuckburgh Copeman, of Roydon Hall, Diss, Norfolk; 4 da (1 s decd); *Heir* none; *Career* Flying Officer RAFVR, late Lt 4/5th Bn Black Watch (TA); *Clubs* Brooks's, Carlton, Pratt's, New (Edinburgh); *Style* - The Rt Hon the Lord Kinnaird; Rossie Priory, Inchture, Perthshire (☎ Inchture 246)

KINNAIRD, Hon Anna; da of 13 Lord Kinnaird; *b* 1952; *Style* - The Hon Anna Kinnaird

KINNAIRD, Lady (Germaine) Elizabeth Olive; *née* Eliot; da of 8 Earl of St Germans, KCVO, OBE (d 1960) and Helen, nee Post; *b* 1911; *m* 1, 1932 (m dis 1940) Thomas James (d 1976), s of Hon Cuthbert James, CBE, MP (s of 2 Baron Northbourne); m 2, 1950 (m dis 1963), Hon (Kenneth) George Kinnaird (d 1973), s of late 12 Lord Kinnaird; *Style* - Lady Elizabeth Kinnaird; New York

KINNAIRD, Hon Mary Clare; da of 13 Lord Kinnaird; *b* 1960; *Style* - The Hon Mary Kinnaird

KINNAIRD, Hon Susan; da of 13 Lord Kinnaird; *b* 1956; *Style* - The Hon Susan Kinnaird

KINNOULL, 15 Earl of (S 1633); Arthur William George Patrick Hay; Viscount Dupplin and Lord Hay (S 1627, 1633, 1697), Baron Hay (GB 1711); s of 14 Earl of Kinnoull (d 1938); *b* 26 March 1935; *Educ* Eton; *m* 1961, Gay Ann, da of Sir Denys Colquhoun Flowerdew Lowson, 1 Bt (d 1975); 1 s, 3 da; *Heir* s, Viscount Dupplin; *Career* memb Agricultural Valuers' Assocn, memb Roy Co of Archers (Queen's Bodyguard for Scotland) 1965-, pres Nat Council on Inland Transport 1964-76, Jun Conservative Whip House of Lords 1966-68, pres Scottish Clans Assocn 1970, vice-pres Nat Assocn of Parish Councils 1971, chm Property Owners' Building Soc FRICS; *Clubs* Turf, Pratt's, White's, MCC; *Style* - The Rt Hon the Earl of Kinnoull; 5 Verulam Bldgs, Grays Inn, WC1 (☎ 01 242 5038); 15 Carlyle sq, SW3; Pier House, Seaview, IOW

KINROSS, 4 Baron (UK 1902); David Andrew Balfour; OBE (1968), TD (1943) & 2 Bars (1953), DL (Edinburgh 1966); s of 2 Baron Kinross and Caroline, da of Arthur Douglas, DL (gn of 6 & 7 Marquesses of Queensberry); suc bro, 3 Baron Kinross (aka Patrick Balfour) 1976; *b* 29 March 1906; *Educ* Sherborne, Edinburgh U; *m* 1, 1936 (m dis 1941), Araminta, 2 da of Lt-Col Willoughby Peel, DSO, JP, DL, late of the Camel Corps (1 cous thrice removed of Sir Robert Peel, the erstwhile PM) and maternal ggda of Sir Edward Hunter Blair, 4 Bt, JP, DL; 1 da; m 2, 1948, Helen (d 1969), da of Alan Hog and formerly w of Lt-Col Patrick Perfect; 1 s; m 3, 1972, Ruth, da of William Mill, of Edinburgh, and formerly w of Kenneth Middleton; *Heir* s, Hon Christopher Balfour; *Career* served WW II UK & Burma, memb Roy Co of Archers (Queen's Bodyguard for Scotland); WS; Col RA (TA); *Clubs* Army & Navy, New (Edinburgh); *Style* - The Rt Hon Lord Kinross OBE TD** DL; The Forge Cottage, Humbie, E Lothian (☎ 277); 58 India st, Edinburgh EH3 6HD (☎ 031 225 2651)

KINROSS, John; s of James Kinross (d 1961); *b* 4 May 1922; *Educ* County Boys' Sch Windsor; Southall Tech Coll; *m* 1947, Marie, da of Arthur Horace Lucas; 1 s, 1 da; *Career* Chartered Engr; with Lancerboss Gp 1959-; dir 1961-; *Recreations* conservation & preservation, wildlife & countryside; *Style* - John Kinross Esq; Papplewick, Oldhill Wood, Studham, Beds LU6 2NF (☎ Whipsnade 872391)

KINTORE, 12 Earl of (S 1677); Sir James Ian Keith; 3 Bt (UK 1897); Lord Keith of Inverurie and Keith Hall (S 1677), Baron Stonehaven (UK 1925), Viscount Stonehaven (UK 1938); s of 1 Viscount Stonehaven, GCMG, DSO, PC (d 1941), and Lady Ethel Sydney Keith-Falconer, da of late 9 Earl of Kintore, KT, GCMG, PC (she suc bro, 10 Earl 1966, as Countess of Kintore, 11 in line, and d 1974); *b* 25 July 1908; *Educ* Eton, Roy Sch of Mines; *m* 1935, Delia, da of late William Lewis Brownlow Loyd, of Upper House, Shamley Green, Guildford; 2 s, 1 da; *Heir* s, Lord Inverurie, Master of Kintore; *Career* changed his name and arms from Baird to Keith by Interlocutor Lyon Court 1967; suc mother as chief of the name of Keith 1974; 1939-45 War as Maj RM, memb Roy Co of Archers, UK Delegate to Council of Europe and Western European Union 1954-64, Cllr Grampian Region (chm Water Service Ctee) 1974-78, DL Kincardineshire 1959, Vice-Lt 1965-76; AIStructE; *Clubs* Beefsteak, Rank; *Style* - The Rt Hon Earl of Kintore DL; Glenton House, Rickarton, nr Stonehaven, Kincardineshire (☎ Stonehaven 63071)

KIRBY, Sir Arthur Frank; GBE (1969, KBE 1957), CMG (1945); s of George Kirby (d 1959); *b* 13 July 1899; *Educ* LSE; *m* 1935, Winifred Kate; 1 da; *Career* FCIT, traffic man Gold Coast Railway 1935-38, assist supt of the line Kenya and Uganda Railways 1938-42, gen man Palestine Railways 1942-48, supt of the line E African Railways 1948, cmmr for transport 1949-53, gen man E African Railways 1953-55, cmmr for E Africa in

London 1958-62, chm British Transport Docks Bd 1962-67, chm Nat Ports Cncl 1967-71; *Recreations* bowls; *Clubs* Roy Commonwealth Soc; *Style* - Sir Arthur Kirby GBE CMG; 6 Baltimore ct, 74 The Drive, Hove, Sussex (☎ 0273 776528)

KIRBY, Hon Mrs (Cecilia Alice); *née* Clifford; da of 13 Baron Clifford of Chudleigh; *b* 1945; *m* 1968, Lt Nicholas Breakspear Kirby, RN; 1 s, 3 da; *Style* - The Hon Mrs Kirby; Langtrees, Landford, Salisbury, Wilts

KIRKE, Rear-Adm David Walter; CB (1967), CBE (1962, OBE 1945); s of Percy St George Kirke (d 1966); *b* 13 March 1915; *Educ* RNC Dartmouth; *m* 1956, Marion Margaret Gibb; 2 s, 1 da; *Career* Rear-Adm, chm Mercantile Airship Transportation Ltd, dir Thermo Skyship (UK) Ltd, dir Airship Industries Ltd, Technical Services Ltd, BRIM Exports Ltd; *Recreations* golf; *Clubs* Army & Navy, Roy Commonwealth Soc; *Style* - Rear-Adm David Kirke, CB, CBE; Lismore House, Pluckley, Kent (☎ 439)

KIRKHAM, Hon Mrs (Pamela Vivien); da and co-heiress of Baroness Berners, *qv*; *b* 30 Sept 1929; *m* 1952, Michael Joseph Sperry Kirkham; 2 s, 1 da; *Style* - The Hon Mrs Kirkham; Parwich Lees, Derbyshire

KIRKHILL, Baron (Life Peer UK 1975); John Farquharson Smith; s of Alexander Findlay Smith; *b* 7 May 1930; *Educ* Robert Gordon's Colls Aberdeen; *m* 1965, Frances Mary Walker Reid; 1 step-da; *Career* Lord Provost of the City and Royal Burgh of Aberdeen 1971-75, Min of State Scottish Office 1975-78, chm North of Scotland Hydro-Electric Bd 1979-; Hon LLD Aberdeen; *Style* - The Rt Hon the Lord Kirkhill; 3 Rubislaw Den North, Aberdeen (☎ Aberdeen 34167)

KIRKPATRICK, Sir Ivone Elliott; 11 Bt (NS 1685), of Closeburn, Dumfriesshire; s of Sir James Alexander Kirkpatrick, 10 Bt (d 1954); *b* 1 Oct 1942; *Educ* Wellington Coll, St Mark's Coll Adelaide U; *Heir* bro, Robin Kirkpatrick; *Style* - Sir Ivone Kirkpatrick, Bt; c/o ANZ Banking Group Ltd, 32 Grenfell st, Adelaide, SA 5000, Australia

KIRKPATRICK, Robin Alexander; s of Sir James Alexander Kirkpatrick, 10 Bt, and hp of bro, Sir Ivone Elliott Kirkpatrick, 11 Bt; *b* 19 March 1944; *Educ* Wellington; *Style* - Robin Kirkpatrick Esq

KIRKWOOD, 3 Baron (UK 1951); David Harvie Kirkwood; s of 2 Baron Kirkwood (d 1970, s of 1 Baron, PC, JP, MP Clydebank 1922-50, who as David Kirkwood was deported for being the ringleader in a protest against rent increases); *b* 21 Nov 1931; *Educ* Rugby, Trin Hall Cambridge; *m* 1965, Judith, da of John Hunt, of Leeds; 3 da; *Heir* bro, Hon James Kirkwood; *Career* sr lecturer metallurgy 1976- Sheffield U, Warden Stephenson Hall 1974-79; chartered engr; *Style* - The Rt Hon Lord Kirkwood; 56 Endcliffe Hall av, Sheffield, S10 3EL (☎ 663107)

KIRKWOOD, Hon Anne Judith; da of 3 Baron Kirkwood; *b* 1969; *Style* - The Hon Anne Kirkwood

KIRKWOOD, Eileen, Baroness; Eileen Grace; da of late Thomas Henry Boalch, of Pill, Bristol; *m* 1931, 2 Baron Kirkwood (d 1970); *Style* - The Rt Hon Eileen, Lady Kirkwood; 25 The Dale, Keston, Kent

KIRKWOOD, Hon James Stuart; s of 2 Baron Kirkwood (d 1970), and hp of bro, 3 Baron; *b* 19 June 1937; *Educ* Rugby, Trin Hall Cambridge; FRICS; *m* 1965, Alexander Mary, da of late Alec Dyson, of Holt, Norfolk; 2 da; *Style* - The Hon James Kirkwood; The Cearne, Kent Hatch, Crockham Hill, Edenbridge, Kent

KIRKWOOD, Hon James Smith; s of 1 Baron Kirkwood, PC (d 1955); *b* 1912; *Educ* Allan Glens Sch Glasgow; *m* 1944, Mary Helen (d 1970), da of late James Marshall, of Elgin; 2 s, 1 da; *Career* 1939-45 War as Capt RE in N Africa, Sicily and Middle East, JP Dunbartonshire; ARIBA; *Style* - The Hon James Kirkwood JP; 26 Glenburn rd, Bearsden, Dunbartonshire

KIRKWOOD, Hon Lucy Jennifer; da of 3 Baron Kirkwood; *b* 1972; *Style* - The Hon Lucy Kirkwood

KIRKWOOD, Hon Ruth Emily; da of 3

Baron Kirkwood; *b* 1966; *Style* - The Hon Ruth Kirkwood

KISSEN, Lady; Victoria; *m* 1, Prof Edward Solomons, of New York (decd); m 2, 1964, Hon Lord Kissen (Scottish Ld of Session, d 1981); *Style* - Lady Kissen; 22 Braid av, Edinburgh EH 10 6EE (☎ 031 447 3000)

KISSIN, Baron (Life Peer UK 1974); Harry Kissin; s of Israel Kissin; *b* 23 Aug 1912; *Educ* Danzig (now Gdansk), Basle U; *m* 1, 1935, Ruth Deborah, da of Siegmund Samuel; 1 s, 1 da; *Career* chm Lewis & Peat Ltd 1961-72, Guinness Peat Group 1973-79, pres Guinness Peat Group 1979-, chm Linfood Holdings 1974-, Esperanza Ltd 1972-, dir Royal Opera House Covent Garden 1973-, chm Royal Opera House Trust 1974-; *Clubs* Reform, E India Devonshire Sports & Public Schs; *Style* - The Rt Hon Lord Kissin; 44 Frognal Lane, NW3 (☎ 01 435 8711)

KISSIN, Hon Robert David; s of Baron Kissin (Life Peer); *b* 1947; *m* 1976, Lesley Chapman; *Style* - The Hon Robert Kissin; Avenue de Champel 79, 1206 Geneva, Switzerland

KISTER, Hon Mrs (Jane Elizabeth); *née* Bridge; da of Baron Bridge of Harwich, PC; *b* 1944; *m* 1978, Prof J K Kister; *Style* - The Hon Mrs Kister

KITCHENER OF KHARTOUM AND OF BROOME, 3 Earl (UK 1914); Henry Herbert Kitchener; TD, DL (Cheshire 1972); also Viscount Kitchener of Khartoum (UK 1902), Viscount Broome (UK 1914) and Baron Denton (UK 1914); s of Viscount Broome (d 1928, s of 2 Earl and nephew of the general who won his reputation at the recapture of Khartoum after the Gordon débacle, was nearly made Viceroy of India, and drowned off the Orkneys en route to Russia 1916; Walter Page, then American Ambass, wrote of him: ...'The Cabinet Minister with whom it was impossible...to get along...He did much in raising the army, but his name did more...The Cabinet could not tell the truth about him...'); suc gf 1937; *b* 24 Feb 1919; *Educ* Winchester, Trin Cambridge; *Heir* bro, Hon Charles Kitchener; *Career* Maj (ret) Roy Signals (TA); *Clubs* Brooks's; *Style* - The Rt Hon The Earl Kitchener of Khartoum, TD, DL; 56 Elm Park rd, SW3 (☎ 01 352 5468)

KITCHENER, Hon Charles Eaton; s of Viscount Broome (d 1928; only s of 2 Earl) and hp of bro, 3 Earl; *b* 11 March 1920; *Educ* Winchester, Trin Cambridge; *m* 1959, Ursula Hope, da of late Capt C M Luck, CMG, DSO; 1 da; *Career* sometime Signalman Roy Corps of Signals; raised to the rank of an Earl's son 1938; *Style* - The Hon Charles Kitchener; Croylands, Old Salisbury Lane, Romsey, Hants

KITCHING, Henry Alan; s of Noel Kitching, JP (d 1975); *b* 9 Feb 1936; *Educ* Leighton Park Reading, Peddie Inst Hightstown NJ USA; *m* 1962, Gillian Joyce Guthrie; 2 s; *Career* Sub-Lt RN, stockbroker, co dir; *Recreations* tennis, shooting, fishing; *Style* - Henry Kitching Esq; The Grange, Ayton, Middlesbrough, Cleveland

KITSON, Hon Mrs (Ginette Molesworth); da of 2 Baron Kindersley, CBE, MC (d 1976); *b* 1924; *m* 1, 1945 (m dis 1949), Dominick Moore Sarsfield; 2 s; m 2, 1953, Henry James Buller Kitson; *Style* - The Hon Mrs Kitson; Olives Manor, Churchsettle Lane, Wadhurst, Kent

KITSON, Hon Verona Vandeleur; MBE (Mil 1960), TD; da of 3 Baron Airedale, DSO, MC; *b* 28 Sept 1920; *Career* served WW II as Jr Cdr ATS; Maj WRAC (TA); formerly JP Liberty of Peterborough; *Style* - The Hon Verona Kitson, MBE, TD; Pasture House, N Luffenham, Oakham, Rutland

KITZINGER, Uwe; CBE (1980); *b* 12 April 1928; *Educ* Watford G S, Balliol & New Coll Oxford; *m* 1952, Sheila Helena Elizabeth, nee Webster; 5 da; *Career* Pres of the Union Oxford U, fell of Nuffield Coll 1956-, prof at Paris U 1970-73, advisor to v-pres of EEC Cmmn in charge of External Relations Brussels 1973-75, dean of European Inst of Business Administration Fontainebleau 1976-80, dir Oxford Centre Mgmnt Studies 1980- *Recreations* sailing (ketch 'Anne of Cleves');

Clubs Reform, Roy Solent, SN le Golfe, Ajaccio; *Style* - Uwe Kitzinger Esq, CBE; Standlake Manor, Witney, Oxon, (☎ 086 731 266); La Rivière, 11100 Bages, France (☎ 68 324755)

KLEEMAN, David George; s of Jack Kleeman; *b* 20 Aug 1948; *Educ* St Paul's School, Trinity Hall Camb; *m* 1968, Manuela Rachel, da of Edouard Cori, Avenue de Wagram, Paris; 4 da; *Career* slr and co dir; *Recreations* fishing, reading; *Clubs* MCC; *Style* - David Kleeman Esq; 141 Hamilton ter, London NW8 9QS (☎ 01 624 2335)

KLEEMAN, Harry; s of Max Kleeman (d 1947); *b* 2 March 1928; *Educ* Westminster Sch; *m* 1955, Avril, da of Dr Maurece Lees (d 1974); 2 s (John, Daniel), 2 da (Jacqueline, Amanda); *Career* chm Kleeman Plastics Group, past pres British Plastics Federation, chm Nedo Sector Working Party on Plastics Processing, chm Polymer Engrg Management Ctee; *Recreations* amateur radio, riding; *Clubs* City Livery Club; *Style* - Harry Kleeman Esq; 41 Frognal, NW3 (☎ 01 794 3366), High Trees, Friday st, Dorking, Surrey (☎ 0306 730 678)

KLEINWORT, Sir Alexander Santiago; 2 Bt (UK 1909), of Bolnore, Cuckfield, Sussex; s of Sir Alexander Drake Kleinwort, 1 Bt (d 1935); *b* 31 Oct 1892; *Educ* St John's Coll Oxford; *m* 1938, Yvonne, da of late John Bloch; *Heir* n, Kenneth Kleinwort; *Style* - Sir Alexander Kleinwort, Bt; 1 Third av, Hove, E Sussex (☎ Hove 71752)

KLEINWORT, Kenneth Drake; s of late Ernest Greverus Kleinwort (2 s of 1 Bt); hp of unc, Sir Alexander Kleinwort, 2 Bt; *b* 28 May 1935; *Educ* Eton, Grenoble U; *m* 1, 1959, Lady Davina Rose Pepys (d 1973), da of 7 Earl of Cottenham (d 1968); 1 s, 1 da; m 2, 1973, Madeleine Hamilton, da of Ralph Taylor, of Larrea 1152, Buenos Aires; 2 s; *Style* - Kenneth Kleinwort Esq; Ermitage Ste-Hélène, 06 Plan de Grasse, Alpes Maritimes, France; 3 Balfour Place, W1

KLIMES, Michal Vladimir; s of Prof Vladimir Klimes of Prague; *b* 9 July 1944; *Educ* Inst of Chemical Tech Prague; *m* 1966, Radana Zdena, nee Egermeyer; 2 c; *Career* gp tech dir Thomas & Green Holdings Ltd, dir Fourstones Paper Mills Co Ltd, dir Thomas Green Ltd; *Recreations* tennis; *Style* - Michal Klimes Esq; The Cedars, Stratford dve, Wooburn Green, Bucks (☎ 06285 26576)

KNAPMAN, Paul Anthony; s of Frederick Ethelbert Knapman; *b* 5 Nov 1944; *Educ* Epsom Coll, King's Coll London U, St George's Hospital Medical Sch; *m* 1970, Penelope Jane, da of Lt-Cdr Michael Cox; 1 s, 3 da; *Career* DMJ Soc of Apothecaries, barr, HM Coroner Inner W London, Westminster Coroners Ct 1980-; honorary lectr in Medical Jurisprudence to St George's, St Thomas's Westminster and Middlesex Medical Schs; *Recreations* squash, sailing; *Clubs* St Stephen's Constitutional, Roy Torbay Yacht; *Style* - Paul Knapman Esq; c/o Westminster Coroners Ct, Horseferry rd, SW1 (☎ 01 834 6515)

KNATCHBULL, Hon Nicholas Louis Charles Norton; s and h of Lord Romsey and gs of Countess Mountbatten of Burma; *b* 15 May 1981; *Style* - The Hon Nicholas Knatchbull

KNEBWORTH, Viscount; John Peter Michael Scawen Lytton; s and h of 4 Earl of Lytton; *b* 7 June 1950; *Educ* Downside, Reading U; *m* 1980, Ursula, da of Anton Komoly, of Vienna; *Career* ARICS 1976; *Style* - Viscount Knebworth; Lillycombe, Porlock, Somerset (☎ Porlock 862353)

KNIGHT, Sir Arthur William; s of Arthur Frederick Knight; *b* 29 March 1917; *Educ* Tottenham County Sch, LSE; *m* 1, 1945, Beatrice, nee Oppenheim (d 1968); 1 s, 3 da; m 2, 1972, Sheila Whiteman; *Career* chm NEB 1979-, Courtaulds 1975-79; dir Dunlop Hldgs 1981-, Courtaulds; memb Cncl RIIA; kt 1975; *Style* - Sir Arthur Knight; Charlton End, Singleton, W Sussex

KNIGHT, Geoffrey Egerton; s of Arthur Egerton Knight; *b* 25 Feb 1921; *Educ* Stubbington House, Brighton Coll Sussex; *m* 1947, Evelyn Bugle; 2 da; *Career* Royal Marines 1939-46, joined Bristol

Aeroplace Co Ltd 1953, dir Bristol Aircraft Ltd 1956, dir BAC Ltd 1964-77, vice-chm 1972-76, dir Guinness Peat Group Ltd 1970-, chm: Guinness Peat Aviation 1976-, St Mary at Hill Properties Ltd 1977-, Fenchurch Insurance Holdings Ltd 1979-, dir Trafalgar House Ltd 1980-; Books *Concorde: the Inside Story* 1976; *Clubs* Boodle's; *Style* - Geoffrey Knight Esq; 33 Smith Terrace, SW3 (☎ 01 352 5391)

KNIGHT, Hon Mrs - Hon Priscilla; *née* Dodson; da of 2 Baron Monk Bretton, CB (d 1933); *b* 1914; *m* 1935, Maj Claude Thorburn Knight; 1 s, 3 da; *Style* - The Hon Mrs Knight; Lower Stoneham, Lewes

KNILL, Sir John Kenelm Stuart; 4 Bt (UK 1893), of The Grove, Blackheath, Kent (but his name does not appear on the Official Roll of Baronets); s of Sir (John) Stuart Knill, 3 Bt (d 1973); *b* 8 April 1913; *Educ* Downside; *m* 1951, Violette Maud Florence, da of Leonard Martin Barnes, of Durban, S Africa; 2 s; *Heir* s, Thomas Knill; *Career* Lt RNVR 1940-45, MOD 1963-77; *Clubs* Victory Services; *Style* - Sir John Knill, Bt; Canal Cottage, Bathampton, Somerset (☎ Bath 63603)

KNILL, Thomas John Pugin Bartholomew; s and h of Sir John Kenelm Stuart Knill, 4 Bt; *b* 23 Aug 1952; *m* 1977, Kathleen Muszynski; *Style* - Thomas Knill Esq

KNOLLYS, 3 Viscount (UK 1911); David Francis Dudley Knollys; Baron Knollys (UK 1902); s of 2 Viscount Knollys, GCMG, MBE, DFC (d 1966), and Margaret, da of Sir Stuart Coats, 2 Bt; *b* 12 June 1931; *Educ* Eton; *m* 1959, Hon Sheelin Virginia, da of late Lt-Col the Hon Somerset Arthur Maxwell, MP, and sis of 12 Baron Farnham; 3 s, 1 da; *Heir* s, Hon Patrick Knollys; *Career* late 2 Lt Scots Gds; *Style* - The Rt Hon the Viscount Knollys; Bramerton Grange, Norwich NR14 7HF (☎ Surlingham 266)

KNOLLYS, Hon Christopher Edward; s of 3 Viscount Knollys; *b* 1964; *Style* - The Hon Christopher Knollys

KNOLLYS, Hon Clarinda Susan; da of 3 Viscount Knollys; *b* 1960; *Style* - The Hon Clarinda Knollys

KNOLLYS, Hon Michael James George; s of 3 Viscount Knollys; *b* 1968; *Style* - The Hon Michael Knollys

KNOLLYS, Margaret, Viscountess; Margaret Mary Josephine; da of late Sir Stuart Auchinloss Coats, 2 Bt; *b* 1902; *m* 1928, 2 Viscount Knollys, GCMG, MBE, DFC (d 1966); *Style* - The Rt Hon Margaret, Viscountess Knollys; 20 Laxford House, Cundy st, SW1; Old White's Farm, Forest Row, Sussex

KNOLLYS, Hon Patrick Nicholas Mark; s and h of 3 Viscount Knollys; *b* 11 March 1962; *Style* - The Hon Patrick Knollys

KNOWLES, Sir Charles Francis; 7 Bt (GB 1765), of Lovell Hill, Berkshire; s of Sir Francis Gerald Knowles, 6 Bt, FRS (d 1974); *b* 20 Dec 1951; *Educ* Marlborough, Oxford Sch of Architecture (BA, DipArch, RIBA); *m* 1979, Amanda Louise Margaret, da of Lance Bromley, MChir, FRCS, of Molyneux st, W1; *Heir* kinsman, Peter Knowles; *Style* - Sir Charles Knowles, Bt; Merlin Haven House, Wotton-under-Edge, Glos

KNOWLES, Hon Mrs (Lorraine Charmian Gabrielle); *née* Carleton; da of 2 and last Baron Dorchester; *b* 1919; *m* 1947, James Metcalfe Knowles, FRIBA; 1 s, 1 da; *Style* - The Hon Mrs Knowles; 9 St Leonards ter, SW3

KNOWLES, Peter Cosby; s of late Robert Cosby Knowles (5 s of 4 Bt); hp of kinsman, Sir Charles Francis Knowles, 7 Bt; *b* 27 June 1930; *m* 1957, Gloria, da of H Oaten; 1 s, 3 da; *Style* - Peter Knowles Esq; Namarva, Winton, Queensland, Australia

KNOWLES, Timothy; s of Cyril William Knowles (d 1966); *b* 17 May 1938; *Educ* Bishop Gore G S Swansea; *m* 1967, Gaynor, da of Edgar Ernest Hallett, of Llandaff, Cardiff; 1 da; *Career* CA; commercial/financial dir HTV Gp Ltd 1976-; financial dir HTV Ltd 1975-81, assist md 1981-; memb South Wales

Electricity Bd 1981-; *Style* - Timothy Knowles Esq; 9 Ger-y-Llan, St Nicholas, Cardiff CFS 6SY (☎ Peterston-super-Ely 760726)

KNOX, Lt-Cdr Gerald Francoys Needham; s of Capt John Needham Knox, RN (ret; ggs of Hon John Knox, 3 s of 1 Earl of Ranfurly, by Hon John's w, Lady Mabella Needham, da of 1 Earl of Kilmorey); hp of kinsman, 6 Earl of Ranfurly, KCMG; *b* 4 Jan 1929; *Educ* Wellington; *m* 1955, Rosemary, da of Air Vice-Marshal Felton Vesey Holt, CMG, DSO; 2 s, 2 da; *Career* RN (ret); *Style* - Lt-Cdr Gerald Knox, RN; Maltings Chase, Nayland, Colchester, Essex

KNUTSFORD, 5 Viscount (UK 1895); Sir Julian Thurstan Holland-Hibbert; 6 Bt (UK 1853), CBE (1957); Baron Knutsford (UK 1888); s of 4 Viscount Knutsford (d 1976); *b* 3 May 1920; *Educ* Eton, Trin Cambridge; *Heir* cous, Michael Holland-Hibbert; *Career* 1939-45 War with Coldstream Gds, memb Nat Advisory Council on Employment of the Disabled; JP Herts 1953, OStJ; *Style* - The Rt Hon Viscount Knutsford CBE JP; Munden, Watford, Herts (☎ Garston 72002)

KOLLITSIS, Hon Mrs; Hon Rosemary; da of 1 and last Baron Inman, PC (d 1979); *b* 1933; *m* 1955, Nickolas Kollitsis, MD, FRCS; 1 s, 2 da; *Style* - The Hon Mrs Kollitsis; 11 Stasinou st, Engomi, Nicosia, Cyprus

KOMIEROWSKI, Hon Mrs (Katharine Mary); *née* Godley; da of 2 Baron Kilbracken, CB, KC (d 1950); *b* 1923; *m* 1944, Capt Peter Komierowski; 1 s, 1 da; *Career* BSc (Soc); *Style* - The Hon Mrs Komierowski; 4 Stanley Mansions, Park Walk, SW10

KOPPEL, Hon Mrs (Jessica Gwendolen); *née* St Aubyn; da of late 3 Baron St Levan and Hon Clementina, nee Nicolson, da of 1 Baron Carnock; Mrs Koppel is hence 1 cous of Nigel Nicolson the writer; *b* 8 Feb 1918; *m* 1939, John Patrick Koppel, late Maj Welsh Gds; 1 s, 2 da; *Recreations* gardening; *Clubs* Army & Navy; *Style* - The Hon Mrs Koppel; Goodworth House, Goodworth Clatford, Andover, Hants (☎ 0264 66539)

KORNBERG, Justin Anthony; s of Isaac Eugene Kornberg; *b* 16 Aug 1928; *Educ* Bronx H S of Science, Clifton, Trin Cambridge, Bradford Tech, LSE; *m* 1961, Elizabeth Ann, nee Oppenheim; 3 children; *Career* md Lister & Co Ltd, memb of Cncl Anglo-Israel Chamber of Commerce, Aims for Free Enterprise Org, the Freedom Assoc Ltd; *Recreations* reading; *Clubs* Athenaeum; *Style* - Justin Kornberg Esq; 11 Harley st, W1 (☎ 01 580 6474)

KORNICKI, Lady Lepel (Sophia); *née* Phipps; da of 4 Marquess of Normanby, CBE; *b* 1952; *m* 1975, Richard Kornicki; 2 s, 1 da; *Style* - Lady Lepel Kornicki

KRASNER, Alex; Campaign medals, 1943, 1945; s of Isaac Krasner (d 1957); *b* 25 Jan 1923; *Educ* Central Foundation G S for Boys, London; *m* 1947, Rose; 2 s; *Career* Sergeant, Royal Artillery, North Africa, Sicily, Austria & Egypt; CA, (Fellow); Senior Ptnr in professional firm, 1978; ptnr 24 yrs; *Recreations* golf, music, bridge, tennis, charity work; *Clubs* Filey, Leeds bridge, Cunard; *Style* - Alex Krasner Esq; 18 Sycamore av, Filey, N Yorks; 6 Linton rd, Leeds 17, Yorkshire (☎ 691542)

KRETSCHMER, John Martin; s of Dr Eric Kretschmer (d 1954); *b* 1 April 1916; *Educ* Ottershaw Coll, King's Coll London; *m* 1943, Noel Mary, nee Tapsfield; 2 s (Robin James, Richard Andrew), 1 da (Katharine Anne Dures); *Career* Maj RE, CEng, FICE, FIStructE, chm- Reed & Mallik Ltd, Reed & Stuart (Pty) Ltd, dir Rush & Tompkins Gp Ltd 1978-, memb of cncl Inst of CEng 1979, memb of cncl Federation of CE Contractors; *Recreations* mountaineering, natural history; *Clubs* Alpine; *Style* - John Kretschmer Esq; Tower House, Redlynch, Salisbury, Wilts (☎ Downton 20401)

KWIATKOWSKI, Lady Barbara; *née* Legge; da of late 7 Earl of Dartmouth; *b* 1916; *m* 1945, Adam Kwiatowski, Lt Polish Army; 4 s; *Career* formerly in First Aid Nursing Yeo; *Style* - Lady Barbara Kwiatkowski; Butler's House, Patshull

Park, Wolverhampton, W Midlands

KYNNAIRD, Viscount; Prince Filippo Giambattista Camillo Francesco Aldo Mana Rospigliosi; s and h of 11 Earl of Newburgh; *b* 4 July 1942; *m* 1972, Baronessa Donna Luisa, da of Count Annibale Caccia Dominioni; 1 da (Princess Benedetta Francesca Marian b 1974); *Style* - Viscount Kynnaird; Via Modestino 3, Milan, Italy

L

LABOUCHERE, Sir George Peter; GBE (1964), KCMG (1955, CMG 1951); s of late Frank Anthony Labouchere; *b* 1905; *Educ* Charterhouse; *m* 1943, Rachel Katharine MacGregor, da of Hon Eustace Hamilton-Russell (d 1962, 6 s of 8 Viscount Boyne); *Career* FO 1929, Cnsllr Nanking 1946, Buenos Aires 1948; Min Vienna 1950-53, Hungary 1953-55; Ambass to Belgium 1955-60, Spain 1960-66 (ret); *Style* - Sir George Labouchere, GBE, KCMG; Dudmaston, Bridgnorth, Salop

LACEY, Graham Ferguson; *Career* chm Bernard Wardle & Co Ltd, chm Rivington Reed Ltd; dir Ferguson Lacey gp of cos, and Birmingham & Midland gp of cos; dir Axebridge Ltd, Berkeley Insurance Brokers Ltd, Edinburgh & General Investments Ltd, Foxhall Securities Ltd, F W Henry Ltd, Lacey Wills Ltd, Lentronics (Labs) Ltd, Hamilborne Ltd, Hamilton & Ferguson Properties Ltd, Harcourt Lacey Ltd, J A Peden Ltd, Killead Investment & Trading Co Ltd, Meara Gibson Ltd, Marchelm Ltd, Multi-National Real Estate Services Ltd, National Carbonising Co Ltd, Paragon Courtney Paint & Varnish Co Ltd, Porters (Croydon) Ltd, St James's Perfumery Co Ltd, Timber Developments Ltd, World Travel Service (NI) Ltd, Energy Investments Ltd, and others; *Style* - Graham Lacey Esq; 8-9 Buckingham pla, SW1

LACHS, His Honour Judge; Henry Lazarus; s of Samuel Lachs (d 1960); *b* 31 Dec 1927; *Educ* Liverpool Institute H S, Pembroke Cambridge; *m* 1959, Edith (Dr Edith Lachs, JP), da of Ludwig Bergel; 4 da; *Career* a recorder of the Crown Court 1972-79, circuit judge 1979-; regional chm Mental Health Review Tribunal 1968-79; *Style* - His Honour Judge Lachs; 41 Menlove Gdns West, Liverpool, L18 (☎ 051 722 5936)

LACON, Edmund Richard Vere; s and h of Sir Edmund Vere Lacon, 8 Bt; *b* 1967; *Style* - Edmund Lacon Esq; Milbrook, Holton St Peter, Halesworth, Suffolk

LACON, Sir Edmund Vere; 8 Bt (UK 1818); s of Sir George Vere Francis Lacon, 7 Bt (d 1980), by his 1 w Hilary; *b* 3 May 1936; *Educ* Woodbridge Sch Suffolk; *m* 1963, Gillian, da of Jack Henry Middleditch, of Wrentham, Suffolk; 1 s, 1 da; *Heir* s, Edmund Richard Vere *Career* marketing manager Rothmans/ Carreras, Kent; *Style* - Sir Edmund Lacon, Bt; c/o Abdul Assiz Al-Babtain, PO Box 559 Safat, Kuwait; c/o Barclays Bank, Thoroughfare, Halesworth, Suffolk; Milbrook, Holton St Peter, Halesworth, Suffolk (☎ 2536)

LACROIX, Hon Mrs (Susan Gina); *née* Weinstock; da of Baron Weinstock; *b* 1955; *Educ* Cranborne Chase, St Hilda's Oxford, LSE; *m* 1980, Laurent Lacroix; *Style* - The Hon Mrs Lacroix

LACY, G A; *Career* md Chrysler United Kingdom Ltd; *Style* - G A Lacy Esq; Chrysler United Kingdom Ltd, Abbey rd, Whitley, Coventry, W Midlands

LACY, Sir Hugh Maurice Pierce; 3 Bt (UK 1921); s of Sir Maurice John Pierce Lacy, 2 Bt (d 1965); *b* 3 Sept 1943; *Educ* Aiglon Coll Switzerland; *m* 1968, Deanna, da of Howard Bailey; *Heir* bro, Patrick Bryan Finucane Lacy; *Style* - Sir Hugh Lacy Bt

LACY, Nansi, Lady; Nansi; da of late Myrddin Evans; *m* 1940, as his 2 w, Sir Maurice John Pierce Lacy, 2 Bt (d 1965); *Style* - Nansi, Lady Lacy; Dormers, Hadlow Down, Sussex

LACY, Patrick Bryan Finucane; s of Sir Maurice John Pierce Lacy, 2 Bt (d 1965); and hp to Btcy of bro, Sir Hugh Maurice Pierce Lacy, 3 Bt; *b* 18 Apr 1948; *Educ* Downside; *m* 1971, Phyllis Victoria, da of Edgar P H James; 1 s, 1 da; *Style* - Patrick Lacy Esq; 11 Tudor Gdns, Barnes, SW13

LAGDEN, Ronald Gordon; s of Reginald Bousefield Lagden, OBE, MC (d 1944); *b* 4 Sept 1927; *Educ* RMC Sandhurst, Harvard U; *m* 1951, Elizabeth Veronica, da of John Kenneth Mathews (d 1972); 2 s, 1 da; *Career* Lt Italy (Queen's Own Cameron Highlanders); v-pres and dir Europe for Quaker Oats Co (Chicago) 1971, chm Quaker Oats Ltd (UK), chm Golf Development International (Brussels); *Style* - Ronald Lagden Esq; 13 Ave de Mercure, 1180 Brussels (☎ 02 374 4011); Spear Hill Cottage, Ashington, Sussex (☎ 0903 892 551)

LAGESEN, Air Marshal Sir Philip Jacobus; KCB (1979, CB 1974) DFC (1945), AFC (1959); *Career* Air Cdre RAF 1970, SASO Strike Command 1972, Air Vice-Marshal 1972, Dep Cdr RAF Germany 1973-75, AOC No 1 Gp, RAF Strike Command 1975-78; air officer commanding 18 Gp, Northwood 1978-; *Style* - Air Marshal Sir Philip Lagesen KCB DFC AFC; c/o Lloyds Bank, 6 Pall Mall, SW1

LAIDLAW, Christopher Charles Fraser; s of late Hugh Alexander Lyon Laidlaw; *b* 9 Aug 1922; *Educ* Rugby, St John's Cambridge; *m* 1952, Nina Mary Pritchard; 1 s, 3 da; *Career* dir Commercial Union Assur 1978-, dep chm British Petroleum Co Ltd 1980-81 (dir of operations 1971-72, md 1972), chm BP Oil 1977-81; exec chm ICL 1981-; *Style* - Christopher Laidlaw Esq; ICL House, Putney High st, SW15 (☎ 01 788 7272)

LAIDLAW, Lady; Elizabeth Henderson; da of late John N Haran; *m* 1957, as his 2 w, Sir George (Palmer) Laidlaw, OBE (d 1969); *Style* - Lady Laidlaw; 55 Gilburn rd, Kilmacolm, Renfrewshire

LAIDLAW, Bt-Col John Andrew Mitchell; TD (1949), DL (Essex 1963); s of Austin Laidlaw (d 1963); *b* 20 Aug 1916; *Educ* Malvern; *m* 1943, Sonia, da of late P M Haines; 2 da; *Career* served in 1939-45 War in AA Command and in N W Europe, cmd 118 Regiment RA 1945-46, cmd 452 Regiment RA 1953-55; *Style* Col John Laidlaw, TD, DL; Old House, Little Baddow, Chelmsford, Essex (☎ Danbury 3204)

LAINE, Cleo (Mrs John Dankworth); OBE (1979); *b* 28 Oct 1927; *m* 1, 1947, George Langridge (m dis 1957); 1 s; m 2, 1958, John Philip William Dankworth; 1 s, 1 da; *Career* vocalist; *Style* - Miss Cleo Laine, OBE; International Artistes Representation, Regent House, 235 Regent st, WC1 (☎ 01 439 8401)

LAING, Austen; CBE (1973); s of William Laing (d 1940); *b* 1923; *Educ* Bede Coll Sunderland, Durham U; *m* 1945, Kathleen, da of Alfred Pearson; *Career* served in 1939-45 War, Lt (A) RNVR in Atlantic, NE Arctic, E Indies and Pacific; economics lecturer, Durham U 1950-57, Dir-Gen British Fishing Federation Ltd 1962-; *Style* - Austen Laing Esq CBE; Boulder Cottage, 7 West End, Swanland, N Ferriby, N Humberside

LAING, Sir Hector; s of Hector Laing; *b* 12 May 1923; *Educ* Loretto, Jesus Cambridge; *m* 1950, Marian Clare Laurie; 3 s; *Career* served with Scots Gds 1942-47, Capt; chm McVitie & Price 1963- (dir 1947-63), chm United Biscuits Ltd 1972- (dir 1953-64, md 1964-72); dir: Court of Bank of England 1973-, Royal Insurance Gp 1970, Allied Breweries Ltd; chm Food & Drink Industries Council 1977-79; kt 1978; *Style* - Sir Hector Laing; High Meadows, Windsor rd, Gerrards Cross, Bucks (☎ 49 82437); Dunphail House, Dunphail, Forres, Morayshire

LAING, Sir (William) Kirby; JP (Middx 1965), DL (1978); s of Sir John Laing, CBE; *b* 21 July 1916; *Educ* St Lawrence Coll Ramsgate, Emmanuel Cambridge; *m* 1939, Joan Dorothy Bratt (d 1981); 3 s; *Career* chm Laing Properties Ltd 1978-, dir John Laing Ltd 1939-80; pres: National Federation of Building Trades' Employers 1965 and 1967, Instn of Civil Engrs 1974, and Royal Albert Hall 1979; kt 1968; *Style* - Sir Kirby Laing, JP, DL; John Laing Ltd,

Page st, NW7 (☎ 01 959 3636)

LAING, Hon Mrs; Hon Lucy Ann Anthea; da of 1 Baron Aldington, KCMG, CBE, DSO, TD, PC; *b* 1956; *Educ* Cranborne Chase Sch; *m* 1979, Alastair North Grant Laing; *Style* - The Hon Mrs Laing

LAING, Sir (John) Maurice; s of Sir John Laing, CBE; *b* 1 Feb 1918; *Educ* St Lawrence Coll Ramsgate; *m* 1940, Hilda Violet, da of William Tom Steeper Richards, of Ramsgate; 1 s; *Career* served in RAF 1941-45, chm John Laing & Son Ltd and John Laing Construction Ltd, dir Bank of England; v-pres Federation of Civil Engineering Contractors, pres British Employers Confederation 1964-65, Govr Administration Staff Coll 1966-72, National Institute of Economic & Social Research 1964-; *Style* - Sir Maurice Laing; Reculver, 63 Totteridge Village, N20

LAING, Peter Anthony Neville Pennethorne; s of Lt-Col Neville Ogilvie Laing, DSO (d 1950); *b* 12 March 1922; *Educ* Eton, Paris U; *m* 1958, Penelope Lucinda, da of Sir William Pennington-Ramsden, 7 Bt, of Muncaster Castle, Cumberland; 2 da; *Career* attaché British Embassy, Madrid 1944-46, int marketing consultant in Western Europe, US, the Caribbean and Latin America, dir ITC Project for UN 1975-; *Style* - Peter Laing Esq; Corton Denham House, Corton Denham, Sherborne, Dorset (☎ 0963 22 205); Sotogrande, Guadiaro, Cadiz, Spain

LAING, Percy Lyndon; CMG (1970); s of Percy William Laing; *b* 12 July 1909; *Educ* Otago Boys H S NZ, Canterbury U; *m* 1937, Mabel Collis, da of John Wood, of Wellington; 1 s; *Career* pres NZ Institution of Engineers 1962, Commissioner of Works NZ 1965-69, chm NZ Natural Gas Corpn 1969, dir NZ Forest Products Ltd; *Style* - Percy Laing Esq CMG; 53 Chesham av, Taupo, New Zealand

LAING, Ronald David; s of D P M Laing; *b* 7 Oct 1927; *Educ* Glasgow U; *Career* MB, ChB, DPM; Dept of Psychological Med, Glasgow U 1953-56, Tavistock Clinic 1956-60, fell Foundations Fund for Research in Psychiatry 1960-67, dir Langham Clinic for Psychotherapy 1962-65, chm Philadelphia Assoc Ltd 1964-; *Books* The Divided Self (1960); The Self and Others (1961); The Politics of Experience and the Bird of Paradise (1967); Knots (1970); The Politics of the Family (1971); The Facts of Life (1976); Do You Love Me (1977); Conversations with Children (1978); *Style* - Ronald Laing Esq; 2 Eton rd, SW3 (☎ 01 722 9448)

LAIRD, Hon Mrs; Hon Caroline (Kirsty); da of Baron Ferrier (Life Peer); *b* 1934; *m* 1957, Michael Laird, ARIBA, FRIAS; *Style* - The Hon Mrs Laird; 22 Moray pla, Edinburgh 3

LAIRD, Edgar Ord; CMG (1969), MBE (1958); s of Edgar Balfour Laird (d 1945), of Monifieth, Angus; *b* 16 Nov 1915; *Educ* Rossall, Emmanuel Cambridge; *m* 1940, Heather Lonsdale, da of Arthur Eric Forrest (d 1971); 4 da; *Career* entered Colonial Service 1939; HM Forces 1939-46, sec to Govt Fedn of Malaya 1953, dep sec PM's Dept F of M 1957, dep high commissioner Nigeria 1965-69, Foreign and Commonwealth Off 1969-72, British Govt rep Associated States, West Indies 1972-75; *Style* - Edgar Laird Esq CMG MBE; Clarendon House, 33 The Strand, Topsham, Exeter, Devon

LAIRD, Gavin Harry; s of James Laird; *b* 14 March 1933; *Educ* Clydebank H S; *m* 1956, Catherine Gillies Campbell; 1 da; *Career* full-time Trade Union Official 1971-; memb Scottish Industrial Development Advisory Bd 1975-; memb Executive Council, Amalgamated Union of Engineering Workers 1975-; dir British National Oil Corpn 1976-; memb TUC General Council 1979-; *Style* - Gavin Laird Esq; 24C Castleton ct, Castleton Drive, Newton Mearns, Glasgow

LAISTER, Peter; s of late Horace Laister; *b* 24 Jan 1929; *Educ* King Edward's Sch Birmingham, Manchester U Coll of Technology; *m* 1, 1951, Barbara Cooke; 1 s, 1 da; m 2, 1958, Eileen Alice Goodchild (nee Town); 1 da; *Career* gp md British Oxygen Co Ltd (BOC Int Ltd) 1969-79, Ellerman Lines Ltd 1976-79, and Thorn EMI 1979-; chm BOC Financial Corpn (USA) 1974-75, Tollemache and

Cobbold Breweries 1978-79, London and Hull Insurance Co 1976-79; memb Indust Dvpt Advsy Bd 1981-, council memb Industrial Society 1971, memb council UCL 1978; *Style* - Peter Laister Esq; Thatches, 92 Staines rd, Wraysbury, Bucks

LAKE, Sir (Atwell) Graham; 10 Bt (GB 1711); s of Capt Sir Atwell Henry Lake, 9 Bt, CB, OBE, RN (d 1972); *b* 6 Oct 1923; *Educ* Eton; *Heir* bro, Willoughby Alfred Lake; *Career* served in Gilbert & Ellice Military Forces 1944-45, Col Admin Service 1945-55, Sec to Govt of Tonga 1950-53, Br High Cmmr New Delhi 1966-68, FCO 1969-72; *Style* - Sir Graham Lake, Bt

LAKE, Lady; Kathleen Marion; da of late Alfred Morrison Turner; *m* 1922, Capt Sir Atwell Henry Lake, 9 Bt, CB, OBE, RN (d 1972); *Style* - Lady Lake; Ford Hill, Little Hadham, Ware, Herts

LAKE, Norman Cecil; CBE (1971); s of Francis C J Lake; *b* 29 Apr 1905; *Educ* Newcastle under Lyme & Longton Staffs; *m* 1930, Nellie Gertrude, da of Thomas Dowler; 2 s, 2 da; *Career* dir and gen man Head Wrightson Machine Co Ltd 1946-51; dep md Head Wrightson & Co Ltd; founder pres Metallurgical Plantmakers Fedn 1967-69; pres Iron and Steel Inst 1970-71; part-time dir Northern Gas Board 1971; *Style* - Norman Lake Esq, CBE; 121 Guisborough Road, Nunthorpe, Middlesbrough, Teesside (☎ 0642 35769)

LAKE, Willoughby Alfred; s of Capt Sir Atwell Henry Lake, 9 Bt, CB, OBE, RN (d 1972); hp to Btcy of bro, Sir (Atwell) Graham Lake, 10 Bt; *b* 31 Aug 1935; *Educ* Eton; *m* 1952, Elizabeth Elsie Faith, da of Sir Rupert Turner Havelock Clarke, 2 Bt; 2 da; *Style* - Willoughby Lake Esq; Manor Cottage, Much Hadham, Herts

LAKEMAN, Enid; da of Horace B Lakeman; *b* 28 Nov 1903; *Educ* Tunbridge Wells G S, Bedford Coll, London U; *Career* WAAF 1941-45; Electoral Reform Soc 1945- (dir 1960-); parliamentary candidate (L) St Albans 1945, Brixton 1950, Aldershot 1955 and 1959; *Clubs* National Liberal; *Style* - Miss Enid Lakeman; 37 Culverden ave, Tunbridge Wells, Kent, TN4 9RE (☎ Tunbridge Wells 21674)

LAKER, Sir Frederick Alfred; *b* 6 Aug 1922; *Educ* Simon Langton Sch Canterbury; *Career* Short Bros Rochester 1938-40, General Aircraft 1940-41, Air Transport Auxiliary 1941-46, Aviation Traders 1946-60, British United Airways 1960-65, chm and md Laker Airways Ltd 1966-; kt; *Clubs* Eccentric and Little Ship; *Style* - Sir Freddie Laker; c/o Laker Airways, Gatwick Airport, Horley, Surrey (☎ 01 668 9363 and Crawley 31222)

LAKIN, Grace, Lady; Grace; da of John Kyme, of Manchester; *m* 1965, as his 2 w, Sir Henry Lakin, 3 Bt (d 1979); *Style* - Grace, Lady Lakin; Torwood, Post Office, Rosetta, Natal, S Africa

LAKIN, Hon Mrs - Hon (Helena Daphne); *née* Pearson; da of 2 Viscount Cowdray (d 1933); *m* 1939, Lt-Col John Lakin, TD, late Warwickshire Yeo; *Style* - Hon Mrs Lakin; Hammerwood House, Iping, Midhurst, Sussex

LAKIN, Sir Michael; 4 Bt (UK 1909); s of Sir Henry Lakin, 3 Bt (d 1979); *b* 28 Oct 1934; *Educ* Stowe; *m* 1, 1956 (m dis 1963), Margaret, da of Robert Wallace, of Mount Norris, Co Armagh; m 2, 1965, Felicity, da of Anthony Denis Murphy, of Londiani, Kenya; 1 s, 1 da; *Heir* s, Richard Lakin; *Style* - Sir Michael Lakin, Bt; Torwood, Post Office, Rosetta, Natal, S Africa

LAKIN, Richard Anthony; s and h of Sir Michael Lakin, 4 Bt; *b* 26 Nov 1968; *Style* - Richard Lakin Esq

LALL, Kanai; *Career* chm Consolidated Pneumatic Tool Co Ltd; *Style* - Kanai Lall Esq

LAMB, Lady; Ada Henderson; da of late James Henry Langlands, JP; *b* 14 Nov 1898; *m* 1923, Lt-Col Sir Thomas Lamb (d 1943); *Style* - Lady Lamb; 23, Camperdown st, Broughty Ferry, Dundee, DD5 3AA (☎ Dundee 79038)

LAMB, Sir Albert Larry; *b* 15 July 1929;

m Joan Mary Denise, nee Grogan; 2 s, 1 da; *Career* editor (Manchester) Daily Mail 1968-69, dir News Int Ltd 1970-, editorial dir 1971-, dep chm News Group 1979-, ed The Sun 1969-72 and 1975-; kt 1980; *Style* - Sir Larry Lamb; 5 Durward House, 31 Kensington Court W8

LAMB, Sir Albert Thomas; KBE (1979, MBE 1953), CMG (1974), DFC (1945); s of Reginald Selwyn Lamb (d 1972); *b* 23 Oct 1921; *Educ* Swansea G S; *m* 1944, Christina Betty Wilkinson; 1 s, 2 da; *Career* entered Foreign Office 1938; served with RAF (1941-46); Foreign Office 1946, counsellor 1965, Diplomatic Service inspr 1968, sr inspr 1971; Ambass to Kuwait 1974-77, Ambass to Norway 1978-; *Style* - Sir Albert Lamb, KBE, CMG, DFC; c/o Foreign and Commonwealth Office, SW1

LAMB, Hon David Charles; s and h of 2 Baron Rochester; *b* 1944; *Educ* Shrewsbury Sch and U of Sussex; *m* 1969, Jacqueline Agnes, yr da of John Alfred Stamp; 2 s; *Career* journalist; *Style* - The Hon David Lamb; 24 Albany ter, Richmond, Surrey (☎ 01 940 7029)

LAMB, Air Vice-Marshal George Colin; CB (1977), CBE (1966), AFC; s of George Lamb; *b* 23 July 1923; *Educ* Lancaster Royal G S; *m* 1, 1945, Nancy Mary, da of Ronald Godsmark; 2 s; m 2, 1981, Mrs Maureen Margaret Mepham; *Career* assist cmdt RAF Coll Cranwell 1964-65, Air Cdre 1968; Royal College of Defence Studies 1971-72; dir of Control (Operations) National Air Traffic Services 1972-74, Cdre Southern Maritime Air Region 1974-75, ch of staff No 18 Gp 1975-78; ch exec Badminton Assoc of England 1978-; Int Rugby Football Referee 1967-72; *Style* - Air Vice-Marshal George Lamb CB CBE AFC; 15 Rushington ave, Maidenhead, Berks (☎ 22624)

LAMB, Hon Kenneth Henry Lowry; s of 1 Baron Rochester, CMG (d 1955); *b* 1923; *Educ* Harrow, Trin Oxford; *m* 1952, Elizabeth Anne Saul; 1 s, 2 da; *Career* pres Oxford Union 1944; sr lecturer History and English, Royal Naval Coll Greenwich 1947-53; head of Religious Broadcasting, BBC 1963-66, sec BBC 1967-68, dir Public Affairs BBC 1969-77; special adviser Broadcasting Research 1977-80; sec to Church Commissioners 1980-; *Style* - The Hon Kenneth Lamb; 25 South ter, Thurloe sq, SW7 (☎ 01 584 7904)

LAMB, Sir Lionel (Henry); KCMG (1953), OBE (1944); s of Sir Harry Harling Lamb, GBE, KCMG (d 1948); *b* 1900; *Educ* Winchester, Queen's Oxford; *m* 1927, Jean Fawcett, da of late Dr William MacDonald, of Sydney, Australia; 1 s; *Career* entered HM Consular Service in China 1921, superintending consul & assist Chinese sec Shanghai 1940-41, consul St Paul-Minneapolis, USA 1943-45; Ambass Switzerland 1953-58, ret 1958; *Style* - Sir Lionel Lamb, KCMG, OBE; Roxford Barn, Hertingfordbury, Hants

LAMB, Lady (Margaret) Pansy Felicia; da of 5 Earl of Longford, KP, MVO (killed in action 1915); *b* 1904; *m* 1928, Henry Lamb, MC, RA (d 1960); 1 s, 2 da; *Style* - Lady Pansy Lamb; 23 Denbigh ter, W11

LAMB, Lady; Rose; da of late Samuel Brooks; *m* 1927, Sir Walter Rangeley Maitland Lamb, KCVO (d 1961); *Style* - Lady Lamb; c/o Barclays Bank, Northwood, Middx

LAMB, Rev Hon Roland Hurst Lowry; s of 1 Baron Rochester, CMG (d 1955); *b* 1917; *Educ* Mill Hill, Jesus Cambridge; *m* 1943, Vera Alicia, da of Arthur Morse, of Walton-on-Naze, Essex; 1 s, 3 da; *Career* chaplain RAF 1942, Middle East 1944, supt Aberystwyth English Methodist Circuit 1955-61, Callington 1961, resigned Methodist Ministry 1967; gen sec British Evangelical Council 1967-; *Style* - Rev the Hon Roland Lamb; 21 Woodstock rd North, St Albans, Herts (☎ 55655)

LAMB, Hon Timothy Michael; s of 2 Baron Rochester; *b* 1953; *Educ* Shrewsbury, Queen's Oxford; *Style* - The Hon Timothy Lamb

LAMB, Capt William John; CVO (1947), OBE (1944); s of Sir Richard A Lamb, KCSI, CIE (d 1923); *b* 1906; *Educ* RN Colls Osborne, Dartmouth; *m* 1948, (Lilian) Bridget, widow of Lt-Cdr G S Salt, RN, and da of late Frederick Stewart

Francis, of Thakeham, Sussex; 2 da; *Career* Capt Supt Admiralty Signal and Radar Establishments 1952-54, cmd HMS 'Cumberland' 1955, ret 1957; *Style* - Capt William Lamb, CVO, OBE; Westons, Bank, Lyndhurst, Hants (☎ Lyndhurst 2620)

LAMBART, Lady; Kathleen Barbara Sophia; da of late Col John Arthur Henry Moore Brabazon; *m* 1911, Lt-Col Sir (Gustavus) Francis William Lambart, 1 Bt, CVO (d 1926); *Style* - Lady Lambart; Beau Parc, Co Meath

LAMBART, Sir Oliver Francis; 2 Bt (UK 1911); s of Lt-Col Sir (Gustavus) Francis William Lambart, 1 Bt, CVO (d 1926); *b* 6 April 1913; *Career* 1 Lt R Ulster Rifles 1932-33, served with RASC; *Style* - Sir Oliver Lambart, Bt; Beau Parc, Co Meath

LAMBART, Roger Cavan; s (by 2 m) of late Frederick Cavan Lambart and presumed hp of 12 Earl of Cavan; *b* 1944; *Style* - Roger Lambart Esq; 34 Woodleigh gdns, SW16

LAMBE, Lady; Lesbia; da of Sir Walter Orlando Corbet, 4 Bt (d 1910); *b* 1905; *m* 1, 1927, Lt Victor Ivor Henry Mylius, formerly RN; m 2, 1940, Adm of the Fleet Sir Charles Edward Lambe, GCB, CVO (d 1960); 2 s, 1 da; *Style* - Lady Lambe; Knockhill House, Newport-on-Tay, Fife; 21 Stafford pla, SW1

LAMBERT, 2 Viscount (UK 1945); George Lambert; TD; s of 1 Viscount, PC (d 1958); *b* 27 Nov 1909; *Educ* Harrow, New Coll Oxford; *m* 1939, Patricia, da of J F Quinn, of London; 1 s (decd), 1 da; *Heir* bro, Hon Michael John Lambert *Career* served 1939-45 TA, Lt-Col 1942, MP (Lib Nat) South Molton 1945-50, Torrington (Nat Lib & C) 1950-58; DL (Devon) 1969-70, v-pres for life Nat Fedn Young Farmers' Clubs 1970-; *Clubs* Carlton, Army & Navy; *Style* - The Rt Hon Viscount Lambert TD; Les Fougères, 1806 St Légier, Switzerland (☎ 021 53 1063)

LAMBERT, Sir Anthony Edward; KCMG (1964, CMG 1955); s of Reginald Everitt Lambert (d 1968); *b* 1911; *Educ* Harrow, Balliol Oxford; *m* 1948, Ruth Mary, da of Sir Arthur P M Fleming, CBE (d 1960); 2 da; *Career* entered Foreign Service 1934, counsellor British Embassy, Athens 1952-58, min to Bulgaria 1958-60, Ambass to Tunisia 1960-63, Ambass to Finland 1963-66, Ambass to Portugal 1966-70; *Clubs* Travellers'; *Style* - Sir Anthony Lambert, KCMG; 28 Victoria rd, W8 (☎ 01 937 0640)

LAMBERT, Senator Charles Gordon; PC (Peace Commissioner - equivalent to JP in UK); s of Robert Hamilton Lambert MRCVS (d 1956); *b* 9 April 1919; *Educ* Rossall Sch Lancashire, Trin Coll Dublin; *Career* FCA, memb Seanad Eireann (Irish Senate) 1977-, chm: W & R Jacob & Co Ltd, Irish Biscuits Ltd and subsidiaries, Variety Foods Ltd; dir: Hibernian Insurance Co Ltd, Mitchell & Son (Wine Merchants) Ltd; cncl memb Irish Management Inst, bd memb: Int Cncl Museum of Modern Art New York, Arts Cncl of N Ireland, chm Contemporary Irish Art Soc; *Recreations* golf, theatre, modern art collector; *Clubs* Royal Dublin Society, Royal Irish Automobile Club, Castle Golf Club; *Style* - Senator Charles Lambert, PC; 15 Hillside Drive, Rathfarnham, Dublin, Ireland

LAMBERT, Sir Edward Thomas; KBE (1958), CVO (1957); s of Brig-Gen Thomas Stanton Lambert, CB, CMG (d 1921); *b* 19 June 1901; *Educ* Charterhouse, Trin Coll Cambridge; *m* 1936, Rhona Patricia Gilmore, da of late Harold St George Gilmore and of late Mrs J H Molyneux; 1 s, 1 da; *Career* entered HM Foreign Service 1926, served at Bangkok, Batavia, Medan, Curacao and at Foreign Office; Consul-Gen Geneva 1949-53, Paris 1953-59; *Style* - Sir Edward Thomas, KBE, CVO; c/o Lloyds Bank Ltd, 16 St James's st, SW1

LAMBERT, Eric Thomas Drummond; CMG (1969), OBE (1946); s of late Septimus Drummond Lambert, of Dublin Ireland; *b* 3 Nov 1909; *Educ* Royal Sch Dungannon; *Career* King's Police Medal 1943, Foreign and Commonwealth Office 1947-68, trustee National Library of Ireland; *Style* - Eric Lambert Esq, CMG,

OBE; Drumkeen, Glenamuck, Carrickmines, Co Dublin, Ireland

LAMBERT, Sir Greville Foley; 9 Bt (GB 1711); s of Lionel Foley Lambert (d 1934, 4 s of 6 Bt); suc cousin, Sir John Foley Grey, 8 Bt, 1938, but name does not appear on the Official Roll of Baronets; *b* 17 Aug 1900; *Educ* Rugby; *m* 1932, Edith Roma, da of Richard Batson; 3 da; *Heir* kinsman, Peter John Biddulph Lambert; *Style* - Sir Greville Lambert, Bt; 12 Newborough rd, Shirley, Solihull, Warwicks

LAMBERT, Hon Grace Mary; da of 1 Viscount Lambert, PC (d 1958); *Style* - The Hon Grace Lambert; 1 St Germans, Exeter, Devon (☎ 74219)

LAMBERT, Henry Uvedale Antrobus; s of Roger Uvedale Lambert MBE (himself s of Sir Henry Lambert KCMG CB) and Muriel (da of Sir Reginald Antrobus KCMG CB); *b* 9 Oct 1925; *Educ* Winchester Coll, New Coll Oxford; *m* 1951, Diana Elsworth, da of Capt Henry Eric Dumbell (d 1957); 2 s (Michael Uvedale b 1952, Roger Mark Uvedale b 1959), 1 da (Jennifer b 1955); *Career* 1939-45 Lt-Cdr (ret) RNR, chm Barclays Bank Int Ltd 1979- (joined Barclays 1948, dir 1966, v-chm 1973, dep chm 1979), v-chm Sun Alliance & London Insurance Group 1978, dep chm Agricultural Mortgage Corpn Ltd 1977, Fell Winchester Coll 1979; *Recreations* fishing, gardening, golf, naval history; *Clubs* Brooks's, MCC; *Style* - Henry Lambert Esq; c/o Barclays Bank International Ltd, 54 Lombard st, EC3

LAMBERT, Sir John Henry; KCVO (1980), CMG (1975); s of Col R S Lambert MC; *b* 8 Jan 1921; *Educ* Eton, Sorbonne, Trin Cambridge; *m* 1950, Jennifer Ann, da of Sir Robert Urquhart, KBE, CMG; 1 s, 2 da; *Career* served 1940-45 with Grenadier Gds, entered Foreign Service 1945, Counsellor Stockholm 1964, Commercial Counsellor and Consul-Gen Vienna 1971-74, Min and Dep Cmdt British Military Govt Berlin 1974-77; Ambass to Tunisia 1977-81; *Style* - Sir John Lambert, KCVO, CMG; c/o FCO, Whitehall, SW1; 16 Woodfall st, SW3 (☎ 01 730 3222)

LAMBERT, Hon Margaret Barbara; CMG (1965); da of 1 Viscount Lambert, PC (d 1958); *b* 1906; *Educ* Lady Margaret Hall Oxford, London Sch of Economics; *Career* served 1939-45 in European Service of BBC; assist editor British Documents of Foreign Policy 1946-50; lecturer in modern history Univ Coll of South West 1950-51; editor-in-ch of German Diplomatic Archives Foreign Office 1951- and lecturer in modern history St Andrews U 1956-60; *Style* - The Hon Margaret Lambert, CMG; 39 Thornhill rd, N1 (☎ 01 607 2286)

LAMBERT, Hon Michael John; s of 1 Viscount Lambert, PC (d 1958); *b* 1912; *Educ* Harrow, New Coll Oxford; *m* 1939, Florence Dolores, da of Nicholas Lechmere Cunningham Macaskie, QC; 3 da; *Style* - The Hon Michael Lambert; 2 Aubrey rd, W8

LAMBERT, Peter John Biddulph; s of John Hugh Lambert (d 1977); h to Btcy of kinsman, Sir Greville Foley Lambert, 9 Bt; *b* 5 Apr 1952; *Educ* Upper Canada Coll, Trent U Peterborough, U of Manitoba; *m* 5 Apr 1952; *Style* - Peter Lambert Esq; c/o 483 Spadina rd, Toronto, Canada

LAMBERT, Thomas Peter; s of Thomas Lambert (d 1938); *b* 7 Oct 1927; *Educ* Stowe, RMA Sandhurst; *m* 1956, Davinia Margaret, nee Walford; 4 children; *Career* Capt Inniskilling Dragoon Gds; pres Bradford Chamber of Commerce 1975-77, regional dir Nat West Bank Ltd 1977, jt md John Foster & Son Ltd 1980, chm Wool Industry Research Assoc 1981; *Recreations* shooting, tennis, gardening; *Style* - Thomas Lambert Esq; The Old Vicarage, S Stainley, Harrogate, N Yorks (☎ 770169)

LAMBERT, Verity; *Career* ch exec Euston Films Ltd (subsid of Thames TV); former producer BBC 2 (work included 'Shoulder to Shoulder' series about suffragettes); *Style* - Miss Verity Lambert; c/o Euston Films Ltd, 365 Euston rd, NW1 (☎ 01 387 0911)

LAMBERT, Hon Mrs; Hon Zita Elaine; da of 1 and last Baron Austin, KBE (d 1941); *b* 8 Oct 1902; *m* 1928, Charles

Powell Lambert (m dis 1948); 1 s; *Style* - The Hon Mrs Zita Lambert; Cruachan, Horsebridge rd, Broughton, Hants

LAMBIE, Alexander Ogilvie; s of the late J M S Lambie; *b* 24 Oct 1938; *Educ* Mill Hill Sch, Durham U; *m* 1969, Diana Margaret, nee Owen; 1 da; *Career* md Cammell Laird Shipbuilders Ltd 1979-, chm Cammell Laird (Training) Ltd 1976-; *Style* - Alexander Lambie Esq; St Nicholas House, Burton, South Wirral, Cheshire

LAMBIE, David; MP (L) Ayrshire and Bute (Central Ayrshire Div) 1970; s of Ex-Provost Robert Lambie, JP, of Saltcoats, Ayrshire; *b* 1925; *Educ* Ardrossan Academy, Glasgow U, Geneva U; *m* 1954, Netta, da of Alexander Merrie; 1 s, 4 da; *Career* teacher; chm Scottish Labour Party 1965-66; *Style* - David Lambie Esq MP; 11 Ivanhoe Drive, Saltcoats, Ayrshire (☎ 0294 64843)

LAMBIE, John; *Career* AIM; chm and md Carron Co Ltd; v-chm and md Carron Co (Holdings); dir ADA Engineering Ltd, Aryx X-Rays Ltd, Assoc Metal Works Glasgow Ltd, Topbrick Builders, H C Wilson Bennetts Ltd, The Standard Gas Fittings Co Ltd, Calrad Panel Radiators Ltd, Charles Henshaw & Sons Ltd, DA Radiator Sales Ltd, Duct & Access Covers Ltd, Islands in the Sky Ltd, Lynda Line Kitchens Ltd, Nationwide Plastics Ltd, Torwood Design & Marine Enterprises Ltd, Torland Investments Ltd; *Style* - John Lambie Esq; Carron Co Ltd, Carron, Falkirk, Stirlingshire

LAMBOLL, Alan Seymour; JP (1965 Inner London); s of late Frederick Seymour Lamboll, of Mark Cross, Sussex; *b* 12 Oct 1923; *Educ* Ascham St Vincents, Eastbourne Prep Sch, Marlborough Coll; *Career* Lloyd's underwriter, dir Slack & Lamboll Ltd 1947-54, Lloyd's Insurance broker 1954-57, dir Ellinger Heath Western (Underwriting Agencies) Ltd, High Tower Construction Co Ltd, S Westminster PSD (chm 1978-80), dep chm City of London 1979-; sec The Ross McWhirter Foundation & The Dicey Tst 1980-; chm Council Drama Centre London Ltd 1975-, vice-chm Roy Gen Theatrical Fund Assoc 1967-, 1965, Common Council Ward of Langbourn 1949-70, Alderman Ward of Castle Baynard 1970-78, Sheriff City of London 1976-77; CStJ 1973; FRSA; *Style* - Alan Lamboll Esq JP; E4 Albany, Piccadilly, WI (☎ 01 734 0364)

LAMBORN, Henry George; MP (L) Southwark (Peckham) 1974-; s of late Cecil Lamborn; *b* 1 May 1915; *Educ* LLC Secondary Sch; *m* 1938, Lilian Ruth, da of J Smith, of Southwark; 2 s, 1 da; *Career* mayor Camberwell Borough Council 1963-64, chm Health Ctee 1962-65, memb GLC 1964-, Govr King's Coll and Bethlem Royal Maudsley Hospitals, PPS to Chancellor of the Exchequer 1974-79; *Style* - Henry Lamborn Esq MP; 53 Farne Close, Hempstead Lane, Hailsham, E Sussex

LAMBTON, Antony Claud Frederick; s of 5 Earl of Durham (d 1970, himself ggs of 1 Earl, Creevey's 'King Jog' - so called because he was supposedly author of the remark that one could jog along very comfortably on £40,000 a year) by his 1 w Diana (da of Granville Farquhar, 4 s of Sir Walter Farquhar, 3 Bt); 1 cous of Lord Home of the Hirsel, 6 Duke of Sutherland and 4 Baron Joicey; *b* 10 July 1922; *m* 1942, Belinda, da of Maj Douglas Holden Blew-Jones, of Westward Ho N Devon; 1 s, 5 da; *Career* MP (C) Northumberland (Berwick-on-Tweed) 1951-73; PPS to Min of Supply 1954, parly under-sec of State for Defence (RAF) 1970-73; disclaimed Earldom (of which he would otherwise continue to be the sixth holder, as technically he was for the short period between his f's death and his disclaimer) of Durham for life 1970, along with Barony of Durham (UK 1828) and Viscountcy of Lambton (1833); *Style* - Antony Lambton Esq; Biddick Hall, Lambton Park, Chester-le-Street, Durham; Lambton Castle, Fence Houses, Durham (☎ Fence Houses 36)

LAMBTON, Lady Beatrix Mary; da of Antony Lambton; *b* 1949; *Style* - Lady Beatrix Lambton; Wooler, Northumberland (☎ Wooler 312); Lambton Castle, Fence Houses, Durham (☎ Fence Houses 36)

LAMBTON, Lady Elizabeth Mary; da

of 6 Marquess of Lansdowne, DSO, MVO (d 1936); *b* 1927; *m* 1950, Maj Charles William Lambton; *Style* - Lady Elizabeth Lambton; The Old Rectory, Calstone, Calne, Wilts

LAMBTON, Viscount; Edward Richard Lambton; s of Antony Lambton, *qv*, and heir to disclaimed Earldom of Durham; *b* 19 Oct 1961; *Style* - Viscount Lambton

LAMBTON, Hon John George; s of 5 Earl of Durham; *b* 1952; *Style* - The Hon John Lambton; Fenton, Wooler, Northumberland (☎ Wooler 12); Lambton Castle, Fence Houses, Durham (☎ Fence Houses 36)

LAMBTON, Hon Mrs; Hon Monica Dorothy; *née* Brand; da of 3 Viscount Hampden, GCVO, KCB, CMG (d 1958); *b* 1914; *m* 1933, D'Arcy Lambton (d 1938); *Style* - The Hon Mrs Lambton; Green close, Copdock, Ipswich, Suffolk

LAMBTON, Lady Mary Gabrielle Anne; da of Antony Lambton; *b* 1954; *Style* - Lady Mary Lambton

LAMOND, James Alexander; JP Aberdeen, MP (L) Oldham (East) 1970-; s of Alexander Lamond (d 1965), of Burrelton, Perthshire; *b* 29 Nov 1928; *Educ* Burrelton Sch, Coupar Angus; *m* 1954, June Rose, da of Joseph Wellburn, of Aberdeen; 3 da; *Career* draughtsman, Lord Provost of Aberdeen 1970, former Lord Lieut Aberdeen; *Style* - James Lamond Esq, JP, MP; 15 Belvidere st, Aberdeen (☎ Aberdeen 51074)

LAMOND, William; s of Robert Lamond (d 1973); *b* 26 Apr 1925; *Educ* Shawlands Acad; *m* 1950, Kathleen Mary; 2 s, 1 da; *Career* CA (Scotland), fin dir James Finlay & Co Ltd; *Recreations* golf, tennis; *Clubs* Oriental (London), Western (Glasgow); *Style* - William Lamond Esq; Windward, Ferniegair Av, Helensburgh, Scotland (☎ 0436 5014)

LAMONT, Noel Brian Lamont of that Ilk; s of late Edward Louis Lamont; succeeded his uncle, Alfred Granville Lamont of Lamont, 1954, as Chief of Clan Lamont, MPS, PhC, JP; *b* 1928; *m* 1954, Anne Paulette Fause; *Heir* s, Peter Noel, b 1955; *Style* - Noel Lamont of that Ilk; 63 Patrick st, Blacktown, Sydney, NSW

LAMONT, Norman Stewart Hughson; MP (C) Kingston upon Thames 1972-; s of Daniel Lamont; *b* 8 May 1942; *Educ* Loretto Sch, Fitzwilliam Cambridge; *m* 1971, Alice Rosemary, da of Lt-Col Peter White, of Hall Farm, Thorp Arch, Boston Spa, Yorks; 1 s; *Career* Parliamentary Under-Secretary of State, Dept of Energy 1979-, PPS to Minister for the Arts 1974, Opposition Spokesman on Prices and Consumer Affairs 1975-76, Industry 1976-79; *Style* - Norman Lamont Esq, MP; House of Commons, SW1

LAMPARD, Martin Robert; s of Austin Hugo Lampard (d 1964); *b* 21 Feb 1926; *Educ* Radley, Ch Ch Oxford; *m* 1957, Felice, da of John MacLean (d 1944); 4 da; *Career* Sub-Lt RNVR North Atlantic; slr 1952, ptnr Ashurst Morris Crisp & Co 1957, sr ptnr 1974; dir Allied Breweries, Laird Gp, Canadian Overseas Packaging Industries Ltd; *Recreations* farming in E Anglia, sailing, shooting; *Clubs* Roy Yacht Squadron, Roy Ocean Racing; *Style* - Martin Lampard Esq; c/o Ashurst Morris Crisp & Co, 17 Throgmorton av, EC2 (☎ 01 283 1070); 40 Canonbury Park North, London N1 (01 226 6107); Theberton House, Theberton, nr Leiston, Suffolk (☎ Leiston 830510)

LAMPERT, Hon Mrs; Hon Jill Mary Joan; da of 3 Baron Acton, CMG, MBE, TD; *b* 1947; *m* 1970, Nicholas Lampert; *Style* - The Hon Mrs Lampert; 26 Lonsdale rd, Harborne, Birmingham 17

LAMPSON, Hon Victor Miles George Aldous; s of 1 Baron Killearn, GCMG, CB, MVO, PC (d 1964), by his 2 w Jacqueline (herself da of Marchese Senator Aldo Castellani, KCMG, FRCP, FACP, DSc, MD); hp of half-bro, 2 Baron; *b* 9 Sept 1941; *Educ* Eton Coll; *m* 1971, Melita Amaryllis Pamela Astrid; da of Rear-Adm Morgan Charles Morgan Giles, DSO, OBE, GM, lately MP Winchester; 1 s, 2 da; *Career* late Capt Scots Guards; *Style* - The Hon Victor Lampson; Franchise Manor, Burwash, Sussex

LANCASTER, Bt-Col Aubrey John; TD (1947), DL (London 1958); s of John T Lancaster (d 1979); *b* 29 May 1915; *Educ* Merchant Taylors' Sch; *m* 1942, Joan Elizabeth, da of Albert W Crofts (d 1969); 2 s, 1 da; *Career* Lt 1933, RAF 1939-45, War Crimes Cmmn 1945-46, Lt-Col cmding 568 (St Pancras) Regt 1952-55; chm Dep Lt Ctee Deptford 1958-6 and Lewisham 1965-; *Style* - Col Aubrey Lancaster, TD, DL; Spinneys, 22 Condover Park, Condover, Shrewsbury, Shropshire (☎ Dorrington 674)

LANCASTER, Jeremy; *Career* chm and md Wolseley Hughes Ltd; dir Rotork Ltd; chm Tomkinsons Carpets Ltd, chm and md Wolseley-Hughes (Gp Services) Ltd; *Style* - Jeremy Lancaster Esq; Wolseley Hughes Ltd, PO Box 18, Vines Lane, Droitwich, Worcs

LANCASTER, Dame Jean; DBE (1963); da of Richard C Davies, of Blundellsands, Lancs; *b* 11 Aug 1909; *Educ* Merchant Taylors' Sch Crosby Lancs; *m* 1967, Roy Cavander Lancaster; *Career* dir WRNS 1961-64; *Style* - Dame Jean Lancaster DBE; Greathed Manor, Dormansland, Lingfield, Surrey

LANCASTER, Vice-Adm Sir John Strike; KBE (1961), CB (1958); s of George Henry Lancaster, of Plymouth; *b* 26 June 1903; *Educ* King Edward VI Sch Southampton; *m* 1927, Edith, da of Ernest Robert Jacobs; 2 da; *Career* Rear-Adm Personnel, Home Air Command 1956-59, Vice-Adm 1959, Dir-Gen of Manpower Admty & Ch Naval Supply & Secretariat Officer 1959-62, ret 1962; *Style* - Vice-Adm Sir John Lancaster, KBE, CB; Moorings, 59 Western Way, Alverstoke, Gosport, Hants (☎ Gosport 84172)

LANCASTER, Sir Osbert; CBE (1953); *b* 1908; *Career* cartoonist Daily Express; artist, writer; kt 1975; *Clubs* Brooks's, Pratt's, Beefsteak and Garrick; *Style* - Sir Osbert Lancaster CBE; 78 Cheyne Court, Royal Hospital rd, SW3

LAND, Peter Anthony; s of Anthony Land (d 1973); *b* 14 April 1927; *Educ* Bemrose School Derby; *m* 1952, Dorothy Jessica, nee Pritchard; 1 s, 2 da; *Career* Capt Sherwood Foresters; CA; md British Transport Hotels 1978; md Nat Carriers 1967-77; ch acct BR Western Region 1963-67; ch acct BTR Industries 1958-63; *Recreations* cricket, golf, work; *Clubs* MCC; *Style* - Peter Land Esq; South Riding, Bisham rd, Marlow, Bucks (☎ 2898)

LANDER, Maxwell; s of the late Gustave Lander; *Educ* 10 May 1914; *m* 1939, Helena Margaret, nee Halon; 1 da; *Career* Colonel, GHQ India Command, consulting actuary, joint senior partner Duncan C Fraser & Co 1950-, assistant secretary Admiralty 1947-50; *Recreations* fast cars, reading; *Clubs* RAC, Ferrari Owners'; *Style* - Maxwell Lander Esq; Flat 124, 25 Porchester Place, W2 (☎ 01 262 4119); 83 Waterloo rd, Hillside, Southport, Merseyside (☎ Southport 67408)

LANDMAN, Rowland Harold; *Career* barr; chm London Scottish Banking Corpn Ltd, London Scottish Finance Corpn Ltd; dir Bunhill Insurance Brokers Ltd, Candcroft Ltd, Chevron Foods Ltd, D B Pension Investments Ltd, Dupont Bros Ltd, Glengall Estates Ltd, Hightrust Ltd, Lancing Automation Ltd, Lenahurst Ltd, London Scottish Computer Services Ltd, London Scottish Investment Co Ltd, London Scottish Securities Ltd, Sylviro Estates Ltd, TVH (Electrical) Ltd; memb IOD; *Style* - Rowland Landman Esq; 62 Queen Anne st, London W1

LANDON, Lady; Aethel Mary; da of late Thomas Sampson, of Lenton, Nottingham; *m* 1934, as his 2 w, Maj-Gen Sir Frederick William Bainbridge London, KCMG, CB (d 1937); *Style* - Lady Landon; 40 Hyde Park Gate, SW7

LANDON, Theodore Luke Giffard; s of Rev Sylvanus Luke Landon, late Vicar of Marldon, Devon; *b* 10 Oct 1926; *Educ* Blundell's, London U; *m* 1956, Joan, da of Frederic Parker, of Alresford (s of Rev Hon Archibald Parker, sometime Rural Dean of Wem, Salop, by his w Hon Maud Bateman-Hanbury, da of 2 Baron Bateman; the Dean was 9 s of 6 Earl of Macclesfield); 3 s (Mark b 1958, Philip b 1962, Benjamin b 1967), 2 da (Felicity b

1960, Rohais b 1964); *Career* dep chm & md Terra Nova Insur 1970-79, dep chm C T Bowring Underwriting Hldgs 1979-; memb Lloyd's 1961-, govr Kelly Coll Tstee Huguenot Soc 1973-; *Recreations* genealogical research; *Clubs* E India, The Gresham; *Style* - Theodore Landon Esq; Tower House, 38 Trinity sq, EC3 (☎ 01 626 7361/283 3100); Great Bromley House, Great Bromley, Colchester, Essex (☎ 0206 230385)

LANDON, Vivian James; *Career* jt chm Wigglesworth & Co Ltd; dir Amboni Ltd, Tanzani, Fibre Investment Ltd (Guernsey CI), G C Williams & Co Ltd, Haines & Isaacs Ltd, Produce Agencies Ltd, Samar Ltd; *Style* - Vivian Landon Esq; Wigglesworth House, 69 Southwark Bridge rd, SE1

LANE, Baron (Life Peer UK 1979); Geoffrey Dawson Lane; AFC (1943), PC (1974), QC (1962); s of late Percy Albert Lane; *b* 17 July 1918; *Educ* Shrewsbury, Trin Cambridge; *m* 1944, Jan, da of Donald Macdonald; 1 s; *Career* served RAF 1939-45, Sqdn Ldr 1942; barr 1946, Bencher 1966, dep chm Beds Quarter Sessions 1960-66, Recorder of Bedford 1963-66, a Judge of the High Court of Justice Queen's Bench Div 1966-74, a Lord Justice of Appeal 1974-79, Lord Chief Justice 1980-, Hon Master of the Bench Inner Temple 1980; kt 1966; *Style* - The Rt Hon Lord Lane, AFC, PC, QC; Royal Courts of Justice, Strand, WC2; House of Lords, SW1

LANE, Maj-Gen Barry; *Career* Dir Army Quartering MOD 1981-; *Style* - Maj-Gen Barry Lane; c/o MOD, SW1

LANE, Dame Elizabeth; Hon Mrs Justice Lane; Elizabeth Kathleen; DBE (1965); da of Edward Alexander Coulborn (d 1934); *b* 9 Aug 1905; *Educ* Malvern Girls' Coll, privately; *m* 1926, late Henry J R Lane, CBE; 1 s (decd); *Career* barr Inner Temple 1940, QC 1960, Bencher 1965, assistant recorder of Birmingham 1953-60, chm Birmingham Region Mental Health Review Tribunal 1960-62, commissioner of Crown Court at Manchester 1961, a judge of High Court of Justice (Probate Divorce and Admiralty Div, now Family Div) 1965-79; *Style* - Dame Elizabeth Lane, DBE; Hillcrest, 60 Chilbolton ave, Winchester, Hants

LANE, Kenneth Alexander; s of Lt Alexander William Lane, RN (d 1970); *b* 20 March 1924; *Educ* Peter Symonds Sch, Winchester, Christ's Cambridge; *m* 1, 1945, Peggy (d 1973), da of Patrick Murphy (d 1942); m 2, 1975, Delma, da of Walter Garrod, of Kings Lynn; 2 s, 3 da; *Career* service Admiralty 1943-45, Avon Rubber Co 1946-53, English Electric Co 1953, dir various subsidiaries until 1969, dep man dir Bowthorpe Holdings Ltd 1970-72, md Porvair 1973-75, exec chm Kearney and Trecker Marwin Ltd 1976-, chm Kemptown Conservative Assoc; *Style* - Kenneth Lane Esq; 6 Court Royal Mansions, Paston pla, Brighton (☎ Brighton 607 068)

LANE, Lady Lettice; da of late Sir Charles William James Orr, KCMG; *m* 1941, Sir Allen (Lane Williams) Lane, CH (d 1970); *Style* - Lady Lane; Priory Farm, Beech Hill, Berks

LANE, Countess; Margaret; da of late H G Lane; *b* 23 June 1907; *Educ* St Stephen's Folkestone, St Hugh's Oxford; *m* 1, 1934, Bryan, s of Edgar Wallace (m dis 1939); m 2, 1944, 15 Earl of Huntingdon; 2 da; *Career* novelist, biographer, journalist; *Style* - The Rt Hon Countess Lane; Blackbridge House, Beaulieu, Hants

LANE, Hon Mrs; Hon Miriam Louisa; da of Hon Nathaniel Charles Rothschild (d 1923), and sis of 3 Baron Rothschild, GBE, GM; *b* 1908; *m* 1943, George H Lane, MC (m dis 1956); 1 s, 3 da; *Career* trustee British Museum, prof Royal Free Hospital; granted 1938 the title, rank and precedence of a Baron's da, which would have been hers had her father survived to succeed as Baron Rothschild; *Style* - The Hon Mrs Lane; Ashton Wold, Oundle, Peterborough, Northants (☎Oundle 2125)

LANE, Peter Stewart; s of Leonard George Lane (d 1950); *b* 29 Jan 1925; *Educ* Sherborne; *m* Doris Florence (d 1969), da of Robert Simpson Botsford; 2 da; *Career* sr ptnr Binder Hamlyn CAs, ptnr Int

Worldwide Binder Dijker Otte & Co; v-chm Nat Union of Conservative & Unionists Assoc 1981-; *Clubs* Boodles, City of London, St Stephens; *Style* - Peter Lane Esq; Holywell, Hook Heath, Woking, Surrey (☎ Woking 61858)

LANE, Hon Richard; s of Baron Lane (Life Peer); *b* 1948; *Style* - The Hon Richard Lane

LANE, Rear-Adm Walter Frederick Boyt; CB (1960), DSC (1940); s of W H Lane; *b* 7 Feb 1909; *Educ* RN Engrg Coll and RN Coll; *m* 1931, Anne, da of Edwin Littlecott; 1 s; RN 1924, HMS 'Cossack' and HMS 'Warspite' WW II, Rear-Adm 1957; dir Marine Engrg 1958-61, ret; *Style* - Rear-Adm Walter Lane, CB, DSC; Foxleaze, Limpley Stoke, Wilts

LANE FOX, Hon Mrs; Hon Janet; *née* Hamilton; da of 3 Baron Hamilton of Dalzell, MC, JP; *b* 8 Sept 1936; *m* 1960, Richard Sackville Lane Fox, 2 s of Lt-Col Francis Lane Fox (né Ward Jackson), RHG, by Hon Marcia Lane Fox, da of 1 Baron Bingley (Barony extinct 1947); 1 s, 1 da; *Style* - The Hon Mrs Lane Fox; 17 Princedale rd, W11 (☎ 01 727 4330)

LANE-FOX, Baroness (Life Peeress UK 1981); Felicity; OBE (1976); 3 da of Capt Edward Lane Fox, JP (2 s of Capt James Lane Fox, JP, DL, sometime Capt Grenadier Gds, and Lucy, da of Humphrey St John-Mildmay, MP, s of Sir Henry St John-Mildmay, 3 Bt, by Humphrey's 2 w, Marianne; Marianne was da of Granville Harcourt-Vernon, 6 s of Most Rev and Rt Hon Edward Harcourt-Vernon, DD, sometime Archbishop of York; the Archbishop was 3 s of 1 Baron Vernon by his 2 w, suc to the Harcourt estates, and m Lady Anne, 3 da of 1 Marquess of Stafford); *b* 22 June 1918; *Career* Patron Handicapped Adventure Playground Assoc 1978-; broadcaster & journalist; V-Pres Roy Assoc of Disability and Rehabilitation; chm Phipp's Respiratory Unit Patients' Assoc, St Thomas's Hosp; *Recreations* racing & drama on TV, cricket, conversation; *Style* - The Rt Hon Lady Lane-Fox, OBE; 30 Marlborough Court, Pembroke rd, W8

LANE-FOX, Hon Mrs (Marcia Agnes Mary); da of 1 Baron Bingley (d 1947); *b* 1904; *m* 1929, Lt-Col Frances Gordon Ward Jackson, Roy Horse Guards, who assumed by deed poll 1937 the names Lane Fox in lieu of his patronymic; 2 s, 1 da; *Style* - The Hon Mrs Lane-Fox; The Little House, Bramham Park, Wetherby, Yorks

LANESBOROUGH, 9 Earl of (1756); Denis Anthony Brian Butler; TD, JP (Leics 1967), DL (1962); also Baron of Newtown-Butler (I 1715, but eldest s & h usually styled Lord Newtown-Butler) and Viscount Lanesborough (I 1728); s of 8 Earl of Lanesborough (d 1950) by his 2 w Grace, da of Sir Anthony Abdy, 3 Bt; *b* 28 Oct 1918; *Educ* Stowe; *m* 1939 (m dis 1950), Bettyne Ione, da of Sir Lindsay Everard, JP, DL, MP (d 1949); 2 da (1 decd); *Heir* 1 cous, Terence Butler; *Career* Lt Leics Yeo 1939, Maj RA (TA) 1945, memb Nat Gas Consumers' Cncl 1973-78, Trent RHA 1974-; chm Loughborough & Dist Housing Assoc 1978-; *Style* - The Rt Hon Earl of Lanesborough TD JP DL; Alton Lodge, Kegworth, Derby (☎ 2243)

LANESBOROUGH, Grace, Countess of; Grace Lilian; da of Capt Sir Anthony C S Abdy, 3 Bt (d 1921); *b* 1887; *m* 1917, 8 Earl of Lanesborough (d 1950); 2 s (1 ka 1944); *Style* - The Rt Hon Grace, Countess of Lanesborough; Swithland Hall, Loughborough, Leics (☎ Rothley 2001)

LANG, Hon Mrs (Alexandra Rose); *née* Alport; da of Baron Alport, PC (Life Peer); *b* 3 Sept 1946; *Educ* County High Sch Colchester, Arundel Sch Salisbury Rhodesia; *m* 1969, Rev Geoffrey Wilfrid Francis Lang, MA, s of Frederick Lang of Croxley Green, Herts; 1 s; *Style* - The Hon Mrs Lang; St Margaret's Vicarage, Kings Lynn, Norfolk

LANG, Lt-Gen Sir Derek (Boileau); KCB (1967), DSO (1944), MC (1941); s of Lt-Col C F G Lang, IA (d 1961), of Whytegates, Church Crookham, Hants; *b* 7 Oct 1913; *Educ* Wellington Coll, RMC Sandhurst; *m* 1, 1942, Morna Helena Casey (d 1953), da of Charles Massy-Dawson, of Sussex; 1 s, 1 da; m 2, 1953 (m dis 1969), Anita Lewis da of Lewis Shields, of Philadelphia, USA; m 3, 1969, Mrs Elizabeth H Balfour; *Career* 2 Lt Cameron Highlanders 1933, Brig 1958, ch of staff Scottish Command 1960-61, dir Army Training, MOD 1964-66, GOC-in-C Scottish Command and govr of Edinburgh Castle 1966-69, Lt-Gen 1966, ret 1969; DL Edinburgh 1978; Associate Consultant, PA Management Consultants Ltd 1975-, OStJ; *Style* - Lt-Gen Sir Derek Lang, KCB, DSO, MC, DL; 4 Belford Place, Edinburgh, EH4 3DH (☎ 031 332 2364)

LANG, Ian Bruce; MP (C) Galloway 1979-; s of James Fulton Lang, DSC; *b* 27 June 1940; *Educ* Lathallan Sch Kincardineshire, Rugby Sch, Sidney Sussex Coll Cambridge (BA); *m* 1971, Sandra Caroline, da of John Alastair Montgomerie, DSC; 2 da; *Career* dir Hutchison and Craft Ltd 1975-, Hutchison and Craft (Underwriting Agents) Ltd, Lloyd's 1976-, memb Roy Co of Archers 1974- (Queen's Bodyguard for Scotland), dir Glasgow Chamber of Commerce 1978-, trustee West of Scotland Trustee Savings Bank 1974-; contested (Con) Central Ayrshire 1970, Glasgow Pollok 1974; OStJ 1974; *Clubs* Western (Glasgow), Glasgow Art, Prestwick Golf; *Style* - Ian Lang Esq, MP; Kersland, Monkton, Ayrshire, KA9 2QU (☎ Symington 830231)

LANG, Sir John Gerald; GCB (1954); s of George Lang (d 1907); *b* 1896; *Educ* Aske's Haberdashers' Sch Hatcham; *m* 1, 1922, Emilie (d 1963), da of Henry Shelley Goddard, of Eastbourne; 1 da; m 2, 1970, Kathleen Winifred, widow of C Edmeades; *Career* Admiralty 1914, assist princ 1930, princ 1935, assist sec 1939, princ assist sec 1942, under-sec 1946, sec 1947, ret 1961; princ adviser on sport to Rt Hon Quintin Hogg, QC, MP 1964, and subsequently princ adviser on sport to the Govt to 1972; VP Roy Naval Assoc, tres Roy Inst of Naval Architects; *Style* - Sir John Lang, GCB

LANGDON, Michael Charles Selfe; s of Rev Charles Godfrey Langdon (d 1941); *b* 13 April 1915; *Educ* Hurstpierpoint Coll; *m* 1944, Kathleen Marjorie, nee Fane; 2 s (Christopher Michael, Patrick John); *Career* Maj Royal Sussex Regt Burma 1944-46; slr and notary public Young Coles & Langdon, chm Stables Trust Ltd, local bd Guardian Royal Exchange Assurance; *Style* - Michael Langdon Esq; 6 Branksome rd, St Leonards-on-Sea, Sussex (☎ Hastings 424946, office 437878)

LANGDON-DAVIES, Robin Harry; DFC (1944); s of John Eric Langdon-Davies (d 1971); *b* 9 Sept 1920; *Educ* Leighton Park; *m* 1942, Cicely Frances, nee Dyer; 1 s, 1 da; *Career* Sqdn Ldr (Middle East, Mediterranean, Balkan Air Force); chartered accountant 1951, honorary tres Oxfam 1961-73, chm Bristol Area Soc of Chartered Accountants 1973-74, pres West of Eng Soc of Chartered Accountants 1980-81; *Recreations* travel, lawn tennis, walking, bird watching; *Clubs* Royal Commonwealth Society, Bristol Commercial Rooms; *Style* - Robin Langdon-Davies Esq, DFC; 14 Knoll Hill, Bristol (☎ 0272 684443)

LANGE, Frederick Matthew; s of Mark Lange (decd); *b* 12 Nov 1898; *Educ* Dickinson Coll, Int Free Protestant Episcopal U, Atlanta Law Sch (USA), Oxford; *m* 1944, Blanche, nee Swanzy; *Career* philanthropic administrator: dir Salvation Army (Texas div) 1933-40, pres Dallas Community Chest Trust Fund 1968- (exec v pres 1957-68); lecturer All Souls Coll, tstee Hardin-Simmons U (Texas); Consul-Gen (hon) of Dominican Rep 1964-; Order of Merit of the Italian Republic; has raised over a quarter of a billion dollars for community, charitable & philanthropic works; *Style* - Frederick Lange Esq; Fred M Lange Center, 4605 Live Oak Dallas, USA

LANGFORD, 9 Baron (I 1800); Col Geoffrey Alexander Rowley-Conwy; OBE (1943), DL (Clwyd 1977); s of Maj Geoffrey Seymour Rowley-Conwy (ka 1915, himself ggs of 1 Baron, who in his turn was 4 s of 1 Earl of Bective, the Earldom of the same now forming one of the subsidiary dignities of the Marquesses of Headfort), of Bodrhyddan, Flintshire; suc 2 cous once removed, 8 Baron Langford, 1953; *b* 8 March 1912; *Educ* Marlborough, RMA Woolwich; *m* 1, 1939 (m dis 1956), Ruth St John, da of late Albert St John Murphy; m 2, 1957, Grete (d 1973), da of Col E T von Freiesleben; 3

s; m 3, 1975, Susan, da of C Denham, of Wrexham; 1 s, 1 da; *Heir* s, Hon Owen Rowley-Conwy; *Career* Constable of Rhuddlan Castle & Lord of the Manor of Rhuddlan; served 1939-45, with RA in Singapore (POW escaped) and Burma, Lt-Col 1945, ret 1957, Hon Col 1967; *Style* - The Rt Hon Lord Langford OBE DL; Bodrhyddan, Rhuddlan, Clwyd

LANGFORD, Audrey; da of Richard Langford Brown (d 1937); *b* 28 June 1912; *Educ* Runton Hill Sch Norfolk, Roy Coll of Music; *m* 1; m 2, 1949, Andrew Field; 2 da; *Career* principal soprano Roy Opera House Covent Garden 1936-39, sr lecturer Roy Northern Coll of Music 1975, voice coach Santa Fe Apprentice Programme USA 1970-, vocal faculty (voice related studies) Manhattan Sch of Music NY 1980-, voice coach Lyric Opera Sch of Chicago USA 1978-80, private Int Studio in London Cantica Voice Studio, conductor Bromley Philharmonic Choir 1950-80; *Style* - Miss Audrey Langford

LANGFORD, Florence, Baroness; Florence Eileen O'Donovan; da of Isaac Shiel, of Dublin; *m* 1922, 7 Baron Langford (d 1952); *Style* - The Rt Hon Florence, Lady Langford; Rose Cottage, Waldemar rd, Wimbledon SW19 (☎ 01 947 3206); Peppard's Cottage, Kilmuckridge, Co Wexford

LANGFORD, Ruth, Lady; Ruth St John; da of Albert St John Murphy, of The Island House, Little Island, Co Cork; *m* 1939 (m dis 1956), 9 Baron Langford; *Style* - Ruth, Lady Langford; Somerdale, Midleton, Co Cork, Eire

LANGFORD-HOLT, Sir John, Anthony; MP (C) Shropshire (Shrewsbury Div) 1945-; s of late Ernest Langford-Holt; *b* 1916; *Educ* Shrewsbury Sch; *m* 1, 1953 (m dis 1969), Flora Evelyn Innes, da of late Ian St Clair Stuart; 1 s, 1 da; m 2, 1971, Maxine, da of H Maxworthy, of Bexhill on Sea; *Career* air branch RN 1939, Lt-Cdr 1944; freeman and liveryman of City of London, Court of Worshipful Co of Horners; dir Authority Investments Ltd, Siebe Gorman Holdings Ltd; kt 1962, Austrian Grand Decoration in Gold (Cdr 1 Class 7 Austria), Order of Civic Merit (France); *Style* - Sir John Langford-Holt, MP; House of Commons, London, SW1

LANGHAM, Sir James Michael; 15 Bt (E 1660); s of Sir John Charles Patrick Langham, 14 Bt (d 1972); *b* 24 May 1932; *Educ* Rossall; *m* 1959, Marion Audrey Eleanor, da of Oswald Barratt; 2 s, 1 da; *Heir* s, John Stephen Langham; *Style* - Sir James Langham, Bt; Claranagh, Tempo, Enniskillen, Co Fermanagh, N Ireland

LANGHAM, John Michael; CBE (1976); s of George Langham (d 1951); *b* 12 Jan 1924; *Educ* Bedford Sch, Cambridge U; *m* 1949, Irene Elizabeth, nee Morley; 2 s, 1 da; *Career* Sub Lieut (E) RN Mediterranean Fleet, exec chm Stone Manganese Marine Ltd 1967, divisional chm Stone-Platt Industries Ltd 1967, chm and md Vacu-Lug Traction Tyres Ltd 1973, dir BPB Industries Ltd 1976; *Recreations* skiing, sailing (50 ft motor yacht 'Lady of Rudding', 40 ft aux cutter 'Campari'); *Clubs* Brooks's, RMYC; *Style* - John Langham Esq, CBE; Bingham's Melcombe, Dorchester, Dorset (☎ Milton Abbas (0258) 880808)

LANGHAM, John Stephen; s and h of Sir James Michael Langham, 15 Bt; *b* 14 Dec 1960; *Style* - John Langham Esq; Claranagh, Tempo, Enniskillen, Co Fermanagh

LANGHAM, Rosamond, Lady; Rosamond Christabel; da of late Arthur Rashleigh; *m* 1930, Sir John Charles Patrick Langham, 14 Bt (d 1972); *Style* - Rosamond, Lady Langham; Tempo Manor, Enniskillen, Co Fermanagh

LANGKER, Sir Erik; OBE (1955); *b* 1898; *Educ* Fort St H S; *Career* painter, pres Royal Art Society NSW 1946-, trustee Art Gallery of NSW 1947, pres 1961-; kt 1968; *Style* - Sir Erik Langker, OBE; Lombardy, Eastview st, Wollstonecraft, NSW 2005, Australia

LANGLAIS, Hon Mrs (Joanna Harriet Nevill); da of 7 Baron Latymer, *qv*; *b* 1928; *m* 1951, Pierre Langlais; 1 s, 4 da; *Style* - The Hon Mrs Langlais; 1340 Avenue Patenaude, Sillery, Province of

Quebec, Canada

LANGLANDS, John David; *Career* chm and md Pattullo, Higgs & Co; chm Baxter & Guion Ltd, chm Charles Wimble Sons & Co Ltd, Chemicals & Feeds Ltd, chm Springfield Produce Ltd, md RW Green Ltd; memb IOD; *Style* - John Langlands Esq; Pattullo, Higgs & Co Ltd, Hast Hill, Hayes, Bromley, Kent BR2 7AJ

LANGLANDS, Hon Mrs (Selena Mary); da of 5 Baron Manners; *b* 1952; *m* 1974, Capt Christopher Jeremy George Langlands, 1 The Queen's Dragoon Gds; 1 da; *Style* - The Hon Mrs Langlands; Box Cottage, Long Sutton, Basingstoke, Hants

LANGLEY-TAYLOR, Lady; Phyllis; da of Ernest Charles Allen; *m* 1922, Sir George Langley-Taylor (d 1968); *Style* - Lady Langley-Taylor; 105 Gloucester ct, Kew Gardens, Surrey

LANGMAN, Sir John Lyell; 3 Bt (UK 1906); s of Sir Archibald Lawrence Langman, 2 Bt, CMG (d 1949); *b* 9 Sept 1912; *Educ* Eton, Ch Ch Oxford; *m* 1936, Pamela Gaskell, da of Capt Spencer Gaskell Kennard, formerly of Purslow Hall, Craven Arms, Shropshire; 3 da (1 decd); *Career* Maj N Somerset Yeo; *Style* - Sir John Langman, Bt; Perrotts Brook Farm, nr Cirencester, Glocs (☎ N Cerney 283)

LANGRISHE, Hon Lady - Hon Grania Sybil Enid; *née* Wingfield; da of 9 Viscount Powerscourt (d 1973); *b* 1934; *m* 1955, Sir Hercules Ralph Hume Langrishe, 7 Bt; *Style* - The Hon Lady Langrishe; Knocktopher Abbey, Co Kilkenny; Ringlestown House, Kilmessan, Co Meath

LANGRISHE, Sir Hercules Ralph Hume; 7 Bt (I 1777); s of Capt Sir Terence Hume Langrishe, 6 Bt (d 1973), of Knocktopher Abbey, Co Kilkenny; *b* 1927; *Educ* Summerfields (St Leonards), Eton; *m* 1955, Hon Grania Sybil Enid, *qv*, da of 9 Viscount Powerscourt; 1 s, 3 da; *Heir* s, James Hercules Langrishe; *Career* 2 Lt 9 Lancers 1947, Lt 1948, ret 1953; *Style* - Sir Hercules Langrishe, Bt; Ringlestown House, Kilmessan, Meath, Ireland (☎ Navan 25243)

LANGRISHE, James Hercules; s and h of Sir Hercules Ralph Hume Langrishe, 7 Bt; *b* 3 March 1957; *Style* - James Langrishe Esq

LANGTON, Col Roland Stephen; MVO (1953), MC (1945); s of late Leslie Langton; *b* 1921; *Educ* Radley, Jesus Cambridge; *m* 1948, Pamela Elvira, da of Kenneth Headington, MC; 3 s, 1 da; *Career* served 1939-45 with Irish Gds, cmd 1 Bn Irish Gds 1961-64, AAG Min of Defence (PS12 Army) 1964-66, sr Army representative Defence Operational Analysis Establishment 1966-69, underwriting memb Lloyd's, dir Langton Underwriting Agents Ltd, and Milestone Underwriting Management Ltd, memb Court of Assistants of Worshipful Co of Merchant Taylors 1971; *Style* - Col Roland Langton MVO MC; Dial House, Peppard Common, Henley-on-Thames, Oxon (☎ Rotherfield Greys 204)

LANGTON-JONES, Hon Mrs (Annie Forrestdale); *née* Weir; da of 1 Baron Inverforth; *b* 1891; *m* 1949, Cdr Ronald Langton-Jones, DSO, RN (ret) (d 1967); *Style* - The Hon Mrs Langton-Jones; Flat F, 36 Eaton sq, SW1

LANGTON-LOCKTON, Lady Emma Bridget; da of 12 Earl of Carlisle, MC *qv*; *b* 1952; *m* 1974, John Philip Charles Langton-Lockton; 1 da; *Style* - Lady Emma Langton-Lockton; 91 Kelmscott rd, SW11

LANSDOWNE, 8 Marquess of (GB 1784); Maj George John Charles Mercer Nairne Petty-Fitzmaurice; PC (1964), JP (Perthshire 1950); also Baron Kerry and Lixnaw (I 1295?), Earl of Kerry, Viscount Clanmaurice (both I 1723), Viscount FitzMaurice, Baron Dunkeron (both I 1751), Earl of Shelburne (I 1753), Lord Wycombe, Baron of Chipping Wycombe (GB 1760), Earl Wycombe, and Viscount Calne and Calston (both GB 1784); s of late Maj Lord Charles Mercer-Nairne, MVO (ka 1914, himself 2 s of the 5 Marquess, sometime Viceroy of India and For Sec, also noted for enjoying a Peerage in the S, I and GB Peerages (a rare occurrence) and a wife (Lady Maud Hamilton, 7 da of 1 Duke of Abercorn) each of whose six elder sisters was married to a Peer (a still rarer one); the 7 Marquess's gf, the 3 Marquess, in refusing a Dukedom (*see* Earl of Derby) provoked in Punch the lines 'Lord Lansdowne won't be Duke of Kerry-/Lord Lansdowne is a wise man - very/Punch drinks his health in Port and Sherry'; he was, at 26, one of the younger Chancellors of the Exchequer; his f (1 Marquess) was PM in 1782-83), by Lady Violet Mary Elliot Murray-Kynynmound, da of 4 Earl of Minto; suc 1 cous, 7 Marquess (ka 1944); *b* 27 Nov 1912; *Educ* Eton, Ch Ch Oxford; *m* 1, 1938, Barbara (d 1965), da of Harold Stuart Chase, of Santa Barbara, California; 2 s, 1 da (& 1 decd); m 2, 1969, Hon Selina Polly Dawson, da of 1 Viscount Eccles, KCVO, PC (m dis 1978); m 3, 1978, Gillian Anna, da of Alured Morgan; *Heir* s, Earl of Shelburne; *Career* served WW II Capt Scots Greys & Maj Free French; Priv Sec to Duff Cooper (1 Viscount Norwich) when Ambass in Paris 1944; memb Roy Co Archers (Queen's Bodyguard for Scotland); assumption of additional surnames of Petty-Fitzmaurice recognised by decree of Lord Lyon 1947; chm Franco-British Soc 1972-, Pres Franco-Br Soc; 2 Lt Scottish Horse (TA), a Lord-in-Waiting to HM the Queen 1957-58, Jt Parly Under-Sec of State Foreign Office 1958-62, Min of State for Colonial Affairs 1962-64, DL (1952-73) Wilts, sec Junior Unionist League for E Scotland 1939; Patron of two livings; *Clubs* Turf, New (Edinburgh); *Style* - The Most Hon the Marquess of Lansdowne, PC, JP; Meikleour House, Perthshire (☎ Meikleour 210)

LANSDOWNE, Selina, Marchioness of; Selina Polly Dawson; da of 1 Viscount Eccles, KCVO, PC, *qv*; *b* 1937; *Educ* Sherborne Sch for Girls, London U; *m* 1, 1962 (m dis 1968), Robin Andrew Duthac Carnegie, late Capt Queen's Dragoon Gds; m 2, 1969 (m dis 1978), 8 Marquess of Lansdowne; 1 s (by 1 m); *Style* - Selina, Marchioness of Lansdowne; 63 Warwick sq, SW1

LAPSLEY, Air Marshal Sir John Hugh; KBE (1969), CB (1966), DFC (1940), AFC (1950); s of Edward John Lapsley (d 1918); *b* 24 Sept 1916; *Educ* Wolverhampton Sch, RAF Coll Cranwell; *m* 1, 1942, Jean Margaret (d 1979), da of Douglas Tait MacIvor, of Gravesend; 1 s, 1 da; m 2, 1980, Mrs Millicent Rees (nee Beadnell) widow of T A Rees; *Career* RAF 1933, awarded Lord Wakefield Scholarship to RAF Coll Cranwell 1936, 1939-45 War (Egypt, UK, France and Germany), Gp-Capt 1956, Air Cdre 1961, Dep Ch Staff (Air) 2 TAF 1961-62, Air V-Marshal 1965, sec to Chs of Staff Ctee, MOD 1964-66; Air Marshal 1968, head of British Defence Staff, Washington 1970, ret 1973; dir-gen Save the Children Fund 1974-75, dir Falkland Is R and D Assoc Ltd 1978-; Cllr Suffolk Coastal Disaster Cncl 1979-; *Style* - Air Marshal Sir John Lapsley KBE CB DFC AFC; c/o Lloyds Bank, Pall Mall, SW1

LAPUN, Sir Paul; *b* 1923; *Educ* Catholic Mission Vunapope; *m* 1951, Lois; 2 s, 1 da; *Career* memb S Bougainville Papua New Guinea House of Assembly 1964-, fndr Pangu Party 1967, ldr 1967-68, dep Parliamentary Ldr 1968-; kt 1974; *Style* - Sir Paul Lapun; c/o House of Assembly, Port Moresby, Papua New Guinea

LARCOM, Aileen, Lady; Aileen Monica Royde; da of late Rev Arthur George Colbeck; *m* 1920, Sir Philip Larcom, 4 Bt (d 1967); *Style* - Aileen, Lady Larcom; Bridge View Cottage, Blandford St Mary, Dorset

LARCOM, Sir (Charles) Christopher Royde; 5 Bt (UK 1868); s of Sir Philip Larcom, 4 Bt (d 1967); *b* 11 Sept 1926; *Educ* Radley, Clare Coll Cambridge; *m* 1956, Barbara Elizabeth, da of Balfour Bowen; 4 da; *Career* memb The Stock Exchange London 1959-, memb cncl 1970-, ptnr Grieveson Grant and Co stockbrokers 1960-; *Style* - Sir Christopher Larcom, Bt; Butlers, Hatfield Peverel, Essex (☎ 508)

LARKIN, M W; *Career* chm Motorola Ltd; *Style* - M W Larkin Esq; Motorola Ltd, York House, Empire Way, Wembley, Middx

LARKINS, Hon Mrs; Hon Miranda; da (by 1 m) of Baroness Sharples, *qv*; *b* 1951; *m* 1981, Nicholas Larkins; *Style* - The Hon Mrs Larkins

LARMOR, Lady; Barbara; da of late Maj H Dixon, of Keighley, Yorks; *m* 1962, as his 2 w, Sir (John) Graham Larmor (d 1968); *Style* - Lady Larmor; 3 St Stephen's Close, Skipton, Yorks

LARMOUR, Sir Edward Noel; KCMG (1977, CMG 1966); s of Edward Larmour; *b* 25 Dec 1916; *Educ* Royal Belfast Academical Institution, Trin Dublin, Sydney U; *m* Agnes Margaret, da of Thomas Bill; 1 s, 2 da; *Career* served 1940-46 with R Inniskilling Fus and 15 Indian Corps in Burma, joined Commonwealth Relations Office 1948, British High Commissioner Jamaica and Ambass (non resident) to Haiti 1970-73, British High Commissioner for New Hebrides (resident in London) 1973, dep under-sec of State FCO 1975-76; *Style* - Sir Edward Larmour, KCMG; 68 Wood Vale, N10 (☎ 01 444 9744)

LASCELLES, Rt Hon Sir Alan Frederick; GCB (1953), GCVO (1947), CMG (1933), MC, PC (1943); s of Cdr Hon Frederick Lascelles RN (2 s of 4 Earl of Harewood); *b* 1887; *Educ* Marlborough, Trin Oxford; *m* 1920, Hon Joan Frances Thesiger (d 1971), da of 1 Viscount Chelmsford, GCSI, GCMG, GCIE, GBE (d 1933); 1 s (decd), 2 da; *Career* Capt Bedfordshire Yeo 1916, assist private sec to HRH Prince of Wales (King Edward VIII) 1920-29, sec to Govr-Gen Canada 1931-35, assist private sec to King George V 1935-36, to King Edward VIII 1936, to King George VI 1937-43, private sec 1943-52, private sec to HM the Queen 1952-53, chm Historic Buildings Council for England 1953-63, past dir Midland Bank, chm Pilgrim Trust 1954-59; *Style* - The Rt Hon Sir Alan Lascelles GCB GCVO CMG MC PC; Kensington Palace, London W8 (☎ 01 937 2142)

LASCELLES, Hon Benjamin George; s of Viscount Lascelles *qv*; *b* 9 Sept 1978; *Style* - The Hon Benjamin Lascelles

LASCELLES, Viscount; David Henry George Lascelles; s of 7 Earl of Harewood; *b* 21 Oct 1950; *Educ* The Hall Sch Westminster; *m* 1979, Margaret Rosalind Messenger; 2 s, 1 da; *Style* - Viscount Lascelles; 2 Orme sq, W2

LASCELLES, Lady; Esmée Marion; da of late C A Bury, of Downings, Co Kildare; *m* 1924, Sir Francis (William) Lascelles, KCB, MC (d 1979); *Style* - Lady Lascelles; Field House, Orford, Suffolk

LASCELLES, Hon Emily Tsering; da of Viscount Lascelles *qv*; *b* 23 Nov 1975; *Style* - The Hon Emily Lascelles

LASCELLES, Hon Gerald David; s of 6 Earl of Harewood, KG, GCVO, DSO and Bar, TD (d 1947) and of HRH The Princess Royal (d 1965); *b* 1924; *Educ* Eton; *m* 1952, Angela Dowding, da of Charles Stanley Dowding (d 1972) and of Lady Fox (d 1959) (m dis 1978); 1 s; m 2, 1978, Mrs Elizabeth Evelyn Colvin, da of Brig Sydney Collingwood CMG CBE MC; *Career* pres British Racing Drivers Club 1964-, dir Silverstone Circuits Ltd and Green Crop Conservation Ltd, dir Smith & Grace (Sales) Ltd and subsidiaries, dir Silverstone Leisure Ltd, pres Institute of the Motor Industry 1969-73 and 1975-77; *Style* - The Hon Gerald Lascelles; Cliffordine House, Rendcomb, Cirencester GL7 7ER

LASCELLES, Hon James Edward; s of 7 Earl of Harewood *qv*; *b* 5 Oct 1953; *Educ* Westminster; *m* 1973, Fredericka Ann, da of Prof Alfred Duhrrson, of Deya, Majorca; 2 c; *Style* - The Hon James Lascelles; 1 Orme lane, W2

LASCELLES, Hon Mark Hubert; s of 7 Earl of Harewood *qv*; *b* 5 July 1964; *Style* - The Hon Mark Lascelles

LASCELLES, Hon Robert Jeremy Hugh; s of 7 Earl of Harewood; *b* 14 Feb 1955 *Style* The Hon Robert Lascelles

LASKEY, Sir Denis Seward; KCMG (1974, CMG 1957), CVO (1958); s of Francis Seward Laskey, MC (d 1972); *b* 18 Jan 1915; *Educ* Marlborough, CCC Oxford; *m* 1947, Perronnelle Mary Gemma, da of Col Sir Edward Le Breton,

MVO (d 1961); 1 s, 3 da; *Career* entered FO 1939, principal private sec to Sec State for Foreign Affairs 1956-59, Minister British Embassy Rome 1960-64, in Bonn 1967-68; Ambass to Romania 1969-71, to Austria 1971-75; *Style* - Sir Denis Laskey, KCMG, CVO; Loders Mill, Nr Bridport, Dorset

LASSENIUS, Tor-Erik; *Career* LLB, EDHC; chm Star Paper Mills Ltd; v-chm Pargas Kalk Ab; *Style* - Tor-Erik Lassenius Esq; Star Paper Ltd, Feniscowles, nr Blackburn, Lancs

LATEY, Hon Mr Justice; Hon Sir John Brinsmead; MBE (1943), QC; s of William Latey, CBE, QC (d 1976); *b* 7 Mar 1914; *Educ* Westminster Sch, Ch Ch Oxford; *m* 1938, Betty Margaret, da of Dr Edwyn Henry Beresford of London; 1 s, 1 da; *Career* served 1939-45, barr Middle Temple 1936, a judge of High Court of Justice (Probate, Divorce and Admiralty Div) (now Family Div) 1965-, chm Lord Chancellor's Ctee on Age of Majority 1965-67, dep chm Oxfordshire quarter sessions 1966 kt 1965; *Style* - The Hon Mr Justice Latey MBE QC; 16 Daylesford ave, Roehampton, SW15

LATHAM, 2 Baron (UK 1942); Dominic Charles Latham; er twin s of Hon Francis Latham (d 1959) by his 3 w Gabrielle and gs of 1 Baron Latham (d 1970) by his 1 w Maya; *b* 20 Sept 1954; *Educ* NSW U; *Heir* bro, Anthony Latham; *Career* part-time post-grad student in civil engrg NSW U, BEng; civil engineer with Electricity Commission of New South Wales 1979-; *Style* - The Rt Hon the Lord Latham; 6/226 Rainbow st, Coogee, Sydney 2034, Australia

LATHAM, Anthony Michael; s of Hon Francis Charles Allman Latham (d 1959 - s of 1 Baron Latham), and hp of twin bro, 2 Baron; *b* 20 Sept 1954; *Style* - Anthony Latham Esq

LATHAM, Edward Michael Locks; s of Edward Bryan Latham, CBE (d 1980); *b* 7 Jan 1930; *Educ* Stowe Sch, Clare Cambridge; *m* 1955, Joan Doris, da of Charles Ellis Merriam Coubrough (d 1967); *Career* chm James Latham Ltd 1973-, dir Trebartha Estates Ltd, chm Hackney Business Promotion Centre, dep chm N E London Employment Gp, pres UCBT (Federation of Tropical Timber Trades in the EEC); *Recreations* riding, tennis, the countryside, classic cars and books; *Style* - Edward Latham Esq; Leeside Wharf, E5 (☎ 01 806 3333)

LATHAM, Hon Mrs Francis; Gabrielle; da of Dr S M O'Riordan; *m* 1951, as his 3 w, the Hon Francis Charles Allman Latham (d 1959); *Style* - The Hon Mrs Francis Latham; 6/226 Rainbow st, S Googee 1034, Sydney, NSW, Australia

LATHAM, Lady Gwendoline Lucy Constance Rushworth; da of Adm of the Fleet 1 Earl Jellicoe, GCB, OM, GCVO (d 1935); *b* 14 Apr 1903; *m* 1935, Lt-Col Edward Latham, MC (d 1957); 2 s, 1 da; *Style* - Lady Gwendoline Latham; Oak Knoll, Sunningdale, Berks (☎ Ascot 22842)

LATHAM, Sir Joseph; CBE (1950); s of John Latham; *b* 1 July 1905; *Educ* Stand G S; *m* 1932, Phyllis Mary, da of R H Fitton, of Prestwich; 1 s, 1 da; *Career* chartered accountant 1926, chm Metal Industries Ltd 1968-72, formerly dep chm and md Associated Electrical Industries Ltd, dir Thorn Electrical Industries Ltd and George Wimpey & Co; kt 1960; *Style* - Sir Joseph Latham, CBE; 25 Badingham dve, Leatherhead, Surrey (☎ Leatherhead 72433)

LATHAM, James Miles; s of Maj James Francis Latham, TD, JP (d 1966); *b* 24 Jan 1940; *Educ* Haileybury Coll; *m* 1968, Margaret Eleanor, nee Gray; 2 s; *Career* wood merchant, dir James Latham Ltd, chm Richard Graefe Ltd, memb cncl Timber Trade Fedn of UK 1974-, Timber Research and Dvpt Assoc 1975-, Assoc of Br Plywood & Veneer Manufacturers, memb of Lloyd's; *Recreations* shooting, golf, gardening, racing; *Clubs* Royal Worlington & Newmarket Golf, Chigwell Golf, Thorpeness Golf; *Style* - James Latham Esq; Gills Farm, Epping Upland, Essex (☎ 0378 75878)

LATHAM, Michael Anthony; MP (C)

Leicestershire (Melton Div) 1974-; s of Wing-Cdr Stanley Hugh Latham, RAF, of Deane, Hants; *b* 20 Nov 1942; *Educ* Marlborough, King's Cambridge, Dept of Education Oxford U; *m* 1969, Caroline Susan, da of Maj T A Terry, RE (d 1971); *Career* memb Westminster City Council 1968-71, dir & ch exec House Builders Fedn 1971-73, memb Expenditure Ctee 1974-, memb Ecclesiastical Ctee of Parliament 1974-, dir Lovell Homes Ltd 1975-; memb bd of Management, Shelter 1976-, C of E Delegate to BBC 1977-; *Style* - Michael Latham Esq MP; House of Commons, SW1

LATHAM, Sir Richard Thomas Paul; 3 Bt (UK 1919); s of 2 Bt (d 1955); *b* 1934; *Educ* Eton, Trin Cambridge; *m* 1958, Marie Louise Patricia, da of Frederick H Russell, of Vancouver, Canada; 2 da; *Heir* none; *Clubs* Cavalry; *Style* - Sir Richard Latham, Bt; 830 Rockbridge rd, Santa Barbara, Calif 93108, USA

LATHAM, Baroness; Sylvia May; da of Alexander Newmark, of London; *b* May 1907; *m* 1, 1931, Alec Kennard (d 1948); m 2, 1957, as his 2 w, 1 Baron Latham (d 1970); *Style* - The Rt Hon the Lady Latham; 170 Chiltern Court, Baker st, NW1 (☎ 01 493 0137)

LATHBURY, Lady; Mairi Zoë; *m* 1, Patrick Somerset Gibbs (decd); m 2, 1972, Gen Sir Gerald William Lathbury, GCB, DSO, MBE, DSC (d 1978); *Style* - Lady Lathbury; Casa San Pedro, Gata de Gorgos, Prov Alicante, Spain

LATIEF, Hon Mrs (Annette Yvonne); *née* Curzon; da (by 1 m) of 3 Viscount Scarsdale; *b* 1953; *m* 1979, Capt Hani Talaat Latief, of Cairo; *Style* - The Hon Mrs Latief

LATIMER, Sir Courtenay Robert; CBE (1958); s of Sir Courtenay Latimer, KCSI, CIE (d 1944); *b* 13 July 1911; *Educ* Rugby, Ch Ch Oxford; *m* Elizabeth Jane Gordon, da of W M Smail; 1 s, 1 da; *Career* HM Overseas Service 1948-64, Min (Territories) British Embassy Pretoria 1964-66, registrar Kingston Polytechnic 1967-76 kt 1966; *Style* - Sir Courtenay Latimer, CBE; Benedicts, Old Ave, Weybridge, Surrey

LATOUR-ADRIEN, Hon Sir (Jean Francois) Maurice; s of late Louis Constant Emile Adrien; *b* 4 Mar 1915; *Educ* Royal Coll Mauritius, Univ Coll London; *Career* Ch Justice of Mauritius 1970-77; kt 1971; *Style* - The Hon Sir Maurice Latour-Adrien; Vacoas, Mauritius

LATTEY, Col (Henry) James Cumming; TD (1945), DL (Worcs 1955); s of Maj James Cumming Lattey, RA (d 1918); *b* 1907; *Educ* Downside, RMC Sandhurst; *m* 1933, Edith Marjorie, da of Sydney Martineau; *Career* served 1939-45 War, Lt-Col 1945, reformed 7 Bn Worcs regt 1947, High Sheriff 1964; *Clubs* Army and Navy, Worcestershire County; *Style* - Col James Lattey TD DL; Hallow Mount, Hallow, Nr Worcester (☎ Hallow 256)

LATYMER, 7 Baron (E 1431-32); Thomas Burdett Money-Coutts; s of 6 Baron (d 1949, great nephew of Baroness (Angela) Burdett-Coutts, the Victorian philanthropist, and ggs of Sir Francis Burdett, 5 Bt, the radical nineteenth century MP); *b* 6 Aug 1901; *Educ* Radley, Trin Oxford; *m* 1925, Patience Margaret, da of late William Courtenay-Thompson and step da of Maj-Gen Herbert C Money, CB; 1 s, 2 da; *Heir* s, Hon Hugo Nevill Money-Coutts; *Career* dir Coutts & Co 1927-72, chm Investment Trust Corpn Ltd to 1972, Metropolitan Trust to 1972, chm London Ctee of Ottoman Bank 1948-75, dir National & Grindlays Bank Ltd to 1972 OStJ; title called out of abeyance in 1913; *Style* - The Rt Hon the Lord Latymer; San Rebassa, Moscari, Mallorca

LAUDERDALE, 17 Earl of (S 1624); Sir Patrick Francis Maitland; 13 Bt (NS 1680); also Lord Maitland of Thirlestane (S 1590), Viscount of Lauderdale (S 1616), Viscount Maitland, and Lord Thirlestane and Boltoun (both S 1624); s of Rev Hon Sydney George William Maitland (d 1946, 2 s of 13 Earl, himself ggggg nephew of 2 Earl and 1 Duke of Lauderdale, the 'L' of Charles II's acronymic CABAL and according to Macaulay the most dishonest man in it; though Pepys said of him he 'had rather hear a cat mew than the best music in the world; and the better the music the more sick it made him', he was an able linguist; his 2 w, to whom belonged Ham House (now Nat Tst owned) at Richmond, was thought to have been Oliver Cromwell's mistress); suc bro, 16 Earl, 1963; f of Lady Olga Maitland (*see* Lady Olga Hay) the gossip columnist; *b* 17 March 1911; *Educ* Lancing, Brasenose Oxford; *m* 1936, Stanka, da of Prof Milivoje Lozanitch, of Belgrade U; 2 s, 2 da; *Heir* s, Master of Lauderdale, Viscount Maitland; *Career* journalist 1933-, founder and sometime editor 'Fleet Street Letter Service', sometime editor 'The Whitehall Letter', war correspondent The Times (Central Europe) 1939-41, News Chronicle Pacific 1941-43, MP (C) Lanarkshire (Lanark Div) 1951-59, founder and chm Expanding Commonwealth Gp at the House of Commons 1955-59, re-elected chm 1959; dir Elf Aquitaine UK Hldgs; FRGS; memb Coll Guardians Nat Shrine of Our Lady of Walsingham 1955-; *Clubs* New (Edinburgh); *Style* - The Rt Hon the Earl of Lauderdale; 12 St Vincent st, Edinburgh (☎ 031 556 5692); 10 Ovington sq, SW3 (☎ 01 589 7451)

LAUDERDALE, Irene, Countess of Lauderdale; Irene Alice May; da of late Rev C P Shipton, of Halsham, Yorks; *m* 1940, as his 2 w, 16 Earl (d 1968); *Style* - The Rt Hon Irene, Countess of Lauderdale; S Raphael, 91 North Lane, E Preston, Littlehampton, Sussex

LAUGHLAND, Graham Franklyn Bruce; s of Andrew Percy Laughland, of Birmingham (d 1962); *b* 18 Aug 1931; *Educ* King Edward's Sch Birmingham, Ch Ch Oxford; *m* 1969, Victoria Nicola Christina, da of A S Jarman, of Brighton; *Career* barr Inner Temple 1958, standing council to the Queen's Proctor 1968-; prosecuting council to Inland Revenue (Midland Oxford circuit) 1973-77; a recorder of Crown Court 1972-; *Style* - Graham Laughland Esq; 4 King's Bench Walk, Temple, EC4 (☎ 01 353 3581); 20 Bryanston Mews East, W1 (☎ 01 262 5713)

LAURENCE, Hon Mrs; Hon Kathleen; da of 1 Baron Iliffe, GBE (d 1960); *b* 1904; *m* 1926, Leslie Frederick Laurence; 1 da; *Style* - The Hon Mrs Laurence; Calle Ferreres, 1 Las Palmas, Canary Islands

LAURENCE, Sir Peter Harold; KCMG (1981, CMG 1976), MC (1944); s of Rev George Laurence (d 1954); *b* 18 Feb 1923; *Educ* Radley Coll, Ch Ch Oxford; *m* 1948, Elizabeth Aida, da of H C B Way; 2 s, 1 da; *Career* HM Diplomatic Service; political adviser Berlin 1967-69; counsellor (commercial) HM Embassy Paris 1970-74; ch inspector HM Diplomatic Service 1974-78; ambass to Ankara; *Style* - Sir Peter Laurence, KCMG, MC; c/o FCO, SW1; Ley Marden, Yarnscombe, Barnstaple, N Devon (☎ 07696 337)

LAURIE, Maj-Gen Sir John Emilius; 6 Bt (UK 1834), CBE (1940), DSO (1916) and Bar (1918); s of Sir Wilfrid Emilius Laurie, 5 Bt, JP (d 1936); *b* 12 Aug 1892; *Educ* Eton, RMC; *m* 1922, Evelyn Clare, da of late Lt-Col L J Richardson Gardner; 1 s, 2 da; *Heir* s, Robert Bayley Emilius Laurie; *Career* joined Seaforth Highlanders 1912, served in Great War 1914-19 (despatches 5, wounded), Maj-Gen 1941, ret 1945, Col Seaforth Highlanders 1947-57; *Style* - Maj-Gen Sir John Laurie Bt CBE DSO*; Crossford, Bulstrode way, Gerrards Cross, Bucks

LAURIE, Robert Bayley Emilius; s and h of Sir John Emilius Laurie, 6 Bt, CBE, DSO; *b* 8 March 1931; *Educ* Eton; *m* 1968, Laurelie Meriol Winifrida, da of late Sir Reginald Lawrence William Williams, 7 Bt, MBE, ED; 2 da; *Style* - Robert Laurie Esq; The Old Rectory, Little Tey, Colchester, Essex

LAURISTON, His Honour Judge; Alexander Clifford; QC (1972); s of Alexander Lauriston, MBE (d 1960); *b* 2 Oct 1927; *Educ* Coatham Sch Redcar, Trin Cambridge; *m* 1954, Inga Louise, da of E Gregor of Tunbridge Wells; 2 da; *Career* barr Inner Temple 1952, recorder of the Crown court 1972-76, a circuit judge 1976-; *Clubs* Berkshire Golf; *Style* - His Honour Judge Lauriston; 74 King's rd, Windsor, Berks

LAURITZEN, Lady Rose (Deirdre Margaret); *née* Keppel; da of Viscount

Bury (d 1968) and gda of 9 Earl of Albemarle, MC (d 1979); *b* 11 Dec 1943; *Educ* Heathfield; *m* 1975, Peter Lanthorp, s of George Lauritzen, of Chicago; 1 s; *Career* raised to the rank of an Earl's da 1980; *Style* - Lady Rose Lauritzen; Palazzo Da Silva, Cannareggio 1468 B, Venice, Italy (☎ 715006)

LAUTERPACHT, Lady; Rachel; da of Michael Steinberg; *m* 1923, Sir Hersch Lauterpacht, QC, (d 1960); *Style* - Lady Lauterpacht; 1 Essex court, Temple, EC4; 6 Cranmer rd, Cambridge

LAVAN, Hon Mr Justice; Sir John Martin; s of late M G Lavan, KC; *b* 5 Sept 1911; *Educ* Aquinas Coll Perth, Xavier Coll Melbourne; *m* 1939, Leith, da of W E Harford; 1 s, 3 da; *Career* Justice of Supreme Court of W Australia 1969-, pres law Soc WA 1964-66, chm Parole Bd WA 1969-76; kt 1980; *Style* - The Hon Mr Justice Lavan; 165 Victoria ave, Dalkeith, WA 6009, Australia

LAVINGTON, His Honour Judge; Cyril Michael; MBE (1940), JP Cornwall (1974); s of Cyril Claude Lavington, of Bristol; *b* 21 June 1912; *m* 1950, Frances Anne (m dis 1968), da of Colston Wintle, MD, JP; 1 s; *Career* barr Middle Temple 1936 (Western Circuit), served in 1939-45 War, recorder of Barnstaple 1964-71, a county court judge (Circuit 54) 1971-72, circuit judge 1972-; *Style* - His Honour Judge Lavington, MBE; Stockadon Villa, St Mellion, Saltash, Cornwall (☎ St Dominick 50259)

LAW, Hon Andrew Bonar; s of late 1 Baron Coleraine, PC; *b* 1933; *Educ* Rugby, Trin Coll, Dublin; *m* 1961, Joanna Margarette, da of Raymond Neill, of Fairview, Delgany, Co Wicklow, Ireland; *Style* - The Hon Andrew Law; Shankill Castle, Shankill, Co Dublin, Ireland

LAW, Hon Charles Adrian Christian Towry; s of 8 Baron Ellenborough; *b* 7 Nov 1960; *Style* - The Hon Charles Law

LAW, Hon Cecil Towry Henry; s of 7 Baron Ellenborough, MC (d 1945); *b* 1931; *Educ* Eton; *m* 1957, (Daphne Mary) Jean, da of Hon Laurence Paul Methuen (d 1970), of Starlings, Sutton Benger, Nr Chippenham, Wilts; 1 s, 3 da; *Career* 2 Lt 1 King's Dragoon Gds 1950-52; Lloyd's Insurance broker 1952, chm Towry Law (Holdings) Ltd, and other Cos; *Style* - The Hon Cecil Law; 6 Sussex sq, W2 (☎ 01 262 4823)

LAW, Hon Mr Justice; Sir Eric (John Ewan); s of late Sir Charles Ewan Law; *b* 10 June 1913; *Educ* Wrekin Coll, St Catharine's Cambridge; *m* 1948, Patricia Constance Elizabeth, da of CWS Seed, CBE; 2 s, 1 da; *Career* barr Middle Temple 1936; Justice of Appeal, Court of Appeal for E Africa 1965-77; Appeal Judge, Court of Appeal Kenya 1977-; kt 1979; *Style* - The Hon Mr Justice Law; c/o Court of Appeal for Kenya, PO Box 30187, Nairobi, Kenya

LAW, Hon Edmund Ivor Cecil; s of 8 Baron Ellenborough; *b* 21 Dec 1956; *Style* - The Hon Edmund Law

LAW, Hon Elizabeth Mary; da (by 1 m) of 2 Baron Coleraine; *b* 1961; *Style* - The Hon Elizabeth Law

LAW, Hon Mrs (Grania Janet Gray); da of Baron Boardman Life Peer); *b* 1955; *m* 1981, Capt Hon Rupert Law, s & h of 8 Baron Ellenborough; *Style* - The Hon Mrs Law

LAW, Hon Henrietta Margaret; da (by 2 m) of 2 Baron Coleraine; *b* 1968; *Style* - The Hon Henrietta Law

LAW, Adm Sir Horace Rochford; GCB (1972), OBE (1951), DSC (1941); s of Sir Horace Law (d 1940), of Dublin; *b* 23 June 1911; *Educ* Sherborne; *m* 1941, Heather Valerie, da of Rev Hayworth Coryton; 2 s, 2 da; *Career* joined RN 1929, Capt Britannia RN Coll Dartmouth 1960, controller of the Navy 1965-70, C-in-C naval Home Command 1970-72, ret 1972; chm Hawthorn Leslie 1973-; first and principal naval ADC to HM the Queen 1970-72, pres Roy Institute of Naval Architects 1975-77; *Style* - Adm Sir Horace Law, GCB, OBE, DSC; West Harting, Petersfield, Hants

LAW, Hon Juliana Caroline Matilda; da (by 2 m) of 2 Baron Coleraine; *b* 1971; *Style* - The Hon Juliana Law

LAW, Hon James Peter Bonar; s (by 2 m) and h of 2 Baron Coleraine; *b* 1975; *Style* - The Hon James Law

LAW, Hon Rupert Edward Henry; s & h of 8 Baron Ellenborough; *b* 28 March 1955; *Educ* Eton; *m* 1981, Hon Grania, da of Baron Boardman; *Career* Capt Coldstream Gds; *Style* - The Hon Rupert Law

LAW, Hon Sophia Anne; da (by 1 m) of 2 Baron Coleraine; *b* 1964; *Style* - The Hon Sophia Law

LAW-SMITH, Sir Richard Robert; CBE (1965), AFC; s of W Law-Smith; *b* 9 July 1914 *Educ* St Edward's Sch Oxford, Adelaide U; *m* 1941, Joan, da of Harold Gordon Darling; 2 da; *Career* chm National Bank of Australasia 1978-; vice-chm Qantas Airways 1961-, Australian Nat Airlines Commission 1975-; dir Broken Hill Pty Co Ltd 1961-, Australian Mutual Provident Soc (Vic), Massey-Ferguson Holdings(Australia) Ltd 1955-, Chrysler Australia Ltd 1975- and others; dir Roy Flying Doctor Service 1956-; kt 1980; *Style* - Sir Richard Law-Smith, CBE, AFC; Bolobek, Macedon, Vic 3440, Australia

LAWES, Sir (John) Michael Bennet; 5 Bt; s of Sir John Claude Bennet Lawes, 4 Bt (d 1979); *b* 24 Oct 1932; *Educ* Elizabeth Coll Guernsey; *Style* - Sir Michael Lawes, Bt; c/o Barclays Bank, Lymington, Hants

LAWES, Lady; Naomi Constance Helen; da of late Lancelot Wykeham Badnall; *m* 1938, as his 2 w, Sir John Claude Bennet Lawes, 4 Bt (d 1979); *Style* - Lady Lawes; Le Clos du Coudré, St Pierre du Bois, Guernsey, Channel Islands

LAWLER, Sir Peter James; OBE; *Career* sec Dept of Administrative Services 1975-; kt 1981; *Style* - Sir Peter Lawler, OBE; 6 Tennyson cres, Forrest, ACT 2603, Australia

LAWRENCE, 5 Baron (UK 1869); Sir David John Downer Lawrence; 5 Bt (UK 1858); s of 4 Baron (d 1968) by his 1 w, Margaret; *b* 4 Sept 1937; *Educ* Bradfield; *Heir* none; *Style* - The Rt Hon the Lord Lawrence; c/o Bird & Bird, 2 Gray's Inn sq, WC1

LAWRENCE, Hon Mrs; Hon (Christine) Alexandra Canning; da of 5 Baron Garvagh; *b* 20 Sept 1949; *Educ* Roy Naval Sch Haslemere, Guildford Tech Coll; *m* 1971, Louis David Lawrence; *Style* - The Hon Mrs Lawrence

LAWRENCE, Hon Catherine Dorina Mary; da of 3 Baron Lawrence (d 1947); *b* 1910; *Style* - The Hon Catherine Lawrence; 14 Juxon Close, Chichester

LAWRENCE, Clive Wyndham; s of Lt-Col Sir Roland Lawrence, 2 Bt, MC and hp to Btcy of bro, Sir David Lawrence, 3 Bt; *b* 6 Oct 1939; *Educ* Gordonstoun; *m* 1966, Sophia Annabel Stuart, da of Ian Hervey Stuart Black; 3 s; *Career* late Lt Coldstream Gds; *Style* - Clive Lawrence Esq; Brandfold Edge, Goudhurst, Kent

LAWRENCE, Derek Howard; s of Eric Lawrence (d 1940); *b* 11 Oct 1925; *Educ* Bradfield Coll, Exeter U, Faraday House; *m* 1952, Ann Margaret, da of James Percival Bristow, of Aldeburgh; 3 s, 1 da; *Career* Lt Royal Signals; md Engineering and Overseas London Brick Co; dir London Brick Landfill Ltd, Midland Structures Ltd, Iran Pressed Brick Co Ltd; *Style* - Derek Lawrence Esq; 22 Mariners Way, Aldeburgh, Suffolk (☎ 072 885 2881)

LAWRENCE, Sir David Roland Walter; 3 Bt (UK 1906); s of Lt-Col Sir (Percy) Roland (Bradford) Lawrence, 2 Bt, MC (d 1950); *b* 8 May 1929; *Educ* Radley, RMC; *m* 1955, Audrey (formerly w of 11 Duke of Leeds), da of Brig Desmond Young, CIE, OBE, MC; *Heir* bro, Clive Wyndham Lawrence; *Career* late Capt Coldstream Gds; *Style* - Sir David Lawrence, Bt; 28 High Town Rd, Maidenhead, Berks

LAWRENCE, Col Frank Hamer; CBE (1949), MC (1918), DL (Warwickshire

1937); s of William Lawrence; *b* 1894; *Educ* Ch Ch Sch Cheltenham; *m* 1917, Hilda Dorothy, da of late Edward E Pearson, of Birmingham; 1 da; *Career* joined RA 1915, served in 1914-18 War, Maj 1920, Bt Lt-Col 1939-45, Col 1945; mil memb Warwickshire TA Assoc 1934-60; pres Roy Artillery Assoc Midland District and F Ambulance Corps, St John Ambulance Bde, Birmingham Co 1932-63; OStJ; *Recreations* gardening and watching cricket; *Style* - Col Frank Lawrence, CBE, MC, DL; Restharrow, Shipston, Stratford-upon-Avon, Warwickshire (☎ 3361)

LAWRENCE, George Alexander Waldemar; s of Sir Alexander Waldemar Lawrence, 4 Bt, and hp of bro, Sir John Waldemar Lawrence, 6 Bt, OBE; *b* 22 Sept 1910; *Educ* Eton, Trin Cambridge; *m* 1949, Olga, da of Peter Schilovsky; 1 s, 2 da; *Style* - George Lawrence Esq; Brockham End, Bath

LAWRENCE, Sir Guy Kempton; DSO (1943), OBE (1945), DFC (1941); s of Albert Edward Lawrence (d 1951); *b* 5 Nov 1914; *Educ* Marlborough Coll; *m* 1947, Marcia Virginia, da of Prof Harold Clark Powell; 2 s, 1 da; *Career* chm Findus (UK) Ltd 1967-75, dep chm Spillers French Holdings Ltd 1972-75, dep chm J Lyons & Co Ltd 1950-75, chm Food and Drink Industries Council 1973-77, dir Eagle Aircraft Services Ltd 1977, chm Eggs Authority 1978-; kt 1976; *Clubs* RAF; *Style* - Sir Guy Lawrence DSO OBE DFC; Food & Drink Industries Council, 1-2 Castle lane, SW1 (☎ 01 834 7554); Courtlands, Kier Park, Ascot, Berks (☎ Ascot 21074)

LAWRENCE, Gerard Ronald; *Career* md The Lummus Co Ltd; memb IOD; *Style* - Gerard Lawrence Esq; The Lummus Co Ltd, 100 Fetter lane, EC4

LAWRENCE, Ivan John; QC (1981), MP (C) Staffordshire 1974-; s of Leslie Lawrence; *b* 24 Dec 1936; *Educ* Brighton, Hove & Sussex G S, Ch Ch Oxford; *m* 1966, Gloria Helene; 1 da; *Career* v-chm Conservative Parly Legal Ctee, pres Nat Assoc of Approved Driving Instructors; *Style* - Ivan Lawrence Esq, QC, MP; Dunally Cottage, Lower Halliford Green, Shepperton, Middlesex (☎ Walton-on-Thames 24692); Grove Farm, Drakelow, Burton-on-Trent, Staffs (☎ 44360)

LAWRENCE, Sir John Waldemar; 6 Bt (UK 1858), OBE (1945); s of Sir Alexander Waldemar Lawrence, 4 Bt (d 1939); suc bro, Sir Henry Eustace Waldemar Lawrence, 5 Bt, 1967; *b* 27 May 1907; *Educ* Eton, New Coll Oxford; *m* 1947, Jacynth Mary, da of late Rev F G Ellerton; *Heir* s, George Alexander Waldemar Lawrence; *Career* press attaché Moscow 1942-45, chm Centre for Study of Religion and Communism (now Keston Coll) 1969, chm Gt Britain-USSR Assoc 1970-, editor of Frontier 1958-75; *Books* A History of Russia; *Style* - Sir John Lawrence Bt, OBE; 24 St Leonards ter, SW3

LAWRENCE, Hon Mrs; Hon Louise Eleanor Alice; da of 5 Baron Garvagh; *b* 1951; *m* 1975, Mark Lawrence; *Style* - The Hon Mrs Lawrence

LAWRENCE, Lady; Marjorie Avice; da of late Charles Angelo Jones, of Bodney Hall, Norfolk; *m* 1941, Hon Mr Justice (Sir Frederick) Geoffrey Lawrence (d 1967); *Style* - Lady Lawrence; Bridge Farm, Burgess Hill, Sussex

LAWRENCE, Hon Patrick John Tristram; s and h of 4 Baron Trevethin and 2 Baron Oaksey; *b* 29 June 1960; *Style* - The Hon Patrick Lawrence

LAWRENCE, Sir Robert Leslie Edward; CBE (1975, OBE 1944); s of Robert Riach Lawrence (d 1971); *b* 29 Oct 1915; *Educ* Dulwich Coll; *m* 1940, Joyce Marjorie, da of John Alfred Ricketts (d 1967); 1 s, 1 da; *Career* v-chm British Railways Board 1975-, chm Nat Freight Corpn 1978-, chm and gen man London Midland Region British Railways 1968-71, v-pres London Cornish Assoc 1979-; kt 1980; *Clubs* MCC, Army & Navy; *Style* - Sir Robert Lawrence, CBE; 37 Oakfield gdns, SE19 (☎ 01 670 7649); Clifford Cottage, Polgigga, St Levan, Cornwall (☎ 073 687 297)

LAWRENCE, Susan, Lady; Susan; da of Sir Charles Stewart Addis, KCMG; *m*

1925, Lieut-Col Sir (Percy) Roland (Bradford) Lawrence, 2 Bt, MC (d 1950); *Style* - Susan, Lady Lawrence; 33 Edith Grove, SW10

LAWRENCE, Hon Sara Honoria Angel; da of 3 Baron Lawrence (d 1947); *b* 1912; *Style* - The Hon Sara Lawrence; 14 Juxon Close, Chichester

LAWRENCE, Hon Sara Victoria; da of 4 Baron Trevethin and 2 Baron Oaksey; *b* 1961; *Style* - The Hon Sara Lawrence

LAWRENCE, Sir William; 4 Bt (UK 1867); s of Sir William Matthew Trevor, 3 Bt, JP (d 1934); *b* 1913; *Educ* Bradfield Coll; *m* 1, 1940, Zoë (m dis 1945), da of Henry Stedham Pether; m 2, 1945, Pamela, da of J Edgar Gordon; 1 s, 2 da; *Heir* s, William Fettiplace Lawrence; *Career* Lt E Surrey Regiment 1940, Maj 1944; sr exec Wilmot Breeden Ltd, ret 1974; sales consultant Long & Hambly Ltd; FRHS, v-pres Stratford on Avon and Warwicks Con Assoc; *Style* - Sir William Lawrence, Bt; The Knoll, Walcote, nr Alcester, Warwicks (☎ 078 981 303)

LAWRENCE, William Fettiplace; s and h of Sir William Lawrence, 4 Bt; *b* 23 Aug 1954; *Educ* King Edward VI Sch Stratford on Avon; *Career* assist financial accountant W B Bumpers Ltd, Rockwell Int 1980-; *Recreations* horse racing, philately; *Style* - William Lawrence Esq; The Knoll, Walcote, nr Alcester, Warwickshire

LAWRENCE-JONES, Sir Christopher; 6 Bt (UK 1831); s of Cdr Bertram Edward Jones, RN (d 1958) and n of Sir Lawrence Evelyn Jones, 5 Bt, MC, TD (d 1969); *b* 19 Jan 1940; *Educ* Sherborne, Gonville and Caius Cambridge, St Thomas' Hospital; *m* 1967, Gail, da of C A Pittar, FRACS; 2 s; *Heir* s Mark Christopher Lawrence-Jones; *Career* Industrial Medical Adviser 1967-, ICI Dyestuffs Divn 1967-70, BP Co Ltd 1970-73, Health and Safety Executive 1973-75, ICI Paints Divn 1975-79, ICI Central Medical Adviser Millbank SW1 1979-; *Recreations* cruising under sail (Yacht- 'Clairvoyance'); *Clubs* Royal Cruising, United Oxford & Cambridge U; *Style* - Sir Christopher Lawrence-Jones, Bt; Silwood House, London rd, Ascot, Berks

LAWRENCE-JONES, David; s of Lawrence Jones (d 1930); *b* 16 Aug 1919; *Educ* Charterhouse; *m* 1949, Gwynnyth Anne, nee Logan; 3 s; *Career* Lt RNVR, Home Fleet, Mediterranean Fleet, despatches 1942, slr 1949; *Recreations* shooting, fishing; *Clubs* Army and Navy; *Style* - David Lawrence-Jones Esq; Rettendon Old Hall, Chelmsford, Essex (☎ Wickford 3360)

LAWRENCE-JONES, Mark Christopher; s and h of Sir Christopher Lawrence-Jones, 6 Bt; *b* 28 Dec 1968; *Style* - Mark Lawrence-Jones Esq

LAWRENCE-PRICE, Christopher; s of Howard Sydney Lawrence-Price; *b* 9 Sept 1946; *Educ* Malvern Coll, Aston U Birmingham, London; *m* 1971 (m dis 1973); *Career* currently md Advertising Consultancy, previously gen administrator English Music Theatre Covent Garden, assoc dir Bland Payne (UK) Ltd; *Recreations* squash, tennis, music - opera/dance; *Style* - Christopher Lawrence-Price Esq; 19 Cambridge st, SW1 (☎ 01 834 6217)

LAWSON, Hon Alma; da of 1 Baron Lawson (d 1965); *b* 1920; *Style* - The Hon Alma Lawson

LAWSON, Hon Mrs; Hon Carole; da of Baron Samuel of Wych Cross (Life Peer); *b* 1942; *m* 1963, Geoffrey Clive Henry Lawson (b 19 June 1940, educ Stowe, Harvard Business Sch; is slr Supreme Court 1963-, chm Magnatex Hldgs and memb Court of Common Cncl Portsoken Ward 1971-; likes polo & hunting, and is a memb of Carlton & City Livery Clubs); 2 s; *Style* - The Hon Mrs Lawson; Innisfree, Woodland dve, East Horsley, Surrey (☎ 2144)

LAWSON, His Honour Judge; Charles; QC (1961); s of Barnet Lawson, of London; *b* 23 Feb 1916; *Educ* Grocers' Company Sch, Univ Coll London; *m* 1943, Olga Daphne (Bobbie), da of John J Kay, of

Hildenborough, Kent; 3 da; *Career* barr Inner Temple 1938, QC 1961, bencher 1968, a recorder of the Crown Court 1972, a Circuit Judge 1972- (salary to be £23,250 pa from 1981); *Style* - His Hon Judge Lawson QC; Mayes Green Cottage, Ockley, Surrey (☎ Forest Green 317)

LAWSON, Charles John Patrick; s and h of Sir John Charles Arthur Digby Lawson, 3 Bt, DSO, MC; *b* 19 May 1959; *Educ* Harrow; *Style* - Charles Lawson Esq; Abbey Hill, Jervaulx, Ripon, Yorks

LAWSON, Mrs E D; *Career* chm Fuerst Day Lawson Holdings Ltd; *Style* - Mrs E D Lawson; Fuerst Day Lawson Holdings Ltd, 1 Leadenhall st, EC3 (☎ 01 626 7773)

LAWSON, Hon Hugh John Frederick; s of 4 Baron Burnham, CB, DSO, MC (d 1963), and hp of bro, 5 Baron Burnham; *b* 1931; *Educ* Eton, Balliol Coll Oxford; *m* 1955, Hilary, da of Alan Hunter, of Huntingtowerfield House, Almondbank, Perthshire; 1 s, 2 da; *Career* Lt Scots Gds (SR) 1952; *Style* - The Hon Hugh Lawson; Woodlands Farm, Beaconsfield, Bucks

LAWSON, Hon Harriet Mary; da of 5 Baron Burnham; *b* 1954; *Style* - The Hon Harriet Lawson

LAWSON, Hon Mrs; Hon Irene; da of 1 Baron Lawson (d 1965); *b* 1909; *m* 1935, Charles Frederick Campbell Lawson; 3 da; *Style* - The Hon Mrs Lawson; Dourene, Park rd North, Chester-le-Street, Co Durham

LAWSON, Hon Jenefer Anne; da of 5 Baron Burnham; *b* 1949; *Educ* The Downs, Seaford; Heathfield Sch Ascot; *Style* - The Hon Jenefer Lawson; Hall Barn, Beaconsfield, Bucks (☎ 3315)

LAWSON, Col Sir John Charles Arthur Digby; 3 Bt (UK 1900), DSO (1943), MC 1940); s of Maj Sir Digby Lawson, 2 Bt, TD, JP (d 1959) and Mrs Gerald Wallis (d 1940); *b* 24 Oct 1912; *Educ* Stowe, RMC; *m* 1, 1945, Rose (m dis 1950, she d 1972 and had m 1, 1933, 7 Earl of Warwick, m dis 1938; m 2, Pilot Officer William M L Fiske, ka 1940), da of David Cecil Bingham (gs of 4 Earl of Lucan) and Lady Rosabelle Millicent, nee St Clair-Erskine, da of 5 Earl of Rosslyn; m 2, 1954, Tresilla Ann Eleanor (who m 1, John de Pret Roose, m dis 1954), da of Maj E Buller Leyborne Popham, MC; 1 s; *Heir* s Charles John Patrick Lawson; *Career* Lt-Col 11 Hussars;, Cdr Inns of Court Regt 1945-47, ret 1947; Col 11 Hussars 1965-69; md Fairbairn Lawson Ltd and subsidiaries Leeds 1966-68, chm 1968-; *Style* - Col Sir John Lawson, Bt, DSO, MC; Abbey Hill, Jervaulx, Ripon, N Yorks (☎ Jervaulx 209)

LAWSON, Lady; Mona Lilian; da of Dr B Thorne Thorne, of Woking; *m* 1930, Sir Henry (Brailsford) Lawson (d 1978); *Style* - Lady Lawson; Churchmead, Pirbright, Surrey

LAWSON, Rt Hon Nigel; PC (1980), MP (C) Blaby 1974-; s of Ralph Lawson; *b* 11 Mar 1932; *Educ* Westminster, Ch Ch Oxford; *m* 1955, Vanessa Mary Addison, da of late Felix Addison Salmon; 1 s, 3 da; *Career* Sub-Lieut RNVR 1954-56, memb editorial staff Financial Times 1956-60, City editor Sunday Telegraph 1961-63, editor of The Spectator 1966-70, opposition whip 1976-77, opposition spokesman on Treasury and Economic Affairs 1977-79, Financial Sec to the Treasury 1979-; *Style* - The Rt Hon Nigel Lawson PC MP; 32 Sutherland Walk, SE17

LAWSON, Hon Mr Justice; Hon Sir Neil; s of late Robb Lawson; *b* 1908; *Educ* Hendon County Sch, London U; *m* 1933, Gweneth Clare, da of late Sidney Wilby, FCA, of Leicester; 1 s, 1 da; *Career* served with RAFVR 1940-45, barr Inner Temple 1929, QC 1955, bencher 1961, High Court Judge (Queen's Bench) 1971-; kt 1971; *Style* - The Hon Mr Justice Lawson; 30a Heath dve, Hampstead NW3 (☎ 01 794 2585)

LAWSON, Lt-Gen Sir Richard George; DSO(1962), OBE (1968); s of John Lawson; *b* 24 Nov 1927; *Educ* St Alban's Sch, Birmingham U; *m* 1956, Ingrid; 1 s; *Career* assist Military Deputy to Head of Defence Sales 1975-77, GOC 1 Armoured Divn 1977-79, GOC Northern Ireland

1979- kt 1979; *Books* Strange Soldiering, All The Queen's Men, Strictly Personal; *Style* - Lt-Gen Sir Richard Lawson, DSO, OBE; HQ N Ireland, Lisburn, Co Antrim

LAWSON, Lady; Susan Elisabeth; da of F E Bay; *m* 1931, Sir William Halford Lawson, CBE (d 1971); *Style* - Lady Lawson; Sands Lodge, Leich lane, Farnham, Surrey

LAWSON, Hon Sarah Jane; da of 5 Baron Burnham; *b* 1955; *Style* - The Hon Sarah Lawson

LAWSON, Lady Grant; Virginia; da of late Sidney Butler Dean, of St Paul, Minnesota, USA; *m* 1940, Col Sir Peter Grant Lawson, 2 Bt (d 1973); *Style* - Lady Grant Lawson; Dorridge Farm, Fordingbridge, Hants

LAWSON, Sir William Howard; 5 Bt (UK 1841), DL (Cumberland 1963); s of Sir Henry Joseph Lawson, 3 Bt (d 1947), of Brough Hall, Catterick, Yorks; suc bro, Sir Ralph Henry Lawson, 4 Bt, 1975; *b* 15 July 1907; *Educ* Ampleforth; *m* 1933, Joan Eleanor, da of Arthur C Stamer, CBE (d 1944); 3 s, 1 da; *Heir* s John Philip Howard Lawson; *Career* kt of Malta 1965; *Style* - Sir William Lawson, Bt, DL; Wood House, Warwick Bridge, Carlisle, Cumbria

LAWSON-JOHNSTON, Hon Arthur Charles St John; s and h of 2 Baron Luke, KCVO, TD, by his w Barbara, da of Sir FitzRoy Hamilton Anstruther-Gough-Calthorpe, 1 Bt; *b* 13 Jan 1933; *Educ* Eton, Trin Cambridge; *m* 1, 1959 (m dis 1971), Silvia Mary, da of Don Honorio Roigt, former Argentine Ambass at The Hague; 1 s, 2 da; m 2, 1971, Sarah Louise, da of Richard Hearne, OBE; 1 s; *Career* CC Beds 1966-70 (chm of Staffing Ctee 1967-70), High Sheriff of Beds 1969-70, pres of Nat Assoc of Warehouse-keepers, dir Pronantica Ltd, and Bunhill Holdings Ltd; OStJ; Cmmr St John Ambulance Bde in Beds 1972-; *Clubs* Jockey (Buenos Aires), Royal Southern Yacht; *Style* - The Hon Arthur Lawson-Johnston; Odell Manor, Beds

LAWSON-JOHNSTON, Hon George Andrew; s of 2 Baron Luke, KCVO, TD; *b* 1944; *m* 1968, Sylvia Josephine Ruth, da of Michael Richard Lloyd Hayes; 3 s, 1 da; *Style* - The Hon George Lawson-Johnston; Hobbs Green Farm, Odell, Beds

LAWSON-JOHNSTON, Hon Hugh de Beauchamp; TD (1951), DL (Beds 1964); s of 1 Baron Luke, KBE (d 1943), by his w Hon Edith Laura St John (d 1941), da of 16 Baron St John of Bletso; *b* 7 April 1914; *Educ* Eton, Chillon Coll, Corpus Christi Cambridge; *m* 1946, Audrey Warren, da of late Col Frederick Warren Pearl; 3 da; *Career* Capt 5 Bn Bedfordshire Regt (TA Reserve), chm Tribune Investment Trust Ltd, Pitman Ltd; chm of ctees, United Soc for Christian Literature; High Sheriff Beds 1961-62; *Style* - The Hon Hugh Lawson-Johnston, TD, DL; Flat 1, 28 Lennox gdns, SW1 (☎ 01 584 1446); Melchbourne Park, Bedfordshire (☎ Riseley 282)

LAWSON-JOHNSTON, Hon Ian Henry Calthorpe; s of 2 Baron Luke, KCVO, TD; *b* 1938; *m* 1970, Lady (Pamela) Lemina Gordon, da of 12 Marquess of Huntly; 1 s, 1 da; *Style* - The Hon Ian Lawson-Johnston; Hawkslaw, Coldstream, Berwickshire

LAWSON-JOHNSTON, Lady (Pamela) Lemina; da of 12 Marquess of Huntly; *b* 1942; *m* 1970, Hon Ian Henry Calthorpe Lawson-Johnston; 1 s, 1 da; *Style* - Lady Lemina Lawson-Johnston; Hawkslaw, Coldstream, Berwickshire

LAWSON-JOHNSTON, Hon Laura Pearl; OBE (1946), JP (Beds 1941), DL (1976); da of 1 Baron Luke, KBE (d 1943); *b* 1916; *Career* county pres St John Ambulance Brigade 1971-; OStJ; *Style* - The Hon Laura Lawson-Johnston OBE, JP, DL; Melchbourne Park, Beds (☎ Riseley 266)

LAWSON-JOHNSTON, Hon Olive Elizabeth Helen; da of 1 Baron Luke, KBE (d 1943); *b* 22 Jan 1904; *m* 1934, Frederick Lothair Lawson-Johnston (d 1963) (m annulled 1936); *Career* Sr Cmdt ATS 1938-40, 2 Officer WRNS 1941-45; *Style* - The Hon Mrs Olive Lawson-Johnston; Shona Beag, Station rd, Dirleton, North Berwick, E Lothian

LAWSON-JOHNSTON, Hon Philip Richard; s of 2 Baron Luke, KCVO, TD; *b* 1950; *Educ* Eton; *m* 1977, Saskia Moyne, da of late Terence George Andrews, MBE; 2 s; *Style* - The Hon Philip Lawson-Johnston; c/o 24a Motcomb st, SW1

LAWSON-TANCRED, Andrew Peter; s and h of Sir Henry Lawson-Tancred, 10 Bt; *b* 18 Feb 1952; *Educ* Eton; *Style* - Andrew Lawson-Tancred Esq

LAWSON-TANCRED, Sir Henry; 10 Bt (E 1662), JP (WR Yorks 1967); s of Maj Sir Thomas Selby Lawson-Tancred, 9 Bt (d 1945); *b* 1924; *Educ* Stowe, Jesus Coll Cambridge; *m* 1, 1950, Jean Veronica (d 1970), da of Gerald Robert Foster (d 1962); 5 s, 1 da; m 2, 1978, Susan Dorothy Marie-Gabrielle, da of late Sir Kenelm Cayley, 10 Bt, and formerly w of Maldwin Drummond; *Heir* s, Andrew Peter Lawson-Tancred; *Career* served with RAFVR 1942-46; *Style* - Sir Henry Lawson-Tancred, Bt, JP; Aldborough Manor, Boroughbridge, Yorks (☎ 2716)

LAWTON, Prof Frank Ewart; s of Hubert Ralph Lawton; *b* 23 Oct 1915; *m* 1943, Muriel Leonora Bacon; 1 s, 1 da; *Career* prof of Operative Dental Surgery Liverpool U 1956-, pres Gen Dental Council 1979-; *Style* - Prof Frank Lawton; 55 Woolton Hill rd, Liverpool L25 6HU (☎ 051 428 1323)

LAWTON, Rt Hon Lord Justice Lawton; Rt Hon Sir Frederick Horace; PC (1972); s of William John Lawton OBE; *b* 21 Dec 1911; *Educ* Battersea GS, CCC Cambridge; *m* 1937, Doreen, da of Richard Maker Wilton, of Bodmin, Cornwall; 2 s; *Career* served 1939-41 with London Irish Rifles, QC (1957), a judge of the High Court 1961-72, a Lord Justice of Appeal 1972-, chm of Standing Ctee for Criminal Law Revision 1977, chm Advisory Ctee on Legal Education 1976-, pres British Academy of Forensic Sciences 1964; kt 1961; *Style* - The Rt Hon Lord Justice Lawton, PC; 2 Harcourt Bldgs, Temple, EC4; Mordryg, Stoptide Rock, nr Wadebridge, Cornwall (☎ Trebetherick 3375)

LAWTON, His Honour Judge; (Kenneth) Keith Fullerton; JP (1969) Lancs; s of John Wlliam Lawton (d 1954); *b* 6 Aug 1924; *Educ* Barrow GS, Trinity Hall Cambridge; *m* 1, 1959, Muriel Iris (d 1974), da of late Moses Hugh Parry; m 2, 1975, Dorothy, da of Harold Rogers of Lancaster; *Career* Lancs, memb SW Lancs Probation Ctee 1973-74, a circuit judge 1972-; *Style* - His Hon Judge Lawton JP; 19 St Anne's rd, Liverpool L17 6BN (☎ 051 427 3339)

LAYCOCK, Lady; Angela Clare Louise; JP (Notts); da of late Rt Hon William Dudley Ward, PC (gn of 1 Earl of Dudley), by Winifred, Marquesa de Casa Maury, *qv*; *b* 1916; *m* 1935, Maj-Gen Sir Robert Edward Laycock, KCMG, CB, DSO, Royal Horse Guards (d 1968, s of Brig-Gen Sir Joseph Laycock, KCMG, DSO, TD, JP, DL, by Katherine, formerly w of 6 Marquess of Downshire and da of Hon Hugh Hare, 4 s of 2 Earl of Listowel, KP); 2 s, 3 da (of whom the yst, Katherine, m David Mlinaric, the interior designer, *qv*); *Career* DStJ, CC Notts; *Style* - Lady Laycock, JP; La Canada Real, Sotogrande, (PA) Cadiz, Spain

LAYCOCK, Sir Leslie Ernest; CBE (1967), JP; s of Ernest B Laycock, of Headingley, Leeds; *b* 4 Sept 1903; *Educ* Uppingham Sch, Leeds U; *m* 1931, Hilda Florence, da of C Ralph Carr, of Harrogate; 2 s; *Career* v-pres Assoc of British Chambers of Commerce 1962-, chm West Riding Branch of Institute of Directors 1959-72, chm Leeds Regional Hospital Board 1963-74, pres Leeds and Holbeck Bldg Soc 1969-71, chm Advisory Ctee to Leeds Prison 1961- kt 1974; *Style* - Sir Leslie Laycock CBE JP; The Gables, Rayleigh rd, Harrogate, North Yorks (☎ 66219)

LAYCOCK, Mrs Peter; Patricia; da of Kenneth Richards, of NSW; *b* 20 Jan 1914; *m* 1, 1932 (m dis 1937), as his 1 w, 9 Earl of Jersey; 1 da (Lady Caroline Ogilvy); m 2, 1937, Maj Robin Filmer-Wilson (k 1944); 1 s, 1 da; m 3, 1953, Lt-Col Peter Laycock (d 1978); *Style* - Mrs Peter Laycock; The Mill House, Sutton Courtenay, Oxon (☎ 023 582 219); 51 Eaton sq, SW1

LAYFIELD, Sir Frank Henry Burland Willoughby; QC (1967); s of Henry Layfield (d 1960); *b* 9 Aug 1921; *Educ* Sevenoaks Sch; *m* 1965, Irene Patricia, da of Capt J D Harvey, RN; 1 s, 1 da; *Career* barr 1954, chm Inquiry into Greater London Plan 1970-72, chm Ctee of Inquiry into Local Govt Finance 1974-76; Recorder of Crown Court 1979-; kt 1976; *Style* - Sir Frank Layfield, QC; 2 Mitre Court Buildings, Temple, London EC4 (☎ 01 236 2246); Maids Moreton Manor, Buckingham, Buckinghamshire (☎ 2419)

LAYLAND, Hon Mrs; Hon Sheila *née* Hamnett; da of Baron Hamnett (Life Peer) by his wife Elsie (d 1970, herself daughter of James Cox); *b* 24 July 1933; *Educ* Levenshulme High School, City of Portsmouth Training College; *m* 1962, Eric Layland; 1 s, 1 da; *Style* - The Hon Mrs Layland; 31 Sevenoaks Avenue, Heaton Moor, Stockport, Cheshire (☎ 061 432 8083)

LAYTON, 2 Baron (UK 1947); Michael John Layton; s of 1 Baron Layton, CH, CBE (d 1966); *b* 28 Sept 1912; *Educ* St Paul's, Gonville & Caius Cambridge; *m* 1938, Dorothy Rose (JP 1954-67 Middx), da of Albert L Cross, of Rugby; 1 s, 1 da; *Heir* s, Hon Geoffrey Michael Layton; *Career* CEng, FIMechE, FIM; formerly with Goss Printing of Chicago, Ibbotson Bros of Sheffield; md Steel Co of Wales, exec bd memb BSC; dir Wolff Steel Hldgs 1977-, Economist Newspaper Ltd 1973-; *Style* - The Rt Hon the Lord Layton; 6 Old Palace Terrace, The Green, Richmond, Surrey (☎ 01 940 0834)

LAYTON, Hon Christopher Walter; s of 1 Baron Layton, CH, CBE (d 1966); *b* 31 Dec 1929; *Educ* Oundle, King's Cambridge; *m* 1, 1952, Anneliese Margarethe, da of Joachim von Thadden, of Hanover (m dis 1957); 1 s, 1 da; m 2, 1961, Margaret, da of Leslie Moon; 3 da; *Career* dir Computer Electronics, Telecommunications and Air Transport Equipment Manufacturing, Directorate-General of Internal Market and Industrial Affairs, Commission of the European Communities 1973-; *Style* - The Hon Christopher Layton; Directorate-General of Internal Market & Industrial Affairs, Commission of the European Communities, 200 rue de la Loi, 1049 Brussels, Belgium; Ave Albert Lancaster, 95B, 1080 Brussels, Belgium

LAYTON, Lt-Col Hon David; MBE (1946); s of 1 Baron Layton, CH, CBE (d 1960); *b* 1914; *Educ* Gresham's Sch, Trin Cambridge; *m* 1, 1939, Elizabeth, da of Rev Robert Millar Gray, of Hampstead; 2 s, 1 da; m 2, 1972, Joy Parkinson; *Career* 2 Lt RE 1939; md Incomes Data Services; *Style* - Lt-Col the Hon David Layton, MBE; 18 Grove ter, Highgate rd, NW5

LAYTON, Hon Geoffrey Michael; s and h of 2 Baron Layton; *b* 19 July 1947; *Educ* St Paul's Sch, Stanford U Calif, The U of Southern Calif; *m* 1969, Viviane (m dis 1971), da of Francois Cracco, of Leuven, Belgium; *Style* - The Hon Geoffrey Layton; 45 Westleigh ave, SW15 (☎ 01 788 3530)

LE BAILLY, Vice-Adm Sir Louis Edward Stewart Holland; KBE (1972), CB (1969); s of Robert Francis Le Bailly; *b* 18 July 1915; *Educ* RN Coll Dartmouth, RN Engineering Coll Devonport; *m* 1946, Pamela Ruth, da of Rear-Adm Charles Pierre Berthon; 3 da; *Career* Joined RN 1929, served in Second World War, Cdr British Navy Staff & Naval Attaché Washington DC 1967-69, dir Service Intelligence MOD 1970, ret 1972, Dep Under-Sec of State 1972, Dir-Gen Intelligence MOD 1972-75; *Style* - Vice-Adm Sir Louis Le Bailly KBE CB; c/o Barclays Bank, Market sq, Chippenham, Wilts

LE CARRÉ, John (David John Moore Cornwell); s of Ronald Cornwell; *b* 19 Oct 1931; *Educ* Sherborne, Berne U, Lincoln Coll Oxford; *m* 1, 1954 (m dis 1971), Alison Ann Veronica Sharp; 3 s; m 2, 1972, Valerie Jane Eustace; 1; *Career* former schoolteacher Eton; Foreign Service 1960-64; novelist, books include *The Spy Who Came In From The Cold* 1963, *Tinker, Tailor, Soldier, Spy* 1974 (TV series), *Smiley's People* 1980; *Style* - David

Cornwell Esq; John Farquharson Ltd, Bell House, Bell Yard, WC2

LE CHEMINANT, Air Chief Marshal Sir Peter de Lacey; GBE (1978), KCB (1972, CB 1968), DFC & Bar (1943, 1951); s of Col Keith Le Cheminant; *b* 17 June 1920; *Educ* Elizabeth Coll Guernsey, RAF Coll Cranwell; *m* 1940, Sylvia, da of J van Bodegom (d 1963); 1 s, 2 da; *Career* joined RAF 1939, Cmdt Joint Warfare Establishment 1968-70, Asst Ch Air Staff (Policy) 1972, memb Permanent Military Deputies Gp Central Treaty Organisation 1972-74, V-Ch of Defence Staff 1974-76, Lt-Gov and C-in-C Guernsey 1980-; *Style* - Air Chief Marshal Sir Peter Le Cheminant, GBE, KCB, DFC and bar; Government House, Guernsey, Channel Islands

le FLEMING, Isabella, Lady; Isabella Annie Fraser; da of late James Craig, of Manaia, Taranaki, NZ; *m* 1921, Sir Frank Thomas le Fleming, 10 Bt (d 1971); *Style* - Isabella, Lady le Fleming; Rydal Lovat, Auroa rd, RD Manaia, Taranaki, New Zealand

le FLEMING, Quentin John; s and h of Sir William Kelland le Fleming, 11 Bt; *b* 27 June 1949; *m* 1971, Judith Ann, da of C J Peck, JP, of Ashhurst, Manawatu, NZ; 1 s, 1 da; *Style* - Quentin le Fleming Esq; 147 Stanford st, Ashhurst, Manawatu, New Zealand

le FLEMING, Sir William Kelland; 11 Bt (E 1705); s of Sir Frank Thomas le Fleming, 10 Bt (d 1971); *b* 27 April 1922; *m* 1948, Noveen Avis, da of C C Sharpe, of Hamilton, NZ; 3 s, 4 da; *Heir* s, Quentin John Le Fleming; *Career* served in 1939-45 War; *Style* - Sir William le Fleming, Bt; Kopane rd, Palmerston North, New Zealand

LE GALLAIS, Sir Richard Lyle; s of William Le Gallais (d 1924); *b* 15 Nov 1916; *Educ* Victoria Coll Jersey, Inns of Court; *m* 1947, Juliette, da of Peter Angus Forsythe (d 1963); 2 s; *Career* barr 1939, mil service 1939-47, pres War Crimes Tribunal Singapore 1946, advocate Royal Court, Jersey 1947, res magistrate Kenya 1949, sr res magistrate N Rhodesia 1958, CJ Aden 1960-67, chm Industrial Tribunals 1968-72, regional chm Industrial Tribunals Bristol 1972-; kt 1965; *Style* - Sir Richard Le Gallais; Bainly House, Bainly, Gillingham, Dorset (☎ Bourton 373)

LE MAITRE, Lady; Evelyn; da of late Ernest Martelli, KC; *m* 1931, Sir Alfred Sutherland Le Maitre, KBE, CB, MC (d 1959); *Style* - Lady Le Maitre; Mill Cottage, Polstead, Suffolk

LE MARCHANT, Sir Denis; 5 Bt (UK 1841); s of Sir Edward Le Marchant, 4 Bt, KCB, CBE, JP, DL (d 1953, of an old Guernsey family whose founder allegedly settled in the Channel Islands from France around the turn of the 12 & 13 centuries); *b* 28 Feb 1906; *Educ* Radley; *m* 1933, Elizabeth Rowena, da of Arthur Hovenden Worth; 2 s (1 decd), 1 da; *Heir* s, Francis Arthur Le Marchant; *Career* Lt Nottingham (Sherwood Rangers) Yeo & Capt late Cheshire Yeo; High Sheriff Lincs 1958; *Style* - Sir Denis Le Marchant, Bt; Hungerton Hall, Nr Grantham, Lincs (☎ Knipton 244)

LE MARCHANT, Francis Arthur; s and h of Sir Denis Le Marchant, 5 Bt, and 1 cous of Spencer Le Marchant, MP, the Comptroller of HM Household; *b* 6 Oct 1939; *Educ* Gordonstoun, Roy Acad Schs; *Career* painter; *Style* - Francis Le Marchant Esq; Hungerton Hall, Grantham, Lincs (☎ Knipton 244)

LE MARCHANT, Spencer; MP (C) Derbyshire (High Peak Div) 1970-; s of Alfred Le Marchant, of Honiton, and nephew of Sir Denis Le Marchant, 5 Bt; *b* 1931; *Educ* Eton; *m* 1955, Lucinda Gaye, da of Brig H N Leveson Gower, of Tilford, Surrey; 2 da; *Career* National Service and Territorial Commissions Sherwood Foresters 1949-54, memb The Stock Exchange 1954, memb Westminster City Council 1956-71, PPS to Ch Sec to the Treasury 1972-74, PPS Dept of Energy 1974, assist opposition whip 1974-79, Comptroller HM Household 1979-; *Style* Spencer Le Marchant Esq, MP; Hillside, Chinley, Derbyshire SK12 6BX; 41 Rivermill, Grosvenor rd, SW1 (☎ 01 821 9191)

LE MASURIER, Sir Robert Hugh; DSC (1942); s of William Smythe Le Masurier (d 1955); *b* 29 Dec 1913; *Educ* Victoria Coll Jersey, Pembroke Oxford; *m* 1941, Helen Sophia Sheringham; 1 s, 2 da; *Career* served in 1939-45 War, Solicitor-General Jersey 1955-58, AG 1958-62, Bailiff of Jersey 1962-74, a judge of Guernsey Court of Appeal 1964-; kt 1966; *Style* - Sir Robert Le Masurier, DSC; La Ville à L'Evêque, Trinity, Jersey, CI

LE POER TRENCH, (Nicholas) Richard Power; s of late Hon Power Edward Ford Le Poer Trench (yst s of 5 Earl of Clancarty); hp of unc, 8 Earl; *b* 1 May 1952; *Educ* Westminster Sch, Ashford G S, Plymouth Polytechnic; *Style* - Richard Le Poer Trench Esq; c/o 55 Shirlock rd, NW3

LE QUESNE, Sir (Charles) Martin; KCMG (1974); s of Charles Thomas Le Quesne, QC (d 1954); *b* 10 June 1917; *Educ* Shrewsbury, Exeter Oxford; *m* 1948, Deidre Noel Fisher; 3 s; *Career* entered Foreign Office 1946; Ambass to Republic of Mali 1961-64, Ambass to Algeria 1968-71, dep under-sec Foreign & Commonwealth Office 1971-74, British High Commisioner in Nigeria 1974-76; memb of the States of Jersey 1978-; *Style* - Sir Martin Le Quesne, KCMG; Beau Desert, St Saviour's, Jersey, Channel Islands (☎ Central 22076)

LEA, His Honour Judge Christopher Gerald; MC; s of late George Percy Lea, of Franche, Kidderminster, Worcs; *b* 27 Nov 1917; *Educ* Charterhouse, RMC Sandhurst; *m* 1952, Susan Elizabeth, da of Maj Edward Pendavies Dorrien Smith; 2 s, 2 da (1 decd); *Career* barr Inner Temple 1948, memb Assistance Board Appeal Tribunal (Oxford Area) 1961-63, memb Mental Health Review Tribunal 1962-68, metropolitan magistrate 1968-72, circuit judge 1972-; *Style* - His Honour Judge Christopher Lea, MC; Simms Farm House, Mortimer, Reading, Berks (☎ Mortimer 332360)

LEA, Sir Frederick Measham; CB (1960), CBE (1952); s of Measham Lea, CIE, OBE (d 1963); *b* 10 Feb 1900; *Educ* King Edward VI Sch Birmingham, Birmingham U; *m* 1938, Eleanor, da of Frank James; *Career* dir Building Research Station, Dept of Scientific and Industrial Research 1946-65, pres Int Council for Bldg Research 1966-57 and 1959-62, pres Int Assoc of Testing and Research Laboratories for Materials and Structures 1958; memb Council, Royal Inst of Chemistry 1943-46 and 1948-51; kt 1966; Walter C Voss Award, American Soc for Testing and Materials 1964; *Style* - Sir Frederick Lea, CB, CBE; Sunnyridge, East Ogwell, Newton Abbot, Devon (☎ Newton Abbot 3269)

LEA, Lt-Gen Sir George (Harris); KCB (1967), DSO (1957), MBE (1950); s of Percy Lea (d 1961); *b* 28 Dec 1912; *Educ* Charterhouse, RMC Sandhurst; *m* 1948, Pamela Elizabeth, da of Brig Guy Lovett-Tayleur; 1 s, 2 da; *Career* Maj-Gen 1962, Cdr British forces, Borneo 1965-66, head of British Defence Staff (Washington) and defence attaché 1968-70, Lt-Gen 1967, ret 1970; md Martin Scott & Co (CI) Ltd 1975-; *Style* - Lt Gen Sir George Lea, KCB, DSO, MBE; Malmaison, Les Ruisseaux, St Brelade, Jersey, CI

LEA, Rear-Adm Sir John Stuart Crosbie; KBE (1979); *b* 4 June 1923; *Career* Capt RN 1966, Rear-Adm 1975, V-Adm 1978, Assist Ch Fleet Support 1976-77, dir Gen Naval Manpower and Training 1977-79; *Style* - Rear-Adm Sir John Lea, KBE; c/o Lloyds Bank, Hayling Island, Hants

LEA, Philip; s of Herbert James Lea (d 1932); *b* 28 July 1915; *Educ* Sandbach Sch Cheshire; *m* 1940, Vera Nadine, nee Cope; 1 s, 1 da; *Career* chm and md Morning Foods Ltd North Western Mills 1942-, dir HJ Lea & Sons, PJ Lea Consulting Servs Ltd, engineering consultant UK Agricultural Supply Trade Assoc; *Recreations* shooting, golf, boar hunting; *Clubs* Farmers', City Livery, RAC; *Style* - Philip Lea Esq; Calveley Court, Tarporley, Cheshire (☎ Wettenhall 222); St Petrock's, Marine Drive, Llandudno (☎ Llandudno 77367)

LEA, Sir Thomas Claude Harris; 3 Bt (UK 1892); s of Sir (Thomas) Sydney Lea, 2 Bt (d 1946); *b* 13 April 1901; *Educ*

Lancing, Clare Cambridge; *m* 1, 1924, Barbara Katharine, OBE, JP (d 1945), da of late Albert Julian Pell, DL; 1 s, 4 da; m 2, 1950, Diana, da of Howard Thompson; *Heir* s, Thomas Julian Lea; *Career* Lt RNVR 1940, Cdr 1945; *Style* - Sir Thomas Lea, Bt; Coneybury, Bayton, nr Kidderminster, Worcs

LEA, Thomas Julian; s and h of Sir Thomas Claude Harris Lea, 3 Bt; *b* 18 Nov 1934; *m* 1970, Gerry Valerie, da of late Capt Gibson Clarence Fahnestock, USAF; Lt RN (ret); 2 s, 2 da; *Style* - Thomas Lea Esq; Batchelors Hall, Hundon, W Suffolk

LEACH, Sir Edmund Ronald; s of William Edmund Leach, of Rochdale, Lancs; *b* 7 Nov 1910; *Educ* Marlborough and Clare Cambridge; *m* 1940, Celia Joyce, da of Henry Stephen Guy Buckmaster, of Fulmer, Bucks; 1 s, 1 da; *Career* lecturer (later reader) in Social Anthropology LSE 1947-53, field research Formosa, Kurdistan, Burma, Borneo, Ceylon, fell King's Cambridge 1960, provost 1966-79, kt 1975; *Style* - Sir Edmund Leach; 11 West Green, Barrington, Cambs (☎ Cambridge 870 675)

LEACH, Adm Sir Henry Conyers; GCB (1978, KCB 1977); s of Capt John Leach, RN; *b* 18 Nov 1923; *Educ* St Peter's Court, RN Coll Dartmouth; *m* 1958, Mary Jean, da of Adm Sir Henry McCall, KCVO, KBE, CB; 2 da; *Career* joined RN 1937, Capt 1961, Vice-Adm 1974, Vice-Chief Defence Staff 1976-77, C-in-C Fleet and Allied C-inc-C Channel and Eastern Atlantic 1977-79, Ch Naval Staff and First Sea Lord 1979-, First and Principal Naval ADC to the Queen 1979; *Style* - Adm Sir Henry Leach, GCB; Wonston Lodge, Sutton Scotney, Winchester, Hants (☎ Sutton Scotney 327)

LEACH, Rodney; s of Edward Leach (d 1951); *b* 3 March 1932; *Educ* Baines G S Lancs, Birmingham U; *m* 1958, Eira Mary, nee Tuck; 3 s, 1 da; *Career* ptnr McKinsey & Co Inc 1965-74, exec dir P & O Steam Navigation Co 1974-, chm P & O Cruises Ltd 1980-, chm North Sea Ferries Ltd 1974-; *Recreations* sailing (yacht: 'Remsad One'), reading, gardening; *Clubs* RAC, Brighton Marina Yacht; *Style* - Rodney Leach Esq; Coombe Side, 15 Grimwade av, Croydon, Surrey

LEACH, Sir Ronald George; GBE (1976); s of William T Leach; *b* 1907; *Educ* Alleyn's Sch; *m* Margaret, da of Henry Binns; *Career* dep fin sec Ministry of Food 1939-46, memb Departmental Ctee on Flooding 1953, chm Consumers Ctee for Great Britain 1957-66, memb Ctee of Inquiry into Shipping 1967, sr ptnr Peat Marwick Mitchell & Co Chartered Accountants 1966-77, dir Samuel Montagu & Co 1977-80, dir Banque Nationale de Paris Ltd 1977-80, dir Jersey Int Bank of Commerce 1980-, kt 1970; *Style* - Sir Ronald Leach, GBE; La Rosière, Mont de la Rosière, St Saviour, Jersey; Limeuil, Dordoyne, France; 10 The Ave, Perth, W Australia

LEADBITTER, Edward; MP (L) Hartlepool 1964-; s of Edward Leadbitter of Easington, Co Durham; *b* 18 June 1919; *Educ* State Sch, Teachers' Training Coll; *m* 1940, Phyllis Irene Mellin; 1 s, 1 da; *Career* served 1939-45 War, teacher, memb W Hartlepool Borough Cncl, organizer of Exhibition on History of Lab Movement 1956; *Style* - Edward Leadbitter Esq MP; 30 Hylton rd, Hartlepool, Cleveland

LEAHY, Sir John Henry Gladstone; KCMG (1981, CMG 1973); s of late William Henry Gladstone; *b* 7 Feb 1928; *Educ* Tonbridge Sch, Clare Cambridge, Yale; *m* 1954, Elizabeth Anne Pitchford; 2 s, 2 da; *Career* HM Diplomatic Service; Ambass Pretoria 1979-; *Style* - Sir John Leahy, KCMG; c/o Personnel Records Section, Foreign and Commonwealth Office, SW1

LEAKEY, Mary Douglas; FBA (1975); da of Erskine Edward Nicol; *b* 6 Feb 1913; *Educ* privately; *m* 1936, Louis Seymour Bazett Leakey, FBA (d 1972); 3 s; *Career* dir Olduvai Gorge Excavations; *Style* - Miss Mary Leakey; c/o The National Museum, Box 30239, Nairobi, Kenya

LEAPMAN, Hon Mrs; Hon Anne Cynthia Veronica Tempest; da of 2 Viscount Plumer (d 1944); *b* 1921; *m* 1952,

John Frederick Martyn Leapman; 3 da; *Style* - The Hon Mrs Leapman; La Houque Grange, Grouville, Jersey

LEARMOND, Hon Mrs; Hon Virginia Mary; da of Baron Marshall of Leeds (Life Peer); *b* 1949; *m* 1971, Nigel James Alexander Learmond; *Style* - The Hon Mrs Learmond; 52 Marryat rd, Wimbledon SW19

LEARMONTH, Lady; Charlotte Newell; da of F G Bundy, of St Johnsbury, Vermont, USA; *m* 1925, Sir James Rögnvald Learmonth, KCVO, CBE (d 1967); *Style* - Lady Learmonth; 17 Oswald Court, South Oswald rd, Edinburgh EH9 2HY

LEAROYD, Lady Mary Sarah Jane Hope; da of 3 Marquess of Linlithgow, MC; *b* 25 May 1940; *Educ* Heathfield Ascot, Paris; *m* 1967, Michael Gordon Learoyd; 1 s; *Style* - Lady Mary Learoyd

LEASK, Lt-Gen Sir Henry Lowther Ewart Clark; KCB (1970), DSO, OBE; s of Rev James Leask; *b* 30 June 1913; *m* 1940, Zöe de Camborne, da of late Col William Patterson Paynter, DSO, RHA; 1 s, 2 da; *Career* served 1939-45 War, served on General staff in Military Operations Dept War Office 1947-49, dep Military Sec to Sec of State for War 1962-64, dir of Army Training, Min of Defence 1966-69, Lt-Gen 1969, GOC Scotland 1969-72, Gov of Edinburgh Castle 1969, ret 1972; *Style* - Lt-Gen Sir Henry Leask KCB DSO OBE; Duchray House, Aberfoyle, Perthsire

LEATHAM, Philip William; s of Maj Patrick Magor Leatham (d 1950); *b* 30 Aug 1946; *Educ* Eton, Magdalene Cambridge; *m* 1971, The Hon Rowena Margaret, da of 9 Baron Hawke; 1 s, 1 da; *Career* chartered accountant, Christie's Rep in Cheltenham; *Recreations* riding, shooting; *Clubs* Boodle's; *Style* - Philip Leatham Esq; Burleigh Hall, Brimscombe, Stroud, Gloucestershire

LEATHAM, Hon Mrs (Rowena Margaret); *née* Hawke; da of 9 Baron Hawke; *b* 1948; *Educ* Hatherop Castle Sch; *m* 1971, Philip William Leatham; 2 s, 1 da; *Style* - The Hon Mrs Leatham; Burleigh Hall, Brimscombe, Glos

LEATHAM, Lady Victoria Diana; da of 6 Marquess of Exeter by his 2 w, Diana, da of late Hon Arnold Henderson, OBE (s of 1 Baron Faringdon, CH); *b* 1947; *m* 1967, Simon Patrick Leatham; 1 s, 1 da; *Style* - Lady Victoria Leatham; Hayes House, Corbridge, Northumberland

LEATHER, Sir Edwin Hartley Cameron; KCMG (1974), KCVO (1975); s of Harold H Leather, MBE; *b* 1919; *Educ* Trinity Coll Sch Ontario, RMC Kingston Ontario; *m* 1940, Sheila Alexie, da of A H Greenlees; 2 da; *Career* dir Hogg Robinson and Capel-Cure Ltd and subsidiary Cos 1950-64, dir William Baird and Co Ltd 1966-73, chm National Union of Conservative Assocs 1969-70, dep chm of Yehudi Menuhin Sch and Orchestra, pres Institute of Marketing 1963-67, MP (C) Somerset (North Div) 1950-64, Gov and C-in-C Bermuda 1973-77, KStJ (1973), kt 1962; *Style* - Sir Edwin Leather, KCMG KCVO; Mangrove View, Paget, Bermuda

LEATHERLAND, Baron (Life Peer UK 1964); Charles Edward Leatherland; OBE (1951), MSM, JP (Essex 1944); s of John Edward Leatherland (d 1945); *b* 18 Apr 1898; *Educ* Birmingham; *m* 1922, Mary Elizabeth, da of Joseph Henry Morgan, of Shareshill, Staffs; 1 s, 1 da; *Career* v-chm Essex CC 1952-55 and 1958-60, chm 1960-61, chm Finance Ctee 1952-55 and 1958-60; Treasurer and memb Essex U Council 1961-73, memb Basildon Development Corpn 1967-71, memb Monopolies Commission To Consider Newspaper Mergers 1969, DL (1963-75); served WW I, CSM Roy Warwicks Regt; *Style* - The Rt Hon Lord Leatherland, OBE, MSM, JP; 19 Starling close, Buckhurst Hill, Essex (☎ 01 504 3164)

LEATHERLAND, Hon John Charles; s of Baron Leatherland, OBE (Life Peer); *b* 2 July 1929; *Educ* Brentwood; *m* 1954, Esther, da of Mrs Dora Steckman, of London; 2 da; *Style* - The Hon John Leatherland; 4 Manor Way, Chingford Hatch, E4 (☎ 01 529 0347)

LEATHERS, 2 Viscount (UK 1954); Frederick Alan Leathers; also Baron Leathers (UK 1941); s of 1 Viscount Leathers, CH, PC (d 1965); *b* 4 April 1908; *Educ* Brighton Coll, Emmanuel Cambridge; *m* 1940, Elspeth Graeme, da of Sir Thomas Alexander Stewart, KCSI, KCIE (d 1964); 2 s, 2 da; *Heir* s, Hon Christopher Graeme Leathers; *Career* memb Baltic Exchange; former chm of various shipping and cement cos; FRPSL, FRSA, MInstPet; dir Nat Westminster Bank (outer London region); *Clubs* RAC; *Style* - The Rt Hon Viscount Leathers; Huntsmore, Shackleford, Godalming, Surrey (☎ Guildford 810359)

LEATHERS, Hon Christopher Graeme; s and h of 2 Viscount Leathers; *b* 31 Aug 1941; *Educ* Rugby; *m* 1964, Maria Philomena, da of Michael Merriman; 1 s, 1 da; *Style* - The Hon Christopher Leathers

LEATHERS, Hon Jeremy Baxter; s of 2 Viscount Leathers; *b* 11 Apr 1946; *Educ* Rugby, Trinity Coll Dublin; *m* 1969, Fiona Lesley, da of George Stanhope Pitt; 1 da; *Style* - The Hon Jeremy Leathers; 1 Burnsall st, SW3 (☎ 01 352 2556)

LEATHERS, Hon Leslie John; s of 1 Viscount Leathers, PC (d 1965); *b* 25 Nov 1911; *Educ* Brighton Coll; *m* 1937, Elizabeth Stella, da of Thomas Stanley Nash (d 1964); 2 s, 1 da; *Career* Lt-Col (AQMG) Staff Coll 1943, slr 1934, memb Council London Chamber of Commerce 1955-65, gen commissioner of income tax 1958-75, memb of Worshipful Co of Coachmakers and Coach Harness Makers; *Clubs* Brooks's, Hurlingham, Rand (Johannesburg); *Style* - The Hon Leslie Leathers; 127 Cranmer Court, Sloane ave, London SW3 (☎ 01 589 0697)

LEAVER, Hon Mrs; Hon Margaret Cavendish; da of 6 Baron Waterpark (d 1949); *b* 1907; *m* 1934, Wallace Thomas Leaver, BSc (d 1972); 2 da; *Style* - The Hon Mrs Leaver; St Benets, Beech Hill, Bridge, Canterbury, Kent

LEAVETT-SHENLEY, John; s of Ernest Leavett-Shenley (d 1974); *b* 21 May 1930; *m* 1961, Alison Yvonne, da of Cdr Hon Henry Cecil (d 1962); 2 s, 1 da; *Career* Welsh Guards 1948-53, farmer and forester, pres Devon Cattle Breeders Soc 1978; *Recreations* racing, breeding, bloodstock, shooting; *Clubs* Cavalry and Guards, Welsh Guards; *Also* John Leavett-Shenley Esq; *Style* - The Holt; Upham, nr Southampton, Hants (☎ Bishops Waltham 3452)

LEAVEY, John Anthony; *Career* chm Wilson (Connolly) Holdings Ltd; dir Smith & Nephew Assoc Co Ltd; dir Flakt Ltd; *Style* - John Leavey Esq; Wilson (Connolly) Holdings Ltd, Thomas Wilson House, Tenter rd, Moulton Park, Northampton NN3 IQT

LEBUS, Hon Mrs; Hon Christina; da of 2 Baron Strathalmond, CMG, OBE, TD (d 1976); *b* 1954; *m* 1974, Timothy Andrew Lebus; *Style* - The Hon Mrs Lebus

LECHMERE, Sir Berwick Hungerford; 6 Bt (UK 1818), JP (Worcs 1966); s of Capt Sir Ronald Berwick Hungerford Lechmere, 5 Bt (d 1965); *b* 1917; *Educ* Charterhouse, Magdalene Cambridge; *m* 1954, Norah Garrett, da of Col C G Elkington, DSO; *Heir* kinsman, Reginald Anthony Hungerford Lechmere; *Career* High Sheriff Worcs 1962, Vice Ld-Lt Hereford and Worcester 1977- (DL 1972), FRICS, CStJ (1980); the estate known as Severn End has been held by the Lechmere family from the close of the eleventh century to the present day; *Style* - Sir Berwick Lechmere, Bt, JP, HM Vice Lord-Lieut for Hereford & Worcester; Severn End, Hanley Castle, Worcester (☎ Upton-on-Severn 2130)

LECHMERE, Reginald Anthony Hungerford; s of late Anthony Hungerford Lechmere (d 1954); hp of kinsman, Sir Berwick Hungerford Lechmere, 6 Bt; *b* 24 Dec 1920; *Educ* Charterhouse, Trin Hall Cambridge; *m* 1956, Anne Jennifer, da of late A C Dind, of Orbe, Switzerland; 3 s, 1 da; *Career* formerly Capt 5 Royal Inniskilling Dragoon Gds; *Style* - Reginald Lechmere

Esq; Primeswell, Evendine Lane, Colwall, nr Malvern, Worcs

LEDGER, Sir Frank (Joseph Francis); s of late Edson Ledger; *b* 29 Oct 1899; *Educ* Perth Boys' Sch; *m* 1923, Gladys Muriel, da of late Charles Oliver Lyons; 1 s, 2 da; *Career* pres J & E Ledger Pty Ltd, J & E Ledger Sales Pty Ltd, Ledger Electrics Pty Ltd, chm Winget Moxey Pty Ltd, governing dir Ledger Investments, chm South Australian Insurance Co (WA), dir Lake View & Star Ltd, Chamber of Manufacturers Insurance Co, A R C Engineering Co WA, chm W Australian Govt Industrial Development Advisory Ctee, past pres W Australian chamber of Manufacturers, pres WA Trotting Assoc, v-pres Australian Trotting Cncl, kt 1963; *Style* - Sir Frank Ledger; 2 The Esplanade, Peppermint Grove, W Australia

LEDWIDGE, Sir William Bernard John; KCMG (1974); s of Charles Bernard Arthur Ledwidge (d 1945); *b* 9 Nov 1915; *Educ* Cardinal Vaughan Sch, King's Cambridge, Princeton U USA; *m* 1, 1948, Anne (m dis 1970), da of George Henry Kingsley (d 1959); 1 s, 1 da; m 2, Flora, da of André Groult (d 1967); *Career* entered India Office 1939, FO 1948, First Secretary Kabul 1952-56, political advsr British Mil Govt Berlin 1956-61, Counsellor Foreign Office 1959, head of Western Dept Foreign Office 1963-65, Min British Embassy Paris 1965-69, Ambass to Finland 1969-72, Ambass to Israel 1972-75, chm United Kingdom Ctee for UNICEF 1976-, memb Police Complaints Board 1977; *Style* - Sir William Ledwidge, KCMG; 54 rue de Bourgogne, 75007 Paris (☎ 705 3026); 19 Queen's Gate ter, SW7 (☎ 01 584 4132)

LEE OF NEWTON, Baron (Life Peer UK 1974); Frederick Lee; PC (1964); s of Joseph William Lee (d 1962); *b* 3 Aug 1906; *Educ* Langworthy Road Sch; *m* 1938, Amelia, da of William Shay; 1 da; *Career* engr; memb Salford City Council, JP (Salford 1946), MP (L) Manchester (Hulme Div) 1945-50, Lancashire (Newton Div) 1950-74, parly sec to Min of Labour and National Service 1950-51, memb UK Delegation to Council of Europe 1949, Min of Power 1964-66, sec of State for the Colonies 1966-67, Chancellor of Duchy of Lancaster 1967-69; *Style* - The Rt Hon Lord Lee of Newton, PC, JP; 52 Ashton rd, Newton-le-Willows, Merseyside (☎ 5012)

LEE OF ASHERIDGE, Baroness (Life Peeress UK 1970); Jennie; PC (1966); da of James Lee, of Fifeshire; *b* 3 Nov 1904; *Educ* Moray House Coll, Beath H S, Edinburgh U; *m* 1934, Rt Hon Aneurin Bevan, MP (d 1960); *Career* MP (L) Lanarkshire (N Div) 1929-31, Staffordshire (Cannock Div) 1945-70, memb Central Housing Advisory Ctee & NEC 1958-70 (Chm 1967-68) Labour Party (V-Chm 1966-67), Parly Sec Miny Public Building and Works 1964-65; Jt Parly Under-Sec of State, Dept of Education and Science 1965-67; Min of State, Dept of Educn and Science 1967-70; dir Tribune; Books *Our Ally Russia* (1941), *My Life with Nye* (1980); *Style* - The Rt Hon Lady Lee of Asheridge, PC; 67 Chester Row, SW1 (☎ 01 730 1758)

LEE, Sir Arthur James; KBE (1966), MC; s of late A J Lee, of Dulwich, S Australia; *b* 1912; *Educ* Collegiate Sch of St Peter's; *m* 1945, Valerie Scanlan; 3 s, 1 da; *Career* served Second World War, Nat Pres Returned Services League Australia 1960-74 (State Pres 1954-60); *Style* - Sir Arthur Lee, KBE, MC; 2 Arthur st, Toorak gdns, S Australia 5065

LEE, Hon Mrs; Hon Doris; da of Baron Williams of Barnburgh (Life Peer; d 1967); *b* 1916; *m* 1939, Robert Kesteven Lee (d 1967); *Style* - The Hon Mrs Lee; 346 Thorne rd, Doncaster

LEE, Air Chief Marshal Sir David John Pryer; GBE (1969), CB (1953); s of late John Lee; *b* 1912; *Educ* Bedford Sch, RAF Coll Cranwell; *m* 1938, Denise, da of late Louis Hartoch; 1 s, 1 da; *Career* joined RAF 1930, served 1939-45 War, Cmdt RAF Staff Coll Bracknell 1962-64, Air Memb for Personnel 1965-68, UK Mil Rep NATO 1968-71; ret 1971; chm Grants Ctee, RAF Benevolent Fund 1971-; exec ctee Nuffield Tst for Armed Forces 1975-; *Style* - Air Chief Marshal Sir David Lee GBE CB; Danemore Cottage, Danemore lane, South Godstone, Surrey (☎ 3162)

LEE, Sir (Henry) Desmond Pritchard; s of late Rev Canon Henry Burgass Lee, of Nottingham; *b* 1908; *Educ* Repton, C C C Cambridge; *m* 1935, Elizabeth, da of late Col A Crookenden; 1 s, 2 da; *Career* U lecturer in Classics Cambridge 1937-48, headmaster Clifton 1948-54, Winchester 1954-68, chm Headmaster's Conference 1959-60 and 1967, memb Secondary Schools Examination Council and Schools Council 1952-68, pres Hughes Hall Cambridge 1974-78; kt 1961 *Style* - Sir Desmond Lee; 8 Barton Close, Cambridge

LEE, David Stanley Wilton; s of Col Kenneth C Lee, TD (d 1964); *b* 17 Sept 1933; *Educ* Uppingham, Queen's Cambridge; *m* 1957, Jennifer Ann, da of Col John P Hunt, TD (d 1971); 3 s, 2 da; *Career* Nat Service and TA, Capt RE, steel manufacturer, dir Arthur Lee & Sons 1965-, Halifax Building Soc 1977-, Iron Trades Insurance 1978-; *Recreations* golf, shooting, fishing, farming; *Clubs* Sheffield; *Style* - David Lee Esq; West Hays, Whiteley, Wood rd, Sheffield (☎ Sheffield 301 633)

LEE, Col Tun Sir Henry Hau Shik; KBE (1957, CBE 1948), JP (Kuala Lumpar 1938); s of K L Lee; *b* 19 Nov 1901; *Educ* Queen's Coll Hong Kong, Cambridge U; *m* 1, 1922 (w d 1926); 1 s; m 2, 1929, Choi Lin (née Kwan); 4 s, 2 da (1 s, decd); *Career* chm Development & Commercial Bank Ltd, China Press Ltd, Chartered Bank (M) Trustee Berhad, KL Golden Castle Finance Corpn (M) Berhad, On Thai Development Sdn Berhad, Board of Governors of Lady Templer Hosp, Kuala Lumpur D&C Monura Merchant Bankers Berhad, Sole Proprietor of H S Lee Tin Mines Malaya, v-chm Inst Bank Malaysia 1977-; *Style* - Col Tun Sir Henry Lee KBE JP; 22 Jalan Langgak Golf, Kuala Lumpur, Malaysia

LEE, John Robert Louis; MP (C) Nelson and Colne 1979-; s of Basil Lee; *b* 21 June 1942; *Educ* William Hulme's G S Manchester; *m* 1975, Anne Monique Bakirgian; 2 da; *Career* founding dir Chancery Consolidated Ltd Investment Bankers, political sec to Rt Hon Robert Carr (now Lord Carr of Hadley) 1974, contested (C) Manchester (Moss Side) Oct 1974, dir Paterson Zochonis (UK) Ltd 1975-76, v-chm NW Conciliation Ctee Race Relations Board 1976-77; *Style* - John Lee Esq, MP; 1 The Gateways, Whitehead's Grove, SW3 (☎ 01 589 6153)

LEE, His Honour Judge John Thomas Cyril; s of Cyril Lee (d 1974); *b* 14 Jan 1927; *Educ* Holly Lodge G S, Emmanuel Cambridge; *m* 1956, Beryl, da of John T Haden (d 1959); 1 s, 3 da; *Career* HM Forces 1945-48, barr Gray's Inn 1952, a circuit judge 1972-; *Style* - His Honour Judge John Lee; The Red House, Upper Colwall, Malvern, Worcs

LEE, Lady; Kathleen Mary; da of late W F Harris; *m* 1937, Rt Hon Sir Frank Godbould Lee, GCMG, KCB (d 1971); *Style* - Lady Lee; Newnham Path, Church Rate Walk, Cambridge

LEE, Sir (George) Wilton; TD (1940); s of Percy W Lee, of Tapton Holt, Sheffield; *b* 8 Apr 1904; *Educ* Uppingham, Queens' Cambridge; *m* 1934, Bettina Stanley, da of Col R B Haywood, TD; 3 s; *Career* chm and md Arthur Lee & Sons Ltd and Gp of Cos 1949-68, pres 1976-; memb Exec Ctee British Iron & Steel Federation 1953-67, chm S Yorks Industrialists' Council, chm S Yorks Board of Eagle Star Insurance Co Ltd 1948-74; Master, Cutlers' Co in Hallamshire 1950-51, JP (1950-64) Sheffield, chm City of Sheffield Conservative & National Liberal Federation 1959-70, v-consul for Norway, Chev Order of St Olav (Norway); *Style* - Sir Wilton Lee, TD; Thornfield, Lindrick Common, Worksop, Notts (☎ Dinnington 2810)

LEE, Col Sir William Allison; OBE (1945), TD (1948), DL (Co Durham 1965) Durham; s of Samuel Lee (d 1939); *b* 31 May 1907; *Educ* Queen Elizabeth G S Darlington; *m* 1, 1933, Elsa Norah (d 1966), da of Thomas Hanning; m 2, 1967, Mollie Clifford, da of Sir Cuthbert Whiteside; *Career* served Roy Signals 1935-53, dep Cdr 151 Inf Bde 1953-58, chm Newcastle Regional Hospital Board 1970-73, chm Northern Regional Health Authority 1973-78; High Sheriff 1978, memb cncl CStJ (1980); kt 1975; *Style* - Col Sir William Lee OBE TD DL; Candle House, Low Row, Richmond, Yorks (☎ Gunnerside 86207); The Woodlands, Woodlands rd, Darlington, Co Durham (☎ 62318)

LEE POTTER, Air Marshal Sir Patrick Brunton; KBE (1958); s of Samuel Lee Potter; *b* 1904; *Educ* Epsom Coll, Sheffield U; *m* 1933, Audrey Mary, da of H Pollock; 2 s; *Career* Joined RAF 1928, served 1939-45 War, Dir-Gen RAF Medical Services 1957-62, KStJ; *Style* - Air Marshal Sir Patrick Lee Potter KBE; Barge Cottage, Rolvenden, Cranbrook, Kent (☎ Wittersham 217)

LEE-BARBER, Rear-Adm John; CB (1959), DSO (1940) and Bar (1941); s of Richard Lee-Barber (d 1960); *b* 16 Apr 1905; *Educ* R N Colls Osborne, Dartmouth; *m* 1939, Suzanne Claude (d 1976), da of Col Albert Le Gallais, ADC, MC; 2 da; *Career* joined RN 1919, served 1939-45 in HMS 'Griffin', 'Opportune' and 'King Alfrd Co', 'St James' 1946-47, sen officer Reserve Fleet Harwich 1948-49, Naval Attaché Chile 1950-52, Co 'Agincourt' and Capt D4 1952-54, Commodore, Inshore Flotilla 1954-56, Adm Supt H M Dockyard, Malta 1957, ret 1959, Polish Cross of Valour 1940; *Style* - Rear-Adm John Lee-Barber CB,DSO,*; Ferry House, The Quay, Wivenhoe, Essex (☎ Wivenhoe 2592)

LEE-STEERE, Sir Ernest (Henry); KBE (1977, CBE 1963), JP; s of Sir Ernest Lee-Steer; *b* 22 Dec 1912; *Educ* Hale Sch Perth, St Peter's Coll Adelaide; *m* 1942, Jessica Margaret, da of Frank Venn; 2 s, 3 da; *Career* Capt Army/Air Liaison Gp AIF, SW Pacific Area 1944-45, Lord Mayor of Perth W Australia 1972-78, co dir, pastoralist and grazier; *Style* - Sir Ernest Lee-Steere KBE JP; Dardanup, 26 Odern cres, Swanbourne, WA 6010, Australia

LEECH, His Honour Judge; Robert Radcliffe; s of Edwin Radcliffe Leech (d 1947); *b* 5 Dec 1919; *Educ* Monmouth Sch, Worcester Oxford; *m* 1951, Vivienne Ruth, da of A J Rickerby; 2 da; *Career* served 1940-44 in Border regiment, barr Middle Temple 1949, a dep chm Cumberland quarter sessions 1966, a county court judge 1970, Circuit judge 1971; *Style* - His Honour Judge Leech; Brackenrigg, Bassenthwaite, Keswick, Cumbria

LEECHMAN, Hon Lord; James Graham Leechman; s of Walter Graham Leechman (d 1943); *b* 1906; *Educ* Glasgow H S, Glasgow U; *m* 1935, Margaret Helen, da of late Thomas Wilson Edgar, of Glasgow; *Career* served 1941-45 with RAF, Socttish advocate 1932, Advocate-Depute 1947, Clerk of Justiciary and KC 1949, Solicitor-Gen for Scotland 1964, a senator of College of Justice in Scotland (with judicial title of Hon Lord Leechman) 1965-76; *Style* - The Hon Lord Leechman; 626 Queensferry rd, Barnton, Edinburgh EH4 6AT (☎ 031 339 6513)

LEEDS, Christopher Anthony; s of late Maj Geoffrey Hugh Anthony Leeds (d 1962); hp of kinsman, Sir Graham Mortimer Leeds, 7 Bt; *b* 31 Aug 1935; *Educ* King's Sch Bruton, London U, U of S Cal USA; *m* 1974, Elaine Joyce, da of late Squadron Leader C H A Mullins; *Style* - Christopher Leeds Esq; Croxton, 39 Rabling rd, Swanage, Dorset

LEEDS, Capt Sir George Graham Mortimer; 7 Bt (UK 1812); s of Cdr Sir Reginald Arthur St John Leeds, 6 Bt, RN (d 1970); *b* 1927; *Educ* Eton; *m* 1954, Nicola (m dis 1965, she d 1972), da of H Pollock; *Heir* cousin, Christopher Anthony Leeds; *Career* Grenadier Gds 1946, memb London Stock Exchange, chm Clive Investments (Jersey) 1977-; *Style* - Capt Sir George Leeds, Bt; Roche Bois, Mont ès Tours, St Aubin, Jersey, CI

LEEPER, Richard John Desmond; *Career* chm and md LEP Gp Ltd; *Style* - Richard Leeper Esq; LEP Gp Ltd, Sunlight Wharf, Upper Thames st, London EC4

LEES, Col Brian Musson; MVO (1979), OBE (1978); s of John Lees (d 1978); *b* 9 Oct 1931; *Educ* Queen Elizabeth G S, Tamworth-Leeds U; *m* 1963, Diana Caroline, da of John Harold Everall; 2 da; *Career* served in Kenya, Cyprus, Arabian

Peninsula; CO 5 Batallion the Light Infantry 1971-73, defence attaché Jedda 1975-79, defence intelligence staff MOD 1979-; publication *The Al Sa'ud, Ruling Family of Saudi Arabia*; *Recreations* music, gardening, reading; *Clubs* Army and Navy, MCC, L'Association Francaise de Frisbee; *Style* - Col Brian Lees, MVO, OBE; The Old Rectory, Kenley, Shropshire (☎ Acton Burnell 281)

LEES, Christopher James; s and h of Sir Thomas Edward Lees, 4 Bt; *b* 4 Nov 1952; *Educ* Eton, Edinburgh U; *m* 1977, Jennifer, da of John Wyllie, of Newton Stewart Wigtownshire; *Style* - Christopher Lees Esq

LEES, His Honour Judge; Charles Norman; s of Charles Lees; *b* 4 Oct 1929; *Educ* Stockport Sch, U of Leeds; *m* 1961, Stella, da of Hubert Swann; 1 da; *Career* barr Lincoln's Inn 1951, a dep chm Cumberland quarter sesiions 1969-72, a recorder of Crown Court 1972-80, a Circuit Judge 1980-, a legal chm of Disciplinary Ctee of the Potato Marketing Board 1965, memb Mental Health Review Tribunal Manchester Region 1971; *Style* - His Honour Judge Lees; 5 Essex Court, Temple EC4; 102 Heathbank rd, Cheadle Hulme, Cheadle, Cheshire (☎ 061 485 3973; 1 Deans Court, Crown sq, Manchester 3

LEES, Lady; Dorothy Gertrude; da of Francis Alexander Lauder; *m* 1930, Sir William Hereward Clare Lees, 2 Bt (d 1976); *Style* - Lady Lees; The Lodge, Beechland, Newick, Lewes, Sussex

LEES, Helen Lady; Helen Agnes Marion; da of late Charles C Chittick and widow of Thomas Orr Gibb; *m* 1927, Sir Arthur Henry James Lees, 5 Bt (d 1949); *Style* - Helen, Lady Lees; 3 Valsayn ave, Valsayn Park, Curepe, Trinidad

LEES, John Cathcart; s of late John Rutherford D'Olier-Lees; hp of kinsman, Sir Thomas Harcourt Ivor Lees, 8 Bt; *b* 12 Nov 1927; *m* 1957, Wendy Garrold, da of late Brian Garrold Groom, of Edinburgh; 2 s; *Career* formerly Lt 12 Bn Border Regiment and SAS Regiment (Artists Rifles) TA; *Style* - John Lees Esq; 5 Pound close, Ringwood, Hants

LEES, Air Marshal Sir Ronald Beresford; KCB (1961, CBE 1943), DFC (1940); s of John Thomas Lees, of Adelaide; *b* 1910; *Educ* St Peter's Coll Adelaide; *m* 1931, Rhoda Lillie, da of Arthur Pank of Adelaide; 1 s, 1 da; *Career* joined RAF 1931, assist Ch of Air Staff (Operations) 1955-58, SASO Fighter Command 1958-60, dep ch of Air Staff 1960, Air Marshal 1961, C-in-C RAF Germany 1963-65, ret 1966, air ADC to HM the King 1943-52, to HM the Queen 1952-53; *Style* - Air Marshal Sir Ronald Lees, KCB, DFC; Jelbra, RMB 367 via Albury, Australia

LEES, Sir Thomas Edward; 4 Bt (UK 1897), JP (Dorset 1951); s of Col Sir John Victor Elliott Lees, 3 Bt, DSO, MC (d 1955); *b* 1925; *Educ* Eton, Magdalene Cambridge; *m* 1949, Faith Justin, JP (1963) Dorset, da of Gaston Jessiman; 1 s, 3 da; *Heir* s, Christopher James Lees; *Career* served with RAF 1943-45, High Sheriff of Dorset 1960; *Style* - Sir Thomas Lees, Bt, JP; Post Green, Lytchett Minster, Dorset (☎ Lytchett Minster 2317)

LEES, Sir Thomas Harcourt Ivor; 8 Bt (UK 1804), of Black Rock, County Dublin; s of Sir Charles Archibald Edward Ivor Lees, 7 Bt (d 1963); *b* 6 Nov 1941; *Heir* kinsman, John Cathcart D'Olier-Lees; *Style* - Sir Thomas Lees, Bt; c/o Mrs Henry Knight; 5 Cricket Field rd, Horsham, Sussex

LEES, Sir William Antony Clare; 3 Bt (UK 1937); s of Sir William Hereward Clare Lees, 2 Bt (d 1976); *b* 14 June 1935; *Educ* Eton, Magdalene Cambridge; *Heir* none; *Style* - Sir William Lees, Bt; Waterside Cottage, New Mill, Pewsey, Wilts

LEES-SPALDING, Rear-Adm Ian Jaffery; CB (1973); s of Frank Souter Lees-Spalding (d 1970); *b* 16 June 1920; *Educ* Blundells; *m* 1946, June Sandys Lyster, da of Maj Warren Lyster Sparkes, of Devon; 2 da; *Career* joined RN 1938, awarded commendation 1940, joined Submarines 1945, ch staff officer (Technical) to C-in-C Fleet and Insp Gen

Fleet Maintenance 1971, ret 1974, ADC 1971, administrator London Int Film Sch 1975-79; *Clubs* Army and Navy; *Style* - Rear-Adm Ian Lees-Spalding, CB; St Olaf's, Wonston, Winchester, Hants (☎ Sutton Scotney 249)

LEESE, Douglas Sims; *Career* chm Cam Gears Ltd, Wraxall Hydraulics Ltd, Wraxall Traders Ltd; dir House of Wraxall Ltd, Moulton Developments Ltd, Sheepbridge Engineering Ltd, Steetley Co Ltd, TRW Valves Ltd, Tornilleria Fina Navaar SA Spain, Ventek Ltd, Wraxall Services Ltd; memb IOD; *Style* - Douglas Leese Esq; South Wraxall Manor, Bradford on Avon, Wilts

LEESE, Sir John Henry Vernon; 5 Bt (UK 1908); s of late Vernon Francis Leese, OBE, 2 s of 1 Bt; suc kinsman, Sir Alexander William Leese, 4 Bt, 1979; *b* 7 Aug 1901; *Heir* none; *Style* - Sir John Leese, Bt

LEFROY, Lady; Callista; da of Leon Courouble, of France; *m* Sir Anthony Langlois Bruce Lefroy, MC (d 1958); *Style* - Lady Lefroy; 258, St George's ter, Perth, W Australia

LEGARD, Charles Thomas; s and h of Sir Thomas Digby Legard, 14 Bt; *b* 26 Oct 1938; *Educ* Eton; *m* 1962, Elizabeth, da of John M Guthrie, of Church Meadows, Hutton Buscel, Scarborough; 2 s, 1 da; *Career* MInstM; *Style* - Charles Legard Esq Bishopton Grange, Ripon, Yorks

LEGARD, Capt Sir Thomas Digby; 14 Bt (E 1660); s of Sir Digby Algernon Hall Legard, 13 Bt (d 1961); *b* 16 Oct 1905; *Educ* Lancing, Magdalene Cambridge; *m* 1935, Mary Helen, JP (E Riding Yorks 1965), da of Lt-Col Edmund L'Estrange-Malone, JP (d 1955), of Scampston Hall, Malton, North Yorkshire; 3 s; *Heir* s, Charles Thomas Legard; *Career* Capt RA; *Style* - Capt Sir Thomas Legard, Bt; Scampston Hall, Malton, North Yorks (☎ Rillington 224)

LEGG, Laurence; s of Samuel Legg (d 1949); *b* 14 Nov 1906; *Educ* Strand; *m* 1950, Margaret, nee Baker; 1 da; *Career* Fl Lt RAF, offr cmding Air Sea Rescue Units Lowestoft, Gt Yarmouth, Ramsgate, Littlehampton and Newhaven, slr pres Sussex Motor Yacht, first Cdre Law Soc Yacht Club, former memb Gen Purposes Ctee Roy Yachting Assoc; *Recreations* yachting ('Solveig'); *Style* - Laurence Legg Esq; Loja, Hurstpierpoint, Sussex (☎ 073 833434); c/o Weeks Legg & Dean, 4 Pavilion Bldgs, Brighton, E Sussex (☎ 27241)

LEGGATT, Lady; Dorothy Meares; Henry Andrews; *m* 1926, Col the Hon Sir William Watt Leggatt, DSO, MC, ED (d 1968); *Style* - Lady Legatt; 36 Herbert st, Mornington, Vic 3931, Australia

LEGGE, Lady Charlotte; da of 9 Earl of Dartmouth; *b* 16 July 1963; *Style* - Lady Charlotte Legge

LEGGE, Hon Henry; s of 9 Earl of Dartmouth; *b* 1968; *Style* - The Hon Henry Legge

LEGGE, Hon Rupert; s of 9 Earl of Dartmouth; *b* 1 Jan 1951; *Educ* Eton, Ch Ch Oxford; *Style* - The Hon Rupert Legge

LEGGE-BOURKE, Lady; Catherine Jean; da of late Col Sir Arthur Grant of Monymusk, 10 Bt, CBE, DSO; *b* 18 Aug 1917; *m* 1938, Maj Sir Harry (Edward Alexander Henry) Legge-Bourke, KBE, MP, DL (d 1973); 2 s (William Nigel Henry, b 1939, m 1964, Hon Shân Baillie, da of 3 Baron Glanusk; Heneage, b 1948, m 1978 Clara Sa Carneiro), 1 da (Victoria, b 1950); *Style* - Lady Legge-Bourke; 121 Dovehouse st, SW3

LEGGE-BOURKE, Hon Mrs; Hon Elizabeth Shân Josephine; da of 3 Baron Glanusk, DSO (d 1948); *b* 1943; *m* 1964, Capt William Nigel Henry Legge-Bourke (s of Sir Harry Legge-Bourke, sometime MP Ely, whose f Nigel Walter Henry, ka 1914, was s of Hon Sir Henry Legge, GCVO (2 s of 5 Earl of Dartmouth), and m Lady Victoria Wynn-Carrington, yst da of 1 & last Marquess of Lincolnshire); *Career* extra Lady-in-Waiting to HRH The Princess Anne, Mrs Mark Phillips 1978-; *Style* - The Hon Mrs Legge-Bourke; Glanusk Park, Crickhowell, Powys

LEGGETT, Sir Clarence Arthur Campbell; *Career* surgeon; kt 1980; *Style* - Sir Clarence Legett

LEGGETT, Sir Frederick William; KBE (1951), CB (1933; s of late Frederick John Leggett; *b* 1884; *Educ* City of London Sch, King's Coll London; *m* 1, 1913, Edith Guinevere (d 1949), da of Henry Kitson; 1 s, 3 da; m 2, 1957, Beatrice Melville (who m 1914, John Mortimer Sheppard, d 1956), da of late Joseph Roe; *Career* entered Civil Service 1904, chm of governing body of Int Labour organisation 1937-38, principal assist sec Min of Lab 1931-39, Ch Industrial Commissioner 1940-42, jt dep sec Min of Lab and Nat Service 1942-45, memb British Reparations Mission Moscow 1945, Anglo-American Palestine Ctee of Inquiry 1946, chm London and South-Eastern Region Board for Industry 1947-49, chm London Docks Disputes Inquiry Ctee 1950, chm Building Apprenticeship and Training Cncl 1953-55; kt 1941; *Style* - Sir Frederick Leggett; Downside Lodge, W Kingston, Sussex

LEGH, Hon David Piers Carlis; s of 4 Baron Newton; *b* 1951; *Educ* Eton, Royal Agricultural Coll Cirencester; *m* 1974, Jane Mary, da of John Roy Wynter Bee, of Heather Hills, West End, Woking, Surrey; 1 da; *Style* - The Hon David Legh; The Round House, Poulton, Cirencester, Glos

LEGH, Maj Hon Sir Francis Michael; KCVO (1968); s of 3 Baron Newton (d 1960); *b* 1919; *Educ* Eton, RMC; *m* 1948, Ruadh Daphne (d 1973), da of late Alan Holmes-Watson; 1 s, 1 da; *Career* Maj Grenadier Gds, served in Italy, GSO (2) British Mil Mission, Greece, assist private sec and equerry to HM Queen Elizabeth the Queen Mother 1956-59, equerry 1956-; private sec to HRH Princess Margaret, Countess of Snowdon 1959-62, private sec and treasurer 1962-71, treasurer 1971-; *Style* - Maj Hon Sir Francis Legh; Orchard House, Littlestone-on-Sea, New Romney, Kent (☎ New Romney 3167)

LEGH, Hon Richard Thomas; s and h of 4 Baron Newton; *b* 11 Jan 1950; *Educ* Eton, Ch Ch Oxford; *m* 1978, Rosemary, da of Herbert Clarke, of Eastbourne; 1 s; *Style* - The Hon Richard Legh; 101 Eton Rise, Eton College rd, NW3

LEHMANN, John Frederick; CBE (1964); s of Rudolph Lehmann and bro of Rosamond Lehmann, *qv*; *b* 2 June 1907; *Educ* Eton, Trin Cambridge; *Career* FRSL; ed London Magazine from founding to 1961, md John Lehmann Ltd from foundation to 1952; founder ed New Writing; ptnr & gen man Hogarth Press 1938-; *Style* - John Lehmann Esq, CBE; 85 Cornwall gdns, SW7

LEHMANN, Rosamond Nina; da of Rudolph Chambers Lehmann and sis of John Lehmann; *Educ* privately and Girton Cambridge; *m* 1, 1923 (m dis 1928), 2 Viscount Runciman of Doxford (then plain Walter Runciman); m 2, 1928 (m dis 1944), as his 1 w, Wogan Philipps (later Hon Wogan Philipps and later still 2 Baron Milford); 1 s (Hon Hugo Philipps), 1 da (Sarah, d 1958 having m the poet and novelist P(atrick) J Kavanagh); *Career* novelist, best known for the markedly autobiographical *Dusty Answer*, also *The Weather in the Streets*; *Style* - Miss Rosamond Lehmann; 70 Eaton sq, SW1

LEICESTER, 6 Earl of (UK 1837); Anthony Lovel Coke; the full designation of the Earldom is Earl of Leicester of Holkham (which prompted the great 19 century Peerage commentator G[eoffrey]E C[okayne] to draw a slighting parallel with Westmorland of Wormwood Scrubs and to apostrophise Simon de Montfort and his Earldom of Leicester); also Viscount Coke (UK 1837); s of Lt Hon Arthur Coke (2 s of 3 Earl, whose gf, before his creation as (1) Earl, was supposedly offered a Peerage no fewer than seven times, by six different Prime Ministers, either as rewards (if by Whigs) or as bribes (if by Tories); the penultimate offer (by Lord Grey) 'Mr Coke of Norfolk', as he was known, accepted; however, on this occasion it was the king (William IV) who did the refusing, feeling incensed at an intemperate reference to George III that Coke had made the previous year when replying to a toast at a public dinner; long dubbed the 'First Commoner of England', he was literally the first such to be honoured with ennoblement by Queen

Victoria; while noted for his good looks and great physical strength, he was also an astute agriculturist, increasing rents from his estates nearly tenfold and making the Holkham area abundant in corn & timber where before it had been an importer of the one & destitute of the other); suc 1 cous 1976; *b* 11 Sept 1909; *Educ* Gresham's; *m* 1, 1934 (m dis 1947), Moyra, da of Douglas Crossley; 2 s, 1 da; m 2, 1947, Vera, da of Herbert Haigh, of Salisbury, Rhodesia (now Zimbabwe); *Heir* s, Viscount Coke; *Career* served WW II RAF; rancher, now farmer; *Style* - The Rt Hon Earl of Leicester; Mhowani, PO Box 529, Plettenberg Bay, Cape Province 6600, S Africa

LEICESTER, Elizabeth, Countess of; Lady Elizabeth Mary Yorke; DCVO (1973); da of 8 Earl of Hardwicke (d 1936); *b* 1912; *Educ* North Foreland Lodge Kent; *m* 1931, 5 Earl of Leicester, MVO (d 1976); 3 da (Lady Anne Tennant, Lady Carey Basset, Lady Sarah Walter); *Career* a lady of the bedchamber to HM the Queen 1953-73; *Style* - The Rt Hon Elizabeth, Countess of Leicester, DCVO; The Parsonage House, Burnham Thorpe, King's Lynn, Norfolk

LEICESTER, Lady; Marthe; da of Louis de Miéville de Rossens; *m* 1930, as his 2 w, Sir Peter Fleming Frederic Leicester, 8 Bt (d 1945); *Style* - Lady Leicester; Shearwater, Downderry, Cornwall

LEIGH, 5 Baron (UK 1839); John Piers Leigh; s of 4 Baron Leigh (d 1979) and Anne, da of Ellis Hicks Beach (himself nephew of 1 Earl St Aldwyn); *b* 11 Sept 1935; *Educ* Eton, Oriel Oxford, London U; *m* 1, 1957, Cecilia Poppy (m dis 1974), da of late Robert Cecil Jackson; 1 s, 1 da (& 1 da decd); m 2, 1976, Susan, da of John Cleave, of Whitnash, Leamington Spa; 1 s; *Heir* s, Hon Christopher Dudley Piers Leigh; *Style* - The Rt Hon the Lord Leigh; Stoneleigh Abbey, Kenilworth, Warwickshire (☎ Kenilworth 53981)

LEIGH, Hon Benjamin Chandos; s of 4 Baron Leigh, TD (d 1979); *b* 1942; *Educ* Eton *m* 1979, Jennifer Vivian, da of late Capt Peter Winser and formerly w of Hon Richard Henry Strutt; 1 da; *Style* - The Hon Benjamin Leigh

LEIGH, Hon Camilla Anne; da of 5 Baron Leigh; *b* 1962; *Style* - The Hon Camilla Leigh

LEIGH, Hon Christopher Dudley Piers; s and h of 5 Baron Leigh; *b* 1960; *Style* - The Hon Christopher Leigh; Stoneleigh Abbey, Kenilworth, Warwicks

LEIGH, Eric; s of Sir John Leigh, 1 Bt (d 1959) and hp of bro Sir John Leigh, 2 Bt; *b* 13 April 1913; *Educ* Radley; *m* 1, 1934, Joan Fitzgerald Lane, da of M C L Freer (m dis 1939); 1 s; m 2, 1939, Mary Babette, da of late J H Jaques; 1 s; *Career* European War 1939-44 as Lt-Cdr RNVR; *Style* - Eric Leigh Esq; Childrey Manor, nr Wantage, Berks

LEIGH, Geoffrey Norman; s of Morris Leigh; *b* 23 March 1933; *Educ* Haberdashers' Aske's; *m* 1976, Sylvia, nee King; 5 c; *Career* industrialist, dep chm and md Allied London Properties Ltd, dir Sterling Homes Holdings Ltd; *Clubs* RAC, Hurlingham; *Style* - Geoffrey Leigh Esq; 3 Manchester sq, W1 (☎ 01 486 1661)

LEIGH, Sir John; 2 Bt (UK 1918); s of Sir John Leigh, 1 Bt (1959); *b* 24 March 1909; *Educ* Eton, Balliol Oxford; *m* 1959, Ariane, da of late Joseph William Allen, of Beverly Hills, Calif, and widow of Harold Wallace Ross, of New York City; *Heir* bro, Eric Leigh; *Style* - Sir John Leigh, Bt; 23 Quai du Mont Blanc, Geneva, Switzerland

LEIGH, John Roland; s of Adam Dale Leigh (d 1978); *b* 11 March 1933; *Educ* Winchester, King's Cambridge; *m* 1957, Rosemary Renée, da of late Capt Gordon Furze, MC; 1 s, 3 da; *Career* merchant banker, ptnr Rathbone Bros & Co 1963-, dir Greenbank Trust Ltd 1969-81, Albany Investment Trust Ltd 1979-, chm Blackburn Diocesan Bd of Fin Ltd 1976-; *Clubs* Flyfishers', Athenaeum (Liverpool); *Style* - John Leigh Esq; Robin Hood Cottage, Blue Stone Lane, Mawdesley, Ormskirk, Lancs (☎ 822641)

LEIGH, Hon Michael James; s of 4 Baron Leigh, TD (d 1979); *b* 1945; *Educ*

Eton, Keble Oxford; *m* 1972, Cherry Rosalind, da of late David Long-Price; *Style* - The Hon Michael Leigh; c/o Stoneleigh Abbey, Kenilworth, Warwicks

LEIGH, Sir Neville Egerton; KCVO (1980, CVO 1967); s of Capt Cecil Egerton Leigh (d 1930); *b* 4 June 1922; *Educ* Charterhouse, abroad; *m* 1944, Denise, da of C D Branch, MC, of Paris, France; 2 s, 1 da; *Career* served in RAFVR 1942-47, barr Inner Temple 1948, legal assist Treasury Solicitor's Dept 1949-51, sr clerk Privy Council Office 1951-65, dep clerk of the Privy Council 1965-74, clerk 1974-; *Style* - Sir Neville Leigh, KCVO; 11 The Crescent, Barnes, SW13 (☎ 01 876 4271)

LEIGH, Hon Piers Henry John; s of 5 Baron Leigh (by 2 m); *b* 1979; *Style* - The Hon Piers Leigh

LEIGH, Hon William Rupert; s of 4 Baron Leigh; *b* 13 Sept 1938; *Educ* Eton, RMA Sandhurst; *m* 1965, Priscilla Elizabeth, da of Lt-Cdr E F P Cooper, of Markree Castle, Collooney, Co Sligo, Ireland; 2 s (and 1 s decd); *Career* Lt 11 Hussars (served Aden, N Ireland), ret 1962; estate agent 1965-66; stud owner; *Style* - The Hon William Leigh; Lower Farm, Adlestrop, Moreton-in-Marsh, Glos

LEIGH FERMOR, Patrick Michael; DSO (1944), OBE (1943); s of Sir Lewis Leigh Fermor, OBE, FRS, DSc; *b* 11 Feb 1915; *Educ* King's Sch Canterbury; *m* 1968, Hon Joan Eyres-Monsell, da of 1 Viscount Monsell; *Career* served WW II Irish Gds, Intell Corps, Greece & Germany, Maj 1943; Dep Dir Br Institute Athens 1936; author; corresponding memb Athens Acad; Hon Citizen Herakleion Crete; *Recreations* travel; *Clubs* Travellers', White's, Pratt's, Beefsteak, Special Forces; *Style* - Patrick Leigh Fermor Esq DSO OBE; c/o Messrs John Murray, 50 Albemarle st, W1

LEIGH-PEMBERTON, Robin (Robert); DL (Kent 1970); s of Capt Robert Leigh-Pemberton, MBE, MC (d 1964, whose gf was Sir Edward Leigh Pemberton, KCB, JP, DL, sometime MP E Kent and n of 1 & last Baron Kingsdown; Sir Edward's w Matilda was niece of 1 Earl of Gainsborough); the Capt's mother, Edith, was da of Robert Hay Murray (himself great nephew of 4 Duke of Atholl); *b* 1 Jan 1927; *Educ* Eton, Trin Oxford; *m* 1953, Rosemary, da of Lt-Col David Forbes, MC, and Diana (gda of 1 Baron Faringdon), now Marchioness of Exeter; 5 s (John b 1955, m 1980 Rosamund Jessel; James b 1956, Edward b 1959, Thomas b 1961, William b 1964); *Career* late Lt Gren Gds, served Palestine 1946-48; chm Nat West Bank 1977- (dir 1972-, dep chm 1974), Vice-Ld-Lt Kent 1972-; Pro-Chllr Kent U 1977-; dir: Birmid Qualcast 1966- (dep chm 1970-, chm 1975-77), Equitable Life Assur Soc 1967-, Redland Ltd 1972-; *Recreations* country life; *Clubs* Brooks's, Cavalry & Guards, Union (New York); *Style* - Robin Leigh-Pemberton Esq, HM Vice-Lord-Lieut for Kent; 66 Marsham Gardens, SW1 (☎ 01 834 1533); Torry Hill, Sittingbourne, Kent (☎ Milstead 258)

LEIGHTON OF ST MELLONS, 2 Baron (UK 1962); Sir John Leighton Seager; 2 Bt (UK 1952); s of 1 Baron, CBE (d 1963); *b* 11 Jan 1922; *Educ* Caldicott Sch, Leys Sch Cambridge; *m* 1953, Elizabeth Rosita, da of late Henry Hopgood, of Cardiff; 2 s, 1 da (& 1 decd); *Heir* s, Hon Robert William Henry Leighton Seager; *Career* dir Principality Bldg Soc; *Style* - Rt Hon Lord Leighton of St Mellons; 185 Lake rd West, Cardiff

LEIGHTON, Kathleen, Lady; Kathleen Irene Linda; da of Maj Albert Ernest Lees, of Rowton Castle, Shrewsbury; *m* 1932, Col Sir Richard Tihel Leighton, 10 Bt, TD (d 1957); *Style* - Kathleen, Lady Leighton; Loton Park, Shrewsbury

LEIGHTON OF ST MELLONS, Marjorie, Baroness; Marjorie; JP (Monmouthshire); da of William Henry Gimson, of Breconshire; *m* 1921, 1 Baron Leighton of St Mellons (d 1963); *Career* Freeman of the City of London; Hon Freedom of Shipwrights' Co; *Style* - The Rt Hon Marjorie, Lady Leighton of St Mellons, JP; Blythwood, St Mellons, Nr Cardiff

LEIGHTON, Sir Michael John Bryan; 11 Bt (E 1693); s of Col Sir Richard Tihel Leighton, 10 Bt, TD (d 1957); *b* 8 March 1935; *Educ* Stowe, Cirencester Coll, Tabley House Agricultural Sch; *m* 1974, Amber Mary Ritchie; *Heir* none; *Style* - Sir Michael Leighton, Bt; Loton Park, Nr Shrewsbury, Salop (☎ Halfway House 232)

LEIGHTON, Ronald; MP (L) Newham North East 1979-; s of Charles Leighton; *b* 24 Jane 1930; *Educ* Monteagle and Bifrons Sch Barking; *m* 1951, Erika Wehkin; 2 s; *Career* chm Labour Common Market Safeguards Ctee; *Books* The Labour Case Against Entry to the Common Market; What Labour Should Do About the Common Market; *Style* - Ronald Leighton Esq, MP; 19 Woodland rd, Fulham SW6 (☎ 01 385 7597)

LEINER, L; *Career* chm P Leiner & Sons Ltd; *Style* - L Leiner Esq; 7 Cleveland Row, SW1

LEINSTER, 8 Duke of (I 1766); Maj Gerald FitzGerald; Premier Duke, Marquess and Earl in the Peerage of Ireland, also Baron of Offaly (I *ante* 1203 restored 1554), Earl of Kildare (I 1316), Viscount Leinster of Taplow (GB 1747), Marquess of Kildare, Earl of Offaly (both I 1761), and Baron Kildare (UK 1870); s of 7 Duke of Leinster (d 1976, descended from common ancestors of (1) The Earls of Plymouth, (2) Giraldus Cambrensis the medieval historian, (3) the Earls of Desmond (now extinct), (4) the hereditary Knights of Glin and Kerry and the (extinct) White Knight, and (5) the Marquesses of Lansdowne) by his 1 w May; *b* 27 May 1914; *Educ* Eton, Sandhurst; *m* 1, 1936, Joane (m dis 1946), da of late Maj Arthur McMorrough Kavanagh, MC; 2 da; m 2, 1946, Anne, da of late Lt-Col Philip Eustace Smith, MC; 2 s; *Heir* s, Marquess of Kildare; *Career* served WW II with 5 Roy Inniskilling Dragoon Gds Normandy, master North Kilkenny Foxhounds 1937-40, West Percy Foxhounds 1945-46, Portman Foxhounds 1946-47 chm CSE Aviation Gp; *Style* - His Grace the Duke of Leinster; Langston House, Chadlington, Oxford (☎ Chadlington 436)

LEINSTER, Dowager Duchess of; Vivien Irene; da of Thomas Albert Felton (d 1957) and his w, Lilian Adshead; *b* 19 Feb 1920; *m* 1, 1937, George William Conner (m dis 1965); 1 s; m 2, 1965, as his 4 w, Edward FitzGerald, 7 Duke of Leinster, Premier Duke, Marquess and Earl of Ireland (d 1976); *Career* pres All Ireland Distress Fund 1975-76, Gift Shop administrator Help the Aged 1976, founder-pres of the charity Stress 1976; *Style* - Her Grace the Dowager Duchess of Leinster; A13 Sloane ave Mansions, Sloane ave, SW3 (☎ 01 589 2151)

LEISHMAN, Hon Mrs; Hon Marista Muriel; da of 1 Baron Reith, KT, GCVO, GBE, CB, TD (d 1971); *b* 10 April 1932; *Educ* St George's Ascot, St Andrew's U; *m* 1960, The Rev Robert Murray Leishman; 1 s, 3 da; *Career* Education Sec Nat Trust for Scotland 1978-; *Recreations* music, painting, walking; *Style* - The Hon Mrs Leishman; Hunter's House, 508 Lanark rd, Edinburgh 14 (☎ 031 441 2216)

LEITH, Hon Alexander Gregory Disney; s and h of 7 Baron Burgh; *b* 16 March 1958; *Style* - The Hon Alexander Leith

LEITH, Hon Eveleigh Julia; da of 5 Baron Burgh (d 1926); *b* 1904; *Style* - The Hon Eveleigh Leith; Sexton's, Speen, Newbury, Berks

LEITH, Hon John Barnabas; s of 6 Baron Burgh (d 1959); *b* 27 Dec 1947; *Educ* Wellington Coll, Exeter U, Birmingham U; *m* 1970, Erica Jane, da of David M Lewis; 1 da; *Style* - The Hon John Leith; 72 Puxton dve, Wolverley Park, Kidderminster, Worcs

LEITH, Lady; Mary (Holroyd); da of late Leonard Asquith, of Brook House, Cleckheaton, Yorks; *m* 1955, as his 2 w, Sir Alexander Leith, 1 Bt, MC (d 1956); *Style* - Lady Leith; 30 Queen's Close, Harrogate, N Yorks

LEITH, Hon Patrick Simon Vincent; s of 7 Baron Burgh; *b* 1964; *Style* - The Hon Patrick Leith

LEITH, Lady; Rhoda Mary; da of

Leonard Asquith; *m* 1955, Alexander Leith, 1 Bt (d 1956); *Style* - Lady Leith; 8 Wentworth ct, Harrogate (☎ 501586)

LEITH-BUCHANAN, Barbara, Lady; Barbara Deane; da of Willard Phelps Leshure, of Springfield, Mass; *b* 29 Feb 1904; *Educ* Emme Willard Sch Troy NY, New England Conservatory of Music Boston; *m* 1933, Sir George Hector Macdonald Leith-Buchanan, 6 Bt (d 1973); *Recreations* music, gardening, youth welfare; *Style* - Barbara, Lady Leith-Buchanan; Drummakill, Alexandria, Dunbartonshire (☎ Gartocharn 232)

LEITH-BUCHANAN, Sir Charles Alexander James; 7 Bt (GB 1775); s of John Wellesley MacDonald Leith-Buchanan (d 1956); suc kinsman Sir George Leith-Buchanan, 6 Bt (d 1973); *b* 1 Sept 1939; *m* 1962, Mary Anne Kelly; 1 s, 1 da; *Heir* s, Gordon Leith-Buchanan; *Style* - Sir Charles Leith-Buchanan, Bt; 9814 Barlow rd, Fairfax, Virginia 22030, USA

LEITH-BUCHANAN, Gordon Kelly McNicol; s and h of Sir Charles Alexander James Leith-Buchanan, 7 Bt; *b* 18 Oct 1974; *Style* - Gordon Leith-Buchanan Esq

LEITRIM, Countess of; Hon Anne Mary Chaloner; da of Hon William Vanneck and sis of 5 Baron Huntingfield; *b* 1893; *m* 1, 1915, (m dis 1939), Maj Percy Rygate Borrett; m 2, 1939, 5 & last Earl of Leitrim (d 1952); raised to rank of Baron's da 1922; *Style* - The Rt Hon the Countess of Leitrim; Mulroy, Co Donegal

LELLEY, Prof Geoffrey Michael; s of Michael Moreland Dessau (d 1941); *b* 16 Nov 1919; *Educ* Isleworth G S, Imperial Coll; *m* 1948, Leslie Marion, da of Leonard Frank Wheeler, of Cranfield Beds (d 1955); 1 s, 2 da; *Career* RAF 1935-36; prof of Aeronautics and Astronautics U of Southampton 1964-; memb Noise Advisory Council 1970-; *Style* - Prof Geoffrey Lelley; Highbury, Pine Walk, Chilworth, Southampton (☎ 0703 769109)

LEMON, Sir (Richard) Dawnay; CBE (1958); s of Lt-Col Frederick Joseph Lemon, CBE, DSO (d 1952); *b* 1912; *Educ* Uppingham, RMC; *m* 1939, Sylvia Marie, da of Lt-Col and Mrs L W Kentish, of Burnham, Bucks; 1 s, 2 da (1 decd); *Career* joined West Yorkshire Regiment 1932, Metropolitan Police 1934-37, Leicestershire Constabulary 1937-39, ch constable East Riding Yorkshire 1939-42, Hants 1942-62; kt 1970; *Style* - Sir Dawnay Lemon, CBE; West Coggers, St Margaret's Bay, Dover, Kent (☎ Dover 852685)

LENNOX-BOYD, Hon Christopher Alan; s of 1 Viscount Boyd of Merton, CH, PC, and Lady Patricia Guinness (da of 2 Earl of Iveagh); (1) bro of Hon Mark Lennox-Boyd, MP, (2) 1 cous of (HRH Princess Antonia von Preussen) Marchioness of Douro and Paul Channon, Min for the Arts, (3) and 1 cous once removed of Maureen Marchioness of Dufferin and Ava; *b* 22 July 1941; *Educ* Eton, Ch Ch Oxford; *Clubs* Carlton, Brooks's; *Style* - The Hon Christopher Lennox-Boyd; c/o Ince Castle, Saltash, Cornwall (☎ 2274)

LENNOX-BOYD, Hon Mark Alexander; MP (C) Morecambe and Lonsdale 1979-; s of 3 Viscount Boyd of Merton; *b* 4 May 1943; *Educ* Eton, Ch Ch Oxford; *m* 1974, Arabella Lacloche; *Career* barr Inner Temple 1968; *Style* - The Hon Mark Lennox-Boyd, MP; Gresgarth Hall, Caton, Lancashire

LENNOX-BOYD, Hon Simon Donald Rupert Neville; s and h of 1 Viscount Boyd of Merton, CH, PC; *b* 7 Dec 1939; *Educ* Eton, Ch Ch Oxford; *m* 1962, Alice Mary, da of Maj Mevsey Deorge Dallas Clive (ka 1943); 2 s, 2 da; *Style* - The Hon Simon Lennox-Boyd; 9 Warwick sq, SW1; Wivelscombe, Saltash, Cornwall (☎ Saltash 2672)

LENTON, Aylmer Ingram; *b* 19 May 1927; *Educ* Leeds G S, Magdalen Coll Oxford, Leeds U; *m* 1951, Ursula Kathleen, da of Cyril Henry Brownlow King (d 1964); 1 s, 1 da; *Career* man dir South African Nylon Spinners 1964-66; dir ICI Fibres 1966-67; dir John Heathcoat & Co 1967-75; chm Bowater UK Paper Co 1976-78; chm Bowater UK Ltd 1979-80; dir Bowater Corp 1979; man dir Bowater

Corp 1981; *Recreations* golf, fencing, walking; *Clubs* Inst of Dirs; *Style* - Aylmer Lenton Esq; Robin Hill, Hockett Lane, Cookham Dean, Berks

LENTON, John Robert; s of Rev Robert Vincent Lenton, Lacock Vicarage, Chippenham, Wilts; *b* 13 May 1946; *Educ* Prince of Wales Sch Nairobi, Exeter Coll Oxford, Harvard Business Sch; *m* 1967, Ann Cathrine, da of Maj E Reece; 1 s, 1 da; *Career* specialist financial marketing; Alex Lawrie Factors Ltd: dir Sales & Marketing 1976, dir Operations 1977; dir Sales & Marketing International Factors Ltd 1979-*Recreations* golf, skiing, bridge; *Style* - John Lenton Esq; 25 Wilbury Ave, Hove, East Sussex (☎ Brighton (0272) 724004)

LEON, Alexander John; s and h of Sir John Ronald Leon, 4 Bt; *b* 3 May 1965; *Style* - Alexander Leon Esq

LEON, Dowager Lady; Alice Mary; da of late Dr Thomas Holt; *b* 10 Sept 1919; *Educ* Queen Ethelburga's Sch Harrogate; *m* 1947, as his 3 w, Sir Ronald George Leon, 3 Bt (d 1964); *Career* served FANY 1941-46; *Style* - Dowager Lady Leon; 83 Lexham Gdns, W8

LEON, Sir John Ronald; 4 Bt (UK 1911); s of Sir Ronald George Leon, 3 Bt (d 1964), by 1 w, Dorothy Katharine, the late Kay Hammond, actress, da of late Cdr Sir Guy Standing, KBE, and who m 2, Sir John Clements, CBE, *qv*; *b* 16 Aug 1934; *Educ* Eton; *m* 1961 (m dis 1972), Jill, da of Jack Melford, actor; 1 s; *Heir* s, Alexander John Leon; *Career* 2 Lt KRRC 1953-55; actor (John Standing); *Style* - Sir John Leon, Bt; 98 Ebury st, SW1

LEONARD, Baron (Life Peer UK 1978); John Denis Leonard,; OBE (1976); s of late Denis Leonard; *b* 19 Oct 1909; *Educ* Manorhamilton Boys' Sch Eire; *m* 1945, Glenys Evelyn Kenny; 1 s, 1 da; *Career* chm Cardiff Sheet Metal & Engineering Co Ltd 1953-, memb Cardiff City Council 1970-76, S Glamorgan County Council 1974-77 (chm 1976-77), a Lord in Waiting (Govt Whip) 1978-79, memb Council U of Wales Inst of Science and Technology 1978; *Style* - The Rt Hon the Lord Leonard, OBE; 19 Queen Anne sq, Cardiff (☎ Cardiff 387109)

LEONARD, Charles; s of Charles Henry Leonard; *b* 14 July 1934; *m* 1969, Lesley, da of Maj Douglas Fox (d 1979); 2 da; *Career* prof philatelist; md Robson Lowe Ltd 1977, md Bournemouth Stamp Auctions 1977, dir Robson Lowe Ltd 1974, dir Robson Lowe Int Ltd 1979, dir Woods of Perth (Printers) Ltd 1976; *Style* - Charles Leonard Esq; West Moors, Wimborne, Dorset

LEONARD, Hon Derek John; s of Baron Leonard (Life Peer); *b* 1956; *Style* - The Hon Derek Leonard

LEONARD, His Honour Judge (Hamilton) John; QC (1969); s of Arthur Leonard (d 1969), of Poole, Dorset; *b* 28 April 1926; *Educ* Dean Close Sch Cheltenham, BNC Oxford; *m* 1948, Doreen Enid, da of late Lt-Col Sidney James Parker, OBE, of Sanderstead, Surrey; 1 s, 1 da; *Career* barr 1951, recorder Crown Court 1972-78, circuit judge 1978-, memb Home Sec Advisory Bd on Restricted Patients 1973-78, memb Judicial Studies Bd 1979-, Common Serjeant in City of London 1979-; liveryman Plaisterers' Co; *Style* - His Honour Judge John Leonard, QC; Field End, Harps Oak Lane, Merstham, Surrey; Central Criminal Court, EC4

LEONARD, His Honour James Charles Beresford Whyte; s of late Hon James Weston Leonard, KC, of Johannesburg; *b* 1905; *Educ* Clifton, Ch Ch Oxford; *m* 1939, Barbara Helen, da of late Capt William Incledon-Webber, of Buckland House, Braunton; *Career* barr Inner Temple 1928, a circuit judge 1972, judge of Mayor's and City of London Court 1973-79, jr counsel Miny of Ag, Fish & Food, Forestry Cmmn and Tithe Redemption Cmmn, chm Statutory Ctee Pharmaceutical Soc of GB 1962-65; *Style* - His Honour James Leonard; Cross Trees, Sutton Courtenay, Berks (☎ 023 582 230); 1 Paper Bldgs, EC4 (☎ 01 583 1870)

LEONARD, Sir Walter McEllister; DFC; s of W Leonard, of Grafton; *b* 22 Feb 1915; *Educ* Cootamundra H S; *m* 1948, Yvonne M, da of J V Brady; 2 s, 3 da;

Career chm Ampol Petroleum Ltd 1970- (gen man 1949-63), Ampol Exploration Ltd 1970-; dir Australian Industry Development Corpn; dir Conzinc Rio Tinto of Australia Ltd 1977-, dir Interscan Pty Ltd; kt 1977; *Style* - Sir Walter Leonard DFC; 51 Cutler rd, Clontarf, NSW 2093, Australia

LERMON, His Honour Judge (Norman); s of Morris Lermon (d 1954), of Cardiff; *b* 12 Dec 1915; *Educ* Clifton, Trin Hall Cambridge; *m* 1939, Sheila Veronica, da of Harold Langton Gilks, of Haslemere; 1 da; *Career* served 1939-46 with S Wales Borderers, Maj 1945; barr Gray's Inn 1943, QC 1966, a county court judge (Guildford Circuit) 1971, a circuit judge 1972-; *Style* - His Honour Judge Lermon, QC; 2 Harcourt Bldgs, Temple, EC4

LESLIE, Hon Alexander John; s of 21 Earl of Rothes; *b* 1962; *Style* - The Hon Alexander Leslie

LESLIE, Capt Alastair Pinckard; TD; s of Hon John Wayland Leslie, qv, s of late 19 Earl of Rothes; *b* 29 Dec 1934; *Educ* Eton; *m* 1963, Rosemary, da of Cdr Hubert Wyndham Barry, RN, of Broughton, Hants; 1 s, 2 da; *Career* formerly Capt Royal Scots Fusiliers (TA) and memb Royal Co of Archers (Queen's Bodyguard for Scotland); dir Willis Faber & Dumas (Agencies) Ltd and other Lloyd's underwriting agencies; *Recreations* fishing, stalking, shooting; *Clubs* Boodles, Pratt's; *Style* - Capt Alastair Leslie, TD; Grays House, Bramley, near Basingstoke, Hampshire

LESLIE, Doris; *see* Fergusson Hannay, Lady

LESLIE, Desmond Arthur Peter; s of Sir Shane Leslie, 3 Bt (d 1971) and hp of bro Sir John Norman Ide Leslie, 4 Bt; *b* 29 June 1921; *Educ* Ampleforth, Trin Coll Dublin; *m* 1, 1945, Agnes, only da of Rudolph Bernauer, of Budapest, Hungary; 2 s, 1 da; m 2, 1970, Helen Jennifer, da of late Lt-Col E I E Strong, of Wiveliscombe, Som; 2 da; *Career* composer, author, film producer, discologist, late Fl Sgt RAF; *Style* - Desmond Leslie Esq; Castle Leslie, Gaslough, Co Monaghan

LESLIE, Lord; James Malcolm David Leslie; s and h of 21 Earl of Rothes; *b* 4 June 1958; *Educ* Eton; *Style* - Lord Leslie; 25B Bolton gdns, SW5 (☎ 01 370 6496)

LESLIE, Sir John Norman Ide; 4 Bt (UK 1876); s of Sir (John Randolph) Shane Leslie, 3 Bt (d 1971); *b* 6 Dec 1916; *Educ* Downside, Magdalene Cambridge; *Heir* bro, Desmond Arthur Peter Leslie; *Career* served in Second World War in Irish Gds (POW 1940-45); KStJ; Kt of Honour and Devotion Sov Mil Order of Malta, and Kt Cdr Order of St Gregory the Great; *Style* - Sir John Leslie, Bt; 19 Piazza in Piscinula, Rome, Italy

LESLIE, Hon John Wayland; s of 19 Earl of Rothes (d 1927); *b* 16 Dec 1909; *Educ* Stowe, CCC Cambridge; *m* 1932, Coral Angela, da of late George Henry Pinckard, JP, of Chiddingfold, Surrey; 1 s, 1 da; *Career* memb Royal Co of Archers (Queen's Bodyguard for Scotland), formerly Fl Lt, invalided 1943; *Recreations* shooting, fishing; *Clubs* Carlton; *Style* - The Hon John Leslie; East Kintrockat, Brechin, Angus (☎ 2739); Guildford House, Castle st, Farnham, Surrey (☎ 0252 716975)

LESLIE, (Percy) Theodore; s of Frank Harvey Leslie (d 1965) and ggs of 4 Bt; *b* 19 Nov 1915; *Educ* London, privately; *Career* engineer British Aerospace, freeman City of London 1978; succession to Leslie of Wardis and Findrassie Btcy (1625) as 10 Bt pending at time of going to press; *Style* - Theodore Leslie Esq; c/o Clydesdale Bank Ltd, 31 St James's st, SW1

LESLIE MELVILLE, Hon Alan Duncan; s of 13 Earl of Leven and (12 of) Melville, KT (d 1947); *b* 1928; *Educ* Eton; *Career* Capt Rifle Bde 1954, ret 1956; *Style* - The Hon Alan Leslie Melville; Fingask, Kirkhill, Inverness

LESLIE MELVILLE, Hon Archibald Ronald; s of 14 Earl of Leven and (13 of)

Melville; *b* 15 Sept 1957; *Educ* Gordonstoun; *Career* 2 Lt Queen's Own Highlanders to 1981, Lt 1981-; *Style* - Lt The Hon Archibald Leslie Melville

LESLIE MELVILLE, Lady Eliza Compton; da of 6 Marquess of Northampton, DSO; *b* 7 Dec 1944; *m* 1968, Ian Hamish Leslie Melville; 1 s; *Style* - Lady Eliza Leslie Melville; 61 Hartington rd, W4 (☎ 01 994 8376)

LESLIE MELVILLE, Hon George David; s of 13 Earl of Leven and (12 of) Melville, KT (d 1947); *b* 13 May 1924; *Educ* Eton, Trin Cambridge; *m* 1955, Diana Mary, da of Brig Sir Henry Houldsworth, KBE, DSO, MC (d 1963); 1 s, 1 da; *Career* late Rifle Bde, served 1942-45 (wounded 1945), Maj Black Watch TA; chartered land agent, FRICS, FLAS, FAI; *Recreations* shooting, skiing; *Clubs* Naval & Military; *Style* - The Hon George Leslie Melville; Kirkton House, Skene, Aberdeenshire, (☎ 204)

LESLIE MELVILLE, Lady Jean Elizabeth; da of 13 Earl of Leven and (12 of) Melville, KT (d 1947); *b* 1921; *Style* - Lady Jean Leslie Melville; Pathways, Sedgeberrow, Evesham, Worcs

LESLIE MELVILLE, Hon Ronald Joscelyn; s of 13 Earl of Leven and (12 of) Melville, KT (d 1947); *b* 1926; *Educ* Eton, Worcester Oxford; *m* 1962, Ruth, da of late Dr John Duckworth; 4 s (1 decd), 1 da; *Style* - The Hon Ronald Leslie Melville; Balgarrock, Aberlemno, Forfar, Angus (☎ Aberlemno 219)

LESSER, C L; *Career* chm J E Lesser & Sons (Holdings) Ltd; *Style* - C L Lesser, Esq; The Lesser Building, Staines rd, Hounslow, Middx

LESSER, Leslie Hugh; s of Isaac Lesser (d 1960); *b* 7 Jan 1934; *Educ* Westcliff High Sch; *m* 1956, Joyce; 1 s (Guy Fenton), 1 da (Vivien Adele); *Career* FCA, dir Greenfields Leisure Ltd, Greenfield Milletts Int Ltd Hong Kong, Llanberis Lake Railway Company, v-chm Southend United Football Club Ltd, Freemason; *Recreations* golf, fishing, Shakespearean theatre; *Style* - Leslie Lesser Esq; 130 Rivermill, SW1; 17 Burlescoombe rd, Thorpe Bay, Essex

LESSOF, Prof Maurice Hart; s of Noah Lessof; *b* 4 June 1924; *Educ* City of London Sch, King's Cambridge; *m* 1960, Leila Liebster; 1 s, 2 da; *Career* prof of medicine London U at Guy's Hospital Medical Sch 1971-, external examiner U of Ibadan 1976, Oxford U 1979, pro-censor and council memb Royal Coll of Physicians; *Style* - Prof Maurice Lessof; 8 John Spencer sq, Canonbury N1 (☎ 01 226 0919)

LESTER, James Theodore; MP (C) Nottingham (Beeston Div) 1974-; s of Arthur Ernest Lester; *b* 23 May 1932; *Educ* Nottingham H S; *m* 1953, Iris; 2 s; *Career* an Opposition Whip 1975-79, Parly Under-Sec of State, Dept of Employment 1979-81; *Style* - James Lester Esq, MP; Flat 7, 37 Smith sq, SW1

LESTOCK REID, Lt-Cdr Christopher Gordon; DL (1971 Northumberland); s of Claud Lestock Reid (d 1954); *b* 12 Oct 1920; *Educ* Pangbourne Coll Berks; *m* 1946, Alwine, da of Richard Straker; 1 da; *Career* served in RN 1938-55; farmer, County Cmmr Northumberland Scouts 1968-, Ch Cmmr for England 1976-; *Style* - Lt-Cdr Christopher Lestock Reid, DL; Low Angerton House, Hartburn, Morpeth, Northumberland (☎ Hartburn 230); c/o Coutts & Co, 440 Strand, WC2

LESTOR, Joan; MP (L) Eton and Slough, 1966-; *b* 1931; 2 adopted children; *Career* Parly Under-Sec of State Dept of Education and Science 1969-70, memb Labour Pty Nat Exec 1967-, Parly Under-Sec of State FCO 1974-75, Dept of Education and Science 1975-76; *Style* - Miss Joan Lestor, MP; House of Commons, SW1

LETANKA, Lady Christina; *nee* Gathorne-Hardy; da of 4 Earl of Cranbrook, CBE; *b* 1940; *m* 1967, Stanley Edward Letanka; 2 da; *Style* - Lady Christina Letanka; Pepsall End, Pepperstock, Luton

LETHBRIDGE, John Francis Buckler Noel; s and h of Sir Thomas Periam Hector Noel Lethbridge, 7 Bt; *b* 10 Mar

1977; *Style* - John Lethbridge Esq

LETHBRIDGE, Sir Thomas Periam Hector Noel; 7 Bt (UK 1804); s of Sir Hector Wroth Lethbridge, 6 Bt (d 1978); *b* 17 July 1950; *Educ* Milton Abbey, RAC Cirencester; *m* 1976, Susan Elizabeth Rocke; 2 s, 1 da; *Heir* s, John Francis Buckler Noel Lethbridge; *Career* artist's promoter, former art gallery dir; *Style* - Sir Thomas Lethbridge, Bt; Long Sutton House, Langport, Somerset (☎ Long Sutton 284); Flat 2, Stanley Mansions, Park Walk, SW1

LETTO, Maurice; s of Henry Elliot Letto of Jersey (d 1968); *b* 5 Aug 1917; *Educ* De La Salle Coll Jersey; *m* 1940, Alice Vera, nee Poyntz; 1 s, 1 da; *Career* FCIS, stockbroker, sr ptnr Trevor Matthews & Carey 1970-79; co dir & chm Jersey Gen Investment Trust Ltd 1970-; *Recreations* travel, reading, crosswords; *Style* - Maurice Letto Esq; Greenacres, St Peter, Jersey, Channel Islands (☎ 0534 81521)

LEUCHARS, Hon Mrs; Hon Gillian Wightman; da of 2 Baron Glendyne (d 1967); *b* 1931; *m* 1953, Maj-Gen Peter Raymond Leuchars, CBE; 1 s; *Style* - The Hon Mrs Leuchars; 5 Chelsea sq, SW3

LEVEN AND MELVILLE, 14 Earl of Leven and 13 of Melville (S 1641); Alexander Robert Leslie Melville; also Lord Melville of Monymaill (S 1616), Lord Balgonie (S 1641), Viscount Kirkaldie, and Lord Raith, Monymaill and Balwearie (both S 1690); s of 13 Earl of Leven (and 12 of) Melville, KT (d 1947, ninth in descent from the celebrated Scottish soldier Sir Alexander Lesley or Leslie, 1 Earl of Leven, one of Gustavus Adolphus's commanders for a while in the Thirty Years War, and thought to have been the chief architect of victory at Marston Moor (though he afterwards supported Charles II at, for instance, Dunbar), by Lady Rosamond Foljambe (da of 1 Earl of Liverpool); *b* 13 May 1924; *Educ* Eton; *m* 1953, Susan, da of late Lt-Col Ronald Steuart-Menzies of Culdares (The Menzies) and sis of The Menzies; 2 s, 1 da; *Heir* s, Lord Balgonie; *Career* chm Cairngorm Chairlift Co; late ADC to Govr-Gen NZ; V-Pres Highland Dist TA, 2 Lt Coldstream Gds 1943, Capt 1947, Lord-Lt Co of Nairn 1969 (DL 1961); *Clubs* Naval & Military, Pratt's; *Style* - The Rt Hon the Earl of Leven and Melville, HM Lord-Lieut for Co of Nairn; Glenferness House, Nairn, Scotland (☎ Glenferness 202)

LEVENE, Peter Keith; s of Maurice Pierre Levene (d 1970); *b* 8 Dec 1941; *Educ* City of London Sch, Manchester U; *m* 1966, Wendy Ann, da of Frederick Fraiman; 2 s, 1 da; *Career* md United Scientific Holdings Ltd 1968-, chm Contracts Ctee Defence Manufacturers' Assoc, memb SEATAG (British Overseas Trade Bd); *Recreations* skiing, swimming; *Style* - Peter Levene Esq; 140 Tottenham Court rd, W1 (☎ 01 387 7224)

LEVENTHAL, Colin; *aet* 34 in June 1981; *Career* Head Copywright BBC to 1981, Head Programme Acquisition IBA Channel 4 TV 1981-; *Style* - Colin Leventhal Esq; IBA Channel 4 TV, 70 Brompton rd, SW3 (☎ 01 584 7011)

LEVER OF MANCHESTER, Baron (Life Peer UK 1979); (Norman) Harold Lever; PC (1969); s of late Bernard Lever, of Manchester; *b* 15 Jan 1914; *Educ* Manchester G S, Manchester U; *m* 1, 1945 (w d 1948); 1 da; m 2, 1962, Mrs Diane Zilkha, da of late Saleh Bashi, of Geneva; 3 da; Lord Lever's daughters include Hon Annabel and Hon Isabel Lever; *Career* barr Middle Temple; MP (L) Manchester Exchange 1945-50, Manchester Cheetham 1950-74, Manchester Central 1974-79; Jt Parly Under-Sec of State, Dept of Economic Affairs 1967, Financial Sec to the Treasury 1967-69, Paymaster Gen 1969-70, chm Public Accounts Ctee 1970-73, treasurer Socialist International 1971-73, Chllr Duchy of Lancaster 1974-79; dir Guardian and Manchester Evening News 1979-; *Style* - The Rt Hon the Lord Lever of Manchester, PC; House of Lords, SW1

LEVER, Hon Bernard Lewis; s of Baron Lever (Life Peer) (d 1977); *b* 1951; *Educ* Clifton, Queen's Oxford; *Career* barr Middle Temple 1975; *Style* - The Hon Bernard Lever; 27 Pine rd, Didsbury, Manchester

LEVER, Sir (Tresham) Christopher Arthur Lindsay; 3 Bt (UK 1911); s of Sir Tresham Joseph Philip Lever, 2 Bt, FRSL, (d 1975); *b* 9 Jan 1932; *Educ* Eton, Trin Cambridge; *m* 1, 1970, Susan Mary (m dis 1974), da of late John A Nicholson, of Crossmolina, Co Mayo; m 2, 1975, Linda Weighton McDowell, da of late James J Goulden, of Tennessee, USA; *Heir* none; *Career* Lt 17/21 Lancers 1949-50; dir John Barran & Sons Ltd 1958-64; author; *Style* - Sir Christopher Lever, Bt; Rye Mead House, Winkfield, nr Windsor, Berks (☎ Winkfield Row 2604)

LEVER, Pamela Lady; Clodagh Pamela; da of late Lt-Col the Hon Malcolm Bowes-Lyon, CBE, and formerly w of late Lord Malcolm Avondale Douglas-Hamilton, OBE, DFC; *m* 1962, as his 2 w, Sir Tresham Joseph Philip Lever, 2 Bt (d 1975); *Style* - Pamela, Lady Lever; Lessudden, St Boswells, Roxburgshire

LEVER, Lady; Phyllis Irene Blok; da of late Frederic Ancill; *m* 1940, as his 2 w, Sir Ernest Harry Lever (d 1970); *Style* - Lady Lever; Blackbrook Farm, Blackbrook, nr Dorking, Surrey

LEVER, Baroness; Ray Rosalia; da of Dr Leonard Levene, of Leicester; *m* 1939, Baron Lever (Life Peer) (d 1977); *Career* JP for Manchester; *Style* - The Rt Hon the Lady Lever, JP; 27 Pine rd, Didsbury, Manchester M20 OUZ

LEVERHULME, 3 Viscount (UK 1922); Sir Philip William Bryce Lever; 3 Bt (1911), TD, JP; also Baron Leverhulme (UK 1917); s of 2 Viscount (d 1949) by his 1 w, Marion; *b* 1 July 1915; *Educ* Eton, Trin Cambridge; *m* 1937, Margaret Ann (d 1973), da of John Moon, of Tiverton, Devon; 3 da (Hon Mrs Susan Pakenham, Hon Mrs Apsion, Hon Mrs Heber-Percy); *Heir* none; *Career* Hon Col Queen's Own Yeo 1979- and RAC, TAVR 1972-; advsy dir Unilever Ltd; KStJ, FRCS; Ld-Lt City & County Chester 1949-; Chllr Liverpool U 1980-; memb Nat Hunt Cttee 1961 (Steward 1965-68), Dep Sr Steward Jockey Club 1970-73, Sr Steward 1973-76; *Clubs* Boodle's, Jockey; *Style* - The Rt Hon Visount Leverhulme TD JP, HM Lord-Lieut for City & County of Cheshire; Thornton Manor, Thornton Hough, Wirral, Merseyside (☎ 051 336 4834); 16 Clarendon rd, W11 (☎ 01 727 1232)

LEVESON, Lord; Granville George Fergus Leveson Gower; s and h of 5 Earl Granville, MC; *b* 10 Sept 1959; *Career* a Page of Honour to HM Queen Elizabeth, the Queen Mother 1973-; *Style* - Lord Leveson

LEVESON GOWER, Lady Marcia Rose Aileen; da of 5 Earl Granville, MC; *b* 10 Feb 1961; *Style* - Lady Marcia Leveson Gower

LEVESON GOWER, Hon Niall James; s of 5 Earl Granville, MC; *b* 24 Aug 1963; *Style* - The Hon Niall Leveson Gower

LEVEY, Sir Michael Vincent; MVO (1965); s of O L H Levey; *b* 8 June 1927; *Educ* Oratory Sch, Exeter Coll Oxford; *m* 1954, Brigid Brophy, *qv*; 1 da; *Career* served with Army 1945-48; assist keeper National Gallery 1951-66, dir 1973-; Slade Prof of Fine Art Cambridge 1963-64, hon fell Exeter Oxford 1973; FRSL; kt 1980; *Style* - Sir Michael Levey MVO; 185 Old Brompton rd, SW5

LEVINE, Sir Montague (Bernard); s of late Philip Levine; *b* 15 May 1922; *Educ* Royal Coll of Surgeons in Ireland, Royal Coll of Physicians in Ireland; *m* 1959, Dr Rose Gold; 1 s, 1 da; *Career* gen practitioner; assist dep coroner Inner South London 1974-, clinical tutor in gen practice St Thomas' Hospital 1972-; kt 1979; *Style* - Sir Montague Levine; Gainsborough House, 120 Ferndene rd, Herne Hill, SE24 (☎ 01 274 5554)

LEVINGE, Richard George Robin; s and h of Maj Sir Richard Levinge, 11 Bt, MBE; *b* 18 Dec 1946; *m* 1969, Hilary Jane, da of Dr Derek Mark; m 2, 1978, Donna Maria d'Ardia Caracciolo, da of Prince Frederico Caracciolo; *Style* - Richard Levinge Esq

LEVINGE, Maj Sir Richard Vere Henry; 11 Bt (I 1704), MBE (1941); s of Sir Richard William Levinge, 10 Bt (ka 1914) and Irene, da of late John H C Pix; *b* 1911; *Educ* Eton, Balliol Oxford; *m* 1, 1935, Barbara, da of George Jardine

Kidston CMG (d 1954); 2 s, 3 da; m 2, 1976, Jane Millward; *Heir* s, Richard George Robin Levinge; *Career* 2 Lt Lovat Scouts TA 1934, Maj 1944, served in Burma 1944-45 (despatches); dir GEI Int and Tobenoil Ltd, chm Ctee of Management Atlantic Salmon Research Trust, and of Salmon and Trout Assoc; *Style* - Maj Sir Richard Levinge, Bt, MBE; Spindles, 27 The Grove, Radlett, Herts

LEVY, Sir Enoch Bruce; OBE (1950), DSC; s of William Levy (d 1936); *b* 1892; *Educ* Victoria U; *m* 1925, Phyllis Rosa Kate, da of G H Mason; *Career* formerly dir Grasslands Div Dept of Scientific and Industrial Research; kt 1953; *Style* - Sir Enoch Levy, OBE, DSC; 217 Fitzherbert ave, Palmerston North, New Zealand

LEVY, Sir Ewart Joseph Maurice; 2 Bt (UK 1913), JP (Leics 1934); s of 1 Bt, JP, DL (d 1933); *b* 1897; *Educ* Harrow; *m* 1932, Hylda Muriel (d 1970), da of late Sir Albert Levy; 1 da; *Heir* none; *Career* served 1940-45 Roy Pioneer Corps (despatches), Lt-Col 1944, High Sheriff 1937; *Style* - Sir Ewart Levy, Bt, JP; Welland House, Weston-by-Welland, Market Harborough, Leics

LEVY, George Joseph; s of Percy Levy (d 1967); *b* 21 May 1927; *Educ* Oundle Sch; *m* 1952, Wendy Yetta, da of Philip Blairman (d 1972); 1 s, 3 da; *Career* chm H Blairman & Sons Ltd 1965- (dir 1955), pres British Antique Dealers Assoc 1974-76; chm Grosvenor House Antiques Fair 1978-79, chm Somerset House Art Treasures Exhibition 1979, chm Friends of Kenwood 1979-, chm Burlington Fine Art and Antique Dealers Fair 1980; *Recreations* photography, theatre, tennis; *Style* - George Levy Esq; 27 Oakhill Ave, NW3 (☎ 01 435 9528)

LEWANDO, Sir Jan Alfred; CBE (1968); s of Maurice Lewando, of Manchester; *b* 31 May 1909; *Educ* Manchester G S, Manchester U; *m* 1948, Nora, da of William Slavouski; 3 da; *Career* joined Marks & Spencer Ltd 1929, (dir 1954-70); past chm Carrington Viyella Ltd and other cos; pres British Textile Confederation 1972-74; chm Heal and Son Holdings Ltd 1975-; dir Bunzl Pulp and Paper Ltd & others; kt 1974; *Style* - Sir Jan Lewando, CBE; Davidge House, Knotty Green, Beaconsfield, Bucks (☎ Beaconsfield 4987)

LEWIN, George Ronald; s of Frank Lewin (d 1957); *b* 11 Oct 1914; *Educ* Heath G S Halifax and Queen's Oxford; *m* 1938, Sylvia Lloyd, da of Philip Maximilian Sturge (d 1935); 2 s, 1 da (1 s decd); *Career* Capt RA 1939-45, BBC Home Talks dept 1946, head of Home Serv 1957, ret 1965; author of books on military subjects: *Rommel as Military Commander; Freedom's Battle, The War on Land 1939-45; Churchill as War Lord; Slim the Standard-Bearer, The Life and Death of the Afrika Korps; Ultra goes to War; The Chief, Field Marshal the Viscount Wavell, Commander-in-Chief and Viceroy*; *Clubs* Army and Navy; *Style* - George Lewin Esq; Camilla House, Forest rd, E Horsley, Surrey KT24 5BB (☎ E Horsley 3779)

LEWIN, Adm of the Fleet Sir Terence Thornton; GCB (1976, KCB 1973), MVO (1959), DSC (1942); s of E Lewin (d 1963); *b* 19 Nov 1920; *Educ* Judd Sch Tonbridge; *m* 1944, Jane, da of Rev C Branch-Evans, 2 s, 1 da; *Career* joind RN 1939, C-in-C Fleet, Allied C-in-C Channel and C-in-C Eastern Atlantic Area 1973-75, C-in-C Naval Home Command 1975-77, Ch Naval Staff & First Sea Lord 1977-79, Naval ADC to HM the Queen 1967-68, flag ADC to HM the Queen 1975-; *Style* - Admiral of the Fleet Sir Terence Lewin GCB MVO DSC; MOD, SW1

LEWIN-HARRIS, Col Carrique Edgar Lewin; OBE (1957); s of Edgar Henry Lewin-Harris (d 1940), of Clifton, Glos; *b* 27 Nov 1899; *Educ* Clifton, RMC Sandhurst; *m* 1, 1934, Leila Northup (d 1939), da of Sidney B Dean, of St Paul, Minnesota, USA; 1 s; m 2, 1950, Prunella Peel, da of Harry Grendon Bentley, of Crossways, Burnham-on-Sea, Somerset; *Career* 2 Lt DCLI 1919, served with Iraq Army 1925-28, served 1939-45 (France, Middle East, N Africa, Italy and India), instructor Staff Coll 1942-43, ret 1947, DL (1957) Somerset; OStJ; *Style* - Col Carrique Lewin-Harris OBE DL; Copper

Hill, Kingston-St-Mary, Taunton, Somerset (☎ Kingston St Mary 370)

LEWIS, Sir (William) Arthur; s of George Ferdinand Lewis, of Castries, St Lucia, W Indies; *b* 23 Jan 1915; *Educ* St Mary's Coll Castries, London Sch of Economics; *m* 1947, Gladys Isabel, da of William Jacobs, of Grenada; 2 da; *Career* lecturer London Sch of Economics 1938-47; Vice-Chancellor U of West Indies 1960-63, Prof of Economics and Int Affairs Princeton U 1963-68; James Madison Prof of Political Economy, Princeton U 1968-; kt 1963; *Style* - Sir Arthur Lewis; Woodrow Wilson School, Princeton University, Princeton, NJ, USA

LEWIS, Prof Sir Anthony Carey; CBE (1967); s of Col Leonard Lewis, OBE (d 1952); *b* 1915; *Educ* Wellington Coll, Peterhouse Cambridge; *m* 1959, Lesley Lisle, da of Frank Lisle Smith (d 1974); *Career* prof of Music Birmingham U 1947-68, principal of Royal Academy of Music 1968-; kt 1972; *Style* - Prof Sir Anthony Lewis CBE; 47 York Terrace East, NW1

LEWIS, Sir Allen Montgomery; s of late George Ferdinand Montgomery Lewis; *b* 26 Oct 1909; *Educ* St Mary's Coll St Lucia, Middle Temple London; *m* 1936, Edna Leofrida, da of late Thomas Alexander Theobalds; 3 s, 2 da; *Career* MLC St Lucia 1943-51, barr St Lucia 1931, chm Nat Development Corpn St Lucia 1972-74, Govr St Lucia 1974-79, Govr-Gen St Lucia 1979-80, Chancellor U of W Indies 1975-; KStJ 1975, kt 1968; *Style* - Sir Allen Lewis; Beaver Lodge, The Morne, Castries, St Lucia (☎ 2281)

LEWIS, Adm Sir Andrew Mackenzie; KCB (1971); s of late Rev Cyril F Lewis, of Gilston, Herts; *b* 24 Jan 1918; *Educ* Haileybury; *m* 1943, Rachel Elizabeth, da of Vice-Adm Eustace La Trobe Latham, CB (d 1935); 2 s; *Career* Capt RN 1955, C-in-C Naval Home Command and Flag Officer Portsmouth area 1972-74, ADC to HM the Queen 1972-74, DL (1975) Essex, Lord-Lt 1978-; *Style* - Adm Sir Andrew Lewis KCB, HM Lord-Lieut for Essex; Coleman's Farm, Finchingfield, Essex

LEWIS, Hon Antony Thomas; s of 3 Baron Merthyr, KBE, PC (d 1977); *b* 1947; *Educ* Eton; *m* 1974, Mary Carola Melton, da of Rev Humphrey John Paine; *Career* barr Inner Temple 1971; *Style* - The Hon Antony Lewis; Croesleiky Cottage, St Bride's-super-Ely, Cardiff

LEWIS, Arthur William John; MP (L) Newham (North-West) 1974-; s of J Lewis (d 1958); *b* 1917; *Educ* Elementary Sch, Borough Polytechnic; *m* 1940, Lucy Ethel, da of J Clack (d 1956); 1 da; *Career* formerly trade union official Nat Union of Gen and Municipal Workers, MP (L) W Ham (Upton) 1945-50, West Ham (North) 1950-74; *Style* - Arthur Lewis Esq, MP; 1 Doveridge Gdns, Palmers Green, N13

LEWIS, His Honour Bernard; s of late Solomon Lewis of London; *b* 1906; *Educ* Trin Hall Cambridge; *m* 1934, Harriette, da of late I Waine, of Dublin; 1 s; *Career* barr Lincoln's Inn 1929, a county court judge 1966, circuit judge 1972-80; *Style* - His Honour Bernard Lewis; Trevelyan House, Arlington rd, St Margarets, Middx

LEWIS, Col David Henry; OBE (1954), TD (1948); s of David Lewis, JP (d 1942); *b* 23 Feb 1914; *Educ* King Edward's Sch Birmingham, St John's Cambridge; *m* 1943, Denise Esmé, da of Col W J Beddows MC TD DL (d 1962); 2 da; *Career* served in 1939-45 War with RA (France, RWAFF BAOR, despatches); DL (1958) Staffs; engineer; dir John Harper & Co Ltd Willenhall 1948-69; *Style* - Col David Lewis OBE TD DL; Holdgate House, Stanton Long, nr Much Wenlock, Salop (☎ Ditton Priors 256)

LEWIS, David Trevor; s and h of Trevor Oswin Lewis (4 Baron Merthyr, who disclaimed his Peerage for life 1977); *b* 21 Feb 1977; *Style* - David Lewis Esq

LEWIS, Elizabeth Anne; da of Trevor Oswin Lewis (4 Baron Merthyr, who disclaimed his Peerage for life 1977); *b* 1970

LEWIS, Lady; Geraldine Susan Maud; da of Prof James Edward Geoffrey de Montmorency (d 1934); *Educ* Blackheath H S, Cheltenham Ladies' Coll, U of

London; *m* 1957, as his 2 w, Sir (William) Hawthorne Lewis, KCSI, KCIE (d 1970); *Career* awarded UNESCO Travelling Fellowship 1952; *Recreations* travel, reading, gardening; *Clubs* English Speaking Union; *Style* - Lady Lewis; The Bridge House, Wilton, Salisbury

LEWIS, Hon Mrs; Hon Hilary Zaraz; da of 1 Baron Morris of Kenwood (d 1954); *b* 1932; *m* 1964, Ronald Graham Lewis (b 5 June 1919, educ London U, served WW II Maj M East, is ch exec Grand Met Hotels & Catering, and enjoys bridge); 1 s (Ross Graham, m 1974 Carol), 1 da (Mrs (Beryl Anne) John Badger); *Style* - The Hon Mrs Lewis; Zaraz, Littlewick Green, Maidenhead, Berks (☎ 062 882 3183)

LEWIS, His Honour Judge Sir Ian Malcolm; QC (1961); *b* 14 Dec 1925; *Educ* Clifton Coll, Trin Hall Cambridge; *m* 1955, Marjorie, da of W G Carrington, of Cleethorpes, Lincs; 1 s; *Career* barr Middle Temple 1951, a justice of Supreme Court of Nigeria 1966-72, adviser to sec of State NI 1975, circuit judge 1973-; kt 1964; *Style* - His Honour Judge Sir Ian Lewis QC; 10 Southfield rd, Westbury-on-Trym, Bristol (☎ 0272 626942)

LEWIS, Hon John Frederick; s of 3 Baron Merthyr, KBE, PC (d 1977); *b* 30 Dec 1938; *Educ* Eton, St John's Cambridge; *m* 1966, Gretl, twin da of Lt-Col J W Lewis-Bowen; 1 s, 2 da; *Career* organiser Citizens' Advice Bureau; *Recreations* DIY; *Clubs* Island Sailing; aircraft- Cessna (shared); *Style* - The Hon John Lewis

LEWIS, Jessamay Jane; da of Trevor Oswin Lewis (4 Baron Merthyr, who disclaimed his Peerage for life 1977); *b* 1972

LEWIS, Kenneth; MP (C) Lincolnshire 1959-; s of late William Lewis, of Jarrow, Co Durham; *b* 1916; *Educ* Jarrow, Edinburgh U; *m* 1948, Jane, da of S Pearson; 1 s, 1 da; *Career* served in 1939-45 War, DL (1973) Rutland; chm Conservative Back Bench Labour Ctee, 1963-64, chm and ch exec Business and Holiday Travel Ltd; *Style* - Kenneth Lewis Esq, DL, MP; 96 Green Lane, Northwood, Middx; Dale Cottage, Preston, Uppingham, Leicestershire; c/o House of Commons, SW1

LEWIS, Lucy Delia; da of Trevor Oswin Lewis (4 Baron Merthyr, who disclaimed his Peerage for life 1977); *b* 1967; *Style* - Miss Lucy Lewis; c/o Trevor Lewis, Esq, JP, Hean Castle, Saundersfoot, Dyfed (☎ Saundersfoot (STD Code 0834) 812222)

LEWIS, Hon Peter Herbert; s of 3 Baron Merthyr, KBE, PC (d 1977); *b* 1937; *Educ* Eton; *m* 1974, Caroline Monica, da of Erik Cadogan; 1 da; *Career* Maj 15/19 Hussars; *Style* - The Hon Peter Lewis; c/o Hean Castle, Saundersfoot, Pembrokeshire (☎ 2222)

LEWIS, Ronald Howard; MP (L) Carlisle 1964-; s of Oliver Lewis; *b* 16 July 1909; *Educ* Elementary Sch, Cliff Methodist Coll; *m* 1947, Edna, da of Arthur Cooke, of Pleasley, Mansfield; 2 s; *Career* served in H M Forces Aug 1940-46; C C (1949) Derbyshire; pres Pleasley Co-operative Soc; *Style* - Ronald Lewis Esq, MP; 22 Alandale ave, Langwith Junction, Nr Mansfield, Notts (☎ Shirebrook (STD Code 062 385) 2460)

LEWIS, Hon Robin William; s of 3 Baron Merthyr, KBE, PC (d 1977); *b* 1941; *Educ* Eton, Magdalen Oxford; *m* 1967, Judith Ann, da of Arthur Giardelli, of Llethr, Pendine, Carmarthenshire 1 s, 1 da; *Style* - The Hon Robin Lewis; Orchard House, Llanstephan, Carmarthenshire (☎ 254)

LEWIS, Trevor Oswin; s of 3 Baron Merthyr, KBE, TD, PC (d 1977); *b* 29 Nov 1935; *Educ* Downs Sch, Eton, Magdalen Oxford, Magdalene Cambridge; *m* 1964, Susan Jane, da of A J Birt-Llewellin; 1 s, 3 da; *Heir* to Btcy & disclaimed Barony, s, David Trevor Lewis; *Career* suc as 4 Baron Merthyr (UK 1911) but disclaimed his Peerage for life 1977, and does not use title of Bt (UK 1896); memb Countryside Commission 1973- (dep chm Cttee for Wales 1980-); Dept of Transport Landscape Advisory Ctee 1968; JP (Dyfed) 1969; *Style* - Trevor Lewis, Esq, JP; Hean

Castle, Saundersfoot, Dyfed (☎ Saundersfoot 812222)

LEWIS-BOWEN, His Honour Judge; Thomas Edward Ifor; s of Lt-Col J W Lewis-Bowen; *b* 20 June 1933; *m* 1965, Gillian Brett; 1 s, 2 da; *Career* barr Middle Temple 1958, a recorder of Crown Court 1974-80, a circuit judge (Wales and Chester) 1980-; *Style* - His Honour Judge Lewis-Bowen; Clynfiew, Boncath, Dyfed; 90 Eaton cres, Swansea, W Glamorgan (☎ Swansea 59736)

LEWISHAM, Viscount; William Legge; s and h of 9 Earl of Dartmouth by Raine, now Countess Spencer; half-nephew of Ian McCorquodale, chm of Debrett's Peerage Ltd, and maternal gs of Barbara Cartland; *b* 23 Sept 1949; *Educ* Eton, Ch Ch Oxford; *Career* contested (C) Leigh Lancs 1974, Stockport South, 1974; *Style* - Viscount Lewisham; The Manor House, Chipperfield, King's Langley, Herts

LEWISOHN, His Honour Judge; Anthony Clive Leopold; s of John Lewishon (d 1939); *b* 1 Aug 1925; *Educ* Stowe, Trin Oxford; *m* 1957, Lone Jurgensen; 2 s; *Career* Lt Oxfordshire & Bucks LI 1946-47, barr Middle Temple 1951, a circuit judge 1974-; *Style* - His Honour Judge Lewisohn; 4 Brick Court, Temple, EC4

LEWTHWAITE, Brig Rainald Gilfrid; CVO (1975), OBE (1974), MC; s of Sir William Lewthwaite, 2 Bt, JP (d 1933) and hp of bro, Sir William Anthony Lewthwaite, 3 Bt; *b* 21 July 1913; *Educ* Rugby and Trin Cambridge; *m* 1936, Margaret Elizabeth, MBE, da of Harry Edmonds, of New York, USA; 2 s, 1 da; *Career* Brig late Scots Gds; Military Attaché 1964 and Defence Attaché at British Embassy, Paris, 1964-68; 1939-45 War in Middle East; ret 1968; dir Protocol Hong Kong 1969-76; *Recreations* country life; *Style* - Brig Rainald Lewthwaite, CVO, OBE, MC; 14 Edwardes sq, W8

LEWTHWAITE, Sir William Anthony; 3 Bt (UK 1927); s of Sir William Lewthwaite, 2 Bt, JP (d 1933); *b* 26 Feb 1912; *Educ* Rugby, Trin Cambridge; *m* 1936, Lois Mairi, da of late Capt Struan Robertson Kerr Clark (bro of 1 Baron Inverchapel, GCMG, PC) and Lady Beatrice Minnie Ponsonby Moore (d 1966, having m 2, 1941, 1 Lord Rankeillour; she was da of 9 Earl of Drogheda); 2 da (1 adopted, 1 decd); *Heir* bro, Brig Rainald Gilfrid Lewthwaite, CVO, OBE, MC; *Career* slr 1937, memb Ctee of Westminster Law Soc 1964-73, Lt Grenadier Gds 1943-46; memb Council, Country Landowners Assoc 1948-64; *Style* - Sir William Lewthwaite, Bt; 73 Dovehouse st, SW3 (☎ 01 352 7203)

LEY, Sir Francis Douglas; 4 Bt (UK 1905), MBE (1961), TD, JP (Derbyshire 1939), DL (1957); s of Maj Sir Henry Gordon Ley, 2 Bt (d 1944); *b* 1907; *Educ* Eton, Cambridge; *m* 1931, Violet Geraldine, da of Maj Gerald Johnson, of Foston, Derbyshire; 1 s, 1 da; *Heir* s, Ian Francis Ley; *Career* chm Ley's Malleable Castings Co Ltd, Ewart Chainbelt Co Ltd, Ley's Foundries & Engineering Ltd, High Sheriff Derbyshire 1956; *Style* - Sir Francis Ley, Bt, MBE TD JP DL; Shirley House, Shirley, Derby (☎ 033528 327)

LEY, Ian Francis; s and h of Sir Francis Douglas Ley, 4 Bt, MBE TD JP DL; *b* 12 June 1934; *Educ* Eton; *m* 1957, Caroline, da of Maj George H Errington, MC, of Rhodesia (now Zimbabwe); 1 s, 1 da; *Career* dep chm Ley's Foundries & Engrg; md Ley's Malleable Castings, Ewart Chainbelt Co, Beeston Boiler Co Ltd (and chm), W Shaw & Co; *Recreations* tennis, shooting; *Clubs* White's, Buck's; *Style* - Ian Ley Esq; 23 Bywater st, SW3 (☎ 01 584 4125); Fauld Hall, Tutbury, Staffs (☎ 0283 812266)

LI, Choh-Ming; Hon KBE (1973, CBE 1967); s of Kanchi Li; *b* 17 Feb 1912; *Educ* Berkeley, Calif; *m* 1938, Sylvia Chi-Wan Lu; 2 s, 1 da; *Career* V-Chllr Chinese U of Hong Kong 1964-78; *Style* - Choh-Ming Li Esq, KBE; 81 Northampton ave, Berkley, Calif 94707, USA

LICHFIELD, 5 Earl of (UK 1831); (Thomas) Patrick John Anson; also Viscount Anson & Baron Soberton (both UK 1806); s of Lt-Col Viscount Anson (d

1958, s & h of the 4 Earl, who he predeceased, and sixth in descent from Janette Adams, sis of that celebrated circumnavigator of the globe Lord Anson, who died even as a patent of Viscountcy was being made out in his favour) by his 1 w Anne (who later m HH Prince Georg of Denmark), da of Hon John Bowes-Lyon (s of 14 Earl of Strathmore and bro of HM Queen Elizabeth the Queen Mother); hence Lord Lichfield is 2 cous of HRH The Prince of Wales & his siblings; suc gf 1960; *b* 25 April 1939; *Educ* Harrow, RMA Sandhurst; *m* 1975, Lady Leonora Mary Grosvenor, da of 5 Duke of Westminster and sis of Duchess of Roxburghe; 1 s, 2 da; *Heir* s, Viscount Anson; *Career* photographer and ptnr in Tai-Pan Gourmet (Chinese restaurant, 8 Egerton Gdns, SW3; T 01 589 8287); family estate owns at least 8,000 acres in Staffs as of July 1981; served in Grenadier Gds 1959-62; fell Royal Photographic Soc, fell Institute of Incorporated Photographers; *Recreations* arboriculture; *Clubs* White's; *Style* - The Rt Hon the Earl of Lichfield; 44 Edwardes sq, W8 (☎ 01 603 7875); 80 Eaton sq, SW1; Shugborough Hall, Stafford (☎ Little Haywood 881454); (studio) 20 Aubrey Walk, W8 (☎ 01 727 4468)

LICHFIELD, 96 Bishop of (656) 1975-; Rt Rev Kenneth John Fraser Skelton; CBE (1972); s of Henry Edmund Skelton (d 1957); *b* 16 May 1918; *Educ* Dulwich Coll, CCC Cambridge; *m* 1945, Phyllis Barbara, da of James Emerton; 2 s, 1 da; *Career* patron of 134 livings, the Canonries & Prebends in the Cathedral, and the Archdeaconries of Stafford, Salop and Stoke-upon-Trent; ordained 1941, Bp of Matabeleland 1962-70; assist Bp of Durham, Rural Dean Wearmouth and Rector Bishopwearmouth 1970-75; see founded by Oswy, king of Mercia; removed to Chester 1075, to Coventry 1102, and eventually back to Lichfield again; *Style* - The Rt Rev the Bishop of Lichfield CBE; Bishop's House, The Close, Lichfield, Staffs

LICHFIELD, Margaret, Countess of; Violet Margaret (Philips); da of late Henry Dawson Dawson-Greene, JP, of Slyne, and Whittington Hall, Lancs; *m* 1949, as his 2 w, 4 Earl of Lichfield (d 1960); *Style* - The Rt Hon Margaret Countess of Lichfield; 17 Strand Court, Topsham, Devon

LICHT, Leonard Samuel; s of Bernhard Licht; *b* 15 March 1945; *Educ* Christ's Coll Finchley London; *m* 1973, Judith, da of Albert Grossman (d 1980); 1 s, 1 da; *Career* merchant banker; dir Warburg Investment Management Ltd 1976-, Mercury Fund Managers Ltd 1974-; *Recreations* philately, tennis; *Style* - Leonard Licht Esq; 35 Sheldon ave, Highgate, London N6

LIDBURY, Sir John (Towersey); s of John Lidbury (d 1950); *b* 25 Nov 1912; *Educ* Owen's Sch; *m* 1939, Audrey Joyce, da of Harold Wigzell; 1 s, 2 da; *Career* joined Hawker Aircraft Ltd 1940; JP (1952-62) Royal Borough of Kingston-upon-Thames; dir and ch exec Hawker Siddeley Aviation Ltd 1961, chm Hawker Siddeley Dynamics Ltd 1971-77, chm High Duty Alloys Castings Ltd 1978-79; dir Smith Industries Ltd 1978-, Carlton Industries Ltd 1978- & others; kt 1971; *Style* - Sir John Lidbury; 18 St James's sq, SW1 (☎ 01 930 6177)

LIDDELL, Douglas Gerard; s of Gen Sir Clive Liddell, KBE, CMG, DSO; *b* 2 Sept 1919; *Educ* Wellington Coll, Peterhouse Coll Cambridge; *m* 1940, Doreen Joyce, nee Ducker; 3 c (Simon Ingrid, Serena Louise, Anita Helen); *Career* Maj WW II, md Spink & Son Ltd; *Recreations* reading, theatre, cricket; *Clubs* Oxford & Cambridge University, Institute of Directors; *Style* - Douglas Liddell Esq; 11A Gloucester Walk, W8 (☎ 01 937 3581); Rose Cottage, Church st, Henfield, Sussex (☎ Henfield 2758)

LIDDELL, Hon Jane Alice; da of 8 Baron Ravensworth; *b* 1952; *Style* - The Hon Jane Liddell; Eslington Park, Whittingham, Alnwick, Northumberland

LIDDELL, Hon Sophie Harriet; da of Hon Cyril Arthur Liddell (d 1932) and sister of 8 Baron Ravensworth; *b* 1927; *Educ* King's Coll Durham U; granted 1951 title, rank and precedence of a Baron's da which would have been hers had her father survived to succeed to title of Baron Ravensworth; *Style* - The Hon Sophie Liddell

LIDDELL, Hon Thomas Arthur Hamish; s and h of 8 Baron Ravensworth; *b* 27 Oct 1954; *Style* - The Hon Thomas Liddell

LIDDELL-GRAINGER, David Ian; s of Capt Henry Liddell-Grainger, JP, DL, and Lady Muriel Bertie (da of 12 Earl of Lindsey & Abingdon); *b* 26 Jan 1930; *Educ* St Peter's Coll Adelaide, Eton; *m* 1957, Anne, da of Col Sir Henry Abel Smith, KCMG, KCVO, DSO, DL, and Lady May Cambridge (da of 1 Earl of Athlone by HRH Princess Alice, gda of Queen Victoria through the Queen's 4 s, the Duke of Albany); 4 s (Ian Richard Peregrine b 1959, Charles Montague b 1960, Simon Rupert b 1962, Malcolm Henry b 1967), 1 da (Alice Mary b 1965); these children are fourth cousins of HRH The Prince of Wales and his siblings; *Career* property developer & farmer; KStJ *Recreations* shooting, gliding, model engineering; *Clubs* New (Edinburgh), MCC; *Style* - David Liddell-Grainger Esq; Ayton Castle, Berwicks (☎ 03902 212)

LIDDERDALE, Sir David William Shuckburgh; KCB (1975); s of late Edward Wadsworth Lidderdale; *b* 30 Sept 1910; *Educ* Winchester, King's Cambridge; *m* 1943, Lola, da of late Rev Thomas Alexander Beckett; 1 s; *Career* served in 1939-45 War; Assist Clerk House of Commons 1934, Clerk 1974-76; memb Pilgrims Soc; *Style* - Sir David Lidderdale, KCB; 46 Cheyne Walk, SW3

LIDDLE, Maj Sir Donald Ross; s of Thomas Liddle; *b* 11 Oct 1906; *Educ* Provanside, Allen Glen's Sch Glasgow; *m* 1933, May, da of R Christie; 1 s, 2 da; *Career* served in 1939-45 War; DL (1963) Co of Glasgow, Lord Provost 1969-72; chm Cumbernauld Development Corpn 1972-78; V-Lord-Lt City of Glasgow, Strathclyde Region 1978-; kt 1971; *Style* - Maj Sir Donald Liddle, HM Vice-Lord-Lieut for City of Glasgow; 15 Riddrie cres, Glasgow, G33 2QG (☎ 041 770 4310)

LIFFORD, 8 Viscount (I 1781); Alan William Wingfield Hewitt; also Baron Lifford (I 1768); 2 s but only surviving s (Lord Lifford's er bro, Denis, was ka 1917 and was a VC) of Hon George Wyldbore Hewitt (d 1924, 7 s of 4 Viscount by his 2 w, Lydia, nee Digby, herself gda of Lady Charlotte Digby, who was in her turn da of 1 Earl Digby); suc 1 (half) cous, 7 Viscount, DSO, 1954; *b* 11 Dec 1900; *Educ* Winchester, RMC Sandhurst; *m* 1935, Alison Mary Patricia, da of Thomas Wingrave Ashton; 1 s (Hon James H), 3 da (Hon Mrs Swann, da-in-law of Sir Anthony Swann, Bt; Hon Mrs Warburton; Hon Mrs Henderson); *Heir* s, Hon Edward James Wingfield Hewitt; *Career* sometime Lt Hants Regt; *Style* - The Rt Hon the Viscount Lifford; Field House, Hursley, Winchester, Hants (☎ Hursley 75203)

LIGGINS, Sir Edmund Naylor; TD; s of Arthur William Liggins; *b* 21 July 1909; *Educ* King Henry VIII Sch Coventry, Rydal Sch; *m* 1952, Celia Jean Lawrence, da of William Henry Lawrence; 3 s, 1 da; *Career* slr 1931, pres Law Soc 1975-76, sr ptnr Liggins & Co (slrs); kt 1976; *Style* - Sir Edmund Liggins, TD; Hareway Cottage, Hareway Lane, Barford, Warwickshire (☎ Barford 246)

LIGHTFOOT, George Cecil; CBE (1968), DL (Suffolk 1970); s of Ernest William Lightfoot (d 1943); *b* 25 March 1906; *Educ* Cheltenham Coll, Wadham Oxford; *m* 1935, Ghetal Angelita Emerson, da of Arnold Herschell; 1 s, 1 da; *Career* slr, clerk East Suffolk CC; ret 1971; *Recreations* golf; *Clubs* Woodbridge Golf Club; *Style* - George Lightfoot Esq, CBE, DL; Penrith House, Woodbridge

LIGHTHILL, Sir (Michael) James; s of E B Lighthill; *b* 23 Jan 1924; *Educ* Winchester, Trin Cambridge; *m* 1945, Nancy Alice Dumaresque; 1 s, 4 da; *Career* Lucasian Prof of Mathematics Cambridge U 1969-79; Provost U Coll London 1979-; kt 1971; *Style* - Sir James Lighthill; University College London, Gower st, WC1

LIGHTON, Lt-Col Sir Christopher Robert; 8 Bt (I 1791), of Merville, Dublin, MBE (1945), JP (Somerset); s of Sir Christopher Lighton, 7 Bt, JP, DL (d

1929); *b* 1897; *Educ* Eton, RMC; *m* 1, 1926, Rachel Gwendoline (m dis 1953), da of late Rear-Adm Walter S Goodridge, CIE; 2 da; m 2, 1953, Horatia Edith (d 1981), da of A T Powlett; 1 s; *Heir* s, Thomas Lighton; *Career* served in Great War 1914-18 with KRRC, re-employed 1939-45 on staff; *Style* - Lt-Col Sir Christopher Lighton, Bt, MBE, JP; Elphinstone House, North Berwick, East Lothian

LIGHTON, Thomas Hamilton; s and h of Sir Christopher Robert Lighton, 8 Bt, MBE, TD; *b* 4 Nov 1954; *m* Eton; *Style* - Thomas Lighton Esq; c/o Elphinstone House, Berwick, E Lothian

LILEY, Sir Albert William; KCMG (1973), DSC; s of Albert Liley (d 1976); *b* 12 March 1929; *Educ* Roy Oak Sch, Auckland G S, Auckland and Otago Us, Australian Nat U; *m* 1953, Helen Margaret Irwin, da of William Hunt; 2 s, 4 da; *Career* Prof perinatal physiology Postgraduate Sch of Obstetrics and Gynaecology Auckland U; *Style* - Sir Albert Liley, KCMG, DSC; 19 Pukenui rd, Epsom, Auckland, New Zealand

LILFORD, 7 Baron (GB 1797); George Vernon Powys; s of Robert Horace Powys (d 1940, gggs of 2 Baron Lilford); suc 6 Baron (2 cous twice removed) 1949; *b* 8 Jan 1931; *Educ* St Aidan's Coll, Grahamstown, S Africa; Stonyhurst; *m* 1, 1954, Mrs Eveline Bird (m dis); m 2, 1957, Anuta (m dis 1958), da of L F Merritt, of Jo'burg; m 3, 1958, Norma Yvonne (m dis 1961), da of V Shell, of Jo'burg, m 4, 1961, Mrs Muriel Spottiswoode, nee Cooke (m dis 1969); 2 da; m 5, 1969, Margaret, da of A Penman, of Roslin, Midlothian; 1 s, 2 da; *Heir* s, Hon Mark Vernon Powys; *Style* - The Rt Hon the Lord Lilford; PO Box 177, Constantia, Cape 7848, S Africa

LILL, John Richard; OBE (1978); s of G R Lill; *b* 17 March 1944; *Educ* Leyton County High, Royal Coll Music; *Career* concert pianist, soloist with leading orchestras, worldwide TV and radio appearances, prof Royal Coll Music, winner of International Tchaikowsky competition, Moscow 1970; *Recreations* amateur radio, chess, physchic research; *Style* - John Lill Esq, OBE; c/o Harold Holt Ltd, 134 Wigmore street, W1 (☎ 01 935 2331)

LILLEY, Prof Geoffrey Michael; s of Michael Moreland Dessau (d 1941); *b* 16 Nov 1919; *Educ* Isleworth G S, Imperial College; *m* 1948, Leslie Marion, da of Leonard Wheeler, of Cranfield, Beds; 1 s, 2 da; *Career* RAF 1935-36, prof Aeronautics and Astronautics U of Southampton 1964-, Experimental Fluid Mechanics Coll of Aeronautics 1962-, memb Noise Advisory Council (chm Noise from Air Traffic) 1970-; *Recreations* walking, music, chess; *Style* - Prof Geoffrey Lilley; Highbury, Pine Walk, Chilworth, Southampton (☎ 0703 769109)

LILLINGSTON, Lady Vivienne Margaret *née* Nevill; da of 5 Marquess of Abergavenny; *b* 1941; *m* 1962, Alan Lillingston; 1 s, 1 da; *Style* - Lady Vivienne Lillingston; Mount Coote, Kilmallock, Co Limerick

LILLIS, Anthony Percival Noel; s of the late Capt Percival Joseph Lillis; *b* 25 Dec 1916; *Educ* King Edward VI G S Totnes; *m* 1940, Beryl, nee Bruton; 2 da; *Career* Lt RNVR: Mediterranean, N Africa, Italy, Pacific; chm Severn Valley Woodworks Ltd, Bennett Transport Ltd; dir H J Heinz Co Ltd 1966-70; *Recreations* sailing, motoring, (Yacht 'Shantimere'); *Clubs* Inst of Directors; *Style* - Anthony Lillis Esq; Underdean House, Blakeney, Glos (☎ Blakeney 236)

LIM, Sir Han-Hoe; CBE (1941), JP; s of late Lim Cheng Sah; *b* 27 Apr 1894; *Educ* St Andrew's Sch, Raffles Institution, Edinburgh U; *m* 1920, Chua Seng Neo; 2 s, 2 da; *Career* Pro-Chllr Malaya U 1949-59; kt 1946; *Style* - Sir Han-Hoe Lim, CBE, JP; 758 Mountbatten rd, Singapore 15 (☎ 40655)

LIMERICK, 6 Earl of (I 1803); Patrick Edmund Pery; also Baron Glentworth (I 1790; from 1834 the gs and h of the 1 Earl was designated - unjustifiably except insofar as lengthening usage legitimates - 'Viscount' Glentworth; this is now the style of the eldest s & h), Viscount Limerick (I 1800), and Baron Foxford (UK 1815, which sits as); s of 5 Earl of Limerick, GBE, CH, KCB, DSO, TD (d 1967), by his w Angela, GBE, DStJ (da of Lt-Col Sir Henry Trotter, KCMG, CB); *b* 12 April 1930; *Educ* Eton, New Coll Oxford; *m* 1961, Sylvia Rosalind, da of Brig Maurice S Lush, CB, CBE, MC; 2 s, 1 da; *Heir* s, Viscount Glentworth; *Career* dir Kleinwort Benson Ltd, Union Minière SA, Tanks Consolidated Investments Ltd, Internat Investment Tst; chm Mallinson-Denny Ltd; Parly Under Sec State DTI 1972-74; Pres SCGB; pres Assoc of British Chambers of Commerce 1974-77, v-pres 1977-; chm Ctee for Middle East Trade 1975-79; chm British overseas Trade Bd 1979-; *Style* - The Rt Hon the Earl of Limerick; Chiddinglye, W Hoathly, E Grinstead, W Sussex (☎ Sharpthorne 810214); 30 Victoria rd, W8 (☎ 01 937 0573)

LIMERICK, Countess of; Sylvia Rosalind Pery; da of Maurice Stanley Lush, CB, CBE, MC; *b* 7 Dec 1935; *Educ* St Swithun's Sch Winchester, Lady Margaret Hall Oxford; *m* 1961, 6 Earl of Limerick; 2 s, 1 da; *Career* pres Nat Assoc for Maternal & Child Welfare 1973-, UK Ctee for UN Children's Fund 1972-79; v-chm Foundation for the Study of Infant Deaths 1971-; memb Kensington, Chelsea and Westminster Area Health Authority 1977-; Ctee of Management, Inst of Child Health 1976-, council and ctee of Management King Edward's Hospital Fund 1977-; *Recreations* skiing, music; *Style* - The Rt Hon the Countess of Limerick; 30 Victoria rd, W8 (☎ 01 937 0573); Chiddinglye, W Hoathly, E Grinstead, W Sussex (☎ 0342 810214)

LINACRE, John Gordon Seymour; CBE (1979), AFC (1943), DFM (1941); s of John James Linacre, of Norton Woodseats, Sheffield (d 1957); *b* 23 Sept 1920; *Educ* Firth Park G S Sheffield; *m* 1943, Irene Amy, da of Alexander Gordon (d 1946); 2 da; *Career* served 1939-46 War, RAF; md Yorkshire Post Newspapers Ltd 1965-; *Recreations* golf, cricket, squash, country walking; *Style* - John Linacre Esq, CBE, AFC, DFM; White Windows, Staircase Lane, Bramhope, Leeds LS16 9JD (☎ Arthington 842 751)

LINCOLN, 69 Bishop of (1072) 1974-; Rt Rev Simon Wilton Phipps; MC (1945); s of Capt William Duncan Phipps, CVO, RN (d 1967); *b* 6 July 1921; *Educ* Eton, Trin Cambridge; *m* 1973, Mary, widow of Rev Dr James Welch and da of Sir (Charles) Eric Palmer (d 1948); *Career* patron of 154 livings & 21 alternately and 14 by turns or jointly, the Canonries, Precentorship, Chllrship, Sub-Deanery, and the Archdeaconries of Stow, Lincoln and Lindsey, also Prebendal stalls in the cathedral; ordained 1950, Chaplain Trin Cambridge 1953-58, first Bp Suffragan of Horsham (dioc of Chichester) 1968-74; formerly chaplain Trin Cambridge, also Coventry Cathedral; see founded from two more ancient ones (Lindisfan, see at Sidnacester, and Middle Angles at Leicester; united in one Diocese under see of Leicester, the new entity was removed (1) to Dorchester and (2), after the Conquest, to Lincoln); *Style* - The Rt Rev the Bishop of Lincoln, MC; Bishop's House, Eastgate, Lincoln (☎ 34701)

LINCOLN, Hon Mr Justice; Hon Sir Anthony (Leslie Julian); s of Samuel Lincoln; *b* 7 Apr 1920; *Educ* Highgate, Queen's Oxford; *Career* served in Somerset LI and RA 1941-45; barr Lincoln's Inn 1949, QC 1968, recorder of Crown Court 1974-79; High Court Judge (Family Div) 1979-; chm Harrison Homes for the Elderly; kt 1979; *Style* - The Hon Mr Justice Lincoln; Heale Park Cottage, Upper Woodford, Salisbury, Wilts (☎ Middle Woodford 312); 9 Paultons sq, SW3

LINCOLN, Sir Anthony Handley; KCMG (1965), CVO (1957); s of John Bebrouth Lincoln, OBE (d 1938); *b* 2 Jan 1911; *Educ* Mill Hill Sch, Magdalene Cambridge; *m* 1948, Lisette Marion, da of late A E Summers, of Buenos Aires; *Career* formerly counsellor British Embassy Copenhagen, Ambass to Venezuela 1964-69; *Style* - Sir Anthony Lincoln, KCMG, CVO

LINCOLN, His Honour John Francis; s of John Lincoln (d 1916); *b* 30 July 1916; *Educ* Newington College Australia, Balliol Oxford; *m* 1952, Joan Alison, da of Harold Robert Lionel Scott (d 1977); 1 s, 1 da;

Career barr Lincoln's Inn, acting judge Supreme Court of New South Wales 1967, judge District Court of New South Wales 1968-, dep-chancellor Macquarie U 1976-, chancellor Diocese of Newcastle NSW 1978-; formerly mayor of North Sydney 1956-58, NSW state treasurer Liberal Party of Australia 1966-68; *Recreations* swimming; *Style* - His Honour John Lincoln; Stone Lodge, 30-34 Stanley st, St Ives NSW 2075, Australia

LINCOLN, Sir Norman; s of Thomas Cox Lindop; *b* 1921; *Educ* Northgate Sch Ipswich, Queen Mary Coll; *m* 1974, Jenny Caroline Quass; 1 s; *Career* head of Dept of Chemistry and Geology, Kingston Coll of Technology 1957-63; dir Hatfield Polytechnic 1969-; chm Council for Professions Supplementary to Medicine 1973-, memb Science Research Council 1974-78, chm Data Protection Ctee 1976-78; kt 1973; *Style* - Sir Norman Lincoln; Hatfield Polytechnic, PO Box 109, Hatfield, Herts (☎ Hatfield 68100)

LINDA, Lady Isobel Mackenzie; da of Countess of Cromartie (d 1962); *b* 1911; *m* 1947, Capt Oscar Linda; *Style* - Lady Isobel Linda; Assynt House, Evanton, Ross-shire

LINDESAY-BETHUNE, Hon Caroline Janet; da of Viscount Garnock; *b* 7 July 1957; *Style* - The Hon Caroline Lindesay-Bethune

LINDESAY-BETHUNE, Hon John Martin; s of 14 Earl of Lindsay; *b* 1929; *Educ* Eton, Trin Hall Cambridge; *m* 1, 1953, Enriqueta Mary Jeanne, (m dis 1976), da of Peter Koch de Gooreynd (and through him 1 cous of Peregrine Worsthorne, *qv*) by Joan, nee Douglas (1 cous four times removed of 6 & 7 Marquesses of Queensberry); 3 s, 1 da; m 2, 1977, Jean Maxwell, da of Brig Eric Brickman, and formerly w of Stephen John Younger; *Career* late Lt Scots Gds; *Style* - The Hon John Lindesay-Bethune; Flat 3, 4 Halkin st, SW1 (☎ 01 235 7699)

LINDGREN, Baroness; Elsie Olive; da of Frank Reed, of Chishill, Herts; *m* 1926, Baron Lindgren (Life Peer) (d 1971); 1 s; *Style* - The Rt Hon the Lady Lindgren; 4 Attimore Close, Welwyn Garden City, Herts (☎ 22669)

LINDGREN, Hon Graham Alastair; s of Baron Lindgren (Life Peer) (d 1971); *b* 25 July 1928; *Educ* Welwyn Garden City G S; *m* 1953, Gwendolyne Mary, da of late A W Miller, of Coleford Glos; 1 s; *Style* - The Hon Graham Lindgren; 43 Westly Wood, Welwyn Garden City, Herts (☎ Welwyn Garden 26706)

LINDLEY, Sir Arnold Lewis George; s of George Dilnot Lindley (d 1927); *b* 13 Nov 1902; *Educ* Woolwich Polytechnic; *m* 1, 1927, Winifred (d 1962), da of Francis Cowling, of Somerset; 1 s, 1 da; m 2, 1963, Phyllis, da of Walter Burns, of Lincoln; *Career* v-chm General Electric Co Ltd 1959, md 1961-62, chm 1961-64; chm Engineering Industry Training Bd 1964-74; v-chm Motherwell Bridge (Holdings) Ltd 1965; chm Council of Engineering Institutions 1971-73; memb of Design Council 1972-74; kt 1964; *Style* - Sir Arnold Lindley; Heathcote House, 18 Nab Lane, Shipley, W Yorks

LINDLEY, Raymond Peter; s of Frederick George Lindley; *b* 26 May 1929; *Educ* fell Chartered Insurance Inst; *m* 1953, Lilian May, nee Scales; 1 da; *Career* insurance broker, dir Reed Stenhouse Ltd 1979- (dir Reed Stenhouse UK Ltd 1969); *Recreations* fishing, music, collecting porcelain; *Style* - Raymond Lindley Esq; Springrove House, Redwings Lane, Pembury, Tunbridge Wells, Kent

LINDON, Sir Leonard Charles Edward; s of James Hemery Lindon (d 1897); *b* Feb 1896; *Educ* Geelong G S, St Peter's Coll Adelaide, Adelaide and Oxford Us; *m* 1921, Jean Monteith, da of late R Humphrey Marten, MD; 2 s, 1 da; *Career* served 1914-16 with AIF and 1939-41 with AAMC; hon surgeon and neuro-surgeon Roy Adelaide Hosp, assoc lecturer in Surgery Adelaide U, pres Roy Australasian Coll of Surgeons 1959-61; kt 1964; *Style* - Sir Leonard Lindon; 222 Brougham pla, N Adelaide 5006, Australia

LINDOP, David Harry; s of Col Carl Arthur Boys Lindop (d 1968); *b* 17 July

1928; *Educ* Sedburgh Sch, Birmingham U; *m* 1952, Heather Margaret Murray, nee Lambert; 3 s; *Career* chartered engineer, liveryman of Worshipful Co of Founders, Freeman of City of London, chm and md FJ Whittle Metal Productions Ltd 1973-; *Recreations* golf, gardening; *Clubs* Little Aston GC; *Style* - David Lindop Esq; Evista, Endwood dr, Little Aston Park, Sutton Coldfield (☎ W Midlands)

LINDSAY OF BIRKER, 2 Baron (UK 1945); Michael Francis Morris Lindsay; s of 1 Baron, CBE (d 1952); *b* 24 Feb 1909; *Educ* Gresham's, Balliol Oxford; *m* 1941, Hsiao Li, da of Li Wen-chi, of the Chinese Army, of Lishih, Shansi; 1 s, 2 da; *Heir* s, Hon James Francis Lindsay; *Career* sinologist and economist; economics lecturer at Yenching U, Peking 1937; Press Attaché British Embassy, Chunking 1940; has taught at various universities in UK, USA; now Prof Emeritus Sch of Internat Serv, American U, Washington DC; served with 18 Gp Army N China 1942-45; *Style* - The Rt Hon the Lord Lindsay of Birker; 6812 Delaware st, Chevy Chase, Maryland 20015, USA (☎ 656 4245)

LINDSAY, 14 Earl of (S 1633); Maj William Tucker Lindesay-Bethune; DL (Fife 1956); also Lord Lindsay of the Byres (S 1445), Lord Parbroath (S 1633), Viscount Garnock, and Lord Kilbirnie, Kingsburn and Drumry (both S 1703); s of 13 Earl (d 1943) and Ethel, nee Tucker, of Boston; *b* 28 April 1901; *Educ* Groton USA, BNC Oxford; *m* 1925, Marjory, DStJ, da of late Arthur G Cross and late Lady Hawke; 2 s, 2 da; *Heir* s, Viscount Garnock; *Career* late Maj Scots Gds, served in Norwegian Campaign 1940; KStJ, Prior of Order of St John of Jerusalem in Scotland 1947-50; memb Queen's Bodyguard for Scotland, Roy Co of Archers; Scottish Rep Peer 1947-59; Zone Commissioner N Civ Def Zone Scotland 1963-69; assumed additional surname of Bethune 1939; pres Shipwrecked Fishermen and Mariner Roy Benevolent Soc 1966-76; *Clubs* Guards & Cavalry, Leander; *Style* - The Rt Hon the Earl of Lindsay DL; Lahill, Upper Largo, Fife (☎ 251)

LINDSAY, Hon Mrs; Hon Anne Bradbury; da of 2 Baron Bradbury; *b* 1947; *m* 1970, Alastair James Ker-Lindsay; 4 s; *Style* - The Hon Mrs Lindsay; 15 Grosvenor sq, W1

LINDSAY, Hon Mrs; Hon Audrey Lavinia Lyttelton; da of 9 Viscount Cobham, KCB, TD (d 1949); *b* 1918; *m* 1950, David Edzell Thomas Lindsay (d 1968); 3 s, 1 da; *Style* - The Hon Mrs Lindsay; Sea Cottage, Fore st, Budleigh Salterton, Devon

LINDSAY, Lady Amabel Mary Maud Yorke; da of 9 Earl of Hardwicke (d 1974); *b* 1935; *m* 1955, Hon Patrick Lindsay; *Style* - Lady Amabel Lindsay; 12 Lansdowne rd, W11

LINDSAY, Hon Alexander Walter; s of Earl of Crawford and Balcarres; *b* 1961; *Style* - The Hon Alexander Lindsay

LINDSAY, Hon Mrs; Hon Bronwen Mary; da of 8 Baron Howard de Walden and Seaford (d 1946); *b* 1912; *m* 1933, Hon James Louis Lindsay; *Style* - The Hon Mrs Lindsay; Spring Farm, Colemans Hatch, Hartfield, Sussex

LINDSAY, Lady Clare Rohais Antonia Elizabeth; *née* Giffard; da of 3 Earl of Halsbury; *b* 1944; *m* 1964, Maj Oliver John Martin Lindsay (b 30 Aug 1938, s of Sir Martin Alexander Lindsay of Dowhill, 1 Bt, CBE, DSO, educ Eton & Sandhurst, Lt-Col Gren Gds, GSO 1 Def Policy Staff MOD; author; memb Roy Co of Archers - Queen's Bodyguard for Scotland - and Boodle's); *Style* - Lady Clare Lindsay; Brookwood House, Brookwood, Surrey

LINDSAY, Hon Erica Susan; da of 2 Baron Lindsay of Birker; *b* 1942; *Educ* Canberra H S Australia, Sch of Int Service, American U Washington DC, LMH Oxford; *Style* - The Hon Erica Lindsay; 6812 Delaware st, Chevy Chase 15, Maryland, USA (☎ 656 4245); Gillbank, Boot, Holmrook, Cumberland

LINDSAY, Hon Iona Sina; da of Rt Hon Lord Balniel, PC, MP; *b* 10 Aug 1957; *Style* - The Hon Iona Lindsay

LINDSAY, Hon James Francis; s and h

of 2 Baron Lindsay of Birker; *b* 29 Jan 1945; *Educ* Canberra H S, Geelong G S Victoria, Bethesda-Chevy Chase H S, U of Keele; *Career* formerly lecturer Dept of Physics Tunghai U Taichung Taiwan Republic of China; 2 Sec Australian Embassy, Santiago, Chile 1973-76; *Style* - The Hon James Lindsay; Australian Foreign Service, Dept of Foreign Affairs, Canberra, ACT, Australia

LINDSAY, Sir James Harvey Kincaid Stewart; s of Arthur Harvey Lindsay; *b* 31 May 1915; *Educ* Highgate Sch; *m* Marguerite Phyllis Bondville (1 s, 1 da by previous m); *Career* formerly chm and md The Metal Box Co of India Ltd; chm Henley Training Ltd 1980-, tstee Inst of Family and Environmental Res 1971-; dir Nimbus Int Development Ltd 1975-; kt 1966; *Style* - Sir James Lindsay; Christmas Cottage, Lower Shiplake, Oxon (☎ Wargrave 2859)

LINDSAY, Hon James Louis; s of 27 Earl of Crawford and (10) Balcarres (d 1940); *b* 1909; *Educ* Eton, Magdalen Oxford; *m* 1933, Hon Bronwen Mary, da (twin) of 8 Baron Howard de Walden (d 1946); 3 s, 1 da; *Career* formerly Maj KRRC; MP (C) North Devon 1955-59; *Style* - The Hon James Lindsay; Spring Farm, Coleman's Hatch, Hartfield, E Sussex

LINDSAY OF DOWHILL, James Martin Evelyn; s and h of Sir Ronald Lindsay of Dowhill, 2 Bt; *b* 1968

LINDSAY OF DOWHILL, Hon Lady; Hon Loelia Mary Ponsonby; da of 1 Baron Sysonby, GCB, GCVO (d 1935); *b* 1902; *m* 1, 1930, as his 3 w, 2 Duke of Westminster (m dis 1947) (he d 1953); m 2, 1969, as his 2 w, Sir Martin Alexander Lindsay of Dowhill, 1 Bt, CBE, DSO (d 1981); *Style* - The Hon Lady Lindsay of Dowhill; The Old Vicarage, Send, Woking, Surrey

LINDSAY, Hon Mary Muriel; da of 2 Baron Lindsay of Birker; *b* 1951; *Educ* Chevy Chase Elementary and H S, Bethesda and Leland Junior H S, Case-Western Reserve U Cleveland USA; *Style* - The Hon Mary Lindsay

LINDSAY, Hon Patrick; s of 28 Earl of Crawford and (11) Balcarres, KT, GBE; *b* 14 Nov 1928; *Educ* Eton, Magdalen Oxford; *m* 1955, Lady Amabel Mary Maud Yorke, da of 9 Earl of Hardwicke; 3 s, 1 da; *Career* dir Christie's Internat Ltd; late 2 Lt Scots Gds; *Recreations* veteran cars; *Clubs* White's, Roy Yacht Sqdn; *Style* - The Hon Patrick Lindsay; 12 Lansdowne rd, W 11 (☎ 01 727 6006)

LINDSAY, Ronald Alexander; s and h of Sir Martin Alexander Lindsay of Downhill, 1 Bt, CBE, DSO; *b* 6 Dec 1933; *m* 1968, Nicoletta, da of Capt Edgar Storich, Italian Navy (ret); *Career* memb Queen's Body Guard for Scotland (Royal Co of Archers); *Style* - Ronald Lindsay Esq; Courleigh, Colley ave, Reigate, Surrey

LINDSAY OF DOWHILL, Sir Ronald Alexander; 2 Bt (UK 1962); s of Sir Martin Alexander Lindsay of Dowhill, 1 Bt, CBE, DSO (d 1981) by 1 w, Joyce, da of late Maj the Hon Robert Hamilton Lindsay, s of late 26 Earl of Crawford; *b* 6 Dec 1933; *m* 1968, Nicoletta, da of Capt Edgar Storich, Italian Navy (ret); 3 s, 1 da; *Heir* s, James Lindsay of Dowhill; *Career* memb Queen's Body Guard for Scotland (Roy Co of Archers); *Style* - Sir Ronald Lindsay of Dowhill, Bt; Courleigh, Colley av, Reigate, Surrey

LINDSAY, Robert Keith; s of Robert Lindsay (d 1978); *b* 15 Nov 1936; *Educ* Lancing, Magdalene Cambridge; *m* 1961, Elisabeth, nee Smith; 2 s, 1 da; *Career* chartered (chemical) engineer, md New Metals and Chemicals Holdings Ltd 1979-, dir Tennant Trading Ltd 1974-79; *Recreations* squash, gardening; *Clubs* United Oxford and Cambridge, Purley Cricket; *Style* - Robert Lindsay Esq; Lilac Wood, 114 Foxley Lane, Purley, Surrey (☎ 01 660 8531)

LINDSAY, Hon Thomas Martin; MBE (1946); s of 1 Baron Lindsay of Birker, CBE (d 1952); *b* 1915; *Educ* Sidcot Sch, Edinburgh U; *m* 1, 1939, Denise Theresa (m dis 1951), da of Gerald Albert Vaughan; 2 s, 1 da; m 2, 1951, Felicitas (m dis 1961), da of Dr Martin Lange; 2 s; m 3, Erica, da of Maj Eric Thirkell-Cooper; 2 s;

Career served 1939-45 War (despatches), Maj Sherwood Rangers; *Style* - The Hon Thomas Lindsay, MBE; rue de Toulouse 17, 1040 Brussels, Belgium

LINDSAY, Hon Thomas Richard; s of 28 Earl of Crawford and (11) Balcarres, KT, GBE; *b* 18 Feb 1937; *Educ* Eton; *m* 1961, Sarah Virginia, da of (George) Nigel Capel Cure, TD, JP, DL, of Blake Hall, Ongar, Essex; 3 s, 2 da; *Career* picture restorer; 2 Lt Scots Gds (Nat Service); *Clubs* Brooks's; *Style* - The Hon Thomas Lindsay; The Old Rectory, Ashmore, Salisbury, Wilts (☎ 0747 811278)

LINDSAY, Sir William; CBE (1956); s of James R Lindsay (d 1940) of Tower of Lethendy, Meikleour, Perthshire; *b* 22 Mar 1907; *Educ* Trin Coll Glenalmond, Ch Ch Oxford; *m* 1936, Anne Dianna, da of Arthur Morley, OBE, KC; 1 s, 2 da; *Career* barr Inner Temple 1931; Admin Officer HM Treasury 1940-45; memb Cuckfield UDC 1946-67, chm 1951-54; DL (1970), CC (1949), E Sussex; v-chm 1958, memb Countryside Commission 1962-71; kt 1963; *Style* - Sir William Lindsay, CBE; Wickham Farm, Hayward's Heath, W Sussex (☎ 50371)

LINDSAY-HOGG, Edward William; s of late Sir Lindsay Hogg, 1 Bt and hp of n, Sir William Lindsay-Hogg, 3 Bt; *b* 23 May 1910; *m* 1, 1936, Geraldine (m dis 1946) da of C M Fitzgerald; 1 s; m 2, 1957, Mrs Kathleen Mary Cadell, da of James Cooney, of Carrick-on-Suir, Co Tipperary; *Clubs* St Stephen's Green (Dublin); *Style* - Edward William Lindsay-Hogg Esq

LINDSAY-HOGG, Sir William Lindsay; 3 Bt (UK 1905); s of Sir Anthony Henry Lindsay-Hogg, 2 Bt (d 1968); *b* 12 Aug 1930; *Educ* Stowe; *m* 1961, Victoria (m dis 1967), da of John Pares, of Kingsclere, Hants; 1 da; *Heir* unc, Edward William Lindsay-Hogg; *Career* md Roebuck Air Charter Ltd 1967-70 (chm 1970-74; *Style* - Sir William Lindsay-Hogg, Bt; Underwoods, Edgefield, Melton Constable, Norfolk NR24 2AR

LINDSAY-MACDOUGALL OF LUNGA, Hon Mrs; Hon Frances Phoebe; da of Capt Hon Anthony Francis Phillimore, (ka), of Coppid Hall; *b* 1938; *m* 1961, Colin John Francis Lindsay-MacDougall of Lunga; *Career* granted 1949, title, rank and precedence of a Baron's da, which would have been hers had her father survived to succeed to title of Baron Phillimore; *Style* - The Hon Mrs Lindsay-MacDougall of Lunga; Lunga, Ardfern Lochgilphead, Argyll

LINDSAY-SMITH, Iain-Mór; s of Edward Duncanson Lindsay-Smith (d 1951); *b* 18 Sept 1934; *Educ* High Sch of Glasgow, London U Extension Diploma Course; *m* 1960, Carol Sara, da of Edward Philip Paxman (d 1948); 1 s; *Career* command 1 Bn Cameronians (Scottish Rifles) 1935-55; journalist Scottish Daily Record 1951-57, Daily Mirror 1957-60; dep editor Yorkshire Post 1971-74, editor Glasgow Herald 1974-77, exec editor The Observer 1977-; *Style* - Iain-Mór Lindsay-Smith Esq; The Observer, St Andrew's Hill, EC4 (☎ 01 236 90202); Old Hall Farm, Little Horkesley, Colchester, Essex (☎ 0206 271035)

LINDSEY AND ABINGDON, 14 and 9 Earl of (E 1626 & 1682); Richard Henry Rupert Bertie; also Baron Norreys of Ryecote (E 1572); s of Lt-Col Hon Arthur Michael Bertie, DSO, MC (d 1957), and cousin of 13 Earl of Lindsey and 8 Earl of Abingdon (d 1963); *b* 28 June 1931; *Educ* Ampleforth; *m* 1957, Norah Elizabeth Farquhar-Oliver, da of Mark Oliver, OBE, by Norah (da of Maj Francis Farquhar, DSO, 2 s of Sir Henry Farquhar, 4 Bt, JP, DL, by the Maj's w Lady Evelyn Hely Hutchinson, da of 5 Earl of Donoughmore); 2 s, 1 da; *Heir* s, Lord Norreys of Rycote; *Career* Lt Roy Norfolk regiment 1951-52; underwriting memb of Lloyds 1958; high steward of Abingdon 1963; *Clubs* Turf, White's; *Style* - The Rt Hon the Earl of Lindsey and Abingdon; Gilmilnscroft, Sorn, Mauchline, Ayrshire

LING, Arthur George; s of George Frederick Lind (d 1957); *b* 20 Sept 1913; *Educ* Christ's Hospital, Univ Coll London; *m* 1939, Marjorie, da of Robert John Tall (d 1962); *Career* sr lecturer, Dept of Town Planning London U 1947-55, project man UN Habitat Project Physical Perspective

Plan for Libya 1977-80; private practice, Arthur Ling & Associates, Architects & Town Planners 1965-77; v-pres RIBA 1963-64, pres Roy Town Planning Inst 1968-69, pres Commonwealth Assoc of Planners 1970-75; memb Sprorts council 1967-71; *Style* - Arthur Ling Esq; The Old Rectory, Howell, Sleaford, Lincs (☎ 0529 60142)

LINGARD, Lady Caroline Flower Erskine; da of 16 Earl of Buchan; *b* 1935; *m* 1963, John Robin William Lingard; 2 da; *Style* - Lady Caroline Lingard; Burnt Oak House, East Bergholt, Suffolk

LINLEY, Viscount; *see* Royal Family section

LINLITHGOW, 3 Marquess of (UK 1902); Sir Charles William Frederick Hope, MC; 11 Bt (NS 1698), MC (1945), TD (1973); also Earl of Hopetoun, Viscount Aithrie, Lord Hope (all S 1703), Baron Hopetoun (UK 1809), and Baron Niddry (UK 1814); er (twin) s (Lord Linlithgow's yr bro is Lord Glendevon) of 2 Marquess, KG, KT, GCSI, GCIE, OBE, TD, PC, DL, FRS (d 1952), by his w Doreen, CI (yr da of Rt Hon Sir Frederick Milner, 7 Bt, GCVO, PC); 1 cous of Lord (17 Earl of) Pembroke; *b* 7 April 1912; *Educ* Eton, Ch Ch Oxford; *m* 1, 1939, Vivien (d 1963), da of Capt Robert Orlando Rodolph Kenyon-Slaney (paternal gggs of 1 Baron Kenyon and maternal gs of 3 Earl of Bradford) by his w Lady Mary Hamilton, da of 3 Duke of Abercorn and subsequently step mother to Ian Gilmour (now Sir Ian Gilmour, Bt, Lord Privy Seal); 1 s, 1 da; m 2, 1965, Judith, formerly w of John Radway and widow of Esmond Charles Baring (OBE, d 1963), also da of late Stanley Matthew Lawson, of Cincinnati, Ohio; *Heir* s, Earl of Hopetoun; *Career* formerly Lt Scots Gds, Capt Lothian and Border Horse, served 1939-45 War, Lord Lt West Lothian 1964-; dir Eagle Star Insurance Co Ltd; *Clubs* Turf and White's Clubs; *Style* - The Most Hon the Marquess of Linlithgow MC TD, HM Lord-Lieut for W Lothian; Hopetoun House, South Queensferry, West Lothian (☎ 031 331 1169)

LINNELL, David Gerald; s of Rev Gerald Hislop Linnell (d 1944); *b* 29 Dec 1934; *Educ* Christ's Hosp, Roy Tech Coll Salford; *m* 1959, Enid, da of Horace Smith; 2 s, 1 da; *Career* md Cableform Ltd; *Recreations* gardening, reading, photography, travel; *Style* - David Linnell Esq; Pickerings Bridge Cottage, Crowton, Cheshire

LINNELL, David George Thomas; *Career* md Linfood Holdings Ltd, dir A F H Gimens & Cia, SA, Linfood Overseas Ltd; chm Barham Bodies Ltd, Linfood Ltd; *Style* - David Linnell Esq; Linfood Holdings Ltd, Brettenham House, 14 Lancaster pla, WC2

LINSTEAD, Sir Hugh Nicholas; OBE (1937); s of late Edward Flatman Linstead, of Winchmore Hill; *b* 1901; *Educ* City of London Sch, Birkbeck Coll, U British Columbia, U Toronto; *m* 1928, Alice Winifred, da of Charles Henry Freke; 2 da; *Career* sec Pharmaceutical Soc of GB 1926-64; MP (C) Wandsworth (Putney) 1942-64; chm Macarthys Pharmaceuticals Ltd 1965-79; kt 1953; *Clubs* Athenaeum; *Style* - Sir Hugh Linstead, OBE; 15 Somerville House, Manor Fields, Putney, SW15

LINTOTT, Sir Henry John Bevis; KCMG (1957); *m* 1940, Margaret Orpen; 1 da; *Career* entered Civil Service 1932, under-sec Board of Trade 1946, dep Sec-Gen Organization for European Economic Co-Operation 1948-56, dep under-sec of State Commonwealth Relations Office 1956-63, British High Commissioner in Canada 1963-68; co dir; *Style* - Sir Henry Lintott, KCMG; 12 Willow walk, Cambridge (☎ Cambridge 312410)

LINZEE, Hon Mrs; Hon Ellinor Aileen Cecil Craig; da of 1 Viscount Craigavan (d 1940); *b* 1907; *m* 1929, Capt Robert Gordon Hood Linzee, CB, CBE, RN (m dis 1943); 1 s; *Style* - The Hon Mrs Linzee; West Lodge, Cluny Castle, Sauchen, Aberdeenshire

LIPFRIEND, His Honour Judge; Alan; s of Israel Lipfriend (d 1931); *b* 6 Oct 1916; *Educ* Central Foundation Sch London, Queen Mary Coll London; *m*

1948, Adele Burke; 1 s; *Career* barr Middle Temple 1948; pres Appeal Tribunal (England and Wales) under Wireless and Telegraphy Act (1949) 1971-73, a circuit judge 1973-; *Recreations* theatre, sport; *Style* - His Honour Judge Lipfriend; 10 Woodside ave, N6 (☎ 01 883 4420)

LIPPINCOTT, Hon Mrs; Hon Caroline Seebohm; da of Baron Seebohm (Life Peer); *b* 1940; *m* 1, 1962, Roger John Smith (m dis 1967); m 2, 1974, Walter H Lippincott; *Style* - The Hon Mrs Lippincott; 315 East 56 st, New York, NY 10022, USA

LISBURNE, 8 Earl of (I 1776); Capt John David Malet Vaughan; also Viscount Lisburne and Baron Fethard (I 1695); the eldest s & h appears to have been styled Lord Vaughan since 1776; s of 7 Earl of Lisburne (d 1965, seventh in descent from the union of the 1 Viscount L with Lady Mallet Wilmot, herself da of 2 Earl of Rochester, a poet, according to Horace Walpole, whom the muses inspired but were ashamed to own, since his works had more obscenity than wit, more wit than poetry, and more poetry than politeness); *b* 1 Sept 1918; *Educ* Eton, Magdalen Oxford; *m* 1943, Shelagh, da of late T A Macauley, of Montreal, Canada; 3 s; *Heir* s, Viscount Vaughan; *Career* barr Inner Temple; 2 Lt Welsh Gds 1939, Capt 1943, served 1939-45 War; dir British Home Stores Ltd, S Wales Regional Bd Lloyds Bank Ltd 1978-, Westward TV (dep chm to 1980); *Clubs* Buck's and Pratt's; *Style* - The Rt Hon the Earl of Lisburne; Cruglas, Ystrad Meurig, Dyfed (Pontrhydfendigaid 230); Sloane Sq House, Holbein pla, SW1; 22 York House, Kensington Church st, W8 (☎ 01 937 3043)

LISLE, 7 Baron (I 1758); John Nicholas Horace Lysaght; s of Horace George Lysaght (d 1918) and Alice (da of Sir John Wrixon-Becher, 3 Bt); gs of 6 Baron (d 1919); *b* 10 Aug 1903; *m* 1, 1928, Vivienne (m dis 1939, she d 1948), da of Rev M Brew; m 2, 1939, Marie, da of A D Purgold, of Salop; *Heir* n, Patrick Lysaght; *Style* - The Rt Hon the Lord Lisle; 4 Bramerton st, SW3

LISSAUER, Franz A; *Career* chm Leopold Lazarus Ltd; chm Spartan Redheugh Ltd; dir Associated Metals & Minerals Corpn (New York); *Style* - Franz Lissauer Esq; Leopold Lazarus Ltd, Gotch House, 20-34 St Bride st, EC4

LISSER, Hon Mrs; Hon June Lisette May; da of 2 Baron May (d 1950); *b* 1929; *Educ* St Paul's Sch; *m* 1958, Raymond Charles Lisser; 1 s; *Style* - The Hon Mrs Lisser; 6H Hyde Park Mansions, NW1; School House, Stanton, Broadway, Worcs

LISTER, Laurier; OBE (1976); s of George Daniel Lister (d 1962); *b* 22 Apr 1907; *Educ* Dulwich Coll; *Career* actor, dramatist, deviser and dir of successful revues including- Penny Plain, Airs on a Shoestring, Joyce Grenfell Requests the Pleasure (all presented under own management) and Tuppence Coloured 1947-56; appointed artistic dir to Sir Lawrence Olivier's Co 1959 and later his assist for Chichester Festivals; dir and administrator Yvonne Arnaud Theatre Guildford 1964-75; *Recreations* gardening, music, travelling; *Style* - Laurier Lister Esq, OBE; c/o National Westminster Bank Ltd, 57 Aldwych, WC2

LISTER, Noel Arthur Vaughan; *Career* md MFI Furniture Gp Ltd; *Style* - Noel Lister, Esq; North End rd, Wembley, Middx

LISTER, Sir (Charles) Percy; s of Charles Ashton Lister, CBE (d 1965); *b* 1897; *Educ* Mill Hill Sch, RMC; *m* 1; 1 s; m 2, 1953, Mrs Geraldine Bigger; *Career* served 1914-18 War; formerly chm and md R A Lister & Co Ltd and Blackstone & Co Ltd; memb Capital Issues Ctee 1946-67, UK Commercial Corp 1940-45, Dollar Exports Councils 1949-64, Iron and Steel Bd 1953-58; DL (1960) Glos; kt 1947; *Style* - Sir Percy Lister DL; Stinchcombe Hill House, Dursley, Glos (☎ Dursley 2030)

LISTER, Raymond George; s of Horace Lister (d 1971); *b* 28 Mar 1919; *Educ* St John's Coll Sch Cambridge; *m* 1947, Pamela Helen, da of Frank Bishop Brutnell; 1 s, 1 da; *Career* author, artist, co dir; dir George Lister & Sons Ltd 1941-, John P Gray & Sons Ltd 1978-; pres royal

Soc of Miniature Painters, Sculptors and Gravers 1970-; chm bd of govs Federation of British Artists 1976-80; pres Architectural Metalwork Assoc 1975-77; liveryman Blacksmiths' Co 1957-; *Clubs* Athenaeum, City Livery, Sette of Odd Volumes; *Style* - Raymond Lister Esq; Windmill House, Linton, Cambs (☎ 0223 891 248)

LISTER, Dame Unity Viola; DBE (1972); da of Dr Arthur S Webley; *b* 19 June 1913; *Educ* St Helens; *m* 1940, Samuel William Lister; *Career* v-chm European Union of Women 1963-69, memb exec 1969; chm Horniman Museum 1967-; memb Inner London Advisory Ctee on Appointment of Magistrates; chm Nat Union of Conservative and Unionist Assocs 1970-71, Women's Nat Advisory Ctee (Conservatives) 1966-69; memb of exec European Union of Women 1971-, European Movement 1970-, Conservative Gp for Europe 1970-; *Style* - Dame Unity Lister, DBE; 32 The Court Yard, Eltham SE9 (☎ 01 850 7038)

LISTER-KAYE, Sir John Christopher Lister; 7 Bt (UK 1812), of Grange, Yorkshire; s of 6 Bt (d 1962); *b* 1913; *Educ* Oundle, Loughborough Coll; *m* 1, 1942, Audrey Helen (d 1979) da of late Edwin James Carter; 1 s, 1 da; m 2, 1980, Margaret Isabelle, da of Barnaby Duke, TD, JP (d 1959); *Heir* s, John Phillip Lister Lister-Kaye; *Career* dir Bath and Portland Gp 1967-75; *Style* - Sir John Lister-Kaye, Bt; Glebe House, Piddlehinton, Dorchester

LISTER-KAYE, John Philip Lister; s and h of Sir John Christopher Lister Lister-Kaye, 7 Bt; *b* 8 May 1946; *Educ* Allhallows Sch; *m* 1972, Sorrel Deirdre, da of Count Henry Noel Bentinck, s of Capt Count Robert Charles Aldenburg-Bentinck (Mediatised Count of the Holy Roman Empire), a descendant of late Hon William Bentinck, s of 1 Earl of Portland; 1 s, 2 da (twins); *Career* naturalist, author, lecturer, farmer, founder dir Scottish Conservation Charity The Aigas Trust 1980; author of *The White Island* 1972, *Seal Cull* 1979, *The Seeing Eye* 1980; *Recreations* figure skating, breeding and showing pedigree highland cattle; *Clubs* Caledonian; *Style* - John Lister-Kaye Esq; Aigas House, Beauly, Inverness-shire

LISTON-FOULIS, Sir Ian Primrose; 13 Bt (NS 1634); s of Lt-Col James Alastair Liston Foulis (d 1942), s of late Lt-Col Archibald Primrose Liston-Foulis, 4 s of 9 Bt; suc kinsman, Sir Archibald Charles Liston-Foulis, 12 Bt (d 1962); *b* 9 Aug 1937; *Educ* Stonyhurst; *Heir* none; *Career* Nat service Argyll and Sutherland Highlanders 1957-59, Cyprus 1958; language teacher Madrid 1959-61 and 1966-; trainee-exec Bank of London and S America 1962, Bank of London and Montreal Ltd Nassau and Guatemala 1963-64; *Style* - Sir Ian Liston-Foulis, Bt; Menendez Pelayo 13, Piso 7, Izqda, Madrid, Spain

LISTOWEL, 5 Earl of (I 1822); William Francis Hare; GCMG (1957), PC (1946); also Baron Ennismore (I 1800), Viscount Ennismore and Listowel (I 1816, usually shortened to Viscount Ennismore when used as courtesy title for eldest s and h), and Baron Hare of Convamore (UK 1869, which sits as); s of 4 Earl (d 1931) by his w Hon Freda Vanden-Bempde-Johnstone (da of 2 Baron Derwent); er bro of Lord (1 Visc) Blakenham and unc of Lord (3 Earl of) Iveagh; *b* 28 Sept 1906; *Educ* Magdalene Cambridge; *m* 1, 1933, Judith (m dis 1945), da of Raoul de Marffy-Mantuano, of Budapest; 1 da (Lady Grantley); m 2 1958, Stephanie Sandra Yvonne, formerly w of Hugh Wise and da of Sam Wise, of Toronto (m dis 1963); 1 da; m 3, 1963, Pamela, da of Francis Day, of Croydon, and formerly w of John Read; 2 s, 1 da; *Heir* s, Viscount Ennismore; *Career* memb LCC 1937-58; late Lt Intelligence Corps; Parly Under-Sec of State India Off 1944-45, also Dep Leader House of Lords 1944-45 (Lab Whip 1941-44); Sec State India 1947, Burma 1947-48, Min State Colonial Affrs 1948-50, Jt Parly Sec Min Ag & Fish 1950-51; Gov-Gen Ghana 1957-60; Chm Cttees Ho Lds 1965-76; *Clubs* Athenaeum; *Style* - The Rt Hon the Earl of Listowel, GCMG, PC; 7 Constable close, Wildwood rd, NW11 (☎ 01 458 8692)

LITCHFIELD, Dame Ruby Beatrice; DBE (1981); *Career* honoured for services to the performing arts and to the community; *Style* - Dame Ruby Litchfield, DBE

LITHGOW, James Frank; s and h of Sir William James Lithgow, 2 Bt; *b* 13 June 1970

LITHGOW, Sir William James; 2 Bt (UK 1925), of Ormsary, Co Argyll, DL (Renfrewshire 1970); s ' of Sir James Lithgow, 1 Bt, GBE, CB, MC, TD, JP, DL (d 1952); *b* 10 May 1934; *Educ* Winchester; *m* 1, 1964, Valerie Helen (d 1964), da of Denis Scott, CBE (d 1958); m 2, 1967, Mary Claire, da of Col F M Hill, CBE, of East Knoyle, Wilts; 2 s, 1 da; *Heir* s, James Frank Lithgow; *Career* shipbuilder; former chm Lithgows (Holdings) Ltd, Scott Lithgow Drydocks Ltd, Campbeltown Shipyard Ltd, Western Ferries Ltd and others; memb Scottish Regent Council of CBI 1969-76; memb Queen's Bodyguard for Scotland (Royal Co of Archers); memb British Inst of Patentees and Inventors; *Style* - Sir William Lithgow, Bt, DL; Ormsary, Lochgilphead, Argyllshire (☎ Ormsary 252); Drums, Langbank, Renfrewshire (☎ 606)

LITTLE, Capt Alec Haines; CBE (1973), RN; s of Cdr H A K Little, RD, RNR (d 1932); *b* 1920; *Educ* Lucton Sch, RNC Keyham; *m* 1945, Pamela, da of Lt-Col R P W Bolt; 1 s, 1 da; *Career* served 1939-45 War in Atlantic, Indian and Pacific Oceans; ch Staff Officer (tech) to flag off Medway 1968-70; dir of Quartering 1970- 73; welfare offr Metropolitan Police 1973; *Recreations* tennis, squash, sailing; *Clubs* Naval and Military Club; *Style* - Capt Alec Little, CBE, RN; Pepys Cottage, 5 The Close, Brambridge Park, Nr Eastleigh, Hampshire

LITTLE, Hon Sir Douglas Macfarlan; QC (Australia 1954); s of John Little; *b* 1904; *Educ* Wangoom State Sch, Scotch Coll, Ormond Coll Melbourne U; *m* 1931, Ida Margaret, da of Edward Chapple; 1 da; *Career* served in 1939-45 War; barr and slr Victoria 1929, judge of Supreme Court Victoria 1959-74; kt 1973; *Style* - The Hon Sir Douglas Little, QC; 2 Lansell cres, Camberwell, Melbourne, Victoria 3124, Australia

LITTLEJOHN, Alistair George; s of James Davidson Littlejohn (d 1970); *b* 17 Feb 1935; *Educ* Aberdeen G S, Aberdeen U; *m* 1962, Mairwen Lloyd, da of Capt Henry Lloyd Jones (d 1971); 1 s, 1 da; *Career* civil engr; dir Cementation Building Ltd, Trollope & Colls Ltd; *Style* - Alistair Littlejohn Esq; Harlyn, 14 Hempstead Lane, Potten End, Berkhamsted, Herts (☎ Berkhamsted 3706)

LITTLER, Sir Emile; *b* 9 Sept 1903; *m* 1933, Cora, nee Goffin; 2 da; *Career* chm and md London Entertainments Ltd, chm Palace Theatre London; dir Eagle Star Insurance Co; govr Memorial Theatre Stratford-on-Avon; theatrical impresario, producer and author; memb of Lloyd's; freeman City of London; kt 1974; *Style* - Sir Emile Littler; Palace Theatre, W1 (☎ 01 734 9691-2)

LITTLETON, Hon Hester Mary Modwena; da of 4 Baron Hatherton (d 1944); *b* 1912; *Career* 1939-45 with WTS/FANY; *Style* - The Hon Hester Littleton; Pitt Manor Cottage, Winchester, Hants (☎ 4898)

LITTLETON, Hon Jonathan Lloyd; s of 6 Baron Hatherton (d 1973); *b* 1949; *m* 1970, Maxine Elizabeth, da of Alistair Brough Mills; 1 s, 2 da; *Style* - The Hon Jonathan Littleton; Plum Tree Cottage, Acton Scott, Church Stretton, Salop

LITTLETON, Hon Moonyeen Meriel; da of 6 Baron Hatherton (by 1 m) (d 1973); *b* 1933; *Style* - The Hon Moonyeen Littleton

LITTLETON, Hon Richard Brownlow; s of 6 Baron Hatherton (by 2 m) (d 1973); *b* 1949; *m* 1975, Shirley Margaret Adamson; *Style* - The Hon Richard Littleton; Gardner's Cottage, Alice Holt Lodge, Wrecclesham, Surrey

LITTLEWOOD, Rear-Adm Charles; CB (1954), OBE (1942); s of Alfred

Littlewood (d 1929); *b* 1902; *Educ* Falconbury Preparatory Sch, RN Colls Osborne and Dartmouth; *m* 1924, Doris Helen, da of William Mackean, of London; *Career* joined RN 1915, served 1933-44, man Engineering Dept Malta Dockyard, sqdn engrg officer escort Vessels Normandy Invasion 1944, engineering officer HMS 'Howe' British Pacific Fleet, Okinawa operations 1944-46, Rear-Adm 1952, assist dir of Dockyards 1952-55, ret 1955; *Style* - Rear-Adm Charles Littlewood, CB, OBE; Saddlers Mead, Sid rd, Sidmouth, Devon (☎ 5482)

LIVERMORE, Sir Harry; s of Jack Livermore; *b* 1908; *Educ* Roy G S Newcastle-upon-Tyne, Durham U; *m* 1940, Esther, da of Samuel Angelman; *Career* slr 1930; formerly chm Royal Liverpool Philharmonic Soc and Everyman Theatre Liverpool; chm Merseyside Arts Assoc; chm Roy Court Theatre and Arts Trust Ltd; Lord Mayor of Liverpool 1958-59; kt 1973; *Style* - Sir Harry Livermore; 18 Burnham rd, Liverpool L18 6JU

LIVERPOOL, 5 Earl of (UK 1905); Edward Peter Bertram Savile Foljambe; also Baron Hawkesbury (UK 1893) and Viscount Hawkesbury (UK 1905); s of Capt Peter George William Savile Foljambe (ka Italy 1944) and great n of 4 Earl of Liverpool (d 1969, himself ggs of half-bro of the nineteenth century PM); *b* 14 Nov 1944; *Educ* Shrewsbury; *m* 1970, Lady Juliana Mary Alice Noel, da of 5 Earl of Gainsborough; 2 s; *Heir* s, Viscount Hawkesbury; *Clubs* Turf and Pratt's; *Style* - The Rt Hon the Earl of Liverpool; Flat 4, 27 Holland Park ave, W11 (☎ 01 221 5045); The Grange Farm, Exton, nr Oakham, Leics

LIVERPOOL, 10 Archbishop of (RC, 1911 by Letters Apostolic 'Si qua est' of Pius X); Most Rev Derek John Harford Worlock; also Metropolitan of Northern Province with Suffragan Sees, Hexham, Lancaster, Leeds, Middlesbrough and Salford; s of Capt Harford Worlock and Dora, nee Hoblyn; *b* 4 Feb 1920; *Educ* St Edmund's Coll Ware; *Career* Priv Sec to ArchBp Westminster 1945-64, Dean Stepney 1964-65, Bp Portsmouth 1965-76, translated Liverpool 1976; ordained 1944; *Style* - Most Rev Archbishop Worlock; 87 Green Lane, Mossley Hill, Liverpool. L18 2EP (☎ 051 722 2379)

LIVERPOOL, 6 Bishop of (1880) 1975; Rt Rev David Stuart Sheppard; s of Stuart Sheppard (d 1937); *b* 6 Mar 1929; *Educ* Sherborne Sch, Trin Hall Cambridge; *m* 1957, Grace, da of Rev B R Isaac; 1 da; *Career* served Roy Sussex Regiment 1947-49; ordained 1955, Bp Suffragan of Woolwich 1969-75, Bp of Liverpool 1975-; *Style* - The Rt Rev the Bishop of Liverpool; Bishop's Lodge, Woolton Park, Liverpool L25 6DT

LIVESEY, Geoffrey Colin; MBE (1968); *b* 21 Dec 1943; *m* 1969, Elisa Jane Pullen; 2 s; *Career* 2 Sec and Vice-Consul at Abidjan 1977-81, Vice Consul for Niger and Upper Volta 1981-; *Style* - Geoffrey Livesey Esq, MBE; c/o Foreign and Commonwealth Office, SW1

LIVINGSTON, Air Marshal Sir Philip Clermont; KBE (1950), CB (1948), AFC (1942); s of Clermont Livingston, of Cowichan Bay; *b* 1893; *Educ* Cambridge U, London Hosp; *m* 1920, Lorna Muriel, da of C W Legassicke Crespin, of London; 2 s (1 decd); *Career* joined RNVR 1915, transferred RAF 1919, head of the Eye Dept RAF Medical Branch 1934-46, DGMS RAF 1948-51, ret 1951; *Style* - Air Marshal Sir Philip Livingston KBE CB AFC; Maple Bay, RR1 Duncan, BC, Canada

LIVINGSTONE, David Willmott; s of late George Blair Livingstone; *b* 3 Feb 1926; *Educ* Haberdashers' Aske's Hampstead Sch, Ch Ch Oxford; *m* 1950, Jane Margaret; 1 s, 3 da; *Career* Sub Lieut RNVR, dep chm and md Albright & Wilson Ltd (md 1972, dep chm md 1977),dir IMI Ltd, v-pres Chemical Industries Assoc, memb Ec Dvpt for Chemical Industry, memb Council CBI, life govr Birmingham U, hon tres-govr Fircroft Coll Birmingham; *Recreations* squash, golf, reading, music; *Clubs* Athenaeum, Edgbaston Priory Club, Edgbaston Golf Club; *Style* - David Livingstone Esq; 87 Harborne rd,

Edgbaston, Birmingham (☎ (021) 454 2087)

LIVINGSTONE, Lady Jeanne Doreen; *née* Fox-Strangways; da of 8 Earl of Ilchester (d 1970); *b* 1931; *m* 1, 1958 (m dis 1969), Peter Skelton, publisher; 1 da; m 2, 1978, John Livingstone; *Style* - Lady Jeanne Livingstone; St Anthony, Higher Woodfield rd, Torquay, Devon

LLANSO, Hon Mrs; Hon Mary Rose Pellew; da of 9 Viscount Exmouth (d 1970); *b* 1938; *m* 1974, D Roman Llanso, of Madrid; *Style* - The Hon Mrs Llanso

LLEWELLYN, Hon Lady; Hon Christine Saumarez; da of 5 Baron de Saumarez (d 1969); *b* 1916; *m* 1944, Lt-Col Sir Henry (Harry) Morton Llewellyn, 3 Bt, CBE, DL, *qv*; *Career* served 1943-45 War with WRNS; *Style* - The Hon Lady Llewellyn; Llanvair Grange, nr Abergavenny, Gwent

LLEWELLYN, David St Vincent; s and h of Sir Henry (Harry) Morton Llewellyn, 3 Bt, CBE; *b* 2 Apr 1946; *Educ* Eton; *m* 1980, Vanessa Mary, da of Lt-Cdr Theodore Bernard Peregrine Hubbard, RN; 1 da; *Style* - David Llewellyn Esq

LLEWELLYN, Sir David Treharne; s of Sir David Richard Llewellyn, 1 Bt (d 1940) and bro of Sir Henry (Harry) Llewellyn, 3 Bt, CBE, *qv*; *b* 1916; *Educ* Eton, Trin Cambridge; *m* 1950, Joan Anne, OBE, da of Robert H Williams; 2 s, 1 da; *Career* served 1939-45 War; MP (C) Cardiff (North) 1950-59, parly under-sec of State Home Office 1951-52, resigned; formerly memb Broadcasting Council for Wales; journalist; author of 'Nye the Beloved Patrician' and 'The Adventures of Arthur Artfully'; kt 1960; *Style* - Sir David Llewellyn; The Old Rectory, Yattendon, nr Newbury, Berks

LLEWELLYN, David Walter; s of Eric Gilbert Llewellyn; *b* 13 Jan 1930; *Educ* Radley Coll; *m* 1955, Josephine Margaret Buxton; 3 s; *Career* md Walter Llewellyn & Sons Ltd and other cos in the Llewellyn Gp 1953-, chm Building Regulations Advisory Ctee 1977-, dep chm Nat Building Agency 1977-; Lloyd's Underwriter 1978-; trustee Queen Alexandra Cottage Homes Eastbourne 1973-; *Style* - David Llewellyn Esq; The Spinney, 20 Southdown rd, Willingdon, Eastbourne, E Sussex (☎ Eastbourne 31717)

LLEWELLYN, Col Sir (Robert) Godfrey; 1 Bt (UK 1959), of Baglan, CB (1950), CBE (1942, OBE 1927), MC, TD, JP (Glam Co 1934), DL (Gwent 1974); s of Robert William Llewellyn, JP, DL, of Cwrt Colman, Bridgend and Baglan Hall, Briton Ferry, Glamorgan; *b* 13 May 1893; *Educ* R N Colls Osborne and Dartmouth; *m* 1920, Frances Doris (d 1969), da of Rowland S A Kennard; 1 s, 1 da; *Heir* s, Michael Rowland Godfrey Llewellyn; *Career* joined RN 1906, resigned 1914, served in 1914-19 War with Montgomeryshire Yeo Cav, formerly Hon Col 16 (Welsh) Bn The Parachute Regiment (TA); High Sheriff Glamorganshire 1947; DL Monmouthshire 1960, High Sheriff Monmouthshire 1963; chm Glamorgan TA and AF Assoc 1953-58, pres Nat Union of Conservative and Unionist Assocs 1962; chm Welsh Hospital Bd 1959-65; KStJ; kt 1953; *Style* - Col Sir Godfrey Llewellyn, Bt CB, CBE, MC, TD, JP, DL; Tredilion Park, Abergavenny, Gwent (☎ Abergavenny 2178)

LLEWELLYN, Sir Henry (Harry) Morton; 3 Bt (UK 1922), of Bwllfa, Aberdare, Co Glamorgan, CBE (1953, OBE Mil 1945), DL (Monmouthshire 1952); s of Sir David Richard Llewellyn, 1 Bt, (d 1940); *b* 18 July 1911; *Educ* Oundle, Trin Cambridge; *m* 1944, Hon Christine, da of 5 Baron de Saumarez (d 1969); 2 s (David St Vincent and Roderic Victor, *qqv*), 1 da (Anna Christina); *Heir* s, David St Vincent Llewellyn; *Career* joined Warwickshire Yeo 1939; chm Davenco (Engineers) Ltd, pres Whitbread Wales Ltd, chm Grid Management & Finance Ltd; dir Chepstow Racecourse Co Ltd, pres British Equestrian Federation; pres British Show Jumping Assoc 1967-69, memb Nat Hunt Ctee 1946-; riding 'Ego', came 1st Grand Nat 1936, Chm Sports Council for Wales; v-chm Civic Trust for Wales; chm Nationwide Building Soc Wales; JP 1953-67, High Sheriff 1966

Monmouthshire; Grand Prix des Nations (Equestrian) Gold Medal, Olympic Games, Helsinki 1952; Roy Humane Soc Medal 1956; *Style* - Sir Henry Llewellyn, Bt, CBE, DL; Llanvair Grange, nr Abergavenny, Gwent (☎ Nantyderry 88022)

LLEWELLYN, Lady Honor Morvyth Malet Vaughan; da of 7 Earl of Lisburne (d 1965); *b* 1919; *m* 1943, Maj William Herbert Rhidian Llewellyn, MC; *Career* JP (Cardiganshire); *Style* - Lady Honor Llewellyn, JP; Brynreithin, Ffair Rhos, Ystrad Meurig, Dyfed

LLEWELLYN, Sir (Frederick) John; KCMG (1974), DSC; s of Reginald George Llewellyn (d 1965), of Dursley, Glos; *b* 29 April 1915; *Educ* Dursley G S, Birmingham U; *m* 1939, Joyce Barrett; 1 s, 1 da; *Career* prof of Chemistry Auckland U (NZ) 1947-55; chm N Z Univ Grants Ctee 1961-66, chm N Z Broadcasting Corpn 1962-65; v-chancellor Exeter U 1966-72; dir-gen British Council 1972-80; *Style* - Sir John Llewellyn, KCMG, DSC; 10 Spring Gdns, SW1

LLEWELLYN, His Hon Judge Seys; John Desmond Seys Llewellyn; s of Charles Ernest Llewellyn (d 1957); *b* 3 May 1912; *Educ* Cardiff H S, Jesus Oxford; *m* 1939, Elaine, nee Porcher; 3 c; *Career* barr 1945, dep chm Cheshire Quarter Sessions 1968, County Court Judge 1971, Circuit Judge 1972; *Recreations* travel, art, archaeology, dog; *Clubs* Athenaeum (Liverpool); *Style* - His Hon Judge Seys Llewellyn; Chetwyn House, Gresford, Clwyd (☎ Gresford 2419)

LLEWELLYN, Rev John Francis Morgan; s of Canon David Leonard John Llewellyn (d 1966); *b* 4 June 1921; *Educ* King's Coll Sch Wimbledon, Pembroke Cambridge, Ely Theological Coll; *m* 1955, Audrey Eileen, da of Frederick James Binks; *Career* served 1941-45 War; headmaster Cathedral Choir Sch and minor canon of St Paul's Cathedral 1958-74; sacrist and warden of Coll of Minor Canons 1968-74; priest in ordinary to HM the Queen 1970-74 (formerly dep); chaplain of the Chapel Roy of St Peter ad Vincula within HM Tower of London 1974-; chaplain of the City Solicitors Co 1974-; *Style* - Rev John Llewellyn; Chaplain's Residence, HM Tower of London, EC3

LLEWELLYN, Michael Rowland Godfrey; s and h of Col Sir (Robert) Godfrey Llewellyn, 1 Bt, CB, CBE, MC, TD; *b* 15 June 1921; *Educ* Harrow; *m* 1, 1946, Bronwen Mary (m dis 1951), da of Sir (Owen) Watkin Williams-Wynn, 8 Bt; m 2, 1956, Janet Prudence, da of Lt-Col Charles Thomas Edmondes, DL, JP, of Bridgend, Glamorgan; 3 da; *Career* Capt, Grenadier Guards (Reserve); *Style* - Michael Llewellyn Esq; Glebe House, Penmaen, nr Swansea, Glamorgan

LLEWELLYN, Roderic (Roddy) Victor; 2 s of Sir Henry (Harry) Llewellyn, 3 Bt, CBE, JP, DL, and Hon Christine Saumarez, yr da of 5 Baron de Saumarez; *b* 9 Oct 1947; *Educ* Shrewsbury, Aix-en-Provence; *m* 1981, Tatiana, da of Paul Soskin, the film producer; *Career* landscape gardener, author; *Recreations* philately, jig-saw puzzles; *Style* - Roderic Llewellyn Esq; Llanvair Grange, Abergavenny, Gwent

LLEWELYN DAVIES, Hon Harriet Lydia Rose; da of Baron Llewelyn-Davies (Life Peer); *b* 1955; *Style* - The Hon Harriet Llewelyn Davies

LLEWELYN DAVIES, Hon Rebecca; da of Baron Llewelyn-Davies, PC (Life Peer); *b* 1957

LLEWELYN-DAVIES OF HASTOE, Baroness (Life Peeress UK 1967); Patricia; PC (1975); da of C P Parry; *b* 16 July 1915; *Educ* Liverpool Coll Huyton, Girton Cambridge; *m* 1943, Baron Llewelyn-Davies (Life Peer); 3 da; *Career* dir African Educational Trust 1960-69, chm Great Ormond St Hosp for Sick Children to 1969; a Baroness in Waiting to HM the Queen 1969-70; Opposition Dep Ch Whip House of Lords 1972, Opposition Ch Whip 1973-74 and 1979-; chm Women's Nat Cancer Control Ctee 1972; *Style* - The Rt Hon the Lady Llewelyn-Davies of Hastoe, PC; 36 Parkhill rd, NW3

LLEWELYN-DAVIES, Baron (Life Peer UK 1963); Richard; s of Crompton Llewelyn Davies; *b* 24 Dec 1912; *Educ* Trin Cambridge, Ecole des Beaux Arts Paris; *m* 1943, Annie Patricia (now Baroness Llewelyn-Davies of Hastoe, *qv*), da of C P Parry (d 1951); 3 da; *Career* architect and town planner; architect British Railways (London Midland and Scottish Railway Co) 1942-48; dir Investigation into Function and Design of Hosps 1948-60; private practice as sr ptnr Llewelyn-Davies Weeks (architects and planners); prof of architecture Univ Coll London 1960-69; prof Urban Planning UCL, head of Sch of Environmental Studies; emeritus prof Urban Planning UCL; *Style* - The Rt Hon the Lord Llewelyn-Davies; Carpenters Yard, Tring, Herts (☎ Tring 2233); 36 Parkhill rd, London NW3 (☎ 485 6575)

LLOYD, 2 Baron (UK 1925); Alexander David Frederick Lloyd; MBE (1945), DL (Herts 1963); s of Rt Hon 1 Baron Lloyd, GCSI, GCIE, DSO (d 1941), by his w Blanche Lascelles, niece of 5 Earl of Harewood, great niece of 1 Earl of Ravensworth and ggda of 1 Marquess of Clanricarde; *b* 30 Sept 1912; *Educ* Eton, Trin Cambridge; *m* 1942, Lady (Victoria) Jean Marjorie Mabell, da of 12 Earl of Airlie, KT, GCVO, MC (d 1968), and sis of Hon Angus Ogilvy; (1 s decd); 2 da; *Heir* none; *Career* 2 Lt Warwick Yeo 1935, Capt 1941; a Lord in Waiting to HM the Queen 1952; Jt Parly Under-Sec of State Colonial Office 1954-57; pres Commonwealth and British Empire Chambers of Commerce 1957; dir Lloyds Bank, Lloyds Bank Unit Tst Managers, Beehive Life Insur; chm London Bd Nat Bank of New Zealand 1978-; with Br Cncl formerly; *Clubs* White's; *Style* - The Rt Hon Lord Lloyd, MBE, DL; Clouds Hill, Offley, Hitchin, Herts (☎ Offley 350)

LLOYD OF HAMPSTEAD, Baron (Life Peer UK 1965); Dennis Lloyd; QC (1975); s of Isaac Lloyd, of 22 Stourcliffe close, W1; *b* 22 Oct 1915; *Educ* Univ Coll Sch, Univ Coll London, Gonville and Caius Coll Cambridge; *m* 1940, Ruth Emma Cecilia, da of Carl Tulla; 2 da; *Career* served in RA & RAOC 1939-45 War; barr Inner Temple 1936; head of Dept of Law Univ Coll London, Quain Prof of Jurisprudence 1965-, chm Bd of Govrs Nat Film Sch, chm Council Univ Coll Sch 1971-79, gov British Film Institute 1968-76; *Style* - The Rt Hon the Lord Lloyd of Hampstead, QC; 84 Hawtrey rd, NW3; 6 Pump Court, Temple EC4 (☎ 01 236 3938)

LLOYD OF KILGERRAN, Baron (Life Peer UK 1973); Rhys Gerran Lloyd; CBE (1953), QC (1961), JP (Surrey 1953); s of late James G Lloyd, of Kilgerran, Pembs; *b* 12 Aug 1907; *Educ* Sloane Sch, Selwyn Cambridge; *m* 1940, Phyllis Mary, da of late Ronald Shepherd, JP, of Chilworth, Southampton; 2 da; *Career* barr Gray's Inn 1939, Middle Temple 1955, QC 1961; hon fell Selwyn Cambridge 1967-; served WW II as sci researcher; stood for Parl (Lib) Anglesey 1959, Pres Welsh Lib Pty 1971-74, UK Lib Pty 1973-74, Jt Tres 1977-; Pres Inst Patentees & Inventors 1975-, V-Chm Ho Lds Select Cttee Sci & Technology, Parly Cttee Info Technology 1979-; specialist in Patent Law; dir Terrapin Internat Ltd, Target Unit Tst Mans (Wales), Strayfield Ltd; chm Educn Tst; *Style* - The Rt Hon the Lord Lloyd of Kilgerran CBE QC JP; 15 Haymeads dve, Esher, Surrey

LLOYD, Hon Mr Justice; Hon Sir Anthony John Leslie; s of Edward John Boydell Lloyd, of Little Bucksteep, Dallington, Sussex; *b* 9 May 1929; *Educ* Eton, Trin Cambridge; *m* 1960, Jane Helen Violet, da of C W Shelford, of Chailey Place, Lewes, Sussex; *Career* Nat Service in 1 Bn Coldstream Gds 1948; barr Inner Temple 1955, QC 1967; attorney-gen to HRH the Prince of Wales 1969-77; judge of the High Court of Justice, Queen's Bench Div 1978-; chm Chichester Diocesan Bd of Finance 1972; kt 1978; *Style* - The Hon Mr Justice Lloyd; Ludlay, Berwick, E Sussex (Alfriston 204); 68 Strand-on-the-Green, W4

LLOYD, Maj-Gen Cyril; CB (1948), CBE (1944, OBE 1943), TD (1945) and 2 Bars; s of late A H Lloyd; *b* 1906; *Educ* Brighton G S, London and Cambridge Us; *Career* dep ch of staff 21 Army Gp 1943-45, dir-gen Army Education and Technical Training 1945-49; FRSA, FRGS, MRST;

lecturer and teacher, former research worker in Science; past memb numerous education councils; dir-gen City and Guilds of London Inst 1949-62, consultant 1968- (dir 1949-62), chm Associated Examining Bd for GCE 1970-; Liveryman Goldsmiths' Co and Freeman of City of London; *Style* - Maj-Gen Cyril Lloyd, CB, CBE, TD**; The Pheasantry, Colgate, Horsham, W Sussex

LLOYD, Hon Corinne Deborah; da of Baron Lloyd of Hampstead (Life Peer); *b* 1951; *Educ* City of London Sch for Girls, Camberwell Sch for Arts & Crafts; *Style* - The Hon Corinne Lloyd; 20 Howard House, Cleveland st, W1 (☎ 01 387 1151)

LLOYD, Hon Davina Margaret; da of 2 Baron Lloyd, MBE; *b* 13 Mar 1943; *Style* - The Hon Davina Lloyd; Clouds Hill, Offley, Hitchin, Herts (☎ Offley 350); 12 St Leonards ter, SW3

LLOYD, Frederick John; CBE (1977); s of Frederick James Lloyd (d 1952); *b* 22 Jan 1913; *Educ* Ackworth Sch Yorkshire, Liverpool U; *m* 1942, Catherine Johnson, da of Cecil Herbert Parker (d 1942); 1 s, 1 da; *Career* ch operating man London Red Buses 1961-65; ch commercial and planning officer London Transport 1965-69; dir-gen W Midlands Passenger Transport Exec 1969-78; chm Road Transport Industry Training Bd 1978-; *Clubs* Birmingham Rotary, Whittingham Barracks Golf; *Style* - Frederick Lloyd Esq, CBE; 8 Cliveden Coppice, Sutton Coldfield, W Midlands (☎ 021 308 5683)

LLOYD, Lady; Gladys Margery; da of late Col H W A F Crichton-Browne, of Buildwas Park, Cressage, Salop; *m* 1932, as his 2 w, Capt Sir Humphrey Clifford Lloyd, KCVO, MC (d 1966); *Style* - Lady Lloyd; Fotheringay House, 14 Montpelier Row, Twickenham, Middx

LLOYD, Maj Sir (Ernest) Guy Richard; 1 Bt (UK 1960), DSO (1917), DL (Dunbartonsire 1953); s of Maj Ernest Thomas Lloyd, late of Bengal Civil Service; *b* 7 Aug 1890; *Educ* Rossall, Keble Oxford; *m* 1918, Helen Kynaston, da of late Col E W Greg, CB, VD, of Norcliffe Hall, Styal, Cheshire; 1 s, 4 da (1 decd); *Heir* s, Richard Ernest Butler Lloyd; *Career* served 1914-19; MP (C) Renfrewshire (Eastern Div) 1940-59; kt 1953; *Style* - Maj Sir Guy Lloyd, Bt, DSO, DL; Rhu Cottage, Carrick, Lochgoilhead, Argyll

LLOYD, Dame Hilda Nora; DBE (1951); da of late John Shufflebotham, of Birmingham; *b* 1891; *Educ* King Edward's Sch Birmingham, Birmingham U; *m* 1, 1930, Bertram Lloyd (d 1948); m 2, 1949, Baron Rose; *Career* emeritus prof of Obstetrics and Gynaecology Birmingham U and United Birmingham Hosp; pres Roy Coll of Obstetricians and Gynaecologists 1949-52; *Style* - Dame Hilda Lloyd, DBE; Broome House, Clent, Worcs

LLOYD, Lt-Col Humphrey William; JP (Glos 1950), DL (1963); s of late Brig-Gen Arthur Henry Orlando Lloyd, CB, CMG, MVO; *b* 1903; *Educ* Eton, RMC; *m* 1938, Diana, da of Capt Robert Bingham Brassey (d 1946); 2 s; *Career* RAC WW II, Capt 1930, Lt-Col 1942, Reserve of Offrs 1945; *Style* - Lt-Col Humphrey Lloyd, JP, DL; Pasture Farm, Oddington, Moreton-in-Marsh, Glos (☎ Stow-on-Wold 203)

LLOYD, Hon Joanna Elizabeth; da of Baron Selwyn-Lloyd (Life Peer) (d 1978); *b* 1952; *Style* - The Hon Joanna Lloyd; 5a Gladys rd, NW6

LLOYD, Baroness; Lady (Victoria) Jean Marjorie Mabell; *née* Ogilvy; da of 12 Earl of Airlie, KT, GCVO, MC, and Lady Alexandra Coke, da of 3 Earl of Leicester; *b* 21 Sept 1918; *m* 1942, 2 Baron Lloyd, MBE; 2 da (and 1 s decd); *Style* - The Rt Hon The Lady Lloyd; Clouds Hill, Offley, Hitchin, Herts (☎ Offley 350)

LLOYD, Hon Laura Blanche Bridget; da of 2 Baron Lloyd, MBE; *b* 7 Mar 1960; *Style* - The Hon Laura Lloyd

LLOYD, Sir (John) Peter (Daniel); s of D J Lloyd, of Swansea; *b* 1915; *Educ* Rossall Sch, Brasenose Oxford; *m* 1947, Gwendolen, da of W N Molesworth, of Lytham, Lancs; 2 s, 4 da; *Career* served with RA 1940-46; chm Cadbury Fry Pascall Australia Ltd 1953-71; memb

Commonwealth Banking Corpn Bd 1967- and Australian Mutual Provident Soc Bd 1970; kt 1971; *Style* - Sir Peter Lloyd; Stonecrest, Sorell, Tasmania 7172, Australia

LLOYD, Patrick John; s of Edmund Commeline Lloyd (d 1936); *b* 20 March 1925; *Educ* Clifton, Magdalene Cambridge; *m* 1956, Margaret, da of Claude Douglas-Pennant (d 1955) gs of 1 Baron Penrhyn; 1 s, 1 da; *Career* Capt RA, wine merchant, purchasing dir IDV Home Trade Ltd; *Recreations* hunting, shooting; *Style* - Patrick Lloyd Esq; Yew Tree Farm, Stebbing, Dunmow, Essex

LLOYD, Reginald Arthur Harris; ED with Clasp (1980), DL (Shropshire 1979); s of The Rev Richard Harris Lloyd (d 1952); *b* 24 Jan 1913; *Educ* Hull G S, Scarborough Coll; *m* 1946, Maureen, da of John Thelwall (d 1946); 4 s, 1 da; *Career* Co Cncllr 1961, vice chm 1977; chm Shropshire co Cncl 1981-; gen cmmr of Taxes 1975-; Head Office Management Sun Alliance London to 1973 (ret); *Recreations* riding, tennis; *Clubs* Carlton, MCC; *Style* - Reginald Lloyd Esq, ED with Clasp, DL; Acrebatch, Lower Wood, All Stretton, Shropshire (☎ Leebotwood 233)

LLOYD, Richard Ernest Butler; s and h of Sir (Ernest) Guy (Richard) Lloyd, 1 Bt, DSO; *b* 6 Dec 1928; *Educ* Wellington, Hertford Coll Oxford; *m* 1955, Jennifer, da of Brig Ereld Cardiff, of Easton Court, nr Ludlow, Shropshire; 3 da; *Career* late Capt Black Watch; *Style* - Richard Lloyd Esq; Sundridge Place, Sundridge, Sevenoaks, Kent

LLOYD, Richard Hey; s of Charles Yates Lloyd (d 1969); *b* 25 June 1933; *Educ* Lichfield Cathedral Sch; Rugby Sch; Jesus Cambridge; *m* 1962, Morwenna, da of Rev Oliver Leonard Willmott; 4 da; *Career* sub-organist Salisbury Cathedral 1957-66; organist Hereford Cathedral 1966-74; master of the choristers and organist Durham Cathedral 1974-; *Style* - Richard Lloyd Esq; 6 The College, Durham (☎ 64766)

LLOYD, Brig Thomas Ifan; CBE (1957), DSO (1944), MC (1940); s of Rev David Lloyd (d 1921), of Weston-super-Mare, Somerset; *b* 1903; *Educ* Westminster, RMA; *m* 1927, Irene Mary, da of Prof A Fullerton, CB, CMG, (d 1932); 1 s, 1 da; *Career* 2 Lt RE 1923, served in 1939-45 War, dep engineer-in-ch War Office 1955-57, Brig 1955, ret 1957; hon founder-pres, Railway Conversion League; *Style* - Brig Thomas Lloyd, CBE, DSO, MC; 24 Grove rd, Merrow, Guildford, Surrey

LLOYD, Hon Mrs; Hon Victoria Mary; *née* Ormsby-Gore; da of 5 Baron Harlech, KCMG, PC (by 1 m); *b* 1946; *m* 1972, Julian Richard Leslie Lloyd; 4 da; *Style* - The Hon Mrs Lloyd

LLOYD GEORGE OF DWYFOR, 3 Earl (UK 1945); Owen Lloyd George; also Viscount Gwynedd (UK 1945); s of 2 Earl Lloyd George of Dwyfor (d 1968, s of the celebrated PM 1916-22) by his 1 w, Roberta (herself da of Sir Robert McAlpine, 1 Bt, of the family of civil engineering contractors); *b* 28 Apr 1924; *Educ* Oundle; *m* 1949, Ruth Margaret, da of Richard Coit (d 1960); 2 s, 1 da; *Heir* s, Viscount Gwynedd; *Career* Capt Welsh Gds 1942, served 1944-45 in Italy; carried the Sword of investiture of HRH The Prince of Wales, Caernarvon Castle 1969; underwriting memb of Lloyd's; dir Sedgwick Forbes Bland Payne Ltd, Marchwiel Ltd, Sir Alfred McAlpine & Son Internat; memb Historic Buildings Council for Wales; *Clubs* White's, Pratt's, City of London; *Style* - The Rt Hon the Earl Lloyd George of Dwyfor; Brimpton Mill, nr Reading, Berks (☎ Woolhampton 2328); 43 Cadogan sq, SW1 (☎ 01 235 1050)

LLOYD GEORGE, Lady Julia Margaret Violet; da of 3 Earl Lloyd-George of Dwyfor; *b* 1958; *Style* - Lady Julia Lloyd George

LLOYD GEORGE, Hon Robert John Daniel; s of 3 Earl Lloyd-George of Dwyfor; *b* 1952; *Educ* Eton and Univ Coll, Oxford; *Style* - Hon Robert Lloyd George

LLOYD GEORGE, Hon William; s of 1 Viscount Tenby, TD, PC (d 1967), and hp of bro, 2 Viscount; *b* 7 Nov 1927; *Educ* Eastbourne Coll, St Catharine's Cambridge (BA); *m* 1955, Ursula, da of late Lt-Col Henry Edward Medlicott, DSO; 1 s, 2 da; *Career* Capt RWF (TA); JP (Hants); *Style* - The Hon William Lloyd George, JP; Triggs, Crondall, nr Farnham, Surrey

LLOYD GEORGE OF DWYFOR, Winifred, Countess of; Winifred Emily; da of late Thomas William Peedle, and formerly w of Henry Michael Calve; *m* 1935, as his 2 w, 2 Earl Lloyd George of Dwyfor (d 1962); *Style* - The Rt Hon Winifred, Countess of Lloyd George of Dwyfor

LLOYD HUGHES, David; s of Trevor Lloyd Hughes, of Leeds; *b* 12 Aug 1941; *Educ* Leeds G S; *m* 1965, Jean, da of William Kenny; 1 s; *Career* FCA; co sec Stylo Shoes Ltd (Stylo PLC from July 1981-) & dir of each of its trading subsids; *Style* -David Lloyd Hughes Esq; 5 Holly gdns, Leeds LS16 5NL (☎ 0532 758478)

LLOYD MOSTYN, Hon Llewellyn Roger Lloyd; s and h of 5 Baron Mostyn, MC; *b* 26 Sept 1948; *Educ* Eton; *m* 1974, Denise Suzanne, da of Roger Duvanel; 1 da; *Career* late Capt Army Legal Servs, barr Middle Temple 1973, in chambers Gray's Inn; *Style* - The Hon Llewellyn Lloyd Mostyn; 9 Sloane av, SW3

LLOYD OWEN, Maj-Gen David Lanyon Lloyd; CB (1971), DSO (1945), OBE (1954), MC (1942); s of Capt Reginald Charles Lloyd Owen, OBE, RN (d 1945); *b* 10 Oct 1917; *Educ* Winchester, RMC Sandhurst; *m* 1947, Ursula Evelyn, da of Evelyn Hugh Barclay (d 1956), of Colney Hall, Norwich; 3 s; *Career* 2 Lt The Queen's Roy Regt, served 1939-45 War, mil assist to High Cmmr in Malaya 1951-53, GOC Cyprus District 1966-67 and NEARELF 1967-69, Maj-Gen 1966, pres Regular Commissions Bd 1969-72; ret 1972; chm Wildfowlers Assoc of Gt Britain & Ireland for Conservation and Research 1979-; *Style* - Maj-Gen David Lloyd Owen, CB, DSO, OBE, MC; Violet Bank, Swainsthorpe, Norwich (☎ Swainsthorpe 470468)

LLOYD PHILLIPS, Ivan; CBE (1963, OBE 1959); s of late Rev A Lloyd Phillips; *b* 25 June 1910; *Educ* Worksop Coll, Selwyn Cambridge, Balliol Oxford; *m* 1941, Faith MacLeay, da of late Brig-Gen G M Macarthur Onslow, CMG, DSO; 1 s; *Career* appointed Colonial Admin Service 1934, Gold Coast 1934-38, Palestine 1938-47; district cmmr Gaza-Beersheba 1946-47, Colonial Office 1947-48, Cyprus 1948-51, cmmr Nicosia-Kyrenia 1950-51, Singapore 1951-53, dep sec for Defence 1952-53, Malaya 1953-62, sec to Ch Min 1955-57, sec to Min of the Interior 1957-62; *Style* - Ivan Lloyd Phillips Esq, CBE; Cranmer Cottage, Dorchester-on-Thames, Oxford (☎ Oxford 340026)

LLOYD-DAVIES, (John) Robert; CMG (1953); s of John (Robert) Lloyd-Davies (d 1971); *b* 24 Mar 1913; *Educ* Highgate Sch, Oriel Oxford; *m* 1943, Margery (d 1978), da of late William McClelland; 1 s, 1 da; *Career* Lt RNVR 1942-45; sr civil servant and memb of HM Diplomatic Service; priv sec to Sir Thomas Phillips, KCB (Employment Dept) 1940; labour counsellor HM Embassies Paris (1956-60) and Washington DC (1972-73); principal Training Services Agency 1973-79; natural therapist since retirement from HM Gov Service; *Recreations* keyboard music; *Style* - Robert Lloyd-Davies Esq, CMG; Stepping Stones, 35 Grange gdns, Pinner, Middx (☎ 01 866 9526)

LLOYD-EDWARDS, Norman; RD (1971) and Bar (1980), DL; s of Evan Stanley Edwards; *b* 13 June 1933; *Educ* Monmouth Sch, Quakers Yard G S, Bristol U; *Career* Cdr RNR, cmding offr HMS Cambria, S Wales Div, Roy Naval Reserve 1981-, slr, memb Cardiff City Cncl 1963-, dep Lord Mayor 1973-74, chapter clerk Llandaff Cathedral 1975-, ptnr Cartwrights 1960-; *Recreations* opera, music, theatre, books; *Clubs* Army and Navy, Cardiff and County; *Style* - Norman Lloyd-Edwards Esq, RD*, DL; 169 Pencisely rd, Llandaff, Cardiff (☎ 566107)

LLOYD-JOHNES, Herbert Johnes; OBE (1973), TD (1950); s of Herbert T C Lloyd-Johnes, MC (d 1958); *b* 9 Dec 1900; *Educ* St Andrew's Sch Eastbourne, Malvern; *m* 1942, Margaret Ruth, da of

Edgar Samuel Edgar; 2 da; *Career* Maj RA, mil mission to Poland 1939, sr liaison officer to Polish Forces 1940-46; chm Historic Buildings Council to Wales (1967-77), memb 1954-; memb of Court and Council Nat Museum of Wales 1949- and of Nat Library of Wales; memb Court of Govrs U of Wales 1952-78; Gov U of South Wales Cardiff; memb of council Nat Trust of Gt Britain 1967-74; jt author of 'Welsh Furniture' 1950; *Recreations* shooting, gardening, reading; *Clubs* Boodles; *Style* - Herbert Lloyd-Johnes Esq, OBE, TD; Fosse Hill, Coates, nr Cirencester, Glos (☎ Kemble 279)

LLOYD-MOSTYN, Hon Llewellyn Roger Lloyd; s and h of 5 Baron Mostyn, MC, by his 1 w Yvonne; *b* 26 Sept 1948; *Educ* Eton; *m* 1974; *Career* late Capt Army Legal Services; barr Middle Temple 1973; *Style* - The Hon Llewellyn Lloyd-Mostyn; 9 Sloane ave, SW3 (☎ 01 589 2288)

LLOYD-WORTH, Hon Mrs Frances; Hon Frances Patricia; da of 3 Baron Tollemache (d 1955); *b* 1908; *m* 1949, Charles Edward Lloyd-Worth (m dis 1964); *Style* - The Hon Mrs Frances Lloyd-Worth; Duntisbourne Leer, Cirencester, Glos (☎ Miserden 354)

LO, Ping-Yan; s of Lo Siu-Nam (d 1968); *b* 12 Nov 1933; *Educ* Lingnam U; *m* 1966, Yee-Ling, da of Koo Kim-Por; *Career* hon consul Republic of Nicaragua in Hong Kong; *Clubs* The Chinese Recreation Club, Chinese Club; *Style* - Ping-Yan Lo Esq; 13/A 21 Breamar Hill rd, Hong Kong

LOBANOV-ROSTOVSKY, Prince Dimitry; s of Prince John Lobanov-Rostovsky, *qv*; *b* 14 Sept 1962; *Style* - Prince Dimitry Lobanov-Rostovsky

LOBANOV-ROSTOVSKY, Princess Helena; da of Prince John Lobanov-Rostovsky, *qv*; *b* 7 Sept 1964; *Style* - Princess Helena Lobanov-Rostovsky

LOBANOV-ROSTOVSKY, Prince John; s of Prince Constantine Lobanov-Rostovsky, of Hove; *m* 1956, Princess Roxane Bibica Rosetti (*see* Bibica Rosetti, Princess Raoul); 2 s, 1 da; *Style* - Prince John Lobanov-Rostovsky; Swallowdale, 67 Woodruff av, Hove 4, Sussex

LOBANOV-ROSTOVSKY, Princess John - Roxane; da of Prince Raoul Bibica Rosetti and Dorothy, nee Acton (*see* Princess Raoul Bibica Rosetti); *b* 3 Oct 1932; *m* 1956, Prince John Lobanov-Rostovsky, yr s of Prince Constantine Lobanov-Rostovsky, of Hove; 2 s, 1 da; *Style* - Princess John Lobanov-Rostovsky; Swallowdale, 67 Woodruff av, Hove 4, Sussex

LOBANOV-ROSTOVSKY, Prince Paul; s of Prince John Lobanov-Rostovsky, *qv*; *b* 23 Oct 1956; *Style* - Prince Paul Lobanov-Rostovsky

LOBB, Eric; s of William Hunter Lobb (d 1946); *b* 3 March 1907; *Educ* Oxford; *m* (m dis); 1 s, 1 da; *Career* Private in the Home Guard; master bootmaker; chm and md John Lobb Ltd; pres West End Master Bootmakers Assoc; *Recreations* small farming; *Clubs* Little Ship; *Style* - Eric Lobb Esq; Newlands, Radlett, Herts WD7 8EH (☎ Radlett 6311)

LOBB, Howard Leslie Vicars; CBE (1952); s of Hedley Vicars Lobb (d 1950); *b* 9 Mar 1909; *Educ* privately, Regent Street Polytechnic Sch of Architecture; *m* 1949, Charmian Isobel, da of Charles Oliver Callcott Reilly, MBE (d 1970); 3 s; *Career* chartered architect, chartered engineer, assoc of Institute of Structural Engrs; fell Roy Soc of the Chartered Institute of Arbitrators; secretary Architects' Benevolent Soc; chm Council for Architecture, Town Planning and Building Research of The Festival of Britain, and later controller of Construction of the South Bank Exhibition 1951; architect British Pavilion, Brussels Expo 1958, gold medal award; architect for numerous schools, nuclear and oil fired stations, motorway service areas, offices, flats and other buildings; *Style* - Howard Lobb Esq, CBE; 2 Admiral's Wharf, Cowes, Isle of Wight (☎ 0983 292414); Black Hill, 18 Blackhills, Esher, Surrey (☎ Esher 63092)

LOBBAN, Albert Sinclair; *Career* FCMA; md British Enkalon; dir Brank

Rex Ltd; dir Wellman Internat Ltd; memb IOD; *Style* - Albert Lobban Esq; British Enkalon, Enkalon House, Regent rd, Leics

LOCH, 3 Baron (UK 1895); Maj George Henry Compton Loch; s of Maj-Gen 2 Baron Loch, CB, CMG, MVO, DSO (d 1942), and Lady Margaret Compton, herself da of 5 Marquess of Northampton; *b* 3 Feb 1916; *Educ* Eton, RMC Sandhurst; *m* 1, 1942, Leila Mary Grace Isabel Hill Mackenzie (m dis 1946), da of Robert Duncanson Mackenzie, of Montreal, Canada; m 2, 1946, Mrs Betty Castillon du Perron (m dis 1952); m 3, 1952, Joan Dorothy Hawthorn Binns; m 4, 1975, Mrs Sylvia Beauchamp-Wilson, da of A G Beauchamp Cameron, of Dalmahoy, Midlothian; *Heir* bro, Hon Spencer Douglas Loch, MC; *Career* late Maj 11 Hussars; chm of Sea Lord Shipping 1969; dressage instructor; *Recreations* equitation; *Style* - The Rt Hon the Lord Loch; Green Farm House, Stoke-by-Clare, Suffolk; Stoke College, Stoke-by-Clare, Suffolk (☎ 266)

LOCH, Hon Spencer Douglas; MC (1945); s of 2 Baron Loch, CB, CMG, DSO, MVO (d 1942); hp to Barony; *b* 12 Aug 1920; *Educ* Wellington, Trin Cambridge; *m* 1, 1948, Hon Rachel (d 1976), da of 9 Baroness Lucas and Dingwall (d 1958) and Gp Capt Howard Lister Cooper, RAF, AFC; 1 s, 1 da (and 1 s decd); m 2, 1979, Davina Julia, formerly w of Sir Richard James Boughey, 10 Bt; *Career* barr Lincoln's Inn 1948; Maj Gren Gds, NW Europe 1944-45; *Clubs* Travellers'; *Style* - The Hon Spencer Loch, MC; Lochluichart by Garve, Ross-shire; 51 Lennox gdns, SW1

LOCK, Lt-Cdr Sir (John) Duncan; RN; s of Brig-Gen FRE Lock, DSO; *b* 5 Feb 1918; *Educ* RN Coll Dartmouth; *m* 1947, Alice Eileen Smith; 3 da; *Career* served as regular offr in RN 1931-58, chm Assoc of District Cncls of England and Wales 1974-79 kt 1978; *Style* - Lt-Cdr Sir Duncan Lock, RN; Fen Court, Oval Way, Gerrards Cross, Bucks SL9 8QD (☎ Gerrards Cross 82467)

LOCK, George David; s of George Wilfred Lock (d 1943); *b* 24 Sept 1929; *Educ* Haileybury and ISC, Queens' Cambridge; *m* 1965, Ann Elizabeth, da of Sidney Harold Biggs; 4 s, 1 da; *Career* British Tabulating Co Ltd (now ICL) 1954-59, Save & Prosper Gp Ltd 1959-69, American Express 1969-74, Private Patients Plan (md 1975-); *Recreations* bridge, music, entertaining, family activities; *Clubs* Institute of Directors, Roy Soc of Medicine; *Style* - George Lock Esq; Buckhurst Place, Horsted Keynes, Sussex (☎ Danehill 790599)

LOCK, John Robert; s of Harry Lock (d 1935); *b* 31 March 1923; *m* 1952, Joyce; 1 s, 2 da; *Career* dir Vectis Stone Group Ltd, md Vectis Stone Ltd, dir I W Cast Concrete Ltd; *Style* - John Lock Esq; West Standen, Newport, Isle of Wight (☎ Newport 523722)

LOCKHART, Angus Hew Lockhart of the Lee; s of Maj Simon Foster Macdonald-Lockhart of the Lee; *b* 1946; *Educ* Rannoch Sch Perthshire; *m* 1970, Susan Elizabeth, da of Hon William Normand (d 1967, s of late Baron Normand, Life Peer); *Career* recognised as Chief of the name of Lockhart by Lord Lyon, 1957; *Style* - Angus Lockhart of the Lee; Newholme, Dunsyre, Lanark

LOCKHART, Brian Alexander; s of John Arthur Hay Lockhart; *b* 1 Oct 1942; *Educ* Glas Acad, Glasgow U; *m* 1967, Christine Ross, nee Clark; 2 s, 2 da; *Career* solicitor, ptnr Robertson Chalmers & Auld 1964-79, Sheriff North Strathclyde 1979; *Recreations* fishing, golf, family; *Clubs* Roy Scottish Auto; *Style* - Brian Lockhart Esq; 18 Hamilton ave, Glasgow (☎ 041 427 1921)

LOCKHART, Hon Christine Anne; sis of 22 Baron Gray, *qv*; *b* 1938; *m* 1960, Brian Joseph Lockhart, Blues and Royals; 1 s; *Style* - The Hon Christine Lockhart; Hawkesbury, South dve, Wokingham, Berks

LOCKHART, Lady Bruce; Frances Mary; da of Maj-Gen Edward Archibald Beck, CB, DSO; *m* 1948, Sir Robert Hamilton Bruce Lockhart, KCMG (d 1970); *Style* - Lady Bruce Lockhart; 20 Elmside, Budleigh Salterton, Devon

LOCKHART, James Duncan; s of James Jackson Lockhart (d 1974); *b* 3 Oct 1933; *Educ* High Sch of Glasgow, Glasgow U; *m* 1964, Joyce, da of Harold Walter Oakley (d 1955); 2 da; *Career* Capt Army; md Transport Development Gp Ltd 1979-; *Style* - James Lockhart Esq; c/o Transport Development Gp Ltd, 66-74 Victoria st, SW1E 6SR (☎ 01-828 5051)

LOCKHART, Stephen Alexander; CMG (1960), OBE (1949); s of late Capt Murray McGregor Lockhart RN; *b* 19 March 1905; *Educ* Harrow, Cambridge; *m* 1944, Angela, da of Col George Watson; 2 s, 2 da (1 s decd); *Career* Foreign Service 1940-65, chm Executive Committee Anglo-Portuguese Society 1976-79; *Clubs* United Oxford and Cambridge Univ; *Style* - Stephen Lockhart Esq, CMG, OBE; Tite st, SW3 (☎ 352 8514)

LOCKHART, Major Simon Foster Macdonald; s of John Ronald Moreton Macdonald (d 1921), of Largie Castle, Tayinloan, Argyllshire; *b* 1916; *Educ* Winchester and Magdalen Coll Oxford; *m* 1942, Ella Caitriona, da of Seton Gordon, of Upper Duntulm, Portree; 3 s, 1 da; *Career* served 1939-45 with The Lovat Scouts (Italy, wounded), Maj 1946, served with Lanarkshire Yeo (TA) 1947-49; DL (1950), JP (Lanarks 1950); assumed surname of Lockhart in lieu of Macdonald by declaration 1946 on succeeding to estates of Lee, Carnwath and Dryden; *Style* - Maj Simon Lockhart JP DL; Dunsyre House, Dunsyre, Lanark (☎Dunsyre 260)

LOCKHART-MUMMERY, Sir Hugh Evelyn; KCVO (1980); s of John Percy Lockhart-Mummery, FRCS; *b* 28 April 1918; *Educ* Stowe, Trin Cambridge, Westminster Hosp Med Sch; *m* 1946, Elizabeth Jean, da of Sir James Crerar, KCSI, CIE; 1 s; *Career* Sq Ldr RAF 1943-46; Consultant Surgeon St Thomas' 1960-; King Edward VII's Hosp for Offrs 1968-; Surgeon to HM Household 1969-75; to HM the Queen 1974-75; RAF 1975-; Consulting Surgeon St Mark's Hosp 1951-78; MD, MChir, FRCS; *Recreations* golf, fishing, music; *Clubs* RAF; *Style* - Sir Hugh Lockhart-Mummery, KCVO; 5 Hereford sq, SW7 4TT (☎ 01 373 3630); 149 Harley st, WIN 2DE (☎ 01 935 4444)

LOCKHART-MUMMERY, Hon Mrs; Hon (Elizabeth) Rosamund Elles; da of Baroness Elles (Life Peeress) and Neil Patrick Moncrieff Elles; *b* 15 May 1947; *m* 1971, Christopher John Lockhart-Mummery; *Style* - The Hon Mrs Lockhart-Mummery; 127 Abbotsbury rd, W14

LOCKSPEISER, Sir Ben; KBE (1950); s of L Lockspeiser, of London; *b* 1891; *Educ* Grocers' Sch, Cambridge U; *m* 1, 1920, Elsie (d 1964), da of Alfred Shuttleworth, of Bury, Lancs; 1 s, 2 da; m 2, 1966, Mary Alice Heywood; *Career* dir of Scientific Research MAP 1943, ch scientist Miny of Supply 1946-49, sec dept of Scientific and Industrial Research 1949-56, dir and scientific advr Staveley Industries 1956-71; pres Council of European Organisation for Nuclear Research 1954-57; hon fell Sidney Sussex Coll Cambridge; kt 1946; *Clubs* Athenaeum; *Style* - Sir Ben Lockspeiser, KBE; 15 Waverley rd, Farnborough, Hants (☎ 43021)

LOCKWOOD, Baroness (Life Peeress UK 1978); Betty; da of late Arthur Lockwood; *b* 22 Jan 1924; *Educ* Eastborough Girls' Sch, Ruskin Coll Oxford; *m* 1978, Lt-Col Cedric Hall, s of late George Hall; *Career* Yorkshire Regional Women's Offr, Lab Party 1952-67, ch woman offr and assist National Agent Lab Party 1967-75, chm Equal Opportunities Cmmn 1975-; *Clubs* U Women's; *Style* - The Rt Hon the Lady Lockwood; 12 Fairdale gdns, London, SW15 (☎ 01 789 1782)

LOCKWOOD, Arthur William; s of William Storm Lockwood (d 1971); *b* 11 May 1924; *Educ* Denstone Coll Staffs; *m* 1948, Heather, da of Maj William Rogerson, OBE, MC (d 1961); 1 s, 2 da; *Career* landowner; farmer; chm Humberoak Gp Ltd, Castle Hill Holdings Ltd, Master Burton Hunt 1959-, memb Lloyd's; *Recreations* hunting, shooting, yachting; *Clubs* Carlton, RSYC; *Also* owner TSDY 'Island Fox'; *Style* - Arthur Lockwood Esq; Cammeringham Manor, nr Lincoln, Lincs (☎ 052271 342)

LOCKWOOD, Sir Joseph Flawith; *b* 14 Nov 1904; *Career* dir EMI Ltd, chm 1954-74; dir Smiths Industries Ltd 1959-79; dir Beecham Gp 1966-75; dir Hawker Siddeley Gp 1964-77, Laird Gp Ltd 1970-; dir National Research Development Corpn 1951-67; memb Industrial Reorganisation Corporation 1966-71; chm Royal Ballet Sch Endowment Fund and Governors 1960-78, Royal Ballet Sch 1960-78; chm The Royal Ballet; memb Council Imperial Society of Knights Bachelor; memb Arts Council 1965-70; vice-pres Central Sch of Speech and Drama; dir Young Vic Co, chm 1974-75; Companion Inst of Electrical Engrs; dir Racecourse Holdings Trust Ltd 1969; dir United Racecourse; knighted 1960; *Clubs* Carlton; *Style* - Sir Joseph Lockwood; 33 Grosvenor sq, WI

LOCKWOOD, Lady; Marjorie; da of William Basil Clitheroe; *Educ* 1929, Sir John Francis Lockwood (d 1965); *Style* - Lady Lockwood; Compton Mount Compton,Winchester

LOCKWOOD, Philip Barton; *Career* chm Lockwoods Foods Ltd; *Style* - Philip Lockwood Esq; c/o Lockwoods Foods Ltd, Bridge rd, Long Sutton, Spalding, Lincs PE12 9EQ

LOCKWOOD, Robert; *b* 14 April 1920; *Educ* Columbia U and Columbia Law Sch; *m* 1947, Phyllis M Laing; 1 s, 1 da; *Career* vice-pres General Motors Overseas Corpn; gen man Japan Br 1974-76; exec v-pres Isuzi Motors Ltd Tokyo 1976; chm General Motors European Advisory Council 1977; *Clubs* Hurlingham and Roehampton; *Style* - Robert Lockwood Esq; Flat J, Upper Feilde, 71 Park st, WIY 3HB (☎ 01 499 2160)

LOCKWOOD, William Philip; *Career* jt md Lockwoods Foods Ltd; *Style* - William Lockwood Esq; Lockwoods Foods Ltd, Bridge rd, Long Sutton, Spalding, Lincs

LODER, Hon Christina Anne; da of 3 Baron Wakehurst, *qv*; *b* 1959; *Style* - The Hon Christina Loder

LODER, Edmund Jeune; s and h of Sir Giles Rolls Loder, 3 Bt; *b* 26 June 1941; *Educ* Eton; *m* 1966, Penelope Jane (m dis 1971), da of Ivo Forde; 1 da; *Career* FCA; *Style* - Edmund Loder Esq; Eyrefield Lodge, The Curragh, Co Kildare

LODER, Sir Giles Rolls; 3 Bt (UK 1887), JP (Sussex), DL (W Sussex 1977); s of late Capt Robert Egerton Loder, s of 2 Bt; suc gf, Sir Edmund Giles Loder, 2 Bt, 1920; *b* 1914; *Educ* Eton, Trin Cambridge; *m* 1939, Marie, only da of Capt Bertram Hanmer Bunbury Symons-Jeune, of Runnymede House, Old Windsor; 2 s; *Heir* s, Edmund Jeune Loder; *Career* 2 Lt 98 Surrey and Sussex Yeo Field Bde RA 1935, Lt 1938; High Sheriff 1948-49; *Clubs* Junior Carlton and Royal Yacht Squadron (Cowes); *Style* - Sir Giles Loder, Bt, JP, DL; Leonardslee, Horsham, West Sussex (☎ Lower Beeding 305)

LODER, Lady (Jean Arnot); *née* Maxwell; da of G Arnot Maxwell, QC; *m* 1924, Sir Louis Francis Loder (d 1972); *Style* - Lady Loder; 20 Hillcrest Ave, Kew, Victoria, Australia 3101

LODER, Hon James David Gerald; s of 2 Baron Wakehurst, KG; *b* 1928; *Educ* Geelong Church of England GS; Victoria and Trin Cambridge; *Career* Coldstream Gds RARO; barr Inner Temple 1953; OstJ; *Style* - The Hon James Loder; 31 Lennox gdns, SWI

LODER, Hon Robert Beauclerk; s of 2 Baron Wakehurst KG; *b* 1934; *Educ* Eton and Trin Cambridge; *m* 1973, Josette, da of Joseph Bromovsky, of Ottmanach, Pisheldorf, Kaernten, Austria; 1 s; *Career* md Esperanzo Trade and Transport Ltd; *Style* - The Hon Robert Loder; 14 Ladbroke Grove, WII

LODER, Brigadier Robert Eric; CBE (1965), DL (Sussex 1972); s of Basil Loder (d 1934); *b* 23 March 1911; *Educ* Lancing and RMC Sandhurst; *Career* 2 Lt R Sussex Regt 1931, served in 1939-45 War in 2 Bn R Sussex Regt; Lt-Col 1950, cmdt Royal Mil Sch of Music, Kneller Hall 1958-61 head of Commonwealth Mission, Korea and mil attaché Korea 1962, ret 1965; Dep Col (Sussex) The Queen's Regt 1968-75; *Clubs* Naval and Military, and Buck's; *Style* - Brigadier Robert

Loder CBE, DL; c/o Lloyds Bank Ltd, Cox's & King's Branch, 6 Pall Mall, London SWI; The White Cottage, Slaugham, Haywards Heath, West Sussex (☎ Handcross 368)

LODER, Hon Timothy Walter; s and h of 3 Baron Wakehurst, *qv*; *b* 1958; *Style* - The Hon Timothy Loder

LODGE, John Stuart; s of Edmund Roy Lodge (d 1961); *b* 30 April 1938; *Educ* Cranbrook Sch Sydney; *m* 1962, Peta, da of Sir Albert Robinson KBE; 1 s, 2 da; *Career* Lt Far East 1958-59, International Security Specialist; *Recreations* hunting, tennis; *Clubs* Brooks's; *Style* - John Lodge Esq; 48 Holland st, W8

LODGE, Sir Thomas; s of James Lodge (d 1936), of Sheffield; *b* 25 Nov 1909; *Educ* Sheffield U; *m* 1940, Aileen, da of James Corduff, of Co Donegal; 1 s, 1 da; *Career* medical practioner, (ret); consultant radiologist United Sheffield Hospitals 1946-74; clinical lectr Sheffield U 1963-66; knighted 1974; *Books* 'Recent Advances in Radiology', 3rd, 4th, 5th editions (1955), (1964), (1974); *Clubs* Royal Society of Medicine; *Style* - Sir Thomas Lodge; 44 Sussex sq, Brighton, East Sussex, BN2 5AA (☎ 64242)

LODHI, Taltif Ahmad Tausif; *b* 1 Sept 1923; *Educ* Punjab U Lahore; *m* 1947, Zohra; 2 s, 1 da; *Career* md The Attock Oil Co Ltd, md Attock Oil Serv (UK) Ltd, chm Attock Int Oil Corpn NV, dir Attock Oil Exploration (UK) Ltd, dir Pakistan Oilfields Ltd, dir Attock Refinery Ltd, dir Attock Oil (Overseas) Ltd, dir Anvil Petroleum Ltd; *Recreations* tennis; *Clubs* Oriental, The Roy Overseas League; *Style* - Taltif Lodhi Esq; 65 The Ridgeway, Golders Green, NW11 (☎ 455 3465)

LOEHNIS, Anthony David; s of Cdr Sir Clive Loehnis, KCMG, RN (ret), and Rosemary, da of Hon Robert Ryder (ka 1917, s of 2 Earl of Harrowby, KG, PC, and Lady Mary Cecil, da of 2 Marq of Exeter); *b* 12 March 1936; *Educ* Eton, New Coll Oxford; *m* 1965, Jennifer, da of Sir Donald Anderson; 2 s; *Career* with FCO to 1966, Schroder Wagg 1966-, assoc dir Bank of England 1980-81, exec dir 1981-; *Style* - Anthony Loehnis Esq; 8 St Peter's Sq, W6

LOEWEN, Gen Sir Charles Falkland; GCB (1957), KBE (1951), DSO (1945); s of Charles Loewen, MA, of Vancouver, British Columbia; *b* 1900; *Educ* Haileybury and RMC Kingston, Canada; *m* 1928, Kathleen, da of Maj-Gen J M Ross CMG DSO, of London, Ontario; 2 s; *Clubs* Army and Navy and Vancouver; *Style* - Gen Sir Charles Loewen, GCB, KBE, DSO

LOEWENTHAL, Sir John; CMG (1975), ED (1965); s of A M Loewenthal; *b* 22 Dec 1914; *Educ* Sydney GS and Sydney Univ, MB BS; MS (Melbourne); *m* 1944, Anne June, da of Dr James Stewart; 2 s, 2 da; *Career* served war 1939-46, AIF, Middle East and SW Pacific, Maj AAMC; FRCS, FRACS, FACS; prof and chm dept ofSurgery, Sydney Univ 1956-79, now Emeritus; *Clubs* Australian, Legacy, Roy C'wlth, Bowral G C; *Style* - Sir John Loewenthal, CMG, ED; Robertson Park, Glenquarry, via Bowral, NSW 2576, Australia (☎ 048 871 207)

LOFTHOUSE, Geoffrey; JP (Pontefract 1970), MP (L) Pontefract and Castleford 1978-; s of Ernest Lofthouse; *b* 18 Dec 1925; *Educ* Featherstone Primary and Secondary Schs; *m* 1952, Sarah; 1 da; *Career* personnel man NCB Fryston 1970-78; memb Wakefield Metropolitan District Council 1974; *Style* - Geoffrey Lofthouse Esq JP MP; 28 The Circle, Pontefract, W Yorkshire (☎ Pontefract 704275)

LOFTHOUSE, Reginald George Alfred; *b* 30 Dec 1916; *m* 1939, Ann Bernardine, nee Bannan; 3 da; *Career* FRICS, ch surveyor Miny of Ag Fish & Food 1973-76, convenor Standing Conference on Countryside Sports 1978-; adviser: Nature Conservancy Cncl 1978-, Cncl for Environmental Conservation 1980-, memb Bd Govrs Coll of Estate Management 1963- (chm 1972-77); *Clubs* Athenaeum, MCC; *Style* - Reginald Lofthouse Esq; c/o College of Estate Management, Whiteknights, Reading RG6, Berks (☎ 0734 861101)

LOFTUS, Viscount; Charles John

Tottenham; s and h of 8 Marquess of Ely by 1 w, Katherine, da of Lt-Col W H Craig; *b* 2 Feb 1943; *Educ* Trin Coll Sch Port Hope Ont, Ecole Internationale de Genève, Toronto U (MA); *m* 1969, Judith Marvelle, da of Dr J J Porter, of Calgary, Alberta, Canada; 1 s, 1 da; *Heir* s, Hon Andrew Tottenham; *Career* Head of Dept of French, Strathcona-Tweedsmuir Sch, Calgary, Alberta; *Style* - Viscount Loftus; 1424 Springfield Place SW, Calgary, Alberta, T2W OY1 Canada

LOGAN, Andrew David; s of William H Logan; *b* 11 Oct 1945; *Educ* Oxford Sch of Architecture; *Career* sculptor and artist; *Style* - Andrew Logan Esq; 34 Cranbourn st, WC2 (☎ 01 836 5909)

LOGAN, Lieut-Col John; TD (1948; s of Crawford Logan, of Gribton, Dumfries; *b* 25 May 1907; *Educ* Eton; *m* 1937, Rosaleen Muriel (d 1967), da of Frederick William O'Hara, of Cooperhill, Co Sligo, Eire; 1 s, 1 da; *Career* served 1939-45 with 7 Bn Argyll & Sutherland Highlanders (Fr), Lt-Col 1949, OC 7 1949-50; County Cadet Cmdt Stirlingshire 1956-58; DL (1956) Stirlingshire, Vice-Lieut 1965-79; *Style* - Lt-Col John Logan, TD, DL; Weser Craigend, by Stirling (☎ Stirling 5025)

LOGAN, Lady; Janet Colville; da of John McIntyre; *m* 1920, Sir William Marston Logan, KBE, CMG (d 1968); *Style* - Lady Logan; Ann st, Gatehouse-of-Fleet, Kircudbrightshire

LOGIE, Ian Thomas Hold; *Career* chm Gillett Brothers Discount Co Ltd; dep md European Banking Co Ltd; *Style* - Ian Logie Esq; European Banking Co Ltd, 150 Leadenhall st, EC3

LOGUE, Christopher; s of John Logue; *b* 23 Nov 1926; *Educ* Prior Park Coll, Bath; *Career* journalist, poet, writer, actor; *Style* - Christopher Logue; 18 Denbigh Close, London, WII

LOISEAU, Hon Mrs; Eliza; da of Baron Hutchinson of Lullington, *qv*; *b* 1941; *m* 1974, Pierre Loiseau; *Style* - The Hon Mrs Loiseau; Les Bouleaux, 2 Rue de Gazet, Seine Port, 77 France

LOKOLOKO, Sir Tore; GCMG (1977), OBE; s of Loko Loko Tore; *b* 21 Sept 1930; *Educ* Sogeri High Sch, Papua New Guinea; *m* 1950, Lalahaia Meakoro; 4 s, 6 da; *Career* Govr-Gen Papua New Guinea from 1977; *Style* - Sir Tore Lokoloko, GCMG, OBE; Government House, Port Moresby, Papua New Guinea (☎ 25 9366)

LOLLEY, Hon Mrs Elizabeth Hamilton; da of Baron Keith of Avonholm (d 1964); *b* 1916; *m* 1945, Raymond Alan Lolley; *Style* - The Hon Mrs Lolley; 17 Cromer Hyde, Lemsford, Welwyn Garden City, Herts AL8 7XE

LOLLI, Ettore; *Career* chm British Olivetti Ltd, v-chm Manufacturers Hanover Ltd, dir British Reserve Insurance Co Ltd, dir Euromobiliare Ltd, dir London & New York Investment SA; *Style* - Ettore Lolli Esq; 115-207 Summerlee st, Glasgow E3

LOMAS, Alfred; MEP (L) London NE 1979-; s of Alfred Lomas; *b* 30 April 1928; *Educ* St Paul's Elementary Sch Stockport and further education; *Career* polit sec London Co-op 1975-79; *Style* - Alfred Lomas Esq, MEP; 23 Hatcliffe Close, London, SE3 9UE (☎ 01 852 5433)

LOMAS, Gerald Alexander; *Career* chm: J & J Dyson Ltd, Diamond Refractories Ltd, Refractory Clays Ltd, Yorkshire Testing Works; dir: Beecroft & Ptnrs (Metallurgists) Ltd, Builders Centre (Sheffield) Ltd, Dyson Refractories Ltd, Island Securities Ltd, James Dougall & Sons Ltd, John Knowles & Co (Wooden Box) Ltd, M & G Tankers Ltd, M & G Trailer (Lye) Ltd, Pickford Holland & Co Ltd, Price Pearson Holdings Ltd, Price-Pearson Refractories Ltd, Sandygate Motor Services Ltd, Whitrigg Fireclay Co Ltd; *Style* - Gerald Lomas Esq; J & J Dyson Ltd, Griffs Works, Stannington, nr Sheffield

LOMAX, Hon Mrs; Hon Elizabeth Margaret; *née* Brand; da of 3 Viscount Hampden GCVO KCB CMG (d 1958); *b* 1911; *m* 1935, Cecil Lomax; 3 da; *Style* - The Hon Mrs Lomax; Codicote Mill, Hitchin, Herts, (☎ Codicote 206)

LOMAX, Sir John Garnett; KBE (1953), CMG (1944), MC (1917); s of Rev Canon Edward Lomax, of Liverpool Cathedral; *b* 27 August 1896; *Educ* Liverpool Coll and Liverpool U; *m* 1922, Feridah Yvette, da of Leon Krajewski, of Paris; 2 s; *Career* served in Great War 1914-18 with RA; Consular Service 1920: commercial sec Rome 1935-38, British commercial agent Jerusalem 1938-40, commercial counsellor Madrid 1940-41, Berne 1941-42, Angora 1943-46, HM Minister (commercial) Buenos Aires 1946-49, Ambass to Bolivia 1949-56; *Clubs* Reform and Royal Automobile; *Style* - Sir John Lomax, KBE, CMG, MC; 803 Nelson Hse, Dolphin sq, SWI (☎ 01 828 3800, ext 803 Nelson); Tanterfyn, Llanelian, Anglesey, Gwynedd (Amlwch 493)

LOMBARD KNIGHT, Eric John Percy Crawford; s of late Herbert John Charles Knight; *Educ* Ashford GS; *m* 1933, Peggy Julia, nee Carter; 1 s, 1 da; *Career* chm: Automobile Bank and Credit Corporation Ltd, Kellock Factors Ltd, Oakwood Securities Ltd, Young Advertising Ltd, Prime Marketing Ltd; dir: Estates and General Investments Ltd, Kellock Holdings Ltd, VIP Travel Ltd, Allscope Ltd; *Clubs* Caledonian and Addington Golf Clubs; *Style* - Eric Lombard Knight Esq; The White House, 18 Limpsfield rd, Sanderstead Village, Surrey (☎ 01 657 2021)

LONDESBOROUGH, 9 Baron (UK 1850); Richard John Denison; s of 8 Baron Londesborough, TD, AMICE (d 1968, gs of Lord Albert Denison, né Conyngham, 2 s of 1 Marquess Conyngham), by his 2 w Ann; *b* 2 July 1959; *Educ* Wellington Coll, Exeter U; *Heir* none; *Style* - The Rt Hon the Lord Londesborough; Dragon House, Edgioak, Redditch, Worcs

LONDESBOROUGH, Ann, Baroness; (Elizabeth) Ann; da of late Edward Little Sale, ICS, and formerly w of Thomas Chambers Windsor Roe; *m* 1957, as his 2 w, 8 Baron (d 1968); *Style* - The Rt Hon Ann Lady Londesborough; Dragon House, Edgioak, nr Redditch, Worcs

LONDESBOROUGH, Jocelyn, Baroness; Jocelyn Helen; da of late Lt-Cdr Hugh Duppa Collins, RN; *m* 1952, as his 3 w, 7 Baron (d 1967); *Style* - The Rt Hon Jocelyn Lady Londesborough; Anchor Cottage, Bembridge, Isle of Wight

LONDON, 116 Bishop of (dates from establishment of Christianity in Br) 1981-; Rt Rev Graham Douglas Leonard; s of Rev Douglas Leonard; *b* 8 May 1921; *Educ* Monkton Combe Sch, Balliol Oxford; *m* 1943, Vivien, da of Dr Swann, Fellow of Gonville & Caius Cambridge; 2 s; *Career* Dean of HM's Chapels Royal 1981- & Prelate of Order of the British Empire 1981-; served WW II Oxford & Bucks LI as Capt; ordained 1948, Archdeacon Hampstead, Bp Suffragan of Willesden 1964-73, delegate 5 Assembly WCC Nairobi 1975, in Ho of Lds 1977-, Bp of Truro 1973-81; *Clubs* Army & Navy; *Also* patron of 160 livings, 18 alternately with others, all Prebendal stalls, Archdeaconries of London, Middx, Hampstead, Hackney and Northolt, the Precentorship, the Chllrship and the Treasureship; *Style* - The Rt Rev Bishop of London; London House, 8 Barton st, SW1 (☎ 01 222 8661)

LONDONDERRY, 9 Marquess of (I 1816); Alexander Charles Robert Vane-Tempest-Stewart; also Baron Londonderry (I 1789), Viscount Castlereagh (I 1795), Earl of Londonderry (I 1796), Baron Stewart (UK 1814), Earl Vane (UK 1823), Viscount Seaham (UK 1823); s of 8 Marquess of Londonderry (d 1955, gggs of half-bro of the famous For Sec (Viscount Castlereagh) during the last years of the Napoleonic Wars and the early ones of peace (1812-22); Marchionesses of Londonderry tend to have been more notable than their Lords: the wife of the afore mentioned For Sec had her husband's Garter set in diamonds and wore it as a tiara during the Congress of Vienna; she was also said to be so rude when she intended to be polite that it was speculated how rude she would be if she tried; the 3 Marquess's wife was long a leader of London fashionable life and was portrayed by her friend Disraeli as Lady Deloraine in *Sybil*; the 4 Marquess's w went over to Rome in 1855, four years behind Manning and ten behind Newman but anticipating Lord Bute by 13 years; the 7 Marquess's w revived the tradition of being a leader of fashion and was known in the earlier years of the twentieth century as 'Circe'); *b* 7 Sept 1937; *Educ* Eton; *m* 1, 1958 (m dis 1971), Nicolette, da of Michael Harrison, of Netherhampton, Wilts; 2 da; m 2, 1972, Doreen Wells, the former ballerina with the Royal Ballet and recipient of the Adeline Genée Gold Medal; 2 s; *Heir* s, Viscount Castlereagh; *Style* - The Most Hon the Marquess of Londonderry; Wynyard Park, Billingham, Cleveland TS22 5NF (☎ Wolviston 317)

LONG, 4 Viscount (UK 1921); Richard Gerard Long; s of 3 Viscount Long, TD, JP, DL (d 1967); *b* 30 Jan 1929; *Educ* Harrow; *m* 1957, Margaret, da of Ninian Frazer; 1 s, 2 da; *Heir* s, Hon James Long; *Career* Pres Bath & Wilts Gliding Club, V-Pres Wilts Roy Br Legion; Opposition Whip 1974-79, Lord-in-Waiting 1979-; *Recreations* hunting, shooting, gardening; *Style* - The Rt Hon Viscount Long; The Lodge, Coppice Hill, Bradford-on-Avon, Wilts (☎ 6454)

LONG, Hon Mrs - Hon (Anne) Cathrine; *née* Parnell; da of 8 Baron Congleton; *b* 1956; *m* 1980, (Michael) Robin Long; *Style* - The Hon Mrs Long

LONG, Hon Charlotte Helen; da of 4 Viscount Long; *b* 1965

LONG, Hon Mrs; Jean; da of Baron Douglas of Cleveland (d 1978); *b* 1928; *m* 1952, Garry Long, FCIS; *Style* - The Hon Mrs Long; 8 The Avenue, Hatch End, Pinner, Middlesex

LONG, Hon John Hume; s of 3 Viscout Long; *b* 1930; *Educ* Harrow; *m* 1957, Averil Juliet (marr dis 1969), da of Henry Stobart; 1 da; *Style* - The Hon John Long; Swyre Farm Cottage, Aldsworth, Glos

LONG, Hon James Richard; s and h of 4 Viscount Long; *b* 31 Dec 1960; *Style* - The Hon James Long

LONG, Sir Ronald; s of Sydney Richard Long, of Halstead, Essex; *b* 5 Sept 1902; *Educ* Earls Colne G S and Stamford Sch; *m* 1931, Muriel Annie, da of F.J. Harper, of Wimbledon; 1 s, 2 da; *Career* pres Law Soc 1963-64; chm Stansted Airport Consultative Ctee; knighted 1964; *Style* - Sir Ronald Long; Ayletts Farm, Halstead, Essex (☎ 2072)

LONG, Hon Sarah Victoria; da of 4 Viscount Long; *b* 1958; *Style* - The Hon Sarah Long

LONG, Lady (Tessie); da of late Patrick Lonergan; *m* 1925, Sir James Long (d 1928); *Style* - Lady Long; c/o Mrs Blanchard, 2 The Crescent, Cobh, Co Cork

LONG, William Casson; s of Capt Clifford Long (d 1974); *b* 25 Aug 1923; *Educ* Sedburgh, St John's Cambridge; *m* 1949, Joan Cantrill, da of Maj Norman Feather, MC; 1 s, 1 da; *Career* Capt RA (Burma cmd), CA; *Recreations* gardening, woodcarving, motorsport, photography; *Clubs* Bradford; *Style* - William Long Esq; 132 Banks Lane, Riddlesden, Keighley, Yorks (☎ 603530)

LONGBOTHAM, Maj Samuel s of George Longbotham, of Elgin, Morayshire; *b* 19 March 1908; *Educ* Elgin; *m* 1941, Elizabeth Rae, da of Donald Davidson, of Glasgow; 2 s; 1 da; *Career* served 1940-46 with RA and Intelligence Corps, commissioned 1944; Maj Lovat Scouts, TA (RA) 1952-60; JP, DL (1964) Ross and Cromarty; Lord Lieut Islands Area Western Isles from 1975; man dir Stornoway Gazette Ltd, Stornoway, Isle of Lewis; *Style* - Maj Samuel Longbotham, JP, HM Lord-Lieut for Islands Area, Western Isles; 25 Lewis st Stornoway, Isle of Lewis

LONGBOTTOM, Charles Brooke; s of William Ewart Longbottom (d 1943); *b* 22 July 1930; *Educ* Uppingham Sch; *m* Anita, da of Guilio Trapani of Sorrento Italy; 2 da; *Career* barr Inner Temple, contested (C) Stockton on Tees 1955, MP (C) York 1959-66, parly private sec to Chancellor of Duchy of Lancaster 1961-63, chm Austin & Pickersgill Shipbuilders Sunderland 1966-72, chm A & P Appledore Ltd 1970-78, Seascape Hldgs Ltd 1970-, Ariel Foundation 1960-, memb General Advisory Council BBC 1965-75,

Community Relations Commission 1968-70; *Style* - Charles Longbottom Esq; 66 Kingston House North, Princes gate, SW7

LONGDEN, Sir Gilbert; s of Lt-Col James Longden; *b* 1902; *Educ* Haileybury, Emmanuel Cambridge; *Career* admitted slr 1927, sec ICI (India) Ltd 1930-38, MP (C) SW Hertfordshire 1950-74; kt 1972; *Clubs* Travellers', Hurlingham and Yorkshire; *Style* - Sir Gilbert Longden; 89 Cornwall gdns, SW7

LONGDEN, Henry Alfred; s of late Geoffrey Appleby Longden; *b* 8 Sept 1909; *Educ* Oundle, Birmingham U; *m* 1935, Ruth, nee Gilliat; 1 s, 4 da; *Career* mining engr, dir Blackwell Colliery Co 1940-, dir Briggs Collieries 1941-, New Hucknall Colliery 1941; production dir NE, NCB 1948-, chm W Midlands NCB 1960-, chm & ch exec Cementation Co 1961-70, dir Trafalgar House 1970-76, ret; *Recreations* rugby, cricket, tennis, shooting, fishing, sailing; *Style* - Henry Longden Esq; Raeburn, Northdown rd, Woldingham, Surrey (☎ Woldingham 2245)

LONGE, Desmond Evelyn; MC (1944); s of late Rev John Charles Longe, MA, of Spixworth Park, Norfolk; *b* 8 August 1944; *Educ* Woodbridge; *m* 1944, Isla, da of R M Bell, of London; 1 s, 1 da; *Career* served with Sharp-shooters Co of London Yeo 1936-38; Royal Norfolk Regt 1940-46 (W Africa, Middle East, Far East and N W Europe); Special Operations Exec (MC, Croix de Guerre avec Palme 1944); chm Norwich Union Life Insurance Soc 1964; chm Scottish Union and Nat Insurance Co 1968, Maritime Insurance Co 1968, & various other cos; dir Eastern Counties Newspapers Ltd 1970-76; memb Australian Ctee of British Nat Export Council 1968; part-time memb British Railways Eastern Region 1969; chm D E Longe & Co Ltd and East Coast Grain Silos Ltd; DL (1971); High Sheriff Norfolk 1975-76; *Style* - Desmond Longe Esq, MC, DL; Woodton Grange, Bungay, Suffolk

LONGFORD, 7 Earl of (I 1785); Francis Aungier Pakenham; KG (1971), PC (1948); also Baron Longford (I 1756), Baron Silchester (UK 1821), Baron Pakenham (UK 1945); sits as Baron Pakenham; s of 5 Earl of Longford, KP, MVO (ka 1915), by his w, Lady Mary Julia Child-Villiers (d 1933; da of late 7 Earl of Jersey); suc bro, 6 Earl, 1961; *b* 5 Dec 1905; *Educ* Eton, New Coll Oxford; *m* 1931, Elizabeth, CBE (Lady Longford the biographer and historian), da of Nathaniel Bishop Harman, FRCS; 4 s, 3 da (among whom is Lady Antonia Pinter) (and 1 da decd); *Heir* s, Thomas Pakenham; *Career* Lord-in-Waiting to HM 1945-46, Parly Under-Sec of State for War 1946-47, Chllr of Duchy of Lancaster 1947-48, Min of Civil Aviation 1948-51, First Lord of the Admiralty May-Oct 1951 and Lord Privy Seal 1964-65, Sec of State for the Colonies 1965-66, again Lord Privy Seal 1966-68, chm Nat Youth Employment Council 1968-71, and of Sidgwick & Jackson 1970-; *Clubs* Garrick; *Style* - The Rt Hon the Earl of Longford, KG, PC; Bernhurst, Hurst Green, East Sussex (☎ Hurst Green 248); 18 Chesil Court, Chelsea Manor st, SW3 (☎ 01 352 7794)

LONGFORD, Countess of; Elizabeth; CBE (1974); da of late N B Harman, FRCS; *b* 30 August 1906; *Educ* Headington Sch, Oxford; LMH Oxford; *m* 1931, Hon Francis Pakenham, now 7 Earl of Longford; 4 s, 3 da (1 decd); *Career* Lectr for WEA and U Extension Lectr 1929-35, Contested (L) Cheltenham 1935, Oxford 1950, candidate for King's Norton, Birmingham, 1935-43, memb Rent Tribunal Paddington and St Pancras 1947-54, Trustee National Portrait Gallery 1968-78, memb advsy cncl V & A Museum 1969-75, advsy bd Br Library 1976-; Hon DLitt Sussex 1970; *Style* - The Rt Hon the Countess of Longford CBE; Bernhurst, Hurst Green, E Sussex (☎ Hurst Green 248); 18 Cheshil Court, Chelsea Manor St, London SW3 (01 352 7794)

LONGLAND, Sir Jack John Laurence; s of Rev Ernest Longland (d 1956); *b* 26 June 1905; *Educ* King's Sch Worcester, Jesus Cambridge; *m* 1934, Margaret Lowrey, da of Arthur Harrison (d 1936); 2 s, 2 da; *Career* lecturer Durham U 1930-36, educn offr & labour dir Community Service Council for Durham County 1936-40, dep educn offr Hertfordshire 1940-42, county educn offr Dorset 1942-49, dir of educn Derbyshire 1949-70; broadcaster; pres Alpine Club 1974-76, dvpt cmmr 1946-76 Roy Cmmn of Local Gov 1966-69, Countryside Cmmn 1966-72, v-chm Sports Council 1970-74; kt 1970; *Style* - Sir Jack Longland; Bridgeway, Bakewell, Derbyshire (☎ Bakewell 2252)

LONGLEY, Sir Norman; CBE (1954); s of Charles John Longley (d 1931); *b* 14 Oct 1900; *Educ* Clifton College; *m* 1925, Dorothy Lilian, da of George Baker (d 1951); 2 s, 1 da; *Career* special constabulary W Sussex (Div Commandant); chm and md James Longley & Co Ltd Crawley 1931-65; pres Nat Federation of Building Trades Employers 1949-50 and pres Int Federation of Building & Public Works Employers 1975-77, chm Construction Industry Training Bd 1964-70, memb W Sussex Co Cncl 1946-61; kt 1966; *Style* - Sir Norman Longley, CBE; The Beeches, East Park, Crawley, W Sussex (☎ Crawley 0293 20253)

LONGLEY-COOK, Vice-Adm Eric William; CB (1950), CBE (1943), DSO (1945); s of Herbert William Cook (d 1966); *b* 6 Oct 1898; *Educ* RNC Osborne and Dartmouth, Christ's Coll Cambridge; *m* 1, 1920, Helga, nee Lowles (d 1962); 1 da; m 2, 1965, Elizabeth, widow of Sir Ulick Blake, 16 Bt; *Career* Vice-Adm; served 1915-51 (retired), md Fairfield Shipbuilding & Engineering Co 1952-59; dir Lithgow Gp 1959-63, Export Cncl for Europe 1965-66; *Recreations* golf, gardening; *Clubs* Naval & Military; *Style* - Vice-Adm Eric Longley-Cook CB CBE DSO; c/o Lloyds Bank, Chichester, W Sussex; Cordwainers, Titchfield, Hants (☎ 0329444

LONGMAN, Lady Elizabeth Mary; *née* Lambart; da of 10 Earl of Cavan; *b* 1924; *m* 1949, Mark Fredric Kerr Longman (d 1972); 3 da; *Style* - Lady Elizabeth Longman; 64 Rutland Gate, London, SW7

LONGMORE, Charles John Nigel; DL (Herts 1971); s of Brig J Longmore, CB, CBE, TD, DL (d 1973); *b* 2 April 1933; *Educ* Harrow; *m* 1973, Celia Jane, nee Walker; 1 da; *Career* solicitor; OStJ (1969), CStJ (1975), KStJ (1980); County Cmmr 1969 and cdr 1971 St John Ambulance 1971, Life Govr Haileybury and Imperial Serv Coll 1966-; *Recreations* shooting, painting, watching cricket; *Clubs* Arts, MCC, Bergeo Working Men's (pres); *Style* - Charles Longmore Esq, DL; The Bury Farm, Hertingfordbury, nr Hertford, Herts (☎ Hertford 52829)

LONGMORE, Lady; Enid; da of late Col Murray Ray de Bruyne James, CMG; *m* 1, Lt-Col Geoffrey Hadden Bolster, OBE, (decd); m 2, 1960, Air Chief Marshal Sir Arthur Murray Longmore, GCB, DSO (d 1970); *Style* - Lady Longmore; Little Trees, Broomfield Park, Sunningdale, Berks

LONGMORE, Lady Felicity Ann; da of 1 Earl of Wavell; *b* 1921; *m* 1947, Maj Peter Maitland Longmore, MC, RA; 1 s; *Style* - Lady Felicity Longmore; Rook Farm, Funtington, Chichester

LONGMORE, Hon Mrs (Jean Mary); da of 2 Baron Forres; *b* 1919; *m* 1941, Wing Cdr William James Maitland Longmore, CBE; 3 da; *Style* - The Hon Mrs Longmore; Strete End House, Bishop's Waltham, Hants

LONGMORE, (William) James Maitland; CBE (1972); 2 s of Air Chief Marshal Sir Arthur Murray Longmore, GCB, DSO (d 1970); *b* 1919; *Educ* Eton; *m* 1941, Hon Jean Mary, *qv*, only da of 2 Baron Forres (d 1954); 3 da; *Career* joined RAF 1938, Wing Cdr 1945, ret 1946, RAFO; dir Lloyds Bank Int Ltd until 1975; *Clubs* Royal Yacht Squadron; *Style* - James Longmore Esq, CBE; Strete End House, Bishop's Waltham, Hants (☎ 2794)

LONGRIGG, John Stephen; CMG (1973), OBE; s of Brig Stephen H Longrigg, OBE; *b* 1923; *Educ* Rugby, Magdalen Oxford; *m* 1, 1953 (m dis 1965), Lydia Meynell; m 2, 1966, Ann Virginia, da of Joseph O'Reilly; *Career* FO 1948; counsellor FCO 1969-73, HQ Br Forces Hong Kong (on secondment) 1974-76, counsellor FCO 1976-; *Style* - John Longrigg Esq, CMG, OBE; c/o FCO, SW1

LONSDALE, 7 Earl of (UK 1807); Sir James Hugh William Lowther; 8 Bt (GB

1764); also Viscount and Baron Lowther (GB 1797); s of Viscount Lowther (d 1949, himself n of the 5 ('The Yellow' - after the Lowther family colours) Earl, one of the last of the great English sporting Peers, who went a few rounds with Gene Tunney and even reportedly floored him (and after whom Boxing's Lonsdale Belt is named), who incessantly smoked a large cigar and who was a constant theatre goer between the Wars); suc gf, 6 Earl 1953; *b* 3 Nov 1922; *Educ* Eton; *m* 1, 1945 (m dis 1954), Tuppina Cecily, da of late Capt C H Bennett; 1 s, 1 da; m 2, 1954 (m dis 1962), Hon Jennifer Lowther, da of late Maj the Hon Christopher William Lowther (himself s of 1 Viscount Ullswater); 1 s, 2 da; m 3, 1963, Nancy Ruth (Stephenson), da of late Thomas Cobbs, of Pacific Palisades, Calif, USA; 1 s; m 4, 1975, Caroline Sheila, da of Sir Gerald Gordon Ley, 3 Bt, TD; 1 s, 1 da; *Heir* s, Viscount Lowther; *Career* RAC 1939-45, Capt E Riding Yeo (despatches); FBIM; structural engrg 1947-50, farmer, forester, dir of assoc and local cos in Cumberland & Westmorland; dir: Cannon Assur Ltd, Border Television, N Housing Gp Ltd; chm Lakeland Investments Ltd and nine associated or subsid cos, chm Plan Investment Gp Ltd; memb Sports Cncl 1971-74, Eng Tourist Bd 1971-75, Cncls CLA & Timber Growers' Org, Court Newcastle U; pres Cumberland & Westmorland Nat Playing Fields Assoc; *Clubs* Carlton, Brooks's, Nat Sporting, Northern Counties (Newcastle); *Style* - The Rt Hon the Earl of Lonsdale; Askham Hall, Penrith, Cumbria (☎ Hackthorpe 208)

LOOKER, Sir Cecil Thomas; s of late Edward William Looker, of Sydney; *b* 11 April 1913; *Educ* Fort St High Sch and Sydney U; *m* 1941, Jean Leslyn, da of late Ernest Edward Withington, of Melbourne; 1 s, 2 da; *Career* private sec to Prime Minister (Rt Hon Sir Robert Menzies) 1939-41; partner Ian Potter & Co 1953, and senior partner 1967-76; chm Stock Exchange of Melbourne 1966-72; pres Australian Associated Stock Exchanges 1968-71; dir Papua New Guinea Development Bank 1966-74; memb Immigration Planning Council 1968-74; ctee memb Stock Exchange of Melbourne 1962-78, chm 1966-72; chm Australian United Corporation Ltd (Group), dep chm Ansett Transport Industries Ltd, chm Plessey Pacific Pty Ltd, dir Southern Cross Properties Ltd and Herald Development Ltd; kt 1969; *Clubs* Australian, RAC Victoria; *Style* - Sir Cecil Looker; 26 Thormey st, N Balwyn, Vict, Australia (☎ 857 9316)

LOPES, Hon George Edward; s of 2 Baron Roborough; *b* 1945; *Educ* Eton, Roy Agricultural Coll Cirencester; *m* 1975, Hon Sarah Violet Astor, *qv* da of 2 Baron Astor of Hever; 1 s; *Style* - The Hon George Lopes; Gnaton Hall, Yealmpton, S Devon (☎ Plymouth 880237)

LOPES, Hon Henry Massey; s and h of 2 Baron Roborough; *b* 2 Feb 1940; *Educ* Eton; *m* 1968, Robyn, da of John Bromwich, of Stamford Hill, Bacchus Marsh, Melbourne, Australia; 2 s, 2 da; *Style* - The Hon Henry Lopes; Bickham House, Roborough, Plymouth

LOPES, Hon Mrs Sarah Violet; da of 2 Baron Astor; *b* 1953; *m* 1975, Hon George Edward Lopes, *qv*; 1 s; *Style* - The Hon Mrs Lopes; Gnaton Hall, Yealmpton, S Devon

LORD, Lady; Doris; daughter of Ernest Jones, of Sheffield; *m* 1928, Sir Percy Lord (d 1968); *Style* - Lady Lord; 10 Yewlands Drive, Fulwood, Preston

LORD, His Honour Judge; John Herent; s of Sir Frank Lord KBE JP DL (d 1974); *b* 5 Nov 1928; *Educ* Manchester G S, Merton Oxford; *m* 1959, June Ann, da of George Caladine (d 1973); 3 s; *Career* barr Inner Temple 1951, Junior of Northern Circuit 1952, Recorder of Crown Court 1972-78, a Circuit Judge 1978-; *Recreations* photography, shooting; *Clubs* Leander, St James's; *Style* - His Honour Judge Lord; Three Lanes, Greenfield, Oldham (☎ 04577 2198)

LORD, P S; *Career* md Wates Construction Ltd; *Style* - P S Lord Esq; Wates Construction Ltd, 1260 London rd, Norbury, SW16

LORD, Richard Thomas Geoffrey; s of

Sam Lord; *b* 29 Mar 1934; *Educ* Giggleswick Sch, Leeds U; *m* 1959, Elizabeth Logie, nee Forrester; 1 s, 2 da; *Career* chartered textile technologist, md Scapa-Porritt Ltd 1970-, dir and divisional ch exec Scapa Gp Ltd 1976-; *Recreations* golf, local politics, old maps; *Clubs* District & Union (Blackburn), Pleasington GC; *Style* - Richard Lord Esq; Cuerden Lodge, Bamber Bridge, Preston

LORD, William Burton Housley; CB 1979; s of Arthur James Lord (d 1931); *b* 22 March 1919; *Educ* King George Sch Southport, London U, Trin Cambridge; *m* 1942, Helena Headon, da of Douglas Jaques (d 1957); 2 da; *Career* Capt, South Lancashire Regiment Middle East, North Africa; consulting scientist Head of Metallurgy, Atomic Weapons Research Establishment 1964, assist ch scientific adviser Ministry of Defence 1964-68, dep ch scientist Army 1968-71, dir gen of Establishments Resources & Programmes MOD 1971-76, dir of the Roy Armament Research & Development Establishment 1976-79; *Recreations* walking, various water sports, amateur radio; *Style* - William Lord Esq, CB; Fort Halstead, Sevenoaks, Kent

LORIMER, Sir (Thomas) Desmond; s of Thomas Berry Lorimer (d 1952); *b* 20 Oct 1925; *Educ* Belfast Tech H S; *m* 1975, Patricia Doris, da of Ernest Samways; 2 da; *Career* fellow of Inst of Chartered Accountants in Ireland, chm Lamont Holdings Ltd 1973, chm Northern Ireland Housing Exec 1970-75, pres Inst of Chartered Accountants in Ireland 1968-69; late ptnr Deloitte Haskins & Sells; kt 1976; *Recreations* gardening, golf; *Clubs* Carlton, Roy Co Down Golf, Roy Belfast Golf; *Style* - Sir Desmond Lorimer; Windwhistle House, Circular Road West, Cultra, Holywood, Co Down (☎ 02317 3323)

LORNE, Marquess of; Torquhil Ian Campbell; s and h of 12 Duke of Argyll; *b* 29 May 1968; *Style* - Marquess of Lorne

LOTHIAN, 12 Marquess of (S 1701); Peter Francis Walter Kerr; also Lord Newbottle (S 1621), Lord Jedburgh (S 1622), Earl of Lothian, Lord Ker of Newbattle (both S 1631), Earl of Ancram, Viscount of Briene, Lord Ker of Newbottle, Oxnam, Jedburgh, Dolphinstoun and Nisbet (all S 1701), and Baron Ker of Kersheugh (UK 1821); s of Capt Andrew William Kerr, RN, JP (d 1929) and cousin of 11 Marquess (d 1940); *b* 8 Sept 1922; *Educ* Ampleforth, Ch Ch Oxford; *m* 1948, Antonella, da of Maj-Gen Sir Foster Reuss Newland, KCMG, CB (d 1943), and Mrs William Carr, of Ditchingham Hall, Norfolk; 2 s, 4 da (who include Lady Mary von Westenholz, Lady Cecil Cameron of Lochiel, and Countess of Euston - da-in-law of 11 Duke of Grafton); *Heir* s, Earl of Ancram, MP; *Career* FRSA; Lt Scots Gds 1943; memb Roy Company of Archers (Queen's Bodyguard for Scotland); DL (1962) Roxburghshire, Cmmdt Roxburgh Selkirk & Berwicks Special Constabulary, kt Sov Mil Order Malta; Jt Parly Sec Min of Health April-Oct 1964; a Lord-in-waiting to HM the Queen 1972-73; chm of Council, Scottish Red Cross 1976; Lord Warden of the Stanneries and Keeper of Privy Seal of Duke of Cornwall 1977-; *Clubs* Boodle's, Beefsteak, New (Edinburgh); *Style* - The Most Hon the Marquess of Lothian DL; 54 Upper Cheyne Row, SW3; Monteviot, nr Jedburgh, Roxburghshire (☎ Ancrum 288); Melbourne Hall, Derby (☎ 2163)

LOUDON, Lady Prudence Katharine Patton; da of 1 Earl Jellicoe (d 1935); *b* 1913; *m* 1936, Francis William Hope Loudon; 1 s, 2 da; *Career* JP (Kent); *Style* - Lady Prudence Loudon, JP; Little Olantigh, Wye, nr Ashford, Kent

LOUDOUN, Countess of (13 holder of S Earldom 1633); Barbara Huddleston; also Lady Campbell of Loudoun (S 1601), and Lady Tarrinzean and Mauchline (S 1633); da of Countess of Loudoun (d 1960, herself da of Hon Paulyn Rawdon-Hastings, who changed his name from Abney-Hastings and was in his turn yr bro of 11 Earl of Loudoun who also enjoyed the Baronies of Botreaux, Hungerford, De Moleyns, and Hastings in the Peerage of England; Paulyn and the 11 Earl were gs of 4 and last Marquess of Hastings) by her husb Maj Reginald Abney-Hastings, né Huddleston; co-heiress with sisters to Baronies of Botreaux (E 1368), Stanley (E

1456), and Hastings (E 1461), abeyant since death of her mother, Countess of Loudoun; *b* 3 July 1919; *m* 1, 1939 (m dis 1945), Capt Walter Strickland Lord; 1 s; m 2, 1945, Capt Gilbert Greenwood (d 1951); 1 s, 1 da; m 3, 1954, Peter, s of William Griffiths, who changed his name to Abney-Hastings; 3 da; *Heir* s, Lord Mauchline; *Career* Hereditary Govr Repton Sch and Etwall Hosp; *Style* - The Rt Hon The Countess of Loudoun; Mount Walk, Ashby-de-la-Zouch, Leics (☎ 5844)

LOUGHBOROUGH, Archdeacon of; Ven Harold Lockley; s of Harry Lockley (d 1936); *b* 16 July 1916; *Educ* Hinckley G S, London U, Westcott House Cambridge, Nottingham U; *m* 1947 Ursula Margaret Anneliese, da of Rev Dr Hans Wedell (d 1964); 3 s; *Career* deacon 1946, priest 1947, chaplain and lecturer Loughborough College 1946-51, vicar of South Wigston 1951-58, residentiary canon and chancellor of Leicester Cathedral 1958-63, vicar All Saints Leicester 1936-77, examining chaplain to Bishop of Leicester 1951-79, diocesan dir of training 1951-, proctor in Convocation 1960-80; *Recreations* walking, foreign travel, antiquarian interests; *Clubs* Nat Liberal, Leicestershire Club; *Style* - The Ven the Archdeacon of Loughborough; 1 Knighton Grange rd, Leicester LE2 2LF (☎ Leicester 707328); Edgehill Cottage, Loxley, Warwicks

LOUIS, His Excellency John J; *aet* 55 in May 1981; *m* Jo; at least 1 da (Kimberley, *aet* 24 in May 1981); *Career* an heir to the Johnson's Wax fortune; US Ambass to UK 1981-; late chairman Combined Communications (subsid of the Gannett Corpn); *Style* - HE Mr John J Louis; The American Embassy, 24 Grosvenor sq, W1 (☎ 01 499 9000)

LOUIS-DREYFUS, Jean; *Career* chm Louis Dreyfus & Co Ltd; dir SA Louis Dreyfus & Cie, Paris; *Style* - Jean Louis-Dreyfus Esq; Louis-Dreyfus & Co Ltd, City Gate House, Finsbury sq, London E2

LOUTH, 16 Baron (I 1541); Otway Michael James Oliver Plunkett; s of 15 Baron (d 1950); *b* 19 Aug 1929; *Educ* Downside; *m* 1951, Angela, da of William Cullinane, of Jersey; 3 s, 2 da; *Heir* s, Hon Jonathan Plunkett; *Style* - The Rt Hon Lord Louth; Gardone, Holmfield Drive, St Brelade, Jersey, CI

LOUTH, Ethel, Baroness; Ethel Molly; da of Walter John Gallichen, of Jersey; *m* 1927, 15 Baron (d 1950); *Style* - The Rt Hon Ethel, Lady Louth

LOUTIT, John Freeman; CBE (1957); s of John Freeman Loutit (d 1950); *b* 1910; *Educ* St John's Oxford; *m* 1941, Thelma, da of J Thelwall Salusbury; 1 s, 2 da; *Career* dir of S London Blood Supply Depot 1940-47, dir Radiobiology Unit Med Reserch Council Harwell 1947-69, external staff Med Research Council 1969-75; *Recreations* gardening, cooking; *Style* - John Loutit Esq, CBE; c/o Barclays Bank, 2 The Square, Abingdon, Oxon (☎ Abingdon 831279)

LOVAT, 15 Lord (S 1458-64); Simon Christopher Joseph Fraser; DSO (1942), MC (1942), TD (1945); 24 Chief of Clan Fraser of Lovat; *de facto* 15 Lord, 17 but for the attainder; Baron Lovat of Lovat (UK 1837); s of 14 Lord Lovat, KT, GCVO, KCMG, CB, DSO, TD (d 1933), by his w Hon Laura Lister, herself da of 4 Baron Ribblesdale; er bro of Rt Hon Hugh Fraser MP and ex-bro-in-law of Lady Antonia Pinter; bro-in-law of Sir Fitzroy Maclean, 1 Bt; 1 cous of 5 Earl of Eldon; *b* 9 July 1911; *Educ* Ampleforth, Magdalen Oxford; *m* 1938, Rosamond, da of Sir Henry John Delves Broughton, 11 Bt (d 1942); 4 s, 2 da; *Heir* s, Master of Lovat; *Career* 2 Lt Lovat Scouts 1930, Brig 1944, served with Commandos 1941; OStJ; proprietor of around 190,000 acres; Jt Parly Under-Sec of State Foreign Office 1945; DL (1942), JP (1944) Inverness-shire; CStJ; Offr Légion d'Honneur, Croix de Guerre (Fr); Norwegian Cross; Order of Suvarov (Soviet Union); Kt Sov Mil Order of Malta; *Style* - The Rt Hon Lord Lovat DSO MC TD JP DL; Balblair House, Beauly, Inverness-shire

LOVAT, Master of; Hon Simon Augustine Fraser; s and h of 17 Lord Lovat; *b* 1939; *Educ* Ampleforth; *m* 1972, Virginia, da of David Grose; 1 s, 1 da; *Career* Lt Scots Gds 1960; *Style* - Master of Lovat; Beaufort Castle, Beauly, Inverness-

LOVEDAY, Bt-Col George Arthur; TD (1952); s of Arthur Frederick, OBE (d 1968); *b* 13 May 1909; *Educ* Winchester College, Magdalen College Oxford; *m* 1, 1935, Sylvia Mary, daughter of Antony Edmund Gibbs (d 1924); 2 s; m 2, 1967, Penelope Elton (Dugdale), da of Cyril Grant Cunard (d 1914); *Career* Maj RA Northwest Europe 1944-45, Brevet-Col RA (TA) 1956; memb London Stock Exchange 1945, dep chm The Stock Exchange 1971-73, chm 1973-75, ret 1975; *Recreations* golf, gardening; *Clubs* Boodles; *Style* - Colonel George Loveday, TD; Bushton Manor, Wootton Bassett, Swindon

LOVELACE, 5 Earl of (UK 1838); Peter Axel William Locke King; also Lord King, Baron of Ockham (GB 1725), and Viscount Ockham (UK 1838); s of 4 Earl (d 1964, seventh in descent from the sis of John Locke, the philosopher); through his paternal grandmother, Lady Edith Anson, the present Lord Lovelace is 2 cous once removed of Lord (5 Earl of) Lichfield; *b* 26 Nov 1951; *Educ* privately; *Heir* none; *Style* - The Rt Hon the Earl of Lovelace; Torridon House, Torridon, Ross-shire (☎ 228)

LOVELACE, Countess of; Manon Lis; da of Axel Sigurd Transo, of Copenhagen, Denmark, and wid of Baron von Blixen Finecke; *m* 1951, as his 2 w, 4 Earl (d 1964); *Style* - The Rt Hon The Countess of Lovelace; Torridon House, Torridon, Ross-shire

LOVELL-DAVIS, Baron (Life Peer UK 1974); Peter Lovell-Davis; s of William Lovell Davis (d 1974); *b* 8 July 1924; *Educ* Elementary Sch, Christ's Finchley, King Edward VI G S Stratford-on-Avon, Jesus Oxford; *m* 1950, Jean, da of late Peter Foster Graham; 1 s, 1 da; *Career* memb Bd C'wlth Devpt Corpn 1978-, London Consortium 1978-md Central Press Features Ltd 1950-70; dir Newspaper & Printing Cos 1950-70, chm Davis & Harrison Ltd 1970-73, chm The Features Syndicate Ltd 1971-74; a Lord in Waiting to HM the Queen 1974-75, Parly Under-Sec of State Dept of Energy 1975-76; *Style* - The Rt Hon the Lord Lovell-Davis; 80 North rd, Highgate, N6 (☎ 01 345 3919)

LOVELOCK, James Ephraim; s of Tom Arthur Lovelock (d 1957); *b* 26 July 1919; *Educ* Strand Sch Brixton, Manchester, London; *m* 1942, Helen Mary, da of David Manson Hyslop (d 1967) 2 s, 2 da; *Career* independent scientist and fell of the Roy Soc of London, formerly staff member of the Nat Inst for Medical Research 1941-61, prof Baylor Coll of Medicine Texas 1961-64; *Recreations* growing trees, mathematical puzzles; *Style* - James Lovelock Esq; Coombe Mill, St Giles on the Heath, Launceston, Cornwall

LOW, Hon Charles Howard Stuart; s and h of 1 Baron Aldington, KCMG, CBE, DSO, TD, PC; *b* 22 June 1948; *Educ* Winchester, New Coll Oxford; *Style* - The Hon Charles Low; 9 Warwick sq, SW1

LOW, William; JP (1971); s of William Low (d 1957); *b* 12 Sept 1921; *Educ* Merchiston Castle Edinburgh; *m* 1949, Elizabeth Ann Stewart, nee Redwood; 2 s; *Career* textile manufacturer, chm & ch exec Don Bros Buist & Co Ltd, chm Low Bros & Co (Dundee) Ltd, chm J & J Smart (Brechin) Ltd, chm Don & Low Ltd, chm Strathmore Woollen Co Ltd, chm Don Coatings (Scotland) Ltd; *Recreations* shooting, fishing, golf; *Clubs* Naval and Military; *Style* - William Low Esq, JP; Herdill Court, Kirriemuir, Angus (☎ 05752 2215)

LOWE, Lady Elisabeth Olive; da of 5 Earl Cairns; *b* 1944; *m* 1965, Capt Martin Ralph Lowe; 1 s; *Style* - Lady Elisabeth Lowe; Castle End, Ross-on-Wye

LOWE, Sir Francis Reginald Gordon; 3 Bt (UK 1918); s of Sir Francis Gordon Lowe, 2 Bt (d 1972); *b* 8 Feb 1931; *Educ* Stowe, Clare Cambridge; *m* 1, 1961 (m dis 1971), Francesca Cornelia, da of Siegfried Steinkopf, of Berlin; 2 s; m 2, 1971, Helen Suzanne, da of late Sandys Stuart Macaskie, solicitor; *Heir* s, Thomas William Gordon Lowe; *Career* barr 1959; *Style* - Sir Francis Lowe, Bt; 4 New sq, Lincoln's Inn, WC2 (☎ 01 242 8508); Bagwich, Godshill, Isle of Wight

LOWE, Robson; s of John Boyd Lowe (d 1950); *b* 7 Jan 1905; *m* 1928, Winifred (d 1972); 2 da; *Career* philatelist (founded business 1920), publisher 1930-, auctioneer 1937- (merged with Christies Int 1980), editor The Philatelist 1933-72, philatelic advr Nat Postal Museum 1964-, pres Br Philatelic Federation 1979-, exposed 1937 Coronation forgeries, 1953 Sperati forgeries and 1980 Gee-Ma forgeries, chm Br Philatelic Assoc Expert Cttee 1941-65; *Recreations* postal history, postage stamps; *Clubs* East India, Devonshire, Sports and Public Schools; *Style* - Robson Lowe Esq; c/o East India Club, 16 St James sq, SW1 (☎ 930 1000); St Cross, Bodorgan rd, Bournemouth (☎ 0202 25150)

LOWE, Thomas William Gordon; s and h of Sir Francis Reginald Gordon Lowe, 3 Bt; *b* 14 Aug 1963; *Style* - Thomas Lowe Esq

LOWEIN, John Charles; *Career* chm Mobil Oil Co Ltd; dir Mobil Services Co Ltd; dir Mobil Data Services Ltd; dir Mobil Europe Inc; *Style* - John Lowein Esq; Mobil Europe Inc, Mobil Court, 3 Clements Inn, WC2

LOWELL, Lady Caroline Maureen; da of 4 Marquess of Dufferin and Ava; *b* 1931; *m* 1, 1953, Lucian Michael Freud (m dis 1957); m 2, 1959, Israel Citkowitz (d 1974); m 3, Robert Lowell, (d 1977); 1 s; *Style* - Lady Caroline Lowell; Castletown House, Celbridge, Co Kildare

LOWRY, Baron (Life Peer UK 1979); Robert Lynd Erskine Lowry; PC (1974), PC (NI 1971); s of late William Lowry (Rt Hon Mr Justice Lowry); *b* 30 Jan 1919; *Educ* Roy Belfast Academical Institution, Jesus Cambridge; *m* 1945, Mary Audrey, da of John Martin; 3 da; *Career* served WW II N Africa Roy Irish Fusiliers, ending as Hon Col; barr NI 1947, QC (NI) 1956; chm NI Constitutional Convention 1975; Lord Ch Justice of N Ireland 1971-; kt 1971; *Clubs* Roy & Ancient (St Andrews), MCC, Army & Navy; *Style* - The Rt Hon the Lord Lowry, PC; White Hill, Crossgar, Co Down (☎ Crossgar 830397)

LOWRY, Hon Anne Lynd; da of Baron Lowry (Life Peer); *b* 1952; *Style* - The Hon Anne Lowry

LOWRY-CORRY, Frederick Henry; s of late Lt-Col Sir Henry Charles Lowry-Corry and Betty, da of late Col Douglas Proby, who assumed surname Proby by Roy Licence 1904 in lieu of patronymic Hamilton (n of 1 Duke of Abercorn); hp of 8 Earl Belmore; *b* 23 Dec 1926; *Educ* Eton; *m* 1949, Hon Rosemary Diana Lavinia, da of 2 Viscount Plumer; 2 s; *Career* Lt RN (ret); *Style* - Frederick Lowry-Corry Esq; Edwardstone Hall, Boxford, Suffolk (☎ 210233)

LOWRY-CORRY, Hon Mrs Mary Constance; da of 2 Baron Biddulph (d 1949); *b* 1906; *m* 1929 (m dis 1938), as his 1 w, Capt Montagu William Lowry-Corry (d 1977, s of Brig Noel Lowry-Corry, gn of 3 Earl Belmore, by the Brig's 2 w, Hon Clare O'Brien, da of 14 Baron Inchiquin); 1 da (HSH Princess Rupert zu Löwenstein-Wertheim-Freudenberg, *qv*); *Style* - The Hon Mrs Mary Lowry-Corry; 39 Bury Walk, SW3

LOWSLEY-WILLIAMS, Hon Mrs; Hon Olivia; *née* Bootle-Wilbraham; da of 6 Baron Skelmersdale, DSO, MC, and Ann, da of Percy Quilter and gda of Sir Cuthbert Quilter, 1 Bt; *b* 31 Dec 1938; *m* 1961, Anthony John Hoole Lowsley-Williams (maternal gs of Sir Paul Makins, 2 Bt, JP); 3 s; *Style* - The Hon Mrs Lowsley-Williams; The Square House, Harrow Barrow, near Callington, Cornwall

LOWSON, Hon Lady; Hon Ann Patricia; da of 1 Baron Strathcarron (d 1937); *b* 1919; *m* 1936, Sir Denys Colquhoun Flowerdew Lowson, Bt (d 1975); *Career* OStJ; *Style* - The Hon Lady Lowson; Oratory Cottage, 33 Ennismore Gdns Mews, SW7; Carmurie, Elie, Fife (☎ 330223)

LOWSON, Henry William; s and h of Sir Ian Lowson, 2 Bt; *b* 10 Nov 1980

LOWSON, Sir Ian Patrick; 2 Bt (UK

1951), of Westlaws, Co Perth; s of Sir Denys Colquhoun Flowerdew Lowson, 1 Bt (d 1975); *b* 4 Sept 1944; *Educ* Eton, Duke U USA; *m* 1979, Mrs Tanya Theresa H Du Boulay, da of R F A Judge; 1 s; *Heir* s, Henry William Lowson; *Style* - Sir Ian Lowson, Bt; Bandirran, Balbeggie, Perthshire

LOWTHER, Lady Barbara; da of 6 Earl of Lonsdale, OBE (d 1953); *b* 1890; *m* 1914, as his second w, Col James Archibald Innes, DSO (d 1948) (m dis 1921); 1 s (has resumed the surname of Lowther in lieu of Innes); *Style* - Lady Barbara Lowther; Lowther, Penrith

LOWTHER, Hon Benjamin James; s and h of 2 Viscount Ullswater; *b* 26 Nov 1975; *Style* - The Hon Benjamin Lowther; Knoyle Down Farm, Hindon, Salisbury

LOWTHER, Lady Caroline; da of 7 Earl of Lonsdale; *b* 1959; *Style* - Lady Caroline Lowther; Askham Hall, Penrith, Cumberland

LOWTHER, Hon Charles Alexander James; s of 7 Earl of Lonsdale; *b* 1978; *Style* - The Hon Charles Lowther; Askham Hall, Penrith, Cumberland

LOWTHER, Charles Douglas; s and h of Sir William Guy Lowther, 5 Bt, OBE; *b* 22 Jan 1946; *m* 1, 1969, Melanie Pensee Fitzherbert (m dis 1975), da of late Roderick Christopher Musgrave; m 2, 1975, Florence Rose, da of Col Alexander James Henry Cramsie, OBE, of Ballymoney, Co Antrim; 1 s; *Career* Major, Queen's Royal Irish Hussars; *Style* - Charles Lowther Esq; 10 Henning st, SW11 (☎ 01 223 3601)

LOWTHER, Hon Clare Priscilla; da of 2 Viscount Ullswater; *b* 1970; *Style* - The Hon Clare Lowther; Knoyle Down Farm, Hindon, Salisbury

LOWTHER, Hon Emma Mary; da of 2 Visount Ullswater; *b* 1968; *Style* - The Hon Emma Lowther; Knoyle Down Farm, Hindon, Salisbury

LOWTHER, Viscount; Hugh Clayton Lowther; s and h of 7 Earl of Lonsdale; *b* 27 May 1949; *m* 1971, Pamela Middleton; *Style* - Viscount Lowther; Parkside, Lowther, Penrith, Cumbria

LOWTHER, Hon James Nicholas; s of 7 Earl of Lonsdale; *b* 1964; *Style* - The Hon James Lowther; Askham Hall, Penrith, Cumberland

LOWTHER, Lady Miranda; da of 7 Earl of Lonsdale; *b* 1955; *Style* - Lady Miranda Lowther; Askham Hall, Penrith, Cumbrland

LOWTHER, Lady Marie-Louisa; da of 7 Earl of Lonsdale; *b* 1976; *Style* - Lady Marie-Louisa Lowther; Askham Hall, Penrith, Cumberland

LOWTHER, Hon Timothy Lancelot Edward; s of 6 Earl of Lonsdale, OBE (d 1953); *b* 1925; *Educ* RN Coll Dartmouth; *m* 1, 1966, Margaret, Baroness Testaferrata-Abela, da of late John Herring, MC (m dis 1976); m 2, 1977, Susan Ann, da of Capt Leonard Stephen Smallwood, of Jersey; 1 da; *Style* - The Hon Timothy Lowther; Ivystone, Rue de la Croix, St Clements, Jersey

LOWTHER, Sir William Guy; 5 Bt (UK 1824), OBE (1952), DL (Denbighshire, now Clwyd 1969); s of Lt-Col Sir Charles Bingham Lowther, 4 Bt, CB, DSO (d 1949); *b* 9 Oct 1912; *Educ* Winchester; *m* 1939, Grania Suzanne, da of late Maj Archibald James Hamilton Douglas Campbell, OBE, of Blythswood House, Renfrew, and Hon Anna, da of late 5 Baron Clarina; 1 s, 1 da; *Heir* s, Charles Douglas Lowther; *Career* Lt 8 Hussars 1932 (despatches and prisoner WW II), Lt-Col late commanding, ret 1954; memb Hon Corps of Gentlemen-at-Arms; KStJ; High Sheriff Denbighshire 1959; *Style* - Lt-Col Sir William Lowther Bt OBE DL; Erbistock Hall, nr Wrexham (☎ Overton 244)

LOWTHER, Hon William James; s of 7 Earl of Lonsdale; *b* 1957; *Style* - The Hon William Lowther; Askham Hall, Penrith, Cumberland

LOYD, Christopher Lewis; MC (1943), JP (1950) Berks, DL (1954); s of Arthur

Thomas Loyd, OBE, JP (d 1944); *b* 1923; *Educ* Eton, King's Cambridge; *m* 1957, Joanna, da of Capt Arthur Turberville Smith-Bingham; 2 s, 1 da; *Career* served 1942-46 Coldstream Gds; High Sheriff 1961; chartered surveyor, trustee Wallace Collection 1973-; *Clubs* Boodle's, Bucks and Jockey Club; *Style* - Christopher Loyd Esq, MC, JP, DL; Lockinge, Wantage, Oxfordshire (☎ 023 588 265)

LOYD, Lady Moyra; da of 1 Earl of Midleton (d 1942); *b* 1897; *m* 1922, Gen Sir Henry Charles Loyd, GCVO, KCB, DSO, MC, DL (d 1973); 1 s; *Style* - Lady Moyra Loyd; Mettingham Pines, Bungay, Suffolk

LUARD, Hon Mrs; Hon Philippa Mary Agnes Joan; da of 9 Viscount Chetwynd (d 1965); *b* 1930; *m* 1959, Maj John Anthony Hawtrey Luard; 1 s, 1 da; *Style* - The Hon Mrs Luard; Ford House, Eversley, nr Basingstoke, Hants

LUBBOCK, Sir Alan; s of Frederic Lubbock (d 1927; 6 s of Sir John Lubbock 1 Bt, and yr bro of 1 Baron Avebury); *b* 13 Jan 1897; *Educ* Eton, King's Coll Cambridge; *m* 1918, Helen Mary, nee Bonham-Carter; 2 s; *Career* RA 1915-19 and Maj 1939-45, chm Hants CC 1955-67, chm CC Assoc 1965-69, Pro-Chancellor Southampton U 1967-; kt (1963); *Clubs* United Oxford and Cambridge University; *Style* - Sir Alan Lubbock; Adhurst St Mary, Petersfield, Hants

LUBBOCK, Christopher William Stuart; s of late Capt Rupert Egerton Lubbock (3 s of Henry Lubbock JP, DL, himself 2 s of Sir John Lubbock, 3 Bt and yr bro of 1 Baron Avebury); *b* 4 Jan 1920; *Educ* Charterhouse, BNC Oxford; *m* 1947, Hazel Gordon, nee Chapman; 1 s, 1 da; *Career* Lieutenant RNVR 1939-45, Master of the Supreme Court of Judicature appointed 1970; *Clubs* Pratt's; *Style* - Christopher Lubbock Esq; Great Horkesley, Essex

LUBBOCK, Hon Mrs; Hon Helen Anne Boyd; da of 1 Baron Boyd-Orr (d 1971); *b* 1919; *m* 1939, David Miles Lubbock; *Style* - The Hon Mrs Lubbock; Farnell, Brechin, Angus

LUBBOCK, Hon Lyulph Ambrose Jonathan; s and h of 4 Baron Avebury; *b* 15 June 1954; *Style* - The Hon Lyulph Lubbock; Combe House, Sundridge, Kent

LUBBOCK, Hon Maurice Patrick Guy; s of 4 Baron Avebury; *b* 1955; *Style* - The Hon Maurice Lubbock; Combe House, Sundridge, Kent

LUBBOCK, Roy; s of Frederic Lubbock (6 s of Sir John Lubbock, 3 Bt, and yr bro of 1 Baron Avebury) by his w Catherine, da of John Gurney, of Earlham Hall, Norfolk (of the extensive family of that name); bro of Percy Lubbock, the author and critic; *b* 1 Oct 1892; *Educ* Eton, King's Cambridge; *m* 1919, Yvonne, da of Sidney Vernham; 2 s (Jocelyn Roy, b 1920, m (1) 1948 Georgette Ashmead-Bartlett; 1 s (decd), 1 da; m (2) 1976 Adriana Camarca; Hubert Timothy, b 1923, m 1959 Anne Caruth); *Career* lecturer engrg Cambridge 1919-60; Fellow Peterhouse 1919-60; *Style* - Roy Lubbock Esq; Riding Oaks, Hildenborough, Tonbridge, Kent (☎ Hildenborough 833502)

LUBBOCK, Hon Victoria Sarah Maria; da of 4 Baron Avebury; *b* 1959; *Style* - The Hon Victoria Lubbock; Combe House, Sundridge, Kent

LUBIENSKI BODENHAM, Count Charles Henry; s of Count Stanislas Lubienski Bodenham (twin s of Count Louis Lubienski, himself gs of Count Heinrich, who was in his turn 5 s of Felix, the 1 Count, sometime Minister of Justice in the Grand Duchy of Warsaw and, according to Ruvigny, a descendant of Hebda Pomian, a feudal Count *temp* 1357; Felix had the title of Count conferred on him by Frederick William III of Prussia 1798, and this was confirmed by Tsar Nicholas I 1844; Louis married, in 1895, May, da of Lady Victoria Rawdon-Hastings (herself 3 da of Barbara, Baroness Grey de Ruthyn, by her 1 husb, 2 Marquess of Hastings); accordingly Charles (the subject of this article) is co-heir, to the extent of one quarter share, to the Barony of Grey de Ruthyn (E 1324), which became abeyant 1963 with the death of the 25 Baron; Louis (Charles's gf) became a naturalised Br subject 1876 and added the name Bodenham by Deed Poll 1897); *b* 1935; *Educ* Beaumont, Gordonstoun; *m* 1964, Lia Zappala; 1 s (Paul b 1965), 2 (twin) da (Elizabeth b 1972, Monica also b 1972); *Style* - Count Charles Lubienski Bodenham; Little Odiam, Bethersden, Ashford, Kent

LUCAN, 7 Earl of (I 1795); Sir Richard John Bingham; 13 Bt (S 1634); also Baron Lucan (I 1776) and Baron Bingham (UK 1934); s of 6 Earl, MC (d 1964, himself ggs of the Crimean War General who gave the order for the Charge of the Light Brigade, though the multiplicity of the factors concerned in the fiasco (*see* among other books Cecil Woodham-Smith's *The Reason Why*) still furnishes matter for much argument as to whether Lord Lucan, Lord Cardigan or Nolan should bear the principal blame), by his w Kaitilin, paternal gda of 1 Earl of Dartrey; *b* 18 Dec 1934; *Educ* Eton; *m* 1936, Veronica, da of late Maj C M Duncan, MC; 1 s, 2 da; *Heir* s, Lord Bingham; *Career* patron of one living; Lt Coldstream Gds; since an incident (7 Nov 1974) in which Lord Lucan's children's nanny was found dead, the 7 Earl has been missing, though unconfirmed sightings have been reported from various corners of the globe, including Zimbabwe; from 7 Nov 1981 legal proceedings to have him declared dead are permissible; in July 1981 an article in a computer magazine suggested that he might be in Mozambique; *Style* - The Rt Hon the Earl of Lucan

LUCAN, Kaitilin, Countess of; Kaitilin Elizabeth Anne; *née* Dawson; da of late Capt the Hon Edward Stanley Dawson, RN (2 s of late 1 Earl Dartrey); *b* 1900; *m* 1929, 6 Earl of Lucan (d 1964); 2 s, 2 da; *Style* - The Rt Hon Kaitilin, Countess of Lucan; 23 Lords View, NW8

LUCAS OF CRUDWELL, Baroness (10 holder of E Barony of 1663) and Lady Dingwall (6 holder of S Lordship 1609); Anne Rosemary; da of Baroness Lucas also Lady Dingwall (d 1958, 12 holder of Lordship but for the attainder of 1715 whereby her ggggg unc, the Jacobite 2 Duke of Ormonde, was stripped of all Scottish & English honours) and Gp Capt Howard Lister Cooper (d 1972); co-heiress to Barony of Butler (abeyant since death in 1905 of her great unc, 7 & last Earl Cowper); also 2 cous once removed of Auberon Waugh, 2 cous of Lord (6 Earl of) Carnarvon, and descended from the extinct Dukes of Kent and Ormonde and the equally extinct Earls of Desmond and Grantham and Earls Cowper; *b* 28 Apr 1919; *m* 1950, Maj Hon Robert Jocelyn Palmer, MC, JP, s of 3 Earl of Selborne, CH, PC; 2 s, 1 da; *Heir* s, Hon Ralph Matthew Palmer; *Style* - The Rt Hon the Lady Lucas of Crudwell, and Dingwall; The Old House, Wonston, Winchester, Hants (☎ Sutton Scotney 323)

LUCAS OF CHILWORTH, 2 Baron (UK 1946); Michael William George Lucas; s of 1 Baron Lucas of Chilworth, sometime Lord in Waiting to George VI & Parly Sec to Min of T'port (d 1967), by his w Sonia (d 1979), herself da of Marcus Finkelstein, of Latvia; *b* 26 April 1926; *Educ* Peter Symonds Sch Winchester, Luton Tech Coll; *m* 1955, Ann-Marie, only da of Ronald Buck, of Southampton; 2 s, 1 da; *Heir* s, Hon Simon William Lucas; *Career* served with Roy Tank Regt; pres-Inst of Traffic Admin 1980-, League of Safe Drivers 1976-; *Style* - The Rt Hon the Lord Lucas of Chilworth; Constables, Knapp, Hants

LUCAS, Sir Cyril Edward; CMG (1956); s of Archibald Lucas (d 1970); *b* 30 July 1909; *Educ* Hull G S, Univ Coll of Hull; *m* 1934, Sarah Agnes, da of Henry Alfred Rose; 2 s, 1 da; *Career* head of Dept of Oceanography, Univ Coll of Hull 1942-48; entered Civil Service 1948; dir Fishery Research in Scotland, Dept of Agriculture and Fisheries for Scotland 1948-70; memb Council for Scientific Policy 1969-70; memb Natural Environment Research Council 1970-78; fell of the Roy Society 1966-; kt 1976; *Style* - Sir Cyril Lucas, CMG; 16 Albert ter, Aberdeen (☎ Aberdeen 25568)

LUCAS, Hon Ivor Thomas Mark; CMG (1980); s of 1 Baron Lucas of Chilworth (d 1967); *b* 25 July 1927; *Educ* St Edward's Sch Oxford, Trin Oxford; *m* 1954, Christine Mallorie, twin da of Cdr A M Coleman, OBE, DSC, RN (ret); 3 s; *Career* served with RA; entered

Diplomatic Service 1951, formerly dep high commr Kadun, Nigeria; counsellor British Embassy Copenhagen 1972-75; head of Middle East Dept, FCO 1975-79; Ambassador to Oman 1979-; *Recreations* music, cricket, tennis; *Clubs* Roy C'wlth Soc; *Style* - The Hon Ivor Lucas, CMG; c/o FCO King Charles st, SW1

LUCAS, Hon Mrs; Hon Madelina Victoria Margaret; da of 1 Baron Grenfell (d 1925); *b* 1904; *m* 1937, Archibald Julian Lucas (d 1946); 2 da; *Style* - The Hon Mrs Lucas; Mount Pleasant, Goudhurst, Cranbrook, Kent

LUCAS, Hon Rachel Ann; da of 2 Baron Lucas of Chilworth; *b* 1963; *Style* - The Hon Rachel Lucas; Connaught Lodge, 59 Brownhill rd, Chandlers Ford, Hants

LUCAS, Stephen Ralph James; s and h of Sir Thomas Edward Lucas, 5 Bt; *b* 11 Dec 1963; *Educ* Wellington; *Style* - Stephen Lucas Esq

LUCAS, Hon Simon William; s and h of 2 Baron Lucas of Chilworth; *b* 6 Feb 1957; *Style* - The Hon Simon Lucas; Connaught Lodge, 59 Brownhill rd, Chandlers Ford, Hants

LUCAS, Sir Thomas Edward; 5 Bt (UK 1887); s of late Ralph John Scott Lucas, gs of 1 Bt; suc cousin, Maj Sir Jocelyn Morton Lucas, 4 Bt, KBE, MC, 1980; *b* 16 Sept 1930; *Educ* Wellington, Trin Hall Cambridge; *m* 1, 1958, Charmian Margaret (d 1970), da of late Col James Stanley Powell, of Drayton Court, SW10; 1 s; m 2, 1980, Mrs Ann J Graham Moore; *Heir* s, Stephen Lucas; *Style* - Sir Thomas Lucas, Bt; c/o Williams & Glyn's Bank, 22 Whitehall, SW1

LUCAS, Hon Timothy Michael; s of 2 Baron Lucas of Chilworth; *b* 1959; *Style* - The Hon Timothy Lucas; Connaught Lodge, 59 Brownhill rd, Chandlers Ford, Hants

LUCAS-TOOTH, Hon Mrs - Hon Caroline; da of 1 Baron Poole, CBE, TD, PC; *b* 1934; *m* 1955, Hugh John Lucas-Tooth, s of Sir Hugh Vere Huntly Duff Munro-Lucas-Tooth, 1 Bt; *Style* - The Hon Mrs Lucas-Tooth; 21 Faroe Road, West Kensington, London W14 (☎ 01 602 4620); Parsonage Farm, East Hagbourne, Didcot, Berkshire (☎ Didcot (STD Code 0235) 813101)

LUCAS-TOOTH, Hugh John; s and h of Sir Hugh Vere Huntly Duff Munro-Lucas-Tooth, 1 Bt; *b* 20 Aug 1932; *Educ* Eton, Balliol Coll Oxford; *m* 1955, Hon Caroline Poole, eld da of 1 Baron Poole; 3 da; *Career* physicist; late Lt Scots Guards; *Clubs* Brooks's; *Style* - Hugh Lucas-Tooth Esq; 21 Faroe Road, W14 (☎ 01 602 4620); Parsonage Farm, East Hagbourne, Didcot (☎ 0235 813101)

LUCY, Hon Mrs; Hon Audrey Elizabeth Paget; da of 1 Baron of Queenborough (d 1949); *b* 1922; *m* 1, 1945, Commandant Christian Martell, DFC, French Air Force (d 1945); m 2, 1946, Roman Nelson (m dis 1956); m 3 1956, Lt Cdr Claud Peter Harcourt Lucy, RN (m dis 1974); 1 s, 2 da; *Style* - The Hon Mrs Audrey Lucy

LUCZYC-WYHOWSKI, Hon Mrs; Hon Oriel Annabelle Diana Skeffington; da of 13 Viscount Massereene and Ferrard; *b* 6 Feb 1950; *Educ* Downham, Tunbridge Wells Tutors, Sorbonne Paris; *m* 1971, Dominik, s of Stanislaus Luczyc-Wyhowski; 2 da; *Style* - The Hon Mrs Luczyc-Wyhowski; Annagh House, Chilham Castle Grounds, near Canterbury, Kent (☎ Chilham (STD Code 022 776) 496)

LUDLOW, Michael Basil; s of George Rex Ludlow; *b* 1 Oct 1928; *Educ* Prior Park Coll Bath; *m* 1958, Anne, da of William F P Bull (decd); 1 s, 2 da; *Career* md Devenish Redruth Brewery Ltd; dir J A Devenish & Co Ltd, Greenbank Hotel Co (Falmouth) Ltd; *Recreations* sailing, gardening; *Clubs* Roy Cornwall Yacht Club; *Style* - Michael Ludlow Esq; The Bluff, Restronguet Hill, Mylor, Falmouth, Cornwall (☎ Penryn (STD Code 0326) 73785)

LUFF, Graham Oliver; s of John

Graham Luff; *b* 7 Sept 1923; *Educ* Swansea G S; *m* 1946, Jeanne Iris; 2 da; *Career* gp md Bifurcated Eng Ltd, chm of many subsidiaries, v-chm Production Engrg Research Assoc, fndr & chm Black & Luff Ltd; *Recreations* painting, gardening; *Club* RAF; *Style* - Graham Luff Esq; The Bend House, Wendover, Bucks (☎ 0296 622389); Nat West Bank, High st, Wendover, Bucks

LUFF, Robert Charles William; s of Robert Hill Luff (d 1955); *b* 7 July 1914; *Career* Maj; chm Robert Luff Gp, Robert Luff Foundation; v-pres Cystic Fibrosis Research Trust, Lloyd's underwriter; *Recreations* golf; *Clubs* RAC; *Style* - Robert Luff Esq; 294 Earls Court rd, London SW5 (☎ 01 373 7003)

LUKE, 2 Baron (UK 1929); Ian St John Lawson-Johnston; KCVO (1976), TD (1949), JP (Beds 1939), DL (1938); s of 1 Baron, KBE, JP (d 1943) and Hon Edith Laura (d 1941), da of 16 Baron St John of Bletso; *b* 7 June 1905; *Educ* Eton, Trin Cambridge; *m* 1932, Barbara, da of Sir FitzRoy Hamilton Anstruther-Gough-Calthorpe, 1 Bt, JP (d 1957); 4 s; 1 da; *Heir* s, Hon Arthur Charles St John Lawson-Johnston; *Career* life-pres Electrolux Ltd 1978-, chm Gateway Building Soc 1978-, chm Bovril Ltd 1943-70, dir Ashanti Goldfields Corpn Ltd, Lloyds Bank, Lloyds Bank Internat, IBM UK, IBM UK Hldgs, Aktiebolaget Electrolux, Bunhill Hldgs; V-Pres Nat Playing Fields Assoc 1977- (late Pres); chm governing body of Queen Mary Coll U of London 1963-, memb Internat Olympic Ctee 1951-, pres Inst of Export 1973, pres London Chamber of Commerce 1952-55; late MFH Oakley Hunt; one of HM's Lts for City of London; CStJ; *Clubs* Carlton; *Style* - The Rt Hon Lord Luke KCVO TD JP, HM Lieut for City of London; Odell Castle, Odell, Beds (☎ Bedford 720 240)

LUKE, Hon Mrs; Hon Oenone Clarissa; da of 3 Viscount Chaplin; *b* 1934; *m* 1958, Michael Charles Deane Luke, s of Sir Harry Charles Luke, KCMG; 1 s, 3 da; *Style* - The Hon Mrs Luke; 22 Eaton sq, SW1

LUMLEY, Richard Edward Walter; s of Edward Lumley Lumley (d 1960); *b* 7 July 1923; *Educ* Eton; *m* 1953, Josephine Mary, nee Harvey; 7 children (and 1 decd); *Career* Capt Coldstream Gds WW II, CA, Lloyd's underwriter 1945-, chm and md Edward Lumley & Sons Ltd 1960-80 (dir 1951-), chm Edward Lumley Holdings Ltd 1974-, dir Edward Lumley (Australia) Ltd 1974-; *Recreations* family pursuits, walking in country, skiing; *Clubs* Boodle's, Cavalry and Guards, E India and Devonshire, MCC, Berks GC, Cook Soc; *Style* - Richard Lumley Esq; St Annes, Titlarks Hill, Sunningdale, Berks (☎ Ascot 23230)

LUMLEY, Viscount; Richard Osbert Lumley; s and h of 12 Earl of Scarbrough; *b* 18 May 1973; *Style* - Viscount Lumley

LUMLEY, Hon Thomas Henry; s of 12 Earl of Scarbrough; *b* 1980; *Style* - The Hon Thomas Lumley

LUMLEY-SAVILE, Hon Henry Leoline Thornhill; s of 2 Baron Savile, KCVO (d 1931), and hp of bro, 3 Baron; *b* 2 Oct 1923; *Educ* Eton; *m* 1, 1946, Presiley June (m dis 1951), da of Maj G H E Inchbald; m 2, 1961, Caroline Jeffie (d 1970), da of Peter Clive; m 3, 1972, Margaret Ann (nee Phillips), widow of Peter Bruce; 4 s; *Career* served with Grenadier Gds (wounded), demobilized 1947; *Style* - The Hon Henry Lumley-Savile; 38 Carlyle sq, SW3

LUMSDEN, James Alexander; MBE (1945), TD (1962), DL (Dunbartonshire 1966); s of Sir James Lumsden, CBE (d 1970); *b* 24 Jan 1915; *Educ* Cargilfield Sch, Rugby Sch, CCC Cambridge; *m* 1947, Sheila, da of late Malcolm Cross, of Glasgow; 3 s; *Career* slr Glasgow; ptnr Maclay, Murray & Spens; dir Bank of Scotland 1958, Weir Gp Ltd 1957, William Baird & Co Ltd 1959, Scottish Western Investment Co Ltd and other cos Scottish Provident Inst 1968-, Burmah Oil Co Ltd 1957-76; *Recreations* shooting, fishing and country pursuits; *Style* - James Lumsden Esq, MBE, TD, DL; Bannachra, By Helensburgh, Dunbartonshire (☎ Arden 653)

LUNCH, John; CBE (1975), VRD (1965); s of Percy Valentine Lunch (d 1974); *b* 11 Nov 1919; *Educ* Roborough Sch Eastbourne; *m* Joyce Barbara, da of Arnold Basil O'Connell Clerke (d 1959); 2 s; *Career* Lt Cdr RNR 1939-69 (ret), served Second World War, Col (TA) Engineer & Railway Staff Corps; dir-gen of the Port of London Authority and Bd Memb 1971-76; chm Comprehensive Shipping Gp 1973-75, Transcontinental Air Ltd 1973-75; pres Inst of Freight Forwarders 1972-73; council memb Inst of Chartered Accountants 1970-77, Chartered Inst of Transport 1973-76; Ctee of Management RNLI 1977-; pres Hayling Island RNLI Station 1978-, RNLI Manhood Branch 1978-; *Style* - John Lunch Esq, CBE, VRD; Twittens, Itchenor, Chichester, W Sussex (☎ 0243 512105)

LUNN, Peter; CMG (1957), OBE (1951); s of Sir Arnold Lunn, the father of British skiing, and Lady Mabel Northcote, sis of 3 Earl of Iddesleigh; *b* 15 Nov 1914; *Educ* Eton; *m* 1939, Hon Antoinette Preston, da of 15 Viscount Gormanston; 4 s, 2 da; *Career* For Serv to 1972; *Recreations* skiing; *Clubs* SCGB; *Style* - Peter Lunn Esq, CMG, OBE; c/o Westminster Bank, 1 St James's sq, SW1

LUNT, Maj-Gen James Doiran; CBE (1964, OBE 1958); s of Brig Walter Lunt, MBE; *b* 13 Nov 1917; *Educ* King William's Coll IOM, RMC Sandhurst; *m* 1940, Muriel, da of A H Byrt, CBE; 1 s, 1 da; *Career* 2 Lt Duke of Wellington's Regt 1937, dir of Administrative Planning (Army) MOD 1964-66, defence advr to British High Cmmr in India 1966-68, ch of staff Contingencies Planning SHAPE 1968-70, V-Adj-Gen MOD 1970, ret 1972; fell and domestic bursar Wadham Coll Oxford 1973-; author; FRGS; *Style* - Maj-Gen James Lunt, CBE; Hilltop House, Little Milton, Oxon (☎ Gt Milton 242)

LUPTON, Thomas; s of Thomas Lupton (d 1956); *b* 4 Nov 1918; *Educ* Ruskin Oxford, Oriel Oxford, U of Manchester; *m* 1963, Constance Shirley, da of Sydney Herbert Wilson (d 1949); 1 s, 2 da; *Career* Corporal Roy Engineers; prof of Industrial Relations U of Leeds 1964-66, prof of Ogranisation Behaviour Manchester Business Sch 1966, dir Manchester Business Sch 1977 (dep 1967); *Recreations* golf, talking, writing; *Style* - Thomas Lupton Esq; 8 Old Broadway, Manchester M20 9DF

LURGAN, 4 Baron (UK 1839); William George Edward Brownlow; s of 3 Baron, KCVO, JP, DL (d 1937), by his w Lady Emily Cadogan, da of 5 Earl Cadogan, KG; *b* 22 Feb 1902; *Educ* Eton, Oxford U; *Heir* 1 cousin, John Desmond Cavendish Brownlow, OBE; *Clubs* Turf; *Style* - The Rt Hon the Lord Lurgan; c/o Messrs Lee and Pembertons, 45 Pont st, SW1

LUSH, Christopher Duncan; s of Eric Duncan Thomas Lush (d 1980); *Educ* Sedbergh, Magdalen Oxford; *m* 1967, Marguerite Lilian, da of Frederick William Bolden (d 1975); *Career* barr 1953-59, assist legal adviser Foreign Office 1959-62, First Sec West Berlin 1962-66, FO 1966-69, Amman 1969-71, Counsellor FCO 1971-73, Canadian Nat Defence Coll 1973-74, Paris 1974-78, Vienna 1978; *Clubs* Travellers'; *Style* - Christopher Lush Esq; c/o FCO, SW1

LUSH, Brig Maurice Stanley; CB (1944), CBE (1942), MC (1916) and Bar (1917); s of late Hubert S Lush; *b* 1896; *Educ* Tonbridge, RMA; *m* 1930, Diana Ruth, da of Charles Alexander Hill; 1 s, 2 da; *Career* served in 1914-19 War, served in Second World War as Brig in Ethiopia, Madagascar, North Africa, Italy; Sudan Political Service 1919-41, exec commissioner Allied Control Commission Italy, chm Int Refugee Organisation United Nations 1946-50, md Shell Pakistan 1956-59, dep chm Neptune Ctee Nat Tst 1963-68; v-pres British & Foreign Bible Soc; *Style* - Brig Maurice Lush, CB, CBE, MC*; 3 Carlton Mansions, Holland Park gdns, London W14 (☎ 01 603 4425)

LUSHINGTON, Sir Henry Edmund Castleman; 7 Bt (GB 1791), of South Hill Park, Berkshire; s of Sir Herbert Castleman Lushington, 6 Bt (d 1968); *b* 2 May 1909; *Educ* Dauntsey's Sch, Birkbeck Coll London U; *m* 1937, Pamela Elizabeth Daphne, da of A R Hunter; 1 s, 2 da; *Heir*

s, John Richard Castleman Lushington; *Career* Flight Lt RAFVR 1941-46; supt Metropolitan Police 1935-58, legal exec Amery-Parkes and Co 1959, ret 1968; *Style* - Sir Henry Lushington, Bt; Carfax, Crowthorne, Berks (☎ 2819)

LUSHINGTON, John Richard Castleman; s and h of Sir Henry Edmund Castleman Lushington, 7 Bt; *b* 28 Aug 1938; *Educ* Oundle; *m* 1966, Bridget Gillian Margaret, da of Col John Foster Longfield; 3 s; *Style* - John Lushington Esq; Standen, Longbottom, Seer Green, Bucks

LUTTRELL, Lady Elizabeth Hermione; da of 12 Earl Ferrers (d 1954); *b* 1923; *m* 1959, John Fownes Luttrell; 1 s; *Career* formerly with WRNS; *Style* - Lady Elizabeth Luttrell; Waterwynch, Itchen Abbas, nr Winchester

LUTTRELL, Geoffrey Walter Fownes; MC (1945), JP (Somerset 1961); s of Geoffrey Luttrell, of Dunster Castle (which until recently had been in the Luttrells' possession from 1404) and Alys, da of Rear-Adm Walter Bridges, of Trewalla, Victoria, Australia; *b* 2 Oct 1919; *Educ* Eton, Exeter Coll Oxford; *m* 1942, Hermione Hamilton, da of Capt Cecil Gunston, MC (er bro of Sir Derrick Gunston, 1 Bt), and Lady Doris Hamilton-Temple-Blackwood, da of 2 Marquess of Dufferin and Ava; *Career* Lt-Col & Hon Col 6 Bn Light Infantry 1977-; Ld-Lt Som 1978- (V-Ld Lt 1966-78); Regnl Dir Lloyds Bank 1972-; memb Wessex Regnl Cttee Nat Tst 1970-; High Sheriff Som 1960; DL 1958; *Recreations* fishing, gardening; *Clubs* Cavalry & Guards; *Style* - Lt-Col Geoffrey Luttrell MC JP, HM Lord-Lieut for Somerset; Court House, East Quantoxhead, Bridgwater, Somerset (☎ Holford 242)

LUTYENS, (Agnes) Elisabeth; CBE (1969); da of Sir Edwin Landseer Lutyens, OM, KCIE, PRA, the noted architect, and Lady Emily Lytton (*see* Mary Lutyens, Elisabeth's sis, for details); *b* 1906; *m* 1, 1939 (m dis 1941), Ian Glennie; 1 s, twin da; m 2, 1942, Edward Clarke; *Career* composer; *Style* - Miss Elisabeth Lutyens CBE; 13 King Henry's rd, NW3

LUTYENS, Mary; da of Sir Edwin Lutyens, OM, KCIE, PRA, the celebrated architect (particularly of New Delhi) and Lady Emily Lytton, da of 1 Earl of Lytton (s of the novelist Bulwer Lytton) by Edith (da of Hon Edward Villiers, yr bro of 4 Earl of Clarendon, the Victorian Foreign Sec); sis of Elisabeth Lutyens, the composer, and aunt of Lord Ridley; *b* 31 July 1908; *Educ* Queen's Coll London and abroad; *m* 1, 1930 (m dis 1945), Anthony Sewell (decd); 1 da (Amanda, b 1935, m 1954 John Pallant; 2 da); m 2, 1945, Joseph Gluckstein Links, OBE, s of Calman Links; *Career* writer, especially on the Lyttons, Ruskin, Venice and Krishnamurti; FRSL; *Style* - Miss Mary Lutyens; 2 Hyde Park st, W2 (☎ 01 262 0455)

LUXMOORE, Edmund; DL (Durham 1978); s of Allan Aylmer Luxmoore, DL (d 1969); *b* 21 Sept 1914; *Educ* Stowe Sch, Trin Coll Cambridge; *m* 1946, Diana Jean, MBE, da of John Methuen Coote, OBE (d 1967, 2 s of Sir Algernon Coote, 12 Bt); 2 s (Michael John, Richard Aylmer), 1 da (Elizabeth Jean Abbott); *Career* Fl Lt RAF Gibralter and N Africa; slr Clayhills Lucas & Co, Under-Sheriff Co Durham & Co Cleveland (Durham dep with his father 1937-65 and solely since 1965, Cleveland since formation), dir Middleton Hall Ltd as of 1974; *Recreations* shooting, fishing, stalking (author *Deer Stalking* 1980); *Clubs* Oxford and Cambridge, Durham County (chm), Yorkshire Fly Fishers; *Style* - Edmund Luxmoore Esq, DL; Staindrop Hall, Staindrop, Darlington, Co Durham (☎ Staindrop 60331); Crackenthorpe Hall, Appleby-in-Westmorland, Cumbria (☎ Appleby 51409); Tom-Na-Moine, Roybridge, Inverness-shire

LYALL, Eric; CBE; s of Alfred Lyall, of Essex; *b* 12 May 1924; *Educ* Chigwell, King's Cambridge; *m* 1952, Joyce, da of Sydney Edward Smith; 1 s; *Career* formerly slr, ptnr Slaughter & May; former ptnr Guinness Mahon; chm Rocla GB Ltd, Br Hartford Fairmont Ltd; Gen Commissioner Income Tax; chm Con Pty E Area, Frewen Educnl Tst; dir Tricentrol, Clarke Nickolls & Coombs; *Recreations* Oriental, City of London, MCC; *Clubs* philately, tennis; *Style* - Eric Lyall Esq,

CBE; Riders Grove, Old Hall Green, Ware, Herts (☎ 821370)

LYALL, Ian Alastair; DSC (1944), VRD (1952); s of William Lyall (d 1937); *b* 16 Mar 1917; *Educ* Hillhead H S, Glasgow; *m* 1947, Eileen Patricia, da of Capt Bennett, HAC; 1 da; *Career* Lieut-Commander RNR; shipping co chm and man dir 1978-79; Pres Glasgow Chamber of Commerce; chm: Port Employers Assoc 1970-80, Nat Dock Labour Board (Clyde) 1978-80 and others; *Recreations* sailing, shooting, fishing; *Clubs* RNYC, CCC, RNSA, Naval & Military; *Style* - Ian Lyall Esq, DSC, VRD; Rimsdale, Helensburgh, Dunbartonshire (☎ 0436 3976)

LYALL GRANT, Maj-Gen Ian Hallam; MC (1944); s of Col Henry Frederick Lyall Grant, DSO, (d 1958); *b* 4 June 1915; *Educ* Cheltenham Coll, Gonville & Caius Cambridge; *m* 1951, Mary Jennifer, da of Norman Moore (d 1980); 1 s, 2 da; *Career* joined Army 1935, Cmdt Royal Sch of Military Engineering 1965-67, Dep Quartermaster-Gen MOD (1967-70), Civil Service 1970-1975, Dir Gen of Supply Co-Ordination 1976-; consultant Defence and Gemmology; *Recreations* sailing, painting, gemmology; yacht 'Starfire'; *Clubs* Naval & Military; *Style* - Maj-Gen Ian Lyall Grant, MC; Kingswear House, Kingswear, Dartmouth, Devon

LYCETT, Lady (June) Wendy; *née* Pelham; JP; da of 5 Earl of Yarborough, MC (d 1948) and co-heiress to Baronies of Fauconberg and Conyers (*see* Lady Diana Miller); *b* 6 June 1924; *m* 1959, Maj Michael Hildesley Lycett; 1 adopted da (the er child of Lady Wendy's sis, Lady Diana Miller, *qv*); *Career* late 3 Officer WRNS; *Style* - Lady Wendy Lycett, JP; West Grange, Scots Gap, Morpeth, Northumberland

LYELL, 3 Baron (UK 1914); Sir Charles Lyell; 3 Bt (UK 1894); s of 2 Baron, VC (ka 1943, VC awarded posthumously) by his w Sophie, nee Trafford (whose family, of Wroxham Hall, Norfolk, were a cadet branch of the Traffords now represented by the de Trafford Bts), whose mother was Lady Elizabeth Bertie, OBE, yst da of 7 Earl of Abingdon; *b* 27 March 1939; *Educ* Eton, Ch Ch Oxford; *Heir* none; *Career* CA; 2 Lt Scots Gds 1957-59; Oppn Whip House of Lords 1974-79, Lord in Waiting (Govt Whip) 1979-; memb Roy Co of Archers (Queen's Bodyguard for Scotland); *Clubs* White's, Turf; *Style* - The Rt Hon the Lord Lyell; Kinnordy House, Kirriemuir, Angus (☎ Kirriemuir 2848); 20 Petersham Mews, SW7 (☎ 01 584 9419)

LYELL, Hon Lady; Hon Katherine; da of 1 Viscount Runciman of Doxford (d 1949); *b* 1909; *m* 1, 1931, 4 Baron Farrer (d 1954); m 2, 1955, Hon Sir Maurice Lyell (d 1975); *Style* - The Hon Lady Lyell; Puddephat's Farm, Markyate, Herts

LYELL, Baroness; Sophie Mary; da of Maj Sigismund William Joseph Trafford, JP, DL (d 1953), of Wroxham Hall, Norfolk and Honington Hall, Grantham and of Lady Elizabeth Bertie, OBE, da of 7 Earl of Abingdon (d 1928); *b* 1916; *m* 1938, 2 Baron Lyell, VC (ka 1943); 1 s; *Style* - The Rt Hon the Lady Lyell; Sheil Hill House, by Forfar, Angus (☎ Foreside 209 and 212); Kinnordy, Kirriemuir, Angus (☎ Kirriemuir 2848)

LYGON, Lady Dorothy; da of 7 Earl Beauchamp KG, KCMG, TD, PC (d 1938); *b* 1912; *Career* late Section Officer WAAF; *Style* - Lady Dorothy Lygon; c/o Messrs C Hoare and Co, 37 Fleet st, EC4

LYGON, Lady Mary; da of 7 Earl Beauchamp KG, KCMG, TD, PC (d 1938); *b* 1910; *m* 1939, HH Prince Vsevolode Joannovitch of Russia (d 1973) (m dis 1956); resumed the surname of Lygon 1956; *Style* - Lady Mary Lygon; 46 Redcliffe gdns, SW10

LYLE, Hon Mrs; Hon Elizabeth; *née* Sinclair; da of 1 Viscount Thurso, KT, CMG, PC (d 1970); *b* 5 June 1921; *m* 1942, Lt Col Archibald Michael Lyle, yst s of Sir Archibald Lyle, 2 Bt; 2 da (Veronica b 1943, m 1967 Magnus Linklater; Janet b 1944, m 1975 Richard Cooper); *Style* - The Hon Mrs Lyle; Riemore Lodge, Dunkeld, Perths

LYLE, Sir Gavin Archibald; 3 Bt (UK 1929), of Glendelvine, Co Perth; s of Capt

Ian Archibald de Hoghton Lyle (ka 1942), s of 2 Bt; suc gf, Col Sir Archibald Moir Park Lyle, 2 Bt, MC, TD, 1946; *b* 14 Oct 1941; *m* 1967, Susan Cooper; 4 s, 1 da; *Heir* s, Ian Abram Lyle; *Career* estate man; farmer; co dir; *Style* - Sir Gavin Lyle, Bt; Glendelvine, Caputh, Perthshire

LYLE, Ian Abram; s and h of Sir Gavin Archibald Lyle, 3 Bt; *b* 25 Sept 1968; *Style* - Ian Lyle Esq

LYLE, Robert David Lyle; s of Robert Harvey Lyle Wyatt; *b* 20 March 1915; *Educ* Eastbourne Coll; *m* 1945, Irene Joyce, nee Francis; 1 s, 1 da; *Career* Major RASC, memb London Stock Exchange, memb Cncl Br Diabetic Assoc, memb Bd Management The Duchy Hosp Cornwall, dir Poldhu Hotel Mullion, dir Woodrow Wyatt Hldgs Ltd, dir Br Industrial & Gen Trust; *Clubs* Mullion Golf, City of London, Landsdowne, MCC; changed surname from Wyatt to Lyle by deed poll (1949) as result of inheriting family estate; *Style* - Robert Lyle Esq; 20 Princes Gate Mews, SW7 (☎ 584 6910); Bonython Manor, nr Helston, Cornwall (☎ 032 6240 234)

LYLE, Thomas Keith; CBE (1949); *b* 26 Dec 1903; *Educ* Dulwich Coll, Sidney Sussex Cambridge; *m* 1949, Jane Bouverie, da of late Maj Nigel Maxwell; 1 s, 3 da; *Career* consulting opthalmic surgeon King's Coll Hospital, Moorfields Eye Hospital, Nat Hospital; dir orthoptic dept Moorfields Eye Hosp 1947-69; dean of Inst of Opthalmology, British post-graduate Med Fedn London U 1959-67; teacher opthalmology London University; *Clubs* Bath, RAF, Ski Club of GB; *Style* - Thomas Lyle Esq CBE; Kingsley, Crowsley rd, Shiplake, nr Henley-on-Thames (☎ Wargrave 2832); 23 Harley House, Marylebone rd, NW1 (☎ 01 935 5213)

LYMINGTON, Viscount; Oliver Kintzing Wallop; s of 9 Earl of Portsmouth by his 1 w Mary; *b* 14 Jan 1923; *Educ* Eton; *m* 1, 1952, Maureen (m dis 1954), da of Lt-Col Kenneth B Stanley, MBE; m 2, 1954, Ruth Violet (m dis 1974) (she d 1978), da of Brig-Gen Gerald Carew Sladen, CB, CMG, DSO, MC (d 1930); 1 s, 2 da; m 3, 1974, Julia Kirwan-Taylor, da of Graeme Ogden, DSO, and formerly w of Peter Kirwan-Taylor; *Career* Lt RNVR 1943, ret; *Clubs* Buck's, RAC; *Style* - Viscount Lymington; 11 Douro Place, W8 (☎ 01 937 3212/4914); The Old Rectory, Aldon Lane, Offham, Maidstone, Kent (☎ West Malling 842322)

LYNCH-BLOSSE, Elizabeth Lady; Elizabeth; da of Thomas Harold Payne, of Welwyn Garden City; *m* 1950, Sir David Edward Lynch-Blosse, 16 Bt (d 1971); *Style* - Elizabeth, Lady Lynch-Blosse; Meriden, Todenham, Moreton-in-Marsh, Glos

LYNCH-BLOSSE, (Eric) Hugh; OBE (1953); s of late Maj Cecil Eagles Lynch-Blosse and hp of kinsman, Sir Richard Hely Lynch-Blosse, 17 Bt; *b* 30 July 1917; *m* 1946, Jean Evelyn, da of Cdr Andrew Robertson Hair, RD, RNR; 1 s, 1 da; *Career* standards engr Rank Xerox 1969-74; Sec Wyedean Tourist Bd, man Tourist Info Centre Ross on Wye 1974-80; Gp Capt, RAF (ret); *Clubs* RAF; *Style* - Hugh Lynch-Blosse Esq OBE; 17 Queens Acre, Newnham, Glos (☎ 335)

LYNCH-BLOSSE, Sir Richard Hely; 17 Bt (I 1622), of Castle Carra, Galway; s of Sir David Edward Lynch-Blosse, 16 Bt (d 1971); *b* 26 Aug 1953; *Educ* Roy Free Hosp Sch of Medicine; *m* 1976, Cara, only da of G L Sutherland, of Welwyn Garden City; *Heir* kinsman, Hugh Lynch-Blosse, OBE; *Career* Capt, commissioned RAMC 1975; LRCP, MRCS 1978; *Recreations* shooting, flying, sailing; *Style* - Sir Richard Lynch-Blosse, Bt; c/o Nat West Bank, 15 Stonehills, Welwyn Garden City, Herts

LYNCH-ROBINSON, Dominick Christopher; s and h of Sir Niall Bryan Lynch-Robinson, 3 Bt, DSC; *b* 30 July 1948; *Style* - Dominick Lynch-Robinson Esq

LYNCH-ROBINSON, Sir Niall Bryan; 3 Bt (UK 1920), of Foxrock, Co Dublin, DSC (1941); s of Sir Christopher Henry Lynch-Robinson, 2 Bt (d 1958); *b* 24 Feb 1918; *Educ* Stowe; *m* 1940, Rosemary Seaton, da of Mrs M S Eller; 1 s, 1 da; *Heir*

s, Dominick Christopher Lynch-Robinson; *Career* Sub-Lt RNVR 1939, Lt 1940; chm Leo Burnett Ltd; *Style* - Sir Niall Lynch-Robinson, Bt, DSC; The Old Parsonage, East Clandon, Surrey

LYNE, Air Vice-Marshal Michael Dillon; CB (1968), AFC (1943) and bars (1947 and 1955), DL (1973); s of Robert Lyne, d 1943; *b* 23 March 1919; *Educ* Imperial Serv Coll, RAF Coll Cranwell; *m* 1943, Avril, da of Lt-Col A Buckley, CBE, DSO, (d 1965), of Liverpool; 2 s, 2 da; *Career* Air V-Marshal Fighter Command Middle East and North Atlantic; sec Diocese of Lincoln 1971-76, dir gen of training RAF (1970-71), sr RAF instructor Imperial Defence Coll 1968-69, AOC 23 Gp 1965 and 67, Cmdt RAF College Cranwell 1963-64, Air Attaché Moscow 1961-63; v-chm Govrs Bishop Grosseteste Coll Lincoln, founder & chm of Lincolnshire Microprocessor Soc, memb council British Computer Soc, pres 54 Squadron Assoc; *Recreations* cruising, photography, writing; yacht: 'Aries of Anglia'; *Clubs* RAF, Cruising Assoc; *Style* - Air Vice-Marshal Michael Lyne CB AFC ** DL; 9 Far Lane, Coleby, Lincoln (☎ 0522 810468)

LYON, Lady Mary; da of 11 Earl of Wemyss (d 1937); *b* 1895; *m* 1, 1915, Algernon Walter Strickland (d 1938); m 2, 1943, Maj John George Lyon, RA; *Style* - Lady Mary Lyon; Apperley Court, Gloucester

LYONS, Hon Deborah; da of Baron Lyons of Brighton (d 1978); *b* 1965; *Style* - The Hon Deborah Lyons

LYONS, Hamilton; s of Richard Lyons; *b* 3 Aug 1918; *Educ* Gourock H S, Greenock H S, Glasgow U; *m* 1943, Jean Cathro Blair; 2 s; *Career* Sheriff of N Strathclyde (formerly Renfrew & Argyll, and Ayr & Bute) 1968-; *Style* - Sheriff Lyons; 14 Cloch rd, Gourock, Inverclyde (☎ Gourock 32566)

LYONS, Hon Rodney; s and h of Baron Lyons of Brighton (d 1978); *b* 1941; *m* 1963, Cory Frances, da of William Owen Hassall, of the Manor House, Wheatley, Oxford; *Style* - The Hon Rodney Lyons; 54 Fore st, Bradninch, Exeter, Devon

LYONS, Hon William; s of Baron Lyons of Brighton (d 1978); *b* 1945; *m* 1963, Petra Deanna, da of William Tibble; *Style* - The Hon William Lyons; 15 Lower Town, Sampford Peverell, Devon

LYSAGHT, Patrick James; s of late Horace James William Lysaght (bro of 6 Baron Lisle); hp to Barony of Lisle; *b* 1 May 1931; *Educ* Shrewsbury; *m* 1957, Mary Louise, da of late Lt-Col Geoffrey Reginald Devereux Shaw and formerly wife of Euan Guy Shaw-Stewart (now 10 Bt); 2 s, 1 da; *Career* late Lt Gren Gds; *Style* - Patrick Lysaght Esq; 52 Wardo ave, SW6

LYTTELTON, Hon Christopher Charles; s of 10 Viscount Cobham, KG, GCMG, GCVO, TD, PC (d 1977); *b* 23 Oct 1927; *Educ* Eton; *m* 1973, Tess Mary, da of late Col Alexander George Jeremy Readman, DSO; 1 s, 1 da; *Style* - The Hon Christopher Lyttelton; 28 Abbey gdns, NW8

LYTTELTON, Hon Deborah Clare; da of 2 Viscount Chandos; *b* 1963; *Style* - The Hon Deborah Lyttelton; The Vyne, Sherborne St John, Basingstoke, Hants

LYTTELTON, Humphrey Richard Adeane; s of Hon George Lyttelton (2 s of 8 Viscount Cobham) by his w Pamela (da of Charles Adeane, CB, JP, and Madeline Wyndham, gda of 1 Baron Leconfield); 2 cous of Baron Adeane; *b* 23 May 1921; *Educ* Eton; *m* 1, 1948 (m dis 1952), Patricia, da of J Wellesley Gaskell and Mrs David Braithwaite, of Hampstead; 1 da; m 2, 1952, Elizabeth, 2 da of Albert Richardson, of Bournemouth; 2 s, 1 da; *Career* jazz musician, writer; served WW II Gren Gds; cartoonist Daily Mail 1949-53; *Style* - Humphrey Lyttelton Esq; Alyn Close, Barnet rd, Arkley, Herts

LYTTELTON, Hon Laura Katherine; da of 2 Viscount Chandos; *b* 1950; *Educ* Cranborne Chase Sch, St Anne's Oxford, London U; *Style* - The Hon Laura Lyttelton; The Vyne, Sherborne St John, Basingstoke, Hants

LYTTELTON, Hon Matthew

Peregrine Antony; s of 2 Viscount Chandos (d 1980), and hp of bro, 3 Viscount; *b* 21 April 1956; *Educ* Eton, Trin Cambridge; *Style* - The Hon Matthew Lyttelton; The Vyne, Sherborne St John, Basingstoke, Hants

LYTTELTON, Hon Nicholas Adrian Oliver; s of 1 Viscount Chandos, KG, DSO, MC, PC (d 1972); *b* 1937; *Educ* Eton; *m* 1960, Margaret, da of Harold Hobson; 1 s, 1 da; *Style* - The Hon Nicholas Lyttelton; 30 Paulton's sq, SW3

LYTTELTON, Hon Nicholas Makeig; s of 10 Viscount Cobham, KG, GCMG, GCVO, TD, PC (d 1977); *b* 1951; *Educ* Shiplake Court Oxon; *m* 1980, June Carrington; *Style* - The Hon Nicholas Lyttelton

LYTTELTON, Hon Richard Cavendish; s of 10 Viscount Cobham, KG, GCMG, GCVO, TD, PC (d 1977); *b* 1949; *Educ* Eton; *m* 1971, Romilly, da of Michael Barker; 1 da; *Style* - The Hon Richard Lyttelton; Aidasmäentle 34a, 00650, Helsinki 65, Finland

LYTTON, 4 Earl of (UK 1880); Sir Noel Anthony Scawen Lytton; 5 Bt (UK 1838), OBE (1945); also 17 Baron Wentworth (E 1529-48), Baron Lytton (UK 1866), and Viscount Knebworth (UK 1880); s of 3 Earl of Lytton, OBE (d 1951, a portraitist, landscape painter & gs of Bulwer Lytton, the novelist who romanced about his paternal ancestors (Wiggett, and not even armigerous) no less than about the Pompeiians and the Rienzi; his political career suffered less from the opposition of a mad wife on the hustings than might be thought) and Baroness Wentworth (d 1957, da of Anne Isabella Noel, Baroness Wentworth and gda of Lord Byron, by her husb Wilfrid Scawen Blunt, another poet; Anne Isabella's mother, whose "favourite science was the mathematical" & who has been considered by some the first computer programmer inasmuch as she devised problems for Babbage's calculating machine, was less at home with applied mathematics, for her losses on the turf, despite an 'infallible system' she invented, were prodigious; it would seem that the horse she backed each time was, like Doña Inez, "a *walking* calculation"); cous of Elisabeth Lutyens, the composer; *b* 7 April 1900; *Educ* Downside, Sandhurst; *m* 1946, Clarissa Mary, da of Brig-Gen Cyril Eustace Palmer, CB, CMG, DSO, RA (d 1939); 2 s, 3 da; *Heir* s, Viscount Knebworth; *Career* added name Milbanke to Lytton by Deed Poll 1925 but removed it in 1951; sits on Cross Benches in Ho of Lds; Lt Rifle Brig 1921, served as Lt-Col in N Africa, Italy, Greece and Austria, ret 1946; author; farmer; *Style* - The Rt Hon the Earl of Lytton, OBE; Keeper Knights, Pound Hill, Crawley, Sussex; Lillycombe House, Porlock, Somerset (☎ 353)

LYTTON, Lady Caroline Mary Noel; da of 4 Earl of Lytton, OBE; *b* 1947; *Educ* St Teresa's Minehead, St Mary's Shaftesbury, Birmingham U; *Style* - Lady Caroline Lytton; Lillycombe House, Porlock, Somerset (☎ Porlock 353)

LYTTON, Lady Lucy Mary Frances; da of 4 Earl of Lytton, OBE; *b* 29 Jan 1957; *Educ* St Teresa's Minehead, Woldingham; *Style* - Lady Lucy Lytton

LYTTON, Sandra, Countess of; Rosa Alexandrine Fortel; *m* 1924, as his 2 w, 3 Earl of Lytton, OBE, Legion of Honour (d 1951); 1 da; *Style* - The Rt Hon Sandra, Countess of Lytton; 8 Rue du Val de Grace, Paris V, France

LYTTON, Hon (Thomas) Roland Cyril Lawrence; s of 4 Earl of Lytton, OBE; *b* 10 Aug 1954; *Educ* St Teresa's Minehead, Worth, Downside; *Style* - The Hon Roland Lytton

LYTTON COBBOLD, Hon David Antony Fromanteel; s of 1 Baron Cobbold KG GCVO PC, of Knebworth House, Herts; *b* 14 July 1937; *Educ* Eton, Trin Cambridge; *m* 1961, Christine Elizabeth, da of Maj Sir Dennis Frederick Bankes Stucley, 5 Bt, of Hartland Abbey, N Devon; 3 s, 1 da; *Career* served in RAF 1955-57; assumed by deed poll 1960 the additional surname of Lytton before his patronymic; *Style* - The Hon David Lytton Cobbold; Knebworth House, Knebworth, Herts

LYVEDEN, 6 Baron (UK 1859); Ronald Cecil Vernon; s of 5 Baron Lyveden (d 1973); *b* 10 Apr 1915; *m* 1938, Queenie Constance, da of Howard Ardern; 3 s; *Heir* s, Hon Jack Leslie Vernon; *Style* - The Rt Hon the Lord Lyveden; 20 Farmer st, Te Aroha, New Zealand (☎ 410)

LYVEDEN, Dowager Baroness; Ada; da of late Arthur Hodgkinson, of Accrington; *m* 1, 1910, Richard Springate; m 2, 1925, as his 2 w, 3 Baron Lyveden (d 1926); *Career* actress (Lynda Martell); *Style* - The Rt Hon the Dowager Lady Lyveden

LYVEDEN, Doris, Baroness; Doris Violet; da of late Henry Francis Coghlan White, of W Hoathly, Sussex; *m* 1, Capt Eric Paterson (decd); m 2, 1949, 4 Baron Lyveden (d 1969); *Style* - The Rt Hon Doris, Lady Lyveden; Hunnersley, Burley, Ringwood, Hants

LYVEDEN, Gladys, Baroness; Gladys; *m* 1, John Cassidy (decd); m 2, 1957, as his 2 w, 5 Baron Lyveden (d 1973); *Style* - The Rt Hon Gladys, Lady Lyveden; Day's Bay, nr Wellington, New Zealand

M

MABANE, Baroness; Stella Jane; da of late Julian Duggan; *m* 1944, 1 and last Baron Mabane, KBE, PC (d 1969); *Style* - The Rt Hon the Lady Mabane; 11 Stanhope gdns, SW7

MACADAM, Sir Peter; s of late Francis Macadam; *b* 9 Sept 1921; *Educ* Buenos Aires Argentina, Stonyhurst Coll Lancs; *m* 1949, Ann Musson; 3 da; *Career* chm BAT Industries Ltd 1976-; kt 1981; *Style* - Sir Peter Macadam; 34 Campden Hill ct, Campden Hill rd, W8

McALPINE OF MOFFAT, Baron (Life Peer UK 1979); (Robert) Edwin; s of William Hepburn McAlpine (d 1951); hp to Baronetcy of bro, Sir Thomas McAlpine, 4 Bt; *b* 23 April 1907; *Educ* Oundle; *m* 1930, Ella Mary Gardner, da of James Garnett, formerly of Vancouver; 3 s, 1 da; *Career* ptnr Sir Robert McAlpine & Sons Ltd 1928-; dep chm British Nuclear Associates 1973-; chm Greycoat London Estates 1978-; kt 1963; *Clubs* Garrick, Buck's, Caledonian, Jockey; *Style* - The Rt Hon Lord McAlpine of Moffat; Benhams, Fawley Green, nr Henley-on-Thames, Oxon (☎ Hambleden 246)

McALPINE, Hon (Robert) Alistair; s of Baron McAlpine of Moffat (Life Peer); *b* 1942; *m* 1, 1964 (m dis 1979), Sarah Alexandra, da of late Paul Hillman Baron; 2 da; m 2, 1980, Romilly T, only da of A T Hobbs, of South House, Knowle Lane, Cranleigh, Surrey; *Career* Hon Treasurer (1975-) & Dep Chm (1979-) Con Pty; chm Arts Cncl's touring advsy cttee 1981-; Hon Treasurer Europe Democratic Union 1978-, V-Pres European League for Econ Co-opn 1975-, Friends of Ashmolean Museum 1969-, Gter London Arts Assoc 1971-77; dir George Weidenfeld Hldgs 1975-, Sir Robert McAlpine & Sons; *Style* - The Hon Alistair McAlpine; West Green House, Hartley Wintney, Hants

McALPINE, Alfred James; *Career* dir Alfred McAlpine & Son; Alfred McAlpine & Son (Pty) Ltd, Johannesburg; Marchwiel Ltd; Sir Alfred McAlpine & Son (Northern) Ltd; United Gravel Co Ltd; *Style* - Alfred McAlpine Esq; Sir Alfred McAlpine & Son Ltd, Hooton, South Wirral, Cheshire L66 7ND

MACALPINE, Hon Mrs; Hon Dorothy Frances; da of 1 Baron Bethell (d 1945); *b* 1897; *m* 1930, Lt-Col Ian Ferguson Macalpine (m dis 1957) and re-married 1966; *Style* - The Hon Mrs Macalpine; 17 Grosvenor sq, W1

McALPINE, Hon David Malcolm; s of Baron McAlpine of Moffat (Life Peer); *b* 1946; *m* 1971, Jennifer Anne, da of Eric Hodges, of Fawley Cottage, Fawley Green, Henley-on-Thames; 2 da; *Career* dir Sir Robert McAlpine & Sons; *Style* - The Hon David McAlpine; Fawley House, Fawley Green, Henley-on-Thames RG9 6JA

McALPINE, Kenneth; DL (Kent 1976); s of Sir Thomas Malcolm McAlpine, KBE (d 1967); *b* 21 Sept 1920; *Educ* Charterhouse; *m* 1955, Patricia Mary, da of Capt Francis William Hugh Jeans, CVO, RN (d 1968); 2 s; *Career* flying offr RAFVR; dir Newarthill Ltd, Sir Robert McAlpine & Sons Ltd, London Brick Co Ltd; High Sheriff Kent 1973-74; gov Roy Hosp of St Bartholomew 1972-74; v-chm Eastbourne Coll 1970-; *Clubs* Roy Yacht Sqdn; *Style* - Kenneth McAlpine Esq, DL; The Priory, Lamberhurst, Kent

McALPINE, Malcolm Hugh Dees; *Career* dir, Sir Robert McAlpine & Sons Ltd; dir: Bank of Nova Scotia Canada, Newarthill Ltd; dep chm, Royal Insurance Co; *Style* - Malcolm McAlpine, Esq; Sir Robert McAlpine & Sons Ltd, 40 Bernard st, WC1N ILG

McALPINE, Robert James; *Career* vice-chm: Sir Alfred McAlpine & Son Ltd, Marchwiel Ltd, Sir Alfred McAlpine & Son (Northern) Ltd; dir: McAlpine Somerville Pipeline Ltd, Minch Shipping & Trading Co Ltd, Penrhyn Quarries Ltd, Pochins (Joinery) Ltd, United Asphalt Co Ltd, Westminster Property Group Ltd; IOD, FIOB; *Style* - Robert McAlpine Esq; Sir Alfred McAlpine & Son Ltd, Hooton, South Wirral, Cheshire L66 7ND

McALPINE, Sir Thomas George Bishop; 4 Bt (UK 1918), of Knott Park, Co Surrey; s of William Hepburn McAlpine (d 1951); suc cousin, Sir (Alfred) Robert McAlpine, 3 Bt, 1968; *b* 3 Oct 1901; *m* 1, 1934, Doris Frew (d 1964), da of late D C Campbell, of Roseneath, Gosforth, Newcastle upon Tyne; m 2, 1965, Mrs Kathleen Mary Blackshaw; *Heir* bro Baron McAlpine of Moffat; *Style* - Sir Thomas McAlpine, Bt; The Manor House, Stanford-in-the-Vale, nr Faringdon, Oxon

McALPINE, Hon William Hepburn; s of Baron McAlpine of Moffat (Life Peer); *b* 12 Jan 1936; *Educ* Charterhouse; *m* 1959, Jill Benton, da of late Lt-Col Sir Peter Fawcett Benton Jones, 3 Bt, OBE; 1 s, 1 da; *Career* FRSE, FCIT; dir: Sir Robert McAlpine & Sons Ltd, Newarthill Ltd; chm Transport Tst; memb Cncl Zoological Soc; *Clubs* Garrick, Caledonian; *Style* - The Hon William McAlpine; Fawley Hill, Fawley Green, Henley-on-Thames RG9 6JA

McANALLY, (Arthur) Patrick; s of Sir Henry William Watson McAnally, CB (d 1952); *b* 14 March 1909; *Educ* Charterhouse, Ch Ch Oxford, LSE; *m* 1935, Basil Hamilton Stuart, nee Knight; 1 s, 1 da; *Career* principal Admiralty 1940-42 (Assistant Sec 1943-45), John Lewis Partnership Head of Res 1933-40 & 1951-79, former dir Peter Jones Ltd, Waitrose Ltd 1960-79; *Recreations* graphic arts, writing, author of *The Economics of the Distributive Trades* 1971; *Clubs* Royal Naval 1970-; *Style* - Patrick McAnally; Point Wharf House, 23 Bath sq, Old Portsmouth, Hants (☎ 0705 814521)

MacANDREW, 2 Baron (UK 1959); Colin Nevil Glen MacAndrew; s of 1 Baron MacAndrew, TD, PC (d 1979); *b* 1 Aug 1919; *Educ* Eton, Trin Cambridge; *m* 1943, Ursula Beatrice, da of Capt Joseph Steel; 2 s, 1 da; *Heir* s, Hon Christopher Anthony Colin MacAndrew; *Career* served 1939-45 War; *Style* - The Rt Hon the Lord MacAndrew; Dilston House, Aldborough St John, Richmond, Yorks (☎ Piercebridge 272)

MacANDREW, Hon Christopher Anthony Colin; s and h of 2 Baron MacAndrew; *b* 16 Feb 1945; *Educ* Malvern; *m* 1975, Sarah Helen, da of Lt-Col Peter Hendy Brazier, of Nash Court, Marnhill, Dorset; 1 da; *Style* - The Hon Christopher MacAndrew; Hall Farm, Archdeacon Newton, Darlington

MacANDREW, Mona, Baroness; Mona; da of J A Ralston Mitchell, of Perceton House, by Irvine, Ayrshire; *m* 1941, as his 2 w, 1 Baron MacAndrew, TD, PC (d 1979); *Style* - The Rt Hon Mona, Lady MacAndrew; The Terrace House, Kelso, Roxburghshire

McANDREW, Nicolas; s of Robert Louis McAndrew; *b* 9 Dec 1934; *Educ* Winchester Coll; *m* 1960, Diana Leonie, nee Wood; 3 c; *Career* Capt Black Watch (Army) Kenya 1954-55, memb of the Inst of Chartered Accountants of Scotland since 1962, currently md NM Rothschild & Sons; *Recreations* shooting, fishing, golf, skiing; *Clubs* City of London, Swinley Forest Golf Club; *Style* - Nicolas McAndrew Esq; White Lodge, Twyford, Winchester, Hants (☎ 0962 713305); 36 Fabian rd, SW6 (☎ 01 381 1924)

MacANDREW, Hon Nicholas Rupert; s of 2 Baron MacAndrew; *b* 1947; *Educ* Eton; *m* 1975, Victoria, da of George Patrick Renton, of Kington Close, Alton, Hants; 1 s, 1 da; *Style* - The Hon Nicholas MacAndrew; 40 Doneraile st, SW6 (☎ 01 736 4218)

MACARA, Sir (Charles) Douglas; 3 Bt (UK 1911), of Ardmore, St Anne-on-the-Sea, Co Lancaster; s of Sir William Cowper Macara, 2 Bt (d 1931); *b* 19 April 1904; *Educ* Fettes; *m* 1926, Quenilda Mary (m dis 1945), da of late Herbert Whitworth; 1 s (decd); 2 da; *Heir* bro, Hugh Kenneth Macara; *Style* - Sir Douglas Macara, Bt; Hill House, New Town, Uckfield, Sussex

MACARA, Hugh Kenneth; s of late Sir William Macara, 2 Bt; hp of bro, Sir (Charles) Douglas Macara, 3 Bt; *b* 17 Jan 1913; *Style* - Hugh Macara Esq

MACARTNEY, Sir John Barrington; 6 Bt (I 1799), of Lish, Armagh; s of late John Barrington Macartney and nephew of 5 Bt (d 1960); *b* 1917; *m* 1944, Amy Isobel Reinke; 1 s; *Heir* s, John Ralph Macartney; *Career* dairy farmer; *Style* - Sir John Macartney, Bt; 37 Meadow st, North Mackay, Queensland 4740, Australia

MACARTNEY, John Ralph; s and h of Sir John Barrington Macartney, 6 Bt; *b* 1945; *m* 1966, Suzanne Marie Fowler, of Nowra, NSW; 3 da; *Career* Petty Officer RAN (ret); *Style* - John Macartney Esq; PO Box 589, Quean Beyan, NSW 2620, Australia

MACASKILL, Malcolm; *Career* dir, Halifax Building Society; MA, ACIS; *Style* - Malcolm Macaskill Esq; Halifax Building Society, Trinity rd, Halifax, Yorks HX1 2RG

MACAULEY, Hon Mrs; Hon Diana Phyllis; da of 1 Viscount Camrose (d 1954); *b* 1924; *m* 1948, William Perine Macauley; 3 s, 3 da; *Style* - The Hon Mrs Macauley; Ballyward House, Blessington, Co Wicklow

McAULIFFE, Thomas Vincent; s of William McAuliffe (d 1940); *b* 19 July 1935; *Educ* Presentation Brothers Coll Cork; *m* 1959, Audrey Ann, da of Robert Malyon; 2 s; *Career* chm Argos Distributors Ltd; *Recreations* golf, rugby; *Clubs* Harpenden Common Golf Club, Porters Park Golf Club; *Style* - Thomas McAuliffe Esq; Glenanaar, 15 West Common Grove, Harpenden, Herts (☎ Harpenden 64777)

McAULIFFE, William Trinder; *Career* chm Argos Distributors Ltd; dir Sunbeam Ltd; *Style* - William McAuliffe Esq; Argos Distributors Ltd, 112 Station rd, Edgware, Middlesex

McBAIN OF McBAIN, Hughston Maynard; recognised as Chief of Clan McBain by Lord Lyon 1959; s of late (William) Frederick McBain; *b* 1902; *Educ* Phillips Exeter Academy Exeter New Hampshire, U of Michigan, Northwestern U; *m* 1927, Margaret, da of Carl Keith, of Kenilworth, Ill; c; *Heir* s, James Hughston, b 1928; *Career* dir: Marshall Field & Co (chm and ch exec offr 1943-58), First Nat Bank of Chicago Illinois Bell Telephone Co of Chicago, Trans World Airlines of NY; a trustee of Field Museum of Natural History, Children's Memorial Hosp Chicago Illinois, St Andrew's Soc of Chicago; *Clubs* Chicago, Commercial, Puffin's (Edinburgh); *Style* - Hughston McBain of McBain

McBEATH, Hon Mrs; Hon Janet Mary; da of 1 Baron Ebbisham, GBE (d 1953); *b* 1916; *m* 1952, Rear-Adm John Edwin Home McBeath, CB, DSO, DSC, DL; 1 s, 1 da; *Style* - The Hon Mrs McBeath; Woodbury House, Churt, Surrey

McCALL, Hon Mrs; Hon Gillian Patricia Denman; da of 5 Baron Denman, CBE, MC; *b* 1944; *m* 1971, William K McCall; 1 s; *Style* - The Hon Mrs McCall;

Upper Old Park Farm, Farnham, Surrey

McCALLUH, Georgette Lizette; da of Edgar Clements Withers, CIE, CBE (d 1951); *b* 12 March 1917; *Educ* Fredville Park Nonnington Kent, Sch of the Holy Family London; *m* 1948, John Neil, s of John Neil; 1 s, 2 da; *Career* actress; *Recreations* reading, interior decorating; *Clubs* Queen's Sydney; *Style* - Miss Georgette McCalluh; 1740 Pittwater rd, Bayview, NSW 2104, Australia

McCALLUM, Lady Charlotte Mary; da of 6 Earl Cathcart, CB, DSO, MC; *b* 29 Oct 1951; *Educ* Woldingham; *m* 1972, Capt Anthony C McCallum, 1 the Queen's Dragoon Gds; 2 s, 1 da; *Style* - Lady Charlotte McCallum; 14 Eaton Mews South, SW1

McCARRAHER, David; VRD (1964); s of Colin McCarraher (d 1960); *b* 6 Nov 1922; *Educ* King Edward VI Sch Southampton, Magdalene Coll Cambridge; *m* 1950, Betty, nee Haywood; 2 da, 1 step s, 1 step da; *Career* Capt RNR 1969, WW II Indian Ocean NW Europe, CO Solent Div (HMS Wessex) 1969-72, ADC to HM The Queen 1972-73, barr (Lincoln's Inn) Western Circuit 1948-52, slr 1955, Crown Court Recorder 1979-; *Recreations* family, golf, sailing (owner of yacht 'Hestia of Hamble'); *Clubs* Stoneham Golf, Royal Naval Sailing Association, Royal Southern Yacht Club, Naval Club; *Style* - David McCarraher Esq, VRD; 3 College Place, London rd, Southampton (☎ 0703 32733)

McCARTHY, Baron (Life Peer UK 1975); William Edward John McCarthy; s of Edward McCarthy; *b* 30 July 1925; *Educ* Ruskin Coll in Oxford, Merton & Nuffield Colls Oxford; *m* 1957, Margaret, da of Percival Godfrey; *Career* formerly worker in men's outfitters and clerk; lecturer Industrial Relations Oxford U, fell Nuffield Coll and Oxford Management Centre 1969-; dir Harland & Wolff Ltd 1976-; special commissioner Equal Opportunities Commission 1977-; chm Railway Staff Nat Tribunal 1974-; research dir Roy Commission on Trade Unions and Employers Associations 1965-68; *Recreations* theatre, ballet, gardening; *Clubs* Reform; *Style* - The Rt Hon the Lord McCarthy; 4 William Orchard Close, Old Headington, Oxford (☎ 62016)

MacCARTHY, Charles Joseph Finnin; s of Thomas J MacCarthy, FJI (d 1949); *b* 23 May 1912; *Educ* Presentation Coll Cork, Univ Coll Cork; *m* 1942, Elizabeth, nee O'Donovan; 3 s, 3 da; *Career* Irish Defence Forces Operations Offr 1940-45, Gp Sec Dwyer Group Cork 1958-72, currently dir Guardian Securities Ltd, pres Assoc of Certified Accountants (Irish Region) 1974, pres Bd of Visitors Nat Museum of Ireland 1974-77, PC (Peace Commissioner); *Recreations* antiquary; *Clubs* Army; *Style* - Charles MacCarthy Esq PC; 10 Carrigdubh Estate, Blackrock rd, Cork, Eire (☎ 021 961242)

McCARTHY, C M A; *Career* md: McCain International Ltd; memb IOD; *Style* - C M A McCarthy Esq,; McCain International Ltd, Havers Hill, East Field, Scarborough, N Yorks

McCARTNEY, Robert; OBE (1968), QPM (1962); s of Arthur McCartney (d 1920); *b* 15 Aug 1912; *Educ* Queen Elizabeth's G S Blackburn; *m* 1937, Marjorie, nee Grayston; 1 s, 1 da; *Career* OStJ (1962), Lancashire Constabulary 1932-54, dep Ch Constable of Monmouthshire 1955-58, Ch Constable Herefordshire 1958-67, dep govr HM Tower of London 1968-71; *Recreations* golf, lectures for charities; *Style* - Robert McCartney Esq OBE QPM; 11 Weatherby gdns, Hartley Wintney, Hants (☎ Hartley Wintney 2045)

McCAUSLAND, Lady Margaret Louisa; da of 6 Earl of Mount Edgcumbe (d 1965); *b* 21 March 1912; *m* 1932, Lt-Col Conolly Robert McCausland, MC, JP, DL (d 1968); 3 s, 2 da; *Style* - Lady Margaret McCausland; Drenagh, Limavady, Co Londonderry, N Ireland

MACCLESFIELD, 8 Earl of (GB 1721); George Roger Alexander Thomas Parker; JP (Oxon 1955), DL (1965); also Lord Parker, Baron of Macclesfield, Co Chester (GB 1716), and Viscount Parker

(GB 1721); s of 7 Earl of Macclesfield (d 1975); *b* 6 May 1914; *Educ* Stowe; *m* 1938, Hon Valerie, da of 4 Baron Sandhurst, OBE (d 1964); 2 s; *Heir* s, Viscount Parker; *Career* Lt RNVR, served WW II; *Style* - The Rt Hon the Earl of Macclesfield, JP, DL; Shirburn, Watlington, Oxon

MACCLESFIELD, Countess of; Hon Valerie; *née* Mansfield; da of 4 Baron Sandhurst, OBE (d 1964); *b* 1918; *m* 1938, 8 Earl of Macclesfield; *Career* chm CC Oxon 1970; *Style* - The Rt Hon The Countess of Macclesfield; Shirburn Castle, Watlington, Oxon

McCLINTOCK-BUNBURY, Hon George Andrew Kane; s of 5 Baron Rathdonnell; *b* 26 July 1968; *Style* - The Hon George McClintock-Bunbury

McCLINTOCK-BUNBURY, Hon James Alexander Hugh; s of 5 Baron Rathdonnell; *b* 21 Feb 1972; *Style* - The Hon James McClintock-Bunbury

McCLINTOCK-BUNBURY, Hon Hermione Jane; da of 4 Baron Rathdonnell (d 1959); *b* 11 Aug 1943; *Style* - The Hon Hermione McClintock-Bunbury; Lisnavagh, Rathvilly, Co Carlow; c/o Wright, Stephenson & Co Ltd, PO Box 1895, Wellington, New Zealand

McCLINTOCK-BUNBURY, Hon Pamela Rosemary; da of 4 Baron Rathdonnell (d 1959); *b* 30 July 1948; *Educ* Lawnside, Great Malvern; Millfield Sch; *Style* - The Hon Pamela McClintock-Bunbury

McCLINTOCK-BUNBURY, Hon William Leopold; s and h of 5 Baron Rathdonnell; *b* 6 July 1966; *Style* - The Hon William McClintock-Bunbury

McCLURE, Alexander Logan; WS; *Career* chm American Trust Co Ltd, Crescent Japan Investment Trust Ltd, Crescent Life Assurance Co Ltd, Crescent Unit Trust Managers Ltd, Edinburgh Fund Managers Ltd, Edinburgh Securities Co Ltd, St Andrew Trust Ltd, Scottish Eastern Investment Trust, Stantrust Securities Ltd, vice-chm Clydesdale Bank Finance Corpn, joint dep chm Clydesdale Bank Ltd; dir Cairngorm Investment Co Ltd, Messrs Brodies; *Style* - Alexander McClure Esq WS; Messrs Brodies, 7 Rothesay Terrace, Edinburgh EH3 7SD

McCLURE, Wing Cdr Charles George Buchanan; AFC (1944), AE (1943), DL (1976); s of George Buchanan McClure (d 1955); *b* 20 Apr 1916; *Educ* Winchester, Trin Oxford, de Havilland Tech Sch; *m* 1943, Helen Margaret Gilloch, da of Maj John Whyte, MBE; 1 s, 1 da; *Career* Wing Cdr 1945, ch test pilot RAC Farnborough 1945-46, operations offr Miny of Civil Aviation 1946, head of flight Cranfield Coll of Aeronautics 1949, prof of flight Cranfield Inst of Technology 1973; *Recreations* golf, gardening; *Clubs* RAF, Leander; *Style* - Wing Cdr Charles McClure, AFC, AE, DL; The Shrubbery, Aspley Guise, Milton Keynes, Bucks (☎ 583126)

McCLUSKEY, Baron (Life Peer UK 1976); John Herbert McCluskey; QC (Scotland 1967); s of F J McCluskey (d 1961), of Edinburgh; *b* 12 June 1929; *Educ* St Bede's G S Manchester, Holy Cross Academy Edinburgh, Edinburgh U; *m* 1956, Ruth Friedland, of Manchester; 2 s, 1 da; *Career* advocate 1955, advocate-depute 1964; QC 1967, Sheriff Principal of Dumfries and Galloway 1974; Slr Gen for Scotland 1974-79; *Style* - The Rt Hon the Lord McCluskey QC; Parliament House, Edinburgh (☎ 031 226 5071); 11 Cluny ave, Edinburgh 10 (☎ 031 447 3880)

McCLUSKEY, Hon Catherine Margaret; da of Baron McCluskey, QC; *b* 1962; *Style* - The Hon Catherine McCluskey; 11 Cluny ave, Edinburgh EH10 4RN

McCLUSKEY, Hon David Francis; s of Baron McCluskey, QC; *b* 1963; *Style* - The Hon David McCluskey; 11 Cluny ave, Edinburgh EH10 4RN

McCLUSKEY, Hon John Mark; s of Baron McCluskey, QC; *b* 1960; *Style* - The Hon John McCluskey; 11 Cluny ave, Edinburgh EH10 4RN

MacCOLL, David Ferguson; MC; *Career* chm Corrie MacColl & Son Ltd; dir: Anglo-American Corpn Sdn Bhd Singapore, Anglo-American Corpn (M) Sdn Bhd Malaysia, Imperial Commodities Corpn USA, LM Fischel & Co Ltd, NV Deli Maatschappij Rotterdam, Windmill Windows (Aust) Pty Ltd Australia; *Style* - David MacColl Esq, MC; Corrie MacColl & Son Ltd, Dunster House, Mincing Lane, EC3R 7AX (☎ 01 623 2691)

McCOLL, Ian; s of late John McColl; *b* 22 Feb 1915; *Educ* Hillhead High Sch, Glasgow; *m* 1968, Brenda, da of late Thomas McKean, of Glasgow; 1 da; *Career* served RAF 1940-46 (despatches, 1945); chm Scottish Express Newspapers Ltd 1975-; dir Express Newspapers Ltd 1971-; *Style* - Ian McColl Esq; Scottish Express Newspapers Ltd, Park House, Park Circus Place, Glasgow G3 6AF

McCOMB, Yvonne Muriel Renee; OBE (1977); da of Lt-Col Percy David Jones, MC, ED (d 1979); *b* 23 Nov 1920; *Educ* State Commercial H S; *m* 1946, John Franklyn (d 1972), s of Lt Frank McComb (d 1978); 2 s, 1 da; *Career* Wing Cmdt Women's Air Training Corps (voluntary org); public relations dir McComb 1976-; Roy Flying Doctor Service of Australia (Queensland Section) PR Consultant 1973-; federal v-pres Liberal Party Australia 1974-79, state pres (Queensland) 1976-80; founder/pres Home Management Advisory Service 1972-; patron Amnesty Int (Queensland) 1978-, trustee Australian War Memorial Canberra 1978-; *Recreations* music, politics, theatre, travel; *Clubs* United Service, U of Queensland Staff Club; *Style* - Mrs Frank McComb, OBE; Galileo Tower, 22 Mullens st, Hamilton, Brisbane, Queensland, Australia (☎ 2683061)

McCONNACHIE, Charles Petrie; CBE; s of David McConnachie (d 1937); *b* 28 June 1906; *m* 1935, Levia; 1 s; *Career* mining co dir 1946, ret 1966; *Clubs* Roy Commonwealth Soc; *Style* - Charles McConnachie Esq, CBE; Mary's Acre, Laurieston, Castle Douglas, Scotland

McCONNELL, Hon Mrs; Hon Elizabeth Millicent; da of 2 Viscount Selby (d 1923); *b* 1917; *m* 1948, Clarence Henry Quentin McConnell (d 1972); 1 s, 1 da; *Style* - The Hon Mrs McConnell; PO Box 43148, Nairobi, Kenya

McCONNELL, Joyce Marion; OBE (1976); da of Lawrence Joseph Smith, of Sydney (d 1928); *b* 21 Aug 1916; *Educ* N Sydney Girls' H S, Sydney U; *m* 1939, Hugh Graham Douglas McConnell; 2 s, 2 da; *Career* Queen's Jubilee Medal 1977, hon life v-pres Nat Cncl of Women of Australia 1979-, memb Nat Women's Advisory Cncl 1978-80, pres Nat Cncl of Women of Australia 1973-78; *Recreations* gardening, golf; *Clubs* Roy Canberra GC, Women's Int; *Style* - Mrs Hugh McConnell, OBE; 95 Stonehaven cres, Deakin, ACT, Australia (☎ 81 2458)

McCONNELL, Sir Robert Melville Terence; 3 Bt (UK 1900), VRD; s of Sir Joseph McConnell, 2 Bt (d 1942); *b* 7 Feb 1902; *Educ* Trin Coll Glenalmond, St John's Cambridge, Coll of Estate Management London; *m* 1, 1928, Rosamond Mary Elizabeth (m dis 1954), da of James Stewart Reade, JP, of Clonmore, Lisburn, Co Antrim; 3 s, 1 da; m 2, 1967, Mrs Alice A M Hills; *Heir* s, Robert Shean McConnell; *Career* Cdr VRD, RNVR, ret; consultant R J McConnell & Co, estate agents; *Style* - Commander Sir Robert McConnell, Bt, VRD; Pigeon Hill, Island rd, Killyleagh, Co Down, N Ireland

McCONNELL, Robert Shean; s and h of Sir Robert Melville Terence McConnell, 3 Bt, VRD; *b* 23 Nov 1930; *Educ* Stowe, Queens' Cambridge, British Columbia U; *Style* - Robert McConnell, Esq

McCORMACK, Thomas; CBE (1980, MBE 1959); s of John McCormack; *b* 13 March 1911; *Educ* De La Salle Coll NSW, St Joseph's Coll Nudgee Queensland Australia; *m* 1963, Yvonne, da of late Archibald McSween, of Brisbane; 1 s, 2 da; *Career* slr of Supreme Ct of Queensland 1934, pres Australian Rugby Union Football 1955-61, pres Queensland Rugby Union Football 1949-62; *Recreations* rugby, horseracing; *Clubs* Queensland Rugby, Queensland Turf,

Tattersall's *Style* - Thomas McCormack Esq, CBE; 48 Oriel rd, Clayfield, Brisbane, Queensland, Australia (☎ 262 4937)

McCORQUODALE, Alastair; *Career* chm McCorquodale & Co Ltd; dir: British Sugar Corpn Ltd, McCorquodale & Blades Trust Ltd, McCorquodale (Scotland) Ltd; *Style* - Alastair McCorquodale Esq; McCorquodale & Co Ltd, 15 Cavendish Sq, W1M GHT

McCORQUODALE, Hon Mrs; Hon Charlotte Enid; da of 1 Baron Luke, KBE (d 1943); *b* 1910; *m* 1933, George McCorquodale; 1 s, 3 da; *Style* - The Hon Mrs McCorquodale; Dunan Lodge, Rannoch, Perth

McCORQUODALE, Ian; s of Hugh McCorquodale, MC, and Barbara Cartland, *qv*; half-bro of Countess Spencer and 1 cous of Neil McCorquodale (husb of HRH The Princess of Wales's sis, Lady Sarah, nee Spencer) and 1 and last Baron McCorquodale of Newton, KCVO, PC; descended, through paternal grandmother Grace, *née* Granville (*sic*), from Sir Richard Grenville, the Elizabethan sea dog famed for his defence of 'The Revenge', and Lady Mary Boleyn (sis of Anne; Ian is hence 1 cous thirteen times removed of Queen Elizabeth I); also 3 cous twice removed of P G Wodehouse; *b* 11 Oct 1937; *Educ* Harrow, Magdalene Cambridge; *m*; 2 da; *Career* chm Debrett's Peerage Ltd; ptnr Cartland Promotions 1976-; dir: Moorside Tst, Energy Finance & Gen Tst, Roy Exchange Art Gallery; late commercial & export man BPC, chm Hatfield S Con Assoc; *Recreations* fishing, shooting, gardening, tennis; *Style* - Ian McCorquodale Esq

McCORQUODALE, Lady (Elizabeth) Sarah Lavinia; da (by 1 m) of 8 Earl of Spencer, MVO, JP, DL, *qv*; sis of HRH The Princess of Wales (*see* Royal Family); *b* 19 March 1955; *Educ* West Heath (Sevenoaks); Le Vieux Chalet, Château d'Oex, Switzerland; *m* 1980, Neil Edmund, s of Alastair McCorquodale (himself 1 cous of Ian McCorquodale, *qv*, and 2 cous of the present Countess Spencer, *qv*) by his w Rosemary, whose mother was Lady Enid Vane (da of 13 Earl of Westmorland); *Style* - Lady Sarah McCorquodale; Stoke Rochford, Grantham, Lincs

McCOSH, Bryce Knox; JP (Lanark); s of Robert McCosh of Hardington, OBE, MC, WS, JP (d 1959); *b* 30 Mar 1920; *Educ* Loretto; *m* 1948, Sylvia Mary (Lady of the Manor of Dalemain and of the Barony of Barton And Dacre, Cumberland), da of Edward William Hasell of Dalemain, JP, DL (d 1972); 3 s; *Career* Lt-Cdr RNVR WW II, sr ptnr SM Penney & Macgeorge (stockbrokers: Glasgow, Edinburgh, London) 1944-56; pres & chm Cncl Thistle Foundation; dir Target Trust Managers (Scotland) Ltd, Rachan Investment Trust, farmer; *Recreations* shooting; *Style* - Bryce McCosh Esq, JP; Huntfield, Biggar, Scotland (☎ 20208); Dalemain, Penrith, Cumbria (☎ Pooley Bridge 450)

McCOWAN, Hon Mr Justice; Hon Sir Anthony James Denys; s of John McCowan, MBE, of Georgetown, Br Guiana; *b* 12 Jan 1928; *Educ* Epsom, BNC Oxford; *m* 1961, Sue, da of Reginald Harvey, of Braiseworth Hall, Tannington, Suffolk; 2 s, 1 da; *Career* barr 1951, QC 1972; Ldr SE Circuit 1978-81; High Court Judge (Queen's Bench) 1981-; Crown Court Recorder 1972-81; kt 1981; *Club* Hurlingham; *Style* - The Hon Mr Justice McCowan; Southernwood, Crendell, Cranborne, Dorset (☎ 393); 48 Sussex st, SW1 (☎ 01 834 1626)

McCOWAN, David William Cargill; s of Sir David James Cargill McCowan, 2 Bt (d 1965); hp of bro, Sir Hew Cargill McCowan, 3 Bt; *b* 28 Feb 1934; *Style* - David McCowan Esq

McCOWAN, Sir Hew Cargill; 3 Bt (UK 1934); s of Sir David James Cargill McCowan, 2 Bt (d 1965); *b* 26 July 1930; *Heir* bro, David William Cargill McCowan; *Style* - Sir Hew McCowan, Bt

McCOWAN, Hon Mrs; Hon Mary Walkden; da of 1 and last Baron Walkden (d 1951); *b* 1907; *m* 1924, Duncan Matheson McCowan (d 1969); 1 s, 1 da; *Style* - The Hon Mrs McCowan

McCRAITH, Col Patrick James Danvers; MC (1943), TD, DL (Notts 1965); s of late Sir Douglas McCraith; *b* 21 June 1916; *Educ* Harrow; *m* 1946, Hon Philippa Ellis, da of 1 and last Baron Robins KBE DSO, of Rhodesia and Chelsea; 1 s, 1 da; *Career* 2 Lt Sherwood Rangers Yeomanry 1935, served 1939-45 (N Africa and NW Europe), Bt Col 1958, Hon Col B (Sherwood Rangers Yeomanry) Sqdn, The Roy Yeomanry 1968-79, High Sheriff Notts 1963; *Clubs* Special Forces (London & Nottingham), Notts United Serv; *Style* - Col Patrick McCraith MC TD DL; Cranfield House, Southwell, Notts (☎ Southwell 812129)

McCRAITH, Hon Mrs; Hon Philippa Mary Ellis; da of 1 Baron Robins (d 1962); *b* 1923; *m* 1946, Col Patrick Danvers McCraith, MC, TD, DL; 1 s, 1 da; *Style* - The Hon Mrs McCraith; Cranfield House, Southwell, Notts

McCRIRIE-HALLMAN, Hon Mrs; Hon Anne Sheridan; da of Baron Walston (Life Peer); *b* 1937; *m* 1, 1960, Charles Brewin (m dis 1972); 1 s, 4 da; m 2, 1978, Edward McCririe-Hallman *Style* - The Hon Mrs McCririe-Hallman

McCULLOCH, Robert Brownlie; s of Robert McCulloch (d 1969); *b* 13 Dec 1939; *Educ* Victoria Drive and Hyndland Schs, Glasgow U; *m* 1964, Lilias Stewart, nee Cuthbertson; 1 s, 1 da; *Career* CA (Scottish Inst), FBIM, fin dir GTE Sylvania (UK) Ltd 1976-, sec & ch accountant Bridon Engrg 1973-76, plant accountant Leyland Nat Co 1971-73, co sec Smith & McLaurin 1966-71; *Recreations* tennis, squash, badminton, gardening; *Style* - Robert McCulloch Esq; 27 Dalesway, Tranmere Park, Guiseley, W Yorks (☎ 76685)

McCULLOUGH, Hon Mr Justice; Hon Sir (Iain) Charles Robert; QC (1971); s of Thomas McCullough, CB, OBE, sometime of Miny of Labour; *b* 31 July 1931; *Educ* Taunton Sch, Trin Hall Cambridge; *m* 1965, Margaret Joyce, JP, da of David Patey, FRCS, and Gladys, nee Summers; 1 s, 1 da; *Career* kt 1981; served RA (TA) 1952-54; barr 1956, Crown Court Recorder 1972-81; High Court Judge (Queen's Bench) 1981-; *Style* - The Hon Mr Justice McCullough; 2 Crown Office Row, Temple, EC4 (☎ 01 353 1365)

McCURRACH, David Fleming; OBE, LLD, BL; *Career* chairman of The Alliance Trust Company Ltd; dir of Scottish Mortgage & Trust Co Ltd; *Style* - David McCurrach Esq, OBE; Alliance Trust Co Ltd, 64 Reform st, Dundee DDI ITJ

MacDERMOT, The; Sir Dermot; KCMG (1962), CBE (1947); Prince of Coolavin; s of Charles Edward, The MacDermot, Prince of Coolavin, of Coolavin (d 1947); suc bro as 36 Chief 1979; *b* 14 June 1906; *Educ* Stonyhurst, Trin Coll Dublin; *m* 1934, Betty Caroline, da of Joseph William Steel, of Hong Kong (d 1917); 3 s; *Heir* s, Niall Anthony MacDermot; *Career* HBM Foreign Service 1929-65; Min to Romania 1954-56, HM Ambass to Indonesia 1954-56, to Thailand 1961-65; *Clubs* Kildare Street, Univ Club Dublin; *Style* - The MacDermot, Prince of Coolavin, KCMG, CBE; Aughmanure Lodge, Oughterard, Co Galway, Ireland (☎ Galway 82318)

McDERMOTT, Sir (Lawrence) Emmet; KBE (1972); s of O J McDermott; *b* 6 Sept 1911; *Educ* St Ignatius Coll Riverview, U of Sydney, Northernwestern U Chicago; *m* 1939, Arline Beatrice, da of William Albertus Hagon, of Sydney (d 1940); 1 s, 1 da; *Career* Hon consulting dental surgn Roy Prince Alfred Hosp 1942; Bd of Control United Dental Hosp 1960-79, pres 1967-79, dental bd of NSW 1967-79, pres Australian Dental Assoc (NSW 1960-61); cllr Australian Dental Assoc 1962-66; memb state council Liberal Party of NSW; memb Sydney Cove Redevelopment Authority 1971-76; v-pres Australia-Britain Soc (NSW) 1972-77; dir City Mutual Life Assurance Soc Ltd 1970, dep chm 1972; Lord Mayor of Sydney 1969-72, cllr Sydney CC 1973, chm 1976, dep chm 1975; *Recreations* golf, bowls, swimming; *Clubs* Roy Sydney Golf, Elanora Country, Australia Jockey; *Style* - Sir Emmet McDermott, KBE; 20 Carnarvon rd, Roseville, NSW 2069, Australia (☎ 46 2086)

MacDERMOTT, Baroness; Louise Palmer; da of Rev J C Johnston; *m* 1926, Baron MacDermott, MC, PC (d 1979); 2 s, 2 da; *Style* - The Rt Hon Lady MacDermott; Glenburn, 8 Cairnburn rd, Belfast BT4 2HR

MACDONALD, 8 Baron (I 1776); Godfrey James Macdonald of Macdonald; Chief of the Name and Arms of Macdonald; s of 7 Baron Macdonald, MBE (d 1970); *b* 28 Nov 1947; *Educ* Belhaven Hill Sch Dunbar, Eton; *m* 1969, Claire, da of Cdre Thomas Catlow, CBE, RN; 3 da; *Heir* bro, Hon Alexander Donald Archibald Macdonald; *Clubs* Turf, New (Edinburgh); *Style* - The Rt Hon the Lord Macdonald; Ostaig House, Isle of Skye (☎ Ardvasar 226)

MACDONALD OF GWAENYSGOR, 2 Baron (UK 1949); Gordon Ramsay Macdonald; s of 1 Baron, KCMG, PC (d 1966); *b* 16 Oct 1915; *Educ* Upholland G S and Manchester U; *m* 1941, Leslie Margaret, da of John Edward Taylor; 3 da; *Heir* bro, Hon Kenneth Lewis Macdonald; *Career* served 1940-46 with RA, Maj GSO; joined Bd of Trade 1946; UK Trade Cmmr Australia 1947-53; md Tube Investments (Export) Ltd 1953-64; ch exec UK Operations Hayek Engineering (AG Zurich), Ferro Metal & Chemical Co, Satra Consultants (UK); *Style* - The Rt Hon the Lord Macdonald of Gwaenysgor; Littleworth House, Littleworth Common, Bucks; Boynton House, Manor rd, Penn, Bucks

MACDONALD, Anne, Baroness; Anne; da of late Alfred Whitaker, of Pembroke, Itchenor, Sussex; *m* 1945, 7 Baron Macdonald, MBE, TD (d 1970); 2 s, 1 da; *Style* - The Rt Hon Anne, Lady Macdonald; Armadale Castle, Isle of Skye; Ostaig House, Isle of Skye

MACDONALD, Hon Alexander Donald Archibald; s and h of 7 Baron Macdonald, MBE (d 1953); *b* Eton; *Style* - The Hon Alexander Macdonald; Armadale Castle, Isle of Skye

MACDONALD, Hon Alexandra Louisa; da of 8 Baron Macdonald; *b* 1973; *Style* - The Hon Alexandra Macdonald

MacDONALD, Alexander MacLeod; CBE (1954); s of John Murdo MacDonald; *b* 10 Oct 1915; *Educ* Inverness Roy Academy; *m* 1939, Joyce Isobel Mary, da of Maj William Ross Mileham; 1 s; *Career* Indian Imperial Police 1935; head of Special Branch Bombay Province 1941-47; entered War Office 1947, seconded as intelligence advr to Govt of Kenya 1952-54 and advr to sec of State for Colonies 1954-57, advr to Supreme Allied Cdr NATO Forces in Europe 1963-65, under-sec MOD 1965-71; *Recreations* cooking; *Style* - Alexander MacDonald Esq, CBE; Les Bellugues, ave des Chênes, 06140 Vence, France

MACDONALD, Hon Mrs; Hon Elspeth Ruth; da of 2 Baron Craigmyle (d 1944); *b* 1921; *m* 1945, Archibald James Florence Macdonald, JP; 2 s; *Style* - The Hon Mrs Macdonald; 22 Heath dve, Hampstead, NW3

McDONALD, Brig Harvey William Donald; s of Albert William Harvey (d 1917); *b* 9 Sept 1906; *Educ* Imperial Serv Coll Windsor, Sandhurst; *m* 1950 (m dis 1960), Rosita Latalina, da of late Victor Escala of Venezuela; 1 s, 1 da; *Career* Brig 1945-48, Colonial Service Nigeria 1957-65, Administrator Ascension Island 1968-73, ret 1973; *Recreations* golf; *Clubs* Naval & Military; *Style* - Brig Harvey McDonald, DSO, OBE; c/o Grindlays Bank Ltd, 13 St James's sq, SW1; c/o Beaufort, Sheep st, Stow on the Wold, Glos

MACDONALD, Hon Isabella Claire; da of 8 Baron Macdonald; *b* 1975; *Style* - The Hon Isabella Macdonald

MacDONALD, Hon Mrs; Hon Jennifer; da of 1 Baron Renwick, KBE (d 1973); *b* 1932; *m* 1, 1954, Anthony Duncan Rowe (m dis 1967); 1 s, 1 da; m 2, 1973, Roy Philip Arthur; m 3, 1978, Robert Ian MacDonald; *Style* - The Hon Mrs MacDonald; Gulett Farm, South Pool, Kingsbridge, S Devon

MACDONALD, Hon Janet Anne; da of 7 Baron Macdonald, MBE (d 1970); *b* 1946; *Style* - The Hon Janet Macdonald; Armadale Castle, Isle of Skye

MacDONALD, Hon Mrs; Hon Jacaranda Fiona; da of 2 Viscount Craigavon; *b* 8 Jan 1949; *Educ* Dixon & Wolfe Tutors; *m* 1972, Dudley Francis MacDonald; 1 s (Toby b 1975), 1 da (Rose b 1978); *Career* co dir & jewellery designer; *Recreations* tennis, racing, ballet; *Clubs* Roehampton, Emsworth Sailing; *Style* - The Hon Mrs Macdonald; 27 Launceston pla, W8 (☎ 01 937 6056)

MACDONALD, Maj John Lachlan; s of Col Kenneth Macdonald, DSO (d 1938); *b* 22 Dec 1919; *Educ* Ampleforth, Trin Cambridge; *m* 1961, Mary Imogen, da of R G Micklethwait; 2 s, 1 da; *Career* served in Lovat Scouts and GHQ Liaison Regt in Faroes, N Africa and Europe 1939-46; memb Inverness Rating Appeals Ctee; gov N of Scotland Agric Coll 1959-61; DL Inverness-shire (1971); *Clubs* New (Edinburgh), Turf; *Style* - Maj John Macdonald, DL; Tote House, Skeabost Bridge, Isle of Skye (☎ 203); 50 Chelsea Park gdns, SW3 (☎ 01 352 1925)

MACDONALD, Hon Mrs; Hon Joan Marquerite; da of 1 & last Baron Lambury (d 1967); *b* 1927; *m* 1, 1951, Miles Lucas Breeden (m dis 1965); 1 s, 1 da; m 2, 1966, Angus James Macdonald; *Style* - The Hon Mrs Macdonald; 113 Century Court, St John's Wood rd, NW8

MACDONALD, Hon Kenneth Lewis; s of 1 Baron Macdonald of Gwaenysgor (d 1966); hp to bro, 2 Baron; *b* 1921; *m* 1952, Maureen Margaret, da of D Watson-Allan, of Churston Ferrers, Devon; 2 da; *Career* served 1940-46 with RAFVR; priv sec and ADC to Govr and C-in-C Newfoundland, Canada 1946-50; *Style* - The Hon Kenneth Lewis; 5 Thornby ave, Solihull, Warwickshire

MACDONALD, Hon Meriel Iona; da of 8 Baron Macdonald; *b* 1978; *Style* - The Hon Meriel Macdonald

McDONALD, Hon Mrs; Hon Margaret Joan; da of Baron Fraser of Lonsdale (d 1974); *b* 1920; *m* 1939, Arthur Edward McDonald; *Style* - The Hon Mrs McDonald; Tal Marruxa, Safi, Malta

MACDONALD, Hon Mrs; Hon Patricia Joan Kathleen, *née* Tryon; da of 2 Baron Tryon, GCVO, KCB, DSO, PC (d 1976); *b* 1942; *m* 1973, C Ranald Macdonald; 1 s; *Style* - The Hon Mrs Macdonald; 8 Gordon Grove, S Yarra, Victoria 3141, Australia

MACDONALD, Hon Mrs; Hon Rosemary; da of 1 Viscount Alanbrooke, KG, GCB, OM, GCVO, DSO (d 1963); *b* 1918; *m* 1945, Capt Ronald Alastair Macdonald, RA; 1 s, 1 da; *Style* - The Hon Mrs Macdonald; Bottom Farm, Berkhamsted, Herts

McDONALD, Hon Lord; Robert Howat McDonald; MC (1944); s of Robert Glassford McDonald (d 1965); *b* 15 May 1916; *Educ* John Neilson Inst Paisley, Glasgow U; *m* 1949, Barbara, da of John Mackenzie, of Ross-shire; *Career* served WW II Maj NW Europe; advocate 1946, QC 1956, Sheriff Ayr & Bute 1966-71, Pres Industl Tbnl Scotland 1971-73; Senator Coll Justice (Scottish Ld of Session) 1973-; *Recreations* gardening; *Clubs* New (Edinburgh); *Style* - The Hon Lord McDonald, MC; 5 Doune ter, Edinburgh EH3 6EA (☎ 031 225 3586)

MACDONALD-BUCHANAN, Alexander James; s of Maj Sir Reginald Macdonald-Buchanan, KCVO, MBE, MC, DL, of Cottesbrooke Hall, Northampton; *b* 21 April 1931; *Educ* Eton; *m* 1960, Elizabeth, da of Hon Hugh Vivian Smith, MBE, of Souldern Manor, Bicester, Oxon; 4 s; *Career* Nat Service Scots Gds (Capt); dir Macdonald-Buchanan Trustees Ltd, Colonial Mutual Life Assurance Soc Ltd; High Sheriff Northants 1972; *Clubs* White's, Turf; *Style* - Alexander Macdonald-Buchanan Esq; Strathconon, Muir of Ord, Ross-shire; Baynton House, Coulston, Westbury, Wilts (☎ Bratton 273)

MACDONALD-BUCHANAN, Hon Lady (Catherine); da of 1 Baron Woolavington (d 1935); *b* 1895; *m* 1922, Maj Sir Reginald Narcissus Macdonald-Buchanan, KCVO, MBE, MC (who assumed by deed poll 1922 the additional name of Buchanan); 2 s, 2 da; *Career* CStJ; *Style* - The Hon Lady Macdonald-Buchanan; Egerton House, Newmarket,

Suffolk; Scatwell, Muir-of-Ord, Ross-shire; Cottesbrooke Hall, Northants (☎ 060124 732)

MACDONALD-BUCHANAN, Capt John; MC (1945), DL (Northamptonshire 1978); s of Sir Reginald Macdonald-Buchanan, KCVO, MBE, MC, DL, of Cottesbrooke Hall, Northamptonshire; *b* 15 March 1925; *Educ* Eton, RMC; *m* 1, 1950, Lady Rose Fane (m dis 1969), da of 14 Earl of Westmorland (d 1948); 1 s, 2 da; m 2, 1969, Mrs Jill Salusbury-Trelawney; 2 da; *Career* 2 Lt Scots Gds 1943, served 1944-45 N W Europe, Malaya 1948-50, Capt 1948, ret 1952; High Sheriff Northants 1963-64; steward Jockey Club 1969-72; memb Horserace Betting Levy Bd 1973-76; *Clubs* Turf, White's; *Style* - Capt John Macdonald-Buchanan MC DL; The Stone House, Lower Swell, Stow-on-the-Wold, Glos (☎ Stow 30622); 22 Cadogan pla, SW1 (☎ 01 235 8615)

McDONNELL, Lady Alice Angela Jane; da of 9 Earl of Antrim; *b* 1964; *Style* - Lady Alice McDonnell

McDONNELL, Lady Flora Mary; da of 9 Earl of Antrim; *b* 1963; *Style* - Lady Flora McDonnell

McDONNELL, Hon Hector John; s of 8 Earl of Antrim (d 1977); *b* 1 March 1947; *Educ* Eton, Ch Ch Oxford; *m* 1969, Catherine Elizabeth, da of Ronald Chapman, of Buttermilk Hall, Brill, Bucks; 1 s, 1 da; *Career* Master of Hounds 1966-69; *Style* - The Hon Hector McDonnell; 51 Lyndhurst Way, SE15

McDONNELL, Hon James Angus; MBE (1946); s of 7 Earl of Antrim (d 1932); *b* 1917; *Educ* Eton; *m* 1939, Jeanne Irene, da of Col Stanley Leonard Barry, CMG, CBE, DSO, MVO, JP, DL; 1 s, 1 da; *Career* 2 Lt 5 Bn Roy Norfolk Regt 1939; *Style* - The Hon James McDonnell MBE; 36 Farley Court, Melbury rd, W14

McDONNELL, Lady Rachel; da of 9 Earl of Antrim; *b* 1978; *Style* - Lady Rachel McDonnell

McDONNELL, Hon Randal Alexander St John; s and h of 9 Earl of Antrim; *b* 2 July 1967; *Style* - The Hon Randal McDonnell

MacDOUGALL, Lady; Agnes; da of Edward McGuire, of Glasgow (d 1930); *b* 11 Nov 1890; *m* 1917, Sir Raibeart MacIntyre MacDougall, KCMG, CIE (d 1949); 1 s, 4 da (and 1 s decd); *Style* - Lady MacDougall; 11 Winchester ct, St Michael's rd, Worthing (☎ Worthing 200916)

MacDOUGALL OF MacDOUGALL, Madam; Coline Helen Elizabeth; 30 Chief of Clan MacDougall; da of Col MacDougall of MacDougall, CMG, 29 Chief, of Dunollie Castle (d 1953); *b* 17 Aug 1904; *Educ* St James W Malvern; *m* 1949, Leslie Grahame Thomson (assumed name MacDougall 1953), FRIBA, RSA, PPRIAS, FSA, s of Patrick Thomson, of Edinburgh; *Career* late 2 Offr WRNS, Fleet Air Arm; occupied with Clan MacDougall membs & overseas societies; *Recreations* gardening, painting, hill walking; *Style* - Madam MacDougall of MacDougall; Dunollie Castle, Oban, Argyll

MacDOWEL, Hon Mrs; Hon Angela Christine; da of 2 Baron Hazlerigg, MC; *b* 1946; *m* 1969, Timothy Effingham MacDowel; 2 s; *Style* - The Hon Mrs MacDowel; Moat House, Grandborough, Rugby

MACDUFF, Earl of; David Charles Carnegie; s and h of 3 Duke of Fife; *b* 3 March 1961; *Educ* Eton; *Style* - Earl of Macduff

McEWEN, Lady; Brigid Cecilia; *née* Laver; da of James Laver CBE; *m* 1954, Sir Robert Lindley McEwen, 3 Bt (d 1980); *Style* - Lady McEwen; Marchmont, Greenlaw, Berwickshire

McEWEN, Sir James Francis Lindley; 4 Bt (UK 1953), of Marchmont, Co Berwick and Bardrochat, Co Ayr; s of Sir Robert Lindley McEwen, 3 Bt (d 1980); *b* 24 Aug 1960; *Educ* Eton; *Style* - Sir James McEwen, Bt; Marchmont, Greenlaw, Berwickshire

McEWEN, John Roderick Hugh; yr s of

Sir Robert Lindley McEwen, 3 Bt, (d 1980); hp of bro, Sir James Francis Lindley, 4 Bt; *b* 4 Nov 1965; *Style* - John McEwen, Esq

MACEY, Rear-Adm David; *Career* Dep Assist Ch of Staff (Ops) Supreme Allied Cdr Europe's Staff 1981-; *aet* 51 in 1981; *Style* - Rear-Adm David Macey; c/o MOD, SW1

McFADZEAN OF KELVINSIDE, Baron (Life Peer UK 1980); Frank (Francis) Scott; *b* 26 Nov 1915; *Educ* Glasgow U, LSE; *Career* kt 1975; Bd of Trade 1938, treas 1939; chm Shell Transport and Trading Co Ltd 1972-75, Shell Int Marine Ltd 1966-76, Shell Canada Ltd 1970-76, Shell Petroleum Co Ltd 1972-76 (dir 1964); chm British Airways 1976-79, Rolls Royce Ltd 1980 (salary as of June 1981 £60,000 pa); *Clubs* Caledonian; *Style* - The Rt Hon the Lord McFadzean of Kelvinside; 65 Buckingham Gate, SW1; Shell Centre, SE1

McFADZEAN, Baron (Life Peer UK 1966); William Hunter McFadzean; KT (1976); s of Henry McFadzean (d 1918); *b* 17 Dec 1903; *Educ* Stranraer Academy and H S, Glasgow U; *m* 1933, Eileen, da of Arthur Gordon, of Blundellsands, Lancs; 1 s, 2 da (1 adopted); *Career* Hon Life Pres BICC; dir Midland Bank 1959-; dep chm Canada Life Assur, Nat Nuclear Corpn Ltd 1973-; chm BICC 1954-73; chm British Insulated Callender's Construction Co Ltd 1952-64; dir Midland Bank Ltd 1959-, dep chm 1968, dir Midland Bank Trust Co Ltd 1959-67; dir Canadian Imperial Bank of Commerce 1967-74, dep chm RTZ/BICC Aluminium Hldgs Ltd 1967-73; dir Anglesey Aluminium Ltd 1968-73; dir Canada Life Assurance Co 1969; chm Canada Life Unit Trust Managers Ltd 1971; dir Steel Co of Wales Ltd 1966-67; dir English Electric Co Ltd 1966-68; chm Standard Broadcasting Corpn (UK) Ltd 1972; chm Home Oil (UK) Ltd 1972; chm Scurry Rainbow (UK) Ltd 1974; pres FBI 1959-61; pres British Electrical Power Convention 1961-62; memb Court of British Shippers' Council 1964, pres 1968-71; memb Advsy Ctee for the Queen's Award to Industry 1965-67; kt 1960; *Recreations* gardening, golf, travel; *Clubs* MCC, Carlton; *Style* - The Rt Hon the Lord McFadzean, KT; Garthland, Woldingham, Surrey (☎ 3222); 114 Whitehall Court, SW1 (☎ 01 930 3160)

McFADZEAN, Hon (Gordon) Barry; s of Baron McFadzean (Life Peer); *b* 14 Feb 1937; *Educ* Winchester, Ch Ch Oxford; *m* 1968, Julia Maxine, da of Max Dillon, of Sydney, NSW, Australia; 2 da; *Career* served in RA 1955-57 as 2 Lt (Nat Service); chartered accountant 1963, exec dir S G Warburg & Co Ltd, Merchant Bankers; exec dir Australian United Corpn; dir S G Warburg & Co Int Ltd; *Style* - The Hon Barry McFadzean; Bourne House, Woldingham, Surrey

McFARLAND, Sir Basil Alexander Talbot; 2 Bt (UK 1914), of Aberfoyle, Co Londonderry, CBE (1954), ERD (1954); s of Sir John McFarland, 1 Bt (d 1926); *b* 1898; *Educ* Neuwied-on-Rhine Germany, Brussels, Bedford Sch; *m* 1, 1924, Annie Kathleen (d 1952), da of late Andrew Henderson, JP, of Belfast; 1 s, 1 da (decd); m 2, 1955, Mary Eleanor (d 1973), da of late William Dougan, of Londonderry; *Heir* s, John Talbot McFarland; *Career* served 1918-19 with Artists Rifles; chm Co Derry TA and AF Assoc 1947-62; ADC to HM the King 1950, to HM the Queen 1952-60; HM Lt City of Londonderry to 1975; High Sheriff City of Londonderry 1930-38 and Co Londonderry 1952, freeman 1944, mayor 1939 and 1949-50; chm Londonderry Port and Harbour Commissioners 1952-67; chm Lane's (Derry) Ltd, John W Corbett & Sons, Alexander Thompson & Co Ltd; dir Lanes (Fuel Oils) Ltd, Lanes (Patent Fuels) Ltd, Holmes Coal Ltd, R C Malseed & Co Ltd, J & R Waterson Ltd; memb N Ireland Air Advisory Council 1946-65; memb London Midland Area Bd, British Transport Commn 1955-61; pres N Ireland TA & VR Assoc 1968-70; trustee of Magee Univ Coll 1962-65; CStJ; *Recreations* bridge; *Clubs* Bath, Northern Counties; *Style* - Sir Basil McFarland, Bt, CBE, ERD; Aberfoyle, Londonderry, N Ireland (☎ Londonderry 62881)

McFARLAND, John Talbot; TD, DL (Londonderry 1962); s and h of Sir Basil

Alexander Talbot McFarland, 2 Bt, CBE, ERD; *b* 3 Oct 1927; *Educ* Marlborough, Trin Oxford; *m* 1957, Mary Scott, da of Dr W Scott Watson; 2 s, 2 da; *Career* Capt RA, ret; High Sheriff Co Londonderry 1958; memb Londonderry Co Borough Council 1955-69; High Sheriff City of Co of Londonderry 1965-67; memb NW HMC 1960-73; jt chm Londonderry & Foyle Coll 1976; dir Lanes (Derry) Ltd, Lanes Fuel Oil Ltd, Lanes Patent Fuels Ltd, Lanes Business Equipment Ltd, Holmes Coal Ltd, J N Corbett Ltd, Alexander Thompson & Co, Londonderry Gaslight Co Ltd, Donegal Holdings Ltd, Wattersons Ltd; *Style* - John McFarland Esq, TD, DL; Dunmore, Carrigans, Lifford, Co Donegal, Ireland (☎ Carrigans 6)

McFARLANE OF LLANDAFF, Baroness (Life Peer UK 1979); Jean Kennedy; da of James McFarlane (d 1963); *b* 1 Apr 1926; *Educ* Howell's Sch Llandaff, Bedford and Birkbeck Colls London U; *Career* chm English Bd for Nursing, Midwifery and Health Visiting 1980-; formerly sr lecturer, now prof and head Dept of Nursing Manchester U; SRN, SCM, FRCN; *Recreations* photography, walking, music, travel; *Clubs* Roy Commonwealth and VAD *Style* - The Rt Hon The Lady McFarlane of Llandaff; 5 Dovercourt ave, Heaton Mersey, Stockport, Cheshire; Dept of Nursing, U of Manchester, Manchester M13 9PT

McGEE, Darryll St John; s of Henry John McGee (d 1966); *b* 15 Nov 1939; *Educ* Emanuel Sch London, King's Cambridge; *m* 1979, Christine Mary, nee Castle; 3 s; *Career* dir ICI Fibres Ltd, chm Camtex Fabrics Ltd; *Recreations* squash, running, politics; *Style* - Daryll McGee Esq; 52 The Oval, Harrogate, N Yorks

McGILL, Robert Hampton Robertson; s of William McGill (d 1956); *b* 22 March 1913; *Educ* Oundle Sch, Cambridge U; *m* 1936, Amelia May, da of Sir David Robertson former MP for Caithness & Sutherland (d 1970); 1 da (Rosemary Nichol); *Career* Maj Scottish Horse, 4 years with SOE, ptnr Turner Peacock (Solicitors), exec and fin dir Power Securities and Balfour Beatty Gp 1956-70, dir (and for 2 yrs chm) Nigerian Electricity Supply Co Ltd 1971-80, chm KCA Drilling Gp Ltd 1974-76, chm Inst of Laryngology 1976-79; *Recreations* golf, fishing, swimming; *Clubs* City of London, Army and Navy, Royal St George's Golf Club, Hawks Club (Cambridge); *Style* - Robert McGill Esq; Little Court, Sandwich, Kent (☎ 030 461 7280)

McGILLYCUDDY OF THE REEKS, The, (Mac Giolla Chuda) Richard Denis Wyer McGillycuddy; *b* 1948; *Heir* cousin, Donough McGillycuddy, born 1939; *Career* succeeded 1959; *Clubs* Pratt's; *Style* - The McGillycuddy of the Reeks; The Reeks, Beaufort, Co Kerry

McGILVRAY, Lady; Anne; *née* Forster; da of late Robert Forster; *m* 1927, Sir William McGilvray, CBE (d 1956); *Style* - Lady McGilvray; 8 Fairmile Court, Henley-on-Thames, Oxon

McGONIGAL, Lady; Patricia; *née* Taylor; only da of Robert Taylor; *m* 1941, Rt Hon Lord Justice McGonigal, MC and Bar (d 1979); 2 s, 2 da; *Style* - Lady McGonigal; Bishops Court House, Bishops Court, Co Down

McGONNIGILL, Hon Mrs (Jean Brown); da of 1 Baron Kirkwood, PC (d 1955); *b* 1917; *m* 1943, William Henderson McGonnigill; 3 da; *Style* - The Hon Mrs McGonnigill; Poolfield Farm, Charfield, Wotton-under-Edge, Glos

McGOVERN, Hon Mrs (Florence Evelyn); *née* Kitson; da of 2 Baron Airedale (d 1944); *b* 1893; *m* 1, 1919, Harold Oscar Nevett, MC (d 1940); m 2, 1967, Capt Francis Joseph McGovern MC (d 1975); 2 s, 3 da; *Style* - The Hon Mrs McGovern; Leslie Manor, Camperdown, Victoria, Australia

McGOWAN, 3 Baron (UK 1937); Harry Duncan Cory McGowan; s of 2 Baron McGowan (d 1966) and Carmen, herself da of Sir Herbert Cory, 1 Bt, JP, DL, by Sir Herbert's 2 w Elizabeth, nee Walker, CBE, JP; *b* 20 July 1938; *Educ* Eton; *m* 1962, Lady Gillian Angela Pepys, da of 7 Earl of Cottenham (d 1968); 1 s, 2 da; *Heir* s, Hon Harry John Charles McGowan; *Career* ptnr Panmure Gordon & Co 1971-; *Clubs* Boodle's; *Style* - The Rt Hon the Lord McGowan; 33 Thurloe st, SW7 (☎ 01 584 9986); Highway House, Lower Froyle, Alton, Hants (☎ Bentley 2104)

McGOWAN, Hon Annabel Kate Cory; da of 3 Baron McGowan; *b* 1965; *Style* - The Hon Annabel McGowan

McGOWAN, Dowager Baroness; Carmen; da of Sir Herbert Cory; *b* 1914; *m* 1937, 2 Baron McGowan (d 1966); 3 s, 2 da; *Style* - The Rt Hon Dowager Lady McGowan; Bragborough Hall, Braundston, Northants (☎ 210)

McGOWAN, Hon Catriona Carmen Harriet; da of 2 Baron McGowan (d 1966); *b* 8 Jan 1953; *Style* - The Hon Catriona McGowan

McGOWAN, Hon Dominic James Wilson; s of 2 Baron McGowan (d 1966); *b* 26 Nov 1951; *Educ* Bradfield Coll; *Style* - The Hon Dominic McGowan; Bragborough Hall, Braundston, Daventry, Northants

McGOWAN, Hon Emma Louise Angela; da of 3 Baron McGowan; *b* 1963; *Style* - The Hon Emma McGowan

McGOWAN, Baroness; Lady Gillian Angela; *née* Pepys; da of late 7 Earl of Cottenham; *b* 1941; *m* 1962, 3 Baron McGowan; 1 s, 2 da; *Style* - The Rt Hon the Lady McGowan

McGOWAN, Hon Harry John Charles; s and h of 3 Baron McGowan; *b* 23 June 1971; *Style* - The Hon Harry McGowan

MACGOWAN, Hon Mrs (Jane Alice); *née* Casey; da of Baron Casey (Life Peer) (d 1976); *b* 1928; *m* 1955, Murray W Macgowan; *Style* - The Hon Mrs Macgowan

McGOWAN, Hon Mungo Alexander Cansh; s of 2 Baron McGowan (d 1966); *b* 10 Dec 1966; *Style* - The Hon Mungo McGowan

McGRADY, Alexander Hughes; TD (1945); s of the late C A McGrady; *b* 14 April 1916; *Educ* Merchiston Castle; *m* 1946, Vivian Jytte, of Copenhagen; 1 s, 2 da; *Career* chm Bell & Sime Ltd, ret 1981; *Recreations* motoring; *Clubs* Bentley Drivers; *Style* - Alexander McGrady Esq, TD; Brackenbrae, West Ferry, Dundee (☎ 0382 79732)

McGREGOR OF DURRIS, Baron (Life Peer UK 1978); Oliver Ross McGregor; s of late William McGregor; *b* 25 Aug 1921; *Educ* Worksop Coll, U of Aberdeen; *m* 1944, Nellie Weate; 3 s; *Career* chm Advertising Standards Authority 1980-, Pres Nat Cncl for One Parent Families; prof of Social Institutions in the U of London 1964-; head of dept of Sociology at Bedford Coll 1964-77; joint dir Rowntree Legal Research Unit 1966-; *Clubs* Garrick; *Style* - The Rt Hon Lord McGregor of Durris; Far End, Wyldes Close, NW11 (☎ 01 458 2856)

McGREGOR, Hon Alistair John; s of 2nd s of Baron McGregor of Durris (Life Peer); *b* 1950; *Style* - The Hon Alistair McGregor; c/o Far End, Wyldes Close, NWII

MACGREGOR, Sir Edwin Robert; 7 Bt (UK 1828), of Savile Row, Middlesex; s of Sir Robert James McConnell Macgregor, 6 Bt (d 1963); *b* 4 Dec 1931; *Educ* U of British Columbia; *m* 1952, Margaret Alice Jean, da of Arthur Peake, of Haney, BC, Canada; 2 s (1 decd), 2 da; *Heir* s, Ian Grant Macgregor; *Career* assist dep minister Ministry of Energy, Mines & Petroleum Resources, Province of BC, Victoria; *Style* - Sir Edwin Macgregor, Bt; 6136 Kirby rd, RR3, Sooke, BC V0S 1NO, Canada

Mac GREGOR OF Mac GREGOR, Brig Sir Gregor; 6 Bt (GB 1795), of Lanrick, Co Perth; 23 Chief of Clan Gregor; s of Capt Sir Malcolm Mac Gregor of Mac Gregor, 5 Bt, CB, CMG, JP, DL, RN (d 1958), and Hon Gylla Rollo, OBE, sis of 12 Lord Rollo; *b* 22 Dec 1925; *Educ* Eton; *m* 1958, Fanny, da of Charles H A Butler, of Newport Essex & sometime High Sheriff for that county; 2 s; *Heir* s, Malcolm Gregor Charles Mac Gregor of Mac Gregor, yr; *Career* Scots Gds: WW II, Palestine 1947-48, Malaya 1950-51, Borneo 1965; Staff Coll Course 1960; Jt Services Staff Coll 1965; cmd 1 Bn Scots Gds 1966-69, British liaison offr US Army Infantry Centre 1969-71, Col A Recruiting HQ Scotland 1971, Lt-Col cmdg Scots Gds 1971-74; Defence & Military Attaché British Embassy Athens 1975-78; Brig Lowlands 1978-80; ADC to HM the Queen 1979; dir MacGregor Centrex Ltd; memb Roy Co of Archers (Queen's Bodyguard for Scotland); *Clubs* Buck's and Pratt's; *Style* - Brig Sir Gregor Mac Gregor of Mac Gregor, Bt; Edinchip, Lochearnhead, Perthshire (☎ 05673 204)

McGREGOR, Hon Gregor Wheate; 3 s Baron McGregor of Durris (Life Peer); *b* 1952; *m* 1978, Wendy Elizabeth, da of Sydney Carlisle, of Yorkshire; *Style* - The Hon Gregor McGregor; c/o Far End, Wyldes Close, NWI 7JB

McGREGOR, Brig Herbert James Dacre Lacy; CBE (1952); s of James McGregor (d 1943); *b* 14 Aug 1899; *Educ* Merchiston Castle Sch, RMC Sandhurst; *m* 1926, Audrey Skasenniio, nee Reeves; 2 s (and 1 decd); *Career* brig, QO Cameron Highlanders WW I, WW II, on staff 1943-52, Kent CCllr 1961-74, county alderman Kent CC 1966-74; *Recreations* fishing; *Style* - Brig Herbert McGregor, CBE; Greathed Manor, Dormansland, Lingfield, Surrey (☎ 834186)

MacGREGOR, Ian; *b* 21 Sept 1912; *Educ* George Watson's Coll Edinburgh, Hillhead High Sch Glasgow, Glasgow U; *m* Sibyl, nee Spencer; 1 s, 1 da; *Career* chm and ch exec Amax Inc 1966-77 (hon chm 1977-), dep chm BL Ltd 1977-80, ptnr Lazard Freres & Co New York 1978-, pres Int Chamber of Commerce 1978, chm and ch exec Br Steel Corp 1980- (salary £48,500 pa as of June 1981); *Style* - Ian MacGregor Esq; c/o BSC, 33 Grosvenor Place, SW1 (☎ 01 235 1212)

MACGREGOR, Ian Grant; s and h of Sir Edwin Robert Macgregor, 7 Bt; *b* 22 Feb 1959; *Style* - Ian Macgregor Esq

McGREGOR, Lady; Jean; da of William Martin, MD, FRCS, of Penarth, Glam; *m* 1931, Air Marshal Sir Hector Douglas McGregor, KCB, CBE, DSO (d 1973); *Style* - Lady McGregor; Bull's Cottage, Old Bosham, W Sussex

Mac GREGOR OF Mac GREGOR, yr, Malcolm Gregor Charles; s and h of Brig Sir Gregor Mac Gregor of Mac Gregor, 6 Bt; *b* 23 March 1959; *Style* - Malcolm Mac Gregor of Mac Gregor, yr

MACGREGOR, Thomas Robert; s of Thomas Low Macgregor (d 1953); *b* 28 Jan 1916; *Educ* Rugby, Clare Cambridge; *m* 1940, Vivien, da of Dr L W Sharp (d 1953); 1 s, 1 da; *Career* served 1939-45 War; Lt RA (Japanese POW 1942-45); man The Scottish Investment Trust 1953-80; dir 1969-; dir The Scottish Mortgage & Trust Co Ltd 1969-, chm 1976-*Recreations* golf, fishing, ornithology, gardening; *Clubs* Hawks; *Style* - Thomas Macgregor Esq; North Berwick, East Lothian

McGREGOR, Hon William Ross; eld s of Baron McGregor of Durris (Life Peer); *b* 1948; *Educ* Haberdashers' Aske's Sch; *Style* - The Hon William McGregor; c/o Far End, Wyldes Close, NWII 7JB

MacGREGOR-DOWSETT, James Harvey Hamilton; CBE (1976, OBE 1972); s of Frank Herbert Dowsett (d 1934); *b* 14 Aug 1897; *Educ* Geelong Church of England G S, Gordon Inst of Technology; *m* 1928, Jessie Margaret, da of William McCowell; 2 s, 4 da (twins decd); *Career* Capt served WW I and WW II; civil servant Territorial Papua New Guinea 1921-26, mining engr 1926-31, cocoa planter TPNG 1931-46; mayor Geelong Victoria 1971-73; memb Cncl Roy C'wlth Soc Victoria 1961-, life v-pres 1977; life memb Victorian section of Australian Assoc of the Order of the British Empire, life governor Royal Freemasons' Homes, Victoria; *Recreations* music, coin collecting, books, and gardening; *Clubs* Royal Commonwealth Soc; *Style* - James MacGregor-Dowsett Esq, CBE; 9 Paterson st, East Geelong, Victoria 3219, Australia (☎ Geelong 94631)

McGRIGOR, Sir Charles Edward; 5 Bt (UK 1831), of Campden Hill, Middlesex; s of Lt-Col Sir Charles Colquhoun McGrigor, 4 Bt (d 1946); *b* 5 Oct 1922; *Educ* Eton; *m* 1948, Mary Bettine, da of Sir Archibald Edmonstone, 6 Bt (d 1954), of Duntreath Castle, Blanefield, Stirlingshire; 2 s, 2 da; *Heir* s, James Angus Rhoderick Neil Mcgrigor; *Career* 2 Lt Rifle Bde 1942, Capt 1943, served in N Africa and Italy (despatches); ADC to HRH the Duke of Gloucester KG 1945-47 (Australia and England); memb Roy Co of Archers; Exon of the Queen's Bodyguard of Yeomen of the Guard 1970-; *Style* - Sir Charles McGrigor, Bt; Upper Sonachan, by Dalmally, Argyll

McGRIGOR, James Angus Rhoderick Neil; s and h of Sir Charles Edward McGrigor, 5 Bt; *b* 19 Oct 1949; *Style* - James McGrigor Esq

McHALE, Henry; s of Henry McHale (d 1980); *b* 12 Sept 1934; *Educ* Queens' Cambridge; *Career* FCA, barr; dir of Grundy (Teddington) Gp Ltd, Envopak Ltd; *Recreations* golf, tennis, field sports; *Clubs* Carlton; *Style* - Henry McHale Esq; 44 Cadogan sq, SW1

McHARG, Bt-Col William Wilson; OBE (1960), MC (1944), TD (1954), DL (Ayrshire 1970); s of Alexander McHarg; *b* 29 Aug 1918; *Educ* Irvine Roy Academy, Glasgow U; *m* 1947, Janet, nee Gommer; 1 s, 1 da; *Career* maj MEF, CMF, TA 1938-46 and 1947-61 Col; slr, racecourse man, Clerk of the Course; *Clubs* Ayr County; *Style* - Col William McHarg, OBE, MC, TD, DL; 29 Earls Way, Doonfoot, Ayr, Ayrshire (☎ Alloway 41350)

McILROY, Hon Mrs (Elizabeth Mary); da of 2 Baron Rochester; *b* 1951; *m* 1974, Thomas Meredith McIlroy; 2 s; *Style* - The Hon Mrs McIlroy

McILROY, Harry (Alexander); s of Henry McIlroy of Dublin; *b* 17 May 1940; *Educ* Model Belfast, Swinton Coll; *m* 1971, Winifred Una, nee McKeown; 1 s, 1 da; *Career* chm and owner Unico Gp Ltd, chm Unico Finance Ltd, underwriting Memb Lloyd's, hon treasurer Friends of Ulster Museum, liveryman Basketmakers Co, Freeman City of London; *Clubs* Carlton, City Livery, E India, Ulster; *Style* - Harry McIlroy Esq; 9 Raglan House, Ballsbridge ct, Dublin 4, Eire; Haven Court, Derbyhaven, Castletown, Isle of Man

McINDOE, Lady; Constance (Belchem); yr da of late John Hutton; *m* 1954, as his 2 wife, Sir Archibald Hector McIndoe, CBE (d 1960); *Style* - Lady McIndoe; 53 Glebe Place, Chelsea, SW3

MacINNES, Kenneth; CBE (1970), JP (Herts, Middlesex 1951), DL (Herts 1969); s of Rev John MacInnes (d 1917); *b* 12 July 1905; *Educ* Rugby, Trin Cambridge; *m* 1934, Helen, da of late Sir Douglas Gordon; 3 s; *Career* chm Central Cncl Probation Aftercare 1964-69; *Recreations* country life; *Style* - Kenneth MacInnes Esq, CBE, JP, DL; Pound House, Shenley, Herts (☎ Radlet 6623)

McINTOSH, Lady; Doris Hutchinson Pow; *m* 1934, Sir Alister Donald McIntosh, KCMG, (d 1978); 1 s; *Style* - Lady McIntosh; 11 Wesley rd, Wellington, New Zealand

McINTOSH, Douglas Moul; CBE (1961); s of Simon McIntosh (d 1957); *b* 27 Sept 1909; *Educ* Dundee Harris Academy, St Andrews U, Edinburgh U; *m* 1939, Jean Blair, nee Paterson; *Career* FRSE 1945, FEIS 1949, dir educn Fife 1944-66, princ Moray House Coll Educn 1966-74; *Recreations* golf; *Style* - Douglas McIntosh Esq, CBE; Tigh an Droma, 22 Balwearie gdns, Kirkcaldy, Fife (☎ 60895)

McINTOSH, Ian Alexander Neville; s of Alexander McIntosh; *b* 24 Sept 1938; *Educ* Bradford G S, Edinburgh U; *m* 1965, Gillian Mary Sophia, nee Cropp; 1 s, 1 da; *Career* exec dir Samuel Montagu & Co Ltd, non-executive dir of Capel Court Corp Ltd, Hampton Gold Mining Areas Ltd, Ruberoid Ltd; *Recreations* golf; *Clubs* MCC, Mid Herts GC; *Style* - Ian McIntosh Esq; 11 Berkley rd, NW1 (☎ 01 722 3229)

McINTOSH, Prof Naomi Ellen; da of Tom Sargant; *b* 10 Dec 1933; *Educ* Friends Sch Saffron Walden, Bedford Coll London; *m* 1, 1954, Peter

Kelly; 1 s; m 2, 1962, Andrew Robert McIntosh; 2 s; *Career* sr commissioning ed Channel Four 1981-, Prof Applied Social Res The Open Univ 1978-81, Pro V-Chancellor Student Affairs The Open Univ 1974-78, chm Nat Gas Consumers Cncl 1977-80, memb Nat Consumer Cncl 1978-, Cmmn on Energy and Environment 1978-, pres Nat Soc for Clean Air 1981-; *Recreations* gardening, photography; *Style* - Prof Naomi McIntosh; 4 Talbot rd, N6 (☎ 01 340 1496)

MACINTYRE, Lady; Blanche Gwendoline Fikuart; *née* Horn; *m* 1976, as his 2 wife, the late Hon Sir Donald Macintyre, CBE; *Style* - Lady Macintyre

MACK, Lady; Ida; da of H W Mocatta; *m* 1937, Hon Sir William (George) Mack, KBE (d 1979); 1 s, 1 da; *Style* - Lady Mack; 60 Alexandra rd, Ascot, Queensland 4007, Australia

MACK, Lady; Winifred Helen; da of late Percy Frank Trevelyan Campion; *m* 1, Philip Crutchfield (decd); 1 s, 1 da; m 2, 1958, as his 2 w, Hon Sir Ronald William Mack (d 1968); 1 step s; *Career* associate Australian Soc of Accountants; memb Victoria League for Commonwealth Friendship in Victoria, memb RAC Aust; *Style* - Lady Mack; 15/152 Power st, Hawthorn, Victoria 3122, Australia

MACKANESS, John Howard; s of Alfred James Mackaness (d 1964); *b* 11 Oct 1915; *Educ* Oakham Sch, Wye Coll London U; *m* 1940, Marjorie, nee Andrews; 4 s; *Career* chm Mixconcrete Holdings Ltd, chm AJ Mackaness Ltd; *Recreations* hunting, shooting, walking, travel; *Style* - John Mackaness Esq; Boughton Hall, Northampton; (☎ 843221) Rudding Gates, Harrogate (☎ 879604)

MACKANESS, Mark; 4 and yst s of John Howard Mackaness, of Boughton Hall, jt MFH Pytchley 1968-; *b* 20 Jan 1952; *Educ* Oundle, RAC Cirencester; *Career* ARICS, land agent, dir AJ Mackaness Ltd, dir Billing Aquadrome Ltd; *Recreations* shooting, flying, squash; *Clubs* Northampton and County; *Style* - Mark Mackaness Esq; Rudding Park, Harrogate, N Yorks (☎ 871350); Boughton Hall, Northampton

MACKAY OF CLASHFERN, Baron (Life Peer UK 1979); James Peter Hymers Mackay; PC (1979), QC (1965); s of James Mackay (d 1958); *b* 2 July 1927; *Educ* George Heriot's Sch Edinburgh, Edinburgh U, Trin Cambridge; *m* 1958, Elizabeth Gunn Hymers, da of D D Manson; 1 s, 2 da; *Career* Sheriff Pncpl Renfrew and Argyll 1972-74, V-Dean Faculty of Advocates 1973-76, Dean 1976-79; advocate 1955; part-time member Scottish Law Commission 1976-79; dir Stenhouse Hldgs 1976-78; memb Insur Brokers' Registration Cncl 1978-79; Lord Advocate 1979-; Commissioner Northern Lighthouses 1975-; *Clubs* New (Edinburgh); *Style* - The Rt Hon the Lord Mackay of Clashfern PC QC; 34 Dick pla, Edinburgh EH9 2JB (☎ 031 667 5995)

MACKAY, Hon Asia Brooke; da of Baron Tanlaw (Life Peer); *b* 1980; *Style* - The Hon Asia Mackay

MACKAY, Hon Ailsa Fiona; da of Viscount Glenapp; *b* 1977; *Style* - The Hon Ailsa Mackay

MACKAY, Hon Alan John Francis; s of 2 Earl of Inchape (d 1939); *b* 1919; *Educ* Eton and Trin Coll, Camb; *m* 1, Janet Mary Wallis, of Elvendon Priory, Goring-on-Thames (m dis 1947); m 2, 1948, Sonia Cecilia Helen (m dis 1953), da of Capt James Richard Tylden, of Milsted Manor, Kent, and of Lady Tower, of Mansters, Sway, Hants; 2 da; m 3, 1955, Countess Lucie Cathinka Christiane (who m 1936 John Boswell, m dis 1955), da of Count Curt Haugwitz-Hardenberg-Reventlow, of Korinth, Fyn, Denmark; *Career* served with Cameronians 1939-40; Mercantile Marine 1941-46; *Clubs* Oriental; *Style* - The Hon Alan Mackay; Enterkine, Annbank, Ayrshire (☎ 223); Inishanboe, Oughterard, Co Galway, Eire

McKAY, Maj-Gen Alexander Matthew; CB (1975); s of Colin McKay, of Canada (d 1978); *b* 14 Feb 1921; *Educ* Portsmouth Poly; *m* 1949, Betty Margaret; 1 s (and 1 da decd); *Career* Maj-Gen, despatches 1944 and Palestine 1948, chartered engineer, sec Inst of Mechanical Engineers 1976-, gen sec Inst of Chemical Engineers 1975-76, chm Stock Lake Holdings Ltd 1975-, v-chm Mechanical Engineering Publications Ltd 1976-; *Recreations* collecting and restoring antique furniture, gardening, outdoor activities; *Clubs* Caledonian, Inst of Dirs; *Style* - Maj Gen Alexander McKay, CB; Church Cottage, Martyr Worthy, Winchester, Hants

MACKAY, Baron (and Hon) Alexander William Rynhard; s of 12 Lord Reay (d 1921), and Baroness Maria Johanna Bertha Christina Van Dedem (d 1932); *b* 1907; *Career* dir Bank of the Netherlands; *Style* - Baron Alexander Mackay; De Lindelaan, 76 Schapendrift, Blaricum (NH), Netherlands

MACKAY, Hon Mrs; Hon Cynthia; *née* Vansittart; da of 1 Baron Vansittart (d 1957); *b* 1922; *m* 1, 1942 Frederick C Whitman (m dis 1954) 3 s, 1 da; m 2, 1955 Edward Hart Mackay; 2 s; *Style* - The Hon Mrs Mackay

McKAY, Douglas Henry; CBE (1977, OBE 1966); s of Oswald Henry McKay (d 1942); *b* 5 Sept 1923; *Educ* Masonic Sch NSW Australia, Sydney U; *m* 1947, Ruth Alison, nee Irwin; 3 da; *Career* ag rep Australian High Cmmn London 1959-62, dir Bureau of Ag Economics 1963-68, dep sec Dept of Trade and Industry 1968-71, permanent sec Dept of Trade 1978-80, permanent sec Dept of Primary Industry; *Recreations* fishing; *Clubs* Commonwealth (Canberra); *Style* - Douglas McKay Esq, CBE; 8 St Jackson st, Campbell, Canberra, ACT, Australia (☎ 062 4983 42)

MACKAY, Baron Donald Theodore; s of Baron Daniel Mackay (d 1962, s of Baron Theodoor Mackay, unc of 12 Lord Reay, by Baroness Juliana Anna van Lynden, da of Baron Constantijn van Lynden) by his 1 w, Helene Hommel; *b* 23 Feb 1910; *m* 1, 1939 (m dis 1945), Jonkvrouwe Alexandra Frederica de Savornin Lohman, da of Jonkheer Bonifacius Christiaan de Savornin Lohman; m 2, 1945, Kathleen, da of Percy Shaw Pearce; 1 s (Baron Niall Mackay, b 1956), 1 da (Baroness Moira Mackay, b 1952); *Career* Lt-Cdr (ret) Roy Netherlands Navy, served WW II with RN (subs); LRCP, LRCS, LRFP&S; *Style* - Baron Donald Mackay; c/o Nat West Bank, High Street, Barnstaple, N Devon

MACKAY, Hon Edward Andrew; s of 14 Lord Reay; *b* 1974; *Style* - The Hon Edward Mackay

MACKAY, Hon Elizabeth Janet; da of Baron Mackay of Clashfern (Life Peer); *b* 1961; *Style* - The Hon Elizabeth Mackay

MACKAY, Hon Elspeth Pease; da of Viscount Glenapp; *b* 1972; *Style* - The Hon Elspeth Mackay

MACKAY, Hon Fergus James Kenneth; s and h of Viscount Glenapp; *b* 9 July 1979; *Style* - The Hon Fergus Mackay

McKAY, Lady; Honor E; da of W Deans; *m* 1934, Sir Charles Holly McKay, CBE (d 1972); *Style* - Lady McKay; 2 Banfield st, Ararat, Victoria, Australia 3377

MACKAY, Hon Ivan Cholmeley; s of 3 Earl of Inchape; *b* 1976; *Style* - The Hon Ivan Mackay

MACKAY, Hon James; s of Baron Mackay of Clashfern (Life Peer); *b* 1958; *Style* - The Hon James Mackay

MACKAY, Hon James Brooke; s of Baron Tanlaw (Life Peer); *b* 1961; *Style* - The Hon James Mackay

MACKAY, Hon James Jonathan Thorn; s of 3 Earl of Inchcape; *b* 1947; *Educ* Eton and Trin Coll Camb (MA); *m* 1970, Mary Caroline, eld da of Peter Joyce of Becklands Farm, Whitchurch Canonicorum, Dorset; 1 s, 1 da; *Style* - The Hon James Mackay; 6 Tivoli rd, N8

MACKAY, Hon Laura Elizabeth; da of 14 Baron Reay; *b* 1966; *Style* - The Hon Laura Mackay

MACKAY, Lady Lucinda Louise; da of 3 Earl of Inchcape; *b* 1941; *Educ* Chatelard Sch; Edinburgh U; Edinburgh Art Coll;

Style - Lady Lucinda Mackay; 11 Queens gdns W2

MACKAY, Baroness (and Hon) Maria Christina Elisabeth; da of 12 Baron Reay (d 1921), and Baroness Maria Johanna Bertha Christina Van Dedem (d 1932); *b* 1904; *Style* - Baroness Maria Mackay; De Eeckwal, Dalfsen, Holland

MACKAY, Hon Rebecca Alexandra; da of Baron Tanlaw (Life Peer); *b* 1967; *Style* - The Hon Rebecca Mackay

MACKAY, Hon Shane Lyle; s of 3 Earl of Inchcape; *b* 1967; *Style* - The Hon Shane Mackay

MACKAY, Hon Shona Ruth; da of Baron Mackay of Clashfern (Life Peer); *b* 1958; *Style* - The Hon Shona Mackay

McKEE, Lady; Mary K Wallace; da of late Eli Dalton; *m* 1970, as his 2 w, His Honour Sir Dermot St Oswald McKee (d 1980); *Style* - Lady McKee; Thatched Cottage, Tockwith, York

McKENNA, Lady Cecilia Elizabeth; *née* Keppel; da of 9 Earl of Albermarle, MC, (d 1979); *b* 1910; *m* 1934, David McKenna CBE, s of late Rt Hon Reginald McKenna; 3 da; *Style* - Lady Cecilia McKenna; Rosteague, Portscatho, Truro, Cornwall; 67 Hamilton Terr, London NW8

McKENNA, Hon Mrs (Emily Dunbar); *née* Burns; OBE (1919); da of 3 Baron Inverclyde (d 1956); *b* 1891; *m* 1922, Lt-Cdr Gerald Morell McKenna, RN (d 1949); *Style* - The Hon Mrs McKenna; Kirtling Tower, Newmarket, Suffolk

McKENNA, Lady Pleasance Elizabeth; *née* Rous; da of 3 Earl of Stradbroke, KCMG, CB, CVO, CBE, (d 1947); *b* 1899; *m* 1923, Owen McKenna; 1 s, 1 da; *Style* - Lady Pleasance McKenna; 56 St James's Gdns, Holland Park, WII

MACKENZIE, Sir (Alexander George Anthony) Allan; 4 Bt (UK 1890), of Glen Muick, Aberdeen, CD; s of Capt Allan Keith Mackenzie (ka 1916), by Hon Alexandra L E, da of 1 Viscount Knollys, GCB, PC, and nephew of 3 Bt, DSO, MVO (d 1944); *b* 4 Jan 1913; *Educ* Stowe; *m* 1937, Marjorie McGuire, of Alberta, Canada; 4 da; *Heir* cousin, James William Guy Mackenzie; *Career* memb Roy Canadian Mounted Police 1932-37; page of honour to late King George V; enlisted Calgary Highlanders 1939, Lt Seaforth Highlanders of Canada 1941, Capt Black Watch of Canada, ret 1961; *Style* - Sir Allan Mackenzie, Bt, CD; RRI, Cobble Hill, Vancouver Island, BC, Canada

MACKENZIE, Angus Alexander; s of Murdo J Mackenzie; *b* 15 Jan 1917; *Educ* in Br Columbia; *m* 1939; 2 s, 2 da; *Career* served WW II Fl Lt RCAF in W Europe & N Atlantic; chm Sceptre Resources Ltd, Scarboro Resources Ltd, Scimitar Oils SA; *Recreations* golf, reading; *Clubs* Deep Dale (NY State), Calgary Golf & Country (Calgary), Sunningdale Golf (Berks), Annabel's, Harry's Bar (London), Mark's; *Style* - Angus Mackenzie Esq; 110 Mount Street, W1 (☎ 01 492 0315/499 9140)

MACKENZIE, Lady Anne Mildred Ismay; *née* Fitzroy; da of 10 Duke of Grafton (d 1970); *b* 1920; *m* 1947, Maj Colin Dalzell Mackenzie, MBE, MC, DL, *qv*, late Seaforth Highlanders; 1 s, 3 da (1 s decd); *Clubs* Turf; *Style* - Lady Anne Mackenzie; Farr House, Inverness-shire; Bergh Apton Manor, Norwich

MACKENZIE, Maj Colin Dalzell; MBE (1945), MC, DL (Inverness-shire 1976); s of Lt-Col (Douglas William) Alexander Dalzell Mackenzie, CVO, DSO (d 1955); *b* 23 March 1919; *Educ* Eton, RMC; *m* 1947, Lady Anne Mildred Ismay FitzRoy, da of 10 Duke of Grafton; 2 s, (1 decd), 3 da; *Career* page of honour to HM King George V 1932-36; joined Seaforth Highlandrs 1939, ret 1950; ADC to Viceroy of India 1945-46; dep mil sec to Viceroy 1946-47; CCllr 1950 Inverness-shire; memb Roy Co of Archers; *Recreations* shooting, fishing; *Clubs* Turf, New (Edinburgh); *Style* - Maj Colin Mackenzie, MBE, MC, DL; Farr House, Inverness (☎ Farr 202)

MacKENZIE, Lady; Doris Agnes; da of Harcourt Sawyer, of Springhill, Windsor Forest, Berks; *m* 1919, Sir Clutha Nantes

MacKenzie (d 1966); *Style* - Lady MacKenzie; 561 Weymouth rd, Manurewa, New Zealand

MACKENZIE, (James William) Guy; s of late Lt-Col Eric Dighton Mackenzie, CMG, CVO, DSO and hp of cousin, Sir (Alexander George Anthony) Allan Mackenzie, 4 Bt, CD; *b* 6 Oct 1946; *Educ* Stowe; *m* 1972, Paulene Patricia Simpson; 1 da; *Style* - Guy Mackenzie Esq; 1 Molerun, Pheasant Drive, High Wycombe, Bucks

MACKENZIE, Col Hector Andrew Courtney; OBE (1969), MC (1945), TD (1951); s of Maj W F Mackenzie, of Dalmore, Alness, Ross-shire; *b* 19 July 1919; *Educ* Cargilfield Midlothian, Edinburgh Academy; *m* 1954, Daphne Florence Elizabeth, da of late H James, of Johannesburg; 3 s, 1 da; *Career* TA Commission 1938, served 1939-45 War; Scotch whisky distiller; part time memb N Scotland Hydro-Electric Bd and Highlands and Islands Development Bd 1970-75; gen commr Income Tax 1977-; *Recreations* skiing, sailing; *Clubs* Roy Scottish Automobile, Royal Overseas League; *Style* - Hector Mackenzie Esq, OBE, MC, TD; Dalmore, Alness, Ross-shire (☎ Alness 0349 882362)

MACKENZIE, Lady Jean Leslie; da of 20 Earl of Rothes (d 1975); *b* 1927; *m* 1949, Roderick Robin Mackenzie, s of Capt Roderick Kilgour Mackenzie (d 1937); *Style* - Lady Jean Mackenzie; Kingfisher House, Ampfield, Hants

MACKENZIE, Kenneth Edward; CMG (1970); s of Alexander Edward Mackenzie, of Dundee and Calcutta; *b* 28 April 1910; *Educ* India, Australia, Scotland, England, Univ Coll London; *m* 1934, Phyllis Edith, da of Francis Hamley Fawkes, of Prestbury, Glos; 1 s; *Career* engineering industry 1926-29, with Inst Civil Engrs 1933-34, Dept Overseas Trade 1934-36; British Embassy, Brussels 1936-40; interned Germany 1940-41; British Embassy Tehran 1942-45; trade cmmr India 1946-48, Malaya 1949-53, assist sec Bd of Trade 1953-66; cnsllr Br Embassy Stockholm 1966-70, (Investment) British Embassy Stockholm 1973; consultant on Inward Investment to Dept Industry 1974-75; cnsllr (Investment) British Embassy Copenhagen 1974-75; chm John Mackenzie Models Ltd; *Clubs* Roy Commonwealth Soc; *Style* - Kenneth Mackenzie Esq, CMG; Prestbury, Middle Hill, Englefield Green, Surrey (☎ Egham 37877)

MACKENZIE, Kenneth William Stewart; CMG (1958), CVO (1975; s of Stewart Mackenzie (d 1950); *b* 30 July 1915; *Educ* Whitcliffe Mount G S Cleckeaton, Downing Cambridge; *m* 1939, Kathleen Joyce, da of John Douglas Ingram, of Dewsbury Yorks; 1 s, 1 da; *Career* entered Colonial Service 1938, assist sec 1940, Mauritius 1944, Kenya 1948; sec to Treasury Kenya 1955, min for Finance 1959-62; MLC Kenya 1955-62; ret 1962; princ Colonial Office 1963, HM Treasury 1966; assist sec Dept of Environment 1970, ret 1975; dir of studies Roy Inst of Public Administration (Overseas Unit) 1976-; *Recreations* reading, gardening, travel; *Clubs* Roy Overseas League, Nairobi; *Style* - Kenneth Mackenzie Esq, CMG, CVO; Beaumont, 28 Greenhurst Lane, Oxted, Surrey (☎ Oxted 3848)

MACKENZIE, Lady; Lilian; da of Malcolm MacSween; *m* 1965, as his 3 w, Sir (Edward Montague) Compton Mackenzie, OBE (d 1972); *Style* - Lady Mackenzie; 31 Drummond pla, Edinburgh

MACKENZIE, Lady; Margaret Patricia (Smail); da of Brig-Gen Horace Cobham, CMG, DSO; *m* 1947, as his 2 w, Sir Duncan George Mackenzie, KCIE (d 1965); *Style* - Lady Mackenzie; The Manor, Wyke Champflower, Bruton, Somerset

MACKENZIE, Sir Roderick Campbell; 10 Bt (NS 1703), of Scatwell Ross-shire; s of late Kenneth Roderick Mackenzie and kinsman of Sir (Lewis) Roderick Kenneth Mackenzie, 9 Bt (d 1972); *b* 15 Nov 1954; *Educ* U of Virginia; *Heir* kinsman, Capt Roderick Mackenzie, CBE, DSC, RN (ret); *Career* student of foreign languages; *Recreations* tennis, canoeing; *Style* - Sir Roderick Mackenzie, Bt; 120

Church st, Clifton Forge, Virginia 24422, USA

MACKENZIE, Sir Robert Evelyn; 12 Bt (NS 1673), of Coul Ross-shire; s of Sir Arthur George Ramsay Mackenzie, 11 Bt, JP, DL (d 1935); *b* 15 Feb 1906; *Educ* Eton, Trin Cambridge; *m* 1, 1940, Mrs Jane Adams-Beck (d 1953); m 2, 1963, Mrs Elizabeth Campbell; *Heir* cousin, Rev Ramsay Malcolm Bolton Mackenzie; *Career* Capt Gen List 1939, Maj Intelligence Corps 1942; 1 sec British Embassy Paris 1945, Foreign Office 1947, British Embassy Washington 1948; memb Lloyd's 1932-71; *Style* - Sir Robert Mackenzie, Bt; 18 Melton Court, Old Brompton rd, SW7

MACKENZIE, Capt Roderick Edward François McQuhae; CBE (1945), DSC (1915), RN (ret); s of John Roderick Kenneth Mackenzie (d 1958); hp of kinsman, Sir Roderick Mackenzie, 10 Bt; *b* 1894; *Educ* RN Colls Osborne and Dartmouth; *m* 1938, Marie Evelyn Campbell, da of late W Ernest Parkinson, of Farnham, Surrey; 1 s, 2 da; *Career* served 1914-19 War, Capt Roy Navy; Medal of Freedom with Silver Palm (US) 1944; *Recreations* golf; *Clubs* Naval & Military; *Style* - Capt Roderick Mackenzie, CBE, DSC, RN

MACKENZIE, Rev Ramsay Malcolm Bolton; s of Henry Augustin Ornano Mackenzie (d 1909, s of 7 Bt); hp of kinsman, Sir Robert Mackenzie, 12 Bt; *b* 7 Aug 1893; *Educ* Lancing Coll, Trin Oxford; *m* 1, 1920, Margaret Cecilia (d 1965), da of late Rev George Augustus Seymour Metford; m 2, 1971, Joan Mary, da of Henry James Davey (d 1909); *Career* Lt RNVR, Capt RAF 1914-18; vicar St Mary's Shrewsbury 1938-55, Rural Dean of Shrewsbury 1952-55, Rector of Edgmond Shropshire 1955-60, sec Additional Curates Soc 1932-34, sec Central Bd of Finance, ret 1960; *Recreations* reading, walking, music; *Style* - Rev Ramsay Mackenzie; 6 Pearl Court, Devonshire Place, Eastbourne, E Sussex BN21 4AB (☎ Eastbourne 23200)

MACKENZIE CROOKS, Air Vice-Marshal Lewis; CBE (1964, OBE 1951); s of David Mackenzie Crooks, MB (d 1953); *b* 20 Jan 1909; *Educ* Epworth Coll Rhyl, Liverpool U; *m* 1936, Mildred, da of Albert John Gwyther (d 1938); 2 s, 1 da; *Career* RAF 1935, served WW II Far East, Middle East and Europe, surgeon RAF 1935-71, consultant adviser in Orthopaedics 1965-71, Locum Consultant in Orthopaedics in Cornwall 1970-, South Western Regional Hosp Bd 1971-; *Recreations* golf, gardening; *Clubs* Revose Golf and Country Club; *Style* - Air Vice-Marshal Lewis Mackenzie Crooks, CBE; Trelawney, Harlyn Bay, Padstow, Cornwall (☎ Padstow 520631)

MACKERETH, Lady; Muriel; da of late David Jouffroy Watson; *m* 1921, Sir Gilbert Mackereth, KCMG, MC (d 1962); *Style* - Lady Mackereth; 188 Cooden Sea rd, Bexhill-on-Sea, E Sussex

MACKESON, Hon Camilla, Lady; Hon Camilla Margaret; da of Baron Keith of Castleacre (Life Peer); *b* 1947 (twin); *m* 1968 (m dis 1972), Sir Rupert Henry Mackeson, 2 Bt; *Style* - The Hon Camilla, Lady Mackeson

MACKESON, Sir Rupert Henry; 2 Bt (UK 1954), of Hythe Co, Kent; s of Brig Sir Harry Ripley Mackeson, 1 Bt (d 1964); *b* 16 Nov 1941; *Educ* Harrow, Trin Coll Dublin; *m* 1968, (m dis 1972) Hon Camilla Margaret, da of Baron Keith of Castleacre; *Heir* none; *Career* Capt RHG, ret 1968; *Clubs* White's; *Style* - Sir Rupert Mackeson, Bt

MACKESSACK, Douglas; MBE (1945), JP (Morayshire 1954), DL (1962); s of George Ross Mackessack (d 1935); *b* 7 Oct 1903; *Educ* Rugby, Oxford U; *m* 1935, Janet, da of D Connel; 2 da; *Career* staff offr 51 Highland Div 1939 (POW 1940-45); md Glen Grant Distillery Rothes 1929-78; *Recreations* golf, shooting, fishing; *Style* - Douglas Mackessack Esq, MBE, JP, DL; Inverugie, Hopeman, Morayshire (☎ 253)

MACKIE OF BENSHIE, Baron (Life Peer UK 1974); George Yull Mackie; CBE (1971), DSO (1944), DFC (1944); s of Maitland Mackie, OBE, and bro of Baron John-Mackie and Maitland Mackie, the Ld-Lt for Aberdeenshire; *b* 10 July 1919; *Educ* Aberdeen G S & U; *m* 1944, Lindsay, da of Alexander & Isabella Sharp, OBE, of Aberdeen; 3 da (and 1 s decd); *Career* chm Mackie Yule & Co, Caithness Glass Ltd 1966-, Caithness Pottery Co, Benshie Cattle Co; Rector Dundee U 1980-; served WW II Bomber Cmmd; farmer 1945-; MP (Lib) Caithness & Sutherland 1964-66; stood for Parl (Lib) Angus S 1959 & (for Euro Parl) Scotland NE 1979; chm Scot Lib Pty 1965-70; Lib Spokesman Ho Lds: Devolution, Ag, Scotland, Indust; *Recreations* golf, tennis, shooting; *Clubs* Garrick, Farmers', RAF; *Style* - Rt Hon Lord Mackie of Benshie CBE DSO DFC; Ballinshoe, Kirriemuir, Angus (☎ 2270)

MACKIE, Baron (Life Peer UK 1981); John; s of Maitland Mackie; *b* 1909; *Educ* Aberdeen G S, N of Scotland Coll of Agriculture; *m* 1934, Jeannie Inglis, da of Mrs Milne, of Carcary, Brechin, Angus; 3 s, 2 da; *Career* farmer; MP (L) Enfield (East) 1959-74, Parly Sec Miny Agriculture, Fisheries and Food 1964-70; chm Forestry Commission 1976-79; *Style* - The Rt Hon the Lord Mackie; Harold's Park Farm, Nazeing, Essex (☎ 2202)

MACKIE, Hon Jeannie Felicia; da of Baron Mackie of Benshie (Life Peer); *b* 1953; *Style* - The Hon Jeannie Mackie; c/o Ballinshoe, Kirriemuir, Angus, DD8 5Q9

MACKIE, Hon Lindsay Mary; da of Baron Mackie of Benshie (Life Peer); *b* 1945; *Style* - The Hon Lindsay Mackie; c/o Ballinshoe, Kirriemuir, Angus DD8 5Q9

MACKIE, Maitland; CBE (1965), JP (Aberdeen 1959); s of Maitland Mackie and bro of Baron Mackie of Benshie and of Baron John-Mackie; *b* 16 Feb 1912; *Educ* Aberdeen G S & U; *m* 1, 1935, Isobel Ross (d 1960); 2 s, 4 da; m 2, 1963, Martha Turner; *Career* farmer 1932-; Ld-Lt Aberdeenshire 1975-; chm Jt Advsy Cttee Scot Farm Bldgs Investigation Unit 1963-, Aberdeen Milk Mktng Bd 1965-, Peterhead Bay Management Co 1975; memb Bd Scot Cncl Devpt & Indust 1975- & chm Oil Policy Cttee 1975-; dir Scot Telecommunications 1969, Hanover Housing Assoc 1978, Highland Hydrocarbons 1978; KStJ 1977; *Style* - Maitland Mackie Esq, CBE, JP, HM Lord-Lieut for Aberdeenshire; Cramond House, 17 Rubislaw Den N, Aberdeen (☎ 33587)

MACKIE, Dr Margaret Alison; CMG (1975); da of David Ross Mackie (d 1937); *b* 6 Nov 1910; *Educ* Presbyterian Ladies' Coll Melbourne; *Career* medical practitioner, Obstetrician and Gynaecologist, In-patient Gynaecologist Queen Victoria Memorial Hosp Melbourne 1952-59, In-patient Obstetrician Roy Women's Hosp Melbourne 1959-70, Consultant Obstetrician 1970-; *Recreations* photography, gardening, travel; *Clubs* Lyceum, Roy Auto; *Style* - Dr Margaret Mackie CMG; Unit 2/11 Albany rd, Toorak, Victoria, Australia (☎ 20 7556)

MACKILLIGIN, Robert Guy Walter; MC (1944, and Bar 1945); s of the late Hector Rennie Mackilligin; *b* 11 Oct 1918; *Educ* Charterhouse, Camborne Sch of Mines; *m* 1949, Daphne Gwendoline, nee Cooper; 3 da; *Career* petroleum engr Shell International Petroleum Co Ltd 1946-53, man Shell Internat Ltd 1954-73, md Bisichi Tin Co Ltd 1974-, dir and chm Bisichi Jantar (Nigeria) Ltd 1974-; *Recreations* genealogy, gardening, ornithology; *Style* - Robert Mackilligin Esq, MC*; Walnut Tree Cottage, Woodlands, Pembury rd, Tunbridge Wells (☎ 0892 30392 and 01 248 2850)

McKINNA, John Gilbert; CMG (1973), CBE (1967), DSO (1945), MVO (1963), ED (1947); s of Rev John McKinna (d 1964); *b* 11 Dec 1906; *Educ* Prince Alfred Coll, Adelaide U; *m* 1937, Elizabeth Mary, da of Col Sydney Edwin Beach (d 1933); 2 da; *Career* Brig WW II; gen man Quarry Industries 1949-56, Hon ADC to Govr Gen 1953-56; commissioner of police South Australia 1957-72; pres Roy Automobile Assoc of SA 1975-78; *Clubs* Adelaide Club, Naval, Military & Air Force Club (Australia); *Style* - Brig John McKinna CMG CBE DSO MVO ED; 12 McKenna st, Kensington Park, S Australia 5068 (☎ 31 4606)

MacKINNON OF MACKINNON, The; Alasdair Neil Hood MacKinnon; s of Cdr Arthur Avalon MacKinnon of MacKinnon, OBE; suc as Ch of Clan MacKinnon 1964; *b* 1926; *Educ* Wellington, Edinburgh U; *m* 1949, Patricia, da of E W Reading; *Heir* da; *Career* Lt RN (ret); *Style* - The MacKinnon of MacKinnon; Field End, Nailsbourne, Taunton

McKINNON, David Douglas; s of John McKinnon; *b* 18 July 1926; *Educ* H S of Stirling, Glasgow U; *m* 1960, Edith June; 1 s, 2 da; *Career* asst, maths dept, Glasgow U 1946-48; Fellow of Faculty of Actuaries 1951; pres of Faculty of Actuaries 1979-81; dep gen man, Scottish Mutual Assurance Society 1979; *Clubs* Western (Glasgow); *Style* - David McKinnon Esq; Kinburn, 4 Carronvale rd, Larbert, Stirlingshire (☎ 032 45 2373)

MACKINNON, Hon Mrs Eva Constance Edith; *née* Best; da of 6 Baron Wynford, DSO (d 1940); *b* 1909; *m* 1932 (m dis 1961), Philip Valentine Mackinnon, s of late Rt Hon Sir Frank Douglas Mackinnon, Lord Justice of Appeal; 1 s; *Style* - The Hon Mrs Eva Mackinnon

MACKINNON, Hon Mrs (Patricia Ann); *née* Souter; da and coheiress of 25 Baron Audley; *b* 10 Aug 1946; *m* 1969, Carey Leigh Mackinnon; 1 s, 1 da; *Style* - The Hon Mrs Mackinnon; Scollops Oast, Ide Hill, Sevenoaks, Kent

MACKINNON, Hon Mrs; Hon Patricia Clare; da of 1 Baron Glentoran, OBE, PC (d 1950); *b* 1919; *m* 1940, Lt-Cdr Adam McLeod Mackinnon, RN; 2 s, 3 da; *Style* - The Hon Mrs Mackinnon; The Cottage Inn, Maidens Green, Winkfield, Windsor, Berks

MACKINTOSH OF HALIFAX, 3 Viscount (UK 1957); Sir (John) Clive Mackintosh; 3 Bt (UK 1935); s of 2 Viscount Mackintosh of Halifax, OBE, BEM (d 1980), by his 2 w, Gwynneth, *see* Viscountess Mackintosh of Halifax; *b* 9 Sept 1958; *Educ* The Leys Sch, and Oriel Oxford; *Heir* bro, Hon Graham Charles Mackintosh; *Style* - The Rt Hon the Viscount Mackintosh of Halifax; The Old Hall, Barford, Norwich (☎ Barnham Broom 271)

MACKINTOSH, Hon Diana Mary; da of 2 Viscount Mackintosh of Halifax (d 1980); *b* 14 Sept 1947; *Educ* Riddlesworth Hall, Harrogate Coll; *Career* children's nursing; *Style* - The Hon Diana Mackintosh; The Grange, Elmfield Park, Gosforth, Newcastle upon Tyne (☎ Gosforth 52972)

MACKINTOSH, Hon Graham Charles; s of 2 Viscount Mackintosh of Halifax (d 1980), and hp of bro, 3 Viscount; *b* 12 March 1964; *Style* - The Hon Graham Mackintosh

MACKINTOSH OF HALIFAX, Viscountess; Gwynneth Charlesworth; da of Charles Gledhill, of Halifax; *m* 1956, as his 2 w, 2 Viscount Mackintosh of Halifax, OBE, BEM (d 1980); 2 s (3 Viscount, Hon Graham Mackintosh); *Style* - Rt Hon Viscountess Mackintosh of Halifax; The Old Hall, Barford, Norwich (☎ Barnham Broom 271)

MACKINTOSH OF MACKINTOSH, The; Lt-Cdr Lachlan Ronald Duncan; OBE (1972), DL (Inverness-shire 1965), RN; 30 Chief of the Clan Mackintosh; s of Vice-Adm Lachlan Donald Mackintosh of Mackintosh, CB, DSO, DSC (d 1957); *b* 27 June 1928; *Educ* Elstree, RN Coll Dartmouth; *m* 1962, Mabel Cecilia Helen (Celia), da of Capt Hon John Bernard Bruce, RN (d 1971); 1 s, 3 da (1 decd); *Heir* s, John Lachlan, b 1969; *Career* Flag Lt to First Sea Lord 1951, specialised in communications 1954, served in HM Yacht Britannia 1957, ret 1963; chm Highland Exhibitions Ltd 1964-; v-pres Scottish Conservative and Unionist Assoc 1969-71; CC Inverness-shire 1970-75, V-Lt 1971-; *Clubs* Naval & Military; *Style* - The Mackintosh of Mackintosh OBE RN, HM Vice-Lieut for Inverness-shire, Moy Hall, Tomatin, Inverness-shire (☎ 211)

MACKINTOSH, (John) Malcolm; CMG (1975); s of Dr James Macalister Mackintosh, MD (d 1966); *b* 25 Dec 1921; *Educ* Mill Hill, Edinburgh Academy, Glasgow U; *m* 1946, Elena, da of late Capt Philip Grafov; 1 s, 1 da (and 1 s decd);

Career Lt British Army Allied Control Cmmn Bulgaria 1944-46; programme organiser BBC Overseas Service 1948-60; research offr FCO 1960-68; assist sec Cabinet Office 1968-; author; *Recreations* walking, climbing; *Clubs* Garrick; *Style* - Malcolm Mackintosh Esq, CMG; 21 Ravensdale ave, London N12 9HP (☎ 01 445 9714)

MACKLIN, Sir Bruce Roy; *Career* honoured for services to commerce, charity and cultural affairs in Australia; kt 1981; *Style* - Sir Bruce Macklin

MACKLIN, Lady; Lilian Margaret Herring; *m* 1972, as his 2 w, Sir (Albert) Sortain Romer Macklin (d 1976); *Style* - Lady Macklin; 32 St John's rd, Eastbourne, Sussex (☎ 31588)

McKNIGHT, David Lawrence; s of Richard McKnight; *b* 13 Sept 1933; *Educ* Wallace H S Lisburn, Queen's U Belfast; *m* 1974, Rosemary, da of Joseph Edward Wood; 4 s; *Career* md: T W Smith (Timber) Ltd and T W Smith (Cheltenham) Ltd 1976-, Hollis (Hull) Ltd 1978-, Hollis Bros Ltd 1980-; *Recreations* flying (light aircraft), photography, golf; *Clubs* Fulford Golf, Middleton St George Aero, RAC; *Style* - David McKnight Esq; 5 New Walk, Beverley, N Humberside (☎ 0482 862071)

MACKWORTH, Cdr Sir David Arthur Geoffrey; 9 Bt (GB 1776), RN (ret); s of Vice-Adm Geoffrey Mackworth, CMG, DSO (d 1952), 5 s of 6 Bt; suc nephew , sir Harry Llewellyn Mackworth, 8 Bt, CMG, DSO, 1952; *b* 13 July 1912; *Educ* Farnborough Sch Hants, RN Coll Dartmouth; *m* 1, 1941, Mary Alice (m dis 1971), da of late Harry Grylls; 1 s; m 2, 1973, Beryl Joan, formerly w of late E H Sparkes and da of late Pembroke Henry Cockayn Cross; *Heir* s, Digby John Mackworth; *Career* joined RN 1926, served 1939-45 in HMS 'Eagle' and HMS 'Suffolk', Cdr 1948; naval advr to dir of Guided Weapon Research and Development, Miny of Supply 1945-59, ret 1956; md South Coast Rod Rigging Co Ltd; *Clubs* Roy Naval (Portsmouth), Roy Ocean Racing and Roy Corinthian Yacht (Cowes), Roy Naval Sailing Assoc; *Style* - Cdr Sir David Mackworth, Bt, RN; 30 Wittering rd, Hayling Island, Hants

MACKWORTH, Digby John; s and h of Cdr Sir David Mackworth, 9 Bt, RN; *b* 2 Nov 1945; *Educ* Wellington; *m* 1971, Antoinette Francesca, da of Henry James McKenna, of Ilford, Essex; *Career* late Lt AAAC in Malaysia and Vietnam; with Iranian Helicopters Ltd; *Style* - Digby Mackworth Esq; PO Box 2898, Tehran, Iran

MACKWORTH-YOUNG, Lady Evelyn; *née* Leslie; da of 20 Earl of Rothes (d 1975); *b* 11 March 1929; *m* 1949, Gerard William Mackworth Mackworth-Young, *qv*, s of late Gerard Mackworth Mackworth-Young; *Style* - Lady Evelyn Mackworth-Young; 21 St Petersburgh pla, W2 (☎ 01 229 4270); Barrs Lodge, Taynuilt, Argyll

MACKWORTH-YOUNG, Gerard William; 2 s of Gerard Mackworth-Young (d 1965, gs of Sir George, 2 Bt); yr bro of Sir Robert Mackworth-Young, *qv*; also 2 cous of Sir George Young, 6 Bt and Parly Und-Sec DHSS; *b* 10 Oct 1926; *Educ* Eton; *m* 1949, Lady Evelyn, da of 20 Earl of Rothes (d 1975); 4 da; *Career* Lt Welsh Guards, ptnr Rowe & Pitman stockbrokers 1953-1973, v-chm Morgan Grenfell Holdings Ltd, dep chm and ch exec Morgan Grenfell & Co Ltd 1975-79, chm Morgan Grenfell & Co Ltd 1980-, dir Union Discount Co of London, Willis Faber Ltd, London Bd Halifax Building Soc, Lloyds Bank Ltd; chm: Industrial Development Advisory Bd 1980, Black Horse Life Assurance Co Ltd 1981; *Recreations* deerstalking; *Clubs* Boodle's, Pratt's, Union (Sydney); *Style* - Gerard Mackworth-Young Esq; 21 St Petersburgh pla, W2 (☎ 01 229 4270)

MACKWORTH-YOUNG, Sir Robin (Robert Christopher); KCVO (1975, CVO 1968, MVO 1961); s of Gerard Mackworth-Young, CIE (d 1965, s of Sir William Mackworth Young, KCSI, himself 3 s of Sir George Young, 2 Bt, by Susan, da of William Mackworth-Praed and sis of Winthrop M-P, the MP and poet); *b* 12 Feb 1920; *Educ* Eton, King's Cambridge; *m* 1953, Helen Rosemarie, da of Werner Charles Rudolf Aue (d 1978), of Menton, France; 1 s; *Career* served RAFVR as Sqdn Ldr UK, M East, Normandy; For Serv 1948-55, Dep Librarian Windsor Castle 1955-58, Librarian & Assist Keeper The Queen's Archives 1958-; *Recreations* music, skiing, electronics; *Clubs* Roxburghe; *Style* - Sir Robin Mackworth-Young, KCVO; Garden House, Windsor Castle, Berks

MACLACHLAN, George Styles Rome; s of S G Rome, of Bentfield, Gullane, East Lothian; *b* 1921; *Educ* Rugby, Cambridge U; *m* 1948, Marjorie Susan Mary Maclachlan of Maclachlan, Chief of the Clan of Maclachlan, da of (John) Maclachlan of Maclachlan, 23 of that Ilk (d 1942); 3 s, 3 da; *Career* served 1940-46 with Argyll and Sutherland Highlanders; assumed name of Maclachlan 1948; *Style* - George Maclachlan Esq; Castle Lachlan, Strathlachlan, Argyl (☎ Strachur 244)

MACLACHLAN OF MACLACHLAN, Madam; Marjorie Susan Mary; Lady of the Barony (territorial) Strathlachlan, Chief of the Clan of Machlachlan; da of John Maclachlan of Maclachlan, 23 of that Ilk (d 1942); *b* 1920; *m* 1948, George Styles Rome, *qv*; 3 s, 3 da; *Heir* s, Euan John, b 1949; *Style* - Madam Maclachlan of Maclachlan; Castle Lachlan, Strathlachlan, Argyll

McLACHLAN CLARK, Donald Mitchell; s of Thomas William Clark (d 1954); *b* 25 June 1928; *Educ* Dulwich Coll; *m* 1955, Jean Mary, nee Meredith; 1 s, 1 da; *Career* grain merchant and dir Henry W Peabody Grain Ltd 1962-, dir Baltic Mercantile & Shipping Exchange 1979-, pres Grain & Feed Trade Assoc 1978-79; *Recreations* golf, walking; *Clubs* Caledonian, North Downs Golf; *Style* - Donald McLachlan Clark Esq; Toby Cottage, Bough Beech, nr Edenbridge, Kent (☎ Four Elms 233)

McLAGGAN, Lady; Elsa Violet; da of William E Adams; *m* 1928, Sir (John) Douglas McLaggan, KCVO (d 1967); *Style* - Lady McLaggan; Daws Wood, Frensham, Surrey

McLAREN, Hon Caroline Mary; da of 3 Baron Aberconway; *b* 1944; *Style* - The Hon Caroline McLaren

McLAREN, Hon Christopher Melville; s of 2 Baron Aberconway, CBE (d 1953); *b* 1934; *Educ* Eton, King's Cambridge; *m* 1973, Jane Elizabeth, da of James Barrie; 1 s, 1 da; *Career* business consultant; *Recreations* local politics, gardening, walking; *Style* - The Hon Christopher McLaren; 31 Upper Addison Gdns, W14

MACLAREN, Derek Anthony Ewen; s of late John Ewen Maclaren; *b* 19 Jan 1925; *Educ* Cranbrook (Sydney Australia), Sydney U; *m* 1951, Pamela Ann, da of Harold Miller; 2 s, 1 da; *Career* FIMC; dir PA Int Management Consultants 1971, chairman PA Computers and Telecommunications 1976, memb CSERB 1976-78, Computing Servs Assoc Cncl 1975-76; *Recreations* history, architecture, skiing; *Clubs* Hurlingham; *Style* - Derek Maclaren Esq; The Manor House, West Coker, Somerset; 2 Westminster gdns, Marsham st, SW1 (☎ 01 828 3552)

MacLAREN OF MacLAREN, The; Donald MacLaren of MacLaren and Achleskine; s of late Donald MacLaren of MacLaren; suc his father 1966 as Chief of Clan Labhran; *b* 1954; *m* 1978, Maida Jane, da of late Robert Paton Aitchison; *Heiress* half-sis, Veronica Barbara Allen; *Style* - The MacLaren of MacLaren; Flat 7, 75 Harrington gdns, SW7

MACLAREN, Lady Edith Huddleston Griffiths; da of Countess of Loudoun (d 1960); co-heiress to the Baronies of Botreaux, Stanley and Hastings; *b* 1925; *m* 1947, Maj David Kenneth Maclaren; 2 s; *Style* - Lady Edith Maclaren

McLAREN, Hon Henry Charles; s and h of 3 Baron Aberconway; *b* 26 May 1948; *Educ* Eton; *Style* - The Hon Henry McLaren

McLAREN, Ian Francis; OBE (1959); s of Alexander Morrison McLaren (d 1951); *b* 30 March 1912; *Educ* Melbourne U; *m* 1941, Eileen Adele, da of John Henry Porter (d 1971); 3 s, 1 da; *Career* Lt RANVR (New Guinea and Philippines); chartered accountant 1945-; MP Victorian

Parliament 1945-47 and 1965-79, dep speaker 1964-69; *Style* - Ian McLaren Esq, OBE; 237 Waverley rd, East Malvern, Victoria 3145, Australia (☎ 01 211 6897)

McLAREN, Hon Julia Harriet; da of 3 Baron Aberconway; *b* 22 Sept 1942; *Style* - The Hon Julia McLaren

McLAREN, Hon Michael Duncan; s of 3 Baron Aberconway; *b* 29 Nov 1958; *Educ* Eton, Christ's Cambridge; *Career* reading for Bar; *Recreations* skiing, shooting; *Style* - The Hon Michael McLaren; 25 Egerton ter, SW3 (☎ 01 589 4369)

McLAREN, Hon Mrs; Hon Rosemary Jean; da of 2 Baron Kinross, KC; *b* 1910; *m* 1, 1934, Alec M Mitchell (m dis 1958); 1 s, 3 da; m 2, 1958, Robert Monteath McLaren (d 1969); *Style* - The Hon Mrs McLaren; 7B Gloucester sq, Edinburgh EH3

McLAREN, Lady Rose Mary Primrose *née* Paget; da of 6 Marquess of Anglesey, GCVO (d 1947); *b* 1919; *m* 1940, Hon John McLaren (d 1953, s of 2 Baron Aberconway); 2 da; *Style* - Lady Rose McLaren; Old Bodnod, Tal-y-Cafn, Denbighshire (☎ Tyn-Groes 251)

MACLAY, 3 Baron (UK 1922); Sir Joseph Paton Maclay; 3 Bt (UK 1914); s of 2 Baron Maclay, KBE (d 1969); *b* 11 April 1942; *Educ* Winchester; *m* 1976, Elizabeth, da of George Buchanan, of Pokataroo, NSW; 1 s, 1 da; *Heir* s, Hon Joseph Maclay; *Career* md Denholm Maclay Ltd, Triport Ferries Management, Denholm Maclay Offshore Ltd; dir Milton Shipping, Br Steamship Short Trades Assoc, N of Eng Protection & Indemnity Assoc 1976-; *Recreations* gardening, fishing; *Clubs* Western; *Style* - The Rt Hon Lord Maclay; Duchal, Kilmacolm, Renfrewshire (☎ 2255)

MACLAY, Hon Angus Grenfell; s of 2 Baron Maclay, KBE (d 1969); *b* 11 Aug 1945; *Educ* Winchester, Royal Agricultural Coll Cirencester; *m* 1970, Hon Elizabeth Victoria Baillie, da of 3 Baron Burton; 1 s, 1 da; *Recreations* shooting, skiing; *Style* - The Hon Angus Maclay; Westruther Mains, Gordon, Berwickshire (☎ 207)

MACLAY, Hon David Milton; s of 2 Baron Maclay, KBE (d 1969); *b* 1944; *Educ* Winchester; *m* 1968, Valerie, da of late Lt-Cdr J P Fyfe, of Kinkell, St Andrews, Fife; 1 s; *Style* - The Hon David Maclay; 12 Langton st, SW10

MACLAY, Hon Mrs; Hon Elizabeth Victoria; *née* Baillie; da of 3 Baron Burton; *b* 24 March 1950; *Educ* West Heath, Edinburgh U; *m* 1970, Hon Angus Grenfell Maclay, 2 s of 2 Baron Maclay; 1 s, 1 da; *Style* - The Hon Mrs Maclay; Westruther Mains, Gordon, Berwickshire (☎ Westruther 207)

MACLAY, Hon Joseph Paton; s and h of 3 Baron Maclay; *b* 6 March 1977; *Style* - The Hon Joseph Maclay

MACLAY, Nancy, Baroness; Nancy Margaret; da of Robert C Greig, of Hall of Caldwell, Uplawmoor, Renfrewshire; *m* 1936, 2 Baron Maclay, KBE (d 1969); 3 s, 2 da; *Style* - The Rt Hon Nancy, Lady Maclay; Milton, Kilmacolm, Renfrewshire (☎ 2255)

MACLAY, Hon Mrs Walter - Dorothy; da of late William Lennox, WS; *m* Hon Walter Symington Maclay, CB, OBE, MD (d 1964); 3 s, 2 da; *Style* - The Hon Mrs Walter Maclay; 40 Kensington sq, W8

MACLEAN, Baron (Life Peer UK 1971); Sir Charles Hector Fitzroy Maclean; 11 Bt (NS 1631), KT (1969), GCVO (1971), KBE (1967), PC (1971), JP (Argyll 1955); also 27 Chief of Clan Maclean; 2 but only surviving s of Maj Hector Fitzroy Maclean, Scots Gds, himself eldest s of Sir Fitzroy Maclean, 10 Bt, KCB, JP, DL (d 1936, ggs through his mother's f of 2 Baron Romney); *b* 5 May 1916; *Educ* Canford Sch Wimborne; *m* 1941, Elizabeth, da of Frank Mann, of Wilts; 1 s, 1 da; *Heir* (to Btcy only) s, Hon Lachlan Maclean; *Career* Lord Chamberlain of HM Household 1971-, Chllr Roy Victorian Order 1971-, Ld-Lt Argyll 1954-, Lt Roy Co Archers (Queen's Bodyguard for Scotland); served WW II Maj Scots Gds; Pres Argyll T & AFA, Convenor Standing Cncl Scottish Chiefs;

memb Cncl RZS, memb Roy Ag Soc England; former Ch Scout C'wlth; patron of various charities; *Clubs* Puffin's, Pratt's, Cavalry & Guards, Roy Highland Yacht (Oban), Roy C'wlth Soc (memb Cncl); *Style* - The Rt Hon Lord Maclean KT GCVO KBE PC JP, HM Lord-Lieut for Argyll; Duart Castle, Isle of Mull (☎ Craignure 309); St James's Palace, SW1 (☎ 01 930 4010)

MACLEAN, Charles Edward; s and h of Sir Fitzroy Hew Royle Maclean, 1 Bt, CBE; *b* 31 Oct 1946; *Educ* Eton, New Coll Oxford; *Style* - Charles Maclean Esq

MACLEAN, Donald Buchanan; s of Donald Maclean, MBE (d 1949); *b* 3 Feb 1924; *Educ* Queen's Park Glasgow; *m* 1954, Isabella Forrester, da of Sir John Henderson; *Career* CA, fin dir H D Symons & Co Ltd 1966-; *Recreations* golf, bridge, reading; *Clubs* Inst of Dirs; *Style* - Donald Maclean Esq; Dolphin Den, Den Close, Beckenham, Kent

MACLEAN, Sir Fitzroy Hew Royle; 1 Bt (UK 1957), CBE (1944); s of Maj Charles Maclean, DSO (whose paternal grandmother was Elizabeth, ggda of 5 Duke of Beaufort, while his paternal great grandmother was da of 2 Earl of Hopetoun); *b* 11 March 1911; *Educ* Eton, King's Cambridge; *m* 1946, Hon Veronica, nee Fraser, 2 da of 14 Lord Lovat and widow of Lt Alan Phipps (gggs of 1 Earl of Mulgrave, f of 1 Marquess of Normanby); 2 s; *Heir* s, Charles Maclean; *Career* Brig Cmmdg Br Mil Mission to Yugoslav Partisans 1943-45; has Order of Kutuzov (USSR), Partisan Star 1 Class (Yugoslavia); late For Serv & SAS; MP (C) Lancaster 1941-59, Bute & N Ayrshire 1959-74; Parly Under-Sec & Fin Sec War Off 1954-57; *Clubs* White's, Pratt's, Puffin's, New (latter two Edinburgh); *Style* - Sir Fitzroy Maclean, Bt, CBE; Strachur House, Strachur, Argyll (☎ 036986 242)

MACLEAN, Ian Albert Druce; s of Alec Henry Herbert Maclean (d 1947); *b* 23 June 1902; *Educ* Marlborough, Pembroke Cambridge; *m* 1, Diana Futvoye (decd), da of John Bertram Marsden Smedley (d 1959); 2 s; m 2, Margaret Heather, da of Andrew Ronald Mackenzie (d 1964); *Career* chm Halifax Bldg Soc 1962-75; dir Halifax Bldg Soc 1953-77; dir Barclays Bank and other cos; chm John Smedley Ltd 1959-81; *Recreations* yachting (yacht: 'Ethie 11'); *Clubs* Roy Southern Yacht, Roy Windemere, Lansdowne; *Style* - Ian Maclean Esq; Bay Trees, River Green, Hamble, Hampshire

McLEAN, Ivor Drury; s of the late George McLean; *b* 4 Aug 1921; *Educ* St Paul's; *m* 1964, Jacqueline Ann, nee Binns; 1 s; *Career* Major Middlesex Regt 1940-46, fellow of Inst Chartered Accountants in England and Wales 1948, dir Mallinson-Denny Ltd 1975-; *Style* - Ivor McLean Esq; Harewood Cottage, Kingston Vale, London SW15

MACLEAN, Lowry Druce; s of Ian Albert Druce Maclean; *b* 22 July 1939; *Educ* Eton, Pembroke Cambridge; *m* 1967, Anne Francis, da of Henry Crawford, of USA; 2 s, 1 da; *Career* gp ch exec Tomkinsons Ltd 1979-, dir John Crossley & Sons Ltd 1972-79, dir Karastan Inc 1970-72; *Recreations* entertaining my wife, business schools, (yacht 'Ethie II'); *Clubs* Lansdowne House; *Style* - Lowry Maclean Esq; The Pound, Old Colwall, Gt Malvern, Worcs (☎ 0684 40426)

MACLEAN, Maj Hon Lachlan Hector Charles; s & h (to Btcy only) of Baron Maclean, KT, GCVO, KBE (Life Peer); *b* 25 Aug 1942; *Educ* Eton; *m* 1966, Mary Helen, da of William Gordon Gordon, of Lude, Blair Atholl, Perthshire; 2 s, 2 da (1 decd); *Career* Maj Scots Gds; *Style* - Maj the Hon Lachlan Maclean; Arngask House, Glenfarg, Perthshire

McLEAN, Lt-Col Neil Loudon Desmond; DSO (1943); s of Neil McLean (d 1964); *b* 28 Nov 1918; *Educ* Eton, RMC Sandhurst; *m* 1949, Daška Maria, da of Dr Ivan Richard Ivanovič (memb of Croat Parl 1905-1918 and memb Nat Assembly of Serbs, Croats and Slovenes 1918, d 1949); *Career* 1938 2 Lt Royal Scots Greys, 1938-39 Palestine Campaign, 1939-45 Mid East & Far East (1944 Cdr first mil mission to Albania), 1943 Lt-Col, 1954-64 MP (C) Inverness - Ross & Cromarty, 1954-64 memb Highlands & Islands Advisory Panel, 1964- freelance journalist and lecturer; member Royal Co of Archers (Queen's Bodyguard for Scotland); *Recreations* travel, shooting, underwater fishing; *Clubs* White's, Guards and Cavalry, Buck's, Pratt's, Highland (Inverness), Beefsteak, Shikar; *Style* - Lt-Col Neil McLean DSO; 17 Eaton sq, SW1

MACLEAN, Sir Robert Alexander; KBE (1973), DL (Renfrewshire 1970); s of Andrew Johnston Maclean, JP (d 1924); *b* 11 Apr 1908; *Educ* Glasgow H S; *m* 1938, Vivienne Neville, da of Capt Bertram Walter Bourke, JP (ka 1915) and half-sis of Eileen, Countess of Mount Charles; 2 s, 2 da; *Career* chm Scottish Ctee Council of Industrial Design 1949-58, regional controller (Scot) Bd of Trade 1944-46, dir Nat Freight Corpn 1969-72, memb Export Council for Europe 1960-64, memb British Nat Export Ctee 1966-70, chm Scottish Industrial Estates Corpn 1955-72, chm Scottish Exports Ctee, pres Glasgow Chamber of Commerce 1956-58, chm Council of Scottish Chambers of Commerce 1960-62, pres Assoc of British Chamber of Commerce 1966-68, dir Norwich Union Insurance Gp, chm Stoddard Holdings Ltd, & associated cos; kt 1955; *Recreations* golf, fishiing; *Clubs* Carlton; *Style* - Sir Robert Maclean, KBE, DL; Woodend House, Houston, Renfrewshire

MACLEAN, Hon Mrs; Hon Sarah Elizabeth Cameron; da of 3 Baron Rowallan; *b* 1949; *m* 1968, (Lachlan) Roderick Maclean; 2 da; *Style* - The Hon Mrs Maclean; Erland House, Crondall, Surrey

MACLEAN, Lady Sarah Elizabeth Jane; *née* Finch-Knightley; da of 11 Earl of Aylesford; *b* 14 July 1950; *Educ* Abbot's Hill Hemel Hempstead; *m* 1974, Angus Nigel Garnet, s of Maj Lachlan Gordon Maclean, MC, 11 of Hynish; 2 s (Angus Charles, Ian Andrew); *Style* - Lady Sarah Maclean; c/o Child & Co, Fleet st, EC4

MACLEAN, Hon Lady; Hon Veronica Nell; da of 15 Lord Lovat (17 but for the attainder) KT, GCVO, KCMG, CB, DSO, TD (d 1933); *b* 1920; *m* 1, 1940, Lieut Alan Phipps, RN (d 1943); 1 s, 1 da; m 2, 1946, Brig Sir Fitzroy Hew Royle Maclean, Bt, CBE, MP; 2 s; *Style* - The Hon Lady Maclean; Strachur House, Argyll

McLEAVY, Hon Frank Waring; s of Baron McLeavy (Life Peer); *b* 1925; *Educ* Wirral G S, Liverpool U, Leeds U; *m* 1954, Verena, da of Emil Lüsher, of Unterkulm, Switzerland; *Career* headmaster of Clayton Junior H S Bradford Yorks; *Style* - The Hon Frank McLeavy; 23 West End Rise, Horsforth, Leeds

McLEAVY, Hon Mrs Douglas; Janet Elizabeth; da of Harry Ogden; *b* 14 Jan 1934; *Educ* Bingley G S, St Osyth's Coll; *m* 1958, Hon Douglas John McLeavy (d 1969), s of Baron McLeavy (Life Peer, d 1975); 1 s (Mark b 1969), 1 da (Ruth b 1964); *Career* school mistress; *Style* - The Hon Mrs Douglas McLeavy; 40 Ruskin Drive, Morecambe, Lancs

McLEAVY, Baroness; Mary; da of late George Waring, of Rock Ferry, Birkenhead; *m* 1924, Baron McLeavy (Life Peer) (d 1976); *Style* - The Rt Hon The Lady McLeavy; 9 Sheridan ter, Whitton Av West, Northolt, Middx

MacLELLAN, Kenneth; s of the late Peter MacLellan, JP; *b* 8 Dec 1889; *Educ* Clifton Coll; *m* 1914, Rachel Madeleine, nee Withy; 4 s; *Career* rubber manufacturer, also rubber plantation director; *Recreations* rugby at school, golf; *Clubs* New (Glasgow); *Style* - Kenneth MacLellan Esq; Harwood, 9 Upper Glenburn rd, Bearsden, Glasgow

MacLENNAN, Ronald George MacLennan of MacLennan; Chief of Clan MacLennan; *b* 1925; *Educ* Boroughmuir and Copenhagen; *Heir* s, Ruairich Donald George; *Career* lecturer and teacher Roy H S Edinburgh 1949-51; Sch of Physiotherapy Glasgow 1952-54 and Coll of Physical Education Fredensborg Denmark 1955-56; recognised as Chief of Clan MacLennan by Lord Lyon 1978; *Style* - Ronald MacLennan of MacLennan; Clachan, Lochbroom, Ullapool, Ross-shire

MACLEOD OF BORVE, Baroness (Life Peeress UK 1971); Evelyn Hester; *née* Blois; JP (Middx 1955), DL (Gter London 1977); da of Rev Gervase Vanneck Blois (d 1916, yst s of Sir John Blois, 8 Bt, DL) and Hon Hester Pakington, da of 3 Baron Hampton; *b* 19 Feb 1915; *Educ* Lawnside Gt Malvern; *m* 1, 1937, Mervyn (k by enemy action 1940), s of Alwyne Humfrey-Mason, JP, formerly of Foxley Manor Malmesbury and Necton Hall Norfolk; m 2, 1941, Rt Hon Iain Macleod, PC, MP (d 1970), s of Dr Norman Macleod, of Isle of Lewis; 1 s, 1 da; *Career* memb IBA 1972-76, chm Nat Gas Consumers Cncl 1972-77, Nat Assoc Leagues Hosp Friends 1976-; Gov Queenswood Sch 1977-; Pres Nat Assoc of Widows 1976-; *Recreations* family, music; *Style* - Rt Hon Lady Macleod of Borve JP DL; Luckings Farm, Coleshill, Amersham, Bucks (☎ 5158)

MacLEOD OF FUINARY, Baron (Life Peer UK 1967); Very Rev Sir George Fielden MacLeod; 4 Bt (UK 1924), MC (1917); 2 s of Sir John MacLeod, 1 Bt, JP, DL, sometime MP Glasgow Centl & Glasgow Kelvingrove (d 1934); suc n, 3 Bt, 1944; *b* 17 June 1895; *Educ* Winchester, Oriel Oxford; *m* 1948, Lorna Helen Janet, da of Rev Donald MacLeod, of Balvonie of Inshes, Inverness; 2 s, 1 da; *Heir* (to Btcy only) s, Hon John Maxwell Norman MacLeod; *Career* DD; served in 1914-18 War, Capt 1917; Min of St Cuthbert's Edinburgh 1926-30 and of Govan Old Parish Church 1930-38, leader of Iona Community 1938-67; select preacher Cambridge U 1943 and 1963; chaplain to HM the Queen in Scotland 1956-65, extra chaplain 1965-; moderator of Gen Assembly Church of Scotland 1957-58; *Style* - The Rt Hon Lord MacLeod of Fuinary MC; 23 Learmonth ter, Edinburgh EH4 1PG (☎ 031 332 3262)

McLEOD, Sir Charles Henry; 3 Bt (UK 1925), of the Fairfields, Cobham, Surrey; s of Sir Murdoch Campbell McLeod, 2 Bt (d 1950); *b* 7 Nov 1924; *Educ* Winchester; *m* 1957, Anne Gillian (d 1978), da of Henry Bowlby, of London; 1 s, 2 da; *Heir* s, James Roderick Charles McLeod; *Clubs* Brooks's; *Style* - Sir Charles McLeod, Bt; Gilhams House, Lynchmere, Haslemere, Surrey

MacLEOD, Hon Eva Mary Ellen; da of Baron MacLeod of Fuinary, MC (Life Peer); *b* 1950; *Style* - The Hon Eva MacLeod; 23 Learmonth ter, Edinburgh 4

MacLEOD OF MacLEOD, John MacLeod of MacLeod; s of late Capt Robert Wolridge-Gordon, MC; suc grandmother Dame Flora MacLeod of MacLeod, DBE, 1976, as Chief of Clan MacLeod; *b* 1935; *Educ* Eton; *m* 1, 1961, Drusilla Mary, da of Sebastian Shaw; m 2, 1973, Melita, da of Duke Kolin, of Sofia, Bulgaria; children; *Heir* s, Hugh Magnus, b 1973; officially recognised in the name of Macleod of MacLeod, Younger, by decree of Lyon Court 1951; *Style* - John MacLeod of MacLeod; Dunvegan Castle, Isle of Skye

MacLEOD, Hon John Maxwell Norman; s of Baron MacLeod of Fuinary, MC (Life Peer); h to Btcy of MacLeod, (cr 1924); *b* 23 Feb 1952; *Educ* Gordonstoun; *Style* - The Hon John MacLeod

McLEOD, James Roderick Charles; s and h of Sir Charles Henry McLeod, 3 Bt; *b* 26 Sept 1946; *Style* - James McLeod Esq

MacLEOD, Hon Neil David; s of Baron MacLeod of Fuinary, MC (Life Peer); *b* 1959; *Style* - The Hon Neil MacLeod

McLEOD, Robert; s of Robert Frew McLeod (d 1973); *b* 1 Oct 1928; *Educ* Alloa Academy & Royal Tech College (Glasgow); *m* 1954, Agnes Myrtle; 1 s, 1 da; *Career* dep chm Scottish Bus Group 1979-; *Recreations* gardening, travel, golf; *Style* - Robert McLeod Esq; Rozelle, 4 Briarhill av, Dalgety Bay, Fife KY11 5UR

MACLEOD, Hon Torquil Anthony Ross; s of Baroness Macleod of Borve; *b* 1942; *Educ* Harrow; *m* 1967, (Elizabeth) Meriol (m dis 1973), da of Brig Arthur Pelham Trevor, DSO; 1 s; *Style* - The Hon Torquil Macleod

McLINTOCK, Hon Mrs (Carla Ann); da of Baron Hill-Norton, GCB (Life Peer); *m* 1, 1966, Christopher Thomas Jowett; m

2, 1973, Graeme McLintock; *Style* - The Hon Mrs McLintock; 34 Ebury Mews, SW1

McLINTOCK, Charles Alan; s of Charles Henry McLintock (d 1947); *b* 28 May 1925; *Educ* Rugby; *m* 1955, Sylvia Mary, nee Taylor; 1 s, 3 da; *Career* CA, ptnr Thomson McLintock & Co 1954-, dep chm Ecclesiastical Insurance Office Ltd, dep chm Woolwich Equitable Building Soc, chm Stockholders Investment Trust Ltd and others, dir Nat West Bank Ltd and others, governing body memb Rugby Sch; *Recreations* music, family life; *Style* - Charles McLintock Esq; Burford House, Kingswood, Surrey (☎ 073 783 2447); Little Cottage, Oddington, Stow-on-the Wold, Glos (☎ 30404)

McLINTOCK, David; *Career* dir The Appleyard Gp of Cos; *Style* David McLintock Esq; Appleyard Ltd, 47 Kirklee rd, Glasgow 12

McLINTOCK, Jean, Lady; Jean; da of late Robert Traven Donaldson Aitken, of Newcastle, New Brunswick, Canada; *m* 1929, Sir Thomson McLintock, 2 Bt (d 1953); *Style* - Jean, Lady McLintock; 10 Avenue ct, Draycott ave, SW3

McLINTOCK, Michael William; s and h of Sir William Traven McLintock, 3 Bt; *b* 13 Aug 1958; *Style* - Michael McLintock Esq

McLINTOCK, Sir William Traven; 3 Bt (UK 1934), of Sanquhar, Co Dumfries; s of Sir Thomson McLintock, 2 Bt (d 1953); *b* 4 Jan 1931; *Educ* Harrow; *m* 1, 1952 (m dis), André, da of Richard Lonsdale-Hands, of Lausanne; 3 s; m 2, Heather Homfray-Davies*Heir* s, Michael William McLintock; *Style* - Sir William McLintock, Bt; Villa Kavalliori, St Andrews rd, Swiegi, Malta, GC

McLOUGHLIN, Donald; OBE (1977); s of James Archibald McLoughlin (d 1951); *b* 13 March 1926; *Educ* Perth Modern Sch W Australia, U of W Australia; *m* 1960, Elizabeth Anne, da of Philip Hagan; 1 s (decd), 7 da; *Career* Flight Lt RAAF Australia and Pacific Ocean; private legal practice W A 1951-56; magistrate Fiji 1956-63; slr-gen Fiji 1963-71, legal consultant Fiji 1971-80, Papua New Guinea 1972-75; legal advr to Govr of Pitcairn Island Colony 1964-80; *Recreations* swimming, fishing, boating; *Clubs* Swan Yacht Club (Fremantle W A); *Style* - Donald McLoughlin Esq, OBE; 8 James rd, Swanbourne, W Australia 6010 (☎ 09 384 7042)

MACLURE, Elspeth, Lady; Elspeth King; da of Alexander King Clark, of Wykeham Hatch, W Byfleet (1 cous of Sir George Clark, 1 Bt); *b* 1908; *m* 1929, Sir John Maclure, 3 Bt, OBE (d 1980); 2 s (Sir John Maclure, 4 Bt; Patrick Maclure), 1 da (Mrs (Elspeth) Michael Matthews); *Style* - Elspeth, Lady Maclure; Flat 2, 25 Christchurch rd, Winchester, Hants (☎ 0962 4147)

MACLURE, John Mark; s and h of Sir John Maclure, 4 Bt; *b* 27 Aug 1965; *Style* - John Maclure Esq

MACLURE, Sir John Robert Spencer; 4 Bt (UK 1898), of The Home, Whalley Range, near Manchester, Co Palatine of Lancaster; s of Lt-Col Sir John Maclure, 3 Bt, OBE (d 1980), and Elspeth, Lady Maclure, *qv*; *b* 12 March 1934; *Educ* Winchester; *m* 1964, Jane, da of Rt Rev Thomas Savage, Bishop of Zululand & Swaziland; 4 s; *Heir* s, John Mark Maclure (b 27 Aug 1965); *Career* Headmaster Croftinloan Sch 1978-, previously with KRRC as 2 Lt 2 Bn, BAOR 1953-55, Lt Roy Hants Airborne Regt TA; assist master Horris Hill 1955-66 & 1974-78, teacher in NZ, and at St Edmund's Hindhead 1971-74; *Style* - Sir John Maclure, Bt; Croftinloan School, Pitlochry, Perthshire (☎ 2837)

McMAHON, Sir Brian Patrick; 8 Bt (UK 1817); s of Sir (William) Patrick McMahon, 7 Bt (d 1977); *b* 9 June 1942; *Educ* Wellington, Wednesbury Tech Coll (BSc, AIM); *Heir* bro, Shaun Desmond McMahon; *Style* - Sir Brian McMahon, Bt; 1 Draycot rd, Chiseldon, Wilts

McMAHON, Stella, Lady; Ruth Stella; da of late Maj Percy Robert Kenyon-

Slaney; *m* 1, 1928 (m dis 1939), Lt-Cdr John Francis Crofton Barker Hahlo, RN (d 1941); m 2, 1939, Sir (William) Patrick McMahon, 7 Bt (d 1977); *Style* - Stella, Lady McMahon; 2 Townlands, Willand Old Village, Cullompton, Devon

McMAHON, Shaun Desmond; s of Sir (William) Patrick McMahon, 7 Bt (d 1977); h to Btcy of bro, Sir Brian Patrick McMahon, 8 Bt; *b* 29 Oct 1945; *Educ* Wellington Coll; *m* 1971, Antonia Noel, da of Antony James Adie, of Rowington, Warwicks; *Style* - Shaun McMahon Esq; 28 Mathew rd, Claremont, Cape Town, S Africa

MacMANUS, Hon Mrs (Emma Mary); *née* Soames; da of Baron Soames, GCMG, GCVO, CH, CBE, PC, *qv*; *b* 1949; *m* 1981, James, s of Dr Niall MacManus, of Warwick sq, SW1; *Career* journalist New (formerly Evening) Standard; *Style* - The Hon Mrs MacManus; c/o New Standard, Fleet st, EC4 (☎ 01 353 8000)

McMICHAEL, Hon Mrs; Hon Paquita Mary Joanna; da of Baron Florey (Life Peer) (d 1968); *b* 1929; *m* 1955, John McMichael; *Style* - The Hon Mrs McMichael; 90 Inverleith pla, Edinburgh EH3

MACMILLAN, Alexander Daniel Alan; s of Rt Hon Maurice Victor Macmillan, PC, MP and Hon Dame Katherine, DBE, former owner of Highgrove, now the residence of HRH The Prince of Wales; also gs of Rt Hon Harold Macmillan, PM 1956-63, and Lady Dorothy, nee Cavendish, da of 9 Duke of Devonshire; *b* 10 Oct 1943; *Educ* Eton, Ecole Politique U de Paris, Strathclyde U; *m* 1970, Hélène Birgitte, nee Hamilton; 1 s (Daniel Maurice Alan b 1974), 1 da (Rebecca Elizabeth b 1980); *Career* book and magazine publisher, chm Macmillan Publishing Ltd 1980-, 1965-66 journalist Glasgow Herald, 1967 reporter Daily Telegraph, 1968-69 foreign correspondent Daily Telegraph, 1969-70 ch European correspondent Sunday Telegraph, 1972-80 dep chm Macmillan Ltd, 1979- govr Archbishop Tenison's G S, 1980- govr Merchant Taylor's Sch, 1978- govr English Speaking Union; *Recreations* shooting, fishing, photography, conversation; *Clubs* Beefsteak, Buck's, Carlton, RYA; *Style* - Alexander Macmillan Esq; 51 Chelsea sq, SW3 (☎ 01 352 7596), Pooks, Chelwood Gate, nr Haywards Heath, Sussex (☎ 082 574 554)

MACMILLAN, Hon Dame Katharine Margaret Alice; *née* Ormsby-Gore; DBE (1974); da of 4 Baron Harlech, KG, GCMG, PC (d 1964); *b* 4 Jan 1921; *m* 1942, Rt Hon Maurice Victor Macmillan, PC, MP; *Career* v-chm Conservative Party 1968-71; *Style* - The Hon Dame Katharine Macmillan DBE; 9 Warwick sq, SW1 (☎ 01 834 6004)

MACMILLAN, Robert Hugh; s of Hugh Robert Munro Macmillan (d 1934); *b* 27 June 1921; *Educ* Felsted Sch, Emmanuel Cambridge; *m* 1950, Anna Christina, da of Christian Roding, of Amsterdam (d 1935); 3 da; *Career* Flight Lt 1945; chartered engineer, Prof of Mechanical Engineering U of Wales 1956, dir Motor Industry Research Assoc 1964, prof of Vehicle Design Cranford Inst of Technol 1977; *Recreations* music, painting, philately; *Clubs* RAF; *Style* - Robert Macmillan Esq; 18 The Mount, Aspley Guise, Beds (☎ 0908 584011)

McMULLEN, Robert Peter; DSO (1944) and Bar (1945), MBE (1938), TD, DL (Herts 1959); s of Lt-Col O R McMullen, CMG, TD, DL (d 1946), of Presdales Hall, Ware, Herts; *b* 1914; *Educ* Rugby; *m* 1939, Rosemary Hazel Wodehouse, da of Robert Montgomery Burch Parker (d 1941); 2 s, 1 da; *Career* 2 Lt Hertfordshire Regt 1932, Capt 1938, served 1939-45 Special Forces, Lt-Col 1943; JP Herts 1948-70; High Sheriff Herts 1955; chm McMullen & Sons Ltd; *Recreations* fishing; *Clubs* Special Forces *Style* - Robert McMullen Esq, DSO* MBE TD DL; Westmillbury Wing, Westmill, Buntingford, Herts (☎ Royston 72903)

McMURTRIE, Robert Peter Lax; VRD; s of Donald Scott Anderson McMurtrie; *b* 24 March 1926; *Educ* Marlborough Coll, St John's Cambridge; *m* 1953, Margaret Jane, da of Lancelot

Edwin Lax Wright; 3 da; *Career* Lt-Cdr with RN Volunteer Res 1943-46; dir: Plantation Hldgs 1978-79, Phicom Ltd 1979-; md: Fractional HP Motors Ltd 1964-67, Hills (Patents) Ltd 1967-74, Southern Instrument Hldgs 1974-76, Consumer & Video Hldgs Ltd 1976-78; chm: Imhof-Bedco Special Products Ltd 1976-, I-B Precision Engrg Ltd, Skinners (Electro-Platers) Ltd, and I-B Gerard SA (France) 1978-; *Recreations* shooting, gardening, countryside; *Clubs* Naval; *Style* - Robert McMurtrie Esq, VRD; St Ibbs Bush, nr Hitchin, Herts

MACNAB OF MACNAB, Hon Mrs (Diana Mary); *née* Anstruther-Gray; da of Baron Kilmany, MC, PC, DL; *b* 16 June 1936; *m* 1959, James Macnab, yr of Macnab (now The Macnab, *qv*); 2 s, 2 da; *Style* - The Hon Mrs Macnab of Macnab; Finlarig, Killin, Perthshire (☎ 259)

MACNAB, Hon Mrs; Hon Elisabeth Jocelyn; da of Baron Arwyn (Life Peer) (d 1978); *b* 1938; *m* 1962, John Robb Macnab; 1 s, 1 da; *Style* - The Hon Mrs Macnab; 186 Sedlescombe rd North, St Leonards-on-Sea, E Sussex

MACNAB, The; James Charles Macnab of Macnab; JP (Stirling); 23 Chief of Clan Macnab; s of Lt-Col James Alexander Macnab, MBE, of Bramerton st, Chelsea; suc great unc, Archibald Macnab of Macnab, CIE (to whom Col Macnab had previously made over his rights); *b* 14 April 1926; *Educ* Radley, Ashbury Coll Ottawa; *m* 1959, Hon Diana (*see* Hon Mrs Macnab of Macnab); 2 s, 2 da; *Heir* s, James Macnab of Macnab, yr (b 22 March 1963); *Career* late CCllr Perth, formerly served as Lt Seaforth Highlanders, and RAF and Scots Gds; Offr with Malayan Police 1948-57; memb Roy Co of Archers (Queen's Bodyguard for Scotland); memb Centl Regional Cncl 1978; *Clubs* New, Puffin's (Edinburgh); *Style* - The Macnab, JP; Finlarig, Killin, Perthshire (☎ 259)

MACNAB, Hon Mrs; Hon Sarah Margaret; da of 10 Lord Polwarth, TD; *b* 1944; *m* 1977, John Alexander Hamish Macnab; 1 da; *Style* - The Hon Mrs Macnab; c/o Bank of Scotland, 16/13 Piccadilly, W1

MACNAGHTEN, Magdalene, Lady; Magdalene; da of late Edmund Fisher; *m* 1926, Sir Antony Macnaghten, 10 Bt (d 1972); *Style* - Magdalene, Lady Macnaghten; Dundarave, Bushmills, Co Antrim

MACNAGHTEN, Sir Patrick (Alexander); 11 Bt (UK 1836), of Bushmills House, Co Antrim; s of Sir Antony Macnaghten, 10 Bt (d 1972); *b* 24 Jan 1927; *Educ* Eton, Trin Cambridge; *m* 1955, Marianne, da of Dr Eric Schaefer, of Cambridge; 3 s; *Heir* s, Malcolm Francis Macnaghten; *Career* project man Cadbury Schweppes Foods Ltd; *Style* - Sir Patrick Macnaghten, Bt; Dundarave, Bushmills, Co Antrim, NI; Crofton Crest, Cherry Hill dve, Barnt Green, Birmingham B45 8JY (☎ 021 445 2341)

MACNAGHTEN, (Steuart) Patrick; s of Capt Steuart Cecil Macnaghten (d 1918, ggs of Sir Francis Macnaghten, 1 Bt); *b* 5 April 1917; *Educ* Sherborne; *m* 1961, Beatrix Amy Howard, da of Lt-Col Sir Francis Metford, KCB, DL (d 1958); *Career* Maj 8 Army Mid East NW Europe; company director, author and expert on antiques; *Recreations* travel; *Clubs* Carlton; *Style* - Patrick Macnaghten Esq; South Wing, Rodmarton Manor, Cirencester, Gloucestershire

MACNAGHTEN, Robin Donnelly; s of Sir Henry Pelham Wentworth Macnaghten (d 1949); *b* 3 Aug 1927; *Educ* Eton, King's Cambridge; *m* 1961, Petronella Anne Card; 2 s (adopted), 1 da (adopted); *Career* assist Mackinnon Mackenzie & Co Bombay 1949-54, assist master Eton Coll 1954-65, housemaster 1965-74; headmaster Sherborne 1974; author; *Recreations* gardening, walking; *Clubs* Roy Western India Turf; *Style* - Robin Macnaghten Esq; Ferry Cottage, Bury, nr Pulborough, W Sussex; Abbey Grange, Sherborne, Dorset (☎ 2025)

McNAIR, 2 Baron (UK 1955); (Clement) John McNair; s of 1 Baron McNair, CBE, QC (d 1975); *b* 11 Jan 1915; *Educ* Shrewsbury, Balliol Oxford; *m*

1941, Vera, da of Theodore J Faithfull; 2 s, 1 da; *Heir* s, Hon Duncan James McNair; *Career* served in Tunisia and Italy 1940-46, Maj RA; author; memb Gen Advisory Council IBA 1978-; substitute memb Council of Europe and WEU 1979-; *Style* - The Rt Hon the Lord McNair; House of Lords, Westminster, SW1

McNAIR, Archibald Alister Jourdan; s of Donald McNair (1975); *b* 16 Dec 1919; *Educ* Blundells; *m* 1954, Catherine Alice Jane, da of late John Fleming, of Ireland; 1 s, 1 da; *Career* chm Mary Quant Gp 1955-; chm Thomas Jourdan Ltd 1971-; *Recreations* tennis, fruit farming, chess, backgammon; *Clubs* Turf; *Style* - Archibald McNair Esq; 26 Frances rd, Windsor, Berkshire, SL4 3AA (☎ Windsor 57951)

McNAIR, Hon Duncan James; s and h of 2 Baron McNair; *b* 26 June 1947; *Educ* Bryanston; *Style* - The Hon Duncan McNair

McNAIR, Hon Josephine Margaret; da of Baron McNair (Life Peer); *b* 1949; *Style* - The Hon Josephine McNair

MACNAIR, Lady; Marion Aitken; da of James Wylie, MD, of Glasgow; *m* 1918, Sir Robert Hill Macnair (d 1959); *Style* - Lady Macnair; West Rockmount, Barrhead, Renfrewshire

McNAIR, Hon William Samuel Angus; s of Baron McNair (Life Peer); *b* 1958; *Style* - The Hon William McNair

McNALLY, Jack Reginald Moore; MBE (1963), JP (Fife 1965); *b* 15 Dec 1916; *m* 1939, Lena; *Career* Lt Home Guard; author, winner Queen's Award to Industry (Export) 1975; engr Dental Mfrg, Telephone Mfrg Co; with Sunvic Controls Ltd, Electrothermal Engrg Ltd; md Beckman Instruments Ltd 1963-76, chm 1976-80; dir Beckman Int Operations, chm Beckman Instruments (Hldg) Ltd 1970-80; chm Scientific Documentation Centre Ltd 1960-, Vivian Industries Ltd 1960-, chm G & R Int Electronics Ltd 1980-, chm Triad Tech & Industrial Services Ltd 1980-; memb CBI (London) Regional Development and European Ctee; *Clubs* Livery, RAC; *Style* - Jack McNally Esq, MBE, JP; Suite 205, Glenrothes House, Glenrothes; Roseacre, Orchard dve, Glenrothes

MacNALLY, Peter; s of Gp Capt Patrick MacNally; *b* 16 March 1933; *Educ* Stonyhurst; *m* 1969, Edmée Maria, da of Egon Carmine Del Sasso; 2 s; *Career* CA 1955; dir of LWT (Holdings) Ltd, Hutchinsons Ltd, Page and May (Holdings) Ltd and other cos; *Recreations* shooting, fishing and skiing; *Clubs* RAC; *Style* - Peter MacNally Esq; 9 Addison av, London, W11 (☎ 603 3726)

MacNAUGHTON, Hon Mrs; Hon Liza Jane Pearson; da of 3 Viscount Cowdray; *b* 30 March 1942; *Educ* Cheltenham Ladies' Coll, Brondesbury-at-Stocks, Paris, Madrid; *m* 1967, Malcolm MacNaughton; 1 s, 1 da; *Style* - The Hon Mrs MacNaughton; 1302 Canada rd, Woodside, Calif 94062, USA

McNEAL, Hon Mrs; Hon Julia; da of Baroness Gaitskell (Life Peeress); *b* 1939; *Educ* Somerville Oxford; *m* 1969, George Peter McNeal; *Style* - The Hon Mrs McNeal; 35 Newstead rd, SE12

McNEE, Sir David Blackstock; QPM (1975); s of John McNee; *b* 23 March 1925; *Educ* Woodside Senior Secdy Sch Glasgow; *m* 1952, Isabella Clayton, da of Robert Hopkins; 1 da; *Career* RN 1943-46; ch constable Glasgow 1971-75, Strathclyde 1975-77, cmmr of Metropolitan Police 1977-; kt 1978; DStJ; *Recreations* fishing, golf, music; *Clubs* Royal Commonwealth Soc, RSAC; *Style* - Sir David McNee, QPM; New Scotland Yard, SW1

McNEICE, Sir (Thomas) Percy Fergus; CMG (1953), OBE (1947); s of Canon W G McNeice; *b* 1901; *Educ* Bradford G S, Keble Oxford; *m* 1947, Yuen Peng Loke; 1 s, 1 da; Colonial Serv Malaya 1925; pres Singapore City Cncl 1949-55; kt 1956; *Style* - Sir Percy McNeice CMG OBE

McNEIL, Lady; Barbara J; da of late P S Turner; *m* 1939, Sir Hector McNeil, CBE (d 1978); 1 s, 1 da; *Style* - Lady McNeil; Bramber, St George's Hill, Weybridge, Surrey (☎ Weybridge 48484)

MACNEIL OF BARRA, The; Ian Roderick Macneil of Barra; Chief of Clan Neil; s of Robert Lister Macneil of Barra, of Kisimul Castle, Isle of Barra (d 1970); *b* 20 June 1929; *Educ* Scarborough Sch, Vermont U, Harvard; *m* 1952, Nancy, da of James Wilson, of Ontario; 2 s, 1 da (and 1 s decd); *Heir* s, Roderick Macneil of Barra, yr (b 1954); *Career* Wigmore Prof of Law Northwestern U 1980-, Ingersoll Prof of Law Cornell 1976-80; *Recreations* tennis; *Style* - The Macneil of Barra; Kisimul Castle, Isle of Barra (☎ Castlebay 300); 3500 North Lake Shore Dve, Illinois 60657, USA

McNICOL, George Paul; s of Martin Wilkinson McNicol (d 1956); *b* 24 Sept 1929; *Educ* Hillhead H S Glasgow, Glasgow U; *m* 1959, Susan Moira, nee Ritchie; 3 c; *Career* MBChB, MD, PhD, FRCP, FRCPath, FACP, honorary consultant physician Makerere U Coll Medical Sch Nairobi 1965-66; Prof; appointments in Glasgow Teaching Hospitals and Glasgow U 1952-81, princ Aberdeen U 1981, regius princ Aberdeen U 1981; *Recreations* skiing, gardening; *Clubs* Caledonian; *Style* - Prof George McNicol; The Chanonry Lodge, 13 The Chanonry, Old Aberdeen, AB2 1RP (☎ 40241)

McNICOLL, Vice-Adm Sir Alan Wedel Ramsay; KBE (1966, CBE 1954), CB (1965), GM (1941); s of Brig-Gen Sir Walter Ramsay McNicoll, KBE, CMG, DSO, VD; *b* 3 April 1908; *Educ* Scotch Coll Melbourne, RAN Coll; *m* 1, 1937, Ruth, nee Timmins; 2 s, 1 da; m 2, 1957, Frances, da of late J Chadwick; *Career* RAN 1922; ch of Naval Staff 1965-68, Australian Ambass to Turkey 1968-73; *Style* - Vice-Adm Sir Alan McNicoll, KBE, CB, GM; 6 Hutt st, Yarralumla, ACT 2600, Australia

McNULTY, Lady Sarah Lillian; *née* Lowry-Corry; da of 7 Earl Belmore (d 1960); *b* 31 March 1945; *Educ* Manor House Sch Armagh N Ireland, Florence Italy; *m* 1979, Gary McNulty; *Style* - Lady Sarah McNulty; 4131 County rd 103, Carbondale, 81623 Colorado, USA

MACPHAIL, Bruce Dugald; s of Dugald Ronald Macphail; *b* 1 May 1939; *Educ* Haileybury, Balliol Oxford, Harvard Business Sch; *m* 1963, Susan Mary (d 1975), da of late Col T Gregory, MC, TD; 3 s; *Career* FCA, dir Sterling Guarantee Trust 1969-74, md Town & City Properties Ltd 1976-; *Style* - Bruce Macphail Esq; 13 West Heath rd, NW3 (☎ 01 435 9412)

MACPHERSON OF DRUMOCHTER, 2 Baron (UK 1951); (James) Gordon Macpherson; s of 1 Baron (d 1965); *b* 1924; *Educ* Wells House Malvern, Loretto; *m* 1, 1947, (Dorothy) Ruth (d 1974), da of late Rev Henry Coulter, of Bellahouston, Glasgow; (1 s decd), 2 da; m 2, 1975, Catherine Bridget, da of Dr Desmond MacCarthy, of Brentwood; 1 s, 2 da; *Heir* s, Hon James Anthony Macpherson; *Career* chm A J Macpherson & Co, bankers, fndr chm & pres Br Importers Confedn 1972-; FRSA; Ch Scottish Clans Assoc London 1972-74, JP Essex 1961-76; served with RAF 1941-45; fell Roy Entomological Soc 1940 and Zoological Soc of London 1966; memb Council of London Chamber of Commerce 1958; memb Exec Ctee of W India Ctee 1959; chm and md of Macpherson, Train and Co Ltd, Food and Produce Importers and Exporters; memb Council E European Trade Council 1969-72; freeman City of London 1969; memb Butchers Co 1969; chm W India Ctee 1973; memb Essex Magistrates' Courts Ctee 1974-75; *Clubs* Boodle's; *Style* - The Rt Hon the Lord Macpherson of Drumochter; Kyllachy, Tomatin, Inverness-shire (☎ Tomatin 212); Drumochter, 69-85 Old st, EC1 (☎ 01 253 9311)

MACPHERSON OF DRUMOCHTER, Lucy, Baroness; da of late Arthur Butcher, of Maldon, Essex; *b* 3 Jan 1897; *m* 1920, 1 Baron Macpherson of Drumochter (d 1965); 1 s, 2 da; *Style* - The Rt Hon Lucy, Lady Macpherson of Drumochter; Drumochter, Wickham Bishops, Witham, Essex

MACPHERSON, Hon Anne Alexandra; da of 2 Baron Macpherson of Drumochter by his 2 w Catherine; *b* 1977; *Style* - The Hon Anne Macpherson

MACPHERSON, Hon Andrew Charles James; s of 2 Baron Strathcarron; *b* 1959; *Style* - The Hon Andrew Macpherson

MACPHERSON, Donald Charles; s of Donald Hugh Macpherson (d 1947); *b* 3 Jan 1932; *Educ* Winchester College; *m* 1962, Hilary Clare; *Career* Captain, Black Watch; dir Hogarth Shipping Co & Subsidiaries 1972; dir Lyle Shipping Co 1980; *Recreations* golf, tennis, travel; *Style* - Donald Macpherson Esq; 22 Campden Hill Square, London W8 (☎ 01 727 8292); Willow Cottage, East Lavington, nr Petworth, West Sussex (☎ 07986 266)

MACPHERSON, Hon Ian David Patrick; s and h of 2 Baron Strathcarron; *b* 31 March 1949; *Style* - The Hon Ian Macpherson; Otterwood, Beaulieu, Hants (☎ 334)

MACPHERSON, Hon James Anthony; s & h of 2 Baron Macpherson of Drumochter; *b* 27 Feb 1979; *Style* - The Hon James Macpherson

MACPHERSON, Lady; Joan Frances Brownfield; da of late Dr W E Fry; *m* 1928, Sir John Stuart Macpherson, GCMG (d 1971); *Career* CStJ; *Style* - Lady Macpherson; 141 Marsham Court, Westminster, SW1

MACPHERSON, Hon Jennifer Margaret; da of 2 Baron Macpherson of Drumochter by his 2 w Catherine; *b* 1976; *Style* - The Hon Jennifer Macpherson

MACPHERSON, Hon Mrs; Hon Sarah Catherine; *née* Conolly-Carew; da of 6 Baron Carew, CBE; *b* 1944; *m* 1966, Ian Arthur Cluny Macpherson; 1 s, 2 da; *Style* - The Hon Mrs Macpherson; 6 Parkgate Close, Kingston Hill, Surrey

MACPHERSON, CLUNY; Lt-Col William Alan Macpherson of Cluny and Blairgowrie; TD (1965), QC (1971); 27 Chief of Clan Macpherson; s of Brig Alan David Macpherson of Cluny and Blairgowrie DSO MC (d 1969); *b* 1 April 1926; *Educ* Wellington, Trin Oxford; *m* 1962, Sheila, da of Thomas Brodie; 2 s, 1 da; *Heir* s, Alan Macpherson of Cluny and Blairgowrie, yr (b 1965); *Career* Capt Scots Gds 1944-47, Lt-Col 21 SAS Regt (TA) 1965, barr 1952, Crown Court Recorder 1971; memb Roy Co of Archers (Queen's Bodyguard for Scotland); *Recreations* fishing, golf; *Clubs* Caledonian, London Scottish Football (Pres 1972-79); *Style* - Lieutenant-Colonel Cluny Macpherson, TD, QC; Newton Castle, Blairgowrie, Perthshire (☎ 2097)

MACPHERSON-GRANT, Sir Ewan George; 6 Bt (UK 1838), of Ballindalloch, Elgin, DL (Banffshire 1952); s of Capt George Bertram Macpherson-Grant, OBE, JP, DL (d 1932); suc cousin, Sir George Macpherson-Grant, 5 Bt, 1951; *b* 1907; *Educ* Winchester, Ch Ch Oxford; *m* 1937, Evelyn Nancy Stopford, da of Maj E S Dickin, of Loppington House, Loppington, Salop; 1 da; *Heir* none; *Career* memb Scottish Faculty of Advocates; formerly Maj RA; memb Roy Co of Archers; Hon Sheriff Substitute Perth and Angus; *Style* - Sir Ewan Macpherson-Grant, Bt, DL; Ballindalloch Castle, Banffshire (☎ 206); Craigo, by Montrose, Angus (☎ Hillside 207)

McPHIE, John Kent; TD and Clasp (1945); s of John Kent McPhie (d 1919); *b* 8 Nov 1918; *Educ* Glasgow Academy; *m* 1943, Elsie May; 1 s, 1 da; *Career* exec dir Robinson & Sons Ltd 1964-, dir Robinson-Eirecot Ltd 1967-, dir Edward Taylor Ltd 1964-, Pressure Sealed Plastics Ltd 1970-, chm Disposable Baby Napkin Mfrs Assoc 1977-81, chm Inst of Marketing, Nat Fellowship Panel 1968-; Junior Warden Worshipful Co of Marketers 1980-81; Vice Pres High Peak Hunt Club; *Recreations* riding and hunting; *Clubs* Army & Navy; *Style* - John McPhie Esq, TD and Clasp; Holme Farm, Wilday Green, Barlow, Sheffield S18 5SH (☎ 0742 890387)

MacRAE, Lady Phyllis; *née* Hervey; da of 4 Marquess of Bristol, MVO (d 1951); *b* 30 Nov 1899; *m* 1921, Capt (John) Duncan George MacRae, Seaforth Highlanders (d 1966); 1 s (John), 2 da (Merelina; (Jean) Countess of Northesk); *Career* Company Cdr ATS 1940-48; md MacRae Farms Ltd; *Style* - Lady Phyllis MacRae; 19 Coleherne Mews, SW10 (☎ 01 373 8878); Hatchery House, Barrow, Bury St

Edmunds, Suffolk (☎ 810442)

MacRAE, Hon Mrs; Hon Susan Mary; *née* Southwell; da of 6 Viscount Southwell (d 1960); *b* 1926; *m* 1951, Keith Francis MacRae; 2 s; *Style* - The Hon Mrs MacRae; 27 Dennis rd, Slacks Creek, via Brisbane, Queensland, Australia

MACREADY, Charles Nevil; s and h of Sir Nevil John Wilfrid Macready, 3 Bt; *b* 19 May 1955; *Style* - Charles Macready Esq

MACREADY, Sir Nevil John Wilfrid; 3 Bt (UK 1923), of Cheltenham, Co Gloucester; s of Lt-Gen Sir Gordon Nevil Macready, 2 Bt, KBE, CB, CMG, DSO, MC (d 1956); *b* 7 Sept 1921; *Educ* Cheltenham, St John's Oxford; *m* 1949, Mary, da of Sir (John) Donald Balfour Fergusson, GCB (d 1963); 1 s, 3 da; *Heir* s, Charles Nevil Macready; *Career* served 1942-47 with RA, Staff Capt 1945; md Mobil Oil Co Ltd 1975-; *Clubs* Boodle's, Naval and Military, Jockey (Paris); *Style* - Sir Nevil Macready, Bt; Langley House, Pirbright, Surrey (☎ Brookwood 2172)

MacSWINEY OF MASHANAGLAS, Marquis (Papal cr of Leo XIII 1896); Owen Charles Alexander Patrick Evelyn Diego de Avila; s of Valentine Emmanuel Patrick, 1 Marquis, *camérier secret* to Pope Leo XIII, Kt of Malta & Chllr Order of Malta in Ireland, of Dublin (d 1945, himself s of Valentine MacSwiney, a banker of Paris, who m a da of Count Alexander Konarski, presumably of the family cr Count in the autonomous Galician part of the Habsburg Domains by Emperor Joseph II 1783), by his w, Her Illustrious Highness Countess Anna (d 1938, herself da of HIllH Emil, Sovereign Count & Lord of Schlitz *dit* von Görtz, a mediatised Sovereign Count of the HRE; cr of Count of HRE 1726 by Charles VI (with qualification *Hoch und Wohlgeboren*), admission to Wetteravien College of Counts of Empire 1804, designation of 'Illustrious Counts' (*Erlaucht*) recognised by the post-Congress of Vienna German Diet (*Bundestag*) 1829); the 2 Marquis's maternal grandmother was Sophie Cavalcanti de Albuquerque de Villeneuve, da of Count Cavalcanti etc; *b* 30 July 1916; *Educ* Catholic University Sch Dublin, U Coll Dublin, King's Inns Dublin; *m* 1954, Thaddäa Maria-Theresia Huberta, da of Clemens Paul, Count Gorff *dit* von Schmising; 1 s (Patrick); *Heir* s, Patrick MacSwiney; *Career* barr, industl design consultant; *Recreations* horses & equine behavioural studies, writing; *Style* - Marquis MacSwiney of Mashanaglas; Haus Ermelinghoff, 4700 Hamm 4, W Germany (☎ Hamm 71220)

MacTAGGART, Lady; Irene; da of late Ferdinand Richard Holmes Meyrick; *m* 1, 1939, 6 Earl of Craven (m dis 1954, he d 1965); m 2, 1961, Sir Andrew MacTaggart (d 1978); *Style* - Lady MacTaggart; Clatfields, Marsh Green, Edenbridge, Kent (☎ Edenbridge 2819)

MACTAGGART, Sir Ian (John) Auld; 3 Bt (UK 1938), of King's Park, City of Glasgow; s of Sir John (Jack Auld) Mactaggart, 2 Bt (d 1960); *b* 19 April 1923; *Educ* Oundle, Clare Cambridge; *m* 1946, Rosemary (m dis 1969), da of Sir Herbert Williams, 1 Bt, MP (d 1954); 2 s, 2 da; *Heir* s, John Auld Mactaggart; *Career* Lt RE 1942-45; md Western Heritable Investment Co Ltd; memb LCC 1949-52; *Clubs* ESU, Royal Thames Yacht Club; *Style* - Sir Ian Mactaggart, Bt; 2a Westmoreland ter, SW1 (☎ 01 834 8062)

MACTAGGART, John Auld; s and h of Sir Ian (John) Auld Mactaggart, 3 Bt; *b* 21 Jan 1951; *m* 1977, Patricia, da of late Maj Harry Alastair Gordon, MC; *Style* - John Mactaggart Esq; 16 Bryanston Mews East, W1

MacTHOMAS OF FINEGAND, Andrew Patrick Clayhills; s of Capt Patrick Watt MacThomas of Finegand (d 1970), whom suc 1970 as 19 Chief of Clan MacThomas; *b* 28 Aug 1942; *Educ* St Edward's Sch Oxford; *Heiress* sis, Elizabeth Gillian MacThomas; *Career* sr exec Barclaycard/Visa; dir Scotsworld Servs Ltd 1979-; memb Standing Cncl of Scottish Chiefs; pres Clan MacThomas Soc; *Recreations* horse racing, travel; *Clubs* New (Edinburgh) and Puffin's (also Edinburgh); *Style* - Andrew

MacThomas of Finegand; 22 India st, Edinburgh EH3 6HB

McVEIGH, Lady; Mary Elizabeth Mabel; da of late Adam Reade, of Portstewart, Co Londonderry; *m* 1940, Rt Hon Sir Herbert Andrew McVeigh, PC, QC (d 1977); *Style* - Lady McVeigh; 25 Crambourne Park, Belfast 9, N Ireland (☎ 660927)

McVEY, Lady; Margaret Gardiner; da of Thomas Packman, of Brisbane; *m* 1919, Sir Daniel McVey, CMG (d 1972); *Style* - Lady McVey; 12 Cleeve Court, Toorak, Victoria, Australia

McWATTERS, Hon Mrs; Hon Veronica; *née* Stamp; 2 da of 2 Baron Stamp; *b* 25 May 1934; *Educ* Queenswood Sch Hatfield, Roy Free Hosp Med Sch; *m* 1961, Richard Alfred Hugh McWatters, s of late Sir Arthur Cecil McWatters, CIE; 1 s, 2 da; *Career* doctor (MRCS, LRCP), part-time GP Bristol; *Recreations* bee keeping; *Clubs* Br Bee Keepers Assoc; *Style* - The Hon Mrs McWatters; The Grove, Dundry, Bristol (☎ 641334)

MADDEN, Rear-Adm Colin Duncan; CB (1966), CBE (1964), MVO (1954), DSC (1940) and Bar; s of Archibald Maclean Madden, CMG (d 1928); *b* 19 Aug 1915; *Educ* R N Coll Dartmouth; *m* 1943, Agnes Margaret, da of H K Newcombe, OBE (d 1949), of Aldingbourne, W Sussex, and Canada; 2 da; *Career* joined RN 1928, world wide war service at sea, naval attaché Rome 1955, dir Navigation and Direction, Admiralty 1961, Rear-Adm 1965, sr naval memb directing staff Imperial Defence Coll 1965-67, formerly Cdr (N) HM Yacht Britannia, Capt HMS Crossbow, HMS Albion; dir Nat Trade Development Assoc 1967, Brewers Soc 1969-8; *Recreations* sailing, gardening, embroidery, tapestry; *Clubs* Royal Ocean Racing, Army and Navy; *Style* - Rear-Adm Colin Madden, CB, CBE, MVO, DSC*; c/o Coutts & Co, 440 Strand, London WC2

MADDEN, Adm Sir Charles Edward; 2 Bt (UK 1919), of Kells, Co Kilkenny; GCB (1965), DL (Gtr London 1969); s of Adm of the Fleet Sir Charles Edward Madden, 1 Bt, GCB, OM, GCVO, KCMG (d 1935); *b* 15 June 1906; *m* 1942, Olive, da of late G W Robins; 1 da; *Heir* bro, Lt-Col John Wilmot Madden, MC; *Career* joined RN 1920, ch of naval staff N Zealand 1953-55, naval ADC to HM the Queen 1955, C-in-C Plymouth 1959-62, Adm 1961, C-in-C Eastern Atlantic 1963-65, ret 1965; chm Roy Nat Mission to Deep Sea Fishermen 1971; a trustee of Nat Maritime Museum 1968 (chm 1972-77), chm Standing Council of the Baronetage 1975-77; Vice Lord-Lt Greater London 1969; *Clubs* Arts club; *Style* - Adm Sir Charles Madden, Bt, GCB, HM Vice Lord-Lieut for Greater London; 21 Eldon rd, W8 (☎ 01 937 6700)

MADDEN, Lt-Col John Wilmot; MC (1943); s of Adm of the Fleet Sir Charles Edward Madden, GCB, OM, GCVO, KCMG, (d 1935); h to Btcy of bro, Sir Charles Edward Madden, 2 Bt, GCB; *b* 20 Dec 1916; *m* 1941, Beatrice Catherine, JP, da of late W Sievewright, WS, of St Andrews, Fife; 2 s, 1 da; *Career* Lt-Col (ret) RA, Burma 1944 (despatches, MC); chm Warminster and Westbury RDC 1969-72; *Style* - Lt-Col John Madden, MC; Manor House, Upton Lovell, Warminster, Wilts (☎ Codford St Mary 252)

MADDOCKS, Henry John; s of Henry Hollingdrake Maddocks (d 1969); *b* 18 Nov 1928; *Educ* St Edward's Sch Oxford, London U; *m* 1956, Joyce, nee Reah; 1 s, 1 da; *Career* slr 1954, sr ptnr Hunters 1978 (ptnr 1954), clerk to the Worshipful Co of Masons 1969-; *Recreations* travel, philately, model railways; *Clubs* RAC; *Style* - Henry Maddocks Esq; 7 Fairfax ave, Ewell, Epsom, Surrey (01 393 2084)

MADDOCKS, Sir Kenneth Phipson; KCMG (1958, CMG 1956), KCVO (1963); s of Arthur P Maddocks; *b* 8 Feb 1907; *Educ* Wadham Oxford; *m* 1, 1951, Elnor Radcliffe (d 1976), da of Sir E John Russell, OBE, FRS (d 1965); m 2, 1980, Patricia Josephine, nee Duke; *Career* HM Overseas Serv, civil sec Northern Region Nigeria 1955-57, Dep Govr 1957-58, acting Govr Northern Region Nigeria 1956 & -57, Govr & Commander-in-Chief of Fiji 1958-63, dir and sec East Africa and Mauritius Assoc 1964-69; KStJ; *Recreations* gardening; *Clubs* Athenaeum;

Style - Sir Kenneth Maddocks, KCMG, KCVO; 11 Lee rd, Aldeburgh, Suffolk (☎ Aldeburgh 3443)

MADOC, Maj-Gen Reginald William; CB (1959), DSO (1957), OBE (1951); s of Lt Col Henry William Madoc, CBE, MVO (d 1937); *b* 15 Aug 1907; *Educ* King William's Coll Isle of Man; *m* 1938, Rosemary, da of late Dr Cyril Shepherd, of Sydney, Australia; 1 da; *Career* 2 Lt RM 1926, HMS Rodney 1929-31, HMS Royal Oak 1932-34 and others, instructor for officers Staff Coll Camberley 1947, ch instructor Sch of Amphibious Warfare 1953-55, ADC to HM the Queen 1955-57, Maj-Gen RM, ret 1961; *Recreations* travel, walking; *Clubs* Army and Navy; *Style* - Maj-Gen Reginald Madoc, CB, DSO, OBE; The Malthouse, Meonstoke, by Southampton (☎ Droxford 323)

MADOCKS, John Edward; CBE (1965, MBE 1956), DL (Notts 1978); s of Sidney George Robert Madocks (d 1935); *b* 14 March 1922; *Educ* King Edward VI Sch Lichfield, Birmingham U; *m* 1945, Jessica Kinross, da of Andrew Davidson (d 1939); 2 c; *Career* Maj Europe and Middle East; HM Overseas Civil Serv, permanent sec 1946-65, Bursar of Nottingham U 1965-, nat chm Assoc of British Chambers of Commerce 1980-, dir ATV Network Ltd 1979-, board member British Rail (London Midland) 1979-, chm Notts Economic Planning Forum 1980-, East Midlands Economic Planning Council 1975-79; *Recreations* books, pictures, sport; *Clubs* Roy Commonwealth; *Style* - John Madocks Esq, CBE, DL; 7 Middleton cres, Beeston, Nottingham (☎ 0602 256592)

MAELOR, Baron (Life Peer UK 1966); Thomas William Jones; s of James Jones; *b* 10 Feb 1898; *Educ* Poncian Boys' Sch, Bangor Normal Coll; *m* 1928, Flossy, da of Jonathan Thomas, of Birkenhead; 1 s, 1 da; *Career* welfare offr and education offr (N Wales) Merseyside and N Wales Electricity Bd; JP (1937) Denbighshire; MP (L) Merioneth 1951-66; *Style* - The Rt Hon the Lord Maelor JP; Ger-y-Llyn, Poncian, nr Wrexham, Clwyd (☎ Wrexham 144)

MAFFEY, Hon Alicia Dorothy; da of 2 Baron Rugby; *b* 14 Jan 1960; *Style* - The Hon Alicia Maffey

MAFFEY, Hon Christopher Alan; s of 2 Baron Rugby; *b* 1955; *m* 1977, Barbara Anne, da of Guthrie Stewart, of Auckland, New Zealand; *Style* - The Hon Christopher Maffey

MAFFEY, Hon John Richard; s and h of 2 Baron Rugby; *b* 28 Aug 1949; *Educ* Harrow, Univ Coll Buckland; *Style* - The Hon John Maffey; Grove Farm, Frankton, nr Rugby, Warwickshire (☎ Marton 286)

MAFFEY, Hon Mark Andrew; s of 2 Baron Rugby; *b* 1956; *Style* - The Hon Mark Maffey

MAFFEY, Hon Robert Charles; s of 2 Baron Rugby; *b* 1951; *m* 1974, Anne Penelope, da of David Hale, of Somerden, Chiddingstone, Kent; 2 s; *Style* - The Hon Robert Maffey; Grove Farm Cottage, Frankton, Rugby

MAFFEY, Hon Simon Chelmsford Loader; s of 1 Baron Rugby, GCMG, KCB, KCVO, CSI, CIE (d 1969); *b* 1919; *Educ* Rugby; *m* 1949, Andrée Norma (m dis 1962), da of George Middleton; 1 da; *Career* Lt Coldstream Gds 1937, served 1939-42, served Merchant Navy 1942-45; *Style* - The Hon Simon Maffey; 56 John st, Cottesloe, W Australia

MAFFEY, Hon Selina Penelope; da of 2 Baron Rugby; *b* 1952; *Style* - The Hon Selina Maffey

MAGAN, George Morgan; FCA; s of Brig William Morgan Magan CBE; *b* 14 Nov 1945; *Educ* Winchester College; *m* 1972, Wendy, da of Maj Patrick Chilton MC; 1 s, 1 da; *Career* dir Morgan Grenfell & Co Ltd; dir Asprey & Co Ltd and others; *Clubs* Turf, City of London; *Style* - George Magan Esq; 23 Great Winchester st, EC2; St Michael's House, Nr Tonbridge, Kent

MAGEE, Lady; Joan; da of M Simmons; *m* 1938, Sir Cuthbert Gaulter Magee, CBE (d 1963); *Style* - Lady Magee; Stoke Grange, Guildford, Surrey

MAGGS, Air Vice-Marshal William Jack; CB (1967), OBE (1943); s of Frederick Wilfrid Maggs (d 1959); *b* 2 Feb 1914; *Educ* Bristol G S, St John's Oxford; *m* 1940, Margaret Grace, da of Thomas Liddell Hetherington (d 1975); 1 s, 1 da; *Career* joined RAF 1939, Air Vice-Marshal 1967; served WW II in UK, N Africa, Sicily, Italy; sr staff officer RAF Maintenance Command 1967-69; official fellow and domestic bursar Keble Oxford 1969-77; *Recreations* golf, gardening; *Clubs* Royal Air Force; *Style* - Air Vice-Marshal William Maggs, CB, OBE; Hillside, Noke, Oxford (☎ 086 75 3139)

MAGINNESS, Lady; Kathleen May; da of Alfred Neale; *m* 1928, Sir Greville Simpson Maginness, KBE (d 1961); *Style* - Lady Maginness; The Court, Kent's Green, Callow End, nr Worcester

MAGNIAC, Rear-Adm Vernon St Clair Lane; CB (1961); s of Maj Francis Arthur Magniac (d 1951); *b* 21 Dec 1908; *Educ* Clifton Coll; *m* 1947, Eileen Eleanor, da of Herbert William Witney (d 1951); 1 s, 1 da (1 da decd); *Career* joined RN 1926, served in 1939-45 War, Rear-Adm Mediterranean, South East Asia Command, ret 1962; *Recreations* golf, fishing; *Style* - Rear-Adm Vernon Magniac, CB; Marlborough, Yelverton, Devon (☎ Yelverton 2076)

MAGNUS, Hilary Barrow; TD, QC (1957); s of Laurie Magnus; hp to Btcy of bro, Sir Philip Magnus-Allcroft, 2 Bt; *b* 3 March 1909; *Educ* Westminster, Ch Ch Oxford; *m* 1950, Rosemary Vera Anne, da of George Henry Masefield (d 1969); 1 s, 1 da; *Career* Lt Col Rifle Bde (TA), Western Desert and Europe 1939-45, Nat Insurance Cmmr 1980, barr Lincoln's Inn 1934, bencher 1963, JP 1948-77; *Recreations* gardening, reading, haute cuisine; *Clubs* Garrick, Beefsteak; *Style* - Hilary Magnus Esq, TD, QC; Cragmore House, Church st, Wye, Ashford, Kent (☎ 0233 812 036)

MAGNUS-ALLCROFT, Sir Philip Montefiore; 2 Bt (UK 1917), of Tangley Hill, Wonersh, Co Surrey, CBE (1971); s of Laurie Magnus (d 1933) and Dora, da of Sir Isidore Spielmann, CMG, the art expert, by his w Emily (da of Sir Joseph Sebag-Montefiore and niece of Lady Swaythling (w of 1 Baron) and Sir Benjamin Cohen, 1 Bt); Sir Philip is 2 cous once removed to Sir Bernard Waley-Cohen, 1 Bt; gs of Sir Philip Magnus, 1 Bt (d 1933); *b* 8 Feb 1906; *Educ* Westminster, Wadham Oxford; *m* 1943, Jewell, da of late Herbert J Allcroft (proprietor of Stokesay Castle, Shropshire, the oldest example of a fortified manor house in England, now owned by Sir Philip and Lady M-A) and Margaret (da of Gen Sir William Russell, 2 Bt, CB, and Lady of the Manor of Ashley, Charlton Kings); *Heir* bro Hilary Barrow Magnus, TD, QC; *Career* Civil Service 1928-33 & 1946-51; Lt RA 1939, Maj 1943; CC (1952), CA (1968) Salop; biographer (notably of Gladstone and Edward VII) and historian, writes as 'Philip Magnus'; trustee of Nat Portrait Gallery 1970-77, memb W Midlands Regnl Ctee Nat Trust; assumed additional name of Allcroft by Deed Poll 1951; *Clubs* Athenaeum, Brooks's, Beefsteak and Pratt's; *Style* - Sir Philip Magnus-Allcroft Bt CBE; Stokesay Court, Onibury, Shropshire (☎ Bromfield 372)

MAGOR, Maj (Edward) Walter Moyle; CMG (1960), OBE (1956); s of Edward John Penberthy Magor (d 1941); *b* 1911; *Educ* Marlborough, Magdalen Oxford, Magdalene Cambridge; *m* 1939, Daphne Davis, da of Hector Robert Lushington Graham (d 1960); 2 da; *Career* Maj The Poona Horse Indian Army 1934-47, RARO 10 Roy Hussars 1949-61 Indian Political Serv 1937-39, 1943-47, Colonial Service Kenya 1947-61, permanent sec Ministry of Defence 1954, sec to the Cabinet 1958, Home Civil Serv, Bd of Trade 1961-71, then assist sec; ret 1971; DL Cornwall 1974, High Sheriff 1981; *Recreations* gardening; *Clubs* Army & Navy; *Style* - Maj Walter Magor, CMG, OBE, DL; Lamellen, St Tudy, Bodmin, Cornwall (☎ St Tudy 207)

MAGUIRE, Air Marshal Sir Harold John; KCB (1966), DSO (1946), OBE (1949); s of Michael Maguire, of Maynooth, Ireland, and Bulawayo, Zimbabwe; *b* 12 April 1912; *Educ* Wesley Coll, Trin Coll Dublin; *m* 1940, Mary Elisabeth, da of George H Wild, of Dublin;

1 s; 1 da; *Career* RAF 1933; late Dep Ch of Defence Staff, ret 1968; Dir-Gen Intelligence MOD 1968-72; now dir Commercial Union Assur Co; *Style* - Air Marshal Sir Harold Maguire KCB DSO OBE; c/o Lloyds Bank, 6 Pall Mall, SW1

MAHER, Terence Anthony; s of the late Herbert Maher; *b* 5 Dec 1935; *Educ* Xaverian Coll Manchester; *m* 1960, Barbara, da of the late Dr Franz Max Greenbaum; 3 s; *Career* chm Pentos Ltd; *Recreations* skiing, football; *Style* - Terence Maher Esq; Ferniehurst, 85 Hampstead Way, NW11 (☎ 01 458 6749)

MAHON, Sir George Edward John; 6 Bt (UK 1819), of Castlegar, Co Galway; s of Sir William Mahon, 5 Bt, DSO, JP, DL (d 1926, descended from Capt Bryan Mahon, whose company of Grenadiers suffered devastating losses in holding Oldbridge Ford for James II at the Battle of the Boyne), and Hon Edith Dillon, 2 da of 4 Baron Clonbrock; *b* 1911; *Educ* Eton, Trin Cambridge; *m* 1, 1938, Audrey Evelyn (d 1957), da of late Walter Jagger and late Mrs Maxwell Coote; 2 s, 1 da; m 2, 1958, Suzanne, da of late Thomas Donnellan; 1 da; *Heir* s, Lt-Col William Walter Mahon; *Career* merchant banker (ret), practitioner of Christian Science; *Recreations* gardening; *Clubs* Kildare Street & University; *Style* - Sir George Mahon, Bt; Greeninch, Enniskerry, Co Wicklow, Republic of Ireland

MAHON, William Walter; s and h of Sir George Edward George Mahon, 6 Bt; *b* 4 Dec 1940; *Educ* Eton; *m* 1968, Rosemary Jane, da of Lt-Col Michael Ernest Melvill, OBE, of Symington, Lanarkshire; 1 s 2 da; *Career* Irish Guards 1960-; Command and Staff Coll, Quetta, Pakistan 1973; Commandant Guards Depot 1980-; *Recreations* military history, badge collecting; *Clubs* Army & Navy; *Style* - Lt-Col William Mahon Esq; c/o Lloyds Bank Ltd, 111 High st, Eton, Windsor, Berks

MAHONY, David Arthur; s of late A Mahony; *b* 10 Feb 1944; *m* 1976, Adrienne, nee Kerr; 2 c; *Career* dir: Applied Chromatography Systems Ltd; chm Barwell Machine and Rubber Group; dir: Continental Microwave Hldgs, Custom Synthetics Ltd, Data Card Internat, David Scott Gp, Dawview Plant Hire, Hambros Industrial Management Ltd, Harland Simon (1980) Ltd, Kennetside Holdings Ltd, Keywealth Ltd, D A Mahony & Co, The Tower Mint Greenwich (Medallions) Ltd, Ward Bros (Wolverhampton) Ltd; *Recreations* shooting, golf, fishing, politics, economics; *Clubs* Carlton, Inst of Directors; *Style* - David Mahony Esq; Toft Manor, Toft, Cambs (☎ Comberton 3839)

MAIDSTONE, Viscount; Daniel James Hatfield Finch Hatton; s and h of 16 Earl of Winchilsea; *b* 7 Oct 1967; *Style* - Viscount Maidstone

MAIN, His Honour Judge; John Roy; s of Alfred Charles Main (d 1968); *b* 21 June 1930; *Educ* Portsmouth G S, Hotchkiss Sch USA, Brasenose Oxford; *m* 1955, Angela de la Condamine, da of Robert William Home Davies (d 1970); 2 s, 1 da; *Career* Lt Roy Naval Reserve; barr Inner Temple 1954, memb special panel Transport Tribunal 1970-76, dep chm Isle of Wight Quarter Sessions 1971, recorder Crown Court 1972-76, QC 1974, circuit judge 1976-; *Recreations* boating, gardening, music; *Style* - His Honour Judge Main; 4 Queen Anne dve, Claygate, Surrey (☎ Esher 66380)

MAIN, Peter Tester; ERD (1964); s of Peter Main (d 1977); *b* 21 March 1925; *Educ* Robert Gordon's Coll Aberdeen, Aberdeen U; *m* 1952, Margaret Fimister, nee Tweddle; 2 s, 1 da; *Career* MD 1963, MBChB 1948, MRCPEd 1981, Lt-Col RAMC (AER); chm The Boots Co Ltd 1981- (res dept 1957, dir of res 1968, dir 1973, v-chm 1980-81); *Recreations* fly fishing, shooting, Scottish music; *Clubs* Naval & Military; *Style* - Peter Main Esq, ERD; Limehurst, Halam rd, Southwell, Notts (☎ Nottingham 56111), Lairig Ghru, Dulnain Bridge, Grantown-on-Spey, Moray

MAIR, Duncan Carswell; s of David Mair (d 1975); *b* 20 May 1928; *Educ* Dumbarton Academy; *m* 1959, Elizabeth Anne; 3 c; *Career* director House of Fraser 1972; *Recreations* Golf; *Style* - Duncan Mair Esq; 36 Trevor Square, SW 7

MAIR, Hon Mrs; Hon Elizabeth Smith; da of 1 Baron Kirkwood, PC (d 1955); *b* 1908; *m* 1944, John Archibald Dugald Mair, ARIBA; 1 s, 2 da; *Style* - The Hon Mrs Mair; Shieldaig, 12 Iain rd, Bearsden, Dunbartonshire

MAIS, Baron (Life Peer UK 1967); Alan Raymond Mais; GBE (1973, OBE 1944), ERD (1958), TD (1944), JP (City of London 1962), DL (Kent 1976, Co of London subsequently Gter London 1951-76); s of late Capt Ernest Mais, of Mornington Court, Kensington; *b* 7 July 1911; *Educ* Banister Court Hants, College of Estate Management U of London; *m* 1936, Lorna Aline, da of Stanley Aspinall Boardman, of Addiscombe, Surrey; 2 s, 1 da; *Career* 2 Lt Roy W Kent Regt 1919; Lt City of London 1963, Lord Mayor of London 1972-73; memb of the Court City U 1973, pres London Chamber of Commerce & Industry 1975-78, memb Commonwealth Scholars Cmmn 1978, past pres London Master Builders' Assoc, memb Govt Ctees for Works and Buildings Emergency Organisation; .v-pres Inst of Structural Engineers; Govr Hurstpierpoint Coll; formerly with Richard Costain, late dir Trollope & Colls; Commissioner of Income Tax 1972-; Alderman Walbrook Ward, Sheriff 1969-70; FICE, FRICS; dir Roy Bank of Scotland 1969, Slag Reduction Co; chm Raymond Mais & Assoc; chm City of London Insurance Co, William Sindalls Ltd 1969-, Hay Consultants 1969-; chm Peachey Property Corpn 1977-; KStJ; *Style* - The Rt Hon Lord Mais GBE ERD TD JP DL; Griffins, Sundridge Avenue, Bromley, Kent; 19 Sloane st, SW1 (☎ 01 235 2080); Chesham House, Wilderness rd, Chislehurst, Kent (☎ 01 467 0735)

MAIS, Hon Jonathan Robert Neal; s of Baron Mais, OBE (Life Peer); *b* 1954; *Educ* Hurstpierpoint Coll, City of London Coll of Commercial Law; *m* 1978, Frances Louise, da of late Robert Mark Barrington Brown; *Style* - The Hon Jonathan Mais; Chesham House, Wilderness rd, Chislehurst, Kent

MAIS, Hon Richard Jeremy Ian; s of Baron Mais, OBE (Life Peer); *b* 2 Nov 1945; *Educ* Stowe Sch, Ewell Technical Coll; *m* 1972, Janice, da of Ralph Dean, of Hurley, Berks; 1 s, 1 da; *Career* property developer; dir Attbarn Properties Ltd, CNC Properties Ltd, Waterden Surveys Ltd; MIOB; *Recreations* motor sport, badminton, DIY; *Clubs* Br Automobile Racing; *Style* - The Hon Richard Mais; 79 Seal Hollow rd, Sevenoaks, Kent (☎ 0732 54886)

MAISNER, Air Vice-Marshal Aleksander; CB (1977), CBE (1969), AFC (1955); s of the late Henryk Maisner; *b* 26 July 1921; *Educ* High Sch and Lyceum Czestochowa Poland, Warsaw U; *m* 1946, Mary, nee Coverley; 1 s, 1 da; *Career* served WWII Polish Artillery and Polish Air Force, joined RAF 1946, dir RAF Staff Coll, CO RAF Seletar, Asst Cmdt RAF Coll Cranwell, ret as Dir Gen Personnel Management 1977, personnel exec Reed International Ltd 1977-, governer Shiplake Coll 1978-, memb Hon Ctee and Trustee of Polish Air Force Assoc; *Recreations* reading, music, walking; *Clubs* RAF; *Style* - Air-Vice Marshal Aleksander Maisner CB CBE AFC; 14 Orchard Close, Shiplake Cross, Henley on Thames (☎ Wargrave 2671)

MAITLAND, Lady; Bridget; da of Henry Denny, of Staplefield Place, Sussex; *m* 1930, Cdr Sir John Francis Whitaker Maitland, RN (d 1977); *Style* - Lady Maitland; Harrington Hall, Spilsby, Lincs (☎ 2281)

MAITLAND, Lady Caroline Charlotte Militsa; da of 17 Earl of Lauderdale; *b* 18 Nov 1946; *Educ* Queen's Gate Sch London, SS Mary and Anne Abbots Bromley Rugeley, Lycée Français de Londres and London U; *Career* teacher 1970-77; *Recreations* T'ai Chi, dance, travel;*Style* - Lady Caroline Maitland; 12 St Vincent st, Edinburgh (☎ 031 556 5692)

MAITLAND, Lady Elizabeth Sylvia; da of Viscount Maitland (ka 1943); *b* 1943; *Career* granted 1953, title, rank and precedence of an Earl's da which would have been hers had her father survived to succeed to Earldom of Lauderdale; *Style* - Lady Elizabeth Maitland; 4 Chelsea Towers, Chelsea Manor st, SW3

MAITLAND, Helena, Viscountess; Helena Ruth; da of Col Sir Herbert Charles Perrott, 6 and last Bt, CH, CB (d 1922); *b* 14 Aug 1912; *m* 1936, Viscount Maitland (s & h of 15 Earl of Lauderdale; ka 1943 predeceasing his f); 3 da (Lady Biddulph, Lady Anne Eyston, Lady Elizabeth Maitland, all raised to rank of Earl's da); *Style* - Helena, Viscountess Maitland; Flat E, 34 Cadogan sq, SW1 (☎ 01 584 9920); Park House, Makerstoun, nr Kelso, Roxburghshire (☎ Smailholm 248)

MAITLAND, Viscount; Ian Maitland; Master of Lauderdale; s and h of 17 Earl of Lauderdale; *b* 4 Nov 1937; *Educ* Radley, Brasenose Oxford; *m* 1963, Ann Paule, da of Geoffrey Clark, of London; 1 s, 1 da; *Heir* s, Master of Maitland; *Career* Lt RNR 1963-73, Int Banking Div Nat Westminster Bank Ltd 1975-, Lay Reader C of E; *Style* - Viscount Maitland; 150 Tachbrook st, SW1

MAITLAND, Master of; Hon John Douglas Maitland; s and h of Viscount Maitland; *b* 29 May 1965; *Style* - Master of Maitland

MAITLAND, Jean Lady; Jean Hamilton; MBE; da of late Robert Findlay, of Easterhill, Lanarkshire; *m* 1919, Lt-Col Sir George Ramsay Maitland, 7 Bt, DSO (d 1960); *Style* - Jean, Lady Maitland, MBE; Reswallie, Forfar, Angus

MAITLAND, Lady; Lavender Mary Jex; da of late Francis William Jex Jackson, of Kirkbuddo, Forfar; *m* 1951, Maj Sir Alexander Keith Maitland, 8 Bt (d 1963); *Style* - Lady Maitland; Burnside, Forfar, Angus

MAITLAND, Lady Olga, *see* Lady Olga Hay

MAITLAND, Hon Mrs (Rosemary Coupar); da of 1 Baron Abertay (d 1940); *b* 1931; *m* 1952, John Stuart Maitland; 3 s, 1 da; *Style* - The Hon Mrs Maitland; Alkerton Grange, Eastington, nr Stonehouse, Glos

MAITLAND, Sir Richard John; 9 Bt (UK 1818), of Clifton, Midlothian; s of Maj Sir Alexander Maitland, 8 Bt (d 1963, sixth in descent from Gen Hon Sir Alexander Maitland, 1 Bt, 5 s of 6 Earl of Lauderdale); *b* 24 Nov 1952; *Educ* Rugby, Exeter U, Edinburgh Sch of Agriculture; *Heir* bro, Robert Ramsay Maitland; *Career* farmer; *Recreations* skiing, shooting, fishing, travel; *Style* - Sir Richard Maitland, Bt; Burnside, Forfar, Angus

MAITLAND, Robert Ramsay; s of Maj Sir Alexander Keith, 8 Bt (d 1963); hp of bro, Sir Richard John Maitland, 9 Bt; *b* 14 July 1956; *Style* - Robert Maitland Esq

MAITLAND, Hon Sarah Caroline; da of Viscount Maitland; *b* 1964; *Style* - The Hon Sarah Maitland

MAITLAND, Hon Sydney Milivoye Patrick; s of 17 Earl of Lauderdale; *b* 23 June 1951; *Educ* Hill House London, Summer Fields Oxford, Eton, Edinburgh U (BSc), Strathclyde U (Dip TP); *m* 1974, (Dorothy) Eileen, da of A R Bedell, of Strathaven Lanarkshire; *Style* - The Hon Sydney Maitland; 14 Kersland st, Glasgow, G12 8BL

MAITLAND BIDDULPH, Hon Anthony Nicholas Colin; s and h of 4 Baron Biddulph by Lady Mary Maitland (gda of 15 Earl of Lauderdale, DL); *b* 8 April 1959; *Style* - The Hon Anthony Maitland Biddulph

MAITLAND BIDDULPH, Hon William Ian Robert; 2 s of 4 Baron Biddulph by Lady Mary Maitland (gda of 15 Earl of Lauderdale, DL); *b* 27 March 1963; *Style* - The Hon William Maitland Biddulph

MAITLAND-CAREW, Hon Gerald Edward Ian; s of 6 Baron Carew, CBE; *b* 1941; *Educ* Harrow; *m* 1972, Rosalind Averil, da of Lt-Col Neil Hanning Reed Speke, MC; 1 s, 1 da; *Career* 2 Lt 15/19 Hussars 1961, Capt 1965, formerly ADC to GOC 44 Div Dover Castle; name changed to Maitland-Carew by deed poll 1971; *Clubs* Cavalry; *Style* - The Hon Gerald Maitland-Carew; Thirlestane Castle, Lauder, Berwickshire

MAITLAND-SMITH, Geoffrey; s of Philip John Maitland-Smith; *b* 27 Feb 1933; *Educ* University Coll Sch, Lndon; *m* 1, 1956 (m dis); 3 s (Philip, Kevin Charles, Anthony Edward b 1962), 1 da (Katrina); m 2, 1967, Gabriella Rosa; 1 s (Guy Charles Armandi b 1971), 1 da (Geraldine Carlotta b 1974); *Career* C A; dir Sears Holdings Ltd 1971-; dep chm & chief executive, Sears Holdings Ltd 1978-; *Recreations* opera, music; *Clubs* Cripplegate Ward, Worshipful Co of Gardeners; *Style* - Geoffrey Maitland-Smith Esq; 40 Duke st, WIA 2HP (☎ 01 408 1180)

MAKGILL, Hon Diana Mary Robina; MVO (1971); da of 12 Viscount Oxfuird; *b* 4 Jan 1930; *Educ* Strathcona Lodge Sch Vancouver Island BC Canada; *Career* Ceremonial Offr Protocol Dept FCO 1961-, Hon Steward of Westminster Abbey 1978, Jubilee Medal 1977; *Style* - The Hon Diana Makgill, MVO; Clouds Lodge, E Knoyle, Nr Salisbury, Wilts; 15 Inverna ct, W8

MAKGILL, George Hubbard; s of late Sqdn Ldr Richard Makgill (yr s of Sir George Makgill, 11 Bt); hp of unc, 12 Viscount Oxfuird; *b* 7 Jan 1934; *m* 1967 (m dis), Alison Campbell, da of Neils Max Jensen, of Randers, Denmark; 3 s, 1 da; *Style* - George Makgill Esq; The Cottage, Bishop's Green, Newbury, Berks

MAKGILL, Hon Harriet Frances Janet; da of *de jure* 11 Viscount Oxfuird (d 1926) and sis of 12 Viscount; *b* 1893; *Style* - The Hon Harriet Makgill

MAKGILL CRICHTON MAITLAND, Maj John David; s of Col Mark Edward Makgill Crichton Maitland, CVO, DSO, JP, DL (d 1972), of The Island House, Wilton, Salisbury, Wilts; *b* 1925; *Educ* Eton; *m* 1954, Jean Patricia, da of Maj-Gen Sir Michael Creagh, KBE, MC (d 1970), of Pigeon Hill, Homington, Salisbury, Wilts; 1 s, 1 da; *Career* served 1944-57 with Gren Gds, Temp Maj 1952, ret 1957 with rank of Capt (Hon Maj), DL (Renfrewshire 1962), Vice-Lt 1972, Ld-Lt Strathclyde Regn (Renfrew district) 1980-; *Clubs* Guards'; *Style* - Major John Makgill Crichton Maitland, HM Lord-Lieut for Strathclyde Region; Houston House, Houston, by Johnstone, Renfrewshire (☎ Bridge of Weir 612545)

MAKINS, Hon Christopher James; s and h of 1 Baron Sherfield, GCB, GCMG; *b* 23 July 1942; *Educ* Winchester, New Coll Oxford; *m* 1975, Wendy Cortesi; *Career* Fell All Souls' Coll Oxford 1963, HM Diplomatic Serv 1964-74; *Style* - The Hon Christopher Makins; 3034, P st NW, Washington DC, USA

MAKINS, Hon Dwight William; s of 1 Baron Sherfield, GCB, GCMG; *b* 2 March 1951; *Educ* Winchester, Ch Ch Oxford; *Career* dir John Govett and Co, Tesel Services Ltd; *Recreations* shooting; *Style* - The Hon Dwight Makins; Beaurepaire House, Bramley, Basingstoke, Hants; 51 Ennismore Gdns, SW7 (☎ 01 589 8434)

MAKINS, Jean, Lady; Jean; da of Capt Lord Arthur Hay (2 s of 10 Marquess of Tweeddale; *m* 1932, Lt-Col Sir William Makins, 3 Bt (d 1969); *Style* - Jean, Lady Makins; Martyrwell, Cheriton, Hants

MAKINS, Sir Paul Vivian; 4 Bt (UK 1903), of Rotherfield Court, Henley-on-Thames, Co Oxford; s of Sir Paul Augustine Makins, 2 Bt (d 1939), and bro of Lt-Col Sir William Vivian Makins, 3 Bt (d 1969); *b* 12 Nov 1913; *Educ* Eton, Trin Cambridge; *m* 1945, Maisie, da of Maj Oswald Henry Pedley and widow of Maj Cecil Leander John Bowen; *Heir* none; *Career* formerly JP Gibraltar; Maj Welsh Gds (ret); *Style* - Sir Paul Makins, Bt; c/o Barclays Bank International Ltd, 84-90 Main st, Gibraltar

MAKOWER, Arthur Denis; s of Walter Makower, OBE (d 1945); *b* 6 Oct 1917; *Educ* St Paul's Sch, Trin Cambridge; *Career* scientist Ministry of Supply 1940-45, scientist Lobitas Oilfield Ltd 1945-50, dir of scientific control Nat Coal Bd 1977- (scientist 1950-60, assist dir of scientific control 1960-66, dep dir of scientific control 1966-77); *Recreations* golf, chess, bridge; *Clubs* Wildernesse GC; *Style* - Arthur Makower Esq; 2 Hollington, 73 Bradbourne Park rd, Sevenoaks, Kent (☎ 53621)

MALAN, Mrs Daniel; Dorothy Elise;

née Henry; da of James Raymond Henry (whose mother was Evelyn, da of Sir John Pelly, 2 Bt, by his 1 w Johanna), through whom Mrs Malan is 2 cous once removed of the present (29) Earl of Crawford & Balcarres, and Josine Du Toit, of a family of Huguenot origin; *b* 31 Aug 1908; *m* Daniel François Malan (nephew of Dr Malan, sometime PM of S Africa); 1 s (James b 1941), 1 da (Françoise b 1948); *Style* - Mrs Daniel Malan; 42 Paradise rd, Newlands 7700, Cape Town, S Africa

MALCOLM, Alastair Richard; s of the late Colin Ronald Malcolm; *b* 20 Oct 1947; *Educ* Eton, New Coll Oxford; *m* 1971, Elizabeth Anne, da of Edward Wilfred George Joicey-Cecil; 2 s; *Career* barrister, Inner Temple 1971; *Recreations* shooting, country pursuits; *Style* - Alastair Malcolm Esq; Hart Hill Farm, Woodfalls, Salisbury, Wilts

MALCOLM, Lt-Col Arthur William Alexander; CVO (1954, MVO 1949); s of Maj Charles Malcolm, bro of 9 Bt; hp of kinsman, Sir David Malcolm, 11 Bt; *b* 31 May 1903; *Educ* Repton; *m* 1928, Hester Mary, da of Samuel Furneaux Mann, of Victoria, Australia; 2 s; *Career* Lt-Col (ret 1952) Welsh Gds, assist mil attaché Paris 1950-52, private sec to Govr S Australia 1953-55, Queen's Messenger 1955-68; *Style* - Lt-Col Arthur Malcolm, CVO; Faraday, Sandwich Bay, Kent

MALCOLM, Sir David Peter Michael; 11 Bt (NS 1665), of Balbedie and Innertiel, Co Fife; s of Maj Sir Michael Albert James Malcolm, 10 Bt (d 1976); *b* 7 July 1919; *Educ* Eton, Magdalene Cambridge; *Heir* kinsman, Lt-Col Arthur William Alexander Malcolm, CVO; *Career* chartered accountant; dir James Capel & Co; memb Stock Exchange 1956, Stock Exchange Council 1971; *Clubs* Pratt's, City of London and New (Edinburgh) *Style* - Sir David Malcolm, Bt; 15 Cromwell cres, SW5

MALCOLM, Hon Mrs (Elizabeth Frances); da of Baron Byers, OBE, PC (Life Peer); *b* 1941; *m* 1961, Charles Alasdair Ronald Malcolm; *Style* - The Hon Mrs Malcolm; Achadh Nan Sgiath, Duror of Appin, Argyll

MALCOLM, Kathleen, Lady; Kathleen; da of late Cdr George Jonathan Gawthorne, RN, and formerly w of James Melvin; *m* 1947, as his 2 w, Maj Sir Michael Albert James Malcolm, 10 Bt (d 1976); *Style* - Kathleen, Lady Malcolm; 6 Northumberland st, Edinburgh 3

MALDEN, Viscount; Frederick Paul de Vere Capell; s and h of 10 Earl of Essex; *b* 29 May 1944; *Educ* Lancaster Roy G S, Didsbury Coll of Educn, N Sch of Music; *Career* actg head teacher March County Jr Sch 1974-77; Head Teacher Cockerham C of E Sch 1979-80; Head Curriculum Devpt Skerton County Jr Sch Lancaster 1981-; LCM, FRSA, ACP; *Recreations* classical music; *Style* - Viscount Malden; 'Lindisfarne', Pinewood av, Brookhouse, Lancaster, Lancs

MALET, Col Sir Edward William St Lo; 8 Bt (GB 1791), of Wilbury Wiltshire; OBE (1953); s of Lt-Col Sir Harry Charles Malet, 7 Bt, DSO, OBE, JP (d 1931); *b* 1908; *Educ* Dover Coll, Ch Ch Oxford; *m* 1935, Baroness Benedicta (d 1979), da of Baron Wilhelm von Maasburg, of Vienna, 1 s, 2 da; *Heir* s, Harry Douglas St Lo Malet; *Career* Capt 8 Hussars 1938, served in Palestine 1935, Middle East 1940; dep ch civil affairs offr HQ, Br troops Egypt 1953-55; pres Bridgwater Con Assoc 1959, ret; High Sheriff Somerset 1966; *Clubs* Cavalry and Guards; *Style* - Col Sir Edward Malet, Bt, OBE; Chargot, Washford, Somerset (☎ 371)

MALET, Harry Douglas St Lo; s and h of Sir Edward William St Lo Malet, 8 Bt, OBE; *b* 26 Oct 1936; *Educ* Downside, Trinity Oxford; *m* 1967, Julia Gresley, da of Charles Harper, of Perth, W Australia; 1 s; *Career* late Queen's Royal Irish Hussars; *Style* - Harry Malet Esq; Langham Farm, Luxborough, Watchet, Somerset

MALET, Hon Mrs (Margaret Cherry); da of 2 Baron Wigram, MC; *b* 24 April 1942; *m* 1972, Maj Greville J W Malet; *Style* - The Hon Mrs Malet; Vale House, Little Somerford, Chippenham, Wilts

MALIN, Marilyn Ann; *Career* dir Associated Book Publishers (UK) Ltd, md Methuen Children's Books, chm Methuen Educational Ltd; *Style* - Miss Marilyn Malin; Associated Book Publishers (UK) Ltd, 11 New Fetter Lane, EC4

MALLABY, Lady; Elizabeth Greenwood; *née* Brooke; *m* 1, J W D Locker, OBE (decd); m 2, 1955, Sir (Howard) George (Charles) Mallaby, KCMG, OBE (d 1978); *Style* - Lady Mallaby; Down The Lane, Chevington, W Suffolk (☎ Chevington 308)

MALLALIEU, Lady; Betty Margaret Oxley; da of Dr Pride, of Bridlington, and gda of J W Oxley, of Leeds; *m* 1934, Sir Edward Lancelot (Sir Lance) Mallalieu, QC (d 1979); *Style* - Lady Mallalieu; 5 Woodstock Close, Oxford

MALLALIEU, Lady; Harriet Rita Riddle Tinn; *m* 1945, Sir Joseph Percival William Mallalieu (d 1980); *Style* - Lady Mallalieu; Village Farm, Boarstall, Aylesbury, Bucks (☎ Brill 454)

MALLET, Lady; Christiana Jean; da of Herman Andreae, of Moundsmere Manor, Basingstoke; *m* 1925, Sir Victor Alexander Louis Mallet, GCMG, CVO (d 1969); *Style* - Lady Mallet; The Homestead, Wittersham, Tenterden, Kent

MALLETT, Michael John; s of Albert William Mallett (d 1972); *b* 14 Dec 1931; *Educ* Devonport H S Plymouth and Penzance; *m* 1956, Joan Barbara, nee Ayre; 1 s, 2 da; *Career* FCA, ptnr Noel Lewis & Co (Liverpool) 1957-60; sec James Neill Holdings Ltd 1960, dir Corporate Dvpt 1970, dep ch exec 1974, chm and ch exec Neill Tool Gp Ltd 1981, chm Radio Hallam Ltd 1979, chm Yorks & Humberside Regional Cncl 1979-81, memb Economic & Financial Policy Ctee, master Co of Cutlers in Hallamshire 1979-80; *Recreations* riding; *Style* - Michael Mallett Esq; 106 Ivy Park rd, Sheffield, S Yorks (☎ 305166)

MALLINSON, Sir (William) Paul; 3 Bt (UK 1935), of Walthamstow, Co Essex; s of Sir William Mallinson, 2 Bt, JP, DL, sometime High Sheriff Surrey (d 1944); *b* 6 July 1909; *Educ* Westminster, Ch Ch Oxford, St Thomas's Hosp; *m* 1, 1940, Eila Mary (m dis 1967), da of R G Guy, of Hastings, NZ; 1 s, 2 da; m 2, 1968, Dr Margaret Cooper, da of S A Bowden; *Heir* s, William John Mallinson; *Career* hon consulting psychiatrist to St George's Hosp SW1, civilian consultant in Psychiatry to the Roy Navy 1967-78; chm William Mallinson and Denny Mott Ltd 1962-73; surgeon Lt-Cdr RNVR 1940-46; *Clubs* Athenaeum, Roy Thames Yacht, MCC; *Style* - Sir Paul Mallinson, Bt; Flat 4, 25 Wimpole st, W1 (☎ 01 580 7919); Meadow Lea, North Close rd, Bembridge, Isle of Wight (☎ 2239)

MALLINSON, William John; s and h of Sir (William) Paul Mallinson, 3 Bt, by his 1 w, Eila; *b* 8 Oct 1942; *Educ* Charterhouse; *m* 1968, Rosalind Angela, da of Rollo Hoare (one of the Hoares of Stourton, being 2 s of Henry Hoare, JP, and Lady Geraldine Hervey, sis of 4 Marquess of Bristol), of Dogmersfield, Hants; 1 s, 1 da; *Style* - William Mallinson Esq

MALLOWAN, Lady; Barbara Parker; *m* 1977, as his 2 w, Sir Max Mallowan, CBE (d 1978); *Style* - Lady Mallowan; Winterbrook House, Wallingford, Oxon

MALMESBURY, 6 Earl of (GB 1800); William James Harris; TD (1944) (2 clasps), JP (Hants 1950); also Baron Malmesbury (GB 1788) and Viscount FitzHarris (GB 1800); s of 5 Earl of Malmesbury, JP, DL (d 1950, gs of the Victorian For Sec, who, unlike Lord Monmouth and Basil Seal, condescended to the artifice of the toilet, for Disraeli once noted:"M was skilfully rouged"; his gf was Special Envoy to Brunswick to negotiate the marriage of the future George IV with Caroline of Brunswick; 'Prinny' never forgave him this rôle as architect of his matrimonial miseries, though even had Lord M not died as his master ascended the throne in 1820, it is doubtful if he would have suffered what Thomas Cromwell did some three centuries earlier in the similar affair of Anne of Cleves; Lord M was the last Earl created (3 days before the Union with Ireland) in the GB Peerage and the tutor of Palmerston in diplomacy;

his mane of white hair and striking eyes, faithfully recorded by Sir Thomas Lawrence, led to his being called 'The Lion'; the 2 Earl also dabbled in international relations, but got no further than Under Sec of State); *b* 18 Nov 1907; *Educ* Eton, Trin Cambridge; *m* 1932, Hon Diana Carleton, da of 2 and last Baron Dorchester, OBE (d 1963); 1 s, 2 da; *Heir* s, Viscount FitzHarris; *Career* Professional Assoc RICS; formerly Hon Col 65 Signal Regt; Gold Staff Offr at coronation of King George VI; DL (1957), Vice-Lt 1960, CCllr Hants 1952-, Lord Lt Hampshire 1973-; chm Hampshire Branch Country Landowners' Assoc 1954-56; chm Eastern Wessex TA & VR Assoc 1968-70; KStJ 1973; official verderer of the New Forest 1966-74; *Recreations* rural life, sailing; *Clubs* Roy Yacht Sqdn; *Style* - The Rt Hon Earl of Malmesbury TD JP, HM Lord-Lieut for Hampshire; Greywell Hill, nr Basingstoke, Hants (☎ Odiham 2033)

MALMESBURY, Countess of; Hon Diana Claudia Patricia; *née* Carleton; da of 2 and last Baron Dorchester; *b* 1912; *m* 1932, 6 Earl of Malmesbury; *Style* - The Rt Hon the Countess of Malmesbury

MALPAS, Prof James Spencer; s of Tom Spencer Malpas (d 1972); *b* 15 Sept 1931; *Educ* Sutton County G S, St Bartholomew's Hosp London U, Oxford U; *m* 1957, Joyce May, da of Albert Edward Cathcart (d 1962); 2 s; *Career* Flight Lt RAF; prof of medical oncology St Bartholomew's Hosp London U, dir Imperial Cancer Research Fund Unit of Med Oncology, consultant physician St Bartholomew's Hosp, Dean of Medical Coll 1969-72, formerly assist registrar Roy Coll of Physicians 1975-80; *Recreations* skiing, sailing, history, painting, travel; *Style* - Prof James Malpas; 14 Carlisle Mansions, Carlisle Place, SW1 (☎ 01 828 0042)

MALTBY, Lady; Elizabeth M; da of late John McDonald, of Melbourne, Victoria; *m* 1914, (Hon) Sir Thomas Karran Maltby (decd); *Style* - Lady Maltby; 10 Culbin ave, Belmont, Geelong, Victoria, Australia

MALTBY, John Newcombe; s of Sir Paul Copeland Maltby, KCVO, CB, DSO, DSO, AFC, DL (d 1971); *Educ* Wellington, Clare Cambridge; *m* 1956, Lady Sylvia Veronica Anthea, da of 6 Earl of Malmesbury; 1 s, 2 da; *Career* md Panocean Anco Ltd; *Clubs* Bath; *Style* - John Maltby Esq; Broadford House, Basingstoke, Hants (☎ 882265)

MALTBY, Lady Sylvia Veronica Anthea; *née* Harris; da of 6 Earl of Malmesbury, TD; *b* 17 May 1934; *Educ* Croft House Dorset; *m* 1956, John Newcombe Maltby, s of late Air V-Marshal Sir Paul Copeland Maltby, KCVO, KBE, CB, DSO, AFC, DL; 1 s, 2 da; *Style* - Lady Sylvia Maltby; Broadford House, Stratfield Turgis, Basingstoke, Hants (☎ 0256 882265)

MALTBY, Lady; Winifred Russell; da of late James H Paterson, of 6 Moray Place, Edinburgh; *m* 1921, Air Vice-Marshal Sir Paul Copeland Maltby, KCVO, KBE, CB, DSO, AFC (d 1971); *Style* - Lady Maltby; Froglanes, Rotherwick, Basingstoke

MALTWOOD, Hon Mrs (Nancy Margaret); *née* Lyle; da of 1 Baron Lyle of Westbourne (d 1954); *b* 26 Feb 1910; *m* 1, 1938, Capt Philip Foster Glover, RN (d 1957); 1 s, 1 da; m 2, 1969, Ryder Gardyne Maltwood; *Style* - The Hon Mrs Maltwood; Lande à Geon, Beaumont, Jersey, C I

MALVERN, 3 Viscount (UK 1955); Ashley Kevin Godfrey Huggins; s of 2 Viscount Malvern (d 1978); *b* 26 Oct 1949; *Heir* unc, Hon (Martin) James Huggins; *Style* - The Rt Hon Viscount Malvern; c/o Standard Bank, Cecil sq, Salisbury, Zimbabwe

MALVERN, Viscountess; Patricia Margery; da of Frank Renwick-Bower, of Durban; *m* 1949, 2 Viscount Malvern (d 1978); *Style* - The Rt Hon Viscountess Malvern; c/o Standard Bank, Cecil sq, Salisbury, Zimbabwe

MANASSEI DI COLLESTATTE, Countess John; Hon Susan Barbara; *née* Addington; da of 7 Viscount Sidmouth; *b* 1944; *m* 1965, Count John Paul James Alessandro Camillo Manassei di

Collestatte, s of Count Alessandro Manassei di Collestatte and Lady Maryel de Wichfield, nee Drummond, da of 16 Earl of Perth and Hon Angela Constable-Maxwell, da of 11 Lord Herries of Terregles; 1 s, 1 da; *Style* - Countess John Manassei di Collestatte; 27 Ellerby st, SW6

MANCE, Lady; Joan Erica Robertson; *née* Baker; *m* 1940, Sir Henry Mance (d 1981, dep chm & treasurer Lloyd's Register Shipping 1979-81); 1 s, 3 da; *Style* - Lady Mance; Gatefield Cottage, Okehurst, Billingshurst, W Sussex (☎ 2155)

MANCHESTER, 11 Duke of (GB 1719); Sidney Arthur Robin George Drogo Montagu; also Baron Kimbolton of Kimbolton (E 1620; some sources, starting with Collins, have 'Baron Montagu of Kimbolton', but *The Complete Peerage* says the former; moreover the 2 Earl of Manchester was called to Parl in his f's Barony of 'Lord Kimbolton' 1626-42, the fact of his being styled also Viscount Mandeville not affecting the designation of the Barony), Viscount Mandeville (also E 1620; this cr occasioned the lines: "Adding the honour, as he rolled down hill,/Of Viscount to the name of Mandeville,/Which crowned his cadency with empty fame/But brought him nothing to support the same"; tho' their author was dismissed as poetaster by the Peerage commentator Vicary Gibbs, the age that fawns on Ayres and James might deliver a different verdict), and Earl of Manchester (E 1626, created only three days after Charles I's coronation); s of 10 Duke, OBE (d 1977), himself tenth in descent from the 2 Earl of Manchester, a Parliamentary Commander in The Great Rebellion, being Cromwell's immediate superior at Marston Moor, and a five times married man (Sir John Bramston observed: "He married the Earl of Warwick's daughter, the Earl of Warwick's niece...and the Earl of Warwick's wife...could any but a Presbyterian do this?"); His Grace is s of the 10 Duke's 1 w, Nell; *b* 5 Feb 1929; *m* 1, 1955, Adrienne Valerie (m dis 1978), da of J K Christie, of Cape Province S Africa; m 2, 1978, Andrea, da of Cecil Alexander Joss, of Johannesburg, and formerly wife of G J W Kent; *Heir* bro, Lord Angus Charles Drogo Montagu; *Career* farmer; *Style* - His Grace the Duke of Manchester; PO Box 24667, Karen, Kenya

MANCHESTER, Elizabeth, Duchess of; Elizabeth; da of Samuel Clyde Fullerton, of Miami; *m* 1, W Crocker; m 2, 1969, as his 2 w, 10 Duke of Manchester (d 1977); *Style* - Her Grace Elizabeth, Duchess of Manchester; PO Box 303, Pebble Beach, Calif 93953, USA

MANCHESTER, 9 Bishop of (1847); Rt Rev Stanley Eric Francis Booth-Clibborn; s of Eric Booth-Clibborn; *b* 20 Oct 1924; *Educ* Highgate Sch, Oriel Oxford, Westcott House Cambridge; *m* 1958, Anne Roxburgh Forrester; 2 s, 2 da; *Career* Bp of Manchester 1979-; *Style* - The Rt Rev the Lord Bishop of Manchester; Bishopscourt, Bury New Road, Manchester M7 OLE (☎ 061 792 2096/1779)

MANCROFT, 2 Baron (UK 1937); Sir Stormont Mancroft Samuel Mancroft; 2 Bt (UK 1932), KBE (1958, MBE 1945), TD (1950); s of 1 Baron (d 1942), among other things an author whose books included a biography of Piranesi and *The Herring: Its Effect on the History of Britain*; *b* 27 July 1914; *Educ* Winchester, Ch Ch Oxford; *m* 1951, Diana Elizabeth, da of Lt-Col Horace Lloyd, DSO, and formerly w of Richard Quarry (by whom she had at least 1 da, Venetia, who m Capt Frederick Barker); 1 s, (Hon Benjamin Lloyd Stormont M), 2 da (Princess Nicholas von Preussen, sis-in-law of Marchioness of Douro; Hon Jessica Rosetta M); *Heir* s, Hon Benjamin Lloyd Stormont Mancroft; *Career* joined TA 1937, Lt-Col 1945, Hon Col Cmdt RA 1970-80, served WW II RA (TA); late Pres Inst Mktg, St Marylebone Con Assoc; chm Incentive Investments, E S Schwab & Co, Wallis Fashion Gp; dep chm Group 4 Total Security; dir Ashbourne Investments, Bank Leumi (UK), Garrott Dorland & Crawford Hldgs; barr 1938; a Lord in Waiting to HM the Queen 1952-54; jt parly under sec of State Home Office 1954-57, Parly Sec MOD 1957, Min Without Portfolio 1957-58; dir Cunard 1966-71, GUS; pres London Tourist Bd

1963-73; chm Ctee for Exports to USA 1967-70, Horserace Totalisator Bd 1972-76, British Greyhound Racing Federation 1977-; took surname Mancroft by Deed Poll 1925; *Clubs* Pratt's; *Style* - The Rt Hon Lord Mancroft KBE TD; 29 Margaretta ter, SW3 (☎ 01 352 7674)

MANCROFT, Hon Benjamin Lloyd Stormont; s and h of 2 Baron Mancroft, KBE, TD; *b* 16 May 1957; *Educ* Eton; *Style* - The Hon Benjamin Mancroft

MANCROFT, Hon Jessica Rosetta; da of 2 Baron Mancroft, KBE, TD; *b* 10 May 1954; *Style* - The Hon Jessica Mancroft

MANCUSO, Lady Patricia; *née* Pelham-Clinton-Hope; da of 9 Duke of Newcastle, OBE; *b* 20 July 1949; *m* 1, 1971 (m dis 1974), Alan Pariser; resumed surname of Pelham-Clinton-Hope 1974; m 2, 1981, Nick Mancuso, of Toronto; *Style* - Lady Patricia Mancuso; 12302 3rd Helena, Los Angeles, Calif, USA

MANDELSON, Hon Mrs (Mary Joyce); da of Baron Morrison of Lambeth (Life Peer) (d 1965); *b* 1921; *m* 1, 1941 (m dis 1948), Horace Williams (later The Hon Horace Williams), s of Baron Williams of Barnburgh (Life Peer); m 2, 1948, George Mandelson; *Style* - The Hon Mrs Mandelson; 12 Bigwood rd, NW11

MANDER, Sir Charles Marcus; 3 Bt (UK 1911), of the Mount, Tettenhall, Co Stafford; s of Maj Sir Charles Mander, 2 Bt, TD, JP, DL (d 1951); *b* 22 Sept 1921; *Educ* Eton, Trin Cambridge; *m* 1945, Maria Dolores Beatrice, da of late Alfred Brödermann, of Gross Fontenay, Hamburg; 2 s, 1 da; *Heir* s, Charles Nicholas Mander; *Career* Capt Coldstream Gds; served 1939-45 War; dir Mander Bros Ltd 1948-57, Headstaple Ltd 1976; chm Arlington Securities; High Sheriff Staffs 1962; underwriting memb of Lloyd's; *Recreations* yachting, shooting, music; *Clubs* Roy Thames Yacht, Boodle's, Mark's; *Style* - Sir Charles Mander, Bt; Little Barrow, Moreton-in-Marsh, Glos (☎ Stow-on-the-Wold (0451) 30265/30791); 6 Greville House, Kinnerton st, SW1 (☎ 01 235 1669)

MANDER, Charles Nicholas; s and h of Sir Charles Marcus Mander, 3 Bt; *b* 23 March 1950; *Educ* Downside, Trin Cambridge; *m* 1972, Karin Margareta, da of Gustav Arne; 3 c; *Career* co dir (publishing and land cos); farming and forestry, Lloyd's underwriter, founder ptnr of Mander Portman Woodward (private tutors) in Kensington; *Recreations* humane letters and arts; *Clubs* Boodle's; *Style* - Charles Mander Esq; 8 Cornwall Mews West, London SW7 (☎ 01 370 3544); Owlpen Manor, nr Uley, Gloucestershire

MANDER, Lady; Mary Rosalie Glynn; da of A C Grylls; *Educ* Queen's Coll London, LMH Oxford; *m* 1930, as his 2 w, Sir Geoffrey Le Mesurier Mander (d 1962); (1 s decd), 1 da (Anthea, m 1963 John Lahr); *Career* author & lecturer; *Style* - Lady Mander; Wightwick Manor, Wolverhampton

MANDL, George Thomas; s of Dr Gottfried Mandl (d 1941); *b* 8 Aug 1923; *Educ* Secdy Schs in Czechoslovakia Switzerland, England; Prague U; *Career* chm Thomas & Green Holdings Ltd and subsidiary cos, Thomas & Green Ltd, Soho Paper Mills, Fourstones Paper Mills Co Ltd, South Tyne Mill, dep chm Papierfabrik Netstal AG Switzerland, chm GT Mandl & Co Denmark; *Recreations* skiing, collection of books, manuscripts, paper making, history; *Clubs* City Livery; *Style* - George Mandl Esq; c/o Thomas & Green Ltd, Soho Mills, Wooburn Green, Bucks (☎ 062 85 22881); CH-8754 Netstàl, Switzerland (☎ 058-61 38 36)

MANGRIOTIS, Hon Mrs (Anne Margaret); da of Maj Sir Arthur Lindsay Grant, 11 Bt (ka 1944), and Baroness Tweedsmuir of Belhelvie (Life Peeress d 1978); *b* 1937; *Educ* Lady Margaret Hall Oxford; *m* 1965, Nicolas Mangriotis; 2 s; *Style* - The Hon Mrs Mangriotis; 57 Ypsilantou st, Athens 140, Greece

MANIFOLD, Lady; Gwenda; da of Maj-Gen H W Grimwade; *m* 1923, Hon Sir (Thomas) Chester Manifold, KBE (d 1979); *Style* - Lady Manifold; Talindert, Camperdown, Victoria 3260, Australia

MANKIEWICZ, Joseph Leo; s of Prof Frank Mankiewicz; *b* 11 Feb 1909; *Educ* Columbia USA, Yale U; *m* 1, 1939, Rosa Stradner (d 1958); 2 s, (1 s by previous m); m 2, 1962, Rosemary Helen Joan, da of John Matthews, Archdeacon of Hampstead 1950-62 (d 1971); 1 da; *Career* writer, film director 1929-, pres of Screen Dir Guild (1950), first award for direction and screenplay Motion Picture Academy 1949 and 1950, screen dir award 1949 and 50, British Film Academy 1950, NY Critics Award 1950, dir *La Bohème* for Metropolitan Opera 1952; films include *Philadelphia Story*, *Keys of the Kingdom*, *A Letter to Three Wives*, *All About Eve*, *Suddenly Last Summer*, *Guys and Dolls*, *Sleuth* and others; *Recreations* theatrical history, golf, travel; *Clubs* Bedford Golf and Tennis Club, NY; *Style* - Joseph Mankiewicz Esq

MANN, Alexander Rupert; s and h of Sir Rupert Edward Mann, 3 Bt; *b* 6 April 1978; *Style* - Alexander Mann Esq

MANN, Clare, Lady; Clare Helen; CBE (1962); da of late Robert Graham Dryden Alexander, of Brentwood; *m* 1951, Sir (Edward) John Mann, 2 Bt (d 1971); *Style* - Clare, Lady Mann, CBE; The Moat House, Scole Common, Diss, Norfolk

MANN, Lady; Evelyn Aimée; da of late Charles Richard Hughes; *m* 1958, as his 2 w, Sir James Gow Mann, KCVO (d 1962); *Style* - Lady Mann; 23 Chapel st, SW1

MANN, Felix Bernard; s of Leo William Mann (d 1956); *b* 10 April 1931; *Educ* Christ's Cambridge, Westminster Hosp; *Career* doctor, founder of the Medical Acupuncture Soc; *Recreations* walking in the countryside; *Style* - Dr Felix Mann; 15 Devonshire pla, London W1 (☎ 01 935 7575)

MANN, Sir Rupert Edward; 3 Bt (UK 1905), of Thelveton Hall, Thelveton, Norfolk; s of Edward Charles Mann, DSO, MC (d 1959), and great nephew of Sir John Mann, 2 Bt (d 1971); *b* 11 Nov 1946; *Educ* Malvern; *m* 1974, Mary Rose, da of Geoffrey Butler, of Springhill, Widdington, Saffron Walden, Essex; 1 s; *Heir* s, Alexander Rupert Mann; *Career* farmer; *Clubs* Norfolk and MCC; *Style* - Sir Rupert Mann, Bt; Billingford Hall, Diss, Norfolk (☎ Scole 314)

MANN, Lady; Yvonne Ella; da of late William Stanley Stanton, of Melbourne; *Educ* Tintern C of E Grammar Sch, Melbourne U; *m* 1940, Hon Mr Justice (Sir Alan Harbury) Mann, MBE, QC (d 1970); *Career* slr Victoria 1938; chm UNICEF Papua New Guinea, dir YWCA Papua New Guinea 1966-69; council memb Emily McPherson Coll Melbourne 1971; *Style* - Lady Mann; Harbury, Charles st, Mount Eliza, Victoria 3930, Australia

MANNERS, 5 Baron (UK 1807); John Robert Cecil Manners; s of 4 Baron Manners, MC, JP, DL (d 1972, himself ggs of 1 Baron, who was in his turn 5 s of Lord George Manners-Sutton, 3 s of 3 Duke of Rutland, KG), by his w Mary, twin da of Rt Rev Lord William Gascoyne-Cecil, DD, 65 Bp of Exeter and 2 s of 3 Marquess of Salisbury (the great Conservative PM); *b* 13 Feb 1923; *Educ* Eton, Trin Oxford; *m* 1949, Jennifer Selena, da of Stephen Fairbairn (whose w Cynthia was gggda of Sir William Arbuthnot, 1 Bt); 1 s, 2 da; *Heir* s, Hon John Hugh Robert Manners; *Career* slr to Supreme Court 1949, ptnr Osborne Clarke & Co (Slrs) Bristol; joined RAFVR, flying offr 1942, Flight Lt 1944; *Clubs* Brooks's; *Style* - The Rt Hon the Lord Manners; Wortley House, Wotton-under-Edge, Glos (☎ 3174)

MANNERS, Lady Charlotte Louisa; da of 10 Duke of Rutland, CBE,; *b* 1947; *Style* - Lady Charlotte Manners; Belvoir Castle, Grantham (☎ Knipton 246); Haddon Hall, Derbyshire (☎ Bakewell 2014)

MANNERS, Lord Edward John Francis; s of 10 Duke of Rutland, CBE; *b* 1965; *Style* - Lord Edward Manners

MANNERS, Lady Helen Teresa Margaret; da of 10 Duke of Rutland CBE; *b* 11 Nov 1962; *Style* - Lady Helen Manners

MANNERS, Hon John Hugh Robert; s and h of 5 Baron Manners by his w Jennifer, through whose maternal gf's mother, John is 2 cous twice removed to Sir

Iain Moncreiffe of that Ilk, 11 Bt; *b* 5 May 1956; *Style* - The Hon John Manners

MANNERS, Lord John Manners; s of 9 Duke of Rutland (d 1940); *b* 1922; *Educ* Eton, New Coll Oxford; *m* 1957, Mary Diana, da of late Lt-Col L Geoffrey Moore, DSO; 1 s, 2 da; *Career* 2 Lt Life Gds 1941; High Sheriff Leics 1973-74; *Clubs* Pratt's and White's; *Style* - Lord John Manners; Haddon Hall, Derbyshire (☎ Bakewell 2014); Reservoir Cottage, Knipton, Grantham, Lincs (☎ Knipton 225)

MANNERS, Lady; Kathleen Mary; da of James Miller Johnson, of Newcastle, NSW; *m* 1927, as his 2 w, Rear-Adm Sir Errol Manners, KBE (d 1953); *Style* - Lady Manners; Flat 53, 17 Wylde st, Potts Point, Sydney, NSW

MANNERS, Mary, Baroness; Mary Edith; twin da of Rt Rev Lord William Gascoyne Cecil, Bishop of Exeter (d 1936); *b* 1900; *m* 1921, 4 Baron Manners, MC (d 1972); 3 s, 1 da; *Style* - The Rt Hon Mary, Lady Manners; North End House, Avon, Christchurch, Hants (☎ Bransgore 72317)

MANNERS, Lord Roger David; s of 9 Duke of Rutland (d 1940); *b* 1925; *m* 1965, Finola St Lawrence, only da of T Daubeney; *Career* 2 Lt Grenadier Gds 1944; *Style* - Lord Roger Manners; Belcombe Court, Bradford-on-Avon

MANNERS, Hon Thomas Jasper; s of 4 Baron Manners, MC (d 1972); *b* 1929; *Educ* Eton; *m* 1955, Sarah, eld da of Brig Roger Peake, DSO, OBE (d 1959), of Little Missenden, Bucks; 3 s; *Style* - The Hon Thomas Manners; c/o Wortley House, Wotton-under-Edge, Glos

MANNERS, Hon Venetia Jane; da of 5 Baron Manners; *b* 1950; *Style* - The Hon Venetia Manners; c/o Wortley House, Wotton-under-Edge, Glos (☎ 3174)

MANNING, Air Cdre Frederick John; CB (1954), CBE (1948); s of Frederick Manning; *b* 5 May 1912; *Educ* Colchester; *m* 1937, Elizabeth Anwyl, da of Rev Æ Ruthven-Murray (d 1949); 1 s (decd), 4 da; *Career* Sqdn Ldr M East 1939-40, Gp Capt N Africa and Italy 1942-43, Acting Air Cdre Air Ministry 1943-45, sr air adviser and dep head of Mission, British Services Mission, Burma 1949-52, SOA Transport Command 1952-56, dep dir Work Study, Air Ministry 1956, dir of Manning (2) Air Ministry 1960-63, Air Cdre 1961, AOA NEAF 1963-65, AOA Fighter Command 1965, ret 1967; *Recreations* gardening, military history; *Clubs* RAF; *Style* - Air Cdre Frederick Manning, CB, CBE; Myrtle Cottage, Eynsham, Oxford (☎ Oxford 881301)

MANNING, Lady; Olga Mary; da of Herbert Sefton-Jones; *m* 1920, as his 2 w, Brig-Gen Sir William Henry Manning, GCMG, KBE, CB (d 1932); *Style* - Lady Manning; Hampton Court Palace, East Molesey, Surrey

MANNING, Lady; Sarah Edith; da of Edgar Willmore, of Birmingham; *m* 1923, Sir George Manning, CMG (decd); *Style* - Lady Manning; 7 Bletsoe ave, Christchurch 2, New Zealand

MANNINGHAM-BULLER, Hon Anne Constance; da of 1 Viscount Dilhorne, PC, (d 1980); *b* 1951; *Educ* Leelands Sch Walmer Kent and Benenden Sch; *Style* - The Hon Anne Manningham-Buller; Horninghold Manor, Market Harborough, Leics

MANNINGHAM-BULLER, Hon Elizabeth Lydia; da of 1 Viscount Dilhorne, PC, (d 1980); *b* 1948; *Educ* Benenden Sch and Lady Margaret Hall, Oxford; *Style* - The Hon Elizabeth Manningham-Buller; Horninghold Manor, Market Harborough, Leics

MANNINGHAM-BULLER, Hon James Edward; s and h of 2 Viscount Dilhorne; *b* 1956; *Career* Lt Welsh Guards; *Style* - The Hon James Manningham-Buller

MANNINGHAM-BULLER, Hon Mary Louise; da of 2 Viscount Dilhorne; *b* 1970; *Style* - The Hon Mary Manningham-Buller

MANNINGHAM-BULLER, Hon Mervyn Reginald; s of 2 Viscount

Dilhorne; *b* 1962; *Style* - The Hon Mervyn Manningham-Buller

MANSEL, Sir Philip; 15 Bt (E 1622), of Muddlescombe, Carmarthenshire; s of Sir John Mansel, 14 Bt (d 1947); *b* 3 March 1943; *Educ* Grosvenor Coll Carlisle, Carlisle G S; *m* 1968, Margaret, da of Arthur Docker; 1 da; *Heir* unc, Regnier Ranulf Dabridgecourt Mansel; *Career* md Eden-Vale Engineering Co Ltd; *Style* - Sir Philip Mansel, Bt; 4 Redhill dve, Fellside Park, Whickham, Newcastle upon Tyne

MANSEL, Regnier Ranulf Dabridgecourt; s of late Sir Courtenay Mansel, 13 Bt; hp of n, Sir Philip Mansel, 15 Bt; *b* 6 July 1919; *m* 1941, Mary Germaine, da of Wing Cdr W St J Littlewood, OBE; 3 s, 2 da; *Career* formerly Signaller RA; *Style* - Regnier Mansel Esq; Taliaris, Maesycrugiau, Carmarthenshire

MANSEL LEWIS, David Courtenay; JP (1969), DL (1971); s of Charlie Ronald Mansel Lewis (d 1960); *b* 25 Oct 1927; *Educ* Eton, Keble Oxford; *m* 1953, Lady Mary Rosemary Marie Gabrielle Montagu-Stuart-Wortley-Mackenzie, da of 3 Earl of Wharncliffe; 1 s, 2 da; *Career* High Sheriff Carmarthenshire 1965, HM Lt 1973-74, HM Lt of Dyfed 1974-79, Lord Lt 1979-; *Recreations* sailing, music; *Clubs* Lansdowne and Cruising Assoc; *Style* - David Mansel Lewis Esq, JP, HM Lord-Lieut for Dyfed; Stradey Castle, Llanelli, Dyfed (☎ Llanelli 4626)

MANSELL, Gerard Evelyn Herbert; s of Herbert Goodinge Mansell (d 1968); *b* 16 Feb 1921; *Educ* Lycée Hoche Versailles, Lycée Buffon Paris, Ecole Libre des Sciences Politiques Paris, Chelsea Sch of Art London; *m* 1956, Diana Marion Sherar; 2 s; *Career* served 1940-46 War; joined BBC European Services 1951; controller Radio 4 and music programme BBC 1965-69, dir Programmes (Radio) 1970-71, md External Broadcasting 1972-, Dep Dir-Gen BBC 1977-; Books *Tragedy in Algeria*; *Style* - Gerard Mansell Esq; BBC, Bush House, Strand WC2 (☎ 01 240 3456); 46 Southway, NW11

MANSERGH, Lady; Violet Elsie; da of late Bernard Hillman; *m* 1921, Adm Sir Maurice James Mansergh, KCB, CBE (d 1966); *Style* - Lady Mansergh; 48 Bilton Towers, Great Cumberland pla, W1

MANSFIELD, Hon Guy Rhys John; s and h of 5 Baron Sandhurst, DFC; *b* 3 March 1949; *Educ* Harrow and Oriel Coll Oxford (BA); *m* 1976, Philippa St Clair, da of Digby Everard Verdon-Roe, of Le Cannet, France; 1 da (Alice Georgina b 1980); *Career* barr Middle Temple 1972; *Recreations* cricket; *Clubs* Leander and MCC; *Style* - The Hon Guy Mansfield; 63 Burnfoot Ave, SW6 5EB

MANSFIELD, Hon Ralph Geoffrey Knyvet; s of 4 Baron Sandhurst, OBE (d 1964); *b* 1926; *Educ* Haileybury; *m* 1, 1952, Helene Gertrude (m dis 1960), da of James Montague Coutts Duffus of Dalclaverhouse (d 1947); m 2, 1961, Evelyn Cecil, da of Sir Ronald Barry Keefe (d 1967); 1 da; *Career* served with Fleet Air Arm 1944-47, PO (A); chm and md Hatch, Mansfield and Co Ltd; county dir (Oxford) St John Ambulance Assoc 1970-72; dir Grants of St James's Ltd; OStJ; *Clubs* Carlton; Pratt's; *Style* - The Hon Ralph Mansfield; Millington House, Thorpe Green, Thorpe Le Soken, Essex (☎ 025 584 423)

MANSFIELD AND MANSFIELD, 8 Earl of (GB 1776 and 1792); William David Mungo James Murray; JP (Perth & Kinross 1975); also Lord Scone (S 1605), Viscount Stormont (S 1621) and Lord Balvaird (S 1641); s of 7 Earl of Mansfield, JP, DL (d 1971, whose family were long the owners of Robert Adam's neo-classical Kenwood; Lord Mansfield is sixth in descent from the bro of the celebrated Lord Ch Justice and 1 Earl (Pope's "silver-tongued Murray"), whose lenience towards Catholic priests arraigned before him on charges of saying Mass was rewarded by the rabble destroying his house (with its fine library) during the Gordon Riots; his broad Scotch accent allegedly caused his birth place (Perth) to be mistaken for Bath), by Dorothea, da of Rt Hon Sir Lancelot Carnegie, GCVO, KCMG, PC (2 s of 9 Earl of Southesk, by his 2 w); *b* 7 July 1930; *Educ* Wellesley House, Eton, Ch Ch

Oxford; *m* 1955, Pamela Joan, da of W N Foster, CBE; 2 s, 1 da; *Heir* s, Viscount Stormont; *Career* Hon Sheriff Perths; hereditary keeper of Bruce's Castle of Lochmaben; Lt Scots Gds RARO 1949-50; barr 1958-71; dir General Accident Fire & Life Assurance Corpn and other cos 1972-75; an opposition front bench spokesman in the House of Lords 1975-79; Min of State Scottish Office 1979-; Pres Scottish Assoc of Boys' Clubs 1976-79; Pres Roy Scottish Country Dance Soc & Fédération des Associations de Chasse de l'Europe 1977-; memb Br Delegn to Euro Parl 1973-75; chm of Historic Houses Assoc Scotland 1976-79 CCllr Perths, Hon Sheriff 1974; *Clubs* Turf, White's, Pratt's and Beefsteak; *Style* - The Rt Hon the Earl of Mansfield and Mansfield, JP; 16 Thorburn House, Kinnerton st, SW1 (☎ 01 235 7645); 2 Harcourt Bldgs, Temple, EC4 (☎ 01 353 2817); Scone Palace, Perthshire (☎ Scone 51416)

MANSFIELD AND MANSFIELD, Dorothea Countess of; Dorothea Helena; da of Rt Hon Sir Lancelot Douglas Carnegie, GCVO, KCMG (d 1933); *b* 1906; *m* 1928, 7 Earl of Mansfield and Mansfield (d 1971); 1 s, 2 da (1 decd); *Style* - The Rt Hon Dorothea, Countess of Mansfield and Mansfield; Scone Palace, Perthshire; Comlongon Castle, Ruthwell, Dumfriesshire; 1 Sloane gdns, SW1

MANSON-BAHR, Lady - Edith Mary Grossmith; *m* 1950, as his 2 w, Sir Philip Henry Manson-Bahr, CMG, DSO (d 1966); *Style* - Lady Manson-Bahr; 2 Wykeham House, 14 Chesterfield rd, Eastbourne

MANT, Prof Arthur Keith; s of George Arthur Mant (d 1967); *b* 11 Sept 1919; *Educ* Enstone Coll, London U; *m* 1947, Heather Olive Emma, da of John William Smith (d 1974); 2 s, 1 da; *Career* prof of forensic medicine Guy's Hosp U of London 1974-; formerly research fell, lecturer, reader in dept of forensic medicine Guy's Hosp; hon consultant in forensic medicine King's Coll Hosp 1967; visiting lecturer in forensic medicine St Mary's Hosp 1955; *Clubs* Athenaeum; *Style* - Prof Arthur Mant; 29 Ashley dve, Walton-on-Thames, Surrey (☎ Walton-on-Thames 25005)

MANTON, 3 Baron (UK 1922); Joseph Rupert Eric Robert Watson; s of 2 Baron Manton, JP (d 1968), by his 1 w, Alethea (gggda of 17 Baron Stourton); *b* 22 Jan 1924; *Educ* Eton; *m* 1951, Mary Elizabeth, twin da of Maj T D Hallinan; 2 s, 3 da; *Heir* s, Hon Miles Ronald Marcus Watson; *Career* joined army 1942, Lt Life Gds 1943, transferred 7 (QO) Hussars 1951 Capt; ret 1956; DL (Humberside) 1980 landowner & farmer; *Clubs* Jockey and White's; *Style* - The Rt Hon the Lord Manton DL; Houghton Hall, Sancton, York (☎ Market Weighton 3234)

MANVERS, Countess; Marie-Louis Roosevelt; da of Sir Frederick W L Butterfield (d 1943), of Cliffe Castle, Keighley, Yorks; *b* 1890; *m* 1918, 6 and last Earl Manvers, MC (d 1955); 1 s (decd), 2 da (1 decd); *Style* - The Rt Hon Countess Manvers; 22 Woodfall st, Chelsea SW3; Thoresby Park, Ollerton, Notts (Edwinstowe 315)

MANZONI, Lady; Lilian May; da of late Albert Newton Davies, of Birkenhead; *m* 1923, Sir Herbert John Baptista Manzoni, CBE (d 1972); *Style* - Lady Manzoni; 20 Viceroy Close, Bristol rd, Birmingham 5

MAR, Countess of (31 holder of S Earldom, precedence of 1404); Margaret; *née* of Mar; also Lady Garioch (an honour originally held together with the ancient territorial Earldom of Mar and which was therefore restored to the then Earl of Mar by the Act of Parliament of 1885 which settled the problem of the succession after the death of the 26 Earl; the 11 Earl of Mar & (13 of) Kellie was thereby considered to enjoy an Earldom of Mar of a Scottish cr of 1565, while his 1 cous once removed, 27 Earl of Mar (whose mother Lady Frances was sis of 26 Earl) was confirmed in his position as Premier Earl of Scotland; the Lordship of Garioch is thought, on balance, not to have been an actual S Lordship as such); da of 30 Earl of Mar (d 1975, paternal gs of Alice, herself niece through her mother, Lady Frances Goodeve-Erskine, of 27 Earl; the latter was fifth in descent from the Jacobite 23 Earl, cr titular Duke of Mar by The Old Pretender; His Titular Grace's s, when a schoolboy, rounded on a General Stanhope, who admonished him to mind his book rather than be a rebel like his father, with the riposte that the matter was not yet decided, who were the rebels; the predecessors of the original Earls of Mar were Mormaers in pre-Feudal Scotland long before the term 'Earl' came to be used); *b* 19 Sept 1940; *Educ* Lewes County G S for Girls Sussex; *m* 1, 1959 (m dis 1976), Edwin Noel of Mar (his adoption of the surname 'of Mar' was recognised by the Lord Lyon 1969), s of Edward Artiss; 1 da (Lady Susan Helen, Mistress of Mar, b 31 May 1963); m 2, 1976, John (also recognised in the surname 'of Mar' by Warrant of Lord Lyon 1976), s of Norman Salton; *Heiress* da, Mistress of Mar; *Career* holder of Premier Earldom of Scotland; PO telecommunications sales rep; *Recreations* gardening, painting, interior decoration; *Style* - The Rt Hon The Countess of Mar; 41 Penbury st, Worcester, Worcs WR3 7JD

MAR, Mistress of; Lady Susan Helen; *née* of Mar; da of Countess of Mar in her own right (31 holder of S Earldom) by her 1 husb Edward (or Edwin) Artiss (later 'of Mar'); *b* 31 May 1963; *Educ* Kidderminster H S for Girls; *Style* - Mistress of Mar

MAR AND KELLIE, 13 & 15 Earl of (S 1565, 1619); John Francis Hervey Erskine; JP (Clackmannanshire 1971); also Lord Erskine (S 1426), Baron Erskine of Dirletowne (*sic* as stated by 'The Complete Peerage', S 1604), and Viscount of Fentoun and Lord Dirletoun (S 1619, whereby Lord Mar and Kellie is premier Viscount of Scotland); also Hereditary Keeper of Stirling Castle; s of Lord Erskine, GCSI, GCIE (d 1953), and Lady Marjorie Hervey (er da of 4 Marquess of Bristol); suc gf, 12 Earl, KT, 1955; *b* 15 Feb 1921; *Educ* Eton, Trin Cambridge; *m* 1948, Pansy Constance, JP, da of Gen Sir Andrew Nicol Thorne, KCB, CMG, DSO (d 1970); 3 s, 1 da; *Heir* s, Lord Erskine; *Career* farmer; served 1939-45 War, Maj 1950, ret 1954; chm T and AF Assoc Clackmannanshire 1961-68; Scottish Rep Peer 1958-63; DL (1954), KStJ 1966, CCllr (1955-75); chm Forth Conservancy Bd 1957-68; Ld-Lt Clackmannanshire 1966- (V-Lt 1957-66); Elder Church of Scotland 1958-; Pres UNICEF 1980-; memb Roy Co Archers (Queen's Bodyguard for Scotland); *Clubs* New (Edinburgh); *Style* - Rt Hon Earl of Mar and Kellie JP, HM Lord-Lieut for Clackmannanshire; Claremont House, Alloa, Clackmannanshire (☎ 0259 212020)

MARCH AND KINRARA, Earl of; Charles Henry Gordon-Lennox; DL (W Sussex 1975); s and h of 9 Duke of Richmond and (4 of) Gordon; *b* 19 Sept 1929; *Educ* Eton, William Temple Coll Rugby; *m* 1951, Susan Monica, da of Col Cecil Grenville-Grey, CBE, by his w, Louise, gda of Sir Charles Morrison-Bell, 1 Bt; 1 s, 2 da; *Heir* s, Lord Settrington; *Career* late 2 Lt KRRC; CA, memb House of Laity Gen Synod Chichester Diocese, Centl & Exec Cttee World Cncl Churches; Church Commissioner; chm Bd for Mission and Unity Gen Synod 1972-; chm Goodwood Gp of Cos 1969-, Sussex Heritage Tst 1978-; Pres Sussex Rural Community Cncl 1973-; V-Pres SE England Tourist Bd 1974-; Treasurer Sussex U 1979-, (Hon) HHA 1975-; dir CGA 1975-; *Style* - Earl of March and Kinrara DL; Goodwood House, Chichester, W Sussex (☎ 527107 office, 527312 home)

MARCHAMLEY, 3 Baron (UK 1908); John William Tattersall Whiteley; s of 2 Baron (d 1949); *b* 24 April 1922; *m* 1967, Sonia Kathleen Pedrick; 1 s; *Heir* s, Hon William Francis Whiteley; *Career* served WW II Lt RAC, attached Indian Army, Capt 19 King George V Own Lancers; *Style* - The Rt Hon Lord Marchamley; Whetcombe, N Huish, S Brent, Devon (☎ Gara Bridge 231)

MARCHANT, Lady; Hilda Constance; da of late Ebenezer Holyman; *m* 1915, Sir Stanley Robert Marchant, CVO (d 1949); *Style* - Lady Marchant; White Cottage, Blythburgh, Halesworth, Suffolk

MARCHWOOD, 3 Viscount (UK 1945); Sir David George Staveley Penny; 3 Bt (UK 1933); also Baron Marchwood (UK 1937); s of 2 Viscount Marchwood, MBE (d 1979); *b* 22 May 1936; *Educ* Winchester; *m* 1964, Tessa

Jane, da of W F Norris; 3 s; *Heir* s, Hon Peter George Worsley Penny; *Career* 2 Lt, Roy Horse Gds (The Blues) 1955-57; dir (UK and Cyprus) Schweppes Internat Ltd, Cadbury-Schweppes Europe, L Rose & Co; *Recreations* cricket, shooting, racing; *Clubs* White's, Twelve, MCC; *Style* - The Rt Hon the Viscount Marchwood; Glebe Park, Lurgashall, Midhurst, Sussex; Filberts, Aston Tirrold, nr Didcot, Oxon (☎ 0235 850386)

MARCOW, Hon Mrs; Hon Hannah Olive; da of 1 Baron Marks of Broughton (d 1964); *b* 1918; *m* 1, 1941, Alec Lerner (m dis 1959); 1 s, 2 da; m 2, 1960, Gerald William Harold Marcow; *Style* - The Hon Mrs Marcow; The White House, Westwood rd, Windlesham, Surrey

MARCUS, Martin Alan; s of Sydney Victor Marcus; *b* 12 Jan 1948; *Educ* Wanstead County H S; *m* 1971, Cheryl Natalie, da of Dr Benjamin Green MRCS LRCP; 1 s; *Career* Fellow of Institute of Chartered Accountants England and Wales, joint md Queens Moat Houses Ltd; *Recreations* golf, tennis, badminton, table tennis; *Clubs* Abridge G C , Woodford G C, Woodford Wells Crostyx and Tennis; *Style* - Martin Marcus Esq; Little Moat, 25 Linden Crescent, Woodford Green, Essex (☎ 01 504 9488)

MARDON, Lt-Col John Kenric La Touche; DSO (1945), TD (1943), JP (Somerset 1948), DL (1962); s of Evelyn John Mardon (d 1958); *b* 1905; *Educ* Clifton, Christ's Cambridge; *m* 1933, Dulcie Joan, da of Maj-Gen K M Body, CB, CMG, OBE (d 1973); 2 s, 1 da; *Career* 2 Lt Roy Devon Yeo 1925, served 1939-45 War; chm Mardon Son & Hall Ltd 1962-69; High Sheriff 1956, Vice-Lord Lt Avon 1974-80; dir Bristol & West Building Soc; Govr Clifton Coll 1957, pres YMCA Bristol 1969-79; *Recreations* shooting, lawn tennis, squash rackets; *Style* - Lt-Col John Mardon, DSO, TD, JP, DL; Hemington House, Hemington, Bath (☎ Faulkland 592)

MARETT, Sir Robert Hugh Kirk; KCMG (1964, CMG 1955), OBE (1942); s of Dr Robert Ranulph Marett, late Rector of Exeter Coll Oxford (d 1942); *b* 20 April 1907; *Educ* Dragon Sch Oxford, Winchester Coll; *m* 1935, Piedad, nee Gavito; 1 da (Suzanne Elizabeth m 1968); *Career* businessman in Latin America 1927-38, Miny Information 1939-45, HM Diplomatic Serv 1946, Assist Under-Sec of State in Foreign Office 1959-63, HM Ambass Peru 1963-67, Dep in States of Jersey 1971-, Seigneur du Franc Fief en St Brelade (Norman feudal title in Jersey in family since 17th century); *Recreations* author, country life in general; *Clubs* Travellers'; *Style* - Sir Robert Marett, KCMG, OBE; Mon Plaisir, La Haule, Jersey (☎ 0534 34577)

MARGADALE, 1 Baron (UK 1964); John Granville Morrison; TD (1944), JP (Wilts 1936); s of Hugh Morrison, MP, JP, DL (d 1931), and Lady Mary Leveson-Gower (d 1934, 2 da of 2 Earl Granville by his 2 w Castalia, yst da of Walter Campbell of Islay); *b* 16 Dec 1906; *Educ* Eton, Magdalene Cambridge; *m* 1928, Hon Margaret Esther Lucie Smith, JP (d 1980), da of 2 Viscount Hambleden (d 1928); 3 s (including Hon Peter & Hon Charles Morrison, both MPs), 1 da (Hon Mary Morrison, Woman of the Bedchamber to HM), *qqv*; *Heir* s, Maj Hon James Ian Morrison, TD; *Career* Hon Col Roy Wiltshire Yeo, RAC (TA) 1960-72; late Cmdt Yeomanry; jt master South and W Wilts Foxhounds; JP (1933) Argyllshire, DL (1950-69); High Sheriff 1938, Lord Lt Wilts 1969-; MP (C) Wilts (Salisbury) Div 1942-64, chm 1922 Cttee 1955-64; served WW II M East; pres British Field Sports Soc 1980-; KStJ; *Recreations* hunting, shooting, fishing, racing; *Clubs* Pratt's, White's, Turf, Jockey; *Style* - The Rt Hon Lord Margadale TD JP, HM Lord-Lieut for Wiltshire; Islay House, Bridgend, Islay, Argyll; Fonthill House, Tisbury, Wilts (☎ Tisbury 202)

MARGAI, Lady; Gladys; da of Edward Gosman; *m* 1924, Rt Hon Sir Milton Augustus Strieby Margai, MBE (d 1964); *Style* - Lady Margai; The Lodge, Hill Station, Freetown, Sierra Leone

MARGESSON, 2 Viscount (UK 1942); Francis Vere Hampden Margesson; s of 1 Viscount, MC, PC (d 1965, whose mother was Lady Isabel Hobart-Hampden, JP, 3 da of 7 Earl of Buckinghamshire); *b* 1922; *Educ* Eton, Trin Oxford; *m* 1958, Helena Backstrom, of Oulu, Finland; 1 s, 3 da; *Heir* s, Hon Richard Francis David Margesson; *Career* late ADC to Govr Bahamas, dir Thames & Hudson Publications Inc of New York; Sub-Lt RNVR 1942-45; information offr British Consulate-Gen N Y 1964-70; *Style* - The Rt Hon the Viscount Margesson; Stone Ridge, New York, NY 12484, USA

MARGESSON, Hon Jane Henrietta; da of 2 Viscount Margesson; *b* 20 Oct 1965; *Style* - The Hon Jane Margesson

MARGESSON, Hon Rhoda France; s of 2 Viscount Margesson; *b* 31 May 1962; *Style* - The Hon Rhoda Margesson

MARGESSON, Hon Richard Francis David; s and h of 2 Viscount Margesson; *b* 25 Dec 1960; *Style* - The Hon Richard Margesson

MARGESSON, Hon Sarah Helena; da of 2 Viscount Margesson; *b* 18 Oct 1963; *Style* - The Hon Sarah Margesson

MARJORAM, Michael Warren; s of Derrick Noel Marjoram (d 1962); *b* 14 Jan 1932; *Educ* Framlingham College; *m* 1960, Margaret Eileen, da of John McLea (d 1965); 2 s; *Career* chm Malaysian Tobacco Co 1975-77; dir British American Tobacco Co Ltd 1978-; *Recreations* golf, tennis, waterskiing; *Clubs* Lansdowne, Roehampton; *Style* - Michael Marjoram Esq; 5 Beverley Close, SW13 OEH

MARKHAM, Alfred Langton; s of John Hatton Markham (d 1960); *b* 19 Feb 1923; *Educ* Haberdashers' Aske's; London Poly; *m* 1948, Marian Audrey; 5 c (1 decd); *Career* late plant man Common Cars; md Chubb & Sons Lock & Safe Co 1970-75; md Chubb & Sons 1974-; *Recreations* gardening; *Clubs* MCC; *Style* - Alfred Markham Esq; Windy Ridge, Grubbins Lane, Speen, Aylesbury, Bucks (☎ 024 028 229)

MARKHAM, Betty, Lady; (Frederica) Betty Cornwallis (Crawford); da of Hon Christian Eliot (gs of 3 Earl of St Germans) OBE; *m* 1942, as his 3 w, Sir Charles Markham, 2 Bt (d 1952); *Style* - Betty, Lady Markham; P O Box 583, Mbabane, Swaziland

MARKHAM, Sir Charles John; 3 Bt (UK 1911), of Beachborough Park, Newington, Kent; s of Sir Charles Markham, 2 Bt (d 1952); *b* 2 July 1924; *Educ* Eton; *m* 1949, Valerie, da of Lt-Col E Barry-Johnston, of Kenya; 2 s, 1 da; *Heir* s, (Arthur) David Markham; *Career* served 1943-47, Lt 11 Hussars (despatches); KStJ; *Clubs* Cavalry; *Style* - Sir Charles Markham, Bt; PO Box 42263, Nairobi, Kenya

MARKHAM, (Arthur) David; s and h of Sir Charles John Markham , 3 Bt; *b* 6 Dec 1950; *m* 1977, Carolyn, da of Capt Mungo Park, of Carraig, Breac, Baily, Co Dublin; *Style* - David Markham Esq

MARKS OF BROUGHTON, 2 Baron (UK 1961); Michael Marks; s of 1 Baron Marks of Broughton, sometime chm & jt md Marks & Spencer (d 1964), by his w Miriam, sis of Joseph Edward Sieff (Hon Pres of M & S) and late Baron Sieff (Life Peer, who m (the first) Lord Marks of Broughton's sis) and aunt of Baron Sieff of Brimpton; *b* 27 Aug 1920; *Educ* St Paul's, CCC Cambridge; *m* 1, 1949, Ann Catherine (m dis 1958), da of Maj Richard James Pinto, MC; 1 s, 2 da; m 2, 1960, Helene (m dis 1965), da of Gustav Fischer; *Heir* s, Hon Simon Richard Marks; *Style* - The Rt Hon Lord Marks of Broughton; Michael House, Baker st, W1

MARKS, Hon Mrs; Hon Adrianne Barbara Ellis; da of Baron Stone, MB (Life Peer); *b* 1934; *m* 1957, Clive M Marks; *Style* - The Hon Mrs Marks; 39 Farm ave, NW2

MARKS, John Graham; s of Lt-Col Sydney John Marks (d 1980); *b* 29 Sept 1930; *Educ* Oundle, Caius Cambridge; *m* 1957, Ann Morwenna, da of Dr T Simpson (d 1956); 4 s; *Career* chm Trebor Gp Ltd; *Recreations* motor racing; *Clubs* Bugatti Owners' Club; owner of yachts: 'Moffat Maid', 'Peppermint'; *Style* - John Marks Esq; New Hall, Mulberry Green, Old Harlow, Essex (☎ 0279 29454)

MARKS, Paul; s of Sidney Marks OBE, Brecon House, The Close, Totteridge; *b* 16 Sept 1935; *Educ* Acton G S; *m* 1960, Patricia Susan; 3 c; *Career* ch exec M Y Dart Ltd, v-pres English Table Tennis Association, council memb British Toy and Hobby Mfrs Association; *Recreations* tennis, table tennis; *Style* - Paul Marks Esq; Hortsedge, Pine Grove, Totteridge, London N20

MARKS, Hon Simon Richard; s and h of 2 Baron Marks of Broughton; *b* 3 May 1950; *Educ* Eton, Balliol Oxford; *Style* - The Hon Simon Marks; c/o Michael House, Baker st, W1

MARLBOROUGH, 11 Duke of (E 1702); John George Vanderbilt Henry Spencer-Churchill; JP (Oxon 1962), DL (1974); also Baron Spencer (E 1603), Earl of Sunderland (E 1643), Baron Churchill of Sandridge (E 1685), Earl of Marlborough (E 1689), Marquess of Blandford (E 1702), Prince of the Holy Roman Empire (1704), and Prince of Mindelheim (1705, cr of the Emperor Joseph); s of 10 Duke of Marlborough (d 1972), by his 1 w, Hon Alexandra Cadogan, CBE, da of Viscount Chelsea and gda of 5 Earl Cadogan; seventh cous once removed of HRH The Princess of Wales and 1 cous twice removed of Sir Winston Churchill; also 2 cous of Lady Soames and late Randolph Churchill and 3 cous of Winston Churchill, MP; *b* 13 April 1926; *Educ* Eton; *m* 1, 1951, Susan Mary (m dis 1960, she m 1962 Alan Cyril Heber-Percy), da of Michael Charles St John Hornby, of Pusey House Berks; 1 s, 1 da (1 s decd); m 2, 1961, Mrs Tina (Athina) Livanos (m dis 1971, she d 1974), da of Stavros G Livanos, of Paris, and formerly w of late Aristotle Onassis; m 3, 1972, (Dagmar) Rosita (Astri Libertas), da of late Count Carl Ludwig Douglas; 1 s, 1 da (and 1 s decd); *Heir* s, Marquess of Blandford; *Career* proprietor of Blenheim Palace, probably England's largest domestic building and one of the masterpieces of Sir John Vanbrugh (tho' Voltaire remarked that had the rooms been as wide as the walls were thick the château would have been convenient enough; *noblesse oblige* attained its most inconvenient form at mealtimes, for the kitchens were 400 yards from the dining room); formerly Capt Life Gds; chm Martini & Rossi Ltd, London Paperweights Ltd; pres Thames & Chilterns Tourist Bd, Oxon Assoc Boys' Clubs; CCllr (1960) Oxon; *Clubs* White's, Portland; *Style* - His Grace the Duke of Marlborough JP DL; Lee Place, Charlbury, Oxon (☎ 0608 810244); Blenheim Palace, Woodstock, Oxon (☎ Woodstock 811666); 1 Shepherd's Place, Upper Brook st, W1 (☎ 01 629 7971)

MARLBOROUGH, Laura, Duchess of; (Frances) Laura; da of Capt Hon Guy Lawrence Charteris (d 1967, 2 s of 11 Earl of Wemyss, and unc of Baron Charteris of Amisfield) by his 1 w, Frances Tennant, niece of 1 Baron Glenconner and Margot Asquith; *b* 10 Aug 1915; *m* 1, 1933, 2 Viscount Long (m dis 1943) (killed in action 1944); 1 da; m 2, 1943, 3 Earl of Dudley (m dis 1954); m 3, 1960, Michael Temple Canfield (decd); m 4, 1972, as his 2 w, 10 Duke of Marlborough (d 1972); *Style* - Her Grace Laura, Duchess of Marlborough; Coutts & Co, 15 Cavendish sq, London, W1 (☎ 01 935 3006 & Chalfont St Giles 2141)

MARLER, Dennis Ralph Greville; s of Greville Sidney Marler (d 1952); *b* 15 June 1927; *Educ* Marlborough; *m* 1952, Angela; 1 s, 1 da; *Career* Lt Palestine (MELF); CA, FRICS since 1969; md Capital and Counties Property Co Ltd; *Recreations* golf, travel, reading; *Clubs* Roy Thames Yacht, Roehampton; *Style* - Dennis Marler Esq; Woolborough House, 40 Roedean Crescent, SW15 (☎ 01 876 4182)

MARLEY, 2 Baron (UK 1930); Maj (Godfrey) Pelham Leigh Aman; s of 1 Baron, DSC, JP, DL, Under-Sec State War Off in Ramsay Macdonald's 1930-31 Govt (d 1952), by his w Octable, da of Sir Hugh Gilzean-Reid, DL, of Tenterden Hall, Hendon, Middx; *b* 6 Sept 1913; *Educ* Bedales, Grenoble U; *m* 1, 1938 (m dis 1946), Lilian, da of James Chrystal; m 2, 1956, Catherine Doone, da of Frank Angwyn Beal, of Eden, France; *Heir* none; *Career* 2 Lt RM 1939; served 1939-45 War, Acting Maj 1944; *Style* - The Rt Hon the Lord Marley; 104 Ebury Mews, SW1 (☎ 01 730 4844)

MARLING, Sir Charles William Somerset; 5 Bt (UK 1882), of Stanley Park and Sedbury Park, Co Gloucester; s of Lt-Col Sir John Stanley Marling, 4 Bt, OBE (d 1977); *b* 2 June 1951; *m* 1979, Judi P, adopted da of Thomas W Futrille; *Style* - Sir Charles Marling, Bt; Woodcray Manor Farm, Wokingham, Berks

MARLING, Marjorie, Lady; Marjorie Frances Esclair-Monde; da of late Sir Francis Hugh Stewart, CIE, and widow of Maj Gustavus March-Philipps; *m* as his 2 w, Sir John Marling, 4 Bt, OBE (d 1977); *Style* - Marjorie, Lady Marling; Woodcray Manor Farm, Wokingham, Berks

MARLOW, Hon Mrs; Hon Teresa; *née* Sackville-West; da (by 1 m) of 6 Baron Sackville; *b* 1954; *m* 1979, Alastair Rupert Marlow; *Style* - The Hon Mrs Marlow

MARPLES, Baroness; Ruth; da of late F W Dobson, JP, FSA, of Nottingham; *m* 1956, as his 2 w, Baron Marples, PC (Life Peer) (d 1978); *Style* - The Rt Hon Lady Marples; 33 Eccleston st, SW1

MARQUES, Reginald William David; JP; s of Charles Albert Marques MBE (d 1967); *b* 9 Dec 1932; *Educ* Tonbridge and Queens' Cambridge; *m* 1965, Janet Isabel; 3 s; *Career* 2 Lt, Royal Engineers; md Concrete Utilities Ltd 1979-; *Clubs* Harlequins & British Sportsman's; *Recreations* (past) played rugby for England & British Lions; sailing on Sovereign in America's Cup '64; *Style* - Reginald Marques Esq JP; Cockhamsted, Ware, Herts (☎ 027974 312)

MARQUIS, Lady Alexandra Susan; da of 3 Earl of Woolton (d 1969); *b* 12 Jan 1961; *Style* - Lady Alexandra Marquis

MARR, Allan James; CBE (1965); s of late William Bell Marr, s of 1 Bt; hp of kinsman, (Sir) Leslie Marr (2 Bt); *b* 6 May 1907; *Educ* Oundle, Durham U; *m* 1935, Joan de Wolf, da of John Ranken, of Sunderland; 1 s, 2 da; *Career* chm Sir James Laing & Sons Ltd 1960-73 (dir 1933-73), dir and chm EGS Ltd, former pres Shipbuilding Conference, and of NEC Inst of Eng Shipbuilders, chm Cncl of Br Ship Research Assoc 1965-73; *Style* - Allan Marr Esq, CBE; Dalesford, Thropton, Morpeth, Northumberland

MARR, (Sir) Leslie Lynn; (2 Bt, UK 1919, of Sunderland, Co Palatine of Durham); s of late Col John Lynn Marr, OBE, TD, s of 1 Bt; suc gf, Sir James Marr, 1 Bt, CBE, JP, 1932, but does not use title; *b* 1922; *Educ* Shrewsbury, Pembroke Cambridge; *m* 1948, Dinora Delores Mendelson (m dis 1956); 1 da (adopted); m 2, 1962, Lynn Heneage; 2 da; *Heir* kinsman, Allan James Marr, CBE; *Career* Pilot Offr RAF 1942, Fl Lt; *Style* - Leslie Lynn Esq; c/o Lloyds Bank, Holt, Norfolk

MARR-JOHNSON, Hon Mrs (Diana Julia); *née* Maugham; da of 1 Viscount Maugham (d 1958); *m* 1932, Kenneth Marr-Johnson; 3 s; *Style* - The Hon Mrs Marr-Johnson; Flat 3, 14 Onslow sq, SW7

MARRIS, David Drummond; s of Adam Denzil Marris, CMG; *b* 5 May 1942; *Educ* Winchester; *m* 1978, Clare Katrina, nee Mayers; *Career* banker, dir Barclays Bank Ltd Manchester (Chelmsford 1973-77) 1977-; *Recreations* country pursuits, sailing (boat: 'Naivasha'); *Clubs* Boodle's; *Style* - David Marris Esq; Foxhill, Start Lane, Whaley Bridge, Stockport, Cheshire (☎ Whaley Bridge 2530)

MARSDEN, Sir John Denton; 2 Bt (UK 1924), of Grimsby, Co Lincoln, JP (City of Liverpool 1969); s of Sir John Denton Marsden, 1 Bt (d 1944); *b* 25 Aug 1913; *Educ* Downside, St John's Cambridge; *m* 1939, Hope, da of late G E Llewelyn; 2 s, 2 da; *Heir* s, Nigel John Denton Marsden; *Career* Lt RA; JP (1950) Parts of Lindsey, Lincs, High Sheriff Lincs 1955; chm and md Consolidated Fisheries Ltd Grimsby; *Style* - Sir John Marsden, Bt, JP; White Abbey, Linton-in-Craven, Skipton, North Yorks

MARSDEN, Lady; Joyce Winifred; da of William Alfred Chote, of Wellington, New Zealand; *m* 1958, as his 2 w, Sir Ernest Marsden, CMG, CBE, MC, FRS (d 1970); *Style* - Lady Marsden; 104 Winara ave, Waikanae, Wellington, New Zealand

MARSDEN, Nigel John Denton; s and h of Sir John Denton Marsden, 2 Bt; *b* 26

May 1940; *m* 1961, Diana Jean, da of Air Marshal Sir Patrick Hunter Dunn, KBE, CB, DFC; 3 da; *Style* - Nigel Marsden Esq; 1 Grimsby rd, Waltham, Lincs

MARSDEN, Hon Mrs; Hon Vere Mary; da of Hon Conrad Adderley Dillon (d 1901) and sister of 19 Viscount Dillon, CMG, DSO (d 1946); *m* 1911, Reginald Edward Marsden (d 1960); 3 s, 3 da; granted 1934 title, rank and precedence of a Viscount's da, which would have been hers had her father survived to succeed to Viscountcy of Dillon; *Style* - The Hon Mrs Marsden; Bishopsgate Place, Englefield Green, Egham, Surrey (☎ Egham 3034)

MARSH, Baron (Life Peer UK 1981); Richard William; PC (1966); s of William Marsh, of Belvedere, Kent; *b* 14 March 1928; *Educ* Jennings Sch Swindon, Ruskin Oxford; *m* 1, 1950, Evelyn Mary (m dis 1973), da of Frederick Andrews, of Southampton; 2 s; m 2, 1973, Caroline Dutton (d 1975); m 3, Hon Felicity, *qv*, da of Baron McFadzean of Kelvinside; *Career* health services offr Nat Union of Public Employees 1951-59; memb Clerical and Admin Whitley Cncl for Health Service 1953-59; MP (L) Greenwich 1959-71; memb Nat Exec Fabian Soc; Jt Parly Sec Miny Labour 1964-65; Jt Parly Sec Miny of Technology 1965-66, Min of Power 1966-68; chm British Railways Bd 1971-76; chm Newspaper Publishers Assoc 1976-; kt 1976; *Style* - The Rt Hon the Lord Marsh, PC; c/o 6 Bouverie st, EC4

MARSH, Baroness; Hon Felicity Carmen Francesca; da of Baron McFadzean of Kelvinside (Life Peer); *b* 26 April 1946; *Educ* St Paul's Girls' Sch, Sch Oriental and African Studies London U; *m* 1979, as his 3 w, Rt Hon Sir Richard Marsh, PC, now Baron Marsh, *qv*; *Career* investment analyst/portfolio manager, Robert Fleming 1974-79, assist v-pres Rowe Price-Fleming Int Inc 1979-; *Recreations* oriental antiques, classic cars, windsurfing, photography; *Style* - The Rt Hon Lady Marsh; Lloyds Bank Ltd, South Bank Branch, 2 York rd, SE1

MARSH, Laurie Peter; s of Davis Marsh; *b* 23 Oct 1930; *Educ* Perse Sch, Cambridge U; *m* 1961 (m dis); 1 s, 2 da; *Career* md LP Marsh Properties Ltd 1958-, md John Laurie & Co Ltd 1961-64, jt md English Property Corpn 1965-70, chm and ch exec Intereuropean Properties Ltd (formerly Tigon Gp) 1969-, merged with Assoc Communications Coprn 1979, dir ACC 1979-, chm and ch exec Laurie Marsh Gp, Shaftesbury Theatre Ltd and others 1980-; *Recreations* travel, theatre, music, literature; *Style* - Laurie Marsh Esq; 30 Grove End rd, NW8 (☎ 01 289 6081), 244 East 48th st, New York

MARSHALL OF LEEDS, Baron (Life Peer UK 1980); Frank Shaw Marshall; s of Charles William Marshall, of Wakefield (d 1961); *b* 26 Sept 1915; *Educ* Queen Elizabeth's Sch Wakefield, Downing Cambridge; *m* 1941, Mary, da of Robert Barr, of Shadwell; 2 da; *Career* served Capt RAC & War Off Staff Capt; slr; V-Chm Con Pty; Special Advsr to Govt Third London Airport; chm Maplin Devpt Corpn 1973-74, Municipal Mutual Insur Ltd; V-Pres Leeds & Holbeck Bldg Soc 1977-, Bldg Socs Assoc, Barr & Wallace Arnold Tst; FRSA; kt 1971; dir: AA, B & WAT Pensions, Evan Evans Ltd, Fanum Ltd, Highfield Travel, Leeds & Holbeck Pension, London Cremation Ltd, MLA Unit Tst Management, OQS Property Management, Wallace Arnold Travel; *Recreations* reading, working; *Clubs* Carlton, Athenaeum; *Style* - Rt Hon Lord Marshall of Leeds; Holtby, N Yorks

MARSHALL, Geoffrey Wyndham; s of W J Marshall; *b* 5 March 1937; *Educ* King Edward VI Sch Birmingham, Jesus Oxford, Harvard Business Sch; *m* 1960, Sally Rose, nee Gerard; 2 s (Andrew b 1965, Julian b 1969), 1 da (Miranda b 1964); *Career* shoemaker, dir Somerville Brothers Ltd 1972-75, md: Bally Shoe Factories (Norwich Ltd), Bally Shoe Co Ltd, Bally London Shoe Co 1975-; gp md Bally (UK) Ltd 1979-; pres Norwich & Norfolk Chamber of Commerce & Industry 1981-; *Recreations* squash, rugby football, gardening, travel; *Clubs* United Oxford and Cambridge; *Style* - Geoffrey Marshall Esq; Salle Place, Reepham, Norfolk (☎ 060 526 638)

MARSHALL, Lady; Meta; da of William Hawke, of Bugle, Cornwall; *m* 1926, Hon

Mr Justice (Sir Archie Pellow) Marshall (d 1966); *Style* - Lady Marshall; Penlea, Penwinnick rd, St Austell, Cornwall

MARSHALL, Thomas Elder; s of John Marshall; *b* 16 Nov 1939; *Educ* Govan Sr Secdy Sch, Glasgow & Strathclyde Us; *m* 1963, Jessie Paton Hamilton; 3 da; *Career* chartered engr, dir Haden Young Ltd, md Haden Robertson, govr dir Scottish Engrg Training Scheme Ltd, pres Electrical Contractors Assoc of Scot 1975-77; *Recreations* riding, hill walking, vintage cars; *Clubs* Western, Roy Scottish Auto; *Style* - Thomas Marshall Esq; Duirinnis, Davieland rd, Whitecraigs, Glasgow; Milverton, North Connel, by Oban

MARSHALL, Mrs A R; Valerie Margaret; da of Ernest Knagg; *b* 30 March 1945; *Educ* Brighton, Hove H S, Girton Cambridge, London Graduate Sch of Business Studies; *m* 1972, Alan Roger Marshall; 1 s, 1 da; *Career* financial controller Industrial and Commercial Finance Corpn 1970-79, memb investment exec Scottish Development Agency 1979-, Monopolies and Mergers Commission 1977-, Scottish Design Council 1974-77; *Recreations* music, ballet, drama, golf; *Style* - Mrs A R Marshall; Valhalla, Garth Estate, by Fortingall, Perthshire; Kilmore, 16 Dalkeith ave, Dumbreck Glasgow (☎ 041 427 0096)

MARSHAM, Lady Anne Rhoda; da of Lt-Col Hon Reginald Hastings Marsham, OBE, and sis of 7 Earl of Romney; *b* 1909; *Career* raised to the rank of an Earl's da, 1976; served 1939-45 war as Section Officer, WAAF; Kenya Police Reserve 1952-60; *Style* - Lady Anne Marsham; PO Box 31, Gilgil, Kenya

MARSHAM, Julian Charles; JP; s of Col Peter Marsham, MBE (s of Hon Sydney Marsham, yst s of 4 Earl of Romney), and Hersey, da of Maj Hon Richard Coke (3 s of 2 Earl of Leicester, KG, JP, DL, by his 2 w, Hon Georgina Cavendish, da of 2 Baron Chesham); hp of 1 cous once removed, 7 Earl of Romney; *b* 28 March 1948; *Educ* Eton; *m* 1975, Catriona, da of Robert Stewart (nephew through his mother of Sir Christopher Lighton, 8 Bt, MBE); 2 s (David Charles b 1977, Michael Julian b 1979); *Career* land agent; *Recreations* shooting, fishing, silviculture, gardening; *Style* - Julian Marsham Esq, JP; Gayton Hall, King's Lynn, Norfolk (☎ Gayton 259)

MARSTON, Hon Mrs (Vanessa Mary); *née* Cawley; da of 3 Baron Cawley; *b* 30 Dec 1951; *Educ* Downe House; *m* 1971, Dr John Anthony, s of Donald Marston, of the Br Embassy, Beirut; 4 da (Cicely b 1973, Emma b 1975, Camilla b 1977, Annabel b 1979); *Style* - The Hon Mrs Marston; Gorwell House, Barnstaple, N Devon (☎ 75499)

MARTELL, Vice-Adm Sir Hugh Colenso; KBE (1966, CBE 1957), CB (1963); s of Engr Capt A Martell, DSO, RN (ret); *b* 6 May 1912; *Educ* Edinburgh Acad, RNC Dartmouth; *m* 1941, Marguerite, da of Sir Dymoke White, 2 Bt; 5 s, 1 da; *Career* Ch Allied Staff Med Aegean & Black Sea 1965-67, ret; *Style* - Vice-Adm Sir Hugh Martell KBE CB; Long Beach, Bosham Hoe, Chichester, Sussex

MARTEN, Hon Mrs; Hon Mary Anna Sibell Elizabeth; da of 3 Baron Alington (d 1940); *b* 1929; *m* 1949, George Gosselin Marten, MVO, DSC, s of late V-Adm Sir Francis Arthur Marten, KBE, CB, CMG, CVO; 1 s, 4 da; *Style* - The Hon Mrs Marten; Crichel, Wimborne, Dorset

MARTIN, Alan Gould; s of Arthur Herbert Martin (d 1962); *b* 19 Jan 1920; *Educ* Monkton Combe Sch, Harvard Business Sch; *m* 1953, Barbara Goodier, nee Haworth (d 1929); 2 s; *Career* chartered accountant, dir Industrial and Commercial Finance Corpn 1976-81, chm Frank Horsell Gp 1980-, chm Singleton Birch 1979-; dir Provincial Bldg Soc, W Yorks Ind Hosp, W Yorks Chemicals, Robert Glew & Co, Rainford Venture Capital; *Recreations* idleness; *Clubs* Leeds, Nat Liberal; *Style* - Alan Martin Esq; Huby House, Strait Lane, Huby, Leeds (☎ 0423 74254)

MARTIN, Douglas Whitwell; s of Rev Thomas Henry Martin (d 1955); *b* 17 Feb 1906; *Educ* Rossall Sch, Lausanne U; *m* 1, 1931, Jessie Milroy (d 1965), da of Dr John

Lowrie,(d 1952); 3 s; m 2, 1967, Margaret Helen, da of Edwin James Simms (d 1964); *Career* chm Gill & Duffus Ltd, 1964-70, pres 1973-; Lloyd's underwriter 1950-59; *Recreations* reading, theatre; *Clubs* Boodle's; *Style* - Douglas Martin Esq; 74 Fort George; St Peter Port, Guernsey, CI (☎ Guernsey 25381)

MARTIN, Lady; Gladys; *m* 1919, late Hon Sir Norman Angus Martin; *Style* - Lady Martin; Longleat, 133 Alexandra ave, South Yarra, Vic 3141, Australia

MARTIN, Hugh Hutton; s of Hugh Lumsden Martin (d 1968); *b* 26 Nov 1940; *Educ* Merchiston; *m* 1964, Kay Roberta, nee Calder; 2 c; *Career* chm Martins (Dundyvan) Ltd, dir Martin-Black Ltd; *Recreations* skiing; *Style* - Hugh Martin Esq; Abbygreen, Carmunnock, Glasgow (☎ home: 041 644 2153; office: 0236 3360)

MARTIN, Hubert Sinclair; CBE (1945), DL (Sussex 1960); *b* 6 Sept 1891; *m* 1, 1920, Margaret (d 1961), nee Hawksley; 1 s; m 2, 1963, Joan L J, nee Abraham; *Career* served WW I; clerk of peace & CCllr E Sussex 1939-59; *Clubs* Athenaeum; *Style* - Hubert Martin Esq, CBE, DL; Field Cottage, Belgrave rd, Seaford, Sussex (☎ 892183)

MARTIN, Lady; Jean Macgaradh; da of Thomas Hay Wilson, of Edinburgh; *m* 1943, Sir David Christie Martin, CBE (d 1976); *Style* - Lady Martin; Flat 1, 6 Carlton House ter, SW1 (☎ 01 839 5266)

MARTIN, Lady; Margaret; da of Alfred Roberts; *m* 1930, Sir Charles Carnegie Martin, CBE (d 1969); *Style* - Lady Martin; Flat 5, 241 Alcester Road South, King's Heath, Birmingham

MARTIN, Lady; Nina Margherita; da of late Francesco Michele Amadini; *m* 1938, as his 3 w, Sir Ernest Martin (d 1957); *Style* - Lady Martin; 1 Redcliffe sq, SW10

MARTIN, Maj-Gen Peter Lawrence De Carteret; CBE (1968, OBE 1964); s of the late Col Charles De Carteret Martin, MD, CRD, IMS; *b* 15 Feb 1920; *Educ* Wellington, Sandhurst; *m* 1, 1949, Elizabeth Felicia, da of the late Col C M Keble, OBE; 1 s, 1 da; m 2, 1973, Valerie Elizabeth, nee Brown; 2 s (step); *Career* dir Personal Services (Army) 1971-74, Col the 22 (Cheshire) Regt 1971-78, Col Cmdt Miliary Provost Staff Corps 1972-74, chm Lady Grover's Hospital Fund for Officers' Families 1975-, National Exec Ctee Forces Help Society 1975-, Gen Ctee Ex-Services Mental Welfare Society 1977-, Services Liaison Officer Variety Club of Great Britain 1976-, head of admin Smith & Williamson 1976-; *Recreations* golf, tennis, walking, reading; *Clubs* Army & Navy; *Style* - Maj-Gen Peter Martin, CBE; Faircrosse, Brimpton Common, Berks (☎ Tadley 5274)

MARTIN, Col Robert Andrew St George; OBE (1959, MBE 1949); s of Maj William Francis Martin (ka 1915); *b* 23 April 1914; *Educ* Eton, Sandhurst; *m* 1950, Margaret Grace, da of John V Buchanan (d 1966); 1 s; *Career* served in S Africa 1939-40, UK 1940-44, North West Europe 1944-45; ADC to Govr-Gen S Africa 1938-40, AMS HQ BAOR 1952-55, mil sec to Govr-Gen Australia 1955-57, 1 Oxford and Bucks LI 1934-38 and CO 1 Green Jackets 1957-59, Bde Col Green Jackets 1959-62, CRLS HQ Western Command 1962-65, Ld-Lt Leics 1965-; *Recreations* hunting, shooting, gardening; *Clubs* Army & Navy, MCC *Style* - Col Robert Martin OBE, HM Lord-Lieut for Leicestershire; The Brand, Woodhouse Eaves, Loughborough, Leicestershire (☎ Woodhouse Eaves 890269)

MARTIN, Robin Frank; s of Robert George Martin; *b* 25 March 1938; *Educ* Sevenoaks Sch; *Career* Fl Lt RAF, chm East Grinstead Securities Ltd 1972-, chm Forest Row Properties 1972-, chm Forest Row Investments Ltd 1972-, chm Oceanclean Ltd 1974-, Ellis Hearing Aid Services Ltd 1974- FInstD, MInstAM, FAAI; *Recreations* skiing; *Clubs* RAF, Ski Club of Great Britain; *Style* - Robin Martin Esq; Chequers Mead, Forest Row, Sussex (☎ Forest Row 2795)

MARTIN, Lady; Thelma Idina; da of James Martin Stander; *m* 1961, as his 2 w, Sir Albert Victor Martin, CBE (d 1968);

Style - Lady Martin; Little Dalby Hall, Melton Mowbray, Leics

MARTIN-BATES, James Patrick; JP (1961); s of Robert Martin-Bates JP (d 1950); *b* 17 April 1912; *Educ* Glenalmond, Worcester Coll Oxford; *m* 1939, Dorothy Clare, da of Prof James Miller (d 1962); 1 s, 2 da; *Career* md PE Mgmnt Gp 1938-61, princ admin Staff Coll 1961-72, dir WS Atkins Gp 1970-, dir Averys 1970-77, dir Charringtons Industrial Hldgs 1972-77, dir Hutchinson 1958-78, Cncl Univ Coll Buckingham 1977-; *Recreations* golf, fishing; *Clubs* Caledonian, Roy & Ancient St Andrews, Leander; *Style* - James Martin-Bates Esq, JP; Ivy Cottage, Fingest, nr Henley-on-Thames

MARTIN-JENKINS, Timothy Dennis; s of Lt-Col Dennis Frederick Martin-Jenkins; *b* 26 May 1947; *Educ* St Bede's Sch Eastbourne, Marlborough, Cambridge U, Harvard U; *Career* chm Ellerman Commercial Holdings Ltd 1980-, dir Ellerman Lines Ltd 1978-; *Recreations* golf, skiing, tennis, music; *Clubs* Woking Golf, Ganton Golf, Pacific (Hull); *Style* - Timothy Martin-Jenkins Esq; 20 Pembridge Crescent, W11

MARTONMERE, 1 Baron (UK 1964); (John) Roland Robinson; GBE (1973), KCMG (1966), PC (1962); s of Roland Walkden Robinson; *b* 22 Feb 1907; *Educ* Trin Hall Cambridge; *m* 1930, Maysie, da of late Clarence Warren Gasque; 1 da (1 s, decd); *Heir* gs, John Stephen Robinson; *Career* Flying Offr RAFVR 1941; MP (C) Lancashire 1931-35, Blackpool 1935-45, Blackpool (South) 1945-64; past pres Assoc of Health and Pleasure Resorts; chm Conservative Party Commonwealth Affairs Ctee 1954-6; Govr and C-in-C Bermuda 1964-72; kt 1954; KStJ; *Style* - The Rt Hon the Lord Martonmere, GBE, KCMG, PC; El Mirador, Lyford Cay PO Box 7776, Nassau, Bahamas; Romay House, Tuckers Town, Bermuda

MARTYN-HEMPHILL, Hon Angela Mary Martyn; da of 5 Baron Hemphill; *b* 26 Jan 1953; *Style* - The Hon Angela Martyn-Hemphill

MARTYN-HEMPHILL, Hon Charles Andrew Martyn; s and h of 5 Baron Hemphill; *b* 8 Oct 1954; *Educ* Downside; *Style* - The Hon Charles Martyn-Hemphill

MARTYN-HEMPHILL, Hon Mary Anne Martyn; da of 5 Baron Hemphill; *b* 29 Nov 1958; *Style* - The Hon Mary Martyn-Hemphill

MARYON-WILSON, Lady; Janet Mary; da of late Rev E A Moxon; *m* 1923, Sir Hubert Guy Maryon-Wilson, 13 & last Bt (d 1978); *Style* - Lady Maryon-Wilson; The Grange, Great Canfield, Essex

MASEFIELD, Hon Mrs; Hon Veronica Margery; da of 9 Baron Hawke (d 1939); *b* 1915; *m* 1940, Jack Briscoe Masefield; 1 da; *Style* - The Hon Mrs Masefield; Down Lodge, East Harting, Petersfield, Hants

MASHAM OF ILTON, Baroness (Life Peeress UK 1970); Susan Lilian Primrose; da of Maj Sir Ronald Norman Sinclair, 8 Bt; *b* 14 April 1935; *Educ* Heathfield Ascot, London Poly; *m* 1959, 2 Earl of Swinton; 1 s, 1 da (both adopted); *Career* memb Bd Visitors Wetherby Borstal; Pres N Yorks Red Cross, Chartered Soc Physiotherapy, Spinal Injuries Assoc (chm); *Recreations* swimming, breeding Highland ponies; *Style* - Rt Hon Countess of Swinton; Dykes Hill House, Masham, Ripon, Yorks (☎ 241)

MASON, David; s of George Edward Mason; *b* 3 Nov 1944; *Educ* Deacon's G S Peterborough, RAC Cirencester; *m* 1970, Shirley Ann, nee Adams; 2 s, 1 da; *Career* trials offr Rotherwell Plant Breeders 1968-73, cereal trials coordinator N American Plant Breeders 1973-75, dir Rothwell Plant Breeders 1975-79, md Mickerson RPB Ltd 1979-; *Recreations* gardening, family; *Style* - David Mason Esq; 5 St James rd, Brigg, S Humberside (☎ 56210)

MASON, Hon Mrs; Hon Elizabeth; da of 7 Baron Auckland (d 1955); *b* 1928; *Educ* Brondesbury; *m* 1954, Maj Frederic Edward Isdale (Robin) Mason; 2 s, 1 da; *Style* - The Hon Mrs Mason; Reed Hall, Holbrook, nr Ipswich, Suffolk (☎ Ipswich 328327)

MASON, Hon Elizabeth-Anne; da of 3 Baron Blackford (d 1977); *b* 1965; *Style* - The Hon Elizabeth-Anne Mason

MASON, Hon Mrs; Hon Frieda; da of 1 Baron Essendon (d 1944); *m* 1, 1927, Ian Patrick Robert Napier, MC (m dis 1940); 2 s; m 2, 1940, Cecil Warde Mason (m dis 1947); *Style* - The Hon Mrs Frieda Mason; 90k Eaton sq, SW1

MASON, James Neville; s of John Mason (d 1972), of Huddersfield; *b* 15 May 1909; *Educ* Marlborough Coll, Peterhouse Cambridge; *m* 1, 1941, Pamela Kellino (m dis 1965); 1 s, 1 da; m 2, 1971, Clarissa Grace, da of Austin Knipe (d 1979); *Career* actor; *Recreations* painting, tennis; *Clubs* Garrick; *Style* - James Mason Esq; c/o Mrs Al Parker, 55 Park Lane, W1 (☎ 01 499 3080)

MASON, Hon Mrs; Hon Kristina Elizabeth; da of Baroness Robson of Kiddington (Life Peeress); *b* 1946; *m* 1967, Iain McLaren Mason; *Style* - The Hon Mrs Mason; The Dower House, Kiddington, Woodstock, Oxon

MASON, His Honour Judge; (George Frederick) Peter Mason; QC (1963); s of George Mason, of Keighley; *b* 11 Dec 1921; *Educ* Lancaster Roy G S, St Cat's Cambridge; *m* 1, 1950 (m dis 1977); 2 s, 2 da (and 1 da decd); m 2, 1981, Sarah, da of Sir Robert Ricketts, 7 Bt, and Anne (da of Rt Hon Sir Stafford Cripps, CH, PC, QC, sometime Chllr of the Exchequer and 4 s of 1 Baron Parmoor, KCVO, PC, JP); *Career* served WW II RA M East & Italy; barr 1947, dep chm Ag Land Tbnl W Yorks & Lancs 1962, Circuit Judge 1970-; *Style* - His Honour Judge Mason QC; Central Criminal Court, EC4 (☎ 01 248 3277)

MASON, Lady; Roberta; da of late J Lorn McDougall, KC, of Ottawa; *m* 1938, Sir Paul Mason, KCMG, KCVO (d 1978); *Style* - Lady Mason; Morton Hall, Retford, Notts

MASON, Sydney; s of Jack Mason (d 1936); *b* 30 Sept 1920; *m* 1945, Rosalind, da of Victor Woolf (d 1975); *Career* man Land Securities Investment Trust Ltd 1943-49, md Hammerson Property & Investment Trust Ltd 1949- (chm 1958-); *Recreations* sailing, riding, painting; *Clubs* Naval, Roy Thames Yacht, City Livery; race horses: 'Brentex' (Flat), 'Trace of Gold' (Nat Hunt); *Style* - Sydney Mason Esq; 100 Park Lane, W1 (☎ 01 629 9494)

MASSEREENE AND FERRARD, 13 & 6 Viscount (I 1660 & 1797); John Clotworthy Talbot Foster Whyte-Melville Skeffington; also Baron of Loughneagh (I 1660), Baron Oriel of Collon (I 1790), and Baron Oriel of Ferrard (UK 1821, which sits as); s of 12 (& 5) Viscount, DSO, JP, DL (d 1956, himself ggs of Harriet, w of 2 Viscount Ferrard and Viscountess Massereene in her own right; Harriet's f was the 4 & last Earl of Massereene, while her unc, the 2 Earl, was imprisoned for 18 years in France prior to the Revolution for running up debts while speculating in salt (then of course relatively heavily taxed and therefore, although a necessity, a dear one); whether 18 years in prison unhinged his wits or no must remain a matter for conjecture, but a Carrickfergus jury certainly considered him insane when invalidating his will; over the water, in cynophile Albion, the Earl's orders that 50 dogs should attend his favourite hound's funeral clad in white scarves, and that all the parish dogs should be present, would have excited less censure); *b* 23 Oct 1914; *Educ* Eton; *m* 1939, Annabelle Kathleen, da of late Henry Lewis, of Combwell Priory, Hawkhurst; 1 s, 1 da; *Heir* Hon John David Clotworthy Whyte-Melville Skeffington; *Career* 2 Lt Black Watch 1933-36 and briefly WW II; FZS; patron of one living; Cross of Cdr Order of Merit Sov Mil Order Malta; dir of cos; freeman City of London, memb Worshipful Co of Shipwrights; chm Victoria League for Kent; Commodore House of Lords Yacht Club; master Ashford Valley Foxhounds 1953-54; driver leading British car Le Mans Grand Prix 1937; Gold Staff Offr Coronation of HM the Queen 1953; memb Inter-Parliamentary Union Delegation to Spain 1960; ch London Scottish Clans Assoc; pres Kent Hotels & Restaurants Assoc and other socs; DL (1957) Co Antrim; Book *The Lords*; *Clubs* Carlton, Roy Yacht Sqdn, Turf, Carlton, Pratt's;

Style - The Rt Hon the Viscount Massereene and Ferrard DL; Knock, Isle of Mull, Oban (Aros 56); Chilham Castle, Canterbury, Kent (☎ Chilham 319)

MASSEY, Lady; Dorothy Blanche Ince; da of late Rev H H T Cleife; *m* 1924, Sir Arthur Massey, CBE (d 1980); *Style* - Lady Massey; 93 Bedford gdns, W8 (☎ 01 727 6591)

MASSEY, Hon Mrs; Hon Lavinia; da of 6 Baron Skelmersdale (d 1973); *b* 1937; *m* 1969, Robert Brian Noel Massey; 2 s; *Style* - The Hon Mrs Massey; Melbury, Kingston Hill, Kingston-upon-Thames, Surrey

MASSIMO, Prince Cesare Camillo Ivan Vittorio Alessandro; 2 s of Prince Stefano Massimo by his w Atalanta, da of Maj Ivan Foxwell and Lady Edith, nee Lambart, gda of 9 Earl of Cavan, KP, PC, DL; *b* 1977; *Style* - Prince Cesare Massimo

MASSIMO, Prince Stefano; *m* 1973, Atalanta Edith, da of Lady Edith Sybil, nee Lambart (da of Capt Hon Lionel Lambart, DSO, RN, 2 s of 9 Earl of Cavan, KP, PC, DL, sometime MP Somerset S), by her husb, Maj Ivan Foxwell; 2 s; *Style* - Prince Stefano Massimo; 44 Fernshaw rd, SW6

MASSIMO, Prince Valerio Stefano Francesco Zaffiro; er s of Prince Stefano Massimo by his w Atalanta, 2 da of Maj Ivan Foxwell and Lady Edith, nee Lambart, gda of 9 Earl of Cavan, KP, PC, DL; *b* 1973; *Style* - Prince Valerio Massimo

MASSINGBERD-MUNDY, Adrian John; DL (Lincs 1971); s of Godfrey Massingberd-Mundy, JP, DL (d 1935; Godfrey's paternal gf, Charles Massingberd-Mundy, JP, DL, was ggs through his m, Harriet, of William Massingberd; the latter's w, Anne, was gggda through the Armytage Bts of Catherine Danby, through whom Mr Massingberd-Mundy is co-heir to the Barony of Scrope of Masham, abeyant 1517), by his w, Margaret, 2 da of Stephen Schilizzi, of Loddington Hall, Kettering, and Guilsborough Court, Northants (sometime sr male rep in England of the Schilizzis, originally of Byzantium, membs of which family were officials under Emperors Nicephorus III, who reigned 1078-81, and Isaac Comnenus II, who reigned 1085-95); *b* 10 Feb 1927; *Educ* RNC Dartmouth; *Career* Lt RN (ret), late CC Lindsey and chm Lincs Branch CLA; Lord of the Manor of S Ormsby; patron of livings of S Ormsby with Ketsby, Calceby and Driby, and Whixley with Green Hammerton; *Style* - Adrian Massingberd-Mundy Esq, DL; Ormsby Hall, Lincs

MASSY, 9 Baron (I 1776); Hugh Hamon John Somerset Massy; s of 8 Baron (d 1958); *b* 11 June 1921; *Educ* Clongowes Wood Coll, Clayesmore Sch; *m* 1943, Margaret Elizabeth, da of late John Flower; 4 s, 1 da; *Heir* s, Hon David Hamon Somerset Massy; *Career* served 1940-45 War, Private RAOC; *Style* - The Rt Hon the Lord Massy

MASSY, Hon David Hamon Somerset; s and h of 9 Baron Massy; *b* 4 March 1947; *Educ* St George's Coll Weybridge; *Career* serving with Merchant Navy; *Style* - The Hon David Massy

MASSY, Hon Graham Ingoldsby Somerset; s of 9 Baron Massy; *b* 1952; *Style* - The Hon Graham Massy

MASSY, Hon John Hugh Somerset; s of 9 Baron Massy; *b* 1950; *m* 1978, Andrea, da of Alan West, of Leicester; *Style* - The Hon John Massy

MASSY, Hon Muriel Olive; da of 7 Baron Massy; *b* 1892; *Style* - The Hon Muriel Massy

MASSY, Hon Paul Robert; s of 9 Baron Massy; *b* 1953; *m* 1976, Anne Bridget, da of James McGowan, of Leicester; 1 s; *Style* - The Hon Paul Massy

MASSY, Hon Sheelagh Marie Louise; da of 9 Baron Massy; *b* 1958; *Style* - The Hon Sheelagh Massy

MASTERMAN, Hon Mrs; Hon Elizabeth Trilby Charity; da of Baron Taylor (Life Peer); *b* 1943; *Educ* Sussex U; *m* 1971, Paul Stephen Masterman; *Style* -

The Hon Mrs Masterman; 16 Ladbroke gdns, W11

MATARASSO, Hon Mrs; Hon Pauline Maud; da of 1 Baron Sanderson of Ayot (d 1971); *b* 1929; *Educ* Oxford, Dr de L'Université de Paris; *m* 1952, Robert Henry Matarasso; 3 s, 1 da; *Style* - The Hon Mrs Matarasso; Church Hill House, Burton Dassett, Leamington Spa

MATHER, Hon Mrs; Hon Philippa Selina; da of 5 Baron Cromwell, DSO, MC (d 1966); *b* 1925; *m* 1951, Lt-Col David Carol MacDonell Mather, MC, MP; 1 s, 3 da; *Style* - The Hon Mrs Mather; Brookfield, Horton, Bucks

MATHER-JACKSON, Sir Anthony Henry Mather; 6 Bt (UK 1869), of The Manor House, Birkenhead, JP (Notts 1938), DL (1942); s of late W B M Jackson, of Glapwell Hall, Chesterfield, and bro of Sir George Christopher Mather-Jackson, 5 Bt (d 1976); assumed additional surname Mather 1976; *b* 9 Nov 1899; *Educ* Harrow; *m* 1923, Evelyn Mary, da of Lt-Col Sir H K Stephenson, 1 Bt, DSO, of Hassop Hall, Bakewell; 3 da; *Heir* kinsman, William Jackson; *Career* Gren Gds 1918-20; *Style* - Sir Anthony Mather-Jackson Bt JP DL; Archway House, Kirklington, Newark, Notts (☎ Southwell 2070)

MATHER-JACKSON, Victoria, Lady; Victoria Emily Ford; da of Indick Freyberg, of Mitau, Latvia; *m* 1941, Sir (George) Christopher Mather Mather-Jackson, 5 Bt (d 1976); *Style* - Victoria, Lady Mather-Jackson; West Court, Crondall, nr Farnham, Surrey

MATHERS, Baroness; Jessie Newton; da of late George Graham, JP, of Peebles and Edinburgh; *m* 1940, as his 2 w, 1 and last Baron Mathers, KT, PC, DL (d 1965); *Style* - The Rt Hon Lady Mathers; 50 Craiglea Drive, Edinburgh 10 (☎ 031 4477 555)

MATHERS, Sir Robert William; *Career* kt 1981 for service to the retail industry and the community; *Style* - Sir Robert Mathers

MATHESON, Lady; Elsie Kate; da of William Cocks and widow of Maj Robert Scott; *m* 1946, as his 2 w, Cdr Sir Charles George Matheson, DSO, RD (d 1948); *Style* - Lady Matheson; c/o Barclays Bank, 189 Terminus rd, Eastbourne, Sussex

MATHESON, Lady Elizabeth Mary Gertrude; ARRC ; da of 8 Earl of Albemarle (d 1942); *b* 1890; *m* 1923, as his 2 w, Gen Sir Torquhil George Matheson, of Matheson, KCB, CMG (d 1963); 2 s; *Career* served in World War I as VAD nurse in France (1915 Star, 2 Medals, despatches); *Style* - Lady Elizabeth Matheson, ARRC; Cedar House, Woodbridge, Suffolk

MATHESON, Maj Fergus John; s of Gen Sir Torquhil Matheson of Matheson, KCB, CMG (d 1963); h to Btcy & Chiefship of bro, Sir Torquhil Alexander Matheson of Matheson, 6 Bt; *b* 22 Feb 1927; *Educ* Eton; *m* 1952, Hon Jean Elizabeth Mary Willoughby, da of 11 Baron Middleton; 1 s, 2 da; *Career* Maj Coldstream Gds Reserve, Hon Corps of Gentlemen at Arms 1979; *Style* - Maj Fergus Matheson; Hedenham Old Rectory, Bungay, Suffolk

MATHESON, Hon Mrs; Hon Jean Elizabeth Mary; da of 11 Baron Middleton (d 1970); *b* 1928; *m* 1952, Major Fergus John Matheson; 1 s, 2 da; *Style* - The Hon Mrs Matheson; Hedenham Old Rectory, Bungay, Suffolk

MATHESON, Margaret; *aet* 34; *Career* formerly BBC secretary, story ed, producer Play Dept, ATV Controller Drama 1981-; *Style* - Miss Margaret Matheson; c/o ATV, ATV House, Gt Cumberland Place, W1

MATHESON OF MATHESON, Maj Sir Torquhil Alexander; 6 Bt (UK 1882), of Lochalsh, Co Ross; s of Gen Sir Torquhil George Matheson of Matheson, 5 Bt, KCB, CMG (d 1963); *b* 15 Aug 1925; *Educ* Eton; *m* 1954, Serena Mary Francesca, da of Lt-Col Sir (James) Michael Peto, 2 Bt; 2 da; *Heir* bro, Maj Fergus John Matheson; *Career* served 1939-45 with 5 Bn Coldstream Gds, Maj 1959, seconded KAR (Kenya) 1961-64, ret 1964; Wilts Regt (TA) 1965-67; one of HM Body Guard of Hon Corps of Gentlemen at

Arms 1977-; suc as Chief of Clan Matheson 1975; *Style* - Maj Sir Torquhil Matheson of Matheson, Bt; Standerwick Court, Frome, Somerset

MATHEW, HSH Princess Olga Romanoff, Mrs Thomas; Olga; da of HH Prince Andrew Romanoff (eldest s of HIH The Grand Duke Alexander, 4 s of HIH The Grand Duke Mikhail, 4 s of Tsar Nicholas I of Russia) by his 2 w, Nadine, da of Lt-Col Herbert McDougall, of Belgravia; *b* 8 April 1950; *m* 1975, Thomas Mathew, 2 s of Francis Mathew, formerly with The Times; 1 s and at least 1 da; *Style* - Her Serene Highness Princess Olga Romanoff, Mrs Thomas Mathew; Welford House, nr Rugby, Northants

MATHEW, Lady; Phyllis Helen; da of late Cyril Russell and gda of late Lord Russell of Killowen; *b* 1897; *m* 1923, Sir Theobald Mathew, KBE, MC (d 1964); *Style* - Lady Mathew; 65 Cornwall gdns, SW7

MATHEW, Theobald David; s of Robert Mathew (d 1942); *b* 7 April 1942; *Educ* Downside, Balliol Oxford; *Career* Windsor Herald of Arms 1978-, Green Staff Offr at Investiture of HRH Prince of Wales 1969, Rouge Dragon Pursuivant of Arms 1970, dep treasurer of the College of Arms; *Recreations* sailing (yacht: 'Tinker Liz'), cricket, music, sketching; *Clubs* Athenaeum, MCC, Middlesex CCC, Roy Harwich Yacht; *Style* - Theobald Mathew Esq; 76 Clifton Hill, NW8 (☎ 01 624 8448)

MATHEWSON, Lady; Iris; da of late R M Christie, of Dunblane; *m* 1935, Sir Alexander Robert Mathewson, CBE, CA (d 1968); *Style* - Lady Mathewson; 12 Drummond pla, Edinburgh

MATHIAS, Sir Richard Hughes; 2 Bt (UK 1917), of Vaendre Hall, St Mellons, Co Monmouth; s of Sir Richard Mathias, 1 Bt (d 1942); *b* 6 April 1905; *Educ* Eton, Balliol Oxford; *m* 1, 1937, Gladys Cecilia Turton (m dis 1960), da of Edwin Hart, of New Hextalls, Bletchingley, Surrey; 2 da; m 2, 1960, Mrs Elizabeth Baird Murray (d 1972), da of Dr Miles, of Hendrescythan, Glamorgan; m 3, 1973, Mrs Hilary Mary Vines (d 1975), da of William Howells, of Cardiff; *Heir* none; *Career* RAF 1940-46; memb London Stock Exchange; memb Council of Roy Nat Mission to Deep Sea Fishermen 1953-54, Council of Hurstpierpoint Coll 1965, chm 1967-74; fell of Corpn of SS Mary and Nicolas (Woodard Schools) 1965; *Clubs* Reform; *Style* - Sir Richard Mathias, Bt; 8 Oakwood Court, Abbotsbury rd, W14

MATTHEWMAN, Keith; QC (1979); s of Lt Frank Matthewman (d 1976); *b* 8 Jan 1936; *Educ* Long Eaton G S, Univ Coll London; *m* 1962, Jane, da of Thomas Maxwell (d 1957); 1 s; *Career* barr Middle Temple 1960, recorder of the Crown Court 1979; *Recreations* gardening, cine photography; *Style* - Keith Matthewman Esq, QC; 24 The Ropewalk, Nottingham (☎ Nottingham 42581)

MATTHEWS, Baron (Life Peer UK 1980); Victor Collin Matthews; s of A Matthews; *b* 5 Dec 1919; *Educ* Highbury; *m* 1942, Joyce Geraldine (nee Pilbeam); 1 s; *Career* served RNVR 1939-45; chm & ch exec Express Newspapers Ltd 1977-, gp md Trafalgar House Ltd 1968-77, dep chm 1973-, gp ch exec 1977-; chm Cunard Steam-ship Co Ltd 1971-, Cunard Cruise Ships Ltd 1978-, Cunard Line Ltd 1978-, Trafalgar Ho Construction Holdings Ltd 1977- & T H Devpts, Fleet Publishing Internat Holdings Ltd 1978-, Eastern Int Investment Trust Ltd 1974-, The Ritz Hotel (London) Ltd 1976-; dir Associated Container Transportation (Australia) Ltd 1972-, Cunard Crusader World Travel Ltd 1974-, Racecourse Holdings Trust Ltd 1977-, Assoc Cummunications Corpn Ltd 1977, Goldquill Ltd 1979-, Darchart Ltd, Garmaine Ltd (both 1980-); FIOB, FRSA, CBIM; *Clubs* MCC, RAC; *Style* - The Rt Hon the Lord Matthews; Trafalgar House Ltd, 1 Berkeley st, W1 (☎ 01 499 9020)

MATTHEWS, Dr Aubrey Royston; s of Douglas Royston Matthews; *b* 14 Nov 1931; *Educ* Queen Elizabeth's Hospital Bristol, Bristol U; *m* 1960, Hazel, nee Ellis; 3 c; *Career* Shell International Petroleum Ltd (Venezuela) 1958-62, (Trinidad) 1962-66, (USA) 1967-68, (UK) 1968-73, (Netherlands) 1973-74, dir Dr Colin Phipps & Ptnrs Ltd (Consultants) 1974-79, tech dir Clyde Petroleum Ltd 1979-;

Recreations opera, cricket; *Clubs* Reform, MCC; *Style* - Dr Aubrey Matthews; Folly End, Cook's Folly rd, Sneyd Park, Bristol (☎ 0272 683282)

MATTHEWS, Sir Peter Alec; AO (1980); s of Maj Alec Matthews; *b* 21 Sept 1922; *Educ* Vancouver, Oundle; *m* 1946, Sheila Bunting; 4 s, 1 da; *Career* chm Vickers 1980- (md 1970-79), Pegler-Hattersley 1979- (dir 1977-); dir Vickers Australia 1971-, Lloyds Bank 1974-, Br Electric Traction 1976-, Sun Alliance & London Insur 1979-; FBIM, FRSA; served WW II Maj RE; chm Engrg Industs Cncl 1980-, Lloyds Bank Centl London Regnl Bd 1978-; *Style* - Sir Peter Matthews AO; Vickers House, Millbank Tower, SW1 (☎ 01 828 7777)

MATTHEWS-MAXWELL, Maj Christopher Richard George; TD (1979); s of Lt-Col A C Matthews-Maxwell, of Mounton (d 1958); *b* 28 June 1945; *Educ* King's Sch, Skerry's Coll, Newcastle Poly; *Career* commissioned Roy Northumberland Fusiliers 1967, transfd T & AVR 1970, Maj 1970, Hon Artillery Co 1981; farmer, property developer and manager; *Recreations* hunting, shooting, skiing, equestrian sports; *Clubs* Constitutional; *Style* - Maj Christopher Matthews-Maxwell TD; Williams and Glyn's Bank, Grey st, Newcastle upon Tyne

MATUSCH, Antony Hugh; s of Frederick Hugh Matusch (d 1964); *b* 9 Oct 1940; *Educ* Stowe; *m* 1972, Helen Mary, nee Blakesley; 1 s; *Career* FCA, chm and md F Bender Ltd 1964-; *Recreations* yachting; *Clubs* Roy Yacht Sqdn, Roy Thames Yacht, MCC; *Style* - Antony Matusch Esq; 23 Maunsel st, SW1

MAUCHLINE, Lord; Michael Edward Abney-Hastings; s of Capt Walter Strickland Lord and 13 Countess of Loudoun; h to Earldom of mother; *b* 22 July 1942; *Educ* Ampleforth; *m* 1969, Noelene, da of W J McCormick; 1 s, 3 da; assumed by deed poll 1946 surname of Abney-Hastings; *Style* - Lord Mauchline; 74 Coreen st, Jerilderie, NSW 2716, Australia

MAUD, Hon Humphrey John Hamilton; s of Baron Redcliffe-Maud (Life Peer); *b* 1934; *m* 1963, Maria-Eugenia Gazitua; *Style* - The Hon Humphrey Maud

MAUDE, Hon Henry Cornwallis; s of 7 Viscount Hawarden (d 1958); *b* 3 March 1928; *Educ* Marlborough Coll, Worcester Coll Oxford; *m* 1964, Elizabeth Georgina, da of David McNaught Lockie, of Grasse, France; 2 s, 2 da; *Career* schoolmaster, farmer; *Recreations* swimming, shooting, reading; *Style* - The Hon Henry Maude; Wingham Well House, Wingham, Canterbury, Kent

MAUDE, Hon Robert Connan Wyndham Leslie; s and h of 8 Viscount Hawarden; *b* 23 May 1961; *Style* - The Hon Robert Maude

MAUDE, Hon Sophia Rose Eileen; da of 8 Viscount Hawarden; *b* 20 Jan 1959; *Style* - The Hon Sophia Maude

MAUDE, Hon Thomas Patrick Cornwallis; s of 8 Viscount Hawarden; *b* 1 Oct 1964; *Style* - The Hon Thomas Maude

MAUDE-ROXBY, Richard Gay; s of John Henry Maude-Roxby; *b* 7 June 1947; *Educ* Dauntsey's Sch; *m* 1971, Lynda Helena Marjorie, nee Sanders; 1 c; *Career* marketing dir Booker Belmont Retail Ltd 1978, dir Produce Importers Alliance 1978; *Recreations* shooting, fishing; *Style* - Richard Maude-Roxby; Charmandean, Green Lane, Prestwood, Great Missenden, Bucks (☎ Great Missenden 2566)

MAURICE, Hon Mrs; Hon Pamela Mary Violet; JP (Wilts), da of Baron Goddard (Life Peer) (d 1971); *b* 1907; *m* 1934, James Burdett Maurice, MRCS, LRCP; 2 s, 2 da; *Style* - The Hon Mrs Maurice JP; Batt's Farm, Wilton, Marlborough, Wilts

MAWBY, Lady; Lena Lillian; da of Fred White, of Broken Hill, NSW; *m* 1929, Sir Maurice Alan Edgar Mawby, CBE (d 1977); *Style* - Lady Mawby; 102 Mont Albert rd, Canterbury, Vic 3126, Australia

MAXEY, Peter Malcolm; *b* 26 Dec 1930; *Educ* Bedford Sch, CCC Cambridge; *m* 1, 1955, Joyce Marshall; 2 s, 2 da; m 2, Christine Spooner; *Career* For Serv, Br Ambass E Germany 1981-; Under Sec Cabinet Off 1978-81; formerly Head UN Dept FCO 1974-77; with Lazard Bros 1971-72; *Style* - Peter Maxey Esq; c/o FCO, SW1

MAXWELL, Sir Aymer; 8 Bt (NS 1681), of Monreith, Wigtownshire, JP (Wigtownshire 1939); s of Lt-Col Aymer Edward Maxwell (d 1914) and Lady Mary, da of 7 Duke of Northumberland, and gs of Rt Hon Sir Herbert Eustace Maxwell, 7 Bt, KT, PC (d 1937); *b* 1911; *Educ* Eton, Magdalene Cambridge; *Heir* nephew, Michael Eustace George Maxwell; *Career* Hon Capt Scots Gds; *Clubs* Boodle's; *Style* - Sir Aymer Maxwell, Bt, JP; Monreith, Wigtownshire (☎ Portwilliam 248); Katounia, Limni, Euboea, Greece; Lansdowne House, Holland Park, W11 (☎ 01 727 6394)

MAXWELL, Lady Avena Margaret Clare; *née* Stanhope; da of 11 Earl of Harrington; *b* 1944; *m* 1969, Adrian J Maxwell, s of Maj James Maxwell, of Buckby; 1 da; *Style* - Lady Avena Maxwell; South Lodge, Carrick-on-Suir, Co Tipperary, Ireland

MAXWELL, Hon Diana Elizabeth; da of Cdr John David Maxwell, RN (ret) and 27 Baroness de Ros; *b* 6 June 1957; *Educ* Godstowe Sch High Wycombe Bucks; *Style* - The Hon Diana Maxwell

MAXWELL, Lady; Helen Hood; da of late W K Findlay, of Barncailzle Hall, Kircudbrightshre; *m* 1914, as his 2 w, Sir John Maxwell, CMG (d 1946); *Style* - Lady Maxwell; Belmont, Dumfries

MAXWELL, Michael Eustace George; s of Maj Eustace Maxwell (d 1971); hp to Btcy of unc, Sir Aymer Maxwell, 8 Bt; *b* 28 Aug 1943; *Educ* Eton; *Style* - Michael Maxwell Esq; 24 Draycott pla, SW3

MAXWELL, Hon Lord; Peter Maxwell; s of Cdr Desmond Herries Maxwell, RN, of Munches, Dalbeattie, Kirkcudbrightshire; *b* 21 May 1919; *Educ* Wellington, Balliol Oxford, Edinburgh U; *m* 1941, Alison, da of James Readman; 1 s, 2 da (and 1 da decd); *Career* served WW II Capt Argyll & Sutherland Highlanders & RA; advocate Scotland 1951, QC 1961, Sheriff Pncpl Dumfries & Galloway 1970-73, Senator Coll Justice (Lord of Session) 1973-; *Style* - The Hon Lord Maxwell; 1c Oswald rd, Edinburgh EH9 2HE

MAXWELL, Hon Peter Trevor; s and h of Baroness de Ros by her husb Cdr David Maxwell, RN (ret); *b* 23 Dec 1958; *Educ* Headford Sch Kells Co Meath, Stowe; *Style* - The Hon Peter Maxwell

MAXWELL, (Ian) Robert; MC (1945); s of Michael Hoch; *b* 1923; *m* 1945, Elisabeth, nee Meynard; 3 s, 4 da; *Career* fndr and chm Pergamon Press and other publishing cos, ch exec BPC, MP (L) Buckingham 1964-70; *Style* - Robert Maxwell Esq, MC; Headington Hill Hall, Oxford (☎ 64881)

MAXWELL, Hon Simon Kenlis; s of Lt-Col Hon Somerset Arthur Maxwell, MP (d of wounds 1942); *b* 12 Dec 1933; *Educ* Eton; *m* 1964, Karol Anne, da of Maj-Gen G E Prior-Palmer, CB, DSO; 2 s, 1 da; granted 1959, title, rank and precedence of a Baron's s which would have been his had his father survived to succeed to Barony of Farnham; *Style* - The Hon Simon Maxwell; The Dower House, Westcote, Kingham, Oxon

MAXWELL, Hon Lady; Theodora Mary; da of Arthur Hickling, of Wing Old Hall, Rutland; *m* 1923, V-Adm Hon Sir Denis Crichton Maxwell, KCB, CBE (d 1970); 1 da; *Style* - The Hon Lady Maxwell; 1 Arlington Row, Umtali, Zimbabwe

MAXWELL-SCOTT, Dominic James; s and h of Sir Michael Maxwell-Scott, 13 Bt; *b* 22 July 1968; *Style* - Dominic Maxwell-Scott Esq

MAXWELL-SCOTT, Sir Michael Fergus Constable; 13 Bt (E 1642), of Haggerston, Northumberland; s of late Rear-Adm Malcolm Joseph Raphael Constable Maxwell-Scott, DSO, RN, gs of

Lord Herries of Terregles, ggs of 3 Bt; suc kinsman, Sir Ralph Stanley de Marie Haggerston, 12 Bt 1972; *b* 23 July 1921; *Educ* Ampleforth, Trin Cambridge; *m* 1963, Deirdre Moira, da of late Alexander McKechnie; 2 s, 1 da; *Heir* s, Dominic Maxwell-Scott; *Style* - Sir Michael Maxwell-Scott, Bt; 10 Evelyn Mansions, Carlisle Place, SW1 (☎ 01 828 0333)

MAY, 3 Baron (UK 1935); Sir Michael St John May; 3 Bt (1931); s of 2 Baron (d 1950) by his 2 w Ethel; *b* 26 Sept 1931; *Educ* Wycliffe Coll, Magdalene College Cambridge; *m* 1, 1958, Dorothea Catherine Ann (m dis 1963), da of Charles McCarthy; m 2, 1963, Jillian Mary, da of Albert Edward Shipton; 1 s, 1 da; *Heir* s, Hon Jasper Bertram St John May; *Career* late Lt Roy Corps of Signals; *Style* - The Rt Hon the Lord May; Gautherns Farm, Sibford Gower, Oxfordshire (☎ Swalcliffe 696)

MAY, Denis Ronald William; s of Fredrick William May (d 1944); *b* 4 July 1940; *Educ* Kingston Tech, Surrey U; *m* 1968, Margaret, nee Bond; 1 c; *Career* PhD, external examiner and visiting lectr Surrey U 1966, tech dir J E Hanger & Co Ltd; *Recreations* riding; *Clubs* BHS; *Style* - Denis May Esq; Baronsmead, Wayneflete Tower av, Esher, Surrey

MAY, Hon Jasper Bertram St John; s and h of 3 Baron May; *b* 24 Oct 1965; *Style* - The Hon Jasper May

MAY, Miranda Jane; da of 3 Baron May; *b* 1968; *Style* - The Hon Miranda May

MAY, Hon Mrs Patrick - (Audrey) Gillian (Jackson); da of Edward Bagot, of Cross Farm, West Coker, Somerset; *m* 1951, as his 2 w, Hon Patrick William May (d 1956); 2 da, 2 step da; *Style* - The Hon Mrs Patrick May; Preston Place Cottage, 28 Worthing rd, East Preston, Sussex

MAYALL, Hon Lady; Hon Mary Hermione *née* Ormsby-Gore; da of 4 Baron Harlech KG GCMG PC (d 1964); *b* 1914; *m* 1, 1936, Capt Robin Francis Campbell DSO (m dis 1946), s of late Rt Hon Sir Ronald Hugh Campbell GCMG; 2 s; m 2, 1947, Sir Alexander Mayall KCVO CMG; 1 s, 2 da; *Style* - The Hon Lady Mayall; Sturford Mead, Warminster, Wilts

MAYBRAY-KING, Baron (Life Peer UK 1971); Horace Maybray Maybray-King; PC (1965), DL (Hants 1975); s of John William King (d 1964); *b* 25 May 1901; *Educ* Stockton-on-Tees Secdy Sch, King's Coll London; *m* 1, 1924, Victoria Florence, OBE (d 1966), da of George David Harris; 1 da; m 2, 1967, Una Porter (d 1978); m 3, 1981, Mrs Ivy Forster (widow), of Darlington; *Career* headmaster Regent's Pk Sch 1946-50. head Eng Dept Taunton's Sch 1922-46; MP (L) Southampton 1950-55, Southampton (Itchen) 1955-71; dep speaker of House of Lords 1971-; chm Ways and Means 1964-65; speaker of House of Commons 1965-71; freeman of Southampton 1967 and of Stockton-on-Tees 1968; *Clubs* Farmers' *Style* - The Rt Hon Lord Maybray-King PC DL; 37 Manor Farm rd, Bitterne Park, Southampton, Hants (☎ 555884)

MAYBURY, Lady; Katharine Mary; da of S W Pring, of Winchester; *m* 1942, as his 2 w, Brig-Gen Sir Henry Percy Maybury, GBE, KCMG, CB (d 1943); *Style* - Lady Maybury; 4 Quarry pla, Shrewsbury

MAYHEW, Baron (Life Peer UK 1981); Christopher Paget; s of Sir Basil Mayhew, KBE, and Dorothea, da of Stephen Paget and gda of Sir James Paget, 1 Bt, whereby His Lordship is 2 cous of Sir Julian Paget, 4 Bt, (Gentleman Usher to HM), and Paul Paget, the architect, also great nephew to two Bishops (Francis, sometime Bp of Oxford, and Henry, sometime Bp of Chester); *b* 12 June 1915; *Educ* Haileybury, Ch Ch Oxford; *m* 1949, Cicely Ludlam; 2 s, 2 da; *Career* served Surrey Yeo RA WW II, Maj; MP (L) S Norfolk 1945-50, Woolwich E (subsequently Greenwich, Woolwich E) 1951- June '74 (when resigned from L Pty and joined Libs), MP (Lib) July-Oct 1974; stood (Lib) for Bath 1974 & 1979, Min Def (RN) 1964-66, Lib Spokesman Def 1974; stood (Lib) for Surrey as prospective MEP 1979, London SW Sept 1979; chm Middle East Internat (Publishers), ANAF Fndn; *Style* - The Rt Hon the Lord

Mayhew; 39 Wool rd, SW20 (☎ 01 946 3460)

MAYHEW, Lady; Beryl Caroline Rees; da of Russell James Colman (Lord Lieut of Norfolk, 1929-44); *m* 1932, as his 2 w, Sir Basil Edgar Mayhew, KBE (d 1966); *Style* - Lady Mayhew; The Old Manor Farm, Framingham Pigot, Norwich

MAYHEW, Hon Mrs; Hon Margaret Louise; da of Baron Brock (Life Peer) (d 1980); *b* 1936; *Educ* Malvern Girls' Coll; *m* 1962, (John Alexander) Simon Cary Mayhew; *Style* - The Hon Mrs Mayhew; Ivy Farm, Waldron, Heathfield, Sussex

MAYHEW, Patrick Barnabas Burke; QC (1972), MP (C) Tun Wells Feb 1974-; s of A Mayhew, MC; *b* 11 Sept 1929; *Educ* Tonbridge, Balliol Oxford; *m* 1963, Jean, 2 da of John Gurney, *qv*, of Walsingham Abbey, Norfolk; 4 s; *Career* Parly Under Sec Dept Employment 1979-; barr 1955; contested Camberwell & Dulwich 1970; *Style* - Patrick Mayhew Esq, QC, MP; House of Commons, SW1

MAYHEW-SANDERS, John Reynolds; s of Jack Mayhew-Sanders; *b* 25 October 1931; *Educ* Royal Naval Coll Dartmouth; Jesus Cambridge; *m* 1958, Sylvia Mary; 4 c; *Career* chm & chief executive John Brown & Co Ltd 1978-; dir BL Ltd 1980-; *Recreations* fishing, shooting, music, gardening; *Style* - John Mayhew-Sanders Esq; Earlstone House, Burghclere, nr Newbury, Berkshire (☎ Burghclere 288)

MAYNE, Hon Mrs; Hon Helena Stewart; da of Baron Keith of Avonholm (Life Peer) (d 1964); *b* 1919; *m* 1943, Gerald Outram Mayne, MB, ChB; *Style* - The Hon Mrs Mayne; 47B Fairdene rd, Coulsdon, Surrey

MAYNE, James Edward Mosley; s of Rupert Eric Mosley Mayne; *b* 16 July 1944; *Educ* Wellington Coll, Pembroke Oxford; *m* 1970, Patricia Ann Mary, nee Mayer; 1 s, 2 da; *Career* barrister, chm Habit Precision Engrg PLC 1979-, chm Wymanor Investments Ltd 1976-; *Recreations* shooting, fishing, skiing; *Clubs* United Oxford and Cambridge Univ; *Style* - James Mayne Esq; The Manor House, Wycomb, Melton Mowbray, Leics

MAYO, 10 Earl of (I 1785); Terence Patrick Bourke; also Baron Naas (I 1776) and Viscount Mayo (I 1781); s of Hon Bryan Longley Bourke (d 1961) and nephew of 9 Earl (d 1962); *b* 26 Aug 1929; *Educ* St Aubyn's Rottingdean, RN Coll Dartmouth; *m* 1952, Margaret Jane Robinson, da of Gerald Harrison, DL (d 1954); 3 s; *Heir* Lord Naas; *Career* Lt RN 1952, served Suez 1956; Solo Aerobatic Displays, Farnborough 1957; md Irish Marble Ltd, Merlin Park, Galway; memb Lib Pty 1963-65, stood for Dorset S as Lib candidate 1964; memb Gosport Borough Council 1961; *Clubs* Naval and County Galway; *Style* - The Rt Hon the Earl of Mayo; Doon House, Maam, Co Galway, Eire

MAYO, Lady; Gwen Alister Brookes; da of John MacInnes, of Naracoorte, S Australia; *m* 1958, as his 2 w, Hon Sir Herbert Mayo (d 1972); *Style* - Lady Mayo; 90 Northgate st, Unley Park, S Australia

MAYO, John William; s of Malcolm Guy Mayo (d 1968); *b* 8 Oct 1920; *Educ* St Paul's Sch; *m* 1959, Susan Margaret; 3 s, 1 da; *Career* Capt RN; Hon FRCGP; sr ptnr Linklaters & Paines, Solicitors (qualified 1947, joined firm 1947, ptnr 1952); *Recreations* bridge, golf; *Clubs* Royal Wimbledon GC Hunstanton GC, Ealing FC (RN); *Style* - John Mayo Esq; 38 Marryat rd, Wimbledon, SW19 (☎ 01 946 1537); The Mill Cottage, Ringstead, Hunstanton, Norfolk (☎ Holme 391)

MAYO, Countess of; Noël Jessie Haliburton; da of William James Wilson (d 1904); *m* 1937, 9 Earl of Mayo (d 1962); *Career* served WW I 1914-18 in WRNS and WRAF, Red Cross nurse; *Style* - The Rt Hon Countess of Mayo; Active Truth Academy, 140 Princes st, Edinburgh

MAYO, Rear-Adm Robert William; CB (1965), CBE (1962); s of Frank Mayo (d 1934); *b* 9 Feb 1909; *Educ* Weymouth Coll, HMS Conway; *m* 1942, Sheila (d 1974), da of late John Colvill, JP; 1 s; *Career* joined RN 1937, Korea 1952, Capt 1953,

Rear-Adm 1964, naval dep Allied Forces N Europe 1964-66, ret 1966; Hon Sheriff Substitute Campbeltown 1971; *Recreations* gardening, sailing; *Clubs* Roy Scottish Automobile, Roy Naval Sailing Assoc; *Style* - Rear-Adm Robert Mayo, CB, CBE; Rose Cottage, Silverless st, Marlborough (☎ 53951); Bellgrove, Campbeltown, Argyll (☎ 2101)

MAYON-WHITE, Hon Mrs; Hon Mary Angela; da of 2 Viscount Daventry; *b* 1919; *m* 1, 1940, Maj Anthony Dermot Melloney Musker (d 1959); 3 s, 2 da; m 2, 1962, Richard Mayon Mayon-White, MD, PhD, FRCP; *Style* - The Hon Mrs Mayon-White; Baylham House, Baylham, Ipswich

MAYWARD, Frederick Gerard; s of Edwin Maynard (d 1951); *b* 9 Oct 1924; *Educ* Westminster; *m* 1956, Olivia Jane, nee Reed; 2 da; *Career* Croix de Guerre (Fr 1944), Capt Special Air Serv (Fr, Germany, South East Asia), chm Maynard, Reeve & Wallace Ltd 1961-80, Lloyd's Underwriter; *Clubs* City of London, Special Forces; *Style* - Frederick Mayward Esq; 4 Queen's Elm sq, Old Church st, SW3

MBONIMPA, His Excellency Cyprien; *Career* Burundi Ambass to UK 1981-; *Style* - H E Mr Cyprien Mbonimpa

MEADE, Lady Julia Elizabeth; da of 6 Earl of Clanwilliam; *b* 31 Dec 1953; *Style* - Lady Julia Meade

MEADE, John Herbert; s of late Adm the Hon Sir Herbert Meade-Fetherstonhaugh, GCVO, CB, DSO (s of 4 Earl of Clanwilliam); hp to Earldom of Clanwilliam; *b* 27 Sept 1919; *m* 1956, Maxine, nee Hayden Scott; 1 s, 2 da; *Clubs* Turf; *Style* - John Meade Esq; 28 Yeoman's Row, SW3

MEADE, Lady Katharine Anne; da of 6 Earl of Clanwilliam; *b* 10 Aug 1959; *Style* - Lady Katharine Meade

MEADE, Lady Mary Jane; da of 6 Earl of Clanwilliam; *b* 12 July 1952; *Style* - Lady Mary Meade

MEADE, Lady Sophia Catherine Gathorne-Hardy; da of 4 Earl of Cranbrook, CBE; *b* 1936; *m* 1957, Simon Robert Jasper Meade; *Style* - Lady Sophia Meade

MEADE, Lady Sophia Hester; da of 6 Earl of Clanwilliam; *b* 14 Oct 1963; *Style* - Lady Sophia Meade

MEADOWS, Robert Ian Shaw; s of A Gordon Meadows (d 1978); *b* 5 Feb 1946; *Educ* Loretto; *m* 1974, Patricia Anne, nee Adnitt; *Career* md R S Clare & Co Ltd, dir Wilson & Scott (Highways) Ltd, dir Plastaspray International, Liverpool Personal Serv Soc (Fin Cttee); *Recreations* sailing, ornithology, amateur dramatics; *Clubs* Lyceum (Liverpool), Institute of Directors; *Style* - Robert Meadows Esq; Windward, Beacon dve, W Kirby, Merseyside

MEAGER, Hon Mrs; Hon Joan Beryl; da of 5 Baron Henley; *b* 1893; *m* 1914, Kildare Stucley Meager; 1 s, 1 da; *Style* - The Hon Mrs Meager; 117 Brighton rd, Worthing, Sussex

MEANEY, Patrick Michael; s of the late Joseph Francis Meaney; *b* 6 May 1925; *Educ* Wimbledon Coll, Northern Poly; *m* 1967, Mary June, nee Kearney; 1 s; *Career* dir Thomas Tilling 1964-, md Thomas Tilling 1973-, dir: Midland Bank Ltd 1980-, Rank Organisation Ltd 1979-, Cable & Wireless Ltd 1978-; *Recreations* sport, music, travel; *Clubs* British Sportsman's, Harlequin Football; *Style* - Patrick Meaney Esq; Stambourne House, Totteridge Village, N20 (☎ 01 445 9576)

MEARS, Lady; Margaret Mary; da of Charles Ernest Tempest, JP; *m* 1951, as his 2 w, Sir (Edward) Grimwood Mears, KCIE (d 1963); *Career* author and illustrator of children's books; *Style* - Lady Mears; St Edmund's rd, Ipswich

MEASURES, Lady; Muriel Steventon; *m* 1935, Sir Philip Herbert Measures, CBE (d 1961); *Style* - Lady Measures; Point House, Port St Mary, IOM

MEATH, 14 Earl of (I 1627); Anthony Windham Normand Brabazon; also

Baron Ardee (I 1616) and Baron Chaworth (UK 1831); s of 13 Earl, CB, CBE (d 1949), by his w Lady Aileen Wyndham Quin (da of 4 Earl of Dunraven); *b* 3 Nov 1910; *Educ* Eton, RMC Sandhurst; *m* 1940, Elizabeth Mary, da of late Capt Geoffrey and Hon Mrs Bowlby, CVO (4 da of 11 Viscount Valentia), of Middleton Stoney, Bicester, Oxon; 2 s, 2 da; *Heir* s, Lord Ardee; *Career* ADC to Govr Bengal 1936; Capt Gren Gds 1938, Maj 1941, ret 1946; *Style* - The Rt Hon The Earl of Meath; Killruddery, Bray, Co Wicklow, Ireland

MEATH, Bishop of (RC); Most Rev John McCormack; s of Peter McCormack, of Moynalty, Kells, Co Meath; *b* 25 May 1921; *Educ* St Finian's Coll Mullingar, Maynooth Coll, Lateran U; *Career* ordained 1946, Bp of Meath 1968-; *Style* - The Most Rev the Bishop of Meath; Bishop's House, Dublin rd, Mullingar, Co Westmeath, Ireland (☎ Mullingar 8841)

MEDD, William Gordon; s of William Thomas Medd (d 1959); *b* 30 Dec 1920; *Educ* Scarborough H S, Liverpool U; *m* 1943, Joan, nee Fenwick; 1 s; *Career* biochemist, biscuit manufacturer, dir Assoc Biscuit Manufacturers (ABM) 1967, W & R Jacob (Dublin) 1976, O P Chocolate 1973, CBI Regional Cncllr 1975-81; *Recreations* golf; *Clubs* Sonning Golf; *Style* - William Medd Esq; The Barn, Highmoor, Henley-on-Thames, Oxon (☎ Nettlebed 641283)

MEDHURST, Brian; s of Eric Gilbert Medhurst; *b* 18 March 1935; *Educ* Godalming G S, Trin Coll Cambridge; *m* 1960, Patricia Anne, nee Beer; 2 s, 1 da; *Career* jt sec & ch investment man The Prudential Assur Co Ltd 1981- (dep investment man 1972, investment man 1975); *Recreations* squash, golf, music; *Clubs* North Hants Golf; *Style* - Brian Medhurst Esq; Longacre, Fitzroy rd, Fleet, Hants (☎ 025 14 4159)

MEDHURST, Lady; Christabell Elizabeth; da of late Rev T E B Guy, Canon of York; *m* 1919, Air Chief-Marshal Sir Charles Edward Hastings Medhurst, KCB, OBE, MC (d 1954); *Style* - Lady Medhurst; Woodstock House, Woodstock, Oxford; c/o Barclays Bank, Parliament st, York

MEDLICOTT, Lady; Helen Elizabeth; da of late Rev Walter T Penny, of Acton; *m* 1931, Sir Frank Medlicott, CBE (d 1972); *Style* - Lady Medlicott; 186 Ashley gdns, SW1

MEDLYCOTT, Sir (James) Christopher; 8 Bt (UK 1808), of Ven House, Somerset; s of Sir Hubert Mervyn Medlycott, 7 Bt (d 1964); *b* 17 April 1907; *Educ* Harrow, Magdalene Cambridge; *Heir* nephew, Mervyn Tregonwell Medlycott; *Style* - Sir Christopher Medlycott, Bt; The Yard House, Milborne Port, Sherborne, Dorset (☎ Milborne Port 312)

MEDLYCOTT, Mervyn Tregonwell; s of late Thomas Anthony Hutchings Medlycott (2 s of Sir Hubert Medlycott, 7 Bt); hp of unc, Sir Christopher Medlycott, 8 Bt; *b* 21 Feb 1947; *Style* - Mervyn Medlycott Esq; The Manor House, Sandford Orcas, Sherborne, Dorset

MEDVEI, Victor Cornelius; CBE (1965); s of Maurice William Cornelius Medvei (d 1941); *b* 6 June 1905; *Educ* Prince Eszterhazy Gymnasium Vienna, U of Vienna, Medical Coll of St Bartholomew's Hosp London; *m* 1946, Sheila Mary, da of John Morgan Wiggins (d 1969); 1 s, 2 da; *Career* MD, FRCP; consultant physician (principal med offr TMS) in charge of Foreign Service Med Service 1958-65; consultant (examining) physician UN (London) Assoc, ch assist Endocrine Dept St Bartholomew's Hosp London; *Recreations* reading, travel, study of history (med history); *Clubs* Garrick, Royal Commonwealth Soc; *Style* - Victor Medvei Esq, CBE; 38 Westmoreland ter, London SW1

MEDWAY, Lord; John Jason Gathorne-Hardy; s and h of 5 Earl of Cranbrook, *qv*; *b* 26 Oct 1968; *Style* - Lord Medway

MEECH, Lady; Rachel Crease; da of Robert Anderson, of Wellington, NZ; *m*

1938, late Sir John Valentine Meech, KCVO; *Style* - Lady Meech; 205 Barhard st, Highland Park, Wellington, New Zealand

MEEK, Hedley Jack; s of Leonard Meek (d 1939); *b* 8 May 1925; *Educ* Purley Secdy Sch, Calne Secdy Sch Wilts; *m* 1948 (m dis 1972) -- , nee Walker; 1 s, 2 da; *Career* chm & md Nevill Long Gp 1959-, pres Southall Chamber of Commerce 1971-72, pres MBRE Bldg Board Federation 1976-78, vice-chm Suspended Ceilings Assoc 1980-81; *Recreations* horticulture, photography; *Clubs* Institute of Directors; *Style* - Hedley Meek Esq; Little Bekkons, Westfield rd, Beaconsfield, Bucks (☎ Beaconsfield 2505)

MEEK, Hon Mrs (Jane Maureen Thérèse); da of late 15 Baron Dormer; *b* 1945; *m* 1, 1966, H A Samuel Sandbach; 1 s, 1 da; m 2, 1980, Sqdn Ldr Geoffrey E Meek, RAF; *Style* - The Hon Mrs Meek; Fox Cottage, Kineton, Warwicks

MEERS, John Laurence; s of Laurence Wilfred Meers; *b* 4 Feb 1941; *Educ* Westcliff H S Essex, London U; *m* 1961, Pamela Mary, nee Thornes; 1 s, 1 da; *Career* research and dvpt dir J E Sturge Ltd 1978, tech dir Sturge Enzymes 1979; *Recreations* preservation of rare breeds of farm-stock; *Clubs* Fauna and Flora Preservation Soc, Rare Breeds Survival Trust; *Style* - John Meers Esq; Carr Lodge, Ampleforth, York YO6 4ED (☎ Coxwold 339)

MEGAW, Rt Hon Sir John; CBE (1956), TD (1951), PC (1969); 2 s of Hon Mr Justice Megaw, of Belfast; *b* 16 Sept 1909; *Educ* Roy Acad Inst Belfast, St John's Cambridge, Harvard Law Sch; *m* 1938, Eleanor Chapman; 1 s, 2 da; *Career* kt 1961, barr 1934, QC (1953 & NI 1954), High Court Judge (Queen's Bench) 1961-69, Ld Justice of Appeal 1969-80, chm Ind Inquiry into Civil Serv Pay Dispute 1981; last judge to pass death sentence (1964; it was later commuted to life imprisonment); *Style* - Rt Hon Sir John Megaw CBE TD PC QC; 14 Upper Cheyne Row, SW3 (☎ 01 352 7855)

MEINERTZHAGEN, Daniel; s of Louis Meinertzhagen (gs of Daniel Meinertzhagen, who settled in London from Bremen 1826; Johann de Meinertzhagen, Cllr of Cologne 1464-75, was his ancestor); bro of Sir Peter, unc of Nicholas Meinertzhagen and 1 cous of Lady Rothschild, *qqv*; *b* 2 March 1915; *Educ* Eton, New Coll Oxford; *m* 1940, Marguerite, da of A Leonard; 2 s; *Career* chm Roy Insur Co 1974; dep chm Alexanders Discount Co; dir Costain Gp, Tozer Kemsley & Millbourn Hldgs, Brixton Estate; *Clubs* White's; *Style* - Daniel Meinertzhagen Esq; Bramshott Vale, Liphook, Hants (☎ 723243)

MEINERTZHAGEN, Luke; 2 s of Louis Meinertzhagen by Gwynedd, da of Sir William Llewellyn, GCVO; bro of Daniel and f of Nicholas, *qqv*; *b* 9 Dec 1916; *Educ* Eton, New Coll Oxford; *m* Sheila, da of Neil Macnamara, CBE, and gda of Rt Hon Thomas Macnamara, PC, MP, sometime Min of Labour; 1 s (Nicholas), 1 da; *Career* served WW II as Maj RM; late sr ptnr Cazenove & Co (stockbrokers); dir N M Rothschild & Sons 1981-; *Style* - Luke Meinertzhagen Esq; 46 Victoria rd, W8

MEINERTZHAGEN, Nicholas Neil; s of Luke Meinertzhagen (*see* Daniel Meinertzhagen) and Sheila (da of Neil Macnamara, CBE, and gda of Rt Hon Thomas Macnamara, PC, MP, sometime Min of Labour); *b* 26 Aug 1943; *Educ* Eton, New Coll Oxford; *m* 1966, Erzsébet Sarolta, da of Janos von Kenyeres and Countess Eva Toldalagi de Nagy Ertse; 1 da; *Career* antiquarian bookseller, whose finest coup was nevertheless in the field of objets d'art, when he purchased a bust of Pope Gregory XV in a Clapham antique dealer's for £240, which was identified as being by Bernini and sold in the sale room for £114,000 (bought at auction for £85 in 1978 from 9 Earl of Lanesborough on occasion of his removal to a smaller house); *Style* - Nicholas Meinertzhagen Esq; 24 Clareville Grove, SW7

MEINERTZHAGEN, Sir Peter; CMG (1966); s of Louis Meinertzhagen and yr bro of Daniel and Luke, *qqv*; *b* 24 March 1920; *Educ* Eton; *m* 1949, Dido, da of William Pretty, of Malta; 1 s (Simon m 1980 Sarah Hilton), 1 da (Tana); *Career* kt

1980; served WW II Maj Europe & Far East; gen man C'wlth Devpt Corpn 1973-; *Clubs* Muthaiga Country (Nairobi); *Style* - Sir Peter Meinertzhagen CMG; Pas de Molle, Eymet, 24500, France; 59 Cleaver sq, SE11 (☎ 01 735 6263)

MELCHETT, 4 Baron (UK 1928); Sir Peter Robert Henry Mond; 4 Bt (UK 1910); s of 3 Baron Melchett (d 1973, himself gs of 1 Baron, better known as Sir Alfred Mond, first chm of ICI and Min of Health 1921-22, mentioned in terms of surprising intimacy by his fellow banker T S Eliot in *A Cooking Egg*); *b* 24 Feb 1948; *Educ* Eton, Pembroke Cambridge, Keele U Staffordshire; *Heir* none; *Career* a Lord in Waiting to HM the Queen 1974-75, chm Community Industry 1979-, Working Party on Pop Festivals 1975-76; memb Friends of Release; Parly Under-Sec of State, Indust 1975-76, N Ireland 1976-79; *Style* - The Rt Hon the Lord Melchett; 14 Allcroft rd, NW5 (☎ 01 267 0619)

MELCHETT, Gwen, Baroness; (Amy) Gwen; da of late E J Wilson, of Klerksdorp, Transvaal; *m* 1920, 2 Baron Melchett (d 1949); 2 s (elder killed on active service 1945); 1 da; *Style* - The Rt Hon Gwen, Lady Melchett; Coppinton Stud, Lambourne, Berks

MELCHETT, Baroness; Sonia Elizabeth; da of late Col Roland Harris Graham, RAMC (ret), of the Lodge, Bridge, Kent; *m* 1947, 3 Baron Melchett (d 1975); *Style* - The Rt Hon Lady Melchett; 16 Tite st, Chelsea, SW3

MELDON, Hon Mrs (Dorothy Albreda); da of late Gen Sir Robert C A Bewicke-Copley, KBE, CB (d 1923), and sis of 5 Baron Cromwell, DSO; *m* 1926, Lt-Col Philip Albert Meldon, DSO, RA, MA (d 1942); *Style* - The Hon Mrs Meldon; 7 Editha Mansions, Edith Grove, SW10

MELGUND, Viscount; Gilbert Timothy George Lariston Elliot-Murray-Kynymound; s and h of 6 Earl of Minto, MBE; *b* 1 Dec 1953; *Educ* Eton; *Career* Lt Scots Gds 1972-76; *Clubs* Turf *Style* - Viscount Melgund; Minto, Hawick, Roxburghshire (☎ Denholm 321)

MELLOR, Frank Edward; JP (Liverpool 1961), DL (Merseyside 1976); s of Robert Mellor (d 1928); *b* 27 Jan 1912; *Educ* Waterloo G S, Liverpool Polytechnic; *m* 1963, Mavis, da of Gavin Black (d 1957); *Career* Flying Offr 1940-46; FRSA 1940, Fellow Inst of Marketing 1965; sr mktg exec Pharmaceutical & Fine Chemicals Indust, ret 1973; memb Liverpool Regional Hosp Bd 1969-73, Mental Health Review Tbnl 1967-, Supplementary Benefits Tbnl 1976-, parole bd H M Prison Liverpool 1967-69, Industrial Tribunals 1976-, chm St Helens and Knowsley Area Health Authority 1973-78; *Recreations* point to point and Nat Hunt racing, golf; *Style* - Frank Mellor Esq, JP, DL; Lapsley, Bleak Hill rd, Windle, St Helens, Merseyside WA10 6DW (☎ St Helens 21508)

MELLOR, John Francis; s and h of Sir John Mellor, 2 Bt; *b* 9 March 1925; *Educ* Eton; *m* 1948, Alix Marie, da of late Charles François Villaret; *Career* 1939-45 War with RASC and Int Corps; accountant; *Style* - John Mellor Esq; Birchlea, Lone Oak, Redenhall rd, Smallfield, Horley, Surrey

MELLOR, Sir John Serocold Paget; 2 Bt (UK 1924), of Culmhead, Somerset; s of Sir John Paget Mellor, 1 Bt (d 1929); *b* 6 July 1893; *Educ* Eton, New Coll Oxford; *m* 1, 1922, Rachel Margaret (m dis 1937), da of Sir Herbert Frederick Cook, 3 Bt; 1 s; m 2, 1937, Mrs Raie Mendes (d 1965), da of late Samuel Moses; m 3, 1971, Mrs Jessica de Pass, da of late Clarence de Sola, of Montreal; *Heir* s, John Francis Mellor; *Career* served 1914-19 War, Capt Somerset LI, re-employed 1939; barr Inner Temple 1920; dir Prudential Assurance Co Ltd 1946, dep chm 1959, chm 1965-70, pres 1972; dir of other cos; MP (C) Warwickshire (Tanworth Div) 1935-45, (Sutton Coldfield Div) 1945-55; *Clubs* Carlton; *Style* - Sir John Mellor, Bt; 16 Chesterfield House, W1; Binley House, nr Andover, Hants

MELLOR, Maj James Thomas Paulton; MC (1946), TD (1948), DL (Argyll (1964); s of Maj James Mellor, MC (d 1950); *b* 15 March 1918; *Educ* Eton; *m* 1946, Eve, da of Lt Col Walter Thomas

Holland AFC (d 1976); 1 s, 1 da; *Career* served 1939-40 Argyll & Sutherland Highlanders, POW 1940-45 (Colditz 43-45); Maj TA 1946; with Walpamur Co, Darwen, 1946-58; landowner, farmer 1958-; *Recreations* shooting, fishing, curling, ski-bobbing; *Style* - Maj James Mellor, MC, TD, DL; Barndromin Farm, Knipoch, by Oban, Argyll (☎ Kilninver 273)

MELLOWS, Professor Anthony Roger Mellows; TD (1969); s of Laurence Beresford Mellows; *b* 30 July 1936; *Educ* King's Coll London; *m* 1973, Elizabeth Angela, nee Fox; *Career* solicitor Messrs Alexanders 1962, professor of the Law of Property London U 1974-, chm London Law International Ltd 1973-; *Clubs* Athenaeum; *Style* - Professor Anthony Mellows, TD; 22 Devereux Court, Temple Bar, WC2

MELVILLE, 9 Viscount (UK 1802); Robert David Ross Dundas; also Baron Duneira (UK 1802); s of Hon Robert Maldred St John Melville Dundas (ka 1940), and nephew of 8 Viscount Melville (d 1971); *b* 28 May 1937; *Educ* Cargilfield, Wellington; *Heir* kinsman, Hugh McKenzie Dundas; *Career* served in Scots Gds (Nat Service); Lt Ayrshire Yeo (TA); *Clubs* Turf, Cavalry & Guards; *Style* - The Rt Hon the Viscount Melville; Esk Cottage, Melville Castle, Lasswade, Midlothian (Lasswade 3162); Keltie Castle, Dunning, Perthshire (☎ 208)

MELVIN, Air Cdre James Douglas; CB (1956), OBE (1947); s of William Adamson Melvin (d 1954); *b* 20 Feb 1914; *Educ* Turriff Secondary Sch, RAF Halton, RAF Coll Cranwell; *m* 1946, Mary, da of Dr Alfred Wills, of Old Cross Keys, Princes Risborough (d 1935); 1 da (and 1 s decd); *Career* Air Cdre, dir Organization Air Ministry; property man Coutts and Co 1961-70; *Recreations* sailing (yacht: 'John Dory'); *Clubs* RAF, Bosham Sailing Club; *Style* - Air Cdre James Melvin, CB, OBE; Kyrenia Cottage, Old Bosham, Chichester (☎ Bosham 572337)

MENPES, Hon Mrs; Hon Marjorie; da of Baron Cooper of Stockton Heath (Life Peer); *b* 1941; *m* 1, 1959 (m dis 1969) Neville Finch; m 2, 1974, Robert Dennis Menpes; *Style* - The Hon Mrs Menpes; 12 Kings Drive, Thames Ditton, Surrey K7 OTH

MENSFORTH, Sir Eric; CBE (1945), DL (W R Yorks 1971); s of Sir Holberry Mensforth, KCB, CBE (d 1951); *b* 17 May 1906; *Educ* Altrincham H S, Univ Coll Sch, King's Cambridge; *m* 1934, Betty, JP, da of late Rev Picton W Francis; 3 da; *Career* V-Ld-Lt S Yorks 1974-81; dir and pres Westland Aircraft Ltd, dir John Brown & Co Ltd, Boddy Industries Ltd; Master Co of Cutlers in Hallamshire 1965-66, gen tres Br Assoc for Science 1971-76, kt 1962; *Style* - Sir Eric Mensforth, CBE, DL; 3 Belgrave dve, Fulwood, Sheffield (☎ 307737)

MENZIES, Lady; Audrey Clara Lilian; da of late Sir Thomas Paul Latham, 1 Bt; *b* 1899; *m* 1, 1921, Sir Henry Ralph Stanley Birking, Bt (m dis 1927, he d 1933); m 2, 1928, as his 2 w, Lt-Col Lord Edward Douglas John Hay (d 1944); m 3, 1948, Hon Niall Greville Chaplin (m dis 1952, he d 1963); m 4 1952, Maj-Gen Sir Stewart Graham Menzies, KCB, KCMG, DSO, MC (d 1968); *Style* - Lady Menzies; The Manor, Davies Street, W1

MENZIES, Lady; Jenny Hamilton; da of late Thomas Young, of Edinburgh; *m* 1932, Sir Robert Menzies, VC, OBE (d 1967); *Style* - Lady Menzies; Heather Wells, Lightwater, Surrey

MENZIES ANDERSON, Lady; Ivy Beryl Shairp; *née* Chadwick; *m* 1943, Sir Gilmour Menzies Anderson, CBE (d 1977); *Style* - Lady Menzies Anderson; Craigievern Cottage, Balfron Station, Glasgow (☎ Drymen 320)

MERCER, Lady; Helen Margaret; da of George Lunan, MPS; *m* 1923, Sir Walter Mercer (d 1971); *Style* - Lady Mercer; 2 Henderland rd, Edinburgh 12

MERCER NAIRNE, Lord Robert Harold; s of 8 Marquess of Lansdowne, PC; *b* 1947; *Educ* Gordonstoun, U of Kent at Canterbury, U of Washington Graduate Sch of Business Administration; *m* 1972, Jane Elizabeth, da of Lt-Col Lord Douglas

Gordon; 2 s, 1 da; *Style* - Lord Robert Mercer Nairne; 51 Tregunter rd, SW10

MEREDITH, Lady; Lorna; da of R D Sandes; *m* 1929, Sir Herbert Ribton Meredith (d 1959); *Style* - Lady Meredith

MEREDITH, Richard Alban Creed; s of Rev Canon Ralph Creed Meredith (d 1970); *b* 1 Feb 1935; *Educ* Stowe Sch Bucks, Jesus Cambridge; *m* 1963, Hazel Parry; 1 s, 1 da; *Career* assist master King's Sch Canterbury 1957-70, house master 1962-70, headmaster Giggleswick Sch 1970-78, headmaster Monkton Combe Sch 1978-; *Recreations* music, gardening, walking; *Style* - Richard Meredith, Esq; Head Master's House, Shaft rd, Monkton Combe School, Bath (☎ Limpley Stoke 3278)

MEREDITH-HARDY, Michael Francis; s of Howard Meredith Hardy (decd); *b* 12 May 1923; *Educ* Eton, Pembroke Cambridge; *m* 1955, Penelope Jane, da of Hon Bartholomew Pleydell-Bouverie (3 s of 6 Earl of Radnor) by his 1 w Lady Doreen, *née* Hely-Hutchinson (da of 6 Earl of Donoughmore); 4 s; *Career* 5 Roy Inniskilling Dragoon Gds 1942, Maj 1947; barr 1951-76, chm Nat Insurance Appeal Tribunal DHSS 1967-, Nat Insurance Appeal Tribunal Dept Employment and Social Security 1967-, Appeal Bd Road Traffic Act (1967) Dept Employment 1969-; examiner High Court of Justice 1969-, sr examiner 1978-; High Sheriff Herts 1980; *Recreations* painting; *Style* - Michael Meredith-Hardy Esq; Radwell Mill, Baldock, Herts (☎ Hitchin 730 242)

MERIVALE-AUSTIN, Hon Mrs Alison Mary; da of 2 Baron Rankeillour, GCIE, MC (d 1958); *b* 1927; *m* 1, 1945 (m dis 1959) Maj Bruce Gardiner Merivale-Austin; 2 da; m 2 1960, Maj Cyril Ernest Stearns, OBE (m annulled 1963); *Style* - The Hon Mrs Alison Merivale-Austin; 7 Cheyne Court, SW3 (☎ 01 353 4430)

MERRIAM, Lady Marjory; *née* Kennedy; da of 3 Marquess of Ailsa (d 1938); *b* 1898; *m* 1921, Sir Laurence Pierce Brooke Merriam, MC, JP, DL (d 1966); 2 s; *Style* - Lady Marjory Merriam; South Cottage, Dedham, Gloucester

MERRILLS, Austin; s of Austin Merrills; *b* 15 April 1928; *Educ* King Edward VII Sheffield, Sheffield U; *m* 1953, Daphne Olivia, nee Coates; 1 s, 2 da; *Career* chm and ch exec Ireland Alloys (Hldgs) Ltd (Scotland); *Recreations* skiing, squash, rugby (spectator), gardening, painting, food & wine; *Clubs* Caledonian; *Style* - Austin Merrills Esq; Clyde House, Kirkfieldbank, Lanark (☎ 0555 3664)

MERRIMAN, Hon Violet Grace; OBE (1948); da of 1 and last Baron Merriman, GCVO, OBE, PC (d 1962); *b* 1911; *Educ* Bedgebury Park and in France; *Career* joined ATS 1938, Ch Cdr 1943; *Style* - The Hon Violet Merriman, OBE; c/o Westminster Bank, 195 Earls Ct rd, SW5

MERRIVALE, 3 Baron (UK 1925); Jack Henry Edmond Duke; s of 2 Baron, OBE (d 1951); *b* 1917; *Educ* Dulwich, Ecole des Sciences Politiques Paris; *m* 1, 1939, Colette Wise (m dis 1974); 1 s, 1 da; m 2, 1975, Betty, widow of Paul Baron; *Heir* s, Hon Derek John Philip Duke; *Career* joined RAF 1940, Flight Lt 1944; chm Scotia Investments Ltd, Anglo-Malagasy Soc; past pres Inst of Traffic Admin; pres Railway Development Assoc; chm British Ctee for the Furthering of Relations with French-Speaking Africa; Chevalier Nat Order of Malagasy; *Style* - The Rt Hon the Lord Merrivale; 16 Brompton Lodge, 9-11 Cromwell rd, SW7 (☎ 01 589 4111)

MERRIVALE, Dowager Baroness; Meta Therese; da of Joseph Wolczon, of Danzig; *b* 1900; *m* 1939, as his 2 w, 2 Baron Merrivale, OBE (d 1951); *Style* - The Rt Hon Dowager Lady Merrivale

MERSEY, 4 Viscount (UK 1916); Richard Maurice Clive Bigham; also Master of Nairne (*see below*) and Baron Mersey (UK 1910); s of 3 Viscount Mersey (d 1979), himself gs of the 1 Viscount, who allegedly chose that particular title (he was a shipping lawyer) 'because he was leaving the Atlantic to F E Smith', (who 2 years later was indeed to take the title of Birkenhead, first as a Barony and later as an Earldom); the 3 Viscount m Lady Katherine Evelyn Constance Petty-

Fitzmaurice (since her f's death Lady Nairne in her own right), da of 6 Marquess of Lansdowne; ha to Lordship of Nairne; *b* 8 July 1934; *Educ* Eton, Balliol Oxford; *m* 1961, Joanna Dorothy Corsica Grey, da of John Grey Murray, CBE; 1 s; *Heir* s, Hon Edward John Hallam Bigham; *Career* Lt Irish Gds (Nat Service) Germany and Egypt; film producer (documentary); *Recreations* mountaineering, music; *Style* - The Rt Hon the Viscount Mersey; 1 Rosmead rd, London W11 (☎ 727 5057)

MERTHYR, Barony of; *see* Lewis, JP, Trevor

MERTHYR, Baroness; Violet; da of Brig-Gen Sir Frederick Charlton Meyrick, 2 Bt, CB, CMG; *m* 1932, 3 Baron Merthyr, KBE, TD, PC (d 1977); *Style* - The Rt Hon Lady Merthyr; Churchton, Saundersfoot, Dyfed

MERTON, John Ralph; MBE (1942); s of Sir Thomas Ralph Merton, KBE (d 1969); *b* 7 May 1913; *Educ* Eton, Balliol Oxford; *m* 1938, Viola Penelope, da of Adolf von Bernd (d 1975); 3 da, (1 decd); *Career* portrait painter; *Recreations* music, making things, underwater photography; *Clubs* Garrick; *Style* - John Merton Esq, MBE; Fourth Floor, 50 Cadogan sq, London SW1; Pound House, Oare, nr Marlborough, Wiltshire (☎ Pewsey 3539)

MERTON, Robert Ralph; s of Sir Thomas Ralph Merton, KBE, (d 1969); *b* 26 April 1914; *Educ* Eton, Balliol Oxford; *m* 1950, Esther Frances, da of Cdr John Leslie Whitehead Allison; 1 s, 1 da; *Career* served in 1939-45 War, Maj 1944; md Alginate Industries Ltd 1950-80; High Sheriff Berks 1964; *Recreations* shooting, country life; *Clubs* Garrick; *Style* - Robert Merton Esq; The Old Rectory, Burghfield, Berks (☎ Burghfield Common 2206)

MERTON, Air Chief Marshal Sir Walter Hugh; GBE (1963, OBE 1941), KCB (1959); s of late Gerald R Merton; *b* 29 Aug 1905; *Educ* Eastbourne, RAF Cadet Coll Cranwell; *m* 1938, Margaret Ethel, da of J C Macro Wilson, of Cossington Manor, Somerset; 1 s; *Career* joined RAF 1925, dir staff and assist Cmdt RAF War Staff Coll 1943-44, dir of organization Air Ministry 1944-45, Air Attaché Prague 1947-48, Air Vice Marshal 1953, Ch of Air Staff RNZAF 1953, AOA Bomber Command 1956-59, Ch of Staff AAFCE 1959, Air Marshal 1959, air memb for Supply and Organisation 1960-63, Air Ch Marshal 1961, ret 1963; Inspector Gen of Civil Defence 1964-68; Air ADC to HM the Queen 1962-63; *Recreations* shooting, fishing; *Clubs* Roy Air Force; *Style* - Air Chief Marshal Sir Walter Merton, GBE, KCB; Hart House, Martin, Fordingbridge Hants (☎ Martin Cross 237)

MESSEL, Hon Mrs (Judith Horatia Maud); da of Field Marshal 1 Baron Birdwood, GCB, GCSI, GCMG, GCVO, CIE, DSO (d 1951); *b* 5 March 1910; *m* 1, 1939 (m dis 1947, he d 1959) Roger William Colville-Wallis; m 2, 1947, Rudolph Putnam Messel (d 1958); *Style* - The Hon Mrs Messel; 1 Broad Lane, Haslingfield, Cambridge CB3 7JF

MESSER, Cholmeley Joseph; s of Col Arthur Albert Messer, CBE, DSO, Woking, Surrey (d 1934); *b* 20 March 1929; *Educ* Wellington Coll; *m* 1956, Ann Mary; 1 s, 1 da; *Career* 2 Lt KRRC M East; chm: Code of Advertising Practice Committee 1976-78, Unit Trust Association 1979-81; *Recreations* golf, gardening, armchair sport, history; *Clubs* City of London; *Style* - Cholmeley Messer Esq; The Manor House, Normandy, Guildford, Surrey (☎ Normandy 3304)

MESTON, 2 Baron (UK 1919); Dougall Meston; s of 1 Baron, KCSI (d 1943); *b* 17 Dec 1894; *Educ* Charterhouse, RMA Woolwich; *m* 1947, Diana Mary Came, da of Capt O S Doll; 2 s; *Heir* s, Hon James Meston; *Career* served WW I, Afghan War 1919, Waziristan 1919-20, Capt RA 1917, ret 1922; Pres Br Soc Commerce; stood for Parl as Lib Candidate Southend 1927 & 1929; barr Lincoln's Inn 1924; *Clubs* Reform Club; *Style* - The Rt Hon the Lord Meston; Hurst Place, Cookham Dene, Berks (☎ Bourne End 23962); Queen Elizabeth Bldg, Temple, EC4 (☎ 01 353 3911)

MESTON, Hon James; s and h of 2 Baron Meston; *b* 10 Feb 1950; *Educ* Wellington, St Catharine's Cambridge; *m*

1974, Jean Rebecca Anne, da of John Carder, of Stud Farm House, Chalvington, Sussex; 1 s (Thomas James Dougall b 1977), 1 da (Laura Anne Rose b 1980); *Career* barr Middle Temple 1973; *Clubs* Hawks; *Style* - The Hon James Meston; c/o Coutts & Co, 188 Fleet st, EC4

MESTON, Hon William Dougall; s of 2 Baron Meston; *b* 17 May 1953; *Educ* Wellington; *Style* - The Hon William Meston

METCALF, John; s of John Metcalf (d 1967); *b* 31 Dec 1922; *Educ* Univ Coll Sch, Downing Coll Cambridge; *m* 1955, Shelagh, nee Branagan; 1 s, 1 da; *Career* chm Dorland Advertising Ltd 1971-, dep chm and jt man dir Hobson Bates & Ptnrs Ltd 1955-68; *Recreations* gardening, writing; *Clubs* Garrick, RAF; *Style* - John Metcalf Esq; Brookland, Wisborough Green, W Sussex (☎ Wisborough Green 700325); A13 Albany, Piccadilly, W1 (☎ 439 7600)

METCALF, Malcolm; MC (1944), DL (1979); s of Charles Almond Metcalf (1976); *b* 1 Dec 1917; *Educ* Merchant Taylors Sch Crosby; *m* 1945, Charis, da of Edward Thomas (d 1959); 2 s; *Career* Capt Middle East and Italy; chartered sec; memb Surrey CC 1965-, leader 1973-77, v-chm 1977-78, chm 1978-; memb Metropolitan Water Bd 1965-74, v-chm 1971-72; memb Thames Conservancy 1970-74, Thames Water Authority 1973-78, Assoc of CCs 1975-; *Recreations* golf; *Clubs* MCC, Burhill Golf Club; *Style* - Malcolm Metcalf Esq, MC DL; Linden, Clive rd, Esher, Surrey (☎ Esher 64476)

METCALFE, Lady Alexandra Naldera; da of 1 and last Marquess Curzon of Kedleston (d 1925); *b* 1904; *m* 1925, Maj Edward Dudley Metcalfe, MVO, MC (d 1957); 1 s, 2 da; *Style* - Lady Alexandra Metcalfe; 65 Eaton Place, SW1

METCALFE, Lady; Dorothea; da of Charles Edwin Gibbs; *m* 1947, as his 2 w, Sir Ralph Ismay Metcalfe (d 1977); *Style* - Lady Metcalfe; Elmtree, West Mersea, Essex (☎ 2934)

METCALFE, David Patrick; s of Major Edward Dudley Metcalfe, MVO, MC; *b* 8 July 1927; *Educ* Eton; *m* 1, 1957, Alexandra; 2 s, 1 da; m 2, 1974, Countess Anne Chauvigny De Blot, 1 s; m 3, 1979, Sally Cullen Howe, da of Edward Everett Cullen III, of Pennsylvania USA; *Career* Lt Irish Guards Germany 1945-48, dir Wigham Poland Holdings Ltd, memb Lloyd's; *Recreations* skiing, tennis, shooting, golf; *Clubs* White's, Buck's, Travellers' (Paris), The Brook (New York); *Style* - David Metcalfe Esq; 15 Wilton st, SW1 (☎ 01 235 1833)

METHERELL, Hon Mrs (Rosamond Ann); da of Rt Hon John Emerson Harding Harding-Davies, who was nominated a Life Peer 16 June 1979, but who d 4 July 1979 before the Peerage was cr; *b* 1946; *m* 1968, Charles Martin Metherell; raised to the rank of a Baron's da 1980; *Style* - The Hon Mrs Metherell; 79 Rivermead Court, SW6

METHUEN, 6 Baron (UK 1838); Anthony John Methuen; s of 5 Baron Methuen (d 1975, himself s of Field Marshal Lord Methuen who commanded in S Africa during the Boer War and who was in his turn sixth in descent from the yr bro of the Ambass to Portugal who negotiated the treaty with that country which bears his name) and Grace, JP, da of Sir Richard Durning Holt, 1 Bt; *b* 26 Oct 1925; *Educ* Winchester, Roy Agricultural Coll Cirencester; *Heir* bro Hon Robert Alexander Holt Methuen; *Career* ARICS; served Scots Gds and Roy Signals 1943-47; lands offr Air Min 1951-62; QALAS 1954; *Clubs* Lansdowne, Roy Ocean Racing and Roy Motor Yacht (Bole); *Style* - The Rt Hon the Lord Methuen; Corsham Court, Corsham, Wilts (☎ 0249 712214)

METHUEN, Lady Maureen Margaret; da of late 13 Earl of Meath; *b* 1908; *m* 1950, Hon Laurence Paul Methuen (d 1970, s of late 3 Baron Methuen); 1 da; *Style* - Lady Maureen Methuen; Starlings, Sutton Benger, Chippenham, Wilts

METHUEN, Hon Robert Alexander Holt; s of 5 Baron Methuen (d 1975), and hp of bro, 6 Baron; *b* 22 July 1931; *Educ* Shrewsbury, Trin Cambridge; *m* 1958, Mary Catherine Jane, da of Ven Charles

German Hooper, Archdeacon of Ipswich; 2 da; *Style* - The Hon Robert Methuen; Stoneycroft Farm, Kniveton, Ashbourne, Derbys

METHVEN, Lady; Karen Jane Caldwell; *m* 1977, Sir (Malcolm) John Methven (d 1980); *Style* - Lady Methven; 20 Bushwood rd, Richmond, Surrey

MEXBOROUGH, 8 Earl of (I 1766); John Christopher George Savile; also Baron Pollington (I 1753) and Viscount Pollington (I 1766); s of 7 Earl (d 1980, himself gs of the 4 Earl; the latter, portrayed as Lord Gaverstock, featured in Disraeli's *Coningsby*, converted to Roman Catholicism in 1894 (his s by his 1 w, the 5 Earl, went one stage further and joined the Buddhists), and for the last seven and a half months of his life enjoyed the distinction of being the last surviving ex-member of the unreformed (pre-1832) House of Commons); *b* 16 May 1931; *Educ* Eton, Worcester Coll Oxford; *m* 1, 1958, Lady Elisabeth Hariot Grimston (m dis 1972), da of 6 Earl of Verulam; 1 s, 1 da; m 2, 1972, Catherine Joyce, da of James Kenneth Hope, CBE, DL, and formerly wife of Maj the Hon Nicholas Crespigny Laurence Vivian; 1 s, 1 da; *Heir* s, Viscount Pollington; *Career* late 2 Lt Gren Gds; *Clubs* Turf, Bath and All England Lawn Tennis clubs; *Style* - The Rt Hon the Earl of Mexborough; 28 Walpole st, SW3 (☎ 01 730 1166); Arden Hall, Hawnby, York (☎ Bilsdale 348)

MEXBOROUGH, Dowager Countess of; Josephine Bertha Emily; da of late Capt Andrew Mansel Talbot Fletcher; *m* 1930, John Raphael Wentworth Savile, 7 Earl of Mexborough (d 1980); *Style* - The Rt Hon Dowager Countess of Mexborough; The Dower House, Arden Hall, Helmsley, Yorks

MEYER, Anthony Ashley Frank; s and h to Sir Anthony John Charles Meyer, 3 Bt, MP; *b* 23 Aug 1944; *Educ* Eton; *m* 1966, Susan Mathilda, da of John Freestone; 1 da; *Style* - Anthony Meyer Esq

MEYER, Sir Anthony John Charles; 3 Bt (UK 1910), of Shortgrove, Newport, Essex, MP (C) Flintshire 1970-; s of Sir Frank Meyer, 2 Bt, MP (d 1935); *b* 27 Oct 1920; *Educ* Eton, New Coll Oxford; *m* 1941, Barbadee Violet, da of A Charles Knight, JP (d 1958); 1 s, 3 da; *Heir* s, Anthony Ashley Frank Meyer; *Career* Lt Scots Gds WW II; For Serv 1947, First Sec Paris 1956, Moscow 1957, at FO 1958-62, PPS to Ch Sec of Treasury 1970-72 and to Sec of State for Employment 1972-74 (both Rt Hon Maurice Macmillan, MP), v-chm Franco-British Parly Relations Ctee, MP (C) Eton and Slough 1964-66, founder and dir of 'Solon' 1969, tstee Shakespeare Nat Memorial Theatre; *Clubs* Beefsteak; *Style* - Sir Anthony Meyer, Bt, MP; Rhewl House, Llanasa, Flints; Cottage pla, Brompton Sq, SW3 (☎ 01 589 7416)

MEYER, James Henry Paul; s of late Leo Henry Paul Meyer; *b* 5 Nov 1938; *Educ* Hilton Coll S Africa, Millfield Sch Somerset; *m* 1964, Janet, nee Baker; 3 c; *Career* chm and md Federated Land Ltd 1959-; *Recreations* squash, showjumping, flying; *Clubs* RAC; *Style* - James Meyer Esq; Keston Stud, Downs Lane, Leatherhead, Surrey (☎ Dorking 5995)

MEYER, Montague John; s of John Mount Montague Meyer, CBE (decd); *b* 18 Dec 1944; *Educ* Cranleigh; *m* 1972, Diana Ruth, da of William Edward Curtis Offer; 2 da; *Career* timber merchant; chm and md Montague L Meyer Ltd 1979- (previously dir of operations 1977-79, dir 1974); md MacMillan Bloedel Meyer Ltd 1979-, dir MacMillan Bloedel Ltd Vancouver BC 1980-; *Recreations* sports, reading, charity works; *Clubs* MCC; *Style* - Montague Meyer Esq; 24 Kensington Park Road, London, W11 (☎ 01 299 5303)

MEYER, Peter John Herman; *b* 29 Apr 1936; *Educ* Cardiff H S, U of Wales; *m* 1962, Elisabeth Ann; 1 s, 1 da; *Career* FCA; in practice at Caerphilly, dir Nova (Jersey) Knil Ltd, councillor S Glamorgan CC, memb Business Educn Cncl; *Recreations* skiing; *Style* - Peter Meyer Esq; 167 Pencisely rd, Cardiff (☎ 561637)

MEYNELL, Hon Mrs; Hon Alexandra Rachel Catherine Mary; *née* Lampson; da of 2 Baron Killearn; *b* 1947; *m* 1966, Nicholas Edward Hugo Meynell; 2 da;

Style - The Hon Mrs Meynell; Ladysmith Farm, Hoar Cross, Burton-on-Trent

MEYNELL, Hon Mrs (Elizabeth Margaret); *née* Gretton; da of 2 Baron Gretton, OBE; *b* 25 July 1945; *Educ* Downham Sch and Switzerland and Italy; *m* 1968, Christopher Mark, s of Canon Mark Meynell; 2 s (Mark John Henrik, Guy Francis); *Style* - The Hon Mrs Meynell; c/o Stapleford Park, Melton Mowbray, Leics (☎ Wymondham 229)

MEYRICK, David John Charlton; s and h of Sir Thomas Frederick Meyrick, 3 Bt, TD; *b* 2 Dec 1926; *Educ* Eton and Trin Hall Cambridge; *m* 1962, Penelope Anne, da of late Cdr John Bertram Aubrey Marsden-Smedley, RN; 3 da; *Career* chartered surveyor and land agent; *Style* - David Meyrick Esq; Great Wedlock, Gumfreston, Tenby, Dyfed

MEYRICK, Col Sir Thomas Frederick; 3 Bt (UK 1880), TD, JP (Pembrokeshire), DL; s of Brig-Gen Sir Frederick Charlton Meyrick, 2 Bt, CB, CMG (d 1932); *b* 28 Nov 1899; *Educ* Eton; *m* 1, 1926, Ivy Frances (d 1947), da of Lt-Col Frederick Charles Pilkington, DSO; 3 s, 3 da; m 2, 1951, Gladice Joyce (d 1977), da of Bertram W Allen; 1 s; m 3, 1978, Suzanne, da of late David Arthur Evans, of Clifton, Bristol; *Heir* s, David John Charlton; *Career* Capt (ret) 15/19 King's Roy Hussars, Maj (ret) 102 (Pembrokeshire Yeo) Field Regt RA (TA), High Sheriff Pembrokeshire 1938, pres Roy Welsh Ag Soc 1955, Hon Col 302 (Pembrokeshire Yeo) Field Regt RA (TA) 1955-59, sometime instructor in equitation at Weedon and RMC; *Style* - Col Sir Thomas Meyrick, Bt, TD, JP, DL; Gumfreston, Tenby, Dyfed

MEYSEY-THOMPSON, Sir (Humphrey) Simon; 4 Bt (UK 1874), of Kirby Hall, Yorkshire; s of Guy Herbert Meysey-Thompson (d 1961) and kinsman of Sir Algar de Clifford Charles Meysey-Thompson, 3 Bt (d 1967); *b* 31 March 1935; *Style* - Sir Simon Meysey-Thompson, Bt; 39 Chesham st, SW1 (☎ 01 235 5806); 10 Church st, Woodbridge, Suffolk (☎ Woodbridge 2144)

MICHELHAM, 2 Baron (UK 1905); Sir Herman Alfred Stern; 2 Bt (UK 1905); also Baron de Stern in the Peerage of Portugal (cr of King Luiz 1864); s of 1 Baron, KCVO (d 1919, through whose mother Julia the present Lord Michelham is great great nephew of Sir Isaac Goldsmid, 1 Bt); *b* 5 Sept 1900; *Educ* Malvern; *m* 1, 1919, Berthe (d 1961), sis of Capt Arthur Capel, CBE; m 2, 1980, Marie-José, nee Dupas (Prof of History, Université de Béthune, France); *Heir* none; *Style* - The Rt Hon the Lord Michelham

MICHELL, Francis Victor; CMG (1955); s of Pierre William Michell (d 1939); *b* 17 Jan 1908; *Educ* Barry Sch, Jesus Oxford; *m* 1943, Betty Enid Tempest, da of William Tempest Olver, JP (d 1958); *Career* entered Foreign Office 1941, British Embassy Rio de Janeiro 1941-46, British Consulate-General Istanbul 1947-51, memb UK Commission-Gen Singapore 1951-53, Foreign Office 1953-65; *Clubs* Travellers'; *Style* - Francis Michell Esq, CMG; Nettlesworth Farm, Vines Cross, Heathfield, East Sussex (☎ Heathfield 2695)

MICHIE, Hon Mrs Anne Laura Dorinthea; da of 2 Baron Aberconway, CBE (d 1953); *b* 1927; *Educ* Lady Margaret Hall Oxford; *m* 1952, Donald Michie (m dis 1959); 1 s, 2 da; *Style* - The Hon Mrs Anne Michie; 9 Steele's rd, NW3

MICHIE, Hon Mrs; Hon Janet Ray Bannerman; da of Baron Bannerman of Kildonan OBE (Life Peer) (d 1969); *b* 1934; *m* 1957, Lt-Col Iain Michie, MB, MRCPEd, RAMC; *Style* - The Hon Mrs Michie; Tigh an Eas, Oban, Argyll

MIDDLEDITCH, Hon Mrs Grace; da of 1 Baron Bethell (d 1945); *b* 1898; *m* 1, 1927, Frederick Joseph Parsons (m dis 1956); 1 s, 1 da; m 2, 1958, Henry Seton Middleditch (m dis 1963); *Style* - The Hon Mrs Grace Middleditch

MIDDLEMISS, Prof Sir John Howard; CMG (1968); s of Thomas Middlemiss, of Northumberland; *b* 14 May 1916; *Educ* Repton, Durham U; *m* 1942, Isobel Mary, da of Ivan Pirrie, MC, MD; 1 s, 2 da;

Career MD, DMRD, FFR, MRCP, FRCP, FRCS; prof of Radiodiagnosis U of Bristol, dir of Radiology United Bristol Hosps 1949-, dean Faculty of Medicine Bristol U 1978-; kt 1981; *Style* - Prof Sir John Middlemiss, CMG; 48 Pembroke rd, Clifton, Bristol (☎ Bristol 38553)

MIDDLEMORE, Sir William Hawkslow; 2 Bt (UK 1919), of Selly Oak, Northfield, Co Worcs; s of Sir John Throgmorton Middlemore, 1 Bt (d 1924); *b* 10 April 1908; *m* 1934, Violet Constance (d 1976), da of Andrew Kennagh; *Heir* none; *Style* - Sir William Middlemore, Bt; St Joseph's, 87 Shurdington rd, Cheltenham, Glos (☎ Cheltenham 25414)

MIDDLETON, 12 Baron (GB 1711); Sir (Digby) Michael Godfrey John Willoughby; 13 Bt (E 1677), MC (1945), DL (N Yorks); s of 11 Baron Middleton, KG (d 1970, descended from 4 Baron Willoughby de Eresby and hence distant cousin of the Earls of Ancaster and Lords Willoughby de Broke, but enjoying unbroken descent in the male line whereas those of the two latter pass through the female); *b* 1 May 1921; *Educ* Eton, Trin Cambridge; *m* 1947, Janet, JP, da of Gen Sir James Marshall-Cornwall KCB CBE DSO MC; 3 s; *Heir* s, Hon Michael Willoughby; *Career* JP & DL E Riding Yorks & Kingston upon Hull 1964-74; 2 Lt Coldstream Gds 1940, temp Maj, NW Europe 1944-45; land agent 1951-; CCllr N Yorks 1974-77; memb Yorks & Humberside Economic Planning Council; Hon Col 2 Bn Yorks (TAVR) Vols 1976-; *Clubs* Boodle's; *Style* - The Rt Hon Lord Middleton MC DL; Birdsall House, Malton, North Yorks (☎ North Grimston 202)

MIDDLETON, Lawrence Monck; s of late Lieut Hugh Jeffery Middleton, RN (3 s of 7 Bt); *b* 23 Oct 1912; *Educ* Eton, Edinburgh, (BSc Forestry); *Career* hp to Btcy of bro, Sir Stephen Hugh Middleton, 9 Bt; *Style* - Lawrence Middleton Esq; Winterhayes, South Perrott, Beaminster, Dorset

MIDDLETON, Sir Stephen Hugh; 9 Bt (E 1662), of Belsay Castle, Northumberland; s of Lt Hugh Jeffery Middleton, RN (d 1914, s of 7 Bt); suc unc, Sir Charles Arthur Middleton, 8 Bt, 1942; *b* 20 June 1909; *Educ* Eton, Magdalene Cambridge; *m* 1962, Mary (d 1972), da of Richard Robinson (d 1933); *Heir* bro, Lawrence Monck Middleton; *Style* - Sir Stephen Middleton, Bt; Belsay Castle, Newcastle upon Tyne

MIDLETON, 11 Viscount (I 1717); Trevor Lowther Brodrick; also Baron Brodrick of Midleton (I 1715) and Baron Brodrick of Peper Harow (GB 1796); the full designation of the Viscountcy is 'Midleton of Midleton'; s of William John Henry Brodrick, OBE (d 1944, himself gs of 7 Viscount, who in his turn was gggs of the 1 Viscount; in 1719 the latter joined with the 2 Duke of Bolton and the 3 Baron Barry of Santry in publicly urging the castration of every unregistered priest & friar in Ireland with a view to promoting the conversion of the common laity there to Protestantism); suc to Viscountcy of cous, 2 Earl of Midleton, MC, who d 1979, when the Earldom became ext; *b* 7 March 1903; *Educ* privately; *m* 1940, Sheila Campbell MacLeod, da of late Charles Campbell MacLeod; *Heir* n, Alan Brodrick; *Recreations* photography, gardening; *Style* - The Rt Hon the Viscount Midleton; Frogmore Cottage, 105 North rd, Bourne, Lincs PE10 9BU

MIDLETON, Countess of; Irène Lilian (Rène Ray); da of late Alfred Creese, of Ewell, Surrey; *b* 22 Sept 1917; *m* 1975, as his 3 w, 2 Earl of Midleton (d 1979 when the Earldom became extinct and the Viscountcy passed to a kinsman); *Style* - The Rt Hon the Countess of Midleton; Martello Lodge, St Brelade's Bay, Jersey

MIDWOOD, Hon Mrs Antonia Catherine; da of Baron Caccia (Life Peer); *b* 15 Feb 1947; *m* 1970 (m dis 1974), Barton Midwood; *Style* - The Hon Mrs Antonia Midwood; 21 Westwood rd, Barnes, SW13

MIECZKOWSKI, Hon Mrs; Hon Caroline Sarah Aline; da of 2 Baron Grenfell, TD (d 1976); *b* 1933; *m* 1965, Zbyszek L Mieczkowski; 1 s, 1 da; *Style* - The Hon Mrs Mieczkowski; Rose Cottage, Henley Park, Henley-on-Thames

MIERS, Rear-Adm Sir Anthony Cecil Capel; VC (1942), KBE (1959), CB (1958), DSO (1941); s of Capt D N C C Miers; *b* 1906; *Educ* Edinburgh Academy, Stubbington House, Wellington; *m* 1945, Patricia Mary, da of late D M Miller; 1 s, 1 da; *Career* special entry cadet 1924, joined submarines as Sub Lt 1929, Lt 1930, commanded HM Submarine L54 1936-37, HMS Iron Duke 1937-388, Lt-Cdr 1938, commanded HM Submarine Torbay 1940-42, Commander 1942, Staff of Fleet Adm C W Nimitz (C-in-C US Pacific Fleet in Pearl Harbour 1942-44), Capt 1946, commanded HMS Forth and 1 Submarine Flotilla in Mediterranean Fleet 1950-52, Capt RN Coll Greenwich 1952-54, Rear Adm 1956; ret 1959; Nat Pres Submarine Old Comrades Assoc 1967-, Hon Life Councillor of Lawn Tennis Assoc 1979-, pres RN Squash Rackets Assoc 1960-70, Govr of Star and Garter Home Richmond 1970-76, chm Hudson's Offshore Ltd 1972-73, Freeman City of London 1966-; Jubilee Medal 1977, fell of Inst of Directors 1960-, pres Coral Yacht Club Newhaven 1978-80; *Recreations* swimming, table tennis; *Clubs* Army and Navy, British Sportsman's, MCC; *Style* - Rear Adm Sir Anthony Miers, VC, KBE, CB, DSO; 8 Highdown rd, Roehampton, London SW15 (☎ 01 788 6863)

MIERS, Henry David Alastair Capel; CMG (1979); s of Col R D M C Miers DSO (d 1974); *b* 6 Jan 1937; *Educ* Winchester Coll Oxford; *m* 1966, Imelda Maria Emilia, nee Wouters; 2 s, 1 da; *Career* HM Diplomatic Serv, head M East Dept Foreign and C'wlth Office 1980-, private sec Min of State FO 1968 (Paris 1972, Cnsllr Tehran 1977-80); *Style* - Henry Miers Esq CMG; c/o FCO, King Charles st, SW1

MIGHELL, Lady; Marjorie; da of late Alexander Draper; *m* 1920, Sir Norman Rupert Mighell, CMG (d 1955); *Style* - Lady Mighell; 90 Collins st, Melbourne, Australia

MIHALOP, Paul Bradley; s of Paul Mihalop; *b* 20 July 1943; *Educ* Portsmouth G S, Birmingham U; *m* 1968, Judith Margaret, nee Eaves; 1 s, 2 da; *Career* md South Crofty Ltd 1980-, gen man Queensload Mines 1978-80, metallurgical man Rossing Uranium 1976-78, process metallurgist Anglo American 1968-7; *Style* - Paul Mihalop Esq; Scarcewater House, Higher St Clements, Truro (☎ 0872 76940)

MILBANK, Anthony Frederick; s and h of Sir Mark Vane Milbank, 4 Bt, KCVO, MC; *b* 16 Aug 1939; *Educ* Eton; *m* 1970, Belinda Beatrice, da of Brig Adrian Clements Gore, DSO; 2 s, 1 da; *Style* - Anthony Milbank Esq; Barningham Park, Richmond, N Yorks

MILBANK, Maj Sir Mark Vane; 4 Bt (UK 1882), of Well, Co York and of Hart, Co Durham, KCVO (1962), MC (1944); s of Sir Frederick Milbank, 3 Bt (d 1964), and Dorothy, eldest da of John Wilson, CB, JP, DL, and Angelina, da of Rev Hon Henry O'Brien (bro of 13 Baron Inchiquin); *b* 11 Jan 1907; *Educ* Eton, Sandhurst; *m* 1, 1930, Lady Angela Isabel Nellie Lanarch-Nevill (m dis 1933), da of 4 Marquess of Abergavenny; m 2, 1938, Hon Verna Aileen (widow of Charles Crawley), da of 11 Baron Farnham (d 1957); 2 s; *Heir* s, Anthony Frederick Milbank; *Career* Maj Coldstream Gds (RARO), ADC to Govr Bombay 1933-38; Comptroller to Govr-Gen Canada 1946-52, Master of HM's Household 1954-67; an Extra Equerry to HM the Queen 1954-; *Style* - Maj Sir Mark Milbank, Bt, KCVO, MC; Gate House, Barningham, Richmond, N Yorks (☎ Teesdale 21269)

MILBANK, Hon Lady; Hon Verena Aileen; da of 11 Baron Farnham, DSO (d 1935); *b* 1907; *m* 1, 1934, Charles Lambart Crawley (d 1935); m 2, 1938, as his 2 w, Maj Sir Mark Vane Milbank, 4 Bt, KCVO, MC; *Style* - The Hon Lady Milbank; The Gate House, Barningham, Richmond, N Yorks

MILBORNE-SWINNERTON-PILKINGTON, Richard Arthur; s and h of Sir Thomas Henry Milborne-Swinnerton-Pilkington, 14 Bt; *b* 4 Sept 1964; *Style* - Richard Milborne-Swinnerton- Pilkington Esq

MILBORNE-SWINNERTON-PILKINGTON, Sir Thomas Henry; 14

Bt (NS 1635); s of Sir Arthur W Milborne-Swinnerton-Pilkington, 13 Bt (d 1952); *b* 10 March 1934; *Educ* Eton; *m* 1961, Susan, da of Norman Stewart Rushton Adamson, of Durban, S Africa; 1 s, 2 da; *Heir* s Richard Arthur Milborne-Swinnerton-Pilkington; *Career* chm Thos & James Harrison Ltd 1980-, chm Charente Steamship Co Ltd 1977-, formerly in Roy Scots Greys; *Clubs* White's; *Style* - Sir Thomas Milborne-Swinnerton-Pilkington, Bt; King's Walden Bury, Hitchin, Herts

MILBURN, Anthony Rupert; s of late Maj Rupert Leonard Eversley Milburn (yr s of 3 Bt) and hp to Btcy of unc, Sir John Milburn, 4 Bt; *b* 17 April 1947; *Educ* Eton and RAC Cirencester (ARICS, MRAC); *m* 1977, Olivia Shirley Catlow; *Style* - Anthony Milburn Esq; 5 Billing St, SW10

MILBURN, Sir John Nigel; 4 Bt (UK 1905), of Guyzance, Parish of Shilbottle Northumberland; s of Sir Leonard John Milburn, 3 Bt (d 1957); *b* 22 April 1918; *Educ* Eton, Trin Cambridge; *m* 1940, Joan, da of Leslie Butcher (d 1969), of Dunholme, Lincs; *Heir* nephew, Anthony Rupert Milburn; *Career* jt-master West Percy Foxhounds 1955-59 and 1963-; late Capt Northumberland Hussars; *Style* - Sir John Milburn, Bt; Brainshaugh, Acklington, Northumberland (☎ Shilbottle 631)

MILBURN, Very Rev Robert Leslie Pollington; s of George Leslie Milburn (d 1961); *b* 28 July 1907; *Educ* Oundle, Sidney Sussex Coll Cambridge, New Coll Oxford; *m* 1944, Margery Kathleen Mary, nee Harvie; 1 da (1 s decd); *Career* Assist Master Eton 1930-32, Fellow and Chaplain Worcester Coll Oxford 1934-57 (Domestic Bursar 1936-47, Estates Bursar 1947-57, Tutor), Dean of Worcester 1957-68, Master of the Temple 1968-80; *Clubs* Athenaeum; *Style* - The Very Rev Robert Milburn; Wallcroft, Bromyard, Herefordshire (☎ Bromyard 3469)

MILDMAY-WHITE, Hon Mrs; Hon Helen Winifred Mildmay; JP (Devon 1952); da of 1 Baron Mildmay of Flete (d 1947); *b* 12 Aug 1907; *m* 1945, Lt-Cdr (Richard) John Bramble Mildmay-White, DL (d 1969); 2 s, 1 da; *Career* AARC; Devon County Pres Girl Guides 1962-65; *Style* - The Hon Mrs Mildmay-White; Pamflete, Holbeton, Plymouth, Devon

MILES, Baron (Life Peer UK 1979); Bernard James Miles; CBE (1953); s of Edwin James Miles; *b* 27 Sept 1907; *Educ* Uxbridge Co Sch, Pembroke Oxford, City Univ; *m* 1931, Josephine Wilson; 1 s, 2 da; *Career* actor; founder with his w of the Mermaid Theatre, Puddle Dock, EC4 1959; author; kt 1969; Books *The British Theatre, God's Brainwave, Favourite Tales from Shakespeare*; *Style* - The Rt Hon the Lord Miles, CBE; Mermaid Theatre, Puddle Dock, Blackfriars, EC4

MILES, Anthony John; s of Alfred Paul Miles (d 1946); *b* 18 July 1930; *Educ* High Wycombe Roy G S; *m* 1975, Anne Elizabeth, nee Bishop; *Career* chm & editorial dir Mirror Gp Newspapers Ltd 1980-, editor Daily Mirror 1971-74, dir Reuters Ltd 1978-, memb Press Council 1975-78; *Clubs* Reform; *Style* - Anthony Miles Esq; Mirror Group Newspapers Ltd, Holborn Circus, EC1

MILES, Hon Mrs; Hon Julian Isabella Joan; da of 9 Viscount Chetwynd (d 1965); *b* 1932; *m* 1960, Maj Philip David Miles, s of Maj W H Miles, MBE; 1 s, 1 da; *Style* - The Hon Mrs Miles; Hinton Hall, Lea Cross, Shrewsbury, Salop

MILES, Lady; Lilian Hope; da of late H J Sykes; *m* 1926, Sir Charles Watt Miles, OBE (d 1970); *Style* - Lady Miles; 5 Courtfield Mews, Courtfield rd, SW5

MILES, Philip John; s and h of Sir William Napier Maurice Miles, 6 Bt; *b* 10 Aug 1953; *Style* - Philip Miles Esq

MILES, Sir William Napier Maurice; 6 Bt (UK 1859), of Leigh Court, Somersetshire; s of Lt-Col Sir Charles William Miles, 5 Bt, OBE (d 1966); *b* 19 Oct 1913; *Educ* Stowe, Jesus Cambridge; *m* 1946, Pamela Dillon; 1 s, 2 da; *Heir* s, Philip John Miles; *Style* - Sir William Miles, Bt; Flat 59, Fort Picklecombe, Maker, Torpoint, Cornwall; Old Rectory House, Walton-in-Gordano, nr Clevedon, Avon (☎ Clevedon 873365)

MILFORD, 2 Baron (UK 1939); Sir Wogan Philipps; 2 Bt (UK 1919); s of 1 Baron Milford (d 1962; 6 s of Rev Sir James Philipps, 12 Bt, by Hon Mary Best, sis of 5 Baron Wynford; also yst bro of 1 Viscount St Davids) by Ethel Speke, niece of the African explorer John Speke (discoverer of Lake Victoria and, with Sir Richard Burton, Lake Tanganyika); *b* 25 Feb 1902; *Educ* Eton, Magdalen Oxford; *m* 1, 1928 (m dis 1944), the novelist Rosamond Lehmann; 1 s (and 1 da decd); m 2, 1944, as her 2 husb, Cristina (d 1953; former w of 15 Earl of Huntingdon and da of the Marchese Casati by his w, the Marchesa, subject of the celebrated portrait by Augustus John); m 3, 1954, Tamara, nee Kravetz, widow of William Rust, sometime ed The Daily Worker; 1 s; *Heir* s, Hon Hugo Philipps; *Career* farmer, painter, trades unionist, former memb Henley & Cirencester RDCs, late Internat Brigade; *Style* - The Rt Hon Lord Milford; Butler's Farm, Colesbourne, Cheltenham, Glos (☎ Coberley 260)

MILFORD HAVEN, 4 Marquess of (UK 1917); George Ivar Louis Mountbatten; also Earl of Medina and Viscount Alderney (both UK 1917); s of 3 Marquess of Milford Haven, OBE, DSC (d 1970, himself gs of HSH Prince Louis of Battenberg, who was forced by anti-German hysteria in 1917 to anglicise his name; the Battenbergs have been traced to Duke Ydulf, who flourished in the area covered by modern Benelux in the sixth century AD, and are thus one of the most ancient houses in the West); Lord Milford Haven is, through his paternal great grandmother's mother (Princess Alice, da of Queen Victoria) 4 cous of HRH The Prince of Wales, while through his great aunt Alice (sis of 2 Marquess and mother of HRH The Duke of Edinburgh) he is even more closely related, being 2 cous to HRH; also great nephew to late Earl Mountbatten of Burma and, through his paternal grand mother (Nada), ggggs of Tsar Nicholas I of Russia and 2 cous of the Duchesses of Abercorn and Westminster; *b* 6 June 1961; *Heir* bro, Lord Ivar Alexander Michael Mountbatten; *Style* - The Most Hon the Marquess of Milford Haven; Moyns Park, Birdbrook, Essex; Flat 2, 2 Wilton ter, SW1

MILFORD HAVEN, Janet Marchioness of; Janet Mercedes; JP (Inner London 1979); da of late Maj Francis Bryce, OBE; *b* 29 Sept 1937; *Educ* Trafalgar School for Girls, Montreal; *m* 1960, 3 Marquess of Milford Haven, OBE, DSC (d 1970); 2 s; *Style* - The Most Hon Janet Marchioness of Milford Haven, JP

MILLAIS, Geoffroy Richard Everett; s and h of Sir Ralph Regnault Millais, 5 Bt; *b* 27 Dec 1941; *Educ* Marlborough; *Career* 5 in descent from Sir John Millais, 1 Bt, Artist and Pres RA; *Style* - Geoffroy Millais Esq

MILLAIS, Sir Ralph Regnault; 5 Bt (UK 1885), of Palace Gate, Kensington, Co Middlesex and of St Ouen, Jersey; s of Sir Geoffroy William Millais, 4 Bt (d 1941); Sir John Everett Millais, 1 Bt, was the Victorian artist; *b* 4 March 1905; *Educ* Marlborough, Trin Cambridge; *m* 1, 1939, Felicity Caroline Mary Ward Robinson (m dis 1947), da of Brig-Gen William Ward Warner, CMG (d 1950); 1 s, 1 da; m 2, 1947, Irene Jessie (m dis 1971), da of late E A Stone, of St Anne's Mont à l'Abbé, St Helier, Jersey; m 3, 1975, Mrs Babette Sefton-Smith, da of late Maj-Gen H F Salt, CB, CMG, DSO; *Heir* s, Geoffroy Richard Everett Millais; *Career* joined RAFVR 1939, Sqdn Ldr 1940, Wing Cdr 1941; *Style* - Sir Ralph Millais, Bt; Gate Cottage, Winchelsea, E Sussex

MILLAR, Hon Alastair James Harold Hoyer; s of 1 Baron Inchyra, GCMG, CVO; *b* 13 Nov 1936; *Educ* Eton; *m* 1974, Virginia Margaret Diana, da of William Perine Macauley; 1 s, 1 da; *Career* late Scots Gds; *Style* - The Hon Alastair Millar; 16 Pembridge Villas, W11

MILLAR, Ian Alastair Duncan; CBE (1978), MC (1945), JP (Perths 1952), DL (1960); s of Sir James Millar; *b* 22 Nov 1914; *Educ* Gresham's, Cambridge U; *m* 1945, Louise Reid, da of W McCosh (d 1937); 2 s, 2 da; *Career* served Corps of Roy Engineers 1940-45, Maj; stood (Lib) for Parl Banff 1945 and Kinross and W Perthshire 1949 and 1963; CCllr 1946-79 (Perthshire and Kinross), Convener 1975-78; Regnl Cllr Tayside 1974-78; memb N of Scotland Hydro Electric Bd 1956-70, dep chm 1970-72; chm United Auctions (Scotland) Ltd 1967-74; dir Macdonald Fraser & Co 1961-; *Recreations* learning about & catching salmon, meeting people; *Clubs* Roy Perth Golfing Soc & Club; *Style* - Ian Millar Esq, CBE, MC, JP, DL; Remony, Aberfeldy, Perthshire (☎ Kenmore 209)

MILLAR, John Harold Derek; MBE (1944), DL (Humberside 1981); s of James Charles Millar (d 1947); *b* 23 Jan 1914; *Educ* The Edinburgh Acad, Edinburgh U; *m* 1947, Isobel Margaret da of John Jardine CB, OBE, MD; 1 s, 1 da; *Career* sr consultant physician Scunthorpe Gp of Hosps 1948-79 (now Hon Consultant), civilian medical offr Rapier Barracks Kirton-in-Lindsey, consultant physician Grimsby Gen Hosp 1948-60; *Recreations* golf, fishing; *Clubs* Army and Navy; *Style* - John Millar Esq, MBE, DL; Garden Cottage, Low st, Winterton, Scunthorpe (☎ Scunthorpe 732371)

MILLAR, Lady; Noreen Winifred; da of Edward Glynn; *m* 1920, Col Sir Jackson Millar, CBE (d 1958); *Style* - Lady Millar; 34 Station rd, Killearn, Stirlingshire

MILLAR, Hon Robert Charles Reneke Hoyer; s and h of 1 Baron Inchyra, GCMG, CVO; *b* 4 Apr 1935; *Educ* Eton, New Coll Oxford; *m* 1961, Fiona Mary, da of Edmund C R Sheffield, of Normanby Park, Scunthorpe, Lincs; 1 s, 2 da; *Career* late Scots Gds; *Style* - The Hon Robert Millar; Rookley Manor, King's Somborne, Stockbridge, Hants

MILLER, Alan John McCulloch; DSC (1941), VRD (1950); s of Louis McEwan Miller (d 1950); *b* 21 Apr 1914; *Educ* Kelvinside Academy, Strathclyde U; *m* 1940, Kirsteen Ross, da of Frank George Orr, CBE (d 1945); 3 s, 1 da; *Career* commanded RNVR (Clyde Div) 1938; served RN 1939-45; chm and md Bestobell Ltd 1965-73, chm Low and Bonar Gp Ltd 1978-, chm BNEC Southern Africa Ctee 1970; *Recreations* sailing, skiing, golf, shooting; *Clubs* Army & Navy, Roy Thames Yacht, Roy Cruising, Roy and Ancient (St Andrews) and Sunningdale Golf; *Style* - Alan Miller Esq, DSC, VRD; 3 Windlesham ct, Windlesham, Surrey (☎ Bagshot 72980 and 74720)

MILLER, Hon Mrs; Hon Ann Kathleen; da of 12 Baron Aylmer; *b* 1941; *Educ* Mount Douglas HS, Victoria Coll; *m* 1972, Gregor Byron Miller, s of late John Brown Miller, 1 s, 2 step da; *Recreations* tennis, cycling, music; *Style* - The Hon Mrs Miller; 2765 Skilift pla, W Vancouver, BC, Canada

MILLER, Lady Diana Mary; *née* Pelham; da of 5 Earl of Yarborough, MC, DL (d 1948), and Nancye, nee Brocklehurst, niece of 1 and last Baron Ranksborough; co-heiress to Baronies of Fauconberg (E *ante* 24 June 1295) and Conyers (E 1509), through her paternal grandmother, who brought 153 quarterings into the Pelham family and in whose favour they were brought out of abeyance 1903 and 1892 respectively, only to lapse into it again on the 5 Earl of Yarborough's death in 1948; *b* 5 July 1920; *m* 1952, Robert Miller, s of Capt Gordon Molineux Miller (d 1952); 2 da (Marcia Anne b 1954, adopted by Maj Michael H L Lycett, whose surname she assumed, but retains right of succession to the Baronies; Beatrix Diana b 1955); *Career* SRN; *Style* - Lady Diana Miller; c/o Rhobank Corpn Ltd, Box 2270, Salisbury, Zimbabwe

MILLER, Lady; Elizabeth; da of C E Barberie; *m* 1957, Sir Roderick William Miller, CBE (d 1971); *Style* - Lady Millar; 9 Hillside ave, Vaucluse, NSW 2030, Australia

MILLER, Lady; Ella Jane; JP (Edinburgh); da of John Stewart, of Edinburgh; *m* 1933, Sir James Miller, GBE, LLD (d 1977); *Style* - Lady Miller, JP; Belmont, Ellersly rd, Edinburgh EH12 65A

MILLER OF GLENLEE, Sir Frederick William MacDonald; 7 Bt (GB 1788), of Glenlee, Kirkcudbrightshire; s of Sir Alastair George Lionel Miller, 6 Bt, (d 1964); *b* 21 March 1920; *Educ* Tonbridge; *m* 1947, Marion Jane Audrey, da of R S Pettit, of Sudbury, Suffolk; 1 s, 1 da; *Heir* s, Stephen William Macdonald Miller of Glenlee; *Career* served 1939-43, Beds and

Herts Regt 1940, Black Watch 1941-42, RAC 1943; conservative agent for Whitehaven Div of Cumberland 1947-50, for Wembley North 1950-52, for North Norfolk 1952-65, for Lowestoft 1965- and Suffolk Conservative Euro agent 1980-; dep Traffic Cmmr 1974-, memb Suffolk CC 1977-, Gov Reydon HS 1980-; *Recreations* gardening; *Style* - Sir Frederick Miller of Glenlee, Bt; Ivy Grange Farm, Westhall, Halesworth, Suffolk

MILLER, Harry Holmes; s of Sir Ernest Henry John Miller, 10 Bt (d 1960); hp to Btcy of bro, Sir John Miller, 11 Bt; *b* 1927; *m* 1954, Gwynedd Margaret, da of R P Sherriff, of Paraparauma, New Zealand; 1 s, 2 da; *Style* - Harry Miller Esq; Komako, RD, Ashurst, New Zealand

MILLER, Hon Mrs (Honor Leslie); *née* Brooke; da of Baron Brooke of Cumnor, CH, PC (Life Peer) and Baroness Brooke of Ystradfellte, OBE (Life Peeress); *b* 1941; *m* 1966, Dr (Thomas) Nigel Miller; 1 s, 1 da; *Style* - The Hon Mrs Miller; Laurel Hill, Repton, Derby

MILLER, Maj-Gen Joseph Esmond; MC (1943); s of Col John Francis Xavier Miller, OBE (d 1960); *b* 22 Sept 1914; *Educ* St George's Coll Weybridge, U of London (St Bartholomew's Hosp Med Sch); *m* 1946, Kathleen Veronica, da of Louis Lochée Bayne (d 1919); 1 s; *Career* served in N Africa, Sicily and Italy 1943, Holland and Germany 1944; CO British Mil Hosp Hong Kong 1965-68; dir Medical Services UK Land Forces 1973-76, dep dir Medical Services UKLF 1972-73, dep dir Medical Services HQ Scotland 1971-72, dep dir Med Services HQ BAOR 1969-71, ret 1973; CStJ; MRCS, LRCP, MBIM; *Recreations* golf, gardening; *Style* - Maj-Gen Joseph Miller, MC; 17 Norton Green close, Norton, Sheffield (☎ 748694)

MILLER, Lady; Jane Elizabeth Simson; da of Francis Elliott; *m* 1925, Lt-Col Sir James MacBride Miller, MC, TD (d 1977); *Style* - Lady Miller; Duneaton, West Bay rd, North Berwick, E Lothian

MILLER, Sir John Holmes; 11 Bt (E 1705), of Chichester, Sussex; s of Sir Ernest Henry John Miller, 10 Bt (d 1960); *b* 1925; *m* 1950, Jocelyn Edwards; 2 da; *Heir* bro, Harry Holmes Miller; *Style* - Sir John Miller, Bt; Te Whare, Kohinui, Pahiatua, New Zealand

MILLER, Michael George; s of George James Miller (d 1977); *b* 19 Sept 1927; *Educ* Cirencester G S, Roy Agricultural Coll; *m* 1957, Elizabeth Mary, nee Todd; 4 c; *Career* sales man Stita Farm Tours 1977-, dir Furness Travel Ltd 1973-77; *Recreations* squash, tennis, swimming, walking; *Style* - Michael Miller Esq; 36 High st, Cheltenham (☎ 0242 24548)

MILLER, Michael George; s of Robert Miller; *b* 17 June 1925; *Educ* Torquay G S, Wales U; *m* 1, 1948, Elizabeth Jane (d 1971); 2 da; m 2, 1972, Sadie Lorna; *Career* chartered engineer, dir in charge Racal-Decca Serv Ltd 1981-, dir Decca Radar Ltd 1965-80, serv man BAC (GW Div) 1958-63, reg offr REME 1944-58; *Recreations* golf; *Clubs* Directors'; *Style* - Michael Miller Esq; 11 Lyne Place Manor, Bridge Lane, Virginia Water, Surrey (☎ Chertsey 65532)

MILLER, Mahala, Lady; Mahala Netta Bennett; *m* 1920, Sir Ernest Henry John Miller, 10 Bt (d 1960); *Style* - Mahala, Lady Miller; 19 Huiast, Pahiatua, New Zealand

MILLER, Hon Mrs; Hon Patricia; *née* Makins; da of 1 Baron Sherfield, GCB, GCMG; *b* 1946; *m* 1966, Michael Ordway Miller, s of Albert O Miller, of Carmel, California; *Style* - The Hon Mrs Miller; 3 Sunset Way, Muir Beach, Calif, USA; 1655 Sequoia, Tahoe City, Calif, USA

MILLER, Lady (Beatrix) Patricia; *née* de la Poer Beresford; da of 6 Marquess of Waterford (d 1911); *b* 1902; *m* 1926, Lynden Roberts Miller (d 1973); 1 s, 1 da; *Style* - Lady Patricia Miller; Georgestown House, Kilmacthomas, Co Waterford

MILLER, Roger Geoffrey; s of Robert Ralph Miller; *b* 5 Aug 1952; *Educ* St Dunstans College, London; Trinity College Cambridge; *m* 1971, Diana Evelyn, da of late Brig Henry Latham; 3

children; *Career* man consultant, md RTZ Computer Services Ltd 1978-; *Recreations* sailing; *Style* - Roger Miller Esq; 18 Bramcote rd, SW15

MILLER, Robert Michael; s of Hugh Begg Miller (d 1979); *b* 4 April 1943; *Educ* Hamilton Acad; *m* 1972, Janis, nee Fleming; 2 children; *Career* chartered accountant 1968, md The Blackie Publishing Group 1978-; *Recreations* golf, reading; *Clubs* Caledonian; *Style* - Robert Miller Esq; 2 Glenburn rd, Hamilton, Lanarkshire

MILLER, Stephen William Macdonald; s and h of Sir (Frederick William) Macdonald Miller of Glenlee, 7 Bt; *b* 20 June 1953; *Educ* Rugby, St Bart's Hospital; *m* 1978, Mary Owen; *Career* MB, LMSSA; *Style* - Stephen Miller Esq; 45 Dover st, Norwich

MILLES-LADE, Lady Diana; da of Hon Henry Augustus Milles-Lade JP (d 1937) and sis of 4 Earl Sondes; *b* 1919; *Career* granted 1942, rank, title and precedence as an Earl's da which would have been hers had her father survived to succeed to the title; *Style* - Lady Diana Milles-Lade; 37 Lennox gdns, SW1

MILLETT, Anthony Derek; s of Denis Millett; *b* 20 April 1936; *Educ* Harrow; *Career* dir Millett Stores, dir Black & Edgington Ltd, dir Gaiety Theatre Inc Player's Theatre; *Recreations* cricket, theatre, old cinema, reading, writing; *Clubs* MCC, Harrow Wanderers, Gentlemen of Leicester; *Style* - Anthony Millett Esq; Barclays Bank Ltd, 9 Portman sq, WlA 3AL

MILLIGAN, Lady; Muriel Jean; da of James MacLehose (d 1943); *b* 10 April 1899; *m* 1925, late Rt Hon Lord (William Rankine) Milligan (Senator of College of Justice in Scotland), s of Very Rev George Milligan; 1 s, 3 da; *Style* - Lady Milligan; 39 Lauderdale st, Edinburgh (☎ 447 2839)

MILLING, Henry Miles; s of the late Henry Robert Milling; *b* 30 Nov 1934; *Educ* Oundle Sch, Cambridge, Imperial Coll London; *m* 1968, Ann Cartledge, nee Bradbury; 2 da; *Career* marketing dir Fairey Engineering 1978-, head of sales and marketing NEI International Combustion 1975-78, proposals man GEC Power Station Projects 1970-75; *Recreations* sailing, tennis, golf, skiing; *Style* - Henry Milling Esq; Beech Tree House, Davenport Lane, Mobberley, Knutsford, Cheshire

MILLINGTON-DRAKE, Lady Effie; *née* Mackay; da of 1 Earl of Inchcape; *b* 1895; *m* 1920, Sir (John Henry) Eugen (Vanderstegen) Millington-Drake, KCMG (d 1972); 2 s (James, *qv*, Teddy), 3 da decd; *Career* OStJ *Style* - Lady Effie Millington-Drake; Palazzo Taverna, via di Monte Giordano 36, 00186 Rome, Italy

MILLINGTON-DRAKE, James Mackay Henry; s of Sir Eugen Vanderstegen Millington-Drake, Min to Uruguay 1934-41, who played a major role in the events leading to the scuttling of the Graf Spee in the mouth of the River Plate by continuously sending messages, as if to acquaint a fleet over the horizon with the position of the German pocket battleship, thus engendering a sense of hopelessness in German breasts at Montevideo; Sir Eugen m Lady Effie Mackay, da of 1 Earl of Inchcape; Sir Eugen's paternal great grandmother was Frances, nee Vanderstegen, ggda of Henri, whose er bro was cr Count van der Stegen 1688 and has descendants still extant; Henri & the Count were ggs of Nicolas van der Stegen, Burgomaster of Bois-le-Duc, memb Cncl of Brabant, Treasurer of the Order of the Golden Fleece and Receiver-Gen of the Emperor Charles V & the Archduchess Isabella; *b* 10 Jan 1928; *Educ* RNC Dartmouth; *m* 1953, Manon, da of Reginald Redvers-Bate; 2 s, 2 da; *Career* Lt RN ret; dir: Bahrein Slipway Co Ltd, C'wlth Devpt Corpn, Dilmun Navigation, Gray Dawes Tstee & Nominee Co, Gray Mackenzie & Co, Inchcape & Co, Nat Bank of Australasia, Ocean Inchcape, Peschaud et Cie Internat, St Mary Axe Securities; *Style* - James Millington-Drake Esq; Manor House, Shepperton-on-Thames, Middx (☎ Walton-on-Thames 28762)

MILLIS, Derek Maunsell; s of Arthur Hugh Millis (d 1962); *b* 27 Feb 1927; *Educ* Eastbourne G S & Coll; *m* 1951, Constance Mary, da of Percy Durrant; 2 ch; *Career* formerly Sergeant Instructor RA (Instruments); CA; co dir; advr to ptnrs J Henry Schroder & Co 1957-60; area controller British Petroleum 1962-65; financial controller British Aluminium 1961-62; dir Slough Estates Ltd 1975-; *Recreations* fishing, music, motoring; *Style* - Derek Millis Esq; Chaldon, Oval Way, Gerrards Cross, Bucks (☎ Gerrards Cross 83402)

MILLN, Hon Mrs (Susan Margaret); da of 14 Viscount Valentia, MC, MRCS, LRCP; *b* 18 Feb 1931; *m* 1954, Peter Lindsay Milln, s of Alexander Lindsay Milln (d 1932); 1 s, 3 da; *Career* British Horse Soc's Bridleway Offr for Cornwall (Hon Appt); *Recreations* riding, sailing (yacht: 'Thunderpaws'); *Style* - The Hon Mrs Milln; Bosinver, St Austell, Cornwall (☎ St Austell 2128)

MILLNER, Brian David; s of Edwin Millner (d 1932); *b* 7 Oct 1930; *Educ* Scarborough H S; *m* 1956, Adina Josephine, nee Tonn; 1 s, 1 da; *Career* govt relations advr Pilkington Bros Ltd 1980-, dir Chance Pilkington Ltd 1979-80 (Japan 1977-80), dir Chance (Optical) Ltd 1976-80, marketing man Chance Pilkington 1973-79 (N Reg man 1970-73), marketing administrator Sundry Pilkington Gp Appointments Prod 1954-70; *Recreations* motoring, gardening, reading, travel; *Style* - Brian Millner Esq; 3 Church Walk, Tarleton, Lancs (☎ 077 473 4811)

MILLS, 2 Viscount (UK 1962); Sir Roger Clinton Mills; 2 Bt (UK 1953); also Baron Mills (UK 1957); s of 1 Viscount Mills, KBE, PC (d 1968); *b* 14 June 1919; *Educ* Canford, Jesus Cambridge; *m* 1945, Joan Dorothy, da of James Shirreff, of London; 1 s, 2 da; *Heir* s, Hon Christopher Mills; *Career* served 1940-46 with RA, Maj; admin offr Kenya 1947; barr Inner Temple 1958; admin offr HM Overseas Civil Service 1946-63; now business exec; *Style* - The Rt Hon the Viscount Mills; Whitecroft, 24 Abbey rd, Knaresborough, N Yorks (☎ Harrogate 866201)

MILLS, Hon Catherine Gray; da of 4 Baron Hillingdon; *b* 18 Sept 1963; *Style* - The Hon Catherine Mills

MILLS, Lady; Carola Marshall; JP (Hants); da of late Judge Somerville Pinkney Tuck; *m* 1918, Col Sir John Digby Mills, TD (d 1972); *Style* - Lady Mills, JP; White House, Hangersley, Ringwood, Hants

MILLS, Hon Christopher Philip Roger; s and h of 2 Viscount Mills; *b* 20 May 1956; *m* 1980, Lesley, da of Alan Bailey, of Lichfield, Staffs; *Style* - The Hon Christopher Mills

MILLS, Edward David William; CBE (1959); s of late Edward Mills; *b* 19 Mar 1915; *Educ* Regent St Polytechnic Sch of Architecture; *m* 1939, Elsie, da of late W Bryant; 1 s, 1 da; *Career* chartered architect and design consultant, fell of Soc of Industrial Artists, Alfred Bossom Research fell of Roy Inst of British Architects, Churchill Fell 1969; sr ptnr Edward D Mills and Ptnrs Architects; pres Soc of Architectural Illustrators 1975-; chm Faculty of Architecture British Sch at Rome; author; *Recreations* photography, writing, travel; *Style* - Edward Mills Esq, CBE; Gatehouse Farm, Newchapel, Lingfield, Surrey

MILLS, Lady; Hilda Grace Shirley; da of H Gavin Young; *m* 1940, as his 2 w, Maj-Gen Sir Arthur Mordaunt Mills, CB, DSO (d 1964); *Style* - Lady Mills; 29 Normans, Norman rd, Winchester

MILLS, Hon Jessica Anne; da of 4 Baron Hillingdon; *b* 1 April 1957; *Style* - The Hon Jessica Mills

MILLS, John Alfred; *b* 7 Nov 1924; *Educ* City Boys Sch Leicester, Univ of London; *m* 1950, Noreen Mary, 1 s, 1 da; *Career* md Churchill Gear Machines Newcastle 1959-67, md B Elliott Group and main board dir 1967-71, md of main division Molins Ltd 1971-77, group md Molins Ltd 1977-; *Recreations* music, squash, bridge, gardening; *Clubs* Institute of Mechanical Engineers; *Style* - John Mills Esq; Cullford, Coombe Park, Kingston on Thames, Surrey

MILLS, Major John Rice Francis; s of Lt Col Frank Mills, DSO (d 1945); *b* 18 Jan 1921; *Educ* Harrow; *m* 1968, Matilda, da of Lt Col William Warburton Hayes, DL, JP (d 1953); *Career* Royal Welch Fusiliers 1941-42, Kings African Rifles 1942-47, Game Warden and National Park Warden Uganda 1948-62, High Sheriff Anglesey 1966; *Recreations* training and working labrador retrievers, fishing; *Style* - Major John Mills; Rhiwlas, Pentraeth, Anglesey, Gwynedd (☎ Pentraeth 204)

MILLS, Lady; Mary Austen; da of Sydney Austen Smith; *m* 1926, Air Chief Marshal Sir George Holroyd Mills, GCB, DFC (d 1971); *Style* - Lady Mills; c/o Lloyds Bank, 6 Pall Mall, SW1

MILLS, Michael Victor Leighton; s and h of Sir Peter Frederick Leighton Mills, 3 Bt; *b* 30 Aug 1957; *Style* - Michael Mills Esq

MILLS, Peter Francis; *b* 20 Sept 1945; *Educ* Liverpool Coll & U; *m* 1969, Rosemary Grace; 1 s, 1 da; *Career* chartered accountant, fin dir Cow & Gate Ltd, dir Cow & Gate (Kenya) Ltd; *Recreations* microprocessors; *Style* - Peter Mills Esq; 20 Ivybank pk, Bath, Avon (☎ Avon 833794)

MILLS, Sir Peter Frederick Leighton; 3 Bt (UK 1921), of Ebbw Vale, Co Monmouth; s of Sir (Frederick Leighton) Victor Mills, 2 Bt, MC (d 1955); *b* 9 July 1924; *Educ* Eastbourne Coll, Cedara Agricultural Coll, Natal U; *m* 1954, Pauline Mary, da of L R Allen, of Calverton, Notts; 1 s; *Heir* s, Michael Victor Leighton Mills; *Career* served 1943-44 with R Corps of Signals, Lt 5 R Gurkha Rifles 1946-47; entered Fedn of Rhodesia Nyasaland Civil Service 1953, with Rhodesia Govt 1964-; *Style* - Sir Peter Mills, Bt; Henderson Research Station, P Bag 222a, Salisbury, Zimbabwe

MILLS, Ronald Stephen; s of Peter Mills; *b* 2 March 1947; *Educ* Glaisdale Sch; *m* 1969, Jean, nee Marshall; 2 da; *Career* chartered accountant 1968, dir William Lawrence & Co Ltd; *Recreations* church, walking, gardening; *Style* - Ronald Mills Esq; 229 Oxclose lane, Arnold, Nottingham (☎ 0602 263231)

MILLS, Hon Ursula Sybil; da of 3 Baron Hillingdon (d 1952); *b* 1918; *Style* - The Hon Ursula Mills

MILMAN, Sir Dermot Lionel Kennedy; 8 Bt (GB 1800), of Levaton-in-Woodland, Devonshire; s of Sir Lionel Charles Patrick Milman, 7 Bt, CMG (d 1962); *b* 24 Oct 1912; *Educ* Uppingham, CCC Cambridge; *m* 1941, Muriel, da of J E S Taylor, of King's Lynn; 1 da; *Heir* bro, Malcolm Douglas Milman; *Career* served in 1939-45 War with RASC; Maj British Council Service Overseas and Home 1946-76; *Style* - Sir Dermot Milman, Bt; 7 Old Westhall close, Warlingham, Surrey

MILMAN, Marjorie, Lady; Marjorie Aletta; da of late Col Arthur Harry Clark-Kennedy; *m* 1911, Brig-Gen Sir Lionel Charles Patrick Milman, 7 Bt, CMG, (d 1962); *Style* - Marjorie, Lady Milman; 15 Rectory rd, Beckenham, Kent

MILMAN, Malcolm Douglas; s of Brig-Gen Sir Lionel Charles Patrick Milman, 7 Bt, CMG (d 1962); hp of bro, Sir Dermot Lionel Kennedy Milman, 8 Bt; *b* 18 May 1915; *Educ* Canford, Worcester Oxford; *m* 1940, Sheila Maud (m dis 1949), da of Albert Maurice Dudeney; 2 da; *Career* served 1939-45 War; Malaya 1952-57; *Style* - Malcolm Milman Esq; 15 Rectory rd, Beckenham, Kent

MILNE, 2 Baron (UK 1933); George Douglass Milne; s of Field Marshal 1 Baron, GCB, GCMG, DSO (d 1948); *b* 10 Feb 1909; *Educ* Winchester, New Coll Oxford; *m* 1940, Cicely, da of Ronald Leslie; 2 s, 1 da; *Heir* s, Hon George Alexander Milne; *Career* Maj (TA) 1940; memb Inst of Chartered Accountants of Scotland; master Worshipful Co of Grocers 1961-62; ptnr Arthur Young McClelland Moores, CA 1947-72; dir London & Northern Gp, Oxo (UK) Ltd; *Style* - The Rt Hon the Lord Milne; 33 Lonsdale rd, Barnes, SW13 (☎ 01 748 6421)

MILNE, Hon George Alexander; s and h of 2 Baron Milne; *b* 1 April 1941; *Educ* Winchester; *Style* - The Hon George

Milne; 188 Broom rd, Teddington, Middx (☎ 01 977 9761)

MILNE, Hon Iain Charles Luis; s of 2 Baron Milne; *b* 16 Sept 1949; *Educ* Oundle; *Style* - The Hon Iain Milne

MILNE HOME, John Gavin; TD, DL; s of Sir John Hepburn Milne Home (d 1963); *b* 20 Oct 1916; *Educ* Wellington Coll, Trin Coll Cambridge; *m* 1942, Rosemary Honor Croad, da of Capt Godfrey Gervase Elwes (d 1959); children; *Career* Capt KOSB, chartered surveyor, agent for Buccleuch Estates Ltd 1949-74; *Style* - John Milne Home Esq, TD DL; Kirkside of Middlebie, Lockerbie, Dumfriesshire (☎ Ecclefechan 204)

MILNE-WATSON, Sir David Ronald; 2 Bt (UK 1937), of Ashley, Longbredy, Co Dorset; s of Sir David Milne-Watson, 1 Bt, TD (d 1945); *b* 15 July 1904; *Educ* Glenalmond, Balliol Oxford; *Heir* bro, Sir Michael Milne-Watson; *Career* Capt IA 1942-45; *Clubs* Travellers' and MCC; *Style* - Sir David Milne-Watson, Bt; 38 Hugh st, SW1 (☎ 01 834 5166); The Stables, Oakfield, Mortimer, Berks

MILNE-WATSON, Sir Michael; CBE (1953); s of Sir David Milne-Watson, 1 Bt (d 1945); hp to bro, Sir Ronald Milne-Watson, 2 Bt; *b* 16 Feb 1910; *Educ* Eton, Balliol Oxford; *m* 1940, Mary Lisette, da of late H C Bagnall; 1 s; *Career* Sub-Lt RNVR; joined Gas Light & Coke Co 1933, md 1945; gov North Thames Gas Bd 1946-49, chm 1949-64; Liveryman Grocers' Co 1947; dir Industrial & Commercial Finance Corpn Ltd 1963-80; chm Richard Thomas & Baldwins Ltd 1964-67; dep chm British Steel Corpn 1967-69; dir Commercial Union Assurance Co 1968-81, Northern Assurance Co Ltd 1960-65, Northern & Employers Assurance Co Ltd 1961-68; chm The William Press Gp of Cos 1969-74; pres Council of Reading U 1975-80; dir Finance Corpn for Industry Ltd 1974-80; gov British United Provident Assoc Ltd 1975, chm 1976-81; kt 1969; *Recreations* fishing, walking; *Clubs* MCC, Leander; *Style* - Sir Michael Milne-Watson, CBE; Oakfield, Mortimer, Berks (☎ Burghfield Common 2200)

MILNER OF LEEDS, 2 Baron (UK 1951); Arthur James Michael Milner; AE (1952); s of 1 Baron Milner of Leeds, MC, PC (d 1967); *b* 12 Sept 1923; *Educ* Oundle, Trin Hall Cambridge; *m* 1951, Sheila Margaret, da of late Gerald Hartley, of North Hill Court, Leeds; 1 s, 2 da; *Heir* s, Hon Richard James Milner; *Career* Oppn Whip 1971-74; joined RAFVR 1942, served 1942-46, commissioned 1943; served with RAUXAF 609 (W Riding) Sqdn 1947-52, Flight Lt; slr 1951; ptnr Milners, Curry & Gaskell (Legal firm), and J H Milner & Son; *Style* - The Rt Hon Lord Milner of Leeds AE; 2 The Inner Court, Old Church st, SW3 (☎ 01 352 7588)

MILNER, Andrew; s of Thomas Milner; *b* 2 Feb 1951; *Educ* Guthlaxton G S, Hull Coll of Higher Education; *m* 1978, Lynda, nee Fullam; 1 c; *Career* md Humber Manures Ltd, national officer British Junior Chamber; *Recreations* gardening, jogging, British Junior Chamber; *Style* - Andrew Milner Esq; Lawsonia, 53 Station rd, Noth Ferriby (☎ 0482 631620)

MILNER, Lady Charlene Mary Olivia; *née* French; da of 3 Earl of Ypres; *b* 17 May 1946; *m* 1965, Charles Mordaunt Milner, yr s of Sir George E M Milner, 9 Bt; 3 s; *Style* - Lady Charlene Milner; Nun Appleton, PO Windmill, Cape, S Africa

MILNER, Sir George Edward Mordaunt; 9 Bt (GB 1717), of Nun Appleton Hall, Yorkshire; s of Brig-Gen George Francis Milner, CMG, DSO (d 1921), and cousin of 8 Bt (d 1960); *b* 7 Feb 1911; *Educ* Oundle; *m* 1, 1935, Barbara (d 1951), da of H N Belsham, of Hunstanton, Norfolk; 2 s, 1 da; m 2, 1953, Katherine Moodie Bisset Hoey, of Dunfermline; *Heir* s, Timothy William Lycett Milner; *Career* served in 1939-45 War with RA (Capt); stipendiary steward of the Jockey Club (SA) 1954-59, exec steward 1977-80; steward Cape Turf Club 1959-76; memb Council of Thoroughbred Breeders Assoc (SA) 1976-; author; *Books* Inspired Information, Vaulting Ambition, The Last Furlong; *Recreations* writing, racing; *Clubs* Rand; *Style* - Sir George Milner, Bt; Natte Valleij, Klapmuts, Cape Province, S Africa (☎0251 5171)

MILNER OF LEEDS, Lois, Baroness; Lois Tinsdale; da of Thomas Brown, of Roundhay, Leeds; *m* 1917, 1 Baron Milner of Leeds, MC, PC (d 1967); 1 s, 2 da; *Style* - The Rt Hon Lois, Lady Milner of Leeds; The Grove, Roundhay, Leeds 8 (☎ 657488)

MILNER, Hon Meredith Ann; da of 2 Baron Milner of Leeds; *b* 1956; *Style* - The Hon Meredith Milner

MILNER, Hon Richard James; s and h of 2 Baron Milner of Leeds; *b* 16 May 1959; *Style* - The Hon Richard Milner

MILNER, Timothy William Lycett; s and h of Sir George Edward Mordaunt Milner, 9 Bt; *b* 11 Oct 1936; *Style* - Timothy Milner Esq

MILNER, Hon (Lois Elizabeth Florence) Zaidée; da of 1 Baron Milner of Leeds, MC, PC (d 1967); *b* 1921; *Educ* Roundhay High Sch, Switzerland; *Style* - The Hon Zaidée Milner; Whitehall ct, SW1 (☎ Whitehall 3160); The Grove, Roundhay, Leeds 8 (☎ 657488)

MILNER-BARRY, Sir (Philip) Stuart; KCVO (1975), CB (1962), OBE (1946); s of late Prof E L Milner-Barry; *b* 20 Sept 1906; *Educ* Cheltenham, Trin Cambridge; *m* 1947, Thelma Tennant, da of Charles Tennant Wells; 1 s, 2 da; *Career* stockbroker L Powell Sons & Co 1929-38; chess correspondent The Times 1938-45; temporary civil servant Foreign Office 1940-55; prin HM Treasury 1945, assist secretary 1947, under-sec 1954, dir Establishments & Organisation Miny of Health 1958-60, under sec HM Treasury 1966, Civil Service Dept 1968-77; *Clubs* Brooks's; *Style* - Sir Stuart Milner-Barry, KCVO, CB, OBE; 43 Blackheath Park, SE3 (☎ 01 852 5808)

MILNES COATES, Anthony Robert; s and h of Sir Robert Edward James Clive Milnes Coates, 3 Bt, DSO; *b* 8 Dec 1948; *Educ* Eton, St Thomas' Hospital; *m* 1978, Harriet, da of Raymond Burton, of The Old Rectory, Slingsby, York; *Career* MRCS, LRCP; *Style* - Anthony Milnes Coates Esq

MILNES COATES, Lt-Col Sir Robert Edward James Clive; 3 Bt (UK 1911), of Helperby Hall, Helperby, N Riding of Yorkshire, DSO (1945), JP (N R Yorks 1960); s of Capt Sir Clive Milnes Coates, 2 Bt, OBE, JP (d 1971); *b* 1907; *Educ* Harrow, RMC, Queens' Cambridge; *m* 1945, Lady Patricia (who m 1936, Lt-Col Charles Thomas Milnes Gaskell (ka 1943); 3 s), da of 4 Earl of Listowel (d 1931); 1 s, 1 da; *Heir* s, Dr Anthony Robert Milnes Coates; *Career* Lt Coldstream Gds 1930, Capt 1938, seconded Trans-Jordan Frontier Force 1937-39, served in Italy 1944-45, ret 1947; patron of two livings; *Clubs* Pratt's; *Style* - Lt-Col Sir Robert Milnes Coates, Bt, DSO, JP; Moor House Farm, Helperby, Yorks (☎ Helperby 662)

MILNES COATES, Lady Celia Hermione; JP (NR Yorks 1933); da (twin) of 1 and last Marquess of Crewe, KG, PC (d 1945); *b* 1884; *m* 1906, Capt Sir Edward Clive Milnes Coates, 2 Bt, OBE (d 1971) (assumed additional surname of Milnes 1946); 2 s (1 ka 1944), 2 da; *Style* - Lady Celia Milnes Coates, JP; Helperby Hall, Helperby, York (☎ Helperby 204)

MILNES COATES, Lady (Ethel) Patricia Hare; da of 4 Earl of Listowel (d 1931); *b* 1912; *m* 1, 1936, Lt-Col Charles Thomas Milnes Gaskell (k on active service 1943); 3 s; m 2, 1945, Lt-Col Sir Robert Edward James Clive Milnes Coates, 3 Bt, DSO, *qv*; 1 s, 1 da; *Style* - Lady Patricia Milnes Coates; Moor House Farm, Helperby, York

MILSOM, Hon Mrs (Penelope Jane); *née* Kaldor; da of Baron Kaldor, FBA (Life Peer); *b* 1942; *m* 1964, Robert Charles Milsom; *Style* - The Hon Mrs Milsom; 27 The Dreel, Norfolk Park, Edgbaston, Birmingham 15

MILTON, Maj Robert Nicholas Manning; CVO (1962), OBE (1960); s of Ralph Stanley Milton; *b* 16 Sept 1915; *Educ* Bedford, St Catharine's Cambridge; *m* 1940, Elizabeth Newnham, da of Col H N Sealy; 2 s, 1 da; *Career* Maj late IA; Colonial Administrative Service 1947, perm sec 1957-61; exec dir of development Kaiser Engineers, Oakland Calif 1961-72; consultant on admin and control to

Channel Tunnel Project 1972-73; freeman Clockmakers Co 1978; freeman City of London 1979; *Style* - Maj Robert Milton, CVO, OBE; Coombe Hayes, Pebble Hill, Betchworth, Surrey

MILVERTON, 2 Baron (UK 1947); Rev Fraser Arthur Richard Richards; s of 1 Baron Milverton, GCMG (d 1978); *b* 21 July 1930; *Educ* Ridley Coll, Ontario, Clifton Coll, Egerton Agricultural Coll Njovo Kenya, Bishop's Coll Cheshunt Herts; *m* 1957, Mary Dorothy, da of Leslie Fly, of Bath; 2 da; *Heir* bro, Hon Michael Hugh Richards; *Career* Roy Signals 1949-50; Kenya Police 1952-53; Deacon 1957, rector of Christian Malford with Sutton Benger and Tytherton Kellaways 1967-, chaplain Wilts ACF; *Style* - The Rev the Rt Hon the Lord Milverton; The Rectory, Christian Malford, Chippenham, Wilts (☎ Seagry 720466)

MILVERTON, Noelle, Baroness; Noelle Benda; da of Charles Basil Whitehead of Torquay; *m* 1927, 1 Baron Milverton, GCMG (d 1978); *Style* - The Rt Hon Noelle, Lady Milverton

MINNITT, Hon Mrs (Primrose Keighley); *née* Balfour; da of 1 Baron Riverdale, GBE (d 1957); *b* 20 April 1913; *m* 1, 1933, Oliver Grahame Hall (who assumed by deed poll 1945 the christian name of Claude in lieu of Oliver and the surname of Muncaster in lieu of his patronymic) (d 1974); 2 s; m 2, 1975, Robert John Minnitt, CMG, s of late Charles Frederick Minnitt; *Clubs* Lansdowne; *Style* - The Hon Mrs Minnitt; Whitelocks, Sutton, Pulborough, Sussex (☎ Sutton 216)

MINNITT, Robert John; CMG (1955); s of late Charles Frederick Minnitt; *b* 2 April 1913; *Educ* Marlborough, Trin Cambridge; *m* 1, 1943, Peggy Christine (d 1973), da of Eric William Sharp; 1 s, 2 da; m 2, 1975, Hon Primrose Keighley Muncaster (nee Balfour), da of 1 Baron Riverdale, GBE (d 1957) and widow of Claude Muncaster (d 1974); *Career* entered Colonial Service (Hong Kong) 1935, ch sec Western Pacific High Commission 1952, ret 1958; furniture designer and craftsman 1960; civil service Commonwealth Office 1966; ret 1969; *Recreations* furniture making; *Clubs* Lansdowne; *Style* - Robert Minnitt Esq, CMG; Whitelocks, Sutton, nr Pulborough, Sussex (☎ Sutton (Sussex) 216)

MINOPRID, Frank Charles; s of Charles Anthony Minoprid; *b* 9 Aug 1939; *Educ* Harrow, Grenoble U; *m* Patricia Mary, nee Dixon; 3 children; *Career* Lt Royal Artillery Germany, wine merchant, sales dir Hatch Mansfield & Co, Master of Wine; *Recreations* tennis, squash, gardening; *Clubs* memb of Champagne Academy; *Style* - Frank Minoprid Esq; The Manor House, Milton Ernest, Bedford (☎ 0230 22237)

MINTO, 6 Earl of (UK 1813); Sir Gilbert Edward George Lariston Elliot-Murray-Kynynmound; 9 Bt (S 1700), MBE (1955); also Baron Minto (GB 1797) and Viscount Melgund (UK 1813); s of 5 Earl of Minto (d 1975, himself s of the 4 Earl who was Viceroy of India 1905-10 and who is commemorated in the Morley-Minto Reforms; the most memorable of their provisions was the introduction of a native member into the Viceregal Executive Cncl; like other reformers of the period he was the victim of an assassination attempt made with a bomb, but escaped with his life, continuing to enjoy the good fortune he had had as a gentleman rider (he made five attempts on the Grand National): Sir James Paget, who once attended upon him following a nasty tumble by his Lordship at Valentine's Brook, diagnosed a broken neck; the 4 Earl's ggf, the 1 Earl, did a similar spell as Govr-Gen of India in the early nineteenth century (allegedly returning £245,000 the richer) and was educated at Fontainbleau (at the suggestion of the philosopher David Hume, a friend of the family) where a schoolfellow was Mirabeau); *b* 19 June 1928; *Educ* Eton, RMA Sandhurst; *m* 1, 1952, Lady Caroline Child-Villiers (m dis 1965), da of 9 Earl of Jersey; 1 s, 1 da; m 2, 1965, Mary Elizabeth, da of late Peter Ballantine, of Gladstone, New Jersey USA; *Heir* s, Viscount Melgund; *Career* 2 Lt Scots Gds 1948, served Malaya 1949-51; ADC to CIC FarELF 1951, to CIGS 1953-55, to Govr Cyprus 1955; RARO 1956; Brig Queen's Bodyguard Scotland (Roy Co of

Archers); JP (1961) Roxburghshire; memb Borders Regional Council 1974; chm Scottish Council on Alcoholism 1973-, dep Traffic Commr Scotland 1975-; exec v-pres Scotland Chamber of Commerce 1978-; *Clubs* Puffin's; *Style* - The Rt Hon Earl of Minto, MBE, JP; Minto, Hawick, Roxburghshire (☎ Denholm 321)

MISHCON, Baron (Life Peer UK 1978); Victor Mishcon; DL (Gter London); s of Rabbi Arnold Mishcon; *b* 15 Aug 1915; *Educ* City of London Sch; *m* 1, Beryl Honor, da of J E Posnansky; 2 s, 1 da; m 2, 1976, Joan, da of Bernard Monty; *Career* slr 1937, sr ptnr Victor Mishcon & Co, memb Nat Theatre Bd 1968-, S Bank Theatre Bd 1977-; late memb LCC, GLC, ILEA; stood for NW Leeds 1950, Bath 1951, Gravesend 1955 & 1959, all in Lab interest; memb Ho Lds European Communities Cttee Law Sub-Cttee 1978-; chm Inst Jewish Studies UCL; *Style* - Rt Hon Lord Mishcon DL; 12 Chelwood House, Gloucester sq, W2; Threeways, Bighton rd, Medstead, Hants (☎ Alton 62161); 125 High Holborn, WC1 (☎ 01 405 3711/1236)

MISHCON, Hon Peter Arnold; s of Baron Mishcon (Life Peer); *b* 1946; *m* 1967, Penny Green; *Style* - The Hon Peter Mishcon

MISHCON, Hon Russell Orde; s of Baron Mishcon (Life Peer); *b* 1948; *m* 1975, Marcia Leigh; *Style* - The Hon Russell Mishcon

MISSEN, Leslie Robert; CMG (1956), MC (1918); s of Robert Symonds Missen (d 1915); *b* 2 May 1897; *Educ* Perse Sch, Christ's Cambridge; *m* 1932, Muriel, da of Robert Alstead, OBE (d 1946); 2 s; *Career* Capt 1916-19 War; ch education offr Wigan 1930-36, E Suffolk 1936-62, commissioner for Local Govt 1962-66; chm of Working Party Trinidad 1954; chm trustees of Homerton Cambridge 1946-61; pres Association of Ch Ed Offrs 1952, pres Ed Section British Assoc 1957; *Recreations* writing, music; *Clubs* National Liberal; *Style* - Leslie Missen Esq, CMG, MC; 34 Saxmundham rd, Aldeburgh, Suffolk

MITCHELL, Lt-Col Brian Granville Blayney; DSC (1940), DL (1956) RM (ret); s of William Blayney Mitchell (d 1917); *b* 14 Mar 1900; *Educ* King's Sch Bruton; *m* 1937, Violet Gwyndolin, da of Maj Sir Charles Price, DL (d 1954); 2 da; *Career* 2 Lt RM 1917, served 1917-18 (UK) Grand Fleet 1919, served 1939-45 RM Div as CSO Commando Gp, Lt-Col 1940, Acting Col 1945, ret 1945; memb Governing Body Church in Wales; High Sheriff 1959 (Pembs); *Clubs* Victory Services; *Style* - Lt-Col Brian Mitchell, DSC, DL, RM; Manor House, Wiston, Haverfordwest, Dyfed (☎ Clarbeston 258)

MITCHELL, Air Cdre Sir (Arthur) Dennis; KBE (1977), CVO (1961), DFC (1944) and Bar (1945), AFC (1943); s of late Col A Mitchell, DSO, RA; *b* 26 May 1918; *Educ* Nautical Coll Pangbourne, RAF Coll Cranwell; *m* 1949, Mireille Caroline, da of Comte Henri Cornet de Ways Ruart; 1 s; *Career* joined RAF 1936, served in 1939-45 War, Dep Capt The Queen's Flight 1956-59, Capt 1962-64; ADC to HM the Queen 1958-62, extra equerry 1962-; md Aero Systems (SA); founder of Brussels Airways (SA), Aero Distributors (SA); *Recreations* golf; *Clubs* Naval & Military, Anglo Belgian , RAF; *Style* - Air Cdre Sir Dennis Mitchell KBE, CVO, DFC*, AFC; 8 Chemin des Chasseurs, 1328 Ohain, Belgium (☎ 02 653 13 01)

MITCHELL, Lady; Elizabeth; da of late Charles Leigh Pemberton; *m* 1945, Sir George Irvine Mitchell, CB, QC (d 1978); *Style* - Lady Mitchell; 14 Rodway rd, Roehampton, SW15

MITCHELL, Lady; Elizabeth Jane Mitchell; da of Rev William Innes, of Aberdeenshire; *m* 1927, as his 2 w, Sir Thomas Gillan Mitchell (d 1954); *Style* - Lady Mitchell; 6 Belvidere st, Aberdeen

MITCHELL, Lady; Edith Theresa; da of James Henry Bona; *m* 1935, Sir James Mitchell (d 1968); *Style* - Lady Mitchell; Flat 5, 11 Grand ave, Hove, Sussex

MITCHELL, Harold Charles; CIE (1948); s of late Daniel Charles Mitchell; *b* 1896; *Educ* Fairfield Sch; *m* 1923, Edna Evadne, nee Bion; 1 da; *Career* RNVR

WW I, Indian Police 1920, central intelligence officer Ajmer 1937, dep inspector gen of Police HQ and Railways, ret 1949; *Clubs* Naval and Camberley Heath GC; *Style* - Harold Mitchell Esq, CIE; Camber Cottage, Camberley, Surrey (☎ 22675)

MITCHELL, Col Sir Harold Paton; 1 Bt (UK 1945), of Tulliallan, Co Fife, and of Luscar, Province of Alberta, Canada, JP (Clackmannanshire 1941, and Fifeshire 1943), DL (Clackmannanshire 1942); s of Col Alex Mitchell, TD, JP, DL (d 1935); *b* 21 May 1900; *Educ* Eton, RMC, Univ Coll Oxford; *m* 1947, Mary, CStJ, da of late William Pringle; 1 da; *Heir* none; *Career* Command Welfare Offr AA Command 1940-48; lecturer Stanford U California 1959-65; chm and ch exec coal and oil Cos Canada; contested Clackmannan and East Stirlingshire (C) 1929; MP (C) Middlesex 1931-45; PPS to Rt Hon John Colville Dept of Overseas Trade 1931-35, to Rt Hon Ralph Assheton Miny of Labour 1939-40; v-chm Con Party 1942-45; hon fell Univ Coll Oxford; KStJ; *Clubs* Roy Bermuda Yacht Club; *Style* - Col Sir Harold Mitchell, Bt, JP, DL; Maison Silence, 3920 Zermatt, Switzerland

MITCHELL, James Alexander Hugh; s of the late William Moncur Mitchell; *b* 20 July 1939; *Educ* Winchester, Trinity Cambridge; *m* 1962, Janice Page, nee Davison; 3 s; *Career* chm Mitchell Beazley Ltd, senior V-pres American Express Company Communications Division; *Recreations* fishing, shooting, gardening; *Clubs* Garrick; *Style* - James Mitchell Esq; Teasel, Wilsford-cum-Lake, Nr Amesbury, Wilts

MITCHELL, James Lachlan Martin; RD (1969); s of Lachlan Martin Victor Mitchell OBE, MB (d 1956); *b* 13 June 1929; *Educ* Cargilfield, Sedbergh, Edinburgh U; *Career* Cdr RNR (ret 1974), advocate 1957-74, standing junior cnsl in Scotland to Admty Bd 1963-74, Sheriff Lothians & Peebles 1974, Floating Sheriff 1974-78), Sheriff at Edinburgh 1978; *Recreations* fishing, photography, the gramophone; *Clubs* New (Edinburgh); *Style* - James Mitchell Esq, RD; 3 Great Stuart st, Edinburgh (☎ 031 225 3384)

MITCHELL, William Vernon; s of Peter Mitchell (d 1976); *b* 1 May 1923; *Educ* Dollar Acad Scotland; *m* 1945, Muriel Olive Cooke; 2 c; *Career* tech dir Lever Brothers Ltd; *Recreations* golf; *Style* - William Mitchell Esq; 15 Uplands Way, Sevenoaks, Kent (☎ 0732 56887)

MITCHELL-INNES, Alistair Campbell; s of Peter Campbell Mitchell-Innes (d 1960); *b* 1 March 1934; *Educ* Charterhouse; *m* 1957, Penelope Ann, nee Hill; 1 s, 2 da; *Career* dir Brooke Bond Liebig Ltd 1979-, v-chm Walls Meat Co Ltd 1975-77, dir Macfisheries Ltd 1971-75, Lt Queens Own Roy West Kent Parachute Regt 1953-54; *Recreations* golf; *Clubs* Caledonian; *Style* - Alistair Mitchell-Innes Esq; Langton Lodge, Sunningdale, Berks (☎ 0990 24993)

MITCHELL-THOMSON, Hon Callum Malcolm McEacharn; s and h of 3 Baron Selsdon; *b* 7 Nov 1969; *Style* - The Hon Callum Mitchell-Thomson

MITCHISON, Dr Hon Denis Anthony; s of Baron Mitchison, CBE (Life Peer, d 1970); *b* 6 Sept 1919; *Educ* Abbotsholme Sch, Trin Cambridge, Univ Coll Hosp London; *m* 1940, Ruth Sylvia, da of Hubert Gill; 2 s, 2 da; *Career* Prof of Bacteriology, Roy Postgraduate Med Sch 1971-; dir Medical Research Council Unit for Laboratory Studies of Tuberculosis 1956-; *Style* - Dr the Hon Denis Mitchison; 14 Marlborough rd, Richmond, Surrey (☎ 01 940 4751)

MITCHISON, Prof Hon John Murdoch; s of Baron Mitchison, CBE, QC (Life Peer) (d 1970); *b* 11 June 1922; *Educ* Winchester Coll, Trin Cambridge; *m* 1947, Rosalind Mary Wrong; 1 s, 3 da; *Career* prof of zoology Edinburgh U 1963-; memb Science Board SRC 1977-; author; *Style* - Prof the Hon John Murdoch; Great Yew, Ormiston, E Lothian (☎ Pencaitland 340530)

MITCHISON, Prof Hon Nicholas Avrion; s of Baron Mitchison, CBE, QC (Life Peer) (d 1970); *b* 5 May 1928; *Educ* Leighton Park Sch, New Coll Oxford; *m* 1957, Lorna Margaret, da of Maj-Gen J S S Martin, CSI; 2 s, 3 da; *Career* Prof of zoology and comparative anatomy UCL 1970-; *Style* - Prof the Hon Nicholas Mitchison; 14 Belitha Villas, London N1

MITCHISON, Baroness; Naomi Margaret; da of late John Scott Haldane, CH, FRS; *b* 1 Nov 1897; *Educ* Dragon Sch Oxford; *m* 1916, Baron Mitchison, CBE, QC (Life Peer) (d 1970); 3 s (*see* Dr Hon Denis, Prof Hon John and Prof Hon Nicholas Mitchison), 2 da (*see* Hon Mrs Godfrey, Hon Mrs Arnold-Forster); *Career* authoress of many books; fell St Anne's College Oxford; *Style* - The Rt Hon the Lady Mitchison; Carradale House, Carradale, Campbeltown, Kintyre, Scotland

MITFORD, Hon Emma; da of 5 Baron Redesdale; *b* 1959; *Style* - The Hon Emma Mitford

MITFORD, Hon Georgina Clementine; da of 5 Baron Redesdale; *b* 1968; *Style* - The Hon Georgina Mitford

MITFORD, Hon Georgina Kathryn Mercia; da of 5 Baron Redesdale; *b* 1961; *Style* - The Hon Georgina Mitford

MITFORD, Hon Henrietta Jane; da of 5 Baron Redesdale; *b* 4 Aug 1965; *Style* - The Hon Henrietta Mitford

MITFORD, Jessica Lucy, *see* Hon Mrs Treuhaft

MITFORD, Hon Rupert Bertram; s and h of 5 Baron Redesdale; *b* 18 July 1967; *Style* The Hon Rupert Mitford

MITFORD, Hon Tessa; da of 5 Baron Redesdale; *b* 1960; *Style* - The Hon Tessa Mitford

MITFORD, Hon Victoria-Louise; da of 5 Baron Redesdale; *b* 1962; *Style* - The Hon Victoria-Louise Mitford

MITFORD-SLADE, Patrick Buxton; s of Col Cecil Townley Mitford-Slade; *b* 7 Sept 1936; *Educ* Eton, Sandhurst; *m* 1964, Anne Catherine, nee Stanton; 1 s, 2 da; *Career* Capt Green Jackets, memb Stock Exchange 1972, Assistant Sec Panel on Takeovers and Mergers 1970-72, ptnr Cazenove & Co 1973, memb Cncl Stock Exchange 1976; *Recreations* shooting, fishing, riding, gardening; *Clubs* Naval & Military, City; owner of racehorse 'Double Past'; *Style* - Patrick Mitford-Slade; 6 Queensberry Place, SW7 (☎ 581 2285); Damales House, West Green, Hartley Wintney, Hampshire (☎ Hartley Wintney 2640)

MLINARIC, David; *m* 1969, (Katherine) Martha, da of Sir Robert Laycock (d 1968) and Lady Laycock, *qv*; *Career* interior designer; *Style* - David Mlinaric Esq; 33 Tite st, SW3

MOBBS, Gerald Nigel; s of Gerald Aubrey Mobbs (d 1976); *b* 22 Sept 1937; *Educ* Marlborough, Ch Ch Oxford; *m* 1961, Hon Pamela Jane, nee Berry da of Viscount Kemsley and Lady Hélène Hay, da of 11 Marquess of Tweeddale; 1 s, 2 da; *Career* chm & ch exec Slough Estates Ltd 1976-, chm Charterhouse Group Ltd 1977-, chm Property Serv Agency Advsy Board 1980-, dir Barclays Bank Ltd 1979-, dir Barclays Trust Co Ltd 1973-, dep chm Charterhouse Japhet Ltd, pres Br Prop Fed 1979-81, chm assoc of Br Chambers of Commerce 1974-76; *Recreations* riding, hunting, travel, skiing; *Style* - Gerald Mobbs Esq; Widmer Lodge, Lacey Green, Aylesbury, Bucks

MOBBS, John Graham; s of E N Mobbs, CBE, of Stoke Poges; *b* 13 March 1935; *Educ* Wellington; *m* 1960, Marina Nicole, da of Visconde de Pereira Machado (title originally 1861 conferred for life by King Peter V of Portugal, later renewed), of Passadena, Estoril; 2 s, 1 da; *Career* chm Amberush Ltd; dir ML Hldgs; *Recreations* golf, tennis, squash; *Clubs* Thurlestone Golf; *Style* - John Mobbs Esq; Stoneridge, Tapps Lane, Brixton, Plymouth, Devon (☎ 880301)

MOBBS, Hon Mrs (Pamela Jane Margaret); *née* Berry; da of 2 Viscount

Kemsley; *b* 27 May 1937; *m* 1961, Gerald Nigel Mobbs; 1 s, 2 da; *Style* - The Hon Mrs Mobbs; Widmer Lodge, Lacey Green, Aylesbury

MOFFATT, Hon Mrs (Ruth Lesley); *née* Jackson; da of Baron Jackson of Burnley (Life Peer) (d 1970); *b* 22 May 1945; *Educ* Sutton High Sch, U of Wales, Bangor and Aberdeen; *m* 1970, David John Moffatt; 1 da; *Style* - The Hon Mrs Moffatt; 26 Townsend Lane, Upper Boddington, Daventry, Northants

MOGGRIDGE, Hon Mrs (Catherine Grevile); *née* Herbert; da of 2 Baron Hemingford; *b* 1942; *m* 1962, Harry Treherne Moggridge; 2 s, 1 da; *Style* - The Hon Mrs Moggridge; The New House, Shilton, Oxon

MOIR, Christopher Ernest; s and h of Sir Ernest Ian Royds Moir, 3 Bt; *b* 22 May 1955; *Style* - Christopher Moir Esq

MOIR, Sir Ernest Ian Royds; 3 Bt (UK 1916), of Whitehanger, Fernhurst, Co Sussex; s of Sir Arrol Moir, 2 Bt (d 1957); *b* 9 June 1925; *Educ* Rugby, Caius Cambridge; *m* 1954, Margaret Hanham, da of George Carter, of Huddersfield, Yorks; 3 s; *Heir* s, Christopher Ernest Moir; *Style* - Sir Ernest Moir, Bt; Three Gates, Coombe lane West, Kingston upon Thames, Surrey (☎ 01 942 7394)

MOLE, Arthur Charles; s of Sir Charles Johns Mole, KBE, MVO, (d 1962); *b* 25 Feb 1926; *Educ* St George's Coll Weybridge, King's Coll London; *m* 1957, Hon Susan Mary, da of Baron Hinton of Bankside OM KBE (Life Peer); 2 s; *Career* project design engineer Atomic Power Constructions Ltd 1957-65, gen man Engineering Morganite Carbon Ltd 1972-, dir Morgan Electrical Carbon Ltd 1973-, MB Metals Ltd 1976; *Style* - Arthur Mole Esq; 2 Second av, Charmandean, Worthing, W Sussex (☎ 209122); 32 Devon ct, Freshwater E, Dyfed (☎ Lamphey 2467)

MOLE, Lady; Marjorie; da of late Capt Frederick William Butt-Thompson; *m* 1962, as his 2 w, Sir Charles Johns Mole, KBE, MVO (d 1962); *Style* - Lady Mole; The Bucknalls, Westbourne, Emsworth, Hants

MOLE, Hon Mrs (Susan Mary); da of Baron Hinton of Bankside OM KBE (Life Peer); *b* 6 Feb 1932; *m* 1957, Arthur Charles Mole, *qv*, s of late Sir Charles John Mole, KBE, MVO; 2 s; *Style* - The Hon Mrs Mole; Polurrian, 2 Second av, Charmandean, Worthing, Sussex BN14 9NX (☎ 209122); 32 Devon ct, Freshwater East, Dyfed, Wales (☎ Lamphey 672467)

MOLESWORTH, 11 Viscount (I 1716); Richard Gosset Molesworth; also Baron Philipstown (I 1716); s of 10 Viscount (d 1961); *b* 31 Oct 1907; *Educ* Lancing; *m* 1958, Anne Florence, da of John Mark Freeman Cohen; 2 s; *Heir* s, Hon Robert Bysse Kelham Molesworth; *Career* formerly farmer; Freeman City of London 1978; served 1939-45 with RAF (Middle East Forces); *Style* - The Rt Hon the Viscount Molesworth; Garden Flat, 2 Bishopswood rd, Highgate, N6 (☎ 01 348 1366)

MOLESWORTH, Allen Henry Neville; s of Col Roger Bevil Molesworth (d 1974); *b* 20 Aug 1931; *Educ* Wellington, Trin Cambridge; *m* 1970, Gail Cheng Kwai, da of Chan Lum Choon (Singapore); *Career* Lt Queen's Own Hussars, chartered accountant, management consultant 1967-76, fin & admin controller Crown Agents 1976-; *Recreations* skiing, shooting, restoring antiques; *Style* - Allen Molesworth Esq; c/o Lloyds Bank, 6 Pall Mall, SW1

MOLESWORTH, Hon Robert Bysse Kelham; s and h of 11 Viscount Molesworth; *b* 4 June 1959; *Style* - The Hon Robert Molesworth

MOLESWORTH, Hon William John Charles; s of 11 Viscount Molesworth; *b* 20 Oct 1960; *Style* - The Hon William Molesworth

MOLESWORTH-ST AUBYN, Sir John; 14 Bt (E 1689), CBE (1968), JP (Cornwall 1942, Devon 1941); s of Sir Hugh Molesworth-St Aubyn, 13 Bt, JP (d 1942), and Emma, da of Adm Charles Wake (bro of Sir William Wake, 11 Bt)

by his w Emma (da of Sir Edward St Aubyn, 1 Bt, and sis of 1 Baron St Levan); *b* 12 Jan 1899; *Educ* Eton, Ch Ch Oxford; *m* 1926, Celia Marjorie, JP (d 1965), da of Lt-Col Valentine Vivian, CMG, DSO, MVO (d 1948), by Lady Aline Mary, da of 5 Earl of Portarlington; 1 s, 2 da; *Heir* s, Lt-Col John Arscott Molesworth-St Aubyn, MBE; *Career* pilot offr RAF 1940, flying offr 1940, Flight-Lt 1941; High Sheriff Cornwall 1948; chm Cornwall Ag Ctee; local dir Lloyds Bank Ltd; *Style* - Sir John Molesworth-St Aubyn, Bt CBE JP; Pencarrow, Washaway, Bodmin, Cornwall (☎ St Mabyn 277)

MOLESWORTH-ST AUBYN, Lt-Col John Arscott; MBE (1963), JP (Devon 1971), DL (Cornwall 1971); s and h of Sir John Molesworth-St Aubyn, 14 Bt, CBE; *b* 15 Dec 1926; *Educ* Eton; *m* 1957, Iona, da of Adm Sir Francis Loftus Tottenham, KCB, CBE; 2 s, 1 da; *Career* served KRRC & Roy Green Jackets 1945-67, Lt-Col 1967; High Sheriff Cornwall 1975; chm SW Water Authority 1974-, v-chm S Regn HHA 1979-, memb Nat Cncl CLA 1974- & Exec Cttee CLA 1979-, v-chm SW Regn Timber Growers Assoc 1978-; *Recreations* shooting, ornithology; *Clubs* Army & Navy; *Style* - Lt-Col John Molesworth-St Aubyn MBE JP DL; Pencarrow, Bodmin, Cornwall; Tetcott Manor, Holsworthy, Devon (☎ North Tamerton 220)

MOLLOY, Baron (Life Peer UK 1981); William John; *b* 28 Oct 1918; *Educ* Elementary Sch Swansea, Univ Coll Swansea; *m* Eva Lewis; 1 da; *Career* served 1939-46 with RE; Foreign Office 1946-52; MP (L) Ealing (North) 1964-; memb Estimates Ctee 1965-70; parl advr London Trades Council Transport Ctee 1967-69 and 1970; Govr Holland Pk Co-Ed Comprehensive Sch 1958-64; memb Assemblies Council of Europe and Western European Union 1969-73; memb Ct Reading U; Govr Northolt Grouped Governing Body Secondary Schs; PPS to Min of Posts and Telecommunications 1969-70; memb European Parliament 1976-79; memb Council of Roy Geographical Soc 1976-79; *Style* - The Rt Hon the Lord Molloy; 2a Uneeda dve, Greenford, Middlesex (☎ 01 578 7736)

MOLONY, Alexandra, Lady; Alexandra Campbell; da of late John Alexander Todd, MRCVS, of Glasgow; *m* 1, Myles Cooper (decd), of Argentina; m 2, 1936, Sir Hugh Francis Molony, 2 Bt (d 1976); *Style* - Alexandra Lady Molony; Hobson's Croft, W Chiltingdon, Pulborough, Sussex

MOLONY, Lady; Carmen Mary; da of late Frankland Dent; *m* 1936, Sir Joseph Thomas Molony, KCVO, QC (d 1978); *Style* - Lady Molony; 4 Parkside gdns, Wimbledon Common, SW19

MOLONY, (Sir) (Thomas) Desmond; 3 Bt (UK 1925), of the City of Dublin (but does not use title); s of Sir Hugh Francis Molony, 2 Bt (d 1976); *b* 13 Mar 1937; *Educ* Ampleforth, Trin Coll Dublin; *m* 1962, Doris, da of late E W Foley, of Cork; 4 da; *Heir* unc, Sir Joseph Thomas Molony, KCVO, QC; *Style* - Desmond Molony Esq; 3164-66 Hampton Court rd, Carlton, NSW 2218, Australia

MOLONY, Peter John; s of late Sir Josephy Molony, KCVO, QC and gs of Rt Hon Sir Thomas Molony, 2 s of 1 Bt; h to Btcy of kinsman (Sir) (Thomas) Desmond Molony, 3 Bt (but does not use title); *b* 17 Aug 1937; *Educ* Downside and Trin Cambridge; *m* 1964, Elizabeth Mary, da of Henry Clevaux Chaytor, of Cambridge; 4 s, 1 da; *Style* - Peter Molony Esq; 23 Blacket pla, Edinburgh 9

MOLSON, Baron (Life Peer UK 1961); (Arthur) Hugh Elsdale Molson; PC (1956); s of late Maj John Elsdale Molson, MD, MP, of Goring Hall, Worthing; *b* 29 June 1903; *Educ* R N Colls Osborne and Dartmouth, Lancing and New Coll Oxford; *m* 1949, Nancy, da of late W H Astington; *Career* barr; served 36 Searchlight Regt RA 1939-41, MP (U) W R Yorks (Doncaster Div) 1931-35 and Derbyshire (High Peak Div) 1939-61, parly sec Miny of Works 1951-53, jt parly sec Miny of Transport & Civil Aviation 1953-57, Miny of Works 1957-59; memb Monckton Commission of Privy Counsellors on Buganda-Bunyoro Dispute 1962; chm council for the Protection of

Rural England 1968-71, pres 1971-80; *Style* - The Rt Hon the Lord Molson, PC; Cherrytrees, Kelso, Roxburghshire (☎ Yetholm 204); 14 Wilton cres, SW1 (☎ 01 235 3948)

MONAHAN, Lady; Lillie Elevia; da of Peter Donald Bowman, of Adelaide; *m* 1929, Hon Sir Robert Vincent Monahan (decd); *Style* - Lady Monahan; 99 Spring st, Melbourne, Vic 3000, Australia

MONBIOT, Raymond Geoffrey; MBE (1981); s of Maurice Ferdinand Monbiot (d 1976); *b* 1 Sept 1937; *Educ* Westminster Sch, London Business Sch; *m* 1961, Rosalie Vivien Gresham, da of R G Cooke CBE MP (d 1970); 3 c; *Career* pres S Oxon Conservative Assoc 1980- (chm 1974-78), chm Wessex Industrial Panel 1980-, chm Duke of Edinburgh Award Berks Industrial Scheme 1980, md Assoc Biscuits Ltd 1978-, chm BIM Westminster Branch 1978-, J Lyons & Co Ltd 1956-78; *Recreations* writing, sports admin, charity work, cooking; *Clubs* Institute of Directors, Leander; *Style* - Raymond Monbiot Esq, MBE; Peppard House, Peppard Common, Henley-on-Thames, Oxon (☎ 04917 424)

MONCK, 6 Viscount (I 1801); Henry Wyndham Stanley Monck; OBE (1961), JP (1944 Hampshire), DL (1973); also Baron Monck (I 1797) and Baron Monck (UK 1866); s of Hon Charles H S Monck (d 1914) by Mary, da of Sir William Portal, 2 Bt; suc gf, 5 Viscount (d 1927, himself eleventh in descent from the yr bro of the ancestor of George Monck, who for his services in bringing about the Restoration in 1660 was cr Duke of Albemarle); *b* 11 Dec 1905; *Educ* Eton, Sandhurst; *m* 1, 1937, Eva Baroness Vreto (m dis 1951), da of Prof Zaunmüller-Freudenthaler, of Vienna; m 2, 1951, Brenda Mildred, da of George William Adkins (d 1952); 3 s; *Heir* s, Hon Charles Stanley Monck; *Career* formerly memb S Gas Bd and Lt Coldstream Gds; formerly co dir; v-chm Nat Assoc of Boys' Clubs 1938-78; sits as Baron Monck; *Clubs* MCC; *Style* - The Rt Hon Viscount Monck OBE JP DL; Hurstbourne Priors House, Whitchurch, Hants (☎ 2277)

MONCK, Hon Charles Stanley; s and h of 6 Viscount Monck, OBE; *b* 2 April 1953; *Educ* Eton; *Style* - The Hon Charles Monck

MONCK, Hon George Stanley; s of 6 Viscount Monck, OBE; *b* 12 April 1957; *Educ* Eton; *Style* - The Hon George Monck

MONCK, Hon James Stanley; s of 6 Viscount Monck, OBE; *b* 5 July 1961; *Style* - The Hon James Monck

MONCK, Hon Mrs (Margaret St Clair Sydney); *née* Thesiger; da of 1 Viscount Chelmsford, GCSI, GCMG, GCIE, GBE (d 1933); *b* 1911; *m* 1934, John Monck (who assumed surname of Monck in lieu of Goldman by deed poll), s of Maj Charles Sydney Goldman (d 1958); 1 s; *Style* - The Hon Mrs Monck; Aldern Bridge House, Newbury, Berks

MONCK, Hon Mrs; Hon (Isolde) Sheila Tower; *née* Butler; da of 27 Baron Dunboyne (d 1945); *b* 1925; *m* 1949, Cdr Penryn Victor Monck, RNVR; 1 s, 2 da; *Style* - The Hon Mrs Monck; Yaverland Manor, Sandown, I O W

MONCKTON OF BRENCHLEY, 2 Viscount (UK 1957); Maj-Gen Gilbert Walter Riversdale Monckton; CB (1966), OBE (1956), MC (1940), DL (Kent 1970); s of 1 Viscount, GCVO, KCMG, PC, MC, QC (d 1965); *b* 3 Nov 1915; *Educ* Harrow, Trin Cambridge; *m* 1950, Marianna Laetitia, OStJ, Dame of Honour & Obedience Sov Mil Order Malta and da of Cdr and Hon Mrs Robert Tatton Bower, of Gatto-Murina Palace, Mdina, Malta; 4 s, 1 da; *Heir* s, Hon Christopher Walter Monckton; *Career* landowner and farmer (400 acres); High Sheriff Kent 1981; served 1939-45 War, dep dir Personnel Admin 1962, DPR War Office (Maj-Gen) 1963-65, Ch of Staff HQ, BAOR 1965-67; dir Monckton Equities Ltd, United & General Trust, Ransome Hoffmann Pollard Ltd, Crosswall Reinsurance; liveryman Broderers' Co 1962; pres Kent Assoc of Boys Clubs 1965, Inst of Heraldic and Genealogical Studies 1965, Kent Archaeological Assoc 1968-75, Medway Productivity Assoc 1968-74,

Maidstone and District Football League 1968; v-chm Scout Assoc Kent 1968-74; pres Anglo-Belgian Union 1974; chm Council of the Order of St John for Kent 1969-74; KStJ; Bailiff Grand Cross Obedience (Pres Br Assoc 1974-) Sov Mil Order Malta, Grand Cross Merit 1980; *Clubs* Brooks's, MCC, Cavalry & Guards; *Style* - The Rt Hon the Viscount Monckton of Brenchley, CB, OBE, MC, DL; Runhams Farm, Runham Lane, Harrietsham, Maidstone, Kent (☎ 0627 87 313)

MONCKTON, Hon Anthony Leopold Colyer; s of 2 Viscount Monckton of Brenchley, CB, OBE, MC; *b* 25 Sept 1960; *Educ* Ladycross, Harrow; *Style* - The Hon Anthony Monckton

MONCKTON, Alan Stobart; s of Maj R F P Monkton TD DL (d 1975); *b* 5 Sept 1934; *Educ* Eton; *m* 1961, Joanna Mary, nee Bird; 2 s, 2 da (1 c decd); *Career* chartered surveyor, dir Halifax Bldg Soc and various companies, landowner, farmer, forester; *Recreations* bridge, shooting; *Style* - Alan Monckton Esq; Horsebrook Hall, Brewood, Stafford (☎ Brewood 850239)

MONCKTON, Hon Christopher Walter; s and h of 2 Viscount Monckton of Brenchley, CB, OBE, MC; *b* 14 Feb 1952; *Educ* Harrow, Churchill Cambridge, Univ Coll Cardiff; *Career* leader-writer Yorkshire Post Newspapers Ltd Leeds 1975-77; press offr Conservative Central Office 1977-78; editor The Universe 1979-81; sec Economic Accounting Study Gp, Centre for Policy Studies 1980-; man ed The Sunday Telegraph Magazine 1981-; freeman City of London; liveryman of Broderers' Co; Kt Sov Mil Order of Malta 1973, OStJ 1973; *Clubs* Beefsteak, Brooks's; *Style* - The Hon Christopher Monckton; 71 Albert rd, Richmond, Surrey (☎ 01 940 6528); Runhams Farm, Harrietsham, Maidstone, Kent (☎ Ulcombe 310/313)

MONCKTON, Herbert Anthony; s of Francis Guy Monckton (d 1969); *b* 13 July 1923; *Educ* Malvern; *m* 1948, Peggy, nee Bunting; 2 da; *Career* chm & md Publishing & Literary Serv Ltd Sheffield 1980-, assist md Whitbread East Pennines Ltd Sheffield 1968-80, assist md Flower & Sons Ltd Stratford-upon-Avon 1955-68, memb Institute of Brewing 1949; *Recreations* walking, bird-watching, historical research; *Style* - Herbert Monckton Esq; 6 Whirlow pk rd, Sheffield (☎ 0742 369668)

MONCKTON, Hon Jonathan Riversdale St Quintin; s (twin) of 2 Viscount Monckton of Brenchley, CB, OBE, MC; *b* 15 Aug 1955; *Educ* Ladycross, Worth; *Career* Monk of the Order of St Benedict, Worth Abbey; *Style* - The Hon Jonathan Monckton

MONCKTON, Hon Rosamond Mary; da of 2 Viscount Monckton of Brenchley, CB, OBE, MC; *b* 26 Oct 1953; *Educ* Ursuline Convent Tildonk Belgium; *Style* - The Hon Rosamond Monckton

MONCKTON, Hon Timothy David Robert; s (twin) of 2 Viscount Monckton of Brenchley, CB, OBE, MC; *b* 15 Aug 1955; *Educ* Harrow, Roy Ag Coll Cirencester; *Style* - The Hon Timothy Monckton

MONCKTON-ARUNDELL, Hon Charlotte Anne; da of 9 Viscount Galway; *b* 1955; *Style* - The Hon Charlotte Monckton-Arundell

MONCKTON-ARUNDELL, Hon Rose Wynsome; da of 11 Viscount Galway (d 1980); *b* 1937; *Career* occupational therapist; *Style* - The Hon Rose Monckton-Arundell

MONCREIFF, 5 Baron (UK 1874); Lt-Col Sir Harry Tobert Wellwood Moncreiff; 15 Bt (NS 1626), of Moncreiff, and 5 Bt (UK 1871), of Tulliebole; s of 4 Baron (d 1942); *b* 4 Feb 1915; *Educ* Fettes; *m* 1952, Enid Marion Watson, da of late Maj H W Locke, of Belmont, Dollar, Clackmannan; 1 s; *Heir* s, Hon Rhoderick Harry Wellwood Moncreiff; *Career* 2 Lt RASC 1939, Maj 1943, ret 1958, Hon Lt-Col; *Style* - The Rt Hon the Lord Moncreiff; Tulliebole Castle, Fossoway, Kinross (☎ Fossoway 236)

MONCREIFF, Hon Donald Graham Fitz-Herbert; s of 4 Baron Moncreiff (d 1942); *b* 1919; *Educ* Dollar Academy; *m* 1955, Catriona Sheila, da of James MacDonald, of Devonshaw, Kinross-shire; 1 s, 3 da; *Career* Lt Argyll and Sutherland Highlanders 1940; *Club* New (Edinburgh); *Style* - The Hon Donald Moncreiff; Glenleacnamuidhe, Ballachulish, Argyll (☎ Ballachulish 309)

MONCREIFF, Hon Robert Frederick Arthur; s of 4 Baron Moncreiff (d 1942); *b* 1924; *m* 1951, Aileen Marr, da of Robert Marr Meldrum LLS PhD; 1 s, 1 da; *Style* - The Hon Robert Moncreiff; c/o Royal Hotel, Stow, Midlothian

MONCREIFF, Hon Rhoderick Harry Wellwood; s and h of 5 Baron Moncreiff; *b* 22 March 1954; *Educ* Holt Sch Norfolk; *Style* - The Hon Rhoderick Moncreiff

MONCREIFFE OF MONCREIFFE, Miss (Katharine) Elisabeth; da of Sir Guy Moncreiffe of that Ilk, 9 Bt, and sis of Sir David Moncreiffe of that Ilk, 10 Bt; cous (and h as regards being Chief of the name of Moncreiffe) of Sir Iain Moncreiffe of that Ilk, 11 Bt; *b* 23 May 1920; *Career* served WW II WRNS; *Style* - Miss Elisabeth Moncreiffe of Moncreiffe; Moncreiffe, Perthshire

MONCREIFFE OF THAT ILK, Sir (Rupert) Iain (Kay); 11 Bt (NS 1685), of Moncreiffe, Perthshire, (and 24 Ch 1247), CVO (1980), QC (1980), DL (Perthshire 1961); s of late Lt-Cdr Gerald Moncreiffe, RN (himself gs of Sir Thomas Moncreiffe of that Ilk, 7 Bt, by Sir Thomas's w Lady Louisa Hay, da of 11 Earl of Kinnoull; through this couple's various daughters, Sir Iain is: 1 cous once removed of late 8 & 9 Dukes of Atholl, 2 cous of 6 Marquess of Bath and 1 Viscount Ward of Whitley, and 2 cous once removed of 4 Earl of Dudley and 4 Baron St Oswald); Sir Iain's mother was Hinda (d 1960), da of Frank Meredyth, styled Count de Miremont; Sir Iain suc his 1 cous, the 10 Bt, 1957; *see also* Edward James; *b* 1919; *Educ* Stowe, Heidelberg, Ch Ch Oxford, Edinburgh U; *m* 1, 1946, Diana Denyse Hay, 23 Countess of Erroll (m dis 1964), da of Josslyn, 22 Earl of Erroll (d 1941); 2 s, 1 da; m 2, 1966, Hermione Patricia, da of Lt-Col Walter Douglas Faulkner, MC, Irish Gds (ka 1940) and Patricia (later, as w of 11 Earl, Countess of Dundee), da of Lord Herbert Montagu-Douglas-Scott (d 1944, 5 s of 6 Duke of Buccleuch); *Heir* s, Earl of Erroll; *Career* served 1939-45 War, ADC to Gen Sir Andrew Thorne 1944-45, Mil Liaison Offr to Adm Sir William Whitworth 1945, Attaché and Priv Sec to HBM Ambassador in Moscow 1946; called to Scottish Bar 1950; QC 1980; memb Lloyd's 1952-; Maj Perthshire Home Guard 1953, Memb Roy Co of Archers (Queen's Body Guard for Scotland); Albany Herald 1961; memb Advisory Ctee Scottish Nat Portrait Gallery 1957; Hon Sheriff of Perth and Angus 1958-; author; founder of Puffin's club 1962 ('Puffin' being the nickname of his 1 w); OStJ; chm Debrett's Peerage Ltd 1977-81, Patron 1981-; *Recreations* genealogy; *Clubs* Turf, White's Pratt's, Beefsteak, Puffin's (Edinburgh), New (Edinburgh); *Style* - Sir Iain Moncreiffe of that Ilk, Bt, CVO, QC, DL; Easter Moncreiffe, Perthshire PH2 8QA (☎ Bridge of Earn 2338)

MONCREIFFE, Mary, Lady; Mary; da of late John Balli, of Paris; *m* 1919, Cdr Sir John Robert Guy Moncreiffe, RN, 9 Bt (d 1934); *Career* Offr of Order of Orange Nassau of the Netherlands; *Style* - Mary Lady Moncreiffe; Beau Rivage Palace, Lausanne-Ouchy, Switzerland

MONCREIFFE OF MONCREIFFE, Hon Peregrine David Euan Malcolm; Apparent of that Ilk, Fiar of the Barony of Moncreiffe and Baron (Scottish territorial Barony) of Easter Moncreiffe; 2 s of late Countess of Erroll and Sir Iain Moncreiffe of that Ilk, Bt; hp to Earldom of er bro, 24 Earl of Erroll; *b* 16 Feb 1951; *Educ* Eton (Oppidan Scholar and Capt of the Oppidans), Ch Ch Oxford (rowing blue); *Career* investment banker with Credit Suisse First Boston; *Clubs* White's, Pratt's, Turf, Puffin's (Edinburgh), Roy & Ancient (St Andrews); *Style* - The Hon Peregrine Moncreiffe of Moncreiffe; Easter Moncreiffe, Perth (☎ 073 881 2338)

MONCRIEFF, Lady; Mary Katherine; da of late Ralph Wedmore; *m* 1955, as his 2

w, Prof Sir Alan Aird Moncrieff, CBE, MD (d 1971); *Style* - Lady Moncrieff; Waterford Cottage, Buckland rd, Bampton, Oxon

MOND, Hon Pandora Shelley; da of 3 Baron Melchett (d 1973); *b* 11 Sept 1959; *Style* - The Hon Pandora Mond

MONEY, John Kyrle; s of the late Edward Douglas Money; *b* 21 March 1927; *Educ* Stowe, Trinity Cambridge; *m* 1957, Verena, da of Dr Heinrich Gottfried Mann, of Frankfurt; 2 da; *Career* East India merchant and co dir 1951-79, chm Rubber Growers Assoc 1978; *Clubs* Kandahar, Wentworth; *Style* - John Money Esq; 18 Pembroke Gardens, W8 (☎ 01 602 2211); Log House, West drive, Virginia Water, Surrey. (☎ 09904 3754)

MONEY, Maj-Gen Robert Cotton; CB (1943), MC (1915); s of Col Robert Cotton Money, CMG, CBE (d 1954); *b* 1888; *Educ* Wellington, RMC; *m* 1, 1917, Daphne Dorina (d 1968), da of late Brig-Gen C W Gartside Spaight, of Derry Castle, Killaloe; (1 s ka 1940) 1 da; m 2, 1978, Evelyn, da of late E J Grosstephan; *Career* joined the Cameronians 1909, served in 1914-18 War; Maj-Gen 15 (Scottish) Div 1940, Dist Cdr India 1942, Home Forces 1944, ret 1944; employed Miny Transport, ret 1952; *Clubs* Army & Navy; *Style* - Maj-Gen Robert Money, CB, MC; Moat House, Cholesbury, Tring, Herts (☎ 235)

MONEY, Robert George; s of late Thomas George Money; *b* 18 Feb 1937; *Educ* Polytechnic; *m* 1961, Joan May, 1 c; *Career* dir Freemans Mathews & Milne Ltd; *Recreations* music; *Clubs* Farmers'; *Style* - Robert Money Esq; Conifers, Roselands Avenue, Mayfield, Sussex

MONEY-COUTTS, Lt-Col Hon Alexander Burdett; OBE (1946); s of 6 Baron Latymer (d 1949); *b* 1902; *Educ* Eton, New Coll Oxford; *m* 1930, Mary Elspeth, da of Sir Reginald Arthur Hobhouse, 5 Bt (d 1947); 1 s, 2 da (adopted); *Career* served with Royal Scots Fus; Lt-Col 1944; Master Tobacco Pipe Makers and Tobacco Blenders Co 1964; *Style* - Lt-Col the Hon Alexander Money-Coutts OBE; Askett House, Askett, nr Aylesbury (☎ Princes Risborough 5498)

MONEY-COUTTS, Hon Mrs (Penelope) Ann Clare; da of Thomas Addis Emmet (d 1934) and Baroness Emmet of Amberley (Life Peeress); *b* 1932; *m* 1951, Hon Hugo Nevill Money-Coutts (m dis 1965); 2 s, 1 da *Career* Govr Cobham Hall, Cobham, Kent 1962; *Style* - The Hon Mrs Ann Money Coutts; Flat 9, 34 Sloane Court West, SW1; Naldrett House, Bucks Green, Rudgwick, Sussex

MONEY-COUTTS, David Burdett; s of Hon Alexander B Money-Coutts (2 s of 6 Baron Latymer, great nephew of the Victorian millionairess and philanthropist Baroness Burdett-Coutts and ggs of Sir Francis Burdett, 5 Bt, the *quondam* Radical MP (he leant increasingly towards Conservatism after the Reform Bill), whose heavy expenses in the disputed Middx election of 1802-06 must have been more than recouped by his m to Sophia, da of the banker Thomas Coutts) and Mary, da of Sir Reginald Hobhouse, 5 Bt (d 1947, gn of (Sir) John Cam Hobhouse (2 Bt, cr Baron Broughton), Byron's friend); *b* 19 July 1931; *Educ* Eton, New Coll Oxford; *m* 1958, Penelope Utten Todd; 1 s, 2 da; *Career* Nat service 1 Roy Dragoons 1950-51, Roy Glos Hussars, TA 1951-67; md Coutts & Co 1970-, chm 1976-; dir and dep chm Gerrard & Nat Discount Co 1969-; dir Charities Investment Managers (Charifund) 1964-; regional dir SE Region Nat West Bank 1969-; dir Nat West Bank 1976-, Dun & Bradstreet 1973-, Phoenix Assurance 1978-; chm Middx Hosp Med Sch 1974; v-chm Kensington & Chelsea & Westminster AHA 1978-; *Clubs* Leander; *Style* - David Money-Coutts Esq; Magpie House, Peppard Common, Henley-on-Thames, Oxon

MONEY-COUTTS, Hon Hugo Nevill; s and h of 7 Baron Latymer; *b* 1 March 1926; *Educ* Eton; *m* 1, 1951, Hon (Penelope) Ann Clare (m dis 1965), da of Thomas Addis Emmet (d 1934) and Lady Emmet of Amberley (Life Peeress); 2 s (Crispin b 1955, Giles b 1957), 1 da (Clare b 1952); m 2, 1965, Jinty (b 30 Oct 1940), da of Peter Calvert (d 1970); 1 s (Henry b 1967), 2 da (Vera b 1972, Fanny b 1973);

Career gardener; *Style* - The Hon Hugo Money-Coutts; Vivero Hortus, Santa Maria, Mallorca

MONIBA, His Excellency Dr Harry Fumba; *Career* Liberian Ambass to UK 1981-; *Style* - HE Dr Harry Fumba Moniba; The Liberian Embassy, 21 Princes Gate, SW7 (☎ 01 589 9405)

MONIER-WILLIAMS, His Honour Judge; Evelyn Faithfull; s of Roy Monier-Williams, OBE; *b* 29 April 1920; *Educ* Charterhouse, Univ Oxford; *m* 1948, Maria-Angela, da of Rudolf Oswald, of Oberhausen; 1 s (Christopher), 1 da (Hon Mrs Mark (Vivien Angela) Piercy, sis-in-law of 3 Baron Piercy); *Career* served RA Mediterranean & NW Europe as Capt; barr 1948, Circuit Judge 1972-; *Style* - His Hon Judge Monier-Williams; 1 Temple Gardens, Temple, EC4; 73 Christchurch rd, SW14

MONK BRETTON, 3 Baron (UK 1884); John Charles Dodson; s of 2 Baron, CB, JP, DL (d 1933), by his w Ruth (herself da of Hon Charles Brand and gda of 1 Viscount Hampden & 23 Baron Dacre); *b* 17 July 1924; *Educ* Westminster, New Coll Oxford; *m* 1958, Zoë Diana, da of Ian Douglas Murray Scott (d 1974); 2 s; *Heir* s, Hon Christopher Mark Dodson; *Career* farmer; *Clubs* Brooks's; *Style* - The Rt Hon The Lord Monk Bretton; Shelley's Folly, Cooksbridge, nr Lewes, E Sussex (☎ Barcombe 231)

MONKSWELL, Barony of (UK 1885); *see* Collier, William Adrian Larry

MONKSWELL, Baroness; Katherine Edith; da of William Shaw Harris Gastrell, of Rockbeare Grange, Devon; *m* 1925, as his 2 w, 3 Baron Monkswell (d 1964); 1 s (decd); *Style* - The Rt Hon Lady Monkswell; 49 Novello st, SW6 (☎ 01 736 7326)

MONRO, Hon Mrs; Hon Mary Katharine; *née* Lampson; da of 1 Baron Killearn, GCMG, CB, MVO, PC (d 1964); *b* 1915; *m* 1952, as his 2 w, Lt-Col Alexander George Falkiner, s of Maj G Nowlan Monro, DL (d 1933); 1 s (adopted); *Career* a Lady-in-waiting to HRH the late Princess Royal 1948-51; *Style* - The Hon Mrs Monro; Balnain, Cononbridge, Easter Ross

MONSELL, 2 Viscount (UK 1935); Lt-Col Henry Bolton Graham Eyres Monsell; s of 1 Viscount Monsell, GBE, PC (d 1969); *b* 21 Nov 1905; *Educ* Eton; *Heir* none; *Career* served in N Africa with Intelligence Corps (despatches) 1939-45; Medal of Freedom with Bronze Palm (USA); *Clubs* Travellers'; *Style* - The Rt Hon the Viscount Monsell; The Mill House, Dumbleton, Evesham, Worcs

MONSELL, Viscountess; Essex Leila Hilary; da of Lt-Col Hon Edward Gerald French, DSO; *b* 1907; *m* 1, 1929, Vyvyan Drury (m dis 1935); 1 da; m 2, 1950, as his 2 w, 1 Viscount Monsell, GBE, PC (d 1969); *Style* - The Rt Hon Viscountess Monsell; 78 Whitehall Court, SW1

MONSLOW, Baroness; Jean Baird; da of Rev Angus Macdonald; *m* 1960, as his 2 w, Baron Monslow (Life Peer) (d 1966); *Style* - The Rt Hon the Lady Monslow; 30 Clarence Drive, Glasgow

MONSON, 11 Baron (GB 1728); Sir John Monson; 15 Bt (E 1611); s of 10 Baron (d 1958); *b* 3 May 1932; *Educ* Eton, Trin Cambridge; *m* 1955, Emma, da of Anthony Devas (d 1958) and Mrs Rupert Shephard; 3 s; *Heir* s, Hon Nicholas John Monson; *Style* - The Rt Hon the Lord Monson; The Manor House, South Carlton, nr Lincoln (☎ Scampton 263)

MONSON, Hon Andrew Anthony John; s of 11 Baron Monson; *b* 12 May 1959; *Style* - The Hon Andrew Monson

MONSON, Hon Anthony John; s of 10 Baron Monson (d 1958); *b* 1944; *Educ* Malvern; *Style* - The Hon Anthony Monson; 35 Lynwood Grove, Orpington, Kent

MONSON, Maj Hon Jeremy David Alfonso John; s of 10 Baron Monson (d 1958); *b* 1934; *Educ* Eton, RMA Woolwich; *Career* 2 Lt Grenadier Gds 1954, served in Cyprus Emergency 1956-57, Capt 1959, Maj 1964, military assist to Defence Services Secretary 1964-66; *Style*

- Maj the Hon Jeremy Monson; Southlake House, Shurlock Row, nr Twyford, Berks (☎ Shurlock Row 485)

MONSON, Hon Nicholas John; s and h of 11 Baron Monson; *b* 19 Oct 1955; *Educ* Eton; *Style* - The Hon Nicholas Monson

MONSON, Hon Stephen Alexander John; s of 11 Baron Monson; *b* 5 Jan 1961; *Style* - The Hon Stephen Monson

MONTAGU OF BEAULIEU, 3 Baron (UK 1885); Edward John Barrington Douglas-Scott-Montagu; s of 2 Baron, KCIE, CSI, VD, JP, DL, sometime MP New Forest (d 1929, gs of 5 Duke of Buccleuch and Queensberry, KG, KT), by his 2 w Clara Alice; *b* 20 Oct 1926; *Educ* Eton, New Coll Oxford; *m* 1, 1959, Belinda (m dis 1974), da of Capt Hon John de Bathe Crossley, JP (d 1935, yr bro of 2 Baron Somerleyton); 1 s, 1 da; m 2, 1974, Fiona, da of R L D Herbert; 1 s; *Heir* s, Hon Ralph Douglas-Scott-Montagu; *Career* as proprietor of Beaulieu Abbey (originally a Cistercian foundation of 1204), has been one of the most successful in attracting visitors to a 'stately home'; figures for 1980 (565,000 visitors) show that Lord Montagu of Beaulieu's is still at the top of the 'league table' for privately owned establishments; served with Gren Gds 1945-48; editor and publisher of the Veteran and Vintage Magazine; founded Montagu Motor Museum 1952, which became the Nat Motor Museum at Beaulieu July 1972, as a charitable foundation; author and lecturer on Historic Houses Assoc, pres 1973-78; memb Development Commission 1980-; *Recreations* shooting, water sports; *Style* - The Rt Hon the Lord Montagu of Beaulieu; Palace House, Beaulieu, Brockenhurst, Hants (☎ 0590 612345); Flat 11, Wyndham House, Bryanston sq, W1 (☎ 01 262 2603)

MONTAGU, Lady Anne; *née* Cavendish; MBE (1952), JP; da of late 9 Duke of Devonshire, KG, GCMG, GCVO, TD, PC; *b* 1909; *m* 1, 1929 (m dis 1945), Lt-Col Henry Philip Hunloke (d 1978); 2 s, 1 da; m 2, 1949, Christopher John Holland-Martin, MP (d 1960); m 3, 1962 (m annulled 1965), Alexander Victor Edward Paulet Montagu, 10 Earl of Sandwich until he disclaimed his titles 1964; *Style* - Lady Anne Montagu, MBE, JP; Kilmore House, Bampton, Oxon

MONTAGU, Lord Angus Charles Drogo; s of 10 Duke of Manchester, OBE (d 1977), and hp of bro, 11 Duke; *b* 9 Oct 1938; *Educ* Gordonstoun; *m* 1961 (m dis 1970), Mary Eveleen, da of Walter Gillespie McClure, of Geelong, Victoria, Australia; 2 s, 1 da; *Style* - Lord Angus Montagu

MONTAGU, Hon Anthony Trevor Samuel; s of 3 Baron Swaythling, OBE; *b* 1931; *Educ* Eton; *m* 1962, Deirdre, da of Ronald Henry Senior, DSO, TD; 2 s, 1 da; *Career* chm Abingworth Ltd; *Style* - The Hon Anthony Montagu; 78 Chelsea Park Gdns, SW3 (☎ 01 352 1834)

MONTAGU, Hon David Charles Samuel; s and h of 3 Baron Swaythling, OBE; *b* 6 Aug 1928; *Educ* Eton, Trin Cambridge; *m* 1951, Christiane Françoise (Ninette), da of Edgar Dreyfus (d 1976); 1 s, 2 da; *Career* chm Samuel Montagu & Co Ltd 1970-73; chm and ch exec Orion Bank Ltd 1974-79; dir Trades Union Unit Trust Managers Ltd, Carreras Rothmans Ltd, chm United British Securities Trust Ltd, dir Drayton Commercial Investment Co Ltd, Rothmans Int Ltd, London Weekend Television Ltd, Standard Telephones & Cables, Philip Hill Investment Trust Ltd, ITT (UK) Ltd; chm Derby Trust Ltd, Merrill Lynch Int Bank Ltd 1980-; *Style* - The Hon David Montagu; The Kremlin, The Severals, Newmarket, Suffolk; 25 Kingston House South, Ennismore gdns, SW7 (☎ 01 581 2549)

MONTAGU, Lady Elizabeth; da of 9 Earl of Sandwich (d 1962); *b* 1917; *Style* - Lady Elizabeth Montagu; La Respelido, Mougins, France, AM

MONTAGU, Hon Ewen Edward Samuel; CBE (1950, OBE 1944), QC (1939), DL (Hants 1953); s of 2 Baron Swaythling; *b* 29 March 1901; *Educ* Westminster, Trin Cambridge, Harvard U USA; *m* 1923, Iris Rachel, da of late Solomon J Solomon, RA ; 1 s, 1 da; *Career* barr; Lt-Cdr RNVR 1939-45, Judge

Advocate of the Fleet 1945-73; Hon Capt RNR 1973; dep chm quarter sessions 1948-51, chm 1951-60, dep chm 1969-71; dep chm Middlesex quarter sessions 1954, chm 1956-65, chm Middlesex Area Greater London quarter sessions 1965-69; judge 1969; v-chm Central Council of Magistrates' Courts Ctees 1954-63, chm 1963-70, pres United Synagogue 1954-62; *Clubs* Roy Ocean and Bar Yacht; *Style* - The Hon Ewen Montagu CBE QC DL; Warren Beach, Beaulieu, Hants (☎ Buckler's Hard 239); 24 Montrose Court, Exhibition rd, SW7 (☎ 01 598 9999)

MONTAGU, Hon Ivor Goldsmid Samuel; s of 2 Baron Swaythling (d 1927); *b* 23 April 1904; *Educ* Westminster, Roy Coll of Science London, King's Cambridge; *m* 1927, Eileen, da of late Francis Anton Hellstern; *Career* author; life v-pres English Table Tennis Assoc 1970-, life founder pres Int Table Tennis Assoc 1967, pres Soc for Cultural Relations with USSR 1973-; Lenin Peace Prize 1959; *Style* - The Hon Ivor Montagu; Old Timbers, Verdure Close, Watford

MONTAGU, John Edward Hollister; s and h of Alexander Montagu (10 Earl of Sandwich; Earldom disclaimed for life 1964); *b* 11 April 1943; *Educ* Eton, Trin Cambridge; *m* 1968, Caroline, da of Canon P E C Hayman; 2 s, 1 da; *Career* jounalist; information officer Christian Aid 1974-; does not use courtesy title Viscount Hinchingbrooke; *Style* - John Montagu Esq; 69 Albert Bridge rd, SW11 (☎ 01 223 0997)

MONTAGU, Hon (George Charles) Robert; s of Victor Edward Paulet Montagu (disclaimed Earldom of Sandwich for life 1964); *b* 1949; *Educ* Eton; *m* 1970, Donna Marzia Brigante Colonna, da of Conte Brigante Colonna; 1 s, 2 da; *Style* - The Hon Robert Montagu; 16 Brook Green, W6 7BL (☎ 01 603 0845)

MONTAGU, (Alexander) Victor Edward Paulet; s and h of 9 Earl of Sandwich (d 1962, himself tenth in descent from Sir Sidney Montagu, who purchased from his er bro, 1 Earl of Manchester, Hinchingbrooke (a house that the fastidious Horace Walpole later much approved of and the property, a short while before Sir Sidney bought it, of the unc of Sir Oliver Cromwell); Mr Montagu is sixth in descent from the 4 Earl, whose tenure of the Admiralty as First Lord was considered so discreditable for its corruption, though again Horace Walpole was relatively complimentary about his period in office; the 4 Earl (who in 1762 spent 24 hours gaming without food save 'a little something' between two slices of bread; thus was born the sandwich) sponsored Captain Cook's voyages and gave his name to the Sandwich Islands); Mr Montagu disclaimed his Peerages (besides the Earldom they are the Viscountcy of Hinchingbrooke and the Barony of Mountagu (*sic*) of Saint Neots, both E cr of 1660) for life 1964; *b* 22 May 1906; *Educ* Eton, Trin Cambridge; *m* 1, 1934 (m dis 1958), Rosemary, da of late Maj Ralph Harding Peto (gs of Sir Morton Peto, 1 Bt); 2 s, 4 da; m 2, 1962 (m annulled 1965), Lady Anne, nee Cavendish, MBE (d 1981), da of 9 Duke of Devonshire, KG, PC (d 1938), and widow of Christopher Holland-Martin, MP; *Heir* to disclaimed peerages, s, John Edward Hollister Montagu; *Career* joined Northamptonshire Regt (TA) 1926, served in France 1940 and afterwards Gen Staff Home Forces, priv sec to Rt Hon Stanley Baldwin MP 1932-34; tres Junior Imperial League 1934-35, MP (C) Dorset (Southern Div) 1941-62; chm Tory Reform Ctee 1943-44; v-chm Conservative Parly Foreign Affairs Ctee 1957-58; pres Anti-Common Market League 1962-; chm Conservative Trident Gp 1973-; contested Lancs (Accrington Div) at gen election 1964; *Clubs* Carlton, Brooks's; *Style* - Victor Montagu Esq; Mapperton, Beaminster, Dorset

MONTAGU DOUGLAS SCOTT, Lord Damian Torquil Francis Charles; s of 9 and 11 Duke of Buccleuch and Queensberry, KT, VRD, JP; *b* 1969; *Style* - Lord Damian Montagu Douglas Scott

MONTAGU DOUGLAS SCOTT, Lord George Francis John; s of 7 and 9 Duke of Buccleuch and Queensberry, KT, GCVO (d 1935), and Lady Margaret Bridgeman (da of 4 Earl of Bradford by his w, Lady Ida Lumley, da of 9 Earl of Scarbrough); *b*

8 July 1911; *Educ* Eton, Ch Ch Oxford; *m* 1938, Molly (Mary Wina Mannin), da of Lt-Col Harry Bishop, of Harewood, Andover; 1 s, 2 da; *Career* farmer, co dir; Bt-Col TA Reserve ; memb Roy Co of Archers (Queen's Bodyguard for Scotland); *Recreations* racing, gardening; *Clubs* Cavalry; *Style* - Lord George Montagu Douglas Scott; 60 Glebe Place, SW3; The Old Almshouse, Weekley, Kettering, Northants

MONTAGU DOUGLAS SCOTT, Lord William Henry John; s of 9 and 11 Duke of Buccleuch and Queensberry, KT, VRD, JP; *b* 6 Aug 1957; *Style* - Lord William Montagu Douglas Scott

MONTAGU DOUGLAS SCOTT, Lady Charlotte-Anne; da of 9 and 11 Duke of Buccleuch and Queensberry, KT, VRD, JP; *b* 9 Jan 1966; *Style* - Lady Charlotte-Anne Montagu Douglas Scott

MONTAGU DOUGLAS SCOTT, Lady William; Lady Rachel; *née* Douglas-Home; da of 13 Earl of Home, KT, TD (d 1951), and Lady Lilian Lambton (da of 4 Earl of Durham); is sis of Baron Home of the Hirsel, KT, PC; *b* 10 April 1910; *m* 1937, Lord William Walter Montagu Douglas Scott, MC, MP Roxburgh and Selkirk 1935-50 (d 1958), 2 s of 7 and 9 Duke of Buccleuch and Queensberry, KT, GCVO; 1 s, 4 da; *Style* - Lady William Montagu Douglas Scott; Beechwood, Melrose, Roxburghshire

MONTAGU-POLLOCK, Giles Hampden; s and h of Sir George Seymour Montagu-Pollock, 4 Bt; *b* 19 Oct 1928; *Educ* Eton, de Havilland Technical Sch; *m* 1963, Caroline Veronica, da of Richard F Russell, of London; 1 s, 1 da; *Career* with Airspeed Ltd 1949-51, Lloyd's 1951-52, de Havilland Engine Co Ltd 1952-56, Bristol Aeroplane Co Ltd 1956-59 (advertising man), dir 119 Pall Mall Ltd 1972-78, Acumen Marketing Gp Ltd 1971-75, C Vernon & Sons Ltd 1969-71; assist dir J Walter Thompson Co Ltd 1961-69; *Recreations* water-skiing, skiing, photography; *Style* - Giles Montagu-Pollock Esq; The White House, 7 Washington rd, SW13 (☎ 01 748 8491)

MONTAGU-POLLOCK, Sir George Seymour; 4 Bt (UK 1872), of the Khyber Pass; s of Sir Montagu Frederick Montagu-Pollock, 3 Bt (d 1938); *b* 14 Sept 1900; *Educ* RN Colls Osborne and Dartmouth; *m* 1927, Karen-Sofie, da of Hans Ludwig Dedekam, of Norway; 1 s, 1 da; *Heir* s, Giles Hampden Montagu-Pollock; *Career* joined RN 1913, served in HMS 'Royal Oak' 1916-18, served in RN WW II, Lt Cdr ret; Medal of Freedom with Bronze Palm (USA); Haakon VII Liberty Cross (Norway); *Recreations* shooting, fishing; *Clubs* Army and Navy, Special Forces; *Style* - Sir George Montagu-Pollock, Bt; Brooke House, Swallowcliffe, nr Salisbury, Wilts (☎ Tisbury 220)

MONTAGU-POLLOCK, Sir William Horace; KCMG (1957, CMG 1946); 3 s of Sir Montagu Montagu-Pollock, 3 Bt, by his w Margaret, nee Bell, sis of late Countess of Glasgow (w of 8 Earl); Sir William's 1 cous, William Bell, m Belinda, da of Geoffrey Dawson, former ed The Times; *b* 12 July 1903; *Educ* Marlborough, Trin Cambridge; *m* 1, 1933, Frances (m dis 1945), da of Sir John Fischer Williams, CBE, KC; 1 s, 1 da; m 2, 1948, Barbara, da of late Percy Jowett, CBE, FRCA, RWS, and formerly w of Thomas Gaskell (maternal gs of Lt-Col Josceline Bagot, DL, of Levens Hall in what is now Cumbria), by whom she had a da Josceline, who m David Dimbleby, the TV personality; 1 s, 1 da; *Career* For Serv to 1962, Ambass to Damascus 1952-53, Peru 1953-58, Switzerland 1958-60, Denmark 1960-62; *Style* - Sir William Montagu-Pollock KCMG; Playa Blanca, Yaiza, Lanzarote, Canary Islands; 28 Drayton gdns, SW10 (☎ 01 373 3685)

MONTAGU-SMITH, Arthur; DL (1970); *b* 17 July 1915; *Educ* Whitgift Sch, RAF Staff Coll; *m* 1942, Elizabeth Hood, da of the late T H W Alexander, JP; 1 s, 1 da; *Career* Group Captain Battle of Britain, served 1939-45 War NW Europe, N Africa, Mediterranean, dep dir RAF Training USA 1944, OC 104 Wing (France) 1945, Air Adviser New Delhi 1949-50, RAF Rep COS Ctee United Nations New York 1951-53, HM Air Attaché Budapest 1958-60, retd 1961; memb Elgin District Council 1967-75, regional exec Small Industries Council and Scottish Development Agency 1962-80, former chm Moray Assoc of Youth Clubs, chm SSPCA Elgin & Lossiemouth Branch 1971-, dir Elgin & Lossiemouth Harbour Co 1966-, HM Dep-Lt Morayshire 1970-; *Clubs* RAF; *Style* - Arthur Montagu-Smith Esq, DL; Woodpark, Elgin, Moray (☎ 034 384 2220)

MONTAGU-STUART-WORTLEY, Alan Ralph; s of Ralph Montagu-Stuart-Wortley (s of Hon Ralph M-S-W, yr bro of 2 Earl of Wharncliffe); hp of kinsman, 4 Earl of Wharncliffe; *b* 27 July 1927; *m* 1952, Virginia, da of William Claybaugh; 2 s, 1 da; *Style* - Alan Montagu-Stuart-Wortley Esq; 532 Oakridge drive, Cheshire, Conn, USA

MONTAGU-STUART-WORTLEY-MACKENZIE, Lady Joanna Margaret; da of 4 Earl of Wharncliffe; *b* 15 July 1959; *Style* - Lady Joanna Montagu-Stuart-Wortley-Mackenzie

MONTAGU-STUART-WORTLEY-MACKENZIE, Lady Rowena; da of 4 Earl of Wharncliffe; *b* 14 June 1961; *Style* - Lady Rowena Montagu-Stuart-Wortley-Mackenzie

MONTAGUE, Hon Keith Norman; s and h of 2 Baron Amwell; *b* 1943; *Educ* Ealing Grammar Sch, Nottingham U (BSc), CEng, MICE, MIHE, FGS; *m* 1970, Mary, da of Frank Palfreyman of Potters Bar, Herts; 2 s; *Style* - The Hon Keith Montague

MONTAGUE, Hon Sheila Elizabeth; da of 2 Baron Amwell; *b* 1949; *Style* - The Hon Sheila Montague; 34 Halliford rd, Sunbury-on-Thames, Middlesex

MONTAGUE-BARLOW, Lady; Doris Louise; da of H Edward Reed, of Sandwich Kent; *b* 3 June 1894; *Educ* St Helen's; *m* 1934, Rt Hon Sir (Clement) Anderson Montague-Barlow, 1 Bt, KBE (d 1951); *Style* - Lady Montague-Barlow; 20 Charles st, W1 (☎ 01 499 9600)

MONTEAGLE OF BRANDON, 6 Baron (UK 1839); Gerald Spring Rice; s of 5 Baron (d 1946); *b* 5 July 1926; *Educ* Harrow; *m* 1949, Anne, da of Col Guy James Brownlow, DSO, DL (d 1960); 1 s, 3 da; *Heir* s, Hon Charles James Spring Rice; *Career* Capt Irish Gds, ret 1955; memb of London Stock Exchange 1957-76, Lloyd's 1978-, HM Body Guard of Hon Corps of Gentlemen-at-Arms 1978-; *Clubs* Cavalry & Guards, Pratt's; *Style* - The Rt Hon Lord Monteagle of Brandon; Templenoe House, Fermoy, Co Cork, Ireland; Brandon, 242A Fulham rd, London SW10 (☎ 351 3455)

MONTEATH, Lady; Mary Lindsay; da of late Kenneth Eady, of Market Harborough; *m* 1933, Sir David Taylor Monteath, KCB, KCSI, KCMG, CVO, OBE (d 1961); *Style* - Lady Monteath; The Limes, 76 High st, Sutton Courtenay, Abingdon, Berks

MONTEFIORE VITO, John; s of Victor Montefiore Vito (d 1962); *b* 25 Oct 1918; *Educ* Milan U; *m* 1943, Margaret, nee Simans; *Career* dir H W Chapman Ltd (Wilkinson Sword Gp), dir Constant Printing Co Ltd (Lipton Int); *Clubs* Rutland Polo, Wellingborough Golf; *Style* - John Montefiore Vito Esq; 21 Hatton pk rd, Wellingborough, Northants (☎ 0933 223457)

MONTEITH, Charles Montgomery; s of James Monteith (d 1965); *b* 9 Feb 1921; *Educ* Roy Belfast Academical Institution, Magdalen Oxford (MA, BCL); *Career* served war Roy Inniskilling Fusiliers, India and Burma (Maj) 1940-45; barr Gray's Inn 1949; joined Faber & Faber 1953, dir 1954, v-chm 1974-76, chm 1977-81; sr editorial consultant 1981-; sub-warden All Souls Coll Oxford 1967-69, fell 1948; *Clubs* Beefsteak, Garrick, Travellers'; *Style* - Charles Monteith Esq; c/o Faber & Faber Ltd, 3 Queen sq, WC1 (☎ 01 278 6881)

MONTEITH, Lt-Col Robert Charles Michael; MC (1943), TD (1945), JP (1957), DL (Lanarkshire 1955); s of Maj Joseph Basil Monteith, CBE, JP, DL (d 1960); *b* 1914; *Educ* Ampleforth; *m* 1950, Mira Elizabeth, da of late John Fanshawe; 1 s; *Career* served 1939-45 with Lanarkshire Yeo, Lt-Col 1945; memb

Queen's Bodyguard for Scotland (Roy Co of Archers); CC (1940-64 and 1967) Lanarkshire, Vice-Lt 1964; chm Lanark District Council 1974; part time commissioner Mental Welfare Commission for Scotland 1962; memb East Kilbride Development Corpn 1972-76; memb British Assoc Sovereign Mil Order of Malta 1956; OStJ 1974; *Recreations* field sports; *Clubs* New Club (Edinburgh) and Puffin's (Edinburgh); *Style* - Lt-Col Robert Monteith, MC, TD, JP, DL; Cranley, Cleghorn, Lanarkshire (☎ Carstairs 330)

MONTESQUIEU (ET DE ROQUEFORT), Baron; Henri de Secondat; s of Baron de Montesquieu et de Roquefort (d 1926, fifth in descent from the celebrated 18 century *philosophe* and historian, author of the *Lettres Persanes* and *L'Esprit des Lois*, who himself inherited the title from an uncle (Président à Mortier in the Parlement of Bordeaux); the title of Baron was cr 1606; the family, essentially of the *noblesse de robe*, first gained prominence in the person of a *trésorier* at Bordeaux in 1544); *b* 30 Oct 1925; *Educ* St Joseph de Tivoli Bordeaux, Ecole Speciale Militaire St Cyr Coëtquidan; *m* 1949, Baronne Colette, da of Baron Charles Halna du Fretay (d 1972; the family of Halnat (*sic*) du Fretay has, according to the *Catalogue de la Noblesse Française Contemporaine*, been traced to 1532 and is of Breton extraction); 3 s (Charles-Henri m 1981 Milto Graham-Stuart, Alexandre b 1960, Hubert-Cecil b 1963), 1 da (Corinne m 1975 Patrick Baseden); *Career* late cavalry offr; with Societé Solex as internat co-ordinator to 1975; internat manager Moët-Hennessy 1975-; dir Moët et Chandon (London) Ltd, Ditta Claretta Torino, Rozes Ltda Villa Nova de Faia Portugal; *Recreations* hunting, riding, waterskiing; *Clubs* Jockey (Paris), Travellers', Polo de Bagatelle, Gentlemen Riders, St Moritz Tobogganing; *Style* - Baron de Montesquieu et de Roquefort; Château de Fougères, Labrède, Gironde (☎ 33 (56) 20 20 13); 26 Rue de l'Yvette, 75016 Paris, France (☎ 010 331-527 1815)

MONTGOMERIE, Lord; Hugh Archibald William Montgomerie; s and h of 18 Earl of Eglinton and Winton; *b* 24 July 1966; *Style* - Lord Montgomerie

MONTGOMERIE, Hon James David; s of 18 Earl of Eglinton and Winton; *b* 1972; *Style* - The Hon James Montgomerie

MONTGOMERIE, Hon Roger Hugh; DFC; s of 16 Earl of Eglinton (d 1945); *b* 1923; *Educ* Eton, New Coll Oxford; *Career* served in RAF 1943-46; *Style* - The Hon Roger Montgomerie, DFC; Rudgwick Manor, nr Horsham, Sussex

MONTGOMERIE, Hon Robert Seton; s of 18 Earl of Eglinton and Winton; *b* 1975; *Style* - The Hon Robert Montgomerie

MONTGOMERIE, Hon William John; s of 18 Earl of Eglinton and Winton; *b* 4 Oct 1968; *Style* - The Hon William Montgomerie

MONTGOMERY OF ALAMEIN, 2 Viscount (UK 1946); David Bernard Montgomery; CBE (1975); s of 1 Viscount Montgomery of Alamein, KG, GCB, DSO (d 1976); *b* 1928; *Educ* Winchester, Trin Cambridge; *m* 1, 1953, Mary Raymond (m dis 1967), da of Sir Charles Connel (d 1973); 1 s, 1 da; m 2, 1970, Tessa, da of Lt-Gen Sir Frederick A M Browning, GCVO, KBE, CB, DSO (d 1965) and Lady Browning, DBE (Daphne du Maurier); *Heir* s, Hon Henry David Montgomery; *Career* md Terimar Services Ltd (Overseas Trade Consultancy) 1974; editorial advisory bd *Vision Interamericana* 1974; councillor Roy Borough of Kensington & Chelsea 1974-78, chm Hispanic & Luso Brasilian Council Canning House 1978-1980, chm Antofagasta (Chile) & Bolivia Railway Co and subsids 1980-; non-exec dir KCA Internat 1981-; dir Yardley Internat 1963-74; Pres Anglo-Argentine Soc, chm Brazilian Chamber Commerce GB 1980-; Patron D-Day & Normandy Fellowship 1980-; Pres Redgrave Theatre Farnham; *Recreations* sailing; *Clubs* Roy Fowey Yacht Club; *Style* - The Rt Hon Viscount Montgomery of Alamein, CBE; Isington Mill, Alton, Hampshire (☎ Bentley 23126)

MONTGOMERY, Hon Arabella Clare; da of 2 Viscount Montgomery of Alamein, CBE; *b* 1956; *Style* - The Hon Arabella Montgomery

MONTGOMERY, Sir (Basil Henry) David; 9 Bt (UK 1801), of Stanhope, Peeblesshire, JP (Kinross-shire 1966), DL (Kinross and Perth 1960 and 1975); s of Lt Col Henry Keith Purvis-Russell-Montgomery, OBE (d 1954), and nephew of 8 Bt (d 1964); *b* 20 March 1931; *Educ* Eton; *m* 1956, Delia, da of Adm Sir (John) Peter Lorne Reid, GCB, CVO; 2 s (1 decd), 3 da; *Heir* s, James David Keith Montgomery; *Career* Vice-Lt 1966-74 Kinross-shire; chm Forestry Commission 1979-; *Style* - Sir David Montgomery, Bt, JP, DL; Kinross House, Kinross

MONTGOMERY, Gp Capt George Rodgers; CBE (1946), DL (Norfolk 1979); s of John Montgomery (d 1956); *b* 1910; *Educ* Roy Academy Belfast; *m* 1932, Margaret McHarry, da of late William J Heslip; *Career* served in 1939-45 War; Gp Capt ret RAF; Civil Air Attaché & Air Advr Tokyo 1948-49; Cmdt RAF Sch of Admin 1950-52; Cmdt RAF Hednesford 1953-54; dep dir Organisation (Estab) Air Min and chm RAF W European Establishments Ctee Germany 1955-57; organizing sec Friends of Norwich Cathedral 1959-62; sec Norfolk Naturalists Trust 1963-75 (hon v-pres 1976-); memb Court and Hon Appeal sec U of E Anglia; memb Norfolk Naturalists Trust Council; *Recreations*river cruising, gardening, nature conservation; *Clubs* Roy Air Force; *Style* - Gp Capt George Montgomery, CBE, DL; 24 Cathedral Close, Norwich, Norfolk (☎ Norwich 28024)

MONTGOMERY, Hon Henry David; s of 2 Viscount Montgomery of Alamein, CBE; *b* 2 April 1954; *m* 1980, Caroline J, da of Richard Odey, of Hotham Hall, York; *Style* - The Hon Henry Montgomery

MONTGOMERY, Lady; Joan; da of late W Christopherson, of Ipswich; *m* 1925, Sir Frank Percival Montgomery, MC (d 1972); *Style* - Lady Montgomery; 19 Broomhill Park, Belfast, BT9 5JB

MONTGOMERY, James David Keith; s and h of Sir (Basil Henry) David Montgomery, 9 Bt; *b* 6 June 1957; *Style* - James Montgomery Esq

MONTGOMERY CUNINGHAME, Sir John Christopher Foggo; 12 Bt (NS 1672), of Corsehill, Ayrshire; s of 10 Bt, DSO, JP (d 1945), and bro of 11 Bt (d 1959); *b* 24 July 1935; *Educ* Fettes, Worcester Oxford; *m* 1964, Laura Violet, da of Sir Godfrey Nicholson, 1 Bt; 3 da; *Heir* none; *Career* 2 Lt Rifle Bde (Nat Service); dir Artemis Corpn, Claneil Enterprises Inc, Remington Business Systems and other cos; *Style* - Sir John Montgomery Cuninghame, Bt; 52 Scarsdale Villas, W8 (☎ 01 937 9935)

MONTGOMERY CUNINGHAME, Barbara, Lady; Barbara; MBE; da of late Lt-Col Hugh Annesley Gray-Cheape, DSO, of Forfar, Co Angus; *m* 1934, Lt-Col Alexander William James Henry Montgomery Cuninghame, DSO, Roy Scots Fusiliers (ka Normandy 1944); raised to rank of Baronet's widow 1948; *Style* - Barbara, Lady Montgomery Cuninghame MBE; Yalford Kelly, Lifton, Devon, PL16 0HQ

MONTROSE, 7 Duke of (S 1707); Sir James Angus Graham; 11 Bt (S 1625); also Lord Graham (S 1445), Earl of Montrose (S 1505), Marquess of Montrose (S 1644, new charter granted 1706), Marquess of Graham and Buchanan, Earl of Kincardine, Viscount Dundaff, Lord Aberuthven, Mugdock and Fintrie (all S 1707), Earl Graham and Baron Graham (GB 1722); also Hereditary Sheriff of Dunbartonshire; s of 6 Duke, KT, CB, CVO, VD (d 1954), by his w Lady Mary Douglas-Hamilton (da of 12 Duke of Hamilton); *b* 2 May 1907; *Educ* Eton, Ch Ch Oxford; *m* 1, 1930, Isobel Veronica (m dis 1950), da of Lt-Col T B Sellar, CMG, DSO (d 1924); 1 s, 1 da; m 2, 1952, Susan Mary Jocelyn (who m 1949 Michael Raleigh Gibbs), da of John Mervyn Semple; 2 s, 2 da; *Heir* s, Marquess of Graham; *Career* Lt RNVR 1930, ret, rejoined 1939, Lt-Cdr RNVR; memb Federal Parliament of Rhodesia and Nyasaland 1958; Min of Agriculture Lands and Natural Resources S Rhodesia 1962-64; Rhodesia Min of Defence and External

Affairs 1965-68; *Style* - His Grace the Duke of Montrose; Auchmar, Drymen, Glasgow; PO Box A252, Avondale, Salisbury, Zimbabwe

MONTWILL, Andrew Theodore; s of Theodore Montwill (d 1940); *b* 9 Nov 1921; *Educ* St Andrews U; *m* 1947, Olive Mary Donaldson, nee Buchanan; 1 da; *Career* dir Simons & Co Ltd, dir Harry M Beames & Co Ltd, dir UFS (Western) Ltd, dir United Fruit Shippers Ltd, dir William Hardy Caterers Ltd, dir William Hardy & Co (Newcastle) Ltd, dir William Hardy & Sons (Middlesbrough) Ltd; *Recreations* golf, bridge, dining out; *Clubs* Cranbrook Golf; *Style* - Andrew Montwill Esq; Fair Winds, Tongswood dve, Hawkhurst, Kent (☎ Hawkhurst 2683)

MOODIE, David Garrioch; s of the late Peter Alexander Moodie; *b* 19 May 1926; *m* 1952, Mary Smith Hunter, nee Williamson; 1 s, 1 da; *Career* md Black & Edgington Ltd 1973-; *Recreations* sailing, golf, skiing, (yacht: 'Stringalong'); *Clubs* Caledonian; *Style* - David Moodie Esq; Barnbeth, Bridge of Weir, Renfrewshire (☎ Bridge of Weir 612201)

MOODY, Lady; Rosalind Ley; da of R E Mitcheson; *m* 1924, Adm Sir Clement Moody, KCB (d 1960); *Style* - Lady Moody; Rushgrove, Fleet, Hants

MOODY STUART, Lady; Judith; da of late Leonard Isaac Henzell, OBE; *m* 1925, Sir Alexander Moody Stuart, OBE, MC (d 1971); *Style* - Lady Moody Stuart; Grey House Cottage, High st, Albrighton, Wolverhampton

MOON, Sir Edward; 5 Bt (UK 1887), of Copsewood, Stoke, Co Warwick; s of Jasper Moon (gs of 1 Bt) (d 1975); suc kinsman, Sir John Arthur Moon, 4 Bt, 1979; *b* 23 Feb 1911; *Educ* Sedbergh; *m* 1947, Mary, da of late Capt B Conolly, RAMC; *Heir* bro, Roger Moon; *Career* served 1939-45 King's African Rifles (Maj); farmer; *Style* - Sir Edward Moon, Bt; c/o Midland Bank Ltd, Oswestry, Salop

MOON, Gertrude, Lady; Mary Gertrude; da of late Herbert E Waggoner, of Bowen, Illinois, USA; *m* 1954, as his 2 w, Sir Richard Moon, 3 Bt (d 1961); *Style* - Gertrude, Lady Moon

MOON, Roger; s of Jasper Moon (d 1975, gs of 1 Bt); h to Btcy of bro, Sir Edward Moon, 5 Bt; *b* 17 Nov 1914; *m* 1950, Meg, da of late Col Arthur Mainwaring Maxwell, DSO, MC; 3 da; *Recreations* golf, shooting; *Style* - Roger Moon Esq; Mill House, Ruyton-xi-Towns, Shropshire (☎ Baschurch 260354)

MOORE, Viscount; Henry Dermot Ponsonby Moore; s and h of 11 Earl of Drogheda, KG, KBE; *b* 1937; *Educ* Eton, Trin Cambridge; *m* 1, 1968, Eliza (m dis 1972), da of Stacy Barcroft Lloyd, Jr, of Philadelphia; m 2, 1978, Alexandra, da of Sir Nicholas Henderson; *Career* Lt LG 1957; *Style* - Viscount Moore; 40 Warwick ave, W9

MOORE, Lady; Catherine Harlow; da of late Richard Austin Harlow and widow of V-Adm T S Wilkinson, USN; *m* 1948, as his 2 w, Adm Sir Henry Ruthven Moore, GCB, CVO, DSO, DL (d 1978); *Style* - Lady Moore; The Beck, Wateringbury, Kent

MOORE, Christopher M; s of Sir Harry Moore; *b* 1 Dec 1944; *Educ* Winchester, Cambridge; *m* 1972, Charlotte, nee Glessing; 3 c; *Career* banker, merchant dir Jardine Fleming & Co Ltd 1973-76, dir Robert Fleming & Co Ltd 1977-; *Recreations* hunting, tennis, flying; *Clubs* White's, Pratt's, Leander; *Style* - Christopher Moore Esq; Thornborough Grounds, Bourton, Buckingham (☎ Buckingham 2170)

MOORE, Hon Mrs (Constance Sheila); da of 11 Baron Digby, KG (d 1964); *b* 1921; *m* 1945, Charles Arthur Moore; *Career* in ATS 1939-40, with British Security Co-Ordination 1943-45; *Style* - The Hon Mrs Moore; 135 East 71st st, New York City, USA; Bearforest, Mallow, Co Cork

MOORE, Air Vice-Marshal Charles Stuart; CB (1962), OBE (1945); s of Ernest A Moore (d 1950); *b* 27 Feb 1910; *Educ* Sutton Valence Sch, RAF Coll

Cranwell; *m* 1, 1937, Anne (d 1957), da of late Alfred Rogers; m 2, 1961, Jean Mary, da of late J C Wilson; 1 da; *Career* served 1930-39 in UK and Middle East and 1939-45 in Egypt, Sudan and UK, Gp Capt 1947; dep dir Plans, Air Ministry 1947-49; served Washington DC and Air U Alabama USA 1949-53, AOC No 66 (Scottish) Gp 1953-55, Air Cdre 1954, Dir of Intelligence Air Ministry 1955-58, AOA NEAF 1958-62, Acting Air Vice-Marshal 1960, ret 1962; first sec (temp) Foreign Office 1962-69; *Recreations* travelling, photography, music; *Clubs* Roy Air Force; *Style* - Air Vice-Marshal Charles Moore CB OBE; The Avenue, Crowthorne, Berkshire (☎ Crowthorne 2300)

MOORE, Lady; Daphne; da of late William John Benson, CBE; *m* 1921, Sir Henry Monck-Mason Moore, GCMG (d 1964); *Career* CStJ; *Style* - Lady Moore; 409 Grosvenor sq, Rondebosch, Cape Province, S Africa

MOORE, Bt-Col Dudley Frank; TD, DL (Merseyside 1975); s of John Whitelock Moore, MBE; *b* 20 June 1917; *Educ* Alleyne's Stone; *m* 1940, Barbara, da of George Granville Page (d 1932); *Career* formerly Capt Roy Artillery, Western Desert, Italy, & NW Europe; bank man, formerly with District Bank Ltd, Nat Westminster Bank Ltd Southport 1968-; *Recreations* golf; *Clubs* Formby Golf Club, Union Club; *Style* - Bt-Col Dudley Moore, TD, DL; 18 Dunes dve, Freshfield, Merseyside (☎ Formby 79062)

MOORE, Maj-Gen Denis Grattan; CB (1960), DL (Co Tyrone 1973); s of Col Frederick Moore; *b* 15 March 1909; *Educ* Wellington, RMC Sandhurst; *m* 1, 1932, Alexandra, da of William Harland Wann; 2 da; m 2, 1947, Beatrice, da of William Sproat Williamson; 1 da; *Career* 2 Lt Inniskilling Fus 1929, served 1939-45 War, Lt-Col 1949, Col 1953, Brig 1967, dir Weapons and Development War Office (Maj-Gen) 1968-60, dir Equipment Policy War Office 1960-61, Ch Jt Services Liaison Staff BAOR 1961-63, ret 1963; Col Roy Inniskilling Fus 1960-66; chm Ulster Timber Growers Organisation 1965; High Sheriff Co Tyrone 1969; *Recreations* field sports, forestry; *Clubs* Naval & Military; *Style* - Maj-Gen Denis Moore, CB, DL; Pooks Hill, Alton Lane, Four Marks, Hants (☎ 096277 3331)

MOORE, Lt-Col Darrell John Robert; DL (Cambs 1972); s of William John Moore (d 1939); *b* 19 May 1908; *Educ* Bedford Sch, Sandhurst; *m* 1947, Hilda Irene, da of Edmund Bland Hammond OBE MC (d 1971); 1 s, 2 da; *Career* served 1939-45 war, commanded 1 Bn Gurkhas 1945-47; farmer; chm Anglo-American Civil Liaison Cttee Alconbury 1967-73; High Sheriff Huntingdon and Peterborough 1970-71; *Recreations* golf, gundogs; *Clubs* Army & Navy; *Style* - Lt-Col Darrell Moore DL; 22 De Vere Close, Hemingford Grey, Huntingdon, Cambs (☎ St Ives 65775)

MOORE, Edwin Hardwick; s of Edwin Eastwood Moore (d 1951); *b* 6 Oct 1910; *Educ* Repton, Christ's Coll Cambridge; *m* 1938, Phyllis Mary, nee Underwood; 2 da; *Career* chm and md Alfred Adams & Co West Bromwich 1937-80, High Sheriff West Midlands 1975-76, Warwickshire CC 1959-74 (alderman 1967-74), memb Severn River Authority 1965-74; chm Alfred Adams & Co Ltd 1937-80; *Recreations* farming, shooting, fishing; *Clubs* Birmingham Club; *Style* - Edwin Moore Esq; Ashfurlong Hall, Sutton Coldfield, West Midlands (☎ 021 308 0007)

MOORE, Sir Edward Stanton; 2 Bt (UK 1923), of Colchester, Essex, OBE (1970); s of Maj Edward Cecil Horatio Moore (ka 1917), and gs of 1 Bt (d 1923); *b* 28 Dec 1910; *Educ* Mill Hill; *m* 1946, Margaret, da of late T J Scott-Cotterell; *Career* served in RAF 1940-46, Wing Cdr; dir European British Chambers of Commerce 1970-72, pres British Chamber of Commerce Spain 1969-72; md Spain & Western Mediterranean, BEA 1965-72, and dir Gibraltar Airways, v-pres British Chamber of Commerce Belgium & Luxembourg 1963-64; *Recreations* sea cruising, walking, gardening, ornithology, yacht 'John Gaunt'; *Clubs* Chichester Yacht Club, Roy Yachting Assoc, Cruising Assoc; *Style* - Sir Edward Moore, Bt, OBE; Church House, Sidlesham, W Sussex (☎ Sidlesham 369)

MOORE, Gladstone Eugene; s of Thomas Moore (d 1965); *b* 20 Feb 1905; *Educ* Whitgift Mid Sch; *m* 1934, Edith Muriel, nee Burch; 2 s; *Career* v-chm Gateway Bldg Soc 1978-, consultant A T Underwood & Co Chartered Surveyors (Three Bridges and Crawley, W Sussex; prev sr ptnr) 1976-, pres Incorporated Soc of Auctioneers and Landed Property 1952-53; *Recreations* photography; *Style* - Gladstone Moore Esq; Sunlea, Highcroft rd, Sharpthorne, East Grinstead, W Sussex (☎ 0342 810287)

MOORE, Sir Harry (Henry Roderick); CBE (1971); s of Roderick Edward Moore (d 1946); *b* 19 Aug 1915; *Educ* Malvern Coll, Pembroke Coll Cambridge; *m* 1944, Beatrice Margaret, da of Maj J W Seigne (d 1955); 1 s 1 da; *Career* kt 1978, Lt-Col (N Africa Italy N Europe) 1939-46, chartered accountant 1939, dir Hill Samuel Gp Ltd 1949-79, chm Associated Engrg Ltd 1955-75, chm Staveley Industries Ltd 1970-79, chm Molins Ltd 1978-, chm N E Thames Regional Health Authority 1974-, chm Bd Govrs The London Hosp 1960-74, High Sheriff Bucks 1966; *Recreations* shooting, racing (racehorse owned 'Perlesse'); *Clubs* White's, Pratt's, Leander, Rand Club (Johannesburg); *Style* - Sir Harry Moore CBE; Bourton Grounds, nr Buckingham (☎ Buckingham 2241); 70 Chesterfield House, Chesterfield gdns, W1 (☎ 01 492 0666)

MOORE, Hon Mrs (Janie St George); *née* Caulfield; da of 11 Viscount Charlemont (d 1971); *b* 1921; *m* 1942, David Dominic Moore; 2 da; *Style* - The Hon Mrs Moore; 30 Maxwell st, Turramurra, Sydney, NSW, Australia

MOORE, (Sir) Norman Winfrid; 3 Bt (UK 1919), of Hancox, Whatlington, Sussex (but does not use title); s of Sir Alan Hilary Moore, 2 Bt, MB (d 1959); *b* 1923; *Educ* Eton, Trin Cambridge; *m* 1950, Janet, da of late Mrs Phyllis Singer; 1 s, 2 da; *Heir* s, Peter Alan Cutlack Moore; *Career* Lt RA, served 1942-45; princ scientific offr Nature Conservancy 1958-, sr princ scientific offr 1965-; *Style* - Norman Moore Esq; The Farm House, Swavesey, Cambs

MOORE, Lady; Penelope; da of late Lt-Col Samuel Gurney Sheppard, DSO; *m* 1, Robert Lawrence Angus, DL (decd), of Ladykirk, Monkton, Ayrshire; m 2, as his 2 w, Sir Thomas (Cecil Russell) Moore, 1 and last Bt, CBE (d 1971); *Style* - Lady Moore; Bogside House, Monkton, Ayrshire

MOORE, Peter Alan Cutlack; s and h of (Sir) Norman Winfrid Moore, 3 Bt (does not use title); *b* 21 Sept 1951; *Educ* Eton; *Style* - Peter Moore Esq

MOORE, Lady; Rose Sarah; da of Henry Howlett, of S Australia; widow of Rev H H Fennell; *m* 1952, as his 2 w, Sir Richard Greenslade Moore (d 1967); *Style* - Lady Moore; 169 Egan st, Kalgoorlie, W Australia

MOORE, Richard William; s and h of Sir William Roger Clotworthy Moore, 3 Bt, TD; *b* 8 May 1955; *Educ* Portora Sch; *Career* Lt Royal Scots Gds 1974; *Style* - Richard Moore Esq

MOORE, Sir William Roger Clotworthy; 3 Bt (UK 1932), of Moore Lodge, Co Antrim, TD; s of Sir William Samson Moore, 2 Bt (d 1978); *b* 17 May 1927; *Educ* Marlborough Coll, RMC Sandhurst; *m* 1954, Gillian, da of John Brown; 1 s, 1 da; *Heir* s, Richard William Moore; *Career* served War 1939-45, Lt Roy Inniskilling Fusiliers; Maj North Irish Horse; High Sheriff Co Antrim 1964; *Recreations* shooting, racing, tennis, travel; *Clubs* Naval & Military; *Style* - Sir William Moore, Bt, TD; Moore Lodge, Ballymoney, N Ireland; Ellenbank, Kircudbright, Galloway

MOOREHEAD, Hon Kerena Ann; *née* Mond; da of 3 Baron Melchett (d 1973); *b* 17 May 1951; *Educ* Heathfield Sch Ascot; *m* 1980, Richard Moorehead; *Style* - The Hon Mrs Moorehead

MOORES, Peter; Gold Medal of the Italian Republic (1974); s of Sir John Moores CBE; *b* 9 April 1932; *Educ* Ch Ch Oxford; *m* 1960, Luciana, da of Salvatore Pinto, of Naples; 2 c; *Career* dir the Littlewoods Organisation 1965; dir Singer and Friedlander 1978; Trustee Tate

Gallery 1978; *Recreations* waterskiing, windsurfing, shooting, opera; *Style* - Peter Moores Esq; Parbold Hall, Nr Wigan, Lancaster

MOORFOOT, Frederick James; s of Jesse Moorfoot (d 1957); *b* 10 Sept 1916; *Educ* Scunthorpe G S, Pembroke Coll Cambridge; *m* 1939, Cynthia Patricia, nee Read; 2 s, 1 da; *Career* dir and manufacturing man Kodak Ltd 1968-71, chm and md Kodak Ltd 1971-79, chm Kodak Ltd 1979-; *Recreations* golf, bridge, music, theatre; *Style* - Frederick Moorfoot Esq; 7 Lower Plantation, Sarratt lane, Loudwater, Rickmansworth, Herts (☎ Rickmansworth 71291)

MOORHOUSE, Lady Diana Merial Coke; da of late Hon Arthur George Coke (2 s of 3 Earl of Leicester) and sis of 6 Earl; *b* 1907; *m* 1930 (m dis 1938), Trevor Moorhouse (who d 1975); 1 da (1 s decd); *Career* raised to the rank of an Earl's da 1977; *Style* - Lady Diana Moorhouse; 1 Stoke Green Cottages, Stoke Poges, Slough, Bucks

MORAN, 2 Baron (UK 1943); (Richard) John McMoran Wilson; KCMG (1980, CMG 1970); s of 1 Baron, MC (d 1977, best known as Sir Winston Churchill's doctor during WW II); *b* 22 Sept 1924; *Educ* Eton, King's Cambridge; *m* 1948, Shirley Rowntree, da of George Harris, MC, of Bossall Hall, York; 2 s, 1 da; *Heir* s, Hon James Wilson; *Career* served WW II RNVR; For Serv 1945-, Ambass: Chad 1970-73, Hungary 1973-76, Portugal 1976-81; Br High Commissioner Canada 1981-; Book: *C.B.- A Life of Sir Henry Campbell-Bannerman* (1973); *Style* - The Rt Hon Lord Moran, KCMG; c/o British High Commission, Ottawa, Canada; Llewelyn House, Aberedw, Radnorshire (☎ Erwood 257)

MORAN, Dorothy, Baroness; Dorothy; MBE; da of late Samuel Felix Dufton, DSC; *m* 1919, 1 Baron Moran (d 1977); *Style* - The Rt Hon Dorothy, Lady Moran MBE; The Manor House, Newton Valence, Alton, Hants

MORAN, Peter Myles; s of Myles Moran (d 1957); *b* 3 Aug 1936; *Educ* St Edwards Coll, Liverpool U; *m* 1963, Miriam Rosemary, nee Macey; 2 da; *Career* LLB, solicitor, dir of Beatson Clark & Co Ltd and others; *Recreations* tennis, squash; *Clubs* Carlton; *Style* - Peter Moran Esq; Langton House, Horncastle, Lincs (☎ 2296)

MORAY, 20 Earl of (S 1562); Douglas John Moray Stuart; also Lord Abernethy and Strathearn (S 1562), Lord Doune (S 1581), Lord St Colme (S 1611), and Baron Stuart of Castle Stuart (GB 1796); s of 19 Earl of Moray (d 1974); *b* 13 Feb 1928; *Educ* Trin Cambridge, Hilton Coll Natal; *m* 1964, Lady Malvina Murray, da of 7 Earl of Mansfield (d 1971); 1 s, 1 da; *Heir* s, Lord Doune; *Career* JP (1968) Perthshire; *Clubs* New (Edinburgh); *Style* - The Rt Hon Earl of Moray JP; Darnaway Castle, Forres, Moray (Forres 72101); Doune Park, Doune, Perthshire (☎ Doune 333)

MORAY, Barbara, Countess of; Barbara; da of John Archibald Murray, of New York; *b* 1903; *m* 1924, 18 Earl of Moray (d 1943); 3 da; *Style* - The Rt Hon Barbara, Countess of Moray; 174 Ebury st, SW1

MORAY, Countess of; Lady Malvina Dorothea; *née* Murray; da of 7 Earl of Mansfield and Mansfield (d 1971); *b* 1936 *see* Moray, Earl of

MORDAUNT, Kim John; s and h of Sir Richard Mordaunt, 14 Bt; *b* 1966; *Style* - Kim Mordaunt Esq

MORDAUNT, Sir Richard Nigel Charles; 14 Bt (E 1611), of Massingham Parva, Norfolk; s of Lt-Col Sir Nigel John Mordaunt, 13 Bt, MBE (d 1979); *b* 12 May 1940; *Educ* Wellington; *m* 1964, Myriam Atchia; 1 s, 1 da; *Heir* s, Kim John Mordaunt; *Style* - Sir Richard Mordaunt, Bt; 12 Ebor rd, Palm Beach, New South Wales, Australia

MORDAUNT-SMITH, Hon Mrs (Kathleen Marcia); da of 3 Baron Oranmore and Browne, KP, PC (d 1927); *m* 1926, Maj Cotterell Boughton Mordaunt-Smith (d 1956); 1 s, 1 da; *Style* - The Hon Mrs Mordaunt-Smith; 73

Onslow Square, SW7

MORE, Sir Jasper; KBE (1980), JP, DL (Salop); s of Thomas Jasper Mytton More (d 1947); *b* 31 July 1907; *Educ* Eton, King's Coll Cambridge; *m* 1944, Clare Mary, nee Coldwell; *Career* kt 1979, Lt-Col MEF, barr of Lincoln's Inn 1930 and Middle Temple (1932), Shropshire CC 1958-70 and 1973-, MP (C) Ludlow Division 1960-79, Vice-Chamberlain of HM Household 1970-71; *Recreations* fishing; *Clubs* Travellers', Brooks's; *Style* - Sir Jasper More KBE JP DL; Linley Hall, Bishop's Castle, Shropshire (☎ Linley 228)

MORE-MOLYNEUX, James Robert; s of Brig-Gen Francis More-Molyneux Longbourne, CMG, DSO, and Gwendoline, da of Sir Robert More-Molyneux, GCB; *b* 17 June 1920; *Educ* Eton, Cambridge; *m* 1948, Susan, da of Capt Frederick Bellinger; 1 s; *Career* served Italy as Maj; landowner; chm Guildway Ltd, Loseley Park Farms Ltd; *Clubs* IOD, Farmers; *Style* - James More-Molyneux Esq; Loseley Park, Guildford, Surrey (☎ 66090)

MORETON, Lady Alison Jeannette; da of 6 Earl of Ducie; *b* 1954; *Educ* Westwings Sch, Thornbury, Glos; *Style* - Lady Alison Moreton

MORETON, Hon Douglas Howard; s of 6 Earl of Ducie; *b* 21 Oct 1958; *Educ* Stouts Hill, Uley, Glos; *Style* - The Hon Douglas Moreton

MORETON, Lord; David Leslie Moreton; s and h of 6 Earl of Ducie; *b* 20 Sept 1951; *Educ* Cheltenham Coll; *m* 1975, Helen, da of M L Duchesne, of Brussels; *Style* - Lord Moreton; Talbots End Farm, Cromhall, Glos

MORETON, Sir John Oscar; KCVO (1976), CMG (1966), MC (1944); s of Rev C O Moreton; *b* 28 Dec 1917; *Educ* St Edward's Sch Oxford, Trin Oxford; *m* 1945, Margaret Katherine, da of Sir John Fryer, KBE (d 1948); 3 da; *Career* served in Second World War with RA, Maj 1945; assist master Uppingham Sch 1946-48; entered Colonial Office 1948, Kenya 1953-55, private sec to Sec of State 1955-59, Commonwealth Relations Office 1960, Nigeria 1961-64, IDC 1965, Asst Under-Sec State, Commonwealth Office 1965-69, Ambass to Vietnam 1969-71, High Commissioner in Malta 1972-74; Dep Permanent Rep (Ambass) UK Mission to UN 1974-75; Min British Embassy Washington 1975-77; dir Wates Foundation 1978-; Gentleman Usher of the Blue Rod, Order of St Michael and St George, 1979-; *Clubs* Army and Navy; *Style* - Sir John Moreton, KCVO, CMG, MC; Woodside House, Woodside rd, Cobham, Surrey (☎ Oxshott 2154)

MORETON, Hon Robert Matthew; s of 6 Earl Ducie; *b* 8 March 1964; *Style* - The Hon Robert Moreton

MORGAN, Hon Mrs; Hon Christine Maralyn Woolley; da of Baron Woolley, CBE (Life Peer); *b* 1946; *m* 1970, Dr Barrie Scott Morgan; *Style* - The Hon Mrs Morgan; Felsberg, Gerard rd, West Kirby, Cheshire

MORGAN, (David) Dudley; s of Thomas Dudley Morgan; *b* 23 Oct 1914; *Educ* Swansea G S, Jesus Cambridge; *m* 1948, Margaret Helen, da of late David MacNaughton Duncan; 2 da; *Career* war service RAF Intelligence Branch, UK 1940-42, Legal Branch India 1942-46; Wing Cdr 1945; solicitor 1939; sr ptnr Theodore Goddard & Co Solicitors 1974-80; now consultant; dir Associated Fisheries Ltd, Crown House Ltd, Francis Industries Ltd and other cos; Lloyd's underwriter; *Clubs* Carlton; *Style* - Dudley Morgan Esq; St Leonard's House, St Leonard's rd, Nazeing, Waltham Abbey, Essex (☎ Nazeing 2124)

MORGAN, Lady; Dorothy Millar; da of James Waite, MBE; *m* 1924, Hon Sir Edward James Ranembe Morgan (decd); *Style* - Lady Morgan; 155 Kermode st, N Adelaide, SA 5006, Australia

MORGAN, Lt-Col David Richard; OBE (1971), TD (1963), DL (Merseyside 1976); s of Samuel Morgan (d 1966); *b* 27 August 1921; *Educ* Neath, St Luke's Exeter; *m* 1955, Sarah Gaynor, nee Roberts; 2 s, 1 da; *Career* Hon Col

Merseyside ACF, schoolmaster, chm Army Benevolent Fund Merseyside; *Recreations* tennis, rugby football; *Clubs* Cardiff and County; *Style* - Lt-Col David Morgan OBE TD DL; Pine Lodge, 22 Knowsley rd, Southport, Merseyside (☎ 0704 35208)

MORGAN, David Reginald; s of the late Reginald Morgan; *b* 28 Jan 1945; *Educ* Monkton Combe Sch; *m* 1968, Annabella, da of the late Dr Thomas Owen Mason; 2 c; *Career* dir Avon Tin Printers Ltd 1974-, Avon Aluminium Co Ltd 1973-, council memb Bristol Chamber of Commerce 1979-, dir Avon Tin Inc (USA) 1979-, ATP Management Ltd; *Recreations* shooting, photography, reading; *Style* - David Morgan Esq; Rock Cottage, Quarry rd, Frenchay, Bristol (☎ 566853)

MORGAN, Eric Albert George; s of the late Albert E Morgan; *b* 24 May 1928; *Educ* Ilford County H S, St Catherine's Oxford; *m* 1952, Mary, nee Evans; 2 da; *Career* Hon Citizen Georgia (USA) 1976, md British-American Cosmetics 1970-; chm: Yardley & Co 1970-, Lentheric 1970-, Germaine Monteil Cosmetiques Corpn (USA) 1970-; *Recreations* management education, writing, TV; *Style* - Eric Morgan, Esq; Sas-sa-Quin, 8 Princes Drive, Oxshott, Surrey (☎ Oxshott 2875)

MORGAN, Lady; Eirene Marjorie; da of late Very Rev Canon L M Hay-Dinwoody and widow of late Capt Cecil Allen, RN; *m* 1962, as his 2 w, Adm Sir (Llewellyn) Vaughan Morgan, KBE, CB, MVO, DSC (d 1969); *Style* - Lady Morgan; Webbs Green Cottage, Soberton, Hants

MORGAN, Hon Mrs Fionn Frances Bride; da of 3 Baron O'Neill (d 1944); *b* 1936; *Educ* Heathfield, St Anne's Coll Oxford; *m* 1961 (m dis 1976), John Albert Leigh Morgan; 1 s, 2 da; *Style* - The Hon Mrs Fionn Morgan; 182 Ebury st, SW1W 8VP (☎ 01 730 1140)

MORGAN, Col Frank Stanley; CBE (1940), ERD (1947), JP (1951), DL (Glamorganshire 1946); s of Frank Arthur Morgan; *b* 1893; *Educ* Marlborough, Ch Ch Oxford; *m* 1, 1918, Gladys Joan (d 1953), da of Lt-Col Henry Murray Ashley Warde, CBE, DL; m 2, 1956, Minnie Helen, MBE, TD, da of Maj Charles Pine, OBE (d 1937); *Career* served in 1914-18 War with Pembroke Yeo and Imperial Camel Corps and 1939-45 Roy Corps of Signals, Col 1940, Brig 1943-44, ret (Col) 1945; *Recreations* country pursuits & travel; *Style* - Col Frank Morgan, CBE, ERD, JP, DL; Herbert's Lodge, Bishopston, Swansea (☎ Bishopston 4222)

MORGAN, Col George Frederick Kenneth; OBE, MC, TD, DL (1974) S Glamorgan and (1950) Monmouthshire; s of late George Herbert Morgan; *b* 1912; *Educ* Clifton; *m* 1950, Rosemary Margaret, da of Benjamin Arthur Williams, of Newport, Mon; 1 s, 2 da; *Career* served 1939-45 2 Bn Monmouthshire Regt, Col 1953; chartered accountant 1937; High Sheriff 1974-75; OStJ; company dir; *Recreations* golf, fishing, collecting antiques; *Clubs* Carlton, Army & Navy, Cardiff and County (Cardiff) Club; *Style* - Col George Morgan, OBE, MC, TD, DL; Llantrithyd House, nr Cowbridge, South Glamorgan (☎ Bonvilston 315)

MORGAN, Hugh Travers; CMG (1966); s of Montagu Travers Morgan, CMG, MC (d 1974); *b* 3 Aug 1919; *Educ* Winchester, Magdalene Cambridge; *m* 1959, Alexandra, da of Ilya Belinoff, of Geneva; 2 s, 1 da; *Career* served in WW II with RAF; entered Foreign Service 1945, head of Western Dept Foreign Office 1967-70; Ambass Peru 1970-74; Assist Under-Sec State Foreign and Commonwealth Office 1974-75; Ambass to Austria 1976-79; ret; *Recreations* archaeology, handicrafts; *Style* - Hugh Morgan Esq, CMG; 42 Waldemar ave, London SW6 (☎ 01 731 2720)

MORGAN, Kenneth; OBE (1975); s of Albert Edward Morgan (d 1975); *b* 3 Nov 1928; *Educ* Stockport G S; *m* 1950, Margaret Cynthia, da of Roland Ellis Wilson, of Stockport; 3 da; *Career* served in Army 1946-49; journalist Exchange Telegraph Co 1956-62; Central London sec Nat Union of Journalists 1962-66; nat organiser NUJ 1966-70; gen sec NUJ 1970-77; memb exec ctee Nat Fedn of

Professional Workers 1970-77; consultative memb Press Council 1970-77, jt sec 1977-78, dep dir and conciliator 1978-79, dir 1980; memb Jt Standing Ctee Nat Newspaper Industry 1976-77; Assoc Int Press Inst 1980; *Style* - Kenneth Morgan Esq, OBE; 174 Overhill rd, Dulwich SE22 (☎ 01 693 6585)

MORGAN, Lt-Col Minnie Helen; MBE (1944), TD (1948), DL (W Glamorgan 1974); da of Maj Charles Pine OBE (d 1937); *b* 26 July 1906; *Educ* Braunston House Newport; *m* 1956, Col Frank Stanley Morgan CBE, ERD, DL, JP *qv*; *Career* TA and Reg Army Officer ATS/WRAC 1939-56 (ret), div cmmr W Glamorgan Girl Guides 1956-66; *Recreations* country pursuits, travel; *Style* - Mrs Frank Morgan, MBE, TD, DL; Herbert's Lodge, Bishopston, Swansea (☎ Bishopston 4222)

MORGAN, Lady; Sylvia Axford; *m* 1941, Sir Morien Morgan, CB (d 1978); *Style* - Lady Morgan

MORGAN-EVANS, Hon Mrs Phillida Ann; da of 9 Baron Walpole; *b* 18 Jan 1950; *Educ* Abbots Hill Sch for Girls, Norwich H S for Girls; *m* 1973 (m dis 1981), Clive Grainger Morgan-Evans; 2 s; *Career* schools horses; *Style* - The Hon Mrs Phillida Morgan-Evans; Beck Farm, Calthorpe, Norwich, (☎ Matlaske 309)

MORGAN-GILES, Rear-Adm Morgan Charles; DSO (1944), OBE (1943), GM (1942); s of F C Morgan-Giles, OBE (d 1964); *b* 19 June 1914; *Educ* Clifton Coll; *m* 1, 1946, Pamela (d 1966), da of Philip Bushell; 2 s, 4 da; m 2, 1968, Mrs Marigold Steel, da of late Percy Lowe; *Career* served in 1939-45 War, Capt 1953, pres Roy Naval Coll Greenwich 1962-64, Rear-Adm 1963, ret 1964; MP (C) Hampshire (Winchester Div) 1964-79, chm HMS Belfast Trust 1971-78, management ctee RNLI, Worshipful Co of Shipwrights; *Recreations* sailing and country pursuits, yacht: 'Melita'; *Clubs* Roy Yacht Sqdn, Carlton, Australian (Sydney) *Style* - Rear-Adm Morgan Morgan-Giles DSO OBE GM; Upton Park, Alresford, Hants (☎ 2443)

MORGAN-GRENVILLE, Capt Hon Robert William; JP (Sussex 1963); s of (Mary) Lady Kinloss (d 1944); *b* 1892; *Educ* Cheltenham; *m* 1, 1915, Irene A G (d 1916), da of Sir Robert Grenville Harvey, 2 Bt, of Langley Park, and The Hon Emily (da of 1 Viscount Elibank); 1 s; m 2, 1922, Elizabeth (d 1969), da of Sir Charles Bine Renshaw, 1 Bt (d 1918), & widow of Maj F W Lindley Gull; 2 s; *Career* served in 1914-18 War; *Style* - Capt the Hon Robert Morgan-Grenville, JP; Lower Burgate, Loxhill, Godalming, Surrey (☎ 048 632 375)

MORGAN-WITTS, Maxwell; s of George Frederick Vincent Lionel Morgan-Witts (d 1944); *b* 27 Sept 1931; *Educ* Mount Roy Coll Calgary, Academy of TV and Film Arts Toronto; *m* 1958, Pauline Ann Lynette, da of Alan Lawson, of Humberside; 1 s, 1 da; *Career* BBC TV actor and presenter 1952; radio writer and producer India, Ceylon, Australia and Canada 1953-55; Granada TV exec producer 1956-66; BBC TV documentary services exec-editor 1962-69; exec producer BBC TV 1966-76; author 1970-; *Recreations* sailing, swimming, skiing, theatre, travel; *Clubs* Hurlingham Racquet Club; *Style* - Maxwell Morgan-Witts Esq; 3 Place du Lac, Le Village, Les Hauts de Vaugrenier, 06270 Villeneuve-Loubet, Nice, France (☎ 93 20 18 68)

MORIARTY, Michael John Patrick; s of Alexander Hugo Moriarty; *b* 22 Nov 1942; *Educ* St Stephens, Welling, Kent; *m* 1965, Pearl Joy; 1 s, 2 da; *Career* Memb of the Stock Exchange 1977; dir Shaw & Marvin Ltd 1978-80; *Recreations* gardening; *Style* - Michael Moriarty Esq; Woodside, Foxendown Lane, Meopham, Kent (☎ 0474 812232)

MORLAND, Lady; Alice; da of late Rt Hon Sir F O Lindley GCMG PC; *m* 1932, Sir Oscar Charles Morland, GBE, KCMG (d 1980); *Style* - Lady Morland; The High Hall, Thornton-le-Dale, Pickering, N Yorks (☎ Thornton-le-Dale 371)

MORLEY, 6 Earl of (UK 1815); Lt-Col John St Aubyn Parker; JP (Plymouth 1972); Viscount Boringdon (UK 1815), Baron Boringdon (GB 1784); s of Hon

John Holford Parker (d 1955) and nephew of 5 Earl (d 1962); *b* 29 May 1923; *Educ* Eton; *m* 1955, Johanna Katherine, da of Sir John Molesworth-St Aubyn, 14 Bt, CBE; 1 s, 1 da; *Heir* s, Viscount Boringdon; *Career* 2 Lt KRRC 1942, served in NW Europe 1944-45, served in Korea 1952-53 and Middle East 1953-55 and 1956 commanding 1 Bn Roy Fus 1965-67, ret 1970; pres Plymouth Inc Chamber of Trade and Commerce 1970-; pres W Country Tourist Bd 1971-; chm Farm Industries Ltd Truro 1970; memb Devon and Cornwall Regional Ctee of the Nat Trust 1969-; regional dir Devon and Cornwall Regional Bd of Lloyds Bank 1971, chm and dir Lloyds Bank Ltd 1974-78; govr Seale-Hayne Ag Coll 1973; pres Fedn of Chambers of Commerce & Trader Assoc of the Co of Cornwall 1972-79; chm Plymouth Sound Ltd 1974-; Vice-Ld Lt Devon 1978-, Pres W Country Tourist Bd, Cncl OStJ Devon 1979, Devon County FA; Hon Col Devon ACF; *Style* - The Rt Hon the Earl of Morley JP, HM Vice Lord-Lieut for Devon; Pound House, Yelverton, S Devon (☎ 3162)

MORLEY, Cecil Denis; CBE (1967); s of late Cornelius Cecil Morley; *b* 1911; *Educ* Clifton, Trin Cambridge; *m* 1936, Lily Florence, da of Edward Albert Younge; *Career* served in 1939-45 War as Maj RA (TA); slr 1935; sec to Council of Stock Exchange London 1949-65, Sec-Gen 1965-71; *Recreations* gardening, travel; *Style* - Cecil Morley Esq, CBE; 17A Eldon rd, W8 (☎ 01 937 8383)

MORLEY, Sir Godfrey William Rowland; OBE (1944), TD (1946); s of Sir Arthur Morley OBE KC (d 1946); *b* 15 June 1909; *Educ* Westminster, Ch Ch Oxford; *m* 1, 1934, Phyllis Dyce (d 1963), da of Sir Edward Duckworth, 2 Bt (d 1945); 2 s, 2 da; m 2, 1967, Sonia Gisèle, nee Ritchie; 2 s; *Career* kt 1971, solicitor (ret), sr ptnr Allen & Overy 1960-75, pres The Law Soc 1970-71, hon memb Canadian Bar Assoc; *Clubs* Athenaeum, Boodle's, City of London; *Style* - Sir Godfrey Morley OBE TD; Hunters Lodge, Warren dve, Kingswood, Surrey (☎ 604 2485)

MORLEY, Lady; Hedy Katharina; da of late Prof Julius von Landesberger-Antburg, of Vienna; *m* 1939, Sir Alexander Francis Morley, KCMG, CBE (d 1971); *Style* - Lady Morley; 47 Campden Hill sq, W8

MORNINGTON, Earl of; Arthur Gerald Wellesley; s and h of Marquess of Douro by HRH Princess Antonia von Preussen; gs of 8 Duke of Wellington, 4 cous once removed of HRH The Prince of Wales, and gggs of last German Kaiser Wilhelm II; *b* 31 Jan 1978; *Style* - Earl of Mornington

MORO, Hon Mrs (Anne Margaret Theodosia); da of 5 Baron Huntingfield, KCMG (d 1969); *b* 1918; *m* 1940, Peter Moro, FRIBA; 3 da; *Style* - The Hon Mrs Moro; 20 Blackheath Park, Greenwich, SE3 (☎ 01 852 0250)

MORPETH, Sir Douglas Spottiswoode; TD; s of Robert Spottiswoode Morpeth; *b* 6 June 1924; *Educ* George Watson's Coll Edinburgh, Edinburgh U; *m* 1951, Anne Rutherford, da of Ian C Bell, OBE, MC; 2 s, 2 da; *Career* ptnr Touche Ross & Co; sr ptner Touche Ross; kt 1981; *Style* - Sir Douglas Morpeth, TD; Summerden House, Shamley Green, nr Guildford, Surrey

MORPETH, Viscount; George William Beaumont Howard; s and h of 12 Earl of Carlisle, MC; *b* 15 Feb 1949; *Educ* Eton, Balliol Oxford; *Career* Maj 9/12 Roy Lancers (Prince of Wales) 1967, Lt 1970, Capt 1974; *Clubs* Beefsteak, Brooks's; *Style* - Viscount Morpeth; 34 Epirus rd, London SW6; Gate House, Naworth Castle, Cumbria

MORRELL, Lady; Audrey Louise; da of Louis Alston, of Port of Spain, Trinidad; *m* 1924, Capt Sir Arthur Routley Hutson Morrell, KBE (d 1968); *Style* - Lady Morrell; Saffrons Court, Compton pla, Eastbourne

MORRIS OF GRASMERE, Baron (Life Peer UK 1967); Charles Richard Morris; KCMG (1936); s of M C Morris (d 1954); *b* 25 Jan 1898; *Educ* Tonbridge, Trin Oxford; *m* 1923, Mary, da of Prof de

Selincourt; 1 s, 1 da; *Career* Lt RGA 1916-19, served 1939-45 War; fell and tutor Balliol Coll Oxford 1921-43, v-chancellor U of Leeds 1948-63; chm Council for Training of Health Visitors and Council for Training in Social Work 1963-71; pro-chancellor of Bradford U 1966; chm Local Govt Training Bd 1968-75; kt 1953; *Clubs* Athenaeum; *Style* - Rt Hon Lord Morris of Grasmere KCMG; Ladywood, White Moss, Ambleside, Cumbria (☎ 286)

MORRIS, 3 Baron (UK 1918); Michael David Morris; s of (twin) 2 Baron Morris (d 1975); *b* 9 Dec 1937; *Educ* Downside; *m* 1, 1959, Denise Eleanor (m dis 1962), da of Morley Richards; m 2, 1962, Jennifer (m dis 1969), da of Tristram Gilbert; 2 da; m 3, 1980, Juliet Susan, da of Anthony Buckingham; 1 da; *Heir* bro, Hon Edward Patrick Morris; *Career* fell Inst of Chartered Accountants in England & Wales; *Style* - The Rt Hon Lord Morris; 8 Carlos Place, W1 (☎ 01 499 2807)

MORRIS OF KENWOOD, 2 Baron (UK 1950); Philip Geoffrey Morris; JP (Inner London 1967); s of 1 Baron (d 1954); *b* 18 June 1928; *Educ* Loughborough Coll Sch, Loughborough Coll; *m* 1958, Hon Ruth Joan Gertrude Rahle, da of Baron Janner (Life Peer); 1 s, 3 da; *Heir* s, Hon Jonathan David Morris; *Career* served 1946-49 with RAF, rejoined 1951-55, Flying Offr 1953; *Style* - The Rt Hon Lord Morris of Kenwood, JP; Lawn Cottage, Orchard Rise, Kingston, Surrey (☎ 01 942 6321)

MORRIS, Hon Charles Christopher; s of Baron Morris of Grasmere, KCMG (Life Peer); *b* 24 May 1929; *Educ* Keswick Sch, Balliol Coll Oxford; *m* 1951, Cynthia Prudence, da of Sir Alan Parsons, KCIE (d 1964); 2 s, 2 da; *Career* assist Youth Employment Officer Newcastle upon Tyne 1952-54, teacher at Wilsthorpe County Sec and Melton Mowbray Modern Boys' Schs 1955-63, assist then head of Liberal Studies Mid Herts Coll Further Educn 1963-67, V-Princ Sutton Coldfield Coll 1967-; *Style* - The Hon Charles Morris; 170 Station rd, Wylde Green, Sutton Coldfield, Warwickshire (☎ 021 354 7821)

MORRIS, Hon Caroline Harriet; da of 2 Baron Morris of Kenwood; *b* 23 April 1961; *Style* - The Hon Caroline Morris

MORRIS, Sir Cedric Lockwood; 9 Bt (UK 1806), of Clasemont, Glamorganshire; s of Sir George Lockwood Morris, 8 Bt (d 1947); *b* 11 Dec 1889; *Educ* Charterhouse, Paris, Rome; *Heir* kinsman, Robert Byng Morris; *Career* served 1914-18 War; artist; Int Exhibitor Venice, Brussels, Pittsburg, Chicago, Buenos Aires etc; lecturer on design Roy Coll of Art 1950-53; pres South Wales Art Soc; v-pres Contemporary Art Soc for Wales; *Style* - Sir Cedric Morris, Bt; Benton End, Hadleigh, Ipswich (☎ Hadleigh Suffolk 3222)

MORRIS, Hon Mrs (Caroline Madge Warrand); *née* de Montmorency; da of 7 Viscount Mountmorres (d 1951); *b* 1920; *m* 1947, Douglas Osmond Morris; *Career* 1939-45 war in WAAF, physiotherapist; *Style* - The Hon Mrs Morris; Danebury Hill, Lilliput, Poole, Dorset

MORRIS, Hon Diane Susan; da of 2 Baron Morris of Kenwood; *b* 25 Jan 1960; *Style* - The Hon Diane Morris

MORRIS, Hon Mrs; Hon Elizabeth; *née* Hill; da of Baron Hill of Luton, PC, MD (Life Peer); *b* 1935; *m* 1964, David Maxwell Morris; 2 s, 1 da; *Style* - The Hon Mrs Morris; 9 St Leonards rd, Exeter

MORRIS, Hon Edward Patrick; s of 2 Baron Morris (d 1975), and hp of bro, 3 Baron; *b* 9 Dec 1937; *Educ* Downside; *m* 1963, Mary Beryl, da of Lt-Col D H G Thrush, of Canterbury; 1 s, 1 da; *Career* co dir (export) Barrow Hepburn 1973-75, export man Portex Ltd Hythe Kent 1976; *Style* - The Hon Edward Morris; Hornsdown Cottage, Elham, Canterbury, Kent (☎ 030-384 575)

MORRIS OF KENWOOD, Florence, Baroness; Florence; da of Henry Isaacs, of Leeds; *b* 1896; *m* 1924, 1 Baron Morris of Kenwood (d 1954); 1 s, 1 da; *Style* - The Rt Hon Florence, Lady Morris of Kenwood; 21 Wendover Court, NW2

MORRIS, Hon Jonathan David; s and h

of 2 Baron Morris of Kenwood; *b* 5 Aug 1968; *Style* - The Hon Jonathan Morris

MORRIS, Hon John Martin; s (twin) of 3 Baron Killanin, MBE, TD; *b* 4 April 1951; *Educ* Ampleforth, St Conleth's Coll Dublin; *m* 1972, Thelma, da of Mrs Mansfield, of Monkstown, co Dublin; 2 s; *Career* photographer; *Recreations* falconry, fishing; *Style* - The Hon John Morris; 5 Rus-in-Urbe, Lower Glenageary rd, Dun Laoghaire, co Dublin

MORRIS, James Nathaniel; s of Arthur Russel Morris (d 1977); *b* 6 Nov 1942; *Educ* Wycliffe Coll Glos, Birmingham U; *m* 1965, Barbara, nee Goldstaub; 2 s, 2 da; *Career* md Electrothermal Engrg Ltd (London) 1976; *Recreations* squash, music; *Style* - James Morris Esq; 18 Snakes Lane, Woodford Green, Essex (☎ 504 2365/472 9911)

MORRIS, Hon Lucy; da of 3 Baron Morris by his 3 w Juliet, nee Buckingham; *b* 18 June 1981; *Style* - The Hon Lucy Morris

MORRIS, Hon Linda Jane; da of 2 Baron Morris of Kenwood; *b* 28 April 1965; *Style* - The Hon Linda Morris

MORRIS, Mary, Baroness; Mary; da of late Rev Alexander Reginald Langhorne; *m* 1, Anthony Robert Agate, MRCS, LRCP; m 2, 1960, 2 Baron Morris (d 1975); *Style* - The Rt Hon Mary, Lady Morris; The Old Farmhouse, Lower Denford, Hungerford, Berks

MORRIS, Hon Michael Francis Leo; s (twin) of 3 Baron Killanin, MBE, TD; *b* 1951; *Educ* Ampleforth, St Conleth's Coll Dublin; *m* 19--, Susannah; *Style* - The Hon Michael Morris; Lakefield Gate Lodge, Lisronagh, co Tipperary, Eire (☎ Fethard 162)

MORRIS, Lady; Mary Louisa; da of Peter McDermott; *m* 1930, Hon Sir John Demetrias Morris KCMG (d 1956); *Style* - Lady Morris; Winmarleigh, Brown's River rd, Hobart, Tasmania, Australia

MORRIS, Hon Michaela Mary; da of 3 Baron Morris; *b* 1965; *Style* - The Hon Michaela Morris

MORRIS, Lady Olive Irene; da of William Davies, of Swansea; *m* 1938, Sir Herbert Edward Morris, 7 Bt (d 1947); *Style* - Lady Morris; 29 Belle Vue rd, West Cross, Swansea

MORRIS, Quentin Mathew; s of John Eric Morris (d 1942); *b* 28 March 1930; *Educ* St Clement Dane's Sch; LSE; BSc (Econ); *m* 1950, Eva; 1 s, 1 da; *Career* Inland Revenue 1952-64; The British Petroleum Co Ltd 1964-; dir BP International Ltd 1977-; dir the Granada Group Ltd 1981-; special trustee the Middlesex Hospital 1980-; *Recreations* skiing, shooting, squash, reading; *Clubs* Reform; *Style* - Quentin Morris Esq; Britannic House, Moor Lane, EC2Y 9BU (☎ 920 6879)

MORRIS, Robert Byng; s of late Percy Byng Morris, gs of 2 Bt; hp of kinsman, Sir Cedric Morris, 9 Bt; *b* 25 Feb 1913; *m* 1947, Christine Kathleen, da of Archibald Field, of Toddington, Glos; 1 s, 3 da; *Style* - Robert Morris Esq; RR2 Norton Creek rd, St Chrysostome, Quebec, Canada

MORRIS, Hon (George) Redmond Fitzpatrick; s and h of 3 Baron Killanin, MBE, TD; *b* 26 Jan 1947; *Educ* Gonzaga Coll Dublin, Ampleforth, Trin Coll Dublin; *m* 1972, Pauline, da of Geoffrey Horton, of The Lawns, Cabinteely, co Dublin; 1 s, 1 da; *Style* - The Hon Redmond Morris; 22 West Park rd, Richmond, Surrey

MORRIS OF KENWOOD, Baroness; Hon Ruth Joan Gertrude Rahle; da of Baron Janner (Life Peer); *b* 1932; *m* 1958, 2 Baron Morris of Kenwood; *Career* slr 1956; *Style* - The Rt Hon the Lady Morris of Kenwood; Lawn Cottage, Orchard Rise, Kingston upon Thames, Surrey

MORRIS, Sir Thomas Gwilym; CBE (1974), QPM (1968), DL (1972) Glamorgan; s of William David Morris (d 1957); *b* 1913; *Educ* Swansea G S; *m* 1940, Mair Eluned (CStJ), da of Daniel Williams (d 1938); 1 s, 1 da; *Career* Ch Constable Cardiff 1963, dep Ch Constable S Wales Constabulary 1969, Ch Constable 1971-79;

CStJ 1970, kt 1979; *Recreations* golf, rugby football, motoring; *Clubs* County Club Cardiff; *Style* - Sir Thomas Morris, CBE, DL; Erw Deg, 39 Llantrisant rd, Llandaff, Cardiff (☎ Cardiff 551877)

MORRIS, Lady Victoria Audrey Beatrice; da of late Charles John Alton Chetwynd, Viscount Ingestre, MVO (d 1915) and sis of 21 Earl of Shrewsbury and Waterford (d 1980); *b* 1910; *m* 1, 1932 (m dis 1936), 6 Baron Sheffield (d 1972); m 2, 1945, His Honour Judge Gwyn Morris, QC *qv*; *Career* raised to the rank of an Earl's da 1921; *Style* - Lady Victoria Morris; Carpmael Building, Temple, EC4; Penylan Hall, Llechryd, Cardiganshire

MORRIS, Rev William James; JP (Aberdeenshire 1963 and Glasgow 1971); s of William John Morris; *b* 22 Aug 1925; *Educ* Cardiff H S, U of Wales, Edinburgh U; *m* 1952, Jean Daveena Ogilvy, da of Rev David Porter Howie, of Kilmarnock, Ayrshire; 1 s; *Career* ordained 1951, min St David's Buckhaven 1953-57, Peterhead Old Parish 1957-67; chaplain HM Prison Peterhead 1963-67, memb Convocation of U of Strathclyde, Scottish Ctee Br Sailors' Soc, Bd of Quarriers' Homes, Bridge of Weir; chm Council Soc of Friends of Glasgow Cathedral, min of Glasgow Cathedral 1967-; chaplain to the Lord High Commissioner 1975-; memb IBA Scotland 1979-; chaplain to the Queen in Scotland 1969-; *Recreations* being a paternalistic do-gooder; gardening, sunbathing in SW France; *Clubs* New (Edinburgh); *Style* - Rev William Morris, JP; 94 St Andrews dve, Glasgow (☎ 041 427 2725)

MORRIS-EYTON, Lt-Col Robert Charles Gilfrid; TD, DL (Salop 1973); s of Robert Edward Morris-Eyton (d 1936); *b* 8 May 1921; *Educ* Bilton Grange, Rugby, Shrewsbury Sch, Trin Cambridge; *m* 1956, Jean Jocelyn, da of Maj-Gen E G Miles, CB, DSO, MC; 1 s, 1 da; *Career* 2 Lt to Lt 75 Shropshire Yeo RA (Mid East and Italy) 1942-45; Lt to Lt-Col Shropshire Yeo (TA) 1947-67; Bd memb Telford Development Corpn 1968; chm CC Salop 1974-77; chm W Mercia Police Authority 1978-79; pres Wrekin Div Con Assoc 1978-80; High Sheriff Salop 1980-81; *Recreations* shooting; *Style* - Lt-Col Robert Morris-Eyton, TD, DL; Calvington, Newport, Salop (☎ Sambrook 316)

MORRIS-JONES, Lady; Leila Augusta Paget; da of Samuel Manning Crosby, & widow of J Ilidge Marsland; *m* 1931, Sir (John) Henry Morris-Jones, MC, LRCP, LRCS, DL (d 1972); *Style* - Lady Morris-Jones; c/o Maj F P U Phillips, The Orchard, Linney, Ludlow, Salop

MORRISH, David Bruce; s of the late James Morrish; *b* 17 Dec 1940; *Educ* St Albans' Sch, Oriel Coll Oxford; *m* 1965, Helena Jane, nee Wilsdon; 2 c; *Career* dir James Halstead Ltd; *Recreations* squash; *Style* - David Morrish Esq; North Haven, 3 Blueberry rd, Bowden, Cheshire (☎ 061 941 3293)

MORRISH, John Sutherland Cavers; s of Capt Leo Grafton Morrish; *b* 4 Nov 1946; *Educ* George Watson's Coll, Edinburgh U; *m* 1977, Elspeth Joan, da of Robert Leslie Findlay; 2 c; *Career* fin dir GEC Medical Equipment Ltd 1976-81, fin & invest man Small Business Div Scottish Dvpt Agency 1981-; *Recreations* golf; *Style* - John Morrish Esq; Ardeonaig, 38 Dukes Wood Ave, Gerrards Cross, Bucks (☎ 83076)

MORRISON, 2 Baron (UK 1945); Dennis Glossop Morrison; s of 1 Baron, PC (d 1953); *b* 21 June 1914; *Educ* Tottenham County Sch; *m* 1, 1940 (m dis 1958), Florence, da of Augustus Hennes, of Tottenham; m 2, 1959, Joan, da of William Meech, of Acton; *Heir* none; *Career* formerly with Metal Box Co; Ld-Lt's rep for Tottenham 1955-, V-Pres Acton Chamber Commerce; *Style* - The Rt Hon Lord Morrison; 7 Ullswater Avenue, Felixstowe, Suffolk (☎ 77405)

MORRISON, Hon Alasdair Andrew Orr; s of 1 Viscount Dunrossil GCMG MC PC QC (d 1961); *b* 25 March 1929; *Educ* Fettes, Balliol Oxford, Chicago U; *m* 1958, Frances Mary, da of late Wilfrid Rippon Snow, of Adelaide, S Australia; 1 s, 2 da; *Style* - The Hon Alasdair Morrison; Maisemore Park, nr Gloucester

MORRISON, Hon Alasdair Godfrey; s of 2 Viscount Dunrossil; *b* 4 April 1962; *Style* - The Hon Alasdair Morrison

MORRISON, His Honour Judge; Alexander John Henderson; s of Dr Alexander Morrison, of Derby; *b* 16 Nov 1927; *Educ* Derby Sch, Emmanuel Cambridge; *m* 1978, Hon Philippa Hives, da of 1 Baron Hives; *Career* barr Gray's Inn 1951, dep chm Derbyshire quarter sessions 1964-71; Crown Court Recorder 1972-80; chm Industl Tbnls; Circuit Judge 1980-; *Recreation* golf; *Style* - His Honour Judge Morrison; 17 Eastwood dve, Littleover, Derby (☎ 45376)

MORRISON, Alastair McLeod; MC (1944); s of Brig Hugh McLeod Morrison, MC; *b* 2 March 1924; *Educ* Imperial Service Coll; *m* 1957, Diana Elizabeth, da of late Col Forester Metcalfe Griffin-Griffin, MC; 1 s, 2 da; *Career* Capt 4/7 Roy Dragoon Gds; dir Howard Machinery Ltd (overseas md France 1953-57, USA 1957-60); chm J Mann & Son Ltd 1973 (md 1970-73); dir AO Smith Harvestore Inc USA 1979-; *Recreations* field sports; *Clubs* Cavalry & Guards; *Style* - Alastair Morrison Esq, MC; Field House, Little Saxham, Bury St Edmunds, Suffolk (☎ 810513)

MORRISON, Hon Charles Andrew; MP (C) Wiltshire (Devizes Div) 1964-; s of 1 Baron Margadale, TD, JP; bro of Hon Peter Morrison, MP; gs of 2 Viscount Hambleden; *b* 25 June 1932; *Educ* Eton; *m* 1954, Hon (Antoinette) Sara Frances Sibell (dir Abbey Nat Bldg Soc 1979-, Fourth Channel TV 1980-), da of 2 Viscount Long (ka 1944) and Laura, Duchess of Marlborough; 1 s, 1 da; *Career* chm Br Tst Conservation Volunteers; V-Chm Game Conservancy, 1922 Cttee 1974-; memb Cncl Salmon & Trout Assoc; 2 Lt Life Gds 1951-52, Capt Roy Wilts Yeo 1952-66; *Clubs* White's and Pratt's; *Style* - The Hon Charles Morrison, MP; Upper Farm, Milton Lilbourne, Pewsey, Wilts (☎ 3438); 45 Westminster gdns, Marsham st, SW1 (☎ 01 834 8608)

MORRISON, Hon Catriona Mary; da of 2 Viscount Dunrossil; *b* 10 July 1952; *Educ* Cheltenham Ladies' Coll; *Style* - The Hon Catriona Morrison

MORRISON OF LAMBETH, Baroness; Edith; da of late John Meadowcroft; *m* 1955, as his 2 w, Baron Morrison of Lambeth, PC (Life Peer) (d 1965); *Career* dir FCI Ltd and BNEIS; *Style* - The Rt Hon Lady Morrison of Lambeth; 5 St Albans st, Rochdale, Lancs

MORRISON, Grace, Baroness; Grace; da of late Thomas Glossop; *m* 1910, 1 Baron Morrison PC (d 1953); 2 s (1 decd); *Style* - The Rt Hon Grace, Lady Morrison; Ullswater ave, Felixstowe, Suffolk

MORRISON, Hon Godfrey Donald; s of 1 Viscount Dunrossil, GCMG, MC, PC, QC (d 1961); *b* 11 April 1937; *Educ* Stowe, Balliol Oxford; *Style* - The Hon Godfrey Morrison; 19 Lloyd Baker st, WC1

MORRISON, Hon Joanna Catherine; da of 2 Viscount Dunrossil; *b* 25 April 1971; *Style* - The Hon Joanna Morrison

MORRISON, Maj Hon James Ian; TD (1963), DL (Wilts 1977); s and h of 1 Baron Margadale; *b* 17 July 1930; *Educ* Eton, RAC Cirencester; *m* 1952, Clare, da of Anthony Lister Barclay, of Broad Oak End, Hertford; 2 s, 1 da (Hon Mrs Hugh Trenchard); *Career* memb Roy Co Archers (Queen's Bodyguard for Scotland); 2 Lt Life Gds 1949-50, Maj Roy Wilts Yeo, ret; chm W Wilts (Westbury) Conservative Assoc 1967-71, pres 1972; CCllr 1955 & 1973-77 Wilts, Alderman 1969, High Sheriff 1971, chm Wilts CLA 1978-, Tattersall's Ctee 1969-71; farmer, co dir; *Clubs* White's and Jockey; *Style* - Maj the Hon James Morrison, TD, DL; Hawking Down, Hindon, Salisbury, Wilts; 13 Kingston House South, SW7 (☎ 01 589 3283)

MORRISON, Hon Mary Anne; CVO (1970); da of 1 Baron Margadale; *b* 17 May 1937; *Educ* Heathfield Sch Ascot, abroad; *Career* a woman of the bedchamber to HM the Queen 1960-; *Style* - The Hon Mary Morrison, CVO; Islay House, Bridgend, Islay, Argyll (☎ Bowrore 223); Fonthill House, Tisbury, Wilts (☎ Tisbury 202)

MORRISON, Hon Mary Allison; da of 2 Viscount Dunrossil; *b* 12 Dec 1972; *Style* - The Hon Mary Morrison

MORRISON, Rev Hon Nial Ranald; s of 1 Viscount Dunrossil, GCMG, MC, PC, QC (d 1961); *b* 27 July 1932; *Educ* Fettes and Jesus Oxford; *m* 1959, Sheila Mary, da of Alexander Forbes, of Gloucester; 3 s, 2 da; *Career* ordained 1956, assistant curate St Catharine's Gloucester 1956-58, Stroud Parish Church 1959-62, vicar of Randwick, Stroud 1962-; *Style* - The Rev Hon Nial Morrison; c/o C Hoare and Co, 37 Fleet st, EC4; The Vicarage, Randwick, Stroud, Glos (Stroud 4727)

MORRISON, Hon Mrs (Phillippa Ann); da of 1 Baron Hives, CH, MBE (d 1965); *b* 1928; *m* 1978, Alexander J H Morrison; *Style* - The Hon Mrs Morrison

MORRISON, Hon Peter Hugh; MP (C) Chester 1974-; s of 1 Baron Margadale; *b* 2 June 1944; *Educ* Eton, Keble Oxford; *Career* a Lord Commissioner of HM Treasury and Govt Whip 1979-81; Parly Under-Sec of State for Employment 1981-; formerly PA to Peter Walker, investment man, ind businessman; Oppn Whip 1976-79; *Clubs* White's, Pratt's; *Style* - The Hon Peter Morrison, MP; 81 Cambridge st, SW1 (☎ 01 828 8228); Islay House, Bridgend, Islay, Argyll; Stable House, Puddington, Wirral, Cheshire (☎ 051 336 2330)

MORRISON, Lady; Rosemary; *m* 1, E H U de Groot (decd); 2 da; m 2, 1959, Sir Nicholas Morrison, KCB, sometime PUS Scottish Off and chm Local Govt Boundary Commission for Eng (d 1981); *Style* - Lady Morrison; Gosse Ford, Clare, Suffolk (☎ 200)

MORRISON, Hon Ranald John; s of 2 Viscount Dunrossil; *b* 19 Dec 1956; *m* 1979, Henrietta F, da of late J H Wilson, of Halewell, Withington, Glos; *Style* - The Hon Ranald Morrison

MORRISON, Hon Mrs; Hon (Antoinette) Sara (Frances Sibell) Long; da of 2 Viscount Long (d 1944) and of Laura, Duchess of Marlborough; *b* 9 Aug 1934; *Educ* England, France; *m* 1954, Hon Charles Andrew Morrison, *qv*; 1 s, 1 da; *Career* GEC 1975-; dir Abbey Nat Bldg Soc 1979-; chm Cncl Soc Serv 1977-, v-chm 1970-77; *Style* - The Hon Mrs Morrison; 45 Westminster gdns, SW1; Upper Farm, Milton Lilbourne, Pewsey, Wilts (☎ Pewsey 3438)

MORRISON, William McKenzie Meek; s of William Morrison (d 1968); *b* 6 Sept 1925; *Educ* Charles Adams G S Wem Salop, Birmingham Tech Coll; *m* 1, 1950, Margaret Millicent Hinton (d 1978); 2 s; m 2, 1980, Irmgard Anne, widow of Martin Adelheid and da of William Karl Körner, of W Germany; 1 step s from previous m; *Career* Awarded Crompton-Lanchester Medal Inst of Mechinical Engineers 1974, former chm (Midlands Branch) Inst of Marine Engineers, dir Turner MFG Co Ltd 1955-79, dir Hydraulics & Pneumatics Ltd 1957-72, tech dir Turner-Spicer Drivetrain Products 1980-; *Recreations* oil painting, motoring; *Style* - William Morrison Esq; 57 Seagar st, Sandwell, W Bromwich, W Midlands (☎ 021 525 1142)

MORRISON-BELL, Julian Francis Tarret; s of Capt Sir Charles Morrison-Bell, 3 Bt (d 1967); *b* 14 Feb 1959; *Career* heir presumptive to Btcy of brother, Sir William Hollis Dayrell Morrison-Bell, 4 Bt; *Style* - Julian Morrison-Bell Esq c/o 38 Tournay rd, SW6

MORRISON-BELL, Hon Lady; Hon Lilah Katherine Julia; da of 7 Viscount Powerscourt (d 1904); *b* 1888; *m* 1912, Sir (Arthur) Clive Morrison-Bell, 1 and last Bt (d 1956); 2 da; *Style* - The Hon Lady Morrison-Bell; 11 Cumberland Mansions, W1

MORRISON-BELL, Sir William Hollin Dayrell; 4 Bt (UK 1905); s of Capt Sir Charles Reginald Francis Morrison-Bell, 3 Bt (d 1967); *b* 21 June 1956; *Educ* Eton, St Edmund Hall Oxford; *Heir* bro, Julian Francis Tarret Morrison-Bell; *Style* - Sir William Morrison-Bell, Bt; 38 Tournay rd, SW6; Highgreen, Tarset, Northumberland

MORRISON-LOW, Sir James Richard; 3 Bt (UK 1908), of Kilmaron, Co Fife, DL (Fife 1978); s of Sir Walter John Morrison-Low, 2 Bt (d 1955); *b* 3 Aug 1925; *Educ* Merchiston, Faraday House; *m* 1953, Ann Rawson, da of Air Cdre R Gordon, CB, CMG, DSO (d 1954); 1 s, 3 da; *Heir* s, Richard Walter Morrison-Low; *Career* served 1943-47 with Roy Corps of Signals, Capt; electrical engineer Osborne & Hunter Ltd Glasgow 1952, dir 1956; *Style* - Sir James Morrison-Low, Bt, DL; Kilmaron Castle, nr Cupar, Fife (☎ 2248)

MORRISON-LOW, Richard Walker; s and h of Sir James Richard Morrison-Low, 3 Bt; *b* 4 Aug 1959; *Style* - Richard Walker Morrison-Low Esq

MORRISON-LOW, Dowager Lady; (Henrietta) Wilhelmina Mary; da of late Maj Robert Walter Purvis, of Gilmerton, Fife; *m* 1948, as his 2 w, Sir Walter John Morrison-Low, 2 Bt (d 1955); *Style* - Dowager Lady Morrison-Low; Kingsbarns House, Kingsbarns, Fife

MORRISON-SCOTT, Sir Terence Charles Stuart; DSC (1944); s of R C S Morrison-Scott, DSO (d 1940); *b* 24 Oct 1908; *Educ* Eton, Ch Ch Oxford and Roy Coll of Science; *m* 1935, Rita, da of E J Layton; *Career* served 1939-45 War with RN; on scientific staff British Museum (Nat History) 1966, dir Science Museum 1960-68; memb Properties Ctee Nat Trust 1968-, chm Nature Conservation Panel 1970-, Architectural Panel 1973-; kt 1965; *Clubs* Athenaeum, Brooks's; *Style* - Sir Terence Morrison-Scott, DSC; Upperfold House, Fernhurst, Haslemere, Surrey (☎ Haslemere 53046)

MORRISSEY, Lady Joanna Agnes; *née* Townshend; da of 7 Marquess Townshend; *b* 1943; *m* 1, 1962, Jeremy George Courtenay Bradford (m dis 1968); 1 s; m 2, 1978, James Barry Morrissey; *Style* - Lady Joanna Morrissey

MORRISSEY, Patrick John; s of Martin Morrissey (d 1959); *b* 4 March 1941; *Educ* Salesian Coll London, Nottingham U; *m* 1964, Diane, nee Kennedy; 3 s, 2 da; *Career* md Beecham Products Overseas (Beecham Gp) 1971-, marketing controller Sterling-Winthrop (UK) 1969-71, marketing mgmnt Lyons Bakery 1963-69; *Recreations* football coach and referee, cricket; *Style* - Patrick Morrissey Esq; 45 Woodlands ave, New Malden, Surrey (☎ 942 6179)

MORSE, Hon Mrs; Hon Jennifer; da of Baron Delfont (Life Peer); *b* 1949; *m* 1974, Andrew Morse; *Style* - The Hon Mrs Morse; Cheglinch Farm, Ilfracombe, Devon

MORSHEAD, Lady; Myrtle; da of late William Woodside, of Melbourne, Australia; *m* 1921, Lt-Gen Sir Leslie James Morshead, KCB, KBE, CMG, DSO, ED (d 1959); *Career* formerly v-pres of Ladies Assoc, of Dr Barnardo's Homes in Aust, memb NSW Cncl of Dr Barnardo's Homes, patron Sydney Hosp Graduate Nurses Assoc and Sydney Nurses Memorial Club, memb ctees Day Nursery and Dist Nursing Assocs; *Clubs* Queen's (Sydney); *Style* - Lady Morshead; 69 Wolseley rd, Point Piper, Sydney, NSW, Australia

MORTENSEN, Cdr Axel S; JP (1972), DL (Notts 1974); s of Andreas Mortensen (d 1923); *b* 11 Aug 1919; *m* 1955, Juliet Lilias, da of Rear-Adm R St V Sherbrooke VC DSO (d 1972); 3 da; *Career* served RN 1939-63 (ret), landowner, farmer, Freeman City of London, Liveryman Farmers Co, Cdr St John Ambulance Notts 1973, Cdr Order St John 1979; *Recreations* shooting; *Clubs* Brooks's, Farmers'; *Style* - Cdr Axel Mortensen JP DL RN; Church Farm House, Oxton, Southwell, Notts (☎ Notts 652085); 40 Westminster Gardens, Marsham st SW1

MORTIMER, David John; s of Eric Richardson Mortimer (d 1976); *b* 3 May 1938; *Educ* The King's Sch Canterbury, St John's Coll Oxford; *m* 1965, Sheila Gail, nee Ross; 2 s; *Career* publisher, dir Longman Gp Ltd 1972, dir Wolters Noordhoff-Longman 1969, pres dir gen Armand Colin-Longman 1972-77, jt md Langenscheidt-Longman 1980 (dir 1972-80); *Recreations* music, sport, walking, reading; *Clubs* MCC; *Style* - David Mortimer Esq; 46 Parkgate ave, Hadley Wood, Herts (☎ 449 8000)

MORTON, 21 Earl of (S 1458); John Charles Sholto Douglas; also Lord Aberdour (no actual cr, but designation of the eldest s & h, incorporated with the Earldom in a charter of 1638, where the Earls of Morton are described as *domini Abirdour*); s of Hon Charles William Sholto Douglas (d 1960, 2 s of 19 Earl of Morton); suc cous, 20 Earl 1976; *b* 19 March 1927; *m* 1949, Mary Sheila, da of late Rev Canon John Stanley Gibb, MC, of Didmarton House, Badminton, Glos; 2 s, 1 da; *Heir* s, Lord Aberdour; *Career* md Dalmahoy Country Club, Scottish dir Bristol & W Building Soc, partner Dalmahoy Farms, chm Edinburgh Polo Club; *Clubs* Edinburgh Polo, Dalmahoy Country; *Style* - The Rt Hon the Earl of Morton; Dalmahoy, Kirknewton, Midlothian

MORTON, Rev Arthur; CVO (1979), OBE (1961); s of Arthur Morton; *b* 29 June 1915; *Educ* Imperial Service Coll Windsor, Jesus Cambridge, Wycliffe Oxford; *m* 1940, Medora Gertrude Harrison; 2 da; *Career* Clerk in Holy Orders; dir NSPCC 1954-79; *Recreations* gardening, reading; *Clubs* MCC; *Style* - The Rev Arthur Morton CVO OBE; 25 Cottes Way, Hillhead, Fareham, Hants (☎ Stubbington 3511)

MORTON, Air Cdre Crichton Charles; CBE (1946); s of Charles Crichton Morton (d 1953); *b* 26 July 1912; *Educ* King William's Coll Isle of Man, RAF Coll Cranwell; *m* 1956, Diana Yvonne, da of Maj-Gen R C Priest CB and widow of Gp Capt N D Gilbart-Smith RAF; *Career* joined RAF 1930, served WW II, Air Cdre 1959, Inspector Radio Serv 1955-58, Ch Signals Offr HQ SHAPE, Chm Br Jt Communications Electronics Bd 1960-62, Cmd Electronics Offr HQ Bomber Cmd 1962-66 (ret); *Recreations* voluntary work; *Clubs* RAF; *Style* - Air Cdre Crichton Morton CBE; 102 Torre Tramontana, Apartado De Correos 50, Playa De Aro, Gerona, Spain

MORTON, David; *b* 31 Oct 1929; *Educ* Devonport H S Plymouth, Pembroke Coll Cambridge; *m* 1954, Bess; 2 c; *Career* md and ch exec Alcan Aluminium (UK) Ltd, v-pres Alcan Aluminium (Europe) SA; *Style* - David Morton Esq; 61 Raynham, Norfolk cres, W2 (☎ 723 2115); Brickwheat Bottom, Blandford Forum, Dorset (☎ 0258 52376)

MORTON, Lady; Doreen Elizabeth; da of late Lt-Col Frederick O'Kinealy, CIE, CVO, IMS; *m* 1929, Sir George Bond Morton, OBE, MC (d 1954); *Style* - Lady Morton; Rectory House, Ogbourne St George, Marlborough, Wilts

MORTON, Lady; Hilda Sherwood; JP; da of Robert John Calver, SSC, of Edinburgh; *m* 1927, as his 2 w, Sir George Morton, KBE, QC (d 1953); *Style* - Lady Morton, JP; 37 Moray pla, Edinburgh, EH3 6BT

MORTON, John Percival; CMG (1965), OBE (1946); s of Henry Percy Dee Morton (d 1933); *b* 15 May 1911; *Educ* Bedford Modern Sch; *m* 1939, Leonora Margaret, da of Hon Justice Stephen Leonard Sale (d 1958); 1 s, 1 da; *Career* Indian (Imperial) Police 1930-47, Medal for Gallantry 1935 and Bar 1940; principal Min of Defence 1947, civil assist to AOC, RAF Iraq 1947-49, counsellor Commission-Gen SE Asia 1949-52, dir of Int Fedn of Malaya 1952-54, Assist Sec Miny Defence 1954-59, Imp Defence Coll 1959, Colonial Office 1961-65; dir MOD 1968-71; chm Aviation Industry Security T'ning Steering Gp 1978-80; panel chm CS Commission Selection Bd 1974-80; *Style* - John Morton Esq, CMG, OBE; Temple End House, 27 Temple End, Great Wilbraham, Cambridge (☎ Cambridge 880691)

MORTON, Kenneth John; *Career* FCA; chm Reed Properties Ltd, treasurer Reed Internat, fin dir & memb exec cttee 1981-; *Style* - Kenneth Morton Esq; c/o Reed Properties Ltd, Reed House, 83 Piccadilly, W1 (☎ 01 499 4020)

MORTON OF HENRYTON, Baroness; Margaret Greenless; da of late James Begg; *m* 1914, Baron Morton of Henryton (Life Peer) (d 1973); *Style* - The Rt Hon Lady Morton of Henryton; 78 Melton Court, SW7

MORTON, Lady; Maureen Norman; da of Ralph Francis Ley, RN, & widow of John Garratt, of Plymouth; *m* 1937, as his 2 w, Sir Charles Henry Morton (d 1939); *Style* - Lady Morton

MOSLEY, Hon Clare; da of 3 Baron Ravensdale, MC; *b* 1959; *Educ* Bedales Sch; *Style* - The Hon Clare Mosley

MOSLEY, Hon Lady; Hon Diana; *née* Freeman-Mitford; da of 2 Baron Redesdale, JP (d 1958); sis of late Nancy Mitford (the novelist and biographer), Jessica Mitford (also a writer), (Debo) Duchess of Devonshire, and Unity Mitford, the friend of Adolf Hitler; *b* 17 June 1910; *m* 1, 1929, Hon Bryan Walter Guinness (m dis 1934) (afterwards 2 Baron Moyne); 2 s (Hon Jonathan and Hon Desmond Guinness, *qqv*); m 2, 1936 (at which wedding the late Herr Reichskanzler Adolf Hitler was, though not best man (as some aver), at any rate principal guest), as his 2 w, Sir Oswald Ernald Mosley, 6 Bt (d 1980); 2 s (Alexander, publisher, and Max, qualified as barr and sometime racing driver); *Style* - The Hon Lady Mosley; 1 Rue des Lacs, 91400, Orsay, France (☎ 010 336 010 4211)

MOSLEY, Hon Ivo Adam Rex; s of 3 Baron Ravensdale, MC; *b* 1951; *Educ* Bryanston Sch, New Coll Oxford; *m* 1977, Xanthe Jennifer Greville, da of Sir Michael Bernard Grenville Oppenheimer, 3 Bt; *Style* - The Hon Ivo Mosley

MOSLEY, Hon Marius; s of 3 Baron Ravensdale, MC; *b* 1976; *Style* - The Hon Marius Mosley

MOSLEY, Hon Michael; s of Sir Oswald Ernald Mosley, 6 Bt (d 1980), by his 1 w Lady Cynthia Curzon (da of 1 & last Marquess Curzon of Kedleston); n of Baroness Ravensdale (d 1966); *b* 1932; *Educ* Eton, London Sch of Econ; *Career* granted 1967, title, rank and precedence of the son of a Baroness which would have been his had his mother survived to succeed to Barony of Ravensdale; *Style* - The Hon Michael Mosley; Durham Cottage, Christchurch st, Chelsea, SW3 (☎ 01 352 5409)

MOSLEY, Nicholas; *Style* - *see* 3 Baron Ravensdale

MOSLEY, Hon Robert; s of 3 Baron Ravensdale, MC; *b* 1955; *Educ* Bedales; *m* 1980, Victoria McBain; *Style* - The Hon Robert Mosley

MOSLEY, Simon James; s of John Arthur Noel Mosley (3 s of Sir Oswald Mosley, 5 Bt, by his w Katharine, da of Capt Justinian Edwards-Heathcote, whose maternal grandmother (Richard Heathcote's 2 w) was Lady Elizabeth Lindsey, da of 23 Earl of Crawford & 6 Balcarres); *b* 8 April 1927; *Educ* Eton, Ch Ch Oxford; *m* 1957, Maria, da of Iraklis Zeris (d 1980); 1 s, 1 da; *Career* slr 1956-, Pres Holborn Law Soc 1967-68, memb Cncl Law Soc 1969; *Clubs* Cavalry and Guards; *Style* - Simon Mosley Esq; 23 The Little Boltons, SW10 (☎ 01 373 1701)

MOSLEY, Hon Shaun Nicholas; s and h of 3 Baron Ravensdale, MC; *b* 5 Aug 1949; *Educ* Bryanston Sch and Hertford Coll Oxford; *m* 1978, Theresa Clifford; *Style* - The Hon Shaun Mosley; c/o 9 Church Row, Hampstead, NW3 (☎ 01 435 8222)

MOSS, Lady; Monica; *née* Meriton-Reed; *m* 1919, Sir Eric de Vere Moss, CIE, formerly ICS (d 1981); 1 s, 3 da; *Style* - Lady Moss; Bracken Lodge, Brookside Close, Runcton, Chichester, W Sussex (☎ 784521)

MOSS, Montague George; s of Harry Neville Moss; *b* 21 April 1924; *Educ* Harrow, New Coll Oxford; *m* 1955, Jane, nee Levi; 2 s, 1 da; *Career* chm Moss Bros 1981-, pres Federation of Merchant Tailors of Gt Br 1965-66, pres Tailors' Benevolent Institute 1980-; *Recreations* public speaking, music, golf, lawn tennis; *Clubs* Jesters, Old Harrovian Eton Fives; *Style* - Montague Moss Esq; 25 Edmunds Walk, N2 (☎ 883 1668)

MOSSE, Richard Hugh; s of The Rev Charles Herbert Mosse (d 1970); *b* 30 May 1924; *Educ* Radley; *m* 1954, Barbara Mary; 3 da; *Career* Captain Welsh Guards, France and Germany 1944-45, Palestine 1946-48; Solicitor 1957; President Chichester & District Law Society 1978-79;

Sec to Board of Chichester Festival Theatre 1966; *Recreations* golf, sailing; *Clubs* RAC; *Style* - Richard Mosse Esq; Cedar Cottage, Creek End, Fishbourne, Chichester, West Sussex (☎ 0243 785996)

MOSSELMANS, Carel Maurits; TD; s of Adriaan Willem Mosselmans; *b* 9 March 1929; *Educ* Stowe, Trin Cambridge; *m* 1962, Hon Prudence, da of 1 and last Baron McCorquodale of Newton (d 1971) and 2 cous of Ian McCorquodale, chm Debrett's Peerage Ltd, *qv*; 2 s; *Career* Lt-Col Inns of Court & City Yeo (TA); Lloyd's Insur Broker; dir: Coutts & Co 1981-, Sedgwick Gp; chm Sedgwick Ltd, Sedgwick Forbes (Lloyd's Underwriters Agents); dep chm Sedgwick Forbes Bland Payne 1979; *Recreations* shooting, fishing, golf; *Clubs* White's, Cavalry & Guards; *Style* - Carel Mosselmans Esq, TD; Seameads, Sandwich Bay, Kent (☎ 030461 3558); 15 Chelsea sq, SW3 (☎ 01 352 0621)

MOSSELMANS, Hon Mrs (Prudence Fiona); da of 1 and last Baron McCorquodale of Newton (d 1971); *b* 1936; *m* 1962, Carel Maurits Mosselmans, TD; 2 s; *Style* - The Hon Mrs Mosselmans; 15 Chelsea Square, SW3

MOSSOP, Lady; Jean Maud Bennett; MBE (1945); da of A B Paton & widow of Lt-Cdr William Alexander Elliot, RN; *m* 1950, as his 2 w, Sir Allan George Mossop (d 1965); *Career* served WW II as 1 Offr WRNS; *Style* - Lady Mossop MBE; Henli, Hont Bay, Cape Province, S Africa

MOSTYN, 5 Baron (UK 1831); Capt Sir Roger Edward Lloyd Lloyd-Mostyn; 6 Bt (GB 1778), MC (1942); s of 4 Baron (d 1965); *b* 17 April 1920; *Educ* Eton, RMC Sandhurst; *m* 1, 1943, Yvonne Margaret, da of A Stuart Johnson, of Henshall Hall, Congleton, Cheshire; 1 s, 1 da; m 2, Mrs Sheila Edmondson Shaw, da of Maj Reginald Fairweather; *Heir* s, Hon Llewellyn Roger Lloyd Lloyd-Mostyn; *Career* 2 Lt 9 Lancers 1939 (despatches 1940), temp Maj 1945; *Style* - The Rt Hon the Lord Mostyn, MC; Mostyn Hall, Mostyn, Clwyd, N Wales (☎ Mostyn 222)

MOSTYN, Hon Dorothy Alice; da of 7 Baron Vaux of Harrowden (d 1935); *b* 1893; *Educ* Farnborough Convent, Bedford Coll London; *Career* a Religious of Inst of Christian Ed; *Style* - The Hon Dorothy Mostyn; Lafosse, Ship Lane, Farnborough, Hants

MOSTYN, Sir Jeremy John Anthony; 14 Bt (E 1670), of Talacre, Flintshire; s of Sir Basil Antony Trevor Mostyn, 13 Bt (d 1956); *b* 24 Nov 1933; *Educ* Downside, S Rhodesia; *m* 1963, Signorina Christina Orengo, da of Marchese Pier Paolo Vladimiro Orengo, of Turin, Italy; 1 s, 2 da; *Heir* s, William Basil John Mostyn; *Career* formerly in RN; contested Ealing South in Liberal interest Gen Election 1959; contested Cities of London and Westminster in LCC elections 1961; a Green Staff Offr at Investiture of HRH Prince of Wales 1969; fell of Roy Soc of Arts 1974; assoc memb of Roy Soc of Health 1980; Kt of Hon & Devotion SMO Malta; ptnr Mostyn & Co Estate Agents, Woodstock, Oxford; *Recreations* study of history, sailing, shooting, squash; *Style* - Sir Jeremy Mostyn, Bt; 29 Aynhoe rd, W14; The Manor House, Lower Heyford, Oxon

MOSTYN, Margery, Lady; Margery; da of late Alfred Stanley Marks, of Sydney, NSW; *m* 1927, Capt Sir Pyers George Joseph Mostyn, 11 Bt, MC (d 1937); *Style* - Margery, Lady Mostyn; c/o Midland Bank, 69 Pall Mall, SW1

MOSTYN, William Basil John; s and h of Sir Jeremy John Anthony Mostyn, 14 Bt; *b* 15 Oct 1975; *Style* - William Mostyn Esq

MOTION, Hon Mrs (Penelope Mary); da of 2 Viscount Harcourt, KCMG, OBE (d 1979); *b* 1933; *m* 1954, Capt Anthony David Motion; 1 s; *Style* - The Hon Mrs Motion; 7 Jaraba ave, Kalamunda, W Australia

MOTT, David Hugh; s and h of Sir John Harmar Mott, 3 Bt; *b* 1 May 1952; *Educ* Shrewsbury, Sussex U (BSc), Birbeck Coll London U (MSc); *m* 1980, Amanda Jane, da of Lt-Cdr D W D Fryer, RN (ret), of Fleet, Hants; *Career* res asst, Queen Mary

Coll, London University; *Style* - David Mott Esq

MOTT, Sir John Harmar; 3 Bt (UK 1930), of Ditchling, Co Sussex; s of Sir Adrian Spear Mott, 2 Bt (d 1964); *b* 21 July 1922; *Educ* Radley, New Coll Oxford; *m* 1950, Elizabeth, da of Hugh Carson; 1 s, 2 da; *Heir* s, David Hugh Mott; *Career* served 1939-45 with RAF, flying offr 1943-46; regional medical offr Dept of Health and Social Security; *Style* - Sir John Mott, Bt; 64 Hodge Lane, nr Northwich, Cheshire (☎ Northwich 77021)

MOTT-RADCLYFFE, Sir Charles Edward; DL (Norfolk 1977); s of Lt-Col Charles Edward Radclyffe, DSO; *b* 1911; *Educ* Eton, Balliol Oxford; *m* 1, 1940, Diana (d 1955), da of Lt-Col William Gibbs, CVO, JP (d 1963); 3 da; m 2, 1956, Stella Constance, da of Lionel G S Harrisson (d 1953); *Career* Capt Rifle Bde (RARO); Hon Attaché HM Diplomatic Corps Athens 1936, Rome 1936-38; MP (C) Berks 1942-70; chm Conservative Party Foreign Affairs Ctee 1951-59; memb Historic Buildings Council for England 1962-70, Plowden Ctee on Overseas Representational Services 1962-63; High Sheriff Norfolk 1974-75, kt 1957; *Recreations* cricket, shooting; *Clubs* Turf, MCC; *Also* assumed additional surname of Mott 1927; *Style* - Sir Charles Mott-Radclyffe, DL; Barningham Hall, Matlaske, Norfolk (☎ Matlaske 250)

MOTTERSHEAD, Frank William; CB (1957); s of Thomas Hastings Mottershead (d 1969); *b* 7 Sept 1911; *Educ* King Edward's Sch Birmingham, St John's Coll Cambridge; *Career* civil servant, princ private sec 1 Lord of the Admiralty 1944-46, dep sec MOD 1958-65, dep sec Dept Health and Soc Security 1965-71; *Clubs* United Oxford and Cambridge; *Style* - Frank Mottershead Esq, CB; Old Warden, Grevel Lane, Chipping Campden, Glos

MOTTISTONE, 4 Baron (UK 1933); David Peter Seely; DL (IOW 1981); s of 1 Baron Mottistone, CB, CMG, DSO, TD, PC (d 1947); *b* 1920; *Educ* RN Coll Dartmouth; *m* 1944, Anthea Christine, da of Victor McMullan, of Bangor; 2 s, 3 da (1 decd); *Heir* s, Hon Peter John Philip Seely; *Career* Cdr RN 1955, Capt 24 Escort Squadron 1963-65; ret at own request 1967; dir personnel training Radio Rentals Ltd 1967-69, dir Distributive Industry Training Bd 1969-75; dir Cake & Biscuit Alliance 1975-; fell Inst of Electronic & Radio Engineers; fell Roy Commonwealth Soc; memb British Inst of Management and Inst of Personnel Managers; *Clubs* Roy Cruising and Island Sailing (Cowes), Roy Commonwealth Soc; *Style* - The Rt Hon the Lord Mottistone, DL; The Old Parsonage, Mottistone, Isle of Wight

MOULD, Air Cdre John Edwin Michael; CBE (1964); s of Clifford Mould (d 1968); *b* 12 Nov 1914; *Educ* Farnham G S; *m* 1945, Molly, da of Richard Bateman; 1 s, 1 da; *Career* Artists' Rifles 1937-38, RAF Equipment Branch 1939, served in 1939-45 War, dir staff RAF Staff Coll 1951-53, Air Cdre 1965, Dir of Equipment 2 (RAF) Miny Defence 1965-67; Dep Ch of Staff (Logistics & Administration) HQ 2 ATAF 1937-69; ret 1970; v-pres Surrey Trust for Nature Conservation 1977-; *Style* - Air Cdre John Mould, CBE; Limes, Middle ave, Farnham, Surrey (☎ Farnham 715418)

MOULTON, Hon Mrs Hugh - Marie Josephine; da of late Sebastian Bergaentzle; *m* 1937, as his 2 w, Hon Hugh Fletcher Moulton, MC (d 1962); *Style* - The Hon Mrs Hugh Moulton; 16 Argyll rd, W8

MOULTON, Hon Sylvia May Fletcher; CBE (1961), JP (1949); da of Baron Moulton, PC (Life Peer, who d 1921); *b* 1902; *Educ* Girton; *Career* barr Middle Temple 1929; sometime regional administrator for Women's Vol Services for Civil Defence Midland Region; *Style* - The Hon Sylvia Moulton, CBE, JP; Court House, Barcombe, Sussex (☎ 235)

MOUNSEY, Michael Fryer; s of George Fryer Mounsey (d 1961); *b* 12 Sept 1915; *Educ* Leighton Park Sch Reading, King's Coll Cambridge; *m* 1945, Ola Blanche, nee Jack; 1 da; *Career* dir Barclays Bank Ltd Notts 1956-79, dir Barclays Bank (UK) Ltd 1971-79; *Recreations* gardening; *Clubs* United Services Notts; *Style* - Michael

Mounsey Esq; Bassingfield House, Tollerton Village, Notts (☎ Plumtree 2603)

MOUNT, Air Cdre Christopher John; CBE (1956), DSO (1943), DFC (1940); s of Francis Mount (d 1915); *b* 14 Dec 1913; *Educ* Eton, Trin Coll Oxford; *m* 1947, Audrey Mabel, da of Lt-Col Marshal Falconer Clarke, DSO (d 1953); 2 s (David Richard, Anthony Francis); *Career* Air Cdre RAF served in UK Middle East and Europe, slr, ptnr CR Thomas and Son Solicitors Maidenhead 1970-78; consultant 1978-; *Recreations* gardening; *Style* - Air Cdre Christopher Mount, CBE, DSO, DFC; Garden House, Bagshot rd, Ascot, Berks (☎ Ascot 22225); c/o Barclays Bank Ltd, 74 Kensington High st, W8

MOUNT, (William Robert) Ferdinand; s of late Robert Francis Mount (himself 2 s of Sir William Mount, 1 Bt, CBE; the latter's paternal grandmother's paternal grandmother was Anne, da of that Viscount Folkestone whose male descendants in the sr line became Earls of Radnor; Anne's husb George was 3 s of 1 Baron Talbot, Lord High Chancellor of England under George II; through him Ferdinand is thirteenth in descent from Sir Gilbert Talbot, who commanded Henry Tudor's right wing at Bosworth Field, fifteenth from the 1 Earl of Shrewsbury who fell at Chastillon, the last battle of The Hundred Years War, and in direct line from Richard de Talbot, who was a sub-tenant of Walter Giffard, Earl of Buckingham, at the time of Domesday Book to the extent of 9 hides of land) and Lady Julia Pakenham, through whom Ferdinand is nephew of Lord (7 Earl of) Longford, nephew by marriage of Anthony Powell, and 1 cous of Lady Antonia Pinter; hp of unc, Sir William Mount, 2 Bt; *b* 2 July 1939; *Educ* Eton, Vienna U, Ch Ch Oxford; *m* 1968, Julia Margaret, twin da of Archibald Julian Lucas; 2 s, 2 da; *Career* sometime with CRD; political correspondent of The Spectator; *Style* - Ferdinand Mount Esq; 17 Ripplevale Grove, N1 (☎ 01 607 5398)

MOUNT, Lt-Col Sir William Malcolm; 2 Bt (UK 1921), of Wasing Place, Reading, Berks, ED (1942), DL (Berks 1946); s of Sir William Arthur Mount, 1 Bt, CBE, MP, JP, DL (d 1930); *b* 28 Dec 1904; *Educ* Eton, New Coll Oxford; *m* 1929, Elizabeth Nance, JP, da of Owen John Llewellyn; 3 da; *Heir* n, (William Robert) Ferdinand Mount; *Career* Lt 99 (Bucks and Berks) Yeo, Field Bde RA (TA) 1926, Capt 1937, Maj 1938, transfd Reconnaissance Corps 1941; jt master S Berks Foxhounds 1935-39, CC (1938) Berks; vice-chm CC 1960, High Sheriff 1947, Vice-Lieut 1960-75; *Clubs* Cavalry; *Style* - Lt-Col Sir William Mount, Bt, ED, DL; Wasing Place, Aldermaston, Berks (☎ Woolhampton 3398)

MOUNT CHARLES, Earl of; Henry Vivian Pierpoint Conyngham; s & h of 7 Marquess Conyngham; *b* 23 May 1951; *Educ* Harrow, Harvard U; *m* 1971, Juliet Ann, da of Robert R B Kitson, of Churchtown, Morval, Cornwall; 1 s, 1 da; *Heir* s, Viscount Slane; *Style* - Earl of Mount Charles; Slane Castle, Slane, Co Meath, Eire

MOUNT EDGCUMBE, 7 Earl of (GB 1789); Edward Piers Edgcumbe; also Viscount Mount Edgcumbe and Valletort (GB 1781) and Baron Edgcumbe of Mount Edgcumbe (GB 1742); s of George Valletort Edgcumbe (d 1947) and cousin of 6 Earl (d 1965); *b* 13 July 1903; *Educ* Normal Sch, Auckland G S; *m* 1944, Victoria Effie (d 1979), widow of John Warbrick and da of Robert Campbell, of Lisburn, Ireland, and New Zealand; *Heir* nephew, Robert Charles Edgcumbe; *Career* farmer; *Style* - The Rt Hon the Earl of Mount Edgcumbe; Mount Edgecumbe, Plymouth, Devon (☎ Millbrook 311)

MOUNTAIN, Doris Lady; Doris Elsie; da of late Eric Charles Edward Lamb; *m* 1926, Sir Brian Edward Stanley Mountain, 2 Bt (d 1977); *Style* - Doris Lady Mountain; Dunley Manor, Whitchurch, Hants; 75 Eaton sq, SW1

MOUNTAIN, Sir Denis Mortimer; 3 Bt (UK 1922), of Oare Manor, Co Somerset, and Brendon, Co Devon; s of Lt-Col Sir Brian Edward Stanley Mountain, 2 Bt (d 1977); *b* 2 June 1929; *Educ* Eton; *m* 1958, (Helene) Fleur Mary, da of John Kirwan-Taylor, of Switzerland; 2 s, 1 da; *Heir* s,

Edward Brian Stanford Mountain; *Career* chm and md Eagle Star Insurance Co Ltd 1974-, Eagle Star Insurance Corpn of America 1978-, Eagle Star Holdings Ltd 1979-; chm Home & Overseas Insurance Co Ltd and other cos; dir Compagnie de Bruxelles English Property Corpn Ltd; chm Australian Eagle Insurance Co Ltd; dir Masters Ltd of Bermuda and other cos; chm Ashdale Land Property Co Ltd 1975; dir Rank Organisation Ltd, Philip Hill Investment Trust Ltd, Bank of Nova Scotia (Toronto); *Recreations* fishing, shooting; *Clubs* Derby, Nat Sporting, Blues & Royals; *Style* - Sir Denis Mountain, Bt; 12 Queen's Elm sq, Old Church st, SW3 (☎ 01 352 4331); Shawford Park, Shawford, nr Winchester, Hants (☎ Twyford Hants 712289)

MOUNTAIN, Edward Brian Stanford; s and h of Sir Denis Mortimer Mountain, 3 Bt; *b* 19 March 1961; *Style* - Edward Mountain Esq

MOUNTBATTEN OF BURMA, Countess (UK 1947); Patricia Edwina Victoria Knatchbull; CD (1976), JP (Kent 1971), DL (Kent 1973); Viscountess Mountbatten of Burma (UK 1946), Baroness Romsey (UK 1947); da of Adm of the Fleet 1 Earl Mountbatten of Burma, KG, GCB, OM, GCSI, GCIE, GCVO, DSO, PC (assassinated 1979) and Hon Edwina Ashley, CI, GBE, DCVO (d 1960, da of 1 and last Baron Mount Temple, himself gs of the 7 Earl of Shaftesbury, the philanthropist whose influence over the London rabble was invoked to maintain calm in the tumultuous year 1848; Shaftesbury's mother was sis of Lord Melbourne the PM and their mother was Elizabeth, nee Milbanke, who, as 'the best friend I ever had in my life' to Byron, allowed concern for his finances to outrun her judgement so far as to saddle him with her niece Anna Isabella, with results from which matrimony as an institution is still reeling); Edwina's mother was Amalia, da of Sir Ernest Cassel, the opulent banker and friend of Edward VII; Lady Mountbatten of Burma is sis-in-law of David Hicks, the interior decorator; *b* 14 Feb 1924; *Educ* Malta, England, NYC; *m* 1946, 7 Baron Brabourne; 4 s, 2 da (1 s decd); *Heire* s, Lord Romsey; *Career* V-Pres SSAFA 1981-; served 1943-46 WRNS; magistrate 1971; Col-in-Ch Princess Patricia's Canadian Light Infantry 1974-; v-chm of Council BRCS; dep v-chm NSPCC; chm Sir Ernest Cassel Educational Trust; pres PNEU; SOS Children's Villages; Kent East Girl Guides Assoc; v-pres FPA; Nat Childbirth Trust; Govr Ashford Sch Kent; memb British Legion; *Style* - The Rt Hon the Countess Mountbatten of Burma, CD, JP, DL; New House, Mersham, Ashford, Kent (☎ 23466); 39 Montpelier Walk, SW7 (☎ 01 589 8829)

MOUNTBATTEN, Lord Ivar Alexander Michael; s of 3 Marquess of Milford Haven, OBE, DSC (d 1970); hp of bro, 4 Marquess; *b* 9 March 1963; *Style* - Lord Ivar Mountbatten

MOUNTBATTEN, Lady (Elizabeth) Tatiana; da of 2 Marquess of Milford Haven, GCVO (d 1938); *b* 17 Dec 1917; *Style* - Lady Tatiana Mountbatten

MOUNTEVANS, 3 Baron (UK 1945); (Edward Patrick) Broke Andvord Evans; s of 2 Baron Mountevans (d 1974); *b* 1 Feb 1943; *Educ* Rugby, Trin Oxford; *m* 1974, Johanna, da of Antonius Keyzer, of The Hague; *Heir* bro, Hon Jeffrey de Corban Richard Evans; *Career* Lt (ret 74) MC Regt Roy Corps of Transport, AER 1966; on mgmnt Consolidated Gold Fields Ltd 1966; joined British Tourist Authority 1972, man Sweden and Finland 1973, man Promotion Services 1976; *Recreations* reading, travel; *Style* - The Rt Hon the Lord Mountevans; 86 Portland Place, W1

MOUNTEVANS, Deirdre, Baroness; Deirdre Grace; da of John O'Connell, of Buxton Hill, Co Cork; *m* 1940, 2 Baron Mountevans (d 1974); *Style* - The Rt Hon Deirdre, Lady Mountevans; 5 Campden House Court, 42 Gloucester Walk, W8

MOUNTGARRET, 17 Viscount (I 1550); Richard Henry Piers Butler; also Baron Mountgarret (UK 1911), which sits as in House of Lords; s of 16 Viscount Mountgarret (d 1966); *b* 8 Nov 1936; *Educ* Eton, Sandhurst; *m* 1, 1960, Gillian (m dis 1969), da of Cyril Buckley, of Chelsea; 2 s, 1 da; m 2, 1970, Mrs Jennifer Fattorini, da of Capt D Wills, of Wrington, Somerset; *Heir* s, Hon Piers Butler; *Career* formerly Capt Irish Gds; hp to Earldoms of Ossory and Ormonde, also Chief Butlership of Ireland, as descendant of Hon Richard Butler, yr s of 8 Earl of Ormonde and 1 Earl of Ossory, cr Viscount Mountgarret 1550; *Recreations* shooting, stalking; *Clubs* White's, Pratt's; *Style* - The Rt Hon The Viscount Mountgarret; Stainley House, South Stainley, Harrogate, Yorks (☎ 0423 770087); Wyvis, Evanton, Ross-shire; 29 Trevor Place, SW7 (☎ 01 589 9846)

MOUTAFIAN, Princess Helena; *née* Gagarin; MBE (1976); da of Prince Alexei Grigorievitch Gagarin (descended ultimately from the Grand Prince Rurik who founded the Russian monarchy in c 879, the first to be named Gagara being Prince Mikhail Ivanovitch, er s of Prince Ivan Lapin-Golibessovski, c 1500) and an Austrian mother; *b* 2 May 1930; *m* 1955, Artin Moutafian; 2 s; *Career* V-Pres St John Ambulance London Dist, Hon V-Pres Women's Cncl 1981-, Pres Friends of Unicorn Theatre 1981-; Friend Utd Roy (Atlantic) Colls; OStJ; Patron Utd Kingston Charities; freelance memb IOJ; Hampstead Pres NSPCC (Hon Memb Cncl & Life Patron); Freedom of City of Paris; *Recreations* painting, writing; *Clubs* Hurlingham, Eng Speaking Union; *Style* - Princess Helena Moutafian, MBE; 12 Greenaway gdns, NW3

MOVERLEY, Rt Rev Gerald; s of William Joseph Moverley; *b* 9 April 1922; *Educ* St Bede's G S Bradford, Ushaw Coll Durham, Anglican U Rome; *Career* Priest 1946, Titular Bishop in Proconsulari, Domestic Prelate to HH Pope Paul VI 1965-78, Bishop Auxiliary of Leeds (RC) 1968-; *Style* - The Right Reverend Gerald Moverley; Quarters, Carsick Hill Way, Sheffield S10 3LT (☎ Sheffield 301596)

MOWAT, John Frederick Michael; MBE (1933); s of Martin James Mowat (d 1952); *b* 18 April 1911; *Educ* Haileybury, Univ Coll Oxford; *m* 1939, Elizabeth Rebecca, nee Murray (d 1977); 2 s, 2 da; *Career* Major RA 1939-45, dir and dep chm Br Tar Prods 1960-81, chm Lichfield Diocesan Bd Fin 1970-79, JP 1949-81 Denbighshire and Salop, memb W Mercia Police Authority 1970-81; *Recreations* farming; *Clubs* Army & Navy; *Style* - John Mowat Esq, MBE; Lake House, Ellesmere, Salop (☎ Ellesmere 2538)

MOWBRAY, Dowager Lady; Diana Margaret; da of late Sir Robert Heywood Hughes, 12 Bt; *m* 1927, Sir George Robert Mowbray, 5 Bt, KBE (d 1969); *Style* - Dowager Lady Mowbray; Starvehill House, Mortimer, Berks

MOWBRAY, Sir John Robert; 6 Bt (UK 1880), of Warennes Wood, Berkshire, JP (W Suffolk 1972); s of Sir George Robert Mowbray, 5 Bt, KBE (d 1969); *b* 1 March 1932; *Educ* Eton, New Coll Oxford; *m* 1957, Lavinia Mary, da of Lt-Col Francis Edgar Hugonin, OBE; 3 da; *Heir* none; *Style* - Sir John Mowbray, Bt, JP; Hunt's Park, Great Thurlow, Haverhill, Suffolk (☎ Thurlow 232)

MOWBRAY, SEGRAVE AND STOURTON, 26, 27 & 23 Baron (E 1283, 1295 & 1448 respectively); Charles Edward Stourton; Premier Baron of England; s of 25 Baron Mowbray, 26 Segrave and 22 Stourton, MC, JP (d 1965, himself gs of 23, 24 & 20 Baron M, S & S, who had inherited the Barony of Stourton from his f, and had the abeyance of the Baronies of Mowbray and Segrave (operative from the death in 1777 of the 9 Duke of Norfolk) terminated in his favour 1878) and of Sheila, da of Hon Edward W K Gully, CB (d 1931, who in his turn was 2 s of 1 Viscount Selby); *b* 11 March 1923; *Educ* Ampleforth, Ch Ch Oxford; *m* 1952, Hon Jane Faith de Yarburgh-Bateson, da of 5 Baron Deramore (d 1964), by his w Nina Macpherson-Grant; 2 s; *Heir* s, Hon Edward William Stephen Stourton; *Career* Lt Gren Gds 1943; memb of Lloyd's 1952; dir Securicor (Southern) Ltd 1965-66, Securicor (Scotland) 1966-70; a Conservative Whip in House of Lords and Front Bench Spokesman 1967-70 and 1974-78; a Lord in Waiting 1970-74 and 1979-80; Dep Ch Opposition Whip House of Lords 1978-79; Chancellor of The Primrose League 1974-79; hon pres Safety Glazing Assoc 1975-78; *Style* - The Rt Hon the Lord Mowbray, Segrave and Stourton; Marcus, by Forfar, Angus (☎ Finavon 219); 23 Warwick sq, SW1

MOWBRAY, SEGRAVE AND STOURTON, Baroness; Hon Jane Faith; *née* de Yarburgh-Bateson; da of late 5 Baron Deramore; *b* 1933; *m* 1952, 26 Baron Mowbray, Segrave and Stourton, *qv*; *Style* - The Rt Hon Lady Mowbray, Segrave and Stourton

MOXHAM, Lady; Marjorie; da of late Arthur Julien, LLD, of Cornwall; *m* 1938, as his 2 w, Sir Harry Cuthbertson Moxham (d 1965); *Style* - Lady Moxham; 609 NS Head rd, Rose Bay, Sydney, NSW, Australia

MOXON, Hon Mrs (Jennifer Julia); da of 3 Baron de Ramsey, KBE; *b* 1940; *m* 1964, John Frederick Moxon; 3 s, 2 da; *Style* - The Hon Mrs Moxon; Roundwood, Bury rd, Ramsey, Huntingdon

MOYLE, Baroness; Lena; da of William Henry Bassett, of Tunbridge Wells; *m* 1951, as his 2 w, Baron Moyle (Life Peer) (d 1974); *Style* - The Rt Hon Lady Moyle; Hafod, Grassy Lane, Sevenoaks, Kent

MOYNE, 2 Baron (UK 1932); Bryan Walter Guinness; s of Rt Hon 1 Baron Moyne, DSO, TD, PC (assas Cairo 1944; né Hon Walter Guinness, 3 s of 1 Earl of Iveagh, KP, GCVO), and Lady Evelyn Erskine (da of 14 Earl of Buchan); *b* 27 Oct 1905; *Educ* Eton, Ch Ch Oxford; *m* 1, 1929, Hon Diana Freeman Mitford (m dis 1934; she is da of 2 Baron Redesdale, sis of the writers (Hon) Jessica and late (Hon) Nancy Mitford and the Duchess of Devonshire, and widow of Sir Oswald Mosley, 6 Bt, whom she m as his 2 w 1936); 2 s; m 2, 1936, Elisabeth, da of Thomas Nelson; 3 s (and 1 s decd), 5 da; *Heir* s, Hon Jonathan Guinness; *Career* late Maj M East, France; poet, novelist, playwright; FRSL, memb Irish Acad of Letters; V-Chm Arthur Guinness Son & Co 1949-79; barr; Tstee Iveagh & Guinness Tsts; *Recreations* wood cutting, travel, gardening; *Clubs* Athenaeum, Carlton, University & Kildare Street (Dublin); *Style* - The Rt Hon The Lord Moyne; Knockmaroon House, Castleknock, Co Dublin, Eire; Biddesden House, Andover, Hants (☎ 790237)

MOYNIHAN, 3 Baron (UK 1929); Sir Antony Patrick Andrew Cairnes Berkeley Moynihan; 3 Bt (UK 1922); s of 2 Baron Moynihan, sometime Chm Exec Cttee Liberal Pty (d 1965), by his 1 w Ierne; *b* 2 Feb 1936; *Educ* Stowe; *m* 1, 1955, Ann (m dis 1958), da of Reginald Herbert; m 2, 1958, Shirin Berry (m dis 1967); 1 da; m 3, 1968, Luthgarda Maria (m dis 1979), da of Alfonzo Fernandez; 2 da; *Heir* half-bro, Hon Colin Berkeley Moynihan; *Career* dog breeder; *Style* - The Rt Hon the Lord Moynihan

MOYNIHAN, Hon Aurora Luzon Maria Dolores; da of 3 Baron Moynihan; *b* 1971; *Style* - The Hon Aurora Moynihan

MOYNIHAN, Hon Antonita Maria Carmen; da of 3 Baron Moynihan; *b* 31 March 1969; *Style* - The Hon Antonita Moynihan

MOYNIHAN, Hon Colin Berkeley; s of 2 Baron Moynihan (d 1965), and hp of half-bro, 3 Baron; *b* 13 Sept 1955; *Style* - The Hon Colin Moynihan

MOYNIHAN, Hon Dorothy Wellesley; da of 1 Baron Moynihan, KCMG, CB (d 1936); *b* 1897; *Style* - The Hon Dorothy Moynihan; 42 Warwick rd, Beaconsfield, Bucks (☎ 3395)

MOYNIHAN, Ierne, Baroness; Ierne Helen; da of Cairnes Candy (d 1949), of Mt Barker, W Australia; *b* 1910; *m* 1931, 2 Baron Moynihan (m dis 1952) (he died 1965); 1 s, 2 da; *Clubs* Hurlingham and Queen's; *Style* - Ierne, Lady Moynihan; 81 Sussex Square, W2 (☎ 01 723 9818)

MOYNIHAN, Hon Kathleen Maynila Helen Imogen Juliet; da of 3 Baron Moynihan; *b* 1974; *Style* - The Hon Kathleen Moynihan

MOYNIHAN, Hon Miranda Dorne Ierne; da of 3 Baron Moynihan; *b* 1959; *Style* - The Hon Miranda Moynihan

MOYNIHAN, Hon Melanie June; da of 2 Baron Moynihan (d 1965); *b* 19 Aug 1957; *Style* - The Hon Melanie Moynihan

MOYNIHAN, Sir Noël Henry; s of Dr Edward B Moynihan; *b* 24 Dec 1916; *Educ* Ratcliffe, Downing Cambridge; *m* 1941, Margaret Mary, JP, da of William Lovelace; 2 s, 2 da; *Career* qualified as doctor St Thomas' Hosp 1954 family dr; chm Save The Children Fund 1977-; CStJ; Kt Sov Order of Malta; kt 1979; *Recreations* Save The Children Fund, studying the rock art of the Sahara; *Clubs* Carlton, MCC, Hawks, Achilles; *Style* - Sir Noël Moynihan; 25-27 Sloane Court W, SW3; Herstmonceux Place, Flowers Green, E Sussex

MOYOLA, Baron (Life Peer UK 1971); James Dawson Chichester-Clark; PC (NI 1966), DL (Co Derry 1954); s of Capt James L C Chichester-Clark, DSO and Bar (d 1933), and Mrs C E Brackenbury, of Moyola Park, Castle Dawson, Co Derry, N Ireland; *b* 12 Feb 1923; *Educ* Eton; *m* 1959, Moyra Maud, widow of Capt T Haughton & da of Brig Arthur de Burgh Morris, CBE, DSO; 1 step s, 2 da; *Career* memb N Ireland Parl 1960, Chief Whip 1963-67; Leader of the House and Ch Whip 1966-67, Prime Minister 1969-71; *Recreations* shooting, fishing, gardening; *Style* - The Rt Hon the Lord Moyola PC DL; Moyola Park, Castledawson, Co Derry, N Ireland

MUDDIMAN, Colin Trevor; s of Arthur Edgar Lanwer Muddiman (d 1961); *b* 4 June 1929; *Educ* Wellington Coll; *m* 1962, Stella Pillans; *Career* farmer; memb of Eastern Electricity Board 1973-78 & 1980, chm Eastern Electricity Consultative Council 1973-78; memb Lloyd's; memb of Worshipful Company of Farmers 1960, memb of Court 1975; chm of Grainec (UK) Ltd (Grain Traders of Woburn, Beds); *Clubs* Farmers (chm 1981), Royal London Yacht; *Style* - Colin Muddiman Esq; Gade House, Little Gaddesden, Berkhamsted, Herts

MUDGE, Hon Mrs (Maureen Ann); da of Baron Wigg, PC (Life Peer); *b* 1934; *m* 1964, Alfred John Mudge; *Style* - The Hon Mrs Mudge; 1580 Mississauga Valley Bvd, Mississauga, Ont, Canada

MUFF, Hon Jonathan Edward ; s and h of 3 Baron Calverley; *b* 16 April 1975; *Style* - The Hon Jonathan Muff

MUFF, Hon Peter Raymond; s of 2 Baron Calverley (d 1971); *b* 12 August 1953; *Educ* Grange Boys' Sch Bradford; *Career* assist engineer (instruments) Central Electricity Generating Bd, T Eng, (CEI), MITE; *Recreations* squash, electronics, domestic cat shows; *Clubs* Abyssinian Cat; *Style* - The Hon Peter Muff; 18 Brackendale av, Thackley, W Yorks

MUIR, Frank; CBE (1980); s of Charles James Muir; *b* 5 Feb 1920; *Educ* Chatham House Ramsgate, Leyton County H S; *m* 1949, Polly McIrvine; 1 s, 1 da; *Career* served RAF 1940-46; writer and broadcaster with Denis Norden 1947-64; collaborated for 17 yrs writing comedy scripts; resident in TV and Radio Panel Games; assist head of BBC Light Entertainment Gp 1964-67; head Entertainment LWT 1968-69; resumed TV Series Call My Bluff 1970; *Recreations* sitting quietly collecting dust; *Club* Savile; *Style* - Frank Muir Esq CBE; Anners, Thorpe, Surrey (☎ 09328 62759)

MUIR, Hon Mrs; Hon Helen; da of Baron du Parcq (d 1949) (Life Peer); *m* 1, 1935, William Farr (m dis 1948); m 2, 1948, Alec Andrew Muir, CBE; *Style* - The Hon Mrs Muir

MUIR, Sir John (Harling); 3 Bt (UK 1892), of Deanston, Perthshire, TD, DL (Perthshire 1966); s of James Finlay Muir (d 1948) and nephew of 2 Bt (d 1951); *b* 7 Nov 1910; *Educ* Stowe; *m* 1936, Elizabeth Mary, da of late Frederick James Dundas; 5 s, 2 da; *Heir* s, Richard James Kay Muir; *Career* served 1939-45 War; dir James Finlay & Co Ltd Glasgow 1946-, Grindlay's Hldgs Ltd, Roy Insurance Co Ltd, Scottish Investors Ltd; memb Roy Co of Archers (Queen's Body Guard for Scotland); memb Fourth Dist Salmon Fishery Bd; *Clubs* Oriental and Western (Glasgow); *Style* - Sir John Muir, Bt, TD, DL; Bankhead House, Blair Drummond, Perthshire (☎ Doune 207)

MUIR, Lady Linda Mary, da of 6 Earl of Enniskillen, MBE; *b* 1944; *m* 1975, as his 2 w, Richard James Kay Muir, *qv*, s of Sir John Muir, 3 Bt, TD, DL; *Style* - Lady Linda Muir; Box 72244, Nairobi, Kenya

MUIR, Richard James Kay; s and h of Sir John Muir, 3 Bt, TD; *b* 25 May 1939; *m* 1, 1965, Susan Elizabeth Gardner (m dis 1974); 2 da; m 2, 1975, Lady Linda Mary Cole, da of 6 Earl of Enniskillen; 1 da; *Style* - Richard Muir Esq; Box 72244, Nairobi, Kenya

MUIR, Lady Rosemary Mildred; *née* Spencer-Churchill; da of 10 Duke of Marlborough (d 1972); *b* 1929; *m* 1953, Charles Robert Muir (d 1972); 2 s, 1 da; *Style* - Lady Rosemary Muir; Billingbear House, Binfield, Bracknell, Berks

MUIR, William Archibald Gordon; s of William John Inglis Muir; *b* 4 Feb 1931; *Educ* Glasgow Acad, Trin Coll Glenalmond, St John's Coll Cambridge; *m* 1956, Joanna Margaret, nee Calverley; 2 s, 2 da; *Career* chartered surveyor, memb Sco Housing Advsy Ctee 1970 (chm 1978-79), Nat Housebldg Cncl Scot 1970- (chm 1981-), chm Sco Special Housing Assoc 1972-76, dir Nat Bldg Agency 1976-, dir Housing Corpn 1980-, dir Merchants House of Glasgow 1981-; *Recreations* gliding, satiable curiosity; *Clubs* Caledonian, Roy Scot Auto; owner of glider 'Skylark 4' BG 1044; *Style* - William Muir Esq; The White House, Cardross, Dunbarton, Scotland

MUIR MACKENZIE, Sir Alexander Alwyne Brinton; 7 Bt (UK 1805), of Delvine, Perthshire; s of Sir Robert Henry Muir Mackenzie, 7 Bt (d 1970); *b* 8 Dec 1955; *Educ* Eton, Trin Cambridge; *Heir* none; *Career* 2 Lt 16/5 Lancers; *Style* - Sir Alexander Muir Mackenzie, Bt; Park Hall, nr Kidderminster, Worcs; Sunderland Hall, nr Galashiels, Selkirkshire

MUIR MACKENZIE, Lady; Mary Teresa; da of late Dr James Matthews and widow of John Geoffrey Turner, of Farnham, Surrey; *m* 1963, as his 2 w, Capt Sir Robert Henry Muir Mackenzie, 6 Bt (d 1970); *Style* - Lady Muir Mackenzie; Flat A, 62 Pont st, SW1

MUIRHEAD, Hon Lady (Elspeth Rachel Marianne Winifred Hope); da of 2 Baron Hollenden, JP (d 1977); *b* 1917; *m* 1942, Sir David Francis Muirhead, KCMG, CVO; 2 s, 1 da; *Style* - The Hon Lady Muirhead; 16 Pitt st, W8

MUIRHEAD, William Mortimer; s of Denis Butler Muirhead; *b* 11 July 1947; *Educ* The Armidale Sch NSW, St Dunstan's Coll SE6; *m* Jeanne Elizabeth, nee Meins; 2 s; *Career* advertising; formerly dir Saatchi & Saatchi Garland-Compton, dir Saatchi & Saatchi Compton 1980-; *Recreations* rugby, tennis, squash, skiing; *Clubs* RAC, Zanzibar, Mortons; *Style* - William Muirhead Esq; Ightham, Merlewood Drive, Chislehurst, Kent; Tramontana, Encounter Bay, Victor Harbour, S Australia

MUIRSHIEL, 1 Viscount (UK 1964); John Scott Maclay; KT (1973), CH (1962), CMG (1944), PC (1952), JP (Renfrewshire 1968), DL (Renfrewshire 1981); 5 s of 1 Baron Maclay (d 1951); *b* 26 Oct 1905; *Educ* Winchester, Trin Cambridge; *m* 1930, Betty L'Estrange (d 1974), da of Maj Delaval Astley, CB, JP, DL (d 1951, g nephew of 16 Baron Hastings); *Heir* none; *Career* Capt 57 Searchlight Regt RA; dir Clydesdale Bank 1970-; memb British Shipping Mission to USA 1941, head of Mission 1944; MP (Lib Nat) Montrose District of Burghs 1940-50, (Nat Lib & C) Renfrewshire (Western Div) 1950-64; parly sec Miny of Production 1945; Min of Transport and Civil Aviation 1951-52, Min of State for Colonial Affairs 1956-57; Sec of State for Scotland 1957-62; chm Jt Exchequer Bd for N Ireland; Ld-Lt of Renfrewshire 1967-80; *Clubs* Boodle's, Western (Glasgow) and Roy Yacht Sqdn; *Style* - The Rt Hon the Viscount Muirshiel KT, CH, CMG, PC, JP, DL; Knapps, Kilmacolm, Renfrewshire (☎ Kilmacolm 2770)

MULCAHY, Geoffrey John; s of the late Maurice Frederick Mulcahy; *b* 7 Feb 1942; *Educ* King's Sch Worcester, Manchester U, Harvard U; *m* 1964, Valerie Elizabeth, nee Ison; 1 s, 1 da; *Career* finance dir British Sugar Corporation Ltd 1977-; *Recreations* squash, sailing; *Clubs* Lansdowne; *Style* - Geoffrey Mulcahy Esq; 50 Stamford rd, Oakham, Rutland (☎ 0572 55822)

MULGRAVE, Earl of; Constantine Edmund Walter Phipps; s & h of 4

Marquess of Normanby, CBE; *b* 24 Feb 1954; *Educ* Eton, Worcester Coll Oxford; *Style* - Earl of Mulgrave; Mulgrave Castle, Whitby, N Yorks

MULHALLEN, Lady Katherine Lilian; *née* Edgcumbe; da of 6 Earl of Mount Edgcumbe, TD (d 1965); *b* 1910; *m* 1, 1936, Gp Capt Francis Campbell de la Poer Beresford-Peirse (m dis 1957); m 2, Cdr R Gabbett Mulhallen, CBE, RN; *Style* - Lady Katherine Mulhallen; 9 St Michael's ter, Stoke, Plymouth

MULHOLLAND, Brian Henry; s and h of Sir Michael Henry Mulholland, 2 Bt; *b* 25 Sept 1950; *Educ* Eton; *m* 1976, Mary Joana, da of Maj R J F Whistler of Camberley, Surrey; *Style* - Brian Mulholland Esq

MULHOLLAND, Maj Sir Michael Henry; 2 Bt (UK 1945), of Ballyscullion Park, Co Derry; s of Rt Hon Sir Henry Mulholland, 1 Bt (d 1971); hp to Barony of Dunleath; *b* 15 Oct 1915; *Educ* Eton, Pembroke Coll Cambridge; *m* 1, 1942, Rosemary (m dis 1949), da of late Maj David Ker, OBE; m 2, 1949, Elizabeth, da of Laurence Hyde; 1 s; *Heir* s, Brian Henry Mulholland; *Career* 2 Lt Oxford and Bucks LI 1936, served 1939-45 War, Maj 1946; *Style* - Maj Sir Michael Mulholland, Bt; Storbrooke, 31 Massey ave, Belfast (☎ 63394)

MULHOLLAND, Hon Dame; Hon Olivia Vernon; DCVO (1971); da of 1 Viscount Harcourt (d 1922); *b* 1902; *Educ* Notting Hill H S, Lady Margaret Hall Oxford; *m* 1923, Hon (Godfrey) John Arthur (d 1948), s of 2 Baron Dunleath (d 1931); 1 s, 2 da; *Career* v-chm Roy Free Hosp 1950-62; chm Elizabeth Garrett Anderson Hosp 1945-72; woman of the bedchamber to HM Queen Elizabeth, the Queen Mother 1950-; *Style* - The Hon Dame Olivia Mulholland, DCVO; Weston Mark, Upton Grey, Basingstoke, Hants (☎ Long Sutton 429)

MULHOLLAND, Hon Lady; Sheelah; da of Sir Arthur Douglas Brooke, 4 Bt; aunt of 2 Viscount Brookeborough; *m* 1914, Rt Hon Sir Henry George Hill Mulholland, 1 Bt (d 1971), 3 s of 2 Baron Dunleath; *Style* - The Hon Lady Mulholland; Ballyscullion Park, Bellaghy, Co Derry

MULJI, Hon Mrs; Hon Rosaleen Elisabeth; *née* Guinness; da of 2 Baron Moyne; *b* 1937; *Educ* St Anne's Coll Oxford (MA); *m* 1965, Sudhir Mulji; 2 s, 2 da; *Style* - The Hon Mrs Mulji; 150 Malcha Marg, New Delhi, 110021

MULLAN, Charles Heron; CBE (1979), VRD, JP, DL (Co Down 1974); s of Frederick Heron Mullan, DL (d 1972);*b* 1912; *Educ* Rossall School, Clare Cambridge; *m* 1940, Marcella Elizabeth Sharpe, da of J A McCullagh, of Ballycastle, Co Antrim; 1 s; *Career* joined RNVR 1936, Lt 1940, RN 1939-45, retired as Lt-Cdr; solicitor 1948; MP (U U) Imperial Parliament Co Down 1946-50; memb Ulster Unionist Council 1946-60; resident magistrate N Ireland 1960, stipendiary magistrate Belfast 1964-79; *Recreations* walking, boating; *Clubs* Naval (London); *Style* - Charles Mullan Esq, CBE, VRD, JP, DL; Casanbarra, Ballycastle, Co Antrim, N Ireland (Ballycastle 6323); Cairn Hill, Newry, Co Down, N Ireland (☎ Newry 2003)

MULLETT, Arthur Reginald Haden; s of late Arthur Mullett; *b* 21 April 1915; *Educ* King Edward VI G S Stourbridge; *m* 1946, Florence Joan, nee Weaver; 3 da; *Career* chartered accountant, ptnr Gough & Aright 1946-62, md Midland Bright Group Ltd 1962-67, dep financial dir British Steel Constructions (Birmingham) Ltd 1967-69, financial dir 1969-73; chm Foster Bros Ltd 1973-; *Recreations* golf; *Style* - Arthur Mullett Esq; Keble House, Fockbury, Bromsgrove, Worcs (☎ 71972); Tradyddan, Ynyslas, Borth, Dyfed (☎ 256)

MULLINS, Leonard; CMG (1976); s of Robert Mullins (d 1964); *b* 21 May 1918; *Educ* Eltham Coll, Univ Coll London U; *m* 1943, Freda Elaine, nee Churchouse; 2 da; *Career* physicist, dir of research Malaysian Rubber Producers' Research Assoc 1962-, Commander Malaysian Order of Chivalry JMN (Hon) 1975; *Clubs* Athenaeum; *Style* - Leonard Mullins Esq,

CMG; 32 Sherrardspark rd, Welwyn Garden City, Herts (☎ Welwyn Garden 23633)

MUNDY, Lady Bridget; da of 5 Earl of Minto (d 1975); *b* 1921; *m* 1, 1944, Lt-Col James Averell Clark, Jr, DFC, USAF; 1 s; m 2, 1954, Maj Henry Claude Lyon Garnett, CBE (m dis 1963); m 3, 1966, Maj (Edward) Peter Godfrey Miller Mundy, MC (m dis 1970); *Style* - Lady Bridget Mundy

MUNN, Rear-Adm William James; CB (1962), DSO (1941), OBE (1946); s of late Lt-Col R G Munn, CMG; *b* 15 July 1911; *Educ* Britannia RN Coll Dartmouth; *m* 1940, Susan Astle, da of late St J V H Sperling, of Teviot Bank, Hawick, Roxburghshire; 2 s; *Career* served 1939-45 War, Capt 1951, CO RN Coll Dartmouth 1956-58, commanding HMS Gambia 1958, Rear-Adm 1960, ch of staff to C-in-C Home Fleet 1961, ret 1963; sec St John Council for Suffolk 1973-; *Recreations* golf; *Clubs* Roy Worlington GC; *Style* - Rear-Adm William Munn, CB, DSO, OBE; The Old Rectory, Langham, Bury St Edmunds, Suffolk (☎ Walsham le Willows 234)

MUNRO, Alasdair Thomas Ian; s and h of Sir (Thomas) Torquil Alphonso Munro of Lindertis, 5 Bt; *b* 6 July 1927; *Educ* Landon Sch USA, Georgetown U Washington, Pennsylvania U; *m* 1954, Marguerite Lillian, da of late Franklin R Loy, of Ohio, USA; 1 s, 1 da; *Style* - Alasdair Munro Esq; River Ridge, Waitsfield, Vermont, USA

MUNRO, Lady; Beryl; da of James Nicholson, of Esk, Qld; *m* 1921, Sir Alan Whiteside Munro, KBE (d 1968); *Style* - Lady Munro; c/o E W Munro Esq, A W Munro and Co, Empire House, Queen and Wharf sts, Brisbane 4000, Australia

MUNRO, Hon Mrs (Diana Mary); *née* Colville; da of 2 Baron Clydesmuir, KT, CB, MBE, TD; *b* 1947; *m* 1973, Christopher I C Munro; 1 da; *Style* - The Hon Mrs Munro; 26 Pembroke Square, W8 6PB

MUNRO, Sir Ian Talbot; 15 Bt (NS 1634), of Foulis-Obsdale, Ross-shire; s of Robert Hector Munro and first cousin once removed of Sir Arthur Herman Munro, 14 Bt (d 1972); *b* 18 Dec 1929; *Educ* Bradfield Sch Berks; *Heir* unc, Malcolm Munro; *Career* marine consultant; *Style* - Sir Ian Munro, Bt; 38 Clarence Gate gdns, NW1

MUNRO, Kenneth John; s of the late Robert Clarke Munro; *b* 7 Feb 1926; *Educ* St George's Sch Herts; *m* 1948, Nerys Edith, nee Eatwell; 4 c; *Career* chm T Wheeler Ltd and R W Munro Ltd; *Recreations* walking; *Style* - Kenneth Munro Esq; 54 Lower Luton rd, Harpenden, Herts

MUNRO, Malcolm; s of Charles Munro, FAA, FLAA (d 1959); hp to Btcy of n Sir Ian Talbot Munro, 15 Bt; *b* 24 Feb 1901; *m* 1931, Constance, da of William Carter; 1 da; *Style* - Malcolm Munro Esq; Whitegates, Rock, Wadebridge, Cornwall

MUNRO, Robert Wilson; CMG (1967); s of John Sutherland Munro (d 1948); *b* 21 Jan 1915; *Educ* Otago Boys' H S (NZ), Otago U, London U; *m* 1946, Annette, nee Kilroy; 2 s; *Career* scientist, New Zealand Dept of Agriculture 1938-40, Sudan Civil Service 1945-52, HM Foreign (later Diplomatic) Serv 1952-74, Middle East Adv NZ Meat Producers Bd 1978-80, Order of Nilein 1965; *Recreations* fishing; *Clubs* The Wellington; *Style* - Robert Munro Esq, CMG; 7 Lynmouth ave, Karori, Wellington, New Zealand (☎ 769591)

MUNRO OF LINDERTIS, Sir (Thomas) Torquil Alphonso; 5 Bt (UK 1825), of Lindertis, Forfarshire, JP (Angus 1932); s of Sir Hugh Thomas Munro of Lindertis, 4 Bt (d 1919); *b* 7 Feb 1901; *Educ* Winchester, Cambridge U; *m* 1, 1925, Beatrice Maude (m dis 1932), da of late Robert Sanderson Whitaker, of Villa Sofia, Palermo; 1 s; m 2, 1934, Averil Moira Katharine, da of Kenneth Hunter; 1 s, 1 da; *Heir* s, Alasdair Thomas Ian Munro; *Career* 2 Lt Gren Gds 1922-23; served in Gren Gds and Underground Army 1942; *Style* - Sir Torquil Munro of Lindertis, Bt, JP; Lindertis, Kirriemuir, Co Angus (☎ Craigton 209)

MUNRO, Lady; Violet Beatrice; da of late Henry Powles; *m* 1919, Sir Arthur Herman Munro, 14 Bt (d 1972); *Style* - Lady Munro

MUNRO-FERGUSON OF RAITH AND NOVAR, Arthur Brocklehurst Luttrell; s of Ralph Munro-Ferguson (s of Alice Munro Ferguson, eld da of Col Robert M-F, JP, DL, and sis of 1 and last Viscount Novar and late Maj Hector M-F, who m a gda (Henrietta) of 6 Baron Howard de Walden, GBE; Alice's husb was Alexander, eld s of George Fownes Luttrell, JP, DL, of the ancient Somerset family, proprietors of Dunster Castle since the 14th century); *b* 10 Nov 1921; *Educ* Stowe, Trin Cambridge; *m* 1952, Jane, da of Lewis Reynolds, of Natal; 2 s, 2 da; *Career* recognised by Lord Lyon in designation 'of Raith and Novar' 1951; served WW II RCS; *Style* - Arthur Munro-Ferguson of Raith and Novar; Novar, Evanton, Ross-shire

MUNRO-LUCAS-TOOTH, Sir Hugh Vere Huntly Duff; 1 Bt (UK 1920), of Bught, Inverness; s of Maj H M Warrand, of Bught, Inverness, by Beatrice Maud, da of Sir Robert Lucas Lucas-Tooth, 1 & penultimate Bt (d 1915, Btcy extinct 1918); *b* 13 Jan 1903; *Educ* Eton, Balliol Oxford; *m* 1925, Laetitia Florence, OBE (1958), JP (d 1978), da of Sir John Findlay, 1 Bt, KBE, JP, DL (d 1930); 1 s, 2 da; *Heir* s, Hugh John Lucas-Tooth; *Career* changed name to Lucas-Tooth 1920, added Munro 1965; MP (C) Isle of Ely 1924-29, Hendon (South) 1945-70, parly under-sec of state Home Office 1952-55; barr Lincoln's Inn 1933; Lt-Col Queen's Own Cameron Highlanders; memb Nat Wales Council 1973-76; *Style* - Sir Hugh Munro-Lucas-Tooth, Bt; Burgate Court, Fordingbridge, Hants

MUNSTER, 6 Earl of (UK 1831); Edward Charles Fitz-Clarence; also Viscount Fitz-Clarence and Baron Tewkesbury (both UK 1831); s of Brig-Gen Charles Fitz-Clarence, VC (ka 1914) and 1 cousin once removed of 5 Earl of Munster (d 1975), also ggs of King William IV by the actress 'Mrs Jordan' (nee Dorothy Bland, gda of Nathaniel Bland, an Irish judge; mistress alike of the arts of comedy and the Duke of Clarence (as he was known before ascending the throne); besides her 10 children by the latter she gave proof of having granted her favours elsewhere in the 4 da she bore Sir Richard Ford - a police magistrate - and the one she had by Richard Daly, manager of the Cork theatre; Mr Jordan was as real as Mrs Gamp's friend Mrs Harris); Lord Munster's mother was Violet, da of Lord Alfred Spencer Churchill, 2 s of 6 Duke of Marlborough; hence Lord Munster is 2 cous to late Sir Winston Churchill and 3 cous twice removed of HM The Queen; *b* 3 Oct 1899; *Educ* Eton; *m* 1, 1925, Monica Sheila Harrington (m dis 1930 and who d 1958), da of Lt-Col Sir Henry Mulleneux Grayson, 1 Bt, KBE; 1 s, 1 da; m 2, 1939, Mrs Vivian Schofield, da of late Benjamin Schofield, JP; *Heir* s, Viscount Fitz-Clarence; *Style* - The Rt Hon the Earl of Munster; 99 Whitelands House, Cheltenham ter, SW3 (☎ 01 730 1301)

MUNTHE, Hon Mrs (Ann Felicity); da of 2 Baron Rea, OBE, PC; *b* 1923; *m* 1945, Malcolm Grane Ludovic Martin Munthe, MC, s of late Dr Axel Munthe; 2 s, 1 da; *Career* European War 1941-5 as 3 Offr WRNS; *Style* - The Hon Mrs Munthe; Southside House, Wimbledon Common; Much Marcle, Herefordshire

MURDOCH, Lady; Barbara Marshall; da of late James Cameron; *m* 1962, as his 2 w, Prof Sir Walter Murdoch, KCMG, CBE (d 1970); *Style* - Lady Murdoch; Blithedale, S Perth, W Australia

MURGATROYD, F Bruce; s of the late Thomas Murgatroyd; *b* 17 Sept 1917; *Educ* Keighley G S, Leeds U; *m* 1941, Marjorie Hannah, nee Holmes; 1 s, 1 da; *Career* served in North Africa, Italy, Greece, chm Courtaulds Woollens Division Ltd 1969-, md Henry Lister & Sons 1958-; *Recreations* golf, travel; *Clubs* Harrogate; *Style* - Bruce Murgatroyd Esq; Millcrest, Fulwith Mill Lane, Harrogate, North Yorkshire

MURISON, Robert Fraser; OBE (1978), QPM (1971), DL (Fife 1975); s of William Murison (d 1937); *b* 15 Feb 1919; *Educ* Dunfermline H S, Glasgow U; *m* 1948, Isobel Stirrat, nee Tennent; 2 da;

Career police officer Lanarkshire Constabulary 1937-42 and 1946-63, Dep Cmdt Scottish Police Coll 1963-65, Ch Constable Fife 1965-, North Zone Home Defence Police Cdr Designate 1974-; *Recreations* gardening; *Style* - Robert Murison Esq OBE QPM DL; 2 Abbots Walk, Kirkcaldy, Fife (☎ 0592 62436)

MURPHY, Lady; Betty Mary; MBE; da of late Col the Rev Thomas Ormsby, DSO, of Milford, Co Mayo; *m* 1922, Sir William Lindsay Murphy, KCMG (d 1965); *Style* - Lady Murphy MBE; Killallagh, PO Bromley, Zimbabwe

MURPHY, Graham Claude; OBE (1971), TD (1952), JP (1957), DL (Salop 1972); s of Owen Downey Murphy (d 1943); *b* 14 March 1911; *Educ* Adams G S Salop; *m* 1955, Joyce, da of Herbert W Baker; 1 da; *Career* served WW II; chartered accountant; dir The Wrekin Brewery Co Ltd 1936-66; memb Wellington (Salop) UDC 1947-65, chm 1955-56; chm Orthopaedic Hosp Oswestry HMC 1964-74; v-chm Salop Area Health Authority 1974-79; *Recreations* golf, breeding race horses; *Style* - Graham Murphy Esq, OBE, TD, JP, DL; Shray Hill, Telford, Salop (☎ Great Bolas 260)

MURPHY, Michael Joseph; s of Joseph (d 1972); *b* 10 Dec 1919; *Educ* Christian Brothers Coll Dun-Laoghaire; *m* 1941, Joan (d 1980); 6 c; *Career* company director; pres Golfing Union of Ireland 1963-65; chm Council of National Golf Unions 1969; dir Ulster Bank Ltd 1969; *Recreations* reading and golf administration; *Clubs* United Services, Dublin, Royal & Ancient Golf; *Style* - Michael Murphy Esq; Hilltop, Ballina, Co Mayo, Ireland (☎ (096) 2174)

MURPHY, Lady Sophia Louise Sydney; *née* Cavendish; da of 11 Duke of Devonshire, MC, PC; *b* 1957; *m* 1979, Anthony William Lindsay Murphy; *Recreations* hunting, hang gliding; *Style* - Lady Sophia Murphy

MURRAY OF NEWHAVEN, Baron (Life Peer UK 1964); Keith Anderson Hope Murray; KCB (1963); s of Rt Hon Lord Murray, CMG, PC, a Scottish Lord of Session (d 1936); *b* 28 July 1903; *Educ* Edinburgh Academy, Edinburgh U, Cornell U NY, Oriel Oxford; *Career* late JP Oxford; formerly dir Bristol Aircraft and Metal Box Co, late Chm U Grants Cttee; Agricultural Economics Research Inst 1929-32; Miny of Food 1939-40; RAF 1949, seconded as dir of food and agriculture Middle East Supply Centre 1942-45; fell and bursar Lincoln Coll Oxford 1937, rector 1944-53; chancellor U of Southampton 1964-74; dir Leverhulme Trust 1965-72; hon fell Oriel and Lincoln Colls Oxford, Downing Cambridge and Birkbeck Coll London; kt 1955; *Style* - The Rt Hon Lord Murray of Newhaven, KCB; 224 Ashley gdns, SW1

MURRAY, Angus; CBE; *Career* dir: Prudential Assurance Co, Rugby Portland Cement Co Ltd, Mercantile Investment Tst Ltd, Talbot Ltd; *Style* - Angus Murray Esq, CBE; Prudential Assurance Co Ltd, 142 Holborn Bars, EC1 (☎ 01 405 9222)

MURRAY, Athol Hollins; s of Richard Hollins Murray, ACA (d 1957); *b* 27 Jan 1922; *Educ* Shrewsbury; *m* 1947, Sheila, da of late Herman Edward Hulme, MBE; 1 s, 1 da; *Career* incorporated valuer, pres Incorporated Soc of Valuers & Auctioneers 1972-73, chm Barrowmore Village Settlement Chester 1979-; *Recreations* golf; *Style* - Athol Murray Esq; Somerville, Hargate dve, Hale, Altrincham, Cheshire (☎ 061 980 3443)

MURRAY, Lady; Christine; da of late J J Auld, of Glasgow; *m* 1939, Brig Sir George David Keith Murray, OBE, MC, TD, JP (d 1965); *Style* - Lady Murray; Borgie House, Castletown, Caithness

MURRAY, Hon Catherine Anne; da of Baron Murray of Gravesend (Life Peer) (d 1980); *b* 1964; *Style* - The Hon Catherine Murray

MURRAY, Maj Charles Graham; MBE (1945), JP (1975), DL (South Yorks 1965); s of Charles Graham Murray (d 1946); *b* 28 Jan 1920; *Educ* St Cyprian's Sch Eastbourne, Stowe; *m* 1949, Susan

Madeleine, da of Willaim Raymond Stephenson of Bennet Grange, Sheffield; 3 da; *Career* Capt RA 1940-46, Maj RA (TA) 1947-52; md Tempered Spring Co Sheffield; *Recreations* walking, gardening; *Clubs* Sheffield; *Style* - Maj Charles Murray, MBE, JP, DL; 545 Fulwood rd, Sheffield (☎ 0742 30 2123)

MURRAY OF OCHTERTYRE, Lady; Deirdra; da of Norman Wood, of Crail, Fife; *m* 1975, Sir William Patrick Keith Murray of Ochtertyre, 11 Bt (d 1977); *Career* folk singer (Dee Dee Woods); *Style* - Lady Murray of Ochtertyre

MURRAY, Hon Mrs (Dinah Karen Crawshay); da of Baron Greenwood of Rossendale, PC, (Life Peer); *b* 1946; *m* 1970, David Murray; *Style* - The Hon Mrs Murray; 62 Belsize Park, NW3

MURRAY, Hon Mrs Diana Lucy; da of Baron Home of the Hirsel, KT, PC, (Life Peer); *b* 1940; *m* 1936, James Archibald Wolfe Murray (m dis 1976); *Style* - The Hon Mrs Diana Murray

MURRAY, Hon Geoffrey Charles; 2 s of 11 Earl of Dunmore; *b* 1949; *m* 1974, Margaret Irene, da of H Bulloch, of Blackwall, Tasmania; *Style* - The Hon Geoffrey Murray; 73 Pomona rd, Riverside, Tasmania

MURRAY, Lady Georgina Dorothea Mary; da of 8 Earl of Mansfield; *b* 10 March 1967; *Style* - Lady Georgina Murray

MURRAY, Hon Mrs (Greta Sheira Bernadette); *née* Grant-Ferris; da of Baron Harvington, PC (Life Peer); *b* 1937; *m* 1, John Frederick Edward Trehearne; m 2, Christopher Mark Henry Murray; *Style* - The Hon Mrs Murray

MURRAY, John Grey; CBE (1975, MBE 1945); s of Thomas Robinson Grey and Dorothy (da of Sir John Murray, KCVO, JP, DL, himself gs of John Murray, the friend and publisher of Byron, who commemorated his connection with the noble poet by christening his suburban villa at Wimbledon 'Newstead' after His Lordship's former country seat); added the name 'Murray' by Deed Poll 1930; *b* 22 Sept 1909; *Educ* Eton, Magdalen Oxford; *m* 1939, Diana, da of Col Bernard James and Hon Angela Kay-Shuttleworth (da of 1 Baron Shuttleworth); 2 s (John b 1941, m Virginia Lascelles; Hallam b 1950), 2 da (Joanna b 1940, m 4 Viscount Mersey, *qv*; Mrs Nigel (Freydis Marianne) Campbell); *Career* late Maj RA, served WW II; publisher, sr dir John Murray (Publishers) 1968-; *Recreations* Byron, archives, music; *Clubs* Brooks's, Pratt's, Beefsteak; *Style* - John Murray Esq, CBE; Cannon Lodge, Cannon Place, NW3 (☎ 01 435 6537)

MURRAY, James Patrick; CMG (1958); s of Brig-Gen E R B Murray (d 1942); *b* 10 Oct 1906; *Educ* St Edward's Sch Oxford, Ch Ch Oxford; *m* 1934, Margaret Ruth, da of late Rev A E Buchanan; 3 s; *Career* formerly sr provincial commissioner N Rhodesia, for N Rhodesia in UK 1961-64 (became Zambia 1964) ret; *Style* - James Murray Esq, CMG; Trewen, Shaftesbury rd, Woking, Surrey (☎ 61988)

MURRAY, Hon James William; s of Earl of Mansfield; *b* 7 June 1969; *Style* - The Hon James Murray

MURRAY, Kenneth Alexander George; CB (1977); s of late George Dickie Murray; *b* 17 June 1916; *Educ* Skenest, Central Schools Aberdeen, Aberdeen U; *m* 1942, Elizabeth Ward Simpson; 1 da; *Career* dir civil Service Selection Bd and Civil Service Commissioner 1964-77; special adviser to the Home Office on Police Service, Prison Service, and Fire Service Selection 1977-; div Home Office Unit 1977-80; *Style* - Kenneth Murray Esq, CB; 15 Melvinshaw, Leatherhead, Surrey (☎ Leatherhead 72995)

MURRAY, Kenelm Gerald Digby; s of Sir Alan John Digby Murray of Blackbarony, 14 Bt; hp of bro, Sir Nigel Murray of Blackbarony, 15 Bt; *b* 9 June 1946; *Educ* St Paul's Sch Argentina, Birmingham U; *m* 1973, Jolande St Clare Byrne, da of Mrs Francis Mellor; 1 s, 1 da; *Style* - Kenelm Murray Esq; 3 Stringham's Copse, Sendmarsh, Ripley, Surrey

MURRAY, Lady Kate Rodel; da of 9 Earl of Dunmore; *b* 9 May 1969; *Style* - Lady Kate Murray

MURRAY, Kenneth Randolph; s of late Arthur Charles Murray (ggs of 4 Earl of Dunmore) and hp to Earldom of bro, 10 Earl; *b* 6 June 1913; *m* 1938, Margaret Joy, nee Cousins; 2 s; *Career* late Sergeant 12/50 Bn Australian Inf; *Style* - Kenneth Murray Esq; Gravelly Beach, W Tamar, Tasmania, Australia

MURRAY OF GRAVESEND, Baroness; Margaret Ann; da of Frederick Charles Wakeford, of Crayford; *m* 1960, Baron Murray of Gravesend (Life Peer) (d 1980); 1 s, 1 da; *Style* - The Rt Hon Lady Murray of Gravesend; 13 Parrock rd, Gravesend, Kent (☎ Gravesend 65958)

MURRAY OF BLACKBARONY, Lady; Mabel Elisabeth; da of late Arthur Bernard Schiele, of Arias, Argentina; *m* 1943, Sir Alan John Digby Murray of Blackbarony, 14 Bt (d 1972); *Style* - Lady Murray of Blackbarony

MURRAY OF BLACKBARONY, Sir Nigel Andrew Digby; 15 Bt (NS 1628), of Blackbarony, Peeblesshire; s of Sir Alan John Digby Murray of Blackbarony, 14 Bt (d 1978); *b* 15 Aug 1944; *Educ* St Paul's Sch Argentina, Salesian Agric Tech Sch, Roy Agricultural Coll Cirencester; *Heir* bro, Kenelm Gerald Digby Murray; *Style* - Sir Nigel Murray of Blackbarony, Bt; Estancia Tinamú, CC5, Arias, FCBM, Provincia de Córdoba, Argentina

MURRAY, Lady; Ottilie Grahame; da of late Tom Anderson, of Glasgow; *m* 1924, Sir (Robert) Alistair Murray, OBE (d 1973); *Style* - Lady Murray; 10 Beechwood ct, Bearsden, by Glasgow

MURRAY OF OCHTERTYRE, Sir Patrick Ian Keith; 12 Bt (NS 1673), of Ochtertyre, Perthshire; s of Sir William Patrick Keith Murray of Ochtertyre, 11 Bt (d 1977); *b* 22 March 1965; *Educ* Christ Coll Brecon Powys; *Heir* kinsman, Maj Peter Keith-Murray; *Style* - Sir Patrick Murray of Ochtertyre, Bt; Old Fford Fawr, Hay-on-Wye, Powys (☎ Hay-on-Wye 736)

MURRAY, Ruby, Lady; Ruby; da of S Hearn, of Helmdon, Northants; *m* 1938, as his 2 w, Lieut-Col Sir Edward Robert Murray, 13 Bt, DSO (d 1958); *Style* - Ruby, Lady Murray

MURRAY, Lady Rebecca Moulin; da of 9 Earl of Dunmore; *b* 11 Dec 1970; *Style* - Lady Rebecca Murray

MURRAY, Rowland William; s and h of Sir Rowland William Patrick Murray, 14 Bt; *b* 22 Sept 1947; *Style* - Rowland Murray Esq

MURRAY, Sir Rowland William Patrick; 14 Bt (NS 1630), of Dunerne, Fifeshire; s of Rowland William Murray (d 1946) and nephew of 13 Bt, DSO (d 1958); *b* 26 Oct 1910; *Educ* U of Georgia; *m* 1944, Josephine Margaret, da of Edward D Murphy; 4 s, 2 da; *Heir* s, Rowland William Murray; *Career* enlisted US Army 1942, 2 Lt 1943, served with 84 Div 335 Inf Regt, ret Capt 1946; *Style* - Sir Rowland Murray, Bt; 239 Kenlock pla, NE, Atlanta, Georgia 30305, USA

MURRAY, Hon Mrs; Hon Sally Ann Hale; *née* Willis; da of Baron Willis (Life Peer); *b* 8 Jan 1951; *Educ* Chislehurst & Sidcup Girls' G S, Crownwoods Sch; *m* 1974, Robin James, s of James Patrick Murray, of Bexley; 1 s (James Edward b 1980); *Career* Civ Serv 1974-77, advice worker (Citizens Advice Bureau) 1977-80; *Recreations* cooking, embroidery, needlework; *Style* - The Hon Mrs Murray; 24 Thirlmere Rise, Bromley, Kent (☎ 01 464 9135)

MURRAY, Brig (Arthur) Stewart Pakington; s of Brevet-Col Arthur Murray, CB, MVO (gs of Rt Rev George Murray, DD, sometime Bp of Sodor and Man, by his w, Lady Sarah Hay, da of 10 Earl of Kinnoull; the Bishop was s of Rt Rev Lord George Murray, DD, himself sometime Bishop of St David's and 2 s of 3 Duke of Atholl, KT) by his 2 w Mabel, da of Frederick Nicolson; hp of 1 cous, twice removed, 10 Duke of Atholl; *b* 9 Sept 1899; *Educ* Eton, Sandhurst; *m* 1961, Winifreda, da of Edmund Bevan, of Hilston Park, Monmouth; *Career* late Gren Gds, served WW II, ret from army 1948; *Style* - Brig

Stewart Murray; Hazelwood Hall, Friston, Saxmundham, Suffolk

MURRAY, Hon Timothy John; s of Baron Murray of Gravesend (Life Peer) (d 1980); *b* 1966; *Style* - The Hon Timothy Murray

MURRAY, Hon Mrs - Hon Virginia; da of Baron Bowden (Life Peer); *b* 3 April 1943; *Educ* E Anglian Girls' Sch, Reading and Manchester Us; *m* 1967, David Ian Murray; *Style* - The Hon Mrs Murray; 61 Woburn Drive, Hale, Cheshire

MURRAY, Hon Mrs (Winifred Mary); *née* Hardinge; da of 2 Baron Hardinge of Penshurst, GCB, GCVO, MC, PC (d 1960); *b* 1923; *m* 1943, Major John Anthony Herningham Murray; 1 s; *Career* late WRNS; *Style* - The Hon Mrs Murray; Woodmancote Manor, Cirencester, Glos

MURRAY-AYNSLEY, Lady; Annamaria Eleanor; da of late Judge Emil Curth, of Trebnitz, Silesia; *m* 1, 1934, Dr Erich Goldberg (d 1942); m 2, 1952 as his 2 w, Sir Charles Murray Murray-Aynsley (d 1967); *Career* MD Heidelberg and Pisa, specialist in children's diseases, hon memb German Paediatric Soc & dist surg St John Ambulance Bde Singapore, prisoner Sumatra 1942-45; *Style* - Lady Murray-Aynsley; 5 Piazza Conti, Florence, Italy

MURTON OF LINDISFARNE, Baron (Life Peer UK 1979); (Henry) Oscar; OBE (1946), TD & Clasp (1947 & 1951), PC (1976), JP (Poole 1963); s of Henry Murton, of Hexham; *b* 8 May 1914; *Educ* Uppingham; *m* 1, 1939, Constance (d 1977), da of Fergus O'L Connell, of Co Durham; 1 s, 1 da; m 2, 1979, Pauline, da of Thomas Keenan, of Jo'burg; *Career* served Roy N'umberland Fusiliers (TA) 1934-39, 1939 Staff Coll Camberley, Lt-Col Gen Staff; dep-sec N Div NCB 1947-49, md Dept Stores NE England 1949-57, MP (C) Poole 1964-79, Assist Govt Whip 1971-72, Ld Commissioner Treasury 1973-76, Dep Spkr & Chm Ways & Means 1976-79; *Recreations* sailing, painting, reading history; *Style* - Rt Hon Lord Murton of Lindisfarne, OBE, TD & Clasp, PC, JP; 5 Seaview Court, 125 North rd, Poole, Dorset (☎ 0202 730243); 49 Carlisle Mansions, Carlisle pla, SW1 (☎ 01 834 8226)

MURTON, Hon Henry Peter John Connell; s of Baron Murton of Lindisfarne (Life Peer); *b* 1941; *m* 1962, Louisa, da of late Major Percy Montagu Nevile, of Skelbrooke Park, Yorks; *Style* - The Hon Henry Murton

MUSGRAVE, Christopher John Shane; s and h of Sir Richard James Musgrave, 7 Bt; *b* 23 Oct 1959; *Style* - Christopher Musgrave Esq

MUSGRAVE, Sir Christopher Patrick Charles; 15 Bt (E 1611), of Hartley Castle, Westmorland; s of Sir Charles Musgrave, 14 Bt (d 1970); *b* 14 Apr 1949; *m* 1978, Megan, da of Walter Inman; *Heir* bro, Julian Nigel Chardin Musgrave; *Style* - Sir Christopher Musgrave, Bt; c/o Williams & Glyn's Bank Ltd, Silver st, Kingston upon Hull, E Yorks

MUSGRAVE, Julian Nigel Chardin; s of Sir Charles Musgrave, 14 Bt (d 1970); h to Btcy of bro, Sir Christopher Patrick Charles Musgrave, 15 Bt; *b* 8 Dec 1951; *Style* - Julian Musgrave Esq

MUSGRAVE, Hon Mrs - Hon Rosemary Jane; *née* Watkinson; da of 1 Viscount Watkinson, CH, PC; *b* 1947; *m* 1976, Barrie Musgrave, 1 s; *Style* - The Hon Mrs Musgrave; Tredown Farm, S Petherwin, Launceston, Cornwall

MUSGRAVE, Sir Richard James; 7 Bt (I 1782), of Tourin, Waterford; s of Sir Christopher Norman Musgrave, 6 Bt, OBE (d 1956); *b* 10 Feb 1922; *Educ* Stowe; *m* 1958, Maria, da of late Col M Cambanis, of Athens; 2 s, 4 da; *Heir* s, Christopher John Shane Musgrave; *Career* 2 Lt 1940, served 1940-45 (India, Middle East), Capt Poona Horse, 17 Queen Victoria's Own Cavalry; *Recreations* shooting, bridge; *Clubs* Kildare Street (Dublin); *Style* - Sir Richard Musgrave, Bt; Riverstown, Tara, Co Meath, Eire (☎ Balrath 21)

MUSKER, Lady Rose Diana; *née* Lambton; da of Antony Lambton (6 Earl of Durham, peerages disclaimed 1970); *b* 1952; *m* 1979, Herbert Oliver Fitzroy Musker; *Style* - Lady Rose Musker

MUSKERRY, 8 Baron (I 1781); Sir Hastings Fitzmaurice Tilson Deane; 13 Bt (I 1710); s of 3 (but only surviving) s of 7 Baron Muskerry (d 1966); *b* 12 March 1907; *Educ* Sandford Park Sch Dublin, Trin Coll Dublin; *m* 1944, Betty Fairbridge, da of late Wilfred George Reckless Palmer, of S Africa; 1 s, 1 da; *Heir* s, Hon Robert Fitzmaurice Deane; *Career* Capt SAMC; held various Hosp appointments 1934-39, specialised in Radiology, London U 1946-49, consultant radiologist Transvaal Admin to Eastern Transvaal Hospitals 1949-57, radiologist to The Limerick Regional Health Authority 1961-77 and to Mid-Western Health Bd; *Style* - The Rt Hon the Lord Muskerry; Springfield Castle, Drumcollogher, Co Limerick, Ireland (☎ 5)

MUSKERRY, Muriel, Baroness; Muriel Doreen Sellars; da of late Arthur Gibson Simpson, of Carlisle; *m* 1964, as his 2 w, 7 Baron Muskerry (d 1966); *Clubs* Cowdray and Irish; *Style* - The Rt Hon Muriel, Lady Muskerry; 44 Woodlands rd, Liverpool 17

MUSPRATT, Lady; Rosamonde; da of late Sir Edward Arthur Barry, 2 Bt; *b* 1901; *m* 1925, Gen Sir Sydney Frederick Muspratt, KCB, CIE, DSO (d 1972); 2 s; *Style* - Lady Muspratt; 40 Broad st, Alresford, Hants

MUSSELL, Hon Mrs; Hon (Margaret) Jean; *née* Shaw; da of 2 Baron Craigmyle (d 1944); *b* 20 Feb 1915; *m* 1949, (Laurence) Shirl Mussell (d 1956); 3 da (1 adopted); *Style* - The Hon Mrs Mussell; Dyke Croft, Ravenglass, Cumberland

MUSSON, Hon Lady; Hon Elspeth Lorraine; *née* Bailey; da of late Hon Herbert Crawshay Bailey (4 s of 1 Baron Glanusk) and sis of 4 Baron; *b* 1915; *m* 1939, Gen Sir Geoffrey Randolph Dixon Musson, GCB, CBE, DSO, *qv*; 1 s 1 da; raised to the rank of a Baron's da 1948; *Style* - The Hon Lady Musson; Provost Hill, Hurstbourne Tarrant, Andover

MUSSON, Gen Sir Geoffrey Randolph Dixon; GCB (1970), CBE (1945), DSO (1944); s of Robert Dixon Musson (d 1957); *b* 9 June 1910; *Educ* Shrewsbury, Trin Hall Cambridge; *m* 1939, Hon Elspeth Lorraine (granted title, rank and precedence of a Baron's da which would have been hers had her father survived to succeed to the title of Baron Glanusk), da of Hon Herbert Crawshay Bailey, JP (d 1936) and Hon Mrs Bailey (d 1948); 1 s, 1 da; *Career* 2 Lt KSLI 1930, Brig 1944, cmd Commonwealth Forces in Korea 1954-55, Maj-Gen 1958, ch of staff MELF 1959-61, Miny of Defence 1967-70, Gen 1968, ret 1970; Col KSLI 1963-68; Col Light Inf 1968-72; v-chm Nat Savings Ctee, chm HM Forces Savings Ctee 1970-78, v-pres Roy Patriotic Fund Corpn; pres Victory (Services) Club 1970-80; *Style* - Gen Sir Geoffrey Musson GCB CBE DSO; Barn Cottage, Hurstbourne Tarrant, Andover, Hants (☎ Hurstbourne Tarrant 354); Provost Hill, Hurstbourne Tarrant, Andover, Hants

MUSSON, Samuel Dixon; CB (1963), MBE (1943); s of Robert D Musson; *b* 1 April 1908; *Educ* Shrewbury Sch, Trin Hall Cambridge; *m* 1949, Joan Isabella da Col Delme Davis-Evans; *Career* barr 1930, princ assist slr Miny of Health 1958-63, ch registrar Friendly Societies and Industrial Assur Cmmn 1963-72; *Recreations* country pursuits, farming, gardening and racing; *Clubs* Savile; owner of racehorse 'Holsworthy'; *Style* - Samuel Musson Esq, CB, MBE; Prospect Hill Farm, Headley, Bordon, Hants (☎ Headley Down 713183)

MYDDELTON, Lady Mary Margaret Elizabeth; da of late Major Lord Charles George Francis Mercer Nairne, MVO (2 s of 5 Marquess of Lansdowne) and sis of 8 Marquess; *b* 1910; *m* 1931, Lt-Col Ririd Myddelton, CVO; 2 s 1 da; *Style* - Lady Mary Myddelton; Chirk Castle, nr Wrexham, N Wales

MYDDELTON, Hon Mrs (Sarah Cecily); *née* Allsopp; da of 5 Baron Hindlip; *b* 1944; *m* 1967, Hugh Robert Myddelton, s of Lt-Col Ririd Myddelton and Lady Mary Myddelton, *qv* (sis of 8 Marquess of Lansdowne); *Style* - The Hon Mrs Myddelton; 139 Holland Park Ave, W11

MYERS, Lady; Elsie; *m* 1917, Sir James Eckersley Myers, OBE (d 1958); *Style* - Lady Myers; 28 Victoria Park, Colwyn Bay, Denbighshire

MYERS, Prof Sir Rupert Horace; KBE (1981, CBE 1976); s of H Myers; *Educ* Melbourne H S, Melbourne U; *m* 1944, Io Edwina King; 1 s, 3 da; *Career* Vice-Chllr and Principal U of New South Wales 1969-81, Fndn Prof of Metallurgy 1969-81; Hon LLD Strathclyde 1973, Hon DSc Wollongong 1976; FTS 1979; *Style* - Prof Sir Rupert Myers, KBE; 135 Neerim rd, Castlecove, NSW 2069, Australia

MYNORS, Sir Humphrey Charles Baskerville; 1 Bt (UK 1964) of Treago, Co Hereford; s of Rev A B Mynors, of Langley Burrell, Wilts; *b* 28 July 1903; *Educ* Marlborough, CCC Cambridge; *m* 1939, Lydia Marian, da of Prof Sir Ellis H Minns; 1 s, 4 da; *Heir* s, Richard Baskerville Mynors; *Career* joined Bank of England 1933, sec 1939, dir 1949, dep govr 1954-64; chm Finance Corpn for Industry Ltd 1964-74; formerly dir Pilkington Bros Ltd; *Style* - Sir Humphrey Mynors, Bt; Treago, St Weonards, Hereford (☎ St Weonards 208)

MYNORS, Sir Roger (Aubrey Baskerville); s of Rev Aubrey Baskerville Mynors (d 1937) and Margery Musgrave, nee Harvey, sis of Sir Ernest Harvey, 1 Bt; er bro of Sir Humphrey Mynors, 1 Bt; *b* 28 July 1903; *Educ* Eton, Balliol Coll Oxford; *m* 1945, Lavinia Sybil, sis of Lady Home of the Hirsel and da of Very Rev Cyril Argentine Alington, Dean of Durham and sometime Headmaster of Eton (d 1955); *Career* kt 1963, FBA 1944, Fellow of Balliol Coll Oxford 1926-44, Principal HM Treasury 1940-44; Professor of Latin Cambridge 1944-53, Oxford 1953-70; *Style* - Sir Roger Mynors; Treago, St Weonards, Hereford

MYNORS, Richard Baskerville; s and h of Sir Humphrey Charles Baskerville Mynors, 1 Bt; *b* 5 May 1947; *Educ* Marlborough Coll, Corpus Christi Coll Cambridge; *m* 1970, Fiona Bridget, da of Rt Rev George Edmund Reindorp, DD, Lord Bishop of Salisbury; 2 da (Alexandra Fiona b 1975, Frances Veronica b 1978); *Career* Dir of Music Wolverhampton GS 1973-81, Dir of Music Merchant Taylors' Sch Crosby 1981-; *Recreations* gardening, DIY, building pipe organs; *Style* - Richard Mynors Esq; Beggars Roost, Cross rd, Albrighton, Wolverhampton (☎ Albrighton 3645)

MYRDDIN-EVANS, George Watkin; s of Sir Guildhaume Myrddin-Evans KCMG, CB (d 1964); *b* 26 March 1924; *Educ* Rugby, Ch Ch Oxford; *m* 1966, Anna Katharine, nee Buxton; 1 s; *Career* memb Lloyd's 1951-, chm Gardner Mountain & Capel-Cure Agencies 1973-, dir M C Winn Agencies, dir C R Hill Agencies 1978; *Recreations* shooting, fishing, real tennis; *Clubs* White's, Pratt's, City of London, Cardiff & County; *Style* - George Myrddin-Evans Esq; 8 Pembridge Place, W2 (☎ 229 9809); Church House, Llandefalle, Brecon, Powys (☎ Llyswen 210)

N

NAAS, Lord; Charles Diarmuidh John Bourke; s and h of 10 Earl of Mayo; *b* 11 June 1953; *Educ* St Aubyn's Rottingdean, Portora Roy Sch Enniskillen, Queen's U Belfast, Bolton St Coll of Technology Dublin; *m* 1975, Marie Antoinette Cronnelly; 1 da; *Style* - Lord Naas; Doon House, Maam, Co Galway, Eire

NABARRO, Eric John Nunes; JP (1972); s of Joseph Nunes Nabarro (d 1948); *b* 5 Apr 1917; *Educ* Clifton Coll; *m* 1947, Cecily, da of Henry Orenstein (d 1937); 1 s, 1 da; *Career* Capt RA Iceland, N Africa, Italy, sr ptnr G Nabarro & Co 1960-, tres Bd of Deps of British Jews 1973-79; *Recreations* travel, golf, jogging; *Clubs* MCC, RAC; *Style* - Eric Nabarro Esq, JP; 11 The Marlowes, NW8 (☎ 01 586 1240)

NABARRO, Dr John David Nunes; s of Dr David Nunes Nabarro (d 1958); *b* 21 Dec 1915; *Educ* Oundle, U Coll London; *m* 1948, Joan Margaret, nee Cockrell; 2 s, 2

da; *Career* acting Lt-Col RAMC, TA, physician, consultant physician Middlesex Hospital, honorary consultant physician Roy Prince Alfred Hospital Sydney, dir Cobbold Laboratories, dir Middlesex Hospital Medical Sch, fell U Coll London, chm Jt Consultants Ctee; *Recreations* gardening; *Style* - Dr John Nabarro; 33 Woodside av, N12 (☎ 01 445 7925)

NAGDA, Kanti; s of Vershi Bhoja Nagda of India; *b* 1 May 1946; *Educ* City H S Kampala Uganda, Coll Further Education Chippenham, E African U Uganda; *m* 1972, Bhagwati, nee Desai; 2 children; *Career* accountant Hollander Hyams Ltd 1972-, sec gen Confederation of Indian Org (UK) 1975-, pres Anglo-Indian Circle 1973-, hon editorial consultant Int Asian Guide and Who's Who 1975-, assist ed Oshwah News 1975-; *Recreations* cricket, photography; *Style* - Kanti Nagda Esq; 11 North av, Harrow, Middlesex, HA2 7AE (☎ 01 427 0696)

NAGGAR, Hon Mrs - Hon Marion; *née* Samuel; da of Baron Samuel of Wych Cross (Life Peer) ; *b* 1944; *m* 1964, Guy Antony Naggar; *Style* - The Hon Mrs Naggar; 61 Avenue rd, NW8

NAIRAC, Lady Jane Fortune Margaret; *née* Ogilvy; da of 13 Earl of Airlie, DL; *b* 24 June 1955; *m* 1980, François Nairac; *Style* - Lady Jane Nairac

NAIRN, Sir (Michael) George; 3 Bt (UK 1904), TD; s of Sir Michael Nairn, 2 Bt, JP, DL (d 1952); *b* 30 Jan 1911; *Educ* Trin Coll Glenalmond; *m* 1936, Helen, da of Maj Ernest Bruce, MC; 2 s; *Heir* s, Michael Nairn; *Career* DL Fife 1955-70; memb Roy Co Archers (Queen's Bodyguard for Scotland); chm Michael Nairn & Greenwich 1958-62, Nairn Williamson Hldgs 1962-70; *Clubs* Caledonian; *Style* - Sir George Nairn, Bt, TD; Pitcarmick, Bridge of Cally, Blairgowrie, Perths (☎ Strath Ardle 214)

NAIRN, Michael; s and h of Sir (Michael) George Nairn, 3 Bt, TD; *b* 1 July 1938; *Educ* Eton and INSEAD; *m* 1972, Diana Gordon, da of F Leonard Bligh, of Pejar Park, Woodhouselee, NSW; 2 s, 1 da; *Style* - Michael Nairn Esq; 39 Ann st, Edinburgh

NAIRNE, Lady (12 holder of S Lordship cr 1681); Lady Katherine Evelyn Constance Bigham; *née* Mercer Nairne; da of 6 Marquess of Lansdowne DSO MVO (d 1936) by his w Elizabeth, da of Sir Edward Hope, KCB (ggs of 2 Earl of Hopetoun); suc bro, 7 Marquess (ka 1944), in the Lordship of Nairne; *b* 22 June 1912; *m* 1933, 3 Viscount Mersey (d 1979); 3 s (including 4 Viscount); *Heir* s, 4 Viscount Mersey; *Style* - The Rt Hon Katherine, Viscountess Mersey; Bignor Park, Pulborough, Sussex

NAIRNE, Sir Patrick Dalmahoy; GCB (1981, KCB 1975, CB 1971), MC (1943); s of Lt-Col C Nairne (d 1966), of Plover Hill, Compton, Winchester; *b* 15 Aug 1921 *Educ* Radley Coll, Univ Coll Oxford; *m* 1948, Penelope Chauncy, da of Lt-Col R F Bridges, of Oxford; 3 s, 3 da; *Career* priv sec to First Lord Admiralty 1958-60; private sec to Sec of State for Defence 1965-67; Dep Under-Sec of State Defence 1965-67; Permanent Sec Dept Health and Social Security 1975-81, ret; *Style* - Sir Patrick Nairne, GCB, MC; South Lodge, Knipp Hill, Cobham, Surrey (☎ Cobham 2401)

NALL, Edward William Joseph; s and h of Sir Michael Joseph Nall, 2 Bt; *b* 24 Oct 1952; *Educ* Eton; *Career* Capt 13/18 Roy Hussars; *Style* - Edward Nall Esq; c/o Hoveringham Hall, Nottingham

NALL, Sir Michael Joseph; 2 Bt (UK 1954), of Hoveringham, Co Nottingham, DL (Notts 1970); s of Col Sir Joseph Nall, 1 Bt, DSO, TD (d 1958); *b* 6 Oct 1921; *Educ* Wellington; *m* 1951, Angela Loveday Hanbury, da of Air Chief Marshal Sir Alex Coryton, KCB, KBE, MVO, DFC; 2 s; *Heir* s, Edward William Joseph Nall; *Career* joined RN 1939, served 1939-45, Lt Cdr 1950, ret 1961; gen man Guide Dogs for the Blind Assoc 1961-64; High Sheriff Notts 1971; pres Nottingham Chamber of Commerce & Industry 1972-74; banker; *Style* - Sir Michael Nall, Bt, DL; Hoveringham Hall, Nottingham (☎ Lowdham 3634)

NALL-CAIN, Hon David Lawrence Robert; s of 2 Baron Brocket (d 1967); *b* 1930; *Educ* Eton and Magdalene Coll, Cambridge; *m* 1958, Hon Katherine Elizabeth Palmer, da of Maj Visc Wolmer (d on active service 1942); 1 s, 2 da; *Career* 2 Lt 12 Royal Lancers 1949; JP (Cheshire 1964); *Clubs* Cavalry; *Style* - The Hon David Nall-Cain JP; Crosby Farm, Bride, IOM

NALL-CAIN, Hon David Michael Anthony; s of Hon Ronald Charles Manus Nall-Cain (d 1961) and gs of 2 Baron Brocket (d 1967); *b* 5 April 1953; *Educ* Harrow; granted precedence of a Baron's son 1969; *Style* - The Hon David Nall-Cain

NALL-CAIN, Hon Mrs (Katherine Elizabeth); *née* Palmer; da of Major Viscount Wolmer (s and heir of 3 Earl of Selborne but who was killed in action 1942, predeceasing his f) by Priscilla (who m 2 the 4 Baron Newton), da of Capt John Egerton Warburton; also sister of 4 Earl of Selborne; *b* 24 July 1938; *m* 1958, Hon David Lawrence Robert Nall-Cain, qv; *Style* - The Hon Mrs Nall-Cain; Crosby Farm, Bride, Isle of Man (☎ Kirk Andreas (STD Code 062 488) 514)

NALL-CAIN, Hon Richard Philip Christopher; s of Hon Ronald Charles Manus Nall-Cain (d 1961) and gs of 2 Baron Brockett (d 1967); *b* 5 April 1953; *Educ* Eton; *m* 1978, Juliet, da of J E V Forester; *Career* late 2 Lt, 12 Roy Lancers; granted precedence of a Baron's son 1969; *Style* - The Hon Richard Nall-Cain; Mells Park, Frome, Somerset

NANCE, His Honour Judge; Francis James; JP (Lancs 1963); s of Herbert James Nance of S Africa (d 1922); *b* 5 Sept 1915; *Educ* St Francis Xavier's Coll Liverpool, Liverpool U; *m* 1943, Margaret Gertrude, nee Roe; 2 s; *Career* Capt Roy Signals NW Europe 1940-45, barr 1936, dep chm Lancs Quater Session 1963-66, cmmr Liverpool and Manchester Crown Cts 1966-71, county ct judge 1966-, circuit judge 1972-; *Recreations* chess, travel; *Clubs* Athenaeum (Liverpool); *Style* - His Hon Judge Nance, JP; 37 Warren Drive, Wallasey, Merseyside, L45 0JW (☎ 051 639 2915)

NANDA, Pramod Kumar; s of late M L Nanda; *b* 28 Sept 1932; *Educ* Agra U (BCom); *m* 1962, Asha, da of H L Sibal, sr advocate, of Chandigarh; 1 child; *Career* dir Metal Box 1981, chm Metal Box Overseas Ltd 1981-; dir Bata India Ltd 1973-81, chm 1976-81; FCA, FCS; *Clubs* Oriental, Bengal (Calcutta), Delhi Gymkhana; *Style* - Pramod Nanda Esq; 19 Randolph ave, W9 (☎ 01 289 3654); Metal Box Ltd, Queens House, Forbury rd, Reading (☎ 581177)

NAPIER OF MAGDALA, 5 Baron (UK 1868); Brig Robert John Napier; OBE (1944); s of 4 Baron (d 1948); *b* 16 June 1904; *Educ* Wellington; *m* 1939, Elizabeth Marion, da of late Edmund Henderson Hunt, FRCS; 3 s, 2 da; *Heir* s, Hon Robert Alan Napier; *Career* Lt RE 1926, attached training Bn KGO Bengal Sappers and Miners 1934, Capt 1935, Lt-Col 1942, Col 1951, served in Waziristan 1936-37 & Italy 1944-45, Brig 1956, ret 1959; *Recreations* fishing, shooting, skiing; *Style* - Brig The Rt Hon the Lord Napier of Magdala, OBE; 8 Mortonhall rd, Edinburgh EH9 3HW (☎ 031 667 1687)

NAPIER, Maj Hon Alastair John George Malcolm; TD (1947); s of 12 Lord Napier and (3) Ettrick (d 1941); *b* 1909; *Educ* Merchiston and Sherborne; *m* 1933, Geraldine, da of late Jas Dunlop; 1 da; *Career* Lt 51 (Highland) divnl engrs (TA) 1931, Capt RE 1940; Maj 1944; Kenya Min of Works (formerly PWD) 1950-65; *Style* - Major The Hon Alastair Napier; P O Box 14222, Nairobi, Kenya

NAPIER, Hon Andrew Perceval; s of 5 Baron Napier of Magdala, OBE; *b* 1947; *Educ* Winchester and Imperial Coll; *Style* - The Hon Andrew Napier; 8 Mortonhall rd, Edinburgh EH9 2HW (☎ 031 667 1687)

NAPIER, Barbara Langmuir; OBE (1975); da of the late James Langmuir Napier; *b* 21 Feb 1914; *Educ* Hillhead H S Glasgow, Glasgow U; *Career* JP 1955-80, oganising secretary Redlands Hospital Glasgow 1937-41, warden Queen Margaret Hall Glasgow U 1941-44, gen advisor to Women Students 1942-64, senior tutor to Women Students 1964-74, retd 1974; *Recreations* books, radio, cats, dogs; *Clubs* College (Glasgow); *Style* - Miss Barbara Napier OBE; 67 Brisbane st, Largs, Ayrshire (☎ Largs 675495)

NAPIER, Hon Charles Malcolm; s of 13 Lord Napier and 4 Ettrick, TD (d 1954); *b* 1933; *Educ* Canford; *m* 1969, Lady Mariota Cecilia Murray, da of 7 Earl of Mansfield and Mansfield (d 1971); 3 da; *Career* formerly Lt 1 Roy Dragoons, served 1952-53; chm Iyati Gold Mining Co (Pty) Ltd; dir Caravan Manufacturers Ltd, Viking Travel Ltd and General Belting Ltd; founder-memb of Council of Anglo-Rhodesian Soc; *Clubs* Cavalry, Pratt's, Turf; *Style* - The Hon Charles Napier; Hanover pla, 314 Rhodes ave, Salisbury, Zimbabwe; Bardmony House, Alyth, Perthshire

NAPIER, Hon Ermine Maude; da of 4 Baron Napier of Magdala (d 1948); *b* 1907; *Style* - The Hon Ermine Napier; c/o Barclays Bank Ltd, 30 Sloane Sq, SW1; Jack's Piece, Ogdens, nr Fordingbridge, Hants

NAPIER, Master of; Hon Francis David Charles Napier; s and h of 14 Lord Napier and (5) Ettrick; *b* 3 Nov 1962; *Style* - The Master of Napier

NAPIER, Hon Georgina Helena Katherine; da of 14 Lord Napier and (5) Ettrick; *b* 21 Feb 1969

NAPIER, Hon Hugh Lenox; s of 13 Lord Napier and (4) Ettrick, TD (d 1954); *b* 1943; *Educ* privately; *Style* - The Hon Hugh Napier; Glenfarg House, Dron, Perthshire (☎ Abernethy 233)

NAPIER, Hon Mrs - Hon Jean; da of 21 Baron Hastings (d 1956); *b* 1917; *m* 1945, Lt-Cdr Mark Napier, RN (ret) (d 1962); 1 s ; *Style* - The Hon Mrs Napier; 13 Harding rd, Langley Vale, Epsom Downs, Surrey

NAPIER, John Archibald Lennox; s and h of Sir William Archibald Napier of Merchistoun, 13 Bt; *b* 6 Dec 1946; *Educ* St Stithians, Witwatersrand U Johannesburg; *m* 1969, Erica, da of late Kurt Kingsfield, of Johannesburg; 1 s, 1 da; *Style* - John Napier Esq; Merchiston Croft, PO Box 65177, Benmore 2010, Transvaal, S Africa

NAPIER, Hon John Greville; s of 13 Lord Napier and (4 Baron) Ettrick; *b* 3 Jan 1939; *Educ* Fettes; *m* 1968, Juliet Elizabeth Hargreaves, da of Sir Alexander Durie, CBE; 2 da; *Career* joined Christie Manson & Woods Ltd 1958; man of H W Keil Ltd 17th & 18th Century Furniture 1960-68; md Napier Antiques Ltd 17th, 18th & 19th Century Furniture; *Recreations* travel, genealogy, swimming, shooting; *Style* - The Hon John Napier; Underhill, Treyford, nr Midhurst, Sussex (☎ Harting 470)

NAPIER, Sir Joseph William Lennox; 4 Bt (UK 1867), of Merrion Sq, Dublin, OBE (1944); s of Lt-Col Sir William Lennox Napier, 3 Bt (ka at the Dardanelles 1915); *b* 1895; *Educ* Rugby, Jesus Cambridge; *m* 1931, Isabel Muriel, da of Maj Henry Siward Balliol Surtees, JP, DL (d 1955), of Redworth Hall, Darlington; 2 s; *Heir* s, Robert Surtees Napier; *Career* served WW I & II, Lt-Col AQMG, HQ Staff E Command; *Club* Alpine; *Style* - Sir Joseph Napier, Bt, OBE; Berystede Cottage, S Ascot, Berks (☎ 22300); 17 Cheyne gdns, SW3 (☎ 01 352 4968)

NAPIER, Hon Louisa Mary Constance; da of 14 Lord Napier and (5) Ettrick; *b* 5 Feb 1961; *Style* - The Hon Louisa Napier

NAPIER, Lady Mariota (Cecilia); *née* Murray; da of 7 Earl of Mansfield and Mansfield (d 1971); *b* 1945; *m* 1969, Hon (Charles) Malcolm Napier, *qv*; *Style* - Lady Mariota Napier; Bardmony House, Alyth, Perthshire; Hanover Place, 314 Rhodes ave, Salisbury, Zimbabwe

NAPIER, Hon Michael Elibank; s of 5 Baron Napier of Magdala, OBE; *b* 1953; *Educ* Trinity Coll Glenalmond; *Style* - The Hon Michael Napier

NAPIER, Hon Nicholas Alexander

John; s of 14 Lord Napier and Ettrick; *b* 27 Feb 1971

NAPIER, Hon Mrs Neville - Helen Catherine; *née* Sanderson; *m* 1967, as his 2 w, Cdr Hon Neville Napier RN (d 1970, s of 12 Lord Napier & Ettrick); *Style* - The Hon Mrs Neville Napier; Kippilaw, St Boswells, Roxburghshire

NAPIER, Hon Robert Alan; s and h of 5 Baron Napier of Magdala, OBE; *b* 1940; *Educ* Winchester and St John's Coll, Cambridge; *m* 1964, Frances Clare, da of A F Skinner; 1s, 1 da; *Clubs* Leander; *Style* - The Hon Robert Napier; 1 Thames st, Hampton, Middx TW12 2EW

NAPIER, Robert Surtees; s and h of Sir Joseph William Lennox Napier, 4 Bt, OBE; *b* 5 March 1932; *Educ* Eton; *m* 1971, Jennifer Beryl, da of late H Warwick Daw; 1 s; *Career* dir Charterhouse Japhet Ltd, Merchant Bankers; assumed forename of Surtees in lieu of those of Aubone Siward; *Style* - Robert Napier Esq; 107 Woodsford sq, W14; Rose Tree Cottage, Lowar Upham, nr Southampton

NAPIER, Brig Vivian John Lennox; MC (1919), DL (Brecknock 1958); 3 s of Maj Sir William Lennox Napier, 3 Bt (ka 1915); *b* 13 July 1898; *Educ* Uppingham, RMC Sandhurst; *m* 1958, Marion Avis, da of Lt-Col Sir John Lloyd, MC; *Career* Brig E Africa, district cmmr Kenya, V-Lt Brecknock 1964-74, OStJ; *Recreations* fishing; *Style* - Brig Vivian Napier, MC, DL; Ty Nant, Groesffordd, Brecon, Powys

NAPIER OF MERCHISTOUN, Sir William Archibald; 13 Bt (NS 1627), of Merchistoun; s of Sir Robert Archibald Napier, 12 Bt (d 1965); *b* 19 July 1915; *Educ* Cheam Sch, Stowe; *m* 1942, Kathleen Mabel, da of late Reginald Greaves, of Tafelberg, Cape, S Africa; 1 s; *Heir* s, John Archibald Lennox Napier; *Career* consulting engineer; served 1939-45 War as Capt S African Engineers in Middle East; *Clubs* Carlton (London), Johannesburg Country, Rand and Wanderers; *Style* - Sir William Napier of Merchistoun, Bt; Merchiston Croft, PO Box 65177, Benmore, Transvaal 2010, S Africa (☎ Johannesburg 7832651); c/o Nat Westminster Bank Ltd, Kensington High st, W8

NAPIER AND ETTRICK, 14 Lord (Napier S 1627) & 5 Baron (Ettrick UK 1872); Sir Francis Nigel Napier; 11 Bt (S 1666), of Thirlestane, MVO (1980), DL (Selkirk 1974, Ettrick and Lauderdale 1975); s of 13 Lord Napier and Ettrick, TD, JP, DL (d 1954, eleventh in descent from 1 Lord, himself s of John Napier of Merchistoun; the latter combined the callings of engineer (his screw for ridding coal mines of water was invaluable), theologian (his *Plaine Discovery of the Whole Revelation of St John* was far in advance of anything by contemporaries), agriculturist (he did useful work on manures), thaumaturge (he entered into a compact to discover buried treasure by his arts), man of property (he had amassed a considerable estate by his death), and, chiefly, mathematician (he invented logarithms); when these rôles are taken together with his part as experimenter with secret weapons for use against the Spaniards, it only remains to ponder whether he more resembles the Sage of Syracuse or of Vinci, and be known as the Archimedes, or the Leonardo, of the North; the Napiers of Merchistoun are co-heirs general of the ancient Celtic Earls of Lennox); *b* 5 Dec 1930; *Educ* Eton, RMA Sandhurst; *m* 1958, Delia, da of Archibald Pearson, of Upper Sattenham, Surrey; 2 s, 2 da; *Heir* s, Master of Napier; *Career* Maj Scots Gds, Malaya 1950-51; Adj 1 Bn Scots Gds 1955-57, ret 1960; Equerry to late Duke of Gloucester 1958-60, to HRH the Princess Margaret, Countess of Snowdon 1973- & Private Sec Comptroller and Equerry 1974-; in the City 1960-62; Dep Ceremonial and Protocol Secretary Commonwealth Relations Office 1962-66; memb Roy Co of Archers (Queen's Bodyguard for Scotland) 1953-; Pres St John Ambulance Assoc & Bde London 1975-; Conservative Whip House of Lords 1970-71; hon treasurer People's Dispensary for Sick Animals; liveryman of Worshipful Co of Grocers 1963; *Clubs* White's, Pratt's; *Style* - The Rt Hon the Lord Napier and Ettrick, MVO, DL; Forest Lodge, The Great Park, Windsor (☎ 61262); Thirlestane, Ettrick,

Selkirkshire; Apartment 2, St James's Palace, SW1 (☎ 01 930 0242)

NAPIER AND ETTRICK, Dowager Lady; (Violet) Muir; da of Sir Percy Wilson Newson, 1 & last Bt (d 1950); *b* 1909; *m* 1958, 13 Lord Napier and (4) Ettrick, TD (d 1954); 4 s; *Career* Nat Pres YWCA Scotland; *Style* - The Rt Hon The Dowager Lady Napier and Ettrick; Glenfarg House, Dron, Perthshire (☎ Abernethy 233)

NAPOLITAN, Leonard; CB (1970); s of the late Domenic Napolitan; *b* 9 April 1919; *Educ* Highbury County Sch, London U; *m* 1945, Dorothy, nee Laycock; 2 da; *Career* assist agricultural economist, U of Bristol 1947-48; entered Miny of Ag and Fish 1948, and ret in 1977 as dir of Economics & Statistics; *Style* - Leonard Napolitan Esq, CB; High Lee, Sandford av, Church Stretton, Shropshire (☎ Church Stretton 722303)

NAPPER, Capt Derek William; CBE (1973, MBE 1946); s of William Ernest Napper (d 1974); *b* 28 Aug 1922; *Educ* RN Coll Dartmouth, RN Coll Greenwich; *m* 1945, Isobel, nee Cowie; 4 s; *Career* Capt RN (Cdre) 1936-73, despatches 1942, Ch of Staff to Cdr Far East Fleet, Dir Defence Operational Plans MOD, dir of customer training Racal Electronics, gen man administration West of England Ship Owners Mutual Insurance Assoc 1973-79; *Recreations* rugby football, boxing, judo, karate; *Clubs* Army and Navy, Roy Commonwealth Soc; *Style* - Capt Derek Napper CBE RN; Thorn, Melton, Woodbridge, Suffolk (☎ 2448)

NASH, (Denis Frederic) Ellison; AEA (1944); s of the late Frederic Arthur Nash; *b* 10 Feb 1913; *Educ* Dulwich Coll, St Bartholomew's Hospital Med Coll, London U; *m* 1938, Joan Mary, nee Andrew; 2 s, 2 da; *Career* consulting surgn St Bartholomew's Hosp; late Dean of Medical Coll, University of London; *Recreations* gardening, photography, work with disabled; *Clubs* Guild of Freemen, City of London; *Style* - Ellison Nash Esq, FRCS; 28 Hawthorne rd, Bickley, Kent (☎ 01 467 1142)

NASH, John Edward; s of Joseph Ronald Nash (d 1977); *b* 25 June 1925; *Educ* Sydney U, Balliol Coll Oxford; *m* 1947, Ralda Everard Tyndall, nee Herring; 2 s (Antony James, Jeremy Robert), 2 da (Regina Jane, Camilla Kate); *Career* chm SG Warburg Bank AG Zurich 1977-, dir SG Warburg & Co Ltd London 1977-, dir Reckitt & Colman Ltd 1966-73 and 1977-, chm Mercury Money Market Trust 1978-, dir Monetary Affairs EEC Cmmn 1973-1977; *Recreations* golf, skiing, horse racing, music; *Clubs* Turf, Buck's, MCC; *Style* - John Nash Esq; Chalet Gstelli, CH-3781 Gsteig-bei-Gstaad, Switzerland (☎ Gstaad 51162)

NASH, Thomas Arthur Manly; CMG (1959), OBE (1944); s of Col Llewellin Thomas Nash CMG (d 1928); *b* 18 June 1905; *Educ* Wellington Coll, London U; *m* 1930, Marjorie Wenda, nee Wayte; 1 s; *Career* entomologist, dir W African Institute for Trypanosomiasis Research 1954-59, dir Tsetse Research Laboratory Bristol U Langford 1962-71; *Recreations* fishing, gardening; *Style* - Thomas Nash Esq, CMG, OBE; Spring Head Farm, Upper Langford, nr Bristol (☎ Churchill 852 321)

NATHAN, 2 Baron (UK 1940); Capt Roger Carol Michael Nathan; s of 1 Baron, PC (d 1963); bro of Hon Lady Waley-Cohen; *b* 5 Dec 1922; *Educ* Stowe, New Coll Oxford; *m* 1950, Philippa, da of Maj Joseph Bernard Solomon, MC, of Sutton End, Pulborough, Sussex; 1 s, 2 da; *Heir* s, Hon Rupert Harry Bernard Nathan; *Career* master Gardeners' Co 1963; slr, assoc memb Bar Assoc of City of New York; FSA, FRSA, FRGS; pres Jewish Welfare Bd 1967-71; chm exec ctee Cancer Research Campaign 1970-75; chm Central British Fund for Jewish Relief and Rehabilitation 1971-77; chm RSA 1975-77; v-pres 1977; chm exec ctee British Empire Cancer Campaign 1970-75; hon treasurer 1979-; *Clubs* Athenaeum, Calvary; *Style* - The Rt Hon the Lord Nathan; 20 Copthall ave, EC2 (☎ 01 628 9611); Collyers Farm, Lickfold, Petworth, W Sussex (☎ Lodsworth 284)

NATHAN, Hon Jennifer Ruth; da of 2 Baron Nathan; *b* 4 June 1952; *Style* - The

Hon Jennifer Nathan; Collyers Farm, Lickfold, Petworth, Sussex

NATHAN, Hon Nicola Jane Eleanor; da of 2 Baron Nathan; *b* 18 May 1954; *Style* - The Hon Nicola Nathan

NATHAN, Hon Rupert Harry Bernard; s and h of 2 Baron Nathan; *b* 26 May 1957; *Style* - The Hon Rupert Nathan

NATHANSON, Hon Mrs (Victoria Elizabeth Anne); *née* Thorneycroft; da of Baron Thorneycroft, CH, PC, by his 2 w, Carla, da of Conte Malagola-Cappi, of Ravenna, and formerly w of Conte Giorgio Roberti (presumably of the family, originally of Bassano, ennobled by the Venetian Doge Francesco Loredan 1757 and confirmed by the Austrian Emperor Francis I 1830 and Victor Emmanuel III of Italy 1909); *b* 25 June 1951; *Educ* St Mary's Convent Ascot; *m* 1975, Richard H Nathanson; *Style* - The Hon Mrs Nathanson; 7 Broadbent st, W1 (☎ 01 629 1300)

NAYLOR, Lady Mary (Millicent Rachel); *née* Byng; da of 6 Earl of Strafford; *b* 1899; *m* 1927, Maj-Gen Robert Francis Brydges Naylor, CB, CBE, DSO, MC (d 1971); 2 s, 1 da; *Style* - Lady Mary Naylor; Dancers Hill House, Barnet, Herts (☎ 6789)

NAYLOR-LEYLAND, Lady Isabella; da of Antony Lambton, *qv* (6 Earl of Durham, who disclaimed his peerage); *b* 1958; *m* 1980, Philip Naylor-Leyland, *qv*; *Style* - Lady Isabella Naylor-Leyland

NAYLOR-LEYLAND, Philip Vyvyan; s and h of Sir Vivyan Edward Naylor-Leyland, 3 Bt; *b* 9 Aug 1953; *Educ* Eton; *m* 1980, Isabella, da of Antony C F Lambton, *qv* (6 Earl of Durham, who disclaimed his peerage); *Career* 2 Lt, LG; *Style* - Philip Naylor-Leyland Esq

NAYLOR-LEYLAND, Sir Vivyan Edward; 3 Bt (UK 1895), of Hyde Park House, Albert Gate, Co London; s of Sir Albert Edward Herbert Naylor-Leyland, 2 Bt (d 1952); *b* 5 March 1924; *Educ* Eton, Oxford U, Roy Agricultural Coll Cirencester; *m* 1, 1952, Hon Elizabeth Anne (m dis 1960), da of 2 Viscount FitzAlan of Derwent (d 1962); 1 s; m 2, 1967, (Noreen) Starr Anker Simmons (m dis 1975), da of late Wing-Cdr Peter Anker Simmons, DFC, RAF; 1 da; *Heir* s, Philip Vyvyan Naylor-Leyland; *Career* Lt-Gren Gds 1943-47; *Style* - Sir Vivyan Naylor-Leyland, Bt; 6 Harbour mews, Nassau, Bahamas (☎ Nassau 77523)

NEAGLE, Dame Anna (Dame Marjorie Wilcox); DBE (1969, CBE 1952); da of the late Herbert William Robertson; *b* 20 Oct 1904; *Educ* St Albans H S; *m* 1943, the late Herbert Sidney Wilcox, CBE; *Career* actress, films include *Victoria the Great*, *Odette*, *Sixty Glorious Years*, *Nurse Edith Cavell* and *Nell Gwyn*, *Spring in Park Lane* with Michael Wilding 1948; their films won them 13 awards, including the Gold Cup of All Nations at the Venice Film Festival for the film of Queen Victoria; stage rôles included Peter Pan, Rosalind, Olivia, Jane Austen's Emma and *Glorious Days*; 2,062 performances in *Charlie Girl* at the Adelphi Theatre, which qualified her for inclusion in The Guiness Book of Records; Book: *There's Always Tomorrow* 1974 (autobiog); *Recreations* reading; *Clubs* FANY Regimental; *Style* - Dame Anna Neagle, DBE; 117b Hamilton ter, St John's Wood, NW8 (☎ 01 328 7698)

NEAL, Harry Morton; s of Godfrey French Neal; *b* 21 Nov 1931; *Educ* Uppingham Sch, London U, City and Guilds Coll; *m* 1954, Cecilia Elizabeth, da of Col Mervyn Crawford, DSO (d 1977); 1 s (Michael Harry Walker b 1956), 3 da (Camilla Jane b 1960, Janet Carolyn b 1961, Alexandra Cecilia Martha b 1967); *Career* Flying Offr RAF, md Harry Neal Ltd Building and Civil Engineering Contractors 1963-, chm Connaught Hotel Ltd 1980-, chm City and Guilds of London Institute 1979-; *Recreations* gardening, shooting; *Style* - Harry Neal Esq; Great Sarratt Hall, Sarratt, nr Rickmansworth, Herts (☎ Kings Langley 64321)

NEAME, Lady; H Alberta Drew; *m* 1934, Lt-Gen Sir Philip Neame, VC, KBE, CB, DSO (d 1978); 3 s, 1 da; *Style* - Lady Neame; The Kintle, Selling Court, Faversham, Kent

NEATE, Alfred; s of William Neate (d 1945); *b* 29 Jan 1909; *Educ* Sutton Valence, Oriel Oxford; *m* 1933, Olga Margaret, nee Spall; 1 s, 1 da; *Career* memb Willesden Borough Cncl 1932-39, regional controller (NW) Miny of Aircraft Prodn 1942-45, Miny of Supply 1946-51; dir gen of Machine Tools, Miny of Supply 1951, dir Wickman Ltd and subsidiaries 1953-58; *Recreations* · rowing and gardening; *Clubs* Carlton, Naval and Military, Oriental, Rand Club (Johannesburg); *Style* - Alfred Neate Esq; The Spinney, London Road, Boxmoor, Hemel Hempstead, Herts (☎ 52882)

NEAVE, Maj Sir Arundell Thomas Clifton; 6 Bt (GB 1795), of Dagnam Park, Essex, JP (Anglesey 1950); s of Sir Thomas Lewis Hughes Neave, 5 Bt (d 1940); *b* 31 May 1916; *Educ* Eton; *m* 1946, Richenda Alice Ione, da of Sir Robert Joshua Paul, 5 Bt (d 1955); 2 s, 2 da; *Heir* s, Paul Arundell Neave; *Career* served 1939-45 (Dunkirk), Maj Welsh Gds 1945, ret 1947; *Clubs* Carlton, Pratt's; *Style* - Maj Sir Arundell Neave, Bt, JP; Greatham Moor, Liss, Hants

NEAVE, Julius Arthur Sheffield; CBE (1978, MBE 1944), JP (Brentwood); s of late Col Richard Neave; *b* 17 July 1919; *Educ* Sherborne Sch; *m* 1951, Helen Margery, da of the late Col P M Acton-Adams, DSO; 3 da; *Career* served in 13/18 Royal Hussars, joined Mercantile & General Reinsurance Co Ltd 1938, gen man 1966, md 1980, first chm Reinsurance Offices Assoc, now Hon Pres, received Founders Award Gold Medal of International Insurance Seminars 1977, pres of The Insurance Inst London 1976-77, v-pres Geneva Assoc; *Recreations* golf, shooting, fishing, tennis, needlework; *Clubs* Cavalry & Guards; *Style* - Julius Neave Esq, CBE, JP; Mill Green Park, Ingatestone, Essex (☎ Ingatestone 3036)

NEAVE, Paul Arundell; s and h of Sir Arundell Thomas Clifton Neave, 6 Bt; *b* 13 Dec 1948; *m* 1976, Coralie Jane Louise, da of Sir Robert George Caldwell Kinahan, ERD; 1 s; *Style* - Paul Neave Esq; 7 Franconia rd, SW4

NEAVE, Hon Richard Patrick Sheffield; s of Baroness Airey of Abingdon (Life Peeress), and of Airey Middleton Sheffield Neave, DSO, OBE, MC, TD, MP (assas 1979); *b* 1947; *m* 1980, Elizabeth Mary Catherine, da of Cuthbert Edward Riddell, of Hermeston Hall, Worksop, Notts; *Style* - The Hon Richard Neave

NEAVE, Hon William Robert Sheffield; s of Baroness Airey of Abingdon (Life Peeress), and of Airey Middleton Sheffield Neave, DSO, OBE, MC, TD, MP (assas 1979); *b* 1953; *Style* - The Hon William Neave

NEDEN, Lady; L Violet; *m* 1967, as his 2 w, Sir Wilfred John Neden, CB, CBE (d 1978); *Style* - Lady Neden

NEEDHAM, Hon Andrew Francis; s of Richard Francis Needham (6 Earl of Kilmorey, but does not use title); *b* 7 March 1969

NEEDHAM, Lady Christina Clare; da of Richard Francis Needham, 6 Earl of Kilmorey (but does not use the title); *b* 1977; *Style* - Lady Christina Needham

NEEDHAM, Hon Christopher David; s of 5 Earl of Kilmorey (d 1977); *b* 30 July 1948; *Educ* Milton Abbey; *m* 1974, Marina, da of Rodi Malvezzi, of Milan; *Style* - The Hon Christopher Needham; Villa Kilmorey, Pineta di Roccamare 58043, Castiglione-della-Pescia, Grosseto, Italy

NEEDHAM, Hon Patrick Jonathan; s of 5 Earl of Kilmorey; *b* 30 July 1951; *Style* - The Hon Patrick Needham; Villa Kilmorey, Pineta de Roccamare, 58043 Castiglione-della-Pescia, Grosseto, Italy

NEEDHAM, Hon Mrs Peter - Janet Beatrice Winifred; da of late Capt George Taylor Ramsden, MP; *m* 1951, Hon (Arthur) Peter Needham (d 1979), s of late Maj Hon Francis Edward Needham, MVO (2 s of 3 Earl of Kilmorey); 2s, 1 da; *Style* - The Hon Mrs Peter Needham; The Old Manor House, Helmsley, York

NEEDHAM, Peter Southwood; s of William Needham, of Hobart, Tasmania;

b 9 Jan 1924; *Educ* Hobart H S; *m* 1, 1945, Anne Louise; 2 da (Mrs (Elizabeth Anne) McCormick, Mrs (Rosemary Jane) Buckle); m 2, 1971, Susan Augusta, da of Philip H Band, of Westhampton Beach, NY; 3 step children; *Career* business consultant; dir Wilkins & Mitchell Ltd 1974-77, Venesta Ltd 1961-68; *Clubs* Hurlingham, RAC; *Style* - Peter Needham Esq; c/o Barclays Bank, 9 Gracechurch st, EC3

NEEDHAM, Richard Francis; MP (C) Chippenham 1979-; also Hereditary Abbot of the Exempt Jurisdiction of Newry and Mourne, Viscount Kilmorey (I 1625) and Viscount Newry and Morne (I 1822); s of 5 Earl of Kilmorey (d 1977, I Earldom cr 1822) and Helen, da of Sir Lionel Faudel-Phillips, 3 & last Bt; does not use titles (nor did he use courtesy title of Viscount Newry and Morne 1969-77); *b* 29 Jan 1942; *Educ* Eton; *m* 1965, Sigrid Juliana, da of late Ernest Thiessen and Mrs John Gairdner; 2 s; *Heir* s, Viscount Newry and Morne; *Career* formerly CCllr Somerset, chm RGM Print Holdings Ltd, personal assist to Rt Hon James Prior MP 1974-79, conservative sec Employment Ctee 1979-; memb Slade Art Union; used title of Viscount Newry and Morne to Dec 1968; *Clubs* Buck's; *Style* - Richard Needham Esq, MP; House of Commons, SW1

NEGRETTI, Antony Simon Timothy; s of Paul Antony Negretti, *qv*; *b* 2 Dec 1945; *Educ* Eton; *Career* bill broker, banker, dir of Page & Gwyther Holdings Ltd, Page & Gwyther Ltd, Page & Gwyther Investments Ltd; *Recreations* tennis, golf, skiing, shooting; *Clubs* Boodle's; *Style* - Antony Negretti Esq; 15 Roland Way, SW7 (☎ 01 370 1887)

NEGRETTI, Paul Anthony; s of Paul Ernest Negretti, of Lane House, Lodsworth (d 1954), gs of Enrico Negretti, who was naturalised in UK 1826 and who was s of Paolo Negretti, of Como, by his 1 w; *b* 26 April 1912; *Educ* Oundle; *m* 1943, Audrey Elsie Townsend, da of Sir Grey Humberston d'Estoteville Skipwith (d 1950); 1 s, 1 da; *Career* Maj Black Watch (RHR), served France, Gibraltar, N Africa, Sicily, Italy, Germany; dir Negretti & Zambra 1948-81, chm 1954-71, dep chm 1971-81; mayor Westminster 1963-64; *Recreations* formerly tennis, cricket, skiing, lawn tennis; *Clubs* Brooks's; *Style* - Paul Negrett Esq; 6 Conway House, Ormonde Gate, SW3; Thornborough Manor, Buckingham

NEGUS, Arthur George; s of the late Arthur George Negus; *b* 29 March 1903; *Educ* Reading Sch; *m* 1926, Irene Amy, nee Hollett; 2 da; *Career* fine art appraiser, BBC Radio and TV 1966-, Freeman of The City of London 1976, Liveryman of The Plaisterers' Company 1977; *Recreations* philately, sport; *Clubs* New, Cheltenham, Lord's Taverners; *Style* - Arthur Negus Esq; 31 Queens Court, Cheltenham, Glos (☎ Cheltenham 45696)

NEIDPATH, Lord; James Donald Charteris; full title Lord Douglas of Neidpath, Lyne and Munard; s and h of 12 Earl of Wemyss and (8 of) March, KT, JP; *b* 22 June 1948; *Educ* Eton, Univ Oxford; *Career* Page of Honour to HM Queen Elizabeth The Queen Mother 1962-64, memb Roy Co of Archers (Queen's Body Guard for Scotland); trainee land agent; *Recreations* history; *Clubs* Brocks's, Pratt's, Puffin's, Ogniesko Polskie; *Style* - Lord Neidpath; Stanway, Cheltenham, Glos (☎ Stanton 469)

NEILL, The Very Rev Ivan Delacherois; CB (1963), OBE (1958); s of Robert Richard Neill (d 1951); *b* 10 July 1912; *Educ* St Dunstan's Coll, Jesus Cambridge; *m* 1938, Enid Eyre Godson, nee Bartholomew; 1 s, 1 da; *Career* ordained 1936, Army Chaplains Dept 1939-66, despatches 1945, provost of Sheffield 1966-74, provost Emeritus 1974-, Hon Chaplain to HM The Queen 1962-66, govr Monkton Combe Sch 1964-, chm Govrs 1969-81, pres C of E Foundation St Paul & St Mary Cheltenham 1978-; *Recreations* trying not to retired, off shore boating, photogaphy; *Style* - The Very Rev Ivan Neill, CB, OBE; Rodborough Crest, Rodborough Common, Stroud, Glos (☎ Amberley 3224), Churchtown, Broadway, Co Wexford (☎ Wexford 31221)

NEILL, Lt-Col James Hugh; CBE (1969), TD (1950), DL (S Yorks 1974); s of

Col Sir Frederick Neill, CBE, DSO, TD; *b* 29 March 1921; *Educ* Rugby; *m* 1943, Jane Margaret (d 1980), nee Shuttleworth; 2 da (and 1 decd); *Career* Lt-Col WW II Norway, India, Burma, Germany; chm James Neill Hldgs 1963-, Master Cutler of Hallamshire 1958-59, High Sheriff Hallamshire 1971-72; *Recreations* golf, racing, horse trials; *Clubs* Roy and Ancient of St Andrews, Sheffield, E India and Sports; *Style* - Lt-Col James Neill, CBE, TD, DL; Lindrick Lodge, Woodsetts, Worksop, Notts (☎ Dinnington 2806)

NEILL-FRASER, Lady Sarah (Louisa); *née* Erskine; da of 16 Earl of Buchan; *b* 1931; *m* 1957 (m dis 1972), Maj Norman Neill-Fraser; 1 s; *Style* - Lady Sarah Neill-Fraser; Willow Cottage, S Hay, Kingsley, Bordon, Hants

NELSON, 8 Earl (UK 1805); George Joseph Horatio Nelson; also Baron Nelson of the Nile & of Hilborough (UK 1801) and Viscount Merton of Trafalgar & of Merton (UK 1805); s of 5 Earl Nelson (d 1951, himself ggn of both 1 Earl and the naval hero Horatio Nelson, 1 Baron & Viscount and Duke of Bronte - the latter title being now held by Viscount Bridport); suc bro, 7 Earl Nelson, 1972; *b* 20 April 1905; *Educ* Ampleforth; *m* 1945, Winifred Mary, da of W Bevan, of Swansea; 1 da; *Heir* nephew, Peter John Horatio Nelson; *Career* former FCA; *Style* - The Rt Hon the Earl Nelson; 9 Pwlldu lane, Bishopston, Swansea (☎ Bishopston 2682)

NELSON OF STAFFORD, 2 Baron (UK 1960); Sir Henry George Nelson; 2 Bt (UK 1955); s of 1 Baron, sometime chm English Electric Co (d 1962); *b* 2 Jan 1917; *Educ* Oundle, King's Coll Cambridge; *m* 1940, Pamela Roy, da of Ernest Roy Bird, MP (d 1933); 2 s, 2 da; *Heir* s, Hon Henry Roy George Nelson; *Career* Chancellor of Aston U Birmingham; Lord High Steward of borough of Stafford 1966-71; dir English Electric Co Ltd 1943, deputy md 1949, md 1956, chm 1962-68; chm General Electric Co 1968-; dep chm British Aircraft Corpn 1960-77, Roy Worcester Ltd; dir Bank of England and Int Nickel Co of Canada; dir London Bd of Advice of Nat Bank of Australia; pres Soc of British Aircraft Constructors 1960-63, Orgalime 1968-70; pres Inst of Electrical Engineers 1970-71; chm Defence Industries Council 1971-77; chm British Nat Ctee World Energy Conference 1971-74; pres Sino-British Trade Council; freeman City of London; Benjamin Franklin Medal 1959, Roy Soc of Arts; *Clubs* Carlton, Hurlingham; *Style* - The Rt Hon Lord Nelson of Stafford; Wincote Farm, Eccleshall, Stafford; 8 Carlton Lodge, 37 Lowndes st, SW1

NELSON, Cathleen Lady (Annie Cathleen Elizabeth); da of Lt-Col Loftus Bryan, DL; *m* 1923, as his 2 w, Sir James Hope Nelson, 2 Bt (d 1960); *Style* - Cathleen Lady Nelson

NELSON, Campbell Louis; s of George Francis Nelson (d 1913); *b* 14 Dec 1910; *Educ* Seaford Coll, King's Coll London; *m* 1939, Pauline Frances (d 1978), nee Blundell; 1 s (Richard Campbell), 1 da (Jane Frances); *Career* Lt KRRC (Motor Bns) 1941-44, FCA, chm Ultramar Co Ltd 1971- (md 1960, dir 1947), chm British-Borneo Petroleum Syndicate Ltd 1957- (exec dir 1948), chm Gellatly Hankey & Co Ltd 1976- (dir 1970-), chm Scottish Offshore Investors Ltd 1975-, memb of Cncl of the Maritime Trust 1979-; *Recreations* golf, bridge; *Clubs* City of London, Royal and Ancient (St Andrews) Golf Club, Sunningdale Golf, Royal Wimbledon Golf; *Style* - Campbell Nelson Esq; 2 Chelsea House, 26 Lowndes st, SW1 (☎ 01 235 8260); Queenshill, Ridgemount rd, Sunningdale, Berks (☎ 0990 20088)

NELSON, Hon Lady (Elizabeth Ann Bevil); *née* Cary; da of 14 Visc Falkland; *b* 1927; *m* 1945, Sir William Vernon Hope Nelson, 3 Bt, OBE; *Style* - The Hon Lady Nelson; White House Farm, Holnest, Sherborne, Dorset

NELSON, Lady Geraldine Mary Diana; da of 5 Earl Nelson (d 1951); *Educ* St Anthony's Convent, Sherborne; *Career* served 1939-46 with RAF as Nursing Sister; *Style* - Lady Geraldine Nelson; Richmond House, 27 Rabling rd, Swanage, Dorset

NELSON, Hon Harry (Henry) Roy George; s and h of 2 Baron Nelson of

Stafford; *b* 26 Oct 1943; *Educ* Ampleforth and King's Coll, Cambridge; *m* 1968, Dorothy, da of Leslie Caley, of Tibthorpe Manor, Driffield, E Yorks; 1 s, 1 da; *Style* - The Hon Harry Nelson; Ackworth Grove, Pontefract rd, High Ackworth, nr Pontefract, Yorks

NELSON, Lady (Margaret) Jane; *née* Fitzroy; da of William Henry Alfred, Visc Ipswich, and sis of 9 Duke of Grafton (d 1936); *b* 1916; *m* 1936, Maj-Gen Sir Eustace John Blois Nelson, KCVO, CB, DSO, MC; 2 da ; *Style* - Lady Jane Nelson; Tigh Bhaan, Appin, Argyll

NELSON, Jamie Charles Vernon Hope; s and h of Sir William Vernon Hope Nelson, 3 Bt, OBE; *b* 23 Oct 1949; *Style* - Jamie Nelson Esq

NELSON, Hon James Jonathan; s of 2 Baron Nelson of Stafford; *b* 17 June 1947; *Educ* Ampleforth and McGill U; *m* 1977, Lucille Mary, da of Roger Gopsill Brown, of Albrighton, Salop; *Style* - The Hon James Nelson; 44 Lamont rd, SW10

NELSON, Hon Mrs John - Kathleen Mary; *née* Burr; *m* 1941, Capt Hon John Nelson (d 1970, s of 5 Earl Nelson); 2 s, 1 da; *Style* - The Hon Mrs John Nelson; Dunbar Cottage, Potten End, Berkhamsted, Herts

NELSON, Michael Edward; s of Thomas Alfred Nelson (d 1977); *b* 30 April 1929; *Educ* Latymer Upper Sch, Magdalen Coll Oxford; *m* 1960, Helga Johanna, nee den Ouden; 2 s (Patrick b 1961, Paul b 1963), 1 da (Shivaun b 1967); *Career* journalist, Reuters Economic Servs (joint man 1960-61, man 1962-73), Reuters Ltd (assist gen man 1967-73, joint dep md and gen man 1976-81, dep md and gen man 1981-); *Clubs* Garrick; *Style* - Michael Nelson Esq; 2 Foxgrove rd, Beckenham, Kent (☎ 01 650 2639)

NELSON, Lady Mary Winefride; da of 5 Earl Nelson (d 1951); *Educ* Roehampton; *Clubs* Challoner; *Style* - Lady Mary Nelson; Richmond House, 27 Rabling rd, Swanage, Dorset BH19 1ED

NELSON, Peter John Horatio; s of late Capt John Marie Joseph Horatio Nelson (s of 5 Earl Nelson); hp to Earldom of Nelson; *b* 9 Oct 1941; *m* 1969, Maureen Diana, da of Edward Patrick Quinn, of Kilkenny; 1 s, 1 da; *Style* - Peter Nelson Esq; 7 Chiltern Park av, Berkhampstead, Herts

NELSON, Maj Sir William Vernon Hope; 3 Bt (UK 1912), of Acton Park, Acton, of Denbigh, OBE (Mil 1952); s of William Hope Nelson (d 1953) and nephew of 2 Bt (d 1960); *b* 25 May 1914; *Educ* Beaumont, RMC Sandhurst; *m* 1945, Hon Elizabeth Ann Bevil Cary, da of 14 Viscount Falkland; 3 s, 3 da; *Heir* s, Jamie Charles Vernon Hope Nelson; *Career* 2 Lt 8 Hussars 1934, Palestine 1936-39 (despatches, medal with clasp), Korea 1950-51; *Style* - Maj Sir William Nelson, Bt, OBE; c/o Hoare & Co, Aldford House, Park lane, W1

NELSON-SMITH, David Austin; s of Adrian Nelson-Smith (d 1978); *b* 6 April 1936; *Educ* Brighton Coll, CCC Cambridge; *m* 1965, Joyce Yvonne, nee Naef; 1 s (Mark b 1966), 1 da (Nicola b 1968); *Career* chm and md Tradax England Ltd 1978-; *Style* - David Nelson-Smith Esq; c/o Chase Manhattan Bank, Coleman st, EC2

NELTHORPE, Lt-Col Roger Sutton; MBE (1945), TD (1949) and 3 clasps, JP (1947), DL (Lincs 1950); s of Col Oliver Sutton Nelthorpe; *b* 5 Mar 1918; *Educ* Eton, RAC Cirencester; *Career* Lt-Col 1959 with TA, landowner and farmer; *Recreations* shooting, forestry, agriculture; *Style* - Lt-Col Roger Nelthorpe, MBE, TD***, JP, DL; Scawby Hall, Scawby Brigg, S Humberside, DN20 9LX

NEPEAN, Lt-Col Sir Evan Yorke; 6 Bt (UK 1802), of Bothenhampton, Dorsetshire; s of Maj Sir Charles Evan Molyneux Yorke Nepean, 5 Bt (d 1953); *b* 23 Nov 1909; *Educ* Winchester, Downing Cambridge; *m* 1940, (Georgiana) Cicely, da of late Maj N E G Willoughby; 3 da; *Heir* none; *Career* served 1939-45 with Roy Signals (UK and Middle East), Lt-Col 1943, ret 1957; *Style* - Lt-Col Sir Evan Nepean, Bt; Goldens, Teffont, Salisbury, Wilts (☎ Teffont 275)

NESBITT, Hon Mrs (Patricia Catherine); da of 2 Baron Bethell (d 1965); *b* 1933; *m* 1956, Michael William Nesbitt, DFC; 1 s, 2 da; *Style* - The Hon Mrs Nesbitt; Rotherwood, Fittleworth, Pulborough, Sussex

NESS, Lady Brigid (Katharine Rachel); *née* Guinness; da of 2 Earl of Iveagh, KG, CB, CMG (d 1967); *b* 1920; *m* 1 1945, HRH Prince Friedrich Georg Wilhelm Christoph of Prussia (d 1966); 3 s, 3 da (*see* Douro, Marquess of); m 2, 1967, Maj Anthony Patrick Ness ; *Style* - Lady Brigid Ness; Patmore Hall, Hadham, Herts; Letterellan, by Aberfeldy, Perths; 7 Iveagh House, Ormond Yard SW1

NETHERTHORPE, 2 Baron (UK 1959); James Andrew Turner; s of 1 Baron (d 1980); *b* 23 July 1936; *Educ* Rugby, Pembroke Cambridge; *m* 1960, Belinda, da of F Hedley Nicholson (d 1980); 2 s, 2 da; *Heir* s, Hon James Turner; *Career* CA; ch exec Dalgety Ltd 1978-; dir Lazard Bros & Co Ltd 1961-; dir Babcock Int Ltd 1971-; *Style* - The Rt Hon the Lord Netherthorpe; Boothby Hall, Boothby Pagnell, Grantham, Lincs (☎ Ingoldsby 374); I 2 Albany, Piccadilly, W1 (☎ 01 734 7894)

NETHERTHORPE, Margaret, Baroness; Margaret Lucy; da of James Arthur Mattock, of Barnet, Herts; *m* 1935, 1 Baron (d 1980); *Style* - The Rt Hon Margaret, Lady Netherthorpe; Hadley Hurst, Hadley Common, Barnet, Herts

NETTLESHIP, Brig Rev Charles; OBE (1944), TD (1943), DL (Warwicks 1970); s of the late William Nettleship; *b* 7 July 1908; *Educ* Bridlington Sch; *m* 1945, Mireille (d 1978), nee Abecasis; 2 da; *Career* army officer seniority 1933, Chief Signal Officer 1 (BR) Corps BAOR 1956-58, CSO Western Command 1958-61, ret 1962, clerk in Holy Orders 1962, secretary Coventry Diocese Pastoral Ctee 1969-77, Vicar Leek Wootten 1965-; *Recreations* off-shore fishing, hunting (now by car); *Clubs* 2 Div Dinner; *Style* - Brig Rev Charles Nettleship, OBE, TD; The Vicarage, Leek Wootten, Warwick (☎ Kenilworth 52319)

NEVILL, Lady Anne (Camilla Eveline); *née* Wallop; da of 9 Earl of Portsmouth; *b* 1925; *m* 1944, Lord Rupert Charles Montacute Nevill, *qv*; *Style* - Lady Anne Nevill; Horsted Place, Uckfield, Sussex; 30B St James's Palace, SW1

NEVILL, Maj-Gen Cosmo Alexander Richard; CB (1958), CBE (1954), DSO (1944); s of Maj Cosmo Nevill, DSO, OBE (d 1940), of Eccleston, Leamington Spa, gs of Charles Nevill by Lady Georgiana Bingham (yst da of 2 Earl of Lucan); the General's gf, Richard, served in the 7 Hussars of the Austrian Army and the Nizam of Hyderabad's Imperial Forces, and m Giulia, da of Charles Lever, the picaresque novelist (who, though typifying Irish character in his novels and life, was wholly English), friend of Oscar Wilde's f Sir William and sometime Consul in Trieste (where he was only a little less wretched than Stendhal in Civita Vecchia, though less indigent than Joyce, who lacked the resources of the Consular service, a couple of generations later); General Nevill's line are thought to be Lever's only descendants; *b* 14 July 1907; *Educ* Harrow, Sandhurst (Sword of Honour & King's Medal); *m* 1934, Grania, da of Maj Guy Goodliffe, MC, of Birdstown, Co Donegal; 1 s (Capt Richard Nevill m 1961 Caroline, da of Adm Sir Guy Grantham, GCB, CBE, DSO), 1 da (Charmian m 1965 Capt David James); *Career* served WW II Staff India (2 Lt Roy Fusiliers 1927), Cmmd 2 Bn Devonshire Regt 1944 D-Day Normandy, UN New York 1946-48; GOC 2 Inf Div 1956-58, Brig 1956, Maj-Gen 1957, ret 1960; Hon Lay Canon St Edmundsbury Cathedral 1969; *Recreations* shooting, painting; *Clubs* Army & Navy; *Style* - Maj-Gen Cosmo Nevill CB CBE DSO; Holt, Edwardstone, Boxford, Suffolk (☎ 0787 210428)

NEVILL, Lady Rose; da of 5 Marq of Abergavenny; *b* 15 July 1950

NEVILL, Lord Rupert Charles Montacute; CVO (1979), JP (Sussex 1953), DL (Sussex 1960); s of 4 Marquess of Abergavenny; hp to bro, 5 Marquess; *b* 29 Jan 1923; *Educ* Eton; *m* 1944, Lady Anne Wallop, da of 9 Earl of Portsmouth; 2 s

(Guy Rupert Gerard, b 29 March 1945, educ Eton, Page of Honour to HM 1958-61; Christopher George Charles, b 23 April 1955, educ Harrow), 2 da (Angela Isabel Mary, b 2 Jan 1948; Henrietta Emily Charlotte, b 21 June 1964); *Career* Capt late Life Gds; served WW II ADC to Lt-Gen Sir Brian Horrocks; Sec to HRH The Duke of Edinburgh 1975- (Treasurer 1970-); chm Courier Printing & Publishing Co; v-chm Sun Life Assur Soc; dir Daily Mail Tst, Owners of the Middlesbrough Estate Ltd; *Clubs* White's, Buck's, Beefsteak; *Style* - Lord Rupert Nevill CVO JP DL; Horsted Place, Uckfield, Sussex (☎ Isfield 315); 30b St James's Palace, SW1 (☎ 01 839 7206)

NEVILLE, Air Cdre Christopher Roger Gartside; CBE (1972); s of Gp Capt R N G Neville, OBE, MC; *b* 10 Sept 1924; *Educ* Malvern Coll, Oxford U; *m* 1958, Shelagh Maureen, da of late Lt-Col H H Mulholland; 2 s, 1 da; *Career* Air Cdre RAF 1975, Middle East NATO (Europe) UK, cmdg RAF Coningsby 1970-72, princ SO to Dep Saceur 1972-74, dir RAF Command Control and ADP 1975-79; *Recreations* athletics, golf; *Clubs* RAF; *Style* - Air Cdre Christopher Neville, CBE; Orchard Lea, Wiggaton, Ottery St Mary, Devon (☎ Ottery St Mary 2497)

NEVILLE, Lt-Col Sir (James) Edmund Henderson; 2 Bt (UK 1927), of Sloley, Co Norfolk, MC; s of Sir Reginald James Neville, 1 Bt, JP (d 1950); *b* 5 July 1897; *Educ* Eton, RMC; *m* 1932, Marie Louise (d 1980), da of Charles Pierson, of Vale Lodge, Weston, Bath; 2 da; *Heir* half-bro, Richard Lionel John Baines Neville; *Career* served in WW I 1916-18 with 2 Bn Oxford and Bucks LI, and in N Russia 1919 with 1 Bn; re-employed 1939-45; master Bowyers Co 1936-38; prime warden Fishmongers' Co 1958; *Clubs* Army & Navy; *Style* - Lt-Col Sir Edmund Neville, Bt, MC; Sloley Old Hall, Norwich, Norfolk (☎ Swanton Abbot 232)

NEVILLE, Hon Grey Aldworth; s of late Rev the Hon Grey Neville and bro of 9 Baron Braybrooke; *b* 20 Sept 1900; *Educ* RNC Dartmouth; *m* 1930, Margaret Emily Cortlandt, da of late Rev Henry Cortlandt Stokes; *Career* Cdr RN WWI and II; *Style* - The Hon Grey Neville; Kingsdown, King's rd, St Peter Port, Guernsey

NEVILLE, Hon Robin Henry Charles; DL (Essex 1980); s and h of 9 Baron Braybrooke; *b* 29 Jan 1932; *Educ* Eton, Magdalene Cambridge; *m* 1, 1955 (m dis 1974), Robin Helen Brockhoff; 4 da (and 1 decd); m 2, 1974, Linda, da of Arthur Norman; 2 da; *Style* - The Hon Robin Neville, DL; Abbey House, Audley End, Saffron Walden, Essex

NEVILLE, Richard Lionel John Baines; s of Sir Reginald James Neville, 1 Bt (d 1950); h to Btcy of half-bro, Sir (James) Edmund Henderson Neville, 2 Bt, MC; *b* 15 July 1921; *Educ* Eton, Trin Cambridge; *Career* Burma 1943-45 as Capt Oxford and Bucks, and W African Frontier Force; *Style* - Richard Neville Esq; Sloley Hall, Norwich

NEVIN, His Hon Judge; Thomas Richard Nevin; TD (1949) and Bar, JP (1965); s of late Thomas Nevin, JP, of Mirfield, Yorks; *b* 9 Dec 1916; *Educ* Bilton Grange, Shrewsbury Sch, Leeds U (LLB); *m* 1955 (m dis 1979), Brenda Micaela, da of Dr B Andrade-Thompson, MC; 1 s (and 1 decd); *Career* Lt-Col London Bombardment, India and Burma; barr NE Circuit for 19 years, asst recorder of Leeds 1961-64, recorder of Doncaster 1964-67, dep chm Quarter Sessions Yorks W Riding 1965-71, E Riding 1968-71, chm Ag Lands Tribunal 1963-67 (dep chm 1961-63), a Circuit Judge and Crown Court Liaison Judge (formerly Judge of County Courts) 1967-, a Dep High Court Judge 1974-; Freeman of City of London; *Recreations* numismatics and our past; *Style* - His Hon Judge Nevin, TD*, JP; c/o 11 King's Bench Walk, Temple, EC4 (☎ 01 236 3337)

NEWALL, 2 Baron (UK 1946); Francis Storer Eaton Newall; s of Marshal of the RAF 1 Baron Newall, GCB, OM, GCMG, CBE, AM (d 1963); *b* 23 June 1930; *Educ* Eton, Sandhurst; *m* 1956, Pamela, da of Edward Rowcliffe, TD, of Pinkney Park, Malmesbury (d 1978), by his 1 w, Margaret (da of Sir Henry Farrington, 6 Bt); 2 s, 1 da; *Heir* s, Hon Richard Newall; *Career* Capt 11 Hussars, served Germany,

Malaya, Singapore, NI; Adj Roy Glos Hussars; consultant & co dir; Con Whip & Oppn Front Bench Spokesman 1976-79 Ho Lds; Fndr Memb Ho Lds All Party Def Study Gp; *Recreations* shooting, travel; *Clubs* Cavalry & Guards; *Style* - The Rt Hon Lord Newall; Wotton Underwood, Aylesbury, Bucks; 81 Lennox gdns, SW1 (☎ 01 589 9370)

NEWALL, Hon David William Norton; s of 2 Baron Newall; *b* 2 July 1963; *Style* - The Hon David Newall

NEWALL, Hon Georgiana; da of Marshal of the RAF 1 Baron Newall GCB OM GCMG CBE AM (d 1963); *b* 1926; *Style* - The Hon Georgiana Newall; Catridge Farm, Lacock, Chippenham, Wilts

NEWALL, Hon Miranda Jane; da of 2 Baron Newall; *b* 25 Feb 1959; *Style* - The Hon Miranda Newall

NEWALL, Olivia, Baroness; Olive; da of Horace Tennyson Foster, of USA, and Mrs Francis Storer Eaton, of Boston; *b* 19 July 1891; *Educ* USA (Boston Conservatory of Music), Germany, Paris; *m* 1925, Marshal of the RAF 1 Baron Newall, GCB, OM, GCMG, CBE, AM (d 1963); 1 s, 2 da; *Career* DStJ; *Recreations* fishing, tennis, travel, racing; *Clubs* Oriental, Guards & Cavalry, Anglo-Belgian with Roy Thames Yacht, Commonwealth; *Style* - The Rt Hon Olivia Lady Newall; c/o Coutts & Co, 1 Old Park Lane, W1

NEWALL, Hon Richard Hugh Eaton; s and h of 2 Baron Newall; *b* 19 Feb 1961; *Style* - The Hon Richard Newall

NEWBIGGING, David Kennedy; s of David Locke Newbigging, CBE, MC (d 1948); *b* 19 Jan 1934; *Educ* Oundle Sch; *m* 1968, Carolyn Susan, nee Band; 1 s, 2 da; *Career* 2 Lt (Nat Serv), chm and ch exec Jardine Matheson & Co Ltd 1975- (joined 1954, md 1970), dir Hongkong & Shanghai Banking Corp Ltd 1975-; *Recreations* most outdoor sports; *Clubs* Turf, The Royal Hongkong Jockey; *Style* - David Newbigging Esq; 35 Mt Kellett rd, The Peak, Hong Kong (☎ 5-96334)

NEWBOROUGH, 7 Baron (I 1776); Sir Robert Charles Michael Vaughan Wynn; 9 Bt (GB 1742), DSC (1942); s of 6 Baron Newborough, OBE, JP, DL (d 1965); *b* 24 April 1917; *Educ* Oundle; *m* 1, 1945 (m dis 1971), Rosamund, da of Maj Robert Barbour, of Bolesworth Castle, Tattenhall, Cheshire; 1 s, 2 da; m 2, 1971, Jennifer, yst da of late Capt Cecil Allen, RN; *Heir* s, Hon Robert Wynn; *Career* farmer, High Sheriff Merioneth 1963; served 2 Lt 9 Lancers, 5 Inniskilling Dragoon Gds & Lt 16/5 Lancers 1935-39, invalided 1940, RNVR Cmmn, commanded MTB 74 St Nazaire raid 1942, POW Colditz, escaped; *Recreations* sailing, fishing, shooting; *Clubs* Naval & Military; *Style* - The Rt Hon Lord Newborough DSC; Rûg, Corwen, Clwyd (☎ Corwen 2510)

NEWBURGH, 11 Earl of (S 1660); Giulio Cesare Taddeo Cosimo Rospigliosi; also Viscount Kynnaird and Lord Levingston (S 1660), Prince Rospigliosi (HRE & Papal, 1668 & 1854 respectively, bestowed by Emperor Leopold I & Pope Pio Nono, also respectively), 13 Prince of Castiglione (by the Sicilian cr of 1602, which as being then under Spanish suzerainty carries the status of Grandeeship; a further cr of the kingdom of Italy occurred 1897), 10 Duke of Zagarolo (Papal title of 1668), Marquis of Giuliana (Sicily 1543, It 1897), Count of Chiusa (Sic 1535, It 1897), Baron di Valcorrente e della Miraglia (Sic 1780, It 1897), Lord (Signore) of Aidone, Burgio, Contessa, and Trappeto (1854), conscribed Roman noble (1854), and Patrician of Venice (1667), Genoa (1786) and Pistoia; s of Prince Giambattista Rospigliosi (d 1956) and Ethel Bronson (d 1924); suc cousin Maria Sofia Giuseppina, nee Giustiniani-Bandinini, Countess of Newburgh in her own right (d 1977), da of 9 Earl of Newburgh (d 1941); *b* 26 Oct 1907; *Educ* CCC Cambridge; *m* 1940, Donna Giulia, da of Don Guido Carlo dei Duchi Visconti di Modrone, Count of Lonate Pozzolo; 2 s (Viscount Kynnaird, also Prince Filippo Rospigliosi; Prince Francesco Rospigliosi); *Heir* Viscount Kynnaird; *Style* - The Rt Hon the Earl of Newburgh; Via Corridoni 3, 20122 Milan, Italy

NEWBURY, Hon Mrs (Julia Elizabeth Heather); *née* Hamilton; da of 13 Lord Belhaven and Stenton; *b* 1956; *m* 1975, Richard Newbury; *Style* - The Hon Mrs Newbury

NEWBY, Hon Mrs (Ailsa Ballantyne); da of Baron Thomson of Monifieth (Life Peer); *b* 1956; *m* 1978, Richard Newby; *Style* - The Hon Mrs Newby

NEWCASTLE, 9 Duke of (GB 1756); Henry Edward Hugh Pelham-Clinton-Hope; OBE (1945); also Earl of Lincoln (E 1572); s of 8 Duke (d 1941, ggs of the 4 Duke, after whom the Newcastle Scholarship at Eton is named; though in other respects his existence bore less resemblance to Madeline Usher's than a brother Duke (the fifth of Portland)'s did to that of *her* brother Roderick (His Grace & the latter shared an obsession with vaults and seclusion), he was once nearly buried alive when in a coma after a bout of typhus; on another occasion his seat of Nottingham Castle was burnt to the ground by a rabble which he imprudently goaded to fury by justifying the eviction of some tenants with the words "Shall I not do what I like with my own?"); *b* 1907; *Educ* Eton, Magdalene Cambridge; *m* 1, 1931, Eugenia Van Voorhees (m dis 1940), adopted da of David Banks, of Park Ave, New York USA; m 2, 1946, Lady (Mary) Diana Montagu-Stuart-Wortley-Mackenzie (m dis 1959), da of 3 Earl of Wharncliffe (d 1953); 2 da; m 3, 1959, Mrs Sally Ann Wemyss Hope (Jamal), da of Brig John Henry Anstice, DSO; *Heir* cousin, Edward Charles Pelham-Clinton; *Career* Flying Offr 1936-38, Sqdn Ldr AAF 1938-39; served 1939-45 War in Middle East, Mornady and Norway; Wing Cdr 1947-48; JP Notts (1933-48), DL (1937-48); *Style* - His Grace the Duke of Newcastle, OBE; 5 Quay Hill, Lymington, Hants

NEWCASTLE, 10 Bishop of (1882) 1981-; Rt Rev Andrew Alexander Kenny Graham; s of late Andrew Graham; *b* 7 Aug 1929; *Educ* Tonbridge, St John's Oxford; *Career* Bp Suffragan of Bedford 1977-81; Warden Lincoln Theological Coll 1970-77; *Recreations* hill walking; *Clubs* Oxford and Cambridge; *Style* - The Rt Rev The Bishop of Newcastle; 29 Moor Road South, Gosforth, Newcastle upon Tyne NE3 1PA (☎ 0632 852220)

NEWCASTLE, Diana, Duchess of; Lady (Mary) Diana; *née* Montagu-Stuart-Wortley-Mackenzie; da of 3 Earl of Wharncliffe; *b* 2 June 1920; *m* 1946 (m dis 1959), 9 Duke of Newcastle, OBE; 2 da; *Career* served WW II Mechanised T'port Corps; *Style* - Diana, Duchess of Newcastle; Cortington Manor, Warminster, Wilts

NEWENS, (Arthur) Stanley; MP (L/Co-op) Harlow 1974-; s of late Arthur Ernest Newens; *b* 4 Feb 1930; *Educ*Buckhurst Hill County H S, Univ Coll London; *m* 1 1954, Ann, nee Sherratt (d 1962), 2 da; m 2, 1966, Sandra Christina, nee Frith; 2 da; *Career* MP (Lab) Epping 1964-70; pres London Co-operative Society 1977-81, dir London Co-op Society 1971-77, chm Liberation 1967-; *Recreations* family, reading, historical research, gardening; *Style* - Stanley Newens Esq, MP; The Leys, 18 Park Hill, Harlow, Essex (☎ 0279 20108)

NEWMAN, Hon Lady; Hon Ann Rosemary Hope; da of Capt Hon Claude Hope Hope-Morley (d 1968), and sis of 3 Baron Hollenden; *m* 1946, Sir Ralph Alured Newman, 5 Bt (d 1968); raised to the rank of a Baron's da; *Style* - The Hon Lady Newman; Blackpool House, Dartmouth, S Devon

NEWMAN, Francis Hugh Cecil; s and h of Sir Gerard Robert Henry Sigismund Newman, 3 Bt; *b* 12 June 1963; *Style* - Francis Newman Esq

NEWMAN, Sir Geoffrey Robert; 6 Bt (UK 1836), of Mamhead, Devonshire; s of Sir Ralph Alured Newman, 5 Bt (d 1968); *b* 2 June 1947; *Educ* Heatherdown, Ascot, Kelly Coll; *m* 1980, Mary Elizabeth, da of Col Martin St John Valentine Gibbs, CB, DSO, TD; *Heir* bro, Richard Claude Newman; *Career* 1 Bn Gren Gds 1967-70; *Clubs* Guards; *Style* - Sir Geoffrey Newman, Bt; Blackpool House, Dartmouth, S Devon

NEWMAN, Sir Gerard Robert Henry Sigismund; 3 Bt (UK 1912), of Cecil Lodge, Newmarket, Co Cambridge; s of Sir Cecil Gustavus Jacques Newman, 2 Bt (d 1955); *b* 19 July 1927; *Educ* Eton, Jesus Oxford; *m* 1960, Caroline Philippa, da of Brig Alfred Geoffrey Neville, CBE, MC (d 1955); 3 s, 1 da; *Heir* s, Francis Hugh Cecil Newman; *Career* co dir; *Clubs* Boodle's; *Style* - Sir Gerard Newman, Bt; Burloes, Royston, Hertfordshire (☎ Royston (STD Code 0763) 42150); 27 Bloomfield Terrace, London SW1 (☎ 01 730 7540)

NEWMAN, John Francis; s of Sir Cecil Gustavus Newman, 2 Bt (d 1955), and Joan, CBE (d 1969), da of Canon Hon Robert Grimston (s of 2 Earl of Verulam); *b* 25 Jan 1930; *Educ* Eton, Sandhurst; *m* 1963, Caroline, da of Lt-Col Angus Rose, of Perthshire (d 1981); 1 s, 2 da; *Career* late Lt RHG; chm Rom River Co, Hayman Engrg Ltd; *Recreations* shooting, farming, golf; *Clubs* White's, MCC; *Style* - John Newman Esq; 28 St Luke's st, SW3 (☎ 01 352 7808); Compton Park, Compton Chamberlayne, Salisbury, Wilts (☎ Fovant 294)

NEWMAN, Hon Mrs (Jean Sybil); *née* Loch; da of 2 Baron Loch, CB, CMG, MVO, DSO (d 1942); *b* 18 May 1908; *m* 1930, Guy Arthur Newman, s of late Sir Sigmund Neumann, 1 Bt (who anglicised his name to Newman 1936); 3 da; *Style* - The Hon Mrs Newman; Stanners Hill Manor, Chobham, Surrey (☎ Chobham (STD Code 099 05) 8808)

NEWMAN, Karl Max; CB (1979); s of Dr Karl Neumann (d 1978); *b* 26 March 1919; *Educ* Ottershaw Coll, Ch Ch Oxford; *m* 1952, Annette Muriel, nee Sheen; 1 s, 1 da; *Career* barr 1946-49, Lord Chancellor's Office: legal assist 1949-56, sr legal assist 1956-62, Under-Sec 1972-; legal adviser European Unit Cabinet Office 1972-; *Recreations* travelling, philately, visiting picture galleries; *Clubs* United Oxford and Cambridge U; *Style* - Karl Newman Esq, CB; 17 Marryat rd, Wimbleton, SW19 (☎ 01 946 3430)

NEWMAN, Peter John; s of Peter Laurence Newman; *b* 5 July 1938; *Educ* St John's Johannesburg, St John's Cambridge; *m* 1963, Patricia Anne, nee Wright; 3 s; *Career* operations man Davy-United 1975, gen man Loewy Robertson Engineering Co 1979-, Queen's Award for Export 1980; *Recreations* sailing, gardening; *Clubs* Parkstone Yacht; *Style* - Peter Newman Esq; 11 Greenwood av, Parkstone, Poole, Dorset (☎ 708578)

NEWMAN, Richard Claude; s of Sir Ralph Alured Newman, 5 Bt (d 1968); hp of bro, Sir Geoffrey Robert Newman, 6 Bt; *b* 2 May 1951; *Style* - Richard Newman Esq

NEWMAN, Lady Selina (Mary); *née* Abney-Hastings; da of Countess of Loudoun; *b* 1946; *m* 1967, William Newman; 1 s, 1 da; *Style* - Lady Selina Newman

NEWNS, Sir (Alfred) Foley (Francis Polden); KCMG (1963, CMG 1957), CVO (1961); s of Rev Alfred Newns (d 1930); *b* 30 Jan 1909; *Educ* Christs' Hospital, St Catharine's Cambridge; *m* 1936, Emma Jean, nee Bateman; 1 s, 1 da; *Career* Colonial Administrative Serv Nigeria 1932, sec to Cncl of Ministers 1951-54, sec to Govr-Gen and Cncl of Minsters 1955-59, Dep Govr Sierra Leone 1960, Actg Govr 1960, adviser to Govr 1961-63, sec to Cabinet Govt of Bahamas 1964-71; *Recreations* nature study, gardening; *Style* - Sir Foley Newns, KCMG, CVO; Caxton Lane, Foxton, Cambridge, CB2 6SR (☎ 870629)

NEWNS, George Henry; s of George Newns (d 1916); *b* 27 July 1908; *Educ* Whitgift Sch, King's Coll London, King's Coll Hosp Med Sch; *m* 1936, Eileen Deirdre, da of late Lawrence Kenny; 1 s, 1 da; *Career* MD, FRCP; chm Leukaemia Research Fund 1962-, Civilian Paediatric Consultant to Admiralty 1962-74, Hon Consultant in Paediatrics to the Army 1966-74, Dean Inst of Child Health London U 1949-73, Dean Emeritus 1974-, Consultant Paediatrician-Physician Hosp for Sick Children Gt Ormond St 1946-73, Hon Consulting Physician 1974-; *Recreations* walking, reading, music; *Style*

- Dr George Newns, MD; 12 Milborne Grove, SW10 (☎ 01 373 2011)

NEWPORT, Viscount; Richard Thomas Orlando Bridgeman; s and h of 6 Earl of Bradford, TD; *b* 3 Oct 1947; *Educ* Harrow, Trin Cambridge; *m* 1979, Joanne Elizabeth, da of Benjamin Miller; 1 s; *Career* company dir, proprietor Porters Restaurant in Covent Garden; *Style* - Viscount Newport; 32 Westbridge rd, SW11

NEWRY AND MORNE, Viscount; Robert Francis John; s and h of Richard Needham, 6 Earl of Kilmorey (who does not use the title); *b* 30 May 1966; *Style* - Viscount Newry and Morne

NEWSOME, Dr David Hay; s of Capt C T Newsome, OBE (d 1972); *b* 15 June 1929; *Educ* Rossall Sch Fleetwood, Emmanuel Cambridge (MA, LittD); *m* 1955, Joan Florence, da of Lt-Col L H Trist, DSO, MC (d 1979); 4 da; *Career* fell 1959-70 and sr tutor 1965-70 Emmanuel Coll Cambridge, lectr Ecclesiastical History Cambridge 1966-70, headmaster Christ's Hospital 1970-79, Master Wellington 1980-; *Recreations* fell-walking, music; *Clubs* East India Sports & Public Schools, MCC, Nobody's Friend; *Style* - Dr David Newsome; Master's Lodge, Wellington Coll, Crowthorne, Berks (☎ 2353); The Retreat, Thornthwaite, Keswick, Cumbria (☎ Braithwaite 372)

NEWSON-SMITH, Sir John Kenneth; 2 Bt (UK 1944), of Totteridge, Co Hertford, DL (City of London); s of Sir Frank Newson-Smith, 1 Bt (d 1971); *b* 9 Jan 1911; *Educ* Dover Coll, Jesus Cambridge; *m* 1, 1945, Vera Margaret (m dis 1971), da of late Dr Wilfred Greenhouse Allt, CVO, CBE; 1 s, 2 da; m 2, 1972, Anne, da of Harold Burns; *Heir* s, Peter Frank Graham Newson-Smith; *Career* joined HAC 1933, RN 1939, Lt RNVR 1941; memb Court of Common Council 1945, dep 1961-, memb HM Cmmn of Lieutenancy for City of London (HM Lt 1947); chm London United Investments Ltd 1968-71, dep chm 1971-; *Clubs* City Livery and Naval; *Style* - Sir John Newson-Smith, Bt, DL; 39 Godfrey st, SW3 (☎ 01 352 0722)

NEWSON-SMITH, Peter Frank Graham; s and h of Sir John Kenneth Newson-Smith; *b* 8 May 1947; *Educ* Dover Coll; *m* 1974, Mary-Ann, da of Cyril C Collins and formerly w of Anthony Owens; 1 s, 1 da; *Style* - Peter Newson-Smith Esq

NEWTON, 4 Baron (UK 1892); Peter Richard Legh; JP (Hants 1951); s of 3 Baron (d 1960); *b* 6 April 1915; *Educ* Eton, Ch Ch Oxford; *m* 1948, Priscilla (who had m, 1936, Capt Viscount Wolmer, s & h of 3 Earl of Selborne and who was k accidentally while on active serv 1942; 2 s, 1 da), da of Capt John Egerton-Warburton (d 1915) and Hon Mrs Waters (d 1968, herself da of 2 Baron Newton); 2 s; *Heir* s, Hon Richard Thomas Legh; *Career* 2 Lt Gren Gds 1937, Capt 1941, Maj 1945; MP (C) Hants 1951-60; Assistant Govt Whip 1953-55, Lord Cmmr Treasury 1955-57, Vice-Chamberlain HM Household 1957-59, Treasurer 1959-60; Joint Parly Sec Miny of Health 1962-64; memb Hants CC 1949-52 and 1954-55; *Clubs* Carlton, Constitutional, Pratt's; *Style* - The Rt Hon the Lord Newton, JP; Vernon Hill House, Bishop's Waltham, Hants (☎ 2301)

NEWTON, Alice, Lady (Alice Mary); da of late Henry Barber, of Surbiton, and widow of Glyn Rosser; *m* 1968, as his 2 w, Sir Edgar Henry Newton, 2 Bt (d 1971); *Style* - Alice, Lady Newton; Barn Cottage, Griggs Farm Court, Liphook, Hants

NEWTON, George Peter Howgill; s and h of Sir Harry Michael Rex Newton, 3 Bt; *b* 26 March 1962; *Style* - George Newton Esq

NEWTON, Sir Hubert; s of Joe Newton (d 1935); *b* 2 Sept 1904; *Educ* Burnley G S; *m* 1931, Elsie, da of late James Wilson; 1 da; *Career* chm Britannia Building Soc 1976- (formerly gen man, then chm and md Leek and Morlands Building Soc, former md and chm Leek and Westbourne Building Soc, former jt dep chm Leek Westbourne and Eastern Counties Building Soc, which became Britannia Building Soc); chm Building Socs of GB 1952-54; Liveryman Gold and Silver Wire Drawers' Co; kt 1968; *Recreations* golf, travel; *Clubs* English-Speaking Union; *Style* - Sir Hubert Newton; Birchall Lane, Birchall, Leek, Staffs

NEWTON, Sir Harry Michael Rex; 3 Bt (UK 1900), of The Wood, Sydenham Hill, Lewisham, Kent and Kottingham House, Burton-on-Trent, Co Stafford; s of Sir Harry Kottingham Newton, 2 Bt, OBE (d 1951); *b* 7 Feb 1923; *Educ* Eastbourne Coll; *m* 1958, Pauline Jane, da of Richard John Frederick Howgill, CBE, of Branscombe, Sullington Warren, Storrington, Sussex; 1 s, 3 (adopted) da; *Heir* s, George Peter Howgill Newton; *Career* served 1941-46 with KRRC; memb Girdlers' Co; freeman City of London; dir Thomas Parsons & Sons Ltd; *Clubs* Bath, Roy Ocean Racing; *Style* - Sir Harry Newton, Bt; Weycroft Hall, nr Axminster, Devon (☎ 3232)

NEWTON, John Garnar; s and h of Sir Kenneth Garnar Newton, 3 Bt, OBE, TD; *b* 10 July 1945; *Educ* Reed's Sch Cobham; *Style* - John Newton Esq

NEWTON, Lt-Col Sir Kenneth Garnar; 3 Bt (UK 1924), of Beckenham, Co Kent, OBE (1969), TD; s of Sir Edgar Henry Newton, 2 Bt (d 1971); *b* 4 June 1918; *Educ* Wellington; *m* 1, 1944, Margaret Isabel (d 1979), da of Rev Dr George Blair, of Dundee; 2 s; m 2, 1980, Pamela, widow of F T K Wilson; *Heir* s, John Garnar Newton; *Career* served 1939-45, Lt-Col 1944; gen cmmr for Income Tax 1961-; md Garnar Scotblair Ltd 1961-, chm 1972; pres British Leather Fedn 1968-69; pres Int Council of Tanners 1972-78; master of Leathersellers' Co 1977-78; memb Court of Assistants, Feltmakers' Co; *Style* - Lt-Col Sir Kenneth Newton, Bt, OBE, TD; Whitebeams, Beech ave, Effingham, Surrey

NEWTON, Hon Mrs - Hon Ursula Helen Rank; da of 1 and last Baron Rank (d 1972); *b* 1919; *m* 1952, Robert Lancelot Newton (d 1969); 1 s, 2 da; *Style* - The Hon Mrs Newton; Church Farm, Saltby, Melton, Mowbray, Leics

NICHOLL, Anthony John David; s of Brig David William Dillwyn Nicholl (d 1972); *b* 3 May 1935; *Educ* Eton, Pembroke Coll Oxford; *m* 1961, Hermione Mary, nee Palmer; 1 s, 2 da; *Career* barr, Recorder of the Crown Court 1978-; *Recreations* history, horses, gardening; *Style* - Anthony Nicholl Esq; 2 Fountain ct, Stealhouse lane, Birmingham, B4 6DR

NICHOLL, Henry Rice; s of Major Basil Rice Nicholl; *b* 28 April 1909; *Educ* Winchester, Sandhurst; *m* 1936, Marjorie Joicey, nee Dickenson; 2 s, 1 da; *Career* officer Rifle Brigade, comd 7 Btn Rifle Brigade 1946, retd 1948, High Sheriff Northumberland 1969, MFH Haydon 1959-67; *Recreations* foxhunting, stalking, shooting, painting, glass engraving; *Style* - Henry Nicholl Esq; High Lipwood, Haydon Bridge, Hexham, Northumberland (☎ Haydon Bridge 205)

NICHOLLS, David Alan; s of Thomas Edward Nicholls (d 1971); *b* 28 Aug 1931; *Educ* Cheshunt G S, St John's Cambridge; *m* 1955, Margaret; 2 da (Amanda, Camilla b 1961); *Career* Home Civil Service 1954, Assist Sec MOD 1969-75, Cabinet Office 1975-77, Und-Sec MOD 1977-80, Assist Sec-Gen NATO 1980; *Recreations* sketching, printmaking; *Style* - David Nicholls Esq; c/o Midland Bank, Church Stretton, Salop

NICHOLLS, David Jermyn Brasted; s of Ernest James Nicholls, CBE (1978); *b* 27 July 1932; *Educ* Uppingham, Christ's Cambridge; *m* 1956, Gillian Mary, nee Gibbard; 1 s, 2 da; *Career* Maj Kenya 1955-56; tea broker, dir Gow Wilson Ltd, Tea Brokers Publications Ltd; *Recreations* sailing, bellringing; *Clubs* Nairobi, Little Ship; *Style* - Maj David Nicholls; Portmark House, 55 High st, Manningtree Essex (☎ 3680)

NICHOLLS, Philip; CB (1976); s of William Herbert Nicholls (d 1960); *b* 30 Aug 1914; *Educ* Malvern, Pembroke Coll Cambridge; *m* 1955, Sue, nee Shipton; 2 s (Mark William, Paul Conolly); *Career* Maj 8 Bn Worcestershire Regt HQ E Africa Cmmd (Mil Asst to GOC-in-C), Allied Commission for Austria; Foreign Office (German section) 1940-46; asst master Malvern Coll 1936 (Sr Master 1939, resigned 1947); HM Treasury 1949-70; Forestry Cmmn (Fin and Admin)

1970-75, memb of Cncl for Malvern Coll 1960- (v-chm 1963-); *Style* - Philip Nicholls Esq, CB; Barnard's Green House, Malvern, Worcestershire (☎ Malvern 4446)

NICHOLLS, Hon Susan Frances; da of Baron Harmar-Nicholls (Life Peer and 1 Bt); *b* 1943; *Style* - The Hon Susan Nicholls

NICHOLLS, Hon Mrs (Virginia Jean Furse Maud); da of Baron Redcliffe-Maud, GCB, CBE (Life Peer); *b* 1943; *m* 1970, Roger Frank Nicholls; *Style* - The Hon Mrs Nicholls

NICHOLS, William Henry; CB (1974); s of William Nichols (d 1955); *b* 25 March 1913; *Educ* Owens Sch; *Career* entered Inland Revenue 1930, Exchequer and Audit Dept 1935, Dir of Audit 1963, Dir of Establishments and Accounts 1967, Dep Sec 1972, Sec 1973-75; *Style* - William Nichols Esq CB; 17 Park House, Winchmore Hill rd, N2 (☎ 01 886 4321); 11 Old st, Haughley, Stowmarket, Suffolk

NICHOLSON, Hon Mrs (Ariadne Maria); *née* Balfour; da of 4 Baron Kinross, OBE, TD; *b* 31 Jan 1939; *m* 1961, Richard, s of late Robert Nicholson and Mrs Kenneth Seth-Smith (stepmother of Viscountess Buckmaster); 3 s, 1 da; *Style* - The Hon Mrs Nicholson; Ochiltree Cottage, Linlithgow, W Lothian

NICHOLSON, Bryan Hubert; s of Reginald Hubert Nicholson (d 1977); *b* 6 June 1932; *Educ* Palmers Sch, Grays, Essex; Oriel Oxford; *m* 1956, Mary Elizabeth Harrison; 2 c; *Career* Lt (Nat Serv); chm Rank Xerox (UK) Ltd 1980- (dir 1972-80); dir Rank Xerox Ltd 1977-, Sperry Rand Ltd 1969-72, dir Sperry Rand (Australia) Pty Ltd 1966-69; *Recreations* tennis, bridge; *Clubs* RAC; *Style* - Bryan Nicholson Esq; Point Piper, Lilley drive, Kingswood, Surrey

NICHOLSON, Charles Christian; s and h of Sir John Norris Nicholson, 2 Bt, KBE, CIE; *b* 15 Dec 1941; *Educ* Ampleforth, Magdalen Oxford; *m* 1975, Martha Rodman, da of Stuart Warren Don and widow of Niall Hamilton Anstruther-Gough-Calthorpe; *Style* - Charles Nicholson Esq; Turners Green Farm, Elvetham, Hants

NICHOLSON, Hon Mrs (Diana Mary); *née* Seely; da of 4 Baron Mottistone; *b* 1954; *m* 1977, Edward Anthony Spours Nicholson; *Style* - The Hon Mrs Nicholson; 171 E 74th st, New York, NY 10021, USA

NICHOLSON, Lady; Evelyn Odell; da of late Capt R G Westropp (late RA), of Camberley; *m* 1926, Gen Sir Cameron Gordon Graham Nicholson, GCB, KBE, DSO, MC (d 1979); *Style* - Lady Nicholson; Greyhayes, St Breward, Bodmin, Cornwall

NICHOLSON, Sir Godfrey; 1 Bt (UK 1958), of Winterbourne, Roy Co of Berks, FSA (1961); s of Richard Francis Nicholson (d 1940), of Woodcott, Hants; *b* 9 Dec 1901; *Educ* Winchester, Ch Ch Oxford; *m* 1936, Lady Katharine Constance (d 1972), da of 27 Earl of Crawford and 10 Balcarres (d 1940); 4 da; *Heir* none; *Career* served with Roy Fus 1939-42; MP (C) Morpeth 1931-35 and (C) Surrey 1937-66; *Clubs* Pratt's; *Style* - Sir Godfrey Nicholson, Bt; Bussock Hill House, Newbury, Berks (☎ Chieveley 260)

NICHOLSON, (Charles) Gordon (Brown); s of William Addison Nicholson, OBE; *b* 11 Sept 1935; *Educ* George Watson's Coll, Edinburgh U; *m* 1963, Hazel Mary, nee Nixon; 2 s (David Charles b 1964, Robin Graeme b 1966); *Career* Lt Queen's Own Cameron Highlanders (Nat Service). Advocate 1961-70, Sheriff of Dumfries and Galloway at Dumfries 1970-76, Sheriff of Lothian and Borders at Edinburgh 1976-; *Recreations* golf, philately; *Clubs* New (Edinburgh); *Style* - Sheriff Nicholson; 23 Lennox st, Edinburgh EH4 1PY (☎ 031 332 5861)

NICHOLSON, Lady - Jean; da of late Alexander Landles; *m* 1927, Sir Harold Stanley Nicholson, 14 Bt (d 1961 when the title became dormant); *Style* - Lady Nicholson; Brough Lodge, Fetlar, Shetland; Grimista, Shetland

NICHOLSON, Col John Aubrey Hastings; MC (1944), TD (1955) & 2 bars, DL (S Yorks 1974); s of Cyril Aubrey Nicholson (d 1974); *b* 27 March 1920; *Educ* Uppingham, Queens' Cambridge; *m* 1946, Dawn Eanswythe Lillian, nee Leighton; 1 s, 2 da; *Career* Col, NW Europe; stockbroker, dir JW Nicholson & Sons, Don Trust Ltd, Pegler-Hattersley Ltd; *Recreations* shooting, fishing, sailing, golf; *Clubs* Hawks (Cambridge), Sheffield, Lindrick GC; *Style* - Col John Nicholson, MC, TD**, DL; Quinton, Saltergate, Bamford in the Peak, Sheffield S30 2BE (☎ Hope Valley 51429)

NICHOLSON, Sir John Charles; 3 Bt (UK 1859), of Luddenham, NSW; s of Sir Charles Nicholson, 2 Bt (d 1949, sometime consulting architect to Wells and other cathedrals), by his 1 w, Evelyn, nee Olivier (sis of 1 & last Baron Olivier of the 1924 cr, and through whom the present Sir John is 1 cous of Lord (Laurence) Olivier the actor); *b* 10 Jan 1904; *Educ* Brighton Coll, New Coll Oxford, Bart's Hosp; *m* 1928, Caroline, da of Rt Rev John MacNeice, DD, sometime Bp of Down, Connor and Dromore; *Heir* none; *Career* consulting surgeon, ret 1969, FRCS; *Style* - Sir John Nicholson, Bt; Thames Cottage, Thames st, Sunbury-on-Thames, Middx (☎ 82148)

NICHOLSON, Sir John Norris; 2 Bt (UK 1912), of Harrington Gdns, Roy Borough of Kensington, KBE (1971), CIE (1946); s of Capt George Crosfield Norris Nicholson, (ka 1916), s of 1 Bt, and Hon Evelyn Izme, JP (who m 2 1917, as his 2 w, 1 Baron Mottistone, CB, CMG, DSO), da of (10 Lord and) 1 Viscount Elibank; gs of Sir Charles Norris Nicholson, 1 Bt (d 1918); *b* 19 Feb 1911; *Educ* Winchester, Trin Cambridge; *m* 1938, (Vittoria) Vivien, da of Percy Trewhella, of Villa St Andrea, Taormina, Sicily; 2 s, 2 da; *Heir* s, Charles Christian Nicholson; *Career* Lt 4 Bn Cheshire regt 1939, Capt 1940, Miny of Shipping 1941, rep Miny of War Transport in Delhi; formerly chm Ocean Steamship Co Ltd; dir Barclays Bank, Roy Insurance Co; pres Chamber of Shipping 1970; JP and Vice Ld-Lt Isle of Wight 1974-80; Keeper of the Rolls Isle of Wight 1974-, Ld-Lt 1980-; *Style* - Sir John Nicholson, Bt, KBE, CIE, HM Lord-Lieut for the Isle of Wight; Mottistone Manor, Isle of Wight

NICHOLSON, Paul Douglas; s of Frank Douglas Nicholson TD DL; *b* 7 March 1938; *Educ* Harrow, Clare Coll Cambridge; *m* 1970, Sarah, da of Sir Edmund Bacon, 13 Bt, KG, KBE, TD, of Raveningham Hall, Norfolk; 1 da; *Career* Lt Coldstream Gds; chm Vaux Breweries Ltd 1976-; chm Northern region of CBI 1977-79; chm Northern Bd of Nat Enterprise Bd 1979-; High Sheriff of Co Durham 1980-81; DL of Co Durham 1980; *Recreations* shooting, deerstalking, flying; *Clubs* Boodle's, Northern Counties; *Style* - Paul Nicholson Esq DL; Quarry Hill, Brancepeth, Durham (☎ 780 275)

NICOL, Claude Scott; CBE (1977), TD (1950); s of Claude Gordon Nicol (d 1931, barr Lincoln's Inn); *b* 23 Feb 1914; *Educ* Harrow, London U, Oxford; *m* 1939, Janet Wickham, da of Nigel Bosworth Smith, Dep Cmmr Indian Civil Service; 1 s (Alasdair), 2 da (Judy, Melany); *Career* Col TAVR: RAMC BEF 1939, 9 Army 1944; MD, FRCP, physician-consultant in genito-urinary medicine (1946 LU and London Hosp, 1947 St Bartholomews Hosp, 1956 St Thomas Hosp), adviser to the Army, adviser to Dept of Health and Social Security, pres of Medical Society of Venereal Diseases, retired 1977; *Recreations* squash, racquets, tennis, walking; *Style* - Claude Nicol Esq, CBE, TD; Spring Grove (West Wing), Milverton, Taunton, Somerset

NICOLL, Lady; Irene; da of Maj J D Lenagan, MBE; *m* 1939, Sir John Fearns Nicoll, KCMG (d 1981); *Style* - Lady Nicoll

NICOLSON, Hon David Henry Arthur; s and h of 3 Baron Carnock, DSO; *b* 1920; *Educ* Winchester, Balliol Oxford; *Career* served 1940-46 with R Devon Yeo, Artillery and Staff, Maj 1945, slr 1949, ptnr Clifford, Turner and Co 1955; *Style* - The Hon David Nicolson; 11 Old Jewry, London EC2; 90 Whitehall Court SW1 (☎ 01 930 3160); Ermewood House, Harford, Ivybridge, Devon (☎ 075 54 2519)

NICOLSON, Ian Norman Carmichael Nicolson; Chief of the Hebridean Clan of MacNicol (Nicolson); s of late Norman Alexander Nicolson of Scorrybreck; *b* 1921; *Educ* Scotch Coll Tasmania; *m* 1946, Pamela Savigny, da of Philip Oakley Fysh; *Heir* Philip John Lyne Nicolson; *Career* dir Grazier and Co, served 1939-45 War; *Style* - Ian Nicolson of Scorrybreck; Murrumbateman, New South Wales, Australia

NICOLSON, Hon Mrs (Katharine Ingrid Mary Isabel); *née* Ramsay of Mar; da and heiress of Lady Saltoun, *qv*, by her husb Capt Alexander Ramsay of Mar, Grenadier Gds; assumed surname and arms of Fraser by Warrant of Lord Lyon Kings of Arms 1973; through her f's mother (late Lady Patricia Ramsay, da of HRH The Duke of Connaught, 3 s of Queen Victoria), Mrs Nicolson is 3 cous of HM The Queen; *b* 11 Oct 1957; *m* 1980, Capt Mark Malise Nicolson, Irish Gds; *Style* - The Hon Mrs Nicolson

NICOLSON, Malise Allen; MC; s of Sir Kenneth Nicolson, MC (d 1974), of Norton Bavant Manor, Warminster; *b* 31 Oct 1921; *Educ* Eton; *m* 1946, Vivien, da of Arthur Ridley, CBE (d 1974), of Hexham; 1 s (Mark Malise, m 1980, Hon Katherine Fraser, da of Lady Saltoun), 2 da (Mrs (Dinah) Henry Verey, The Hon Mrs (Emma) James Bethell, who m 1974 the 2 s of 5 Baron Westbury); *Career* served WW II Maj Burma; chm Booker Line 1968-, Coe Metcalf Shipping 1977-; dir Booker McConnell 1968-, Mersey Docks & Harbours 1974-80; *Recreations* racing, farming; *Clubs* Cavalry & Guards; *Style* - Malise Nicolson Esq MC; Frog Hall, Tilston, Malpas, Cheshire (☎ 082 98 320)

NICOLSON, Nigel; MBE (1945); s of Hon Sir Harold Nicolson, KCVO, CMG, sometime MP Leics W (d 1968, the biographer, critic and broadcaster, 3 s of 1 Baron Carnock), and Hon Vita (Victoria) Sackville-West, CH, JP (also a writer, authoress of *The Edwardians*), only child of 3 Baron Sackville; bro of late Benedict Nicolson, the art critic; *b* 19 Jan 1917; *Educ* Eton, Balliol Oxford; *m* 1953, Philippa, da of Sir Eustace Tennyson d'Eyncourt, 2 Bt; 1 s, 2 da (Juliet, the er, b 9 June 1954 and m James Macmillan Scott, is publicity man Hamish Hamilton); *Career* author, notably of *Harold Nicolson: Diaries and Letters, 1930-39, 1939-45, 1945-62* (three vols) and *Portrait of a Marriage* (making his parents' life together one of the most fully scrutinised of any ever); MP (C) Bournemouth E & Christchurch 1952-59; dir Weidenfeld & Nicolson 1946-, FRSL; *Recreations* archaeology; *Clubs* Beefsteak; *Style* - Nigel Nicolson Esq, MBE; Sissinghurst Castle, Kent (☎ 0580 712850)

NIDDITCH, Prof Peter Harold; s of Lazarus Nidditch, Monte Carlo; *b* 15 Sept 1928; *Educ* Clifton Coll, Birkbeck Coll London U; *m* 1951, Bridget Veronica, nee McDonnell; *Career* writer and prof of Philosophy; academic appointments at Univs of London, Belfast, Liverpool, Bristol, Sussex 1953-69, Prof U of Sheffield 1969- (Dean Faculty of Arts 1977-79, chm University Library Ctee 1979-, Academic Staffing Ctee 1980-), gen ed Clarendon Edition of the Works of John Locke 1974-; *Style* - Prof Peter Nidditch; Sparlands, Grindleford, Derbyshire (☎ 0433 30670)

NIGHTINGALE, Sir Charles Manners Gamaliel; 17 Bt (E 1628), of Newport Pond, Essex; s of Sir Charles Athelstan Nightingale, 16 Bt (d 1977); *b* 21 Feb 1947; *Educ* St Paul's; *Heir* 2 cous, Edward Lacy George Nightingale; *Career* higher exec offr DHSS 1977-; *Style* - Sir Charles Nightingale, Bt; 14 Frensham Court, 27 Highbury New Park, N5

NIGHTINGALE, Hon Mrs (Evelyn Florence Margaret Winifred); *née* Gardner; da of Baron Burghclere (d 1921); *b* 1903; *m* 1, 1928 (m dis 1930), Evelyn Waugh (the writer); m 2 1930 (m dis 1936), John Edward Nourse Heygate (later 4 Bt and who d 1976); m 3, 1937, Ronald Nightingale (d 1977); 1 s, 1 da; *Style* - The Hon Mrs Nightingale; Orchard Cottage, Ticehurst, Wadhurst, Sussex (☎ 509)

NIGHTINGALE, Edward Humphrey; CMG (1955); s of Rev Edward Charles Nightingale (d 1938); *b* 19 Aug 1904; *Educ* Emmanuel Cambridge; *m* 1944, Evelyn Mary, da of Mervyn Swire Ray; 3 s, 1 da;

Career Sudan Political Serv 1926-54, dep Civil Sec Sudan Govt 1951-52, Govr Equatoria Province Sudan 1952-56; farmer Kenya 1956-; *Recreations* polo, photography; *Clubs* Muthaiga Co Club (Nairobi), Rift Valley Sports (Nakuru); *Style* - Edward Nightingale Esq, CMG; Nunjoro Farm, PO Box 100, Naivasha, Kenya

NIGHTINGALE, Edward Lacy George; s of late Manners Percy Nightingale, MNRCS, LRCP; hp of 2 cous, Sir Charles Manners Gamaliel Nightingale, 17 Bt; *b* 11 May 1938; *Educ* Exeter Sch; *Career* Master Mariner 1966, left Merchant Navy 1974, final rank Ch Offr Cunard Cargo 1956-74; now Sub Postmaster Lynmouth; *Recreations* all types of sport (non contestant); *Style* - Edward Nightingale Esq; Kneesworth, Lynton, N Devon (☎ 05985 2204)

NIGHTINGALE, John; JP (1953), DL (1981); s of James Nightingale (d 1963); *b* 16 July 1914; *Educ* Arnold Sch, Manchester U; *m* 1940, Helen Burton, nee Fearnley; 1 s, 1 da (decd); *Career* solicitor (retd), JP 1953-, DL Greater Manchester 1981-; *Recreations* fly fishing, gardening; *Style* - John Nightingale Esq, JP, DL; Topeka, Bridge End drive, Prestbury, Macclesfield (☎ Prestbury (0625) 829000)

NIGHTINGALE, Michael David; OBE (1960); s of Victor Nightingale, of Wormshill, Kent (d 1951), Lord of the Manors of Wormshill, Bobbing, Ayington, and Bedmonton in Kent, stockbroker, and co-owner (with Hilaire Belloc) of the magazine 'The Weekly Review', by his w Bathsheba, da of Manheim Buhay, of Montreal; *b* 6 Dec 1927; *Educ* Winchester, Wye Coll, Magdalen Oxford; *m* 1956, Hilary, da of John Eric Jones, of Swansea; 2 s, 3 da; *Career* dep steward, Roy Manor of Wye 1954-; late sec Museums' Assoc, ed Museums' Journal, investment advsr London U, dir Charterhouse Japhet; chm Anglo-Indonesian Corpn 1971-, Churches Cttee Kent Archaeological Soc 1973-; memb Gen Synod Church of England 1979-; Baron (territorial, by tenure) of Cromarty; *Clubs* Athenaeum; *Style* - Michael Nightingale Esq, OBE; Cromarty House, Ross and Cromarty (·03817 265); Wormshill Court, Sittingbourne, Kent (☎ 062784 235)

NIGHTINGALE, Lady; Nadine; da of late Arthur Diggens; *m* 1932, Sir Charles Athelstan Nightingale, 16 Bt (d 1977); *Style* - Lady Nightingale; 12 Jacob's Pool, Okehampton, Devon

NIMMO, Lady; Dorothy Wordsworth; da of Walter Gillies; *m* 1922, Sir Robert Nimmo (d 1979); *Style* - Lady Nimmo; 8 Anderson Drive, Perth

NISSEN, George Maitland; s of Col Peter Norman Nissen (d 1930); *b* 29 March 1930; *Educ* Eton, Trin Coll Cambridge; *m* 1956, Jane Edmunds, nee Bird; 2 s, 2 da; *Career* 2 Lt KRRC, Capt Royal Greenjackets TA; dep chm Stock Exchange 1978- (memb 1956; cncl memb 1973); *Recreations* music, railways, walking; *Style* - George Nissen Esq; Swan House, Chiswick Mall, W4 (☎ 01 994 8203)

NIVEN, Sir (Cecil) Rex; CMG (1954), MC (1918); s of late Rev Dr George Cecil Niven; *b* 20 Nov 1898; *Educ* Blundell's Sch Tiverton, Balliol Coll Oxford; *m* 1, 1925, Dorothy Marshall (d 1977), da of D M Mason, formerly MP Coventry and E Edinburgh; 1 da (and 1 da decd); m 2, 1980, Pamela Mary Catterall, nee Leach; *Career* kt 1960; 2 Lt RFA 1918-19; Administration Officer Nigeria 1921-54, Speaker N Nigeria Assembly 1953-60, Special Commissioner N Nigeria 1960-62; life memb BRCS, FRGS, author of several books on Africa; *Clubs* Royal Over-Seas League; *Style* - Sir Rex Niven, CMG, MC; West Hill House, Finglesham, Deal, Kent (☎ Sandwich 611317)

NIVISON, Hon John; s and h of 3 Baron Glendyne; *b* 18 Aug 1960; *Style* - The Hon John Nivison

NIXON, Maj Cecil Dominic Henry Joseph; MC; s of late Maj Sir Christopher William Nixon, 2 Bt, & hp of bro, Rev Sir Kenneth Michael John Basil Nixon, 4 Bt, SJ; *b* 5 Feb 1920; *Educ* Beaumont Coll; *m* 1953, Brenda, da of late Samuel Lycett Lewis & widow of Maj M F McWhor; 2 s, 1

da; *Career* Maj, Roy Ulster Rifles; *Style* - Maj Cecil Nixon, MC; 9 Larpent ave, SW15

NIXON, Howard Millar; s of Rev Leigh H Nixon, MVO, Precentor, Westminster Abbey (d 1941); *b* 3 Sept 1909; *Educ* Marlborough, Oxford; *m* 1951, Enid Dorothy, nee Bromley; 3 s (John Leigh, David Howard, Anthony Alexander); *Career* Maj AA Command 1939-44; librarian Westminster Abbey since 1974, assist cataloguer Printed Books Dept Br Museum 1936-46, assist keeper 1946-59, dep keeper 1959-74; Sandars Reader in Bibliography Cambridge U 1967-68, pres of Bibliographical Soc 1972-74, Lyell Lecturer in Bibliography Oxford U 1978-79, Officier de l'Ordre de la Couronne (Belgium) 1979; *Recreations* golf; *Clubs* Grolier (New York); *Style* - Howard Nixon Esq; 4A Little Cloister, Westminster Abbey, SW1 (☎ 01 222 6428)

NIXON, Lady; Joan Lucille Mary; da of Robert Felix Mervyn Brown; *m* 1949, Maj Sir Christopher John Louis Joseph Nixon, 3 Bt, MC, (d 1978); *Style* - Lady Nixon; c/o Lloyds Bank, 6 Pall Mall, SW1

NIXON, Rev Sir Kenneth Michael John Basil; 4 Bt (UK 1906), of Roebuck Grove, Milltown, Co Dublin and Merrion Sq, City of Dublin, SJ; s of late Sir Christopher William Nixon, 2 Bt, DSO, and bro of 3 Bt (d 1978); *b* 22 Feb 1919; *Educ* Beaumont Coll, Heythrop Coll Oxon; *Heir* bro, Maj Cecil Dominic Henry Joseph Nixon, MC; *Career* catholic priest; ordained 1952; teaching memb of the Jesuit Community at St George's Coll Salisbury 1954-; *Style* - Rev Sir Kenneth Nixon, Bt, SJ; St George's Coll, PB 7727, Causeway, Zimbabwe (☎ Salisbury 24650)

NOBLE, Cdr The Rt Hon Sir Allan Herbert Percy; KCMG (1959), DSO 1943), PC (1956), DL (Suffolk 1973); s of Adm Sir Percy Noble GBE KCB CVO (d 1955); *b* 2 May 1908; *Educ* Radley Coll; *m* 1938, Barbara Janet Margaret, da of Brig Kenneth Joseph Gabbett, Indian Army (d 1948); *Career* entered RN 1927, Cdr RN, ADC Viceroy of India 1936-38, Cdr destroyers 1940-42, Naval Staff Quebec & Yalta Conferences, ret 1945; MP (C) Chelsea 1945-59, PPS to Anthony Eden 1947-51, Parly and Fin Sec The Admiralty 1951-55, Parly Und-Sec of State Commonwealth Relations 1955-56, Min of State for Foreign Affairs 1956-59; *Clubs* White's; *Style* - Cdr The Rt Hon Sir Allan Noble, KCMG, DSO, PC, DL; Troston Cottage, Bury St Edmunds, Suffolk (☎ 035 96 250)

NOBLE, Sir Andrew Napier; 2 Bt (UK 1923), of Ardkinglas, Co Argyll, KCMG (1954); s of Sir John Noble, 1 Bt (d 1938, himself 3 s of Sir Andrew Noble, 1 Bt, of the 1902 cr of Ardmore); *b* 16 Sept 1904; *Educ* Eton, Balliol Oxford; *m* 1934, Sigrid, da of Johan Michelet, of the Norwegian Diplomatic Serv; 2 s, 1 da; *Heir* s, Ian Noble; *Career* For Serv, Ambass Warsaw 1954-56, Mexico 1956-60, The Hague 1960-64 (ret 1964); *Recreations* various, formerly genealogy; *Clubs* Boodle's; *Style* - Sir Andrew Noble, Bt, KCMG; 11 Cedar House, Marloes rd, W8 (☎ 01 937 7952)

NOBLE, Dowager Lady; Celia; da of late Capt Stewart Carmac Weigall, RN; *m* 1926, Sir Humphrey Brunel Noble, 4 Bt, MBE, MC (d 1968); *Style* - Dowager Lady Noble; The Old Vineyard, Ticehurst, Wadhurst, Sussex

NOBLE, David Brunel; s and h of Sir Marc Brunel Noble, 5 Bt; *b* 25 Dec 1961; *Style* - David Noble Esq

NOBLE, Ian Andrew; s and h of Sir Andrew Napier Noble, 2 Bt, KCMG; *b* 8 Sept 1935; *Educ* Eton, Univ Coll Oxford (BA); *Career* Scottish Cncl (Development and Industry) Edinburgh 1964-69; jt founder md Noble Grossart Ltd, Merchant Bankers of Edinburgh 1969-72; dir Lyle Shipping Ltd of Glasgow, Seaforth Maritime Ltd of Aberdeen (chm 1972-76), Sgiath Bheinn Ltd and Muileann Beag a' Chrotail Ltd of Skye and other cos; Govr Sabhal Mor Ostaig (Gaelic Coll) and Fir Chlis Ltd (Repertory Drama Co); *Recreations* New (Edinburgh); *Style* - Ian Noble Esq; Lamraig, Eilean Iarmain, Isle of Skye

NOBLE, Sir Marc Brunel; 5 Bt (UK 1902), of Ardmore and Ardardan Noble,

Cardross, Co Dumbarton; s of Sir Humphrey Noble, 4 Bt, MBE, MC (whose great aunt Georgina, nee Noble, m Isambard, eldest s of Isambard Kingdom Brunel, the celebrated Victorian engineer, hence the prevalence of the names in the Noble family); *b* 8 Jan 1927; *Educ* Eton; *m* 1956, Jennifer, da of John Mein-Austin, of Northants; 2 s, 1 da (and 1 da decd); *Heir* s, David Brunel Noble; *Career* Maj (ret) King's Dragoon Gds & Roy Dragoons; *Clubs* Guards & Cavalry; *Style* - Maj Sir Marc Noble, Bt; Deerleap House, Knockholt, Sevenoaks, Kent (☎ Knockholt 33222)

NOBLE, Hon Mrs Mary Myfanwy; da of 1 Baron Davies (d 1944); *b* 1923; *m* 1958 (m dis 1979), Hugh McAskill Noble; 1 s; *Career* formerly in Women's Roy Canadian Naval Serv; CStJ; *Style* - The Hon Mrs Mary Noble; 17 Dick pla, Edinburgh

NOEL, Lady Celestria (Magdalen Mary); da of 5 Earl of Gainsborough; *b* 27 Jan 1954; *Educ* St Mary's Convent Ascot, St Hilda's Coll Oxford; *Style* - Lady Celestria Noel

NOEL, Hon Edward Andrew; s of 5 Earl of Gainsborough; *b* 22 Oct 1960; *Educ* Farleigh House Sch Basingstoke, Ampleforth; *Style* - The Hon Edward Noel

NOEL, Hon Gerard Edward Joseph; s of 5 Earl of Gainsborough; *b* 23 Jan 1955; *Educ* Ampleforth, London U; *Style* - The Hon Gerard Noel

NOEL, Hon Gerard Eyre Wriothesley; s of 4 Earl of Gainsborough, OBE (d 1927); *b* 1926; *Educ* Georgetown USA, Exeter Coll Oxford; *m* 1958, Adèle Julie Patricia, da of Maj Vivian Bonville Were, of Carrington House, Hertford st, W1; 2 s, 1 da; *Career* barr Inner Temple 1952; author; publisher; contested (Lib) Argyll 1959; editorial dir Catholic Herald 1976-; memb exec Ctee Council of Christians and Jews 1974-; liveryman Co of Stationers and Newspapermakers; freeman City of London; Books: *Paul VI, The Path from Rome, Goldwater, Harold Wilson, Princess Alice*; *Clubs* Garrick, Beefsteak; *Style* - The Hon Gerard Noel; 105 Cadogan gdns, SW3; Westington Mill, Chipping Campden, Glos (☎ Evesham 840240)

NOEL, Hon Thomas; s of 5 Earl of Gainsborough; *b* 9 March 1958; *Educ* Ampleforth, Roy Ag College Cirencester; *Style* - The Hon Thomas Noel

NOEL-BAKER, Baron (Life Peer UK 1977); Philip John; PC (1945); s of J Allen Baker, MP (d 1918); *b* 1889; *Educ* Bootham, King's Cambridge; *m* 1915, Irene (d 1956), da of Frank Noel, of Euboea, Greece; 1 s; *Career* 1 Cdr Friends Ambulance Unit 1914; hon fell King's Cambridge; Cassel Prof Int Relations London U 1924-29; personal assist to pres Disarmament Conference 1932-33, Dodge Lecturer Yale U 1934; MP (L) Coventry 1929-31, Derby 1936-50 and 1950-70; PPS to Sec State Foreign Affairs 1929-31, Sec State for Air 1946-47; Sec State for Commonwealth Relations 1947-50, Min of Fuel and Power 1950-51; chm Foreign Affairs Gp of Parly Lab Party 1964-70; Nobel Peace Prize 1959; assumed surname of Noel in addition to that of Baker by deed poll 1921; *Style* - The Rt Hon the Lord Noel-Baker PC; 16 South Eaton pla, SW1 (☎ 01 730 5377)

NOEL-BAKER, Hon Francis Edward; s of Baron Noel-Baker, PC; *b* 1920; *Educ* Westminster, King's Cambridge; *m* 1957, Barbara Kristina, da of late Josef Sonander, of Norrköping, Sweden; 4 s, 1 da; *Career* joined Roy Tank Regt 1940, transferred Intelligence Corps 1941, Capt 1942; MP (L) Middx 1945-50, Swindon 1955-69; chm UN Parly Ctee 1966-69; chm Parly Lab Party Overseas Development Ctee 1964-68; chm British Greek Parly Gp 1958-69; chm North Euboean Enterprises Ltd 1963-; hon pres Union of Forest Owners of Greece 1968-; gov Campion Sch Athens 1974-78; dir Fini Fisheries, Cyprus 1976-; memb Ecology Party 1978-, Soil Assoc 1979-; *Clubs* Travellers'; *Style* - The Hon Francis Noel-Baker; Sisini 13, Athens 612, Greece

NOEL-BUXTON, 3 Baron (UK 1930); Martin Connal; s of 2 Baron (d 1980); *b* 8 Dec 1940; *Educ* Bryanston, Balliol Oxford; *m* 1, 1964, Miranda Mary (m dis 1968), da of H A Chisenhale-Marsh, of Gaynes Park, Epping, Essex; m 2, 1972, Sarah Margaret Surridge, da of Neil Charles Wolseley Barrett, of Twickenham rd, Teddington; 1 s, 1 da; *Heir* s, Hon Charles Noel-Buxton; *Career* slr 1966, ptnr Speechly Bircham; resumed surname Noel-Buxton by deed poll 1964 (his father having substituted the names Rufus Alexander Buxton for those of Noel Alexander Noel-Buxton in 1944); *Style* - The Rt Hon the Lord Noel-Buxton; c/o Speechly Bircham, Bouverie st, EC4; 14 Grange rd, Kingston upon Thames

NOEL-BUXTON, Hon Charles Connal; s and h of 3 Baron Noel-Buxton; *b* 17 April 1975; *Style* - The Hon Charles Noel-Buxton

NOEL-BUXTON, Hon Lucy Margaret; da of 3 Baron Noel-Buxton; *b* 1977; *Style* - The Hon Lucy Noel-Buxton

NOEL-BUXTON, Hon Michael Barnett Noel; s of 1 Baron Noel-Buxton, PC (d 1948); *b* 1920; *Educ* Harrow, Balliol Coll Oxford; *Career* served with RA 1940-46, with colonial civil service (Gold Coast) 1947-59; *Clubs* Flyfishers'; *Style* - The Hon Michael Noel-Buxton; Stretchney, Diptford, S Devon (☎ Garabridge 342)

NOEL-PATON, Hon Frederick Ranald; s of Baron Ferrier (Life Peer); *b* 7 Nov 1938; *Educ* Rugby, Haverford Coll Pennsylvania, McGill U Montreal (BA); *m* 1973, Patricia, da of late Gen Sir William Gurdon Stirling, GCB, CBE, DSO; *Career* assist planning man British United Airways Ltd; *Style* - The Hon Frederick Noel-Paton; 40 Stockwell Park cres, SW9

NOLAN, Sir Sidney Robert; CBE (1963); s of the late Sidney Nolan; *b* 22 April 1917; *Educ* Melbourne State & Tech Schs; *m* 1948, Cynthia Hansen (d 1976); 1 da; *Career* represented in Tate Gallery London, Museum of Modern Art NY, & Australian Nat Galleries; kt 1981; *Style* - Sir Sidney Nolan CBE; c/o Bank of NSW, 9 Sackville st, London W1

NORBURY, 6 Earl of (I 1827); Noel Terence Graham-Toler; also Baron Norwood (I 1797), Baron Norbury (I 1800), and Viscount Glandine (I 1827); s of 5 Earl (d 1955); *b* 1 Jan 1939; *m* 1965, Anne, da of late Francis Mathew; 1 s, 1 da; *Heir* s, Viscount Glandine; *Style* - The Rt Hon the Earl of Norbury; c/o Stock Exchange, EC2

NORBURY, Margaret, Countess of; Margaret L; da of John Kevan Greenhalgh, of Hoylake, Cheshire; *m* 1933, 5 Earl of Norbury (d 1955); 2 s; *Style* - The Rt Hon Margaret, Countess of Norbury; Barn Cottage, The Pound, Cookham, Berks (☎ Bourne End 21640)

NORCROSS, Lawrence John Charles; s of Frederick Marshall Norcross (d 1934); *b* 14 April 1927; *Educ* Ruskin Coll Oxford, U of Leeds; *m* 1958, Janet Margaret, nee Wallace; 3 s (Matthew, Alastair b 1960, Daniel b 1969), 1 da (Joanna b 1962); *Career* RN 1942-49 (E Indies Fleet 1944-45 HMS Nigeria); Headmaster Highbury Grove Sch 1975-; *Recreations* cricket, music, bridge, talking; *Clubs* Surrey County Cricket Club; *Style* - Lawrence Norcross Esq; 17 Devereux rd, SW11 (☎ 01 228 8478)

NORFOLK, 17 Duke of (Premier E Dukedom 1514 with precedence 1397); Miles Francis Fitzalan Howard; CB (1966), CBE (1960), MC (1949), DL (W Sussex 1977); also Earl of Arundel (E 1139 if the claim by tenure, which was admitted by the Crown in 1433, is recognised; otherwise 1292; either way, the Premier E Earldom), Baron Beaumont (E 1309), Baron Maltravers (E 1330), Earl of Surrey (E 1514), Baron FitzAlan, Baron Clun, Baron Oswaldestre (all E 1627), Earl of Norfolk (E 1644), and Baron Howard of Glossop (UK 1869); Earl Marshal and Hereditary Marshal of England and Chief Butler of England 1975-; s of 3 Baron Howard of Glossop (d 1972) and Baroness Beaumont (d 1971); suc 2 cous once removed (16 Duke) 1975; His Grace is thirteenth in descent from the courtier poet the Earl of Surrey, who himself was 1 cous of Queens Anne Boleyn and Catherine Howard; the execution of all three by Henry VIII is ironic in view of Surrey's son's marriage with the representative of the Fitzalan Earls of Arundel, for one of their subsidiary titles was the Barony of Maltravers, whose first holder, Lord Maltravers, was, if not directly responsible, undoubtedly an agent in the murder of Edward II; *b* 21 July 1915; *Educ* Ampleforth, Ch Ch Oxford; *m* 1949, Anne Mary Teresa, da of Wing Cdr Gerald Constable-Maxwell, MC, DFC, AFC, through whom she enjoys the same degree of kinship with the 16 Duke as her husb; 2 s, 3 da; *Heir* s, Earl of Arundel; *Career* Maj-Gen (ret) Gren Gds; Kt Sov Mil Order of Malta; Head Br Mil Mission to Russian Forces Germany 1957-59; dir Robert Fleming & Co 1969-; served WW II Europe, N Africa; dir Serv Intelligence MOD 1966-67; chm Arundel Castle Tstees Ltd; *Clubs* Turf, Pratt's; *Style* - His Grace The Duke of Norfolk CB CBE MC DL; Carlton Towers, Goole, Humberside (☎ 860 243); Bacres House, Hambleden, Henley-on-Thames, Oxon (☎ Hambleden 350); Arundel Castle, Sussex (☎ 882173)

NORFOLK, Lavinia Duchess of; Hon Lavinia Mary; *née* Strutt; CBE (1971); da of 3 Baron Belper; *b* 22 March 1916; *m* 1937, 16 Duke of Norfolk KG GCVO GBE TD PC (d 1975); *Career* bore Queen's Canopy at George VI's Coronation; Ld-Lt W Sussex 1975-; *Style* - Her Grace Lavinia, Duchess of Norfolk CBE, HM Lord-Lieut for W Sussex; Arundel Park, West Sussex

NORMAN, Nigel James; s and h of Sir Mark Annesley Norman, 3 Bt; *b* 5 Feb 1956; *Style* - Nigel Norman Esq

NORMAN, Hon Mrs Barbara Jacqueline; *née* Boot; da of 2 and last Baron Trent, KBE (d 1956); *b* 1915; *m* 1934 (m dis 1973), Maj Willoughby Rollo Norman, 2 s of Maj Rt Hon Sir Henry Norman, 1 Bt (d 1939); *Style* - The Hon Mrs Barbara Norman; 31 Milner st, SW3

NORMAN, Hon Mrs; Doreen Albinia de Burgh; *née* Gibbs; da of 1 Baron Wraxhall (d 1931); *b* 1913; *m* 1937, Charles Bathurst Norman; 1 s, 1 da; *Style* - The Hon Mrs Norman; Villa Villetri, Vallee des Vaux, Jersey

NORMAN, Sir Mark Annesley; 3 Bt (UK 1915), of Honeyhanger, Parish of Shottermill, Co Surrey; s of Air Cdre Sir Nigel Norman, 2 Bt, CBE (d 1943), and Lady Perkins, *qv*; *b* 8 Feb 1927; *Educ* Winchester; *m* 1953, Joanna, da of Lt-Col Ian Kilgour and Aura (ggda of Gen Sir George Walker, 1 Bt, GCB, KCTS); 2 s (Nigel James b 5 Feb 1956, Antony Rory b 9 Sept 1963), 1 da (Lucinda Fay b 7 Dec 1965); *Heir* s, Nigel Norman; *Career* chm IU Europe Ltd 1978- (dir 1974-); dir Gotaas-Larsen Shipping Corpn 1979-, IU Liberian Finance Corpn 1980-, chm Gotaas-Larsen (Europe) Ltd 1980-; dir IMS Lyerete Inc 1975-, PIE Internat Inc 1978-, VSI (Valve Systems Internat) Ltd 1973-; late Lt Coldstream Gds & Flying Offr 601 (London) Sqdn RAAF; *Recreations* gardening, shooting, workshop, people; *Clubs* White's, Pratt's, Travellers', MCC; *Style* - Sir Mark Norman, Bt; Wilcote Manor, Charlbury, Oxon (☎ Ramsden 357)

NORMAN, Nigel James; s and h of Sir Mark Norman, 3 Bt; *b* 5 Feb 1956; *Style* - Nigel Norman Esq

NORMAN, Baroness; Priscilla; CBE (1963), JP (Co of London 1944); da of late Maj Robert Reyntiens and late Lady Alice Bertie; *b* 1899; *m* 1, 1921, Col Alexander Koch de Gooreynd (who assumed surname of Worsthorne by deed poll 1923; m dis 1929); 2 s; m 2, 1933, 1 and last Baron Norman, DSO, PC (d 1950); *Career* VP Roy Coll of Nursing; vice-chm Women's Voluntary Services for Civil Defence 1938-41; *Style* - The Rt Hon Baroness Norman, CBE, JP; Aubrey Lodge, Aubrey rd, Campden Hill, W8 (☎ 01 727 6266)

NORMAN, Hon Mrs; Stella Maria; da of Baron Zuckerman, OM, KCB, FRS (Life Peer); *b* 1947; *Educ* Cranborne Chase Sch; E Anglia U, London U; *m* 1977, Dr Andrew R Norman; *Style* - The Hon Mrs Norman

NORMAN, Willoughby Rollo; s of Rt Hon Sir Henry Norman, 1 Bt, by his 2 w, Hon Florence McLaren CBE, yr da of 1 Baron Aberconway; half-unc to Sir Mark Norman, 3 Bt; *b* 12 Oct 1909; *Educ* Eton, Magdalen Coll Oxford; *m* 1, 1934, Hon Barbara Jacqueline Boot, da of 2 Baron Trent (d 1956); 1 s (Jeremy), 2 da (Sarah, Roselle); m 2, 1973, Caroline Haskard, da of Capt and Lady Diana Worthington (both d 1942); *Career* Maj Grenadier Guards 1939-45, chm The Boots Co Ltd 1961-72 (v-chm 1954-61), dir English China Clays, dir National Westminster Bank 1963-79 (chm Eastern region until 1979), dir Sheepbridge Engrg Ltd 1961-79, dir Guardian Royal Exchange Assurance until 1979, High Sheriff of Leicestershire 1960; *Recreations* shooting, deer stalking, gardening; *Clubs* White's, Pratt's; *Style* - Willoughby Norman Esq; Hurst Mill, Petersfield, Hants (☎ Harting 216); 28 Ranelagh House, Elystan place, SW3 (☎ 01 584 9410)

NORMAN-WALKER, Sir Hugh Selby; KCMG (1966, CMG 1964), OBE (1961); s of the late Col John Norman-Walker, CIE; *b* 17 Dec 1916; *Educ* Sherborne Sch, C C C Cambridge; *m* 1948, Janet, nee Baldock; *Career* KStJ 1967, C-in-C (honorary title) as Governor of Seychelles and when acting as Governor in Hong Kong, Colonial Administrative Service 1949, development secretary Nyasaland 1954, secretary to the Treasury Nyasaland 1960-64, Malawi 1964-65, HM Commissioner Bechuanaland 1965-66; *Recreations* sailing, bridge; *Clubs* East India, Devonshire, Sports and Public Schools; *Style* - Sir Hugh Norman-Walker, KCMG, OBE; Houndwood, Farley, Nr Salisbury, Wilts (☎ 072 272 214)

NORMANBY, 4 Marquess of (UK 1838); Oswald Constantine John Phipps; CBE (1974), JP (North Riding Yorks 1937); Baron Mulgrave (I 1767), Baron Mulgrave (GB 1794), Earl of Mulgrave and Viscount Normanby (UK 1812); s of Rev the 3 Marquess (d 1932); *b* 29 July 1912; *Educ* Eton, Ch Ch Oxford; *m* 1951, Hon Grania Maeve Rosaura, JP, da of 1 Baron Moyne, DSO, PC (assass 1944); 2 s, 5 da; *Heir* s, Earl of Mulgrave; *Career* chm Nat Art Collections Fund 1980-; High Steward York Minster 1980-; Lt 5 Bn Green Howards 1939; PPS to Sec of State for Dominion Affairs 1944-45, to Lord Pres of the Council 1945; a lord in waiting to HM the King 1945; chm King's Coll Blind and Council of St John for North Yorks 1950 and memb Council St John; Ld-Lt N Yorks 1955-74; Ld-Lt N Yorkshire 1974-; pres TA & VR Assoc for N England 1971-74; memb Council St Dunstan's; memb Ctee of Management RNLI; memb Gen Council of King Edward VII Hosp Fund; KStJ; *Style* - The Most Hon the Marquess of Normanby CBE JP, HM Lord-Lieut for N Yorks; Mulgrave Castle, Whitby, N Yorks (Sandsend 233); Argyll House, 211 King's rd, SW3

NORMANBY, Marchioness of - Hon Grania Maeve Rosaura; *née* Guinness; da of 1 Baron Moyne, DSO, TD, PC (assassinated 1944); *b* 1920; *Educ* Hon LLD Dublin; *m* 1951, 4 Marquess of Normanby; *Career* formerly Section Officer, WAAF; JP North Yorks; *Style* - The Most Hon the Marchioness of Normanby JP; Mulgrave Castle, Whitby; Argyll House, 211 King's rd, SW3 (☎ 01 352 5154)

NORMAND, Sir Charles (William Blyth); CIE (1938); s of John Hodge Normand (d 1912); *b* 10 Sept 1889; *Educ* Royal HS Edinburgh, Edinburgh U; *m* 1920, Alison, nee MacLennan; 1 s (and 1 decd); *Career* kt 1945, Lt IARO Mesopotamia 1916-19, research scholar Edinburgh 1911-13, Imperial Meteorologist India 1913-15 and 1919-27, dir gen of Observatories India 1927-44, on special duty Govt of India 1944-45, chm Meteorological research Ctee 1955-58 (memb 1945-58), pres Royal Met Soc 1951-53, sec Int Ozone Cmmn 1948-60; *Style* - Sir Charles Normand CIE; 23 St Thomas st, Winchester

NORMAND, Hon Mrs William; Elizabeth Ann; da of James Cumming, of Biggar, Lanarkshire; *m* 1945, Hon William Normand (d 1967); *Style* - The Hon Mrs William Normand; 15 Ravelston Heights, Edinburgh

NORMANTON, 6 Earl of (I 1806); Shaun James Christian Wellbore Ellis Agar; also Baron Mendip (GB 1794), Baron Somerton (I 1795 & UK 1873, which sits as), and Viscount Somerton (I 1800); s of 5 Earl of Normanton (d 1967) by his 2 w, Lady Fiona Pratt, da of 4 Marquess Camden; *b* 21 Aug 1945; *Educ* Eton; *m* 1970, Victoria, da of John Beard, of Guernsey; 2 da; *Heir* bro, Hon Mark Agar; *Career* Capt Blues & Royals to 1972, served N Ireland; farmer; *Recreations* motor racing, shooting, skiing; *Clubs* White's, Roy Yacht Sqdn; *Style* - The Rt Hon Earl of Normanton; Somerley, Ringwood, Hants (☎ 3253)

NORMANTON, Fiona, Countess of - Lady Fiona; *née* Pratt; da of late 4 Marquess Camden; *b* 1911; *m* 1, 1931 (m dis 1944), Maj Sir (John) Gerard Henry Fleetwood Fuller, 2 Bt, Life Gds (ret); 2 s; m 2, 1944, 5 Earl of Normanton (d 1967); 2 s; *Style* - The Rt Hon Fiona, Countess of Normanton; North End Park, Harbridge Green, Ringwood, Hants (☎ Fordingbridge 52968)

NORREYS OF RYCOTE, Lord; Henry Mark Willoughby Bertie; s and h of 14 (and 9) Earl of Lindsey and Abingdon; *b* 6 June 1958; *Educ* Eton, Edinburgh U; *Heir* bro, Hon Alexander Bertie; *Clubs* Brooks's, Puffin's (Edinburgh); *Style* - Lord Norreys of Rycote; Gilmilnscroft, Sorn, Mauchline, Ayrshire

NORRIE, 2 Baron (UK 1957); George Willoughby Moke Norrie; s of 1 Baron, GCMG, GCVO, CB, DSO, MC (d 1977); *b* 27 April 1936; *Educ* Eton, RMA Sandhurst; *m* 1964, Celia Marguerite, da of John Pelham Mann, MC, of Brimpton House, Reading, Berks; 1 s, 2 da; *Heir* s, Mark Willoughby John Norrie; *Career* 11 Hussars (PAO), 2 Lt 1956, Lt 1958, Acting Capt 1960-61, Capt 1962, GSO 3 Fourth Gds Bde 1967-69, Actg Maj Roy Hussars 1969-70; pres Roy British Legion (Newbury) 1972; ptnr Fairfield Nurseries (Hermitage) Ltd, nr Newbury; *Clubs* MCC, Cavalry; *Style* - The Rt Hon the Lord Norrie; Henwick Old Farm, Newbury, Berks (☎ Thatcham 62808)

NORRIE, Hon Annabel Mary Adelaide; da of 1 Baron Norrie, GCMG, GCVO, CB, DSO, MC (d 1977); *b* 23 Dec 1945; *Educ* Downham Herts, Blois France; *Style* - The Hon Annabel Norrie; 124 Swan Court, Chelsea Manor st, SW3

NORRIE, Hon Clare Marguerite; da of 2 Baron Norrie; *b* 1966; *Style* - The Hon Clare Norrie

NORRIE, Hon Guy Bainbridge; s of 1 Baron Norrie, GCMG, GCVO, CB, DSO, MC; *b* 3 May 1940; *Educ* Eton; *m* 1968, Sarah Georgina, da of Maj George Fielding, DSO (fifth in descent from Henry Fielding, the magistrate and novelist, author of *Tom Jones* etc; Henry himself was gs of Rev Hon John Fielding, DD, Chaplain to William III and yr bro of (2) Earl of Desmond & (3 Earl of) Denbigh); 2 s; *Career* ret Lt-Col Roy Hussars, GSO (3) HQ 1 British Corps 1966-67; RN Staff Coll 1972; GSO (2) MOD (Directorate of Army Training) 1973-74; GSO (1) (DS) Staff Coll, Camberley 1977-78; Lloyd's Underwriter; dir Willis Faber & Dumas (Agencies) Ltd 1980-; *Recreations* fishing, stalking, shooting, skiing; *Clubs* City of London; *Style* - The Hon Guy Norrie; 21 Radipole rd, SW6 (☎ 01 731 1645)

NORRIE, Hon Julia Jocelyn; da of 2 Baron Norrie; *b* 1968; *Style* - The Hon Julia Norrie

NORRIE, Hon Mark Willoughby John; s and h of 2 Baron Norrie; *b* 31 March 1972; *Style* - The Hon Mark Norrie

NORRIE, Patricia Baroness; Patricia Merryweather; da of late Emerson Bainbridge, MP, of Auchnashellach, Ross-shire; *m* 1938, as his 2 w, 1 Baron Norrie, GCMG, GCVO, CB, DSO (d 1977); *Style* The Rt Hon Patricia, Lady Norrie; The Ham, Wantage, Oxon

NORRIS, Dame Ada May; DBE (1976, OBE 1954), CMG (1969); da of Alan Herbert Bickford (d 1911); *b* 28 July 1901; *Educ* Melbourne HS, Melbourne U; *m* 1929, John Gerald Norris; 2 da (Rosemary Anne Balmford, Elizabeth Jane); *Career* teacher 1925-29, pres Australian Advsy Cncl for Physically Handicapped 1955-57, Australian rep UN Cmmn Status Women 1961-63, exec ctee Melbourne Cncl of Women 1966-79, pres Australian Nat Cncl Women 1967-70, chm Nat Ctee for Int Women's Year 1974-76, chm Nat Status of Women Ctee 1976-80, UN Peace Medal 1975; *Clubs* Melbourne Lyceum; *Style* - Dame Ada Norris, DBE, CMG; 10 Winnifred cres, Toorak, Victoria, Australia (☎ 241 5166)

NORTH, Barony of (E 1554); abeyant

1942; *see* Hon Mrs Bowlby and Hon Mrs North-Beauchamp

NORTH, Hon Mrs; Hon Carolyn; da of 2 Baron Banbury of Southam; *b* 1947; *m* 1977, Christopher J A North; *Style* - The Hon Mrs North

NORTH, Hon Charles Evelyn; s of 8 Earl of Guilford (d 1949); *b* 1918; *Educ* Eton, London U; *m* 1, 1942, Maureen O'Callaghan (m dis 1957), da of Maj F C B Baldwin; 1 s, 1 da; m 2, 1959, Joan Aston, da of Maj F B Booker (d 1954), of Edenmore House, Raheny, Co Dublin; *Career* Pilot Offr RAFVR 1940, Flight Lt 1942, staff Air Miny and Miny of Aircraft Production; dir J M W North and Co Ltd London; professional engr with Dept of the Environment; *Style* - The Hon Charles North; Park End House, Eythorne, Dover, Kent (☎ Shepherdswell 830368)

NORTH, Lt-Col Geoffrey Edward Ford; MC (1943), JP (Devon 1970); s of Stephen North (d 1963); *b* 21 Jan 1917; *Educ* Winchester, New Coll Oxford; *m* 1950, Hon Margaret Isolda de Grey, da of late Lt-Col 8 Baron Walsingham; 1 s, 3 da; *Career* 10 Roy Hussars WW II, dispatches, Lt-Col Middle East, Italy; barr 1939, chm City Offices Co Ltd 1978-; *Recreations* stalking, fishing, shooting, skiing; *Clubs* Cavalry and Guards; *Style* - Lt-Col Geoffrey North, MC, JP; Colleton Hall, Rackenford, Tiverton, Devon (☎ Rackenford 300); La Farigoulette, Le Rey d'Agneou, 83550 Vidauban, Var, France

NORTH, Sir (William) Jonathan Frederick; 2 Bt (UK 1920), of Southwell, Co Nottingham; s of Hon John Montagu William North (s of 8 Earl of Guilford); suc maternal gf (Sir William Hicking, 1 Bt) 1947 by special remainder; *b* 6 Feb 1931; *Educ* Marlborough; *m* 1956, Sara Virginia, da of Air Ch Marshal Sir Donald Hardman GBE KCB DFC; 1 s, 2 da; *Heir* s, Jeremy William Francis North; *Style* - Sir Jonathan North, Bt; Frogmore, Weston-under-Penyard, Herefordshire (☎ Lea 214)

NORTH, Hon John Montagu William; s of 8 Earl of Guilford (d 1949); *b* 1905; *Educ* R N Colls Osborne and Dartmouth; *m* 1, 1927, Muriel Norton (m dis 1938), da of Sir William Hicking, 1 Bt (d 1947); 1 s, 1 da; m 2, 1939, Marion Dyer, da of F E Chase; *Style* - The Hon John North; 57 Montagu sq, W1

NORTH, Jeremy William Francis; s and h of Sir (William) Jonathan Frederick North, 2 Bt; *b* 5 May 1960; *Style* - Jeremy North Esq

NORTH, Hon Mrs; Margaret Isolda; *née* de Grey; da of 8 Baron Walsingham, DSO, OBE (d 1965); *b* 1926; *m* 1950, Maj Geoffrey Edward Ford North, MC; 1 s, 3 da; *Style* - The Hon Mrs North; Colleton Hall, Rackenford, Tiverton, Devon

NORTH, Lord; Piers Edward Brownlow North; s & h of 9 Earl of Guilford; *b* 9 March 1971; *Style* - Lord North

NORTH, Dr Peter Machin; s of Geoffrey Machin North (d 1974); *b* 30 Aug 1936; *Educ* Oakham Sch, Keble Coll Oxford; *m* 1960, Stephanie Mary, da of Thomas Chadwick (d 1963); 2 s (Nicholas Machin b 1964, James William Thomas b 1971), 1 da (Jane Amanda b 1962); *Career* Lt Royal Leicestershire Regt Cyprus 1955-56; teaching assist Northwestern U Sch of Law Chicago 1960-61, lecturer U College of Wales Aberystwyth 1961-63, Nottingham 1963-65, tutor in law Keble Coll Oxford 1965-76, Fellow of Keble Coll 1976-, Law Commissioner for England and Wales 1976-; *Recreations* locking; yacht: 'Topper' *Style* - Dr Peter North; Law Commission, Conquest House, 37-38 John st, Theobald's rd, WC1 (☎ 01 242 0861)

NORTH, Roger; s of Frederick Keppel North (d 1948, gggggs of Hon Roger North KC, MP, himself 6 s of 4 Baron North, bro of 1 Baron Guilford & a memorist) by his w Grace, da of Gen Hon Sir Percy Fielding, KCB (2 s of 7 Earl of Denbigh); Frederick's mother Augusta was gda of 4 Earl of Albemarle; *b* 10 Dec 1901; *Educ* Eton, Cambridge; *m* 1934, Pamela Susan, da of Rev Henry William Leycester O'Rorke (d 1940); 1 s (Thomas Frederick m 1974), 3 da (Christine m 1963, Valerie Susan m 1967, Grace Elisabeth m 1975); *Career* barrister-at-law, Recorder of the Crown

Court 1969-73; *Recreations* vintage motors; *Clubs* Royal Institution, Norfolk; *Style* - Roger North Esq; Rougham Hall, Rougham, Kings Lynn, Norfolk (☎ Weasenham St Peter 230)

NORTH, Hon Mrs; Rosemary Victoria; *née* Orde-Powlett; da of 7 Baron Bolton; *b* 1952; *m* 1974, John Richard Bentley North; 1 s, 1 da; *Style* - The Hon Mrs North; Disi Cottage, PB63, Umvukwes, Zimbabwe

NORTH, Lady; Thelma Grace; *née* Dawson; *m* 1924, Rt Hon Sir Alfred North, KBE, PC, sometime Chm NZ Press Cncl & Pres NZ Court of Appeal (d 1981); 2 s, 1 da; *Style* - Lady North; 28 Mahoe av, Remuera, Auckland, New Zealand

NORTH-BEAUCHAMP, Hon Mrs (Susan Silence); da of late Hon Dudley William John North MC and sis of 13 Baron North (d 1941); *b* 19 Jan 1920; *m* 1944, Frederick Guy Beauchamp, MD, MRCS; 3 da; co-heiress to abeyant Barony of North; took by deed poll 1943 additional surname Beauchamp; *Style* - The Hon Mrs North-Beauchamp; 19 Beaumont St, W1

NORTHAMPTON, 7 Marquess of (UK 1812); Spencer Douglas David Compton; DL (Northants 1979); also Earl of Northampton (UK 1618), Earl Compton, and Baron Wilmington (both UK 1812); s of 6 Marquess of Northampton, DSO (d 1978), by his 2 w Virginia, nee Rimington; *b* 2 April 1946; *Educ* Eton; *m* 1, 1967, Henriette Luisa Maria (m dis 1973), da of late Baron Bentinck, sometime Netherlands Ambass to France; 1 s, 1 da; m 2, 1974 (m dis 1977), Annette Marie, da of C A R Smallwood; m 3, 1977, Rosemary, da of P Hancock and formerly w of Hon Charles Dawson-Damer (bro of 7 Earl of Portarlington); *Heir* s, Earl Compton; *Career* as proprietor of both Compton Wynyates (built 1480-1520; the garden is noted for its topiary) and Castle Ashby (constructed 1574; Inigo Jones frontage of 1635), Lord Northampton is probably unique in possessing two important examples of the Tudor mansion, one built at the beginning of the dynasty's reign, the other towards the close; patron of nine livings; *Clubs* Turf; *Style* - The Most Hon The Marquess of Northampton DL; Compton Wynyates, Tysoe, Warwick (☎ 029 588 229/629); Castle Ashby, Northampton (☎ Yardley Hastings 232/332)

NORTHBOURNE, 4 Baron (UK 1844); Sir Walter Ernest Christopher James; 5 Bt (GB 1791); s of 3 Baron (d 1932); *b* 18 Jan 1896; *Educ* Eton, Magdalen Oxford; *m* 1925, Katherine Louise, JP (d 1980), da of late George A Nickerson, of Boston, Mass, and Hon Lady Hood; 1 s, 4 da; *Heir* s, Hon Christopher George Walter James; *Career* late Lt 4 Bn The Buffs; chm Kent Agriculture Exec Ctee 1946-57; *Clubs* Farmers', Leander; *Style* - The Rt Hon the Lord Northbourne; Northbourne Court, Deal, Kent (☎ Deal 4617)

NORTHBROOK, 5 Baron (UK 1886); Sir Francis John Baring; 7 Bt (GB 1793), JP (Hants 1954), DL (1972); s of 4 Baron (d 1947); *b* 31 May 1915; *Educ* Winchester, Trin Oxford; *m* 1951, Rowena Margaret, da of Brig-Gen Sir William Henry Manning, GCMG, KBE, CB (d 1932); 1 s, 3 da; *Heir* s, Hon Francis Thomas Baring; *Style* - The Rt Hon Lord Northbrook, JP, DL; East Stratton House, East Stratton, Winchester, Hants (☎ Micheldever 469)

NORTHCHURCH, Baroness (Life Peeress UK 1963); *see* Davidson, DBE, Dowager Viscountess

NORTHCOTE, Lady Catherine Cecilia Mary; da of 3 Earl of Iddesleigh (d 1970); *b* 1931; *Educ* Univ Coll London; *Style* - Lady Catherine Northcote; c/o Pynes, Exeter, Devon

NORTHCOTE, Cecil Henry Stafford; s of Capt (Hon Maj) Cecil Stafford Northcote (d 1912); *b* 8 June 1912; *Educ* Douai Sch, Queen's Oxford; *m* 1936, Winifreda Marguerite Ida, nee Williams; 2 s, 1 da; *Career* Kt of Malta (1957), Kt St Gregory (1976), headmaster Bishton Hall Prep Sch 1936-78, chm Stafford & Stone Conservative Div 1972-81, Staffordshire County Cllr 1958-81, High Sheriff Staffordshire 1981; *Recreations* walking, gardening (assistant), cricket (watching);

Clubs Staffordshire County; *Style* - Cecil Northcote Esq; Bishton Hall, Wolseley Bridge, nr Stafford; Ucheldir, Sarnau, Llandyssul, Dyfed

NORTHCOTE, Donald Henry; s of Frederick Northcote; *b* 27 Dec 1921; *Educ* George Monoux G S, London U, Cambridge; *m* 1948, Eva Marjorie, nee Mayo; 2 da; *Career* Prof Plant Biochemistry Cambridge 1972-, Master Sidney Sussex Coll, Cambridge 1976-; *Recreations* sailing (yacht: 'Sprite'); *Style* - Donald Northcote Esq; The Masters Lodge, Sidney Sussex Coll, Cambridge (☎ 0223 355860)

NORTHCOTE, Hon Edward Frederic; s of 3 Earl of Iddesleigh; *b* 1934; *Educ* Downside and Trin Oxford; *m* 1963, Vivien Sheena, da of Col Robert J A Hornby, OBE; 2 s, 1 da; *Career* served with Oxford U OTC 1953-55; Maj Intelligence Corps; principal offr HM Treasury 1969; *Style* - The Hon Edward Northcote; 91 Cottenham Park rd, Wimbledon SW20

NORTHCOTE, Hon Mrs; Mary Betty; da of 1 Baron Cunliffe (d 1920); *b* 1898; *m* 1921, Lt-Col Otho Stuart Irwin Northcote (d 1966); 1 da; *Style* - The Hon Mrs Northcote; 24 Broadway ave, Newlands, Cape, S Africa

NORTHCOTE, Lady Mary Louise; da of 4 Earl of Iddesleigh; *b* 14 April 1959; *Style* - Lady Mary Northcote

NORTHCOTE, His Hon Judge; Peter Colston Northcote; s of the late William George Northcote; *b* 23 Oct 1920; *Educ* Ellesmere Coll, Bristol U; *m* 1947, Patricia Elizabeth, nee Bickley; 2 s; *Career* Circuit Judge 1973, chm National Insur Tribunal, West Midland Rent Tribunal, Ag Land Tribunal; *Recreations* travel, music; *Clubs* Army & Navy; *Style* - His Hon Judge Northcote; Wroxeter Grange, Shrewsbury, Salop (☎ 074 375 279)

NORTHESK, 13 Earl of (S 1647); Robert Andrew Carnegie; also Lord Rosehill and Inglismaldie (S precedence 1639); s of 12 Earl of Northesk (d 1975) and Dorothy (da of Col Sir William Campion, KCMG, DSO, DL, himself s of Col William Campion, CB, VD, JP, DL, and Hon Gertrude Brand; she was da of 1 Viscount Hampden & 23 Baron Dacre, GCB, PC; Dorothy's mother was Katherine, aunt of 11 Baron Byron); the 1 Earl of Northesk was yr bro of 1 Earl of Southesk; *b* 24 June 1926; *Educ* Pangbourne, Tabor Naval Acad, Mass, USA; *m* 1949, Jean, yr da of Capt John MacRae, of Argyll, by Lady Phyllis Hervey (da of 4 Marquess of Bristol); 1 s, 2 da (and 1 s decd); *Heir* s, Lord Rosehill; *Career* landowner & farmer; served RN 1942-45; memb Br Racing Drivers Club 1957-; dir Internat Fedn Charolais Cattle, Cncl Br Charolais Cattle Soc 1972-; chm Midhurst RDC 1972-74; dir Chandler Hargreaves Whittall (IOM) 1979-, IOM Bank 1980-, Buchan Sch (IOM) 1980-; *Recreations* gardening, shooting, motor racing, silversmithing; *Style* - The Rt Hon Earl of Northesk; Springwaters, Ballamodha, IOM

NORTHESK, Betty, Countess of; Elizabeth; da of late Anthony A Vlasto; *m* 1929, 11 Earl of Northesk (d 1963); 1 da (adopted); *Style* - The Rt Hon Betty, Countess of Northesk; Bear Farm, Binfield, Bracknell, Berks (☎ Shurlock Row 286); Glenley Farm House, Glenogil, by Forfar, Angus (Fern 216)

NORTHFIELD, Baron (Life Peer UK 1975); (William) Donald Chapman; s of W H Chapman of Barnsley, Yorks; *b* 25 Nov 1923; *Educ* Barnsley G S, Emmanuel Cambridge; *Career* formerly memb Cambridge Borough Council; gen sec Fabian Soc 1949-53; MP (L) Birmingham (Northfield) 1951-70; research fell Nuffield Coll Oxford 1971-73; visiting fell Centre for Contemporary European studies U of Sussex 1973; chm HM Development Commissioners 1974; chm Telford New Town Development Corpn 1975; co dir; economist, writer, braoadcaster; *Clubs* Reform; *Style* - The Rt Hon the Lord Northfield; Dale End House, Ironbridge, Telford, Salop

NORTHUMBERLAND, 10 Duke of (GB 1776); Sir Hugh Algernon Percy; 13 Bt (E 1660), KG (1959), GCVO (1981), TD (1961), PC (1973), JP

(Northumberland 1946); also Baron Percy (GB 1723), Earl of Northumberland and Baron Warkworth (GB 1749), Earl Percy (GB 1776), Earl of Beverly (GB 1790), and Lord Lovaine, Baron of Alnwick (GB 1784); s of 8 Duke, KG, CBE, MVO (d 1930), and Lady Helen Gordon-Lennox, GCVO, CBE, JP (da of 7 Duke of Richmond); suc bro, 9 Duke (ka 1940); *b* 6 April 1914; *Educ* Eton, Ch Ch Oxford; *m* 1946, Lady Elizabeth Diana Montagu Douglas Scott, da of 8 Duke of Buccleuch, KT, GCVO, TD, PC; 3 s, 3 da; *Heir* s, Earl Percy; *Career* Lt Northumberland Hussars 1936, RA 1940, Capt 1941; Lord Steward of HM's Household 1973-, chm Court of U of Durham 1956-64; chancellor U of Newcastle upon Tyne 1964-; chm Agricultural Research Council 1958-68; Ld-Lt & Custos Rotulorum Northumberland 1956-; MFH Percy Foxhounds 1940-; Hon assist RCVS 1967; pres Wild Fowl Trust 1969-72, chm Departmental Ctee Slaughter of Horses 1952, Border Forest Park Ctee 1956-68; chm Independent Ctee of Inquiry on Foot and Mouth Disease 1968; Hon treas Roy Nat Life-Boat Institution; chm Medical Research Council 1969-77; KStJ; *Clubs* Boodle's, Turf; *Style* - His Grace the Duke of Northumberland KG GCVO TD PC JP, HM Lord-Lieut for Northumberland; Alnwick Castle, Northumberland (☎ 2456); Syon House, Brentford (☎ Isleworth 2353); Clive Lodge, Albury Park, Guildford (☎ Shere 2695)

NORTON, 7 Baron (UK 1878); Maj John Arden Adderley; OBE (1964); s of 6 Baron (d 1961); *b* 24 Nov 1915; *Educ* Radley, Magdalen Oxford; *m* 1946, Betty Margaret, JP, da of late James McKee Hannah, of Domaine de Fontvieille, Aix-en-Provence; 2 s; *Heir* s, Hon James Nigel Arden Adderley; *Career* Lt RE 1940, served 1940-45, Maj 1944; Oxford U Greenland Expedition 1938, assist master Oundle Sch 1938-39; *Style* - The Rt Hon the Lord Norton, OBE; Fillongley Hall, Coventry, W Midlands (☎ Fillongley 40303)

NORTON, Hon Adam Gregory; s of 2 Baron Rathcreedan; *b* 1952; *m* 1980, Hilary Shelton, da of Edmon Ryan, of Anchorage, Kentucky, USA; *Style* - The Hon Adam Norton

NORTON, Hon Christopher John; s and h of 2 Baron Rathcreedan, TD; *b* 3 June 1949; *Educ* Wellington Coll; *m* 1978, Lavinia Anne Ross, da of Alan George Ross Ormiston, of Holford House, N Chailey, Sussex; *Style* - The Hon Christopher Norton

NORTON, Hon Elizabeth Ann; da of 2 Baron Rathcreedan; *b* 1954; *Style* - The Hon Elizabeth Ann Norton

NORTON, Hon Francis John Hilary; s of 7 Baron Grantley, MC; *b* 28 Sept 1960; *Style* - The Hon Francis Norton

NORTON, James William; CBE (1965); s of William Francis Duesbury Norton (d 1949); *b* 22 Feb 1918; *Educ* Marlborough, Dresden, Nottingham U; *m* 1952, Mary Helen, da of late William Reeves of Arkansas USA; *Career* Capt WW II, Dunlop Rubber Co Ltd 1937, resident rep Iran 1948-65; local rep in Iran Fedn of British Industs (now CBI) 1961-65; dir and jt md F Longdon & Co Ltd 1969-78; *Recreations* gardening, golf, tennis, travel, cars; *Clubs* E India Devonshire, Roy Soc of St George, Turf (Cairo), Imperial Iranian Sports (Teheran); *Style* - James Norton Esq, CBE; Random House, Hob Hill, Hazlewood, Derbys (☎ Derby 840822)

NORTON, Hon Michael Adrian; s of 1 Baron Rathcreedan (d 1930); *b* 1907; *Educ* Wellington, Trinity Coll Cambridge; *Clubs* Reform; *Style* - The Hon Michael Norton; 6 Carisbrooke Court, Weymouth St, WI

NORTON, Hon Richard William Brinsley; s of 7 Baron Grantley, MC; *b* 30 Jan 1956; *Style* - The Hon Richard Norton

NORTON, Tom; TD (1966), JP (1961), DL (Radnorshire 1962); s of Tom Norton JP (d 1955); *b* 15 April 1920; *Educ* Hanley Castle, Birmingham U; *m* 1948, Pauline Fane, nee Evans; 3 s, 1 da; *Career* Capt RA; chm & md Automobile Palace Hldg Ltd (dir 1947-); High Sheriff Radnorshire 1966; *Recreations* gardening, old cycles; *Clubs* Roy Automobile; *Style* - Tom Norton Esq, TD, JP, DL; Sargodha, Brookfields, Cefnllys Lane, Llandrindod

Wells, Powys (☎ 0597 2079)

NORTON-GRIFFITHS, John; s and h of Sir Peter Norton-Griffiths, 2 Bt; *b* 4 Oct 1938; *Educ* Eton; *m* 1964, Marilyn Margaret, da of Norman Grimley of Liverpool; *Career* late Sub-Lt RN; chartered accountant, pres Main Street Computers Inc 1980-; FCA; *Style* - John Norton-Griffiths Esq; 17 Royal Drive, Bricktown, NJ 08723, USA

NORTON-GRIFFITHS, Sir Peter; 2 Bt (UK 1922), of Wonham, Betchworth, Co Surrey; s of 1 Bt, KCB, DSO (d 1930); *b* 1905; *Educ* Eton, Magdalen Oxford; *m* 1935, Kathryn (d 1980), da of late George F Schrafft, of Mass USA; 2 s, 1 da; *Heir* s, John Norton-Griffiths; *Career* served with Intelligence Corps 1940-45, Maj 1941-42; barr Inner Temple 1931; gen man Shell Co of Portugal 1951-53, admin délégué and dir gen Belgian Shell Co 1953, ret 1960; *Clubs* Boodle's; *Style* - Sir Peter Norton-Griffiths, Bt; c/o Williams & Glyn's Bank Ltd, Kirkland House, Whitehall, SW1

NORWICH, 2 Viscount (UK 1952); John Julius Cooper; s of Rt Hon 1 Viscount Norwich, GCMG, DSO, PC (Duff Cooper), Min of Information 1940-41, Br Envoy to French Nat Cttee N Africa 1943-44 and Ambass to France 1944-47, by Lady Diana Cooper, *qv*; *b* 15 Sept 1929; *Educ* Upper Canada Coll Toronto, Eton, Strasbourg U, New Coll Oxford; *m* 1952, Anne Frances May, da of Hon Sir Bede Clifford, GCMG, CB, MVO (yst s of 10 Baron Clifford of Chudleigh by his 1 w Catherine), and Alice, nee Gundry, of Cleveland Ohio; 1 s, 1 da; *Heir* s, Hon Jason Cooper; *Career* writer and (as John Julius Norwich) broadcaster; with FO 1952-64; FRSL; chm Venice in Peril Fund, Serenissima Travel Ltd; memb Exec Cttee Nat Tst 1969-; *Style* - The Rt Hon The Viscount Norwich; 24 Blomfield rd, W9 (☎ 01 286 5050)

NORWICH, 69 Bishop of (diocese est 1088 by Herbert de Lozinga, Bp of Thetford, of the See founded at Dunwich AD 630 by Felix of Burgundy) 1971-; **Rt Rev Maurice Arthur Ponsonby Wood**; DSC (1944); s of Arthur Wood; *b* 26 Aug 1916; *Educ* Monkton Combe Sch, Queens' Cambridge; *m* 1, 1947, Marjorie, nee Pennell (d 1954); 2 s, 1 da; m 2, 1955, Margaret, da of Rev E Sandford; 2 s, 1 da; *Career* patron of some 81 livings, alternately of 3, and of one every third turn, and of the Archdeaconries of Norwich, Norfolk and Lynn; is Titular Abbot of St Benet's; took seat in House of Lords 1975; Rural Dean Islington 1952-61; owner yacht: 'Telscombe'; *Style* - The Rt Rev The Bishop of Norwich DSC; The Bishop's House, Norwich (☎ 29001)

NOTT, Brig Donald Harley; DSO (1941), OBE (1954), MC (1939) & Bar (1942); s of the late John Harley Nott; *b* 27 April 1908; *Educ* Marlborough, Sandhurst; *m* 1, 1933, Eve, nee Harben (m dis); 1 da; m 2, 1947, Elfriede Eugenie, da of Maj Eugen August von Kahler; 1 s, 1 da; *Career* assistant Civil Defence Offr Worcs 1959-69, OStJ, DL 1963 Worcs; *Recreations* archery, fishing, shooting, painting; *Style* - Brig Donald Nott, DSO, OBE, MC*, DL; Four Seasons, Battenhall av, Worcester (☎ Worcester 354402)

NOTT, Miss Kathleen Cecilia; da of Philip Nott (d 1931); *Educ* Mary Datchelor Sch, Somerville Coll Oxford, King's Coll London; *m* (m dis); *Career* author (poet, novelist, philosopher), critic (Observer, Times, TLS, BBC, Encounter and others), FRSL 1977, pres English PEN 1974-75; *Recreations* walking, playing the piano; *Clubs* PEN, Society of Authors, University Women's; *Style* - Miss Kathleen Nott; 5 Limpsfield ave, Thornton Heath, Surrey (☎ 01 684 2889)

NOWELL-SMITH, Simon Harcourt; s of Nowell Charles Smith (d 1961); *b* 5 Jan 1909; *Educ* Sherborne Sch, New Coll Oxford; *m* 1938, Marion Sinclair, nee Crichton; 2 s (Geoffrey Simon, John Colin), 1 da (Elizabeth Campbell); *Career* editorial staff The Times 1932-40, Intelligence Division Naval Staff 1940-45, librarian and sec London Library 1950-56, Lyell reader in Bibliography Oxford U 1965-67; author; OStJ 1959; *Recreations* book collecting; *Clubs* Athenaeum, Roxburghe, Savage; *Style* - Simon Nowell-

Smith Esq; 7 Beaumont rd, Headington, Oxford (☎ Oxford 61688)

NUGEE, Edward George; TD (1964), QC (1977); s of Brig George Travers Nugee, CBE, DSO, MC, RA (d 1977); *b* 9 Aug 1928; *Educ* Radley, Worcester Coll Oxford; *m* 1955, Rachel Elizabeth (central pres of the Mothers' Union), da of John M Makower, MBE, MC; 4 s; *Career* barr Inner Temple 1955, Bencher 1976, *ad eundem* Lincoln's Inn 1968, Conveyancing Counsel of the Court 1967-77, v-chm Cncl of Legal Educn 1976- (memb 1967-), chm Bd of Studies 1976-, Lord Chllr's Law Reform Ctee 1973-, Advsy Ctee on Legal Educn 1971-; *Recreations* - travel, cooking, the family; *Style* - Edward Nugee Esq, TD, QC; 3 New sq, Lincoln's Inn, WC2 (☎ 01 405 9204); 10 Heath Hurst rd, NW3 (☎ 01 435 9204)

NUGENT OF GUILDFORD, Baron (Life Peer UK 1966); Sir (George) Richard Hodges Nugent; 1 Bt (UK 1960), PC (1962), JP (Surrey 1941); s of late Col George H Nugent, RA, of Churt, Surrey; *b* 1907; *Educ* Imperial Service Coll, RMA; *m* 1937, Ruth, da of late Hugh G Stafford, of Tilford, Surrey; *Heir* none; *Career* CC (1942), County Alderman (1951-52) Surrey; MP (C) Surrey 1950-66; jt parly sec Min of Agriculture, Fisheries and Food 1951-57; parly sec Min of Transport 1957-59; chm Thames Conservancy 1961-74; chm Select Ctee for Nationalised Industries 1961-64; past pres Assoc of River Authorities 1965-74; chm Standing Conference on London and South E Regional Planning; chm Nat Water Council 1973-78; dep speaker House of Lords; hon doctor U of Surrey; *Clubs* RAC; *Style* - The Rt Hon Lord Nugent of Guildford PC JP; Blacknest Cottage, Dunsfold, nr Godalming, Surrey (☎ Dunsfold 210)

NUGENT, Christopher George Ridley; s and h of Sir Robin George Colborne Nugent, 5 Bt; *b* 5 Oct 1949; *Educ* Eton, E Anglia U; *Style* - Christopher Nugent Esq

NUGENT, Lady; Cynthia Maud; da of late Capt Frederick William Ramsden; *m* 1917, Rt Hon Sir Roland Thomas Nugent, 1 Bt (d 1962, when title became extinct); *Style* - Lady Nugent; Quinton Castle, Portaferry, Co Down

NUGENT, Baron (7 of Austrian cr of 1859); David James Douglas Nugent; s of Baron Nugent (5 of Austrian cr, d 1938) and Frances, da of Lt Robert Campbell, RN (bro of 1 & 2 Barons Blythswood and 4 s of Archibald Douglas, 17 Laird of Mains, who assumed the name Campbell on succeeding as 12 Laird of Blythswood); paternally the present Baron descends from Andrew Nugent, bro of 11 Baron Delvin (which dignity later became merged in the Earldom of Westmeath) and beyond Andrew from Foulke de Nogent, who accompanied William The Conqueror to England 1066; suc bro (6 Baron, ka Italy 1944); *b* 24 Nov 1917; *Educ* Lancing; *m* 1, 1958 (m dis 1960), Rosemary, da of William Edwards, of St John's Wood; m 2, 1968, Mary, JP (d 1975), da of late William Wroth, of Bigbury Court, Devon, and widow of Howard Seys-Phillips; m 3, 1979, Evelyn, da of Lt-Col Frank Noel, OBE (gs of Capt Frederic Noel, RN, half-bro of 1 Earl of Gainsborough of the 2 cr), and formerly w of (1) Maj John Bailey, (2) Sir Hector Lethbridge, 6 Bt; *Heir* (Baron) Charles Nugent (b 26 June 1942, educ Brickwall, gs of (Baron) Frank Burnell-Nugent, CB, DSO, OBE, yr bro of (Baron) Albert Nugent , f of the present Baron); *Career* bookseller; *Recreations* historical research, genealogy, writing; *Style* - Baron Nugent; Alford House, Castle Cary, Somerset (☎ Wheathill 315)

NUGENT, Lady Elizabeth Maria; *née* Guinness; da of Maj Arthur Onslow Edward Guinness, Viscount Elveden, and sis of 3 Earl of Iveagh; *b* 1939; *m* 1960, David Hugh Lavallin Nugent, s of Sir Hugh Nugent, 6 Bt; raised to the rank of an Earl's daughter 1969; *Style* - Lady Elizabeth Nugent; Chaddleworth House, Chaddleworth, Newbury; Ross Castle, Mount Nugent, Co Cavan

NUGENT, Sir Hugh Charles; 6 Bt (I 1795), of Ballinlough, Westmeath; Count of the Holy Roman Empire; s of late Charles Hugh Nugent, only s of 5 Bt; suc gf 1927; *b* (posthumous) 26 May 1904; *Educ* Stonyhurst; *m* 1931, Margaret Mary Lavallin, da of late Rev Herbert Lavallin Puxley; 2 s; *Heir* s, John Edwin Lavallin Nugent; *Career* formerly Flying Offr RAFVR, despatches WW II; Kt of Sov

Order of Malta; *Style* - Sir Hugh Nugent, Bt; Ballinlough Castle, Clonmellon, Co Westmeath, Ireland (☎ Trim 33135)

NUGENT, John Edwin Lavallin; JP (Berks); s and h of Sir Hugh Charles Nugent, 6 Bt; *b* 16 March 1933; *Educ* Eton; *m* 1959, Penelope Anne, da of Brig Richard Nigel Hanbury, CBE, TD, DL (d 1972); 1 s, 1 da; *Career* Lt Irish Gds; chm and md light and mechanical engineering cos: md Lambourn Engrg Ltd, Lambourn Coachbuilders Ltd and others (Roy Warrant Grantee, Lambourn Ridgeway Transport Ltd); High Sheriff of Berkshire 1981; *Recreations* gardening, shooting, fishing; *Clubs* Kildare St and University Club (Dublin); *Style* - John Nugent Esq, JP; Limes Farm, Upper Lambourn, Newbury, Berks (☎ home Lambourn 71369, office 71111)

NUGENT, Maisie Lady; Maisie Esther; da of late Jesse Arthur Bigsby; *m* 1921, Capt Sir (George) Guy Bulwer Nugent, 4 Bt (d 1970); *Style* - Maisie Lady Nugent; Bannerdown House, Batheaston, Bath

NUGENT, Oliver; CBE (1975); s of the late George Oliver Nugent, of Antigua, W Indies; *b* 15 June 1915; *Educ* Antigua, Queens' Coll Cambridge; *m* 1943, Mary Tudor, nee Witty; 1 s, 2 da; *Career* barr 1938, Supreme Court of Windward and Leeward Islands 1939, Dept of Dir of Public Prosecutions 1946-75, assist dir 1971-75; *Recreations* philately, genealogy, travel; *Style* - Oliver Nugent Esq, CBE; 19 Scotts Lane, Shortlands, Bromley, Kent (☎ 01 460 8008)

NUGENT, Hon Patrick Mark Leonard; 2 s of 13 Earl of Westmeath; *b* 6 April 1966; *Educ* Douai; *Style* - The Hon Patrick Nugent

NUGENT, Sir Peter Walter James; 5 Bt (UK 1831), of Donore, Westmeath; s of Sir Walter Richard Nugent, 4 Bt (d 1955); *b* 26 July 1920; *Educ* Downside; *m* 1947, Anne Judith, da of Maj Robert Smyth, of Gaybrook, Mullingar, Co Westmeath; 2 s, 2 da; *Heir* s, Walter Richard Middleton Nugent; *Career* 2 Lt Hampshire Regt 1941, and with 10 Baluch Regt in India, Maj 1945; *Style* - Sir Peter Nugent, Bt; Bay Bush, Straffan, Co Kildare

NUGENT, Baroness; Rosalie; da of late Brig-Gen Hon Charles Strathavon Heathcote-Drummond-Willoughby, CB, CMG, 2 s of 1 Earl of Ancaster by his w, Lady Evelyn Gordon (2 da of 10 Marquess of Huntly); Brig-Gen Hon Charles Heathcote-Drummond-Willoughby m Lady Muriel Erskine (da of 14 Earl of Buchan); *m* 1935, 1 and last Baron Nugent (d 1973); is in remainder to Barony of Willoughby de Eresby, held by 3 Earl of Ancaster, *qv*; *Style* - The Rt Hon Lady Nugent; 40 Bramerton st, SW3 (☎ 01 352 8861)

NUGENT, Sir Robin George Colborne; 5 Bt (UK 1806), of Waddesdon, Berkshire; s of Sir George Guy Bulwer Nugent, 4 Bt (d 1970), of Bannerdown House, Bath; *b* 11 July 1925; *Educ* Eton, RWA Sch of Architecture; *m* 1947, Ursula Mary, da of Lt-Gen Sir Herbert Cooke, KCB, KBE, CSI, DSO (d 1936); 2 s, 1 da; *Heir* s, Christopher George Ridley Nugent; *Career* Lt Gren Gds 1944-48; ARIBA; *Clubs* Cavalry and Guards; *Style* - Sir Robin Nugent, Bt; Bannerdown House, Batheaston, Bath, Avon (☎ Bath 858481)

NUGENT, Sean Charles Weston; s and h of 13 Earl of Westmeath; *b* 16 Feb 1965; does not use title of Lord Delvin; *Style* - Sean Nugent Esq

NUGENT, Walter Richard Middleton; s and heir of Sir Peter Walter James Nugent, 5 Bt; *b* 15 Nov 1947; *Style* - Walter Nugent Esq

NUNAN, Manus; QC (1962); s of Manus Timothy Nunan, Justice of the Irish Dist Court (d 1979); *b* 26 March 1926; *Educ* St Mary's Coll Dublin, Trin Coll Dublin; *m* 1960, Anne Monique, da of Jean Fradin of French Colonial Service (d 1978); 1 s (Manus b 1972), 1 da (Nathalie b 1961); *Career* barr, King's Inns 1950, Gray's Inn 1956, Recorder of Crown Court since 1978, memb of Colonial Legal Services 1953-64, Crown Counsel Nigeria 1953-62, Solicitor-General Northern Nigeria 1962-64, Min of Govt and memb Exec Cncl of Northern Nigeria 1962; *Clubs* Kildare Street and University (Dublin), Racquet (Liverpool);

Style - Manus Nunan Esq, QC; 35 Elmswood Court, Palmerston rd, Liverpool (☎ 051 724 5373); 16 Belgrave Mews, Belgrave sq, Dublin

NUNBURNHOLME, 4 Baron (UK 1906); Ben Charles Wilson; s of 3 Baron Nunburnholme (d 1974) and Lady Mary Thynne (herself da of 5 Marquess of Bath); *b* 16 Jan 1928; *Educ* Eton; *m* 1958, Ines Dolores, da of Gerard Walravens, Belgian Ambass to Turkey; 4 da; *Heir* bro, Hon Charles Thomas Wilson; *Career* Capt RHG 1953, Maj 1962, resigned 1969; *Style* - The Rt Hon the Lord Nunburnholme; Lake Cottage, Shillinglee Park, Chiddingfold, Surrey (☎ Northchapel 461)

NUNN, Antony Stuart; s of C Stuart Nunn (d 1974); *b* 24 May 1927; *Educ* Haileybury Coll; *m* 1956, Pamela May, da of late William Hall, MBE; 2 da; *Career* Marine underwriter, dep chm Inst of London Underwriters 1980-81, dir Malvern Insurance Co Ltd 1978-, dir Kyoei Marine & Fire Insurance Co (UK) Ltd 1971-, dir Sirius Insurance Co (UK) Ltd 1978-, dep underwriter Lloyd's Syndicate, memb Lloyd's 1970-71; *Recreations* golf, cricket, hockey; *Clubs* MCC, Sloane; *Style* - Antony Nunn Esq; Shirlands, 158 Old Woking rd, Pyrford, Surrey

NUSSEY, Lady; Viva Frances; da of late Benjamin Talbot; *m* 1941, Sir Thomas (Moore) Nussey, 2 Bt (d 1971); *Style* - Lady Nussey; Rushwood, East Tanfield, Ripon, Yorks

NUTT, John Allister; *Career* FCA, memb IOD; chm Booker McConnell Engrg 1981- (dep chm to 1981 when replaced F Doyle, *qv*, who became ch exec SPD), APG Integrated Projects, Sigmund Pulsometer Projects, Sigmund Pulsometer Pumps, R G Brown Ltd, SPP Gp (also ch exec), Tangye Ltd; *Style* - John Nutt Esq; c/o Booker McConnell Engrg Ltd, 709-731 Oxford rd, Reading, Berks (☎ Gerrards Cross 88161)

NUTTALL, Beris Muriel; DL (Stafford 1974); da of Fred Nuttall; *b* 8 July 1924; *Educ* Holme Valley G S Huddersfield, Avery Hill Coll London; *Career* sch teacher, dep head Longton H S Stoke on Trent, on mgmnt Leonard Cheshire Home Sandbach 1970-; *Recreations* philately, collector commemorative ware, help with animals, children, OAPs, owner 1911 Swift Car 2 seater touber; *Clubs* Veteran Car Club of GB, Antique Automobile Club of America, Potteries Philatelic Soc (Stoke on Trent); *Style* - Miss Beris Nuttall, DL; Holme View, 50 Delph Lane, Netherton, Huddersfield; 14 Little-Field, Trent Vale, Stoke on Trent (☎ 46162)

NUTTALL, Harry; s and h of Sir Nicholas Keith Lillington Nuttall, 3 Bt; *b* 2 Jan 1963; *Style* - Harry Nuttall Esq

NUTTALL, Lawrence S D; s of Frank Nuttall (d 1977); *b* 26 Sept 1936; *Educ* St Christopher Sch Letchworth, Christ's Cambridge, Edinburgh U; *m* 1967, Lynda, nee Wilson; 1 s; *Career* northern princ Diverco Ltd 1979-, dir gen Nuttals Airport Serv 1980-, chm and md TRS Ltd 1978, dir Cash Mgmnt Ltd 1970-79, dir Telefusion (Blackburn) Ltd 1957-79; *Clubs* Cambridge Union, CUCA, No 10; *Style* - Lawrence Nuttall Esq; PO Box 99, Altrincham, Cheshire

NUTTALL, Sir Nicholas Keith Lillington; 3 Bt (UK 1922), of Chasefield, Parish of Bowdon, Co Chester; s of Lt-Col Sir (Edmund) Keith Nuttall, 2 Bt (d 1941); *b* 21 Sept 1933; *Educ* Eton, RMA Sandhurst; *m* 1, 1960, Rosemary Caroline (m dis 1971), da of Christopher York, of Long Marston; 1 s, 1 da; m 2, 1971, Julia Beresford, da of Thomas Williamson; m 3, 1975, Miranda Elizabeth Louise, da of Richard Quarry, and former w of the late Peter Sellers, CBE, actor; 1 da; *Heir* s, Harry Nuttall; *Career* Maj RHG, ret 1968; *Clubs* White's; *Style* - Sir Nicholas Nuttall, Bt; Lyford Cay, PO Box N7776, Nassau, Bahamas

NUTTING, Rt Hon Sir (Harold) Anthony; 3 Bt (UK 1902), of St Helens, Booterstown, Co Dublin, PC (1954); s of Lt-Col Sir Harold Stansmore Nutting, 2 Bt (d 1972); *b* 11 Jan 1920; *Educ* Eton, Trin Cambridge; *m* 1, 1941, Gillian Leonora (m dis 1959), da of Edward Strutt; 2 s, 1 da; m 2, 1961, Anne Gunning, da of Arnold Barthrop Parker, of Cuckfield Sussex; *Heir* s, John Grenfell Nutting; *Career* served in Leicestershire Yeo 1939-40, served in HM Foreign Service in France, Spain and Italy 1940-45; MP (C) Leicestershire 1945-56, Jt Parly Under-Sec of State Foreign Affairs 1951-54, Min of State 1954-56, leader UK Delegation to UN Assembly and to UN Disarmament Commission 1954-56; resigned 1956; chm Young Conservative Movement 1946; special writer New York Herald Tribune 1957-59; author; *Style* - The Rt Hon Sir Anthony Nutting, Bt, PC; 1 1/2 Disbrowe rd, W6

NUTTING, John Grenfell; s and h of Rt Hon Sir (Harold) Anthony Nutting, 3 Bt; *b* 28 Aug 1942; *Educ* Eton, McGill U Canada; *m* 1973, Diane, da of John Rutherford Blundell, of Havant, Hants, adopted da of Capt Duncan Kirk and widow of 2 Earl Beatty; 1 s, 1 da; *Career* barr Middle Temple 1968; elected to Senate of Inns of Court and Bar 1975; chm Young Bar 1978; *Style* - John Nutting Esq; Chicheley Hall, Newport Pagnall, Bucks; 2 Justice Walk, Lawrence St, SW3

NUTTING, Peter Robert; JP (Inner London 1978); s of Capt Arthur Ronald Stansmore Nutting, OBE, MC (d 1964); *b* 22 Oct 1935; *Educ* Eton; *m* 1965, Cecilia Hester Marie-Louise, nee Russell; 2 s, 1 da; *Career* Lt Irish Guards Suez Canal 1955-56, business & fin consultant, ptnr W I Carr & Sons Co Stockbrokers 1963-67, chm E & J Burke Ltd 1965-68, dir Wm Brandt & Sons Co Ltd 1968-73, numerous pt-time corpn appointments 1973-; *Recreations* shooting, tennis, golf, fishing, sailing; *Clubs* Royal Yacht Squadron, Boodle's, Pratt's; part owner yacht 'Dauntless'; *Style* - Peter Nutting Esq JP; 8 Holland pk rd W14 (☎ 603 0383); North Breache Manor, Ewhurst, Surrey (☎ Ewhurst 328)

O

O'BRIEN OF LOTHBURY, Baron (Life Peer UK 1973); Leslie Kenneth O'Brien; GBE (1967), PC (1970); s of Charles John Grimes O'Brien; *b* 8 Feb 1908; *Educ* Wandsworth Sch; *m* 1932, Isabelle, da of Francis Pickett, MBE; 1 s (Hon Michael John O'Brien, b 1933, m 1964 Marion, da of Walter Blackie; The Lodge, Thursley, Godalming, Surrey); *Career* private in Artists Rifles 1928-32; Govr Bank of England 1966-73, Pres Br Bankers Assoc 1973-80; dir Prudential Corpn 1979-, Saudi Internat Bank 1975-; *Recreations* music, theatre, tennis; *Clubs* Athenaeum, Boodle's, Garrick, Grillions, MCC, All England Lawn Tennis; *Style* - The Rt Hon The Lord O'Brien of Lothbury GBE PC; 23 Burghley House, Somerset rd, SW19 (☎ 01 946 7749)

O'BRIEN, Conor Myles John; s of Hon Fionn Maryons O'Brien (yst s of late 15 Baron Inchiquin); hp of 17 Baron; *b* 17 July 1943; *Educ* Eton; *Career* late Capt 14/20 Hussars; *Style* - Conor O'Brien Esq

O'BRIEN, Sir David Edmond; 6 Bt (UK 1849), of Merrion Sq, Dublin and Boris-in-Ossory, Queen's County; s of Edmond Lyons O'Brien (d 1948) and bro of Sir John Edmond Noel O'Brien, 5 Bt, MC (d 1969); *b* 19 Feb 1901; *Educ* Oratory Sch; *m* 1927, Mary Alice (d 1974), da of Sir Henry Foley Grey, 7 Bt (d 1914); 1 s, 1 da (1 s decd); *Heir* gs, Timothy John O'Brien; *Style* - Sir David O'Brien, Bt; Salisbury, Clonmel, Co Tipperary, Ireland

O'BRIEN, Hon Mrs Fionn - Josephine Reine; da of late Joseph Eugene Bembaron, of Herne Cottage, Long Ditton, Surrey; *m* 1939, Hon Fionn Myles Maryons O'Brien (d 1977, s of 15 Baron Inchiquin); 1 s, 3 da; *Style* - The Hon Mrs O'Brien; Falkners Down Cottage, Andover, Hants SP11 6L2

O'BRIEN, Hon Mrs Henry - Edith Lawrie; widow of T M Steele; *m* 1964, as his 2 w, Capt the Hon Henry Barnaby O'Brien (d 1969, s of late 14 Baron Inchiquin); *Style* - The Hon Mrs Henry O'Brien; 3 Ibris Place, N Berwick, E Lothian

O'BRIEN, Hon Michael John; s of Baron O'Brien of Lothbury, GBE, PC (Life Peer); *b* 1933; *m* 1964, Marion Sarah, da of late Walter Graham Blackie; *Style* - The Hon Michael O'Brien; The Lodge, Thursley, nr Godalming, Surrey

O'BRIEN, Timothy John; s of late John David O'Brien (s of Sir David O'Brien, 6 Bt); h to Baronetcy of grandfather; *b* 1958; *Style* - Timothy O'Brien Esq

O'BRIEN, (Michael) Vincent; s of Daniel Patrick O'Brien (d 1943); *b* 9 April 1917; *Educ* Mungret Jesuit Coll Limerick; *m* 1951, Jacqueline, nee Wittenoom; 2 s (David, Charles b 1967), 3 da (Elizabeth McClory, Susan Magnier, Jane Myerscough); *Career* racehorse trainer, began training 1944 Co Cork, Co Tipperary 1951, won all major English and Irish steeple-chases (3 consec Grand Nationals, Gold Cups, Champion Hurdles), trainer of 'Nijinsky', trained winners of 13 English classics (incl 5 Derbys), 3 Irish Derbys, 3 Prix de l'Arc de Triomphe and Washington Int; *Recreations* golf, fishing; *Style* - Vincent O'Brien Esq; Ballydoyle House, Cashel, Co Tipperary, Ireland

O'CALLAGHAN, The; Don Juan O'Callaghan; recognised as Chieftain by Chief Herald, Dublin Castle 1944; *b* 1903; *m* 1934, Enriquetta Casas; *Heir* s, Juan, b 1934; *Style* - The O'Callaghan; Calle Genoveses, Tortosa, Spain

O'COCK, Brig Michael James Palmer; CBE (1974), MC (1945); s of Wilfred Palmer O'Cock (d 1947); *b* 19 June 1919; *Educ* Harrow, Trin Cambridge; *m* 1, 1943, Elizabeth Jane (d 1970), nee Hall; 2 da; m 2, 1975, Helen Jane Sibbald, da of Capt Henry Mangles Denham, CMG, RN; 2 s, 1 da (all step); *Career* Brig, NW Europe 1944-45, Lt-Col Cmdg Irish Gds 1964-66, defence attaché Bonn 1968-70, ch of Staff London District 1972-74; *Recreations* shooting, skiing; *Clubs* Cavalry and Guards, MCC; *Style* - Col Michael O'Cock, CBE, MC; Church Farm, Kington Langley, Chippenham, Wilts (☎ Kington Langley 264)

O'CONNELL, Sir Morgan Donal Conail; 6 Bt (UK 1869), of Lakeview, Killarney, Co Kerry, and of Ballybeggan, Tralee, Co Kerry; s of Capt Sir Maurice James Arthur O'Connell, 5 Bt, MC (d 1949); *b* 29 Jan 1923; *Educ* Abbey Sch Fort Augustus Inverness-shire; *m* 1953, Elizabeth, da of late Maj John MacCarthy O'Leary, of Coomlegane, Millstreet, Co Cork; 2 s, 4 da; *Heir* s, Maurice James Donagh MacCarthy O'Connell; *Career* served 1943-46 with Roy Corps of Signals; *Style* - Sir Morgan O'Connell, Bt; Lakeview House, Killarney, Co Kerry, Ireland (☎ 31845)

O'CONNELL, Maurice James Donagh MacCarthy; s and h of Sir Morgan Donal Conail O'Connell, 6 Bt; *b* 10 June 1958; *Style* - Maurice O'Connell Esq

O'CONNOR, Lady; Dorothy; *m* 1, Brig Hugh Russell, DSO (decd); m 2, 1963, as his 2 w, Gen Sir Richard Nugent O'Connor, KT, GCB, DSO, MC, JP (d 1981); *Style* - Lady O'Connor; Flat 3, 28 Lennox gdns, SW1

O'CONNOR, Hon Mr Justice (Rory); s of James Edward O'Connor (d 1956); *b* 26 Nov 1925; *Educ* Blackrock Coll, Univ Coll Dublin; *m* 1963, Elizabeth, nee Dew; 1 s (Rory Brendan b 1967), 1 da (Fiona b 1964); *Career* barr, King's Inns 1949, Resident Magistrate Kenya 1956, Magistrate Hong Kong 1962, Dist Judge 1970, Supreme Court Judge Hong Kong 1977-; *Recreations* travel, reading; *Clubs* Royal Hong Kong Jockey, United Services Recreation (Hong Kong); *Style* - Hon Mr Justice O'Connor; 30 Kings Park Rise Flats, Kowloon, Hong Kong (☎ 850575)

O'DONOGHUE OF THE GLENS, The; Geoffrey Vincent Paul O'Donoghue; *b* 1937; *m* Frances Kelly; *Heir* s, Conor, b 1964; *Style* - The O'Donoghue of the Glens; Glas Choill, Screggan, Tullamore, Co Offaly; The Glens, Flesk, Co Kerry

O'DONOVAN, Timothy Charles Melville; s of John Conan Marshall Thornton O'Donovan (d 1964); *b* 10 Feb 1932; *Educ* Marlborough Coll Wiltshire; *m* 1958, Veronica Alacoque, nee White; 2 s; *Career* chm Eckersley Hicks & Co Ltd Lloyd's Brokers 1979-, dir Peek Puckle Ltd 1976-, dir common Cause Ltd 1964-, steward St George's Chapel Windsor Castle 1978-, trustee Br Monarchy Museum Trust 1979-; *Recreations* watching cricket, collecting Royal Memorabilia, reading The Court Circular; *Clubs* MCC; *Style* - Timothy O'Donovan Esq; Mariners, The Avenue, Datchet, nr Windsor, Berkshire

O'FERRALL, Lady Elizabeth (Cecilia); *née* Hare; da of 4 Earl of Listowel (d 1931); *b* 1914; *m* 1, 1936, Maj Viscount Elveden, RA (TA) (d 1945), s of 2 Earl of Iveagh; m 2, 1947, Edward Rory More O'Ferrall; *Style* - Lady Elizabeth O'Ferrall; The Old Rectory, Elveden, Suffolk; Gloucester Lodge, Regent's Park, NW1

O'GRADY OF KILBALLYOWEN, The; Lt-Col Gerald Vigors de Courcy O'Grady; MC (1945); s of late Lt-Col Standish de Courcy O'Grady, CMG, DSO; *b* 1912; *Educ* Arnold House, Wellington Coll, RMA; *m* 1, 1941, Pamela Violet (m dis 1961), da of Lt-Col T A Thornton, CVO, DL, of Brockhall, Northampton; 1 s, 1 da; m 2, 1961, Mollie, da of Robert Mclean, of Gibson Island, Maryland USA; 2 da; *Career* joined RA 1932, Lt 1935, ADC to C-in-C India 1939, Maj 1940, instructor RMA Sandhurst 1947, ret 1947; chm Limerick Show Soc 1975-78; *Style* - The O'Grady of Kilballyowen, MC; Kilballyowen, Bruff, Co Limerick, Ireland (☎ 061 82213)

O'HAGAN, 4 Baron (UK 1870); Charles Towneley Strachey; MEP (C) Devon 1979-; s of Hon Thomas Strachey (d 1955), who assumed the surname 'Strachey' *vice* 'Towneley-O'Hagan' 1938 and added the forename 'Towneley'; s of 3 Baron O'Hagan (d 1961) by his 1 w, Hon Frances Strachey (da of 1 Baron Strachie), whereby Lord O'Hagan is (1) 1 cous once removed to John St Loe Strachey, the Socialist polemicist who was both Sec of State for War in Attlee's 1950-51 Govt and the author of *On the Prevention of War* (2) in the same degree of kinship towards Lady Williams-Ellis, w of the creator of Port Meirion (3) 1 cous twice removed of (i) Lytton Strachey (ii) Dorothy or Dorothea Bussy, authoress, under the *nom de plume* 'Olivia', of the delicately sapphic novel of the same name (iii) Pernel Strachey, sometime Principal of Newnham College Cambridge (4) 3 cous of Charlotte, sometime w of Anthony Blond, the publisher; Thomas's w was Lady Mary-Sophia Palmer, yst da of 3 Earl of Selborne; *b* 6 Sept 1945; *Educ* Eton, New Coll Oxford; *m* 1967, HSH Princess Tamara, former w of Lt-Cdr Thomas Smith-Dorrien-Smith, of Tresco Abbey, Isles of Scilly, and er da of HSH Prince Michael Imeterinsky (of the Princely family of Bagration, sometime rulers of an independent Georgia), RAFVR, of Menton; 1 da; *Heir* bro, Hon Richard Strachey; *Career* Page of Honour to HM 1959-62; Independent memb European Parl 1973-75, Jr Oppn Whip Ldr 1977-79; *Clubs* Newton Abbot Constitutional, Pratt's; *Style* - The Rt Hon Lord O'Hagan, MEP; Sutton Court, Stowey, Pensford, Avon (☎ Chew Magna 2933)

O'KELLY, Hon Mrs (Mary Gail); *née* Mitchell-Thomson; da of 3 Baron Selsdon; *b* 1939; *m* 1963, Patrick John O'Kelly, MB, BCH; 3 s; *Style* - The Hon Mrs O'Kelly; 10 Parkview pla, Staten Island, New York, 10310, USA

O'LOGHLEN, Sir Colman Michael; 6 Bt (UK 1838), of Drumconora, Ennis; s of Henry Ross O'Loghlen (d 1944) and nephew of 5 Bt (d 1951); *b* 6 April 1916; *Educ* Xavier Coll Melbourne, Melbourne U; *m* 1939, Margaret, da of Francis O'Halloran of Melbourne; 6 s, 2 da; *Heir* s, Michael O'Loghlen; *Career* served 1942-45 with AIF New Guinea, Capt 1945; LLB, stipendiary magistrate Lae New Guinea, former acting judge of Supreme Court of Territory of Papua New Guinea; *Style* - Sir Colman O'Loghlen, Bt; 98 Williamsons rd, Doncaster, Vic 3108, Australia

O'LOGHLEN, Michael; s and h of Sir

Colman O'Loghlen, 6 Bt, LLB; *b* 21 May 1925; *Style* - Michael O'Loghlen Esq

O'MORCHOE, The; (of Oulartleigh and Monamolin); Maj-Gen David Nial Creagh O'Morchoe; CB (1979), MBE (1966); s of Col Nial Creagh O'Morchoe (d 1970); *b* 17 May 1928; *Educ* St Columba's Coll Dublin, Sandhurst; *m* 1955, Margaret, da of George Brewitt, of Cork; 2 s (Dermot b 1956, Kevin b 1958), 1 da (Maureen b 1964); *Career* Maj-Gen ret 1979; served Roy Irish Fusiliers from 1948 in M East, Mediterranean, NW Europe, Kenya, Oman, late Cdr Sultan of Oman's forces; *Recreations* sailing (Westerly Renown ketch: 'Skillara'); *Clubs* Friendly Brothers, Roy Cork Yacht, Cruising Association; *Style* - Maj-Gen The O'Morchoe CB MBE; c/o Williams & Glyn's Bank, Kirkland House, SW1

O'NEILL, 3 Baron (UK 1868); Raymond Arthur Clanaboy O'Neill; TD (1970), DL (Co Antrim 1967); s of 3 Baron O'Neill (ka in Italy 1944, just as his f was (only in Flanders) in 1914; his f was Capt Hon Arthur O'Neill, JP, DL, MP, 2 s of 2 Baron, and the first MP to fall in WW I), whose mother was Lady Annabel Crewe-Milnes, da of 1 & last Marquess of Crewe, through whom Lord O'Neill is half-nephew to Quentin Crewe; Lord O'Neill's own mother was Mrs Ian Fleming; the O'Neills stem from the most ancient family in Europe that it has been possible to tabulate; *b* 1 Sept 1933; *Educ* Eton, RAC Cirencester; *m* 1963, Georgina, da of Lord George Montagu-Douglas-Scott, 3 s of 7 Duke of Buccleuch; 3 s; *Heir* s, Hon Shane O'Neill; *Career* Lt-Col RARO, served with 11 Hussars Prince Albert's Own, also NI Horse (TA); chm Fin Ctee Roy Ulster Ag Soc 1975-; memb NI Tourist Bd 1973-(chm 1975-80), NI Nat Tst Ctee 1980-, Tstee Ulster Folk & T'port Museum 1969-; *Recreations* railways, vintage motoring, gardening; *Clubs* Turf, Ulster; *Style* - Rt Hon Lord O'Neill TD DL; Shanes Castle, Antrim, N Ireland (☎ Antrim 3264)

O'NEILL OF THE MAINE, Baron (Life Peer UK 1970); Hon Terence Marne O'Neill; PC (NI 1956), DL (Co Antrim 1948); s of Capt Hon Arthur O'Neill, of Shanes Castle, Co Antrim, and bro of 3 Baron O'Neill, *qv*; *b* 10 Sept 1914; *Educ* Eton; *m* 1944, Katherine, da of William Whitaker, DL, of Pylewell Park, Lymington, by his w Hon Hilda Guilhermina, DGStJ, da of 6 Viscount Melville; 2 s, 1 da; *Career* late Capt Irish Gds; PM NI 1963-69; MP (U) NI Parl Bannside 1946-70, also Min Home Affrs 1956, Finance 1956; dir S G Warburg & Co, Internat Hldgs, Phoenix Assur 1969-; High Sheriff Co Antrim 1953; *Clubs* Brooks's; *Style* - Rt Hon Lord O'Neill of the Maine PC DL; Lisle Court, Lymington, Hants (☎ 72010)

O'NEILL, Hon Sir Con Douglas Walter; GCMG (1972, KCMG 1962, CMG 1953); 2 s of 1 Baron Rathcavan, PC; *b* 3 June 1912; *Educ* Eton, Balliol Oxford; *m* 1, 1940 (m dis 1954), Rosemary, da of late Dr Harold Pritchard, FRCP; 1 s, 1 da; m 2, 1954, Baroness Mady (Carola Hertha Adolfine Emma Harriet Luise, d 1960), da of late Baron Max von Holzing-Berstett, and widow of Baron Wilhelm Pleikart Marschall von Bieberstein; m 3, 1961, Mrs Anne-Marie Lindberg, of Helsinki; *Career* barr 1936, FO (later FCO) 1936-72; Chargé d'Affaires Peking 1955-57, Ambass Finland 1961-63, EEC 1963-65, Dep Under-Sec FCO & Leader Br Delegn to negotiate EEC entry 1969-72, Dir Br in Europe Campaign 1974-75; dir Unigate Ltd 1974-; *Style* - The Hon Sir Con O'Neill GCMG; 37 Flood st, SW3

O'NEILL, Hon Patrick Arthur Ingham; s of Baron O'Neill of the Maine (Life Peer); *b* 1945; *Educ* Eton; *m* 1975, Anne, da of Douglas Lillecrapp, of Adelaide, S Australia; 1 da (Sophie b 1976); *Career* Lt QRI Hussars; *Style* - The Hon Patrick O'Neill; 87 Hewitt av, Toorak gdns, Adelaide, S Australia

O'NEILL, Rt Hon Phelim Robert Hugh; PC (NI 1969); s and h of 1 Baron Rathcavan, PC; *b* 2 Nov 1909; *Educ* Eton; *m* 1, 1934 (m dis 1944), Clare Désirée (d 1956), da of Detmar Blow, JP, and Winifred Tollemache (gda of 1 Baron Tollemache); 1 s, 1 da; m 2, 1953, Bridget, da of Maj Hon Richard Coke (3 s of 2 Earl of Leicester, KG, JP, DL, by his 2 w Hon Georgina Cavendish, da of 2 Baron Chesham) and former w of Thomas Edwards-Moss (bro of Sir John Edwards-Moss, 4 Bt); 3 da (and 1 da decd); *Career* MP (UU) N Antrim 1952-59 (NI Parl as U 1959-72, Min (N Ireland): Educn 1969, Ag 1969-71); late Maj RA; *Style* - The Rt Hon Phelim O'Neill, PC; Lizard Manor, Aghadowey, Londonderry, N Ireland

O'NEILL, Hon Rory St John; s of 4 Baron O'Neill; *b* 20 Dec 1968; *Style* - The Hon Rory O'Neill

O'NEILL, Hon Shane Sebastian Clanaboy; s and h of 4 Baron O'Neill; *b* 25 July 1965; *Style* - The Hon Shane O'Neill

O'NEILL, Hon Tyrone Alexander; s of 4 Baron O'Neill; *b* 24 June 1966; *Style* - The Hon Tyrone O'Neill

O'NEILL, Hon Mrs Nial; Virginia Lois; da of John Douglas Legge, MC, late Capt Coldstream Gds (s of Lt-Col Hon Edward Legge, sometime Assist Serjeant-at-Arms House of Commons and 3 s of 4 Earl of Dartmouth); *b* 5 May 1922; *m* 1966, Hon Nial O'Neill (d 1980), 3 and yst s of 1 Baron Rathcavan, PC; *Style* - The Hon Mrs Nial O'Neill; The Great House, Layer-de-la-Haye, Colchester, Essex

O'RORKE, Timothy Mawdesley; s of Michael Sylvester O'Rorke, CBE; *b* 10 July 1929; *Educ* Haileybury and ISC, Queens' Coll Cambridge; *m* 1964, Anne Patricia, da of Brig Theodore Edward Dudley Kelly, CBE; 1 s (Nicholas John Mawdesley b 1968), 2 da (Kelly Anne Frances b 1966, Patricia Elizabeth b 1969); *Career* CA with Imperial Continental Gas Assoc 1956, sec 1969, fin dir 1972, md 1979-; *Recreations* tennis, gardening, skiing; *Clubs* Anglo Belgian; *Style* - Timothy O'Rorke Esq; Denstone, Wadhurst, Sussex (☎ 0892 88 2282)

O'SHAUGHNESSY, Hon Mrs (Maud Elizabeth); *née* Grosvenor; da of late 4 Baron Ebury, DSO, MC; *b* 1909; *m* 1, 1931 (m dis 1942), 2 Viscount Harcourt (d 1978); 2 da; m 2, 1942, Lt-Col Edward O'Shaughnessy; 2 da (twins); *Style* - The Hon Mrs O'Shaughnessy; Marylea, Coombe Cres, Bury, W Sussex

O'SHEA, David Michael; s of Francis Edward O'Shea (d 1954); *b* 27 Jan 1927; *Educ* St Ignatius Coll, London; King's Coll, London U (LLB); *m* 1953, Sheila Winifred, da of late Reginald Charles Polking Horne; 2 s; *Career* slr 1954, dep slr Metropolitan Police 1976- (joined Police Slr's Dept 1956); *Style* - David O'Shea Esq; 55 Northey ave, Cheam, Surrey (☎ 01 642 4862)

O'SULLEVAN, Peter John; OBE (1977); s of Col John Joseph O'Sullevan DSO (decd); *b* 3 March 1918; *Educ* Hawtreys, Charterhouse, Collège Alpin Switzerland; *m* 1951, Patricia, da of late Frank Duckworth, of Manitoba, Canada; *Career* racing correspondent Daily Express 1950-, commentator BBC TV 1946- (including Australia, S Africa, Italy, USA;) *Recreations* racehorses, travel, reading, art, food and wine; *Style* - Peter O'Sullevan Esq OBE; 37 Cranmer ct, Sloane av, SW3 (☎ 01 584 2781)

O'SULLIVAN, Carrol Austin John Naish; CB (1973); s of Dr Carrol Naish O'Sullivan (d 1929); *b* 24 Jan 1915; *Educ* Mayfield Coll, London U; *m* 1939, Lillian Mary, nee Molineux; 1 s, 1 da; *Career* slr 1936, assist Public Trustee 1966-71, Public Trustee 1971-75; *Recreations* golf, family history, listening to radio; *Style* - Carrol O'Sullivan Esq CB; 3 The Leeway, Hopping Jack's Lane, Danbury, Chelmsford, Essex (☎ Danbury 3829)

O'SULLIVAN, Rev Mgr James; CBE (1973); s of Richard O'Sullivan; *b* 2 Aug 1917; *Educ* St Finnbarr's Coll, Cork; All Hallows Coll, Dublin; *Career* officiating chaplain (RC) RAMC Depot & T'ning Centre 1973-; *Style* - The Rev Monsignor James O'Sullivan CBE; Osgil, Vicarage Lane, Ropley, Alresford, Hants

O'TOOLE, Peter; s of Patrick Joseph O'Toole; *b* 1932; *Educ* RADA; *m* Sian Phillips (m dis); 2 da; *Career* actor; with Bristol Old Vic Co 1955-58; artistic dir Royal Alexander Theatre Co 1978; *Clubs* Garrick; *Style* - Peter O'Toole Esq; c/o

Veerline Ltd, 54 Baker st, W1 (☎ 01 486 5888)

OAKELEY, Sir (Edward) Atholl; 7 Bt (GB 1790), of Shrewsbury; s of Maj Edward Francis Oakeley, JP (d 1954), and cousin of 6 Bt (d 1959); *b* 31 May 1900; *Educ* Clifton, RMC; *m* 1, 1922, Ethyl Felice (m dis 1926), da of T O'Coffey; m 2, 1930, Patricia Mabel Mary (m dis 1951), da of Lionel Birtchnell, of Slough Bucks; 1 s; m 3, 1952, Doreen (m dis 1959), da of Stanley Wells, of Sholing, Hants; m 4, 1960, Shirley, da of Herbert W Church, of Tonbridge, Kent; 1 da; *Heir* s, John Digby Atholl Oakeley; *Career* served 1919-23 in S Ireland; ch advertising contact for Sir Charles Higham; champion Army Marathon and 10 Mile Track 1920-22; Heavyweight Wrestling Champion of Gt Britain 1930-35, Europe 1932; *Style* - Sir Atholl Oakeley, Bt; Nomad, Lynton, N Devon

OAKELEY, Anne-Marie, Lady - Anne-Marie (Rudd); da of Etienne Dennis, of Le Havre, Seine Maritime, France; *m* 1957, as his 3 w, Sir Charles Richard Andrew Oakeley, 6 Bt (d 1959); *Style* - Anne-Marie, Lady Oakeley; 31 Résidence de la Garoupe, Blvd de la Garoupe, 066 00 Cap d'Antibes, France

OAKELEY, Ida, Lady - Ida Margaret Elena; da of late Col John MacGregor Kerr; *b* 1885; *m* 1934, as his 2 w, Sir Charles John Oakeley, 5 Bt (d 1938); *Style* - Ida, Lady Oakeley; Holly Lodge, Firlands ave, Camberley, Surrey

OAKELEY, John Digby Atholl; s and h of Sir Atholl Oakeley, 7 Bt; *b* 27 Nov 1932; *m* 1958, Maureen, da of John Cox, of Hamble, Hants; 1 s, 1 da; *Style* - John Oakeley Esq; 22 Sydney ave, Hamble, Hants

OAKES, Sir Christopher; 3 Bt (UK 1939), of Nassau, Bahama Islands; s of Sir Sydney Oakes, 2 Bt (d 1966); *b* 10 July 1949; *Educ* Bredon Tewkesbury, Georgia Military Academy USA; *m* 1978, Julie Dawn, da of Donovan Cowan, of Canada; 1 da; *Heir* unc, Harry Philip Oakes; *Style* - Sir Christopher Oakes, Bt; PO Box 1002, Nassau, Bahamas

OAKES, Harry Philip; s of late Sir Harry Oakes, 1 Bt, & hp of nephew, Sir Christopher Oakes, 3 Bt; *b* 30 Aug 1932; *m* 1958, Christiane, da of Rudolf Botsch, of Hamburg, Germany; 3 s, 1 da; *Style* - Harry Oakes Esq; P O Box 1002, Nassau, Bahamas

OAKES, Stephen Rodney; s of Brian Ernest Oakes; *b* 24 Oct 1948; *Educ* Alcester G S; *m* 1969, Rina Margaret, nee Lovett; 1 s (Mark Alan b 1976), 1 da (Lyndsay Marie b 1973); *Career* fin accountant, co sec, fin dir; *Recreations* golf, DIY, chess; *Style* - Stephen Oakes Esq; 62 Gerard rd, Kinwarton Park, Alcester, Warwicks (☎ 762601)

OAKSEY, 2 Baron (UK 1947), 4 Baron Trevethin (UK 1921); John Geoffrey Tristram Lawrence; known as Lord Oaksey; s of 3 & 1 Baron Trevethin and Oaksey, DSO, TD (d 1971); *b* 21 March 1929; *Educ* Horris Hill, Eton, New Coll Oxford, Yale Law Sch; *m* 1959, Victoria Mary, da of Maj John Dennistoun, MBE (d 1980); 1 s, 1 da; *Heir* s, Hon Patrick John Tristram Lawrence; *Career* late P/O RAFVR and Lt 9 Lancers; Racing Correspondent to Daily Telegraph (as 'Marlborough') 1957-, to Sunday Telegraph 1961-, to Horse and Hound (as 'Audax') 1959-, Commentator for ITV on Racing (World of Sport) 1969-; JP; Pres Amateur Boxing Assoc, York U Turf Club; *Recreations* riding, skiing; *Clubs* Brooks's; *Style* - The Rt Hon the Lord Oaksey JP; Hill Farm, Oaksey, Malmesbury, Wilts (☎ Crudwell 303)

OAKSEY, Marjorie, Baroness - Marjorie; OBE (1941), TD; da of late Cdr Charles Napier Robinson, RN; *m* 1921, 3 Baron Trevethin and 1 Baron Oaksey DSO, TD, PC (d 1971); *Career* late Controller ATS; JP Wilts; *Style* - The Rt Hon Marjorie, Lady Oaksey OBE TD JP; Flintham Cottage, Oaksey, Wilts

OAKSHOTT, Hon Sir Anthony Hendrie; 2 Bt (UK 1959), of Bebington, Co Palatine of Chester; s of Baron (& 1 Bt) Oakshott, MBE (Life Peer d 1975); *b* 10 Oct 1929; *Educ* Rugby; *m* 1965, Valerie, formerly w of (1) Donald Ross and (2) Michael de Pret-Roose and da of Jack

Vlasto, of Hurst, Berks; *Heir* bro, Hon Michael Oakshott; *Clubs* White's; *Style* - The Hon Sir Anthony Oakshott, Bt; 42 Eaton Square, London SW1 (☎ 01 235 2107)

OAKSHOTT, Joan, Baroness - Joan; da of Marsden Withington, of London and Buenos Aires; *m* 1928, 1 and last Baron Oakshott (d 1975); *Style* - The Rt Hon Joan, Lady Oakshott; The Mount, Broxton, Cheshire; Flat D, 42 Eaton sq, SW1

OAKSHOTT, Hon Michael Arthur John; s of Baron Oakshott (Life Peer) and 1 Bt (d 1975); hp to Baronetcy of bro, Hon Sir Anthony Oakshott, 2 Bt; *b* 12 April 1932; *Educ* Rugby; *m* 1957, Christina Rose Methuen, da of late Thomas Banks, of Solai, Kenya; 3 s; *Style* - The Hon Michael Oakshott; Barwhinnock, Twynholm, Kirkcudbrightshire

OATLEY, Clive; s of James William Oatley, OBE; *b* 3 April 1938; *Educ* St Paul's, St Catharine's Cambridge; *m* 1; 1 s (Maxwell James); m 2, 1980, Brooke Randolph, da of Joseph Simpson Farland, former US Ambassador to Iran and Panama; 1 da (Virginia Lawson); *Career* Lt 5 Royal Inniskilling Dragoon Guards; pres Tampimex Oil Int Ltd, chm and md Tampimex Oil Ltd and Tampimex Europe Ltd, chm Tampimex Houston, chm Trans National Trading Ltd, dir Ingram Corpn; *Recreations* golf; *Clubs* Eccentric, Hawks, Royal Wimbledon Golf; *Style* - Clive Oatley Esq; 21 Ilchester Place, London W14 (☎ 01 602 2195)

OF MAR, Lady Janet Helen; da of 30 Earl of Mar; *b* 31 Jan 1946; *Educ* St Andrews U; *m* 1969, Instructor-Lieutenant Laurence of Mar (who was formerly Laurence Duncan McDiarmid Anderson, of Winton Castle, East Lothian); recognised in the surname 'of Mar' by warrant of Lord Lyon 1969; 2 da (Elizabeth b 1970 and Catherine b 1971); *Style* - Lady Janet of Mar; c/o Bank of Scotland, Haddington, East Lothian; Princes Court, Brompton rd, SW3

OFFALY, Earl of; Thomas FitzGerald; s and h of Marquess of Kildare and gs of 8 Duke of Leinster; *b* 12 Jan 1974; *Style* - Earl of Offaly

OFFICER, Maj-Gen William James; CB (1962), CBE (1959); s of John Liddell Officer, OBE, WS; *b* 24 Aug 1903; *Educ* Edinburgh Acad, Durham Sch, Edinburgh U; *m* 1934, Doris, nee Mattinson; 3 da; *Career* RAMC 1929; Maj-Gen 1960; dir Medical Services FARELF 1960-63, QHS 1961-63, ret; *Style* - Maj-Gen William Officer, CB, CBE; c/o Williams & Glyn's Bank Ltd, Kirkland House, SW1

OGDEN, Eric; MP (L) Liverpool West Derby 1964-; s of Robert Ogden (d 1959); *b* 23 Aug 1923; *Educ* Queen Elizabeth's GS Middleton, Wigan Tech Coll; *m* 1; 1 s (David Norman); m 2, 1964, Marjorie, nee Smith; 2 s (Mark Robert b 1966, Martin Branston b 1967), 2 step da (Christine Davies, Deborah Birtles); *Career* Br Dutch and US Mercantile Marines 1942-46, coal miner, sponsorship as MP by NUM; *Recreations* gardening, motoring, surviving; *Clubs* Europe House, Gillmoss & Dovecot; *Style* - Eric Ogden Esq, MP; House of Commons, Westminster, SW1 (☎ 01 219 5201)

OGDEN, Maj Frank Collinge; CBE (1956); s of Paul Ogden (d 1932); *b* 13 March 1907; *Educ* Manchester G S, King's Cambridge; *m* 1944, Margaret, nee Greenwood; 1 s, 2 da (and 1 decd); *Career* Maj (Gen Staff Intelligence), HM Diplomatic Serv (ret), Vice-Consul Cairo, Alexandria, Baghdad, Damascus 1930-40; General HQ Middle East 1941-42; Tabriz 1942, Bogota 1944, Chargé d'Affaires 1945, Shiraz 1947, Consul-Gen Seattle 1952, Basra 1953, Gothenburg 1955, Libya 1958, Chargé d'Affaires 1958-59, Counsellor and Consul-Gen British Embassy Buenos Aires 1960-65; *Recreations* swimming, motoring and appalling snooker; *Clubs* RAC, Civil Serv; *Style* - Maj Frank Ogden, CBE; Yellow Sands, 2 Thorney dve, Selsey, Chichester, W Sussex (☎ Selsey 2163)

OGDEN, (Edward) Michael; QC (1968); s of Edward Cannon Ogden (d 1933); *b* 9 April 1926; *Educ* Downside, Jesus Coll Cambridge; *m* 1951, Joan Kathleen, nee Brodrick; 2 s, 2 da; *Career* barr, Lincoln's Inn 1950, Capt 16/5 Lancers 1944-47,

Inns of Court Regt (TA) 1950-56, Recorder of Hastings 1971, Recorder of the Crown Court 1972-, chm Criminal Injuries Compensation Bd 1975- (memb of Bd 1968-), Assessor for the Home Sec of compensation for persons wrongly convicted or charged 1978-; *Style* - Michael Ogden Esq, QC; 2 Crown Office Row, Temple, EC4 (☎ 01 353-9337/937-6275)

OGILVIE THOMPSON, Julian; s of Hon Mr Justice Ogilvie Thompson (Ch Justice SA to 1974), of Cape Province; *b* 27 Jan 1934; *Educ* Diocesan Coll, Rondebosch, Cape; Worcester Coll Oxford; *m* 1956, Hon Tessa Brand (*see* Hon Mrs O T); 2 s (Christopher William b 1958, Anthony Thomas b 1964), 2 da (Rachel Amanda b 1960, Leila Katharine b 1965), all four of whom are in remainder to the Barony of Dacre; *Career* exec dir Anglo American Corpn SA; chm Anglo American Gold Investment Tst, Barclays Nat Bank; dir De Beers Consolidated Mines, Consolidated Goldfields, Charter Consolidated, Minerals & Resources Corpn; *Recreations* shooting, fishing, golf; *Clubs* White's, Rand (Jo'burg), Kimberley; *Style* - Julian Ogilvie Thompson Esq; Froome, Froome st, Athol Ext 3, Johannesburg, S Africa (☎ 011 784 3925)

OGILVIE THOMPSON, Hon Mrs (Tessa Mary); *née* Brand; da of late 4 Viscount Hampden and sis of Baroness Dacre, *qv*; *b* 1934; *m* 1956, Julian Ogilvie Thompson, *qv*; 2 s, 2 da; *Style* - The Hon Mrs Ogilvie Thompson; Froome, Froome st, Athol Extension, Johannesburg, S Africa (☎ 011 784 3925)

OGILVIE-GRANT, Hon Alexander Derek Henry; s (by 1 m) of 13 Earl of Seafield; *b* 1966; *Style* - The Hon Alexander Ogilvie-Grant

OGILVY, Hon Angus James Bruce; 2 s of 12 Earl of Airlie, KT, GCVO, MC (d 1968); *b* 14 Sept 1928; *Educ* Eton, Ch Ch Oxford; *m* 1963, HRH Princess Alexandra of Kent, GCVO; 1 s, 1 da; *Career* Scots Gds 1946-48; pres Imperial Cancer Research Fund; pres Nat Assoc of Youth Clubs; memb British Rheumatism and Arthritis Assoc; dir Sotheby's, Gen Electric Co ltd, London Trust Co Ltd, MEPC Ltd, Rank Organisation Ltd (dir Lonhro to 1973); hon pres The Scottish Wildlife Trust; *Style* - The Hon Angus Ogilvy; Thatched House Lodge, Richmond Park, Surrey (☎ 01 546 8833)

OGILVY, Hon Bruce Patrick; s of 13 Earl of Airlie, DL; hp of bro, Lord Ogilvy; *b* 7 April 1959; *Style* - The Hon Bruce Ogilvy

OGILVY, Lady Caroline; *née* Child-Villiers; da of 9 Earl of Jersey; *b* 1934; *m* 1, 1952 (m dis 1965), Viscount Melgund, MBE (now 6 Earl of Minto); 1 s, 1 da; m 2, 1969 (m dis 1972), the Hon John Douglas Stuart, s of 1 Viscount Stuart of Findhorn, CH, MVO, MC (d 1971); m 3, 1980, Hon James Donald Diarmid Ogilvy, s of 12 Earl of Airlie; *Style* - Lady Caroline Ogilvy; Sedgebrook Manor, nr Grantham, Lincs

OGILVY, Lord; David John Ogilvy; s and h of 13 Earl of Airlie; *b* 9 March 1958; *m* 1981, Hon Geraldine Harmsworth, da of 3 Viscount Harmsworth; *Career* Page of Honour to HM 1971-; *Style* - Lord Ogilvy

OGILVY, Sir David John Wilfrid; 13 Bt (NS 1626), of Inverquharity, Forfarshire, JP (E Lothian 1957), DL (1971); s of Gilbert Francis Molyneux Ogilvy, JP (4 s of Sir Reginald Ogilvy, 10 Bt, JP, DL, by Hon Olivia, da of 9 Lord Kinnaird, KT), and his w Marjory (da of Charles Clive and Lady Katharine Feilding, da of 7 Earl of Denbigh); suc unc, Sir Herbert Ogilvy, 12 Bt, 1956; *b* 3 Feb 1914; *Educ* Eton, Trin Oxford; *m* 1966, Penelope, da of Arthur Hills, of White Court, Tonbridge, and Moira (da of Henry Seymour Guinness, of the extensive Co Kildare brewing and banking family, & sis to Princess John de Mahé, also 1 cous once removed to Sir Hugh Greene's 1 w, Helga); 1 s; *Heir* s, Francis Gilbert Arthur Ogilvy; *Career* farmer & landowner; *Recreations* forestry; *Clubs* New (Edinburgh); *Style* - Sir David Ogilvy, Bt, JP, DL; Winton House, Pencaitland, E Lothian (☎ 340222)

OGILVY, Lady Elizabeth Clementina; 3 da of 13 Earl of Airlie, DL; *b* 4 June 1965; *Style* - Lady Elizabeth Ogilvy

OGILVY, Francis Gilbert Arthur; s and h of Sir David John Wilfrid Ogilvy, 13 Bt; *b* 22 April 1969

OGILVY, Lady; Hon Geraldine Theodora Mary Gabriel; *née* Harmsworth; da of 3 Viscount Rothermere; *b* 25 July 1957; *m* 1981, Lord Ogilvy, s and h of 13 Earl of Airlie; *Style* - Lady Ogilvy

OGILVY, Hon James Donald Diarmid; s of 12 Earl of Airlie, KT, GCVO, MC, and Lady Alexandra Coke, da of 3 Earl of Leicester; *b* 28 June 1934; *Educ* Eton; *m* 1, 1959, June, da of Robert Ducas, of New York, by his 1 w, Magdalen, da of Maj Herbert Stourton, OBE (gs of 19 Baron Stourton, DL), and Hon Frances, only da of 4 Viscount Southwell; 2 s, 2 da; m 2, 1980, Lady Caroline, nee Villiers, da of 9 Earl of Jersey and former w of (1) Viscount Melgund, MBE (now 6 Earl of Minto), (2) Hon John Stuart (s of 1 Viscount Stuart of Findhorn); *Career* Lt Scots Gds 1952-54; memb Roy Co of Archers (Queen's Bodyguard for Scotland); Page of Honour to King George VI 1947-51; Govr Queen Charlotte's & Chelsea Hosps 1966; *Clubs* White's, New (Edinburgh); *Style* - The Hon James Ogilvy; Canal House, 23 Blomfield rd, Little Venice, W9 (☎ 01 286 9913)

OGILVY, Hon Patrick Alexander; s of 13 Earl of Airlie, DL; *b* 24 March 1971; *Style* - The Hon Patrick Ogilvy

OGILVY-WEDDERBURN, Capt Sir Andrew John Alexander; 7 Bt (UK 1803), of Balindean, Perthshire; s of Sir (John) Peter Ogilvy-Wedderburn, 7 Bt (d 1977); *b* 4 Aug 1952; *Educ* Gordonstoun; *Heir* cousin, Caryl Eustace Wedderburn-Ogilvy; *Career* Capt Black Watch (Roy Highland Regiment); *Recreations* bobsleighing, ski-ing, shooting; *Style* - Capt Sir Andrew Ogilvy-Wedderburn, Bt; Silvie, Alyth, Perthshire (☎ Alyth 2362)

OGILVY-WEDDERBURN, Lady; Elizabeth Katharine; da of John Cox; *m* 1946, Cdr Sir Peter Ogilvy-Wedderburn, 6 Bt (d 1977); 1 s (7 Bt), 3 da (Mrs Sebastian Thewes, Jean & Elizabeth O-W); *Style* - Lady Ogilvy-Wedderburn; Silvie, Alyth, Perthshire

OGMORE, 2 Baron (UK 1950); Gwilym Rees Rees-Williams; s of 1 Baron Ogmore (d 1976); *b* 5 May 1931; *Educ* Mill Hill; *m* 1967, Gillian, da of Maurice Slack, of Hindley, Lancs; 2 da; *Heir* bro, Hon Morgan Rees-Williams; *Career* with Dept of Environment; *Recreations* watching rugby, walking; *Style* - The Rt Hon Lord Ogmore; 4 Foster rd, W4 (☎ 01 995 0775)

OGMORE, Constance, Baroness - Alice Alexandra Constance; da of late Alderman Walter Robert Wills, Lord Mayor of Cardiff 1945-46; *m* 1930, 1 Baron Ogmore, TD, PC (d 1976); *Style* - The Rt Hon Constance, Lady Ogmore; 48 Cheyne Court, Royal Hospital rd, SW3 (☎ 01 352 6131)

OHLSON, Brian Eric Christopher; s and h of Sir Eric (James) Ohlson, 2 Bt; *b* 27 July 1936; *Educ* Harrow and RMA; *Career* late Coldstream Gds; *Style* - Brian Ohlson Esq

OHLSON, Sir Eric James; 2 Bt (UK 1920), of Scarborough, North Riding of Co of Yorkshire; s of 1 Bt (d 1934); *b* 1915; *m* 1935, Marjorie Joan, da of late C H Roosmale-Cocq, of Dorking, Surrey; 2 s, 1 da; *Heir* s, Brian Eric Christopher Ohlson; *Career* consul for Romania at Hull 1936; *Style* - Sir Eric Ohlson, Bt; Belvedere House, Esplanade, Scarborough, N Yorks

OLDFIELD, Lady (Mary) Elisabeth; *née* Murray; da of late 8 Earl of Dunmore, VC, DSO, MVO; *b* 1918; *m* 1937, Major Peter Carlton Oldfield, OBE, Warwicks Yeo; 1 da; *Style* - Lady Elisabeth Oldfield, OBE; Ham Cottage, Sydmonton, Newbury, Berks

OLDFIELD, Brig John Briton; OBE (1980), DL (Hants 1973); s of William Aitken Oldfield, JP (d 1966); *b* 28 April 1918; *Educ* Repton, RMC Sandhurst; *m* 1949, Pamela Carrol, nee Ward; 1 s, 1 da; *Career* Brig Green Howards, Palestine 1938-39, France and Western Desert, despatches 1945, Malaya 1951-52, despatches 1953, Int Standing Gp NATO Washington DC 1957-59, cmdg offr 1

Green Howards 1960-62, staff NATO Defence Coll Paris (Col) 1962-64, cdr TA 1965-67, dep cdr Aldershot district 1967-69, ret 1969, Col Green Howards 1975-, Hon Col 2 Bn Wessex Regt 1980-; *Recreations* field sports, painting; *Clubs* Army and Navy; *Style* - Brig John Oldfield, OBE, DL; Paddock Cottage, Bramshaw, Lyndhurst, Hants (☎ Earldoms 233)

OLDHAM, Stanley Clifford; s of Harry Robert Oldham (d 1945); *b* 8 Aug 1920; *Educ* Moseley; *m* 1947, Patricia Spedding, da of Michael Spedding Fox (d 1963); 5 c (1 decd); *Career* Lieut, Middle East, Italy, India; md Fox's Biscuits Ltd 1955-; *Recreations* sports; *Style* - Stanley Clifford Esq; 'Cranleigh', Alton Lodge, Batley, W Yorkshire

OLDROYD, James Gardner; s of Harry Oldroyd (d 1947); *b* 25 April 1921; *Educ* Bradford G S, Trin Cambridge; *m* 1946, Marged Katryn, nee Evans; 3 s; *Career* applied mathematician, research in Theoretical Rheology, fell Trin Cambridge 1947-51, prof of applied maths Wales U Swansea 1953-65, Liverpool U 1965-; *Style* - James Oldroyd Esq; Ardenmohr, Graham rd, W Kirby, Wirral (☎ Merseyside)

OLIVER, Col Claude Danolds; OBE (Mil 1945), TD (1942), DL (Leics 1950); s of Col Sir Frederick Oliver, TD, JP, DL (d 1939); *b* 29 Dec 1903; *Educ* Rugby; *Career* Col, joined TA 1922, UK and Burma RA 1939-45, co cmdt Leics & Rutland ACF 1949-53, chm Leics and Rutland T and AF Assoc 1957-68, Hon Col Roy Leics Regt (Territorial) 1967-72; chm George Oliver (Footwear) Ltd (md 1945-73) 1973-78; *Recreations* shooting, fishing, gardening; *Clubs* Army and Navy; *Style* - Col Claude Oliver, OBE, TD, DL; Whitecroft, 4 The Fairway, Oadby, Leicester

OLIVER, Brig James Alexander; CB (1957), CBE (1945), DSO (1942) and Bar (1943), TD; s of Adam Oliver (d 1944); *b* 19 March 1906; *Educ* Trin Coll Glenalmond; *m* 1932, Margaret, nee Scott; *Career* commanded 152 Infantry Brigade (Highland Div) 1943 (154 Inf Brig 1944-45), ADC to HM 1953-63, V-Lt County of Angus 1967, chm Angus & Dundee TA Assoc 1945-59, chm Earl Haig Fund (Scotland) 1972-73 (v-pres 1973), Hon Col 1960-70; *Clubs* Naval and Military; *Style* - Brig James Oliver CB CBE DSO* TD, HM Vice-Lieut for Angus; West Newton, Arbroath, Angus (☎ Arbroath 72579)

OLIVER, Prof Michael Francis; s of Capt Wilfrid Francis Lenn Oliver, MC (d 1940); *b* 3 July 1925; *Educ* Marlborough Coll, Edinburgh U; *m* 1947 (dis 1979), Margaret Yool, da of Maj James Yool Abbey, DSO, MC (d 1932); 2 s (and 1 s decd), 1 da; *Career* FRCP, FFCM, FACC, Duke of Edinburgh Prof of Cardiology 1979, convener: Ctee for Education in Health Roy Coll of Physicians Edinburgh 1978-, Cardiology Ctee of Scottish Roy Colls 1978-; chm: BBC Medical Advisory Gp Scotland 1975-, Science Ctee Fondation Cardiologique Princess Lilian Brussels 1976-, UK rep Advisory Panel for Cardiovascular Diseases WHO 1972-, memb Cncl and Research Funds Ctee of British Heart Foundation 1976-, examiner Cambridge; *Clubs* Athenaeum, New (Edinburgh); *Style* - Prof Michael Oliver; Ladyurd House, Blythebridge, Peeblesshire

OLIVIER, Baron (Life Peer UK 1970); Laurence Kerr Olivier; OM (1981); s of Rev Gerard Kerr Olivier, of Dorking, Surrey; *b* 22 May 1907; *Educ* St Edward's Sch Oxford; *m* 1, 1930, Jill Esmond (m dis 1940); 1 s; m 2, 1940, Vivien Leigh (m dis 1961 and who d 1967), da of Ernest Hartley (d 1959); m 3, 1961, Joan Plowright, CBE; 1 s, 2 da; *Career* actor, film producer, director; dir of Nat Theatre 1963-73; kt 1947; *Style* - The Rt Hon the Lord Olivier, OM; 33/34 Chancery Lane, WC2

OLIVIER, Brig Charles Harold Arthur; CBE (1959); s of Capt Robert Harold Olivier (ka 1914); *b* 29 Aug 1912; *Educ* Wellington, RMA Woolwich; *m* 1, 1937, Lois Mary (d 1959), nee James; 1 s, 2 da; m 2, 1960, Evelyn Elizabeth, da of Sir Norman Stronge, Bt, MC, PC (assas 1981); *Career* Brig, chm (Col) Planning Staff SHAPE 1956-58, Ch Staff (Brig) NI Command 1958-60, Brig-Author War Off 1962-63;

W Command 1966-67, ADC to HM the Queen 1964-67; dep cmdt, assist Ch Constable Police Coll Bramshill 1968-71; cncllr Test Valley Borough Cncl 1973-, Winchester Diocesan Synod 1976-; govr Cricklade Tertiary Coll 1977-; memb exec ctee Southern Tourist Board 1978-; *Recreations* travel, cricket, astronomy; *Clubs* Army and Navy, MCC; *Style* - Brig Charles Olivier CBE; Rosemary Cottage, The Green, Amport, Andover, Hants (☎ Weyhill 2602)

OLIVIER, Hon Julie Kate; da of Baron Olivier (Life Peer); *b* 1966; *Style* - The Hon Julie Olivier

OLIVIER, Hon Richard; s of Baron Olivier; *b* 1961; *Style* - The Hon Richard Olivier

OLIVIER, Hon (Simon) Tarquin; s of Baron Olivier (Life Peer); *b* 1936; *m* 1965, Riddelle, da of Patrick Boyce Riddell Gibson; 1 da; *Style* - The Hon Tarquin Olivier; 31 Queensdale rd, W11

OLIVIER, Hon Tamsin; da of Baron Olivier; *b* 1963; *Style* - The Hon Tamsin Olivier

OLNEY, Robert C; s of Herbert M Olney, of USA; *b* 19 Aug 1926; *Educ* Cornell; *m* 1948, Wanda, nee Gasch; 3 c; *Career* md 3M UK Ltd 1980-, v-pres and gen man Nat Adv Co Chicago 1976 (division dir 1973, marketing dir 1969, gen sales man 1959); *Recreations* golf swimming; *Clubs* Mid-America (Chicago), Hinsdale Golf (Illinois), St Paul Athletic (Minnesota); *Style* - Robert Olney Esq; 23 Albury rd, Walton-on-Thames, Surrey

OMAN, Julia Trevelyan; da of Charles Chichele Oman (see Lord Trevelyan); *b* 11 July 1930; *Educ* Roy Coll of Art; *m* 1971, Dr Roy Colin Strong; *Career* Roy Designer for Indsutry (RDI), dir Oman Productions Ltd; designer: BBC TV, *The Charge of the Light Brigade* 1967, *The Enigma Variations* (for the Roy Ballet) 1968, production designer *The Merchant of Venice* National Theatre 1970, Samuel Pepys Exibition Nat Portrait Gallery 1971, *A Month in the Country* (Roy Ballet) 1976 and others; *Style* - Mrs Roy Strong; c/o London Management, 235/241 Regent st, W1

ONSLOW, 7 Earl of (UK 1801); Sir Michael William Coplestone Dillon Onslow; 11 Bt (E 1674, of 2 cr, with precedency 1660); also Baron Onslow (GB 1716), Baron Cranley (GB 1776), and Viscount Cranley (UK 1801); s of 6 Earl, KBE, MC, TD (d 1971), by his w Pamela, Countess of Onslow, *qv*; bro-in-law of Auberon Waugh; the Onslows were formerly proprietors of Clandon Park (Palladian, built c 1730 by Giacomo Leoni, and with fine plasterwork) before it was acquired by the Nat Tst; *b* 28 Feb 1938; *Educ* Eton, Sorbonne; *m* 1964, Robin, da of Maj Robert Lee Bullard III, of Atlanta, Ga (Lady Onslow's mother subsequently m Lord Aberconway as his 2 w); 1 s, 2 da; *Heir* s, Viscount Cranley; *Career* insur broker, farmer; served Life Gds M East; *Style* - The Rt Hon Earl of Onslow; Temple Court, Clandon Park, Guildford, Surrey

ONSLOW, Lady Arabella Ann Teresa; da of 7 Earl of Onslow; *b* 1970

ONSLOW, Lady Charlotte Emma Dorothy; da of 7 Earl of Onslow; *b* 1977

ONSLOW, Lady June Ann; *née* Hay; da of 14 Earl of Kinnoull (d 1938); *b* 1932; *m* 1955, Cranley Gordon Douglas Onslow, MP; 1 s, 3 da; *Style* - Lady June Onslow; Highbuilding, Fernhurst, Sussex

ONSLOW, Sir John Roger Wilmot; 8 Bt (GB 1797), of Althain, Lancashire; s of Sir Richard Wilmot Onslow, 7 Bt, TD (d 1963); *b* 21 July 1932; *Educ* Cheltenham; *m* 1, 1955 (m dis 1973), Catherine Zoia, da of Henry Atherton Greenway, of The Manor, Compton Abdale, nr Cheltenham; 1 s, 1 da; m 2, 1976, Susan Fay, da of E M Hughes, of Victoria, Australia; *Heir* s, Richard Onslow; *Style* - Sir John Onslow, Bt; c/o Barclays Bank Ltd, Fowey, Cornwall

ONSLOW, Mary, Lady - Mary; da of late H R Russell, JP, of Belfast; *m* 1961, as his 2 w, Sir Richard Wilmot Onslow, 7 Bt, TD (d 1963); *Style* - Mary, Lady Onslow; 1 Strathearn House, New Forge Lane, Belfast BT9 5NU

ONSLOW, Jo, Countess of - Nina; MBE (1953); da of Thomas Sturdee; *m* 1962, 6 Earl of Onslow, KBE, MC, TD (d 1971); *Style* - The Rt Hon Jo, Countess of Onslow, MBE; Sturdee's, Freeland, Oxford

ONSLOW, Pamela, Countess of - Hon Pamela Louisa Ellinor; JP (Guildford 1952); da of 19 Viscount Dillon, CMG, DSO (d 1946); *b* 1915; *m* 1936, (m dis 1962, he d 1971) 6 Earl of Onslow, KBE, MC; 1 s, 1 da; *Style* - Pamela, Countess of Onslow, JP; 12 Callcott st, W8

ONSLOW, Richard Paul Atherton; s and h of Sir John Roger Wilmot Onslow, 8 Bt; *b* 16 Sept 1958; *Style* - Richard Onslow Esq

OPPENHEIM, Lady Bridget Sarah; da (by 2 m) of late 19 Earl of Caithness; *b* 1947; *m* 1976, Nicholas Anthony Oppenheim (s of Sir Duncan Oppenheim); 1 da; *Style* - Lady Bridget Oppenheim

OPPENHEIMER, Sir Michael Bernard Grenville; 3 Bt (UK 1921), of Stoke Poges, Co Bucks; s of Sir Michael Oppenheimer, 2 Bt (d 1933 after a flying accident), by his w Caroline (da of Sir Robert Harvey, 2 & last Bt, and sis of Diana, Lady Balfour of Inchrye (divorced w of 1 Baron); Caroline m 2, as his 2 w, Sir Ernest Oppenheimer, f by his 1 w of Harry Oppenheimer, the present chm of De Beers); *b* 27 May 1924; *Educ* Charterhouse, Ch Ch Oxford; *m* 1947, Laetitia, da of Sir Hugh Munro-Lucas-Tooth, 1 Bt; 3 da (Henrietta, b 1954, m 1978 Adam Scott; Matilda, b 1956, m 1978 Neil King; Xanthe, b 1958, m 1977 Hon Ivo Mosley, *qv*); *Heir* none; *Career* late Lt SA Artillery, served M East & Italy WW II; university lecturer in politics (Lincoln Coll Oxford 1955-68, Magdalen 1966-68); *Clubs* Kimberley (S Africa), Victoria (Jersey); *Style* - Sir Michael Oppenheimer, Bt; L'Aiguillon, Grouville, Jersey, CI

ORAM, Baron (Life Peer UK 1975); Albert Edward Oram; s of Henry Oram (d 1963); *b* 1913; *Educ* Burgess Hill Elementary Sch, London Sch of Economics; *m* 1956, Joan, da of Charles Barber, of Lewes, Sussex; 2 s; *Career* served 1942-45 War; research offr Co-operative Party 1946-55; MP (L and Co-op) East Ham (South) 1955-74; a Lord in Waiting to HM the Queen (Govt Whip) 1976-78; chm Co-Operative Development Agency 1978-; *Style* - The Rt Hon the Lord Oram; 19 Ridgeside ave, Patcham, Brighton, E Sussex (☎ Brighton 505333)

ORAM, Hon Mark; s of Baron Oram (Life Peer); *b* 1967

ORAM, Hon Robin; s of Baron Oram (Life Peer); *b* 1968

ORANMORE AND BROWNE, 4 Baron (I 1836); Geoffrey Edward Browne; also 2 Baron Mereworth (UK 1926, which sits as); s of 3 Baron, KP, PC (d 1927), by his w Lady Olwen Ponsonby, herself da of 8 Earl of Bessborough, KP; *b* 21 Oct 1901; *Educ* Eton, Ch Ch Oxford; *m* 1, 1925, Mildred Helen (m dis 1936 and who d 1980 having m as her 2 husb Hon Hew Dalrymple, 2 s of 12 Earl of Stair), da of Hon Thomas Egerton (d 1953, 3 s of 3 Earl of Ellesmere & unc of 6 Duke of Sutherland) by Thomas's w Lady Bertha, nee Anson, da of 3 Earl of Lichfield; 2 s, 3 da (1 decd); m 2, 1936, Oonagh (m dis 1950), da of Hon Arthur Ernest Guinness (d 1949), gda of 1 Earl of Iveagh and sis of Maureen Marchioness of Dufferin and Ava; 3 s (2 decd); m 3, 1951, the actress Sally Gray (otherwise Constance Vera, da of Charles Stevens); *Heir* s, Hon Dominick Geoffrey Thomas Browne; *Career* 2 Lt Gren Gds 1922-23; *Style* - The Rt Hon the Lord Oranmore and Browne; 52 Eaton pla, SW1

ORCHARD, Hon Mrs - Hon Modwena Louise; da of 6 Baron Hatherton (d 1973); *b* 1947; *m* 1, 1968 (m dis 1974), Edward Willison; 2 da; m 2, 1978, Peter Fleming Orchard; *Style* - The Hon Mrs Orchard; 18 Church rd, Buckhurst Hill, Essex

ORCHARD, Peter Francis; s of Edward Henslowe Orchard (d 1958); *b* 25 March 1927; *Educ* Downside Sch, Magdalene Coll Cambridge; *m* 1955, Helen, da of Sir Joseph Sheridan (d 1964); 2 s (Rupert b 1957, Timothy b 1963), 2 da (Marianne b 1959, Josephine b 1964); *Career* Capt 60 Rifles 1944-48, Sch of Infantry instructor, ch exec The De La Rue Co Ltd since 1977, chm: Crosfield Business Machines Ltd, Crosfield Electronics Ltd, Thomas De La Rue (Security Systems Print) Ltd, Thomas De La Rue Holdings; dir: Anglo-Swiss Engrg Ltd, Federated Banknote Printing Co Ltd, Security Express Ltd, Vebass Ltd, Westwood Instruments Ltd; *Recreations* gardening, swimming, building, cricket; *Clubs* Travellers', MCC; *Style* - Peter Orchard Esq; Willow Cottage, Little Hallingbury, Bishop's Stortford, Herts (☎ 0279 54101)

ORDE, His Hon Judge (Denis Alan); s of John Orde CBE; *b* 28 Aug 1932; *Educ* Oxford; *m* 1961, Jennifer Jane, nee Longworth; 2 da; *Career* barr 1956, Recorder 1972-79, Circuit Judge 1979-; *Recreations* cricket, fishing, music, biography, nineteenth century oil paintings *Clubs* Carlton; *Style* - His Hon Judge Orde; Chollerton Grange, Chollerton, nr Hexham, Northumberland

ORDE-POWLETT, Hon Harry Algar Nigel; s and h of 7 Baron Bolton by his 1 w, Hon Christine Weld-Forester, da of 7 Baron Forester; *b* 14 Feb 1954; *Educ* Eton; *m* 1977, Philippa, da of Maj Peter Tapply, of Essex; 2 s (Thomas, William Benjamin); *Style* - The Hon Harry Orde-Powlett

ORFORD, Countess of; Emily Gladys; da of Rev Thomas Oakes; *m* 1917, as his 2 w, 5 and last Earl of Orford, JP, DL (d 1931); 1 da (Lady Anne Palmer, *qv*; also 1 da decd); *Style* - The Rt Hon Countess of Orford; Rosemoor, Torrington, Devon

ORIGO, Marchesa Iris; DBE (1977); da of W Bayard Cutting, of New York (d 1910), sometime attached to the American Embassy in London, and Lady Sybil Cuffe (da of 5 & last Earl of Desart by his w Lady Margaret Lascelles, herself da of 5 Earl of Harewood and sis of Lady Wenlock, w of 3 Baron); *b* 15 Aug 1902; *Educ* privately in Florence; *m* 1924, Marchese Antonio Origo, s of Marchese Clemente Origo, of Rome and Florence; 2 da (Benedetta Lysy, Donata Migone), & 1 child decd; *Career* biographer (notably of Leopardi) & historian; Pres Internat Soc Serv for 1 year, memb exec ctee 1958-68, formerly liaison between American & Italian Red Cross; FRSL; fndr Hosp for Tubercular Children near Florence; *Recreations* farming, gardening, travel; *Style* - Marchesa Antonio Origo, DBE; c/o Williams & Glyn's Bank Ltd, 20 Bride's Lane, EC3; Via di Monte Sarello 30, Rome 00186 (☎ 06 6511327)

ORKNEY, 8 Earl of (S 1696); Cecil O'Bryen Fitz-Maurice; also Viscount Kirkwall and Lord Dechmont (both S 1696); s of late Douglas Frederick Harold Fitz-Maurice (himself gs of Cdr Hon Frederick Fitz-Maurice, who was in turn 3 s of 5 Earl); suc kinsman, 7 Earl, 1951; *b* 3 July 1919; *m* 1953, Rose Katherine Durk, da of late J W D Silley; *Heir* kinsman, Peter Fitz-Maurice; *Career* joined RASC 1939, served 1939-45 (N Africa, Italy, France, Germany and Holland) and 1950-51 (Korea); *Style* - The Rt Hon Earl of Orkney; 4 Summerland, Princes rd, Ferndown, Dorset (☎ 893178)

ORLEBAR, Richard Astry Bourne; s of Lt-Col Richard Rouse-Boughton whose mother was 5 da of Sir William Boughton, 10 Bt; *b* 7 Oct 1894; *Educ* Rugby Sch, Pembroke Coll Cambridge; *m* 1935, Barbara, da of Capt Frederick Charles Pilcher (d 1953); 2 s (Richard Michael b 1938, Robert John b 1944), 1 da (Lucy Mary Forster b 1942); *Career* Capt France 1914, Salonika 1914-17, landowner; *Recreations* shooting; *Style* - Richard Orlebar Esq; Hinwick House, nr Wellingborough, North Hants (☎ Rushden 53624)

ORMATHWAITE, 6 Baron (UK 1868); Sir John Arthur Charles Walsh; 7 Bt (UK 1804); s of 5 Baron (d 1944), and Lady Margaret Jane, da of 12 Earl of Home, KT; *b* 25 Dec 1912; *Educ* Eton, Trin Cambridge; *Heir* none; *Career* farmer; *Style* - The Rt Hon the Lord Ormathwaite; Pen-y-Bont Hall, Llandrindod Wells, Powys (☎ Pen-y-Bont 228)

ORME-SMITH, Hon Mrs (Teresa Caroline); *née* Shaw; da of Baron Kilbrandon, PC (Life Peer); *b* 1940; *m* 1969, Christopher Orme-Smith; *Style* - The Hon Mrs Orme-Smith

ORMONDE, 7 Marquess of (I 1825); James Hubert Theobald Charles Butler; MBE (1921); also Earl of Ormonde (I 1328), Earl of Ossory (I 1527), Viscount Thurles (I 1536), Baron Ormonde (UK 1821), and 31 Hereditary Ch Butler of Ireland (1177); s of Rev Lord James Butler (4 s of 2 Marquess, KP, and Frances, gda of 1 Earl of Uxbridge); suc 1 cous, 6 Marquess, 1971; *b* 19 April 1899; *Educ* Haileybury, Sandhurst; *m* 1, 1935, Nan (d 1973), da of Garth Gilpin, of USA; 2 da; m 2, 1976, Elizabeth, da of Charles Rarden, of USA; *Heir* to Marquessate, Viscountcy and Barony: none; to Earldoms of Ormonde and Ossory, and Hereditary Chief Butlership: 17 Viscount Mountgarret; *Career* late Lt KRRC WW I; US businessman; *Style* - The Most Hon Marquess of Ormonde MBE; 10 N Washington Apartment 120, Hinsdale, Ill 60521, USA

ORMROD, Hon Mrs (Barbara Helen); *née* FitzRoy; da of 2 Viscount Daventry; *b* 1928; *m* 1952, Maj Peter Charles Ormrod, MC, 8 King's Roy Irish Hussars; 2 da; *Style* - The Hon Mrs Ormrod; Pen-y-Lan, Ruabon, Wrexham, Clwyd

ORMROD, Maj Peter Charles; MC (1951), DL (Clwyd 1972); s of Maj James Ormrod (d 1945); *b* 31 Aug 1922; *Educ* Harrow, Sandhurst; *m* 1952, Hon Barbara Helen, da of 2 Viscount Daventry; 2 da; *Career* land use and forestry consultant, Maj NW Europe 1944-45, Korea 1950-51; memb Inst Civil Engrs and Inst Foresters, Magistrate 1958, High Sheriff 1962; *Recreations* shooting, sailing, photography; *Clubs* Army & Navy; *Style* - Maj Peter Ormrod, MC, DL; Pen-y-Lan, Ruabon, Wrexham, Clwyd (☎ Ruabon 823336)

ORMSBY-GORE, Hon Alice Magdalen Sarah; da of 5 Baron Harlech, KCMG, PC; *b* 22 April 1952; *Style* - The Hon Alice Ormsby-Gore

ORMSBY-GORE, Hon Francis David; s and h of 5 Baron Harlech, KCMG, PC; *b* 13 March 1954; *Style* - The Hon Frances Ormsby-Gore

ORMSBY-GORE, Hon John Julian; 2 surv s of 4 Baron Harlech, KG, GCMG, PC (1964); *b* 1925; *Educ* Eton, New Coll Oxford; *Career* Capt Coldstream Gds 1944; *Style* - The Hon John Ormsby-Gore; 14 Ladbroke rd, WII

ORMSBY-GORE, Hon Pandora Beatrice; da of 5 Baron Harlech, KCMG, PC; *b* 19 April 1972; *Style* - The Hon Pandora Ormsby-Gore

ORR, John Carmichael; *Career* exec dir S G Warburg & Co, fin dir Grand Metropolitan Ltd 1981-; *Style* - John Carmichael Esq; 11/12 Hanover sq, W1 (☎ 01 629 7488)

ORR, Robin (Robert Kemsley); CBE (1972); s of Robert Workman Orr (d 1942); *b* 2 June 1909; *Educ* Loretto Sch, Roy Coll of Music, Pembroke Cambridge; *m* 1, 1937 (m dis 1979), Margaret Ellen, nee Mace; 1 s, 2 da; m 2, 1979, Doris Ruth, da of late Leo Meyer-Bechtler, of Zürich; *Career* composer, organist St John's Cambridge 1938-51, U lectr Cambridge 1947-56, prof of Music Glasgow U 1956-65, prof of Music Cambridge U 1965-76 (Emeritus 1976-), chm Scottish Opera 1962-76; *Recreations* gardening, mountain walks; *Style* - Robin Orr Esq, CBE; 16 Cranmer rd, Cambridge (☎ 353858); Chesa Maya, Rüefaweg 4, 7250 Klosters, Switzerland (☎ 083 43467)

ORR EWING, Archibald Donald; s and h of Sir Ronald Orr Ewing, 5 Bt; *b* 20 Dec 1938; *Educ* Gordonstoun, Trin Coll Dublin; *m* 1, 1965 (m dis 1972), Venetia, da of Maj Richard Turner; m 2, 1972, Nicola, da of Reginald Black, of Creagh Castle, Doneraile, Co Cork, and Eloise, nee Innes-Ker, niece of 8 Duke of Roxburghe; *Career* memb Roy Co Archers (Queen's Bodyguard for Scotland); *Clubs* Brooks's, New (Edinburgh); *Style* - Archibald Orr Ewing Esq; Sandyholes, Arnprior, Kippen, by Stirling

ORR EWING, Maj Edward Stuart; DL (Wigtownshire 1971); s of Capt David Orr Ewing, DSO, RN (ret) (d 1964, s of Charles Orr Ewing, MP Ayr & himself 5 s of Sir Archibald O E, 1 Bt, by Charles's 2 w, Lady Augusta Boyle, da of 7 Earl of Glasgow); *b* 28 Sept 1931; *Educ*

Sherborne; *m* 1958, Fiona Anne Bowman, da of Anthony Hobart Farquhar, of Hastingwood House; 1 s, 2 da; *Career* Maj, Black Watch, ret 1969; *Style* - Major Edward Orr Ewing, DL; Dunskey, Portpatrick, Wigtownshire (☎ Portpatrick 211)

ORR EWING, Major Sir Ronald Archibald; 5 Bt (UK 1886), JP (Perthshire 1956), DL (1963); s of Sir Norman Orr Ewing, 4 Bt, CB, DSO (d 1960); *b* 14 May 1912; *Educ* Eton and Sandhurst; *m* 1938, Marion Hester, da of late Col Sir Donald Walter Cameron of Lochiel, KT, CMG, and Lady Hermione Cameron of Lochiel, da of 5 Duke of Montrose, KT; 2 s, 2 da; *Heir* s Archibald Donald Orr Ewing; *Career* Scots Guards, 1932-53, Major; served World War II, Middle East (POW 1942); Grand Master Mason of Scotland 1965-69; *Clubs* Army and Navy, and New (Edinburgh); *Style* - Major Sir Ronald Orr Ewing, Bt, JP, DL; Cardross, Port of Menteith, Stirling (☎ Port of Menteith 220)

ORR-EWING, Baron (Life Peer UK 1971); Sir (Charles) Ian Orr-Ewing; 1 Bt (UK 1963), OBE (1945); s of Archibald Ian Orr-Ewing (d 1942, s of Capt John Orr-Ewing, 4 s of Sir Archibald Orr Ewing, Bt (of the 1886 cr), and the Capt's 1 w, Ellen, da of Howard Kennard, and 2 cous once removed of Sir Coleridge Kennard, 1 Bt); *b* 10 Feb 1912; *Educ* Harrow, Trin Oxford; *m* 1939, Joan Helen, da of Gordon McMinnies, of Stoke Orchard, nr Cheltenham; 4 s; *Heir* to Btcy only, s Hon Alistair Simon Orr-Ewing; *Career* served World War II with RAF, Wing Cdr 1941, ch radar offr Gen Eisenhower's staff 1945; employed BBC (TV) 1937-39 and 1946-49; MP (C) Hendon 1950-70; PPS to Min of Labour 1951-55, Parly Under-Sec State Air Miny 1957-59, Parly & Financial Sec to the Admiralty 1959, Civil Lord of the Admiralty 1959-63; a vice-chm Conservative 1922 Ctee 1966-70; chm Ultra Electric Hldgs 1965-79; chm Clayton Dewandre Ltd; dir MK Hldgs 1977-, Dowty 1978-; chm MK Switchgear 1980-; former chm Metrication Bd; *Recreations* part owner of race-horse: 'Proper Gentleman'; *Clubs* Boodle's, MCC, Harrow Wanderers (chm), Vincent's (Oxford); *Style* - The Rt Hon the Lord Orr-Ewing, OBE; The Old Manor, Little Berkhamsted, nr Hertford, Herts (☎ 284 5962); Flat 2, 9 Cheyne Gdns, SW3 (☎ 01 730 3728)

ORR-EWING, Hon Alistair Simon; s of Baron Orr-Ewing, OBE (Life Peer and 1 Bt); ha to Baronetcy; *b* 10 June 1940; *Educ* Harrow and Trin, Oxford; ARICS; *m* 1968, Victoria, da of late Keith Cameron; 2 s, 1 da; *Style* - The Hon Alistair Orr-Ewing; 44 Paultons sq, SW3

ORR-EWING, Hamish; s of Capt Hugh Eric Douglas Orr-Ewing (gs of James Ewing, yr bro of Sir Archibald Orr Ewing, 1 Bt, JP, DL, MP); Hamish is 3 cous of Baron Orr-Ewing, the Life Peer and former chm of the Metrication Bd, while his mother (the Capt's 2 w) was sis of Sir Kenneth Stewart, 1 Bt, GBE; *b* 17 Aug 1924; *Educ* Heatherdown and Eton; *m* 1, 1948 (m dis 1954), Morar Margaret, sis of the TV journalist Ludovic Kennedy, *qv*, and da of late Capt Edward Kennedy, RN (ggs of Hon Robert Kennedy and 3 s of 11 Earl of Cassillis); 1 s (1 da decd); m 2, 1954, Ann Mary Teresa, da of late Frederick Terry; *Career* Capt Black Watch 1942-47; chm Rank Xerox Ltd 1980-; dir Tricentrol Ltd 1975-; *Recreations* mechanics, country life, the Roman Empire; *Style* - Hamish Orr-Ewing Esq; 51 Clifton Hill, NW8 (☎ 01 624 5702); Fox Mill, Purton, nr Swindon, Wilts (☎ 0793 770496)

ORR-EWING, Hon Ian Colin; s of Baron Orr-Ewing, OBE (Life Peer); *b* 1942; *Educ* Harrow, Trin Oxford; *m* 1973, Deirdre, da of Lance Japhet; 1 s, 1 da; *Style* - The Hon Ian Orr-Ewing; 9 Trevor Place, SW1

ORR-EWING, Hon Malcolm Archie; s of Baron Orr-Ewing, OBE (Life Peer); *b* 1946; *Educ* Harrow and Munich; *m* 1973, Clare Mary, da of Brig George Robert Flood, MC; 2 da; *Style* - The Hon Malcolm Orr-Ewing; Far Oakridge House, Stroud, Glos

ORR-EWING, Hon Robert James; s of Baron Orr-Ewing, OBE (Life Peer); *b*

1953; *Educ* Harrow; *Career* barr, Inner Temple 1976; *Style* - The Hon Robert Orr-Ewing

ORSON, Rasin Ward; FSS; s of Rasin Nelson Orson; *b* 16 April 1927; *Educ* Stratford G S; LSE; *m* 1950, Marie Goodenough; 2 s; *Career* memb The Electricity Council 1976-; dir Chloride Silent Power Ltd 1974-; *Style* - Rasin Orson Esq, FSS; 128 De Beauvoir rd, N1 (☎ 01 254 7784)

OSBORN, Sir Danvers Lionel Rouse; 8 Bt (E 1662); s of Sir Algernon K B Osborn, 7 Bt, JP (d 1948); *b* 31 Jan 1916; *Educ* Eton and Magdalene Cambridge; *m* 1943 (m dis 1979), Constance Violette, JP, SSStJ, da of late Maj Leonard Frank Rooke, KOSB; 1 s, 1 da (1 s and 1 da decd); *Heir* s, Richard Henry Danvers Osborn; *Career* employed as Civil Assistant in Intelligence Dept of War Office, 1940-45; Joined Spicers Ltd, 1955; dir of two picture galleries; *Clubs* MCC; *Style* - Sir Danvers Osborn, Bt; The Dower House, Moor Park, Farnham, Surrey

OSBORN, Fuller Mansfield; CBE (1972); s of Fuller Mansfield Osborn; *b* 1915; *Educ* Grocers' Co Sch, Hackney Downs; *m* 1949, Mary Armstrong, da of William James Auld; *Career* served in 1939-45 War as Maj RA SEAC; md Northern Rock Building Soc; chm Council of Building Socs Assocn 1969-71; DL (1975), High Sheriff co of Tyne and Wear 1974-75; *Clubs* Northern Counties and Union (Newcastle upon Tyne) ; *Style* - Fuller Osborn Esq, DL; Arundel, 9 Furzefield rd, Gosforth, Newcastle upon Tyne NE3 4EA

OSBORN, Harold Ernest; CBE (1963); s of Albert George Osborn (d 1956); *b* 25 Dec 1909; *Educ* Finchley County Sch and LSE; *m* 1949, Gerda Ilse, da of Curt Treitel, of Berlin; *Career* CA 1933; joined service of London Passenger Transport Bd 1936; on formation of British Transport Commission appointed dir of accounts 1948, financial controller 1962; comptroller Transport Holding Co 1963-73; comptroller National Freight Corpn 1969; vice-chm Exec Nat Freight Corpn 1972-73; special adviser to chm NFC 1974; *Style* - Harold Osborn Esq, CBE; 6 Park ave, Golders Green, NW11 (☎ 01 455 2566); Chiltern Meadow, Cadmore End, High Wycombe, Bucks (☎ High Wycombe 881 623)

OSBORN, John Holbrook; MP; s of Samuel Eric Osborn; *b* 14 Dec 1922; *Educ* Rugby and Trinity Hall, Cambridge; Nat Foundry Coll; *m* 1 1952 (m dis), Molly Suzanne Marten; 2 da; m 2, 1976, Joan Mary MacDermot, nee Wilkinson; *Career* MP (C) (NL and U 1959-64) Hallam Div of Sheffield, 1959-; MEP 1975-79; dir, Samuel Osborn & Co Ltd and assoc cos, 1951-79; *Style* - John Osborn Esq, MP; Folds Head Close, Calver, Sheffield S30 1XJ; Flat 13, 102 Rochester Row, SW1 (☎ 01 799 5932)

OSBORN, Richard Henry Danvers; s and h of Sir Danvers Lionel Rouse Osborn, 8 Bt; *b* 12 Aug 1958; *Educ* Eton; *Style* - Richard Osborn Esq; c/o The Dower House, Moor Park, Farnham, Surrey

OSBORNE, Sir Basil; CBE (1962); s of late Alderman W W Osborne, MBE; *b* 19 April 1907; *Educ* Metropolitan Business Coll ; *m* 1934, Esma, da of late T Green; 1 s; *Career* Lord Mayor of Hobart, Tasmania, 1959-70; Alderman 1952-76; chm Metropolitan Transport Trust 1971-78; business administrator; knighted 1967; *Style* - Sir Basil Osborne, CBE; 6 Myella Drive, Chigwell, Tasmania 7011, Australia

OSBORNE, Maj-Gen the Rev Coles Alexander; CIE (1945); s of late W E Osborne; *b* 29 July 1896; *Educ* Dover County Sch; *m* 1930, Joyce, da of late R H Meares; 2 da; *Career* Indian Army, retired; chm Freedom from Hunger Campaign NSW 1970-72; *Style* - Major-Gen the Rev Coles Osborne, CIE; 126 Hopetown ave, Vaucluse, NSW 2030, Australia (☎ 337 2969)

OSBORNE, Charles Thomas; s of Vincent Lloyd Osborne; *b* 24 Nov 1927; *Educ* Brisbane State H S; *m* 1970 (m dis 1975), Marie Korbelarova; *Career* author; literature dir Arts Council of Gt Britain 1971-; *Style* - Charles Osborne Esq; 26 Evelyn Mansions, SW1P 1NH

OSBORNE, Hon Frederick Meares; CMG (1969), DSC, VRD, BA, LLB; s of late W A Osborne; *b* 20 Jan 1909; *Educ* N Sydney H S, Sydney C of E G S and St Andrew's Coll, Sydney U; *m* 1944, Elizabeth, da of C C H Drake; 2 s, 2 da; *Career* slr 1934; MHR Australia 1949-61; Min Customs and Excise 1956; Min for Air 1956-60; Min Repatriation 1960-61; pres NSW div Liberal Party 1967-70; *Style* - The Hon Frederick Osborne, CMG; 9 Mary st, Longueville, NSW 2066, Australia

OSBORNE, Gideon Oliver; s and h of Sir Peter George Osborne, 17 Bt; *b* 23 May 1971

OSBORNE, John (James); s of Thomas Godfrey Osborne; *b* 12 Dec 1929; *Educ* Belmont Coll, Devon; *m* 1 (m dis 1957) Pamela Elizabeth Lane; m 2, 1957 (m dis 1963) Mary Ure (d 1975); m 3, 1963 (m dis 1968) Penelope Gilliatt; m 4, 1968 (m dis 1977) Jill Bennett; m 5, 1978, Helen Dawson; *Career* dramatist and actor; dir of Woodfall Films; *Clubs* Garrick; *Style* - John Osborne Esq; 18 Elm Tree rd, NW8

OSBORNE, Col John Lander; CBE (1969), TD (1947); s of Frank John Osborne, MC, FRIBA (d 1959), of Solihull, Warwickshire; *b* 30 June 1917; *Educ* Solihull Sch; Villars, Switzerland; Birmingham Sch of Architecture; *m* 1, 1942, Kate Honour (d 1980), da of late Col Duncan Cameron; 1 da; m 2, 1981, Phyllis Mary Tipper, nee James; *Career* Lt-Col Div Engrs N Africa, Italy 1942-46; ch engr W Midlands Dist 1958-66; Hon Col 48 divnl engrs 1957-66; pres Birmingham & Five Counties Architectural Assoc 1962-64; chm W Midlands Region RIBA 1970-72; (FRIBA); partner John P Osborne & Son, Architects, 1949; DL (1975) W Midlands; ADC to the Queen 1968-72; *Recreations* sailing, skiing, golf, horticulture; *Clubs* Army & Navy, Royal Thames Yacht, Birmingham, Little Aston Golf; *Style* - Colonel John Osborne, CBE, TD, DL; The Elms, Copt Heath, Knowle, Solihull, W Midlands (☎ Knowle 2573); Maidenwell, Broad Campden, Chipping Campden, Glos (☎ Evesham 840772)

OSBORNE, Kenneth Hilton; QC (Scot); s of Kenneth Osborne; *b* 9 July 1937; *Educ* Larchfield Sch, Helensburgh; Merchiston Castle Sch, Edinburgh; Edinburgh U; *m* 1964, Clare Ann Louise Lewis; 1 s, 1 da; *Career* admitted to Faculty of Advocates in Scotland, 1962; QC (Scot) 1976; chm, Disciplinary Ctee, Potato Marketing Bd, 1975-; chm, Supreme Court Legal Aid Ctee, 1979-; *Clubs* New (Edinburgh); *Style* - Kenneth Osborne Esq, QC; 11 Ann st, Edinburgh EH4 1PL (☎ 031 332 1455); Primrose Cottage, Bridgend of Lintrathen, by Kirriemuir, Angus DD8 5JH

OSBORNE, Surgeon Rear-Admiral (D) Leslie Bartlet; CB (1956); s of late Rev Joseph Osborne, MA ; *b* 16 Sept 1900; *Educ* Caterham Sch; Guy's Hosp; LDS, RCS, FDS, RCS (Edinburgh); *m* 1929; 2 s, 1 da; *Career* Dep Dir-Gen Dental Services in the Royal Navy, 1954-57, ret; *Style* - Surgn Rear-Admiral Leslie Osborne, CB; 4 Westbourne Court, Cooden Drive, Cooden Beach, Bexhill-on-Sea, E Sussex TN39 3AA (☎ Cooden 4431)

OSBORNE, Mary, Lady - Mary Grace; da of late C S Horn, of Goring-by-the-Sea, Sussex; *m* 1938, Lt-Col Sir George Francis Osborne, 16 Bt, MC (d 1960); *Style* - Mary, Lady Osborne; 4 Herbert Mansions, 35 Sloane st, SW1

OSBORNE, Sir Peter (George); 17 Bt (I 1629); s of Lt-Col Sir George Osborne, 16 Bt, MC (d 1960); *b* 29 June 1943; *Educ* Wellington, Ch Ch Oxford; *m* 1968, Felicity, da of Grantley Loxton-Peacock; 3 s; *Heir* s, Gideon Oliver Osborne; *Style* - Sir Peter Osborne, Bt; 36 Porchester Terrace, W2 (☎ 01 402 3903)

OSIFELO, Sir Frederick (Aubarua); MBE (1972); s of Paul Iromea; *b* 15 Oct 1928; *Educ* Torquay Technical Coll; *m* 1949, Margaret Tanai; 3 s, 3 da; *Career* speaker of Legislative Assembly, Solomon Islands, 1974-; chm, Public Service Commission, 1975-; knighted 1977; *Style* - Sir Frederick Osifelo, MBE; PO Box 548, Honiara, Solomon Islands (☎ 01 25)

OSMAN, Sir (Abdool) Raman (Mahomed); GCMG (1973), CBE (1963); *b* 29 Aug 1902; *Educ* Royal Coll, Mauritius; Inns of Court, London; *Career* Governor-General of Mauritius, 1972-77; *Style* - Sir Raman Osman, GCMG, CBE; Le Goulet Terrace, Tombeau Bay, Mauritius

OSMOND, Sir Douglas; CBE (1968), QPM; *Career* Chief Constable, Shropshire, 1946-62, Hampshire, 1962-77; memb, Roy Commn on Criminal Procedure, 1978-; kt 1971; *Style* - Sir Douglas Osmond, CBE, QPM; Cygnet House, Martyr Worthy, Winchester, Hants

OSMOND, Michael William Massy; CB (1977); s of Brig WRF Osmond, CBE (d 1952); *b* 20 Nov 1918; *Educ* Winchester, Ch Ch Oxford; *m* 1943, Jill Stephanie, nee Ramsden; 1 s, 1 da; *Career* barr 1941, assist princ Miny of Production 1941-43, housemaster HM Borstal Usk 1943-45, legal assist Miny of Nat Insurance 1946, sr legal assist 1948, assist slr Miny of Pensions & Nat Insurance 1958, princ assist slr DHSS 1969, legal advisor to DHSS and to Office of Population Censuses and Surveys and to Gen Register Office 1974-78; *Recreations* music; *Clubs* United Oxford and Cambridge U; *Style* - Michael Osmond Esq, CB; Waylands, Long Newnton, Tetbury, Glos (☎ 53308)

OSMOND, Sir (Stanley) Paul; CB (1966); s of late Stanley C Osmond; *b* 13 May 1917; *Educ* Bristol G S; Jesus Coll, Oxford; *m* 1942, Olivia Sybil, JP, da of late Ernest E Wells, JP; 2 s; *Career* served war of 1939-45 in Army (Gloucestershire Regt and Staff); Home Civil Service, 1939-75; sec to the Church Commissioners, 1975-80; knighted 1980; *Style* - Sir Paul Osmond, CB; 20 Beckenham Grove, Bromley, Kent BR2 OJU (☎ 01 460 2026)

OSMOND-CLARKE, Sir Henry; KCVO (1969), CBE (1947), FRCS; s of W J Clarke; *Educ* Clones H S; Trinity Coll, Dublin U; Vienna, Bologna, New York, Boston, London; BA, MB, BCh, FRCSIre, FRCS; *m* Freda, da of Richard Hutchinson; 2 da; *Career* consulting orthopaedic surgeon- London Hosp, E1 (orthopaedic surgeon, 1946-70); Robert Jones and Agnes Hunt Orthopaedic Hosp, Oswestry (sr visiting surgeon, 1930-70); hon civilian consultant in Orthopaedics, RAF, 1946-; orthopaedic surgeon to the Queen, 1965-73 ; *Clubs* RAF; *Style* - Sir Henry Osmond-Clarke, KCVO, CBE, ; 46 Harley House, Marylebone rd, NW1 5HJ (☎ 01 486 9975)

OSSORY, Earl of; title which would be borne by eld s, if any living, of Marquess of Ormonde

OSTENFELD, D W; *Career* chm, Joseph Stocks & Sons (Holdings) Ltd; *Style* - D W Ostenfeld Esq; c/o Joseph Stocks & Sons (Hldgs) Ltd, 57 Stanley rd, Whitfield, Manchester M25 6QP

OSWALD, Lady Angela Mary Rose; *née* Cecil; da of 6 Marquess of Exeter KCMG by his 1 w, Lady Mary Montagu Douglas Scott, da of 7 Duke of Buccleuch; *b* 1938; *m* 1958, William Oswald, MVO, MA; 1 s, 1 da; *Style* - Lady Angela Oswald; Flitcham Hall, King's Lynn, Norfolk; Hampton Court Palace, E Molesey, Surrey

OSWALD, Maj-Gen Marshall St John; CB (1965), CBE (1961), DSO (1945), MC (1943); s of William Whitehead Oswald; *b* 13 Sept 1911; *Educ* Rugby and RMA Woolwich; *Career* command RA 1931; served in RHA and Field Artillery, UK and India, 1931-39; served war of 1939-45 (despatches, MC, DSO); DMI, War Office, Ministry of Defence (Army) 1964-65; ret 1966; *Clubs* Army and Navy; *Style* - Major-General Marshall Oswald, CB, CBE, DSO, MC; Eastfield House, Longparish, nr Andover, Hants (☎ Longparish 228)

OSWALD, Dr Neville Christopher; TD (1946), MD, FRCP (1947); s of Late Col Christopher Percy Oswald, CMG; *b* 1 Aug 1910; *Educ* Clifton, Queens' Coll Cambridge; *m* 1, 1941, Patricia Rosemary Joyce Cooke (d 1947); 1 s, 1 da; m 2, 1948, Marjorie Mary Sinclair; 1 da; *Career* formerly consultant physician: St Bart's Hosp, Brompton Hosp, King Edward VII Hosp for Officers London, King Edward VII's Hosp, Midhurst; ret 1975; DL

(Greater London) 1973-78; *Style* - Dr Neville Oswald, TD; 2 The Old Rectory, Thurlestone, South Devon (☎ Thurlestone 555)

OSWALD, William Richard Michael, MA; s of Lt-Col William Alexander Hugh Oswald, MS (d 1974), of Little Orchard, St George's Hill, Weybridge, Surrey; *b* 21 April 1934; *Educ* Eton and King's Coll, Cambridge; *m* 1958, Lady Angela Mary Rose, da of 6 Marquess of Exeter, KCMG, of Burghley House, Stamford, Lincs; 1 s, 1 da; *Career* 2 Lt 1 Bn King's Own Royal Regt 1953-54 (Korea); Capt 8 Bn Royal Fus (TA) 1960-61; memb, Council of The Thoroughbred Breeders Assocn, 1964; Manager HM Thoroughbred Studs, 1970; *Style* - William Oswald Esq; Flitcham Hall, King's Lynn, Norfolk (☎ Hillington 319); Apt 8a Hampton Court Palace, East Molesey, Surrey (☎ 01 977 5673)

OTTER, Air Vice-Marshal Victor Charles; CBE (1967); s of Robert Otter; *b* 9 Feb 1914; *Educ* Weymouth G S; *m* 1943, Iris Louise Dykes; *Career* Air Officer Engrg Air Support Command Royal Air Force, 1966-69; ret; *Clubs* RAF; *Style* - Air Vice-Marshal Victor Otter, CBE; Harpenden, 21 Keats ave, Littleover, Derby (☎ Derby 512048)

OTTLEY, Warner Herbert Taylor; CB (1945); *b* 1899; *Educ* Malvern; St John's Coll, Cambridge; *m* 1921, Hilda Mary Edwards; 2 s; *Career* higher division clerk, War Office, 1913; dir of finance, War Office, 1942; ret 1949; *Style* - Warner Ottley Esq, CB; 14 Medlow Court, Eversfield Place, St Leonards-on-Sea, East Sussex

OTTON, Sir Geoffrey (John); KCB (1980, CB 1978); s of late John Alfred Otton; *b* 10 June 1927; *Educ* Christ's Hosp; St John's Coll, Cambridge (MA); *m* 1952, Hazel Lomas, nee White; 1 s, 1 da; *Career* Under-Sec DHSS 1971-75, Dep Sec 1975-79, Second Permanent Sec 1979-; chief advr to Supplementary Benefits Cmmn, 1976-; *Style* - Sir Geoffrey Otton, KCB; 72 Cumberland rd, Bromley, Kent (☎ 01 460 9610)

OTTON, Philip Howard; QC; s of H A Otton; *b* 28 May 1933; *Educ* Bablake Sch, Coventry; Birmingham U (LLB); *m* 1965, Helen Margaret, da of late P W Bates; 2 s, 1 da; *Career* barr, Gray's Inn, 1955; dep chm, Beds QS 1970-72; jr counsel to the Treasury (Personal Injuries) 1970-75; a Recorder of Crown Court, 1972-; QC 1975; govr, Nat Heart and Chest Hosps, 1979-; *Style* - Philip Otton Esq, QC; 6 Parkmead, SW15 5BS (☎ 01 789 6262); 2 Crown Office Row, Temple, EC4Y 7HJ (☎ 01 353 9337)

OUBRIDGE, Victor William; BA, CEng, FIMechE, FIProdE, FBIM; s of William Arthur Oubridge, JP (d 1942); *b* 1 April 1913; *Educ* Oundle and Jesus Coll, Cambridge; *m* 1937, Ruth Louise, da of late Thomas Carpenter; 1 s, 1 da; *Career* visiting research fell, U of Aston; memb Warwickshire Area Health Authority; visiting prof of Business Administration U of Aston 1969-73; memb, Management Ctee, S Warwickshire Hosp Group 1971-74; Industrial Adviser to Dept of Economic Affairs 1967-69; dir, Associated Engineering Ltd, 1947-67; memb Council of CBI 1956-67; memb Council of Engineering Employers' Fedn 1963-65; pres Coventry and District Engineering Employers' Assocn 1963-65; memb Council of BIM, 1962-67; pres Coventry North Conservative Assocn 1956-65; memb Coventry Cathedral Reconstruction Ctee 1956-63; High Sheriff Warwicks 1966; *Style* - Victor Oubridge Esq, ; 21 Wasperton, Warwick (☎ Barford 240)

OUGHTRED, Brian Norman; MA; *Career* jt md William Jackson & Son; chm, Automatic Information Management Ltd; dir Associated & Independent Merchandisiers (Holdings) Ltd; *Style* - Brian Oughtred Esq; William Jackson & Son, 40 Derrington st, Hull

OUGHTRED, Peter B; *Career* chm and jt md, William Jackson & Son; dir, Associated & Independent Merchandisers (Holdings) Ltd; trustee, Trustee Savings Bank of Yorkshire and Lincoln; *Style* - Peter Oughtred Esq; c/o William Jackson & Son, 40 Derrington st, Hull

OULTON, Antony Derek Maxwell; CB (1979); s of late Charles Cameron

Courtenay Oulton; *b* 14 Oct 1927; *Educ* St Edward's Sch, Oxford; King's Coll, Cambridge (BA, MA, PhD); *m* 1955, Margaret Geraldine, da of late Lt-Col G S Oxley, MC; 1 s, 3 da; *Career* barr, Gray's Inn, 1952; dep sec, Lord Chancellor's Office, 1976-; Dep Clerk the Crown in Chancery, 1977-; *Style* - Antony Oulton Esq, CB; 35 St John's Wood Terrace, NW8 6JL (☎ 01 586 1555)

OULTON, John Desmond Calverley; s of John George Oulton (d 1952), of Clontarf Castle, Dublin; *b* 1921; *Educ* St Columba's Coll and Dublin U; *m* 1958, Moyra Ann, da of Col J H Graham-Hunter, RAMC; 2 s, 1 da; *Career* commissioned London Irish Rifles 1940, invalided (ill-health), co dir; *Style* - John Oulton Esq; 83 Goldstone Crescent, Hove, Sussex (☎ Brighton 51801); Muxna House, Kenmare, Co Kerry, Irish Republic

OULTON, Air Vice-Marshal Wilfrid Ewart; CB (1958), CBE (1953), DSO (1943), DFC (1943); s of Llewellin Oulton; *b* 27 July 1911; *Educ* U College, Cardiff; Cranwell; CEng, FRIN, FIERE; *m* 1935, Sarah, da of Rev E Davies; 3 s; *Career* cmmnd 1931; dir, Joint Anti-Submarine Sch, 1946-48; Joint Services Staff Coll, 1948-50; Air Attaché, Buenos Aires, Montevideo, Asuncion, 1950-53; idc 1954; Dir Operations, Air Ministry, 1954-56; commanded Joint Tast Force 'Grapple' for first British megaton weapon tests in the Pacific, 1956-58; sr Air Staff Officer, RAF Coastal Command, HQ, 1958-60; chm, Medsales Ltd and Medfurn Ltd; *Clubs* RAF; *Style* - Air Vice-Marshal Wilfrid Oulton, CB, CBE, DSO, DFC; Farthings, Hollywood Lane, Lymington, Hants (☎ Lymington 3498)

OUTERBRIDGE, Col Hon Sir Leonard Cecil; CC (Canada) 1967, CBE (1926), DSO (1919), CD (1954); s of late Sir Joseph Outerbridge; *b* 1888; *Educ* Marlborough; Toronto U (BA, LLB, Hon LLD), Hon LLD- Laval U and Memorial U of Newfoundland; *m* 1915, Dorothy Winifred (d 1972), da of late John Alexander Strathy; *Career* Lieutenant-Governor of Newfoundland, 1949-57; dir Harvey & Co Ltd and other cos, St John's, Newfoundland; knighted 1946; *Style* - Col Hon Sir Leonard Outerbridge; Littlefield, Pringle Place, St John's, Newfoundland

OUTRAM, Sir Alan James; 5 Bt (UK 1858); s of late James Ian Outram (gs of 2 Bt); suc great-uncle, Sir Francis Davidson Outram, 4 Bt, OBE, 1945; *b* 15 May 1937; *Educ* Marlborough, St Edmund Hall Oxford; *m* 1976, Victoria Jean, da of George Dickson Paton; 1 s, 1 da (Alison Catharine b 1977); *Heir* s, Douglas Benjamin James Outram; *Career* Lt-Col TAVR; housemaster of Druries (winner of Torpids Finals summer 1981) Harrow Sch 1979-; formerly assistant master; *Recreations* bridge, golf, tennis, cycling; *Style* - Sir Alan Outram, Bt; Harrow School, Harrow-on-the-Hill, Middlesex

OUTRAM, Douglas Benjamin James; s and h of Sir Alan James Outram, 5 Bt; *b* 15 March 1979

OVENS, Maj-Gen Patrick John; OBE (1968), MC (1951); s of late Edward Alec Ovens; *b* 4 Nov 1922; *Educ* King's Sch, Bruton; *m* 1952, Margaret Mary White; 1 s, 2 da; *Career* cmmnd into Roy Marines, 1941; C-in-C Fleet Staff, 1968-69; Cdr 3 Commando Bde, 1970-72; RCDS 1973; COS to Comdt Gen, RM, MOD, 1974-76; Commandant, Joint Warfare Establishment, 1976-79; *Style* - Major-General Patrick Ovens, OBE, MC; Virginia House, Netherhampton, Salisbury, Wilts SP2 8PU (☎ Wilton 3113)

OVERALL, Sir John (Wallace); CBE (1962), MC and bar; s of late W Overall; *b* 19 July 1913; *Educ* Sydney Tech Coll; *m* 1943, Margaret J, da of C W Goodman; 4 s; *Career* principal, John Overall & Partners, 1973-; dir: CSR Ltd 1973-, Land Lease Corpn Ltd 1973-, Alliance Holdings Ltd 1975-, Gen Property Trust 1976-; memb, Parliament House Construction Authority (Commonwealth Govt of Australia), 1979-; knighted 1968; *Style* - Sir John Overall, CBE, MC*; 10 Wallaroy rd, Double Bay, NSW 2028, Australia (☎ 367719)

OVEREND, Douglas; CB (1965); s of Simeon Overend; *b* 22 Nov 1914; *Educ*

Leeds G S; Queen's Coll, Oxford; *Career* Assist Under-Sec State DHSS 1968-75; *Style* - Douglas Overend Esq, CB; 2 The Orchard, Tayles Hill, Ewell, Surrey (☎ 01 394 0094)

OVERTON, Hugh Thomas Arnold; CMG (1975); s of late Sir Arnold Overton, KCB, KCMG, MC; *b* 2 April 1923; *Educ* Dragon Sch, Oxford; Winchester; Clare Coll, Cambridge; *m* 1948, Claire-Marie Binet; 1 s, 2 da; *Career* Royal Signals, 1942-45; HM Diplomatic Service; Min (economic) Bonn, 1975-; *Style* - Hugh Overton Esq, CMG; c/o Barclays Bank, 276 Kensington High st, W8

OWEN, Hon Mrs (Ardyne Mary); da of 2 Viscount Knollys, GCMG, MBE, DFC (d 1966); *b* 1929; *m* 1958, Ronald James Owen; *Style* - The Hon Mrs Owen; Paradise Wood, Upper Hartfield, Sussex

OWEN, Cicely Elizabeth; CBE (1969); da of Late Rev Ernest Owen, MA, of Boys Hall, Ashford, Kent; *b* 1911; *Career* memb Conservative Commonwealth Council 1953; chm E Central African Group, 1960-67; vice pres Royal Commonwealth Soc 1962; dep chm 1972-5; *Clubs* Royal Commonwealth Society; *Style* - Miss Cicely Owen; 83 Burton Court, SW3

OWEN, (Alfred) David; *b* 26 Sept 1936; *Educ* Brocksford Hall; Oundle; Emmanuel Coll, Cambridge; *m* 1966, Ethne, nee Sowman; 2 s, 1 da; *Career* md, Rubery Owen Holdings Ltd, 1969-; chm, 1975-; trustee, Community Projects Foundn, 1978-; *Style* - David Owen Esq; Mill Dam House, Mill Lane, Aldridge, Walsall, W Midlands (☎ 021 353 1221)

OWEN, Rt Hon David Anthony Llewellyn; PC (1976), MP; s of Dr John William Morris Owen; *b* 2 July 1938; *Educ* Bradfield Coll; Sidney Sussex Coll, Cambridge (Hon Fell 1977); St Thomas' Hosp (BA, MB, BChir, MA); *m* 1968, Deborah Schabert; 2 s, 1 da; *Career* St Thomas's Hosp: house appts 1962-64, neurological and psychiatric registrar 1964-66, research fell medical unit 1966-68; contested (L) Torrington 1964; PPS to MOD, Administration, 1967; Parly Under-Sec of State for Defence for RN, 1968-70; resigned over EEC, 1972; MP (L) Plymouth, Devonport, 1974- (Plymouth, Sutton, 1966-74); Parly Under Sec of State, DHSS, 1974; Min of State DHSS 1974-76; FCO 1976-77; Sec of State for Foreign and Commonwealth Affairs, 1977-79; opposition spokesman on energy, 1979-81, founder memb SDP 1981; *Style* - The Rt Hon David Owen, PC, MP; 78 Narrow st, Limehouse, E14 (☎ 01 987 5441); Castlehayes, Plympton, Plymouth, Devon (☎ Plymouth 336130); House of Commons, SW1 (☎ 01 219 4203)

OWEN, David Elystan; CBE (1972); s of John Griffith Owen (d 1916); *b* 27 Feb 1912; *Educ* The Leys Sch, Cambridge; King's Coll, London U; *m* 1936, Pearl, da of George Edward Jennings (d 1925); *Career* war service, 1939-45, in Artillery (Major, RA); museum curator (ret); author; Keeper, Dept of Geology, Liverpool Museum, 1935-47; dir Leeds City Museums 1947-57 and Manchester Museum, 1957-76; *Style* - David Owen Esq, CBE; 9 Carleton rd, Higher Poynton, Cheshire SK12 1TL (☎ Poynton 872924)

OWEN, Eirwen Mary; CBE (1973), BA; da of Richard John Owen (d 1951); *b* 24 Nov 1914; *Educ* U of Wales, Aberystwyth; *Career* dep regnl commr Wales, 1939-45; head of Overseas Dept, WVS 1944-56; memb Council for U Coll of S Wales and Mon 1946-52; memb Royal Cmmn on the Press 1947-50; dir Admin Zoological Soc of London, 1957; *Style* - Miss Eirwen Owen, CBE; 13 Brook Mews North, W2

OWEN, Lt-Col Garth Henry; TD; s of Henry Owen (d 1964); *b* 4 May 1924; *Educ* Rugeley G S; *m* 1948, Madeleine, nee Day; *Career* served in 1939-45 War with RN, 1941-46; RAFVR 1948-53; 639 Heavy Field Regt RA (TA) 1953-57; 125 (Staffordshire) Engineer Regt (TA) 1957-67; Hon Col 125 (Staffordshire) Field Support Sqdn, RE (V) and The 143 Plant Sqdn RE (V) T & AVR; DL (1967) Staffs; *Style* - Lt-Col Garth Owen, TD, DL; Carioca Cottage, Brackenridge, Fair Oak, Slitting Mill, Rugeley Staffs (☎ Rugeley 2875)

OWEN, Gerald Victor; QC; *b* 29 Nov 1922; *Educ* Kilburn G S; St Catharine's

Coll, Cambridge; *m* 1946, Phyllis, nee Ladsky; 1 s, 1 da; *Career* barr, Gray's Inn, 1949; ad eundem Inner Temple, 1969; QC 1969; a dep Circuit Judge, 1971; a Recorder of the Crown Court, 1979-; *Style* - Gerald Owen Esq, QC; Wellington House, Eton rd, NW3; 3 Paper Buildings, Temple EC4 (☎ 01 353 1182)

OWEN, Maj-Gen Harry; CB (1972); *b* 17 July 1911; *Educ* Univ Coll, Bangor (BA); *m* 1952, Maureen, nee Summers; 1 s, 1 da; *Career* dir Army Legal Services 1969-71; chm Medical Appeal Tribunal 1972-; *Style* - Major-General Harry Owen, CB; Clavering, 40 North Park, Gerrards Cross, Bucks (☎ Gerrards Cross 86777)

OWEN, Sir Hugh (Bernard Pilkington); 5 Bt (UK 1813); s of Sir John Arthur Owen, 4 Bt; *b* 28 March 1915; *Educ* Chillon Coll, Switzerland; *Heir* bro, John William Owen; *Style* - Sir Hugh Owen, Bt; 63 Dudsbury rd, Ferndown, Dorset

OWEN, Harold; s of Owen William Owen, slr (d 1939); *b* 7 July 1909; *Educ* Rossall; *m* 1934, Doris Melhuish, da of William Melhuish Thomas; 3 da; *Career* served 1939-45 RA; Maj; admitted slr 1932, ret; memb, Liverpool Stock Exchange 1948-72; High Sheriff Anglesey 1957; *Style* - Harold Owen Esq; Llynon Hall, Llanddesusant, Anglesey

OWEN, Idris Wyn; *b* 1912; *Educ* Stockport Sch and Coll of Technology; Manchester Sch of Commerce; *m*; *Career* MP (C) Stockport N 1970-Feb 1974 (contested the same Oct 1974), former Mayor of Stockport; company dir (construction industry); *Style* - Idris Owen Esq; Gawsworth Old Rectory, Cheshire

OWEN, John Arthur Dalziel; QC; s of late R J Owen; *b* 22 Nov 1925; *Educ* Solihull Sch; Brasenose, Oxford (MA, BCL); *m* 1952, Valerie, da of W Ethell; 1 s, 1 da; *Career* barr, Gray's Inn, 1951; dep chm, Warwickshire QS, 1967-71; QC 1970; Recorder of Crown Court, 1972-; memb Senate of the Inns of court and the Bar, 1977-80; dep leader Midland & Oxford Circuit, 1979-; Dean of the Arches & Auditor of the Chancery Court of York, 1980-; *Style* - John Owen Esq, QC; Lansdowne House, Shipston-on-Stour, Warwicks (☎ Shipston-on-Stour 61521)

OWEN, Maj Gen John Ivor Headon; OBE (1963); s of Maj William Headon Owen, MC (d 1954); *b* 22 Oct 1922; *Educ* St Edmund's Sch Canterbury; *m* 1948, Margaret Jean; 3 da; *Career* 1942 Roy Marines, commando Far East 1942-46, constable Metropolitan Police 1946-47, rejoined Roy Marines, regimental serv to 1955, Staff Coll Camberley 1956, Bde Maj, MOD (Admlty) 1962-64, Roy Coll Defence Studies 1971-72, Maj-Gen Commando Forces RM Plymouth 1972-73, Maj-Gen 1972, treasurer Clergy Orphan Corporationn Committee, with Thomson McLintock & Co (Accountants); Publications: *Brassey's Infantry Weapons of the World, Brassey's NATO Infantry Weapons*, contributions to the Contemporary Review; *Recreations* woodworking, gardening; *Clubs* Army and Navy; *Style* - Maj-Gen John Owen, OBE; 6 Campden Hill Mansions, Edge st, W8 (☎ 01 727 6361); Pollards Down, Rushlake Green, Heathfield, E Sussex

OWEN, John Tudor; MB, BS; s of William Seth Owen; *b* 16 Sept 1924; *Educ* Guys Hosp Med Sch; *m* 1951, Heather, da of John Young Sangster; 2 s, 2 da; *Career* past pres Roy Welsh Ag Soc; High Sheriff Anglesey 1965; *Style* - John Owen Esq; Dinam Hall, Llangaffo, Gaerwen, Anglesey (☎ Newborough (Anglesey) 228)

OWEN, John William; s of Capt Sir John Arthur Owen, 4 Bt (d 1973) & hp of bro, Sir Hugh Bernard Pilkington Owen, 5 Bt; *b* 7 June 1917; *Educ* Charterhouse; *m* 1963, Gwenllian Mary, Wing Officer, MBE, WRAF, da of late E B Phillips, of Barry, Glam; *Career* late Capt 4/7 Roy Dragoon Gds; *Style* - John Owen Esq; 12 Elizabeth ave, St Brelade, Jersey

OWEN, Lady - Lucy Fletcher; da of Fred William Pilkington, of Kencott House, nr Lechlade; *m* 1914, Capt Sir John Arthur Owen, 4 Bt (d 1973); *Style* - Lady Owen; 63 Dudsbury rd, Ferndown, Dorset

OWEN, Peter Granville; CMG (1965),

QPM (1960); s of Walter Lincoln Owen; *b* 28 Oct 1918; *Educ* Grove House Sch, Highgate; City of Norwich Sch; *m* 1943, Mercia Louvaine Palmer; 1 s, 1 da; *Career* Gt Yarmouth Borough Police, 1938-42; RAF/FO, 1942-46; Adjudication Officer, Cadastral Surveys, British Virgin Is, 1971, Cayman Is, 1973, Blantyre, Malawi, 1976; dep dir, Fund Raising, Save the Children Fund, 1978-; *Clubs* Royal Commonwealth Soc and MCC; *Style* - Peter Owen Esq CMG QPM; 7 Thakeham Close, Lawrie Park Gardens, SE26 6HN

OWEN, Philip Loscombe Wintringham; TD (1950), QC, JP; s of Rt Hon Sir Wintringham Stable, MC ; assumed surname of Owen by deed poll, 1942; *b* 10 Jan 1920; *Educ* Winchester; Christ Church, Oxford (MA); *m* 1949, Elizabeth Jane, da of late Lewis Trelawny Widdicombe; 3 s, 2 da; *Career* served WW II, Roy Welch Fusiliers; Maj TARO; barr, Middle Temple, 1949; Bencher, 1969; QC, 1963; memb, Gen Council of the Bar of England and Wales, 1971-77; a deputy chm of QS Montgomeryshire, 1959-71; Cheshire, 1961-71; a Recorder of Merthyr Tydfil, 1971; Leader, Wales and Chester circuit, 1975-77; Legal Assessor to Gen Med Council 1970-, Gen Dental Council 1970-; member of RICS, 1970-; contested (C) Montgomeryshire, 1945; JP (Montgomeryshire) 1959; JP (Cheshire) 1961; *Style* - Philip Owen Esq, TD, QC, JP; 51 Hartington rd, Chiswick, W4 (☎ 01 994 0415); Llwyn Owen, Llanbrynmair, Powys (☎ 229)

OWEN, Prof Paul Robert; CBE (1974), FRS (1971); s of Joseph Owen; *b* 24 Jan 1920; *Educ* Queen Mary Coll, London U (BSc, London, MSc, Manchester) CEng, FRAeS, FRMetrS; *m* 1958, Margaret Ann, da of Herbert Baron; 2 s, 2 da; *Career* Zaharoff Prof of Aviation, London U, at Imperial Coll of Science and Technology, 1963-; *Style* - Professor Paul Owen, CBE, FRS; 1 Horbury Crescent, W11 (☎ 01 229 5111)

OWEN, Sir Ronald (Hugh); FIA; s of late Owen Hugh Owen; *b* 2 June 1910; *Educ* King's Coll Sch, Wimbledon; *m* 1939, Claire May Tully; 1 s; *Career* served war of 1939-45 52 Field Regt, RA (Maj); Bde Maj RA, 8 Ind Div, Middle East and Italy; chm: Prudential Corpn Ltd 1978-, Prudential Assurance Co Ltd 1975-; knighted 1980; *Clubs* Hurlingham and Royal Wimbledon Golf; *Style* - Sir Ronald Owen; 110 Rivermead Court, Hurlingham, SW6 (☎ 01 736 4842)

OWEN, Rear-Adm Richard Arthur James; CB (1963); s of late Capt Leonard E Owen OBE, JP; *b* 26 Aug 1910; *Educ* Sevenoaks Sch; *m* 1941, Jean Sophia, nee Bluett; 1 s, 2 da; *Career* joined RN 1927; Cdr (S) 1945; Capt, 1954; Rear-Adm, 1961; dir-gen, Personal Services, Admiralty, 1962-64, ret; *Style* - Rear-Admiral Richard Owen, CB; High Bank, Martin, nr Fordingbridge, Hants (☎ Martin Cross 295)

OWEN, Robert Davies; CBE (1962), FRCS, FRCSE; s of late Capt Griffith Owen; *b* 8 May 1898; *Educ* Towyn G S; *m* 1928, Janet Miles; 2 da; *Career* sr Ear and Throat Surgeon, Cardiff Roy Infirmary, 1928-64, ret; lecturer in Oto-Laryngology, Welsh Nat Sch of Medicine, 1929-64, ret; *Style* - Robert Owen Esq, CBE; 1 The Mount, Cardiff rd, Llandaff, Cardiff (☎ Cardiff 568739)

OWEN, Col Richard Edward; OBE, TD; *Career* DL (Greater London 1967); *Style* - Colonel Richard Owen, OBE, TD, DL; The Pines, 1 Hartfield Crescent, West Wickham, Kent

OWEN, Rowland Hubert; CMG (1948); s of William Rowland Owen (d 1924); *b* 3 June 1903; *Educ* Royal Sch, Armagh and Trinity Dublin (BA, LLB); *m* 1, 1930, Kathleen Margaret Evaleen Scott (d 1965); m 2 1966, Shelagh Myrle, da of Kenneth Nicholson (d 1924); *Career* civil servant; sr British Trade Commissioner in India 1945-52; Comptroller-General, Export Credits Guarantee Dept, 1953-58; dep Controller, HM Stationery Office, 1959-64; organist and choirmaster, St Luke's, Grayshott; sec, Surrey Organists Assoc; *Style* - Rowland Owen Esq, CMG; Oak Tree Cottage, Holdfast Lane, Haslemere, Surrey GU27 2EU (☎ Haslemere 3748)

OWEN, Samuel Griffith; CBE (1977), MD, FRCP; s of late Rev Evan Lewis Owen; *b* 3 Sept 1925; *Educ* Dame Allen's Sch; Durham U; *m* 1954, Ruth, da of Merle W Tate; 2 s, 2 da; *Career* Hon Consultant Royal Victoria Infirmary, Newcastle upon Tyne, 1960-68; Clinical Sub-Dean Med Sch, U of Newcastle-upon-Tyne, 1960-68; Examiner in Medicine Liverpool U 1966-68; Second Sec Medical Research Council 1968-, memb Scientific Co-ordinating Ctee Arthritis and Rheumatism Council 1978-; NW Thames RHA 1978-; govr Queen Charlotte's Hosp for Women 1979-; *Style* - Samuel Owen Esq, CBE; 20 Park Crescent, W1; 60 Bath rd, Chiswick, W4 (☎ 01 636 5422)

OWEN, Thomas Arfon; s of Hywel Peris Owen, of Tumble; *b* 7 June 1933; *Educ* Ystalyfera G S and Magdalen Coll Oxford (William Doncaster Scholar); *m* 1955, Mary Joyce, da of Tom Ellis Phillips; 3 s, 1 da; *Career* registrar Univ Coll of Wales, Aberystwyth 1966; High Sheriff Dyfed 1976-77; *Style* - Thomas Owen Esq; Bryn-Derw, Llanbadarn Fawr, Aberystwyth, Dyfed

OWEN, Thomas Joseph; s of late Richard Owen; *b* 3 Nov 1903; *m* 1935, Marjorie Ethel Tilbury; *Career* Town Clerk Nottingham 1951-66; DL Notts 1966; *Style* - Thomas Owen Esq, DL; Woodlands, Sherwood, Nottingham (☎ Nottingham 61767)

OWEN, Miss Veronica; da of Cdr J H Owen, RN (d 1970), of Chichester; *b* 26 Jan 1925; *Educ* Sherborne and King's Coll London; *Career* served in WRN 1942-46; history mistress St Felix Sch, Southwold 1951-55; history mistress Cambridgeshire H S for Girls 1955-60; headmistress Limur Girls' Sch, Kenya 1960-68; headmistress Malvern Girls' Coll 1968-; *Clubs* Royal Commonwealth Society; *Style* - Miss Veronica Owen; Malvern Girls' College, Malvern, Worcs

OWEN-JONES, John Eryl; CBE (1969); s of John Owen-Jones (d 1962); *b* 19 Jan 1912; *Educ* Portmadoc G S; Univ Coll of Wales, Aberystwyth (LLB); Gonville & Caius Coll, Cambridge (MA); *m* 1944, Mabel Clara, da of Grant McIlvride; 1 s, 1 da; *Career* admitted slr 1938; asst slr Chester Corpn 1939; dep clerk Caernarvonshire CC 1946; clerk Caernarvonshireshire CC 1956-74; Clerk of the Peace 1956-72; clerk N Wales Combined Probation Ctee; dep clerk Snowdonia Park Jt Advsy Ctee; dep clerk Gwynedd Police Authority 1967; Clerk of Lieutenancy; memb Gorsedd Roy Nat Eisteddfod of Wales; JP 1974; DL Caernarvonshires 1971, Gwynedd 1974; memb Central Cncl Magistrates' Courts Ctees; *Style* - John Owen-Jones Esq, CBE, JP, DL; Rhiw Dafnau, Caernarvon, Gwynedd (☎ Caernarvon 3370)

OWEN-SMITH, Hon Mrs (Rose Magdalen); *née* Ponsonby; da of 2 Baron Ponsonby of Shulbrede (d 1976); *b* 1940; *m* 1966, Brian David Owen-Smith, MB, MRCP, DPhysMed; 1 s, 1 da; *Style* - The Hon Mrs Owen-Smith; 48 Westgate, Chichester, Sussex

OWENS, Ernest Stanley; CBE (1979); s of Rev William James Owens; *b* 22 Sept 1916; *Educ* The King's Sch, Parramatta, NSW; *m* 1943, Margaret Clara Brown; 1 s, 1 da; *Career* chartered accountant and co dir 1947-; chm Enterprise Australia 1976-, dir Bank of New South Wales 1978-; *Style* - Ernest Owens Esq, CBE; 11/576 Pacific Highway, Killara, NSW 2071, Australia (☎ 498 8990)

OWENS, Frank Arthur Robert; CBE (1971); s of Arthur Oakes Owens; *b* 31 Dec 1912; *Educ* Hereford Cathedral Sch; *m* 1, 1936, Ruby Lilian Long; 2 s; m 2, Olwen Evans, BSc; 1 s, 1 da; *Career* served with RAF, 1940-46 (despatches); editor Birmingham Evening Mail 1956-74; dir Birmingham Post & Mail Ltd 1964-75; memb Press Council 1976-; *Style* - Frank Owens Esq, CBE; Fox Hill, 30 Linden rd, Bournville, Birmingham B30 1JU (☎ 021 472 1509)

OXBURY, Harold Frederick; CMG (1961); s of Fredric Thomas Oxbury (d 1964); *b* 11 Nov 1903; *Educ* King Edward VI Sch Norwich, and Trin Cambridge; *m* 1, 1928, Violet Bennets (d 1954); 1 s, 1 da; m 2, 1954, Helen Shipley (d 1975), da of Amos Perry, FLS, VMH; *Career* Indian Civil Service 1928-47; dir Colonies

Dept, British Council, 1947; controller finance 1956; assist dir-gen 1959; dep dir-gen, 1964-66; *Style* - Harold Oxbury Esq, CMG; Huntersmoon, Horton-cum-Studley, Oxon

OXFORD, 40 Bishop of (1542) 1978-; Rt Rev Patrick Campbell Rodger; s of Patrick Wylie Rodger; *b* 28 Nov 1920; *Educ* Rugby, Ch Ch Oxford; *m* 1952, Margaret, da of Dr William Menzies Menzies, of Edinburgh; 2 s; *Career* served in WW II; formerly Canon & V-Provost St Mary's Cathedral Edinburgh then Provost; 8 Bp of Manchester 1970-78; patron of over 116 livings and the Archdeaconries of Oxford, Buckingham and Berks; the Bishopric was originally endowed with lands of dissolved monasteries by Henry VIII, but in Elizabeth I's reign much of these were removed from it; *Style* - The Rt Rev Bishop of Oxford; Bishop's House, 27 Linton rd, Oxford

OXFORD, Kenneth Gordon; QPM (1976); s of Ernest George Oxford; *b* 25 June 1924; *Educ* Caldecot Sch, Lambeth; *m* 1954, Muriel, nee Panton; *Career* RAF, 1942-47; Chief Constable, Merseyside Police, 1976-; chm, Crime Ctee, Assoc of Chief Police Officers of Eng, Wales and NI, 1977-; pres, NW Police Benevolent Fund, 1978-; chm Merseyside BIM 1978-; FBIM 1977; OStJ 1977; *Style* - Kenneth Oxford Esq, QPM; Chief Constable's Office, PO Box 59, Liverpool L69 1JD (☎ 051 709 6010)

OXFORD, Samuel; *Career* chm and ch exec, Magnet & Southerns Ltd; chm and jt md Southerns-Evans Ltd and dir Magnet & Southerns Trustees Ltd; *Style* - Samuel Oxford Esq; c/o Magnet & Southerns Ltd, Sasco House, Mill Lane, Widnes, Cheshire WA8 OUJ

OXFORD AND ASQUITH, 2 Earl of (UK 1925); Julian Edward George Asquith; KCMG (1964, CMG 1961); also Viscount Asquith (UK 1925); s of late Raymond Asquith (ka The Somme 1916) and gs of the Lib PM Rt Hon Sir Herbert Asquith, KG, 1 Earl (d 1928), by his 1 w Helen; nephew of Herbert Asquith, the barrister, novelist and versifier, Lord Asquith of Bishopstone, and Lady Asquith of Yarnbury (better known as Lady Violet Bonham Carter); half-nephew of Anthony Asquith (dir of such films as *The Winslow Boy*, *The Millionairess* and *The Yellow Rolls-Royce*) and Princess Antoine (Elizabeth) Bibesco, who featured in Proust's parody of Saint-Simon in *Pastiches et Mélanges*; also 1 cous of (Hon) Mark Bonham Carter and Mrs Jo (Laura) Grimond; *b* 22 April 1916; *Educ* Ampleforth and Balliol, Oxford; *m* 1947, Anne Mary Celestine, CStJ, da of late Sir Michael Palairet, KCMG; 2 s, 3 da; *Heir* s, Viscount Asquith; *Career* 2 Lt RE 1940; assist dist cmmr Palestine administration 1942-48, dep chief sec British Administration, Tripolitania 1949; dir of the Interior, Tripolitanian Govt 1951; advsr to Prime Minister of Libya 1952; admin sec Zanzibar 1955; Administrator St Lucia 1958-61; Govr and C-in-C Seychelles 1962-67, and Commissioner British Indian Ocean Territory 1965-67; Constitutional Cmmr Cayman Islands 1971; Constitutional Cmmr Turks and Caicos Islands 1973-74; KStJ; *Clubs* Bath; *Style* - The Rt Hon the Earl of Oxford and Asquith KCMG; The Manor House, Mells, Frome, Somerset (☎ Mells 812324)

OXFUIRD, 12 Viscount of (S 1651); Sir (John) Donald (Alexander Arthur) Makgill; 12 Bt (NS 1627); also Lord Makgill of Cousland (S 1651); s of Sir George Makgill, 11 Bt (*de jure* 11 Viscount) (d 1926); *b* 31 Dec 1899; *Educ* Eton; *m* 1, 1927 (m dis 1943), Esther Lilian, da of late Sir Robert Bromley, 6 Bt; 1 da; m 2, 1955, Maureen, da of late Lt-Col Arthur Tilson Shaen Magan, CMG, and formerly wife of Col John Herbert Gillington, OBE, MC; *Heir* n, George Hubbard Makgill (Master of Oxfuird), b 7 Jan 1934; *Career* claim to Viscountcy admitted by Ctee for Privileges, House of Lords 1977; *Clubs* New (Edinburgh); *Style* - The Rt Hon the Viscount of Oxfuird; The Flat, Blairquhan, Maybole, Ayrshire (☎ Straiton 278)

OXLADE, Zena Elsie; da of James Oxlade; *b* 26 April 1929; *Educ* Latymer G S, Univ of London; *Career* state registered nurse and registered nurse tutor, memb Gen Nursing Cncl for England and Wales 1975-, chm Nursing Cncl 1977-, Area

Nursing Officer Suffolk 1978-, Regional Nursing Officer East Anglia 1981-; *Recreations* motoring, reading, handicrafts; *Clubs* Soroptomist International; *Style* - Miss Zena Oxlade; 29 Ballater Close, Ipswich, Suffolk (☎ Ipswich 43354)

OXLEY, Humphrey Leslie Malcolm; CMG (1966), OBE (1956); s of W H F Oxley, MRCS, LRCP, FRCOG; *b* 9 Oct 1909; *Educ* Epsom Coll; *m* 1945, Frances Olga, da of George Bowden; twin s; *Career* admitted slr 1933; junior legal assist India Office 1933; Commissioner for Oaths 1934; assist slr 1944; Commonwealth Relations Office 1947; assist legal advsr Commonwealth Relations Office 1961; Diplomatic Service 1965; dep legal advsr 1967-69; legal advsr to HM's Commissioner & magistrate Anguilla 1971-72; *Style* - Humphrey Oxley Esq CMG; Sandpipers, Crooked Lane, Birdham, Chichester, W Sussex

OXMANTOWN, Lord; (Lawrence) Patrick Parsons; s and h of 7 Earl of Rosse; *b* 31 March 1969; *Style* - Lord Oxmantown

P

PACE, Franco Giustino; s of Edmondo Pace (d 1959); *b* 28 Sept 1927; *Educ* Bologna U (doctorate in industl engrg), Milan U (post grad specialisation in chemistry); *m* 1955, Maria Vittoria, da of Dr Ing Salvatore Picchetti, of Italy; 1 s (1 s decd); *Career* md Montedison UK Ltd, 1973-, dir Polyamide Intermediates Ltd, 1974-, dir ACNA UK Ltd 1976-; Counsellor Italian Chamber of Commerce GB 1974; *Clubs* Hurlingham; *Style* - Franco Pace Esq; 10 Kensington Court gdns, W8 5QE (☎ 01-937 7143)

PACK, Prof Donald Cecil; CBE (1978, OBE 1969), MA, DSc, FIMA, FRSE, FEIS; s of late John Cecil Pack; *b* 14 April 1920; *Educ* Wellinborough Sch, New Coll, Oxford; *m* 1947, Constance Mary Gillam; 2 s, 1 da; *Career* Prof of Mathematics, U of Strathclyde, Glasgow, 1953-, Vice-Principal, 1968-72; memb, various Govt Scientific Cmtees, 1952-, memb Council, *Gesellschaft für Angewandte Mathematik und Mechanik* 1977-; chm Nat Youth Orchestra Scotland; Govr Hamilton Coll Education 1977-; *Style* - Professor Donald Pack, CBE; 3 Horseshoe rd, Bearsden, Glasgow (☎ 041-942 5674)

PACKARD, Lt-Gen Sir (Charles) Douglas; KBE (1957, CBE 1945, OBE 1942), CB (1949), DSO (1943); s of Capt Charles Turner Packard, MC (d 1944), of Copdock, Ipswich; *b* 17 May 1903; *Educ* Winchester and RMA, Woolwich; *m* 1937, Marion Cargill Thomson, da of Dr James Lochhead, CBE, of Edinburgh; 1 s, 2 da; *Career* DMI War Office 1948-49, Maj-Gen 1948, Cdr British Military Mission in Greece 1949-51, Ch of Staff MELF 1951-53, Vice QMG War Office 1953-56, mil advsr to W African Govts 1956, Lt-Gen 1957, GOC N Ireland District 1958-59, GOC-in-C N Ireland Command 1959-61, ret 1961; Colonel Commandant RA 1957-62; *Style* - Lieutenant-General Sir Charles Packard, KBE, CB, DSO; 103a Thoro'fare, Woodbridge, Suffolk IP12 1AS (☎ Woodbridge 4729)

PACKER, Kerry Francis Bullmore; s of late Sir Douglas Frank Hewson Packer, KBE; *b* 17 Dec 1937; *Educ* Cranbrook Sch, Sydney, NSW; Geelong C of E G S; *m* 1963, Roslyn Redman Weedon; 1 s, 1 da; *Career* chm and md, Consolidated Press Holdings Ltd, Publishing and Broadcasting Ltd; chm, Australian Consolidated Press Ltd and Conpress Printing Ltd; dir, Gen Television Corpn Ltd, 1974-; *Style* - Kerry Packer Esq; 168 Castlereagh st, Sydney, NSW 2000, Australia (☎ 02-20666)

PACKETT, Charles Neville; MBE (1974), JP (1964); s of Sydney Packett, JP (d 1980); *b* 25 Feb 1922; *Educ* Ashville Coll Harrogate Yorks; *m* 1969, Audrey Winifred, da of Frank Vincent Clough (d 1975); *Career* md Sydney Packett & Sons, V-Pres Insurance Inst of Bradford 1960-, Hon V-Pres The United Commercial Travellers' Assoc 1976- (Nat Pres 1975-

76), Govr Ashville Coll Harrogate 1970- (Chm House Ctee 1977-), Master Worshipful Co of Woolmen 1979-80 (Liveryman 1959-), FRSA, FRGS, FCIB, ACII, CStJ (1975); *Recreations* travel, amateur cine, heraldry, writing; *Clubs* City Livery (London), Nat Liberal, Bradford, Otley Golf; *Style* - Charles Packett Esq, MBE, JP; San Marino, 15 Fairway, Tranmere Park, Guiseley (nr Leeds), W Yorks LS20 8JT (☎ Guiseley 73596; (office) Bradford 308755)

PADMORE, Sir Thomas; GCB (1965, KCB 1953, CB 1947), MA, FCIT; s of Thomas William Padmore; *b* 23 April 1909; *Educ* Central Sch Sheffield, Queens' Coll Cambridge; *m* 1, 1934, Alice (d 1963), da of Robert Alcock; 2 da (1 s decd); m 2, 1964, Rosalind Culhane; *Career* Princ Priv Sec to Chllr of Exchequer 1943-45, Second Sec 1952-62, Perm Sec Miny of Transport 1962-68; dir: Metropolitan Cammell Ltd 1969-, Laird Group Ltd 1970-79; chm Handel Opera Soc 1963-; Hon Tres Inst of Cancer Res 1973-; *Clubs* Reform; *Style* - Sir Thomas Padmore, GCB; 39 Cholmeley Crescent, Highgate, N6 (☎ 01-340 6587)

PADOVAN, John Mario Faskally; s of Dr Umberto Mario Padovan (d 1966); *b* 7 May 1938; *Educ* St George's Coll Weybridge, King's Coll London (LLB), Keble Oxford (BCL); *m* 1963, Sally Kay; 3 s; *Career* CA 1963; ch exec County Bank Ltd 1976-; *Clubs* City of London; *Style* - John Padovan Esq; White House, Church rd, Milford, Surrey (☎ Godalming 5728)

PAFFARD, Rear-Adm Ronald Wilson; CB (1960), CBE (1943); s of late Murray Paffard, of Headcorn, Kent; *b* 14 Feb 1904; *Educ* Maidstone GS; *m* 1933, Nancy Brenda, da of J C Malim, MBE, MICE, of Weymouth; 1 s, 1 da; *Career* joined RN 1922; served 1939-45 as Sec to Adm of the Fleet Lord Tovey (Mediterranean and Home Fleets); Capt 1951, Rear-Adm 1957, Ch Staff Offr (admin) Portsmouth 1957-60, ret 1960; *Style* - Rear-Admiral Ronald Paffard, CB, CBE; 2 Little Green Orchard, Alverstoke, Hants (Gosport 82932)

PAGAN, Brig Sir John Ernest; CMG (1969), MBE (1945), ED; s of late D C Pagan, of Hay, NSW; *b* 13 May 1914; *Educ* St Peter's Coll, Adelaide; *m* 1948, Marjorie, da of late Sir Cecil Harold Hoskins; 1 s, 2 da; *Career* served in Second World War with AIF (Middle East, Papua and New Guinea), Lt-Col 1948, Brig 1958; Rep Col Cmmdt in Australia, Roy Regt Australian Artillery 1974-78; Hon ADC to Govr of NSW 1950-55; chm P Rowe Holdings Pty Ltd 1958-, Associated Nat Insurance Co Ltd 1973-, Medical Journal Pty Ltd; dep chm NSW Permanent Building Soc Ltd; dir D J Properties Ltd; Fedl Pres Liberal Party Australia 1966-70; Agent-Gen for NSW in London 1970-72; freeman, City of London, 1973; kt 1971; CStJ (1972); *Style* - Brig Sir John Pagan, CMG, MBE, ED; 2 Lincoln Place, Edgecliff, NSW 2027, Australia; Kennerton Green, Mittagong, NSW 2575, Australia

PAGE, Annette (Mrs Ronald Hynd); da of James Lees and Margaret Page; *b* 18 Dec 1932; *Educ* Royal Ballet Sch; *m* 1957, Ronald Hynd; 1 da; *Career* ballerina of the Royal Ballet, 1959-67; memb, Arts Council of Gt Britain, 1976-; *Style* - Miss Annette Page

PAGE, Col Alfred John; CB (1964), TD; s of Harry Gould Page; *b* 1912; *Educ* Westminster; *m* 1, 1941 (m dis 1966), Sheila Margaret Aileen, da of Charles Skinner Wilson; 1 s, 2 da; m 2, 1969, Margaret Mary Juliet, widow of Harold Driver; *Career* 2 Lt 19 London Regt (TA) 1931, served 1939-45 with RA in ADGB, Bt-Col 1952; ADC to HM the Queen 1961-66, chm Co of London T and AF Assoc 1957-68, Hon Col 300 Regt RA (TA) 1963-67, Hon Col Greater London Regt RA (Territorials) 1967-71; Master Co of Watermen and Lightermen of the River Thames 1966-67; Master the Worshipful Co of Pattenmakers 1973-74; chm Greater London TA & VR Assoc 1968-71; DL (1951) Co of London, (1965) Greater London; *Style* - Col Alfred Page, CB, TD, DL; 66 Iverna Court, W8 (☎ 01 937 2590)

PAGE, Sir Alexander Warren (Sir Alex Page); MBE (1943); s of Sydney E Page; *b* 1 July 1914; *Educ* Tonbridge, Clare Coll Cambridge; *m* 1940 (m dis), Anne Lewis Hickman; 2 s, 1 da; *Career* ch exec Metal

Box Ltd 1970-77, chm 1970-79; chm Electrolux 1978-, GT Pension Services Ltd; dir Shiphams Chichester; memb Food Science and Technology Bd 1973-, Govr Colfe's G S Lewisham 1977-; FIMechE, FBIM, kt 1977; *Style* - Sir Alex Page, MBE; 2 Montagu sq, W1 (☎ 01-935 9894); Merton Place, Dunsfold, Godalming, Surrey (☎ Dunsfold 211)

PAGE, Bruce; s of Roger Page; *b* 1 Dec 1936; *Educ* Melbourne H S, Melbourne U; *m* 1, 1964 (m dis 1969), Anne Gillison; m 2, 1969, Anne Louise Darnborough; 1 s, 1 da; *Career* with Melbourne Herald 1956-60, Evening Standard 1960-62, Daily Herald 1962-64, Sunday Times 1964-76, Daily Express 1977, editor The New Statesman, 1978-; *Style* - Bruce Page Esq; 35 Duncan Terrace, N1 8AL (☎ 01 359 1000)

PAGE, Maj-Gen Charles Edward; CB (1974), MBE (1944); s of late Sir (Charles) Max Page, KBE, CB, DSO, FRCS; *b* 23 Aug 1920; *Educ* Marlborough and Trin, Cambridge; FIEE 1968; *m* 1948, Elizabeth Marion, da of late Sir William Smith Crawford, KBE; 2 s, 1 da; *Career* CCR Signals 1 (BR) Corps 1966-68, Sec NATO Mil Ctee, Brussels, 1968-70, DCD(A) MOD 1971-74, ret 1974; Col Cmmdt Royal Corps of Signals 1974-; Independent Telecommunications Consultant; *Clubs* Bath; *Style* - Major-General Charles Page, CB, MBE; 6 Cheyne gdns, SW3 5QU (☎ 01-352 5674)

PAGE, Lady Cecilia Norah; *née* Stopford; da of late 7 Earl of Courtown; *b* 1917; *m* 1947, Cdr Thomas Philip Frederick Urquhart Page, RN, s of Sir Leo Francis Page; 1 s, 2 da; *Style* - Lady Cecilia Page; Toller Porcorum, Dorchester, Dorset

PAGE, Ewan Stafford; PhD, MA, BSc; s of late Joseph William Page; *b* 17 Aug 1928; *Educ* Wyggeston G S Leicester and Christ's Coll, Cambridge (MA, PhD, Raleigh Prize 1952); London U (BSc); *m* 1955, Sheila Margaret Smith; 3 s, 1 da; *Career* Instr RAF Tech Coll 1949-51, Lectr in Statistics Durham Colls 1954-57, dir: Durham U Computing Lab 1957-63, Newcastle U Computing Lab 1963-78; Visiting Prof U of N Carolina 1962-63; Prof of Computing and Data Processing U of Newcastle upon Tyne 1965-78, Pro-Vice Chancellor 1972-78 (Acting Vice-Chancellor 1976-77); Vice-Chancellor U of Reading 1979-; *Style* - Ewan Page Esq; University of Reading, Whiteknights, Reading, Berks (☎ Reading 85123)

PAGE, Sir Frederick (William); CBE (1961), FRS (1978), FEng, FRAeS; s of Richard Page; *b* 20 Feb 1917; *Educ* Rutlish Sch, Merton; St Catharine's Coll, Cambridge; *m* 1940, Kathleen Edith de Courcy; 3 s, 1 da; *Career* appt to bd of Panavia Aircraft GmbH 1969, chm 1977; chm BAC Ltd 1977, chm and ch exec Aircraft Gp of British Aerospace 1977-; knighted 1979; *Style* - Sir Frederick Page, CBE, FRS; Renvyle, 60 Waverley Lane, Farnham, Surrey (☎ Farnham 4999)

PAGE, Sir Harry (Robertson); s of late Henry Page; *b* 14 April 1911; *Educ* Manchester G S, Manchester U; IPFA 1938; *m* 1937, Elsie Dixon; 2 s; *Career* Sr Hon Financial Adviser to Assoc of Municipal Corpns 1962-71, chm Chancellor's ctee to review Nat Savings 1971-73; consultant Butler Till Ltd; chm Nat Transport Tokens Ltd; kt 1968; *Style* - Sir Harry Page; 205 Old Hall Lane, Fallowfield, Manchester M14 6HJ (☎ 061-224 2891)

PAGE, (Arthur) John; MP (C) Harrow West 1960-; s of Sir Arthur Page, QC (d 1959); *b* 16 Sept 1919; *Educ* Harrow and Magdalene Cambridge; *m* 1950, Anne, da of Charles Micklem, DSO, JP, DL (d 1957); 4 s; *Career* chm Bethnal Green and E London Housing Assoc 1957-, contested (C) Eton and Slough Gen Election 1959, sec Con Parly Labour Affairs Ctee 1960-61 & 1964- (vice-chm 1964-69, chm 1970-74); memb British Delegn to Council of Europe and WEU 1972-; pres Independent Schools Assoc 1971-, chm Council for Ind Educn 1974; *Style* - John Page Esq, MP; Hitcham Lodge, Taplow, Bucks (☎ Burnham 5056)

PAGE, (Charles) James; CBE (1978), QPM (1971); s of Charles Page; *b* 31 May 1925; *Educ* Sloane G S Chelsea; *m* 1, 1947, Margaret Dobson; 2 s; m 2, 1971, Shirley

Marina Woodward; *Career* HM Inspector of Constabulary, 1977-; vice-pres, Police Athletic Assoc, 1977; FBIM 1975; CStJ 1974; Officer of Legion d'Honneur 1976; *Clubs* City Livery; *Style* - James Page Esq, CBE, QPM; Government Buildings, Ovangle rd, Lancaster

PAGE, Sir John (Joseph Joffre); OBE (1959); s of late William Joseph Page; *b* 7 Jan 1915; *Educ* Emanuel Sch; *m* 1939, Cynthia Maynard, da of late L M Swan, CBE; 2 s; *Career* FCIT; RAF, 1933-38 and 1939-46 (despatches, 1943), Group Capt; Iraq Petroleum Gp of Cos, 1938-39 and 1946-70; gen man, 1955-58, ch rep, 1961-70, chm, 1972-77 and ch exec, 1975-77, Mersey Docks and Harbour Co; dep chm, British Ports Assoc, 1974-77; chm, Nat Ports Council, 1977-; kt 1979; *Style* - Sir John Page, OBE; Springhill, Hill rd, Helsby, Cheshire (☎ Helsby 2994)

PAGE, John Brangwyn; s of late Sidney John Page, CB, MC; *b* 23 Aug 1923; *Educ* Highgate Sch (Foundation Schol), King's Cambridge; *m* 1948, Gloria Vail; 1 s, 1 da; *Career* RAF 1942-46; Cambridge, 1946-48; 1 Dep Chief Cashier, Bank of England, 1968, Chief Cashier, 1970-; FIB, FBIM; *Style* - John Page Esq; Bank of England, EC2

PAGE, Maj-Gen John Humphrey; CB (1977), OBE (1967), MC (1952); s of Capt W J Page, JP; *b* 5 March 1923; *Educ* Stonyhurst; *m* 1956, Angela Mary Bunting; 3 s, 1 da; *Career* dir of Personal Services (Army), Min of Defence, 1974-78, ret 1978; *Style* - Major-General John Page, CB, OBE, MC; c/o Midland Bank, 221 Fleet rd, Fleet, Hants

PAGE, Norman John; MC (1945), FCCA; s of John Francis Page; *b* 11 June 1920; *Educ* Harrow County G S for Boys; *m* 1949, Valerie Gascoine; 2 da; *Career* Sec-Gen, Institute of Actuaries, 1977-; *Style* - Norman Page Esq, MC, FCCA; 17 Grange rd, Bushey, Watford, Herts WD2 2LQ (☎ Watford 34177)

PAGE, Rt Hon Sir R(odney) Graham; MBE (1944), PC (1972), MP (C) Crosby 1953-; s of Lt-Col Frank Page, DSO and bar; *b* 30 June 1911; *Educ* Magdalen Coll Sch Oxford, London U; *m* 1934, Hilda Agatha Dixon; 1 s, 1 da; *Career* slr. 1934; chm, Select Ctee on Statutory Instruments, 1964-70, 1974-79; an Opposition Front Bench Spokesman on Housing and Land, 1965-70; Min of State, Miny of Housing & Local Govt, June-Oct 1970; Min for Local Govt and Development, DOE, 1970-74; sec, Parly All-Party Slr's Gp; dir, United Real Property Trust Ltd, John Howard (Northern) Ltd; Privy Council Appeal Agent; kt 1980; *Style* - The Rt Hon Sir Graham Page, MBE; 21 Cholmeley Lodge, Cholmeley Park, N6 5EN (☎ 01 340 3579)

PAGE, Richard Lewis; MP (C) Hertfordshire South West 1979-; s of Victor Charles Page; *b* 22 Feb 1941; *Educ* Hurstpierpoint Coll, Luton Tech Coll; *m* 1964, Madeleine Ann Brown; 1 s, 1 da; *Career* dir of family co 1964-; MP (C) Workington Nov 1976-79; *Style* - Richard Page Esq, MP; Brook Cottage, Gomshall, Surrey

PAGE CROFT, Hugo Douglas; s of Richard Arthur Fitzroy Page Croft, of The Round House, Ware, Herts; *b* 23 May 1944; *Educ* Shrewsbury; *m* 1969, Dawn, da of William Pryde (d 1980); 3 s, 1 da; *Career* Home Grown Cereals Authority 1978-; md Moray Firth Maltings 1980-; *Club* Pilgrims; *Style* - Hugo Page Croft Esq; Murlingden, Brechin, Angus

PAGE WOOD, Sir Anthony John; 8 Bt (UK 1837); s of Sir David John Hatherley Page Wood, 7 Bt (d 1955); *b* 6 Feb 1951; *Educ* Harrow; *Heir* unc, Matthew Page Wood; *Style* - Sir Anthony Page Wood, Bt

PAGE WOOD, Lady - Evelyn Hazel Rosemary; da of late Capt George Ernest Bellville; assumed by deed poll 1956 the additional surname of Page; *m* 1947, Sir David John Hatherley Page Wood, 7 Bt (d 1955); *Style* - Lady Page Wood; The Old Cottage, Wolverton, Basingstoke, Hants

PAGE WOOD, Matthew; s of Sir John Stuart Page Wood, 6 Bt (d 1955) and hp of nephew, Sir Anthony Page Wood, 8 Bt; assumed by deed poll 1955 the additional surname of Page before his patronymic; *b* 13 Aug 1924; *m* 1947,

Betsann, da of Lt-Col Francis Christesson Darby Tothill; 2 da; *Career* Capt Coldstream Gds; *Style* - Matthew Page Wood Esq; 31 Halsey st, SW3 (☎ 01 584 6008)

PAGE-WOOD, Sir Anthony John; 8 Bt (UK 1837), of Hatherley House, Gloucestershire; s of Sir David John Hatherley Page Wood, 7 Bt (d 1955); *b* 6 Feb 1951; *Educ* Harrow; *Heir* unc, Matthew Page, b 13 Aug 1924; *Style* - Sir Anthony Page-Wood, Bt; 22 Godfrey st, SW3

PAGET OF NORTHAMPTON, Baron (Life Peer UK 1974); Reginald Thomas Guy Des Vœux Paget; QC (1947); s of late Maj Thomas Guy Frederick Paget, of Sulby Hall, Northants, by his w Emma, through whom Lord Paget of Northampton is gggs of Sir Charles Des Vœux, 1 Bt; Sir Charles's w was herself ggda of 3 Earl of Granard, from whom therefore Lord P of N also descends, and a collateral descendant of William of Wykeham; through Emma's mother Lord P of N is also 2 cous once removed to 3 Baron Pender, while through his f's paternal grandmother he is kin to Basil Rathbone, the actor; *b* 2 Sept 1908; *Educ* Eton and Trin, Cambridge; *m* 1931, Sybil Helen, da of late Sills Clifford Gibons, widow of Sir John Bridger Shiffner, 6 Bt and formerly wife of Sir Victor Basil John Seely, 4 Bt; *Career* barr 1934; Lt RNVR 1940-43; contested Northampton 1935; MP (L) Northampton 1945-74; Hon Sec, UK Council of European Movement, 1954; Master, Pytchley Hounds, 1958-71; *Style* - The Rt Hon the Lord Paget of Northampton; 9 Grosvenor Cottages, SW1 (☎ 01 730 4034)

PAGET, Hon Mrs Audrey Elizabeth; da of 1 and last Baron Queenborough (d 1949); *b* 1922; *m* 1, Jan 1945, Cmdt Christian Martell, DFC, French Air Force (d Aug 1945); m 2, 1946 (m dis 1956), Ronan Nelson; 1 s, 2 da; m 3, 1956 (m dis 1974) Lt-Cdr Claud Peter Harcourt Lucy, RN; *Career* resumed the surname of Paget; *Style* - The Hon Mrs Audrey Paget

PAGET, Lady Amelia Myfanwy Polly; da of 7 Marquess of Anglesey, DL; *b* 12 Sept 1963; *Style* - Lady Amelia Paget

PAGET, Hon Mrs (Enid Louise); da of 1 and last Baron Queenborough (d 1949); *b* 1923; *m* 1947 (m dis) Count (Roland) de la Poype; 1 da; *Career* resumed the surname of Paget; *Style* - The Hon Mrs Paget

PAGET, Grace, Lady - Grace Hartley; da of late Walter Herbert Glover, of Birkdale and Grasmere; *m* 1939, as his 2 w, Sir Richard Arthur Surtees Paget. 2 Bt (d 1955); *Style* - Grace, Lady Paget; 8 Iverna Ct, Kensington, W8

PAGET, Lady Henrietta Charlotte Eiluned; da of 7 Marquess of Anglesey, DL; *b* 31 July 1949; *Style* - Lady Henrietta Paget

PAGET, Henry James; s and h of Sir Julian Tolver Paget, 4 Bt; *b* 2 Feb 1959; *Style* - Henry Paget Esq; c/o 4 Trevor st, SW7 1DU

PAGET, Sir John Starr; 3 Bt (UK 1886); s of Sir Richard Paget, 2 Bt (d 1955); *b* 24 Nov 1914; *Educ* Oundle, Chateau D'Oex, Trin Cambridge; *m* 1944, Nancy Mary Parish, JP, da of late Lt-Col Francis Parish, DSO, MC; 2 s, 5 da; *Heir* s, Richard Herbert Paget, b 2 Feb 1959; *Career* CEng, FIMechE; dir Glacier Metal Gp 1963-65, Hilger & Watts 1965-68, Rank Precision Industries Ltd 1968-70; chm Thermal Syndicate Ltd Wallsend 1973-; *Clubs* Athenaeum and Northern Counties (Newcastle upon Tyne); *Style* - Sir John Paget, Bt; Haygrass House, Taunton, Somerset (☎ Taunton 81779); 20 Marloes rd, W8 (☎ 01 373 9760)

PAGET, Lt-Col Sir Julian Tolver; 4 Bt (UK 1871); s of Gen Sir Bernard Paget, GCB, DSO, MC (d 1961) and nephew of Sir James Francis Paget, 3 Bt (d 1972); *b* 11 July 1921; *Educ* Radley, Ch Ch Oxford; *m* 1954, Diana Frances, da of late F S H Farmer; 1 s, 1 da; *Heir* s, Henry James Paget; *Career* joined Coldstream Gds 1940, served NW Europe 1944-45, ret as Lt-Col 1968; Gentleman Usher to HM The Queen 1971-; author; public relations officer Strutt and Parker 1968-; *Clubs* Cavalry and Guards, Pratt's and Flyfishers'; *Style* - Lt-Col Sir Julian Paget,

Bt; 4 Trevor st, SW7 (☎ 01 584 3524)

PAGET, Lady Mary Patricia Beatrice Rose; 3 da of 6 Marquess of Anglesey, GCVO; *b* 19 Jan 1918; *Style* - Lady Mary Paget; Orchard Lea, Churchill, Somerset

PAGET, Lord Rupert Edward Llewellyn; 2 s of 7 Marquess of Anglesey, DL; *b* 21 July 1957; *Educ* Westminster; *Style* - Lord Rupert Paget

PAGET, Richard Herbert; s and h of Sir John Starr Paget, 3 Bt; *b* 17 Feb 1957; *Style* - Richard Paget Esq; c/o Haygrass House, Taunton, Somerset

PAGET, Lady (Elizabeth) Sophia Rhiannon; da of 7 Marquess of Anglesey, DL; *b* 14 May 1954; *Style* - Lady Sophia Paget

PAGET, Winifred, Lady - Winifred Norah; da of late Sir John Rahere, 2 Bt, KC; *b* 1896; *m* 1918, Gen Sir Bernard Charles Tolver Paget, GCB, DSO, MC (d 1961); mother of Sir Julian Paget, 4 Bt; *Style* - Winifred, Lady Paget; The Old Orchard, Heath rd, Petersfield, Hants

PAIGE, Rear-Adm Richard Collings; CB (1967); s of Herbert Collings Paige; *b* 4 October 1911; *Educ* Blundell's Sch, Tiverton; RNE Coll, Keyham; *m* 1937, Sheila Brambles Ward, da of late Dr Ernest Ward; 2 s; *Career* joined Navy 1929, Capt 1957, Commanding Officer RNE Coll 1960-62, Cdre Supt HM Naval Base Singapore 1963-65, Adm Supt HM Dockyard Portsmouth 1966-68, Rear-Adm 1965; *Style* - Rear-Admiral Richard Paige, CB

PAIGE, Victor Grellier; CBE (1978); s of Victor Paige; *b* 5 June 1925; *Educ* East Ham G S, Nottingham U; CIPM, FCIT, FBIM; *m* 1948, Kathleen Winifred, da of Arthur Harris; 1 s, 1 da; *Career* dep chm National Freight Corpn 1977, memb Manpower Services Cmmn 1974; chm Port of London Authority 1980; *Style* - Victor Paige, Esq, CBE; 1 Seeleys Close, Beaconsfield, Bucks (☎ Beaconsfield 4647)

PAIN, Barry Newton; CBE (1979), QPM (1976); s of Godfrey William Pain; *b* 25 Feb 1931; *Educ* Waverley G S Birmingham; *m* 1952, Marguerite Agnes King; 1 s, 1 da; *Career* Ch Constable of Kent 1974-; *Style* - Barry Pain Esq, CBE, QPM; c/o Kent Police HQ, Maidstone, Kent ME15 9BZ (☎ Maidstone 65432)

PAIN, Beville Wheeler; s of Douglas Wheeler Pain (d 1951); *b* 27 April 1918; *Educ* Lancing Coll, Trin Cambridge (MA); *m* 1949, Patience, da of Col J Maitland-Addison, RA (d 1954); *Career* Lt-Col Burma 1944-45, Assist Mil Attaché Br Embassy Paris 1947-50; dir Charter Consolidated 1967, Anglo-American Corpn of S Africa 1976; chm European Mining Cos Gp 1975-80; pres Mining Assoc UK 1977; *Recreations* shooting, travel; *Clubs* Boodle's, Travellers' (Paris), Inanda (Johannesburg); *Style* - Beville Pain Esq; Preston House, Firle, nr Lewes, Sussex (☎ Glynde 245)

PAIN, Hon Mr Justice - Hon Sir Peter (Richard); s of Arthur Richard Pain; *b* 6 Sept 1913; *Educ* Westminster and Ch Ch Oxford; *m* 1941, Barbara Florence Maude Riggs; 2 s; *Career* barr, Lincoln's Inn, 1936, Bencher 1972; QC 1965; a Judge of the High Court of Justice, Queen's Bench Div, 1975-; chm: Race Relations Bd Conciliation Ctee for Greater London, 1968-, South Metropolitan Conciliation Ctee 1971-73; memb Parole Bd 1978-; pres Holiday Fellowship 1977; kt 1975; *Style* - The Hon Mr Justice Pain; Loen, St Catherine's rd, Frimley, Surrey (☎ 02516 5639)

PAIN, Lt-Gen Sir (Horace) Rollo (Squarey); KCB (1975, CB 1974), MC (1945); s of late Horace Davy Pain; *b* 11 May 1921; *m* 1950, Denys Sophia, nee Chaine-Nickson; 1 s, 2 da; *Career* farmer; late 4/7 Roy Dragoon Gds; Head of British Defence Staff, Washington, 1975-78, ret; Col Cmmdt, Mil Provost Staff Corps, 1974-, Col 4/7 Roy Dragoon Gds 1979-; *Clubs* Cavalry and Guards; *Style* - Lt-Gen Sir Rollo Pain, KCB, MC; Eddlethorpe Hall, Malton, N Yorkshire (☎ Burythorpe 218)

PAINE, George; CB (1974), DFC (1944); s of late Jack Paine; *b* 14 April 1918; *Educ* Bradfield Coll and Peterhouse, Cambridge; *m* 1969, Hilary, nee Garrod, widow of Dr A C Frazer; *Career* dir of Statistics and Intelligence, Bd of Inland Revenue, 1957-72; dir OPCS and Registrar Gen for England and Wales 1972-78; Hon Treasurer Royal Statistical Soc 1974-78; *Style* - George Paine Esq, CB, DFC; Springield House, Broad Town, nr Swindon, Wilts SN4 7RU (☎ Broad Hinton 377)

PAINE, Peter Stanley; CBE (1980), DFC (1944); s of Arthur Bertram Paine; *b* 19 June 1921; *Educ* King's Sch, Canterbury; *m* 1942, Sheila Mary, da of late Frederick Wigglesworth; 2 s, 2 da; *Career* served 1940-46; Fl-Lt 2 Gp RAF; Punch Publishing Office 1948-52; sales promotion manager Newnes Pearson 1948-52, Odhams Press 1948-52, sales dir and dir of Tyne Tees Television 1958-67; sales dir and dir of Yorkshire Television 1967; md Tyne Tees Television and dir Trident Television; memb Council of Independent Television Cos Assoc; *Style* - Peter Paine Esq, DFC; Whitegates, Meadowfield rd, Stocksfield, Northumberland (☎ Stocksfield 3143); Briarfield, Ashwood rd, Woking, Surrey (☎ 048 62 73183)

PAISLEY, Rev Ian Richard Kyle; MP (Democratic Unionist) North Antrim, 1974-; s of late Rev J Kyle Paisley; *b* 6 April 1926; *Educ* Ballymena Model Sch, Ballymena Tech H S, S Wales Bible Coll, Reformed Presbyterian Theol Coll Belfast; *m* 1956, Eileen Emily Cassells; 2 s, 3 da; *Career* ordained 1946; MP (Prot U) N Antrim 1970-74; MEP (Democratic Unionist) Northern Ireland 1979-; Minister, Martyrs Memorial Free Presbyterian Church, Belfast, 1946-; *Style* - The Rev Ian Paisley MP MEP; House of Commons, SW1; The Parsonage, 17 Cyprus ave, Belfast BT5 5NT

PAISLEY, John Lawrence; CB (1970), MBE (1946); s of J R Paisley; *b* 4 Sept 1909; *Educ* King George V Sch, Southport; Liverpool U; FICE, FInstHE; *m* 1937, Angela Dorothy Catliff; 3 da; *Career* War Service with Royal Engineers, 1939-46; Chief Highway Engr Miny of Transport 1966-70; consultant with L G Mouchel & Partners, Consulting Engineers, 1971-; *Style* - John Paisley Esq, CB, MBE; Weybrook, Warren rd, Guildford, Surrey (☎ Guildford 62798)

PAKENHAM, Hon Kevin John Toussaint; s of 7 Earl of Longford, KG, PC ; *b* 1947; *Educ* Ampleforth and New Coll Oxford; *m* 1972, Ruth Lesley, da of Leslie Douglas Colbeck Jackson; 1 s, 1 da; *Style* - The Hon Kevin Pakenham; 103 Lansdowne rd, W11

PAKENHAM, Hon Michael Aidan; s of 7 Earl of Longford KG PC; *b* 1943; *Educ* Ampleforth and Trinity Cambridge; *Style* - The Hon Michael Pakenham

PAKENHAM, Hon Patrick Maurice; s of 7 Earl of Longford, KG, PC; *b* 1937; *Educ* Ampleforth and Magdalen Coll, Oxford; *m* 1968, Mary Elizabeth, da of Maj H A J Plummer, of Winchester; 3 s; *Career* barr, Inner Temple, 1962; *Style* - The Hon Patrick Pakenham; Little Meadow, London rd, Sunningdale, Berks

PAKENHAM, Hon Mrs (Susan Elizabeth Moon); *née* Lever; da of 3 Viscount Leverhulme, TD; *b* 1938; *m* 1957 (m dis 1973) Hercules Michael Roland Pakenham; *Style* - The Hon Mrs Pakenham; Oaklands, Lower Common rd, W Wellow, Romsey, Hants

PAKENHAM, Thomas Frank Dermot; s and h of 7 Earl of Longford, KG, PC , but does not use courtesy title of Lord Pakenham; *b* 14 Aug 1933; *Educ* Ampleforth and Magdalen Coll, Oxford; *m* 1964, Valerie Susan, da of Maj Ronald Guthrie McNair Scott; 2 s, 2 da; *Style* - Thomas Pakenham Esq; Tullynally, Castelpollard, Co Westmeath, Eire

PAKINGTON, Hon Anne ; da of 5 Baron Hampton, OBE (d 1919); *b* 1919; *Educ* Somerville Oxford; *Style* - The Hon Anne Pakington; Cherry Tree Cottage, Holt Heath, Worcs (☎ 0905 620280)

PAKINGTON, The Hon Auriol Mary Grace; da of 5 Baron Hampton, OBE (d 1919) ; *b* 1922; *Style* - The Hon Auriol Pakington; The Old Rectory, Holt, Worcester (☎ Ombersley 243)

PAKINGTON, Hon Catherine Mary

Grace; da of 6 Baron Hampton; *b* 1960; *Style* - Hon Catherine Pakington

PAKINGTON, Hon John Humphrey Arnott; s and h of 6 Baron Hampton; *b* 24 Dec 1964; *Style* - The Hon John Pakington

PAKINGTON, Hon Sarah Jane Auriol; da of 6 Baron Hampton; *b* 25 Nov 1961; *Educ* Ellerslie Sch Malvern; Worcester Tech; Bedford Coll, London U; *Style* - The Hon Sarah Pakington

PALAMOUNTAIN, Edgar William Irwin; s of William Bennett Palamountain (d 1958); *b* 24 December 1917; *Educ* Charterhouse, St John's Oxford; *m* 1948, Eleanor Mary Aylward, da of Maj-Gen Sir Richard Lewis, KCMG; 1 s, 2 da; *Career* served War, Army, 1941-47 (despatches); RHA and staff, Capt 1943, Maj 1945, Acting Lt-Col 1946; Allied Cmmn for Austria, 1945-47; md, M & G Group 1968-77, chm 1977-79; chm Unit Trust Assoc 1977-79; chm Wider Share Ownership Council 1969-; chm of Council U College Buckingham 1979-; dir Esmée Fairbairn Charitable Trust 1980-; *Clubs* Boodle's, City of London and MCC; *Style* - Edgar Palamountain Esq; Duns Tew Manor, Oxford (☎ Steeple Aston 40332); 5 Regency Terrace, SW7 3QW

PALING, Helen Elizabeth (Mrs W J S Kershaw); da of A Dale Paling; *b* 25 April 1933; *Educ* Prince Henry's G S Otley and LSE; *m* 1961, William John Stanley Kershaw; 1 s, 3 da; *Career* barr, Lincoln's Inn, 1955; a recorder of the Crown Court, 1972-; *Style* - Mrs William Kershaw; 46 Grainger st, Newcastle upon Tyne (☎ Newcastle upon Tyne 21980/22392)

PALLISER, Sir (Arthur) Michael; GCMG (1977, KCMG 1973, CMG 1966); s of Adm Sir Arthur Palliser, KCB, DSC, of S Kensington (d 1972); *b* 9 April 1922; *Educ* Wellington, Merton Oxford; *m* 1948, Marie Marguerite, da of late Paul-Henri Spaak, of Belgium; 3 s; *Career* Capt Coldstream Gds, Perm Und-Sec and Head of Diplomatic Serv Foreign & Commonwealth Office 1975-, Ambass and UK Perm Rep to European Communities 1973-75, Ambass and Head of UK Delegation to European Communities 1971, Min Paris 1969, Private Sec to PM 1966; *Clubs* Buck's; *Style* - Sir Michael Palliser, GCMG; c/o Foreign & Commonwealth Office, SW1 (☎ 01 233 4740)

PALLOT, Arthur Keith; CMG (1966); s of Harold Pallot, La Tourelle, Jersey; *b* 25 Sept 1918; *Educ* Newton Coll; *m* 1945, Marjorie, da of J Smith, of Rugby; 2 da; *Career* RN 1936, ret as Lt-Cdr, 1947; dir of Finance and Establishment, 1956-75, sec and dir-gen, 1975-, Commonwealth War Graves Commission; *Style* - Arthur Pallot Esq, CMG; Northways, Stubbles Lane, Cookham Dean, Berks (☎ Marlow 6529)

PALMAR, Derek James; s of Lt-Col Frederick James Palmar (d 1978); *b* 25 July 1919; *Educ* Dover Coll; *m* 1946, Edith, da of William Brewster (d 1948); 1 s, 1 da; *Career* served RA and Staff, 1941-46; psc; Lt-Col 1945; chm and ch exec Bass Ltd 1976- (fin dir 1970-); chm Rush & Tompkins Group Ltd 1974-; dir Grindlays Bank Ltd, Grindlays Holdings Ltd, Howard Machinery Ltd; Trustee, Civic Trust; chm, The Brewers' Soc, 1980-; FCA, FBIM; *Clubs* Boodle's; *Style* - Derek Palmar Esq; 30 Portland Place, W1 (☎ 01 637 5499)

PALMER, 3 Baron (UK 1933); Sir Raymond Cecil Palmer; 3 Bt (UK 1916), OBE (1968); s of 2 Baron Palmer (d 1950, gs of Samuel Palmer, a fndr of Huntley & Palmers, the purveyors of biscuits); *b* 24 June 1916; *Educ* Harrow and Univ Coll, Oxford; *m* 1941, Victoria Ellen, da of late Capt J A R Weston-Stevens, Maidenhead; 2 da (1 da decd); *Heir* bro, Col Hon Gordon William Nottage Palmer; *Career* Lt, Grenadier Gds, 1940-43; dir, Associated Biscuit Manufacturers Ltd to 1980; chm: Huntley & Palmers Ltd, 1969-80, Huntley Boorne & Stevens Ltd, Reading, 1956-80 (dep chm, 1948); pres, Berks CC; *Recreations* music; *Clubs* Cavalry and Guards; *Style* - The Rt Hon the Lord Palmer, OBE; Higher Moor, North Hill, Minehead, Somerset (☎ 2360); Farley Hill House, Farley Hill, Reading, Berkshire (☎ Eversley 732260)

PALMER, Hon Anthea Amabel; da of Baroness Lucas of Crudwell, and Dingwall; *b* 1956; *Career* assumed by deed poll 1963 additional forename of Amabel; *Style* - The Hon Anthea Palmer

PALMER, Arthur Montague Frank; MP (L and Co-op) Bristol North East, 1974-; s of late Frank Palmer; *b* 4 Aug 1912; *Educ* Ashford GS, Brunel Tech Coll (now Brunel U); CEng, FIEE, FInstF; *m* 1939, Dr Marion Ethel Frances Woollaston; 2 da; *Career* MP (L) for Wimbledon 1945-50, MP (L and Co-op) for Cleveland Div of Yorks Oct 1952-Sept 1959; MP (L and Co-op) Bristol Central 1964-74; chm, Co-operative Parly Gp, 1970-; *Style* - Arthur Palmer Esq, MP; 14 Lavington Court, Putney, SW15 (☎ 01 789 1967); Hill Cottage, Charlcutt, nr Calne, Wilts (☎ Kellaways 653)

PALMER, Lady Anne Sophia; *née* Walpole; da of 5 Earl of Orford (fifth in descent from bro of Sir Robert Walpole, the 1 PM & 1 Earl of Orford of 1 cr, and 1 cous four times removed of the litterateur Horace Walpole, 4 and last Earl of Orford of the 1 cr); *b* 11 Dec 1919; *m* 1939, Col Joseph Palmer, CBE, TD, DL (d 1980); 2 s; *Style* - Lady Anne Palmer; Rosemoor, Torrington, Devon

PALMER, Anthony Wheeler; QC; s of late Philip Palmer; *b* 30 Dec 1936; *Educ* Wrekin Coll, Salop; *m* Jacqueline, da of Reginald Fortnum, of Taunton; 1 s, 2 da; *Career* barr Gray's Inn 1962, QC (1979), a recorder of the Crown Court 1980-; *Style* - Anthony Palmer Esq, QC; 17 Warwick ave, Coventry CV5 6DJ (☎ Coventry 75340)

PALMER, Bernard Harold Michael; s of late Christopher Harold Palmer; *b* 8 Sept 1929; *Educ* St Edmund's Sch, Hindhead, Eton (King's Scholar), King's Cambridge; *m* 1954, Jane Margaret, da of late E L Skinner; 1 s, 1 da; *Career* editor of the Church Times 1968-; *Style* - Bernard Palmer Esq; 143 Bradbourne Vale rd, Sevenoaks, Kent (☎ Sevenoaks 53327)

PALMER, Charles Alan Salier; CBE (1969), DSO (1945); s of late Sir (Charles) Eric Palmer; *b* 23 Oct 1913; *Educ* Harrow; Exeter Coll, Oxford; *m* 1939, Auriol Mary, da of late Brig-Gen Cyril R Harbord, CB, CMG, DSO; *Career* vice-chm Associated Biscuit Manufacturers Ltd 1963, chm 1969-72; pres Reading Conservative Assoc 1946-; *Style* - Charles Palmer Esq, CBE, DSO; Forest Edge, Farley Hill, Reading, Berks (☎ Arborfield Cross 760223)

PALMER, Hon Lady (Catherine Elizabeth); *née* Tennant; da of 2 Baron Glenconner by his 2 w; *b* 10 Nov 1947; *m* 1976, Sir Mark Palmer, 5 Bt; 1 da; *Style* - The Hon Lady Palmer; Mill Hill Farm, Sherborne, Northleach, Glos (☎ Windrush 395); 15 Bramerton st, SW3

PALMER, Charles Graham; *Career* chm: Gill & Duffus Ltd, Peek Puckle Holdings Ltd; dir: British Cocoa Mills (Hull) Ltd, René Weil SA, Gill & Duffus Group Ltd; *Style* - Charles Palmer Esq; Gill & Duffus Group Ltd, 201 Borough High st, SE1

PALMER, Charles Lionel; s of Capt Lionel Hugo Palmer (6 s of 1 Bt) (d 1914) and hp of kinsman, Sir Mark Palmer, 5 Bt; *b* 7 Feb 1909; *Educ* Cheltenham Coll and Trent Coll; *m* 1937, Karoline, LRAM, da of late Maj Carl Gach, of Vienna; 2 da; *Career* formerly Capt Roy Canadian Army Serv Corps; *Style* - Charles Palmer Esq; 52 Patika ave, Weston, Ont, Canada

PALMER, Hon Mrs (Dorothy Cecily Sybil); *née* Loder; da of 1 Baron Wakehurst and Lady Louise Beauclerk, da of 10 Duke of St Albans; *b* 1896; *m* 1922, Hon Lewis Palmer (d 1971), yst s of 2 Earl of Selborne, KG, GCMG, PC, by Lady Beatrix Cecil, da of 3 Marquess of Salisbury (the Con PM); 1 s, 1 da; *Style* - The Hon Mrs Palmer; St Michel, Rue à l'Or, St Saviours, Guernsey, CI

PALMER, Edward Hurry; CB (1972); s of late Harold G Palmer; *b* 23 Sept 1912; *Educ* Haileybury; *m* 1940, Phyllis Eagle; *Career* dir Defence Land Services, Property Services Agency, DOE 1972-73; dir Estate Surveying Services 1973-74; *Style* - Edward Palmer Esq, CB; 49 Paines Lane, Pinner, Middlesex (☎ 01 866 5961)

PALMER, Hon Mrs Edward; Joanna

Constance; JP (Inner London); da of Sir Edmund Bacon, 13 Bt, KG, KBE, TD; *m* 1957, Hon Edward Roundell Palmer, s of 3 Earl of Selborne; 2 s, 2 da; *Style* - The Hon Mrs Palmer, JP; 3 Holland pk, W11

PALMER, Lady Emily Sophia; da of 4 Earl of Selborne, *qv*; *b* 1978

PALMER, Felicity Joan; *b* 6 April 1944; *Educ* Erith G S, Guildhall Sch of Music and Drama; AGSM, FGSM; *Career* soprano; Kathleen Ferrier Memorial Prize 1970; major appearances at concerts in Britain, America, Belgium, France, Germany, Italy and Spain; *Style* - Miss Felicity Palmer; 7 Bayham rd, W4 1BJ (☎ 01 995 1291)

PALMER, Sir Geoffrey Christopher John; 12 Bt (E 1660); s of Lt-Col Sir Geoffrey Frederick Neill Palmer, 11 Bt (d 1951); *b* 30 June 1936; *Educ* Eton; *m* 1957, Clarissa Mary, da of Stephen Villiers-Smith; 4 da; *Heir* bro, Jeremy Charles Palmer; *Career* is a patron of two livings; *Style* - Sir Geoffrey Palmer, Bt; Carlton Curlieu Hall, Leicestershire (☎ Great Glen 2656)

PALMER, Hon George Horsley; s (twin) of 4 Earl of Selborne; *b* 1974

PALMER, Hon Gordon William Nottage; OBE (1957, MBE 1944), TD (1950); s of 2 Baron Palmer (d 1950) and hp of bro, 3 Baron Palmer, OBE; *b* 18 July 1918; *Educ* Eton and Ch Ch Oxford; *m* 1950, Lorna Eveline Hope, da of Maj C W H Bailie; 2 s; *Career* served war of 1939-45, with Berks Yeo, 1939-41, staff Capt RA, HQ 61 Div, 1941, DAQMG Malta, 1942, GSO2, Ops, GHQ Middle East 1943-44, GSO2 HQ Div 1944-45; dir of cos and part-time soldier; commanded Berkshire Yeo 1954-56; md, Huntley & Palmers Ltd, 1959-69; chm, Associated Biscuit Manufacturers, 1978-; pres, Reading U, 1954-79; DL (1960) Berks, JP 1956, High Sheriff 1965; Vice-Lord Lt 1976, Lord-Lt 1978-; chm of Council, Roy Coll of Music, 1974-; *Style* - The Hon Gordon Palmer OBE TD JP, HM Lord-Lieut for Berkshire; Harris House, Mortimer, Berks (☎ 332317); Edrom Newton, Duns, Berwicks (☎ Chirnside 292)

PALMER, Hon Henry William; s of Viscount Wolmer (s of 3 Earl of Selborne, k on active service 1942) and Priscilla (*see Baron Newton*), and bro of 4 Earl; *b* 1941; *Educ* Eton, Ch Ch Oxford; *m* 1968, Minette, da of Sir Patrick Donner, of Hurstbourne Park, Whitchurch, Hants; 3 s, 1 da; *Career* dep dir Centre for Interfirm Comparison 1975-; *Style* - The Hon Henry Palmer; 10 Crescent Grove, SW4

PALMER, Jeremy Charles; s of Lt-Col Sir Geoffrey Frederick Neill Palmer, 11 Bt (d 1951); hp of bro, Sir Geoffrey Palmer, 12 Bt; *b* 16 May 1939; *Educ* Eton; *m* 1968, Antonia, da of late Astley Dutton; 2 s; *Style* - Jeremy Palmer Esq; 8 Ashchurch Park Villas, W12

PALMER, Sir John Chance; s of Ernest Clephan Palmer (d 1954); *b* 21 March 1920; *Educ* St Paul's and St Edmund Hall, Oxford; *m* 1945, Mary Winifred, da of Arthur Sidney Ellyatt, OBE (d 1973); 4 s; *Career* served war RNVR, Atlantic and Mediterranean 1939-46, slr 1948, partner Ashford Sparkes and Harward, of Tiverton, Exeter and Crediton 1950-, elected council of Law Soc 1963, Govr Coll of Law 1965, pres Devon and Exeter Law Soc 1972, pres S Western Law Soc 1973, pres The Law Soc 1978-79, Govr Coll of Law 1965, chm Govrs Blundell's Sch, memb Criminal Injuries Compensation bd 1981-; kt 1979; *Style* - Sir John Palmer; Hensleigh, Tiverton, Devon EX16 5NJ (☎ Tiverton 2114); Sunnycote, Riverside, Shaldon, Devon (☎ 062687 2350); Flat 317 Queens Quay, Upper Thames st, EC4 (☎ 01 248 6132)

PALMER, Sir John Edward Somerset; 8 Bt (GB 1791); s of Sir John Palmer, 7 Bt, DL (d 1963); *b* 27 Oct 1926; *Educ* Canford, Pembroke Coll Cambridge and Durham U; *m* 1956, Dione Catharine, da of Charles Duncan Skinner; 1 s, 1 da; *Heir* s, Robert John Hudson Palmer; *Career* Lt RA served India; Colonial Ag Serv N Nigeria 1952-61; sr exec R A Lister & Co Ltd Dursley Glos 1962-63; Miny Overseas Devpt 1964-68; memb American Soc Ag Engrs; MIAgrE; dir Sir John Palmer Ltd & independent consultant 1976-; *Recreations* sailing; *Clubs* IOD, C'wlth

Soc; *Style* - Sir John Palmer, Bt; Gayton House, Gayton, Northampton (☎ 0604 858336); 14 Hale st, Cambridge (☎ 0223 521929)

PALMER, Maj-Gen Joseph Michael; s of late Lt-Col William Robert Palmer, DSO; *b* 17 Oct 1928; *Educ* Wellington; *m* 1953, Jillean Monica Sherston; 2 s, 1 da; *Career* dir, Royal Armoured Corps, 1978; Col, 14/20 King's Hussars 1981-; AMBIM; *Clubs* Cavalry and Guards; *Style* - Major-General Joseph Palmer; 103 Albert Palace Mansions, Lurline gdns, SW11 (☎ 01 720 5506)

PALMER, Kathleen, Lady - Kathleen; da of late Herbert Smith; *m* 1922, Sir John Archdale Palmer, 7 Bt (d 1963); *Style* - Kathleen, Lady Palmer; The Green, Uley, nr Dursley, Glos

PALMER, Hon Luke James; s (twin) of 4 Earl of Selborne; *b* 1974

PALMER, Leslie Robert; CBE (1964); s of Robert Palmer; *b* 21 Aug 1910; *Educ* Battersea GS, London U; *m* 1937, Mary Crick; 2 s, 1 da; *Career* hon treasurer and chm, Finance and Admin Dept, United Reformed Church, 1973-; dir-gen, Defence Accounts, MOD, 1969-72; *Style* - Leslie Palmer Esq, CBE; High Meadow, Upper Limpley Stoke, Nr Bath (☎ Limpley Stoke 3308)

PALMER, Sir (Charles) Mark; 5 Bt (UK 1886); s of Sir Anthony Frederick Mark Palmer, 4 Bt (d 1941); *b* (posthumous) 21 Nov 1941; *Educ* Eton; *m* 1976, Hon Catherine Tennant, 2 da of 2 Baron Glenconner; 1 da; *Heir* kinsman, Charles Lionel Palmer; *Career* was a Page of Honour to HM 1956-59; *Style* - Sir Mark Palmer, Bt; Mill Hill Farm, Sherborne, Northleach, Glos (☎ Windrush 395)

PALMER, Hon Mrs; Hon Pamela; da of late 1 Baron Forster of Harraby; *b* 1921; *m* 1948, Peter Hitcham Palmer; *Style* - The Hon Mrs Palmer; 84 Albemarle rd, Beckenham, Kent

PALMER, Maj-Gen Philip Francis; CB (1957), OBE (1945), MB, BCh; s of Lt-Col Francis James Palmer (d 1950); *b* 8 Aug 1903; *Educ* Trin Coll Dublin and Durham U; *Career* Lt RAMC 1926, served 1939-45 with RAMC, Brig, 1955, DMS MELF (temp Maj-Gen) 1955-56, DDMS Northern Command, ret 1960; QHS 1956-60; Col Cmdt RAMC 1963-68; *Style* - Maj-Gen Philip Palmer, CB, OBE; c/o Williams & Glyn's Bank Ltd, Whitehall, SW1

PALMER, Hon Mrs (Patricia Margaret); da of Baron Feather (Life Peer, d 1976); *b* 1934; *m* 1957, Stanley Lawrence Palmer; *Style* - The Hon Mrs Palmer

PALMER, His Honour Judge - Robert Henry Stephen; s of Henry Alleyn Palmer; *b* 13 Nov 1927; *Educ* Charterhouse and Univ Coll, Oxford; *m* 1955, Geraldine Elizabeth Ann, da of George Evan Evens (d 1950); 1 s, 2 da; *Career* barr 1950; dep chm, Berks QS 1970; a Recorder of the Crown Court, 1972-78; a Circuit Judge, 1978-; *Style* - His Honour Judge Palmer; 44 Staveley rd, Chiswick W4 3ES (☎ 01 994 3394)

PALMER, Hon Robert Jocelyn; MC, JP (Hants); s of 3 Earl of Selborne by his 1 w, Hon Grace, da of 1 Viscount Ridley and Hon Mary Marjoribanks, da of 1 Baron Tweedmouth; *b* 1919; *Educ* Winchester, Balliol Oxford; *m* 1950, Baroness Lucas of Crudwell (in her own right), *qv*; 2 s, 1 da; *Career* late Maj Coldstream Gds, Italy (despatches, MC) 1939-45; *Style* - The Hon Robert Palmer, MC, JP; The Old House, Wonston, Winchester, Hants

PALMER, Richard John; JP (1961); s of Reginald Howard Reed Palmer (d 1970); *b* 5 Nov 1926; *Educ* Eton; *m* 1951, Sarah Faith Georgina, da of 1 Viscount Churchill, GCVO (d 1934); 3 s, 1 da; *Career* dir Associated Biscuit Mfrs, High Sheriff of Berks 1979-80; *Recreations* shooting, fishing; *Clubs* White's; *Style* - Richard Palmer Esq, JP; Queen Anne's Mead, Swallowfield, Berks (☎ Reading 883264)

PALMER, Robert John Hudson; s and h of Sir John Edward Somerset Palmer, 8 Bt; *b* 20 Dec 1960; *Style* - Robert Palmer Esq; Newland, nr Coleford, Glos

PALMER, Hon Ralph Matthew; s and h of Baroness Lucas of Crudwell, and Dingwall; *b* 7 June 1951; *Educ* Eton and Balliol, Oxford; *m* 1978, Clarissa Marie, da of George Vivian Lockett, TD, of Stratford Hills, Stratford St Mary, Colchester; *Style* - The Hon Ralph Palmer

PALMER, Hon Mrs (Sarah Faith Georgina); *née* Spencer; da of late 1 Viscount Churchill, GCVO; *b* 1931; *m* 1951, Richard John Palmer, JP; 3 s, 1 da; *Style* - The Hon Mrs Palmer; Queen Anne's Mead, Swallowfield, Berks

PALMER, Sidney John; CB (1972), OBE (1953); s of Sidney Palmer (d 1919); *b* 29 Nov 1913; *Educ* Royal Dockyard Sch and RNC Greenwich; *m* 1941, Mavis Beatrice Blennerhassett, da of Jeremiah Hallett, of Plymouth; 4 s; *Career* Ch Constructor, Sydney 1945, Hong Kong 1946; Prof of Naval Architecture, RNC 1952-57; dir Ship Production 1966-67; memb Council RINA 1960; Liveryman, Shipwrights Co 1968; dep dir-gen Ships, MOD 1968-73; Head of Royal Corps of Naval Constructors 1968-74; Management Ctee RNLI 1975; *Style* - Sidney Palmer Esq, CB, OBE; Bloomfield ave, Bath, Avon (☎ Bath 312592)

PALMER, Hon Timothy John; s of Baroness Lucas of Crudwell, and Dingwall; *b* 1953; *Educ* Eton and Balliol, Oxford; *Style* - The Hon Timothy Palmer

PALMER, Hon Mrs; Hon Veronica; *née* Saumarez; da of late 5 Baron de Saumarez; *b* 1915; *m* 1945, Brig Anthony William Allen Llewellen Palmer, DSO, MC, King's Dragoon Gds; *Career* ATS 1943-45; *Style* - The Hon Mrs Palmer; Clos du Menage, Sark, Channel Islands

PALMER, William Alexander; s of Reginald Howard Reed Palmer (d 1970); *b* 21 June 1925; *Educ* Eton; *m* 1949, Cherry Ann, da of late Arthur Gibbs; 2 s, 2 da; *Career* dir Huntley & Palmers Ltd 1951, chm 1980-, dir The Associated Biscuit Manufacturers Ltd 1971-, Pres Flour Milling and Baking Research Assoc 1971, Pres Royal Warrant Holders Assoc 1976-77, Chm Cake & Biscuit Alliance 1980, High Sheriff Berkshire 1974-75; Govr Malvern Girls' Coll 1965, memb Reading U Council 1980; *Recreations* shooting, tennis, gardening; *Clubs* Cavalry and Guards; *Style* - William Palmer Esq; Phillips Hill, Snelsmore Common, nr Newbury, Berks (☎ Chieveley 203)

PALMER, William John; CBE (1973); s of late William Palmer; *b* 25 April 1909; *Educ* Pate's GS, Cheltenham; Christ's, Cambridge (Lady Margaret Scholar); *m* 1, 1935, Zenaida Nicolaevna (d 1944), da of late Nicolai Maropoulo, of Yalta, Russia; m 2, 1949, Vanda Ianthe Millicent, da of late William Matthew Cowton, of Queensland; 1 s, 2 da; *Career* barr, Gray's Inn; joined Indian Civil Service, 1932, ret 1949; joined Colonial Legal Serv as Magistrate, Nigeria, 1950; Judge, 1958; Judge of HM Chief Court for the Persian Gulf, 1967-72; memb, Court of Appeal for Anguilla, 1973-; *Style* - William Palmer Esq, CBE; Guys Farm, Icomb, Glos GL54 1JD (☎ Stow-on-the-Wold 30219)

PANCKRIDGE, Surgeon Vice-Adm Sir (William) Robert (Silvester); KBE (1962), CB (1960); s of W P Panckridge, OBE, MB, MRCS, LRCP; *b* 11 Sept 1901; *Educ* Tonbridge Sch, Middx Hosp; FRSM (1955), QHP (1958); *m* 1932, Edith Muriel, da of Sir John Crosbie, St John, Newfoundland; 1 da; *Career* PMO RN Coll, Dartmouth, 1948, Medical Officer-in-Charge, RN Hosp, Hong Kong, 1952, RN Hosp Chatham, 1958, Surgeon Capt 1952, Surgeon Rear-Adm, 1958, Surgeon Vice-Adm, 1960, QHP, 1958-63, Medical dir-gen of the Navy, 1960-63; CStJ 1959; *Style* - Surgeon Vice-Admiral Sir Robert Panckridge, KBE, CB; Waterfall Lodge, Oughterard, Co Galway, Eire (☎ Galway 82168)

PANKHURST, Air Vice-Marshal Leonard Thomas; CB (1955), CBE (1944); s of Thomas Pankhurst; *b* 26 Aug 1902; *Educ* Hampton G S; *m* 1939, Ruth, da of Alexander Phillips; 1 s, 2 da; *Career* joined RAF 1925, Gp Capt 1942, Air Cdre 1947, Actg Air Vice-Marshal 1954; served WW II (despatches); Dir-Gen Personnel (I) Air Miny 1954-57, ret; *Style* - Air Vice-Marshal Leonard Pankhurst, CB, CBE; Earl's Eye House, 8 Sandy Lane, Chester CH3 5UL (☎ Chester 20993)

PANNELL, Hon Hilary; da of Baron Pannell, PC (Life Peer) (d 1980); *b* 1940; *Style* - The Hon Hilary Pannell

PANNELL, Baroness; Lilian Maud; da of Edward William Francis Frailing, of Islington; *m* 1929, Baron Pannell, PC (Life Peer, d 1980); *Style* - The Rt Hon The Lady Pannell; 159 Glenview, Abbey Wood, SE2

PANTCHEFF, Theodore Xenophon Henry; CMG (1977); s of Sophocles Xenophon Pantcheff, of Buckhurst Hill, Essex (d 1949); *b* 29 Dec 1920; *Educ* Merchant Taylors' Sch, Gonville and Caius Cambridge; *m* 1954, Patricia Mary, nee Tully; 2 s; *Career* Maj Europe 1941-47; Control Commission for Germany 1948-51; HM Diplomatic Serv 1951-77, Vice-Consul Munich 1954-56, 1 Sec Lagos 1958-60, 1 Sec Leopoldville 1961-63; seconded MOD 1969-71; FCO 1971-77, ret; Jurat of the Court of Alderney 1979; *Clubs* Carlton; *Style* - Theodore Pantcheff Esq, CMG; Butes Cottage, Alderney, Channel Islands (☎ 3169)

PANTON, Air Cdre Alastair Dyson; CB (1969), OBE (1950), DFC (1939); s of William Dickson Panton; *b* 2 Nov 1916; *Educ* Bedford Sch, RAF Coll Cranwell; *m* 1939, Eileen Isabel Lumley; 3 s (and 1 s decd); *Career* Provost Marshal and dir of RAF Security 1968-71; *Style* - Air Commodore Alastair Panton, CB, OBE, DFC; Penrhyn Castle, Bangor, Gwynedd (☎ Bangor 53084)

PANTON, Dr Francis Harry; MBE (1948); s of George Emerson Panton; *b* 25 May 1923; *Educ* City Sch, Lincoln; Univ Coll and Nottingham U; *m* 1952, Audrey Mary, nee Lane; 2 s; *Career* dir of Propellants, Explosives and Rocket Motor Establishment, Waltham Abbey and Westcott, and Head of Rocket Motor Exec MOD 1976-80, dir Roy Armament Res and Devpt Establishment MOD 1980-; *Clubs* Reform; *Style* - Dr Francis Panton, MBE; 1 St Peter's Lane, Canterbury, Kent (☎ Canterbury 52902)

PAO, Sir Yue-Kong; CBE (1976), JP; s of Sui-Loong Pao; *b* Chekiang, China, 10 Nov 1918; *Educ* Shanghai, China; *m* 1940, Sue-Ing Haung; 4 da; *Career* chm: World-Wide Shipping Group 1974-, World Finance Int Ltd, IBJ Finance (HK) Ltd, Eastern Asia Navigation Co Ltd, World Int (Hldgs) Ltd; dir: Hongkong & Shanghai Banking Corpn, Mercantile Bank Ltd, South China Morning Post, Inchcape Far East Ltd and other cos; JP Hong Kong 1971; kt 1978; *Style* - Sir Yue-Kong Pao, CBE, JP; World-Wide Shipping Agency Ltd, Prince's Building, 20/21st Floors, Hong Kong (☎ H-242111)

PAOLOZZI, Eduardo Luigi; CBE (1968); s of Rudolpho Antonio Paolozzi (d 1940); *b* 7 March 1924; *Educ* Edinburgh Sch of Art, Slade Sch; *m* 1951, Freda, da of Ernest George Elliott (d 1959); *Career* sculptor; tutor ceramics RCA 1968-; prof Fachhochschule Cologne 1977-; RA *Style* - Eduardo Paolozzi Esq, CBE; 107 Dovehouse st, SW3; Landermere, Thorpe-le-Soken, Essex (☎ Thorpe-le-Soken 210)

PAPADOPOULOS, Achilles Symeon; CMG (1980), MVO (1972), MBE (1954); s of Symeon Papadopoulos (d 1971); *b* 16 Aug 1923; *Educ* The English Sch, Nicosia, Cyprus; *m* 1954, Joyce Martin, nee Stark; 1 s, 2 da; *Career* HM Diplomatic Ser, HM Ambass to Mozambique 1979, British High Cmmr to Bahamas 1981; *Style* - Achilles Papadopoulos Esq, CMG, MVO, MBE; 5 Lansdowne Close, Wimbledon, SW20; c/o Barclays Bank, 160 Piccadilly, W1

PAPE, Hon Sir George (Augustus); s of late George Frederick Pape; *b* 29 Jan 1903; *Educ* All Saints GS, St Kilda, Melbourne U; *m* 1952, Mabel, da of Alfred Lloyd; *Career* RAAF 1940-46; QC 1955; Judge of Supreme Court of Victoria, 1957-75, ret; kt 1968; *Style* - The Hon Sir George Pape; 146 Kooyong rd, Toorak, Victoria 3142, Australia (☎ 20-6158)

PAPWORTH, Frank; s of James Papworth (d 1977); *b* 11 Jan 1926; *Educ* Bacup Central Sch; *m* 1950, Alice; 3 s; *Career* gp finance dir Biddle Holdings, jt md Bennie Lifts Ltd; part-time lecturer on English Company Law; FCIS, FBIM, Associate Inst of Co Accountants; *Style* - Frank Papworth Esq; Shalom, 6 Manor Drive, Baston, Peterborough PE6 9PQ (☎ 077 86 328)

PARARAJASINGAM, Sir Sangarapillai; s of late W Sangarapillai; *b* 25 June 1896; *Educ* St Thomas' Coll, Mt Lavinia; *m* 1916, Padmavati, da of Sir Ponnambalam Arunachalam; 1 s, 1 da; *Career* Senator Ceylon 1954-59; chm Bd of Dirs Colonial Motors Ltd 1961-74, former memb Bd of Trustees, Ceylon Social Service League; kt 1955; *Style* - Sir Sangarapillai Pararajasingam; No 50 Pathmalaya, Flower rd, Colombo 7, Sri Lanka (☎ 23159)

PARBO, Sir Arvi Hillar; s of Aado Parbo; *b* 10 Feb 1926; *Educ* Clausthal Mining Acad, Germany; Adelaide U; *m* 1953, Saima Soots; 2 s, 1 da; *Career* chm and md Western Mining Corp Ltd 1974-, chm Alcoa of Australia Ltd 1978-; kt 1978; *Style* - Sir Arvi Parbo; Western Mining Corporation Ltd, 360 Collins st, Melbourne, Vic 3000, Australia; GPO Box 860K, Melbourne, Vic 3001 (☎ 67 7556)

PARDOE, Hon Mrs (Anna Josephine Bridget); da of 2 Baron Darling; *b* 1946; *m* 1971, Anthony Robert Pardoe; 1 s, 1 da; *Style* - The Hon Mrs Pardoe; Sharow Cottage, Sharow, Ripon, N Yorks

PARDOE, John Wentworth; s of Cuthbert B Pardoe; *b* 27 July 1934; *Educ* Sherborne, Corpus Christi Cambridge; *m* 1958, Joyce R Peerman; 2 s, 1 da; *Career* MP (Lib) Cornwall N 1966-79; jt md Sight and Sound Education Ltd 1979-; sr research fell of Policy Studies Inst 1979-; presenter 'Look Here' London Weekend Television 1979-; *Style* - John Pardoe Esq; Chy-an-Porth, Trevone, Padstow, Cornwall

PARGETER, Ronald Albert; s of Albert Henry Pargeter (d 1963); *b* 3 Oct 1919; *Educ* Archbishop Tenison's Grammar; *m* 1, 1943, Edna Margaret; 1 s, 1 da; m 2, 1978, Iva Patricia, nee Stones; 2 da; *Career* Fl Lt RAF 1939-45, chm Rapadex Ltd 1980-; dir Dalgety Chem Ltd 1978-; dep chm K & K Greeff Chem Ltd 1976-; pres Fed Euro Commerce Chimique 1980-; chm BCDTA 1973-75; *Recreations* golf, cricket, travelling; *Clubs* St Stephen's, RAF, Inst of Dirs; *Style* - Ronald Pargeter Esq; Mill Hill, Rodmell, East Sussex (☎ 079 16 2912); 63 Park West, W2 (☎ 723 1982)

PARGITER, Baron (Life Peer UK 1966); George Albert Pargiter; CBE (1961); s of late William Russell Pargiter, of Green's Norton, Northants; *b* 16 March 1897; *Educ* Towcester G S; *m* 1919, Dorothy Maud, da of Roger Woods; 2 s, 1 da; *Career* 1914-18 War, Gallipoli; MP (L) Spelthorne Div of Middx 1945-50, Southall 1950-66; memb Middx CC 1934-65, County Alderman 1946 (chm 1959-60); Mayor of Southall 1938-40; DL Middx 1953, Greater London 1965-76; v-chm CCs Assoc 1960-63, chm 1963-65, v-pres 1965-; *Style* - The Rt Hon the Lord Pargiter, CBE; 190 Whyteleafe rd, Caterham, Surrey CR3 5ED (☎ Caterham 45588)

PARGITER, Hon Donald; s of Baron Pargiter, CBE (Life Peer); *b* 1921; *m* 1947; *Style* - The Hon Donald Pargiter; 68 Tonbridge rd, Maidstone, Kent

PARGITER, Hon Russell Ashby; s of Baron Pargiter, CBE (Life Peer); *b* 1924; *m* 1954, Elizabeth Edwina, da of John George Jamieson Coghill; *Career* MB, BS London; fell Roy Australian and NZ Coll of Psychiatrists; DPM England; FRC Psych; sr hon psychiatrist Roy Hobart Hosp; *Style* - The Hon Russell Pargiter; Grays rd, Ferntree 7101, Tasmania

PARGITER, Maj-Gen Robert Beverley; CB (1942), CBE (1945); s of late F E Pargiter, ICS; *b* 11 July 1889; *Educ* Rugby; RMA Woolwich; *m* 1, 1917, Muriel Huxley (d 1971); 1 s, 2 da; m 2, 1973, Elaine Ilma, widow of Colin Gulliland; *Career* war service 1939-45; Cdr 1 AA Brigade, 4, 7 and 5 AA Divisions, 3 AA Group; Maj-Gen Anti-Aircraft Allied Force HQ, N Africa and Central Mediterranean Forces, ret 1945; *Style* - Major-General Robert Pargiter CB, CBE; The Dye House, Biddenden, Kent

PARHAM, Adm Sir Frederick Robertson; GBE (1959, CBE 1949), KCB (1955, CB 1951), DSO (1944); s of late Frederick James Parham; *b* 9 Jan 1901; *Educ* RNCs Osborne and Dartmouth; *m* 1, 1926, Kathleen Dobree (d 1973), da of Eugene Carey, of Guernsey; 1 s; m 2, 1978, Mrs Joan Saunders, nee Charig;

Career Cdr 1934, Rear-Adm 1949, Vice-Adm 1952; a Lord Commissioner of the Admiralty, Fourth Sea Lord and Ch of Supplies and Transport 1954-55; Cdr-in-Chief The Nore 1955-58, ret 1959; *Style* - Admiral Sir Frederick Parham, GBE, KCB, DSO; The Coach House, Church rd, West Lavington, Midhurst, W Sussex GU29 OEH (☎ Midhurst 3183)

PARIS, Sir Edward (Talbot); CB (1947); s of late Edward Paris; *b* 23 Jan 1889; *Educ* Dean Close Sch, Cheltenham; Imperial Coll of Science; Univ Coll London; *m* 1925, Eveline Amy (d 1968), da of late J W Shortt, MD; 3 da; *Career* Principal Dir of Scientific Research (Defence) Miny of Supply 1946; Ch Scientific Adviser Home Office 1948-54; US Medal of Freedom with Bronze Palm 1947; kt 1954; *Style* - Sir Edward Paris, CB; Lavender Cottage, Crazy Lane, Sedlescombe, Sussex (☎ Sedlescombe 261)

PARISH, Sir David (Elmer Woodbine); CBE (1964); s of late Walter Woodbine Parish; *b* 29 June 1911; *Educ* Sandroyd, Eton, Lausanne, Switzerland; *m* 1939, Mona Blair McGarel, da of late Charles McGarel Johnston; 2 da; *Career* chm City and Guilds of London Inst 1967-79, life vice-pres 1979; dep chm Marine and General Mutual Life Assurance Soc 1976-; FIOB 1940, FRSA 1953, FBIM 1957; Fell Imperial Coll 1976; Hon LLD Leeds 1975; kt 1980; *Style* - Sir David Parish, CBE; The Glebe Barn, Pulborough, W Sussex RH20 2AF (☎ Pulborough 2613); 5 Lurgan Mansions, Sloane sq, SW1W 8BH (☎ 01 730 6512)

PARISH, Hon Mrs (Elizabeth Campbell); *née* Boot; da of 2 and last Baron Trent (d 1956); *b* 1927; *m* 1947, Maj Michael Woodbine Parish, MC, Notts Yeo; 1 s, 3 da; *Style* - The Hon Mrs Parish; Walcot Hall, North Lydbury, Salop

PARISH, Hon Mrs Monica Esmé Ebba; *née* Suenson-Taylor; da of 1 Baron Grantchester, OBE; *b* 17 Jan 1926; *Educ* Queen's Coll London, Newnham Cambridge; *m* 1951 (m dis 1965), Graham, s of George Parish, of The Manor House, Cossington, Somerset; 1 da; *Style* - The Hon Mrs Monica Parish; 71 Prince's House, Kensington Park rd, W11

PARISH, Robert James; CMG (1980), OBE (1975); s of L R Parish; *b* 7 May 1916; *Educ* Melbourne C of E G S; *m* 1939, Nannette I, da of E L Lewis; 2 s, 1 da; *Career* chm Australian Cricket Bd 1975-, memb 1957-; man Macmillan Bloedel Pty Ltd Melbourne 1969-; *Style* - Robert Parish Esq, CMG, OBE; 1 Lawrenny Ct, Toorak, Victoria 3142, Australia

PARK, Andrew Edward Wilson; QC; s of late Dennis Edward Park; *b* 27 Jan 1939; *Educ* Leeds G S, Univ Coll Oxford; *m* 1962, Ann Margaret Woodhead; 2 s, 1 da (and 1 s decd); *Career* barr Lincoln's Inn 1964, practice at Revenue Bar 1965-, QC 1978; *Style* - Andrew Park Esq, QC; Blandford Cottage, Weston Green rd, Thames Ditton, Surrey (☎ 01 398 5349)

PARK, Hon Mrs (Christine Coleman); da of Baron Cohen of Brighton (Life Peer, d 1966); *b* 1942; *m* 1965, David Maxwell Park, MRCP; *Style* - The Hon Mrs Park

PARK, Daphne Margaret Sybil Desiree; CMG (1971), OBE (1960); *b* 1 Sept 1921; *Educ* Rosa Bassett Sch, Somerville Coll Oxford; *Career* HM Diplomatic Service; Consul-Gen Hanoi 1969-70; temp Chargé d'Affaires Ulan Bator Apr-June 1972; FCO 1973-79, ret; *Style* - Miss Daphne Park, CMG, OBE; c/o National Westminster Bank, 121 High st, Oxford

PARK, George Maclean; JP, MP (L) Coventry North East Feb 1974-; s of James McKenzie Park; *b* 27 Sept 1914; *Educ* Onslow Drive Sch Glasgow; Coventry Tech Coll; *m* 1941, Joyce, da of Robert Holt Stead; 1 da; *Career* PPS to Dr J Gilbert Min for Transport 1975-76; PPS to Sec of State for Industry 1976-79; chm W Midland Gp Labour MPs; JP Coventry 1961; *Style* - George Park Esq, JP, MP; 170 Binley rd, Coventry CV3 1HG (☎ Coventry 458589)

PARK, Hon Mr Justice - Hon Sir Hugh (Eames); s of late William Robert Park; *b* 24 April 1910; *Educ* Blundell's; Sidney

Sussex Cambridge (Hon Fell 1968); *m* 1938, Beryl Josephine, da of late Joseph Coombe; 3 da; *Career* barr Middle Temple 1936, QC 1960, Bencher 1965, Presiding Judge Western Circuit 1970-75, Judge of the High Court of Justice Queen's Bench Division 1973- (Family Div 1965-73); kt 1965; *Style* - The Hon Mr Justice Park; Royal Courts of Justice, Strand, WC2; 34 Ordnance Hill, St John's Wood, NW8 (☎ 01 586 0417); Gorran Haven, Cornwall (☎ Mevagissey 2333)

PARK, Ian Grahame; JP; s of William Park; *b* 15 May 1935; *Educ* Lancaster Roy G S, Queens' Cambridge; *m* 1965, Anne Turner; 1 s; *Career* md and ed-in-chief Liverpool Daily Post and Echo Ltd 1972-; JP Liverpool 1975; *Style* - Ian Park Esq, JP; Church Cottage, Green Lane, Formby, Liverpool

PARK, Hon Mrs (Joanna MacAlister); JP (Warwicks); da of Baron Baker, OBE (Life Peer); *b* 1933; *m* 1962, Dr David Park; *Style* - The Hon Mrs Park JP; 42 Leam ter, Leamington Spa, Warwicks

PARK, Merle Florence (Mrs Sidney Bloch); CBE (1974); da of P J Park, of Eastlea, Salisbury, Zimbabwe; *b* 8 Oct 1937; *Educ* Elmhurst Ballet Sch; *m* 1, 1965 (m dis 1970), James Monahan; 1 s; m 2, 1971, Sidney Bloch; *Career* joined Sadler's Wells Ballet 1955, Principal Royal Ballet, founded Ballet Sch St Peter's sq W6, 1977; *Style* - Mrs Sidney Bloch, CBE; Chiswick Mall, W4

PARKER, Anthony; OBE (1972); s of Albert Sydney Parker; *b* 3 Oct 1929; *Educ* Sutton G S; *m* 1955, Jean Betty Mary, nee Ede; 1 da; *Career* banker Bank of England 1949-73, dir Foreign Exchange Dept Bank of Uganda 1965-66, controller Foreign Exchange Bermuda 1968-71, md Bermuda Monetary Authority 1969-71, dir West of England Trust Ltd 1976-81, dir Globe Financial Services Ltd 1981-; *Recreations* walking, music, reading, writing; *Style* - Anthony Parker Esq, OBE; Beckwood, Dolphin Close, Haslemere, Surrey (☎ 0428 2973)

PARKER, Hon Mrs (Audrey Joan); *née* Vernon; da of 5 Baron Lyveden (d 1973); *b* 1922; *m* 1940, Russell Parker; 3 s, 1 da; *Style* - The Hon Mrs Parker

PARKER, Christopher William Oxley; JP (Essex 1952), DL (Essex 1972); s of Lt-Col John Oxley Parker (d 1979); *b* 28 May 1920; *Educ* Eton, Trin Oxford; *m* 1947, Jocelyn Frances Adeline, da of Col C G Arkwright MC (d 1980); 1 s, 2 da; *Career* served World War II with 147 Field Regt (Essex Yeo) RA 1939-42; dir: Barclays Bank (Chelmsford Local Bd) 1950-81, Strutt and Parker (Farms) Ltd, Lord Rayleighs Farms Inc, dir Lavenham Fen Farms Ltd, High Sheriff 1961; *Recreations* shooting, golf; *Clubs* Boodle's, MCC; *Style* - Christopher Parker Esq JP DL; Faulkbourne Hall, Witham, Essex (☎ Witham 513385)

PARKER, Rear-Adm Douglas Granger; CB (1971), DSO (1945), DSC (1945), AFC (1952); s of R K Parker; *b* 21 Nov 1919; *Educ* W Hartlepool Tech Coll; *m* 1953, Margaret Susan, da of late Col W Cooper; 1 s, 1 da; *Career* joined RN 1940, Capt 1959, Rear-Adm 1969; Assist Ch of Naval Staff (Operations & Air) 1969-71, retired; *Style* - Rear-Admiral Douglas Parker CB DSO DSC AFC; High Meadow, Walhampton, Lymington, Hants (☎ Lymington 3259)

PARKER, Hon David Jonathan Geoffrey; s of 8 Earl of Macclesfield; *b* 1945; *m* 1968, Lynne Valerie, da of George Butler; 1 s, 2 da; *Style* - The Hon David Parker

PARKER, Sir Douglas William Leigh; OBE (1954); s of W Parker; *b* 12 July 1900; *Educ* Sydney U, Liverpool U; MB, ChM, FRCSEd, MChOrth, FRACS; *m* 1933, Hilary, da of S Secretan; 2 s, 1 da; *Career* formerly Dir of Orthopaedic Services, Tasmanian Govt Health Dept, ret 1966 ; kt 1966; OStJ; *Style* - Sir Douglas Parker, OBE; 30 Fisher ave, Lower Sandy Bay, Hobart, Tasmania, Australia

PARKER, Eric Wilson; s of Wilson Parker; *b* 8 June 1933; *Educ* Priory Sch Shrewsbury; *m* 1954, Marlene Teresa, da of Michael Neale (d 1941); 2 s, 2 da; *Career* Sgt Pay Corps Cyprus; group md Trafalgar House Ltd; dir Sealink UK Ltd; FICA; *Style* - Eric Parker Esq; Thresholds, The Drive, Tyrrells Wood, nr Leatherhead (☎ Surrey)

PARKER, Geoffrey; CB (1966); *b* 17 Jan 1917; *Educ* Hulme G S Oldham; New Coll and Queen's Coll, Oxford, Us of Berlin and Berne; *m* 1942, Janet Crawford Chidley; 2 s, 1 da; *Career* Under-Sec Dept of Trade and Industry, now Dept of Industry, 1970-76; *Style* - Geoffrey Parker Esq, CB; 5 Hove Court, Raymond rd, Wimbledon SW19 4AG (☎ 01 946 9300)

PARKER, Hugh; s of Ross Parker; *b* 12 June 1919; *Educ* Tabor Acad, Trin Hall Cambridge, Massachusetts Inst of Technology; *m* 1957, Elsa del Carmen Mijares Osorio; 1 s, 1 da; *Career* sr dir McKinsey & Co (UK); pres American Chamber of Commerce (UK) 1976; memb Council of Management, Oxford Centre for Management Studies; *Style* - Hugh Parker Esq; 9 Cheyne Walk, SW3 (☎ 01 352 9592)

PARKER, Iain George McKim; s of Ernest Parker, of Harrogate (d 1971); *b* 29 Dec 1937; *Educ* Ashville Coll Harrogate, Emmanuel Cambridge; *m* 1964, Judith Taylor; 1 s, 1 da; *Career* Lt IPWO Nat Service; chm: Otter Controls Ltd, Montgomery Thermostats Ltd, St Davids Assemblies Ltd, Tarka Controls Ltd, dir Otter Controls (NZ) 1967 Ltd; *Recreations* mountain walking, photography, orchids; *Clubs* Oxford & Cambridge; *Style* - Iain Parker Esq; Cherry Trees, Chapel En Le Frith, Via Stockport, SK12 6UP

PARKER, John; CBE (1965), MP (L) Barking, Dagenham, 1974-; s of Capt H A M Parker; *b* 15 July 1906; *Educ* Marlborough, St John's Oxford; *m* 1943, Zena Mimardiere; 1 s; *Career* MP (L) Romford Essex 1935-45, Dagenham 1945-74; pres Fabian Soc 1980-; Govr LSE 1949-; Father of the House of Commons 1979-, Hon Sec Webb Trustees; *Style* - John Parker Esq, CBE, MP; 4 Essex Court, Temple, EC4 (☎ 01 353 8521)

PARKER, Sir John (Edward); s of late Matthew Parker; *b* 28 Sept 1904; *Educ* Wesley Coll, Melbourne, Queen's Coll, Melbourne U; *m* 1932, Winifred Mary Becher; 2 s, 1 da; *Career* BCEng, FIEAust; dep dir Works, Public Works Dept Perth WA 1953-62, dir Engrg PWD Perth WA 1962-69, chm State Electricity Cmmn of WA 1969-74; kt 1975; *Style* - Sir John Parker; 11 Hopetoun st, South Perth, WA 6151, Australia (☎ Perth 67 1272)

PARKER, Vice-Adm Sir (Wilfred) John; KBE (1969, OBE 1953), CB (1965), DSC (1943); s of Henry Edmond Parker; *b* 12 Oct 1915; *Educ* RNC Dartmouth; *m* 1943, Marjorie Stuart Jones; 2 da; *Career* Flag Officer Medway and Adm Supt HM Dockyard Chatham 1966-69, ret 1969; chm Seven Seas Dredging 1974-; *Style* - Vice-Admiral Sir John Parker, KBE, CB, DSC; Nyewood Oaks, Rogate, Petersfield, Hants

PARKER, Jonathan Frederic; QC; s of late Sir Edmund Parker; *b* 8 Dec 1937; *Educ* Winchester, Magdalene Cambridge; *m* 1967, Maria-Belen Burns; 3 s, 1 da; *Career* barr Inner Temple 1962; QC 1979; *Clubs* Garrick; *Style* - Jonathan Parker Esq, QC; The Grange, Radwinter, Saffron Walden, Essex (☎ Radwinter 375); 11 Old sq, Lincoln's Inn WC2A 3TS (☎ 01 405 5243)

PARKER, Hon Jocelyn George Dudley; s of 7 Earl of Macclesfield (d 1975); *b* 1920; *m* 1948, Daphne, da of late Maj G Cecil Whitaker, of Britwell House, Watlington, Oxon; 1 s, 1 da; *Career* European War 1939-45 as Lt RNVR; *Style* - The Hon Jocelyn Parker; Pyrton Field Farm, Watlington, Oxon

PARKER, James Roland Walter; CMG (1978), OBE (1968); s of late Alexander Roland Parker, ISM; *b* 20 Dec 1919; *m* 1941, Deirdre Mary Ward; *Career* HM Diplomatic Serv: Govr and Cdr-in-Chief Falkland Islands and Dependencies, and High Cmmr British Antarctic Territory 1977-80, ret; *Style* - James Parker Esq, CMG, OBE; 1 St Edmund's Court, NW8

PARKER, Sir Karl (Theodore); CBE (1954); s of late Robert William Parker, FRCS; *b* 1895; *Educ* Bedford, Paris, Zurich; MA, PhD, FBA; *m* Audrey (d 1976), da of Henry Ashworth James; 2 da;

Career Keeper of Ashmolean Museum Oxford U, ret 1962; a Trustee of Nat Gallery 1962-69, Hon Fell Oriel Coll Oxford 1962; kt 1960; *Style* - Sir Karl Parker, CBE; 4 Saffrons Court, Compton Place rd, Eastbourne

PARKER, Hon Kathrine Anne; twin da of Viscount Parker; *b* 1973; *Style* - The Hon Kathrine Parker

PARKER, Kenneth Alfred Lamport; CB (1959); s of A E A Parker; *b* 1 April 1912; *Educ* Tottenham G S and St John's Cambridge; *m* 1938, Freda Silcock, OBE; 1 s, 1 da; *Career* Receiver for the Metropolitan Police District 1967-74; *Style* - Kenneth Parker Esq, CB; 18 Lichfield rd, Kew, Surrey (☎ 01 940 4595)

PARKER OF WADDINGTON, Baroness - Loryn; da of Oscar Tilton Bowser, of Kentucky, USA; *Educ* 1924, Hon Sir Herbert Lister Parker, PC, later Baron Parker of Waddington (Life Peer 1958, d 1972); *Style* - The Rt Hon the Lady Parker of Waddington; 20 Dunraven st, W1

PARKER, Laurence Edmond Hyde; s of Laurence Hyde Parker (5 s of 9 Bt) (d 1950); hp to Baronetcy of kinsman, Sir Richard Parker, 12 Bt; *b* 24 Feb 1912; *m* 1953, Margarethe Van Thorne; 2 s, 1 da; *Career* late Fl Lt RAFVR 1939-45 War; *Style* - Laurence Parker Esq; Smeetham Hall, Bulmer, Sudbury, Suffolk

PARKER, Cdr (John) Michael (Avison); CVO (1957, MVO 1953); s of late Capt C A Parker, CBE; *b* 23 June 1920; *Educ* Xavier Coll, Melbourne; *m* 1, 1943 (m dis 1958), Eileen Margaret Anne, nee Allan; 1 s, 1 da; m 2, 1962 (m dis, she d 1977), Carol, da of Sir Ivo Thomson, 2 Bt; 1 s, 1 da; m 3, 1976, Mrs Jean Ramsay; *Career* RN (ret); chm Mann's Transport, In-Situ Mining Consultants, Treglor Pty Ltd; dir Leo Burnett-Australia; *Style* - Cdr Michael Parker, CVO; Santosa, 33 Albany rd, Toorak, Victoria 3142, Australia

PARKER, Dame Marjorie Alice Collett; DBE (1977); da of W Shoppee, of Ballarat; *Educ* Ballarat State Sch; *m* 1926, Max Parker; 1 s; *Career* welfare worker Tasmania; dep-chm Australian Nat Council of Women 1960-64, life-memb 1974-; *Style* - Dame Marjorie Parker, DBE; Apsley, 5 Croydon Grove, Cypress st, Launceston, Tasmania 7250, Australia

PARKER, His Honour Judge - Michael Clynes; QC; s of Herbert Parker; *b* 2 Nov 1924; *Educ* City of London Sch and Pembroke Cambridge; *m* 1950, Molly Leila Franklin; 1 s, 2 da; *Career* barr, Gray's Inn, 1949, QC 1973, a Recorder of the Crown Court 1972-78, a Circuit Judge 1978-; contested (L) S Kensington, 1951; *Style* - His Hon Judge Parker QC; 17 Courtnell st, W2 (☎ 01 229 5249)

PARKER, Hon Marian Jane; twin da of Viscount Parker; *b* 1973; *Style* - The Hon Marian Parker

PARKER, Hon Mrs (Marjory Katharine Elizabeth Alexandra); *née* St Aubyn; da of 2 Baron St Levan (d 1940); *b* 1893; *m* 1919, Hon John Holford Parker (d 1955); 3 s (*see* Earl of Morley); *Style* - The Hon Mrs Parker; Saltram, Plympton, Plymouth, Devon

PARKER, Hon Nigel Geoffrey; s of late Hon John Holford Parker and bro of 6 Earl of Morley; *b* 1931; *Educ* Eton and Trin Cambridge; *m* 1965, Georgina Jane, da of Sir Thomas Gordon Devitt, 2 Bt; 1 s, 1 da; *Career* late Grenadier Gds; with Shell Petroleum Co Ltd; *Style* - The Hon Nigel Parker; Combe Lane Farm, Wormley, Godalming, Surrey

PARKER, Sir Peter; MVO (1957); s of late Tom Parker; *b* 30 Aug 1924; *Educ* Bedford Sch, London U and Lincoln Coll Oxford; *m* 1951, Gillian Rowe-Dutton, da of late Sir Ernest Rowe-Dutton, KCMG, CB; 3 s, 1 da; *Career* Maj Intelligence Corps 1943-47; contested (L) Bedford 1951; chm British Rail Bd 1976-, memb British Airways Bd 1971-; kt 1978; *Style* - Sir Peter Parker, MVO; British Railways Board, Rail House, Euston sq, NW1 12Z; 222 Marylebone rd, NW1 (☎ 01 262 3232)

PARKER, Hon Mr Justice - Hon Sir Roger (Jocelyn); s of Capt Hon T T

Parker, DSC, RN (ret) (d 1975); *b* 25 Feb 1923; *Educ* Eton and King's Cambridge; *m* 1948, Ann Elizabeth Frederika, nee White; 1 s, 3 da; *Career* barr Lincoln's Inn 1948, QC 1961, Bencher 1969; a Judge of the High Court, Queen's Bench Div, 1977-, Judge of the Courts of Appeal, Jersey and Guernsey, 1974-; kt 1977; *Style* - The Hon Mr Justice Parker; The Old Rectory, Widford, nr Ware, Herts (☎ Much Hadham 2593)

PARKER, Sir Richard (William) Hyde; 12 Bt (E 1681); s of Sir William Stephen Hyde Parker, 11 Bt (d 1951); *b* 5 April 1937; *Educ* Millfield and Roy Agricultural Coll Cirencester; *m* 1972, Jean, da of late Sir Lindores Leslie, 9 Bt; 3 da; *Heir* kinsman, Laurence Edmond Hyde Parker; *Style* - Sir Richard Parker, Bt; Melford Hall, Long Melford, Suffolk

PARKER, Hon Robin Michael; s of late Hon John Holford Parker and bro of 6 Earl of Morley; *b* 1925; *Educ* Eton; *Career* Col KRCC; Palestine 1946-48 (despatches) cmdg 2 Bn R Green Jackets 1967-69; final rank Brigadier; ret 1980; raised to the rank of an Earl's son 1963; *Style* - The Hon Robin Parker; Saltram, Plympton, Devon

PARKER, Viscount; Richard Timothy George Parker; s and h of 8 Earl of Macclesfield; *b* 31 May 1943; *Educ* Stowe and Worcester Coll Oxford; *m* 1967, Tatiana Cleone, da of Maj Craig Wheaton-Smith; 3 da; *Style* - Viscount Parker; Portobello Farm, Shirburn, Watlington, Oxon

PARKER, Rear-Adm Robert William; CBE (1954), JP; s of Col W F Parker; *b* 1902; *Educ* RN Colls Osborne and Dartmouth; *m* 1935, Noemi Vyvian, da of C V Espeut; *Career* Rear-Adm (E) 1952; dep Engineer-in-Chief of the Fleet 1935-55, ret 1955; JP Somerset 1961; *Style* - Rear-Admiral Robert Parker, CBE, JP; The Hermitage, Freshford, nr Bath, Avon (☎ Limpley Stoke 3220)

PARKER, Ronald William; CBE (1959), JP; s of late Ernest Edward Parker, MBE; *b* 21 Aug 1909; *Educ* Royal H S Edinburgh; *m* 1937, Phyllis Mary, nee Sherren; 2 s; *Career* CA 1933; regional chm Scottish Region, Nat Coal Bd, 1967-68; chm Scottish Gas Region (formerly Scottish Gas Bd) 1968-74; JP City and County of Edinburgh 1972; *Style* - Ronald Parker Esq, CBE, JP; Claremont, 3 South Lauder rd, Edinburgh EH9 2LL (☎ 031 667 7666)

PARKER, Timothy James; s of Malcolm Topsfield Parker (d 1978); *b* 28 Oct 1942; *Educ* London Coll of Printing, Bath U; *m* 1970, (m dis 1980), Patricia May, da of John Percy Robert Smith, of Dartmouth; 2 da; *Career* dir Capper Neill PLC 1976, Aqua Logistics (Int), British Ropeway Engrg, Capper Injection Moulding, Capper Neill Controls, Capper Neill Plastics, Capper Neill Plastic Fabrications, Capper Neill (Refrigeration Services), Custom Coils, Glover Bros (Mossley), Paterson Hughes Engrg, UDEC Refrigeration 1979, Allied Nuclear Inc 1980; *Recreations* squash, skiing, sailing, theatre; *Clubs* Roy Automobile, St James', Aston Martin Owners'; *Style* - Timothy Parker Esq; Keepers Cottage, Antrobus, Cheshire CW9 6JZ (☎ Arley 304)

PARKER, Thomas John; s of Robert Parker (d 1957); *b* 8 April 1942; *Educ* Newcastle, Belfast Coll of Technology (CEng, FRINA, FIMarEng); *m* 1967, Emma Elizabeth, da of Alexander Blair, of Ballymena, N Ireland; 1 s, 1 da; *Career* shipbuilder and engineer; md Austin & Pickersgill (Shipbuilders), Sunderland 1974-78, bd memb for shipbuilding British Shipbuilders Corpn 1978-80, dep ch exec British Shipbuilders Corpn 1980; *Recreations* reading, walking in the countryside, motoring; *Style* - Thomas Parker Esq; Inglefield, Sunniside ter, Cleadon Village, Sunderland, Tyne and Wear

PARKER, Hon Tanya Susan; da of Viscount Parker; *b* 1971

PARKER, Lady Venetia Katherine; da of 6 Earl of Morley; *b* 1960; *Style* - Lady Venetia Parker

PARKER, Sir William Alan; 4 Bt (UK 1844); s of Sir William Lorenzo Parker, 3 Bt, OBE (d 1971); *b* 20 March 1916; *Educ* Eton, New Coll Oxford; *m* 1946,

Sheelagh Mary, da of late Dr Sinclair Stevenson; 1 s, 1 da; *Heir* s, William Peter Brian Parker; *Career* served World War II, RE (Capt), Middle East 1941-45; *Style* - Sir William Parker, Bt; Apricot Hall, Sutton-cum-Beckingham, Lincoln (☎ Fenton Claypole 322)

PARKER, William Peter Brian; s and h of Sir William Alan Parker, 4 Bt; *b* 30 Nov 1950; *Educ* Eton; *m* 1976, Patricia Ann, da of R Filtness; 1 da; *Career* ACA; *Style* - William Parker Esq; The Cottage, Kirklington rd, Hockerton, Southwell (☎ Notts)

PARKER BOWLES, Dame Ann; DCVO (1977), CBE (1972); da of Sir Humphrey de Trafford, 4 Bt, MC (d 1971); *b* 14 July 1918; *m* 1939, Derek Henry Parker-Bowles (d 1977); 3 s, 1 da; *Career* County Cmmr Girl Guides (Berkshire) 1959-64; Dep Ch Cmmr Girl Guides 1962-66; Ch Cmmr 1966-75; *Style* - Dame Ann Parker Bowles, DCVO, CBE; Forty Hill, Highclere, Newbury, Berks (☎ Highclere 253735)

PARKES, Sir Alan (Sterling); CBE (1956), FRS (1933), MA, PhD, DSc, ScD; s of E T Parkes, of Purley; *b* 1900; *Educ* Willaston Sch; Christ's Cambridge, Manchester U, Univ Coll London; *m* 1933, Ruth, da of Edward Deanesly, FRCS; 1 s, 2 da; *Career* Fell Christ's Coll Cambridge 1961-69, Hon Fell 1970; Fell UCL; chm Galton Foundation 1969-; kt 1968; *Style* - Sir Alan Parkes, CBE; 1 The Bramleys, Shepreth, Royston, Herts SG8 6PY

PARKES, Sir Basil (Arthur); OBE (1966), JP; s of late Sir Fred Parkes; *b* 20 Feb 1907; *Educ* Boston G S, Lincs; *m* 1933, May Lewis McNeill; 2 s, 1 da; *Career* chm Boston Deep Sea Fisheries Ltd 1962-, Belgian Consul in Humberside 1974-, pres United Towing Ltd 1960-; JP Hull 1966; kt 1971; *Style* - Sir Basil Parkes OBE JP; Loghan-y-Yuiy, The Garey, Lezayre, Isle of Man

PARKES, Francis Patrick; s of Alfred Herbert Parkes (d 1978); *b* 26 March 1932; *Educ* Bryanston, Aiglon Coll Switzerland; *m* June, da of James Alfred Coltas (d 1976); 1 s, 1 da; *Career* md Don International (formerly Small and Parkes Ltd) 1965-70, dir Cape Industries 1970-; *Recreations* travel, gardening; *Style* - Francis Parkes Esq; Cherry Trees, Lane End, nr Reading, Berks (☎ Kidmore End 3416)

PARKES, Geoffrey; CMG (1947); s of late Harry Clement Parkes, JP; *b* 24 April 1902; *Educ* Clifton Coll; L'Institut Technique, Roubaix; *m* 1925, Marjorie Syddall (d 1976); *Career* dep chm Nat Westminster Bank Ltd, North Region, 1969-72; JP Manchester 1949-65; *Style* - Geoffrey Parkes Esq, CMG; Berth-y-Coed, Colwyn Bay, N Wales (☎ Colwyn Bay 30377)

PARKES, John Hubert; s of Frank Hubert Parkes; *b* 1 Oct 1930; *Educ* George Dixon Sch Birmingham, Magdalen, Oxford; *m* 1956, Elsie Griffiths Henderson; 2 s; *Career* Permanent Sec Dept of Education N Ireland 1979-; *Style* - John Parkes Esq; c/o Dept of Education, Rathgael House, Balloo rd, Bangor, Co Down, N Ireland

PARKES, Norman James; CBE (1976, OBE 1960); s of Ernest William Parkes; *b* 29 July 1912; *Educ* Victorian State Schs; *m* 1937, Maida Cleave, da of James Nicholas Silk; 2 s; *Career* Clerk of the Australian House of Representatives 1971-76; *Style* - Norman Parkes Esq, CBE; 3/3 Nuyts st, Red Hill, Canberra, ACT 2603, Australia

PARKINSON, Cecil Edward; MP (C) Hertfordshire South, 1974-; s of Sidney Parkinson, of Carnforth, Lancs; *b* 1 Sept 1931; *Educ* Roy Lancaster G S, Emmanuel Cambridge; *m* 1957, Ann Mary, da of F A Jarvis, of Harpenden Herts; 3 da; *Career* founded Parkinson Hart Securities Ltd 1967; MP (C) Enfield West Nov 1970-74; Min of State Dept of Trade 1979-; chm Anglo-Swiss Parly Gp; *Style* - Cecil Parkinson Esq, MP; The Old Vicarage, Northaw, Potters Bar, Herts

PARKINSON, Cyril Northcote; MA, PhD, FRHistS; s of late W Edward Parkinson, ARCA; *b* 30 July 1909; *Educ* St Peter's Sch York, Emmanuel Cambridge

(Fell 1935) and King's Coll, London; *m* 1, 1943 (m dis) Ethelwyn Edith Graves; 1 s, 1 da; m 2, 1952, Elizabeth Ann Fry; 2 s, 1 da; *Career* author, historian and journalist; Seigneur of Anneville, Mauxmarquis and Beavoir; Professor Emeritus Troy State U Alabama, 1970-; chm Leviathan House (Publishers) 1972-; *Style* - Cyril Parkinson Esq; 18 Hauteville, St Peter Port, Guernsey, CI

PARKINSON, Desmond Frederick; CMG (1975); s of Lt-Col Percy Willoughby Parkinson (d 1941); *b* 26 Oct 1920; *Educ* Winchester Coll and RMC Sandhurst; *m* 1, 1947 (m dis 1957), Ann Deborah Durnford; 2 s, 1 da; m 2, 1970, Heather Marguerite, da of Brig Ivor Douglas-Brown, OBE; 1 da; m 3, 1977, Patricia Jean Campbell Taylor; *Career* HM Diplomatic Serv (ret); FCO 1967-78; *Style* - Desmond Parkinson Esq, CMG; Woodrow, Silchester, Nr Reading (☎ Reading 700257)

PARKINSON, Dr David Hardress; s of E R H Parkinson; *b* 9 March 1918; *Educ* Gravesend County G S, Wadham Oxford; FInstP; *m* 1, 1944, Muriel Gwendoline Patricia (d 1971), da of Capt P W Newenham; 2 s; m 2, 1974 (m dis 1978) Daphne Margaret Scott-Gall; *Career* RA, 1939-45 (Major); Dir-Gen Establishments Resources and Programmes (A) MOD 1973-77; *Style* - Dr David Parkinson; South Bank, 47 Abbey rd, Great Malvern, Worcs WR14 3HH (☎ Malvern 5423)

PARKINSON, Lady Elizabeth Mary; *née* Murray; da of 10 Earl of Dunmore; *b* 1951; *m* 1973, John Michael Parkinson; 1 s, 2 da; *Style* - Lady Elizabeth Parkinson; RD Tasman Highway, Cambridge, Hobart, Tasmania 7170, Australia

PARKINSON, His Excellency Sir Nicholas; s of late Rev C T Parkinson; *b* 5 Dec 1925; *Educ* Sydney U; *m* 1952, Roslyn, da of late A D Campbell; 2 da; *Career* RAAF 1943-46; Sec Dept of Foreign Affairs Canberra 1977-79, Ambass for Australia to the US 1979-; kt 1980; *Style* - His Excellency Sir Nicholas Parkinson; c/o Dept of Foreign Affairs, Canberra, ACT 2600, Australia

PARKINSON, Norman; CBE (1980); *b* 21 April 1913; *Educ* Westminster; *m* 1945, Wenda, nee Rogerson; 1 s; *Career* photographer; *Style* - Norman Parkinson Esq, CBE; Tobago, W Indies

PARKINSON, Thomas Harry; CBE (1972), DL; s of G R J Parkinson; *b* 25 June 1907; *Educ* Bromsgrove and Birmingham U; *m* 1936, Joan Catherine, da of C J Douglas-Osborn; 2 s, 1 da; *Career* admitted slr 1930; RAF 1939-45; Town Clerk 1960-72, Clerk of the Peace 1970-72 Birmingham; DL (Warwickshire) 1970; Hon DSc Aston 1972; *Style* - Thomas Parkinson Esq, CBE, DL; Stuart House, Middlefield Lane, Hagley, Worcs (☎ Hagley 2422)

PARKS, Sir Alan (Guyatt); MD, FRCS, FRCP, PRCS; s of Harry Parks; *b* 19 Dec 1920; *Educ* Epsom Coll, Brasenose Oxford, Johns Hopkins U Med Sch, Guy's Hosp Med Sch; *m* 1956, Caroline Jean Cranston; 3 s, 1 da; *Career* Capt RAMC, 1950-52; Consultant Surgeon to the London Hosp and St Mark's Hosp 1959-, Hon Consultant in Colon and Rectal Surgery to the Army 1974-; Hunterian Prof RCS 1965, memb council RCS 1971- (vice pres 1979-); kt 1977; *Style* - Sir Alan Parks; 33 Alwyne rd, N1 2HW (☎ 01 226 8045)

PARMOOR, 4 Baron (UK 1914); (Frederick Alfred) Milo Cripps; s of 3 Baron Parmoor, DSO, TD, DL (d 1977) and of Violet Mary Geraldine, da of Sir William Nelson, 1 Bt; *b* 18 June 1929; *Educ* Ampleforth and Corpus Christi Oxford; *Heir* cous, (Matthew) Anthony Leonard Cripps, *qv*; *Style* - The Rt Hon the Lord Parmoor; Manor House, Sutton Veny, Wilts

PARNELL, Hon Elizabeth Dagny; da of 8 Baron Congleton; *b* 1960; *Style* - The Hon Elizabeth Parnell

PARNELL, Hon John Patrick Christian; s and h of 8 Baron Congleton; *b* 17 March 1959; *Style* - The Hon John Parnell

PARNELL, Hon Mrs Lionel - Marjorie Gore; da of William Millar; *m* 1899, Hon

Lionel Charles Nugent Parnell (d 1940); 1 s, 2 da; *Style* - The Hon Lionel Parnell

PARNELL, Hon Mary Clare; da of 8 Baron Congleton; *b* 1965; *Style* - The Hon Mary Parnell

PARNELL, Hon Thomas David Howard; s of 8 Baron Congleton; *b* 1963; *Style* - The Hon Thomas Parnell

PARNIS, Alexander Edward Libor; CBE (1973); s of Alexander T J Parnis; *b* 25 Aug 1911; *Educ* Malvern Coll and London U; *Career* Sec Church's Main Ctee 1973-81; *Style* - Alexander Parnis Esq, CBE; 26 Ardilaun rd, N5 2QR (☎ 01 226 2688)

PARR, Hon Mrs (Caroline Mary); *née* Renton; da of Baron Renton, KBE, TD, PC, QC, DL; *b* 22 Nov 1948; *m* 1, 1970 (m dis 1974), Peter Dodds Parker; m 2, 1977, Robin Parr; has 1 child by each marriage; *Style* - The Hon Mrs Parr; Port Mary House, Dundrennan, Kirkcudbright (☎ 05575 229)

PARR, Martin Willoughby; CBE (1944, OBE 1929); s of Rev Willoughby Chase Parr; *b* 22 Nov 1892; *Educ* Winchester and BNC Oxford; *Career* Govr Upper Nile 1934-36, Govr Equatoria 1936-42, ret 1942; Fndn Ctee Gordon Boys' Sch Woking; *Style* - Martin Parr Esq, CBE; 11 Edith rd, W14 (☎ 01 603 6729)

PARR, Stanley; CBE (1975), QPM (1968); s of Thomas W Parr; *b* 14 July 1917; *Educ* St Helens, Lancs; *m* 1943, Charlotte Lilian Wilson; 3 s; *Career* Ch Constable of Lancashire 1972-78; DL Lancs 1976-78; OStJ 1970; *Style* - Stanley Parr Esq, CBE, QPM

PARRIS, Matthew Francis; MP (C) West Derbyshire 1979-; s of Leslie Francis Parris; *b* 7 Aug 1949; *Educ* Waterford Sch Swaziland, Clare Cambridge, Yale USA; *Career* FO 1974-76; Con Research Dept 1976-79; *Style* - Matthew Parris Esq, MP; 41 Bramfield rd, SW11

PARROT, Hon Mrs (Deirdre Barbara Elland); *née* Lumley-Savile; da of late 2 Baron Savile, KCVO (who assumed by Roy Licence surname Savile after that of Lumley) by 2 w, Esmé, nee Wolton; *b* 1928; *m* 1948, Col Kent Kane Parrot, US Air Force (ret); 2 s, 1 da; *Style* - The Hon Mrs Parrot; 5506 Grove st, Chevy Chase, Maryland, USA

PARROTT, Sir Cecil (Cuthbert); KCMG (1964, CMG 1953), OBE (1947); s of Engr Capt Jasper W A Parrott, RN; *b* 29 Jan 1909; *Educ* Berkhamsted Sch and Peterhouse Cambridge (MA); *m* 1935, Ellen Julie, da of Hermann Matzow, of Trondhjem, Norway; 3 s; *Career* Prof Emeritus in Central and South-Eastern European Studies Lancaster U, Founder and Hon Pres Comenius Centre Lancaster U (Dir 1968-76); FRSL, Hon FIL 1968; *Style* - Sir Cecil Parrott, KCMG, OBE; c/o University of Lancaster, Bailrigg, Lancaster LA1 4YN

PARRY, Baron (Life Peer UK 1975); Gordon Samuel David Parry; s of Thomas Lewis Parry; *b* 30 Nov 1925; *Educ* Neyland Board Sch, Pembroke County Intermediate Sch, Trinity Coll Carmarthen, Liverpool U; *m* 1948, Glenys Catherine, da of Jack Leslie Incledon; 1 da; *Career* house master and librarian Co Secondary Sch Haverfordwest 1952-68, and warden of Pembrokeshire Teachers' Centre 1968-78; chm Wales Tourist Bd 1978-, memb British Tourist Authority, memb Council Open U 1978- (chm of Educn Advsy Ctee 1979-), pres of Spastic Soc Wales 1977-; *Style* - The Rt Hon the Lord Parry; Marlborough House, 164 Marlborough rd, Roath, Cardiff (☎ Cardiff 41397)

PARRY, Hon Mrs Anna Josephine; *née* Banbury; da of 2 Baron Banbury of Southam, DL (d 1981); *b* 1950; *m* 1970, Michael Parry (m dis 1981); *Style* - The Hon Mrs Anna Parry; 26 Gowan av, SW6

PARRY, Hon Catherine Anne; da of Baron Parry (Life Peer); *b* 1955; *Style* - The Hon Catherine Parry

PARRY, Emyr Owen; s of Ebenezer Owen Parry; *b* 26 May 1933; *Educ* Caernarfon G S; Univ Coll of Wales Aberystwyth; *m* 1959, Enid Griffiths; 1 s, 1 da; *Career* admitted slr 1957; Dep Circuit

Judge 1975; a Recorder of the Crown Court 1979-; chm Nat Insurance Appeals Tribunal Holyhead Area 1969-; slr memb Ld Chllr's County Ct Rule Ctee 1975; *Style* - Emyr Parry Esq; Bryn Meillion, Rhosmeirch, Llangefni, Anglesey, Gwynedd (☎ Llangefni 722469)

PARRY, Sir Hugh (Nigel); CBE (1954); s of Charles Frank Parry; *b* 26 Aug 1911; *Educ* Cheltenham Coll, Balliol Oxford; *m* 1945, Ann Maureen Forshaw; 2 da; *Career* entered Colonial Administrative Serv 1939, Miny of Overseas Devpt 1965, Acting Head Middle East Devpt Div 1969-71, ret 1971; kt 1963; *Style* - Sir Hugh Parry, CBE; c/o Grindlays Bank, 13 St James's Sq, SW1

PARRY, Prof John Horace; CMG (1960), MBE (1942); s of late Walter Austin Parry; *b* 26 April 1914; *Educ* King Edward's Sch Birmingham, Clare Cambridge (Fell, 1938) and Harvard U; *m* 1939, Joyce, da of Rev H C Carter; 1 s, 3 da; *Career* Prof of Oceanic History and Affairs Harvard U 1965-; *Style* - Professor John Parry, CMG, MBE; Widener 45, Cambridge, Mass 02138, USA

PARRY, Robert; MP (L) Liverpool, Scotland Exchange, 1974-; s of Robert Parry; *b* 8 Jan 1933; *Educ* Bishop Goss RC Sch Liverpool; *m* 1956, Marie, nee Hesdon; *Career* MP (L) Liverpool, Liverpool Exchange, 1970-74; chm Merseyside Gp of Labour MPs 1976-; *Style* - Robert Parry Esq, MP; House of Commons, SW1

PARRY, Mrs Raymond - Margaret Joan; da of W J Tamplin; *b* 27 Nov 1919; *Educ* Howell's Sch Llandaff; U of Wales; *m* 1946, Raymond Howard Parry; 2 s, 1 da; *Career* headmistress of Heathfield Sch Ascot 1973-; *Style* - Mrs Raymond Parry; 5 Gulliver's, Eton College, Windsor, Berks (☎ Windsor 60902)

PARRY, Sir Thomas; s of Richard Parry, of Carmel, Caernarvonshire; *b* 14 Aug 1904; *Educ* Pen-y-groes G S; Univ Coll of N Wales, Bangor (MA, DLitt Wales); *m* 1936, Enid, da of Picton Davies, of Cardiff; *Career* Vice-Chllr U of Wales 1961-63, 1967-69, Pres Nat Library of Wales 1969-77, Principal of the Univ Coll of Wales, Aberystwyth, 1958-69; Pres Hon Soc of Cymmrodorion 1978- (Cymmrodorion Medal 1976), Hon Professorial Fell Univ Coll of Wales 1971, Hon DLitt Celt NUI, Hon LLD Wales, FBA 1959; kt 1978; *Style* - Sir Thomas Parry; Gwyndy, 2 Victoria av, Bangor, Gwynedd (☎ Bangor 4460)

PARRY EVANS, Mary Alethea (Lady Hallinan); da of Dr Evan Parry Evans, MD, JP; *b* 31 Oct 1929; *Educ* Malvern Girls' Coll, Somerville Oxford; *m* 1955, Sir (Adrian) Lincoln Hallinan, *qv*; 2 s, 2 da; *Career* barr Inner Temple 1953, Wales and Chester Circuit, a Recorder of the Crown Court 1978-; memb S Glamorgan Health Authority 1977-, Lady Mayoress of Cardiff 1969-70; *Style* - Lady Hallinan; 63 Cathedral rd, Cardiff (☎ Cardiff 20511); (chambers) 33 Park Place, Cardiff (☎ Cardiff 33313)

PARRY-EVANS, Air Vice-Marshal David; CBE; *Career* RAF 1956, MOD 1977-81 (Air Cdre); Cmdt RAF Staff Coll Bracknell 1981-; *Style* - Air Vice-Marshal David Parry-Evans, CBE; 47 Pound Lane, Marlow, Bucks (☎ 3405)

PARSHALL, Horace Field; TD (1947); s of late Horace Field Parshall, DSc; *b* 16 June 1903; *Educ* Eton, New Coll Oxford; *m* 1, 1929 (m dis 1942), Hon Ursula Mary Bathurst, da of 1 Viscount Bledisloe; 1 s; m 2, 1953, Margaret Savage, MB, BS, DPH (d 1961), da of late Capt Philip Alcock, JP, DL; 1 s, 2 da; m 3, 1965, Lady (Phyllis Gabrielle) Gore, da of M von den Porten, of New York; *Career* barr Inner Temple; Chllr Venerable Order of St John of Jerusalem 1961-66, Receiver-Gen 1968-72; GCStJ 1960; *Style* - Horace Parshall Esq, TD; Flat 8, 51 Onslow sq, SW7 (☎ 01 589 3371)

PARSONS, Sir Anthony (Derrick); KCMG (1975, CMG 1969), MVO (1965), MC (1945); s of late Col H A J Parsons, MC; *b* 9 Sept 1922; *Educ* King's Sch Canterbury and Balliol Oxford; *m* 1948, Sheila Emily Baird; 2 s, 2 da; *Career* HM Diplomatic Serv; Ambass to Iran 1974-79, UK Perm Rep to the UN 1979-; *Style* - Sir Anthony Parsons, KCMG, MVO, MC; c/o Foreign and Commonwealth Office, SW1

PARSONS, Hon Mrs (Alice Esmeralda); *née* O'Neill; da of 2 Baron O'Neill (d 1928); *b* 1886; *m* 1909, John Randal Parsons (d 1967), s of Hon Richard Clere Parsons, 3 s of 3 Earl of Rosse; *Style* - The Hon Mrs Parsons; Little Gillions, Croxley Green, Herts

PARSONS, Andrew Peter Harold; s of Thomas Edward Thornborough Parsons (d 1950); *b* 30 July 1940; *Educ* Millfield (Army Staff Coll); *m* 1962, Rosemary Jane, da of Ralph Arthur Hubbard; 2 s, 1 da; *Career* Maj Scots Gds; *Clubs* Cavalry and Guards;*Style* - Major Andrew Parsons; Rectory Cottage, East Worldham, Alton, Hants (☎ Alton 82415)

PARSONS, Lady Alicia Siobhan Margaret Nasreen; da of 7 Earl of Rosse; *b* 1971; *Style* - Lady Alicia Parsons

PARSONS, Hon Desmond Oliver Martin; 2 s of 6 Earl of Rosse, KBE, and Anne, Countess of Rosse, *qv*; *b* 23 Dec 1938; *Educ* Eton, Aiglon Coll Switzerland; *m* 1965, Aline, da of Dr George Macdonald, of Rugby; 2 s; *Style* - The Hon Desmond Parsons; Womersley Park, Doncaster

PARSONS, Geoffrey Penwill; OBE (1977); s of Francis Hedley Parsons; *b* 15 June 1929; *Educ* Canterbury H S, Sydney and State Conservatorium of Music (with Winifred Burston), Sydney; *Career* concert accompanist; Harriet Cohen Int Music Award 1968; Hon RAM 1975; *Style* - Geoffrey Parsons Esq, OBE; 176 Iverson rd, NW6 2HL (☎ 01 624 0957)

PARSONS, Kenneth Charles; CMG (1970), OBE (1962); s of late W S Parsons, of Cardigan; *b* 9 Jan 1921; *Educ* Haverfordwest G S, Exeter Coll Oxford; *m* 1977, Mary Woolhouse; *Career* Oxfordshire and Buckinghamshire LI 1941-46; Counsellor HM Diplomatic Serv served FO Moscow, Tokyo, Rangoon and Athens 1951-72, FCO 1972-77, with HQ British Forces Hong Kong 1977-; *Style* - Kenneth Parsons Esq, CMG, OBE; Grove End, Lower Park rd, Chipstead, Surrey (☎ Downland 53907)

PARSONS, Sir (John) Michael; s of late Rt Rev Richard Godfrey Parsons, DD, Bishop of Hereford; *b* 29 Oct 1915; *Educ* Rossall Sch, Univ Coll Oxford; *m* 1, 1946 (m dis 1964), Hilda Mary Frewen; 1 s, 2 da; m 2, 1964, Caroline Inagh Margaret Frewen; *Career* dir Inchcape & Co Ltd 1971-, sr md 1976-, dep chm and ch exec 1979-; chm and dir Assam Investments 1976-, dir Commonwealth Development Finance Co Ltd 1973-; chm Council Royal Commonwealth Soc 1976-; kt 1970; *Style* - Sir Michael Parsons; 38 Barrie House, Lancaster Gate, W2 (☎ 01 262 4365); Tall Trees, Warren Hill Lane, Aldeburgh, Suffolk IP15 5QB (☎ Aldeburgh 2917)

PARSONS, Richard Edmund (Clement Fownes); CMG (1977); s of Dr R A Parsons; *b* 14 March 1928; *Educ* Bembridge Sch and Brasenose Oxford; *m* 1960, Jenifer Jane Mathews; 3 s; *Career* HM Diplomatic Serv, Ambass Hungary 1976-79, Ambass Spain 1979-; *Style* - Richard Parsons Esq, CMG; c/o Foreign and Commonwealth Office, King Charles st, SW1

PART, Sir Antony (Alexander); GCB (1974, KCB 1966, CB 1959), MBE (1943); s of late Alexander Francis Part; *b* 28 June 1916; *Educ* Wellesley House Broadstairs, Harrow, Trinity Cambridge; *m* 1940, Isabella Bennett; *Career* chm Orion Insurance Co; dir: Debenhams, EMI, Life Assoc of Scotland, Lucas Industries, Metal Box and Savoy Hotel Gp; Perm Sec MPBW 1965-68, BOT 1968-70, DTI 1970-74, DOI 1974-76; FBIM 1972; Hon DTech Brunel 1966, Hon DSc Aston 1974, Cranfield 1976; *Style* - Sir Antony Part, GCB, MBE; Flat 5, 71 Elm Park gdns, SW10 (☎ 01 352 2950)

PARTRIDGE, Sir (Ernest) John; KBE (1971); s of William Henry Partridge; *b* 18 July 1908; *Educ* Queen Elizabeth's Hosp Bristol; *m* 1, 1934, Madeline Fabian (d 1944); 1 s, 1 da; m 2, 1949, Joan Johnson, MBE; 1 s, 1 da; *Career* chm Imperial Group Ltd (formerly Imperial Tobacco Group Ltd) 1964-75; dir: Dunlop Holdings Ltd 1973-, Delta Metal Co Ltd 1973-; chm Educn Fndn CBI 1976-81 (pres CBI 1970-72); pres Fndn for Management Educn 1972-, and Nat

Council of Voluntary Orgs 1973-80; FBIM 1963, Hon LLD Bristol 1972, Hon DSc Cranfield Inst of Technology 1974; *Style* - Sir John Partridge, KBE; Wildwood, Haslemere, Surrey (☎ Haslemere 51002)

PASCO, Richard Edward; CBE (1977); s of Cecil George Pasco; *b* 18 July 1926; *Educ* Colet Court, King's Coll Sch Wimbledon; *m* 1 (m dis), Greta, nee Watson; 1 s; m 2, 1967, Barbara, nee Leigh-Hunt; *Career* actor; Associate Artist Royal Shakespeare Co; *Style* - Richard Pasco Esq, CBE; c/o M L Representation Ltd, 194 Old Brompton rd, SW5

PASLEY, John Malcolm Sabine; s and h of Sir Rodney Marshall Sabine Pasley, 4 Bt; *b* 5 April 1926; *Educ* Sherborne and Trin Oxford; *m* 1965, Virginia Killigrew, da of Peter Lothian Killigrew Wait, of Kew, Surrey; 2 s; *Career* fell Magdalen Coll Oxford; *Style* - John Pasley Esq; 25 Lathbury rd, Oxford

PASLEY, Sir Rodney Marshall Sabine; 4 Bt (GB 1794); s of late Capt Malcolm Sabine Pasley, RN (2 s of late Capt Thomas Malcolm Sabine Pasley, RN, eld s of 2 Bt); n of 3 Bt (d 1947); *b* 22 Feb 1899 (twin); *Educ* Sherborne, Univ Coll Oxford; *m* 1922, Aldyth Werge, da of late Maj Lancelot Cecil Bray Hamber; 1 s, 1 da; *Heir* s, John Malcolm Sabine Pasley; *Career* headmaster Central G S Birmingham 1943-59; *Style* - Sir Rodney Pasley, Bt; Hazel Cottage, Peaslake, Surrey

PASMORE, (Edwin John) Victor; CH (1980), CBE (1959); s of late E S Pasmore; *b* 3 Dec 1908; *Educ* Harrow and LCC Central Sch of Arts & Crafts; *m* 1940, Wendy Blood; 1 s, 1 da; *Career* artist; visiting teacher LCC Camberwell Sch of Art 1945-49, Central Sch of Arts and Crafts 1949-53, Master of Painting Durham U 1954-61, consultant urban and architectural designer SW area Peterlee New Town 1955-77; *Style* - Victor Pasmore Esq, CH, CBE; Dar Gamri, Gudja, Malta; 12 St Germans Place, Blackheath, SE3

PASTON BROWN, Dame Beryl; DBE (1967); da of Paston Charles Brown; *b* 7 March 1909; *Educ* Streatham Hill H S and Newnham Cambridge; *Career* Principal of City of Leicester Training Coll 1952-61, Principal Homerton Coll Cambridge 1961-71; chm Assoc of Teachers in Colleges and Depts of Educn 1965-66; *Style* - Dame Beryl Paston Brown, DBE; 21 Keere st, Lewes, E Sussex (☎ Lewes 3608)

PASTON-BEDINGFELD, Sir Edmund George Felix; 9 Bt (E 1660); s of Sir Henry Edward Paston-Bedingfeld, 8 Bt (d 1941); *b* 2 June 1915; *Educ* Oratory Sch, New Coll Oxford; *m* 1, 1942 (m dis 1953), Joan Lynette (d 1965), da of Edgar G Rees, of Llwyneithin, Llanelly; 1 s, 1 da; m 2, 1957, Agnes Danos (d 1974), da of late Miklos Gluck, of Budapest, Hungary; m 3, 1975, Mrs Peggy Hannaford-Hill, of Fort Victoria, Rhodesia (now Zimbabwe); *Heir* s, Henry Edgar Paston-Bedingfeld; *Career* co-heir to Barony of Grandison (abeyant since *temp* Edward III; Maj Welsh Gds; md Handley Walker (Europe) Ltd 1969-; *Recreations* ornithology, heraldry; *Style* - Sir Edmund Paston-Bedingfeld, Bt; Arundell House, Brettenham, Ipswich, Suffolk (☎ Rattlesden 607); Oxburgh Hall, King's Lynn, Norfolk

PASTON-BEDINGFELD, Henry Edgar; s (by 1 m) and h of Sir Edmund Paston-Bedingfeld, 9 Bt; *b* 7 Dec 1943; *Educ* Ampleforth; *m* 1968, Mary, da of late Brig Robert Denis Ambrose, CIE, OBE, MC; 2 s, 2 da; *Career* chartered surveyor; Kt of Sov Mil Order of Malta; v-pres Norfolk Heraldry Soc (chm 1975-80), memb Cncl Heraldry Soc 1976; *Clubs* Norfolk (Norwich); *Style* - Henry Paston-Bedingfeld Esq; Paston House, Litcham, King's Lynn, Norfolk

PASTON-BEDINGFELD, Dowager Lady; Sybil; da of late Henry Alexander Lyne Stephens; *m* 1904, Sir Henry Paston-Bedingfeld, 8 Bt (d 1941); *Style* - Dowager Lady Paston-Bedingfeld; Oxburgh Hall, King's Lynn, Norfolk

PATCH, Air Chief Marshal Sir Hubert Leonard; KCB (1957, CB 1952), CBE (1942); s of late Capt Leonard W Patch, RN (ret); *b* 16 Dec 1904; *Educ* Stonyhurst,

RAF Coll Cranwell Lincs; *m* 1960, Claude Renée, da of Maj Jean-Marie Botéculet (ka 1925); *Career* joined RAF 1925; Gp Capt 1946, Air Cdre 1947, Air Vice-Marshal 1951, Acting Air Marshal 1956, Air Marshal 1957, Air Ch Marshal 1959, ret 1961; rep of British Aircraft Corpn to the NATO countries 1961-63; *Style* - Air Chief Marshal Sir Hubert Patch, KCB, CBE; Loma de Rio Verde, Marbella, Spain; c/o Barclays Bank, Colchester, Essex

PATEL, Ambalal Bhailalbhai; CMG (1949); s of late Bhailalbhai Dharamdas Patel; *b* 1 May 1898; *Educ* Petlad H S, Baroda Coll, Bombay U; *m* Gangalaxmi Patel (decd); 4 s, 1 da; *Career* barr Lincoln's Inn 1923; memb E African Central Legislative Assembly 1948-52; Min without Portfolio Govt of Kenya 1954-56, ret; *Style* - Ambalal Patel Esq, CMG; c/o Sri Aurobindo Ashram, Pondicherry, via Madras, India

PATEMAN, Jack Edward; CBE (1970); s of William Edward Pateman; *b* 29 Nov 1921; *Educ* Gt Yarmouth G S; *m* 1949, Cicely Hope Turner; 1 s, 1 da; *Career* dir GEC Computers Ltd 1971-, chm 1978-, md Marconi Avionics Ltd 1971-, dir Canadian Marconi Co 1971-, Elliott Bros (London) Ltd 1979-; *Style* - Jack Pateman Esq, CBE; 20 Lyndhurst Drive, Sevenoaks, Kent (☎ Sevenoaks 54390)

PATER, John Edward; CB (1953); s of Edward Rhodes Pater; *b* 15 March 1911; *Educ* King Edward VI Sch Retford, Queens' Cambridge; *m* 1938, Margaret Anderson, da of M C Furtado; 2 s, 1 da; *Career* Under-Sec Miny of Health, and DHSS 1947-73 (ret); Govr Kingswood Sch; *Style* - John Pater Esq, CB; 22 Manor Way, South Croydon CR2 7BR (☎ 01 688 0349)

PATERSON, Dame Betty Fraser Ross; DBE (1981, CBE 1973), JP (1950), DL (Herts 1980); da of Robert Ross Russell (d 1934); *b* 14 March 1916; *Educ* Harrogate Coll, Western Infirmary Glasgow; *m* 1940, Ian Douglas Paterson; 1 s, 1 da; *Career* chm Herts CC 1969-73, memb Cmmn for the New Towns 1961-74 (dep chm 1970-74), chm NW Thames Regional Health Authority 1973-, chm Nat Staff Ctee (nurses and midwives) 1974-; *Recreations* music, cooking, foreign travel; *Style* - Dame Betty Paterson, DBE, JP, DL; Twyford Bury, Bishop's Stortford, Herts (☎ 53184)

PATERSON, Colin Walter; MC; *Career* dep chm and managing director British Home Stores Ltd; *Style* - Colin Paterson Esq, MC; British Home Stores Ltd, Marylebone House, 129-137 Marylebone Road, NW1

PATERSON, Sir Dennis Craig; s of Lt-Col Gilbert Charles Paterson (d 1962); *b* 14 Oct 1930; *Educ* Collegiate Sch of St Peter's Adelaide and Adelaide U; *m* 1955, Mary Mansell, da of Frederick Hardy; 1 s (Thomas), 3 da (Cecily, Mrs Mark Goedecke, Lucy); *Career* MB, BS; FRCS 1958, FRACS 1961, kt 1976, Queen's Silver Jubilee Medal 1977; Capt Australian Citizens Military Force; dir and chief orthopaedic surgn Adelaide Children's Hosp 1970-; consultant orthopaedic surgeon Queen Victoria Hospital 1968-, Regency Park Centre for Physically Handicapped Children Adelaide 1976-, Roy Adelaide Hosp Adelaide 1964-; pres Crippled Children's Association of South Australia 1970-; *Recreations* golf, tennis, gardening; *Clubs* Adelaide, Royal Adelaide Golf, Kooyong Golf; *Style* - Sir Dennis Paterson; 31 Myall Avenue, Kensington Gardens, Adelaide, South Australia 5068 (☎ 08 3323364)

PATERSON, Hon Mrs; Hon Fiona; da (by 1 m) of Baroness Sharples, *qv*; *b* 1949; *m* 1981, Alexander Paterson; *Style* - The Hon Mrs Paterson

PATERSON, His Honour Judge - Frank David; s of David Paterson, of Liverpool (d 1956); *b* 10 July 1918; *Educ* Quarry Bank H S Liverpool and Liverpool U (LLB); *m* 1953, Barbara Mary, da of Oswald Ward Gillow, of Formby, Lancashire (d 1949); 1 s (David), 2 da (Rachel Elizabeth, Angela Mary); *Career* barrister Gray's Inn 1941, Assistant Deputy Coroner Liverpool 1960-68, chm Ministry of Pensions and National Insurance Tribunal Liverpool 1957-68, chairman of Mental Health Review Tribunal for South-West Lancs and Cheshire 1963-68, Circuit Judge (formerly County Court Judge) 1968-; *Style* - His Honour Judge Paterson; Vailima, 2 West Lane, Formby, Liverpool L37 7BA (☎ Formby 74345)

PATERSON, Sir George (Mutlow); OBE (1946), QC; s of late Dr G W Paterson; *b* 3 Dec 1906; *Educ* Grenada Boys' Sch and St John's Cambridge; *m* 1935, Audrey Anita, da of late Maj C C B Morris, CBE, MC; 1 s, 2 da; *Career* barr Inner Temple 1933, QC (Sierra Leone) 1950; Attorney-Gen Sierra Leone 1949, Ghana 1954-57; Ch Justice of N Rhodesia 1957-61, ret 1961; chm Industrial Tribunals 1965-79; kt 1959; *Style* - Sir George Paterson, OBE, QC; Buckshaw House, Sherborne, Dorset DT9 5LD (☎ Bishop's Caundle 318)

PATERSON, Sqdn Ldr Ian Veitch; CBE (1969), JP (Hamilton), DL (Lanarkshire 1963); s of Andrew Wilson Paterson; *b* 17 Aug 1911; *Educ* Lanark G S and Glasgow U; *m* 1940, Anne Weir, da of Thomas Brown; 2 s, 1 da; *Career* Dep Chm Local Govt Boundary Commission 1974-; *Style* - Squadron Leader Ian Paterson, CBE, JP, DL; 35 Stewarton Drive, Cambuslang, Glasgow

PATERSON, James Alexander; s of Col Alexander Thomas Paterson, DSO*, OBE (d 1955); *b* 6 Feb 1926; *Educ* Trin Coll Port Hope Ontario, Roy Canadian Naval Coll, McGill U Montreal, Balliol Oxford; *m* 1948, Rosalie Anne, da of Maj Charles Thomas Ballantyne, QC (d 1962); 1 s, 2 da; *Career* Cadet RCN (invalided from serv 1944); barr Lincoln's Inn; chm and ch exec RTZ Industries Ltd 1974-, main bd dir Rio Tinto-Zinc Corpn Ltd 1970-, founding chm (now non-exec dir) Indal Ltd Toronto, dir of other cos within RTZ Gp, memb Advsy Bd of Centre of Advanced Business Studies, U of Dalhousie Halifax NS; *Recreations* reading; *Clubs* City of London, Mount Royal, St James', Forest and Steam (Montreal), University (Toronto); *Style* - James Paterson Esq; Saraguay, Fifield, Milton under Wychwood, Oxon; 12 Kinnerton st, SW1

PATERSON, Prof James Ralston Kennedy; CBE (1949), MC (1917); s of Rev David Paterson; *b* 21 May 1897; *Educ* George Heriot's Sch Edinburgh and Edinburgh U; *m* 1930, Edith Isabel Myfanwy Irvine-Jones; 2 s, 1 da; *Career* Prof Emeritus of Radiotherapeutics Manchester U 1960-, dir of Radiotherapy Christie Hosp and Holt Radium Institute 1931-62; *Style* - Professor James Paterson, CBE, MC; Stenrieshill, Moffat, Scotland (☎ Johnstone Bridge 221)

PATERSON, James Veitch; s of John Robert Paterson; *b* 16 April 1928; *Educ* Peebles H S, Edinburgh Acad, Lincoln Coll Oxford, Edinburgh U; *m* 1956, Ailie, da of Lt-Cdr Sir (George) Ian Clark Hutchison; 1 s, 1 da; *Career* admitted Faculty of Advocates 1953; Sheriff of the Lothian and Borders (formerly Roxburgh, Berwick and Selkirk) at Jedburgh, Selkirk and Duns 1963-; *Style* - Sheriff Paterson; Sunnyside, Melrose, Roxburghshire (☎ Melrose 2502)

PATERSON, Noel Kennedy; CIE (1947), OBE (1943); s of Rev David Paterson, of Edinburgh; *b* 25 Dec 1905; *Educ* George Heriot's Sch, Edinburgh U, St John's Cambridge; *m* 1934, Margaret Winifred Schreiber; 2 s, 2 da; *Career* ICS 1929, Ch Cmmr Andaman and Nicobar Islands 1944-47; former UK Trade Cmmr Dublin; *Style* - Noel Paterson Esq, CIE, OBE; Chestnut Cottage, Gabriels Farm, Park Lane, Twyford, Hants (☎ Twyford 713116)

PATERSON, Hon Mrs (Rose Emily); *née* Ridley; da of 4 Viscount Ridley, TD, JP, DL; *b* 13 Aug 1956; *m* 1980, Owen William Paterson; *Style* - The Hon Mrs Paterson

PATON, Sir (Thomas) Angus (Lyall); CMG (1960); s of Thomas Lyall Paton; *b* 10 May 1905; *Educ* Cheltenham Coll and Univ Coll London (Fell); *m* 1933, Eleanor Joan Delmé-Murray (d 1964); 2 s, 2 da; *Career* kt 1973; sr ptnr Sir Alexander Gibb & Partners 1955-77, sr consultant 1977-; FICE (Hon FICE 1975), FIStructE; FRS (& v-pres Roy Soc 1977-78), FRSA, Fell Imperial Coll London 1978, Hon

DSc London 1978; *Style* - Sir Angus Paton CMG; 45 Richmond Hill Ct, Richmond-on-Thames, Surrey (☎ 01 940 1270)

PATON, George Campbell Henderson; QC (Scot); s of George Grieve Paton; *b* 6 Aug 1905; *Educ* Glasgow Acad, Glasgow U; *m* 1950, Eva French, da of David French Cranston, of Edinburgh; 2 da; *Career* slr 1931, advocate 1951, QC (Scotland) 1967, reader in Scots Law Edinburgh U 1967-75; *Style* - George Paton Esq, QC; 163 Colinton rd, Edinburgh EH14 1BE (☎ 031 443 1660)

PATON, Sir George Whitecross; s of Rev Frank H L Paton; *b* 16 Aug 1902; *Educ* Scotch Coll Melbourne, Melbourne U, Magdalen Oxford; *m* 1931, Alice Watson, CBE; 1 s, 3 da; *Career* barr Gray's Inn 1929, Vice-Chllr Melbourne U 1951-68; kt 1957; *Style* - Sir George Paton; Dunraven av, Toorak, Vic 3142, Australia (☎ 240 1034)

PATON, His Honour Harold William; DSC (1943); s of late Clifford James Paton; *b* 6 Oct 1900; *Educ* Winchester and Ch Ch Oxford; *m* 1947, Joan Orby, da of late Lt-Col Cecil Gascoigne, DSO; 1 da; *Career* 1939-45 RNVR, Lt-Cdr 1944; barr Inner Temple 1923, Judge of County Courts Circuit No 54 1950-71, chm Somerset QS 1965-71; *Style* - His Honour Harold Paton, DSC; Ardullie Farmhouse, Dingwall, Ross-shire

PATON, Sir Leonard (Cecil); CBE (1944), MC (1915); s of John Paton, of Dunfermline, Fife; *b* 7 May 1892; *Educ* George Watson's Coll, Edinburgh U, Ch Ch Oxford; *m* 1917, Muriel, da of William Searles; 1 s, 1 da; *Career* chm Harrisons & Crosfield Ltd 1957-62; kt 1946; *Style* - Sir Leonard Paton, CBE, MC; 63 Woodland Court, Dyke rd av, Hove, E Sussex

PATON, Hon Mrs (Rachel Audrey); *née* Eden; da of 9 Baron Auckland; *b* 9 June 1959; *m* 1981, Bramwell, s of John Paton, of Maidenhead; *Style* - The Hon Mrs Paton

PATON, Sir Stuart (Henry); KCVO (1965), CBE (1945); s of William Henry Paton; *b* 9 July 1900; *Educ* Hillside Godalming, RN Colls Osborne and Dartmouth; *m* 1925, Dorothy Morgan; 2 s, 2 da; *Career* Capt RN 1940; Dep Dir Administrative Planning 1945-46, Cmd HMS Newcastle, Mediterranean Fleet 1948-49; ADC to King George VI 1949, ret 1950; *Style* - Sir Stuart Paton, KCVO, CBE; West Stroud, Grayswood, Haslemere, Surrey (☎ Haslemere 3973)

PATON, Prof Sir William (Drummond Macdonald); CBE (1968); s of late Rev William Paton, DD; *b* 5 May 1917; *Educ* Winchester House Sch Brackley, Repton, New Coll Oxford, Univ Coll Hosp Med Sch (BA, BM, BCh Oxon, MA, DM); *m* 1942, Phoebe Margaret, da of Thomas Rooke; *Career* house physician UCH Med Unit 1942, pathologist King Edward VII Sanatorium 1943-44, memb scientific staff Nat Inst for Medical Research 1944-52, Reader in Pharmacology Univ Coll and UCH Med Sch 1952-54, Prof of Pharmacology RCS 1954-59, Prof of Pharmacology in the U of Oxford 1959-, Fell Balliol 1959-; FRS, FRCP; JP St Albans 1956; kt 1979; *Style* - Professor Sir William Paton, CBE, JP; 13 Staverton rd, Oxford

PATRICK, Graham McIntosh; CMG (1968), DSC (1943); *b* 17 Oct 1921; *Educ* Dundee H S and St Andrews U; *m* 1945, Barbara Worboys; 2 s; *Career* Under-Sec DOE 1971-; dir Scottish Services, Property Services Agency 1975-; *Style* - Graham Patrick Esq, CMG, DSC; c/o Argyle House, 3 Lady Lawson st, Edinburgh

PATRICK, John Bowman; s of late John Bowman Patrick; *b* 29 Feb 1916; *Educ* Greenock Acad, Edinburgh U, Glasgow U; *m* 1945, Sheina Struthers McCrea; 1 da; *Career* slr (Sco) 1947, advocate 1956, Sheriff of Inverness, Moray, Nairn, Ross and Cromarty at Fort William and Portree (Skye) 1961-68, Sheriff of N Strathclyde (formerly Renfrew and Argyll) at Greenock 1968-; *Style* - Sheriff Patrick; 77 Union st, Greenock, Renfrewshire (☎ 20712)

PATRICK, Margaret Kathleen; OBE (1976); da of late Roy Patrick; *b* 5 June 1923; *Educ* Godolphin and Latymer Sch London and Guy's Hosp Sch of Physiotherapy; *Career* District/ Superintendent Physiotherapist Central Health District, Birmingham Area Health Authority (Teaching) (formerly United Birmingham Hospitals Hosp Management Ctee) 1951-; *Style* - Miss Margaret Patrick, OBE; 7 Hawthorn Coppice, Hagley, W Midlands DY9 OPE

PATRICK, Nigel Dennis Wemyss; s of Charles Wemyss and Dorothy Turner; *b* 2 May 1913; *Educ* privately; *m* 1951, Beatrice Josephine Campbell (d 1979); 1 s, 1 da; *Career* actor; *Clubs* Garrick; *Style* - Nigel Patrick Esq; 54 Ovington st, Chelsea, SW3 (☎ 01 589 4385)

PATRON, Sir Joseph; OBE (1945), MC (1917), JP (Gibraltar 1948); s of late Joseph Armand Patron, CMG, OBE; *b* 19 Jan 1896; *Educ* Harrow; *m* 1924, Emily Isham, da of John Maxwell Vaughan; *Career* md Saccone and Speed 1927-45; Speaker of the Legislative Council Gibraltar 1958-64; kt 1961; *Style* - Sir Joseph Patron, OBE, MC, JP; 10 Calle Avila, Sotogrande, Prov de Cadiz, Spain

PATTEN, Christopher Francis; MP (C) Bath 1979-; s of late Francis Joseph Patten; *b* 12 May 1944; *Educ* St Benedict's Sch Ealing and Balliol Oxford; *m* 1971, Mary Lavender St Leger Thornton; 2 da; *Career* Dir Con Research Dept 1974-79, PPS to Patrick Jenkin, Sec of State for Soc Servs 1981-; *Style* - Christopher Patten Esq, MP; 8 Avenue rd, N6 (☎ 01 348 2694); Cromwell's Rest, 207 Conkwell, nr Winsley, Wilts (☎ Limpley Stoke 3378)

PATTEN, John Haggitt Charles; MP (C) City of Oxford 1979-; s of Jack Patten; *b* 17 July 1945; *Educ* Wimbledon Coll and Sidney Sussex Cambridge (PhD); *m* 1978, Louise Alexandra Virginia, da of John Rowe; *Career* PPS to Leon Brittan and Timothy Raison, Mins of State, Home Office, 1980-81, Parly Under-Sec of State NI 1981-; *Style* - John Patten Esq, MP; 176a Ashley gdns, SW1P 1PD

PATTERSON, Arthur; CMG (1951); s of late Alexander Patterson; *b* 24 June 1906; *Educ* Methodist Coll Belfast, Queen's U Belfast and St John's Cambridge; *m* 1942, Mary Ann Stocks, da of late J L Stocks; 2 s, 1 da; *Career* Assist Sec DHSS 1968-71; *Style* - Arthur Patterson Esq, CMG; 42 Campden Hill sq, W8 (☎ 01 229 3894)

PATTERSON, Maj-Gen Arthur Gordon; CB (1969), DSO (1964), OBE (1961), MC (1945); s of late Arthur Abbey Patterson, ICS; *b* 24 July 1917; *Educ* Tonbridge Sch and RMC Sandhurst; *m* 1949, Jean Mary Grant; 2 s, 1 da; *Career* Dir of Army Training 1969-72, ret; *Clubs* Naval and Military; *Style* - Maj-Gen Arthur Patterson, CB, DSO, OBE, MC; Burnt House, Benenden, Cranbrook, Kent

PATTERSON, Rt Rev Cecil John; CMG (1958), CBE (1954); *b* 9 Jan 1908; *Educ* St Paul's Sch, St Catharine's Cambridge (Hon Fell 1963), Bishop's Coll Cheshunt; *Career* Archbishop of W Africa 1961-69, Rep for the Archbishops of Canterbury and York for Community Relations 1970-72, Hon Assist Bishop Diocese of London 1970-76; *Style* - The Right Rev Cecil Patterson CMG CBE; 6 High Park rd, Kew, Surrey (☎ 01 876 1697)

PATTERSON, Hon Mrs (Fiona Elizabeth Cameron); *née* Corbett; da of 2 Baron Rowallan, KT, KBE, MC, TD; *b* 14 Nov 1942; *m* 1, 1966 (m dis 1972), as his 1 w, David Cecil, yr twin s of Hon Henry Cecil (bro of 3 Baron Amherst of Hackney; David and his twin bro Henry are both racehorse trainers); 2 s; m 2, 1974, W Patterson; *Style* - The Hon Mrs Patterson; 43 Holland Villas, W 14

PATTERSON, George Benjamin; MEP (C) Kent West 1979-; s of Prof Eric James Patterson (d 1972); *b* 21 April 1939; *Educ* Westminster, Trinity Cambridge; *m* 1970, Felicity Barbara Anne, da of Gordon Raybould; 1 s, 1 da; *Career* Dep Head London Office of European Parl 1974-79; dir Wiltenbridge Ltd 1979-; *Style* - George Patterson Esq, MEP; Birchenholt, Wellingtonia ave, Crowthorne, Berks RG11 6AF (☎ Crowthorne 4611)

PATTERSON, Mrs Thomas - (Constance) Marie; CBE (1978, OBE 1973); da of Dr Richard Swanton Abraham; *b* 1 April 1934; *Educ* Pendleton H S, Bedford Coll London U; *m* 1960 (m dis 1976), Thomas Michael Valentine Patterson; *Career* Nat Woman Officer TGWU 1963-76, Nat Officer 1976-, chm Gen Council of TUC 1974-75 and 1977, memb 1963-; *Style* - Mrs Thomas Patterson, CBE; 15 Mackeson rd, NW3 (☎ 01 485 1327)); Transport House, Smith sq, SW1 (☎ 01 828 7788

PATTERSON, Hon Mrs (Mary Ann); da of Baroness Stocks (Life Peeress, d 1975) and late Prof John Leofric Stocks, DSO; *b* 1915; *m* 1942, Arthur Patterson, CMG; 2 s, 1 da; *Style* - The Hon Mrs Patterson; 42 Campden Hill sq, W3

PATTERSON, Hon Mrs Sandra Debonnaire; *née* Monson; da of 10 Baron Monson (d 1958); *b* 1937; *m* 1958 (m dis 1971), Maj William Garry Patterson; 1 s, 3 da; *Style* - The Hon Mrs Sandra Patterson; The Old Vicarage, Aston Rowant, Oxon

PATTIE, Geoffrey Edwin; MP (C) Chertsey and Walton Feb 1974-; s of Alfred Edwin Pattie; *b* 17 Jan 1936; *Educ* Durham Sch, St Catharine's Cambridge; *m* 1960, Tuëma Caroline, nee Eyre-Maunsell; 1 s, 1 da; *Career* Parly Under-Sec of State Def & RAF 1979-81, Procurement (MOD) 1981-; barr Gray's Inn 1964, contested (C) Barking, 1966 and 1970, V-Chm Con Parly Defence Ctee 1978-79, V-Chm All Party Ctee on Mental Health 1977-79; *Style* - Geoffrey Pattie Esq, MP; Terrington House, 15 College rd, Dulwich Village, SE21 7BG (☎ 01 693 5131)

PATTINSON, Hon Sir Baden; KBE (1962); *b* 22 Dec 1899; *m* 1926, Florence, da of T A Doman; *Career* Min of Education S Australia 1953-65; memb legal firm Pattinson, McLaughlin & Reid Smith; *Style* - The Hon Sir Baden Pattinson, KBE; 12 Maturin rd, Glenelg, Adelaide, SA 5045, Australia

PATTULLO, (David) Bruce; s of Colin Arthur Pattullo; *b* 2 Jan 1938; *Educ* Rugby and Hertford Coll Oxford; *m* 1962, Fiona Jane Nicholson; 3 s, 1 da; *Career* gen man Bank of Scotland 1978-, dep treasurer 1978-79, treasurer 1979-; *Style* - Bruce Pattullo Esq; 6 Cammo rd, Edinburgh EH4 8BB (☎ 031 339 6012)

PAUL, Geoffrey David; s of Reuben Goldstein; *b* 26 March 1929; *Educ* Liverpool, Kendal, Dublin; *m* 1, 1952 (m dis 1972) Joy Stirling; 1 da; m 2, 1974, Rachel Mann; 1 s; *Career* editor Jewish Chronicle 1977-; *Style* - Geoffrey Paul Esq; 25 Furnival st, EC4A 1JT (☎ 01 405 9252)

PAUL, Air Cdre Gerard John Christopher; CB (1956), DFC (1944); s of E W Paul, FRCS; *b* 31 Oct 1907. *Educ* Cheltenham Coll and St John's Cambridge; *m* 1937, Rosemary, da of Rear-Adm H G E Lane, CB; 2 s, 1 da; *Career* RAF 1929, Fleet Air Arm 1931-36, 1939-45 War in England and N W Europe, Commandant Central Flying Sch 1954-56, ret 1958; Sec-Gen Air League 1958-71, Pres Popular Flying Assoc 1969-78; FRAeS; *Style* - Air Commodore Gerard Paul, CB, DFC; Wearne House, Old Alresford, Hants

PAUL, Sir John (Warburton); GCMG (1965, KCMG 1962), OBE (1959), MC (1940); s of Walter George Paul; *b* 29 March 1916; *Educ* Weymouth Coll Dorset and Selwyn Cambridge; *m* 1946, Kathleen Audrey, CStJ, da of Dr A D Weeden, of Weymouth; 3 da; *Career* barr Inner Temple 1947; Govr-Gen of The Gambia 1965-66, Govr & C-in-C British Honduras 1966-72, The Bahamas 1972-73, Govr-Gen The Bahamas July-Oct 1973, Lt-Govr of the Isle of Man 1974-80; KStJ 1962; *Style* - Sir John Paul, GCMG, OBE, MC; Sherrens Mead, Sherfield-on-Loddon, Hampshire (☎ Turgis Green 331)

PAUL, Noel Strange; CBE (1978); s of late S Evan Paul; *b* 1914; *Educ* Kingston G S; *m* 1950, Mary, da of Philip J Bone; *Career* dir The Press Council 1976-79; *Style* - Noel Paul Esq, CBE; Plummers Farmhouse, Fordham, Colchester, Essex (☎ Colchester 240388); Camus Lusta, Loch Bay, Waternish, Isle of Skye

PAUL, Swraj; s of Payare Lal (d 1944); *b* 18 Feb 1931; *Educ* Punjab U, Massachusetts Inst of Technology; *m* 1956, Aruna; 3 s, 1 da; *Career* chm Caparo Gp Ltd, chm Indo-British Assoc; *Clubs* MCC, Oriental; *Style* - Swraj Paul Esq; 6 Ambika House, 9a Portland Place, WIN 3AA (☎ 01 637 5525)

PAULET, Lord Richard George; 2 s of 18 Marquess of Winchester; *b* 1971; *Style* - Lord Richard Paulet

PAULET, Lady Susan; da of 18 Marquess of Winchester; *b* 1976; *Style* - Lady Susan Paulet

PAULET, Lord Timothy Guy; s of George Paulet and bro of 18 Marquess of Winchester; *b* 1944; *m* 1974, Jill; at least 1 s and another child; raised to the rank of Marquess's s 1970; *Style* - Lord Timothy Paulet

PAULL, Sir Gilbert (James); s of Alan Paull, FSI, JP; *b* 18 April 1896; *Educ* St Paul's Sch and Trin Cambridge; *m* 1922, Maud Winifred (d 1978), da of Charles Harris; 1 s, 1 da; *Career* barr Inner Temple 1920, QC 1939, Judge of High Court of Justice, Queen's Bench Division, 1957-71; kt 1957; *Clubs* Athenaeum; *Style* - Sir Gilbert Paull

PAULSON, Godfrey Martin Ellis; CB (1966), CMG (1959), OBE (1945); s of late Dr W H Ellis; *b* 6 July 1908; *Educ* Westminster, Peterhouse Cambridge; *m* 1936, Patricia Emma, da of late Sir Hugh Murray, KCIE, CBE; 1 s, 1 da; *Career* slr 1936; served 1939-45, Manchester Regt and on Gen Staff in Africa, UK and NW Europe; Lt-Col 1945, Control Cmmn for Germany 1945, for Austria 1947-48; joined Foreign Service 1948 (Venice, Stockholm, Far East, Beirut, Rome, Nice and FO), ret 1970; *Style* - Godfrey Paulson Esq, CB, CMG, OBE; Eastley House, Brightwalton, nr Newbury, Berks (☎ Chaddleworth 226)

PAUNCEFORT-DUNCOMBE, David Philip Henry; s and h of Sir Philip Digby Pauncefort-Duncombe, 4 Bt; *b* 21 May 1956; *Style* - David Pauncefort-Duncombe Esq

PAUNCEFORT-DUNCOMBE, Evelyn, Lady - Evelyn Elvira; da of late Frederick Anthony Denny; *m* 1922, Maj Sir Everard Philip Digby Pauncefort-Duncombe, 3 Bt, DSO (d 1971); *Style* - Evelyn, Lady Pauncefort-Duncombe; Lane End, Great Brickhill, Bletchley, Bucks

PAUNCEFORT-DUNCOMBE, Sir Philip Digby; 4 Bt (UK 1859), of Great Brickhill, Buckinghamshire, DL (Bucks 1971); s of Maj Sir Everard Philip Digby Pauncefort-Duncombe, 3 Bt, DSO (d 1971); *b* 18 May 1927; *Educ* Stowe; *m* 1951, Rachel Moyra, da of Maj Henry Gerald Aylmer, gggs of 2 Baron Aylmer; 1 s, 2 da; *Heir* s, David Philip Henry Pauncefort-Duncombe; *Career* 2 Lt Gren Gds 1946; Hon Maj, ret 1960, Reg Army Reserve; County Cmdt Bucks ACF 1967-70; memb HM Body Guard (Hon Corps of Gentlemen-at-Arms); *Style* - Sir Philip Pauncefort-Duncombe Bt DL; Great Brickhill Manor, Milton Keynes, Bucks (☎ Gt Brickhill 205)

PAVITT, Laurence Anstice; MP (L and Co-op) Brent South 1974-; s of George Anstice Pavitt; *b* 1 Feb 1914; *Educ* Central Sch West Ham; *m* 1937, Rosina, nee Walton; 1 s, 1 da; *Career* MP (L and Co-op) Willesden West Oct 1959-74, Assist Govt Whip 1974-76; *Style* - Laurence Pavitt Esq, MP; House of Commons, SW1 (☎ 01 219 5225)

PAWLE, Lady Mary Clementine; da (by 1 m) of 5 Marq Camden; *b* 1921; *m* 1, 1940, Fl Lt the Hon (Herbert) Oswald Berry (d 1952); m 2, 1953, (Shafto) Gerald Strachan Pawle; *Style* - Lady Mary Pawle; Trehiven House, Madron, Penzance, Cornwall

PAWSEY, James Francis; MP (C) Rugby 1979-; s of William Pawsey; *b* 21 Aug 1933; *Educ* St Osburg's Sch Coventry, Coventry Tech Sch, Coventry Tech Coll; *m* 1956, Cynthia Margaret Francis; 6 s; *Career* chm and ch exec Autobar Machine Div; dir: Autobar Ltd, Autobar Manufacturing Ltd, Autobar Contract Maintenance Ltd, Vend Finance Ltd, Freshbrew Machines Ltd; memb Warwickshire CC 1975-79; *Style* - James Pawsey Esq, MP; Shilton House, Shilton,

Warwicks (☎ Coventry 612922); Flat 4, Sheriden House, Wincott st, London (☎ 01 735 4499)

PAWSON, Albert Guy; CMG (1935); s of Albert Henry Pawson; *b* 30 May 1888; *Educ* Winchester and Ch Ch Oxford; *m* 1917, Helen Humphrey Lawson; 2 s; *Career* Sec-Gen International Rubber Study Group 1948-60; *Style* - Albert Pawson Esq, CMG; Warleigh House, Tamerton Foliot, Plymouth, Devon PL5 4LN

PAWSON, Kenneth Vernon Frank; s of Capt Arnold Gilderdale Pawson (d 1937); *b* 24 Sept 1923; *Educ* Rugby and Trin Hall Cambridge; *m* 1950, Nicolette Vivian, da of Mervyn Thoresby (d 1965); 1 s, 2 da; *Career* barr Gray's Inn 1949; md Joseph Hobson & Son Ltd (Brewers) 1954-74, chm and md Gale Lister & Co Ltd 1975-, exec dir Mount Charlotte Investments Ltd 1974-; *Recreations* shooting, fishing, farming and old cars; *Style* - Kenneth Pawson Esq; Haggas Hall, Weeton, nr Leeds, Yorkshire (☎ Harrogate 74200); 45 Elystan Place, SW3 (☎ 01 589 8584); 4 Le Blaireau, Verbier, Switzerland

PAXTON, John; *b* 23 Aug 1923; *m* 1950, Joan Thorne; 1 s, 1 da; *Career* author, also writing as Jack Cherrill; editor The Statesman's Year-Book 1969-, ch consultant editor Reference Book Div The Macmillan Press Ltd, dir Linolite Ltd; *Style* - John Paxton Esq; Moss Cottage, Hardway, Bruton, Somerset BA10 OLN (☎ Bruton 3423)

PAYNE, Maj-Gen George Lefevre; CB (1966), CBE (1963); s of Dr E L Payne, MRCS, LRCP; *b* 23 June 1911; *Educ* The King's Sch Canterbury, RMC Sandhurst; *m* 1938, Betty Maud, da of Surgn Capt H A Kellond-Knight, RN; 3 s; *Career* Dir of Ordnance Services MOD 1964-68, ret 1968; *Style* - Maj-Gen George Payne, CB, CBE; 17 Highridge Court, Downs ave, Epsom, Surrey

PAYNE, Hon Mrs - Hon Joan; *née* Spring Rice; da of 5 Baron Monteagle of Brandon (d 1946); *b* 1928; *m* 1953, Michael Shears Payne, MC; 1 s, 1 da; *Style* - The Hon Mrs Payne; Scotlands Farm, Cockpole Green, nr Wargrave, Berks

PAYNE, Hon Mrs (Jacqueline Faith); *née* Addison; da of 2 Viscount Addison; *b* 2 March 1944; *m* 1966, Jeremy Payne, assist lecturer in German Heriot Watt U; 2 da; *Style* - The Hon Mrs Payne; 11 Canaan Lane, Edinburgh EH10 4SZ

PAYNE, Keith; VC (1969); s of Henry Thomas Payne; *b* 30 Aug 1933; *Educ* State Sch Ingham N Qld; *m* 1954, Florence Catherine Payne, nee Plaw; 5 s; *Career* Australian Army Trng Team Vietnam 1969 (Warrant Officer), WO Instructor RMC Duntroon ACT 1970-72, 42 Bn Roy Qld Regt Mackay 1973-75, Capt Oman Army 1975-76; *Style* - Keith Payne Esq, VC; St Bees ave, Bucasia, via Mackay, Qld 4741, Australia (☎ 079 546125)

PAYNE, Leonard Sidney; s of Leonard Sydney Payne; *b* 16 Dec 1925; *Educ* Woodhouse G S; *m* 1944, Marjorie Vincent; 2 s; *Career* dir J Sainsbury Ltd, 1974-; FCCA, MBIM, FCIT, MBCS; *Style* - Leonard Payne Esq; Wisley, Gills Hill Lane, Radlett, Herts

PAYNE, Norman John; CBE (1976, OBE 1956, MBE 1944); s of late F Payne, of Folkestone; *b* 9 Oct 1921; *Educ* Lower Sch of John Lyon Harrow, City and Guilds Coll London; *m* 1946, Pamela Vivien Wallis; 4 s, 1 da; *Career* ch exec British Airports Authority 1972-77, chm 1977- (salary as of June 1981 £34,000 pa); FBIM 1975; *Style* - Norman Payne Esq, CBE; Summer Meadow, Shamley Green, Guildford, Surrey (☎ Guildford 2515)

PAYNE, Sir Robert (Frederick); s of late Frederick Charles Payne; *b* 22 Jan 1908; *Educ* Hymers Coll, Hull; *m* 1, 1937, Alice Marguerite, da of William Sydney Cussons; 1 s, 1 da; m 2, 1951, Maureen Ruth, da of William Charles Walsh; 1 s; *Career* slr 1931; RAF 1940-44; pres The Law Society 1969-70, principal in Payne & Payne, Solicitors, Hull; founder memb British Acad of Forensic Sciences 1959; Sheriff of Kingston-upon-Hull 1957, Hon Fell Victoria Coll of Music; kt 1970; *Style* - Sir Robert Payne; High Woodgates, North Ferriby, North Humberside (☎ Hull 631533)

PAYNTER, Air Cdre Noel Stephen; CB (1946), DL (Bucks, 1963); s of late Canon F S Paynter; *b* 26 Dec 1898; *Educ* Haileybury, RMC Sandhurst; *m* 1925, Barbara Grace Haagensen; 1 s, 1 da; *Career* Ch Intelligence Officer Bomber Command 1942-45, Directorate of Intelligence Air Miny 1946; High Sheriff Bucks 1965; *Style* - Air Commodore Noel Paynter, CB, DL; Lawn House, Edgcott, nr Aylesbury, Bucks (☎ Grendon Underwood 238)

PAYTON, Stanley Walden; CMG (1965); s of late Archibald Walden Payton; *b* 29 May 1921; *Educ* Monoux Sch; *m* 1941, Joan, nee Starmer; 1 s, 1 da; *Career* Ch of Overseas Dept Bank of England 1975-; *Style* - Stanley Payton Esq, CMG; Pollards Park House, Chalfont St Giles, Bucks

PAYTON, Rev Wilfred Ernest Granville; CB (1965); s of Wilfred Richard Daniel Payton; *b* 27 Dec 1913; *Educ* Nottingham H S, Emmanuel, Cambridge, Ridley Hall Cambridge; *m* 1946, Nita Mary Barber; 1 s, 1 da; *Career* ord 1938, Archdeacon Prebendary and Canon of St Boltolph, Lincoln Cathedral 1965-69, Vicar of Abingdon 1969-79, Rural Dean of Abingdon 1976-79, Hon Chaplain to the Queen 1965-69; *Style* -The Reverend Wilfred Payton, CB; Westwood, Nailsworth, Gloucester

PEACOCK, Hon Andrew Sharp; MP (Lib) Kooyong 1966-; s of late A S Peacock; *b* 13 Feb 1939; *Educ* Scotch Coll Melbourne and Melbourne U; *Career* Min for Foreign Affairs Australia 1975-80, Min for Industrial Relations Commonwealth of Australia 1980-81; *Style* - The Hon Andrew Peacock, MP; 4 Treasury Place, Melbourne, Vic 3002, Australia (☎ 633417)

PEACOCK, Sir Geoffrey Arden; CVO (1977); s of Warren Turner Peacock; *b* 7 Feb 1920; *Educ* Wellington, Jesus Cambridge; *m* 1949, Mary Gillian Drew, da of Dr Harold Drew Lander, of Cornwall; 2 da; *Career* barr Inner Temple; Remembrancer City of London 1968-; kt 1981; *Style* - Sir Geoffrey Peacock, CVO; Cowfold Lodge, Cowfold, West Sussex (☎ Cowfold 237)

PEACOCK, (Ian) Michael; s of Norman Henry Peacock; *b* 14 Sept 1929; *Educ* Kimball Union Acad USA, Welwyn Garden City G S, LSE; *m* 1956, Daphne Lee; 2 s, 1 da; *Career* md Video Arts Television Ltd 1978-, chm Monitor Enterprises Ltd 1970-; dir Video Arts Ltd, Greater Manchester Independent Radio Ltd; *Style* - Michael Peacock Esq; 21 Woodlands rd, Barnes, SW13 (☎ 01 876 2025)

PEAKE, David Alphy Edward Raymond; s of Sir Harald Peake (d 1978); *b* 27 Sept 1934; *Educ* Ampleforth and Ch Ch Oxford; *m* 1962, Susanna, da of Sir Cyril Kleinwort; 1 s, 1 da; *Career* 2 Lt Roy Scots Greys 1953-55; banker; chm Hargreaves Gp Ltd; dir: Kleinwort Benson Ltd, BNP Ltd and M & G Group (Holdings) Ltd; *Clubs* Brooks's, and Cavalry and Guards; *Style* - David Peake Esq; Sezincote House, Moreton In Marsh, Glos (☎ Blockley 444); 15 Ilchester Place, W 14 (☎ 01 602 2375)

PEAKE, Sir Francis; s of late John Henry Hill Peake; *b* 31 Jan 1889; *Educ* Tottenham G S; *m* 1914, Winifred Marie, da of late Thomas McKinnon Clark; 2 da; *Career* barr Lincoln's Inn 1915, Controller of Death Duties 1948-51; kt 1951; *Style* - Sir Francis Peake; 5 Churchfield House, Guessens rd, Welwyn Garden City, Herts (☎ Welwyn Garden 20456)

PEAKE, Air Cdre Dame Felicity (Hyde), (Lady Peake); DBE (1949, MBE 1941), AE, JP; da of late Col Humphrey Watts, OBE, TD; *b* 1 May 1913; *Educ* St Winifred's, Eastbourne; Les Grands Huguenots, Vaucresson, Seine et Oise, France; *m* 1, 1935, John Charles Mackenzie Hanbury (k on active serv 1939); m 2, 1952, Sir Harald Peake (d 1978); 1 s; *Career* Dir WAAF 1946-49, Dir WRAF 1949-50, ret 1950; a Vice-Pres RAF Benevolent Fund, 1978-, Hon ADC to King George VI 1949-50; *Style* - Dame Felicity Peake, DBE, AE, JP; 2 Shepherd's Close, Shepherd's Place, Upper Brook st, W1 (☎ 01 629 1264); Court Farm, Tackley, Oxford OX5

3AQ (☎ Tackley 221)

PEAKE, Hon Henrietta Cecilia Imogen; da of 2 Viscount Ingleby; *b* 1961; *Style* - The Hon Henrietta Peake

PEAKE, Hon Katherine Emma Charlotte; da of 2 Viscount Ingleby; *b* 1963; *Style* - The Hon Katherine Peake

PEAKE, Hon Sarah Rachel; da of 2 Viscount Ingleby; *b* 1958; *Style* - The Hon Sarah Peake

PEARCE, Baron (Life Peer UK 1962); Edward Holroyd Pearce; PC (1957); s of late John W E Pearce; *b* 9 Feb 1901; *Educ* Charterhouse and Corpus Christi Oxford (Hon Fell 1950); *m* 1927, Erica, da of late Bertram Priestman, RA; 2 s; *Career* barr Lincoln's Inn and Middle Temple 1925; QC 1945, Bencher Hon Soc of Lincoln's Inn 1948, Treasurer 1966; Judge of High Court of Justice, Probate, Divorce and Admiralty Div 1948-54, Queen's Bench Div 1954-57; a Lord Justice of Appeal 1957-62, A Lord of Appeal in Ordinary 1962-69, chm of the Press Council 1969-74, chm Appeals Ctee Takeover Panel 1969-76; RBA 1940, kt 1948; *Style* - The Rt Hon the Lord Pearce, PC, QC; Sweethaws, Crowborough, Sussex (☎ 61520)

PEARCE, Andrew; MEP (C) Cheshire West, 1979-; s of Henry Pearce (d 1964); *b* 1 Dec 1937; *Educ* Durham U; *m* 1966, Myra, da of Kevin Whelan, of Co Wexford, Eire; 3 s, 1 da; *Career* formerly Management Services Exec; Principal Administrator Cmmn of the European Communities Brussels 1974-79, contested (C) Islington North 1969 and 1970; *Style* - Andrew Pearce Esq, MEP; (Home) Harley Hall, 76 Eastham Village rd, Eastham, Wirral, Merseyside L62 0AW; (Office) 30 Grange rd, W Kirby, Wirral, Merseyside L48 4HA (☎ 051 625 1896)

PEARCE, Sir Austin William; CBE (1974); s of William Thomas Pearce (d 1970); *b* 1 Sept 1921; *Educ* Devonport H S for Boys, Birmingham U; *m* 1, 1947, Maglona Winifred Twinn (d 1975); 3 da; m, 2, Dr Florence Patricia Grice, da of John Walter Forsythe; *Career* dir Williams & Glyn's Bank 1974, Royal Bank of Scotland Gp 1978, chm and ch exec Esso Petroleum Co Ltd 1972-80, chm British Aerospace 1980- (salary as of June 1981 £48,000 pa); kt 1980; *Clubs* Athenaeum and Royal Wimbledon Golf; *Style* - Sir Austin Pearce, CBE; c/o British Aerospace, Brooklands rd, Weybridge, Surrey KT13 OSJ (☎ Weybridge 45522)

PEARCE, Hon Mrs (Constance Ada); *née* Caulfield; da of late 11 Viscount Charlemont; *b* 1918; *m* 1943, Henry Edward Pearce; 2 s, 3 da; *Style* - The Hon Mrs Pearce; 254 Mooroondu rd, Thorneside, Queensland 4158, Australia

PEARCE, Clifford James; CB (1974); s of late Samuel Lightfoot Pearce; *b* 14 Aug 1916; *Educ* Strand Sch, King's Coll London and LSE; *m* 1946, Elaine Hilda, nee Baggley; 1 s, 1 da; *Career* Under-Sec (Local Govt) DOE (formerly Miny of Housing and Local Govt) 1968-76; Hon Res Fell Birmingham U 1976-78; *Style* - Clifford Pearce Esq, CB; Elm Cottage, The Street, Boxgrove, Chichester

PEARCE, Sir Eric (Herbert); OBE (1970); s of Herbert Clement Pearce; *b* 5 March 1905; *Educ* Raynes Sch, Hants; *m* 1956, Betty Constance Ham; 1 da; *Career* Dir of Community Affairs Gen Television Corpn, Channel Nine, Melbourne, Australia 1979-; kt 1979; *Clubs* Athenaeum and Toorak Services (Melbourne); *Style* - Sir Eric Pearce, OBE; 48 Lansell rd, Toorak, Vic 3142, Australia

PEARCE, Hon James Edward Holroyd; QC (1979); s of Baron Pearce (Life Peer) *qv*; *b* 18 March 1934; *Educ* Charterhouse and Corpus Christi Oxford; *m* 1969, Julia, da of late C D Hill; 2 s, 2 da; *Career* Mil Serv RE, 2 Lt 1953-54; barr Middle Temple 1960, NI 1974; Hon Legal Adviser to Nat Skating Assoc 1970-, Memb Council Artists' Gen Benevolent Instn 1978-, Renter Warden Skinners' Co, 1979; *Clubs* Athenaeum; *Style* - The Hon James Pearce, QC; Turf Lodge, Slaugham Ghyll, Crowborough, Sussex TN6 3ST (☎ Crowborough 5505)

PEARCE, John Trevor Archdall; CMG (1964); s of late Rev W T L A Pearce, of

NSW, Australia; *b* 7 May 1916; *Educ* The King's Sch Parramatta Australia, Keble Oxford; *m* 1948, Isabel Bundey Rankine; *Career* Perm Sec (Admin) Office of the V-Pres 1961 Tanganyika, Chm Public Service Cmmn Basutoland 1963, Swaziland 1965; Registrar Papua and New Guinea U of Technology 1969-73; *Style* - John Pearce Esq, CMG; Clippings, Ferguson ave, Buderim, Qld 4556, Australia

PEARCE, Maj-Gen Leslie Arthur; CB (1973), CBE (1971, OBE 1964, MBE 1956); *b* 22 Jan 1918; *Educ* N Zealand; *m* 1944, Fay Mattocks, of Auckland, NZ; 2 s, 1 da; *Career* Ch of Gen Staff, NZ Army, 1971-73; chm, Vocational Training Council 1975-; *Style* - Maj-Gen Leslie Pearce, CB, CBE; 13 Stapleford Crescent, Browns Bay, Auckland, New Zealand

PEARCE, Malcolm Arthur Fraser; CVO (1954), CBE (1946); s of late J S Pearce, of Kapunda; *b* 19 April 1898; *Educ* Kapunda H S, SA; *m* 1, 1922, Gladys M (d 1958), da of J Green; 1 s, 1 da; m 2, 1959, Ivy, widow of Rev F V Duffy; *Career* Under-Sec State of SA; Sec to Min of Health Clerk of Exec Council 1954-61; Chm State Bank Bd 1948-61; *Style* - Malcolm Pearce Esq, CVO, CBE; 10 Newcastle st, Heathpool, Adelaide, SA 5068, Australia (☎ 316371)

PEARCE, (Ann) Philippa, (Mrs M J G Christie); da of Ernest Alexander Pearce; *Educ* Perse Girls' Sch, Cambridge, and Girton, Cambridge; *m* 1963, Martin James Graham Christie (decd); 1 da; *Career* producer/scriptwriter Sch Broadcasting BBC Radio 1945-58; editor Educn Dept Clarendon Press 1958-60, Children's Editor André Deutsch Ltd 1960-67, children's fiction writer 1967-; *Style* - Miss Philippa Pearce; c/o Kestrel Books, 17 Grosvenor gdns, SW1W OBD

PEARCE, Hon Richard Bruce Holroyd; QC (1969); s of Baron Pearce (Life Peer) *qv*; *b* 12 May 1930; *Educ* Charterhouse and Corpus Christi Oxford; *m* 1958, Dornie Smith-Pert; 1 s, 1 da; *Career* HM Forces 1949-56, RE and E African Engrs 1949-50, 119 Field Engr Regt RE, TA 1950-56; barr Lincoln's Inn 1955, a Recorder of the Crown Court 1972-, Legal Assessor to GMC 1974-, GDC 1974-, GNC 1975-; *Style* - The Hon Richard Pearce, QC; Sweethaws, Crowborough, E Sussex (☎ Crowborough 3888)

PEARD, Rear-Adm Sir Kenyon (Harry Terrell); KBE 1958 (CBE 1951); s of Henry T Peard; *b* 1902; *Educ* RNCs Osborne and Dartmouth; *m* 1935, Mercy Leila Bone; 1 s, 1 da; *Career* Dir, Naval Electrical Dept, Admiralty, 1955-58, ret 1958; *Style* - Rear-Admiral Sir Kenyon Peard, KBE; Finstead, Shorefield Crescent, Milford-on-Sea, Hants

PEARL, David Brian; s of Leonard Pearl, barr-at-Law; *b* 6 Aug 1944; *Educ* Wellington Coll; *m* 1972, Rosamond Mary Katharine, da of Lt-Cdr C G de L'isle Bush, of Frampton-upon-Severn, Glos; 2 s; *Career* Lloyd's Underwriter; md Meru Group Ltd and assoc cos 1970, dir Explaura Gold Ltd 1980-; Westminster City Council 1974-, Dep Lord Mayor 1979-80, Ch Whip 1980-81, V-Chm Finance & Scrutiny 1981-; Chm St Marylebone Con Assoc 1981-, London Tourist Bd 1980; FCA 1980; *Recreations* riding; *Clubs* Reform, MCC, Guards' Polo, Royal St George's Golf; *Style* - David Pearl Esq; Hedsor Court, Hedsor, Nr Burnham, Bucks SL1 8PE (☎ Bourne End 26312)

PEARL, Prof Valerie Louise; da of Cyril R Bence; *b* 31 Dec 1926; *Educ* King Edward VI H S Birmingham and St Anne's Oxford (BA, MA, DPhil); *m* 1949, Morris Leonard Pearl; 1 da; *Career* Prof of the History of London at Univ Coll London 1976-, Pres New Hall Cambridge 1981-; FSA 1976; *Style* - Professor Valerie Pearl; 11 Church Row, Hampstead, NW3 6UT (☎ 01 794 6055)

PEARMAN, Sir James (Eugene); CBE (1960); s of Eugene Charles Pearman; *b* 24 Nov 1904; *Educ* Saltus G S Bermuda, Bromsgrove Sch Worcs, Merton Coll Oxford and Middle Temple; *m* 1, 1929, Prudence Tucker Appleby (d 1976); 2 s; m 2, 1977, Mrs Antoinette Trott, da of Dr James Aiguier, of Philadelphia, Pa; *Career* memb Colonial Parl Bermuda 1943-72,

MLC 1972-, sr partner Conyers, Dill & Pearman, Hon Consul for Bolivia; kt 1973; *Style* - Sir James Pearman, CBE; Tideway, Point Shares, Pembroke, Bermuda (☎ 1-3029)

PEARS, His Honour Judge - Harold Snowden; s of late Harold Pears; *b* 21 April 1926; *Educ* Dauntsey's Sch and Emmanuel Cambridge; *m* 1960, Inge Haumann; *Career* barr, Inner Temple, 1948, NE Circuit 1948-71, Dep Chm W Riding QS 1967-71, Recorder of Doncaster 1968-71, a Circuit Judge (formerly Judge of County Courts) 1971-; *Style* - His Honour Judge Pears; 35 Whirlow Park rd, Sheffield S11 9NN (☎ Sheffield 366244)

PEARS, Sir Peter; CBE (1957); s of Arthur Pears; *b* 22 June 1910; *Educ* Lancing, Oxford and RCM; *Career* tenor; BBC Singers 1934-37, New English Singers 1936-38, began American and European tours with Benjamin Britten 1939, with Julian Bream 1956, with Osian Ellis 1972, Sadler's Wells Opera 1943-46, Co-Founder of Aldeburgh Festival 1948 kt 1978; *Style* - Sir Peter Pears, CBE; The Red House, Aldeburgh, Suffolk

PEARSON, Brig Alastair Stevenson; CB (1958), DSO, OBE (1953), MC,TD; *b* 1 June 1915; *Educ* Kelvinside Acad Sedbergh; *m* 1944, Mrs Joan Morgan Weld-Smith; 3 da; *Career* farmer; Ld-Lt of Dunbartonshire 1979-; KStJ 1980 Keeper Dumbarton Castle 1981-; *Style* - Brig Alastair Pearson CB DSO OBE MC TD, HM Lord-Lieut for Dunbartonshire; Tullochan, Gartocharn, By Alexandria, Dunbartonshire (☎ Gartocharn 205)

PEARSON, Bertram Lamb; CB (1947), DSO (1917), MC; s of late William Pearson; *b* 1893; *Educ* Bedford G S, Wakefield G S and Queen's Oxford; *m* 1920, Gladys Mary, da of John Stewart; *Career* Under-Sec Miny of Education 1946-55; *Style* - Bertram Pearson Esq, CB, DSO, MC; 15 Queen's Court, Queen's rd, Cheltenham, Glos GL50 2LU

PEARSON, Hon Charles Anthony; s (by 2 m) of 3 Viscount Cowdray, TD; *b* 1956; *Style* - The Hon Charles Pearson

PEARSON, Sir (James) Denning; JP; s of James Pearson; *b* 8 Aug 1908; *Educ* Canton Secdy Sch Cardiff and Cardiff Tech Coll (BSc Eng); *m* 1932, Eluned Henry; 2 da; *Career* consultant chm and ch exec Rolls-Royce Ltd 1969-70, chm Gamma Associates 1972-; pres SBAC 1963, memb NEDC 1964-67; kt 1963; *Clubs* Athenaeum; *Style* - Sir Denning Pearson, JP; Green Acres, Holbrook, Derbyshire (☎ Derby 881137)

PEARSON, David; s of Maurice Judge Pearson, of Saltburn, Cleveland; *b* 7 March 1942; *Educ* Sir William Turner's Sch Redcar Yorks, King's Coll London; *m* 1972, Christine Faith, da of Douglas Littlejohn, of Wadhurst, Sussex; 3 c; *Career* md Chetwynd Haddons Ltd; MIPA; *Recreations* skiing; *Style* - David Pearson Esq; 6 Spenser rd, Harpenden, Herts (☎ Harpenden 4303)

PEARSON, Derek Leslie; CB (1978); s of late George Frederick Pearson; *b* 19 Dec 1921; *Educ* William Ellis Sch and LSE; *m* 1956, Diana Mary, da of late Sir Ralph Freeman; *Career* Dep Sec, Miny of Overseas Development 1977-; *Style* - Derek Pearson Esq, CB; Hadlow, Hazelwood Lane, Chipstead, Surrey

PEARSON, Dominic Michael; s of Arthur Anselm Pearson (d 1954); *b* 18 Sept 1921; *Educ* Ampleforth and Peterhouse Cambridge (MA, CEng, FIMechE, FIL); *m* 1955, Carmen, da of Manuel Sanfeliu Galceran (d 1968); 3 s, 3 da; *Career* served UK and India 1941-46, Capt REME; Sovex Ltd 1949, British Belting & Asbestos Ltd 1951, chm of BBA Group Ltd 1974-, chm of various operating cos of BBA Gp Ltd; *Style* - Dominic Pearson Esq; Daisy Hill, Cliffe Drive, Rawdon, Leeds LS19 6LL (☎ Rawdon 502501)

PEARSON, Lady Frances Elizabeth Ann; *née* Hay; da of 11 Marquess of Tweeddale (d 1967); *b* 1926; *m* 1956, Nigel Arthur Pearson (d 1975), s of Sir Neville Arthur Pearson, 2 Bt; *Style* - Lady Frances Pearson; Dovecote Farm, Nutley, Sussex

PEARSON, Sir Francis Fenwick; 1 Bt (UK 1964), JP (Lancs 1952), DL (Co Palatine of Lancaster 1971); s of Frank

Pearson; *b* 13 June 1911; *Educ* Uppingham, Trinity Hall Cambridge; *m* 1938, Katharine Mary Fraser; 1 s, 1 da; *Heir* s, Francis Nicholas Fraser Pearson; *Career* farmer and landowner; Maj 1 Gurkha Rifles 1931-34, ADC to Viceroy of India 1934-36, Under-Sec 1942-45 and Ch Min Maipur State 1945-47, Assist Govt Whip (unpaid) 1960-62, a Lord Cmmr of the Treasury 1962-63, and PPS to PM 1963-64, MP (C) Clitheroe Div of Lancs 1959-70, chm Central Lancs New Town Devt Corpn 1971-; *Clubs* Carlton; *Style* - Sir Francis Pearson, Bt, MBE, JP, DL; Gressingham Hall, Hornby, Lancs (☎ Hornby 21288)

PEARSON, Hon Mrs (Francesca Mary); *née* Charteris; da of Baron Charteris of Amisfield (Life Peer); *b* 1945; *m* 1977, Malcolm Everard MacLaren Pearson; *Style* - The Hon Mrs Pearson; 3 Shepherd's Close, W1

PEARSON, Francis Nicholas Fraser; s and h of Sir Francis Fenwick Pearson, 1 Bt, MBE; *b* 28 Aug 1943; *m* 1978, Henrietta, da of Cdr Henry Pasley-Tyler, of Coton Manor, Guilsborough, Northants; *Career* Capt Rifle Bde; *Style* - Francis Pearson Esq

PEARSON, Hon Graham Thomas; s of Baron Pearson, CBE, PC (Life Peer) (d 1980); *b* 1935; *m* 1963, Diana, da of Vice-Adm Sir Maxwell Richmond, KBE, CB, DSO; *Style* - The Hon Graham Pearson; Manor House, Manor Lane, Old Basing, Basingstoke

PEARSON, Air Cdre Herbert Macdonald; CBE (1944); s of John Charles Pearson; *b* 17 Nov 1908; *Educ* Cheltenham Coll, Cranwell; *m* 1939, Jane Leslie; 1 s, 2 da; *Career* Commanding RAF, Kai Tak, Hong Kong 1951-53, Assist Ch of Staff Intelligence, Headquarters of Allied Air Forces, Central Europe 1953-55, Air Cdre 1953, ret 1955; *Style* - Air Commodore Herbert Pearson, CBE; Mapleridge Barn, Horton, Glos

PEARSON, Hon Michael Orlando Weetman; s and h of 3 Viscount Cowdray, TD, DL, by his 1 w, Lady Anne Bridgeman (da of 5 Earl of Bradford); *b* 17 June 1944; *Educ* Gordonstoun; *m* 1977, Ellen, da of Hermann Erhardt, of Munich; *Career* bought one million shares at 30p each in Bardsey Gp from John Bentley, *qv*, 1981; non-exec dir Bardsey Gp; *Style* - The Hon Michael Pearson

PEARSON, Sir Neville Arthur; 2 Bt (UK 1916); s of Sir Arthur Pearson, GBE, 1 Bt (d 1921); *b* 13 Feb 1898; *Educ* Eton; *m* 1, 1922 (m dis 1928, she m 1928, C Willoughby Hordern and d 1937) Hon Mary Mond, da of 1 Baron Melchett; 1 da (1 s decd); m 2, 1928 (m dis 1937, she m 1937 Philip Merivale) Gladys Cooper, later Dame Gladys Cooper, DBE; 1 da; m 3, 1943, Mrs Anne Davis Elebash, da of late David Montgomery Davis, of Richmond, Virginia, USA; *Career* RFA European War 1917-18, 1939-45 War as Maj Anti-Aircraft Regt RA; C Arthur Pearson Ltd, Publishers, to 1968; *Style* - Sir Neville Pearson, Bt; Meadow Lake, Hightstown, NJ 08520, USA

PEARSON, Hon Rosanna; da (by 2 m) of 3 Viscount Cowdray, TD; *b* 1959; *Style* - The Hon Rosanna Pearson

PEARSON, Sir (James) Reginald; OBE (1950); s of George Henry Pearson; *b* 17 Nov 1897; *Educ* Dudley, Worcs; *m* 1925, Nellie Rose Vittery (d 1977); 1 da; *Career* exec assist to md Vauxhall Motors Ltd 1953-62, dep chm 1958-62; High Sheriff of Bedfordshire 1964, DL (Beds) 1968-78; FIMechE, MIProdE; kt 1959; *Style* - Sir Reginald Pearson, OBE; 45 Bloomfield rd, Harpenden, Herts (☎ Harpenden 3052)

PEARSON, Baroness - Sophie Grace Hermann; da of Arthur Hermann Thomas, MC, LLD, of Worthing; *m* 1931, Baron Pearson, CBE, PC (Life Peer) (d 1980); 1 s, 1 da; *Style* - The Rt Hon the Lady Pearson

PEARSON, Gen Sir Thomas (Cecil Hook); KCB (1967, CB 1964), CBE (1959, OBE 1953), DSO 1940, and Bar 1943; s of late Vice-Adm J L Pearson, CMG; *b* 1 July 1914; *Educ* Charterhouse and Sandhurst; *m* 1947, Aud, da of late Alf Skjelkvale, of Oslo; 2 s; *Career* C-in-C, Allied Forces, Northern Europe 1972-74, ret 1974; psc 1942, jssc 1950, ndc Canada 1957; ADC

Gen to the Queen 1974-, Col Cmmdt Royal Green Jackets 1973-77; *Style* - General Sir Thomas Pearson, KCB, CBE, DSO*; Streete House, Weston under Penyard, Ross on Wye, Herefordshire HR9 7NY

PEART, Baron (Life Peer UK 1976); (Thomas) Frederick Peart; PC (1964); s of Emerson Featherstone Peart, of Durham; *b* 30 April 1914; *Educ* Crook Cncl Sch, Wolsingham G S, Henry Smith Secdy Hartlepool, Bede Coll Durham U, Inner Temple, Inns of Court; *m* 1945, Sarah Elizabeth Lewis; 1 s; *Career* MP (L) Workington Div of Cumberland, 1945-76, Lord Privy Seal and Leader of the House of Lords 1976-79, Leader of the Opposition in the House of Lords 1979-; chm Retail Consortium, 1979-, Advsy Council for Applied R&D 1976-; pres British Karate Bd 1979-, Hon DSc Cranfield 1977; *Style* - The Rt Hon the Lord Peart, PC; House of Lords, SW1

PEART, Hon Emerson Frederick; s of Baron Peart, PC (Life Peer); *b* 1948; *Style* - The Hon Emerson Peart

PEASE, Dowager Lady; Emily Elizabeth; JP (N Yorks); adopted da of late James Smith, of Thornaby; *m* 1922, as his 3 w, Sir Alfred Edward Pease, 2 Bt (d 1939); *Style* - Dowager Lady Pease JP; Baysdale Cottage, Pinchinthorpe, Guisborough, Cleveland

PEASE, Hon Mrs (Elizabeth Jane); *née* Ormsby-Gore; da of 4 Baron Harlech, KG, GCMG, PC (d 1964); *b* 1929; *m* 1962, the Hon William Simon Pease, s of 1 Baron Wardington (d 1950); *Style* - The Hon Mrs Pease; 72 Ladbroke rd, W11

PEASE, Hon George; s of 2 Baron Gainford, TD, and Veronica, Baroness Gainford, *qv*; hp of bro, 3 Baron Gainford; *b* 20 April 1926; *Educ* Eton; *m* 1958, Flora, da of Dr Neville Dyce Sharp; 2 s, 2 da; *Career* ARIBA, MRTPI, served WW II RNVR, County Planning Offr Ross & Cromarty; *Style* - The Hon George Pease; Blairhill Cottage, Rumbling Bridge, Kinross

PEASE, Joseph Gurney; s of Sir Alfred Edward Pease, 2 Bt (d 1939), & hp of bro, Sir (Alfred) Vincent Pease, 4 Bt; *b* 16 Nov 1927; *Educ* Bootham Sch, York; *m* 1953, Shelagh Munro, da of Cyril G Bulman; 1 s, 1 da; *Career* memb of Guisborough Urban District Council 1950-53; *Style* - Joseph Pease Esq; The Woolpack Inn, Eskdale, via Holmrook, Cumbria

PEASE, Hon John Michael; s of 2 Baron Gainford, TD, and Veronica, Baroness Gainford, *qv*; *b* 22 Sept 1930; *Educ* Gordonstoun; *m* 1962, Catherine, da of Duncan Shaw; 3 s; *Style* - The Hon John Pease; Auchentenavil, Tayvallich, Lochgilphead, Argyll

PEASE, Hon Joanna Ruth Miriam; da of 3 Baron Gainford; *b* 22 Aug 1959; *Style* - The Hon Joanna Pease

PEASE, Hon Phyllis Helen; da of 1 Baron Daryngton, PC (d 1949); *b* 12 Sept 1904; *Educ* Beaufort Sch, Cambridge U, LSE; *Career* head almoner Bethnal Green Hosp 1935-41, head medical social worker St Stephen's Hosp 1942-65; *Clubs* University Women's; *Style* - The Hon Phyllis Pease; 7 Stocks Mead, Washington, Pulborough, W Sussex RH20 4AD (☎ Ashington 892246)

PEASE, Hon Mrs - Hon Rosemary; *née* Portman; da of 5 Viscount Portman (d 1942); *b* 1931; *m* 1951, Derrick Allix Pease, s of Sir Richard Arthur Pease, 2 Bt (d 1969); 3 s, 1 da; *Style* - The Hon Mrs Pease; 2 Britten st, SW3; Upper Woodcott, Whitchurch, Hants

PEASE, Richard Peter; s and h of Sir Richard Thorn Pease, 3 Bt; *b* 4 Sept 1958; *Style* - Richard Pease Esq; c/o Hindley House, Stocksfield-on-Tyne, Northumberland

PEASE, Dr Rendel Sebastian; s of Michael Stewart Pease; *b* 1922; *Educ* Bedales, Trin Cambridge; *m* 1952, Susan Spickernell; 2 s, 3 da; *Career* dir Culham Laboratory UKAEA 1968-; Pres Inst of Physics 1978-; FRS 1977; *Style* - Dr Rendel Pease; The Poplars, West Ilsley, Newbury, Berks RG16 OAW

PEASE, Sir Richard Thorn; 3 Bt (UK 1920); s of Sir Richard Arthur Pease, 2 Bt (d 1969); *b* 20 May 1922; *Educ* Eton; *m* 1956, Anne, da of late Lt-Col Reginald Francis Heyworth; 1 s, 2 da; *Heir* s, Richard Peter Pease; *Career* 60 Rifles 1941-46; v-chm Barclays Bank Ltd 1970-, Barclays Bank UK Management 1971-; *Style* - Sir Richard Pease, Bt; Hindley House, Stocksfield-on-Tyne, Northumberland

PEASE, Sir (Alfred) Vincent; 4 Bt (UK 1882); s of Sir Alfred (Edward) Pease, 2 Bt (d 1939) and half-bro of Sir Edward Pease, 3 Bt (d 1963); *b* 2 April 1926; *Educ* Bootham Sch York; *Heir* bro, Joseph Gurney Pease; *Style* - Sir Vincent Pease, Bt; The Woolpack Inn, Boot, Eskdale, Cumbria CA19 1TH (☎ Eskdale 230)

PEASE, Hon Virginia Claire Margaret; da of 3 Baron Gainford; *b* 13 Oct 1960; *Style* - The Hon Virginia Pease

PEASE, Hon William Simon; s of 1 Baron Wardington (d 1950), and hp of bro, 2 Baron; *b* 15 Oct 1925; *Educ* Eton, New Coll Oxford, St Thomas's Hosp Medical Sch (MB, BS); *m* 1962, Hon Elizabeth Jane Ormsby-Gore, da of 4 Baron Harlech; *Career* late Capt Gren Gds; consulting surg ENT Dept Central Middx and Northwick Park Hosps; FRCS; *Clubs* Royal Yacht Sqdn, Royal Ocean Racing, Royal and Ancient; *Style* - Dr The Hon William Pease; 72 Ladbroke rd, W11

PEAT, Sir Henry; KCVO (1980, CVO 1973), DFC; s of late Sir Harry (William Henry) Peat, GBE, KCVO; *b* 1913; *Educ* Eton and Trin, Oxford; *Career* served in 1939-45 War as Fl Lt RAF Bomber Command in Europe; FCA; *Clubs* United Oxford and Cambridge University; *Style* - Sir Henry Peat, KCVO, DFC; Gothic Cottage, Bath rd, Littlewick, Maidenhead, Berks SL6 3QR

PEAT, William Wood Watson; CBE (1972), JP (Stirlingshire 1963); s of William Peat; *b* 14 Dec 1922; *Educ* Denny Public Sch; *m* 1955, Jean Frew Paton McHarrie; 2 s, 1 da; *Career* farmer; dir FMC Ltd; broadcaster; V-Pres Scottish Advsy Ctee Assoc of Agriculture 1979-, memb British Ag Council 1974-; *Style* - William Peat Esq, CBE, JP; Carbro, 61 Stirling rd, Larbert, Stirlinghsire FK5 4SG (☎ Larbert 2420)

PECHELL, Doris Lady - Doris Margery; da of late T Drewitt Lobb, of Kent, and formerly w of Lt-Col Arthur Thomas Begg Green; *m* 1971, as his 2 w, Sir Paul Pechell, 8 Bt, MC (d 1972); *Style* - Doris, Lady Pechell; Flat 1, 35 Talbot ave, Talbot Woods, Bournemouth

PECHELL, Sir Ronald (Horace); 9 Bt (GB 1797); s of Maj Hugh Charles Pechell and ggs of Cdr Charles Pechell, bro of 5 Bt; suc kinsman, Sir Paul Pechell, 8 Bt, MC, 1972; *b* 4 June 1918; *Educ* St Paul's Sch, HMS Worcester; *m* 1949, Dora Constance, da of late John Crampthorne; *Heir* none; *Career* late RAF Marine Craft Section; Royal Humane Soc Medal 1950; *Style* - Sir Ronald Pechell, Bt; c/o Childe & Co, 1 Fleet st, EC4

PECK, Antony Dilwyn; CB (1965), MBE (1945); s of late Sir James Peck, CB; *b* 10 April 1914; *Educ* Eton and Trin Oxford; *m* 1, 1939, Joan de Burgh Whyte (d 1955); 1 s, 1 da; m 2, 1956, Sylvia Glenister; 1 s, 2 da; *Career* Dep Sec Dept of Trade and Industry 1970-73, ret; *Style* - Antony Peck Esq, CB, MBE; 45 Argyll rd, W8 (☎ 01 937 2869)

PECK, His Honour Judge - David (Edward); s of late William Edward Peck; *b* 6 April 1917; *Educ* Charterhouse and Balliol Oxford; *m* 1, 1950 (m dis), Rosina Seton Glover Marshall; 1 s, 3 da; m 2, 1973, Frances Deborah Redford, nee Mackenzie; 1 s; *Career* barr Middle Temple 1949, a Circuit Judge (formerly Judge of County Courts) 1969-, memb County Court Rule Ctee 1978-; *Style* - His Honour Judge Peck; 8 New Square, Lincoln's Inn, WC2A 3QP

PECK, Sir Edward (Heywood); GCMG (1974, KCMG 1966, CMG 1957); s of Lt-Col Edward Surman Peck, IMS; *b* 5 Oct 1915; *Educ* Clifton Coll, Queen's Oxford; *m* 1948, Alison Mary MacInnes; 1 s, 2 da; *Career* Entered Consular Ser 1938, British High Cmmr in

Kenya 1966-68, Dep Under-Sec of State, FCO 1968-70, British Perm Rep to North Atlantic Council 1970-75, ret; Hon Visiting Fell in Defence Studies Aberdeen U 1976-; *Style* - Sir Edward Peck, GCMG; Easter Torrans, Tomintoul, Banffshire

PECK, Sir John (Howard); KCMG (1971, CMG 1956); s of late Howard Peck; *b* 16 Feb 1913; *Educ* Wellington College, CCC Oxford; *m* 1939, Mariska Caroline (d 1979), da of Josef Somlo; 2 s; *Career* UK Perm Rep to the Council of Europe, Consul-Gen Strasbourg 1959-62, Ambass to Senegal 1962-66, and Mauritania 1962-65, Assist Under-Sec of State FO then FCO 1966-70, Ambass to the Republic of Ireland 1970-73; dir Irish Dunlop Ltd, Edward Dillon & Co Ltd Dublin; *Style* - Sir John Peck KCMG; 4 Eglinton Park, Dun Laoghaire, Co Dublin (☎ Dublin 806315)

PECK, Stanley Edwards; CBE (1974), BEM (1954), QPM (1964), DL (Staffs 1962); s of late Harold Edwards Peck; *b* 1916; *Educ* Solihull Sch and Birmingham U; *m* 1939, Yvonne Sydney Edwards, da of late John Edwards Jessop, LDS; 2 s, 2 da; *Career* HM Inspector of Constabulary 1964-78, OStJ; *Style* - Stanley Peck Esq, CBE, BEM, QPM, DL; Lodge gdns, Walnut Grove, Radcliffe-on-Trent, Notts

PEDDER, Vice-Adm Sir Arthur (Reid); KBE (1959), CB (1956); s of late Sir John Pedder, KBE, CB; *b* 6 July 1904; *Educ* Osborne and Dartmouth; *m* 1934, Dulcie, da of O L Bickford; 2 s; *Career* Cdr Admiralty 1937-40, Capt 1944, Rear-Adm 1953, Vice-Adm 1956, Cdr Allied Naval Forces Northern Europe 1957-59; *Clubs* Athenaeum; *Style* - Vice-Adm Sir Arthur Pedder, KBE, CB; Langhurst, Hascombe, Godalming, Surrey (☎ Hascombe 294)

PEDDER, Air Vice-Marshal Ian Maurice; OBE (1963), DFC (1949); s of Maurice Albert Pedder (d 1967); *b* 2 May 1926; *Educ* Royal G S High Wycombe and Queen's, Oxford; *m* 1949, Jean Mary, da of Thomas Kellett; *Career* served in sqdns in Far East, Germany and UK 1944-64, directing staff of RAF Staff Coll 1964-67, Staff and Command Appts 1967-80, Dep Controller Nat Air Traffic Services 1977-; *Style* - Vice-Adm Sir Arthur Pedder, OBE, DFC; Pilton, Barnstaple, N Devon

PEDDIE, Maj-Gen Graham; CB (1959), DSO (1945), MBE (1941); s of late Graham Peddie; *b* 15 Oct 1905; *Educ* Sherborne Sch and RMA Woolwich; *m* 1, 1937, Dorothy Mary Humfress (decd); 1 s, 1 da; 2, 1959, Alexandra Mavrojani; *Career* RA 1926, BAOR 1953-56, dir of Manpower Planning War Office 1957-60, ret 1960; *Style* - Maj-Gen Graham Peddie, CB, DSO, MBE; Sundridge, Stratton, Cirencester, Glos GL7 2LJ

PEDDIE, Baroness - Hilda Mary Alice; da of Henry James Ernest Bull, of Lowestoft and Hull; *m* 1931, Baron Peddie, MBE (Life Peer) (d 1978); *Style* - The Rt Hon the Lady Peddie; 20 The Ridings, Epsom, Surrey

PEDDIE, Hon Ian James Crofton; s of Baron Peddie (Life Peer) (d 1978); *b* 1945; *Educ* Gordonstoun, U College London (LLB); *m* 1976, Susan Renee, da of Edmund John Brampton Howes; *Career* barr Inner Temple 1971; *Style* - The Hon Ian Peddie; 13 Tavistock Terrace, Islington, N19

PEDLER, Sir Frederick (Johnson); s of Charles Henry Pedler; *b* 10 July 1908; *Educ* Watford G S, Caius Cambridge; *m* 1935, Esther Ruth Carling; 2 s, 1 da; *Career* Ch Brit Econ Rep Dakar 1942, Finance Dept Colonial Office 1944; dep chm United Africa Co 1965-68, dir Unilever Ltd and NV 1956-68, William Baird Ltd 1969-75; treasurer Sch of Oriental and African Studies London U 1969-; kt 1969; *Style* - Sir Frederick Pedler; 36 Russell rd, Moor Park, Northwood, Middx

PEECH, Neil Malcolm; s of Albert Orlando Peech; *b* 27 Jan 1908; *Educ* Wellington, Magdalen Oxford; *m* 1932, Margaret Josephine, da of late R C Smallwood CBE; 1 s, 1 da; *Career* md The Steetley Co Ltd 1935-68 (chm 1935-76, pres 1976-), dir Albright & Wilson Ltd 1958-, Lloyd's Underwriter 1950-69, High Sheriff of Yorkshire 1959; *Style* - Neil

Peech Esq; Park House, Firbeck, Worksop (☎ Worksop 730338)

PEEK, Sir Francis Henry Grenville; 4 Bt (UK 1874); s of Sir Wilfrid Peek, 3 Bt, DSO (d 1927); *b* 16 Sept 1915; *Educ* Eton, Trin Cambridge; *m* 1, 1942 (m dis 1949), Ann, da of late Capt Gordon Duff and widow of Sir Charles Mappin (she m 1951, Sir William Rootes, later 1 Baron Rootes); m 2, 1949 (m dis 1967), Marilyn, da of Dr Norman Kerr (she m 1967, Peter Quennell); 1 s (decd); m 3, 1967, Mrs Caroline Kirkwood, da of Sir Robert Lucien Morrison Kirkwood; *Heir* kinsman, William Grenville Peek; *Career* ADC to Govr of Bahamas 1938-39, served Irish Guards 1939-46; *Style* - Sir Francis Peek, Bt; Los Picos, Nagueles, Marbella, Spain (☎ 774736); 60 Grosvenor Close, Nassau, Bahamas

PEEK, Vice-Adm Sir Richard Innes; KBE (1972, OBE 1944), CB (1971), DSC (1945); s of late James Norman Peek; *b* 30 July 1914 *Educ* Roy Australian Naval Coll; *m* 1, 1943, Margaret Seinor, nee Kendall (d 1946); 1 s; m 2, 1952, Mary Catherine Tilley, nee Stops; 2 da; *Career* 2 Naval memb Australian Naval Bd 1968-70, Ch of Naval Staff Australia 1970-73; Legion of Merit (USA); *Style* - Vice-Adm Sir Richard Peek, KBE, CB, DSC; Rothlyn, RMB, Monaro Highway, via Cooma, NSW 2630, Australia

PEEK, William Grenville; s of late Capt Roger Grenville Peek (2 s of 2 Bt) and hp of kinsman, Sir Francis Peek, 4 Bt; *b* 15 Dec 1919; *Educ* Eton; *m* 1950, Lucy Jane, da of late Maj Edward Dorrien-Smith; 1 s, 3 da; *Career* Capt late 9th Lancers; 1939-45 War (despatches); *Style* - William Peek Esq; Hazelwood, Loddiswell, S Devon

PEEL, 3 Earl (UK 1929); Sir William James Robert Peel; 8 Bt (GB 1800); Viscount Peel (UK 1895) and Viscount Clanfield (UK 1929); s of 2 Earl Peel (d 1969, himself gs of 1 Viscount, who was in turn 5 s of Sir Robert Peel, 2 Bt, the distinguished statesman); *b* 3 Oct 1947; *Educ* Ampleforth, Tours U, RAC Cirencester; *m* 1973, Veronica Naomi Livingston, da of Alastair Timpson; 1 s, 1 da; *Heir* s, Viscount Clanfield; *Clubs* Turf; *Style* - The Rt Hon the Earl Peel; Gunnerside Lodge, Richmond, N Yorks

PEEL, Lady - Beatrice Gladys; da of late John Lillie; *m* 1920, Sir Robert Peel, 5 Bt (d 1934); *Style* - Lady Peel; c/o Barclays Bank, 415 Strand, WC2

PEEL, Lady Iona Joy Julia; da of 3 Earl Peel; *b* 1978; *Style* - Lady Iona Peel

PEEL, Sir (William) John; s of late Sir William Peel, KCMG, KBE; *b* 16 June 1912; *Educ* Wellington, Queens' Cambridge; *m* 1936, Rosemary Mia Minka, da of Robert Readhead; 1 s, 3 da; *Career* Contested (C) Meriden Div of Warwicks 1955, MP (C) Leicester SE 1957-Feb 1974, PPS to Economic Sec to the Treasury 1958-59, to Min of State BOT 1959-60, Assistant Govt Whip 1960-61, a Lord Cmmr of the Treasury Nov 1961-Oct 1964, hon dir Con Party International Office 1975-76; kt 1973; *Style* - Sir John Peel; 51 Cambridge st, SW1 (☎ 01 834 8762)

PEEL, Jack Armitage; CBE (1972), DL (W Yorks, 1971); s of George Henry Peel; *b* 8 Jan 1921; *Educ* Ruskin Coll, Oxford; *m* 1950, Dorothy Mabel Dobson; 1 s, 1 da; *Career* dir Industrial Relations in the Social Affairs Directorate EEC 1973-79, ch adviser 1979-; JP Bradford 1960-72; *Style* - Jack Peel Esq, CBE, DL; 21 Fitzroy rd, Bradford Moor, Bradford, W Yorks

PEEL, Sir John Harold; KCVO (1960); s of Rev J E Peel; *b* 10 Dec 1904; *Educ* Manchester G S, Queen's, Oxford, King's Coll Hosp Med Sch; *m* 1947, Freda Margaret Mellish; 1 da; *Career* Surgeon-Gynaecologist to the Queen 1961-73, Consulting Obstetric and Gynaecological Surgeon King's Coll Hosp 1969-, Emeritus Consulting Gynaecologist Princess Beatrice Hosp 1965-; FRCP, FRCS, FRCOG; *Style* - Sir John Peel KCVO; Warren Court Farm, West Tytherley, Salisbury, Wilts

PEEL, Capt Jonathan Sidney; MC; s of Maj David Arthur Peel (ka 1944 - s of late Rev the Hon Maurice Berkeley Peel MC, 4 s of 1 Visc Peel); *b* 1937; *Educ* Norwich Sch, Eton Coll and St John's Coll

Cambridge; *m* 1965, Jean Fulton, da of Air Ch Marshal Sir Denis Hensley Fulton Barnett, GCB, CBE, DFC; 1 s, 4 da; *Career* formerly Capt Rifle Bde Malaya 1957, Congo 1960-61; a Page of Honour to HM 1951-53; dir Norwich Union Insurance Gp, Vice Ld-Lt for Norfolk 1980-; JP, CCllr; *Style* - Captain Jonathan Peel, MC, JP, HM Vice Lord-Lieut for Norfolk; Barton Hall, Barton Turf, Norwich NR12 8AU

PEEL, Hon Robert Michael Arthur; s of 2 Earl Peel (d 1969); *b* 5 Feb 1950; *Educ* Eton, Hertford Oxford; *m* 1973, Fiona Natalie, da of Charles Davidson, of Dunhampstead House, Droitwich, Worcs; 2 da; *Style* - The Hon Robert Peel

PEEL, Hon Mrs (Sara Carola); *née* Vanneck; da of 5 Baron Huntingfield, KCMG (d 1969); *b* 1913; *m* 1936, Major David Arthur Peel, MC (ka 1944); *Style* - The Hon Mrs Peel; Huntingfield Hall, Halesworth, Suffolk IP19 OQA

PEET, Ronald Hugh; CBE (1974); s of Henry Leonard Peet; *b* 12 July 1925; *Educ* Doncaster G S, Queen's Oxford; *m* 1949, Winifred Joy (d 1979), da of late Ernest Adamson; 2 s, 2 da; *Career* chm Legal and General Assurance Soc Ltd 1979-, dir and gp ch exec Legal & General Gp 1979-, chm Aviation & General Assurance Soc Ltd 1978-80, dir Watling Street Properties 1971-, chm City Arts Trust Ltd 1980-, dir Roy Philharmonic Orchestra Ltd 1977-, English Nat Opera 1978-; FIA; *Recreations* music, opera; *Clubs* Hurlingham; *Style* - Ronald Peet Esq CBE; 83 Deodar rd, Putney SW15, (☎ 01 874 9694)

PEGNA, Hon Mrs Elizabeth Ruth Frances; da of 1 Baron Layton (d 1966); *b* 1923; *m* 1944 (m dis 1965), Bobbie Pegna; 2 s, 1 da; *Style* - The Hon Mrs Elizabeth Pegna; Whitegates, Chedworth, Cheltenham, Glos

PEIERLS, Sir Rudolf Ernst; CBE (1946); s of H Peierls; *b* Berlin, 5 June 1907; *Educ* Humboldt Sch Oberschöneweide Berlin, Us of Berlin, Munich, Leipzig; MA (Cantab), DSc Manchester, DPhil Leipzig; *m* 1931, Eugenia, da of late N Kannegiesser; 1 s, 3 da; *Career* Wykeham Prof of Physics Oxford U, Fell New Coll Oxford 1963-74, now Emeritus Fell; Prof of Physics (part-time) Washington U, Seattle 1974-77; FRS 1945, kt 1968; *Clubs* Athenaeum; *Style* - Sir Rudolf Peierls, CBE; Farleigh, Orchard Lane, Old Boar's Hill, Oxford OX1 5JH

PEILE, Vice-Adm Sir Lancelot Arthur Babington; KBE (1960), CB (1957), DSO (1941), MVO (1947), DL (Devon 1969); s of late Basil Wilson Peile; *b* 22 Jan 1905; *Educ* RNC's Osborne and Dartmouth; *m* 1928, Gertrude Margaret, nee Tolcher; 2 s; *Career* Cdr (E) 1939, Capt (E) 1947, Rear-Adm 1955, Vice-Adm 1958, Adm Superintendent Devonport Dockyard 1957-60, ret 1960; *Style* - Vice-Adm Sir Lancelot Peile, KBE, CB, DSO, MVO, DL; Strawberry How, Thurlestone, Kingsbridge, Devon (☎ Thurlestone 209)

PELHAM, Lady Arabella; 2 da of 7 Earl of Yarborough, JP; *b* 20 Jan 1960; *Style* - Lady Arabella Pelham

PELHAM, Hon Mrs Anthony Barbara Clare; da of late Col J E D Tanton, late DQMG, Australian Mil Forces; *m* 1928, as his 2 w, Hon Anthony Ashley Ivo Pelham (s of late 5 Earl of Chichester and who d 1951); *Style* - The Hon Mrs Anthony Pelham; Halland, Clyst St Mary, Exeter, Devon (☎ Topsham 3010)

PELHAM, Sir (George) Clinton; KBE (1957), CMG (1949); s of George Pelham; *b* 20 May 1898; *Educ* privately; *m* 1930, Jeanie Adelina Morton; 2 da; *Career* Ambass to Saudi Arabia 1951-55, to Czechoslovakia 1955-57, ret; FRGS; *Clubs* Carlton; *Style* - Sir Clinton Pelham, KBE, CMG; Belcroute, Boughton Hall ave, Send, Surrey GU23 7DP

PELHAM, Lady Georgina Joceleyn; da of late 8 Earl of Chichester; *b* 1942; *Style* - Lady Georgina Pelham

PELHAM, Richard Anthony Henry; s of late Maj Anthony George Pelham; hp of kinsman, 9 Earl of Chichester; *b* 1 Aug 1952; *Educ* Eton; *Recreations* vintage motor cycle racing; *Clubs* Vintage Motor

Cycle; *Style* - Richard Pelham Esq; c/o Coutts & Co, 162 Brompton rd, SW3

PELHAM, Lady Sophia; da of 7 Earl of Yarborough, JP; *b* 15 Oct 1958; *Style* - Lady Sophia Pelham

PELHAM, Hon Mrs; Hon Valerie; da of Baron Segal (Life Peer); *b* 1943; *m* 1967, Paul Nicholas David Pelham; children; *Style* - The Hon Mrs Pelham; Creaseys Farm, Hutton, Essex; 24 Frognal Lane, NW3

PELHAM, Lady Vanessa Petronel; 3 da of 7 Earl of Yarborough, JP; *b* 21 Sept 1961; *Style* - Lady Vanessa Pelham

PELHAM BURN, Angus Maitland; s of Brig-Gen Henry Pelham Burn, CMG, DSO (d 1958); *b* 13 Dec 1931; *Educ* Harrow, N of Scotland Coll of Agriculture; *m* 1959, Anne Rosdew, da of Sir Ian Forbes-Leith, 2 Bt (d 1973); 4 da; *Career* farmer, Vice Ld-Lt for Kincardineshire 1978-, dir Bank of Scotland 1977-, dir: Aberdeen and Northern Marts Ltd 1970-, Aberdeen Meat Marketing Co Ltd 1973-, MacRobert Farms (Douneside) Ltd 1970-, Jessfield Ltd 1970-, Scottish Provident Institution 1975- (dep chm 1980-), Pelett Admin Ltd 1973-, Prime Space Design (Scotland) Ltd 1981-; memb, Roy Co of Archers (Queen's Body Guard for Scotland) 1968-, DL Kincardineshire 1978, OStJ 1978; *Recreations* fishing stalking, photography, shooting; *Clubs* Caledonian, Roy Northern (Aberdeen) *Style* - Angus Pelham Burn Esq, HM Vice Lord-Lieut for Kincardineshire; Knappach, Banchory, Kincardineshire AB3 3JS (☎ Crathes 555)

PELHAM-CLINTON, Edward Charles; s of late Capt Guy Edward Pelham-Clinton, MC (s of Lord Charles Pelham-Clinton, 2 s of 4 Duke of Newcastle, KG) by his w Hermione, ggda of Hon Arthur Tollemache (3 s of William, Lord Huntingtower, whose eldest s was 8 Earl of Dysart) hp of 9 Duke of Newcastle, OBE; *b* 18 Aug 1920; *Educ* Eton, Cambridge; *Career* assist keeper Roy Scottish Museum Edinburgh; Capt RA 1939-45 *Style* - Edward Pelham-Clinton Esq; Gillerhill, Winchburgh, West Lothian

PELLEW, Hon Alexander Paul; s (younger twin, by 2 m) of 10 Viscount Exmouth; *b* 30 Oct 1978

PELLEW, Hon Edward Francis; s (twin, by 2 m) and h of 10 Viscount Exmouth; *b* 30 Oct 1978

PELLEW, Hon Peter Irving; s of late 9 Viscount Exmouth & Maria Luisa (Marquesa e Olias), da of late Marqués de Amurrio, of Madrid; *b* 1942; *Educ* Downside; *Style* - The Hon Peter Pellew

PELLEW, Hon Patricia Sofia; da (by 1 m) of 10 Viscount Exmouth; *b* 1966; *Style* - The Hon Patricia Pellew

PELLEW, Hon Mrs Rose Mary; *née* Pellew; da of late 8 Visc Exmouth, OBE, MRCS, LRCP; *b* 1903; *m* 1942 (m dis 1949), Maurice Van de Goor; 2 da (twins); *Career* resumed surname Pellew 1949; *Style* - The Hon Mrs Rose Pellew; Le Boué, Jurançon, Pau, Basses Pyrénées, France

PELLY, Cornelius James; CMG (1952), OBE (1944); s of Hyacinth Albert Pelly; *b* 8 April 1908; *Educ* Clongowes Wood Coll Co Kildare, Trin Coll Dublin; *m* 1949, Una O'Shea, da of Patrick Seaborn O'Shea; 1 s, 1 da; *Career* ICS 1930; Sec for Financial Affairs Sultanate of Muscat and Oman 1968-70; *Style* - Cornelius Pelly Esq, CMG, OBE; 12 Stoke Water House, Beaminster, Dorset (☎ 862807)

PELLY, Sir John Alwyne; 6 Bt (UK 1840), of Upton, Essex, JP (Hants 1969), DL (Hants); s of Sir (Harold) Alwyne Pelly, 5 Bt, MC (d 1981), and Caroline (d 1976), da of Richard Heywood-Jones, of Badsworth Hall, Yorks; *b* 11 Sept 1918; *Educ* Canford and RMC; *m* 1, 1945, Ava Barbara Anne, da of Brig Keith Frederick William Dunn, CBE; m 2, 1950, Elsie May, da of late L Thomas Dechow, of Rhodesia (now Zimbabwe); 1 da (and 1 da decd); *Heir* bro, Richard Pelly; *Career* Maj Coldstream Gds (Reserve of Officers), 1939-45 War; High Sheriff Hants 1970-71; *Clubs* Guards; *Style* - Sir John Pelly, Bt, JP, DL; Preshaw House, Upham, Nr Southampton

PELLY, Richard Heywood; 2 s of Sir

Alwyne Pelly, 5 Bt, MC (d 1981); hp to bro, Sir John Pelly, 6 Bt, JP, DL; *b* 25 April 1920; *Educ* Wellington; *m* 1948, Mary, da of John Luscombe, of N Huish, Devon; 1 s (Richard John b 10 April 1951, educ Wellington & Wadham Oxford), 1 da (Jane Carol b 18 May 1949); *Career* FRICS, FLAS; served WW II temp Capt RASC; *Style* - Richard Pelly Esq; Loup House, Lyme rd, Axminster, Devon (☎ 32298)

PEMBERTON, Sir Francis Wingate William; CBE (1970); s of late Dr William Warburton Wingate (assumed Arms of Pemberton, by Roy Licence, 1921) and Viola Patience Campbell Pemberton; *b* 1 Oct 1916; *Educ* Eton, Trin Cambridge; *m* 1941, Diana Patricia, da of Reginald Salisbury Woods and late Irene Woods, CBE, TD; 2 s; *Career* sr ptnr Bidwells (Chartered Surveyors), dir Agricultural Mortgage Corpn Ltd 1969-, Barclays Bank UK Management Ltd 1977-, High Sheriff Cambridgeshire and Isle of Ely 1965-66, kt 1976, FRICS; *Style* - Sir Francis Pemberton CBE; Trumpington Hall, Cambridge (☎ Cambridge 841941)

PEMBROKE AND MONTGOMERY, 17 Earl of (E 1551) and 14 Earl of (E 1605) respectively; Henry George Charles Alexander Herbert; also Baron Herbert of Cardiff (E 1551), Baron Herbert of Shurland (E 1605), and Baron Herbert of Lea (UK 1861); s of 16 Earl of Pembroke and Montgomery, CVO (d 1969) and of Mary Countess of Pembroke; *b* 19 May 1939; *Educ* Eton and Oxford U; *m* 1966 (m dis 1981), Claire Rose, da of Douglas Pelly; 1 s, 3 da; *Heir* s, Lord Herbert; *Career* Hereditary Grand Visitor of Jesus Coll Oxford, Roy Horse Gds 1958-60; *Also* owner of Wilton House (Inigo Jones, built around 1650, with additonal work by James Wyatt 1810); *Style* - The Rt Hon the Earl of Pembroke and Montgomery; Wilton House, Salisbury, Wilts (☎ Wilton 3211)

PEMBROKE AND MONTGOMERY, Mary, Countess of - Lady Mary Dorothea; *née* Hope; CVO (1947); da of 1 Marquess of Linlithgow, KT, GCMG, GCVO, PC (d 1908); *m* 1936, 16 Earl of Pembroke and Montgomery, CVO (d 1969); *Career* Hon 1 Officer WRNS; a Lady-in-Waiting to HRH the Duchess of Kent 1934-49 and an Extra Lady-in-Waiting 1949-68; *Style* - The Rt Hon Mary, Countess of Pembroke and Montgomery CVO; The Old Rectory, Wilton, Salisbury

PENDER, 3 Baron (UK 1937); John Willoughby Denison-Pender; s of 2 Baron Pender CBE (d 1965); *see* Lord Paget of Northampton; *b* 6 May 1933; *Educ* Eton; *m* 1962, Julia, da of Richard Nevill Cannon OBE, of Coombe Place, Lewes; 1 s, 2 da; *Heir* s, Hon Henry John Richard Denison-Pender; *Career* formerly Lt 10 Roy Hussars and Capt City of London Yeo; *Clubs* White's and Pratt's; *Style* - The Rt Hon the Lord Pender; North Court, Tilmanstone, Kent

PENDER, Camilla, Baroness - Camilla Lethbridge; da of late Willoughby Arthur Pemberton; *m* 1930, 2 Baron Pender, CBE (d 1965); *Style* - The Rt Hon Camilla, Lady Pender; 151 Cranmer Court, SW3

PENDER, Reginald Robinson; s of Reginald George Pender (d 1967); *b* 23 March 1934; *Educ* Harrow; *m* 1958, Elizabeth, da of Charles Joseph Meager (d 1968); 2 s, 1 da; *Career* Capt (Army) Nat Service 1952-54; md Stag Line Ltd, chm Marine Shipping Mutual Insurance Co Ltd 1978-; Fell Inst of Chartered Ship Brokers 1958; *Recreations* gardening; *Clubs* Challoner; *Style* - Reginald Pender Esq; 10 Beverley gdns, Cullercoats, Northumberland (☎ 0632 521282); Bark Mill, West Hall, Brampton, Cumbria (☎ 06972 289)

PENDRED, Air Marshal Sir Lawrence Fleming; KBE (1954, MBE 1933), CB (1947), DFC, DL (Warwickshire 1959); s of Dr B F Pendred (d 1948); *b* 5 May 1899; *Educ* Epsom Coll; *m* 1923, Nina, da of M Chour, of Tiflis, S Russia; 2 s; *Career* RAF 1917, Wing Cdr 1938, Actg Air Cdre 1942, Assist Cmdt RAF Staff Coll 1944, Air Vice-Marshal 1948, Cmdt Sch of Land-Air Warfare Old Sarum 1950-52, AOC-in-C Flying Training Command 1952-55, Air Marshal 1953, ret 1955; dir Civil Defence Midland Region 1955-6; *Style* - Air

Marshal Sir Lawrence Pendred, KBE, CB, DFC, DL; 13 Lansdowne Circus, Leamington Spa, Warwicks (☎ Leamington Spa 23559)

PENDRY, Thomas; MP (L) Stalybridge and Hyde 1970-; *b* 10 June 1934; *Educ* St Augustine's Ramsgate, Oxford U; *m* 1966, Moira Anne Smith; 1 da; *Career* Lord Cmmr of the Treasury and Govt Whip 1974-77, Parly Under-Sec of State, NI Office 1978-79, Opposition Spokesman on NI 1979-; *Style* - Thomas Pendry Esq MP; Chapel House, Gorsey Brow, Broadbottom, Cheshire

PENFOLD, Maj-Gen Robert Bernard; CB (1969), MVO (1957); s of late Bernard Hugh Penfold; *b* 19 Dec 1916; *Educ* Wellington, RMC Sandhurst; *m* 1940, Ursula, da of Lt-Col E H Gray; 2 da; *Career* Ch of Defence Staff Kenya 1966-69, GOC S E District 1969-72, gen man Royal Hong Kong Jockey Club 1972-; *Style* - Maj-Gen Robert Penfold, CB, MVO; c/o Grindlays Bank, 13 St James's sq, SW1

PENHALIGON, David Charles; MP (Lib) Truro, Oct 1974-; s of late Robert Charles Penhaligon; *b* 6 June 1944; *Educ* Truro Sch, Cornwall Tech Coll (CEng, MIMechE); *m* 1968, Annette Lidgey; 1 s, 1 da; *Career* Liberal Party Spokesman on Transport and Energy; *Style* - David Penhaligon Esq MP; 54 Daniell rd, Truro, Cornwall (☎ Truro 70977)

PENISTON, Hon Mrs (Zoe Leighton); *née* Seager; da of 1 Baron Leighton of St Mellons, CBE (d 1963); *b* 1928; *m* 1955, Malcolm James Peniston; 1 s, 2 da; *Style* - The Hon Mrs Peniston; The Fishermans, King st, Emsworth

PENLEY, William Henry; CB (1967), CBE (1961); s of late William Edward Penley; *b* 22 March 1917; *Educ* Wallasey G S, Liverpool U; *m* 1, 1943, Raymonde Evelyn (d 1975), da of late Frederick Richard Gough; 2 s, 1 da; m 2, 1977, Marion Claytor, da of late Joseph Enoch Airey; *Career* Controller R & D Establishments, and Research, MOD, and Professional Head of Science Gp of the Civil Service 1976-77, dep dir Under Water Weapons, Marconi Space and Defence Systems Ltd 1979-, chm Appleton Laboratory Establishment Ctee 1977-; *Style* - William Penley Esq, CB, CBE; 93 Manor rd, Barton-le-Clay, Beds MK45 4NR (☎ Luton 881880)

PENN, Christopher Arthur; s of Lt-Col Sir Eric Penn, GCVO, OBE, MC; *b* 13 Sept 1950; *Educ* Wellesley House, Eton Coll; *m* 1976, Sabrina Mary, da of Timothy Colman, of Bixley Manor, Norwich; *Career* Chartered Surveyor; *Clubs* Bucks; *Style* - Christopher Penn Esq; 46 Hazlebury rd, SW6 (☎ 01 736 1872)

PENN, Lt-Col Sir Eric; GCVO (1980, KCVO 1972), OBE (1960), MC (1944); s of Capt Eric F Penn (ka 1915); *b* 9 Feb 1916; *Educ* Eton, Magdalene Cambridge; *m* 1947, Prudence Stewart-Wilson, da of late Aubyn Wilson; 2 s, 1 da; *Career* Comptroller Lord Chamberlain's Office 1964-, Extra Equerry to HM the Queen 1963-; *Clubs* Turf and White's; *Style* - Lt-Col Sir Eric Penn GCVO OBE MC; Sternfield House, Saxmundham, Suffolk (☎ Saxmundham 2456); St James's Palace, SW1 (☎ 01 839 3936)

PENNANT, His Honour Judge (David Edward Thornton); s of David Falconer Pennant, JP, DL (d 1938); *b* 2 Aug 1912; *Educ* Charterhouse, Trin Cambridge; *m* 1938, Alice Catherine, da of John Frederick Randall Stainer MBE; 3 s, 1 da; *Career* barr Inner Temple 1935; Roy Signals (TA) 1939-45, OC Signals Officers' Training Sch Mhow India 1944-45; Chllr Dioc Monmouth 1949-77, chm Radnorshire QS 1962-64, dep chm Brecknockshire QS 1956-64, Flintshire QS 1962-71, Dorset QS 1971, a Circuit Judge 1961-; *Style* - His Honour Judge Pennant; Parkbury, Balcombe rd, Branksome Park, Poole, Dorset (☎ Bournemouth 765614)

PENNELL, Montague Mattinson; CBE (1970); s of F M S Pennell; *b* 20 March 1916; *Educ* Liverpool U; *m* 1945, Helen Williams; 1 s, 2 da; *Career* Roy Corps of Signals 1939-46, md British Petroleum Co Ltd 1972- (dep chm 1975-), dir Cadbury-

Schweppes Ltd 1979-, memb Advsy Cncl for Applied R&D 1976-; *Clubs* MCC; *Style* - Montague Pennell Esq CBE; 52 Onslow sq, SW7 3NX; Rushdens Farm, Stanford Dingley, Berks

PENNEY, Baron (Life Peer UK 1967); William George Penney; OM (1969), KBE (1952, OBE 1946); s of W A Penney; *b* 24 June 1909; *Educ* Sheerness Tech Sch, Imperial Coll London, London U (PhD, DSc) Cambridge (PhD), Wisconsin (MA), Melbourne Universities (hon LLD); FRS *m* 1, 1935, Adele Minnie Elms (decd); 2 s; m 2, 1945, Eleanor Joan Quennell; *Career* director Atomic Weapons Research Establishment Aldermaston 1953-59, member for Weapon Research & Devpt, UKAEA 1954-59, memb for Research UKAEA 1959-61, (deputy chairman 1961-64, chm 1964-67); dir Tube Investments 1968-79, Standard Telephones and Cables 1971-, Treasurer, Royal Society 1956-60, (V-Pres 1957-60), Rector of the Imperial Coll of Science and Technology 1967-73; *Style* - The Rt Hon Lord Penney OM KBE; Cat st, East Hendred, Wantage, Oxon OX12 8JT

PENNEY, Hon Christopher Charles; s of Baron Penney, OM, KBE, FRS (Life Peer); *b* 1941; *Educ* Cranleigh, Gonville and Caius Cambridge; Guy's Hosp; MRCP, FRCR; *m* 1968, Margaret, da of Henry Bell Fairley, of Stockport; 1 s; *Style* - The Hon Christopher Penney; 39 Beaulieu ave, Sydenham, SE26

PENNEY, Hon Martin Charles; s of Baron Penney, OM, KBE, FRS (Life Peer); *b* 1938; *Educ* Cranleigh, Gonville and Caius Cambridge; *m* 1961, Margaret Heather, da of Sqdn-Ldr H Almond, DSO, DFC, of Basingstoke; 2 da; *Style* - The Hon Martin Penney; Ellesmere College, Ellesmere, Salop

PENNINGTON-RAMSDEN, Major Sir (Geoffrey) William; 7 Bt (E 1689); s of Sir John Frecheville Ramsden, 6 Bt (d 1958); *b* 28 Aug 1904; *Educ* Ludgrove, Eton, Jesus Cambridge; *m* 1927, Veronica Prudence Betty, da of F W Morley, formerly of Biddestone Manor, Chippenham, Wilts; 3 da; *Heir* kinsman, Caryl Oliver Imbert Ramsden; *Career* assumed by deed poll 1925, surname of Pennington in lieu of his patronymic, and the arms of Pennington quartered with those of Ramsden; resumed surname of Ramsden after that of Pennington by deed poll 1958; 11 Hussars 1925, transferred Life Gds 1927-38, served War of 1939-45, seconded to Provost Branch, APM 9 Armd Div and APM 14 Army, Maj 1942. High Sheriff Cumberland 1962-63, patron of four livings; *Style* - Major Sir William Pennington-Ramsden, Bt; Versions Farm, Brackley, Northants (☎ Brackley 702412); Ardverikie, Newtonmore, Scotland; Muncaster Castle, Ravenglass, Cumberland (☎ Ravenglass 203)

PENNOCK, Sir Raymond William; s of Frederick Henry Pennock; *b* 16 June 1920; *Educ* Coatham Sch, Merton, Oxford (Hon Fell 1979); *m* 1944, Lorna Pearse; 1 s, 2 da; *Career* Capt RA 1941-46; dep chm ICI 1975-80, chm 1980-, pres CBI 1980-82; memb Doctors' and Dentists' Pay Review Bd 1977-; kt 1977; *Style* - Sir Raymond Pennock; Imperial Chemical Industries Ltd, Imperial Chemical House, Millbank, SW1P 3JF

PENNY, Hon Edward James Frederick; s of 3 Viscount Marchwood; *b* 1970

PENNY, Francis David; s of late David Penny; *b* 20 May 1918; *Educ* Bromsgrove County H S and Univ Coll London (Fell 1973); *m* 1949, Betty E Smith, da of late Oswald C Smith; *Career* dep chm Y-ARD Ltd, md Yarrow & Co Ltd, a v-pres IMechE 1977-; FRSE, FIMarE, FIMechE; *Style* - Francis Penny Esq; Forefaulds, East Kilbride, Glasgow (☎ East Kilbride 20102)

PENNY, Joseph Noel Bailey; QC (1971); s of Joseph A Penny, JP; *b* 25 Dec 1916; *Educ* Worksop Coll, Ch Ch Oxford; *m* 1, 1947, Celia (d 1969), da of R H Roberts; 3 s, 1 da; m 2, 1972, Sara Margaret, da of Sir Arnold France; 1 da; *Career* Maj Roy Signals 1939-46; barr Gray's Inn 1948, a Nat Insurance Cmmr 1977-; *Style* - Joseph Penny Esq QC; Fair Orchard, Lingfield, Surrey (☎ Lingfield 191)

PENNY, Hon Nicholas Mark Staveley; s of 3 Viscount Marchwood; *b* 1967

PENNY, Hon Patrick Glyn; s of 2 Viscount Marchwood, MBE (d 1979); *b* 1939; *m* 1, 1968 (m dis 1974), Sue Eleanor Jane, da of late Charles Phipps Brutton, CBE; 1 da; m 2, 1979, Mrs Lynn Vanessa Knox, da of John Leslie Wyles, of Wimbledon; *Style* - The Hon Patrick Penny

PENNY, Hon Peter George Worsley; s and h of 3 Viscount Marchwood; *b* 8 Oct 1965; *Style* - The Hon Peter Penny

PENNYBACKER, Joseph Buford; CBE (1967); s of Claude Martin Pennybacker; *b* 23 Aug 1907; *Educ* Tennessee and Edinburgh Us; FRCS 1935; *m* 1941, Winifrid Dean; 1 s; *Career* dir Dept of Neurological Surgery Radcliffe Infirmary Oxford 1954-71; *Style* - Joseph Pennybacker Esq CBE; Creagandarraich, Tighnabruaich, Argyll (☎ 260)

PENNYCUICK, Rt Hon Sir John; PC (1974); s of late Col John Pennycuick, CSI; *b* 6 Nov 1899; *Educ* Winchester, New Coll Oxford; *m* 1930, Lucy Johnstone (d 1972); 1 s, 1 da; *Career* barr Inner Temple 1925, QC 1947, Bencher 1954, Treasurer 1978, Judge of High Court of Justice, Chancery Div 1960-74, Vice-Chllr 1970-74; *Style* - The Rt Hon Sir John Pennycuick PC; Old Manor House, Maids Moreton, Buckingham (☎ Buckingham 2249); 2 Harcourt Buildings, Temple, EC4 (☎ 01 583 1815)

PENRHYN, 6 Baron (UK 1866); Malcolm Frank Douglas-Pennant; DSO (1945), MBE (1943); s of 5 Baron Penrhyn (d 1967, himself gn of 17 Earl of Morton and ggs of Lady Frances Lascelles, da of 1 Earl of Harewood) and Alice Nellie (d 1965), da of Sir William Charles Cooper, 3 Bt; *b* 11 July 1908; *Educ* Eton and RMC Sandhurst; *m* 1954, Elisabeth Rosemary, da of late Brig Sir Percy Laurie, KCVO, CBE, DSO, JP; 2 da; *Heir* bro, Hon Nigel Douglas-Pennant; *Career* Col (ret) KRRC, 1939-45 in N Africa and NW Europe; *Style* - The Rt Hon the Lord Penrhyn, DSO, MBE; Littleton Manor, Winchester, Hants (☎ 880205)

PENRICE, Geoffrey; CB (1978); s of Harry Penrice; *b* 28 Feb 1923; *Educ* Thornes House G S, LSE; *m* 1947, Janet Gillies Allardice; 3 s; *Career* Dir of Statistics and Dep Sec Dept of Employment 1978-; *Style* - Geoffrey Penrice Esq CB; 10 Dartmouth Park ave, NW5 (☎ 01 267 2175)

PENROSE, George William; QC (1978); s of George W Penrose; *b* 2 June 1938; *Educ* Glasgow U; *m* 1964, Wendy Margaret Cooper; 1 s, 2 da; *Career* CA; Advocate 1964; *Style* - George Penrose Esq, QC; 5 Cobden rd, Edinburgh EH9 2BJ (☎ 031 667 1819)

PENROSE, Sir Roland Algernon; CBE (1961); s of James Doyle Penrose; *b* 14 Oct 1900; *Educ* Leighton Park Sch Reading, Queens' Cambridge; *m* 1, 1925, Valentine Andrée Boue; m 2, 1947, Lee Miller (d 1977); 1 s; *Career* chm ICA 1947-69, pres 1969-76; kt 1966; *Style* - Sir Roland Penrose CBE; Farley Farm, Chiddingly, nr Lewes, E Sussex (☎ Chiddingly 308)

PENRUDDOCK, Sir Clement Frederick; CBE (1954); s of Rev Frederick Fitzpatrick Penruddock; *b* 30 Jan 1905; *Educ* Marlborough Coll, Keble Coll Oxford; *m* 1945, Philippa Mary Tolhurst; 1 s, 3 da; *Career* slr 1931, chm Atlanta Baltimore & Chicago Investment Trust Ltd, Channel Islands & Int Investment Trust Ltd, Paten & Co (Peterborough) Ltd, West Coast and Texas Regional Investment Trust Ltd; dir Save & Prosper Gp Ltd, Ocean Wilsons (Holdings) Ltd, Lancashire & London Investment Trust Ltd, sr partner Lawrance, Messer & Co Slrs 1947-; kt 1973; *Style* - Sir Clement Penruddock CBE; Venars, Nutfield, Redhill, Surrey (☎ Nutfield Ridge 2218)

PENRY, William Cedric Rhys; s of Benjamin William Penry (d 1978); *b* 21 June 1927; *Educ* Gowerton G S, U of Wales, Swansea and Stanford-INSEAD Fontainebleau France; *m* 1952, Margaret Winifred, da of Charles Starvington, late Royal Marines; 1 s, 1 da; *Career* dir Halivourgiki Athens 1963-69, dir British Steel Corpn (Int) Ltd and British Steel Corpn (Overseas Services) 1976-, dir Slater Steel Industries of Canada 1977-;

FIM; *Recreations* golf, squash, chess; *Clubs* Directors'; *Style* - William Penry Esq; 1 Amberley Court, Maidenhead, Berks (☎ Maidenhead 72701)

PENTIN, David John; s of Sydney Edward Pentin, of Mayfield, Hackington Close, Canterbury (d 1971); *b* 26 June 1935; *Educ* Kent College, London U (LLB); *m* 1960, Alicia Henrietta Althea; 3 s, 1 da; *Career* National Service RAF; chartered accountant (FCA), admitted 1959; partner Pentin Neame & Co Chartered Accountants; *Recreations* walking, squash, cycling, music; *Clubs* Forest of Blean Rotary; *Style* - David Pentin Esq; Ashley Hse, Brewery Lane, Bridge, Canterbury (☎ Bridge 830278)

PENTLAND, 2 Baron (UK 1909); Henry John Sinclair; s of 1 Baron Pentland (d 1925) and Lady Marjorie Gordon, DBE, JP (d 1970, da of 1 Marquess of Aberdeen and Temair); *b* 6 June 1907; *Educ* Cargilfield, Wellington, and Trin Cambridge; *m* 1941, Lucy Elisabeth, da of late Sir Henry Babington Smith, GBE, CH, KCB, by Sir Henry's w Lady Elisabeth Bruce (eldest da of 9 Earl of Elgin & 13 of Kincardine); 1 da; *Heir* none; *Career* assist sec Miny of Production and CPRB Washington 1944-45, dir and v-pres American British Electric Corpn (New York), and of Hunting Surveys Inc (New York); *Style* - The Rt Hon the Lord Pentland; 131 East 66th st, New York, NY 10021, USA

PEPPER, Brig Ernest Cecil; CMG (1967), CBE (1943, OBE 1940), DSO (1944); s of W E Pepper; *b* 3 Oct 1899; *Educ* RMC Sandhurst; *m* 1929, Margaret, da of A W Allan, MD; 2 s; *Career* Bde-Cdr Normandy 1944-45, Cmdt Sch of Infantry 1945, ret 1946; DL Co of London, later Greater London 1948-76; *Style* - Brig Ernest Pepper, CMG, CBE, DSO; Flat 1, Nutcombe Height, Portsmouth rd, Hindhead, Surrey (☎ Hindhead 4644)

PEPPER, Kenneth Bruce; CB (1965); s of late E E Pepper; *b* 11 March 1913; *Educ* County H S Ilford, LSE; *m* 1945, Irene Evelyn Watts; 2 s; *Career* Cmmr of HM Customs and Excise 1957-73; *Style* - Kenneth Pepper Esq CB; Fairfield, Cae Mair, Beaumaris, Gwynedd

PEPPIATT, Sir Kenneth Oswald; KBE (1941), MC; s of late W R Peppiatt; *b* 25 March 1893; *Educ* Bancrofts; *m* 1929, Pamela, da of late Capt E W Carter MC; 2 s, 1 da; *Career* ch cashier Bank of England 1934-49, exec dir 1949-57, dir Coutts and Co 1958-69; *Style* - Sir Kenneth Peppiatt, KBE, MC; 7 Harvey Orchard, Beaconsfield, Bucks (☎ Beaconsfield 3158)

PEPPITT, John Raymond; QC (1976); s of late Reginald Peppitt; *b* 22 Sept 1931; *Educ* St Paul's Sch, Jesus Cambridge; *m* 1960, Judith Penelope James; 3 s; *Career* barr, Gray's Inn 1958, a Recorder of the Crown Court 1976-; *Style* - John Peppitt Esq QC; Stanton House, Romford rd, Pembury, Kent TN2 4AY (☎ Pembury 2482)

PEPYS, Charles Donald Leslie; s of late Col Gerald Pepys, CB, DSO and ggs of 1 Earl of Cottenham; hp of kinsman, 8 Earl of Cottenham; *b* 25 Sept 1909; *Educ* Radley; *m* 1941, Hon (Pamela Sophia) Nadine Stonor, da of 5 Baron Camoys; *Career* Lt-Col King's Own Yorkshire Light Infantry; *Style* - Charles Pepys Esq; Old Tiles, Catts Hill, Mark Cross, Crowborough, E Sussex

PEPYS, Hon Mrs - (Pamela Sophia) Nadine; *née* Stonor; da of late 5 Baron Camoys; *b* 1917; *m* 1941, Lt-Col Charles Donald Leslie Pepys, King's Own Yorkshire LI; *Style* - The Hon Mrs Pepys; Old Tiles, Catts Hill, Mark Cross, Crowborough, Sussex

PEPYS, Lady Rachel; Lady (Mary) Rachel; *née* Fitzalan Howard; DCVO (1968, CVO 1954); da of 15 Duke of Norfolk, KG, GCVO, PC (d 1917); *b* 27 June 1905; *m* 1, 1939, Lt-Col Colin Keppel Davidson, CIE, OBE, RA (ka 1943), s of Col Leslie Davidson, CB, RHA, and Lady Theodora, da of 7 Earl of Albermarle; 1 s, 1 da; m 2, 1961, Brig Anthony Hilton Pepys, DSO (d 1967); *Career* Lady-in-Waiting to HRH Princess Marina, Duchess of Kent 1943-68; *Style* - Lady Rachel Pepys, DCVO; Highfield House, Crossbush, Arundel, W Sussex (☎ Arundel 883158)

PEPYS, Lady Rose Edith Idina; da of late 6 Earl of Cottenham; *b* 1927; *Style* - Lady Rose Pepys; Flat B, 101 Earls Court rd, W8

PERCEVAL, Lady Geraldine Elizabeth Ursula; da of 11 Earl of Egmont; *b* 1939; *Style* - Lady Geraldine Perceval

PERCEVAL, Hon Mrs - Hon Joanna Ida Louisa; da of 5 Baron Hatherton (d 1969); *b* 1926; *m* 1948, Robert Westby Perceval; 1 s, 2 da; *Style* - The Hon Mrs Perceval; Pillaton Hall, Penkridge, Stafford

PERCEVAL, Viscount; Thomas Frederick Gerald Perceval; s of 11 Earl of Egmont; *b* 17 Aug 1934; *Style* - Viscount Perceval

PERCIVAL, Allen Dain; CBE (1975); s of Charles Percival; *b* 23 April 1925; *Educ* Bradford G S, Magdalene Cambridge; *m* 1952, Rachel Hay; *Career* Principal Guildhall Sch of Music and Drama 1965-78, exec chm Stainer & Bell Publishers 1978-, professional continuo playing, broadcasting and conducting; *Style* - Allen Percival Esq CBE; 7 Park Parade, Cambridge (☎ 353953)

PERCIVAL, Sir Anthony Edward; CB (1954); *b* 23 Sept 1910; *Educ* Manchester G S, Cambridge U; *m* 1935, Doris Cuff; 1 da; *Career* Und-Sec BOT 1949-58, Export Credits Guarantee Dept 1962-71, chm Gordon & Gotch Holdings Ltd 1971-, Brameast Gotch 1972-, dir Simon Engineering Ltd 1971-, Bank of Adelaide 1971-, Switzerland (General) Insurance Co 1971-, Trade Indemnity Co 1973-; kt 1966; *Style* - Sir Anthony Percival CB; 16 Hayes Way, Beckenham, Kent (☎ 01 650 2648)

PERCIVAL, Sir Ian; QC (1963), MP (C) Southport 1959-; s of Eldon Percival; *b* 11 May 1921; *Educ* Latymer Upper Sch, St Catharine's Cambridge; *m* 1942, Madeline Buckingham Cooke; 1 s, 1 da; *Career* barr Inner Temple 1948, Bencher 1970, Recorder of Deal, later of the Crown Court 1971-, Slr-Gen 1979-; kt 1979; *Style* - Sir Ian Percival, QC, MP; 9 King's Bench Walk, Temple, EC4 (☎ 01 583 2939)

PERCY, Earl; Henry Alan Walter Richard Percy; s and h of 10 Duke of Northumberland, KG, TD, PC, and Lady Elizabeth Montagu Douglas Scott (da of 8 Duke of Buccleuch); *b* 1 July 1953; *Educ* Eton, Ch Ch Oxford; *Style* - Earl Percy; Alnwick Castle, Northumberland

PERCY, Lady Julia Helen; da of 10 Duke of Northumberland, KG, TD, PC; *b* 1950; *Style* Lady Julia Percy

PERCY, Lord James William Eustace; s of 10 Duke of Northumberland, KG, TD, PC; *b* 1965

PERCY, Hon Mary Edith; da of 1 and last Baron Percy of Newcastle (d 1958); *b* 1919; *Educ* Bristol U; *Style* - The Hon Mary Percy; Glebe Orchard, Etchingham, Sussex

PERCY, His Honour Judge (Rodney Algernon); s of Hugh James Percy; *b* 15 May 1924; *Educ* Uppingham and BNC Oxford; *m* 1948, Mary Allen, da of late J E Benbow; 1 s, 3 da; *Career* barr, Middle Temple 1950, dep Coroner N Northumberland 1957, assist Recorder Sheffield QS 1964, dep chm Co Durham QS 1966-71, a Recorder of the Crown Court 1972-79, a Circuit Judge 1979-; *Style* - His Honour Judge Percy; Brookside, Lesbury, Alnwick, Northumberland NE66 3AT (☎ Alnmouth 326)

PERCY, Lord Richard Charles; s of 8 Duke of Northumberland, KG, CBE, MVO (d 1930) and Lady Helen Gordon-Lennox, da of 7 Duke of Richmond (d 1965, as Dowager Duchess of Northumberland, GCVO, CBE, JP); *b* 11 Feb 1921; *Educ* Eton, Ch Ch Oxford and Durham U; *m* 1, 1966, Sarah Jane Elizabeth (d 1978), da of Petre Norton, of the Manor House, Whalton, Northumberland; 2 s; m 2, 1979, Hon Clayre Ridley, da of 4 Baron Stratheden and Campbell, CBE and formerly w of Hon Nicholas Ridley, MP; *Career* Lt-Col cmding Northumberland Hussars (TA) 1959-61, late Capt Gren Gds; lecturer, Dept of Zoology U of Newcastle upon Tyne; *Style* - Lord Richard Percy; Dept of Zoology, The University, Newcastle upon Tyne NE1 7RU; Lesbury House, Alnwich,

Northumberland NE66 3PT (☎ Alnmouth 330), 58 Woodsford sq, W14 8DS (☎ 01 603 2220); Kirkville, Fochabers, Morayshire IV32 7DQ (☎ Fochabers 820269)

PERCY, Lord Ralph George Algernon; s of 10 Duke of Northumberland, KG, TD, PC; *b* 1956; *m* 1979, Jane, da of John W M M Richard; *Style* - Lord Ralph Percy

PERCY, Lady Richard - Hon Clayre; *née* Campbell; da (by 1 m) of 4 Baron Stratheden and Campbell, CBE; *b* 1927; *m* 1, 1950 (m dis 1974), Hon Nicholas Ridley, MP; 3 da; m 2, 1979, as his 2 w, Lord Richard Charles Percy, *qv*; *Style* - Lady Richard Percy; 212 Lambeth rd, SE1

PERCY OF NEWCASTLE, Baroness - Stella Katherine; da of late Maj-Gen Laurence George Drummond, CB, CBE, MVO; *b* 1895; *m* 1918, 1 Baron Percy of Newcastle (d 1958, when the title became extinct); *Style* - The Rt Hon the Lady Percy of Newcastle; The Glebe Orchard, Etchingham, Sussex

PEREIRA, Sir (Herbert) Charles; s of Herbert John Pereira (d 1952); *b* 12 May 1913; *Educ* St Albans Sch, London U (BSc, PhD, DSc); *m* 1941, Irene Beatrice, da of David James Sloan (d 1915); 3 s, 1 da; *Career* dir ARC of Rhodesia and Nyasaland 1961-63, dir ARC of Central Africa (Rhodesia, Zambia and Malawi) 1963-67, chm ARC of Malawi 1967-74, dir E Malling Research Station 1969-72, ch scientist (dep sec) Miny of Agriculture, Fisheries and Food 1972-77, Research Consultant in Tropical Agriculture to World Bank and other organisations; FRS 1969, Haile Selassie Prize for Research in Africa 1966; kt 1977; *Style* - Sir Charles Pereira; Peartrees, Fairlawn, Teston, Kent ME18 5AD (☎ Maidstone 813333)

PERHAM, Dame Margery Freda; DCMG (1965), CBE (1948); da of Frederick Perham; *b* 1895; *Educ* St Anne's Sch Abbots Bromley and St Hugh's Oxford (DLitt), St Andrews U (hon LLD), Cambridge (hon LittD); *Career* dir Oxford U Inst of Colonial Studies 1945-48, reader in Colonial Admin Oxford U 1939-48, Fell Nuffield Coll and St Hugh's Coll Oxford 1939-63, Hon Fell 1963-, editor *Colonial and Comparative Studies* 1946-; *Style* - Dame Margery Perham, DCMG, CBE; 5 Rawlinson rd, Oxford

PERKINS, Francis Layton; CBE (1977), DSC (1940); s of Montague Thornton Perkins; *b* 7 Feb 1912; *Educ* Charterhouse; *m* 1, 1941 (m dis 1971), Josephine Brice Miller; 1 s, 2 da; m 2, 1971, Jill Patricia Greenish; *Career* slr 1937; chm Insur Brokers' Registration Cncl 1977-; *Style* - Francis Perkins Esq, CBE, DSC; Flat 18, 7 Princes Gate, SW7 (☎ 01 589 9438); The Dunes, Sandwich Bay, Kent (☎ Sandwich 612832)

PERKINS, Maj-Gen Kenneth; CB (1977), MBE (1955), DFC (1953); s of George Samuel Perkins; *b* 15 Aug 1926; *Educ* Lewes County Sch for Boys, New Coll Oxford; *m* 1949, Anne Theresa, da of John Barry (d 1960); 3 da; *Career* Cmd 1st Regiment Roy Horse Artillery 1967-69, Cmd 24 Airportable Bde 1971-72, Cmd Sultan of Oman's Armed Forces 1975-77, assist Ch of Defence Staff (Operations) 1977-79, dir of Military Assistance Office 1980-, Col Cmdt RA 1980-; *Style* - Maj-Gen Kenneth Perkins, CB, MBE, DFC; c/o National Westminster Bank, Seaford, Sussex

PERKINS, Air Vice-Marshal Maxwell Edmund Massy; CB (1962), CBE (1957); s of late Donald Maxwell Perkins; *b* 22 Aug 1907; *Educ* Portsmouth Coll, London U; *m* 1, 1934, Helena Joan Penelope (d 1973), da of Herbert John Newberry; 1 s, 2 da; m 2, 1974, Sylvia Mary, widow of Willson Gatward; *Career* RAF 1929, Air Cdre 1957, Air Vice-Marshal 1961, Dir-Gen of Engrg, Air Miny 1961-64; dir of Engrg Aviation Div Smiths Industries Ltd, ret; *Style* - Air Vice-Marshal Maxwell Perkins CB CBE; Little Court, London rd, Hitchin, Herts

PERKINS, Lady; Patricia Moyra; da of Lt-Col James Howard Adolphus Annesley, CMG, DSO, and 2 cous of late 9 Earl Annesley; *b* 26 April 1904; *m* 1, 1926, Air Cdre Sir Nigel Norman, 2 Bt, CBE (k on active serv 1943); 3 s (including Sir Mark,

3 Bt); m 2, 1944, Sir Walter Robert Perkins, sometime MP (C) Stroud & Thornbury & Parly Sec Miny Aviation; *Style* - Lady Perkins; The Manor House, Downton, Wilts

PERKINS, Sir Robert Dempster; s of late W Frank Perkins; *b* 1903; *Educ* Eton, Trin Cambridge; *m* 1944, Lady Norman, widow of Sir Nigel Norman, 2 Bt; *Career* MP (C) Stroud 1931-45, MP (C) Stroud and Thornbury Div of Gloucestershire 1950-55, Parly Sec Miny Civil Aviation 1945; kt 1954; *Style* - Sir Robert Perkins; The Manor House, Downton, Wilts

PERKS, His Honour Judge (John Clifford); MC (1944); s of late John Hyde Haslewood Perks; *b* 20 March 1915; *Educ* Blundell's, Balliol Oxford; *m* 1940, Ruth Dyke, nee Appleby; 2 s (1 s 2 da decd); *Career* barr, Inner Temple 1938, dep chm Devon QS 1965-71, a Circuit Judge 1970-; *Style* - His Honour Judge Perks, MC; 32 Melbury Close, Chislehurst, Kent

PEROWNE, Rear-Adm Benjamin Cubitt; CB (1978); s of late Bernard Cubitt Perowne; *b* 18 Feb 1921; *Educ* Culford Sch; *m* 1946, Phyllis Marjorie, da of late Cdre R D Peel; 2 s, 1 da; *Career* Dir Management and Support Intelligence 1976-78, Ch Naval Supply and Secretariat Officer 1977-78; gen sec Roy United Kingdom Beneficent Assoc 1978-; *Style* - Rear-Adm Benjamin Perowne CB; c/o Barclays Bank, Haslemere, Surrey

PEROWNE, Maj-Gen Lancelot Edgar Connop Mervyn; CB (1953), CBE (1945); s of late Col Woolrych Perowne; *b* 11 June 1902; *Educ* Wellington and RMA Woolwich; *m* 1927, Gertrude Jenny Johanna Stein, of Cologne, Germany; 1 da; *Career* 2 Lt RE 1923, Maj-Gen Brigade of Gurkhas 1952-55, ret 1955; Col The Gurkha Engrs 1957-66; MIEE, KStJ; *Style* - Maj-Gen Lancelot Perowne CB CBE; Benfleet Hall, Green Lane, Cobham, Surrey KT11 2NN

PERRETT, Desmond Seymour; QC (1980); s of His Honour Judge Perrett, *qv*; *b* 22 April 1937; *Educ* Westminster; *m* 1961, Pauline Merriel, da of late Paul Robert Buchan May, ICS; 1 s, 1 da; *Career* RN 1955-57; barr Gray's Inn 1962, Recorder of the Crown Court 1978-; *Style* - Desmond Perrett Esq, QC; The Old Tap House, Upper Wootton, Basingstoke, Hants (☎ Basingstoke 850027); 2 Crown Office Row, Temple EC4Y 7HJ (☎ 01 353 9337)

PERRETT, His Honour Judge; John Perrett; JP (Warwicks 1970); s of late Joseph Perrett; *b* 22 Oct 1906; *Educ* St Anne's RC and Stratford rd Schs Birmingham, King's Coll London; *m* 1933, Elizabeth Mary, da of late William Seymour; 2 s, 2 da; *Career* RAPC 1939-45, RASC 1945; barr, Gray's Inn 1946, dep chm Warwicks QS 1970-71, a Circuit Judge 1969-; *Style* - His Honour Judge Perrett JP; 9 The Close, Lichfield, Staffs (☎ Lichfield 52320); Farrar's Building, Temple, EC4 (☎ 01 583 9241)

PERRIN, Arthur Stanley; s of Walter William Perrin (d 1961); *b* 7 April 1920; *Educ* Southgate County Sch; *m* 1954, Enid Beatrice, nee Harvey; 1 s, 1 da; *Career* Sergeant RASC 1939-45 War; md: Diecasting Machine Tools Ltd 1973-, Lone Star Products Ltd 1973-; chm Californian Screen Blocks Ltd 1974-, Eaglet Industries Ltd 1975-, Br Toy & Hobby Manufacturer's Assoc 1980-; *Recreations* golf; *Clubs* Brookman's Park Golf, Mayfield Athletic, The Sportsman's; *Style* - Arthur Perrin Esq; 34 Claremont rd, Hadley Wood, Herts, EN4 0HP (☎ 01 440 2309)

PERRIN, Sir Michael Willcox; CBE (1952, OBE 1946), FRSC; s of late Bishop W W Perrin; *b* 13 Sept 1905; *Educ* Winchester and New Coll Oxford, Toronto and Amsterdam Us; *m* 1934, Nancy May, da of late Bishop C E Curzon; 1 s, 1 da; *Career* chm The Wellcome Foundation Ltd 1953-70, dir Inveresk Research International 1961-74 (chm 1971-73), dir Radiochemical Centre Ltd 1971-75; kt 1967; *Clubs* Athenaeum; *Style* - Sir Michael Perrin, CBE; 14 Christchurch Hill, Hampstead NW3 1LB (☎ 01 794 3064)

PERRING, John Raymond; TD (1965); s and h of Sir Ralph Edgar Perring, 1 Bt; *b* 7 July 1931; *Educ* Stowe; *m* 1961, Ella Christine, da of late Maj Anthony George

Pelham; 2 s, 2 da; *Career* vice-chm Perring Furnishings Ltd 1972-, one of HM Lts of City of London 1963-; FRSA; *Style* - John Perring Esq TD, HM Lieut for the City of London; 21 Somerset rd, Parkside, SW19 (☎ 01 946 8971)

PERRING, Sir Ralph Edgar; 1 Bt (UK 1963) JP (London 1943); s of late Col Sir John Perring, JP, DL; *b* 23 March 1905; *Educ* Univ Coll Sch London; *m* 1928, Ethel Mary, OStJ, da of late Henry T Johnson; 2 s (and 1 s decd); *Heir* s John Raymond Perring; *Career* Lt RA (TA) 1938-40; memb Court of Common Council (Ward of Cripplegate) 1948-51, Alderman of City of London (Langbourn Ward) 1951-75, one of HM Lts of City of London and Sheriff 1958-59, Lord Mayor of London 1962-63; chm Perring Furnishings Ltd, Bd of Govrs English-Speaking Union 1976-, dir Confederation Life Insurance Co of Canada 1969-, v-pres Roy Bridgwell Hosp, Trustee Morden Coll Blackheath 1970- (chm 1979-); FRSA, KStJ, kt 1960; *Style* - Sir Ralph Perring, Bt, JP; 15 Burghley House, Somerset rd, Wimbledon SW19 (☎ 01 946 3433)

PERRIS, Sir David Arthur; MBE (1970), JP (Birmingham 1961); s of Arthur Perris; *b* 25 May 1929; *Educ* Sparkhill Commercial Sch Birmingham; *m* 1955, Constance Parkes, BPharm, FPS; 1 s, 1 da; *Career* chm W Midlands Regional Health Authority 1974-, sec TUC W Midlands Regional Council 1974-, sec Birmingham Trades Council 1966-, chm Nat Health Service Nat Training Council 1975-, v-chm ATV Midlands Ltd 1980-; kt 1977; *Style* - Sir David Perris, MBE, JP; 24 Mayfield rd, Moseley, Birmingham B13 9HJ (☎ 021 449 3652)

PERROTT, Sir Donald Cyril Vincent; KBE (1949); s of late Frederick John Perrott; *b* 12 April 1902; *Educ* Tauntons' Sch Southampton, Univ Coll Southampton; *m* 1, 1925, Marjorie May (d 1969), da of late William Holway; 1 s; m 2, 1969, Mrs L L Byre; *Career* Sec Dept of Atomic Energy 1954 and Memb for Finance and Admin of Atomic Energy Authority 1954-60, Memb Governing Bd of Nat Inst for Research in Nuclear Science 1957-60; *Style* - Sir Donald Perrott KBE; 5 Plane Tree House, Duchess of Bedford's Walk, W8 7QT

PERRY OF WALTON, Baron (Life Peer UK 1979); Walter Laing Macdonald Perry; OBE (1957); s of Fletcher S Perry; *b* 16 June 1921; *Educ* Ayr Acad, Dundee H S, St Andrews U, Edinburgh U; MRCP, FRCPE, FRCP; *m* 1, 1946 (m dis 1971) Anne Grant; 3 s; m 2, 1971, Catherine Hilda Crawley; 2 s, 1 da; *Career* dir Dept of Biological Standards, Nat Inst for Medical Research 1952-58; Prof of Pharmacology U of Edinburgh 1958-68 (Vice-Pncpl 1967-68), Vice-Chllr The Open U 1969-80, Fell 1981-; dep leader SDP House of Lds; FRSE, kt 1974; *Style* - The Rt Hon the Lord Perry of Walton OBE; The Open University Finance Division, Sherwood House, Sherwood Drive, Bletchley, Milton Keynes

PERRY, Hon Alan Malcolm; s of Baron Perry of Walton (Life Peer); *b* 1950; *m* Naomi Freedman; *Style* - The Hon Alan Perry

PERRY, Barrie Edward; s of Edward Perry; *b* 5 June 1933; *Educ* Surbiton Modern Sch, King's Coll Durham; *m* 1961 (m dis); 1 s; *Career* naval architect, chm and md Proctor Masts; *Recreations* sailing; *Clubs* Roy Southern Yacht; *Style* - Barrie Perry Esq; c/o Proctor Masts, Duncan rd, Swanwick, Southampton, Hants

PERRY, Hon Sir (Alan) Clifford; s of George Perry; *b* 10 July 1907; *Educ* Hornby Primary Sch, Christ's Coll Christchurch, Canterbury Univ Coll, U of NZ; *m* 1943, Barbara Jean Head; 2 s, 1 da; *Career* barr and slr 1928, Sr Puisne Judge Supreme Court of New Zealand 1976-79 (Judge 1962); kt 1976; *Style* - The Hon Sir Clifford Perry; 54 Mountain rd, Epsom, Auckland 3, New Zealand (☎ 601 035)

PERRY, Hon Colin Stuart Macdonald; s of Baron Perry of Walton (Life Peer); *b* 1979; *Style* - The Hon Colin Perry

PERRY, David Howard; s of Howard Dace Perry; *b* 13 April 1931; *Educ* Berkhamsted Sch, Pembroke Coll Cambridge; *m* 1961, Rosemary Grigg; 1

s, 2 da; *Career* Dir-Gen Future Projects, Procurement Exec MOD 1978-; *Style* - David Perry Esq; 23 Rectory rd, Farnborough, Hants (☎ Farnborough 41117)

PERRY, Hon Jenifer Joan; da of Baron Perry of Walton (Life Peer); *b* 1981; *Style* - The Hon Jenifer Perry

PERRY, Hon Michael John; s of Baron Perry of Walton (Life Peer); *b* 1948; *m* 1970, Kathleen Elliott; *Style* - The Hon Michael Perry; 5 Corstorphine Park gdns, Edinburgh

PERRY, Sir Norman; MBE; *Career* chm of dirs, Opotiki Textiles Ltd, Opotiki; consultant Whakatohea Maori Trust Board and Coast Resource Developments; kt 1977; *Style* - Sir Norman Perry, MBE; Waiotahi, Opotiki, New Zealand (☎ Opotiki 961)

PERRY, Hon Niall Fletcher; s of Baron Perry of Walton (Life Peer); *b* 1953; *Style* - The Hon Niall Perry; 34 Dundas st, Edinburgh

PERRY, Hon Robin Charles Macdonald; s of Baron Perry of Walton (Life Peer); *b* 1973; *Style* - The Hon Robin Perry

PERRY, Lt-Col Robert Stanley Grosvenor; DSO (1943), DL (Dorset 1962); s of late Robert Grosvenor Perry, CBE; *b* 1909; *Educ* Harrow, RMC Sandhurst; *m* 1937, Margaret Louisa Elphinstone, da of Horace Czarnikow; 1 s; *Career* 2 Lt 9 Lancers 1929, Maj 1941, Adj Cheshire Yeo 1938-40, Cmdg 2 Lothians and Border Yeo 1943, 9 Lancers 1944-45, served War of 1939-45 Palestine, Western Desert, N Africa, Italy, Cmdt RACOCTU 1945-48; One of HM Bodyguard of Hon Corps of Gentlemen at Arms 1959-79, High Sheriff of Dorset 1961, memb British Olympic Yachting Team Helsinki 1952; *Style* - Lt-Col Robert Perry, DSO, DL; Crendle Court, Purse Caundle, Sherborne, Dorset (☎ Milborne Port 250364)

PERRY-KEENE, Air Vice-Marshal Allan Lancelot Addison; CB (1947), OBE (1940), RAF (ret); s of late L H A Perry-Keene; *b* 10 Nov 1898; *Educ* Wolverley, King Edward's Birmingham; *m* 1923, Katrine Lucy, da of late Charles Silberrad, ICS; *Career* Air Cdr Royal Pakistan Air Force 1947-49; *Style* - Air Vice-Marshal Allan Perry-Keene CB, OBE; Wayfarers Cottage, St Mary Bourne, Andover, Hants SP11 6AR (☎ St Mary Bourne 210)

PERT, Maj-Gen Claude Ernest; CB (1947), CVO (1976), DSO (1945); s of F J Pert, late ICS; *b* 26 Sept 1898; *Educ* RNC Osborne, Clifton Coll; *m* 1922, Lilian Katherine Nicolls (d 1980); *Career* cmd 255 Indian Tank Bde in 14 Army Burma, cmd 1 Indian Armoured Div 1945-48; *Style* - Maj-Gen Claude Pert, CB, CVO, DSO; Garden House, Ribblesdale Park, Ascot, Berks (☎ Ascot 22973)

PERTH, 17 Earl of (S 1605); John David Drummond; PC (1957); also Lord Drummond of Cargill and Stobhall (S 1488), Lord Maderty (S 1609), also Viscount Strathallan (S 1686), Lord Drummond of Cromlix (S 1686); s of 16 Earl of Perth, GCMG, CB, PC (d 1951) and Hon Angela Constable-Maxwell (d 1965), da of 11 Lord Herries of Terregles; *b* 13 May 1907; *Educ* Downside and Cambridge U; *m* 1934, Nancy Seymour, da of Reginald Fincke, of New York City; 2 s; *Heir* s Viscount Strathallan; *Career* a Representative Peer for Scotland 1952-63, Hereditary Thane of Lennox and Hereditary Steward of Menteith and Strathearn, late Lt Intelligence Corps, seconded to War Cabinet Offices 1942-43 and to Miny Production 1944-45, Min of State for Colonial Affairs 1957-62, First Crown Estate Cmmr 1962-77, Chm of the Reviewing Ctee on the Export of Works of Art 1972-76, Trustee of Nat Library of Scotland; memb of Court St Andrew's U; Hon FRIBA 1978; *Clubs* White's,Puffin's; *Style* - The Rt Hon the Earl of Perth PC; 14 Hyde Park Gardens Mews, W2 (☎ 01 262 4667); Stobhall by Perth

PERTWEE, Anthony Nigel Ferens; s of Norman Frank Pertwee; *b* 4 Nov 1942; *Educ* Tonbridge Kent; *m* 1965, Margaret Joan, da of Ronald George Gammer; 1 s, 2

da; *Career* chm Pertwee Anfood Ltd, dir Pertwee Holdings Ltd, dir New World Plants Ltd; *Recreations* sailing, hot air ballooning, water sports; *Style* - Anthony Pertwee Esq; St Patricks, Third ave, Frinton-on-Sea, Essex (☎ Frinton-on-Sea 3709)

PERTWEE, Desmond Brian; s of Frank Pertwee (d 1964); *b* 26 April 1911; *Educ* King's Sch Canterbury; *m* 1, 1935 (w d 1949); m 2, 1950, Margaret Angela Clare, da of Vice-Adm Charles Round-Turner (d 1952); 5 c; *Career* chm Frank Pertwee & Sons Ltd, Stimpson Pertwee Ltd, dir Pertwee Holdings Ltd; *Recreations* ocean racing, sailing, horse trials; *Style* - Desmond Pertwee Esq; Rookery House, Gt Horkesley, nr Colchester C06 4EJ (☎ 271213)

PERUTZ, Gerald; s of Dr Georg Perutz (d 1935); *b* 9 Aug 1929; *Educ* Loughborough Coll; *m* 1953, Dinah Fyffe, nee Pope; 3 c; *Career* gen man Rank Precision Industs 1957-63, dir and exec v-pres Bell & Howell Co Chicago USA; *Recreations* tennis, skiing; *Clubs* Glenview; *Style* - Gerald Perutz Esq; c/o Nat West Bank Ltd, 115 Old Brompton rd, SW7; 223 Melrose, Kenilworth, Illinois USA

PERUTZ, Max Ferdinand; CH (1975), CBE (1963), FRS (1954); s of Hugo and Adele Perutz; *b* 19 May 1914; *Educ* Theresianum Vienna, Vienna U, Peterhouse Cambridge (Hon Fell 1962); *m* 1942, Gisela Peiser; 1 s, 1 da; *Career* chm Medical Research Council Laboratory of Molecular Biology Cambridge 1962-79, memb Scientific Staff 1979-, Fullerian Prof of Physiology at the Royal Institution 1973-79, Nobel Prize for Chemistry 1962, Roy Medal of Roy Society 1971; *Style* - Professor Max Perutz, CH, CBE, FRS; 42 Sedley Taylor rd, Cambridge

PERY, Lady Alison Dora; da of 6 Earl of Limerick; *b* 1964; *Style* - Lady Alison Pery

PERY, Hon Adrian Patrick; s of 6 Earl of Limerick; *b* 1967; *Style* - The Hon Adrian Pery

PESTELL, Catherine Eva; da of Edmund Ernest Pestell; *b* 24 Sept 1933; *Educ* Leeds Girls' H S, St Hilda's Oxford; *Career* Counsellor E Berlin 1975-78, Cabinet Office 1978-80, Diplomatic Service Inspector 1980-; *Style* - Miss Catherine Pestell; c/o Cabinet Office, SW1

PESTELL, Sir John Richard; KCVO (1969); s of late Lt-Cdr Frank Lionel Pestell, RN; *b* 21 Nov 1916; *Educ* Portsmouth Northern Secdy Sch; *m* 1951, Betty, nee Parish; 3 da; *Career* British South Africa Police S Rhodesia 1939-65, Sec/Controller to Govr S Rhodesia (Rt Hon Sir Humphrey Gibbs) 1965-69; Adjudicator Immigration Appeals Harmondsworth 1970-; *Style* - Sir John Pestell, KCVO; Monks Walk, Ferry Lane, Medmenham, Marlow, Bucks

PETCH, Barry Irvine; s of Charles Reginald Petch; *b* 12 Oct 1933; *Educ* Doncaster G S; *m* 1966, Anne Elisabeth, nee Johannessen; 2 s, 1 da; *Career* FCA 1967, Finance Dir, IBM United Kingdom Holdings Ltd and subsidiaries 1971-; *Clubs* Reform; *Style* - Barry Petch Esq; Hoevringen, Coombe Park, Kingston Hill, Surrey (☎ 01 549 4778)

PETERBOROUGH, 35 Bishop of (cr 1541) 1972-; Rt Rev Douglas Russell Feaver; s of late Ernest Henry Feaver, of Bristol; *b* 22 May 1914; *Educ* Bristol G S, Keble Coll Oxford (Scholar, 1 cl Hons Mod Hist 1935, 1 cl Hons Theology 1937, Liddon Student 1935-37, MA); *m* 1939, Katharine, da of Wilfrid Thomas Stubbs (d 1968); 1 s, 2 da; *Career* Canon and Sub-Dean of St Albans 1946-58, Vicar and Rural Dean of Nottingham 1958-72; patron of 101 livings, the Chllrship, the Archdeaconries of Northampton and Oakham, and the Canonries of his Cathedral; Bishopric set up by Henry VIII from the proceeds of the dissolved land holdings of the Abbey of St Peter's (founded by Saxulf, a Thane of Mercia, 653), whose last abbot was the first Bp of the new see; *Style* - The Rt Rev the Bishop of Peterborough; The Palace, Peterborough (☎ Peterborough 62492)

PETERKEN, Hon Mrs - Hon Hyacinthe Ann; da of 7 Baron Hatherton, TD; *b* 1934; *m* 1954, Patrick Peterken; 2 s,

1 da; *Career* LLB Newcastle, slr 1978; *Style* - The Hon Mrs Peterken; Claypool Farm, Hutton Henry, Castle Eden, Durham

PETERS, Brian Henry; s of Harry Peters; *b* 13 June 1933; *Educ* Edmonton County G S; *m* 1957, Moyra Bowes; 2 s; *Career* admin dir Allied Hambro Unit Trust Gp; *Recreations* badminton, motoring, compiling crossword puzzles; *Style* - Brian Peters Esq; 74 Mayfield rd, Writtle, Chelmsford, Essex (☎ 0245 420936)

PETERS, Kenneth Jamieson; CBE (1979), JP (City of Aberdeen 1961), DL (Aberdeen 1978); s of William Jamieson Peters (d 1966); *b* 17 Jan 1923; *Educ* Aberdeen G S, Aberdeen U; *m* 1951, Arunda Merle Jane Jones; *Career* 1939-45 War, final rank Capt/Adj 2 Bn King's Own Scottish Borderers; editor Evening Express Aberdeen 1953-56, The Press and Journal Aberdeen 1956-60; dir Highland Printers Ltd (Inverness) 1968-, md Aberdeen Journals Ltd 1960-80 (chm 1980-), dir Thomson Regnl Newspapers 1974-; *Style* - Kenneth Peters Esq, CBE, JP, DL; 47 Abergeldie rd, Aberdeen AB1 6ED (☎ Aberdeen 27647)

PETERS, Michael Edmund; s of Edmund Lind du Thon Peters, of Rugby; *b* 19 March 1939; *Educ* Clayesmore Sch, Dorset Coll of Ag NCA; *m* 1964, Judith Joy, da of Donald George Harris; 2 da; *Career* founder and jt md Agripress Publicity Ltd 1963-70, relinquished directorship 1972, md A O Smith Harvestore Products Ltd 1971-; *Style* - Michael Peters Esq; Mead House, Drinkstone Green, Bury St Edmunds, Suffolk IP30 9TL (☎ Rattlesden 570)

PETERS, Sir Rudolph Albert; MC and bar (1917), MD, FRCP, FRS, FRSE (hon), MD (hon), Liège and Amsterdam DSc (hon), Cincinnati, London, Leeds and Australia Nat U, Dr (hon) Paris, LLD (hon) Glasgow; s of Albert Edward Duncan Ralph Peters, MRCS, LRCP (d 1945); *b* 1889; *Educ* Wellington, King's Coll London, Gonville and Caius Coll Cambridge; *m* 1917, Frances Williamina, da of Francis William Verel; 2 s; *Career* memb Staff of Agricultural Research Council 1954-59, Whitley Prof of Biochemistry Oxford U 1923-54, Hon Fell Gonville and Caius Coll Cambridge and Trin Oxford, hon memb Assoc Clinical Biochemists, hon Fell RSM and Assoc of Physicians, hon memb of Biochemical Soc and Physiological Soc and of American Inst of Nutrition, hon memb Celer et Audaz Club, Pres Int Council of Scientific Unions 1958-61, Pres Cambridge Philosophical Soc 1965-67, Hon Fell Coll of Pathologists 1967, Nutrition prize 1972, kt 1952; *Style* - Sir Rudolph Peters, MC*; 3 Newnham Walk, Cambridge (☎ 50819)

PETERS, Theophilus; CMG (1967); s of late Mark Peters; *b* 7 Aug 1921; *Educ* Exeter Sch, St John's Cambridge; *m* 1953, Lucy Bailey Summers, da of late Lionel Morgan Summers; 2 s, 3 da; *Career* Counsellor and Consul-Gen Buenos Aires 1971-73, Consul-Gen Antwerp 1973-78, dir Theophilus Knapman & Co 1979; *Style* - Theophilus Peters Esq, CMG; c/o National Westminster Bank Ltd, Stamford, Lincs

PETERS, William; CMG (1980), MVO (1961), MBE (1959); s of John William Peters; *b* 28 Sept 1923; *Educ* King Edward VI G S Morpeth, Balliol Oxford; *m* 1944, Catherine B Bailey; *Career* Dep High Cmmr Bombay 1974-77, Ambass to Uruguay 1977-80, High Cmmr in Malawi 1980-, memb Nat Preservation Soc of Malawi; *Style* - William Peters Esq, CMG, MVO, MBE; c/o Foreign and Commonwealth Office, SW1A 2AH

PETERSEN, Sir Jeffrey Charles; KCMG (1978, CMG 1968); s of Charles Petersen; *b* 20 July 1920; *Educ* Westcliff H S, LSE; *m* 1962, Karin Kristina Hayward; 2 s, 4 da; *Career* Ambass to Republic of Korea 1971-74, to Romania 1975-77, to Sweden 1977-80, ret; *Style* - Sir Jeffrey Petersen, KCMG; 32 Longmoore st, SW1 (☎ 01 834 8262); Crofts Wood, Petham, Kent

PETERSHAM, Viscount; Charles Henry Leicester Stanhope; s and h of 11 Earl of Harrington; *b* 20 July 1945; *Educ* Eton; *m* 1966, Virginia Alleyne Freeman, da of Capt Harry Freeman Jackson, of

Cool-na-Grena, Co Cork; 1 s, 1 da; *Style* - Viscount Petersham; c/o Greenmount, Patrickswell, Co Limerick, Ireland

PETERSON, Alexander Duncan Campbell; OBE (1946); s of late J C K Peterson, CIE; *b* 13 Sept 1908; *Educ* Radley, Balliol Oxford; *m* 1946, Corinna May, da of late Sir Arthur Cochrane, KCVO; 2 s, 1 da; *Career* Contested (Lib) Oxford City 1966, V-Pres International Council of United World Colleges 1980-; *Style* - Alexander Peterson Esq OBE; 47 Belsize Park, NW3 (☎ 01 722 9044)

PETERSON, Sir Arthur William; KCB (1973, CB 1963), MVO (1953); s of J C K Peterson; *b* 22 May 1916; *Educ* Shrewsbury, Merton Coll Oxford; *m* 1940, Mary Isabel Maples; 1 s, 2 da; *Career* Perm Under-Sec of State Home Office 1972-77; chm Family Service Units 1978-, National Ports Council 1980-, Jt Ctee on Refugees from Vietnam 1979-; Hon Fell Inst of Local Govt Studies Birmingham U; *Style* - Sir Arthur Peterson, KCB, MVO; 7 Lincoln House, Basil st, SW3 (☎ 01 589 2237)

PETERSON, Christopher Matthew; TD (1956), JP (1973), DL (S Glam 1978); s of Oscar Peterson (d 1923); *b* 22 Feb 1918; *Educ* St Illtyd's Coll Cardiff; *m* 1945, Grace Winfred, da of John McNeil (d 1940); 3 c (1 c decd); *Career* co dir; Lloyd's Underwriter, High Sheriff S Glamorgan 1981; *Clubs* Cardiff County, Army & Navy; *Style* - Christopher Peterson Esq, TD, JP, DL; 15 Llandennis ave, Cyncoed, Cardiff (☎ 754062); 15 Castle Dill Crescent, Milford Haven, Dyfed

PETERSON, Colin Vyvyan; s of late Sir Maurice Drummond Peterson GCMG; *b* 24 Oct 1932; *Educ* Winchester, Magdalen Oxford; *m* 1966, Pamela Rosemary Barry; 2 s, 2 da; *Career* HM Treasury 1959, Sec for Appointments to the Prime Minister and Ecclesiastical Sec to the Lord Chancellor 1974-; *Style* - Colin Peterson Esq; 87 Christchurch rd, Winchester, Hants (☎ Winchester 3784)

PETHERICK, Hon Mrs (Bridget Frances Kate); da of late 1 Baron Cornwallis; *b* 1900; *m* 1921, Lt-Col John Cecil Petherick, OBE, MC, 3 Hussars (ret); 2 da; *Style* - The Hon Mrs Petherick; Hextall Court, Peckham Bush, nr Tonbridge, Kent

PETHYBRIDGE, Frank; CBE (1977); s of Frank Pethybridge; *b* 19 Jan 1924; *Educ* William Hulme's G S Manchester, Manchester U; *m* 1947, Jean Ewing; 1 s, 1 da; *Career* Regional Administrator North Western Regional Health Authority 1973-; FHA, FRSH; *Style* - Frank Pethybridge Esq CBE; 31 Lullington rd, Pendleton, Salford M6 8GW (☎ 061 736 5697)

PETIT, Sir Dinshaw Manockjee; 3 Bt (UK 1890); s of Sir Dinshaw Manockjee Petit, 2 Bt (d 1933) and Dinbai, da of Sir J Jeejeebhoy, 3 Bt; *b* 24 June 1901; *Educ* St Xavier's Bombay, Trinity Hall Cambridge; *m* 1928, Sylla (d 1963), da of late R D Tata; 1 s, 1 da; *Heir* s, Nasserwanjee Dinshaw Petit; *Career* barr, Inner Temple 1925, Pres SPCA Bombay, Petit Boys' Sch Poona, Petit Girls' Sch Pali Hill Bombay, Petit Sanatorium Cumballa Hill Bombay, Hon Life Memb RSPCA, V-Pres British Assoc of Riviera, Citizen of Honour of France; *Style* - Sir Dinshaw Petit, Bt; Petit Hall, 66 Nepean Sea rd, Bombay, India; Savaric, 06 Eze-Village, France; 8 Mount Row, W1

PETIT, Joseph Adrien Letiere; s of Capt Joseph Paris Sydney Petit (d 1966); *b* 6 May 1921; *Educ* Warwick Sch, Nottingham U, Birmingham U; *m* 1959, Carroll Foster, da of Henry Alan Gould; 1 s, 1 da; *Career* management consultant 1952-73; regnl dir 1971-73; chm Brandauer Holdings Ltd 1965-, chm C Brandauer & Co Ltd 1964-; dir Assmann Electronics Ltd 1976-; Pres Inst of Management Consultants 1979-80; *Recreations* music, genealogy, inventing, swimming, sailing; *Clubs* Inst of Directors; *Style* - Joseph Petit Esq; The Close, Cloister Crofts, Leamington Spa (☎ Leamington 23912); Gable Cottage, Plas Maen Drive, Cefn-y-bedd, N Wales (☎ 0978 760 535)

PETIT, Naswanji; s and h of Sir Dinshaw Manockjee Petit, 3 Bt; *b* 13 Aug 1934; *m* 1964, Nirmala Nanavati; 2 s; *Style* - Naswanji Petit Esq; Petit Hall, Nepean Sea rd, Bombay

PETO, Barbara, Lady - Barbara; da of Edwyn Thomas Close, of Woodcote, Camberley, Surrey; *m* 1935, Sir Christopher Henry Maxwell Peto, 3 Bt, DSO (d 1980); *Style* - Barbara, Lady Peto; Lockeridge House, nr Marlborough, Wilts SN8 4EL

PETO, Francis Michael Morton; s and h of Sir Henry George Morton Peto, 4 Bt; *b* 1949; *m* 1974, Felicity Margaret, da of Lt-Col John Alan Burns, of Godminster Wood House, Bruton, Som; 1 s; *Style* - Francis Peto Esq; Sorrowlessfield, Earlston, Berwicks

PETO, Henry Christopher Morton Bampfylde; s and h of Sir Michael Henry Basil Peto, 4 Bt; *b* 8 April 1967; *Style* - Henry Peto Esq

PETO, Sir Henry George Morton; 4 Bt (UK 1855); s of Cdr Sir Henry Francis Morton Peto, 3 Bt, RN (d 1978); *b* 29 April 1920; *Educ* Sherborne, Corpus Christi Cambridge; *m* 1947, Frances Jacqueline, JP, da of late Ralph Haldane Evers; 2 s; *Heir* s, Francis Michael Morton Peto; *Career* RA 1939-46; company dir & consultant; *Style* - Sir Henry Peto, Bt; Stream House, Selborne, Alton, Hants (☎ Selborne 246)

PETO, Sir Michael Henry Basil; 4 Bt (UK 1927); s of Brig Sir Christopher Henry Maxwell Peto, 3 Bt, DSO (d 1980); *b* 6 April 1938; *Educ* Eton and Ch Ch Oxford; *m* 1, 1963, Sarah Susan (m dis 1970), da of Maj Sir Dennis Stucley, 5 Bt; 1 s, 2 da; m 2, 1971, Lucinda Mary, da of Maj Sir Charles Douglas Blackett, 9 Bt; 2 s; *Heir* s, Henry Christopher Morton Bampfylde Peto; *Career* barr Inner Temple 1960, memb Stock Exchange 1965-; *Clubs* Turf; *Style* - Sir Michael Peto, Bt; Cliddesden Down House, Basingstoke, Hants

PETO, Hon Mrs (Selina Lillian); *née* Hughes-Young; da of late 1 Baron St Helens, MC; *b* 1944; *m* 1969, Jonathan Basil Morton Peto (gs of Sir Basil Edward Peto, 1 Bt); 2 s, 2 da; *Style* - The Hon Mrs Peto

PETRE, 17 Baron (E 1603); Joseph William Lionel Petre; s of 16 Baron Petre (d 1915, seventh in descent from the 7 Baron, on whom a contemporary (Lord Berkeley of Stratton) pronounced the epitaph 'Much lamented, tho' a Papist'; he figured as the Baron in Pope's *Rape of the Lock*, while his widow was considered as a possible bride for the Old Pretender) and Catherine, herself da of Hon John Boscawen (3 s of 6 Viscount Falmouth); John's w was Lady Margaret Byng (da of 2 Earl of Strafford) who later m, as her 2 husb, Sir Frederic Carne Rasch, 2 Bt, TD; *b* 5 June 1914; *Educ* Eton; *m* 1941, Marguerite, da of late Ion Wentworth Hamilton; 1 s; *Heir* s, Hon John Patrick Lionel Petre; *Career* Capt Essex Regt, patron of 3 livings (but being a Roman Catholic cannot present); *Style* - The Rt Hon the Lord Petre; Writtle Park, Essex; Ingatestone Hall, Essex

PETRE, His Honour Judge; Francis Herbert Loraine; s of late Maj-Gen R L Petre, CB, DSO, MC; *b* 9 March 1927; *Educ* Downside, Clare Cambridge; *m* 1958, Mary Jane, da of Everard White, of Masterton, NZ; 3 s, 1 da; *Career* barr Lincoln's Inn 1952, dep chm E Suffolk QS 1970, dep chm Agricultural Lands Tribunal (Eastern Area) 1972, a Circuit Judge 1972-; *Style* - His Honour Judge Petre; Colneford House, Earls Colne, nr Colchester, Essex

PETRE, Hon John Patrick Lionel; s and h of 17 Baron Petre; *b* 4 Aug 1942; *Educ* Eton, Trin Oxford; *m* 1965, Marcia Gwendolyn, da of Alfred Plumpton; 2 s, 1 da; *Style* - The Hon John Petre; Writtle Park, Essex

PETRIE, Edward James; CMG (1955); *b* 1907; *m* (wife decd 1960); 2 s, 1 da; *Career* Sec to Treasury Kenya 1953-56, ret; *Style* - Edward Petrie Esq, CMG; 19 Stirling rd, Edinburgh EH5 3JA

PETRIE, Cecilia, Lady; Jessie Cecilia; da of late Frederick James George Mason; *m* 1926, as his 2 w, Sir Charles Petre, 3 Bt, CBE (d 1977); 1 s; *Career* memb Kensington Borough Council (Queen's Gate Ward) 1946-62, Alderman 1965-71, Freeman 1971, Mayor of the Royal Borough of Kensington 1954-56, memb

(C) LCC for S Kensington 1949-65; *Style* - Cecilia, Lady Petrie; 31 Queen's Gate Terr, SW7 5PP (☎ 01 581 0112)

PETRIE, Peter Charles; CMG (1980); s of Sir Charles Petrie, 3 Bt (d 1977) and of Cecilia, Lady Petrie *qv*; hp of half-bro, Sir Richard Petrie, 3 Bt; *b* 7 March 1932; *Educ* Westminster, Ch Ch Oxford; *m* 1958, Countess Lydwine Maria Fortunata, da of Count Charles Alphonse van Oberndorff, of The Hague and Paris; 2 s, 1 da; *Career* 2 Sec UK Del NATO Paris 1958-61, 1 Sec New Delhi 1961-64, Chargé d'Affaires Katmandu 1963, Cabinet Office 1965-57, UK Mission to UN, NY 1969-73, Counsellor (Head of Chancery) Bonn 1973-76, Head of European Integration Dept (Int) FCO 1976-79, Minister Paris 1979-; *Style* - Peter Petrie Esq CMG; 40 rue Lauriston, 75116 Paris, France

PETRIE, Sir (Charles) Richard Borthwick Petrie; 4 Bt (UK 1918), TD; s of Sir Charles Alexander Petrie, 3 Bt, CBE (d 1977); *b* 19 Oct 1921; *Educ* Radley, Heidelberg U, New Coll Oxford; *m* 1962, Jessie Ariana Borthwick, da of late Cdr Patrick Straton Campbell, RN; *Heir* half-bro, Peter Charles Petrie, CMG; *Career* Lt-Col REME (RARO) 1939-45; dir Richard Petrie Ltd Audio-Visual Programme Production; *Style* - Sir Richard Petrie, Bt, TD; 3 Northmoor rd, Oxford (☎ Oxford 56081)

PETTINGELL, Sir William Walter; CBE (1965, OBE 1959); s of H G W Pettingell, of Cootamundra, NSW; *b* 4 Sept 1914; *Educ* Wollongong H S, Sydney U; *m* 1942, Thora M , da of J Stokes; 1 s, 2 da; *Career* gen man The Australian Gas Light Co 1952-74, dep chm 1974-, chm Hanimex Corpn 1978-, Leighton Holdings Ltd, Prudential Cornhill Insurance, Blackwood Hodge Ltd, dep chm Australian Consolidated Industries, Foreign Investment Review Bd; kt 1972; FAIM, FIAM, FInstF, MInstGasE; *Style* - Sir William Pettingell CBE; 54 Linden Way, Castlecrag, NSW 2068, Australia (☎ 95 1976)

PETTIT, Sir Daniel Eric Arthur; s of Thomas Edgar Pettit; *b* 19 Feb 1915; *Educ* Quarry Bank H S Liverpool, Fitzwilliam Coll Cambridge; *m* 1940, Winifred, da of William Bibby; 2 s; *Career* chm Post Office Staff Superannuation Fund 1979-, memb Nat Ports Council 1971-80, chm Birmingham & W Midlands Bd Lloyds Bank Ltd 1978-, chm Lloyds Bank (UK) Ltd 1979-, Bransford Farmers Ltd, chm Incpen 1979-; FBIM, FCIT, FRSA, MIPM; kt 1974; *Style* - Sir Daniel Pettit; Bransford Court, Worcester

PETTIT, Richard William; s of Sir Daniel Pettit; *b* 11 Nov 1941; *Educ* Westminster, Oxford U; *m* 1967, Jane Anne, da of Wing Cdr Duncan Basset McGill, of Ruthin Castle, Clwyd; 2 c; *Career* dir Operations Vaux Brewery Sunderland 1977-, memb CBI Northern Region Council 1978-; MIMechE, MIProdE, MBIM; *Recreations* farming, fishing, model railways, horses; *Clubs* RAC; *Style* - Richard Pettit Esq; Hill End Farm, Bransford, Worcester; West Lodge, Tunstall rd, Sunderland (☎ Sunderland 51748

PETTY, Hon Sir Horace Rostill; *b* 29 March 1904; *Educ* S Yarra Sch, Univ H S, Melbourne U; *m* 1, 1930 (m dis) Mary Margaret, da of P S Watt; 2 s, 2 da; m 2, 1959, Beryl Anne Hoelter; *Career* Agent-Gen for State of Victoria in London 1964-69; BCom, FASA, RSSAILA; kt 1964; *Style* - The Hon Sir Horace Petty; 593 Toorak rd, Toorak, Vic 3142, Australia

PETTY-FITZMAURICE, Lady Arabella Helen Mary; da of Earl of Shelburne, *qv*; *b* 1966

PETTY-FITZMAURICE, Lady Rachel Barbara Violet; da of Earl of Shelburne, *qv*; *b* 1968

PETTY-FITZMAURICE, Hon William Nicholas Charles; s of Earl of Shelburne, *qv*; *b* 1973

PEVSNER, Dieter; s of Sir Nikolaus Pevsner, CBE; *aet* 48 in June 1981; *Career* jt dep md André Deutsch Ltd Aug 1981-; formerly sr ed at Penguin; fndr and jt owner Wildwood House (publishers) 1971-81; *Style* - Dieter Pevsner Esq; c/o André Deutsch Ltd, 105 Gt Russell st, WC1 (☎ 01 580 2746)

PEVSNER, Prof Sir Nikolaus Bernhard Leon; CBE (1953), FBA, FSA, Hon FRIBA, Hon ARCA, Hon FNZIA; s of Hugo Pevsner, of Leipzig; *b* 30 Jan 1902; *Educ* Leipzig U (PhD), and Hon Dr Leicester, York, Leeds, Oxford (MA), E Anglia, Zagreb, Keele, Warwick and London; *m* 1923, Carola, da of Alfred Kurlbaum, of Leipzig; 2 s (one of whom is Dieter P, *qv*), 1 da; *Career* Prof of History of Art Birkbeck Coll London U 1947-67, Emeritus Prof 1967-, Roy Gold Medal for Architecture 1967; kt 1969; author, best known for his architectural guides to Br Counties; *Style* - Professor Sir Nikolaus Pevsner CBE; 2 Wildwood Ter, North End, NW3 (☎ 01 455 9369)

PEYRONEL, Mrs Daniel; Alexandra Louise; *née* Rubens; da of Col Ralph Rubens by his w (he being her 3 husb) Lady Rosemary, *née* Eliot, da of 6 Earl of St Germans, whose w was Lady Blanche Somerset, da of 8 Duke of Beaufort; through Lady Blanche Mrs Peyronel is co-heiress presumptive to the Baronies of Botetourt and Herbert, at present held by 10 Duke of Beaufort, KG, GCVO, PC; *b* 9 Oct 1951; *Educ* St Martin's & Byam Shaw Schs of Art; *m* 1976, Daniel Augusto, s of Vice-Adm Aldo Peyronel, of Buenos Aires & Mar del Plata; 1 s; *Recreations* tennis, swimming, riding, hunting; *Style* - Mrs Daniel Peyronel; 12 Eleanor Grove, SW13 (☎ 01 876 8126)

PEYTON, Rt Hon John Wynne William; PC (1970), MP (C) Yeovil Div of Somerset 1951-; s of late Ivor Eliot Peyton; *b* 13 Feb 1919; *Educ* Eton, Trin Oxford; *m* 1, 1947 (m dis 1966), Diana Clinch; 1 s, 1 da (and 1 s decd); m 2, 1966, Mrs Mary Cobbold; *Career* 15/19 Hussars 1939, POW Germany 1940-45; barr Inner Temple 1945, Parly Sec Miny of Power 1962-64, Min of Transport 1970, Min for Transport Industries DOE 1970-74; chm Texas Instruments Ltd 1974-; *Style* - The Rt Hon John Peyton PC MP; The Old Malt House, Hinton St George, Somerset (☎ Crewkerne 73618); 6 Temple West Mews, West sq, SE11 (☎ 01 582 3611)

PEYTON-JONES, Jeremy Norman; s of Jeremy Peyton-Jones (d 1930); *b* 7 March 1919; *Educ* Dragon Sch, Eton; *m* 1963, Eva Louise, da of Prof Singdahl Kjaer, of Norway; 6 da (inc twins); *Career* Lt-Col Roy Artillery; dep chm H Clarkson Holdings Ltd, chm H Clarkson Insurance Holdings Ltd; on cncl Open U 1971-; JP 1968-, memb of Lloyd's; *Recreations* shooting, golf, tennis; *Clubs* White's, Boodle's, Pratt's; *Style* - Jeremy Peyton-Jones Esq JP; Rodsall Manor, Puttenham, Guildford, Surrey

PHELAN, His Honour Judge; Andrew James; s of Cornelius Phelan, of Clonmel, Ireland; *b* 25 July 1923; *Educ* Clongoweswood, Co Kildare, Nat U of Ireland, Trin Cambridge; *m* 1950, Joan Robertson, da of John McLagan (d 1978), of Callander, Perthshire; 1 s, 2 da; *Career* barr (I) King's Inn 1945, barr Gray's Inn 1949; Jr Fell Bristol U 1948-50; a Circuit Judge 1974-; *Style* - His Honour Judge Phelan; 17 Hartington rd, Chiswick, W4 1PD (☎ 01 994 6109)

PHELPS, Anthony John; CB (1976); s of John Francis Phelps, of Oxford; *b* 14 Oct 1922; *Educ* City of Oxford H S, Univ Coll Oxford; *m* 1, 1949, Sheila Nan Rait (d 1967), da of late Colin Benton Rait, of Edinburgh; 1 s, 2 da; m 2, 1971, Janet M T, da of late Charles R Dawson, of Edinburgh; *Career* Dep Chm Bd of Customs and Excise 1973-; *Style* - Anthony Phelps Esq CB; 1 Woodsyre, Sydenham Hill, SE26 6SS (☎ 01 670 0735)

PHELPS, Hon Mrs (Helen Rosemary); da of 3 Baron Cozens-Hardy; *b* 1918; *m* 1953, Brig Douglas Vandeleur Phelps, TD, JP, DL; *Style* - The Hon Mrs Phelps; Bayfield Hall, Holt, Norfolk

PHELPS, Howard Thomas Henry Middleton; s of Ernest Henry Phelps, of Gloucester; *b* 20 Oct 1926; *Educ* Crypt G S Gloucester, Hatfield Coll Durham U; *m* 1949, Audrey, nee Ellis; 1 da; *Career* memb British Airways Bd 1973-, Operations Dir 1979-; FIPM, FCIT, CBIM; *Style* - Howard Phelps Esq; Littlecroft, Heathside rd, Woking, Surrey (☎ Woking 62027)

PHELPS, Maj-Gen Leonard Thomas Herbert; CB (1973), OBE (1963); s of Abijah Phelps; *b* 9 Sept 1917; *m* 1945, Jean Irene, da of R Price Dixon; 1 s, 1 da;

Career 2 Lt RAOC 1941, Brig 1967, Cdr Base Organisation RAOC 1970-71, Maj-Gen 1970, DOS MOD 1971-73, ret, Col Cmdt RAOC 1976-78; dir Leon Davis & Co Ltd, FBIM, CBI; *Style* - Maj-Gen Leonard Phelps, CB, OBE; South Port Cottage, Sutton Courtenay, Oxon; 2 Glebe House, Fitzroy Mews, WIP 5DQ

PHILIP, Sir William Shearer; CMG (1961), MC (1918); s of Capt William Philip; *b* 18 Aug 1891; *Educ* Scotch Coll Melbourne; *m* 1920, Irene Laura (d 1960), da of William Cross; 2 s, 2 da; *Career* memb Bd of Management Alfred Hospital 1935, Hon Treasurer 1939-48, Pres 1948-, co dir; kt 1975; *Style* - Sir William Philip, CMG, MC; Glenshee, No 1 Macquarie rd, Toorak, Vic 3142, Australia (☎ 20 3973)

PHILIPPE, André J; Hon GCVO 1972; *b* Luxembourg City 28 June 1926; *Career* barr Luxembourg 1951-52, Luxembourg Ambass to UK, Perm Rep to Council of WEU, and concurrently Ambass to Ireland and Iceland 1972-78, Ambass to France 1978-; Cdr Order of Adolphe Nassau and Order of Oaken Crown (Lux), Cdr Légion d'Honneur (Fr); *Style* - HE Monsieur André Philippe, GCVO; The Luxembourg Embassy, 33 avenue Rapp, 75007 Paris, France (☎ 555 13 37)

PHILIPPS, Hon Colwyn Jestyn John; s (by 1 m) and h of 2 Viscount St Davids, *qv*; *b* 30 Jan 1939; *Educ* Sevenoaks Sch; *m* 1965, Augusta Victoria Correa Larrain, da of late Don Estantislao Correa Ugarte, of Santiago, Chile; 2 s; *Career* late 2 Lt Welsh Gds; *Style* - The Hon Colwyn Philipps; 14a Alwyne pla, N1

PHILIPPS, Hon Mrs (Elizabeth Joan); da of 1 Baron Kindersley GBE (d 1954); *b* 1911; *m* 1930, Maj the Hon James Perrott Philipps TD; *Style* - The Hon Mrs Philipps; Dalham Hall, Newmarket, Suffolk

PHILIPPS, Hon Eiddwen Sara; da (by his 1 wife) of 2 Viscount St Davids, *qv*; *b* 1948; *Style* - The Hon Eiddwen Philipps; Roch Cottage, 15 Newton Toney, nr Salisbury, Wilts

PHILIPPS, Hon Gwenllian; OBE (1962); da of 1 Baron Milford (d 1962); *b* 1916; *Career* formerly Subaltern ATS; JP Radnorshire, CC Radnorshire 1959-64, High Sheriff 1970-71; *Style* - The Hon Gwenllian Philipps OBE JP; The Old Rectory, Boughrood, Llyswen, Brecon

PHILIPPS, Hon (Richard) Hanning; MBE (1945); s of 1 Baron Milford (d 1962); *b* 14 Feb 1904; *Educ* Eton; *m* 1930, Lady Marion Violet Dalrymple JP, da of 12 Earl of Stair; 1 s; *Career* NW Europe, 1944-45, Maj Welsh Gds (Reserve), Hon Col Pembroke Yeo; hon pres of Schweppes Ltd; chm Northern Securities Trust Ltd 1950-80, and Milford Haven Conservancy Bd 1963-75; memb Civic Trust for Wales; JP; HM-Lt for Pembrokeshire 1958-74, Ld-Lt for Dyfed 1974-79, Keeper of the Rolls for Dyfed 1974-, contested (Nat) Brecon and Radnor 1939; *Recreations* painting, forestry, gardening; *Clubs* Boodle's; *Style* - The Hon Richard Philipps MBE JP; Picton Castle, Haverfordwest, Pembrokeshire; 5 Connaught Place, W2

PHILIPPS, Hon Hugo John Laurence; s and h of 2 Baron Milford; *b* 27 Aug 1929; *Educ* Eton, King's Coll Camb; *m* 1, 1951 (m dis 1958), Margaret, da of Capt Ralph Heathcote, DSO, RN; 1 da; m 2, 1959, the Hon Mary Makins, da of 1 Baron Sherfield; 3 s, 1 da; *Career* memb Lloyd's; farmer; *Style* - The Hon Hugo Philipps; Llanstephan House, Llanstephan, Brecon, Powys

PHILIPPS, Lady Jean (Meriel); *née* McDonnell; da of 7 Earl of Antrim (d 1932); *b* 1914; *m* 1939, Capt the Hon William Speke Philipps, CBE (d 1975); 2 s, 2 da; *Style* - Lady Jean Philipps; Slebech Park, Haverfordwest, Dyfed

PHILIPPS, Hon James Perrott; TD; s of 1 Baron Milford (d 1962); *b* 25 Nov 1905; *Educ* Eton and Ch Ch Oxford; *m* 1930, the Hon Elizabeth Joan Kindersley, da of 1 Baron Kindersley; 1 s, 2 da; *Career* Maj TA Reserve; farmer; High Sheriff of Suffolk 1955, chm Dalham Farms Ltd; *Clubs* Turf and Jockey; *Style* - The Hon James Philipps TD; Dalham Hall, Newmarket, Suffolk (Ousden 242)

PHILIPPS, Hon Mrs; Hon Mary; *née* Makins; da (twin) of 1 Baron Sherfield, GCB, GCMG; *b* 1935; *m* 1959, as his 2 w, Hon Hugo John Laurence Philipps, *qv*; *Style* - The Hon Mrs Philipps; Llanstephan House, Llanstephan, Brecon, Powys

PHILIPPS, Lady Marion Violet; *née* Dalrymple; JP (Pembrokeshire); da of late 12 Earl of Stair, KT, DSO; *b* 1908; *m* 1930, Maj the Hon Richard Hanning Philipps, MBE, *qv*; *Style* - Lady Marion Philipps, JP; 5 Connaught pla, W2; Picton Castle, Haverfordwest, Pembrokeshire

PHILIPS, Prof Sir Cyril Henry; s of William Henry Philips; *b* 27 Dec 1912; *Educ* Rock Ferry H S, Liverpool U (MA), London U (PhD); *m* 1, 1939, Dorcas (d 1974), da of John Rose Wallasey; 1 da (& 1 s decd); m 2, 1975, Joan Rosemary, da of William George Marshall; *Career* Prof of Oriental History London U 1946-, dir Sch Oriental and African Studies London 1957-76, Dep Vice-Chllr London U 1969-70, Vice-Chllr 1972-76; kt 1974; *Clubs* Athenaeum; *Style* - Professor Sir Cyril Philips; School of Oriental & African Studies, Malet st, WCIE 7HP (☎ 01 637 2388)

PHILIPSON, Garry; DFC (1944); s of George Philipson; *b* 27 Nov 1921; *Educ* Stockton G S, Durham U; *m* 1949, June Mary Miller Somerville; 1 da; *Career* md Aycliffe and Peterlee Development Corpns 1974-; *Style* - Garry Philipson Esq DFC; Tunstall Grange, Tunstall, Richmond, N Yorks (☎ Richmond 833327); 12 Glebe Place, SW3 (☎ 01 352 0131)

PHILIPSON, Sir Robin (Robert James); s of James Philipson; *b* 17 Dec 1916; *Educ* Whitehaven Secdy Sch, Dumfries Acad, Edinburgh Coll of Art; *m* 1, 1949, Brenda Mark; m 2, 1962 (m dis 1975), Thora Clyne; m 3, 1976, Diana Mary Pollock; *Career* Head of the Sch of Drawing and Painting, The College of Art, Edinburgh 1960-; Pres Royal Scottish Academy 1973-; FRSA, FRSE, Doctorate Stirling U 1976, Hon LLD Aberdeen 1977; kt 1976; *Style* - Sir Robin Philipson; 23 Crawfurd rd, Edinburgh EH16 5PQ (☎ 031 667 2373)

PHILIPSON-STOW, Christopher; DFC; s of late Henry Matthew Philipson Philipson-Stow (3 s of 1 Bt) and hp of kinsman, Sir Edmond Cecil Philipson-Stow, 4 Bt MBE; *b* 13 Sept 1920; *Educ* Winchester; *m* 1952, Elizabeth Nairn, da of late James Dixon Trees and widow of Maj F G McLaren; 2 s; *Career* late Fl Lt RAFVR; *Style* - Christopher Philipson-Stow DFC; 32 John st, Thornhill, Ontario, Canada

PHILIPSON-STOW, Lady; Cynthia Yvette; da of late William Robertson Jecks, of Johannesburg, S Africa, and formerly w of Francis Romaine Govett; *m* 1951, as his 2 w, Sir Frederic Lawrence Philipson-Stow, 3 Bt (d 1976); *Style* - Lady Philipson-Stow; Na Xencha, Villa Carlos, Menorca, Spain; Apartado 211, Mahon, Menorca, Spain

PHILIPSON-STOW, Sir Edmond Cecil; 4 Bt (UK 1907), of Cape Town, Colony of Cape of Good Hope and Blackdown House, Lodsworth, Co Sussex; MBE (1946); s of Sir Elliot Philipson Philipson-Stow, 2 Bt, and bro of Sir Frederic Lawrence Philipson-Stow, 3 Bt (d 1976); *b* 25 Aug 1912; *Educ* Malvern Coll, RMC Sandhurst; *Heir* kinsman, Christopher Philipson-Stow DFC; *Career* Maj late DCLI, 1939-45 War (Burma 1943-45); *Style* - Sir Edmond Philipson-Stow, Bt MBE; Cloonaghmore, Crossmolina, Co Mayo

PHILLIMORE, 3 Baron (UK 1918); Sir Robert Godfrey Phillimore; 4 Bt (UK 1881); s of Capt Hon Anthony Francis Phillimore (ka 1940) and gs of 3 Baron Phillimore (d 1947); *b* 24 Sept 1939; *Educ* Winchester; *Heir* unc, Maj Hon Claud Stephen Phillimore; *Career* late 2 Lt 9/12 Roy Lancers; *Style* - The Rt Hon the Lord Phillimore; Coppid Hall, Henley-on-Thames, Oxon

PHILLIMORE, Hon Claud Stephen; s of 2 Baron Phillimore, MC (d 1947); hp of n, 3 Baron; *b* 15 Jan 1911; *Educ* Winchester, Trin Camb; *m* 1944, Anne Elizabeth, da of late Maj Arthur Algernon Dorrien-Smith, DSO; 1 s, 1 da;

Career Capt and Acting Maj 11 (City of London Yeo) Light Anti-Aircraft Brig RA (TA); *Style* - The Hon Claud Phillimore; 39 Ashley gdns, SW1; Raymans Tower, Apuldram, Chichester

PHILLIMORE, John Gore; CMG (1946), DL (Kent 1979); s of late Adm Sir Richard Phillimore; *b* 16 April 1908; *Educ* Winchester and Ch Ch Oxford; *m* 1951, Jill Irene, da of late Capt Mason Scott, RN (ret) and of Hon Mrs Scott; 2 s, 2 da; *Career* md Baring Bros & Co Ltd 1949-72; dir Commonwealth Development Finance Co Ltd 1967, Tribune Investment Trust Ltd; High Sheriff of Kent 1975; *Style* - John Phillimore Esq, CMG, DL; The Postern, Tonbridge, Kent (☎ 352178)

PHILLIMORE, Hon Mrs Miles - Margaret; da of late Gibson Lamb Caldwell, of Kenwood Place, Wheeling, W Virginia; *m* 1946, Hon Miles Phillimore (d 1972, s of 2 Baron Phillimore); 1 da; *Style* - The Hon Mrs Miles Phillimore; 264 Glenwood rd, Wheeling, W Virginia, USA

PHILLIMORE, Hon Robert George Hugh; OBE (1945, MBE 1941); s of 2 Baron Phillimore, MC (d 1947); *b* 1913; *Educ* Winchester Trin Cambridge; *m* 1944, Sheila Bruce, da of John Farquhar MacLeod, JP, MB, ChB; 3 da; *Career* Col RE (ret); JP Oxon; 1939-45 war in Middle East (despatches); *Style* - The Hon Robert Phillimore OBE JP; The Mill House, Shiplake, Oxon

PHILLIPS, Baroness (Life Peeress UK 1964); Norah Phillips; JP (Co of London); da of William Lusher, of Fulham; *b* 1910; *Educ* Marist Convent, Hampton Training Coll; *m* 1930, Morgan Phillips, sometime Gen Sec Labour Pty (d 1963); 1 s, 1 da; *Career* Ld-Lt Greater London 1978-, Dir Assoc for the Prevention of Theft in Shops, Pres Nat Assoc of Women's Clubs, Inst of Shops, Health and Safety Acts Admin, Assoc for Research into Restricted Growth, Keep Fit Assoc; V-Pres Nat Assoc of Local Councils, Pre-Retirement Assoc, Nat Chamber of Trade; chm Beatrice Webb House Trust; a Baroness in Waiting (Govt Whip) 1965-70; *Style* - Rt Hon Baroness Phillips JP, HM Lord-Lieut for Greater London; 115 Rannoch rd, W6 (☎ 01 828 8889/0781)

PHILLIPS, Arthur; OBE (1957), JP (Hants); s of Albert William Phillips (d 1955); *b* 29 May 1907; *Educ* Highgate Sch and Trin Oxford; *m* 1934, Kathleen, da of Thomas Henry Hudson (d 1938); 2 s, 2 da; *Career* Maj E African Campaign; barr Middle Temple, HM Colonial Serv (Kenya) 1931-47; Prof of English Law Southampton U 1956-67, Dep Vice-Chllr 1961-63; dep chm Hants QS 1956-71, a Recorder 1972-79, Chllr Diocese of Winchester 1964-; *Clubs* Royal Commonwealth Soc; *Style* - Arthur Phillips Esq, OBE, JP; Church Cottage, Compton, nr Winchester, Hants (☎ Twyford 713295)

PHILLIPS, (David) Alan; s of Stephen Thomas Phillips; *b* 21 July 1926; *Educ* Llanelli G S, Univ Coll Oxford; *m* 1960, Jean Louise, nee Godsell; 2 s; *Career* barr Gray's Inn 1960, a Recorder of the Crown Court 1974-, Stipendiary Magistrate for Mid-Glamorgan 1975-; *Style* - Alan Phillips Esq; The Magistrates' Court, Union st, Pontypridd, Mid-Glamorgan

PHILLIPS, Brian Harold; s of Charles Douglas Phillips (d 1958); *b* 30 Aug 1930; *Educ* Luton G S; *m* 1952, Margaret June, da of Stanley Archibald Wilkins (d 1977); 1 s, 1 da; *Career* sr local govt financial appts to 1967, finance controller Nationwide Building Soc 1967-71, gen man (finance) 1971-; FRSA; *Style* - Brian Phillips Esq; Treetops, 17 Silverthorn Drive, Longdean Park, Hemel Hempstead, Herts HP3 8BU

PHILLIPS, Maj-Gen Charles George; CB (1944), DSO (1919) and bar (1940), MC (1915); s of late Lt-Col George Edward Phillips; *b* 1889; *Educ* Repton and RMC; *m* 1924, Norah, da of F P Butler; 3 da; *Career* Maj-Gen 1942, cmdg Gambia area 1942-43, Sierra Leone area 1943-44 (despatches), ret; *Style* - Maj-Gen Charles Phillips CB, DSO*, MC; P O Box 42370, Nairobi, Kenya

PHILLIPS, Prof Sir David Chilton; s of Charles Harry Phillips (d 1963); *b* 7 March 1924; *Educ* Oswestry Boys' H S,

Univ Coll Wales (BSc, PhD); *m* 1960, Diana Kathleen, da of Maj Edward Maitland Hutchinson; 1 da; *Career* Sub-Lt RNVR 1944-47, Post-Doctoral Fell Nat Research Council of Canada 1951-53, Research Officer Nat Research Labs Ottawa Canada 1953-55, Research Worker Roy Institution London 1956-66, Prof of Molecular Biophysics Oxford U 1966-, Fell Corpus Christi Oxford 1966-, Biological Sec of The Royal Soc 1976-, memb Medical Research Council 1974-78; FInstP, FRS 1967, kt 1979; *Style* - Professor Sir David Phillips; 3 Fairlawn End, Upper Wolvercote, Oxford OX2 8AR (☎ Oxford 55828)

PHILLIPS, Eric Lawrance; CMG (1963); s of L Stanley Phillips; *b* 23 July 1909; *Educ* Haileybury Coll, Balliol Oxford; *m* 1938, Phyllis Bray; 2 s, 1 step-da; *Career* Under-Sec BOT 1964-69, Sec Monopolies Cmmn 1969-74, consultant to Monopolies and Mergers Cmmn 1974-75; *Style* - Eric Phillips Esq CMG; 46 Platts Lane, NW3 (☎ 01 435 7873)

PHILLIPS, Edwin William; MBE (1946); s of Charles Edwin Phillips (d 1979), of Chiswick; *b* 29 Jan 1918; *Educ* Latymer Upper Sch; *m* 1951, Pauline Mary Matusch; 2 s; *Career* dir: Lazard Bros & Co Ltd 1960-, BR Property Bd 1970, Phoenix Assurance 1975, Woolwich Equitable Building Soc 1977; chm Friends Provident Life Office 1968-, Higgs and Hill 1975-; *Style* - Edwin Phillips Esq MBE; Send Barns, Send, Surrey (☎ Guildford 223305)

PHILLIPS, Sir Fred Albert; CVO (1966); s of Wilbert A Phillips, of Brighton, St Vincent; *b* 14 May 1918; *Educ* London U (LLB), Toronto U, McGill U (MCL); *Career* barr Middle Temple, Govr St Kitts/Nevis/Anguilla 1967-69, special rep Cable and Wireless (W Indies); KStJ 1968, kt 1967; *Style* - Sir Fred Phillips CVO; Chambers, Kingstown, St Vincent, West Indies; PO Box 206, Bridgetown, Barbados

PHILLIPS, Sir Horace; KCMG (1973, CMG 1963); s of Samuel Phillips; *b* 31 May 1917; *Educ* Hillhead H S Glasgow; *m* 1944, Idina Doreen Morgan; 1 s, 1 da; *Career* Ambass to Indonesia 1966-68, High Cmmr in Tanzania 1968-72, Ambass to Turkey 1973-77, Resident Rep (Iran) Taylor Woodrow Ltd 1978-79, Hong Kong 1979-, Hon LLD Glasgow 1977, Order of the Taj (Iran) 1961; *Style* - Sir Horace Phillips, KCMG; 34a Sheridan rd, Merton Park, SW19 3HP (☎ 01 542 3836)

PHILLIPS, Sir Henry Ellis Isidore; CMG (1960), MBE (1946); s of late Harry J Phillips, MBE; *b* 30 Aug 1914; *Educ* Haberdashers' Sch Hampstead, UCL (BA, MA); *m* 1, 1941 (m dis 1965), Vivien Hyamson; 2 s, 1 da; m 2, 1966, Philippa Cohen; *Career* Colonial Admin Serv (Nyasaland) 1946-65, Financial Sec Nyasaland Govt 1957-64 and Min of Finance 1961-64; md Standard Bank Finance and Development Corpn 1966-72, memb Civil Aviation Authority 1975-80, Hon Treasurer Stonham Memorial Trust 1977-; kt 1964; *Style* - Sir Henry Phillips, CMG, MBE; 34 Ross Court, Putney Hill, SW15 (☎ 01 789 1404)

PHILLIPS, Herbert Moore; CMG (1949); s of Herbert Charles Phillips; *b* 7 Feb 1908; *Educ* St Olave's and Wadham Coll Oxford; *m* 1, 1934, Martha (decd), da of Karl Löffler, of Graz, Austria; 1 da; m 2, 1952, Doris Rushbrooke; *Career* Assist Sec Miny Labour 1942, Counsellor for Economic and Social Affairs to Perm UK Delegation to UN 1946-49, memb of UK Delegation to various int organisations, consultant to OECD, UNESCO, UN, UNICEF, World Bank 1968-; *Style* - Herbert Phillips Esq CMG; 9 rue de Mézières, 75006 Paris, France

PHILLIPS, John Francis; CBE (1977, OBE 1957), QC (1981); s of late F W Phillips; *b* 1911; *Educ* Cardinal Vaughan Sch, London U, Trinity Hall Cambridge (LLB, LLM); *m* 1937, Olive M Royer; 1 s, 2 da; *Career* arbitrator, barr Gray's Inn 1944, chm Provident Assoc for Medical Care (Private Patients Plan) 1977-, dep chm Eggs Authority 1971-; *Clubs* Athenaeum; *Style* - John Phillips Esq, CBE, QC; 17 Ossulton Way, Hampstead Gdn Suburb, N2 (☎ 01 455 8460)

PHILLIPS, John Fleetwood Stewart; CMG (1965); s of late Maj Herbert

Stewart Phillips; *b* 16 Dec 1917; *Educ* Brighton, Worcester Coll Oxford; *m* 1948, Mary Gordon Shaw, MB, BS; 2 s, 2 da; *Career* Ambass to S Yemen 1969-70, to Jordan 1970-72, to Sudan 1973-77, ret; *Clubs* Travellers'; *Style* - John Phillips Esq CMG; Southwood, Gordon rd, Horsham, Sussex (☎ Horsham 2894)

PHILLIPS, Sir John Grant; KBE (1972, CBE 1968); s of Oswald Phillips, of Sydney; *b* 13 March 1911; *Educ* C of E G S Sydney, Sydney U (BEc); *m* 1935, Mary W Debenham; 2 s, 2 da; *Career* Govr & Chm Reserve Bank of Australia 1968-75; dir Lend Lease Corpn Ltd 1976-, chm Australian States Advsy Cncl 1976-; *Style* - Sir John Phillips, KBE; 2/25 Marshall st, Manly, NSW 2095, Australia

PHILLIPS, John George Crispin; QC (1980); s of George Godfrey Phillips, CBE (d 1965); *b* 27 Oct 1938; *Educ* Harrow, Trin Cambridge; *Career* Nat Service Scots Gds 1956-58, barr Gray's Inn 1962; *Clubs* White's; *Style* - John Phillips Esq QC; 1 Brick Court, Temple, EC4Y 9BY

PHILLIPS, Lady Katherine (Mary); *née* Fitzalan-Howard; da of 15 Duke of Norfolk, KG, CVO, PC (d 1917); *b* 1912; *m* 1940, Lt-Col Joseph Anthony Moore Phillips, DSO, MBE, DL; 1 s; *Career* Order of Mercy; *Style* - Lady Katherine Phillips; Lund House, Lund, Driffield, Yorks

PHILLIPS, Hon Mrs (Laura Claire); *née* Grenfell; da of 2 Baron St Just by his 1 w Leslie (da of Condé Nast); *b* 17 July 1950; *m* 1980, Hayden Phillips; 1 da (Florence Leslie, christened 1 June 1981, godparents include: Lord Harris of Greenwich, Jane Bonham Carter, Mrs Dermot Gleeson); *Style* - The Hon Mrs Phillips

PHILLIPS, Sir Leslie Walter; CBE (1947); s of late Charles Phillips; *b* 12 Aug 1894; *m* 1, 1915, Mary (d 1971), da of late John Corby; 1 s; m 2, 1972, Patricia, da of late Claude Palmer; *Career* vice-chm Baltic Exchange 1961-63, chm 1963-65; kt 1962; *Style* - Sir Leslie Phillips CBE; 18 The Village, Meads, Eastbourne, E Sussex (☎ Eastbourne 37624)

PHILLIPS, Hon Mrs (Margaret Askew Alexander); da of 2 Baron Harmsworth; *b* 1928; *m* 1960, Frank Gibson Phillips; 2 s *Style* The Hon Mrs Phillips

PHILLIPS, Capt Mark Anthony Peter; CVO (1974), ADC(P); s of P W G Phillips, MC; *b* 22 Sept 1948; *Educ* Marlborough, RMA Sandhurst; *m* 1973, HRH The Princess Anne; 1 s, 1 da; *Career* Queen's Dragoon Gds 1969, regimental duty 1969-74, Co Instructor RMA Sandhurst 1974-77, Army Trg Directorate MOD 1977-78, ret; student RAC Cirencester 1978-; Personal ADC to HM the Queen 1974-; in Three Day Equestrian Event, GB winning teams, Team Championships: World 1970, European 1971, Olympic Gold Medallists (Team) Olympic Games Munich 1972, memb Equestrian Team (Reserve) Olympic Games Mexico 1968 and Montreal 1976; Liveryman Farriers' Co, Farmers' Co, Saddlers' Co, Freeman Loriners Co, City of London; *Clubs* Buck's (Hon memb); *Style* - Captain Mark Phillips, CVO, ADC(P); Gatcombe Park, Cirencester, Glos

PHILLIPS, Hon Morgan David; s of Baroness Phillips; *b* 1939; *Educ* St Paul's, Downing Cambridge and London U; *Style* - The Hon Morgan Phillips

PHILLIPS, Michael George; s of Walter George Phillips (d 1958); *b* 31 Oct 1931; *Educ* Steyning G S; *m* 1957, Elizabeth Ann, da of Harold Stanley Batten (d 1959); 1 da; *Career* chm UBM Group Ltd 1975-, dir MK Electric Holdings Ltd 1976-; *Style* - Michael Phillips Esq; Maysmead Place, Langford, nr Bristol BS18 7HX (☎ Wrington 862343)

PHILLIPS, Lady Marion Violet; *née* Dalrymple; JP (Dyfed 1965); da of 12 Earl of Stair, KT, DSO (d 1961); *b* 1 Feb 1908; *Educ* privately; *m* 1930, Hon Hanning Philipps; 1 s, 1 da; *Career* memb Narberth Rural Dist Council 1970-73; chm Picton Land & Investment Pty Ltd WA; trustee, Picton Castle Trust (Graham Sutherland Gallery) 1976-; founder memb and first pres British Polled Hereford Soc 1950; FRAgS 1973, CStJ, Order of Mercy 1926; *Style* - Lady Marion Phillips JP; Picton Castle, The Rhos, Haverfordwest, Dyfed (☎ Rhos 201); 5 Connaught Place, W2

PHILLIPS, Nicholas Addison; QC (1978); *b* 21 Jan 1938; *Educ* Bryanston Sch, King's Cambridge; *m* 1972, Christylle Marie-Thérèse Rouffiac, nee Doreau; 2 da, and 1 step s, 1 step da; *Career* RNVR 1956-58, barrister Middle Temple (Harmsworth Scholar) 1962, Junior Counsel to Miny of Defence and to Treasury in Admiralty matters 1973-78, Govr Bryanston 1975-; *Style* - Nicholas Phillips Esq, QC; 28 Chalcot sq, NW1 (☎ 01 586 2813)

PHILLIPS, Prof Neville Crompton; CMG (1973); s of Samuel Phillips, of Christchurch, NZ; *b* 7 March 1916; *Educ* Dannevirke H S, Palmerston North Boys' H S, Canterbury Univ Coll, Merton Oxford, NZ Univ; *m* 1940, Pauline Beatrice, da of Selby Palmer, of NZ; 1 s, 2 da; *Career* Vice-Chllr and Rector, Univ of Canterbury, Christchurch, NZ 1966-77, ret; chm Management Ctee Canterbury Archaeological Trust 1980-; *Style* - Professor Neville Phillips, CMG; Tyle House, Hackington rd, Tyler Hill, Canterbury, Kent CT2 9NF (☎ Blean 708)

PHILLIPS, Prof Owen Hood; *b* 30 Sept 1907; *Educ* Weymouth Coll, Merton Oxford; *m* 1949, Lucy, da of Arnold Philip; *Career* late Barber Prof of Jurisprudence Birmingham U; *Style* - Prof Owen Phillips

PHILLIPS, Percy; s of Harry Phillips (d 1963); *b* 1 May 1900; *Educ* Grove Park County Sch Wrexham; *m* 1924, Gertrude, nee Nelken; 2 children; *Career* certified accountant and chartered sec, co dir; *Recreations* reading, bridge; *Style* - Percy Phillips Esq; Bracken Knoll, Courtenay av, N6

PHILLIPS, Hon Mr Justice; Hon Sir (John) Raymond; MC (1945); s of David Rupert Phillips; *b* 20 Nov 1915; *Educ* Rugby, Balliol Oxford; *m* 1951, Hazel Bradbury, da of T John Evans, of Cyncoed, Cardiff; 2 s; *Career* barr Gray's Inn 1939, Bencher 1965, QC 1968, dep chm Glamorgan QS 1964-71, a Justice of the High Court Queen's Bench Division 1971-, Presiding Judge Wales and Chester Circuit 1980-; kt 1971; *Style* - The Hon Mr Justice Phillips, MC; The Elms, Park rd, Teddington, Middx (☎ 01 977 1584)

PHILLIPS, Reginald Arthur; CMG (1965), OBE (1951); s of late James Phillips; *b* 31 Jan 1913; *Educ* Tredegar G S, Balliol Oxford; *Career* Dep Dir-Gen British Council 1966-73, ret; *Recreations* Athenaeum; *Style* - Reginald Phillips Esq, CMG, OBE; 76 Chiltley Way, Liphook, Hants (☎ Liphook 722610)

PHILLIPS, Sir Robin Francis; 3 Bt (UK 1912); s of Sir Lionel Francis Phillips, 2 Bt (d 1944); *b* 29 July 1940; *Educ* Aiglon Coll Switzerland; *Heir* none; *Style* - Sir Robin Phillips, Bt; 12 Manson Mews, Queen's Gate, SW7

PHILLIPS, Surgeon Rear-Adm Rex Philip; CB (1972), OBE (1963); s of William John Phillips; *b* 17 May 1913; *Educ* Epsom Coll, Coll of Med Newcastle upon Tyne, Durham U (now U of Newcastle upon Tyne); *m* 1939, Gill Foley; 2 s; *Career* Medical Officer-in-Charge RN Hosp Plymouth 1969-72, QHS 1969-72, CStJ 1970; *Style* - Surgeon Rear-Admiral Rex Phillips CB OBE; Langstone House, Langstone Village, Havant, Hants (☎ Havant 484668)

PHILLIPS, Sian; da of D Phillips; *Educ* Pontardawe G S, U of Wales (Cardiff Coll), RADA; *m* 1, 1960 (m dis 1979) Peter O'Toole; 2 da; m 2, 1979, Robin Sachs; *Career* actress, BBC Radio Wales mid 1940s-, BBC TV Wales early 1950s-, Newsreader and Announcer, and memb Rep Co BBC 1953-55; Critics Circle Award, New York Critics Award and Famous 7 Critics Award for *Goodbye Mr Chips* 1969, BAFTA Award for *How Green Was My Valley* and *I, Claudius* 1978, Roy Television Soc Award for *I, Claudius* 1978; memb Gorsedd of Bards 1960 (for services to drama in Wales); *Style* - Miss Sian Phillips; c/o Saraband Ltd, 348 Upper st, Islington, N1 OPD

PHILLIPS, Sydney William Charles; CB (1955); s of late Frederick Charles Phillips; *b* 1 Dec 1908; *Educ* Bridport G S, UCL (Fell 1969); *m* 1932, Phyllis, da of late James Spence; 2 s; *Career* Second Civil Service Cmmr 1968-70, a part-time Cmmr 1970-72; *Style* - Sydney Phillips Esq, CB;

Innisfree, Higher Drive, Purley, Surrey (☎ 01 660 8617)

PHILLPOTTS, Christopher Louis George; CMG (1957); s of Adm Edward Montgomery Phillpots CB; *b* 23 April 1915; *Educ* RNC Dartmouth; *m* 1942, Vivien Chanter-Bowden; 1 s, 1 da; *Career* RN 1932-43; Counsellor HM Embassy Paris 1957, FO 1962, Cnsllr Washington 1964-66, FCO 1966-70; *Clubs* White's, Pratt's, Army and Navy; *Style* - Christopher Phillpotts Esq, CMG; 27 Merrick sq, SE1 (☎ 01 407 5995)

PHILO, Gordon Charles George; CMG (1970), MC (1944); s of Charles Gilbert Philo; *b* 8 Jan 1920; *Educ* Haberdashers' Aske's Sch, Wadham Oxford; *m* 1952, Mavis (Vicky) Ella, da of John Ford Galsworthy; *Career* Consul-Gen Hanoi 1968-69, FCO 1969-78, ret; *Clubs* Athenaeum; *Style* - Gordon Philo Esq, CMG; 10 Abercorn Close, NW8 (☎ 01 286 9597)

PHILPOT, Oliver Lawrence Spurling; MC (1944), DFC (1941); s of Lawrence Benjamin Philpot; *b* 6 March 1913; *Educ* Queen Mary Sch, N Vancouver, Aymestrey Court Worcester, Radley, Worcester Coll Oxford; *m* 1, 1938 (m dis 1951); 1 s, 2 da; m 2, 1954, Rosl Widhalm; 1 s, 1 da; *Career* md Remploy Ltd 1974-78, dir Arthur Woollacott & Rappings Ltd 1953, chm and md Spirella Co of Gt Britain Ltd 1956, md Venesta (later Aluminium) Foils Ltd 1959; memb Nat Advsy Cncil on Employment of Disabled People 1978; *Style* - Oliver Philpot Esq, MC, DFC; 30 Abingdon Villas, Kensington W8 6BX (☎ 01 937 6013)

PHILPOTT, Air Vice-Marshal Peter Theodore; CB (1966), CBE (1954, OBE 1945); s of Rev R Philpott, of Worcester; *b* 20 March 1915; *Educ* Malvern Coll, RAF Coll Cranwell; *m* 1942, Marie, da of Charles Griffin, of Malvern; 2 da; *Career* Dir of Service Intelligence MOD 1968-70; *Style* - Air Vice-Marshal Peter Philpott CB CBE; c/o Lloyds Bank Ltd, 6 Pall Mall, SW1

PHIPPS, Lady Anne Elizabeth Grania; da of 4 Marquess of Normanby, CBE; *b* 1965; *Style* - Lady Anne Phipps

PHIPPS, Colin Barry; s of Edgar Reeves Phipps; *b* 23 July 1934; *Educ* Acton County Sch, Swansea G S, UCL, Birmingham U; *m* 1956, Marion May, da of Clifford Harry Lawrey; 2 s, 2 da; *Career* MP (L) Dudley W Feb 1974-79; dep chm and ch exec Clyde Petroleum Ltd 1979-; memb Council of Europe 1976-79, Western European Union 1976-79; FGS 1956, FInstPet 1972, memb Inst of Geologists 1978; *Clubs* Reform; *Style* - Colin Phipps Esq; Mathon Ct, Mathon, Malvern WR13 5NZ, (☎ Malvern 5606); 38 Cheyne Walk, SW3 (☎ 01 352 5381)

PHIPPS, Lady Evelyn Rose; da of 4 Marquess of Normanby; *b* 1955; *Style* - Lady Evelyn Phipps

PHIPPS, Lady Henrietta Laura; da of 4 Marquess of Normanby; *b* 1962; *Style* - Lady Henrietta Phipps

PHIPPS, Lord Justin Charles; s of 4 Marquess of Normanby; *b* 1958; *Style* - Lord Justin Phipps

PHIPPS, Air Vice-Marshal Leslie William; AFC (1959); s of late Frank Walter Phipps; *b* 17 April 1930; *Educ* SS Philip and James Sch Oxford; *Career* Dir of Air Def and Overseas Ops 1978-79, Dir-Gen Personnel Management (RAF) 1980-; *Style* - Air Vice-Marshal Leslie Phipps, AFC; 33 Knole Wood, Sunningdale, Berks

PHIPPS, Vice-Adm Sir Peter; KBE (1964, CBE 1962), DSC (1941, Bar 1943), VRD (1945); *b* 7 June 1909; *Educ* Sumner Primary Sch, Christchurch Boys' H S; *m* 1937, Jean Hutton; 2 s, 1 da; *Career* Ch of Defence Staff NZ 1963-65, Vice-Adm 1964, ret 1965; *Style* - Vice-Admiral Sir Peter Phipps KBE, DSC*, VRD; 126 Motuhara rd, Plimmerton, New Zealand (☎ Plimmerton 331240)

PHIPPS, Lady Phoebe; *née* Pleydell-Bouverie; 3 da of 7 Earl of Radnor, KG, KCVO, JP, DL, by his 1 w; *b* 25 Jan 1932; *Educ* Greenvale Sch, Long Island, USA; Godolphin Sch Salisbury, Queen's Secretarial Coll, Powderham Castle Sch of Domestic Science; *m* 1955 (m dis 1963), Hubert Beaumont Phipps, of Long Island;

1 s, 1 da; *Style* - Lady Phoebe Phipps; The Bothy, Longford Park, Salisbury, Wilts

PHIPPS, Lady Peronel Katharine; da of 4 Marquess of Normanby; *b* 1959; *Style* - Lady Peronel Phipps

PHIPPS, Lady Sybil Anne; *née* Montagu Douglas Scott; da of 7 & 9 Duke of Buccleuch & Queensberry, KT, GCVO, and Lady Margaret Bridgeman (da of 4 Earl of Bradford by his w, Lady Ida Lumley, 2 da of 9 Earl of Scarbrough); *b* 14 July 1899; *m* 1919, Charles Bathurst Hele Phipps, Lt 1 Life Gds (d 1960); 1 s, 3 da; *Style* - Lady Sybil Phipps; 8 Cumberland Mansions, George st, W1 (☎ 01 723 3339)

PICK, Charles Samuel; s of Samuel Pick; *b* 22 March 1917; *Educ* Masonic Sch Bushey; *m* 1938, Hilda Beryl Hobbs; 1 s, 1 da; *Career* founder memb Michael Joseph Ltd 1935, jt md 1959-62, md William Heinemann Ltd 1962, dir Heinemann Gp of Publishers 1962, md 1979-, dir Pan Books 1968, chm Secker & Warburg 1973, memb Council Publishers' Assoc 1980-; *Style* - Charles Pick Esq; Littlecot, Lindfield, Sussex (☎ 2218); 2 Hyde Park st, W2 (☎ 01 402 8043)

PICK, Hon Mrs (Rachel Ann); *née* Bridge; 2 da of Baron Bridge of Harwich, PC; *b* 1946; *m* 1975, Martin Pick; *Style* - The Hon Mrs Pick

PICK, Werner Rolf Theodor; s of Arthur Pick, MRCP, LRCS (d 1956); *b* 25 Aug 1913; *Educ* Schulpforta, Germany, Freiburg and Munich Universities; *m* 1937, Margaret Hermine, da of Walter Fischer (d 1936); 1 s, 1 da; *Career* chm E G Cornelius & Co Ltd and associated cos in the Cornelius Group; *Recreations* travel, golf, gardening; *Style* - Werner Pick Esq

PICKARD, Sir Cyril Stanley; KCMG (1966, CMG 1964); s of G W Pickard; *b* 18 Sept 1917; *Educ* Alleyn's Sch Dulwich, New Coll Oxford; *m* 1941, Helen Elizabeth Strawson; 3 s, 1 da (and 1 s decd); *Career* RA 1940-41, Capt; British High Cmmr Pakistan 1966-71, British High Cmmr in Nigeria 1971-74, ret; *Style* - Sir Cyril Pickard, KCMG; 37a Brodrick rd, SW17

PICKARD, John Michael; s of John Stanley Pickard (d 1979), of Epsom, Surrey; *b* 29 July 1930; *Educ* Oundle; *m* 1959, Penelope Jane, da of Christopher Catterall; 4 c; *Career* FCA, md Trust House Forte 1958-71, chm Grattan Warehouses Ltd, St Paul's Finance Investment Co Ltd, Michael Pickard Ltd; dep chm British Printing Corpn; chm Happy Eater Ltd; memb BTA 1958-71; *Recreations* sport, education; *Clubs* Bath and MCC; *Style* - John Pickard Esq; Meadow House, Meadow Walk, Walton-on-the-Hill, Tadworth, Surrey (☎ Tadworth 3103)

PICKARD, Michael John; s of Denis Luther Pickard; *b* 9 July 1939; *Educ* Christ's Hosp; *m* 1965, Heather Jill, da of John Hallsworth (d 1969); 1 s, 1 da; *Career* actuary 1974- and dir 1977- The Royal London Mutual Insurance Soc Ltd; FIA; *Recreations* squash, golf, reading; *Style* - Michael Pickard Esq; Tyndals, Groton, nr Boxford, Suffolk CO6 5EE (☎ Boxford 210692)

PICKAVANCE, Thomas Gerald; CBE (1965); s of William Pickavance; *b* 19 Oct 1915; *Educ* Cowley Sch St Helens, Liverpool U (BSc, PhD); *m* 1943, Alice Isobel, nee Boulton; 2 s, 1 da; *Career* Atomic Energy Research Establishment Harwell, dir of Nuclear Physics SRC 1969-72, FRS 1976, Hon DSc City U 1969, Fell St Cross Coll Oxford 1967-; *Style* - Thomas Pickavance Esq, CBE; 3 Kingston Close, Abingdon, Oxon OX14 1ES (☎ Abingdon 23934)

PICKERILL, Dame Cecily Mary Wise; DBE (1977, OBE 1958); da of Rev Percy Wise Clarkson; *b* 9 Feb 1903; *Educ* Diocesan H S for Girls Auckland NZ, Otago U Med Sch Dunedin NZ (MB, ChB); *m* 1934, Henry Percy Pickerill, CBE, MD, MDS (d 1956); 1 da; *Career* specialist plastic surgeon Wellington NZ 1935-68; *Style* - Dame Cecily Pickerill, DBE; Beech Dale, 50 Blue Mountains rd, Silverstream, New Zealand (☎ Upper Hutt 284542)

PICKERING, Derek (Frederick Derwent); CBE (1974), DL (Berks 1978); s of Frederick Owen Pickering; *b* 28 Nov

1909; *Educ* Bedford House Sch Oxford; *m* 1935, Marjorie Champion, nee Shotter (d 1980), JP; 1 s; *Career* chm Local Authorities Mutual Investment Trust 1975-, memb Conference of Local and Regional Authorities of Europe 1977-, CC Berks 1961-; *Style* - Derek Pickering Esq, CBE, DL; 5 Scotswood, Devenish rd, Sunningdale, Berks SL5 9QP (☎ Ascot 24884)

PICKERING, Sir Edward Davies; s of George Pickering; *b* 4 May 1912; *Educ* Middlesbrough H S; *m* 1, 1936 (m dis 1947), Margaret Soutter; 1 da; m 2, 1955, Rosemary Whitton; 2 s, 1 da; *Career* chm IPC Newspaper Div 1968-70, IPC Magazines 1970-74, Mirror Gp Newspapers 1975-77; dir Times Newspapers Ltd 1981-; v-chm Press Council 1977-, memb council Royal Opera House Covent Garden 1978-; kt 1977; *Clubs* Garrick; *Style* - Sir Edward Pickering; Little Tangley Lodge, Wonersh, Guildford, Surrey

PICKERING, His Honour Judge; John Robertson; s of late J W H Pickering; *b* 8 Jan 1925; *Educ* Winchester, Magdalene Cambridge; *m* 1951, Hilde, widow of E M Wright; 1 s, 2 step s; *Career* barr Inner Temple 1949, dep chm NE London Q S 1971, a Circuit Judge 1972-; *Clubs* MCC; *Style* - His Honour Judge Pickering; 35 Eaton Terrace, SW1 (☎ 01 730 4271)

PICKERING, His Honour Judge Richard Edward Ingram; s of Richard Pickering; *b* 16 Aug 1929; *Educ* Birkenhead Sch, Magdalene Cambridge; *m* 1962, Jean Margaret Eley; 2 s; *Career* barr Lincoln's Inn 1953, a Recorder of the Crown Court 1977-81; Circuit Judge (N Circuit) 1981-; *Style* - His Hon Judge Richard Pickering; Trelyon, Croft Drive, Caldy, Wirral L48 2JN (☎ 051 625 7043); 54 Castle st, Liverpool L2 7LQ

PICKERING, Hon Mrs (Veronica Mary); da of Baroness Fisher of Rednal (Life Peeress) and Joseph Fisher; *b* 1945; *m* 1968, John Adrian Pickering; *Style* - The Hon Mrs Pickering; 63 Warwick av, Bromsgrove, Worcs

PICKERING, William Roy; s of Ernest Stanley Pickering (d 1977); *b* 21 Feb 1927; *Educ* Merchant Taylors' Sch Gt Crosby Lancs, U Coll of N Wales Bangor; *m* 1949, Carmen Fay, da of late Herbert Hawley, OBE, MSc, FRIC, of India; 1 s, 3 da; *Career* dir of Tube Production Planning, Tube Investments STD 1962-64; dir and gen man Parkinson Cowan Appliances Ltd 1967-70; chm and md Bryan Donkin Ltd 1970-79, md Hopkinsons Ltd 1977-79, chm and md Padley & Venables Ltd 1979-; chm Bedford Steels Ltd 1979-; *Recreations* skiing, swimming, shooting; *Style* - William Pickering Esq; Honley House, Honley, Huddersfield, Yorks (☎ 661896)

PICKETT, Hon Mrs (Patricia Margaret); da of 2 Baron Kershaw (d 1961); *b* 1943; *m* 1968, David Anniss Pickett, BSc, BMus; 2 da; *Style* - The Hon Mrs Pickett; 13 Wood End, Park st, St Albans, Herts

PICKETT, Thomas; CBE (1972); s of John Joseph Pickett; *b* 22 Nov 1912; *Educ* Glossop G S, London U; *m* 1940, Winifred Irene, da of late Benjamin Buckley; *Career* barr Lincoln's Inn 1948, Sr Regional Chm NW Area Industrial Tribunals (England and Wales) 1975-; *Style* - Thomas Pickett Esq, CBE; Oakmere, Chester rd, Mere, Cheshire (☎ Bucklow Hill 830040)

PICKFORD, David Michael; s of Aston Charles Corpe Pickford (d 1945); *b* 25 Aug 1926; *Educ* Emanuel Sch London, Coll of Estate Management; *m* 1956, Elizabeth Gwendoline, da of John Hooson, of Segrwyd Hall, Denbigh (d 1972); 3 c; *Career* chartered surveyor; dir Bellwood Properties Ltd, Bishopswood Properties Ltd, Brigade House Ltd, Carlos Estates Ltd, The Faircliffe Finance Co Ltd, Kenda Investments Ltd and Haslemere Estates Ltd; pres Boys' Bde London; *Recreations* farming, youth work; *Clubs* RAC, Farmers'; *Style* - David Pickford Esq; Elm Tree Farm, Mersham, nr Ashford, Kent (☎ Aldington 200); 33 Grosvenor sq, W1

PICKFORD, Hon Mrs (Felicity Jane); *née* Mills; da of 2 Viscount Mills; *b* 1947; *m* 1970, Roger B Pickford; *Style* - The Hon Mrs Pickford

PICKLES, His Honour Judge; James; s of Arthur Pickles, OBE, JP; *b* 18 March 1925; *Educ* Worksop Coll, Leeds U, Ch Ch Oxford; *m* 1948, Sheila Ratcliffe; 2 s, 1 da; *Career* barr Inner Temple 1948, a Recorder of the Crown Court 1972-76, a Circuit Judge 1976-, contested (Lib) Brighouse and Spenborough 1964; *Style* - His Honour Judge Pickles; c/o Sheffield Crown Court, Sheffield S1 1EH

PICKSTOCK, Sam (Samuel) Frank; *Career* md John McLean & Sons Land Ltd 1981-; dir Gotheridge & Sanders, Groveside Devpts, Island Pools, McLean Estates, McLean Investments, Tarmac Homes, Tarmac Properties, Thomas Lowe & Sons, W Mercian Property Co; *Style* - Sam Pickstock Esq; c/o John McLean & Sons, Crestwood House, Birches Rise, Willenhall, Staffs (☎ 68511)

PICKTHORN, Sir Charles William Richards; 2 Bt (UK 1959); s of Rt Hon Sir Kenneth William Murray Pickthorn, 1 Bt (d 1975); *b* 3 March 1927; *Educ* Eton, Corpus Christi Cambridge; *m* 1951, Helen Antonia, da of late Sir James Mann, KCVO; 1 s, 2 da; *Heir* s, James Francis Mann Pickthorn; *Career* barr Middle Temple 1952, dir J Henry Schroder Wagg & Co Ltd 1971-79; *Style* - Sir Charles Pickthorn, Bt; Manor House, Nunney, nr Frome, Somerset (☎ Nunney 574); 3 Hobury st, SW10 (☎ 01 352 2795)

PICKTHORN, James Francis; s and h of Sir Charles William Richards Pickthorn, 2 Bt; *b* 18 Feb 1955; *Educ* Eton; *Style* - James Pickthorn Esq; c/o Manor House, Nunney, nr Frome, Som

PICKTHORN, Nancy, Lady - Nancy Catherine Lewis; da of late Lewis Matthew Richards; *m* 1924, the Rt Hon Sir Kenneth William Murray Pickthorn, 1 Bt (d 1975); *Style* - Nancy, Lady Pickthorn; Rose Cottage, Orford, Suffolk

PIERCY, 3 Baron (UK 1945); James William Piercy; s of 2 Baron Piercy (d 1981); *b* 19 Jan 1946; *Educ* Shrewsbury and Edinburgh U (BSc); *Heir* bro, Hon Mark Edward Pelham Piercy; *Style* - The Rt Hon The Lord Piercy

PIERCY, Hon Henrietta Jane; da of 2 Baron Piercy; *b* 1951; *Educ* Badminton Sch, and St Andrew's U; *Style* - The Hon Henrietta Piercy

PIERCY, Hon Mark Edward Pelham; s of 2 Baron Piercy (d 1981) and hp of bro, 3 Baron; *b* 1953; *Educ* Shrewsbury and New Coll Oxford; *m* 1979, Vivien Angela, da of His Honour Judge Monier-Williams; *Style* - The Hon Mark Piercy

PIERCY, Baroness - Oonagh Lavinia; JP; da of late Maj Edward John Lake Baylay, DSO; *m* 1944, 2 Baron Piercy (d 1981); 2 s, 3 da; *Style* - The Rt Hon The Lady Piercy, JP; The Old Rectory, Elford, Tamworth, Staffs

PIERCY, Hon Penelope Katharine; CBE (1968); da of 1 Baron Piercy, CBE (d 1966); *b* 1916; *Educ* St Paul's and Somerville Oxford; *Career* Under-Sec, Miny Technology (ret); *Style* - The Hon Penelope Piercy, CBE; Southside, Hinton Martell, Wimborne, Dorset

PIERCY, Veronica, Baroness - Veronica; da of late John Hordley Warham; *m* 1964, as his 2 w, 1 Baron Piercy, CBE (d 1966); *Style* - The Rt Hon Veronica, Lady Piercy; 7 Milborne Grove, SW10

PIERPOINT, Robert Brian; s of Robert Sidney Pierpoint; *b* 25 March 1936; *Educ* Liverpool Coll; *m* 1963, Margaret Mary, nee Healy; 2 s, 2 da (1 decd); *Career* Lt-Cdr RN 1959-60, FIQS, FCIOB, quantity surveyor, ch surveyor Unit Construction Co Ltd 1974; dir Booth Mechanical Services Ltd 1975; *Recreations* golf, gardening; *Clubs* Bluecoat; *Style* - Robert Pierpoint Esq; Amberley Ridge, Church rd, Woolton Park, Liverpool L25 6DD (☎ 428 4019)

PIERRE, Sir (Joseph) Henry; s of Charles Henry Pierre; *b* 28 Oct 1904; *Educ* Queen's Roy Coll Trinidad, St Bartholomew's Hosp London, London U, Roy Coll of Surgeons Edinburgh; *m* 1, 1939; 1 s; m 2, 1962, Marjorie Boös; 1 s; *Career* Consultant Surgeon Gen Hosp Port of Spain Trinidad 1950-, hon surgn Caura Tuberculosis Sanatorium Trinidad, hon surgn Mental Hosp Trinidad; CMT, FRCS, kt 1957; *Style* - Sir Henry Pierre; St Florian, Fishery rd, Bray, Nr Maidenhead, Berks SL6 1UN

PIERS, Sir Charles Robert Fitzmaurice; 10 Bt (I 1661); s of Sir Charles Piers, 9 Bt (d 1945); *b* 30 Aug 1903; *Educ* RNCs Osborne and Dartmouth; *m* 1936, Ann Blanche Scott (d 1975), da of late Capt Thomas Ferguson; 1 s, 1 da; *Heir* s, James Desmond Piers; *Career* man Midland Doherty Ltd, of Duncan, BC, Canada; *Style* - Sir Charles Piers, Bt; RR no 1, Duncan, BC, Canada

PIERS, Rear-Adm Desmond William; DSC (1943), CD, RCN; s of William Harington Piers; *b* 12 June 1913; *Educ* Halifax County Acad, RMC of Canada, RN Staff Coll, Nat Defence Coll of Canada; *m* 1941, Janet, da of Dr Murray Macneill, of Halifax, NS; 1 step da; *Career* Chm Canadian Def Liaison Staff Washington DC, Canadian Rep NATO Mil Ctee 1962-66, ret 1967; Agent Gen Nova Scotia in UK & Europe 1977-79; *Style* - Rear-Admiral Desmond Piers, DSC; The Quarter Deck, Chester, Nova Scotia BOJ IJO, Canada (☎ 902 275 4462)

PIERS, James Desmond; s and h of Sir Charles Robert Fitzmaurice Piers, 10 Bt; *b* 24 July 1947; *Style* - James Piers Esq

PIESOLD, David Daniel August; s of Max Emil Piesold (d 1937), of Bristol; *b* 22 May 1923; *Educ* Standerton H S, U of Witwatersrand; *m* 1948, Eva, da of Alexander John Brownlee (d 1948), of Colinton, Scotland; 2 s, 2 da; *Career* consulting civil engineer, partner in Watermeyer, Legge, Piesold & Uhlmann 1952-, sr partner 1975-; Fell Inst of Civil Engineers 1959; *Recreations* swimming; *Clubs* St Stephen's, RAC; *Style* - David Piesold Esq; 45 Smith st, SW3 (☎ 01 352 7561); Sheerland House, Pluckley, Ashford, Kent (☎ Pluckley 633)

PIGGOTT, Donald James; s of James Piggott; *b* 1 Sept 1920; *Educ* Bradford G S, Christ's Coll Cambridge, LSE; *m* 1974, Kathryn Courtenay-Evans; *Career* Dir-Gen, British Red Cross Soc 1980-; *Style* - Donald Piggott Esq; 18 Elm Lodge, River Gardens, SW6 (☎ 01 385 5588); Beech Tree House, Tostock, Bury St Edmunds, Suffolk (☎ Beyton 70589)

PIGGOTT, Maj-Gen Francis James Claude; CB (1963), CBE (1961), DSO (1945); s of late Maj-Gen F S G Piggott, CB, DSO; *b* Tokyo 11 Oct 1910; *Educ* Cheltenham, RMC Sandhurst; *m* 1940, Muriel Joan, da of late Wilfred E Cottam, of Rotherham; 1 s, 1 da; *Career* Assistant Ch of Staff (Intelligence) SHAPE 1961-64; *Style* - Major-General Francis Piggott CB CBE DSO; The Old Forge, Long rd, Croscombe, Wells, Somerset

PIGOT, George Hugh; s and h of Sir Robert (Anthony) Pigot, 7 Bt, CB, OBE; *b* 28 Nov 1946; *m* 1967 (m dis 1973), Judith Sandeman, da of late Maj John Hele Sandeman-Allen, RA; 1 da; *Style* - George Pigot Esq; The Mill House, Padworth, Berks

PIGOT, Maj-Gen Sir Robert Anthony; 7 Bt (GB 1764), CB (1964), OBE (1959), DL (IOW 1978); s of George Douglas Hugh Pigot (2 s of 5 Bt) (d 1959); suc unc, Sir Robert Pigot, 6 Bt, DSO, MC (d 1977); *b* 6 July 1915; *Educ* Stowe; *m* 1, 1942, Honor, da of late Capt Wilfred St Martin Gibbon; 1 s, 1 da; m 2, 1968, Sarah Anne, da of Mr David and Lady Joan Colville; 1 s, 1 da; *Heir* s, George Hugh Pigot; *Career* Maj-Gen RM, ret; Dep Standing Gp NATO, Rep with N Atlantic Council Paris 1958-59, Ch of Staff RM 1960-64; md Bone Bros Ltd 1964-66; dir Exec Appointments Ltd 1968-70; High Sheriff IOW 1978-79; OStJ 1981; *Style* - Major-General Sir Robert Pigot, Bt, CB, OBE, DL; Yew Tree Lodge, Bembridge, Isle of Wight

PIGOT, His Honour Judge; Thomas Herbert; QC (1967); s of late Thomas Pigot; *b* 19 May 1921; *Educ* Manchester G S, BNC Oxford; *m* 1950, Zena Marguerite, da of late Tom Wall; 3 da; *Career* barr Inner Temple 1947, Circuit Judge 1972-, Dep Sr Judge SBA Cyprus 1974-; *Recreations* golf; *Clubs* Vincent's (Oxford), United Oxford & Cambridge; *Style* - His Honour Judge Pigot, QC;

Fairfields, Dunsden Green, nr Reading, Berks RG4 9QD (☎ Reading 478730)

PIGOTT, Major Sir Berkeley; 4 Bt (UK 1808); s of Charles Pigott (s of 3 Bt); suc gf, Sir Charles Robert Pigott, 3 Bt, 1911; *b* 29 May 1894; *Educ* Wellington; *m* 1919, Christabel (d 1974), da of late Rev F H Bowden-Smith; 1 s, 2 da; *Heir* s, Berkeley Henry Sebastian Pigott; *Career* pres Nat Pony Soc 1948, chm 1961-62, chm County Polo Assoc 1948, Verderer of the New Forest 1955-68; *Style* - Major Sir Berkeley Pigott, Bt; 86 Admirals Walk, Bournemouth

PIGOTT, Berkeley Henry Sebastian; s and h of Sir Berkeley Pigott, 4 Bt; *b* 24 June 1925; *Educ* Ampleforth; *m* 1954, Jean, da of J W Balls, of Holly Lodge, Surlingham, Norfolk; 2 s, 1 da; *Career* European War 1944-45 with RM; *Style* - Berkeley Pigott Esq; Brook Farm, Shobley, Ringwood, Hants

PIGOTT, Air Vice-Marshal Michael Joseph; CBE (1956); *b* 16 May 1904; *Educ* Blackrock Coll Dublin, Nat U of Ireland, Nat Dental Hosp of Ireland; *m* 1938, Ethel Norah, da of Alfred Sutherland Blackman; 1 da; *Career* dir of Dental Serives RAF 1954-58, ret; *Style* - Air Vice-Marshal Michael Pigott, CBE; 18 Duck st, Cerne Abbas, Dorchester, Dorset DT2 7LA (☎ Cerne Abbas 538)

PIGOTT-BROWN, Sir William Brian; 3 Bt (UK 1902); s of Sir John Pigott-Brown, 2 Bt (ka 1942); *b* 20 Jan 1941; *Style* - Sir William Pigott-Brown, Bt; Orchard House, Aston Upthorpe, Oxon; 25 Chapel st, SW1

PIHL, Brig Hon Dame Mary Mackenzie (Fru Mary Pihl); *née* Anderson; DBE (1970, MBE 1958); da of 1 Viscount Waverley, GCB, OM, GCSI, GCIE, PC, FRS (d 1958); *b* 3 Feb 1916; *Educ* Sutton H S, Villa Brillantmont Lausanne; *m* 1973, Frithjof Pihl; *Career* Dir WRAC 1967-70, ret; Hon ADC to the Queen 1967-70; *Style* - The Hon Dame Mary Pihl, DBE; Engö, 3145 Tjöme, Norway

PIKE, Baroness (Life Peeress UK 1974); Irene Mervyn Parnicott Pike; DBE (1981); da of I S Pike, of Okehampton, Devonshire; *b* 16 Sept 1918; *Educ* Hunmanby Hall, Reading U; *Career* MP (C) Melton, Leics Dec 1956-Feb 1974, Assist Postmaster-Gen 1959-63, Jt Parly Under-Sec of State Home Office 1963-64, dir Watts Blake Bearne & Co Ltd, Dunderdale Investments, chm IBA Gen Advsy Cncl 1974-79, chm WRVS 1974-81; chm Broadcasting Complaints Ctee 1981-; *Style* - The Rt Hon the Lady Pike, DBE; 25 Chester Row, SW1 (☎ 01 730 8778); Hownam, nr Kelso, Roxburghshire

PIKE, Andrew Hamilton; CMG (1956), OBE (1945); s of late Canon William Pike; *b* 26 Aug 1903; *Educ* The Abbey Tipperary, Trin Coll Dublin, Univ Coll Oxford; *m* 1951, Catherine Provan, da of late Prof E P Cathcart, CBE; 4 s; *Career* Min for Lands and Mineral Resources Tanganyika 1957-59, ret; *Style* - Andrew Pike Esq, CMG, OBE; Blatchfeld, Blackheath, nr Guildford, Surrey (☎ Guildford 892358)

PIKE, Air Cdre James Maitland Nicholson; CB (1963), DSO (1942), DFC (1941), RAF, ret; s of late Frank Pike, of Co Mayo, Eire; *b* 8 Dec 1916; *Educ* Stowe, RAF Coll Cranwell; *m* 1, 1942; 1 da; m 2, 1955, Amber Pauline Bettesworth Hellard; 1 s, 1 step da; m 3, 1972, Dorothy May Dawson, nee Holland; 1 step da; *Career* MOD 1969-78; *Style* - Air Commodore James Pike CB DSO DFC; Glendarary, Christmas Common, Watlington, Oxford

PIKE, Lady Romayne (Aileen); *née* Brabazon; da of 14 Earl of Meath; *b* 1943; *m* 1968, Capt Robert Eben Neil Pike; 1 s, 1 da; *Style* - Lady Romayne Pike; Kidborough House, Danehill, Sussex

PIKE, Sir Philip Ernest Housden; s of Rev Ernest Benjamin Pike; *b* 6 March 1914; *Educ* De Carteret Sch, Munro Coll Jamaica, Middle Temple London; *m* 2, 1959, Millicent Locke Staples; 1 s, 1 da (by 1 m); *Career* barr 1938, Ch Justice High Ct in Borneo 1965-68, Judge High Ct of Malawi 1969-70, Actg Ch Justice 1970, Ch Justice Swaziland 1970-72, ret; kt 1969; *Style* - Sir Philip Pike; 30 Berg rd, Fish

Hoek, Cape, S Africa

PIKE, Marshal of the Royal Air Force Sir Thomas Geoffrey; GCB (1961, KCB 1955, CB 1946), CBE (1944), DFC (1942 and Bar 1942), DL (Essex 1973); s of late Capt S R Pike, RA; *b* 29 June 1906; *Educ* Bedford Sch, RAF Coll Cranwell; *m* 1930, Kathleen Althea, da of Maj H Elwell; 1 s, 2 da; *Career* RAF 1923, Sqdn Ldr 1937, Gp Capt 1941, Air Cdre 1944, Air Vice-Marshal 1950, Air Marshal 1955, Air Ch Marshal 1957, Marshal of the RAF 1962, Dep Supreme Allied Cdr Europe 1964-67; Officer Legion Merit (USA); *Style* - Marshal of the Royal Air Force Sir Thomas Pike, GCB, CBE, DFC*, DL; Little Wynters, Hastingwood, Harlow, Essex

PIKE, Sir Theodore Ouseley; KCMG (1956, CMG 1953); s of late Canon W Pike, of Co Tipperary; *b* 1904; *Educ* The Abbey Tipperary, Trin Coll Dublin, Univ Coll Oxford; *m* 1934, Violet F, da of late Sir William Robinson, JP, DL; 2 s, 1 da; *Career* Govr & C-in-C Somaliland Protectorate 1954-59; Hon LLD Dublin; *Style* - Sir Theodore Pike, KCMG; c/o Grindlay's Bank, 23 Fenchurch st, EC3

PIKE, Rt Rev Victor Joseph; CB (1953), CBE (1950, OBE 1944), DD 1955; s of late Canon William Pike; *b* 1 July 1907; *Educ* Bishop Foy Sch Waterford, Trin Coll Dublin; *m* 1937, Dorothea Elizabeth Frend, da of late Capt W R Frend; 1 s, 2 da; *Career* Chaplain-Gen to the Forces 1951-60 (Archdeacon 1958-60), Prebend of Fordington with Writhlington in Salisbury Cathedral 1960, Bishop Suffragan of Sherborne 1960-76, Hon Canon of Canterbury 1951-60, QHC 1948-53, Chaplain to the Queen 1953-60, Chaplain to retired Clergy in Archdeaconry of Sarum 1978-; *Style* - The Right Rev Victor Pike, CB, CBE; 53 The Close, Salisbury, Wilts (☎ Salisbury 5766)

PIKE, Lt-Gen Sir William Gregory Huddleston; KCB (1961, CB 1956), CBE (1952), DSO (1943); s of late Capt Sydney Royston Pike, RA; *b* 24 June 1905; *Educ* Bedford Sch, Marlborough Coll, RMA Woolwich; *m* 1939, Josephine Margaret, da of late Maj-Gen R H D Tompson, CB, CMG, DSO; 1 s, 2 da; *Career* Ch of Staff Far East Land Forces 1957-60, V-Ch of the Imperial Gen Staff 1960-63, Col Cmdt RA 1962-70, Lt of HM Tower of London 1963-66, Ch Cdr St John Ambulance 1969-7; Legion Merit (USA) 1953, GCStJ 1976; *Style* - Lieutenant-General Sir William Pike KCB CBE DSO; Ganwells, Bentley, Hants; Rhos-y-Bayvil, Velindre, Crymych, Dyfed

PILBROW, Richard Hugh; s of Arthur Gordon Pilbrow; *b* 28 April 1933; *Educ* Cranbrook Sch, Central Sch of Speech and Drama; *m* 1, 1958, Viki Brinton; 1 s, 1 da; m 2, 1974, Molly Friedel; 1 da; *Career* chm Theatre Projects Group of Cos 1957-; *Clubs* Garrick; *Style* - Richard Pilbrow Esq; Theatre Projects Ltd, 10 Long Acre, WC2E 9LN (☎ 01 240 5411)

PILCH, Anthony Michael; s of Lt-Col George Harold Pilch (d 1943); *b* 6 July 1927; *Educ* Shrewsbury and Balliol Oxford; *m* 1950, Betty Christine, da of Franklin John Skinner (d 1976); 1 da; *Career* dir Noble Lowndes & Partners Ltd 1968-; V-Pres Nat Assoc of Pension Funds 1981-; *Recreations* theatre, photography, writing; *Clubs* Inst of Directors; *Style* - Anthony Pilch Esq; 12 Taunton av, Caterham, Surrey CR3 5EB (☎ Caterham 46671)

PILCHER, Sir (Charlie) Dennis; CBE (1968); s of Charlie Edwin Pilcher; *b* 2 July 1906; *Educ* Clayesmore Sch; *m* 1929, Mary Allison, da of William Aumonier; 2 da; *Career* chm Commission for the New Towns 1971-78, consultant and late sr partner Graves, Son & Pilcher (Chartered Surveyors); dir Save and Prosper Gp Ltd 1970-80; memb Cncl Glyndebourne Festival Opera 1969-; kt 1974, FRICS; *Clubs* Garrick; *Style* - Sir Dennis Pilcher, CBE; Brambles, Batts Lane, Mare Hill, Pulborough, W Sussex (☎ Pulborough 2126)

PILCHER, Sir John Arthur; GCMG (1973, KCMG 1966, CMG 1957); s of late Lt-Col A J Pilcher; *b* 16 May 1912; *Educ* Shrewsbury, Clare Cambridge; *m* 1942, Delia Margaret Taylor; 1 da; *Career* Ambass to Austria 1965-67, to Japan 1967-72; dir Foreign & Colonial Investment

Trust 1973-; chm Brazil Fund 1975-, Fleming Japan Fund SA 1976-; adviser on Far Eastern affairs Robert Fleming & Co 1973-; *Clubs* Brooks's; *Style* - Sir John Pilcher, GCMG; 33 The Terrace, SW13 (☎ 01 876 9710)

PILDITCH, James George Christopher; s of Frederick Henry Pilditch; *b* 7 Aug 1929; *Educ* Slough G S, Reading U, INSEAD; *m* 1, 1952 (m dis) Molly; m 2, 1970, Anne Elisabeth Johnson; *Career* chm Allied International Designers 1963-; FRSA, ASIAD; *Style* - James Pilditch Esq; 62 Cadogan sq, SW1 (☎ 01 584 9279)

PILDITCH, John Richard; s and h of Sir Richard Edward Pilditch, 4 Bt; *b* 24 Sept 1955; *Style* - John Pilditch Esq; c/o 4 Fisherman's Bank, Mudeford, Christchurch, Dorset

PILDITCH, Sir Richard Edward; 4 Bt (UK 1929); s of Sir Philip Harold Pilditch, 2 Bt, and bro of Sir Philip John Frederick Pilditch, 3 Bt (d 1954); *b* 8 Sept 1926; *Educ* Charterhouse; *m* 1950, Pauline Elizabeth Smith; 1 s, 1 da; *Heir* s, John Richard Pilditch; *Career* RN 1944-45 India and Ceylon; *Style* - Sir Richard Pilditch, Bt; 4 Fishermans Bank, Mudeford, Christchurch, Hants

PILE, Colonel Sir Frederick Devereux; 3 Bt (UK 1900), MC (1945); s of Gen Sir Frederick Alfred Pile, 2 Bt, GCB, DSO, MC (d 1976); *b* 10 Dec 1915; *Educ* Weymouth Coll, RMC Sandhurst; *m* 1940, Pamela, da of late Philip Henstock; 2 da; *Career* 1939-45 War Col Royal Tank Regt, British Jt Serv Mission Washington DC 1957-60, Cmdt RAC Driving and Maintenance Sch 1960-62; *Clubs* MCC; *Style* - Colonel Sir Frederick Pile, Bt; Harriet House, Sedlescombe, Battle, Sussex (☎ Sedlescombe 240)

PILE, Sir John Devereux; s of Gen Sir Frederick A Pile, 2 Bt, GCB, DSO, MC (d 1976) and hp to bro, Col Sir Frederick Pile, 3 Bt; *b* 5 June 1918; *Educ* Weymouth Coll Dorset, Trin Cambridge; *m* 1946, Katharine Mary Shafe; 2 s, 2 da; *Career* chm Imperial Gp Ltd 1975-80, dir Nat West Bank 1977-, memb Council Industry for Management Educn 1975-, FBIM 1973-80; Freeman of City of London; kt 1978; *Style* - Sir John Pile; Munstead, Godalming, Surrey (☎ Godalming 4716)

PILE, Molly, Lady - Molly Eveline Lousie Mary; da of late Ralph Smyth, of Newtown, Drogheda, Co Louth, & widow of Brig Francis Wyville Home; *m* 1951, as his 3 w, Gen Sir Frederick Alfred Pile, 2 Bt, GCB, DSO, MC (d 1976); *Career* late Ch Cdr ATS; *Style* - Molly, Lady Pile; Broom Manor, Cottered, nr Buntingford, Herts

PILE, Sir William Dennis; GCB (1978, KCB 1971, CB 1968), MBE (1944); s of James Edward Pile; *b* 1 Dec 1919; *Educ* Royal Masonic Sch, St Catharine's Cambridge; *m* 1, 1939 (m dis 1947), Brenda Skinner; m 2, 1948, Joan Marguerite Crafter; 1 s, 2 da; *Career* chm Board of Inland Revenue 1976-79, dir Nationwide Building Soc 1980-, Distillers' Co Ltd 1980-; *Clubs* United Oxford & Cambridge, Hawks (Cambridge); *Style* - Sir William Pile, GCB, MBE; The Manor House, Riverhead, nr Sevenoaks, Kent (☎ Sevenoaks 54498)

PILKINGTON, Baron (Life Peer UK 1968); Harry (William Henry) Pilkington; s of Richard Austin Pilkington and Hon Hope, da of late 1 Baron Cozens-Hardy, PC; *b* 19 April 1905; *Educ* Rugby, Magdalene Cambridge; *m* 1, 1930, Rosamond Margaret Rowan (d 1953); 1 s, 1 da (and 1 da decd); m 2, 1961, Mrs Mavis Wilding; *Career* chm Pilkington Bros Ltd 1949-73, Hon Life-Pres 1973-; Vice Lord-Lt Merseyside 1974-; chm NW Regional Sports and Recreations Council 1976-, Chllr Loughborough U of Technology 1966-80; DL Lancs 1968; Hon FIOB 1974, Hon LLD Manchester 1959, Liverpool 1963, Hon DSc Loughborough 1966, Hon DCL Kent 1968, Freeman St Helens 1968; kt 1953; *Style* - The Rt Hon the Lord Pilkington, HM Vice Lord-Lieut for Merseyside; Windle Hall, St Helens, Lancs (☎ 23423)

PILKINGTON, Sir Alastair (Lionel Alexander Bethune); s of late Col L G Pilkington; *b* 7 Jan 1920; *Educ* Sherborne and Trin Cambridge; *m* 1, 1945, Patricia

Nicholls, nee Elliott (d 1977); 1 s, 1 da; m 2, 1978, Kathleen, widow of Eldridge Haynes; *Career* chm Pilkington Bros Ltd 1973-80, dir 1980-; chm Chloride Group Ltd 1979-, a dir of Bank of England 1974-, dir British Petroleum 1976-; Pro-Chllr Lancaster U 1980-, Hon FUMIST 1969, Hon Fell Imperial Coll 1974, LSE 1980; FBIM 1971, Hon DTech Loughborough 1968, CNAA 1976, Hon DEng Liverpool 1971, Hon LLD Bristol 1979, Hon DSc (Eng) London 1979; kt 1970; FRS 1969; *Clubs* Athenaeum; *Style* - Sir Alastair Pilkington; Goldrill Cottage, Patterdale, nr Penrith, Cumbria (☎ Glenridding 263)

PILKINGTON, Rev the Hon John Rowan; s of Baron Pilkington (Life Peer); *b* 1932; *Educ* Rugby and Magdalene, Cambridge (MA); *m* 1964, Celia Collison; *Career* R of Farlington (Portsmouth), 1975-; *Style* - The Reverend the Hon John Pilkington; 27 Farlington av, Cosham, Portsmouth

PILKINGTON, Lawrence Herbert Austin; CBE (1964), JP; s of Richard Austin Pilkington and Hon Hope, da of late 1 Baron Cozens-Hardy, PC; *b* 13 Oct 1911; *Educ* Bromsgrove Sch, Magdalene Cambridge; *m* 1936, Norah Holden; 2 da; *Career* dir Pilkington Bros Ltd 1935-, JP Lancs 1942, Hon LLD Sheffield 1956, Hon DSc Salford 1970; *Style* - Lawrence Pilkington Esq, CBE, JP; Coppice End, Colborne rd, St Peter Port, Guernsey, CI

PILKINGTON, Rev Canon Peter; s of Frank Pilkington; *b* 5 Sep 1933; *Educ* Dame Allans Sch Newcastle on Tyne, Jesus Cambridge; *m* 1966, Helen, nee Wilson; 2 da; *Career* Hon Canon Canterbury Cathedral 1975-, master St Joseph's Coll Chidya Tanganyika 1955-58, ordained 1959, curate Bakewell Derbys 1959-62, master Eton 1962-75 (Master in College 1965-75), headmaster King's Sch Canterbury 1975-; *Clubs* Athenaeum; *Style* - The Rev Canon Peter Pilkington; 14 the Precincts, Canterbury, Kent (☎ 62963)

PILKINGTON, Thomas Alec; s of Charles Carlisle Pilkington (d 1950); *b* 30 Nov 1906; *Educ* Eton, Oxford; *m* 1936, Susan Lucy, nee Hollebone; 3 s (and 1 decd); *Career* Major RA, memb & ptnr Stock Exchange 1930-40; chm River Plate & General Investment Trust Co Ltd, Vantage Securties; *Recreations* fishing, shooting, racing, cricket, racquets; *Clubs* White's, Pratt's; *Style* - Thomas Pilkington Esq; 26 West place, Wimbledon Common (☎ 946 0595)

PILL, Malcolm Thomas; QC (1978); s of Reginald Thomas Pill; *b* 11 March 1938; *Educ* Whitchurch G S, Trin Cambridge; *m* 1966, Roisin, nee Riordan; 2 s, 1 da; *Career* barr Gray's Inn 1962, a Recorder of the Crown Court 1976-; chm UNA (Wales) Trust 1969-77 1980-; chm UK Ctee Freedom from Hunger Campaign 1978-; *Style* - Malcolm Pill Esq, QC; 9 Westbourne Crescent, Whitchurch, Cardiff CF4 2BL (☎ Cardiff 65961)

PILLAI, Sir (Narayana) Raghavan; KCIE (1946, CIE 1939), CBE (1937); s of M C Narayana Pillai; *b* 24 July 1898; *Educ* Madras U, Trin Hall Cambridge (Hon Fell 1970); *m* 1928, Edith Minnie Arthurs (d 1976); 2 s; *Career* Sec Gen, Miny of External Affairs, New Delhi 1952-60; *Style* - Sir Raghavan Pillai, KCIE, CBE; 1022 St James's Court, SW1

PILLAI, Raghavan Sushil; s of Sir (Narayana) Raghavan Pillai, KCIE, CBE; *b* 6 April 1936; *Educ* Rugby and Trin Hall Cambridge; *m* 1959, Nita, da of Sir Birendra (Nath) Mookerjee; 1 s, 1 da; *Career* marketing dir Hoskins Ltd 1975-, marketing and sales dir Hoskins Ltd 1978-, dir Hoskins and Horton Ltd 1979-; *Style* - Raghavan Pillai Esq; 30 Serpentine rd, Selly Park, Birmingham B29 7HV (☎ 021 472 6049)

PILLAR, Vice-Adm Sir William Thomas; KCB (1980); s of William Pillar; *b* 24 Feb 1924; *Educ* Blundell's Sch Tiverton; RNEC; *m* 1946, Ursula Ransley; 3 s, 1 da; *Career* RN 1942, Capt RNEC 1973-75, Port-Adm Rosyth 1976-77, Assist Ch of Fleet Support 1977-79, Ch 1979-; FIMechE, FIMarE; *Style* - Vice-Admiral Sir William Pillar, KCB; Selwood, Zeals Row, Zeals, Warminster, Wilts (☎ Bourton 577)

PIM, Captain Sir Richard Pike; KBE (1960), VRD, DL (City of Belfast 1957); s of late Cecil Pim; *b* 1900; *Educ* Lancing Coll Sussex, Trin Coll Dublin; *m* 1925, Marjorie Angel, da of late John Young; 2 s; *Career* formerly Inspector-Gen Roy Ulster Constabulary; Nat Govr North Ireland BBC 1962-67, memb Council Winston Churchill Memorial Trust 1965-69, memb Ulster Transport Authority 1962-64; kt 1945; *Style* - Captain Sir Richard Pim, KBE, VRD, DL; Mullagh, Killyleagh, Co Down, N Ireland (☎ Killyleagh 267)

PINCHER, (Henry) Chapman; s of Maj Richard Chapman Pincher (d 1963), E Surrey Regt; b Ambala India 29 March 1914; *Educ* Darlington G S, King's London; *m* 1965, Constance Wolstenholme; 1 s, 1 da (by previous m); *Career* journalist; assist ed Daily Express & ch def correspondent Beaverbrook Newspapers 1972-79; *Style* - Chapman Pincher Esq; 16 Church st, Kintbury, Hungerford, Berks (☎ 04885 8855)

PINCKNEY, Jeremy Gerald; s of Gerald Henry Pinckney; *b* 17 Oct 1935; *Educ* Eton; *m* 1960, Helen Belinda, da of Maj M H Gold, MC; 2 s, 1 da; *Career* dir Cowley Investments Ltd, English Nat Investment Co Ltd, The Mining Investment Corpn Ltd, North Sea & National Gas Investments Ltd, Oil & Energy Securities Ltd and other cos; *Style* - Jeremy Pinckney Esq; 45 Black Lion Lane, W6

PINCOTT, Leslie Rundell; CBE (1978); s of Hubert George Pincott; *b* 27 March 1923; *Educ* Mercers' Sch Holborn; *m* 1944, Mary Mae Tuffin; 2 s, 1 da; *Career* v-chm Remploy Ltd 1979-, chm Stone-Platt Industries 1980-; dir: George Wimpey & Co Ltd 1978-, Canada Permanent Trust Co (UK) Ltd 1978-; memb BR SR Bd 1977-; v-pres English Schs Athletics Assoc 1977-; *Style* - Leslie Pincott Esq, CBE; 132 Woodsford sq, Kensington W14 8DT

PINDLING, Rt Hon Lynden Oscar; PC (1976); s of Arnold Franklin Pindling; *b* 22 March 1930; *Educ* Western Sr Sch, Nassau Govt H S, London U; *m* 1956, Marguerite McKenzie; 2 s, 2 da; *Career* barr Middle Temple 1953, Prime Minister and Min of Economic Affairs of the Commonwealth of The Bahamas 1969-; *Style* - The Rt Hon Lynden Pindling; Office of the Prime Minister, Rawson sq, Nassau, Bahamas

PINE, Leslie Gilbert; s of Henry Moorshead Pine, of Bristol; *b* 22 Dec 1907; *Educ* Tellisford House Sch Bristol, SW London Coll Barnes, London U; *m* 1948, Grace V Griffin; 1 s; *Career* author and lecturer, barr Inner Temple 1953, Editor The National Message 1977-, Chm Covenant Publishing Co Ltd 1978-79, Freeman City of London, Liveryman of the Glaziers' Co 1954; formerly: editor *Burke's Peerage* and *Landed Gentry*, man ed The Shooting Times and Shooting Times Library, *International Who's Who of the Arab World*; dir L & G Pine & Co Ltd; FRSA 1961, FRGS 1969, FRAS 1970; *Clubs* Press, Wig and Pen; *Style* - Leslie Pine Esq; Hall Lodge Cottage, Brettenham, Suffolk (☎ 04493 402)

PINK, Lady Dora Elizabeth; JP (London); da of George Leonard Tottenham, ggs of Rt Rev Lord Robert Ponsonby Tottenham, Bishop of Clogher (s of 1 Marquess of Ely); sis of 8 Marquess; *b* 1919; *Educ* Queen's U Kingston Ontario (BA); *m* 1, 1946, Lt (E) Bernard Edgar Hall, RN (d 1947); m 2, 1950, Sir Ivor Thomas Montague Pink, KCMG (d 1966); 1 da; *Career* Lt WRCNS 1939-45; raised to the rank of a Marquess's da 1973; *Style* - Lady Dora Pink, JP; 24 The Gateways, SW3

PINK, Ralph Bonner; CBE (1961), VRD (1951), JP (Portsmouth 1950), MP (C) Portsmouth South 1966-; s of Frank Pink; *b* 30 Sept 1912; *Educ* Oundle Sch; *m* 1939, Marguerite Nora Bannar-Martin; 1 s, 1 da; *Career* Portsmouth City Council 1948-, Lord Mayor of Portsmouth 1961-62; *Recreations* yachting; *Style* - Ralph Pink Esq, CBE, VRD, JP, MP; House of Commons, SW1A OAA

PINKER, George Douglas; s of late Ronald Douglas Pinker; *b* 6 Dec 1924; *Educ* Reading Sch, St Mary's Hosp London U (MB, BS), DObst; *m* Dorothy

Emma, nee Russell; 3 s, 1 da; *Career* Surgeon-Gynaecologist to HM the Queen 1973-, Consulting Gynaecological Surgn & Obstetrician St Mary's Hosp Paddington and Samaritan Hosp 1958-, Consulting Gynaecological Surgeon Middx and Soho Hosps 1969-, Consultant Gynaecologist King Edward VII Hosp for Officers 1974-; MRCOG 1954, FRCS(Ed) 1957, FRCOG 1964, FRSocMed; *Clubs* Bath; *Style* - George Pinker Esq; Medley, Kingston Hill, Kingston-on-Thames, Surrey KT2 7IU; 96 Harley st, W1N 1AF (☎ 01 935 2292)

PINN, Denniss Arthur Joseph; s of Thomas Arthur Pinn (d 1938); *b* 29 Aug 1914; *Educ* Ratcliffe Coll; *m* 1943, Iris Lorna, da of Edward Groves (d 1967); 1 s, 2 da; *Career* late Maj RA, chm Alcan Aluminium (UK) Ltd 1978-; *Recreations* sailing, music, reading, gardening; *Clubs* MCC, Roy NZ Yacht Sqdn, Roy Cornwall Yacht, Northern (Auckland NZ); *Style* - Denniss Pinn Esq; Chylowen, Tredenham rd, St Mawes, Cornwall TL2 5AN (☎ St Mawes 223)

PINNINGTON, Geoffrey Charles; s of Charles Pinnington; *b* 21 March 1919; *Educ* Harrow County Sch, Rock Ferry H S Birkenhead, King's Coll London; *m* 1941, Beryl, da of Edward Clark; 2 da; *Career* editor Sunday People 1972-, dir Mirror Gp Newspapers 1976-; *Style* - Geoffrey Pinnington Esq; Sunday People, 9 New Fetter Lane, EC4A 1AR (☎ 01 353 0246)

PINNINGTON, Roger Adrian; TD; s of William Austin Pinnington (decd); *b* 27 Aug 1932; *Educ* Rydal Sch Colwyn Bay, Lincoln Coll Oxford; *m* 1943, Marjorie Ann, da of George Alan Livingstone Russell, of Beverley, Yorks; 1 s, 3 da; *Career* md CAM Gears Ltd, chm TRW (South Africa) Pty Ltd, pres TRW Italia Spa; *Recreations* golf, gardening; *Style* - Roger Pinnington Esq; Church End Cottage, Rushden, Nr Buntingford, Herts (☎ (home) 076 388 243; (office) 0462 5751)

PINSENT, Sir Christopher Roy; 3 Bt (UK 1938); s of Sir Roy Pinsent, 2 Bt (d 1978); *b* 2 Aug 1922; *Educ* Winchester; *m* 1951, Susan Mary, da of John Norton Scorer, of Fotheringhay; 1 s, 2 da; *Heir* s, Thomas Benjamin Roy Pinsent; *Career* portrait painter; lecturer Camberwell Sch of Art; *Style* - Sir Christopher Pinsent, Bt; The Chestnuts, Castle Hill, Guildford, Surrey

PINSENT, Thomas Benjamin Roy; s and h of Sir Christopher Roy Pinsent, 3 Bt; *b* 21 July 1967

PINSON, Barry; QC (1973); s of Thomas Alfred Pinson; *b* 18 Dec 1925; *Educ* King Edward's Sch, Birmingham U; *m* 1, 1950, Miriam Mary; 1 s, 1 da; m 2, 1977, Anne Kathleen Golby; *Career* barr Gray's Inn 1949, trustee RAF Museum; *Style* - Barry Pinson Esq, QC; 11 New sq, Lincoln's Inn, WC2 (☎ 01 242 3981)

PINTER, Harold; CBE (1966); s of J Pinter; *b* 10 Oct 1930; *Educ* Hackney Downs G S; *m* 1, 1956 (m dis 1980), Viven Merchant; 1 s; m 2, 1980, Lady Antonia Fraser, *qv*; *Career* actor, playwright and director; Assoc Dir Nat Theatre 1973-; Hon DLitt Reading 1970, Birmingham 1971, Glasgow 1974, East Anglia 1974; *Clubs* City Livery; *Style* - Harold Pinter Esq, CBE; c/o ACTAC Ltd, 16 Cadogan Lane, SW1

PIPER, John Egerton Christmas; CH (1972); s of late C A Piper; *b* 13 Dec 1903; *Educ* Epsom Coll, RCA; *m* 1935, Mary Myfanwy Evans; 2 s, 2 da; *Career* painter & writer, memb Oxford Docesan Advsy Ctee 1950-; Hon ARIBA 1957, Hon FRIBA 1971, Hon ARCA 1959, Hon DLitt Leicester 1960, Oxford 1966, Sussex 1974, Reading 1977; *Clubs* Athenaeum; *Style* - John Piper Esq, CH; Fawley Bottom Farmhouse, nr Henley-on-Thames, Oxon

PIPER, Peter (Bright Harold); CBE (1979); s of Robert Harold Piper; *b* 22 Sept 1918; *Educ* Maidstone G S; *m* 1, 1945, Marjorie Joyce, da of Capt George Arthur; 1 s, 1 da; m 2, 1979, Leonie Mary, da of Maj C V Lane; *Career* ch exec Lloyds Bank Gp 1973-78, dir 1970-, Freeman City of London, Liveryman Spectacle Makers' Co; *Style* - Peter Piper Esq, CBE; Greenways, Hawkshill Close, Esher, Surrey

PIPPARD, Prof Sir (Alfred) Brian; s of late Prof A J S Pippard; *b* 7 Sept 1920; *Educ* Clifton Coll, Clare Cambridge (Hon Fell 1973); *m* 1955, Charlotte Frances Dyer; 3 da; *Career* Cavendish Professor of Physics Cambridge U 1971-; FRS 1956, kt 1975; *Style* - Professor Sir Brian Pippard; 30 Porson rd, Cambridge

PIRIE, Group Captain Gordon Hamish; CBE (1946), JP, DL (London 1962); s of Harold Victor Campbell Pirie; *b* 10 Feb 1918; *Educ* Eton, RAF Coll Cranwell; *m* 1953, Margaret Joan Bomford (d 1972); *Career* RAF 1938, Gp Capt 1946, ret; Dep High Bailiff of Westminster 1978-, memb Westminster City Council 1949-, Mayor 1959-60, Leader of Council 1961-69, Alderman 1963-78, Lord Mayor 1974-75; chm Services Kinema Corpn 1979-, dir Parker Gallery; *Clubs* Carlton, RAF; *Style* - Group Captain Gordon Pirie CBE JP DL; Cottage Row, Tarrant Gunville, Blandford, Dorset (☎ Tarrant Hinton 212)

PIRIE, Henry Ward; s of William Pirie (d 1922), of Leith; *b* 13 Feb 1922; *Educ* George Watson's Coll Edinburgh, Edinburgh U; *m* 1948, Jean Marion, da of late Frank Jardine (d 1956); 4 s; *Career* advocate 1947, Sheriff-Substitute of Lanarkshire at Airdrie 1954-55, Sheriff-Substitute (later Sheriff) of Lanarkshire at Glasgow 1955-74, ret 1974; now crossword compiler, journalist and broadcaster; OStJ 1967; *Recreations* golf, curling, bridge; *Style* - Henry Pirie Esq; 16 Poplar Drive, Lenzie, Glasgow G66 4DN (☎ 041 776 2494)

PIRIE, Iain Gordon; s of Charles Fox Pirie; *b* 15 Jan 1933; *Educ* Harris Acad Dundee, St Andrews U; *m* 1960, Sheila Brown Forbes, MB, ChB; *Career* Procurator Fiscal Dumfries 1971-76, Ayr 1976-79, Sheriff of South Strathclyde, Dumfries and Galloway at Airdrie 1979-; *Style* - Sheriff Pirie; 56 Aytoun rd, Glasgow G41 5HE

PITBLADO, Sir David Bruce; KCB (1967, CB 1955), CVO (1953); s of Robert Bruce Pitblado; *b* 18 Aug 1912; *Educ* Strand Sch, Emmanuel Cambridge (Hon Fell 1972), Middle Temple; *m* 1941, Edith (d 1978), da of Capt J T and Mrs Rees Evans; 1 s, 1 da; *Career* memb Council Davies Educational Services 1975-, chm 1979-; consultant, Inst of Directors 1977-, Comptroller and Auditor-Gen 1971-76; *Clubs* Athenaeum; *Style* - Sir David Pitblado, KCB, CVO; 23 Cadogan st, SW3; Pengoitan, Borth, Dyfed

PITCHER, Desmond Henry; s of George Charles Pitcher; *b* 23 March 1935; *Educ* Liverpool Coll of Technology; *m* 2 1978, Carol, nee Rose; 1 s and 1 step s (and twin da by former m); *Career* md Plessey Telecommunications and Office Systems 1978-, dir Plessey Co 1979-, dir CEI 1979-; V-Pres TEMA 1978; *Style* - Desmond Pitcher Esq; Hough Hall, Hough, Nantwich, Cheshire (☎ Nantwich 67865)

PITCHFORD, His Honour Judge; Charles Neville; *Career* barr Middle Temple 1948, a Circuit Judge, Wales and Chester Circuit 1972-; *Style* - His Honour Judge Pitchford; Old Vicarage, Taliaris, Llandeilo, Dyfed

PITCHFORD, John Hereward; CBE (1971); s of John Pitchford; *b* 30 Aug 1904; *Educ* Brighton Coll, Christ's Coll Cambridge; *m* 1930, Teresa Agnes Mary Pensotti; 1 s, 2 da; *Career* chm Ricardo Consulting Engineers Ltd 1962-76, pres 1976-; *Clubs* Athenaeum, Roy Automobile; *Style* - John Pitchford Esq, CBE; Byeways, Ditchling, East Sussex (☎ Hassocks 2177)

PITHER, Jon Peter; s of Philip John Pitcher (d 1965); *b* 15 June 1934; *Educ* Dauntsey's, Queens' Coll Cambridge; *m* 1961, Karin Jutta, da of Werner Gropp; 1 s, 1 da; *Career* md Amari Ltd 1970-, memb Inst of Management Consultants; *Recreations* sailing, skiing, tennis; *Clubs* Royal Thames; *Style* - Jon Pither Esq; South House, Claremont Park, Esher, Surrey (☎ 01 493 9371)

PITHER, Hon Mrs (Pauline Ruth); da of 1 Baron Lambury (d 1967); *b* 1931; *m* 1954, John Pither; 2 s; *Style* - The Hon Mrs Pither; Appletree Farmhouse, Chorleywood Common, Herts

PITMAN, Sir Hubert; OBE (1953); s of

W H Pitman, JP; *b* 19 Aug 1901; *Educ* Repton; *Career* memb Lloyd's 1926-, chm H Pitman & Co Ltd, London; OStJ, kt 1961; *Clubs* Carlton; *Style* - Sir Hubert Pitman, OBE; 57 Porchester Ter, W2 (☎ 01 262 6593); Danemore Park, Speldhurst, Kent (☎ Langton 2829); 11/12 Blomfield st, EC4 (☎ 01 588 1852)

PITMAN, Sir (isaac) James; KBE (1961); s of late Ernest Pitman and gs of late Sir Isaac Pitman; *b* 14 Aug 1901; *Educ* Eton, Ch Ch Oxford; *m* 1927, Hon Margaret Beaufort Lawson-Johnston, da of 1 Baron Luke & sis of 2 Baron; 3 s, 1 da; *Career* Charter Pro-Chllr Bath U, V-Pres British and Foreign Sch Soc, British Assoc for Commercial Land Industrial Education; memb NUT; proponent and designer of Initial Teaching Alphabet; chm Sir Isaac Pitman and Sons Ltd 1934-66; MP (C) Bath 1945-64; Hon DLitt Strathclyde and Bath; *Clubs* Carlton, Harlequins, Achilles; *Style* - Sir James Pitman, KBE; 58 Chelsea Park gdns, SW3 6AE (☎ 01 352 7004); Holme Wood, Chisbridge Cross, Marlow, Bucks (☎ High Wycombe 881260)

PITMAN, Hon Lady - Hon Margaret Beaufort; *née* Lawson-Johnston; da of 1 Baron Luke, KBE (d 1943); *b* 1907; *m* 1927, Sir (Isaac) James Pitman, KBE; 3 s, 1 da; *Clubs* Carlton; *Style* - The Hon Lady Pitman; 58 Chelsea Park gdns, SW3 6AE; Holme Wood, Chisbridge Cross, Marlow, Bucks

PITOI, Sir Sere; CBE (1975); s of Pitoi Sere; *b* 11 Nov 1935; *Educ* Sogeri, Queensland U, Birmingham U; *m* 1957, Daga Leva; 2 s, 3 da; *Career* chm Public Services Commission of Papua New Guinea 1971-; Fell PNG Inst of Management, MACE; kt 1977; *Style* - Sir Sere Pitoi, CBE; PO Box 6029, Boroko, Papua New Guinea

PITT OF HAMPSTEAD, Baron (Life Peer UK 1975); David Thomas Pitt; JP (1966); s of Cyril S L Pitt, of St David's Grenada, WI; *b* 3 Oct 1913; *Educ* St David's RC Sch Grenada, Grenada Boys' Secdy Sch, Edinburgh U; *m* 1943, Dorothy Elaine Alleyne; 1 s, 2 da; *Career* GP London 1947-, pres W Indian Nat Party (Trinidad) 1943-47, memb LCC 1961-64, GLC 1964-77, for Hackney (dep chm 1969-70, chm 1974-75), chm Campaign Against Racial Discrimination 1965, chm Community Relations Commission 1977, memb Standing Advsy Cncl on Race Relations 1977-, part time memb PO Bd 1975-77, chm Shelter 1979, contested (L) Hampstead 1959, Clapham (Wandsworth) 1970; Hon DSc U of WI 1975, Hon DLitt Bradford 1977, Hon LLD Bristol 1977; *Style* - The Rt Hon Lord Pitt of Hampstead JP; 6 Heath Drive, NW3

PITT, Hon Amanda; da of Baron Pitt of Hampstead (Life Peer); *Style* - The Hon Amanda Pitt

PITT, Hon Bruce Michael David; s of Baron Pitt of Hampstead (Life Peer); *Style* - The Hon Bruce Pitt

PITT, Sir Harry Raymond; BA, PhD, FRS (1957); s of H Pitt; *b* 3 June 1914; *Educ* King Edward's Sch Stourbridge, Peterhouse Cambridge; *m* 1940, Clemency Catherine, da of H C E Jacoby, MIEE; 4 s; *Career* Dep Vice-Chllr Nottingham U 1959-62, Visiting Prof Yale U 1962-63, Vice-Chllr Reading U 1964-79, chm UCCA 1975-78; Hon LLD Aberdeen 1970, Nottingham 1970, Hon DSc Reading 1978; kt 1978; *Style* - Sir Harry Pitt; 46 Shinfield rd, Reading, Berks RG2 7BW (☎ Reading 82962)

PITT, Hon Phyllis Leonora; da of Baron Pitt of Hampstead (Life Peer); *Style* - The Hon Phyllis Pitt

PITT-RIVERS, Dr Rosalind Venetia; da of Hon Anthony Morton Henley, CMG, DSO (d 1925) and late Hon Sylvia Laura Henley, nee Stanley; *b* 4 March 1907; *Educ* Notting Hill H S, Bedford Coll London U (MSc, PhD); *m* 1931, Capt George Henry Lane Fox Pitt-Rivers (d 1966); 1 s; *Career* Head of Chemistry Div, Nat Inst for Medical Research 1969-72 FRS 1954; *Style* - Dr Rosalind Pitt-Rivers; 23a Lyndhurst rd, Hampstead, NW3 5NX

PITTOM, L(ois) Audrey; CB (1979); da of Thomas Pittom; *b* 4 July 1918; *Educ* Laurels Sch, Wroxall Abbey Warwick, St Anne's Oxford; *Career* Under Sec Health and Safety Executive, Dept of Employment 1975-78, ret; *Style* - Miss Audrey Pittom, CB; 1 Rectory Lane, Barby, Rugby, Warwicks (☎ Rugby 890424)

PITTS, Sir Cyril Alfred; s of late T H Pitts; *b* 21 March 1916; *Educ* St Olave's, Jesus Cambridge; *m* 1942, Barbara; 2 s, 1 da; *Career* pres British and South Asian Trade Assoc 1978-, chm Process Plant EDC 1979-, Peter Brotherhood 1980-; dep chm London Sch of Hygiene and Tropical Medicine; kt 1968; *Style* - Sir Cyril Pitts; 11 Queensmead, St John's Wood Park, NW8 (☎ 01 586 0871)

PITTS, John Kennedy; s of Thomas Alwyn Pitts (d 1968); *b* 6 Oct 1925; *Educ* Trowbridge, Bristol U; *m* 1957, Joan Iris, da of Henry Charles Light (d 1963); *Career* chm Richardson Fertilizers Ltd 1972-76, dep chm ICI Agricultural Div 1972-77, v-pres Compagnie Neerlandaise de l'Azote 1975-77, chm Hargreaves Fertilizers Ltd 1975-77, chm and ch exec Tioxide Group Ltd 1978-; memb Tees & Hartlepool Port Authority 1976-78; *Clubs* RAC; *Style* - John Pitts Esq; 74 Dorset House, Gloucester Place, NW1 5AF (☎ 01 935 9413)

PITTS, James Michael; s of James Walter Pitts (d 1956); *b* 20 June 1929; *Educ* Shrewsbury; *m* 1955, Jean Hilarie; 2 s, 1 da; *Career* chartered accountant, senior ptnr Chalmers; Pres Birmingham & West Midlands Society of Chartered Accountants 1979-80; memb of the court of Birmingham University 1980; churchwarden St Laurence's Rowington; *Recreations* gardening, golf, sailing; *Clubs* The Birmingham; *Style* - James Pitts Esq; Hickecroft, Mill Lane, Rowington, Warwick

PITTS-TUCKER, Robert St John; CBE (1975); s of Walter Greame Pitts-Tucker (d 1978); *b* 24 June 1909; *Educ* Haileybury (Schol), Clare Cambridge (Schol) (1 class tripos); *m* 1942, Joan Margery, da of Frank Furnivall (d 1936); 3 s, 1 da; *Career* assist master Shrewsbury 1931-44, headmaster Pocklington Sch 1945-66, Gen Sec of HMC and HMA 1966-74; *Recreations* gardening, music, country walks; *Clubs* Royal Commonwealth Soc; *Style* - Robert Pitts-Tucker Esq, CBE; 59 Kings rd, Berkhamsted, Herts HP4 3BP, 04427 3841

PIXLEY, Sir Neville Drake; MBE (1944), VRD (1941); s of Arthur Pixley; *b* 21 Sept 1905; *Educ* C of E G S Brisbane; *m* 1938, Lorna, da of Llewellyn Stephens; 3 da; *Career* dir Burns Philp & Co 1962-; chm Australian Cttee Lloyd's Register of Shipping; ADC to King George VI and to the Queen 1951-54; Vice-Chllr 1978- and Receiver-Gen 1963, Order of St John in Australia; chm Roy Humane Soc of NSW; KStJ 1963, FCIT, kt 1976; *Style* - Sir Neville Pixley, MBE; Koiyong, 335 New South Head rd, Double Bay, Sydney, NSW 2028, Australia (☎ 3262676)

PIZEY, Admiral Sir (Charles Thomas) Mark; GBE (1957, KBE 1953), CB (1942), DSO (1942), idc, RN ret, DL (Somerset 1962); s of late Rev C E Pizey; *b* 1899; *m* Phyllis, da of Alfred D'Angibau; 2 da; *Career* Ch of Naval Staff and Cdr-in-Chief Indian Navy 1951-55, Admiral 1954, Cdr-in-Chief Plymouth 1955-58, ret; *Style* - Admiral Sir Mark Pizey GBE CB DSO DL; 1 St Ann's Drive, Burnham on Sea, Somerset

PLACE, Rear-Admiral (Basil Charles) Godfrey; VC (1944), CB (1970), DSC (1943); s of late Maj C G M Place, DSO, MC; *b* 19 July 1921; *Educ* The Grange Folkestone, RNC Dartmouth; *m* 1943, Althea Annington, da of late Harry Tickler; 1 s, 2 da; *Career* Capt 1958, Adm Cmdg Reserves, Dir-Gen Naval Recruiting 1968-70, chm VC and GC Assoc 1971-, Lay Observer 1975-78; Polish Cross of Valour 1941; *Style* - Rear-Admiral Godfrey Place VC CB DSC; 87 Bishop's Mansions, SW6; The Old Bakery, Corton Denham, Sherborne, Dorset

PLACE, Michael Macgregor; *b* 15 March 1936; *Educ* Oundle, LSE; *m* 1963, Pauline Ann; 3 s; *Career* md Grattan Warehouses Ltd 1976-; *Clubs* RAF; *Style* - Michael Place Esq; Beech House, Lady Lane, Bingley, W Yorkshire (☎ Bingley 5109)

PLAISTER, Sir Sidney; CBE (1972); s of Herbert Plaister; *b* 15 Jan 1909; *Educ*

Acton and Chiswick Polytechnic, Coll of Estate Management; *m* 1937, Coralie Fraser Steele; 1 s, 1 da; *Career* chartered quantity surveyor 1930-, Pres West Midlands Con Council 1980-, Chm Midlands Central Con Euro-Constituency Council 1978-, memb exec cttee Nat Union of Con Assocs 1967-; FRICS, kt 1980; *Clubs* Carlton; *Style* - Sir Sidney Plaister, CBE; Turnpike Close, Old Warwick rd, Lapworth, Warwicks B94 6AP (☎ Lapworth 2792)

PLANK, Hon Mrs (Marion Rose); *née* Blyton; da of Baron Blyton (Life Peer); *b* 1926; *m* 1948, John Plank; children; *Style* - The Hon Mrs Plank; 36 Gerald st, S Shields, Tyne & Wear

PLANT, Baron (Life Peer UK 1978); Cyril Thomas Howe Plant; CBE (1975, OBE 1965); s of late Sidney Plant; *b* 27 Aug 1910; *Educ* Leek H S; *m* 1931, Gladys Mayers; 2 s, 1 da; *Career* Gen Sec Inland Revenue Staff Fedn 1960-76, Chm Post Office and Civil Service Sanatorium Soc 1950-75, memb Gen Council TUC 1964-76, chm 1976; memb Southern Water Bd 1977-, Treasurer Workers' Educational Assoc 1969-, Trustee Brighton and Hove Enginerium 1980-; *Clubs* English-Speaking Union; *Style* - The Rt Hon the Lord Plant, CBE; Longridge, 19 Montacute rd, Lewes, E Sussex (☎ Lewes 2556)

PLANT, Hon Christopher Victor Howe; s of Baron Plant (Life Peer); *b* 1945; *m* 1966, Marian, da of John Parkes; *Style* - The Hon Christopher Plant; 22 Roslyn av, Eastbourne, E Sussex

PLANT, Hon John Sydney Sampson; s of Baron Plant (Life Peer); *b* 1931; *m* 1953, Mary, da of John Clayton; *Style* - The Hon John Plant; 6 Swallow Croft, Leek, Staffs

PLASKETT, Maj-Gen Frederick Joseph; CB (1980), MBE (1966); s of Frederick Joseph Plaskett; *b* 23 Oct 1926; *m* 1950, Heather, nee Kington; 4 da; *Career* Dir Gen Transport and Movements (Army) 1978-81, ret 1981; FCIT, RCDS (1975); *Clubs* Army and Navy; *Style* - Major-General Frederick Plaskett CB MBE; c/o National Westminster Bank Ltd, Minster st, Salisbury, Wilts

PLASTOW, David Arnold Stuart; s of James Stuart Plastow, of Grimsby, S Humberside; *b* 9 May 1932; *Educ* Culford Sch Bury St Edmunds; *m* 1954, Barbara Ann, da of Ralph May, of Luton, Beds; 1 s, 1 da; *Career* marketing dir Motor Car Div Rolls-Royce Ltd 1967-70, md 1971, md Rolls-Royce Motors Ltd 1972, group md 1974-80, dir Vickers Ltd 1975-80, ch exec 1980-, dir GKN Ltd 1978-, pres Soc of Motor Manufacturers & Traders 1976-78, pres Motor Industry Res Assoc 1978-; Hon DSc Cranfield 1978; *Recreations* golf, music; *Clubs* Royal and Ancient (St Andrews); *Style* - David Plastow Esq; Eaton Cottage, Congleton, Cheshire (☎ Congleton 3462)

PLATER-ZYBECK, Countess (patent of nobility granted by Empress Maria-Teresa of Austria 1774) Christina; title of Staroste (roughly 'mayor' or 'chief executive') conferred on leading rep of family, then domiciled in Dinebourg E Prussia, by Tsar Ivan the Terrible 1578; da of Count Jan Plater-Zyberk (d 1980; the family migrated from Westphalia to the Baltic coast region with the Teutonic Knights in the 14th century); *b* 11 April 1947; *Educ* Lausanne U, U of Paris; *Career* res scientist INSERM Paris 1976-78, UCL 1978-79, Kennedy Res Inst Hammersmith; *Recreations* skiing, travel; *Style* - Countess Christina Plater-Zyberk; 20 av de Chailly, 1012 Lausanne, Switzerland (☎ 21 - 32 56 15); 37 Courtfield rd, SW7 (☎ 01 370 1820)

PLATT OF WRITTLE, Baroness (Life Peeress UK 1981); Beryl Catherine; CBE (1978); da of Ernest Myatt (d 1950); *b* 18 April 1923; *Educ* Westcliff H S for Girls, Girton Cambridge; *m* 1949, Stewart Sydney, s of Sydney Rowland Platt (d 1946); 1 s (Hon Roland Francis Platt), 1 da (Hon Victoria Catherine Platt); *Career* aeronautical engr, tech assist Hawker Aircraft Ltd 1943-46, BEA 1946-49; V-Chm Essex CC 1980- & Tech Educn Cncl, formerly chm Essex Educn Cttee; memb Court Essex U and Cambridge U Appointments Bd; memb Assoc of CCs and ILEA; *Recreations* reading, gardening, cooking; *Style* - Rt Hon Lady Platt of Writtle CBE; Greenbury House, The Green, Writtle, Essex (☎ Chelmsford 420337)

PLATT, Frank Lindsey; s and h of Sir Harry Platt, MD, MS, FRCS, 1 Bt; *b* 16 Jan 1919; *Educ* Stowe, Magdalen Oxford and the Sorbonne; *m* 1951, Johanna Magdalena Elizabeth, da of late Friedrich Wilhelm Laenger, of Westphalia; *Career* 1939-45 War as Maj Intelligence Corps; barr, Inner Temple 1954; *Style* - Frank Platt Esq; 3 Sherwood ave, Fallowfield, Manchester 14

PLATT, Sir Harry; 1 Bt (UK 1958); s of Ernest Platt; *b* 7 Oct 1886; *Educ* Manchester U (MB, ChB, MD); *m* 1916, Gertrude Sarah (d 1980), da of Richard Turney; 1 s, 4 da; *Heir* s, Frank Lindsey Platt; *Career* Prof Orthopaedic Surgery Manchester U 1939-41, now Emeritus; pres Nat Fund for Res into Crippling Diseases 1970-, hon pres Internat Fedn of Surgical Colls, Société Internationale de Chirurgie Orthopédique et de Traumatologie, pres Central Council for the Disabled 1969; MS, FRCS, KStJ 1972, kt 1948; *Style* - Sir Harry Platt, Bt; 14 Rusholme gdns, Platt Lane, Manchester M14 5LS (☎ 061 224 2427)

PLATT, Martin Philip; s and h of Hon Sir Peter Platt, 2 Bt; *b* 9 March 1952; *m* 1971, Frances Corinne Moana, da of Trevor Samuel Conley; 1 s, 2 da; *Style* - Martin Platt Esq; 25 Manchester st, Dunedin, New Zealand

PLATT, Norman; s of Edward Turner Platt; *b* 29 Aug 1920; *Educ* Bury G S, King's Cambridge; *m* 1, 1942, Diana Franklin Clay; 1 s, 1 da; m 2, 1963, Johanna Sigrid Bishop; 1 s, 2 da; *Career* artistic dir Kent Opera 1969-; *Style* - Norman Platt Esq; Pembles Cross, Egerton, Ashford, Kent TN27 9EN (☎ Egerton 406)

PLATT, Hon Sir Peter; 2 Bt (UK 1959); s of Baron Platt (Life Peer and 1 Bt) (d 1978); *b* 6 July 1924; *Educ* Abbotsholme Sch Derbyshire, Magdalen Oxford, RCM (BMus, MA, BLitt Oxon); *m* 1948, Jean Halliday, da of late Charles Philip Brentnall, MC; 1 s, 2 da; *Heir* s, Martin Philip Platt; *Career* Prof of Music Otago U NZ 1957-75, Sydney U 1975-; *Style* - The Hon Sir Peter Platt, Bt; 1 Ellison Place, Pymble, NSW 2073, Australia

PLATT, Hon Mrs (Pauline Mary); da of Baroness Fisher of Rednal and Joseph Fisher; *b* 1940; *m* 1961, Michael James Platt; *Style* - The Hon Mrs Platt; 19 Woodfields Drive, Lichfield, Staffs

PLATT, Sylvia, Baroness; Sylvia Jean; da of Sydney Charles Caveley, and formerly w of John Alfred Haggard; *m* 1974, as his 2 w, 1 Baron Platt (Life Peer and 1 Bt) (d 1978); *Style* - The Rt Hon Sylvia, Lady Platt; 53 Heathside, Hinchley Wood, Esher, Surrey

PLATTS-MILLS, John Faithful Fortescue; QC (1964); s of John F W Mills and Dr Daisy Platts-Mills, NZ; *b* 4 Oct 1906; *Educ* Nelson Coll, Victoria U, NZ, Balliol Oxford (Rhodes Scholar); *m* 1936, Janet Katherine Cree; 6 s; *Career* barr, bencher Inner Temple 1970, MP (L) Finsbury 1945-48, (Ind L) 1948-50, pres Haldane Soc, v-pres Int Assoc of Democratic Lawyers, memb TGWU; *Clubs* Athenaeum, Vincent's (Oxford), Hampshire (Winchester), Leander; *Style* - John Platts-Mills Esq, QC; Cloisters, Temple, EC4 (☎ 01 583 9526); Terrible Down Farm, Halland, E Sussex (☎ Halland 310)

PLATZER, Dr Wilfried; Hon GCVO (1969); s of Karl Platzer; *b* 5 April 1909; *Educ* Vienna U, Foreign Service Coll; *m* 1939, Edith von Donat; 1 s, 1 da; *Career* Ambass of Austria to the Court of St James's 1970-74; Gold Cross of Commander, Order of Merit (Austria) 1968; *Style* - Dr Wilfried Platzer, GCVO

PLAYFAIR, Sir Edward Wilder; KCB (1957, CB 1949); s of late Dr Ernest Playfair; *b* 17 May 1909; *Educ* Eton and King's Cambridge; *m* 1949, Dr Mary Lois Rae; 3 da; *Career* Perm Sec MOD 1960-61, chm Int Computers and Tabulators Ltd 1961-65, dir Equity and Law Life Assurance Soc Ltd, Govr Imperial Coll Science and Technology 1958- (fell 1972), hon fell UCL 1969, Hon FBCS; *Clubs*

Brooks's; *Style* - Sir Edward Playfair, KCB; 12 The Vale, Chelsea SW3 6AH (☎ 01 352 4671)

PLEASS, Sir Clement John; KCMG (1955, CMG 1950), KCVO (1956), KBE (1953); s of J W A Pleass, of Tiverton, Devon; *b* 19 Nov 1901; *Educ* Royal Masonic Sch, Selwyn Cambridge; *m* 1927, Sybil, da of Alwyn Child, of Gerrard's Cross; 1 s; *Career* Lt-Govr E Region Nigeria 1952-54, Govr 1954-56; *Clubs* Royal Commonwealth Society; *Style* - Sir Clement Pleass, KCMG, KCVO, KBE; Higher Barton, Marlborough, nr Kingsbridge, S Devon

PLEWMAN, Thomas Langford; s of Frank Victor Plewman (d 1952); *b* 9 April 1912; *Educ* Portora Roy Sch, Trin Coll Dublin; *m* 1950, Betty, da of William Herbert Ainsworth; 1 s, 1 da; *Career* partner A C Palmer & Co (now Ernst & Whinney) 1950-70; chm Richards (Leicester) Ltd 1974-, Diana Shoemakers Ltd 1977-80; *Style* - Thomas Plewman Esq; Hythe House, Woodmarket, Lutterworth, Leics (☎ Lutterworth 2737)

PLEYDELL-BOUVERIE, Hon Mrs Edward; Alice Pearl; da of Maj Edward Barrington Crake by his 2 w, Clara (da of George Plunkennet Woodroffe, RHG); *m* 1, 1920 (as his 2 w), 2 Baron Montagu of Beaulieu, KCIE, CSI, JP, DL (d 1929); 1s (3 Baron Montagu of Beaulieu), 3 da (of which the yst, Mary-Clare, m (David) Viscount Garnock, s and h of 14 Earl of Lindsay); m 2, 1936, Hon Edward Pleydell-Bouverie, MVO, DL, (d 1951) 2 s of 6 Earl of Radnor; 1 s; *Style* - The Hon Mrs Edward Pleydell-Bouverie; The Lodge, Beaulieu, Hants

PLEYDELL-BOUVERIE, Lady Belinda; da of 8 Earl of Radnor by his 2 w Margaret; *b* 9 Nov 1966; *Style* - Lady Belinda Pleydell-Bouverie

PLEYDELL-BOUVERIE, Lady Elizabeth; da of 6 Earl of Radnor, CIE, CBE, JP; *b* 27 June 1897; *Career* Co Assist ATS 1940-41; *Style* - Lady Elizabeth Pleydell-Bouverie; Ducarts, Stanford Dingley, Berks (☎ Bradfield 291)

PLEYDELL-BOUVERIE, Lady Frances; da of 8 Earl of Radnor by his 2 w Margaret; *b* 1973; *Style* - Lady Frances Pleydell-Bouverie

PLEYDELL-BOUVERIE, James; s of Hon Peter Pleydell-Bouverie by his 2 w; b 1950; *Educ* Eton; *Style* - James Pleydell-Bouverie Esq

PLEYDELL-BOUVERIE, Lady Lucy; twin da of 8 Earl of Radnor by his 2 w Margaret; *b* 6 May 1964; *Style* - Lady Lucy Pleydell-Bouverie

PLEYDELL-BOUVERIE, Lady Martha; twin da of 8 Earl of Radnor by his 2 w Margaret; *b* 6 May 1964; *Style* - Lady Martha Pleydell-Bouverie

PLEYDELL-BOUVERIE, Hon Peter; s of 6 Earl of Radnor, CIE, CBE, JP, by Julian (da of Charles Balfour, DL); *b* 19 Oct 1909; *Educ* Harrow, Trin Cambridge; *m* 1, 1938 (m dis 1946), Audrey (d 1968), formerly w of Marshall Field and da of William Dodge James, CVO, JP, DL, of West Dean Park, Sussex, also sister of Edward James, the collector of Surrealist paintings, *qv*; *m* 2, 1947, Audrey, youngest daughter of Captain Archibald Glen Kidston, JP, of Builth Wells, Radnorshire, and Breconshire (Audrey's former husband was Anthony Seymour Bellville; 1 s; *Career* Maj KRRC, late 2 Lt Roy Wilts Yeomanry; chm Calor Gas Hldg Co, Western Gazette Co; dir Bristol Evening Post Ltd; *Clubs* White's; *Style* - Major The Hon Peter Pleydell-Bouverie; Landford Lodge, Salisbury, Wiltshire (☎ Earldoms (STD Code 079 439) 247)

PLEYDELL-BOUVERIE, Hon Peter John; 2 s of 8 Earl of Radnor by his 1 w Anne; *b* 14 Jan 1958; *Educ* Harrow, Trin Cambridge; *Career* Far Eastern analyst, Grieveson Grant & Co (stockbrokers); *Recreations* fishing, skiing, shooting, photography; *Style* - The Hon Peter Pleydell-Bouverie; Longford Castle, Salisbury, Wilts; 115 Flood st, SW3 (☎ 01 352 4195)

PLEYDELL-BOUVERIE, Hon Reuben; 2 s of 7 Earl of Radnor, KG,

KCVO, JP, DL, by his 1 w Helena; *b* 30 Dec 1930; *Educ* Harrow; *m* 1956, Bridget, da of Maj John Fowell Buxton (gggs of Sir Thomas Buxton, 1 Bt); 2 s, 1 da; *Career* late 2 Lt Roy Scots Greys; *Style* - The Hon Reuben Pleydell-Bouverie; The Dower House, Slindon, Arundel, Sussex

PLEYDELL-BOUVERIE, Hon Richard Oakley; s of 7 Earl of Radnor, KG, KCVO, JP, DL, by his 2 w Isobel, OBE (da of Lt-Col Richard Oakley, DSO, JP); *b* 25 June 1947; *Educ* Harrow, RAC Cirencester; *m* 1978, Victoria, yr da of Frank Waldron; 1 s; *Style* - The Hon Richard Pleydell-Bouverie; Lawrence End, Peters Green, Luton, Beds

PLIATZKY, Sir Leo; KCB (1977, CB 1972); *b* 1919; *Educ* Manchester G S, City of London Sch, Corpus Christi Oxford (hon fell 1980); *m* 1948, Marian Jean Elias (d 1979); 1 s, 1 da; *Career* Permanent Sec Dept of Trade 1977-79, ret, retained for special duties 1979-80; part-time memb British Airways Board 1980-, dir Associated Communications Corpn Ltd 1980-; Visiting Prof City U 1980-; FRSA; *Clubs* Reform; *Style* - Sir Leo Pliatzky, KCB; 27 River Court, Upper Ground, SE1 (☎ 01 928 3667)

PLIMMER, Sir Clifford Ulric; KBE (1967); s of late Arthur Bloomfield Plimmer; *b* 25 July 1905; *Educ* Scots Coll Wellington, Victoria U of Wellington; *m* 1935, Letha May, nee Port; 3 s (and 1 s decd); *Career* chm Lion Breweries Ltd, United Dominions Corpn Finance Ltd; chm and md Wright, Stephenson & Co Ltd to 1970; dir Cable Price Downer Ltd, McKechnie Bros (NZ) Ltd; Nat Patron Intellectually Handicapped Children's Soc Inc, memb: Dr Barnardo's in NZ, Wellington Med Res Foundn; *Style* - Sir Clifford Plimmer, KBE; PO Box 106, Wellington, New Zealand

PLOUVIEZ, Peter William; s of Charles Plouviez; *b* 30 July 1931; *Educ* Sir George Monoux G S, Hastings G S; *m* 1978, Alison Dorothy Macrae; 2 da (by former m); *Career* Gen Sec British Actors' Equity Assoc 1974-, contested (L) St Marylebone by-election 1963, Councillor St Pancras 1962-65, chm Radio and Television Safeguards Ctee 1974-, Sec Fedn of Theatre Unions 1974-, Vice-Chm Confedn of Entertainment Unions 1974-; *Style* - Peter Plouviez Esq; 8 Harley st, W1 (☎ 01 637 9311)

PLOWDEN, Baron (Life Peer UK 1959); Edwin Noel Plowden; KCB (1951), KBE (1946); s of late Roger H Plowden; *b* 6 Jan 1907; *Educ* Switzerland, Pembroke Coll Cambridge (hon fell 1958); *m* 1933, Bridget Horatia (*see* Plowden, Baroness); 2 s, 2 da; *Career* Ch Planning Officer and Chm of Economic Planning Bd HM Treasury 1947-53; chm Atomic Energy Authority 1954-59; Visiting Fell Nuffield Coll 1956-64; chm Ctees of Inquiry 1959-; chm Equity Capital for Industry Ltd 1976-; chm Police Complaints Bd 1976-, independent chm Police Negotiating Bd 1979-; pres Tube Investments 1976; chm Top Salaries Review Body 1981-; Pres London Graduate Sch of Business Studies 1976-; Hon DSc Pennsylvania State U 1958, U of Aston 1972, Hon DLitt Loughborough 1976; *Style* - The Rt Hon the Lord Plowden, KCB, KBE; Martels Manor, Dunmow, Essex (☎ Great Dunmow 2141); 7 Cottesmore gdns, W8 (☎ 01 937 4238)

PLOWDEN, Hon Anna Bridget; da of Baron Plowden (Life Peer); *b* 1938; *Educ* Newhall, Chelmsford, and Inst of Archeology London U; *Style* - The Hon Anna Plowden

PLOWDEN, Baroness; Bridget Horatia; DBE (1972); da of late Adm Sir Herbert Richmond, KCB, by his w Florence (2 da of Sir Hugh Bell, 2 Bt, CB, JP, DL, by his 2 w Florence, DBE, JP, who in her turn was da of Sir Joseph Olliffe); *Educ* Downe House; *m* 1933, Baron Plowden; 2 s, 2 da; *Career* dir Trust Houses Forte Ltd 1961-72; Govr and Vice-Chm BBC 1970-75, chm IBA 1975-80; v-chm ILEA Schools Sub-Ctee 1967-70, pres Pre-School Playgps Assoc 1972-, Nat Assoc of Adult Educn 1980-; memb Nat Theatre Bd 1976-; Liveryman Goldsmiths' Co 1979-, JP Inner London Area Juvenile Panel 1962-71, Fell Royal TV Soc 1980, Hon LLD Leicester 1968, Reading 1970, London 1976, Hon DLitt

Loughborough 1976, DUniv Open 1974; *Style* - The Rt Hon the Lady Plowden, DBE; Martels Manor, Dunmow, Essex (☎ Great Dunmow 2141); 7 Cottesmore gdns, W8 (☎ 01 937 4238)

PLOWDEN, Hon Francis John; s of Baron Plowden (Life Peer); *b* 1945; *Educ* Eton and Trin, Cambridge; *Style* - The Hon Francis Plowden

PLOWDEN, Hon William Julius Lowthian; s of Baron Plowden (Life Peer); *b* 1935; *Educ* Eton, King's Cambridge and California U; *m* 1960, Veronica Mary, da of Lt-Col Derek Ernest Frederick Orby Gascoigne; 2 s, 2 da; *Career* Under-Sec Dept of Industry 1977-78, Dir-Gen Royal Inst of Public Administration 1978-, Hon Prof Dept of Politics Warwick U 1977-; *Style* - The Hon William Plowden; 49 Stockwell Park rd, SW9 (☎ 01 274 4535)

PLOWMAN, Sir (John) Anthony; s of late John Tharp Plowman; *b* 27 Dec 1905; *Educ* Highgate Sch, Gonville and Caius Cambridge; *m* 1933, Vernon, da of late A O Graham; 3 da; *Career* barr Lincoln's Inn 1931, QC 1954, Bencher 1961, Judge of the High Court of Justice (Chancery Div) 1961-76, Vice-Chllr 1974-76; kt 1961; *Style* - Sir Anthony Plowman; Lane End, Bucks

PLOWMAN, Sir John Robin; CBE (1970, OBE 1949), MLC (1966); s of Owen Plowman; *b* Bermuda 18 Sept 1908; *Educ* Bermuda and England; *m* 1936, Marjorie Hardwick; 2 s; *Career* Min of Marine and Air Services Bermuda 1977-, Govt Leader on Legislative Council 1968-; kt 1979; *Style* - Sir John Plowman, CBE, MLC; Chiswick, Paget, Bermuda

PLOWRIGHT, David Ernest; s of William Ernest Plowright; *b* 11 Dec 1930; *Educ* Scunthorpe G S; *m* 1953, Brenda Mary, nee Key;1 s, 2 da; *Career* jt md Granada Television Ltd 1976-; *Style* - David Plowright Esq; Granada TV Ltd, Manchester M60 9EA (☎ 061 832 7211); Granada TV, 36 Golden sq, W1 (☎ 01 734 8080)

PLOWRIGHT, Joan Ann; (Lady Olivier), CBE (1970); da of William Ernest Plowright; *b* 28 Oct 1929; *Educ* Scunthorpe G S, Laban Art of Movement Studio, Old Vic Theatre Sch; *m* 1, 1953 (m dis) Roger Gage; m 2, 1961, Sir Laurence Olivier, later Baron Olivier; 1 s, 2 da; *Career* leading actress with the National Theatre 1963-74, memb RADA Council; *Recreations* reading, music, entertaining; *Style* - Miss Joan Plowright, CBE; c/o LOP Ltd, 33-34 Chancery Lane, WC2A 1EN (☎ 01 836 7932)

PLOWRIGHT, Walter; CMG (1974); s of Jonathan Plowright; *b* 20 July 1923; *Educ* Moulton and Spalding G Ss, RVC London; MRCVS, DVSc; *m* 1959, Dorothy Joy, nee Bell; *Career* Prof of Vet Microbiology RVC 1971-78, Head of Dept of Microbiology, Inst for Research on Animal Diseases 1978-; FRCVS (1977); *Style* - Walter Plowright Esq, CMG; Institute for Research on Animal Diseases, Compton, Newbury, Berks (☎ Compton 411)

PLUMB, Sir (Charles) Henry; DL (Warwick 1977), MEP (C) The Cotswolds 1979-; s of Charles Plumb; *b* 27 March 1925; *Educ* King Edward VI Sch Nuneaton; *m* 1947, Marjorie Dorothy Dunn; 1 s, 2 da; *Career* Pres Nat Farmers Union 1970-79, chm British Ag Council 1975-79, Pres Warwicks County Fedn of Young Farmers' Clubs 1974-, Pres Int Fedn of Ag Producers 1979-, chm Ag Comittee European Parliament 1979-; FRSA 1970, FRAgS 1974, kt 1973; *Style* - Sir Henry Plumb, DL, MEP; Southfields Farm, Coleshill, Birmingham B46 3EJ (☎ Coleshill 63133); 35 Belgrave sq, SW1X 8QN (☎ 01 245 9382)

PLUMB, John Harold; s of late James Plumb, of Leicester; *b* 20 Aug 1911; *Educ* Alderman Newton's Sch Leicester, Univ Coll Leicester, Christ's Cambridge (PhD, LittD); *Career* historian, Master of Christ's Coll Cambridge 1978-, Prof of Modern English History Cambridge U 1966-74, Chm Centre of E Anglian Studies 1979-, Trustee Nat Portrait Gallery 1961-; FRHistS, FSA, FRSL 1969, Hon DLitt Leicester U 1968, E Anglia 1973, Bowdoin Coll 1974, U of S Calif 1978; *Clubs* Brooks's, Beefsteak, Century Assoc (NY); *Style* - John Plumb Esq; Master's Lodge,

Christ's College, Cambridge (☎ 67641); The Old Rectory, Westhorpe, Stowmarket, Suffolk (☎ Bacton 235)

PLUMMER OF ST MARYLEBONE, Baron (Life Peer UK 1981); (Arthur) Desmond Herne Plummer; TD (1950), JP (London 1958), DL (Greater London 1970); s of late Arthur Herne Plummer; *b* 25 May 1914; *Educ* Hurstpierpoint Coll, Coll of Estate Management; *m* 1941, Pat Holloway; 1 da; *Career* Mayor St Marylebone Borough Council 1958-59 (memb 1952-65), LCC St Marylebone 1960-65, ILEA 1964-76, Leader of Council GLC 1967-73, dep chm Nat Employers' Mutual Gen Insurance Assoc 1973-, chm: Horserace Betting Levy Bd 1974-, Epsom and Walton Downs Trg Grounds Mgmnt Bd 1974-, National Stud 1975-; vice-chm Portman Building Soc 1979-; Pres London Anglers' Assoc 1976-; FAI 1948, FRICS 1970, FRSA 1974, Hon FFAS 1966, CStJ 1981; kt 1971; *Clubs* Carlton, Royal Automobile; *Style* - The Rt Hon The Lord Plummer of St Marylebone, TD, JP, DL; 4 The Lane, St Johns Wood, NW8 OPN

PLUMMER, Hon Sally Jane; da of Baron Plummer of St Marylebone (Life Peer); *Style* - The Hon Sally Plummer

PLUMPTON, Alan; CBE (1980), JP (Mon 1971); s of late John Plumpton; *b* 24 Nov 1926; *Educ* Sunderland Technical Sch, Durham U; *m* 1950, Audrey Smith; 1 s, 1 da; *Career* chm London Electricity Bd 1976, dep chm Electricity Council 1981-; *Style* - Alan Plumpton Esq, CBE, JP; Lockhill, Stubbs Wood, Amersham, Bucks HP6 6EX (☎ Amersham 3791)

PLUMPTRE, Hon Francis Charles; s of 21 Baron FitzWalter; *b* 30 May 1963; *Style* - The Hon Francis Plumptre

PLUMPTRE, Hon Henry Bridges; s of 21 Baron FitzWalter; *b* 18 Feb 1954; *m* 1981, Susie, nee Payne; *Style* - The Hon Henry Plumptre

PLUMPTRE, Hon Julian Brook; s and h of 21 Baron FitzWalter; *b* 18 Oct 1952; *Educ* Radley; *Style* - The Hon Julian Plumptre

PLUMPTRE, Hon William Edward; s of 21 Baron FitzWalter; *b* 23 July 1959; *Style* - The Hon William Plumptre

PLUMPTRE, Hon Wyndham George; s of 21 Baron FitzWalter; *b* 24 April 1956; *Style* - The Hon Wyndham Plumptre

PLUMTREE, Air-Vice-Marshal Eric; CB (1974), OBE (1946), DFC (1940); s of William Plumtree; *b* 9 March 1919; *Educ* Eckington G S; *m* 1942, Dorothy Patricia, nee Lyall; 2 s (and 1 s decd); *Career* Dir Air Plans MOD (Air) 1968-69, AOC 22 Group RAF 1970-71, Air Vice-Marshal 1971, Cdr Southern Maritime Air Region 1971-73, Economy Project Officer (RAF) MOD 1973-74, Co-ordinator of Anglo-American Relations MOD (Air) 1977-; *Style* - Air Vice-Marshal Eric Plumtree CB OBE DFC; Wings Cottage, Ditchling, Sussex (☎ Hassocks 5539)

PLUNKET, 8 Baron (UK 1827); Robin Rathmore Plunket; s of 6 Baron Plunket (d 1938) and bro of 7 Baron (d 1975); *b* 3 Dec 1925; *Educ* Eton; *m* 1951, Jennifer, da of late Bailey Southwell, of S Africa; *Heir* bro, Hon Shaun Albert Frederick Sheridan Plunket; *Career* formerly Capt Rifle Brigade; *Style* - The Rt Hon the Lord Plunket; Rathmore, Melsetter, Zimbabwe; 39 Lansdowne gdns, SW8 (☎ 01 622 6049)

PLUNKET, Hon Mrs (Denis) Kiwa - Pamela Mary; da of late James Watherston, of Christchurch, NZ; *m* 1962, the Hon (Denis) Kiwa Plunket (d 1970), s of 5 Baron Plunket, GCMG, KCVO, KBE (d 1920); *Style* - The Hon Mrs Kiwa Plunket; 16 Town Hill, W Malling, Kent ME19 6QN

PLUNKET, Hon Shaun Albert Frederick Sheridan; s of 6 Baron Plunket and hp of bro, 8 Baron Plunket; *b* 5 April 1931; *Educ* Eton and L'Institut de Touraine; *m* 1, 1961, Judith Ann, da of late Gerard Patrick Power; 1 s (Tyrone Shaun Terence b 1966, Page of Honour to HM 197?-79), 1 da (Loelia Dorothé Alexandra b 1963); m 2, 1980, Mrs Elizabeth de Sancha, da of Gunar Danielson; *Career* formerly Lt Irish Gds and Dist Cmdt, Kenya Police (Reserve); *Clubs* White's; *Style* - The Hon Shaun Plunket; Hollonds,

Langton Green, near Tunbridge Wells, Kent

PLUNKETT, Hon Beatrice Mary; da of 19 Baron Dunsany by his 2 w, Sheila Victoria Katrin; *b* 1948; *Style* - The Hon Beatrice Plunkett

PLUNKETT, Hon Edward John Carlos; s and h of 19 Baron Dunsany by his 1 w Vera, da of Senhor de Sà Sottomaior, of São Paolo, Brazil, and formerly w of -- Bryce; *b* 10 Sept 1939; *Educ* Eton and Slade School of Fine Art; *Style* - The Hon Edward Plunkett; c/o The Rt Hon The Lord Dunsany, Dunsany Castle, Co Meath, Republic of Ireland (☎ 046 25198)

PLUNKETT, Hon Jonathan Oliver; s and h of 16 Baron Louth; *b* 4 Nov 1952; *Educ* BSc; *Style* - The Hon Jonathan Plunkett; c/o The Rt Hon The Lord Louth, Gardone, Holmfield Drive, St Brelade, Jersey, Channel Islands

PLUNKETT, Hon Olivia Jane; da of 16 Baron Louth; *b* 1953; *Style* - The Hon Olivia Plunkett

PLUNKETT, Hon Otway Jeremy Oliver; s of 16 Baron Louth; *b* 1954; *Style* - The Hon Otway Plunkett

PLUNKETT, Hon Mrs Randal - Gwendoline Mary; da of E A Cowling, of Torquay; *m* (Feb) 1936, the Hon Randal Patrick Ralph Oliver Plunkett (d July 1936, s of 14 Baron Louth); *Style* - The Hon Mrs Randal Plunkett

PLUNKETT, Hon Stephanie Patricia; da of 16 Baron Louth; *b* 1963; *Style* - The Hon Stephanie Plunkett

PLUNKETT, Hon Timothy James Oliver; s of 16 Baron Louth; *b* 1956; *Style* - The Hon Timothy Plunkett

PLUNKETT-ERNLE-ERLE-DRAX, Lt-Cdr Henry Walter; JP (1971), DL (1979); only s of Admiral The Hon Sir Reginald Aylmer Ranfurly Plunkett-Ernle-Erle-Drax, KCB, DSO, JP, DL (2 s of 17 Baron Dunsany); *b* 18 March 1928; *Educ* RNC Dartmouth; *m* 1957, The Hon Pamela Rose, da of 1 Baron Weeks (d 1960); *Career* RN 1945-68, co dir, landowner, farmer, forester, Govr Milton Abbey Sch; *Recreations* skiing, shooting, fishing, tennis; *Clubs* Naval; *Style* - Lt-Cdr Henry Plunkett-Ernle-Erle-Drax, JP, DL; Charborough Park, Wareham, Dorset (☎ Sturminster Marshall 368)

PLUNKETT-ERNLE-ERLE-DRAX, Hon Mrs (Pamela Rose); *née* Weeks; da of Lt-Gen 1 and last Baron Weeks, KCB, CBE, DSO, MC, TD (d 1960); *b* Nov 1931; *m* 1957, Lt-Cdr Henry Plunkett-Ernle-Erle-Drax, RN (ret, n of 18 Baron Dunsany, DL, the author and playwright); 4 s; *Style* - The Hon Mrs Plunkett-Ernle-Erle-Drax; Charborough Park, Wareham, Dorset

PLURENDEN, Baroness - Dorothée Monica; da of Maj Robert Bateman Prust, OBE, of Vancouver, BC, Canada; *m* 1951, 1 and last Baron Plurenden (d 1978); *Style* - The Rt Hon the Lady Plurenden; Plurenden Manor, High Halden, Kent; 79b Elizabeth st, SW1

PLYMOUTH, 3 Earl of (UK 1905); Other Robert Ivor Windsor-Clive; DL (Salop 1961); also Baron Windsor (E 1529) and Viscount Windsor (UK 1905); s of 2 Earl of Plymouth, DL (d 1943, ggs of the Hon Robert Clive (s of 1 Earl of Powis and gs of Clive of India) by his w Baroness Windsor (da of 6 (and last but two) Earl of Plymouth of the 2 cr, a previous cr having been made for an illegitimate s of Charles II in 1675); she was twenty fifth in descent from William Fitz Walter (among whose bros were the ancestors of the Dukes of Leinster), castellan of Windsor Castle *temp* Maud, and from which office the first half of the family name derives); the 2 Earl's w was Lady Irene Charteris, 3 da of 11 Earl of Wemyss; *b* 9 Oct 1923; *Educ* Eton, Trin Cambridge; *m* 1950, Caroline, da of Edward Rice, of Dane Court, Eastry, Kent (Edward's mother was Hon Helen Godley, da of 1 Baron Kilbracken); 3 s, 1 da; *Heir* s, Viscount Windsor; *Career* late Capt Coldstream Gds; KStJ, FRSA; memb Standing Commission on Museums & Galleries; *Style* - The Rt Hon Earl of Plymouth DL; 48 Burton Court, Franklins

Row, SW3 (☎ 01 730 7115); Oakly Park, Ludlow, Salop

PLYMOUTH, Dowager Countess of - Lady Irene Corona; *née* Charteris; da of 11 Earl of Wemyss (d 1937); *b* 1902; *m* 1921, 2 Earl of Plymouth, PC (d 1943); 3 s, 1 da; *Career* formerly sr Cmdt ATS; DStJ; *Style* - The Rt Hon the Dowager Countess of Plymouth; 12 Kings gdns, Hove 3, E Sussex

POANANGA, Maj-Gen Brian Matauru; CB (1980), CBE (1977, OBE 1967, MBE 1962); s of Henare Poananga; *b* 2 Dec 1924; *Educ* RMC Duntroon Australia; *m* 1948, Doreen Mary Porter; 2 s, 1 da; *Career* Ch of Gen Staff New Zealand Army 1978-; *Style* - Major-General Brian Poananga, CB, CBE; c/o Ministry of Defence, Wellington, New Zealand (☎ Wellington 722 760)

POCHIN, Sir Edward Eric; CBE (1959); s of Charles Davenport Pochin; *b* 22 Sept 1909; *Educ* Repton, St John's Cambridge; *m* 1940, Constance Margaret Julia (d 1971), da of T H Tilly; 1 s, 1 da; *Career* memb Scientific Staff of MRC 1941, dir Dept of Clinical Research UCH Med Sch 1946-74, Horton Smith Prize 1945, Antoine Bédère Lectr 1979, memb Int Cmmn on Radiological Protection 1959, chm 1962-69, emeritus memb 1977; rep UN Scientific Ctee on Effects of Atomic Radiation, memb Nat Radiological Protection Bd; FRCP 1946, kt 1975; *Clubs* Athenaeum, Oriental; *Style* - Sir Edward Pochin, CBE; c/o National Radiological Protection Board, Harwell, Didcot, Oxon

POCOCK, Air Vice-Marshal Donald Arthur; CBE (1975, OBE 1957); s of late A Pocock; *b* 5 July 1920; *Educ* Crouch End; *m* 1947, Dorothy Monica Griffiths; 2 s, 3 da; *Career* Cmdt-Gen RAF Regt 1973-75; gen man Iran British Aerospace Dynamics Gp 1976-79; dir Metallurgical Plantmakers' Fedn, British Metalworking Plantmakers' Assoc, Ironmaking and Steelmaking Plant Contractors' Assoc 1980-; *Style* - Air Vice-Marshal Donald Pocock, CBE; Brincliffe, Dence Park, Herne Bay, Kent (☎ Herne Bay 4773)

POCOCK, Gordon James; s of Leslie Pocock; *b* 27 March 1933; *Educ* Royal Liberty Sch Romford, Keble Oxford; *m* 1959, Audrey Singleton; *Career* sr dir marketing British Telecom 1979-; *Style* - Gordon Pocock Esq; 2 Queensberry Place, Friars Lane, Richmond, Surrey TW9 1NW (☎ 01 940 7118)

POETT, Gen Sir (Joseph Howard) Nigel; KCB (1959, CB 1952), DSO* (1945), idc, psc; s of late Maj-Gen J H Poett, CB, CMG, CBE; *b* 20 Aug 1907; *Educ* Downside, RMC Sandhurst; *m* 1937, Julia, da of E J Herrick, of NZ; 2 s, 1 da; *Career* Maj-Gen 1951, Lt-Gen 1958, Gen 1962, Gen Officer Cmdg-in-Chief Southern Command 1958-61, C-in-C Far East Land Forces 1961-63; *Clubs* Army and Navy; *Style* - General Sir Nigel Poett, KCB, DSO*; Swaynes Mead, Great Durnford, Salisbury, Wilts

POIRIER, Lady Anne Thérèse; *née* Bennet; da of 9 Earl of Tankerville (d 1980); *b* 18 Oct 1956 (twin sis of 10 Earl); *m* 1981, Timothy, s of Joseph Poirier, of Comox, BC, Canada; *Style* - Lady Anne Poirier

POLAND, Rear-Adm Edmund Nicholas; CB (1967), CBE (1962); s of late Maj Raymond A Poland, RMLI; *b* 19 Feb 1917; *Educ* RNC Dartmouth; *m* 1941, Pauline Ruth Margaret Pechell; 3 s, 1 da (and 1 da decd); *Career* Cdr 1950, Capt 1956, Rear-Adm 1965, Dir of Under Sea Warfare (Naval) MOD 1962, Ch of Staff to C-in-C Home Fleet 1965-68, ret; v-pres Scottish Assoc for the Care and Resettlement of Offenders 1979-; *Clubs* New (Edinburgh); *Style* - Rear-Admiral Edmund Poland, CB, CBE; Bryant's Cottage, Burgate Cross, nr Fordingbridge, Hants

POLAND, Richard Domville; CB (1973); s of late Maj R A Poland, RMLI; *b* 22 Oct 1914; *Educ* RNC Dartmouth; *m* 1948, Rosalind Frances, da of late Surgeon-Captain H C Devas; 1 s, 1 da; *Career* Under-Sec Miny Transport 1964-70, DOE 1970-74, Sec Int Maritime Industry Forum 1976-78; chm Kent Branch CPRE 1980-; *Style* - Richard Poland Esq, CB; Downs House, Blunden

Lane, Yalding, Kent ME18 6JD (☎ Hunton 337)

POLE, *see* Carew Pole

POLE, Peter John Chandos; s and h of Sir Peter Van Notten Pole, 5 Bt; *b* 27 April 1952; *m* 1973, Suzanne Norah, da of Harold Raymond Hughes; *Style* - Peter Pole Esq; 49 Doonan rd, Nedlands 6009, W Australia

POLE, Sir Peter Van Notten; 5 Bt (GB 1791); s of late Arthur Chandos Pole and kinsman of Sir Cecil Pery Van-Notten-Pole, 4 Bt (d 1948); *b* 6 Nov 1921; *Educ* Guildford G S; *m* 1949, Jean Emily, da of late Charles Douglas Stone; 1 s, 1 da; *Heir* s, Peter John Chandos Pole; *Career* 1939-45 war as Flt-Sgt RAAF, accountant FASA, ACIS; *Style* - Sir Peter Pole, Bt; 5 Sandpiper Mews, 10 Perina Way, City Beach, WA 6015, Australia

POLLARD, Maj-Gen (Charles) Barry; s of Leonard Charles Pollard (d 1980); *b* 20 April 1927; *Educ* Ardingly and Selwyn Cambridge; *m* 1954, Mary, da of Jack Sydney Weyes (d 1970); 3 da; *Career* RE 1947, GSO 1 MOD 1967, directing staff, Staff Coll 1967-68, CRE 3 Div 1969-71, Col GS 3 Div 1971-72, CCRE 1 (Br) Corps 1972-74, RCDS 1975, Ch Engr BAOR 1976-79, Nat Dir Project Trident (Trident Trust) 1980-; *Recreations* ocean sailing, golf, squash; *Clubs* Army & Navy; *Style* - Major-General Barry Pollard; Yateley, Coombe rd, Salisbury (☎ Salisbury 5493)

POLLARD, Sir (Charles) Herbert; CBE (1957, OBE 1946, MBE 1943); s of late Charles Pollard; *b* 23 Oct 1898; *Educ* Blackpool; *m* 1, 1922, Elsie (d 1970), da of Charles Crain; 1 da; m 2, 1971, Hilda M Levitch; *Career* City Treasurer Kingston upon Hull 1929-61, fin adviser to Assoc of Municipal Corpns 1951-61, memb ctees and working parties arranged by govt depts on education, housing, police and local authority finance; OStJ 1962, kt 1962; *Style* - Sir Herbert Pollard, CBE; Hale Barns, Elloughton, Brough, N Humberside (☎ Brough 667206)

POLLEN, Hon Mrs; Hon Daphne; *née* Baring; da of 3 Baron Revelstoke (d 1934); sis-in-law of late Guy Liddell, CB, CBE, MC; *b* 15 Feb 1904; *m* 1926, Arthur (d 1968), er s of Arthur Pollen (n of Sir Richard Pollen, 3 Bt); 2 s, 4 da; *Style* - The Hon Mrs Pollen; Cray Cottage, Harpsden, Henley-on-Thames, Oxon

POLLEN, Sir John Michael Hungerford; 7 Bt (GB 1795); s of late Lt-Cdr John Francis Hungerford Pollen RN and kinsman of Sir John Lancelot Hungerford Pollen, 6 Bt (d 1959); *b* 6 April 1919; *Educ* Downside, and Merton Oxford; *m* 1, 1941 (m dis 1956), Angela Mary Oriana, da of Maj F J Russi, MC; 1 s, 1 da; m 2, 1957, Diana Alice, da of late A E Timbrell; *Heir* s, Richard John Hungerford Pollen; *Career* Capt RA; *Style* - Sir John Pollen, Bt; Manor House, Rodbourne, Malmesbury, Wilts; Lochportain, Isle of North Uist, Outer Hebrides

POLLEN, Peregrine Michael Hungerford; s of late Sir Walter Michael Hungerford Pollen, MC, JP; *b* 24 Jan 1931; *Educ* Eton, and Ch Ch Oxford; *m* 1958, Patricia Helen Barry; 1 s, 2 da; *Career* Exec Dep Chm Sotheby Parke Bernet & Co 1975-; *Clubs* Brooks's; *Style* - Peregrine Pollen Esq; Norton Hall, Mickleton, Glos (☎ Mickleton 218)

POLLEN, Richard John Hungerford; s and h of Sir John Michael Hungerford Pollen, 7 Bt; *b* 3 Nov 1946; *m* 1971, Christianne, da of Sir (William) Godfrey Agnew, KCVO; 1 s, 1 da; *Style* - Richard Pollen Esq

POLLINGTON, Elisabeth, Viscountess; Lady Elisabeth Hariot; *née* Grimston; da of 6 Earl of Verulam (d 1973), and hp to Lordship of Forrester of Corstorphine; *b* 1939; *m* 1958 (m dis 1972), Viscount Pollington (now 8 Earl of Mexborough), s & h of 7 Earl of Mexborough (d 1980); *Style* - Elisabeth, Viscountess Pollington; 75 Cadogan sq, SW1

POLLINGTON, Viscount; John Andrew Bruce Savile; s and h of 8 Earl of Mexborough; *b* 30 Nov 1959; *Style* - Viscount Pollington; Arden Hall, Helmsley, Yorks

POLLOCK, Alexander; MP (C) Moray and Nairn 1979-; s of Robert Faulds Pollock, OBE; *b* 21 July 1944; *Educ* Rutherglen Acad, Glasgow Acad, BNC Oxford, Edinburgh U (LLB); *m* 1975, Verena Francesca Gertraud Alice Ursula Critchley; 1 s, 1 da; *Career* slr, advocate Scottish Bar 1973-, memb Commons Select Ctee on Scottish Affairs 1979-; *Style* - Alexander Pollock Esq, MP; Drumdarrach, Forres, Moray, Scotland IV36 ODW

POLLOCK, David Frederick; s and h of Sir George Frederick Pollock, 5 Bt; *b* 13 April 1959; *Style* - David Pollock Esq

POLLOCK, Hon David Stephen Geoffrey; s of 2 Viscount Hanworth; *b* 16 Feb 1946; *Educ* Wellington Coll; Guildford Technical Coll; Sussex U; *m* 1968, Elizabeth Vambe; 1 da; *Style* - The Hon David Pollock; Folly Hill, Ewhurst, Surrey

POLLOCK, Sir George; QC (1951); s of William Mackford Pollock; *b* 15 March 1901; *m* 1, 1922, Doris Evelyn Main (d 1977); 1 s, 1 da; m 2, 1977, Mollie, nee Pedder, widow of J A Van Santen; *Career* barr Gray's Inn 1928, Bencher 1948, Recorder of Sudbury 1946-51, dir British Employers' Confedn 1954-65, sr consultant to CBI on Int Labour Affairs 1965-69; kt 1959; *Style* - Sir George Pollock, QC; 62 Saffrons Court, Eastbourne, East Sussex

POLLOCK, Sir George Frederick; 5 Bt (UK 1866); s of Sir (Frederick) John Pollock, 4 Bt (d 1963); *b* 13 Aug 1928; *Educ* Eton and Trin Cambridge; *m* 1951, Doreen Mumford, da of late Norman Ernest Keown Nash, CMG; 1 s, 2 da; *Heir* s, David Frederick Pollock; *Career* 2 Lt 17/21 Lancers 1948-49, slr 1956, artist-photographer 1963-; Hon FRPS (Pres 1978), FIIP, FRSA; *Style* - Sir George Pollock, Bt; Netherwood, Stones Lane, Westcott, nr Dorking, Surrey (☎ Dorking 5447)

POLLOCK, Adm of the Fleet Sir Michael Patrick; GCB (1971, KCB 1969, CB 1966), MVO (1952), DSC (1944); s of late C A Pollock; *b* 19 Oct 1916; *Educ* RNC Dartmouth; *m* 1, 1940, Margaret Steacy (d 1951); 2 s, 1 da; m 2, 1954, Marjory Helen Reece, nee Bisset; 1 step da; *Career* RN 1930, Cdr 1950, Capt 1955, Rear-Adm 1964, Vice-Adm 1968, Adm 1970, Controller of the Navy 1970-71, Ch of Naval Staff and First Sea Lord 1971-74, First and Principal Naval ADC to the Queen 1972-74; Bath King of Arms 1976-; *Style* - Admiral of the Fleet Sir Michael Pollock, GCB, MVO, DSC; The Ivy House, Churchstoke, Montgomery, Powys SY15 6DU (☎ Churchstoke 426)

POLLOCK, Hon Richard Charles Standish; s of 2 Viscount Hanworth; *b* 1951; *Educ* Wellington Coll and Trinity Coll Cambridge; *Career* Capt Roy Yeo TAVR (General List); *Style* - The Hon Richard Pollock; Folly Hill, Ewhurst, Cranleigh, Surrey

POLLOCK, Hon Mrs (Rosemary Tyrwhitt); da and co-heiress of Baroness Berners, *qv*; *b* 20 July 1931; *m* 1959, Kelvin Alexander Pollock; 2 s; *Style* - The Hon Mrs Pollock; Malt House, Hollingbourne, Kent

POLLOCK, Lady Zinnia (Rosemary); *née* Denison; da of 4 Earl of Londesborough (d 1937); *b* 1937; *m* 1, 1957 (m dis 1961) Peter Comins; 1 s; m 2, 1961 (m dis 1964), John David Leslie Melville; m 3, 1964 (m dis 1967), Maj Hugh Cantlie; 1 s; m 4, 1968, Ralph John Hamilton Pollock ; *Style* - Lady Zinnia Pollock; Grove Farm, Stoke Hammond, Milton Keynes, Bucks

POLTIMORE, 7 Baron (UK 1831); Sir Mark Coplestone Bampfylde; 12 Bt (E 1641); s of Capt the Hon Anthony Gerard Hugh Bampfylde (d 1969) and gs of 6 Baron (d 1978); *b* 8 June 1957; *Educ* Radley; *Heir* unc Hon David Cecil Warwick Bampfylde; *Style* - The Rt Hon the Lord Poltimore; Boyton House, Woodbridge, Suffolk

POLTIMORE, Baroness - Margaret Mary; da of 4 Marquis de la Pasture (cr France 1768); *m* 1918, 6 Baron Poltimore (d 1978); *Style* - The Rt Hon the Lady Poltimore; c/o Coombe Lea, Malmesbury, Wilts

POLWARTH, 10 Lord (S 1690); Henry Alexander Hepburne-Scott; TD, DL (Roxburgh 1962); s of Master of Polwarth, JP, DL (d 1942), and Elspeth, JP (da of Rt Rev Archibald Campbell, DD, DCL, sometime Bp of Glasgow and Galloway, by his w, Hon Helen, nee Brodrick, da of 8 Viscount Midleton, JP); suc gf (9 Lord Polwarth, CBE, JP, DL, who m Edith, da of Sir Thomas Buxton, 3 Bt, GCMG) 1944; descended from Sir David Home, of Wedderburn, who *floruit* c 1418, and whose bro Sir Alexander Home of that Ilk was ancestor of Lord Home of the Hirsel; *b* 17 Nov 1916; *Educ* Eton, King's Cambridge; *m* 1, 1943, Caroline (m dis 1969), da of Capt Robert Hay (d 1939), er bro of Sir Bache Hay, 11 Bt (d 1966, since when Btcy dormant); 1 s, 3 da; m 2, 1969, Jean, da of Adm Sir Angus Cunninghame Graham of Gartmore and of Ardoch, KBE, CB, and formerly w of Charles Jauncey, QC; 2 step s, 1 step da; *Heir* s, Master of Polwarth; *Career* Maj Lothians & Border Horse NW Europe 1944-45; CA, Govr Bank of Scotland 1966-72, dir 1974-, chm Gen Accident Gp 1968-1972; Min of State Scotland 1972-74; dir: ICI 1974-, Canadian Pacific Ltd 1975-, Sun Life Assur of Canada 1975-, Halliburton Co (USA) 1974-; Chllr Aberdeen U 1966, Hon LLD St Andrews, Aberdeen, Hon DLitt Heriot-Watt, DUniv Stirling, FRSE, FRSA; *Recreations* country pursuits and the arts; *Clubs* Brooks's, Pratt's, New (Edinburgh); *Style* - The Rt Hon The Lord Polwarth, TD, DL; Harden, Hawick, Roxburghshire (☎ 2069); 37 St James's Place, SW1 (☎ 01 499 9789)

POLWARTH, Master of; Hon Andrew Walter Hepburne-Scott; s and h of 10 Lord Polwarth; *b* 30 Nov 1947; *Educ* Eton and Trin Hall Cambridge; *m* 1971, Isabel Anna, da of Maj John Freville Henry Surtees, OBE, MC; 2 s, 1 da; *Style* - The Master of Polwarth; 72 Cloncurry st, SW6

POMEROY, Hon Rosamond Mary; da of 8 Viscount Harberton, OBE (d 1956); *Clubs* Sailing; *Style* - The Hon Rosamond Pomeroy; 38 Thurloe sq, SW7; The Cottage in the Lane, Swaines Lane, Bembridge, IOW

POMEROY, Maj Hon Robert William; s of 8 Viscount Harberton, OBE (d 1956); bro of 9 Viscount (d 1980) and bro & hp of 10 Viscount; *b* 1916; *Educ* Eton; *m* 1953, Anne, da of Sir Arthur Colegate, MP (d 1956); 2 s; *Career* Major Welsh Gds 1945, ret 1960; *Clubs* Boodle's; *Style* - Maj the Hon Robert Pomeroy; Rockfield House, Nunney, nr Frome, Somerset (☎ Nunney 208)

POMFRET, Surgn Rear-Adm Arnold Ashworth; CB (1957), OBE (1941); s of John Pomfret; *b* 1 June 1900; *Educ* Manchester U, Postgrad at London, Capetown and Oxford; *m* 1928, Carlene Blundstone; 1 s, 2 da; *Career* Surgn Cdr 1934, Surgn Capt 1944, Surgn Rear-Adm 1954, MO i/c RN Hosp Plymouth, and Command MO Plymouth 1954-57; QHS 1954-57; CStJ 1957; *Style* - Surgeon Rear-Admiral Arnold Pomfret CB OBE; Passlands, Forton, Chard, Somerset

POND, Prof Sir Desmond Arthur; s of Thomas Arthur Pond; *b* 2 Sept 1919; *Educ* John Lyons's Harrow, St Olave's SE1, Clare Cambridge, Univ Coll Hosp; *m* 1945, Margaret Helen, MD, nee Jordan; 3 da; *Career* sr lectr Dept Clinical Neurophysiology Maudsley Hosp & consulting psychiatrist UCH 1952-66, memb MRC 1968-72, HB Williams Visiting Prof Australian & NZ Coll Psychiatrists 1968, Riddell Memorial Lectr Newcastle U 1971; Pres RCPsych 1978-; kt 1980; *Style* - Professor Sir Desmond Pond; 5 Arlesey Close, Lytton Grove, SW15 2EX (☎ 01 788 2903)

PONSONBY OF SHULBREDE, 3 Baron (UK 1930); Thomas Arthur Ponsonby; s of 2 Baron Ponsonby of Shulbrede (d 1976, whose f, the 1 Baron, was bro of 1 Baron Sysonby, n on his f's side to 1 Baron de Mauley, and paternally ggs of 3 Earl of Bessborough), and of Hon Elizabeth Bigham, da of 2 Visc Mersey, PC, CMG, CBE (d 1956); *b* 23 Oct 1930; *Educ* St Ronan's Sch, Bryanston, Hertford Coll Oxford; *m* 1, 1956 (m dis 1973), Ursula Mary, da of Cdr Thomas Stanley Lane Fox-Pitt, OBE, RN; 1 s, 3 da; m 2, 1973, Maureen Estelle Campbell-Tiech, da of Alfred William Windsor; *Heir* s Hon Frederick Matthew Thomas Ponsonby; *Career* Councillor 1956-65, Alderman

1964-74, Roy Borough of Kensington and Chelsea, Leader Labour Gp 1968-73, Chm of Council GLC 1976-77, Chm London Convention Bureau 1977-, Bd of Trustees Community Projects Foundn 1978-, Tourism Soc 1980-, Gen Sec Fabian Soc 1964-76, Pres Galleon World Travel Assoc Ltd 1977-, Govr LSE 1970-; contested (L) Heston and Isleworth gen election 1959; Opposition Spokesman and Whip, House of Lords; *Style* - The Rt Hon the Lord Ponsonby of Shulbrede; 19 Morpeth Mansions, Morpeth Terrace, SW1P 1ER (☎ 01 828 0164)

PONSONBY, Sir Ashley Charles Gibbs; 2 Bt (UK 1956), MC (1945); s of Col Sir Charles Edward Ponsonby, 1 Bt, TD (d 1976) and of Hon Winifred, da of 1 Baron Hunsdon (d 1935); *b* 21 Feb 1921; *Educ* Eton and Balliol Oxford; *m* 1950, Lady Martha Butler, da of 6 Marquess of Ormonde, CVO, MC (d 1971); 4 s; *Heir* s, Charles Ashley Ponsonby; *Career* md Schroder Wagg & Co Ltd; chm Colville Estate Ltd, Trans-Oceanic Trust Ltd; vice-pres Equitable Life Assurance Soc 1980-; dir Rowntree Mackintosh Ltd and other cos; Ld-Lt of Oxfordshire 1980-; DL (Oxon 1974); *Clubs* Brooks's; *Style* - Sir Ashley Ponsonby, Bt, MC, HM Lord-Lieut for Oxfordshire; Woodleys, Woodstock, Oxon (☎ 811422)

PONSONBY, Arthur Mountifort Longfield; s of late Maj the Hon Cyril Myles Brabazon Ponsonby, MVO, Gren Gds (2 s of 8 Earl of Bessborough) by his 1 w, Rita, da of Lt-Col Mountifort John Courtenay Longfield; hp (to Irish Earldom and UK Barony only) of 10 Earl of Bessborough; *b* 11 Dec 1912; *Educ* Harrow, Trin Cambridge; *m* 1, 1939, Patricia (d 1952), da of Col Fitzhugh Lee Minnigerode, of Virginia, USA; 1 s, 1 da; m 2, 1956 (m dis 1963), Anne Marie, formerly w of Prince George Galitzine and da of Lt-Gen (Baron) Sir Rudolf Carl (von) Slatin (Pasha) GCVO KCMG CB; m 3, 1963, Madeleine Lola Margaret, da of Maj-Gen Laurence Douglas Grand CB CIE CBE; 2 s; *Career* Capt Welsh Gds WW II; *Style* - Arthur Ponsonby Esq; Castle Mary, Cloyne, Co Cork, Eire

PONSONBY, Charles Ashley; s and h of Sir Ashley Charles Gibbs Ponsonby, 2 Bt, MC; *b* 10 June 1951; *Educ* Eton; *Style* - Charles Ponsonby Esq

PONSONBY, Hon Carolyn Mary; da of late 2 Baron Sysonby, DSO; *b* 1938; *Style* - The Hon Carolyn Ponsonby

PONSONBY OF SHULBREDE, Elizabeth, Baroness - Hon Elizabeth Mary; *née* Bigham; da of 2 Viscount Mersey, CMG, CBE, PC (d 1956); *b* 1905; *m* 1929, 2 Baron Ponsonby of Shulbrede (d 1976); *Style* - The Rt Hon Elizabeth, Lady Ponsonby of Shulbrede; Shulbrede Priory, Lynchmere, Haslemere, Surrey; 17 South End, Kensington sq, W8

PONSONBY, Hon Frederick Matthew Thomas; s and h of 3 Baron Ponsonby of Shulbrede; *b* 27 Oct 1958; *Educ* Holland Park Sch and Cardiff U; *Style* - The Hon Frederick Ponsonby; 95 Elgin Cres, W11

PONSONBY, Hon Julia Mary; da of 3 Baron Ponsonby of Shulbrede; *b* 1960; *Style* - The Hon Julia Ponsonby; c/o 63 Marine Parade, Brighton, E Sussex

PONSONBY, Hon Laura Mary; da of 2 Baron Ponsonby of Shulbrede (d 1976); *b* 1935; *Style* - The Hon Laura Ponsonby

PONSONBY, Lady Martha; *née* Butler; da of 6 Marquess of Ormonde, CVO, MC (d 1971); *b* 1926; *m* 1950, Capt Sir Ashley Charles Gibbs Ponsonby, MC, 2 Bt; *Style* - Lady Martha Ponsonby; Woodleys, Woodstock, Oxon

PONSONBY, Hon Rachael Elizabeth Emma; da of 3 Baron Ponsonby of Shulbrede; *b* 1964; *Style* - The Hon Rachel Ponsonby; c/o 63 Marine Parade, Brighton, E Sussex

PONSONBY, Hon Thomas Maurice; TD, DL (Glos); s and h of 6 Baron de Mauley; *b* 2 Aug 1930; *Educ* Eton; *m* 1956, Maxine Henrietta, da of late William Dudley Keith Thellusson; 2 s; *Career* High Sheriff of Glos 1978, Lt-Col The Wessex Yeo; *Style* - The Hon Thomas Ponsonby, TD, DL; The Common, Little Faringdon, Lechlade, Glos

PONSONBY, Hon Lady; Hon Winifred Marian; *née* Gibbs; da of 1 Baron Hunsdon of Hunsdon (d 1935); *b* 1886; *m* 1912, Col Sir Charles Edward Ponsonby, 1 Bt TD (d 1976); *Style* - The Hon Lady Ponsonby; Garrett House, Woodstock, Oxon

PONTÉ, Lady Jennifer Jane; *née* Curzon; da of 6 Earl Howe, CBE; *b* 1941; *m* 1962, Alan Joseph Ponté; 4 s, 1 da; *Style* - Lady Jennifer Ponté; Ardeley Bury, nr Stevenage, Herts

PONTIN, Sir Frederick William (Sir Fred Pontin); *b* 24 Oct 1906; *Educ* Sir George Monoux G S Walthamstow; *m* Dorothy Beatrice Mortimer; 1 da; *Career* founder Pontins Ltd 1946, Pontinental Ltd 1963, chm and jt md Pontins Ltd 1946-79, Pontinental (HS) Ltd 1972-79; kt 1976; *Style* - Sir Fred Pontin; 55 Park Lane, W1 (☎ 01 499 1205)

POOLE, 1 Baron (UK 1958); Oliver Brian Sanderson Poole; CBE (1945), TD, PC (1963); s of late Donald Louis Poole, whose family connections with Lloyd's stretch back two centuries to when Henry Poole (d c 1793) did business at Lloyd's Coffee House; *b* 11 Aug 1911; *Educ* Eton, Ch Ch Oxford; *m* 1, 1933 (m dis 1951), Betty Margaret, da of Capt Dugald Gilkison and Janet, nee Harcourt Vernon (ggggda of 1 Baron Vernon); 1 s, 3 da; m 2, 1952 (m dis 1965), Daphne Wilma Kenyon, da of late Eustace Bowles (himself gs of 6 Earl of Macclesfield), and formerly w of Brig Algernon Heber Percy, DSO; m 3, 1966, Barbara Ann, da of E A Taylor; *Heir* s Hon David Charles Poole; *Career* Warwicks Yeo 1934, MP (C) Oswestry Div of Salop 1945-50, chm Con Party Organisation 1955-57, vice-chm 1963-64, memb of Lloyds, formerly dir S Pearson & Son Ltd, Trustee Nat Gallery 1973-; Hon DSc City U 1970; *Style* - The Rt Hon the Lord Poole, CBE, TD, PC; 24 Campden Hill Gate, Duchess of Bedford's Walk, W8 (☎ 01 937 6466)

POOLE, Hon Mrs (Anne Rosemary Dorothea); da of 1 Baron Croft, CMG, TD, PC, (d 1947) and Hon Nancy, da of 1 Baron Borwick; *b* 1918; *m* 1946, Fl Lt Herbert Edmund Poole, RAF; 3 s; *Style* - The Hon Mrs Poole; Knight's Hill, Sawbridgeworth, Herts

POOLE, Hon David Charles; s and h of 1 Baron Poole, CBE, TD, PC; *b* 6 Jan 1945; *m* 1, 1967, Fiona, da of John Donald; 1 s; m 2, 1975, Philippa, da of Mark Reeve, of King's Somborne, Hants; *Style* - The Hon David Poole; 30 Avenue D'Elyau, Paris 75116, France

POOLE, Isobel Anne; da of John Cecil Findlay Poole; *b* 9 Dec 1941; *Educ* Oxford H S for Girls, Edinburgh U; *Career* Advocate 1964, Sheriff of the Lothian and Borders (travelling commission) 1979-; *Style* - Sheriff Poole; 5 Randolph Place, Edinburgh EH3 7TQ (☎ 031 225 1931)

POOLE, Michael John Ruscombe; s of John Chichester Poole, MC, CBE (d 1968); *b* 15 March 1930; *Educ* Downside; *m* 1959, Pamela Nicola, da of Evan Jones (d 1967); 2 c; *Career* dir Hawkes Wills Ltd; *Recreations* tennis, gardening; *Style* - Michael Poole Esq; 11 Courtfield gdns, W13 OEY (☎ 01 997 7392)

POORE, Lady; Amelia; da of Senor Santiago Guliemone, of Estancia La Blanca, Estacion Acuna, Corrientes, Argentine Republic; *m* 1922, Sir Edward Poore, 5 Bt (d 1938); *Style* - Lady Poore; Curuzu Cuatia, Corrientes, Argentina

POORE, Sir Herbert Edward; 6 Bt (GB 1795); s of Sir Edward Poore, 5 Bt (d 1938); *b* April 1930; *Heir* unc, Nasionceno Poore; *Style* - Sir Herbert Poore, Bt; Curuzu Cuatia, Corrientes, Argentine Republic

POORE, Nasionceno; s of Herbert Poore (d 1905) and bro of 5 Bt (d 1938); hp of n, Sir Herbert Edward Poore, 6 Bt; *b* 1900; *m* Juana Borda (d 1943); 3 s, 3 da; *Style* - Nasionceno Poore Esq

POORE, Roger Dennistoun; s of Lt-Col Roger Alvin Poore DSO; *b* 19 Aug 1916; *Educ* Eton, King's Cambridge; *m* 1949, Mrs Peta Farley; 1 da; *Career* chm and md Norton Villers Triumph Ltd 1973-, Federated Trust Corpn Ltd 1967-; chm: Manganese Bronze Holdings Ltd 1963-,

The Scottish & Mercantile Investment Trust Ltd 1971-, dir Scottish Cities Investment Trust Ltd 1953-, memb Lloyd's 1950-; *Style* - Roger Poore Esq; 33 Phillimore gdns, W8 (☎ 01 937 1384)

POPE, Anthony; s of Lt-Col Albert Victor Pope (d 1976); *b* 25 April 1933; *Educ* Melbourne G S Victoria Australia; *m* 1965, Cynthia, nee Walker; 1 s, 1 da; *Career* dir: Eldridge Pope & Co Ltd 1960-, Hants & Dorset Mineral Water Co Ltd 1977-, Barnham Broom Golf & Country Club 1979-; *Recreations* shooting, farming; *Clubs* Cavalry & Guards; *Style* - Anthony Pope Esq; Hamlet House, Chetnole, Sherborne, Dorset (☎ Yetminster 872325)

POPE, Andrew Lancelot; CMG (1972), CVO (1965), OBE (1959); s of Maj Andrew Noble Pope, OBE (d 1941); *b* 27 July 1912; *Educ* Harrow; *m* 1, 1938 (m dis); m 2, 1948, Ilse, da of late K Pipperger, of Frayn, Austria; 1 step da; *Career* Counsellor Bonn 1962-72, dir Conf Bd NY, Gerling Global Gen and Reinsurance Co Ltd; *Style* - Andrew Pope Esq, CMG, CVO, OBE; Goldhill Grove, Lower Bourne, Farnham, Surrey (☎ Farnham 21662)

POPE, Sir (Sidney) Barton; s of Henry Pope; *b* 18 Feb 1905; *Educ* Pulteney G S, S Australia; *m* 2, 1944, Ada Lilian, da of late J BHawkins; 2 s, 2 da; *Career* formerly md Pope Products Ltd S Aust, chm Pope Industries Ltd, pres S Aust Chamber of Manufacturers 1947-49, patron SA Assoc for Mental Health; kt 1959; *Style* - Sir Barton Pope; Swan Reach, SA 5354, Australia

POPE, Vice-Adm Sir (John) Ernle; KCB (1976); s of Cdr R K C Pope; *b* 22 May 1921; *Educ* RNC Dartmouth; *Career* RN 1935, Capt 1960, Flag Offr Flotillas Western Fleet 1969-71, Ch of Staff to C-in-C Western Fleet 1971-74, Rear-Adm 1969, Vice-Adm 1972, Ch of Staff to Cdr Allied Naval Forces S Europe 1974; *Clubs* Army and Navy; *Style* - Vice-Adm Sir Ernle Pope, KCB; Homme House, Much Marcle, Herefordshire

POPE, Geoffrey George; s of Sir George Reginald Pope; *b* 17 April 1934; *Educ* Epsom Coll, Imperial Coll London; *m* 1961, Rosemary Frances Harnden; 2 s; *Career* Dep Dir (Weapons) Roy Aircraft Establishment 1979-; FRAeS; *Style* - Geoffrey Pope Esq; 22 Rosemary Lane, Rowledge, Farnham, Surrey (☎ Frensham 2426)

POPE, Sir George Reginald; s of George James Pope (d 1930); *b* 25 March 1902; *Educ* Clapham Parochial Sch; *m* 1930, Susie Annie, da of John O Hendy; 1 s; *Career* gen man The Times 1965-67, dir Times Newspapers Ltd 1967-76, Kingsway Press Ltd; kt 1967; *Style* - Sir George Pope; 57 West Drive, Cheam, Surrey (☎ 01 6424754)

POPE, Sir Joseph Albert; s of Albert Henry Pope; *b* 18 Oct 1914; *Educ* Sch of Arts and Crafts Cambridge, King's Coll London; *m* 1940, Evelyn Alice, da of Rev Robert Henry Gallagher; 1 s, 2 da; *Career* Prof of Mech Engineering Nottingham U 1949-60, Vice-Chllr U of Aston in Birmingham 1969-79, chm TecQuipment Gp Nottingham 1975-, dir John Brown & Co Ltd 1970-, Royal Worcester Ltd 1979, chm W Midlands Econ Planning Council 1977-, gen tres British Assoc 1975-; Hon LLD Birmingham 1979, Hon DUniv Heriot-Watt 1979, Hon DSc Aston 1979, Belfast 1980, Salford 1980; kt 1980; *Style* - Sir Joseph Pope; 3 Mapperley Hall Drive, Nottingham NG3 5EP (☎ Nottingham 621146)

POPE, Air Vice-Marshal John Clifford; CB (1963), CBE (1959); s of George Newcombe Pope (d 1938); *b* 27 April 1912; *Educ* Tiverton Sch, RAF Coll Cranwell; *m* 1950, Christine Agnes, da of Alfred Hames; 1 s, 2 da; *Career* RAF 1931, Group Capt 1956, Air Cdre 1961, CE Flying Training Command 1960-61, AOC and Cmdt RAF Tech Coll Henlow 1961-63, Sr Tech Staff Officer Transport Command 1963-66, Air Vice-Marshal 1964, life v-pres RAF Boxing Assoc; *Style* - Air Vice-Marshal John Pope, CB, CBE; Dilston, 47 Oxford rd, Stone, nr Aylesbury, Bucks (☎ Aylesbury 748467)

POPE, Hon Mrs (Jacqueline Dorothy Mametz); *née* Best; da of 8 Baron Wynford, MBE, DL; *b* 9 Nov 1946; *Educ* St Mary's Wantage; *m* 1969, Jeremy James Richard, s of Philip Pope, of Dorchester; 3 s; *Career* Social Sec to Lady Erskine of Rerrick 1966-68 (wife of former Govr NI); *Recreations* gardening, skiing, squash; *Style* - The Hon Mrs Pope; Field Cottage, Compton Abbas West, Maiden Newton, Dorset (☎ Maiden Newton 20469)

POPE-HENNESSY, Sir John Wyndham; CBE (1959, MBE 1944); s of late Maj-Gen Ladislaus Herbert Richard Pope-Hennessy, CB, DSO (d 1942) and late Dame Una Pope-Hennessy DBE; *b* 13 Dec 1913; *Educ* Downside, Balliol Oxford; *Career* dir and sec Victoria and Albert Museum 1967-73, dir British Museum 1974-76, Consultative Chm Dept of European Paintings Metropolitan Museum New York 1977-, Prof of Fine Arts New York Univ 1977-; FBA 1955, FSA, FRSL, kt 1971; *Style* - Sir John Pope-Hennessy, CBE; 1130 Park ave, New York, NY 10028, USA

POPHAM, Maj-Gen Christopher John; s of late Gordon F B Popham; *b* 2 April 1927; *Educ* Merchant Taylors' Sch; *m* 1950, Heather Margaret, da of late Lt-Col H R W Dawson; 2 s; *Career* Assist Ch of Staff (Intelligence) Supreme Headquarters Allied Powers Europe 1979-; *Style* - Maj-Gen Christopher Popham; B7010, SHAPE, Belgium

POPPER, Prof Sir Karl Raimund; s of Simon Siegmund Carl Popper, of Vienna; *b* 28 July 1902; *Educ* Vienna U; *m* 1930, Josefine Anne, da of Josef Henniger, of Vienna; *Career* Prof of Logic and Scientific Method LSE London U 1949-69, Emeritus Prof 1969-; pres Aristotelian Soc 1958-59 and British Soc for the Philosophy of Science 1959-61, Membre de l'Institut de France, Fell Int Academy for Philosophy of Science, Hon Memb Roy Soc of NZ, Foreign Hon Memb American Acad of Arts and Sciences, Hon Fell LSE, Grand Decoration of Honour in Gold (Austria); author of books on various philosophical problems; Hon LLD, Hon DLitt, Hon LittD, FBA, FRS, kt 1965; *Style* - Sir Karl Popper; Fallowfield, Manor rd, Penn, Bucks (☎ Penn 2126)

POPPLEWELL, Hon John Arnold; s of Baron Popplewell (Life Peer) (d 1977); *b* 1928; *m* 1951; *Style* - The Hon John Popplewell

POPPLEWELL, Baroness - Lavinia; da of Samuel Rainbow, of Sherburn-in-Elmet; *m* 1922, Baron Popplewell (Life Peer) (d 1977); *Style* - The Rt Hon the Lady Popplewell; North View, Moor Lane, Sherburn-in-Elmet, Leeds

POPPLEWELL, Oliver Bury; QC (1969); s of late Frank Popplewell; *b* 15 Aug 1927; *Educ* Charterhouse, Queens' Cambridge; *m* 1954, Catharine Margaret Storey; 4 s (and 1 s decd); *Career* barr Inner Temple 1951, Bencher 1978, Recorder Burton-on-Trent 1970-71, Dep Chm Oxon QS 1970-71, a Recorder of the Crown Court 1972-, chm & independent memb Wages Cncls, memb MCC Ctee; *Clubs* MCC, Hawks (Cambridge), Blakeney Sailing; *Style* - Oliver Popplewell Esq QC; 2 Crown Office Row, Temple, EC4 (☎ 01 353 9337); Lime Tree Farm, Chartridge, Bucks (☎ The Lee 356)

PORBANDAR, Maharaja of; Lt-Col HH Maharaja Rana Saheb, Shri Sir Natwarsinhji Bhavsinhji; KCSI (1929); s of HH the Rana Saheb Shri Bhavsinhji Bahadur of Porbandar; *b* 30 June 1901; *Educ* Rajkumar Coll, Rajkot; *m* 1, 1920, Princess Rupaliba MBE (d 1943), da of late Thakore Saheb of Limbdi KCSI KCIE; m 2, 1954, Anantkunver; *Career* captained first All-India Cricket Team (toured England 1932), composer, author; *Style* - Lt-Col HH the Maharaja of Porbandar; Porbandar, Saurashtra, India; Firgrove, Ootacamund, S India

PORCHER, Michael Somerville; CMG (1962), OBE (1960); s of late Geoffrey Lionel Porcher; *b* 9 March 1921; *Educ* Cheltenham Coll, St Edmund Hall Oxford; *m* 1955, Mary Lorraine, nee Tweedy; 2 s; *Career* Dep Ch Sec British Guiana 1956, Colonial Sec British Honduras 1960, Ch Sec 1961, ret 1964; Sec (Operations Div) Royal Nat Life-Boat Institution 1964-; *Style* - Michael Porcher

Esq, CMG, OBE; Bladon, Worth Matravers, nr Swanage, Dorset

PORCHESTER, Lord; Henry George Reginald Molyneux Herbert; KBE (1976), DL (Hants 1965); s and h of 6 Earl of Carnarvon; *b* 19 Jan 1924; *Educ* Eton; *m* 1956, Jean Margaret, da of Hon Oliver Malcolm Wallop (s of late 8 Earl of Portsmouth); 2 s, 1 da; *Career* late Lt Roy Horse Gds; Hon Col 115 (Hants Fortress) Engineer Regt (TA) 1963; appointed Racing Manager to HM the Queen 1970; former Pres Thoroughbred Breeders' Assoc, Chm Agricultural Research Cncl 1978-, V-Pres Game Research Assoc 1967-, Chm Stallion Advsy Ctee Betting Levy Bd 1974-, Pres Roy Ag Soc 1980-, CC Hants 1954, County Alderman 1956-74, V-Chm County Council 1971-74; *Clubs* White's, Portland; *Style* - Lord Porchester KBE DL; Milford Lake House, Burghclere, Newbury, Berks (☎ Highclere 253387)

PORRITT, Baron (Life Peer UK 1973); Brigadier Sir Arthur Espie Porritt; 1 Bt (UK 1963), GCMG (1967), GCVO (1970), CBE (1945); s of Ernest E Porritt, VD, MD, FRCS (d 1950), of NZ; *b* 10 Aug 1900; *Educ* Wanganui Collegiate Sch NZ, Otago U NZ, Magdalen Oxford, St Mary's Hosp London; *m* 1946, Kathleen Mary, da of late A S Peck and Mrs Windley; 2 s, 1 da; *Heir* (to Btcy) s, Hon Jonathon Espie Porritt; *Career* Sergeant Surgn to HM the Queen 1952-67, Govr-Gen of New Zealand 1967-72; Pres RSM 1966-67, RCS 1960-63, BMA 1960-61; formerly Hon Surgn St Mary's Hosp, Roy Masonic Hosp, King Edward VII Hosp for Officers and Hosp of St John and Elizabeth; Consulting Surgn King Edward VII Convalescent Home for Officers, Osborne and Roy Hosp Chelsea, Hon Consulting Surgn to the Army 1954-67; Chm Medical Advisory Ctee Miny of Overseas Dvpt, memb International Olympic Ctee 1934, Chm Empire Games Fedn 1948-67, V-Pres 1968-, Red Cross Commr for NZ in UK, Chm African Medical and Research Foundn 1973-, Arthritis and Rheumatism Council 1973-, Roy Masonic Hosp 1973-; KStJ, Legion of Merit (USA); *Clubs* Buck's; *Style* - Brig The Rt Hon the Lord Porritt, GCMG, GCVO, CBE; 57 Hamilton Ter, NW8 (☎ 01 286 9212)

PORRITT, Hon Jeremy Charles; s of Baron Porritt, GCMG, GCVO, CBE (Life Peer and 1 Bt); *b* 1953; *Educ* Eton; *m* 1980, S Penny, da of J H Moore, of London, Ontario; *Style* - The Hon Jeremy Porritt

PORRITT, Hon Jonathon Espie; s and h of Baron Porritt, GCMG, GCVO, CBE (Life Peer and 1 Bt); *b* 6 July 1950; *Educ* Eton, Magdalen Oxford; *Style* - The Hon Jonathon Porritt

PORTAL OF HUNGERFORD, Baroness (UK 1945); Rosemary Ann Portal; da of 1 Viscount Portal of Hungerford, KG, GCB, OM, DSO, MC (d 1971, when the Viscountcy became extinct) and of Joan Margaret, da of late Sir Charles Glynn Welby, 5 Bt; *b* 12 May 1923; *Heiress* sis, Hon Mavis Elizabeth Alouette Portal; *Career* formerly Section Officer WAAF; *Style* - The Rt Hon the Lady Portal of Hungerford; West Ashling House, Chichester, West Sussex

PORTAL, Sir Francis Spencer; 5 Bt (UK 1901), DL (Hants 1967); s of Sir Spencer John Portal, 4 Bt (d 1955); *b* 27 June 1903; *Educ* Winchester, Ch Ch Oxford, McGill U Montreal; *m* 1, 1930, Rowena (d 1948), da of late Paul Selby, of Johannesburg; 2 da; m 2, 1950, Jane Mary, da of late Albert Henry Williams, OBE; 2 s, 1 da; *Heir* s, Jonathan Francis Portal; *Career* Capt late Welsh Gds, Gds Armoured Div (Belgian Croix de Guerre, 2 cl); chm YMCA Nat Commission 1968, dep chm Winchester Diocesan Bd of Finance, memb Bishop's Council Diocese of Winchester, Pres Portals Holdings Ltd, Master Clothworkers' Co 1970, High Sheriff Hants 1963; *Style* - Sir Francis Portal, Bt, DL; Burley Wood, Ashe, nr Basingstoke, Hants (☎ Basingstoke 770269)

PORTAL, Jonathan Francis; s and h of Sir Francis Spencer Portal, 5 Bt; *b* 13 Jan 1935; *Educ* Marlborough, Edinburgh U; *Style* - Jonathan Portal Esq; c/o Burley Wood, Ashe, nr Basingstoke, Hants RG25 3AG

PORTAL OF HUNGERFORD,

Viscountess - Joan Margaret; da of late Sir Charles Glynne Earle Welby, 5 Bt, CB; *b* 1898; *m* 1919, 1 Viscount Portal of Hungerford (d 1971, when the Viscountcy became ext); *Style* - The Rt Hon the Viscountess Portal of Hungerford; West Ashling House, nr Chichester, Sussex

PORTAL, Hon Mavis Elizabeth Alouette; da of Viscount Portal of Hungerford (d 1971 when Viscountcy became ext) and sis of Baroness Portal of Hungerford; *b* 13 June 1926; heiress to Barony of Portal of Hungerford; *Style* - The Hon Mavis Portal

PORTAL, Admiral Sir Reginald Henry; KCB (1949, CB 1946), DSC (1916); s of late Edward Robert Portal, JP, DL; *b* 6 Sept 1894; *Educ* RNC Dartmouth; *m* 1926, Helen, da of late Frederick Anderson; 2 s, 2 da; *Career* Naval Rep on Joint Chiefs of Staff Ctee (Australia) 1946-47, Flag Officer Air (Home) 1947-51, ret 1951; *Style* - Admiral Sir Reginald Portal, KCB, DSC; Overton House, Queen Camel, Yeovil, Somerset

PORTARLINGTON, 7 Earl of (1 1785); George Lionel Yuill Seymour Dawson-Damer; also Baron Dawson (I 1770), Viscount Carlow (I 1776); s of Air Cdre Viscount Carlow (k on active serv 1944) and gs of 6 Earl of Portarlington (d 1959); *b* 10 Aug 1938; *Educ* Eton; *m* 1961, Davina, da of late Sir Edward Windley, KCMG, KCVO; *Heir* s, Viscount Carlow; *Career* Page of Honour to HM the Queen 1953-55; dir: G S Yuill & Co Ltd Sydney, Cold Storage Holdings Ltd London, Queensland Trading Holding Co Ltd (Brisbane), Australian Stock Breeders Co Ltd (Brisbane); Pres Aust Malaysia Singapore Assoc; *Clubs* Union (Sydney); *Style* - The Rt Hon the Earl of Portarlington; 19 Coolong rd, Vaucluse, NSW 2030, Australia (☎ Sydney 337 3013)

PORTEOUS, Colonel Patrick Anthony; VC (1942); s of the late Brig-Gen C Porteous; *b* 1 Jan 1918; *Educ* Wellington, RMA Woolwich; *m* 1955, Deirdre, da of late Eric King; 3 da; *Career* AMS HQ Southern Cmd 1959-60, Col Junior Leaders Regt RA 1960-63, Col Gen Staff War Office later MOD 1963-66, Cdr Rheindahlen Garrison 1966-69, ret 1970; *Style* - Colonel Patrick Porteous, VC; Flat 1, Binderton House, Lavant, nr Chichester, W Sussex (☎ Chichester 528169)

PORTER, Alfred Ernest; CSI (1947), CIE (1942); s of late F L Porter; *b* 2 Nov 1896; *Educ* Manchester G S, Corpus Christi Oxford; *Career* Manchester Regt 1915, Machine Gun Corps 1916, ICS 1922-48; *Style* - Alfred Porter Esq, CSI, CIE; The Old Hall, Chawleigh, Chulmleigh, Devon EX18 7HH (☎ Chulmleigh 280)

PORTER, Prof Sir George; s of late John Smith Porter; *b* 6 Dec 1920; *Educ* Thorne G S, Leeds U (BSc), Emmanuel Cambridge (MA, PhD, ScD); *m* 1949, Stella Jean, da of late G A Brooke; 2 s; *Career* dir Royal Institution of Gt Britain, Fullerian Prof of Chemistry 1966-, Hon Prof of Chemistry 1966-, Hon Prof of Physical Chemistry U of Kent at Canterbury 1966-, Visiting Prof Dept of Chemistry UCL 1967- and Imperial Coll London 1978-, memb Council and Science Bd SRC 1976-, Pres Nat Assoc for Gifted Children 1975-, R & D Soc 1977-, Jt Nobel Prize for Chemistry 1967; FRS 1960, FRIC, kt 1972; *Clubs* Athenaeum; *Style* - Professor Sir George Porter; The Royal Institution, 21 Albemarle st, W1X 4BS (☎ 01 409 2992)

PORTER, George Barrington; MP (C) Bebington and Elesmere Port 1979-; s of Kenneth William Porter; *b* 11 June 1939; *Educ* Birkenhead Sch, Univ Coll Oxford; *m* 1965, Susan Carolyn James; 2 s, 2 da; *Career* slr 1965; Councillor Birkenhead County Borough Council 1967-74, Wirral Borough 1975-79; *Style* - George Porter Esq, MP; 42 Village rd, Oxton, Birkenhead, Merseyside L43 6TY (☎ 051 652 1006)

PORTER, Ivor Forsyth; CMG (1963), OBE (1944); s of Herbert Porter; *b* 12 Nov 1913; *Educ* Barrow G S, Leeds U; *m* 1951, Ann (m dis 1961), da of late Dr John Speares; m 2, 1961, Katerina, da of A T Cholerton; 1 s, 1 da; *Career* formerly Dir Atlantic Region Research Dept FCO,

Ambass UK Delegation to Geneva Disarmament Conf 1968-71, Ambass to Senegal, Guinea, Mali and Mauritania 1971-73; *Clubs* Travellers', PEN; *Style* - Ivor Porter Esq, CMG, OBE; 17 Redcliffe rd, SW10

PORTER, John Andrew; JP (1952); s of late Horace Augustus Porter, DFC, JP; *b* 18 May 1916; *Educ* Radley, Sidney Sussex Cambridge; *m* 1941, Margaret Isobel Wisnom; 2 da; *Career* chm: Hastings & Thanet Building Soc 1972-78, Anglia Building Soc 1978-; chm Gravesham Div of JPs 1975-, pres Gravesend Con Assoc 1966-78; *Style* - John Porter Esq JP; Leaders, Hodsoll st, nr Wrotham, Kent TN15 7LH (☎ Fairseat 822260)

PORTER, James Forrest; s of Ernest Porter; *b* 2 Oct 1928; *Educ* Salford G S, Dudley Training Coll, LSE, London U Inst of Educn; *m* 1952, Dymphna, da of Leo Francis Powell; 2 da; *Career* dir Adult Literacy Support Services Fund 1977-, dir Commonwealth Institute 1978-, chm World Education Fellowship 1979-; C'wlth Fell Australia 1977, FRSA 1978, Hon FCP 1978; *Clubs* Royal Commonwealth Society; *Style* - James Porter Esq; Commonwealth Institute, Kensington High st, W8 6NQ (☎ 01 602 3252); House by the Water, Bolney ave, Shiplake, Oxon (☎ Wargrave 2187)

PORTER, Air Marshal Sir (Melvin) Kenneth Drowley; KCB (1967, CB 1959), CBE (1945, OBE 1942); s of late Edward Ernest Porter; *b* 19 Nov 1912; *Educ* No 1 Sch of Technical Training Halton, RAF Coll Cranwell; *m* 1940, Elena, da of F W Sinclair; 2 s, 1 da; *Career* RAF 1928, served 1939-45, actg Air Cdre 1944, Air Cdre 1958, CSO Fighter Command 1956-59, IDC 1959, Cmdt No 4 Sch of Technical Training RAF St Athan and Air Offr Wales 1960, Dir-Gen of Ground Training Air Miny 1961-63, Air V-Marshal 1962, Dir-Gen of Signals (Air) MOD 1963-66, AOC-in-C Maintenance Command 1966-70, Air Marshal 1966, ret 1970; dir Technical Educational Projects Dept of Education Univ Coll Cardiff 1970-74, conslt 1975; Legion of Merit (USA); *Style* - Air Marshal Sir Kenneth Porter KCB, CBE; c/o Lloyds Bank Ltd, Redland Branch, 163 Whiteladies rd, Clifton, Bristol BS8 8RW

PORTER, Leslie; s of Henry Alfred Porter; *b* 10 July 1920; *Educ* Holloway County Sch; *m* 1949, Shirley Cohen; 1 s, 1 da; *Career* chm Tesco Stores (Holdings) Ltd 1973-, memb Lloyd's 1964- (John Poland Syndicate); *Style* - Leslie Porter Esq; 19 Chelwood House, Gloucester sq, W2 2SY (☎ 01 262 2911)

PORTER, Hon Sir Murray Victor; s of late V Porter; *b* 20 Dec 1909; *Educ* Brighton (Victoria) G S Australia; *m* 1932, Edith Alice Johnston, da of late C A Johnston; 2 da; *Career* 2 AIF 1941-45, MLA (Lib) Sandringham Victoria 1955-70, Govt Whip 1955-56, Assist Min 1956-58, Min for Forests 1958-59, Local Govt 1959-64, Public Works 1964-70, Agent-Gen for Victoria in London 1970-76; kt 1970; *Clubs* Melbourne Cricket, Roy Melbourne Golf, Roy Automobile of Victoria; *Style* - The Hon Sir Murray Porter; Flat 7, The Point, 405 Beach rd, Beaumaris, Vic 3193, Australia

PORTER, Sir Robert Evelyn; s of Frederick Windmill Porter; *b* 10 July 1913; *Educ* St Peter's Collegiate Sch Adelaide SA, Adelaide U; *m* 1942, June Leah, da of late Stanley Perry, OBE, of Perth, WA; *Career* Partner F W Porter & Co (memb of Stock Exchange of Adelaide) 1937-; dir: Standard Chartered Australia Ltd, Castalloy Ltd, Freeman Motors Ltd; Lord Mayor of Adelaide 1968-71, Pres RSPCA SA 1956-, Consul of Belgium for SA and Northern Territory 1949-; kt 1978; *Style* - Sir Robert Porter; 1 Edwin Ter, Gilberton, SA 5081, Australia (☎ 44 1455)

PORTER, Robert Stanley; CB (1972), OBE (1959); s of S R Porter; *b* 17 Sept 1924; *Educ* St Clement Danes Holborn Estate G S, New Coll Oxford; *m* 1, 1953 (m dis 1967), Dorothea Naomi, da of Rev Morris Seale; 1 da; m 2, 1967, Julia Karen, da of Edmund A Davies; *Career* Dir-Gen Economic Planning, Overseas Dvpt Administration FCO 1969-; *Clubs* Athenaeum; *Style* - Robert Porter Esq CB, OBE; Morland Cottage, Sheepstead, Marcham, Abingdon, Oxon (☎ Frilford

Heath 390458)

PORTER, Rt Hon Sir Robert Wilson; PC (NI 1969), QC (NI 1965); s of late Joseph Wilson Porter; *b* 23 Dec 1923; *Educ* Model Sch, Foyle Coll Londonderry, Queen's U Belfast; *m* 1953, Margaret Adelaide, da of late F W Lynas; 1 s, 1 da (and 1 da decd); *Career* barr (NI) 1950, Counsel to Attorney-Gen for NI 1963-64 and 1965, V-Chm 1959-61, Chm 1961-66 War Pensions Appeal Tribunal for NI, MP (U) Queen's U of Belfast 1966-69, Lagan Valley 1969-73, County Court Judge NI 1978-; kt 1971; *Style* - The Rt Hon Sir Robert Porter, PC, QC; Ardkeen, Marlborough Park North, Belfast, N Ireland BT9 6HL (☎ 666761)

PORTLAND, 9 Duke of (GB 1716); (Victor Frederick) William Cavendish-Bentinck; CMG (1942); also Baron Cirencester, Viscount Woodstock, Earl of Portland (E 1689), and Marquess of Titchfield (GB 1716); s of Frederick Cavendish-Bentinck (himself gs of Maj-Gen Lord Frederick Cavendish-Bentinck, CB, MP, 4 s of 3 Duke; His Grace was twice PM (1783 & 1807-09), though arguably his main achievement was as Home Sec 1794-1801; his f, the 2 Duke, was said to be the handsomest man in England, while his ggf, the 1 Earl of Portland who was such a favourite of William III, was, while also favoured with good looks, reputedly the richest subject in Europe; His (present) Grace is 1 cous twice removed of the recluse 5 Duke, who twice refused the Garter ("I knew I could not be a Knight of the Garter, or a member of White's - the only two things an Englishman cannot command" says St Barbe, Disraeli's caricature of Thackeray) and was a noted catacomb constructor at his seat, Welbeck Abbey; also of the 5 Duke's bro, Lord George Bentinck, the chief ally of Disraeli in the early years after the split from the Peelites); suc bro, 8 Duke of Portland, KBE, CMG, MC (d 1980); *b* 18 June 1897; *Educ* Wellington; *m* 1, 1924 (m dis 1948), Clothilde Bruce, da of late James Bruce Quigley, of Dallas, Texas; 1 da; m 2, 1948, Kathleen Elsie, da of Arthur Barry, of Montreal, and formerly w of Arthur Ritchie Tillotson; *Heir* (to all honours save the Dukedom and Marquessate), kinsman, Count (Henry Noel) Bentinck; *Career* late 2 Lt Gren Gds, entered Diplomatic Serv 1919, 1 Sec 1929 and Counsellor 1942, Chm Joint Intelligence Sub-Ctee on Chs of Staff 1939-45, Foreign Office Adviser to Dir of Plans 1942-45, Ambass to Poland 1945-47, ret 1947; chm of Council British Nuclear Forum; Grosses Verdienstkreuz, Germany; *Clubs* Turf, Beefsteak; *Style* - His Grace the Duke of Portland CMG; 21 Carlyle sq, SW3

PORTLAND, Gwyneth, Duchess of; Gwyneth Ethel; MBE; da of late John Wesley Edward, of Chettlewood Estate, and Montpelier, Jamaica, BWI, and widow of Col David Alexander John Bowie, MC, RA; *m* 1950, as his 2 w, 8 Duke of Portland, KBE, CMG, MC (d 1980); *Style* - Her Grace Gwyneth, Duchess of Portland MBE; Muthaiga, PO Box 47311, Nairobi, Kenya

PORTLAND, Ivy, Duchess of - Hon Ivy; DBE (1958); da of late Lord Algernon Charles Gordon-Lennox; *b* 1887; *m* 1915, 7 Duke of Portland, KG (d 1977); *Career* a Maid of Honour to Queen Alexandra 1912-15, Chm of Council Nat Assoc for Prevention of Tuberculosis; *Style* - Her Grace Ivy, Duchess of Portland DBE; Welbeck Woodhouse, Worksop, Notts; Langwell, Berriedale, Caithness

PORTLOCK, Rear-Adm Ronald Etridge; CB (1961), OBE (1947), DL (Greater London 1967); s of late Henry Portlock; *b* 28 June 1908; *Educ* RNC Dartmouth; *m* 1939, Angela, da of late Gerard Kirke Smith; *Career* RN 1922, Lt-Cdr 1938, Cdr 1943, Capt 1949, Rear-Adm 1959, Ch of Staff to C-in-C Far East Station 1959-61, ret 1961; ADC to the Queen 1958; *Style* - Rear-Adm Ronald Portlock, CB, OBE, DL; 1 Swan Court, Chelsea, SW3 (☎ 01 352 4390)

PORTMAN, 9 Viscount (UK 1873); Edward Henry Berkeley Portman; also Baron Portman (UK 1873); s of late Hon Michael Berkeley Portman (d 1959) (yr so f 7 Viscount); n of 8 Viscount (d 1967); *b* 22 April 1934; *Educ* Canford, RAC Cirencester; *m* 1, 1956 (m dis 1965) Rosemary Joy, da of Charles Farris; 1 s, 1 da; m 2, 1966, Penelope Anne Hassard, da of Trevor Allin; 4 s; *Heir* s, Hon Christopher Edward Berkeley Portman; *Career* farmer; *Clubs* White's; *Style* - The Rt Hon the Viscount Portman; Clock Mill, Clifford, Herefordshire (☎ Clifford 235)

PORTMAN, Hon Alexander Michael Berkeley; s of 9 Viscount Portman; *b* 1967; *Style* - The Hon Alexander Portman

PORTMAN, Hon Claire Elizabeth; da of 9 Viscount Portman; *b* 1959; *Style* - The Hon Claire Portman

PORTMAN, Hon Christopher Edward Berkeley; s and h of 9 Viscount Portman; *b* 30 July 1958; *Style* - The Hon Christopher Portman; c/o Clock Mill, Clifford, Hereford

PORTMAN, Hon Justin Trevor Berkeley; s of 9 Viscount Portman; *b* 1969; *Style* - The Hon Justin Portman

PORTMAN, Hon Matthew Gerald Berkeley; s of 9 Viscount Portman; *b* 1973; *Style* - The Hon Matthew Portman

PORTMAN, Hon Mrs Michael - Marjorie Karr; da of late Frederick William Harris; *m* 1938, as his 2 w, the Hon Michael Berkeley Portman (d 1959); 1 s, 1 da; *Style* - The Hon Mrs Michael Portman; Portman Lodge, Durweston, Blandford, Dorset

PORTMAN, Nancy, Viscountess - Nancy Maureen; da of Capt Percy Herbert Franklin, RN (ret); *m* 1946, as his 2 w, 8 Viscount Portman (d 1967); *Style* - The Rt Hon Nancy, Viscountess Portman; Sutton Waldron House, Blandford, Dorset

PORTMAN, Hon Piers Richard Berkeley; s of 9 Viscount Portman; *b* 1971; *Style* - The Hon Piers Portman

PORTSMOUTH, 9 Earl of (GB 1743); Gerard Vernon Wallop; also Baron Wallop (GB 1720), Viscount Lymington (GB 1720); s of 8 Earl of Portsmouth (d 1943) by his w Marguerite, nee Walker, originally of Kentucky and Chicago; *b* 16 May 1898; *Educ* Winchester and Balliol Oxford; *m* 1, 1920 (m dis 1936, she m 2, 1938, E J B How), Mary Lawrence, da of Waldron Kintzing Post, of Bayport, Long Island; 1 s, 1 da; m 2, 1936, Bridget (d 1979), da of late Capt Patrick B Crohan, RN, of Owlpen Manor, Glos; 1 s, 2 da; *Heir* s, Viscount Lymington; *Career* Hereditary Bailiff of Burley, New Forest; MP (U) Basingstoke Div of Hants 1929-34, V-Chm Hants War Ag Ctee 1939-47, V-Pres and Chm Country Landowners Assoc 1947-48, Pres Electors Union Kenya 1953-55, MLC Kenya (Corporate Memb for Ag) 1957-60, V-Chm East African Natural Resources Research Cncl 1963-; *Clubs* Buck's; *Style* - The Rt Hon the Earl of Portsmouth; c/o Estate Office, Farleigh Wallop, Basingstoke, Hants

PORTSMOUTH, 6 Bishop of (cr 1927) 1975-; Rt Rev Archibald Ronald McDonald Gordon; s of late Sir Archibald Gordon, CMG; *b* 19 March 1927; *Educ* Rugby Sch, Balliol Oxford, Cuddesdon Theological Coll; *Career* Deacon 1952, Priest 1953, Curate of Stepney 1952-55, Chaplain Cuddesdon Coll 1955-59, Vicar of St Peter Birmingham 1959-67, Res Canon Birmingham Cathedral 1967-71, Vicar of Univ Church of St Mary the Virgin with St Cross and St Peter in the East Oxford 1971-75, memb Church Assembly and Gen Synod, and Proctor in Convocation 1965-71, Chm Advsy Cncl for Church's Miny 1976-; *Style* - The Rt Rev the Lord Bishop of Portsmouth; Bishopswood, Fareham, Hants

PORTSMOUTH, Hon Mrs (Gladys Irene); da of Hon Sydney Byng (d 1920); *b* 1891; *m* 1910, Henry Portsmouth (d 1933); 1 s, 1 da; granted 1945 title, rank and precedence of a Viscount's da which would have been hers had her father survived to succeed to title of Viscount Torrrington; *Style* - The Hon Mrs Portsmouth; 6 The Drive, Oakley, nr Basingstoke, Hants (☎ Oakley 533)

POSFORD, John Albert; s of Capt Benjamin Ashwell Posford (d 1915); *b* 3 Sept 1914; *Educ* The Oratory Sch, King's Cambridge; *m* 1, 1940, Nell Margaret (d 1966), da of Capt Augustus Knight (d 1950); 1 s, 4 da; m 2, 1970, Jean Davidson, da of Col Alastair Gordon, MC, Roy Scots

Fus (d 1968); 2 s; *Career* sr partner and founder (1944) Posford, Pavry & Partners, Consulting Engineers to the ports of Felixstowe, Milford Haven and Sheerness; Queen's Award for Export Achievement 1979; chm Maritime Gp British Consultants Bureau 1979; FRSA; *Recreations* gardening; *Clubs* United Oxford and Cambridge; *Style* - John Posford Esq; Falkenham Lodge, Ipswich, Suffolk (☎ 039 48 246); 49 Eaton Mews South, SW1 (☎ 01 235 7446)

POSNETT, Sir Richard Neil; KBE (1980, OBE 1963), CMG (1976); s of Rev Charles Walker Posnett; *b* 19 July 1919; *Educ* Kingswood, St John's Cambridge; *m* 1; 2 s, 1 da; m 2, 1959, Shirley Margaret Hudson; 2 s, 1 da; *Career* barr Gray's Inn 1951, Colonial Office London 1958, FO 1964, Govr and C-in-C of Belize 1972-76, Dependent Territories Advr FCO 1977-79, British High Cmmr Kampala 1979, Govr and C-in-C of Bermuda 1980-; UK Cmmr British Phosphate Cmmrs 1978, Pres Kingswood Assoc 1980, KStJ 1972; *Style* - Sir Richard Posnett, KBE, CMG; Government House, Hamilton, Bermuda; Timbers, Northway, Godalming, Surrey (☎ Godalming 6869)

POSTAN, Lady Cynthia Rosalie; *née* Keppel; da of 9 Earl of Albemarle, MC, by his 1 w, Lady Judith Carington (*see* Keppel, Hon Walter); *b* 25 June 1918; *m* 1944, Prof (now Sir) Michael Moissey Postan, *qv*; 2 s (Basil David, b 9 June 1946, m 1968 Maria Carr; 1 s, 2 da; Alexander Henry Keppel, b 25 Aug 1948); *Style* - Lady Cynthia Postan; Penrallt Goch, Ffestiniog, Gwynedd; 2 Sylvester rd, Cambridge (☎ 0223 353314)

POSTAN, Sir Michael Moissey; s of Efim Postan, of Bessarabia; *b* Sept 1899; *m* 1, 1937, Eileen Power (d 1940); m 2, 1944, Lady Cynthia Rosalie Keppel, da of 9 Earl of Albemarle, MC (d 1979); 2 s; *Career* Lecturer in History UCL 1927-31, Lecturer in Economic Hist LSE 1931-35 (Hon Fell 1974), Lecturer in Econ Hist Cambridge U 1935-38, Prof of Econ Hist Cambridge U 1938-65, now Emeritus; Fell of Peterhouse 1935-65 (Hon Fell 1965-); FBA 1959, kt 1980; *Style* - Sir Michael Postan; 2 Sylvester rd, Cambridge; Penrallt Goch, Ffestiniog, Gwynedd

POTT, Sir Leslie; KBE (1962, CBE 1957); s of Charles Groves Pott; *b* 4 July 1903; *Educ* Manchester G S, Gonville and Caius Cambridge; *m* 1937, Norma (d 1978), da of Capt Kynaston Lyons-Montgomery; 1 s; *Career* Levant Consular Service 1924, Dep High Cmmr for the UK at Bombay 1950-52, Consul-Gen at Istanbul 1952-55, at Marseilles 1955-61, to Monaco 1957-61, ret 1962; *Style* - Sir Leslie Pott, KBE; Becking Spring, Hudnall Common, nr Berkhamsted, Herts HP4 1QJ (☎ Little Gaddesden 3409)

POTTER, Arthur Kingscote; CMG (1957), CBE (1946); s of late Richard Ellis Potter; *b* 7 April 1905; *Educ* Charterhouse, New Coll Oxford; *m* 1950, Hilda, da of late W A Butterfield, OBE; 1 da; *Career* ICS 1928, Ch Financial Officer (Brig) Mil Admin of Burma 1944-47, HM Treasury Rep in India, Pakistan and Burma 1947-50, Assist Sec HM Treasury 1950-56, Counsellor UK Deleg to NATO Paris 1956-65; *Style* - Arthur Potter Esq, CMG, CBE; Lower House, Bepton, Midhurst, W Sussex GU29 0JB

POTTER, Donald Charles; QC (1972); s of late Charles Potter; *b* 24 May 1922; *Educ* St Dunstan's Coll, LSE; *Career* barr Middle Temple 1948, Bencher Lincoln's Inn 1979, assist lectr in Law LSE 1947-49; *Clubs* Garrick; *Style* - Donald Potter Esq, QC; 37 Tufton st, SW1P 3QL

POTTER, His Honour Douglas Charles Loftus; s of John Charles Potter; *b* 17 Dec 1903; *Educ* Radley, Trin Oxford; *m* 1, 1934, Margaret Isabel (d 1979), da of Dr William Savile Henderson; 1 da; m 2, 1980, Nicole, da of Dr Eugene Charles Joseph Kayser; *Career* barr Inner Temple 1928, SE Circuit Herts and Essex Sessions; Judge of County Courts 1959-71, Willesden, Croydon and Kingston upon Thames; a Circuit Judge 1972-78; *Style* - His Honour Douglas Potter

POTTER, Ernest Frank; s of Frank William Potter; *b* 29 April 1923; *Educ* Dr Challoner's G S Amersham; *m* 1945,

Madge, nee Arrowsmith; 1 s; *Career* dir of finance and corporate planning Cable & Wireless Ltd 1977-79, dir of finance 1979-; FCMA, FCIS, MIMC; *Style* - Ernest Potter Esq; Long Meadow, Gorse Hill rd, Virginia Water, Surrey GU25 4AS

POTTER, Hon Mrs Elizabeth Sarah; da of Baroness David (Life Peer); *b* 1947; *m* 1966 (m dis 1977), Martin Anthony Potter; *Style* - The Hon Mrs Sarah Potter; Sedgwick Cottage, Dent, Cumbria

POTTER, His Honour Judge; Francis Malcolm; s of Francis Martin Potter; *b* 28 July 1932; *Educ* Rugby, Jesus Coll Oxford; *m* 1970, Bertha Villamil; 1 s, 1 da; *Career* barr Lincoln's Inn 1956, a Recorder of the Crown Court 1974-78, a Circuit Judge 1978-; *Style* - His Honour Judge Potter; 5 Fountain Court, Steelhouse Lane, Birmingham B4 6DR

POTTER, Sir (William) Ian; s of James William Potter; *b* 25 Aug 1902; *Educ* Sydney U; *m* 1975, Primrose C Dunlop; 2 da (by former m); *Career* principal ptnr Ian Potter & Co 1935-67, founder and govr of Ian Potter Foundn Ltd, chm Aust Elizabethan Theatre Trust 1968-, economist Fed Treasury Canberra 1933-35; chm: ASEA Electric (Aust) Pty Ltd, Atlas Copco Aust Pty Ltd, Associated Steamships Pty Ltd, Aust United Investment Co Ltd, Bulkships Ltd, McIlwraith McEacharn Ltd, Time-Life Int (Aust) Pty Ltd, Tricontinental Ltd; kt 1962; *Style* - Sir Ian Potter; 30 Sargood st, Toorak, Victoria 3142, Australia (☎ 24 4308)

POTTER, Maj-Gen Sir (Wilfrid) John; KBE (1968, CBE 1963, OBE 1951), CB (1966); s of late Maj Benjamin Henry Potter, OBE, MC; *b* 18 April 1913; *m* 1, 1943, Vivienne Madge (d 1973), da of late Capt Henry D'Arcy Medlicott Cooke; 1 s, 1 da; m 2, 1974, Mrs D Ella Purkis; 1 step s, 1 step da; *Career* Maj-Gen 1962, Transport Officer in Chief (Army) 1965-66, Dir of Movements (Army) MOD 1966-68, ret; Chm Traffic Cmmrs and Licensing Authority Western Traffic Area 1973-; *Style* - Major-General Sir John Potter KBE CB; Orchard Cottage, The Orchard, Freshford, Bath, Avon

POTTER, (Ronald) Jeremy; s of Alistair Richardson Potter; *b* 25 April 1922; *Educ* Clifton Coll, Queen's Oxford; *m* 1950, Margaret, da of Bernard Newman; 1 s, 1 da; *Career* formerly dep chm New Statesman, md Independent Television Publications Ltd 1970-79, chm Independent Television Books Ltd 1971-79, gp dir of Corporate Affairs London Weekend Television 1979-; dir Hutchinson Ltd 1978-, dep chm 1980-; pres Periodical Publishers Assoc 1978-79, chm Richard III Soc 1971-; FRSA; *Style* - Jeremy Potter Esq

POTTER, Mark Howard; QC (1980); s of Prof Harold Potter, LLD, PhD; *b* 27 Aug 1937; *Educ* Perse Sch Cambridge, Gonville and Caius Cambridge; *m* 1962, Undine Amanda Fay Miller; 2 s; *Career* assist supervisor Legal Studies Gonville and Caius, Queens' and Sidney Sussex Colls 1961-68; barr Gray's Inn 1961, memb Senate of Inns of Court and Bar 1976-79, Senate Law Reform Ctee 1976-; *Style* - Mark Potter Esq, QC; 6 St Mary's Grove, N1 2NT; Fountain Court, Temple, EC4 9DH (☎ 01 353 7356)

POTTER, Sir (Joseph) Raymond Lynden; s of Rev Henry Lynden; *b* 21 April 1916; *Educ* Haileybury Coll (now Life-Govr), Clare Cambridge; *m* 1939, Daphne Marguerite, da of Sir Crawford Douglas-Jones, CMG; 3 s, 1 da; *Career* dir Halifax Building Soc 1968-, chm 1974-; memb bd Warrington New Town Devpt Corpn 1969-, Wakefield Diocesan Bd of Finance 1960-; kt 1978; *Clubs* Hawks (Cambridge); *Style* - Sir Raymond Potter; 1 Prince's Gate, Halifax, W Yorks HX3 OEH, Halifax 61017

POTTER, Hon Mrs (Vanessa Jane); *née* Robson; da of Baroness Robson of Kiddington, JP; *b* 1949; *m* 1973, Jonathan Martin Potter; *Style* - The Hon Mrs Potter; Wood Farm House, Woodleys, Woodstock, Oxon

POTTS, Francis Humphrey; QC (1971); s of late Francis William Potts; *b* 18 Aug 1931; *Educ* Roy G S Newcastle upon Tyne, St Catherine's Soc Oxford; *m* 1971, Philippa Margaret Campbell, da of late J C H Le B Croke; 2 s, 2 step s; *Career* barr

Lincoln's Inn 1955, Bencher 1979, N Eastern Circuit 1955, a Recorder of the Crown Court 1972-; *Style* - Francis Potts Esq, QC; 11 King's Bench Walk, Temple, EC4 (☎ 01 353 3337)

POULETT, Countess - Margaret Christine; da of Wilfred John Peter Ball, of Reading; *m* 1968, as his 3 w, 8 Earl Poulett (d 1973, when the Earldom became ext, and the Barony became ext or dormant); *Style* - The Rt Hon the Countess Poulett; Ker du Pons, Route de Petit Port, St Brelade, Jersey

POUNCEY, Philip Michael Rivers; s of Rev George Ernest Pouncey; *b* 15 Feb 1910; *Educ* Marlborough, Queens' Coll Cambridge; *m* 1937, Myril Gros; 2 da; *Career* a dir Sothebys 1966-, Hon Keeper of Italian Drawings Fitzwilliam Museum 1975- FBA 1975; *Style* - Philip Pouncey Esq; 5 Lower Addison gdns, W14 8BG

POUND, Joan, Lady; Joan Amy; da of James Woodthorpe; *m* 1942, Sir Derek Allen Pound, 4 Bt (d 1980); *Style* - Joan, Lady Pound; Saham Grove Hall, Shipdham, Thetford, Norfolk

POUND, Sir John David; 5 Bt (UK 1905); s of Sir Derek Allen Pound, 4 Bt (d 1980); *b* 1 Nov 1946; *m* 1, 1968 (m dis 1978), Heather Frances O'Brien, da of Harry Jackson; 1 s; m 2, 1978, Penelope Ann, da of Grahame Rayden; *Heir* s, Robert John Pound; *Style* - Sir John Pound, Bt; 54 Lime Tree av, Findon Valley, Worthing, Sussex

POUND, Robert John; s and h of Sir John David Pound, 5 Bt; *b* 1973; *Style* - Robert Pound Esq

POUNDER, Rafton John; s of Cuthbert C Pounder; *b* 13 May 1933; *Educ* Charterhouse, Christ's Coll Cambridge; *m* 1959, Valerie Isobel, da of late Robert Stewart, MBE; 1 s, 1 da; *Career* MP (UU) Belfast S Oct 1963-Feb 1974; sec N Ireland Bankers' Assoc 1977-; *Style* - Rafton Pounder Esq; 29 Coastguard Lane, Orlock, Groomsport, Co Down

POUNDS, Maj-Gen Edgar George Derek; CB (1975); s of Edgar Henry Pounds, MBE, MSM; *b* 13 Oct 1922; *Educ* Reading Sch; *m* 1944, Barbara Winifred May Evans; 1 s, 1 da; *Career* Capt RM 1952, Maj 1960, Col 1970, Actg Maj-Gen 1973, Maj-Gen 1974, Cmdt Commanding Commando Forces RM 1973-76, ret; ch exec Br Friesian Cattle Soc 1976-, memb Exec Ctee Nat Cattle Breeders' Assoc 1978-; *Style* - Major-General Edgar Pounds, CB; Langdon, Burtons Way, Chalfont St Giles, Bucks HP8 4BW

POUT, Harry Wilfred; CB (1978), OBE (1959); *b* 11 April 1920; *Educ* East Ham G S, Imperial Coll London; *m* 1949, Margaret Elizabeth, nee Nelson; 3 da; *Career* Dep Controller Guided Weapons 1973, Guided Weapons and Electronics 1973-75, Air Systems 1975-79, Aircraft Weapons and Electronics 1979-80 MOD, defence consultant 1980-; *Style* - Harry Pout Esq, CB, OBE; Oakmead, Fox Corner, Worplesdon, Surrey (☎ 2223)

POWELL, Arthur Barrington; CMG (1967); s of late Thomas Powell; *b* 24 April 1918; *Educ* Cowbridge, Jesus Coll Oxford; *m* 1945, Jane, da of late Gen Sir George Weir, KCB, CMG, DSO; 4 s, 1 da; *Career* ICS 1939-47; Petroleum Attaché HM Embassy Washington 1962-64, Gas Div 1968-72, Reg Finance Div DOI 1972-76; exec dir Welsh Devpt Agency 1976-; *Clubs* United Oxford and Cambridge U; *Style* - Arthur Powell Esq, CMG; Croesllanfro House, Rogerstone, Gwent

POWELL, Anthony Dymoke; CBE (1956); s of late Lt-Col P L W Powell, CBE, DSO (of an ancient Welsh family claiming descent from the 'Second Royal Tribe' of Wales, and ninth in descent from one Roger Powell, who m Fortune, *née* Hakluyt, of the family that produced the geographer; Roger in turn was sixth in descent from Llywelyn ap Philip ap Meurig, whose yr bro was ancestor of Dr John Dee, another geographer (in a minor way) but better known as alchemist & wizard - he certainly looked the part, judging from Aubrey; how influential the Dr's naming (at Lord Dudley's request) of a propitious day for Elizabeth I's coronation was in bringing about the glories of the reign is, tho' a puzzling question, not beyond all conjecture;)

Mr Powell's mother was Maud, da of Edmund Wells-Dymoke (whose paternal great grandmother was a Dymoke of Scrivelsby); *b* 21 Dec 1905; *Educ* Eton, Balliol Oxford (Hon Fell 1974); *m* 1934, Lady Violet Pakenham, da of 5 Earl of Longford KP MVO (ka 1915) and aunt of Lady Antonia Fraser, *qv*; 2 s (Tristram, the TV director, and John Marmion Anthony Powell); *Career* author (notably of the *Dance to the Music of Time* sequence of novels); trustee Nat Portrait Gallery 1962-76; hon memb American Acad of Arts and Letters 1977; Hon DLitt Sussex 1971, Leicester 1976, Kent 1976, Oxon 1980; *Clubs* Travellers', Pratt's; *Style* - Anthony Powell Esq CBE; The Chantry, Frome, Somerset (☎ Nunney 314)

POWELL, Alice, Lady; Alicia Maria; da of Wilhelmus den Bode, of Utrecht; *m* 1980, as his 2 w, Sir Richard Powell, 3 Bt, MC (d 1980); *Style* - Alice, Lady Powell; Mackney, Brightwell-cum-Sotwell, Oxon (☎ Wallingford 37245)

POWELL, Albert Paul; s of late Albert Edward Powell; *b* 1 March 1940; *Educ* St Luke's Portsmouth, Law Society's Coll; *m* 1972, Avril Moira, nee Wylie; 1 s, 2 da; *Career* Capt Mid & Near East; slr; co dir: Cleveland Hldgs Ltd, Cleveland Bridge & Engrg Co Ltd, Cleveland Offshore Ltd, Robert Stevenson Ltd, Hughes & Ellison Ltd; *Recreations* rifle shooting, medal collecting; *Clubs* English XX; *Style* - Albert Powell Esq; 20 Edinburgh dve, Darlington, Co Durham (☎ 0325 57909)

POWELL, Hon Mrs; Hon Beryl; *née* Davies; da of Baron Davies of Penrhys (Life Peer); *b* 1947; *m* 1965, Colin James Powell; children; *Style* - The Hon Mrs Powell; Maesgwyn, Ton Pentre, Rhondda

POWELL, Brian David; s of T D L Powell (d 1970); *b* 20 Feb 1970; *Educ* Saltley Birmingham, Coleshill Warwicks, Trin Cambridge, U of New South Wales Australia; *m* 1957, Jean Mary, nee Stephenson; 3 da; *Career* fell Roy Soc of Chemistry 1962, fell Inst of Food Science & Technology 1971, mastership in Food Control 1980; dir Cadbury Ltd 1969, dir (Int Scientific Standards) Cadbury Schweppes Ltd 1980, chm Cocoa Growing Research Assoc, v-pres Int Office of Cocoa & Chocolate; *Recreations* silversmithing, industrial archaeology, walking, photography; *Style* - Brian Powell Esq; 427 Heath rd S, Northfield, Birmingham B31 2BB (☎ 475 4983)

POWELL, (Elizabeth) Dilys; CBE (1974); da of late Thomas Powell; *Educ* Bournemouth H S, Somerville Coll Oxford; *m* 1, 1926, Humfry Payne (d 1936); m 2, 1943, Leonard Russell (d 1974); *Career* film critic The Sunday Times 1939-76, TV film critic 1976-, film critic Punch 1979-; FRSL; *Style* - Miss Dilys Powell, CBE; 14 Albion st, Hyde Park, W2 (☎ 01 723 9807)

POWELL, His Honour Judge Watkin; Dewi Watkin; JP (Dyfed); s of W H Powell, AMICE; *b* 29 July 1920; *Educ* Penarth G S, Jesus Coll Oxford; *m* 1951, Alice, da of William Williams; 1 da; *Career* barr Inner Temple 1949; dep chm Merioneth and Cardigan QS 1966-71, Dep Recorder of Cardiff, Birkenhead, Merthyr Tydfil and Swansea 1965-71; Liaison Judge for Dyfed; a Circuit Judge 1972-; *Style* - His Honour Judge Watkin Powell, JP; Crown Court, Law Courts, Cathays Park, Cardiff

POWELL, Rt Hon (John) Enoch; MBE (1943), PC (1960), MP (UU) South Down 1974-; s of Albert Enoch Powell; *b* 16 June 1912; *Educ* King Edward's Birmingham, Trin Cambridge; *m* 1952, Margaret Pamela, nee Wilson; 2 da; *Career* MP (C) Wolverhampton SW 1950-74, Parly Sec Miny of Housing and Local Govt 1955-57, Fin Sec to the Treasury 1957-58, Min of Health 1960-63; *Style* - The Rt Hon Enoch Powell, MBE, MP; 33 South Eaton Place, SW1 (☎ 01 730 0988)

POWELL, James Richard Douglas; s and h of Sir Nicholas Folliott Douglas Powell, 4 Bt; *b* 17 Oct 1962; *Style* - James Powell Esq

POWELL, Sir Nicholas Folliott Douglas; 4 Bt (UK 1897); s of Sir Richard George Douglas Powell, MC, 3 Bt (d 1980); *b* 17 July 1935; *Educ* Gordonstoun; *m* 1960, Daphne Jean, da of Maj George Errington, MC; 1 s, 1 da; *Heir* s, James

Richard Douglas Powell; *Career* Lt Welsh Gds 1953-57; co dir; *Style* - Sir Nicholas Powell, Bt; Petrunella Coffee Estate, Box 58, Chipinga, Zimbabwe

POWELL, Sir Philip; OBE (1957); s of late Canon A C Powell; *b* 15 March 1921; *Educ* Epsom Coll, AA Sch of Architecture; *m* 1953, Philippa, da of Lt-Col C C Eccles; 1 s, 1 da; *Career* ptnr Powell & Moya (architects) 1946-, also Powell Moya & Partners 1976-; Roy Gold Medal for Architecture RIBA 1974, memb Roy Fine Art Commission 1969-, RA 1977, FRIBA, kt 1975; *Style* - Sir Philip Powell, OBE; 16 The Little Boltons, SW10 9LP (☎ 01 373 8620); 21 Upper Cheyne Row, SW3 (☎ 01 351 3881)

POWELL, Raymond; MP (L) Ogmore 1979-; s of Albert Powell; *b* 19 June 1928; *Educ* Pentre G S, Nat Council of Labour Colls, LSE; *m* 1951, Marion Grace Evans; 1 s, 1 da; *Career* memb S Wales Euro-Constituency Labour Party 1979-; *Style* - Raymond Powell Esq, MP; 8 Brynteg gdns, Bridgend, Mid-Glam (☎ Bridgend 2159)

POWELL, Sir Richard Royle; GCB (1967, KCB 1961, CB 1951), KBE (1954), CMG (1946); s of Ernest Hartley Powell; *b* 30 July 1909; *Educ* Queen Mary's G S Walsall, Sidney Sussex Coll Cambridge (Hon Fell 1972); *Career* Dep Sec Admiralty 1948-50, Dep Sec MOD 1950-56, Perm Sec MOD 1956-59, BOT 1960-68, dep chm Perm Ctee on Invisible Exports 1968-76; chm Alusuisse (UK) Ltd and subsid cos 1969-, Wilkinson Match Ltd 1979-80, Hon Pres 1981-; dir Philip Hill Investment Trust, Whessoe Ltd 1968-; chm Sandoz Gp of cos 1972-; dir Clerical, Medical & Gen Life Assurance Soc 1972-, BPB Industries Ltd 1973-; *Clubs* Athenaeum; *Style* - Sir Richard Powell, GCB, KBE, CMG; 56 Montagu sq, W1 (☎ 01 262 0911)

POWELL, Roger Stuart; s of Charles William Powell; *b* 14 April 1948; *Educ* King Alfred Coll Winchester; *m* 1969, Jane Mary, da of Bernard Wilfred Earley; 2 c; *Career* personal assist to Conrad Swan, York Herald of Arms, and R O Dennys, OBE, Somerset Herald, both 1965-69, to P Gwynne-Jones, Blue Mantle Pursuivant, 1975-78; genealogist Debrett's Ancestry Research 1978-; *Recreations* tennis, athletics; *Style* - Roger Powell Esq; 28 Loughwood Close, Boyatt Wood, Eastleigh, Hants (☎ 615843)

POWELL, Tim (Harry Allan Rose); MBE (1944), TD (1973); s of William Allan Powell (d 1954); *b* 15 Feb 1912; *Educ* Winchester, Pembroke Cambridge; *m* 1936, Elizabeth North, da of Leonard W North Hickley (d 1932); 2 da; *Career* Herts Yeo 1938, Col 1944-45 S E Asia (Head of Secretariat to Supreme Allied Cdr); md Massey-Ferguson Holdings Ltd 1962-78, chm 1970-80; vice-chm Holland & Holland Ltd; *Recreations* fishing, lapidary; *Clubs* Bucks, Bath, MCC; *Style* - Tim Powell Esq, MBE, TD; Ready Token, nr Cirencester, Glos (☎ Bibury 219); 12 Shafto Mews, Cadogan sq, SW1 (☎ 01 235 2707)

POWELL, Lady Violet (Georgiana); *née* Pakenham; da of 5 Earl of Longford, KP, MVO (d 1915); *b* 1912; *m* 1934, Anthony Dymoke Powell, CBE; 2 s; *Style* - Lady Violet Powell; The Chantry, Nr Frome, Somerset

POWELL, Victor George Edward; s of George Richard Powell; *b* 1 Jan 1929; *Educ* Beckenham G S, Durham U, Manchester U; *m* 1956, Patricia Copeland Allen; 3 s, 1 da; *Career* sr partner Victor G Powell Associates, Management Consultants, 1963-; dir and ch adviser ILO 1977-, dir Mosscare Housing Assoc Ltd 1974-; associate memb BIM 1957, Memb Inst Management Consultants 1968; *Style* - Victor Powell Esq; Inglewood, Coppice Lane, Disley, Stockport, Cheshire SK12 2LT (☎ Disley 2011)

POWELL-COTTON, Christopher; CMG (1961), MBE (1951), MC (1945), JP; s of Maj P H G Powell-Cotton; *b* 23 Feb 1918; *Educ* Harrow, Trin Cambridge; *Career* Uganda Admin: District Cmmr 1950, Provincial Cmmr 1955, Min of Security and External Relations 1961, ret; dir Powell-Cotton Museum of Nat History and Ethnography; landowner; *Clubs* MCC; *Style* - Christopher Powell-Cotton

Esq CMG MBE MC JP; Quex Park, Birchington, Kent (☎ Thanet 41836)

POWELL-JONES, John Ernest; CMG (1974); s of late Walter James Powell-Jones; *b* 14 April 1925; *Educ* Charterhouse, Univ Coll Oxford; *m* 1, 1949 (m dis 1967), Ann Murray; 2 s, 1 da; m 2, 1968, Pamela Sale; *Career* HM Foreign Service 1949, Ambass at Phnom Penh 1973-75, RCDS 1975, Ambass to Senegal, Guinea, Mali, Mauritania and Guinea-Bissau 1976-79, to Cape Verde 1977-79, Ambass and Perm Rep UN Conference on Law of the Sea 1979-; *Clubs* Travellers'; *Style* - John Powell-Jones Esq, CMG; c/o Foreign and Commonwealth Office, SW11; Gaston Gate, Cranleigh, Surrey (☎ Cranleigh 4313

POWER, Alastair John Cecil; s and h of Sir John Patrick McLannahan Power, 3 Bt; *b* 15 Aug 1958; *Style* - Alastair Power Esq; c/o Ashwick House, Dulverton, Som

POWER, Vice-Adm Sir Arthur Mackenzie; KCB (1974), MBE (1952); s of Admiral of the Fleet Sir Arthur Power, GCB, GBE, CVO; *b* 18 June 1921; *Educ* Rugby; *m* 1949, Marcia Helen Gell; 2 s, 1 da; *Career* RN 1938, Capt 1959, ADC to the Queen 1968, Rear-Adm 1968, Vice-Adm 1971, Flag Officer Plymouth, Port Adm Devonport, Cdr Central Sub Area E Atlantic, and Cdr Plymouth Sub Area Channel 1973-75, Sec to the Senate of the Inns of Court and the Bar 1975-; *Clubs* Army and Navy; *Style* - Vice-Admiral Sir Arthur Power, KCB, MBE; Gunnsmead, South rd, Liphook, Hants

POWER, Eugene Barnum; Hon KBE (1977); s of Glenn Warren Power; *b* 4 June 1905; *Educ* Michigan U; *m* 1929, Sadye L Harwick; 1 s; *Career* microphotographer, ret 1970; founder Universal Microfilms (merged with Xerox Corpn 1962) 1938, Universal Microfilms London 1952, dir Xerox Corpn 1962-68; chm Michigan Co-ordinating Council for State Higher Educn; Hon Fell Magdalene Coll Cambridge 1967, Northwestern Michigan Coll 1967, Hon LHD St John's U 1966, Michigan U 1971; *Style* - Eugene Power Esq KBE; 989 Forest rd, Barton Hills, Ann Arbor, Mich 48105, USA (☎ 313-662 2886)

POWER, John Christopher; TD (1980); s of Geoffrey William Power; *b* 7 Dec 1945; *m* 1969, Ann Marie; 1 da; *Career* formerly dir NEI Parsons Peebles Transformers Ltd, dir Hawker Siddeley Petter Diesels Ltd 1980-; FBIM, FAMEME; *Recreations* squash, running, swimming, parachuting, shooting; *Style* - John Power Esq, TD; Harwood, 2 Oakwood av, Purley, Surrey (☎ 01 660 3735)

POWER, Sir John Patrick McLannahan; 3 Bt (UK 1924); s of Sir Ivan McLannahan Cecil Power, 2 Bt (d 1954); *b* 16 March 1928; *Educ* Pangbourne Coll; *m* 1, 1957 (m dis 1967), Melanie, adopted da of Hon Alastair Erskine (s of 15 Earl of Buchan, d 1960); 2 s, 1 da; m 2, 1970 (m dis 1974), Tracey, da of George Cooper; *Heir* s, Alastair John Cecil Power; *Career* RN 1946-48, rep The Cunard Steamship Co Ltd 1945-58, chm Arthur Beale Ltd; *Clubs* Arts, Roy Ocean Racing, Roy London Yacht, RN Sailing Assoc, Island Sailing; *Style* - Sir John Power, Bt; Ashwick House, Dulverton, Som (☎ Dulverton 488)

POWERSCOURT, 10 Viscount (I 1743); Mervyn Niall Wingfield; also Baron Wingfield (I 1743) and Baron Powerscourt (UK 1885), which sits as; s of 9 Viscount Powerscourt (d 1973); *b* 3 Sept 1935; *Educ* Stowe, Trin Cambridge; *m* 1, 1962 (m dis 1974), Wendy Ann Pauline, da of Ralph C G Slazenger; 1 s, 1 da; m 2, 1978, Pauline, da of W P Vann, of San Francisco, Calif; *Heir* s Hon Mervyn Anthony Wingfield; *Career* late Lt Irish Gds; *Style* - The Rt Hon the Viscount Powerscourt

POWERSCOURT, Sheila, Viscountess - Sheila Claude; da of late Lt-Col Claude Beddington; *m* 1932, 9 Viscount Powerscourt (d 1973); *Career* writer (as Sheila Wingfield); *Style* - The Rt Hon Sheila, Viscountess Powerscourt; Palma au Lac, 6600 Locarno, Switzerland

POWIS, 6 Earl of (UK 1804); Christian Victor Charles Herbert; also Baron Clive of Plassey (I 1762), Baron Clive of Walcot (GB 1794), Baron Powis of Powis Castle,

Baron Herbert of Chirbury, and Viscount Clive of Ludlow (all UK 1804); s of Col Edward Herbert, CB (d 1924, gs of 2 Earl of Powis, KG, himself gs of Clive of India and bro of the Robert Clive who m Baroness Windsor and was ancestor of the present Earls of Plymouth; the 1 Earl of Powis's w was Lady Henrietta Herbert, da of 1 Earl of Powis of the previous (& second) cr by his distant cous Barbara Herbert; Barbara was niece of 3 & last Marquess of Powis and descended from the 2 s of the 1 Earl of Pembroke of the *second* Herbert cr of 1551; her husb (1) descended through his paternal gf from a yr bro of the 1 Earl of Pembroke of the *first* Herbert cr, (2) through his paternal grandmother & gf was respectively gggs & 1 cous thrice removed of the Lord Herbert of Chirbury who united the callings of Ambassador, Deist, poet, Cambridge Platonist, soldier, historian, traveller, linguist and marriage broker (he negotiated the alliance of Charles I & Henrietta Maria) and was bro of George Herbert, the poet); suc bro (5 Earl) 1974; *b* 28 May 1904; *Educ* Oundle, Trin Cambridge, UCL; *Heir* cous, George William Herbert; *Career* barr Inner Temple 1932, Priv Sec to Gov and C-in-C British Honduras 1947-55, to Gov of British Guiana 1955-64; patron of twelve livings; *Clubs* Brooks's, MCC; *Style* - The Rt Hon the Earl of Powis; Powis Castle, Welshpool, N Wales (☎ 3360)

POWIS, Countess of - Ella Mary; da of late Col William Hans Rathborne; *m* 1932, 5 Earl of Powis, CBE, TD (d 1974); *Style* - The Rt Hon the Countess of Powis; The Garden House, Powis Castle, Welshpool; 4 Green st, W1

POWLES, Sir Guy Richardson; KBE (1961), CMG (1954), ED (1944); s of late Col C G Powles, CMG, DSO, NZ Staff Corps; *b* 5 April 1905; *Educ* Wellington Coll NZ, Victoria U; *m* 1931, Eileen, da of A J Nicholls; 2 s; *Career* barr Supreme Court NZ 1929, High Cmmr Western Samoa 1949-60, for NZ in India 1960-62, Ceylon 1960-62; Ambass of NZ to Nepal 1960-62; first Ombudsman of NZ 1962-75, Ch Ombudsman 1975-77, pres NZ Inst of Int Affairs 1967-71, NZ Cmmr Cmmn of the Churches on Int Affairs, World Council of Churches 1971-, Cmmr Int Cmmn of Jurists Geneva 1975-; *Style* - Sir Guy Powles, KBE, CMG, ED; 34 Wesley rd, Wellington, New Zealand

POWLETT, Rear-Adm Philip Frederick; CB (1961), DSO (1941) and Bar (1942), DSC (1941), DL (Norfolk 1974); s of late Vice-Adm F A Powlett, CBE; *b* 13 Nov 1906; *Educ* RNC Osborne and Dartmouth; *m* 1935, Frances Elizabeth Sykes, nee Elwell; 2 s, 1 da; *Career* Dir (RN) Joint Anti-Submarine Sch, and Sr Naval Officer N Ireland 1956-58, Flag Officer and Adm Superintendent Gibraltar 1959-62, ret 1962; *Style* - Rear-Admiral Philip Powlett CB, DSO*, DSC, DL; The Mill House, Lyng, Norwich, Norfolk NR9 5QZ

POWLETT SMITH, Joye; da of Hubert Cecil Nicholson; *b* 18 Oct 1925; *Educ* Hawnes Sch Haynes Park Beds; *m* 1946, Sydney Powlett Smith, s of Godfrey Smith, the Ven the Archdeacon of Furness; 1 s, 1 da; *Career* JP Hallamshire 1961-68, Rotherham 1968, High Sheriff of S Yorks 1981-; *Recreations* gardening, fishing; *Style* - Mrs Sydney Powlett Smith, JP; Lake House, Firbeck, nr Worksop, Notts

POWNALL, Henry Charles; QC (1979); s of John Cecil Glossop Pownall CB (d 1967); *b* 25 Feb 1927; *Educ* Rugby, Trin Cambridge; *m* 1955, Sarah Bettine, da of Maj John Latham Deverell (d 1978); 1 s, 1 da (and 1 da decd); *Career* barr Inner Temple 1954, Bencher 1976, Junior Prosecuting Counsel to the Crown at the Central Criminal Court 1964-71, a Sr Prosecuting Counsel 1971-79, a Recorder of the Crown Court 1972-, Hon Legal Adviser ABA 1976-, pres Orders and Medals Research Soc 1971-75, 1977-81, Judge of the Court of Appeal of Jersey and Guernsey; *Recreations* travel, medals and medal ribbons; *Clubs* Pratt's, Hurlingham, Ebury Court; *Style* - Henry Pownall Esq, QC; 69 Eaton Ter, SW1W 8TN; 2 Harcourt Buildings, Temple, EC4Y 9DB

POWYS, Hon Clare Lynette; da of 7 Baron Lilford; *b* 1962

POWYS, Hon Emma-Jane; da of 7 Baron Lilford; *b* 1964

POWYS, Hon Hanna Victoria; da of 7 Baron Lilford; *b* 1974

POWYS, Hon Mark Vernon; s of 7 Baron Lilford; *b* 16 Nov 1975; *Style* - The Hon Mark Powys

POWYS, Hon Sarah Margaret; da of 7 Baron Lilford; *b* 1971

POYNTON, Hon Finola Dominique; *née* Fitz-Clarence; da (by 1 m) of Viscount Fitz-Clarence (s and h of 6 Earl of Munster); *b* 6 Dec 1953; *m* 1981 Jonathan Poynton; *Style* - The Hon Mrs Poynton

POYNTON, Sir (Arthur) Hilton; GCMG (1964, KCMG 1949, CMG 1946); s of late Arthur Blackburne Poynton, formerly Master of Univ Coll Oxford; *b* 20 April 1905; *Educ* Marlborough, BNC Oxford (Hon Fell 1964); *m* 1946, Elisabeth Joan, da of late Rev Edmund Williams; 2 s, 1 da; *Career* Perm Under-Sec of State Colonial Office 1959-66; KStJ 1968; *Clubs* Athenaeum; *Style* - Sir Hilton Poynton, GCMG; Craigmillar, 47 Stanhope rd, Croydon CRO 5NS

PRAG, Derek Nathan; MEP (C) Hertfordshire 1979-; s of Abraham J Prag; *b* 6 Aug 1923; *Educ* Bolton Sch, Emmanuel Cambridge; *m* 1948, Dora Weiner; 3 s; *Career* dir London Information Office of European Communities 1965-73, ran consultancy on relations with EEC 1973-79; *Style* - Derek Prag Esq, MEP; Pine Hill, 47 New rd, Digswell, Herts AL6 OAQ

PRAGNELL, Anthony William; OBE (1960), DFC (1944); s of William Hendley Pragnell; *b* 15 Feb 1921; *Educ* Cardinal Vaughan Sch London; *m* 1955, Teresa Mary, da of Leo Monaghan; 1 s, 1 da; *Career* Dep Dir-Gen IBA 1961-; Fell Roy Television Soc 1980; *Style* - Anthony Pragnell Esq, OBE, DFC; Ashley, Grassy Lane, Sevenoaks, Kent (☎ Sevenoaks 51463)

PRAIN, Sir Ronald Lindsay; OBE (1946); s of Arthur Lindsay Prain; *b* 3 Sept 1907; *Educ* Cheltenham Coll; *m* 1938, Esther Pansy, da of late Norman Brownrigg; 2 s; *Career* ch exec RST Int Gp of cos 1943-68, chm 1950-72; dir Seltrust Investments Ltd, Monks Investment Trust Ltd, Pan-Holding SA and other cos; pres British Overseas Mining Assoc 1952; kt 1956; *Style* - Sir Ronald Prain, OBE; Waverley, St George's Hill, Weybridge, Surrey KT13 OQJ (☎ Weybridge 42776); 43 Cadogan sq, SW1X OHX (☎ 01 235 4900)

PRATT, Michael John; QC (1976); s of W Brownlow Pratt; *b* 23 May 1933; *Educ* West House Sch Edgbaston, Malvern Coll (LLB Birmingham); *m* 1960, Elizabeth Jean Hendry; 2 s, 3 da; *Career* barr Middle Temple 1954, a Recorder of the Crown Court 1974-; *Clubs* Cavalry and Guards, Birmingham Conservative; *Style* - Michael Pratt Esq, QC; South Hill, 170 Oak Tree Lane, Bournville, Birmingham B30 1TX (☎ 021 472 2213)

PRATT, Lord Michael John Henry; s (by 2 m) of 5 Marquess Camden; *b* 1946; *Educ* Eton, Balliol Oxford; *Career* author and researcher; *Clubs* White's, Pratt's, MCC; *Style* - Lord Michael Pratt; 16 Coulson st, SW3

PRATT, Lord Roderic Arthur Nevill; s of 4 Marquess Camden; *b* 1915; *Educ* Eton, Trinity Cambridge; *m* 1945, Ursula Eva, da of Capt the Hon Valentine Maurice Wyndham-Quin, RN (s of late 5 Earl of Dunraven and Mount-Earl); 1 s, 1 da; *Career* Maj late Life Gds; chm Roderic Pratt Underwriting Agencies Ltd; dir Tennant Budd & Roderic Pratt Ltd; underwriting memb Lloyd's; *Style* - Lord Roderic Pratt; Saxonbury House, Frant, Tunbridge Wells, Kent

PRATT, Lady Samantha Caroline; da of Earl of Brecknock; *b* 1964; *Style* - Lady Samantha Pratt

PRENDERGAST, (Christopher) Anthony; CBE (1980); s of Maurice Prendergast; *b* 4 May 1931; *Educ* Falmouth G S; *m* 1959, Simone Ruth Laski, JP, DL, OStJ; 1 s; *Career* chm Dolphin Sq Trust Ltd 1967-, Lord Mayor and Dep High Steward of Westminster 1968-69, High Sheriff of Greater London 1980, Lloyd's underwriter; *Clubs* Carlton, Brooks's, Irish, MCC; *Style* - Anthony

Prendergast Esq, CBE; 51 Sutherland st, SW1V 4JX (☎ 01 821 7653)

PRENDERGAST, Sir John Vincent; KBE (1977, CBE 1960), CMG (1968), GM (1955); s of late John Prendergast; *b* 11 Feb 1912; *Educ* Ireland, London U (external); *m* 1943, Enid Sonia, da of Percy Speed; 1 s, 1 da; *Career* Colonial Police Service Kenya 1953-58 (Dir of Intelligence and Security 1955-58), Ch of Intelligence Cyprus 1958-60, Dir Special Branch Hong Kong (ret as Dep Cmmr of Police) 1960-66, Dir of Intelligence Aden 1966-67, Dep Cmmr and Dir of Operations Independent Cmmn Against Corruption, Hong Kong 1973-77; Colonial Police Medal 1955, QPM 1963; *Style* - Sir John Prendergast KBE CMG GM QPM; 20 Westbourne Ter, W2 3UP

PRENTICE, John Oscar; s of Oscar Prentice (d 1957); *b* 15 Dec 1925; *Educ* Bardfield Coll, Clare Cambridge; *m* 1954, Geraldine Ildiko, da of Humphrey Ridley Tomalin (d 1978); 3 da; *Career* Lloyd's insurance broker and underwriter; dep chm Willis Faber Ltd; FRGS; *Recreations* yachting, fishing, farming; *Clubs* Royal Thames Yacht, City of London; yacht: 'Battlecry', racehorse 'Sagittario'; *Style* - John Prentice Esq; 29 Wilton Row, SW1 (☎ 01 235 7594); Gentilshurst, Fernhurst, Haslemere, Surrey

PRENTICE, Rt Hon Reginald Ernest; PC (1966), JP, MP (C) Daventry 1979-; s of Ernest George Prentice; *b* 16 July 1923; *Educ* Whitgift Sch, LSE; *m* 1948, Joan Godwin; 1 da; *Career* MP (L) East Ham North 1957-74, Newham North East 1974-77, MP (C) Newham North East 1977-79, Min of State (Min for Social Security) DHSS 1979-81; JP (Croydon 1961); *Clubs* Reform, Addington Palace Golf; *Style* - The Rt Hon Reginald Prentice, JP, MP; 5 Hollingsworth rd, Croydon CR0 5RP

PRENTICE, Thomas; MC (1945); s of Alexander Prentice; *b* 14 Oct 1919; *Educ* McLaren H S Callander Perthshire; *m* 1949, Peggy Ann Lloyd; 2 s, 2 da; *Career* dir Harrisons & Crosfield Ltd 1967-, chm 1977-; *Style* - Thomas Prentice Esq, MC; Eveley, Standford, nr Bordon, Hants (☎ Passfield 228)

PRENTICE, Dame Winifred Eva; DBE (1977, OBE 1972); da of Percy John Prentice; *b* 2 Dec 1910; *Educ* Northgate Sch for Girls Ipswich, E Suffolk and Ipswich Hosp, W Middx Hosp, Queen Elizabeth Coll London U; *Career* Principal Tutor Stracathro Hosp Brechin Angus 1947-61, Matron 1961-72, Pres Roy Coll of Nursing 1972-76; *Clubs* VAD Ladies; *Style* - Dame Winifred Prentice, DBE, SRN; Marleish, 4 Duke st, Brechin, Angus (☎ Brechin 2606)

PRENTICE, Hon Sir William Thomas; MBE (1945); s of Claud Stanley Prentice (d 1931); *b* 1 June 1919; *Educ* St Joseph's Coll Sydney, Sydney U; *m* 1946, Mary Elizabeth Beresford, da of Frank Beresford Dignam (d 1946); 3 s, 1 da; *Career* Staff Capt 7 Aust Inf Bde Bougainville Campaign 1944-45; barr NSW 1947, Judge Supreme Court Papua New Guinea 1970, Sr Puisne Judge 1975, Dep Ch Justice on independence PNG 1975, Ch Justice 1978-80; kt 1977; *Recreations* bush walking, swimming, reading; *Clubs* Tattersall's (Sydney); *Style* - The Hon Sir William Prentice, MBE; 16 Olympia rd, Naremburn, NSW 2065, Australia

PRESCOT, Kenrick Warre; s of the late Brig C P Prescot, CBE; *b* 21 Nov 1920; *Educ* Eton, Worcester Coll Oxford; *m* 1948, Angharad Joanna, da of Brig C R M Hutchison, DSO, MC (ka 1942); 2 s, 1 da; *Career* Captain RA, India, Burma and UK 1942-46, Bank of England 1947-59, v-pres Bankers Trust Company 1959-, dir Amev Life Assurance Ltd 1973-80, dir Amev Ltd 1980-; *Recreations* tennis, beagling; *Clubs* Gresham, MCC; *Style* - Kenrick Prescot Esq; 13 The Little Boltons, SW10

PRESCOTT, John Leslie; MP (L) Kingston upon Hull (East) 1970-; s of John Herbert Prescott, JP; *b* 31 May 1938; *Educ* Ellesmere Port Secdy Modern Sch, WEA, Ruskin Coll Oxford, Hull U; *m* 1961, Pauline Tilston; 2 s; *Career* Contested (L) Southport 1966, PPS to Sec of State for Trade 1974-76, Leader Labour Party Delegn Euro Parliament 1976-79, Opposition Spokesman transport 1979-; *Style* - John Prescott Esq, MP; 365

Saltshouse rd, Sutton-on-Hull, North Humberside

PRESCOTT, Sir Mark; 3 Bt (UK 1938); s of late Maj (William Robert) Stanley Prescott (yr s of Col Sir William Prescott, 1 Bt) and n of Sir Richard Prescott, 2 Bt (d 1965); *b* 3 March 1948; *Educ* Harrow; *Career* racehorse trainer; *Style* - Sir Mark Prescott, Bt; Heath House, Moulton rd, Newmarket, Suffolk CB8 8DU (☎ Newmarket 2117)

PRESLAND, John David; s of Leslie Presland; *b* 3 July 1930; *Educ* St Albans Sch, LSE; *m* 1969, Margaret Brewin; *Career* exec vice-chm Port of London Authority 1978-; FCA, IPFA, MBCS; *Clubs* Oriental; *Style* - John Presland Esq; c/o Port of London Authority, London Dock House, 1 Thomas More st, E1 (☎ 01 476 6900)

PRESS, Dr Robert; CB (1972), CBE (1962); s of William J Press; *b* 22 Feb 1915; *Educ* Regent House Secdy Sch Co Down, Queen's U Belfast, Trin Coll Dublin; *m* 1946, Honor Elizabeth Tapp; *Career* Dep Sec Science and Technology Cabinet Office 1974-76, ret; adviser in the Cabinet Office 1976-; FPhysS 1950, FInstP 1961, FRSA 1967; *Clubs* Army and Navy; *Style* - Dr Robert Press, CB, CBE; 8 Ardross ave, Northwood, Middx (☎ Northwood 23707)

PRESTON, Bryan Nicholas; s of Bryan Wentworth Preston, MBE (d 1965); *b* 6 Feb 1933; *Educ* Eton, RAC Cirencester; *m* 1955, Elsbeth, nee Hostettler; 1 s, 2 da; *Career* farmer; mktg dir SMM Propellers Ltd, chm Br Marine Equipment Cncl 1966-68 & 1976-78; memb BOTB European Tde Ctee, memb BOTB E European Tde Cncl; *Recreations* field sports, skiing; *Clubs* Boodle's, Farmers'; *Style* - Bryan Preston Esq; Park Farm House, Beverston, nr Tetbury, Glos (☎ Tetbury 52688)

PRESTON, Ella, Lady; Ella Henrietta; da of late Friedrich von Shikendantz; *m* 1913, Sir Thomas Hildebrand Preston, 6 Bt, OBE (d 1976); *Style* - Ella, Lady Preston; Beeston Hall, Beeston St Lawrence, Norwich, Norfolk NR12 8YS

PRESTON, Sir Kenneth Huson; s of late Sir Walter Preston; *b* 19 May 1901; *Educ* Rugby, Trin Oxford; *m* 1922, Beryl Wilmot, da of Sir William Wilkinson; 1 s, 1 da; *Career* dir Midland Bank Ltd 1945-76, Pres Stone-Platt Industries Ltd 1968-, memb S Area Bd BR; memb British Olympic Yachting team 1936 and 1952, Capt 1960; kt 1959; *Clubs* Roy Yacht Sqdn (V-Cdre 1965-71), Thames Yacht (V-Cdre 1953-56); *Style* - Sir Kenneth Preston; Ilsom, Tetbury, Glos (☎ Tetbury 52348)

PRESTON, Philip Charles Henry Hulton; s of late Lt-Col Philip Henry Herbert Hulton Preston, OBE, MC (gggs of 1 Bt); hp of kinsman, Sir Ronald Preston, 7 Bt; *b* 31 Aug 1946; *Educ* Nautical Coll Pangbourne; *Style* - Philip Preston Esq

PRESTON, Peter John; s of John Whittle Preston; *b* 23 May 1938; *Educ* Loughborough G S, St John's Coll Oxford; *m* 1962, Jean Mary Burrell; 2 s, 2 da; *Career* editor The Guardian 1975-; *Style* - Peter Preston Esq; The Guardian, 119 Farringdon rd, EC1

PRESTON, Sir Peter Sansome; KCB (1978, CB 1973); s of Charles Guy Preston; *b* 18 Jan 1922; *Educ* Nottingham H S; *m* 1951, Marjory Harrison; 2 s, 3 da; *Career* Dep Sec Dept of Trade 1972-76, Perm Sec Overseas Dvpt Admin, FCO 1976-; *Style* - Sir Peter Preston, KCB; 5 Greville Park av, Ashtead, Surrey (☎ Ashtead 72099)

PRESTON, Sir Ronald Douglas Hildebrand; 7 Bt (UK 1815); s of Sir Thomas Hildebrand Preston, 6 Bt, OBE (d 1976); *b* 9 Oct 1916; *Educ* Westminster, Trin Cambridge, Ecole des Sciences Politiques Paris; *m* 1, 1954 (m dis 1971) Smilya Stefanovic; m 2, 1972, Pauleen Jane, da of late Paul Lurcott; *Heir* kinsman, Philip Charles Henry Hulton Preston; *Career* 1939-45 War in ME and Italy (8 Army), Austria and Allied Control Cmmn to Bulgaria, late Maj Intelligence Corps, Reuters Correspondent in Belgrade 1948-53, Times Correspondent in Vienna and E Europe 1953-60, and in Tokyo 1960-63, HM Diplomatic Serv 1963-76; *Clubs* Travellers', Norfolk (Norwich), Tokyo

(Tokyo); *Style* - Sir Ronald Preston, Bt; Beeston Hall, Beeston St Lawrence, Norwich (☎ Horning 630771)

PRESTON, Timothy William; s of Charles Frank Preston LDS RCS; *b* 3 Nov 1935; *Educ* Haileybury, Jesus Coll Oxford; *m* 1965, Barbara Mary Haygarth; *Career* barr Inner Temple 1964, a Recorder of the Crown Court 1979-; *Clubs* Cavalry and Guards; *Style* - Timothy Preston Esq; 2 Temple gdns, EC4Y 9AY (☎ 01 583 6041)

PRESTT, His Honour Judge; Arthur Miller; QC (1970); s of Arthur Prestt (d 1959); *b* 23 April 1925; *Educ* Bootham Sch York, Trin Hall Cambridge; *m* 1949, Jill Mary, da of Graham Richards Dawbarn, CBE, FRIBA, FRAeS (d 1977); 1 s, 1 da; *Career* barr Middle Temple 1949, dep chm Cumberland QS 1966-69, chm 1970-71, a Circuit Judge 1971-; JP Cumberland 1966, has held various appts in Scout Assoc (Silver Acorn 1970); *Recreations* golf, gardening; *Style* - His Honour Judge Prestt QC; Glebe House, Eccleston, Chorley, Lancs (☎ 0257 451397)

PRESTWOOD, Viscount; John Richard; s and h of 2 Earl Attlee; *b* 3 Oct 1956; *Style* - Viscount Prestwood

PRETYMAN, Hon Mrs; Hon Camilla; *née* Gurdon; da of late 2 Baron Cranworth, KG, MC; *b* 1909; *m* 1932, George Marcus Tomline Pretyman (d 1979); 1 da; *Style* - The Hon Mrs Pretyman; Orwell Park House, Ipswich

PRETYMAN, Sir Walter Frederick; KBE (1972); s of Rt Hon E G Pretyman; *b* 17 Oct 1901; *Educ* Eton, Magdalen Oxford; *m* 1, 1929, Margaret Cunningham (d 1942); 1 da; m 2, 1947, Vera de Sa Sotto Maior; 2 s; *Career* RAFVR 1943-45, despatches 1946, ret with rank of Sq Ldr; pres Usina Santa Cruz; *Style* - Sir Walter Pretyman, KBE; 90 Rua Mexico, Rio de Janeiro, Brazil (☎ 232 8197)

PREVETTE, Kenneth George Charles; s of George William Prevette (d 1966); *b* 17 May 1917; *Educ* Cottingham College (private); *m* 1946, Sheila; 1 s, 1 da; *Career* Territorial Army 1939-46; dir: The London Cremation Company Ltd 1971, Kent County Crematorium Ltd 1973; Freeman of the City of London 1974; dir Norwich Crematorium Ltd 1978; *Recreations* photography, collecting car road tests, growing trees from seeds; *Clubs* formerly RAC, Pall Mall; *Style* - Kenneth Prevette Esq; 80 Ware Street, Bearsted Green, Maidstone, Kent ME14 4PG (☎ 0622 38034)

PREVITÉ, Hon Mrs; Hon Phyllida; *née* Browne; da of 6 Baron Kilmaine, CBE (d 1978); *b* 1935; *m* 1959, John Edward Previté; 2 s; *Style* - The Hon Mrs Previté; The Wilderness, Hampton Wick, Kingston upon Thames, Surrey

PREVOST, Christopher Gerald; s and h of Sir George James Augustine Prevost, 5 Bt; *b* 25 July 1935; *Educ* Cranleigh Sch; *m* 1964, Dolores Nelly, da of Dezo Hoffman; 1 s, 1 da; *Career* late 60 Regt; *Style* - Christopher Prevost Esq

PREVOST, Capt Sir George James Augustine; 5 Bt (UK 1805); s of Sir Charles Thomas Keble Prevost, 4 Bt (d 1939); *b* 16 Jan 1910; *Educ* Repton; *m* 1, 1935, Muriel Emily (d 1939), da of late Lewis William Oram; 1 s, 1 da; m 2, 1940 (m dis 1949), Phyllis Catherine Mattock; m 3, 1952, Patricia Betty Porter; 2 s; *Heir* s, Christopher Gerald Prevost; *Career* formerly Staff Capt, HQ N Command India; Lord of the Manor of Stinchcombe, Glos; *Style* - Captain Sir George Prevost, Bt; 12 Chiltern rd, Pinner, Middx

PRICE, Arnold Justin; QC (1976); s of late Sydney Walter Price; *b* 16 Aug 1919; *Educ* St Christopher's Sch Liverpool, Kingsmead Sch Meols, Liverpool Coll, Liverpool U; *m* 1948, Ruth Corinne, da of Ralph Marks; 4 da; *Career* barr Middle Temple 1952, Actg Ch Magistrate and Judge High Court N Nigeria 1957-60, Wales and Chester Circuit 1960, Northern Circuit 1969, a Recorder of the Crown Court 1972-, Adjudicator Immigration Appeals 1970-, CC Chester 1963-68; *Style* - Arnold Price Esq, QC; Thicket Ford, Thornton Hough, Wirral (☎ 051 336 4444); 13 Castle st, Liverpool (☎ 051 236

5072); 2 Pump Court, Temple, EC4 (☎ 01 353 3106)

PRICE, Hon Mrs (Anne Margaret); *née* Younger; 2 da of 2 Viscount Younger of Leckie, DSO, TD, JP, DL; *b* 10 March 1920; *m* 1943, Capt James Price, RA (ret), s of Capt James Price, MC (ka 1916), and Mariquita (3 da of Sir Timothy O'Brien, 3 Bt, JP, DL, and Gundrede, da of Sir Humphrey de Trafford, 2 Bt); 2 s, 3 da; *Style* - The Hon Mrs Price; The Moorings, Port Lewaigue, Ramsey, IOM

PRICE, Christopher; MP (L) Lewisham West 1974-; s of Stanley Price; *b* 26 Jan 1932; *Educ* Leeds G S, Queen's Oxford; *m* 1956, Annie Grierson Ross; 2 s, 1 da; *Career* MP (L) Perry Barr Div of Birmingham 1966-70, PPS to Sec of State Education & Science 1966-67 & 1975-76, Chm Select Committee on Education, Science and the Arts 1980, European Parl 1977-78; *Style* - Christopher Price Esq, MP; 30 Horniman Drive, SE23 3BP (☎ 01 699 2335)

PRICE, Cyril; s of Ieuan Penry Price (d 1975); *b* 26 Feb 1924; *Educ* Cathays Sch Cardiff; *m* 1946, Nancy Joy, da of Fredric Seaton, JP, of Australia (d 1966); 2 c; *Career* dir Tennant Guaranty Ltd 1964-, Orford Trading Co Ltd 1964-, Tennant Guaranty Int Ltd 1976-, Tennant Guaranty Trust Ltd 1969-; *Clubs* Royal Inst of International Affairs; *Style* - Cyril Price Esq; Stratfords Cottage, Church rd, Penn, Bucks (☎ Penn 3528)

PRICE, Rear-Adm Cecil Ernest; CB (1978), AFC (1953); s of Ernest C Price; *b* 29 Oct 1921; *Educ* Bungay G S; *m* 1946, Megan Morgan; 1 s, 1 da; *Career* RN 1941, Capt 1966, Rear-Adm 1976, Dep Assist Ch of Staff (Operations) SHAPE 1976-80; *Style* - Rear-Admiral Cecil Price, CB, AFC; Low Farm, Mendham, Harleston, Norfolk (☎ Harleston 852676)

PRICE, C L; *Career* md I(nter)Q(uest Accounts) Ltd (advertising agency; accounts include Liberty's) 1980-; *Style* - C L Price Esq; 19 Cambridge st, SW1 (☎ 01 834 6217)

PRICE, Maj-Gen Cedric Rhys; CB (1951), CBE (1945, OBE 1943); s of late Col Sir Rhys H Price, KBE, CMG; *b* 13 June 1905; *Educ* Wellington Coll, RMA Woolwich, Trin Cambridge; *m* 1935, Rosamund, da of late Arthur W Clifford; 2 da; *Career* Dir of Military Intelligence War Office 1956-59, Principal Staff Officer to Sec of State for Commonwealth Relations 1959-64, ADC to the Queen 1954-57; *Clubs* Army and Navy; *Style* - Major-General Cedric Price, CB, CBE; Furze Field Cottage, Hoe Lane, Peaslake, Guildford, Surrey (☎ Dorking 730586)

PRICE, Maj-Gen (Maurice) David; CB (1970), OBE (1956); s of Edward Allan Price; *b* 13 Feb 1915; *Educ* Marlborough, RMA Woolwich; *m* 1, 1938, Ella Lacy (d 1971), da of late H L Day; 2 s, 2 da; m 2, 1972, Mrs Olga Marion Oclee; *Career* Vice-Quartermaster-Gen MOD (Army) 1967-70, ret, Col Cmdt Roy Corps of Signals 1967-74; *Clubs* Army and Navy; *Style* - Major-General David Price, CB, OBE; The Cross, Chilmark, Salisbury, Wilts (☎ Teffont 212)

PRICE, Sir David Ernest Campbell; MP (C) Eastleigh Div Hampshire 1955-; s of Maj Villiers Price; *b* 20 Nov 1924; *Educ* Eton, Trin Cambridge, Yale U USA; *m* 1960, Eugénie Evelyn, da of late Cyril Johnston, OBE; 1 da; *Career* ICI 1949-62, Parly Sec BOT 1962-64, Opposition Front-Bench spokesman on Science and Technology 1964-70, Parly Sec Miny of Technology June-Oct 1970, Parly Sec Miny of Aviation Supply 1970-71, Parly Under-Sec of State Aerospace DTI 1971-72; dir T W Downs Ltd 1973-, Aberdeen Cold Storage Co Ltd 1977-, Linear Shipping Agencies Ltd; kt 1980; *Clubs* Beefsteak; *Style* - Sir David Price, MP; 36 Sloane Court West, SW3 (☎ 01 730 3326); Lepe House, Exbury, Southampton

PRICE, David William James; s of R J E Price, of Portugal; *b* 11 Jun 1947; *Educ* Ampleforth, CCC Oxford; *m* 1971, Shervie Ann Lander, da of Sir James Whitaker, Bt, of Babworth Hall, Retford; 1 s, 1 da; *Career* merchant banker SG Warburg & Co Ltd; dir Warburg Investment Management Ltd 1979-, Moorside Tst 1979-, cllr London Borough Lambeth 1979-; *Clubs* Oriental, Brooks's;

Style - David Price Esq; 39 Old Town, Clapham, SW4

PRICE, Lady; Eva Mary Dickson; *m* 1939, as his 2 w, Sir Henry Philip Price, 1 and last Bt (d 1963); *Style* - Lady Price; c/o Midland Bank, 60 Broadway, Hayward's Heath, Sussex

PRICE, Sir Francis Caradoc Rose; 7 Bt (UK 1815); s of Sir Rose Francis Price, 6 Bt (d 1979); *b* 9 Sept 1950; *Educ* Eton, Trin Coll Melbourne U, U of Alberta; *m* 1975, Marguerite Jean, da of Roy S Trussler; 2 da; *Heir* bro, Norman William Rose Price; *Career* barr and slr Canada; *Style* - Sir Francis Price, Bt; 9677 95th av, Edmonton, Alberta, Canada T6C 2A3

PRICE, Sir Frank Leslie; DL (Hereford and Worcester and Co of W Midlands, 1977); s of George Frederick Price; *b* 26 July 1922; *Educ* St Matthias Church Sch Birmingham, Vittoria st Arts Sch; *m* 1944, Maisie Edna (m dis), da of Albert Davis; 1 s; *Career* sr partner Comprehensive Development Associates 1968-, Chm British Waterways Bd 1968-, Eurotech (Int) Ltd 1980-, Pres BAIE 1979; FSVA, FCIT, FRSA, kt 1966; *Clubs* Reform; *Style* - Sir Frank Price, DL; New Oxford House, 16 Waterloo st, Birmingham B2 5UG

PRICE, Henry Alfred; CBE (1962); s of James William Price; *b* 3 January 1911; *Educ* Holloway County Sch; *m* 1938, Ivy May Trimmer; 1 s, 1 da; *Career* MP (C) West Lewisham 1950-64, md Grove Paper Co Ltd; *Style* - Henry Price Esq, CBE; 22 Cator rd, Sydenham SE26 (☎ 01 778 3838)

PRICE, John Alan; QC (1980); s of Frederick Leslie Price (d 1976); *b* 11 Sept 1938; *Educ* Stretford G S, Manchester U; *m* 1964, Elizabeth Myra, da of Stanley Priest; 1 s, 1 da; *Career* barr Gray's Inn 1961, in practice on Northern Circuit, Dep Circuit Judge 1975-, a Recorder of the Crown Court 1980-; *Recreations* tennis, squash, golf, football; *Clubs* Northern Lawn Tennis, Wilmslow Golf; *Style* - John Price Esq, QC; 15 Carrwood rd, Wilmslow, Cheshire (☎ Wilmslow 523532); Byrom House, Quay st, Manchester (☎ 061 834 5238); 5 Essex Ct, Temple

PRICE, Hon Mrs (Joanna Mary); *née* Cavendish; da of 5 Baron Chesham; *b* 1938; *m* 1960, Peter Henry Mabille Price; 1 s, 1 da; *Style* - The Hon Mrs Price; The Mill House, Itchen Abbas, Winchester, Hants

PRICE, J(ohn) Maurice; QC (1976); s of Edward Samuel Price; *b* 4 May 1922; *Educ* Grove Park Sch Wrexham, Trin Cambridge; *m* 1945, Mary, da of Dr Horace Gibson, DSO*; 2 s; *Career* RN 1941-46, Lt RNVR, barr Gray's Inn 1949, memb Senate of Inns of Court and the Bar 1975-78; *Clubs* Flyfishers'; *Style* - J Maurice Price Esq, QC; Bowzell Place, Weald, Sevenoaks, Kent TN14 6NF; 2 New sq, Lincoln's Inn, WC2A 3RU (☎ 01 242 6201)

PRICE, June, Lady; Kathleen June; da of late Norman W Hutchinson, of Toorak, Melbourne, Australia; *m* 1949, Sir Rose Francis Price, 6 Bt (d 1979); 2 s; *Style* - June, Lady Price; Dormer Cottage, Park rd, Stoke Poges, Bucks

PRICE, (Arthur) Leolin; QC (1968); s of late Evan Price; *b* 11 May 1924; *Educ* Judd Sch Tonbridge, Keble Oxford; *m* 1963, Hon Rosalind Helen Penrose Lewis, da of 1 Baron Brecon, PC (d 1976); 2 s, 2 da; *Career* barr Middle Temple 1949, Bencher 1970, barr Lincoln's Inn 1959, QC Bahamas 1969, Chm Ctee of Management Inst of Child Health 1976-, dir Child Health Res Investment Trust Co Ltd 1980-; *Clubs* Carlton; *Style* - Leolin Price Esq, QC; 32 Hampstead Grove, NW3 6SR (☎ 01 435 9843); 10 Old sq, Lincoln's Inn, WC2A 3SU (☎ 01 405 0758); Mrs Price's Cottage, Cross Oak, Talybont-on-Usk, Brecon LD3 7UQ (☎ Talybont-on-Usk 248)

PRICE, Sir Leslie Victor; OBE (1971); s of late H V L Price; *b* Qld 30 Oct 1920; *m* 1941, Lorna D Collins; 1 s, 2 da; *Career* chm Australian Wheat Bd 1977- (memb 1971-); kt 1976; *Clubs* Queensland, Melbourne; *Style* - Sir Leslie Price, OBE; 80 Studley park rd, Kew, Vic 3101, Australia

PRICE, Margaret Berenice; da of late Thomas Glyn Price; *b* 13 April 1941; *Educ* Pontllanfraith Secdy Sch, Trin Coll of Music London; *Career* opera singer; Hon FTCL, Elisabeth Schumann Prize for Lieder, Ricordi Prize for Opera, Silver Medal Worshipful Co of Musicians; *Style* - Miss Margaret Price; c/o Harrison/Parrott Ltd, 22 Hillgate st, W8

PRICE, Hon Mrs (Margaret Joan); *née* Nelson; JP (Warwicks); da of 1 Baron Nelson of Stafford (d 1962); *b* 1915; *m* 1941, Edward Michael Price; 3 da; *Style* - The Hon Mrs Price, JP; Frankton Manor, Frankton, Warwickshire

PRICE, Hon Mrs (Maureen Maude Tower); *née* Butler; da of late 27 Baron Dunboyne; *b* 1919; *m* 1946, Lt-Col Robert Caradoc Rose Price, DSO, OBE, late Welsh Gds; 1 s, 1 da; *Style* - The Hon Mrs Price; Tetworth Hall, Ascot, Berks

PRICE, Sir Norman Charles; KCB (1975, CB 1969); s of Charles William Price; *b* 5 Jan 1915; *Educ* Plaistow G S; *m* 1940, Kathleen Beatrice, nee Elston; 2 da; *Career* dep chm Bd of Inland Revenue 1968-73, chm 1973-76, memb European Court of Auditors 1977-; *Style* - Sir Norman Price, KCB; Résidence Belairizon-Arlingten, 100 Route d'Arlon, Luxembourg (☎ Luxembourg 446531)

PRICE, Norman George; JP (1961); s of George Strongitharm Price (d 1942); *b* 14 Nov 1922; *Educ* Rockferry H S, Liverpool U; *m* 1945, Grace Dorothy, nee Melling; 2 da; *Career* served Merchant Navy 1940-46, Ministry of Supply 1950-54, Colonial Service Fiji 1954-58; with Granada Gp Ltd 1958-62, personnel dir Carreras Ltd 1962-71, J Bibby Sons Ltd 1971-81; educational consultant to Assoc of Business Execs 1981; *Recreations* racing, gardening, walking, reading; *Clubs* Reform; *Style* - Norman Price Esq, JP; Boleyns, Duton Hill, Dunmow, Essex (☎ 037 184 419)

PRICE, Norman Stewart; CMG (1959), OBE (1946); s of late Lt-Col Ivon Henry Price, DSO, LLD; *b* 9 Aug 1907; *Educ* Portora Roy Sch Enniskillen, Exeter Sch, Trin Coll Dublin, Queen's Oxford; *m* 1933, Rosalind Evelyn Noelle, nee Ormsby (d 1973); 2 da; *Career* Provincial Cmmr N Rhodesia 1951-59; *Style* - Norman Price Esq, CMG, OBE; Overton Rise, 6 Wavell rd, Highlands, Salisbury, Zimbabwe (☎ Salisbury 46350)

PRICE, Norman William Rose; s of Sir Rose Francis Price, 6 Bt (d 1979), & hp of bro, Sir Francis Caradoc Rose, 7 Bt; *b* 17 March 1953; *Educ* Eton; *Style* - Norman Price Esq

PRICE, Peter Nicholas; s of Rev Dewi Emlyn Price, of Worcester; *b* 19 Feb 1942; *Educ* Worcester Roy G S, Aberdare Boys' G S, Southampton U; *Career* slr, assist slr Glamorgan County Council 1967-68, sr partner Peter Price & Partners 1969-; MEP (C), vice-chm Budgetary Control Ctee European Parliament; *Recreations* theatre, music, photography; *Clubs* Europe House; *Style* - Peter Price Esq, MEP; 13 Orchard Dene, Rainhill, Prescot, Merseyside L35 OLT (☎ 051 430 7936); 37 Heol St Denys, Lisvane, Cardiff CF4 5RU (☎ 0222 761792)

PRICE, Sir (James) Robert; KBE (1976); s of Edgar James Price; *b* 25 March 1912; *Educ* St Peter's Coll Adelaide, Adelaide U, Oxford U; *m* 1940, Joyce Ethel, nee Brooke; 1 s, 2 da; *Career* Chm of the Exec, CSIRO 1970-77; FAA 1959; *Clubs* Melbourne (Melb); *Style* - Sir Robert Price, KBE; Yangoora, 2 Ocean View av, Red Hill South, Vic 3936, Australia

PRICE, (Llewelyn) Ralph; CBE (1972); s of Llewelyn David Price (d 1962); *b* 23 Oct 1912; *Educ* Quarry Bank Sch Liverpool; *m* 1939, Vera Patricia, da of C H Harrison (d 1935); 1 s, 2 da; *Career* chm Honeywell Ltd 1972-, ML Holdings Ltd 1975-, dir American Chamber of Commerce, memb NEDC Electronics Ctee, Pres British Industrial Measurement and Control Trade Assoc 1972-77; FCA, FBIM; *Style* - Ralph Price Esq, CBE; Nascot, Pinkneys Drive, Pinkneys Green, Maidenhead, Berks (☎ Maidenhead 28270)

PRICE, Roy Kenneth; CB (1980); s of Ernest Price; *b* 16 May 1916; *Educ* Eltham

Coll; *m* 1948, Martha, nee Dannhauser; 1 s, 1 da; *Career* slr 1937, Under-Sec (Legal) in office of HM Treasury Solicitor 1972-; *Clubs* Law Society; *Style* - Roy Price Esq, CB; 6 Old Palace Lane, Richmond, Surrey (☎ 01 940 6685)

PRICE, Lady Susan; *née* Murray; da of 10 Earl of Dunmore; *b* 1949; *m* 1980, Graham Price, of Bunbury, W Australia; *Style* - Lady Susan Price

PRICE, Vivian William Cecil; QC (1972); s of late Evan Price; *b* 14 April 1926; *Educ* Judd Sch Tonbridge, Trin Cambridge, Balliol Oxford; *m* 1961, Elizabeth Anne, da of late Arthur Rawlins; 3 s, 2 da; *Career* RN 1946-49, barr Middle Temple 1954, Hong Kong 1975, Singapore 1979, bencher Middle Temple 1979, Dep High Court Judge (Chancery Div) 1975; *Clubs* Travellers'; *Style* - Vivian Price Esq, QC; Redwall Farmhouse, Linton, Kent (☎ Maidstone 43682); New Court, Temple, EC4 (☎ 01 353 1769)

PRICHARD, Brian Justin; s of Bernard A'Bear Prichard (d 1957); *b* 2 Sept 1925; *Educ* Wimbledon Coll, Keble Oxford, King's Coll London (LLB); *m* 1954, Patricia Margaret Oldham, da of Reginald Garforth Cooke; 1 s, 3 da; *Career* slr; dir Walter Lawrence Ltd, S W Farmer Gp Ltd and other cos; *Recreations* gardening, travel; *Clubs* Royal Overseas League; *Style* - Brian Prichard Esq; Little Hill, St George's Hill, Weybridge, Surrey (☎ Weybridge 46216)

PRICHARD, Sir Montague Illtyd; CBE (1965), MC (1944); s of late George Montague Prichard; *b* 26 Sept 1915; *Educ* Felsted Sch Essex; *m* 1942, Kathleen Georgana Hamill; 2 s, 1 da; *Career* chm McKee Bros Ltd Ontario 1976-, Brown Bros Corpn Ltd 1979-; memb Council of Advisors AMF Inc White Plains, NY; dir Polysius Ltd, Tozer Kemsley & Millbourn (Holdings) Ltd; formerly chm and ch exec Perkins Engines Gp Ltd and subsidiaries; FinstMSM, kt 1972; *Style* - Sir Montague Prichard, CBE, MC; Monte Kay, Mijas, Malaga, Spain (☎ Malaga 485085)

PRICHARD, Robert David Caradoc; s of Lt-Col David Prichard and Elizabeth , 2 da of Sir David Llewellyn, 1 Bt, whereby Robert is 1 cous to Roddy and Dai Llewellyn, Jennifer Loehnis (w of Anthony, an assoc dir of the Bank of England), and the Countess of Darnley; he is also nephew by marriage of Lady Honor Llewellyn; Col Prichard is ninth in descent from Matthew Prichard, whose epitaph claims him to be desended from "Cradocke Vraich Vras, Earle of Hereford, and Prince between Wye and Seaverne"; *b* 17 Nov 1947; *Educ* Wellington, CCC Cambridge; *Career* merchant banker; assist dir Kleinwort Benson Investment Management 1981-; *Recreations* bridge, croquet; *Style* - Robert Prichard Esq; 25 Longmoore st, SW1 (☎ 01 828 0919)

PRICHARD, Air Cdre Richard Julian Paget; CB (1963), CBE (1958), DFC (1942), AFC (1941); s of Maj W O Prichard; *b* 4 Oct 1915; *Educ* Harrow, St Catharine's Cambridge; *Career* RAF 1937, Dir Air Plans Air Ministry 1960-63, AOC No 13 Scottish Sector Fighter Command 1963-64, AOC Northern Sector of Fighter Command 1965-66; US Legion Merit; *Clubs* RAF; *Style* - Air Commodore Richard Prichard CB CBE DFC AFC; c/o Lloyds Bank Ltd, 6 Pall Mall, SW1Y 5NH

PRICHARD-JONES, David John Walter; s and h of Sir John Prichard-Jones, 2 Bt; *b* 14 March 1943; *Educ* Ampleforth, Ch Ch Oxford; *Style* - David Prichard-Jones

PRICHARD-JONES, Sir John; 2 Bt (UK 1910); s of Sir John Prichard-Jones, 1 Bt, JP, DL (d 1917); *b* 20 Jan 1913; *Educ* Eton, Ch Ch Oxford; *m* 1, 1937, Heather (m dis 1950), da of late Sir Walter Nugent, 4 Bt; 1 s; m 2, 1959, Helen Marie Thérèse, da of J F Liddy; 1 da; *Heir* s, David John Walter Prichard-Jones; *Career* barr Gray's Inn 1936, Capt late The Queen's Bays; *Style* - Sir John Prichard-Jones, Bt; Allenswood House, Lucan, Co Dublin

PRICKETT, Air Chief Marshal Sir Thomas Other; KCB (1965, CB 1957), DSO (1943), DFC (1942); s of late E G Prickett; *b* 31 July 1913; *Educ* Stubbington House Sch, Haileybury Coll; *m* 1942, Elizabeth Gratian, da of late William

Galbally, of Calif, USA; 1 s, 1 da; *Career* RAF 1937, AOC-in-C NEAF, Cdr British Forces Near East and Administrator Sovereign Base Area 1964-66, AOC-in-C RAF Air Support Command 1967-68, Air Memb for Supply and Organisation MOD 1968-70, ret; *Clubs* RAF; *Style* - Air Chief Marshal Sir Thomas Prickett KCB DSO DFC; 3 Grange House, Aldwick Grange, Bognor, Sussex

PRICKMAN, Air Cdre Thomas Bain; CB (1953), CBE (1945); s of Thomas Prickman; *b* 1902; *Educ* Blundell's and RAF Coll Cranwell; *m* 1, 1938, Ethel Serica (d 1949), da of John Cubbon; m 2, 1952, Dorothy (who m 1946, Group Capt Frederick Charles Read, d 1949), da of John Charles Clarke; *Career* RAF 1923, AOA RAF Home Command 1950-54, ret; *Style* - Air Commodore Thomas Prickman CB, CBE; Well Cottage, New Pond Hill, Cross-in-Hand, E Sussex

PRIDDEN, Lady Maria; *née* Noel; da of 5 Earl of Gainsborough, JP; *b* 3 Feb 1951; *Educ* St Mary's Convent, Ascot; *m* 1971, Robert Pridden; 1 s, 1 da; *Style* - Lady Maria Pridden; Fort Henry House, Exton, Oakham, Leics

PRIDE, John Charles Blackwell; s of John Oswald Pride (d 1959); *b* 19 Nov 1929; *Educ* Oundle; *m* 1951, Jill da of Col F Jordan; 1 s, 1 da; *Career* dir Pride & Clarke Ltd 1962-, dir Toyota (GB) Ltd 1967-78, md Toyota (GB) Ltd 1978-; *Recreations* skiing (snow & water), model engrg; *Style* - John Pride Esq; Little Green ct, Sandown ave, Esher, Surrey (☎ Esher 62946)

PRIDEAUX, Sir Humphrey Povah Treverbian; OBE (1945); s of Walter Treverbian Prideaux; *b* 13 Dec 1915; *Educ* St Aubyns Rottingdean, Eton, Trin Oxford; *m* 1939, Cynthia, da of late Lt-Col H Birch Reynardson, CMG; 4 s; *Career* Jt Planning Staff War Office 1945, Naval Staff Coll 1948, Cmdt Sch of Administration 1948, Chiefs of Staff Secretariat 1950-53, ret; dir The London Life Assoc Ltd 1964, v-pres 1965-72, pres 1973-; dir W H Smith & Son Ltd 1969-77, v-chm 1977-; chm Lord Wandsworth Foundn 1966-; kt 1971; *Clubs* Cavalry & Guards; *Style* - Sir Humphrey Prideaux, OBE; Summers Farm, Long Sutton, Basingstoke, Hants (☎ Long Sutton 295)

PRIDEAUX, Sir John Francis; OBE (1945), DL (Surrey 1976); s of Walter Treverbian Prideaux; *b* 30 Dec 1911; *Educ* St Aubyns Rottindean, Eton; *m* 1934, Joan, da of late Capt Gordon Hargreaves Brown, MC; 2 s, 1 da; *Career* dir National Westminster Bank Ltd 1955-, chm 1971-77, International Westminster Bank Ltd 1955-, chm 1969-77, dir Arbuthnot Latham Holdings Ltd, chm 1969-74; chm Victoria League for Commonwealth Friendship 1977-, memb Lambeth, Southwark and Lewisham AHA(T); US Leg of Merit 1945, kt 1974; *Clubs* Brooks's, Overseas Bankers (pres 1976-77); *Style* - Sir John Prideaux, OBE, DL; Elderslie, Ockley, Surrey (☎ Dorking 711263)

PRIDEAUX, Walter Arbuthnot; CBE (1973), MC (1945), TD (1948); s of Walter Treverbian Prideaux; *b* 4 Jan 1910; *Educ* Eton, Trin Cambridge; *m* 1937, Anne, da of Francis Stewart Cokayne; 2 s, 2 da; *Career* slr 1934, Clerk of the Goldsmiths' Co 1953-75, chm City Parochial Foundn 1972-80, Kent Yeo 1936-4; *Style* - Walter Prideaux Esq, CBE, MC, TD; Saykers, Rusper, Horsham, W Sussex RH12 4RF (☎ Rusper 331)

PRIDHAM, Kenneth Robert Comyn; CMG (1976); s of late Col G R Pridham, CBE, DSO; *b* 28 July 1922; *Educ* Winchester, Oriel Coll Oxford; *m* 1965, Ann Rosalind, da of late E Gilbert Woodward; *Career* Assist Under Sec of State FCO 1974-78, Ambass to Poland 1978-81; *Clubs* Travellers'; *Style* - Kenneth Pridham Esq, CMG; c/o Foreign and Commonwealth Office, SW1

PRIESTLEY, J(ohn) B(oynton); OM (1977); s of Jonathan Priestley (d 1924); *b* Bradford 13 Sept 1894; *Educ* Belle Vue Bradford , Trin Hall Cambridge (Hon Fell 1978); *m* Jacquetta Hawkes; 1 s, 4 da by previous marrs; *Career* author and dramatist; served with Duke of Wellington's and Devon Regts 1914-19, UK Delegate to UNESCO Conferences 1946-47, chm of Int Theatre Conf Paris 1947, and Prague 1948, chm British

Theatre Conf 1948, Pres Int Theatre Inst 1949, memb Nat Theatre Bd 1966-67, freeman City of Bradford 1973; *Style* - J B Priestley Esq, OM; Alveston, Stratford-upon-Avon, Warwicks

PRIMROSE, Alasdair Neil; s and h of Sir John Ure Primrose, 3 Bt; *b* 11 Dec 1935; *m* 1958, Elaine Noreen, da of Edmund Cecil Lowndes, of Buenos Aires, Argentina; 2 s, 2 da; *Style* - Alasdair Primrose Esq; Ada Elflein 3155, Boulogne, Buenos Aires, Argentina

PRIMROSE, Lady Caroline Sara Frances; da of 7 Earl of Rosebery, DL; *b* 20 Nov 1964; *Style* - Lady Caroline Primrose

PRIMROSE, Lady Emma Elizabeth Anne; da of 7 Earl of Rosebery, DL; *b* 12 Sept 1962; *Style* - Lady Emma Primrose

PRIMROSE, Lady Jane Margaret Helen; da of 7 Earl of Rosebery, DL; *b* 11 July 1960; *Style* - Lady Jane Primrose

PRIMROSE, Sir John Ure; 3 Bt (UK 1903); s of Sir William Louis Primrose, 2 Bt (d 1953); *b* 15 April 1908; *Educ* Rugby, Sandhurst; *m* 1933, Enid, da of James Evans Sladen, of BC, Canada; 1 s; *Heir* s, Alasdair Neil Primrose; *Career* Lt Queen's Own Cameron Highlanders 1928-33, farmer; *Style* - Sir John Primrose, Bt; Puerto Victoria, Alto Parana, Misiones, Argentina

PRINCE, William Herbert Carriss; s of Charles William Carriss Prince (d 1972); *b* 8 Feb 1934; *Educ* Denstone Coll, Birmingham U; *m* 1959, Janet Christine Mary, nee Haworth; 1 s, 1 da; *Career* Lt REME during National Service BAOR; production director Walsall Conduits Ltd 1978-; *Recreations* sailing, squash; *Style* - William Prince Esq; 125 Little Sutton Road, Four Oaks, Sutton Coldfield, (☎ 021 308 5174)

PRINCE-SMITH, James William; s and h of Sir (William) Richard Prince-Smith, 4 Bt; *b* 2 July 1959; *Style* - James Prince-Smith Esq

PRINCE-SMITH, Sir (William) Richard; 4 Bt (UK 1911); s of Sir William Prince-Smith, 3 Bt, OBE, MC (d 1964); *b* 27 Dec 1928; *Educ* Charterhouse, Clare Coll Cambridge; *m* 1, 1955, Margaret Ann, da of late Dr John Carter; 1 s, 1 da; m 2, 1975, Ann Christina Faulds; *Heir* s, James William Prince-Smith; *Career* landowner; *Style* - Sir Richard Prince-Smith, Bt; Augres House, Trinity, Jersey

PRING, David Andrew Michael; CB (1980), MC (1943); s of late Capt John Arthur Pring; *b* 6 Dec 1922; *Educ* King's Sch Rochester, Magdalene Cambridge; *m* 1962, Susan Brakspear; 1 s, 1 da; *Career* RE 1941-46, a Clerk of the House of Commons 1948-, Clerk of Committees House of Commons 1976-; *Clubs* Athenaeum; *Style* - David Pring Esq, CB, MC; Bushy Platt, Stanford Dingley, Berks RG7 6DY (☎ Woolhampton 2585)

PRINGLE, Air Marshal Sir Charles Norman Seton; KBE (1973, CBE 1967); s of late Seton Pringle, OBE, FRCSI; *b* 6 June 1919; *Educ* Repton, St John's Cambridge; *m* 1946, Margaret, da of late B Sharp; 1 s; *Career* RAF 1941, Dir-Gen of Engineering (RAF) MOD 1969-70, Air Officer Engineering Strike Command 1970-73, Dir-Gen Engineering (RAF) 1973, Controller Engineering and Supply (RAF) 1973-76, sr exec Rolls Royce Ltd 1976-78, dir Soc of British Aerospace Cos 1979-; CEI; *Style* - Air Marshal Sir Charles Pringle, KBE; 8 Strangways Ter, W14 (☎ 01 602 3356)

PRINGLE, Dr Mia Lilly Kellmer; CBE (1975); da of late Samuel Kellmer; *Educ* Birkbeck Coll London U (Hon Fellow 1980); *m* 1, 1946, William Joseph Sommerville Pringle (d 1962); m 2, 1969, William Leonard Hooper (d 1980); *Career* dir National Children's Bureau 1963-; *Style* - Dr Mia Pringle, CBE; 68 Wimpole st, W1

PRINGLE, Dr Robert William; OBE (1967); s of late Robert Pringle; *b* 2 May 1920; *Educ* George Heriot's Sch Edinburgh, Edinburgh U; *m* 1948, Carol Stokes; 3 s, 1 da; *Career* pres Nuclear Enterprises Ltd Edinburgh 1976-, memb bd Edinburgh U Centre for Industrial Liaison and Consultancy 1968-, Scottish

Sch Business Studies 1972-; FInstP, FRSC, FRSE, Fell American Inst Physics, Hon Fell Roy Scottish Soc Arts; *Clubs* Athenaeum, English-Speaking Union; *Style* - Dr Robert Pringle OBE; 27 avenue Princesse Grace, Monaco

PRINGLE, Simon Robert; s and h of Sir Steuart Robert Pringle, 10 Bt; *b* 6 Jan 1959; *Style* - Simon Pringle Esq; c/o Seymour House, Mount Wise, Plymouth

PRINGLE, Lt-Gen Sir Steuart Robert; 10 Bt (NS 1683); s of Sir Norman H Pringle, 9 Bt (d 1961); *b* 21 July 1928; *Educ* Sherborne; *m* 1953, Jacqueline Marie, da of Wilfrid Hubert Gladwell; 2 s, 2 da; *Heir* s, Simon Robert Pringle; *Career* Lt RM 1949, Capt 1957, Maj 1964, Lt-Col 1971, Col 1975, Maj-Gen RM Commando Forces 1978-79, Ch of Staff to Cmdt Gen RM 1979-81, Cmdt Gen RM 1981-; *Style* - Lt-Gen Sir Steuart Pringle, Bt; 76 South Croxted rd, Dulwich, SE21 (☎ 01 670 1389)

PRIOR, Ven Christopher; CB (1968); s of late Ven W H Prior; *b* 2 July 1912; *Educ* King's Coll Taunton, Keble Oxford, Cuddeston Coll; *m* 1945, Althea Stafford, nee Coode; 2 da; *Career* Chaplain RN 1941-, Archdeacon of Portsmouth 1969-71, Archdeacon Emeritus 1977-; *Style* - The Venerable Christopher Prior CB; Ponies End, West Melbury, Shaftesbury, Dorset SP7 OLY (☎ 0747 811239)

PRIOR, Rt Hon James Michael Leathes; PC (1970), MP (C) Lowestoft Div of Suffolk 1959-; s of late C B L Prior, of Norwich; *b* 11 Oct 1927; *Educ* Charterhouse, Pembroke Coll Cambridge; *m* 1954, Jane Primrose Gifford, da of late Air Vice-Marshal O G Lywood, CB, CBE; 3 s, 1 da; *Career* farmer and land agent in Norfolk and Suffolk; PPS to Pres of BOT 1963, to Min of Power 1963-64, to Mr Edward Heath (Leader of the Opposition) 1965-70; Min of Ag Fish & Food 1970-72, Lord Pres of Council and Leader of House of House of Commons 1972-74, Opposition Front Bench Spokesman on Employment 1974-1979, Sec State Employment 1979-81, Sec State NI 1981-; dep chm Con Party 1972-74 (v-chm 1965); *Style* - The Rt Hon James Prior PC MP; Old Hall, Brampton, Beccles, Suffolk (☎ Brampton 278); 36 Morpeth Mansions, SW1 (☎ 01 834 5543)

PRIOR-PALMER, Lady Doreen (Hersey Winifred); *née* Hope; da of 2 Marquess of Linlithgow, KG, KT, GCSI, GCIE, OBE, TD (d 1952); *b* 1920; *m* 1948, Maj-Gen George Erroll Prior-Palmer, CB, DSO (d 1977); 1 s, 1 da; *Style* - Lady Doreen Prior-Palmer; Appleshaw House, Andover, Hants

PRIOR-PALMER, Lucinda Jane; MBE (1978); da of late Maj-Gen George Erroll Prior-Palmer CB DSO (yr bro of Sir Otho Prior-Palmer, *qv*), by his 2 w, Lady Doreen, nee Hope, da of 2 Marquess of Linlithgow; Miss Prior-Palmer is hence 7 cous of Felix Hope-Nicholson, *qv*; *b* 7 Nov 1953; *Educ* St Mary's, Wantage, and Idbury Manor Oxon; *Career* dir Bacon Everitt Morris & Associates Ltd 1979-; winner Badminton Horse Trials Championships 1973, 1976, 1977, 1979, Individual European Championships 1975, 1977, memb Olympic Team Montreal 1976, winning European Championship Team Burghley 1977, World Championship Team Kentucky 1978; *Style* - Miss Lucinda Prior-Palmer MBE; Appleshaw House, Andover, Hants (☎ Weyhill 2333)

PRIOR-PALMER, Brig Sir Otho Leslie; DSO (1945); s of late Prior Spunner Prior-Palmer; uncle of Miss Lucinda Prior-Palmer, *qv*; *b* 28 Oct 1897; *Educ* Wellington, RMC Sandhurst; *m* 1964, Elizabeth, da of late Harold Henderson; 2 s; *Career* commanded 7 Armoured Bde 1943-45, ret 1946 with hon rank of Brig; MP (C) Worthing Div W Sussex 1945-50, Worthing 1950-64; kt 1959; *Clubs* Royal Yacht Squadron (Cowes), Pratt's; *Style* - Brigadier Sir Otho Prior-Palmer DSO; Grange, Honiton, Devon (☎ Broadhembury 377)

PRISINZANO, Hon Mrs (Helen Margaret); *née* Macdonald; da of 2 Baron Macdonald of Gwaenysgor; *b* 1950; *m* 1974, James Edward Richard Prisinzano; *Style* The Hon Mrs Prisinzano

PRITCHARD, Baron (Life Peer UK 1975); Derek Wilbraham Pritchard; DL (Northants 1974); s of Frank Wheelton

Pritchard; *b* 8 June 1910; *Educ* Clifton Coll Bristol; *m* 1941, Denise Arfor, da of Frank Huntbach; 2 da; *Career* dir J & W Nicholson (Holdings) Ltd 1952-, Midland Bank Ltd 1968-, Samuel Montagu Ltd 1969-, Adelaide Associates Ltd 1970-, Rothmans Internat Ltd 1972-, Rothmans Group Services SA 1972-, Rothmans of Pall Mall (London) Ltd 1980-, Carreras Gp (Jamaica) Ltd 1972-, Paterson, Zochonis & Co Ltd 1977-, Philips Electronic & Associated Industries Ltd 1978-, Templeton Investments Internat Inc 1980-, Templeton Investments Internat Ltd 1980-; chm Dorchester Hotel Bd of Trustees 1980-, Advsy Bd Rothmans World Gp 1980-; pres British Export Houses Assoc 1976-; v-pres Inst of Export 1976-, Wine and Spirit Assoc of GB 1964-; kt 1968; *Style* - The Rt Hon the Lord Pritchard DL; West Haddon Hall, Northampton NN6 7AU (☎ West Haddon 210)

PRITCHARD, Arthur Alan; CB (1979); s of Arthur Henry Standfast Pritchard; *b* 3 March 1922; *Educ* Wanstead H S Essex; *m* 1949, Betty Rona Nevard, nee Little; 2 s, 1 da; *Career* BOT 1939, RAF 1941-46, RAFVR 1947-52, Admiralty 1952, Asst Under-Sec of State Naval Personnel and Ops Requirements MOD 1972-76, seconded as Dep Sec NI Office 1976-78, Dep Under Sec of State (Navy) MOD 1978-; *Style* - Arthur Pritchard Esq CB; Ministry of Defence, SW1A 2HB

PRITCHARD, Sir Asa Hubert; s of William Edward Pritchard, of the Bahamas; *b* 1 Aug 1891; *Educ* Queen's Coll Bahamas; *m* 1915, Maud Pyfrom (d 1978); 2 s, 2 da; *Career* MHA Bahamas 1925-62, speaker 1946-62; pres Asa H Pritchard Ltd Nassau; kt 1965; *Style* - Sir Asa Pritchard; Breezy Ridge, P O Box 6218 ES, Nassau, Bahamas

PRITCHARD, Sir Fred Eills; MBE (1942); s of late Fred Pritchard, of Liverpool; *b* 23 June 1899; *Educ* Shrewsbury, Liverpool U; *m* 1931, Mabel Celia, da of late F W Gaskin, of Liverpool; 1 da; *Career* barr Middle Temple 1923, Master of the Bench 1946-, Treasurer 1964, RMA 1917-19, KC (1937), RA 1939, Maj and Deputy Judge Advocate 1939-42, Lt-Col and Assist Judge Advocate-Gen 1942-45, Judge of the Salford Hundred Court of Record 1944-47, Judge of Queen's Bench Div of High Court of Justice 1947-53, resigned; Hon Bencher Gray's Inn 1965-, dir Inns of Court Sch of Law 1958-68; kt 1947; *Style* - Sir Fred Pritchard MBE; 3 Pump Court, Temple, EC4Y 7AJ (☎ 01 353 4962); Tye Cottage, Mill rd, Slindon, W Sussex (☎ Slindon 404)

PRITCHARD, Rear-Adm Gwynedd Idris; CB (1980); s of Cyril Idris Pritchard; *b* 18 June 1924; *Educ* Wyggeston Sch; *m* 1975, Mary Theresa, nee Curtin; 3 s (by previous m); *Career* RN 1942, Sub-Lt 1944, Lt 1946, Lt-Cdr 1954, Cdr 1959, Capt 1967, Rear-Adm 1976, Flag Officer Gibraltar 1979-80; *Style* - Rear-Adm Gwynedd Pritchard CB; Hoofprints, Beach rd, Burton Bradstock, Dorset

PRITCHARD, John Michael; CBE (1962); s of Albert Edward Pritchard; *b* 5 Feb 1921; *Educ* Sir George Monoux Sch London, privately; *Career* Ch Conductor Cologne Opera 1978-, Ch Guest Conductor BBC Symphony Orchestra 1979-; *Clubs* Spanish; *Style* - John Pritchard Esq CBE; c/o Artists International Management, 3/4 Albert Ter, NW1

PRITCHARD, Hon Mrs (Mary Patricia); *née* Monck; da of late Capt the Hon Charles Henry Stanley Monck and sis of 6 Viscount Monck OBE; *b* 1911; *m* 1935, Brig (Charles) Hilary Vaughan Pritchard, DSO, JP, DL (d 1976); 4 da; *Career* raised to the rank of a Viscount's da, 1928; *Style* - The Hon Mrs Pritchard; Maesbryner, Dolgellau, Gwynedd

PRITCHARD, Sir Neil; KCMG (1962, CMG 1952); s of late Joseph Pritchard; *b* 14 Jan 1911; *Educ* Liverpool Coll, Worcester Coll Oxford; *m* 1943, Mary Burroughes, of Pretoria; 1 s; *Career* Br High Cmmr Tanganyika 1961-63, Dep Under-Sec of State Commonwealth Office 1963-67, Ambass in Bangkok 1967-70, ret; *Style* - Sir Neil Pritchard KCMG; Little Garth, Daglingworth, Cirencester, Glos GL7 7AQ

PRITCHETT, Sir Victor Sawdon; CBE (1968); s of Sawdon Pritchett; *b* 16 Dec 1900; *Educ* Alleyn's Sch; *m* 1936, Dorothy, da of Richard Samuel Roberts; 1 s, 1 da; *Career* author and literary critic; Christian Gauss Lectr Princeton U 1953, Beckman Prof California U Berkeley 1962, Writer-in-Residence Smith Coll Mass 1966; Visiting Prof Brandeis U Mass, Columbia U, Clark Lectr 1969; foreign memb American Acad & Inst 1971, American Acad Arts & Sciences 1971; pres Int PEN 1974-76, Soc of Authors 1977-; Hon LittD Leeds, Hon DLitt Columbia & Sussex; FRSI; kt 1975; *Clubs* Savile, Beefsteak; *Style* - Sir Victor Pritchett, CBE; 12 Regent's Park Ter, NW1

PRITTIE, Hon Henry Francis Cornelius; s and h of 6 Baron Dunalley; *b* 30 May 1948; *Educ* Gordonstoun, Trin Coll Dublin (BA); *m* 1978, Sally Louise, nee Vere; 1 da; *Style* - The Hon Henry Prittie; Jacob's Cottage, Middle Barton, Oxon

PRITTIE, Hon Michael Philip St John; s of 6 Baron Dunalley; *b* 31 Oct 1961; *Educ* Stowe; *Style* - The Hon Michael Prittie

PRITTIE, Hon Mary Rose Madeline; da of 6 Baron Dunalley; *b* 1953; *Style* - The Hon Mary Prittie

PRITTIE, Hon Terence Cornelius Farmer; MBE (1945); s of 5 Baron Dunalley, DSO; *b* 15 Dec 1913; *Educ* Stowe, Ch Ch Oxford; *m* 1946, Laura, da of late Charles Dundas, of Colombia; 2 s; *Career* 2 Lt Rifle Bde 1938, Lt 1940, POW 1939-45 War, Germany Correspondent Manchester Guardian 1946-63, Dip Correspondent The Guardian 1963-70, editor Britain and Israel 1970-; *Recreations* cricket, shooting, reading, and writing books; *Clubs* Travellers', Royal Greenjackets, MCC; *Style* - The Hon Terence Prittie, MBE; 9 Blithfield st, W8 (☎ home 01 937 0164; office 486 414314)

PROBY, Sir Peter; 2 Bt (UK 1952), DL (Cambs 1980); s of Sir Richard George Proby, 1 Bt, MC (d 1979); *b* 4 Dec 1911; *Educ* Eton and Trin Oxford; *m* 1944, Blanche, da of Lt-Col Henry Harrison Cripps, DSO (d 1960); 1 s, 3 da (and 1 s decd); *Heir* s, William Henry Proby, ACA; *Career* 1939-45 War, Capt Irish Gds; Bursar of Eton College 1953-71, land agent; Lord-Lt Cambridgeshire 1981; FRICS; *Clubs* Travellers', Pall Mall; *Style* - Sir Peter Proby, Bt, HM Lord-Lieut for Cambridgeshire; Pottle Green, Elton, Peterborough, Cambs (☎ Elton 434)

PROBY, William Henry; s and h of Sir Peter Proby, 2 Bt; *b* 13 June 1949; *m* 1974, Meredyth Anne Brentnall, da of Dr Timothy David Brentnall; 1 da; *Style* - William Proby Esq

PROBY, Yvonne, Lady; (Eileen) Yvonne; da of Walter Helps, of Trevath Manor, Gwennap, Cornwall, and widow of Fl Lt Reginald Harris, RAF; *m* 1972, as his 2 w, Sir Richard Proby, 1 Bt, MC (d 1979); *style* - Yvonne, Lady Proby; The Dial House, 12 Middle st, Elton, Peterborough, Cambs

PROBYN, Air Cdre Harold Melsome; CB (1944), CBE (1943), DSO (1917); s of late William Probyn; *b* 8 Dec 1891; *m* 1920, Marjory (d 1961), da of late Francis Evance Savory; *Career* commanded RAF Station Cranwell 1940-44, ret; *Clubs* Naval and Military, Nairobi (Kenya); *Style* - Air Commodore Harold Probyn, CB, CBE, DSO; The Cottage, PO Box 61, Nyeri, Kenya (☎ 2248)

PROBYN-JONES, Lady; Eileen; da of late James Evans, of The Old Hall, Helsby, Cheshire; *m* 1919, Sir Arthur Probyn Probyn-Jones, 2 and last Bt (d 1951); *Style* - Lady Probyn-Jones; Spur Cottage, South Lodge, Ham Common, Surrey

PROCKTOR, Patrick; s of Eric Christopher Procktor (d 1940); *b* 12 March 1936; *Educ* Highgate Sch, Slade Sch of Fine Art, UCL; *m* 1973, Kirsten Bo, nee Andersen; 1 s; *Career* painter, etcher, illustrator, stage designer; *Recreations* bridge, Russian ballet; *Style* - Patrick Procktor Esq; 26 Manchester st, WI (☎ 01 486 1763)

PROCTER, Sidney; s of Robert Procter; *b* 10 March 1925; *Educ* Ormskirk G S; *m*

1952, Isabel, nee Simmons; 1 da; *Career* RAF 1943-47; dir Williams & Glyn's Bank Ltd 1976-, ch exec 1978-; dir Royal Bank of Scotland Gp 1978-, dep gp md 1979-; dir Royal Bank of Scotland Ltd 1979-; FCIS, FIB; *Clubs* Royal Automobile, Overseas Bankers; *Style* - Sidney Procter Esq; 40 Moss Close, Pinner, Middlesex (☎ 01 868 3965)

PROCTOR, Sir (Philip) Dennis; KCB (1959, CB 1946); s of late Sir Philip Proctor, KBE; *b* 1 Sept 1905; *Educ* Falconbury, Harrow, King's Cambridge (Hon Fell 1968); *m* 1, 1936, Dorothy Varda (d 1951); m 2, 1953, Barbara, da of Sir Ronald Adam, Bt; 2 s, 1 da; *Career* Miny of Health 1929, Treasury 1930; Dep Sec Miny of Transport and Civil Aviation 1953-58, Perm Sec Miny of Power 1958-65; dir Williams Hudson Ltd 1966-71; *Style* - Sir Dennis Proctor, KCB; 102 High st, Lewes, Sussex

PROCTOR, (Keith) Harvey; MP (C) Basildon 1979-; s of Albert Proctor; *b* 16 Jan 1947; *Educ* H S for Boys Scarborough, York U; *Career* Assist Dir Monday Club 1969-71, Research Officer Con 1970s Parly Gp 1971-72, exec dir Parliamentary Digest Ltd 1972-74, sec British Paper & Board Industry Fedn 1978-79; *Style* - Harvey Proctor Esq, MP; House of Commons, SW1 (☎ 01 219 3000)

PROCTOR, Ian Douglas Ben; s of Douglas McIntyre Proctor; *b* 12 July 1918; *Educ* Gresham's Sch Holt, London U; *m* 1943, Elizabeth Anne Gifford Lynwood, da of Air Vice-Marshal O G Lynwood, CB, CBE; 3 s, 1 da; *Career* md Gosport Yacht Co 1947-48, jt ed Yachtsman Magazine 1948-50, Daily Telegraph Yachting Correspondent 1950-64, Yachtsman of the Year 1965, dir Ian Proctor Metal Masts Ltd 1959-, freelance industrial designer 1950-; RDI, FSIAD, FRSA; *Style* - Ian Proctor Esq; Ferry House, Duncannon, Stoke Gabriel, nr Totnes, Devon

PROCTOR, Sir (George) Philip; KBE (1971, CBE 1961); s of late C A Proctor; *b* 8 June 1902; *Educ* Cheltenham Coll, Liverpool U; *m* 1, 1926, Mary Turney (d 1939), da of late K W Monsarrat; 1 s, 2 da; m 2, 1939, Hilary Frances, da of late F S Clark; 1 s, 2 da; *Career* chm and md Dunlop (NZ) Ltd 1945-65, chm NZ Industrial Design Council 1968-79, chm NZ Heart Foundn 1968-78; nat co-ordinator and chm Duke of Edinburgh Award in NZ 1963-69; KStJ 1976; *Style* - Sir Philip Proctor, KBE; Flat 5, Landscape Apartments, 123 Austin st, Wellington 1, New Zealand

PROCTOR, Sir Roderick Consett; MBE (1946); s of Frederick William Proctor; *b* 28 July 1914; *Educ* Hale Sch Perth WA, Melbourne C of E G S; *m* 1943, Kathleen Mary Murphy (d 1978); 4 s; *Career* joined Clarke & Son, Chartered Accountants, Brisbane, Qld, 1937 (merged with Hungerfords 1960), sr partner 1966-76; FCA; kt 1978; *Clubs* Queensland, Brisbane, Roy Queensland Golf, Southport Golf; *Style* - Sir Roderick Proctor, MBE; Unit 102, The Gardens, Alice st, Brisbane, Qld 4000, Australia

PROCTOR-BEAUCHAMP, Charles Barclay; s and h of Sir Christopher Radstock Proctor-Beauchamp, 9 Bt; *b* 7 July 1969; *Style* - Charles Proctor-Beauchamp Esq

PROCTOR-BEAUCHAMP, Caroline, Lady - Caroline Muriel; da of late Frank Densham; *m* 1933, Rev Sir Ivor Cuthbert Proctor-Beauchamp, 8 Bt (d 1971); *Style* - Caroline, Lady Proctor-Beauchamp

PROCTOR-BEAUCHAMP, Sir Christopher Radstock; 9 Bt (GB 1745); s of Rev Sir Ivor Cuthbert, 8 Bt, MB, BCh, (d 1971); *b* 30 Jan 1935; *Educ* Rugby, Trin Cambridge; *m* 1965, Rosalind Emily Margot, da of Gerald Percival Wainwright, of St Leonard's-on-Sea; 2 s, 1 da; *Heir* s, Charles Barclay Proctor-Beauchamp; *Style* - Sir Christopher Proctor-Beauchamp, Bt; The White House, Harpford, nr Sidmouth, Devon

PRODGER, John Alan; ERD (1964); s of Alan St George Cuthbert Prodger; *b* 19 Jan 1932; *Educ* Merchant Taylors' Sch Northwood, Worchester Coll Oxford; *m* 1971, Tessa Mary Colthurst, nee Davies; 1 s, 1 da; *Career* dir personnel & bd memb Carreras Rothmans Ltd 1973-, chm Tobacco Indust Employers' Assoc 1979-, memb CBI Cncl & Southern Region Cncl; with Tate & Lyle Ltd 1957-73; *Recreations* fishing, cricket, gardening, watching rugby; *Clubs* Marylebone Cricket, Vincent's; *Style* - John Prodger Esq, ERD; Granborough Lodge, Granborough, Buckingham (☎ North Marston 349)

PROFFITT, Adrian Roland; s of Arthur Proffitt; *b* 5 Feb 1934; *Educ* King Edward VI Roy G S Guildford; *m* 1955, Joan Beryl, da of James Blanchard Downton; *Career* dir/co sec: Dzus Fastener Europe Ltd, Dzus Int Products Ltd, Dzus Warrior Leisure Ltd, Just Fasteners Ltd; dir Dzus France S A; *Style* - Adrian Proffitt Esq; Abdera, Folly Hill, Farnham, Surrey (☎ 0252 721491)

PROFUMO, John Dennis; CBE (1975, OBE 1944); 5 Baron of the late United Kingdom of Italy; s of late Baron Albert Profumo, KC; *b* 30 Jan 1915; *Educ* Harrow, BNC Oxford; *m* 1954, Valerie Hobson; 1 s; *Heir* s, David Profumo; *Career* MP (C) Kettering Div Northants 1940-45, MP (C) Stratford-on-Avon Div of Warwicks 1950-63, dir Provident Life Assoc of London 1975-, dep chm 1978-; *Clubs* Boodle's; *Style* - John Profumo Esq, CBE

PROPPER, Arthur; CMG (1965), MBE (1945); s of late I Propper; *b* 3 Aug 1910; *Educ* Owen's Sch, Peterhouse Cambridge; *m* 1941, Erica Mayer; 1 da; *Career* Under-Sec Miny of Agriculture, Fisheries and Food 1964-70, Common Market advr Unigate Ltd 1970-73, sec Food Panel Price Cmmn 1973-76; *Clubs* United Oxford and Cambridge University; *Style* - Arthur Propper Esq, CMG, MBE; 3 Hill House, Stanmore Hill, Stanmore, Middx (☎ 01 954 1242)

PROSSER, (Elvet) John; QC (1978); s of David Prosser; *b* 10 July 1932; *Educ* Pontypridd G S, King's Coll London; *m* 1957, Mary Louise Cowdry; 2 da; *Career* barr Gray's Inn 1956; Fl Lt RAF 1957-59; a Recorder of the Crown Court 1972-, Part-time Chm of Industrial Tribunals 1975-, an Assist Boundary Cmmr Wales 1977-; *Style* - John Prosser Esq, QC; 78 Marsham Court, Westminster, SW1 (☎ 01 834 9779); Hillcroft, Mill rd, Lisvane, Cardiff CF4 5XJ (☎ Cardiff 752380)

PROSSER, Raymond Frederick; CB (1973), MC (1942); s of Frederick Charles Prosser; *b* 12 Sept 1919; *Educ* Wimbledon Coll, Queen's Coll Oxford; *m* 1949, Fay Newmarch Holmes; 2 s, 3 da; *Career* RA 1939-45, Under-Sec Marine Div BOT, later DTI 1968-72, Dep Sec Regional Industrial Organisation and Policy DTI, later DOI 1972-77, Principal Establishment and Finance Officer Depts of Industry, Trade, and Prices and Consumer Protection 1977-79, part-time memb Civil Aviation Authority 1980-; *Style* - Raymond Prosser Esq, CB, MC; Juniper House, Shalford Common, Shalford, Guildford, Surrey (☎ Guildford 66498)

PROSSER, (Albert) Russell Garness; CMG (1967), MBE (1953); s of late Thomas Prosser; *b* 8 April 1915; *Educ* Godlys Sch, LSE; *m* 1957, Ruth Avalon Moore; 1 s (and 1 s decd); *Career* Sr Adviser Social Development, Overseas Development Administration 1967-80; *Style* - Russell Prosser Esq, CMG, MBE; 18b Wray Park rd, Reigate, Surrey (☎ Reigate 42792)

PROSSER, Thomas Vivian; CBE (1963); s of T V Prosser; *b* 25 April 1908; *Educ* Old Swan Tech Inst, Coll of Technology Liverpool; *m* 1935, Florence Minnie (Billie), da of W J Boulton; 1 s, 1 da; *Career* architect 1924, chm T V Prosser & Son (Estates) Ltd, Consultant Dir Proteus-Bygging Ltd LRIBA; *Clubs* Lyceum; *Style* - Thomas Prosser Esq, CBE; Faraway Meadow, Cross o' th' Hill rd, No Man's Heath, Malpas, Cheshire SY14 8NN (☎ Hampton Heath 344)

PROSSER, William David; QC (S (1974); s of David G Prosser; *b* 23 Nov 1934; *Educ* Edinburgh Acad, Corpus Christi Oxford, Edinburgh U; *m* 1964, Vanessa, da of Sir William O'Brien Lindsay, KBE; 2 s, 2 da; *Career* advocate 1962, vice-dean of the Faculty of Advocates 1979-; *Clubs* New, Scottish Arts (Edinburgh); *Style* - William Prosser Esq, QC; 7 Randolph Crescent, Edinburgh (☎ 031 225 2709); Netherfoodie, Dairsie, Fife (☎ Balmullo 438)

PROTHEROE, Alan Hackford; MBE (1980), TD; s of Rev B P Protheroe (d 1971); *b* 10 Jan 1934; *Educ* Maesteg G S Glamorgan; *m* 1956, Anne Miller, da of late Mrs P M Watkins and H M Watkins; 2 s; *Career* 2 Lt The Welch Regt - Nat Serv 1954-56, Lt-Col TA, currently serving HQUKLF, reporter Glamorgan Gazette 1951-53, reporter BBC Wales 1957-59, industrial correspondent Wales BBC 1959-64, ed Wales News and Current Affairs 1964-70, asst ed BBC TV News 1970-72, dep ed 1972-77, ed 1977-80, asst dir BBC News and Current Affairs 1980-, FBIM; *Recreations* writing, pistol and rifle shooting; *Style* - Alan Protheroe Esq, MBE, TD; c/o Broadcasting House, W1A 1AA (☎ 01 580 4468)

PROUD, Sir John Seymour; s of William James Proud; *b* 9 Aug 1907; *Educ* Sydney U; *m* 1964, Laurine, da of M Ferran; *Career* chm Peko-Wallsend Ltd to 1978, (dir 1958-), dir/consultant 1978-; dir Electrical Equipment Ltd 1943-, chm 1978-; dir Oil Search Ltd 1974-, chm 1978-; chm Oil Co of Australia NL 1979-; MIMM, AMIE(Aust), M(Aust)IMM; kt 1978; *Style* - Sir John Proud; 9 Finlay rd, Turramurra, NSW 2074, Australia (☎ 44 3860)

PROUDFOOT, (George) Wilfred; *b* 19 Dec 1921; *Educ* Crook Council Sch, Scarborough Coll; *m* 1950, Margaret Mary, da of Percy Clifford Jackson; 2 s, 1 da; *Career* owner self service stores; consultant in distribution; MP (C) Cleveland Div of Yorkshire 1959-64, Brighouse and Spenborough 1970-74, md Radio 270 1975-, chm Cleveland European Constituency Con Assoc; *Style* - Wilfred Proudfoot Esq; 278 Scalby rd, Scarborough, N Yorkshire (☎ Scarborough 67027)

PROUT, Christopher James; MEP (C) Shropshire and Stafford 1979-; s of late Frank Yabsley Prout, MC*; *b* 1 Jan 1942; *Educ* Sevenoaks Sch, Manchester U, Queen's Coll Oxford; *Career* barr Middle Temple 1972, English-Speaking Union Fell Columbia U 1963-64, staff memb World Bank Gp (UN) Washington DC 1966-69, Leverhulme Fell and Lectr in Law Sussex U 1969-79, Reserve Officer 16/5 The Queen's Roy Lancers 1974-; *Clubs* Roy Armoured Corps Yacht; *Style* - Christopher Prout Esq, MEP; 54 Broad st, Ludlow, Shropshire (☎ Ludlow 2187)

PROUTEN, Leonard William; s of Alfred Prouten (d 1964); *b* 27 March 1917; *Educ* Clapham Central; *m* 1939, Janet Alison Goodwin; 1 s, 1 da; *Career* Captain RA, World War II RE (TA) and RA, ADGB and on staff in South Asia; Solicitor 1951; partner in Stephenson Harwood 1956; senior partner 1973-81; *Recreations* reading and travel; *Clubs* The Gresham, Lansdowne; *Style* - Leonard Prouten Esq; 4 Iverna Court, London W8

PROVAN, James Lyal Clark; MEP (C) NE Scotland 1979-; s of John Provan; *b* 19 Dec 1936; *Educ* Ardvreck Sch Crieff, Oundle, RAC Cirencester; *m* 1960, Roweena Adele Lewis; twin s, 1 da; *Career* memb Tayside Regional Council 1978-, founder vice-chm East of Scotland Grassland Soc 1972-; *Style* - James Provan Esq, MEP; Wallacetown, Bridge of Earn, Perth, Scotland (☎ Bridge of Earn 2243)

PROWTING, Peter Brian; s of Arthur Edwin Alfred Prowting (d 1977); *b* 19 Dec 1924; *Educ* Frays Coll Uxbridge; *m* 1966, Elizabeth Anne, da of Wing Cdr Leslie Mobsby (d 1966); 1 da (by former m); *Career* chm Prowting Holdings Ltd 1955-, dir Estates & General Investments Ltd 1974-; *Recreations* gardening, golf, jazz; *Clubs* Gerrards Cross Golf; *Style* - Peter Prowting Esq; Old House Farm, Fulmer, Bucks (☎ Fulmer 2213)

PRYCE, George Terry; s of Edwin Pryce (d 1961); *b* 26 March 1934; *Educ* Welshpool G S, Nat Coll of Food Technology; *m* 1957, Thurza Elizabeth, da of Capt Arthur Denis Tatham (d 1942); 2 s, 1 da; *Career* dir Dalgety Ltd 1972-, md 1978-, chm Dalgety (UK) Ltd 1978-, Dalgety Spillers Ltd 1980-; FIFST, FBIM; *Style* - George Pryce Esq; 89 Brookmans av, Brookmans Park, nr Hatfield, Herts (☎ Potters Bar 42039)

PRYCE-JONES, Hon Mrs (Clarissa Sabina); da of Baron Caccia (Life Peer); *b* 26 May 1939; *m* 1959, David Eugene Henry Pryce-Jones; 3 da; *Style* - The Hon Mrs Pryce-Jones; 1 Phillimore Lodge, Phillimore ter, W8

PRYCE-JONES, Lady; Syra Roantree; da of late Francis O'Shiel, of Omagh, Co Tyrone; *m* 1938, Capt Sir Pryce Victor Pryce-Jones, 2 and last Bt (d 1963); *Style* - Lady Pryce-Jones; The Manor House, Great Ryburgh, Norfolk

PRYKE, Sir David Dudley; 3 Bt (UK 1926); s of Sir (William Robert) Dudley Pryke, 2 Bt (d 1959); *b* 16 July 1912; *Educ* St Lawrence Coll Ramsgate; *m* 1945, Doreen Winifred, da of late Ralph Bernard Wilkins; 2 da; *Heir* bro, William Dudley Pryke; *Career* late Common Councilman, City of London, Liveryman Turners' Co 1961; *Style* - Sir David Pryke, Bt; Flatholme, Brabant rd, North Fambridge, Chelmsford, Essex (☎ Maldon 740227)

PRYKE, William Dudley; s of Sir (William Robert) Dudley Pryke, 2 Bt (d 1959) and hp of bro, Sir David Pryke, 3 Bt; *b* 18 Nov 1914; *Educ* Highgate Sch; *m* 1940, Lucy Irene (Peggy), da of late Frank Madgett, of Whetstone; 1 s, 1 da; *Career* formerly Capt Duke of Cornwall's LI; a Liveryman of Plumbers' Co (Master 1969-70); *Clubs* United Sports; *Style* - William Pryke Esq; 4 Parkgate Cres, Hadley Wood, Barnet, Herts

PUDNEY, Hon; Hon Carolyn; da of late Baron Delacourt-Smith (Life Peer, d 1972); *b* 1944; *m* 1969, Roger Martin Pudney; *Style* - The Hon Mrs Pudney; 10 Mulgrave rd, Ealing, W5

PUGH, Alastair Tarrant; s of Sqdn Ldr Rev Herbert Cecil Pugh, GC; *b* 16 Sept 1928; *Educ* Tettenhall Coll Staffs, De Havilland Aeronautical Tech Sch; *m* 1957, Sylvia Victoria Marlow; 2 s, 1 da; *Career* md British Caledonian Airways 1978-FRAeS, FCIT, FRSA; *Style* - Alastair Pugh Esq; England's Cottage, Sidlow Bridge, Reigate, Surrey (☎ Reigate 43456)

PUGH, Hon Mrs (Caroline Mary Stewart); *née* Maud; da of Baron Redcliffe-Maud, GCB, CBE; *b* 1939; *m* 1967, Very Rev Dean Joel Pugh; *Style* - The Hon Mrs Pugh; Trinity Cathedral, Little Rock, Arkansas, USA

PUGH, Sir Idwal Vaughan; KCB (1972, CB 1967); s of late Rhys Pugh; *b* 10 Feb 1918; *Educ* Cowbridge G S, St John's Oxford (Hon Fell 1979); *m* 1946, Mair Lewis; 1 s, 1 da; *Career* 2 Perm Sec DOE 1971-76, Parly Cmmr for Admin and Health Serv Cmmr for England, Wales & Scotland 1976-79, chm Chartered Trust Ltd 1979-; dir: Standard Chartered Bank 1979-, Halifax Building Soc 1979-; chm Development Corpn of Wales 1980-; *Clubs* Brooks's, Cardiff and County (Cardiff); *Style* - Sir Idwal Pugh, KCB; Nant-y-Garreg, Bontddu, Gwynedd

PUGH, Hon Mrs; Hon Jane; *née* Lyon-Dalberg-Acton; da of 3 Baron Acton, CMG, MBE, TD; *b* 25 Jan 1954; *m* 1975, Charles Thomas Pugh; 1 da; *Style* - The Hon Mrs Pugh

PUGH, John Stanley; s of John Albert Pugh; *b* 9 Dec 1927; *Educ* Wallasey G S; *m* 1953, Kathleen Mary; 2 s, 1 da; *Career* ed Liverpool Daily Post 1969-78, ed Liverpool Echo 1978-; *Style* - John Pugh Esq; 26 Westwood rd, Noctorum, Birkenhead, Merseyside

PUGH, Lionel Roger Price; CBE (1975), VRD (1953); s of late Henry George Pugh, of Cardiff; *b* 9 May 1916; *Educ* Clifton; *m* 1942, Joyce Norma Nash; 1 s, 1 da; *Career* dir Bridon Ltd 1973-, dep chm 1977-, dir L Ryan Holdings 1979-, pres Iron and Steel Inst 1973, DL S Glamorgan 1963-78; Gold Cross of Merit (Poland) 1942; *Style* - Lionel Pugh Esq, CBE, VRD; Brook Cottage, Bournes Green, Oakridge, Glos (☎ Bisley 554)

PUGH, Hon Mrs (Petrina Frances Anne); *née* Mitchell-Thomson; da of 3 Baron Selsdon; *b* 1945; *Educ* Queens Gate London; *m* 1967, James Geoffrey Lennox Pugh, late Gren Gds; 1 s, 1 da; *Career* co dir & co sec T & J Grain Ltd (ag merchants/ cereal mktg); *Recreations* real tennis; *Style* - The Hon Mrs Pugh; Whitelands, Rudford, Glos (☎ 045 279 204)

PUGH-COOK, Richard Gerald; s of Cdr George Garnet Pugh-Cook, OBE, RN (d 1969); *b* 15 Dec 1937; *Educ* Felsted Sch; *m* 1963, Elizabeth Ann, da of Capt Michael William Allday; 2 s, 1 da; *Career* dir Mid-Wales Yarns Ltd, Steeles Carpets Ltd, gp marketing dir Tomkinsons Carpets Ltd; *Recreations* tennis, cricket; *Style* - Richard Pugh-Cook Esq; The Old Vicarage, Elmbridge, Droitwich, Worcs

PUGSLEY, Rear-Adm Anthony Follett; CB (1944), DSO (1943); s of late J Follett Pugsley; *b* 7 Dec 1901; *Educ* RNCs Osborne and Dartmouth; *m* 1931, Barbara, da of late J Byam Shaw; 1 s; *Career* Midshipman 1918, Cdr 1936, Capt 1942, Rear-Adm 1952, Flag Officer Malayan Area 1951-53, ret 1954; *Style* - Rear-Admiral Anthony Pugsley, CB, DSO; Javelin, Milverton, Taunton, Somerset (☎ Milverton 400355)

PUGSLEY, Sir Alfred Grenvile; OBE (1944); s of H W Pugsley; *b* May 1903; *Educ* Rutlish Sch, London U; *m* 1928, Kathleen M Warner (d 1974); *Career* Prof of Civil Engineering Bristol U 1944-68 (now Emeritus), Pro-Vice-Chllr 1961-64; Hon FRAeS 1963, Hon DSc Belfast 1965, Cranfield 1978, Hon DUniv Surrey 1968, Structural Engrs' Gold Medal 1968, Civil Engrs Ewing Gold Medal 1979, FRS 1952; kt 1956; *Clubs* Athenaeum; *Style* - Sir Alfred Pugsley, OBE; 4 Harley Court, Clifton Down, Bristol BS8 3JU

PUGSLEY, Peter Vivian Rupert; s of Vivian Stanley Pugsley; *b* 2 March 1933; *Educ* Cranleigh; *m* 1971, Carolyn, da of Sidney Francis Morgan; 1 c; *Career* chm and md Premier Gold Trading Stamp Co Ltd, Performance Awards (1980) Ltd, Phoenix Promotions Ltd, Edgware Travel Ltd; *Recreations* hockey, golf; *Clubs* MCC; *Style* - Peter Pugsley Esq; 28 Penny st, Old Portsmouth, Hants (☎ Portsmouth 25189)

PULAY, George; s of Dr Erwin Pulay (d 1951); *b* 5 March 1923; *Educ* Manchester G S, London U; *m* 1, 1953, Lilette Anna (d 1962), da of late George Callil; m 2, 1965, Katharine Frances Goddard, da of Rt Hon Sir Eric Sachs, MBE, TD (d 1979), and of Hon Margaret, da of Baron Goddard of Aldbourne, GCB; 2 da; *Career* editorial staff Daily Telegraph 1950-59, City Editor The Times 1966-68; founder dir Charles Barker City Ltd 1968-, chm 1977-; chm Charles Barker Lyons Ltd 1977-, dir Charles Barker ABH Int Ltd 1972-; *Recreations* skiing, tennis, music; *Clubs* City of London, Hurlingham; *Style* - George Pulay Esq; 83 Dovehouse st, SW3 (☎ 01 351 1342)

PULLEN, Leslie Robert; s of Robert Victor Pullen (d 1975); *b* 15 June 1921; *Educ* Wakefield, Sch of Architecture Regent St Poly; *m* 1946, Lorna Ada, da of Stanley Peirce (d 1945); 3 s; *Career* sales dir KDG Instruments Ltd 1956-64, gen man 1964-74, md 1974-; gp bd dir Bath & Portland Gp Ltd 1968-; *Recreations* cricket, soccer, rugby, golf; *Clubs* Wig and Pen; *Style* - Leslie Pullen Esq; Misteltoe Cottage, Common Lane, Ditchling, Sussex (☎ Hassocks 4260)

PULLINGER, Sir (Francis) Alan; CBE (1970); s of William Pullinger; *b* 22 May 1913; *Educ* Marlborough, Balliol Oxford; *m* 1, 1946, Felicity Charmian Gotch Hobson (decd); 2 s, 1 da; m 2, 1966, Jacqueline Louise Anne Durin; *Career* chm Haden Carrier Ltd 1961-79, pres Instn of Heating and Ventilating Engrs 1972-73; Hon FCIBS 1977, kt 1977; *Recreations* mountaineering, sailing, beagling; *Clubs* Alpine, Travellers'; *Style* - Sir Alan Pullinger, CBE; Barnhorn, Meadway, Berkhamsted, Herts (☎ Berkhamsted 3206)

PUMPHREY, Christopher Jonathan; TD; s of Col Jonathan Moberly Pumphrey, OBE, TD, DL; *b* 2 Nov 1933; *Educ* Winchester, Magdalene Cambridge; *m* 1960, Joanna Jane, da of Frederic Howard Aykroyd (d 1978); 2 s, 1 da; *Career* partner Wise Speke & Co, Stockbrokers, 1960-; dir Newcastle Building Soc; *Clubs* Northern Counties (Newcastle upon Tyne); *Style* - Christopher Pumphrey Esq, TD; Bolam West Houses, Middleton, Morpeth, Northumberland (☎ Belsay 232)

PUMPHREY, Sir (John) Laurence; KCMG (1973, CMG 1963); s of late Charles Ernest Pumphrey; *b* 22 July 1916; *Educ* Winchester, New Coll Oxford; *m*

1945, Jean, da of Sir Walter Buchanan Riddell, 12 Bt; 4 s, 1 da; *Career* Foreign Serv 1945, Dep High Cmmr Nairobi 1965-67, British High Cmmr Zambia 1967-71, Ambass to Pakistan 1971-76; *Style* - Sir Laurence Pumphrey, KCMG; Caistron, Thropton, Morpeth, Northumberland NE65 7LG

PURBECK, Luca; s of Herbert Gutmann (d 1942); *b* 13 July 1914; *Educ* Realgymnasium, Berlin U; *m* 1954, Vera (d 1979), da of Arthur Doughty, of London (d 1961); 1 s (and 1 s decd); *Career* news editor Associated Press of America, London 1944-46; founder md Mayborn Products Ltd London and Dylon Int Ltd; pres Dylon-France SA FCO SA, dir Dylon-Japan KK, Dylon-Nederland NV 1946-79, non exec v-chm 1980-; FInstM; *Recreations* golf, painting, sculpting; *Clubs* Wentworth, RAC, Directors'; *Style* - Luca Purbeck Esq; 14 Langford Place, St Johns Wood, NW8 (☎ 01 624 9492)

PURBRICK, Tony; *Career* formerly with the Police; with Pinkerton's detective agency 1968-, md Pinkerton UK; *Style* - Tony Purbrick Esq; c/o Pinkerton's of the UK Ltd, Ferrari House, 102 College rd, Harrow HA1 1BQ (☎ 01 427 1077)

PURCELL, Robert Michael; s of late Lt-Col Walter Purcell; *b* 22 Oct 1923; *Educ* Ampleforth; *m* 1965, Julia Evelyn, da of late Brig Edward Marsh-Kellett; 2 da; *Career* Counsellor and Dep High Cmmr Malta 1977-80, Ambass to Somali Democratic Republic 1980-; KSG 1976; *Clubs* Naval and Military; *Style* - Robert Purcell Esq; c/o Foreign and Commonwealth Office, SW1; Lythe House, Selborne, Hants (☎ Selborne 231)

PURCHAS, Hon Mr Justice; Hon Sir Francis Brooks; s of late Capt Francis Purchas; *b* 19 June 1919; *Educ* Summerfields Sch Oxford, Marlborough, Trin Cambridge; *m* 1942, Patricia Mona Kathleen, da of Lt R Milburn; 2 s; *Career* barr Inner Temple 1948, QC 1965, Bencher 1972, Recorder of the Crown Court 1972-74, a Judge of the High Court of Justice, Family Div 1974-, Presiding Judge South Eastern Circuit 1977; kt 1974; *Recreations* shooting, golf, fishing; *Clubs* Hawks (Cambridge); *Style* - The Hon Mr Justice Purchas; Parkhurst House, nr Haslemere, Surrey GU27 3BY (☎ North Chapel 280); 1 Mitre Court Buildings, Temple, EC4Y 7BS (☎ 01 353 5124)

PURDY, Robert John; CMG (1963), OBE (1954); s of late Lt-Col Thomas Woods Purdy; *b* 2 March 1916; *Educ* Haileybury, Jesus Coll Cambridge; *m* 1957, Elizabeth, da of Richard Matthew Sharp (d 1975); 2 s, 1 da; *Career* Maj 3 and 4 Burma Campaigns 1943-45, Colonial Admin Serv N Nigeria 1939, Sr Resident Sokoto Province 1961-63; bursar Gresham's Sch Holt 1965-81; *Style* - Robert Purdy Esq, CMG, OBE; Spratt's Green House, Aylsham, Norwich NR11 6TX (☎ Aylsham 2147)

PURLEY, David Charles; s of Charles Reginald Chenies Purley; *b* 26 Jan 1945; *Educ* Dartington Hall, RMA Sandhurst; *m* 1969 (m dis 1975), Jane Alexandra, da of late Sqdn Ldr Richard Garvey, DFC & Bar; 2 da; *Career* Lt, George Medal 1973, co dir of Lec Refrigeration Ltd 1973; *Recreations* aerobatic flying, enduro motorcycle racing; *Clubs* British Automobile Racing, British Racing Drivers; *Style* - David Purley Esq; Summersday, Spinney Lane, Itchenor, Chichester, W Sussex

PURSEGLOVE, John William; CMG (1973); s of late Robert Purseglove; *b* 11 Aug 1912; *Educ* Lady Manners Sch Bakewell, Manchester U, Gonville and Caius Cambridge, Imperial Coll of Tropical Agric Trinidad; *m* 1947, Phyllis Agnes Adèle, da of late George Turner; 1 s, 1 da; *Career* tropical crops specialist; Overseas Dvpt Admin at East Malling Research Station Kent 1967-75; FLS 1944, FIBiol 1970; *Style* - John Purseglove Esq, CMG; Walnut Trees, Sissinghurst, Cranbrook, Kent TN17 2JL (☎ Cranbrook 712836)

PURSSELL, Anthony John Richard; *b* 5 July 1926; *Educ* Oriel Oxford; *m* 1952, Ann Margaret Batchelor; 2 s, 1 da; *Career* md Arthur Guinness Son & Co Ltd 1975-; memb IBA 1976-; *Clubs* Leander (Henley); *Style* - Anthony Purssell Esq; c/o Arthur Guinness Son & Co Ltd, 10

Albemarle st, W1X 4AJ (☎ 01 493 6747)

PURVES, Dame Daphne Helen; DBE (1979); da of Irvine Watson Cowie; *b* 8 Nov 1908; *Educ* Otago Girls' H S Dunedin NZ, Otago U; *m* 1939, Herbert Dudley Purves; 1 s, 2 da; *Career* Sr Lecturer in French, Dunedin Teachers Coll 1967-73, pres Int Fedn of Univ Women 1977-80, v-pres for Women, Global Cooperation Soc Club 1980; *Style* - Dame Daphne Purves, DBE; 11 Falkland st, Dunedin, New Zealand (☎ Dunedin 779 105)

PURVES, James Grant; CMG (1971); s of Alexander Murray Purves; *b* 15 May 1911; *Educ* St Andrews U, U of Freiburg-im-Breisgau; *m* 1947, Mary Tinsley; 3 s, 1 da; *Career* Counsellor HM Embassy Berne 1965-67, HM Consul-Gen Hamburg 1967-71; *Style* - James Purves Esq, CMG; Long Roof, Walberswick, Southwold, Suffolk (☎ Southwold 722242)

PURVIS, John Robert; MEP (C) Mid-Scotland and Fife 1979-; s of Lt-Col Robert William Berry Purvis, MC; *b* 6 July 1938; *Educ* Cargilfield Barnton Edinburgh, Trin Coll Glenalmond Perths, St Salvator's Coll St Andrews U; *m* 1962, Louise S Durham; 1 s, 2 da; *Career* md Gilmerton Management Services Ltd 1973-, dir and sec Brigton Farms Ltd Cupar; *Clubs* Cavalry and Guards, Farmers', New (Edinburgh), Royal and Ancient (St Andrews); *Style* - John Purvis Esq, MEP; Gilmerton, Dunino, St Andrews, Fife, Scotland KY16 8NB (☎ St Andrews 73275)

PUSINELLI, Frederick Nigel Molière; CMG (1966), OBE (1963), MC (1940); s of S Jacques Pusinelli; *b* 28 April 1919; *Educ* Aldenham Sch, Pembroke Cambridge; *m* 1941, Joan Mary Chaloner, da of Cuthbert B Smith; 1 s, 1 da; *Career* Dir of Establishments 1962-68, & Assist High Cmmr 1963-68, Aden and Fedn of S Arabia; *Style* - Frederick Pusinelli Esq CMG OBE MC; Routledge Cottage, Westbourne, Emsworth, Hants PO10 8SE (☎ Emsworth 2915)

PUTTICK, Richard George; s of late George Frederick Puttick; *b* 16 March 1916; *Educ* St Mark's Teddington; *m* 1943, Betty Grace Folbigg; 2 s; *Career* c[illegible] Taylor Woodrow Ltd 1974-, ch exec 1978-, pres NW Middx Branch BIM; FIOB, CBIM, FRSA, Liveryman Worshipful Co of Joiners and Ceilers; *Style* - Richard Puttick Esq; Woodlawn, Hanger Hill, Weybridge, Surrey

PYBUS, William Michael; s of Sydney James Pybus (d 1972); *b* 7 May 1923; *Educ* Bedford Sch, New Coll Oxford; *m* 1959, Elizabeth Janet, da of Peter Percy Whitley (ka 1942); 2 s, 2 da; *Career* partner Herbert Oppenheimer, Nathan & Vandyk 1953-; chm: AAH Ltd 1968-, British Fuel Co 1968-, Inter Continental Fuels Ltd 1975-, Overseas Coal Developments Ltd 1979-, Siebe Gorman Holdings Ltd 1980 (dir 1972-); dep chm R Mansell Ltd 1980-, chm BR Midlands and N Western Bd 1977-, dir Nat West Bank Ltd (Outer London Region) 1977-, Coal Trade Benevolent Association 1969-, Cornhill Insurance Company Ltd 1977-, pres Coal Industry Society 1976-81, master of Pattenmakers' Co 1972-73; *Recreations* fishing; *Clubs* Cavalry & Guards, MCC; *Style* - William Pybus Esq; Beades, Old Malden Lane, Worcester Park, Surrey (☎ 01 337 1496); Higher Shilstone, Throwleigh, nr Okehampton, Devon (064 723 396)

PYKE, Sir Louis Frederick; ED (1946); s of late J M Pyke; *b* 21 Nov 1907; *Educ* Melbourne C of E G S; *m* 1936, Sierlah, da of H J Cohen; 2 s, 1 da; *Career* md Costain (Aust) Pty Ltd 1965-73, chm and md 1971-77; dir: Costain Investments (Aust) Pty Ltd 1977-, Steel Deck Industries Pty Ltd 1978-, Davis Vindin Pty Ltd 1978-; FAIB, FAIM, kt 1978; *Style* - Sir Louis Pyke, ED; 419 Wattletree rd, East Malvern, Vic 3145, Australia (☎ 25 6961)

PYM, Rt Hon Francis Leslie; MC (1945), PC (1970), DL (Cambs 1973), MP (C) Cambridgeshire 1961-; s of late Leslie Pym, JP, DL, MP, sometime Sr Lord of the Treasury (whose paternal grandmother's mother was Hon Margaret, da of 12 Baron St John of Bletso, while his paternal grand*father's* mother was Lady Jane Melville, 2 da of 7 Earl of Leven and Melville); *b* 13 Feb 1922; *Educ* Eton, Magdalene Cambridge; *m* 1949, Valerie

Fortune, da of Francis Daglish; 2 s (Jonathan b 1952, m 1981 Laura da of Robin Wellesley, *qv*; Andrew b 1954), 2 da (Charlotte b 1950, Sarah b 1958); *Career* Parly Sec to the Treasury and Govt Ch Whip 1970-73, Sec of State for NI 1973-74, Opposition Spokesman on Agriculture 1974-76, House of Commons Affairs & Devolution 1976-78, For & C'wlth Affairs 1978-79, Sec of State for Defence 1979-81, Chllr of the Duchy of Lancaster, Leader of the House of Commons and Paymaster Gen 1981; Lord of the Manor of Sandy and Girtford, patron of 1 living (Sandy); served WW II Capt 9 Queen's Roy Lancers; *Clubs* Cavalry and Guards, Buck's; *Style* - The Rt Hon Francis Pym MC PC DL MP; Everton Park, Sandy, Beds

PYMAN, Lancelot Frank Lee; CMG (1961); s of late Dr F L Pyman, FRS; *b* 8 Aug 1910; *Educ* Dover Coll, King's Cambridge; *m* 1936, Sarah Woods Gamble; *Career* Levant Consular Serv 1933; HM Consul-Gen Zagreb 1957-61, Basra March-Dec 1961; Ambass to the Somali Republic 1961-63, Consul-Gen San Francisco 1963-66; *Style* - Lancelot Pyman Esq, CMG; c/o Foreign and Commonwealth Office, SW1

Q

QUANT, Mary (Mrs A Plunket Greene); OBE (1966); da of Jack Quant; *b* 11 Feb 1934; *Educ* Goldsmiths' Coll of Art; *m* 1957, Alexander Plunket Greene; 1 s; *Career* fashion designer; dir Mary Quant Gp of Cos 1955-, memb Design Council; RDI 1969; *Style* - Miss Mary Quant, OBE; 3 Ives st, SW3 (☎ 01 584 8781)

QUARMBY, David Anthony; s of Frank Reginald Quarmby; *b* 22 July 1941; *Educ* Shrewsbury, King's Cambridge, Leeds U (PhD, Dip Indust Management Studies); *m* 1968, Hilmary, da of Denis Hilton Hunter; 4 da; *Career* memb London Transport Executive 1975-, md (Buses) LTE 1978-; FCIT; *Recreations* music, singing; *Style* - David Quarmby Esq; 13 Shooters Hill rd, Blackheath SE3 7AR (☎ 01 858 7371)

QUARREN EVANS, His Honour Judge; John Kerry; s of Hubert Royston Quarren Evans, MC (d 1967); *b* 4 July 1926; *Educ* King Henry VIII Sch Coventry, Cardiff H S, Trinity Hall Cambridge (MA, LLB); *m* 1958, Jane Shaw, da of Neil Lawson; 1 s, 1 da; *Career* slr of Supreme Court 1953; partner Lyndon Moore & Co, of Newport, Gwent 1954-71, partner T S Edwards & Son 1971-80, Recorder Wales & Chester Circuit 1974-80; a Circuit Judge, South Eastern Circuit 1980-; *Recreations* music, golf, rugby football; *Clubs* Newport Golf; *Style* - His Honour Judge Quarren Evans; c/o Acton Crown Court, Armstrong rd, W3 7BJ (☎ 01 740 8888)

QUAYLE, (John) Anthony; CBE (1952); s of Arthur Quayle; *b* 7 Sept 1913; *Educ* Rugby; *m* 1947, Dorothy Hyson; 1 s, 2 da (of whom 1, Rosanna, m Richard Astley, ggs of Francis L'Estrange Astley, bro of 16 Baron Hastings; 2 s, 1 da); *Career* actor, served War 1939-45 RA, dir Shakespeare Memorial Theatre 1948-56; *Style* - Anthony Quayle Esq, CBE; 49b Elystan Place, SW3 3JY

QUEENSBERRY, 12 Marquess of (S 1682); Sir David Harrington Angus Douglas; 11 Bt (S 1668); also Viscount Drumlanrig, Lord Douglas of Hawick and Tibbers (both S 1628), and Earl of Queensberry (S 1633); s of 11 Marquess (d 1954, himself n of Lord Alfred Douglas, the poet and friend of Oscar Wilde) by his 2 w Cathleen, nee Mann; *b* 19 Dec 1929; *Educ* Eton; *m* 1, 1956 (m dis 1969), Ann, da of Maurice Jones and formerly w of George Radford; 2 da; m 2, 1969, Alexandra, da of Guy Wyndham Sich; 2 s, 1 da; *Heir* s, Viscount Drumlanrig; *Career* late 2 Lt RHG; Prof Ceramics RCA 1959-; Pres Design & Industs Assoc 1976-78; *Style* - Prof The Most Hon The Marquess of Queensberry; c/o Royal College of Art, Kensington Gore, SW7 (☎ 01 589 3886)

QUEENSBERRY, Dowager Marchioness of; Muriel Beatrice

Margaret (Chunn); da of late Arthur John Rowe Thornett; *m* 1947, as his 3 wife, 11 Marquess of Queensberry (d 1954); *Style* - The Most Hon the Dowager Marchioness of Queensberry; Jesmond, 1 Port Lewaigue Close, Maughold, IOM

QUENINGTON, Viscount; Michael Henry Hicks Beach; s and h of 2 Earl St Aldwyn, KBE, TD, PC; *b* 7 Feb 1950; *Style* - Viscount Quenington

QUIBELL, Baroness; Catherine Cameron Rae; *m* 1954, as his 2 w, 1 Baron (d 1962, when title became extinct); *Career* pres Scunthorpe and Dist Spastic Soc; *Style* - The Rt Hon The Lady Quibell; 38 Exeter rd, Scunthorpe, Lincs

QUICK, Brian; s of Stanley James Quick (d 1973); *b* 26 May 1933; *Educ* Devonport H S; *m* 1964, Anne Vivien, nee Fowler; 1 s, 2 da; *Career* dir: Hill Samuel & Co Ltd, Hill Samuel & Co (Ireland) Ltd, Lambert Bros Shipping Ltd, Nat Bank of Ras Al Khaima; chm London Bridge Finance Ltd, Universal Credit Ltd; *Recreations* tennis, golf; *Style* - Brian Quick Esq; 2 Wheatfield rd, Harpenden, Herts (☎ 4425)

QUICK-SMITH, George William; CBE (1959); s of George Windsor Smith (d 1954); *b* 23 Aug 1905; *Educ* London U; *m* 1934, Ida Muriel; *Career* barr, memb Br Rd Serv 1948-59, advr Br T'port Cmmn 1959-62, ch exec T'port Hldg Co 1963-69, dep chm & ch exec Nat Freight Corp 1968-71; *Clubs* Royal Motor Yacht; *Style* - George Quick-Smith Esq, CBE; 6 Martello Towers, Ravine rd, Canford Cliffs, Poole, Dorset (☎ 0202 708 127)

QUICKE, John Godolphin; CBE (1978); s of Capt Noel Arthur Godolphin Quicke (d 1943); *b* 20 Apr 1922; *Educ* Eton, New Coll Oxford; *m* 1953, Prudence Tinné, da of late Rear-Adm Charles Pierre Berthon; 6 c; *Career* farmer and landowner, chm Min of Ag's SW Regional Panel 1972-75, pres Country Landowners' Assoc 1975-77, memb of SW Regional Bd Nat West Bank 1974-, chm Commercial Union JNS Co (Exeter Local Bd) 1980-; *Recreations* music, trees; *Clubs* Boodle's; *Style* - John Quicke Esq, CBE; Sherwood, Newton St Cyres, Exeter (☎ Newton St Cyres 216)

QUILLEY, Denis; s of Clifford Charles Quilley (d 1968); *b* 26 Dec 1927; *Educ* Bancroft's Sch; *m* 1949, Stella Jean, nee Chapman; 1 s, 2 da; *Career* actor; *Clubs* St James'; *Style* - Denis Quilley Esq; 22 Willow rd, NW3; (☎ 01 435 5976) Sea Venture, Lyme Regis, Dorset (☎ 2397)

QUILTER, Sir Anthony Raymond Leopold Cuthbert; 4 Bt (UK 1897); s of Sir (John) Raymond Cuthbert Quilter, 3 Bt (d 1959); *b* 25 March 1937; *Educ* Harrow; *m* 1964, (Mary) Elise, da of Col Brian Sherlock Gooch, DSO, TD, of Tannington Hall, Woodbridge; 1 s; *Heir* s, Guy Quilter; *Style* - Sir Anthony Quilter, Bt; The Applehouse, Methersgate, Sutton, Woodbridge, Suffolk

QUILTER, David Cuthbert Tudway; DL (Somerset 1970); s of Percy Cuthbert Quilter (d 1947); *b* 26 March 1921; *Educ* Eton; *m* 1953, Elizabeth Mary, da of Sir John Carew Pole, Bt; 1 s, 2 da; *Career* Vice Lord-Lieut Somerset 1978-; dir Barclays Bank UK Ltd 1971- (local dir Pall Mall 1957, Bristol 1962), JP London Juvenile Courts 1959-62, High Sheriff Somerset 1974-75, Mayor of Wells 1974-75, tres Bristol U 1976-, memb Cncl Outward Bound Trust 1959-; *Recreations* gardening, shooting, tennis, golf; *Clubs* Boodle's; *Style* - David Quilter Esq, HM Vice Lord-Lieut for Somerset; Milton Lodge, Wells, Somerset (☎ Wells 72168)

QUILTER, Guy Raymond Cuthbert; s and h of Sir Anthony Quilter, 4 Bt; *b* 13 April 1967

QUINLAN, Michael Edward; CB (1980); s of Gerald Andrew Quinlan; *b* 11 Aug 1930; *Educ* Wimbledon Coll, Merton Oxford; *m* 1965, Margaret Mary, nee Finlay; 2 s, 2 da; *Career* Civil Serv 1954-, defence counsellor UK Delegation to NATO 1970-73, Und-Sec Cabinet Office 1974-77, Dep Und-Sec of State (Policy & Programmes) MOD 1977-; *Recreations* cricket, squash, listening to music; *Clubs* RAF; *Style* - Michael Quinlan Esq, CB; c/o Ministry of Defence, Whitehall, SW1 (☎ 01 218 2135)

QUINN, James Charles Frederick; s of Rev Chllr James Quinn; *b* 23 Aug 1919; *Educ* Shrewsbury, Trin Coll Dublin, Christchurch Oxford; *m* 1941, Hannah, da of Rev Robert Malcolm Gwynn, V-Provost Trin Coll Dublin; 1 s, 1 d; *Career* Chevalier dans l'Ordre des Arts et des Lettres (France 1979); film producer and exibitor; dir British Film Inst 1955-64, trustee Imperial War Museum 1968-78, chm Nat Panel for Film Festivals 1974-; *Recreations* lawn tennis, sleeping; *Clubs* Cavalry and Guards, Vincent's Oxford; *Style* - James Quinn Esq; 7 Tregunter rd, SW10; (☎ 01 373 7354) Cresent Cottage, 108 Marine Parade, Brighton, Sussex

QUINN, Sheila Margaret Imelda; CBE (1978); da of Wilfred Amos Bairstow Quinn (d 1963); *b* 16 Sept 1920; *Educ* Layton Hill Convent Sch Blackpool, London U; *Career* Regional Nursing Offr Wessex Regional Health Authority 1978-, dep pres Roy Coll of Nursing (chm of cncl 1974-79) 1980-82, UK rep Standing Ctee Nurses of ECC 1972-, pres EEC Advisory Ctee Training in Nursing (v-pres 1979) 1980-81, memb bd dirs Int Cncl of Nurses 1977-81; *Recreations* reading, walking, gardening; *Clubs* VAD; *Style* - Miss Sheila Quinn CBE; Far Close, Wickham Lodge, Wickham, Fareham, Hants

QUINNELL, Air Cdre John Charles; CB (1943), DFC (1918); s of late John Busteed Quinnell; *b* 7 Jan 1891; *Educ* Royal School, Dungannon, Co Tyrone; *m* m 1, 1923, Atwell, nee McFarlane (d 1945); m 2 1948, Mildred Joan (d 1976), nee Humphreys, widow of Major Cyril Drummond; *Career* Air Cdre, AOC No 6 Aux Gp 1935-38 & No 6 Gp 1939, Sr Air Offr Advanced Air Striking Force (France) 1939-40, AOC Gp & RAF 1942, retired 1945; Pres Solent Cruising & Racing Assoc 1947-79 & Hon Life Pres 1979; *Recreations* horses, shooting, fishing, yachting; *Clubs* Royal Yacht Sqdn, Turf, Army & Navy, Royal Thames Yacht; *Style* - Air Cdre John Quinnell, CB, DFC; Nelson's Place, Fawley, Southampton, Hants (☎ 0703 891 002)

QUINTON, Anthony Meredith; s of Capt Richard Frith Quinton, RN (d 1935); *b* 25 March 1925; *Educ* Stowe, Ch Ch Oxford; *m* 1952, Marcelle, da of late Maurice Wegier, of New York; 1 s, 1 da; *Career* fell of All Souls Coll Oxford 1949-55, fell of New Coll Oxford 1955-78, pres Trin Oxford 1978-; memb of Arts Cncl of GB 1979-; *Clubs* Garrick, Beefsteak; *Style* - Anthony Quinton Esq; President's Lodgings, Trinity Coll, Oxford (☎ 42888)

QUIRK, Hon Mrs (Carol Ann); *née* Penny; da of 2 Viscount Marchwood, MBE (d 1979); *b* 1948; *m* 1978, Patrick J Quirk; 1 s; *Style* - The Hon Mrs Quirk; 9 Lambourn rd, SW4

QUITMAN, Harold Channing; s of Ernest Arthur Quitman (d 1944); *b* 28 May 1918; *Educ* Malvern; *m* 1950, Jean Jacqueline, da of Lt-Col Sir Roland Lawrence, Bt, MC; 1 s 1 da; *Career* Major BEF 1940, 21 Army Gp 1944-46; chm Aquis Securities Ltd 1960-, md Aquis Securities Ltd 1960-79, Immediate Past Master Worshipful Co Haberdashers (Master 1979-80); *Recreations* riding, skiing, painting; *Clubs* Marylebone Cricket; *Style* - Harold Quitman Esq; Rookley Farmhouse, Upper Somborne, Stockbridge, Hampshire (☎ Kings Somborne 338)

R

RABEN-LEVETZAU, Baroness Paul; Lady Rosanagh Mary; *née* Crichton; da of late 5 Earl of Erne and Lady Davidema, da of 2 Earl of Lytton; *b* 1932; *m* 1956, Baron (Michael) Paul Raben-Levetzau, of Rathmore Park, Tullow, Co Carlow; 4 s; *Style* - Baroness Paul Raben-Levetzau; Rathmore Park, Tullow, Co Carlow

RADCLIFFE, Viscountess; Hon Antonia Mary Roby; *née* Benson; da of late 1 Baron Charnwood; *b* 1903; *m* 1, 1929 (m dis 1939), Maj John Tennant, TD, late RA (d 1967, n of 1 Baron Glenconner); 2 s (Anthony, m Rosemary, da of Lt-Col Henry Stockdale, bro of Sir Edmund

Stockdale, 1 Bt; Mark, m Lady Harriet Pleydell-Bouverie, yst da of 7 Earl of Radnor, KG, KCVO); m 2, 1939, 1 Viscount Radcliffe (d 1977, when title became extinct); *Style* - The Rt Hon the Viscountess Radcliffe; 5 Campden Hill Gate, Duchess of Bedford's Walk, W8 (☎ 01 937 0321); Hampton Lucy House, Warwick

RADCLIFFE, Hugh John Reginald Joseph; MBE (1944); s of late Sir Everard Radcliffe, 5 Bt; hp of nephew, Sir Sebastian Radcliffe, 7 Bt; *b* 3 March 1911; *Educ* Downside; *m* 1937, Marie Thérèse, da of Maj-Gen Sir Cecil Edward Pereira, KCB, CMG; 5 s, 1 da; *Career* company dir; Kt Cdr Order of St Silvester (Papal); Lt-Col London Scottish WW II; *Style* - Hugh Radcliffe Esq, MBE; The White House, Stoke, Andover, Hants

RADCLIFFE, Julian Guy Yonge; s of Maj G L Y Radcliffe MBE; *b* 29 Aug 1948; *Educ* Eton, New Coll Oxford; *Career* Lloyd's broker and underwriting memb of Lloyd's, dir Hogg Robinson Overseas (and subsid), md Investment Insurance International 1973, md Control Risks Ltd, dir Credit Insurance Assoc Ltd 1975; *Recreations* farming, shooting, military and strategic studies; *Clubs* City of London, Carlton, Cavalry & Guards; *Style* - Julian Radcliffe Esq; 32 Brynmaer rd, SW11; Lower Stanway, Much Wenlock, Shropshire (☎ Longville 223)

RADCLIFFE, Sir Sebastian Everard; 7 Bt (UK 1813); s of Capt Sir (Joseph Benedict) Everard Henry, 6 Bt, MC (d 1975); *b* 8 June 1972; *Heir* unc, Hugh Radcliffe, MBE; *Style* - Sir Sebastian Radcliffe, Bt

RADFORD, (Guy) Harold (Richard); s of Walter Guy Wolfe Radford (d 1947); *b* 26 Sept 1908; *Educ* Marlborough; *m* 1948, Joanna Laetitia, nee Wardle-Smith; *Career* owner Harold Radford & Co Ltd (mfr private fleet of vehicles for Special Branch Combined Forces of the Secret Service, WWII), chm & dir Harold Radford & Co Ltd memb of Lloyd's, consultant to motor industry; *Recreations* lawn tennis, rackets, squash rackets, horse riding & driving in harness; *Clubs* Bath, RAC, Queen's, Jesters; *Style* - Harold Radford Esq; The Old Forge Farm, Conford, Liphook, Hants (☎ 0428 77 214)

RADNOR, 8 Earl of (GB 1765); Sir Jacob Pleydell-Bouverie; 11 Bt (GB 1714); also Viscount Folkestone, Lord Longford (both GB 1747), and Baron Pleydell-Bouverie (GB 1765); s of 7 Earl of Radnor, KG, KCVO (d 1968), by his 1 w, Helena, da of late Charles Adeane, CB (whose w Madeline, CBE, JP, was gda of 1 Baron Leconfield); *b* 10 Nov 1927; *Educ* Harrow, Trin Cambridge; *m* 1, 1953 (m dis 1962), Anne, da of Donald Seth-Smith, MC; 2 s; m 2, 1963, Margaret, da of Robin Fleming, of Catter House, Drymen; 4 da; *Heir* s, Viscount Folkestone; *Career* landowner & farmer; chm Br Dyslexia Assoc 1971-76, Pres Dyslexia Inst 1975-; patron of one living; *Recreations* field sports, fly tying; *Clubs* White's, Farmers; *Style* - The Rt Hon The Earl of Radnor; Longford Castle, Salisbury, Wilts (☎ 29732)

RADNOR, Dowager Countess of; Anne Isobel Graham; OBE (1961); da of Lt-Col Richard Oakley, DSO, JP, by his w Enid Elizabeth (da of James Noble Graham, JP, DL, of the oldest cadet branch of the Montrose (Duke of) family); *b* 6 Sept 1908; *m* 1, 1931, Richard Sowerby (d 1939), er s of Lt-Col Thomas Sowerby, JP, of The Manor House, Lilley, Herts; m 2, 1943, as his 2 w, 7 Earl of Radnor, KG, KCVO, JP, DL (d 1968); 1 s; *Career* Pres Health Visitors' Assoc; memb Cncl Historic Churches Preservation Tst, Soc for Protection Ancient Bldgs; *Style* - Rt Hon Dowager Countess of Radnor OBE; Avonturn, Alderbury, Salisbury

RADOMIR, Hon Mrs (Sarah Elizabeth); *née* Marks; da of 2 Baron Marks of Broughton; *b* 1953; *m* 1979, Nicholai Radomir; *Style* - The Hon Mrs Radomir

RADWAN, Aziz Kordy; s of Kordy Bey Radwan (himself s of Abdel-Aziz Pasha Radwan, which dignity of Pasha was conferred by King Fwad of Egypt 1923); *b* 12 April 1941; *Educ* privately in UK, St Cat's Oxford, LSE; *Career* dir Sceptre Resources (Abu Dhabi), Scarborough Resources; consultant Scimitar Oils

SA; *Recreations* reading, music; *Clubs* Gezira Sporting (Cairo), Automobile (Cairo), Annabel's, Harry's Bar, Aspinall's, Bath; *Style* - Aziz Radwan Esq; PO Box 4311, Deira, Dubai, United Arab Emirates (☎ Dubai 94 56234)

RAEBURN, Maj-Gen Sir (William) Digby Manifold; KCVO (1979), CB (1966), DSO (1945), MBE (1941); s of late Sir Ernest Manifold Raeburn, KBE, s of 1 Bt; hp of kinsman, (Sir) Michael Raeburn (4 Bt, but does not use his title); *b* 6 Aug 1915; *Educ* Winchester, Magdalene Cambridge; *m* 1960, Adeline Margaret, da of late Thomas Selwyn Pryor, MC; *Career* Maj-Gen (ret) late Scots Gds; Dir of Combat Dvpt (Army) 1963-65, Ch of Staff Allied Forces N Europe 1965-68, Ch Army Instructor Imperial Defence Coll 1968-70, Resident Govr & Keeper of Jewel House of HM Tower of London 1971-79; *Style* - Maj-Gen Sir Digby Raeburn, KCVO, CB, DSO, MBE; 25 St Ann's ter, NW8

RAEBURN, (Sir) Michael Edward Norman; (4 Bt, UK 1923, but does not use his title); s of Sir Edward Alfred Raeburn, 3 Bt (d 1977); *b* 12 Nov 1954; *m* 1979, Penelope, nee Penn, of Tunbridge Wells; *Heir* kinsman, Maj-Gen Sir (William) Digby Manifold, KCVO, CB, DSO, MBE; *Style* - Michael Raeburn Esq; Fourways, Turners Green, Wadhurst, E Sussex

RAGLAN, 5 Baron (UK 1852); FitzRoy John Somerset; JP (Mon, now Gwent 1958), DL (1971); s of 4 Baron Raglan, JP (d 1964; he descended from the 5 Duke of Beaufort), by Hon Julia Hamilton, da of 11 Lord Belhaven and Stenton; *b* 8 Nov 1927; *Educ* Westminster, Magdalen Oxford; *m* 1973, Alice, yr da of Peter Bailey, of Gt Whittington, Northumberland; *Heir* bro, Hon Geoffrey Somerset; *Career* Capt Welsh Gds; chm Cwmbran New Town Devpt Corpn, Courtyard Arts Tst 1974-, Bath Soc 1977-; Pres Bath Centre Nat Tst; Patron Raglan Baroque Players; *Style* - The Rt Hon The Lord Raglan JP DL; Cefntilla House, Usk, Gwent (☎ 2050)

RAHMAN PUTRA, Tunku (Prince) Abdul; CH (1961); *b* 1903; *Educ* Bangkok, St Cat's Cambridge, Inner Temple London; *m* 1; 1 s, 1 da; m 2; m 3, 1939, Puan Sharifah Rodziah binti Syed Alwi Barakhbah; 1 s, 3 da (all adopted); *Career* Sec Gen Islamic Conference of Foreign Ministers 169-73, Premier of Malaysia 1963-70; *Style* - Tunku Abdul Rahman Putra, CH; 16 Ayer Rajah rd, Penang, Malaysia

RAINEY, Hon Mrs (Jane Teresa Denyse); *née* Ormsby Gore; da of 5 Baron Harlech, KCMG, PC; *b* 1942; *m* 1966, Michael Sean O'Dare Rainey; 2 s, 2 da; *Style* - The Hon Mrs Rainey; Ty Baen, Llanfechain, Montgomeryshire (☎ Llansantffraid 482)

RAISON, Patrick Nicolas; s of Rev Herbert Chaplin Raison (d 1952); *b* 30 Oct 1933; *Educ* Harrow, Magdalen Oxford, Sch of Business Stanford U USA; *m* 1962, Françoise Yvonne, da of Maître Fernand Haissly, of Switzerland; 1 s, 2 da; *Career* barr at Law (Gray's Inn) not practising, man dir Oxford Controls Co Ltd; *Recreations* travel, aviation (Cessna GBFGY); *Clubs* Carlton; *Style* - Patrick Raison Esq; Farncombe Hill, Broadway, Worcs (☎ 852465)

RALLI, David Charles; s and h of Sir Godfrey Ralli, 3 Bt, TD; *b* 5 April 1946; *Educ* Eton; *m* 1975, Jacqueline Cecilia, da of David Smith; 1 da; *Style* - David Ralli Esq

RALLI, Sir Godfrey Victor; 3 Bt (UK 1912), TD; s of Sir Strati Ralli, 2 Bt, MC (d 1964); *b* 9 Sept 1915; *Educ* Eton; *m* 1, 1937 (m dis 1947), Nora Margaret, da of late Charles Forman, of Lodden Court, Spencers Wood, nr Reading; 1 s, 2 da; m 2, 1949, Jean, da of late Keith Barlow; *Heir* s, David Ralli; *Style* - Sir Godfrey Ralli, Bt, TD; Great Walton, Eastry, Sandwich, Kent

RAMSAY, Hon Anthony; s of 16 Earl of Dalhousie, KT, GCVO, GBE, MC; *b* 1949; *Educ* Ampleforth, Magdalen Oxford; *m* 1973 (m dis), Georgina Mary, da of the late the Hon Michael Langhorne Astor (s of late 2 Visc Astor); 1 s; *Style* - The Hon Anthony Ramsay

RAMSAY, Alexander David; s and h of

Sir Alexander Ramsay, 7 Bt; *b* 20 Aug 1966

RAMSAY, Hon Alice Elizabeth Margaret; da of Lady Saltoun, *qv*; *b* 8 July 1961; *Style* - The Hon Alice Ramsay

RAMSAY, Hon Alice Magdalene; da of Lord Ramsay, s and h of 16 Earl of Dalhousie, KT, GCVO, GBE, MC; *b* 1977

RAMSAY, Sir Alexander William Burnett; 7 Bt (UK 1806); s of late Sir Alexander Burnett Ramsay, 6 Bt (d 1965); is the presumed heir to the Baronetcy of Burnett of Leys (cr 1626); *b* 4 Aug 1938; *m* 1963, Neryl Eileen, da of J C Smith Thornton, of Trangie, NSW; 2 s; *Heir* s, Alexander David Ramsay; *Style* - Sir Alexander Ramsay, Bt; 30 Brian st, Balgownie, NSW 2519, Australia

RAMSAY, Hon Elizabeth Alexandra Mary; da of Lady Saltoun, *qv*; *b* 15 April 1963; *Style* - The Hon Elizabeth Ramsay

RAMSAY, Lord; James Hubert Ramsay; s and h of 16 Earl of Dalhousie, KT, GBE, MC, by his w Margaret, da of late Brig-Gen Archibald Stirling of Keir (2 s of Sir John Stirling-Maxwell, 10 Bt, KT, DL, which Btcy has been dormant since 1956) and Hon Margaret Fraser, OBE, da of 13 Lord Lovat; *b* 17 Jan 1948; *Educ* Ampleforth; *m* 1973, Marilyn, yr da of Maj David Butter, MC, and Myra (da of Sir Harold Wernher, 3 and last Bt, GCVO, TD, by his w Lady Zia, nee Countess Anastasia Mikhailovna, er da of HIH Grand Duke Mikhail of Russia; Lady Ramsay is hence 1 cous of the Duchesses of Abercorn and Westminster, *qqv*); 2 da; *Career* dir Hambros Bank 1981-; Cmd 2 Bn Coldstream Gds 1968-71, RARO 1971; *Clubs* White's, Pratt's, Turf; *Style* - Lord Ramsay; Dalhousie Lodge, Edzell, Angus; 3 Vicarage gdns, W8

RAMSAY, Hon John Patrick; s of 16 Earl of Dalhousie, KT, GCVO, GBE, MC; *b* 1952; *Style* - The Hon Patrick Ramsay

RAMSAY, Hon Lorna Theresa; da of Lord Ramsay (s and h of 16 Earl of Dalhousie, KT, GCVO, GBE, MC); *b* 1975

RAMSAY, Hon Mrs (Mary Margaret Hastings); *née* MacAndrew; da of 1 Baron MacAndrew, TD, PC (d 1979); *b* 1942; *m* 1967, Lt-Col Charles Alexander Ramsay, s of late Adm Sir Bertram Home Ramsey, KCB, KBE, MVO (d 1945); 1 s, 2 da; *Style* - The Hon Mrs Ramsay; Rughtrig, Coldstream, Berwickshire

RAMSAY, Sir Neis Alexander; 12 Bt (NS 1666); s of Col Sir James Douglas Ramsay, 11 Bt, MVO, TD (d 1959); *b* 4 Oct 1909; *Educ* Winchester, Trin Cambridge; *m* 1, 1940 (m dis 1951), Edith Alix Ross, da of C F Hayes, FCIS; m 2, 1952, Rachel Leonore Beatrice (Drummond), da of late Col Edward Brabazon Urmston, CB; *Career* formerly Lt Gordon Highlanders; Lt S African Engineering Corps WW II; *Style* - Sir Neis Ramsay, Bt; Bamff, Alyth, Perthshire

RAMSAY, Norman James Gemmill; s of James Ramsay (d 1940); *b* 26 Aug 1916; *Educ* Merchiston Castle Sch, Edinburgh U; *m* 1952, Rachael Mary Berkeley, da of Sir Herbert Charles Fahie Cox (d 1973); 22; *Career* Writer to the Signet 1939, advocate 1956, Administrator-Gen North Rhodesia 1947-56, Resident Magistrate 1958-64, Puisne Judge High Court of North Rhodesia (later Zambia) 1964-68; Sheriff South Strathclyde, Dumfries and Galloway 1971-; *Recreations* gardening; *Clubs* Roy C'wlth Soc; *Style* - Norman Ramsay Esq, WS; Mill of Borgue, Kirkcudbright

RAMSAY-FAIRFAX-LUCY, Hon Lady; Hon Alice Caroline Helen; *née* Buchan; da of 1 Baron Tweedsmuir, GCMG, GCVO, CH (d 1940); *b* 1908; *m* 1933, Maj Sir Brian Fulke Ramsay-Fairfax-Lucy, 5 Bt (d 1974); *Style* - The Hon Lady Ramsay-Fairfax-Lucy; 41 College Lane, Stratford-upon-Avon; Charlecote Park, Warwick

RAMSAY-FAIRFAX-LUCY, *see also* Fairfax-Lucy

RAMSAY-STEEL-MAITLAND, Lady; Matilda Brenda; da of late Thomas Doughty, of Coalbrookdale; *m* 1942, as his 2 w, Sir (Arthur) James (Drummond) Ramsay-Steel-Maitland, 2 Bt (d 1960);

Style - Lady Ramsay-Steel-Maitland; Castle Gogar, Edinburgh 12

RAMSBOTHAM, Hon Sir Peter Edward; GCMG (1978, KCMG 1972, CMG 1964), GCVO (1976); s of late 1 Viscount Soulbury, GCMG, GCVO, OBE, MC, PC; hp of bro, 2 Viscount; *b* 8 Oct 1919; *Educ* Eton, Magdalen Oxford; *m* 1941, Frances Marie, da of Hugh Massie Blomfield; 2 s, 1 da; *Career* FO 1950 (formerly in Foreign Service), Br High Cmmr Cyprus 1969-71, Ambass to Iran 1971-73, Ambass to USA 1974-77, Govr Bermuda 1977-80; dir Lloyds Bank; KStJ 1976; *Style* - The Hon Sir Peter Ramsbotham, GCMG, GCVO; East Lane, Ovington, nr Alresford, Hants

RAMSDEN, Caryl Oliver Imbert; CMG (1965), CVO (1966); s of Lt-Col Josslyn Vere Ramsden, CMG, DSO (d 1952); hp of kinsman, Sir Geoffrey William Pennington-Ramsden, 7 Bt; *b* 4 April 1915; *Educ* Eton, New Coll Oxford; *m* 1945, Anne, da of Sir Charles Wickham, KCMG, KBE, DSO; 1 s; *Career* RA 1937-49; FO 1949, private sec to PM 1957, consul-gen Hanover 1957-59, counsellor Rio de Janeiro 1959-62, counsellor Brussels 1962, ret 1967; pro-principal (admin) Univ Coll Bucks 1975; *Style* - Caryl Ramsden Esq, CMG, CVO; The Old Brewery, Helperby, York (☎ Helperby 256)

RAMSEY OF CANTERBURY, Baron (Life Peer UK 1974); Rt Rev & Rt Hon (Arthur) Michael Ramsey; PC (1956); s of Arthur Ramsey, sometime Fellow Magdalene Cambridge; *b* 14 Nov 1904; *Educ* Repton, Magdalene Cambridge; *m* 1942, Joan, da of late Lt-Col Francis Hamilton, MC; *Career* 100 Archbp of Canterbury and Primate of All England and Metropolitan 1961-74 (92 Archbp York 1955-61, 88 Bp Durham 1952-56); Roy Victorian Chain 1974; ordained 1928; Regius Prof Divinity Cambridge 1950-52; *Style* - Rt Rev & Rt Hon Lord Ramsey of Canterbury, PC; 16 South Bailey, Durham (☎ 62934)

RAMSEY, Alexander William; s of Sir William Clark Ramsay, CBE (d 1973); *b* 3 Aug 1931; *Educ* Mill Hill, Brasenose Oxford; *m* 1957, Patricia, 4 c; *Career* Capt Middlesex Regt, Korea 1950; barrister; co dir; Dep Lord Mayor Westminster City Council; High Sheriff of Greater London 1976-77; Pres The Rugby Football Union 1979-80; *Recreations* reading, rugby, fishing, collecting watercolours; *Clubs* Carlton, East India, Cardiff & County, RLYC, City Univ; *Style* - Alexander Ramsay Esq; 15 Brunswick Gdns, London W8 4AS (☎ 01 727 6282)

RAMSEY, Hon Mrs (Cicely Sylvia); *née* Molesworth; da of 9 Viscount Molesworth (d 1947); *b* 1902; *m* 1927 (m dis 1937, he d 1959), Guy Haylett Walker Ramsey; 1 s; *Style* - The Hon Mrs Ramsey; 12 Parkfield, North Parade, Horsham, Sussex

RANDOLPH, Denys; s of Harry Beckham Randolph (d 1980); *b* 6 Feb 1926; *Educ* St Paul's Sch Hammersmith, Queen's U Belfast; *m* 1951, Marjorie, nee Hales; 2 da; *Career* chm Wilkinson Match Ltd, pres Wilkinson Sword 1980- (chm 1972-1980), chm Inst of Dirs 1976-1979, Master Worshipful Co of Scientific Instrument Makers 1977; *Recreations* viticulture, golf, boating ('La Russhe'); *Clubs* Army & Navy, City Livery, Little Ship; *Style* - Denys Randolph Esq; 6 Atherstone Mews, SW7; The Cottages, Rush Court, Wallingford, OX10 8LJ (☎ 01 584 5121)

RANDOLPH, Lady Elisabeth Katharine; *née* Waldegrave; da of 11 Earl Waldegrave; *b* 7 May 1897; *m* 1918, Rev George Randolph (d 1977); 1 s, 2 da; *Style* - Lady Elisabeth Randolph; S Woodside, Corfe, Taunton, Somerset

RANFURLY, 6 Earl of (I 1831); Thomas Daniel Knox; KCMG (1955); also Baron Welles (I 1781), Viscount Northland (I 1791), and Baron Ranfurly (UK 1826, which sits as in House of Lords); s of Capt Viscount Northland (ka 1915, only s of 5 Earl of Ranfurly, GCMG, PC, who d 1933) and Hilda, yr da of Sir Daniel Cooper, 2 Bt, JP, DL, by Harriet (da of Sir James Grant Suttie, 6 Bt); *b* 29 May 1913; *Educ* Eton, Trin Cambridge; *m* 1939, Hermione, OBE, CStJ, da of Griffith Llewellyn, of Baglan Hall, Abergavenny (er bro of Sir Godfrey Llewellyn, 1 Bt, CB,

CBE, MC, TD, JP, DL); 1 da; *Heir* kinsman, Gerald Knox; *Career* KStJ; ADC to Gov-Gen & CIC Australia 1936-38, Gov & CIC Bahamas 1953-56; chm Colonial Mutual Life Assur Soc (London Bd), Bd Govrs London Clinic 1973-, Madame Tussaud's, Inchcape Insur Hldgs; dir Inchcape & Co; memb Lloyd's 1947-; Steward Jockey Club 1973-75; Pres Shaftesbury Homes & Arethusa Training Ship 1959-; *Clubs* White's, Jockey (Newmarket); *Style* - The Rt Hon The Earl of Ranfurly KCMG; Great Pednor, Chesham, Bucks (☎ Gt Missenden 2155)

RANK, Joseph McArthur; s of the late Rowland Rank; *b* 24 April 1918; *Educ* Loretto Sch Musselburgh; *m* 1946, Hon Moira, nee Hopwood, *qv*, da of 3 Baron Southborough; 1 s, 1 da; *Career* Flight Lt RAFVR UK, France & Germany, personal pilot to Air C-in-C; flour miller; chm Ranks Hovis McDougall Ltd 1969-81, pres National Assoc of British & Irish Millers 1981, centenary pres 1978, chm Millers Mutual Assoc 1969-, dir Royal Alexander and Albert Sch 1952-, First High Sheriff East Sussex 1974; *Recreations* boating and travelling; *Clubs* RAF, Bembridge Sailing; *Style* - Joseph Rank Esq; Landhurst, Hartfield, East Sussex (☎ Hartfield 293)

RANK, Hon Mrs; Hon Moira; *née* Hopwood; da of 3 Baron Southborough; *b* 1919; *m* 1, 1940, Peter Anthony Stanley Woodwark, Acting Pilot Offr, RAF Vol Res (ka 1943), s of late Col Sir (Arthur) Stanley Woodwark, CMG, CBE, MD, FRCP; 1 da; m 2, 1946, Joseph McArthur Rank, *qv*; 1 s, 1 da; *Style* - The Hon Mrs Rank; Landhurst, Hartfield, Sussex

RANKEILLOUR, 4 Baron (UK 1932); Peter St Thomas More Henry Hope; s of 3 Baron Rankeillour (d 1967; he descended from Hon Sir Alexander Hope, GCB, 4 s of 2 Earl of Hopetoun, ancestor of the Marquesses of Linlithgow) and Baroness Rankeillour, *qv*; *b* 29 May 1935; *Educ* Ampleforth and privately; *Heir* kinsman, Michael Hope; *Style* - The Rt Hon Lord Rankeillour; Achaderry House, Roy Bridge, W Inverness-shire (☎ Spean Bridge 206)

RANKEILLOUR, Baroness; Mary Sibyl; da of Lt-Col Wilfred Ricardo, DSO (gn of David Ricardo, the celebrated political economist); *b* 5 April 1910; *m* 1933, 3 Baron Rankeillour (d 1967); 1 s (4 Baron), 1 da (Hon Mrs Dobson); *Style* - Rt Hon Lady Rankeillour; Little Orchard, Liphook, Hants (☎ 2177)

RANKIN, Antony Colin Deans; s of Maj-Gen Henry Charles Deans Rankin, CIE, OBE (d 1965); *b* 5 Feb 1923; *Educ* Loretto Sch Musselburgh; *m* 1950, Barbara, nee Vernon; *Career* Capt 12th Lancers 1941-46, dir ICI Ltd (Mond Div) 1970-81, dir Ellis & Everard Ltd 1979-81; *Recreations* gardening, watching sport; *Clubs* MCC, Army & Navy; *Style* - Antony Rankin Esq; 11 Curzon Park North, Chester, CH4 8AP (☎ 676921)

RANKIN, Sir Hugh Charles Rhys; 3 Bt (UK 1898); s of Lt-Col Sir (James) Reginald (Lea) Rankin, 2 Bt (d 1931); *b* 8 Aug 1899; *Educ* Harrow; *m* 1, 1932, Helen Margaret (d 1945), da of late Sir Charles Stewart, KBE, First Public Tstee, and widow of Capt Colin Campbell; m 2, 1946, Robina Kelly (FSA, Scot), of Crieff; assumed by deed poll 1946 use of the additional surname of Stewart; discontinued surname Stewart by deed poll 1946 and assumed name Hugh in lieu of Herbert; *Heir* n, Ian Niall Rankin; *Career* formerly a follower of Kadaria' School of Thought, sr v-pres Western Islamic Assoc (Mohammedan) and Capt RASC; stock breeder and sheep judge; FSA (Scot), memb Welsh Nationalist Plaid Cymru; memb Standing Cncl of Baronetage 1979-; former pres of Muslim Soc of GB, first rep of Gt Britain on All-European Muslim Congress at Geneva 1935, and a permanent memb of fin ctee; town cncllr 1949, co cncllr 1950, ex-vice-pres Scottish Nat Lib Assoc; adopted Mahayana (Theistic) Buddhist Faith 1943; *Style* - Sir Hugh Rankin, Bt; Carterton Cottage, Corrie Common, Lockerbie, Dumfriesshire

RANKIN, Ian Niall; s of late Lt-Col (Arthur) Niall Talbot Rankin, yr s of 2 Bt; hp of unc, Sir Hugh Rankin, 3 Bt; *b* 19 Dec 1932; *Educ* Eton, Ch Ch Oxford; *m* 1, 1959, Alexandra, da of Adm Sir Laurence

George Durlacher, KCB, OBE, DSC; 1 s, 1 da; m 2, 1980, June, da of late Capt Thomas Marsham-Townshend, and formerly w of Bryan Montagu Norman; 1 da; *Career* FRGS; Lt Scots Gds (Res); *Style* - Ian Rankin Esq; Blomfield House, Clifton Villas, W9

RANKIN, Lady Jean Margaret; *née* Dalrymple; DCVO (1969, CVO 1957); da of late 12 Earl of Stair, KT, DSO; *b* 1905; *m* 1931, Lt-Col (Arthur) Niall Talbot Rankin, Scots Gds (d 1965), s of Lt-Col Sir (James) Reginald (Lea) Rankin, 2 Bt; 2 s; *Career* appointed a Woman of the Bedchamber to HM Queen Elizabeth the Queen Mother 1947; *Style* - Lady Jean Rankin, DCVO; 3 Catherine Wheel Yard, St James's st, SW1; House of Treshnish, Calgary, Isle of Mull

RANKIN, Robert Craig McPherson; s of Robert Craig Rankin (d 1943); *b* 15 Aug 1937; *Educ* The Academy Ayr, Roy Coll Science & Technol Glasgow; *m* 1963, Alison Barbara Black, nee Douglas; 1 s, 1 da; *Career* civil engr; dep man Balfour Beatty Construction (Scot) 1974-75, man Balfour Beatty Construction (Eng & Wales) 1975-81, dep exec director Balfour Beatty Construction Ltd 1981-; *Recreations* golf, tennis, skiing, opera and ballet; *Clubs* Wentworth, Les Ambassadeurs; *Style* - Robert Rankin Esq; Kellyside, Dollar, Clackmannanshire, Scotland (☎ Dollar 2454); 604 Willoughby House, Barbican, EC2 (☎ 638 2656)

RANKING, His Hon Judge; Robert Duncan; s of Robert Maurice Ranking MD (d 1939); *b* 24 Oct 1915; *Educ* Cheltenham, Pembroke Cambridge; *m* 1949, Evelyn Mary, nee Walker; 1 da; *Career* County Court Judge 1968, Circuit Judge 1971, dep chm East Sussex Quarter Sessions 1962-68, dep chm Agricultural Land Tribunal SE Area, Judge of The Mayor's & City of London Court 1979-; *Style* - His Hon Judge Ranking; Little Oakfield, Camden Hill, Tunbridge Wells, Kent (☎ Tunbridge Wells 27551)

RANSOME, Hon Mrs; Hon (Shirley) Elizabeth; *née* Macpherson; da of 2 Baron Macpherson of Drumochter by his 1 w Ruth; *b* 31 March 1953; *m* 1978, Mark William Ransome; *Style* - The Hon Mrs Ransome; 101, 18th Street, Parkhurst 2193, Johannesburg, S Africa

RAPER, Alfred Graham; *Career* BSc (Tech), PhD; md Davy Internat (Minerals & Metals); dir Davy Corpn 1981-, Davy Ashmore Canada, Davy Ashmore SA; *Style* - Alfred Raper Esq; c/o Davy International, Ashmore House, Bowesfield Lane, Stockton-on-Tees, Cleveland (☎ 62221)

RAPER, Alan Humphrey; s of Frederick George Raper (d 1977); *b* 11 Aug 1927; *Educ* Acklam Hall Middlesbrough, Leeds U; *m* 1955, Audrey, nee Baker; 1 s, 2 da; *Career* dir Glaxo Holdings Ltd, Glaxo Trustees Ltd, chm Glaxo Operations UK Ltd, chm Vestric Ltd, dir Glaxo Nigeria Ltd, Glaxochem Ltd; memb of cncl Chemical Industries Assoc 1974-77, advisory cncl Industrial Participation Assoc 1978-, Education & Training Ctee CBI 1980-; *Recreations* skiing, hill walking, history; *Style* - Alan Raper Esq; Church Cottage, 126 High st, Lindfield, Sussex; Mews Cottage, Low Startforth Hall, Barnard Castle, Co Durham

RAPLEY, Hon Mrs - Hon Heather; *née* McLeavy; da of Baron McLeavy (Life Peer) (d 1976); *b* 1929; *m* 1955, Patrick William Rapley; *Style* - The Hon Mrs Rapley; 7 Salcombe Drive, Earley, Reading

RASCH, Catherine, Lady - Catherine Margaret; da of late Hon John Boscawen; *b* 1891; *m* 1, 1913, 16 Baron Petre (d 1915); m 2, 1921, Col Sir Frederic Carne Rasch, 2 Bt (d 1963); *Style* - Catherine, Lady Rasch; 9 Trevor st, SW7

RASCH, Sir Richard Guy Carne; 3 Bt (UK 1903); s of late Brig Guy Elland Carne Rasch, CVO, DSO, s of 1 Bt; suc unc, Col Sir Frederic Carne Rasch, 2 Bt, TD, 1963; *b* 10 Oct 1918; *Educ* Eton; *m* 1, 1947 (m dis 1959), Anne Mary, da of late Maj John Henry Dent-Brocklehurst, OBE; 1 s, 1 da; m 2, 1961, Fiona Mary, da of Robert Douglas Shaw, and formerly w of Humphrey Salmon; *Heir* s, Simon Rasch; *Career* Maj late Gren Gds; memb Hon Corps of Gentlemen-at-Arms 1968-;

Style - Sir Richard Rasch, Bt; 30 Ovington sq, SW3; The Manor House, Lower Woodford, Salisbury, Wilts

RASCH, Simon Anthony Carne; s and h of Sir Richard Rasch, 3 Bt; *b* 26 Feb 1948; *Educ* Eton; *Career* Page of Honour to HM 1962-64; *Style* - Simon Rasch Esq

RASHLEIGH, Sir Harry Evelyn Battie; 5 Bt (UK 1831); s of late Harry Rashleigh, JP, 3 s of 3 Bt; suc unc, Sir Colman Battie Walpole Rashleigh, 4 Bt, 1951; *b* 17 May 1923; *Educ* Wellington Sch Somerset; *m* 1954, Honora Elizabeth, da of G S Sneyd, of Downderry, Cornwall; 1 s, 3 da; *Heir* s, Richard Rashleigh; *Career* formerly Sergeant RAC, was engineer in Tanganyika 1948-51 and engineer English Clays Cornwall 1951-52; farmer; *Style* - Sir Harry Rashleigh, Bt; Stowford Grange, Lewdown, Okehampton, Devon

RASHLEIGH, Richard Harry; s and h of Sir Harry Rashleigh, 5 Bt; *b* 8 July 1958; *Style* - Richard Rashleigh Esq

RATHBONE, Bertram Lyle; s of Francis Warre Rathbone (d 1939); *b* 28 June 1913; *Educ* Marlborough, London Sch of Economics; *m* 1, 1939, Joan Duckworth (m dis 1945); 1 da; m 2, 1949, Elizabeth Eleanor, da of Lt-Col Thomas Coulson, RA, DSO and Bar (d 1927); 1 s, 1 da; *Career* ptnr Rathbone Bros & Co 1939-79 (ret); hon tres Liverpool U 1972-; dir Albany Investment Trust, dir Norton Megaw & Co (and assoc cos); *Recreations* travel, horticultural labourer; *Clubs* Travellers', Liverpool Racquet; *Style* - Bertram Rathbone Esq; Park Lodge, Sefton Park rd, Liverpool (☎ 051 727 5006)

RATHBONE, Sebastian David; s of Richard Reynolds Rathbone (d 1969); *b* 6 Jan 1932; *Educ* Rugby, Trin Cambridge; *m* 1964, Susan Kennedy, da of late Robert Kennedy Rathbone; 4 s, 2 da; *Career* CA, ptnr Rathbone Bros & Co 1960-; *Recreations* sport; *Clubs* Athenaeum Liverpool, Nat Lib; *Style* - Sebastian Rathbone Esq; c/o Rathbone Bros & Co, Castle Chambers, Castle st, Liverpool

RATHBONE, Tim (John Rankin); MP (C) Lewes 1974-; s of J Rathbone, MP (ka 1940, 2 cous once removed of Basil Rathbone (the actor noted for his portrayal of Sherlock Holmes) and n of Sir Robert Rankin, 1 Bt, through his mother) and Lady Wright (w of Sir Paul Wright, KCMG); *b* 17 March 1933; *Educ* Eton, Ch Ch Oxford, Harvard Business Sch; *m* 1960 (m dis 1981), Margarita Sanchez y Sanchez; 2 s, 1 da; *Career* served KRRC 1951-53 2 Lt; merchant banker 1956-58, advertising (OB&M) 1958-66; dir Charles Barker ABH Internat 1968-, Ayer Barker Ltd; chm Charles Barker Coulthard 1979-; PPS Min Health 1979-; FRSA; *Style* - Tim Rathbone Esq, MP; 30 Farringdon st, EC4 (☎ 01 236 3011)

RATHCAVAN, 1 Baron (UK 1953); Sir (Robert William) Hugh O'Neill; 1 Bt (UK 1929), PC (I 1921, NI 1922, GB 1937); 3 s of 2 Baron O'Neill, JP, DL (descended from the O'Neills who, as High Kings of Ireland, are the earliest traceable family in Europe), by Lady Louisa Cochrane, da of 11 Earl of Dundonald; *b* 8 June 1883; *Educ* Eton, New Coll Oxford; *m* 1909, Sylvia (d 1972), da of Walter Sandeman, of Morden House, Royston (of the sherry and port family; Walter's m was Maria Carlota Perpetua de Moraes Sarmento, da of Visconde Da Torre de Moncorvo, sometime Portuguese Ambassador to the Court of St James; of Walter's 4 sisters, 3 married; 2 to Baronets - Sir James Malcolm, 9 Bt, and Sir William Leese, 2 Bt - one to the Marchese Lomellini-Tabarca, of Pavia); 2 s (and 1 s decd); *Heir* s, Rt Hon Phelim O'Neill, PC; *Career* MP (U) Mid Antrim 1915-22, Co Antrim 1922-50, Antrim N 1950-52; MP (NI Parl) Co Antrim 1921-29 & First Speaker; stood as Con candidate Stockport 1906; chm 1922 Cttee 1935-39, Under-Sec India & Burma 1939-40; CStJ; barr 1909; served WW I Maj Roy Irish Rifles, Dep Judge Advocate-Gen Palestine 1918; *Style* - The Rt Hon Lord Rathcavan PC; Cleggan Lodge, Ballymena, Co Antrim, (☎ Aughafatten 209); 28 Queen's Gate gdns, SW7 (☎ 01 584 0358)

RATHCREEDAN, 2 Baron (UK 1916); Charles Patrick Norton; TD; s of 1 Baron Rathcreedan (d 1930) by his 2 w,

Marguerite, da of Sir Charles Huntington, 1 Bt (Btcy extinct on death of 3 Bt 1928); *b* 26 Nov 1905; *Educ* Wellington, Lincoln Coll Oxford; *m* 1946, Anne, da of Surgn-Capt William Bastian, RN; 2 s, 1 da; *Heir* s, Hon Christopher Norton; *Career* barr 1931, slr 1936; late Maj 4 Bn Oxford & Bucks LI (TA), POW WW II; Master Founders' Co 1970; *Style* - The Rt Hon The Lord Rathcreedan TD; Church Field, Fawley, Henley-on-Thames, Oxon (☎ 4160)

RATHDONNELL, 5 Baron (I 1868); Thomas Benjamin McClintock-Bunbury; s of 4 Baron Rathdonnell (d 1959); *b* 17 Sept 1938; *Educ* Charterhouse, RNC Dartmouth; *m* 1965, Jessica, da of George Butler (eighth in descent from 2 Baron Dunboyne) by Norah Pomeroy Colley, gggda of 4 Viscount Harberton; 3 s, 3 da; *Heir* s, Hon William McClintock-Bunbury; *Style* - The Rt Hon The Lord Rathdonnell; Lisnavagh, Rathvilly, Co Carlow, Eire (☎ Carlow 55104)

RATTRAY OF RATTRAY, Hon Mrs (Elizabeth Sophia); *née* Sidney; da (by 1 m) of 1 Visc De L'Isle, VC, KG, GCMG, GCVO, PC; *b* 1941; *m* 1, 1959 (m dis 1966), George Silver Oliver Annesley Colthurst; m 2, 1966 (m dis 1971), Sir (Edward) Humphry Tyrell Wakefield, 2 Bt; m 3, 1972, Capt James Silvester Rattray of Rattray; 1 s; *Style* - The Hon Mrs Rattray of Rattray; Craighall-Rattray, Blairgowrie, Perthshire

RAUF, Bayan; Angela Mary; *née* Culme-Seymour; da of Capt George Culme-Seymour, 3 s of Sir Michael Culme-Seymour, 3 Bt, GCB, GCVO, and Mary, da of Hon Richard Watson, of Rockingham Castle (*see* John Churchill for fuller details); *b* 3 Aug 1912; *m* 1, 1934 (m dis 1938), John Churchill (*qv*); 1 da; m 2, 1938 (m dis 1942), 3 Baron Kinross (formerly Hon Patrick Balfour, the author and journalist); m 3, 1948 (m dis), Comte René Guillet de Chatellus, 2 s of late Comte Pierre de Chatellus, of Château de Nogent, Montbard; m 4, 1977, Mehmet Ali Bulent Rauf, Bey of Beylerbeyi, Istanbul; *Style* - Bayan Rauf; 10 Eccleston sq, SW1

RAVEN, Ronald William; OBE (Mil 1946), TD (1953); s of Fredric William Raven (d 1952); *b* 28 July 1904; *Educ* Ulverston G S, St Bartholomew's London U; *Career* OStJ (1946), Chevalier Légion D'Honneur (1952); consulting surgeon; memb Court of Patrons Roy Coll Surgeon of Eng 1976-, cncl 1968-76 & chm Epsom Coll 1954-, chm Marie Curie Memorial Fndn 1957-, founder pres Br Assoc Surgical Oncology 1973-77, Master Worshipful Co Barbers 1980-8l, consulting surgeon Westminster Hosp & Roy Marsden Hosp 1969-; *Recreations* philately (medallist International Stamp Exhibition 1950), music, ceramics, paintings, travel; *Clubs* MCC; *Style* - Ronald Raven Esq, OBE, TD; 29 Harley st, W1 (☎ 580 3765)

RAVENSDALE, 3 Baron (UK 1911); Sir Nicholas Mosley; 7 Bt (GB 1781), of Ancoats, Lancashire, and of Rolleston, Staffordshire, MC (1944); s of Sir Oswald Mosley, 6 Bt (d 1980, sixth in descent from Sir John Mosley, 1 Bt, himself 2 cous of 2 & 3 Bts of the 2 cr (1720); Sir John was fifth in descent from Anthony, yr bro of Sir Nicholas Mosley, Lord Mayor of London 1599 & gf of the 1 Bt of the 1 cr (1640); Nicholas's f Edward was (according to Sir Bernard Burke) descended from Oswald, 2 s of Ernald de Moseley, Lord (a feudal lordship) of Moseley *temp* King John; Moseley is a hamlet in Staffs near Wolverhampton; Moseley Old Hall, now a Nat Tst property having apparently no connection with the family other than the name, hid Charles II after the Battle of Worcester; Sir Oswald was sometime MP Harrow (U, then Ind, then L) and Smethwick (L), Chllr Duchy of Lancaster and leader of the New Party; he m 1, Lady Cynthia Curzon, 2 da of 1 & last Marquess Curzon of Kedleston KG GCSI GCIE PC); suc aunt, Baroness Ravensdale (also cr Life Peeress: Baroness Ravensdale of Kedleston 1958) 1966; *b* 25 June 1923; *Educ* Eton, Balliol Oxford; *m* 1, 1947 (m dis 1974), Rosemary, da of Marshal of the RAF Sir John Salmond GCB CMG CVO DSO by his 2 w, Hon Monica Grenfell (da of 1 Baron Desborough and Ethel, da of Hon Julian Fane, 4 s of 11 Earl of Westmorland, by Julian's w Lady Adine, da of 6 Earl Cowper (his w was Anne, Baroness Lucas *suo jure* & da & coheir of 2 Earl de Grey; Rosemary & her children by Lord

Ravensdale are hence in remainder to the Lordship of Lucas and the Baronies of Butler and Lucas of Crudwell); 3 s, 1 da; m 2, 1974, Verity, 2 da of John Raymond, of Winslade House, Basingstoke, and former w of John Bailey; 1 s; *Heir* s, Hon Shaun Mosley; *Career* Capt Rifle Bde WW II; author (as Nicholas Mosley); books include *Accident* (1964, later filmed by Joseph Losey) and *The Assassination of Trotsky* (1972, also filmed); *Style* - The Rt Hon The Lord Ravensdale, MC; 9 Church Row, NW3 (☎ 01 435 8222)

RAVENSWORTH, 8 Baron (UK 1821); Sir Arthur Waller Liddell; 13 Bt (E 1642), JP (Northumberland 1959); s of Hon Cyril Liddell, JP, DL (2 s of 5 Baron Ravensworth); suc cous, 7 Baron, 1950; is 2 cous once removed of late Guy Liddell, CB, CBE, MC, sometime Civil Assist War Off; *b* 25 July 1924; *Educ* Harrow; *m* 1950, Wendy, adopted da of J Stuart Bell, of Cookham; 1 s, 1 da; *Heir* s, Hon Thomas Liddell; *Career* late Radio Engr BBC; *Style* - The Rt Hon The Lord Ravensworth JP; Eslington Park, Whittingham, Alnwick, Northumberland (☎ 066 574 239)

RAWCLIFFE, James Overbury; s of Brig James Maudsley Rawcliffe, OBE, MC, TD (d 1965); *b* 8 Nov 1930; *Educ* Rossall; *m* 1957, Jutta Maria Edith, nee Heinisch; 1 s, 3 da; *Career* fin dir RHM General Products Ltd, fell Inst of CA, fell Institute of Cost and Management Accountants, chm Maidenhead Coll Trust, councillor Roy Borough of Windsor & Maidenhead; *Clubs* Canning, MCC; *Style* - James Rawcliffe Esq; Alnmouth, Chauntry rd, Maidenhead, Berks

RAWLINS, Peter J; s of Leslie Rawlins; *b* 14 May 1941; *Educ* Warwick Sch Warwick, Nottingham U (BA); *m* 1967, Gillian Lister, da of Cyril Goddard (d 1980); 3 s; *Career* chartered accountant, fin dir Hepworth Iron Co (Hldgs) Ltd; *Recreations* sport; *Style* - Peter Rawlins Esq; The Lodge, Daisy Lee lane, Huddersfield, W Yorks

RAWLINSON OF EWELL, Baron (Life Peer UK 1978); Peter Anthony Grayson Rawlinson; PC (1969), QC (1959, NI 1972); s of Lt-Col Arthur Rawlinson, OBE, by his w Ailsa, eldest da of Sir Henry Grayson, 1 Bt, KBE, and his 1 w, Dora; *b* 26 June 1919; *Educ* Downside, Christ's Cambridge; *m* 1, 1940 (m annulled by Sacred Rota, Rome, 1954), Haidee, da of Gerald Kavanagh, of Dublin; 3 da; m 2, 1954, Elaine, da of Vincent Dominguez, of Rhode Island, and Angela Grayson (6 da of Sir Henry Grayson, 1 Bt, KBE), and hence his 1 cous; 2 s, 1 da; *Career* Maj Irish Gds WW II; barr 1946, Slr-Gen 1962-64, Attorney Gen 1970-74, Recorder Kingston 1975-, Leader Western Circuit 1975-; MP (C) Epsom 1955-74, Epsom & Ewell 1974-78; kt 1962; *Clubs* White's, Pratt's, MCC; *Style* - Rt Hon Lord Rawlinson of Ewell PC QC; 12 King's Bench Walk, Temple, EC4 (☎ 01 353 5892/6)

RAWLINSON, Sir Anthony Henry John; 5 Bt (UK 1891); s of Sir (Alfred) Frederick Rawlinson, 4 Bt (d 1969); *b* 1 May 1936; *Educ* Millfield; *m* 1, 1960 (m dis 1967), Penelope Byng, da of Rear-Adm Gambier John Byng Noel, CB; 1 s, 1 da; m 2, 1977, Helen Leone, da of Thomas Miller Kennedy; 2 s; *Heir* s, Alexander Rawlinson; *Style* - Sir Anthony Rawlinson, Bt; Heath Farm, Guist, Norfolk

RAWLINSON, Hon Angela Lorraine; *née* Rawlinson; da of Baron Rawlinson of Ewell, PC, QC, by his 2 w and 1 cous, Elaine; *b* 3 Sept 1962; *Style* - The Hon Angela Rawlinson

RAWLINSON, Alexander Noel; s and h of Sir Anthony Rawlinson, 5 Bt; *b* 15 July 1964

RAWLINSON, Hon Anthony Richard; 2 s of Baron Rawlinson of Ewell, PC, QC, by his 2 w, Elaine; *b* 28 Dec 1963; *Style* - The Hon Anthony Rawlinson

RAWLINSON, Charles Frederick Melville; s of Capt Rowland Henry Rawlinson (d 1980); *b* 18 March 1934; *Educ* Canford, Jesus Cambridge; *m* 1962, Jill Rosalind, nee Wesley; 3 da; *Career* banker; v-chm Morgan Grenfell & Co Ltd (London) 1980-, dir Morgan Grenfell & Co Ltd (London) 1970-, chm Assoc Paper Industs Ltd 1979-; *Recreations* music, sailing; *Clubs* Brooks's, City of London, Kildare St & University, Dublin, Roy Harwich Yacht; *Style* - Charles Rawlinson Esq; 23 Great Winchester st, EC2 (☎ 588 4545)

RAWLINSON, Hon Mrs (Catherine Julia); da of Baron Trend (Life Peer); *b* 1950; *m* 1966, Colin James Rawlinson; *Style* - The Hon Mrs Rawlinson; 9 Shooter's Hill rd, Blackheath, SE3

RAWLINSON, Hon Michael Vincent; s of Baron Rawlinson of Ewell, PC, QC, and his 2 w, Elaine; *b* 24 Jan 1957; *Style* - The Hon Michael Rawlinson

RAYLEIGH, 5 Baron (UK 1821); John Arthur Strutt; s of 4 Baron Rayleigh, JP, DL, FRS (d 1947; ggs of Lady Charlotte FitzGerald, da of 1 Duke of Leinster and w of Col Joseph Strutt, MP, who was cr Baroness Rayleigh 1821), by his 1 w, Lady Mary Clements, da of 4 Earl of Leitrim, DL, and Lady Winifred Coke (da of 2 Earl of Leicester); *b* 12 April 1908; *Educ* Eton, Trin Cambridge; *m* 1934, Ursula, da of Lt-Col Richard Brocklebank, DSO, JP, DL, and Charlotte Carissima (da of Gen Sir Bindon Blood, GCB, GCVO, himself gs of that Bindon Blood, known as 'The Vampire', who was also fifth in descent from The Very Rev Neptune Blood, unc of the Col Thomas Blood who made an attempt on the Crown Jewels 1671); *Heir* bro, Hon Charles Strutt; *Style* - The Rt Hon The Lord Rayleigh; Terling Place, Chelmsford, Essex (☎ Terling 235 and 01 453 3235)

RAYMOND, Hon Mrs - Hon Gay; da of 4 Visc Hardinge (d 1979); *b* 1938; *m* 1963, Pierre Raymond; 1 s; *Style* - The Hon Mrs Raymond; Warden, Quebec, Canada

RAYNAR, Hon Mrs (Sarah Elizabeth Ann); *née* Butler; da of 16 Viscount Mountgarret (d 1966); *b* 1932; *m* 1955 (m dis 1976), Geoffrey Kenneth Raynar; 2 s; *Style* - The Hon Mrs Raynar; 21 Hollybush Green, Collingham Bridge, Wetherby, Yorks

RAYNE, Baron (Life Peer UK 1976); Max Rayne; s of Phillip Rayne; *b* 8 Feb 1918; *Educ* Central Fndn Sch, UCL; *m* 1, 1941 (m dis 1960), Margaret, da of Louis Marco; 1 s, 2 da; m 2, 1965, Lady Jane Antonia Frances Vane-Tempest-Stewart, da of 8 Marquess of Londonderry; 2 s, 2 da; *Career* kt 1969; chm London Merchant Securities Ltd 1960-, Westpool Investment Tst 1980-, Nat Theatre Bd 1971-; Govr Yehudi Menuhin Sch, Hon V-Pres Jewish Welfare Bd 1966-; Fndr Patron Rayne Fndn 1962-; *Style* - The Rt Hon Lord Rayne; 33 Robert Adam st, W1 (☎ 01 935 3555)

RAYNE, Hon Alexander Philip; s of Baron Rayne by his 2 w, Lady Jane Vane-Tempest-Stewart, da of 8 Marquess of Londonderry; *b* 1973; *Style* - The Hon Alexander Rayne

RAYNE, Baroness - Lady Jane Antonia Frances; *née* Vane-Tempest-Stewart; da of 8 Marquess of Londonderry (d 1955); *b* 1932; *m* 1965, as his 2 w, Baron Rayne (Life Peer); *Style* - The Rt Hon the Lady Rayne; 100 George st, W1H 6DJ

RAYNE, Hon Nicholas Alexander; s of Baron Rayne by his 2 w, Lady Jane Vane-Tempest-Stewart, da of 8 Marquess of Londonderry; *b* 1969; *Style* - The Hon Nicholas Rayne

RAYNE, Hon Natalie Deborah; da of Baron Rayne by his 2 w, Lady Jane Vane-Tempest-Stewart, da of 8 Marquess of Londonderry; *b* 8 March 1966; *Style* - The Hon Natalie Rayne

RAYNE, Hon Robert Anthony; s of Baron Rayne by his 1 w, Margaret; *b* 1949; *Style* - The Hon Robert Rayne

RAYNE, Hon Tamara Annabel; da of Baron Rayne by his 2 w, Lady Jane Vane-Tempest-Stewart, da of 8 Marquess of Londonderry; *b* 1970; *Style* - The Hon Tamara Rayne

RAYNER, Hon Mrs; Hon Madeleine; *née* Rayne; da of Baron Rayne by his 1 w, Margaret; *b* 1943; *m* 1964, Alan Rayner; *Style* - The Hon Mrs Rayner

RAYNES, Lady (Frederica) Rozelle (Ridgway); *née* Pierrepont; da of 6 Earl Manvers (d 1955); *b* 1925; *m* 1, 1953 (m dis 1961), Maj Alexander Mongomerie Greaves Beattie; m 2, 1965, Richard Hollins Raynes, MB, BS, DPH, MFCM; *Career* 1939-45 War as Leading Wren WRNS; writer; *Style* - Lady Rozelle Raynes; Dolphin's Leap, St Margaret's Bay, Kent; 88 Narrow st, E14

RAYNHAM, Viscount; Charles George Townshend; s and h of 7 Marquess Townshend; *b* 6 Sept 1945; *Educ* Eton; *m* 1975, Hermione, da of Lt-Cdr Robert Martin Dominic Ponsonby; 1 s, 1 da; *Heir* s, Hon Thomas Charles Townshend; *Style* - Viscount Raynham; 22 Ebury st, SW1 (☎ 01 730 3388/4466)

RAYNSFORD, Hon Mrs (Joan Rosemary); *née* Wakefield; OBE (1981); da of 1 Baron Wakefield of Kendal; *b* 18 Nov 1920; *Educ* Francis Holland Sch London, Downe House Newbury, Berlin U; *m* 1944, Capt Antony Raynsford, RN, er s of Lt-Col Richard Raynsford, DSO, JP, DL; 1 s, 1 da; *Career* V-Chm Women's Nat Advsy Cttee Con Pty, chm Gter London Women's Advsy Cttee, memb Internat Exec Cttee European Union of Women 1979-81; dir Battlefelds Ltd, Shapland & Petter, Lake District Estates; *Recreations* skiing; *Clubs* Bath, SCGB (chm 1972-75, Pres 1981), Kandahar Ski (chm 1977-), National Ski Fedn of GB (V-Pres 1966-69); *Style* - The Hon Mrs Raynsford OBE; Milton Malsor Manor, Northampton (☎ 0604 858251)

RAZZALL, Edward Timothy; s of Leonard Humphrey Razzall; *b* 12 June 1943; *Educ* St Paul's Sch, Worcester Coll Oxford; *m* (dis); 1 s, 1 da; *Career* slr; chm Greencoat Properties Ltd, councillor London Borough of Richmond upon Thames 1974-; *Recreations* cricket; *Clubs* Nat Liberal; *Style* - Edward Razzall Esq; 28 Lincoln's Inn Fields, WC2 (☎ 01 405 7878)

REA, 3 Baron (UK 1937); Sir (John) Nicolas Rea; 3 Bt (UK 1935); s of Hon James Rea (2 s of 1 Baron Rea), by his 1 w, Betty, nee Bevan; *b* 6 June 1928; *Educ* Dartington Hall, Dauntsey's Sch, Christ's Cambridge, U Coll Hosp London; *m* 1951, Elizabeth, da of William Robinson, of Woking; 4 s; *Heir* s, Hon Matthew Rea; *Career* formerly Actg Sergeant Suffolk Regt; GP (Kentish Town Health Centre), former lecturer in social medicine St Thomas's Hosp Med Sch, Res Fellow Paediatrics Ibadan U Nigeria; MD, DPH, DCH, DObst; *Recreations* music, sailing, winter sports; *Clubs* Roy Soc Medicine; *Style* - The Rt Hon The Lord Rea; 48 Hungerford rd, N7 (☎ 01 607 4415)

REA, Hon Daniel William; s of 3 Baron Rea; *b* 30 Dec 1958; *Style* - The Hon Daniel Rea

REA, Hon Findlay Russell; s of 1 Baron Rea by his 2 w, Isobel, nee Pringle; *b* 25 Sept 1907; *Educ* Westminster, New Coll Oxford; *m* 1, 1932 (m dis 1946), Margaret, da of Lt-Col Kenneth Hope Bruce, DSO; 1 s, 1 da; m 2, 1947 (m dis 1959), Eileen, da of Lt-Col Isaac Wardle and former w of John Clemence; m 3, 1959, Helen, da of Bernard Richardson, of Edinburgh, and former w of Donald Crawford Reid; *Career* IO COI ret; late Lt Intelligence Corps; Cncllr Chelsea 1945-49, St Marylebone 1960-62; *Recreations* cricket & cricket writing, politics (SDP); *Clubs* MCC, Civil Serv, Surrey County Cricket; *Style* - The Hon Findlay Rea; Weald Cottage, Weald, Sevenoaks, Kent (☎ Weald 424)

REA, Hon John Silas Nathaniel; s of 3 Baron Rea; *b* 16 Oct 1965; *Style* - The Hon John Rea

REA, Hon Matthew James; s and h of 3 Baron Rea; *b* 28 March 1956; *Educ* William Ellis Sch; *Style* - The Hon Matthew Rea

REA, Hon Quentin Thomas; s of 3 Baron Rea; *b* 8 March 1961; *Style* - The Hon Quentin Rea

READ, Charles Patrick Wilson; s of Sir Charles Read; *b* 17 March 1957; *Educ* Harrow; *m* 1966, Susan Viner, da of Brian Viner Edsall; 1 s; *Career* md Young & Co Brewery Ltd 1977-; *Style* - Charles Read Esq; Malthouse Cottage, Little Bognor, Fittleworth, Pulborough, W Sussex

READE, Sir Clyde Nixon; 12 Bt (E 1661); s of late Sir George Reade, 10 Bt; suc bro, Sir John Stanhope Reade, 11 Bt,

1958; *b* 1906; *m* 1, 1930, Trilby (d 1958), da of Charles McCarthy; m 2, 1960 (m dis 1968), Alice Martha, da of Joseph Asher, of Ohio; *Heir* kinsman, Robert Reade; *Style* - Sir Clyde Reade, Bt; Box 242, Mason, Michigan 48854, USA

READE, Robert Ward; s of late Leverne Elton Reade, 5 s of 9 Bt; hp of kinsman, Sir Clyde Reade, 12 Bt; *b* 11 Oct 1923; *Style* - Robert Reade Esq

READER-HARRIS, Hon Mrs (Henrietta Marguerite Jean); *née* Loder; da of 2 Baron Wakehurst; *b* 5 Feb 1922; *Educ* Sydney U (Diploma Soc Studies); *m* 1953, John, s of Montgomery Reader-Harris; 1 s (Michael John), 1 da (Sarah Margaret); *Career* housewife & voluntary social worker; *Recreations* visiting places of historical & archaeological interest; *Style* - The Hon Mrs Reader-Harris; 35 The Close, Salisbury, Wilts

READHEAD, (Sir) James Templeman; (3 Bt, UK 1922, has established his claim but does not use his title); s of late Maj Stanley Readhead, MC, 2 s of 1 Bt; suc unc, Sir James Halder Readhead, 2 Bt, 1940; *b* 12 Feb 1910; *Educ* Repton, Lycée de Nice; *m* 1946, Hilda Rosemary, da of G H Hudson, of The Manor, Hatfield, Doncaster; 1 da; *Career* Lt KOYLI (invalided) WW II; *Style* - James Readhead Esq

READING, 4 Marquess of (UK 1926); Simon Charles Henry Rufus Isaacs; also Baron Reading (UK 1914), Viscount Reading (UK 1916), Earl of Reading and Viscount Erleigh (both UK 1917); s of 3 Marquess of Reading, MBE, MC (d 1980); *b* 18 May 1942; *Educ* Eton, Tours U; *m* 1979, Melinda, yr da of Richard Dewar; 1 da; *Heir* bro, Lord Anthony Michael Rufus Isaacs; *Career* memb London Stock Exchange 1971-74; late Lt 1 Queen's Dragoon Gds; *Clubs* Cavalry & Guards, MCC; *Style* - The Most Hon The Marquess of Reading; 3 Charlwood Place, SW1 (☎ 01 821 7185)

READING, Margot, Marchioness of; Margot Irene; da of Percival Augustus Duke, CBE, of Walton-on-the-Hill; *b* 11 Jan 1919; *Educ* Benenden; *m* 1941, 3 Marquess of Reading, MBE, MC (d 1980); 3 s (4 Marquess, Lord Anthony Isaacs and Lord Alexander Isaacs), 1 da (Lady Jacqueline Thomson); *Style* - Most Hon Margot, Marchioness of Reading; 24 Pelham st, SW7 (☎ 01 584 2140)

REARDON-SMITH, (William) Antony John; s and h of Sir William Reardon-Smith, 3 Bt; *b* 20 June 1937; *Educ* Wycliffe Coll; *m* 1962, Susan, da of Henry W Gibson, of Cardiff; 2 s, 1 da; *Style* - Antony Reardon-Smith Esq; Englewick, Englefield Green, Egham, Surrey

REARDON-SMITH, Sir William Reardon; 3 Bt (UK 1920); s of Sir Willie Reardon-Smith, 2 Bt (d 1950); *b* 12 March 1911; *Educ* Blundell's Sch; *m* 1, 1935 (m dis 1954, she d 1959), Nesta, da of Frederick J Phillips; 3 s, 1 da; m 2, 1954, Beryl, da of William H Powell; 1 s, 3 da; *Heir* s, (William) Antony Reardon-Smith; *Career* Maj RA (TA); *Style* - Sir William Reardon-Smith, Bt; Rhode Farm, Romansleigh, South Molton, N Devon

REAY, 14 Lord (S 1628); Sir Hugh William Mackay; 14 Bt (NS 1627), MEP (C) 1979-; also Chief of Clan Mackay, Jonkheer Mackay (Netherlands 1816), Baron Mackay van Ophemert (Netherlands 1822), and Baron Mackay (Netherlands 1858); s of 13 Lord Reay (d 1963, having been naturalised a Br subject 1938) by Charlotte, da of William Younger (bro of 1 Viscount Younger of Leckie); *b* 19 July 1937; *Educ* Eton, Ch Ch Oxford; *m* 1, 1964 (m dis 1978), Hon Annabel Fraser, da of 15 Lord Lovat; 2 s, 1 da; m 2, 1980, Hon Victoria Warrender, da of 8 Baron Bruntisfield; *Heir* s, Master of Reay; *Career* del to Cncl of Europe & WEU 1979-, V-Chm Con Gp European Parl; *Clubs* St James's, Turf, Beefsteak, Puffin's (Edinburgh); *Style* - The Rt Hon The Lord Reay MEP; Kasteel Ophemert, Ophemert in Gelderland, The Netherlands; 11 Wilton Crescent, SW1 (☎ 01 235 7171)

REAY, Master of; Hon Aeneas Simon Mackay; also Baron Aeneas Mackay; s and h of 14 Lord Reay (and h to S Btcy, Netherland Baronies and Jonkheership) by his 1 w, Hon Annabel Fraser, da of 15 Lord Lovat; *b* 20 March 1965; *Style* - The

Master of Reay

REAY, Charlotte, Lady; Charlotte Mary; *née* Younger; da of William Younger, of Ravenswood, Melrose (4 s of James Younger, of Alloa; bro of George Younger, cr a Bt and 1 Viscount Younger of Leckie); sis of Sir William Younger, 1 Bt, DSO, of Fountainbridge, and Maj-Gen Ralph Younger, CB, CBE, DSO, MC, JP, DL; 1 cous twice removed of Rt Hon George Younger, Sec of State for Scotland; *m* 1936, 13 Lord Reay (d 1963); 1 s, 2 da; *Style* - The Rt Hon Charlotte, Lady Reay; Southbank, Melrose, Roxburghshire

REAY, Lt-Gen Sir Hubert Alan John; KBE (1981); s of Rev John Reay; *b* 19 Mar 1925; *Educ* Lancing Coll; Edinburgh U; *m* 1960, Ferelith Haslewood Deane; 2 s, 2 da (1 s decd); *Career* formerly post-graduate dean Roy Army Med Coll, dir Medical Services HQ BAOR 1979-81, Dir Gen Army Medical Services 1981-; *Style* - Lt-Gen Sir Hubert Reay, KBE; DMS, HQ BAOR, BFPO 40

REAY, Annabel, Lady - Hon Annabel Terese; Fraser; s of 17 Lord Lovat, DSO, MC, TD; *b* 1942; *m* 1964 (m dis 1978), 14 Lord Reay; *Style* - Annabel, Lady Reay; 11 Wilton Cres, SW1; Ophemert in Gelderland, Holland

RECKITT, Basil Norman; TD (1946); s of Major Frank Norman Reckitt (d 1940); *b* 12 Aug 1905; *Educ* Uppingham, King's Cambridge, Hull U; *m* 1, 1928, Virginia, da of late Major Meredith Carre-Smith; 3 da; m 2, 1966, Mary, nee Peirce, wid of Paul Holmes, OBE; *Career* Lt-Col Home & Germany (Mil Govt); co dir: chm Reckitt & Colman Ltd 1966-1980; Sheriff of Kingston upon Hull 1970-1971; *Recreations* hunting, ornithology; *Style* - Basil Reckitt Esq, TD; Haverbrack, Milnthorpe, Cumbria; Holoman House, Isle of Raasay, by Kyle of Lochalsh, Ross-shire, Scotland

RECORDON, Hon Mrs - Dinah; da of Baron Baker, OBE (Life Peer); *b* 1936; *m* 1960, Nigel Esmond Recordon; *Style* - The Hon Mrs Recordon; Bush Farm, Colwall, nr Malvern, Worcs

REDCLIFFE-MAUD, Baron (Life Peer UK 1967); John Primatt Redcliffe Redcliffe-Maud; GCB (1955, KCB 1946), CBE (1942); s of Rt Rev John Maud, sometime Bp of Kensington; *b* 3 Feb 1906; *Educ* Eton, New Coll Oxford, Harvard; *m* 1932, Jean, yr da of John Hamilton, of Melrose; 1 s, 2 da (and 1 da decd); *Career* Master Birkbeck Coll London 1939-43, Univ Oxford 1963-76; Perm Sec Min Educn 1945-52, Min Fuel & Power 1952-59; Br Ambass S Africa 1961-63 (High Commissioner 1959-61); chm Exec Bd UNESCO 1949; High Bailiff Westminster & Searcher of the Sanctuary 1967-; *Recreations* golf, cricket, writing; *Clubs* Savile and Eton Ramblers; assumed by deed poll 1967 surname Redcliffe-Maud; *Style* - The Rt Hon Lord The Redcliffe-Maud GCB CBE; 221 Woodstock rd, Oxford (☎ 55354)

REDESDALE, 5 Baron (UK 1902); Clement Napier Bertram Mitford; s of Hon Rupert Freeman-Mitford (d 1939; bro of 2, 3 and 4 Barons); suc unc, 4 Baron, 1963; Lord Redesdale is 1 cous of Nancy and Jessica Mitford, the writers, Unity Mitford, the friend of Adolf Hitler, Hon Lady Mosley, also a writer and widow of Sir Oswald Mosley, 6 Bt, and the Duchess of Devonshire, *qqv*; *b* 28 Oct 1932; *Educ* Eton; *m* 1958, Sarah, da of Brig Alston Cranstoun Todd, OBE; 1 s, 6 da; *Heir* s, Hon Rupert Mitford; *Career* formerly with Erwin Wasey (Advertising); v-pres Corpn Communications Europe & M East Chase Manhattan Bank; govr Yehudi Menuhin Sch 1973-; *Recreations* walking; *Clubs* Lansdowne; *Style* - The Rt Hon The Lord Redesdale; The School House, Rochester, Newcastle upon Tyne; 2 St Mark's sq, NW1 (☎ 01 722 1965)

REDMAYNE, Baron (Life Peer UK 1966); Sir Martin Redmayne; 1 Bt (UK 1964), DSO (1944), TD (1952), PC (1959), DL (Notts 1954); 2 s of Leonard Redmayne and Mildred, nee Jackson; *b* 16 Nov 1910; *Educ* Radley; *m* 1933, Anne, da of John Griffiths; 1 s; *Heir* s (to Btcy only), Hon Nicholas Redmayne; *Career* MP (C) Notts Rushcliffe 1950-66, Ch Govt Whip 1959-64 (Dep 1955-59) & Parly Sec to Treasury; JP Nottingham 1948-66; formed and commanded 66 Inf Bde 1944-45, Hon

Brig 1945; former co dir; *Style* - Rt Hon Lord Redmayne DSO TD PC DL; Flat 1, 18 Hans Place, SW1 (☎ 01 584 1525)

REDMAYNE, Hon Nicholas John; s and h (to Btcy only) of Baron Redmayne, DSO, TD, PC, DL (who is also the 1 Bt); *b* 1 Feb 1938; *Educ* Radley, Sandhurst; *m* 1, 1963 (m dis 1976), Anne, da of Frank Saunders, of Kineton, Warwicks; 1 s, 1 da; m 2, 1978, Mrs Christine Hewitt, da of late Thomas Fazakerley; *Career* stockbroker, dir Scottish & Universal Investments Ltd; commanded Gren Gds 1958-62, ret; *Recreations* shooting, tennis; *Style* - The Hon Nicholas Redmayne; Walcote Lodge, Walcote, Lutterworth, Leics (☎ 2637)

REDWOOD, Sir Peter Boverton; 3 Bt (UK 1911); s of Sir Thomas Boverton Redwood, 2 Bt (d 1974); *b* 1 Dec 1937; *Educ* Gordonstoun; *m* 1964, Gilian Waddington, da of John Lee Waddington Wood, of Limuru, Kenya; 3 da; *Heir* half-bro, Robert Redwood; *Career* Lt-Col KOSB; *Style* - Sir Peter Redwood, Bt; c/o Nat West Bank, Millbank Branch, Thames House, Millbank, SW1

REDWOOD, Robert Boverton; s of late Sir Thomas Boverton Redwood, 2 Bt; hp of half-bro, Sir Peter Redwood, 3 Bt; *b* 24 June 1953; *m* 1978, Mary Elizabeth Wright; *Style* - Robert Redwood Esq

REED, Barry St George Austin; MC (1951), DL (Gtr London 1977, Hackney 1980); s of Douglas Austin Reed; *b* 5 May 1931; *Educ* Rugby Sch; *m* 1956, Patricia, nee Bristow; 1 s, 1 da; *Career* Major (Korea), chm & ch exec Austin Reed Gp Ltd 1973-, dir City & West End Bd Nat West Bank Ltd, pres Men's Assoc of Br 1966-67 & 1980-, Master Worshipful Co Glovers of London 1980-81; *Recreations* gardening, tennis; *Clubs* Bath, Marylebone Cricket; *Style* - Barry Reed Esq, MC, DL; Crakehall House, Bedale, North Yorkshire (☎ 0677 22743)

REED, Lady (Penelope Ann Rachel); *née* Ward; da of Rt Hon William Dudley Ward, PC (gn of 1 Earl of Dudley) and Winifred, Marquesa de Casa Maury, *qv*; *b* 1914; *m* 1, 1930, Anthony (m dis 1944), s of H Pelissier and Fay Compton, the actress; 1 da (Tracy Clare Compton); m 2, 1948, Sir Carol Reed; 1 s (Max); *Style* - Lady Reed; 213 King's rd, SW3

REES, Brian; s of Frederick Thomas Rees; *b* 20 Aug 1929; *Educ* Bede G S Sutherland, Trin Cambridge; *m* 1959, Julia (decd), da of Sir Robert Birley, KCMG; 2 s, 3 da; *Career* assist master Eton 1952-65 (housemaster 1963-65), headmaster Merchant Taylors' 1965-73, headmaster Charterhouse 1973-82; *Recreations* music, travel; *Clubs* Beefsteak, Athenaeum, Savile; *Style* - Brian Rees Esq; Headmaster's House, Charterhouse, Godalming, Surrey

REES, William Linford Llewelyn; CBE (1977); s of Edward Parry Rees (d 1947); *b* 24 Oct 1914; *Educ* Llanelli G S, U Coll Cardifff, Welsh Nat Sch Medicine, London U; *m* 1940, Catherine Magdalen, nee Thomas; 2 s, 3 da; *Career* emeritus prof psychiatry London U, consulting physician Bart's 1980-, civilian consultant in psychiatry to RAF; Pres Roy Coll Psychiatrists 1975-78, Pres Br Medical Assoc 1978-79, Tres of World Psychiatric Assoc 1966-78; *Recreations* photography, grandchildren, gardening, swimming, entertaining; *Clubs* Athenaeum, Liveryman Barber Surgeons' Worshipful Co, Worshipful Soc Apothecaries; *Style* - Prof William Rees, CBE; 62 Oakwood ave, Purley, Surrey; 27 Speed House, Barbican (☎ 588-4881)

REES-MOGG, Sir William; s of late Edmund Fletcher Rees-Mogg, JP (of a Somerset family of landowners extant since the 13 century), and Beatrice (da of Daniel Warren, of New York State, US); *b* 14 July 1928; *Educ* Charterhouse, Balliol Oxford; *m* 1962, Gillian Shakespeare Morris, da of T R Morris; 2 s, 3 da; *Career* dir GEC; V-Chm BBC 1981-; editor The Times 1967-81, dir The Times Ltd 1968-, Times Newspapers Ltd 1978; High Sheriff Somerset 1978; kt 1981; *Style* - Sir William Rees-Mogg; The Old Rectory, Hinton Blewitt, nr Bristol, Avon (☎ Temple Cloud (0761) 52489); 3 Smith sq, SW1

REES-WILLIAMS, Hon Christine Ann; da of 2 Baron Ogmore; *b* 1968

REES-WILLIAMS, Hon Jennet

Elizabeth; da of 2 Baron Ogmore; *b* 1970

REES-WILLIAMS, Hon Morgan; s of 1 Baron Ogmore, TD, PC (d 1976) and hp of bro, 2 Baron; *b* 19 Dec 1937; *Educ* Mill Hill Sch; *m* 1, 1964 (m dis 1970), Patricia, da of C Paris Jones; m 2, 1972 (m dis 1976), Roberta, da of Capt Alec Stratford Cunningham-Reid, DFC; *Career* Lt R Regt of Wales (TA); *Style* - The Hon Morgan Rees-Williams; Flat 6, 98 Elm Park gdns, SW10

REEVE, John Frederick; *Career* FIQS, FCIARB, MBIM, md & chm Costain UK Ltd; *Style* - John Reeve Esq; Costain House, Nicholsons Walk, Maidenhead, Berks

REEVES, Christopher Reginald; s of Reginald Raymond Reeves; *b* 14 Jan 1936; *Educ* Malvern; *m* 1965, Stella Jane, da of Cdr Patrick Whinney RN, of Guernsey; 3 s; *Career* merchant banker, Bank of England 1958-63, Hill Samuel & Co Ltd 1963-67, dep chm and gp ch exec Morgan Grenfell & Co Ltd 1980 (dir 1970, dep chm and dep ch exec 1975); *Recreations* sailing, shooting, skiing; *Clubs* Boodle's, Royal Southern Yacht; *Style* - Christopher Reeves Esq; 15 Woodhall drive, College rd, SE21 (☎ 01 693 2673)

REID, Sir Alexander James; 3 Bt (UK 1897), of Ellon, Aberdeenshire, JP (Cambs and Isle of Ely 1971), DL (1973); s of Sir Edward Reid, 2 Bt, KBE (d 1972, through whose sis, Victoria, Sir Alexander is 1 cous of Richard Ingrams, the ed of Private Eye, and 1 cous once removed to the h of the Barony of Darcy de Knayth), and Tatiana, Lady Reid, *qv*; *b* 6 Dec 1932; *Educ* Eton, Magdalene Cambridge; *m* 1955, Michaela, da of Olaf Kier, CBE, of Royston; 1 s, 3 da; *Heir* s, Charles Reid; *Career* Capt (ret) 3 Bn Gordon Highlanders, served Malaya 1951-53; dir Cristina Securities Ltd, Kingston Ag Servs Ltd 1970-, Quantock Veal Ltd 1974-, Bellinger Bros Ltd 1975-, Ellon Castle Estates, Kingston Wood Farms Ltd; *Style* - Sir Alexander Reid, Bt, JP, DL; Kingston Wood Manor, Arrington, Royston, Herts (☎ Caxton 231)

REID, Andrew Milton; s of The Rev A A R Reid, DD (decd); *b* 21 July 1929; *Educ* Glasgow Academy, Jesus Oxford; *m* 1953, Norma MacKenzie, da of Norman Davidson (decd); 2 s; *Career* assist md John Player and Sons, 1975-77, dir Imperial Gp Ltd 1978- , chm Imperial Tobacco Ltd 1979-; *Recreations* fishing, golf, sailing; *Clubs* Clifton (Bristol); *Style* - Andrew Reid Esq; Parsonage Farm, Publow, Pensford, nr Bristol (☎ Compton Dando 229)

REID, Hon Mrs (Angela Margaret Amherst); *née* Cecil; da of 3 Baron Amherst of Hackney, CBE; *b* 16 May 1955; *m* 1980, Gavin Reid, s of Col Ivo Reid, of Somerton Oxford; *Style* - The Hon Mrs Reid

REID, Charles Edward James; s and h of Sir Alexander Reid, 3 Bt; *b* 24 June 1956; *Educ* Rannoch, RAC Cirencester; *Style* - Charles Reid Esq

REID, Sir Hugh; 3 Bt (UK 1922); s of Sir Douglas Neilson Reid, 2 Bt (d 1971); *b* 27 Nov 1933; *Educ* Loretto; *Style* - Sir Hugh Reid, Bt; Auchterarder House, Perthshire

REID, Lady Laura Louise; *née* Meade; da of 6 Earl of Clanwilliam; *b* 11 March 1957; *m* 1981, (W) Scott (B), s of Howard Reid, of Bronxville New York; *Style* - Lady Laura Reid

REID, Michael Herbert; s of John Lillingstone Reid (d 1958); *b* 25 Feb 1925; *Educ* Radley, Trin Oxford; *m* 1970, Caroline Jane Jefferson, nee Bell; 1 s, 2 da; *Career* RAF & Aux RAF (Middle East); landowner, farmer; cncl memb RASE, S of E Ag Soc, Sussex Cattle Soc; dir John Weston Ltd, South Counties Livestock Suppliers Ltd, Cridmore Farm Co, formerly of SCATS; *Recreations* fishing; *Clubs* RAF; *Style* - Michael Reid Esq; Coopers Farm, Stonegate, Wadhurst, Sussex (☎ 0580 200295)

REID, Robert Basil; CBE 1980; s of Sir Robert Neil Reid, KCSI, KCIE (d 1963); *b* 7 Feb 1921; *Educ* Malvern, Brasenose Oxford; *m* 1951, Isobel Jean, nee McLachlan; 1 s, 1 da; *Career* ch exec (Railways) British Railways Board 1980- (gen man Southern Region 1974-77, bd memb marketing 1977-1980); *Recreations* golf, sailing, shooting, gardening; *Clubs* Naval & Military; *Style* - Robert Reid, CBE; 23 Edgehill rd, Purley, Surrey, CR2 2ND (☎ 01 660 5429)

REID, Tatiana, Lady; Tatiana; da of Col Alexandre Fenoult, late of the Russian Imperial Gd; *m* 1930, Sir Edward Reid, 2 Bt, KBE (d 1972), sometime Page of Honour to George V; 1 s (Sir Alexander Reid, 3 Bt, JP, DL) (1 da decd); *Style* - Tatiana, Lady Reid; 16 Buckingham ter, Edinburgh EH4 3AD

REID, William; s of William Reid (d 1961); *b* 16 Nov 1937; *Educ* Creighton Sch Carlisle, Loughborough U; *m* 1964, Kathleen, nee Morris; 1 s adopted (Paul James), 2 da (Joanne Camille b 1964, Nicola Sydney Mary b 1968); *Career* chemical engineer, md RTZ Chemicals Ltd; dir: RTZ Borax Ltd, Feroxide (Widnes) Ltd, ISC Chemicals Ltd, Manchem Ltd, Nutfield Manufacturing Co Ltd, RTZ Chemical Investments Ltd, RV Chemicals Ltd, Thorium Ltd, Vine Chemicals Ltd, Berk Spenser Acids Ltd, Manox Ltd, Kaylis Chemicals Ltd, Sterling Moulding Materials Ltd, Sterling Petrochemicals Ltd, Sterling Materials Management Ltd, Sterling Labelling Systems Lts, Sterling Coated Materials Ltd; *Recreations* sailing (catamaran 'Kathy's Sable'); *Style* - William Reid Esq; The Old Forge, Blackhorse Lane, Upper Gatton, Reigate, Surrey (☎ Merstham (07374) 2341)

REIDHAVEN, Viscount; Hon James Andrew Ogilvie-Grant; Master of Seafield; s and h of 13 Earl of Seafield by his 1 w; *b* 30 Nov 1963; *Style* - Viscount Reidhaven and Master of Seafield

REIGATE, Baron (Life Peer UK 1970); Sir John Kenyon Vaughan-Morgan; 1 Bt (UK 1960), PC (1961); s of Sir Kenyon Pascoe Vaughan-Morgan, OBE, MP; *b* 2 Feb 1905; *Educ* Eton, Ch Ch Oxford; *m* 1940, Emily, da of William Redmond Cross, of New York; 2 da; *Heir* none; *Career* MP (C) Reigate 1950-70, Min of State BOT 1957-59; served WW II Welsh Gds; late memb LCC and Pres E Fulham Con Assoc; former co dir; *Clubs* Brooks's, Beefsteak, Hurlingham; *Style* - The Rt Hon Lord Reigate PC; 36 Eaton sq, SW1 (☎ 01 235 6506)

REILLY, Baron (Life Peer UK 1978); Paul Reilly; s of Prof Sir Charles Reilly, OBE, FRIBA, sometime Head Liverpool Sch Architecture; *b* 29 May 1912; *Educ* Winchester, Hertford Coll Oxford, LSE; *m* 1, 1939, Pamela Foster; 1 da; m 2, 1952, Annette, da of Brig-Gen Clifton Stockwell, CB, CMG, DSO; *Career* designer; memb Cncl: BTA 1960-70, RCA 1963-80, BBC Genl Advsy 1964-70, BR Bd Design Panel 1966-, Environment Panel 1977-, GLC Historic Bldgs Ctee, PO Stamp Advsy Ctee; former journalist with News Chronicle; dir Conran Assocs, Bldg Tdes Exhibition Ltd, chm Race Internat Designs Ltd; kt 1967; *Style* - Rt Hon Lord Reilly; 3 Alexander Place, SW7 (☎ 01 589 4031)

REILLY, Brian Thomas; s of Thomas Joseph Reilly, OBE (d 1978); *b* 9 Dec 1978; *Educ* Mount St Mary's nr Sheffield; *m* 1952, Jean Cynthia, nee Gilbey; 1 s, 4 da; *Career* md GEC Radio & Television Ltd (assoc dir 1968-74), chm Nat Panasonic UK Ltd 1976-79; *Recreations* golf, bridge, theatre; *Clubs* Annabel's; *Style* - Brian Reilly Esq; Marsham Manor, Marsham Lane, Gerrards Cross, Bucks (☎ 82188)

REITH, Barony of (UK 1940); *see* Reith, Christopher John

REITH, Christopher John; s of 1 Baron Reith, KT, GCVO, GBE, CB, TD, PC (best known as the Dir Gen of the BBC 1926-38); suc f 1971 but disclaimed Peerage for life 1972; *b* 27 May 1928; *Educ* Eton, Worcester Coll Oxford; *m* 1969, Penelope, da of Henry Morris, of Notts; 1 s, 1 da; *Heir* s, Hon James Reith; *Career* served RN 1946-48, subsequently farmer; *Style* - Christopher Reith Esq; Whitebank Farm, Methven, Perths (☎ 333)

REITH, Hon James Harry John; s and h of Christopher Reith (suc as 2 Baron Reith 1971, but disclaimed Peerage for life 1972); *b* 2 June 1971; *Style* - The Hon James Reith

REITH, Hon Julie Katharine; da of

Christopher Reith (suc as 2 Baron Reith 1971 but disclaimed Peerage for life 1972); *b* 1972; *Style* - The Hon Julie Reith

REMNANT, 3 Baron (UK 1928); Sir James Wogan Remnant; 3 Bt (UK 1917), CVO (1978); s of 2 Baron Remnant MBE (d 1967); *b* 23 Oct 1930; *Educ* Eton; *m* 1953, Serena, da of Cdr Sir Clive Loehnis, KCMG, RN (ret), by his w, Rosemary (da of Maj Hon Robert Dudley Ryder, 4 s of 4 Earl of Harrowby, JP, DL, sometime sr ptnr Coutts & Co); 3 s, 1 da; *Heir* s, Hon Philip Remnant; *Career* FCA 1955; chm Roy Jubilee Tsts 1980-, City of London Brewery & Investment Tst; dep chm Ultramar Ltd 1981-, Union Discount Co of London; jt md Touche Remnant & Co; dir Nat Provident Inst, Utd Dominions Tst; Church Commissioner 1976-; *Clubs* White's; *Style* - The Rt Hon Lord Remnant CVO; Bear Ash, Hare Hatch, Reading, Berks

REMNANT, Hon Hugo Charles; 3 s of 3 Baron Remnant CVO; *b* 28 Nov 1959; *Style* - The Hon Hugo Remnant

REMNANT, Hon Melissa Clare; da of 3 Baron Remnant CVO; *b* 20 May 1963; *Style* - The Hon Melissa Remnant

REMNANT, Dowager Baroness; Norah Susan; da of Lt-Col Alexander Wogan-Browne, 33 Indian Cavalry; *b* 18 July 1900; *m* 1924, 2 Baron Remnant MBE; 1 s (3 Baron), 1 da (Hon Mrs Tyser) *qqv*; *Style* - Rt Hon Dowager Lady Remnant; 131 Cranmer Court, Sloane av, SW3 (☎ 01 589 5018)

REMNANT, Hon Philip John; s and h of 3 Baron Remnant CVO; *b* 20 Dec 1954; *Educ* Eton, New Coll Oxford; *m* 1977, Caroline, da of Capt Godfrey Cavendish (ggs of Francis Cavendish by his w Lady Elinor Fitzgibbon, herself da of 3 Earl of Clare and niece of that Lord Clare whose friendship with Lord Byron culminated in the affecting and celebrated meeting on the road between Imola and Bologna; Francis Cavendish was s of Gen Hon Henry Cavendish, who was in his turn s of Lord George Cavendish, 3 s of 4 Duke of Devonshire, KG; Lord George was elevated to the Peerage as 1 Earl of Burlington - of the 2 creation); 1 s (*b* 2 July 1981); *Style* - The Hon Philip Remnant; PO Box 78882, Sandton 2146, Transvaal, S Africa; 2/28 Rosary gdns, SW7 (☎ 01 370 3297)

REMNANT, Hon Robert James; 2 s of 3 Baron Remnant CVO; *b* 10 Oct 1956; *Educ* Eton; *Style* - The Hon Robert Remnant

RENALS, Sir Stanley; 4 Bt (UK 1895); s of Sir Herbert Renals, 3 Bt (d 1961); *b* 20 May 1903; *Educ* City of London Freemen's Sch; *m* 1957, Maria Dolores Rodriguez Pinto, da of late José Rodriguez Ruiz; 1 s; *Heir* s, Stanley Michael Renals; *Career* late Merchant Navy; *Style* - Sir Stanley Renals, Bt; 47 Baden rd, Brighton, Sussex

RENALS, Stanley Michael; s and h of Sir Stanley Renals, 4 Bt; *b* 14 Jan 1958; *Style* - Stanley Renals Esq

RENDLESHAM, 8 Baron (I 1806); Charles Anthony Hugh Thellusson; s of Lt-Col Hon Hugh Thellusson DSO, 3 s of 5 Baron Rendlesham, JP, DL, by his w Lady Egidia Montgomerie (da of 13 Earl of Eglinton and Winton KT); Hugh was bro of 6 and 7 Barons Rendlesham and m Gwynnydd, da of Brig-Gen Sir Robert Colleton, 1 and last Bt, CB; suc unc 1943; the Thellussons descend from an eighteenth century Swiss Ambass to the court of Louis XV of France, one Isaac de Thellusson; *b* 15 March 1915; *Educ* Eton; *m* 1, 1940, Margaret (m dis 1947), da of Lt-Col Robin Rome MC; 1 da (Hon Lady Goring, *qv*); m 2, 1947, Clare, da of Lt-Col Douglas McCririck, of Wiveliscombe, Somerset; 1 s, 3 da; *Heir* s, Hon Charles Thellusson; *Career* Capt late Roy Corps of Signals (WW II); *Style* - The Rt Hon The Lord Rendlesham; 100b Eaton sq, SW1

RENFREW, Glen McGarvie; *aet* 52 in July 1981; *m* Daphne; 1 s (Barry), 3 da (Susan, Judy, Pamela; also 1 da, Ann, decd); *Career* jt dep md Reuters Ltd to 1981 (md Feb 1981-); dir IDR Inc (USA); *Style* - Glen Renfrew Esq; c/o Reuters Ltd, 1700 Broadway, NYC, NY 10019, USA; c/o Reuters Ltd, 85 Fleet st, EC4 (☎ 01 353

6060/836 2567); Shorewood Drive, Sands Point, New York, USA

RENNELL, 3 Baron (UK 1933); (John Adrian) Tremayne Rodd; s of 2 but only surviving s of Cdr Hon Gustaf Rodd (bro of (1) 2 Baron Rennell, KBE, CB, JP, DL, who d 1978, (2) Hon Peter Rodd, who d 1968, was husb of late Nancy Mitford and was allegedly the model for Evelyn Waugh's character Basil Seal, (3) late Baroness Emmet of Amberley, and (4) late Hon Mrs Elwes (w of Lt-Col Simon Elwes, former Official War Artist); *b* 28 June 1935; *Educ* Downside, RNC Dartmouth; *m* 1977, Phyllis, da of Thomas Neill, of Co Armagh; 1 s, 1 da; *Heir* s, Hon James Rodd; *Career* served RN 1952-62; Morgan Grenfell & Co 1963-66, former freelance journalist & Scottish Rugby International; dir Tremayne Ltd 1980-; *Clubs* White's; *Style* - The Rt Hon Lord Rennell; 64 Netherwood rd, W14 (☎ 01 602 4094)

RENNY, Hon Mrs (Nicola Gladys); *née* Moncreiff; da of 4 Baron Moncreiff (d 1942); *b* 1917; *m* 1, 1940, Capt Frederick W Gifford, RA (ka 1943); 1 s; m 2, 1946, Charles John Derek Renny (d 1970); 1 s, 2 da; *Style* - The Hon Mrs Renny; Millbrook, St Peter Port, Guernsey, CI

RENSHAW, John David; s and h of Sir (Charles) Maurice Renshaw, 2 Bt; *b* 9 Oct 1945; *m* 1970, Jennifer, da of Gp Capt F Murray RAF; *Style* - John Renshaw Esq

RENSHAW, Sir (Charles) Maurice Bine; 2 Bt (UK 1903); s of Capt Sir (Charles) Stephen Bine Renshaw, 1 Bt (d 1976); *b* 7 Oct 1922; *Educ* Eton; *m* 1, 1942 (m dis 1947), Isobel Bassett, da of late Rev John L T Popkin; 1 s, 1 da; m 2, 19--, Winifred Mary, da of H F Giddon, and formerly w of of James H T Sheldon; 3 s, 3 da; *Heir* s, John Renshaw; *Career* late Flying Offr RAF; *Style* - Sir Maurice Renshaw, Bt; Tam-na-Margaidh, Balquhidder, Perthshire; Linwood, Instow, N Devon

RENTON, Baron (Life Peer UK 1979); David Lockhart-Mure Renton; KBE (1964), TD, PC (1962), QC (1954), DL (Hunts 1962, Huntingdon & Peterborough 1964, Cambs 1974); s of Dr Maurice Waugh Renton; *b* 12 Aug 1908; *Educ* Oundle, Univ Oxford; *m* 1947, Claire, da of Walter Duncan; 3 da; *Career* barr 1933; MP Hunts (Nat Lib 1945-50, Nat Lib & C 1950-68, C 1968-79); Min of State Home Off 1961-62; Pres Statute Law Soc 1980-, chm Nat Soc Mentally Handicapped Children 1978-; *Recreations* riding, shooting, tennis, gardening; *Clubs* Carlton, Pratt's; *Style* - Rt Hon Lord Renton, KBE, TD, PC, QC, DL; Moat House, Abbots Ripton, Huntingdon, (☎ 227); 22 Old sq, Lincoln's Inn, WC2 (☎ 01 242 8986)

RENTON, Hon Clare Olivia; 2 da of Baron Renton, KBE, TD, PC, QC, DL; *b* 23 Aug 1950; *Educ* St Mary's Wantage, Birkbeck London; *Career* barr; *Recreations* opera, history, the country; *Style* - The Hon Clare Renton; 2 Dr Johnson's Building, Temple EC4

RENTON, Hon Davina Kathleen; da of (Life) Baron Renton, KBE, TD, PC, QC, DL; *b* 1954; *Style* - The Hon Davina Renton

RENTON, (Ronald) Timothy; MP (C) Mid-Sussex 1974-; s of Ronald Kenneth Duncan Renton CBE (d 1980); *b* 28 May 1932; *Educ* Eton, Magdalen Oxford; *m* 1960, Alice Blanche Helen, da of Sir James Fergusson, 8 Bt; 2 s (1 twin), 3 da (1 twin); *Career* PPS to John Biffen when Ch Sec to Treasury 1979-81 & later when Sec State Trade, resigned as PPS 1981; pres Cons Trade Unionists 1980-, memb APEX; dir Silvermines Ltd; *Recreations* gardening, growing amenity trees, tennis; *Clubs* Brooks's, Coningsby; *Style* - Timothy Renton Esq MP; Mount Harry House, Offham, Lewes, East Sussex

RENWICK, 2 Baron (UK 1964); Sir Harry Andrew Renwick; 3 Bt (UK 1927); s of 1 Baron Renwick KBE (d 1973), by his 1 w, Dorothy, nee Parkes; *b* 10 Oct 1935; *Educ* Eton; *m* 1965, Susan, da of Capt Kenneth Lucking; 2 s; *Heir* s, Hon Robert Renwick; *Career* memb Stock Exchange; dir Gen Tehnology Systems 1975-, dir Eurotech Developments 1980-; chm Br Dyslexia Assoc 1977-; *Clubs* White's, Turf; *Style* - The Rt Hon Lord Renwick; 22 Rosslyn Hill, NW3

RENWICK, Charles Richard; s and h of Sir Richard Renwick, 4 Bt; *b* 10 April 1967

RENWICK, Diana, Lady; Diana Mary; da of Col Bernard Cruddas DSO, of Middleton Hall, Morpeth; *m* 1934, Sqdn-Ldr Sir Eustace Renwick, 3 Bt (d 1973); 2 s, 1 da; *Style* - Diana, Lady Renwick; Whalton, Northumberland

RENWICK, Joan, Baroness; (Edith) Joan; da of Sir Reginald Clarke CIE; *m* 1, Maj John Ogilvie Spencer (decd); m 2, as his 2 w, 1953, 1 Baron Renwick KBE (d 1973); *Style* - Rt Hon Joan, Lady Renwick; Herne's Cottage, Windsor Forest, Berks

RENWICK, Hon Michael David; s of 2 Baron Renwick; *b* 26 July 1968; *Style* - The Hon Michael Renwick

RENWICK, Sir Richard Eustace; 4 Bt (UK 1921), of Newminster Abbey, Morpeth, Northumberland; s of Sir Eustace Renwick, 3 Bt (d 1973), and Diana, Lady Renwick, *qv*; *b* 13 Jan 1938; *Educ* Eton; *m* 1966, Caroline, da of Maj Rupert Milburn, JP (2 s of Sir Leonard Milburn, 3 Bt, JP), and Anne, da of Maj Austin Scott Murray, MC; 3 s; *Heir* s, Charles Renwick; *Career* late Capt Northumberland Hussars; md & proprietor Master Saddlers Co; *Recreations* tennis, hunting, point-to-pointing; *Clubs* Northern Counties (Newcastle); *Style* - Sir Richard Renwick, Bt; Whalton House, Whalton, Morpeth, Northumberland (☎ Whalton 383)

RENWICK, Hon Robert James; s and h of 2 Baron Renwick; *b* 19 Aug 1966; *Style* - The Hon Robert Renwick

REPARD, Hon Mrs; Hon Peggy; *née* Bowyer; da of late 1 Baron Denham; *b* 1925; *m* 1947, Cdr John David Latimer Repard, OBE, DSC, RN; 3 da; *Style* - The Hon Mrs Repard; Pheasant Lodge, The Common, Berkhamsted, Herts

REUBEN, Arnold; JP (1971); s of Jack Reuben (d 1971); *b* 19 Dec 1929; *Educ* King George V Sch Southport, Oxford U; *m* 1954, Audrey, nee Cussins; 1 s, 2 da; *Career* dir Waring & Gillow Holdings Ltd, chm Leeds United Dvpt Co, govr Leeds Playhouse, v-pres Leeds Jewish Welfare Bd; *Recreations* theatre, literature, wine & food, travel; *Clubs* Royal Commonwealth; *Style* - Arnold Reuben Esq JP; Stone Acre, Leeds LS17 8EP (☎ 683222)

REVELSTOKE, 4 Baron (UK 1885); Rupert Baring; s of 3 Baron Revelstoke (d 1934, through whose sis Susan the present Lord R is 1 cous once removed to Richard Ingrams, ed of Private Eye); also 1 cous twice removed of HRH The Princess of Wales, n to late Countess (w of 5 Earl) of Kenmare, and bro-in-law of late Guy Liddell, CB, CBE, MC; *b* 8 Feb 1911; *Educ* Eton; *m* 1934 (m dis 1944), Hon Flora Fermor-Hesketh (d 1971; da of 1 Baron Hesketh by his w Florence, gda of Gen J C Breckinridge, sometime Vice-Pres of the USA), sis of Hon Lady Stockdale; 2 s; *Heir* s, Hon John Baring; *Career* late 2 Lt RAC (TA); *Style* - The Rt Hon Lord Revelstoke; Lambay Island, Rush, Co Dublin, Eire

REX-TAYLOR, David; s of William Walter Taylor (d 1953); *b* 25 Jan 1947; *Educ* Jt Servs Sch for Linguists, Birkbeck Coll London; *Career* Fellow Inst of Sales Management, assist man (Russia) BEA 1969-71, Regional Organiser London Nat Fund Research into Crippling Diseases 1971-72, founder Bibliagora (Publishers & Int Book Mail Order Co, 1973) and Lineage Res Unit; *Recreations* bridge (fndr Evening Standard Bridge Congress; Br Rubber Bridge Championship; London bridge clubs); *Clubs* Crockford's, Curzon House, Palm Beach, Int Sporting; *Style* - David Rex-Taylor Esq; PO Box 7, Hounslow (☎ 898 1234, 898 7700, 894 6262; London Radiophone 16605; Telex 935918 Bridge G)

REYNOLDS, Sir David James; 3 Bt (UK 1923); s of Lt-Col Sir John Francis Roskell Reynolds, 2 Bt, MBE (d 1956); *b* 26 Jan 1924; *Educ* Downside; *m* 1966, Charlotte Baumgartner; 1 s, 2 da; *Heir* s, James Reynolds; *Career* Capt 15/19 Hussars Italy WW II; *Style* - Sir David Reynolds, Bt; Blanchepierre House, rue de la Blanchepierre, St Lawrence, Jersey, CI

REYNOLDS, James; s and h of Sir David Reynolds, 3 Bt; *b* 10 June 1971

REYNOLDS, Hon Mrs (Joan Murray); *née* Siddeley; da of 1 Baron Kenilworth CBE (d 1953); *b* 1904; *m* 1926, Eric Austyn Reynolds (d 1969); 3 s, 1 da; *Style* - The Hon Mrs Reynolds; Wyastone Leys, Monmouth, Gwent NP5 3SR

REYNOLDS, Lady Kathleen (Marie Gabrielle); *née* Pelham-Clinton-Hope; da of 9 Duke of Newcastle OBE; *b* 1951; *m* 1970, Edward Reynolds; *Style* - Lady Kathleen Reynolds

REYNOLDS, Patrick John; s of James Reynolds (d 1969); *b* 20 Aug 1969; *Educ* Latymer Sch Edmonton; *m* 1959, Pauline Claire, nee Farmer; 2 da; *Career* chm Reynolds Medical Ltd, winner Queen's Award Exports 1980; *Recreations* cricket, badminton, real tennis; *Style* - Patrick Reynolds Esq; The Wall House, Little Berkhamsted, Herts (☎ Cuffley 4071)

REYNOLDS, Simon; s of Major James Reynolds, of Leighton Hall, Carnforth, Lancs; *b* 20 Jan 1939; *Educ* Ampleforth College, Heidelberg University; *m* 1970, Beata Cornelia, da of Baron Siegfried von Heyl zu Herrnsheim, of Schlosschen, Worms; 2 s, 2 da; *Career* export dir ADP Export Sales Ltd; *Recreations* writing, collecting fine art, travelling; *Style* - Simon Reynolds Esq; Langold House, Birling, Maidstone, Kent

RHEAD, David Michael; s of Harry Bernard Rhead JP; *b* 12 Feb 1936; *Educ* St Philips G S Edgbaston Birmingham; *m* 1958, Rosaleen Loretto, nee Finnegan; 4 da; *Career* FCA, CBIM, Chartered Accountant, memb Worshipful Co of CAs of England & Wales, freeman of City of London; chm LCP Holdings Ltd 1975- (dep chm 1973, fin dir 1968); *Recreations* fishing, assoc football; *Style* - David Rhead Esq; 62 Little Sutton Lane, Sutton Coldfield, W Midlands B75 6PE (☎ 021 308 4762)

RHODES, Baron (Life Peer UK 1964); Hervey Rhodes; KG (1972), DFC and Bar (1918), PC (1969), DL (Lancs 1971); s of John Rhodes; *b* 12 Aug 1895; *Educ* Huddersfield Tech; *m* 1925, Ann Bradbury; 2 da; *Career* MP (L) Ashton-under-Lyne 1945-64, Parly Sec BOT 1950-51 & 1964-66; KStJ; fndr & chm H Rhodes & Bros (woollen mfrs) 1921-61; Ld-Lt Lancs 1968-71; *Style* - The Rt Hon Lord Rhodes, KG, DFC*, PC, DL; Cribbstones, Delph, Oldham, Lancs (☎ Saddleworth 4500)

RHODES, Sir John Christopher Douglas; 4 Bt (UK 1919); s of Lt-Col Sir Christopher George Rhodes, 3 Bt (d 1964); *b* 24 May 1946; *Heir* bro, Michael Rhodes; *Style* - Sir John Rhodes, Bt

RHODES, John Ivor McKinnon; CMG (1971); s of Joseph Thomas Rhodes (d 1922); *b* 6 March 1914; *Educ* Leeds Middle Sch; *m* 1939, Eden Annetta, nee Clark; 1 s, 1 da; *Career* Major Middle East, fin staff War Office 1933-46, princ & assist sec HM Treasury 1947-66, Min UK mission to UN 1966-73, memb UN Committee on Contributary & UN Pensions Bd 1966-71, chm UN Advisory Ctee on Admin & Budget Questions 1971-74, sr consultant (assist sec gen) to administrator UN Dvpt Programme 1979-80; *Recreations* gardening, playing electronic organ; *Clubs* Roy C'wlth Soc; *Style* - John Rhodes Esq CMG; 'Quintins', Watersfield, Pulborough, W Sussex (☎ 079 881 634)

RHODES, Hon Mrs; Hon Margaret; *née* Buller-Fullerton-Elphinstone; da of late 16 Lord Elphinstone KT and Lady Mary Bowes-Lyon DCVO, da of 14 Earl of Strathmore; *b* 1925; *m* 1950, Denys Gravenor Rhodes; 2 s, 2 da; *Style* - The Hon Mrs Rhodes; Spitchwick Farm, Poundsgate, Ashburton, Devon

RHODES, Michael Philip James; s of late Lt-Col Sir Christopher Rhodes, 3 Bt; hp of bro, Sir John Rhodes, 4 Bt; *b* 3 April 1948; *m* 1973, Susan, da of Patrick Roney-Dougal; 1 da; *Style* - Michael Rhodes Esq

RHODES, Zandra Lindsey; da of Albert James; *b* 19 Sept 1940; *Educ* Medway Tech Sch for Girls, Medway Coll of Art; *Career* textile/fashion designer & artist, founded textile printing Co with Alexander MacIntyre, created Sylvia Ayton & Zandra Rhodes Ready to Wear Dress Co 1967/8, founded Zandra Rhodes Co manufacturing fantasy dresses 1969, founded ZR (UK) Ltd & Subsidiary Cos with Anne Knight & Ronnie Sterling 1975, followed by licensing Zandra Rhodes name in USA, UK & Australia & founding shops worldwide; *Clubs* Embassy; *Style* - Miss Zandra Rhodes; 28 St Stephens gdns, W2 (☎ 01 727 1174)

RHYL, Baroness; Hon Esmé Consuelo Helen; *née* Glyn; OBE (1946); 2 da of 4 Baron Wolverton, JP, DL, by his w, Lady Edith Ward CBE (da of 1 Earl of Dudley); sis of 5 Baron Wolverton and late Lady Hyde (mother of 7 Earl of Clarendon); *b* 20 Sept 1908; *m* 1950, Baron Rhyl, OBE, PC (Life Peer, d 1981), s of Gen Sir Noel Birch, GBE, KCB, KCMG, and Florence (3 da of Sir George Chetwode, 6 Bt, and sis of 1 Baron Chetwode; also aunt of Lady Betjeman, w of the Poet Laureate); *Style* - The Rt Hon Lady Rhyl OBE; Holywell House, Swanmore, Hants; 73 Ashley gdns, SW1

RHYS, Lady Anne Maud; *née* Wellesley; da of 5 Duke of Wellington and Hon Lilian Coats, da of 1 Baron Glentanar; *b* 2 Feb 1910; *m* 1933 (m dis 1963), Hon David Rhys, 3 s of 7 Baron Dynevor; 1 s, 1 da; *Career* inherited Duchy (Sp) of Ciudad Rodrigo and Grandeeship of 1 Class on death of her bro, 6 Duke, 1943, but ceded them to unc, 7 Duke, 1949; *Style* - Lady Anne Rhys; Le Bourg, Rue de Tertrie, Castel Parish, Guernsey

RHYS, David Lewellin; OBE (1950), MC (1937), DL (Mon 1965, Gwent 1974); s of Owen Lewellin Rhys MD (d 1963); *b* 2 April 1910; *Educ* Epsom, RMC Sandhurst; *m* 1949, Doreen, nee Giles; 2 s; *Career* CStJ (1975), KStJ (1978); Col (Palestine 1936, Waziristan 1937, Burma 1942-43, Italy 1944-45, Malaya 1955-56), Mil Attaché Netherlands & East Indies 1947-49, Sec Monmouth TAFA 1957-68, Sec Wales TAURA 1968-75, Ch Cmmr St John Ambulance Bde Wales 1975-79; *Recreations* fishing, shooting, golf; *Clubs* Army & Navy, Cardiff & Country; *Style* - David Rhys Esq, OBE, MC, DL; Ty Mawr, Llyswen, Powys (☎ 346), Paradwys, Aberthin, Cowbridge, S Glam (☎ 2056)

RHYS, Hon David Reginald; s of late 7 Baron Dynevor and Lady Margaret Child-Villiers, da of 7 Earl of Jersey; *b* 1907; *Educ* Eton; *m* 1, 1933 (m dis 1963), Lady Ann Maud Wellesley, da of 5 Duke of Wellington; 1 s, 1 da; m 2, 1963, Sheila Mary d'Ambrumenil, da of D J Phillips; 1 s; *Career* late Capt Welsh Gds 1939-45 War (wounded); *Clubs* Guards'; *Style* - The Hon David Rhys; Southwick Court, Trowbridge, Wilts

RHYS, Hon Mrs Elwyn - Diana Sloane; da of Maj Roger Cyril Hans Sloane Stanley JP DL, of Paultons Park, Hants; *m* 1931, Capt the Hon Elwyn Villiers Rhys (2 s of 7 Baron Dynevor and who d 1966); 1 da; *Style* - The Hon Mrs Elwyn Rhys; Beechwood, Burley, Hants

RHYS, Hon Hugo Griffith Uryan; s & h of 9 Baron Dynevor; *b* 19 Nov 1966; *Style* - The Hon Hugo Rhys

RHYS, Hon Miranda Jane Caroline; da of 9 Baron Dynevor; *b* 1960; *Style* The Hon Miranda Rhys

RHYS, Hon Susannah Mair Elizabeth; da of 9 Baron Dynevor; *b* 1964; *Style* - The Hon Susannah Rhys

RHYS, Hon Sarah Sophia Rhiannon; da of 9 Baron Dynevor; *b* 1963; *Style* The Hon Sarah Rhys

RHYS, William Joseph St Ervyl-Glyndwr; s of Edward John Rhys (d 1955); *b* 6 July 1924; *Educ* Newport H S, U of Wales, Guy's Hosp London U, St John's Coll Cambridge; *m* 1961, Ann (MB, BCh, MFCM, DPM), nee Rees; 5 da; *Career* Sqdn Ldr RAF Inst Aviation Medicine & Empire Test Pilot Sch; MOH Cardiganshire 1966-74, Consultant Physician Community Medicine (Dyfed) 1974-, Hon Medical Advsr Welsh Nat Water Dvpt Authority 1966-, Cambridge U Rep on Cncl & Court Govrs U Coll Wales 1979-; chm Ystrad Meurig Community Cncl 1972-, Trustee St John's Coll Dyfed 1979-; High Sheriff Dyfed 1979-80; *Recreations* medical history, genealogy, local history, walking; *Clubs* RAF; *Style* - William Rhys Esq; Plas Bronmeurig, Ystrad Meurig, Dyfed (☎ 097 45 650); Minffordd, Llangadog, Dyfed (☎ 496)

RHYS WILLIAMS, Sir Brandon Meredith; 2 Bt (UK 1918), of Miskin,

Parish of Llantrisant, Co Glamorgan, MP (C) Kensington 1974-, MEP (C then ED) 1973-, for S E London 1979-; s of Sir Rhys Rhys Williams, 1 Bt, DSO, QC, sometime MP (Lib) Oxon and Banbury (d 1955), and Juliette, DBE, DGStJ, late Govr BBC, da of Clayton Louis Glyn JP (gggs of Sir Richard Glyn, 1 Bt, of the 1759 cr); bro of Lady Glyn (w of Sir Anthony Glyn, 2 Bt, *né* Geoffrey Davson); *b* 14 Nov 1927; *Educ* Eton; *m* 1961, Caroline, da of Ludovic Foster, of Greatham Manor, Pulborough; 1 s, 2 da; *Heir* s, Gareth Rhys Williams; *Career* late Lt Welsh Gds; contested (C) Pontypridd 1959, Ebbw Vale 1964 & 66; formerly with ICI; MP (C) S Kensington 1968-74; *Clubs* Pratt's, Cardiff & County; *Style* - Sir Brandon Rhys Williams, Bt, MP, MEP; Miskin Manor, Pontyclun, Mid Glam (☎ 0443 224204); 32 Rawlings st, SW3 (☎ 01 584 0636)

RHYS WILLIAMS, (Arthur) Gareth Ludovic Emrys; s and h of Sir Brandon Rhys Williams, 2 Bt, MP & MEP; *b* 9 Nov 1961; *Educ* Eton, Durham U; *Recreations* climbing, target shooting, OTC, conjuring, travel; *Style* - Arthur Rhys Williams Esq; Miskin Manor, Pontyclun, Mid Glamorgan; 32 Rawlings st, SW3 (☎ 01 584 0636)

RICARDO, Lady Barbara Maureen; *née* Montagu-Stuart-Wortley-Mackenzie; da of 3 Earl of Wharncliffe; *b* 26 Aug 1921; *m* 1943, David Ricardo; 2 s; *Career* served WW II Women's Land Army; *Style* - Lady Barbara Ricardo; The Lodge, Carlton House, Wortley, Sheffield

RICE, Arthur Gorton; s of Arthur Edwin Rice (d 1967); *b* 8 Apr 1929; *Educ* St Georges in Field Birmingham; *m* 1953, Joan, nee Thomas; 5 c; *Career* RAF, Berlin Airlift Flying Offr 1948-49; CA, sr ptnr Rice & Co; *Recreations* squash rackets, golf, tennis; *Style* - Arthur Rice Esq; 'While Gales', Ladywood rd, Four Oaks, Sutton Coldfield (☎ W Midlands)

RICE, His Hon Judge; Gordon Kenneth; s of Victor Rice (d 1947); *b* 16 April 1927; *Educ* BNC Oxford; *m* 1967, Patricia Margaret; *Career* Crown Court Judge; *Style* - His Hon Judge Rice; 83 Beach ave, Leigh-on-Sea, Essex (☎ Southend 73485)

RICE-OXLEY, James Keith; s of Montague Keith Rice-Oxley (d 1956); *b* 15 Aug 1920; *Educ* Marlborough, Trin Oxford; *m* 1949, Barbara Mary Joan, nee Parsons; 2 da; *Career* Maj (despatches 1944); dir gen Cncl of British Shipping 1965-1980, dir Int Shipping Fedn & chm Shipowners Gp ILO 1969-1980, chm Nat Sea Training Trust 1965-1980, chm Merchant Navy Training Bd 1981-; *Recreations* ceramics, squash, tennis; *Style* - James Rice-Oxley Esq; Ox House, Bimport, Shaftesbury, Dorset (☎ 2741)

RICH, Sir Almeric Frederic Conness; 6 Bt (GB 1791); s of Sir Almeric Edmund Frederic Rich, 5 Bt (d 1948); a descendant of Sir Richard Rich, Slr-Gen to Henry VIII and later Lord High Chancellor of England (*see* Guilford, Earl of); *b* 9 Feb 1897; *Career* Lt RGA WW I, HM's Borstal Serv 1932-61; *Style* - Sir Almeric Rich, Bt; c/o Nat West Bank, 1 St James's sq, SW1

RICHARDS, Archibald Banks; s of Charles Richards; *b* 29 March 1911; *Educ* Daniel Stewart's Coll Edinburgh; *m* 1941, Edith Janet, nee Sinclair; 1 s, 1 da; *Career* chartered accountant, ptnr A T Niven & Co 1939-64, ptnr Touche Ross & Co 1964-78, pres Institute Chartered Accountants Scotland 1976-77; *Clubs* Caledonian (London), New (Edinburgh); *Style* - Archibald Richards Esq; 7 Midmar Gardens, Edinburgh (☎ 031 447 1942)

RICHARDS, Hon Mrs (Gillian Mary); da of Baron Hunt of Fawley CBE (Life Peer); *b* 1951; *m* 1972, Paul Andrew Richards; *Style* - The Hon Mrs Richards; 78 Overstrand Mansions, Prince of Wales Drive, SW11

RICHARDS, Hon Mrs Irene Mary; da of Baron Leatherland (Life Peer); *b* 1923; *m* 1961 (m dis 1977), Douglas Richards; *Style* The Hon Mrs Irene Richards

RICHARDS, Lt-Gen Sir John Charles Chisholm; KCB (1980); s of Charles Richards and Alice Milner; *b* 21 Feb 1927; *Educ* Worksop Coll Notts; *m* 1953, Audrey Hidson; 2 s, 1 da; *Career* HM Marshal of the Diplomatic Corps 1 Jan 1982-; Cmdt Gen RM 1977-81 (with RM 1945-), Cdr 3

Commando Bde 1975-76; *Clubs* Roy Thames Yacht; *Style* - Lt-Gen Sir John Richards KCB; c/o Nat West Bank, 48 High st, Egham, Surrey

RICHARDS, Hon Juliet Elizabeth; da of 2 Baron Milverton; *b* 1964 *Style* The Hon Juliet Richards

RICHARDS, Joseph Harold William Garner; OBE (1943), DL (Huntingdon 1952, Cambs 1974); s of Rev Joseph Richards (d 1941); *b* 19 Aug 1897; *Educ* RMA Newcastle; *m* 1932, Enid Clunes, nee Mackay; 1 da; *Career* Brig (France 1917, NWFF 1919 & 1924), Staff Sch Artillery 1928-32, Instructor Gunnery Coast Artillery Sch 1928-32, Cdr Cross Channel Guns of Dover 1942-44, Ch Instructor Sch of AA Artillery 1945-47, Cdr Highlands AA Bde 1947-49, County CD Officer Huntingdon 1952-67, County CD Officer Cambs 1974; *Recreations* heavy horses, gardening, antiques; *Style* - Joseph Richards Esq, OBE, DL; Old House, Brampton, Cambridgeshire (☎ Huntingdon 53677)

RICHARDS, Hon Michael Hugh; s of 1 Baron Milverton GCMG (d 1978); hp of bro, 2 Baron Milverton; *b* 1 Aug 1936; *Educ* Ridley Coll Ontario, Clifton Coll; *m* 1960, Edna Leonie B, da of Col Leo Steveni, OBE, MC, IA (ret); 1 s; *Career* Capt (ret) Rifle Bde; Malaya 1957 (despatches); attached R Nigerian Army 1962; memb UN Congo Force 1963-65; md Philip Morris Nigeria Ltd 1972-; dir Africa Carreras-Rothmans Ltd 1978-; *Clubs* Naval and Military; *Style* - The Hon Michael Richards; Windrush Lodge, Middleton Park, Bicester, Oxon

RICHARDS, Hon Susan Mary; da of 2 Baron Milverton; *b* 1962; *Style* The Hon Susan Richards

RICHARDSON, Baron (Life Peer UK 1979); Sir John Samuel Richardson; 1 Bt (UK 1963), MVO (4 class 1943); s of Maj John Richardson and Elizabeth, da of Sir Samuel Roberts, 1 Bt, PC, JP, DL; *b* 16 June 1910; *Educ* Charterhouse, Trin Cambridge; *m* 1933, Sybil, da of Ronald Trist, of Stanmore; 2 da; *Heir* to Btcy, none; *Career* conslt St Thomas's Hosp 1974- & Metropolitan Police 1957-80; Pres Gen Medical Cncl 1973-80, V-Pres Roy Coll Nursing 1972-; *Style* - Rt Hon Lord Richardson MVO; Windcutter, Lee, Ilfracombe, N Devon (☎ 63198)

RICHARDSON, Hon Mrs (Averil Diana); *née* Betterton; da of 1 Baron Rushcliffe; *b* 1914; *m* 1, 1939, Maj Richard Wyndham-Quin Going KOSB (ka 1944); 1 s, 1 da; m 2, 1946, Col Charles Walter Philipps Richardson, DSO & Bar, KOSB, (b 8 Jan 1905, educ RNCs Osborne & Dartmouth and Sandhurst, served NW Europe WW II and enjoys shooting & fishing); 2 s; *Style* - The Hon Mrs Richardson; Quintans, Steventon, Hants (☎ Dummer 473)

RICHARDSON, Anthony Lewis; s and h of Sir Leslie Richardson, 2 Bt; *b* 5 Aug 1950; *Style* - Anthony Richardson Esq

RICHARDSON, Garry Peter Alan; s of Claud Alan Richardson; *b* 6 Jan 1931; *m* 1961, Jill Rosemary Grenville, da of Robert Grenville Smith, of Vaud, Switzerland; 3 da; *Career* dir: Park Close Estates, Poulten Selfe & Lee Ltd, Stanhope-Seta Ltd; *Recreations* tennis, golf; *Clubs* Lansdowne, Wentworth; *Style* - Garry Richardson Esq; Mount House, Waverley Drive, Virginia Water, Surrey (☎ Wentworth 4473)

RICHARDSON, John Bryson; s of George Bryson Richardson; *b* 17 Dec 1939; *Educ* Halliford Borough Tech; *m* 1962, Julie Mary; 2 s, 1 da; *Career* md GTE Sylvania Ltd; *Recreations* cars, photography, glass; *Style* - John Richardson Esq; Albury, Clarence Drive, Menston, Ilkley, W Yorks (☎ Menston 74325)

RICHARDSON, John David Benbow; MC (1942); s of His Hon Judge Richardson OBE (d 1956); *b* 6 April 1919; *Educ* Harrow, Clare Cambridge; *m* 1946, Kathleen Mildred, nee Turner; 4 s; *Career* Capt 1 King's Dragoon Gds; barrister, dep chm Durham County Quarter Sessions 1964-71, Recorder 1972-73, pres Northern Rent Assessment Panel 1979-; *Recreations* fishing, gardening, golf; *Clubs* Marylebone Cricket, York County Stand, Northern Counties; *Style* - John Richardson Esq MC; Cliffe Lodge,

Corbridge, Northumberland (☎ Corbridge 2101 & 3094)

RICHARDSON, John Francis; s of Francis Richardson (d 1957); *b* 16 June 1934; *Educ* Scarborough Coll, Wadham Coll Oxford; *m* 1960, Jacqueline Mary; 2 c; *Career* joined Burnley Bldg Soc 1959, (assist gen man 1972-76, dep gen man 1976-80, ch general mananager 1980-); *Recreations* golf; *Clubs* Clitheroe Golf; *Style* - John Richardson Esq; 'Hammerton', Old rd, Chatburn, Clitheroe, Lancs

RICHARDSON, Sir Leslie Lewis; 2 Bt (UK 1924); s of Sir Lewis Richardson, 1 Bt CBE (d 1934); *b* 14 Aug 1915; *Educ* Harrow; *m* 1946, Joy Patricia, da of J P Rillstone, of Johannesburg, S Africa; 2 s, 1 da; *Heir* s, Anthony Lewis Richardson; *Career* memb of L Richardson & Co of Port Elizabeth; S African Artillery N Africa WW II; *Style* - Sir Leslie Richardson, Bt; Old Vineyard, Constantia, Cape Town, S Africa

RICHARDSON, Michael John; s of George Richardson; *b* 24 July 1936; *Educ* Heanor G S Derbys; *m* 1955, Janet Ruth, nee Holmes; 2 da; *Career* auctioneer, memb Inst of Motor Auctioneers, former sec Soc of Motor Auctioneers, jt md British Car Auctions Ltd; *Recreations* golf, gliding, yachting (Yacht: 'Umgrummit'); *Clubs* Roy Thames Yacht; *Style* - Michael Richardson Esq; The Hollies, 13 Holly av, Camberley, Surrey (☎ 29039)

RICHARDSON, Hon Mrs (Sarah Amy); da of 13 Baron Clifford of Chudleigh, OBE; *b* 22 June 1956; *Educ* Convent of the Sacred Heart Woldingham; *m* 1981, Robert Carwithen Richardson, s of Christopher Richardson, of Ash, Dartmouth, Devon; *Style* - The Hon Mrs Richardson; Tolchard Cottage, Dean Prior, Buckfastleigh, Devon

RICHARDSON-BUNBURY, Lt-Cdr Sir (Richard David) Michael; 5 Bt (I 1787), of Augher, Co Tyrone, RN; s of Richard Richardson-Bunbury (ggs of Sir James Richardson-Bunbury, 2 Bt); suc kinsman, Sir Mervyn Richardson-Bunbury, 4 Bt (d 1953); the Richardson-Bunburys are a cadet branch of the Bunburys, of whom Sir William Bunbury, 12 Bt, is sr male rep; *b* 27 Oct 1927; *Educ* RNC Dartmouth; *m* 1961, Jane Louise, da of Col Alfred Pulverman; 2 s; *Heir* s, Roger Richardson-Bunbury; *Career* Lt-Cdr RN, ret 1967; computer bureau mgmnt; *Style* - Lt-Cdr Sir Michael Richardson-Bunbury; Woodlands, Mays Hill, Worplesdon, Guildford, Surrey (☎ 232034)

RICHARDSON-BUNBURY, Roger Michael; s and h of Lt-Cdr Sir Michael Richardson-Bunbury, 5 Bt, RN; *b* 2 Nov 1962; *Style* - Roger Richardson-Bunbury Esq

RICHARDSON-HILL, John William; *Career* ACIS, AIB, AMBIM; dir Hill Samuel Securities, dir business dvpt Antony Gibbs & Sons 1981-; *Style* - John Richardson-Hill Esq; c/o Antony Gibbs & Sons, 1 Fredericks Place, EC2 (☎ 01 588 4111)

RICHES, John Dansey Hurry; s of Norman Vaughan Hurry Riches (d 1975); *b* 13 Dec 1920; *Educ* Repton; *m* 1948, Pearl, nee McIlveen; 1 da; *Career* Maj RA WW II; slr, pres Incorporated Law Soc for Cardiff and District 1976; *Recreations* cricket, sports generally; *Clubs* MCC, Cardiff and County; *Style* - John Riches Esq; 9 Brynderwen Close, Cyncoed, Cardiff (☎ 754596)

RICHES, Peter Dennis; s of Walter Riches (d 1972); *b* 21 Apr 1926; *Educ* G S Swansea, Univ of Wales; *m* 1947, Valerie, da of Frank Herbert Mowbray (d 1942); 1 s, 1 da; *Career* Flying Officer, RAFVR; md Plessey Microsystems Ltd 1977-, md Motorola Ltd 1972-76, marketing dir Ampex Int SA 1967-72; *Recreations* music, travel, philately, gardening; *Clubs* RAF; *Style* - Peter Riches Esq; Wicken Manor, Wicken, Northants (☎ 234)

RICHEY, Hon Mrs Mary Teresa; *née* Lister Robinson; da of 1 and last Baron Robinson OBE (d 1952); *b* 1914; *m* 1939 (m dis 1951), Wing Cdr Paul Richey DFC; 2 s, 2 da; *Style* - The Hon Mrs Teresa Richey; 47 Sloane gdns, SW1 (☎

01 730 5530)

RICHMOND, Sir John Frederick; 2 Bt (UK 1929); s of Sir Frederick Henry Richmond, 1 Bt (d 1953); *b* 12 Aug 1924; *Educ* Eton, Jesus Cambridge; *m* 1965, Mrs Anne Moreen Bentley, da of late Dr Robert William Paylor Hall MC; 1 da; *Career* formerly Lt 10 Royal Hussars (seconded Provost Branch); *Style* - Sir John Richmond, Bt; Shimpling Park Farm, Bury St Edmunds, Suffolk

RICHMOND AND GORDON, 9 (and 4 respectively) Duke of (E 1675, UK 1876 respectively); Frederick Charles Gordon-Lennox; also Earl of March, Baron of Settrington (both E 1675), Duke of Lennox, Earl of Darnley, Lord of Torboulton (all S 1675), Duc d'Aubigny (Fr 1684), Earl of Kinrara (UK 1876), and Hereditary Constable of Inverness Castle; s of 8 Duke of Richmond and Gordon, DSO, MVO, JP, DL (d 1935), by his w, Hilda, DBE, JP (da of Henry Brassey, JP, DL, of Preston Hall, Kent, and sis of 1 Baron Brassey of Apethorpe, JP, DL, who m a da of the 7 Duke); His Grace descends from King Charles II by Louise de Kéroualle (da of Guillaume de Penancoet, Comte de Kéroualle, in Brittany), cr Baroness Petersfield, Countess of Fareham and Duchess of Portsmouth for life by HM, and Duchesse d'Aubigny by Louis XIV; *b* 5 Feb 1904; *Educ* Eton, Ch Ch Oxford; *m* 1927, Elizabeth, da of Rev Thomas Hudson, sometime Vicar of Wendover; 2 s; *Heir* s, Earl of March and Kinrara; *Career* served WW II as Fl Lt RAF; patron of five livings; late Lt Roy Tank Corps (TA); bore sceptre with dove at coronations of King George VI and HM Queen Elizabeth II; *Style* - His Grace The Duke of Richmond and Gordon; Carne's Seat, Goodwood, Chichester, Sussex; 29 Hyde Park st, W2; Seat: Goodwood, Chichester

RICHMOND BROWN, Hon Lady; Hon Gwendolen Carlis; *née* Meysey-Thompson; da of 1 Baron Knaresborough (d 1929); *b* 1903; *m* 1951 (m dis 1968), as his 2 wife, Sir Charles Frederick Richmond Brown, 4 Bt; *Career* Lady-in-Waiting to HRH the Duchess of Gloucester 1938-44; *Style* - The Hon Lady Richmond Brown; Estate Office House, Birdsall, Malton, N Yorks

RICKARDS, Hon Mrs (Patience Veronica); *née* French; da of late 6 Baron De Freyne; *b* 1922; *m* 1952, Arthur Rickards, Lt-Cdr, RN (ret); 2 da; *Style* - The Hon Mrs Rickards; The Fishery Office, Strathnaver, Kinbrace, Sutherland; Kirkmichael Old Manse, Ballindalloch, Banffshire

RICKETTS, Cyril Lewis; OBE (1979); s of Matthew Edwin Ricketts (d 1972); *b* 10 March 1972; *Educ* Brentwood Sch; *m* 1939, Margaret Constance, nee Townsend; 2 s, 1 da (decd); *Career* chairman and md Elephant Chemical Co Ltd 1933-72; High Sheriff of the County of Merioneth 1949-50; pres Industrial Assoc of Wales 1958-59, v-pres Dvpt Corpn for Wales 1958 (founder dir), Transport Users Consultative Ctee for Wales 1968-79; *Recreations* cricket, music, gardening; *Style* - Cyril Ricketts Esq OBE; Delfan, Llanbedr, Gwynedd (☎ Llanbedr 253)

RICKETTS, Sir Robert Cornwallis Gerald St Leger; 7 Bt (UK 1828), of The Elms, Gloucestershire, and Beaumont-Leye, Leicestershire; s of Sir Claude Ricketts, 6 Bt (d 1937); *b* 8 Nov 1917; *Educ* Haileybury, Magdalene Cambridge; *m* 1945, Anne, da of Rt Hon Sir Stafford Cripps, CH, PC, QC, the austere Chllr of the Exchequer in Attlee's govt and 4 s of 1 Baron Parmoor, KCVO, PC, JP, by his lordship's 1 w; 2 s, 2 da (*see* His Hon Judge Mason, whom Sarah, the er da, m 1981); *Heir* s, Robert Ricketts; *Career* slr 1949; FRSA; formerly ptnr Wellington and Clifford; Personal Assist to Ch of Staff Gibraltar 1942-45 and ADC to Lt-Govr of Jersey 1945-46; Hon Citizen of Mobile Alabama USA; *Recreations* books, history; *Style* - Sir Robert Ricketts, Bt; Forwood House, Minchinhampton, Stroud, Glos (☎ 0453 882160)

RICKETTS, (Robert) Tristram; s and h of Sir Robert Ricketts, 7 Bt; *b* 17 April 1946; *Educ* Winchester, Magdalene Cambridge; *m* 1969, Ann, yr da of Eric Lewis CB; 1 s, 1 da; *Career* Sec Horserace Betting Levy Bd Jan 1980-; *Style* - Tristram Ricketts Esq; 47 Lancaster av, SE 27 (☎ 01 670 8422)

RIDDELL, Sir John Charles Buchanan; 13 Bt (NS 1628), of Riddell, Roxburghshire; s of Sir Walter Riddell, 12 Bt (d 1934), and Hon Rachel Lyttelton JP (yst da of 8 Viscount Cobham, JP, DL, and Hon Mary Cavendish, da of 2 Baron Chesham); *b* 3 Jan 1934; *Educ* Eton, Ch Ch Oxford; *m* 1969, Sarah, da of Rt Hon Gordon Richardson, MBE, PC, Govr of Bank of England; 2 s; *Heir* s, Walter Riddell; *Career* late 2 Lt KRRC; banker, dep chm IBA 1981-; *Recreations* shooting; *Style* - Sir John Riddell, Bt; Hepple, Morpeth, Northumberland; 31 Woodsford sq, W14

RIDDELL, Walter John; s and h of Sir John Riddell, 13 Bt; *b* 10 June 1974

RIDDIOUGH, Maj Stanley Hyde; MBE (1945), TD (1945), JP (Lancs 1964), DL; s of Walmsley Riddiough JP; *b* 12 Sept 1915; *Educ* Oundle; *m* 1944, Suzanne, nee Reynolds; 3 da; *Career* Major RA 1939-46; chm & md John Riddiough & Co Ltd 1972-, dir Colne Bldg Soc 1970-, Gen Cmmr Income Tax 1975-, High Sheriff of Lancashire 1977-78; *Recreations* cinematography, amateur radio; *Clubs* Rotary; *Style* - Maj Stanley Riddiough, MBE, TD, JP, DL; Noynaroyd, Castle rd, Colne, Lancs (☎ 0282 863404)

RIDGELY, Hon Mrs; Hon Janetta; *née* Somerset; da of 4 Baron Raglan, JP; *b* 8 June 1925; *Educ* St Hugh's Oxford; *m* 1956, Prof Joseph Ridgely; 1 da; *Style* - The Hon Mrs Ridgely; 4819 Keswick rd, Baltimore, Maryland, 21210, USA

RIDLEY, 4 Viscount (UK 1900); Sir Matthew White Ridley; 8 Bt (GB 1756), TD, JP (1957), DL (Northumberland 1968); also Baron Wensleydale (UK 1900); s of 3 Viscount Ridley CBE (d 1964), and Ursula, 2 da of Sir Edwin Lutyens, OM, KCIE, the architect, and Lady Emily Lytton (da of 1 Earl of Lytton, GCB, GCSI, CIE, PC, sometime Viceroy of India and s of the novelist Bulwer Lytton, cr (1) Baron Lytton); *b* 29 July 1925; *Educ* Eton, Balliol Oxford; *m* 1953, Lady Anne Lumley, da of 11 Earl of Scarbrough, KG, GCSI, GCIE, GCVO, PC; 1 s, 3 da; *Heir* s, Hon Matthew Ridley; *Career* chm Northumberland CC 1967-79, Pres Assoc of CCs 1979-; dir: Northern Rock Bldg Soc, Tyne Tees TV, Barclays Bank NE; *Recreations* shooting, fishing, gardening; *Clubs* Turf, Pratt's; *Style* - The Rt Hon The Viscount Ridley TD DL; Blagdon, Seaton Burn, Northumberland (☎ 067089 236)

RIDLEY, Hon Mrs - Hon Annabel; da of 9 Baron Hawke; *b* 27 Aug 1940; *Educ* Hatherop Castle Sch; *m* 1961, Nicholas Adam Ridley, s of Rev Michael Ridley (d 1953); 1 s, 2 da; *Career* artist, glass engraver; *Recreations* singing, tennis; *Style* - The Hon Mrs Ridley; Arsparfel, Kerarbars, Crozon Morgat 29160, Finistère, France; 29 Richmond Hill, Richmond, Surrey (☎ 01 940 1732)

RIDLEY, Viscountess; Lady Anne Katharine; *née* Lumley; da of late 11 Earl of Scarbrough, KG, GCSI, GCIE, GCVO, TD, PC and Katharine, nee McEwen DCVO; *b* 1928; *m* 1953, 4 Viscount Ridley, *qv*; *Style* - The Rt Hon The Viscountess Ridley; Blagdon, Seaton Burn, Northumberland

RIDLEY, Adam Nicholas; s of Lt Jasper Ridley (s of Maj Hon Sir Jasper Ridley, KCVO, OBE, 2 s of 1 Viscount Ridley, by the Maj's w Countess Nathalie, da of Count Benckendorff, sometime Russian Ambass in London) and Hon Helen Bonham Carter (da of Baroness Asquith of Yarnbury and gda of H H Asquith the Liberal PM); nephew by marriage of Rt Hon Jo Grimond, PC, MP; *b* 14 May 1942; *Educ* Eton, Balliol Oxford; *m* 1970 (m dis), Lady Katherine Asquith, da of 2 Earl of Oxford and Asquith and hence his mother's 1 cous; *Career* political adviser to Chllr of the Exchequer 1979-; *Style* - Adam Ridley Esq; 52 Novello st, SW6

RIDLEY, Lt Cdr Charles David Matthew; s of Arthur Ridley CBE (d 1974); *b* 27 June 1928; *Educ* RNC Dartmouth; *m* 1960, Alison Hay, nee Thorburn; 1 s; *Career* Lt Cdr RN Staff: SNO W Indies 1958-60, Flag Offr Sea T'ning 1960-62, HMS Ganges 1962-64, CIC S Atlantic 1964-66; farmer 1966-, High Sheriff Northumberland 1981; *Recreations* shooting; *Style* - Lt Cdr Charles Ridley;

Park End, Simonburn, Hexham, Northumberland (☎ Bellingham 30631)

RIDLEY, Hon Mrs (Julia Harriet); *née* McLaren; da of 3 Baron Aberconway; *b* 22 Sept 1942; *Educ* Grenoble U; *m* 19--, Charles Walter Hayes Ridley; 1 s, 2 da; *Style* - The Hon Mrs Ridley; c/o UPI, Rome, Italy

RIDLEY, Lady Katharine (Rose Celestine); *née* Asquith; da of 2 Earl of Oxford and Asquith KCMG; *b* 16 Oct 1949; *Educ* Mayfield Sussex, King's Coll London; *m* 1970 (m dis), Adam Nicholas Ridley, *qv*, s of late Jasper Alexander Maurice Ridley; *Style* - Lady Katharine Ridley

RIDLEY, Hon Mary Victoria; da of 4 Viscount Ridley, TD, JP, DL; *b* 30 Nov 1962; *Style* - The Hon Mary Ridley

RIDLEY, Hon Matthew White; s and h of 4 Viscount Ridley, TD, JP, DL; *b* 7 Feb 1958; *Style* - The Hon Matthew Ridley

RIDLEY, Hon Nicholas; MP (C) Cirencester & Tewkesbury 1959-; s of 3 Viscount Ridley CBE; *b* 17 Feb 1929; *Educ* Eton, Balliol Oxford; *m* 1, 1950, Hon Clayre Campbell (m dis 1974), da of 4 Baron Stratheden and Campbell, CBE, JP, DL, by his 1 w, Jean, CBE, da of Col William Anstruther-Gray; 3 da; m 2, 1979, Judy, da of Dr E Kendall; *Career* Min of State FCO 1979-, formerly civil engrg contractor; Parliamentary Under-Sec DTI 1970-72; *Style* - The Hon Nicholas Ridley MP; Old Rectory, Naunton, Cheltenham, Glos (☎ Guiting Power 252); 50 Warwick sq, SW1 (☎ 01 828 1816)

RIDLEY, Rear-Adm William Terence Colborne; CB (1954), OBE (1958); s of the late W H W Ridley; *b* 9 March 1915; *Educ* RN College Dartmouth, RN Engineering Coll Keyham; *m* 1938, Barbara, nee Allen; 1 s; *Career* Rear-Adm 1966, served in Atlantic, Mediterranean and Pacific, Captain RN Engineering Coll 1962-64, Adm Superintendent HM Dockyard Rosyth 1966-71, Port Adm Rosyth 1971-72, chm Ex Services Mental Welfare Society 1973-; *Recreations* gardening; *Style* - Rear-Adm William Ridley, CB, OBE; The Green, Brompton Ralph, Taunton, Somerset (☎ Wiveliscombe 23305)

RIGBY, Anthony John; s and h of Sir John Rigby, 2 Bt, ERD; *b* 3 Oct 1946; *Educ* Rugby; *m* 1978, Mary, da of Robert Oliver, of Cheshire; 2 s; *Career* chm Cheshire Car Care (operating Ziebart vehicle rustproofing franchise for Warrington); *Recreations* motor racing, gardening, brood mare; *Clubs* Park Green (Macclesfield); *Style* - Anthony Rigby Esq; Netherton End, Howey Rise, Frodsham, Warrington, Cheshire (☎ Frodsham 31890)

RIGBY, Sir (Hugh) John Macbeth; 2 Bt (UK 1929), of Long Durford, Rogate, Co Sussex, ERD and 2 Clasps; s of Sir Hugh Rigby, 1 Bt, KCVO (d 1944); *b* 1 Sept 1914; *Educ* Rugby, Magdalene Cambridge; *m* 1946, Mary, da of Edmund Erskine Leacock (s of Mary, nee Erskine, gda of Sir David Erskine, 1 Bt); 4 s; *Heir* s, Anthony Rigby; *Career* Lt-Col (ret) RCT, served UK and SEAC; dir Executors of James Mills Ltd to 1977; *Style* - Lt-Col Sir John Rigby, Bt ERD; Casa das Palmeiras, Armação de Pêra, Algarve, Portugal (☎ 082 32548); 5 Park st, Macclesfield, Cheshire (☎ 613959)

RIGBY, Reginald Francis; TD (1950, Clasp 1952); s of the late Reginald Rigby; *b* 22 June 1919; *Educ* Manchester G S; *m* 1949, Joan Edwina, nee Simpson; 2 s; *Career* Major Far East; solicitor, dep circuit judge 1973, recorder 1977; *Recreations* fishing, shooting; *Clubs* Flyfishers; *Style* - Reginald Rigby Esq TD; The Rookery, Woore, Salop (☎ Pipe Gate 414)

RILEY, Norman Robinson; s of James Herbert Riley (d 1979); *b* 20 July 1925; *Educ* Bury H S, Queen Mary Coll London, Oxford U; *m* 1956, Inger Clara, nee Linde; 1 da; *Career* legal adviser The Distillers Co Ltd 1955-62 & Kellogg Int Corpn 1962-65, legal dir Standard Telephone & Cables Ltd 1965-; *Recreations* golf, tennis, wines; *Style* - Norman Riley Esq; 1 Macarthey House, Chesterfield Walk, SE10

RILEY, Hon Mrs (Ruth Margaret); da of 1 Baron Hives, CH, MBE (d 1965); *b* 1922; *m* 1941, Joseph Graham Riley; 3 s; *Style* - The Hon Mrs Riley; 7 Avenue rd, Duffield, Derbys

RIPLEY, Sir Hugh; 4 Bt (UK 1880), of Rawdon, Yorks; s of Sir Henry Ripley, 3 Bt, JP (d 1956), and Dorothy (da of Robert Harley, JP, DL, of a landed family long supposed to be a yr branch of the Harleys who were cr Earls of Oxford; at any rate, Robert was willed the estates of the Oxford Harleys by the sis and co-heiress of the 6 and last Earl of Oxford of that creation; Robert m Hon Patience Rodney, da of 6 Baron Rodney, herself descended collaterally from Sir Robert Harley, 1 Earl of Oxford & Queen Anne's Lord High Treasurer, being ggda of Lady Rodney, who was herself ggda of Edward, yr bro of Sir Robert); *b* 26 May 1916; *Educ* Eton; *m* 1, 1946 (m dis 1971), Dorothy, da of John Cumming Bruce-Jones and Dorothy, da of Sir Thomas Dunlop, 1 Bt, GBE, JP, DL; 1 s, 1 da; m 2, 1972, Susan, da of William Parker, of Keythorpe Grange, E Norton, Leics; 1 da; *Heir* s, William Ripley; *Career* late Maj, served WW II N Africa & Italy; dir John Walker & Sons 1956-; *Recreations* fishing, shooting; *Clubs* Boodle's; *Style* - Sir Hugh Ripley, Bt; The Oak, Bedstone, Bucknell, Salop; 20 Abingdon Villas, W8

RIPLEY, William Hugh; s and h of Sir Hugh Ripley, 4 Bt; *b* 13 April 1950; *Educ* Eton, McGill U Canada; *Recreations* fishing, writing; *Style* - William Ripley Esq; Dove Cottage, Bedstone, Bucknell, Salop

RIPON, 11 Bishop of (See founded AD 678 but merged in York till reconstituted 1836) 1977-; Rt Rev David Nigel de Lorentz Young; s of Brig Keith Young, CIE, MC; *b* 2 Sept 1931; *Educ* Wellington, Balliol Oxford; *m* 1, 1962, Rachel (d 1965), da of Jack Lewis, of Liverpool; 1 s, 1 da; m 2, 1967, Jane, da of Lewis Collison, TD, JP; 2 s; *Career* Lecturer Buddhist Studies Manchester U 1967-70, chm Governing Body SPCK 1978-, Ptnrship World Mission 1978-; Archdeacon Huntingdon & Hon Canon Ely Cathedral 1975-77; patron of 38 livings and 20 alternately with others, all the Canonries in the Cathedral, the Archdeaconries of Richmond and Leeds, and the Chllrship of the diocese; *Recreations* fell walking, sailing; *Clubs* Roy C'wlth Soc; *Style* - The Rt Rev The Bishop of Ripon; Bishop Mount, Ripon, N Yorks

RIPPON, Rt Hon (Aubrey) Geoffrey Frederick; PC (1962), QC (1964), MP (C) Hexham 1966-; s of Arthur Rippon (d 1966); *b* 28 May 1924; *Educ* King's Coll Taunton, BNC Oxford; *m* 1946, Ann Yorke; 1 s, 3 da; *Career* MP Norwich S 1955-64; Minister Public Bldgs & Works 1962-64, Minister Technology 1970, Chllr Duchy Lancester 1970-72, Environment Sec 1972-74; barr 1948; chm Dun & Bradstreet 1976-, Britannia Arrow Hldgs 1977-; *Clubs* White's, Pratt's, MCC; *Style* - The Rt Hon Geoffrey Rippon PC QC MP; Mantle Hill, Hesleyside, Hexham, Northumberland; 21 Caroline Terrace, SW1; 2 Paper Buildings, Temple, EC4 (☎ 01 353 5835)

RISLEY, George Francis; s of Thomas Risley (d 1971); *b* 23 Dec 1929; *Educ* Doncaster G S, Liverpool Tech, IMEDE Lausanne; *m* 1; 2 s, 1 da; m 2, 1976, Wendy, da of Capt Cecil Bell; 1 da; *Career* dir mktg & sales Findus Ltd; dir: Vincent Sorge Ltd, County Frozen Foods, Alpine Refrigerated Deliveries; exec memb Chambourcy Dairy Products, cncl memb Inst Food Distribution; *Recreation* golf; *Club* RAC; *Style* - George Risley Esq; 37 Westview rd, Warlingham, Surrey (☎ 820 6146)

RITCHIE OF DUNDEE, 5 Baron (UK 1905); (Harold) Malcolm Ritchie; s of 2 Baron Ritchie of Dundee; suc bro, 4 Baron, 1978; *b* 29 Aug 1919; *Educ* Stowe, Trin Oxford; *m* 1948, Anne, da of Col Charles Johnstone MC, of Durban; 1 s, 1 da; *Heir* s, Hon Charles Ritchie; *Career* served WW II as Capt KRRC; Headmaster Brickwall House Sch 1965-72; *Style* - Rt Hon Lord Ritchie of Dundee; The Poplars, Beckley, Rye, E Sussex (☎ Beckley 311)

RITCHIE, Hon Allan Graham; s of Baron Ritchie-Calder CBE; *b* 4 Jan 1944; *Educ* New Sherwood Sch, Epsom & Ewell Tech, London U; *m* 1967, Anne, da of Robert Wood; 3 da; *Career* Maths Lecturer London U; *Style* - The Hon Allan

Ritchie; 4 Radnor rd, NW6

RITCHIE, Hon Angus Lindsay; s of Baron Ritchie-Calder CBE; *b* 5 Feb 1942; *Educ* Wallington Co G S, King's Cambridge; *m* 1963, Jennifer, da of Prof David Daiches; 1 s, 1 da; *Career* author; *Style* - The Hon Angus Ritchie

RITCHIE OF DUNDEE, Anne, Baroness; Anne Petronill; da of Henry Burra JP; *b* 13 April 1909; *m* 1, 1935 (m dis 1943), John Huntley, s of Francis Huntley, of Boxwell Court, Glos; m 2, 1943, 4 Baron Ritchie of Dundee (d 1978); *Style* - Rt Hon Anne, Lady Ritchie of Dundee; 5 Fairmeadow, Rye Hill, Rye, Sussex

RITCHIE, Hon Charles Rupert Rendall; s and h of 5 Baron Ritchie of Dundee; *b* 15 March 1958; *Style* - The Hon Charles Ritchie

RITCHIE, Sir James Edward Thomson; 2 Bt (UK 1918), of Highlands, TD (1943 - 2 clasps); s of Sir James William Ritchie, 1 Bt, MBE (d 1937); *b* 16 June 1902; *Educ* Rugby, The Queen's Coll Oxford; *m* 1928, Esme (m dis 1936 - she d 1939), da of late J M Oldham, of Ormidale, Ascot; m 2, 1936, Rosemary, da of late Col Henry Sidney John Streatfeild, DSO, TD; 2 da; *Heir* half-bro, William Ritchie; *Career* chm M W Hardy & Co Ltd 1948-78, dir William Ritchie & Son (Textiles) Ltd, patron of Ashford and Dist Caledonian Soc, memb Court of Assist Merchant Taylors' Co (Master 1963-64), Hon Lt-Col late Inns of Court Regt RAC (TA), a selected Mil memb Kent T & AF Assocn 1953-68, pres Ashford Branch Roy British Legion 1951-75, FRSA, jt Hon Treas and chm of Finance and Gen Purposes Ctee London Sch of Hygiene and Tropical Med London U 1951-61, memb Finance & Gen Purposes Ctee and a co-opted memb of Bd of Management 1964-65; 1939-45 War holding various Staff and Regimental appts (Central Mediterranean Force 1944-45); *Clubs* Army and Navy; *Style* - Sir James Ritchie, Bt; Kirkbank House, High Halden, Ashford, Kent TN26 2JD (☎ Ashford 85249)

RITCHIE, Hon Nigel David; s of Baron Ritchie-Calder CBE; *b* 2 Dec 1931; *Educ* Merchant Taylors', Sidney Sussex Cambridge; *m* 1954, Elisabeth, da of Alfred Palmer; 2 s, 3 da; *Career* ed New Scientist 1962-66, sci correspondent New Statesman, writer and TV scriptwriter; *Style* - The Hon Nigel Ritchie; 8 The Chase, Furnace Green, Crawley, Sussex

RITCHIE, Hon Philippa Jane; da of 5 Baron Ritchie of Dundee; *b* 14 Aug 1954; *Educ* St Mary's Convent Baldslow, UCL (BA Hons Eng Lit); *Career* actress; *Style* - The Hon Philippa Ritchie; 12 Oxford gdns, W4

RITCHIE, William Peter Emerton; s of Sir James William Ritchie, 1 Bt, MBE, and hp of half-bro, Sir James Edward Ritchie, 2 Bt, TD; *b* 15 Sept 1918; *Educ* Canford; *Career* 1939-45 War with Queen's Own Roy W Kent Regt; *Style* - William Ritchie Esq; Pytchley, Main St Holcot, Northampton NN6 9SP

RITCHIE-CALDER, Baron (Life Peer UK 1966); Peter Ritchie-Calder; CBE (1945); s of David Calder, of Forfar; *b* 1 July 1906; *Educ* Forfar Acad; *m* 1927, Mabel, da of Dr David McKail, of Glasgow; 3 s, 2 da; *Career* author and journalist; former sci ed News Chronicle, also on New Statesman, Daily News, Daily Herald; chm Metrication Bd 1969-72; memb Gen Cncl OU; *Style* - Rt Hon Lord Ritchie-Calder CBE; Philipstoun House, Linlithgow, W Lothian (☎ Philipstoun 187)

RITSON, Lady; Norah; da of David Halley, of Broughty Ferry; *m* 1922, Sir Edward Ritson, KBE, CB (d 1981); 1 s; *Style* - Lady Ritson; The Small House, Dinton, Salisbury, Wilts (☎ Teffont 209)

RIVERDALE, 2 Baron (UK 1935); Sir Robert Arthur Balfour; 2 Bt (UK 1929), DL (S Yorks 1959); s of 1 Baron Riverdale GBE (d 1957); *b* 1 Sept 1901; *Educ* Oundle; *m* 1, 1926, Nancy, da of Rear-Adm Mark Rundle DSO; 1 s; m 2, 1933, Christian, da of Maj Arthur Hill (ka 1915, ggggs of Sir Rowland Hill, 1 Bt); 1 s,

1 da; *Heir* s, Hon Mark Balfour; *Career* former co dir; memb Exec Cncl Br Assoc Chambers Commerce; *Style* - Rt Hon Lord Riverdale DL; Ropes, Grindleford, via Sheffield (☎ Hope Valley 30408)

RIVETT-CARNAC, Cdr Miles James; s of late Vice-Adm James Rivett-Carnac and hp of bro, Rev Sir Nicholas Rivett-Carnac, 8 Bt; *b* 7 Feb 1933; *m* 1958, April Sally, da of Maj Arthur Villar; 2 s, 1 da; *Career* Cdr RN, Far East Fleet Patrols and Borneo Territories 1964-65 (despatches); *Style* - Commander Miles Rivett-Carnac, RN; The Manor House, Martyr Worthy, Winchester, Hants

RIVETT-CARNAC, Rev Sir (Thomas) Nicholas; 8 Bt (UK 1836); s of late Vice-Adm James William Rivett-Carnac, CB, CBE, DSC (s of 6 Bt); suc unc 1972; *b* 3 June 1927; *Educ* Marlborough; *m* 1977, Susan Marigold MacTier Copeland; *Heir* bro, Miles James Rivett-Carnac; *Career* ordained 1962, Rural Dean of Lambeth 1978-, Priest-in-Charge St Mark's Kennington Oval 1972-; *Style* - The Rev Sir Nicholas Rivett-Carnac, Bt; St Mark's Vicarage, Kennington Oval, SE11 (☎ 01 735 1801)

RIX, Sir John; MBE (1955); s of the late Reginald Arthur Rix; *b* 30 Jan 1917; *Educ* Imperial Service Coll Haileybury, Southampton U; *m* 1953, Sylvia Gene, nee Howe; 2 s, 1 da; *Career* kt 1977, joined Vosper Ltd 1937, assistant to general works manager 1940, appointed gen man Vosper Ltd 1955, (dir 1958, md 1963), dir Thorneycroft (Malaysia) Ltd 1966, Keith Nelson (Italia) SpA 1972, and David Brown-Vosper (Offshore) Ltd 1974, dep chm and md Vosper Ltd 1978, dir David Brown Gear Industries Ltd 1979, chm Vosper Hovermarine Ltd and Mainwork Ltd 1980, chm of David Brown Corporation Ltd 1980-; *Recreations* sailing, tennis, walking; *Clubs* Royal Thames Yacht, Island Sailing; *Style* - Sir John Rix MBE; Lower Baybridge House, Owslebury, Winchester, Hants (☎ Owslebury 306)

ROBARTS, Anthony Julian; s of Lt-Col Anthony Vere Cyprian Robarts; *b* 6 May 1937; *Educ* Eton; *m* 1961, Edwina Beryl, da of the Rt Hon John Gardiner Sumner Hobson, OBE, TD, PC, QC, MP (d 1967); 2 s, 1 da; *Career* banker, dir Coutts and Co 1963-, now dep man dir, also holds other directorships; *Recreations* shooting, gardening; *Style* - Anthony Robarts Esq; c/o Coutts & Co, 440 Strand, WC2

ROBB, Lady Violet (Cynthia Lilah); *née* Butler; da of 7 Marquess of Ormonde, MBE; *b* 1946; *m* 1971, Donald Leroy Robb; *Style* - Lady Violet Robb; 2734 N Racine, Chicago, Illinois, USA

ROBBINS, Baron (Life Peer UK 1959); Lionel Charles Robbins; CH (1968), CB (1944); s of Rowland Robbins CBE; *b* 22 Nov 1898; *Educ* UCL, LSE; *m* 1924, Iris, da of A Gardiner; 1 s, 1 da; *Career* first Chllr Stirling U, Prof Economics LSE; late chm Financial Times and Ctee on Higher Educn; Dir Ec Section Offices of War Cabinet WW II; dir Roy Opera House Covent Gdn; *Style* - Rt Hon Lord Robbins CH CB; 10 Meadway Close, NW11 (☎ 01 455 4815)

ROBBINS, Hon Richard; s of Baron Robbins, CH, CB; *b* 12 July 1927; *Educ* Dauntsey's Sch, New Coll Oxford; *m* 1, 1952 (m dis 1961), Wendy, da of Brig Nithsdale Dobbs; 2 s; m 2, 1961, Brenda, former w of A Rooker Roberts and da of Douglas Clark, of Hong Kong; *Style* - The Hon Richard Robbins; 50 Highbury Hill, N5

ROBENS OF WOLDINGHAM, Baron (Life Peer UK 1961); Alfred Robens; PC (1951); s of George Robens; *b* 18 Dec 1910; *Educ* Manchester Secondary Sch; *m* 1937, Eva, da of Fred Powell; *Career* chm MLH Consultants 1971-, Johnson Matthey & Co 1971-, St Regis Newspapers Bolton 1975-, St Regis Internat 1976-, Snamprogetti 1980-, Engrg Industs Cncl 1976-, Guy's Hosp Medical & Dental Sch 1974-; dir: Bank of England 1966-, Times Newspapers Hldgs 1980-, Br Fuel Co 1967-, AAH 1971-, St Regis Paper Co (NY) 1976-, Trust Houses Forte Ltd 1971-; MP (L) Northumberland Wansbeck 1945-50, Blyth 1950-60, Min Labour & Nat Serv 1951; *Style* - Rt Hon Lord Robens of Woldingham PC; 100 High st, Southgate, N14

ROBERTHALL, Baron (Life Peer UK 1969); Robert Lowe Roberthall; KCMG (1954), CB (1950); s of Edgar Hall; *b* 6 March 1901, NSW; *Educ* Ipswich G S, Qld U, Magdalen Oxford; *m* 1, 1932, Laura (m dis 1968), da of George Linfoot; 2 da; m 2, 1968, Perilla Thyme, da of Sir Richard Southwell, FRS, and former w of Patrick Nowell-Smith; *Career* assumed name Roberthall by deed poll 1969; economist; ec advr to HM Govt 1953-61, Princ Hertford Coll Oxford 1964-67; *Recreations* gardening; *Clubs* Travellers'; *Style* - Rt Hon Lord Roberthall KCMG CB; Quarry, Trenance, Newquay, Cornwall (☎ St Mawgan 456); 7a Carey Mans, Rutherford st, SW1 (☎ 01 834 7041)

ROBERTS, Andrew Denby; s of Sir James Roberts, 2 Bt, OBE, (d 1973), and hp of bro, Sir William Roberts, 3 Bt; *b* 21 May 1938; *Educ* Rugby, Ch Ch Oxford; *Style* - Andrew Roberts Esq

ROBERTS, Hon Mrs David; Aileen Mary; da of Charles Burrow; *m* 1936, Hon David Roberts (s of 1 Baron Clwyd & d 1956); 2 s, 1 da; *Style* - The Hon Mrs David Roberts; Box Cottage, Box, Stroud, Glos

ROBERTS, Hon Mrs; Hon Elisabeth; da of Baron Edmund-Davies, PC (Life Peer); *b* 1939; *m* 1965, Richard Owen Roberts; *Style* - The Hon Mrs Roberts; 28 Rosehill rd, Burnley, Lancs

ROBERTS, Rt Rev Edward James Keymer; s of Rev Arthur Henry Roberts (d 1952); *b* 18 April 1908; *Educ* Marlborough, CCC Cambridge; *m* 1941, Dorothy Frances, nee Bowser; 3 s, 1 da, 1 step da; *Career* Archdeacon Isle of Wight 1948-52, Archdeacon Portsmouth 1952-56, Bishop Suffragan Malmesbury 1956-62, Bishop Suffragan Kensington 1962-64, Bishop of Ely 1964-77, ret; *Recreations* cycling, walking; *Clubs* Leander, Bembridge Sailing; *Style* - The Rt Rev Edward Roberts; Garden House, Tyne Hall, Bembridge IOW (☎ 2645)

ROBERTS, Sir Gilbert Howland Rookehurst; 7 Bt (UK 1809), of Glassenbury, Kent, of Brightfieldstown, Co Cork and of the City of Cork; s of Sir Thomas Langdon Howland Roberts, CBE, 6 Bt (d 1979); *b* 31 May 1934; *Educ* Rugby, Gonville and Caius Cambridge; *m* 1958, Ines Eleonore, da of late A Labunski; 1 s, 1 da; *Heir* s, Howland Roberts; *Career* MIMechE; served in Kenya with RE (East African GS Medal); *Style* - Sir Gilbert Roberts, Bt; 3340 Cliff Drive, Santa Barbara, Calif 93109, USA

ROBERTS, Howland Langdon; s and h of Sir Gilbert Roberts, 7 Bt; *b* 19 Aug 1961; *Style* - Howland Roberts Esq

ROBERTS, Ian; s of James William Roberts; *b* 23 March 1940; *Educ* Huddersfield Coll, Sheffield U; *m* 1966, Hilda Carole, nee Bramhall; 2 s, 1 da; *Career* chm Wultex Machine Co Ltd 1978 (md from 1974); dir Hampton Gold Mining Areas Ltd 1978-; *Recreations* walking, music, English history; *Clubs* Marsden & Longwood Conservative; *Style* -Ian Roberts Esq; Lower Green Owlers, Marsden, Huddersfield (☎ 843741); 2 The Crescent, Filey, N Yorks (☎ 0723 512834)

ROBERTS, Hon John Anthony; s and h of 2 Baron Clwyd; *b* 2 Jan 1935; *Educ* Harrow, Trin Cambridge; *m* 1969, Geraldine, nee Cannons; 3 s; *Career* barr Gray's Inn 1970; *Style* - The Hon John Roberts; 24 Salisbury av, Cheam, Sutton, Surrey

ROBERTS, Hon Mrs Juliana Eveline; *née* Curzon; da of late 2 Viscount Scarsdale; *b* 1928; *m* 1, 1948 (m dis 1956), George Derek Stanley Smith (d 1963); 1 s, 1 da; m 2, 1953 (m dis 1955), Frederick Nettlefold; 1 da (Viscountess Windsor); m 3, 1956 (m dis 1962), Sir Dudley Herbert Cunliffe-Owen, 2 Bt; 1 da; m 4, 1962 (m dis 1972), as his 2 w, John Roberts; 1 s, 1 da; *Style* - The Hon Mrs Juliana Roberts; Hill Farm, Garsdale, Sedbergh, Cumbria

ROBERTS, Hon Mrs (Jane Elisabeth Sybil); *née* Roskill; da of Baron Roskill, PC, QC, JP, DL; *b* 1948; *m* 1973, David Roberts; *Style* - The Hon Mrs Roberts

ROBERTS, Hon Mrs (Joan Mary); *née* Royle; da of Baron Royle (Life Peer d 1975); *b* 17 Dec 1920; *m* 1, 1942 (m dis 1963), Gordon Dixon; 1 s; m 2, 1975,

Albert Roberts; *Style* - The Hon Mrs Roberts; Abbotswell, Frogham, Fordingbridge, Hants

ROBERTS, Hon Mrs; Hon (Priscilla) Jane Stephanie; *née* Low; da of 1 Baron Aldington, KCMG, CBE, DSO, TD*, PC, DL; *b* 4 Sept 1949; *Educ* Cranborne Chase, Westfield Coll London U; *m* 1975, Hugh Roberts, s of Rt Rev Edward Roberts, sometime Bp of Ely; 1 da; *Style* - The Hon Mrs Roberts; Salisbury Tower, Windsor Castle, Berks (☎ 95 55581)

ROBERTS, Hon (William Herbert) Mervyn; s of late 1 Baron Clwyd; *b* 1906; *Educ* Trin Cambridge (BA); *m* 1947, Eileen Margaret, nee Easom; 1 da; *Career* ARCM, LMusTCL, ALCM; *Style* - The Hon Mervyn Roberts; Arunlea, 41 Worthing rd, Horsham, Sussex

ROBERTS, Peter David Thatcher; s of Leonard Charles Roberts (d 1978); *b* 1 March 1934; *Educ* Alleyn's Sch Dulwich, Sir John Cass Coll London U; *m* 1959, Elizabeth June, nee Dodds; 1 s, 2 da; *Career* Lt RNR; with Leinster/Hispania Maritime Ltd 1960-69 (dir 1963, md 1965), Hays Gp Ltd 1969-, md United Kingdom Cold Storage Ltd 1976, chm Warehousing Div Hays Gp Ltd 1981-; *Recreations* offshore sailing; *Clubs* Roy Ocean Racing, RAC; *Style* - Peter Roberts Esq; Callenders Cottage, Bidborough, nr Tunbridge Wells, Kent (☎ 0892 29053)

ROBERTS, Sir Peter Geoffrey; 3 Bt (UK 1919), of Ecclesall and Queen's Tower, City of Sheffield, and W Riding of Yorkshire; s of Sir Samuel Roberts, 2 Bt (d 1955); *b* 23 June 1912; *Educ* Harrow, Trin Cambridge; *m* 1939, Judith Randell, da of late Randell G Hempson, of Wallingford; 1 s, 4 da; *Heir* s, Samuel Roberts; *Career* barr Inner Temple 1936, Master Cutler of Sheffield 1956-57, MP (C) for Ecclesall Div of Sheffield 1945-50 and for Heeley Div of Sheffield 1950-66, Town Trustee of Sheffield 1958, Town Collector of Sheffield 1971-74, Freeman of Sheffield 1970, High Sheriff of Hallamshire 1970; Maj Coldstream Gds 1939-45 *Style* - Sir Peter Roberts, Bt; Cockley Cley Hall, Swaffham, Norfolk; Stubbin House, Sandygate, Sheffield S10 3LU; 11 Mount st, W1Y 5 RA

ROBERTS, Hon Mrs (Patricia Mairead Janet); *née* Anderson; da of 2 Viscount Waverley; *b* 2 March 1955; *m* 1979, Charles Roberts; *Style* - The Hon Mrs Roberts

ROBERTS, Lady Sarah (Josephine Mary); *née* Nelson; da of 8 Earl Nelson; *b* 1947; *m* 1978, Dr John Clive Roberts, MB, BS; *Style* - Lady Sarah Roberts; Oak End, Chalfont Park, Gerrards Cross, Bucks

ROBERTS, Samuel; s and h of Sir Peter Roberts, 3 Bt; *b* 16 April 1948; *Educ* Harrow, Sheffield U; *m* 1977, Georgina A, da of David Cory, of Peterston-super-Ely, S Glam; *Career* barr Inner Temple 1972; *Style* - Samuel Roberts Esq; 10 Smith Terrace, SW3

ROBERTS, Thomas Somerville; JP (Cardiff 1966); s of Joseph Richard Roberts; *b* 10 Dec 1911; *Educ* Cardiff H S, Balliol Coll Oxford; *m* 1, 1938, Ruth Moira Teasdale; 2 s; m 2, 1950, Margaret Peggy Anderson; *Career* port dir S Wales Ports 1970-75, chm S Wales Port Employers 1962-75, dir Dvpt Corpn Wales 1965-79, v-pres Dvpt Corpn Wales 1979-, chm Milford Haven Conservancy Bd 1976- *Recreations* TV; *Clubs* Cardiff and County; *Style* - Thomas Roberts Esq, JP; Marcross Lodge, 9 Ely rd, Llandaff, Cardiff (☎ Cardiff 561 153)

ROBERTS, Sir William James Denby; 3 Bt (UK 1909), of Milner Field, Bingley, WR of Yorkshire; s of Sir James Denby Roberts, 2 Bt, OBE, (d 1973); *b* 10 Aug 1936; *Educ* Rugby, RAC Cirencester; *Heir* bro, Andrew Roberts; *Career* collector of vintage aircraft; in July 1981 some (25 aeroplanes plus spares) of his collection was sold at auction (for a total of £667,000, only 4 failing to find a buyer), notably a WW II Hawker Hurricane, which was bought by a Roberts family trust for £260,000 (considered a record price for a vintage aircraft); *Style* - Sir William Roberts, Bt; Strathallan Castle, Auchterarder, Perthshire; Combwell Priory, Flimwell, Wadhurst, Sussex

ROBERTSHAW, John Desmond; s of Horace Archibald Robertshaw; *b* 19 Dec 1928; *Educ* Bembridge Sch, Oxford U; *m* 1961, Leslie Lynette, nee Carter; 3 c; *Career* CA, chm United Scientific Holdings Ltd, dir Kode Int Ltd, dir Energy Finance and General Trust Ltd, dir of Rights and Issues Investment Trust Ltd & other cos; *Recreations* golf; *Clubs* MCC; *Style* - John Robertshaw Esq; Birches Farm, Isfield, Sussex (☎ 304)

ROBERTSON OF OAKRIDGE, 2 Baron (UK 1961); Sir William Ronald Robertson; 3 Bt (UK 1919); s of 1 Baron Robertson of Oakridge, GCB, GBE, KCMG, KCVO, DSO, MC (d 1974); *b* 8 Dec 1930; *Educ* Charterhouse; *m* 1972, Celia, da of William Elworthy; 1 s; *Heir* s, Hon William Robertson; *Career* memb London Stock Exchange 1973-, late Maj Roy Scots Greys; *Style* - Rt Hon Lord Robertson of Oakridge; 259 Dover House rd, SW15

ROBERTSON, Alastair Macdonald; s of John Robertson (d 1980); *b* 4 Nov 1930; *Educ* George Heriot's Sch, Edinburgh U; *m* 1969, Avril Margaret, nee Willison; *Career* fell of Faculty of Actuaries, gen man and dir Scottish Equitable Life Assurance Soc; *Recreations* golf, skiing, sailing (yacht: 'Semlas', registered Leith); *Clubs* New (Edinburgh); *Style* - Alastair Robertson Esq; 13 Cumlodden av, Edinburgh (☎ 556 9101)

ROBERTSON, Alan Murray; s of Dr James Robert Robertson (d 1942); *b* 19 Dec 1914; *Educ* Malvern, Pembroke Coll Cambridge; *m* Judith-Anne Ballantyne, nee Russell; 1 s, 2 da; *Career* Maj RASC despatches, exec v-pres BP Oil Corpn New York 1968-70, dir BP Trading Ltd 1970-76, md BP Oil Ltd 1970-76, chm Alexander Duckham & Co 1972-76, memb CBI Cncl 1971-76, dir Motherwell Bridge Holdings Ltd 1976- and subsids, dir Hardcastle & Co 1976; *Recreations* travel, gardening; *Clubs* Caledonian; *Style* - Alan Robertson Esq; Shepherd's Cottage, Shipton under Wychwood, Oxon (☎ 830 696)

ROBERTSON, Duncan; JP (Denbighshire 1953); s of Sir Henry B Robertson, JP, DL (d 1948); *b* 29 April 1900; *Educ* Eton, Trin Cambridge; *m* 1929, Joyce, da of Sir Robert Williams-Wynn, 9 Bt, KCB; 3 da; *Career* barrister, High Sheriff Merioneth 1959, chm Dee & Clwyd River Authority; *Recreations* fishing, shooting, gardening; *Style* - Duncan Robertson Esq, JP; Llantysilio Hall, Llangollen, Clwyd (☎ 0978 860654)

ROBERTSON OF OAKRIDGE, Edith, Baroness; Edith Christina; da of James Macindoe, of Glasgow; *m* 1926, 1 Baron Robertson of Oakridge, GCB, GBE, KCMG, KCVO, DSO, MC (d 1974); 1 s (2 Baron), 2 da (Hon Mrs Cuming, Hon Mrs Chapman, *qqv*); *Career* OStJ; *Style* - Rt Hon Edith Lady Robertson of Oakridge; Iles Green, Far Oakridge, Glos

ROBERTSON, Maj-Gen Ian Argyll; CB (1968), MBE (1947), DL (Nairn 1973); s of John Argyll Robertson (d 1943); *b* 17 July 1913; *Educ* Winchester, Trin Oxford; *m* 1939, Marjorie Violet Isobel, nee Duncan; 2 da; *Career* commissioned Seaforth Highlanders 1934-, cmd Sch Infantry 1963-64, cmd 51 Infantry Div 1964-68 (ret 1968), HM Vice-Lord-Lt Highland Region 1980-; *Recreations* gardening, golf; *Clubs* Army & Navy; *Style* -Maj-Gen Ian Robertson CB MBE, HM Vice-Lord-Lieut for Highland Region; Brackla House, Nairn (☎ Cawdor 220)

ROBERTSON, Sir James Anderson; CBE (1963, OBE 1949, MBE 1942), QPM (1961); s of James Robertson; *b* 8 April 1906; *Educ* Provanside Sch Glasgow, Glasgow U; *m* 1942, Janet MacFarlane; 2 s, 1 da; *Career* kt 1968, Ch Constable Glasgow 1960-71, chm Glasgow Standing Conference Voluntary Youth Orgs; chm Securicor (Scotland) Ltd; *Recreations* golf, gardening; *Style* - Sir James Robertson CBE QPM; 3 Kirklee rd, Glasgow (☎ 041 339 4400)

ROBERTSON, Lady Joan Patricia Quirk; da of 1 Earl Wavell (d 1950); *b* 1923; *m* 1, 1943, Maj Hon Simon Astley (d 1946), s of 21 Baron Hastings and Lady Marguerite Nevill (da of 3 Marquess of Abergavenny); 1 da; m 2, 1948, Maj Harry Gordon, MC (d 1965); 1 da; m 3, 1973, Maj Donald Struan Robertson, Scots Gds, s of Rt Hon Sir Malcolm Robertson, GCMG, KBE (d 1951); *Style* - Lady Joan Robertson; Winkfield Plain Farm, Winkfield, Windsor, Berks

ROBERTSON, John Windeler; s of Major John Bruce Robertson (d 1973); *b* 9 May 1934; *Educ* Winchester; *m* 1959, Jennifer-Ann, da of Gontran Gourdou, of Switzerland; 1 s, 2 da; *Career* dep chm Stock Exchange 1976-79, memb of Stock Exchange 1956-, memb of Stock Exchange Cncl 1966-, sr ptnr Wedd Durlacher Mordaunt & Co 1979-; *Recreations* deer stalking, golf; *Clubs* City of London; *Style* - John Robertson Esq; Grayhurst, Haslemere, Surrey (☎ 2822)

ROBERTSON, Hon Mrs - Hon Lucy; *née* Maclay; da of 2 Baron Maclay, KBE (d 1969); *b* 1938; *m* 1966, James Ian Alexander Robertson; 3 s, 1 da; *Style* - The Hon Mrs Robertson; Glenside Farm, Plean, Stirlingshire

ROBERTSON, Lewis; CBE (1969), s of John Robertson (d 1976); *b* 28 November 1922; *Educ* Trinity College Glenalmond; *m* 1950, Elspeth, nee Badenoch; 3 s, 1 da; *Career* RAF, industrialist, administrator, dir Scottish & Newcastle Breweries 1975-, dep chm & ch exec Scottish Dvpt Agency 1976-81, dep chm & ch exec Grampian Hldgs Ltd 1971-76; *Recreations* reading, classical music; *Clubs* Caledonian, New (Edinburgh); *Style* - Lewis Robertson Esq, CBE; 32 Saxe Coburg Place, Edinburgh (☎ 031 332 5221)

ROBERTSON, Hon Mrs (Myrtle Olive Felix); *née* Arbuthnot; da of Baroness Wharton in her own right (10 holder of the title, cr E 1544-45; she d 1974, since when the Barony has fallen into abeyance between her 2 daughters; *see also* Hon Mrs Appleyard-List) by her 1 husb, David Arbuthnot, s of Maj John Arbuthnot, MVO (gn of Sir Robert Arbuthnot, 2 Bt); *b* 20 Feb 1934; *m* 1958, Henry Robertson; 3 s (including twins), 1 da; *Style* - The Hon Mrs Robertson; 9 Gipsy Lane, SW15

ROBERTSON, Neil; JP, DL (Moray 1970); s of Ian Robertson; *b* 13 March 1921; *Educ* Cargilfield Sch, Loretto Sch; *m* 1948, Marie Forbes, da of Maj Robert Young (d 1957); 1 s, 4 da; *Career* farmer, co dir, councillor: Co 1955-74, Regional 1974- ; chm Manpower Ctee, memb Policy and Resources, Water, and Social Work Ctees; past pres Elgin Branch Nat Farmer's Union, former memb Scottish Agricultural Advisory Ctee; *Recreations* shooting, golf; *Style* - Neil Robertson Esq, JP, DL; Millburn, Linkwood, Elgin, Moray

ROBERTSON, Peter McKellar; JP (Ayrshire 1976), DL (1960); s of John McKellar Robertson CBE (d 1939); *b* 5 June 1923; *Educ* Marlborough, Roy Tech Coll Glasgow; *m* 1951, Elspeth, nee Hunter; 1 s, 2 da; *Career* RN, landowner, County Cncl 1949-75 (Ayrshire), pres Assoc County Cncl Scotland 1974-75, memb Cmmn Local Authority Accounts Scotland 1974-; *Recreations* music, sailing (owner yacht 'Marella'); *Clubs* Western (Glasgow), Prestwick Golf; *Style* - Peter Robertson Esq, JP, DL; Noddsdale, Largs, Ayrshire (☎ Largs 672382)

ROBERTSON, Sidney Park; MBE (1962), TD (1967), JP (1968), DL (Orkney 1968); s of John Davie Manson Robertson; *b* 12 March 1914; *Educ* Kirkwall G S, Edinburgh U; *m* 1940, Elsa Miller, da of James Miller Croy (d 1943); 1 s, 1 da; *Career* Brig 51 Highland Div 1966-67 (cmmn RA 1940, NW Europe 1943-45; Lt-Col cmdg Lovat Scouts 1962-65); Hon Col Cmdt Roy Regt of Artillery 1977-80, Hon Col (Ulster & Scottish) Light Air Defence Regt 1975-80; chm Orkney Hospitals Health Bd 1965-1979, Roy Artillery Cncl of Scotland 1980-; v-pres Nat Artillery Assoc 1977-; Hon Sheriff Grampian Highlands and Islands 1969-, Honorary Area V-Pres Roy British Legion 1975-; *Recreations* travel, fishing; *Clubs* Army and Navy, Caledonian, New Club (Edinburgh); *Style* - Brigadier Sidney Robertson MBE TD JP DL; Daisybank, Kirkwall, Orkney (☎ Kirkwall 2085)

ROBERTSON, Hon William Brian Elworthy; s and h of 2 Baron Robertson of Oakridge; *b* 15 Nov 1975; *Style* - The Hon William Robertson

ROBEY, Ian Crake; JP (1979); s of Lt-

Col A E L Robey OBE (d 1973); *b* 4 July 1927; *Educ* Felsted Sch Essex; *m* 1953, Pamela, nee Elbourne (m dis 1977); 2 s, 2 da; *Career* builders' merchant, chm Cakebread Robey & Co Ltd 1965-, dir Assoc Builders' Merchants Ltd 1964-; v-chm National Home Improvement Cncl; *Recreations* food, music, theatre; *Style* - Ian Robey, Esq, JP; The Willows, High st, Walton-at-Stone, Herts (☎ 0920 830 076)

ROBINS, Hon Mrs (Elizabeth Mary Gerran); *née* Lloyd; da of Baron Lloyd of Kilgerran (Life Peer); *b* 1944; *m* 1968, Daniel Gerard Robins; *Style* - The Hon Mrs Robins; 6 Belvedere Grove, Wimbledon, SW19

ROBINSON, Alwyn Arnold; *b* 15 Nov 1929; *Career* md The Daily Mail; dir Associated Newspapers Group Ltd; dir Harmsworth Publishing Ltd; memb Press Council; *Style* - Alwyn Robinson Esq

ROBINSON, Arthur Geoffrey; CBE (1978); s of Arthur Robinson; *b* 22 Aug 1917; *Educ* Lincoln G S, Cambridge; *m* 1, 1943, Patricia MacAllister (d 1971); 3 s, 1 da; m 2, 1973, Hon Mrs Treeves, da of Baron Salmon (Life Peer) (*see* Hon Mrs (G R) Robinson); *Career* chm English Industrial Estates Corpn, Medway Ports Authority; dep chm Br Ports Assoc, memb Nat Ports Cncl; *Recreations* writing (*Hedingham Harvest* 1977, and many articles); *Clubs* Oxford and Cambridge; *Style* - Arthur Robinson Esq, CBE; West View Cottage, Potto, Northallerton (☎ Hutton Rudby 700134); 19 Millers ct, Chiswick Mall, W4 (☎ 01 748 2997)

ROBINSON, Hon Mrs à COURT; Hon Betty Mary; *née* Holmes à Court; da of 4 Baron Heytesbury (d 1949); *b* 1902; *m* 1, 1923 (m dis 1946), Cdr Vivian John Robinson, RN; 2 s, 1 da; m 2, 1956, Alfred Esmond Robinson, CBE, MC (d 1975); *Career* assumed the additional surname of à Court 1946; *Style* - The Hon Mrs à Court Robinson; Combe House, 62 Church Lane, Backwell, Bristol

ROBINSON, Christopher Philipse; s of late Christopher Robinson, QC; hp of kinsman, Sir John Robinson, 7 Bt; *b* 10 Nov 1938; *m* 1962, Barbara Judith, da of Richard Duncan, of Ottawa; 2 s; *Style* - Christopher Robinson Esq; 5 Bedford Crescent, Ottawa 7, Ontario, Canada

ROBINSON, Maj Edwin Rowland Winwood; MC; s of Capt Claude Robinson, MC; *m* 1953, Hon Prudence Arthur (b 1932, d between 1976 and 1980), da of 3 Baron Glenarthur, OBE, DL, by his 1 w, Audrey (da of George Lees-Milne, formerly of Wickhamford Manor, Evesham, and Crompton Hall, Lancs, by his w Helen, da of Henry Bailey, JP, DL, by Henry's 2 w; Henry was 5 s of Sir Joseph Bailey, 1 Bt, and unc of 1 Baron Glanusk), sis of James Lees-Milne, the expert on historical bldgs, *qv*; landowner; *Style* - Maj Edwin Robinson, MC; Moor Wood, Cirencester, Glos (☎ N Cerney 206/350)

ROBINSON, Hon Mrs (Gai Rencie); da (by 1 m) of Baron Salmon (Life Peer); *b* 1933; *m* 1, 1955, Martin Treves (d 1970); 3 s, 1 da; m 2, 1973, Geoffrey Robinson, CBE; *Style* - The Hon Mrs Robinson; 19 Millers ct, Chiswick Mall, W4 (☎ 01 748 2997); West View Cottage, Potto, Northallerton (☎ Hutton Rudby 700134)

ROBINSON, Sir John Beverley; 7 Bt (UK 1854), of Toronto, Canada; s of Sir John Beverley Robinson, 6 Bt (d 1954); *b* 3 Oct 1913; *Heir* kinsman, Christopher Robinson; *Style* - Sir John Robinson, Bt

ROBINSON, Sir John James Michael Laud; 11 Bt (E 1660), of London; s of Maj Sir Frederick Robinson, 10 Bt, MC (d 1975, descended from Sir John Robinson, 1 Bt, Lord Mayor of London 1662-63 and s of Ven William Robinson, sometime Archdeacon of Nottingham and half-bro of Archbishop Laud); *b* 10 Jan 1943; *Educ* Eton, Trinity Coll Dublin; *m* 1968, Kathryn Gayle, da of Stuart Keyes, of Ontario; 2 s; *Heir* s, Mark Robinson; *Career* financial analyst, landowner; *Style* - Sir John Robinson, Bt; Cranford, Kettering, Northants

ROBINSON, John Stephen; s of late Hon Richard Anthony Gasque Robinson and gs and h of 1 Baron Martonmere, GBE, KCMG, PC; *b* 10 July 1963; *Style* - John Robinson Esq

ROBINSON, Kenneth Paul; s of John Robert Robinson (d 1965); *b* 5 Feb 1925; *Educ* Skegness G S, Hatfield Coll Durham U; *m* 1951, Helen Elizabeth, nee McKissock; 5 s; *Career* CEng, FIEE, FInstP, dir and gen man Marconi Space & Defence Systems Ltd; *Style* - Kenneth Robinson Esq; 9 Grovely av, Boscombe, Bournemouth (☎ 35485)

ROBINSON, Leonard Keith; s of Cuthbert Lawrence Robinson; *b* 2 July 1920; *Educ* Queen Elizabeth's G S Blackburn, Victoria U Manchester; *m* 1948, Susan May, da of the late Vice-Adm W Tomkinson; 2 s, 2 da; *Career* RAFVR Sqdn Leader Coastal Command 1940-46; solicitor; County Chief Executive Hampshire County Council 1973, Town Clerk Stoke-on-Trent City Council 1966-73, Dep Town Clerk Birkenhead Co Borough Council 1955-66; *Recreations* cricket, theatre, cine photography, gardening; *Clubs* National Liberal, MCC; *Style* - Leonard Robinson Esq; Byewood, 21 Hocombe rd, Chandlers Ford, Hants (☎ Chandlers Ford 2081)

ROBINSON, Mark Christopher Michael Villiers; s and h of Sir John Robinson, 11 Bt; *b* 23 April 1972; *Style* - Mark Robinson Esq

ROBINSON, Michael Perkin; TD (1948), DL (W Yorks 1971); s of Cecil Hall Robinson (d 1949); *b* 12 April 1919; *Educ* Stowe; *m* 1946, Barbara Helen, nee Clay; 3 da; *Career* Col, Dep Brigade Cdr 146 Brigade TA; pres Newspaper Soc 1968-69, chm Yorkshire Weekly Newspaper Gp; dep chm Printing & Publishing Indust T'ning Bd 1980-; *Recreations* skiing, travel, photography; *Style* - Michael Robinson Esq TD DL; Carleton Lodge, Carleton, Pontefract, W Yorks (☎ 703818)

ROBINSON, Nicholas Ambrose Eldred; s of Gerard Robinson; *b* 26 July 1941; *Educ* Birkenhead Sch; *m* 1977, Annie Georgette Gabrielle, nee Barada; 2 s, 2 da; *Career* FRICS 1964, chartered surveyor, ptnr Eddisons (Bradford), dir Bradford Property Trust; *Recreations* sailing; *Clubs* Bradford; *Style* - Nicholas Robinson Esq; 8a Hollycroft av, NW3 (☎ 01 431 0176); 3 Hamilton House, 4 Park av, Harrogate (☎ 68820)

ROBINSON, Nicholas Johnson; s of Johnson Robinson; *b* 15 May 1918; *Educ* Loretto Sch Musselburgh, Trin Hall Cambridge; *m* 1948, Dorothy Evelyn, nee Dixon; 3 da; *Career* shipowner: dir Stag Line Ltd 1953-, chm 1976-; pres Tyne & Wear Chamber of Commerce 1973-75, JP for Borough of Tynemouth 1954-66, High Sheriff of County of Tyne & Wear 1981-; *Recreations* gardening, concerts; *Clubs* Army & Navy; *Style* - Nicholas Robinson Esq; 42 The Grove, Gosforth, Newcastle upon Tyne, (☎ Newcastle 851770)

ROBINSON, Peter Frank; s and h of Sir Wilfred Robinson, 3 Bt; *b* 23 June 1949; *Style* - Peter Robinson Esq

ROBINSON, Peter Harry; JP (1975); s of William Norman Robinson (d 1960); *b* 6 May 1930; *Educ* Denstone, Manchester G S; *m* 1956, Margaret, nee Mundell; 1 s, 1 da; *Career* chartered accountant, v-pres Manchester Soc Chartered Accountants 1981-, memb CBI NW Regional Council 1976, dir Manchester Chamber of Commerce 1980, chm & dir of several companies; *Recreations* bridge, shooting, fishing, gardening; *Clubs* St James's, The Manchester, St James's Bridge; *Style* - Peter Robinson Esq, JP; Highrigg, Prestbury, Cheshire (☎ 0625 829495); Mermaids, Rhosneigr, Anglesey (☎ 0704 810270)

ROBINSON, Patrick William; s of Lyell Bryant Robinson (d 1961); *b* 23 July 1927; *Educ* Rugby, Trin Hall Cambridge; *m* 1952, Ann Dorothea, nee Fletcher; 1 s (Fletcher), 2 da (Lorraine, Georgina); *Career* Pilot Offr (post-war Nat Serv); dir Rio Tinto Zinc Corp 1965-68, dir Kleinwort Benson Ltd 1969-72, chm Herbert Morris Ltd 1969-79; *Recreations* fishing, painting; *Clubs* Boodle's, India House (New York), Melbourne (Melbourne); *Style* - Patrick Robinson Esq; Lovington Mill, Castle Cary, Somerset (☎ Wheathill 243); 3 East 71st st, New York 10021, USA (☎ 628-7906)

ROBINSON, Hon Mrs (Stella Hope); da of Hon Claude Hope-Morley (d 1968) and sis of 3 Baron Hollenden; *b* 1919; *m*

1950, Neville Whiteoak Robinson; 2 s, 1 da; *Career* 1939-45 War as 2 Officer WRNS; raised to the rank of a Baron's da; *Style* - The Hon Mrs Robinson; 107 Old Church st, Chelsea, SW3

ROBINSON, Thomas Lloyd; TD (1945); s of Thomas Rosser Robinson (d 1927); *b* 21 Dec 1912; *Educ* Wycliffe Coll Glos; *m* 1939, Pamela Rosemary, nee Foster (d 1960); 1 s, 2 da; *Career* vice-chm Legal & Gen Assurance Soc 1978-, dir W England Trust Ltd 1973-79, dir Bristol Waterworks Co 1978-, dir Van Leer Groep Stichting (Holland) 1977-; chm Legal & Gen Western Adv Bd 1972-, Cncl Govrs Wycliffe 1971; High Sheriff Avon 1979-80; *Recreations* music, golf; *Clubs* Army & Navy, Marylebone Cricket, Roy & Ancient; *Style* - Thomas Robinson Esq, TD; 23 Druid Stoke ave, Stoke Bishop, Bristol (☎ Bristol 681957)

ROBINSON, Sir Wilfred Henry Frederick; 3 Bt (UK 1908), of Hawthornden, Wynberg, Cape Province, S Africa, and Dudley House, City of Westminster; s of late Wilfred Henry Robinson (3 s of 1 Bt); suc unc, Sir Joseph Robinson, 2 Bt, 1954; *b* 24 Dec 1917; *Educ* Diocesan Coll Rondebosch, St John's Coll Cambridge; *m* 1946, Margaret, da of Frank Mellish MC, of Bergendal, Cape Province; 1 s, 2 da; *Heir* s, Peter Robinson; *Career* late Maj Parachute Regt; V-Princ Diocesan Coll Sch Rondebosch 1969-77; fin offr Soc of Genealogists; *Style* - Sir Wilfred Robinson, Bt; 44 Kildare rd, Newlands, Cape Province, S Africa

ROBINSON, William Norman; CBE (1957); s of William Robinson, of Pendleton, Salford, Lancs (d 1949); *b* 1 Aug 1898; *Educ* Earls Colne G S, LSE; *m* 1926, Edna Doris, da of William Baker (d 1957), of Alton, Hants; 1 s; *Career* served 1914-18 War, 3 Afghan War 1919; civil servant (ret) in Miny of Aircraft Production: Dep Dir Labour 1941-45, Dir Materials Production 1945-46, Assist Sec Miny of Supply 1946-63; consultant British Airports Authority 1966-68; *Recreations* canine world (breeding, exhibiting & judging), int judge of Airedale Terriers; *Clubs* Kennel (memb House Ctee); *Style* - William Robinson Esq, CBE; The Cottage, 160 Wood Lane, Osterley, Middx (☎ 560 6756)

ROBOROUGH, 2 Baron (UK 1938); Sir Massey Henry Edgcumbe Lopes; 5 Bt (UK 1905), JP (Devon 1951); s of 1 Baron Roborough (d 1938) and Lady Albertha Edcumbe, da of 4 Earl of Mount Edgcumbe, GCVO, PC, JP, DL, by his w Lady Katherine Hamilton (da of 1 Duke of Abercorn, KG); *b* 4 Oct 1903; *Educ* Eton, Ch Ch Oxford; *m* 1936, Helen, da of Lt-Col Edward Dawson, JP; 2 s; *Heir* s, Hon Henry Lopes; *Career* DL Devon 1946, V-Lt 1951-58, Ld-Lt 1958-78; High Steward Barnstaple; KStJ; served Roy Scots Greys 1925-38 & 1939-45; ADC to Earl of Clarendon as Govr Union of S Africa 1936-37; memb Duchy of Cornwall Cncl 1958-68; *Style* - The Rt Hon Lord Roborough JP; Seat: Maristow, Roborough, S Devon; Residence: Bickham Barton, Roborough, S Devon (☎ Yelverton 2478)

ROBOTHAM, Maj Alpheus John; OBE (1972), JP (Derby 1956), DL (1968); s of late William Blews Robotham; *b* 9 March 1905; *Educ* Clifton Coll Bristol, Jesus Coll Cambridge; *m* 1932, Gwendolyn Constance, nee Bromet; 2 s, 1 da; *Career* Squadron Leader 2 Derbyshire Yeo 1939-45, Major (Alamein, NW Europe; despatches), solicitor; *Clubs* County (Derby); *Style* - Maj Alpheus Robotham Esq, OBE, JP, DL; Holmwood, Burley Lane, Quarndon, Derby (☎ Derby 596558)

ROBOTHAM, John Michael; s of Maj Alpheus Robotham, OBE; *b* 27 March 1933; *Educ* Clifton Coll; *m* 1963, Diana Elizabeth, nee Webb; 2 s; *Career* FCA 1957, memb Stock Exchange 1963, hon tres Inst of Advanced Motorists 1964; *Recreations* shooting, skiing, sailing, tennis, gardening; *Clubs* Cavalry & Guards, HAC; *Style* - John Robotham Esq; The Church Cottages, Bayford, Hertford (☎ 214)

ROBSON OF KIDDINGTON, Baroness (Life Peeress UK 1974); Inga-Stina Robson; JP (Oxon 1955); da of Erik Arvidsson, of Stockholm; *b* 20 Aug 1919; *Educ* Stockholm; *m* 1940, Lawrence Robson, FCS, FCMA, JDipMA; 1 s, 2 da; *Career* chm SW Thames RHA 1974-, Bd

Govrs Queen Charlotte's and Chelsea Hosps, Midwife Teachers T'ning Coll; Swedish Foreign Off 1939-40, Miny Information 1942-43; contested (Lib) Eye 1955 & 59, Gloucester 1964 & 66; Pres Lib Pty Orgn 1970-71; *Recreations* skiing, sailing, fishing; *Clubs* Nat Liberal, Boodle's; *Style* - Rt Hon Lady Robson of Kiddington JP; The Flat, 1 Whitehall Place, SW1 (☎ 01 930 5218); Kiddington Hall, Woodstock, Oxon (☎ Enstone 398)

ROBSON, Hon Erik Maurice William; s of Baroness Robson of Kiddington, JP; *b* 1943; *Style* - The Hon Erik Robson; The Old Rectory, Nether Kiddington, Woodstock, Oxon

ROBSON, Edward Stephen; s of John Arthur Robson (d 1923); *b* 15 July 1923; *Educ* Pitman's Coll Putney; *m* 1968, Joan Barbara; 1 s, 1 da; *Career* Warrant Officer RAF; md: Nickerson Fuel Oils Ltd and Nickerson Lubricants Ltd; dir: Nickerson Investments Ltd & Nickerson Transport Ltd 1971 to date; *Recreations* golf, cricket; *Clubs* Pathfinder, Albany (Halifax), Sicklehome Golf; *Style* - Edward Robson Esq; 'Barnbrook', Hope, via Sheffield, S30 2RA

ROBSON, Hon Mrs Harold (Iris Emmeline); da of Reginald Abel Smith, JP, and Hon Margaret Holland (2 da of 1 Viscount Knutsford, GCMG); through the Abel Smiths, Mrs Robson is 4 cous of the present Lord Carrington, the Foreign Secretary; a cous of Lord Bicester; and a cous of that Sir Henry Abel Smith who m Lady May Cambridge, cous of HM The Queen; *b* 14 Jan 1896; *m* 1922, as his 2 w, Col Hon Harold Robson (d 1964), s of Baron Robson, GCMG, PC (Ld of Appeal and Life Peer, d 1918); 1 s, 1 da; *Style* - The Hon Mrs Harold Robson; Pinewood Hill, Wormley, Surrey

ROBSON, Lawrence William; s of Michael William Robson (d 1947); *b* 8 Aug 1904; *Educ* Stockton G S, RAM; *m* 1940, Inga-Stina, nee Arvidsson (Baroness Robson of Kiddington, *qv*); 3 c; *Career* chartered accountant, sr ptnr Robson Rhodes 1927-72, Knight Cdr Order of North Star (Swedish Order) 1981; *Recreations* yachting, shooting, skiing; *Clubs* Boodle's; *Style* - Lawrence Robson; Kiddington Hall, nr Woodstock; Inverbroom Estate, Wester Ross

ROBSON, Nigel John; s of Col the Hon Harold Burge Robson TD JP DL (d 1964, s of Baron Robson, Life Peer, who d 1918); *b* 25 Dec 1926; *Educ* Eton; *m* 1957, Anne, nee Gladstone; 3 s; *Career* banker, vice pres Institute Bankers 1980-, chm Grindlays Bank Ltd & Grindlays Hldgs Ltd 1977-, dir Arbuthnot Latham Hldgs Co Ltd 1969-, chm Arbuthnot Latham and Co Ltd 1969-75; *Recreations* walking, music, tennis; *Clubs* Brooks's, Marylebone Cricket; *Style* - Nigel Robson Esq; Pinewood Hill, Wormley, Godalming, Surrey; 8 Clareville Grove SW7

ROBSON, William David; s of William Michael Robson; *b* 28 Jan 1944; *Educ* Eton; *m* 1975, Anne Helen, nee Gosling (d 1974); 1 s, 1 da; *Career* Lloyd's underwriter; *Recreations* golf, opera; *Clubs* White's, Pratt's; *Style* - William Robson Esq; The Woods, Hatfield Broad Oak, Bishop's Stortford, Herts (☎ Hatfield Broad Oak 452)

ROBSON, William Michael; s of Col the Hon Harold Burge Robson TD JP DL (d 1964); *b* 31 Dec 1912; *Educ* Eton, New Coll Oxford; *m* 1 1939, Audrey Isobel Wales, nee Dick (d 1964); 2 s, 1 da; m 2 1965, Frances Mary Wyville, nee Dawson & widow of Andrew Alexander Buchanan; *Career* dep chm: The Standard Bank Ltd 1965-, The Chartered Bank 1974-, Standard and Chartered Banking Gp Ltd 1974-; dir: Antony Gibbs 1976-, Antony Gibbs, Sage Ltd 1976-, dir Anton Underwriting Agencies Ltd 1977-, dir Bellfax Internat 1978-; memb Lloyd's 1938-; High Sheriff Kent 1970; *Clubs* Brooks's, MCC, Overseas Bankers; *Style* - William Robson Esq; Hales Place, Tenterden, Kent (☎ 2932)

ROCHDALE, 1 Viscount (UK 1960); John Durival Kemp; OBE (1945), TD (1943), DL (Cumbria 1948); also Baron Rochdale (UK 1913); s of 1 Baron Rochdale, CB (d 1945), and Lady Beatrice Egerton, MBE, da of 3 Earl of Ellesmere, JP, DL, (by his w Lady Katherine Phipps, 2 da of 2 Marquess of Normanby) and aunt of 6 Duke of Sutherland; *b* 5 June 1906; *Educ* Eton, Trin Cambridge; *m* 1931, Elinor, CBE, JP, da of Capt Ernest Pease, of Darlington; 1 s (and 1 da decd); *Heir* s, Hon St John Kemp; *Career* late Col BEF 1940 (Hon Brig); chm Kelsall & Kemp 1952-71; Pres NW Indust Devpt Assoc 1974-; *Recreations* forestry, gardening, music; *Clubs* Lansdowne; *Style* - The Rt Hon Viscount Rochdale OBE TD DL; Lingholm, Keswick, Cumbria (☎ 0596 72003)

ROCHE, Hon Lady; Hon (Helen) Alexandra Briscoe; *née* Gully; da of late 13 Duke of Hamilton and sis of 4 Viscount Selby; *b* 1934; *m* 1, 1952 (m dis 1965), Roger Moreton Frewen (d 1972); 3 s, 1 da; m 2, 1971, Sir David O'Grady Roche, 5 Bt, *qv*; *Style* - The Hon Lady Roche

ROCHE, David Alexander O'Grady; s and h of Sir David Roche, 5 Bt; *b* 28 Jan 1976; *Style* - David Roche Esq

ROCHE, Sir David O'Grady; 5 Bt (UK 1838), of Carass, Limerick; s of Lt-Cdr Sir Standish O'Grady Roche, DSO, RN, 4 Bt (d 1977); *b* 21 Sept 1947; *Educ* Wellington Coll, and Trin Coll Dublin; *m* 1971, Hon Alexandra (*see* Hon Lady Roche), da of 3 Viscount Selby, and formerly wife of late Roger Moreton Frewen; 1 s (and 1 s decd); *Heir* s, David Roche; *Career* ACA; Freeman City of London; *Clubs* Bucks, Kildare St, University (Dublin); *Style* - Sir David Roche, Bt; Bridge House, Starbotton, Skipton, N Yorks; 36 Coniger rd, SW6

ROCHE, Hon Frances Caroline Burke; da of 5 Baron Fermoy; *b* 1965; *Style* - The Hon Frances Roche

ROCHE, Hon (Edmund) Hugh Burke; s of 5 Baron Fermoy; *b* 1972; *Style* - The Hon Hugh Roche

ROCHE, Hon John Fenwick Adair; s of Baron Roche, PC (Life Peer, d 1956); *b* 1903; *Educ* Rugby, Wadham Oxford; *m* 1928, Ethel, da of Kennett Champain Bayley (ggs of Rt Hon Sir John Bayley, 1 Bt, the distinguished lawyer); 2 da (1 decd); *Style* - The Hon John Roche; Hospital rd, Moreton-in-Marsh, Glos

ROCHE, Hon Patrick Maurice Burke; s and h of 6 Baron Fermoy; *b* 11 Oct 1967; *Style* - The Hon Patrick Roche

ROCHE, Hon Thomas Gabriel; QC (1955); s of Baron Roche, PC (Life Peer, d 1956); *b* 1909; *Educ* Rugby, Wadham Oxford; *Career* barr 1932; WW II as Lt-Col RA; Recorder Worcester 1959-71, Church Commissioner 1961-65; *Style* - The Hon Thomas Roche, QC; Ashcroft, Church rd, Chadlington, Oxford

ROCHESTER, 2 Baron (UK 1931); Foster Charles Lowry Lamb; DL (Cheshire 1979); s of 1 Baron Rochester, CMG, JP (d 1955); *b* 7 June 1916; *Educ* Mill Hill, Jesus Cambridge; *m* 1942, Mary, da of Thomas Wheeler, CBE; 2 s, 1 da (and 1 da decd); *Heir* s, Hon David Lamb; *Career* late Capt 23 Hussars WW II; personnel man ICI; Pro-Chllr Keele U 1976; chm S & Mid-Cheshire Dist Manpower Cttee 1980-; *Style* - The Rt Hon Lord Rochester DL; The Hollies, Hartford, Cheshire (☎ Northwich 74733)

ROCHESTER, 104 Bp of (founded by St Augustine some time between AD 597 & 604) 1961-; Rt Rev (Richard) David Say; DD; s of Cdr Richard Say, OBE, RNVR; *b* 4 Oct 1914; *Educ* Univ Coll Sch, Christ's Cambridge; *m* 1943, Irene, OBE, JP, da of Seaburne Rayner, of Exeter; 1 s, 2 da (and 1 s decd); *Career* ordained deacon 1939, priest 1940; Sub-Prelate & Chaplain Order St John Jerusalem; domestic chaplain to Marquess of Salisbury 1955-61, chaplain to Pilgrims of GB 1968-, Lord High Almoner to HM The Queen 1970; Dep-Pro-Chllr Kent U 1977; patron of 76 livings, of the Archdeaconries of Rochester, Tonbridge and Bromley, two residentiary Canonries and all the Hon Canonries; *Recreations* sailing, travel; *Clubs* Oxford & Cambridge; *Style* - Rt Rev Bishop of Rochester; Bishopscourt, Rochester, Kent (☎ Medway 42721)

ROCHESTER, Dorothy, Baroness; Rosa Dorothea; da of William John Hurst, JP, of Co Down; *m* 1913, 1 Baron Rochester, CMG, JP (d 1955); 3 s (2 Baron, Hon Roland Lamb, Hon Kenneth Lamb), 2 da (Hon Mrs Stride, Hon Mrs

Muriel Collier, and 1 da decd); *Style* - The Rt Hon Dorothy, Lady Rochester

ROCKLEY, 3 Baron (UK 1934); James Hugh Cecil; s of 2 Baron Rockley (d 1976, whose f, 1 Baron, was er s of Lord Eustace Cecil, 3 s of 2 Marquess of Salisbury by his 1 w, Frances, the Gascoyne heiress) and Anne, da of Adm Hon Sir Herbert Meade-Fetherstonhaugh, GCVO, CB, DSO, yr bro of 5 Earl of Clanwilliam; *b* 5 April 1934; *Educ* Eton, New Coll Oxford; *m* 1958, Lady Sarah Cadogan, da of 7 Earl Cadogan, MC, DL; 1 s, 2 da; *Heir* s, Hon Anthony Cecil; *Career* dir: Kleinwort Benson 1970-, Equity & Law Life Assur 1980-; Tstee Nat Portrait Gallery 1981-; *Style* - The Rt Hon Lord Rockley; Lytchett Heath, Poole, Dorset (☎ Lytchett Minster 2228); 6 Manresa rd, SW3 (☎ 01 352 5335)

ROCKLEY, Baroness - Lady Sarah Primrose Beatrix; da (by 1 m) of 7 Earl Cadogan; *b* 1938; *m* 1958, 3 Baron Rockley; 1 s, 2 da; *Style* - The Rt Hon the Lady Rockley; 6 Manresa rd, SW3

ROCKSAVAGE, Earl of; David George Philip; s and h of 6 Marq of Cholmondeley, GCVO, MC; *b* 27 June 1960; *Career* a Page of Honour to HM the Queen 1974-76; *Style* - Earl of Rocksavage

RODD, Hon James Roderick David Tremayne; s and h of 3 Baron Rennell; *b* 9 March 1978; *Style* - The Hon James Rodd

RODD, Hon Mrs Gustaf; Yvonne Mary; da of Sir Charles Murray Marling, GCMG, CB (2 s of Sir William Marling, 2 Bt, JP, DL), and Lucia, CBE (da of Maj-Gen Sir John Slade, KCB, by his 2 w, Janet); *b* 6 Dec 1912; *m* 1932 (m dis 1948), as his 1 w, Cdr Hon Gustaf Guthrie Rennell Rodd, OBE, RN, (d 1974) s of 1 Baron Rennell, GCB, GCMG, GCVO, PC; 1 s (3 Baron Rennell) and 1 s decd; *Style* - The Hon Mrs Gustaf Rodd; Flat 53, 47/58 Cheniston gdns, W8

RODEN, 9 Earl of (I 1771); Sir Robert William Jocelyn; 13 Bt (E 1665); also Baron Newport (I 1743) and Viscount Jocelyn (I 1755); s of 8 Earl of Roden, DL (d 1956), by Elinor, da of Joseph Parr, JP, DL (her bro Roger m Lady Julian Jocelyn, the 8 Earl's sis); *b* 4 Dec 1909; *Educ* RNC Dartmouth; *m* 1938, Clodagh, da of Edward Kennedy (gs of Sir John Kennedy, 1 Bt); 3 s; *Heir* s, Viscount Jocelyn; *Career* Capt RN (ret); *Style* - Capt the Rt Hon Earl of Roden RN; 75 Bryansford Village, Newcastle, Co Down, N Ireland (☎ 23469)

RODGERS, Sir John Charles; 1 Bt (UK 1964), of Groombridge, Kent, DL (Kent 1973); s of Charles Rodgers, of York; *b* 5 Oct 1906; *Educ* St Peter's York, Ecole des Roches France, Keble Oxford; *m* 1931, Betsy, JP, da of Francis Aikin-Sneath, JP, late of Burleigh Court, Glos; 2 s; *Heir* s, John Rodgers; *Career* MP (C) Sevenoaks 1950-79, PPS to Rt Hon Viscount Eccles at Minies of Works, Education and BOT 1951-57, Parly Sec BOT and Min Regnl Devpt & Employment 1958-60; formerly FO during WW II; fndn govr Adminve Staff Coll; exec cncl memb Fndn for Management Educn 1959-, memb BBC Gen Advsy Cncl 1946-52, Govr British Film Inst 1958, memb Cncl Nat Trust 1978-; CBIM, FSS, FIS, FRSA; chm: Radio Luxembourg London, Cocoa Merchants Ltd; dir other cos; *Recreations* travel, theatre; *Clubs* Brooks's, Pratt's, Beefsteak, Roy Thames Yacht; *Style* - Sir John Rodgers, Bt, DL; The Dower House, Groombridge, Kent (☎ 213); 72 Berkeley House, Hay Hill, W1 (☎ 01 629 5220)

RODGERS, John Fairlie Tobias; s and h of Sir John Rodgers, 1 Bt, DL; *b* 2 July 1940; *Educ* Eton, Worcester Coll Oxford; *Career* bookseller & publisher; *Clubs* Brooks's, Garrick; *Style* - John Rodgers Esq; 34 Warwick av, W9

RODNEY, 9 Baron (GB 1782); Sir John Francis Rodney; 9 Bt (GB 1764); s of 8 Baron Rodney (d 1973; descended from the celebrated Admiral who won the decisive victory over the French off Dominica in 1782, capturing the enemy's commander, the Comte de Grasse, and five sail and sinking one, an exploit little tarnished by the accusation of Hood, his second in command, of want of energy in pursuit; the Admiral's gggf, Sir John Rodney, m Jane Seymour, niece of the Queen of the same name and 1 cous of King Edward VI) and Lady Marjorie Lowther, da of 6 Earl of Lonsdale, OBE; *b* 28 June 1920; *Educ* Stowe, McGill U Canada; *m* 1951, Régine Elisabeth Lucienne Jeanne Thérèse Marie Ghislaine, yr da of late Chevalier Rogert Egide Marie Ghislain Pangaert d'Opdorp, of Château Rullingfen, Looz, Belgium, and Baronne Pangaert d'Opdorp; 1 s, 1 da; *Heir* s, Hon George Rodney; *Career* served World War II as Lt Commandos; md Vacuumatic Ltd; formerly with Rootes; *Clubs* White's; *Style* - The Rt Hon Lord Rodney; Brizes Park, Kelvedon Hatch, Brentwood, Essex (☎ Coxtie Green 72139); 38 Pembroke rd, W8 (☎ 01 602 4391)

RODNEY, Hon Anne; da of 9 Baron Rodney; *b* 27 June 1955; *Style* - The Hon Anne Rodney

RODNEY, Hon Diana Rosemary; da of 8 Baron Rodney; *b* 19 April 1924; *Educ* McGill U; *Career* served WW II WRCNS; *Style* - The Hon Diana Rodney; 9745-110 st, Edmonton, Alberta, Canada

RODNEY, Hon George Brydges; s and h of 9 Baron Rodney; *b* 3 Jan 1953; *Educ* Eton; *Style* - The Hon George Rodney

RODNEY, Hon Michael Christopher; s of 8 Baron Rodney; *b* 26 June 1926; *Educ* McGill U; *m* 1, 1953 (m dis 1973), Anne, da of David Yuile, of Montreal; 3 da; m 2, 1974, Penelope, da of Eric Gaener, of Edmonton; *Career* barr Canada 1950, served WW II RCN; *Style* - The Hon Michael Rodney; 11683-72 av, Edmonton, Alberta, Canada

ROFF, Hon Mrs Victoria Elizabeth; *née* Mills; da of 4 Baron Hillingdon (d 1978); *b* 1948; *m* 1971 (m dis), Anthony Roff; *Style* - The Hon Mrs Victoria Roff; Myra House, Bisley, Stroud, Glos

ROFFE, Clive Brian; s of Philip Roffe (d 1961); *b* 4 June 1935; *Educ* Brighton Coll; *m* 1966, Jacqueline Carole, nee Branston; 2 da (Danielle Philippa Geraldine b 1970, Natasha Nicole b 1974); *Career* Lloyd's underwriter 1966; financial consultant; chm: Melbo Petroleum Ltd 1970, Edinburgh Insurance Services 1971, Offshore Investments Ltd 1968; dir other companies; Freeman of City of London; *Recreations* organ, philately, jogging; *Clubs* MCC, Guards Polo, Hurlingham, City Livery; *Style* - Clive Roffe Esq; 50 Kingsway ct, Hove, Sussex (☎ 0273 737 044)

ROGERS, Lady; Brenda Mary; CBE (1964); da of late Edward Thomas Sharp; *b* 15 May 1907; *m* 1939, Sir Philip J Rogers, CBE, *qv*; *Career* former gcvr Delamere Girls Sch Kenya and dep pres Kenya Branch Br Red Cross Soc; memb Nat Exec Ctee BRCS 1964-67, 1961-71 and 1973-, dep pres Sussex Counties BRCS 1968-; *Clubs* VAD Ladies; *Style* - Lady Rogers CBE; Church Close, Newick, Sussex (☎ 082 572 2210)

ROGERS, Frank Jarvis; s of Percy Rogers (d 1960); *b* 24 Feb 1920; *Educ* Wolstanton G S; *m* 1949, Esma Sophia, nee Holland; 2 da; *Career* journalist 1937-49, Military Serv 1940-46, gen man Nigerian Daily Times 1949-52, manager Argus Melbourne 1952-55, md Overseas Newspapers 1958-60, dir Daily Mirror 1960-65, md IPC 1965-70, chm Nat Newspaper Steering Gp 1970-72, dir Newspaper Publishers Assoc 1971-73, chm British Exec Ctee Int Press Inst 1978-, chm Exec Ctee Industrial Soc 1976-79, chm E Midland Allied Press 1973-, dir Plessey New Jersey Inc, adviser Corporate Affairs Plessey Co Ltd to 1981, chm Ansaphone Ltd 1981-; *Recreations* golf, travel; *Clubs* Reform; *Style* - Frank Rogers Esq; Greensleeves, Loudwater dve, Loudwater, Rickmansworth, Herts

ROGERS, Air Marshal John Robson; CBE (1971); s of B Rogers; *b* 11 Jan 1928; *Educ* Brentwood Sch, RAF Coll Cranwell; *m* 1955, Gytha Campbell; 2 s, 2 da; *Career* AOC T'ning Units HQ RAF Support Cmd 1979-, Air V-Marshal 1977, Air Marshal 1981; Dir-Gen Org RAF 1977-79; *Clubs* RAF; *Style* - Air Marshal John Rogers CBE; c/o Lloyds Bank, 27 High st, Colchester, Essex

ROGERS, John Willis; QC (1975); s of Reginald John Rogers (d 1940); *b* 7 Nov 1929; *Educ* Sevenoaks Sch, Fitzwilliam Cambridge; *m* 1952, Sheila Elizabeth, nee Cann; 1 s, 1 da; *Career* barrister 1955,

First Prosecuting Counsel 1969-75, Recorder 1974-; *Recreations* cricket, gardening, music, change-ringing; *Clubs* Garrick, MCC, Band of Brothers; *Style* - John Rogers Esq, QC; Carpmael Building, Temple, EC4 (☎ 01 353 5537)

ROGERS, Hon Mrs (Loretta Anne); *née* Robinson; da of 1 Baron Martonmere, GBE, KCMG, PC; *b* 1939; *m* 1963, Edward Samuel Rogers; 1 s, 3 da; *Style* - The Hon Mrs Rogers; 3 Frybrook rd, Toronto 7, Ontario, Canada

ROGERS, Sir Philip; GCB (1975), CMG (1952); s of William Edward Rogers (d 1951); *b* 19 Aug 1914; *Educ* William Hulme's G S, Emmanuel Coll Cambridge; *m* 1940, Heather Mavis, nee Gordon; 1 s, 1 da; *Career* Permanent Sec DHSS 1970-75, chm Outward Bound 1975-80, chm Univ Superannuation Scheme 1975-, chm London Sch Hygiene & Tropical Medicine 1976-, pres Reading U Cncl 1980-; *Recreations* gardening; *Clubs* East India; *Style* - Sir Philip Rogers GCB CMG; Orchard House, Wargrave, Berks

ROGERS, Sir Philip James; CBE (1952); s of late James Henry Rogers; *b* 19 Sept 1908; *Educ* Blundell's Sch; *m* 1939, Brenda Mary, CBE, *qv*; *Career* Capt Frontier Force; kt 1961; chm Tobacco Resource Cncl 1963-72, memb Legislative Cncls Nigeria 1947-51 & Kenya 1957-62, chm of various East & West African and UK bodies; *Style* - Sir Philip Rogers CBE; Church Close, Newick, Sussex (☎ 082 572 2210)

ROGERS, Thomas Edward; CMG (1960), MBE (1945); s of Thomas Edward Rogers, MBE (d 1958); *b* 28 Dec 1912; *Educ* Bedford Sch, Emmanuel Coll Cambridge, London Sch Oriental Studies; *m* 1950, Eileen Mary, nee Speechley; *Career* ICS 1936-41, IPS 1941-47, HM Foreign Service 1949-73, High Cmmr and Min Ottawa 1967-68, Ambassador Colombia 1970-73 (Grand Cross Order of San Carlos 1974); *Recreations* travel; *Clubs* United; *Style* - Thomas Rogers Esq, CMG, MBE; Chintens, Grayshott, Hants

ROGERS, Thomas Gordon Parry; s of Victor Frank Rogers (d 1947); *b* 7 Aug 1924; *Educ* West Hartlepool G S, Oxford U; *m* 1, 1947, Pamela Greene; 1 s, 7 da; m 2, 1973,Patricia Juliet, nee Curtis; 1 s, 1 da; *Career* dir personnel IBM UK 1961-74; dir The Plessey Co Ltd, Plessey N America Corpn, Plessey GmbH, Plessey France, Plessey Pension Trust 1976-; *Recreations* golf, tennis, birdwatching, music; *Clubs* Saville, RAC, Royal Wimbledon; *Style* - Thomas Rogers Esq; St Edward's Chantry, Bimport, Shaftesbury, Dorset (☎ 0747 2789); 32 Romulus Court, Justin Close, Brentford, Middx (☎ 01 568 6060)

ROGERS-COLTMAN, Charles Hugh; s of Lt-Cdr Julian Rogers-Coltman OBE (d 1944); *b* 25 April 1930; *Educ* Radley, Selwyn Coll Cambridge; *m* 1955, Olive Teresa M, da of Lt-Col W H Bamfield; 1 s, 3 da; *Career* land agent, farmer, co dir; High Sheriff Shropshire 1964, governor Wrekin Coll; *Recreations* shooting, fishing, skiing; *Clubs* Turf, Shropshire; *Style* - Charles Rogers-Coltman Esq; The Home, Bishop's Castle, Shropshire (☎ Linley 233)

ROKEBY-JOHNSON, Henry Ralph; s of Henry Spencer Rokeby-Johnson (d 1977); *b* 2 April 1931; *Educ* Eton, Brasenose Oxford; *m* 1, 1958, Rosemary, Halford; m 2, 1965, Billinda Forster, nee Pharazyn; 2 s; m 3, 1979, Cecilia Bridget, nee Cavendish; *Career* non-marine underwriter of R W Sturge & Co 1974-, dir A L Sturge (Management) Ltd 1966-, ptnr RW Sturge & Co 1968, dir A L Sturge (Holdings) Ltd 1971-; *Recreations* motoring, golf; *Clubs* City of London, Mark's, Sunningdale; *Style* - Henry Rokeby-Johnson Esq; 8 Mulberry Walk, SW3 (☎ 01 352 3607)

ROLL OF IPSDEN, Baron (Life Peer UK 1977); Eric Roll; KCMG (1962, CMG 1949), CB (1956); s of Mathias Roll; *b* 1 Dec 1907; *Educ* Birmingham U; *m* 1934, Winifred, da of Elliott Taylor; 2 da; *Career* dir Bank of England 1968-77; Chllr Southampton U; chm S G Warburg & Co 1974-, Mercury Securities 1974-; prof Economics & Commerce U Coll Hull 1935-46; under-sec Treasury 1948, dep sec Miny Ag Fish & Food 1959-61; dep head UK del negotiating EEC entry 1961-63, UK del NATO Paris 1952;

exec dir UK IMF & IBRD 1963-64; hon chm Book Devpt Cncl 1967-; dir Times Newspapers Hldgs 1980-; *Style* - Rt Hon Lord Roll of Ipsden KCMG CB; Fledgers' Wood, Homer Lane, Ipsden, Oxford; D2 Albany, Piccadilly, W1

ROLL, Hon Elizabeth; da of Baron Roll of Ipsden KCMG CB; *b* 1946; *Style* - The Hon Elizabeth Roll

ROLL, Hon Joanna; da of Baron Roll of Ipsden KCMG CB; *b* 1944; *Style* - The Hon Joanna Roll

ROLL, Rev Sir James William Cecil; 4 Bt (UK 1921), of The Chestnuts, Wanstead, Essex; s of Sir Cecil Roll, 3 Bt (d 1938); *b* 1 June 1912; *Educ* Chigwell, Pembroke Oxford, Chichester Theological Coll; *Heir* none; *Career* Vicar of St John The Divine, Becontree; *Style* - The Rev Sir John Roll, Bt; 82 Leighcliff rd, Leigh on Sea, Essex; 34 Castle rd, Dagenham, Essex (☎ 01 592 5409)

ROLLO, 13 Lord (S 1651); Eric John Stapylton Rollo; JP (Perthshire 1962); also Baron Dunning (UK 1869); s of Maj 12 Lord Rollo (d 1947) by his 1 w, Helen, da of Frederick Chetwynd-Stapylton (gggs of 4 Viscount Chetwynd); *b* 3 Dec 1915; *Educ* Eton; *m* 1938, Suzanne, da of William Hatton, of Broome House, Broome, Worcs; 2 s, 1 da; *Heir* s, Master of Rollo; *Career* farmer; *Style* - The Rt Hon Lord Rollo, JP; Pitcairns, Dunning, Perthshire (☎ 202)

ROLLO, Master of; Hon David Eric Howard Rollo; s and h of 13 Lord Rollo, JP; *b* 31 March 1943; *Educ* Eton; *m* 1971, Felicity, da of Lt-Cdr Bruce Lamb, RN, of Cornwall; 3 s; *Heir* s, James Rollo; *Career* late Capt Gren Gds; *Style* - Capt the Master of Rollo; 20 Draycott av, SW3

ROLLO, Hon David Ian; MBE (Mil 1944), MC; 3 s but 2 surviving of 12 Lord Rollo; *b* 29 July 1921; *Educ* Eton; *m* 1948, Bridget, da of Brig James Erskine Stirling, DSO (d 1968), by his w, Evelyn, da of Capt Henry Cavendish, JP, DL, RN (ggs of Lord George Cavendish, 3 s of 4 Duke of Devonshire, who was cr 1 Earl of Burlington), and Lady Harriet Osborne (da of 9 Duke of Leeds); 1 s, 3 da; *Career* late Capt Gren Gds, served WW II N Africa & Italy; *Style* - The Hon David Rollo, MBE, MC

ROLLO, Hon Mrs William (Diana Joan); da of Edward Castell Wrey, 7 s of Sir Henry Wrey, 10 Bt, and bro of 11, 12 and 13 Bts; sis of Sir Castel Wrey, 14 Bt; *b* 190-; *m* 1, 1932 (m dis 1946), Jocelyn Abel Smith (d 1966, of the Abel Smiths of Woodhill); 2 s; m 2, 1946, as his 2 w, Hon William Hereward Charles Rollo, MC (k out hunting 1962), bro of 12 Lord Rollo; *Style* - The Hon Mrs William Rollo; Barleythorpe, Oakham, Rutland

ROLLO, Hon John Dunning; s of 12 Lord Rollo by his 2 w Phyllis; half-bro of 13 Lord Rollo; *b* 16 July 1931; *Style* - The Hon John Rollo

ROLLO, Hon James Malcolm; 2 s of 13 Lord Rollo, JP; *b* 25 Sept 1946; *Educ* Eton, Ch Ch Oxford; *m* 1968, Henrietta, da of Maj Alasdair Boyle (gggs of David Boyle, Lord Justice-Gen of Scotland and gs of 2 Earl of Glasgow); *Style* - The Hon James Rollo; Corwar House, Barrhill, Girvan, Ayrshire

ROLLO, Hon Simon David Paul; s of 12 Lord Rollo by his 3 w Lily, nee Seflow; half-bro of 13 Lord Rollo and Hon David and Hon John Rollo; *b* 4 Oct 1939; *Educ* Eton; *m* 1964, Valerie, da of R Willis, of Sudbury; 2 da; *Style* - The Hon Simon Rollo; Biffens Boatyard, Staines, Middx

ROLLS, John Lawrence; s of Capt George Henry Rolls; *b* 14 Jan 1930; *Educ* Sherborne, Loughborough U; *m* 1970, Maura Catherine, nee Tunney; 5 children; *Career* dep chm Oil Mop (UK) Ltd, chm Aquaflite Ltd, chm Marine Auctions Ltd, chm Ravenscourt Dvpts Ltd; *Recreations* shooting, golf; *Style* - John Rolls Esq; Ravenscourt, Lymington, Hants (☎ 73132)

ROMER, Hon Lady (Frances Evelyn Lebeau); da of Alfred Kemp, of Epping; *m* 1925, as his 2 w, Rt Hon Sir Charles Romer, OBE (d 1969), s of Baron Romer, PC (Life Peer, d 1944); 2 s; *Style* - The

The Hon Lady Romer; Orchard House, Littlestone, Kent

ROMILLY, 4 Baron (UK 1866); William Gaspard Guy Romilly; s of 3 Baron Romilly (d 1905, ggs of that Sir Samuel Romilly, father of the 1 Baron, who incurred Lord Byron's anger for having accepted a retainer only to act in Lady Byron's interests at the time of the separation proceedings; Romilly, be it said, claimed the retainer had been accepted by a clerk without his knowledge; hence the spiteful couplet in *Don Juan* (*see* Treuhaft, Hon Mrs) following Sir Samuel's *felo de se*, which took place four days after the death of his w) by Violet, da of Sir Philip Grey Egerton, 11 Bt, and Hon Henrietta, da of 1 Baron Londesborough; Giles Romilly, the writer, descends from a yr bro of the 1 Baron; the family is originally of Huguenot stock; *b* 8 March 1899; *Educ* Eton, Sandhurst; *m* 1, 1929 (m dis 1944), Hon Diana Sackville-West (d 1975), da of 4 Baron Sackville & 1 cous of Vita Sackville-West, by 4 Baron's 1 w, Maude; m 2, 1944, Dora (d 1960), da of Reginald Morris, of Chelsea; m 3, 1966, Marion, da of Charles Clover, of Blewbury, & widow of Capt Lionel Cecil (ggs of 2 Marquess of Salisbury by his 2 w Lady Mary Sackville-West, herself 2 da of 5 Earl de la Warr); *Heir* none; *Career* served Coldstream Gds WW I (1917-23) & II, ret as Maj (Hon); chm Marlborough & Ramsbury RDC 1964-67; *Style* - The Rt Hon Lord Romilly; Bridge House, Chilton Foliat, Hungerford, Berks (☎ 2328)

ROMNEY, 7 Earl of (UK 1801); Sir Michael Henry Marsham; 13 Bt (E 1663); also Baron of Romney (GB 1716) and Viscount Marsham (UK 1801); s of Lt-Col Hon Reginald Marsham, OBE (2 s of 4 Earl of Romney), and Dora, 4 da of Charles North, JP, DL (5 in descent from Hon Roger North, the memoirist and 6 s of 4 Baron North); suc 1 cous, 6 Earl, 1975; *b* 22 Nov 1910; *Educ* Sherborne; *m* 1939, Frances, da of Lt-Col James Landale; *Heir* 1 cous once removed, Julian Marsham; *Career* late Maj RA, served WW II; *Style* - The Rt Hon The Earl of Romney; Wensum Farm, W Rudham, King's Lynn, Norfolk (☎ E Rudham 249)

ROMSEY, Lord; Norton Louis Philip Knatchbull; s and h of Countess Mountbatten of Burma (da of Earl Mountbatten of Burma and 1 cous of HRH The Duke of Edinburgh) and (also h of) 7 Baron Brabourne; 2 cous of HRH The Prince of Wales; *b* 8 Oct 1947; *Educ* Gordonstoun, Kent U; *m* 1979, Penelope Eastwood; 1 s; *Heir* s, Hon Nicholas Knatchbull; *Career* film producer; dir Capital Radio, Claridge Films; High Steward Romsey 1980-; *Style* - Lord Romsey; Broadlands, Romsey, Hants (☎ 517888); 16 Royal av, SW3

RONALDSHAY, Earl of; Lawrence Mark Dundas; s and h of 3 Marquess of Zetland, DL; *b* 28 Dec 1937; *Educ* Harrow, Christ's Cambridge; *m* 1964, Susan, da of Guy Chamberlin, of Shefford House, Great Shefford, Newbury; 2 s, 2 da; *Heir* s, Lord Dundas; *Career* landowner; dir: Redcar Racecourse, Catterick Racecourse, Tocketts Mill Devpt Co, Escor Toys Ltd, Barony Fishing Co Ltd; late 2 Lt Gren Gds; *Recreations* tennis (Lawn & Royal), squash, racing (racehorses: 'Fogey Buoy', 'Tocketts Mill', 'Chance Command', 'Mister Ketchup'); *Clubs* All England Lawn Tennis; *Style* - Earl of Ronaldshay; 10 Crescent Place, SW3 (☎ 01 584 6840); Copt Hewick Hall, Ripon, N Yorks (☎ 3946)

ROOKE, Sir Denis (Eric); CBE (1970); s of F G Rooke; *b* 2 April 1924; *Educ* Westminster City Sch, Addey and Stanhope Sch, Univ Coll London; *m* 1949, Elizabeth Brenda, nee Evans; 1 da; *Career* kt 1977; Maj REME 1944-49; FRS, FEng; joined S Eastern Gas Bd 1949 (dvpt engr 1959), chm CNAA 1977-, memb Advisory Cncl for R&D 1972-77, Advisory Cncl for Energy Conservation 1974-77, Offshore Energy Tech Bd 1975-78, Br Nat Oil Corpn 1976-, NEDC 1976-, Energy Cmmn 1977-79, pres Instn of Gas Engineers 1975, chm Br Gas Corpn 1976- (dep chm 1972-76, salary as chm £48,000 pa as of June 1981); *Recreations* listening to music, also photography; *Clubs* Athenaeum, English Speaking Union; *Style* - Sir Denis Rooke, CBE; 23 Hardy rd, Blackheath, SE3 (☎ 01 858 6710)

ROOKE, Giles Hugh; TD (1963), QC (1979); s of Charles Eustace Rooke, CMG (d 1947); *b* 28 Oct 1930; *Educ* Stowe, Exeter Coll Oxford; *m* 1968, Anne Bernadette Seymour, da of His Hon Judge Perrett, *qv*; 3 s, 2 da; *Career* Major (TA); barr 1957, Recorder 1975, Hon Recorder of Margate 1980; *Recreations* gardening; *Clubs* Carlton; *Style* - Giles Rooke Esq, TD, QC; St Stephen's Cottage, Bridge, Canterbury (☎ 0227 830298)

ROOKE, James Smith; CMG (1961), OBE (1950); s of Joseph Nelson Rooke (d 1964); *b* 6 July 1916; *Educ* Workington G S, Univ Coll London, Vienna U; *m* 1938, Maria Theresa, da of Franz Rebrec, of Austria; 3 c; *Career* HM Diplomatic Serv 1938-76, ch exec British Overseas Trade Bd 1972-76; company dir; industrial and banking consultant 1976-80, lecturer Diplomatic Academy Vienna 1980-; *Recreations* skiing, tennis, climbing, swimming; *Clubs* Devonshire; *Style* - James Rooke Esq, CMG, OBE; c/o Midland Bank, 165 Kilburn High rd, NW6; Rudolph Bärenhartgasse 20, Vienna XV11, Austria

ROOTES, 2 Baron (UK 1959); (William) Geoffrey Rootes; s of 1 Baron Rootes (d 1964) by his 1 w, Nora; *b* 14 June 1917; *Educ* Harrow, Ch Ch Oxford; *m* 1946, Marian, da of Lt-Col Herbert Hayter, DSO, and widow of Wing Cdr James Slater, AFC; 1 s, 1 da; *Heir* s, Hon Nicholas Rootes; *Career* FBIM, FRSA; chm Chrysler UK (formerly Rootes Motors) 1967-73; late memb NEDC for Motor Mfrg Indust; served WW II RASC; dir Rank Hovis McDougall 1973-, Joseph Lucas Industs 1973-; memb Cncl IOD 1953-; V-Pres Game Conservancy 1979-; County Pres Berks St John Ambulance; *Style* - The Rt Hon Lord Rootes; Glenalmond House, Glenalmond, Perthshire; North Standen House, Hungerford, Berks

ROOTES, Hon Mrs Brian (Elizabeth Margaret); da of Rev Humphrey Barclay, CVO, MC (of the Essex banking family, being s of Henry Barclay, CVO, JP, DL, who was himself gs of Robert Barclay by his w Elizabeth, nee Gurney, a member of the extensive Norfolk family); *b* 11 April 1916; *m* 1, 1939, Norman (ka 1940), s of Brig-Gen Lewis Philips, CB, CMG, CBE, DSO; 1 s; m 2, 1944, Hon Brian Rootes (d 1971), s of 1 Baron Rootes; 1 s; *Style* - The Hon Mrs Brian Rootes; Dallick House, Glenalmond, Perths

ROOTES, Hon Nicholas Geoffrey; s and h of 2 Baron Rootes; *b* 12 July 1951; *Educ* Harrow; *m* 1976, Dorothy, formerly Mrs Burn-Forti and da of Cyril Wood, of Swansea; 1 step s (Dante Burn-Forti b 1966), 1 step da (Lucinda Burn-Forti b 1964); *Career* writer; *Style* - The Hon Nicholas Rootes; 2 Cedars rd, SW13 (☎ 01 879 6965)

ROOTHAM, Col Jasper St John; s of Dr Cyril Bradley Rootham (d 1938); *b* 21 Nov 1910; *Educ* Tonbridge, St John's Coll Cambridge; *m* 1944, Joan, nee McClelland; 1 s, 1 da; *Career* Col Middle East, Yugoslavia, France, Germany, mentioned despatches 1944; Civil Serv 1933-41 (Miny of Ag, Colonial Office, Treasury, 10 Downing St), Bank of England 1946-67 (assist ch cashier, adviser to Govr, assist to Govr), sr banking dir Lazard Bros & Co Ltd 1967-75; poet, published 5 books; *Recreations* music, country life; *Clubs* Oxford & Cambridge, Northern Counties Newcastle; *Style* - Col Jasper Rootham; 7 Watling st, Corbridge, Northumberland (☎ 2992)

ROPER, John Charles Abercromby; CMG (1969), MC (1945); s of Charles Roper (d 1950); *b* 8 June 1915; *Educ* Harrow, Cambridge, Princeton; *m* 1, 1945, Valerie Muir, nee Wilson (m dis) (d 1978); 2 da; m 2, 1960, Kathryn, nee Bibes; *Career* Major Scots Guards, Diplomatic Service 1946 (retired), Dep Cmdt NATO Def Coll 1960-62, Assist Sec Cabinet Office 1962-64, Counsellor UK Delegation OECD 1964-70, Ambassador Luxembourg 1970-75; *Recreations* travel, the arts; *Clubs* Bath, Sepcial Forces; *Style* - John Roper Esq, CMG, MC; Cavallini, 58048 Paganico, Province of Grosseto, Italy; Hydra, Greece

ROPER, Lanning; *Career* landscape gardener; *aet* 60-70 in May 1981; domiciled in UK 1946-; late gardening correspondent Sunday Times, occasional contributor Country Life; sometime advr to Nat Tst on Sir Winston Churchill's old home at Chartwell; landscaper of garden of

HRH Prince of Wales at Highgrove, Glos; *Style* - Lanning Roper Esq; 29 Clarendon gdns, W9 (☎ 01 286 4092)

ROPER, Hon Mrs (Penelope Christina); *née* Plowden; da of Baron Plowden (Life Peer); *b* 1941; *Educ* St Mary's Convent Ascot and New Hall Cambridge; *m* 1965, (m dis 1975), Christopher Roper; *Style* - The Hon Mrs Roper; 43 Lansdowne gdns, SW8

ROPER-CURZON, Hon David Henry Ingham; s and h of 20 Baron Teynham; *b* 5 Oct 1965; *Style* - The Hon David Roper-Curzon

ROPER-CURZON, Hon Emma Elizabeth; da of 20 Baron Teynham; *b* 1966; *Style* - The Hon Emma Roper-Curzon

ROPER-CURZON, Hon Holly Anne-Marie; da of 19 Baron Teynham, DSO, DSC (d 1972); *b* 1963; *Style* - The Hon Holly Roper-Curzon

ROPER-CURZON, Hon Henrietta Margaret Fleur; da of 19 Baron Teynham, DSO, DSC (d 1972); *b* 1955; *Style* - The Hon Henrietta Roper-Curzon

ROPER-CURZON, Hon Hermione Marie Hilda Edith; da of 20 Baron Teynham; *b* 1973; *Style* - The Hon Hermione Roper-Curzon

ROPER-CURZON, Hon Jonathan Christopher James; s of 20 Baron Teynham; *b* 1973; *Style* - The Hon Jonathan Roper-Curzon

ROPER-CURZON, Hon Lucy Elspeth; da of 20 Baron Teynham; *b* 1969; *Style* - The Hon Lucy Roper-Curzon

ROPER-CURZON, Hon Michael Henry; s of 19 Baron Teynham, DSO, DSC (d 1972); *b* 1931; *m* 1964 (m dis 1967), Maria, da of late Maj R V Taylor, 16/5 Queen's Roy Lancers; *Career* Lt (ret) RN; OStJ; *Style* - The Hon Michael Roper-Curzon; 75 Eccleston Sq Mews, SW1

ROPER-CURZON, Hon Peter Michael Alexander; s of 20 Baron Teynham; *b* 1977; *Style* - The Hon Peter Roper-Curzon

ROPER-CURZON, Hon Sophie Patricia; da of 20 Baron Teynham; *b* 1967; *Style* - The Hon Sophie Roper-Curzon

ROPER-CURZON, Hon William Thomas; s of 20 Baron Teynham; *b* 1980; *Style* - The Hon William Roper-Curzon

ROPNER, Sir John Bruce Woollacott; 2 Bt (UK 1952), of Thorp Perrow, N Riding of Yorkshire; s of Sir Leonard Ropner, 1 Bt, MC, TD (d 1977); *b* 16 April 1937; *Educ* Eton, St Paul's Sch USA; *m* 1, 1961 (m dis 1970), Anne Melicent, da of late Sir Ralph Hubert Joan Delmé-Radcliffe; 2 da; m 2, 1970, Auriol Veronica, da of Captain Graham Lawrie Mackeson-Sandbach, of Caerllo, Llnagernyw, Abergele, Denbighshire; 2 da; *Career* dir Ropner Hldgs Ltd; *Clubs* Northern Counties; *Style* - Sir John Ropner, Bt; Thorp Perrow, Bedale, N Yorks

ROPNER, Jeremy Vyvyan; s of John Raymond Ropner; *b* 3 May 1932; *Educ* Harrow, RMC Dartmouth; *m* 1955, Sally, da of late Wing Cdr George Talbot Willcox; 1 s (and 1 decd), 2 da; *Career* shipowner, dir Ropner Holdings, dir Nat West Bank (East Regional Bd), chm Hartlepools Water Co, md Ropner Shipping Co Ltd; *Recreations* forestry, golf; *Clubs* Bath; *Style* - Jeremy Ropner Esq; Firby Hall, Bedale, N Yorks (☎ 22345)

ROPNER, Robert Clinton; s and h of Sir Robert Ropner, 4 Bt; *b* 6 Feb 1949; *Educ* Harrow; *Style* - Robert Ropner Esq

ROPNER, Sir Robert Douglas; 4 Bt (UK 1904), of Preston Hall, Stockton-on-Tees, Co Palatine of Durham, and Skutterskelfe Hall, Hutton Rudby, North Yorks; s of Sir (Emil Hugo Oscar) Robert Ropner, 3 Bt (d 1962); *b* 1 Dec 1921; *Educ* Harrow; *m* 1943, Patricia Kathleen, da of William Edward Scofield, of West Malling, Kent; 1 s, 1 da; *Heir* s, Robert Clinton Ropner; *Career* formerly Capt RA; *Style* - Sir Robert Ropner, Bt

ROSCOE, Sir Robert Bell; KBE (1981); s of T B Roscoe; *b* 7 Aug 1906; *Educ* Central Technical Coll Brisbane; *m* 1931, Daphne, da of G Maxwell; 1 da; *Career* dir Chase NBA Gp Ltd Australia & NZ 1969-; chm Melbourne Underground Rail Loop Authority 1971-; *Style* - Sir Robert Roscoe, KBE; 833 Burwood rd, Hawthorn East, Victoria 3123, Australia

ROSE, Sir Clive Martin; KCMG (1976, CMG 1976); s of Rt Rev Alfred Rose (d 1971); *b* 15 Sept 1921; *Educ* Marlborough, Ch Ch Oxford; *m* 1946, Elisabeth Mackenzie, da of Rev Cyril Lewis; 2 s, 3 da; *Career* Diplomatic Serv: Ambassador & UK Perm Rep The North Atlantic Cncl 1979-, Dep Sec Cabinet Office 1976-79, Head UK Delegation Mutual & Balanced Force Reductions negotiations 1973-, served in Foreign Office 1950-; *Clubs* Army & Navy; *Style* - Sir Clive Rose, KCMG; FCO, SW1

ROSE, David Lancaster; s of late Ronald Paul Lancaster Rose, by his 1 w, Shelagh; hp of kinsman, Sir Philip Rose, 3 Bt; *b* 17 Feb 1934; *m* 1965, Dorothy Whitehead; 1 s; *Style* - David Rose Esq; 20 Kingston Close, Seaford, Sussex

ROSE, Hon Mrs (Irene Phyllis); CBE (1961); da of 1 and last Baron Hirst (d 1943); *b* 1901; *m* 1922, Group Capt Trevor Felix David Rose, RAFVR and late Maj RFA and RHA (d 1946); 2 da; *Career* CC London 1952-58, and 1961-65; *Style* - The Hon Mrs Rose, CBE; Pear Tree Cottage, Cranleigh, Surrey; 54 Marsham Court, SW1

ROSE, Lady Jean (Maule); *née* Ramsay; da of late 14 Earl of Dalhousie; *b* 1909; *m* 1945, Lt-Col David McNeil Campbell Rose, DSO, Black Watch; 1 s, 1 da; *Style* - Lady Jean Rose; Trian, Comrie, Perthshire

ROSE, Sir Julian Day; 4 Bt (UK 1909), of Hardwick House, Whitchurch, Oxon, and 5 Bt (UK 1872), of Montreal, Dominion of Canada; s of Sir Charles Henry Rose, 3 Bt (d 1966), by his w, Hon Phoebe Margaret Dorothy Phillimore, da of 2 Baron Phillimore; also suc kinsman, Sir Francis Rose, 4 Bt, 1979; *b* 3 March 1947; *Educ* Stanbridge Earl's Sch Romsey; *Style* - Sir Julian Rose, Bt; Hardwick House, Whitchurch, Oxon

ROSE, Sir Philip Humphrey Vivian; 3 Bt (UK 1874); s of late Capt Philip Vivian Rose (eld s of 2 Bt); suc gf 1919; *b* 16 March 1903; *Educ* Harrow; *m* 1927, Joan, da of Martin Richardson, MD; 2 da; *Heir* kinsman, David Rose; *Style* - Sir Philip Rose, Bt; Rayners Cottage, High st, Prestwood, Gt Missenden, Bucks

ROSE, Hon Lady - Hon Phoebe Margaret Dorothy; da of 2 Baron Phillimore, MC (d 1947); *b* 1912; *m* 1937, Sir Charles Rose, 3 Bt (d 1966); *Style* - The Hon Lady Rose; Hardwick House, Whitchurch, Oxon

ROSE, (Thomas) Stuart; CBE (1974); s of Thomas Rose; *b* 2 Oct 1911; *Educ* Magdalen Coll Sch Oxford, Central Sch Arts & Crafts; *m* 1940, Dorothea Ebsworth; 2 da; *Career* late print conslt FBI, art ed Design magazine, first design dir GPO; typographical advr Postmaster Gen 1962-68, memb PO Stamp Advsy Ctee 1968-76; *Style* - Stuart Rose Esq CBE; 25 Balcombe st, NW1; Ladyland, Good Easter, Essex

ROSE, Hon Mrs (Susan Jane); *née* James; da of 4 Baron Northbourne; *b* 1936; *m* 1961, Michael Hugh Rose, s of late Rt Rev A C W Rose, Bp of Dover; 1 s, 3 da; *Style* - The Hon Mrs Rose; Le Sirondole, Panzano-in-Chianti, Florence, Italy

ROSEBERY, 7 Earl of (S 1703); Sir Neil Archibald Primrose; 9 Bt (S 1651), DL (Midlothian 1960); also Viscount of Rosebery, Lord Primrose and Dalmeny (both S 1700), Viscount of Inverkeithing, Lord Dalmeny and Primrose (both S 1703), Baron Rosebery (UK 1828), Earl of Midlothian, Viscount Mentmore, and Baron Epsom (all UK 1911); s of 6 Earl of Rosebery, KT, DSO, MC, PC (d 1974, the celebrated race horse owner and s of the Liberal PM by Hannah, da of Baron Meyer de Rothschild, through whom Mentmore came into the family), by his 2 w, Hon Dame Eva, nee Bruce, DBE, JP (da of 2 Baron Aberdare and former w of 3 Baron Belper); *b* 11 Feb 1929; *Educ* Stowe, New Coll Oxford; *m* 1955, Alison, da of Ronald Reid, MS, FRCS, by Elinor, nee Chaytor (ggda of Sir William Chaytor, 1 Bt); 1 s, 4 da; *Heir* s, Lord Dalmeny; *Career* patron of three livings; *Style* - The Rt Hon The Earl of Rosebery DL; Dalmeny House, S Queensferry, W Lothian

ROSEBERY, Eva, Countess of; Hon Dame Eva Isabel Marian; *née* Bruce; DBE (1955), JP (Bucks); da of 2 Baron Aberdare; *b* 17 June 1892; *m* 1, 1911 (m dis 1922), 3 Baron Belper, DL; 2 s (4 Baron Belper and Hon Michael Strutt), 1 da (Lavinia, Duchess of Norfolk, *qv*); m 2, 1924, 6 Earl of Rosebery, KT, DSO, MC, PC (d 1974); 1 s (7 Earl of Rosebery, DL); *Career* Hon LLD; *Style* - The Rt Hon Eva, Countess of Rosebery, DBE, JP; Cleveland House, Old Station, Newmarket, Suffolk (☎ 0638 2483)

ROSEHILL, Lord; David John MacRae Carnegie; s and h of 13 Earl of Northesk; *b* 3 Nov 1954; *Educ* Eton; *m* 1979, Jacqueline, da of David Reid; 1 s; *Heir* s, Hon Alexander Carnegie; *Career* farmer and theatre manager; *Style* - Lord Rosehill; Fair Oak, Rogate, Petersfield, Hampshire (☎ Rogate (STD Code 073 080) 508)

ROSEN, Anthony; s of Maurice Rosen (d 1971); *b* 19 Dec 1930; *Educ* Framlingham Coll; *m* 1954, Hilary June, da of Comyns Mansfield, of Paignton, Devon; 2 s (Andrew b 1956, Howard b 1958), 1 da (Philippa b 1965); *Career* Capt RA 1950-52; chm Fordson Estates Ltd, v-pres Western Agri-Management Co (USA), exec dir Feenix Int Pty Ltd (Australia), ch exec Feenix Farming, managing ptnr Ecro Farming, memb Agricultural Forum, memb BBC Agricultural Advisory Ctee, founder Farm Management Assoc; *Recreations* work, photography, travel; *Clubs* Farmers'; *Style* - Anthony Rosen Esq; Moor Hatches, West Amesbury, Salisbury, Wilts (☎ 098 23594)

ROSEN, Hon Mrs (June Avis); *née* Lever; da of Baron Lever (Life Peer, d 1977); *b* 4 June 1940; *Educ* Cheltenham Ladies' Coll, Sch of Physiotherapy Ancoats Hosp Manchester; *m* 1962, Emanuel Saul, s of Lionel Rosen, MBE (d 1978), of 45 Newland Park, Hull, Yorks; 3 children; *Career* physiotherapist, at present on staff of Cheadle Royal Hospital, Cheshire; *Recreations* choral singing, sewing, reading, committee work; *Style* - The Hon Mrs Rosen; 18a Torkington rd, Wilmslow, Cheshire (☎ 522768)

ROSEVEAR, Donovan Reginald; CBE (1954); s of William Arthur Rosevear (d 1920); *b* 28 Nov 1900; *Educ* Bedford Sch, Christ's Coll Cambridge; *m* 1935, Gerda-Maria Elizabeth, nee Ziegler; 1 s; *Career* forester, zoologist, formerly Inspector Gen Forests Nigeria 1950-54, Stamford Raffles Award for 1970 London Zoological Soc, HH Bloomer Award for 1978 London Linnean Society; *Recreations* gardening, antiques, music, Shakespeare; *Clubs* Linnean; *Style* - Donovan Rosevear Esq CBE; 22 Weatherby Gardens, Hartley Wintney, Hants (☎ Hartley Wintney 2634)

ROSIER, Sir Frederick Ernest; GCB (1972, KCB 1966, CB 1961), CBE (1955, OBE 1943), DSO 1942; s of Ernest George Rosier (d 1941); *b* 13 Oct 1915; *Educ* Grove Park Sch Wrexham; *m* 1939, Hettie Denise, nee Blackwell; 3 s, 1 da; *Career* Air Chief Marshal (UK, Fr, W Desert, USA, Middle East, Turkey), chm Jt Planning Staff 1959-61, Air ADC HM 1972-73, Mil Adv Br Aircraft Corp 1973-77, Dir in Charge BAC Saudi Arabia 1977-80, Dep CIC Allied Forces Central Europe 1970-73; *Clubs* Victory Services (pres 1980-); *Style* - Air Chief Marshal Sir Frederick Rosier, GCB, CBE, DSO; 286 Latymer Court, W6 (☎ 741 0765)

ROSKILL, Baron (Life Peer UK 1980); Eustace Wentworth Roskill; PC (1971), QC (1953), JP (1950), DL (Hants 1972); s of John Roskill, KC, by Sybil (niece of Sir Charles Dilke, 2 Bt, the Victorian radical MP, whose appearance as co-respondent in a divorce case of a particularly unsavoury nature in 1885 ruined his political career); *b* 6 Feb 1911; *Educ* Winchester, Exeter Coll Oxford; *m* 1947, Elisabeth, da of Thomas Jackson; 1 s, 2 da; *Career* barr 1933, chm Hants QS 1960-71, High Court Judge (Queen's Bench) 1962-71, Ld Justice of Appeal 1971-80, chm Commission on Third London Airport 1968-70; *Style* - Rt Hon Lord Roskill PC QC JP DL; New Court, Temple, EC4 (☎ 01 353 8870); Heatherfield, Newtown, Newbury, Berks (☎ 40606)

ROSKILL, Hon Julian Wentworth; s of Baron Roskill PC QC JP DL; *b* 22 July

1950; *Educ* Winchester; *m* 1975, Catherine, 2 da of Maj William Garnett, of Quernmore Park, Lancaster; 2 s (Matthew, Oliver Wentworth b 12 June 1981); *Career* slr 1974; *Recreations* photography, gardening, tennis, squash; *Style* - The Hon Julian Roskill; 32 Remington st, N1 (☎ 01 251 0661)

ROSKILL, Capt Stephen Wentworth; CBE (1971), DSC (1944); s of late John Henry Roskill KC; *b* 1 Aug 1903; *Educ* RN Colls of Osborne, Dartmouth and Greenwich; *m* 1930, Elizabeth Charlotte Henriette, nee Van Den Bergh; 4 s, 3 da; *Career* Captain RN 1939-41, Pacific Theatre 1941-44, British Mission to USA 1944-46, served 5 years in Far East, 2 in West Indies and 8 in Mediterranean between Wars; Cabinet Off 1949-61, Fell Churchill Coll Cambridge 1961-70, (Life Fell 1970), Fell British Academy 1970; *Recreations* painting, all country pursuits; *Clubs* Travellers'; *Style* - Capt Stephen Roskill, CBE, DSC; Frostlake Cottage, Malting Lane, Cambridge (☎ 354705)

ROSPIGLIOSI, Hon Francesco; Prince Francesco Rospigliosi; 2 s of 11 Earl of Newburgh; *b* 1947; *m* 1974, Countess Clothilde, da of Count Henri Rival de Rouville ; 1 s (Prince Alessandro b 1978); *Style* - Prince Francesco Rospigliosi

ROSPIGLIOSI, Princess Helen; Hon Helen Mary Grace; *née* Lyon-Dalberg-Acton; da of 2 Baron Acton KCVO (d 1924); *b* 21 May 1910; *m* 1933 (m dis 1958) Prince Guglielmo Rospigliosi (s of Prince Ludovico Rospigliosi, 4 s of Princess Elena Giustiniani-Bandini, da of Sigismund Prince Giustiniani-Bandini who was also 8 Earl of Newburgh, by her husb Camillo Prince Rospigliosi); 2 s, 1 da; *Style* - Princess Helen Rospigliosi; 602 Park West, W2

ROSPIGLIOSI, Princess Margherita Maria Francesca; da of late Prince Giambattista Pia Sigismondo Francesco Rospigliosi (s of Lady Elena Maria Concetta Isabella Gioacchina Giuseppa Giustiniani-Bandini, Princess Camillo Rospigliosi, 3 da of late 8 Earl of Newburgh) and sister of 11 Earl of Newburgh; *b* 1909; *Style* - Princess Margherita Rospigliosi

ROSS OF MARNOCK, Baron (Life Peer UK 1979); William Ross; MBE (Mil 1945), PC (1964); s of William Ross; *b* 7 April 1911; *Educ* Ayr Acad, Glasgow U; *m* 1948, Elizabeth, da of J Aitkenhead, of Ayr; 2 da; *Career* MP (L) Kilmarnock 1946-79, former schoolmaster; Sec of State Scotland 1964-70 & 1974-76; Hon Pres Scottish FA 1978; *Style* - The Rt Hon Lord Ross of Marnock, MBE, PC; 10 Chapelpark rd, Ayr (☎ 65673)

ROSS, Andrew Charles Paterson; s and h of Sir James Ross, 2 Bt; *b* 18 June 1966; *Style* - Andrew Ross Esq

ROSS, Hon Mrs Charles - Mary Margaret; da of late Thomas Graham; *m* 1953, as his 2 w, Hon Charles Dudley Anthony Ross (s of Una Mary, Baroness de Ros and who d 1976); 1 s; *Style* - The Hon Mrs Charles Ross; 67 Seafield rd, Southbourne, Bournemouth, Hants

ROSS, Carl Philip Hartley; s of John Carl Ross; *b* 3 May 1943; *Educ* Shrewsbury Sch; *m* 1968, Pamela Jean, nee Dixon; 3 da; *Career* chartered accountant, chm Bristol & West Cold Stores Ltd, dir Tempco Severnside Ltd; *Recreations* foxhunting, racehorse breeding (racehorse owned 'Cape Flattery'); *Style* - Carl Ross Esq; The Becklands, Barnoldby-Le-Beck, Grimsby (☎ 0472 822337/825010)

ROSS, Hon Lord; Donald MacArthur Ross; s of John Ross, slr; *b* 29 March 1927; *Educ* Dundee H S, Edinburgh U; *m* 1958, Dorothy, nee Annand; 2 da; *Career* Sen of Coll of Justice, Scotland (Lord of Session) 1977-, QC (Scot) 1964; Sheriff Princ Ayr & Bute 1972-73; Dep Chm Scot Boundary Commission 1977-; *Style* - The Hon Lord Ross; 33 Lauder rd, Edinburgh (☎ 031 667 5731)

ROSS, Sir James Keith; 2 Bt (UK 1960), of Whetstone, Middx, RD (1967); s of Sir James Paterson Ross, 1 Bt, KCVO, FRCS (d 1980); *b* 9 May 1927; *Educ* St Paul's Sch, Middx Hosp; MB BS (1950), MS (1965), FRCS (1956); *m* 1956, Jacqueline Annella Clarke; 1 s, 3 da; *Heir* s, Andrew Ross; *Career* formerly Surgn Lt-Cdr RNR; consultant Cardiac Surgeon Wessex Region 1972-, King Edward VII Hosp

Midhurst 1979-; *Clubs* MCC, Royal Southampton Yacht, Royal Lymington Yacht; *Style* - Sir James Ross, Bt; Moonhills Gate, Beaulieu, Hants SO4 7YS (☎ Beaulieu 612104)

ROSS, John MacDonald; CBE (1968); s of Sir James Stirling Ross KBE CB (d 1961); *b* 31 March 1908; *Educ* Highgate Sch, Wadham Coll Oxford; *m* 1932, Helen Margaret, nee Wallace; 2 s, 3 da; *Career* Assistant Sec General Register Office 1946, Home Office 1951-68; *Recreations* Greek New Testament, piano, bookbinding; *Clubs* Athenaeum; *Style* - John Ross Esq CBE; 64 Wildwood rd, NW11 (☎ 455 7872)

ROSS, John Malcolm Thomas; s of John Carl Ross, of Grimsby; *b* 7 Oct 1934; *Educ* Shrewsbury, Clare Coll Cambridge; *m* 1, 1958, Gillian Mary Hampton; 1 s, 1 da; m 2, 1964, Linda Susan Thomas; 1 s 2 da; m 3, 1981, Jennifer Mary Fawcett, nee Clark; *Career* FCA; chartered accountant Peat Marwick Mitchell & Co, dir Ross Group Ltd 1964-68, md Cosalt Ltd 1968-73, chm and ch exec Cosalt Ltd 1973-; *Recreations* golf, private flying; *Style* - John Ross Esq; Five Gables, 27 Ferriby Lane, Grimsby, South Humberside

ROSS, Lewis Nathan; CMG (1974); s of Robert Ross (d 1945); *b* 7 March 1911; *Educ* Auckland G S, Auckland U; *m* 1937, Ella Myrtle, nee Burns; 2 s, 1 da; *Career* FCA; president New Zealand Society of Accountants 1972-73, chm of dirs: Bank of NZ, NZ Forest Products Ltd, NZ Sugar Co Ltd, Rex Consolidated Ltd; dir NZ Insurance Co Ltd, LD Nathan & Co Ltd, Mainzeal Corpn Ltd, Black & Decker (Australia) Ltd & other cos; *Recreations* gardening, bowls, bridge; *Clubs* Northern (Auckland), Wellington (Wellington); *Style* - Lewis Ross Esq CMG; 11 Rewiti st, Orakei, Auckland, N Zealand (☎ 547 449)

ROSS, Rear-Adm Maurice James; CB (1962), DSC (1940); s of the late Basil James Ross; *b* 31 Oct 1908; *Educ* Charterhouse; *m* 1946, Helen Matheson, nee McCall; 1 da; *Career* joined Royal Navy 1927, served 1939-45 in home and Mediterranean waters, Rear-Adm, ret; 1964; *Recreations* gardening; *Style* - Rear Adm Maurice Ross, CB, DSC; The School House, Chippenham, Ely, Cambs (☎ Newmarket 720 180)

ROSS, Patrick James Forrest; DFC; *Career* dir Croda gp of cos; md Croda Inks Ltd; *Style* - Patrick Ross Esq, DFC; Croda Inks Ltd, 170 Glasgow rd, Edinburgh 12

ROSS, Hon Mrs (Roxana Rose Catherine Naila); *née* Lampson; da of 1 Baron Killearn, GCMG, CB, MVO, PC (d 1964); *b* 1945; *m* 1966, Ian Cowper Ross; 2 s, 2 da; *Style* - The Hon Mrs Ross; 60 Westbourne Park rd, W2

ROSS, Stephen Sherlock; MP (Lib) Isle of Wight Feb 1974-; s of Reginald Sherlock Ross (d 1970); *b* 6 July 1926; *Educ* Bedford Sch; *m* 1949, Brenda Marie, da of late Arthur Ivor Hughes; 2 s, 2 da; *Career* RN 1944-48; FRICS; non-exec dir Polatis Britten-Norman; *Recreations* cricket; *Clubs* Nat Liberal; *Style* - Stephen Ross Esq, MP; 47 Quay st, Newport, Isle of Wight (☎ 522215)

ROSS RUSSELL, Graham; *b* 3 Jan 1933; *Educ* Loretto, Trinity Hall Cambridge, Harvard; *m* 1963, Jean Margaret, da of the late Col K M Symington; 4 c; *Career* partner Laurence Prust & Co, memb Stock Exchange Council 1973-; *Style* - Graham Ross Russell Esq; 30 Ladbroke Square, London W11

ROSSE, 7 Earl of (I 1806); Sir William Brendan Parsons; 10 Bt (I 1677); also Baron Oxmantown (I 1792); s of 6 Earl of Rosse, KBE (d 1979), and Anne, Countess of Rosse; Lord Rosse is half-bro of the Earl of Snowdon and nephew of Oliver Messel, the portraitist and set designer (the Messels were originally bankers in Darmstadt); *b* 21 Oct 1936; *Educ* Eton, Grenoble U, Ch Ch Oxford; *m* 1966, Alison, da of Maj John Cooke-Hurle, of Startforth Hall, Barnard Castle; 1 s, 1 da; *Heir* s, Lord Oxmantown; *Career* late 2 Lt Irish Gds; with UN 1963-, Dep Resident Rep Algeria 1978-80; *Style* - The Rt Hon The Earl of Rosse; Birr Castle, Co Offaly, Eire (☎ Birr 23)

ROSSE, Anne, Countess of; Anne; da of

Lt-Col Leonard Messel, OBE, TD (gs of Simon Messel, a Darmstadt banker, Priv Sec to the Grand Duke of Hesse and Sec of the War Office in Darmstadt), by Maud, MBE (da of Edward Linley Sambourne); sis of Oliver Messel, the portraitist and set designer; *m* 1, 1925 (m dis 1934), Ronald, s of Sir Robert Armstrong-Jones, CBE, of Plas Dinas, Caernarvonshire; 1 s (Earl of Snowdon), 1 da (Viscountess de Vesci, w of 6 Viscount); m 2, 1935, 6 Earl of Rosse, KBE (d 1979, whose mother m, as her 2 husb, 5 Viscount de Vesci); 2 s (7 Earl and Hon Desmond Parsons); *Style* - The Rt Hon Anne, Countess of Rosse; Nymans, Handcross, Sussex

ROSSLYN, 7 Earl of (UK 1801); Sir Peter St Clair-Erskine; 10 Bt (S 1666); also Baron Loughborough (GB 1780), which title he uses in preference to Rosslyn; s of 6 Earl of Rosslyn (d 1977) and Athenais, Countess of Rosslyn, *qv*; *b* 31 March 1958; *Educ* Eton, Bristol U; *Heir* great unc, Hon David St Clair-Erskine; *Career* Tstee Dunimarle Museum, PC with Metropolitan Police 1980-; *Clubs* Clifton (Bristol); *Style (Rosslyn is given as for punctilious usage although this may be theoretical if the subject of this entry prefers to be called Lord Loughborough)* - The Rt Hon The Earl of Rosslyn; Cedar House, Shurlock Row, Berks (☎ 341); 49 Fentiman rd, SW8 (☎ 01 735 0474)

ROSSLYN, Athenais, Countess of; Comtesse Athenais; *née* Mortemart de Rochechouart; da of Louis Victor de Mortemart, Duc de Vivonne, and Mme Michel Valéry Ollivier; *m* 1955 (m dis 1962), 6 Earl of Rosslyn (d 1977); 1 s (7 Earl of Rosslyn), 1 da (Lady Caroline St Clair-Erskine); *Style* - Athenais, Countess of Rosslyn; 64 Avenue Henri-Martin, Paris XVI, France

ROSSMORE, 7 Baron (I 1796 & UK 1838); William Warner Westenra; s of 6 Baron Rossmore (d 1958); *b* 14 Feb 1931; *Educ* Eton, Trin Cambridge; *Heir* none; *Career* 2 Lt Somerset LI; co-founder Coolemine Therapeutic Community Dublin; *Style* - The Rt Hon Lord Rossmore; Rossmore Park, Co Monaghan, Eire (☎ Monaghan 81947)

ROTHERMERE, 3 Viscount (UK 1919); Sir Vere Harold Esmond Harmsworth; 3 Bt (UK 1910); also Baron Rothermere (UK 1914); s of 2 Viscount Rothermere (d 1978) by his 1 w Margaret; *b* 27 Aug 1925; *Educ* Eton, Kent Sch Conn USA; *m* 1957, 'Bubbles' (Patricia Evelyn Beverley), da of John Matthews, FRCS, and former w of Capt Christopher Brooks (gs of 2 Baron Crawshaw); 1 s, 2 da; *Heir* s, Hon Jonathan Harmsworth; *Career* chm & ch exec Associated Newspapers Gp 1971-, chm Daily Mail & Gen Tst 1978-, tstee Reuters, dir Consolidated Bathurst (Canada), tstee Vis-News, Pres London Press Club; FRSA, FBIM; patron of three livings; *Style* - The Rt Hon Viscount Rothermere; Rue du Sentier, Paris 75002; c/o New Carmelite House, Carmelite st, EC4; 86 Eaton sq, SW1

ROTHERMERE, Mary, Viscountess; Mary; da of Kenneth Murchison, of Dallas, Texas, and formerly w of Richard Ohrstrom, of The Plains, Virginia; *m* 1966, as his 3 w, 2 Viscount Rothermere (d 1978); *Style* - The Rt Hon Mary, Viscountess Rothermere; c/o Carmelite House, Carmelite st, EC4

ROTHERWICK, 2 Baron (UK 1939); Sir (Herbert) Robin Cayzer; 2 Bt (UK 1924); s of 1 Baron Rotherwick, JP, DL (d 1958) and Freda, da of Col William Rathborne, of Co Cavan (of an ancient Anglo-Irish family, founder of whose fortunes in Drogheda in the reign of Charles II was one Richard Rathborne, yr bro of William Rathbone (*sic*), ancestor of Basil Rathbone, the actor celebrated for his portrayals of Sherlock Holmes); through his mother (Freda) Lord Rotherwick is 2 cous four times removed of John Wilson Croker (the egregious Rigby of *Coningsby*), friend to Canning and Peel, foe to William IV and Reform; Croker was also author of the celebrated 'slashing' article on Keats's *Endymion* and coined the word 'Conservatives' to describe the Tories; Lord Rotherwick's bro is m to Lord Oranmore and Browne's da, his sis to Lord Boyne's unc; *b* 5 Dec 1912; *Educ* Eton, Ch Ch Oxford; *m* 1952, Sarah Jane, da of Sir Michael Slade, 6 Bt; 3 s, 1 da; *Heir* s, Hon Herbert Cayzer; *Career* late Maj The Greys (Supp Reserve); dep chm Br &

C'wlth Shipping Co & Assoc Cos; *Recreations* racing, shooting; *Clubs* White's, Turf; *Style* - The Rt Hon Lord Rotherwick; Cornbury Park, Charlbury, Oxon (☎ 810311); 50 Eaton Mews North, SW1 (☎ 01 235 6314)

ROTHES, 21 Earl of (S before 1457); Ian Lionel Malcolm Leslie; also Lord Leslie and Ballenbreich (the S Lordship of 1445 being regranted as such 1663); s of 20 Earl of Rothes (d 1975) and Beryl, Countess of Rothes, *qv*; *b* 10 May 1932; *Educ* Eton; *m* 1955, Marigold, da of Sir David Evans-Bevan, 1 Bt; 2 s; *Heir* s, Lord Leslie; *Career* late Sub-Lt RNVR; *Style* - The Rt Hon The Earl of Rothes; Tanglewood, W Tytherley, Salisbury, Wilts

ROTHES, Beryl, Countess of; Beryl Violet; da of James Lionel Dugdale and sis of 1 Baron Crathorne; *m* 1926, 20 Earl of Rothes (d 1975); 1 s (21 Earl), 2 da (Lady Jean Mackenzie, Lady Evelyn Mackworth-Young, *qqv*); *Style* - Rt Hon Beryl, Countess of Rothes; Strawberry House, Chiswick Mall, W 4 (☎ 01 994 3052)

ROTHSCHILD, 3 Baron (UK 1885); Sir Nathaniel Mayer Victor Rothschild; 4 Bt (UK 1847), GBE (1975), GM (1944); also a Baron of the Austrian Empire (1822); s of Hon Nathaniel Rothschild (2 s of 1 Baron, who himself was gs of Baron Nathan von Rothschild, the first of this celebrated family of financiers to settle in the UK, where his raising of loans was a major factor in the eventual Allied triumph over Napoleon; Nathan did not neglect his own enrichment, to which his use of carrier pigeons in obtaining news ahead of rivals contributed substantially, particularly in the depressed state of the market on the eve of the announcement of the victory of Waterloo; the family's original name was Bauer, but Mayer Anselm, Nathan's f, started as money lender at the sign of the Rote Schild, Judengasse, Frankfort); suc unc, 2 Baron, 1937; is 3 cous of 7 Earl of Rosebery; *b* 31 Oct 1910; *Educ* Harrow, Trin Cambridge; *m* 1, 1933 (m dis 1946), Barbara, da of late St John Hutchinson KC; 1 s, 2 da; m 2, 1946, Teresa, MBE, JP, da of Robert Mayor, CB, and Katherine (da of Daniel Meinertzhagen, of Mottisfont Abbey, Romsey, and Brockwood Park, Alresford, sr ptnr of Frederick Huth & Co Merchant Bankers; *see* Nicholas Meinertzhagen); 1 s (and 1 s decd), 2 da; *Heir* s, Hon Nathaniel Rothschild; *Career* zoologist; Dir-Gen & 1 Perm Under-Sec Centl Policy Review Staff Cabinet Off 1971-74; chm: Rothschilds Continuation 1976-, Roy Commission on Gambling 1976-78, N M Rothschild & Sons 1975-76 (still dir); served WW II in Mil Intelligence; former Shell exec; KStJ 1948; FRS; *Style* - The Rt Hon Lord Rothschild GBE GM

ROTHSCHILD, Hon Amschel Mayor James; s of 3 Baron Rothschild, GBE, GM, by his 2 w, Teresa; *b* 18 April 1955; *Educ* Leys Sch Cambridge; *m* 1981, Anita, 3 da of James Guinness (s of Sir Arthur Guinness, KCMG, of the extensive Irish brewing and banking family); *Style* - The Hon Amschel Guinness

ROTHSCHILD, Hon Emma Georgina; da of 3 Baron Rothschild, GBE, GM, by his 2 w, Teresa; *b* 16 May 1948; *Educ* Oxford U; *Style* - The Hon Emma Rothschild

ROTHSCHILD, Edmund Leopold de; TD; s of Maj Lionel de Rothschild, OBE, JP, sometime MP Aylesbury (s of (Austrian) Baron Leopold de Rothschild, CVO, JP, n of 1 Baron Rothschild of UK creation and gs of (Austrian) Baron Lionel de Rothschild, first MP of Jewish faith), by Marie, nee Beer, of Paris; *b* 2 Jan 1916; *Educ* Harrow, Trin Cambridge; *m* 1948, Elizabeth Lentner (d 1980), da of Marcel Lentner, of Vienna; 2 s, 2 da; *Career* Pres N M Rothschild & Sons 1975-, chm Straflo Ltd, Pres Assoc of Jewish Ex-Service Men & Women; served WW II as Maj RA; *Clubs* White's; *Style* - Edmund de Rothschild Esq TD; New Court, St Swithin's Lane, EC4 (☎ 01 626 356)

ROTHSCHILD, Evelyn Robert Adrian de; s of Anthony de Rothschild DL (3 s of Leopold de Rothschild CVO JP *see* Edmund de Rothschild); *b* 29 Aug 1931; *Educ* Harrow, Trin Cambridge; *m* 1, 1966 (m dis 1971), Jeannette, da of Ernest Bishop; m 2, 1973, Victoria, da of Lewis Schott; 2 s, 1 da; *Career* chm N M Rothschild & Sons, Economist Newspaper

1972-, United Racecourses Ltd 1977-; dep chm Milton Keynes Devpt Corpn 1972-; *Style* - Evelyn de Rothschild Esq; Ascott, Wing, Leighton Buzzard, Bedfordshire (☎ Wing (STD Code 029 668) 204 and 390)

ROTHSCHILD, Hon (Nathaniel Charles) Jacob; s and h of 3 Baron Rothschild, GBE, GM, by his 1 w Barbara; *b* 29 April 1936; *Educ* Eton, Christ Church Oxford; *m* 1961, Serena, da of Sir Philip Dunn, 2 Bt, by his wife Lady Mary St Clair-Erskine (da of 5 Earl of Rosslyn); 1 s, 3 da; *Career* chm RIT Ltd (formerly Rothschild Investment Trust); formerly Second Lieutenant The Life Guards; *Style* - The Hon Jacob Rothschild; Doves House, Ham, near Hungerford, Berkshire; 28 Warwick Avenue, London W9 (☎ 01 283 5234)

ROTHSCHILD, Leopold David de; 2 s of Maj Lionel Rothschild OBE (*see* Edmund de Rothschild); *b* 12 May 1927; *Educ* Harrow, Trinity College Cambridge; *Career* director N M Rothschild and Sons 1970-, The Bank of England 1970-; Fellow Royal College of Music 1977; chairman English Chamber Orchestra and Music Society Ltd, also of the Bach Choir; *Style* - Leopold de Rothschild, Esq; c/o N M Rothschild and Sons Ltd; New Court, St Swithin's Lane, London EC4 (☎ 01 626 4356)

ROTHSCHILD, Hon Miranda; da of 3 Baron Rothschild, GBE, GM, by his 1 w, Barbara; *b* 25 Dec 1940; *Style* - The Hon Miranda Rothschild

ROTHSCHILD, Hon Sarah; da of 3 Baron Rothschild, GBE, GM, by his 1 w, Barbara; *b* 13 Sept 1934; *Educ* St Hilda's Oxford; *Style* - The Hon Sarah Rothschild

ROTHSCHILD, Hon Victoria Katherine; da of 3 Baron Rothschild, GBE, GM, by his 2 w, Teresa; *b* 13 Aug 1953; *Style* - The Hon Victoria Rothschild

ROTHSTEIN, Saul; s of Simon Rothstein; *b* 4 July 1920; *Educ* Manchester U; *m* 1949, Judith Katz; 2 da; *Career* slr 1947, slr to the Post Office 1976- (dir Advsy Dept 1972-76); *Style* - Saul Rothstein Esq, 9 Templar's Crescent, N3 (☎ 01 346 3701)

ROUBANIS, Lady Sarah (Consuelo); *née* Spencer-Churchill; da of 10 Duke of Marlborough (d 1972); *b* 1921; *m* 1, 1943 (m dis 1966), Lt Edwin F Russell, US Navy; 4 da; m 2, 1966 (m dis 1967), Guy Burgos, of Santiago, Chile; m 3, 1967, Theodoros Roubanis; *Style* - Lady Sarah Roubanis

ROUS, Lady Catherine Charlotte; OBE (1972); da of late 3 Earl of Stradbroke, KCMG, CB, CVO, CBE, and Dame Helena DBE, da of late Lt-Gen James Fraser CMG; *b* 1900; *Career* Ex-Services War Disabled Help Dept in Suffolk; *Style* - Lady Catherine Rous OBE; Bracondale, 5 Evans Close, Reydon, Southwold, Suffolk

ROUS, Hon George Nathaniel; s of late 3 Earl of Stradbroke, KCMG, CB, CVO, CBE and Dame Helena DBE, da of Lt-Gen James Fraser CMG; *b* 1911; *Educ* Geelong G S, Harrow, Trin Cambridge; *m* 1949, Joyce, da of late Col Charles Harpur OBE; 1 s, 3 da; *Career* Maj (ret) Life Gds; Co Cllr E Suffolk, served with Trans-Jordan Frontier Force 1938-42, Palestine 1936-39 (despatches); *Style* - The Hon George Rous

ROUS, Hon (William) Keith; s of late 3 Earl of Stradbroke, KCMG, CB, CVO, CBE and Dame Helena DBE, da of late Lt-Gen James Fraser CMG; hp of bro, 4 Earl; *b* 10 March 1907; *Educ* Geelong G S; *m* 1, 1935 (m dis 1941), Pamela Catherine Mabell (d 1972), da of late Capt the Hon Edward James Kay-Shuttleworth, s of 1 Baron Shuttleworth, PC, JP; 2 s; m 2, 1943, April Mary, da of late Brig the Hon Arthur Melland Asquith DSO, s of 1 Earl of Oxford and Asquith, KG, PC; 1 s, 3 da; *Career* Lt (E) RN (ret) and Lt RNVR WW II; *Style* - The Hon Keith Rous; Clovelly Court, Bideford, North Devon (☎ Bideford (023 72) 215)

ROUS, Lady Marye Violet Isolde; da of 4 Earl of Stradbroke; *b* 1930; *Style* - Lady Marye Rous; Farm Cottage, Bulcamp White House, Blythburgh, Halesworth, Suffolk (☎ Blythburgh 415)

ROUS, Hon Peter James Mowbray; s of late 3 Earl of Stradbroke, KCMG, CB, CVO, CBE, and Dame Helena, DBE, da of late Lt-Gen James Fraser CMG; *b* 1914; *Educ* Harrow, Melbourne G S; *m* 1942, Elizabeth Alice Mary (d 1968), da of late Maj the Hon Alastair Thomas Joseph Fraser, DSO, (s of 13 Lord Lovat) and Lady Sibyl, nee Grimston, da of 3 Earl of Verulam; 6 s (and 2 decd), 4 da; *Career* Maj (ret) 16/5 Lancers; *Style* - The Hon Peter Rous; Priors Mead, Quality st, Merstham, Surrey

ROUTLEDGE, Alan; CBE (1979); s of George Routledge (d 1954); *b* 12 May 1919; *Educ* Liscard H S Wallasey; *m* 1949, Irene Jessie, nee Hendry; 2 s; *Career* Control Cmmn Germany 1946-51, Head Cypher & Signals Branch Diplomatic Wireless Service Foreign Office 1962-73, Head Communications Planning Staff Foreign & C'wlth Office (FCO) 1973-79, Head of Communications Operations Dept of FCO 1979 (retired); *Recreations* gardening, golf, watching cricket; *Clubs* Civil Service, Orpington Sports; *Style* - Alan Routledge Esq CBE; 10 St Margaret's Close, Orpington, Kent (☎ Orpington 23900)

ROUTLY, Ernest John; s of Ernest Sydney Routly MRCS, LRCP (d 1931); *b* 4 Sept 1914; *Educ* Radley Coll, Gonville & Caius Coll Cambridge; *m* 1939, Alice Janet, nee Bailey; 2 da; *Career* RAFVR; solicitor, dir William Baird & Co to 1966, fin advr Help The Aged & Action Aid 1976-, fin advr Andrews Furnishers Gp 1976-, memb Bucks County Cncl 1965-80, vice-chm Bucks Council 1977-79, chm Ffestiniog Railway Co 1954-, High Sheriff of Bucks 1972-; *Recreations* railways, walking; *Clubs* East India, Sports & Public Schs; *Style* - Ernest Routly Esq; Ormonde House, St John's Hill, Shrewsbury

ROWALLAN, 3 Baron (UK 1911); Arthur Cameron Corbett; s of 2 Baron Rowallan, KT, KBE, MC, TD, DL (d 1977), and Gwyn, da of Joseph and sis of Rt Hon Jo Grimond, PC, MP; *b* 17 Dec 1919; *Educ* Eton, Balliol Oxford; *m* 1, 1945 (m dis 1962), Eleanor, da of George Boyle (ggs of David Boyle, Lord Justice Gen of Scotland and himself gs of 2 Earl of Glasgow) by Mary, 2 da of Sir Peter Mackie, 1 and last Bt; 1 s, 3 da; m 2, 1963 (m annulled 1970), April Ashley (né(e) George Jamieson, sometime merchant seaperson); *Heir* s, Hon John Corbett; *Career* served WW II, Capt Ayrshire Yeomanry; *Style* - The Rt Hon Lord Rowallan; Villa Antoinette, Finca el Capricho, Marbella, Spain

ROWAN, Thomas Stanley; s of Thomas Rowan (d 1965); *b* 11 Apr 1935; *Educ* Wellington Sch, U of Natal, Gonville and Caius Cambridge; *m* 1964, Anne Strafford, nee Sanderson; 1 s, 1 da; *Career* CA 1961, fell Inst of CAs in England & Wales 1971, md Singer & Friedlander Ltd 1975-; *Recreations* golf; *Clubs* Leeds; *Style* - Thomas Rowan Esq; 2 St Leonards Rd, Harrogate, N Yorks (☎ 0423 884588)

ROWE, Jeremy; CBE (1980); s of Col Charles William Dell Rowe, CB, MBE (d 1954); *b* 31 Oct 1928; *Educ* Uppingham, Trin Cambridge; *m* 1957, Susan Mary, da of Cdr Richard Noel Johnstone RN; 4 da; *Career* dep chm Abbey National Building Soc 1978-, chm London Brick Co Ltd 1979-, bd memb Peterborough Dvpt Corpn 1979-; *Recreations* tennis, shooting, travel, music, history; *Clubs* All England Tennis, Buck's; *Style* - Jeremy Rowe Esq CBE; Woodside, Peasmarsh, Rye, Sussex (☎ Peasmarsh 335)

ROWE, Robert Stewart; CBE (1969); s of James Stewart Rowe (d 1960); *b* 31 Dec 1920; *Educ* private tutors, Cambridge U; *m* 1953, Barbara Elizabeth Hamilton, da of late Thomas Austin Hamilton Baynes OBE; 3 c; *Career* assist keeper of art Birmingham Art Gallery 1950-56, dep dir Manchester City Art Galleries 1956-58, dir Leeds City Art Galleries 1958-; *Recreations* reading, gardening; *Style* - Robert Rowe Esq CBE; Grove Lodge, Shadwell, Leeds

ROWELL, Sir John Joseph; CBE (1974); s of Joseph Alfred Rowell (d 1932); *b* 15 Feb 1916; *Educ* Brisbane G S, Queensland U; *m* 1947, Mary Kathleen, nee de Silva; 5 c; *Career* kt 1980; notary public; solicitor; dir Boral Ltd & Boral Resources Ltd, chm Brisbane Gas Co Ltd & Concrete Constructions, chm Legal Aid Cmmn Queensland, past pres Queensland Law Soc, dir Castlemaine Tooheys Ltd; *Recreations* golf, fishing, gardening; *Clubs*

Brisbane, Union (Sydney), Indooroopilly Golf, United Service; *Style* - Sir John Rowell CBE; 'Edgecliffe', 4 Walcott st, St Lucia, Brisbane, Queensland, Australia

ROWETT, Geoffrey Charles; s of Frederick Charles Rowett (d 1953); *b* 1 Aug 1925; *Educ* Roundhay Sch Leeds; *m* 1951, Joyce, nee Eddiford; 2 c; *Career* FCA, FCMA, JDipMA, FIMC, CBIM; man dir Sunday Times 1965-72, dir and gen man Times Newspapers 1967-72, man dir (Corporate Finance) British Steel Corpn 1973-, gp ch exec Charterhouse Gp 1974-; *Recreations* gardening, golf; *Clubs* RAC; *Style* - Geoffrey Rowett Esq; 3 Wilswood rd, NW11 (☎ 01 455 4561)

ROWLAND, (John) David; *Career* chm Stewart Wrightson Hldgs 1981- (dep chm to 1981); chm: J D Rowland Insur Brokers, Matthews Wrightson Underwriting, Nasco Insur Brokers, Prudential Gulf Ltd (Greece), Stewart Wrightson Internat Gp; Pres Cedar Insur Co Bermuda, Crest Insur Hldgs Bermuda; dir: Bankers Assur Co Beirut, Nasco Karoaglan Bermuda, Ras Al Khaima Nat Insur Co UAR, Saudi Gen Insur Bermuda, Stewart Wrightson Australia Pty, S W Gp Bermuda, S W Hldgs (SA) Pty; memb IOD; *Style* - David Rowland Esq; c/o Stewart Wrightson Hldgs, 1 Camomile st, EC3 (☎ 01 623 7511)

ROWLAND, (Roland Walter) 'Tiny'; s of Wilhelm Friederich Furhop, a merchant of Hamburg, and Muriel, nee Carton; *b* Nov 1917; *Educ* Churchers Coll Hants; *m* 1968; *Career* served in Hitler Jugend c 1933; changed name from Furhop to Rowland 1939; RAMC 1940-42, interned in Isle of Man 1942-43; md and ch exec Lonrho (jt md 1961 or 1963), ch proprietor The Observer 1981-, chm: AVP Industs, Firsteel Hadfields Invests, London City and Westcliff Properties, Scottish Universal Investments; dir: Dunford & Elliott, Volkswagen (GB), Willoughby's Consolidated Co; farmer Rhodesia 1947-61; *Style* - Tiny Rowland Esq; Hedsor Wharf, Bourne End, Bucks; c/o Lonrho, Cheapside House, Cheapside, EC2 (☎ 01 606 9898)

ROWLANDS, John; *Career* Dep Keeper Dept Prints & Drawings Br Museum to 1981, Keeper Oct 1981- (salary £14,250-15,748); *Style* - John Rowlands Esq; c/o British Museum, Dept Prints & Drawings, Gt Russell st, WC1 (☎ 01 636 1555)

ROWLANDSON, Hon Mrs (Antonia Jane Hamilla); *née* Inskip; da of 2 Visc Caldecote; *b* 1952; *m* 1972, Piers Rowlandson; 1 s; *Style* The Hon Mrs Rowlandson

ROWLEY, Sir Charles Robert; 7 Bt (UK 1836), of Hill House, Berkshire; s of Lt-Col Sir William Joshua Rowley, 6 Bt (d 1971); *b* 15 March 1926; *Educ* Wellington; *m* 1952, Astrid, da of Sir Arthur Massey, CBE, MD; 1 s, 1 da; *Heir* s, Richard Rowley; *Style* - Sir Charles Rowley, Bt; Naseby Hall, Northants; 21 Teddingworth sq, SW3

ROWLEY, Donald; s of the late Bertram Rowley; *b* 24 June 1926; *Educ* Selwyn Coll Cambridge; *m* 1950, Ruth Mary, nee Dunkley; 1 s, 1 da; *Career* dir British Aircraft Corpn Ltd 1967-77, assistant md 1975-77, dir British Aerospace Dynamics Group 1977-; *Recreations* photography, gardening, music; *Style* - Donald Rowley Esq; Manor Farm House, Northwick, Pilning, Bristol

ROWLEY, Sir Joshua Francis; 7 Bt (GB 1786), of Tendring Hall, Suffolk; s of Col Sir Charles Samuel Rowley, OBE, TD, 6 Bt (d 1962); *b* 31 Dec 1920; *Educ* Eton, Trin Cambridge; *m* 1959, Hon Celia Ella Vere Monckton, da of 8 Viscount Galway; 1 da; *Career* formerly Capt Gren Gds; dep sec Nat Trust 1952-55, chm W Suffolk CC 1971-74, Suffolk CC 1976-78, DL 1968, High Sheriff 1971, Vice Lord-Lieutenant 1973-78, JP 1978 Suffolk, Lord Lieutenant 1978-; *Clubs* Boodle's, Pratt's, MCC; *Style* - Sir Joshua Rowley, Bt, JP, HM Lord-Lieut for Suffolk; Holbecks, Hadleigh, Ipswich, Suffolk (☎ Hadleigh 823211)

ROWLEY, Baroness; Mary Elizabeth; da of Ernest Verrall Barnes, of Finchley; *m* 1, Harold Gliksten (decd); m 2, 1958, Baron Rowley (Life Peer, d 1968); *Style* - The Rt Hon Lady Rowley; PO Box 5, Miami Shores, Fla 33153, USA

ROWLEY, Richard Charles; s and h of Sir Charles Rowley, 7 Bt; *b* 14 Aug 1959; *Style* - Richard Rowley Esq

ROWLEY-CONWY, Hon Christopher Geoffrey Hugh; s of 9 Baron Langford OBE; *b* 1978

ROWLEY-CONWY, Hon Charlotte Susan Gabrielle; da of 9 Baron Langford OBE; *b* 1980

ROWLEY-CONWY, Hon John Seymour; s of 9 Baron Langford OBE; *b* 1955; *Educ* Marlborough, Magdalene Coll Cambridge (BA), Oriel Coll Oxford (MSc); *Style* - The Hon John Rowley-Conwy

ROWLEY-CONWY, Hon Owen Grenville; s and h of 9 Baron Langford OBE; *b* 27 Dec 1958; *Educ* Marlborough and Roy Agric Coll Cirencester; *Style* - The Hon Owen Rowley-Conwy

ROWLEY-CONWY, Hon Peter Alexander; s of 9 Baron Langford OBE; *b* 1951; *Educ* Marlborough and Magdalene Cambridge (BA Archaeology) *Style* The Hon Peter Rowley-Conwy

ROWSON, Peter Aston; s of Lionel Edward Aston Rowson, OBE, FRS, FRCVS; *b* 8 Oct 1942; *Educ* St Edmunds Coll Ware; *m* 1967, Jennifer Mary, nee Smyth; 1 s, 2 da; *Career* accountant, fin dir & co sec: Panther Securities Ltd, J B Jacquemin Bros Ltd, Panther Shop Investments Ltd, Neil Martin Ltd and Ingrams Opticians Ltd; company secretary Yardworth Ltd, Excelchoice Ltd, Snowbest Ltd, Saxonbest Ltd; *Style* - Peter Rowson Esq; 12 Docwras Close, Shepreth, Cambs

ROXBEE COX, Hon Christopher Withers; s of Baron Kings Norton (Life Peer); *b* 1928; *m* 1955, Rosemary, da of late Frederick Day Ardagh; *Style* - The Hon Christopher Roxbee Cox; 43/44 St Dunstans st, Canterbury, Kent

ROXBEE COX, Hon Jeremy William; s of Baron Kings Norton (Life Peer); *b* 1932; *m* 1962, Anne, da of Albert Moore Linton; *Style* - The Hon Jeremy Roxbee Cox; 1 Rectory Barn, Halton, Lancaster

ROXBURGH, Vice-Adm Sir John Charles Young; KCB (1972, CB 1969), CBE (1967), DSO (1943), DSC (1942) & Bar (1945); s of Sir (Thomas) James (Young) Roxburgh (d 1974); *b* 29 June 1919; *Educ* RNC Dartmouth; *m* 1942, Philippa, da of Maj Charles Montague Hewlett MC; 1 s, 1 da; *Career* RN 1933, Vice-Admiral 1970, Flag Officer Plymouth 1969, Flag Officer Submarines 1969-72, retired 1972; chm Grovebell Gp Ltd 1972-75, County Councillor (Surrey) 1977-81, pres RN Benevolent Trust 1978-, memb Cncl & Management Ctee of Freedom Assoc 1977-; *Recreations* golf, sailing, walking, music; *Clubs* Army & Navy; *Style* - Vice-Adm Sir John Roxburgh, KCB, CBE, DSO, DSC*; Wood rd, Hindhead, Surrey (☎ 042 873 5600)

ROXBURGH, Ven James William; s of James Thomas Roxburgh; *b* 5 July 1921; *Educ* Whitgift, St Cat's Cambridge; *m* 1949, Marjorie Winifred, nee Hipkiss; 1 s, 1 da; *Career* Clerk in Holy Orders, ord Priest 1945, Vicar Barking 1965-77, Archdeacon Colchester 1977-, Pro-Prolocutor Convocation of Canterbury 1977-; *Recreations* travel, philately; *Clubs* Rotary; *Style* - The Ven James Roxburgh; Uplands, 25 Powers Hall End, Witham, Essex (☎ 0376 513447)

ROXBURGHE, 10 Duke of (S 1707); Sir Guy David Innes-Ker; 11 Bt (Premier Bt of Scotland or Nova Scotia, S 1625); also Lord Roxburghe (S before 31 March 1600), Earl of Roxburghe, Lord Ker of Cessford and Cavertoun (both S 1616), Marquess of Bowmont and Cessford, Earl of Kelso, Viscount of Broxmouth (S, with the Dukedom the last Peerages cr in the Peerage of Scotland, 1707), and Earl Innes (UK 1837); s of 9 Duke of Roxburghe (d 1974) by his 2 w (now Mrs Jocelyn Hambro, *qv*); *b* 18 Nov 1954; *Educ* Eton, Magdalene Cambridge; *m* 1977, Lady Jane Grosvenor, da of 5 Duke of Westminster by Hon Viola Lyttelton (da of 9 Viscount Cobham) and sis of Countess of Lichfield, *qv*; 1 s, 1 da; *Heir* s, Marquess of Bowmont and Cessford; *Career* formerly Lt RHG/1 Dragoons; landowner and co dir; *Recreations* fishing, shooting, golf, cricket, skiing; *Clubs* White's, Turf; *Style* - His Grace The Duke of Roxburghe;

Floors Castle, Kelso, Roxburghshire (☎ 057 32 2288)

ROXBURGHE, Mary, Duchess of; Lady Mary Evelyn Hungerford; *née* Crewe-Milnes; da (by 1 m) of 1 and last Marquess of Crewe; *b* 1915; *m* 1935 (m dis 1953), 9 Duke of Roxburghe (d 1974); *Career* bore HM the Queen's Canopy at Coronation of King George VI; *Style* - Mary, Duchess of Roxburghe; 15 Hyde Park gdns, W2

ROYDEN, Sir Christopher John; 5 Bt (UK 1905); s of Sir John Royden, 4 Bt (d 1976), by Dolores, da of Cecil Coward, of Lima; *b* 26 Feb 1937; *Educ* Winchester, Ch Ch Oxford; *m* 1961, Diana, da of Lt-Col Joseph Goodhart MC, of Keldholme Priory, Kirkbymoorside, York, by Evelyn (yst da of Henry Beaumont JP DL); 2 s, 1 da; *Heir* s, John Royden; *Career* stockbroker; ptnr Spencer Thornton & Co 1974-; *Recreations* shooting, fishing, gardening; *Clubs* Cavalry & Guards; *Style* - Sir Christopher Royden, Bt; 9 Stanhope gdns, SW7 (☎ 01 370 2665)

ROYDEN, Catherine, Lady (Dolores Catherine); da of Cecil Coward, of Lima; *m* 1936, Sir John Royden, 4 Bt (d 1976); 2 s, 2 da; *Style* - Catherine, Lady Royden; Netherfield Place, Battle, Sussex

ROYDEN, John Michael Joseph; s and h of Sir Christopher Royden, 5 Bt; *b* 17 March 1965; *Style* - John Royden Esq

ROYLE, Timothy Lancelot Fanshawe; s of Sir Lancelot Carrington Royle KBE (d 1978); *b* 24 Apr 1931; *Educ* Harrow, Mons Mil Acad; *m* 1959, Margaret Jill, da of Sir Ivan Rice Stedeford GBE; 2 s, 1 da; *Career* Church Cmmr 1967, chm Lindley Lodge Educational Trust 1970-, man dir Hogg Robinson UK 1972, man dir Hogg Robinson Ltd 1976, man dir Hogg Robinson Gp 1980; *Recreations* country pursuits, real tennis, skiing; *Clubs* Cavalry & Guards, MCC, St Moritz Tobogganing; *Style* - Timothy Royle Esq; 35 Grange Grove, Islington, N1; Ilrington Grange, Shipston on Stour, Warwicks

ROYSTON, Viscountess - Virginia Anne; da of Geoffrey Lyon, of Hambledon, Surrey; *m* 1968, Viscount Royston (d 1973, predeceasing his father, 9 Earl of Hardwicke); 1 s (10 Earl of Hardwicke), 1 da (Lady Jemima Yorke); *Style* - Viscountess Royston; 9 Fernshaw rd, SW10

RUBBRA, Arthor Alexander; CBE (1961); s of Edmund James Rubbra (d 1947); *b* 29 Oct 1903; *Educ* Northampton Sch, Bristol U; *m* 1930, Lilian Agnes, nee Webster; 1 s; *Career* designer Aircraft Engines; ch designer Aero Engine Div Rolls Royce Ltd 1940-44, tech dir Rolls Royce Ltd 1954-65; *Recreations* music, old buildings; *Style* - Arthor Rubbra Esq CBE; 100 Belper rd, Derby, DE1 3EQ (☎ 43107)

RUBIN, Hon Mrs; Hon Susan; *née* Rayne; da of Baron Rayne by his 1 w, Margaret; *b* 1945; *m* 1965, John Rubin; *Style* - The Hon Mrs Rubin

RUCK, Hon Mrs (Catherine Dorothy); *née* Neville; da of 7 Baron Braybrooke, JP, DL, by his 2 w, Dorothy JP, da of late Sir George Lawson KC; *b* 21 Jan 1922; *m* 1954, Gordon Alexander Egerton Ruck (d 1977); 1 da; *Style* - The Hon Mrs Ruck; Asherne, Strete, Dartmouth, Devon

RUDA, Mike; *Career* advertisement dir Times Newspapers 1981-; *Style* - Mike Ruda Esq

RUDD, Hon Mrs (Fiona Catherine); *née* Ritchie; da of Baron Ritchie-Calder, CBE; *b* 10 July 1929; *Educ* LSE, Essex U; *m* 1949, Dr Ernest Rudd; 3 da; *Style* - The Hon Mrs Rudd; 51 High st, Brightlingsea, Essex

RUDD, Hon Mrs Hilary Aileen; *née* Peddie; da of Baron Peddie (Life Peer) (d 1978); *b* 1938; *m* 1959 (m dis), Christopher Geoffrey Rudd; 1 s, 1 da; *Style* - The Hon Mrs Hilary Rudd; 31 Nonsuch Court av, Ewell, Surrey

RUDD, Lewis; *aet* 44; *Career* controller young people's programmes ATV 1981-, assist controller programmes Southern TV to 1981, initiator Rainbow and Magpie Thames TV; *Style* - Lewis Rudd Esq;

c/o ATV Ltd, ATV House, Gt Cumberland pla, W1 (☎ 01 262 8040)

RUDGE, Anthony John de Nouaille; s of John Edward Rudge (d 1970); *b* 17 Feb 1931; *Educ* Eton, Ch Ch Oxford; *m* 1961, Kathleen Jill; 1 s, 1 da; *Career* dir Barclays Bank Ltd 1973; dir Yorkshire Bank Ltd 1980; dir Estate Duties Investment Trust Ltd 1980; *Recreations* sailing, tennis, music, history; *Clubs* Travellers'; *Style* - Anthony Rudge Esq; Church Farm, Churchover, nr Rugby, Warwickshire

RUFF, William Willis; CBE (1973), DL (Surrey 1964); s of William Ruff (d 1957); *b* 22 Sept 1914; *Educ* Durham Sch; *m* 1939, Agnes, nee Nankivell; 2 s; *Career* Major Roy Signal Corp (N Africa & India); solicitor; clerk Surrey County Cncl 1952-74, chm Soc Clerks of Peace and Clerks of County Cncl 1969-74, memb Parly Commission for England 1974; *Recreations* music, watching cricket; *Style* - William Ruff Esq, CBE, DL; 3 Brympton Close, Ridgeway rd, Dorking, Surrey (☎ Dorking 882406)

RUFFER, Jonathan Garnier; s of Maj Jem Ruffer; *b* 17 Aug 1951; *Educ* Marlborough, Sidney Sussex Cambridge; *Career* Myers and Co, Stock Exchange, barr Middle Temple (Jr Harmshorth Exhibitioner); J Henry Schroder Wagg 1977-79, Dunbar Gp Ltd 1980-, dir Dunbar Tower Fund Managers Ltd 1981; author *The Big Shots* (1977, Debrett); *Recreations* shooting, opera, name-dropping; *Clubs* Athenaeum; *Style* - Jonathan Ruffer Esq; 4 Cavendish Mews North, W1 (☎ 01 580 2253)

RUGBY, 2 Baron (UK 1947); Alan Loader Maffey; s of 1 Baron Rugby, GCMG, KCB, KCVO, CSI, CIE (d 1969); *b* 16 April 1913; *Educ* Stowe; *m* 1947, Margaret, da of Harold Bindley; 4 s, 2 da; *Heir* s, Hon Robert Maffey; *Career* served WW II Fl Lt RAF; inventor Foldgate Herd Handler (RASE Silver Award 1974); *Style* - The Rt Hon Lord Rugby; Grove Farm, Frankton, Rugby, Warwicks

RUGGE-PRICE, Sir Charles Keith Napier; 9 Bt (UK 1804); s of Lt-Col Sir Charles James Napier Rugge-Price, 8 Bt (d 1966); *b* 7 Aug 1936; *Educ* Middleton Coll Eire; *m* 1965, Jacqueline Mary, da of Maj Pierre P Loranger, MC, CD; 2 s; *Heir* s, James Keith Peter Rugge-Price; *Career* man Tomenson Alexander Ltd (Toronto) 1971-76, supervisor compensation City of Edmonton; *Style* - Sir Charles Rugge-Price, Bt; 23 Lambert Crescent, St Albert, Alberta T8N 1M1, Canada

RUGGE-PRICE, James Keith Peter; s and h of Sir Charles Keith Napier Rugge-Price, 9 Bt; *b* 8 April 1967; *Style* - James Rugge-Price Esq

RUGGE-PRICE, Maeve, Lady; Maeve Marguerite; da of Edgar Stanley de la Peña, of Hythe, Kent; *m* 1935, Lt-Col Sir Charles James Napier Rugge-Price, 8 Bt (d 1966); *Style* - Maeve, Lady Rugge-Price

RUGGLES-BRISE, Guy Edward; TD, DL (Essex 1967); s of Col Sir Edward Ruggles-Brise, 1 Bt, MC, TD, sometime MP Maldon, JP, DL (d 1942), by his 1 w, Agatha, nee Gurney, of the Norfolk family; hp to bro, Sir John Ruggles-Brise, 2 Bt, CB, OBE, TD; *b* 15 June 1914; *Educ* Eton; *m* 1940, Elizabeth, da of James Knox, of Ayrshire; 3 s; *Career* served WW II as Capt (POW but escaped); sr ptnr Brewin Dolphin & Co (stockbrokers); dir The Investment Co; v-chm Riding for the Disabled Tst; *Recreations* hunting, shooting, fishing; *Clubs* Cavalry & Guards, City of London; *Style* - Guy Ruggles-Brise Esq, TD, DL; Ledgowan Lodge, Achnasheen, Ross-shire (☎ 245); The Manor House, Housham Tye, Harlow, Essex (☎ Matching 236)

RUGGLES-BRISE, Sir John Archibald; 2 Bt (UK 1935), of Spains Hall, Finchingfield, Essex, CB (1958), OBE (Mil 1945), TD, JP (Essex 1946); s of Col Sir Edward Ruggles-Brise, 1 Bt, MC, TD, MP (d 1942); *b* 13 June 1908; *Educ* Eton; *Heir* bro, Guy Ruggles-Brise, TD; *Career* KStJ; Lloyd's Underwriter; formerly Pres CLA, Ld-Lt Essex, chm Standing Cncl Baronetage and Church Cmmr; Pro-Chllr Essex U 1964-; *Style* - Col Sir John Ruggles-Brise, Bt, CB, OBE, TD, JP; Spains Hall, Finchingfield, Essex (☎ Gt Dunmow 810266)

RUHEMANN, Frank Andrew; s of Helmut Moritz Ruhemann CBE, (d 1973); *b* 26 July 1930; *Educ* Stowe, Clare Coll Cambridge; *m* 1958, Marie-Elizabeth, sis of Sherban Cantacuzino (Sec of Roy Fine Art Commission 1979-) & da of Prince Georges Matei Cantacuzino (d 1960, descended from the Byzantine Cantacuzene Emperors (the 'Can-' prefix is thought to be a particule cognate with the French 'de' and the 'Cuzenos' to refer to a mountain in Asia Minor); the Cantacuzinos were styled Princes in Romania (where they eventually settled following the Fall of Constantinople in 1453) from the 15th Century & were confirmed in their local pre-eminence by the Sublime Porte); 2 s (Andrew b 1962, Philip b 1968), 2 da (Ileana b 1961, Alexandra b 1965); *Career* Lt Roy Fusiliers (seconded to Nigeria Regt as Intelligence Offr during state of emergency); personal assist to Lord Plowden when latter chm BA/TI 1960-63; md Aluminium Foils Ltd 1963-69, dir of special assignments TI 1969-74, main bd dir Tube Investments Ltd 1973-, ch exec Tube Investments Engrg Ltd 1974-, non exec director: Midland Aluminium 1970-75, British Aluminium1973-79, Conder Int 1975-; v-chm Cncl OU 1978- & Govrs Purcell Sch, chm Young Music Makers; *Recreations* music, squash, tennis, walking, cross country skiing; *Style* - Frank Ruhemann Esq; 65 Blenheim ter, NW8 (☎ 01 624 4004)

RUMBALL, William Norman; s of the late Arthur Rumball; *b* 16 April 1906; *Educ* Mercers Sch; *m* 1935, Kathleen Ethel, nee Le Rossignol; 1 s, 1 da; *Career* stockbroker Le Masurier James & Chinn (senior ptnr 1957); *Recreations* golf; *Clubs* Victoria (Jersey), La Moye Golf (Jersey), Reform; *Style* - William Rumball Esq; The Elms, Millbrook, Jersey, Channel Islands (☎ 0534 20244)

RUMBOLD, Sir (Horace) Anthony Claude; 10 Bt (GB 1779), of Wood Hall, Watton, Herts, KCMG (1962, CMG 1953), KCVO (1969), CB (1955); s of Rt Hon Sir Horace Rumbold, 9 Bt, GCB, GCMG, MVO (d 1941), by Etheldred, CBE, da of Sir Edmund Fane KCMG, of Boyton Manor; *b* 7 March 1911; *Educ* Eton, Magdalen Oxford; *m* 1, 1937 (m dis 1974), Felicity, da of late Lt-Col Frederick Bailey by Lady Janet, nee Mackay (da of 1 Earl of Inchcape and sis of Lady Effie Millington-Drake, *qv*); 1 s, 3 da; m 2, 1974, Pauline, da of Hon David Tennant (3 s of 1 Baron Glenconner and nephew of Margot (Countess of Oxford and Asquith) by David's w Hermione Baddeley, the actress), and former w of (1) Capt Julian Fox-Pitt-Rivers (bro-in-law of Sonia Orwell, gs through his mother of 1 Baron Forster and 1 cous of 3 Baron Avebury) (2) Euan Graham, n of 6 Duke of Montrose; *Heir* s, Henry Rumbold; *Career* Foreign Serv 1935-70, Ambass Thailand 1965-67, Austria 1967-70; *Clubs* Travellers'; *Style* - Sir Anthony Rumbold, Bt, KCMG, KCVO, CB; Var House, Stinsford, Dorchester, Dorset (☎ 2644)

RUMBOLD, Sir (Horace) Algernon Fraser; KCMG (1960, CMG 1953), CIE (1947); s of Col William Rumbold, CMG, yr bro of Sir Horace Rumbold, 9 Bt; 1 cous of Sir Anthony Rumbold, 10 Bt; *b* 27 Feb 1906; *Educ* Wellington, Ch Ch Oxford; *m* 1946, Margaret, da of Arthur Hughes; 2 da; *Career* India Off 1929-47, CRO 1947-66 (Dep Under-Sec of State 1958-66); advr Welsh Off 1967; *Style* - Sir Algernon Rumbold KCMG CIE; Shortwoods, W Clandon, Surrey (☎ Guildford 222757)

RUMBOLD, Henry John Sebastian; s and h of Sir Anthony Rumbold, 10 Bt, KCMG, KCVO, CB, by his 1 w; *b* 24 Dec 1947; *Educ* Eton, William & Mary U (USA); *m* 1978, Frances, da of Dr A Whitfield Hawkes and formerly w of Julian Berry; *Style* - Henry Rumbold Esq; 19 Hollywood rd, SW10

RUNCHORELAL, Sir Chinubhai Madhowlal; 2 Bt (UK 1913), of Shahpur, Ahmedabad, India; s of Sir Chinubhai Madhowlal Runchorelal CIE (d 1916), whose name he then assumed in place of that of Girjaprasad; *b* 19 April 1906; *m* 1924, Tanumati Zaverilal Mehta, of Ahmedabad, India; 2 s; *Style* - Sir Chinubhai Runchorelal, Bt; Shantikunj, Shahibag, Ahmedabad, India

RUNCHORELAL, Udayan; s and h of Sir Chinubhai Runchorelal, 2 Bt; *b* 25 July 1929; *m* 1953, Muneera Khodadad

Fozdar, of Bombay; 3 children; *Style* - Udayan Runchorelal Esq

RUNCIMAN OF DOXFORD, 2 Viscount (UK 1937); Sir Walter Leslie Runciman; 3 Bt (UK 1906), OBE (1946), AFC (1937), AE, DL (Northumberland 1961); also Baron Runciman (UK 1933); s of 1 Viscount Runciman of Doxford, shipowner, MP, Pres BOT and Head Mission Czechoslovakia 1938 (d 1949) by Hilda Stevenson, MP, JP; bro of Hon Sir Steven Runciman, the historian, *qv*; *b* 26 Aug 1900; *Educ* Eton, Trin Cambridge; *m* 1, 1923 (m dis 1928), Rosamond Lehmann, the writer and da of Rudolph Lehmann as well as sis of John Lehmann, also a writer; m 2, 1932, Katherine Schuyler, da of William Garrison, of New York; 1 s; *Heir* s, Hon Walter Runciman; *Career* shipowner, Pres UK Chamber Shipping 1952; formerly banker; er bro Trin House; *Recreations* sailing (yacht: 'Bondicar II'), shooting; *Clubs* Brooks's, Roy Yacht Sqdn; *Style* - Rt Hon Viscount Runciman of Doxford, OBE, AFC, AE, DL; Doxford, Chathill, Northumberland (☎ Chathill 223); 46 Abbey Lodge, Park rd, NW8 (☎ 01 723 6882)

RUNCIMAN, Hon Sir Steven James Cochran Stevenson; 2 s of 1 Viscount Runciman of Doxford; *b* 7 July 1903; *Educ* Eton, Trin Cambridge; *Career* historian; FBA, kt 1958; Br Cncl Rep Greece 1945-47, Prof Byzantine Hist Istanbul U 1942-45; books include *A History of the Crusades* in three vols; *Clubs* Athenaeum; *Style* - The Hon Sir Steven Runciman; Elsieshields, Lockerbie, Dumfriesshire (☎ 038 781 280)

RUNCIMAN, Hon Walter Garrison; s and h of 2 Viscount Runciman of Doxford, OBE, AFC, AE, DL, by his 2 w, Katherine; *b* 10 Nov 1934; *Educ* Eton, Trin Cambridge; *m* 1963, Ruth, da of Joseph Hellman (d 1941); 1 s, 2 da; *Career* FBA; chm Walter Runciman & Co & subsids 1976-; Fell Trin Cambridge 1971-; sociologist; tres Child Poverty Action Gp 1972-; memb Gen Policy Cttee Gen Cncl Br Shipping 1977-; *Clubs* Brooks's; *Style* - The Hon Walter Runciman; 36 Carlton Hill, NW8 (☎ 01 624 8419)

RUNDALL, Hon Mrs (Rosalthé Frances); da of Viscount Sandon; *b* 1 May 1954; *m* 1976, Francis Richard Seton Rundall; 1 s; *Style* - The Hon Mrs Rundall

RUNGE, Hon Lady; Hon Fiona; *née* Macpherson; da of late 1 Baron Strathcarron, KC, PC and Jill, da of Sir George Wood Rhodes, 1 Bt, JP; *b* 1917; *m* 1935, Sir Peter Francis Runge (d 1970); 3 s, 1 da; *Style* - The Hon Lady Runge; The Brick House, Cadmore Common, High Wycombe, Bucks

RUSHMORE, Frederick Herbert Margetson; CBE (1962, OBE 1956, MBE 1951); s of Frederick Margetson Rushmore, Master of St Catharine's Cambridge (d 1933); *b* 19 May 1915; *Educ* King's Sch Bruton, Christ's Cambridge; *Career* Brig Roy Artillery 1935-70 (Burma 1943-44, Korea 1952-53); dir Nat Assoc of Leagues of Hospital Friends 1970-80, chm General Cmmrs of Income Tax (Holborn Div) 1979-; *Recreations* music, drama; *Clubs* London Rowing; *Style* - Frederick Rushmore Esq CBE; 71 Lakeside House, Eaton Drive, Kingston upon Thames, Surrey (☎ 01 549 1877)

RUSSELL OF KILLOWEN, Baron (Life Peer UK 1975); Hon Charles Ritchie Russell; PC (1962); s of Baron Russell of Killowen (Life Peer, d 1946); *b* 12 Jan 1908; *Educ* Beaumont, Oriel Coll Oxford; *m* 1, 1933, Joan (d 1976), da of Dr James Torrens FRCP; 2 s, 1 da; m 2, 1979, Elizabeth, da of Air Vice-Marshal W Foster, CB, CBE, DSO, DFC, and widow of Judge Edward Laughton-Scott QC; *Career* kt 1960; barr 1931, KC 1948; High Court Judge (Chancery) 1960-62, Lord Justice of Appeal 1962-75, Lord Justice of Appeal in Ordinary 1975-; *Style* - The Rt Hon Lord Russell of Killowen PC; Orchard House, Sheepdown, Petworth, W Sussex (☎ 42657)

RUSSELL, 4 Earl (UK 1861); John Conrad Russell; also Viscount Amberley (UK 1861); s of 3 Earl Russell, OM, FRS (d 1970, otherwise Bertrand Russell, the philosopher, writer and savant; himself ggs of Lord John Russell, of Great Reform Bill fame and twice PM, b 3 s of 6 Duke of Bedford and cr 1 Earl Russell), by his 2 w,

Dora MBE, da of Sir Frederick Black, KCB; *b* 16 Nov 1921; *Educ* Dartington Hall, UCLA, Harvard; *m* 1946 (m dis 1955), Susan Doniphan, da of Vachel Lindsay, the American poet; 1 da (and 1 da decd), 1 adopted child; *Heir* half-bro, Hon Conrad Russell; *Career* late RNVR; admin assist Treasury 1947-49; writer; *Recreations* chess; *Style* - The Rt Hon The Earl Russell; Carn Voel, Porthcurno, Cornwall (☎ St Buryan 391)

RUSSELL OF LIVERPOOL, 3 Baron (UK 1919); Simon Gordon Jared Russell; s of Capt Hon Langley Russell MC, s of 2 Baron Russell of Liverpool, CBE, MC, by his 1 w Constance, nee Gordon; suc gf 1981; *b* 30 Aug 1952; *Educ* Charterhouse; *Heir* bro, Adam Russell; *Style* - Rt Hon Lord Russell of Liverpool

RUSSELL, Hon Mrs (Ann Bridget); *née* Parnell; da of late 6 Baron Congleton; *b* 1927; *m* 1947, Major Derek Campbell Russell RE; *Style* - The Hon Mrs Russell; Lyscombe, Piddletrenthide, Dorset

RUSSELL, Rev Arthur Colin; CMG (1957), ED (1941); s of Arthur Walker Russell OBE, WS (d 1967); *b* 2 Nov 1906; *Educ* Harrow, BNC Oxford; *m* 1939, Elma Isobel (d 1967), nee Strachan; 3 da (and 1 decd); *Career* Capt Gold Coast Regiment, Admin Officer Colonial Service 1929-57 (Gold Coast), Parish Minister Church of Scotland Aberlemno Angus 1959-76, district councillor Angus District Council 1977-; *Recreations* hill walking, bridge, chess; *Clubs* Overseas (Edinburgh); *Style* - Rev Arthur Russell, CMG, ED; The Manse, Aberlemno, Forfar, Angus (☎ Aberlemno 265)

RUSSELL, Hon Anthony John Mark; s of 4 Baron Ampthill; *b* 10 May 1952; *Educ* Stowe; *Style* - The Hon Anthony Russell

RUSSELL, Arthur Mervyn; s of Sir Arthur Russell, 6 Bt (d 1964), and hp of half-bro, Sir George Russell, 7 Bt; *b* 7 Feb 1923; *Style* - Arthur Russell Esq

RUSSELL, Adam Mark Haslingden; s of Capt Hon Langley Russell MC, and gs of 2 Baron Russell of Liverpool, CBE, MC; hp to bro, 3 Baron; *b* 23 Oct 1957; *Style* - Adam Russell Esq

RUSSELL, Charles Dominic; s and h of Sir Charles Russell, 3 Bt; *b* 28 May 1956; *Style* - Charles Russell Esq

RUSSELL, Sir Charles Ian; 3 Bt (UK 1916), of Littleworth Corner, Burnham, Co Buckingham; s of Capt Sir Alec Charles Russell, 2 Bt, MC (d 1938); *b* 13 March 1918; *Educ* Beaumont Coll, Univ Coll Oxford; *m* 1947, Rosemary, da of late Maj Sir John Theodore Prestige, of The Court House, Bishopsbourne, Canterbury, 1 s, 1 da; *Heir* s, Charles Russell; *Career* 1939-45 War as Capt RHA (despatches); slr 1947, sr partner in the firm of Charles Russell & Co, Hale Court Lincoln's Inn WC2; *Clubs* Garrick, Army and Navy; *Style* - Sir Charles Russell, Bt; 35 Coleherne Court, Little Boltons, SW5; Hidden House, Strand st, Sandwich, Kent

RUSSELL, Hon Conrad Sebastian Robert; s of 3 Earl Russell, OM, FRS (otherwise Bertrand Russell), by his 3 w, Patricia; hp to half-bro, 4 Earl; *b* 15 April 1937; *Educ* Eton, Merton Coll Oxford; *m* 1962, Elizabeth, da of Horace Sanders, of France; 2 s; *Career* Reader in History Bedford Coll London; *Style* - The Hon Conrad Russell; 29 Hamilton rd, SW19

RUSSELL, Hon Mrs (Catherine Virgina); *née* Ponsonby; da of 2 Baron Ponsonby of Shulbrede (d 1976); *b* 1944; *m* 1972, Ian Macdonald Affleck Russell; 1 da; *Style* - The Hon Mrs Russell; Shulbrede Priory, Lynchmere, Haslemere, Surrey

RUSSELL, Hon (Francis) Damian; 2 s of Baron Russell of Killowen PC; *b* 8 June 1947; *Educ* Beaumont, Trin Coll Dublin; *Recreations* art, books, skiing, shooting; *Style* - The Hon Damian Russell; 91 Camberwell Grove, SE5 (☎ 01 701 5658)

RUSSELL, David Francis Oliphant; CBE (1969), MC (1942), DL (1955); s of Sir David Russell, LLD (d 1956); *b* 9 Sept 1915; *Educ* Sedbergh Sch, St Andrews U; *m* 1945, Catherine Joan, nee Robinson; 4 da; *Career* DSc, LLD; Major 1939-45 (N Africa, Sicily, France); chm Tullis Russell & Co Ltd, Chancellor's Assessor St

Andrews U 1963-75 (remained ct memb), memb Roy Co of Archers 1949, bd of trustees Nat Museum of Antiquities 1966; FRSE 1974; councillor emeritus Nat Trust for Scotland 1976; *Recreations* sailing, fishing, shooting; *Clubs* RAC, Caledonian, New; *Style* - David Russell, CBE, MC, DL; Rossie, Collessie, Fife (☎ Auchtermuchty 300)

RUSSELL, Hon David Whitney Erskine; s and h of 4 Baron Ampthill by his 1 w, Susan (da of Hon Charles Winn, s of 2 Baron St Oswald, JP, DL); *b* 27 May 1947; *Educ* Stowe; *m* 1980, April, da of Paul Arbon, of New York; *Style* - The Hon David Russell

RUSSELL, Hon Lady; Hon (Helen) Elizabeth; *née* Blades; da (twin) of late 1 Baron Ebbisham GBE; *b* 1908; *m* 1939, Adm the Hon Sir Guy Herbrand Edward Russell, GBE, KCB, DSO (s of late 2 Baron Ampthill, GCSI, GCIE and Lady Margaret Lygon, CI, GCVO, GBE, da of 6 Earl Beauchamp); 2 s, 1 da; *Style* - The Hon Lady Russell; Cleve Cottage, Wisborough Green, Sussex

RUSSELL, Hon Mrs (Elizabeth Mary Gwenllian Lloyd); *née* Lloyd Mostyn; da of 4 Baron Mostyn (d 1965); *b* 1929; *m* 1, 1950 (m dis 1957), David Nicholas Goldsmith Duckham; 1 da; m 2, 1957, John Henry Russell; *Style* - The Hon Mrs Russell; 8 The Vale, Chelsea, SW3

RUSSELL, Hon Edward Wriothesley Curzon; OBE (Mil 1946); s of 2 Baron Ampthill, GCSI, GCIE, and Lady Margaret Lygon, CI, GCVO, GBE, 3 da of 6 Earl Beauchamp; *b* 2 June 1901; *Educ* Eton, Trin Cambridge; *m* 1941, Baroness Barbara Korff, da of late Baron Serge Korff, of Russia; 2 da; *Career* formerly man ed Morning Post; sometime Wing Cdr RAFVR; *Style* - The Hon Edward Russell OBE; Pony's Point, Iona, CB 1, Nova Scotia, Canada (☎ 6 112); Tall Pines, Hearthstone Ridge, Route 1, Landrum, S Carolina, 29356, USA

RUSSELL, Hon Mrs (Frances Marian); da (by 1 m) of Lady Sempill, *qv*; *b* 1942; *m* 1976, David Ian Russell, s of Denis Russell, MBE, TD (unc of Sir Charles Russell, 3 Bt, *qv*); *Style* - The Hon Mrs Russell; 25 Eddiscombe rd, SW10

RUSSELL, Hon Georgiana Adeline Villiers; da of 3 Baron Ampthill CBE, by his 3 w, Adeline; *b* 3 Jan 1952; *Style* - The Hon Georgiana Russell

RUSSELL, Sir George Michael; 7 Bt (UK 1812), of Swallowfield, Berkshire; s of Sir Arthur Edward Ian Montagu Russell, 6 Bt (d 1964); *b* 30 Sept 1908; *Educ* Radley; *m* 1936, Joy Francis Bedford, da of late W Mitchell, of Irwin, W Australia; 2 da; *Heir* half-bro, Arthur Russell; *Style* - Sir George Russell, Bt

RUSSELL, Hon John Edward Southwell; s (by 1 m) and h of 26 Baron De Clifford, OBE, TD; *b* 8 June 1928; *Educ* Eton; *m* 1959, Bridget Jennifer, nee Robertson; *Style* - The Hon John Russell; Cliff House, Sheepy, Atherstone, Warwicks

RUSSELL, Hon John Hugo Trenchard; s of 3 Baron Ampthill, CBE, by his 3 w, Adeline; *b* 13 Oct 1950; *Educ* Eton; *m* 1976, Susanna, da of Peter Merriam (s of Sir Laurence Merriam, MC, JP, DL, and Lady Marjory Kennedy, da of 3 Marquess of Ailsa by his 2 w); 2 s; *Clubs* Turf; *Style* - The Hon John Russell; Pitt Cottage, Ringstead Bay, Dorchester, Dorset; 30 Parma cres, SW11

RUSSELL, Hon Mrs Langley (Kiloran Margaret); da of Hon Sir Arthur Howard, KBE, CVO (bro of 3 Baron Strathcona and Mount Royal), by Lady Lorna Baldwin (da of 1 Earl Baldwin of Bewdley, KG, PC - Stanley Baldwin, the PM); *b* 21 July 1926; *m* 1951, Capt Hon Langley Russell, MC (d 1975), only s of 2 Baron Russell of Liverpool, CBE, MC, by his 1 w; 3 s (the 3 Baron; Adam Russell, hp to the Barony; and Daniel Russell), 2 da (Emma, Annabel); *Style* - Hon Mrs Langley Russell; Ash Farm, Stourpaine, Blandford, Dorset

RUSSELL, Hon Leopold Oliver; CBE (1970, OBE Mil 1944), TD (1945); s of 2 Baron Ampthill, GCSI, GCIE, and Lady Margaret Lygon, CI, GCVO, GBE, da of 6

Earl Beauchamp; *b* 26 Jan 1907; *Educ* Eton; *m* 1935 (m dis 1954), Rosemary, da of Capt Charles Wintour RN; *Career* Hon Brig late Beds & Herts Regt (TA); formerly dir BIM; chm Cement & Concrete Assoc 1976-80 (dir-gen 1958), Cement Makers Fedn 1979-, E Anglian RHA 1973-78; *Clubs* Brooks's, Buck's, Beefsteak, Pratt's; *Style* - Brig Hon Leopold Russell, CBE, TD; Old Rectory, Kettlebaston, nr Bildeston, Suffolk (☎ Bildeston 740314); Flat 2, 17 Onslow sq, SW7 (☎ 01 589 0891)

RUSSELL, Lady Mary Katherine; *née* Baillie-Hamilton; da of 12 Earl of Haddington, KT, MC, TD; *b* 1934; *m* 1, 1954 (m dis 1965), John Adrian Bailey; 2 s, 1 da; m 2, 1965, David, s of Brig H E Russell DSO; 1 s, 1 da; *Style* - Lady Mary Russell; 23 Edwardes sq, W8; Combe Manor, nr Newbury, Berks

RUSSELL, Hon Mrs - Hon Nicole; *née* Yarde-Buller; da (by 1 m) of 4 Baron Churston; *b* 11 March 1936; *m* 1, 1958 (m dis 1962), Richard Wilfred Beavoir Berens; 1 s (Thomas), 1 da (Jessica); m 2, 1963, Michael Russell; 2 s (Francis *aet* 15, Alexander *aet* 11), 1 da (Lorna *aet* 17); *Style* - The Hon Mrs Russell; The Chantry House, Wilton, Salisbury, Wilts

RUSSELL, Lady Patricia Ethel; *née* Hamilton-Temple-Blackwood; da of late 2 Marq of Dufferin and Ava; *b* 1902; *m* 1926, Henry Russell (d 1937); *Style* - Lady Patricia Russell; Aumbry Lodge, Eastry, Sandwich, Kent

RUSSELL, Lady Sarah Elizabeth; da of 4 Earl Russell; *b* 16 Jan 1947; *Style* - Lady Sarah Russell

RUSSELL, Thomas; CMG (1980), CBE (1970, OBE 1963); s of Thomas Russell OBE, MC; *b* 27 May 1920; *Educ* Hawick H S, St Andrews U and Peterhouse Cambridge; *m* 1951, Andrée Irma, nee Desfosses; 1 s; *Career* Capt Parachute Regiment (N Africa, Italy); Colonial Adminve Serv Solomon Islands 1948, District Cmmmr 1948-49 & 1954-56, Seconded Colonial Officer 1956-57, Fin Sec 1965, Ch Sec 1970, Acting High Commissioner for Western Pacific, Governor Cayman Islands 1974-; *Recreations* anthropology, archeology; *Clubs* Roy C'wlth Soc; *Style* - Thomas Russell Esq, CMG, CBE; 49 Trafalgar Court, Farnham, Surrey (☎ Farnham 713363); Govt House, Grand Cayman, Cayman Islands, WI

RUSSELL, Hon Valentine Francis Xavier Michael; s of Baron Russell of Killowen PC; *b* 1938; *Educ* Beaumont, Oriel Oxford; *Style* - The Hon Valentine Russell

RUSSELL, Hon Vanessa Mary Linda; da of 4 Baron Ampthill; *b* 18 Sept 1960; *Style* - The Hon Vanessa Russell

RUSSELL, William George Ainge; s of Albert Frederick Russell (d 1953); *b* 12 March 1903; *Educ* privately; *m* 1956, Sylvia Ellen, JP, OStJ, MB, ChB, nee Leather; 1 da; *Career* CA, founder ptnr Russell Durie Kerr Watson & Co 1930-60 (now Spicer & Pegler), chm Glynwed Ltd 1953-70, dir Legal & General Assurance Soc 1959-73 and other cos, chm Ironbridge Gorge Museum Devpt Trust 1972-77, chm of Exec City of Birmingham Symphony Orchestra 1949-65, govr Birmingham U 1953- (memb of cncl 1956-73), pres W Midlands Council for Disabled 1979-; *Recreations* music, literature; *Clubs* Reform, Birmingham Union; *Style* - William Russell Esq; Pinfield House, Barnt Green, Worcs (☎ 021 445 2534)

RUSSELL, William Robert; s of William Andrew Russell (d 1932); *b* 6 Aug 1913; *Educ* Wakefield Central Sch; *m* 1940, Muriel Faith, nee Rolfe; 1 s, 1 da; *Career* chm Shaw Savill & Albion Co Ltd 1968-73, chairman Europe/Australia/Europe Conference 1957 and 1965-70, chm Cncl of European and Japanese Nat Shipowners Association 1969-71 and 1973-75, chm Australian British Trade Assoc 1966-72 and 1975-77, vice-pres 1980-, chm New Zealand/UK Chamber of Commerce & Industry 1979-, chm Bank of New Zealand 1981-; *Recreations* golf, gardening, sailing (yachts: 'Westland Voyager' Moody 36, 'Westland Mistral' Moody 40); *Clubs* Naval, E India Devonshire Sports & Public Schs; *Style* - William Russell Esq;

Westland, Uvedale rd, Limpsfield, Oxted, Surrey

RUSSELL, Hon William Southwell; s (by 1 m) of 26 Baron de Clifford, OBE, TD; *b* 1930; *Educ* Eton, King's Cambridge; *m* 1961, Jean Brodie, nee Henderson; 1 s, 2 da; *Style* - The Hon William Russell; Five Chimneys, Hadlow Down, Uckfield, Sussex

RUTHVEN OF FREELAND, Lady (11 holder of S Lordship, cr 1651); Bridget Helen Ruthven; CBE (Mil 1947); also Dowager Viscountess Monckton of Brenchley; da of 10 Lord Ruthven of Freeland, CB, CMG, DSO, JP, DL (d 1956), by his 1 w, Jean, da of Norman George Lampson, JP, DL (3 s of Sir Curtis Lampson, 1 Bt); petition as heir of line and heir of tailzie of 1 Lord allowed in Lyon Court 1967, and her succession to the Peerage recognised; *b* 27 July 1896; *m* 1, 1918, 11 Earl of Carlisle (m dis 1947, he d 1965); 1 s (12 Earl of Carlisle), 1 da (Lady Carolyn Howard); m 2, 1947, as his 2 w, 1 Viscount Monckton of Brenchley (d 1965); *Heir* s, 12 Earl of Carlisle; *Career* late sr controller ATS & Dir WAC India; formerly on many hosp governing bds & ctees; *Style* - Rt Hon Lady Ruthven of Freeland CBE; 113 Eaton sq, SW1

RUTLAND, 10 Duke of (E 1703); Charles John Robert Manners; CBE (1962); also Earl of Rutland (E 1525), Baron Manners of Haddon (E 1679), Marquess of Granby (E 1703), and Baron Roos of Belvoir (UK 1896); s of 9 Duke of Rutland (d 1940) and Dowager Duchess of Rutland, *qv*; nephew of Lady Diana Cooper and fifteenth in descent from 1 Earl of Rutland's maternal grandmother Anne Plantagenet (sis of Edward IV); *b* 28 May 1919; *Educ* Eton, Trin Cambridge; *m* 1, 1946 (m dis 1956), Anne, da of Maj William Cumming Bell, of Huddersfield; 1 da; m 2, 1958, Frances, da of Charles Sweeny and Margaret Duchess of Argyll, *qv*; 2 s, 1 da (and 1 s decd); *Heir* s, Marquess of Granby; *Career* proprietor of Belvoir Castle (remodelled by Wyatt in 1816) and the late medieval Haddon Hall in Derbyshire; late Capt Gren Gds; patron of 11 livings, owner of 18,000 acres, and possessor of minerals in Leics & Derbys; *Style* - His Grace The Duke of Rutland CBE; Belvoir Castle, Grantham, Lincs; Haddon Hall, Bakewell, Derbys

RUTLAND, Hon Mrs (Joan Claire Florence); *née* Milne; da of 1 Baron Milne, GCB, GCMG, DSO (d 1948); *b* 1907; *m* 1937, as his 2 w, James Hart Rutland (d 1954); *Style* - The Hon Mrs Rutland; Cromwell Cottage, Church st, Alresford, Hants

RUTLAND, Dowager Duchess of; Kathleen; JP; da of Francis Tennant (bro of 1 Baron Glenconner and Margot Asquith); aunt of Laura, Duchess of Marlborough; *m* 1916, 9 Duke of Rutland (d 1940); 3 s, 2 da (10 Duke, Lord John Manners, Lord Roger Manners; Lady Ursula d'Abo, Lady Isabel Throckmorton, *qqv*); *Career* bore Queen's Canopy at Coronation of King George VI; *Style* - Her Grace The Dowager Duchess of Rutland, JP; 21 Wilton st, SW1

RYAN, Derek Gerald; s and h of Sir Derek Ryan, 3 Bt, by his 1 w, Penelope; *b* 25 March 1954; *Style* - Derek Ryan Esq;

RYAN, Sir Derek Gerald; 3 Bt (UK 1919); s of Sir Gerald Ryan, 2 Bt (d 1947), of Chattisham Hall, Ipswich, and Hilda, da of Maj Spencer Herapath; *b* 9 July 1922; *Educ* Harrow, Sandhurst; *m* 1, 1947 (m dis 1971), Penelope, da of Rex Hawkings, of New York; 1 s, 3 da; m 2, 1972, Katja, da of Ernst Best, of Kassel; *Heir* s, Derek Ryan; *Career* late Lt Gren Gds; admin dir Cabot Corpn Boston 1956-72; *Recreations* yachting, vintage cars, music; *Clubs* Bentley Drivers, Rolls Royce, Sloane; *Style* - Sir Derek Ryan, Bt; 4902 Bad Salzuflen 1, Uhlandstrasse 8, W Germany

RYAN, Peter Henry; s of John Ryan, OBE (d 1975); *b* 1 Oct 1930; *Educ* Harrow, Gonville and Caius Cambridge; *m* (dis 1981); 1 s (Mark Peter), 2 da (Nicola Mary, Jocelyn Jane b 1965); *Career* Flight Offr (Nat Serv); exec dir Thomas Tilling Ltd; chm: Cimex Int Ltd, Gascoigne Gp Ltd, Hansen Transmissions Int Ltd, Pilkington's Tiles Ltd, Rest

Assured Ltd; bd of govrs Roy Nat Orthopaedic Hosp; *Recreations* golf, theatre, travel, gardening; *Clubs* RAF, MCC; *Style* - Peter Ryan Esq; Crewe House, Curzon st, W1 (☎ 01 499 4151)

RYCROFT, Cdr Henry Richard; OBE (1960), DSC, RN; s of Sir Richard Nelson Rycroft, 5 Bt (d 1925); hp of n, Sir Richard Rycroft, 7 Bt; *b* 28 Dec 1911; *m* 1941, Penelope Gwendoline, da of late Lt-Col C S B Evans-Lombe; 1 s, 3 da; *Career* RN WW II (despatches), Lt-Cdr 1942 and Cdr 1947; *Style* - Cdr Henry Rycroft, OBE, DSC, RN; Ganderdown, Smugglers Lane, Bosham, Chichester, Sussex

RYCROFT, Sir Richard Newton; 7 Bt (GB 1784), of Calton, Yorkshire; s of Sir Nelson Edward Oliver Rycroft, 6 Bt (d 1958); *b* 23 Jan 1918; *Educ* Winchester, Ch Ch Oxford; *m* 1947, Ann, da of late Hugh Bellingham Smith; 2 da; *Heir* unc, Cdr Henry Rycroft, OBE, DSC, RN; *Career* WW II as Maj on Special Work in Balkans (despatches, Knight of Order of Phoenix of Greece with Swords); is patron of one living; *Style* - Sir Richard Rycroft, Bt; Winalls Wood House, Stuckton, Fordingbridge, Hants

RYDER OF EATON HASTINGS, Baron (Life Peer UK 1975); Don (Sydney Thomas) Ryder; s of John Ryder; *b* 16 Sept 1916; *Educ* Ealing Co G S; *m* 1950, Eileen, da of William Dodds; 1 s, 1 da; *Career* kt 1972; indust advr to Govt 1974-, chm NEB 1975-77; memb Cncl & Bd Fellows BIM 1970-, Cncl UK S Africa Tde Assoc 1974-, Reserve Pension Bd 1973-, Cncl Indust Soc 1971-; late co dir; *Style* - The Rt Hon Lord Ryder of Eaton Hastings; 12-18 Grosvenor gdns, SW1

RYDER OF WARSAW, Baroness (Life Peeress UK 1978); Sue (Margaret Susan) Ryder; CMG (1976), OBE (1957); da of Charles Ryder; *b* 3 July 1923; *Educ* Benenden; *m* 1959, Gp Capt Leonard Cheshire, VC, OM, DSO, DFC; 1 s, 1 da; *Career* social worker, fndr Sue Ryder Home for Sick & Disabled All Age Gps; served WW II SOE & FANY; Tstee Cheshire Fndn; *Style* - The Rt Hon Lady Ryder of Warsaw CMG OBE; Sue Ryder Home, Cavendish, Suffolk

RYDER, Hon Dudley Adrian Conroy; s and h of Visc Sandon; *b* 18 March 1951; *Educ* Eton; *m* 1977, Sarah Nichola Hobhouse, da of Capt Anthony Denys Phillpotts Payne, of Gt Down Farm, Marnhull, Dorset; *Style* - The Hon Dudley Ryder; 5 Tregunter rd, SW10 (☎ 01 373 9276); Sandon Hall, Stafford

RYDER, Hon Jill Patricia; da of Baron Ryder of Eaton Hastings; *b* 1950; *Style* - The Hon Jill Ryder

RYDER, Hon John Stuart Terrick Dudley; s of 6 Earl of Harrowby; *b* 1924; *Educ* Eton; *m* 1946, Dorothy Ethel, da of J T Swallow, of Mansfield; 2 s; *Career* RAF pilot 1942-46; *Style* - The Hon John Ryder; Sandon Hall, Stafford

RYDER, Hon Michael John; s of Baron Ryder of Eaton Hastings; *b* 1953; *Style* - The Hon Michael Ryder

RYDER, Captain Robert Edward Dudley; VC (1942), RN; s of Col Charles Henry Dudley Ryder CB CIE DSO (d 1945); *b* 16 Feb 1908; *Educ* Cheltenham Coll; *m* 1941, Constance Hilaré Myfanwy, da of Rev Lumley Green-Wilkinson; 1 s, 1 da; *Career* Capt RN, Cdr forces at St Nazaire (despatches 1942), attaché Br Embassy Oslo 1948-50, MP (C) Merton and Morden 1950-55, member Br Graham Land Expdn 1934-37, Legion of Honour, Croix de Guerre (France); *Recreations* yacht cruising (owner of yacht 'Watchdog of Wareham'); *Clubs* Royal Cruising; *Style* - Capt Robert Ryder VC RN; The Cedar House, Inkpen, Newbury

RYECART, Lady Marsha (nee Marcia) Mary Josephine; *née* Fitzalan Howard; da of 17 Duke of Norfolk, CB, CBE, MC; *b* 10 March 1953; *m* 1977, Patrick Geoffrey Ryecart; *Career* actress; as Marsha Fitzalan, has appeared in Upstairs Downstairs and, portraying Miss Bingley ("of a respectable family in the north of England; a circumstance more deeply impressed on their memories than that their fortune . . . had been acquired by trade"); in the BBC production of Pride and Prejudice shown most recently in early summer 1981; *Style* - Lady Marsha Ryecart; 5 Dunsany rd, W14

RYLANDS, George Chapman; OBE (1976), TD (1959), DL (1975); s of Lt Col Geoffrey Glazebrook Rylands JP (d 1957); *b* 16 Jan 1924; *Educ* Bromsgrove Sch Worcs; *Career* JP 1959, CC 1969, chm Cheshire TA Assoc 1974, memb North West England & Isle of Man TA & VR Assoc 1974, chm HM Prison Appleton Thorn Cheshire 1960, chm Cheshire Police Authority 1973, pres Runcorn County Constituency Conservative Assoc 1965-68; *Recreations* golf, reading; *Style* - George Rylands Esq OBE TD JP DL; Woodstock, Tarporley rd, Stretton, nr Warrington, Cheshire (☎ Norcott Brook 378)

RYLANDS, Lt-Col Hon Joseph; DFC (1945); s of Joseph T Rylands; *b* 5 Dec 1914; *Educ* St Bede's Coll, Manchester Coll of Tech; *m* 1947, Lena Mary, da of Adam Goss, of Manchester; 3 s, 4 da; *Career* served in WW II (RA), 7 Cheshire HG 1951-55 Lt-Col (Hon); memb E Lancs TA Assoc 1947; v-chm TAVR Assoc NW and IOM; *Recreations* gardening; *Clubs* Manchester; *Style* - Lt-Col Joseph Rylands, DFC; Brynwood, Wilmslow rd, Alderley Edge, Cheshire (☎ 3233)

RYLE, Lt-Col Ian Nigel; OBE (1961), MC (1945), DL (Kent 1976); s of Arthur Ryle (d 1921); *b* 7 April 1914; *Educ* Epsom Coll; *m* 1, 1959 (m dis 1975), Jytte, da of Christian Skovby, of Denmark; 1 da; m 2, 1976, Joanna (d 1977), nee Hawksworth; *Career* Roy Tank Regt 1946, NW Europe 1944-45, Staff Coll 1947, Lt-Col 1956, ret 1964; sec Worcs Territorial & Auxiliary Forces Assoc 1965-68, sec SE Territorial & Auxiliary Volunteer Reserve Assoc 1968-79; *Recreations* foxhunting, shooting, fishing; *Clubs* Army and Navy; *Style* - Lt-Col Ian Ryle, OBE, MC, DL; Scryals Ct, Matfield, Tonbridge, Kent (☎ Brenchley 2499)

S

SAATCHI, Charles; s of Nathan David Saatchi; *b* 6 Sept 1943; *Educ* Christ's Coll Finchley; *m* 1973, Doris Jean, da of Jack Lockhart, of USA; *Career* dir Saatchi & Saatchi Co 1970- (which 1981 bought Age Synergy & 23.2 percent in Garrott Dorland Crawford Hldgs, whose subsids are-Crawfords, Brockie Haslam, Dorland Advertising; latter's clients include Heinz, PO, Dept National Savings, Cadbury Scweppes, Rolls-Royce); *Style* - Charles Saatchi Esq; 12 Langford pl, NW8 (☎ 01 636 5060)

SACHER, Michael Moses; s of Late Harry Sacher; *b* 17 Oct 1917; *Educ* St Paul's Sch and New Coll Oxford (MA); *m* 1942, Audrey Doreen, da of late Sydney Glucksman; 3 s, 2 da; *Career* Maj RASC 1940-46, Liaison Gen Leclerc's HQ Free French N Africa; v-chm and jt md Marks and Spencer Ltd and dir of associated cos; chm Keren Hayesod Discretionary Trust; pres Jt Israel Appeal (UK); Hon V-Pres Zionist Fedn of GB; *Recreations* philately; *Style* - Michael Sacher Esq; 47 Baker st, W1A 1DN (☎ 01 935 4422)

SACHER, Hon Mrs (Rosalind Eleanor Cameron); *née* Corbett; da of 3 Baron Rowallan by his 1 w, Eleanor; *b* 2 Jan 1958; *m* 1977, Jeremy Sacher; *Style* - The Hon Mrs Sacher; 55 Shawfield st, SW3

SACKS, John Harvey; *b* 29 April 1946; *Educ* Perse School Cambridge; *m* 1969, Roberta Judith, 1 s, 2 da; *Career* dir A Arenson (Holdings) Ltd and Arenson International Ltd 1970-, md 1980-; *Recreations* tennis, bridge, walking; *Style* - John Sacks Esq; Barlogan, Priory Drive, Stanmore, Middx (☎ 01 954 2042)

SACKVILLE, 6 Baron (UK 1876); Lionel Bertrand Sackville-West; s of late Hon Bertrand George Sackville-West (bro of 4 Baron and unc of Vita (Victoria) Sackville-West, w of Hon Sir Harold

Nicholson, KCVO, CMG) and Eva, da of late Maj-Gen Inigo Richmond Jones, CB, CVO; suc cous 1965; *b* 30 May 1913; *Educ* Winchester, Magdalen Oxford; *m* 1, 1953, Jacobine Napier (d 1971), da of J R Menzies-Wilson and widow of Capt John Hitchens, RA; 5 da; m 2, 1974, Arlie Roebuck, da of Charles Woodhead, of Romany Rye, Brisbane, Australia, widow of Maj Hugh Dalzell Stewart and formerly w of Maj-Gen Sir Francis Wilfred de Guingand, KBE, CB, DSO; *Heir* bro, Hugh Sackville-West; *Career* proprietor of Knole, one of the most spacious houses in private hands in the country, started by Thomas Bourchier, then Archbp of Canterbury, around 1456 and expanded in the early seventeenth century by Thomas Sackville, to whom it was made over by Elizabeth I; patron of 11 livings, late Coldstream Gds; memb Lloyd's, POW WWII; *Clubs* Brooks's; *Style* - The Rt Hon The Lord Sackville; Knole, Sevenoaks, Kent

SACKVILLE, Lady Arabella Avice Diana; da of 10 Earl De La Warr; *b* 1958; *Style* - Lady Arabella Sackville

SACKVILLE, Hon Mrs (Mary Teresa); *née* Pearson; da (by 1 m) of 3 Viscount Cowdray, TD; *b* 1940; *m* 1980, as his 2 w, Lionel Geoffrey Stopford Sackville; *Style* - The Hon Mrs Sackville

SACKVILLE, Hon Sophia Anne; da (by 1 m) of 6 Baron Sackville; *b* 1957; *Style* - The Hon Sophia Sackville

SACKVILLE, Hon Thomas Geoffrey; s of 10 Earl De La Warr; *b* 1950; *Educ* Eton; *Style* - The Hon Thomas Sackville

SACKVILLE, Hon Victoria Mary; da (by 1 m) of 6 Baron Sackville; *b* 1959; *Style* - The Hon Victoria Sackville

SACKVILLE, Hon William Herbrand Thomas; s of Lord Buckhurst, *qv*; *b* 13 June 1979

SACKVILLE-WEST, Hugh Rosslyn Inigo; MC; s of late Hon Bertrand Sackville-West (bro of 4 Baron Sackville) and Eva, da of Maj-Gen Inigo Richmond Jones, CB, CVO; hp of bro, 6 Baron; *b* 1 Feb 1919; *Educ* Winchester, Magdalen Oxford; *m* 1957, Bridget Eleanor, da of Capt Robert Lionel Brooke Cunliffe, CBE, RN (ggs of 3 Bt); 2 s, 3 da; *Career* late Capt R Tank Regt; ARICS; Adminve Offr N Nigeria 1946-59, Croix de Guerre WWII; *Style* - Hugh Sackville-West Esq, MC; Knole, Sevenoaks, Kent

SAINER, Leonard; s of Archer Sainer; *b* 12 October 1909; *Educ* Central Foundation Sch, UCL, LSE; *Career* solicitor; former senior ptnr with Titmuss Sainer & Webb; chm Sears Holdings Ltd; *Recreations* golf, horse racing; *Style* - Leonard Sainer Esq; 15 Chesterfield House, S Audley St, London WIY 5TB

SAINSBURY, Baron (Life Peer UK 1962); Alan John Sainsbury; s of John Benjamin Sainsbury; *b* 13 Aug 1902; *Educ* Haileybury; *m* 1, 1925, (m dis 1939), Doreen Davan Adams; 3 s; m 2, 1944, Anne Elizabeth, da of Paul Lewy; 1 da; *Career* jt pres J Sainsbury Ltd 1967 (joined 1921, former chm), contested (Lib) 1929, 1931, 1935, subsequently joined Lab Pty; *Style* - The Rt Hon The Lord Sainsbury; J Sainsbury Ltd, Stamford House, Stamford st, SE1

SAINSBURY, Hon Sir John Davan; s (by 1 m) of Baron Sainsbury; *b* 2 Nov 1927; *Educ* Stowe; *m* 1963, Anya Linden; 2 s, 1 da; *Career* chm J Sainsbury Ltd 1969 (dir 1958-, v-chm 1967-69); dir: Roy Opera House Covent Garden 1969-, chm Friends of Covent Garden 1969-, dir: The Economist 1972-80, Roy Opera House Tst 1974-; tstee Nat Gallery 1976-; kt 1980; *Clubs* Garrick; *Style* - The Hon Sir John Sainsbury; J Sainsbury Ltd, Stamford House, Stamford st, SE1 (☎ 01 921 6000)

SAINSBURY, Jeffrey Paul; s of Capt W R Sainsbury; *b* 27 June 1943; *Educ* Cardiff H S, Cowbridge G S; *m* 1967, Janet Elizabeth, nee Hughes; 1 s, 1 da; *Career* chartered accountant; Dep Lord Mayor City of Cardiff 1977-78; *Clubs* Cardiff & County, Cardiff Exchange; *Style* - Jeffrey Sainsbury Esq; 34 Heol Iscoed, Rhiwbina, Cardiff (☎ 0222 64489)

SAINSBURY, Sir Robert; s of late John Benjamin Sainsbury and bro of Baron

Sainsbury; *b* 24 Oct 1906; *Educ* Haileybury, Pembroke Coll Cambridge; *m* 1937, Lisa Ingeborg, nee Van den Bergh; 1 s, 2 da (and 1 decd); *Career* joined J Sainsbury 1930, dir 1934, jt gen man 1938, dep chm 1956, chm 1967, jt pres 1969, former tstee and chm Tate Gallery, memb Art Panel of Arts Council to 1974, kt 1967; *Style* - Sir Robert Sainsbury; 5 Smith sq, SW1 (☎ 01 222 1752)

SAINSBURY, Hon Simon David Davan; s (by 1 m) of Baron Sainsbury; *b* 1930; *Career* v-chm and dir J Sainsbury Ltd; *Style* - The Hon Simon Sainsbury; J Sainsbury Ltd, Stamford House, Stamford st, SE1

SAINSBURY, Hon Timothy Alan Davan; MP (C) Hove 1973-; s (by 1 m) of Baron Sainsbury; *b* 11 June 1932; *Educ* Eton, Worcester Oxford; *m* 1961, Susan Mary Mitchell; 2 s, 2 da; *Career* dir J Sainsbury Ltd 1962-, PPS to Sec of State for Environment 1979-; *Style* - The Hon Timothy Sainsbury, MP; House of Commons, SW1

SAINT, Lady Josephine Sylvia Rose; *née* Chetwynd-Talbot; da (by 1 m) of late 21 Earl of Shrewsbury and Waterford; *b* 1940; *m* 1965, Stafford Antony Saint; 1 s, 2 da; *Style* - Lady Josephine Saint; The Woodman, Sandridge, St Albans, Herts

SAINT BRIDES, Baron (Life Peer UK 1977); John Morrice Cairns James; GCMG (1975, KCMG 1962, CMG 1957), CVO (1961), MBE (1944); s of late Lewis Cairns James; *b* 30 April 1916; *Educ* Bradfield, Balliol Oxford; *m* 1, 1948, Elizabeth Margaret Roper (d 1966), da of late Francis Piesse; 1 s, 2 da; m 2, 1968, Mme Geneviève Sarasin, da of late Robert Henri Houdin; *Career* Perm Under-Sec of State for Commonwealth Affairs 1968, Br High Cmmr in India 1968-71, in Australia 1971-76; King of Arms Order of St Michael and St George 1975-; *Style* - The Rt Hon The Lord Saint Brides, GCMG, CVO, MBE; Cap Saint-Pierre, 83990 St Tropez, France (☎ 97 14 75)

SALAMAN, Frederick Nicholas Paul; s of Sebastian Max Alexander Clement Salaman (d 1976); *b* 4 Feb 1936; *Educ* Radley and Trinity Oxford; *m* 1960, (m dis 1974), Elisabeth Cecily, da of Francis Sclater; 2 da; *Career* advertising and marketing; dir Connell May & Steavenson Ltd 1976-81 and London Herb & Spice Co Ltd 1978-; *Style* - Frederick Salaman Esq; Flat 9, 92 Elm Park gdns, SW 10 (☎ 01 352 8060)

SALAMAN, Hon Mrs (Nancy Adelaide); da of late 1 Viscount Samuel, GCB, OM, GBE, PC; *b* 1906; *Educ* Oxford U; *m* 1935, Arthur Gabriel Salaman, MB, BCh, MRCS, LRCP; 2 s, 2 da; *Style* - The Hon Mrs Salaman; 1 Belmont Hill, Newport, Saffron Walden, Essex

SALE, Hon Mrs (Ismay Hilda Margaret); *née* FitzRoy; da of late 4 Baron Southampton and late Lady Hilda Mary Dundas, da of 1 Marquess of Zetland; *b* 1908; *m* 1928, Brig Walter Morley Sale, CVO, OBE, late Roy Horse Guards (d 1976); 1 s, 1 da; *Style* - The Hon Mrs Sale; Woodlands, Worlds End rd, Saxtead, Woodbridge, Suffolk

SALEM, Daniel Laurent Manuel; s of Raphael Salem (d 1963); *b* 29 Jan 1925; *Educ* Harvard; *m* 1950, Marie-Pierre, nee Arachtingi; *Career* chm Condé Nast Int Inc 1970-, chm Condé Nast Publications Ltd 1967-; also dir of various other companies; *Recreations* music, chess, bridge, backgammon, golf; *Clubs* White's, Harvard (New York City); *Style* - Daniel Salem Esq; 3 Ennismore gdns, SW7

SALFORD, Bishop of (RC, cr 1850) 1964-; Rt Rev Thomas Holland; DSC (1944); s of late John Holland, of Southport; *b* 11 June 1908; *Educ* Upholland Coll Wigan, Pontifical English Coll Valladolid Spain (PhD), Pontifical Gregorian U Rome (DD); *Career* ordained 1933; former prof English Colls Valladolid, Spain and Lisbon, Portugal; Co-Adjutor Bp of Portsmouth 1960-64; *Recreations* poetry, music, sailing, cricket; *Style* - The Rt Rev The Bishop of Salford, DSC; Wardley Hall, Worsley, Manchester M28 5ND

SALISBURY, 6 Marquess of (GB 1789); Robert Edward Peter Gascoyne-

Cecil; DL (Dorset 1974); also Baron Cecil (E 1603), Viscount Cranborne (E 1604), Earl of Salisbury (E 1605); s of 5 Marquess, KG, PC, FRS, Actg Foreign Sec 1953 (d 1972, himself gs of the 3 Marquess and celebrated PM, who served under Disraeli as Foreign Sec but was privately scathing about his chief; the 3 Marquess was in his turn eighth in descent from Lord Treasurer Robert Cecil (Elizabeth I's 'little man', James I's 'little beagle' & a yr s of the Tudor statesman Lord Burghley); (the present) Lord Salisbury's gggggggf, the 4 Earl of Salisbury, showed a maladroitness (& friendliness to Papistry) untypical of the Cecils by converting to Catholicism some two or three months before The Prince of Orange (William III) arrived in 1688 and on hearing the news cursed "O God O God O God I turn'd too soon, I turn'd too soon") and Elizabeth Vere, da of late Rt Hon Lord Richard Cavendish, CB, CMG, PC, bro of 9 Duke of Devonshire; is 2 cous of Rt Hon Maurice Macmillan, PC, MP; *b* 24 Oct 1916; *Educ* Eton; *m* 1945, Marjorie Olein, da of Capt the Hon Valentine Maurice Wyndham-Quin, RN, s of 5 Earl of Dunraven and Mount-Earl and Lady Eva Constance Aline, da of 6 Earl of Mayo; 4 s (and 2 s decd), 1 da; *Heir* s, Viscount Cranborne, MP; *Career* Capt Gren Gds, MP (C) W Bournemouth 1950-54; patron of seven livings; *Also* 1 cous of 11 Duke of Devonshire and 5 Baron Harlech, also n of Lord David Cecil, the literary critic; *Style* - The Most Hon The Marquess of Salisbury, DL; Manor House, Cranborne, Dorset; Hatfield House, Hatfield, Herts

SALISBURY, Elizabeth, Marchioness of; Elizabeth Vere; da of late Col the Rt Hon Lord Richard Frederick Cavendish, CB, CMG, PC (s of late Rt Hon the Lord Edward Cavendish, PC, MP, s of 7 Duke of Devonshire) and Lady Moyra de Vere Beauclerk, da of 10 Duke of St Albans; *b* 1897; *m* 1915, 5 Marquess (d 1972); *Style* - The Most Hon Elizabeth, Marchioness of Salisbury; Hatfield House, Hatfield; Cranborne Lodge, Cranborne, Dorset

SALISBURY, 76 Bishop of (see founded Sherborne 705) 1981-; Rt Rev John Austin Baker; s of George Baker; *b* 11 Jan 1928; *Educ* Marlborough, Oriel Oxford; *m* 1974, Gillian Leach; *Career* Canon Westminster 1973-81, Sub-Dean & Lector Theologiae 1978-81; Rector St Margaret's Westminster & Speaker's Chaplain 1978-81; Old Testament scholar & specialist in Continental theology; patron of 63 livings & 45 shared, the Precentorship, Chllrship, Treasureship and Succentorship of Salisbury and other Canonries, also Archdeaconries of Dorset, Sarum, Wilts and Sherborne; the see had Wells and Exeter detached 905, removed to Old Sarum 1075, and to Salisbury 1220; *Style* - The Rt Rev The Bishop of Salisbury; Bishop's Office, Church House, Crane st, Salisbury, Wilts; South Canonry, The Close, Salisbury, Wilts (☎ 4031)

SALMON, Baron (Life Peer UK 1972); Cyril Barnet Salmon; PC (1964), JP (Kent 1949); s of late Montagu Salmon; *b* 28 Dec 1903; *Educ* Mill Hill, Pembroke Coll Cambridge; *m* 1, 1929, Rencie (d 1942), da of late Sidney Gorton Vanderfelt, OBE; 1 s, 1 da; m 2, 1946, Jean, Lady Morris, da of late Lt-Col David Edward Maitland-Makgill-Crichton (ggggs of 6 Earl of Lauderdale) and former w of 2 Baron Morris; *Career* barr 1925, QC 1945, a Lord Justice of Appeal 1964-72, a Lord of Appeal in Ordinary 1972-80, kt 1957; *Style* - The Rt Hon The Lord Salmon PC JP; Manwood House, Sandwich, Kent (☎ 2244)

SALMON, Hon David Neville Cyril; s (by 1 m) of Baron Salmon (Life Peer); *b* 1935; *m* 1, 1958 (m dis 1972), Heather Turner-Laing; m 2, 1973, Sarah Harrison; *Style* - The Hon David Salmon; Holne Cottage, Holne, nr Ashburton, Devon

SALMON, Baroness - Jean Beatrice; da of late Lt-Col David Edward Maitland-Makgill-Crichton; *b* 1912; *m* 1, 1933 (m diss 1946, he d 1975), 2 Baron Morris; m 2, 1946, Baron Salmon (Life Peer); *Style* - The Rt Hon the Lady Salmon; Manwood House, Sandwich, Kent

SALMON, Neil Lawson; s of Julius Salmon (d 1940); *b* 17 Feb 1921; *Educ* Malvern, Institut Minerva Zürich; *m* 1944, Yvonne Hélène, da of Arthur Danziger Isaacs; 1 s, 1 da; *Career* dep chm J Lyons & Co Ltd 1972 (gen man 1946, dir 1965, md 1967), dir Allied Breweries Ltd 1978-; *Recreations* music, food, wine, puzzles; *Clubs* Savile; *Style* - Neil Salmon Esq; (business) Cadby Hall, W14 (☎ 01 603 2040)

SALMON, Col William Alexander; OBE (1956); s of Lt-Col William Salmon, Indian Army (d 1962); *b* 16 Nov 1910; *Educ* Haileybury, RMC Sandhurst; *m* 1939, Jean Barbara, da of late Rt Rev John Macmillan, OBE, DD (Bp of Guildford); 1 s, 2 da; *Career* 2 Lt HLI 1930, regular army offr 1930-1963, Col GS SHAPE 1956-59, War Office 1959-63; civil servant 1963-77, Assistant Ecclesiastical Secretary to Lord Chancellor and to PM 1964-77; *Recreations* shooting, fishing, writing, gardening; *Clubs* Army & Navy; *Style* - Col William Salmon, OBE; Little Thorpe, 220 Forest rd, Tunbridge Wells, Kent (☎ 265262)

SALOBREÑA, 1 Marquès de (Spain 1981 by King Juan Carlos); Andres Segovia; *b* 18 Feb 1894; *m* 1; 1 s, 1 da; m 2, 1962, Emilia; 1 s; *Career* guitarist; memb Sp Roy Acad of Fine Arts 1978; Hon DMus Oxon, Hon Doctorate Granada U 1981; *Style* - Marquès de Salobreña; c/o Ibbs & Tillett, 450-452 Edgware rd, W2 (☎ 01 262 2864)

SALT, Sir Anthony Houlton; 6 Bt (UK 1869) of Saltaire, Yorks; s of late Cdr Sir John Salt, 4 Bt, RN; suc bro, Sir David Salt, 5 Bt 1978; *b* 15 Sept 1931; *Educ* Stowe; *m* 1957, Prudence Meath Baker; 4 da; *Heir* bro, Patrick Salt; *Career* memb Stock Exchange, ptnr Hill Chaplin & Co (Stockbrokers) 1957, chm Williams de Broe Hill Chaplin & Co 1981-; *Style* - Sir Anthony Salt, Bt; Dellow House, Ugley Green, Bishop's Stortford, Herts (☎ Bishop's Stortford 813141)

SALT, Anthony William David; s of late Lt-Col Sir Thomas Henry Salt, 3 Bt, JP, DL, and hp of bro, Sir Michael Salt, 4 Bt; *b* 5 Feb 1950; *Educ* Milton Abbey; *m* 1978, Olivia Anne, da of Martin Morgan Hudson; 1 s (Edward James Stevenson Salt, b 11 June 1981); *Career* bank official; *Recreations* veteran/vintage cars; *Clubs* Vintage Car of GB; *Style* - Anthony Salt Esq; 1 Titchwell rd, London SW18 (☎ 01 874 8888)

SALT, Sir (Thomas) Michael John; 4 Bt (UK 1899) of Standon, and of Weeping Cross, Co Stafford; s of Lt-Col Sir Thomas Henry Salt (d 1965); *b* 7 Nov 1946; *Educ* Eton; *m* 1971, Caroline, da of Henry Hildyard; 1 da; *Heir* bro, Anthony Salt; *Style* - Sir Michael Salt, Bt; Shillingstone House, Shillingstone, Dorset

SALT, Meriel, Lady; Meriel Sophia Wilmot; da of late Capt Berkeley Cole Wilmot Williams; *b* 11 Sept 1921; *m* 1943, Sir Thomas Henry Salt, 3 Bt (d 1965); 2 s, 2 da; *Style* - Meriel, Lady Salt; Shillingstone House, Shillingstone, Dorset

SALT, Patrick MacDonnell; younger s of Cdr Sir John William Titus Salt, 4 Bt (d 1953); *b* 25 Sept 1932; *Educ* Stowe; *m* 1976, Ann Elizabeth Mary, nee Maclachlan; *Career* marine underwriter Lloyd's, dir Grayston Rust & Salt Ltd; *Recreations* fishing, gardening; *Clubs* City University; *Style* - Patrick Salt Esq; Hillwatering Farm House, Langham, Bury St Edmunds, Suffolk (☎ Walsham le Willows 367)

SALTOUN, Lady (20 holder of title; S 1445); Flora Marjory; *née* Fraser; Chief of the Clan of Fraser; da of 19 Lord Saltoun, MC (d 1979) and Dorothy, da of Sir Charles Welby, 5 Bt, CB, by Maria, sis of 4 Marquess of Bristol; *b* 18 Oct 1930; *Educ* St Mary's Wantage; *m* 1956, Capt Alexander Ramsay of Mar, Gren Gds, ret, s of late Adm Hon Sir Alexander Ramsay, GCVO, KCB, DSO (s of 13 Earl of Dalhousie) and Lady Patricia Ramsay (da of HRH 1 Duke of Connaught and Strathearn (3 s of Queen Victoria) who on her marriage renounced by Roy permission the style and title of HRH and Princess and adpoted that of Lady); 3 da; *Heiress* da, Hon Mrs Nicolson; *Clubs* Turf; *Style* - The Rt Hon The Lady Saltoun; Flat 4, 21 Cadogan gdns, SW 3; Cairnbulg Castle, Fraserburgh, Aberdeenshire

SALTOUN, Dorothy, Lady; Dorothy Geraldine; da of Sir Charles Glynne Earle Welby, 5 Bt, CB and Lady Mary, da of Lord Augustus Hervey and sis of 4 Marquess of Bristol; *b* 1890; *m* 1920, Lord

Saltoun, MC (19 in line, d 1979); 1 da; *Style* - The Rt Hon Dorothy, Lady Saltoun; Cross Deep, Twickenham, Middx (☎ 01 892 1809)

SALUSBURY-TRELAWNY, Sir John Barry; 13 Bt (E 1628) of Trelawny, Cornwall; s of Sir John William Robin Maurice Salusbury-Trelawny, 12 Bt (d 1956, eighth in descent from Brigadier-General Henry Trelawny, himself younger brother of The Rt Rev Sir John Trelawny, 3 Bt; the latter's imprisonment as one of the seven Bishops (he was successively Bishop of Bristol, Exeter and Winchester) by James II prompted his fellow West Countrymen to demand "And have they fixed the where and when? And shall Trelawny die? Here's twenty thousand Cornish men Will know the reason why" (Only the first line is Hawker's very own). James II's gggggg grandmother's 1 husb, Henry V, was better disposed towards the Trelawnys, for under a figure of him at Launceston was formerly inscribed a couplet "He that will do ought for me, Let him love well Sir John Tirlawnee"); *b* 4 Sept 1934; *m* 1958, Carol Knox, da of C F K Watson; 1 s, 3 da; *Heir* s, John Salusbury-Trelawny; *Career* company director; dir Korn Ferry International Inc 1978-; *Style* - Sir John Salusbury-Trelawny, Bt; The Grange, Grange Road, Saltwood, near Hythe, Kent (☎ 0303 66476)

SALUSBURY-TRELAWNY, John William Richard; s and h of Sir John Salusbury-Trelawny, 13 Bt; *b* 30 March 1960; *Style* - John Salusbury-Trelawny Esq

SALUSBURY-TRELAWNY, Dowager Lady; Rosamund Helen; da of late Arthur Reed Ropes (Adrian Ross); *m* 1937, as his 2 w, Sir John William Robin Maurice Salusbury-Trelawny, 12 Bt (d 1956); *Style* - Dowager Lady Salusbury-Trelawny; 3 The Orchards, Pellingbridge, Scaynes Hill, Sussex (☎ Scaynes Hill (STD Code 044 486) 241)

SAMENGO-TURNER, Fabian Pius; s of the late Joseph Frederick Samengo-Turner; *b* 11 Feb 1931; *Educ* St Benedict's Sch; *m* 1953, Maureen Ursula O'Connor; 3 s, 1 da; *Career* Lt Intelligence Corps; md Laurentide Financial Trust 1962-67, Citibank Financial Trust 1968-72, (chm 1973-74), exec dir Citicorp International Bank Ltd 1975-; *Recreations* squash, tennis, motor racing, sailing (yacht: 'Nicajejo'; *Clubs* RAC, Royal Southern Yacht, Overseas Bankers; *Style* - Fabian Samengo-Turner Esq; Chapel Row Farm, Bucklebury, Reading, Berks

SAMPSON, Maj Richard Claude; s of Evelyn Sampson (d 1923); *b* 5 May 1916; *Educ* St Hugh's Prep Sch, privately, Exeter Coll Oxford; *m* 1947, Rosemary Anne, nee Collingridge; 1 s, 1 da; *Career* charity consultant; Wiltshire Regt 1937, served WW II with KAR, local Lt-Col Br Mil Mission Ethiopia (advsr to Hailé Selassie on Officer Training); personal staff officer and ADC to Govr and C-in-C Nyasaland, Supt of Colonial Police, Field Force & Instruction Mau-Mau Campaign E Africa (ret 1969); *Recreations* shooting, gardening, history and labradors; *Clubs* Naval & Military, Norfolk; *Style* - Maj Richard Sampson; Church Farmhouse, Mileham, Norfolk ; National Westminster Bank, London st, Norwich

SAMUEL, 3 Viscount (UK 1937); David Herbert Samuel; s of 2 Viscount (d 1978, himself gs of Edwin Samuel, whose yr bro Montagu was cr Lord Swaythling; hence the present (3) Viscount Samuel is 2 cous once removed of 3 Baron Swaythling); *b* 8 July 1922; *Educ* Balliol Oxford, Hebrew U (PhD); *m* 1, 1950 (m dis 1957), Esther Berelowitz; 1 da; m 2, 1960 (m dis 1978), Rinna Dafni, nee Grossman; 1 da; m 3, 1980, Veronika Engelhardt Grimm; *Heir* bro, Hon Dan Samuel; *Career* dep chm Lawrence Radiation Lab California U 1965-66; Sherman Prof of Physical Chemistry in Isotope Dept 1967-; dir Centre for Neurosciences and Behavioural Research Weizmann Institute Rehovot Israel 1978-; memb Cncl Israel Chemical Society 1977-; *Style* - The Rt Hon The Viscount Samuel; c/o Isotope Dept, Weizmann Institute of Science, Rehovot, Israel

SAMUEL OF WYCH CROSS, Baron (Life Peer UK 1972); Harold Samuel; s of late Vivian Samuel; *b* 23 April 1912; *Educ* Mill Hill and Coll of Estate Management; *m* 1936, Edna, da of Harry Nedas; 2 da; *Career* chm The Land Securities Investment Trust Ltd, The Central London Housing Trust for the Aged; former memb of Covent Garden Market Authority, v-pres British Heart Foundation; kt 1963, FRICS; *Style* - The Rt Hon The Lord Samuel of Wych Cross; Wych Cross Place, Forest Row, Sussex; 75 Avenue rd, Regent's Park, NW8

SAMUEL, Hon Anthony Gerald; s of 2 Viscount Bearsted, MC; *b* 18 Feb 1917; *Educ* Eton, New Coll Oxford; *m* 1, 1946, Mary (m dis 1961), da of John Higgins, CIE, of Alford, Lincs; 2 da; m 2, 1962 (m dis 1966), Jenifer, da of Maj Kenneth Puckle, of Farnham; m 3, 1966, Mercy, da of M Haystead; *Career* Lt WW II; *Clubs* White's; *Style* - The Hon Anthony Samuel; Arndilly House, Craigellachie, Banffshire (☎ 232); 29 St Leonard's ter, SW1 (☎ 01 730 9089)

SAMUEL, Anthony John Fulton; s and h of Sir John Samuel, 5 Bt; *b* 13 Oct 1972

SAMUEL, Hon Dan Judah; s of late 2 Viscount Samuel and hp of bro, 3 Viscount; *b* 25 March 1925; *Educ* Rugby, Balliol Oxford, Sch of Advanced Internat Studies (Johns Hopkins) Washington DC; *m* 1, 1957 (m dis 1977), Esther Naomi, da of Max Gordon, of Johannesburg; 1 s (Jonathan b 1965), 2 da (Lia b 1961, Maia b 1962); m 2, 1981, Heather, nee Cumming; *Career* late Maj Yorks Hussars; Gp Personnel Co-ordinator Shell Internat Chemical Co London 1976-77, Regional Co-ordinator Western Hemisphere 1977-, dir Shell Internat Petroleum Co 1973-, UK Tstee Asian Inst Technology; *Recreations* sailing (yacht: 'Limajo'); *Clubs* Hurlingham, Chichester Yacht; *Style* - The Hon Dan Samuel; 812 Park av, New York; The Barns, Old Mill Farm, Sidlesham, Sussex; 5 Chesilton rd, SW6

SAMUEL, Hon Mrs (Elizabeth Adelaide); da of late Baron Cohen (Life Peer); *b* 1919; *m* 1, 1940, Capt Arthur John Pearce-Serocold, Welsh Gds (Supp Res) (ka 1942); m 2, 1946, Hon Peter Montefiore Samuel, MC, TD (s of late 2 Visc Bearsted); 2 s, 1 da; *Style* - The Hon Mrs Samuel; 12 Rutland ct, SW7; Farley Hall, Farley Hill, Reading, Berks; Phones, Newtonmore, Inverness-shire

SAMUEL, Hon Godfrey Herbert; CBE (1969); s of late 1 Viscount Samuel, GCB, OM, GBE, PC; *b* 12 Jan 1904; *Educ* Westminster, Balliol Oxford; *Career* architect in private practice 1932-40; Hon Lt-Col RE, FRIBA (ret); an assoc of Town Planning Institute, Sec of Roy Fine Art Cmmn 1948-69; *Clubs* Athenaeum, Reform; *Style* - The Hon Godfrey Samuel, CBE; 15 Hans pla, SW1 (☎ 01 584 7107)

SAMUEL, Hadassah, Viscountess; Hadassah; da of Judah Goor, of Tel Aviv; *m* 1920, 2 Viscount (d 1978); 2 s; *Style* - The Rt Hon Hadassah, Viscountess Samuel; 15 Rashba rd, Jerusalem, Israel

SAMUEL, Hon Judith; da (by 1 m) of 3 Viscount Samuel; *b* 1951; *Style* - The Hon Judith Samuel

SAMUEL, Sir Jon Michael Glen; 5 Bt (UK 1898) of Nevern Square, St Mary Abbots, Kensington; s of Sir John Samuel, 4 Bt (d 1962); *b* 25 Jan 1944; *Educ* Radley, London U; *m* 1966, Antoinette Sandra, da of late Capt Anthony Hewitt RE; 2 s; *Heir* s, Anthony Samuel; *Career* chm Electric Auto Corporation (USA) 1978-; *Style* - Sir Jon Samuel, Bt; Box No 904, Freeport, Grand Bahama

SAMUEL, Michael John; 2 s of Hon Peter Samuel, himself 2 s of 2 Viscount Bearsted MC; *b* 2 Nov 1952; *Educ* Eton; *m* 1980, Julia, da of James Guinness, *qv*; 1 da (b 1981); *Style* - Michael Samuel Esq

SAMUEL, Hon Naomi Rachel; da (by 2 m) of 3 Viscount Samuel; *b* 1962; *Style* - The Hon Naomi Samuel

SAMUEL, Hon Philip Ellis Herbert; s of late 1 Viscont Samuel, GCB, OM, GBE, PC; *b* 1900; *Educ* Westminster, Trin Cambridge; *Career* Hong Kong Vol Defence Corps (prisoner) 1939-45; *Clubs* Royal Institution, Roy Overseas League,

Victory Ex-Services; *Style* - The Hon Philip Samuel

SAMUEL, Hon Peter Montefiore; MC (1943), TD; s of 2 Viscount Bearsted, MC; hp of bro, 3 Viscount Bearsted, TD, DL; *b* 9 Dec 1911; *Educ* Eton, New Coll Oxford; *m* 1, 1939 (m dis 1942), Deirdre du Barry, da of Thomas Marshall du Lavey, of Tiffenden Manor, High Halden, Kent; m 2, 1946, Hon Elizabeth, da of late Baron Cohen, PC (Life Peer), and widow of Capt Arthur Pearce-Serocold, Welsh Gds; 2 s, 1 da; *Career* Maj Warwicks Yeomanry; dep chm Hill Samuel Gp 1935-; chm Dylon Internat 1958-, Hill Samuel & Co (Ireland) 1964-; dir: Shell T'port & Trading 1935-, Samuel Properties 1961-, Trades Union Unit Tst Managers 1961-, Gen Consolidated Investment Tst 1975-; chm Cncl Roy Free Hosp of Medicine; chm Mayborn Products 1946-; *Recreations* golf, fishing, shooting; *Clubs* White's; *Style* - The Hon Peter Samuel, MC, TD; Farley Hall, Farley Hill, nr Reading, Berks (☎ Eversley 733242); Flat 12 Rutland Court, SW7

SAMUELSON, Sir Francis Henry Bernard; 4 Bt (UK 1884) of Bodicote, Banbury, Oxon; s of Sir Francis Samuelson, 3 Bt (d 1946); *b* 22 Feb 1890; *Educ* Eton, Trin Cambridge; *m* 1913, Margaret Kendall, da of late H Kendall Barnes of Orpington, Kent; 3 s, 1 da (and 1 decd); *Heir* s, Michael Samuelson; *Career* Capt Yorkshire Hussars Yeo WWI; *Style* - Sir Francis Samuelson, Bt; Midway House, Partridge Green, Sussex

SAMUELSON, (Bernard) Michael (Francis); s and h of Sir Francis Samuelson, 4 Bt; *b* 17 Jan 1917; *Educ* Eton; *m* 1952, Janet Amy, da of Lt-Cdr Laurence Garrett Elkington; 2 s, 2 da; *Career* Lt RA, Burma 1939-45 (despatches); *Style* - Michael Samuelson Esq

SAMWORTH, David Chetwode; s of Frank Samworth; *b* 25 June 1935; *Educ* Uppingham Sch, Harvard Business Sch; *m* 1969, Rosemary Grace, nee Hobbs; 1 s (Mark b 1970), 3 da (Mary b 1972, Susannah b 1975, Victoria b 1977); *Career* Lt Sudan and Cyprus; chm Meat and Livestock Cmmn appointed 1980, chm Pork Farms Ltd 1968-, dir Northern Foods Ltd 1978-, v-chm Leics Number 3 Hosp Management Ctee 1970-74, memb Cncl of Nottingham U 1975-76, v-chm governing body Uppingham Sch 1980-, *Recreations* swimming, tennis, hunting; *Style* - David Samworth Esq; Markham House, Thorpe Satchville, Melton Mowbray, Leics

SANDELL, Kenneth Edwin; s of Ernest Arthur Sandell (d 1980); *b* 28 April 1929; *Educ* Tollington Sch; *m* 1960, Lillian Rose, nee Buckingham; 1 s (Mark Christopher b 1966), 1 da (Joanne Leslie b 1970); *Career* served Suez 1948-49; insurance broker; dir: Fenchurch Marine Brokers Ltd 1971, Samson Menzies Ltd 1972, Fenchurch Group Int Ltd 1979; *Recreations* reading, youth work; *Style* - Kenneth Sandell Esq; 4 Cranley rd, Westcliff-on-Sea, Essex (☎ 0702 42906)

SANDEMAN, Hon Mrs (Phyllis Elinor); *née* Legh; da of 2 Baron Newton PC (d 1942); *b* 1895; *m* 1918, Henry Gerard Walter Sandeman (d 1953); 2 da; *Style* - The Hon Mrs Sandeman; The Mill House, Melton, Woodbridge, Suffolk

SANDEMAN-ALLEN, Lady Margaret Judith; *née* Marquis; TD; da of 1 Earl of Woolton, CH, PC, JP, DL, by his 1 w, Maud; *b* 21 Aug 1917; *m* 1945, Maj John Sandeman-Allen RA, s of Col J Sandeman-Allen, MC, OBE, TD; 1 s, 2 da (and 1 s decd); *Style* - Lady Margaret Sandeman-Allen TD; 12/85 Cadogan gdns, SW3 (☎ 01 589 0542)

SANDERSON OF AYOT, Barony of (UK 1960); *see* Sanderson, Dr Alan

SANDERSON, Hon Andrea; da of Dr Alan Sanderson, *qv*; *b* 1964; *Style* - The Hon Andrea Sanderson

SANDERSON, Dr Alan Lindsay; s (twin) of 1 Baron Sanderson of Ayot MC (UK 1960); suc father 15 Aug 1971 and disclaimed his peerage for life 28 Sept 1971; *b* 12 Jan 1931; *Educ* Uppingham; *m* 1959, Gertrud, da of Herman Boschler; 1 s, 4 da; *Career* MB, BS London, MRCP London; *Style* - Dr Alan Sanderson; 2 Caroline close, W2 (☎ 01 229 8533)

SANDERSON, Sir (Frank Philip) Bryan; 2 Bt (UK 1920), of Malling Deanery, South Malling, Co Sussex; s of Sir Frank Bernard Sanderson, 1 Bt (d 1965); *b* 18 Feb 1910; *Educ* Stowe, Pembroke Coll Oxford; *m* 1933, Annette Irene Caroline (d 1967), da of late Col Korab Laskowski, of Warsaw; 2 s, 1 da; *Heir* s, Frank Sanderson; *Career* memb Lloyd's, chm Humber Fish Manure Co Ltd (Hull); *Style* - Sir Bryan Sanderson, Bt; Lychgate Cottage, Scaynes Hill, Haywards Heath, W Sussex

SANDERSON, Sir Charles Russell; *b* 30 April 1933; *Educ* Trinity Coll Glenalmond, Bradford U; *m* 1958, Frances Elizabeth; 4 children; *Career* company dir 1980-, ptnr Wool & Yarn Merchants 1958-, vice chairman National Union of Con Assocs 1979-81, chm 1981-; instrumental in unifying Scottish Unionist organisation with English Conservative one based in London, pres Scottish Con Unionist Assoc 1977-79; kt 1981; *Recreations* golf, amateur operatics; *Clubs* Caledonian, Hon Co Edinburgh Golfers, Luffness New Golf; *Style* - Sir Charles Sanderson; Beckettsfield, Bowden, Melrose, TD6 OST (☎ St Boswells 2736)

SANDERSON, Hon Evelyn; da of Dr Alan Sanderson, *qv*; *b* 1961; *Style* - The Hon Evelyn Sanderson

SANDERSON, Hon Frances; da of Dr Alan Sanderson, *qv*; *b* 1963 *Style* The Hon Frances Sanderson

SANDERSON, Frank Linton; s and h of Sir Bryan Sanderson, 2 Bt; *b* 21 Nov 1933; *Educ* Stowe, Salamanca U; *m* 1961, Margaret Ann, da of John C Maxwell, of New York (USA); 2 s, 3 da (inc twins); *Career* memb Lloyd's, RNSVR 1950-65, dir Knott Hotels Co of London Ltd, Humber Fishing & Fish Manure Co Ltd, (Hull); *Style* - Frank Sanderson Esq; Grandturzel Farm, Burwash, Sussex

SANDERSON, Joan, Lady; Joan; da of late Harry Cubberley; *m* 1951, as his 2 w, Sir Frank Bernard Sanderson, 1 Bt; 2 s, 1 da; *Style* - Joan, Lady Sanderson; 12 Connaught House, Mount Row, W1

SANDERSON, Hon Michael; s and h of Dr Alan Sanderson, *qv* (Baron Sanderson of Ayot, who disclamed his peerage for life); *b* 6 Dec 1959; *Style* - The Hon Michael Sanderson

SANDERSON, Hon Murray Lee; s (twin) of 1 Baron Sanderson of Ayot MC (d 1971) and bro of Dr Alan Sanderson, *qv*; *b* 1931; *Educ* Rugby, Trin Oxford, King's Cambridge; *m* 1, 1966 (m dis 1972), Muriel, da of late George Williams; m 2, 1973, Eva, da of Rev David Simfukwe; 1 s, 1 da; *Career* company dir; admin offr Kenya 1956-63; *Style* - The Hon Murray Sanderson; PO Box 2253, Kitwe, Zambia

SANDERSON, Hon Stephanie; da of Dr Alan Sanderson, *qv*; *b* 1970

SANDFORD, 2 Baron (UK 1945); Rev John Cyril Edmondson; DSC (1942); s of 1 Baron (d 1959); *b* 22 Dec 1920; *Educ* Eton, RNC Dartmouth; *m* 1947, Catharine Mary, da of Rev Oswald Hunt; 2 s, 2 da; *Heir* s, Hon James Edmondson; *Career* Cdr RN (ret); chaplain to Bp of St Albans 1965-68, Cons Whip House of Lords 1966-70, Parly Under-Sec of State Dept of Environment 1970-73 and of Dept of Education and Science 1973-74, pres of Cncl for Environmental Education, chm Inst of Environmental Sciences; *Clubs* Ski Club of Great Britain; *Style* - The Rev The Rt Hon The Lord Sandford DSC; 6 Smith sq, SW1 (☎ 01 222 5715)

SANDHURST, 5 Baron (UK 1871); (John Edward) Terence Mansfield; DFC (1944); s of 4 Baron OBE (d 1964); *b* 4 Sept 1920; *Educ* Harrow; *m* 1, 1942 (m dis 1946), Priscilla Ann (d 1970), da of late J Fielder Johnson; m 2, 1947, Janet Mary, da of late John Edward Lloyd, of Long Island, New York; 1 s, 1 da; *Heir* s, Hon Guy Mansfield; *Career* RAFVR WW II; md Leslie Rankin Ltd Jersey, Hon ADC to Lt-Govr of Jersey 1969-74; *Style* - The Rt Hon The Lord Sandhurst DFC; Les Sapins, St Mary, Jersey, CI

SANDILANDS, Hon Margaret Elizabeth Grizel; da of 15 Lord Torphichen; *b* 1979; *Style* - The Hon Margaret Sandilands

SANDON, Viscount; Dudley Danvers

Granville Coutts Ryder; TD (1953); s and h of 6 Earl of Harrowby; *b* 20 Dec 1922; *Educ* Eton; *m* 1949, Jeannette Rosalthé, da of late Capt Peter Johnston-Saint; 1 s, 1 da; *Heir* s, Hon Dudley Ryder; *Career* chm Powell Duffryn Gp 1981- (director 1976-), International Westminster Bank Ltd 1977-, dep chm Nat Westminster Bank Ltd 1971- (dir 1968-), chm Nat Westminster Unit Trust Managers Ltd 1979-, Orion Bank 1979-, dep chm Coutts & Co (formerly md); dir: Saudi Internat Bank 1980-, Orion Pacific Ltd, Orion Pension Tstees Ltd, UK Provident Institution; *Style* - Viscount Sandon; Sandon Hall, Stafford (☎ 08897 338); Burnt Norton, Chipping Campden, Glos (☎ 0386 840 358); 5 Tregunter rd, SW10 (☎ 01 373 9276)

SANDWICH, Earldom of; *see* Montagu, (Alexander) Victor Edward

SANDWICH, Dowager Countess of; Ella Lilian (Amiya); da of late George Sully; *m* 1952, as his 2 w, 9 Earl (d 1962); *Style* - The Rt Hon The Dowager Countess of Sandwich; 24 Monckton ct, Addison rd, W14

SANDYS, 7 Baron (UK 1802); Richard Michael Oliver Hill; DL (Worcs 1968); s of 6 Baron (d 1961); *b* 21 July 1931; *Educ* RNC Dartmouth; *m* 1961, Patricia Simpson, da of late Capt Lionel Hall MC; *Heir* cous, Marcus Hill; *Career* late Lt Roy Scots Greys; patron of one living, FRGS; a Lord-in-Waiting to HM Jan to March 1974, Oppn Whip House of Lords 1974-79, Capt HM Bodyguard of the Yeomen of the Guard 1979; *Clubs* Cavalry; *Style* - The Rt Hon The Lord Sandys DL; Ombersley Court, Droitwich, Worcs (☎ Worcester 620220)

SANDYS, Cynthia, Baroness; Cynthia Mary; da of late Col Frederic Richard Thomas Trench-Gascoigne DSO (gs of Charles Trench, bro of 1 Baron Ashtown); *b* 1898; *m* 1924, 6 Baron Sandys (d 1961); 1 s, 1 da; *Style* - The Rt Hon Cynthia, Lady Sandys; Himbleton Manor, nr Droitwich, Worcs

SANSEVERINO, Hon Mrs (Julia Collbran); *née* Cokayne; da (by 1 m) of 2 Baron Cullen of Ashbourne; *b* 1943; *m* 1968, Don Francesco Costa Sanseverino; 2 s; *Style* - The Hon Mrs Sanseverino; 75 Cadogan gdns, SW3

SARSON, Hon Mrs (Gillian Isolda Josephine); *née* Pollock; da of 2 Viscount Hanworth; *b* 1 April 1944; *m* 1963, Timothy von Weber Sarson; 2 s, 2 da; *Style* - The Hon Mrs Sarson; 8 Gatcombe rd, N19

SAS, Tadeusz Robert; Polonia Restituta decoration (1980); s of Tadeusz Sas, of London (d 1974); *b* 13 Dec 1941; *Educ* Atholl School; *m* 1967, Irena Eugenia; 2 s, 2 da; *Career* JP 1977; dir: Sas Investments, Elektromodul Ltd; *Recreations* work; *Clubs* Carlton, Jockey (Miami); *Style* - Tadeusz Sas Esq; 'Warren End', Long Grove, Seer Green, Beaconsfield, Bucks; 10350 Old Cutler rd, Miami, Fla 33156, USA; Villa Annabel, 2 Atalaya Park, Estepona, Málaga, Spain

SAUMAREZ, Hon Eric Douglas; s (er twin) and h of 6 Baron de Saumarez; *b* 13 Aug 1956; *Style* - The Hon Eric Saumarez

SAUMAREZ, Hon Louisa; da of 6 Baron de Saumarez; *b* 1955; *Style* - The Hon Louisa Saumarez

SAUMAREZ, Hon Victor Thomas; s (yr twin) of 6 Baron de Saumarez; *b* 1956; *Style* - The Hon Victor Saumarez

SAUNDERS, Air Chief Marshal Sir Hugh William Lumsden; GCB (1953, KCB 1950, CB 1943), KBE (1945, CBE 1941), MC, DFC, MM; s of Frederick Saunders, of Transvaal; *b* 1894; *Educ* Marist Brothers' Sch Johannesburg; *m* 1923, Phyllis (d 1980), da of Maj P Mabbett; 1 s (& 1 decd); *Career* Witwatersrand Rifles and S African Horse 1914, RFC 1917; Air Ch Marshal 1950, CIC Air Forces W Europe 1951, Air Dep to Supreme Cdr SHAPE 1951-53, Air Advr Miny Defence Denmark 1954-56, ret; *Style* -Air Chief Marshal Sir Hugh Saunders, GCB, KBE, MC, DFC, MM; c/o Barclays Bank International, 16-18 Brompton rd, SW1

SAVILE, 3 Baron (UK 1888); George Halifax Lumley-Savile; JP (Borough of

Dewsbury 1955), DL (W Yorks 1954); s of 2 Baron (d 1931); *b* 24 Jan 1919; *Educ* Eton; *Heir* bro, Hon Henry Lumley-Savile; *Career* patron of 2 livings; OStJ; formerly Capt Duke of Wellington's Regt, Lincs Regt Burma 1943-44; *Style* - The Rt Hon The Lord Savile, JP, DL; Gryce Hall, Shelley, Huddersfield, W Yorks (☎ Kirkburton 2774)

SAVILE, Hon Alethea Frances Clare; da of 8 Earl of Mexborough; *b* 1963; *Style* - The Hon Alethea Savile

SAVILE, Hon Charles Anthony; s of 7 Earl of Mexborough (d 1980); *b* 1934; *Educ* Eton; *m* 1966, Zita Loretta, da of Leslie White; 2 s; *Career* late Lt Grenadier Guards; *Style* - The Hon Charles Savile; Youngsbury, Ware, Herts

SAVILE, Hon James Hugh Hope John; s of 8 Earl of Mexborough; *b* 1976

SAVILE, Hon Lucinda Sarah Catherine; da of 8 Earl of Mexborough; *b* 1973

SAVILLE, Hon Mrs (Yvonne Catherine); da of Baron Schon (Life Peer); *b* 12 June 1944; *Educ* Badminton Sch Bristol, St Godric's Theological Coll, Montessori Coll London; *m* 1979, Norman, s of Mark Saville, of Hampstead; 1 step s (Daniel); *Career* Montessori teacher 1970-72; *Recreations* theatre, tennis, music, cooking; *Style* - The Hon Mrs Saville; 21a Chesterford gdns, NW3 (☎ 01 435 4551)

SAYE AND SELE, 21 Baron (E 1447 and 1603); Nathaniel Thomas Allen Fiennes; DL (Oxon 1979); s of 20 Baron, OBE, MC (Ivo Murray Twisleton-Wykeham-Fiennes, d 1968) and Hersey, da of late Capt Sir Thomas Dacres Butler KCVO; relinquished by deed poll 1965 the additional surnames of Twisleton and Wykeham; *b* 22 Sept 1920; *Educ* Eton, New Coll Oxford; *m* 1958, Mariette Helena, da of Maj-Gen Sir (Arthur) Guy Salisbury-Jones, GCVO, CMG, CBE, MC and Hilda, da of Rt Hon Sir Maurice de Bunsen, 1 and last Bt, GCMG, GCVO, CB; 3 s, 1 da; *Heir* s, Hon Richard Fiennes; *Career* Rifle Bde (despatches twice) 1939-45; chartered surveyor; *Style* - The Rt Hon The Lord Saye and Sele DL; Broughton Castle, Banbury, Oxon (☎ 2624)

SAYER, Guy Mowbray; CBE (1977); s of the late Geoffrey Robley Sayer; *b* 18 June 1924; *Educ* Shrewsbury Sch; *m* 1951, Marie Anne Sophie, da of the late Arnold Henri-Marie Mertens, of Brussels; 1 s, 2 da *Career* banker, Hong Kong and Shanghai Banking Corporation 1946-77 (dir 1969-, chm 1972-77), tres Hong Kong U 1971-77, memb Legislative and Executive Councils of Hong Kong 1972-77, dir of various shipping and ship finance cos in Hong Kong, Bermuda, and Bahamas; *Recreations* golf, walking; *Clubs* Hong Kong, Royal HK Jockey, Royal HK Golf, MCC, Royal Wimbledon Golf; *Style* - Guy Sayer Esq CBE; c/o Hong Kong & Shanghai Banking Corpn, 99 Bishopsgate, EC2 (☎ 01 638 2300)

SCANLON, Baron (Life Peer UK 1979); Hugh Parr Scanlon; s of Hugh Scanlon; *b* 26 Oct 1913; *Educ* NCLC; *m* 1943, Nora; 2 da; *Career* memb British Gas Corpn 1976-, Pres AEUW 1968-78 (formerly div organiser and memb London Exec Cncl); *Style* - The Rt Hon The Lord Scanlon; 23 Seven Stones Drive, Broadstairs, Kent

SCARBROUGH, 12 Earl of (E 1690); Richard Aldred Lumley; DL (S Yorks 1974); also Viscount Lumley of Waterford (I 1628), Baron Lumley of Lumley Castle (E 1681), and Viscount Lumley of Lumley Castle (E 1690); s of 11 Earl, KG, GCSI, GCIE, GCVO (d 1969); *b* 5 Dec 1932; *Educ* Eton, Magdalen Oxford; *m* 1970, Lady Elizabeth, nee Ramsay, da of 16 Earl of Dalhousie, KT, GCVO, GBE, MC; 1 s; *Heir* s, Viscount Lumley; *Career* late Lt Queen's Own Yorks Dragoons and 2 Lt 11 Hussars, ADC to Govr and CIC Cyprus 1956, Hon Col 1 Bn Yorks Volunteers 1975-; *Style* - The Rt Hon The Earl of Scarbrough DL; Sandbeck Park, Maltby, Rotherham, S Yorks (☎ Doncaster 742210)

SCARBROUGH, Countess of; Lady Elizabeth; *née* Ramsay; da of 16 Earl of Dalhousie, KT, GCVO, GBE, MC; *b* 1941; *m* 1970, 12 Earl of Scarbrough, *qv*;

Style - The Rt Hon The Countess of Scarbrough

SCARLETT, Hon James Harry; s and h of 8 Baron Abinger DL; *b* 28 May 1959; *Style* - The Hon James Scarlett

SCARLETT, His Hon Judge; James Harvey Anglin; s of Lt-Col James Scarlett DSO (d 1925); *b* 27 Jan 1924; *Educ* Shrewsbury Sch, Ch Ch Oxford; *Career* Lt Roy Artillery; barr (Inner Temple) 1950, Malayan Civil Service 1955-58, Recorder of Crown Court 1972-74, Circuit Judge 1974-; *Recreations* fell walking; *Clubs* Athenaeum; *Style* - His Hon Judge Scarlett; Chilmington Green, Great Chart, nr Ashford, Kent

SCARLETT, Maj Hon John Leopold Campbell; CBE (1973); s of 7 Baron Abinger DSO (d 1943); *b* 18 Dec 1916; *Educ* Eton, Magdalene Cambridge; *m* 1947, Bridget, da of late H B Crook, of Kensington; 2 s, 1 da; *Career* formerly Maj RA; Order of St John of Jerusalem; *Style* - Maj The Hon John Scarlett CBE; Bramblewood, Castle Walk, Wadhurst, Sussex

SCARLETT, Hon Peter; s of 8 Baron Abinger DL; *b* 21 March 1961; *Style* - The Hon Peter Scarlett

SCARMAN, Baron (Life Peer UK 1977); Leslie George Scarman; OBE (1944), PC (1973); s of late George Charles Scarman; *b* 29 July 1911; *Educ* Radley, BNC Oxford; *m* 1947, Ruth Clement, da of Clement Wright, ICS; 1 s; *Career* barr 1936, QC 1957, a Judge of the High Court 1961-73, a Lord Justice of Appeal 1973-77, a Lord of Appeal in Ordinary 1977-; Chllr U of Warwick 1977-, former memb Arts Council; kt 1961; *Style* - The Rt Hon The Lord Scarman, OBE, PC; 12 Wellington Court, Knightsbridge, SW1 (☎ 01 584 8302)

SCARSDALE, 3 Viscount (UK 1911); Sir Francis John Nathaniel Curzon; 11 Bt (S 1636); also 7 Baron Scarsdale (GB 1761); 30 Lord (territorial lordship) of Kedleston; s of late Hon Francis Nathaniel Curzon (himself bro of 1 & last Marquess Curzon of Kedleston and s of 4 Baron Scarsdale, who was in turn ggs of 1 Baron, whose yr bro was ancestor of the Earls Howe) and Winifred, da of Capt Christian Combe, by his w, Lady Jane Seymour, da of 3 Marquess Conyngham; *b* 28 July 1924; *Educ* Eton; *m* 1, 1948 (m dis 1967), Solange Yvonne Palmyre Ghislaine (d 1974), da of late Oscar Hanse, of Mont-sur-Marchienne, Belgium; 2 s, 1 da; m 2, 1968, Helene Gladys Frances, da of late Maj William Ferguson Thomson, of Kinellar, Aberdeenshire; 2 s; *Heir* s, Hon Peter Curzon; *Career* late Capt Scots Gds; *Style* - The Rt Hon The Viscount Scarsdale; Kedleston, Derby (☎ 840386)

SCARSDALE, Ottilie, Viscountess; Ottilie Margarete Julie; da of late Charles Pretzlik and former w of James Harris; *m* 1946, as his 2 w, 2 Viscount (d 1977); *Career* formerly Ensign FANY; *Style* - The Rt Hon Ottilie, Viscountess Scarsdale; The Dower House, Rowler Manor, Croughton, Brackley, Northants

SCHÜFFEL, Hon Mrs; Hon Shân; da of Baron Edmund-Davies PC (Life Peer); *b* 1940; *m* 1964, Wolfram Schüffel MD; *Style* - The Hon Mrs Schüffel; 3550 Marburg/Lahn, Kaffweg 17A, W Germany

SCHELLENBERG, Hon Mrs (Margaret de Hauteville); *née* Udny-Hamilton; da of 11 Lord Belhaven and Stenton CIE (d 1950, assumed additional surname of Udny 1934); *b* 1939; *m* 1964, Keith Schellenberg; 1 s, 2 da; *Style* - The Hon Mrs Schellenberg; Udny Castle, Udny, Aberdeenshire (☎ 309)

SCHERGER, Air Chief Marshal Sir Frederick Rudolph Williams; KBE (1958, CBE 1950), CB (1954), DSO (1944), AFC (1940); s of Frederick H Scherger; *b* 18 May 1904; *Educ* Ararat H S, RMC Australia; *m* 1, 1929, Thelma Lilian Harricks (d 1974); 1 da; m 2, 1975, Mrs J Robertson; *Career* RAAF 1925, Ch of Air Staff 1957-61, Chm Chiefs of Staff 1961-66, Air Ch Marshal 1965, chm Australian Nat Airlines 1966-75, company dir; *Style* - Air Chief Marshal Sir Frederick Scherger, KBE, CB, DSO, AFC; 45 Stephens st, N Balwyn, Victoria 3104, Australia

SCHILIZZI, Maj John Stephen; s of Stephen Schilizzi (descended from a family prominent in Byzantium under the Emperors Nicephorus III and Isaac Comnenus II - ie c 1080 - and until the 14th century; the first Schilizzis to settle in England did so after the massacre of Chios 1822); unc of Edmund Brudenell, the proprietor of Deene Park; *b* 15 Dec 1896; *Educ* Eton; *m* 1935, Lady Sophia Waldegrave; 1 s, 2 da; *Career* served WW I Capt Northants Yeo & WW II as Maj RASC; *Clubs* Jockey; *Style* - Maj John Schilizzi; Chacombe House, Banbury, Oxon

SCHILIZZI, Lady (Gabrielle) Sophia Annette; Waldegrave; *b* 7 June 1908; *m* 1935, Maj John Schilizzi, *qv*; 1 s, 2 da; *Style* - Lady Sophia Schilizzi; Chacombe House, Banbury, Oxon

SCHOLES, John Francis Millar; s of Frank Victor Gordon Scholes (d 1954); *b* 7 Apr 1919; *Educ* Melbourne U, Sydney U; *m* 1947, Joyce Bartlett, da of Sidney Frank Henry Laws (d 1973); *Career* Aeronautical Res Laboratory (Melbourne) 1943-49, Roy Aircraft Establishment 1950-58, Int Computers and Tabulators Ltd 1958-65, Nat Res Dvpt Corpn 1965- (memb and ch exec engrg 1977-); *Recreations* genealogy, stamp collecting; *Style* - John Scholes Esq; 30 Lansdowne Av, Orpington, Kent (☎ Farnborough 54641)

SCHON, Baron (Life Peer UK 1976); Frank Schon; s of late Dr Frederick Schon of Vienna; *b* 18 May 1912; *Educ* Rainer Gymnasium Vienna, Vienna and Prague Us; *m* 1936, Gertrude, da of late Abraham Secher; 2 da; *Career* co-founder Marchon Products Ltd 1939, Solway Chemicals Ltd 1943, chm and md of both until 1967; chm NRDC 1969-79, dir Blue Circle Industries 1967-, former memb Northern Economic Planning Cncl and Industrial Reorganisation Corpn, kt 1966; *Recreations* golf, reading; *Style* - The Rt Hon The Lord Schon; Flat 82, Prince Albert Court, 33 Prince Albert rd, NW8 (☎ 01 586 1461)

SCHOOLING, John Duprey; TD (1945), DL (Hereford & Worcester 1972); s of Arthur John Schooling (d 1971); *b* 8 July 1911; *Educ* Dean Close Sch, Sheffield U; *m* 1939, Ursula Mary, nee Taylor; 1 s; *Career* Maj RA(TA) 1931-61; solicitor 1934, assist solicitor Worcs CC 1945-63, assist clerk and dep clerk of the peace Worcs CC 1963-71, dep county sec Hereford and Worcs CC 1974-75, private practice 1975-; *Recreations* beagling, local history; *Clubs* Naval & Military, Union & County (Worcs); *Style* - John Schooling Esq, TD, DL; The Shrubs, Powick, Worcs (☎ Worcs 830236)

SCHREIBER, Mark Shuldham; s of John Shuldham Schreiber (d 1968); *b* 11 Sept 1931; *Educ* Eton, Trin Cambridge; *m* 1969, Gabriella Federica, da of Conte Teodoro Veglio Di Castelletto Uzonne; 2 da; *Career* Fisons Ltd 1957-63, Conservative Research Dept 1963-67, dir Conservative Party Public Sector Research Unit 1967-70, special adviser HM Government 1970-74, special adviser to Leader of the Opposition 1974-75, editorial staff of The Economist 1974-, (Parliamentary Lobby correspondent); *Clubs* Turf, Pratt's; *Style* - Mark Schreiber Esq; Marlesford Hall, Woodbridge, Suffolk; 5 Kersley st, London SW11

SCHRODER, Baron Bruno Lionel; s of Baron Helmut Schroder (s of Baron Bruno Schroder or von Schröder, ch of the London branch of the Banking House of J Henry Schroder & Co, cr Freiherr by Kaiser Wilhelm II aboard the All Highest's yacht 'Hohenzollern' on 27 July 1904; the Baron's er bro Rudolph was cr Freiherr eight months later by the same puissant if withered hand at Berlin) and Margaret (1 da of Sir Lionel Darell, 6 Bt, DSO, JP, DL, and Eleanor, nee Edwards-Heathcote), whereby Bruno is 2 cous of Lord Ravensdale and 1 cous once removed of the late Sir Oswald Mosley, 6 Bt; *b* 17 Jan 1933; *Educ* Eton, Univ Oxford, Harvard Business Sch; *m* 1969, Patricia, da of Maj Adrian Holt; 1 da (Baroness Leonie Kira Emma b 17 April 1974); *Career* late Lt Life Gds; dir Schroders Ltd & J Henry Schroder Wagg & Co; *Recreations* flying, shooting; *Clubs* Brooks's; *Style* - Bruno Schroder Esq; 47 Victoria rd, W8; Dunlossit, Port Askaig, Isle of Islay, Argyll (☎ Port Askaig 664)

SCHUSTER, Hon Lady - Hon Gwendolen; *née* Parker; da of Baron Parker of Waddington (Life Peer) (d 1918); *b* 1888; *m* 1908, Sir George Ernest Schuster, KCSI, KCMG, CBE, MC; *Style* - The Hon Lady Schuster; Nether Worton House, Middle Barton, Oxon

SCHUSTER, Sir (Felix) James Moncrieff; 3 Bt (UK 1906), of Collingham Rd, Roy Boro of Kensington, OBE (Mil 1955), TD; s of Sir (Felix) Victor Schuster, 2 Bt (d 1962); *b* 8 Jan 1913; *Educ* Winchester; *m* 1937, Ragna, da of late Direktor Ole Sundo, of Copenhagen; 2 da; *Heir* none; *Career* Col late Rifle Bde, Hon Col 5 Bn Roy Green Jackets T & AVR 1970-75; *Style* - Sir James Schuster, Bt, OBE, TD; Piltdown Cottage, Piltdown, Uckfield, E Sussex

SCHUSTER, Hon Mrs (Lorna Frances); *née* Hermon-Hodge; da of 2 Baron Wyfold, DSO, MVO; *b* 25 Feb 1911; *m* 1941, John Schuster, TD, DL, eldest s of Sir George Schuster, KCSI, KCMG, CBE, MC; 2 s, 1 da (all adopted); *Style* - The Hon Mrs Schuster; The Manor Farm, Nether Worton, Oxon (☎ Great Tew 254)

SCLATER, John Richard; s of Arthur William Sclater; *b* 14 July 1940; *Educ* Charterhouse, Gonville and Caius Coll Cambridge, Yale, Harvard; *m* 1967, Nicola Mary Gloria, nee Cropper; 1 s, 1 da; *Career* banker, landowner, co dir, md Nordic Bank Ltd 1976-, dir Nordfinanz-Bank Zurich 1979-, trustee The Grosvenor Estate 1972-, dir James Cropper & Co Ltd 1972-, dir Foreign & Colonial Investment Trust Co Ltd 1981-, chm Sclater Farming Ltd 1977-; *Recreations* shooting, fishing, gardening, forestry, running, tennis; *Clubs* Brooks's, University Pitt (Cambridge); *Style* - John Sclater Esq; Sutton Hall, Barcombe, Lewes, Sussex (☎ 0273 400 450)

SCLATER-BOOTH, Hon Neil Lutley; s and h of 4 Baron Basing; *b* 16 Jan 1939; *Educ* Eton, Harvard; *m* 1967, Patricia Ann, nee Whitfield, of New Haven, Conn; 2 s; *Clubs* Harvard, Meadow Brook; *Style* - The Hon Neil Sclater-Booth; 112 E 74th st, NYC, NY 10021, USA (☎ Lehigh 5 1945)

SCOONES, Maj-Gen Sir Reginald Laurence; KBE (1955, OBE 1941), CB (1951), DSO (1945); s of late Maj Fitzmaurice Scoones, Roy Fus; *b* 18 Dec 1900; *Educ* Wellington, RMC Sandhurst; *m* 1933, Isabella Bowie, da of John Nisbet, of Cumbrae Isles, Scotland; 1 da; *Career* late RAC; 2 Lt Roy Fus 1920, Royal Tank Corps 1923, Sudan Defence Force 1926-34, 1939-45 War Middle East and Burma; Lt-Col 1941, Brig 1942, Maj-Gen 1950, Maj-Gen Commanding British Troops Sudan and Commandant Sudan Defence Force 1950-54; dir The Brewers' Soc 1957-69; *Clubs* Oriental; *Style* - Major-General Sir Reginald Scoones, KBE, CB, DSO; 7 Court Royal Mansions, 1 Eastern Terrace, Brighton BN2 1 DJ (☎ Brighton 697141)

SCOTLAND, James; CBE (1975); s of Duncan Anderson (d 1925); *b* 8 Sept 1917; *Educ* Whitehill Sch Glas; *m* 1944, Jean, nee Hamilton; 2 s; *Career* schoolmaster, lecturer and coll principal, head of education Jordanhill Coll Glasgow 1950-61, princ Aberdeen Coll 1961-, chm Gen Teaching Cncl Scot 1976-79; *Recreations* writing, drama; *Clubs* Roy Scots Edinburgh, Business and Professional Aberdeen; *Style* - James Scotland Esq, CBE; 67 Forest rd, Aberdeen (☎ 0224 22 649)

SCOTT, Hon Lady (Anna Drusilla); *née* Lindsay; da of 1 Baron Lindsay of Birker CBE (d 1952); *b* 1911; *m* 1937, Sir Ian Dixon Scott, KCMG, KCVO, CIE; 1 s, 4 da; *Style* - The Hon Lady Scott; Ash House, Alde Lane, Aldeburgh, Suffolk (☎ 2160)

SCOTT, Anthony Douglas; TD (1972); s of the late Douglas Ernest Scott; *b* 6 Nov 1933; *Educ* Gateshead G S; *m* 1962, Irene, nee Robson; 1 s, 1 da; *Career* Major TA; chartered accountant, ch exec and dir Council for Small Industries in Rural Areas 1981-, dir Consumer Credit Office of Fair Trading 1975-80, dir gen Internat Audit Ministry of Defence 1972-74; *Recreations* antique collecting, mountaineering; *Clubs* Army & Navy;

Style - Anthony Scott Esq; 33 Barlings rd, Harpenden, Herts (☎ 058 27 63067)

SCOTT, Anthony Percy; s and h of Col Sir Douglas Scott, 2 Bt; *b* 1 May 1937; *Educ* Harrow, Ch Ch Oxford; *m* 1962, Caroline Teresa Anne, da of Edward Bacon; 2 s, 1 da; *Career* barr 1960; *Style* - Anthony Scott Esq; Older House, Redford, Midhurst, Sussex

SCOTT, Hon Mrs - Hon Cecilia Anne; da of 9 Baron Hawke; *b* 1943; *m* 1, 1963, Peter Tapsell, MP (m dis 1971); 1 s; m 2, 1979, as his 2 w, Nicholas Scott, MBE, JP, MP; *Style* - The Hon Mrs Scott

SCOTT, Christopher James; s and h of Sir Oliver Scott, 3 Bt; *b* 16 Jan 1955; *Style* - Christopher Scott Esq

SCOTT, Dame Catherine Margaret Mary; DBE (1981; conferred for services to ballet); *Style* - Dame Catherine Scott

SCOTT, Sir David Aubrey; GCMG (1979, KCMG 1974, CMG 1966); s of Hugh Scott; *b* 3 Aug 1919; *Educ* Charterhouse, Birmingham U; *m* 1941, Vera, da of Maj G Ibbitson, MBE, RA; 2 s, 1 da; *Career* chm Ellerman Lines 1982- (v-chm 1981-82), Roy Overseas League 1981- (v-chm to 1981); dir: Barclays Bank Internat, Mitchell Cotts Gp, Delta Metal Overseas; Foreign Serv, Ambass S Africa 1976-79, High Commissioner NZ & Govr Pitcairn Islands 1973-75; served WW II RA; *Style* - Sir David Scott GCMG; Wayside, Mousehill Lane, Milford, Surrey

SCOTT, Douglas Francis; s of late Sir Douglas Scott, 7 Bt, and hp of bro, Sir Edward Scott, 8 Bt; *b* 26 Aug 1908; *Style* - Douglas Scott Esq

SCOTT, David Griffiths; *b* 15 Feb 1942; *Educ* Adams G S Newport Salop, Christs' Coll Camb, London Business School; *m* 1969, Alison Jane Fraser, 3 c; *Career* md ISC Alloys Ltd 1965-, Impalloy Ltd 1968-; *Recreations* cricket, gardening, squash; *Style* - David Scott Esq; Meadow Bank, Coventry rd, Berkswell, Nr Coventry (☎ 0676 32836)

SCOTT, Col Sir Douglas Winchester; 2 Bt (UK 1913), of Witley, Surrey; s of Adm Sir Percy Moreton Scott, 1 Bt, KCB, KCVO, LLD (d 1924); *b* 4 Feb 1907; *Educ* Harrow; *m* 1933, Elizabeth Joyce, da of Archibald Lloyd Glanley; 2 s, 1 da; *Heir* s, Anthony Scott, *qv*; *Career* Lt-Col (ret) 9 Lancers and Hon Col Queen's Own Hussars; v-pres of Thomas Coram Foundation; *Style* - Col Sir Douglas Scott, Bt; Pine Trees, West Strand, W Wittering, nr Chichester, Sussex

SCOTT, Sir Edward Arthur Dolman; 8 Bt (UK 1806), of Great Barr, Staffs; s of Sir Douglas Edward Scott, 7 Bt (d 1951); *b* 14 Dec 1905; *m* 1943, Dorothy Elsie, da of W H Winchcombe, of Yorktown, S Australia; *Heir* bro, Douglas Scott; *Career* painter; *Style* - Sir Edward Scott, Bt; 8 Alice st, S Plympton, S Australia

SCOTT, Lady Elizabeth Louise Margaret; *née* Meade; da of 6 Earl of Clanwilliam; *b* 1911; *m* 1933, Lt-Col Charles Rankin Scott KRRC (d 1965); 2 s; *Style* - Lady Elizabeth Scott; Culkerton, Tetbury, Glos

SCOTT, James Jervoise; s and h of Sir James Scott, 2 Bt, DL; *b* 12 Oct 1952; *Style* - James Scott Esq

SCOTT, Sir James Walter; 2 Bt (UK 1962) of Rotherfield Park, Alton, Hants, DL (Hants 1978); s of Col Sir Jervoise Bolitho Scott, 1 Bt (d 1965); *b* 26 Oct 1924; *Educ* Eton; *m* 1951, Anne Constantia, da of late Lt-Col Clive Grantham Austin DL; 3 s, 1 da; *Heir* s, James Scott; *Career* Col (ret) Life Gds, formerly Gren Gds; memb Lloyd's; Master of Mercers' Co 1976; one of HM Body Guard of Hon Corps of Gentlemen-at-Arms 1977-, ADC to Viceroy and Govr-Gen of India 1946-48; *Style* - Sir James Scott, Bt, DL; Rotherfield Park, Alton, Hants (☎ Tisted 204)

SCOTT, John William; s of the late Donald Alan Scott, memb London Stock Exchange; *b* 6 April 1930; *Educ* Marlborough, Worcester Coll Oxford; *m* 1957, Rhoda Janet, da of the late Robert Cecil Mayall CMG DSO MC; 3 s; *Career* solicitor, partner Clifford-Turner 1961-; *Recreations* cricket, golf, family history; *Clubs* City University, MCC; *Style* - John

Scott Esq; Bemerton, Lingfield rd, East Grinstead, West Sussex

SCOTT, Hon Mrs (Mary Cecilia); *née* Berry; da of late 1 Visc Camrose; *b* 1906; *m* 1930, Maj Ronald Guthrie McNair Scott; 2 s, 3 da; *Style* - The Hon Mrs Scott; Huish House, Old Basing, nr Basingstoke, Hants

SCOTT, Nicholas Paul; MBE (1964), JP (London 1961), MP (C) Kensington and Chelsea 1974-; s of P J Scott; *b* 5 Aug 1933; *Educ* Clapham Coll, City of London Coll; *m* 1, 1964 (m dis 1976), Elizabeth, nee Robinson; 1 s, 2 da; m 2, 1979, Hon Mrs Tapsell (Hon Cecilia, *qv*, da of 9 Baron Hawke); *Career* PPS to Rt Hon Iaian Macleod, MP, 1970 and Rt Hon Robert Carr, MP, 1972; Parly Under-Sec of State Dept of Employment 1974, Oppn Spokesman on Housing 1974; company dir; *Style* - Nicholas Scott Esq, MBE, JP, MP; House of Commons, SW1

SCOTT, Sir Oliver Christopher Anderson; 3 Bt (UK 1909), of Yews, Undermilbeck, Westmorland; s of Sir Samuel Haslam Scott, 2 Bt (d 1960); *b* 6 Nov 1922; *Educ* Charterhouse, King's Cambridge; *m* 1951, Phoebe Anne, da of Desmond O'Neill Tolhurst; 1 s, 2 da; *Heir* s, Christopher Scott; *Career* High Sheriff of Westmorland 1966, dir of Research Unit of Radiobiology British Empire Cancer Campaign 1966-69, consultant Inst of Cancer Research 1974; *Clubs* Brooks's; *Style* - Sir Oliver Scott, Bt; 31 Kensington sq, W8

SCOTT, Hon Mrs; Hon Rita; *née* Blyton; da of Baron Blyton (Life Peer); *b* 1930; *m* 1954, Mr Scott; children; *Style* - The Hon Mrs Scott; 67 Australia Grove, S Shields, Tyne & Wear

SCOTT, Hon Simon Peter; s of late 4 Earl of Eldon GCVO and Hon Magdalen Fraser OBE, da of 14 Lord Lovat; *b* 1939; *Educ* Ampleforth, Salamanca and Madrid Us, Sorbonne; *m* 1966, Mary Isabel, da of late Andrew Ramon Dalzell de Bertodano; 3 s, 1 da; *Career* Page of Honour to HM 1953-56; *Style* - The Hon Simon Scott; Howe Hills Farm, Mordon, Sedgefield, Co Durham

SCOTT, Lady Victoria Laura Maria Magdalene; da of 5 Earl of Eldon; *b* 1968; *Style* - Lady Victoria Scott

SCOTT, Sir Walter; 4 Bt (UK 1907), of Beauclere, Bywell St Andrews, Co Northumberland, DL (E Sussex 1975); s of Sir Walter Scott, 3 Bt (d 1967); *b* 29 July 1918; *Educ* Eton, Jesus Cambridge; *m* 1945, Diana Mary, da of James Owen; 1 s, 1 da (*see* Duke of Hamilton and Brandon); *Heir* s, Walter Scott; *Career* Maj late 1 Roy Dragoons; JP (E Sussex 1963); *Style* - Sir Walter Scott, Bt, JP, DL; Eckington Manor, Ripe, E Sussex (☎ 204)

SCOTT, Walter Grant; s of Thomas Scott (d 1979); *b* 13 May 1947; *Educ* Eastwood H S, Edinburgh U, Trin Hall Cambridge; *m* 1973, Rosemary Ann Clark, da of Alfred W C Lobban, of Bedfordshire; 2 c; *Career* md Ivory & Sime (investment managers with portfolio as of mid-summer 1981 c £450,000,000); Ind Investment Co nominee dir Systems Designers International 1981-; dir Integrated Micro Applications Ltd 1981; *Recreations* rowing, gardening; *Clubs* Leander, Edinburgh New; *Style* - Walter Scott Esq; Hillwood, Loanhead, Midlothian EH20 (☎ 031 440 0587); c/o Ivory & Sime, 1 Charlotte sq, Edinburgh (☎ 031 225 1357)

SCOTT, Walter John; s and h of Sir Walter Scott, 4 Bt; *b* 24 Feb 1948; *Style* - Walter Scott Esq

SCOTT, Hon Lady; Winifred Kathleen; *née* Brodrick; *m* 1941, Hon Sir Ernest Stowell Scott, KCMG, MVO (s of 3 Earl of Eldon and who d 1953); 1 da; *Style* - The Hon Lady Scott; The Manor House, Bradford Peverell, Dorchester, Dorset

SCOTT, William Patrick; DL (Orkney 1967); *b* 1 Dec 1910; *Educ* Sedbergh; *m* 1938, Philippa; 1 s 3 da; *Career* dir Highland Distilleries 1938-78, Chairman LEC Orkney 1948-68, RSPB Orkney 1950-64, memb Highland TA & VR Assoc 1950-78; *Recreations* golf, shooting, fishing; *Clubs* New, Royal & Ancient; *Style* - William Scott Esq DL; Kierfiold House, Sandwick, Stromness, Orkney (☎ Sandwick 503)

SCOTT MONCRIEFF, David Charles; CVO (1960), TD, WS; s of John Scott Moncrieff MRCVS & n of Charles Scott Moncrieff, the translator of Proust; *b* 2 July 1915; *Educ* Sedbergh, Edinburgh U; *m* 1948, Ann, da of Sir Kenneth Murray of Geanies (d 1979); 2 s, 1 da; *Career* memb Roy Co of Archers; Bailie of Holyrood 1957-79, Purse-Bearer to Ld High Cmmr to Gen Assembly Church of Scotland 1959 & 1960; *Style* - David Scott Moncrieff Esq CVO TD; 23 Cluny Drive, Edinburgh (☎ 447 2578)

SCOTT-ELLIOT, Aydua Helen; CVO (1969, MVO 1958); da of Lewis Alexander Scott-Elliot (d 1916); *b* 11 Dec 1909; *Educ* St Paul's Girls' Sch and abroad; *Career* Keeper of Prints and Drawings Royal Collection Windsor Castle 1946-69 (ret 1970), temp assist civilian officer Admiralty 1941-45; *Recreations* gardening; *Clubs* University Women's; *Style* - Miss Aydua Scott-Elliot, CVO; Shaldon, Station rd, Mayfield, East Sussex (☎ Mayfield 2079)

SCOTT-HOPKINS, Sir James Sidney Rawdon; MEP (C) Hereford & Worcester 1979-; s of Col R Scott-Hopkins; *b* 29 Nov 1921; *Educ* Eton, Oxford & Cambridge Us; *m* 1946, Geraldine Hargreaves; 3 s, 1 da; *Career* chm European Democratic Gp 1979-; MP (C) N Cornwall 1959-66, W Derbyshire 1967-79; Jt Parly Sec Miny Ag Fish & Food 1962-64; kt 1980; *Style* - Sir James Scott-Hopkins MEP; 602 Nelson House, Dolphin sq, SW1

SCOTT-NOBLE, James Robert; MC (1940), MC (1940), TD, JP (Roxburghshire 1961), DL (1962); *b* 24 Feb 1915; *Educ* Loretto; *m* 1941, Diana, da of Lt-Col W Dickson; 1 s, 2 da; *Career* Lt-Col 1940; farmer; *Recreations* shooting; *Style* - Lt-Col James Scott-Noble MC TD JP DL; Wood Norton, Hawick, Roxburghshire (☎ 0450 2175)

SCOTT-PLUMMER, Hon Mrs (Pamela Lilias); *née* Balfour; da of 2 Baron Kinross, KC (d 1939); *b* 1907; *m* 1933, Humphrey Scott-Plummer; 1 s, 2 da; *Style* - The Hon Mrs Scott-Plummer; Mainhouse, Kelso, Roxburghshire

SCRIVENER, Ronald Stratford; CMG (1965); s of Sir Patrick Stratford Scrivener KCMG (d 1966); *b* 29 Dec 1919; *Educ* Westminster, St Cat's Cambridge; *m* 1, 1947, Elizabeth Drake-Brockman (m dis 1952); m 2, 1962 (as her 2 husb), Mary Alice Olga Sofia Jane (who had m 1 Edward Hohler, whose maternal grand mother was Hon Elizabeth Vereker, da of 4 Viscount Gort and subsequently w of 3 Baron de L'Isle and Dudley; by Mary Edward had 2 s: Frederick b 1943 & Robert b 1947, & 2 da: (Olga) Mrs Godfrey Bland & (Philippa) Mrs William Sanders, all 4 of whom are, as will appear shortly, 5 cousins of HM The Queen); Mary's mother was Olga, herself da of Rear-Adm Sir Adolphus FitzGeorge, KCVO, while the Admiral's paternal ggf was George III (*see* Gen Sir Victor FitzGeorge-Balfour, whose own gf, Col George FitzGeorge, was Sir Adolphus's er bro); 2 step s, 2 step da (*see above*); *Career* exec dir Br-Soviet Chamber of Commerce 1977-, Assist Under-Sec of State Foreign and C'wlth Office 1974-76, Ambassador to Czechoslovakia 1971-74, Ambassador to Panama 1969-70; *Recreations* travel, fishing; *Clubs* White's; *Style* - Ronald Scrivener Esq CMG; 72 Bedford Gardens, W8 (☎ 01 727 1584)

SCROGGIE, Alan Ure Reith; CBE (1973, OBE 1961), QPM (1968); s of Col William Reith John Scroggie (d 1953); *b* 10 March 1912; *Educ* Cargilfield Prep Sch, Fettes Coll, Edinburgh U; *m* 1940, Sheila Catherine, nee Mackenzie; 2 s; *Career* OStJ 1954, Edinburgh Police 1930-47, Assist Chief Constable of Bucks 1947-53, Chief Constable Northumberland 1953-63, HM Inspector of Constabulary 1963-75; *Recreations* golf, fishing; *Clubs* Roy and Ancient (St Andrews), Elie Golf; *Style* - Alan Scroggie Esq, CBE, QPM; Fowler's Cottage, Abercrombie, By St Monans, Fife

SCROPE, Lady Mary; *née* Egerton; da of late 4 Earl of Ellesmere by Lady VioletLambton, da of 4 Earl of Durham; sis of 6 Duke of Sutherland; *b* 1911; *m* 1945, Lt-Col Conyers Scrope MC, s of Stephen Scrope & cous of Richard Scrope, *qv*; 2 da; *Style* - Lady Mary Scrope; Branxton Old Vicarage, Cornhill-on-Tweed, Northumberland (☎ 089 082 278)

SCROPE, Richard Ladislas; s of Henry Aloysius Scrope (whose gf, Simon, in 1859 claimed the Earldom of Wiltshire (extinct 1399) in his capacity as sr male rep of the descendants of the 1 and last Earl's yr bro; the House of Lords Privileges Ctee rightly rejected his claim, but for the wrong reason, confusing remainder to heirs male for ever with remainder to heirs male whatsoever, which latter limitation they ruled invalid, notwithstanding the contrary (and erroneous) verdict in the Devon (*qv*) case; the right reason is: that heirs male for ever means heirs male of the body for ever, which rules out collaterals) by Maria Mercedes, da of Alexander de Laski by Joaquina, Marquesa de Souza Lisboa; of the Scropes, it might be said what Evelyn Waugh wrote of the Crouchbacks, that they "suffered for their Faith and yet retained a round share of material greatness", tho' a family that in its day held the Earldoms of Wiltshire & Sunderland, the Baronies of Scrope of Masham & Scrope of Bolton and the Sovereignty of the Isle of Man must inevitably today seem a little dimmed in its lustre; *b* 22 Aug 1901; *Educ* Oratory Sch Edgbaston, Gonville & Caius Cambridge; *m* 1934, Lady Jane Egerton (d 1978), da of 4 Earl of Ellesmere and his 11 cous once removed (through descent from 1 & last Earl of Sunderland & 11 Baron Scrope of Bolton); 1 s (*see below*), 1 da (Elizabeth Jane, b 5 June 1937); *Career* served Coldstream Gds in M East & Europe as Maj; landowner; *Recreations* shooting, hunting, fishing; *Clubs* Brooks's; *Style* - Richard Scrope Esq; Danby House, Middleham, N Yorks (☎ Wensleydale 23225)

SCROPE, Simon Egerton; s of Richard Ladislas Scrope, *see above*; *b* 23 Dec 1934; *Educ* Ampleforth, Trin Cambridge; *m* 1970, Jennifer Jane, da of Sir Kenneth Wade Parkinson DL (d 1981); 2 children; *Career* late 2 Lt Coldstream Gds; insur broker, memb Lloyd's 1956, chm Richards Longstaff Gp 1974; farmer & landowner; *Recreations* racing, shooting, gardening, fishing; *Clubs* Brooks's; *Style* - Simon Scrope Esq; Danby on Yore, Leyburn, N Yorks (☎ Wensleydale (STD Code 0969) 23297)

SCRYMGEOUR, Lord; Alexander Henry Wedderburn of that Ilk; s and h of 11 Earl of Dundee; *b* 5 June 1949; *Educ* Eton; *m* 1979, Siobhan Mary, nee Llewellyn; 1 da; *Career* Page of Honour to HM the Queen 1964-65, contested (C) Hamilton May 1978; *Style* - Lord Scrymgeour; Birkhill, Cupar, Fife (☎ Gauldry 209)

SCRYMGEOUR-WEDDERBURN, Hon Mrs William - Joyce; da of late Col Robert Henry Jennings, CSI, RE; *m* 1921, Capt the Hon William Ogilvy Scrymgeour-Wedderburn, DSC, RN (ret) (s of *de jure* 9 Earl of Dundee and who d 1958); 1 s, 1 da; *Style* - The Hon Mrs William Scrymgeour- Wedderburn; B13 Sloane Avenue Mansions, Sloane av, SW3

SCURFIELD, William Russell; s of Harold Scurfield, MD, DPH (d 1941); *b* 15 Oct 1908; *Educ* Malvern College, London U; *m* 1931, Elizabeth Morton; 2 s, 2 da; *Career* slr and local govt officer; clerk of the peace 1942-72; clerk of Worcs CC 1942-74; *Style* - William Scurfield Esq; 2 Old Church rd, Colwall, Malvern, Worcs WR13 6ET(☎ Colwall 40270)

SCUTT, Robin Hugh, (known professionally as Scott); CBE (1976); s of the late Rev Arthur Octavius Scutt MA; *b* 24 Oct 1920; *Educ* Bryanston, British Institute Sorbonne Paris, Jesus Cambridge; *m* 1, 1943 (m dis 1960), Judy, nee Watson, 2 s; m 2, 1961, Patricia Anne Marie, nee Pilkington-Smith; *Career* BBC radio producer & exec (European Service) 1942-54, BBC TV producer 1955-58, BBC Paris rep 1958-62, BBC producer 1963-66, controller BBC Radio 1 & 2 1967-68, BBC2 TV 1969-74, Controller Devpt BBC TV 1974-77, dep md BBC TV 1977-80; chm Morning TV 1980-, joint md National Video Corporation and Covent Garden Video Productions 1980-, dir Lella Productions 1980-; pres Radio Industries Club 1980-81; dir Prospect Productions Ltd (The Old Vic); *Recreations* gardening, theatre, travel; *Style* - Robin Scutt Esq

SEABROOK, Air Vice-Marshal Geoffrey Leonard; CB (1965); s of Robert Leonard Seabrook (d 1946); *b* 25 Aug 1909; *Educ* King's Sch Canterbury; *m* 1949, Beryl Mary, nee Hughes; 1 s, 1 da;

Career chartered accountant 1931; RAF 1933 (Iraq & Far East), Air Vice-Marshal, dir of Personnel (G) Air Ministry 1961-63, AOA Tech Training Command 1963-66 (ret); *Recreations* golf, sailing; *Clubs* RAF, Piltdown Golf, Walton & Frinton Yacht; *Style* - Air Vice-Marshal Geoffrey Seabrook CB; Long Pightle, Piltdown, Uckfield, Sussex (☎ Newick 2322)

SEABROOK, Timothy James; s of Frederick James Seabrook (d 1979); *b* 20 May 1940; *Educ* Wellington; *m* 1967, Catherine Marion Jean, da of Cdr Herbert Geoffrey St John Bury; 1 da; *Career* FCA, man of Industrial Subsiduaries & Associates Div 1975-, dep chm Triangle Int Ltd 1980-, dir Shipton Automation Gp 1973-75; *Recreations* golf; *Clubs* MCC; *Style* - Timothy Seabrook Esq; Southfield House, S Warnborough, Basingstoke, Hants (☎ Long Sutton 598)

SEAFIELD, 13 Earl of (S 1701); Ian Derek Francis Ogilvie-Grant; Lord Ogilvy of Cullen and Viscount Seafield (S 1698), Lord Ogilvy of Deskford and Cullen and Viscount Reidhaven (S 1701); s of Countess of Seafield (12 in line, d 1969) and Derek Studley-Herbert (who assumed by deed poll 1939 the additional surnames of Ogilvie-Grant, the present Peer being recognised in those surnames by warrant of Lord Lyon 1971); *b* 20 March 1939; *Educ* Eton; *m* 1, 1960 (m dis 1971), Mary Dawn Mackenzie, da of Henry Illingworth; 2 s; m 2, 1971, Leila, da of Mahmoud Refaat, of Cairo; *Heir* s, Viscount Reidhaven, *qv*; *Style* - The Rt Hon The Earl of Seafield; Kinveachy Forest, Boat of Garten, Inverness-shire; Old Cullen, Cullen, Banffshire

SEAGER, Hon Carole Mary Leighton; da of 2 Baron Leighton of St Mellons; *b* 1958; *Style* The Hon Carol Seager

SEAGER, Hon Douglas Leighton; s of 1 Baron Leighton of St Mellons CBE (d 1963); *b* 1925; *m* 1960, Gillian Claire, da of L W Greenwood, of Pound Piece, Astley, Stourport, Worcs; 3 da; *Style* - The Hon Douglas Seager; Leighton House, 5929 Hudson, Vancouver, BC, Canada

SEAGER, Hon Robert William Henry Leighton; s and h of 2 Baron Leighton of St Mellons; *b* 28 Sept 1955; *Style* - The Hon Robert Seager

SEAGER, Hon Simon John Leighton; s of 2 Baron Leighton of St Mellons; *b* 1957 *Style* The Hon Simon Seager

SEAL, David Herbert; s of Jefferson Seal (d 1977); *b* 7 April 1935; *Educ* Marlborough, Cambridge; *m* 1958, Juliet Rose, da of John Perrot (d 1944); 3 c; *Career* stockbroker; *Recreations* riding, sailing ; *Style* - David Seal Esq; Holmbury, Augres, Trinity, Jersey, CI (☎ 61614)

SEALE, Sir John Henry; 5 Bt (UK 1838) of Mount Boone, Devonshire; s of Sir John Carteret Hyde Seale, 4 Bt (d 1964); *b* 3 March 1921; *Educ* Eton, Ch Ch Oxford; *m* 1953, Ray, da of R G Charters, of Christchurch, NZ; 1 s, 1 da; *Heir* s, John Seale; *Career* Capt late RA; architect; RIBA; sr lectr Plymouth Sch Architecture; patron 1 living; *Style* - Sir John Seale, Bt; Slade, Kingsbridge, Devon (054 855 226)

SEALE, John Robert Charters; s and h of Sir John Seale, 5 Bt; *b* 17 Aug 1954; *Style* - John Seale Esq

SEALY, Hon Mrs (Lavinia Caroline); twin da of 2 Baron Piercy; *b* 1947; *Educ* Badminton Sch, St Hugh's Oxford; *m* 1971, Nicholas John Elliot Sealy; 1 s, 1 da; *Style* - The Hon Mrs Sealy; Timber Hill, Chobham, Surrey

SEARBY, Norman Halifax; CBE (1961); *b* 12 March 1910; *Educ* Bishop Vesey's G S Sutton Coldfield, Birmingham U; *m* 1934, Violet Monk; 1 s, 3 da; *Career* electrical engr Ferranti Ltd 1932-75, ch engr Radio Dept 1940, man Guided Weapons Dept 1951, dir Ferranti 1963-75; *Recreations* organ building, carpentry, gardening, church activities, painting, snooker; *Style* - Norman Searby Esq CBE; Bryancliffe, Wilmslow Park, Wilmslow, Cheshire

SEARLE, Geoffrey William; CBE (1972), DSC (1943); s of William Arthur Searle (d 1957); *b* 11 April 1914; *m* 1940, Constance, nee Tyrrell; 1 s, 1 da; *Career* Lt-Cdr RNVR, chartered accountant 1936, joined BP 1946, dir of Finance & Planning and chm Exec Ctee BP Trading Ltd (ret 1974), md London & Scottish Marine Oil Co Ltd 1974, chm London & Scottish Marine Oil Co Ltd 1978; *Recreations* tennis, golf, music, gardening; *Clubs* Naval, Oriental, RAC; *Style* - Geoffrey Searle Esq, CBE, DSO; 20 Beech rd, Reigate, Surrey (☎ Reigate 45803); 104 Mountjoy House, Barbican, EC2 (☎ 628 7514)

SEATH, Derrick Stephen; s of Bertram Harrison Seath (d 1920); *b* 16 Sept 1918; *Educ* Trawalla Victoria Australia, Shillelagh Wicklow Ireland; *m* 1948, Mildred Lilian Kathleen, nee Browning; 1 s, 1 da; *Career* Freeman City of London 1979, memb Guild of Freemen 1979, dir Carters (merchants) Ltd, dir Rolls & Son (Produce) Ltd, dir Skins Hides & Leather Trades Assoc Ltd; *Recreations* polo; *Style* - Derrick Seath Esq; 75 Chesterton pk, Cirencester, Glos (☎ Cirencester 66245)

SEBAG-MONTEFIORE, Harold Henry; s of late John Sebag-Montefiore (5 s of Arthur Sebag-Montefiore, himself s of Sir Joseph Sebag-Montefiore and gs of Sarah; Sarah was sis of the philanthropist Sir Moses Montefiore, 1 and last Bt); *b* 5 Dec 1924; *Educ* Stowe, Lower Canada Coll Montreal, Pembroke Coll Cambridge; *m* 1968, Harriet, nee Paley; 1 step da (Jennifer Tess); *Career* served with RAF WW II; barr (Lincoln's Inn 1951), stood for N Paddington (C) 1959, Dep Circuit Judge, memb of Bd of National Theatre, Freeman of City of London, Chevalier de la Legion d'Honneur 1973; *Recreations* broadcasting, polo; *Clubs* Carlton, Hurlingham; *Style* - Harold Sebag-Montefiore Esq; 2 Paper Buildings, Temple, EC4 (☎ 01 353 5835)

SEBRIGHT, Sir Hugo Giles Edmund; 14 Bt (E 1626) of Besford, Worcs; s of Sir Giles Edward Sebright, 13 Bt, CBE (d 1954), and Margery, da of late Adm Sir Sydney Fremantle, GCB, MVO; *b* 2 March 1931; *m* 1, 1952 (m dis 1964), Deirdre Ann, da of Maj Vivian Lionel Slingsby Bethell RA (gs of Hon Slingsby Bethell CB, s of 1 Baron Westbury); 1 s; m 2, 1965, Sheila Mary Howard, da of Walter Howard Rocke & widow of Edward George Hervey; *Heir* s, Peter Sebright; *Career* patron of one living; *Clubs* St James'; *Style* - Sir Hugo Sebright, Bt

SEBRIGHT, Peter Giles Vivian; s (by 1 m) and h of Sir Hugo Sebright, 14 Bt; *b* 2 Aug 1953; *m* 1977, Regina Maria, da of Francis Steven Clarebrough, of Melbourne Australia; 1 s; *Style* - Peter Sebright Esq

SECKER, Prof Philip Edward; s of Cyril Edward Secker (d 1980); *b* 28 April 1936; *Educ* Haberdashers' Aske's Hampstead Sch and London U; *m* 1968, Judith Andrea, da of Douglas Eric Lee (d 1981); 2 s; *Career* chartered engr; lecturer London U 1961-64, visiting assist prof Massachusetts Inst of Tech 1964-65, lecturer 1965-69, sr lecturer 1969-73, reader 1973-75, prof 1975-80; md of IDB (UCNW) Ltd 1971-80; engrg dir Royal Doulton Tableware (Holdings) Ltd 1980-; *Recreations* flying light aircraft and gardening; *Style* - Prof Philip Secker; Gwel-y-Don, Awel Menai, Beaumaris, Gwynedd (☎ 0248 810771)

SECOMBE, Sir Harry Donald; CBE (1963); *b* 8 Sept 1921; *Educ* Dynevor Sch Swansea; *m* 1948, Myra Joan Atherton Swansea; 2 s, 2 da; *Career* entertainer, actor, singer, comedian; served WW II in N Africa and Italy; films include: *Song of Norway*, *Doctor in Trouble* and others; radio: *Educating Archie*, *The Goon Show*; author; pres Lord's Taverners 1980-81, barker Variety Club of GB, past chm Stars Organisation for Spastics, pres Panda (World Wildlife) Fund Club; kt 1981; Books: *Twice Brightly*, *Goon For Lunch*, *Welsh Fargo*; *Recreations* photography, cricket, golf; *Clubs* Savage, RAC; *Style* - Sir Harry Secombe CBE; 46 St James's pla, SW1

SECONDÉ, Sir Reginald Louis; KCMG (1981, CMG 1972), CVO (1968, MVO 1957); s of Lt-Col Emile Charles Secondé (d 1952); *b* 22 July 1922; *Educ* Beaumont, King's Cambridge; *m* 1951, Catherine Penelope, da of Thomas Ralph Sneyd-Kynnersley OBE MC (decd); 1 s, 2 da; *Career* Diplomatic Serv 1949, UK Delegation to United Nations and Br Embassies 1949-69, head of S European Dept (FCO) 1969-72, Roy Coll Def Studies

1972-73, Ambassador to Chile 1973-76, Ambassador to Romania 1977-79 and Venezuela 1979-; *Recreations* gardening, shooting; *Clubs* Cavalry and Guards; *Style* - Sir Reginald Secondé, KCMG, CVO; Br Embassy, Caracas, Venezuela; Wamil Hall, nr Mildenhall, Suffolk (☎ 0638 714160)

SEDGWICK, Stanley; s of Adam Edmondson Sedgwick (d 1958); *b* 20 July 1914; *Educ* John Ruskin Sch Croydon; *m* 1939, Constance Elaine, nee Field; 1 da; *Career* chartered accountant, FICA; with Foreign Office WW II, seconded Air Ministry Intelligence; dep chm & md of London Overseas Freighters Ltd, Patron of Bentley Drivers Club; *Recreations* motoring, travel, photography; *Style* - Stanley Sedgwick Esq; Greensleeves, Leigh Place, Cobham, Surrey

SEEAR, Baroness (Life Peeress UK 1971); Beatrice Nancy Seear; da of Herbert Seear, of Croydon; *b* 7 Aug 1913; *Educ* Croydon H S, Newnham Cambridge, LSE; *Career* Pres of Lib Pty Org 1965-66, Reader in Personnel Management 1970-78 (formerly teacher); author of books on working women; *Style* - The Rt Hon The Lady Seear; The Garden Flat, 44 Blomfield rd, W9 (☎ 01 286 5701)

SEEBOHM, Baron (Life Peer UK 1972); Frederic Seebohm; TD (1949); s of Hugh Exton Seebohm; *b* 18 Jan 1909; *Educ* Leighton Park, Trin Cambridge; *m* 1932, Evangeline, da of late Sir Gerald Hurst QC; 1 s, 2 da; *Career* Lt-Col RA; High Sheriff of Herts 1970-71; dir: Technical Dvpt Capital Ltd, Ship Mortgage Finance Co Ltd, Finance for Shipping Ltd, Estate Duties Investment Tst Ltd, Gillett Bros Discount Co Ltd, Barclays Bank Ltd 1947-79 (dep chm 1968-74), Barclays Bank Int Ltd 1951-79 (also sometime v-chm, dep chm, chm); former v-chm Barclays Bank SA, former Pres Inst of Bankers; kt 1972; *Recreations* gardening, painting; *Clubs* Carlton, Hurlingham; *Style* - The Rt Hon The Lord Seebohm TD; Brook House, Dedham, nr Colchester, Essex (☎ Colchester 3372); 28 Marsham Ct, Marsham st, SW1 (☎ 01 828 2168)

SEEBOHM, Hon Richard Hugh; s of Baron Seebohm; *b* 1933; *m* 1966, Margaret Evelyne Hok; *Style* - The Hon Richard Seebohm; Bradfield End, Manningtree, Essex

SEELY, Sir Nigel Edward; 5 Bt (UK 1896), of Sherwood Lodge, Arnold, Notts and Brooke House, Brooke, Isle of Wight; s of Sir Victor Seely, 4 Bt (d 1980), by his 1 w, Sybil, nee Gibbons, widow of Sir John Bridger Shiffner, 6 Bt; *b* 28 July 1923; *Educ* Stowe; *m* 1949, Loraine, da of late W W Lindley-Travis; 3 da; *Heir* half-bro, Victor Seely; *Career* ch exec Dancer Fitzgerald Sample Int; *Style* - Sir Nigel Seely, Bt; 34 Porchester sq, W2

SEELY, Hon Peter John Philip; s and h of 4 Baron Mottistone; *b* 29 Oct 1949; *m* 1972 (m dis 1975), Joyce, da of Mrs Ellen Cairns, of St Ninians, Stirling; 1 s; *Style* - The Hon Peter Seely; 99 Bow Lane, Finchley, N12

SEELY, Hon Patrick Michael; s of 4 Baron Mottistone; *b* 1960; *Style* - The Hon Patrick Seely

SEELY, Hon Victoria Anne; da of 4 Baron Mottistone; *b* 1957; *Style* - The Hon Victoria Seely

SEELY, Victor Ronald; s of late Sir Victor Seely, 4 Bt, by his 2 w, Hon Patience Kemp, herself da of 1 Baron Rochdale and Lady Beatrice Egerton (da of 3 Earl of Ellesmere by Lady Katharine Phipps, da of 2 Marquess of Normanby); hp of half-bro, Sir Nigel Seely, 5 Bt; *b* 1941; *Educ* Eton, RMA; *m* 1972, Annette Bruce, da of Lt-Col J A D McEwen; *Career* Maj The R Hussars (PWO); *Style* - Victor Seely Esq; Highfield House, Somerford rd, Cirencester, Glos

SEFTON OF GARSTON, Baron (Life Peer UK 1978); William Henry Sefton; s of George Sefton; *b* 5 Aug 1915; *Educ* Duncombe Rd Sch Liverpool; *m* 1940, Phyllis, nee Kerr; *Career* Leader Liverpool County Cncl 1964-78, Oppn Leader Merseyside Co Cncl 1977- (formerly Leader); chm Runcorn Dvpt Corpn 1974-, chm North West Planning Corpn 1975-; *Style* - The Rt The Lord Sefton of Garston; 88 Tramway rd, Liverpool L17 7AZ

SEGAL, Baron (Life Peer UK 1964); Samuel Segal; s of late Prof M H Segal; *b* 2 April 1902; *Educ* Roy G S Newcastle, Jesus Oxford, Westminster Hosp (MRCS, LRCP); *m* 1934, Molly, da of Robert J Rolo OBE, of Alexandria, Egypt; 1 s (decd), 2 da; *Career* former casualty surgeon and house physician Westminster Hosp and sr clinical assist Gt Ormond St Children's Hosp, regional med offr Miny of Health 1951-62; MP (L) Preston 1945-50, Dep Speaker and Dep Chm of Ctees House of Lords 1973-; *Recreations* photography, travel; *Clubs* United Universities, RAF, Roy C'Wlth Soc; *Style* - The Rt Hon The Lord Segal; 208 Frobisher House, Dolphin Square, SW1 (☎ 01 828 7172); 2 Park Town, Oxford (☎ 513322)

SEGROVE, Geoffrey Eric; *b* 4 May 1932; *Educ* Oundle; *m* 1960, Robina, 3 da; *Career* dir Y J Lovell (Holdings) 1965- (public construction co); *Recreations* skiing, squash (yacht: TSMY 'Lan'acre'); *Clubs* Bath, City Livery, Livery Co of Painter Stainers; *Style* - Geoffrey Segrove Esq; Ferndown, Saunton, Devon

SEIRADHAKIS, Hon Mrs (Mercy Burdett); *née* Money-Coutts; da of 6 Baron Latymer TD (d 1949); *b* 16 April 1910; *Educ* Lady Margaret Hall Oxford (BA); *m* 1947, Michael Seiradhakis; 1 s, 1 da; *Career* served with British Red Cross Mission in Greece and Central Mediterranean and with UN Relief and Rehabilitation Administration in Crete; *Style* - The Hon Mrs Seiradhakis; 19 Odos Seirenon, Byrona, Athens

SELBORNE, 4 Earl of (UK 1882); John Roundell Palmer; s of Viscount Wolmer (s of 3 Earl, k on active service 1942) and Priscilla (*see* Baron Newton); suc gf 1971; *b* 24 March 1940; *Educ* Eton, Ch Ch Oxford; *m* 1969, Joanna Van Antwerp, da of Evan James, of Upwood Park, Abingdon; 3 s, 1 da; *Heir* s, Viscount Wolmer; *Career* chm Hops Marketing Bd 1978-, former v-chm The Apple and Pear Dvpt Cncl, tres Bridewell Roy Hosp (King Edward's Sch Witley) 1972-, memb Ag Research Cncl 1975-; *Clubs* Brooks's, Farmers'; *Style* - The Rt Hon The Earl of Selborne; Temple Manor, Selborne, Alton, Hants (☎ Bordon 3646)

SELBY, 4 Viscount (UK 1905); Michael Guy John Gully; s of 3 Viscount (d 1959); *b* 15 Aug 1942; *Educ* Harrow; *m* 1965, Mary Theresa, da of Capt Thomas F Powell; 1 s, 1 da; *Heir* s, Hon Edward Gully; *Career* ACA, ATII, chartered accountant, computer consultant, fish farm advr; *Recreations* shooting, sailing; *Style* - The Rt Hon The Viscount Selby; Ardfern House, by Lochgilphead, Argyll; Island of Shuna, Arduaine, by Oban, Argyll

SELBY, Bishop Suffragan of 1972-; Rt Rev Morris Henry St John Maddocks; s of Rev Canon Arthur Maddocks (d 1953); *b* 28 April 1928; *Educ* St John's Sch Leatherhead, Trin Cambridge; *m* 1955, Anne, da of late William Oliver Miles; *Career* curate St Peter's Ealing 1954-55, St Andrew's Uxbridge 1955-58, vicar of Weaverthorpe, Helperthorpe and Luttons Ambo 1958-61, of St Martin-on-the-Hill Scarborough 1961-71, co-chm Churches' Cncl for Health and Healing 1975-; *Recreations* golf, reading, music; *Clubs* Ganton Golf; *Style* - The Rt Rev The Bishop of Selby; Greenriggs, 8 Bankside Close, Upper Poppleton, York (☎ York 795342)

SELBY, Ralph Walford; CMG (1961); s of Sir Walford Selby KCMG, CB, CVO (d 1965); *b* 20 March 1915; *Educ* Eton, Ch Ch Oxford; *m* 1945, Julianna, da of Capt I Snell MC (d 1958); 3 da; *Career* entered HM Diplomatic Service 1938, Capt Grenadier Gds 1939-45, 1 Sec High Cmmr's Office India 1947-50, Consul-General Boston 1966-69, Minister Rome 1969-72, Ambassador Oslo 1972-75; *Recreations* sailing, tennis, beagling, lumberjack; *Clubs* Roy Yacht Squad, Turf; *Style* - Ralph Selby Esq, CMG; Mengeham House, Mengeham Lane, Hayling Island, Hants (☎ 070 16 3833)

SELBY, Dowager Viscountess; Veronica Catherine Briscoe; da of late J George; *m* 1933, 3 Viscount Selby (d 1959); 2 s, 1 da; *Style* - The Rt Hon The Dowager Viscountess Selby; The Dower House, Island of Shuna, Argyll

SELF, Hugh Michael; QC (1973); s of Sir Henry Self, KCMG, KCB, KBE (d 1975); *b* 19 March 1921; *Educ* Lancing,

Worchester Oxford; *m* 1950, Penelope Ann, nee Drinkwater; 2 da; *Career* Lt RNVR, barr 1951, Recorder 1975, Bencher (Lincoln's Inn) 1980; *Recreations* golf, walking, wine; *Clubs* Savile; *Style* - Hugh Self Esq, QC; 59 Maresfield Gardens, Hampstead, NW3 (☎ 435 8311); Christmas Cottage, Ingram's Green, Midhurst, Sussex

SELF, Hon Mrs (Ruth Kathleen); *née* Napier; twin da of 5 Baron Napier of Magdala, OBE; *b* 1947; *m* 1972, John Arthur Self, PhD; *Style* - The Hon Mrs Self; 70 Victoria rd, Hawthorn East, Melbourne, Vic 3123, Australia

SELIGMAN, Sir Peter Wendel; CBE (1969); s of Dr Richard Joseph Simon Seligman (d 1972); *b* 16 Jan 1913; *Educ* Harrow, Caius Coll Cambridge; *m* 1937, Elizabeth Lavinia Mary, da of Prof John Laviers Wheatley, ARA, RWS (d 1955); 2 s, 4 da; *Career* kt 1978; engineer; md APV Hldgs Ltd 1942-65, chm APV Hldgs Ltd 1965-77, chm Br Chemical Plant Manufacturers Assoc 1965-77, chm Nat Ski Federation of GB 1977-; *Recreations* yachting, skiing, carpentry, travel (owner of yacht 'Thornele II'); *Clubs* Athenaeum, Hawks', Island Sailing; *Style* - Sir Peter Seligman CBE; Dagmar House, Birmingham rd, Cowes, Isle of Wight

SELKIRK, 10 Earl of (S 1646); George Nigel Douglas-Hamilton; KT (1976), GCMG (1959), GBE (1963, OBE 1941), AFC, AE, PC (1955), QC (Scot 1959); s of 13 Duke of Hamilton and younger bro of 14 Duke of Hamilton; suc to Earldom under terms of special remainder 1940, the Earldom & Dukedom having been merged from 1886 to 1940; *b* 4 Jan 1906; *Educ* Eton, Balliol Oxford, Paris, Bonn, Vienna and Edinburgh Us; *m* 1949, Audrey Durell, da of late Maurice Drummond-Sale-Barker; *Heir* n, Alasdair Douglas-Hamilton (Master of Selkirk, *qv*); *Career* advocate Scotland 1934, Gp Capt late Auxiliary Air Force, memb of Roy Co of Archers (Queen's Bodyguard in Scotland), UK Cmmr Singapore and Cmmr-Gen S E Asia 1959-63, Scottish Rep Peer 1945-63, Hon Chief Saulteaux Indians 1967; *Style* - The Rt Hon The Earl of Selkirk, KT, GCMG, GBE, AC, AE, PC, QC; 60 Eaton pla, SW1 (☎ 01 235 6926); Rose Lawn Coppice, Wimborne, Dorset (☎ 883160)

SELKIRK, Master of; Alasdair Malcolm Douglas-Hamilton; s of late Lord Malcolm Douglas-Hamilton, OBE, DFC (3 s of 13 Duke of Hamilton), by his 1 w, (Clodagh) Pamela, da of Lt-Col the Hon Malcom Bowes-Lyon (s of 13 Earl of Strathmore); hp of uncle, 10 Earl of Selkirk, KT, GCMG, GBE, AFC, AE, PC, QC; *b* 10 Sept 1939; *Educ* Gordonstoun, Edinburgh U; *m* 1965, Angela Kathleen, da of John Molony Longley; 2 s, 2 da; *Career* with Morgan Guaranty Tst Co of New York 1964-68, Bank of Scotland 1969- *Recreations* mountaineering, skiing, photography; *Clubs* New (Edinburgh); *Style* - The Master of Selkirk; The Old Manse, Fountainhall, Pencaitland, E Lothian (☎ 340244)

SELKIRK, Hon Mrs - Hon Nadia; *née* Lucas; da of 1 Baron Lucas of Chilworth (d 1967); *b* 1923; *m* 1944, Flt Lt Hamish Selkirk, DFC, RAF; 2 s, 1 da; *Style* - The Hon Mrs Selkirk; Saffron Cottage, Northfield rd, Henley-on-Thames, Oxon

SELSDON, 3 Baron (UK 1932); Sir Malcolm McEacharn Mitchell-Thomson; 4 Bt (UK 1900); s of 2 Baron Selsdon, DSC (d 1963); *b* 27 Oct 1937; *Educ* Winchester; *m* 1965, Patricia Anne, da of Donald Smith; 1 s; *Heir* s, Hon Callum Mitchell-Thomson; *Career* Sub Lt RNVR; banker; *Style* - The Rt Hon The Lord Selsdon; 33 Cadogan lane, SW1 (☎ 01 235 8692)

SEMPILL, Lady (20 in line, S 1489); Ann Moira Sempill; *née* Forbes-Sempill; da of 19 Lord Sempill (d 1965), by his 1 w, Eileen, da of Sir John Lavery, RA; niece of Hon Sir Ewan Forbes of Craigievar, 11 Bt, *qv*; *b* 19 March 1920; *Educ* convents in Austria and Germany, Poles' Convent Ware; *m* 1, 1942 (m dis 1945), Capt Eric Holt, Manchester Regt; 1 da; m 2, 1948, Lt-Col Stuart Whitemore Chant-Sempill, OBE, MC, late Gordon Highlanders (who assumed by decree of Lyon Court 1966 the additional name of Sempill); 2 s, 1 da; *Heir* s, Master of Sempill, *qv*; *Career* late Petty Offr WRNS, ctee memb House of Lords, Cons Peer 1966-; *Style* - The Rt

Hon The Lady Sempill; East Lodge, Druminnor, Rhynie, Aberdeenshire (☎ Rhynie 663); 15 Onslow ct, Drayton gdns, SW10

SEMPILL, Cecilia, Lady; Cecilia Alice; da of late B E Dunbar-Kilburn; *m* 1941, as his 2 w, Col (RAF) 19 Lord Sempill AFC (d 1965); 1 da; *Style* - The Rt Hon Cecilia, Lady Sempill; Craigievar Castle, Lumphanan, Aberdeenshire; Sloane Cottage, Long Melford, Suffolk

SEMPILL, Master of; Hon James William Stuart Whitemore Sempill; s and heir of Lady Sempill, *qv*, by her second husband, Lieutenant-Colonel Stuart Whitemore Chant-Sempill, OBE, MC; *b* 25 Feb 1949; *Educ* The Oratory School, St Clare's Hall Oxford (BA Hons History 1971) and Hertford College Oxford; *m* 1977, Josephine Ann Edith, eldest da of Joseph Norman Rees, of Johannesburg, South Africa; 1 s; *Career* regional manager Argus of Ayr Ltd; formerly with Gallagher Ltd and personal assistant to the managing director of Sentinel Engineering Pty Ltd, of Johannesburg; *Clubs* Vincent's, Carlton; *Style* - The Master of Sempill; Pibworth House, Aldworth, Berkshire (☎ Compton (STD Code 063 522) 202); PO Box 31908, Braamfontein, Johannesburg, Transvaal 2107, Republic of South Africa

SENIOR, Hon Mrs (Norah Marguerite); da of 2 Baron Joicey (d 1940); *b* 1905; *m* 1932, Brig Ronald Henry Senior, DSO, TD; 2 da; *Style* - The Hon Mrs Senior; 110 Eaton sq, SW1

SENIOR, Hon Mrs; Hon Rosemary; da of Baron Hunt of Fawley, CBE (Life Peer); *b* 1943; *Educ* St Andrews U (MA); *m* 1974, Dr Clive Malcolm Senior; *Style* - The Hon Mrs Senior; 55 Warwick sq, SW1

SENIOR, William Hirst; CB(1964); s of Capt Arthur Senior (d 1961); *b* 24 August 1904; *Educ* Bradford G S, London U, Reading U; *m* 1930, Olive Kathleen, nee Killick (d 1978); 2 s, 3 da; *Career* Deputy Sec Dept Ag & Fish Scotland 1958-66; memb: Scottish Country Industries Trust 1967-68, Small Industries Cncl for Rural Areas in Scot 1959-; *Clubs* Royal C'wlth Soc; *Style* - William Senior Esq, CB; Manse Wood, Innerwick, Dunbar, East Lothian (☎ Innerwick 278)

SENN, Peter Alexander; *b* 4 Aug 1925; *Educ* King's Sch Macclesfield; *m* 1953, Lilian Ada Margaret, da of Capt James Kinley, of the IOM; 3 s; *Career* chm and md Selectus Ltd; *Style* - Peter Senn Esq; Cloud Park Farm, Dial Lane, Congleton, Cheshire (☎ 02602 2407)

SENTANCE, David Geoffrey; *b* 17 Jan 1930; *Educ* Newark and Grantham Colls, Huddersfield Poly; *m* 1955, Joan Margaret; 2 c; *Career* civil engr, MIMechE, MIProdE, CDipAF, dir Sutcliffe Engrg Holdings Ltd, md Niels Larson & Son Ltd, dir Recticel Sutcliffe Ltd and Sutcliffe Impact Ltd; *Recreations* music, gardening; *Style* - David Sentance Esq; 21 Far View cres, Almondbury, Huddersfield (☎ 0484 27651)

SERGEANT, Patrick John; *b* 17 March 1924; *Educ* Beaumont Coll; *m* 1952, Gillian, nee Wilks; 2 da (Harriet, Emma); *Career* Lt RNVR, dir Associated Newspapers Group, md Euromoney Publications Ltd, City editor Daily Mail 1960-, winner of Wincott Award as Financial Journalist of the Year 1979; *Recreations* tennis, skiing; *Clubs* RAC, Annabel's; *Style* - Patrick Sergeant Esq; No 1 The Grove, Highate Village, N6 (☎ 01 340 1245)

SEROTA, Baroness (Life Peeress UK 1967); Beatrice; JP (Inner London); da of Alexander Katz; *b* 15 Oct 1919; *Educ* LSE; *m* 1942, Stanley Serota, FICE; 1 s, 1 da; *Career* memb LCC 1954-65 (chm Children's Ctee 1958-65) and of GLC (Lambeth) 1964-67, memb Advisory Cncl in Child Care and Central Training Cncl in Child Care 1958-68, Min of State DHSS 1969-70; govr BBC 1977-, pres Nat Cncl for Unmarried Mother & Her Child 1971-; *Style* - The Rt Hon The Lady Serota, JP; The Coach House, 15 Lyndhurst ter, NW3

SEROTA, Hon Judith Alexandra Anne; da of Baroness Serota, *qv*; *b* 1948; *Educ* Roy Coll of Music

Manchester; *Style* - The Hon Judith Serota

SEROTA, Hon Nicholas Andrew; s of Baroness Serota, *qv*; *b* 1946; *Educ* Cambridge U; *Style* - The Hon Nicholas Serota

SERVATIUS, Hon Mrs - Hon Prunella Jane; da of 9 Baron Hawke; *b* 1951; *Educ* Heathfield Sch; *m* 1976, Albert Hendrik Servatius; 1 s; *Style* - The Hon Mrs Servatius; c/o Pierson, Heldring and Pierson, Korte Vijverberg 2, The Hague, The Netherlands

SERVICE, Hon Mrs - Hon Helen; da of 2 Baron Loch, CB, CMG, MVO, DSO (d 1942); *b* 1919; *m* 1947, G Ronald Service (d 1961); 1 s; *Style* - The Hon Mrs Service; Kinfauns House, Kinfauns, by Perth

SERVICE, Louisa Anne; JP (1969); da of Lt-Col Henry Hemming, OBE, MC (d 1976); *b* 13 Dec 1932; *Educ* various schools in North America and England, St Hilda's Oxford; *m* 1959, Alastair Stanley Douglas, son of Lt-Cdr Douglas Service (d 1976); 1 s, 1 da; *Career* publisher, joint chm of Municipal Group 1976-, dep chm Glass's Guide Service Ltd 1976-, chm Hackney Juvenile Court 1975-; *Recreations* opera, friends, travel; *Clubs* Arts; *Style* - Mrs Alastair Service, JP; 47 Boundary rd, NW8 (☎ 01 624 0583); Villa Ligeia, Cersuta, Maratea, Italy

SETH-SMITH, Hon Mrs (Gabrielle Mary); *née* Sclater-Booth; da of 3 Baron Basing, TD (d 1969); *b* 1929; *m* 1953, Cdr Martin Seth-Smith, RN, s of Brig Hugh Seth-Smith, DSO; 1 s, 1 da; *Style* - The Hon Mrs Seth-Smith; The Triangle, Wildhern, Andover, Hants

SETH-SMITH, Lady Jane Annabelle; *née* Howard; da of 12 Earl of Carlisle; *b* 1947; *m* 1968 (m dis 1977), John Vaughan Seth-Smith; 1 da; *Style* - Lady Jane Seth-Smith

SETH-SMITH, Hon Mrs (Moana Elizabeth Jean); *née* McGowan; da of 2 Baron McGowan (d 1966); *b* 1948; *m* 1978, John David Vaughan Seth-Smith; *Style* - The Hon Mrs Seth-Smith

SETON, Sir (Christopher) Bruce; 12 Bt (NS 1663), of Abercorn, Linlithgowshire; s of Charles Henry Seton (d 1917), ggs of 5 Bt; suc kinsman, Sir Bruce Lovat Seton, 11 Bt, 1969; *b* 3 Oct 1909; *Educ* Marlborough, Magdalene Cambridge; *m* 1939, Joyce Vivian, da of late Oliver George Barnard; 2 s (1 twin), 2 da (1 twin); *Heir* s, Iain Seton; *Career* farmer, now retired; *Style* - Sir Bruce Seton, Bt; Bay Laurel, Thorrington rd, Great Bentley, Colchester, Essex (☎ Colchester 250723)

SETON, Iain Bruce; s and h of Sir (Christopher) Bruce Seton, 12 Bt; *b* 27 Aug 1942; *m* 1963, Margaret Ann, da of Walter Charles Faulkner; 1 s, 1 da; *Style* - Iain Seton Esq; PO Box 253, Bridgetown 6255, W Australia

SETON, James Christall; s of late Christall Seton, gs of 7 Bt; hp of kinsman, Sir Robert Seton, 11 Bt; *b* 21 Jan 1913; *m* 1939, Evelyn, da of Ray Hafer; *Career* sometime Private US Army; *Style* - James Seton Esq; 814 Buckeye st, Miamisburg, Ohio, USA

SETON, Sir Robert James; 11 Bt (NS 1683), of Pitmedden, Aberdeenshire; s of Capt Sir John Hastings Seton, 10 Bt (d 1956); *b* 20 April 1926; *Heir* kinsman, James Seton; *Career* Midshipman RNVR (invalided) 1939-45, former banker Hong Kong and Shanghai Bank, ret 1961; *Recreations* philately, steam railway trains, signed prints; *Style* - Sir Robert Seton, Bt; c/o Hong Kong and Shanghai Banking Corporation, 99 Bishopsgate, EC2

SETTRINGTON, Lord; Charles Henry Gordon-Lennox; s and h of Earl of March and Kinrara, DL; *b* 8 Jan 1955; *Educ* Eton; *m* 1976, Sally, da of late Maurice Clayton and Mrs Dennis Irwin; *Style* - Lord Settrington; Goodwood, Chichester, Sussex

SEYMOUR, Lady Anne Frances Mary; da of 18 Duke of Somerset, DL; *b* 1954; *Style* - Lady Anne Seymour

SEYMOUR, Lady Anne Katherine; da of 8 Marquess of Hertford; *b* 1966; *Style* - Lady Anne Seymour

SEYMOUR, Lady Carolyn Mary; da of 8 Marquess of Hertford; *b* 1960; *Style* - Lady Carolyn Seymour

SEYMOUR, Lady Diana Helen; da of 8 Marquess of Hertford; *b* 1963; *Style* - Lady Diana Seymour

SEYMOUR, Lord Francis Charles Edward; 2 s of 18 Duke of Somerset, DL; hp to bro Lord Seymour; *b* 10 Aug 1956; *Educ* Eton, Coll of Law; *Career* slr, memb HAC; *Recreations* shooting, eating, collecting military vehicles; *Clubs* MCC; *Style* - Lord Francis Seymour; 59 Cranbury rd, SW6 (☎ 01 731 2251)

SEYMOUR, George FitzRoy; JP (Notts 1960), DL (1974); s of Richard Seymour MVO (d 1959, himself gggs of 1 Marquess of Hertford) by Lady Victoria FitzRoy, sis of 10 Duke of Grafton; *b* 8 Feb 1923; *Educ* Winchester; *m* 1946, Hon Rosemary Scott-Ellis, da of 8 Baron Howard de Walden; 1 s, 1 da; *Career* High Sheriff Notts 1966, Lord of Manor of Thrumpton & patron of the Living; *Recreations* shooting, deerstalking, tennis; *Clubs* Pratt's, MCC, Brooks's; *Style* - George Seymour Esq JP DL; Thrumpton Hall, Nottingham (☎ 83033); 38 Molyneux st, W1 (☎ 01 262 7684)

SEYMOUR, George Raymond; MVO; s of Sir Reginald Seymour, KCVO (gs of Rt Hon Sir George Seymour, GCB, GCH, PC, and Hon Gertrude, da of 21 Baron Dacre; Sir George was gs of 1 Marquess of Hertford, KG); *b* 5 May 1923; *Educ* Eton; *m* 1957, Hon Mrs Finnis, da of Gen 1 Baron Ismay (extinct 1965); 1 da; *Career* Maj; dep chm Whitbread & Co; *Recreations* sailing; *Clubs* Boodle's; *Style* - Maj George Seymour, MVO; 'Appletrees', Swains rd, Bembridge, IOW (☎ 2760); The Old Vicarage, Bucklebury, Reading, Berks (☎ Woolhampton 2504); Flat 2, 10 Redcliffe Sq, SW10 (☎ 01 373 4678)

SEYMOUR, Lord; John Michael Edward Seymour; s and h of 18 Duke of Somerset; *b* 30 Dec 1952; *Educ* Eton; *m* 1978, Judith-Rose, da of John Hull; *Style* - Lord Seymour; Maiden Bradley, Warminster, Wilts

SEYMOUR, Lady Katharine; *née* Hamilton; DCVO (1961, CVO 1939); da of 3 Duke of Abercorn, KG, KP, PC (d 1953) and Lady Rosalind Bingham, DBE, da of 4 Earl of Lucan; *b* 25 Feb 1900; *m* 1930, as his 2 w, Lt-Col Sir Reginald Seymour, KCVO (d 1938; gs of Rt Hon Sir George Seymour, GCB, GCH, PC, and Hon Gertrude, da of 21 Baron Dacre; Sir George Seymour was s of Lord George Seymour, 7 s of 1 Marquess of Hertford, KG); *Career* Woman of the Bedchamber to HM Queen Mary 1927-30 (Extra Woman of the Bedchamber 1930-53) and HM Queen Elizabeth (subsequently HM Queen Elizabeth The Queen Mother) 1937-60 (Extra Woman of the Bedchamber 1960-); *Style* - Lady Katharine Seymour, DCVO; Strettington House, Chichester, Sussex (☎ Halnaker 265)

SEYMOUR, Hon Mrs (Mary Quenelda); da of 1 Baron Ismay (d 1965); *b* 1929; *m* 1, 1952, Robert Mervyn Fitz Finnis (d 1955); 2 da; m 2, 1957, Maj George Raymond Seymour, MVO; 1 da; *Style* - The Hon Mrs Seymour; 54 Chelsea sq, SW3

SEYMOUR, Hon Mrs (Rosemary Nest); *née* Scott-Ellis; da of 8 Baron Howard de Walden and 4 Baron Seaford (d 1946); *b* 1922; *m* 1946, George FitzRoy Seymour, s of Richard Sturgis Seymour, MVO (d 1959); 1 s, 1 da; *Style* - The Hon Mrs Seymour; Thrumpton Hall, Notts; 38 Molyneux st, W1

SEYMOUR, Lady Susan Mary; da of late 17 Duke of Somerset, DSO, OBE; *b* 1913; *Career* late Div Pres Br Red Cros Soc; *Style* - Lady Susan Seymour; Sunnyside, Maiden Bradley, Wilts

SHACKLETON, Baron (Life Peer UK 1958); Edward Arthur Alexander Shackleton; KG (1974), OBE (1945), PC (1966); s of Sir Ernest Shackleton CVO OBE, the Antarctic explorer; *b* 15 July 1911; *Educ* Radley, Magdalen Oxford; *m* 1938, Betty, da of Capt Charles E Homan, Elder Bro of Trinity House; 1 s (decd), 1 da; *Career* accompanied expeditions to Borneo & Sarawak 1932, Ellesmereland 1934-35; author, lecturer, broadcaster; MP (L) Preston 1946-50, Preston S 1950-

55, Min of Defence for RAF 1964-67, former Min Without Portfolio and Dep Leader House of Lords, Lord Privy Seal 1968-70, Leader of House of Lords 1968-70, Min in charge CSD 1968-70, Oppn Leader House of Lords 1970-74; dep chm RTZ 1975-, former sr exec & dir John Lewis Partnership; *Style* - The Rt Hon Lord Shackleton KG OBE PC; c/o RTZ Corporation, 6 St James's sq, SW1 (☎ 01 930 2399)

SHACKLETON, Lady Caroline Harriet; *née* Hastings; da of 15 Earl of Huntingdon by his 2 w, Margaret; *b* 12 June 1946; *Educ* St Paul's Girls' Sch, Edinburgh & Oxford Us; *m* 1970, Hon Charles Edward Ernest Shackleton (d 1979), s of Baron Shackleton, KG, OBE, PC (Life Peer); *Career* res psychologist; *Style* - Lady Caroline Shackleton; c/o Messrs Coutts & Co, 440 Strand, WC2

SHAFTESBURY, 10 Earl of (E 1672); Sir Anthony Ashley-Cooper; 11 Bt (E 1622); also Baron Ashley of Wimborne St Giles (E 1661) and Baron Cooper of Pawlett (E 1672); s of Lord Ashley (d 1947, s of 9 Earl of Shaftesbury, KP, GCVO, CBE, PC and Lady Constance, da of Earl Grosvenor (s of 1 Duke of Westminster and Lady Constance Leveson-Gower, da of 2 Duke of Sutherland) and Lady Sibell Lumley, da of 9 Earl of Scarbrough; suc gf 1961; *b* 22 May 1938; *Educ* Eton, Ch Ch Oxford; *m* 1, 1966 (m dis 1976), Mrs Bianca Maria Le Vien, da of late Gino de Paolis; m 2, 1976, Mrs Christina Eva Casella, da of Nils Montan; 2 s; *Heir* s, Lord Ashley; *Career* late Lt 10 Hussars, Hon Citizen S Carolina USA, chm London Philharmonic Orchestra; patron of 8 livings; *Style* - The Rt Hon The Earl of Shaftesbury; St Giles's House, Wimborne, Dorset (Cranborne (072 54) 312)

SHAKERLEY, Charles Frederick Eardley; s of late Maj Sir Cyril Shakerley, 5 Bt, & bro of Sir Geoffrey Shakerley, 6 Bt, *qv*; *b* 14 June 1934; *Educ* Harrow, Ch Ch Oxford, Pennsylvania U; *m* 1962, Lucy Carolyn, da of Francis St G Fisher, of Cragg, Cockermouth, Cumbria; 3 da; *Career* chm Provincial Insurance Co Ltd 1977-, dir Williams & Glyn's Bank 1980-, memb Stock Exchange, sr ptnr Roger Mortimer & Co 1970-75; *Recreations* forestry, shooting, fishing; *Clubs* Brooks's; *Style* - Charles Shakerley Esq; Cudworth Manor, Newdigate, Surrey (☎ 030 677 275)

SHAKERLEY, Lady Elizabeth Georgiana; da of Lt-Col Viscount Anson & sis of 5 Earl of Lichfield; *b* 1941; *m* 1972, as his 2 w, Sir Geoffrey Shakerley, 6 Bt; 1 da; *Career* dir Debrett's Peerage Ltd; proprietor Party Planners; *Style* - Lady Elizabeth Shakerley; 56 Ladbroke Grove, W11 2PB (☎ 01 229 9666)

SHAKERLEY, Sir Geoffrey Adam Shakerley; 5 Bt (UK 1838), of Somerford Park, Cheshire; s of Maj Sir Cyril Holland Shakerley, 5 Bt (d 1970), and Elizabeth, MBE, da of Edward Eardley-Wilmot & gggda of Sir John Eardley-Wilmot, 1 Bt; *b* 9 Dec 1932; *Educ* Harrow, Trin Oxford; *m* 1, 1962, Virginia (d 1968), da of W Maskell; 2 s; m 2, 1972, Lady Elizabeth Anson; 1 da; *Heir* s, Nicholas Shakerley; *Career* late 2 Lt KRRC, dir Photographic Records Ltd 1970-; *Style* - Sir Geoffrey Shakerley, Bt; 56 Ladbroke Grove, W11

SHAKERLEY, Nicholas Simon Adam; s & h of Sir Geoffrey Shakerley, 6 Bt; *b* 20 Dec 1963; *Style* - Nicholas Shakerley Esq

SHAKESPEARE, Elizabeth, Lady; Elizabeth; da of Brig-Gen Robert Hare, CMG, DSO (great nephew of 2 Earl of Listowel); *b* 4 May 1914; *m* 1952, as his 2 w, Rt Hon Sir Geoffrey Shakespeare, 1 Bt, PC (d 1980); *Style* - Elizabeth, Lady Shakespeare; Flat 6, Great Ash, Lubbock rd, Chislehurst, Kent

SHAKESPEARE, Thomas William; s & h of Sir William Shakespeare, 2 Bt; *b* 11 May 1966; *Style* - Thomas Shakespeare Esq

SHAKESPEARE, Sir William Geoffrey; 2 Bt (UK 1942), of Lakenham, City of Norwich; s of Rt Hon Sir Geoffrey Shakespeare, 1 Bt, PC (d 1980), by his 1 w, Aimée, da of Walter Loveridge & widow of Cdr Sir Thomas Fisher, RN; *b* 12 Oct 1927; *Educ* Radley, Clare Cambridge; *m* 1964, Susan, da of Douglas Raffel, of Ceylon; 2 s; *Heir* s, Thomas Shakespeare; *Career* MB,

BChir; Dip in Child Health; GP 1968-; clinical assist Manor House Hosp Aylesbury 1972-, Registrar St George's Hosp 1961-63 & Stoke Mandeville Hosp 1964-66; v-pres Physically Handicapped and Able-Bodied 1977-; *Recreations* gardening, reading; *Clubs* MCC, Stewards' Enclosure Henley Regatta; *Style* - Sir William Shakespeare, Bt; Manor Cottage, Stoke Mandeville, Bucks (☎ 0296 61 2601)

SHAMS-UD DOHA, His Excellency A R; *Career* High Commissioner for Bangladesh in UK; chm Bd Tstees Islamic Centre Regent's Pk London 1981-; *Style* - HE Mr A R Shams-ud Doha; Bangladesh High Commission, 28 Queen's Gate, SW7 (☎ 01 584 0081/589 3073)

SHAND, Alexander Thomas Basil; s of Lt-Col T Shand (d 1953); *b* 26 Oct 1925; *Educ* Oundle Shool, Nottingham U; *Career* civil engineer; dir Charter Consolidated Ltd, chm Alexander Shand (Holdings) Ltd, pres Federation of Civil Engrg Contractors; *Recreations* music, opera, old houses; *Clubs* Hurlingham; *Style* - Alexander Shand Esq; Horham Hall, Thaxted, Essex (☎ 0371 830 389)

SHAND, Maj Bruce Middleton Hope; MC (1940) and Bar (1942), DL (Sussex 1962); s of Philip Morton Shand (d 1960); *b* 22 Jan 1917; *Educ* Rugby, RMC Sandhurst; *m* 1946, Hon Rosalind Maud, nee Cubitt, *qv*, da of 4 Baron Ashcombe; 1 s, 2 da; *Career* Maj late 12 Roy Lancers, Ensign Queen's Bodyguard of the Yeomen of the Guard 1978 (Exon 1971), V-Lord Lt E Sussex 1974; *Recreations* hunting and gardening; *Clubs* White's, Cavalry and Guards; *Style* - Maj Bruce Shand, MC*, HM Vice-Lord-Lieut for East Sussex; The Laines, Plumpton, E Sussex (☎ 890248)

SHAND KYDD, Hon Mrs (Frances Ruth Burke); *née* Roche; da of 4 Baron Fermoy; *b* 20 Jan 1936; *m* 1, 1954, 8 Earl Spencer, MVO, DL (m dis 1969); 1 s: Viscount Althorp (and 1 s decd), 3 da: Lady Sarah McCorquodale, Lady Jane Fellowes, HRH The Princess of Wales (*see* Royal Family); m 2, 1969, Peter Shand Kydd; *Style* - The Hon Mrs Shand Kydd; 5 Warwick sq, SW1 (☎ 01 821 8120); Ardencaple, Isle of Seil, by Oban, Argyll (☎ 08523 213)

SHANNON, 9 Earl of (I 1756); Richard Bentinck Boyle; sits as Baron Carleton (GB 1786); also Viscount Boyle and Baron Castle-Martyr (both I 1756); s of 8 Earl (d 1963); *b* 23 Oct 1924; *Educ* Eton; *m* 1, 1947 (m dis 1955), Donna Catherine Irene Helen, da of Marchese Demetrio Imperiali di Francavilla (cr of King Victor Amadeus III of Piedmont 1779); m 2, 1957 (m dis 1979), Susan Margaret, da of late John Russell Hogg; 1 s, 2 da; *Heir* s, Viscount Boyle; *Career* chm Fndn Sci & Technology; dir Cttee Dirs Res Assoc; V-Pres Inland Waterways Assoc, Br Hydromechanics Res Assoc; Pres Kent BIM, FRSA, FBIM, MBHI; Dep Speaker & Dep Chm Ctees Ho Lds 1968-78; late Capt Irish Gds & Roy W African Frontier Force 1942-54, Assist Mil Attaché Dublin 1946-47; co dir; *Recreations* horology, inland waterways; *Clubs* White's; *Style* - The Rt Hon The Earl of Shannon; Palace Chambers, Bridge st, SW1 (☎ 01 930 0777)

SHANNON, Dowager Countess; Marjorie; da of S A Walker of Ootacamund, India; *m* 1923, 8 Earl of Shannon (d 1963); 1 s; *Style* - The Rt Hon The Dowager Countess of Shannon

SHAPIRO, Hon Mrs; Hon Virginia; *née* Makins; da of 1 Baron Sherfield, GCB, GCMG; *b* 1939; *Educ* LMH Oxford; *m* 1972, David Michael Shapiro; *Style* - The Hon Mrs Shapiro; 14 Woodstock rd, W4

SHAPLAND, Richard Guy; s of Thomas John Shapland; *b* 7 Aug 1932; *Educ* Wellington Sch Somerset; *m* 1956, Dorothy, nee Carter; 1 da (Sarah Jane b 1961); *Career* CA, pres South Western Soc of Chartered Accountants 1981-82; *Recreations* sailing (yacht owned: 'Resurrection'); *Clubs* Royal Cornwall Yacht Club, Royal Overseas League; *Style* - Richard Shapland Esq; Nauron, Tregenver rd, Falmouth, Cornwall (☎ 0326 313 634)

SHARKEY, Colum John; MBE (1973); s of late Andrew Sharkey; *b* 9 June 1931; *Educ* St Malachy's Coll Belfast; *m* 1962,

Olivia, nee Brassil; 2 s, 1 da; *Career* Diplomatic Service 1968, Consul-Gen Bilbao 1978-81, Ambass to Rep of Honduras 1981-; *Style* - Colum Sharkey Esq, MBE; c/o FCO, SW1

SHARP, Baroness (Life Peer UK 1966); Evelyn Adelaide Sharp; GBE (1961, DBE 1948); da of late Rev Charles James Sharp, Vicar of Ealing; *b* 25 May 1903; *Educ* St Pauls's Girls' Sch, Somerville Oxford; *Career* Perm Sec Miny of Housing and Local Govt 1955-66, memb Bd of ITA 1966-73, pres London and Quadrant Housing Tst (formerly chm); *Style* - The Rt Hon The Lady Sharp, GBE; The Small House, Dinton, Salisbury, Wilts

SHARP, Adrian; s and h of Sir Edward Sharp, 3 Bt; *b* 17 Sept 1951; *Style* - Adrian Sharp Esq

SHARP, Sir Edward Herbert; 3 Bt (UK 1922), of Warden Court, Maidstone, Kent; s of Sir Herbert Edward, 2 Bt (d 1936, s of Sir Edward Sharp, 1 Bt, founder of Edward Sharp & Sons Ltd, confectioners); *b* 3 Dec 1927; *Educ* Haileybury; *m* 1949, Beryl Kathleen, da of L Simmons-Green; 2 s, 1 da; *Heir* s, Adrian Sharp; *Style* - Sir Edward Sharp, Bt; PO Box 749, Manzini, Swaziland

SHARP, John; s of Alfred Sharp (d 1968); *b* 18 Dec 1927; *Educ* Keighley G S, BNC Oxford; *m* 1950, Jean, nee Prosser; 1 s, 2 da; *Career* assist master Marlborough Coll 1954-62, senior science master Marlborough Coll 1959-62, headmaster Christ Coll Brecon 1962-72, headmaster Rossall 1973-; *Recreations* fishing, photography, roses; *Clubs* East India; *Style* - John Sharp Esq; The Hall, Rossall School, Fleetwood, Lancs (☎ 039 17 3849)

SHARP, Sir Milton Reginald; 3 Bt (UK 1920) of Heckmondwike, W Riding, Co York; s of Sir Milton Sharp, 2 Bt (d 1941); *b* 21 Nov 1909; *Educ* Shrewsbury, Trin Hall Cambridge; *m* 1, 1935, Dorothy Mary, nee McCarrick; m 2, 1951, Marie-Louise de Vignon, of Paris; *Heir* cous, Samuel Sharp; *Career* Capt REME (TA); *Style* - Sir Milton Sharp, Bt; c/o Messrs Redfearns, Midland Bank Chambers, Heckmondwike, Yorks

SHARP, Ronald Landels; Queen's Jubilee Medal; s of Charles Sharp (d 1955); *b* 18 May 1911; *Educ* Daniel Stewart's College, Edinburgh; *m* 1951, Marian Pinkerton, da of John Burns (d 1956); 1 s, 1 da; *Career* co sec Bruce Lindsay Bros Ltd 1950; *Recreations* golf; *Clubs* Royal Overseas, Royal Scots, RSAC; *Style* - Ronald Sharp Esq; Holmcroft, 1 Maybury rd, Edinburgh, EH4 8DX (☎ 031 339 1924)

SHARP, Samuel Christopher Reginald; s of late Reginald Sharp, bro of Sir Milton Sharp, 2 Bt; hp of cous, Sir Milton Sharp, 3 Bt; *b* 1936; *Educ* Rugby; *m* 1, 1958 (m dis 1967); m 2, --; *Style* - Samuel Sharp Esq; 2231 Bancroft pla, NW, Washington DC 20008, USA

SHARP, Thomas Michael Budworth; CBE (1971, OBE 1966); s of John Sharp (d 1943); *b* 29 Sept 1923; *Educ* Tonbridge Sch, Aberdeen U, Queens' Cambridge, London U; *m* 1966, Ellen Jane Luke, nee McCartney; 1 c; *Career* Capt Roy Artillery Burma, Indian Civil Service 1946, Colonial Admin Serv, Dep Perm Sec Ministry for Local Government N Nigeria 1963-68, sec Interim Common Serv Agency 1968-70, principal Admin Officer Shelmersdale Dvpt Corpn 1973-; *Clubs* Army & Navy; *Style* - Thomas Sharp Esq, CBE; 36 Dunbar cres, Southport, Merseyside

SHARPLES, Baroness (Life Peer UK 1973); Pamela; da of Keith William Newall; *b* 11 Feb 1923; *Educ* Southover Manor Lewes; *m* 1, 1946, Sir Richard Christopher Sharples, KCMG, OBE, MC, Governor of Bermuda (assassinated in Bermuda 1973); 2 s, 2 da; m 2, 1977, Patrick de Laszlo (d 1980); *Style* - The Rt Hon The Lady Sharples; Southfield Farm, Chawton, Alton, Hants (☎ Alton 83318)

SHARPLES, Anthony Frederick Gillett; *b* 19 Jan 1936; *Educ* Ratcliffe Coll, Queens' Cambridge; *m* 1969, Anne Elizabeth, da of George Tallenire; 1 da; *Career* dir Gloster Saro Ltd; *Recreations* sailing; *Style* - Anthony Sharples Esq;

Three Elms, Grosvenor rd, Gloucester, (☎ 0452 23077)

SHARPLES, Hon Christopher John; s (by 1 m) of Baroness Sharples, *qv*, and Sir Richard Sharples KCMG OBE MC (assas 1973); *b* 24 May 1947; *Educ* Eton; *m* 1975, Sharon, da of Robert Sweeny, DFC; 3 children; *Career* joint md Inter Commodities Ltd 1973, chm InterCom Videotex Ltd 1981, commodity broker and electronic publisher; *Recreations* sailing, shooting, tennis; *Clubs* Turf, Royal Yacht Squadron, Royal Ocean Racing; *Style* - The Hon Christopher Sharples; 72 Elm Park rd, London SW3 (☎ 01 352 3791); Chavey Down Farm, Ascot, Berks (☎ Winkfield Row 2215)

SHARPLES, Hon David Richard; s (by 1 m) of Baroness Sharples, *qv*; *b* 1955; *Style* - The Hon David Sharples

SHAUGHNESSY, 3 Baron (UK 1916); William Graham Shaughnessy; s of 2 Baron (d 1938); *b* 28 March 1922; *Educ* Bishop's Coll Sch, Bishop's U Lennoxville Canada; *m* 1944, Mary, da of John Whitley; 2 s, 2 da; *Heir* s, Hon Patrick Shaughnessy; *Career* Maj (ret) Canadian Army, exec assist to Canadian Min Finance 1949-51, pres C'wlth Soc of Canada 1959; dir Canada Northwest Land Ltd 1955-, Arbor Capital Resources Inc 1972-; *Style* - Rt Hon Lord Shaughnessy; Apt 1001, 1209 6th st SW, Calgary, Alberta, Canada T2R OZ5

SHAUGHNESSY, Hon Bridget Ann; da of late 2 Baron Shaughnessy; *b* 1916; *Style* - The Hon Bridget Shaughnessy; 235 Heath st E, Toronto, Ontario, Canada

SHAUGHNESSY, Hon Brigid Mary; da of 3 Baron Shaughnessy; *b* 1948; *Style* - The Hon Brigid Shaughnessy

SHAUGHNESSY, Hon Michael James; s of 3 Baron Shaughnessy; *b* 1946; *Style* - The Hon Michael Shaughnessy

SHAUGHNESSY, Hon Marion Kathleen; da of 3 Baron Shaughnessy; *b* 1951; *Style* - The Hon Marion Shaughnessy

SHAUGHNESSY, Hon Patrick John; s and h of 3 Baron Shaughnessy; *b* 23 Oct 1944; *Style* - The Hon Patrick Shaughnessy

SHAW, Hon Alexander Joseph Ranald; s of 3 Baron Craigmyle; *b* 1971; *Style* - The Hon Alexander Shaw

SHAW, Hon Alison Margaret; da of 3 Baron Craigmyle; *b* 1956; *Style* - The Hon Alison Shaw

SHAW, Brian Piers; s of Percy Augustus Shaw; *b* 21 March 1933; *Educ* Wrekin Coll, CCC Cambridge; *m* 1962, Penelope Gay, nee Reece; 3 s; *Career* chm and md Furness Withy & Co 1979- (md 1977-), chm Cncl of European and Japanese Nat Shipowners' Assocs 1979-, dir Grindlays Bank 1979-;, assist to Court, Worshipful Co of Shipwrights 1979-; *Recreations* golf, cricket, music; *Clubs* MCC, Roy Liverpool Golf; *Style* - Brian Shaw Esq; 5 Alleyn pk, Dulwich, SE21 (☎ 01 670 3012)

SHAW, Hon Catriona Mary; da of 3 Baron Craigmyle; *b* 1958; *Style* - The Hon Catriona Shaw

SHAW, Charles de Vere; s of late Capt John Frederick de Vere Shaw, yr s of 6 Bt; hp of unc, Sir Robert Shaw, 7 Bt; *b* 1 March 1957; *Style* - Charles Shaw Esq

SHAW, Hon Elizabeth Cecilia; da of Baron Kilbrandon, PC (Life Peer); *b* 1948; *Style* - The Hon Elizabeth Shaw

SHAW, (John) Giles (Dunkerley); MP (C) Pudsey Feb 1974-; s of Hugh Dunkerley Shaw; *b* 16 Nov 1931; *Educ* Sedbergh Sch, St John's Cambridge; *m* 1962, Dione Patricia Crosthwaite, da of Prof Mervyn Ellison, of Dublin; 1 s, 2 da; *Career* former pres Cambridge Union, marketing dir Confectionary Div Rowntree Mackintosh Ltd 1969-74, Parly Under-Sec of State Northern Ireland Office 1979-; *Style* - Giles Shaw Esq, MP; 20 Parkside, Horsforth, Leeds

SHAW, Hon Justin Edward Magnus; s of 3 Baron Craigmyle; *b* 1965; *Style* - The Hon Justin Shaw

SHAW, James Thomas Durrant; s of Lt-Col Geoffrey Devereux Shaw (d 1960); *b* 14 June 1927; *Educ* Eton, King's Coll Cambridge; *m* 1956, Jennifer June, da of late Christopher Birkbeck, of Hevingham, Norfolk; 1 s 1 da; *Career* chm and md of Scottow Farms Ltd, dir Scottow Management Services; chm Sywell Airport & Sywell Motel Ltd; Master North Norfolk Harriers 1973-78; *Recreations* hunting, shooting, horse breeding; *Clubs* RAC; *Style* - James Shaw Esq; Scottow Hall, Norwich Norfolk (☎ Swanton Abbott 601)

SHAW, Hon Madeleine Claire; da of 3 Baron Craigmyle; *b* 1963; *Style* - The Hon Madeleine Shaw

SHAW, Hon Michael Frank; s of Baron Kilbrandon, PC (Life Peer); *b* 1944; *m* 1978, Catherine Ballantine; *Style* - The Hon Michael Shaw

SHAW, Michael Norman; JP (Dewsbury 1953), DL (W Yorks 1977), MP (C) Scarborough 1974-; s of late Norman Shaw; *b* 9 Oct 1920; *Educ* Sedbergh; *m* 1951, Joan Mary Louise, da of late Sir Alfred Mowat, 2 Bt; 3 s; *Career* MP (Lib and C) Brighouse and Spenborough 1960-64, (C) Scarborough and Whitby 1966-74, PPS to Min of Labour and Nat Service 1962-63, PPS to Min for Trade and Industry 1970-74; *Style* - Michael Shaw Esq, JP, DL, MP; Duxbury Hall, Liversedge, W Yorks (☎ Heckmondwike 402270)

SHAW, Hon Patrick James; s of Baron Kilbrandon, PC (Life Peer); *b* 1938; *m* 1964, Elisabeth Campbell-Gibson; *Style* - The Hon Patrick Shaw; Highfield, Taynuilt, Argyll

SHAW, Sir Robert; 7 Bt (UK 1821), of Bushy Park, Dublin; s of Lt-Col Sir Robert de Vere Shaw, 6 Bt, MC (d 1969); *b* 31 Jan 1925; *Educ* Harrow, Oklahoma and Missouri Us; *m* 1954, Jocelyn Mary, da of late Andrew McGuffie, of Mbabane, Swaziland; 2 da; *Heir* n, Charles de Vere Shaw; *Career* professional engineer (Alberta), Lt RN (ret); *Style* - Sir Robert Shaw, Bt; 234 40th Avenue SW, Calgary, Alberta, Canada

SHAW, Richard John Gildroy; s of Edward Philip Shaw (d 1970); *b* 7 June 1936; *Educ* Dragon Sch Oxford, Eton; *m* 1973, Yvonne Kathleen, nee Maskell; 1 s (Rupert Henry Gildroy b 1974); *Career* dir Hill Samuel Group Ltd, ch exec Lowndes Lambert Group Ltd (insurance brokers); *Recreations* golf, cricket, reading, yachting (MY 'Moonmaiden'); *Clubs* Sunningdale GC, Portland, Clermont, Lloyd's Yacht; *Style* - Richard Shaw Esq; 18 Phillimore gdns, W8 (☎ 01 937 2942)

SHAW, Sinclair; QC (1950); s of late John Beaumont Shaw; *Educ* Stewart Coll Edinburgh, Edinburgh U; *m* 1948, Denise Fanny, nee Mantoux; *Career* advocate, memb French Resistance 1941-45, Croix de Guerre avec Palme, Chevalier Légion d'Honneur, Médaille de la Résistance; chm Scottish Cncl of Labour Party 1947; Sheriff Edinburgh, the Lothians and Peebles, Sheriff of Chancery 1966-73; *Recreations* travel; *Style* - Sinclair Shaw Esq, QC; 5 Randolph Cliff, Edinburgh (☎ 031 225 4445); La Diane, 32 Rue des Eveuses, 78120 Rambouillet, France

SHAW, Sydney Herbert; CMG (1963), OBE (1958); s of the late John Beaumont Shaw; *b* 6 Nov 1903; *Educ* King's College Sch Wimbledon, Imperial Coll London; *m* 1930, Mary Louise, nee Chapman; 1 s, 1 da; *Career* dir Overseas Geological Surveys and Geological Adviser to Secretary of State for the Colonies 1959-68; *Style* - Sydney Shaw Esq, CMG, OBE; Bishamedge, Stoney Ware, Marlow, Bucks (☎ 062 844951)

SHAW, Hon Thomas Columba; s and h of 3 Baron Craigmyle; *b* 19 Oct 1960; *Style* - The Hon Thomas Shaw

SHAW-STEWART, Sir Houston Mark; 11 Bt (NS 1667), of Greenock and Blackhall, Renfrewshire, MC (1950), TD (1968), DL; s of Lt-Col Sir (Walter) Guy Shaw-Stewart, 9 Bt, MC (d 1976); suc bro, Sir Euan Guy Shaw-Stewart, 10 Bt 1976; *b* 24 April 1931; *Educ* Eton; *Heir* kinsman, Donald Stewart; *Career* 2 Lt Roy Ulster Rifles Korea 1950, Ayrshire Yeo 1952, ret 1969 with rank of Major; jt MFH

Lanarkshire and Renfrewshire 1974-78, Vice Lord-Lt Strathclyde Region Dec 1980-; *Recreations* shooting and racing; *Clubs* White's, Turf, Pratt's; *Style* - Sir Houston Shaw-Stewart, Bt, MC, TD, HM Vice-Lord-Lieutenant for Strathclyde; Ardgowan, Inverkip, Renfrewshire

SHAWCROSS, Baron (Life Peer UK 1959); Hartley William Shawcross; GBE (1974), PC (1946), QC (KC 1939), JP (Sussex); s of late John Shawcross; *b* 4 Feb 1902; *Educ* Dulwich Coll and Geneva; *m* 1, 1924, Rosita Alberta (d 1943), da of William Shyvers; m 2, 1944, Joan Winifred (d 1974), da of Hume Mather, of Tunbridge Wells; 2 s, 1 da; *Career* barr 1925, former recorder; dir of EMI Ltd, Rank Hovis Macdougall Ltd, Caffyns Motors Ltd, Morgan et Cie SA; chm Upjohn & Co Ltd; former dir Times Newspapers, former chm Morgan Guaranty Tst Co's Internat Advisory Cncl; MP (L) St Helens 1945-58; kt 1945, Chllr Sussex U 1965-, chm Internat Chamber of Commerce Cmmn on Unethical Practices 1976-; *Clubs* Buck's, White's, Royal Automobile, Roy Cornwall Yacht, Roy Yacht Squadron, New York Yacht, Travellers' (Paris); *Style* - The Rt Hon The Lord Shawcross, GBE, PC, QC, JP; Friston Place, Sussex

SHAWCROSS, Hon Hume; s (by 2 m) of Baron Shawcross (Life Peer); *b* 1953; *Educ* Eton; *Style* - The Hon Hume Shawcross

SHAWCROSS, Hon Joanna; da (by 2 m) of Baron Shawcross (Life Peer); *b* 1948; *Educ* Benenden, London U; *Style* - The Hon Joanna Shawcross

SHAWCROSS, Hon William Hartley Hume; s (by 2 m) of Baron Shawcross (Life Peer); *b* 1946; *Educ* Eton, Univ Coll Oxford; *m* 1972, Marina Warner; *Style* - The Hon William Shawcross; 40 Estelle rd, NW3

SHAWE-TAYLOR, Desmond Christopher; CBE (1965); s of Francis Manley Shawe-Taylor (d 1920); *b* 29 May 1907; *Educ* Shrewsbury, Oriel Oxford; *Career* Capt RA (Anti-Aircraft); music critic: New Statesman and Nation 1945-58, Sunday Times 1958-, New Yorker (guest critic) 1973-74; *Recreations* gramophone, travel, croquet; *Club* Brooks's; *Style* - Desmond Shawe-Taylor Esq CBE; Long Crichel House, Wimborne, Dorset; 15 Furlong rd, N7

SHEA, Michael Sinclair MacAuslan; s of James Michael Shea, BSc, of Lenzie; *b* 10 May 1938; *Educ* Gordonstoun, Edinburgh U (MA, PhD); *m* 1968, Mona Grec Stensen, da of Egil Stensen, of Oslo; 2 da; *Career* Foreign Office 1964, former First Sec Bonn, Head of Chancery Bucharest 1973, Dep Dir Gen Br Info Services New York 1976, Press Secretary to HM the Queen 1978-; author of *Britain's Offshore Islands* 1981; *Recreations* writing, sailing; *Style* - Michael Shea Esq; Wester Grange, North Berwick, Scotland (☎ (0620) 2094); c/o Buckingham Palace, SW1

SHEARER, Col Edgar Donald Reid; CBE (1974, OBE 1945), TD (1950), DL (Co Down 1959); s of Edgar Shearer; *b* 6 June 1909; *Educ* Aldenham Sch; *m* 1935, Hester Helena, nee Cooke; 3 da; *Career* chm Lindsay Bros (Belfast) Ltd & assoc cos 1970-73, dir Sir Alfred McAlpine & Son Ltd 1959-; chm Ulster Sports & Recreation Trust 1977-80, memb Londonderry Dvpt Trust 1968-73, ADC to HM 1960-64, High Sheriff Co Down 1979; *Recreations* shooting, golf, spectator sport; *Clubs* Ulster, Northern Counties, MCC, Friendly Brothers (Dublin); *Style* - Col Edgar Shearer CBE TD DL; Saltwater Cottage, Finnebrogue, Downpatrick, Co Down, N Ireland (☎ 0396 2081)

SHEASBY, John Michael; s of Herbert Sheasby, OBE; *b* 31 May 1936; *Educ* Haileybury; *m* 1961, Juliet Sylvia, da of Dr Edmund Gillett; 1 s; *Career* Fellow Inst of Chartered Accountants in England and Wales, md RCA Ltd 1969-, pres RCA International Finance Ltd 1977-; *Recreations* sailing, golf, gardening; *Clubs* American, Lansdowne; *Style* - John Sheasby Esq; c/o 50 Curzon st, W1 (☎ 01 499 4100)

SHECHTERMAN, Hon Mrs (Judith Hannah); da of Baron Sieff (Life Peer, d 1972) and sis of Baron Sieff of Brimpton; *b* 1921; *m* 1, 1941 (m dis 1947), Konrad

Steiner; children; m 2, 1947 (m dis 1962), Philip Giaquinto; children; m 3, 1962, Abraham Shechterman; *Style* - The Hon Mrs Shechterman; 20 Dubnow st, Tel Aviv, Israel

SHEDDEN, Hon Mrs (Joan Frances); MBE (1946); s of 2 Baron Vestey (d 1954); *b* 1914; *m* 1, 1934 (m dis 1944), Maj John Hammon Paine, formerly King's Roy Rifle Corps; 1 s; m 2, 1954, John Lindesay Compton Shedden; *Career* sometime Lt First Aid Nursing Yeo; *Style* - The Hon Mrs Shedden, MBE; The Manor, Fossebridge, Glos; Greenhill Farm, Chedworth, Glos

SHEEHY, Hon Mrs (Mary Anne); *née* Lyon-Dalberg-Acton; da of 3 Baron Acton, CMG, MBE, TD; *b* 30 March 1951; *m* 1972, Timothy John Sheehy; 2 da; *Style* - The Hon Mrs Sheehy; 27 Baalbec rd, N5

SHEEPSHANKS, Robin John; DL (Suffolk 1979); s of Maj Richard Sheepshanks DSO, MVO (d 1951); *b* 4 Aug 1925; *Educ* Eton; *m* 1951, Lilias Mulgrave, da of Maj Sir Humphrey Noble, 4 Bt, MBE, of Walwick Hall (d 1968); 4 s; *Career* Capt 1 King's Dragoon Guards 1943-52, farmer, E Suffolk CC 1953-74, Suffolk CC 1974-, chm Conservation Group, High Sheriff 1981; *Recreations* shooting, golf, gardening; *Clubs* Cavalry and Guards, Pratt's; *Style* - Robin Sheepshanks Esq, DL; The Rokery, Eyke, Woodbridge, Suffolk

SHEERMAN, Barry John; MP (L) Huddersfield E 1979-; s of Albert Sheerman; *b* 17 Aug 1940; *Educ* Hampton G S, Kingston Tech Coll, LSE; *m* 1965, Pamela Elizabeth, nee Brenchley; 1 s, 2 da; *Career* former lectr; *Style* - Barry Sheerman Esq, MP; c/o House of Commons, SW1

SHEFFIELD, Bishop of (cr 1914) 1980-; Rt Rev David Ramsay Lunn; *b* 1930; *Educ* King's Cambridge, Cuddesdon Coll Oxford; *Career* deacon 1955, Rural Dean of Tynemouth 1975-80; *Style* - The Rt Rev The Lord Bishop of Sheffield; Bishopscroft, Snaithing Lane, Sheffield, S Yorks

SHEFFIELD, John Julian Lionel George; *b* 28 August 1938; *Educ* Eton, Christ's Cambridge; *m* 1961, Carolyn Alexandra, da of the late Brig Sir Alexander Abel-Smith; 3 s, 1 da; *Career* industrialist; chm Portals Holdings Ltd, chm Basingstoke Sports Trust 1978-, dep chm British Water and Effluent Treatment Assoc 1979-, dir Norcos Ltd 1974-, dir Edward Le Bas Ltd 1971-; *Recreations* tennis, golf; *Clubs* White's, MCC; *Style* - John Sheffield Esq; Laverstoke House, Whitchurch, Hants (☎ Basingstoke 770 770)

SHEFFIELD, John Vincent; s of late Sir Berkeley Sheffield, 6 Bt; hp of n, Sir Reginald Sheffield, 8 Bt; *b* 11 Nov 1913; *Educ* Eton, Magdalene Cambridge; *m* 1, 1936, Anne Margaret (d 1969), da of Sir Lionel Lawson Faudel Faudel-Phillips, 3 Bt; 1 s, 3 da; m 2, 1971, France Mary Agnes, da of Brig-Gen Goland Clarke; *Career* OStJ, former Priv Sec to Min of Works, High Sheriff of Lincs 1944-45, chm Atlantic Assets Trust Ltd 1972-, chm Norcros Ltd 1956-; *Style* - John Sheffield Esq; New Barn House, Laverstoke, Whitchurch, Hants (☎ Whitchurch 3187)

SHEFFIELD, Michael Joseph Forster; TD; s of Brigadier Thomas Tredwell Jackson Sheffield, CBE, TD, DL; *b* 11 April 1930; *Educ* Denstone College Staffs, London U; *m* 1958, Joan Margaret, nee Ridley; 2 c; *Career* Commandant Durham Army Cadet Force 1977, Govr Middlesbrough H S 1965-67; LLB; HM Coroner Teesside 1973-, dir Solicitors' Benevolent Association 1973-, Secretary Teesside Cheshire Home 1973-, dir Fabrecon (Sunderland) Ltd 1968-, v-pres Middlesbrough Rugby Club 1965-, chm 1977-80; DL 1975; *Recreations* tennis, squash, rugby, theatre, military affairs, gardening; *Clubs* Lansdowne, Cleveland Middlesbrough; *Style* - Michael Sheffield Esq, TD, DL; East Hambleton, Guisborough Road, Nunthorpe, nr Middlesbrough (☎ 0642 315476)

SHEFFIELD, Sir Reginald Adrian Berkeley; 8 Bt (GB 1755), of Normanby, Lincolnshire; s of late Maj Edmund Sheffield (s of 6 Bt); suc unc, Sir Robert Sheffield, 7 Bt, 1977; *b* 9 May 1946; *Educ* Eton; *m* 1, 1969 (m dis 1975), Annabel

Lucy Veronica, da of Timothy Angus Jones and Hon Mrs Pandora Astor; 2 da; m 2, 1977, Victoria Penelope, da of late Ronald Walker, DFC; *Heir* unc, John Sheffield; *Career* company dir; dir Normanby Estates Co Ltd, chm Aylesford Hdgs Ltd, memb Lloyd's; *Style* - Sir Reginald Sheffield, Bt; The Old Rectory, West Tytherley, Salisbury, Wilts (☎ Lockerley 40345)

SHELBOURNE, Philip; s of late Leslie John Shelbourne; *b* 15 June 1924; *Educ* Radley Coll, CCC Oxford, Harvard Law Sch; *Career* barr (Inner Temple) 1951-62, ptnr N M Rothschild & Sons 1962-70, ch exec Drayton Corpn 1971-72 (chm 1973-74), chm and ch exec Samuel Montagu & Co 1974-80, chm and ch exec Br Nat Oil Corpn 1980- (salary £58,500 pa as of June 1981); *Recreations* music; *Clubs* Brooks's; *Style* - Philip Shelbourne Esq; Theberton House, Theberton, Suffolk

SHELBURNE, Earl of; Charles Maurice Petty-Fitzmaurice; s (by 1 m) and h of 8 Marquess of Lansdowne, *qv*; *b* 21 Feb 1941; *Educ* Eton; *m* 1965, Lady Frances Eliot, da of 9 Earl of St Germans; 2 s, 1 da; *Heir* s, Viscount Calne and Calstone, *qv*; *Career* late Kenya Regt Roy Wilts Yeo and Roy Wessex Yeo, Page of Honour to HM 1956-57, Co Cllr Wilts 1970-, contested (C) Coventry N E 1979; *Style* - Earl of Shelburne; 3 Rutland st, SW7 (☎ 01 584 1714); Bowood House, Calne, Wilts (☎ 813343)

SHELBURNE, Countess of; Lady Frances Helen Mary; *née* Eliot; da (by 1 m) of 9 Earl of St Germans, *qv*; *b* 1943; *m* 1965, Earl of Shelburne, *qv*; *Style* - Countess of Shelburne; Bowood House, Calne, Wilts

SHELDON, Hon Mr Justice; Hon Sir (John) Gervase (Kensington); s of Dr John Henry Sheldon (d 1960); *b* 4 Oct 1913; *Educ* Winchester, Trin Cambridge; *m* 1, 1940, Patricia Mary, da of Lt-Col Arthur Mardon; 1 s; m 2, 1960, Janet Marguerite, da of George Seager; 2 s, 1 da; *Career* barr 1939, bencher 1978, Co Court Judge 1968-72, Circuit Judge 1972-78, Judge of the High Court of Justice (Family Div) 1978-, Presiding Judge Western Circuit 1980-; kt 1978; *Recreations* shooting, stalking, cricket; *Clubs* Oxford and Cambridge; *Style* - The Hon Mr Justice Sheldon; Royal Courts of Justice, Strand, WC2; Hopton, Churt, Surrey

SHELDON, Rt Hon Robert Edward; PC (1977), MP (L) Ashton-under-Lyne 1964-; *b* 13 Sept 1923; *m* 1945, Eileen Shamash (d 1969); 1 s, 1 da; m 2, 1971, Mary Shield; *Career* Min of State CSD 1974, Financial Sec to Treasury 1975-79; *Recreations* arts, crafts; *Style* - The Rt Hon Robert Sheldon, PC, MP; 2 Ryder st, SW1 (☎ 01 839 4533 and 930 1528); 27 Darley av, Manchester M20 8ZD (☎ 061 445 3489)

SHELLEY, Sir John Richard; 11 Bt (E 1611), of Michelgrove, Sussex (Dr John Shelley, does not use his title); s of John Shelley (d 1974); suc gf, Maj Sir John Frederick Shelley, 10 Bt (d 1976); *b* 18 Jan 1943; *Educ* King's Sch Bruton, Trin Cambridge, St Mary's Hosp London; *m* 1965, Clare, da of Claud Bicknell, OBE; 2 da; *Heir* bro, Thomas Shelley; *Career* GP; partner Drs Durstan-Smith, Shelley and Newth (Medical Practitioners), DObstRCOG, MRCGP; farmer; *Style* - Dr John Shelley; Shobrooke Park, Crediton, Devon; Molford House, 27 South st, South Molton, Devon (☎ 076 95 3101)

SHELLEY, Thomas Henry; s of late John Shelley and hp of bro, Sir John Shelley, 11 Bt; *b* 3 Feb 1945; *Educ* King's Sch Bruton, Trin Cambridge; *m* 1970, Katherine Mary Holton; 3 da; *Style* - Thomas Shelley Esq; Heath Cottage, Padworth Common, Reading, Berks

SHELTON, Hon Mrs; Hon Sarah; *née* Fellowes; da of 3 Baron De Ramsey, KBE; *b* 1938; *m* 1972, Peter Shelton; 1 s, 1 da; *Style* - The Hon Mrs Shelton; Can Magret, Capdella, Palma, Mallorca

SHELTON, William Jeremy Masefield; MP (C) Lambeth, Streatham 1974-; s of late Lt-Col R C M Shelton, MBE; *b* 1929; *Educ* Radley, Oxford U; *m* 1960, Anne Patricia, da of John Warder; 1 s, 1 da; *Career* memb GLC 1967; chm Fletcher Shelton Delaney & Reynolds; MP Wandsworth, Clapham

1970-74, former PPS to Min of Posts and Telecommunications, PPS to Rt Hon Margaret Thatcher, MP, 1975; *Style* - William Shelton Esq, MP; The Manor House, Long Crendon, Bucks (☎ 208748); 27 Ponsonby ter, SW1 (☎ 01 821 8204)

SHENTON, Brian; s of late Harry Shenton; *b* 15 March 1927; *Educ* Doncaster G S Yorks; *m* 1971, Jane Mary, da of the late Lt-Cdr J W White; 1 s 2 da; *Career* md Noble Lowndes & Ptnrs, dir Hill Samuel Life Assur Co, dir English Insur Co Ltd, v-pres Noble Lowndes Inc USA, chm Noble Lowndes Personal Financial Servs, chm Noble Lowndes International Holdings Ltd; *Recreations* former Olympic sprinter 1952-56; golf, music, ornithology, walking, gardening; *Clubs* Liveryman Worshipful Co of Marketers; *Style* - Brian Shenton Esq; Orchard House, Tilburstow Hill, South Godstone, Surrey (☎ S Godstone (034 285) 2471)

SHEPARD, Giles Richard Carless; s of Richard Shepard, MC, TD; *b* 1 April 1937; *Educ* Eton, Harvard Business Sch; *m* 1966, Peter Carolyn Fern; 1 s 1 da; *Career* Capt Coldstream Guards; dir: Charrington & Co Ltd 1962-64, H P Bulmer & Co Ltd 1964-70; md: Westminster & Country Properties Ltd 1970-76, Savoy Hotel Ltd 1976-; memb Court Fishmongers' Co; *Recreations* gardening, shooting, tennis; *Clubs* Boodle's, Pratt's; *Style* - Giles Shepard Esq; Wallop House, Nether Wallop, Hants (☎ Wallop 551)

SHEPHARD, Hon Mrs (Belinda Anne); *née* Renwick; da of 1 Baron Renwick, KBE, by his 1 w, Dorothy; *b* 6 March 1934; *m* 1959, John Shephard; 1 s, 1 da; *Style* - The Hon Mrs Shephard; The Old School House, Winkfield, Berks

SHEPHARD, Hon Mrs (Harriet Olivia); *née* Davies; da of Baron Davies of Leek, PC (Life Peer); *b* 1930; *Educ* London U (BScEcon); *m* 1950, Derek Shephard; *Style* - The Hon Mrs Shephard; 36 Clevenden Mansions, Lissenden gdns, NW5

SHEPHARD, Hon Mrs (Mary Anna); *née* Shaw; da of Baron Kilbrandon (Life Peer); *b* 1946; *m* 1971, Thomas H C Shephard; *Style* - The Hon Mrs Shephard

SHEPHERD, 2 Baron (UK 1946); Malcolm Newton Shepherd; PC (1965); s of 1 Baron (d 1954); *b* 27 Sept 1918; *Educ* Friends' Sch Saffron Walden; *m* 1941, Allison, JP, da of Patrick Redmond; 2 s; *Heir* s, Hon Graeme Shepherd; *Career* chm National Bus Co 1979-, Packaging Cncl 1978-, Civil Service Pay Research Unit Bd 1978-, Sterling Gp of Cos 1976-, Medical Res Cncl, Dep Leader House of Lords 1968-70, Lord Privy Seal and Leader of the House of Lords 1974-76, Min of State Commonwealth Office 1967-70; *Style* - The Rt Hon The Lord Shepherd, PC; 29 Kennington Palace Court, Sancroft st, SE11 (☎ 01 582 6772)

SHEPHERD, Hon Douglas Newton; s of 2 Baron Shepherd, PC; *b* 1952; *Style* - The Hon Douglas Shepherd

SHEPHERD, Frank Cavendish; s of William Ewart Shepherd (d 1960); *b* 15 Aug 1918; *Educ* Manchester G S; *m* 1946, Edna, nee Hankinson; 2 da; *Career* slr, part time chm VAT Appeal Tribunals 1976-; *Recreations* philately, photography; *Clubs* Lyceum (Liverpool); *Style* - Frank Shepherd Esq; Thurlestone Valley Drive, Handforth, Wilmslow, Cheshire

SHEPHERD, Hon Graeme George; s and h of 2 Baron Shepherd, PC; *b* 6 Jan 1949; *m* 1971, Eleanor; 1 s (Patrick Malcolm); *Style* - The Hon Graeme Shepherd; Suite 72, Wheelock House, 20 Pedder st C, Hong Kong

SHEPHERD, Richard Charles Scrimgeour; MP (C) Aldridge-Brownhills 1979-; s of Alfred Shepherd; *b* 6 Dec 1942; *Educ* LSE, Johns Hopkins U; *Career* dir Partridges of Sloane St Ltd, Shepherd Foods Ltd; *Style* - Richard Shepherd Esq, MP; c/o House of Commons, SW1

SHEPPARD, Hon Mrs - Hon Angela; *née* Spring Rice; twin da of 6 Baron Monteagle of Brandon; *b* 1950; *m* 1973, Christopher Richard Seton Sheppard; *Style* - The Hon Mrs Sheppard

SHEPPARD, James Lancelot; s of George Sheppard (d 1939); *b* 13 Sept 1926;

Educ St Julian's H S Newport; *m* 1951 Margaret Mary, da of Alfred Harris (decd); 1 s, 1 da; *Career* CA; assist md IMI Santon Ltd 1976- (CA 1950, co sec 1965, fin dir 1970); *Recreations* hill walking, charity work; *Clubs* Rotary; *Style* - James Sheppard Esq; The Croft, Ridgeway Grove, Newport, Gwent (☎ 0633 33744)

SHEPPARD, Sir Richard Herbert; CBE (1964); s of William Sheppard; *b* 2 July 1910; *Educ* Bristol G S; Architectural Assoc Sch of Architecture; *m* 1, 1938, Jean Shufflebotham (d 1974); 1 s, 1 da; m 2, 1976, Marjorie Head; *Career* architect City U London, Brunel U Uxbridge, Manchester Polytechnic and others; kt 1981; *Style* - Sir Richard Sheppard, CBE; 6 Robin's Nest Hill, Little Berkhamsted, Herts (☎ Cuffley 5066)

SHEPPARD, Col William Paine; MC (1951), TD (1978), DL (N Yorkshire 1976); s of Lt-Col William Hutchings Sheppard (d 1970); *b* 19 April 1929; *Educ* Ellesmere Coll Salop, Sandhurst; *m* 1957, Judith, nee Sawkill; 1 s, 3 da; *Career* RA 1947-58 (Korea, Malaya, Austria, Singapore, Hong Kong, UK, BAOR, Aden); farmer 1960-, md Bootham Properties Ltd 1963-, District Councillor 1974-; *Recreations* hunting, shooting, sailing; *Style* - Col William Sheppard MC TD DL; The Old Rectory, Barton-le-Street, Malton, N Yorks (☎ Hovingham 334)

SHEPPERD, Alfred Joseph; s of Alfred Charles Shepperd (d 1939); *b* 19 June 1925; *Educ* Archbishop Tenison's Sch, Univ Coll London; *m* 1950, Gabrielle Marie Yvette, da of late France Bouloux, MRCS, LRCP; 2 da; *Career* Sub-Lt, RNVR UK and Canada; chm & ch exec The Wellcome Fndn Ltd 1977-, fin dir 1972-; dir Anglia Maltings (Holdings) Ltd 1972-, dir Wood Hall Trust Ltd 1974-, dir Mettoy Co Ltd 1979-, Wood Hall Trust Ltd 1974-, md Keyser Ullman Industries Ltd 1967-, fin dir Laporte Industries Ltd 1971-72; *Clubs* Athenaeum, Oriental, Naval; *Style* - Alfred Shepperd Esq; Court Mead, 6 Guildown Avenue, Guildford, Surrey

SHERBORNE, 7 Baron (GB 1784); Charles Dutton; s of 6 Baron, DSO (d 1949); *b* 13 May 1911; *Educ* Stowe; *m* 1943, Joan Molesworth, da of Sir James Dunn, 1 and last Bt, and widow of John Antony Jenkinson; *Heir* 2 cous once removed, Ralph Dutton; *Career* patron of 2 livings; *Style* - The Rt Hon The Lord Sherborne; Lodge Park, Aldsworth, Cheltenham, Glos (☎ Windrush 296)

SHERBROOKE, John Penn; s of Col Nevile Sherbrooke, CBE, DSO (whose mother was Lady Lilias Cairns, da of 1 Earl Cairns), gn of 1 and last Viscount Sherbrooke; *b* 12 July 1917; *Educ* Eton; *m* 1946, Madeleine Mary, da of Francis Constable Maxwell Stuart (gn of 10 Lord Herries of Terregles) and sis of Peter Maxwell Stuart, *qv*, owner of Traquair; 3 s, 1 da; *Career* WW II Capt RA; solicitor; *Recreations* tennis, gardening; *Style* - John Sherbrooke Esq; Churchen Green, E Morden, Wareham, Dorset

SHERFIELD, 1 Baron (UK 1964); Roger Mellor Makins; GCB (1960, KCB 1953), GCMG (1955, KCMG 1949, CMG 1944), DL (Hants 1978); s of late Brig-Gen Sir Ernest Makins, KBE, CB, DSO; *b* 3 Feb 1904; *Educ* Winchester, Ch Ch Oxford; *m* 1934, Alice, da of late Hon Dwight Davis, of Washington DC, USA; 2 s, 4 da; *Heir* s, Hon Christopher Makins; *Career* fellow of All Souls Coll Oxford, barr 1927, joined Foreign Office 1928, Ambass to USA 1953-56, Jt Perm Sec of Treasury 1956-59; former chm UK Atomic Energy Authority, Hill Samuel & Co Ltd; Chllr Reading U 1970-, chm Wells Fargo Ltd 1972-, A C Cossor Ltd, Raytheon Europe Int Co; *Style* - The Rt Hon The Lord Sherfield, GCB, GCMG, DL; 81 Onslow sq, SW7 (☎ 01 589 6295); Sherfield Court, nr Basingstoke, Hants

SHERLOCK, Edward Barry Orton; s of Victor Edward Sherlock (d 1973); *b* 10 Feb 1932; *Educ* Merchant Taylors' Sch, Pembroke Coll Cambridge; *m* 1955, Lucy Trerice, da of Professor Basil Willey (d 1978); 2 da; *Career* Fellow of The Institute of Actuaries; dir, gen man and actuary of The Equitable Life Assurance Society; *Recreations* music; *Style* - Edward Sherlock Esq; 63 Sunnyfield, NW7 (☎ 01 959 5193)

SHERSBY, (Julian) Michael; MP (C) Hillingdon Uxbridge 1974-; s of William Shersby; *b* 17 Feb 1933; *Educ* John Lyon Sch Harrow-on-the-Hill; *m* 1958, Barbara Joan, da of John H Barrow; 1 s, 1 da; *Career* Dir-Gen Br Sugar Bureau (formerly dir), PPS to Min for Aerospace and Shipping 1974, MP Uxbridge 1972-74; *Style* - Michael Shersby Esq, MP; House of Commons, SW1

SHERSTON-BAKER, Sir Humphrey Dodington Benedict; 6 Bt (GB 1796), of Dunstable House, Richmond, Surrey; s of Lt-Col Sir Dodington Sherston-Baker, 5 Bt (d 1944), and Irene, da of Col Sir John Parkington JP DL; *b* 13 Oct 1907; *Educ* Downside, Christ's Cambridge; *m* 1938 (m dis 1952), Margaret Alice, nee Binns; 1 s, 3 da; *Heir* s, Robert Sherston-Baker; *Style* - Sir Humphrey Sherston-Baker, Bt; 22 Frognal ct, NW3

SHERSTON-BAKER, Robert George Humphrey; s and h of Sir Humphrey Sherston-Baker, 6 Bt; *b* 3 April 1951; *Style* - Robert Sherston-Baker Esq

SHEWAN, Henry Alexander; CB (1974), OBE (1946), QC (1949); s of James Smith Shewan (d 1939); *b* 7 Nov 1906; *Educ* Robert Gordon's Coll Aberdeen, Aberdeen U and Emmanuel Cambridge; *m* 1937, Ann Fraser, nee Thomson; 2 s; *Career* Sqdn Ldr RAF, advocate 1933, National Insurance Commissioner (full-time) 1955-79, Nat Insurance Cmmr (part-time) 1979-; *Clubs* New (Edinburgh), Hon Co Edinburgh Golfers; *Style* - Henry Shewan Esq, CB, OBE, QC; 7 Winton Loan, Edinburgh (☎ 031 445 3239)

SHIELDS, Sir Neil Stanley; MC (1946); s of Archie Shields (d 1958); *b* 7 Sept 1919; *m* 1970, (Gloria) Dawn; *Career* kt 1964; Maj NW Europe 1940 & 1944-46, dir Central & Sheerwood Ltd, chm Holcombe Hldgs Ltd, Standard Catalogue Co Ltd, chm London Area National Union of Conservative Unionist Assocs 1961-63, memb Cncl of Aims for Freedom and Enterprise 1975-; *Recreations* reading, music, wining & dining; *Clubs* Carlton, HAC; *Style* - Sir Neil Shields MC; 12 London House, Avenue rd, NW8 (☎ 01 586 4155)

SHIFFNER, George Frederick; s of late Capt Edward Shiffner (gs of 4 Bt) and hp of kinsman, Sir Henry Shiffner, 8 Bt; *b* 3 Aug 1936; *Educ* Wellington; *m* 1961, Dorothea Helena Cynthia, da of late T H McLean; 1 s, 1 da; *Style* - George Shiffner Esq; 14 Coggeshall rd, Braintree, Essex

SHIFFNER, Sir Henry David; 8 Bt (UK 1818) of Coombe, Sussex; s of Maj Sir Henry Burrows Shiffner, 7 Bt, OBE (d 1941); *b* 2 Feb 1930; *Educ* Rugby, Trin Hall Cambridge; *m* 1, 1951 (m dis 1956), Dorothy, da of W G Jackson; 1 da; m 2, 1957 (m dis 1970), Beryl, da of George Milburn; 1 da; m 3, 1971, Joaquina Rames Lopez, of Madrid; *Heir* kinsman, George Shiffner; *Career* company dir; *Style* - Sir Henry Shiffner, Bt

SHINWELL, Baron (Life Peer UK 1970); Emanuel Shinwell; CH (1965), PC (1945); s of late Samuel Shinwell, of Glasgow; *b* 18 Oct 1884; *m* 1, 1903, Fay Freeman (d 1954); 3 s, 1 da; m 2, 1956, Dinah (d 1971), da of late Carol Ludwig Meyer, of Denmark; m 3, 1972, Sarah (d 1977), da of Solomon Stungo and former w of Alfred Hurst; *Career* formerly Nat Organiser Marine Workers' Union, Parly Sec to Dept of Mines 1924, Parly and Fin Sec War Dept 1929-30, Min of Fuel and Power 1945-47, Sec of State for War 1947-50, Min of Defence 1950-51, chm Parly Labour Party 1964-67, MP (L) Linlithgow 1922-24 and 1928-31, for Seaham Div of Durham 1935-50, and for Easington Div of Durham 1950-70; *Style* - The Rt Hon The Lord Shinwell, CH, PC; House of Lords, SW1

SHIPSTER, Col John Neville; CBE (1973), DSO (1944); s of Col George Cecil Shipster MC (d 1941); *b* 31 Jan 1922; *Educ* Marlborough; *m* 1948, Cornelia Margarethe, nee Arends; 2 s, 1 da; *Career* served WW II 2 Punjab Regt Indian Army, Cmdg Offr 1 Bn Middlesex Regt 1965-67, Cdr Br Forces Honduras 1970-73, Cmdt Defence NBC Sch 1974, Dep Col Queen's Regt 1975; *Recreations* golf, sailing; *Clubs* Army & Navy; *Style* - Col John Shipster CBE DSO; Deben House, 41 Cumberland st, Woodbridge, Suffolk (☎ 03943 3957)

SHIRLEY, Hon Andrew John Carr Sewallis; s of 13 Earl Ferrers; *b* 1965; *Style* - The Hon Andrew Shirley

SHIVELY, Jerry; *Career* chm McCann Erickson Advertising Ltd 1981-; *Style* - Jerry Shively Esq; McCann Erickson House, Howland st, W1 (☎ 01 580 6690)

SHORT, Ian Gradon; *b* 24 June 1927; *Educ* Nottingham H S, Hertford G S; *m* 1953, Sheila Ann, nee Mansell; 1 s; *Career* Lloyd's underwriter 1979-, and Lloyd's broker 1955-, now md Cayzer Steel Bowater Holdings Ltd, chm Cayzer Steel Bowater Ltd, chairman Cayzer Steel Reinsurance Brokers Ltd; *Clubs* Oriental; *Style* - Ian Short Esq; 12A Calverley Park, Tunbridge Wells, Kent (☎ 0892 30586)

SHORT, Mrs Renée; MP (L) Wolverhampton North East 1964-; *Educ* Manchester U; *m* ; 2 da; *Career* freelance journalist; memb Watford RDC 1952-64, CC Herts 1952-67; *Style* - Mrs Renée Short, MP; House of Commons, SW1

SHOWERING, Sir Keith Stanley; s of Herbert Showering; *b* 6 Aug 1930; *Educ* Wells Cathedral Sch; *m* 1953, Marie Sadie, da of Charles Golden; 4 s, 2 da; *Career* chm and ch exec Allied Breweries 1975-, v-chm Guardian Roy Exchange Assurance 1974-, dir Midland Bank 1979-, dir Castlemaine Tooheys (Australia) 1978-; kt 1981; *Recreations* music, shooting; *Clubs* Buck's, Garrick, Arts; *Style* - Sir Keith Showering; 156 St John st, EC1 (☎ 01 584 0695)

SHREWSBURY, Bishop of (RC, cr 1851) 1980- ; The Rt Rev Joseph Gray; s of late Terence Gray; *b* 20 Oct 1919; *Educ* St Patrick's Cavan, Oscott Coll Sutton Coldfield, Maynooth Coll, Pontifical U Rome; *Career* Bishop of Shrewsbury (RC) 1980, Auxiliary Bishop of Liverpool 1969-80, Vicar Gen of Birmingham 1960-69, ordained 1943; *Recreations* music, reading, travel; *Style* - The Rt Rev the Bishop of Shrewsbury; The Council House, Shrewsbury (☎ 0743 3513)

SHREWSBURY, Bishop Suffragan of, 1980-; Rt Rev Leslie Lloyd Rees; s of Rees Thomas Rees (d 1939); *b* 14 April 1919; *Educ* Pontardawe G S, Kelham Theological Coll; *m* 1944, Rosamond, da of Thomas Smith; 2 s; *Career* Chaplain Gen of Prisons 1962-80, Chaplain to HM The Queen 1971-80, Hon Canon of Canterbury 1966-80; *Recreations* music; *Style* - The Rt Rev The Bishop of Shrewsbury; Athlone House, 68 London rd, Shrewsbury (☎ 56410)

SHREWSBURY, Nadine, Countess of; Nadine Muriel; da of late Brig-Gen Cyril Randell Crofton, CBE; *m* 1936 (m dis 1963), 21 Earl (d 1980); 2 s, 4 da; *Style* - Nadine, Countess of Shrewsbury; The Annexe, Upper Bolney, Henley-on-Thames, Oxon

SHREWSBURY AND WATERFORD, 22 Earl of (E 1442, I 1446); Charles Henry John Benedict Crofton Chetwynd Chetwynd-Talbot; Premier Earl (on the Roll) in peerages both of England and Ireland; Baron Talbot (GB 1723), Earl Talbot and Viscount Ingestre (GB 1784); Hereditary Lord High Steward of Ireland; patron of 11 livings; s of 21 Earl (d 1980) by his 1 w, Nadine, Countess of Shrewsbury, *qv*; *b* 18 Dec 1952; *Educ* Harrow; *m* 1974, Deborah Jane, da of Noel Staughton Hutchinson of Ellerton House, Sambrook, Salop; 1 s, 1 da; *Heir* s, Viscount Ingestre; *Style* - The Rt Hon The Earl of Shrewsbury; Forton Hall, Newport, Shropshire (☎ 0952 812135)

SHREWSBURY AND WATERFORD, Dowager Countess of; (Doris Aileen) Nina; da of Dr -- Mortlock; *m* 1963, as his 2 w, 21 Earl (d 1980); *Style* - The Rt Hon The Dowager Countess of Shrewsbury and Waterford; Sentier De Priolaz 8, 1802 Corseaux, Vaud, Switzerland

SHRIMPTON, Col George Henry Thomas; CBE (1962), TD (1948) and 4 Bars; s of Henry David Shrimpton (d 1956); *b* 12 Oct 1914; *Educ* Christ's Hosp; *m* 1940, Joyce Margaret, nee Little; 2 s; *Career* Col AER 1959-62, Col TA 1962-69, ADC (TA) to HM 1964-69, Cmdg Offr 11 Anti-Aircraft Signal Regt 1947-51; *Style* - Col George Shrimpton CBE TD****; 24 Walkerscroft Mead, W Dulwich, SE2 (☎ 670 5346)

SHRIMSLEY, Anthony; s of late John Shrimsley; *b* 12 June 1934; *Educ* William Ellis Sch; *m* 1961, Yvonne Ann, nee Ross; 1 s, 1 da; *Career* ed-in-chief Now! 1979-81, dir Cavenham Communications Ltd, former political ed Manchester Evening News, Sunday Mirror, The Sun, Daily Mail 1973-76, political advr News Gp Newspapers 1976-79, chm Parly Lobby Journalists 1975-76; *Recreations* sailing; *Clubs* Reform; *Style* - Anthony Shrimsley Esq; c/o Cavenham Communications Ltd, 161 City rd, EC1 (☎ 01 250 3030)

SHRIMSLEY, Bernard; s of the late John Shrimsley; *b* 13 Jan 1931; *Educ* Kilburn G S; *m* 1952, Norma Jessie Alexandra, nee Porter; 1 da; *Career* editor News of The World, dir News Group Newspapers Ltd 1975; editor: The Sun 1972, Liverpool Daily Post 1968, northern editor Daily Mirror 1962, dep northern editor Sunday Express 1958; *Style* - Bernard Shrimsley Esq; 30 Bouverie st, EC4 (☎ 01 353 3030)

SHUCKBURGH, Sir Charles Gerald Stewkley; 12 Bt (E 1660), of Shuckburgh, Warwickshire, TD, JP (Warwicks 1946), DL (1965); s of Sir Gerald Shuckburgh, 11 Bt (d 1939); *b* 28 Feb 1911; *Educ* Harrow, Trin Oxford; *m* 1, 1935, Remony Dorothy (d 1936), da of late F N Bell; m 2, 1937, Nancy Diana Mary, OBE, da of late Capt Rupert Egerton Lubbock, RN (ret), bro of 1 Baron Avebury and gs of Sir John Lubbock, 1 Bt; 1 s, 2 da; *Heir* s, Rupert Shuckburgh; *Career* Maj 11 City of London Yeo; *Style* - Sir Charles Shuckburgh, Bt, TD, JP, DL; Shuckburgh, Daventry, Northants (☎ 032 72 2523)

SHUCKBURGH, Hon Lady; Hon Nancy Mildred Gladys; *née* Brett; da of late 3 Viscount Esher, GBE; *b* 1918; *m* 1937, Sir (Charles Arthur) Evelyn Shuckburgh, GCMG, CB, former Ambass to Italy; *Style* - The Hon Lady Shuckburgh; High Wood House, Watlington, Oxon (☎ 049 161 2433)

SHUCKBURGH, Rupert Charles Gerald; s (by 2 m) and h of Sir Charles Shuckburgh, 12 Bt, TD, JP, DL; *b* 12 Feb 1949; *m* 1976, Judith, da of W G Mackaness; 1 s; *Style* - Rupert Shuckburgh Esq

SHUTTLEWORTH, 5 Baron (UK 1902); Sir Charles Geoffrey Nicholas Kay-Shuttleworth; 6 Bt (UK 1850); s of 4 Baron, MC (d 1975), by Anne, da of late Col Geoffrey Phillips, CBE, DSO; *b* 2 Aug 1948; *Educ* Eton; *m* 1975, Ann Mary, da of James Whatman and former w of late Daniel Henry Barclay; 3 s; *Heir* s, Hon Thomas Kay-Shuttleworth; *Career* ARICS, chartered surveyor, ptnr Burton Barnes & Vigers 1977-; *Style* - The Rt Hon The Lord Shuttleworth; Leck Hall, Carnforth, Lancs; 14 Sloane av, SW3 (☎ 01 589 8374)

SHUTTLEWORTH, Dowager Baroness; Anne Elizabeth; da of late Col Geoffrey Francis Phillips, CBE, DSO; *m* 1947, 4 Baron (d 1975); 3 s, 1 da; *Style* - The Rt Hon The Dowager Lady Shuttleworth; Heber House, Leck, Carnforth, Lancs

SHUTTLEWORTH, Hon Mrs (Idonea Mary Ellice); da of late 2 Viscount Cross and Maud, da of late Maj-Gen Inigo Richmond Jones, CVO, CB; *b* 1918; *m* 1946, Lt-Col William Preston Ashton Shuttleworth, RCT (gggs of Sir Thomas Preston, 1 Bt); 2 s, 2 da; *Style* - The Hon Mrs Shuttleworth; 8 Culford Mansions, Culford gdns, SW3 (☎ 01 589 3708); Stoke Lodge, Clee Downton, Ludlow, Salop

SICH, Sir Rupert Leigh; CB (1953); s of Alexander Ernest Sich (d 1926); *b* 3 Aug 1908; *Educ* Radley, Merton Oxford; *m* 1933, Elizabeth Mary, nee Hutchison; 1 s, 2 da; *Career* kt 1968, barr 1930, Board of Trade 1932-48, Principal Assist Treasury Solicitor's Dept 1948-56, registrar Restrictive Trading Agreements 1956-73; *Recreations* music, gardening, golf; *Clubs* Oxford and Cambridge, MCC; *Style* - Sir Rupert Sich CB; Norfolk House, The Mall, Chiswick, W4 (☎ 994 2133)

SIDAWAY, Ronald; *b* 19 March 1916; *Educ* Wolverhampton G S; *m* 1969, Irene Mary Catherine; 1 s, 3 da; *Career* chm Ductile Steels Ltd, chm Ironbridge Gorge Museum Dvpt Trust, chairman Advisory Committee of Wolverhampton Nuffield Hospital; *Recreations* golf, skiing, gardening, Wolverhampton Wanderers Football Club; *Style* - Ronald Sidaway

Esq; Meadow House, Oldbury, nr Bridgnorth, Salop (☎ Bridgnorth 3331)

SIDDELEY, Hon Ernest Hall; s of 1 Baron Kenilworth, CBE (d 1953); *b* 1895; *Educ* St Lawrence Coll Ramsgate; *m* 1921, Muriel, da of late John R Quick; 1 da; *Career* formerly dir Armstrong Siddeley Motors Ltd, of Coventry; European War 1914-18 in France with Roy W Kent Regt; *Style* - The Hon Ernest Siddeley; Poynings, Barford rd, Bloxham, Oxon (☎ Banbury (0295) 720628)

SIDDELEY, Hon Mrs Norman - Pamela; da of late G A Williams, of Gorey, Jersey; *m* 1953, as his 2 wife, Hon Norman Goodier Siddeley (d 1971, s of late 1 Baron Kenilworth); *Style* - The Hon Mrs Norman Siddeley; Le Côtil, Rue du Coin, Grouville, Jersey

SIDDELEY, Hon (John) Randle; s & h of 3 Baron Kenilworth; *b* 16 June 1954; *Educ* Northease Manor, London Coll Furniture; *Style* - The Hon Randle Siddeley; 36 Bear Lane, SE1 (☎ 01 633 9816)

SIDEY, John Macnaughton; DSO (1945); s of John Sidey (d 1968); *b* 11 July 1914; *Educ* Exeter Sch; *m* 1941, Eileen, da of Sir George Wilkinson, 1 Bt, KCVO (d 1967); 1 s, 1 da (decd); *Career* WW II Royal Tank Regiment and Westminster Dragoons, Lt-Col cmd 22 Dragoons, P&SNCo and subsids since 1947, dir P&O Steam Navigation Co 1970-77, divisional ch exec 1972-77; British Railways Board 1962-68, chm Southern Regional Board BRB 1962, Board memb 1955-61, Eastern Regional Board BRB 1963-65; *Recreations* golf, gardening, fishing; *Clubs* Woking Golf; *Style* - John Sidey Esq, DSO; Acre Holt, Golf Club rd, Woking, Surrey (☎ 048 62 4788)

SIDMOUTH, 7 Viscount; John Tonge Anthony Pellew Addington; s of 6 Viscount Sidmouth (d 1976, himself fourth in descent from the 1 Viscount, PM from 1801 to 1804 & the subject of the ill-natured doggerel comparing him unfavourably with the younger Pitt ("Pitt is to Addington /As London is to Paddington"); he was dubbed 'the Doctor' (a calling then held in less esteem than now and commemorating his f's practice as a physician - he attended both Pitt the Elder and George III), but the King nevertheless apparently proposed to create him Earl of Banbury after he resigned the Premiership; later Home Sec for a decade (1812-22), during which the smack of firm government was administered by suspending Habeas Corpus, muzzling the Press, and keeping the lower orders (for example at Peterloo in 1819) in their place); *b* 3 Oct 1914; *Educ* Downside, BNC Oxford; *m* 1940, Barbara Mary Angela, da of Bernard Rochford, OBE; 2 s, 5 da; *Heir* s, Hon Christopher Addington; *Career* Colonial Serv E Africa 1938-54, dir John Rochford & Sons Ltd; Kt of Malta 1962; *Style* - The Rt Hon The Viscount Sidmouth; Stivers, Nightingales Lane, Chalfont St Giles, Bucks (☎ Little Chalfont 2192)

SIDMOUTH, Gladys, Viscountess; Gladys Mary Dever; da of late Thomas Francis Hughes, Cmmr of Imperial Chinese Customs; *b* 2 Feb 1886; *m* 1913, 6 Viscount (d 1976); 6 s, 3 da; *Style* - The Rt Hon Gladys, Viscountess Sidmouth; Amesbury Abbey, Amesbury, Wilts (☎ 0980 22895)

SIDMOUTH, Mary, Viscountess; Mary (Murdoch); da of Sir Donald Campbell Johnstone, formerly Ch Judge of Ch Court, Punjab; *m* 1915, 5 Viscount (d 1953); *Style* - The Rt Hon Mary, Viscountess Sidmouth; Netherclay House, Bishops Hull, Taunton, Somerset

SIDNEY, Hon Philip John Algernon; MBE (1977); s and h of 1 Viscount De L'Isle, VC, KG, GCMG, GCVO, PC, by his 1 w, Hon Jacqueline Vereker; through his f Philip is connected with the poets Sir Philip Sidney and Percy Bysshe Shelley, while through his mother he descends from Robert Smith Surtees, the creator of the sporting grocer John Jorrocks; through his father's mother he is related to Douglas James Kinnaird, who was a boon companion of Byron, and who, like Samuel Rogers, T S Eliot & the late Pamela Hansford Johnson, combined banking and literature (at least to the extent of a comedy and pamphlet on India); *b* 21 April 1945; *m* 1980, Isobel, da of Sir Edmond Compton GCB KBE; *Career* Maj Grenadier Guards, ret; *Style* - The Hon Philip Sidney, MBE; Flat 1, Eaton sq, SW1

SIEFF OF BRIMPTON, Baron (Life Peer UK 1980); Hon Marcus Joseph Sieff; OBE (1944); s of Baron Sieff (Life Peer, d 1972); *b* 2 July 1913; *Educ* Manchester G S, St Paul's and CCC Cambridge; *m* 1, 1937 (m dis 1947), Rosalie Fromson; 1 s; m 2, 1951 (m dis 1953), Elsie Florence Gosen; m 3, 1956 (m dis 1962), Brenda Mary Beith; 1 da; m 3, 1963, Mrs Pauline Lily Moretzki, da of Friedrich Spatz; 1 da; *Career* Col RA; chm and md Marks & Spencer Ltd 1972-, assist md 1963, v-chm 1965, jt md 1967, dep chm 1971; memb BNEC 1965-71; kt 1971; *Style* - The Rt Hon The Lord Sieff of Brimpton OBE; St Michael House, Baker st, W1 (☎ 01 935 4422)

SIEFF, Hon Amanda Jane; da (by 3 m) of Baron Sieff of Brimpton (Life Peer), *qv*; *b* 1958; *Style* - The Hon Amanda Sieff

SIEFF, Hon David Daniel; s (by 1 m) of Baron Sieff of Brimpton (Life Peer), *qv*; *b* 1939; *Educ* Repton; *m* 1962, Jennifer, da of H Walton; *Style* - The Hon David Sieff

SIEFF, Hon Daniela Frederica; da of Baron Sieff of Brimpton (Life Peer), *qv*; *b* 1965

SIEFF, Hon Michael David; CBE (1975); s of late Baron Sieff (Life Peer, d 1972) and bro of Baron Sieff of Brimpton; *b* 1911; *Educ* Manchester G S; *m* 1, 1932 (m dis 1975), Daphne Madge Kerin, da of Cyril Michael; 1 s; m 2, 1975, Elizabeth Pitt; 1 s, 1 da; *Career* assist md Marks and Spencer Ltd 1965-71, jt md 1971-73, v-chm and jt md 1973-76; founder fellow and memb of cncl Roy Post-Graduate Med Sch (Hammersmith Hosp); *Style* - The Hon Michael Sieff, CBE; Michael House, Baker st, W1

SIEGER, Joshua; CBE (1981), OBE (1970); s of Maurice Sieger (d 1950); *b* 5 Jan 1907; *Educ* Latymer Sch, London Polytech Sch of Engrg; *m* 1935, Sylvia Doreen de Wilton, nee Tabbernor; 2 da; *Career* vice pres & dir engrg & res Freed Radio Corp (New York) 1947-51, pres J H Bunnell & Co Ltd Communication Engrs (New York) 1952-53, chm & md J & S Sieger Ltd (Poole) 1954-80, dir Polymetron Ltd (Switzerland) 1980-; *Recreations* sailing (TSDY 'Environist'), motoring; *Clubs* Roy Motor Yacht, Poole Harbour Yacht; *Style* - Joshua Sieger Esq, CBE; Tinkers Revel, 8 Crichel Mount rd, Parkstone, Poole, Dorset (☎ Canford Cliffs 707570); Castel du Cap, Boulevard Maréchal Juin, Cap D'Antibes 06600, France

SIEGHART, Paul; s of Ernest Alexander Sieghart (d 1968); *b* 22 Feb 1927; *Educ* Harrow, Berkhamsted, Univ Coll London U; *m* 1, 1954, Rosemary, nee Aglionby (d 1956); 1 s, 1 da; m 2 1959, Felicity Ann, nee Baer; 1 s, 1 da; *Career* law reformer, int arbitrator and consultant, writer and broadcaster; barr 1953-66, chm exec ctee Justice (British section of Int Cmmn of Jurists) 1978-, govr British Inst of Human Rights 1974-, fndr Cncl for Science and Society (v-chm 1972-78), memb Cmmn for Int Justice and Peace 1976-80, tstee European Human Rights Fndn 1980-, Shaw Memorial Lectr 1981; Publications: *Chalmer's Sale of Goods* (13 & 14 edition), *Slaughterhouses* (jointly with J B Whalley), *Privacy and Computers*; *Recreations* music, skiing, sailing, shooting; *Clubs* Brooks's, Bar Yacht; *Style* - Paul Sieghart Esq; 6 Gray's Inn sq, WClR 5AZ (☎ 01 405 1351)

SIEMENS, Herman Werner; s of Herman Werner Siemens & Berta Luise von Müller, of Munich; *m* 1955, Countess Cornélia Schimmelpenninck (b Lausanne 14 Feb 1928), da of Count Herman Constantijn Schimmelpenninck; (one of Mr Siemens' da, Clara Hedwig Frances, m 1981, Richard Charles Furse, eldest s of A W Furse, of Nerquis Hall, Mold, Clwyd, and thought to be of the Furses of Halsdon); *Career* sometime with Aluminium Co of Canada; *see also* Addenda & Corrigenda

SILKIN, Barony of (UK 1950); *see* Silkin, Arthur

SILKIN, Arthur; s (by 1 m) of 1 Baron Silkin, CH, PC (d 1972); suc f as 2 Baron (UK 1950) 11 May 1972, disclaimed Peerage for life 18 May 1972; *b* 20 Oct 1916; *Educ* Dulwich Coll, Peterhouse Cambridge; *m* 1969, Audrey, da of late

Thomas Bennett; *Heir* bro, Rt Hon Samuel Silkin, PC, QC, MP; *Career* First Sec Br Embassy Kinshasa 1964-66, pub admin lectr Civil Service Coll 1971-76, ret; *Style* - Arthur Silkin Esq; Cuzco, 33 Woodnook rd, SW16 (☎ 01 677 8733)

SILKIN, Rt Hon John Ernest; PC (1966), MP (L) Lewisham, Deptford 1974-; s of late 1 Baron Silkin, CH, PC; *b* 18 March 1923; *Educ* Dulwich Coll, Univ of Wales, Trin Hall Cambridge; *m* 1950, Rosamund John (Lloyd), actress, da of Frederick Jones; 1 s; *Career* slr 1950, Min of Public Building and Works 1969-70, Min for Planning and Local Govt DOE 1974-76, Min of Ag Fish and Food 1976-79, MP Deptford 1963-74, Shadow Leader of the House 1980; *Style* - The Rt Hon John Silkin, PC, MP; 29 Tufton st, SW1 (☎ 01 222 3341)

SILKIN, Rt Hon Samuel Charles; PC (1974), QC (163), MP (L) Southwark, Dulwich 1974-; s of late 1 Baron Silkin, CH, PC; *b* 6 March 1918; *Educ* Dulwich Coll, Trin Hall Cambridge; *m* 1941, Elaine Violet, da of late Arthur Stamp; 2 s, 2 da; *Career* barr 1941, Recorder of Bedford 1966-71, MP Camberwell Dulwich 1964-74, Attorney-Gen 1974-79; *Style* - The Rt Hon Samuel Silkin, PC, QC, MP; Lamb Building, Temple, EC4

SILLS, Thomas Herbert; MBE (1946), TD (1958), DL (Beds 1976); s of Walter Sills; *b* 5 Aug 1915; *Educ* Bradfield; *m* 1939, Eileen Mary, nee Yeadon; 1 s, 1 da; *Career* Maj WW II 1939-45; solicitor 1938, dir Sidney C Banks Ltd 1951-80, sec Sandy Building Soc 1939-73, md Sandy Bldg Soc 1973-79; *Recreations* shooting, fishing; *Clubs* Army & Navy; *Style* - Thomas Sills Esq, MBE, TD, DL; Broadlands, Sandy, Bedfordshire (☎ 0767 80229)

SILSOE, 2 Baron (UK 1963); Sir David Malcom Trustram Eve; 2 Bt (UK 1943), QC (1972); s of 1 Baron Silsoe GBE MC TD QC (d 1976) by his 1 w, Marguerite, da of Sir Augustus Meredith Nanton; *b* 2 May 1930; *Educ* Winchester, Ch Ch Oxford; *m* 1963, Bridget Min, da of Sir Rupert Hart-Davis; 1 s, 1 da; *Heir* s, Hon Simon Eve; *Career* barr 1955, Bar Auditor Inner Temple 1965-70, Bencher 1970; *Style* - The Rt Hon The Lord Silsoe, QC; Neals Farm, Wyfold, Reading, Berks

SILSOE, Margaret, Baroness; Margaret Elizabeth; da of late Henry Wallace Robertson, of Ayton, Berwicks; *m* 1946, as his 2 w, 1 Baron Silsoe (d 1976); *Style* - The Rt Hon Margaret, Lady Silsoe; Lower Ballacottier, Kirk Onchan, IOM (☎ Douglas (0624) 5687)

SILVER, Robert Simpson; CBE (1967); s of Alexander Clark Silver (d 1962); *b* 13 March 1913; *Educ* Montrose Acad, Glasgow U; *m* 1937, Jean McIntyre, nee Bruce; 2 s; *Career* engrg scientist, consultant; James Watt Prof Mechanical Engrg Glasgow U 1966 (Emeritus 1979), Prof Mechanical Engrg Heriot-Watt Coll Edinburgh 1962-66; dir G & J Weir Ltd 1958-; *Recreations* fly-fishing; *Clubs* Roy Scottish Auto; *Style* - Prof Robert Silver CBE; 14 Beech ave, Glasgow (☎ 041 427 1322); Oakbank, Tobermory, Isle of Mull (☎ Tobermory 2024)

SILVERMAN, Julius; MP (L) Birmingham, Erdington 1945-55 & 1974-; s of Nathan Silverman; *b* 8 Dec 1905; *Educ* Central H S Leeds; *m* 1959, Eva Price; *Career* barr 1931, MP Aston 1955-74; *Style* - Julius Silverman Esq, MP; House of Commons, SW1

SILVESTER, Frederick John; MP (C) Manchester, Withington, Feb 1974-; s of William Silvester; *b* 20 Sept 1933; *Educ* Sir George Monoux G S, Sidney Sussex Cambridge; *m* 1971, Victoria Ann, nee Davies; 2 da; *Career* former teacher; MP Walthamstow W 1967-70, Oppn Whip 1974-76; sr assoc dir J Walter Thompson; *Style* - Frederick Silvester Esq, MP; House of Commons, SW1

SIMCOX, Richard Alfred; CBE (1975, MBE 1956); s of the late Alfred William Simcox; *b* 29 March 1915; *Educ* Wolverhampton, Gonville and Caius Cambridge; *m* 1951, Patricia Elisabeth, nee Gutteridge; 1 s, 2 da; *Career* British Council 1943-75: representative Jordan 1957-60, Libya 1960, Cultural Attaché British Embassy Cairo 1968-71, rep Iran 1971-75, now governor Gabbitas-Thring Educational Trust; *Style* - Richard Simcox

Esq, CBE; Little Brockhurst, Lye Green rd, Chesham, Bucks (☎ Chesham 3797)

SIMEON, Sir John Edmund Barrington; 7 Bt (UK 1815), of Grazeley, Berkshire; s of Sir John Walter Barrington Simeon, 6 Bt (d 1957); *b* 1 March 1911; *Educ* Eton, Ch Ch Oxford; *m* 1937, Anne Robina Mary, da of Hamilton Dean; 1 s, 2 da; *Heir* s, Richard Simeon; *Career* Fl Lt (ret) RAF, former civil servant; *Style* - Sir John Simeon, Bt; 1704 Wolfe st, N Vancouver, BC V7M 2Z1, Canada

SIMEON, John Power Barrington; OBE (1978); s of Cornwall Barrington Simeon, of Jersey (d 1957); *b* 15 Nov 1929; *Educ* Beaumont Coll, RMA Sandhurst; *m* 1970, Carina Renate Elisabeth, da of late Michael Schüller, of Bonn; 1 s, 2 da; *Career* entered HM Diplomatic Serv 1965, First Sec (Commercial) Colombo 1967, Bonn 1968-70, First Sec and sometime Acting High Cmmr Port of Spain 1970-73, FCO 1973-75, dep High Cmmr and Head of Post Ibadan, Nigeria, 1975-79, HM Consul-Gen W Berlin 1979-; *Recreations* travel, photography, shooting; *Style* - John Simeon Esq, OBE; Foreign & Commonwealth Office, King Charles st, SW1

SIMEON, Richard Edmund Barrington; s and h of Sir John Simeon, 7 Bt; *b* 2 March 1943; *Educ* British Columbia and Yale (MA, PhD) Us; *m* 1966, Agnes Joan, da of George Frederick Weld; 1 s, 1 da; *Style* - Richard Simeon Esq; 95 Mack st, Kingston, Ontario, Canada

SIMEY, Baroness; Margaret Bayne; da of John Alton Todd; *m* 1935, Baron Simey (Life Peer, d 1969); 1 s; *Style* - The Rt Hon The Lady Simey; 3 Blackburne ter, Blackburne Place, Liverpool 8

SIMEY, Hon Thomas Iliff; s of late Baron Simey (Life Peer, d 1969); *b* 1938; *Educ* St Christopher's Sch Letchworth; *m* 1963, Fiona, da of A G Porteous; children; *Career* chartered architect 1965, tree conservationist, memb Simey Reardon Ptnrship; *Style* - The Hon Thomas Simey; Modyn, Eversley Park, Chester

SIMM, Ralph Octavian; s of Eric Simm (d 1935); *b* 6 May 1921; *Educ* City of London Coll, Southampton U; *m* 1963, Ursula, da of George Sornowski (d 1977); *Career* dir Hoechst UK Ltd; chm Harlow Chemical Co Ltd 1975- and Hoechst Fibre Industs 1980-; *Recreations* music, painting; *Style* - Ralph Simm Esq; Bamford Cottage, South Hill Av, Harrow-on-the-Hill, Middlesex

SIMMONDS, Lady Caroline; *née* Knox; da of 6 Earl of Ranfurly, KCMG; *b* 11 Dec 1948; *m* 1975, John Edward Simmonds; 1 da (b 1976); *Style* - Lady Caroline Simmonds

SIMMONDS, Kenneth Willison; CMG (1956); s of William Henry Simmonds (d 1958); *b* 13 May 1912; *Educ* Bedford Modern, Humberstone Sch, St Cat's Cambridge; *m* 1, 1939 (m dis 1974), Ruth Constance (d 1979), da of Thomas Sargant; 2 s; m 2, 1974, Mrs Catherine Lewis, da of Col Francis Brakenridge CMG MRCS; *Career* Colonial Admin Serv, Dist Admin & Secretariat Kenya 1935-48, Dep Fin Sec Uganda 1948-57, Ch Sec Aden 1957-63; *Recreations* painting, angling, gardening; *Style* - Kenneth Simmonds Esq CMG; North Close, Milverton, Taunton, Somerset (☎ Milverton 235)

SIMOGEN, Sir Pita; *Career* kt 1981 for public and community services Papua New Guinea; *Style* - Sir Pita Simogen

SIMON OF WYTHENSHAWE, Barony of; *see* Simon, Roger

SIMON OF GLAISDALE, Baron (Life Peer UK 1971); Jocelyn Edward Salis Simon; PC (1961), DL (N Yorks 1973); s of Frank Simon; *b* 15 Jan 1911; *Educ* Gresham's, Trin Hall Cambridge; *m* 1, 1934, Gwendolen Helen (d 1937), da of E J Evans; m 2, 1948, Fay Elizabeth Leicester, JP, da of Brig H Guy A Pearson of Jersey; 3 s; *Career* barr 1934, KC 1951, MP (C) Middlesborough W 1951-62, Jt Parly Under-Sec of State Home Office 1957-58, Fin Sec to the Treasury 1958-59, Slr-Gen 1959-62, kt 1959, Pres Probate Divorce and

Admiralty Div High Court of Justice 1962-71, a Lord of Appeal in Ordinary 1971-77, Elder Bro Trinity House; *Style* - The Rt Hon The Lord Simon of Glaisdale, PC, DL; Midge Hall, Glaisdale Head, Whitby, N Yorks (☎ 87205)

SIMON, 2 Viscount (UK 1940); John Gilbert Simon; CMG (1947); s (by 1 m) of 1 Viscount, GCSI, GCVO, OBE, PC, QC (d 1954); *b* 2 Sept 1902; *Educ* Winchester, Balliol Oxford; *m* 1930, James Christie, da of William Stanley Hunt; 1 s, 1 da; *Heir* s, Hon Jan Simon; *Career* Ministry of War Transport 1940-47, md P & O Steam Navigation Co 1947-58, chm Port of London Authority 1958-71; *Style* - The Rt Hon The Viscount Simon CMG; 51 The Strand, Topsham, Exeter

SIMON, Hon Brian; 2 s of 1 Baron Simon of Wythenshawe (d 1960); *b* 1915; *Educ* Gresham's, Trin Cambridge; *m* 1941, Joan Home, da of late Capt Home Peel, DSO, MC; 2 s; *Style* - The Hon Brian Simon; 11 Pendene rd, Leicester

SIMON, Hon Benedict Mark Leycester; s (by 2 m) of Baron Simon of Glaisdale (Life Peer); *b* 1953; *Style* - The Hon Benedict Simon

SIMON, Hon Dominic Crispin Adam; s (by 2 m) of Baron Simon of Glaisdale (Life Peer); *b* 1958; *Style* - The Hon Dominic Simon

SIMON, Hon Jan David; s and h of 2 Viscount Simon, CMG; *b* 20 July 1940; *Educ* Westminster; *m* 1969, Mary Elizabeth, da of John Joseph Burns, of Sydney, NSW; 1 da; *Style* - The Hon Jan Simon; Nairn Cottage, Dog Kennel Lane, The Common, Chorleywood, Herts

SIMON, Hon Matthew; s and h of 2 Baron Simon of Wythenshawe (who does not use his title, *see* Roger Simon); *b* 10 April 1955; *Educ* St Paul's Sch; *Style* - The Hon Matthew Simon

SIMON, Hon Margaret; da of 2 Baron Simon of Wythenshawe (who does not use his title, *see* Roger Simon); *b* 1953; *Style* - The Hon Margaret Simon

SIMON, Hon Peregrine Charles Hugo; s (by 2 m) of Baron Simon of Glaisdale (Life Peer); *b* 1950; *Style* - The Hon Peregrine Simon

SIMON, Roger; 2 Baron Simon of Wythenshawe (UK 1947), but does not use title; s of 1 Baron (d 1960); *b* 16 Oct 1913; *Educ* Gresham's, Gonville and Caius Cambridge; *m* 1951, (Anthea) Daphne, da of Sidney May; 1 s, 1 da; *Heir* s, Hon Matthew Simon; *Style* - Roger Simon Esq; Oakhill, Chester av, Richmond, Surrey

SIMONIS, Peter George; *b* 3 June 1926; *Educ* Cranleigh; *m* 1956, Erica, da of Eric Marsden; 1 s, 1 da; *Career* Lt RNVR, dir Burmah Oil Co Ltd 1970-79, chm Haden Carrier Group 1979-, dir Ellerman Lines Ltd 1979-; *Clubs* Naval, Oriental; *Style* - Peter Simonis Esq

SIMONS, Elkan; CBE (1968); s of David Simons (d 1935); *b* 21 March 1902; *Educ* King Edward's Birmingham; *m* 1927, Coralie Ann, nee Hart; 1 s, 1 da; *Career* chm Trade Promotion Servs 1956-, Simons Bros (London) Ltd 1947-, chm John Edgington (Exhibitions) Ltd 1973-, memb BOTB European Cttee 1975-, pres Export Cncl for Jewelley & Gift Industry 1964-; *Recreations* golf, walking; *Clubs* City Livery; *Style* - Elkan Simons Esq, CBE; 10 Park Way, Temple Fortune Lane, NW11 (☎ 01 455 7448)

SIMPSON, Alfred Moxon; AC (1978), CMG (1959); s of A Simpson, CMG, CBE; *b* 17 Nov 1910; *Educ* St Peter's Coll, Adelaide U; *m* 1938, Elizabeth, da of late Prof Sir John Cleland; 1 s; *Career* chm Simpson Hldgs, SA Telecasters; dir Adelaide Steamship Co, Elder Smith Goldsbrough Mort Ltd, QBE Insurance Group Ltd; *Clubs* Adelaide, Mount Lofty Ski (Adelaide), Melbourne, Union (Sydney); *Style* - Alfred Simpson Esq, AC, CMG; 31 Heatherbank Terrace, Stonyfell, SA 5066, Australia (☎ 31 12 85)

SIMPSON, Sir (John) Cyril Finucane; 3 Bt (UK 1935), of Bradley Hall, Ryton, Co Palatine of Durham; s of Sir Frank Simpson, 1 Bt, CB; suc bro, Sir Basil Simpson, 2 Bt, OBE, 1968; *b* 10 Feb 1899; *Educ* Rugby, Queen's Oxford; *m* 1, 1936

(m dis 1944), da of Frank J Lambert; m 2, 1945, Maria Teresa, da of Capt John Sutherland Harvey, of Romerillo, Biarritz; *Heir* none; *Career* RNAS (2 Medals) WW I; stockbroker; *Style* - Sir Cyril Simpson, Bt; Bradley Hall, Wylam, Northumberland (☎ 2246)

SIMPSON, Air Cdre Charles Hunting; CBE (1960); s of Maj John Andrew Simpson (d 1936); *b* 11 Feb 1915; *Educ* Oundle, Pembroke Coll Cambridge; *m* 1945, Beatrice Gillian Patricia; 2 da; *Career* RAF 1937, Bomber & Flying T'ning Commands WW II, Air Attaché Stockholm 1946-48, Gp Capt 1954, Cmd RAF E Africa 1958-60, ret 1961; memb Lloyd's; horse breeder; *Recreations* yachting, racing; *Clubs* Roy Yacht Sqdn, Boodle's, Bath, RAF; *Style* - Air Cdre Charles Simpson CBE; Fugelmere Grange, Fulmer, Bucks (☎ Fulmer 2051)

SIMPSON, Gen Sir Frank Ernest Wallace; GBE (1953, KBE 1947), KCB (1951, CB 1944), DSO (1960); s of Maj Robert Wallace Simpson MC (d 1950); *b* 21 March 1899; *Educ* Bedford Sch, RMA Woolwich, Trin Cambridge; *m* 1934, Charlotte Cooke; 2 da; *Career* joined RA 1916, Gen 1950, Commandant IDC 1952-54, ADC Gen to HM 1951-52, HM The Queen 1952-54; memb Eastern Electricity Bd 1954-63; Govr Roy Hosp Chelsea 1961-69; late Col Cmdt RE; *Recreations* watching cricket; *Clubs* Naval & Mil, MCC, Bath & County; *Style* - Gen Sir Frank Simpson GBE KCB DSO; 5 Northfields Close, Bath, Avon (☎ 0225 316671)

SIMPSON, Gordon Russell; DSO (1944) and bar (1945), MVO (1979), TD (1945); s of Alexander Russell Simpson, WS (d 1928); *b* 2 Jan 1917; *Educ* Rugby; *m* 1943, Marion Elizabeth, nee King (d 1976); 2 s; *Career* Col (TA) UK 1950; stockbroker 1938, sr ptnr Bell Cowan & Co (now Bell, Lawrie, Macgregor) 1955-; chm Gen Accident Fire & Life Assur Co 1969- (dir 1967-); memb Roy Co of Archers (Queen's Bodyguard for Scotland); *Recreations* skiing, archery, music; *Clubs* New (Edinburgh); *Style* - Col Gordon Simpson DSO & Bar, MVO, TD; Arntomie, Port of Menteith, Perthshire

SIMPSON, Lady Juliet; da of late 4 Earl of Cranbrook by his 2 w, Fidelity; *b* 1934; *m* 1958 (m dis 1970), Charles Colin Simpson, TD; 2 s, 2 da; *Style* - Lady Juliet Simpson; The White House, Rooks Hill, Underriver, Sevenoaks, Kent (☎ 61905)

SIMPSON, Ven John; *aet* 48 in July 1981; *Career* Dir Ordinands & Post-Ordination Studies Diocese of St Albans to 1981; Archdeacon Canterbury and Canon Residentiary Canterbury Cathedral 1981-; as possessor *ex officio* of right to enthrone all 29 Bishops in the Province, enthroned Dr Graham Leonard as Bishop of London in St Paul's Sept 1981; *Style* - The Venerable John Simpson, Archdeacon of Canterbury; 29 The Precincts, Canterbury (☎ 63036)

SIMPSON, Jack William; CBE (1976); s of John Sandall Simpson (d 1950); *b* 30 March 1915; *Educ* Leyton Tech Coll, Woolwich Poly, Jt Servs Staff Coll; *m* 1939, Winifred Doris, da of Henry Mitchell; 2 da; *Career* chartered mechanical engineer, exec MOD 1967-76, special advr to Dir-Gen Roy Ordnance Factories; visiting Prof Roy Mil Coll Science 1978-, City & Guilds Engrg Assessor SE Area 1977-, chm Young Enterprise West Kent Area Bd 1978-; *Recreations* golf, gardening; *Clubs* Nevill Golf; *Style* - Jack Simpson Esq CBE; 59 The Ridgeway, Tonbridge, Kent (☎ 357376)

SIMPSON, Leonard Ian; s of late Walter Septimus Simpson; *b* 16 Dec 1904; *Educ* Marlborough; *m* 1937, Ursula Elizabeth, nee Archbald; 3 s, 1 da; *Career* chartered accountant, chm Comtec (UK) Ltd 1969-, chm Alginure Products 1970-, chm Para Telephone Co Ltd 1947-, retired chm rubber estate companies; *Recreations* gardening, modelling; *Style* - Leonard Simpson Esq; Leyswood House, Groombridge, Tunbridge Wells, Kent (☎ Groombridge 314)

SIMPSON, Dr Samuel Leonard; s of Simeon Simpson (d 1932); *b* 6 Oct 1900; *Educ* Westminster City Sch, Downing Cambridge; *m* 1945, Heddy Monique; 1 da; *Career* consultant, endocrinologist, res worker St Mary's Paddington; fndr

Alexander Simpson Lab for Metabolic Research; chm S Simpson Ltd, Simpson (Piccadilly), Daks-Simpson; Pres Simpson Imports Inc, Daks USA Inc, Daks (Canada); fndr chm Jermyn Street Assoc 1978; *Recreations* golf, boxing; *Style* - Dr Leonard Simpson; 28 Hyde Park Gate, SW7

SIMPSON, Stanhope Rowton; CBE (1953); s of Herbert Simpson DL (d 1932); *b* 7 May 1903; *Educ* Rossall Sch, Magdalene Cambridge; *m* 1930, Evelyn Constance, nee Adams; 1 s, 3 da; *Career* barr 1933, Sudan Political Serv 1925-42, Registrar-Gen and Cmmr of Lands Sudan 1943-53, Land Tenure Advr Colonial Office & Ministry Overseas Dvpt 1953-69; *Style* - Stanhope Simpson Esq, CBE; 65 Collington ave, Bexhill-on-Sea, E Sussex (☎ 0424 211858)

SINCLAIR, 17 Lord (S about 1449, confirmed 1488-9); Charles Murray Kennedy St Clair; MVO (1953), DL (Kircudbrightshire 1969); s of 16 Lord, MVO (d 1957); *b* 21 June 1914; *Educ* Eton, Magdalene Cambridge; *m* 1968, Anne Lettice, da of Sir Richard Cotterell, 5 Bt, CBE, TD; 1 s, 2 da; *Heir* s, Master of Sinclair; *Career* Maj late Coldstream Gds, memb Roy Co of Archers (Queen's Bodyguard for Scotland); Portcullis Pursuivant of Arms 1949-57, York Herald 1957-68, Hon Genealogist Roy Victorian Order 1960-68; an Extra Equerry to HM Queen Elizabeth the Queen Mother 1953-; Vice-Ld-Lt Dumfries and Galloway, Stewartry Dist 1977-; Rep Peer for Scotland 1959-63; *Style* - The Rt Hon The Lord Sinclair, MVO, HM Vice-Lord-Lieut for Dumfries & Galloway; Knocknalling, Dalry, Castle Douglas, Kirkcudbrightshire (☎ 221)

SINCLAIR OF CLEEVE, 2 Baron (UK 1957); Lt-Col John Robert Kilgour Sinclair; OBE (1963, MBE 1954); s of 1 Baron, KCB, KBE (d 1979); *b* 3 Nov 1919; *Educ* Winchester, RMC Sandhurst; *m* 1950, Patricia, da of late Maj Lawrence Hellyer; 1 s, 2 da; *Heir* s, Hon John Lawrence Sinclair; *Career* Lt-Col 1960, Mil Attaché Leopoldville 1960-63, Office of Dep Supreme Allied Cdr Europe SHAPE 1964-66, MOD 1967-69, ret; *Style* - The Rt Hon The Lord Sinclair of Cleeve, OBE; Toppinghoe Hall, Hatfield Peverel, Essex (☎ Chelmsford 380862)

SINCLAIR, Lady (Margaret) Alison; da of late Rev the Hon Charles August Sinclair (s of 16 Earl of Caithness); *b* 1910; *Career* raised to the rank of an Earl's daughter 1948; *Style* - Lady Alison Sinclair; Wych Elm, Kennington, Oxford

SINCLAIR, Hon Angus John; s of 1 Viscount Thurso, KT, CMG, PC (d 1970); *b* 1925; *Educ* Eton and New Coll Oxford; *m* 1, 1955 (m dis 1967), Pamela Karen, da of Dallas Bower; m 2, 1968, Judith Anne Percy; 1 s; *Career* formerly Lt Scots Gds, NW Europe 1945, with BBC 1950-54, and Nigerian Broadcasting Corpn 1954-58, is now with Central Office of Information; *Clubs* Pratt's; *Style* - The Hon Angus Sinclair; 2 The Batch, Swainswick, Bath

SINCLAIR, Lady Augusta Lilian Buchan; MBE; da of late 18 Earl of Caithness; *b* 1910; *Career* formerly Food Advice Organizer, W of Scotland Div Min of Food; *Style* - Lady Augusta Sinclair, MBE; 8 Eton ter, Edinburgh

SINCLAIR, Lady Bridget Elinor; da (by 1 m) of late 6 Earl Fortescue; *b* 1927; *m* 1952, Wing Cdr Gordon Leonard Sinclair, DFC; 2 s, 2 da; *Style* - Lady Bridget Sinclair; Mary Monks Close, Whitchurch, Aylesbury, Bucks

SINCLAIR, Hon Camilla Janet; da of 2 Viscount Thurso; *b* 2 Aug 1957; *Educ* Wycombe Abbey; *Style* - The Hon Camilla Sinclair

SINCLAIR, Clive Marles; s of George Sinclair; *b* 30 July 1940; *Educ* Highgate Sch, St George's Coll Weybridge; *m* 1962, Ann, nee Trevor Briscoe; 2 s, 1 da; *Career* ed Bernards (Publishers) 1958-61; chm Sinclair Research Ltd 1979- (Sinclair Radionics 1962-79, the company that produced pocket TV); fndr Sinclair Browne (publishers) 1981, also of £5,000 annual Sinclair Prize for fiction; *Style* - Clive Sinclair Esq; The Stone House, 3 Madingley rd, Cambridge (☎ 353726)

SINCLAIR, Hugh Macdonald; s of Col Hugh Montogomerie Sinclair CB CMG CBE; *b* 4 Feb 1910; *Educ* Winchester Coll Oxford; *Career* hon nutrition consult Control Cmmn for Germany 1945-47, dir

Int Inst Human Nutrition 1972-, dir Laboratory of Human Nutrition Oxford U and reader in Human Nutrition 1947-57, visiting Prof Food Science Reading U 1970-80; *Recreations* medical history, horticulture; *Clubs* Athenaeum, MCC; *Style* - Hugh Sinclair Esq; Lady Place, Sutton Courtenay, Abingdon, Oxon (☎ Sutton Courtenay 246)

SINCLAIR, Lady Iona Alexandra; da of 20 Earl of Caithness; *b* 1978; *Style* - Lady Iona Sinclair

SINCLAIR, Hon Juliet; da of 2 Baron Sinclair of Cleeve, OBE; *b* 1951; *Style* - The Hon Juliet Sinclair

SINCLAIR, Hon Jane; da of 2 Baron Sinclair of Cleeve, OBE; *b* 1955; *Style* - The Hon Jane Sinclair

SINCLAIR, Hon John Lawrence Robert; s and h of 2 Baron Sinclair of Cleeve, OBE; *b* 6 Jan 1953; *Style* - The Hon John Sinclair

SINCLAIR, Sir John Rollo Norman Blair; 9 Bt (NS 1704), of Dunbeath, Caithness-shire; s of Sir Ronald Sinclair, 8 Bt, TD, JP, DL (d 1952) and bro of Baroness Masham of Ilton (Countess of Swinton); *b* 4 Nov 1928; *Educ* Wellington; *Heir* cous, Patrick Sinclair; *Career* Lt Intelligence Corps BA in Austria; author, lecturer, dir Lucis Trust 1957-61, The Human Development Tst 1970-, Natural Health Foundation 1980-, Wrekin Tst; *Recreations* answering correspondence; *Style* - Sir John Sinclair, Bt; Barrock House, Lyth, by Wick, Caithness, Scotland; c/o Messrs Coutts & Co, Trafalgar Branch, 440 Strand, WC2

SINCLAIR, Lady (Euphemia) Meredith; da of late Rev the Hon Charles Augustus Sinclair (s of 16 Earl of Caithness); *b* 1915; *Career* raised to the rank of a Earl's daughter 1948; *Style* - Lady Meredith Sinclair; King John's Thorn, Hethel, Norwich

SINCLAIR, Hon Mary; da of 2 Baron Pentland; *b* 1942; *Educ* Mount Holyoke, USA (BA); *Style* - The Hon Mary Sinclair; 435 East 87th st, New York City, USA

SINCLAIR, Master of; Hon Matthew Murray Kennedy St Clair; s and h of 17 Lord Sinclair, MVO; *b* 9 Dec 1968; *Style* - The Master of Sinclair; c/o The Rt Hon The Lord Sinclair MVO DL, Knocknalling, Dalry, Castle Douglas, Kirkcudbrightshire

SINCLAIR OF CLEEVE, Mary, Baroness; Mary Shearer; da of late Robert Shearer Barclay; *m* 1917, 1 Baron Sinclair of Cleeve (d 1979); 1 s (2 Baron); *Style* - The Rt Hon Mary, Lady Sinclair of Cleeve; Cleeve Court, near Bristol, Avon (☎ Yatton (STD Code 0934) 832124)

SINCLAIR, Hon Patrick James; s of 2 Viscount Thurso; *b* 1954; *m* Carol North; *Style* - The Hon Patrick Sinclair

SINCLAIR, Patrick Robert Richard; s of late Alexander Sinclair, bro of 8 Bt; hp of cous, Sir John Sinclair, 9 Bt; *b* 21 May 1936; *Educ* Winchester, Oriel Oxford; *m* 1974, Susan Catherine Beresford, da of Geoffrey Davies, OBE; *Career* Sub Lt RNVR, barr Lincoln's Inn 1961; *Style* - Patrick Sinclair Esq; 1 New sq, Lincoln's Inn, WC2

SINCLAIR, Lady Sarah Audrey; *née* Lambart; da of 12 Earl of Cavan; *b* 1948; *m* 1968, Capt Alistair Charles Sinclair, 17/21 Lancers; 2 s; *Style* - Lady Sarah Sinclair; Bransbury Manor, Barton Stacey, Winchester, Hants

SINCLAIR, YR OF ULBSTER, Hon John Archibald; s and h of 2 Viscount Thurso; *b* 10 Sept 1953; *Educ* Eton; *m* 1976, Marion Ticknor, da of Louis D Sage, of Connecticut, USA; 1 da (Louisa Ticknor Beaumont b 1980); *Style* - The Hon John Sinclair, yr of Ulbster

SINCLAIR-LOCKHART, Sir Muir Edward; 14 Bt (NS 1636), of Murkle, Co Caithness, and Stevenson, Co Haddington; s of Sir Robert Sinclair-Lockhart, 11 Bt (d 1918); suc bro, Sir John Beresford Sinclair-Lockhart, 13 Bt 1970; *b* 23 July 1906; *Educ* Wanganui Collegiate Sch; *m* 1940, Olga Ann, da of late Claud White-Parsons; 1 s, 1 da; *Heir* s, Simon Sinclair-Lockhart;

Career retired sheep farmer; *Recreations* hunting (harrier); *Style* - Sir Muir Sinclair-Lockhart, Bt; RD 10, Feilding, New Zealand

SINCLAIR-LOCKHART, Simon John Edward Francis; s and h of Sir Muir Edward Sinclair-Lockhart, 14 Bt; *b* 22 July 1941; *m* 1973, Felicity Edith, da of late I L C Stewart, of Havelock North, NZ, and formerly w of Cdr Michael Newcome Waymouth RNZN; 2 s; *Style* - Simon Sinclair-Lockhart Esq; Onga Onga, Waipawa, Hawkes Bay, New Zealand

SINCLAIR-LOCKHART, Winifred, Lady; Winifred Ray (Graham); da of late Tom Ray Cavaghan, of Aglionby Grange, Carlisle; *m* 1949, Sir John Beresford Sinclair-Lockhart, 13 Bt (d 1970); *Style* - Winifred, Lady Sinclair-Lockhart; Woolmer Hill House, Haslemere, Surrey

SINDEN, Donald Alfred; CBE (1979); s of Alfred Edward Sinden (d 1972); *b* 9 Oct 1923; *m* 1948, Diana, nee Mahony; 2 s; *Career* actor, chm Theatre Museum Adv Cncl, Associate Artist Roy Shakespeare Co, pres Federation of Playgoers Soc, vice pres London Appreciation Soc, memb Victoria & Albert Museum Advsy Cncl; *Recreations* theatrical history, architecture, ecclesiology, serendipity; *Clubs* Garrick, Beeksteak, MCC; *Style* - Donald Sinden Esq, CBE; 60 Temple Fortune Lane, NW11; Rats Castle, Ebony, Isle of Oxney, Kent

SINGER, Hon Mrs (Evelyn Anne); da of Baron Kissin (Life Peer); *b* 1944; *m* 1972, Jack Donald Singer, MD, FAAPaed; *Style* - The Hon Mrs Singer; 45 Campden Hill Court, Campden Hill rd, W8

SINGER, Very Rev Samuel Stanfield; s of William Haus Singer (d 1944); *b* 2 May 1920; *Educ* The Academy Banbridge, Trin Coll Dublin; *m* 1942, Helen, da of Michael Naughton; 3 s, 1 da; *Career* Rector St George's Maryhill Glasgow 1952-62, All Saints' Glasgow 1962-75; Synod Clerk & Canon St Mary's Cathedral Glasgow 1966-74, Dean Glasgow & Galloway 1974-, Rector Holy Trinity Ayr with St Oswald's Maybole 1975; *Style* - The Very Rev the Dean of Glasgow and Galloway; 12 Barns Terrace, Ayr, Scotland (☎ 0292 62382)

SINGLETON, Sir Edward Henry Sibbald; s of William Parkinson Singleton JP (d 1960) by Florence Octavia, da of Sir Francis Scott, 5 Bt, of Shrewsbury; *b* 7 April 1921; *Educ* BNC Oxford; *m* 1943, Margaret Vere, nee Hutton; 3 s, 1 da; *Career* kt 1975, Lt RNVR 1941-45, solicitor, memb Cncl of The Law Soc 1961-80 (pres 1974), chm Solicitors' Law Stationery Soc Ltd 1980-; dir Serck Ltd 1977-, trustee Fleet Air Arm Museum and Temple Bar Trust 1976-, memb Cncl Securities Industry 1979-; *Recreations* relaxing; *Clubs* City of London, Vincent's (Oxford); *Style* - Sir Edward Singleton; 57 Victoria rd, W8

SINHA, 3 Baron (UK 1919); Sudhindro Prosanno Sinha; s (by 2 m) of 2 Baron Sinha (d 1967, s in his turn of 1 Baron, who was the first Indian to be raised to the Peerage and the first member of the Viceroy's Executive Cncl in the wake of the Morley-Minto Reforms under the Raj); *b* 29 Oct 1920; *Educ* Bryanston Sch; *m* 1945, Madhabi, da of late Monoranjan Chatterjee, of Calcutta; 1 s, 2 da; *Heir* s, Hon Sushanto Sinha; *Career* chm and md of McNeill and Barry Ltd Calcutta; *Style* - The Rt Hon The Lord Sinha; 7 Lord Sinha rd, Calcutta, India

SINHA, Hon Anjana; da of 3 Baron Sinha; *b* 1950; *Style* - The Hon Anjana Sinha

SINHA, Hon A K; s (by 2 m) of 2 Baron Sinha (d 1967); *b* 1930; *Style* - The Hon A K Sinha

SINHA, Hon Bina; da (by 1 m) of late 2 Baron Sinha; *b* 1917; *Style* - The Hon Bina Sinha

SINHA, Hon Gita; da (by 1 m) of late 2 Baron Sinha; *b* 1918; *Style* - The Hon Gita Sinha

SINHA, Hon Manjula; da of 3 Baron Sinha; *b* 1947; *Style* - The Hon Manjula Sinha

SINHA, Nirupama, Baroness; Nirupama; da of Rai Bahadur Lalit Mohan Chatterjee; *m* 1919, as his 2 w, 2 Baron (d 1967); 2 s, 1 da; *Style* - The Rt Hon Nirupama, Lady Sinha; 7 Lord Sinha rd, Calcutta, India

SINHA, Hon Sushanto; s and h of 3 Baron Sinha; *b* 1953; *Style* - The Hon Sushanto Sinha

SINHA, Hon Sheila; da (by 2 m) of late 2 Baron Sinha; *b* 1923; *Style* - The Hon Sheila Sinha

SINHA, Hon Tarun; s of late 1 Baron Sinha (Rt Hon Sir Satyendra Prasanna Sinha, KCSI, PC, KC, the first Indian to be created a peer); *b* 1899; *Educ* Hertford Oxford; *Style* - The Hon Tarun Sinha

SISMEY, Lt-Col Oliver North Deane; s of George Herbert Sismey (d 1958); *b* 25 Oct 1900; *Educ* Cheam Sch, Eton, Sandhurst; *m* 1, 1931, Anne Laetitia, da of Brig-Gen Lewis Francis Philips CB, CMG, CBE, DSO (d 1935); 1 da (Islay Anne); m 2, 1956, Pauline Vincent, nee Turner; *Career* Lt-Col OC 2 Bn KRRC; DL Huntingdonshire 1952, Cambridgeshire on amalgamation of counties; CCllr Huntingdonshire 1949-, chm Police Authority 1954-64, County Alderman Huntingdonshire 1960-65, Huntingdon & Peterborough 1965-74; *Recreations* formerly: hunting, shooting, polo, rackets, now: gardening; *Style* - Lt-Col Oliver Sismey DL; Offord Cluny Manor, nr Huntingdon (☎ 810 259)

SITWELL, (Sacheverell) Reresby; s and h of Sir Sacheverell Sitwell, 6 Bt; *b* 15 April 1927; *Educ* Eton, King's Cambridge; *m* 1952, Penelope, da of Col the Hon Donald Forbes, DSO, MVO, s of 7 Earl of Granard; 1 da; *Career* Lt Gren Gds, BAOR W Germany 1946-8; advertising and public relations exec 1948-60, wine merchant 1960-72 (as proprietor of Renishaw Hall enjoys the distinction of owning probably the northernmost vineyard in the world), landowner 1965-; *Recreations* travel; *Clubs* White's, Brooks's, Pratt's; *Style* - Reresby Sitwell Esq; Renishaw Hall, nr Sheffield; 4 Southwick pla, W2 (☎ 01 262 3939)

SITWELL, Sir Sacheverell; 6 Bt (UK 1808), of Renishaw, Derbyshire; s of Sir George Sitwell, 4 Bt (d 1943), and Lady Ida Denison (da of 1 Earl of Londesborough (himself s of 1 Baron Londesborough) and Lady Edith Somerset, da of 7 Duke of Beaufort); suc bro, Sir (Francis) Osbert Sacheverell Sitwell, 5 Bt, CH, CBE (the poet and author, notably of the five-volume autobiography starting with *Left Hand, Right Hand!*) 1969; bro of late Dame Edith Sitwell, DBE (the poet, author and critic); for a cruel portrayal of the Sitwell siblings the reader is referred to Wyndham Lewis's *The Apes of God*; *b* 15 Nov 1897; *m* 1925, Georgia, da of late Arthur Doble, of Montreal; 2 s; *Heir* s, (Sacheverell) Reresby Sitwell; *Career* formerly 2 Lt Gren Gds, poet and writer, notably of lives of Mozart and Liszt, also of books on the Gothick (and the Gothic) and Baroque; *Style* - Sir Sacheverell Sitwell, Bt; Weston Hall, Towcester, Northants

SIVEWRIGHT, Brevet-Colonel Robert Charles Townsend; MC (1945), DL (Glos 1965); s of Capt R H V Sivewright DSC RN; *b* 7 Sept 1923; *Educ* Repton, RAC Cirencester; *m* 1951, Pamela Molly Ryder-Richardson; 3 da; *Career* served Italy, NW Europe; ADC to Field Marshal Lord Harding of Petherton 1948-50; farmer; jt principal (with wife) The Talland Sch of Equitation (Glos); chm W Wessex TAVRA 1970-, v-chm Cncl TAVRAs 1970-; High Sheriff Glos 1977; *Recreations* racing (race-horse 'Probable'); *Clubs* Cavalry and Guards; *Style* - Colonel Robert Sivewright MC DL; Talland House, S Cerney, Cirencester, Glos (☎ Cirencester 860209)

SKEFFINGTON, Hon John David Clotworthy Whyte-Melville Foster; s and h of 13 Viscount Massereene and Ferrard; *b* 3 June 1940; *Educ* Millfield and Inst Monte Rosa; *m* 1970, Anne Denise, da of late Norman Rowlandson; 1 s, 1 da; *Career* Gren Gds 1959-61; stockbroker with Walter Ward & Co; *Clubs* Turf; *Style* - The Hon John Skeffington; Scarisdale House, New rd, Esher, Surrey

SKELMERSDALE, 7 Baron (UK 1828); Roger Bootle-Wilbraham; s of Brig 6

Baron Skelmersdale, DSO, MC (d 1973), and Ann (d 1974), da of Percy Quilter and gda of Sir Cuthbert Quilter, 1 Bt; *b* 2 April 1945; *Educ* Eton, Lord Wandsworth Coll; *m* 1972, Christine, da of Philip Morgan, of Hamel Evercreech, Somerset; 1 s, 1 da; *Heir* s, Hon Andrew Bootle-Wilbraham; *Career* horticulturist; md Broadleigh Nurseries; Pres Somerset Tst for Nature Conservation 1980-, a Lord in Waiting to HM 1980-; *Recreations* gardening, reading, bridge; *Style* - The Rt Hon The Lord Skelmersdale; Barr House, Bishops Hull, Taunton, Somerset (☎ 0823 70655)

SKELTON, Joseph Osmotherley; s of Matthew Skelton; *b* 10 May 1929; *Educ* Cockermouth G S, Durham U; *m* 1953, Sheila Daphne Trimble, da of Laurence Trimble Carruthers (d 1976); 2 s; *Career* CA; md Wagon Finance Corpn 1967-; chm Finance Houses Assoc 1978-80; dir HP Information Ltd 1979- and Frilford Heath G C Ltd; cncl memb European Fedn Finance Houses Assoc 1978-; *Recreations* golf, gardening, swimming; *Club* Frilford Heath G C; *Style* - Joseph Skelton Esq; Kinloss, Woodside, Abingdon, Oxon (☎ Frilford Heath 390500)

SKENE, Robert William Dugald; TD; s of Col Philip George Moncrieff Skene OBE JP DL (d 1944); *b* 16 June 1912; *Educ* Eton; *m* 1, 1939, Elizabeth Diana Wolfe, da of Sir George Sutherland (m dis 1964); 1 s; m 2, 1968, Inge, nee Andersen; *Career* Major Black Watch (TA), chartered accountant 1937-, farmer, landowner, memb Roy Co Archers (Queen's Bodyguard for Scotland); *Recreations* golf; *Clubs* Army & Navy, Royal & Ancient (St Andrews), Marylebone Cricket; *Style* - Robert Skene Esq; Pitlour, Strathmiglo, Fife (☎ Strathmiglo 237)

SKIDMORE, Hon Mrs (Felicity Margaret); *née* Roberthall; da of Baron Roberthall, KCMG, CB; *b* 30 June 1936; *Educ* Oxford H S For Girls, LMH Oxford; *m* 1957, Thomas Skidmore; 3 s; *Style* - The Hon Mrs Skidmore; 2025 Chadbourne av, Madison, Wisconsin, 53705 USA

SKILLINGTON, William Patrick Denny; CB (1964); s of S J Skillington (d 1967); *b* 13 Feb 1913; *Educ* Malvern, Exeter Coll Oxford; *m* 1941, Dorin, nee Kahn; 2 da; *Career* Lt-Col WW II, civil servant 1946-73, Under-Sec Miny Public Bldg and Works 1956-64, Assist Under-Sec Home Office 1964-66, Dep Sec Miny Public Bldg & Works 1966-70, Dep Sec Dept of the Environment 1970-73; *Clubs* United Oxford and Cambridge; *Style* - William Skillington Esq, CB; 95A Saint Mark's rd, Henley-on-Thames, Oxon (☎ Henley 3756)

SKINNER, Alan Frank; OBE (1946), DL (Suffolk 1974); s of Wilfrid Skinner CBE; *b* 22 April 1913; *Educ* Trin Cambridge; *m* 1938, Frances West; 2 da; *Career* slr; Clerk of W Suffolk CC 1953-74, chm Anglian Water Authority 1973-78; *Clubs* Oxford and Cambridge Combined University; *Style* - Alan Skinner Esq, OBE, DL; Monks Close, Woolpit, Suffolk (☎ 035940235)

SKINNER, Dennis Edward; MP (L) Bolsover 1970-; *b* 1932; *Educ* Tupton Hall G S, Ruskin Coll Oxford; *m* 1960, Mary, da of James Parker; 1 s, 2 da; *Career* joined Lab Pty 1950, former miner; *Style* - Dennis Skinner Esq, MP; House of Commons, SW1

SKINNER, Sir (Thomas) Keith (Hewitt); 4 Bt (UK 1912), of Pont Street, Borough of Chelsea; s of Sir (Thomas) Gordon Skinner, 3 Bt (d 1972); *b* 6 Dec 1927; *Educ* Charterhouse; *m* 1959, Jill, da of late Cedric Tuckett, of Tonbridge; 2 s; *Heir* s, Thomas Skinner; *Career* chm and ch exec IPC Business Press, dir Reed International, IPC and others; *Style* - Sir Keith Skinner, Bt; Long Acre, West Clandon, Surrey

SKINNER, Hon Mrs (Rose Marian); da of late Maj Geoffrey Seymour Rowley-Conwy and sis of 9 Baron Langford, OBE; *b* 6 June 1915; *m* 1938, Ralph Becher Skinner; 1 s, 2 da; *Career* raised to the rank of a Baron's da, 1955; *Style* - The Hon Mrs Skinner; The Fold, Cwm, Dyserth, Clwyd

SKINNER, Thomas James Hewitt; s and h of Sir (Thomas) Keith Skinner, 4 Bt;

b 11 Sept 1963; *Style* - Thomas Skinner Esq

SKIPPER, David John; s of Herbert Skipper; *b* 14 April 1931; *Educ* Watford G S, BNC Oxford (rugby blue); *m* 1955, Brenda, da of Alfred Williams; 4 c; *Career* headmaster Ellesmere Coll 1969-81, Merchant Taylors' 1982- (assist master Radley 1957-63, Rugby 1963-69); *Style* - David Skipper Esq; Headmasater's House, Merchant Taylors' School, Sandy Lodge, Northwood, Middx (☎ 21850)

SKIPWITH, Alexander Sebastian Grey d'Estoteville; s & h of Sir Patrick Skipwith, 12 Bt; *b* 9 April 1969; *Style* - Alexander Skipwith Esq

SKIPWITH, Sir Patrick Alexander d'Estoteville; 12 Bt (E 1622), of Prestwould, Leicestershire; s of Grey d'Estoteville Townsend Skipwith (ka 1942); suc gf, Sir Grey Skipwith, 11 Bt, 1950; *b* 1 Sept 1938; *Educ* Harrow, Trin Coll Dublin, Imperial Coll London; *m* 1, 1964 (m dis 1970), Gillian Harwood; 1 s, 1 da; m 2, 1972, Ashkhain, da of Bedros Atikian, of Calgary; *Heir* s, Alexander Skipwith; *Career* geological ed Bureau de Recherches Géologiques et Minières, Jeddah, 1973-; marine geologist Directorate Gen Mineral Resources, Jeddah 1970-73; *Recreations* riding, deep sea fishing; *Club* Travellers'; *Style* - Sir Patrick Skipwith, Bt; 94 Frithville gdns, W12; c/o Lloyds Bank, Chelsea, SW3

SKYRME, Hon Mrs (Barbara Suzanne); *née* Lyle; da of 1 Baron Lyle of Westbourne; *b* 1915; *m* 1938 (m dis 1953), William Skyrme CBE TD JP (CB 1966, KCVO 1974); 1 s, 2 da; *Style* - The Hon Mrs Skyrme; Beechwood House, Nettlebed, Oxon; 20 Eaton Place, SW1

SLADE, (Sir) (Julian) Benjamin Alfred; (7 Bt (UK 1831), of Maunsel House, Somersetshire (but does not use title); s of Capt Sir Michael Niall Slade, 6 Bt (d 1962); *b* 22 May 1946; *Educ* Millfield; *m* 1977, Pauline Carol, da of Maj Claude Myburgh; *Heir* kinsman, Gerald Slade; *Career* chm Shirlstar Container Transport Ltd; company dir; *Style* - Benjamin Slade Esq; 164 Ashley gdns, SW1 (☎ 01 828 2809); Maunsel, North Newton, Bridgwater, Somerset

SLADE, Hon Mrs; Hon Constance; *née* Montague; da of 2 Baron Amwell; *b* 2 March 1915; *Educ* N London Collegiate Sch; *m* 1938, Albert Slade; 1 s, 2 da; *Style* - The Hon Mrs Slade; 27 Howitt rd, NW3

SLADE, Hon Mr Justice; Hon Sir Christopher John; QC (1965); s of George Penkivil Slade KC (d 1942); *b* 2 June 1927; *Educ* Eton, Oxford; *m* 1958, Jane Gwenllian Armstrong, da of Rt Hon Sir Denys Buckley MBE; 1 s 3 da; *Career* kt 1975; barr 1951, Attorney-General Duchy of Lancaster 1972-75, Bencher 1973, Judge of High Court of Justice (Chancery Div) 1975-, Judge of the Restrictive Practices Court 1980-; *Clubs* Garrick; *Style* - The Hon Mr Justice Slade; 12 Harley Gardens, SW10 (☎ 373 7695)

SLADE, Gerald Gordon; s of late Henry Adolphus Slade (gs of 1 Bt); hp of kinsman, (Sir) (Julian) Benjamin Slade, (7 Bt, who does not use his title); *b* 27 Oct 1899; *m* 1952, Netta Kathleen, da of Richard Maunsell, CBE; *Career* Cdr RN (ret) WWs I and II; *Clubs* Naval and Military; *Style* - Gerald Slade Esq; Northbrooke, Ashford, Kent

SLADEN, Angus Murray; s of Sqdn Leader Algernon Ivan Sladen DSO (d 1976); *b* 17 Dec 1950; *Educ* Stowe, Texas U; *Career* with Cunliffe-Fraser Bruce & Co Lloyd's underwriting agents; *Recreations* stalking, fishing; *Style* - Angus Sladen Esq; Glencarron Lodge, Achnashellach, Ross-Shire, Scotland; 26 Tite st SW3

SLANE, Viscount; Alexander Burton Conyngham; s and h of Earl of Mount Charles, *qv*; *b* 30 Jan 1975; *Style* - Viscount Slane

SLATER, Hon Brian; s of Baron Slater (Life Peer, d 1977); *b* 1948; *Style* - The Hon Brian Slater

SLATER, Gordon Charles Henry; CMG (1964), CBE (1956); s of Matthew Slater (d 1922); *b* 14 Dec 1903; *Educ*

Croydon Polytech, London U; *m* 1928, Doris Primrose, nee Hammond; 1 s, 1 da; *Career* Ministry of Labour 1928-64 (ret), Assist Sec 1945, Under-Sec 1958-64, dir London Branch Office ILO 1964-70, memb Berks CC 1970, vice-chm 1977-79; *Recreations* gardening, civic affairs mainly concerning environment; *Style* - Gordon Slater Esq, CMG, CBE; White House, 66 Altwood rd, Maidenhead, Berks (☎ Berks 27463)

SLATER, Baroness; Hilda; da of Gilbert James Clement; *m* 1928, Baron Slater (Life Peer, d 1977); 1 s, 1 da; *Style* - The Rt Hon The Lady Slater; 5 Witton rd, Ferryhill, Co Durham

SLATER, Richard Mercer Keene; CMG (1962); s of Samuel Henry Slater CMG, CIE (d 1968); *b* 27 May 1915; *Educ* Eton, Cambridge; *m* 1939, Barbara Janet, da of Lt-Col Clive Murdoch DSO (d 1942); 4 s; *Career* Assistant Under-Sec of State FCO 1973, High Commissioner in Uganda 1970-72, Ambassador to Cuba 1966-70; *Style* - Richard Slater Esq, CMG; Vicary's, Odiham, Hants (☎ Odiham 2648)

SLATTERY, Rear-Adm Sir Matthew Sausse; KBE (1960), CB (1946); s of Henry Francis Slattery (d 1911); *b* 12 May 1902; *Educ* Stonyhurst, RNCs Osborne and Dartmouth; *m* 1925, Mica Mary, da of Lt-Col George Swain CMG (d 1924); 2 s, 1 da; *Career* kt 1955; RN 1916-48 (ret); special advr to the Prime Minister on Transport of Middle East Oil 1957-59, dir National Bank Ltd 1959-60 & 1964-70, chm BOAC-Cunard Ltd 1962-63, dir R & W Hawthorn Leslie & Co Ltd; *Recreations* country pursuits; *Clubs* Naval & Military; *Style* - Rear-Adm Sir Matthew Slattery, KBE, CB; Harvey's Farm, Warninglid, W Sussex (☎ Warninglid 291)

SLATTERY, Peter Anthony; s of Rear-Adm Sir Matthew Slattery, *qv*; *b* 21 Mar 1926; *Educ* Ampleforth, Middle Temple; *m* 1, 1951 (m dis 1979), Joanella Elizabeth Agnes, nee Scrymsour-Nichol; 1 s, 2 da; m 2, 1979, Judith Mary, nee Gilbert; *Career* assistant md Hobbs Savill & Bradford Ltd 1962-67, md 1967-71; md Hobbs Savill Trustees Ltd 1961-71, Williams & Glyn's Insurance Consultants Ltd 1971-75, dep dir Williams & Glyn's Bank 1972-75 fell Corpn of Insurance Brokers 1974-75, Pensions Management Institute 1980; *Recreations* photography, gardening; *Style* - Peter Slattery Esq; 18 Holmwood Rd, Cheam, Sutton, Surrey (☎ 01 393 6018)

SLEEMAN, John Henry; s of Herbert Sleeman (d 1950); *b* 4 May 1922; *Educ* Thorpe Sch; *m* 1945, Elsie; 2 s; *Career* chartered sec; dir: Charterhouse Japhet gp of cos, Criterion Life Assurance Co Ltd, Keyser Ullman Investment Mgmnt Ltd, Keyser Ullman Pensions Mgmnt Ltd, Pension Servs Ltd, Nat Children's Charities Fund Ltd and others; *Style* - John Sleeman Esq; 1 Paternoster Row, EC4 (☎ 01 248 3999)

SLEEMAN, His Hon Judge (Stuart Colin); s of Stuart Bertram Sleeman (d 1970); *Educ* Clifton Coll, Merton Coll Oxford; *m* 1944, Margaret Emily, nee Farmer; 2 s, 1 da; *Career* barr 1938; Lt-Col 16/5 Lancers WW II; adminve offr Prize Dept Ministry of Economic Warfare 1939-40; Bencher 1974, Recorder 1975, Circuit Judge 1976; *Recreations* travel, genealogy; *Style* - His Hon Judge Sleeman; West Walls, Cotmandene, Dorking, Surrey (☎ 0306 883616); 1 Gray's Inn sq, WC1 (☎ 404 0763)

SLEIGHT, Sir John Frederick; 3 Bt (UK 1920) of Weelsby Hall, Clee, Co Lincoln; s of Sir Ernest Sleight, 2 Bt, OBE, TD (d 1946); *b* 13 April 1909; *m* 1942, Jacqueline Margaret, da of Maj H R Carter and widow of Ronald Mundell; 1 s; *Heir* s, Richard Sleight; *Style* - Sir John Sleight, Bt; The Garden House, 15 High st, Thame, Oxon

SLEIGHT, Richard; s and h of Sir John Sleight, 3 Bt; *b* 27 May 1946; *m* 1978, Marie-Thérèse, da of O M Stepan; *Style* - Richard Sleight Esq

SLIGO, 10 Marquess of (I 1800); Denis Edward Browne; sits as Baron Monteagle (UK 1806); Baron Mount Eagle (I 1760), Viscount Westport (I 1768), Earl of Altamont (I 1771), Earl of Clanricarde (I 1543 and 1800, with special remainder); s of late Lt-Col Lord Alfred Eden Browne, DSO (s of 5 Marquess of Sligo); suc unc, 9 Marquess of Sligo 1952; *b* 13 Dec 1908; *Educ* Eton; *m* 1930, José Gauche; 1 s; *Heir* s, Earl of Altamont; *Style* - The Most Hon The Marquess of Sligo; c/o Messrs Trower, Still and Keeling, 5 New sq, Lincoln's Inn (☎ WC2)

SLIM, 2 Viscount (UK 1960); John Douglas Slim; OBE (Mil 1973); s of Field Marshal 1 Viscount (Sir William Joseph) Slim, KG, GCB, GCMG, GCVO, GBE, DSO, MC, sometime GOC Allied Land Forces SE Asia, Govr-Gen Australia and Govr & Constable Windsor Castle (d 1970); *b* 20 July 1927; *Educ* Prince of Wales Roy Indian Mil Coll Dehra Dun; *m* 1958, Elisabeth Spinney, da of late Arthur Rawdon Spinney, CBE; 2 s, 1 da; *Heir* s, Hon Mark Slim; *Career* Lt-Col 1967, commissioned Indian Army 6 Gurkha Rifles 1945-48, Lt Argyll & Sutherland Highlanders 1948, GSO2 HQ Mid East 1966-67, Cdr 22 SAS Regt 1967-70, GSO1 (Special Forces) HQ UK Land Forces 1970-72, ret 1972; v-pres and dir Boyden Int Ltd, dir FO's (Trade Advisory Services), dir H C Sleigh UK Ltd, pres Burma Star Assoc; *Clubs* White's, Special Forces; *Style* - The Rt Hon The Viscount Slim, OBE; c/o Lloyds Bank Ltd, 6 Pall Mall, SW1

SLIM, Aileen, Viscountess; Aileen; da of Rev J A Robertson of Edinburgh; *m* 1926, 1 Viscount Slim, KG, GCB, GCMG, GCVO, GBE, DSO, MC (d 1970); 1 s, 1 da; *Career* DStJ, has Kaisar-i-Hind Medal; *Style* - The Rt Hon Aileen, Viscountess Slim; 18 Stack House, Cundy Street Flats, Ebury st, SW1

SLIM, Hon Hugo John Robertson; s of 2 Viscount Slim, OBE; *b* 1961; *Style* - The Hon Hugo Slim

SLIM, Hon Mary Ann; da of 2 Viscount Slim, OBE; *b* 1964; *Style* - The Hon Mary Slim

SLIM, Hon Mark William Rawdon; s and h of 2 Viscount Slim, OBE; *b* 13 Feb 1960; *Style* - The Hon Mark Slim

SMAIL, Col James Ingram Miles; OBE (1963), MC (1944), TD (1962), DL (Northumberland 1971); s of James Ingram Smail (d 1947); *b* 21 Aug 1921; *Educ* Christ's Coll, Canterbury U New Zealand; *m* 1948, Dorothy Margaret, nee Reese; 2 s, 2 da; *Career* Brigadier, served WW II 1 Canterbury Regt then 2 NZEF (Africa, Tunisia, Italy), proprietor of Tweeddale Press Gp, dir Border TV, dir Borprint Ltd, chm Northumberland Co Plan Ctee, Mayor Berwick upon Tweed 1969-71, Dep Mayor 1971; *Recreations* shooting, gardening; *Clubs* Northern Counties, Newcastle, Lansdowne; *Style* - Col James Smail OBE MC TD DL; Kiwi Cottage, Scremerston, Berwick upon Tweed, Northumberland (☎ 0289 6219)

SMALE-ADAMS, Kenneth Barry; s of Douglas William Smale-Adams; *b* 30 June 1932; *Educ* St John's Coll Johannesburg, Camborne Sch of Mines; *m* 1953, Marion June, nee Whitewalls; 2 s (Mark, Jeremy b 1963), 1 da (Deborah); *Career* mining engr; The Rio Tinto Zinc Corpn Ltd 1967- (exec dir Con Zinc Rio Tinto Malaysia Ltd and Rio Tinto Bethlehem Indonesia 1967-72), gen man and dir Rio Tinto Fin and Exploration Ltd 1973-80, md RTZ Deep Sea Mining Enterprises Ltd 1974-, chm Riofinex Ltd 1980- (md 1976-80); *Recreations* fishing, reading, music, theatre, sports (generally now as spectator); *Clubs* RAC; *Style* - Kenneth Smale-Adams Esq; Cedar Lawn, 15 Queens dve, Thames Ditton, Surrey (☎ 01 398 3163)

SMART, John Dalziel Beveridge; s of George Beveridge Smart; *b* 12 Aug 1932; *Educ* Harrow; *m* 1960, Valerie Bigelow, da of late Col Hugh Kenneth Blaber; 2 s; *Career* Lt Black Watch Korea; dir Don Brothers Buist & Co Ltd 1964, dir J & J Smart (Brechin) Ltd 1954; *Recreations* skiing, shooting; *Style* - John Smart Esq; Woodmyre, Edzell, Angus (☎ 416)

SMART, Maj-Gen Robert Arthur; CBE (1958); s of Arthur Francis Smart (d 1948); *b* 29 April 1914; *Educ* Aberdeen G S, Aberdeen U; *m* 1947, Josephine, nee von Oepen; 1 da; *Career* Maj-Gen RAMC 1938-47, dir Army Health 1964-68, dir Medical Serv Far East land Forces 1968, dir Med Serv Br Army of the Rhine 1970-71; ch medical officer Esso Petroleum Co Ltd 1972-79; *Recreations* reading, music;

Clubs Army & Navy, Caledonian, Roy Northern and University (Aberdeen); *Style* - Maj-Gen Robert Smart CBE; 186 Forest ave, Aberdeen (☎ 0224 322743)

SMEDLEY, (Frank) Brian; QC (1977); s of Leslie Smedley (d 1970); *b* 28 Nov 1934; *Educ* West Bridgford G S, London U; *Career* barr 1960, Recorder of Crown Court 1971-, memb Senate of Inns of Court & The Bar 1973-77; *Recreations* travel; *Clubs* Garrick; *Style* - Brian Smedley Esq, QC; The Barn, Barnes Lane, Wellingore, Lincoln (☎ 0522 810 386); 4 Hale Court, Lincoln's Inn WC1 (☎ 242 4552)

SMILEY, Sir Hugh Houston; 3 Bt (UK 1903), of Drumalis, Larne, Co Antrim and Gallowhill, Paisley, Co Renfrew, JP (Hants 1952), DL (1962); s of Sir John Smiley, 2 Bt (d 1930) and Valerie, da of late Sir Claude Champion de Crespigny, 4 Bt; *b* 14 Nov 1905; *Educ* Eton, RMC Sandhurst; *m* 1933, Nancy Elizabeth Louise, da of late Ernest Walter Hardy Beaton; 1 s; *Heir* s, Maj John Smiley; *Career* Capt Gren Gds NW Europe 1944-5; High Sheriff Hants 1959-60, Vice Ld-Lt Hants 1973-; *Clubs* Cavalry & Guards; *Style* - Sir Hugh Smiley, Bt, JP, HM Vice Lord-Lieut of Hants; Ivalls, Bentworth, Alton, Hants (☎ Alton 63193)

SMILEY, Maj John Philip; s and h of Sir Hugh Smiley, 3 Bt, JP; *b* 24 Feb 1934; *Educ* Eton; *m* 1963, Davina Elizabeth, da of late Denis Griffiths; 2 s, 1 da; *Career* Maj Grenadier Gds, Cyprus 1958, ADC to Govr of Bermuda 1961-62; *Style* - Maj John Smiley; Cornerway House, Chobham, Surrey

SMILEY, Xan de Crespigny; s of David Smiley, MVO, OBE, MC* (3 s of Sir John Smiley, 2 Bt), and Moyra, widow of Maj Hugo Tweedie, and da of Lt-Col Lord Francis Montagu Douglas Scott, KCMG, DSO (6 s of 6 Duke of Buccleuch); *b* 1 May 1949; *Educ* Eton, New Coll Oxford; *Career* journalist (contributes to Spectator on African matters); *Style* - Xan Smiley Esq; c/o The Spectator, 56 Doughty st, WC1 (☎ 01 405 1706)

SMITH, Baron (Life Peer UK 1978); (Edwin) Rodney Smith; KBE (1975); s of Dr Edwin Smith; *b* 10 May 1914; *Educ* Westminster Sch, London U (MB, BS, MRCS, LRCP, FRCS, MS); *m* 1, 1938 (m dis 1971), Mary Rodwell; 3 s, 1 da; m 2, 1971, Susan, da of Dr Rowdon Marrian Fry; *Career* pres Roy Coll of Surgeons 1973-77, chm Conference of Roy Colls (UK) 1976-78, pres Roy Soc of Medicine 1978; examiner in surgery London U, consulting surgeon St George's Hosp (surgeon 1946), Wimbledon Hosp, Roy Prince Alfred Hosp Sydney NSW; *Style* - The Rt Hon The Lord Smith, KBE; 149 Harley st, W1

SMITH, Prof Alwyn; s of Ernest Smith (d 1976); *b* 9 Nov 1925; *Educ* Queen Mary's Sch Walsall, Birmingham U; *m* 1950, Doreen, nee Preston; 1 s, 1 da; *Career* prof Community Medicine Manchester 1967-79, prof Epidemiology and Social Oncology Manchester 1979-, pres Faculty Community Medicine, Roy Coll Physicians 1981-; *Recreations* fishing, music, watching football; *Style* - Prof Alwyn Smith; 66 Kingston rd, Didsbury, Manchester M20; c/o Royal College of Physicians, 11 St Andrews Place, NW1 (☎ 01 935 1174)

SMITH, Ven Arthur Cyril; VRD (1958); s of Arthur Smith (d 1916); *b* 26 Feb 1909; *Educ* St John's Coll Winnipeg, Sheffield U, Westcott Cambridge; *m* 1940, Patricia Marion da of Col Ranolf Greenwood (decd); 2 s, 2 da; *Career* ordained 1934, canon and prebendary of Centum Solidorum, archdeacon of Lincoln 1960-76, now emeritus; dir Ecclesiastical Insurance Office Ltd 1967-77, Church Cmmr 1970-76, consultant Inter-Church Travel; *Recreations* Tennyson Soc, travel; *Clubs* Army & Navy; *Style* - The Ven Arthur Smith VRD; Farthings, Great Rollright, Chipping Norton, Oxon

SMITH, Hon Alexander David; s of 4 Visc Hambleden; *b* 11 March 1959; *Style* - The Hon Alexander Smith

SMITH, Hon Andrew Edward Rodney; s (by 1 m) of Baron Smith, KBE (Life Peer); *b* 1948; *Style* - The Hon Andrew Smith

SMITH, Anthony John Frederick (Tony); *b* 6 Feb 1931; *m* 1969, Hon Myfanwy Ann, *qv*, da of 2 Viscount St Davids; *Career* company general manager; *Style* - Tony Smith Esq; Messrs C Hoare & Company, 37 Fleet St, London EC4

SMITH, Lady Alexandra Mary; da of late 6 Earl Cadogan; *b* 1920; *m* 1, 1940 (m dis 1949) Maj Robert Gilliam Buchanan, King's Own Scottish Borderers; m 2, 1951 (m dis 1973), Norman Hutchison Smith; 1 s, 2 da; *Style* - Lady Alexandra Smith; Reightons, Playden, Rye, Sussex

SMITH, Andrew Thomas; s and h of Sir Gilbert Smith, 4 Bt; *b* 17 Oct 1965; *Style* - Andrew Smith Esq

SMITH, Hon Bernardo James; s of 4 Visc Hambleden; *b* 17 May 1957; *Style* - The Hon Bernardo Smith

SMITH, Lady Corisande; da of 8 Earl of Tankerville (d 1971); *b* 1938; *m* 1963, Lt-Cdr Timothy Bain Smith, RN; 2 s; *Style* - Lady Corisande Smith; Wickens Manor, Charing, Kent

SMITH, Cyril; MBE (1966), MP (Lib) Rochdale 1972-; *b* 28 June 1928; *Educ* Rochdale G S for Boys; *Career* councillor Rochdale 1952-66, ald 1966-74, memb Rochdale Metropolitan Dist Cncl 1974-75, Ch Whip Lib 1975-76; co dir; *Recreations* listening to music, reading, TV; *Clubs* National Liberal; *Style* - Cyril Smith Esq, MBE, MP; 14 Emma st, Rochdale, Lancs (☎ Rochdale 48840)

SMITH, Charles G; *Career* dir Waterford Glass Ltd and The Smith Gp Ltd; *Style* Charles Smith Esq; The Smith Group, 28 Fitzwilliam pla, Dublin, Eire

SMITH, Clifford John; *Career* CA; md Grand Metropolitan Ltd 1981-; dir: Grandmet Information Processing, Grand Metropolitan (Finance) Ltd, Henry Ansbacher Ltd, Henry Ansbacher Hldgs; *Style* - Clifford Smith Esq; 11/12 Hanover sq, W1 (☎ 01 629 7488)

SMITH, Hon Mrs Constantine - Marjorie Methwold; OBE (1957); da of late Arthur Birkett; *m* 1917, Hon (Hubert) Constantine Smith (d 1956); 2 s, 1 da; *Style* - The Hon Mrs Constantine Smith, OBE; Pear Trees Farm, Hermitage Lane, Holmes Chapel, Cheshire

SMITH, Hon Craig Peter; s (by 1 m) and h of 3 Baron Colwyn; *b* 13 Oct 1968; *Style* - The Hon Craig Smith

SMITH, Sir Christopher Sydney Winwood; 5 Bt (UK 1809), of Eardiston, Worcestershire; s of Sir William Sydney Winwood Smith, 4 Bt (d 1953); *b* 20 Sept 1906; *m* 1932, Phyllis Berenice, da of late Thomas Robert O'Grady; 3 s, 2 da; *Heir* s, Robert Sydney Winwood Smith; *Style* - Sir Christopher Smith, Bt; Junction rd, via Grafton, NSW, 2460, Australia

SMITH, David; s of late Horace Smith; *b* 18 July 1927; *Educ* Burton G S, Sheffield U; *m* 1951, Nancy Elizabeth, nee Hawley; 2 s, 3 da; *Career* v-pres Exxon Chemical Co 1971-78, chm & md Esso Chemical Ltd 1979-; *Recreations* golf, cricket; *Clubs* MCC; *Style* - David Smith Esq; Meadowlands, Stockbridge Road, Winchester, Hants (☎ 0962 64880)

SMITH, Wing Cdr Denis Bonham; OBE (1945), DL (Hampshire 1965); s of Frederick Stanley Smith (Judge of The Court of Appeal, Barbados) (d 1947); *b* 11 Aug 1909; *Educ* St Paul's Sch W Kensington, Corpus Christi Coll Oxford; *m* 1935, Lisbeth Lily Lochhead, nee Leitch (d 1979); 3 s, 1 da; *Career* Wing Cdr RAFVR 1930-70 (relinquished cmmn); aeronautical engineer, sr exec Folland Aircraft Ltd Hamble 1952-65, scientific staff MOD & UK Coordinator for NATO Advsy Gp for R & D 1966-70, vice-chm governing body Eastleigh Tech Coll 1961-; *Recreations* flying, sailing, tennis; *Clubs* RAF; *Style* - Wing Cdr Denis Smith OBE DL; Bay Tree Cottage, Bentley, Farnham, Surrey (☎ 04204 3136)

SMITH, Sir (Frank) Ewart; s of Richard Sidney Smith (d 1938); *b* 31 May 1897; *Educ* Christ's Hosp, Sidney Sussex Cambridge; *m* 1924, Kathleen Winifred, nee Dawes (d 1978); 1 s, 1 da; *Career* kt 1946; Lt RA Flanders 1917-18; formerly chm ICI Ltd, chm Br Productivity Cncl & v-pres Instn Mechanical Engrs, ch engr & supt Armament Design Dept Miny Supply

1942-45, formerly memb Scientific Advisory Council Ministry of Fuel and Power, Advisory Council of Scientific Policy and chm National Health Service Advisory Council for Management Efficiency; *Recreations* gardening, cabinet making; *Style* - Sir Ewart Smith; Barclays Bank, Haslemere, Surrey

SMITH, Hon Elinor; da (by 1 m) of Baron Smith, KBE (Life Peer); *b* 1950; *Style* - The Hon Elinor Smith

SMITH, Eric Neville Trevelyan; s of Frederick Bowden-Smith; *b* 6 April 1925; *Educ* various schools, Cambridge U; *m* 1960, Elsie Gillian, nee Walters; 1 s, 2 da; *Career* managing director Tudor Food Products 1967-81 and chairman since 1975, director Smiths Food Group NV (Holdings) 1971-79, director Smiths Food Group Ltd 1973-81; *Recreations* family, gardening, sailing; *Clubs* Essex Yacht, Ullswater Yacht; *Style* - Eric Smith Esq; Greystone, Shadforth, Durham (☎ Durham 720368)

SMITH, Sir (Thomas) Gilbert; 4 Bt (UK 1897), of Stratford Place, St Marylebone, Co London; s of Sir Thomas Turner, 3 Bt (1961); *b* 2 July 1937; *Educ* Huntley Sch, Nelson Coll; *m* 1962, Patricia Christine, da of David Cooper, of Paraparaumu, New Zealand; 2 s, 1 da; *Heir* s, Andrew Thomas Smith; *Career* engineer; *Style* - Sir Gilbert Smith, Bt; PO Box 654, 50 Titoki st, Masterton, New Zealand

SMITH, Sir (William) Gordon; 2 Bt (UK 1945) of Crowmallie, Co Aberdeen, VRD; s of Sir Robert (Workman) Smith, 1 Bt (d 1957); *b* 30 Jan 1916; *Educ* Westminster, Trin Cambridge; *m* 1, 1942, Diana Gundreda, da of late Major Charles Malden, RMLI, of Aquahorthies, Aberdeensire; m 2, 1958, Diana Goodchild; 2 s; *Heir* s, Robert Hill Smith; *Career* barr 1939; Lt-Cdr RNR (ret), despatches WW II; *Style* - Sir Gordon Smith, Bt, VRD; Crowmallie, Pitcaple, Aberdeenshire; 15 Cadogan ct, Draycott av, SW3

SMITH, Lady Helen; *née* Pleydell-Bouverie; OBE (1946); da of late 6 Earl of Radnor; *m* 1931, Maj Hon David Smith, CBE (d 1976), s of 2 Visc Hambleden; 3 s, 1 da; *Style* - Lady Helen Smith, OBE; King's Copse House, Bucklebury, Berks

SMITH, Sir Howard; GCMG (1981, KCMG 1976, CMG 1966); *Educ* Sidney Sussex Cambridge; *m* 1943, Winifred Mary Cropper; 1 da; *Career* formerly Ambass to Moscow; HM Diplomatic Service, ret; *Style* - Sir Howard Smith, GCMG; c/o Foreign and Commonwealth Office, SW1

SMITH, Hugh Charles Vivian; s of late Lt-Col the Hon Stephen Edward Vivian Smith, 2 s of 1 Baron Bicester; hp of bro, 3 Baron; *b* 8 Nov 1934; *Educ* Eton, Worcester Coll Oxford; *Career* late 2 Lt RAC; *Style* - Hugh Smith Esq

SMITH, Lady Helen Dorothy; *née* Primrose; da of 6 Earl of Rosebery, KT, DSO, MC, PC, by his 1 w, Lady Dorothy Grosvenor, sis of 3 Duke of Westminster; half-sis of 7 Earl of Rosebery; *b* 1913; *m* 1933, Hon Hugh Smith (d 1977), 3 s of 1 Baron Bicester; 1 s, 1 da; *Style* - Lady Helen Smith; Souldern Manor, Bicester, Oxon

SMITH, Rt Hon John; PC (1978), MP (L) N Lanarkshire 1970-; s of Archibald Leitch Smith, of Dunoon, Argyll; *b* 13 Sept 1938; *Educ* Dunoon G S, Glasgow U; *m* 1967, Elizabeth Margaret, da of late Frederick William Moncrieff Bennett; 3 da; *Career* advocate 1967, Parly Under-Sec of State for Energy 1974-75, Min of State for Energy 1975-76, Min of State Privy Council Office 1976-78, Sec of State for Trade 1978-79; *Recreations* tennis, hill walking, sailing; *Style* - The Rt Hon John Smith, PC, MP; 21 Cluny dve, Edinburgh 10

SMITH, James Boyd; GM (1943); s of James Hugh Smith (d 1950); *b* 9 Feb 1920; *Educ* George Heriot's Sch Edinburgh, Edinburgh U; *m* 1946, May, nee Campbell; 1 s (Peter James Campbell), 1 da (Pamela May Isabelle); *Career* 1939-45

Capt Corps of Royal Engineers; chartered electrical engineer, chm IEE Scottish Centre 1973-74, asst gen man Ferranti Ltd Edinburgh 1980- (joined Ferranti 1947), dir of various subsidiary companies: Ferranti Offshore Systems Ltd 1974-, Ferranti Cetec Graphics Ltd 1977-, TRW Ferranti Subsea Ltd 1977-; FRSE 1977, memb Edinburgh U Court 1975-; *Recreations* organ playing, orchid growing, gardening; *Style* - James Smith Esq, GM; Brunstane Bank House, 120 Milton Road East, Edinburgh 15 (☎ 031 669 5791)

SMITH, John Foster; s of William John Foster Smith (d 1970); *b* 14 Feb 1945; *Educ* New Town Sch Waterford; *m* 1974, Ann; 3 s; *Career* dir: Musgrave Ltd, Musgrave Export Ltd, Irish Modern Distributors Ltd, Centra (Ireland) Ltd, Frank Ltd, VG Services Ltd; chm VG Ireland; *Recreations* sailing, general sports; *Clubs* Rotary Club of Cork, Cork GC; *Style* - John Smith Esq; Mount Patrick, Glanmire, Cork, Eire

SMITH, Jeremy Fox Eric; s of Capt Evan Cadogan Eric Smith, MC (d 1950); *b* 17 Nov 1928; *Educ* Eton, New Coll Oxford; *m* 1953, Julia Mary Rona, da of Sir Walter Burrell, Bt, CBE, TD, DL; 2 s (Julian, Hugo), 2 da (Dione, now Countess of Verulam m 1976 7 Earl of Verulam, Sarah b 1963); *Career* 2 Lt 9 Queen's Royal Lancers; chm Smith St Aubyn & Co Ltd 1973- (joined 1951, dir 1955), dir: Tech Dvpt Capital Ltd 1962-66, Transparent Paper Ltd 1958-76 and 1980- (chm 1965-76), Ship Mortgage Fin Co 1963-78, dir Br & Rhodesian Discount House Ltd 1959-, Discount House of S Africa Ltd 1961-; chm London Market Assoc 1978-80 (dep chm 1976-78), trustee Henry Smith's Charity 1971-; *Recreations* hunting, shooting, stalking, skiing; *Style* - Jeremy Smith Esq; Balcombe House, Balcombe, Sussex (☎ 044 483 267); 53 Chelsea sq, SW3 (☎01 352 2064)

SMITH, Hon Jacqueline Jane; da (by 1 m) of 3 Baron Colwyn; *b* 1967; *Style* - The Hon Jacqueline Smith

SMITH, John Patrick; s of Col Neville Frederick Smith (d 1979); *b* 25 Aug 1932; *Educ* St Edward's Sch Oxford, Brasenose Oxford; *m* 196l, Ann Felicity, nee Hawker; 2 s, 1 da; *Career* actuary; ch investment man Equity and Law Life Assurance Soc Ltd 1977-; *Recreations* golf; *Clubs* MCC, Dale Hill G C; *Style* - John Smith Esq; Hadlow Lodge, Burgh Hill, Etchingham, Sussex (☎ Hurst Green 282)

SMITH, Kenneth Graeme Stewart; CMG (1958), JP (Dorset 1967); s of Prof Herbert Arthur Smith DCL (1961); *b* 26 July 1918; *Educ* Bradfield, Magdalen Coll Oxford; *Career* Fl Lt RAFVR 1940-46; admin cadet Colonial Serv 1940, district cmmr Zanzibar 1946, Govt Sec Seychelles 1949, Assist Ch Sec Aden 1952, Colonial Sec Gambia 1956, (ret 1962); *Style* - Kenneth Smith CMG JP; The Old House, 64 Newland, Sherborne, Dorset (☎ Sherborne 2754)

SMITH, Hon Mrs (Lois Jean); da of Baron Pearson, CBE, PC (Life Peer) (d 1980); *b* 1938; *m* 1961, the Rev Robin Jonathan Norman Smith; *Style* - The Hon Mrs Smith; St Mary's Vicarage, Chesham, Bucks

SMITH, Hon Lorenzo Patrick Harold; s of 4 Visc Hambleden; *b* 1962; *Style* - The Hon Lorenzo Smith

SMITH, Dame Margôt; DBE (1974); s of Leonard Graham-Brown MC (d 1950); *b* 5 Sept 1918; *Educ* Hilders Hindhead, Westonbirt Glos; *m* 1947, Roy Smith; 2 s, 1 da; *Career* chairman Yorks Conservative Women's Ctee 1963-66, chairman Nat Conservative Women's Ctee 1969-72, chm Nat Assoc of Conservative & Unionist Assoc 1973-74, memb NSPCC Central Exec Ctee 1969-; *Recreations* fox hunting, riding, gardening; *Style* - Dame Margôt Smith DBE; Howden Lodge, Spennithorne, Leybburn, N Yorks (☎ 0969 23621)

SMITH, Hon Mrs (Myfanwy Ann); *née* Philipps; da (by 1 m) of 2 Viscount St Davids; *b* 1944; *m* 1968, Anthony Smith, *qv*; 2 s; *Style* - The Hon Mrs Smith; 23 Pyrland rd, N5

SMITH, His Hon Judge Mark Barnet; s of David Smith (d 1933); *b* 11 Feb 1917; *Educ* Manchester G S, Sidney Sussex Coll

Cambridge; *m* 1943, Edith Winifred, nee Harrison; 2 da; *Career* served WW II; assist examiner HM Patent Office 1939, promoted to examiner 1944; barr 1948, temporary Recorder of Folkestone 1971, Recorder 1972, Circuit Judge since 1972; *Recreations* gardening, spectator sports; *Style* - His Hon Judge Mark Smith; 28 Avenue Elmers, Surbiton, Surrey (☎ 399 0634)

SMITH, Hon Martin Rodney; s (by 1 m) of Baron Smith, KBE (Life Peer); *b* 1942; *Style* - The Hon Martin Smith

SMITH, Hon Lady; Hon Monica Victoria; *née* Crossley; da of late 1 Baron Somerleyton, MP, and Phyllis, CBE, da of late Gen Sir Henry Percival de Bathe, 4 Bt, KCB; *b* 1897; *m* 1918, Lt-Gen Sir Arthur Francis Smith, KCB, KBE, DSO, MC, late Coldstream Gds (gs of 8 Earl of Kintore and who d 1977); 3 da; *Style* - The Hon Lady Smith; Greathed Manor, Lingfield, Surrey

SMITH, Nigel Fearn Clive; s of Bernard Clive Smith (d 1970); *b* 24 Jan 1928; *Educ* Stowe; *m* 1962, Audrey Geraldine, nee Catto; 1 s, 1 da; *Career* underwriter; dir J Compton Sons & Webb (Holdings) Ltd 1967-, Vantona Gp 1978-; *Recreations* skiing, sailing; *Clubs* Special Forces; *Style* - Nigel Smith Esq; Vynes Farmhouse, Staunton, Gloucester

SMITH, Hon Nicolas Robin Bartolomeo; s of 4 Visc Hambleden; *b* 17 Aug 1960; *Style* - The Hon Nicolas Smith

SMITH, Peter Alexander Charles; *b* 18 Aug 1920; *Educ* St Paul's Sch; *m* 1945, Marjorie May, nee Humphrey; 1 s; *Career* solicitor 1948-, chm and md Securicor Group Ltd 1974-, chm British Security Industry Assoc 1977-; *Recreations* golf, music, photography; *Clubs* British Racing Drivers'; *Style* - Peter Smith Esq; c/o Vigilant House, 24 Gillingham st, SW1 (☎ 01 828 5611)

SMITH, Philip John Mytton; s of Herbert George Smith; *b* 6 Jan 1936; *Educ* Uppingham, Aston U Birmingham; *m* 1974, Sarah Anne Ruth, nee Forsyth; 2 da; *Career* dir of Brass Turned Parts Ltd Birmingham 1972-, formerly with General Electric Co 1954-64, Ian Heath Ltd Birmingham 1964-67, P-E Consulting Group 1968-72; *Recreations* sailing, hunting, (yacht: 'Nicola of Bosham'); *Style* - Philip Smith Esq; Old Farmhouse, Barton, Guiting Power, Glos (☎ Guiting Power 480)

SMITH, Hon Philip Reginald; s of 3 Visc Hambleden (d 1948); *b* 7 Sept 1945; *Educ* Eton; *m* 1973, Mary, da of John Roberts, of Checkendon, Oxon; 1 s, 1 da; *Career* Maj Roy Green Jackets; *Style* - The Hon Philip Smith; The Old Rectory, Ewelme, Oxon (☎ 223)

SMITH, Hon Robert Aidan Rodney; s (by 1 m) of Baron Smith, KBE (Life Peer); *b* 1956; *Style* - The Hon Robert Smith

SMITH, Robert Courtney; CBE (1980); s of John Smith, DL, JP (d 1976); *b* 10 Sept 1927; *Educ* Sedbergh, Trin Cambridge; *m* 1954, Moira Rose; 1 s, 2 da, (1 s decd); *Career* OstJ 1976; chartered accountant; chm Scottish United Investors Ltd, chm Sidlaw Industries Ltd, dep chm Standard Life Assurance Co Ltd, vice-chm William Collins & Sons (Holdings) Ltd, dir British Aluminium Company Ltd, dir Volvo Trucks (Great Britain) Ltd; *Recreations* gardening, racing; *Clubs* East India, Western (Glasgow), Hawks (Cambridge); *Style* - Robert Smith Esq, CBE; North Lodge, Dunkeld, Perthshire (☎ Dunkeld 574)

SMITH, Hon Richard Edward; s of 3 Visc Hambleden (d 1948); *b* 1937; *m* 1973, Christine Hickey; 1 s; *Style* - The Hon Richard Smith; 8 Belgravia House, W Halkin st, SW1 (☎ 235 3324)

SMITH, Ronald Frank George; s of Sydney Ernest Smith (d 1948); *b* 14 May 1923; *Educ* Edmund Latymer; *m* 1946, Irene Florence, da of Herbert Holmes (d 1940); 2 da; *Career* Maj The Nigeria Regiment Africa; shipbroker; chm 1974 Brown Jenkinson & Co Ltd; *Recreations* golf; *Clubs* Marine, Lloyds; *Style* - Ronald Smith Esq; 5 Eversley Mount, N21 IJP (☎ 01 360 1890)

SMITH, Robert Hill; s (by 2 m) and h of Sir Gordon Smith, 2 Bt, VRD; *b* 15 April

1958; *Educ* Merchant Taylors', Aberdeen U (is reading Physics as of July 1981); *Recreations* sailing; *Clubs* Roy Thames Yacht; *Style* - Robert Smith Esq; 5 Elmfield av, Aberdeen AB2 3NU (☎ 46103)

SMITH, Robert Sydney Winwood; s and h of Sir Christopher Smith, 5 Bt; *b* 1939; *Style* - Robert Smith Esq

SMITH, Hon Mrs (Sheila Marguerite Evelyn); *née* de Montmorency; da of 7 Viscount Mountmorres (d 1951); *b* 1918; *m* 1950, Robert Vernon Smith; 2 s; *Career* is a Princess Christian Nurse; 1939-45 War as London Ambulance Driver; *Style* - The Hon Mrs Smith

SMITH, Prof Sir Thomas Broun; QC (1956); s of John Smith JP, DL (d 1954); *b* 3 Dec 1915; *Educ* Glasgow H s, Sedbergh School, Christ Church Oxford, Edinburgh U; *m* 1940, Ann Dorothea, da of Christian Tindall, CIE, ICS (d 1951); 1 da (1 s and 1 da decd); *Career* Lt-Col British Expeditionary Force (served 1939-50); barrister 1938, advocate 1947; Prof of Scots Law Aberdeen University 1947-58; Prof of Civil Law Edinburgh University 1958-68, Prof of Scots Law 1968-72; memb of Scottish Law Commission (part-time) 1965-72 (full-time) 1972-80; Professor Emeritus Edinburgh University 1980; author; kt 1981; *Recreations* reading, gardening, foreign travel; *Clubs* Naval and Military, New (Edinburgh); *Style* - Prof Sir Thomas Smith QC; 11 India Street, Edinburgh 3 (☎ 031 225 8030); Kirkton of Morham, Haddington, E Lothian

SMITH, Adm Sir Victor Alfred Trumper; AC (1975), KBE (1968), DSC (1941); s of late George Smith; *b* 9 May 1913; *Educ* Chatsworth Sch, RAN Coll; *m* 1944, Nanette Suzanne, nee Harrison; 3 s; *Career* Dep Ch Naval Staff 1968, Ch of Naval Staff 1970-75, Chm Chiefs of Naval Staff Ctee; *Style* - Adm Sir Victor Smith, AC, KBE, DSC; 15 Fishburn st, Red Hill, ACT 2603, Australia

SMITH, Hon William Henry Bernard; s and h of 4 Visc Hambleden; *b* 18 Nov 1955; *Style* - The Hon William Smith

SMITH, Walter Riddell; CB (1973); s of John Riddell Smith (d 1965); *b* 18 Sept 1914; *Educ* Johnston Tech Sch Durham, Durham U; *m* 1942, Janet Henderson, nee Mitchell; 1 s, 1 da; *Career* dir National Agricultural Advsy Serv 1967-71, dep dir General Agricultural Dvpt and Advsy Serv 1971-75, Welsh Sec to Ministry of Ag 1975-78 (ret 1978); *Recreations* gardening, literature, languages; *Style* - Walter Smith Esq, CB; 14 Westpoint, 49 Putney Hill, SW15

SMITH-CARINGTON, Wing Cdr John Hanbury; AFC (1953), DL (Leics 1972); s of Hamo Folville Smith-Carington (d 1946); *b* 26 Oct 1921; *Educ* Harrow, Oriel Coll Oxford; *m* 1951, Noreen, nee Magee; 1 da; *Career* RAF 1941-71 (ret Wing Cdr), chm Parish Cncl and District Cncllr 1972-, memb Borough Cncl 1972-79, dir Leics Red Cross 1972-, E Leics Community Health Cncl 1973-79, memb Leics Cttee Country Landowners 1973-, High Sheriff Leics 1979-; *Recreations* country pursuits; *Clubs* RAF, Leicestershire, Far and Near; *Style* - Wing Cdr John Smith-Carington, AFC, DL; Ashby Folville Lodge, nr Melton Mowbray, Leics (☎ Gaddesby 293)

SMITH-COX, Sidney Clifton; CBE (1963), JP; s of Sidney Cox (d 1949); *b* 8 Feb 1911; *Educ* Clifton Coll; *m* 1943, Marjorie Joyce, da of Frank Lawrence Payne (d 1980); 2 s; *Career* CA; *Recreations* swimming, golf; *Style* - Sidney Smith-Cox Esq, CBE, JP; Westward Ho, 27 Edgehill rd, Clevedon, Somerset (☎ 872455)

SMITH-DODSWORTH, David John; s and h of Sir John Smith-Dodsworth, 8 Bt; *b* 23 Oct 1963; *Style* - David Smith-Dodsworth Esq

SMITH-DODSWORTH, Sir John (Christopher); 8 Bt (GB 1784), of Newland Park, Yorks; s of Sir Claude Matthew Smith-Dodsworth, 7 Bt (d 1940); *b* 4 March 1935; *Educ* Ampleforth; *m* 1961, Margaret Anne, da of Alfred Jones of Pludds, Glos; 1 s, 1 da; *Heir* s, David Smith-Dodsworth; *Style* - Sir John Smith-Dodsworth, Bt; Thornton Watlass Hall, Ripon, Yorks

SMITH-DORRIEN-SMITH, Lady Emma; *née* Windsor-Clive; da of 3 Earl of Plymouth; *b* 1954; *m* 1975, Robert Arthur

Smith-Dorrien-Smith; 1 s; *Style* - Lady Emma Smith-Dorrien-Smith; Tresco Abbey, Isles of Scilly

SMITH-GORDON, Sir (Lionel) Eldred Peter; 5 Bt (UK 1838); s of Sir Lionel Eldred Pottinger Smith-Gordon, 4 Bt (d 1976); *b* 7 May 1935; *Educ* Eton, Trin Oxford; *m* 1962, Sandra Rosamund Ann, da of late Wing Cdr Walter Farley, DFC; 1 s, 1 da; *Heir* s, Lionel Smith-Gordon; *Style* - Sir Eldred Smith-Gordon, Bt; 13 Shalcomb st, SW10 (☎ 01 352 8506)

SMITH-GORDON, Lionel George Eldred; s and h of Sir Eldred Smith-Gordon, 5 Bt; *b* 1 July 1964; *Educ* Eton; *Recreations* photography; *Clubs* Hurlingham; *Style* - Lionel Smith-Gordon Esq; 13 Shalcomb st, SW10 (☎ 01 352 8506)

SMITH-MARRIOTT, Hugh Cavendish; s (by 1 m) and h of Sir Ralph Smith-Marriott, 10 Bt; *b* 22 March 1925; *m* 1953, Pauline Anne, da of Frank Fawcett Holt, of Bristol; 1 da; *Style* - Hugh Smith-Marriott Esq; 26 Shipley rd, Westbury-on-Trym, Bristol

SMITH-MARRIOTT, Sir Ralph George Cavendish; 10 Bt (GB 1774), of Sydling St Nicholas, Dorset; s of late George Rudolph Wyldbore Smith-Marriott, s of late Rev Hugh Forbes Smith-Marriott, s of 4 Bt; suc unc, Sir Hugh Randolph Cavendish Smith-Marriott, 9 Bt, 1944; *b* 16 Dec 1900; *Educ* Cranleigh, Bristol U; *m* 1, 1924, Phyllis Elizabeth (d 1932), da of Richard Kemp, formerly Govr of HM Prison, Bristol; 2 s, 1 da; m 2, 1933, Doris May (d 1951), da of R L C Morrison; m 3, 1966, Mrs Barbara Mary Cantlay; *Heir* s, Hugh Smith-Marriott; *Style* - Sir Ralph Smith-Marriott, Bt; 28a Westover rd, Westbury-on-Trym, Bristol (☎ Bristol 628827)

SMITH-RYLAND, Hon Mrs (Jeryl Marcia Sarah); *née* Gurdon; da of late Hon Robert Brampton Gurdon (s of 2 Baron Cranworth) and Hon Daisy, nee Pearson, da of 2 Viscount Cowdray and subsequently w of (1) Lt-Col Alistair Gibb and (2) 1 Baron McCorquodale of Newton; sis of 3 Baron; *b* 1932; *m* 1952, Charles Mortimer Tollemache Smith-Ryland; 2 s, 3 da; *Career* CStJ 1981; raised to the rank of a Baron's da 1964; *Style* - The Hon Mrs Smith-Ryland; Sherbourne Park, Warwick

SMITHERS, Prof Sir David Waldron; s of Sir Waldron Smithers JP MP (d 1954); *b* 18 Jan 1908; *Educ* Charterhouse, Clare Coll Cambridge; *m* 1933, Gwladys Margaret, nee Angel; 1 s, 1 da; *Career* kt 1969, Prof Radiotherapy Institute of Cancer Research and Roy Marsden Hosp 1943-72, Hon Consultant Radiotherapist Brompton Hosp Diseases of the Chest and to the RN, Kt Cdr of the Sovereign Mil Order St John of Jerusalem, Kt of Malta 1972; *Recreations* book collecting, growing roses; *Style* - Prof Sir David Smithers; Knockholt, Kent (☎ 0959 32122)

SMOLLETT OF BONHILL, Maj Patrick Tobias Telfer; MC (1940), DL (Dunbartonshire 1957); s of Maj-Gen Alexander Telfer Smollett of Bonhill CB CBE DSO MC (d 1954 & himself gggg nephew of Tobias Smollett, the 18th century novelist); *b* 26 Dec 1914; *m* 1951, Georgina, da of Sir Gifford Fox, 2 & last Bt, MP; 1 s, 1 da; *Career* 2 Lt HLI 1936, served India 1936, Palestine 1938, Eritrea, Egypt, Italy WW II, Mil Mission to Egypt 1942, Allied Kommandatura Berlin 1948-51, Cyprus 1955-56, Egypt 1956, ret 1959; memb Roy Co of Archers (Queen's Bodyguard for Scotland) 1956; pres Balloch Loch Lomond Highland Games, V-Cdre Loch Lomond Rowing Club, V-Pres Loch Lomond Motor Cycle Club; KStJ; *Recreations* skiing, animal husbandry, conserving rare animals; *Style* - Maj Patrick Smollett of Bonhill MC DL; 9 Cleveland Row, SW1 (☎ 01 930 6319); The Downs, Croxton, Cambridgeshire (☎ 048087 228); Cameron House, Alexandria, Dunbartonshire (0389 56226)

SMYLY, (Cecil) William; s of Philip Austin Smyly (d 1968); *b* 29 April 1928; *Educ* Aldenham; *m* 1955, Fiona Daphne, nee Wilson; 4 c; *Career* dir: Billing & Sons Ltd Guildford, Norfolk Printers Ltd; dist cncllr, sch and coll govr; *Recreations* sports generally, tennis particularly; *Clubs* National, Victoria; *Style* - William Smyly Esq; Pathways, Grenofen, Tavistock, Devon (☎ Tavistock 2391)

SMYTH, Brig Rt Hon Sir John George; 1 Bt (UK 1956) of Teignmouth, Co Devon, VC (1915), MC (1920), PC (1962); s of late W J Smyth, ICS; *b* 24 Oct 1893; *Educ* Repton, RMC; *m* 1, 1920 (m dis 1940), Margaret, da of late Charles Lawrence Dundas (s of Hon John Dundas, bro of 1 Marquess of Zetland); 3 s (eldest ka 1944, second d 1974), 1 da; m 2, 1940, Frances Read, da of late Lt-Col Robert Alexander Chambers, OBE, IMS; *Heir* gs, Timothy Smyth; *Career* Brig (ret) Indian Army, raised 19 (Dagger) Div India 1941, Burma 1942 Cmdg 17 Div; author and playwright; freeman City of London and of Farriers' Co (Master 1961-62), Cmdt 45 Rattray's Sikhs 1936-39, GSOI 2 London Div 1939-40, mil correspondent Daily Sketch and Sunday Times 1945-46, lawn tennis corrrespondent Sunday Times 1946-51, MP (C) Norwood Div Lambeth 1950-66, Parly Sec Miny of Pensions and Nat Insurance 1953-55, lawn tennis correspondent News of the World 1956-57, pres VC and GC Assoc, v-pres Int Lawn Tennis Club of Gt Britain; *Style* - Brig the Rt Hon Sir John Smyth, Bt, VC, MC, PC; 807 Nelson House, Dolphin sq, SW1

SMYTH, Hon Mrs (Patricia Margaret); da of Baron Black (Life Peer); *b* 1919; *m* 1942, Leslie John Smyth; *Style* - The Hon Mrs Smyth; Rushtons, Longdown, Guildford, Surrey

SMYTH, Timothy John; s of late Julian Smyth, eld s of 1 Bt; hp of gf, Brig Rt Hon Sir John Smyth VC MC PC; *b* 16 April 1953; *Style* - Timothy Smyth Esq

SNEDDON, Robert; CMG (1976), MBE (1945); s of John Sneddon (d 1928); *b* 8 June 1920; *Educ* Dalziel H S, Kettering G S, Univ Coll Nottingham; *m* 1945, Kathleen Margaret, nee Smith; 2 da; *Career* Maj 8 Army 1940-46, Foreign Serv 1946, 3 Sec Warsaw 1946-50, 2 Sec Stockholm 1950-54, Foreign Office 1954-56, 1 Sec Oslo 1956-61, 1 Sec Berlin 1961-63, Foreign & C'wlth Office 1963-69 & 1971-77, Cnsllr Bonn 1969-71; *Recreations* tennis, golf; *Clubs* Woking Lawn Tennis & Croquet, Westhill Golf; *Style* - Robert Sneddon Esq, CMG, MBE; Windrose, Church rd, Horsell, Woking, Surrey (☎ Woking 4335)

SNELL, John Bernard; s of Harold Emley Snell (d 1966); *b* 28 March 1932; *Educ* Bryanston, Balliol Oxford, Lincoln's Inn; *Career* author; md Romney Hythe & Dymchurch Railway Co 1972-; *Recreations* music, literature and photography; *Style* - John Snell Esq; 15 Tudor av, Dymchurch, Kent (☎ Dymchurch 2789)

SNELUS, Alan Roe; CMG (1960); s of John Ernest Snelus (d 1933); *b* 19 May 1911; *Educ* Haileybury, Cambridge; *m* 1947, Margaret Bird, nee Elliott; 1 s, 1 da; *Career* Sarawak Civil Service 1934, barr Gray's Inn 1934, Colonial Service 1946, Sec of Defence 1951, Dep Chief Sec 1955-64 (ret 1964); *Recreations* gardening and contemplation; *Style* - Alan Snelus Esq, CMG; Cleaveside, Verriotts Lane, Morcombelake, Dorset (☎ Chidcock 509)

SNOW, Philip Albert; MBE (1979), JP (Warwicks and W Sussex 1967); s of William Edward Snow FRCD (d 1955); *b* 7 Aug 1915; *Educ* Alderman Newton's Leicester, Christ's Coll Cambridge; *m* 1940, Mary Anne, nee Harris; 1 da; *Career* Colonial Administrative Service (Fiji and Western Pacific) 1938-52, Bursar (1952-75) and Clerk (1967-75) to Governing Body Rugby Sch, Perm Fiji Rep on Int Cricket Conference 1965-, author and bibliographer; *Clubs* MCC, Hawks' (Cambridge); *Style* - Philip Snow Esq, MBE, JP; Gables, Station rd, Angmering, W Sussex (☎ Rustington 73594)

SNOW, Hon Philip Charles Hansford; s of Baron Snow, CBE (C P Snow, the author, d 1980), and Pamela Hansford-Johnson (d 1981; novelist, Proustian, one of that class of ex-banker poets that has included Samuel Rogers and T S Eliot, and ex-fiancée of Dylan Thomas); *b* 26 Aug 1952; *Educ* Eton, Balliol Oxford; *Style* - The Hon Philip Snow

SNOWDON, 1 Earl of (UK 1961); Antony Charles Robert Armstrong-Jones; GCVO (1969); also Viscount Linley (UK 1961); s of Ronald Owen Lloyd Armstrong-Jones, MBE, QC, DL (d 1966) of Plas Dinas, Caernarvonshire, by Anne (later Countess of Rosse), da of Lt-Col Leonard Messel, OBE; *b* 7 March

1930; *Educ* Eton, Jesus Cambridge; *m* 1, 1960 (m dis 1978), HRH The Princess Margaret (*see* Royal Family); 1 s, 1 da; m 2, 1978, Lucy Mary, da of Donald Brook Davies, of Enniskerry, Co Wicklow, and formerly w of Michael Lindsay-Hogg (film dir and 1 cous of Sir William Lindsay-Hogg, 3 Bt); 1 da; *Heir* s, Viscount Linley (*see* Royal Family); *Career* photographer; Constable of Caernarvon Castle 1963-, pres Eng Ctee International Year for Disabled People 1981; RDI 1978, FRSA, artistic advr to Sunday Times and Sunday Times Publications Ltd 1962-; pres Contemporary Art Soc for Wales, Welsh Theatre Co; (George II's eldest s & h, Prince Frederick (Horace Walpole's "Fred, Who was alive and is dead") was in 1726 cr Baron Snaudon (ie Snowdon) and Duke of Edenburgh (*sic*); after his f became king he was also cr Prince of Wales, so that from 1728 to 1750 the Prince of Wales, Duke of Edinburgh and Lord Snowdon were one and the same person); *Style* - The Rt Hon The Earl of Snowdon GCVO; 22 Launceston Place, W8

SOAMES, Baron (Life Peer UK 1978); (Arthur) Christopher (John); GCMG (1972), GCVO (1972), CH (1980), CBE (1955), PC (1958); s of Capt Arthur Granville Soames, OBE (d 1962); *b* 12 Oct 1920; *Educ* Eton, RMC Sandhurst; *m* 1947, Hon Mary, DBE, da of Rt Hon Sir Winston Leonard Spencer Churchill, KG, OM, CH, PC, FRS, and of Baroness Spencer-Churchill, GBE (*see* Soames, Baroness); 3 s, 2 da (*see* Hambro, Hon Mrs (Charlotte) and Clementine); *Career* Assist Mil Attaché Br Embassy Paris 1946-47 and PPS to PM (Rt Hon Sir Winston Churchill) 1952-55, Parly Under-Sec of State Air Miny 1955-57, Parly and Fin Sec Admiralty 1957-58, Sec of State for War 1958-60, Min of Ag Fish and Food 1960-64, Ambass to France 1968-72, V-Pres Cmmn of European Communities (External Relations) 1973-77, MP (C) Bedford 1950-76, Pres Roy Ag Soc of Eng 1973, non-exec dir N M Rothschild & Sons Ltd 1977-79, dir Nat West Bank Ltd 1978-79, Govr Rhodesia 1979-80, Croix de Guerre 1942, Robert Schuman Prize 1976, GO de La Légion d'Honneur 1972, Lord Pres of the Cncl and Leader of House of Lords 1979-81; *Clubs* White's, Portland, Jockey; *Style* - The Rt Hon The Lord Soames, GCMG, GCVO, CH, CBE, PC; Castle Mill House, North Warnborough, Basingstoke, Hants

SOAMES, Hon Jeremy Bernard; s of Baron Soames, GCMG, GCVO, CH, CBE, PC, *qv*; *b* 1952; *Educ* Eton; *m* 1978, Susanna, da of (James) David Agar Keith; 1 da; *Style* - The Hon Jeremy Soames; W Barsham Hall, Fakenham, Norfolk

SOAMES, Baroness; Hon Mary; DBE (1980, MBE Mil 1945); da of late Rt Hon Sir Winston Leonard Spencer-Churchill, KG, OM, CH, TD, PC, FRS (gs of 7 Duke of Marlborough and who d 1965) and Baroness Spencer-Churchill (Dame Clementine Ogilvy, DBE, cr Life Peeress 1965, da of late Col Sir Henry Montague Hozier, KCB (bro of 1 Baron Newlands) and Lady Henrietta Ogilvy, da of 5 Earl of Airlie, KT); *b* 1922; *m* 1947, Capt Christopher Soames (now Baron Soames, GCMG, GCVO, CH, CBE, PC, *qv*); *Career* formerly Jr Cdr ATS, memb Winston Churchill Memorial Tst Cncl 1978-, pres Nat Benevolent Fund for the Aged 1978-; *Style* - The Rt Hon The Lady Soames, DBE; Castle Mill House, North Warnborough, Basingstoke, Hants

SOAMES, Hon (Arthur) Nicholas Winston; s of Baron Soames, *qv*, and Hon Mary, nee Spencer-Churchill, da of late Sir Winston Churchill by Baroness Spencer-Churchill; seventh cous once removed to HRH The Princess of Wales; *b* 12 Feb 1949; *Educ* Eton; *m* 1981 (at which wedding HRH The Prince of Wales was best man), Catherine, da of Capt Tony Weatherall, of Dumfries; *Career* Lloyd's insurance broker; Extra Equerry to HRH The Prince of Wales; late 11 Hussars; *Style* - The Hon Nicholas Soames

SOAMES, Hon Rupert Christopher; s of Baron Soames, GCMG, GCVO, CH, CBE, PC, *qv*; *b* 1959; *Educ* Eton; *Style* - The Hon Rupert Soames

SODOR AND MAN, 77 Bishop of (cr 447) 1974-; Rt Rev Vernon Sampson Nicholls; s of Ernest C Nicholls (d 1957); *b* 3 Sept 1918; *Educ* Truro Sch, Durham U, Clifton Theological Coll Bristol; *m* 1943, Phyllis, da of Edwin Potter; 1 s, 1 da; *Career* Chaplain to the Forces 1944-46,

Vicar and Rural Dean of Walsall 1956-67, Archdeacon of Birmingham 1967-74; *Clubs* Roy Commonwealth Soc; *Style* - The Rt Rev The Lord Bishop of Sodor and Man; Bishop's House, Quarterbridge rd, Douglas, IOM (☎ 0624 22108)

SOFER, Hon Mrs (Anne Hallowell); da of Baron Crowther (Life Peer, d 1972); *b* 1937; *m* 1958, Jonathan Sofer, barrister; children; *Style* - The Hon Mrs Sofer; 46 Regent's Park rd, NW1

SOLEY, Clive Stafford; MP (L) Hammersmith N 1979-; *b* 7 May 1939; *Educ* Downhill Secdy Sch, Newbattle Abbey Adult Educn Coll, Strathclyde U, Southampton U; *Career* probation offr 1970-75, sr probation offr 1975-79; *Style* - Clive Soley Esq, MP; House of Commons, SW1

SOLOMON, Nathaniel; s of Leopold Solomon; *b* 20 Nov 1925; *Educ* Owen's Sch London, Emmanuel Coll Cambridge; *m* 1951, Patricia Ethel, nee Creak; 2 s, 1 da; *Career* dir United Africa Co Ltd 1964-72, William Baird Ltd 1972-74, md Associated Leisure Ltd 1974-; *Recreations* bridge, tennis, opera, theatre, reading; *Clubs* Reform, The Wimbledon, Harvard Business Sch Club of London; *Style* - Nathaniel Solomon Esq; 76 Limerston st, Chelsea, SW10 (☎ 01 352 3906)

SOLOMON, His Hon Judge; (Alan) Peter Solomon; s of Jacob Ovid Solomon (d 1950); *b* 6 July 1923; *Educ* Mill Hill, Lincoln Coll Oxford; *m* 1, 1954 (m dis 1969), Deirdre Anne Punter; 1 da; m 2, 1973 (m dis 1979), Gloria Turower; 1 da; *Career* barr 1949, a Circuit Judge 1973-; *Recreations* the turf, travel, poetry, burgundy; *Clubs* Garrick; *Style* - His Hon Judge Solomon; Crown Court, Middlesex Guildhall, Parliament Sq, SW1

SOMERLEYTON, 3 Baron (UK 1916); Sir Savile William Francis Crossley; 4 Bt (UK 1863), JP (Lowestoft), DL (Suffolk 1964); s of 2 Baron, MC, DL (d 1959); *b* 17 Sept 1928; *Educ* Eton; *m* 1963, Belinda Maris, da of late Vivian Loyd; 1 s, 4 da; *Heir* s, Hon Hugh Crossley; *Career* Capt Coldstream Gds (ret), former CCllr E Suffolk, a Lord in Waiting to HM The Queen (Permanent) 1978-; farmer and landowner; patron of one living; dir E Anglian Water Co, tstee Tstee Savings Bank of Eastern England; *Recreations* hunting, shooting, fishing, sailing, golf; *Clubs* Turf, White's; *Style* - The Rt Hon The Lord Somerleyton, JP, DL; Somerleyton Hall, Lowestoft, Suffolk (☎ Lowestoft 730 308 and 730 224)

SOMERLEYTON, Bridget, Baroness; Bridget; MBE (1946), JP (Suffolk); da of William Douro Hoare, CBE; *m* 1924, 2 Baron (d 1959); 2 s, 1 da; *Career* Govr Nat Corporation for Care of Old People; *Style* - The Rt Hon Bridget, Lady Somerleyton, MBE, JP; White House, Somerleyton, Lowestoft, Suffolk

SOMERS, 8 Baron (GB 1784); Sir John Patrick Somers Cocks; 8 Bt (GB 1772); s of 7 Baron Somers (d 1953, fifth in descent from the sis of the 1 & last Baron Somers of the 1 cr, the celebrated Lord High Chllr, who was a memb of the Whig Junto in Anne's reign, architect of the Union with Scotland, dedicatee of Swift's *Tale of a Tub*, and, according to Addison, "the chief contriver of the quiet accession of the House of Hanover" - which no more stopped him corresponding covertly with the kings over the water than it did many contemporaries); *b* 30 April 1907; *Educ* privately and at Roy Coll of Music (BMus and ARCM); *m* 1961, Dora Helen, da of late John Mountfort; *Heir* kinsman, Philip Somers Cocks; *Career* organist and professional musician; organist and choirmaster Westonbirt Sch 1935-38, Dir of Music Epsom Coll 1949-53, Prof of Theory and Composition RCM 1967-77; *Recreations* carpentry; *Style* - The Rt Hon The Lord Somers; 35 Links rd, Epsom, Surrey (☎ 26514)

SOMERS, Dowager Baroness; (Daisy) Finola; CBE (1950); da of late Capt Bertram Meeking; *m* 1921, 6 Baron Somers KCMG DSO MC (d 1944); 1 da; *Career* formerly Ch Cmmr Girl Guides' Assoc; *Style* - The Rt Hon The Dowager Lady Somers CBE; Garden Cottage, Eastnor Castle, Ledbury, Herefordshire (☎ 205)

SOMERSET, 18 Duke of (E 1547); Sir Percy Hamilton Seymour; 16 Bt (E

1611), DL (Wilts 1960); also Baron Seymour (E 1547); s of 17 Duke of Somerset, DSO, OBE (d 1954), through whom His Grace is fourteenth in descent from 'Protector' Somerset, who pulled down Old St Paul's Cloisters (including a much admired depiction of the Dance of Death - a favourite theme of the waning Middle Ages) to build Somerset House in the Strand; also 1 cous thirteen times removed of King Edward VI (s of Henry VIII by Jane Seymour, the 1 Duke's sis); the Marquesses of Hertford (who are in remainder to the Dukedom) are half cousins through Sir Edward Seymour the 4 Bt's 2 w; *b* 27 Sept 1910; *Educ* Blundell's, Clare Cambridge; *m* 1951, Gwendoline Collette (Jane), da of late Maj J Thomas, N Staffs Regt; 2 s, 1 da; *Heir* s, Lord Seymour, *qv*; *Career* Maj (ret) Wilts Regt, pres Br Legion for Wilts; patron of 2 livings; *Style* - His Grace The Duke of Somerset, DL; Maiden Bradley, Warminster, Wilts (☎ 098 53 203)

SOMERSET, David Robert; s of Henry Somerset DSO (himself s of Henry Somerset OBE JP DL, by his 1 w, Lady Katherine Beauclerk, da of 10 Duke of St Albans; the elder Henry was s of Rt Hon Lord Henry Somerset PC JP DL, 2 s of 8 Duke of Beaufort KG PC, & sometime MP Glos E; Lord Henry m Lady Isabella, er da & co-heiress of 3 Earl Somers), by Bettine, yr da of Maj Charles Malcolm (bro of Sir James Malcolm, 9 Bt) by his w, Hon Beatrix Hore-Ruthven (only da of 8 Lord Ruthven); hp to cous, 10 Duke of Beaufort, KG, GCVO, PC, in all his Peerages except the Baronies of Botetourt and Herbert; *b* 23 Feb 1928; *Educ* Eton; *m* 1950, Lady Caroline Thynne, da of 6 Marquess of Bath; 3 s, 1 da; *Career* late Lt Coldstream Gds; chm Marlborough Fine Art 1977-; *Clubs* White's; *Style* - David Somerset Esq; The Cottage, Badminton, Glos; 90 Eaton ter, SW1

SOMERSET, Hon Geoffrey; s of 2 surviving s of 4 Baron Raglan, JP (d 1964); bro and hp of 5 Baron Raglan, JP, DL; *b* 29 Aug 1932; *Educ* Westminster, RAC Cirencester; *m* 1956, Caroline, da of Col Roderick Hill, DSO, JP, DL, of St Arvan's Court, Chepstow, by his w Rachel (g niece of 1 Earl St Aldwyn, PC, JP, DL); 1 s, 2 da; *Career* Lt Gren Gds (Reserve), CCllr Berks 1966-75, memb Newbury DC 1979-; *Recreations* shooting; *Style* - The Hon Geoffrey Somerset; Manor Farm, Stanford-in-the-Vale, Faringdon, Oxon (☎ S-in-the-V 569)

SOMERSET-WARD, Richard Adrian; s of Rev Canon A D Somerset-Ward (d 1976); *b* 29 May 1942; *Educ* Charterhouse, CCC Cambridge; *Career* joined BBC 1963, seconded to HM Diplomatic Serv 1964-65, BBC dir in USA 1976-78, Head Music and Arts Programming BBC TV 1981-; *Recreations* opera, music, tennis, golf; *Clubs* Saville; *Style* - Richard Somerset-Ward Esq; 47 Welsby ct, Eaton Rise, W5 (☎ 01 998-5789)

SOMERTON, Viscount; courtesy title which would be born by eldest s & h of Earl of Normanton, if he existed

SOMERVILLE, Sir Robert; KCVO (1961, CVO 1953); s of Robert Somerville, FRSE; *b* 5 June 1906; *Educ* Fettes, St John's Cambridge, Edinburgh U; *m* 1, 1932, Marie-Louise Bergené (d 1976); 1 da; m 2, 1981, Mrs Jessie B Warburton, of Sydney; *Career* FSA, FRHistS; Clerk Cncl Duchy of Lancaster 1952-70 (with Off from 1930); *Style* - Sir Robert Somerville, KCVO; 15 Foxes Dale, Blackheath, SE3

SONDES, 5 Earl (UK 1880); Henry George Herbert Milles-Lade; also Baron Sondes (GB 1760) and Viscount Throwley (UK 1880); s of 4 Earl Sondes (d 1970, descended from 1 Baron Monson through the latter's 2 s, who was cr Baron Sondes) and Pamela, da of Lt-Col Herbert McDougall, of Cawston Manor, Norfolk; *b* 1 May 1940; *Educ* Eton; *m* 1, 1968 (m dis 1969), Primrose, da of Lawrence Cotter (s of Sir James Cotter, 5 Bt); m 2, 1976, (m dis 1980), Altgräfin Sissy, da of Altgraf Niklas zu Salm-Reifferscheidt-Raitz; *Heir* none; *Style* - The Rt Hon The Earl Sondes; Stringman's Farm, Faversham, Kent

SOPE, His Excellency Mr Barak; *Career* High Commissioner of Republic of Vanuatu to UK 1981-; *Style* - HE Mr Barak Sope

SOPER, Baron (Life Peer UK 1965); Rev Donald Oliver Soper; s of Ernest Frankham Soper; *b* 31 Jan 1903; *Educ* Aske's Sch Hatcham, St Cat's Cambridge, Wesley House Cambridge, LSE (PhD); *m* 1929, Marie Gertrude, da of Arthur Dean; 4 da; *Career* Minister S London Mission 1926-29, Central London Mission 1929-36, Superintendent Minister West London Mission 1936-78, chm Shelter 1974-78; *Style* - The Rev The Rt Hon The Lord Soper; Kingsway Hall, Kingsway, WC2

SOPWITH, Thomas Edward Brodie; s of Sir Thomas Octave Murdoch Sopwith CBE; *b* 15 Nov 1932; *Educ* Stowe; *m* 1977, Gina Melissa, nee Hathorn; 1 da; *Career* Lt Coldstream Guards, company chairman; *Recreations* yachting, flying, skiing; *Clubs* Royal Yacht Squad, Corviglia Ski; *Style* - Thomas Sopwith Esq; 67 Clabon Mews, SW1 (☎ 589 3305); Axford House, Axord, nr Basingstoke, Hants (☎ 025 687 221)

SOREL-CAMERON, Air Cdre Robert; CBE (1945), AFC (1943); s of Lt-Col George Cecil Minett Sorel-Cameron CBE (d 1947); *b* 27 Nov 1911; *Educ* Wellington, Edinburgh U; *m* 1939, Henrietta Grace, nee Radford-Norcop; 2 s, 1 da; *Career* joined RAF 1931 (Burma, NE India, Netherlands, East Indies), Air Commodore 1960, Air Attaché Athens 1960-62 (ret 1962); *Recreations* shooting, fishing, flat racing, wildlife; *Clubs* RAF; *Style* - Air Cdre Robert Sorel-Cameron CBE, AFC; The White House, Whitwell, Norwich (☎ 060 544 394)

SORENSEN, Baroness; Muriel; JP (Essex); da of late Rev W Harvey Smith; *m* 1915, Baron Sorensen (Life Peer, d 1971); 1 s, 1 da; *Style* - The Rt Hon The Lady Sorensen, JP; 38 Woodside Park av, Walthamstow, E17

SORENSEN, Hon Michael Malcolm Reginald; s of Baron Sorensen (Life Peer, d 1971); *b* 1919; *m* 1960, Jennifer, da of William Adams; children; *Style* - The Hon Michael Sorensen; 37 Nassington rd, NW3

SORN, Hon Lord; James Gordon McIntyre; MC and Bar; s of late T W McIntyre, of Sorn; *b* 21 July 1896; *Educ* Winchester, Balliol Oxford, Glasgow U; *m* 1923, Madeline (d 1954), da of the late Robert Scott Moncrieff, of Downhill; 1 s, 1 da; *Career* advocate Scotland 1922 (Dean of Faculty 1939-44), KC 1936; Capt Ayrshire Yeo (MC and Bar, French Croix de Guerre), a Lord of Session with title of Lord Sorn 1944-63; *Style* - The Hon Lord Sorn, MC*; Sorn Castle, Mauchline, Ayrshire

SORRELL, Martin Stuart; s of Jack Sorrell, 135 Millway, Mill Hill, London NW7; *b* 14 Feb 1945; *Educ* Haberdashers' Aske's Sch; Ch College Cambridge; Harvard Business Sch; *m* 1971, Sandra Carol Ann; 3 s; *Career* 1977 to date, Group Financial Director, Saatchi & Saatchi Company Ltd; *Recreations* skiing; *Clubs* Reform, Harvard; *Style* - Martin Sorrell Esq; Courtlands, Winnington Road, London N2 OTP (☎ 01 456 6144)

SORSBIE, Sir Malin; CBE (1956, OBE 1942); s of Rev William Francis Sorsbie (d 1944); *b* 25 May 1906; *Educ* Brighton Coll, Manitoba University, Canada; *m* 1955, Constantine Eugenie, nee Johnston; *Career* kt 1965, Roy Canadian Mounted Police 1926-29, RAF 1930-35, Capt Imperial Airways 1935-39, BOAC 1939; man W Africa 1937-41, overseas ops dir 1942, gen man E African Airways 1946-56, pres Munitalp Foundation Kenya 1956; *Clubs* RAF, Bath, RAFYC, Muthaiga Country, Nairobi, Mombasa; *Style* - Sir Malin Sorsbie CBE; PO Box 45337, Nairobi (☎ Nairobi 65331/65343)

SOSKICE, Hon David William; s of Baron Stow Hill, PC, QC (Life Peer, d 1979), and Baroness Stow Hill, *qv*; *b* 1941; *Educ* Winchester, Trin Oxford; *m* 1966, Alison, da of Walter Black, of Nately Scures House, Hook, Hants; 1 s, 1 da; *Career* economist HM Treasury 1965-66, Fell and Praelector in Economics Univ Coll Oxford 1966-; *Style* - The Hon David Soskice; 10 Staverton rd, Oxford

SOSKICE, Hon Oliver Cloudesley Hunter; s of Baron Stow Hill (Life Peer, d 1979) and Baroness Stow Hill, *qv*; *b* 1947; *Educ* Winchester, Trin Hall Cambridge; *Style* - The Hon Oliver Soskice

SOUHAMI, Mark; s of John F Souhami; *b* 25 Sept 1935; *Educ* St Marylebone G S; *m* 1964, Margaret; 2 da; *Career* Lt RA; dir: Dixons Photographic 1970-, Dixons Commercial Properties; chm & md Dixons Photographic UK 1976-; chm: Wallace Heaton, Dixserve Ltd, Dixons Japan, Dixons Photographic HK, Ascotts Ltd, ACE Ltd; *Clubs* Savile, RAC; *Style* - Mark Souhami Esq; 9 Stonehill rd, SW14

SOUKUP, Lady Constance (Ann); *née* Butler; da of 7 Marquess of Ormonde, MBE; *b* 1940; *m* 1965, Henry Lea Soukup; 1 s, 1 da; *Style* - Lady Constance Soukup; 618 North Washington, Hinsdale, Ill, USA

SOULBURY, 2 Viscount (UK 1954); James Herwald Ramsbotham; also Baron Soulbury (UK 1941); s of 1 Baron, GCMG, GCVO, OBE, MC, PC (d 1971); *b* 21 March 1915; *Educ* Eton, Magdalen Oxford; *m* 1949, Anthea Margaret (d 1950), da of late David Wilton; *Heir* bro, Hon Sir Peter Ramsbotham; *Style* - The Rt Hon The Viscount Soulbury; c/o Godden Holme & Co, 5 Upper Belgrave st, SW1

SOUTER, Hon Amanda Elizabeth; da and coheiress presumptive of 25 Baron Audley; *b* 5 May 1958; *Style* - The Hon Amanda Souter

SOUTER, Hon Jennifer Michelle; da and coheiress presumptive of 25 Baron Audley; *b* 23 May 1948; *Style* - The Hon Jennifer Souter

SOUTHAMPTON, Barony of (GB 1780); *see* FitzRoy, Charles

SOUTHBOROUGH, 3 Baron (UK 1917); Francis John Hopwood; s of 1 Baron Southborough, GCB, GCMG, GCVO, KCSI, PC (d 1947) by his 2 w, Florence, da of Lt-Gen Samuel Black, CSI, CIE; suc half-bro, 2 Baron 1960; *b* 7 March 1897; *Educ* Westminster, Ch Ch Oxford; *m* 1918, Audrey Evelyn Dorothy, da of late Edgar George Money; 1 s, 1 da; *Heir* s, Hon (Francis) Michael Hopwood; *Career* Sub-Lt RNVR WW I; md Shell Transport & Trading Co Ltd 1951-70 (dir 1946-51) and of Shell Petroleum Co Ltd and Petroleum NV 1946-57 (dir 1957-70), former dir Canadian Eagle Oil Co, Cdr of Order of Orange-Nassau, kt 1953; *Recreations* reading, furniture, architecture; *Clubs* Brooks's; *Style* - The Rt Hon The Lord Southborough; Flat 3, 33 Chesham pla, SW1 (☎ 01 235 8732)

SOUTHBY, Lady Anne (Adeline); *née* Hope; da of 2 Marquess of Linlithgow, KG, KT, GCSI, GCIE, OBE, TD (d 1952); *b* 1914; *m* 1939, Lt-Cdr Patrick Henry James Southby, RN, s of Cdr Sir Archibald Richard James Southby, 1 Bt, RN (d 1969); 1 s, 1 da; *Style* - Lady Anne Southby; Los Castanos, 48 Casasola, Guadalmina, San Pedro de Alcantara, Malaga, Spain

SOUTHBY, John Richard Bilbe; s (by 2 m) and h of Sir (Archibald) Richard Southby, 2 Bt; *b* 2 April 1948; *Educ* Peterhouse Rhodesia, Loughborough U (BSc); *m* 1971, Victoria, da of John Wilfred Sturrock, of Tettenhall, Wolverhampton; 1 s, 1 da; *Style* - John Southby Esq; 49 Brookfield av, Loughborough, Leics

SOUTHBY, Sir (Archibald) Richard Charles; 2 Bt (UK 1937) of Burford, Co Oxford, OBE (Mil 1945); s of Cdr Sir Archibald Richard James Southby, 1 Bt, RN (d 1969); *b* 18 June 1910; *Educ* Eton, Magdalen Oxford; *m* 1, 1935 (m dis 1947), Joan Alice, da of Reginald Balston; m 2, 1947 (m dis 1964), Olive, da of late Sir Thomas Bilbe-Robinson, GBE, KCMG, and formerly w of Gen Sir (James Newton) Rodney Moore, GCVO, KCB, CBE, DSO; 1 s; m 2, 1964, Hon Ethel Peggy (d 1978), da of 1 Baron Cunliffe and widow of Brig Bernard Lorenzo de Robeck, MC, RA; *Heir* s, John Southby; *Career* Lt-Col (ret) Rifle Bde, has American Medal of Freedom; *Style* - Sir Richard Southby, Bt, OBE; 9 Gleneagles rd, Hurlingham, Johannesburg, Transvaal, 2196, South Africa

SOUTHESK, 11 Earl of (S 1633); Sir Charles Alexander Carnegie; 8 Bt (NS 1663), KCVO (1926), DL (Angus); also Lord Carnegie (S 1616), Baron Balinhard (UK 1869); s of 10 Earl (d 1941, whose f, the 9 Earl, was a poet, antiquary and author of *Herminius*, described as a romance) and Ethel, da of Sir Alexander

Bannerman, 9 Bt; *b* 23 Sept 1893; *Educ* Eton; *m* 1, 1923, HH Princess Alexandra Victoria Georgina Bertha Maud (d 1945), yr da of HRH the late Princess Royal and the 1 Duke of Fife; 1 s; m 2, 1952, Evelyn Julia, da of Lt-Col Arthur Peere Williams-Freeman, DSO, OBE, & widow of Maj Ion Campbell, Duke of Cornwall's LI (gs of Sir Edward Campbell, 2 Bt, of the UK cr of 1815); *Heir* s, Duke of Fife, *qv*; *Career* Maj Scots Gds, ret; *Style* - The Rt Hon The Earl of Southesk KCVO DL; Kinnaird Castle, Brechin, Angus (☎ Bridge of Dun 209)

SOUTHGATE, Ven John Eliot; s of Reginald Henry Southgate; *b* 2 Sept 1926; *Educ* City of Norwich, Durham U; *m* 1958, Patricia Mary, nee Plumb; 2 s, 1 da; *Career* ordained 1955 (Leicester), Vicar of Plumstead (Southwark) 1962, Rector of Charlton (Southwark) 1966, Dean of Geenwich 1968, Archdeacon of Cleveland (York) 1974; *Recreations* music, motorcycling; *Style* - The Ven The Archdeacon of Cleveland; 79 Middleton rd, Pickering, N Yorks (☎ 0751 73605); 4 Minster Yard, York (☎ 0904 23482)

SOUTHWARK, 7 Bishop of (cr 1905) 1980-; Rt Rev Ronald Oliver Bowlby; s of Oliver Bowlby; *b* 16 Aug 1926; *Educ* Eton, Trinity Oxford, Westcott House Cambridge; *m* 1956, Elizabeth Trevelyan Monro; 3 s, 2 da; *Career* curate 1952, Vicar of Croydon 1966-72, Bishop of Newcastle 1973-80; patron of 123 livings, of the Archdeaconries of Southwark, Kingston, Lewisham, and Wandsworth, and of Provostship and 6 Residentiary Canonries in Southwark Cathedral; *Style* - The Rt Rev The Lord Bishop of Southwark; Bishop's House, 38 Tooting Bec gdns, SW16

SOUTHWELL, 7 Viscount (I 1776); Sir Pyers Anthony Joseph Southwell; 10 Bt (I 1662); also Baron Southwell (I 1717); s of late Hon Francis Joseph Southwell, 2 s of 5 Viscount; suc unc 1960; *b* 14 Sept 1930; *Educ* Beaumont Coll, RMA Sandhurst; *m* 1955, Barbara Jacqueline, da of A Raynes; 2 s; *Heir* s, Hon Richard Southwell; *Career* Capt (ret) 8 Hussars, company dir; *Clubs* MCC, Woburn Golf and Country, Diners; *Style* - The Rt Hon The Viscount Southwell; 4 Rosebery av, Harpenden, Herts (☎ 05827 5831)

SOUTHWELL, Hon Charles Anthony John; s of 7 Viscount Southwell; *b* 1962; *Style* - The Hon Charles Southwell

SOUTHWELL, Hon Mrs John - Daphne Lewin; da of Sir Geoffrey Lewin Watson, 3 & last Bt (cr 1918, extinct 1959); *m* 1932, Lt-Cdr the Hon John Michael Southwell, RN (killed on active serv 1944, 3 s of 5 Viscount Southwell); *Style* - The Hon Mrs John Southwell; Buckclose, Longparish, Andover, Hants

SOUTHWELL, 7 Bishop of (cr 1884) 1970-; Rt Rev John Denis Wakeling; MC (1945); s of Rev John Lucas Wakeling; *b* 12 Dec 1918; *Educ* Dean Close Sch Cheltenham, St Cat's Cambridge; *m* 1941, Josephine Margaret, da of Dr Benjamin Broomhall; 2 s; *Career* deacon 1947, priest 1948, former Chaplain of Clare Coll Cambridge, Archdeacon of W Ham 1965-70; patron of 97 livings, and of 5 alternately with the Crown, and the Archdeaconries of Newark and Nottingham; *Style* - The Rt Rev The Lord Bishop of Southwell, MC; Bishop's Manor, Southwell, Notts

SOUTHWELL, Hon Joan Evelyn Mary; da of late 5 Viscount Southwell and Hon Dorothy, nee Walrond, da of 1 Baron Waleran; *b* 24 Sept 1909; *Style* - The Hon Joan Southwell; Orchard Way, Pitminster, Taunton, Somerset (☎ Blagdon Hill 371)

SOUTHWELL, Hon Richard Andrew Pyers; s and h of 7 Viscount Southwell; *b* 15 June 1956; *Style* - The Hon Richard Southwell

SOWDEN, John Percival; s of Percival Sowden (d 1956); *b* 6 Jan 1917; *Educ* Silcoates Sch Wakefield, The Grammar Sch Yorks, Imperial Coll London U; *m* 1969, Joyce Diana Mary, da of Charalambos Hji-Ioannou of Nicosia Cyprus; 1 s; *Career* joined Richard Costain 1948, site manager construction projects including Festival of Britain, Apapa Wharf, Nigeria and Bridgetown Harbour Barbados 1948-60; joint md Richard Costain (Associates) Ltd 1961-62, Costain-

Blankevoort International Dredging Co Ltd 1963-65, man Civil Engrg Division 1965-69, Board memb 1967, ch exec International Area 1969-70, chm & gp executive 1973-75, chm 1975-; *Recreations* reading, joinery; *Clubs* RAC; *Style* - John Sowden Esq; 22 Wildcroft Manor, Putney Heath, SW15 (☎ 01 788 5336)

SPALDING, William Liddell; s of William Liddell Spalding, of Balconnel, Brechin, Angus, Scotland (d 1953); *b* 20 Dec 1911; *Educ* Brechin H S; *m* 1946, Margaret Laing; 2 da; *Career* chartered accountant; Fellow of Institute of Cost and Management Accountants (Pres of Institute of Cost and Management Accountants 1966-67), Fellow of Chartered Institute of Secretaries; secretary & chief accountant Richards Ltd, Aberdeen, 1935-48; secretary and chief accountant Aquascutum & Assocs Ltd 1949-54; an executive of Decca Ltd since 1954, Secretary & Group Comptroller 1967-81, dir since 1976 to date; *Recreations* reading and walking; *Style* - William Spalding Esq; Bankside, 71 Frognal, Hampstead, London NW3 (☎ 01 435 1688)

SPARKES, Kenneth Henry Norman; s of Henry Arthur Sparkes, of Ilford (d 1963); *b* 27 Nov 1932; *Educ* Bancroft's School, Essex; *m* 1959, Pamela Jean, da of William Woods; 2 s, 1 da; *Career* slr; sr ptnr Constant & Constant; farmer; *Recreations* sailing, gardening, farming & forestry; *Club* RAC; yachts: 'Ocean Keveral' (Ocean 80) and 'Solent Keveral' (Moody 40); *Style* - Kenneth Sparkes Esq; 21 Alleyn Park, SE21 (☎ 01 670 3922); Broadleaze Farm, Shrivenham, Oxon (☎ 0793 782868)

SPARKS, Hon Mrs (Juliet Jane Margaretta); *née* Moynihan; da of 2 Baron Moynihan, OBE, TD (d 1965); *b* 1934; *m* 1, 1958, Thomas Edwin Bidwell Abraham (d 1976); 2 s; m 2, 1978, Harry Hougham Sparks; *Style* - The Hon Mrs Sparks; Uplands, Bonnington, W Ashford, Kent

SPARROW, Bryan; *b* 8 June 1933; *Educ* Hemel Hempstead G S, Pembroke Oxford; *m* 1958, Fiona Mylechreest; 1 s, 1 da; *Career* For Serv, Ambass Cameroon 1981-; *Style* - Bryan Sparrow Esq; 35 Linton st, N1; c/o FCO, SW1

SPARROW, Basil Henry George; MC (1944); s of Guy Sparrow, of Ball Copse Hall, Brent Knoll, Somerset (d 1955); *b* 16 April 1921; *Educ* Stowe, Ch Ch Oxford; *m* 1945, Patricia Ina; 1 s; *Career* Capt Coldstream Gds Northern Europe; dir Wavin Overseas Ltd, Wavin Overseas BU (Netherlands), Wavin Plastics; *Recreations* gardening, shooting; *Clubs* Buck's; *Style* - Basil Sparrow Esq MC; Bottle Lane Cottage, Shottesbrooke, Maidenhead, Berks (☎ 062 882 2827)

SPARROW, John; s of Richard Albert Sparrow; *b* 4 June 1933; *Educ* Stationers' Company's Sch, LSE; *m* 1967, Cynthia Naomi, da of John Burnham; *Career* FCA 1957; dir: Morgan Grenfell Hldgs 1971-, Morgan Grenfell & Co 1970-, Coalite Gp 1974-, United Gas Industries 1974-; chm Wormald Int Hldgs (UK) 1979-; *Recreations* reading, walking, looking after horses, crosswords; *Clubs* MCC, City of London; *Style* - John Sparrow Esq; Rushmere House, Leighton Buzzard, Beds (☎ 052 523 201)

SPEAR, Rev Arthur Douglas; CBE (1964, OBE 1952); s of Rev Edwin Arthur Spear (d 1948); *b* 2 July 1907; *Educ* Kingswood Sch Bath, Cambridge U; *m* 1936, Mary Hilary, nee Mitchell; 1 s, 1 da; *Career* Methodist Minister, Chaplain RN 1938-64, Principal Chaplain Church of Scotland & Free Churches 1962-64, apptd Hon Chaplain to HM the Queen 1962, Minister in Aberdeen 1964-70, Sec of RN, Army & RAF Bd of Methodist Church 1970-75; *Recreations* sailing, walking; *Clubs* Army & Navy, Roy Ocean Racing; *Style* - The Rev Arthur Spear CBE; 17 Wadhurst Close,, St Leonards-on-Sea, E Sussex (☎ Hastings 752504)

SPEARMAN, Sir Alexander Young Richard Mainwaring; 5 Bt (UK 1840), of Hanwell, Middlesex; s of Sir Alexander Bowyer Spearman, 4 Bt (d 1977); *b* 3 Feb 1969; *Heir* uncle, Dr Richard Spearman; *Style* - Sir Alexander Spearman, Bt; Windwards, Klein Constantia rd, Constantia, Cape Town, 7800, South Africa

SPEARMAN, Dr Richard Ian Campbell; s of late Sir Alexander Young

Spearman, 3 Bt; hp of nephew, Sir Alexander Spearman, 5 Bt; *b* 14 Aug 1926; *Educ* Clayesmore Sch, Birkbeck Coll London (BSc, PhD); *Career* FLS, FZS, Fell of Inst of Biology, memb Genetical Soc, Anatomical Soc, Soc of Experimental Biology, Fell of Roy Soc of Medicine; *Style* - Dr Richard Spearman; Oaks Bungalow, Oaks av, SE19

SPEED, Sir Robert (William Arney); CB (1946), QC (1963); s of Sir Edwin Arney Speed (d 1941); *b* 18 July 1905; *Educ* Rugby, Trin Cambridge; *m* 1924, Phyllis, nee Armitage; 1 s, (1 da decd); *Career* kt 1954, barr 1928, bencher 1961, principal assist slr HM Procurator Gen & Treasury Slr 1945-48, slr Bd of Trade 1948-60, Consul to the Speaker 1960-80; *Recreations* golf; *Clubs* United Oxford and Cambridge, Hon Company of Edinburgh Golfers, Huntercombe GC; *Style* - Sir Robert Speed, CB, QC; Upper Culham, Wargrave, Reading, Berks (☎ Henley-on-Thames 4271)

SPEELMAN, Jonkheer Sir Cornelius Jacob; 8 Bt (E 1686); s of Jonkheer Sir Cornelius Speelman, 7 Bt (d 1949); *b* 17 March 1917; *Educ* Perth U Western Australia; *m* 1972, Julia Mona Le Besque (d 1978); *Heir* none; *Career* formerly in Education Dept Roy Dutch Army, former master of Geelong G S and Clifton Coll, tutor Exeter Tutorial Coll; British subject; *Style* - Jonkheer Sir Cornelius Speelman, Bt; 29 Blackall rd, Exeter, Devon

SPEIGHT, Stanley Lester; OBE (1976); s of Clifford Speight (d 1945); *b* 20 Dec 1920; *Educ* Firth Park G S; *m* 1947, Barbara Joan, da of John Robert Alborough; 2 children; *Career* chm and md Neepsend Ltd 1972-, dep chm Raine Engineering Industries Ltd, dir Sheffield Refreshment Houses Ltd; *Recreations* golf, football; *Clubs* Army and Navy, Sickleholms G C; *Style* - Stanley Speight Esq, OBE; The Limes, Froggatt Lane, Froggatt, Derbyshire (☎ 0433 31023)

SPENCER, 8 Earl (GB 1765); Edward John Spencer; MVO (4 Class 1954), JP (Norfolk 1970), DL (Northants 1961); also Viscount Spencer, Baron Spencer (both GB 1761), and Viscount Althrop (GB 1765 & UK 1905); s of 7 Earl Spencer, TD (d 1975, seventh in descent from the Great Duke of Marlborough; the f of the 1 Earl d young (even by eighteenth century standards) *aet* 38 "because", said Horace Walpole "he would not be abridged of those invaluable blessings of an English subject, brandy, small-beer, and tobacco"; the 1 Earl, in contrast to his gggggda, got married in complete privacy despite the presence of 500 people in the house; the 2 Earl, said to possess the finest library in Europe, suppressed the mutinies at Spithead and The Nore while First Lord of the Admiralty, helped put the Navy on a war footing in readiness to fight such battles as St Vincent and Camperdown, and pushed Nelson's career; the 5 Earl is said to have precipitated Gladstone's resignation in 1894 by insisting on greater spending on the Navy) and Lady Cynthia Hamilton, DCVO, OBE (da of 3 Duke of Abercorn); *b* 24 Jan 1924; *Educ* Eton; *m* 1, 1954 (m dis 1969), Hon Frances Ruth Roche, da of 4 Baron Fermoy (now Hon Mrs Shand Kydd); 1 s (and 1 s decd), 3 da (Lady Sarah McCorquodale, Lady Jane Fellowes, HRH The Princess of Wales); m 2, 1976, Raine, da of Alexander McCorquodale by his 1 wife Barbara Cartland, *qv*, and half sister of Ian McCorquodale and former w of 9 Earl of Dartmouth; *Heir* s, Viscount Althorp; *Career* late Capt Roy Scots Greys, CCllr Northants (High Sheriff 1959); patron of 12 livings; temp Equerry to HM George VI 1950-52 and to HM 1952-54; ADC to Govr S Australia 1947-50; Dep Hon Col Roy Anglian Regt (TA) 1972-; chm Nene Fndn; memb UK Council European Architectural Heritage Year 1975; *Clubs* Turf, Brooks's, MCC, Roy Overseas League; *Style* - The Rt Hon Earl Spencer MVO JP DL; Althorp, Northampton (☎ E Haddon 200)

SPENCER, Cyril; s of the late Isaac Spencer; *b* 31 Aug 1924; *Educ* Christ Coll Finchley, Univ of London; *m* 1971, Wendy Lois; 3 children, 3 step children; *Career* Evans Outsizes Ltd: md 1956, chm 1969, group md and chief exec 1976, group chm 1980-; chm Burton Gp to Aug 1981 (*see* Halpern, Ralph); *Recreations* tennis, swimming, golf; *Clubs* Marks, Burke's, RAC; *Style* - Cyril Spencer Esq; Eliot

House, The Bishop's Avenue, N2 (☎ 01 455 5186)

SPENCER, Gp Capt Desmond Gerard Heath; CBE (1965, MBE); s of late Arthur Spencer; *b* 18 March 1912; *Educ* Harrow; *m* 1939, Ellen Catherine, da of Maj Capel Adye (d 1940); 1 s, 1 da; *Career* 2 Lt Duke of Cornwall's Light Infantry 1932-33, RAF 1933, NW Frontier 1935-39, Gp Capt (Ops) Air HQ Eastern Mediterranean 1942-44, Sr Air Staff Officer Air HQ Levant Jerusalem 1945, served in Cyprus 1954-56 (ret 1967); *Recreations* cruising; *Clubs* Army & Navy, R Fowey Yacht; *Style* - Gp Capt Desmond Spencer CBE; c/o Gp Capt Chichester, Hayne Manor, Lewdown, Okehampton, Devon (☎ Lewdown 216)

SPENCER, Hon George Charles; s of late 6 Earl Spencer, KG, GCVO, PC and Hon Margaret, nee Baring, da of 1 Baron Revelstoke; *b* 1903; *Educ* RNCs Osborne and Dartmouth; *m* 1, 1931 (m dis 1962), Barbara C, da of Benjamin Blumenthal, of Paris; 1 s, 1 da; m 2, 1966, Mrs Sheila Stuart-French (d 1968); *Career* Capt RA (TA) WW II; *Clubs* Travellers'; *Style* - The Hon George Spencer; 2 Parliament sq, Castletown, IOM

SPENCER, Countess; Raine; da of Alexander McCorquodale (1 cous of 1 Baron McCorquodale of Newton, PC) by his 1 w Barbara Cartland, *qv*; *b* 9 Sept 1929; *m* 1, 1948 (m dis 1976), as his 1 w, 9 Earl of Dartmouth; 3 s (Viscount Lewisham, Hon Rupert & Henry Legge), 1 da (Lady Charlotte Legge); m 2, 1976, as his 2 w, 8 Earl Spencer; *Career* memb GLC (Richmond) 1967-73 (Lewisham W former LCC 1958-1965), GLC Gen Purposes Ctee 1971-73, chm GLC Historic Bldgs 1968-71; chm Covent Gdn Devpt Ctee 1971-75; memb Eng Tourist Bd 1971-75, Advsy Council V&A 1980-, BTA Infrastructure Ctee 1972-; *Style* - The Rt Hon The Countess Spencer; Althorp, Northampton (☎ E Haddon 200)

SPENCER, Richard Harry Ramsay; s of late Col Richard Augustus Spencer, DSO, OBE, and hp (to Barony only), of 3 Viscount Churchill; *b* 11 Oct 1926; *m* 1958, Antoinette Rose-Marie, da of Godefroy de Charrière, of Prévérenges, Lausanne, Switzerland; 2 s; *Career* late Lt Coldstream Gds; ARIBA; *Style* - Richard Spencer Esq; The Old Vicarage, Vernham Dean, Hants

SPENCER, Ritchie Lloyd; s of Capt P Lloyd Spencer; *b* 27 Sept 1942; *Educ* St Bees Sch, Manchester U, LSE; *m* 1965, Catherine Dilys, da of Dr John Naish MD; 3 s (Hal b 1968, Patrick b 1969, James b 1972); *Career* MIPM, md Reliant Motor Co Tamworth Staffs 1977-, dir J F Nash Securities Kettering 1980-, dir Sunderland Shipbuilders Ltd 1972-76; cncl memb: Soc Motor Manufacturers & Traders 1978-, Motor Industry Research Assoc 1979-; *Recreations* theatre, gardening, squash, tennis; *Style* - Ritchie Spencer Esq; 16 London Road, Lichfield, Staffs (☎ Lichfield (05432) 22507); Argyll Terrace, Tobermory, Isle of Mull

SPENCER, Richard Peter Michael; s of Richard Percy Spencer (d 1960); *b* 23 Sept 1920; *Educ* Sedbergh; *m* 1951, Bettyne Ione, da of late Sir Lindsay Everard; 1 s, 1 da; *Career* Maj 1 King's Dragoon Gds, Italy, Greece, Palestine, Middle East; farmer, High Sheriff Leics 1968-69; *Recreations* fishing, shooting; *Clubs* Lansdowne; *Style* - Richard Spencer Esq; 7 Adrian Mews, Ifield rd, SW10 (☎ 01 373 9454); Rotherby Grange, Melton Mowbray, Leics (☎ Rotherby 206)

SPENCER, Thomas Newnham Bayley; MEP (C) Derbyshire 1979-; s of Thomas Newnham Spencer (d 1979); *b* 10 April 1948; *Educ* Nautical Coll Pangbourne, Southampton U; *m* 1979, Elizabeth Nan, nee Bath; 1 step da; *Recreations* fencing, opera; *Clubs* Carlton; *Style* - Thomas Spencer Esq, MEP; 13 Goulton rd, E5 (☎ 01 985 5839); 1 Sant Lane, Doveridge, Derbys

SPENCER-CHURCHILL, Lady Alexandra Elizabeth Mary; da of 11 Duke of Marlborough; *b* 1977

SPENCER-CHURCHILL, Lord Charles George William Colin; s of 10 Duke of Marlborough (d 1972); *b* 1940; *Educ* Eton; *m* 1, 1965 (m dis 1968),

Gillian, da of Andrew Fuller; m 2, 1970, Elizabeth Jane, da of Capt the Hon Mark Hugh Wyndham, MC; 2 s; *Style* - Lord Charles Spencer-Churchill; 8 Bloomfield Terrace, SW1

SPENCER-CHURCHILL, Lord Edward Albert Charles; s of 11 Duke of Marlborough; *b* 1974

SPENCER-NAIRN, James Robert; s and h of Sir Robert Arnold Spencer-Nairn, 3 Bt; *b* 7 Dec 1966; *Style* - James Spencer-Nairn Esq

SPENCER-NAIRN, Sir Robert Arnold; 3 Bt (UK 1933), of Monimail, Co Fife; s of Lt-Col Sir Douglas Leslie Spencer Spencer-Nairn, 2 Bt, TD (d 1970); *b* 11 Oct 1933; *Educ* Eton, Trinity Hall Cambridge; *m* 1963, Joanna Elizabeth, da of late Lt-Cdr George Stevenson Salt, RN, s of 2 Bt (cr 1899); 2 s, 1 da; *Heir* s, James Spencer-Nairn; *Career* late Lt Scots Gds; *Style* - Sir Robert Spencer-Nairn, Bt; Barham, Cupar, Fife

SPENCER-SMITH, Sir John Hamilton; 7 Bt (UK 1804) of Tring Park, Hertfordshire; s of Captain Sir Thomas Cospatric Spencer-Smith, 6 Bt (d 1959); *b* 18 March 1947; *Educ* Milton Abbey, Lackham Coll of Agriculture; *m* 1980, Christine Sandra, da of late John Osborne; *Heir* kinsman, Peter Spencer-Smith; *Career* landscape gardener; agricultural projects management; *Recreations* watching polo; *Clubs* Cowdray Park Polo; *Style* - Sir John Spencer-Smith, Bt; Iping Mill, near Midhurst, W Sussex

SPENCER-SMITH, Peter Compton; s of late Lt-Col Michael Seymour (Hamilton-) Spencer-Smith, DSO, MC (gs of bro of 2 Bt), who did not use surname Hamilton; hp of kinsman, Sir John Spencer-Smith, 7 Bt; *b* 12 Nov 1912; *Educ* Eton, New Coll Oxford; *m* 1950, Philippa Mary, da of late Capt Richard Ford, Rifle Bde; 2 s; *Career* formerly Maj 79 Herts Yeo (Heavy Anti-Aircraft Regt), RA (TA); *Style* - Peter Spencer-Smith Esq; High Down House, Hitchin, Herts

SPENS, 2 Baron (UK 1959); William George Michael Spens; s of 1 Baron Spens, KBE, PC (d 1973), by his 1 w, Hilda, da of Lt-Col Wentworth Bowyer, JP, DL (f of 1 Baron Denham, MC, DL, and ggggs of Sir William Bowyer, 3 Bt); *b* 18 Sept 1914; *Educ* Rugby, New Coll Oxford; *m* 1941, Joan, da of Reginald Goodall; 2 s, 1 da; *Heir* s, Hon Patrick Spens; *Career* barr 1945; late Maj RA; *Style* - The Rt Hon The Lord Spens; Lambden, Pluckley, Ashford, Kent (☎ Pluckley 373

SPENS, Hon Emily Susan; MBE (1970); da of 1 Baron Spens, KBE, PC, by his 1 w; *b* 25 April 1924; *Educ* Heathfield; *Career* WRNS WW II 1941-46; *Style* - The Hon Emily Spens, MBE

SPENS, Dowager Baroness; Kathleen Annie Fedden; da of Roger Dodds, of Bath and Northumberland; *m* 1963, as his 2 w, 1 Baron Spens, KBE, PC (d 1973); *Style* - The Rt Hon Dowager Lady Spens; Gould, Frittenden, Kent

SPENS, Hon Mallowry Ann; da of 2 Baron Spens; *b* 30 Sept 1949; *Style* - The Hon Mallowry Spens; Lambden, Pluckley, Ashford, Kent (☎ Pluckley 373)

SPENS, Hon Patrick Michael Rex; s and h of 2 Baron Spens; *b* 22 July 1942; *Educ* Rugby, CCC Cambridge; *m* 1966, Barbara, da of Rear-Adm Ralph Fisher, CB, DSO, OBE, DSC; 1 s, 1 da; *Career* ACA; dir Morgan Grenfell; *Style* - The Hon Patrick Spens; Gould, Frittenden, Kent

SPENS, Hon William David Ralph; s of 2 Baron Spens; *b* 23 Nov 1943; *Educ* Rugby, CCC Cambridge; *m* 1967, Gillian, da of Albert Jowett, OBE, MD, FRCS; 1 s, 1 da; *Career* barr 1972; *Style* - The Hon William Spens; Marsh Mills Cottage, Over Stowey, Somerset

SPENSER-WILKINSON, Sir Thomas Crowe; s of Prof Henry Spenser-Wilkinson (d 1937); *b* 28 Sept 1899; *Educ* RN Colls Osbourne and Dartmouth, Balliol Coll Oxford; *m* 1930, Betty Margaret, nee Horner (d 1980); 1 s, 1 da; *Career* kt 1959; RN 1915-19; barr 1925, advocate and slr 1927-38, pres District Court Cyprus 1938-41, Ch Legal Advr to Civil Affairs Br Mil

Admin Malaya and Singapore, Supreme Court Judge Malaya 1946-56, Ch Justice Nyasaland 1956-62, chm Medical Appeals Tribunal 1962-72; *Recreations* gardening; *Clubs* Roy C'wlth Soc; *Style* - Sir Thomas Spenser-Wilkinson; Whitecroft, 6 Pentre Close, Ashton, Chester (☎ Kelsall 51531)

SPEYER, Hon Mrs (Beatrice Sophie); *née* Liddell; da of 6 Baron Ravensworth, JP, DL; *b* 23 Sept 1906; *m* 1931, Edward Speyer; 2 da; *Style* - The Hon Mrs Speyer; 39 Rivermead Court, Ranelagh gdns, SW6 (☎ 01 736 1354)

SPICER, Dr Nicholas Adrian Albert; s and h of (Sir) Peter Spicer, 4 Bt, *qv*; *b* 28 Oct 1953; *Style* - Dr Nicholas Spicer

SPICER, (Sir) Peter James; 4 Bt (UK 1906) of Lancaster Gate, Borough of Paddington, but does not use title; s of Sir Stewart Dykes Spicer, 3 Bt (d 1968); *b* 20 May 1921; *Educ* Winchester, Trinity Cambridge, Ch Ch Oxford; *m* 1949, Margaret, da of late Sir (James) Steuart Wilson; 1 s, 3 da (and 1 decd); *Heir* s, Dr Nicholas Spicer; *Career* Lt RNVR (despatches) WW II; on publishing staff Oxford University Press 1947-81, chm Educational Publishers Cncl 1974-76; *Recreations* sailing, walking, gardening, reading, music; *Clubs* United Oxford & Cambridge; *Style* - Peter Spicer Esq; Salt Mill House, Fishbourne, Chichester, W Sussex (☎ 0243 782825)

SPICER, Hon Mrs (Sarah Margaret); *née* Watkinson; da of 1 Viscount Watkinson, CH, PC; *b* 17 April 1944; *m* 1965, David Spicer; 3 da; *Style* - The Hon Mrs Spicer; Shortacre, Park Road, Winchester, Hants

SPICKA, Hon Mrs (Victoria Wentworth); *née* Reilly; da of Baron Reilly; *b* 1941; *m* 1973, Daniel Spicka, of Prague; *Style* - The Hon Mrs Spicka; Ul Mrazovsky 7, Prague 5, Czechoslovakia

SPINKS, Alfred; CBE (1977); s of Alfred Robert Spinks; *b* 25 Feb 1917; *Educ* Soham G S Cambridgeshire, Nottingham U, Imperial Coll London, Worcester Coll Oxford; *m* 1946, Patricia, nee Kilner; 2 da; *Career* scientist/industrialist; ICI Main Board director 1970-79, dep chm AECI Ltd S Africa 1975-79, dir Dunlop Hldgs 1979-, Johnson Matthey 1980-, chm Charter Consolidated 1980-, chm Advsy Cncl for Applied Research and Dvpt 1980; *Recreations* photography, theatre, travel; *Clubs* Athenaeum; *Style* - Alfred Spinks Esq, CBE; Woodcote, Torkington rd, Wilmslow, Cheshire (☎ 0625 522316); 9 Arncliffe, 22 Greville Place, NW6 (☎ 624 5331)

SPIRA, Peter John Ralph; s of Dr Jean-Jacques Spira (d 1970); *b* 2 March 1930; *Educ* Eton, King's Coll Cambridge; *m* 1, 1957, Meriel, nee Gold; m 2, 1969, Anne Marie Marguerite Renée, nee Landon; 6 c; *Career* chartered accountant 1956, fin dir Sotheby Parke Bernet Gp Ltd 1974-, v-chm Sotheby's London 1974-, S G Warburg & Co Ltd 1964-, dir S G Warburg & Co 1974-, dir Mercury Securities Ltd 1970-74; *Recreations* music,reading, photography, tennis; *Clubs* Arts;*Style* - Peter Spira Esq; 63 Bedford Gardens, W8 (☎ 727 5295)

SPITTLE, (Anthony) Trevor; s of Stanley Spittle (d 1958); *b* 25 Dec 1929; *Educ* Lindisfarne Coll, Southampton U; *m* 1955, Jennifer Mae, nee Emery; 2 s (Graham Neville, Robert William b 1962), 2 da (Frances Emma m 1980, Laura Mary b 1964); *Career* CA, ptnr Deloitte Haskins & Sells 1963-1976, fin dir Great Universal Stores Ltd 1976-; *Recreations* gardening, sport as a spectator, particularly Rugby Union; *Clubs* Institute of Directors, Southern RFC; *Style* - Trevor Spittle Esq; Mill House, Ruckhatch Lane, Rettendon Common, Chelmsford, Essex (☎ 0245 400207)

SPOKES, Ann; (Mrs John Symonds); da of Peter Spencer Spokes MA BSc FSA (d 1976); *b* 10 Nov 1925; *Educ* The Masters School, Dobbs Ferry, New York; St Anne's Coll Oxford; *m* 1980, John Richard Symonds, s of late Sir Charles Symonds; twin step s (Jeremy and Peter); *Career* social services administrator until 1980 and organising sec 1968-80 of Age Concern Oxford; dir ATV Network Ltd 1978-; Lord Mayor of Oxford 1976-77; chm Association of County Cncls Soc Servs Committee;

chm Oxfordshire Co Cncl May 1981; Parly candidate Elections of 1959, 1966 and 1970; *Recreations* photography, travel, lawn tennis, swimming; *Clubs* Royal Overseas League; Roy Commonwealth; YWCA; *Style* - Miss Ann Spokes; 43 Davenant Rd, Oxford, OX2 8BU

SPOONER, James Douglas; s of late Vice-Admiral E J Spooner, DSO; *b* 11 July 1932; *Educ* Eton, Ch Ch Oxford; *m* 1958, Jane Alison, da of Sir Gerald Glover; 2 s, 1 da; *Career* chartered accountant; chm: Navy, Army & Air Force Insts 1973-, Vantona Group 1969-, Bentalls 1978-; dep chm: Hogg Robinson Group 1971-, Nat Mutual Life Assurance Soc 1973-; dir John Swire & Sons 1970-; *Recreations* history, music, tennis, shooting, riding; *Clubs* White's, Beefsteak, City of London; *Style* - James Spooner Esq; 52 Clarendon rd, W11 (☎ 01 727 6756); Paddock Cottage, Pytchley, Northants, (☎ 0536 790327)

SPOTSWOOD, Marshal of the Royal Air Force Sir Denis Frank; GCB (1970), CBE (1946), DSO (1943), DFC (1942); s of late Frank Spotswood; *b* 26 Sept 1916; *m* 1942, Ann, da of late Solomon Child; 1 s; *Career* RAF 1936, Ch of Air Staff 1971-74, Marshal of RAF 1974; v-chm Rolls Royce 1974-80, chairman Smith's Industries Aerospace Cos 1980-, dir Dowty Gp 1980-, gov Roy Star and Garter Home 1975- (chm 1980); *Recreations* golf, bridge; *Clubs* RAF, Roy Aeronautical Soc, Leander; *Style* - Marshal of the Royal Air Force, Sir Denis Spotswood, GCB, CBE, DSO, DFC; c/o Williams & Glyn's, Kirkland House, Whitehall, SW1

SPRAGGS, Rear-Adm Trevor O K, *Career* Ch of Staff to CIC Naval Home Cmmd Sept 1981-, Rear-Adm 1981, Ch Naval Instructor MOD 1981, former Dir Studies and Dean RNC Greenwich; *Style* - Rear-Adm Trevor Spraggs; c/o MOD, SW1

SPRING, Hon Mrs (Jane Elizabeth); *née* Henniker-Major; da of 8 Baron Henniker, KCMG, CVO, MC; *b* 1954; *m* 1979, Richard John Grenville Spring; *Style* - The Hon Mrs Spring; 124 Cambridge st, SW1V 4QF

SPRING RICE, Hon Charles James; s and h of 6 Baron Monteagle of Brandon; *b* 24 Feb 1953; *Educ* Harrow; *Style* - The Hon Charles Spring Rice

SPRING RICE, Hon Fiona; da of 6 Baron Monteagle of Brandon; *b* 1957; *Style* - The Hon Fiona Spring Rice

SPRING RICE, Hon Michael; s of 5 Baron Monteagle of Brandon (d 1946); *b* 1935; *Educ* Harrow; *m* 1959, Fiona, da of James Edward Kenneth Sprot; 1 s, 1 da; *Career* late Lt Irish Gds; *Clubs* Boodle's and Royal Norfolk and Suffolk Yacht; *Style* - The Hon Michael Spring Rice; Holly Hall, Chelwood Gate, Sussex

SPRINGER, Sir Hugh Worrell; KCMG (1971), CBE (1961); s of Charles Wilkinson Springer (d 1914); *b* 22 June 1913; *Educ* Harrison Coll Barbados, Hertford Coll Oxford; *m* 1942, Dorothy Drinan, nee Gittens; 3 s, 1 da; *Career* barr 1940-47, C'wlth Assist Sec Gen 1966-70, Sec Gen Assoc of C'wlth Us 1970-80, dir University of W Indies Institute of Education 1963-66; *Clubs* Athenaeum, Roy C'wlth Soc; *Style* - Sir Hugh Springer KCMG CB; Barclays International, Oceanic House, 1 Cockspur st, SW1

SPROT, Lt-Col Aidan Mark; MC (1944), JP (Peeblesshire 1966), DL (1966); s of Maj Mark Sprot JP, DL (d 1946); *b* 17 June 1919; *Educ* Stowe; *Career* Ld Lt of Peeblesshire 1980, Lt-Col served Royal Scots Greys 1940-62, memb Roy Co Archers Queen's Bodyguard for Scotland, landowner, farmer, CC Peeblesshire 1963-75; *Clubs* New (Edinburgh), Cavalry; *Style* - Lt-Col Aidan Sprot, MC, JP, HM Lord-Lieut for Peeblesshire; Crookston, by Peebles (☎ Kirkton Manor 209)

SPYER, David Oswald; s of Samuel Michael Spyer (d 1969); *b* 1 Aug 1927; *Educ* West Ham Secondary; *m* 1957, Janice Ruth, nee Solity; 1 s, 1 da; *Career* Corporal RAF 1945-48, dir Hill Samuel Securities Ltd 1972-80, dir Lynn Regis Finance Ltd 1973-80, dir PHH Leasing Ltd 1975-79, chm PHH Leasing Ltd 1977-79, md C E Coates & Co Ltd 1980-; *Recreations* dramatics, philately, rugby football, cricket, squash, table tennis; *Clubs* MCC, Lensbury; *Style* - David Spyer Esq; 36 The Avenue, Hatch End, Middx HA5 4EY

SQUIBB, George Drewry; QC (1956); s of Reginald Augustus Hodder Squibb (d 1946); *b* 1 Dec 1906; *Educ* King's Sch Chester, Queen's Coll Oxford; *m* 1, 1936, Bessie, nee Whittaker (d 1954); 1 da; m 2, 1955, Evelyn May, nee Higgins; *Career* barr (Inner Temple) 1930, bencher 1951, treasurer 1976, president Transport Tribunal 1962-, Chief Commons Commissioner 1971-; Norfolk Herald Extraordinary 1959-; chm Dorset QS 1953-71; *Recreations* heraldic and genealogical research; *Clubs* Athenaeum, United Oxford and Cambridge; *Style* - George Squibb Esq, QC; The Old House, Cerne Abbas, Dorset (☎ 272); 5 Paper Buildings, Temple, EC4 (☎ 353 3436)

SQUIRRELL, John Gordon; s of Percy Lee Squirrell (d 1968); *b* 30 April 1925; *Educ* Woodbridge Sch, St Edmund Hall Oxford; *m* 1948, Sheila Anne, da of George Holliday; 2 da; *Career* served RAF as Fl Lt; dep md Harveys of Bristol 1978 (UK sales & marketing dir 1976-78, UK sales dir 1969-76); dir Grants of St James's Ltd 1978, A Delor & Cie Bordeaux 1977; *Recreations* tennis, squash, music, art; *Clubs* East India Devonshire Sports & Public Schools; *Style* - John Squirrell Esq; Pagans Hill House, Chew Stoke, nr Bristol (☎ Chew Magna 2793)

ST ALBANS, 13 Duke of (E 1684); Charles Frederic Aubrey de Vere Beauclerk; OBE (Mil 1945); also Baron Heddington and Earl of Burford (E 1676), and Baron Vere of Hanworth (GB 1750); Hereditary Grand Falconer & Hereditary Registrar of the Court of Chancery; s of Aubrey Beauclerk & ggggs of 1 Duke of St Albans, natural s of Charles II by Eleanor (better known as Nell) Gwynn; the 1 Duke m Lady Diana de Vere, da of 20 & last Earl of Oxford, of whom Macaulay said "He derived his title, through an uninterrupted male descent, from a time when the families of Howard and Seymour were still obscure, when the Nevilles and Percies enjoyed only a provincial celebrity, and when even the great name of Plantagenet had not yet been heard in England"; while Chief Justice Crew, sitting in judgement on the claimants to the Earldom in 1625, observed: "I suppose there is no man...but his affection stands to the continuance of so noble a name...yet there must be an end to all temporal things, and why not of de Vere? For where is Bohun? Where's Mowbray? Where's Mortimer? Nay, which is more...where is Plantagenet?"; Pepys, less romantic, once remarked (after visiting the 20 Earl, who was still in bed, tho' it was past 10 am): "Lord helpe us so rude a dirty family I never saw"); suc 2 cous 1964; *b* 16 Aug 1915; *Educ* Eton, Magdalene Cambridge; *m* 1, 1938 (m dis 1947), Nathalie Chatham, da of Percival Walker, of Rythe Court, Thames Ditton; 1 s; m 2, 1947, Suzanne Marie Adèle, da of Emile Fesq, of Vence, France; 3 s, 1 da; *Heir* s, Earl of Burford; *Career* late Col Intelligence Corps, dir Films Div Central Office of Information to 1964; chm Amalgamated Developers Gp; patron of two livings; *Clubs* Brooks's, St James', Beefsteak; *Style* - His Grace The Duke of St Albans, OBE; 432 Palais de la Scala, Monte Carlo, Monaco

ST ALBANS, Archdeacon of, *see* Farmbrough, Ven David

ST ALBANS, 8 Bishop of (cr 1887) 1980-; Rt Rev Bernard Taylor; s of George Ernest Taylor; *b* 6 May 1929; *Educ* Watford G S, Christ's Cambridge, Jesus Cambridge; *m* 1956, Linda Courtenay Barnes; 1 s, 2 da; *Career* former Examining Chaplain to Bishop of Chelmsford, Archdeacon of W Ham 1975-80; patron of 64 livings, and alternately of 6, the Archdeaconries of St Albans and Bedford, and 24 Honorary Canonries; *Style* - The Rt Rev The Lord Bishop of St Albans; Abbey Gate House, St Albans, Herts

ST ALDWYN, 2 Earl (UK 1915); Sir Michael John Hicks Beach; 10 Bt (E 1619), KBE (1964), TD (1949), PC (1959), JP (Glos 1952),; also Viscount St Aldwyn (UK 1906), Viscount Quenington (UK 1915); s of Visc Quenington (ka 1916, s of 1 Earl); suc gf 1916; *b* 9 Oct 1912; *Educ* Eton, Ch Ch Oxford; *m* 1948, Diana Mary Christian, formerly w of Maj Richard Smyly and da of late Henry Mills (gs of 1 Baron Hillingdon); 3 s; *Heir* s, Viscount Quenington, *qv*; *Career* formerly in Miny of Ag Fish and Food; Oppn Ch Whip House of Lords 1964-70 and 1974-78, Govt Ch Whip 1958-64 and 1970-74; Capt Hon Corps of Gentlemen-at-Arms 1958-64 and

1970-74, Vice-Lord-Lt of Glos 1981-, GStJ (Chancellor 1978-); *Recreations* shooting, fishing; *Clubs* Pratt's, Carlton, Beefsteak, Roy Yacht Squadron; *Style* - The Rt Hon The Earl St Aldwyn KBE TD PC JP, HM Vice-Lord-Lieut for Gloucestershire; Williamstrip Park, Cirencester, Glos (☎ 226); 13 Upper Belgrave st, SW1 (☎ 01 235 8464)

ST ANDREWS, Archbishop of (RC) 1951-; His Eminence Cardinal Gordon Joseph Gray; s of Francis Gray; *b* 10 Aug 1910; *Educ* Holy Cross Acad Edinburgh, St Joseph's Seminary Wonersh, St Andrews U; *Career* Cardinal 1969; *Recreations* joinery, gardening; *Style* - His Eminence The Cardinal Archbishop of St Andrews; St Bennet's, 42 Greenhill gdns, Edinburgh EH10 4BJ (☎ 031 447 3337)

ST AUBYN, Hon Giles Rowan; s of late 3 Baron St Levan and Hon Clementina, nee Nicolson, da of 1 Baron Carnock; *b* 11 March 1925; *Educ* Wellington, Glasgow U, Trinity Coll Oxford; *Career* FRSL, assistant master Eton, author; *Clubs* Brooks's, Beefsteak; *Style* - The Hon Giles St Aubyn; Hartland's Quay, Tangier lane, Eton, Berks (☎ Windsor 65635)

ST AUBYN, Hon Hilaria Lily; da of late 2 Baron St Levan, CB, CVO, and Lady Edith, nee Edgcumbe, da of 4 Earl of Mount Edgcumbe by his 1 w, Lady Katherine, nee Hamilton, da of 1 Duke of Abercorn and Lady Louisa, nee Russell, da of 6 Duke of Bedford; *b* 1894; *Style* - The Hon Hilaria St Aubyn; 11 Lancaster ct, Seymour st, W2

ST AUBYN, Hon (Oliver) Piers; MC (1944); s of late 3 Baron St Levan and Hon Clementina, nee Nicolson, da of 1 Baron Carnock and sis of Harold Nicolson, the writer (*see* Nigel Nicolson); hp of bro, 4 Baron St Levan, DSC; *b* 12 July 1920; *Educ* Wellington and St James's Sch Maryland USA; *m* 1948, Mary Bailey, da of Bailey Southwell, of Olievenhoortpoort S Africa; 2 s (James Piers Southwell St A, b 6 June 1950, m 1981 Mary Caroline Bennett; Nicholas Francis St A, b 19 Nov 1955, m 1980 Jane Mary Brooks), 1 da (Fiona Mary, b 1952); *Career* memb Stock Exchange 1949-, ptnr W Greenwell & Co 1957-78; Capt 60 Rifles and Parachute Regt (despatches, MC) 1939-45; *Recreations* sailing; *Clubs* House of Lords Yacht, Brooks's; *Style* - The Hon Piers St Aubyn, MC; 60 Cottesmore ct, W8; Woodside House, Barcombe, Lewes, Sussex (☎ Barcombe 400257)

ST CLAIR, Hon Annabel Lettice; da of 17 Lord Sinclair, MVO; *b* 1973

ST CLAIR, Hon Laura Anne; da of 17 Lord Sinclair, MVO; *b* 1972

ST CLAIR-ERSKINE, Lady Caroline; da of 6 Earl of Rosslyn and Athenaïs, Countess of Rosslyn, *qv*; *b* 7 June 1956; *Style* - Lady Caroline St Clair-Erskine

ST CLAIR-ERSKINE, Hon David Simon; s of 5 Earl of Rosslyn by his 3 w, Vera, nee Bayley; *b* 18 Nov 1917; *Educ* Ampleforth, Merton Oxford; *m* 1948, Antonia (m dis 1959, she d 1965), da of Adm of the Fleet Sir John Kelly, GCB, GCVO; 1 s; *Career* served WW II Maj; *Style* - The Hon David St Clair-Erskine; St Fridewide's Cottage, Knighton, Swindon; 3 Culford gdns, SW3 (☎ 01 589 7339)

ST CLAIR-FORD, Capt Sir Aubrey; 6 Bt (GB 1793), DSO and Bar (1942), RN; s of late Anson St Clair St Clair-Ford, s of late Capt St Clair St Clair-Ford (s of 2 Bt); suc kinsman, Sir (Francis Charles) Rupert Ford, 5 Bt, 1948; *b* 29 Feb 1904; *Educ* RNCs Osborne and Dartmouth; *m* 1945, Anne, da of Harold Christopherson; 1 s, 1 da; *Heir* s, James St Clair-Ford; *Career* Capt RN (ret), Crete and Mediterranean (despatches twice) 1939-45, Korea (despatches twice, Offr of American Legion of Merit) 1951-52; *Style* - Capt Sir Aubrey St Clair-Ford, Bt, DSO*, RN; Corner House, Sandle Copse, Fordingbridge, Hants

ST CLAIR-FORD, James Anson; s and h of Capt Sir Aubrey St Clair-Ford, 6 Bt, DSO*, RN; *b* 16 March 1952; *Educ* Wellington, Bristol U; *m* 1977, Jennifer Margaret, da of Cdre J Robin Grindle, RN; *Style* - James St Clair-Ford Esq

ST CLAIR-FORD, Maj-Gen Sir Peter; KBE (1961, CBE 1953), CB (1954), DSO (1943) and Bar (1943); s of late Anson St

Clair-Ford and bro of Capt Sir Aubrey St Clair-Ford, 6 Bt, *qv*; *b* 25 Nov 1905; *Educ* Dover Coll, RMC Sandhurst; *Career* King's Own Yorkshire LI 1925, GOC 1 Federated Div Malaya 1954-57, Dep Ch of Staff HQ Allied Land Forces Centl Europe 1958-60, ret; *Style* - Maj-Gen Sir Peter St Clair-Ford, KBE, CB, DSO*; Cotswold Lodge, Littlestone, New Romney, Kent (☎ 2368)

ST CYRES, Viscount; John Stafford Northcote; s and h of 4 Earl of Iddesleigh, *qv*; *b* 15 Feb 1957; *Educ* Downside, RAC Cirencester; *Style* - Viscount St Cyres; Shillands House, Upton Pyne Hill, Exeter, Devon

ST DAVIDS, 2 Viscount (UK 1918); Sir Jestyn Reginald Austen Plantagenet Philipps; 14 Bt (E 1621); Baron Strange de Knokin (E 1299), Baron Hungerford (E 1426), Baron de Moleyns (E 1445); s of 1 Viscount (s of Rev Sir James Philipps, 12 Bt, and Hon Mary, da of Rev the Hon Samuel Best and sis of 5 Baron Wynford) by the 1 Viscount's 2 w, Baroness Strange of Knokin, Hungerford and de Moleyns *suo jure*, da of late Maj the Hon Paulyn Rawdon-Hastings & niece of 11 Earl of Loudoun; suc to Viscountcy 1938, to mother's Baronies 1974; *b* 19 Feb 1917; *Educ* Eton, Trin Cambridge; *m* 1, 1938 (m dis 1954), Doreen Guinness, nee Jowett (d 1956); 1 s, 4 da; m 2, 1954 (m dis 1959), Elisabeth Joyce, nee Woolf; m 3, 1959, Evelyn Marjorie, da of late Dr John Harris, of Bray, Berkshire; *Heir* s, Hon Colwyn Philipps; *Career* Lt RNVR; *Style* - The Rt Hon The Viscount St Davids; 15 St Mark's cres, Regent's Park, NW1 (☎ 01 485 9953)

ST EDMUNDSBURY AND IPSWICH, 7 Bishop of (cr 1914) 1978-; Rt Rev John Waine; s of William Waine; *b* 20 June 1930; *Educ* Prescot G S, Manchester U; *m* 1957, Patricia Zena, da of Bertram Stephenson Haikney; 3 s; *Career* consecrated Bp of Stafford (Suffragan for Diocese of Lichfield) 1975, late Pilot Officer RAF; patron of 61 livings, 3 Archdeaconries, and 24 Honorary Canonries; *Style* - The Rt Rev The Lord Bishop of St Edmundsbury and Ipswich; Bishop's House, 4 Park rd, Ipswich

ST GEORGE, Rev Denis Howard; s of Sir Theophilus St George, 6 Bt, and hp of bro, 7 Bt; *b* 6 Sept 1902; *Career* is in Holy Orders RC Church; *Style* - The Rev Denis St George; Emmanuel Cathedral, Durban, Natal, S Africa

ST GEORGE, Sir Robert Alan; 7 Bt (I 1766), of Athlone, Co Westmeath; s of Sir Theophilus St George, 6 Bt (d 1943); *b* 20 March 1900; *Heir* bro, Rev Denis St George; *Career* 2 Lt RAF; religious missionary brother; *Style* - Sir Robert St George, Bt; St Joseph's Scholasticate, Cedara, Natal, S Africa

ST GERMANS, 9 Earl of (UK 1815); Nicholas Richard Michael Eliot; Baron Eliot (GB 1784); s of 8 Earl, KCVO, OBE (d 1960), and Helen, da of Lady Barrymore and late Arthur Post, of New York; *b* 26 Jan 1914; *Educ* Eton; *m* 1, 1939 (m dis 1947), Helen Mary (d 1951), da of late Lt-Col Charles Walter Villiers, CBE, DSO (gs of Rt Rev the Hon Henry Villiers, bro of 4 Earl of Clarendon) and Lady Kathleen, nee Cole, da of 4 Earl of Enniskillen; 1 s, 1 da (Countess of Shelburne, da-in-law of 8 Marquess of Lansdowne); m 2, 1948 (m dis 1959), Mrs Margaret Eyston, da of Lt-Col William Wyndham; m 3, 1965, Mrs Mary Lotinga, da of Sir Shenton Thomas; *Heir* s, Lord Eliot; *Career* Capt Duke of Cornwall's LI (attached Roy Armoured Corps); patron of 3 livings; *Style* - The Rt Hon The Earl of St Germans; Les Arcs, Chemin du Signal, 1807 Blonay, Vaud, Switzerland

ST HELENS, 2 Baron (UK 1964); Richard Francis Hughes-Young; s of 1 Baron, sometime Dep Govt Ch Whip (d 1980), and Elizabeth, da of late Capt Richard Blakiston-Houston (himself ggs of Sir Matthew Blakiston, 2 Bt); *b* 4 Nov 1945; *Educ* Nautical Coll Pangbourne; *Style* - The Rt Hon The Lord St Helens; Marchfield, Binfield, Berks

ST JOHN OF BLETSO, 21 Baron (E 1559); Sir Anthony Tudor St John; 18 Bt (E 1660); s of 20 Baron, TD (d 1978), and Katharine, nee von Berg; *b* 16 May 1957; *Educ* Diocesan Coll Cape Town and Cape Town U, S Africa; *Heir* cous, Edmund St

John; *Career* lawyer; *Style* - The Rt Hon The Lord St John of Bletso; By the Sea, Kalk Bay, Cape Town 8001, S Africa

ST JOHN, Edmund Oliver; WS; s of late Col Edmund Farquhar St John, CMG, DSO, s of late Rev the Hon Edmund Tudor St John (s of 14 Baron St John of Bletso) and Henrietta, da of late Col James Dalmahoy, MVO, WS; hp of cous, 21 Baron; *b* 13 Oct 1927; *Educ* Trin Coll Glenalmond; *m* 1959, Elizabeth Frances, da of Lt-Col H Nicholl, of Lipwood Hall, Haydon Bridge, Northumberland; 1 s, 2 da; *Style* - Edmund St John Esq; Lynedale House, West Linton, Peebles-shire

ST JOHN, Hon Helen Evelyn; da (by 1 m) of late 18 Baron St John; *b* 1906; *Style* - The Hon Helen St John; c/o Balfour & Manson, SSC, 58 Frederick st, Edinburgh 2

ST JOHN, Hon Henry Fitzroy; s (by 1 m) and h of 7 Viscount Bolingbroke and St John; *b* 18 May 1957; *Style* - The Hon Henry St John

ST JOHN OF BLETSO, Baroness; Katharine; da of late Alfred von Berg; *m* 1955, 20 Baron (d 1978); *Style* - The Rt Hon The Lady St John of Bletso; c/o Syfret's Trust Co Ltd, 24 Wale st, PO Box 206, Cape Town 8001, S Africa

ST JOHN, (Oliver) Peter; s of Lt-Col Frederick Oliver St John, DSO, MC (d 1977), and gs of Sir Frederick Robert St John, KCMG (yst s of late Hon Ferdinand St John, 2 s of 3 Viscount Bolinbroke and St John); through Sir Frederick's w, Isabella Fitz-Maurice (gda of 5 Earl of Orkney), Peter is hp to his 2 cous once removed, 8 Earl of Orkney; *b* 27 Feb 1938; *m* 1963, Mary Juliet, da of W G Scott-Brown; 1 s, 4 da; *Career* Assoc Prof Political Science, Manitoba U; *Style* - Peter St John Esq; 200 Dromore av, Winnipeg 9, Manitoba, Canada

ST JOHN, Hon Mrs (Sally Hayter); *née* Rootes; da of 2 Baron Rootes; *b* 12 Sept 1947; *m* 1968, Andrew, s of Cdr Michael St John, DSC, RN (ret), of Bepton Lodge, Midhurst (gn of 15 & 16 Barons St John of Bletso), by Pamela, da of Sir Arthur Guinness, KCMG; *Style* - The Hon Mrs St John; The Old Thatch, Leggs Lane, Heyshott, Midhurst, Sussex

ST JOHN, Hon Mrs (Vanessa Marguerite); *née* Palmer; da of 3 Baron Palmer, OBE; *b* 1954; *m* 1977, Robert William St John; *Style* - The Hon Mrs St John

ST JOHN-STEVAS, Rt Hon Norman Antony Francis; PC (1979), MP (C) Chelmsford 1964-; s of late Stephen Stevas and Kitty St John O'Connor; *b* 18 May 1929; *Educ* Ratcliffe, Fitzwilliam Cambridge; *Career* former Pres Cambridge Union, barr 1952, former jurisprudence tutor; political correspondent The Economist 1959; author, FRSL 1966; contested Dagenham 1951, Min of State for Education and Science with special responsibility for the Arts 1973-74, Oppn Spokesman for the Arts 1974 and Memb Shadow Cabinet; Min for the Arts 1979, Leader of the House of Commons and Chllr of the Duchy of Lancaster 1979-81, OStJ 1980; *Style* - The Rt Hon Norman St John-Stevas, PC, MP; 34 Montpellier sq, SW1

ST JOHNSTON, Colin David; s of James Hallewell St Johnston (d 1963); *Educ* Shrewsbury Sch, Lincoln Coll Oxford; *m* 1958, Valerie, nee Paget; 4 c; *Career* md Ocean Co Ltd 1976-, dir Ocean Transport and Trading Ltd 1974-; 1 Lt Nat Serv Hong Kong 1954-55; *Recreations* squash; *Clubs* MCC; *Style* - Colin St Johnston Esq; 30 Fitzroy rd, NW1 (☎ 722 5932)

ST JUST, 2 Baron (UK 1935); Peter George Grenfell; s of 1 Baron (d 1941, s of Henry Grenfell, sometime MP Stoke & Govr Bank of England, by his w Alethea, nee Adeane) and Florence, nee Henderson; thus Lord St Just is 2 cous to late Julian Grenfell, the poet, while his ggf's half sis m Charles Kingsley, author of *The Water Babies* and also a poet; *b* 22 July 1922; *Educ* Harrow; *m* 1, 1949 (m dis 1955), Leslie, da of Condé Nast (publisher of Vogue), of New York, and Leslie (d 1981), da of Albert Volney Foster and subsequently w of Lt-Col Sir Rex Benson, DSO, MVO, MC; 1 da (Hon Mrs

Phillips); m 2, 1956, Maria Britneva, da of Alexander Britnev, of St Petersburg (now Leningrad), Russia; 2 da; *Heir* none; *Career* Hon Lt King's Roy Rifle Corps, NW Europe 1944-45; *Style* - The Rt Hon The Lord St Just; Wilbury Park, Newton Tony, nr Salisbury, Wilts; 9 Gerald rd, SW1 (☎ 01 730 7621)

ST LEGER, Hon David Hugh; s of 9 Viscount Doneraile; *b* 1950; *Style* - The Hon David St Leger

ST LEGER, Hon Elizabeth Adele; da of 9 Viscount Doneraile; *b* 1953; *Style* - The Hon Elizabeth St Leger

ST LEGER, Hon Edward Hayes; s of 9 Viscount Doneraile; *b* 1960; *Style* - The Hon Edward St Leger

ST LEGER, Hon Karen Jean; da of 9 Viscount Doneraile; *b* 1955; *Style* - The Hon Karen St Leger

ST LEGER, Hon Richard Allen; s and h of 9 Viscount Doneraile; *b* 17 Aug 1946; *Educ* Orange Coast Coll, California; *m* 1969, Kathleen Mary, nee Simcox; 1 s, 1 da; *Career* air traffic control specialist, Missippi U; *Style* - The Hon Richard St Leger; 1044 Fuschia Circle, Placentia, California 92670, USA

ST LEONARDS, 4 Baron (UK 1852); John Gerard Sugden; s of late Arthur Sugden (ggs of 1 Baron) and Julia, nee Wyatt; suc kinsman 1972; *b* 3 Feb 1950; *Heir* unc, Dr Edward Sugden; *Style* - The Rt Hon The Lord St Leonards; 17 Craigford dve, Artane, Dublin 5

ST LEVAN, 4 Baron (UK 1887); Sir John Francis Arthur St Aubyn; 5 Bt (UK 1866), DSC (1942), DL (Cornwall 1977); s of 3 Baron (d 1978) and Hon Clementina Gwendolen Catharine, nee Nicolson, da of 1 Baron Carnock and sis of Harold Nicolson, the author; Lord St Levan is therefore 1 cous of Nigel Nicolson; *b* 23 Feb 1919; *Educ* Eton, Trin Cambridge; *m* 1970, Susan, da of late Maj-Gen Sir John Noble Kennedy, GCMG, KCVO, KBE, CB, MC; *Heir* bro, Hon Piers St Aubyn, MC; *Career* slr 1948, sometime Lt RNVR, High Sheriff of Cornwall 1974, Fell of Roy Soc for Encouragement of Art; *Clubs* Brooks's, Roy Yacht Squadron; *Style* - The Rt Hon The Lord St Levan, DSC, DL; St Michael's Mount, Marazion, Cornwall

ST LEVAN, Dowager Baroness - Hon Clementina Gwendolen Catharine; *née* Nicolson; JP; da of late 1 Baron Carnock; sis of late Sir Harold Nicolson, the author; *b* 3 July 1896; *m* 1916, 3 Baron St Levan (d 1978); *Style* - The Rt Hon the Dowager Lady St Levan, JP; Avallon, Green Lane, Marazion, Cornwall (☎ 0736 710 508)

ST OSWALD, 4 Baron (UK 1885); Rowland Denys Guy Winn; MC (1951), DL (W Riding of Yorks 1962); s of 3 Baron (d 1957); *b* 19 Sept 1916; *Educ* Stowe, Bonn and Freiburg Us; *m* 1, 1952 (m dis 1955), Laurian, da of Sir Roderick Jones, KBE, by his w, late Enid Bagnold, author of *National Velvet*; m 2, 1955, Marie Wanda (d 1981), da of late Sigismund Jaxa-Chamiec, of Filtrowa, Warsaw, Poland; *Heir* bro, Hon Derek Winn; *Career* MEP (C) 1973-79, contested Yorks W for European Parl 1979, a Lord in Waiting to HM the Queen 1959-62, Jt Parly Sec Ministry Ag Fish and Food 1962-64, PPS to Earl Jellicoe (Lord Privy Seal) 1970; v-chm Centl & Eastern European Cmmn European Movement; chm Crabtree Denims Ltd; *Style* - The Rt Hon The Lord St Oswald MC DL; Nostell Priory, Wakefield, W Yorks; White Lodge, Gilston rd, SW10 (☎ 01 373 3660)

ST PIER, Hon Mrs (Margaret Wilmett); da of Baron Helsby (Life Peer d 1978); *b* 1939; *m* 1960, (John Frederick) Keith St Pier; *Style* - The Hon Mrs St Pier; Chadhurst Farm, Coldharbour Lane, Dorking, Surrey

ST VINCENT, 7 Viscount (UK 1801); Ronald George James Jervis; s of 6 Viscount (d 1940, himself ggs of 2 Viscount, who was in his turn n of 1 Viscount and Earl of St Vincent, whose title comemorated his stupendous victory over the Spaniards in 1797 despite being outnumbered 27 sail to 15 - the name title was chosen by George III himself; St Vincent, more modestly, had suggested Yarmouth & Orford, which did not call to mind his successful action so readily) and Marion, nee Brown; *b* 3 May 1905; *Educ* Sherborne; *m* 1945, Constance Phillida Anne, da of Lt-Col Robert Logan OBE, of Taunton; 2 s, 1 da; *Heir* s, Hon Edward Jervis; *Career* acting Lt-Cdr RNVR WWII; patron of one living; *Style* - The Rt Hon The Viscount St Vincent; Les Charrières, St Ouen, Jersey, CI

STAËL VON HOLSTEIN, Baron (Sweden 1675); Robert Alexander Karl Constantin; s of Baron Constantin Staël von Holstein (d 1964 in Dawlish) by his w Countess Sylvia von der Recke von Volmerstein, da of (Karl) 4 Count von der Recke von Volmerstein (of a Prussian cr of 1817 by King Frederick William III, though the family originally hailed from Westphalia); the Baron is *chef de famille* and a direct descendant of Madame de Staël, the French authoress (of *Corinne*, interesting, if for no other reason, as the first 'aesthetic' romance written in a language other than German, and *De l'Allemagne*, an account of Germany), by her husb, Baron S von H, Swedish Ambass to France; the Baron is hence descended from Necker (Mme de S's f), the financier who attempted to introduce order into the French *ancien régime*, and Suzanne Churchod, his w (who is assured a place in history for prompting in Gibbon, an aspirant to her hand but who submitted to the author of his being's veto, the sentence "I sighed as a lover, I obeyed as a son."); *b* 20 Feb 1928; *Educ* Prebendal Sch Chichester; *m* 1978, as her 2 husb, Carol, da of Hon Douglas Westwood (2 s of 1 Baron Westwood) & formerly w of Maj John Ralli (whose f John was 3 cous of Sir Godfrey Ralli, 3 Bt); 3 children (including at least 1 s, Baron Jeremy John Alexander S v H); *Career* exec in construction indust in Africa, S America, M East; consultant in W African ec affrs and planning advsr; *Clubs* Travellers'; *Style* - Baron Staël von Holstein; 4 Palace Court, W2 (☎ 01 229 9121)

STABB, His Honour Judge Sir William Walter; QC (1968); s of late Sir Newton Stabb, OBE; *b* 6 Oct 1913; *Educ* Rugby, Univ Coll Oxford; *m* 1940, Dorothy Margaret Leckie; 4 da; *Career* served RAF 1940-46, ret 1950; sr official referee the Supreme Court; kt 1981; *Style* - His Honour Judge Sir William Stabb, QC; The Pale Farm, Chipperfield, Kings Langley, Herts (☎ 63124)

STABLE, Maj-Gen Hugh Huntington; CB (1947), CIE (1938); s of Alfred Henry Stable (d 1907); *b* 30 April 1896; *Educ* Malvern; *m* 1923, Cyrille Helen Dorothy, nee Bayfield (d 1979); *Career* Maj-Gen Palestine, India (NW Frontier), Mil Sec Cdr-in-Chief India 1933-36, Mil Sec to Viceroy of India 1936-38, Commander 1939-47, QMG India Dec 1947 (ret 1950); Govr Malvern Coll, Emeritus Cmmr Boy Scouts of S Africa; *Clubs* Army & Navy, City & Civil Service (Cape Town); *Style* - Maj-Gen Hugh Stable CB CIE; 810 Rapallo, Sea Point, Cape Town, S Africa (☎ 447981)

STACK, Maurice Neville; s of Maurice Stack (d 1970); *b* 2 Sept 1928; *Educ* Arnold Sch; *m* 1953, Molly, nee Rowe; 1 s, 1 da; *Career* ed-in-ch Leicester Mercury 1974-, ed Stockport Advertiser 1974, Daily Express 1973, northern news ed IPC nat papers 1971, Sheffield Telegraph and Kemsley nat papers 1955, Express & Star 1950; *Recreations* sailing, writing, flying, riding; *Clubs* Rutland Sailing, Leicestershire Aero; owner of boat 'Leisure'; *Style* - Maurice Stack Esq; Fydell's Barn, Back Lane, Morcott, Rutland, Leics (☎ Morcott 330)

STACK, Air Chief Marshal Sir (Thomas) Neville; KCB (1965, CB 1969), CVO (1963), CBE (1965), AFC (1957); s of Thomas Neville Stack, AFC (d 1949); *b* 19 Oct 1919; *Educ* St Edmund's Coll, RAF Coll Cranwell; *m* 1955, Diana Virginia, da of late Oliver Stuart Todd, MBE; 1 s, 1 da; *Career* FRMetS, Air Chief Marshal, Air Sec MOD 1976-78; dir gen Asbestos Int Assoc 1978-; Gentleman Usher to HM the Queen 1978-; memb cncl & exec ctee Cancer Research Campaign 1979-; govr Wellington Coll 1980-; *Recreations* gardening, various outdoor sports; *Clubs* RAF, Boodle's; *Style* - Air Chief Marshal Sir Neville Stack KCB CVO CBE AFC; 4 Perrymead st, SW6 (☎ 01 736 4410)

STACY, Reginald Joseph William; CB 1955; s of Frank Dixon Stacy (d 1972); *b* 1

Jan 1904; *Educ* Sir Walter St John's Sch London, Trin Coll Cambridge; *m* 1932, Nina Grace, nee Holder; 1 s, 1 da; *Career* Under Sec Board of Trade 1949-64, French and Latin Master Parkside Prep School Surrey 1967-69; *Recreations* any foreign language; *Style* - Reginald Stacy Esq, CB; 2 Beech ct, Easington Place, Guildford, Surrey (☎ Guildford 60761)

STAFFORD, 14 Baron (E 1640); Basil Francis Nicholas Fitzherbert; s of Capt Hon Thomas Charles Fitzherbert, AM (descended from the 3 s of the 1 Earl of Norfolk of the 1644 cr); suc unc, 13 Baron, KCB 1941; *b* 7 April 1926; *Educ* Ampleforth; *m* 1952, Morag Nada (serving Sister, Order of St John), da of late Lt-Col Alastair Campbell, of Altries, Milltimber, Aberdeenshire; 3 s, 3 da; *Heir* s, Hon Francis Fitzherbert; *Career* patron of one living (but cannot present, being a Roman Catholic); formerly Lt Scots Gds, local dir Barclays Bank Ltd (Birmingham); *Style* - The Rt Hon The Lord Stafford; Swynnerton Park, Stone, Staffs (☎ Swynnerton 228)

STAFFORD, Hon Mrs (Elizabeth Anne); *née* Richardson; da of Baron Richardson, MVO; *b* 24 July 1937; *m* 1, 1960 (m dis 1970), Angus Jack, s of Brig-Gen James Jack, DSO, DL, by his w, Jeanette, da of Thomas Watson (3 s of Sir John Watson, 1 Bt, JP, DL); 1 s; m 2, 1971, Gregory Stafford; 1 s; *Style* - The Hon Mrs Stafford; 49 Deodar rd, SW15

STAFFORD-KING-HARMAN, Sir Cecil William Francis; 2 Bt (UK 1914) of Rockingham, Co Roscommon; s of Rt Hon Sir Thomas Joseph Stafford, Bt, CB (d 1935); *b* 6 Jan 1895; *Educ* RNCs Osborne and Dartmouth, RMC Sandhurst and Ch Ch Oxford; *m* 1917, Sarah Beatrice (d 1979), da of late Col Alfred Dyke Acland, CBE; 1 da (also 1 s ka, 1 da decd); *Career* Midshipman RN; former Maj and temp Lt-Col King's Roy Rifle Corps; AAG Scottish Command 1942-43; memb of Irish Cncl of State 1956; WW I (despatches); added by Royal licence 1932 surnames of King-Harman; *Recreations* shooting, racing, fishing; *Clubs* Kildare Street, Boodle's, Irish Turf; *Style* - Sir Cecil Stafford-King-Harman, Bt; Catherine's Park, Leixlip, Co Kildare, Eire

STAIR, 13 Earl of (S 1703); Sir John Aymer Dalrymple; 14 Bt of Stair (S 1664) and 10 of Killock (S 1698), KCVO (1978, CVO 1964), MBE (1941); also Viscount Stair, and Lord Glenluce and Stranraer (S 1690), Viscount Dalrymple and Lord Newliston (S 1703), Baron Oxenfoord (UK 1841); s of 12 Earl (d 1961, ggggggn of 1 Earl, better known as Master of Stair; as Jt Sec of State, Scotland, he connived at the Massacre of Glencoe; the theory that the Nine of Diamonds is named the 'Curse of Scotland' because the lozenges on it are represented in the Dalrymple arms is to be preferred to the apocryphal story that the Master of Stair scribbled the authorisation for the atrocity on the back of a playing card of that denomination; yet even Lockhart of Carnwath, who opposed him politically and called him the Judas of his country for doing so much to bring about the Union, admitted that he was "extreamly facetious and diverting...and setting aside his politicks...good natured"; G K Chesterton's Father Brown opined that Stair's refined intellectuality was the stuff of which vendors of souls to the Devil were made, and more likely to deal with His Sable Highness in that commodity than 'Bloody Clavers' (Dundee), but as a priest of the Romish persuasion he may have been partial, for while Stair's victims at Glencoe were Jacobites, Dundee was the scourge of the Covenanters; be that as it may, Stair's mother was known as the 'Witch of Endor'); *b* 9 Oct 1906; *Educ* Eton; *m* 1960, Davina, da of Hon Sir David Bowes-Lyon KCVO (s of 14 Earl of Strathmore) & 1 cous of HM The Queen; 3 s; *Heir* s, Viscount Dalrymple; *Career* Col late Scots Gds, Capt Gen Roy Co of Archers; Gold Stick for Scotland; Ld-Lt Wigtownshire 1961-; *Style* - The Rt Hon The Earl of Stair KCVO MBE, HM Lord-Lieut for Wigtownshire; Lochinch Castle, Stranraer, Wigtownshire (☎ 2110)

STALLYBRASS, Hon Mrs (Agnes Mary); *née* Clifford; da of late 11 Baron Clifford of Chudleigh; *b* 1918; *m* 1944, Robert Weatherhead Stallybrass; 1 s, 2 da; *Style* - The Hon Mrs Stallybrass; The Old Laundry, Oakhill, nr Bath

STAMER, Sir (Lovelace) Anthony; 5 Bt (UK 1809), of Beauchamp, Dublin; s of Sir Lovelace Stamer, 4 Bt (d 1941), and Mary, *née* Otter (whose mother Marianne was seventh in descent from 4 Baron North); *b* 28 Feb 1917; *Educ* Harrow and Trinity College Cambridge; *m* 1, 1948 (m dis 1953), Stella Huguette, da of Paul Burnell Binnie; 1 s, 1 da; m 2, 1955 (m dis 1959), Margaret Lucy, da of late Maj Belben; m 3, 1960 (m dis 1968), Marjorie June, da of T C Noakes; *Heir* s, Fl Lt Peter Tomlinson Stamer, RAF; *Career* PO RAF 1939-41, Offr Air Transport Aux 1941-45; exec dir Bentley Drivers Club Ltd 1969-73, and of Bugatti and Ferrari Owners Clubs 1973-74; hon tres Ferrari Owners Club 1976-; *Style* - Sir Anthony Stamer, Bt; Summer Cottage, Turville Heath, Henley-on-Thames, Oxon

STAMER, Fl Lt Peter Tomlinson; s and h of Sir Anthony Stamer, Bt; *b* 19 Nov 1951; *Career* RAF; *Style* - Flight Lieutenant Peter Tomlinson

STAMLER, Samuel Aaron; QC (1971); s of Herman Stamler (d 1972); *b* 3 Dec 1925; *Educ* Berkhamsted, King's Coll Cambridge; *m* 1953, Vivienne Honor, nee Brotman; 2 s, 1 da; *Career* barr (Middle Temple) 1949, Recorder of Crown Court 1974, Master of Bench Middle Temple 1979; *Recreations* tennis, walking; *Clubs* Athenaeum; *Style* - Samuel Stamler Esq, QC; 47 Forty Ave, Wembley, Middx, (☎ Wembley 904 1714)

STAMP, 3 Baron (UK 1938); Trevor Charles Stamp; s of 1 Baron Stamp, GCB, GBE (d 1941 as a result of enemy action World War II; his son (and the present Lord's bro), the 2 Baron, died with him, but by a decision of the House of Lords analogous to the Property Act 1925 it was presumed that the deaths occurred in order of seniority); *b* 13 Feb 1907; *Educ* Leys Sch, Gonville and Caius Cambridge; *m* 1932, Frances Dawes, da of late Charles Henry Bosworth, of Evanston, Illinois, USA; 2 s; *Heir* s, Dr the Hon Trevor Stamp; *Career* MRCS Eng and LRCP London, FRCPath, Fellow Royal Post-grad Med Sch, Prof Emeritus Bacteriology London U (formerly lectr, then Reader, Prof 1948-70); has American Medal of Freedom with Silver Palm; *Style* - The Rt Hon The Lord Stamp; Pennyroyal, Hedgerley, Bucks (☎ Farnham Common 2737); Middle House, 7 Hyde Park st, W2 (☎ 01 723 8363)

STAMP, Hon Arthur Maxwell; s of 1 Baron Stamp, GCB, GBE (d 1941, as a result of enemy action); *b* 20 Sept 1915; *Educ* Leys Sch, Clare Cambridge (BA, MA); *m* 1, 1938, Janet Tyler (m dis 1943), da of B Tyler Bryan, of Beaumont, Texas; m 2, 1944, Mary Hagon, da of Walter Richards, of Hereford; 1 s, 2 da; *Career* Fin Advsr to John Lewis Ltd 1947-49, to Governors Bank of England 1950-57, Head European Dept IMF 1953, dir Hill Samuel 1958-76; late Lt-Col Intelligence Corps; chm Maxwell Stamp Associates Ltd 1962-79, Bonsach Baths Ltd; dir De La Rue Co Ltd; bd memb Civil Aviation Authority; *Style* - Lt-Col the Hon Arthur Stamp; Mulberry Green Farmhouse, Copford, Essex; 19 Clarence Gate gdns, NW1

STAMP, Hon Jos Colin; s of 1 Baron Stamp, GCB, GBE (d 1941, as a result of enemy action); *b* 1917; *Educ* Leys Sch, Queens' Cambridge; *m* 1, 1940, (m dis 1956), Althea, da of late Mrs William Dawes, of Evanston, Illinois; 4 da; m 2, 1958, Gillian Penelope, da of late Guy St J Tatham, of Johannesburg, SA; 2 s; *Career* late Lt RNVR, late dir Marketing Services for Europe of American Express Internat; *Style* - The Hon Jos Stamp; 12 Ullswater rd, SW13

STAMP, Hon Josiah Richard; s of 3 Baron Stamp; *b* 1943; *Educ* Winchester, Queens' Cambridge; *Style* - The Hon Josiah Stamp

STAMP, John Trevor; CBE (1973); s of Harold Stamp (d 1966); *b* 3 Dec 1915; *Educ* Orme Boys' Sch and County G S Newcastle, Edinburgh U; *m* 1941, Margaret May, nee Scott; 2 s, 1 da; *Career* veterinary surgeon, sr lecturer Edinburgh U 1942-47 and hon lecturer 1947-77; Vet Investigator Offr East of Scotland 1947-53, dir Moredun Research Institute Edinburgh 1953-77, President RCVS 1970-71; *Recreations* sailing, golf, fishing; *Clubs* Farmers', Univ Staff; *Style* - John Stamp Esq, CBE; Valebank, N Berwick, E Lothian (☎ 0620 2595)

STAMP, Katharine, Baroness;

Katharine Mary; da of Tom Wickett; *m* 1929, 2 Baron Stamp (d 1941 as a result of enemy action); 3 da; *Style* - The Rt Hon Katharine, Lady Stamp; 25 Squitchey Lane, Summertown, Oxford

STAMP, Hon Nancy Elizabeth; da of 2 Baron Stamp (d 1941, as a result of enemy action); *b* 1931; *Educ* St Andrews U (MA 1953); *Style* - The Hon Nancy Stamp

STAMP, Dr the Hon Trevor Charles Bosworth; s and h of 3 Baron Stamp; *b* 18 Sept 1935; *Educ* Leys Sch, Gonville and Caius Cambridge; *m* 1, 1963 (m dis 1971), Anne Carolynn, da of John Churchill, of Tunbridge Wells; 2 da; m 2, 1975, Carol Anne, da of Robert Keith Russell, of Farnham, Surrey; 1 s, 1 da; *Career* FRCP London; *Style* - Dr the Hon Trevor Stamp; 14 Doneraile st, SW6

STANBRIDGE, Air Vice-Marshal Sir Brian Gerald Tivy; KCVO (1979, MVO 1958), CBE (1974), AFC (1952); s of Gerald Edward Stanbridge (d 1966); *b* 6 July 1924; *Educ* Thurlestone Coll Dartmouth; *m* 1949, Kathleen Diana, nee Hayes; 2 da; *Career* Air Vice-Marshal Burma Campaign 1944-45, personal pilot and flying instructor to HRH the Duke of Edinburgh 1954-58, sec to Ch of Staff Ctee 1971-73, Defence Serv Sec to the Queen 1975-79 (ret), dir-gen Air Transport Users Comittee 1979-; *Recreations* house maintenance, gardening; *Clubs* RAF; *Style* - Air Vice-Marshal Sir Brian Stanbridge KCVO, CBE, AFC; 9 Paines Lane, Pinner, Middx (☎ 866 6643)

STANDING, John; *see* Leon, Bt, Sir John

STANHOPE, Lady Isabella Rachel; da of 11 Earl of Harrington; *b* 11 Oct 1966; *Style* - Lady Isabella Stanhope

STANHOPE, Hon John Fitzroy; s of 11 Earl of Harrington; *b* 20 Aug 1965; *Style* - The Hon John Stanhope

STANHOPE, Hon Serena Alleyne; da of Viscount Petersham; *b* 1 March 1970; *Style* - The Hon Serena Stanhope

STANHOPE, Hon Steven Francis Lincoln; s of 11 Earl of Harrington; *b* 12 Dec 1951; *Educ* Eton; *m* 1978, Maureen, da of Maj H Cole, of Poundbury, Dorset; 1 s (Ben b 1978), 1 da (Tara b 1979); *Career* stud owner and manager; *Recreations* golf, snooker, racing (race horses in training: 'Rosie Black', 'Brandon Creek'); *Clubs* Turf; *Style* - The Hon Steven Stanhope; Dooneen Stud, Patrickswell, Co Limerick, Eire

STANHOPE, Lady Trina Maria; da of 11 Earl of Harrington; *b* 1947; *Style* - Lady Trina Stanhope; Greenmount, Patrickswell, Co Limerick, Eire

STANHOPE, Hon William Henry Leicester; s and h of Viscount Petersham; *b* 14 Oct 1967; *Style* - The Hon William Stanhope

STANIER, Brig Sir Alexander Beville Gibbons; 2 Bt (UK 1917), of Peplow Hall, Hodnet, Co Salop; DSO (1940) and Bar (1945), MC (1918), JP (Salop 1949), DL (1951); s of Sir Beville Stanier, 1 Bt, MP (d 1921); *b* 31 Jan 1899; *Educ* Eton; *m* 1927, Dorothy Gladys (d 1973), da of Brig-Gen Alfred Douglas Miller CBE DSO; 1 s, 1 da; *Heir* s, Belville Stanier; *Career* served WWI France 1918, WW II also France (despatches, American Silver Star, Cdr Order of Leopold of Belgium with Palms, Belgian Croix de Guerre with Palms); Brig (ret) late Welsh Gds (Cmdg 1945-48); patron of two livings; High Sheriff Salop 1951, CC 1950-58; CStJ; *Style* - Brig Sir Alexander Stanier, Bt, DSO*, MC, JP, DL; Park Cottage, Ludford, Ludlow, Salop (☎ 2675); East Farndon Manor, Market Harborough, Leics (☎ 62104)

STANIER, Beville Douglas; s and h of Sir Alexander Stanier, 2 Bt, DSO*, MC, JP, DL; *b* 20 April 1934; *m* 1963, Shelagh, da of late Maj Sinnott; 1 s, 2 da; *Career* late Capt Welsh Gds; ADC to Govr-Gen of Australia 1959-60; *Style* - Beville Stanier Esq; Kings Close, Whaddon, Bletchley, Bucks

STANIFORTH, John Arthur Reginald; s of Capt Staniforth, MC (decd); *b* 19 Sept 1912; *Educ* Marlborough; *m* 1936, Penelope Cecile, da of the late Maj Gen Sir Henry Freeland; 2 c (1 decd); *Career* dir: John

Brown & Co Ltd, Constructors John Brown Ltd, John Brown Engineering, memb Export Group Advisory Council 1971-76, dep chm 1975-76, founder chm British Chemical Engineering Contracters Assoc 1965-68, Governor Bryanston Sch; *Recreations* golf, fishing, sailing; *Clubs* Flyfishers'; *Style* - John Staniforth Esq; Spindlewood, Bosham Lane, Old Bosham, Chichester (☎ 0243 572401)

STANLEY OF ALDERLEY, 8 Baron (UK 1839); Sir Thomas Henry Oliver Stanley; 14 Bt (E 1660); also Baron Sheffield (I 1783) and Baron Eddisbury of Winnington (UK 1848); s of late Lt-Col the Hon Oliver Hugh Stanley, DSO, JP, DL (s of 4 Baron and who d 1952; descended from Sir John Stanley of Weever, yr bro of 1 Earl of Derby; the 2 Baron S of A was called 'Sir Benjamin Backbite' at Oxford for his mordant remarks, while his s, the 3 Baron, 'went native' in the East, where he travelled dressed in Turkish costume and converted to Islam; though buried according to Moslem rites at Alderley, he supported the Anglican establishment in Wales, where with c 6,000 acres (over a moiety of his total estates in the late nineteenth century) he was a considerable landowner), and Lady Kathleen, nee Thynne, da of 5 Marquess of Bath; suc cous, 7 Baron (who preferred to be known as Lord Sheffield) 1971; *b* 28 Sept 1927; *Educ* Wellington; *m* 1955, Jane Barrett, da of late Ernest George Hartley; 3 s, 1 da; *Heir* s, Hon Richard Stanley; *Career* Capt (ret) Coldstream Gds and Gds Independent Parachute Co; farmer; dir Group Cereal Services and chm Thames Vallley Cereals, govr St Edward's Sch Oxford; *Recreations* sailing, fishing, skiing; *Clubs* Farmers'; *Style* - The Rt Hon The Lord Stanley of Alderley; Trysglwyn Fawr, Rhosy Bol, Amlwch, Anglesey (☎ Amlwch 830 364); Rectory Farm, Stanton St John, Oxford (☎ Stanton St John 214)

STANLEY, Hon Charles Ernest; s of 8 Baron Stanley of Alderley; *b* 1960; *Style* - The Hon Charles Stanley

STANLEY, Hon Harry John; s of 8 Baron Stanley of Alderley; *b* 1963; *Style* - The Hon Harry Stanley

STANLEY OF ALDERLEY, Kathleen (Margaret), Baroness; da of Cecil Wright, of Malden, Surrey, & widow of Sir Edmund Crane; *m* 1961, as his 4 w, 6 Baron Stanley of Alderley (d 1971); *Style* - The Rt Hon Kathleen, Lady Stanley of Alderley; Villa Pax, Grouville, Jersey (☎ 51085)

STANLEY, Hon Lucinda Maria; da of 8 Baron Stanley of Alderley; *b* 1958; *Style* - The Hon Lucinda Stanley

STANLEY, Michael Charles; MBE (Mil 1945), DL (Westmoreland 1964-74, Cumbria 1974); s of Col Rt Hon Oliver Frederick George Stanley, MP, MC, PC (d 1950), 2 s of 17 Earl of of Derby, by his w Lady Maureen Vane-Tempest-Stewart, eldest da of 7 Marquess of Londonderry; *b* 11 Aug 1921; *Educ* Eton, Trin Cambridge; *m* 1951, Aileen Fortune Hugh Smith; 2 s; *Career* chartered electrical engineer, V-Lt Westmoreland 1965-79, High Sheriff Westmoreland 1959-60, Cumbria 1975-76; *Recreations* wine, walking, idleness; *Clubs* White's, Turf, Brooks's; *Style* - Michael Stanley Esq, MBE, DL; 39 Charles st, W1 (☎ 01 499 1477); Halecat House, Witherslack, Grange over Sands, Cumbria (☎ Witherslack 229)

STANLEY, Hon Richard Morgan Oliver; s of Hon Oliver Stanley, DSO, and Lady Kathleen Thynne, da of 5 Marquess of Bath; yr bro of 8 Baron Stanley of Alderley and Sheffield; *b* 30 April 1931; *Educ* Winchester, New Coll Oxford; *m* 1956, Phyllida, da of Lt-Col Clive Austin, of Micheldever, and Lady Lilian Lumley, sis of 11 Earl of Scarbrough; 2 s, 2 da; *Career* late Lt Coldstream Gds; dir Metal Box Ltd (UK Pres); Govr Bradfield; *Style* - The Hon Richard Stanley; Jennetts Hill House, Stanford Dingley, Reading, Berks (☎ Bradfield 744349)

STANLEY, Hon Richard Oliver; s of late Lord Stanley MC PC MP (er s of 17 Earl of Derby) & Hon Sibyl Cadogan (da of Viscount Chelsea); hp of bro, 18 Earl of Derby; *b* 29 Jan 1920; *Educ* Eton, Trinity Cambridge; *m* 1, 1965, Susan Mary Fynvola (d 1976), da of Lt-Col Sir John Henry Lancelot Aubrey-Fletcher, 7 Bt;

m 2, 1979, Mary, da of late Maj Vyvian Alfred Tylor, of Sussex, and widow of William Herbert Harrison; *Career* chm Lancs Playing Fields Assoc, PPS to First Lord of the Admiralty 1951-55, MP (C) N Fylde Lancs 1950-66, jt tres Cons Pty 1963-66; *Style* - The Hon Richard Stanley; New England Stud, Newmarket, Suffolk

STANLEY, Hon Richard Oliver; s and h of 8 Baron Stanley of Alderley; *b* 24 April 1956; *Educ* St Edward's Sch Oxford, Univ Coll London (BSc); *Style* - The Hon Richard Stanley

STANLEY, Hon Mrs - Hon Susan Josephine Gabrielle Haden; da of 3 Baron Haden-Guest; *b* 1930; *m* 1953, John Orr Stanley; 4 s; *Style* - The Hon Mrs Stanley; Granary House, Holly Hill, NW3

STANLEY PRICE, His Hon Judge; Peter; QC (1956); s of Herbert Stanley Price (d 1957); *b* 27 Nov 1911; *Educ* Cheltenham, Exeter Coll Oxford; *m* 1, 1946, Harriett Ella Theresa, nee Pownall (d 1948); 2 s (twin); m 2, 1950, Margaret Jane, widow of William Hebditch; 1 da; *Career* Circuit Judge (formerly Judge of Central Criminal Court) 1969, Recorder of Pontefract 1954, York 1955, Kingston-upon-Hull 1958, Sheffield 1965-69, chm N Riding Yorks QS 1958-70; Judge of Appeal Jersey and Guernsey 1964-69; pres Nat Reference Tribunal for Coal Mining Industry 1979-; *Recreations* nature, gardening, shooting; *Clubs* Brooks's, Pratt's, Yorkshire; *Style* - His Hon Judge Stanley Price QC; Church Hill, Great Ouseburn, York (☎ Green Hammerton 30252)

STANSGATE, Viscountcy of; *see* Benn, Rt Hon Tony (Neil) Wedgwood, MP

STANSGATE, Viscountess; Margaret Eadie; da of late Daniel Turner Holmes, formerly MP for Govan Div of Lanarks; *m* 1920, 1 Viscount (d 1960); 2 s (*see* Rt Hon Tony Benn, MP); *Career* First Pres Congregational Fedn of England 1972-73, now Pres Emeritus; *Style* - The Rt Hon The Viscountess Stansgate; Stansgate Abbey House, nr Southminster, Essex; 10 North Court, Great Peter st, SW1

STANTON, Maj-Gen Anthony Francis; OBE (1955); s of Brig-Gen Francis Henry Guy Stanton (d 1928); *b* 6 Aug 1915; *Educ* Eton, RMA Woolwich; *m* 1943, Elizabeth Mary, nee Blackett-Ord; 1 s, 2 da; *Career* Maj-Gen Commissioned RA 1936, served Middle East & Europe 1939-45, Bt Lt-Col 1955, Brigadier 1959, Maj-Gen 1967 (ret 1970), Col Cmdt 1972-77; *Recreations* country pursuits; *Clubs* Army & Navy, MCC; *Style* - Maj-Gen Anthony Stanton OBE; Wooperton Hall, Alnwick, Northumberland (☎ Wooperton 241)

STANTON, Lt-Col John Richard Guy; MBE (1953), DL (Derbyshire 1973); s of Cdr Henry Guy Stanton RN (d 1960); *b* 28 Nov 1919; *Educ* Hon Co of Skinners Sch, Sandhurst; *m* 1941, Margaret Frances, nee Harries; 2 s, 3 da; *Career* Lt-Col Roy Sussex Regt 1939-67, Queen's Regt 1967-72, High Sheriff Derbyshire 1974-75, chm E Midlands Region National Trust 1975, chm Derbyshire Branch CLA 1980; *Recreations* country pursuits, shooting; *Clubs* Army & Navy; *Style* - Lt-Col John Stanton, MBE, DL; Snelston Hall, Ashbourne, Derbyshire (☎ 2064)

STAPLES, Sir John Richard; 14 Bt (I 1682), of Lissan, Co Tyrone; s of John Molesworth Staples (d 1948) and kinsman to Sir Robert George Alexander Staples, 13 Bt (d 1970); *b* 5 April 1906; *m* 1933, Sybella, da of late Dr Charles Henry Wade; 2 da; *Heir* cous, Thomas Staples; *Style* - Sir John Staples, Bt; Butter Hill House, Dorking, Surrey

STAPLETON, Sir (Henry) Alfred; 10 Bt (E 1679), of The Leeward Islands; s of late Brig Francis Harry Stapleton, CMG, and kinsman to Sir Miles Stapleton, 9 Bt (d 1977); *b* 2 May 1913; *Educ* Marlborough and Ch Ch Oxford; *m* 1961, Rosslyne Murray, da of late Capt Harold Stanley Warren, RN; *Heir* none; *Career* served 1939-45 War as Lt Oxfordshire and Bucks LI; *Recreations* cricket umpiring; *Clubs* Garrick and MCC; *Style* - Sir Alfred Stapleton, Bt; Mereworth, Mill Lane, Donhead St Andrew, Shaftesbury, Dorset

STAPLETON, David Eric Cramer; s of Edward Eric Stapleton (d 1957); *b* 7 Nov 1933; *Educ* Royal Agricultural Coll

Cirencester; *m* 1960, Annabel Allison, da of Sir Gerald Ley, 3 Bt, TD; 4 da; *Career* partner W I Carr, now retired, memb Stock Exchange; chm Pinneys Smokehouses Ltd Dumfriesshire; farmer; *Recreations* shooting, fishing; *Clubs* Buck's; *Style* - David Stapleton Esq; Armathwaite Place, Armathwaite, Carlisle, Cumbria (☎ Armathwaite 225); 24 Parthenia rd SW6 (☎ 731 4944)

STAPLETON-COTTON, Hon David Peter Dudley; s of late 4 Viscount Combermere; *b* 1932; *Educ* Eton; *m* 1955, Susan Nomakepu, da of Sir George Werner Albu, 2 Bt; 2 s, 2 da; *Career* Lt Life Gds (Res); *Style* - The Hon David Stapleton-Cotton; Papenboom, Newlands, Cape Town, S Africa

STAPLETON-COTTON, Hon Sophia Mary; da of 5 Viscount Combermere; *b* 1963; *Style* - The Hon Sophia Stapleton-Cotton

STAPLETON-COTTON, Hon Tara Christabel; da of 5 Viscount Combermere; *b* 1961; *Style* - The Hon Tara Stapleton-Cotton

STAPLETON-COTTON, Hon Thomas Robert Wellington; s and h of 5 Viscount Combermere; *b* 30 Aug 1969; *Style* - The Hon Thomas Stapleton-Cotton

STARKEY, David Robert; s of Robert Starkey; *b* 3 Jan 1945; *Educ* Kendal G S, Fitzwilliam Coll Cambridge; *Career* historian, writer, broadcaster, research fell Fitzwilliam Coll 1970-71, lecturer in History London Sch Economics & Political Science 1972-; *Recreations* talking; *Style* - David Starkey Esq; 19 John Spencer sq, N1 (☎ 01 359 2569)

STARKEY, Henry John; s and h of Sir John Philip Starkey, Bt; *b* 13 Oct 1973; *Style* - Henry Starkey Esq

STARKEY, Sir John Philip; 3 Bt (UK 1935), of Norwood Park, Parish of Southwell and Co of Nottingham; s of Lt-Col Sir William Randle Starkey, 2 Bt (d 1977); *b* 8 May 1938; *Educ* Eton and Ch Ch Oxford; *m* 1966, Victoria Henrietta Fleetwood, da of the late Lt-Col Christopher Herbert Fleetwood Fuller, TD; 1 s, 3 da; *Heir* s, Henry John Starkey; *Recreations* cricket; *Style* - Sir John Starkey, Bt; Norwood Park, Southwell, Notts

STARSKY, Hon Mrs (Alleyne Evelyn Maureen Louisa); da of 5 Viscount Templetown (d 1981, when the title became ext); *b* 1921; *m* 1, 1947, Maj John Hackett, late RAOC; 1 s; m 2, 1961, Michael Starsky; *Career* late ATS; *Style* - The Hon Mrs Starsky; Backstreet, Dalry, Castle Douglas, IOM

STAUGHTON, Hon Mr Justice; Hon Sir Christopher Stephen Thomas Jonathan Thayer Staughton; QC (1970); s of Simon Staughton and Edith Jones; *b* 24 May 1933; *Educ* Eton, Magdalene Cambridge; *m* 1960, Joanna, da of George Burgess; 2 da; *Career* served with 11 Hussars as 2 Lt; barr 1957, Crown Court Recorder 1972-81, High Court Judge (Queen's Bench) 1981-, kt 1981; *Style* - The Hon Mr Justice Staughton; Sarratt Hall, Sarratt, Herts (☎ King's Langley 62698); 11 Wilton st, SW1 (☎ 01 235 5791)

STAVELEY, Vice-Adm Sir William Doveton Minet; KCB (1981); s of late Adm Cecil Minet Staveley, CB, CMG; *b* 10 Nov 1928; *Educ* West Downs Winchester, RN Colls Dartmouth and Greenwich; *m* 1954, Bettina Kirstine Shuter; 1 s, 1 da; *Career* Vice-Ch Naval Staff 1980-; *Style* - Vice-Adm Sir William Staveley, KCB; Ministry of Defence, Main Building, Whitehall, SW1

STEDMAN, Baroness (Life Peeress UK 1974); Phyllis Stedman; OBE (1965); da of Percy Adams; *b* 14 July 1916; *Educ* County G S Peterborough; *m* 1941, Henry William Stedman; *Career* branch librarian 1932-41, memb Bd of Peterborough Dvpt Corpn 1972-75, v-chm Cambs Co Cncl 1973-75; Baroness-in-Waiting & Govt Spokesman Ho of Lds T'port, Environment & Trade 1975-79, Parly Under-Sec Environment 1979; Oppn spokesman Environment, Local Govt, New Towns, T'port 1979-; *Recreations* reading, countryside; *Style* - Rt Hon Lady Stedman OBE; Green Pastures, Longthorpe,

Peterborough, Northants (☎ 266506)

STEEDMAN, Air Chief Marshal Sir Alasdair; GCB (1980, KCB 1976, CB 1973), CBE (1965), DFC (1944); s of James Steedman (d 1953); *b* 29 Jan 1922; *Educ* Hampton G S; *m* 1945, Dorothy Isobel, da of Col Walter Frederick Todd, late Cameronians; 1 s, 2 da; *Career* RAF 1941, Station Cdr RAF Lyneham 1962-65, Ch of Air Staff Roy Malaysian Air Force 1965-67, Assist Ch of Air Staff (Policy) 1969-71, Sr Air Staff Offr RAF Strike Cmmd 1971-72, Cmdt RAF Staff Coll 1972-75, Air Memb of Air Force Bd for Supply and Organisation 1976-77, UK Mil Rep NATO 1977-80, Controller RAF Benevolent Fund 1981-; *Recreations* sport, reading, DIY, motoring; *Clubs* RAF, Roy Selangor; *Style* - Air Chief Marshal Sir Alasdair Steedman, GCB, CBE, DFC; Gatehouse of Fleet, Kirkcudbrightshie (☎ Gatehouse 248); 8 Clarendon close, W2 (☎ 01 262 9353)

STEEL, Antony David; s of Sir James Steel, CBE, JP; *b* 1 May 1938; *Educ* Rugby, Queen's Coll Oxford; *m* 1968, Jane Harriet, da of N C Macpherson, CBE, WS; 1 s, 1 da; *Career* md Coles Cranes Ltd 1978-; dir Acrow Ltd 1980-, dir of Coles Krane GMBH, Coles France SA, Tractors India Ltd; *Recreations* field sports; *Style* - Antony Steel Esq; The Old Vicarage, Hillesden, Bucks (☎ Steeple Claydon 350)

STEEL, Brig Charles Deane; CMG (1957), OBE (1941); s of Dr Gerard Steel, JP (d 1937); *b* 29 May 1901; *Educ* Bedford, RMA Woolwich; *m* 1932, Elizabeth, da of late Col Lawrence Chenevix Trench, CMG, DSO; 2 s; *Career* Brig (E Africa, Abyssinia, Western Desert), dep Mil Sec 1949-51, head of Conference & Supply Dept Foreign Office 1952-64, head of Accomodation Dept FCO 1965-67; *Recreations* golf, gardening; *Clubs* Naval and Military, Shikar; *Style* - Brig Charles Steel, CMG, OBE; Little Hill, Nettlebed, Oxfordshire (☎ 641287)

STEEL, Rt Hon David Martin Scott; PC (1977), MP (Lib) Roxburgh, Selkirk and Peebles 1965-; s of Very Rev Dr David Steel, of Linlithgow; *b* 31 March 1938; *Educ* George Watson's Coll Edinburgh, Edinburgh U (MA, LLB); *m* 1962, Judith Mary, da of W D MacGregor, CBE; 2 s, 1 da; *Career* BBC TV interviewer in Scotland 1964-65, Lib Ch Whip 1970-75, Leader of Liberal Party 1976-, tstee Shelter 1970 (former chm Scotland), pres Anti-Apartheid Movement of GB 1966-69; broadcaster and journalist; author of *No Entry*; *Clubs* Scottish Liberal; *Style* - The Rt Hon David Steel, PC, MP; House of Commons, SW1

STEEL, Maj (Fiennes) Michael Strang; s and h of Sir William Steel, 2 Bt, JP, DL; *b* 22 Feb 1943; *m* 1977, Sarah Jane, da of J A S Russell; 1 s; *Career* Maj 17/21 Lancers; *Style* - Major Michael Steel

STEEL, Richard Hugh Jordan; s of Sir Christopher Steel, GCMG, MVO, of Southrop Lodge, Lechlade; *b* 5 Dec 1932; *Educ* Eton; *m* 1959, Lady Rosemary Villiers (b 29 June 1935), sis of 7 Earl of Clarendon; 2 s, 1 da (*see* Lady Rosemary Steel); *Career* late 2 Lt RHG The Blues; md Lazard Bros 1953-73; corporate fin dir Barclays Bank 1973- (Assist Sec HM Treasury 1969-70); *Recreations* gardening, shooting, fishing; *Clubs* Boodle's; *Style* - Richard Steel Esq; Flat 15, Rupert House, Nevern sq, SW5 (☎ 01 373 5366); The Glebe House, Notgrove, Cheltenham, Glos (☎ Guiting Power 347)

STEEL, Lady Rosemary Verena Edith; *née* Villiers; da of late Lord Hyde; *b* (posthumous) 29 June 1935; *m* 1959, Richard Hugh Jordan Steel, s of Sir Christopher Steel, GCMG, MVO; 2 s (James b 1960, Oliver b 1962), 1 da (Arabella b 1966); *Career* raised to the rank of an Earl's da 1956 after bro suc gf as 7 Earl of Clarendon; *Style* - Lady Rosemary Steel; Glebe House, Notgrove, Cheltenham, Glos

STEEL, Maj Sir (Fiennes) William Strang; 2 Bt (UK 1938),of Philiphaugh, Co Selkirk, JP (1965), DL (Selkirkshire 1955); s of Maj Sir Samuel Steel, 1 Bt (d 1961); *b* 24 July 1912; *Educ* Eton, Sandhurst; *m* 1941, Joan, da of Brig-Gen Sir Brodie Handerson KCMG CB; 2 s (1 da decd); *Heir* s, Fiennes Michael Strang

Steel; *Career* Maj (ret) 17/21 Lancers; convenor of Selkirk Co Cncl and a Forestry Cmmr; *Style* - Maj Sir William Steel, Bt, JP, DL; Philiphaugh, Selkirk

STEELE, Hon Mrs (Caroline Mary); *née* McLaren; da of 3 Baron Aberconway; *b* 24 Oct 1944; *Educ* Imperial Coll London; *m* 1, 1962, Raimund Sargent, of Massachussets; 2 s; m 2, Graham Steele; *Style* - The Hon Mrs Steele; Old School House, Great Raveley, Huntingdon

STEELE, Sir Kenneth Charles; DFC; s of K Steele; *b* 2 March 1913; *Educ* Hawthorn H S; *m* 1947, Barbara Harrison; 1 s, 1 da; *Career* gp chm The Myer Emporium Ltd; kt 1981; *Style* - Sir Kenneth Steele DFC; 212 Doncaster rd, N Balwyn, Victoria 3104, Australia

STEELE, Lt Col Robert; MBE (1955); s of the late Robert Steele; *b* 31 July 1920; *Educ* Marlborough, Freiburg U, Sandhurst; *m* 1946, Gyllian Diane, da of the late Lt-Col Kenneth Greville Williams OBE; 2 s, 1 da; *Career* Gren Guards 1939-60, Dir Staff College Camberley 1956-57, Cmd 1 Bn 1957-60; one of HM Bodyguard of Gentleman-at-Arms 1969-; chm: Boat Showrooms of London 1961-64, Boat Showrooms of Birmingham 1962-66, Speedy Transport (Belgravia) Ltd 1973-; JP (Hants) 1972-79; memb Exec Ctee C of E Children's Society 1966-, vice-chm 1976-; *Recreations* sailing, shooting, riding; *Clubs* White's, Royal Yacht Squadron; *Style* - Lt Col Robert Steele MBE; St Leonards Grange, Beaulieu, Hants (☎ 059063 268)

STEENGRACHT VAN MOYLAND, Mevrouw Jan; Hon Cecily; *née* Somerset; da of 4 Baron Raglan, JP; *b* 10 Aug 1938; *m* 1961, Jonkheer Jan Tewdyr Patrick Steengracht van Moyland, Capt Irish Gds (ret; b 12 March 1933, educ Bradfield; portraitist; memb Guards' Club) and yr s of Baron Steengracht van Moyland, of Pant-y-Goitre, Abergavenny; 1 s (Jonkheer Henry Jan Berrington S v M, b 18 Dec 1963), 1 da (Jonkvrouwe Suzanna Cecily S v M, b 3 Nov 1968); *Style* - Mevrouw Jan Steengracht van Moyland; Lanwecha, Llandenny, Usk, Gwent; 14 Addison av, W11 (☎ 01 603 3522)

STEER, William Reed Hornby; DL (London 1950); s of Rev William Henry Hornby Steer, TD, JP (d 1938); *b* 5 April 1899; *Educ* Eton, Trin Coll Cambridge; *Career* KStJ (1951); Lt-Col RA 1917-19, Dep Judge Advocate Gen Malta 1941-43; barr 1922, Recorder S Molton 1936-51; dep chm LCC 1948-49, Master Worshipful Co of Turners 1949; *Clubs* Roy Corinthian Yacht, Oxford and Cambridge, Carlton, Pratt's, MCC; *Style* - William Steer Esq DL; 71A Whitehall Court, SW1 (☎ 01 930 3160)

STEINBERG, Jack; s of Alexander Steinberg (d 1957); *b* 23 May 1913; *Educ* privately, London; *m* 1938, Hannah Anne, da of Solomon Wolfson (d 1941); 2 da; *Career* underwriting memb of Lloyd's, chm: Steinberg Gp 1966-, Horrockses Fashions Ltd, Butte-Knit (London) Ltd, King's College Hospital Voluntary Research Trust; memb of Plumbers' Livery Co, freeman City of London; *Recreations* farming; *Clubs* Brooks's Portland, Carlton; *Style* - Jack Steinberg Esq; Chartners Farm, Butcherfield Lane, Hartfield, Sussex; 74 Portland pla, W1

STENHAM, 'Cob' (Anthony William Paul); s of Bernard Basil Stenham (d 1972); *b* 28 Jan 1932; *Educ* Eton, Trin Cambridge; *m* 1966 (m dis), The Hon Sheila Marion, da of 1 Baron Poole, CBE, TD, PC; *Career* accountant, FCA 1958; memb Inner Temple 1954; fin dir Unilever Ltd & Unilever NV 1970-, chm Cncl (memb 1978-) & Pro-Provost RCA 1979-, Lloyd's underwriter 1978-, chm ICA 1977-; dir: Equity Capital for Industry 1976-, William Baird & Co 1964-69, Philip Hill Higginson Erlanger 1962-64, Price Waterhouse 1955-61; *Recreations* skiing, cinema, theatre, opera; *Club* Turf; *Style* - Anthony Stenham Esq; 4 The Grove, Highgate, N6 (☎ 01 340 2266)

STENHAM, Hon Mrs Sheila Marian; da of 1 Baron Poole; *b* 1940; *m* 1966 (m dis), Cob Stenham; *Style* - The Hon Mrs Sheila Stenham; 9 Albert Place, W8

STEPHEN, Sir Alastair Edward; s of Sir Colin Campbell Stephen (d 1937); *b* 27 May 1901; *Educ* Tudor House Sch NSW, Geelong Church of Eng G S Victoria, St

Paul's Coll Sydney U; *m* 1, 1942, Diana Heni, nee Allen (d 1943); 1 da; m 2, 1946, Winifred Grace, nee Bonnin; 1 s, 2 da; *Career* kt 1973, solicitor Supreme Court of New South Wales 1926-, chm of dirs Roy Prince Alfred Hosp Sydney 1962-73, pres Australia Hosp Assoc 1969-71 (ret 1976), ptnr Stephen Jaques & Stephen 1926-75; *Recreations* skiing, sailing, fishing, racing; *Clubs* Union, Australian, Roy Sydney Golf, Austrialian Jockey, Turf; *Style* - Sir Alastair Stephen; 60 Fairfax rd, Bellevue Hill, NSW 2023 (☎ Sydney 36 6402)

STEPHEN, Sir James Alexander; 4 Bt (UK 1891), of De Vere Gardens; s of Sir Harry Lushington Stephen, 3 Bt (d 1945, 1 cous of Virginia Woolf and Vanessa Bell; through him Sir James is 2 cous of Prof Quentin Bell, Virginia's biographer; Sir James is also nephew to 'JKS' (James Kenneth Stephen), whose pious memory is toasted at Eton after the Wall Game on St Andrew's Day and who was author of *lapsus calami* ("when the Rudyards cease from kipling and the Haggards ride no more") and tutor to HRH the Duke of Clarence, the er bro of George V who died young; HRH and JKS are both suspects in the endless speculation as to the identity of Jack the Ripper); *b* 25 Feb 1908; *Educ* Eton and Trinity Coll Cambridge; *Heir* none; *Career* served RA 1940-41 (when he was discharged unfit); a land volunteer worker 1941-45; certified insane 1945; franchise restored 1960; discharged from hospital 1972; FRGS; *Recreations* contract bridge; *Style* - Sir James Stephen, Bt; 44 Princess rd, Branksome, Poole, Dorset (☎ 0202 764481)

STEPHENS, Sir David; KCB (1964), CVO (1960); s of Berkeley John Byng Stephens CIE (d 1950); *b* 25 April 1910; *Educ* Winchester, Ch Ch and Queen's Oxford; *m* 1, 1941, Mary Clemency (d 1966), da of Sir Eric Gore Browne DSO OBE TD (d 1964); 3 s, 1 da; m 2, 1967, Charlotte Evelyn, widow of Henry Manisty & da of the late Rev A M Baird-Smith; *Career* Sec for Appointments to Sir Anthony Eden and Mr Harold Macmillan 1955-61, Clerk of the Parliaments House of Lords 1963-74; memb Cotswold Dist Cncl 1976; *Recreations* gardening, tennis, outdoor sports; *Clubs* Brooks's, MCC; *Style* - Sir David Stephens, KCB, CVO; The Old Rectory, Coates, nr Cirencester, Glos (☎ Kemble 258)

STEPHENS, Maj-Gen Keith Fielding; CB (1970), OBE (1957); s of Edgar Percy Stephens (d 1953); *b* 28 July 1910; *Educ* Eastbourne Coll, London U; *m* 1937, Margaret Ann, nee MacGregor; 2 s; *Career* CStJ (1966); RAMC 1936-70: Hon Surgeon to HM The Queen 1964-70, consultant advsr Anaesthetics 1957-66; Cmdt Roy Army Medical Coll London 1966-68, Dep Dir Medical Servs S Cmd UK 1968-70, MO DHSS 1970-; *Clubs* Naval & Military; *Style* - Maj-Gen Keith Stephens, CB, OBE; 3 Carnegie Place, Wimbledon, SW19 (☎ 946 0911)

STEPHENSON, Lt-Col Sir Henry Francis Blake; 2 Bt (UK 1936), of Hassop Hall, Co Derby; OBE (1941), TD, JP, DL (Derbyshire 1948); s of Lt-Col Sir Henry Stephenson, 1 Bt, DSO, VD; *b* 3 Dec 1895; *Educ* Eton; *m* 1925, Joan, da of late Maj John Herbert Upton JP; 1 s; *Heir* s, Henry Upton Stephenson TD; *Career* Lt-Col Yorkshire Dragoons; Pro-Chllr Sheffield U 1947-56; served WW I France and Belgium (1914-15 star, two medals), WW II M East; *Style* - Lt-Col Sir Henry Stephenson, Bt, OBE, TD, JP, DL; Hassop Green, Bakewell, Derbyshire (☎ 062 987 233)

STEPHENSON, Henry Upton; TD; s & h of Lt-Col Sir Henry Stephenson, 2 Bt, OBE, TD, JP, DL; *b* 26 Nov 1926; *Educ* Eton; *m* 1962, Susan, da of Maj J E Clowes; 4 da; *Career* High Sheriff Derbyshire 1975; late Capt Yorkshire Yeo; dir Stephenson, Blake (Holdings) Ltd and Thos Thurton and Sons Ltd; *Style* - Henry Stephenson Esq TD; Tissington Cottage, Rowland, Bakewell, Derbyshire

STEPHENSON, Hon Mrs - Hon Sarah Merryweather; *née* Norrie; da of 1 Baron Norrie, GCMG, GCVO, CB, DSO, MC (d 1977); *b* 1943; *m* 1974, Charles Lyon Stephenson TD; *Style* - The Hon Mrs Stephenson; The Cottage, Great Longstone, Bakewell, Derbys

STERN, Lady; Sybil Grace; da of Sir Adolph Tuck, 1 Bt; *m* 1925, as his 2 w, Sir Edward Stern, 1 Bt (d 1933); *Style* - Lady

Stern; 8 Abbey Lodge, Park rd, Regent's Park, NW8

STERNBERG, Hon Francesca Nicola; da of Baron Plurenden (Life Peer) (d 1978); *b* 1962; *Style* - The Hon Francesca Sternberg

STERNBERG, Hon Rosanne Monica Michelle; da of Baron Plurenden (Life Peer) (d 1978); *b* 1960; *Style* - The Hon Rosanne Sternberg

STEVENS, David Robert; s of Arthur Edwin Stevens CBE; *b* 26 May 1936; *Educ* Stowe Sch, Sidney Sussex College, Cambridge; *m* 1977, Melissa, Countess Andrasssy, & da of Milos Milicevich, of USA; 1 s, 1 da; *Career* Nat Serv: Lt Hong Kong; chm: United Newspapers Ltd 1981, Drayton Consolidated Trust 1980, Drayton Commercial Investments 1980, Triplevest Ltd 1979; *Recreations* golf, reading, music; *Clubs* White's, Sunningdale; *Style* - David Stevens Esq; 117 Old Broad St, EC2 (☎ 01 588 1750)

STEVENS, Hon Mrs (Henrietta Maria); *née* Hughes-Young; da of 1 Baron St Helens MC (d 1980); *b* 1940; *m* 1970, Brian Turnbull Julius Stevens; *Style* - The Hon Mrs Stevens

STEVENS, Jocelyn Edward Greville; s of Maj Charles Greville Bartlett Stewart-Stevens (d 1972); *b* 14 Feb 1932; *Educ* Eton, Trin Cambridge; *m* 1956, Jane Armyne Sheffield (m dis 1979); 2 s, 2 da; *Career* journalist; chm & md Stevens Press Ltd and editor of Queen Magazine 1957-68, dir Beaverbrook Newspapers 1971- (md 1974-77); md Evening Standard Ltd 1969-72, Daily Express 1972-74, Express Newspapers 1977-; *Recreations* shooting, skiing; *Clubs* White's, Buck's, Beefsteak; *Style* - Jocelyn Stevens Esq; Testbourne, Longparish, nr Andover, Hants (☎ 026 472 232); 14 Cheyne Walk, SW3

STEVENS, Peter Rupert; s of Surgn Capt R W Stevens RN; *b* 14 May 1938; *Educ* Winchester, Taft Sch (USA); *m* 1963, Sarah Venetia Mary, da of Air Vice Marshal H A V Hogan, CB, DSO, DFC; 3 c; *Career* 2 Lt KRRC; stockbroker, ptnr Laurie Milbank 1969-, sr ptnr 1981-; memb Stock Exchange Cncl 1974-; *Recreations* cricket, tennis, gardening; *Clubs* Farmers'; *Style* - Peter Stevens Esq; Highmead House, Alton, Hants (☎ Alton 83945)

STEVENS, William David; s of Walter Gerald Stevens, of Corpus Christi, Texas; *b* 18 Sept 1934; *Educ* Texas College of Arts & Industry; *m* 1954, Barbara Ann, nee Duncan; 4 c; *Career* management Exxon Co USA 1958-73, exec assistant to pres 1974-75, dep man Producing Dept 1976-78, v-pres Gas 1978-; md Esso Petroleum Co Ltd 1978-; *Recreations* golf, shooting, hiking; *Clubs* Les Ambassadeurs; *Style* - William Stevens Esq; 24 Harley House, Marylebone rd, NW1 (☎ 01 935 6003)

STEVENSON, Lady; Mary Sturrock Campbell; *née* White; *m* 1937, Sir Matthew Stevenson, KCB, CMG (d 1981), sometime Perm Sec Min Housing & Local Govt; *Style* - Lady Stevenson; Arden, Towncourt cres, Petts Wood, Kent (☎ Orpington 2262)

STEVENSON, Cdr Shannan; s of Ronald Cochran Stevenson (d 1934); *b* 9 March 1903; *Educ* RNC Osborne and Dartmouth; *m* 1929, Daphne Evelyn, da of Capt Albert House (d 1957); 4 s; *Career* joined RN 1916, served WW II, Cdr; md North of England Newspaper Company Ltd 1950-68, dir Westminster Press Provincial Newspapers Ltd 1953-68; pres The Newspaper Soc 1964; High Sheriff Co Durham 1963; *Style* - Cdr Shannan Stevenson; Bolton Old Hall, Bolton-on-Swale, Richmond, N Yorks (☎ Richmond 811315)

STEVENSON, Hon Mrs (Susan Mary); *née* Blades; da of 2 Baron Ebbisham TD; *b* 1951; *m* 1980, Peter D Stevenson; *Style* - The Hon Mrs Stevenson

STEWARD, Stanley Feargus; CBE (1947); s of Arthur Robert Steward (d 1964); *b* 9 July 1904; *Educ* The Paston Sch Norfolk; *m* 1929, Phyllis Winifred, nee Thurlow; 1 s, 1 da; *Career* chartered engineer; dir: General Machine Tools, Miny of Supply 1941-45, Bull Motors Ltd 1937-47; chm: South Western Electricity

Board 1948-55, Lancashire Dynamo Group 1956-59; md British Electrical & Allied Manufacturers Assoc 1959-71; chm: Wm Steward & Co Ltd, George Thurlow & Sons Ltd, Thurlow Nunn & Sons Ltd, Thurlow Wright Ltd; dir ERA Technology Ltd; pres: Organisation de Liaison des Industries Metalliques Européennes 1963-66, Electrical Industries Benevolent Assoc and Assoc of Supervisory & Executive Engineers 1971-73; *Recreations* books, music; *Clubs* Athenaeum; *Style* - Stanley Steward Esq CBE; 41 Fairacres, Roehampton lane, SW15 (☎ 01 876 2457)

STEWART OF ALVECHURCH, Baroness (Life Peeress UK 1974); Mary Elizabeth Stewart; JP (London 1949); da of Herbert Birkinshaw; *Educ* King Edward VI H S Birmingham, Bedford Coll London U; *m* 1941, Baron Stewart of Fulham, CH, PC *qv*; *Career* tutor Workers Educnl Assoc 1945-64; memb Fabian Soc Exec Ctee 1950- (chm 1963); chm Bd Govrs Charing Cross Hosp 1966-74, Fulham Gilliatt Comprehensive Sch 1974-; *Style* - The Rt Hon The Lady Stewart of Alvechurch JP; 11 Felden st, SW6 (☎ 01 736 5194)

STEWART OF FULHAM, Baron (Life Peer UK 1979); (Robert) Michael Maitland Stewart; CH (1969), PC (1964); s of Robert Wallace Stewart DSc (d 1910); *b* 6 Nov 1906; *Educ* Christ's Hosp, St John's Oxford; *m* 1941, Baroness Stewart of Alvechurch, *qv*; 2 da; *Career* MP (L) E Fulham 1945-55, Fulham 1955-79, Sec of State for Education and Science 1964-65, Economic Affairs 1966-67 (the First Sec of State 1967-68), Sec State Foreign & C'wealth Affrs 1968-70; MEP 1975-76; *Recreations* painting; *Style* - The Rt Hon The Lord Stewart of Fulham CH PC; 11 Felden st, SW6 (☎ 01 736 5194)

STEWART, Sir Alan; KBE (1981, CBE 1972); *Career* V-Chllr Massey U New Zealand; *Style* - Sir Alan Stewart KBE

STEWART, Alexander David; MBE (Mil 1945), TD; s of Lt-Col Walter Stewart, DSO, MC (gs of 9 Earl of Galloway and Lady Harriet Somerset, da of 6 Duke of Beaufort), by his w Esmé, er da of Riversdale Grenfell JP (of a jr branch of the Grenfells who became Baron Desborough and Barons Grenfell and St Just and half bro of that Mildred Grenfell who m into the Joly de Lotbinières, *qqv*); hp of cous, 13 Earl of Galloway; *b* 25 Dec 1914; *Educ* Eton, Jesus Cambridge; *m* 1948, Daphne, da of Sir Reginald Bonsor, 2 Bt, and widow of Clyde Graham; 2 s (Andrew Clyde S, b 13 March 1949, educ Eton, m 1977 Sara Pollock; David Mark S, b 28 Jan 1960), 1 da (Rosemary Zara, b 5 March 1952, m 1977 G Ian Fleming); *Career* late Maj City of London Yeomanry, served WW II; *Recreations* golf, shooting; *Clubs* MCC; *Style* - Alexander Stewart Esq, MBE, TD; North Green, Kelsale, Saxmundham, Suffolk

STEWART, Alan D'Arcy; s (by 1 m) and h of Sir Jocelyn Harry Stewart, 12 Bt; *b* 29 Nov 1932; *m* 1952, Patricia, da of Lawrence Turner; 2 s, 2 da; *Style* - Alan Stewart Esq; One Acre House, Church st, Ramelton, Co Donegal

STEWART, Alastair Lindsay; s of Alexander Lindsay Stewart (d 1977); *b* 28 Nov 1938; *Educ* Edinburgh Acad, St Edmund Hall Oxford, Edinburgh U; *m* 1968, Annabel, da of Prof William McCausland Stewart; 2 s; *Career* tutor Faculty Law Edinburgh U 1963-73, standing junior cncl Registrar of Restrictive Trading Agreements 1968-70, Advocate Deputy 1970-73, Sheriff South Strathclyde, Dumfries and Galloway at Airdrie 1973-79, Sheriff Grampian Highland & Islands at Aberdeen 1979-; *Recreations* reading, music; *Style* - Sheriff Stewart; 131 Desswood Place, Aberdeen (☎ 0224 24683)

STEWART, Lady (Christine) Daphne; *née* Hay; da of 11 Marquess of Tweeddale (d 1967); *b* 1919; *m* 1, 1939 (m dis 1947), Lt-Col David Morley-Fletcher TD; 1 s, 1 da; m 2, 1957, Lt-Col Francis Robert Cameron Stewart, late Indian Army, s of late Sir Francis Hugh Stewart CIE; *Style* - Lady Daphne Stewart; Middle Blainslie, by Galashiels, Selkirkshire

STEWART, Sir David Brodribb; 2 Bt (UK 1960), of Strathgarry, Co Perth; s of Sir Kenneth Dugald Stewart, 1 Bt, GBE (d 1972); *b* 20 Dec 1913; *Educ* Marlborough and Manchester Coll of Technol; *m* 1963, Barbara Dykes, da of late Harry Dykes Lloyd and widow of Donald Ian Stewart; *Heir* bro, Robin Alastair Stewart; *Career* md Francis Price (Fabrics) Ltd; late Bt-Col Duke of Lancaster's Own Yeo (TA); *Recreations* gardening; *Style* - Sir David Stewart, Bt; Delamere, Alderley Edge, Cheshire

STEWART, Donald Erskine; s of late Michael Stewart (gs of late Adm of the Fleet Sir Houston Stewart GCB, s of 5 Bt); hp of kinsman, Sir Houston Stewart, 11 Bt; *b* 1905; *m* 1936, Ailsa Violet Annie (d 1970), nee Forbes; 1 s; *Style* - Donald Stewart Esq; Flat 1, 5 Whitby cres, Mairangi Bay, Auckland 10, New Zealand

STEWART, David John Christopher; s (by 1 m) and h of Sir Hugh Charlie Godfray Stewart, 6 Bt; *b* 19 June 1935; *Educ* Bradfield; *m* 1959, Bridget Anne, da of late Patrick W Sim; 3 da; *Career* Capt (ret) Roy Inniskilling Fusiliers; *Style* - David Stewart Esq; High Cross Grange, Claybrooke Magna, nr Lutterworth, Leics

STEWART, Hon Lord; Ewan George Francis Stewart; MC (1945), QC (1960); s of George Duncan Stewart, MA, CA (d 1947); *b* 9 May 1923; *Educ* George Watson's Coll Edinburgh, Edinburgh U (MA, LLB); *m* 1953, Sheila Margaret, da of late Maj Kenneth Gordon Richman; 1 s, 1 da; *Career* Capt Roy Scots Gds N W Europe 1944-45; advocate Scottish Bar 1949, Home Advocate-Depute 1965-67, Slr-Gen for Scotland 1967-70, Scottish Law Cmmr 1971-75, Senator of the Coll of Justice in Scotland 1975-; appointed a Lord of Session with title of Lord Stewart 1975; *Recreations* golf, swimming; *Clubs* Caledonian; *Style* - The Hon Lord Stewart, MC, QC; 5 Munro dve, Edinburgh 13

STEWART, Hon Mrs (Frances Julia); da of Baron Kaldor (Life Peer); *b* 1940; *m* 1962, Michael John Stewart; *Style* - The Hon Mrs Stewart; 39 Upper Park rd, NW3

STEWART, George Girdwood; CB (1979), MC (1945), TD (1954); s of the late Herbert Alexander Stewart; *b* 12 Dec 1919; *Educ* Kelvinside Academy Glasgow, Glasgow and Edinburgh U; *m* 1950, Shelagh Jean Morven, nee Murray; 1 s, 1 da; *Career* pres Scottish Ski Club 1971-75, v-pres National Ski Club of Great Britain 1975-78, representative National Trust for Scotland Perth 1980-, memb Environment Panel, British Railways Board 1980; *Recreations* skiing; *Clubs* Ski Club of Great Britain; *Style* - George Stewart Esq, CB, MC, TD; Branklyn House, Dundee rd, Perth (☎ Perth 25535)

STEWART, George Rex; s of John Stewart (d 1931); *b* 8 May 1912; *Educ* Macdonald's, Rutherglen Academy; *m* 1939, Margaret Elizabeth, nee Murray; *Career* chm Rex Stewart & Associates Ltd UK, and International Markets Advertising Associates Inc New York; *Recreations* golf, opera; *Clubs* Caledonian, Royal Scotland Automobile, '21' Walton Heath & Gullane Golf; *Style* - George Stewart Esq; Old Court House, Old Court Place, London W8 (☎ 01 937 8100); Breezes, Bear Hill, Oxshott, Surrey (☎ Oxshott 2848)

STEWART, Gordon William; CVO (1964); s of James Edward Stewart (d 1913); *b* 13 April 1906; *Educ* Daniel Stewart's Coll, George Heriot's Sch Edinburgh; *m* 1935, Dorothy Swan, nee Taylor; *Career* assistant gen man British Rail Scotland 1956; chm and gen man British Rail Scotland 1967-71, chm and md British Transport Ship Management 1967-71, dir British Transport Hotels Ltd 1968-71; *Recreations* golf, gardening; *Style* Gordon Stewart Esq CVO; Creag Mor, 22 Blairforkie Drive, Bridge of Allan, Stirling (☎ Bridge of Allan 832266)

STEWART, Prof Harold Charles; CBE (1975), DL (Greater London 1967); s of Bernard Halley Stewart (d 1958); *b* 23 Nov 1906; *Educ* Mill Hill, Cambridge, Univ Coll Hosp; *m* 1, 1929, Dorothy Irene, nee Löwen (d 1939); 1 s, 1 da; m 2, 1970, Audrey Patricia Nicolle; *Career* KStJ 1969, Emeritus Prof Pharmacology 1974-, Head Pharmacology Dept St Mary's Hosp Med Sch 1950-74, consultant Miny Defence 1961-74, Gresham Prof Physics City of London 1968-70; dir gen St John Ambulance 1976-78; chm Sir Halley Stewart Trust 1978, chm Battle Trust for

Children 1979, vice-chm Medical Cncl Alcoholism and St Christopher's Hosp for Terminal Cases; *Recreations* genealogy, heraldry, voluntary work; *Clubs* Athenaeum, St John House; *Style* - Prof Harold Stewart CBE DL; 41 The Glen, Green Lane, Northwood, Middx (☎ Northwood 24893)

STEWART, Maj Henry Clark; MC (1945), JP (Stirlingshire 1951), DL (1968); s of Dr G C Stewart, (d 1929); *b* 14 April 1914; *Educ* Craigflower and Glenalmond; *Career* Roy Tank Regiment 1940-45; ironfounder; dir Grahamston Iron Co Ltd; succeeded cousin John Alexander Stewart of Inchmahome 1962; Hon Sheriff 1977; *Recreations* reading, travel; *Style* - Maj Henry Stewart MC JP DL; 12 Wellside Place, Falkirk (☎ Falkirk 23477)

STEWART, Sir Hugh Charlie Godfray; 6 Bt (UK 1803), of Athenree, Tyrone; s of Sir George Powell Stewart, 5 Bt (d 1945); *b* 13 April 1897; *Educ* Bradfield Coll Berkshire, RMC Sandhurst; *m* 1, 1929 (m dis 1942), Rosemary Elinor Dorothy, da of late Maj George Peacocke; 1 s, 1 da; m 2, 1948, Diana Margaret, da of late Capt J E Hibbert, MC, DFC; 1 s, 1 da; *Heir* s by 1 m, Capt David Stewart; *Career* served WW I France (wounded) and WW II: France, Assist Commandant Imperial Forces Transhipment Camp Durban and in Syria; late Maj Roy Inniskilling Fusiliers; *Clubs* Tyrone County; *Style* - Sir Hugh Stewart, Bt; Lough Macrory Lodge, Co Tyrone, N Ireland

STEWART, Ian William; s of late Rev William Stewart; *b* 24 March 1923; *Educ* Merchiston Castle; *m* 1953, Jane Alison, nee Cunningham; 2 c; *Career* formerly Flying Officer Italy; dir William Low & Co Ltd 1981-; *Recreations* shooting, golf, music; *Clubs* New (Edinburgh), Panmure Golf; *Style* - Ian Stewart Esq; Greenbank, Barry, Carnoustie, Angus (☎ 0241 53043)

STEWART, John Allan; MP (C) Renfrewshire 1979-; s of Edward MacPherson Stewart; *b* 1 June 1942; *Educ* Bell Baxter H S Cupar, St Andrews U, Harvard; *m* 1973, Susie, nee Gourlay; 1 s; *Career* university lecturer in Political Economy, lecturer St Andrews U 1965-70, head Regional Dvpt Dept 1971-73 (CBI), dep dir (Economics) 1974, Scottish Sec (CBI) 1976, Scottish dir (CBI) 1978; *Recreations* golf, bridge; *Clubs* St Stephen's Constitutional; *Style* - John Stewart Esq MP; 34 Rowan rd, Dumbreck, Glasgow (☎ 041 427 2173)

STEWART OF ARDVORLICH, John Alexander MacLaren; TD, JP (Perthshire); s of Maj William Stewart of Ardvorlich (d 1918); *b* 25 March 1904; *Educ* Wellington; *m* 1930, Violet Hermione (d 1979), da of late Col Sir Donald Cameron of Lochiel KT CMG JP; 1 s, 1 da; *Career* Major 6 Bn The Black Watch, served France 1939-40, Tunisia 1943, Italy 1944; landowner, farmer; V-Lt Perth & Kinross 1974- (DL 1947); *Clubs* Royal Perth Golfing Soc; *Style* - John Stewart of Ardvorlich TD JP, HM Vice-Lieut for Perth & Kinross; Ardvorlich, Lochearnhead, Perthshire (☎ 218)

STEWART, James Cecil Campbell; CBE (1960); s of late James Stewart; *b* 25 July 1916; *Educ* Armstrong Coll, King's Coll Durham U; *m* 1946, Pamela Rouselle, nee King-Smith; 1 da; *Career* dir National Nuclear Corp 1980-; dep chm Nuclear Power Co Ltd 1975-80; chm: Br Nuclear Forum 1974-, NPC Pension Tstee Ltd 1979-, Centl Electricity Generating Bd 1965-69; dep chm Br Nuclear Design & Construction Ltd 1969-75; *Recreations* gardening; *Clubs* East India; *Style* - James Stewart Esq CBE; 'Whitethorns', Higher Whitley, Warrington, Cheshire (☎ 0925 73377)

STEWART, Sir Jocelyn Harry; 12 Bt (I 1623), of Ramelton, Co Donegal; s of Sir Harry Jocelyn Urquhart Stewart, 11 Bt (d 1945); *b* 24 Jan 1903; *m* 1, Constance Shillaber (d 1940), da of D'Arcy Shillaber; 1 s; m 2, 1946, Katherine Christina Sweeney; 2 s, 2 da; *Heir* s, Alan D'Arcy Stewart; *Style* - Sir Jocelyn Stewart, Bt; Letterkenny, Co Donegal

STEWART, John Keith Watson; s of Sir James Watson Stewart, 3 Bt (d 1955), and hp of bro Sir James Watson Stewart 4 Bt; *b* 25 Feb 1929; *m* 1954, Mary Elizabeth, da of John Moxon; 2 s, 1 da; *Style* - John Stewart Esq; 22 St Petersburgh pla, W2

STEWART, Sir James Watson; 4 Bt (UK 1920), of Balgownie, Bearsden, Co Dumbarton; s of Sir James Watson Stewart, 3 Bt (d 1955); *b* 8 Nov 1922; *Educ* Uppingham and Aberdeen U; *m* 1946, Anne Elizabeth, da of Joseph Greer Glaister; *Heir* bro John Keith Watson; *Career* European War 1941-45 with RA and Parachute Regt; *Style* - Sir James Stewart, Bt; Wellwood, Fairlie, Ayrshire

STEWART, Malcolm; s (by 2 m) of Sir (Percy) Malcolm Stewart, 1 Bt, OBE (d 1951) and hp of half-bro Sir Ronald Compton Stewart, 2 Bt; *b* 20 Dec 1909; *Educ* Harrow, Brasenose Oxford; *m* 1935 (m dis 1957), Mary Stephanie, da of Frederick Ramon de Bertodano, 8 Marqués del Moral (Spain); *Career* European War 1942-45 as Lt RNVR; *Style* - Malcolm Stewart Esq; Hoy Lodge, Orkney

STEWART, Robin Alastair; s of Sir Kenneth Dugald Stewart, 1 Bt (d 1972), and hp of bro Sir David Brodribb Stewart, 2 Bt; *b* 26 Sept 1925; *Educ* Marlborough; *m* 1953, Patricia Helen, da of late John Alfred Merrett; 1 s, 3 da; *Style* - Robin Stewart Esq; Walter's Cottage, Little Baddow, Essex

STEWART, Sir Ronald Compton; 2 Bt (UK 1937), of Stewartby, Co Bedford; DL (Beds 1974); s of Sir Malcolm Stewart, 1 Bt, OBE (d 1951); *b* 14 Aug 1903; *Educ* Rugby, Jesus Cambridge; *m* 1936, Cynthia Alexandra, OBE, JP, da of late Harold Farmiloe; *Heir* half-bro, Malcolm Stewart; *Career* High Sheriff Bedfordshire 1954; *Style* - Sir Ronald Stewart, Bt, DL; Maulden Grange, Maulden, Bedfordshire

STEWART, Sinclair Shepherd; s of late Harold Sinclair Stewart; *b* 10 March 1938; *Educ* Glasgow H S; *m* 1961, Avril Marjorie, nee Gillott; 2 s, 1 da; *Career* 2 Lt Royal Artillery; dir Foote Cone & Belding Ltd 1977-; md: Underline Ltd 1970-, Overlay Studios Ltd 1976-, Richard Heath Ltd 1971-74; *Recreations* trout fishing, gardening; *Clubs* Flyfishers'; *Style* - Sinclair Stewart Esq; 2 Mornington, New rd, Digswell, Welwyn (☎ Welwyn 6509)

STEWART, Prof William Alexander Campbell; DL (Staffs 1972); s of Thomas Stewart (d 1921); *b* 17 Dec 1915; *Educ* Colfe's G S, London U, Ulster U; *m* 1947, Ella Elizabeth, nee Burnett; 1 s, 1 da; *Career* schoolmaster 1938-44, lecturer (Nottingham and Wales Us) 1944-50, Prof 1950-67; Vice Chancellor Keele U 1967-79; *Recreations* music, theatre; *Clubs* Athenaeum, Oriental; *Style* - Prof William Stewart DL; 42 Dean Court rd, Rottingdean, Brighton

STEWART-CLARK, Alexander Dudley; s and h of Sir John Stewart-Clark, 3 Bt; *b* 21 Nov 1960; *Style* - Alexander Stewart-Clark Esq

STEWART-CLARK, Sir John; 3 Bt (UK 1918), of Dundas, W Lothian, MEP (C) 1979-; s of Sir Stewart Stewart-Clark, 2 Bt (d 1971); *b* 17 Sept 1929; *Educ* Eton, Balliol Oxford, Harvard Business Sch; *m* 1958, Lydia Fredericke, da of Jonkheer James William Loudon, of The Netherlands; 1 s, 4 da; *Heir* s, Alexander Stewart-Clark; *Career* dir Cope Allman Internat Ltd, European advsr AT Kearney Management Consultants; memb Cncl Roy Utd Servs Inst; late Lt Coldstream Gds; stood for Parl 1959 C & U Aberdeen N; memb of Roy Co of Archers (Queen's Bodyguard for Scotland); md: J & P Coats (Pakistan) Ltd 1961-67, J A Carp's Garenfabrieken (Helmond Holland) 1967-70, Philips Electrical Ltd 1971-75, Pye of Cambridge Ltd 1975-79, FBIM; *Recreations* golf, tennis, squash, skiing, music, travel, vintage cars; *Clubs* Hon Co Edinburgh Golfers, White's; *Style* - Sir John Stewart-Clark, Bt, MEP; Holmsley House, Holtye Common, nr Cowden, Kent (☎ 034 286 541)

STEWART-CLARK, Jane, Lady; Jane Pamela; da of Maj Arundell Clarke, of Fremington House, N Devon; *m* 1927, Sir Stewart Stewart-Clark, 2 Bt (d 1971); 1 s (Sir John, 3 Bt), 1 da (Mrs Patrick Bowlby); *Style* - Jane, Lady Stewart-Clark; Dundas Castle, S Queensferry, W Lothian

STEWART-LIBERTY, Arthur Ivor; MC (1943/4), TD (1946); s of Ivor Stewart-Liberty, MC, DL (d 1952); *b* 11 Jan 1916; *Educ* Winchester, Ch Ch Oxford; *m* 1, 1942, Rosabel Fremantle, nee Fynn (m dis

1953); 2 s, 1 da; m 2, 1955, Elizabeth Cicely, nee Stuart; 1 da; *Career* Maj, served in France 1940, Assam/Burma 1943-45; chm Liberty & Co Ltd 1953-81, dir Liberty & Co Ltd 1981-; *Style* - Arthur Stewart-Liberty Esq; Pipers, The Lee, Great Missenden, Bucks

STEWART-PATTERSON, Lady Alison Margaret Katherine Antoinette; *née* Bruce; da of late 10 Earl of Elgin and (14 of) Kincardine, KT, CMG, TD, CD and Hon Dame Katherine Cochrane DBE, da of late 1 Baron Cochrane of Cults and Lady Gertrude Boyle OBE, da of 6 Earl of Glasgow; *b* 1931; *m* 1957, Cleveland Stewart-Patterson; 2 s, 1 da; *Career* LRAM; *Style* - Lady Alison Stewart-Patterson; Drishane Farm, 251 Senneville rd, Senneville, PQ, Canada

STEWART-RICHARDSON, Ninian Rorie; s of Sir Ian Stewart Richardson (d 1969) and hp of bro Sir Simon Stewart-Richardson, 17 Bt; *b* 25 Jan 1949; *Career* late commercial air pilot; *Style* - Ninian Stewart-Richardson Esq; Rio de Janeiro, Brazil

STEWART-RICHARDSON, Sir Simon Alaisdair (Ian Neile); 17 Bt (NS 1630), of Pencaitland, Haddingtonshire; s of Sir Ian Rorie Hay Stewart-Richardson, 16 Bt (d 1969); *b* 9 June 1947; *Educ* Trinity Coll Glenalmond; *Heir* bro, Ninian Rorie Stewart-Richardson; *Recreations* music, drama; *Style* - Sir Simon Stewart-Richardson, Bt; Lynedale, Longcross, nr Chertsey, Surrey (☎ Ottershaw (719) 2329)

STEWART-SMITH, Christopher Dudley; s of Ean Kendal Stewart-Smith (d 1964); *b* 21 Jan 1941; *Educ* Winchester, King's Cambridge, Massachusetts Inst of Tech; *m* 1964, Olivia, da of Col John Barstow DSO; 1 s, 1 da; *Career* Sterling Guarantee Trust Ltd 1971-, dir Town & City Properties Ltd, dir Buck & Hickman Ltd, chm: Butler's Warehousing & Distribution Ltd 1971-, chm Earl's Court & Olympia Ltd 1974-, Sterling Gds Ltd 1974-, Sutcliffe Catering Gp Ltd 1975-; *Clubs* Travellers'; *Style* - Christopher Stewart-Smith Esq; 52 Westbourne Terrace, W2 (☎ 262 0514); Bradenham Hill Farm, West Wycombe, Bucks (☎ Naphill 3009)

STIBY, Robert Andrew; JP (1976); s of Arthur Robert Charles Stiby; *b* 25 May 1937; *Educ* Marlborough Coll, London College of Printing; *m* 1980, Heather; 1 s, 1 da; *Career* md Croydon Advertiser Group of Newspapers 1969-75, chm 1975-; dir Capital Radio 1972-, dir Chiltern Radio 1981-, vice pres Newspaper Society 1981; *Recreations* sailing, painting in oils, golf; *Clubs* MCC, Reigate Heath GC; *Style* - Robert Stiby Esq JP; The White House, Reigate Heath, Surrey (☎ Reigate 42281)

STILLWELL, Peter Frederic Thomas Cryer; s of the late Samuel Stillwell, OBE; *b* 13 March 1924; *Educ* Uppingham, Clare Coll Cambridge; *Career* physicist, electronics engr; dir Rank Research Laboratories 1970-, dir Rank Precision Industries Ltd 1975-; FIEE, CEng; *Recreations* gardening, the pursuit of trout; *Style* - Peter Stillwell Esq; The Cedars, Hillside close, Crookham village, Aldershot (☎ Fleet 7167); Flat 12, Corfton Lodge, Corfton rd, W5 (☎ 01 918 6886)

STIRLING, Sir Alexander John Dickson; KBE (1981), CMG (1976); s of late Brig A Dickson Stirling, DSO, MB; *b* 20 Oct 1926; *Educ* Edinburgh Academy, Lincoln Oxford; *m* 1955, Alison Mary, da of Gp Capt A P Campbell CBE; 2 s, 2 da; *Career* formerly HM Ambassador Baghdad; ambass to Tunisia 1981-; *Style* - Sir Alexander Stirling, KBE, CMG; c/o Williams & Glyn's Bank Ltd, Kirkland House, Whitehall, SW1

STIRLING, Duncan Alexander; s of William Stirling, JP, DL, of Fairburn (d 1914); *b* 6 Oct 1899; *Educ* Harrow, New Coll Oxford; *m* 1926, Lady Marjorie Murray, da of 8 Earl of Dunmore VC DSO MVO (d 1962); 2 s; *Career* Coldstream Guards 1918 and 1940-43; dir Westminster Bank 1935-74 (chm 1962-69), dir London Life Assurance 1935-80 (pres 1951-65), Prime Warden Fishmongers Co 1954-55; *Clubs* Brooks's; *Style* - Duncan Stirling Esq; 28 St James's Place, SW1 (☎ 01 629 1225); Lake House, Avington, Winchester, Hants

STIRLING, Lady Marjorie Hilda; *née* Murray; da of late 8 Earl of Dunmore, VC, DSO, MVO; *b* 1904; *m* 1926, Duncan Alexander Stirling, late Capt Coldstream Gds; 2 s; *Career* Order of Mercy; *Style* - Lady Marjorie Stirling; Lake House, Avington, Winchester, Hants; 28 St James's pla, SW1

STIRLING-HAMILTON, Bruce; s and h of Capt Sir Robert William Stirling-Hamilton, 12 Bt; *b* 15 Aug 1940; *m* 1968, Stephanie, da of William Campbell; 1 da; *Career* Capt late Queen's Own Highlanders; *Style* - Bruce Stirling-Hamilton Esq; c/o Glyn, Mills and Co (Holt Branch), Kirkland House, SW1

STIRLING-HAMILTON, Capt Sir Robert William; 12 Bt (NS 1673), of Preston, Haddingtonshire, JP, DL (Sussex 1970); s of Sir William Stirling-Hamilton, 11 Bt (d 1946); *b* 5 April 1903; *Educ* Winchester, Magdalen Oxford; *m* 1930, Eileen, da of Rt Rev Henry Southwell CMG; 1 s, 2 da; *Heir* s, Bruce Stirling-Hamilton; *Career* Capt RN, ret; late Cdre RN Barracks Portsmouth; served WW II (despatches); *Style* - Capt Sir Robert Stirling-Hamilton, Bt, JP, DL; Puriton Lodge, Hambrook, Chichester, W Sussex (024 358 363)

STOCKDALE, Sir Edmund Villiers Minshull; 1 Bt (UK 1960), of Hoddington, Co Southampton, JP (City of London 1948-63, Inner London 1968); s of Maj Henry Stockdale JP, of Mears Ashby Hall, Northants, by his w Florence (gda of Hon Thomas Hyde, MP, yr bro of 4 Earl of Clarendon); *b* 16 April 1903; *Educ* Wellington Coll; *m* 1937, the Hon Louise Fermor-Hesketh, da of 1 Baron Hesketh; 2 s; *Heir* s, Thomas Stockdale; *Career* Church Commissioner England 1962; one of HM's Lts City of London 1948; entered Bank of England 1921; assist to Govrs Reserve Bank of India 1935, assist princ Bank of England 1937, dep princ 1941-45; memb of Court of Common Cncl 1946, Alderman 1948-63, Cmmr of Assize 1948-63, Sheriff 1953 and Lord Mayor 1959-60; chm Holloway Prison 1951-53; Govr of Christ's, Roy Bethlem, Maudsley and Bridewell Hosps 1948-63; KStJ; kt 1955; *Recreations* shooting, drawing; *Clubs* Buck's; *Style* - Sir Edmund Stockdale, Bt, JP; Hoddington House, Upton Grey, Basingstoke (☎ 025 681 437); Delnadamph, Strathdon, Aberdeenshire (☎ 097 54 253)

STOCKDALE, Hon Lady; Hon Louise; *née* Fermor-Hesketh; da of 1 Baron Hesketh JP (d 1944); *b* 15 Dec 1911; *m* 1937, Sir Edmund Stockdale, 1 Bt, JP; 2 s; *Style* - The Hon Lady Stockdale;

STOCKDALE, Thomas Minshull; s and h of Sir Edmund Stockdale, 1 Bt, JP; *b* 7 Jan 1940; *Educ* Eton, Worcester Coll Oxford; *m* 1965, Jacqueline, da of Ha-Van-Vuong, of Saigon (now Ho Chi Minh City); 1 s, 1 da; *Career* barrister 1966; *Recreations* shooting, travel; *Clubs* Turf, MCC; *Style* - Thomas Stockdale Esq; Conington Hall, Cambridge (☎ Elsworth 252)

STOCKEN, Oliver Henry James; s of Henry Edmund West Stocken (d 1980); *b* 22 Dec 1941; *Educ* Felsted, Univ Coll Oxford; *m* 1967, Sally Forbes, da of James Dishon, of Australia, 2 s, 1 da; *Career* associate Institute Chartered Accountants 1967; dir: N M Rothschild & Sons 1972-77, Esperanza Ltd 1977-79, Barclays Merchant Bank Ltd 1979-81 (head of Corporate Advice Division), dir TV-AM Ltd; *Clubs* City University, MCC; *Style* - Oliver Stocken Esq; 25c Marryat rd, SW19 (☎ 01 946 8524)

STOCKENSTRÖM, Lady; Elaine Constance; da of Harold Burnett-Smith, of Johannesburg; *m* 1937, Sir Anders Johan Booysen Stockenström, 4 Bt (d 1957, when title became extinct); *Style* - Lady Stockenström; Maasström Estate, Bedford, Cape Province, S Africa

STOCKENSTRÖM, Dowager Lady; Mabel; da of J H Booysen, of Klip Drift, Graaff Reinet, S Africa; *m* 1896, Sir Andries Stockenström, 3 Bt (d 1922); *Style* - Dowager Lady Stockenstrom; Maasström, Bedford, Cape Province, S Africa

STOCKS, Hon Helen Jane; da of Baroness Stocks (Life Peeress, d 1975) and late Prof John Leofric Stocks DSO; *b* 1920; *Style* - The Hon Helen Stocks

STOCKS, Hon John Rendel; s of Baroness Stocks (Life Peeress, d 1975) and late Prof John Leofric Stocks DSO; *b* 1918; *Educ* Rugby, Liverpool U (BSc); *m* 1946, Beryl, da of Edward Bolton; *Career* RN WW II; *Style* - The Hon John Stocks; Flat 1, 10 The Paragon, Blackheath, SE3

STODART OF LEASTON, Baron (Life Peer UK 1981); (James) Anthony Stodart; PC (1974); s of late Col Thomas Stodart CIE, and Mary Coullie; *b* 6 June 1916; *Educ* Wellington; *m* 1940, Hazel Jean, da of late Lt Ronald James Usher, RN; *Career* farmer; MP (C) Edinburgh W 1959-Oct 1974 (stood as Lib Berwick & E Lothian 1950, C Midlothian & Peebles 1951 and Midlothian 1955), Under-Sec of State for Scotland 1963-64, Min State Ag & Fish 1972-74 (Parly Sec 1970-72); chm Ag Credit Corpn 1975-, Cttee Inquiry Local Govt Scotland; dir FMC 1980-; *Recreations* playing golf and preserving a sense of humour; *Clubs* New (Edinburgh), Hon Co of Edinburgh Golfers; *Style* - Rt Hon Lord Stodart of Leaston PC; Lorimers, N Berwick, E Lothian (☎ 2457)

STODDART, Michael Craig; s of Frank Ogle Boyd Stoddart; *b* 27 Mar 1931; *Educ* Marlborough; *m* 1961, Susan Brigid, nee O'Laccoran; 2 s, 2 da; *Career* CA; dep chm Electra Investment Trust; dir: Globe Investment Trust, J Hepworth & Sons, Bullough Ltd; *Recreations* shooting, fishing, tennis, travel; *Clubs* Boodle's; *Style* - Michael Stoddart Esq; Compton House, Kinver, Worcs; Warwick Lodge, 42 St Georges Drive, SW1

STOKE, Gordon Alexander; MBE (1942), DSC (1941); s of Stephen Stoke (d 1980); *b* 28 June 1921; *Educ* Westcliff H S; *m* 1944, Doreen, da of Engr Capt H E Le Poidevin RN (ret); 3 s; *Career* chm: Preformations Group Ltd, Tower Works Group of Companies, Gamena Ltd, European Investment Consultants Ltd; *Recreations* sailing, (yacht: 'Arbella'), theatre, opera; *Clubs* Royal Corinthian; *Style* - Gordon Stoke Esq MBE DSC; 'Meadowside', Chorleywood rd, Rickmansworth, Herts (☎ Rickmansworth 73301)

STOKER, Robert Burdon; s of Kenneth Stoker JP (d 1979); *b* 12 July 1914; *Educ* Marlborough; *m* 1941, Mildred, da of Rev Prof Allan Cameron MA BD; 1 s, 2 da; *Career* Jubilee Medal; served WW II Miny War T'port N Africa & Mediterranean; chm British Engine Insurance Co; past chm Manchester Liners 1968-79, past pres Manchester Chamber Commerce 1967-68; pres Cheadle Conservative Assoc, pres Outward Bound (Manchester); *Recreations* golf; *Clubs* St James's (Manchester); *Style* - Robert Stoker Esq; 23 Carrwood rd, Wilmslow, Cheshire, (☎ Wilmslow 524916)

STOKES, Baron (Life Peer UK 1969); Donald Gresham Stokes; TD, DL (Lancs 1968); s of late Harry Potts Stokes, of Looe, Cornwall; *b* 22 March 1914; *Educ* Blundell's, Harris Institute of Technology Preston; *m* 1939, Laura Courteney, da of Frederick C Lamb; 1 s; *Career* late Lt-Col REME; gen sales man Leyland Motors Ltd 1950, dir 1954; chm and md Leyland Motor Corpn 1968-75, ch exec 1973-75; pres British Leyland Ltd 1975-79, now consultant; dir: Nat West Bank Ltd 1960-, Opus Public Relations Ltd 1979-, Scottish Universal Investments Ltd 1980-, The Dutton-Forshaw Motor Gp Ltd 1980-; chm Two Counties Radio Ltd 1979-, British Arabian Advsy Co Ltd 1977-, Jack Barclay Ltd 1980-; kt 1965; *Recreations* yachting (motor yacht: 'Speedwell of Leyland'); *Clubs* Brooks's, Roy Motor Yacht (Cdre 1979-); *Style* - The Rt Hon The Lord Stokes, TD, DL; Branksome Cliff, Westminster rd, Poole, Dorset (☎ Bournemouth 0202 763088)

STOKES, Hon Michael Donald Gresham; s of Baron Stokes, TD (Life Peer); *b* 1947; *Educ* Southampton U (BSc); *m* 1970, Inger Anita, da of Douglas Percy; *Style* - The Hon Michael Stokes

STONE, Baron (Life Peer UK 1976); Joseph Ellis Stone; s of late Henry Silverstone; *b* 27 May 1903; *Educ* Llanelli Co Intermediate Sch, Cardiff U, Westminster Hosp (MB, BS); *m* 1932, Beryl Florence, da of late Alexander

Bernstein; 1 s, 1 da; *Career* GP; casualty offr & house surgeon Westminster Hosp 1925-26, sr house surg N Staffs Roy Infirmary 1926-28, MO St George in the East Hosp 1928-32, Capt RAMC, graded Med Specialist UK & Europe WW II; PM's personal physician 1964-70 & 1974-76; kt 1970; *Style* - The Rt Hon Lord Stone; 615 Finchley rd, NW3 (☎ 01 435 7333)

STONE, Hon Mrs (Jane Towneley); *née* Strachey; da of late Hon (Thomas) Anthony Edward Towneley Strachey and sis of 4 Baron O'Hagan; *b* 1953; *m* 1972, William Stone; *Style* - The Hon Mrs Stone

STONE, Philip; s of Carl Stone (d 1939); *b* 17 July 1914; *m* 1949, Gladys Christine, da of the late Captain Richard Stevens, RN (d 1966); *Career* underwriting member of Lloyd's, elected 1965; *Style* - Philip Stone Esq; Flat B, 3 Curzon Place, Park Lane, W1 (☎ 01 499 2646)

STONE, Peter John; s of Dr Thomas Scott Stone, MD, MRCP; *b* 24 June 1946; *Educ* King's Sch Canterbury, Christ's Coll Cambridge; *m* 1972, Alison, da of Robert Smith Moffett, of Emsworth, Hants; 1 s, 1 da; *Career* slr, ptnr Clintons 1972-75; banking dir Close Brothers Ltd 1975-; *Recreations* cricket, hot-air ballooning, tennis, choral singing, travel; *Style* - Peter Stone Esq; c/o Lloyds Bank Ltd; 113-116 Leadenhall st, EC3

STONE, Hon Richard Malcolm Ellis; s of Baron Stone (Life Peer); *b* 1937; *Educ* MA (Jurisprudence) Oxford; *m* 1970, Ruth Perry; *Career* BM, BCh, MRCGP; *Style* - The Hon Richard Stone; 15 Blenheim rd, NW8

STONE, Terence Reginald Stewart; s of Harry Victor Stone; *b* 18 Aug 1928; *Educ* Willesden Tech Coll, Regent St Poly, Coll of Architecture; *m* 1952, Beryl Joan, nee Stewart; 6 c; *Career* chm Terence Stone Group of Companies 1970-81, md-Terence Stone (Development) Ltd 1962-81, Terence Stone (Construction) Ltd 1975-81, chief architect Costain (West Africa) Ltd 1956-60; *Recreations* badminton, swimming, running, motor rallying, sponsorship of sport; *Clubs* Rolls Royce E C; *Style* - Terence Stone Esq; Treston House, Dawlish, Devon (☎ Dawlish 863543); Treston Court, Dawlish, Devon; Stonelands House, Ashcombe rd, South Devon

STONHOUSE, Rev Michael Philip; s and h of Sir Philip Allan Stonhouse, 18 Bt; *b* 4 Sept 1948; *Educ* Wycliffe Coll Toronto; *m* 1977, Colleen Coueill, of Toronto, Canada; 1 s; *Style* - Rev Michael Stonhouse; 521/12 St SW, Medicine Hat, Alberta, Canada

STONHOUSE, Sir Philip Allan; 18 & 15 Bt (E 1628 & 1670), of Radley, Berkshire; s of Sir Arthur Stonhouse, 17 & 14 Bt (d 1967); *b* 24 Oct 1916; *Educ* W Canada Coll, Queen's U, Alberta U; *m* 1946, Winnifred, da of John Shield; 2 s; *Heir* s, Michael Stonhouse; *Career* admin manager; former gold miner, rancher, assessor; *Recreations* golf, skiing, travel, shooting; *Clubs* Medicine Hat Ski, Connaught Golf; *Style* - Sir Philip Stonhouse, Bt; 521, 12th Street South West, Medicine Hat, Alberta, Canada (☎ 403 526 5832)

STONOR, Hon Alina Mary; da of 7 Baron Camoys; *b* 15 May 1967; *Style* - The Hon Alina Stonor

STONOR, Hon Emily Mary Julia; da of 7 Baron Camoys; *b* 6 Oct 1969; *Style* - The Hon Emily Stonor

STONOR, Hon Georgina Mary Hope; da of late 6 Baron Camoys; *b* 8 Nov 1941; *Educ* St Mary's Convent Ascot; *Style* - The Hon Georgina Stonor; Flat 24, 7 Elm Park gdns, SW10 (☎ 01 351 0965); Stonor Park, Stonor, Henley-on-Thames, Oxon (☎ Turville Heath (STD Code 049 163) 645)

STONOR, Hon John Edmund Robert; s of late 6 Baron Camoys; *b* 1946; *Educ* Beaumont and Oscott Coll; *Style* - The Hon John Stonor; The Dower House, Stonor, Henley-on-Thames, Oxon

STONOR, Hon Sophia Ulla; da of 7 Baron Camoys; *b* 29 Sept 1971

STONOR, Hon (Ralph) William

Robert Thomas; s and h of 7 Baron Camoys; *b* 10 Sept 1974; *Style* - The Hon William Stonor

STONOR-SAUNDERS, Hon Mrs Julia Maria Cristina Mildred; *née* Stonor; da of late 6 Baron Camoys; *b* 1939; *Educ* St Mary's Convent Ascot; *m* 1963 (m dis 1977), Donald Robin Slomnicki Saunders; 1 s, 1 da; *Career* assumed additional name of Stonor 1978; *Style* - The Hon Mrs Julia Stonor-Saunders; 90 Burnthwaite rd, Fulham, SW6

STOPFORD, Hon Mrs Arthur - Elsa; da of late William Edward Hinke, of Gothenburg, Sweden, and widow of Carl von Wendt, of Abo, Finland; *m* 1932, as his 2 w, Vice-Adm Hon Arthur Stopford CMG (d 1955, s of 6 Earl of Courtown); *Style* - The Hon Mrs Arthur Stopford; 8 Scotts av, Shortlands, Bromley, Kent

STOPFORD, Hon Edward Richard Barrington; s of late 7 Earl of Courtown; *b* 1914; *Educ* Stowe; *m* 1, 1946, Ann Marie Elizabeth Douglas (d 1976), da of late Brig Harold Gordon Henderson CBE; 2 s, 1 da; m 2, 1978, Mrs Millicent Davies; 1 da; *Career* formerly Capt Roy Norfolk Regt; *Style* - The Hon Edward Stopford; 40 Perry st, Wendover, Bucks

STOPFORD, Hon Jeremy Neville; s of late 8 Earl of Courtown and hp of bro, 9 Earl; *b* 22 June 1958; *Educ* Eton; *Style* - The Hon Jeremy Stopford

STOPFORD, Lady Marjorie Gertrude; da of 6 Earl of Courtown; *b* 1904; *Style* - Lady Marjorie Stopford; 40 Herkomer rd, Bushey, Herts (☎ 01 950 1062)

STOPFORD, Lady Rosemary Katharine; da of late 7 Earl of Courtown; *b* 1911; *Style* - Lady Rosemary Stopford; Bartrum, Mountfield, Robertsbridge, Sussex

STOPFORD, Hon Thomas; s of Baron Stopford of Fallowfield (Life Peer, d 1961); *b* 1921; *Educ* Manchester G S, Manchester U; *m* 1943, Mary Howard, da of late Alfred James Small, of Manchester; 1 s; *Career* Capt RA WW II; *Style* - The Hon Thomas Stopford; 85 Higher Woolbrook Park, Sidmouth, Devon

STOPFORD, Hon Terence Victor; s of late 7 Earl of Courtown; *b* 1918; *Educ* Eton; *m* 1951, Sheila Adèle, nee Page; 3 s, 1 da; *Career* Capt RN (ret); Ch of Staff to CIC Naval Home Command 1965-67, Ch Staff Offr to Flag Offr Gibraltar 1967-69, Naval ADC to HM 1969; *Style* - The Hon Terence Stopford; Lake End House, Dorney, Windsor, Berks

STOREY, Kenelm; s and h of Sir Richard Storey, 2 Bt; *b* 4 Jan 1963; *Educ* Winchester; *Style* - Kenelm Storey Esq

STOREY, Leonard Charles; s of Herbert James Storey (d 1944); *b* 12 Aug 1910; *Educ* LCC Central Sch; *m* 1952, Emily, nee Hodgson; *Career* accountant; LMRSH, FinstD; dir: Collateral Securities Ltd, Dwelling Developments Ltd, 5 Grosvenor Square Management Ltd, Linit Flyte Ltd, Silvermoor Property Co Ltd, Kensington Permanent Building Soc 1954-69; *Recreations* reading, swimming; *Style* - Leonard Storey Esq; 'Kensington', 82 Malvern ave, South Harrow, Middlesex (☎ 01 422 6008)

STOREY, Hon Sir Richard; 2 Bt (UK 1960), of Settrington, Co York; s of Baron Buckton (Life Peer) (d 1978); *b* 23 Jan 1937; *Educ* Winchester and Trinity Coll Cambridge; *m* 1961, Virginia Anne, da of late Sir Kenelm Henry Ernest Cayley, 10 Bt; 1 s, 2 da; *Heir* s, Kenelm Storey; *Career* barr Inner Temple 1962; chm Portsmouth and Sunderland Newspapers Ltd; *Style* - Hon Sir Richard Storey, Bt; 7 Douro pla, W8; Settrington House, Malton, Yorks

STORMONT, Viscount; Alexander David Mungo Murray; s and h of 8 Earl of Mansfield and Mansfield; *b* 17 Oct 1956; *Style* - Viscount Stormont; Scone Palace, Perthshire

STORMONTH-DARLING, Robin Andrew; s of Patrick Stormonth-Darling (d 1926); *b* 1 Oct 1926; *Educ* Abberley Hall, Winchester Coll; *m* 1, 1956 (m dis 1974), Susan Clifford-Turner; 3 s, 1 da; m 2, 1974 (m dis 1979), Harriet, da of Lt-Gen Sir Archibald Nye GCSI GCIE GCMG KCB KBE MC; *Career* late Capt 9 Queen's Roy Lancers; with Laing and Cruickshank (stockbrokers) from 1954 chm 1980- (partner from 1956), memb London Stock Exchange 1955-; dir: British Motor Corpn 1960-68, Br Leyland Motor Corpn 1968-75; *Recreations* shooting, skiing, flying, swimming; *Clubs* White's, City of London, MCC, New (Edinburgh), Hurlingham; *Style* - Robin Stormonth-Darling Esq; Balvarran, by Bridge of Cally, Perthshire, Scotland (☎ 025081 248); 21 Paradise Walk, SW3 (☎ 01 352 4161)

STORRY, Kenneth Charles; *b* 11 July 1923; *Educ* Hull G S; *m* 1959, Patricia Irene Frances, nee McLaughlin; 1 s; *Career* Sub Lt RNVR; dir and md Barclays Unicorn Group Ltd 1977-, gen man Barclays Unicorn Ltd 1974-, district man Barclays Bank London (SW district) 1970-; *Recreations* golf, reading, travel, sailing; *Clubs* Royal Wester Yacht, Royal Plymouth, Corinthian Yacht, Overseas Bankers; *Style* - Kenneth Storry Esq; 96 Higher Drive, Banstead, Surrey (☎ 01 393 2472)

STOTHART, William; *b* 29 Sept 1926; *Educ* Quarry Bank H S Liverpool, Downing Coll Cambridge; *m* 1958, Margaret Elizabeth, nee Bowden; 1 s, 1 da; *Career* company secretary and dir Owen Owen Ltd; *Recreations* golf, fell walking, photography; *Style* - William Stothart Esq; 6 Croome drive, West Kirby, Wirral, Merseyside

STOTHERS, Thomas; s of late Robert James Stothers; *b* 24 July 1926; *Educ* Belfast Tech Coll; *m* 1952, Florence Elizabeth, nee Simms; 2 s; *Career* FCIOB (1976), FCSI (1970), Fellow Inst of Dir (1959), md H & J Martin Ltd (bldg & civil engrg contracting firm); *Recreations* golf, boating, rugby; *Clubs* Roy Belfast Golf, Ulster Arts; *Style* - Thomas Stothers Esq; 8 Cloverhill pk, Belfast, N Ireland (☎ 768964)

STOTT, Alan Edward; JP (Staffordshire 1957), DL (1969); s of Charles Ernest Stott FRES (d 1935); *b* 6 June 1910; *Educ* Repton; *m* 1, 1935, Marguerite (d 1957), da of Thomas Knowles, of Sandon Park, nr Stafford; 3 da (1 s decd); m 2, 1973, Marion, da of Dr Allen Morrow, of San Francisco, & widow of Russell Harriman; *Career* dir 1933 & dep chm 1965 Armitage Shanks Gp of England and Overseas; High Sheriff Staffordshire 1968; pres Br Ceramic Manufacturers Federation 1969 (ret 1972); *Clubs* Leander, Phyllis Court; *Style* - Alan Stott Esq, JP, DL; 8 Rupert Close, Henley-on-Thames, Oxon (☎ Henley 5732); the White Lodge, Milford, Stafford (☎ Stafford 661000)

STOTT, Rt Hon Lord; George Gordon Stott; PC (1964); s of Rev G Gordon Stott; *b* 22 Dec 1909; *Educ* Cramond Sch, Edinburgh Acad, Edinburgh U; *m* 1947, Nancy, da of A D Braggins; 1 s, 1 da; *Career* Scottish Advocate 1936, Advocate-Depute 1947-51, KC 1950, Sheriff Roxburgh, Berwick & Selkirk 1961-64, Ld Advocate 1964-67; Lord of Session 1967-; *Style* - The Rt Hon Lord Stott PC; 12 Midmar gdns, Edinburgh (☎ 031 447 4251)

STOURTON, Hon Charlotte Mary; da of 24 Baron Mowbray, (25) Segrave and (21) Stourton (d 1936); *b* 1904; *Style* - The Hon Charlotte Stourton; 2 Arthington ave, Harrogate, N Yorks

STOURTON, Hon Edward William Stephen; s & h of 26 Baron Mowbray, (27) Segrave and (23) Stourton; *b* 17 April 1953; *Educ* Ampleforth; *m* 1980, Penelope (Nell) Lucy, da of Dr Peter Brunet, of 4 Rawlinson rd, Oxford; *Style* - The Hon Edward Stourton

STOURTON, Lady Joanna; *née* Lambart; da (by 2 m) of late 10 Earl of Cavan; *b* 1929; *m* 1955, Maj Michael Godwin Plantagenet Stourton, Grenadier Gds (ret); *Style* - Lady Joanna Stourton; The Old Rectory, Great Rollright, Chipping Norton, Oxon

STOURTON, Hon James Alastair; s of 26 Baron Mowbray, (27) Segrave and (23) Stourton; *b* 1956; *Educ* Ampleforth; *Style*- The Hon James Stourton

STOURTON, Hon John Joseph; TD; 2 s of 24 Baron Mowbray, (25) Segrave and (21) Stourton (who made a claim, which was rejected, to the Earldom of Norfolk in 1906) by Mary, nee Constable; *b* 5 March 1899; *Educ* Downside; *m* 1, 1923 (m dis 1933), Kathleen, da of Robert

Gunther; 2 s, 2 da (one of whom m the 5 Earl of Gainsborough); m 2, 1934 (m dis 1947), Gladys (d 1953), da of Col Sir William Waldron; *Career* late Lt 18 Hussars, Yorks Hussars (Yeo), 10 Roy Hussars, Maj Roy Norfolk Regt (TA) ret; served with N Russia relief force 1919 and WW II; MP (U) Salford S 1931-45; *Style* - Maj The Hon John Stourton TD; Miniature Hall, Wadhurst, Sussex

STOW, Ralph Conyers; CBE (1981); s of Albert Stow; *b* 19 Dec 1916; *Educ* Woodhouse Sch; *m* 1943, Eleanor; 2 c; *Career* past pres Chartered Building Socs Inst; md Cheltenham & Gloucester Building Soc; FCIS, FCBSI; *Clubs* RAC, Rotary; *Style* - Ralph Stow Esq CBE; Shepherds Fold, Charlton Hill, Charlton Kings, Cheltenham (☎ 0242 87305)

STOW HILL, Baroness; Susan Isabella Cloudesley; da of William Auchterlony Hunter, of Spean Bridge, Inverness-shire; *m* 1940, Baron Stow Hill (formerly Sir Frank Soskice; cr Life Peer, d 1979); 2 s; *Style* - The Rt Hon Lady Stow Hill; 19 Church Row, NW3

STOWASSER, Hon Mrs (Helen Margaret); *née* Platt; da of Baron Platt (Life Peer and 1 Bt) (d 1978); *b* 1933; *m* 1954, Cecil Henry Stowasser; 3 s; *Style* - The Hon Mrs Stowasser; 1 Bird st, Herston, Queensland, Australia

STOWE, Sir Kenneth Ronald; KCB (1980, CB 1977), CVO (1979); s of Arthur Stowe; *b* 17 July 1927; *Educ* Dagenham County H S, Exeter Coll Oxford; *m* 1949, Joan Cullen; 2 s, 1 da; *Career* Perm Sec DHSS 1981-, PUS NI Off 1979-81, formerly with NI Off, UNO, Cabinet Off, and Pncpl Priv Sec to PM 1975-79; *Style* - Sir Kenneth Stowe KCB CVO; Thistlelark, Church rd, Newton, Sudbury, Suffolk

STRABOLGI, 11 Baron (E 1318); David Montague de Burgh Kenworthy; s of 10 Baron (d 1953) by his 1 w, Doris, da of Sir Frederick Whitley-Thomson, JP, MP; co-heir to Barony of Cobham; *b* 1 Nov 1914; *Educ* Gresham's Sch Holt; *m* 1, 1939 (m dis 1946), Denise, da of Jocelyn William Godefroi MVO; m 2, 1947 (m dis 1951), Angela, da of George Street; m 3, 1955 (m dis 1961), Myra Sheila Litewka; m 4, 1961, Doreen, da of late Alexander Morgan of Ashton-under-Lyne, Lancs; *Heir* bro, Rev the Hon Jonathan Kenworthy; *Career* Maj & Acting Lt-Col RAOC WW II, Capt Queen's Bodyguard of Yeomen of the Guard; Dep Ch Govt Whip 1974-, PPS to Leader of House of Lords and Lord Privy Seal 1969-70, Assist Oppn Whip House of Lords 1970-74, Oppn Spokesman on Energy 1979-; *Style* - The Rt Hon The Lord Strabolgi; House of Lords, SW1

STRABOLGI, Doris, Baroness; Doris Whitley; da of late Sir Frederick Whitley Whitley-Thomson, JP, MP; *m* 1913 (m dis 1941), 10 Baron (d 1953); 2 s, 1 da; *Style* - Doris, Lady Strabolgi; 137 Gloucester rd, SW7

STRACEY, Sir John Simon; 9 Bt (UK 1818), of Rackheath, Norfolk; s of late Capt Algernon Augustus Stracey; suc cous, Sir Michael Stracey, 8 Bt, 1971; *b* 30 Nov 1938; *m* 1968, Martha Maria, da of Johann Egger, of Innsbruck; 2 da; *Heir* cous, Henry Mounteney Stracey; *Style* - Sir John Stracey, Bt; 652 Belmont ave, Montreal 217, P Q, Canada

STRACHAN, Keith; s of Edward Gordon Kirkpatrick Strachan; *b* 29 Feb 1940; *m* 1963, Anita, nee Lake; 1 s, 1 da; *Career* dir Hargreaves Vehicle Distributors Ltd; memb Inst of Road Transport Engineers; *Recreations* caravanning; *Style* - Keith Strachan Esq; 17 Dale Park Gardens, Cookridge, Leeds (☎ Leeds 679420)

STRACHAN, Hon Mrs (Katharine Mary); *née* Howard; da (by 1 m) of 4 Baron Strathcona and Mount Royal; *b* 1956; *m* 1975, Gavin Michael Jasper Strachan; *Style* - The Hon Mrs Strachan; 13 Gayfield sq, Edinburgh 1

STRACHEY, Charles; 6 Bt (UK 1801), but does not use title; s of Rt Hon Evelyn John St Loe Strachey (d 1963), and cousin of 2 Baron Strachie (d 1973); *b* 20 June 1934; *Educ* Westminster Sch, Magdalen Oxford; *m* 1973, Janet Megan, da of Alexander Miller; 1 da; *Heir*

kinsman, Richard Philip Farquhar Strachey, b 10 Aug 1902; *Career* district dealer, representative man Ford Motor Co Ltd 1972-75, local govt offr; *Style* - Charles Strachey Esq; c/o National Westminster Bank, Warley, Brentwood, Essex

STRACHEY, Lady Mary Sophia; *née* Palmer; da of late 3 Earl of Selborne by his 1 w, Hon Grace (da of 1 Viscount Ridley by Hon Mary Marjoribanks, da of 1 Baron Tweedmouth); *b* 1920; *m* 1944, Maj the Hon (Thomas) Anthony Edward Towneley Strachey (only s of 3 Baron O'Hagan and who d 1955, having assumed by deed poll surname of mother (Hon Frances, da of 1 Baron Strachie) and additional Christian name of Towneley); 2 s (*see* 4 Baron O'Hagan and Hon Richard Strachey), 2 da (*see* Hon Mrs (F T) Gibson and Hon Mrs (J) Stone); *Style* - Lady Mary Strachey; 8 Pembroke sq, W8

STRACHEY, Hon Nino Natalia O'Hagan; only da of 4 Baron O'Hagan; *b* 1968; *Style* - The Hon Nino Strachey

STRACHEY, Hon Richard Towneley; s of late Hon (Thomas) Anthony Edward Towneley Strachey; hp of bro, 4 Baron O'Hagan; *b* 29 Dec 1950; *Educ* Eton; *Style* - The Hon Richard Strachey

STRADBROKE, 4 Earl of (UK 1821); Sir John Anthony Alexander Rous; 9 Bt (E 1660); also Baron Rous (GB 1796), Viscount Dunwich (UK 1821); s of 3 Earl, KCMG, CB, CVO, CBE (d 1947) and Dame Helena DBE, da of late Lt-Gen James Fraser CMG; *b* 1 April 1903; *Educ* RNCs Osborne and Dartmouth, Ch Ch Oxford; *m* 1929, Barbara (d 1977), da of late Lord Arthur Hugh Grosvenor, s of 1 Duke of Westminster by his 1 w, Lady Constance, nee Leveson-Gower, da of 2 Duke of Sutherland, KG; 2 da; *Heir* bro, Hon (William) Keith Rous; *Career* KStJ, Lay Canon of St Edmundsbury Cathedral, FRSA, Cdr RN (ret), late Hon Col 660 Heavy Anti-Aircraft Regt RA (TA), Lord-Lt of Suffolk 1948-78; agriculturalist and forester; dir Daejan Holdings Ltd, Nat V-Pres Br Legion and Pres E Area; *Style* - The Rt Hon The Earl of Stradbroke; Henham, Wangford, Beccles, Suffolk (☎ Wangford 212/214)

STRAFFORD, 7 Earl of (UK 1847); Robert Cecil Byng; also Baron Strafford (UK 1835), Viscount Enfield (UK 1847); s of late Hon Ivo Francis Byng (s of 5 Earl; the 1 Earl was paternal ggs of 1 Viscount Torrington); suc unc, 6 Earl, 1951; *b* 29 July 1904; *m* 1, 1934 (m dis 1947), Maria Magdalena Elizabeth, da of late Henry Cloete CMG, of Alphen, S Africa; 2 s; m 2, 1948, Clara Evelyn, da of late Sir Nusserwanjee Nowrosjee Wadia, KBE, CIE; *Heir* s, Viscount Enfield; *Style* - The Rt Hon The Earl of Strafford; c/o C Hoare & Co, 37 Fleet st, EC4

STRAIGHT, Lady Daphne Margarita; *née* Finch Hatton; da of 14 (& 9) Earl of Winchilsea and Nottingham by Margaretta, only surviving da of Anthony Joseph Drexel, s of the Anthony Drexel who founded the banks of Drexel, Morgan & Co New York, and Drexel, Harjes & Co Paris, also the Drexel Inst of Art, Science & Industry in Philadelphia with an endowment of two million dollars at 1891 prices; *b* 1913; *m* 1935, Air Cdre Whitney Straight (d 1979, a memb of the celebrated American family of Whitney); 2 da; *Style* - Lady Daphne Straight; 3 Aubrey Walk, W8 (☎ 01 727 7822)

STRAKER, Hon Mrs (Ann Geraldine); *née* Milne; da of 2 Baron Milne; *b* 1946; *m* 1969, Ian Frederick Lawrence Straker; 1 s; *Style* - The Hon Mrs Straker; Kentbrook, Little Browns Lane, Edenbridge, Kent

STRANG, 2 Baron (UK 1954); Colin Strang; s of 1 Baron, GCB, GCMG, MBE (d 1978); *b* 12 June 1922; *Educ* Merchant Taylors', St John's Oxford (MA, BPhil); *m* 1, 1948, Patricia Marie, da of Meiert C Avis, of Johannesburg, S Africa; m 2, 1955, Barbara Mary Hope (Linguistics and Eng Lang Prof Newcastle U), da of Frederick Albert Carr, of Wimbledon; 1 da; *Heir* none; *Career* Prof of Philosophy Newcastle U; *Style* - The Rt Hon The Lord Strang; c/o The University, Newcastle upon Tyne

STRANG, Christopher Forrest; s of John Strang (d 1971); *b* 31 May 1926; *Educ* Glasgow Academy, Glasgow U; *m* 1956, Kathleen Mayfield, nee Fetherston;

1 s, 2 da; *Career* chartered accountant, chm Ault & Wiborg Group Ltd; *Recreations* social charity works, golf; *Clubs* Caledonian, RAC; *Style* - Christopher Strang Esq; Lyncourt, 4 Clifton rd, SW19 (☎ 01 946 5765)

STRANG, Hon Caroline Jane; da (by 2 m) of 2 Baron Strang; *b* 1957; *Style* - The Hon Caroline Strang

STRANG, Hon Jean; da of late 1 Baron Strang, GCB, GCMG, MBE; *b* 1921; *Style* - The Hon Jean Strang; 39 Rutland Gate, SW7

STRANGE, 15 Baron (E 1628); John Drummond of Megginch; 10 of Megginch; s of late Capt Malcolm Drummond, JP, DL, 9 of Megginch and ggs of Lady Charlotte, nee Murray (da of 4 Duke of Atholl and 9 Baron Strange, himself fifth in descent from James Stanley, later 7 Earl of Derby, effectively cr Baron Strange; James's w was Charlotte, da of Claude de la Trémoïlle, Duc de Thouars, whose own w was also named Charlotte and was da of William The Silent, Prince of Orange) who m 2, Adm Sir Adam Drummond of Megginch, KCH; suc 1964, on termination of abeyance; *b* 6 May 1900; *Educ* Eton; *m* 1928, Violet Margaret Florence (d 1975), da of Sir Robert William Buchanan-Jardine, 2 Bt; 3 da (co-heiresses presumptive, *see* Hon Mrs (J C) Drummond of Megginch, Hon Mrs (H M) Currey, Hon Mrs (M A I) Agnew-Somerville); *Career* late Lt Gren Gds, author (as John Drummond) of 10 books of fact and fiction, including *The Bride Wore Black* 1942; *Style* - The Rt Hon The Lord Strange; The Mill House, Santon, Isle of Man

STRANGE, Raymond Charles; s of Harry Charles Strange (d 1974); *b* 4 March 1922; *Educ* Raine's Fndn Sch; *m* 1950, Margaret Helen Gummer; 1 da; *Career* Lt RE; chm Stenhouse Reed Shaw Ltd (underwriting agencies); dir Stenhouse Hldgs Ltd, Reed Stenhouse Cos Ltd; v-pres Société Générale de Courtage d'Assurances, Paris; *Recreations* driving, riding, golf, fishing; *Style* - Raymond Strange Esq; 10 Clarence ter, NWl (☎ 01 723 3703); Lower Farm House, Broadwell, Moreton-in-Marsh, Glos (☎ Stow-on-the-Wold (0451) 30250)

STRATHALLAN, Viscount; John Eric Drummond; s and h of 17 Earl of Perth, PC; *b* 7 July 1935; *m* 1963 (m dis 1972), Margaret Ann, da of Robert Gordon; 2 s; *Heir* s, Hon James Drummond; *Style* - Viscount Strathallan; Stobhall, by Perth

STRATHALMOND, 3 Baron (UK 1955); William Robertson Fraser; s of 2 Baron, CMG, OBE, TD (d 1976); *b* 22 July 1947; *Educ* Loretto; *m* 1973, Amanda Rose, da of Rev Gordon Clifford Taylor, of St Giles-in-the-Fields Rectory, Gower st, WC1; 2 s; *Heir* s, Hon William Fraser; *Style* - The Rt Hon The Lord Strathalmond; 8 Stokenchurch st, SW6 (☎ 01 736 6191)

STRATHALMOND, Letitia, Baroness; Letitia; da of late Walter Martin Krementz, of Morristown, New Jersey, USA; *m* 1945, 2 Baron, CMG, OBE, TD (d 1976); 1 s, 2 da; *Style* - The Rt Hon Letitia, Lady Strathalmond; Hillfields Farm, Lower Basildon, Berks

STRATHAVON AND GLENLIVET, Lord; Alistair Granville Gordon; s and h of Earl of Aboyne, and gs of 12 Marquess of Huntly; *b* 26 July 1973; *Style* - Lord Strathavon and Glenlivet

STRATHCARRON, 2 Baron (UK 1936); Sir David William Anthony Blyth Macpherson; 2 Bt (UK 1933); s of 1 Baron KC PC (d 1937) and Jill, da of Sir George Wood Rhodes, 1 Bt, JP; *b* 23 Jan 1924; *Educ* Eton, Jesus Cambridge; *m* 1, 1947 (m annulled 1947), Valerie Cole; m 2, 1948, Diana Hawtry (d 1973), da of late Cdr R H Deane and formerly w of J N O Curle; 2 s; m 3, 1974, Mary Eve, da of late John Comyn Higgins CIE, and formerly w of Hon Anthony Gerald Samuel, *qv*; *Heir* s, Hon Ian Macpherson; *Career* formerly Fl Lt RAFVR; motoring correspondent of The Field; ptnr Strathcarron & Co; dir: Kirchoffs (London) Ltd, Simpson & Whitelaw Ltd, Seabourne Shipping Co Ltd, Dorada Holdings Ltd; pres Guild of Motor Writers, author of *Motoring for Pleasure*; *Style* - The Rt Hon The Lord Strathcarron; 55 Cumberland ter, Regent's

Park, NW1 (☎ 01 935 5913); Otterwood, Beaulieu, Hants (☎ 612334)

STRATHCLYDE, 1 Baron (UK 1955); Thomas Dunlop Galbraith; PC (1953); s of late William Brodie Galbraith JP, of Overton, Kilmacolm, Renfrewshire; *b* 20 March 1891; *Educ* Glasgow Acad, RNCs Osborne and Dartmouth; *m* 1915, Ida Jean, da of late Thomas Galloway JP, of Auchendrane, Ayrshire; 4 s (and 1 decd), 2 da; *Heir* s, Hon Thomas Galbraith MP, *qv*; *Career* Cdr RN (ret), RN 1903, HMS Audacious and HMS Queen Elizabeth WW I; chartered accountant; MP (Nat C) Pollock Div Glasgow 1940-55, Jt Parly Under-Sec of State for Scotland 1945 and 1951-55, Min of State Scottish Office 1955-58, chm N of Scotland Hydro-Electric Bd 1959-67; *Style* - The Rt Hon The Lord Strathclyde PC; Barskimming, Mauchline, Ayrshire

STRATHCONA AND MOUNT ROYAL, 4 Baron (UK 1900); Donald Euan Palmer Howard; s of 3 Baron Strathcona and Mount Royal (d 1959) and Hon Diana, nee Loder, da of 1 Baron Wakehurst; *b* 26 Nov 1923; *Educ* Eton, Trin Cambridge, McGill U Montreal; *m* 1, 1954 (m dis 1977), Lady Jane Mary, da of 12 Earl Waldegrave, KG, GCVO, TD (*see* McIntosh, Lady Jane); 2 s, 4 da; m 2, 1978, Patricia, da of late Harvey Evelyn Thomas and widow of John Middleton; *Heir* s, Hon Donald Howard; *Career* late Lt RNVR; v-chm Maritime Tst, pres UK Pilots Assoc and Steamboat Assoc of GB, a Lord in Waiting to HM (Govt Whip) 1973-74, Parly Under-Sec of State for RAF 1974, Jt Dep Leader of the Oppn House of Lords 1976-79, Min of State MOD 1979-81; *Style* - The Rt Hon The Lord Strathcona and Mount Royal; 1 Highbury rd, SW19 (☎ 01 947 8157); House of Lords, SW1; Kiloran, Isle of Colonsay, Scotland (Colonsay 301)

STRATHCONA AND MOUNT ROYAL, Diana, Baroness; Hon Diana Evelyn; *née* Loder; da (twin) of late 1 Baron Wakehurst; *b* 1899; *m* 1922, 3 Baron (d 1959); *Style* - The Rt Hon Diana, Lady Strathcona and Mount Royal; The Orchard, School Lane, Headbourne Worthy, Winchester, Hants

STRATHEDEN AND CAMPBELL, 4 Baron (UK 1836, UK 1841); Alastair Campbell; CBE (1964), DL (Roxburgh 1946); s of late Hon John Beresford Campbell DSO and Hon Alice Susan, da of 1 Baron Hamilton of Dalzell; suc gf, 3 Baron, 1918; *b* 21 Nov 1899; *Educ* Eton, Sandhurst; *m* 1, 1923, Jean Helen St Clair, CBE (d 1956), da of Col William Anstruther-Gray, gggs of 2 Bt (Anstruther NS 1694); 3 da; m 2, 1964, Mrs Noël Christabel Vincent, da of late Capt Conrad Viner; *Heir* bro, Hon Gavin Campbell; *Career* Brig (ret), late Coldstream Gds (Col Cmdg 1945-6), Capt Roy Co of Archers (Queen's Body Guard for Scotland); Dep Dir Personal Servs War Office 1949-50; chm Edinburgh & E Scotland Coll of Ag 1956-70; chm Roxburgh, Berwick & Selkirk T&AFA 1958-63, Hill Farming Res Org 1958-69; convener Roxburgh CC 1960-68, pres Assoc of CCs Scotland 1966-68, chm Historic Buildings Cncl Scotland 1969-76; Vice-Lt Roxburgh 1962-75; *Style* - The Rt Hon The Lord Stratheden and Campbell, CBE, DL; Hunthill, Jedburgh, Scotland (☎ Jedburgh 2413)

STRATHMORE AND KINGHORNE, 17 Earl of (S 1606 and 1677); Fergus Michael Claude Bowes Lyon; DL (Angus 1973); also Lord Glamis (S 1445), Earl of Kinghorne (S 1606), Lord Glamis, Tannadyce, Sidlaw and Strathdichtie, Viscount Lyon and Earl of Strathmore and Kinghorne by special charter (S 1677), Baron Bowes (UK 1887), Earl of Strathmore and Kinghorne (UK 1937); s of Hon Michael Claude Hamilton Bowes Lyon (s of 14 Earl and who d 1953), and nephew of HM Queen Elizabeth The Queen Mother (*see* Royal Family); suc cous 1972; *b* 31 Dec 1928; *Educ* Eton, RMA Sandhurst; *m* 1956, Mary Pamela, da of Brig Norman Duncan McCorquodale, MC (himself er bro of 1 Baron McCorquodale of Newton), whereby Lady Strathmore and Kinghorne is 2 cous of Countess Spencer, Ian McCorquodale (chm of Debrett's Peerage Ltd) and Lady Denham, sis-in-law to Mrs Euan McCorquodale (temporary Lady-in-Waiting to Duke and Duchess of Kent), and 2 cous once removed to Lady Sarah McCorquodale's husb Neil (the Neil

McCorquodales being bro-in-law & sis respectively to HRH The Princess of Wales); 1 s, 2 da; *Heir* s, Lord Glamis; *Career* formerly Capt Scots Gds, memb of Roy Co of Archers (Queen's Bodyguard Scotland); memb Edinburgh Stock Exchange; *Style* - The Rt Hon The Earl of Strathmore and Kinghorne DL; Glamis Castle, Forfar, Angus (☎ Glamis 244)

STRATHNAVER, Lord; Alistair Charles St Clair Sutherland; also Master of Sutherland; s (twin) and h of Countess of Sutherland, *qv*; *b* 7 Jan 1947; *Educ* Eton, Ch Ch Oxford; *m* 1, 1968, Eileen Elizabeth, da of Richard W Baker, of Princeton, USA; 2 da; m 2, 1980, Gillian, da of Robert Murray, of Gourock, Renfrewshire; *Career* detective constable CID Metropolitan Police 1969-74; with IBM UK Ltd 1976-; *Style* - Lord Strathnaver; Sutherland Estates Office, Golspie, Sutherland (☎ Golspie 268)

STRATHSPEY, 5 Baron (UK 1884); Sir Donald Patrick Trevor Grant of Grant; 17 Bt (NS 1625); 32 Chief of the Clan Grant, recognised in the surname of Grant of Grant by decree of Lord Lyon 1950; s of 4 Baron Strathspey (d 1948); *b* 18 March 1912; *Educ* Stowe, SE Ag Coll; *m* 1, 1938, Alice (m dis 1951), da of Francis Bowe, of NZ; 1 s, 2 da; m 2, 1951, Olive, da of Wallace Grant, of Norwich; 1 s, 1 da; *Heir* s, Hon James Grant of Grant; *Career* late Lt-Col Gen List, Assist Ch Land Agent Def Land Servs; memb Standing Cncl Scottish Chiefs, Highland Soc London, Clan Grant Socs NZ & America; *Style* - The Rt Hon The Lord Strathspey; Elms Cottage, Elms Ride, W Wittering, Sussex

STRATTON, Vernon Gordon-Lennox; s of Undecimus Stratton; *b* 26 Oct 1927; *Educ* Eton; *m* 1952, Penelope, da of Sir Geoffrey Lowles; 3 s, 1 da; *Career* 2 Lt 11 Hussars 1946-48; Sunday Times advertisement manager 1954-56; retail dir Jaeger 1956-64; chm Vernon Stratton Ltd (ad agency) 1964-, Wilkins Campbell Ltd 1978-; chm & man RYA Olympic Ctee 1977; *Recreations* sailing (Star Class yacht VSOP**), photography; *Clubs* Roy Thames Yacht; *Style* - Vernon Stratton Esq; Binfield Manor, Binfield, Berks (☎ 0344 20946)

STRAUSS, Baron (Life Peer UK 1979); George Russell Strauss; PC (1947); s of late Arthur Strauss MP; *b* 18 July 1901; *Educ* Rugby; *m* 1932, Patricia, da of F O'Flynn; 2 s, 1 da; *Career* MP (L) Vauxhall Div of Lambeth 1929-31, 1934-50 and 1950-79, PPS to Min of Transport 1929-31, Parly Sec Miny Transport 1945-47, Ministry Supply 1947-51; *Style* - The Rt Hon The Lord Strauss PC; 1 Palace Green, W8 (☎ 01 937 1630); Naylands, Slaugham, W Sussex (☎ Handcross 400270)

STRAUSS, Hon Brian Timothy; s of Baron Strauss, PC (Life Peer); *b* 1935; *Style* - The Hon Brian Strauss

STRAUSS, Derek Ronald; s of Ronald Strauss; *b* 16 May 1939; *Educ* Eton; *m* 1967, Nicola Mary, da of Gp-Capt William Blackwood, OBE, DFC; 2 children; *Career* Lt Cdr RNR, dir Strauss Turnbull & Co Stock Exchange; *Recreations* fishing, shooting, skiing; *Clubs* White's, Turf, City of London; *Style* - Derek Strauss Esq; 17 Porchester Terrace, W2

STRAUSS, Hon Hilary Jane; da of Baron Strauss PC (Life Peer); *b* 1937; *Style* - The Hon Hilary Strauss

STRAUSS, Hon Roger Anthony; s of Baron Strauss PC; *b* 1934; *Style* - The Hon Roger Strauss

STREATFEILD, Lady Moyra Charlotte; *née* Stopford; da of late 7 Earl of Courtown; *b* 1917; *m* 1943, Lt-Cdr David Henry Champion Streatfeild RN; 3 s, 1 da; *Style* - Lady Moyra Streatfeild; Redberry House, Bierton, Aylesbury, Bucks

STREET, Alan Thomas; s of the late Thomas Albert Street; *b* 22 Jan 1928; *Educ* Uddingston and Stockport G S; *m* 1953, Betty Diamond, nee Shaw; 3 da; *Career* dir: J D Williams Group 1970, Oxendale & Co Ltd 1968, Heather Valley (Woollens) Ltd 1972, Hilton Mailing Services Ltd 1980; *Recreations* sailing (yacht: 'Milord of Ollerton'), skiing; *Clubs* Royal Welsh Yacht, Manchester Cruising Association;

Style - Alan Street Esq; Ollerton Hall, Knutsford, Cheshire (☎ Knutsford 2740)

STREET, Brian Frederick; s of Frederick Street; *b* 2 June 1927; *Educ* St Phillip's G S Edgbaston, Birmingham U, Harvard; *m* 1951, Margaret Patricia, nee Carleton; (1 s decd), 5 da; *Career* dep chm Air Products Ltd, dir public affairs Air Products Europe 1980- (md Air Products Gases Div 1975-80); dir British Cellophane Ltd; chm and md Shorko Films Ltd; chm HJB Plastics Ltd 1970-75, ch technologist Shell Chemicals UK 1964-68; *Recreations* sailing (sailing cruiser: 'Sarasota'), golf, oil painting; *Clubs* IOD; *Style* - Brian Street, Esq; Weston House, Wonersh, Guildford, Surrey (☎ Guildford (STD Code 0483) 898182)

STRETCH, James Lionel; s of Edwin Frederick Stretch; *b* 16 Feb 1935; *Educ* Tottenham G S; *m* 1961, Pamela Helen, nee Minos; 1 s, 1 da; *Career* chartered accountant, md Century Power & Light Ltd 1980-, dir Oil Operations Imperial Continental Gas Assoc 1980-; *Recreations* squash, walking; *Clubs* City of London, Anglo-Belgian; *Style* - James Stretch Esq; Clibbons, Bulls Green, Datchworth, Herts

STRICKLAND, Hon Mabel; OBE (1944); da (by 1 m) of 1 and last Baron Strickland; *b* 1899; *Career* attached Naval HQ Malta 1917-18, assist sec Constitutional Pty Malta 1921-45, v-chm 1950-52; ed Times of Malta 1935-50, of Sunday Times of Malta 1935-56; chm Xara Palace Hotel Co Ltd Malta 1949-62 and 1966-, dir Allied Malta Newspapers Co Ltd 1938-55, & Progress Press Co Ltd 1957-62, Leader Progressive Constitutional Pty 1953-, chm Allied Malta Newspapers Ltd 1950-55 and 1966-, MLA Malta 1950-53, and 1962-64, MP Malta 1964-66; CStJ; *Style* - The Hon Mabel Strickland OBE; Villa Parisio, Lija, Malta

STRICKLAND-CONSTABLE, Sir Robert Frederick; 11 Bt (E 1641), of Boynton, Yorkshire; s of late Lt-Col Frederick Charles Strickland-Constable (ggs of 7 Bt) and Margaret, da of late Rear-Adm Hon Thomas Pakenham, s of 2 Earl of Longford KP, and bro of 3 and 4 Earls; suc bro, Sir Henry Marmaduke Strickland-Constable, 10 Bt, 1975; *b* 22 Oct 1903; *Educ* Magdalen Oxford (MA, DPhil); *m* 1, 1929 (m annulled 1931), Rosalind Mary, da of Arthur Webster; m 2, 1936, Lettice, da of late Maj Frederick Strickland (2 s of 8 Bt) and Mary, da of late Sir John Isaac Thornycroft, LLD, FRS; 2 s, 2 da; *Heir* s, Frederic Strickland-Constable; *Career* Lt-Cdr RNVR; Reader (Engineering) Imperial Coll London U 1963-71; *Style* - Sir Robert Strickland-Constable, Bt; Combe Wood, Brasted, Westerham, Kent

STRICKLAND-CONSTABLE, Edina, Lady; Countess (Ernestine) Edina; da of late (4) Count von Rex (cr of HRE by Francis I 1764, recognised by Elector Frederick Augustus III of Saxony 1765; the family was from Upper Silesia), former Saxon Min in Vienna; *b* 27 Sept 1905, Vienna; *m* 1929, Sir Henry Marmaduke Strickland-Constable, 10 Bt (d 1975); *Style* - Edina, Lady Strickland-Constable; Wassland Hall, nr Hull, Yorks

STRICKLAND-CONSTABLE, Frederick; s (by 2 m) & h of Sir Robert Strickland-Constable, 11 Bt; *b* 21 Oct 1943; *Educ* Westminster, CCC Cambridge (BA); *Style* - Frederick Strickland-Constable Esq

STRIDE, Hon Mrs (Mary Pleasant Lowry); *née* Lamb; da of 1 Baron Rochester CMG; *b* 13 Oct 1919; *m* 1941, Rev Desmond Stride, Chaplain Heathfield Sch 1967-; *Career* LRAM 1939; *Style* - The Hon Mrs Stride; 16 Asmuns Hill, Hampstead Garden Suburb, NW11 (☎ 01 455 5037)

STRIDE, Hon Mrs - Hon Susan; *née* Macdonald; da of 2 Baron Macdonald of Gwaenysgor; *b* 1947; *m* 1968, David Hensley Adair Stride; 1 s, 1 da; *Style* - The Hon Mrs Stride; 80 Clarendon Drive, Putney SW15 (☎ 01 788 0394)

STRINGER, Frederick Charles; s of late John Stringer; *b* 24 June 1904; *Educ* Taunton Sch; *m* 1, 1966, Elsie, nee Warrington; 1 s, 1 da; m 2, 1973, Joan, nee Trigg; *Career* chm Wadham Stringer Ltd 1969-, Fellow of Inst of Motor Industry 1928-, Memb of Inst of Directors;

Recreations fishing, swimming, bridge; *Clubs* Royal Naval, Portsmouth; *Style* - Frederick Stringer Esq; Meonpool, Tanfield Park, Wickham, Hants (☎ Wickham 833115)

STRONG, John Clifford; CBE (1980); s of Clifford Maurice Strong (d 1967); *b* 14 Jan 1922; *Educ* Beckenham G S, London U; *m* 1942, Janet Doris, nee Browning; 3 da; *Career* Lt RNVR; HM Overseas Civil Serv Tanzania 1946-63, C'wlth Relations Office 1963, First Sec Nairobi 1964-68, Foreign & C'wlth Office 1968-73, Cncllr & Head Chancery Dar-es-Salaam 1973-78, Govr Turks & Caicos Islands 1978-80; *Clubs* Royal Overseas League; *Style* - John Strong Esq CBE; Foreign and Commonwealth Office, SW1

STRONG, Oswald Brian; s of James Beaver Strong; *b* 3 Aug 1918; *Educ* Cranleigh, National Leathersellers Coll London; *m* 1948, Margaret Mary, nee Smee; 1 s, 1 da (1 c decd); *Career* tanner; now consultant; with Strong & Fisher (Holdings) Ltd and subsidiary companies 1949-81, London Heatsave Ltd 1979-81; *Recreations* tennis, golf, gardening; *Style* - Oswald Strong Esq; Southbrook, 115 Sussex rd, Petersfield, Hants

STRONG, Richard Martin; *b* 3 Oct 1929; *Educ* Bedford Sch, Trinity Coll Cambridge; *m* 1971, Venetia Mary, nee Henderson; 1 s, 2 da (step); *Career* National Service 2 Lt, Capt TA; CA (memb Scottish Inst); dir Charterhouse Development Ltd 1965-; *Recreations* golf, photography; *Clubs* Royal Wimbledon Golf; *Style* - Richard Strong Esq; 25 Newstead Way, Somerset rd, SW19

STRONGE, Sir James Anselan Maxwell; 10 Bt (UK 1803), of Tynan, Co Armagh; s of late Maxwell Du Pre James Stronge, and 2 cousin of Capt Sir James Matthew Stronge, 9 Bt (assas 1981); *b* 17 July 1946; *Educ* privately; *Style* - Sir James Stronge, Bt; Raheenduff House, Foulks Mills, Co Wexford

STRUTT, Hon Charles Richard; s of 4 Baron Rayleigh, FRS, JP, DL (d 1947), by his 1 w, Lady Mary Clements (da of 4 Earl of Leitrim); hp of bro, 5 Baron Rayleigh; *b* 25 May 1910; *Educ* Eton, Trin Cambridge; *m* 1952, Hon Jean Davidson, da of 1 Viscount Davidson; 1 s, 2 da; *Career* late Capt RA; sometime V-Pres Church Army, memb Cncl Soc Psychical Res, Govr Felsted; dir Australian Estates Co; *Style* - The Hon Charles Strutt; Berwick Place, Hatfield Peverel, Essex (☎ 321)

STRUTT, Hon Guy Robert; s of 4 Baron Rayleigh, FRS, JP, DL, by his 2 w, Kathleen OBE; *b* 16 April 1921; *Educ* Eton, Trin Cambridge; *Style* - The Hon Guy Strutt; 47 Winchester st, SW1 (☎ 01 828 2633)

STRUTT, Hon Hedley Vicars; s of 4 Baron Rayleigh, JP, DL, FRS, by his 1 w, Lady Mary Clements (da of 4 Earl of Leitrim); *b* 19 Feb 1915; *Educ* Eton, Trin Cambridge; *Career* Capt Scots Gds (ret), served WW II; *Style* - The Hon Hedley Strutt; Mulroy, Co Donegal, Ireland

STRUTT, Hon Mrs (Jean Elizabeth); da of 1 Viscount Davidson; *b* 1924; *m* 1952, Hon Charles Richard Strutt (s of late 4 Baron Rayleigh and hp of bro, 5 Baron); 1 s, 2 da; *Career* late Capt WRAC (TA); *Style* - The Hon Mrs Strutt; Berwick Place, Hatfield Peverel, Chelmsford, Essex

STRUTT, Sir Nigel Edward; TD, DL (Essex 1954); s of E J Strutt (d 1964); *b* 18 Jan 1916; *Educ* Winchester, Wye Agricultural Coll; *Career* kt 1972, Maj Essex Yeomanry Middle East, chm and md Strutt & Parker (Farms) Ltd, md Lord Rayleigh's Farms Inc, memb Eastern Electricity Bd 1964-76, Agricultural Advisory Cncl for Agriculture and Horticulture 1973-80, pres Country Landowners' Assoc 1967-69, High Sheriff of Essex 1966; *Recreations* shooting, skiing; *Clubs* Brooks's, Farmers'; *Style* - Sir Nigel Strutt, TD, DL; Sparrows, Terling, Essex (☎ Terling 213)

STRUTT, Hon Richard Henry; s and h of 4 Baron Belper; *b* 24 Oct 1941; *Educ* Harrow; *m* 1, 1966 (m dis), Jennifer Vivian, da of late Capt Peter Winser; 1 s, 1 da; m 2, 1980, Mrs J M de Jonge; *Style* - The Hon Richard Strutt; Slaughter Farm, Bourton-on-the-Water, Glos

STUART OF FINDHORN, 2 Viscount (UK 1959); David Randolph Moray Stuart; s of 1 Viscount, CH, MVO, MC, PC (d 1971), and Lady Rachel, nee Cavendish, OBE, da of 9 Duke of Devonshire; through his mother Lord S of F is 1 cous of Rt Hon Maurice Macmillan, PC, MP; *b* 20 June 1924; *Educ* Eton; *m* 1, 1945, Grizel Mary Wilfreda (d 1948), da of late Theodore Fyfe and widow of Michael Gillilan; 1 s; m 2, 1951 (m dis 1979), Marian, da of late Gerald Wilson; 1 s, 3 da; m 3, 1979, Margaret Anne, da of Cdr Peter Du Cane, CBE, RN, and Victoria, sis of Sir John Gawen Carew Pole, 12 Bt, DSO, TD; *Heir* s, Hon (James) Dominic Stuart; *Career* late Lt KRRC, Maj 6/7 Roy Welch Fus (TA); FRICS; Page of Honour to HM 1938-40; DL Caernarvonshire 1963-68; land agent; *Style* - The Rt Hon The Viscount Stuart of Findhorn; 63 Winchenden rd, SW6 (☎ 01 736 8760)

STUART, Hon Andrew Moray; s (by 2 m) of 2 Viscount Stuart of Findhorn; *b* 1957; *Style* - The Hon Andrew Stuart

STUART, Viscount; Andrew Richard Charles Stuart; s and h of 8 Earl Castle Stewart; *b* 7 Oct 1953; *Educ* Edgarley Hall, Wynstones Sch, Millfield, Bicton Ag Coll; *m* 1973, Annie Yvette, da of Robert le Poulain, of Paris; 1 da; *Career* farmer; *Recreations* flying (Sportavia RS 180 Sportsman), hiking; *Clubs* Ebury Court; *Style* - Viscount Stuart; Gerway Cottage, Ottery St Mary, Devon (☎ 4160)

STUART, Hon Mrs (Alicia St George); *née* Caulfield; da of late 12 Viscount Charlemont; *b* 1918; *m* 1939, Gp Capt Gordon Hackworth Stuart, MD, RAF; 1 s; *Style* - The Hon Mrs Stuart; 3 Lovel Hill, Windsor Forest, Berks

STUART, Lady Bridget Anne; da of 8 Earl Castle Stewart; *b* 12 Feb 1957; *Educ* Wynstones School Glos, Cannington Coll Somerset; *Career* horticulturalist, working at Welsh Horticultural Coll Mold N Wales 1980-; *Recreations* travel, snorkelling, water skiing, walking; *Style* - Lady Bridget Stuart; Stone House Farm, East Pennard, Shepton Mallet, Somerset

STUART, Hon Chloe Anne-Marie; da (by 2 m) of 2 Viscount Stuart of Findhorn; *b* 1952; *Style* - The Hon Chloe Stuart

STUART, Hon Celia Elizabeth; da of Viscount Stuart; *b* 1976; *Style* - The Hon Celia Stuart

STUART, Charles Murray; *b* 28 July 1933; *Educ* Glasgow U; *m* 1963, Netta Caroline, nee Thomson; 1 s, 1 da; *Career* finance dir International Computers Ltd 1974-, memb bd ICL 1976-, dep md ICL 1978-; *Recreations* golf, reading, theatre; *Style* - Charles Stuart Esq; Greenaway House, Forest rd, Pyrford, Woking (☎ Byfleet 40245)

STUART, Charles Rowell; s of Charles Rowell Stuart, MBE (d 1957); *b* 20 May 1928; *Educ* St Olave's and St Saviours G S, LSE; *m* 1951, Anne Grace, nee Mingo; 1 s, (2 c decd); *Career* FRAeS, FCIT; head of Commercial Development British Airways; dir: Cyprus Airways Ltd, British Airtours Ltd, BA Assoc Companies Ltd, BA Helicopters Ltd, IAL Ltd; *Recreations* marathon running; *Clubs* Oriental, RAC, Road Runner Clubs of UK and New York, Ranelagh; *Style* - Charles Stuart Esq; Hawthorn Hill Cottage, Warfield, Bracknell, Berks (☎ (03447) 2362)

STUART, Hon Charles Rodney Stanford; s of 19 Earl of Moray (d 1974); *b* 1933; *Educ* Stowe and McGill U, Montreal; *m* 1961, Sasha A, da of Lt-Col R G Lewis, of Stow on the Wold; 3 s; *Career* late 2 Lt The Queen's Bays; *Style* - The Hon Charles Stuart; PO Box 900, Beirut, Lebanon

STUART, Hon (James) Dominic; s (by 1 m) and h of 2 Viscount Stuart of Findhorn; *b* 25 March 1948; *Educ* Eton, Thames Poly (Diploma in Estate Management); *m* 1979, Yvonne Lucienne, da of Edgar Deprés, of Ottawa; *Career* ARICS 1974; memb SDP 1981-; *Recreations* walking, gardening, swimming, yoga, metaphysics; *Style* - The Hon Dominic Stuart; 3 Stowe rd, W12

STUART, Hon John Douglas; s of late 1 Viscount Stuart of Findhorn, CH, MVO, MC and Lady Rachel, nee Cavendish, da of 9 Duke of Devonshire; *b* 1925; *m* 1, 1957 (m dis 1958), Mrs Cecile Margaret Tonge, da of G H Barr; m 2, 1969 (m dis 1972), Lady Caroline, nee Child-Villiers, da of 9 Earl of Jersey and formerly w of Gilbert Edward George Lariston, Viscount Melgund MBE, now 6 Earl of Minto, *qv*; *Career* Lt (ret) RN; *Clubs* White's; *Style* - The Hon John Stuart; 57 Shawfield st, SW3 (☎ 01 351 3000)

STUART, Hon James Wallace Wilson; twin s of 19 Earl of Moray (d 1974); *b* 1933; *Educ* Stowe and McGill U, Montreal; *m* 1958, Jane-Scott, da of Group Capt Henry Gordon Richards, of Kentucky USA and Edmonton Alberta Canada; 1 da; *Career* late 2 Lt, 13/18 Hussars; *Clubs* Atlantic Cavalry (Montreal); *Style* - The Hon James Stuart; Cowgreens, Dunphail, Moray

STUART, Lady Louisa Helena; da of 20 Earl of Moray; *b* 1968; *Style* - Lady Louisa Stuart

STUART, Malcolm Moncrieff; CIE (1947), OBE (1944); s of George Malcolm Stuart (d 1952); *b* 21 May 1903; *Educ* Sedbergh, St John's Coll Cambridge, Queen's Coll Oxford; *m* 1928, Grizel, da of Arthur Balfour Paul; 1 s, 1 da; *Career* Indian Civil Service 1927-50, reporter to Sec of State, recorder to Cncl of Lord High Commissioners (Church of Scotland); *Recreations* golf, bridge; *Clubs* New (Edinburgh), Hon Co Edinburgh Golfers; *Style* - Malcolm Stuart Esq, CIE, OBE; Old Manse, Pilmuir, Haddington, East Lothian (☎ Pencaitland 340263)

STUART, Sir Phillip Luttrell; 9 Bt (E 1660), of Hartley Mauduit, Hampshire; s of late Luttrell Hamilton Stuart and nephew of 8 Bt (d 1959); *b* 7 Sept 1937; *m* 1, 1962, Marlene Rose (m dis 1968), da of Otto Muth; 2 da; m 2, 1969, Beverley Claire Pieri; 1 s, 1 da; *Heir* s, Geoffrey Phillip Stuart, b 5 July 1973; *Career* Flying Offr RCAF 1957-62; pres Agassiz Industries Ltd; (his name does not, at time of going to press, appear on the Official Roll of Baronets); *Style* - Sir Phillip Stuart, Bt; 3 Windermere Bay, Winnipeg, Manitoba, Canada

STUART, Hon Rosalie Jane; da (by 2 m) of 2 Viscount Stuart of Findhorn; *b* 1954; *Style* - The Hon Rosalie Stuart

STUART, Lady Sarah; da of 18 Earl of Moray, MC (d 1943); *b* 1928; *m* 1947 (m dis 1977, he d 1978) 4 Baron Hillingdon; *Style* - Lady Sarah Stuart; 28 Queensdale rd, W11 (☎ 01 727 6022)

STUART, Hon Simon Walter Erskine; s of late 7 Earl Castle Stewart; *b* 22 Aug 1930; *Educ* Eton, Trin Cambridge; *m* 1973, Deborah Jane, nee Mounsey; 3 s (Thomas b 4 May 1974, Corin b 12 Nov 1975, Tristram b 16 March 1977); *Career* late 2 Lt Scots Gds, served Malaya 1949-50; assist English master Haberdashers' Aske's Sch 1961-78 (previously at King's Canterbury and Stowe); writer 1978-; *Style* - The Hon Simon Stuart; 16 Neville Drive, N2 (☎ 01 458 4149); Windyridge, Wych Cross, Forest Row, Sussex (☎ 2333)

STUART, Hon Vanessa Mary; da (by 2 m) of 2 Viscount Stuart of Findhorn; *b* 1960; *Style* - The Hon Vanessa Stuart

STUART TAYLOR, Hope, Lady; Ada Hope; da of Forrest Bertram Leeder, MRCS, FRCP, of BC, & widow of Norman Alfred Yarrow; *m* 1959, as his 3 w, Sir Eric Stuart Taylor, 2 Bt, OBE, MD, MRCP, (d 1977); *Style* - Hope, Lady Stuart Taylor

STUART TAYLOR, Lady; Iris Mary; da of Rev Edwin John Gargery; *m* 1950, Sir Richard Laurence Stuart Taylor, 3 Bt (d 1978); *Style* - Lady Stuart Taylor; White Lodge, Hambrook, Chichester, Sussex

STUART-FORBES, Sir Charles Edward; 12 Bt (NS 1626); s of late Sir Charles Hay Hepburn Stuart-Forbes, 10 Bt; suc bro, Sir Hugh Stuart-Forbes, 11 Bt (d 1937); *b* 6 Aug 1903; *Educ* Ocean Bay Coll; *m* 1966, Ijah Leah MacCabe (d 1974), of Wellington, New Zealand; *Heir* kinsman, William Daniel Stuart-Forbes; *Career* former co manager building industry; *Style* - Sir Charles Stuart-Forbes, Bt; 33 Dillons Point rd, Blenheim, S Island, New Zealand

STUART-FORBES, William Daniel; s of late William Kenneth Stuart-Forbes, 3 s of 10 Bt; hp of kinsman, Sir Charles Stuart-

Forbes, 12 Bt; *b* 21 Aug 1935; *m* 1956, Jannette MacDonald; 3 s, 2 da; *Style* - William Stuart-Forbes Esq; Omaka Valley, Marlborough, New Zealand

STUART-KNILL, Eve, Lady; Ruth Evelyn; da of Archibald Barnes; *m* 1941, as his 2 w, Sir (John) Stuart Knill, 3 Bt (d 1973); *Career* assumed surname of Stuart-Knill; *Style* - Eve, Lady Stuart-Knill; 7 Barton Close, Berrow, Burnham-on-Sea, Som

STUART-MENTETH, Charles Grieves; s and h of Sir James Wallace Stuart-Menteth, 6 Bt; *b* 25 Nov 1950; *m* 1976, Nicola Mary Jane, da of Vincent Charles Raleigh St Lawrence; 2 da; *Style* - Charles Stuart-Menteth Esq; Partridge Corner, Crudgington, Salop

STUART-MENTETH, Sir James Wallace; 6 Bt (UK 1838), of Closeburn, Dumfriesshire, and Mansfield, Ayrshire; s of Sir William Frederick Stuart-Menteth, 5 Bt (d 1952); *b* 13 Nov 1922; *Educ* Fettes, St Andrews U, Trin Oxford; *m* 1949, (Dorothy) Patricia, da of late Frank Grieves Warburton, of Thorrington, Stirling; 2 s; *Heir* s, Charles Stuart-Menteth; *Career* sometime Lt Scots Gds; with Paints Div ICI Ltd; *Style* - Sir James Stuart-Menteth, Bt; Broomhurst, Deepcut, Camberley, Surrey

STUART-SMITH, Hon Mr Justice; Hon Sir Murray Stuart-Smith; QC (1970); s of Edward Stuart-Smith and Doris Laughland; *b* 18 Nov 1927; *Educ* Radley, CCC Cambridge; *m* 1953, Joan Motion; 3 s, 3 da; *Career* barr 1952, Crown Court Recorder 1972-81, High Court Judge (Queen's Bench) 1981-; kt 1981; memb Criminal Injuries Compensation Bd 1980-; *Style* - The Hon Mr Justice Stuart-Smith; Serge Hill, Abbots Langley, Herts (☎ King's Langley 62116)

STUCLEY, Sir Dennis Frederic Bankes; 5 Bt (UK 1859), of Affeton Castle, Devonshire, JP (Devon 1937), DL (1955); s of 4 Bt (d 1956); *b* 29 Oct 1907; *Educ* Harrow, RMC; *m* 1932, Hon Sheila Margaret Warwick, da of 4 Baron Poltimore (d 1965); 1 s, 4 da; *Heir* s, Hugh George Coplestone Bampfylde Stucley, b 8 Jan 1945; *Career* Lt Gren Gds 1927-32, Capt Roy Devon Yeo 1938, Maj 1944; master Hartland Harriers 1932-35, jt master W Dulverton foxhounds 1952-54, Co Alderman Devon 1955, High Sheriff 1956; Mayor of Bideford 1954-56; chm South West Advisory Ctee, Forestry Commission 1958-75; chm Timber Growers Organisation Ltd 1965-68; chm Exmoor Nat Park (Devon) Ctee 1968-74; *Clubs* Calvary & Guards'; *Style* - Sir Dennis Stucley, Bt, JP, DL; Hartland Abbey, Bideford, Devon (☎ Hartland 234)

STUCLEY, Hon Lady - Hon Sheila Margaret Warwick; *née* Bampfylde; da of 4 Baron Poltimore (d 1965); *b* 1912; *m* 1932, Maj Sir Dennis Frederic Bankes Stucley, 5 Bt; *Career* Patron of two livings; *Style* - The Hon Lady Stucley; Hartland Abbey, N Devon; Court Hall, N Molton, N Devon

STUDD, Anastasia, Lady; Anastasia; da of Lt-Col Harold Leveson-Gower (sixth in descent from 1 Earl Gower and consequently 5 cous of 5 Duke of Sutherland) by his w Kathleen JP, (da of Sir Murrough Wilson, KBE, JP, DL, sometime MP Richmond (Yorks), by his 1 w, Sybil, 2 da of Sir Powlett Milbank, 2 Bt); *b* 26 Nov 1931; *m* 1958, Capt Sir Kynaston Studd, 3 Bt (d 1977); *Style* - Anastasia, Lady Studd; Manor Farm, Rockbourne, Fordingbridge, Hants

STUDD, Sir Edward Fairfax; 4 Bt (UK 1929), of Netheravon, Wilts; s of Sir Eric Studd, 2 Bt OBE; suc bro, Sir Kynaston Studd, 3 Bt, 1977; *b* 3 May 1929; *Educ* Winchester; *m* 1960, Prudence, da of Alastair Fyfe OBE, of Grey Court, Riding Mill, Northumberland; 2 s, 1 da; *Heir* s, Philip Alastair Studd, b 27 Oct 1961; *Career* subaltern Coldstream Gds, served Malaya 1948-49; dir: Inchcape & Co, Anglo-Thai Corpn, Atkins Kroll & Co, Bain Dawes, Borneo Provident Tst, Dodwell & Co, Dr Graham's Homes, Gray Dawes Travel, Marshall Electronics, Marshall Internat Trading; memb Court Assistants Merchant Taylors Co; *Recreations* rural activities; *Clubs* Boodle's, Pratt's, City of London, Roy

Calcutta Turf; *Style* - Sir Edward Studd, Bt; Danceys, Clavering, Saffron Walden, Essex (☎ 0799 85 444)

STUDER, Keith Ronald; s of Ronald Studer, of Goole; *b* 15 Sept 1945; *m* 1971, Jane Hayton; 1 s, 1 da; *Career* International Freight Forwarder; dir LEP Transport Ltd 1975-, md M M Lilley and Co Ltd 1978-; chm Birmingham Exhibition Freight Ltd 1980-; *Style* - Keith Studer Esq; The Long House, Great Alne, Warwickshire (☎ 078981 201)

STUDHOLME, Sir Henry Gray; 1 Bt (UK 1956), of Perridge, Co Devon, CVO (1953), DL (Devon 1969); s of William Studholme; *b* 13 June 1899; *Educ* Eton, Magdalen Oxford; *m* 1929, Judith, da of Henry Whitbread, one of the brewing family, and himself s of Samuel Whitbread and Lady Isabella Pelham (yst da of 3 Earl of Chichester); 2 s, 1 da; *Heir* s, Paul Studholme; *Career* MP (C) Tavistock 1942-66, Con Whip 1945-46, Jt Hon Treasurer Con Pty 1952-62, V-Chamberlain to HM Household 1951-56, PPS to Cdr Brabner as Under Sec State Air; served WW I Scots Gds & 1940; memb LCC 1931-45; *Style* - Sir Henry Studholme, Bt, CVO, DL; Wembury House, Plymouth (☎ 862210)

STUDHOLME, Paul Henry William; DL (Devon 1981); s and h of Sir Henry Studholme, 1 Bt, CVO, DL; *b* 16 Jan 1930; *Educ* Eton, Sandhurst; *m* 1957, Virginia, yr da of Sir Herbert Palmer, KCMG, CBE; 2 s, 1 da; *Career* Capt Coldstream Gds; farmer, landowner; *Recreations* shooting, genealogy; *Style* - Paul Studholme Esq DL; Perridge House, Longdown, Exeter, Devon (☎ 039 281 237)

STURGE, Arthur Collwyn; MC (1945); s of Arthur Sturge; *b* 27 Sept 1912; *Educ* Harrow, BNC Oxford; *m* 1938, Beryl, da of Thomas Arthur, of Hong Kong; 2 s, 2 da; *Career* chm Lloyd's of London Press Ltd 1973-, pres A L Sturge Hldgs 1978-; dep chm Lloyd's 1969-70, Gen Ctee Lloyd's Register Shipping 1969-78; chm Officers' Families Fund; *Recreations* shooting, fishing; *Clubs* City of London, Flyfishers'; *Style* - Arthur Sturge Esq MC; Faircrouch, Wadhurst, East Sussex (☎ 089 288 2281); 15 Arundel Court, Jubilee Place, SW3 (☎ 01 352 7125)

STURT, Hon Mrs (Penelope Ann); *née* Mills; da of 3 Baron Hillingdon (d 1952); *b* 1917; *m* 1940, Evelyn Lennox Napier Sturt (d 1945); 1 s, 2 da; *Style* - The Hon Mrs Sturt; Thorn Croft, Chawleigh, Chulmleigh, Devon

STUTTAFORD, William Royden; s of Dr William Stuttaford, of Norfolk (d 1956); *b* 21 Nov 1928; *Educ* Gresham's, Trin Oxford; *m* 1, 1958, Sarah, da of Philip Legge, of Sevenoaks; 2 s, 2 da; m 2, 1974, Susan, da of Capt Sir Gerald Curteis KCVO RN; *Career* memb Stock Exchange 1959-; chm Framlington Unit Management 1974-; chm Cons Political Centre 1978-81; *Club* Cavalry & Guards'; *Style* - William Stuttaford Esq; Moulshams Manor, Great Wigborough, Essex (☎ Peldon (020 635) 330)

STYLE, Sir William Montague; 12 Bt (E 1627), of Wateringbury, Kent; s of 11 Bt (d 1943); *b* 21 July 1916; *m* 1941, La Verne, da of T M Comstock; 2 s; *Heir* s, William Frederick Style, b 13 May 1945; *Style* - Sir William Style, Bt; c/o Muehlmeier, Wildwood, 2919 N Mill rd, Oconomowoc, Wisconsin 53066, USA

SUDBURY, John Charles; s of Jonathan Sudbury; *b* 7 March 1944; *Educ* East Ham G S, NE London Poly; *m* 1965, Carol, da of Hugh Auker; 1 s, 2 da; *Career* chartered engr; dir Lex Motor Co; *Recreations* golf, travel, work; *Style* - John Sudbury Esq; Sycamore, Fishery rd, Bray, Berks

SUDDABY, Dominic; *b* 27 Oct 1939; *Educ* St Edward's Sch Oxford; *m* 1964, Sheelagh, da of Reuben Minns; 5 c; *Career* md PHH Servs Ltd, PHH Leasing, Autolease Ltd 1972-74; *Recreations* cricket, shooting, reading; *Style* - Dominic Suddaby Esq; 1 Blacksmiths rd, Longwick, nr Princes Risborough, Bucks (☎ 084 44 6462)

SUDELEY, 7 Baron (UK 1838); Merlin Charles Sainthill Hanbury-Tracy; s of Capt David Hanbury-Tracy (gs of 4

Baron) and Colline (whose 2 husb the Capt was), da of Lt-Col Collis St Hill and Rosie (2 da of Sir Spencer Wilson, 10 Bt); Lord Sudeley is fifth in descent from Henrietta, da of 8 & last Viscount Tracy (tho' there were four claimants to the extinct Viscountcy between 1835 and 1862); although the line of the Tracys may only be charted with certainty to Walter I, Count of Amiens (d between 992 & 998), it is possible that Lord Sudeley descends from the Emperor Charlemagne or the half-bro of Charles Martel, Charlemagne's gf and the saviour of Christendom from the Moslem hordes at Poitiers; either way there would be a connection with Clovis, King of the Franks; his descent from Henry I (through a da of William de Tracy, a natural s of Henry) and Godgifu (sis of Edward the Confessor) is certain; the 1 Baron was instrumental in choosing Barry to design the new Houses of Parliament in 1835; suc kinsman (6 Baron) 1941; *b* 17 June 1939; *Educ* Eton, Worcester Coll Oxford; *m* 1980, Hon Mrs Elizabeth Villiers, da of late Viscount Bury (s of 9 Earl of Albemarle) and formerly w of Alastair Michael Hyde Villiers; *Heir* kinsman, Claud Hanbury-Tracy-Domville; *Career* chm Human Rights Soc, Patron Anglican Assoc, Patron St Peter's (Petersham); v-pres Prayer Book Soc; *Recreations* conversation; *Clubs* Brooks's; Lord Sudeley is noted for the remark that by scrutinising a Peer's physiognomy at (for example) a State Opening of Parliament one can tell whether his Peerage was created before or after 1900; *Style* - The Rt Hon The Lord Sudeley; 25 Melcombe Court, Dorset sq, NW1 (☎ 01 723 7502); c/o Williams & Glyn's Bank, 21 Grosvenor gdns, SW1

SUDLEY, Viscount; Arthur (Desmond) Colquhoun Gore; s and h of 8 Earl of Arran; *b* 14 July 1938; *Educ* Eton, Balliol Oxford; *m* 1974, Eleanor, da of Bernard van Cutsem and Lady Margaret Fortescue, da of 5 Earl Fortescue; 2 da; *Career* served 1 Bn Gren Gds as 2 Lt; assist man Daily Mail 1972-73, md Clark Nelson 1973-74, assist gen man Daily & Sunday Express June-Nov 1974; Co-V-Chm Children's Country Holidays Fund; *Recreations* tennis, golf, shooting, ping pong, market gardening, owner of racehorse 'Border Incident'; *Clubs* Turf; *Style* - Viscount Sudley; Crocker End House, Nettlebed, Henley-on-Thames, Oxon (☎ Nettlebed 641659)

SUENSON-TAYLOR, Hon Christopher John; s and h of 2 Baron Grantchester QC; *b* 8 April 1951; *Educ* Winchester, LSE; *m* 1973, Jacqueline, da of Dr Leo Jaffé; 1 s, 1 da; *Career* dairy farmer & cattle breeder; *Recreations* music; *Style* - The Hon Christopher Suenson-Taylor; Lower House Farm, Black Coole Lane, Audlem, Cheshire (☎ 0270 811363)

SUENSON-TAYLOR, Hon Deborah Katherine Louise; 2 da of 2 Baron Grantchester QC; *b* 9 April 1957; *Style* - The Hon Deborah Suenson-Taylor

SUENSON-TAYLOR, Hon James Gunnar; 3 s of 2 Baron Grantchester QC; *b* 30 Sept 1955; *Educ* Eton, Kingston Poly; *Career* sales planner; *Recreations* rowing, shooting, fishing; *Style* - The Hon James Suenson-Taylor; 31 Cherwell Court, Broom Park, Broom rd, Teddington, Middx (☎ 01 977 9665)

SUENSON-TAYLOR, Hon Jeremy Kenneth; twin s of 2 Baron Grantchester QC; *b* 8 April 1951; *Educ* Winchester; *Style* - The Hon Jeremy Suenson-Taylor

SUENSON-TAYLOR, Hon Kirsten Victoria Mary; 3 da of 2 Baron Grantchester QC; *b* 25 Sept 1961; *Style* - The Hon Kirsten Suenson-Taylor

SUESS, Nigel Marcus; s of Julius Suess; *b* 13 Dec 1945; *Educ* Chigwell Sch, Cambridge U; *m* 1978, Maureen Ferguson; 1 da; *Career* dir British Linen Bank Ltd; *Recreations* mountaineering, chess, ornithology; *Style* - Nigel Suess Esq; Drumornie, 35 Woodhall rd, Edinburgh (☎ 031 441 2543)

SUFFIELD, 11 Baron (GB 1786); Sir Anthony Philip Harbord-Hamond; 12 Bt (GB 1745), MC (1950); s of 10 Baron (d 1951); *b* 19 June 1922; *Educ* Eton; *m* 1952, Elizabeth Eve, da of late Judge (Samuel Richard) Edgedale QC; 3 s, 1 da; *Heir* s, Hon Charles Harbord-Hamond; *Career*

Maj Coldstream Gds (ret), N Africa & Italy WW II, Malaya 1948-50, appointed one of HM Body Guard of Hon Corps of Gentlemen-at-Arms 1973, Officer of the Order of Orange Nassau 1950 *Style* - The Rt Hon The Lord Suffield MC; Langham Lodge, Holt, Norfolk

SUFFOLK AND BERKSHIRE, Earl of, 21 of Suffolk (E 1603), 14 of Berkshire (E 1626); Michael John James George Robert Howard; also Viscount Andover and Baron Howard of Charlton (E 1622); s of 20 Earl (k on active serv 1941); the 1 Earl was 2 s of 4 Duke of Norfolk; the 9 Earl's w was mistress of George II, who built Marble Hill House, on the Thames between Twickenham and Richmond, for her; the style is Palladian, the designer was Lord Pembroke; *b* 27 March 1935; *Educ* Winchester; *m* 1, 1960 (m dis 1967), Mme Simone Paulmier, da of Georges Litman, of Paris; m 2, 1973 (m dis 1980), Anita Robsham, da of Robin Fuglesang, of Cuckfield, Sussex; 1 s, 1 da; *Heir* s, Viscount Andover; *Style* - The Rt Hon The Earl of Suffolk and Berkshire; 8 Ennismore gdns, SW7 (☎ 01 584 4103); Charlton Park, Malmesbury, Wilts

SUGDEN, Dr Edward Charles; s of late Arthur Henry Sugden (gs of 1 Baron St Leonards); hp of n, 4 Baron; *b* 24 July 1902; *Career* late Maj RAMC, MB, BCh, MRCS England, LRCP London; *Style* - Dr Edward Sugden; 4 Half Moon st, W1

SUIRDALE, Viscount; Richard Michael John Hely-Hutchinson; s and h of 7 Earl of Donoughmore; *b* 8 Aug 1927; *Educ* Winchester, New Coll Oxford (MA, BM, BCh); *m* 1951, Sheila, nee Parsons; 4 s; *Career* Capt RAMC; fin consultant; co dir; *Recreations* racing, shooting, fishing; *Clubs* Jockey, Cercle de l'Union Interallié (both Paris), Kildare st (Dublin); *Style* - Viscount Suirdale; Le Pavillon, 13-15 Rue des Huissiers, 92200 Neuilly-sur-Seine, France

SULLIVAN, Lady; Muriel Mary; da of Francis Pineo; *m* 1928, Sir Richard Sullivan, 8 Bt (d 1977); 2 s (Richard, Michael); *Style* - Lady Sullivan; 2 Knowles Close, Mount Pleasant, Salisbury, Zimbabwe

SULLIVAN, Richard Arthur; 9 Bt (UK 1804); s of Sir Richard Sullivan, 8 Bt (d 1977); does not use title; *b* 9 Aug 1931; *Educ* Cape Town U, MIT; *m* 1962, Elenor, da of Kenneth Thorpe, of Somerset W, S Africa; 1 s, 3 da; *Heir* s, Charles Merson Sullivan, b 15 Dec 1962; *Career* civil engr; assoc & man Houston Office Golder Assocs, consulting geotechnical & mining engrs; *Recreations* tennis; *Style* - Richard Sullivan Esq; 11810 Longleat Lane, Houston, Texas 77024, USA (☎ 713 975 0067)

SULYAK, Hon Mrs (Rosamond Sybil); *née* Allen; da of Baron Croham (Life Peer), *qv*; *b* 1942; *m* 1973, Stephen Sulyak; *Style* - The Hon Mrs Sulyak

SUMMERHAYES, David Michael; CMG (1974); s of Sir Christopher Summerhayes; *b* 29 Sept 1922; *Educ* Marlborough, Emmanuel Cambridge; *m* 1959, June, da of late Lt-Col H A G van der Hardt Aberson; 2 s, 1 da; *Career* HM Diplomatic Serv, Ambass UK Delegation to Committee on Disarmament Geneva; *Recreations* mountaineering, sailing; *Clubs* United Oxford and Cambridge, Swiss Alpine, Hurlingham; *Style* - David Summerhayes Esq CMG; 5 Chemin Le Fort, 1223 Cologny, Geneva, Switzerland (☎ 22 36 36 72)

SUMMERS, Eric William; b 10 December 1914; *Educ* Dartford Technical Coll; *m* 1934, Elsie Mabel Arawa; 2 c; *Career* chm Courtney, Pope Hldgs; Pres Lighting Industry Fedn; *Clubs* RAC, Livery; *Style* - Eric Summers Esq; 'Muskoday', 29 The Meadow, Chislehurst, Kent (☎ 01 467 8047)

SUMMERS, Felix Roland Brattan; 2 Bt (UK 1952), of Shotton, Co Flint; does not use title; s of Sir Geoffrey Summers, 1 Bt, CBE, JP, DL (d 1972); *b* 1 Oct 1918; *Educ* Shrewsbury; *m* 1945, Anna Marie Louise, da of late Gustave Demaegd, of Brussels; 1 da; *Heir* none; *Career* served 1939-45 War with 8 Army (Middle East, N Africa, France and Belgium); *Style* - Felix Summers Esq; Warren House, 16 Warren Lane, Friston, Eastbourne, Sussex

SUMMERS, Col Maxwell Hamilton; DSO (1946), OBE (1962), TD (1941) and three bars; s of Gilbert Summers; *b* 12 Sept 1899; *Educ* St Paul's, London U; *m* 1927, Evelyne, da of Rev William Baird, of Edinburgh; 2 s, 1 da; *Career* served WW II Nigeria & NW Europe; OStJ; medical practitioner, house surgeon Middx Hosp 1923, Hon Anaesthetist King Edward VII Hosp Windsor 1928-48, lecturer on industrial first aid for Order of St John and BRCS, pres RBL Burnham Bucks, DL Middx 1948-65 & Gtr London 1965-76; *Recreations* territorials; *Clubs* Roy Soc Medicine; *Style* - Col Maxwell Summers, DSO, OBE, TD***; Cranleigh, Henley rd, Maidenhead, Berks (☎ Littlewick Green 2046)

SUMMERSKILL, Hon Michael Brynmôr; s of Baroness Summerskill, CH, PC (Life Peeress, d 1980), and late Dr William Summerskill; *b* 1927; *Educ* St Paul's Sch, Oxford U; *m* 1, 1951, Florence Elliott; 1 s, 2 da; m 2, 1972, Audrey Alexandra Brontë Blemings; *Career* barr Middle Temple 1952; *Style* - The Hon Michael Summerskill; 40 Cadogan sq, SW1

SUMMERSKILL, Dr the Hon Shirley; MP (L) Halifax 1964-; da of Baroness Summerskill, CH, PC (Life Peeress, d 1980) and late Dr William Summerskill; *b* 9 Sept 1931; *Educ* St Paul's Girls' Sch, Somerville Oxford, St Thomas' Hosp; *m* 1957 (m dis 1971), John Ryman, barr; *Career* Parly Under-Sec of State Home Office 1974-79, Oppn Spokesman on Home Affairs 1979-; *Style* - Dr the Hon Shirley Summerskill MP; House of Commons, SW1

SUMNER-FERGUSSON, William Howard David; *b* 11 March 1946; *Educ* Elston Hall Newark, Oratory Sch Reading; *m* 1979, Lucienne Gay Elizabeth, da of William Hilder; 1 da; *Career* dir: Everard Brewery Ltd (Leicester), John Sarson Ltd, John Sarson Wines Ltd, Anglesey Road Developments, Selincourt Ltd; memb Corpn of Lloyd's of London; *Recreations* gardening, shooting, bridge; *Style* - William Sumner-Fergusson Esq; The Granary, Preston, Uppingham, Rutland (☎ Manton 226)

SUMSION, John Walbridge; s of Dr Herbert Sumsion; *b* 16 Aug 1928; *Educ* Rendcomb Coll, Clare Cambridge, Yale, Cornell; *m* 1, 1961 (m dis 1979), Annette English; 4 c; m 2, 1979, Hazel; *Career* dir K Shoes Ltd 1962-81; Lending Right Registrar (under public lending right scheme) Sept 1981-; *Recreations* tennis, squash, music; *Clubs* IOD; *Style* - John Sumsion Esq; 68 Sedbergh rd, Kendal, Cumbria (☎ 21609)

SUNDERLAND, JP (1978) Eric Edgar; s of Edgar Sunderland; *b* 16 Nov 1927; *Educ* Queen Elizabeth G S, Horncastle; Bradford Inst Technology; *m* 1958, Irene, da of John Beecroft; *Career* gp md Homfray Textile Gp 1972-76, md Henry Mason Ltd 1976-80; gp md E & T Wall Ltd 1980-; chm Contessa Cars Ltd 1976-, v-chm Bradford Hospital Fund (Insur) 1974-; *Recreations* music, cars, chess, railway preservation; *Clubs* Conservative (Bradford); *Style* - Eric Sunderland Esq, JP; Sundial House, 5 Manscombe rd, Allerton, W Yorks

SUNDIUS-HILL, Lady Helen (Maglona); *née* Vane-Tempest-Stewart; da of 7 Marquess of Londonderry, KG, MVO, TD, PC (d 1949), by his wife, Hon Dame Edith Chaplin, DBE, da of 1 Viscount Chaplin; *b* 1911; *m* 1, 1935 (m dis 1960), 2 Baron Jessel; m 2, 1960, Dennis Cecil Whittington Walsh, s of late Sir Cecil Henry Walsh, KC; m 3, 1978, Nigel Sundius-Hill; *Style* - Lady Helen Sundius-Hill; 25 Redington Gardens, Hampstead, NW3

SURRELL, Hon Mrs (Maureen Dawn); *née* Vernon; da of 5 Baron Lyveden (d 1973), by his 1 w, Ruby (d 1932), da of Robert Shandley; *b* 1926; *m* 1946, Noel Surrell; 1 s; *Style* - The Hon Mrs Surrell; 17 Duncan st, Taupo, New Zealand

SURTEES, Maj John Freville Henry; OBE (1975), MC (1940); s of Maj Robert Lambton Surtees OBE JP; *b* 26 Jan 1919; *Educ* Eton, Sandhurst; *m* 1, 1946 (m dis 1967), Audrey, *née* Falkner; 2 da (Isabel m The Master of Polwarth, *qv*; Christian m 1972 Captain James Hepburne Scott);

m 2, 1969, Anne Margaret, da of Sir Edward Brandis Denham GCMG KBE (d 1937); *Career* Major Rifle Brigade 1939-48 (ret), md Garvey (London) Ltd, Master Grocers' Co 1966-67, Govr Oundle Sch, memb Lloyd's, memb Inst of Masters of Wine; *Recreations* fishing, racing, music; *Clubs* Boodle's, Pratt's; *Style* - Maj John Surtees OBE MC; Downs House, West Ilsley, Newbury, Berks (☎ East Ilsley 224)

SURTEES, Col William Francis; OBE (1963), TD (1960), DL (Northumberland 1970); *b* 12 Sept 1920; *Educ* Ashville Coll Harrogate; *m* 1945, Gwendoline, nee Plews; 1 s, 1 da; *Career* branch manager Barclays Bank Ltd, ret 1978; *Recreations* fishing, fell walking; *Style* - Col William Surtees

SUTCLIFFE, Cecilia Mary; *née* Turton; da of Ralph Merdyth Turton and sis of da-in-law of Sir Andrew Horsbrugh-Porter, Bt; *b* 30 Nov 1936; *Educ* St Mary's Wantage; *m* 1959, John Harold Vick; 2 s, 2 da; *Recreations* riding, reading; *Style* - Mrs John Sutcliffe; 25 Pont st, SW1 (☎ 01 235 4075); Great Fosters, Egham, Surrey (☎ 33822); Chapelgarth, Gt Broughton, Middlesbrough (☎ Stokesley 712228)

SUTCLIFFE, Charles Wilfred David; s of Max Sutcliffe (d 1976); *b* 21 June 1936; *Educ* Uppingham Sch, Leeds U; *m* 1960, Hanne, nee Carlsen; 2 s; *Career* Lt 4 Roy Tank Regt, chm & jt md Benson Turner & Son Ltd (Spinners & Dyers) 1978-); chm Benson Turner (Dyers) Ltd 1976-78, (jt md 1968-), dir Bradford Micro-Firms Ltd 1981-; *Recreations* golf, sailing, swimming; *Clubs* Bradford *Style* - Charles Sutcliffe Esq; Ivy House Farm, Kettlesing, Harrogate, Yorkshire (☎ Harrogate 770561)

SUTCLIFFE, Hon Mrs; Helen; *née* Rhodes; da of Baron Rhodes, KG, DFC*, PC, DL; *b* 15 Aug 1929; *m* 1954, John, JP, s of Herbert Sutcliffe, of Colwyn Bay; 2 s, 1 da; *Style* - The Hon Mrs Sutcliffe; Lower Carr, Diggle, Dobcross, Oldham, Lancs

SUTCLIFFE, Ian (Sharp); s of H N Sutcliffe (d 1962); *b* 30 Jan 1931; *Educ* Marlborough, Emmanuel Cambridge; *m* 1960, Anne (Lyon), da of R Lyon Wyllie, CBE, JP, DL; 3 s; *Career* slr 1959, registrar Carlisle Diocese 1962, legal sec to Bishop of Carlisle, registrar to Archdeacons 1962, clerk to Dean and Chapter of Carlisle 1962;*Recreations* golf, lawn tennis, bridge, sailing; *Style* - Ian Sutcliffe Esq; Mulcaster House, Stanwix, Carlisle (☎ 25314)

SUTHERLAND, Countess of (24 in line, S circa 1235); Elizabeth Millicent Sutherland; also Lady Strathnaver (strictly speaking a territorial style, but treated as a Lordship for purposes of use as courtesy title for ha to Earldom since the end of the sixteenth century); da of Lord Alastair St Clair Sutherland-Leveson-Gower, MC (s of 4 Duke of Sutherland, KG, and Lady Millicent St Clair-Erskine, da of 4 Earl of Rosslyn); suc to Earldom of Sutherland held by unc, 5 Duke of Sutherland, KT, PC, 1963 (thus came about precisely the contingency that might have caused objection to be made when the Dukedom was so named on its creation 130 years earlier in 1833, *viz* that because the latter was heritable in tail male while the Earldom not only could be held by a female but actually was (by the 1 Duke's wife) at the time of the cr, the two might become separated; the suggestion of 'Sutherland' was said to be Princess Augusta's (da of the Duke of Cambridge and 1 cous of Queen Victoria); the then Countess of Sutherland in her own right (gggg-mother of present Countess) was known as the 'Duchess-Countess' (though presumably only 1833-39) in a style analogous to that of the Spanish Count-Duke Olivares of the seventeenth century); *b* 30 March 1921; *Educ* Queen's Coll Harley St W1 and abroad; *m* 1946, Charles Noel Janson, DL; 2 s, 1 da; *Heir* s, Lord Strathnaver; *Career* Chief of the Clan Sutherland; Land Army 1939-41, former hosp lab technician; chm Northern Times 1963-, Dunrobin Sch Ltd 1965-72, Trentham Gardens Ltd 1963-; adopted surname of Sutherland under Scots law 1963; *Recreations* reading, swimming; *Style* - The Rt Hon The Countess of Sutherland; 39 Edwardes sq, W8 (☎ 01 603 0659); Dunrobin Castle, Sutherland; House of Tongue, by Lairg, Sutherland

SUTHERLAND, 6 Duke of (UK 1833); Sir John Sutherland Egerton; 13 Bt (E 1620), TD, DL (Berwicks); also 5 Earl of Ellesmere (UK 1846), which known as 1944-63 (when he inherited the Dukedom); also Baron Gower (GB 1703), Earl Gower and Viscount Trentham (GB 1746), Marquess of Stafford (GB 1786), Viscount Brackley (UK 1846); s of 4 Earl of Ellesmere (d 1944) and Lady Violet Lambton, da of 4 Earl of Durham; suc father as 5 Earl 1944, and 3 cous once removed as 6 Duke of Sutherland 1963; His Grace is ggggs of the 1 Duke, who bought the structure now known as Lancaster House (formerly called Stafford House) in 1827 from the Duke of York for £72,000; His Grace's 2 cous twice removed, the 4 Duke, was in the early 1880s the greatest landowner in the UK, with over 1,350,000 acres; he was said to be able to ride 100 miles in a straight line on his Sutherland properties, alternatively from one coast to the other without stepping outside his own domains; His Grace is 1 cous to Lord Home of the Hirsel, Antony Lambton and 4 Baron Joicey; *b* 10 May 1915; *Educ* Eton, Trin Cambridge; *m* 1, 1939, Lady Diana Percy (d 1978), da of 8 Duke of Northumberland; m 2, 1979, Evelyn, da of late Maj Robert Moubray (whose w Claire was gda of Sir Charles Morrison-Bell, 1 Bt); *Heir* Cyril Egerton, *qv*; *Career* late Capt Roy Armoured Corps (TA), prisoner WW II; *Style* - His Grace The Duke of Sutherland, TD DL; Mertoun, St Boswell's, Roxburghshire; Lingay Cottage, Hall Farm, Newmarket, Suffolk

SUTHERLAND, Lady Annabel Elizabeth Hélène; da of Countess of Sutherland in her own right (who adopted surname of Sutherland according to Scots law 1963) by her husb Charles Janson, DL; *b* 16 May 1952; *Style* - Lady Annabel Sutherland

SUTHERLAND, Clare, Duchess of; Clare Josephine; 2 da of late Herbert O'Brien, of Calcutta; *m* 1, Alexander Shakespear, CIE, of Cawnpore (decd); m 2, Col Vincent Blundell Dunkerly (decd); m 3, 1944, as his 2 w, 5 Duke of Sutherland, KT, PC (d 1963); *Style* - Her Grace Clare, Duchess of Sutherland; 14 Hyde Park gdns, W2 (☎ 01 262 3305); ES Carregedur, Capdedera, Mallorca, Spain

SUTHERLAND, (Sir) John Brewer; 3 Bt (UK 1921), of Dunstanburgh Castle, Embleton, Co Northumberland; s of Sir Benjamin Sutherland, 2 Bt (d 1980), by his 1 w Marjorie; has established his claim but does not use his title; *b* 19 Oct 1931; *Educ* Sedbergh Sch, St Cat's Cambridge; *m* 1958, Alice, da of W Stamford Henderson, of Kelso; 3 s, 1 da; *Heir* s, Peter William Sutherland, b 1963; *Style* - John Sutherland Esq; Ross, Belford, Northumberland

SUTHERLAND, Margaret, Lady; Margaret; JP; da of Albert Owen, of Chalfont St Giles; *m* 1944, as his 2 w, Sir Ivan Sutherland, 2 Bt (d 1980); *Style* - Margaret, Lady Sutherland, JP; Dunstan Steads, Embleton, Northumberland

SUTHERLAND, Hon Rachel Elizabeth; da (by 1 m) of Lord Strathnaver; *b* 1970; *Style* - The Hon Rachel Sutherland

SUTHERLAND, Hon Rosemary Millicent; da (by 1 m) of Lord Strathnaver; *b* 1972; *Style* - The Hon Rosemary Sutherland

SUTHERLAND JANSON, Hon Martin Dearman; s (yr twin) of Countess of Sutherland; *b* 1947; *Educ* Eton; *m* 1974, Hon Mary Ann Balfour, da of 1 Baron Balfour of Inchrye, MC, PC; 3 s; *Style* - The Hon Martin Sutherland Janson

SUTTON, Sir Richard Lexington; 9 Bt (GB 1772), of Norwood Park, Nottinghamshire; s of Sir Robert Lexington, 8 Bt (d 1981); *b* 27 April 1937; *Educ* Stowe; *m* 1959, Fiamma, da of G M Ferrari, of Rome; 1 s, 1 da; *Heir* s, David Robert Sutton, b 26 Feb 1960; *Style* - Sir Richard Sutton, Bt; Moor Hill, Langham, Gillingham, Dorset

SWALLOW, Sir William; s of the late W T Swallow; *b* 2 Jan 1905; *m* 1929, Kathleen Lucy, nee Smith; *Career* kt 1967; chm and md: Vauxhall Motors Ltd 1961-66, General Motors Ltd 1953-61; *Recreations* golf; *Style* - Sir William Swallow; Alderton Lodge, Ashridge Park,

Berkhampstead, Herts (☎ Little Gaddesden 2284)

SWAN, Conrad Marshall John Fisher; MVO (1978); s of Dr Henry Swan (né Swenciski or Swiecicki), of Vancouver (whose f, Paul, emigrated from Poland, where the family had long been landed proprietors and from time to time represented in the Senate of pre-Partition Poland); *b* 13 May 1924; *Educ* St George's Coll Weybridge, Sch of African & Oriental Studies London U, W Ontario U, Peterhouse Cambridge; *m* 1957, Lady Hilda Northcote, da of 3 Earl of Iddesleigh; 1 s, 4 da; *Career* York Herald of Arms 1968- (Rouge Dragon Pursuivant 1962-68); KStJ (Genealogist of Grand Priory, Order of St John 1976-); Kt of Honour & Devotion Sov Mil Order Malta 1979; Genealogist of Order of Bath 1972-; FSA; lecturer; *Style* - Conrad Swan Esq, MVO; College of Arms, Queen Victoria st, EC4 (☎ 01 248 1850); Boxford House, Boxford, Colchester, Essex (☎ 210208)

SWAN, Lady Hilda Susan Mary; *née* Northcote; da of late 3 Earl of Iddesleigh; *b* 1937; *m* 1957, Conrad Swan, MVO, PhD, York Herald, *qv*; 1 s (Andrew), 4 da (Elizabeth Magdalen m 1981 Roger Le Strange Herring; Hilda, Catherine, Anastasia); *Style* - Lady Hilda Swan; Boxford House, Boxford, Colchester (☎ 210208)

SWANN, Baron (Life Peer UK 1980); Michael Meredith; s of Meredith Blake Robson Swann, MD; *b* 1 March 1920; *Educ* Winchester, Gonville and Caius Cambridge (MA, PhD); *m* 1942, Teresa Ann, da of Reginald Gleadowe, CVO; 2 s, 2 da; *Career* Lt-Col Iceland, N W Europe WW II; fellow of Gonville and Caius Coll Cambridge 1946-52, Prof of Natural History Edinburgh U 1952-65, Princ and Vice-Chancellor Edinburgh U 1965-73, Chm BBC 1973-80, Chancellor York U 1980-, Provost of Oriel Coll Oxford 1980-; kt 1972, FRS 1962, FRSE 1952; *Recreations* gardening, sailing; *Clubs* Athenaeum, New (Edinburgh); *Style* - The Rt Hon The Lord Swann; Oriel College, Oxford (☎ 0865 41962); Tallat Steps, Coln St Denys, nr Cheltenham, Glos (☎ 0285 72 533)

SWANN, Sir Anthony Charles Christopher; 3 Bt (UK 1906), of Prince's Gardens, Royal Borough of Kensington, CMG (1958), OBE (1950); s of Sir Duncan Swann, 2 Bt (d 1962); *b* 29 June 1913; *Educ* Eton, New Coll Oxford; *m* 1940, Jean, da of John Niblock-Stuart, of Nairobi; 1 s; *Heir* s, Michael Swann; *Career* Maj King's African Rifles, served E Africa, Abyssinia; formerly Min of Def & Home Security Kenya; *Recreations* fishing, racing, reading, music; *Clubs* Army & Navy, Pratt's; *Style* - Sir Anthony Swann, Bt, CMG, OBE; 23 Montpelier sq, SW7 (☎ 01 589 5546)

SWANN, Hon Mrs (Lydia Mary); *née* Hewitt; da of 8 Viscount Lifford; *b* 1938; *m* 1965, Michael Swann, *qv*, s of Sir Anthony Charles Christopher Swann, 3 Bt, CMG, OBE; *Style* - The Hon Mrs Swann; Foxhanger, Burwash, Sussex

SWANN, Michael Christopher; TD; s and h of Sir Anthony Swann, 3 Bt, CMG, OBE; *b* 23 Sept 1941; *Educ* Eton; *m* 1965, Hon Lydia Hewitt, da of 8 Viscount Lifford; 2 s (Jonathan b 1966, Toby b 1971), 1 da (Tessa b 1969); *Career* late 60 Rifles; *Style* - Michael Swann Esq TD; Foxhanger, Burwash, Sussex

SWANN, Hon Peter; s of Baron Swann (Life Peer); *b* 25 April 1955; *Educ* Edinburgh Acad, St Andrews U (MA), Bristol U, LSE; *Career* PhD student in economics LSE; *Recreations* sailing; *Style* - The Hon Peter Swann

SWANN, Hon Richard; s of Baron Swann (Life Peer); *b* 1944; *m* 1969, Julia Coke-Steel; *Style* - The Hon Richard Swann

SWANSEA, 4 Baron (UK 1893); Sir John Hussey Hamilton Vivian; 4 Bt (UK 1882), DL (Powys 1962); s of 3 Baron Swansea, DSO, MVO (d 1934), and Hon Winifred Hamilton, da of 1 Baron Holm Patrick; *b* 1 Jan 1925; *Educ* Eton, Trin Cambridge; *m* 1956, (m dis 1973), Miriam (d 1975), da of Anthony Caccia-Birch, MC (nephew of Baron Caccia, GCMG, *qv*); 1 s, 2 da; *Heir* s, Hon Richard Vivian; *Style* - The Rt Hon Lord Swansea, DL; Glanyrafon, Erwood, Builth Wells, Powys (☎ Erwood 662)

SWARTZ, Col Hon Sir Reginald William Colin; KBE (1972, MBE 1948), ED, JP (Queensland 1947); s of late J Swartz; *b* 14 April 1911; *Educ* Toowoomba G S, Brisbane G S; *m* 1936, Hilda, nee Robinson; 2 s, 1 da; *Career* FBIM, FAIM; formerly (consecutively) Min of State for Repatriation, Health, Social Services, Civil Aviation, Nat Dvpt; MHR (Lib) Darling Downs Queensland 1949-72, Leader of House of Reps Canberra 1971-72; company dir; *Recreations* bowls, boating; *Clubs* United Service and Roy Automobile (Brisbane); Roy Automobile and Australian (Melbourne); Twin Towns Services (Tweed Heads), Southport Yacht, Surfers Paradise Bowls, Darling Downs Aero (Toowoomba); *Style* - Col the Hon Sir Reginald Swartz, KBE, ED, JP; Rylstone, 31 Furlong st, Rio Vista, Surfers Paradise, Queensland 4217, Australia

SWAYTHLING, 3 Baron (UK 1907); Sir Stuart Albert Samuel Montagu; 3 Bt (UK 1894), OBE (1947); s of 2 Baron (d 1927) and Gladys, OBE, da of late Col Albert Goldsmid, MVO; *b* 19 Dec 1898; *Educ* Clifton Coll, Westminster Sch, Trin Cambridge; *m* 1, 1925 (m dis 1942), Mary Violet, da of late Maj Walter Levy, DSO; 2 s, 1 da; m 2, 1945, Mrs Jean Marcia Knox, CBE (Ch Controller and Dir of ATS 1941-43), da of late G G Leith Marshall; *Heir* s, Hon David Montagu; *Career* JP Surrey 1948-80, former dir Samuel Montagu & Co Ltd (bankers), Master of Farmers' Co 1962-63, Pres of English Guernsey Cattle Soc 1950-51 and 1971-72 and of Roy Assoc of British Dairy Farmers 1972-73; Lt Gren Gds 1917-20; *Style* - The Rt Hon The Lord Swaythling, OBE; Le Picquerel, Grand House, St Sampson's, Guernsey, Channel Islands (☎ Guernsey 49104)

SWEETEN, Anthony Ricardo; s of Benjamin Arthur Sweeten (d 1975); *b* 24 Oct 1941; *Educ* Clare Hall Coll Halifax, Tech Coll Halifax, Bradford U; *m* 1966, Marion Brenda Mary, nee Hayter; 2 s, 1 da; *Career* dir T S Harrison & Sons Ltd 1975-; *Recreations* golf, shooting, fishing; *Clubs* Lightcliffe Golf, Leeds Serv Rifle; *Style* - Anthony Sweeten Esq; Green Acre, Bramley Lane, Lightcliffe, Halifax, W Yorkshire (☎ Halifax 201467)

SWEETING, Lt-Col Henry Kennett; s of Henry Carol Sweeting, OBE, JP (d 1956); *b* 13 Aug 1919; *Educ* Eton and Sandhurst; *m* 1945, Aileen, da of Capt Keith Seth-Smith OBE (d 1959); 2 da (1 s decd); *Career* Lt-Col Coldstream Guards 1939-61, Gen Staff Officer (2) HQ London District 1950-53, mil assist to Cmdt Berlin (Br Sector) 1956-58, Cdr 2 Bn Coldstream Guards 1958-60 (ret 1961); memb Lloyd's, memb Institute of Directors; *Clubs* Cavalry & Guards'; *Style* - Lt-Col Henry Sweeting; Ballashamrock House, Port Soderick, Isle of Man (☎ Douglas 4670)

SWETENHAM, Brig John Edmund; DSO (1945); s of Maj Foster Swetenham (d 1914); *b* 11 May 1909; *Educ* Eton, Sandhurst; *m* 1938, Alison Ann, da of late Col the Hon Guy Greville Wilson CMG DSO; 1 s; *Career* 5 Roy Inniskilling Dragoon Gds 1940, Col Roy Scots Greys 1958-67, memb HM Body Guard, Hon Corps Gentlemen-at-Arms 1959-, Order of Crown and Croix de Guerre (Belgium); *Recreations* hunting, shooting, racing; *Clubs* Cavalry & Guards, Pratt's; *Style* - Brig John Swetenham DSO; Green Farm, Brompton By Sawdon, Scarborough, Yorks (☎ Scarborough 85378)

SWIFT, Gp Capt William James; CVO (1961); s of late James Swift; *b* 3 Nov 1915; *Educ* Park High Sch Birkenhead, Univ of Liverpool; *m* 1939, Elspeth Madeleine, nee Bruyn; 2 da; *Career* Red Cross Badge of Honour for Distinguished Service 1980; RAF 1938, Gp Capt European theatre 1943-45, cmd 216 Squadron Middle East 1953-56, Suez Operation 1956, Air Attaché Tehran 1958-61, NATO International Military Staff Washington and Brussels 1966-69, ret 1970; dir British Red Cross Society, Berkshire Branch 1971-; *Recreations* golf; *Clubs* Calcot Park Golf; *Style* - Gp Capt William Swift, CVO, RAF; Clompers, Broadlands Close, Calcot Park, Reading, Berks (☎ Reading 27696)

SWINFEN, 3 Baron (UK 1919); Roger Mynors Swinfen Eady; s of 2 Baron (d 1977) by 1 w, Mary Aline, da of late Col Harold Mynors Farmar, CMG, DSO; *b* 14 Dec 1938; *Educ* Westminster; *m* 1962, Patricia Anne, da of late J D Blackmore, of Dundrum, Dublin; 1 s, 3 da; *Heir* s, Hon

Charles Eady; *Career* late Lt Roy Scots; ARICS; *Style* - The Rt Hon The Lord Swinfen; Dene House, Wingham, Canterbury, Kent

SWINFEN, Averil, Baroness; Averil Kathleen Suzanne; da of late Maj William Marshall Hickman Humphreys and formerly w of Lt-Col Andrew Knowles, TD; *m* 1950, as his 2 w, 2 Baron (d 1977); *Style* - The Rt Hon Averil, Lady Swinfen; Medina House, Spanish Point, Co Clare

SWINNERTON, Lt-Col Iain Spencer; TD, JP, DL (W Midlands 1976); s of James Percy Swinnerton (d 1977); *b* 23 April 1932; *Educ* King Edward VI Sch Stourbridge, RMC Sandhurst; *m* 1958, Angela, nee Sellers; 1 s, 2 da; *Career* md Swinnerton & Co Ltd Stourbridge, pres Birmingham & Midland Soc for Genealogy and Heraldry 1972-, divisional pres St John Ambulance 1977-, fellow of Society of Genealogists 1975, magistrate Worcs 1972, chm British Fedn of Family History Societies 1974-77, pres 1978-; trustee Inst of Genealogical and Heraldic Studies; author; *Recreations* genealogy, heraldry, travel; *Clubs* Army and Navy, Old Edwardian; *Style* - Lt-Col Iain Swinnerton, TD, JP, DL; Owls Barn, Bridgnorth rd, Stourton, Stourbridge, W Midlands

SWINNERTON-DYER, Prof Sir (Henry) Peter Francis; 16 Bt (E 1678), of Tottenham, Middx; s of Sir Leonard Schroeder Swinnerton Dyer, 15 Bt (d 1975); *b* 2 Aug 1927; *Educ* Eton, Trin Cambridge; *Heir* 2 cous once removed, Maj Richard Dyer-Bennet; *Career* Fellow Eton 1981-; dir Prutec Ltd 1981-; FRS; Master St Cat's Cambridge 1973-, Prof Mathematics Cambridge 1971-, V-Chllr 1979-81; *Recreations* tennis, squash; *Style* - Prof Sir Peter Swinnerton-Dyer, Bt; The Master's Lodge, St Catharine's College, Cambridge (☎ 0223 59445)

SWINTON, 2 Earl of (UK 1955); David Yarburgh Cunliffe-Lister; JP (N Yorks 1971), DL (1978); also Viscount Swinton (UK 1935), Baron Masham (UK 1955); s of late Maj the Hon John Yarburgh Cunliffe-Lister, eld s of 1 Earl; suc gf 1 Earl, GBE, CH, MC, MP, 1972; *b* 21 March 1937; *Educ* Winchester, RAC Cirencester; *m* 1959, Susan Lilian Primrose (Baroness Masham of Ilton, *qv*), da of late Sir Ronald Norman John Charles Udny Sinclair, 8 Bt (cr 1704); 1 s, 1 da (both adopted); *Heir* bro, Hon Nicholas Cunliffe-Lister; *Career* CC N Riding of Yorks 1961-74; *Style* - The Rt Hon The Earl of Swinton JP DL; Dykes Hill House, Masham, N Yorks (☎ 241)

SWINTON, Maj-Gen Sir John; KCVO (1979), OBE (1969), DL (Berks 1980); s of Brig A H C Swinton MC (d 1972); *b* 21 April 1925; *Educ* Harrow; *m* 1954, Judith Balfour, nee Killen; 3 s, 1 da; *Career* Maj-Gen; Scots Guards 1944; Brig Lowlands and Cdr Edinburgh and Glasgow Garrisons 1975-76, GOC London District and Maj-Gen Cmding The Household Div 1976-79 (ret); landowner; Brig The Queen's Body Guard for Scotland Roy, Co Archers; *Clubs* New (Edinburgh), Pratt's; *Style* - Maj-Gen Sir John Swinton KCVO OBE DL; Kimmerghame, Duns, Berwicks (☎ 03612 3277)

SWIRE, Lady Judith; *née* Compton; da of 6 Marquess of Northampton, DSO (d 1978); *b* 26 Sept 1943; *m* 1970, Adrian Christopher Swire (dep chm John Swire & Sons & chm China Navigation Co, yr bro of John Anthony Swire, chm of the former, and yr s of John Kidston Swire, DL, former chm); 2 s, 1 da; *Style* - Lady Judith Swire; 14 Phillimore Place, W8 (☎ 01 937 6080)

SYKES, Audrey, Lady; Audrey Winifred; da of Frederick Thompson, of Cricklewood; *m* 1935, Sir Hugh Sykes, 2 Bt (d 1974); *Style* - Audrey, Lady Sykes; 19 Bouverie gdns, Harrow, Middx

SYKES, Sir Francis Godfrey; 9 Bt (GB 1781), of Basildon, Berkshire; s of Francis William Sykes (d 1944) and kinsman of 8 Bt (d 1956); *b* 27 Aug 1907; *Educ* Blundell's and Nelson Coll NZ; *m* 1, 1934, Eira Betty (d 1970), da of G W Badcock, of Hove and Steyning, Sussex; 1 s, 1 da; m 2, 1972, Nesta Mabel, da of late Col Harold Sykes; *Heir* s, Francis John Badcock Sykes, b 7 June 1942; *Clubs* Salop (Shrewsbury); *Style* - Sir Francis Sykes, Bt; White Lodge, Bishop's Castle, Salop (☎ Bishop's Castle 487)

SYKES, Sir John Charles Anthony le Gallais; 3 Bt (UK 1921), of Kingsknowes, Galashiels, Co Selkirk; s of Capt Stanley Sykes (yr s of Sir Charles Sykes, 1 Bt, KBE, JP, sometime MP Huddersfield) and Florence Anaïse, da of François le Gallais, of Jersey; suc unc, Sir Hugh Sykes, 2 Bt, 1974; *b* 19 April 1928; *Educ* Churchers Coll; *m* 1954 (m dis 1969), Aitha Isobel, da of Lionel Dean, of Huddersfield; *Heir* bro, Michael Sykes; *Career* export merchant (textile business); *Clubs* Br Epicure Soc; *Style* - Sir John Sykes, Bt; 58 Alders View dve, E Grinstead, W Sussex (☎ 0342 22027)

SYKES, John Keith; s of late Edgar Sykes; *b* 5 Feb 1933; *Educ* Wrekin Coll, Leeds U; *m* 1958, Undine, nee Hodgetts; 1 s, 4 da; *Career* barr; md Watts, Blake, Bearne & Co Ltd, dir Television South West Ltd; *Recreations* fishing; *Style* - John Sykes Esq; 50 Knowles Hill rd, Newton Abbot, Devon (☎ 0626 5297)

SYKES, Hon Mrs (Laura Catherine); *née* James; da (by 1 m) of Baron Saint Brides (Life Peer); *b* 1948; *m* 1981, Robert L T Sykes, s of Geoffrey Sykes, of Kirribilli, New South Wales; *Style* - The Hon Mrs Sykes

SYKES, Michael le Gallais; s of Capt Stanley Sykes; hp to bro, Sir John Sykes, 3 Bt; *b* 4 Jan 1932; *Educ* Trent Coll; *m* 1, 1953, Joan, da of Cecil Groom, of Nuthall, Notts; 2 s (David Michael b 1954, Christopher Cary b 1959); m 2, 1976, Susan, da of Capt C Melia; *Career* late 2 Lt Duke of Wellington's Regt & Sherwood Foresters; *Style* - Michael Sykes Esq; PO Box 634, Doha, Qatar

SYKES, Hon Mrs (Nicola Mary Caroline); *née* Buxton; 1 da of Baron Buxton of Alsa; *b* 7 July 1947; *m* 1970, Adrian Sykes; 1 s (Samuel b 1974), 1 da (Eleanor b 1972); *Style* - The Hon Mrs Sykes; Cook's Mill, Fordham Heath, Colchester, Essex

SYKES, Lady Pauline Anne; *née* Ogilvie-Grant; da of Countess of Seafield (12 in line) and Derek Studley-Herbert (who assumed by deed poll additional surnames of Ogilvie-Grant); *b* 1944; *m* 1, 1964 (m dis 1970), her brother-in-law, James Henry Harcourt Illingworth (*see* Earl of Seafield); m 2, 1976, Hugh Richard Sykes; 1 s; *Style* - Lady Pauline Sykes; Revack Lodge, Grantown-on-Spey, Morayshire

SYKES, Sir Tatton Christopher Mark; 8 Bt (GB 1783), of Sledmere, Yorkshire; s of Lt-Col Sir (Mark Tatton) Richard Tatton-Sykes, 7 Bt (d 1978); *b* 24 Dec 1943; *Educ* Eton, Université d'Aix France and RAC Cirencester; *Heir* bro, Jeremy John Sykes, b 8 March 1946; *Style* - Sir Tatton Sykes, Bt; Sledmere, Driffield, Yorkshire

SYMES, John; s of Capt John Roy Symes, Oxshott (d 1924); *b* 15 April 1920; *Educ* Merchant Taylors'; *m* 1947, Mary Magdelen, da of Prof Albert Bernard, CBE, MD, DFH, DTM, of Malta; 2 c; *Career* dir Rickman Symes (Export) & Co Ltd; *Recreations* golf; *Clubs* Carlton; *Style* - John Symes Esq; 9/121 Haverstock Hill, NW3

SYMONS, Ernest Vize; CB (1975); s of Ernest William Symons (d 1924); *b* 19 June 1913; *Educ* Stationers' Company's Sch, Univ Coll London; *m* 1938, Elizabeth Megan, nee Jenkins; 1 s, 2 da; *Career* chief inspector of Taxes 1973-75, dir gen Board of Inland Revenue 1975-79, governor of The English Speaking Union, Hon Treasurer of NACRO, memb of Council Univ Coll London, memb Lord Keith's Ctee on Enforcement Powers; *Recreations* chess, bridge; *Clubs* Athenaeum; *Style* - Ernest Symons Esq, CB; 6 Links Drive, Totteridge, N20 (☎ 01 445 3015)

SYNGE, Sir Robert Carson; 8 Bt (UK 1801), of Kiltrough; s of late Neale Hutchinson Synge and nephew of 7 Bt (d 1942); *b* 4 May 1922; *m* 1944, Dorothy Jean, da of Theodore Johnson, of Cloverdale, BC, Canada; 2 da; *Heir* cousin, Neale Francis Synge, b 28 Feb 1917; *Style* - Sir Robert Synge, Bt; 19364 Fraser Valley Highway, RR4 Langley, BC, Canada

SYSONBY, 3 Baron (UK 1935); John Frederick Ponsonby; s of 2 Baron, DSO (d 1956); *b* 5 Aug 1945; *Style* - The Rt Hon The Lord Sysonby; Newby Hall, Ripon, N Yorks

T

TABOR, John Edward; OBE (1944), DL (Essex 1972); s of Edward Henry Tabor; *b* 31 March 1911; *Educ* Westminster, Felsted and Emmanuel Cambridge; *m* 1, 1945, Marjorie, nee Lorenzen (d 1953); 1 s, 3 da; m 2, 1960, Margaret Anne Turner, nee Benson; *Career* Civil Service 1932-45; farmer; landowner; Pro Chancellor and chm Cncl University of Essex, High Sheriff of Essex 1980, memb Essex CC 1952-77, pres Essex National Trust; *Recreations* hunting, travel; *Clubs* Farmers'; *Style* - John Tabor Esq, OBE, DL; Bovingdon Hall, Great Dunmow, Braintree, Essex (☎ Great Dunmow 850205)

TABOR, Mark Sydney; s of Major John Bentley Sydney Tabor TD (d 1968); *b* 6 Aug 1939; *Educ* Stonyhurst Coll, London Graduate Sch of Business Studies; *m* 1972, Jane Louise, da of Brig Robert Louis Hargroves, CBE, DL; 2 s, 1 da; *Career* joined Whitbread & Co Ltd 1962, dir Whitbread (London) Ltd 1974-77, dir W H Brakspear & Sons Ltd 1975-77, regional dir Whitbread Flowers Ltd 1977-; *Recreations* hunting, skiing, gardening; *Clubs* Cavalry & Guards; *Style* - Mark Tabor Esq; The Old Rectory, Skilgate, Taunton, Somerset (☎ Bampton 31357)

TADDEI, Hon Mrs (Charlotte Mary); da of 2 Baron Piercy; *b* 1947; *Educ* Badminton Sch; *m* 1966, Paolo Emilio Taddei; 1 s, 1 da; *Style* - The Hon Mrs Taddei; 70 Via Lorenzo il Magnifico, Florence, Italy

TAIT, Lady Katharine Jane; *née* Russell; da of 3 Earl Russell (Bertrand Russell) by his 2 w, Dora; *b* 29 Dec 1923; *m* 1948, Rev Charles Tait; 4 s, 1 da; *Style* - Lady Katharine Tait; Falls Village, Conn 06031, USA

TAIT, Sir Peter; KBE (1975, OBE 1967); s of John Oliver Tait (d 1947); *b* 5 Sept 1915; *m* 1946, Lilian Jean, nee Dunn; 1 s, 1 da; *Career* stockbroker 1960-76, consultant 1976-; dir Rothman Industries Ltd, dir Financial Enterprises Ltd, dir J Herries Ltd, chm Bowring Burgess Finance Co, chm S Pacific Orchids Ltd, chm Tait Assoc Ltd, chm Princess Alexandra Community Hosp, chm Napier Marineland & Aquarium Trust Bd; *Recreations* bowls, gardening; *Clubs* Napier Lions and Cosmopolitan; *Style* - Sir Peter Tait KBE; 13 Simla Terrace, Napier, New Zealand (☎ 53 894)

TALBOT OF MALAHIDE, 9 Baron (I 1831); Joseph Hubert George Talbot; Hereditary Lord Admiral Malahide and Adjacent Seas; s of John Reginald Charles Talbot (gs of Adm the Hon Sir John Talbot, GCB, 3 s of Baroness Talbot of Malahide, first holder of the title) and of Maria Josephine (d 1939), da of 3 Duc de Stacpoole; suc bro, 8 Baron Talbot of Malahide, MC (d 1975); *b* 22 April 1899; *Educ* Beaumont Coll; *m* 1, 1924, Hélène (d 1961), da of M Gouley, of Bessancourt, Seine-et-Oise, France; m 2, 1962 (m dis 1970), Béatrice Bros, of 20 Rue Frédéric, Passy, Nice; *Heir* cous, Reginald John Richard Arundell; *Career* late Lt Coldstream Gds; *Style* - The Rt Hon the Lord Talbot of Malahide; Malahide Castle, Co Dublin; Oakfield, Forest Row, Sussex

TALBOT, Hon Mrs (Cynthia Edith); *née* Guest; da of 1 Viscount Wimborne, JP, and Hon Alice Grosvenor, da of 2 Baron Ebury; *b* 24 Oct 1908; *m* 1933, Thomas George Talbot, CB, QC, *qv*; *Style* - The Hon Mrs Talbot; Falconhurst, Edenbridge, Kent (☎ Cowden 641)

TALBOT, John Bentley; MC (1946); s of Charles W Talbot (d 1965); *b* 30 April 1917; *Educ* Highgate Sch; *m* 1942, Marguerite Maxwell, nee Townley; 2 s, 1 da; *Career* Maj (RA) NW Europe (despatches); solicitor; sr ptnr Messrs Williams and James; *Recreations* travel, swimming, tennis; *Clubs* Army and Navy, HAC; *Style* - John Talbot Esq, MC; Bools Farm, The Holt, Farnham, Surrey

TALBOT, Hon Rose Maud; da of late Col the Hon Milo George Talbot, CB (4 s of late 4 Baron Talbot de Malahide) and sis of 7 Baron Talbot de Malahide (d 1973, when the UK Barony became ext); *b* 1915; raised to the rank of a Baron's da 1949; *Style* - The Hon Rose Talbot; Malahide, Fingal, Tasmania, Australia 7214

TALBOT, Thomas George; CB (1960), QC (1954); s of Rt Hon Sir George Talbot, PC (gs of Hon John Talbot, QC, 4 s of 2 Earl Talbot, which title is now merged with Earldom of Shrewsbury), by Gertrude, nee Cator; *b* 21 Dec 1904; *Educ* Winchester, New Coll Oxford; *m* 1933, Hon Cynthia Guest (*see* Hon Mrs Talbot); *Career* barr 1929; served WW II Scots Gds; Dep Parly Counsel Treasury 1944-53; Counsel Chm Ctees House of Lds 1953-77, Assist Counsel 1977-; *Clubs* Brooks's; *Style* - Thomas Talbot Esq, CB, QC; Falconhurst, Edenbridge, Kent (☎ Cowden 641)

TALBOT-PONSONBY, Nigel Edward Charles; s of Edward Fitzroy Talbot-Ponsonby (ggs of Adm Sir Charles Talbot, KCB, who was himself s of Very Rev Charles Talbot, Dean of Salisbury, by Lady Elizabeth Somerset, da of 5 Duke of Beaufort; the Dean was n of 3 Baron and 1 Earl Talbot, which (latter two) dignities are now held by the Earl of Shrewsbury); *b* 24 Sept 1946; *Educ* Harrow; *m* 1977, Robina, da of Lt-Cdr Henry Bruce, JP, RN (ret; gs of 9 Earl of Elgin & (13 of) Kincardine), of Barley Down House, Alresford, Hants; *Career* ARICS; chartered surveyor; ptnr Humberts (chartered surveyors); *Recreations* sailing, field sports; *Clubs* Roy Thames Yacht; *Style* - Nigel Talbot-Ponsonby Esq; Langrish Lodge, Langrish, Petersfield, Hants (☎ 3374)

TALBOYS, Rt Hon Brian Edward; CH (1981), PC (1977), MP (Nat) Wallace, NZ 1957-; *b* 1921; *Educ* Wanganui Collegiate Sch, Manitoba U, Victoria U Wellington; *m*; 2 s; *Career* Dep Ldr Nat Pty 1974-, Min Foreign Affrs & Overseas Tde 1975-, late Dep PM NZ; landowner; *Style* - The Rt Hon Brian Talboys, CH, PC, MP; Parliament House, Wellington, New Zealand

TAMWORTH, Viscount; Robert William Saswalo Shirley; s and h of 13 Earl Ferrers; *b* 29 Dec 1952; *Educ* Ampleforth; *m* 1980, Susannah Mary, da of Charles Edward Sheepshanks, of Arthington Hall, Otley, W Yorks; *Career* chartered accountant with Ernst & Whinney; *Recreations* country pursuits; *Style* - Viscount Tamworth; 10 Wetherby gdns, SW5 (☎ 01 370 2971)

TANGLEY, Baroness; Gwendolen Hilda; da of late Thomas Langley Judd, CBE; *m* 1932, Baron Tangley (Life Peer, d 1973); *Style* - The Rt Hon the Lady Tangley; Bramfell, Blackheath, Guildford, Surrey

TANGLEY, Hon Peter Meldrum; s of Baron Tangley (Life Peer, d 1973); *b* 1936; *m* 1961, Annabel Binnie; children; *Style* - The Hon Peter Tangley; Byways, Little London, Witley, Surrey

TANGYE, Lady; Baroness Clarisse Schosberger de Tornya; da of Baron Victor Schosberger de Tornya, of Tura, Hungary; *m* 1924, Sir Basil Tangye, 2 & last Bt (d 1969); 1 da; *Style* - Lady Tangye; 4 Farquhar rd, Edgbaston, Birmingham

TANGYE, Lady Marguerite Rose; *née* Bligh; da of late 9 Earl of Darnley by 1 w, Daphne, da of Hon Alfred Mulholland, s of 1 Baron Dunleath; *b* 1913; *m* 1, 1934 (m dis 1941), Claud Dobreé Strickland (ka 1941); m 2, 1942 (m dis 1951), Wing Cdr Gordon Stanley Keith Haywood, RA; 1 s, 1 da (twins); m 3, 1951 (m dis 1964), as his 2 w, Nigel Trevithick Tangye; *Style* - Lady Marguerite Tangye; 30 Coleherne rd, SW10

TANKERVILLE, 10 Earl of (GB 1714); Peter Grey Bennet; Baron Ossulston (E 1682); s of 9 Earl of Tankerville (d 1980); *b* 18 Oct 1956; *Educ* Grace Cathedral Sch (Chorister) San Francisco, Oberlin Conservatory Ohio (BMus); *Heir* uncle, Rev the Hon George Arthur Grey Bennet; *Career* musician, San Francisco; *Style* - The Rt Hon the Earl of Tankerville; 139 Olympia Way, San Francisco, Calif 94131, USA (☎ 415 826 6639)

TANKERVILLE, Countess of; Georgiana Lilian Maude; da of late Gilbert Wilson, of Vancouver, BC; *m* 1954, as his 2 w, 9 Earl of Tankerville (d

1980); *Style* - The Rt Hon the Countess of Tankerville; 139 Olympia Way, San Francisco, Calif, USA

TANKERVILLE, Dowager Countess of; Violet; da of Erik Pallin, of Stockholm; *m* 1930, as his 2 w, 8 Earl of Tankerville (d 1971); *Career* Order of Vasa of Sweden; *Style* - The Rt Hon the Dowager Countess of Tankerville; Chillingham Castle, Alnwick, Northumberland

TANLAW, Baron (Life Peer UK 1971); Hon Simon Brooke Mackay; yst s of 2 Earl of Inchcape (d 1939); *b* 30 March 1934; *Educ* Eton and Trin Cambridge; *m* 1, 1959, Joanna Susan, da of Maj John Henry Hirsch, of Sungrove Lodge, Newbury; 1 s, 2 da (and 1 s decd); m 2, 1976, Rina Siew Yong, da of late Tiong Cha Tan, of Kuala Lumpur, Malaysia; 1 da; *Career* late 2 Lt 12 Roy Lancers, dir Inchcape & Co Ltd, chm and md of Fandstan Gp of Priv Cos, pres Kensington Liberal Assoc 1971-75, dep chm Scottish Liberal Party 1972, pres Sarawak Assoc 1972-75, chm Building Ctee Univ Coll at Buckingham 1973-78, Liberal Energy Spokesman House of Lds 1979-; *Clubs* White's, Oriental, Buck's; *Style* - The Rt Hon the Lord Tanlaw; Tanlawhill, Eskadalemuir, By Langholm, Dumfries, (☎ Eskdalemuir 273); The Manor House, Little Venice, W9

TANNER, Adrian Christopher; s of Alfred Charles Tanner; *b* 13 Oct 1946; *Educ* Skinners Tunbridge Wells; *m* 1969, Anna Margaret, nee Shepherd; 2 da; *Career* marine insurance broker, dir Alexander Howden Insurance Brokers Ltd 1978-, memb of Lloyd's; *Style* - Adrian Tanner Esq; Finches, Smarden, Kent

TANNER, Howard Montagu Stuart; s of Brian Montagu Tanner, of S Africa; *b* 21 May 1944; *Educ* Stellenbosch U; Imede, Lausanne, Switzerland; *m* (m dis); 1 s, 1 da; *Career* Capt 2 Parachute Bn S Africa; md Cape Asbestos Fibres Ltd, dir Cape Asbestos SA Ltd, dir Marico Fluorspar (Pty) Ltd; *Recreations* skiing, fishing, shooting; *Clubs* Rand (Durban), Johannesburg Country, Inanda, Western Province Sport; *Style* - Howard Tanner Esq; 11 Badgerswood, Farnham Common, Bucks; 2 Wimbourne Close, Gwenn Lane, Sandown, Sandton, S Africa

TAPPS-GERVIS-MEYRICK, George Christopher Cadafael; s and h of Sir George David Eliott Tapps-Gervis-Meyrick, 6 Bt, MC; *b* 10 March 1941; *Educ* Eton, Trin Cambridge; *m* 1968 Jean Louise, da of late Lord William Walter Montagu Douglas Scott, MC, s of 7 Duke of Buccleuch; 2 s, 1 d; *Style* - George Tapps-Gervis-Meyrick Esq; Waterditch House, Bransgore, Christchurch, Hants

TAPPS-GERVIS-MEYRICK, Lt-Col Sir George David Eliott; 6 Bt (GB 1791), of Hinton Admiral, Hants, MC; s of Maj Sir George Llewelyn Tapps-Gervis-Meyrick, 5 Bt (d 1960); *b* 15 April 1915; *Educ* Eton, Trin Cambridge; *m* 1940, Ann, da of Clive Miller (d 1956); 1 s, 1 da; *Heir* s, George Christopher Cadafael Tapps-Gervis-Meyrick; *Career* 2 Lt 9 Queen's Roy Lancers 1936, Capt 1940, Lt-Col, ret 1952; High Sheriff Anglesey 1962; *Clubs* Cavalry; *Style* - Lt-Col Sir George Tapps-Gervis-Meyrick, Bt, MC; Bodorgan, Isle of Anglesey (☎ Bodorgan 204); Hinton Admiral, Christchurch, Hampshire (☎ Highcliffe 72887)

TAPSCOTT, Paul Mais; s of Henry John Tapscott (d 1960); *b* 23 May 1919; *Educ* Uppingham, Trin Cambridge; *m* 1946, Babette Alison, nee Blackham; 1 da; *Career* economist and member Stock Exchange 1956-, chm Lesney Products & Co Ltd 1960-80, chm Associated Fisheries Ltd 1969-78, dir Friends Provident Life Office 1966-, chm and dep chairman Francis Industries Ltd 1964-; *Recreations* swimming, gardening, DIY; *Clubs* City of London, RAF, Phyllis Court; *Style* - Paul Tapscott Esq; Brampton, Green Dene, East Horsley, Leatherhead, Surrey (☎ E Horsley 2058)

TARASSENKO, Lady Ann Mary Elizabeth; da (by 2 m) of late 6 Earl of Craven; *b* 1959; *m* 1978, Lionel Tarassenko; *Style* - Lady Ann Tarassenko; 33 Church rd, Caversham, Reading, Berks

TARBAT, Viscount; John Ruaridh Blunt Grant MacKenzie; s and h of Earl of Cromartie (4 holder of title); *b* 12 June 1948; *Educ* Rannoch Sch Perthshire,

Strathclyde U; *m* 1973, Helen, da of John Murray; 1 s (decd); *Style* - Viscount Tarbat; Castle Leod, Strathpeffer, Ross-shire

TATE, Lt-Col Sir Henry; 4 Bt (UK 1898), TD, DL (Rutland 1964); s of Sir Ernest William Tate, 3 Bt, JP, DL (d 1939); *b* 29 June 1902; *Educ* Uppingham, RMC; *m* 1927, Lilian Nairne, da of late Col Saxon Gregson-Ellis, JP; 2 s; *Heir* s, Henry Saxon Tate; *Career* formerly Lt Gren Gds, Hon Lt-Col RWF, Councillor Rutland CC 1958-69 & 1970-74, High Sheriff of Rutland 1949-50, Jt Master Cottesmore Foxhounds 1946-58, pres Cottesmore Hunt 1974-, dep pres Burghley Horse Trials 1960-, chm Rutland Agricultural Soc 1946-66; *Recreations* hunting, fishing, gardening, shooting; *Clubs* Buck's; *Style* - Lt-Col Sir Henry Tate, Bt, TD, DL; Preston Lodge, Withcote, Oakham, Rutland, Leics LE15 8PP; The Cottage, Galltfaenan, Trefnant, Clwyd

TATE, Henry Saxon; s and h of Sir Henry Tate, 4 Bt, TD, DL; *b* 28 Nov 1931; *Educ* Eton, Ch Ch Oxford; *m* 1, 1953 (m dis 1975), Sheila Ann, da of Duncan Robertson; 4 s (incl twin s); m 2, 1975, Virginia Sturm; *Career* Nat Serv Life Guards 1949-50 (Lt); dir Tate & Lyle Ltd 1956, md 1978-80, v-chm 1980-; Fell American Management Assoc 1972, FBIM 1975; *Clubs* Buck's; *Style* - Henry Tate Esq; 26 Cleaver sq, SE11

TATTERSALL-WALKER, George; s of George Tattersall-Walker (d 1947); *b* 2 Sept 1920; *Educ* The Leys Sch; *m* 1947, Edith; 2 s; *Career* chartered accountant 1949, planning dir John Smith's Tadcaster Brewery Ltd 1969-, chm Anchor Hotels & Taverns Ltd 1977-, chm John Smith's Brewery SA Belgium 1973-; Lay Preacher 1944-, memb Cncl Inst of Chartered Accountants 1966-; *Recreations* gardening, donkey breeding, public speaking; *Clubs* Anglo-Belgian, Overseas; *Style* - George Tattersall-Walker Esq; Woodside, Oaks Lane, Boston Spa, W Yorks (☎ 0937 842250)

TATTON-BROWN, Lady Kenya Eleanor; *née* Kitchener; da of Viscount Broome (d 1928 - only s of 2 Earl Kitchener of Kharthoum and of Broome); *b* 1923; *m* 1947, as his 2 wife, John Stewart Tatton-Brown (s 1971); 3 da; *Career* late 3 Officer WRNS; *Style* - Lady Kenya Tatton-Brown; Westergate Wood, nr Chichester, Sussex

TATUM, Hon Mrs (Marguerite Betty); *née* Cadman; 1 da of 1 Baron Cadman, GCMG, FRS; *b* 1913; *m* 1940, Rev John Tatum (d 1966); 2 s, 1 da; *Style* - The Hon Mrs Tatum; Gorsedown, Birling Gap, Eastbourne, Sussex

TAVENER, Robin Frederick; s of Harold William Tavener (d 1970); *b* 20 Nov 1929; *Educ* Leighton Park Sch Reading; *m* 1955, Pamela Beatrice, nee Austin; 2 s, 1 da; *Career* FCCA, CBIM, IOD; md & ch exec Stone-Platt Industries Ltd 1980-, chm electrical div 1975-79, fin dir electrical div 1969-74; fin dir ITT 1965; *Recreations* theatre, walking, travelling; *Clubs* RAC; *Style* - Robin Tavener Esq; 1/11 Adelaide cres, Hove, Sussex

TAVISTOCK, Marquess of; Henry Robin Ian Russell; s and h of 13 Duke of Bedford; *b* 21 Jan 1940; *Educ* Le Rosey Switzerland, Harvard U; *m* 1961, Henrietta Joan, da of Henry F Tiarks; 3 s; *Heir* s, Lord Howland; *Career* dir: Trafalgar House Ltd 1977-, Touche Remnant & Co 1977-, United Racecourses 1977-; chm Cedar Investment Tst 1977-; *Clubs* Buck's, Jockey; *Style* - Marquess of Tavistock; Woburn Abbey, Woburn, Bedfordshire MK43 (☎ Woburn 666)

TAYLOR OF MANSFIELD, Baron (Life Peer UK 1966); Harry Bernard Taylor; CBE (1966); s of late Henry Taylor; *b* 18 Sept 1895; *Educ* Oxclose Lane Sch, Mansfield Woodhouse; *m* 1921, Clara Annie, da of John Ashley; 1 s; *Career* MP (L) Mansfield Div of Nottinghamshire 1941-66, Parly Priv Sec to Parly Sec Miny of Aircraft Production 1942, to Min of Nat Insurance 1945, Parly Sec Miny of Nat Insurance 1950-51; *Style* - The Rt Hon the Lord Taylor of Mansfield CBE; 47 Shakespeare av, Mansfield Woodhouse, Nottinghamshire

TAYLOR, Baron (Life Peer UK 1958); Stephen James Lake Taylor; s of late John Reginald Taylor, MICE; *b* 30

Dec 1910; *Educ* Stowe, St Thomas's Hosp Med Sch (BSc, BS, MD); MRCS, LRCP, MRCP, FRCP, FRCGP; *m* 1939, May Doris Charity, MB, BS, MRCP, LRCP, da of late Wron George Clifford; 2 s, 1 da; *Career* Surg Lt-Cdr RNVR 2 World War, Dir Home Intelligence 1941-45, Pres and V-Chllr Memorial U of Newfoundland 1967-73, Visiting Prof of Medicine 1973-, formerly med dir Harlow Industrial Health Serv, Consultant in Occupational Health to Richard Costain Ltd, memb Harlow New Town Corpn, Visiting Research Fell Nuffield Provincial Hosps Trust, v-chm British Film Corpn, PPS to Dep PM and Lord Pres of Council 1948-50, Parly Under-Sec Commonwealth Relations and Colonial Offices 1964-65, MP (L) Barnet Div of Herts 1945-50; resigned from Labour Party July 1981 (after 42 years membership), Cross-bencher in House of Lords; *Style* - The Rt Hon the Lord Taylor; Plas y Garth, Glyn Ceiriog, Llangollen, Clwyd

TAYLOR OF GRYFE, Baron (Life Peer UK 1968); Thomas Johnston Taylor; DL (Renfrewshire 1970); s of John Sharp Taylor, of Glasgow; *b* 27 April 1912; *Educ* Bellahouston Acad Glasgow; *m* 1943, Isobel, da of William Wands; 2 da; *Career* chm Economic Forestry Gp 1976-, Morgan Grenfell (Scotland) Ltd 1973-, chm Scottish Railways Bd 1971-80, memb BR Bd 1968-80, memb Bd Scottish Television Ltd 1968-, dir Scottish Civic Trust, Whiteaway Laidlaw & Co Ltd (Bankers) 1971-, Friends' Provident Life Office 1972-, Scottish Metropolitan Property Co Ltd 1972, BR Property Bd 1972; Hon LLD Strathclyde 1974; FRSE 1977; *Clubs* Caledonian and New (Edinburgh); *Style* - The Rt Hon the Lord Taylor of Gryfe, DL; The Cottage, Auchenames, Kilbarchan, Renfrewshire PA10 2PM (☎ Kilbarchan 2648)

TAYLOR OF BLACKBURN, Baron (Life Peer UK 1978); Thomas Taylor; CBE (1974, OBE 1969); s of James Taylor; *b* 10 June 1929; *Educ* Blakey Moor Higher Grade Sch; *m* 1950, Kathleen, da of John Edward Nurton; 1 s; *Career* memb Blackburn Town Council 1954-76 (leader, and chm Policy and Resources Ctee 1972-76), Dep Pro-Chllr Lancaster U 1974-, chm Government Ctee of Enquiry into Management and Govt of Schs, and of Nat Foundation for Visual Aids, past chm of Juvenile Bench, pres Free Church Council 1962-68, memb Norweb Bd and consultant Shorrock Security Systems Ltd and other cos; JP Blackburn 1960; *Style* - The Rt Hon the Lord Taylor of Blackburn CBE JP; 34 Tower rd, Feniscliffe, Blackburn, Lancs

TAYLOR, Anthony Donnithorne; DSO (1944), MC (1940); s of Capt John Taylor (d 1956), of North Aston Manor, Oxford, by his w Sybil, whose mother was Blanche, gda of Rev Lord William Somerset; Lord William was 5 s of 5 Duke of Beaufort; Anthony's sis is the Countess of Devon; *b* 6 Aug 1910; *Educ* Winchester, Sandhurst; *m* 1, 1936, Vanda (d 1978), da of Maj Foster Swetenham, Roy Scots Greys; 1 s (Jeremy b 1942, m 1971 Mary Fern, niece of Peter and Ian Fleming, the writers, and gda through her mother (*see* Hon Mrs Fleming) of 2 Baron Wyfold), 3 da (Mrs Nicholas (Vivien) Ansell, da-in-law of Col Sir Michael Ansell; Mrs Richard (Rosemary) Macaire; Mrs David (Celia) Plunkett); m 2, 1979, Veronica, da of Lionel Whitehead, of Goytre Hall, Abergavenny, and widow of Lt-Col P B Sanger; *Career* 2 Lt 15/19 King's Roy Hussars 1930, served France & Belgium 1940, NW Europe 1944-45, Lt-Col 1942, Cmd 15/19 Hussars 1942-45 & 1947-49, GSO (1) 6 Armoured Div 1951-52, ret 1952, Col KRH (15/19) 1964-70; JP Oxon 1956-72, High Sheriff 1963; *Style* - Lt-Col Anthony Taylor DSO MC; Manor Farm, North Aston, Oxon (☎ Steeple Aston 40260)

TAYLOR, Hon Bernard Alfred; s of Baron Taylor of Mansfield (Life Peer); *b* 1922; *m* 1952; *Style* - The Hon Bernard Taylor; 126 Mansfield st, Sherwood, Nottingham

TAYLOR, Cavan; s of Albert William Taylor; *b* 23 Feb 1935; *Educ* King's Coll Sch Wimbledon, Emmanuel Cambridge; *m* 1962, Helen, da of late Everard Tinling; 1 s, 2 da; *Career* slr, ptnr in Durrant Piesse; chm of governing body of King's Coll Sch Wimbledon 1973-; *Recreations* reading, sailing, gardening; *Clubs*

Gresham; *Style* - Cavan Taylor Esq; Covenham House, Broad Highway, Cobham, Surrey KT11 2RP (☎ 4258)

TAYLOR, Cecil Charlton; s of Percy James Taylor (d 1950); *b* 11 Jan 1916; *Educ* Uppingham; *m* 1940, Joan Mary, nee Snowden; 1 s, 2 da; *Career* Maj RASC, Directorate Gen HQ & War Office; CA, Inst Cncl 1968-77; chm McKechnie Bros Ltd 1976-, Victoria Carpet Hldgs 1977-, John Morrell & Co Ltd 1980-, Mace Marketing Servs Ltd 1959-77, dir N Greening & Sons Ltd 1966-75 (dep chm 1970-); *Recreations* sailing, racing, beagling; *Clubs* Roy Yacht Sqdn, Roy Thames Yacht, Roy Mersey Yacht, Sea View Yacht, Liverpool Racquet; *Style* - Cecil Taylor Esq; Wickens, Seaview, Isle of Wight (☎ 098 371 2255)

TAYLOR, Hon Charles Richard Herbert; s of Baron Taylor (Life Peer); *b* 1950; *Educ* Highgate, King's Cambridge, Queen's and St Anthony's Oxford; *m* 1977, Mary-Ellen, da of John Feeney, of Pa USA; *Career* a development economist, World Bank; *Style* - The Hon Charles Taylor; 1425 Floral st, NW, Washington DC, 20012, USA

TAYLOR, David Mills; s of Donald Charles Taylor (d 1940); *b* 22 Dec 1935; *Educ* Roy Commercial Travellers Sch; *m* 1960, Gillian Irene, nee Washford; 4 da; *Career* FCA; fin dir Trafalgar House Ltd 1979-, The Guthrie Corpn Ltd 1971-79 and Brooke Bond Oxo Ltd 1968-71; *Recreations* squash, golf; *Style* - David Taylor Esq; Fairwood House, Fairmile Park rd, Cobham, Surrey

TAYLOR, Lt-Col George; DSO, TD, DL (W Yorks); s of Thomas Taylor; *b* 31 May 1900; *Educ* Sedbergh; *m* 1924, Margaret, nee Silvester; 2 da; *Career* Lt-Col France, Poland, Germany; former chm Heckmondwike Carpets Ltd; *Clubs* Army and Navy; *Style* - Lt-Col George Taylor, DSO, TD, DL; Lower Hall, Kirkheaton, Huddersfield (☎ 23067)

TAYLOR, Hon Mrs (Joan Evelyn); da of Baron Underhill, CBE (Life Peer); *b* 1944; *m* 1973, Ian Taylor; *Style* - The Hon Mrs Taylor; 22 Royal Oak Drive, Selston, Notts

TAYLOR, John Harris; s of Walter Harris Taylor (d 1956); *b* 13 Jan 1918; *Educ* King's Coll Sch Wimbledon; *m* 1942, Violet May, nee Hamilton; 3 c; *Career* Maj Roy Signals; md RE Hamilton & Co Ltd (Ford distributors) 1954-80, dir Bowmaker (Ulster) Ltd 1969-80; *Recreations* hunting, gardening; *Clubs* Ulster; *Style* - John Taylor Esq; Beltrim, Killinakin, Killinchy, Co Down

TAYLOR, Hon Jeremy Stephen; s of Baron Taylor (Life Peer); *b* 1940; *Educ* Highgate; *m* 1964, Christina, da of late John Bruce Holmes; children; *Career* television executive; *Style* - The Hon Jeremy Taylor; 19 Ayresome av, Leeds LS8 1BB

TAYLOR, Lady; Mary; da of Thomas B Hall, of Barnsley; *m* 1930, Sir William Johnson Taylor, 1 Bt, CBE (d 1972, when the title became ext); *Style* - Lady Taylor; Bentwood, Cawthorne, Barnsley, Yorks; 36 Buckingham Gate, SW1

TAYLOR, Martin Gibbeson; s of Roy Gibbeson Taylor (d 1955); *b* 30 Jan 1935; *Educ* Haileybury and St Catharine's Cambridge; *m* 1960, Gunilla Chaterina, nee Bryner; 2 s; *Career* FCA 1961; Dowchemical UK 1963-69; dir Hanson Trust Ltd 1976; *Clubs* MCC; *Style* - Martin Taylor Esq; c/o 180 Brompton rd, SW3 (☎ 01 589 7070)

TAYLOR, Hon Mrs (Marilyn Ruth); da of Baron Fisher of Camden (Life Peer, d 1979); *b* 1940; *Educ* BA; *m* 1960, Mervyn Taylor, solicitor; *Style* - The Hon Mrs Taylor; 4 Springfield rd, Templeogue, Dublin

TAYLOR, Sir Nicholas Richard Stuart; 4 Bt (UK 1917), of Kennington, Co London; s of Sir Richard Laurence Stuart Taylor, 3 Bt (d 1978); *b* 14 Jan 1952; *Educ* Bradfield; *Heir* none; *Career* slr 1977; *Style* - Sir Nicholas Taylor, Bt; White Lodge, Hambrook, Chichester, Sussex

TAYLOR, Paul Duncan; JP (1969); s of Edward Duncan Taylor; *b* 25 April 1936; *Educ* Mill Hill Sch; *m* 1964, Lindsay

Veronica Moncrieff, nee Smith; 2 s; *Career* chartered accountant, ptnr Spicer and Pegler, dep chm Wagon Industrial Hldgs Ltd; *Clubs* The Leeds; *Style* - Paul Taylor Esq, JP; Oakwood House, Upper Batley, Batley, W Yorks (☎ 0924 473552)

TAYLOR, Hon Mrs (Priscilla Jane); da of 1 Baron Piercy, CBE (d 1966); *b* 1926; *Educ* Downe House and LSE; *m* 1950, Rev Thomas Fish Taylor; 1 s, 3 da; *Style* - The Hon Mrs Taylor; Titcombs, Sheep st, Burford, Oxford

TAYLOR, Hon Paul Nurton; s of Baron Taylor of Blackburn (Life Peer); *b* 1953; *m* 1978, Diane Brindle; *Style* - The Hon Paul Taylor; 601 Preston Old rd, Blackburn, Lancs

TAYLOR, Robert (George); MP (C) NW Croydon 1970-; s of the late Frederick Taylor; *b* 7 Dec 1932; *Educ* Cranleigh; *m* 1964, Rosemary Ann, nee Box; 1 s, 1 da; *Career* memb Select Ctee of Public Accounts 1974-; *Recreations* bridge; *Clubs* Carlton, East India, Devonshire & Public Schools; *Style* - Robert Taylor Esq, MP; Hinterland House, Effingham Common, Surrey

TAYLOR, Lt-Col Richard Ian Griffith; DSO, MC, DL; s of Lt-Col Thomas George Taylor, DSO (d 1946); *b* 5 June 1911; *Educ* Harrow, Oxford U; *m* 1, 1934 (m dis 1951), Hon Sylvia, *qv*, da of late 2 Baron Joicey; 2 s, 1 da; m 2, 1952, Hon Cecily Eveline (d 1975, widow of Patrick Magor Leatham, MC), da of 1 & last Baron Buckland; 2 da; *Career* Lt-Col, Greece, Western Desert, France, Germany; farmer; landowner; *Recreations* shooting, fishing, hunting; *Clubs* White's; *Style* - Lt-Col Richard Taylor DSO MC DL; Chipchase Castle, Wark on Tyne, Northumberland

TAYLOR, Robert Julian Faussitt; s of Col G F Taylor, MBE; *b* 21 June 1929; *Educ* Dragon Oxford, Trin Cambridge; *m* 1967, Jacqueline, nee Castaing; 2 s; *Career* md Manchester Ship Canal Co 1980-, dir Ocean Transport & Trading 1964-79, British Antarctic Survey 1953-57, The Wildfowl Trust Cncl 1973-81, RSPB Cncl 1978-81; *Recreations* the countryside, birds, deer, gardening, climbing, reading; *Clubs* Travellers'; *Style* - Robert Taylor Esq; Bridgewater House, Runcorn, Ches; Home Lodge, Cholderton, Wilts

TAYLOR, Hon Mrs Sylvia Alice; da of 2 Baron Joicey (d 1940); *b* 1908; *m* 1934 (m dis 1951), Lt-Col Richard Taylor, DSO, MC, *qv*; 2 s, 1 da; *Style* - The Hon Mrs Sylvia Taylor; Barelees, Cornhill-on-Tweed, Northumberland

TAYLOR, Lady Ursula Daphne; *née* Brudenell-Bruce; da of 6 Marquess of Ailesbury, DSO, TD (d 1961); *b* 21 Oct 1905; *m* 1944, Alec Taylor; 2 s; *Style* - Lady Ursula Taylor; 2 Howard rd, Newbury, Berks

TAYLOR-JONES, Dr Thomas Henry Edward; DL (Kent 1981); s of Henry Taylor-Jones (d 1939); *b* 6 Feb 1906; *Educ* Dulwich, London U; *m* 1931, Dorothy Amy, da of John Corbett (d 1922); 1 s decd, 1 da; *Career* late Sr Med Offr Belgrave Hosp for Children, MO West View Hosp Tenterden 1960-76; MRCS, LRCP, DCH; *Recreations* gardening, general practice; *Clubs* Naval and Military, Band of Brothers; *Style* - Dr Thomas Taylor-Jones, DL; The Garden, Tenterden, Kent (☎ 3193)

TAYLOUR, Lady Olivia Sheelin Davina Anne; da of 6 Marquess of Headfort; *b* 1963; *Style* - Lady Olivia Taylour

TAYLOUR, Lady Rosanagh Elizabeth Angela Mary; da of 6 Marquess of Headfort; *b* 1961; *Style* - Lady Rosanagh Taylour

TAYLOUR, Lord William Desmond; s of 4 Marquess of Headfort (d 1943); *b* 1904; *Educ* Harrow, Trin Cambridge (BA, MA, PhD); *Career* FSA; late Capt 2 Derbyshire Yeo (TA); *Style* - Lord William Taylour; St Aubyns, 2 Woodlands rd, Great Shelford, Cambridge

TAYSIDE, Baroness; Hilda Gwendoline; BSc; da of John Thomson Harris, of Dundee; *m* 1939, Baron Tayside (Life Peer d 1975); *Style* - The Rt Hon The Lady Tayside; The Manor, Forfar, Angus

TEAGUE, Col John; CMG (1958), CBE (1946, OBE 1925), MC (1916); s of William Teague (d 1913); *b* 16 Nov 1896; *Educ* Portsmouth G S; *m* 1, 1926, Heather (d 1966), nee Fairley; 2 s, 1 da; m 2, Nora Ballard, nee Tourle; *Career* Col 1943 (ret 1946), served in Great War 1914-18, Iraq 1920, Ops Kurdistan 1922, NW Frontier 1930, Palestine & Middle East 1936-45; Foreign Office 1945; dir Passport Control 1953-58; *Recreations* reading, music; *Clubs* RAF; *Style* - Col John Teague CMG CBE MC; 5 Hungershall pk, Tunbridge Wells, Kent (☎ 0892 26959)

TEARLE, Francis John Enoch; CBE (1965); s of John Herbert Tearle (d 1966); *b* 26 July 1902; *Educ* Sir William Borlase's Sch, RNCs Osborne and Dartmouth, Manchester U; *m* 1926, Nettie Liddell, nee McLean; 1 s; *Career* chartered mechanical engr, Fell Inst Mech Engrs; dir AEI Ltd, md AEI Overseas Ltd 1956-66, chm Eutectic Company Ltd 1967-77; *Recreations* golf, gardening, travel; *Style* - Francis Tearle Esq, CBE; Little Knowle, 4 Knowle pk, Cobham, Surrey

TEDDER, 2 Baron (UK 1946); John Michael Tedder; s of Marshal of the RAF 1 Baron Tedder, GCB, AOC-in-C M East 1941-42 & Med 1943, Ch Air Staff 1946-49 and Chllr Cambridge U 1950-67 (d 1967); *b* 4 July 1926; *Educ* Dauntsey's Sch, Magdalene College Cambridge (ScD), Birmingham U (PhD, DSc); *m* 1952, Peggy Eileen, da of Samuel George Growcott, of Birmingham; 2 s, 1 da; *Heir* s, Hon Robin John Tedder; *Career* Purdie Prof of Chemistry St Salvator's Coll St Andrews U 1969-; memb RSC 1980-; FRSE, FRSC; *Style* - The Rt Hon The Lord Tedder; Little Rathmore, Kennedy gdns, St Andrews, Fife, Scotland (☎ St Andrews 3546)

TEDDER, Hon Andrew Jonathan; s of 2 Baron Tedder; *b* 1958; *Style* - The Hon Andrew Tedder

TEDDER, Hon Anne Rosalinde; da of 2 Baron Tedder; *b* 1963; *Style* - The Hon Anne Tedder

TEDDER, Hon Mina Una Margaret; da of 1 Baron Tedder, GCB (d 1967); *b* 1920; *Career* formerly assist librarian British Embassy, Washington, USA; BBC TV 1954-57, Scottish TV Glasgow 1957-65, district cmmr Nat Savings, Alnwick, Northumberland; *Style* - The Hon Mina Tedder

TEDDER, Hon Robin John; s and h of 2 Baron Tedder; *b* 6 April 1955; *m* 1977, Jennifer Mangan (d 1978); *Style* - The Hon Robin Tedder

TEDDER, Hon Richard Seton; s of 1 Baron Tedder, GCB (d 1967); *b* 1946; *m* 1975, Ann-Marie Adams; *Style* - The Hon Richard Tedder

TEGNER, Ian Nicol; s of Sven Stuart Tegner, OBE (d 1971); *b* 11 July 1933; *Educ* Rugby; *m* 1961, Meriel Helen, da of Maurice Stanley Lush, CB, CBE, MC; 1 s, 1 da; *Career* CA (Scotland) 1957, Clarkson Gordon & Co Toronto Canada 1958-59, Barton Mayhew & Co 1959-71 (ptnr 1965), fin dir The Bowater Corpn Ltd 1971; *Recreations* book collecting, shooting, walking, choral singing, family life; *Style* - Ian Tegner Esq; 44 Norland sq, W11 (☎ 01 229 8604); Keepers Cottage, Kilninver, Argyll

TEIGNMOUTH, Baroness; Pamela; s of H Edmonds-Heath; *m* 1, --Meyer; m 2, 1979, as his 2 w, 7 & last Baron Teignmouth, DSC* (d 1981); *Style* - The Rt Hon The Lady Teignmouth; Fourpenny Rock, Thomastown, Co Kilkenny, Eire (☎ (056) 2 41 33)

TELFER, Frederick Charles Edmund; s of Edmund Telfer (d 1953); *b* 10 Nov 1931; *Educ* Pangbourne Coll, Millfield Sch, Pembroke Coll Oxford; *m* 1965, Patricia Mary, da of John George Abraham, TD (d 1973); 3 s, 1 da; *Career* stockbroker 1957; ptnr Joseph Sebag & Co 1965-, ptnr Carr Sebag & Co 1979-; memb Council of Stock Exchange 1975-; *Recreations* sailing, shooting, skiing; *Clubs* Roy Thames Yacht, Roy London Yacht, Roy Southern Yacht; *Style* - Frederick Telfer Esq; West End House, Frensham, Surrey (025125 3549)

TELFORD, Sir Robert; CBE (1967); s of late Robert Telford; *b* 1 Oct 1915; *Educ* Quarry Bank Sch Liverpool, Queen Elizabeth's G S Tamworth, Christ's Cambridge; *m* 1 (m dis); 1 s; m 2, 1958, Elizabeth Mary, da of F Shelley; 3 da; *Career* md GEC-Marconi Electronics Ltd; dir: GEC, Marconi (& Canadian Marconi Co), Fisher Controls Int Inc (USA), amongst others; kt 1978; *Clubs* RAF; *Style* - Sir Robert Telford, CBE; Rettendon House, Rettendon, Chelmsford, Essex

TELLING, Alfred Caleb Victor; *b* 18 Sept 1909; *Educ* Haberdashers' Aske's; *m* 1; 2 s, 1 da; m 2, 1975, Megan, nee Parry; *Career* chm Hat Group Ltd; past Master Plaisterers' Co; FIOB; *Recreations* farming, collecting; *Style* - Alfred Telling Esq; Barley Wood, Wrington, Avon

TELLWRIGHT, Hon Mrs (Caroline Fiona); da of 14 Baron Stafford; *b* 1956; *m* 1981, Kirkland Tellwright, s of William Tellwright; *Style* - The Hon Mrs Tellwright

TEMPLE OF STOWE, 7 Earl (UK 1822); Ronald Stephen Brydges Temple-Gore-Langton; s of Capt Hon Chandos Temple-Gore-Langton (d 1921, gs of Lady Anna Temple, sis of 3 & last Duke of Buckingham and Chandos; her gf, the 1 Duke - himself gs of the PM George Grenville & whose f & uncs, it was calculated, got their hands on c £900,000 of public money in 50 years (Cobbett's figures) - was so created (1822) as a *quid pro quo* for Grenville support for Lord Liverpool; Sir Charles Bagot observed "..the Grenvilles are taken into the Government; and (for Grenvilles) they come tolerably cheap. I see no objection to a Dukedom in the head of the Grenville family, but I see many to giving it to the actual blubber head who now reigns over them." The 2 Duke may to a certain extent be regarded as having recycled the monies of which his relations had mulcted the public purse, for he dissipated his vast patrimony in under a decade; Stowe Park (now the public school) was the Dukes' country residence); suc bro (6 Earl) 1966; *b* 5 Nov 1910; in 1941 was granted rank, title and precedence as an Earl's son which would have been his had his father survived to succeed to the title; *Career* company representative, patron of 5 livings; *Style* - The Rt Hon the Earl Temple of Stowe; c/o National Bank of Australasia Ltd, 11 Nerang st, Southport, Queensland, Australia

TEMPLE, Derek Anthony; s of Oscar Vincent Athelstan Temple; *b* 3 June 1923; *Educ* Salvatorian Coll Harrow Weald, Roy School of Mines London, Trinity Hall Cambridge; *m* 1949, Peggy Jean, nee Dunn; 2 da; *Career* metallurgical engineer, dir and ch exec ISP Ltd (RTZ) Group 1970-, former pres Inst of Mining & Metallurgy 1979-80; *Recreations* domestic; *Style* - Derek Temple Esq; 10b Avon Grove, Bristol (☎ 684278)

TEMPLE, His Honour Judge; Ernest Sanderson; MBE (1946), QC (1969); s of Ernest Temple (d 1957); *b* 23 May 1921; *Educ* Kendal School, Queens Oxford; *m* 1946, June Debonnaire, nee Saunders; 1 s, 2 da; *Career* barr Gray's Inn 1943; dep chm Westmorland QS 1967-68, chm 1968-71; recorder Criminal Court 1971-77, Hon Recorder of Kendal 1972, Circuit Judge and Recorder of Liverpool 1977-; *Recreations* farming and horses; *Clubs* Racquet Liverpool; *Style* - His Honour Judge Temple, MBE, QC; Yealand Hall, Yealand Redmayne, nr Carnforth LA5 9TD (☎ 0524 781200)

TEMPLE, John Meredith; JP (Cheshire 1949), DL (1975); s of Tom Temple (d 1955); *b* 9 June 1910; *Educ* Charterhouse, Clare Coll Cambridge; *m* 1942, Nancy Violet, da of Brig-Gen Robert Hare, CMG, DSO, DL; 1 s, 1 da; *Career* farmer, landowner, memb Lloyd's 1938, MP (C) Chester 1956-74, High Sheriff Cheshire 1980-81, special rep from House of Commons at UN XXVI Gen Assembly 1971, memb NW Bd of The Abbey National Bldg Soc; *Recreations* travel, shooting; *Clubs* Carlton, Army & Navy, Racquet (Liverpool), City (Chester); *Style* - John Temple Esq, JP, DL; Picton Gorse, Chester (☎ 0244 300239)

TEMPLE, Kenneth James Noel; s of Richard James Temple; *b* 10 Dec 1919; *Educ* Godalming, Surrey; *m* 1943, Kathleen Mary, nee Staines; 1 c; *Career* RAF 1940-45 Fl Engineer; sales rep 1951-76; company dir Drake & Son Ltd 1976; md

1980 (Weymouth, Torquay, Exeter, Yeovil); *Recreations* travel; *Style* - Kenneth Temple Esq; 42, Brunel rd, Elberry Cove, Paignton, Devon

TEMPLE, Marie, Lady; Marie Wanda; da of late F C Henderson, of Bombay, India; *m* 1939, as his 2 w, Sir Richard Durand Temple, 3 Bt, DSO (d 1962); *Style* - Marie, Lady Temple

TEMPLE, Richard; s and h of Sir Richard Antony Purbeck Temple, 4 Bt, MC; *b* 17 Aug 1937; *m* 1964, Emma Rose, da of late Maj-Gen Sir Robert Edward Laycock, KCMG, CB, DSO; 3 da; *Style* - Richard Temple Esq; 79 Lansdowne rd, W11

TEMPLE, Sir Richard Anthony Purbeck; 4 Bt (UK 1876), MC (1941); s of Sir Richard Durand Temple, 3 Bt, DSO (d 1962); *b* 19 Jan 1913; *Educ* Stowe, Trin Hall Cambridge; *m* 1, 1936 (m dis 1946), Lucy Geils, da of late Alain Joly de Lotbinière, of Montreal; 2 s; m 2, 1950, Jean, da of late James T Finnie, and widow of Oliver P Croom-Johnson; 1 da; *Heir* s, Richard Temple; *Career* served War of 1939-45 (wounded, MC), sometime Maj King's Roy Rifle Corps; *Style* - Sir Richard Temple, Bt, MC; Idbury Manor, Oxon

TEMPLE, Reginald Robert; CMG (1979); s of Lt-Gen R C Temple CB OBE RM (d 1959); *b* 12 Feb 1922; *Educ* Wellington, Peterhouse Cambridge; *m* 1, 1952, Julia Jasmine Anthony (m dis 1979); 1 s, 1 da; m 2, 1979, Susan McCorquodale, nee Pick; 1 step s, 1 step da; *Career* Maj Middle East 1940-46; stockbroker 1947-51, Foreign Service 1951-79, advr in Palace Office Sultanate of Oman 1979-; *Recreations* sailing; *Clubs* Roy Cruising, Roy Ocean Racing, Army & Navy; *Style* - Reginald Temple Esq, CMG; Lloyd's Bank Ltd, Pall Mall, SW1

TEMPLE-GORE-LANGTON, (Walter) Grenville Algernon; s of late Cdr the Hon Evelyn Arthur Temple-Gore-Langton, DSO, RN (yst s of 4 Earl Temple of Stowe); hp of kinsman, 7 Earl; *b* 2 Oct 1924; *m* 1, 1954, Zillah Ray (d 1966), da of James Boxall, of Tillington, Petworth, Sussex; 2 s, 1 da; m 2, 1968, Margaret Elizabeth Graham, da of late Col Henry William Scarth of Breckness, of Skaill House, Orkney; *Style* - Grenville Temple-Gore-Langton Esq; The Cottage, Easton, Winchester

TEMPLETOWN, Viscountess; Margaret Violet Louisa; da of late Lt-Col Henry Arthur Clowes, 1 Life Guards, and widow of Col Sir Lionel George Archer Cust, CBE; *m* 1975, as his 2 w, 5 Viscount Templetown (d 1981, when the peerage became ext); *Style* - The Rt Hon The Viscountess Templetown; 7 Castle st, Kircudbright (☎ Kircudbright 30502)

TENBY, 2 Viscount (UK 1957); David Lloyd George; s of 1 Viscount Tenby, TD, PC (d 1967 - 2 s of 1 Earl Lloyd George of Dwyfor); *b* 4 Nov 1922; *Educ* Eastbourne Coll, Jesus Cambridge (MA); *Heir* bro, Hon William Lloyd George; *Career* served War 1942-47, Capt RA NW Europe 1944-45; barr Inner Temple 1953; *Clubs* Reform; *Style* - The Rt Hon The Viscount Tenby; Flat 2, 40 Preston Park av, Brighton, E Sussex

TENNANT, Lady Anne (Veronica); *née* Coke; da of 5 Earl of Leicester (d 1976); *b* 1932; *m* 1956, the Hon Colin Christopher Paget Tennant, s of 2 Baron Glenconner; *Career* an Extra Lady-in-Waiting to HRH The Princess Margaret, Countess of Snowdon 1971-; *Style* - Lady Anne Tennant; 27 Eldon rd, W8; The Glen, Innerleithen, Peeblesshire

TENNANT, Hon Colin Christopher Paget; s and h of 3 Baron Glenconner by his 1 w; *b* 1 Dec 1926; *Educ* Eton, New Coll Oxford; *m* 1956, Lady Anne Coke, da of 5 Earl of Leicester; 3 s, twin da; *Career* formerly Lt Irish Gds; governing dir Tennants' Estate 1967-, chm Mustique Co; *Clubs* Bath; *Style* - The Hon Colin Tennant; 27 Eldon rd, W8 (☎ 01 937 6963)

TENNANT, Lady Emma; *née* Cavendish; da of 11 Duke of Devonshire, MC, PC; *b* 1943; *m* 1963, Hon Tobias William Tennant (s by 2 m of 2 Baron Glenconner); 1 s, 2 da; *Style* - Lady Emma Tennant; Shaws, Newcastleton, Roxburghshire

TENNANT, Lady Harriot; *née* Pleydell-Bouverie; da of 7 Earl of Radnor, KG, KCVO, JP, DL, by his 1 w; *b* 18 Dec 1935; *m* 1965, Mark Tennant, yr s of Maj John Tennant, TD (gs of Sir Charles Tennant, 1 Bt), and Viscountess Radcliffe, *qv*; 1 s, 1 da; *Style* - Lady Harriot Tennant; Balfluig Castle, Alford, Aberdeenshire; 30 Abbey gdns, NW8

TENNANT, Hon Mrs (Irene Adelaide); *née* Gage; da of 5 Viscount Gage and Leila, nee Peel, great niece of Sir Robert Peel, the PM; *b* 9 Feb 1898; *m* 1, 1923 (m annulled 1928), Capt Murray Shuldham-Legh; m 2, 1928, Maj Frederick Bull (m dis 1950); 1 s, 1 da; m 3, 1950, Ernest Tennant, OBE (d 1962, kinsman of the Barons Glenconner); *Style* - The Hon Mrs Tennant; Grove House, Great Bardfield, Essex

TENNANT, Capt Iain Mark; JP (Morayshire 1961); s of Col Edward Tennant, DSO, MC, RAFVR (gs of Sir Charles Tennant, 1 Bt, and n of 1 Baron Glenconner), by his 1 w, Georgina, da of Sir George Kirkpatrick, KCB, KCSI; *b* 11 March 1919; *Educ* Eton, Magdalene Cambridge; *m* 1946, Lady Margaret Ogilvy, da of 12 Earl of Airlie, KT, GCVO, MC, and Lady Alexandra Coke, da of 3 Earl of Leicester; 2 s, 1 da; *Career* Capt Scots Gds 1941, served N Africa 1940-42; memb Roy Co of Archers (Queen's Bodyguard for Scotland); HM Ld-Lt for Morayshire 1964- (DL 1954); chm Glenlivet Distillers, Scottish Northern Investment Tst 1964-, Grampian TV; Crown Estate Commissioner 1970-; dir Clydesdale Bank; *Recreations* outdoor pursuits; *Style* - Capt Iain Tennant, JP, HM Lord-Lieut for Morayshire; Lochnabo House, Elgin, Morayshire (☎ 034 384 2228)

TENNANT, Hon James Grey Herbert; 2 s of 2 Baron Glenconner by his 1 w; *b* 5 March 1929; *Educ* Eton, Trin Cambridge; *m* 1, 1955, Emily (m dis 1962), da of George Licos, of Khartoum and Cairo; 1 s; m 2, 1962, Mrs Elizabeth Romer, da of James Dales, of W Vancouver; *Career* formerly 2 Lt RHG; FRGS; chm James Tennant (CM) Ltd Commodity Fund Managers & Consultants; *Recreations* shooting, riding; *Clubs* White's, Buck's, Pitt; *Style* - The Hon James Tennant; 25 St Leonard's ter, SW3 (☎ 01 730 6984)

TENNANT, Julian William Fiaschi; s of Ernest William Dalrymple Tennant (s of William Tennant, who was 4 cous of 1 Baron Glenconner, Margot Asquith, Baroness Elliot of Harwood, late Lady Ribblesdale and late Lady Crathorne); *b* 1 Aug 1924; *Educ* Eton; *m* 1954, Miranda, da of Capt Sidney Fairbairn, of Steventon Rectory (a previous occupant of which was Jane Austen), Steventon, nr Basingstoke; 1 s (Mungo), 2 da (Nell, Angela); *Career* served Capt Coldstream Gds (gds Armoured Div); chm C Tennant & Sons 1973-80, Ingersoll Locks 1956-80, Daphne's Restaurant 1970; *Recreations* gardening, good food; *Clubs* Saints & Sinners; *Style* - Julian Tennant Esq; 112 Draycott av, SW3 (☎ 01 589 9898); Vivenda Miranda, Lagos, Algarve, Portugal (☎ Lagos 63222); Plush Manor, Plush, Dorchester, Dorset (☎ Piddletrenthide 516)

TENNANT, Lady Margaret Isla Marion; *née* Ogilvy; da of 12 Earl of Airlie, KT, GCVO, MC, and Lady Alexandra Coke, da of 3 Earl of Leicester; *b* 23 July 1920; *m* 1946, Capt Iain Mark Tennant, JP, s of Gp Capt John Tennant, DSO, MC, RAFVR (gs of Sir Charles Tennant, 1 Bt, and n of 1 Baron Glenconner), and Georgina, da of Gen Sir George Kirkpatrick, KCB, KCSI; 2 s, 1 da; *Career* formerly with WRNS; *Style* - Lady Margaret Tennant; Lochnabo House, Elgin, Morayshire

TENNANT, Hon Mrs David; Shelagh Anne; da of Maj Sean Rainey and Mrs Marion Wrottesley; *m* 1963, as his 3 w, Hon David Pax Tennant (d 1968; 3 s but 2 surviving of 1 Baron Glenconner, JP), who had m previously (1) Hermione Baddeley, the actress, (2) Virginia, nee Parsons, maternal gda of Sir Herbert Beerbohm Tree; *Style* - The Hon Mrs David Tennant; El Palomar, Mijas, Malaga, Spain

TENNANT, Hon Stephen James Napier; s of 1 Baron Glenconner, JP, and Pamela (who m 2, 1922, 1 Viscount Grey of Fallodon, KG), da of Hon Percy Wyndham, JP, DL, MP (2 s of 1 Baron Leconfield); *b* 21 April 1906; *Style* - The Hon Stephen Tennant; Wilsford Manor, Amesbury, Wilts

TENNANT, Hon Tobias William; s of 2 Baron Glenconner by his 2 w; *b* 1 June 1941; *Educ* Eton, New Coll Oxford; *m* 1963, Lady Emma Cavendish, er da of 11 Duke of Devonshire, MC, DL; 1 s, 2 da; *Career* sometime Pres OU Boat Club; *Style* - The Hon Tobias Tennant; Shaws, Newcastleton, Roxburghshire (☎ Steele Road 241)

TENNYSON, 4 Baron (UK 1884); Harold Christopher Tennyson; s of 3 Baron Tennyson (d 1951, a notable cricketer who captained Hants and (in four Test Matches v Australia in 1921) England; he was in turn gs of the Victorian Poet Laureate & 1 Baron; it was the latter's uncle Charles who, in overstressing his Deincourt descent, gave the lie - at least as far as one member of the family was concerned - to the assertion that simple faith is more than Norman blood), and of the Hon Clarissa, nee Tennant (d 1960), da of 1 Baron Glenconner; *b* 25 March 1919; *Educ* Eton, Trin Cambridge (BA); *Heir* bro, Hon Mark Aubrey Tennyson, DSC, RN (ret); *Career* War Office 1939-46, Hon Freeman City of Lincoln 1964; *Clubs* White's, Royal Automobile, Royal and Ancient; *Style* - The Rt Hon the Lord Tennyson; 18 Rue Galilée, 75016 Paris, France

TENNYSON, Hon Mark Aubrey; DSC (1943); s of 3 Baron Tennyson (d 1951), and hp of bro, 4 Baron; *b* 28 March 1920; *Educ* RNC Dartmouth; *m* 1964, Deline Celeste Budler; *Career* 1939-45 War (despatches, DSC), Cdr RN 1954; *Clubs* White's, Royal Yacht Squadron; *Style* - The Hon Mark Tennyson, DSC; Foston Hall, Foston, Yorks

TENNYSON-D'EYNCOURT, Giles Gervais; s of Sir (Eustace) Gervais Tennyson-d'Eyncourt, 2 Bt (d 1971), and hp of bro, Sir Jeremy Tennyson-d'Eyncourt, 3 Bt; *b* 16 April 1935; *Educ* Eton, Millfield; *m* 1966, Juanita, da of Fortunato Borromeo; 1 s; *Career* late Capt Coldstream Gds; *Style* - Giles Tennyson-d'Eyncourt Esq; 3 Allington st, SW1

TENNYSON-D'EYNCOURT, Sir (John) Jeremy (Eustace); 3 Bt (UK 1930); s of Sir (Eustace) Gervais Tennyson-d'Eyncourt, 2 Bt (d 1971); *b* 8 July 1927; *Educ* Eton, Glasgow U; *m* 1, 1964 (m dis 1972), Sally June, da of Robin Stratford, QC, and formerly wife of Colin Fyfe-Jamieson; m 2, 1972 (m dis 1976), Brenda Mary, da of Austin Stafford, LRCST, LM, and formerly w of Peter Deitsch; *Heir* bro, Giles Gervais Tennyson-D'Eyncourt; *Career* Sub-Lt RNVR 1945-48, former memb Inst of Management Consultants, Liveryman and Freeman Fishmongers' Co, Freeman City of London; *Clubs* Rand (Johannesburg), Inanda (Transvaal); *Style* - Sir Jeremy Tennyson-d'Eyncourt, Bt; 106 Delarey rd, Rivonia, Johannesburg, S Africa

TENNYSON-D'EYNCOURT, Vinnie, Lady; Vinnie Lorraine; da of late Andrew Pearson, of Minneapolis, USA, and widow of Robert J O'Donnell; *m* 1964, as his 2 w, Sir (Eustace) Gervais Tennyson-d'Eyncourt, 2 Bt (d 1971); *Style* - Vinnie, Lady Tennyson-d'Eyncourt; Catalino Pueblo, 2556 Avenida Maria, Tucson, Arizona 85718, USA

TERRINGTON, 4 Baron (UK 1918); James Allen David Woodhouse; s of 3 Baron Terrington, KBE (d 1961); *b* 30 Dec 1915; *Educ* Winchester, RMC Sandhurst; *m* 1942, Suzanne, da of Col T S Irwin, JP, DL, late Roy Dragoons, of Justicetown, Carlisle, and Mill House, Holton, Suffolk; 3 da (Hon Mrs Bolton, Hon Georgina W, Countess Alexander of Tunis); *Heir* bro, Hon Christopher Montague Woodhouse, DSO, OBE; *Career* Maj (ret) Roy Norfolk Regt and Queen's Westminster Rifles (King's Roy Rifle Corps), TA, an ADC to GOC Madras 1940, 1939-45 War in India, N Africa and Middle East (wounded), former memb Stock Exchange, partner in Sheppards and Chase 1952-800, Dep Chm of Ctees House of Lords 1961-63; *Recreations* shooting, racing; *Clubs* Boodle's, Pratt's; *Style* - The Rt Hon the Lord Terrington; The Manor House, Barford St Martin, Salisbury, Wilts (☎ Wilton 2252); 23 Sloane gdns, SW1

TETLEY, Lady Patricia Maud; *née* Bowes-Lyon; da (twin) of late Hon Michael Claude Hamilton Bowes-Lyon, 5 s of 14 Earl of Strathmore and Kinghorne; sis of 17 Earl; raised to the rank of an Earl's da 1974; *b* 1932; *m* 1964 (m dis 1970), Oliver Robin Tetley; 1 s; *Style* - Lady Patricia Tetley; Abbey Lodge, Wymondham, Norfolk

TETT, Sir Hugh Charles; s of James Charles Tett (d 1955); *b* 28 Oct 1906; *Educ* Hele's Sch Exeter, Roy Coll Science, Univ Coll Exeter; *m* 1, 1931, Katie Sargent (d 1948); 1 da; m 2, 1949, Joyce Lilian, nee Mansell (d 1979); 1 da; m 3, 1980, Barbara Mary, nee Mackenzie; *Career* kt 1966; Esso Petroleum Co 1928-, chm Esso Petroleum Co 1959-67, pro chancellor University of Southampton 1967-79; *Recreations* golf; *Clubs* Athenaeum, Bath; *Style* - Sir Hugh Tett; Primrose Cottage, Bosham, Chichester, W Sussex (☎ 0243 572305)

TEVIOT, 2 Baron (UK 1940); Charles John Kerr; s of 1 Baron Teviot, DSO, MC (d 1968, himself ggs of 6 Marquess of Lothian), by his 2 w Florence (d 1979), da of Lt-Col Charles Villiers, CBE, DSO (gn of 4 Earl of Clarendon) by his w Lady Kathleen Cole (2 da of 4 Earl of Enniskillen); *b* 16 Dec 1934; *Educ* Eton; *m* 1965, Patricia Mary, da of late Alexander Harris; 1 s, 1 da; *Heir* s, Hon Charles Robert Kerr; *Career* dir Debrett's Peerage Ltd 1977-, Fell Soc of Genealogists 1975, memb Advsy Council on Public Records 1974-; *Style* - The Rt Hon the Lord Teviot; 12 Grand av, Hassocks, W Sussex (☎ Hassocks 4471)

TEWKESBURY, Derek Terence; MBE (1949), DL (1966); s of Frances Garland Tewkesbury (d 1958); *b* 7 Feb 1914; *Educ* Perse Sch Cambridge, RMC Sandhurst; *m* 1941, Barbara Mary, nee Tuck; 1 s, 1 da; *Career* Col Bedfordshire and Hertfordshire Regt 1934, served 1935-39 India and Palestine, Middle East and NW Europe 1939-45, ret 1958, Dep Hon Col Roy Anglian Regt (Bedfords) TAVR 1972-79; *Style* - Col Derek Tewkesbury, MBE, DL; 57 Queen's Drive, Bedford (☎ 66910)

TEYNHAM, 20 Baron (E 1616); John Christopher Ingham Roper-Curzon; s of 19 Baron Teynham, DSO, DSC (d 1972) by his 1 w Elspeth (m dis 1956, she d 1976, having m 2, 1958, 6 Marquess of Northampton, DSO); *b* 25 Dec 1928; *Educ* Eton; *m* 1964, Elizabeth, da of late Lt-Col the Hon David Scrymgeour-Wedderburn, DSO (k on active serv 1944 & 2 s of 10 Earl of Dundee; his er bro, 11 Earl, later m Patricia as her 3 husb) by his w Patricia Katharine (herself da of Lt-Col Lord Herbert Montagu-Douglas-Scott, CMG, DSO, 5 s of 6 Duke of Buccleuch; 4 s, 4 da (of whom 1 s, 1 da are twins); *Heir* s, Hon David Henry Ingham Roper-Curzon; *Career* a land agent; late Capt The Buffs (TA) and 2 Lt Coldstream Gds, active serv Palestine 1948, ADC to Govr of Bermuda 1953 and 1955 ADC to Govr of Leeward Islands 1955 (Priv Sec and ADC 1956), ADC to Govr of Jamaica 1962, Pres Inst of Commerce 1972-, memb Council Sail Training Assoc 1964; *Clubs* Turf, House of Lords Yacht, Ocean Cruising, Puffins (Edinburgh); *Style* - The Rt Hon the Lord Teynham; The Walton Canonry, The Close, Salisbury, Wilts (☎ Salisbury 6896)

THAIN, Leslie Alister; s of Alexander Simpson Thain (d 1966); *b* 22 Aug 1939; *Educ* Fettes Coll Edinburgh; *m* 1968, Katherine Mary, nee Hudson; 1 s, 1 da; *Career* solicitor, Writer to the Signet; *Recreations* golf, tennis, freemasonry, gardening; *Style* - Leslie Thain Esq, WS; The Dean, Longniddry, E Lothian (☎ 53272)

THELLUSSON, Hon Antonia; (now Hon Mrs Kirby); da of 8 Baron Rendlesham by his 2 w, Clare; *b* 17 Jan 1956; *m* 1981, Hugo Giles Stephen Astley Kirby; *Style* - The Hon Mrs Kirby

THELLUSSON, Hon Cynthia Adeline Elizabeth; da of Lt-Col Hon Hugh Thellusson, DSO; is sis of 8 Baron Rendlesham and was raised to rank of Baron's da 1945; *b* 20 March 1918; *Educ* St George's Ascot and abroad; *Style* - The Hon Cynthia Thellusson; 60 Ladbroke Grove, W11 (☎ Bayswater 6155)

THELLUSSON, Hon Charles William Brooke; s and h of 8 Baron Rendlesham by his 2 w, Clare; *b* 10 Jan 1954; *Educ* Eton;

Style - The Hon Charles Thellusson; c/o Hampton & Sons, 6 Arlington st, SW1

THELLUSSON, Hon Mrs Hugh; Gwynnydd; da of Brig-Gen Sir Robert Colleton, 9 and last Bt, CB (d 1938); *b* 1894; *m* 1914, Lieutenant-Colonel the Hon Hugh Thellusson, DSO, 3 s of 5 Baron Rendlesham, JP, DL; 2 s (8 Baron Rendlesham and Hon Peter Thellusson), 1 da (Hon Cynthia Thellusson, *qqv*); *Style* - The Hon Mrs Hugh Thellusson

THELLUSSON, Hon Jaqumine; da of 8 Baron Rendlesham by his 2 w, Clare; *b* 21 Aug 1960; *Style* - The Hon Jaqumine Thellusson

THELLUSSON, Hon Peter Robert; s of Lt-Col Hon Hugh Thellusson, DSO, by his w Gwynnydd, da of Brig-Gen Sir Robert Colleton, 9 and last Bt, CB; bro of 8 Baron Rendlesham and was raised to rank of a Baron's s 1945; *b* 25 Jan 1920; *Educ* Eton; *m* 1, 1947 (m dis 1950), Pamela (d 1968), da of Oliver Parker (2 s of Hon Francis Parker, 4 s of 6 Earl of Macclesfield by Lady Mary Grosvenor, da of 2 Marquess of Westminster, KG) and former w of Maj Timothy Tufnell, MC; m 2, 1952, Celia, da of James Walsh; 2 s; *Career* Served WW II, Capt KRRC; *Style* - The Hon Peter Thellusson; 29 Bramham gdns, SW5

THELLUSSON, Hon Sarah Ann; da of 8 Baron Rendlesham by his 2 w, Clare; *b* 25 Jan 1949; *Style* - The Hon Sarah Thellusson; 28 Walham Grove, SW6

THEOBALD, Col Frederick Kenneth; MBE (1957), TD (1952) and 2 Bars; s of Capt Frederick Theobald MBE (d 1962); *b* 28 June 1909; *Educ* Whitgift G S; *m* 1934, Anne Amelia, nee Beckenham; *Career* served TA 1927-45, Colonel; DL Kent 1971-73; Kent County Army Cadet Force 1952-70, Assoc Chartered Insurance Inst, pension schemes & house purchase specialist Sun Life Assurance Soc (ret 1970), chm Moretonhampstead History Soc and Emergency Cttee; *Recreations* walking on Dartmoor; *Style* - Col Frederick Theobald MBE, TD**, DL; Keystones, Moretonhampstead, Devon (☎ Moretonhampstead 384)

THEODOROU, Skevos Gregory; s of Gregory Alfred Theodorou (d 1970) and Irene, nee Alakouzos (both of shipping families); *b* 12 Oct 1937; *Educ* Le Rosey Switzerland, Neuchâtel U (Dip Business Admin); *m* 1968, Gillian Geraldine Anne, da of Maj-Gen Sir (Harold) John (Crossley) Hildreth, KBE, and sis of Jan Hildreth (sometime dir gen of IOD); 1 s (Alexander John (Skevos) Hildreth b 1976), 1 da (Charlotte Amanda Joanna Hildreth b 1978); *Career* shipping; memb Baltic Exchange 1964-, md Transmarine SA Paris 1967-79, dir Clarkson & Co Ltd 1975-, dir Asmarine SA Paris 1979-; *Recreations* shooting, sailing; *Clubs* Royal Thames Yacht, Royal Hellenic Yacht (Athens); *Style* - Skevos Theodorou Esq; 7A Vicarage Gate, W8 (☎ 01 937 3362)

THESIGER, Hon Dawn Loraine; da of late 2 Viscount Chelmsford; *b* 1934; *Style* - The Hon Dawn Thesiger

THESIGER, Hon Frederic Corin Piers; s and h of 3 Viscount Chelmsford; *b* 6 March 1962; *Style* - The Hon Frederic Thesiger

THESIGER, Hon Philippa Merryn; da of late 2 Viscount Chelmsford; *b* 1939; *Style* - The Hon Philippa Thesiger

THESIGER, Hon Tiffany Gay; da of 3 Viscount Chelmsford; *b* 1968

THETFORD, Bishop Suffragan of, 1981-; Rt Rev Timothy Dudley-Smith; s of Arthur Dudley-Smith; *b* 26 Dec 1926; *Educ* Tonbridge, Pembroke College Cambridge, Ridley Hall Cambridge; *m* 1959, June MacDonald; 1 s, 2 da; *Career* ordained 1950, Archdeacon of Norwich 1973-81; *Style* - The Rt Rev The Bishop of Thetford; Rectory Meadow, Bramerton, Norwich

THISTLETON-SMITH, Vice-Adm Sir Geoffrey; KBE (1959), CB (1956), GM (1941); s of J Thistleton-Smith (d 1950); *b* 10 May 1905; *Educ* RNCs Osborne & Dartmouth; *m* 1931, Mary Katherine, da of Col R K Harvey (d 1948); 1 s, 1 da; *Career* joined RN 1919; Admiral Commanding Reserves, Admiral British Jt Services Mission Washington 1958-60; W Sussex

County Cncllr 1964-77; *Recreations* painting, gardening, golf; *Style* - Vice-Adm Sir Thistleton-Smith, KBE, CB, GM; Down Place, Harting, Petersfield, Hants (☎ Harting 374)

THOMAS OF SWYNNERTON, Baron (Life Peer UK 1981); Hugh Swynnerton Thomas; s of Hugh Whitelegge Thomas, CMG (himself s of Rev T W Thomas and sometime of the Colonial Serv, Ch Commissioner Ashanti 1932 and UK Rep to League of Nations re Togoland Mandate Report 1931 & 1934) and Margery Angelo Augusta Swynnerton; *b* 21 Oct 1931; *Educ* Sherborne, Queens' Cambridge, Sorbonne; *m* 1962, Hon Vanessa Jebb, da of 1 Baron Gladwyn; 2 s, 1 da; *Career* historian, best known for his book *The Spanish Civil War* (1961, revised edn 1977, illustrated edn 1979); previously a Fabian, now (1980-) consultant dir Internat Affrs CRD; chm Centre Policy Studies 1979-; with FO 1954-57, lecturer Sandhurst 1957, Prof History Reading U 1966-76; *Style* - Rt Hon Lord Thomas of Swynnerton; c/o Centre for Policy Studies, 8 Wilfred st, SW1 (☎ 01 828 1177); 29 Ladbroke Grove, W11 (☎ 01 727 2288)

THOMAS, Ambler Reginald; CMG (1951); s of John Frederick Ivor Thomas OBE (d 1940); *b* 12 Feb 1913; *Educ* Gresham's Sch Holt, Corpus Christi Cambridge; *m* 1943, Diana Beresford, nee Gresham; 2 s, 3 da; *Career* Civil Service 1935, transferred Colonial Office 1936, under-sec Min of Overseas Dvpt 1964-70, under-sec Foreign & C'wlth Office 1970-73, chm Ctee of Inquiry into Dvpt Authority Gilbert Islands 1976, memb Exec Ctee Br Cncl 1965-69; *Recreations* gardening, reading, walking; *Clubs* Oxford and Cambridge; *Style* - Ambler Thomas Esq, CMG; Champlands, N Chideock, Bridport, Dorset (☎ Chideock 314)

THOMAS, Hon Charles Inigo Gladwyn; er s of Baron Thomas of Swynnerton; *b* 11 Oct 1962; *Style* - The Hon Charles Thomas

THOMAS, David Graeme; s of Edgar Henry Edwin Thomas (d 1975); *b* 22 Oct 1925; *Educ* St Paul's; *m* 1961, Muriel, nee Rogers; *Career* chartered accountant 1951, sec Philip Hill Higginson Erlangers 1956-63, dir Robert Fleming 1963-, chm Aberdare Hldgs 1970-73; *Recreations* fox hunting, golf; *Clubs* Pratt's; *Style* - David Thomas Esq; 151 Old Church st, Chelsea, SW3 (☎ 351 2082)

THOMAS, David John Godfrey; s and h of Sir Godfrey Michael David Thomas, 11 Bt; *b* 11 June 1961; *Style* - David Thomas Esq

THOMAS, Diana, Lady; Diana Mary Katharine; da of late Ven Benedict George Hoskyns, Archdeacon of Chichester; *m* 1924, the Rt Hon Sir Godfrey John Vignoles Thomas, 10 Bt, GCVO, KCB, CSI (d 1968); *Style* - Diana, Lady Thomas; Royal Cottage, Kew, Surrey

THOMAS, Derek Walter; s of Walter John Thomas (d 1974); *b* 18 Oct 1936; *Educ* Portsmouth Southern G S; *m* 1960, Maureen Janet, nee Smith; 1 s, 1 da; *Career* Fellow Institute of Actuaries, md Christian Morgan Pension Consultants Ltd, md Christian Morgan Trustees Ltd, cttee memb Assoc Pensioneer Trustees; *Recreations* squash, cricket, singing, music; *Style* - Derek Thomas Esq; Allingtons, 43 Beech rd, Reigate, Surrey

THOMAS, Frederick Maginley; CMG (1962); s of Rev Canon Thomas (d 1951); *b* 1 July 1908; *Educ* Truro Sch, Exeter Coll Oxford; *m* 1940, Dorothea Mary, nee North; 2 da; *Career* Lt-Col E Africa; Colonial Adminve Serv 1931; District Cmmr N Rhodesia 1933, Assist Sec 1949, Provincial Cmmr 1954, Min Native Affairs 1960, Ch Sec 1963, Dep Govr 1964 (ret); *Recreations* field sports, family history; *Style* - Frederick Thomas Esq, CMG; Rock House, Halse, Taunton, Somerset (☎ Bishops Lydeard 432293)

THOMAS, Gervase Alan; s of Alan Ernest Wentworth Thomas, DSO, MC (d 1969); *b* 19 April 1930; *Educ* Eton, Clare Cambridge; *m* 1961, Jane Elizabeth, nee Ross-Lowe; 2 s, 2 da; *Career* 2 Lt Gren Gds; CA; md T & R Theakston, dir Park Place Ltd, Rosedimond Investment Trust; *Recreations* fox hunting, golf; *Clubs* Boodle's, MCC; *Style* - Gervase Thomas Esq; Rings Green Farm, Froxfield, Hants

THOMAS, Sir Godfrey Michael David; 11 Bt (E 1694), of Wenvoe, Glam; s of Rt Hon Sir Godfrey John Vignoles, 10 Bt, GCVO, KCB, CSI (d 1968); *b* 10 Oct 1925; *Educ* Harrow; *m* 1956, Margaret Greta, da of John Cleland, of Stormont Court, Godden Green, Sevenoaks; 1 s, 2 da (of whom 1 s, 1 da are twins); *Heir* s, David John Godfrey Thomas; *Career* The Rifle Bde 1944-56, memb Stock Exchange London 1959-; *Clubs* MCC, Hurlingham; *Style* - Sir Godfrey Thomas, Bt; 2 Napier av, SW6 (☎ 01 736 6896)

THOMAS, Air Vice-Marshal Geoffrey Percy Sansom; CB (1970), OBE (1945); s of Reginald Ernest Sansom Thomas (d 1949); *b* 24 April 1915; *Educ* King's Coll Sch Wimbledon; *m* 1940, Sally, nee Biddle; 1 s, 1 da; *Career* cmd RAF 1939, served with RAAF 1960-62, Air Cdre 1965, Dir of Movements 1965, Air Vice-Marshal 1969, SASO Maintenance Cmd 1969-71 (ret 1971); *Style* - Air Vice-Marshal Geoffrey Thomas CB OBE; Elms Wood House, Elms Vale, Dover, Kent (☎ Dover 206375)

THOMAS, Hon Henry Isambard Tobias; 2 s of Baron Thomas of Swynnerton; *b* 28 Jan 1964; *Style* - The Hon Henry Thomas

THOMAS, Baroness; Hylda Nora; da of late George Church, of Littlemore, Oxon; *m* 1924, Baron Thomas, DFC (Life Peer d 1980); *Style* - The Rt Hon the Lady Thomas; Remenham Court, Henley-on-Thames, Oxon

THOMAS, Hon Isabella Pandora; da of Baron Thomas of Swynnerton; *b* 17 March 1966; *Style* - The Hon Isabella Thomas

THOMAS, Hon Mrs; Hon Jacqueline; da of Baron Cooper of Stockton Heath (Life Peer); *b* 1946; *m* 1972, J Bradford Thomas; *Style* - The Hon Mrs Thomas

THOMAS, John Alan; s of Idris Thomas; *b* 4 Jan 1943; *Educ* Dynevor Sch, Nottingham U; *m* 1966, Angela, nee Taylor; 2 s; *Career* chartered engineer 1972, md Data Logic Ltd 1973-, pres Computing Services Assoc 1980-81, fell Inst of Cost & Management Accountants 1974, memb Inst of Production Engineers 1972; *Recreations* music, sport; *Clubs* Les Ambassadeurs, Annabel's; *Style* - John Thomas Esq; Highwood park, NW7 (☎ 01 486 7288)

THOMAS, Wing Cdr John Worsley; OBE (1967), AE (1953), DL (Westmorland and Cumbria 1973); s of John Oliver Thomas (d 1929); *b* 3 Nov 1912; *Educ* Epworth Coll N Wales; *m* 1939, Greta Beatrice, nee Emery; 1 s, 1 da; *Career* Wing Cdr RAF served 1939-46, RAuxAF 1948-53, CO Cumberland and Westmorland ATC Wing 1953-72; banker, ret 1972; Hon Pres Cumbria and North Lancs Wing ATC; *Clubs* RAF; *Style* - Wing Cdr John Thomas OBE AE DL; Longmynd, Storrs Park, Windermere, Cumbria (☎ Windermere 3300)

THOMAS, Sir (William) Michael Marsh; 3 Bt (UK 1918), of Garreglwyd, Anglesey; s of Major Sir William Eustace Rhyddlad Thomas, 2 Bt, MBE (d 1958); *b* 4 Dec 1930; *Educ* Oundle; *m* 1953, Geraldine, da of Robert Drysdale, of Trearddur Bay, Anglesey; 3 da; *Heir* unc, Robert Freeman Thomas; *Career* formerly md Gors Nurseries Ltd; *Style* - Sir Michael Thomas, Bt; Belan, Rhosneigr, Anglesey

THOMAS, Hon (William) Michael Webster; s of Baron Thomas, DFC (Life Peer, d 1980); *b* 1926; *m* 1952, Ann, da of late Col Philip Kirby-Green; *Style* - The Hon Michael Thomas

THOMAS, Patricia, Lady; Patricia; *née* Larkins; *m* 1957, as his 3 w, Major Sir William Eustace Rhyddlad Thomas, 2 Bt, MBE (d 1958); *Style* - Patricia, Lady Thomas

THOMAS, Rt Hon Peter John Mitchell; PC (1964), QC (1965), MP (C) Barnet, Hendon S, 1974-; s of David Thomas; *b* 31 July 1920; *Educ* Epworth Coll Rhyl, Jesus Oxford; *m* 1947, Frances, da of Basil Dean, CBE, the producer, by his 2 w (it being her 2 m), Lady Mercy Greville (2 da of 5 Earl of Warwick and (Daisy) Countess of Warwick, friend of King Edward VII);

2 s (David Nigel, Huw Maynard), 2 da (Frances Jane, Catherine Clare); *Career* barr 1947, Crown Court Recorder 1974-, MP Hendon S 1970-74, Min State Foreign Affrs 1963-64, Sec State Wales 1970-74; *Style* - The Rt Hon Peter Thomas PC QC MP; Millicent Cottage, Elstead, Surrey (☎ 2052); 145 Kennington rd, SE11 (☎ 01 735 6047)

THOMAS, Sir Patrick Muirhead; DSO (1945), TD (1945), DL (1980); s of Herbert James Thomas (d 1960); *b* 31 Jan 1914; *Educ* Clifton Coll, Corpus Christi Cambridge; *m* 1939, Ethel Elizabeth Mary, nee Sheffield; 1 s, 3 da; *Career* kt 1974, OStJ 1970, md Wm Beardmore & Co Ltd 1954-67 (dir 1967-76), dir Scottish Opera 1965- (chm 1976-), chm Scottish Transport Gp 1968-, Lloyd's Register of Shipping 1967-, Govr Clifton Coll 1979-; *Recreations* golf, gardening; *Style* - Sir Patrick Thomas, DSO, TD, DL; Bemersyde, Kilmacolm, Renfrewshire (☎ 050 587 2710)

THOMAS, Robert Freeman; s of late Sir Robert John Thomas, 1 Bt, and hp of n, Sir Michael Thomas, 3 Bt; *b* 8 Jan 1911; *m* 1947, Marcia, da of Walter Lucas; *Style* - Robert Thomas Esq; Garreglwyd, Holyhead, Anglesey

THOMAS, Hon Mrs (Ursula Nancy); *née* Eden; da of 7 Baron Henley (d 1977); *b* 1950; *m* 1978, William Thomas; *Style* - The Hon Mrs Thomas; 36 Faroe rd, W14

THOMAS, Sir William James Cooper; 2 Bt (UK 1919), of Ynyshir, Co Glamorgan, TD; s of Sir (William) James Thomas, 1 Bt (d 1945); *b* 7 May 1919; *Educ* Harrow, Downing Cambridge; *m* 1947, Freida Dunbar, da of late F A Whyte, of Montcoffer, Banff; 2 s, 1 da; *Heir* s, William Michael Thomas; *Career* World War II with RA; barr Inner Temple 1948; High Sheriff Co Monmouth 1973-74, JP Gwent 1958, DL 1973; *Clubs* Army and Navy; *Style* - Sir William Thomas, Bt, TD, JP, DL; Rockfield Park, Monmouth, Gwent (☎ Monmouth 2757)

THOMAS, William Michael; s and h of Sir William James Cooper Thomas, 2 Bt; *b* 5 Dec 1948; *Educ* Harrow, Ch Ch Oxford; *Style* - William Thomas Esq

THOMAS, Wynne Simpson; OBE (1972), DL(1968); s of Edgar Wynne Thomas, MBE (d 1967); *b* 16 Feb 1912; *Educ* Llanelli G S, Swansea U Law Sch; *m* 1942, Mary Etta, nee Jenkins; *Career* solicitor 1936, slr Carmarthenshire CC 1946-52; Clerk of the Peace, Clerk to Ltcy, Clerk & Ch Exec Carms CC 1952-72, Clerk of Carms & Cardiganshire Police Authority 1952-68, dep clerk Dyfed-Powys Police Authority 1968-72, clerk Magistrates Cts Ctee 1952-72; *Recreations* music, walking; *Clubs* Cefn Sidan Rotary, Llanelli Bowling; *Style* - Wynne Thomas Esq, OBE, DL; St Illtyd Rise, Pembrey, Burry Port, Dyfed (☎ 05546 2542)

THOMAS-EVERARD, Christopher Philip; s of Maj Charles Richard Thomas (ka 1944); *b* 19 March 1941; *Educ* Stowe and Roy Agricultural Coll; *m* 1966, Rohaise Harriet Julia, da of Maj Eudo Tonson-Rye; 1 s, 2 da; *Career* farmer, landowner, chartered surveyor, owner of Miltons Estate and Broford Farm 1966-, chm W Somerset NFU 1978-80, chm Somerset NFU Hill Farming Cttee 1981-, underwriting memb of Lloyd's 1973-; *Recreations* sailing, hunting; *Style* - Christopher Thomas-Everard Esq; Broford Farm, Dulverton, Somerset (☎ 0398 23569)

THOMPSON, Alec Geoffrey; s of Alexander William Thompson (d 1968); *b* 25 April 1926; *Educ* Manchester G S, Preston G S, Manchester U; *m* 1949, Irene Lilian, nee Eatock; 2 s; *Career* md J Bibby & Sons Ltd 1979-, dir J Bibby & Sons Ltd 1977-; *Recreations* fishing, shooting; *Style* - Alec Thompson Esq; Barcaldene, Leighton dve, Beetham, Milnthorpe, Cumbria

THOMPSON, Major Christopher Peile; s and h of Sir Peile Thompson, 5 Bt, OBE; *b* 21 Dec 1944; *Educ* Marlborough; *m* 1969, Anna Elizabeth, da of Maj Arthur G Callander; 1 s, 1 da; *Career* Maj R Hussars (PWO); *Clubs* Army and Navy, Hurlingham; *Style* - Major Christopher Thompson; 17 Daisy Lane, SW6

THOMPSON, Christopher Ronald; s of Col S J Thompson DSO DL (d 1956); *b* 14 Dec 1927; *Educ* Shrewsbury Sch, Trin Coll Cambridge; *m* 1949, Rachael Mary, nee Meynell; 1 s, 1 da (1 s decd); *Career* dir Northern Engrg Industries Ltd, chm Northern Engrg Industs Int Ltd, dir Barclays Bank Ltd, dir Saraswati Syndicate India, memb Br Overseas Trade Bd; *Recreations* flyfishing, shooting, gardening; *Clubs* Brooks's; *Style* - Christopher Thompson Esq; Aldenham Park, Bridgnorth, Salop (☎ Morville 218); 15 Kensington sq, W8 (☎ 937 9326)

THOMPSON, David; s of Bernard Thompson, of Castleford, West Yokshire; *b* 28 Oct 1944; *Educ* King's School Pontefract; *m* 1970, Glenys; 2 s; *Career* chartered accountant admitted 1969; Fellow of Institute of Chartered Accountants in England & Wales 1979; ptnr Buckle, Barton & Co 1978, appointed senior partner 1981; *Recreations* most sports, Castleford Corps of the Salvation Army; *Style* - David Thompson Esq; Stone Lea, Badsworth Court, Badsworth, Pontefract, West Yorkshire

THOMPSON, Sir Edward Hugh Dudley; MBE (1945), TD, DL (Derbyshire 1978); s of Neale Dudley Thompson; *b* 12 May 1907; *Educ* Uppingham, Lincoln Coll Oxford; *m* 1, 1931, Ruth Monica, nee Wainwright; 2 s; m 2, 1947, Doreen Maud, nee Tibbitt; 1 s, 1 da; *Career* kt 1967, Lt-Col 1939-45, solicitor 1931-36, assist md Ind Coope & Co Ltd 1937-39 (chm 1955-62), chm Allied Breweries Ltd 1961-68, chm Brewers Soc 1959-61, High Sheriff Derby 1964; *Recreations* farming; *Clubs* Boodle's; *Style* - Sir Edward Thompson, MBE, TD, DL; Culland Hall, Brailsford, Derby (☎ Brailsford 247)

THOMPSON, Gerald Francis Michael Perronet; s of Sir John Perronet Thompson KCSI KCIE (d 1935); *b* 10 Oct 1910; *Educ* Repton Sch, King's Coll Cambridge; *m* 1944, Margaret Mary Bodenham, nee Smith; 2 s, 1 da; *Career* Wing Cdr RAF 1940-46; merchant banking, entered Kleinwort Sons Co 1933 (dir 1960), dir Kleinwort Benson Lonsdale Ltd 1968-, chm Kleinwort Benson Ltd 1971-75; *Recreations* reading, gardening; *Clubs* United Oxford and Cambridge U, City U; *Style* - Gerald Thompson Esq; Whitewebs, Margaretting, near Ingatestone, Essex (☎ Ingatestone 2002)

THOMPSON, Sir (Joseph) Herbert; CIE (1944); s of James Arnold Thompson JP (d 1946); *b* 9 March 1898; *Educ* Manchester G S, BNC Oxford; *m* 1925, Kathleen, nee Rodier; 3 da; *Career* kt 1947, RN Air Serv (Sub-Lt) 1916-18, Capt RAF 1918-19; ICS 1922-47, Divisional & Sessions Judge NW Frontier Province, Revenue & Divisional Cmmr NW Frontier Province 1943; Resident Kolhapur and Deccan 1944-45, Res Lamore to 1947; Rowing Correspondent Sunday Times 1954-68; *Recreations* rowing; *Clubs* Leander (Henley); *Style* - Sir Herbert Thompson CIE; Fair Acre, Haddenham, Bucks

THOMPSON, Ivor Molineaux; s of William Henry Thompson (d 1969); *b* 1 March 1927; *Educ* Bishop Vesey's G S, Sutton Coldfield; *m* 1948, Kathleen Rosemary, nee Shaw; 1 s, 1 da; *Career* dep chm/ch exec Br Industrial Plastics Ltd 1976, chm Thomas Smith & Sons (Saltley) Ltd Birmingham 1979; *Recreations* ornithology, nature study, motor sport; *Style* - Ivor Thompson Esq; Colly Weston, 36 Walsall Road, Sutton Coldfield, West Midlands ☎ 021 308 0288)

THOMPSON, Joseph Lefroy Courtenay; s of Joseph Matthew Thompson, of Belfast (d 1976); *b* 4 April 1943; *Educ* Rugby, Trin Coll Dublin; *m* 1967, Joan Lesley, nee Love; 1 s, 1 da; *Career* dir Charles Hurst Ltd; chm Charles Commercials Ltd, Hurst Fuels Ltd, Arran Oils Ltd, Thompson Reid Fuels Ltd, dir Industrial Therapy Org (Ulster) Ltd, Govr Princes Gardens Sch; *Clubs* Lansdowne; *Style* - Joseph Thompson Esq; Charleville, 39 Manse rd, Castlereagh, Belfast (☎ 792412)

THOMPSON, Air Cdre John Marlow; CBE (1952), DSO (1943), DFC (1940) and Bar (1942), AFC (1952); s of John Thompson (d 1926); *b* 16 Aug 1914; *Educ* Bristol G S; *m* 1938, Margaret Sylvia Barlow Morris, nee Rowlands; 1 s, 1 da (1

s decd); *Career* RAF 1934-66; Air Cdre 1959; dir Air Defence & Air Miny 1958-60, AOC Mil Air Traffic Ops 1962-65, ret 1966; gen man Airwork Servs 1966-68; *Recreations* golf, travel; *Clubs* RAF; *Style* - Air Cdre John Thompson CBE DSO DFC* AFC; Le Bahia, 39 Avenue Princesse Grace, Monte-Carlo, Monaco

THOMPSON, Sir Kenneth Pugh; 1 Bt (UK 1963), of Walton-on-the-Hill, City of Liverpool; s of Ernest Simpson Thompson (d 1971); *b* 24 Dec 1909; *Educ* Bootle G S, (Liverpool) City Coll of Technology; *m* 1936, Nancy, JP, da of Charles Broome (d 1968), of Walton, Liverpool; 1 s, 1 da; *Heir* s, Paul Anthony Thompson; *Career* Cncllr City of Liverpool 1938-58, Sec of 1922 Ctee 1952-57, Chm Con Nat Advisory Ctee on Local Govt 1956-57, Assist Postmaster Gen 1957-59, Parly Sec Miny of Education 1959-62, MP (C) Walton Div of Liverpool 1950-64, Co Cncllr Merseyside (Leader of Con Gp 1973-, Chm 1977-80), Dep Chm Merseyside Development Corpn 1980-; Books: *Member's Lobby* (1966), *Pattern of Conquest* (1967); *Style* - Sir Kenneth Thompson, Bt; Atherton Cottage, via Kirklake rd, Formby, Merseyside (☎ 070 48 72486)

THOMPSON, Sir (Thomas) Lionel Tennyson; 5 Bt (UK 1806), of Hartsbourne Manor, Hertfordshire; s of Lt-Col Sir Thomas Raikes Lovett Thompson, 4 Bt, MC (d 1964), and of Millicent Ellen Jean, da of late Edmund Charles Tennyson-d'Eyncourt, of Bayons Manor, Lincs; *b* 19 June 1921; *Educ* Eton; *m* 1955 (m dis 1962), Mrs Margaret van Beers, da of late Walter Herbert Browne; 1 s, 1 da; *Heir* s, Thomas d'Eyncourt John Thompson; *Career* 1939-45 War as Flying Officer RAFVR (invalided), and subsequently as Able Seaman Roy Fleet Auxiliary (1939-45 and Aircrew (Europe) Stars; Defence and Victory Medals); barr Lincoln's Inn 1952; *Clubs* Naval and Military; *Style* - Sir Lionel Thompson, Bt; Queen Elizabeth Building, Temple, EC4Y 9BS (☎ 01 353 6453); 16 Old Buildings, Lincoln's Inn, WC2 (☎ 01 405 7929)

THOMPSON, Nicholas Annesley Marler; s and h of Sir Richard Hilton Marler Thompson, 1 Bt; *b* 19 March 1947; *Style* - Nicholas Thompson Esq

THOMPSON, Sir Peile; 5 Bt (UK 1890), of Park Gate, Guiseley, Yorks. OBE (1959, MBE 1950); s of Sir Peile Beaumont Thompson, 4 Bt (d 1972); *b* 28 Feb 1911; *Educ* Canford Sch, St Catharine's Cambridge; *m* 1937, Barbara Johnston, da of late Horace Johnston Rampling, of The Old Manor House, Harston, Cambridge; 1 s, 1 da; *Heir* s, Maj Christopher Peile Thompson; *Career* Lt-Col (ret) The Manchester Regt, served 1939-45 War, commanded 26 Bn KAR Kenya Emergency 1954-56 (despatches); *Style* - Sir Peile Thompson, Bt, OBE; Old Farm, Augres, Trinity, Jersey (☎ Jersey 62289)

THOMPSON, Paul Anthony; s and h of Sir Kenneth Pugh Thompson, 1 Bt; *b* 6 Oct 1939; *m* 1971, Pauline, da of Robert O Spencer, of Tippett House, Smithills, Bolton, Lancs; *Style* - Paul Thompson Esq; Drapers Farmhouse, Finch Lane, Appley Bridge, Wigan, Lancs WN6 9DU

THOMPSON, Prof Raymond; s of William Edward Thompson (d 1946); *b* 4 April 1925; *Educ* Longton H S, Nottingham U; *Career* md Borax Research Ltd, dir Borax Hldgs Ltd, Special Prof Chemistry Nottingham U, Hon Prof Molecular Sciences Warwick U, Vice-Pres Industrial Div Roy Soc Chemistry, Govr Kingston Polytechnic; *Recreations* gardening, ceramics; *Clubs* Athenaeum; *Style* - Prof Raymond Thompson; The Garth, Winchester Close, Esher Place, Esher, Surrey (☎ 397 5141)

THOMPSON, Sir Robert Grainger Ker; KBE (1965), CMG (1961), DSO (1945), MC (1943); s of Canon William Grainger Thompson (d 1966); *b* 12 April 1916; *Educ* Marlborough, Sidney Sussex Coll Cambridge; *m* 1950, Merryn, da of Sir Alec Newboult, KBE, CMG, MC (d 1964); 1 s, 1 da; *Career* Wing Cdr RAF 1939-45; consultant; author; Malayan Civil Serv 1938-61, Sec for Defence 1959-61, Head Br Advsy Mission Vietnam 1961-65; *Recreations* all country pursuits; *Clubs* Special Forces; *Style* - Sir Robert Thompson

KBE, CMG, DSO, MC; Pitcott House, Winsford, Somerset

THOMPSON, Sir Richard Hilton Marler; 1 Bt (UK 1963), of Reculver, Co Kent; s of Richard Smith Thompson (d 1952), of London and Calcutta; *b* 5 Oct 1912; *Educ* Malvern Coll; *m* 1939, Anne Christabel de Vere, da of late Philip de Vere Annesley (5 cous of 11 Viscount Valentia); 1 s; *Heir* s, Nicholas Annesley Marler Thompson; *Career* RNVR 1940-46, commissioned 1941 (despatches 1942), Lt-Cdr 1944; MP (C) Croydon West 1950-55, Assist-Govt Whip 1952, Lord Commissioner of the Treasury 1954, MP (C) Croydon South 1955-66 and 1970-74, Vice-Chamberlain of HM Household 1956, Parly Sec Miny of Health 1957-59, Under-Sec of State CRO 1959-60, Parly Sec Miny of Works 1960-62, Tstee British Museum 1951, memb Council Nat Trust 1978-, dir Rediffusion Television Ltd, Rediffusion Holdings Ltd, chm British Museum Soc 1970-74; *Recreations* gardening, country pursuits, reading; *Clubs* Carlton; *Style* - Sir Richard Thompson, Bt; Rhodes House, Sellindge, Kent; 15 Westminster gdns, SW1 (☎ 01 834 6757)

THOMPSON, Thomas D'Eyncourt John; s and h of Sir Lionel Tennyson Thompson, 5 Bt; *b* 22 Dec 1956; *Educ* Eton; *Style* - Thomas Thompson Esq

THOMPSON-SCHWAB, Lady Hermione Frances; *née* Grimston; da of 6 Earl of Verulam (d 1973); *b* 1941; *m* 1, 1955 (m dis 1971), Richard John Perronet Thompson; m 2, 1971, James Darell Dickson Thompson-Schwab; *Style* - Lady Hermione Thompson-Schwab; Kingfield, Penton, Carlisle, Cumberland

THOMSEN, Leif; s of Orla Thomsen; *b* 15 March 1936; *Educ* Gentofte Statsskole Denmark, Denmark Tech; *m* 1962, Anne Elisabeth, nee Naested; *Career* civil engr Denmark and Peru 1960-63, management and commercial engrg positions F L Smidth & Co A/S (Denmark) 1963-79, md F L Smidth & Co Ltd (UK) 1979-; *Recreations* archaeology; *Style* - Leif Thomsen Esq; 19 St Bernards, Chichester rd, Croydon, Surrey

THOMSON OF MONIFIETH, Baron (Life Peer UK 1977); George Morgan Thomson; PC (1966); s of late James Thomson, of Monifieth, Angus; *b* 16 Jan 1921; *Educ* Grove Acad Dundee; *m* 1948, Grace, da of Cunningham Jenkins, of Glasgow; 2 da; *Career* MP (L) Dundee East 1952-72, Min of State FO 1964-66, Chllr of the Duchy of Lancaster 1966-67 and 1969-70, Joint Min of State FO 1967, Sec of State for Commonwealth Affairs 1967-68, Min Without Portfolio 1968-69, Shadow Defence Min 1970-72; chm: European Movement in Britain 1977-80, Advertising Standards Authority 1977-80; First Crown Estate Cmmr 1978-80, chm Independent Broadcasting Authority 1981-, Chllr Heriot Watt U 1977-; Hon LLD Dundee 1967, Hon DLitt Heriot Watt 1973, Hon DSc Aston 1976; *Clubs* Brooks's; *Style* - The Rt Hon the Lord Thomson of Monifieth, PC; Flat 15, 102 Rochester Row, SW1 (☎ 01 834 1047)

THOMSON OF FLEET, 2 Baron (UK 1964); Kenneth Roy Thomson; s of 1 Baron Thomson of Fleet, GBE (d 1976); *b* 1 Sept 1923; *Educ* Upper Canada Coll, Cambridge U (MA); *m* 1956, Norah Marilyn, da of Albert Vernard Lavis, of Toronto; 2 s, 1 da; *Heir* s, Hon David Kenneth Roy Thomson; *Career* newspaper magnate; chm International Thomson Organisation Ltd 1978-, Thomson Organisation 1976-78, co-pres Times Newspapers Ltd 1971-81, chm of the Board and dir Thomson Newspapers Ltd (Canadian newspaper proprietors), pres and dir Thomson Newspapers Inc (American newspaper proprietors); dir: Toronto Dominion Bank, Scottish and York Ltd, Abitibi Paper Co Ltd, Hudson's Bay Co, Robert Simpsons Ltd (and similarly of a large number of other communications/newspaper cos); *Style* - The Rt Hon the Lord Thomson of Fleet; 8 Kensington Palace gdns, W8; 8 Castle Frank rd, Toronto 5, Ont, Canada M4W 2Z4

THOMSON, Bettina, Lady; Bettina; da of late Lt-Cdr David William Shafto Douglas, RN; *m* 1935, Sir (James) Douglas Wishart Thomson, 2 Bt (d 1972); *Style* - Bettina, Lady Thomson; Old Caberston, Walkerburn, Peeblesshire

THOMSON, Christopher James; s of Ronald Stuart Thomson (d 1948); *b* 30 Jan 1933; *Educ* Wellington Coll, Merton Oxford; *m* 1976, Daphne Moyna, nee Maguire; 2 step da; *Career* 2 Lt Coldstream Guards (Egypt), md Bowater Newsprint Sales; *Clubs* White's; *Style* - Christopher Thomson Esq; 16 Westover rd, SW18 (☎ 870 3167)

THOMSON, Sir (Frederick Douglas) David; 3 Bt (UK 1929), of Glendarroch, Co Midlothian; s of Sir (James) Douglas Wishart, 2 Bt (d 1972); *b* 14 Feb 1940; *Educ* Eton, Univ Coll Oxford; *m* 1967, Caroline Anne, da of Maj Timothy Stuart Lewis, Roy Scots Greys, by his w Lucia, gda of Muriel, nee Douglas-Pennant, who was cr Viscountess Daventry after her husb (Capt Rt Hon Edward Fitz-Roy, PC, MP, sometime Speaker House of Commons) d 1943; 2 s, 1 da; *Heir* s, Simon Douglas Charles Thomson; *Career* md Ben Line Steamers Ltd 1964-, chm Ben Line Ship Management 1972-, memb Queen's Body Guard for Scotland, Roy Co of Archers; *Style* - Sir David Thomson, Bt; Glenbrook House, Balerno, Midlothian (☎ 031 449 4116)

THOMSON, David John; s of David Barrow Thomson (d 1979); *b* 21 Feb 1941; *Educ* Forest Sch London E18, Glasgow U; *m* 1966, Marjorie Rose, nee Utting; 3 children; *Career* marketing dir European Div Rowntree Mackintosh Ltd 1980-, marketing dir Grocery Div 1975-80; *Recreations* golf, gardening, sea fishing, walking, reading, light opera; *Clubs* York GC; *Style* - David Thomson Esq; Ashurst, Usher Park rd, Haxby, York (☎ 769537)

THOMSON, Hon David Kenneth Roy; s and h of 2 Baron Thomson of Fleet; *b* 12 June 1957; *Style* - The Hon David Thomson

THOMSON, David Paget; s of the late Sir George Thomson, FRS, Nobel Laureate; *b* 19 March 1931; *Educ* Rugby, Trinity Coll Cambridge; *m* 1959, Patience Mary, da of the late Sir Lawrence Bragg, CH, MC, FRS, Nobel Laureate; 2 s, 2 da; *Career* Lt Cdr RNR; joined Lazard Bros & Co Ltd 1956, md 1966, seconded HM Foreign Service 1971-73 economic counsellor Bonn; Lazards 1973-; *Clubs* Athenaeum, City Livery; *Style* - David Thomson Esq; Little Stoke House, North Stoke, Oxon (☎ Wallingford 37161)

THOMSON, Ewen Cameron; CMG (1964); s of Francis Murphy Thomson (d 1950); *b* 12 April 1915; *Educ* Forfar Acad, St Andrews U; *m* 1948, Betty, da of Lt-Col James Henry Preston MBE; 1 s, 3 da; *Career* consultant to World Bank on Nutrition Admin 1974-, Colonial Admin Serv 1938-64, Perm Sec and Min for Native Affairs 1962-63, Provincial Cmmr and Sr Provincial Cmmr 1957-64, Perm Sec Miny of Transport and Works Govt of Zambia; *Recreations* winemaking, cooking; *Clubs* Roy C'wlth Soc; *Style* - Ewen Thomson Esq, CMG; Acorns, Roundhill, Woking, Surrey (☎ 73223)

THOMSON, Rev George Ian Falconer; s of Dr George Dornin Thomson (d 1924); *b* 2 Sept 1912; *Educ* Shrewsbury Sch, Westcott House Cambridge, Balliol Coll Oxford; *m* 1, 1938 (m dis 1951), Hon Bridget, nee de Courcy, da of 29 Baron Kingsale DSO; 1 da; m 2, 1952, Mary Josephine Lambart, da of Ven Henry Thomas Dixon DD (d 1939), Archdn of Ludlow; 1 s; *Career* Chaplain of All Souls Coll Oxford 1981-, dir Bible Reading Fellowship 1962-77, Chaplain St Paul's Coll Cheltenham 1962-66, Master Maidstone G S 1951-62, Rector Hilgay Norfolk 1946-51; *Recreations* travel, historical research, writing; *Clubs* Leander, RAF; *Style* - The Rev George Thomson; Jackson's Farm House, Yarnton, Oxford

THOMSON, Sir Ivo Wilfrid Home; 2 Bt (UK 1925), of Old Nunthorpe, Co York; s of Sir Wilfrid Thomson, 1 Bt (d 1939), and of Ethel Henrietta, da of late Hon Reginald Parker (6 s of 6 Earl of Macclesfield); *b* 14 Oct 1902; *Educ* Eton; *m* 1, 1933 (m dis 1954), Sybil Marguerite, da of Claude W Thompson, of The Red House, Escrick, York; 1 s (and 1 s decd); m 2, 1954, Viola Mabel, da of Roland Dudley, of Linkenholt Manor, Andover, Hants, and formerly w of Keith Home Thomson; *Heir* s, Mark Wilfrid Home Thomson; *Career* Sqdn-Ldr RAuxAF 608

Sqdn 1930-35, Sqdn Ldr 1940-45 No 4 Gp Bomber Command, Gp Flying Control Officer; newspaper director; *Recreations* formerly shooting & flying, now fishing; *Style* - Sir Ivo Thomson, Bt; Frilsham Manor, Hermitage, Newbury, Berks

THOMSON, Sir John; KBE (1972), TD (1944); s of late Guy Thomson JP; *b* 3 April 1908; *Educ* Winchester, Magdalen Oxford; *m* 1, 1935, Elizabeth JP, nee Brotherhood (d 1977); m 2, 1979, Eva, da of Marcus Russell & widow of Tom Dreaper; *Career* chm Morland & Co 1979-; dir Barclays Bank Ltd 1947-78, chm 1962-73; dir Union Discount Co of London Ltd 1960-74; High Sheriff Oxon 1957, DL Oxon 1947-57, Ld-Lt Oxon 1963-79; Dep Steward Oxford U; Steward Jockey Club 1973-76; *Recreations* steeplechase horse owner and breeder; *Clubs* Cavalry & Guards'; *Style* - Sir John Thomson, KBE, TD; Manor Farm House, Spelsbury, Oxford (☎ Charlbury 810266); Achnaba, Lochgilphead, Argyll (☎ Lochgilphead 2537)

THOMSON, Lady Jacqueline Rosemary Margot Rufus; *née* Isaacs; da of 3 Marquess of Reading, MBE, MC (d 1980); *b* 10 Nov 1946; *Educ* Southover Manor Lewes, Internat Sch Geneva, Madrid U; *m* 1976, Mark (b 29 Dec 1939), s and h of Sqdn Ldr Sir Ivo Thomson, 2 Bt, by his 1 w, Sybil; 1 s (Bertie, b 1979), 1 da (Daisy, b 1977); *Style* - Lady Jacqueline Thomson; 42 Glebe Place, SW3 (☎ 01 352 5015)

THOMSON, Hon Lesley Lynne; da of 2 Baron Thomson of Fleet; *b* 1959; *Style* - The Hon Lesley Thomson

THOMSON, Mark Wilfrid Home; s and h of Sir Ivo Wilfrid Home Thomson, 2 Bt; *b* 29 Dec 1939; *m* 1976, Lady Jacqueline Rosemary Margot Rufus Isaacs, da of 3 Marquess of Reading (d 1980); 1 da; *Style* - Mark Thomson Esq; 42 Glebe Place, SW3

THOMSON, Hon Peter John; s of 2 Baron Thomson of Fleet; *b* 1965; *Style* - The Hon Peter Thomson

THOMSON, Sue; da of Basil Raymond Hamilton (d 1942); *b* 6 Aug 1938; *Educ* Christ's Hosp; *m* 1978, André Davis; 1 da (Susannah b 1978); *Career* publisher 1971-77, md Octopus Books Ltd 1977-, dep chm Octopus publishing Gp Ltd 1971-, dir Mandarin Publishers Ltd Hong Kong; *Recreations* family life, early domestic architecture; *Clubs* University Women's; *Style* - Mrs André Davis; 59 Grosvenor st, W1 (☎ 01 493 5841)

THOMSON, Simon Douglas Charles; s & h of Sir (Frederick) David Thomson, 3 Bt; *b* 16 June 1969; *Style* - Simon Thomson Esq

THOMSON, Thomas Davidson; CMG (1962), OBE (1959); s of James Allan Thomson (d 1961); *b* 1 April 1911; *Educ* George Watson's Coll, Edinburgh U, Magdalene Cambridge; *m* 1947, Marjorie Constance (d 1980), nee Aldred; 1 s; *Career* served 1940-45 KAR, Maj E Africa and Eritrea, Colonial Admin Serv Nyasaland 1934; cmmr Social Dvpt 1959 (ret 1963), BBC 'Brain of Britain' 1969; *Recreations* philately, contemplative archaeology, reading; *Clubs* Caledonian, Edinburgh; *Style* - Thomas Thomson Esq, CMG, OBE; The Hill, Coldingham, Berwicks (☎ Coldingham 209)

THORLEY, Sir Gerald Bowers; TD; s of Clement Thorley (d 1948); *b* 26 Aug 1913; *Educ* Ratcliffe Coll; *m* 1947, Beryl Preston, nee Rhodes; 1 s, 1 da; *Career* kt 1973; chm Br Sugar Corpn 1968- and MEPC 1975, vice-chm Rockware Gp Ltd, dir: BAT Industries, Fitch Lovell Ltd, Allied Breweries Ltd (chm & ch exec 1970-75); underwriting memb Lloyd's 1952; *Recreations* gardening, golf; *Clubs* Naval & Military; *Style* - Sir Gerald Thorley TD; Church House, Bale, Fakenham, Norfolk (☎ Thursford 314)

THORN, John Leonard; s of Stanley Leonard Thorn (d 1951); *b* 28 April 1925; *Educ* St Paul's Sch, Corpus Christi Cambridge; *m* 1955, Veronica Laura, da of Sir Robert Maconochie OBE QC; 1 s, 1 da; *Career* schoolmaster: assist master Clifton Coll 1949-61, headmaster Repton Sch 1961-68, headmaster Winchester Coll 1968-; dir Royal Opera House Covent Garden 1972-78, trustee Br Museum 1980 on; *Recreations* all the arts; *Clubs* Garrick; *Style* - John Thorn Esq; The Headmaster's House, Winchester College, Winchester, Hants (☎ 4328)

THORNE, Lady Anne (Patricia); *née* Pery; da of 5 Earl of Limerick, KCB, DSO, TD (d 1967); *b* 1928; *Educ* North Foreland Lodge and St Hugh's Coll, Oxford (MA, DPhil); *m* 1959, Lt-Col Peter Francis Thorne, CBE, s of late Gen Sir (Augustus Francis) Andrew Nicol Thorne, KCB,CMG, DSO, DL; 1 s, 3 da; *Career* sr lecturer and sr tutor, Imperial Coll of Science and Tech; *Style* - Lady Anne Thorne; Speaker's Green, House of Commons, SW1

THORNE, Neil Gordon; OBE (1980), TD (1969), MP (C) Redbridge, Ilford South 1979-; s of Henry Frederick Thorne (d 1964); *b* 8 Aug 1932; *Educ* City of London, London U; *Career* Lt-Col RA; chartered surveyor 1961-, sr ptnr Hull & Co 1962-76; cncllr Borough of Redbridge 1965-68, Alderman 1975-78, memb GLC and chm Central Area Bd 1967-73; memb TA 1952-; Silver Jubilee Medal 1977; CO London U OTC; *Clubs* Carlton; *Style* - Neil Thorne Esq, OBE, TD, MP; 60 Gyllyngdune Gardens, Seven Kings, Ilford, Essex (☎ 590 3262)

THORNE, Peter Francis; CBE (1966); s of Gen Sir Andrew Thorne, KCB, CMG, DSO (d 1970); *b* 6 Aug 1914; *Educ* Eton, Trin Coll Oxford; *m* 1959, Lady Anne Pery, da of 5 Earl of Limerick, GBE, CH, KCB, DSO; 1 s, 3 da; *Career* Lt-Col Grenadier Guards 1940; Imperial Chemical Industries Ltd 1946-48; Assist Serjeant-at-Arms House of Commons 1948-57, Dep Serjeant-at-Arms 1957-; *Clubs* Cavalry & Guards', Roy Yacht Sqdn; *Style* - Lt-Col Peter Thorne CBE; Speaker's Green, House of Commons, SW1

THORNE, Robert George; s of Maj George Thorne MC DL; *b* 7 Feb 1943; *Educ* Eton, RAC Cirencester; *Career* dir Barclays Bank Ltd Bristol 1973-76, Newcastle upon Tyne 1977-80, London Northern 1980-; *Recreations* country pursuits; *Style* - Robert Thorne Esq; Blounts Farm, Sonning Common, Reading, Berks

THORNELY, Gervase Michael Cobham; s of Maj John Thornely, OBE, by his w, Hon Muriel (granted rank of Baron's da 1917, although her f did not survive to enjoy the Barony of Cobham called out of abeyance in 1916), nee Disney, yr sis of 12 & 13 (or 15 & 16 but for attainder) Barons Cobham; in remainder to abeyant Barony through his mother (who became a co-heiress after the death of the 13 (or 16) Baron in 1951); *b* 21 Oct 1918; *Educ* Rugby, Trin Hall Cambridge; *m* 1954, Jennifer, da of Sir (Charles) Hilary Scott, a slr & former Pres Law Soc, of Knowle House, Addington, Surrey; 2 s (Richard b 1957, Charles b 1958), 2 da (Elizabeth b 1960, Jacqueline b 1965); *Career* Headmaster Sedbergh Sch 1954-75 (assist master 1940-54); *Recreations* music, fishing; *Clubs* E India; *Style* - Gervase Thornely Esq; High Stangeathwaite, Killington, Sedbergh, Cumbria (☎ 20444)

THORNELY TAYLOR, Edward John; s of John Thornely Taylor JP (d 1960); *b* 27 May 1924; *Educ* Uppingham; *Career* landowner, Lord of The Manors of Scaftworth (Notts), Hoylandswaine, Thurnscoe and Oxspring (Yorks); High Sheriff South Yorkshire 1975-76; *Recreations* shooting, cricket; *Clubs* MCC, I Zingari, Free Foresters; *Style* - Edward Thornely Taylor Esq; Scaftworth Hall, nr Doncaster (☎ Doncaster 710323)

THORNEYCROFT, Baron (Life Peer 1967); (George Edward) Peter Thorneycroft; CH (1979), PC (1951); s of late George Thorneycroft, DSO, of Dunston Hall, Staffs (whose w's maternal gf was Capt George Hope, RN, making Lord Thorneycroft 6 cous of the present (3) Marquess of Linlithgow; the Capt's grandmother was Lady Anne Vane, da of 1 Earl of Darlington, who "whenever he was drunk told all he knew, and when he was sober, *more* than he knew" according to Horace Walpole; through Lord Darlington's w Lord Thorneycroft is ninth in descent from Charles II, while through the Earl he is tenth in descent from one of the few to pay with his head for the severing of Charles the Martyr's, *viz* Sir Harry Vane, "who, skilful in diplomacy, a puritan in religion, efficient in administration (to him may be owed England's triumph over Van Tromp), generous in propagating liberty of conscience, was steadfast in opposition to his king, yet stayed his hand from the awful sacrilege of regicide itself."); *b* 26 July 1909; *Educ* Eton, RMA Woolwich; *m* 1, 1938 (m dis 1949), Sheila Wells, da of E W Page, of Tettenhall; 1 s; m 2, 1949, Countess Carla Roberti, da of late Count Malagola Cappi, of Ravenna, Italy; 1 da; *Career* RA 1930, resigned cmmn 1933; barr Inner Temple 1935; MP (C) Stafford 1938-45, Monmouth 1945-66, Parly Sec Miny War Transport 1945, Pres BOT 1951-57, Chllr of the Exchequer 1957-58 (resigned), Min Aviation 1960-62, Min of Defence 1962-64, Chm of Con Party 1975-81; chm Pirelli General Cable Works Ltd, Pirelli Ltd, Trusthouse Forte Ltd; dir Securicor, chm British Reserve Insurance Co Ltd 1980-; memb Roy Soc of British Artists 1978; *Recreations* painting, fishing; *Clubs* Army and Navy; *Style* - Rt Hon Lord Thorneycroft CH PC; 42c Eaton sq, SW1; House of Lords, SW1 (☎ 01 219 4093)

THORNEYCROFT, Hon John Hamo; s of Baron Thorneycroft, CH, PC (Life Peer), by his 1 w Sheila; *b* 1940; *m* 1971, Delia, da of William Lloyd, of Penallt; children; *Style* - The Hon John Thorneycroft; 21 St Peters st, Islington, N1 8JD (☎ 01 226 0578)

THORNEYCROFT, Malcolm; s of Alec Charles Thorneycroft (d 1974); *b* 7 June 1936; *Educ* Wellingborough G S, Nottingham U; *m* 1960, Margaret Rose, nee Fisher; 1 s, 2 da; *Career* chartered electrical engineer, engineering dir TI Churchill Ltd 1976-; *Recreations* swimming, walking; *Clubs* 41 Club, Whitley; *Style* - Malcolm Thorneycroft Esq; 20 Hawthorn gdns, Whitley Bay, Tyne & Wear, (☎ 527739)

THORNHILL, Lt-Col Edmund Basil; MC (1918), Vice-Lt Cambs, Isle of Ely 1965-75; s of Edmund Henry Thornhill (d 1936); *b* 27 Feb 1898; *Educ* St Bees Cumberland, RMA Woolwich; *m* 1934, Diana Pearl Day, nee Beales; 2 s, 1 da; *Career* Lt-Col RA France 1914-18; France, Western Desert, Italy 1934-45; chm Cambridge and Isle of Ely Territorial Assoc 1957-62; *Clubs* Army & Navy; *Style* - Lt-Col Edmund Thornhill MC; Manor House, Boxworth, Cambridge

THORNTON, Adrian Heber; s of Nigel Heber Thornton (d 1941); *b* 17 March 1937; *Educ* Eton, Pembroke Coll Cambridge; *m* 1972, Margaret Barbara, nee Wales; 1 s, 2 da; *Career* 2 Lt Green Jackets Cyprus 1956-58, md Gallic Management Ltd & Gallic Shipping Ltd; *Clubs* City of London; *Style* - Adrian Thornton Esq; 31 Cheyne Row, SW3 (☎ 352 6290)

THORNTON, Lady; Agnes Margaret; *née* Masson; *m* 1927, Sir Ronald Thornton, late Dir Bank of England (d 1981); 1 s, 1 da; *Style* - Lady Thornton; South Bank, Rectory Lane, Brasted, Westerham, Kent

THORNTON, Col Dudley Edwin; CBE (1967), ERD (1953); s of Edwin Thornton (d 1952); *b* 1 May 1919; *Educ* Bristol G S; *m* 1940, Elizabeth Joan, da of Maj John Humphrey England TD (d 1976); 1 s, 2 da; *Career* Col Welch Regt 1939-45, Sr Assist Emergency Planning Offr Leics, Ch Staff Offr Ops/Plans/Trg ANZUK Force 1972-74, Dep Ch of Staff & Cdr Br Contingent UN Force in Cyprus 1970-72, Col Gen Staff Plans & Policy Div IMS NATO HQ 1968-70; *Recreations* army historical research; *Clubs* Naval & Military; *Style* - Col Dudley Thornton, CBE, ERD; Pepper's Farm, Burton Lazars, Melton Mowbray, Leics (☎ Melton Mowbray 2265)

THORNTON, Dr (Clara) Grace; CBE (1964, OBE 1959), MVO (1957); da of Arthur Augustus Thornton (d 1952); *b* 27 June 1913; *Educ* Kettering H S, Newnham Coll Cambridge; *Career* Danish Freedom Medal 1945, Order of Dannebrog 1957, HM Diplomatic Serv 1945-73, Consul-Gen Lisbon 1965-70, Head Consular Dept FO 1970-73, sec Women's National Cmmn Cabinet Office 1973-78, Fellow Newnham Coll 1972-81; *Recreations* music, embroidery, Scandinavia, cats; *Clubs* University Women's; *Style* - Dr Grace Thornton, CBE, MVO; 17 Onslow Court, Drayton Gardens, SW10 (☎ 373 2965)

THORNYCROFT, Col Guy Mytton;

DL (Shropshire 1967); s of Lt-Col Charles Thornycroft CBE DSO; *b* 1 April 1917; *Educ* Shrewsbury, Sandhurst; *m* 1947, Kathleen, da of Robert Evans MBE, of Eyton Old Hall, Leominster; 2 s; *Career* Col King's Shropshire LI 1937-60, Bde Col LI 1959-60; High Sheriff Salop 1975; *Recreations* shooting, cricket; *Clubs* MCC; *Style* - Col Guy Thornycroft DL; The Mount, Cressage, Shropshire (☎ 310)

THOROLD, Sir Anthony Henry; 15 Bt (E 1642), OBE (1942), DSC (1942), and Bar (1945), JP (Lincs 1961), DL (1959); s of Sir James Thorold, 14 Bt (d 1965); *b* 7 Sept 1903; *Educ* Winchester, RNCs Osborne and Dartmouth; *m* 1939, Jocelyn Elaine Laura, da of Sir Clifford Heathcote-Smith, KBE, CMG (d 1965); 1 s, 2 da; *Heir* s, Anthony Oliver Thorold; *Career* RN 1917, served 1939-45 in Home and Mediterranean Fleets as Staff Officer, Operations in Force 'H' and Western Approaches, Capt 1946, Cdre in Charge Hong Kong 1953-55, ADC to the Queen 1955-56, ret; High Sheriff 1968; CCllr Kesteven 1958-74, Lincs 1973-; chm Grantham Hosp Mgmnt Ctee 1963-74; chm Lincoln Diocesan Tst & Bd Finance 1966-77; *Recreations* shooting; *Clubs* Army and Navy; *Style* - Captain Sir Anthony Thorold, Bt, OBE, DSC*, JP, DL; Syston Old Hall, Grantham, Lincs (☎ Honington 270)

THOROLD, Anthony Oliver; s and h of Sir Anthony Thorold, Bt, OBE, DSC; *b* 15 April 1945; *Educ* Winchester, Lincoln Coll Oxford; *m* 1977, Genevra, da of John L Richardson, of Broads Law, West Calder, Midlothian; *Career* barr Inner Temple 1971; *Style* - Anthony Thorold Esq; 51 De Beauvoir rd, N1

THOROLD, Peter Guy Henry; s of Sir Guy Thorold KCMG (d 1970); *b* 20 April 1930; *Educ* Eton, New Coll Oxford; *m* 1964, Anne, da of Robert Fender AFC; 4 c; *Career* dir Bain Daives Ltd 1972; *Clubs* Buck's, City of London; *Style* - Peter Thorold Esq; 14 Clarendon rd, W11 3AB

THOROLD, Hon Mrs (Phyllis Margaret); *née* Russell; OBE (1946); da of 2 Baron Ampthill, GCSI, GCIE; *b* 3 June 1900; *m* 1940 (m annulled on her petition 1942), Capt William Thorold (d 1943, gggs of Sir John Thorold, 9 Bt, MP); *Style* - The Hon Mrs Thorold; 55 Ebury Mews, SW1

THORPE, Mathew Alexander; QC (1980); s of Alexander Thorpe; *b* 30 July 1938; *Educ* Stowe, Balliol Oxford; *m* 1966, Lavinia, da of Robert Buxton (gggs of Sir Thomas Buxton, 1 Bt); 3 s; *Career* barr 1961 Inner Temple; *Recreations* thoroughbred breeding; *Style* - Mathew Thorpe Esq QC; Seend Green House, Melksham, Wilts (☎ Seend 493)

THROCKMORTON, Anthony John Benedict; s of late Capt Herbert John Anthony Throckmorton RN (3 s of 10 Bt), and hp of cous, Sir Robert Throckmorton, 11 Bt; *b* 9 Feb 1916; *m* 1972, Violet Virginia, da of late Anders William Anderson; *Style* - Anthony Throckmorton Esq; 2006 Oakes Everett, Washington 08201, USA

THROCKMORTON, Lady Isabel Violet Kathleen; *née* Manners; da of 9 Duke of Rutland; *b* 5 Jan 1918; *m* 1, 1936 (m dis 1951), Gp Capt Loel Guinness, OBE, *qv*; 1 s, 1 da (William Loel Seymour Guinness and Marchioness of Dufferin and Ava, *qqv*); m 2, 1953, Sir Robert Throckmorton, 11 Bt; *Style* - Lady Isabel Throckmorton; Molland Bottreaux, S Moulton, N Devon; Coughton Court, Alcester, Warwicks

THROCKMORTON, Sir Robert George Maxwell; 11 Bt (E 1642); s of late Lt-Col Richard Courtenay Brabazon Throckmorton (s of 10 Bt); suc gf Sir Richard Charles Acton Throckmorton, 10 Bt, 1927; *b* 15 Feb 1908; *Educ* Downside; *m* 1, 1942 (m dis 1948), Jean, da of late Charles Garland, and formerly w of Arthur Smith-Bingham (she m 1959, 3 Baron Ashcombe, and d 1973); m 2, 1953, Lady Isabel Violet Kathleen, formerly w of Gp Capt Loel Guinness, and da of 9 Duke of Rutland; *Heir* cous, Anthony John Benedict Throckmorton; *Career* 2 Lt Gren Gds 1928-30, Lt (A) RNVR 1940-44; *Clubs* Army and Navy, White's; *Style* - Sir Robert Throckmorton, Bt; Coughton Court, Alcester, Warwickshire (☎ Alcester

3370); Molland Bottreaux, South Molton, N Devon

THROWER, Frank James; s of Henry James Thrower (decd); *b* 11 April 1932; *Educ* Stationers Co's Sch; *m* 1956 (m dis), Gerd Inga-Lill, da of Eric Sellman, of Göteborg, Sweden; 4 s, 3 da; *Career* glass & ceramic designer (Frank Thrower Designs); dir: Dartington Glass, Portmeirion Potteries, Portmeirion Dartington Sales; *Recreations* gardening, reading, squash, tennis, cricket, snooker, eating, drinking; *Club* MCC; *Style* - Frank Thrower Esq; c/o Lloyds Bank, 263 Tottenham Court rd, Wl

THURLOW, 8 Baron (GB 1792); Francis Edward Hovell-Thurlow-Cumming-Bruce; KCMG (1961, CMG 1957); s of Rev 6 Baron Thurlow (d 1971) by his w Grace, nee Trotter (whose paternal grandmother was Hon Charlotte Liddell, da of 1 Baron Ravensworth, while her maternal grandfather was Pascoe Grenfell (presumably by his 2 w Penelope), whose 4 s by his 1 w was cr Baron Grenfell); suc bro, 7 Baron Thurlow, CB, CBE, DSO, 1971; *b* 9 March 1912; *Educ* Shrewsbury, Trin Cambridge (MA); *m* 1949, Yvonne Diana, da of late Aubyn Wilson, of Westerlees, St Andrews, Fife; 2 s, 2 da; *Heir* s, Hon Roualeyn Robert Hovell-Thurlow-Cumming-Bruce; *Career* Dept Agriculture Scotland 1935-37, sec British High Cmmn NZ 1939-44 and Canada 1944-45, Priv Sec to Sec of State for Commonwealth Relations 1947-49, counsellor British High Cmmn New Delhi 1949-52, adviser to Govr of Gold Coast 1955, Dep High Cmmr in Ghana 1957, in Canada 1958, High Cmmr for UK in NZ 1959-63, and in Nigeria 1963-66, Dep Under-Sec FCO 1964, Govr and C-in-C of Bahamas 1968-72, chm Inst of Comparative Study of History, Philosophy and the Sciences 1975-; KStJ; *Recreations* fishing; *Clubs* Travellers'; *Style* - The Rt Hon the Lord Thurlow KCMG; The Old Vicarage, Mapledurham, Oxon; 16 Warwick av, W2 (☎ 01 723 7525)

THURSBY, Brig Patrick Dehany Francis; OBE (1965); s of Maj Francis Dehany Victor Thursby (d 1973); *b* 29 Dec 1922; *Educ* Cheltenham, Manchester U; *m* 1946, Gay, nee Newman; 2 s; *Career* joined 2 Lt RE 1942, Regimental Col Para Regt 1965-68, cmd 44 Para Bde 1968-70, Brig Gen Staff MOD (ret 1973), Hon Col 10 Bn Para Regt TA 1978-, dir Army Sport Control Bd 1973-; *Recreations* gardening, bird watching; *Clubs* Army & Navy, MCC; *Style* - Brig Patrick Thursby OBE; Tipplers, Tilford, Farnham, Surrey (☎ Frensham 2272)

THURSBY-PELHAM, Vaughan Brian George; s of Brian Thursby-Pelham (d 1958, seventh in descent from Henry Pelham, Clerk of the Pells (one of the great sinecures of state) *ante* 1721, whereby Vaughan is kin to the Dukes of Newcastle and 7 cous to 9 Earl of Chichester); *b* 27 Dec 1932; *Educ* Beaumont; *m* 1969, Brigid Kathleen O'Doherty, da of Edward O'Doherty, of Co Donegal; 2 s, 3 da; *Career* FICA, FCA; Gp Fin Dir The Zockoll Gp; *Recreations* philately; *Style* - Vaughan Thursby-Pelham Esq; 2 Woodlands av, New Malden, Surrey

THURSO, 2 Viscount (UK 1952); Sir Robin Macdonald Sinclair; 5 Bt (GB 1786), JP (Caithness 1959); s of 1 Viscount Thurso, KT, CMG, PC (d 1970, leader, as Sir Archibald Sinclair, of Lib Pty 1935-45), and Marigold (da of Lt-Col James Forbes, gs of Sir Charles Forbes, 3 Bt, by the Col's 1 w Lady Angela St Clair-Erskine, da of 4 Earl of Rosslyn); *b* 24 Dec 1922; *Educ* Eton, New Coll Oxford, Edinburgh U; *m* 1952, Margaret Beaumont, da of late Col Josiah James Robertson, DSO, TD, JP, DL, of Norwood, Wick, Caithness, and widow of Lt Guy Warwick Brokensha, DSC, RN; 2 s, 1 da; *Heir* s, Hon John Archibald Sinclair, yr of Ulbster; *Career* farmer; Fl Lt RAF 1939-45, CC for Caithness 1949-61 and 1965-73, Town Councillor Thurso 1957-61 and 1965-73, Baillie 1960 and 1969, Dean of Guild 1968, Police Judge 1971; chm Sinclair Family Trust Ltd, Lochdhu Hotels Ltd, Thurso Fisheries Ltd, dir Caithness Glass Ltd, Stephens (Plastics) Ltd; Ld-Lt Caithness 1973- (DL 1952, Vice-Lt 1964-73), pres Highland Soc of London 1980-; *Recreations* shooting, fishing, amateur drama; *Clubs* RAF, New (Edinburgh); *Style* - The Rt Hon the Viscount Thurso, JP, HM Lord-Lieut for Caithness; Thurso East Mains, Thurso,

Caithness, Scotland (☎ Thurso 2600); Dalnawillan, Altnabreac, Caithness

THYNN, Hon Ceawlin Henry Laszlo; s and h of Viscount Weymouth; *b* 6 June 1974; *Style* - The Hon Ceawlin Thynn

THYNN, Hon Lenka Abigail; da of Viscount Weymouth; *b* 1969; *Style* - The Hon Lenka Thynn

THYNNE, Lord Christopher John; 2 s of 6 Marquess of Bath, ED, by his 1 w, Hon Daphne Vivian, da of 4 Baron Vivian; *b* 9 April 1934; *Educ* Eton; *m* 1968, Antonia, da of Maj Sir Anthony Palmer, 5 Bt; 1 da; *Career* photographer (illustrator of Candida Lycett Green's *The Adventure of Hadrian Hedgehog*); late 2 Lt Life Gds; *Style* - Lord Christopher Thynne; The Hermitage, Horningsham, Wilts

THYNNE, Lady Valentine; Liese; da of Henry Dennis, of Bristol, & Mrs K Denis, of Essex; *b* 1 May 1945; *Educ* Abbeydale Sch, Sheffield; *m* 1977, as his 3 w, Lord Valentine Thynne (d 1979), s of 6 Marquess of Bath ED, by his 1 w, Hon Daphne Vivian, da of 4 Baron Vivian; *Career* artist; *Recreations* reading, painting, gardening, cooking; *Style* - Lady Valentine Thynne; Bridge House, 5 St John Street, Wells, Somerset (☎ 75015)

THYNNE, Lady Silvy Cerne; da of 6 Marquess of Bath by his 2 w, Virginia; *b* 22 Dec 1958; *Style* - Lady Silvy Thynne

THYSSEN-BORNEMISZA, Baroness Francesca; da of Baron Heinrich von Thyssen, of the German steel family, and Fiona Campbell-Walter, the model; *b* 1958; *Educ* St Martin's Art Sch, ICA; *Career* model; *Style* - Baroness Francesca Thyssen-Bornemisza; 18 Seymour Walk, SW10 (☎ 01 352 7913)

TICKELL, Crispin Charles Cervantes; MVO (1958); s of Jerrard Tickell and Renée, *née* Haynes; *b* 25 Aug 1930; *Educ* Westminster, Ch Ch Oxford; *m* 1, 1954 (m dis 1976), Chloë, da of Sir James Gunn, RA; 2 s, 1 da; m 2, 1977, Penelope, da of Dr Vernon Thorne; *Career* For Serv 1954-; Chef de Cabinet to Pres EEC Cmmn (Roy Jenkins) 1977-81; Br Ambassador Mexico 1981-; *Recreations* cosmology, palaeohistory, art; *Clubs* Brooks's; *Style* - Crispin Tickell Esq MVO; c/o FCO, SW1

TICKELL, Maj-Gen Marston Eustace; CBE (1973, MBE 1955), MC (1945); s of Maj-Gen Sir Eustace Francis Tickell KBE CB MC (d 1972); *b* 18 Nov 1923; *Educ* Wellington, Peterhouse Cambridge; *m* 1961, Pamela Vere, da of Vice-Adm Arthur Duncan Read CB (d 1976); *Career* Maj-Gen RA 1944-77 (ret); Col-Cmdt RE 1978- and President Inst Roy Engrs 1979-, Engr-in-Ch (Army) 1972-74, Cmdt Roy Mil Coll Science 1974-77; *Recreations* sailing; *Clubs* Roy Ocean Racing, Army and Navy; *Style* - Maj-Gen Marston Tickell, CBE, MC; The Old Vicarage, Branscombe, Seaton, Devon (☎ Branscombe 298)

TIDBOROUGH, Hon Mrs (Christine Gray); *née* Addison; da of 2 Viscount Addison; *b* 3 Sept 1946; *m* 1966, Terry Tidborough; *Style* - The Hon Mrs Tidborough; The Flat, 16 High st, Cullompton, Devon

TIGHE, Maj-Gen Patrick Anthony Macartan; CB (1977), MBE (1958); s of Macartan H Tighe (d 1928); *b* 26 Feb 1923; *Educ* Christ's Hosp; *m* 1, 1950, Elizabeth Frazer Stewart (d 1971); 2 s; m 2, 1972, Princine Calitri; *Career* Maj-Gen Roy Signals WW II, Palestine, Malaya, B; Signal Offr in Chief 1974-77, Col Cmdt Roy Signals 1977-; gp personnel man Hong Kong Land Co 1977-; *Recreations* golf; *Clubs* Army & Navy, Hong Kong; *Style* - Maj-Gen Patrick Tighe CB MBE; c/o Lloyds Bank, Cox's & King's Branch, 6 Pall Mall, SW1

TILBURY, Alan George; CBE (1966, OBE 1962); s of George Tilbury (d 1945); *b* 9 Dec 1925; *Educ* Sutton County G S, London U; *m* 1949, Jean-Mary McInnes, nee Pinkerton (d 1965); 3 da; *Career* advocate, entered Colonial Legal Serv 1954, Attorney-Gen Bechuanaland 1963 (Botswana 1966-69), head Legal Dept The Brewers Soc London 1970-72 (dep gen sec 1972-); *Recreations* sailing (yacht: 'Mersea Witch'), music, theatre; *Clubs* Tollesbury Cruising; *Style* - Alan Tilbury Esq CBE; Oakwood, Beckingham Green, Tolleshunt Major, Essex (☎ 062 183 656)

TILLEY, Clifford James; s of Henry James Tilley (d 1952); *b* 23 Oct 1911; *Educ* Wycliffe Coll, St John's Coll Oxford; *m* 1936, Ingeborg Hildegard Erna, nee Hoepker; 2 s; *Career* Maj Roy Artillery 1939-45; chm Willett & Son Ltd Bristol 1962-, Président Comité du Commerce des Céréales et des Aliments du Bétail de la Communauté Européenne Brussels 1978-79, Bourse de Commerce Européenne Strasbourg; *Recreations* gardening, travel, theatre, opera, ballet; *Clubs* Constitutional (Bristol), Baltic Exchange (London); *Style* - Clifford Tilley Esq; 17 Denny View rd, Abbots Leigh, Bristol (☎ Pill 2307)

TILLING, (George) Henry Garfield; s of late T G Tilling; *b* 24 Jan 1924; *Educ* Hardye's Sch Dorchester, Univ Coll Oxford; *m* 1956, Margaret Meriel, da of Rear-Adm Sir Alexander McGlashan, KBE, CB, DSO; 2 s, 2 da; *Career* OStJ 1977; Capt Dorsetshire Regt WW II; with Post Office: Assist Principal 1948, Principal 1953, Private Sec to Postmaster General 1964, Dep Dir Finance 1965, Dir E Postal Region 1967, Secretary 1973, Dir Postal Operations 1975, Chm Scottish Postal Board 1977-; *Recreations* orders and medals, heraldry, uniforms; *Clubs* Royal Overseas League; *Style* - Henry Tilling Esq; 4 Glenorchy terrace, Edinburgh, (☎ 031 668 2460)

TIMMINS, John Bradford; OBE (1973), TD (1968) and Bar (1974), DL (Greater Manchester 1981); s of Capt John James Timmins (d 1972); *b* 23 June 1932; *Educ* Dudley G S Worcs; *m* 1956, Jean, nee Edwards; 5 s, 1 da; *Career* Col; ADC to HM the Queen 1975-80, Hon Col 75 Engineer Regt 1980; civil engineer and chartered builder; dir Sir Robert Lloyd (Construction) Ltd 1975-, chm Warburton Properties Ltd 1973-; *Recreations* sailing (yacht: 'Watchdog'); *Clubs* Army and Navy, Roy Engineer Yacht; *Style* - John Timmins Esq, OBE, TD*, DL; The Old Rectory, Warburton, Lymm, Ches (☎ 3957)

TIMPSON, Lady Selina Catherine; *née* Meade; da of 6 Earl of Clanwilliam; *b* 1950; *m* 1972, Nicholas George Lawrence Timpson; *Style* - Lady Selina Timpson

TINLEY, Gervase Edmund Newport; s of Robert Gervase William Newport Tinley; *b* 16 June 1930; *Educ* HMS Worcester, Master Mariner; *m* 1965, Jean Lengden, nee Allen; 2 s, 2 da; *Career* Merchant Navy 1946-51 and 1956-58; schoolmaster 1959-60; dir Stewart Wrightson Associated Consultants 1973-, dir Naval Dependants Income & Assurance Trust 1976, chm Electoral Reform Soc 1977- (dep chm 1977), dep chm Centurion Housing Assoc 1980-; *Clubs* Reform, British Sub-Aqua, Mensa; *Style* - Gervase Tinley Esq; Trevaldwyn, Alma rd, Reigate, Surrey (☎ 07372 42923)

TIPPET, Rear-Adm Anthony Sanders; s of W Tippet; *b* 2 Oct 1928; *Educ* West Buckland Sch Devon; *m* 1950, Lola Bassett; 2 s, 1 da (and 1 s decd); *Career* Ch Naval Supply and Secretariat Officer 1981-, Flag Offr & Port Admiral Portsmouth 1981-; RN 1946-: Rear-Adm 1979, Assist Ch to Fleet Support MOD 1979-81; V-Cdre RN Sailing Assoc; *Style* - Rear-Admiral Anthony Tippet; Rosemary Cottage, Clayhidon, Cullompton, Devon (☎ Hemyock 082 368 378)

TIPPING, Hon Mrs (Catherine Joy); *née* Davies; da of 2 Baron Darwen; *b* 1948; *m* 1, 1970 (m dis 1976), Robert Nienhuis; m 2, 1976, Richard George Tipping; 1 s; *Style* - The Hon Mrs Tipping; Windhover, Park Way, Droitwich, Worcs

TIRARD, Lady Nesta; *née* FitzGerald; da of 8 Duke of Leinster; *b* 1942; *m* 1977, Philip Tirard; 1 da; *Style* - Lady Nesta Tirard

TITCHENER, John Lanham Bradbury; CMG (1955), OBE (1947); s of Alfred Titchener (d 1956); *b* 28 Nov 1912; *Educ* City of London Sch, RCM; *m* 1, 1937 (m dis 1958), Catherine Clark (decd); m 2, 1958, Britta Frederikke Marian, da of Carl Bendixsen (Hon Consul), of Denmark; 2 step s; *Career* BBC Talks Producer 1938-43; For Serv 1947-56, counsellor 1954-56 (resigned); former dir insur & engrg cos; dir Hagen International A/S; *Recreations* music, gardening, fishing; *Clubs* Travellers'; *Style* - John Titchener Esq CMG OBE; 3 Impasse Du Château, 06190 Roquebrune Village, CM

France (☎ 93 35 07 85); 2/4 Milner Street, London SW3; Weysesgade 13, 2100 Copenhagen (☎ (01) 200 831)

TIVERTON, Viscount; *see* Giffard, A E

TODD, Baron (Life Peer UK 1962); Alexander Robertus Todd; OM (1977); s of Alexander Todd, JP (d 1952); *b* 2 Oct 1907; *Educ* Allan Glen's Sch Glasgow, Glasgow U (DSc), Frankfurt-on-Main U (PhD), Oxford U (DPhil); *m* 1937, Alison Sarah, da of Sir Henry Hallett Dale, OM, GBE, MD, FRCP, FRS (d 1968); 1 s, 2 da; *Career* Prof of Chemistry Manchester U 1938-44, Cambridge U 1944-71, Master of Christ's Coll Cambridge 1963-78, Managing Trustee Nuffield Foundation 1950-79 (chm 1973-79), Chllr Strathclyde U 1964-, chm Croucher Foundation (Hong Kong) 1980-; FRS 1942 (Pres 1975-80), Hon LLD Glasgow, Melbourne, Edinburgh, Manchester and California, Hon DSc Durham, and other Univs, Hon DLitt Sydney; Nobel Prize for Chemistry 1957; kt 1954; *Recreations* golf; *Clubs* Athenaeum; *Style* - The Rt Hon The Lord Todd OM; 9 Parker Street, Cambridge (☎ Cambridge (STD Code 0223) 356688)

TODD, Hon Alexander Henry; s of Baron Todd OM (Life Peer); *b* 1939; *Educ* The Leys Sch Cambridge, Oriel Oxford (DPhil); *m* 1967, Joan Margaret, da of F W Koester, of Campbell, Calif, USA; *Style* - The Hon Alexander Todd; 16 Windermere Drive, Alderley Edge, Cheshire

TODD, Hon Hilary Alison; da of Baron Todd OM (Life Peer); *b* 25 June 1946; *Educ* Perse Sch for Girls Cambridge, Westonbirt, London Acad of Music & Dramatic Art; *Style* - The Hon Hilary Todd

TODD, Col Walter John Cambridge; OBE (1953), TD (1945), DL (Cheshire 1975); s of Ralph Todd (d 1963); *b* 2 Oct 1910; *Educ* Durham Sch, St John's Coll Cambridge; *m* 1950, Sheila Gertrude, nee Macbeth; 1 da; *Career* Col RA 1939-45, Cmdt Cheshire Army Cadet Force 1959-67, Hon Col 1968-79; slr 1935, late Dep Clerk of the Peace and Dep Solicitor Cheshire CC until 1975; *Recreations* rowing, gardening; *Clubs* Army & Navy, Leander; *Style* - Col Walter Todd, OBE, TD, DL; 21 Dee Fords ave, Chester (☎ 0244 24390)

TODHUNTER, Michael John Benjamin; s of Brig Edward Todhunter by Agnes (da of John Swire, of Hillingdon House, Harlow, & sometime MFH Essex Foxhounds); *b* 25 March 1935; *Educ* Eton, Magdalen Oxford; *m* 1959, Caroline Francesca, da of Maj William Dowding (d 1980); 1 s, 2 da; *Career* late 2 Lt 11 Hussars; bill broker; dep chm & md Jessel Toynbee; chm Clyde Shipping Co; dir James Finlay & Co, S H Lock & Co Hldgs; *Recreations* shooting; *Clubs* White's, Pratt's, Western (Glasgow); *Style* - Michael Todhunter Esq; The Old Rectory, Farnborough, Wantage, Oxon (☎ 048 82 298); The Studio, 4 Lowndes st, SW1 (☎ 01 235 6421)

TOFIELD, Terence William; s of Herbert Russel Tofield (d 1981); *b* 5 July 1936; *Educ* Latymer Upper; *Career* public relations dir Rumasa and Augustus Barnett & Son Ltd; *Recreations* tennis, shooting, skiing; *Clubs* Hurlingham, RA; *Style* - Terence Tofield Esq; 77 Swan Court, Chelsea Manor st, SW3

TOGANIVALU, His Excellency Ratu (Chief) Josua Brown; *Career* Fijian High Commissioner to UK 1981-; *Style* - HE Ratu Josua Brown Toganivalu; Fiji High Commission, 34 Hyde Park Gate, SW7 (☎ 01 584 3661/ 589 9309/ 589 9312)

TOLER, Maj-Gen David Arthur Hodges; OBE (1963), MC (1945); s of Maj Thomas Clayton Toler, of Swettenham Hall, Congleton, Cheshire; *b* 13 Sept 1920; *Educ* Stowe, Ch Ch Oxford; *m* 1951, Judith Mary, da of James Garden DSO; 1 s, 1 da; *Career* Maj-Gen Coldstream Guards 1940-73; Deputy Hon Colonel for Lincs, Roy Anglian Regt 1979-; *Recreations* shooting, fishing, gardening; *Clubs* Army & Navy; *Style* - Maj-Gen David Toler, OBE, MC; Grove House, Fulbeck, Grantham, Lincs

TOLLEMACHE, 5 Baron (UK 1876); Timothy John Edward Tollemache; s of 4 Baron Tollemache (d 1975, fifth in descent from Lady Jane Tollemache, da of 4 Earl of Dysart); *b* 13 Dec 1939; *Educ* Eton; *m* 1970, Alexandra Dorothy Jean, da of Col Hugo Meynell, MC, JP, DL, (paternal ggs of 1 Viscount Halifax and maternal gs of 6 Earl of Dartmouth), of Hollybush Park, Burton-on-Trent, Staffs (d 1960); 2 s, 1 da; *Heir* s, Hon Edward John Hugo Tollemache; *Career* dir: Tollemache & Cobbold Brewery 1973-, NRG London Re-Insurance Co Ltd 1976-, Amev Ltd 1980-; farmer in Suffolk and Cheshire; *Recreations* shooting, fishing; *Clubs* White's, Pratt's; *Style* - The Rt Hon The Lord Tollemache; 43 Belgrave Mews N, SW1 (☎ 01 235 1767); Helmingham Hall, Stowmarket, Suffolk (☎ Helmingham 217)

TOLLEMACHE, Dinah, Baroness; Dinah Susan; da of late Sir Archibald Auldjo Jamieson, KBE, MC; *m* 1939, 4 Baron Tollemache MC (d 1975); *Style* - The Rt Hon Dinah, Lady Tollemache; The Home Farm, Peckforton, Tarporley, Cheshire

TOLLEMACHE, Hon Edward John Hugo; s and h of 5 Baron Tollemache; *b* 12 May 1976; *Style* - The Hon Edward Tollemache

TOLLEMACHE, Hon Hugh John Hamilton; s of 4 Baron Tollemache (d 1975); *b* 1946; *Educ* Eton; *Style* - The Hon Hugh Tollemache; 19 Clarendon st, SW1

TOLLEMACHE, Sir Humphry Thomas; 6 Bt (GB 1793), CB (1952), CBE (1950); s of Sir Lyonel Tollemache, 4 Bt (d 1952); suc bro 1969; *b* 10 Aug 1897; *Educ* Eastbourne Coll; *m* 1926, Nora Priscilla, da of John Taylor, of Broomhill, Eastbourne; 2 s, 2 da; *Heir* s, Lyonel Tollemache; *Career* 1914-18 War with Grand Fleet, 1939-45 War Admiralty Middle East and Far East (Brig), Maj-Gen RM; Co Cllr Hants 1957, Alderman 1969, DL 1965; Maj-Gen Commanding Portsmouth Gp RM 1949-52, Hon Col Cmdt Portsmouth Gp RM 1958-60, Col Cmdt RM 1961-62 (Representative 1961); *Clubs* Army and Navy; *Style* - Sir Humphry Tollemache, Bt, CB, CBE, DL; Sheet House, Petersfield, Hants (☎ 3813)

TOLLEMACHE, Hon James Henry Timothy; s of 5 Baron Tollemache; *b* 1980; *Style* - The Hon James Tollemache

TOLLEMACHE, Lynette, Baroness; Lynette; MBE (1944); da of late Alfred Vincent Pawson, of Nynehead Court, Som; *m* 1928, as his 2 w, 3 Baron Tollemache (d 1955); *Career* OStJ; *Style* - The Rt Hon Lynette, Lady Tollemache MBE; Flat 2, Cavendish Court, 14 Blackwater rd, Eastbourne BN21 4JD

TOLLEMACHE, Lyonel Humphry John; s and h of Sir Humphry Tollemache, 6 Bt, CB, CBE; *b* 10 July 1931; *Educ* Uppingham; *m* 1960, Mary Joscelyne, da of Col William Henry Whitbread TD, of Warren Mere, Godalming; 2 s, 2 da; *Career* Maj (ret) Coldstream Gds; High Sheriff Leics 1978-79, DL Leics; FRICS; *Style* - Lyonel Tollemache Esq DL; Buckminster Park, Grantham, Lincs NG33 5RU

TOLLEMACHE, Hon Michael David Douglas; s of 4 Baron Tollemache (d 1975); *b* 1944; *Educ* Eton, Trin Cambridge (MA); *m* 1969, Theresa, da of Peter Bowring, of 77 Campden Court, Campden Hill rd, W8; 2 s (twins), 1 da; *Style* - The Hon Michael Tollemache; Framsden Hall, Stowmarket, Suffolk

TOLLEMACHE, Hon (John) Nicholas Lyonel; s of 4 Baron Tollemache (d 1975); *b* 1941; *Educ* Eton, Trin Cambridge (MA), Harvard U (MBA); *m* 1971 (m dis 1974), Heide Eva Marie, da of Gunther Wiedeck, of Bonn; *Style* - The Hon Nicholas Tollemache; 1114 San Ysidro Drive, Beverley Hills, Los Angeles, Calif 90210, USA

TOLLEMACHE, Hon Selina Karen; da of 5 Baron Tollemache; *b* 1973; *Style* - The Hon Selina Tollemache

TOLSTOY, Count; Dimitry (full surname Tolstoy-Miloslavsky); QC (1959); s of Count (Michael) Tolstoy-Miloslavsky (d 1947); *see* Count Nikolai Tolstoy-Miloslavsky for further details); is sr male rep of Tolstoy family; *b* 8 Nov 1912; *Educ* Wellington, Trin Cambridge; *m* 1, 1934, Frieda Mary (m dis), da of Howard

Wicksteed (decd); 1 s (Count Nikolai T-M, *qv*), 1 da (Natasha or Natalie m 1974 Patrick John Bucknell); m 2, 1943, Natalie, da of Captain Vladimir Deytrikh (d 1951); 1 s (Count Andrei m 1976 Carolinda Beatrice Catherine Pilcher), 1 da (Tania or Tatiana, m 1972 James Henry Harcourt Illingworth); *Career* barr 1937, lecturer in Divorce to Inns of Court 1952-68; *Style* - Count Tolstoy QC; San Spyridon, Javea, Alicante, Spain

TOLSTOY-MILOSLAVSKY, Count Andrei; s of Count (Dmitri) Tolstoy (-Miloslavsky) by his 2 w Natalie; half-bro of Count Nikolai Tolstoy-Miloslavsky, *qqv*; *b* in or after 1943; *m* 1976, Carolinda Pilcher; *Style* - Count Andrei Tolstoy-Miloslavsky; 8 Orlando rd, SW4 (☎ 01 720 6687)

TOLSTOY-MILOSLAVSKY, Count Nikolai Dmitrievich; s and h of Count (Dmitri) Tolstoy-Miloslavsky (the present *chef de famille*, descended from Ivan Tolstoy, of a Boyar family granted a confirmation of nobility by Ukase of Peter The Great 1713 (tantamount to a cr); Ivan d before the full grant was effected, and in 1930 the Grand Duke Kyrill 'ordained' that Pavel Sergeievich T-M be known as Count Pavel etc; his ggs Nikolai is a remote cous of the family of the celebrated novelist, Lev or Leo Tolstoy (descended from Ivan's yr bro Piotr, a diplomat), likewise of the Stalin Prize winner (Count) Alexei Tolstoy and the 19 century satirical and romantic novelist Count Alexei Tolstoy; Tsar Nicholas II granted Count Pavel's branch a Royal License (1910) to assume the additional surname of Miloslavsky, since his branch were the sr male reps of the Miloslavskys, an important Russian family in the 16 & 17 centuries but themselves later extinct in the male line); *b* 23 June 1935; *Educ* Wellington, Trin Coll Dublin; *m* 1971, Georgina Katherine, da of Maj Peter Brown, of Llandeilo, Carmarthenshire; 1 s (Dmitri b 1978), 3 da (Alexandra b 1973, Anastasia b 1975, Xenia b 1980); *Heir* s, Dmitri Nikolaevich Tolstoy-Miloslavsky; *Career* author, historian, biographer; books include *Victims of Yalta* (1978) & *Stalin's Secret War* (1981), also monographs on Celtic studies; sr associate memb St Anthony's Coll Oxford; *Recreations* walking, archery, nostalgia; *Clubs* Brooks's, Beefsteak; *Style* - Count Nikolai Tolstoy-Miloslavsky; Court Close, Southmoor, Abingdon, Berks (☎ 0865 820186)

TOMALIN, Air Cdre Charles Douglas; CBE (1966, OBE 1953), DFC (1943), AFC (1942); s of Frederick Tomalin (d 1933); *b* 20 August 1914; *Educ* William Ellis Sch, RAF Staff Coll, US Armed Forces Staff Coll, Imperial Defence Coll; *m* 1941, Margaret, da of Rev J J Ellis (d 1962); 2 s; *Career* Air Cdre RAF 1936-66, Dir Intelligence (A) 1961-63, head Br Defence Liaison Staff and Air Attaché S Africa 1963-66; *Recreations* swimming, reading, touring; *Clubs* RAF; *Style* - Air Cdre Charles Tomalin, CBE, DFC, AFC; 'Rauceby', Nascot Wood rd, Watford, Herts (☎ Watford 29539)

TOMLIN, Eric Walter Frederick; CBE (1965, OBE 1959); s of Edgar Herbert Tomlin (d 1919); *b* 30 Jan 1913; *Educ* Whitgift Sch Oxford; *m* 1, 1945 Margaret (m dis 1952); 1 s; m 2, 1974, Judith, da of Lt-Gen Sir Euan Miller; *Career* author; cultural cnsllr Br Embassy Tokyo & British Cncl rep Japan 1961-67, France 1969-72; Prof English & Philosophy University of Nice, France, 1972-74, visiting fell Univ Coll Cambridge 1971-72; *Recreations* reading, travel; *Clubs* Athenaeum, Union Soc Oxford; *Style* - Eric Tomlin Esq CBE; Tall Trees, Morwenstow, Cornwall (☎ Morwenstow 206); 31 Redan st, W14 (☎ 602 6414)

TOMLINS, Hon Mrs (Angela Mary); *née* Evans-Freke; da of 11 Baron Carbery; *b* 1954; *m* 1975, Martin David Tomlins; 1 s; *Style* - The Hon Mrs Tomlins; 96 Wormholt rd, W12

TOMLINSON, Elvira Mary; da of Domingo Riccardo Busi (d 1962); *b* 13 Sept 1922; *Educ* Westonbirt; *m* 1947, John Michael Tomlinson; *Career* chm Busi & Stephenson Ltd Liverpool & assoc cos in Germany & Ghana, dir Busi & Stephenson Ltd Nigeria 1968-, chm Singlehurst & Co Ltd Liverpool 1979-; *Clubs* Roy Ocean Racing; *Style* - Mrs John Tomlinson; Elmleigh, Neston, South Wirral (☎ 051 336 4259)

TOMPKINS, Granville (Richard) Francis; s of Richard Tompkins (d 1973); *b* 15 May 1918; *m* 1970, Elizabeth Nancy, nee Duke; 1 da; *Career* fndr & chm Green Shield Trading Stamp Co, fndr pres Argos Distributors Ltd (ret as chm 1980), chm New Day Furnishers Ltd and Goodrich Ltd; *Recreations* golf, shooting, fishing; (own aircraft Hawker Siddeley jet 125); *Style* - Richard Tompkins Esq; 7 Belgrave sq, SW1; Wyld Court House, Hampstead Norreys, Berks; West Grinstead Park, Sussex

TONGE, Hon Mrs (Judith Felicity); *née* Allen; da of Baron Allen of Fallowfield CBE; *b* 1946; *m* 1973, Graham Tonge; *Style* - The Hon Mrs Tonge; 14 Grange gdns, Llantwit Major, S Glam

TOOGOOD, John Michael; s of Charles Dutton Toogood (d 1951); *b* 4 Sept 1928; *Educ* Malvern; *m* 1960, Barbara Grace, da of Maj Walter Grant Fanning (d 1964); 1 s, 1 da; *Career* managing director Lambert Brothers Shipping Ltd; *Recreations* squash, walking; *Style* - John Toogood Esq; 25 Baronsmead rd, SW13 (☎ 01 748 9271)

TOOHEY, Joyce; CB (1977); da of Louis Zinkin (d 1924); *b* 20 Sept 1917; *Educ* Brondesbury and Kilburn H S, Girton Coll Cambridge, London Sch of Economics, Harvard Business Sch; *m* 1947, Monty Isaac Toohey, MD, MRCP, DCH (d 1960); 2 da; *Career* admin civil servant 1941-76 (ret), Under-Sec Dept of Environment 1970-76, Under-Sec Miny of Public Bldg & Works 1964-70 (Assist 1956-64, Princ 1948-56, Assist Princ 1946-48), Assist Princ Miny Supply 1941-46; *Recreations* reading, walking; *Clubs* United Oxford and Cambridge; *Style* - Mrs Monty Toohey CB; 11 Kensington Court Gardens, Kensington Court Place, W8 (☎ 01 937 1559)

TOOTH, Simon John Geoffrey; s of Cyril John Tooth (d 1936); *b* 27 May 1934; *Educ* Downside Coll Bath; *m* 1959, Melissa Mary, da of Col Colwell Carney, USAF (d 1978); 1 s, 3 da; *Career* memb London Stock Exchange 1959-; *Recreations* golf, sailing, deep sea fishing; *Clubs* Institute of Directors, Hurlingham; *Style* - Simon Tooth Esq; 14 St Mary Abbots Court, W14 (☎ 01 603 0789); c/o Pacific Coast Stock Exchange, Los Angeles, Calif, USA

TORBOCK, Cdr Richard Henley; JP (Westmorland 1954), DL (1954); s of Joseph Torbock, of Crossrigg Hall, Penrith; *b* 27 Jan 1904; *Educ* Aysgarth Sch, RNCs Osborne, Dartmouth and Greenwich; *Career* Cdr RN, served WW II HMS Valiant, HMS Chaser; High Sheriff Westmorland 1953; *Recreations* shooting, fishing; *Club* Lansdowne; *Style* - Commander Richard Torbock JP DL; Crossing Hall, Cliburn, Penrith, Cumbria (☎ Morland 287)

TORDOFF, Baron (Life Peer UK 1981); Geoffrey Johnson Tordoff; s of Stanley Tordoff, of Marple, Cheshire; *b* 11 Oct 1928; *Educ* N Manchester G S, Manchester U; *m* 1953, Mary, da of Thomas Swarbrick, of Leeds; 2 s (Hon Nicholas Gregory Tordoff, Hon Mark Edmund Tordoff), 3 da (Hon Mary Catherine Tordoff; Hon Frances Jane Tordoff, b 6 Feb 1962; Hon Paula Mary Tordoff, b 16 June 1960); *Career* fought (Lib) Northwich 1964, Knutsford 1966 & 1970; chm Lib Party 1976-79, now chm Campaigns & Elections Ctee; man Public Affairs (Chemicals) Shell UK; *Style* - The Rt Hon Lord Tordoff

TORLESSE, Rear-Adm Arthur David; CB (1953), DSO (1946); s of Capt Arthur Ward Torlesse (d 1939); *b* 24 Jan 1902; *Educ* Stanmore Park Mddx, RNCs Osborne and Dartmouth; *m* 1933, Sheila Mary Susan, da of Lt-Col Duncan Darroch; 2 s, 1 da; *Career* Officer US Legion Merit 1954; joined RN 1918, Cdr 1935, Rear-Adm 1951, Flag Offr Special Squad Cdr Monte Bello Atomic Trial Expedition 1952 (ret 1954); regional dir Civil Defence N Midlands Region 1955-67; *Recreations* fishing, entomology; *Clubs* Naval & Mil; *Style* - Rear-Adm Arthur Torlesse CB DSO; 1 Sway Lodge, Sway, Lymington, Hants (☎ Lymington 682550)

TORPHICHEN, 15 Lord (S 1564); James Andrew Douglas Sandilands; s of 14 Lord Torphichen (d 1975); *b* 27 Aug 1946; *Educ* King's Sch Canterbury,

Birmingham U; *m* 1976, Margaret Elizabeth, da of William Alfred Beale (d 1967), of Boston, Mass; 1 da; *Heir* 1 cous once removed, Master of Torphichen; *Career* electronics engineer; *Style* - The Rt Hon the Lord Torpichen; Calder House, Mid-Calder, West Lothian EH53 0HN

TORPHICHEN, Master of; Douglas Robert Alexander; s of late Hon Walter Alexander Sandilands (s of 12 Lord Torphichen, d 1966), and hp of cous, 15 Lord Torphichen; *b* 31 Aug 1926; *m* 1, 1949, Ethel Louise Burkitt; 1 s; m 2, Suzette Vera, nee Pernet; 2 s; *Style* - The Master of Torphichen; An Airidh, Carrbridge, Inverness-shire

TORPICHEN, Pamela, Lady; Pamela Mary; da of late John Howard Snow, and widow of Thomas Hodson-Pressinger; *m* 1973, as his 3 w, 14 Lord Torpichen (d 1975); *Style* - The Rt Hon Pamela, Lady Torphichen; 16 Moore st, SW3

TORRADO Y DE FONTCUBERTA, Lady Melissa Geraldine Florence; *née* Bligh; da (by 3 w) of late 9 Earl of Darnley; *b* 1945; *m* 1965, Don Manuel Torrado y de Fontcuberta (d 1980); 1 s, 2 da; *Style* - Lady Melissa Torrado y de Fontcuberta; La Casa, Millas, Madre Maña, Gerona, Spain

TORRENS-SPENCE, Capt Frederick Michael Alexander; DSO, DSC,(1941), AFC,(1944) DFC (Greek, 1943) JP, RN (ret); s of Lt-Col Herbert Frederick Torrens-Spence (d 1937); *b* 10 March 1914; *Educ* RN Coll Dartmouth; *Career* ADC to HM The Queen 1961; Co Commandant Ulster Special Constabulary 1961-70; CO 2 Bn Ulster Defence Regiment 1970-71; High Sheriff Co Armagh 1979; Ld-Lt Co Armagh 1981- (formerly DL); *Clubs* MCC; *Style* - Captain Michael Torrens-Spence DSO DSC AFC JP RN, HM Lord-Lieut for Co Armagh; Drumcullan House, Hollymount, Downpatrick, Co Down, N Ireland

TORRINGTON, 11 Viscount (GB 1721); Sir Timothy Howard St George Byng, 11 Bt (GB 1715); Baron Byng, of Southill (GB 1721); s of Hon George Byng, RN (d on active service 1944, s of 10 Viscount), and gs of 10 Viscount (d 1961); *b* 13 July 1943; *Educ* Harrow, St Edmund Hall Oxford; *m* 1973, Susan Honour, da of Michael George Thomas Webster, of The Vale, Windsor Forest, Berks; 2 da; *Heir* kinsman, John Launcelot Byng, MC; *Career* md Attock Petroleum Ltd 1976-; *Clubs* White's, Muthaiga (Nairobi); *Style* - The Rt Hon the Viscount Torrington; 60 Cumberland st, SW1 (☎ 01 834 3020)

TOTMAN, Grenfell William; CMG (1973), OBE (1963); s of William Totman (d 1968); *b* 24 July 1911; *Educ* Selhurst G S, London U; *m* 1, 1938, Eileen Joan Godley (m dis 1962); 1 s; m 2, 1963, Barbara Florence, nee Cannon; *Career* chartered accountant, controller of finance C'wlth Dvpt Corpn 1955-76 (ret); *Recreations* music, horticulture, philately; *Style* - Grenfell Totmam Esq, CMG, OBE; Gayfere, East Hill, nr Otford, Kent (☎ Otford 3256)

TOTTENHAM, Hon --; da of Viscount Loftus, *qv*

TOTTENHAM, Lady Ann Elizabeth; da (by 1 m) of 8 Marquess of Ely; *b* 1940; *Educ* Trin Coll, Toronto U (BA, STB) and Union Seminary New York (MTB); *Style* - Lady Ann Tottenham

TOTTENHAM, Hon Andrew John; s and h of Viscount Loftus, *qv*

TOTTENHAM, Maj Gen Frederick Joseph Loftus; CBE (1943), DSO (1944) and Bar (1945); s of Frederick William Loftus Tottenham; *b* 4 May 1898; *Educ* St Edmonds Coll Old Hall Herts; *m* 1922, Marjorie Fielden, nee Dare (d 1978); 1 s (2 s decd); *Career* Maj Gen served 1914-50 (3 despatches); in charge of Home Guard N Ireland 1954-56; *Recreations* polo, pigsticking, sun and travel; *Clubs* Naval & Military, Ulster; *Style* - Maj Gen Frederick Loftus Tottenham, CBE, DSO; Duart Cottage, 19 Norton Bavant, Warminster, Wilts (☎ Sutton Veny (098 54) 364)

TOTTENHAM, Lady George - Jane Elizabeth; da of Arthur Martin; *m* 1944, Lord George Robert Tottenham (d 1976), s of George Leonard Tottenham (ggs of Rt Rev Lord Ponsonby Tottenham, Bishop of

Clogher & s of 1 Marquess of Ely), bro of 8 Marquess of Ely and who was raised to the rank of a Marquess's son 1973; 1 da; *Style* - Lady George Tottenham; Trullwell, Box, nr Stroud, Glos

TOTTENHAM, Lord Richard Ivor; s (by 1 m) of 8 Marquess of Ely; *b* 1954; *Educ* U of Western Ontario (BA); *m* 1978, Virginia Murney, da of William Murney Mortis, of Toronto, Ontario; *Style* - Lord Richard Tottenham; 221 Balliol st, Apt 1625, Toronto, Ontario, M45 1C8 Canada

TOTTENHAM, Lord Timothy Craig; s (by 1 w) of 8 Marquess of Ely; *b* 1948; *Educ* Ottawa Teachers' Coll; *m* 1973, Elizabeth Jane, da of Grant McAllister, of Ottawa, Ontario; 1 s; *Style* - Lord Timothy Tottenham

TOUCHE, Sir Anthony George; 3 Bt (UK 1920), of Westcott, Co Surrey; s of Donovan Meredith Touche (d 1952); suc unc, Sir Norman George Touche, 2 Bt, 1977; *b* 31 Jan 1927; *Educ* Eton; *m* 1961, Hester Christina, da of Dr Werner Pleuger; 3 s, 1 da; *Heir* s, William George Touche; *Career* chm Touche Remnant & Co 1971-, dep chm Nat Westminster Bank Ltd 1977-; dir: Investment Trust Cos 1952, Westminster Bank Ltd 1968, Yorkshire Bank 1979, Int Westminster Bank Ltd 1980; FCA; *Clubs* Bath; *Style* - Sir Anthony Touche, Bt; Stane House, Ockley, Dorking, Surrey RH5 5TQ (☎ Oakwood Hill 297)

TOUCHE, Eva, Lady; Eva Maitland; da of Patrick Evan Cameron, of Salachan, Ardour, Argyll; *Educ* Edinburgh U (MA); *m* 1923, Sir Norman George Touche, 2 Bt (d 1977); *Style* - Eva, Lady Touche; Nenthorn, 1 Broomfield Park, Westcott, Dorking, Surrey

TOUCHE, Eric MacLellan; s and h of Sir Rodney Touche, 2 Bt; *b* 22 Feb 1960; *Style* - Eric Touche Esq

TOUCHE, Ruby, Lady; Ruby Anne Hume-Purves; da of late Sir Duncan James Macpherson CIE; *m* 1926, Rt Hon Sir Gordon Cosmo Touche, 1 Bt (d 1972); *Style* - Ruby, Lady Touche; Gable End, Mill rd, Holmwood, Surrey

TOUCHE, Sir Rodney Gordon; 2 Bt (UK 1962), of Dorking, Co Surrey; s of Rt Hon Sir Gordon Cosmo Touche, 1 Bt (d 1972); *b* 5 Dec 1928; *Educ* Marlborough, Univ Coll Oxford; *m* 1955, Ouida Ann, da of late Frederick Gerald MacLellan, of Moncton, New Brunswick, Canada; 1 s, 3 da; *Heir* s, Eric MacLellan Touche; *Career* Pres Village Lake Louise Ltd (Alberta Canada) 1973-; *Clubs* Roy Automobile; *Style* - Sir Rodney Touche, Bt; 707 Prospect av, Calgary, Alberta, Canada (☎ 403 244 6097)

TOUCHE, William George; s and h of Sir Anthony Touche, 3 Bt; *b* 26 June 1962; *Style* - William Touche Esq

TOULMIN, John Kelvin; QC (1980); s of A H Toulmin; *b* 14 Feb 1941; *Educ* Winchester Coll, Trin Hall Cambridge, Michigan U; *m* 1967, Carolyn Merton, nee Gullick; 1 s, 2 da; *Career* barr 1965, memb Bar Cncl/Senate 1971-77 & 1978-, chm Young Barristers Ctee 1973-75; memb Supreme Court Rules Ctee 1976-80; govr The Maudsley and Bethlem Roy Hosps 1979-; *Recreations* cricket, music; *Clubs* MCC, Surrey CC, Reform; *Style* - John Toulmin Esq QC; 4 Paper Bldgs, Temple, EC4 (☎ 353 3366); 18 Crescent Wood rd, SE26 (☎ 693 5033)

TOUT, Herbert; CMG (1946); s of Prof Thomas Frederick Tout (d 1929); *b* 20 April 1904; *Educ* Sherborne, Oxford; *Career* univ teacher economics, instructor Univ of Minnesota 1929-36, lecturer Univ of Bristol 1936-45; Temp Principal Bd of Trade 1940-41, Assist Sec 1941-45; Reader in Political Economy London University 1947-68 (ret); *Recreations* walking, gardening; *Style* - Herbert Tout Esq CMG; Little Greeting, W Hoathly, E Grinstead, W Sussex (☎ Sharpthorne 810400)

TOVEY, Raymond Francis; s of Francis Raymond Tovey (d 1966); *b* 13 Feb 1920; *Educ* Mill Hill 1933-38; Lincoln College Oxford, 1938-40; *m* 1970, Pamela Jean McDowell; *Career* served as Capt Roy Regt Artillery UK 1940-43, India & Burma 1943-46; sr ptnr Field Fisher & Martineau 1977-; Solicitor to the Supreme Court; *Recreations* golf, theatre, philately;

Clubs Law Society; *Style* - Raymond Tovey Esq; 51 Norland Square, London, W11 4PZ (☎ 01 727 1227)

TOWER, Maj-Gen Philip Thomas; CB (1968), DSO (1944), MBE (1942); s of Vice-Adm Sir Thomas Tower KBE CB (d 1964); *b* 1 March 1917; *Educ* Hawtrey's Harrow, RMA Woolwich; *m* 1943, Elizabeth, da of Thomas Sneyd-Kynnersley OBE MC, of Loxley Park, Staffs; *Career* Maj-Gen RA 1937-, GOC MELF 1967, Cmdt RMA Sandhurst 1968-72, Cmmr St John for Norfolk 1975-78, Col Cmdt RA 1970-80; *Recreations* shooting, gardening; *Clubs* Roy Yacht Sqdn, Pratt's, Army & Navy; *Style* - Maj-Gen Philip Tower CB DSO MBE; Blickling Hall, Norfolk (☎ 026373 2439); Studio A, 717 Fulham rd, SW6 (☎ 01 385 8538)

TOWNELEY, Simon Peter Edmund Cosmo William; JP (Lancs 1956); s of Col Alexander Koch de Gooreynd OBE, and Priscilla, nee Reyntiens; is bro of Peregrine Worsthorne, *qv* for fuller family background; sr male rep of the Towneleys of Dyneley, whose ancestors were Lay Deans of Whalley Abbey and were granted lands near Burnley by Roger De Lacy, Earl of Lincoln, c 1200; reps of the Towneleys fought at Agincourt on the winning, and at Marston Moor on the losing sides; the family had a recusant and Jacobite tradition; *b* 14 Dec 1921; *Educ* Stowe, Worcester Coll Oxford; *m* 1955, Mary, 2 da of Cuthbert Fitzherbert (ggs of Basil Fitzherbert, whose bro Thomas was the 1 husb of that Mrs Fitzherbert who m the Prince of Wales, later George IV, in contravention of the Roy Marriages Act); 1 s, 6 da; *Career* late lecturer History of Music Oxford, Gen Commissioner for Income Tax; KStJ, Kt Cdr of St Gregory (Papal Decoration); High Sheriff Lancs 1970-71, Ld-Lieut (DL 1970) & Custos Rotulorum Lancs 1976-; chm Northern Dance Theatre; *Clubs* Beefsteak, Pratt's, Boodle's, Turf; *Style* - Simon Towneley Esq JP, HM Lord-Lieut for Lancs; Dyneley, Burnley, Lancs (☎ 23322)

TOWNEND, Hon Mrs (Katherine Patricia); *née* Smith; da of 3 Viscount Hambleden and Lady Patricia Herbert, da of 15 Earl of Pembroke; *b* 1933; *m* 1961, Ivan Moffat; 2 s; m 2, 1973, Peter Robert Gascoigne Townend; *Style* - The Hon Mrs Townend; Seend Manor, Seend, Melksham, Wilts

TOWNSEND, Lady Juliet Margaret; *née* Smith; MVO (1981); da of 2 Earl of Birkenhead TD (d 1975); *b* 9 Sept 1941; *Educ* Westonbirt, Somerville Coll Oxford; *m* 1970, John Richard Townsend, s of Lt-Col Clarence Henry Southgate Townsend, OBE, MC, TD, MRCVS (d 1953); 3 da; *Career* Lady-in-Waiting to HRH The Princess Margaret, Countess of Snowdon 1965-71, Extra Lady-in-Waiting 1971-; *Style* - Lady Juliet Townsend MVO; Newbottle Manor, Banbury, Oxon (☎ Banbury 811295)

TOWNSEND, Sir (Sydney) Lance; s of Edward Henry Townsend (d 1952); *b* 17 Dec 1912; *Educ* Melbourne & Bairnsdale H S, Melbourne U,; *m* 1943, Jean Campbell, nee Smyth; 1 s, 3 da (1 s decd); *Career* kt 1971; Prof Obstetrics & Gynaecology Melbourne U 1951-77, ret; Dean Faculty of Medicine 1971-77, memb Mgmt Bd Austin Hosp 1966 (pres 1979), memb Cancer Inst Bd of Mgmt, chm Consult Cncl of Maternal & Perinatal Mortality 1951-, chm Health Advsy Cncl Victoria 1979-, fndr chm Victoria Cytology Serv; *Recreations* sailing, golf, philately; *Clubs* Melbourne, Naval & Mil, Roy Melbourne Golf; *Style* - Sir Lance Townsend; 28 Ryeburne ave, Hawthorn E, Victoria 3123 Australia (☎ 823434)

TOWNSHEND, 7 Marquess (GB 1787); Sir George John Patrick Dominic Townshend; 12 Bt (E 1617); Baron Townshend of Lynn Regis (E 1661), Viscount Townshend of Raynham (E 1682); s of 6 Marquess Townshend (d 1921, whose great uncle, Charles Fox Townshend, founded the Eton Society ('Pop') 1811; the present Lord Townshend's ggggggf, the 2 Viscount, was the celebrated agriculturist 'Turnip' Townshend & a political colleague of Sir Robert Walpole (who is supposed to have said "as long as the firm...was Townshend and Walpole, the utmost harmony prevailed; but it no sooner became Walpole and Townshend, than things went wrong"); Lord Hervey remarked of

Townshend: "he was much more tenacious of his opinion than his word; for the one he never gave up, and the other he seldom kept"; his 2 w's ghost was said to haunt the family seat of Raynham as well as Houghton Hall (now Lord Cholmondeley's property) while his daughter-in-law's reputation for loose morals supposedly was reflected in her portrayal as Lady Bellaston in Fielding's *Tom Jones*); *b* 13 May 1916; *Educ* Harrow; *m* 1, 1939 (m dis 1960, she m 1960, Brig Sir James Gault, KCMG, MVO, OBE), Elizabeth Pamela Audrey, da of Maj Thomas Luby, late Judicial Cmmr ICS; 1 s, 2 da; m 2, 1960, Ann Frances, da of late Arthur Pellew Darlow; 1 s, 1 da; *Heir* s, Viscount Raynham; *Career* Scots Gds 1940-45, chm Anglia Television Gp Ltd 1976-, Anglia Television Ltd 1958-, Survival Anglia Ltd 1971-, Anchor Enterprises Ltd 1967-, AP Bank Ltd 1975-, Raynham Farm Co Ltd 1957-, Norfolk Agricultural Station 1974-, Vice-Chm Norwich Union Life Insurance Soc Ltd 1973-, Norwich Union Fire Insurance Soc Ltd 1975-, DL Norfolk 1951-61; *Clubs* White's, Pratt's, MCC, Norfolk (Norwich), Royal Yacht Squadron, House of Lords Yacht; *Style* - The Most Hon The Marquess Townshend; Raynham Hall, Fakenham, Norfolk (☎ Fakenham 2133)

TOWNSHEND, Lady Carolyn Elizabeth Ann; da of 7 Marquess Townshend; *b* 1940; *m* 1962 (m dis 1971), Antonio Capellini; 1 s; has resumed the surname of Townshend; *Style* - Lady Carolyn Townshend

TOWNSHEND, Lord John Patrick; s of 7 Marquess Townshend; *b* 1962; *Style* - Lord John Townshend

TOWNSHEND, Lady Katherine Ann; da of 7 Marquess Townshend; *b* 1963; *Style* - Lady Katherine Townshend

TOWNSHEND, Hon Thomas Charles; s of Viscount Raynham; *b* 2 Nov 1977; *Style* - The Hon Thomas Townshend

TOWNSON, John Rothwell; s of Ernest Townson (d 1956); *b* 17 Aug 1913; *Educ* Rivington G S; *m* 1947, June Beryl, nee Phillips; 4 s, 2 da; *Career* chm Townson Gp of Companies 1946-79 (ret as ch exec); dir Nationwide Building Soc, govr Millfield Sch; *Recreations* sailing, fishing; *Clubs* East India & Sports, Roy Cork Yacht; *Style* - John Townson Esq; Orchard House, Victoria rd, Heaton, Bolton (☎ 0204 43649); 5 Strathearn House, 2 Strathearn Place, W2 (☎ 01 262 9022)

TOYNBEE, Michael Robert; JP; s of Ralph Victor Toynbee (d 1970); *b* 26 Nov 1925; *Educ* Winchester; *m* 1953, Yvonne Norah, nee Cleland; 2 children; *Career* Capt Rifle Bde 1945-48, War Office 1949-52; dir Jessel Toynbee & Co 1953-77, chm 1977-; *Recreations* shooting, fishing, tennis; *Style* - Michael Toynbee Esq JP; Westerleigh, Wadhurst, E Sussex (☎ 3238)

TRAHERNE, Sir Cennydd George; KG (1970), TD (1950); s of late Cdr Llewellyn Edmund Traherne RN; *b* 14 Dec 1910; *Educ* Wellington, BNC Oxford; *m* 1934, Olivera OBE, da of James Binney, of Pampisford Hall, Cambs, & sis of Hector Binney, *qv*; *Career* kt 1964; Ld-Lt Glam 1952, Mid West & S Glam 1974-; Hon Col Signal Regt 1953-75; dir Cardiff Bldg Soc, Commercial Bank of Wales Ltd, Nat Coastal Rescue Trg Centre; memb Gorsedd Bards of Wales; *Recreations* fishing, walking; *Clubs* Athenaeum, Cardiff & County; *Style* - Sir Cennydd Traherne KG TD, HM Lord-Lieut for Mid, West and South Glamorgan; Coedarhydyglyn, nr Cardiff (☎ 0446 760321)

TRANMIRE, Baron (Life Peer UK 1974); Robin (Robert) Hugh Turton; KBE (1971), MC (1942), PC (1955); s of late Maj Robert Bell Turton, of Kildale Hall, York; *b* 8 Aug 1903; *Educ* Eton, Balliol Oxford; *m* 1928, Ruby Christian, da of late Robert Thomas Scott, of Beechmont, Sevenoaks, Kent; 3 s, 1 da; *Career* Lt-Col Green Howards 1939-45 War, barr Inner Temple 1926, MP (C) Thirsk and Malton 1929-74, Parly Sec Miny of Nat Insurance 1951-53, Min of Pensions and Nat Insurance 1953-54, Jt Parly Under-Sec of State for Foreign Affairs 1954-55, Min of Health 1955-57; JP 1936, DL 1962 N Riding Co York; *Style* - The Rt Hon the Lord Tranmire, KBE,

MC, PC, JP, DL; Upsall Castle, Thirsk, N Yorks YO7 2QJ (☎ Upsall 202); 15 Grey Coat gdns, SW1P 2QA (☎ 01 834 1525)

TRAVERS, Lt-Gen Sir Paul Anthony; KCB (1981); s of Michael Travers; *b* 5 Aug 1927; *Educ* Clapham Coll; *m* 1956, Therese Sara Keeley; 1 s, 2 da; *Career* formerly Roy Corps of Transport, Gen Offr Commanding South East District 1981-; *Style* - Lt-Gen Sir Paul Travers KCB; Wellesley House, Aldershot, Hants

TRAVIS, Hon Mrs (Rosemary Gail); *née* Pritchard; da of Baron Pritchard (Life Peer); *b* 1946; *m* 1967, Ernest Raymond Anthony Travis; *Style* - The Hon Mrs Travis

TREACHER, Adm Sir John Devereux; KCB (1975); s of Frank Treacher; *b* 23 Sept 1924, Chile; *Educ* St Paul's; *m* 1, 1953 (m dis 1968), Patcie, da of Dr F McGrath, of Evanston Illinois; 1 s, 1 da; m 2, 1969, Kirsteen, da of D Landale; 1 s, 1 da; *Career* with RN to 1977 (CIC Fleet & Allied CIC Channel & E Atlantic 1975-77); non-press memb Press Cncl 1978-, ch exec & dir Nat Car Parks 1977-81, chm & md Playboy UK Ltd Aug 1981- (salary as of July 1981 c £100,000 pa); dir Westland Aircraft 1978-; *Style* - Adm Sir John Treacher KCB; 19 College Gardens, Dulwich Village, SE21 (☎ 01 693 8603)

TREASURE, James Sadler; s of Frederick Treasure (d 1959); *b* 13 Aug 1921; *Educ* Preston G S, Preston Tech Coll; *m* 1944, Margaret, nee Grundy; 1 s, 2 da; *Career* Capt REME, dir Sadler (Lytham) Ltd (General Engineers) 1975-; *Recreations* cricket, gardening, history; *Style* - James Treasure Esq; 387 Garstang rd, Fulwood, Preston, Lancs

TREASURE, Col Kenneth David; CB (1972), CBE (1965), TD, DL (Monmouthshire 1957); s of the late D J Treasure; *b* 20 Sept 1913; *Educ* Cranbrook, Univ of Wales; *m* 1941, Jean, nee Mitchell; 1 s, 1 da; *Career* served 1939-45 War, Lt Col Monmouthshire Regt (TA) India and Burma, Legal Adviser CCG 1946-49, chm Monmouthshire T & AFA 1960-68, Wales & Monmouthshire TA & VR Assoc 1968-71, memb Cncl TA & VR Assocs and TA Advisory Ctee, MOD; *Recreations* judging show jumping, motoring, work; *Clubs* Army & Navy; *Style* - Col Kenneth Treasure, CB, CBE, TD, DL; The Court, Lower Machen, Newport, Gwent (☎ Machen 258)

TREE, Lady Anne Evelyn Beatrice; *née* Cavendish; da of late 10 Duke of Devonshire, KBE, MBE, TD; *b* 1927; *m* 1949, Michael Lambert Tree; *Style* - Lady Anne Tree; Flat E, 75 Eaton sq, SW1

TREE, Arthur Jeremy; s of Arthur Ronald (d 1976), & bro of Michael Tree, *qv*; *b* 21 Dec 1925; *Educ* Eton; *Career* 2 Lt 1 Household Cavalry 1945-47, owner and trainer of racehorses; *Clubs* Turf; *Style* - Arthur Tree Esq; Beckhampton House, Marlborough, Wilts (☎ Avebury 244 204)

TREE, Michael Lambert; s of (Arthur) Ronald Lambert Field Tree, sometime Jt Master of the Pytchley, Tstee of the Wallace Collection & MP for Harborough (d 1976, whose mother was Ethel, da of Marshall Field, of the Chicago Dept Store family; Ethel's 2 husb was 1 Earl Beatty), of New York, by his 1 w, Nancy, widow of Henry Field (of the same family as Ronald's mother's) and da of Moncure Perkins, of Richmond, Virginia; *b* 5 Dec 1921; *Educ* Eton; *m* 1949, Lady Anne Cavendish, da of 10 Duke of Devonshire; 2 adopted da (Isabelle Elizabeth Nancy b 1964, Esther Anne Mary b 1966); *Career* Capt Household Cavalry, served M East, Italy, Germany WW II; with The Chicago Sun 1947-48, Hambro's Bank 1951-53, Christie's 1966 (dir 1967); *Recreations* shooting, golf; *Clubs* White's, Buck's; *Style* - Michael Tree Esq; 75 Eaton sq, SW1 (☎ 01 235 1320)

TREFGARNE, 2 Baron (UK 1947); David Garro Trefgarne; s of 1 Baron Trefgarne (d 1960); *b* 31 March 1941; *Educ* Haileybury, Princeton U USA; *m* 1968, Rosalie, da of Peter Lane, of Holywell, Hook Heath, Woking; 2 s, 1 da; *Heir* s, Hon George Garro Trefgarne; *Career* awarded Roy Aero Club Bronze Medal for flight UK to Australia and back in light aircraft 1963; Opposition Whip House of Lords 1977-79, a Lord in Waiting (Government Whip) 1979-81,

Under-Sec Dept of Trade 1981-; *Clubs* East India, Devonshire, Sports and Public Schools; *Style* - The Rt Hon the Lord Trefgarne; House of Lords, SW1

TREFGARNE, Hon George Garro; s and h of 2 Baron Trefgarne; *b* 4 Jan 1970; *Style* - The Hon George Trefgarne

TREFGARNE, Hon Gwion George Garro; s of 1 Baron Trefgarne (d 1960); *b* 1953; *Style* - The Hon Gwion Trefgarne

TREFGARNE, Hon Justin Peter Garro; s of 2 Baron Trefgarne; *b* 1973; *Style* - The Hon Justin Trefgarne

TREFGARNE, Hon Mary Elizabeth; da of 1 Baron Trefgarne (d 1960); *b* 1946; *Style* - The Hon Mary Trefgarne

TREFGARNE, Hon Rebecca Rosalie; da of 2 Baron Trefgarne; *b* 1976; *Style* - The Hon Rebecca Trefgarne

TREFGARNE, Hon Trevor Garro; s of 1 Baron Trefgarne (d 1960); *b* 1944; *Educ* Cheltenham; *m* 1, 1967, Diana Elizabeth, da of late Michael Gibb, of Forge House, Taynton, Oxon; 2 s, 1 da; m 2, 1979, Caroline France, da of Michael Gosschalk, of Monte Carlo; *Career* Cranfield Sch of Management 1968-69, dep chm Nesco Investments Ltd; *Style* - The Hon Trevor Trefgarne; 51 Av Hector Otto, Monaco

TREHERNE, Lady Sheelah Annette; *née* Browne; da (twin) of late Lt-Col Lord Alfred Eden Browne DSO, s of 5 Marquess of Sligo; sis of 10 Marquess; raised to the rank of a Marquess's da 1953; *b* 1908; *m* 1930, John Dalrymple Winn Treherne (d 1972); 1 s, 1 da; *Style* - Lady Sheelah Treherne; 7 Shelley ct, Tite st, SW3

TRENCH, Cosby Patrick Musgrave; s of late Capt Charles Sadleir Musgrave Trench and hp of kinsman, 6 Baron Ashtown; *b* 14 Jan 1915; *Educ* Eton, Trin Coll Dublin; *m* 1956, Julia Violetta May, da of late Frank Porch, and widow of Frank Whiting; *Style* - Cosby Trench Esq; Sopwell Hall, Cloughjordan, co Tipperary

TRENCHARD, 2 Viscount (UK 1936); Sir Thomas Trenchard; 2 Bt (UK 1919), MC (1944); also Baron Trenchard (UK 1930); s of Marshal of the RAF 1 Viscount (Sir Hugh) Trenchard, GCB, OM, GCVO, DSO, GOC Mil Wing RFC WW I (d 1956); *b* 15 Dec 1953; *Educ* Eton; *m* 1948, Patricia, da of late Adm Sir Sidney Bailey, KBE, CB, DSO; 3 s; *Heir* s, Hon Hugh Trenchard; *Career* Capt King's Roy Rifle Corps 1939-45; dir: T Wall & Sons Ltd 1953-66, Unilever Ltd and Unilever NV 1967-77, Carpets Internat Ltd 1977-79; chm Wall's Meat Co Ltd 1960-66, chm Sausage and Meat Pie Mfrs Assoc 1959-73, pres Roy Inst Public Health & Hygiene 1970-79, Inst Grocery Distribution 1974-77, Bacon & Meat Mfrs Assoc 1974-79; Min of State Dept Industry 1979-81, Min of State MOD for RN 1981 for a few weeks, then Min of State MOD Defence Procurement May 1981-; *Clubs* Brooks's; *Style* - The Rt Hon The Viscount Trenchard MC; House of Lords, SW1

TRENCHARD, Hon Hugh; s and h of 2 Viscount Trenchard MC; *b* 12 March 1951; *Educ* Eton, Trin Cambridge; *m* 1975, Fiona Elizabeth, da of Hon James Ian Morrison TD, s of 1 Baron Margadale; 1 s, 1 da; *Career* Capt 4 RGJ TAVR; *Style* - The Hon Hugh Trenchard; 43 Radipole rd, SW6 5DN (☎ 01 731 0777)

TRENCHARD, Hon John; s of 2 Viscount Trenchard MC; *b* 1953; *Style* - The Hon John Trenchard

TRENCHARD, Hon Thomas Henry; s of 2 Viscount Trenchard MC; *b* 1966; *Style* - The Hon Thomas Trenchard

TREND, Baron (Life Peer UK 1974); Burke St John Trend; GCB (1968, KCB 1962, CB 1955), CVO (1953), PC (1972); s of late Walter St John Trend; *b* 2 Jan 1914; *Educ* Whitgift, Merton Coll Oxford (Hon Fell); *m* 1949, Patricia Charlotte, da of late Rev Gilbert Shaw; 2 s, 1 da; *Career* Principal Priv Sec to Chllr of Exchequer 1945-49, Under Sec HM Treasury 1949-55, Office of the Lord Privy Seal 1955-56, Dep Sec of the Cabinet 1956-59, Third Sec HM Treasury 1959-60, Second Sec 1960-62, Sec of the Cabinet 1963-73, Chm Trustees British Museum 1979-, Chm

Managing Tstees Nuffield Fndn 1980-, Rector Lincoln Coll Oxford 1973-, Pro-Vice-Chllr Oxford U 1975-; Hon DCL Oxford, Hon LLD St Andrews; *Clubs* Athenaeum; *Style* - The Rt Hon the Lord Trend GCB CVO PC; Lincoln College, Oxford

TREND, Hon Michael St John; s of Baron Trend (Life Peer); *b* 1952; *Style* - The Hon Michael Trend

TREND, Hon Patrick St John; s of Baron Trend (Life Peer); *b* 1955; *Style* - The Hon Patrick Trend

TRENERRY, Hon Mrs; Hon Jennifer; *née* Hill; da of Baron Hill of Luton PC (Life Peer); *b* 1933; *m* 1, 1960 (m dis), Robert Duncan Barnaby Leicester MB; m 2, 1974, Thomas Trenerry; *Style* - The Hon Mrs Trenerry; 33 Day rd, Cheltenham, New South Wales, Australia

TREUHAFT, Hon Mrs (Jessica Lucy); *née* Freeman-Mitford; da of 2 Baron Redesdale, JP, and sis of Nancy Mitford, Hon Lady Mosley, Unity Mitford, and (Debo) Duchess of Devonshire; *b* 11 Sept 1917; *m* 1, 1937, her 2 cous (through common descent from 5 Earl of Airlie, KT) Esmond Romilly, RCAF (ka 1941), bro of Giles Romilly the journalist, critic and novelist, also yr s of Col Bertram Romilly, DSO (the Col's m being Lady Arabella Carnegie, da of 9 Earl of Southesk, KT, and his paternal ggf Sir Samuel Romilly, "the Law's expounder, and the State's corrector, whose suicide was almost an Anomaly", but news of which nevertheless afforded Lord Byron much satisfaction), and Nellie Ogilvy (yr da of Col Sir Henry Hozier, KCB, and sis of Baroness Spencer-Churchill), through whom Esmond was 1 cous of Randolph Churchill; 1 da (and 1 da decd); m 2, 1943, Robert Treuhaft, of New York; 1 s; *Career* authoress (notably of *The American Way of Death*); *Style* - The Hon Mrs Treuhaft; 6411 Regent st, Oakland, Calif, USA

TREVELYAN, Baron (Life Peer UK 1968); Humphrey Trevelyan; KG (1974), GCMG (1965, KCMG 1955, CMG 1951), CIE (1947), OBE (1941); 2 s of late Rev George Philip Trevelyan (s of Rev William Trevelyan and Maria, da of Hon Philip Pleydell-Bouverie, 5 s of 2 Earl of Radnor; William was gs of Sir John Trevelyan, 4 Bt, and yr bro of Sir Charles Trevelyan, cr also a Bt); Lord Trevelyan is (1) yr bro of John Trevelyan, the Sec of the Br Bd of Film Censors (2) 2 cous of the historian G M Trevelyan (3) er bro of the w of Rt Rev Harry Carpenter, the former Bp of Oxford (4) 2 cous of Julia Trevelyan Oman, the theatre and film designer and wife of Dr Roy Strong (5) 3 cous twice removed of present Lord Radnor; *b* 27 Nov 1905; *Educ* Lancing, Jesus Cambridge (Hon Fell 1968); *m* 1937, Peggie (Violet Margaret), da of late Gen Sir William H Bartholomew, GCB, CMG, DSO; 2 da; *Career* ICS 1929, Foreign Serv 1947, Counsellor in Baghdad 1948, Econ and Fin Adviser UK High Cmmn for Germany 1951-53, HM Chargé d'Affaires in Peking 1953-55, Ambass to Egypt 1955-56, Under-Sec at UN 1958, Ambass to Iraq 1958-61, Dep Under-Sec of State FO 1962, Ambass to USSR 1962-65, ret; High Cmmr in S Arabia 1967; dir: British Petroleum Co Ltd 1965-75, British Bank of the Middle East 1965-77, Gen Electric Co Ltd 1967-76, pres Council of Foreign Bondholders; Hon LLD Cambridge, Hon DCL Durham, Hon DLitt Leeds; *Recreations* reading, writing, formerly mountain travel; *Clubs* Beefsteak; *Style* - The Rt Hon the Lord Trevelyan, KG, GCMG, CIE, OBE; c/o Nat West Bank, 1 Grosvenor gdns, SW1; (temporary) 13 Wilton st, SW1 (☎ 01 235 4503)

TREVELYAN, Hon Catherine Mary; OBE (1977); da of Baron Trevelyan (Life Peer); *b* 1943; *Style* - The Hon Mrs Trevelyan OBE

TREVELYAN, Edward Norman; s and h of Sir Norman Trevelyan, 10 Bt; *b* 14 Aug 1955; *Style* - Edward Trevelyan Esq

TREVELYAN, Sir George Lowthian; 4 Bt (UK 1874), of Wallington, Northumberland; s of Rt Hon Sir Charles Philips Trevelyan (d 1958); *b* 5 Nov 1906; *Educ* Sidcot Sch, Trin Cambridge; *m* 1940, Editha Helen, da of Col John Lindsay-Smith CBE; 1 da (adopted); *Heir* bro, Geoffrey Washington Trevelyan; *Career* taught at Gordonstoun Sch and Abinger

Hill Sch 1936-41; served War 1941-45, Home Guard Training (Capt), taught no 1 Army Coll Newbattle Abbey 1945-47; Warden Shropshire Adult Coll Attingham Park Shrewsbury 1947-71, founder and dir Wrekin Trust 1971-; *Style* - Sir George Trevelyan, Bt; The Grove, Taynton, Glos GL19 3AN (☎ Tibberton 559)

TREVELYAN, Geoffrey Washington; s and h of Sir George Trevelyan, 4 Bt; *b* 4 July 1920; *m* 1947, Gillian Isabel, da of late Alexander Wood; 1 s, 1 da; *Style* - Geoffrey Trevelyan Esq; Silkstead, 3 Abbey Mill End, St Albans, Herts

TREVELYAN, Sir Norman Irving; 10 Bt (E 1662), of Nettlecombe, Somerset; s of Edward Trevelyan (gggs of Sir John Trevelyan, 4 Bt); suc 3 cous, Sir Willoughby Trevelyan, 9 Bt, 1976; *b* 29 Jan 1915; *m* 1951, Jennifer Mary, da of Arthur E Riddett, of Long Orchards, Copt Hill Lane, Burgh Heath, Surrey; 2 s, 1 da; *Heir* s, Edward Norman Trevelyan; *Style* - Sir Norman Trevelyan, Bt; 1041 Adella av, Coronada, Calif 92118, USA

TREVOR, 4 Baron (UK 1880); Charles Edwin Hill-Trevor; JP (Clwyd 1959); s of 3 Baron Trevor (d 1950, himself gs of 3 Marquess of Downshire); *b* 13 Aug 1928; *Educ* Shrewsbury; *m* 1967, Susan Janet Elizabeth, da of Ronald Ivor Bence, DSC, VRD, BM, of Birmingham; 2 s; *Heir* s, Hon Marke Charles Hill-Trevor; *Career* is patron of two livings; CStJ; *Clubs* Flyfishers'; *Style* - The Rt Hon the Lord Trevor JP; Brynkinalt, Chirk, Wrexham, Clwyd (☎ Chirk 3425); Auch, Bridge of Orchy, Argyllshire (☎ Tyndrum 282)

TREVOR, Phyllis, Baroness; Phyllis; da of J A Sims, of Ings House, Kirton-in-Lindsey, Lincs; *m* 1927, 3 Baron Trevor (d 1950); *Career* OStJ; *Style* - The Rt Hon Phyllis, Lady Trevor; The Holt, Chirk, Wrexham

TRIER, Peter Eugene; CBE (1980); s of Ernst Joseph Trier (d 1938); *b* 12 Sept 1919; *Educ* Mill Hill Sch, Trin Hall Cambridge; *m* 1946, Margaret Nora, nee Holloway; 3 s; *Career* RN Scientific Serv 1941-50, dir Philips Electronics 1969-, chm Defence Scientific Adv Cncl 1981-, Pro-Chancellor Brunel U 1980-, pres elect Institute Mathematics 1981; *Recreations* travel, sailing, railway history; *Clubs* Athenaeum; *Style* - Peter Trier Esq CBE; Yew Tree House, Bredon, Tewkesbury, Glos (☎ Bredon 72200)

TRIMLESTOWN, 19 Baron (I 1461); Charles Aloysius Barnewall; s of 18 Baron Trimlestown (d 1937); *b* 2 June 1899; *Educ* Ampleforth; *m* 1, 1926, Muriel (d 1937), da of Edward Oskar Schneider, of Mansfield Lodge, Whalley Range, Manchester; 2 s, 1 da; m 2, 1952, Freda Kathleen Watkins, da of late Alfred Watkins, of Ross-on-Wye; *Heir* s, Hon Anthony Edward Barnewall; *Career* formerly Lt Irish Gds; *Style* - The Rt Hon the Lord Trimlestown; Tigley, Dartington, Totnes, Devon

TRIPONEL, Hon Mrs - Hon Angela Caroline; da of Baron Harris of High Cross (Life Peer); *m* 1977, Roland Triponel, of Lyon, France; *Style* - The Hon Mrs Triponel; c/o The Rt Hon The Lord Harris of High Cross, 4 Walmar Close, Beech Hill, Hadley Wood, Barnet, Herts (☎ 01 449 6212)

TRITTON, Major Sir Anthony John Ernest; 4 Bt (UK 1905); s of Maj Sir Geoffrey Ernest Tritton, 3 Bt, CBE (d 1976); *b* 4 March 1927; *Educ* Eton; *m* 1957, Diana, da of Rear-Adm St John Aldrich Micklethwait, CB, DSO; 1 s, 1 da; *Heir* s, Jeremy Ernest Tritton; *Career* farmer; Maj (ret) The Queen's Own Hussars; *Recreations* shooting, fishing; *Clubs* Cavalry and Guards; *Style* - Major Sir Anthony Tritton, Bt; Stanton House, Highworth, Wilts (☎ Highworth 762923)

TRITTON, Hon Mrs (Georgina Anne); *née* Ward; da of 1 Viscount Ward of Witley PC; *b* 12 March 1941; *m* 1, 1966 (m dis 1971), Alastair Forbes, the writer and journalist, s of late James Forbes, of Boston; m 2, Patrick Tritton, *qv*; *Career* reverted to maiden name by deed poll 1971; actress; *Style* - The Hon Mrs Tritton; Quintana 23, Gustavo Madero, La Villa, Mexico City, Mexico

TRITTON, Jeremy Ernest; s and h of Sir Anthony Tritton, 4 Bt; *b* 6 Oct 1961;

Style - Jeremy Tritton Esq

TRITTON, Patrick; 2 s of Patrick Arthur Tritton (gn of Sir Charles Tritton, 1 Bt) by his 1 w, Judith; *b* 18 May 1934; *Educ* Eton, Cambridge; *m* 1, 1962 (m dis), as her 2 husb, Nancy, da of Sir Harry Oakes, 1 Bt (*see* von Hoyningen-Huene, Baroness Nancy); m 2, Hon Georgina Ward, da of 1 Viscount Ward of Witley & former w of Alastair Forbes; *Style* - Patrick Tritton Esq

TRITTON, Hon Mrs (Sally Louise); *née* Nelson; da of 2 Baron Nelson of Stafford; *b* 1955; *m* 1975, Peter Robert Jolliffe Tritton; *Style* - The Hon Mrs Tritton; 132 Clarence Gate gdns, Glentworth st, NW1

TROLLOPE, Sir Anthony Owen Clavering; 16 Bt (E 1642); s of Sir Gordon Clavering Trollope, 15 Bt (d 1958, himself gs of Anthony Trollope, the Victorian writer, best known for the Barchester cycle of novels, also a noted Post Office official); *b* 15 Jan 1917; *m* 1942, Joan Mary Alexis, da of Alexis Gibbs, of Manly, NSW; 2 s; *Heir* s, Anthony Trollope; *Career* served War of 1939-45 2/5 Australian Field Regt, Roy Australian Artillery, Middle East and New Guinea; JP NSW; *Style* - Sir Anthony Trollope, Bt, JP; Clavering, 77 Roseville av, Roseville, NSW 2069, Australia

TROLLOPE, Anthony Simon; s and h of Sir Anthony Trollope, 16 Bt; *b* 1945; *Style* - Anthony Trollope Esq

TROLLOPE, Mary, Lady; Mary Isabel; da of Owen Blacket, of Lindfield, NSW; *m* 1913, Sir Gordon Clavering Trollope, 15 Bt (d 1958); *Style* - Mary, Lady Trollope

TROTTER, Neville Guthrie; JP (Newcastle upon Tyne 1973), MP (C) Tynemouth 1974-; s of Capt Alexander Trotter (d 1940); *b* 27 Jan 1932; *Educ* Shrewsbury Sch, Durham U; *Career* RAF 1955-58; chartered accountant, ptnr Thornton Baker & Co 1962-74 (now consultant), chm Cons Parly Shipping and Shipbldg Cttee 1976-, memb Newcastle City Cncl 1963-74; *Recreations* study of foreign affairs, defence, industry and aviation; *Clubs* Carlton, RAF, Whitley Bay, Tynemouth Conservative; *Style* - Neville Trotter JP MP; Granville House, 12 Granville rd, Newcastle upon Tyne (☎ Newcastle 812916)

TROUBRIDGE, Lady; Lilly; da of Herman Kleinwort, of Belgravia and Wierton Place, Maidstone; *m* 1925, Vice-Adm Sir Thomas Troubridge, KCB, DSO (d 1949); *Style* - Lady Troubridge; Oakshott, Hawkley, Liss, Hants

TROUBRIDGE, Sir Peter; 6 Bt (GB 1799); s of Vice-Adm Sir Thomas Hope Troubridge, KCB, DSO (s of Adm Sir Ernest Charles Thomas Troubridge, KCMG, CB, MVO, 3 s of 3 Bt, by his 1 w, his 2 w being Una, long the doxy of Radclyffe Hall), and Lily, niece of Sir Alexander Kleinwort, 1 Bt; suc kinsman, Lt-Col Sir Thomas St Vincent Wallace, 5 Bt, MBE, 1963; *b* 6 June 1927; *Educ* Eton, Emmanuel Cambridge; *m* 1954, Hon Venetia Daphne Weeks, da of 1 Baron Weeks, KCB, DSO (d 1960); 1 s, 2 da; *Heir* s, Thomas Richard Troubridge; *Career* served Korean War 1952-53, HMS Ocean, ret from RN (Lt-Cdr) 1967; memb Stock Exchange 1970-, partner Hedderwick, Stirling, Grumbar & Co 1974-, vice-chm Standing Council of the Baronetage 1979-81, chm 1981-; OStJ 1973; *Recreations* shooting, gardening, bird watching; *Clubs* White's, City of London, MCC; *Style* - Sir Peter Troubridge, Bt; The Manor House, Elsted, Midhurst, West Sussex (☎ Harting 286)

TROUBRIDGE, Pamela, Lady; Pamela; da of late Percy Clough, of The Knowle, Keighley, Yorks; *m* 1939, Lt-Col Sir Thomas St Vincent Wallace Troubridge, MBE, 5 Bt (d 1963); *Style* - Pamela, Lady Troubridge; Ivy Cottage, Longstock, Stockbridge, Hants

TROUBRIDGE, Thomas; s of Vice-Adm Sir Thomas Troubridge, KCB, DSO, RN (d 1949, gs of Sir Thomas Troubridge, 3 Bt), and Lily, 6 and twin da of Herman Kleinwort and niece of Sir Alexander Kleinwort, 1 Bt; *b* 26 Dec 1939; *Educ* Eton; *m* 1, 1971 (m dis 1977, annulment in Roman Catholic Church 1978), Baroness Marie Christine, da of Baron Günther von Reibnitz (of a noble, though until relatively recently untitled, Junker family, a member of which was cr Baron by King Frederick William III of Prussia some time before 1829; the 1 Baron was gggf of Princess Michael) & now Princess Michael of Kent (*see* Royal Family); m 2, 1981, Mrs Petronella Forgan; *Career* pres & dir Kleinwort Benson Inc New York; dir Sharps Pixley Inc New York; *Recreations* shooting; *Clubs* White's, Turf, The Brook (New York); *Style* - Thomas Troubridge Esq; 45 E 62nd st, New York City, NY 10021, USA (☎ 759 6098); 1b Gertrude st, SW10 (☎ 01 352 6049)

TROUBRIDGE, Thomas Richard; s and h of Sir Peter Troubridge, 6 Bt; *b* 23 Jan 1955; *Style* - Thomas Troubridge Esq

TROUBRIDGE, Hon Lady (Venetia Daphne); *née* Weeks; da of Lt-Gen 1 and last Baron Weeks, KCB, CBE, DSO, MC, TD; *b* 1933; *m* 1954, Lt-Cdr Sir Peter Troubridge, 6 Bt, RN (ret); 1 s, 2 da; *Style* - The Hon Lady Troubridge; The Manor House, Elsted, Sussex

TROWBRIDGE, Hon Mrs (Dorothy Frances Lucy St George); *née* Caulfield; da of 12 Viscount Charlemont; *b* 28 Sept 1915; *Educ* Queens Gate London, Brillantmont Lausanne; *m* 1945, Robert Hender Trowbridge, late Fl Lt RAAF; 2 s; *Clubs* Overseas (St James); *Style* - The Hon Mrs Trowbridge; White Lodge, Alresford, Essex (☎ 020622 5126)

TROWER, Hon Lady; Hon Joan Olivia; da of Baron Tomlin (Life Peer d 1935); *b* 1894; *m* 1920, Sir William Gosselin Trower (d 1963); *Career* JP Herts; *Style* - The Hon Lady Trower, JP; Stansteadbury, Ware, Herts

TRUMPINGTON, Baroness (Life Peeress UK 1980); Jean Alys Barker; da of late Arthur Edward Campbell-Harris, MC; *Educ* privately in England and France; *m* 1954, William Alan Barker; 1 s; *Career* Con Cllr Cambridge City Council Trumpington Ward 1963-73, Mayor of Cambridge 1971-72, Dep Mayor 1972-73, Conservative County Cllr Cambridgeshire Trumpington Ward 1973-75, Hon Cllr of the City of Cambridge 1975-, UK Delegate to UN Status of Women Commission 1979-; Hon Fell Lucy Cavendish Coll Cambridge 1980, JP Cambridge 1972-75, S Westminster 1976-; *Style* - The Rt Hon the Lady Trumpington JP; 5 Redington rd, NW3 7QX (☎ 01 435 2518); Luckboat House, King st, Sandwich, Kent (☎ Sandwich 613007)

TRUSCOTT, Sir George James Irving; 3 Bt (UK 1909); s of Sir Eric Homewood Stanham Truscott, 2 Bt (d 1973); *b* 24 Oct 1929; *Educ* Sherborne; *m* 1, 1954 (m annulled 1958), Irene Marion Craig Barr Brown; m 2, 1962, Yvonne Dora, da of late Frank Edward Nicholson, of Carshalton, Surrey; 1 s, 1 da; *Heir* s, Ralph Eric Nicholson Truscott; *Career* co director; *Style* - Sir George Truscott, Bt; BM Quill, WC1V 6XX

TRUSCOTT, Ralph Eric Nicholson; s and h of Sir George James Irving Truscott, 3 Bt; *b* 21 Feb 1966; *Style* - Ralph Truscott Esq

TRUSCOTT, Renée, Lady; Renée Franklin; da of John William Marshall, and formerly wife of William Archibald Redgrave; *m* 1953, as his 3 w, Sir Eric Homewood Stanham Truscott, 2 Bt (d 1973); *Style* - Renée, Lady Truscott; 3 Letchmore rd, Radlett, Herts

TRUSTRAM EVE, Hon Peter Nanton; OBE (Mil 1978); s of 1 Baron Silsoe, GBE, MC, TD, QC; *b* 2 May 1930; *Educ* Winchester; Ch Ch Oxford; *m* 1961, Petronilla Letiere Sheldon, da of Jannion Steele Elliott; 2 s; *Career* Def Attaché Brussels 1980-; late 2 Lt RWF, Cmdg Offr Oxford U OTC 1973-75; *Recreations* skiing, collecting antiques (particularly 16th & 17th Century maps); *Clubs* SKGB; *Style* - The Hon Peter Trustram Eve OBE; Flat 10, 4 Ennismore gdns, SW7; Avenue Franklin Roosevelt 148a, 1050 Brussels (☎ 02 647 13 71); Priory Court, Duns Tew, Oxon (☎ Steeple Aston 40262)

TRYON, 3 Baron (UK 1940); Anthony George Merrik Tryon; s of 2 Baron Tryon, GCVO, KCB, DSO, PC (d 1976), by his w Ethelreda (da of Sir Merrik Burrell, 7 Bt, CBE); *b* 26 May 1940; *Educ* Eton; *m* 1973, Dale Elizabeth, da of Barry

Harper, of Melbourne, Australia; 2 s, 2 da (of whom 1 s, 1 da are twins); *Heir* s, Hon Charles George Barrington Tryon; *Career* a Page of Honour to HM 1954-56, Capt R Wilts Yeo; dir Lazard Bros & Co 1976-, chm English & Scottish Investors Ltd 1977; *Recreations* fishing, shooting; *Clubs* Boodle's, Pratt's; *Style* - The Rt Hon the Lord Tryon; 30 Walton st, SW3 1RE (☎ 01 589 0967); Ogbury House, Great Durnford, Salisbury

TRYON, Hon Aylmer Douglas; s of 1 Baron Tryon (d 1940); *b* 1909; *Educ* Eton, Trin Cambridge (BA); *Career* formerly Capt Gren Gds; *Clubs* Boodle's; *Style* - The Hon Aylmer Tryon; 41 Dover st, W1

TRYON, Hon Charles George Barrington; s and h of 3 Baron Tryon; *b* 15 May 1976; *Style* - The Hon Charles Tryon

TRYON, Hon Edward Henry; s of 3 Baron Tryon; *b* 1979; *Style* - The Hon Edward Tryon

TRYON, Ethelreda, Baroness; Ethelreda Josephine; da of Sir Merrik Burrell, 7 Bt, CBE, JP, by his 2 w, Coralie (da of John Porter, DL, of Belle Isle, Co Fermanagh and Clonbalt, Co Longford); *b* 20 June 1909; *m* 1939, Brig 2 Baron Tryon, GCVO, KCB, DSO, PC (d 1976); 1 s, 1 da; *Style* - The Rt Hon Ethelreda, Lady Tryon; Church Farm, Great Durnford, Salisbury, Wilts (☎ Middle Woodford 281)

TRYON, Hon Victoria Clementine; da of 3 Baron Tryon; *b* 1979; *Style* - The Hon Victoria Tryon

TRYON, Lady Winifrid; da of 3 Earl of Lytton OBE by his w Baroness Wentworth; *b* 19 March 1904; *Educ* Convent of Our Lady of Good Counsel, Haywards Heath; *m* 1921, Claude Tryon MIME MICE (d 1949); *Style* - Lady Winifrid Tryon; 3 High st, Steyning, Sussex (☎ 812501)

TRYON, Hon Zoë Elizabeth; da of 3 Baron Tryon; *b* 1974; *Style* - The Hon Zoë Tryon

TUCK, Sir Bruce Adolph Reginald; 3 Bt (UK 1910); s of Major Sir (William) Reginald Tuck, 2 Bt (d 1954); *b* 29 June 1926; *Educ* Canford Sch; *m* 1, 1949 (m dis in Jamaica 1964), Luise, da of John C Renfro, of San Angelo, Texas, USA; 2 s; m 2, 1968, Pamela Dorothy Nicholson, da of Alfred Michael Nicholson, of London; 1 da; *Heir* s, Richard Bruce Tuck; *Career* Lt Scots Gds 1945-47; *Clubs* Lansdowne; *Style* - Sir Bruce Tuck, Bt; 95 Eaton sq, SW1; Montego Bay, PO Box 274, Jamaica

TUCK, Richard Bruce; s and h of Sir Bruce Tuck, 3 Bt; *b* 7 Oct 1952; *Style* - Richard Tuck Esq

TUCKER, George; CBE (1952); s of Albert Edward Tucker (d 1954); *b* 13 Nov 1893; *Educ* Strand Sch London, King's Coll London U; *m* 1919, Louisa Mary, nee Hine; 2 s, 2 da; *Career* civil servant, Inland Revenue 1912-38; Principal Air Miny 1938, Assist Sec 1942-53, financial adviser Allied Expeditionary Air Force 1944 and RAF Ferry Cmmd 1942-44; *Clubs* Civil Service; *Style* - George Tucker Esq CBE; 'Cranmer', Upton, Taunton, Somerset

TUCKER, Henry John Martin; QC (1975); s of Percival Albert Tucker LDS, RCS (d 1959); *b* 8 April 1930; *Educ* Downside Sch, Ch Ch Oxford; *m* 1957, Sheila Helen, nee Wateridge; 1 s, 4 da; *Career* barr 1954, dep chm Somerset QS 1971-, Recorder 1972-; *Recreations* walking the dogs; *Clubs* Hampshire (Winchester); *Style* - Henry Tucker Esq QC; Sleepers Hill, Winchester, Hants (☎ Winchester 3927)

TUCKWELL, Sir Edward George; KCVO (1975); s of Edward Henry Tuckwell, MBE, JP, DL (d 1943); *b* 12 May 1910; *Educ* Charterhouse, Magdalen Oxford; *m* 1, 1934, Phyllis Courthope, nee Regester (d 1970); 2 s, 1 da; m 2, 1971, Barbara, widow of Maj A Gordon & da of James Jameson, of Castle Bellingham, Co Louth; *Career* Lt-Col RAMC; surgeon St Bart's 1947-75, ret; Dean Medical Sch 1952-57, surgeon King Edward VII Hosp for Offrs 1961-75, surgeon Roy Masonic Hosp 1958-75, serjeant-surgeon to HM the Queen 1973-75 (surgeon 1968-73); *Recreations* gardening, shooting, travel; *Style* - Lt-Col Sir Edward Tuckwell,

KCVO; Berthorpe, Puttenham, Guildford, Surrey (☎ Guildford 810217)

TUDWAY QUILTER, David Cuthbert; *see* Quilter

TUFF, Col Charles Reginald; DL (Kent 1976); s of Sir Charles Tuff (d 1961); *b* 18 March 1909; *Educ* Malvern, Sandhurst; *m* 1940, Ruth, da of Maj A Hardy; 2 s, 1 da; *Career* 2 Lt The Buffs 1929, Capt instructor Sandhurst 1936, served WW II, Lt-Col 1943, Col 1945; chm Kent County Scout Assoc 1967-77; *Recreations* shooting, fishing; *Clubs* Farmers', Roy C'wlth Soc, MCC; *Style* - Col Charles Tuff DL; Hogs Green, Sandling, Hythe, Kent (☎ Hythe 67837)

TUFNELL, Hon Mrs (Georgina Mary); *née* Cavendish; da of 5 Baron Chesham; *b* 1944; *m* 1967, (Michael) Wynne Tufnell; 3 s; *Style* - The Hon Mrs Tufnell; Riverhill Farm, Binsted, Alton, Hants

TUFTON, Lt-Col George William Anthony; TD, DL (Herts 1962); s of Hon Charles Henry Tufton, CMG (d 1923, 3 s of 1 Baron Hothfield), by his w Stella, herself da of Sir George Faudel-Phillips, 1 Bt, GCIE; hp to 1 cous, 4 Baron Hothfield; *b* 28 Oct 1904; *Educ* Eton, Hertford Coll Oxford; *m* 1936, Evelyn Margarette, da of Eustace Mordaunt (bro of Sir Henry Mordaunt, 12 Bt); 2 s (Anthony, b 1939, m 1975 Lucinda Gurney, 1 s, 1 da; Nicholas b 1946, m 1978 Meriel Acworth, 1 s), 1 da (Mrs (Jennifer) Edward Raikes, 2 s, 1 da); *Career* underwriting memb Lloyd's; *Recreations* tennis, shooting; *Style* - Lt-Col George Tufton, TD, DL; The Red House, Barkway, Royston, Herts (☎ Barkway 266)

TUGHAN, Frederick Charles; CBE (1968); s of William Tughan (d 1912); *b* 24 Dec 1909; *Educ* Bangor G S, Queen's U Belfast; *m* 1935, Mildred, nee Patterson; 2 s, 3 da (1 decd); *Career* solicitor 1930; Mayor of Bangor 1956-60; chm Seed Potato Bd N Ireland 1961-68; dir: Lamont Life Assoc Co, Ulster Scot Friendly Soc, Bangor Provident Trust; *Recreations* golf; *Clubs* Roy Belfast, Ulster Reform, Carlton; *Style* - Frederick Tughan Esq CBE; Glenorie, Worcester ave, Bangor, Co Down (☎ Bangor 60489)

TUITE, Sir Christopher Hugh; 14 Bt (I 1622), of Sonnagh, Westmeath; s of Sir Dennis George Harmsworth Tuite, 13 Bt, MBE (d 1981, descended from the Sir Richard de Tuite or Tuitt, who was one of Strongbow (Richard de Clare, 2 Earl of Pembroke and Strigul)'s followers in his invasion of Ireland in 1172); *b* 3 Nov 1949; *Educ* Wellington Coll, Leeds U (BSc), PhD Bristol; *m* 1976, Deborah Ann, da of A E Martz, of Pittsburg USA; 1 s; *Heir* Thomas Livingstone Tuite, b 24 July 1977; *Style* - Sir Christopher Tuite, Bt; c/o The Wild Fowl Trust, Slimbridge, Glos

TUITE, Margaret, Lady; Margaret Essie; da of Col Walter Leslie Dundas, DSO, of Farnham; *m* 1947, Sir Dennis Tuite, 13 Bt, MBE (d 1981); 3 s; *Style* - Margaret, Lady Tuite; Windhaven, Ladygate Drive, Grayshott, Hindhead, Surrey GU26 6DR (☎ Hindhead 5026)

TULLOCH, Hon Mrs (Marion Hamilton); *née* Wills; da (by 1 m) of 2 Baron Dulverton, CBE, TD; *b* 1940; *m* 1964, John G A Tulloch; 2 s, 1 da; *Style* - The Hon Mrs Tulloch; Courance, Lockerbie, Dumfries-shire

TUNE, Laurence Kenneth; s of E T Tune; *b* 30 Sept 1939; *Educ* Holywell G S, Univ of Wales; *m* 1964, Ann Bridget, nee Jackson; 2 children; *Career* dir PA Management Consultants Ltd 1979-, fell Inst of Management Consultants 1978; *Recreations* literature, theatre, cinema; *Clubs* St James's (Manchester); *Style* - Laurence Tune Esq; 8 Dane Bank rd, Lymm, Ches (☎ 3154)

TUPPER, Sir Charles Hibbert; 5 Bt (UK 1888); s of Sir James Macdonald Tupper, 4 Bt (d 1967); *b* 4 July 1930; *m* 1959 (m dis 1975), Bernice Yvonne Quinn; 1 s; *Heir* s, Charles Hibbert Tupper; *Style* - Sir Charles Tupper, Bt; Suite 1101, 955 Marine Drive, W Vancouver, BC V7T 499, Canada

TUPPER, Charles Hibbert; s and h of Sir Charles Tupper, 5 Bt; *b* 10 July 1964; *Style* - Charles Tupper Esq

TURING, John Ferrier; s of late Julius Mathison Turing, and hp of kinsman, Sir John Turing, 11 Bt; *b* 1 Sept 1908; *m* 1, 1934 (m dis 1960), Joan, da of Robert Humphreys, ICS, of Cork; 3 da; m 2, 1960, Beryl Mary Ada, da of late Herbert Vaughan Hann; 1 s; *Career* slr 1931; Col World War II France, Middle East and India (Queen's Roy Regt); dep dir Claims Commission (India); *Style* - John Turing Esq; 158 Prince George av, Southgate, N14

TURING, Sir John Leslie; 11 Bt (NS 1638), MC; s of late Sir James Walter Turing, 9 Bt, and bro of Sir Robert Andrew Henry Turing, 10 Bt (d 1970); *b* 13 Sept 1895; *Educ* Wellington Coll; *m* 1975, Irene Nina, da of Trevor John Tatham, of Beaconsfield, Manor Way, Lee-on-the-Solent, Hants, and widow of Capt W W P Shirley-Rollison RN; *Heir* kinsman, John Ferrier Turing; *Career* late Lt Seaforth Highlanders 1914-18 War (wounded, MC); *Style* - Sir John Turing, Bt, MC; Green's Barn, 67 Mid Lavant, Chichester, Sussex

TURNBULL, Lawrence; CBE (1978), MC (1943), TD (1951), JP (1959), DL (1963); s of Lawrence Turnbull (d 1943); *b* 14 April 1914; *Educ* Roundhay Sch Leeds; *m* 1941, Betty, nee Adams; *Career* md Turnbulls (Removals) Ltd (Leeds) 1945-; member (C) Leeds City Council 1951-67, alderman 1967-73, hon alderman 1973, dep Lord Mayor of Leeds 1963-64, Lord Mayor of Leeds 1967-68; Col: served in TA 1939-, Cmd 269 Field Regt RA, Dep Cdr 1957-61, Cmdt W Riding ACF 1962-66; chm City of Leeds Con Assoc 1979-, pres Leeds Gp Roy British Legion 1959-; *Recreations* rugby union football; *Clubs* Army and Navy, Leeds; *Style* - Col Lawrence Turnbull, CBE, MC, TD, JP, DL; 3 Scarcroft Grange, Scarcroft, Leeds (☎ 892 330)

TURNBULL, Hon Mrs (Mary Elizabeth); da of late 6 Baron Congleton; *b* 1919; *m* 1956, Percy Turnbull (d 1976); *Style* - The Hon Mrs Turnbull; West Broomers, Broomers Hill, Pulborough, Sussex

TURNER, Hon Anna Elizabeth; da of 2 Baron Netherthorpe; *b* 17 Dec 1961; *Educ* Abbot's Hill Sch; *Style* - The Hon Anna Turner

TURNER, Hon Mrs (Anne Mary Cameron); *née* Corbett; da of 3 Baron Rowallan by his 1 w, Eleanor; *b* 3 Sept 1953; *m* 1972, Rodney Turner; 1 s, 1 da; *Style* - The Hon Mrs Turner; Drift House, Ashampstead, Berks

TURNER, Air Vice-Marshal Cameron Archer; CB (1968), CBE (1960, OBE 1947); s of James Oswald Turner (d 1961); *b* 29 Aug 1915; *Educ* New Plymouth Boys' Sch, Victoria U (NZ), Imperial Defence Coll London; *m* 1941, Josephine Mary, nee Richardson; 2 s; *Career* joined RAF 1936, transfd RNZAF 1938, ret 1969: served Europe 1939, Pacific 1940-45, Ch of Air Staff 1966-69; dir NZ Inventions Dvpt Authority 1969-76; *Recreations* golf, fishing, Polynesian studies; *Clubs* Wellington, Taranaki, United Service Officers'; *Style* - Air Vice-Marshal Cameron Turner CB CBE; 37A Parkvale rd, Wellington 5, New Zealand (☎ 766063); 3 Constance st, Fitzroy, New Plymouth, NZ (☎ 85811)

TURNER, Charles Brian Godsell; s of late Ernest Joseph Turner; *b* 26 Oct 1913; *Educ* Tottenham G S, Inst Chartered Accountants England and Wales; *m* 1941, Helen, nee Slowe; 2 s, 1 da; *Career* chartered accountant City of London 1950-74; chm: Bournemouth & District Water Co 1977, Mid Kent Water Co 1980; *Recreations* gardening, philately; *Clubs* Roy Overseas League; *Style* - Charles Turner Esq; Dellside, Tongswood drive, Hawkhurst, Kent (☎ Hawkhurst 3145)

TURNER, Brig Charles Edward Francis; CBE (1943, OBE 1941), DSO (1943); s of Lt Arthur Edward Turner (d 1907); *b* 23 April 1899; *Educ* Twyford, Wellington, RMA Woolwich, Christ's Coll Cambridge; *m* 1930, Mary Victoria, nee Swift; 1 s, 2 da; *Career* 2 Lt RE 1917-50 (ret), Brig 1944; National Cncl Social Serv 1950-58, sec Iona Appeal Trust 1958-61, appeals Organiser Rainer Fndn and Inst Rural Life at Home and Overseas 1950-64; *Recreations* family history, gardening; *Style* - Brig Charles Turner

CBE, DSO; The Colleens, Lower Cousley Wood, Wadhurst, Sussex (☎ Wadhurst 2387)

TURNER, Hon Mrs Elizabeth Alice; da of 1 Baron Schuster (d 1956); *b* 1902; *Educ* St Paul's Sch for Girls; *m* 1925 (m dis 1949), Theodore Francis Turner QC; 2 s (Christopher Gilbert Turner, *qv*, Headmaster of Stowe, and Michael John Turner, who m 1 (m dis) Hon Susan, nee Money-Coutts, da of 7 Baron Latymer, now Hon Mrs Dipple, *qv*), 1 da; *Style* - The Hon Mrs Elizabeth Turner; The Grange, N Cadbury, nr Yeovil, Somerset

TURNER, Hon Edward Neil; s of 1 Baron Netherthorpe (d 1980); *b* 1941; *Educ* Rugby, Roy Agricultural Coll Cirencester, London U; *m* 1963, Gillian Mary, da of late C J King; 1 s, 1 da; *Career* chm Edward Turner Cos; memb Yorks and Humberside Regional Economic Planning Council 1975-; freeman Co of Cutlers in Hallamshire; *Style* - The Hon Edward Turner; The Limes, S Anston, Sheffield

TURNER, Hon Mrs (Joanna Elizabeth); da of 1 Baron Piercy CBE (d 1966); *b* 10 Jan 1923; *Educ* St Paul's and Somerville, Oxford; *m* 1968, James Francis Turner (er s of late Rev P R Turner, educ Cambridge and dir of Bermaline Ltd, Bermaline Foods, Bloxwich Lock & Stamping, Estate Duties Investment Tst, Henry Boot & Sons); *Career* Classics Teacher Ellesmere Coll Salop 1975-80, Headmistress Badmintob Sch Bristol 1966-69 (assist 1948-65, and at Gordonstoun 1947-48); JP, Inner London Juvenile Courts Panel 1970-75; *Style* - The Hon Mrs Turner JP; The Old Coach House, Burford, Oxon (☎ 099382 2368)

TURNER, Hon James Frederick; s and h of 2 Baron Netherthorpe; *b* 7 Jan 1964; *Educ* Harrow; *Style* - The Hon James Turner

TURNER, James Neil Frederick; s of Thomas Henry Huxley Turner (d 1973); *b* 23 June 1932; *Educ* Shrewsbury, Ch Ch Oxford; *m* 1975, Elizabeth Jillian, nee Wells; 1 da; *Career* Lt RNVR; md E Turner & Sons Ltd; *Recreations* sailing; *Clubs* Cardiff and County; *Style* - James Turner Esq; 2 Kymin Ter, Penarth, S Glamorgan, Wales (☎ Penarth 701732)

TURNER, Hon Kate Belinda; da of 2 Baron Netherthorpe; *b* 12 Oct 1967; *Educ* St Mary's Sch; *Style* - The Hon Kate Turner

TURNER, Hon (Philip Noel) Nigel; s of 1 Baron Netherthorpe (d 1980); *b* 1949; *Educ* Rugby, Worcester Oxford; *m* 1973, Anne Rachel, da of R Brown, of Dovecote Farm, Somerton, Oxon; 1 da; *Career* vice-pres Northern Trust Co; *Style* - The Hon Nigel Turner; 210 Vine ave, Lake Forest, Ill 60045, USA

TURNER, Norman Charles; CBE 1971; s of Charles James Turner (d 1926); *b* 22 March 1907; *Educ* City of London; *m* 1930, Gwenneth Agnes, nee Field; 1 da; *Career* company sec to J Sainsbury Ltd 1938-67 (executive dir 1945-67); memb National Insurance Advsy Committee 1958-74; *Style* - Norman Turner Esq CBE; Uplands, St Mawes, Cornwall (☎ 03266 249)

TURNER, Philip; CBE (1975); s of George Francis Turner (d 1957); *b* 1 June 1913; *Educ* Peter Symonds, Winchester; *m* 1938, Hazel Edith, nee Benda; 1 da (1 da decd); *Career* Lt Cdr RNVR WW II; solicitor 1935, assist solicitor GPO Solicitor Dept 1953-62, princ assist slr GPO 1962-72, solicitor to Post Office 1972-75; chm Civil Serv Legal Soc 1957-58, chm Int Bar Assoc Cttee on Public Utility Law 1972-; *Recreations* piano, golf; *Clubs* Naval, RAC; *Style* - Philip Turner Esq CBE; 27 Westfield, Ashtead, Surrey, (☎ Ashtead 73656)

TURNER, Hon Patrick Andrew; s of 2 Baron Netherthorpe; *b* 4 June 1971; *Educ* Heatherdown Sch Ascot; *Style* - The Hon Patrick Turner

TURNER CAIN, Maj-Gen George Robert; CB (1967), CBE (1963), DSO (1944); s of Wing Cdr George Turner Cain (d 1967); *b* 16 Feb 1912; *Educ* Norwich Sch, Sandhurst; *m* 1938, Lamorna

Maturin, da of Col G B Hingston (ka 1916); 1 s, 1 da; *Career* 2 Lt Norfolk Regt 1932, NW Front 1937, WW II, Malaya 1957-59, Malaysia 1964-66, ADC to HM 1960-64; dir: F & G Smith Ltd Maltsters, Walpole & Wright Ltd, Crisp Maltings Ltd & EDME Ltd, Anglia Maltings Ltd & Hldgs; *Style* - Maj-Gen George Turner Cain, CB, CBE, DSO; Holbreck, Hollowlane, Stiffkey Wells, Norfolk

TURNOUR, (Cecil) Noel; s of Cecil Turnour; bro and hp of 7 Earl Winterton; *b* 11 Dec 1919; *Educ* Nutana Collegiate Sch, Saskatchewan U, Ontario Coll of Optometry; *m* 1941, Evelyn, da of Dr C Oulton; 2 s; *Career* late Fl Lt RCAF; *Style* - Noel Turnour Esq; RR2 Hespeler, Cambridge, Ont, Canada

TURRILL, Hon Mrs (Jean Phyllis); *née* Wise; da of 1 Baron Wise, DL; *b* 11 July 1914; *m* 1939, Lt-Col John Turrill, OBE, TD; 1 s, 2 da; *Style* - The Hon Mrs Turrill; 94 Albert rd, Caversham, Reading

TURTON, Hon Gerald Christopher; s of Baron Tranmire (Life Peer); *b* 1937; *m* 1967, Alexandra Susan, da of Lt-Col S Oliver, of 6 Maison Dieu, Richmond, Yorks; *Style* - The Hon Gerald Turton; Colt House, Feliskirk, Yorks

TURTON, Hon Michael Andrew; s of Baron Tranmire (Life Peer); *b* 1929; *Style* - The Hon Michael Turton

TURTON, Hon Timothy Robert Scott; s of Baron Tranmire (Life Peer); *b* 1934; *Style* - The Hon Timothy Turton

TUTTON, Brig John Theodore Stevenson; CBE (1960); s of Dr Alfred Edwin Howard Tutton (d 1938); *b* 15 Feb 1907; *Educ* Winchester Coll, Trin Cambridge; *m* 1940, Diana Cicely, nee Godfrey-Faussett-Osborne; 2 da; *Career* 2 Lt RE 1926, Lt-Col WW II, Brig 1957, AA & QMG N Malaya 1948-51, CRE Kent 1951-53, Col E War Office 1953-56, ch engr Malaya 1956-59, Dir Equipment War Office 1959-62 (ret); *Recreations* gardening, bell ringing; *Style* - Brig John Tutton CBE; Woodend Cottage, Awre, Newnham, Glos (☎ Blakeney 371)

TWEEDDALE, 13 Marquess of (S 1694); Edward Douglas John Hay; also Lord Hay of Yester (S 1488), Earl of Tweeddale (S 1646), Viscount Walden, Earl of Gifford (S 1694), Baron Tweeddale (UK 1881), Hereditary Chamberlain of Dunfermline and presumed h to baronetcy of Hay of Smithfield and Haystoun (NS 1635); s of 12 Marquess of Tweeddale, GC (d 1979), and of Hon Sonia Mary, da of 1 Viscount Ingleby (d 1966) - she m 2, Maj Michael William Vernon Hammond-Maude, JP; *b* 6 Aug 1947; *Educ* Milton Abbey, Trin Cambridge (BA); *Heir* yr twin bro, Lord Charles David Montagu Hay; *Style* - The Most Hon the Marquess of Tweeddale; 14c Ladbroke Terrace, W11 3PG (☎ 01 229 8270)

TWEEDDALE, Marchioness of; Nella Doreen; da of M Dutton; *m* 1959, as his 2 w, 12 Marquess of Tweeddale, GC (d 1979); *Style* - The Most Hon the Marchioness of Tweeddale; Tweeddale House, Gifford, Haddington, E Lothian

TWEEDIE, Hon Mrs (Prudence Mary); *née* Addington; da of late 6 Viscount Sidmouth; *b* 1916; *m* 1939, Lt-Cdr Hugo Edward Forbes Tweedie, DSC, RN, s of late Adm Sir Hugh Tweedie, KCB; 4 s, 3 da; *Style* - The Hon Mrs Tweedie; PO Box 8245, Nairobi, Kenya

TWEEDIE-SMITH, John Ian; s of Leslie Tweedie-Smith; *b* 17 Feb 1929; *Educ* Stowe School; *m* 1954, Gillian Mary, da of Claude James William Mundy (d 1978); 4 c; *Career* company director: md The Rawlplug Co Ltd 1968-73, group md E H Mundy & Co Ltd 1973-75, chm E H Mundy & Co Ltd 1977-; memb LCC 1961-65; *Recreations* swimming; *Style* - John Tweedie-Smith Esq; Old Barn House, Hoe Lane, Flansham, Bognor, Sussex (☎ Middleton on-Sea 4682)

TWEEDSMUIR, 2 Baron (UK 1935); John Norman Stuart Buchan; CBE (1964, OBE 1945), CD (1964); s of 1 Baron Tweedsmuir, GCMG, GCVO, CH, sometime Govr-Gen Canada (the writer John Buchan, d 1940) and Susan Charlotte (d 1977), da of Hon Norman Grosvenor (who was in his turn s of 1 Baron Ebury); half-bro of late Prof the Hon Alastair

Buchan, CBE, sometime dir Inst Strategic Studies; *b* 25 Nov 1911; *Educ* Eton, BNC Oxford; *m* 1, 1948, Priscilla Jean Fortescue (later Baroness Tweedsmuir of Belhelvie, PC - d 1978); 1 da; m 2, 1980, Jean Margharita, da of late Capt Humphrey Douglas Tollemache, RN (gs of 1 Baron Tollemache), and widow of Capt Sir Francis Cullen Grant, 12 Bt; *Heir* bro, Hon William De L'Aigle Buchan; *Career* late Lt-Col Canadian Infantry Corps; Rector of Aberdeen U 1948-51; chm Jt East and Central African Bd 1950-52; UK Delegate UN Assembly 1951-52, Council of Europe 1952; Pres Commonwealth and British Empire Chambers of Commerce 1955-57; Govr Commonwealth Inst 1958-77, Trustee 1977-; Govr Ditchley Fndn, Pres Inst of Export 1964-67; chm Advertising Standards Authority 1971-74, Council on Tribunals 1973-80; Pres Inst of Rural Life at Home and Overseas 1951-, British Schools Exploring Soc 1964-; chm British Rheumatism and Arthritis Assoc 1971-78, Pres 1978-; Hon LLD Aberdeen, FRSA, FRSE; *Clubs* Carlton, Travellers', Pratt's, Flyfishers'; *Style* - The Rt Hon The Lord Tweedsmuir CBE, CD; 40 Tufton Court, Westminster, SW1 (☎ 01 222 6997); Potterton House, Balmedie, Aberdeenshire (☎ Balmedie 2230)

TWELVETREES, Hon Mrs (Catherine Simonne); *née* du Parcq; da of late Baron du Parcq (Life Peer); *m* 1939, Leslie Twelvetrees; children; *Style* - The Hon Mrs Twelvetrees; 14 Overdale rd, Leicester

TWINE, George Edward; s of late L H M Twine; *b* 29 Oct 1909; *Educ* Hurstpierpoint Coll, St Catherine's Coll Cambridge; *m* 1939, Barbara Opal Onslow, nee Perkins; 2 s; *Career* Major Royal Artillery North Sea and India, solicitor of the Supreme Court; *Recreations* target rifle and match rifle shooting, game shooting; *Style* - George Twine Esq; Kolkinnon House, Up Nately, Basingstoke, Hants (☎ Hook 2273)

TWINING, Hon John Peter; s of Baron Twining (Life Peer d 1967); *b* 1929; *Educ* Charterhouse, BNC Oxford; *m* 1954, Mary Avice, da of Brig Joseph Hector Dealy Bennett, CBE; *Career* Colonial Serv 1953-63, an Admin Officer City of Guilds of London Inst 1963-78, chm Guildford Education Services Ltd; *Clubs* Reform; *Style* - The Hon John Twining; 3 The Ridgeway, Guildford, Surrey

TWINING, Hon William Lawrence; s of Baron Twining (Life Peer d 1967); *b* 1934; *Educ* Charterhouse, BNC Oxford, Chicago U; *m* 1957, Penelope Elizabeth, da of Richard Wall Morris, of Dublin; *Career* Prof of Law Queen's U Belfast 1965-72, Prof of Law Warwick U 1972-; *Style* - Prof The Hon William Twining; c/o Lloyds Bank, 222 Strand, WC2

TWISLETON-WYKEHAM-FIENNES, Sir John Saye Wingfield; KCB (1970, CB 1953), QC (1972); 3 s of Gerald T-W-F, CBE (d 1926, s of Rev Hon Wingfield T-W-F, 4 s of 16 Baron Saye and Sele, by his w Alice, niece of 4 Earl of Hardwicke and gda through her mother of Sir Henry Cunningham Montgomery, 1 Bt); *b* 14 April 1911; *Educ* Winchester, Balliol Oxford; *m* 1937, Sylvia (d 1979), da of Rev Charles McDowall (d 1956); 2 s, 1 da; *Career* barr; Parly Counsel Office 1939-76, First Parly Counsel 1968-72; *Style* - Sir John Twisleton-Wykeham-Fiennes KCB QC; Mill House, Preston St Mary, Sudbury, Suffolk (☎ 0787 247125)

TWISLETON-WYKEHAM-FIENNES, Audrey, Lady; Audrey Joan; da of Sir Percy Wilson Newson, 1 & last Bt; sis of Dowager Lady Napier and Ettrick; *b* 21 July 1912; *Educ* Heathfield Ascot; *m* 1931, Lt-Col Sir Ranulph Twisleton-Wykeham-Fiennes, 2 Bt, DSO (d of wounds received in action 1943), s of Col Hon Sir Eustace T-W-F (2 s of 17 Baron Saye and Sele); 1 s (present Bt), 3 da (Susan, m 1957 Capt John Scott, Blues & Royals; Dr Celia Brown, m 1963 Dr Robert B; Gillian m 1960 Timothy Hoult); *Style* - Audrey, Lady Twisleton-Wykeham-Fiennes; Robins, Church Lane, Lodsworth, W Sussex (☎ 363)

TWISLETON-WYKEHAM-FIENNES, Sir Maurice Alberic; s of Alberic T-W-F (d 1919, himself gs of 16 Baron Saye and Sele) by his w Gertrude, paternal ggda of 4 Viscount Harberton and ggda through her mother of 4 Viscount Powerscourt; *b* 1

March 1907; *Educ* Repton, Armstrong Coll Newcastle; *m* 1, 1932 (m dis 1963), Sylvia, da of Maj David Finlay; 2 s, 3 da; m 2, 1967, Erika, da of Dr Herbert Hueller von Huellenried, of Vienna; *Career* Lt Suffolk Yeo; CEng, FIMechE, lately engr with Armstrong Whitworth, Utd Steel Cos, Brush Electrical Engrg; md & later chm Davy-Ashmore Gp; kt 1965; *Recreations* music; *Clubs* Bath; *Style* - Sir Maurice Twisleton-Wykeham-Fiennes; Gowers Close, Sibford Gower, Banbury, Oxon (☎ 029 578 292)

TWISLETON-WYKEHAM-FIENNES, *see also* Fiennes

TWISLETON-WYKEHAM-FIENNES, Capt Sir Ranulph; 3 Bt (UK 1916); s of Lt-Col Sir Ranulph Twisleton-Wykeham-Fiennes, 2 Bt, DSO (d 1944, gs of 17 Baron Saye and Sele), and Audrey, Lady Twisleton-Wykeham-Fiennes, *qv*; *b* 7 March 1944 (posthumously); *Educ* Eton, Mons; *m* 1970, Virginia, da of Thomas Pepper; *Heir* none; *Career* Capt Roy Scots Greys, ret; author and explorer, leader The Transglobe Expedition expected back in UK in Sept 1982; *Recreations* travel, skiing; *Style* - Capt Sir Ranulph Twisleton-Wykeham-Fiennes, Bt; c/o St Peter's Well, Lodsworth, W Sussex (☎ 079 85 302)

TWYSDEN, Lady; Isla; da of late Alfred Evan Howlett, of Rye; *m* 1949, Lt-Cdr Sir William Adam Duncan Twysden, RN, 12 and last Bt (d 1970); *Style* - Lady Twysden; 26 Hans Crescent, Knightsbridge, SW1 (☎ 01 589 9921)

TYACKE, Maj-Gen David Noel Hugh; CB (1970), OBE (1957); s of Capt Charles Noel Walker Tyacke (ka 1918); *b* 18 Nov 1915; *Educ* Malvern, Sandhurst; *m* 1940, Diana, nee Duke; 1 s; *Career* cmd DCLI 1935 RA, cmd 1 Bn DCLI 1957-59, cmd 130 Infantry Brigade (TA) 1961-63, GOC Singapore District 1966-70; *Recreations* walking, motoring, bird watching; *Clubs* Naval & Mil; *Style* - Maj-Gen David Tyacke CB, OBE; The Old Rectory, Headbourne Worthy, Winchester, Hants (☎ Winchester 882339)

TYLDESLEY, Robert John Ross; s of John Tyldesley; *b* 3 Feb 1935; *Educ* Headlands G S, London School of Economics; *m* (m dis); 1 s, 1 da; *Career* md F Hewitt & Son Ltd, memb Cncl of the Newspaper Soc, memb Council of Commonwealth Press Union; *Recreations* skiing, shooting; *Clubs* Leicestershire, Rutland Sailing; *Style* - Robert Tyldesley Esq; Wayside, Main st, Belton, Uppingham, Rutland

TYLER, Arthur Catchmay (Hugh); CBE (1960), MC (1945), DL (Surrey 1968); s of Hugh Griffin Tyler (d 1953); *b* 20 Aug 1913; *Educ* Allhallows Sch, RMC Sandhurst; *m* 1938, Sheila Maysie, nee Kinloch; 3 s, 1 da; *Career* World War II (despatches), Colonel 1957, Brig 1960, sec British Joint Servs Mission Washington 1952-54, War Office 1957-60, sr UK Liaison Officer and Mil Adviser to High Cmmr Canada 1960-63, Assist Ch of Staff Allied Forces Central Europe 1963-65, sec Cncl of TA and VR Assocs 1965-72, Govr Allhallows Sch 1967 (chm 1976-79), Mil Knight of Windsor 1978-; *Clubs* Army and Navy; *Style* - Brig Arthur Tyler CBE MC DL; 19 Lower Ward, Windsor Castle, Berks (☎ 51471)

TYLER, Lady Elizabeth; *née* Jocelyn; da of 8 Earl of Roden, DL; *b* 28 Jan 1907; *m* 1, 1927 (m dis 1940), Gerald Annesley (s of Gerald Sowerby and Lady Mabel Annesley, da of 5 Earl Annesley); 2 da; m 2, 1940 (m dis 1949), Hon Charles Ross (d 1977, yr s of Una Mary, Baroness de Ros, holder of the Premier Barony of England); 1 s; m 3, 1954, Cdr Warden Gilchrist, RN (d 1958); m 4, 1967, Brig Edward Maxwell Tyler, DSO, MC, late RA (d 1974); *Style* - Lady Elizabeth Tyler; Teviot, Firgrove, Cape Province, S Africa

TYLER, Maj-Gen Sir Leslie Norman; KBE (1961, OBE 1942), CB (1955); s of Maj Norman Tyler, TA (d 1931); *b* 26 April 1904; *Educ* Diocesan Coll S Africa, RNCs Osborne and Dartmouth, King's Coll London U; *m* 1, 1930, Louie Teresa (d 1950), da of Lt-Col R J Franklin; 1 s, 1 da; m 2, 1953, Sheila, widow of Maj-Gen L H Cox CB CBE MC (d 1949); 2 s, 2 step da; *Career* Lt RAOC 1927, REME 1942, Maj-Gen WW II, dir DEME War

Off 1957-60 (ret), regnl dir Miny of Public Bldg and Works Central Mediterranean 1963-69, chm & v-chm Roy Hosp and Home for Incurables Putney 1970-81; *Recreations* music, watching rugby & football, cricket, lawn tennis; *Clubs* Army & Navy; *Style* - Maj-Gen Sir Leslie Tyler, KBE, CB; Higher Combe East, Haslemere, Surrey (☎ 0428 3900)

TYNDALE-BISCOE, Rear-Adm Alec Julian; CB (1959), OBE (1945); s of Lt-Col Arthur Annesley Tyndale-Biscoe (d 1969); *b* 10 August 1906; *Educ* RNCs Osborne and Dartmouth; *m* 1, Emma Winifred, nee Haselden (d 1974); 4 da; m 2, 1974, Elsa Hugolyne, widow of Capt Geoffrey Cooke & da of His Hon Sir Arthur Gwynne-James (d 1935); *Career* joined RN 1920; served 1939-45 Admiralty, HMS Vanguard 1947-49, Assist Engr-in-Ch 1950-53 cmdg RN Air Station Anthorn 1953-55, Fleet Engr Offr Mediterranean 1955-57, Flag Offr Res Aircraft 1957-59, ret; chairman Blaw-Knox Ltd 1965-71; *Recreations* model making, carpentry, gardening; *Clubs* Army & Navy; *Style* - Rear-Adm Alec Tyndale-Biscoe CB OBE; Bunces Farm Gardens, Birch Grove, Haywards Heath, Sussex (☎ Chelwood Gate 389)

TYRELL-KENYON, Hon Katherine; da of 5 Baron Kenyon, CBE; *b* 1959; *Style* - The Hon Katherine Tyrell-Kenyon

TYRELL-KENYON, Hon Lloyd; s and h of 5 Baron Kenyon, CBE; *b* 13 July 1947; *Educ* Eton, Magdalene Cambridge; *m* 1971, Sally Carolyn, da of J F P Matthews, of The Firs, Thurston, Bury St Edmunds; 2 s; *Style* - The Hon Lloyd Tyrell-Kenyon; The Green Cottage, Haughton, Tarporley, Cheshire

TYRELL-KENYON, Hon Richard; s of 5 Baron Kenyon, CBE; *b* 1948; *Educ* Eton, Seale Hayne Coll; *m* 1970 (m dis 1976), Davina Jane, da of David Charles George Jessel; 1 da; *Style* - The Hon Richard Tyrell-Kenyon; The Cumbers, Hanmer, Whitchurch, Salop

TYRELL-KENYON, Hon Thomas; s of 5 Baron Kenyon, CBE; *b* 1954; *Style* - The Hon Thomas Tyrell-Kenyon

TYRONE, Earl of; Henry Nicholas de la Poer Beresford; s and h of 8 Marquess of Waterford by his w Lady Caroline Wyndham-Quin, da of 6 Earl of Dunraven and Mount-Earl; *b* 23 March 1958; *Educ* Harrow; *Style* - Earl of Tyrone

TYRRELL, Lady Caroline Susan Elizabeth; da of late Lt-Col Lord Edward Douglas John Hay (3 s of 10 Marquess of Tweeddale) and sis of 12 Marquess; *b* 1930; *m* 1, 1953 (m dis 1970), Richard Noel Marshall Armitage; 2 s; m 2, 1970, Reginald Charles Tyrrell; raised to the rank of a Marquess's da 1970; *Style* - Lady Caroline Tyrrell; Capplegill, Moffat, Dumfriesshire

TYRRELL, George Edward; s of William George Tyrrell (d 1937); *b* 21 Sept 1920; *Educ* Whitgift Middle Sch Croydon; *m* 1950, Mildred Hilda; 1 s, 1 da; *Career* consulting engineer; dir of John Miles & Partners (London) Ltd; *Recreations* shooting; *Clubs* Institute of Directors; *Style* - George Tyrrell Esq; Rumwood Court, Langley, Kent (☎ Maidstone 861745)

TYRWHITT, John Edward Charles; s of Adm Sir St John Reginald Joseph Tyrwhitt, 2 Bt, KCB, DSO, DSC, and hp of bro, Sir Reginald Tyrwhitt, 3 Bt; *b* 27 July 1953; *m* 1978, Melinda Ngaire, da of Capt Anthony Philip Towell, MC, of Ridge rd, Long Island, NY, USA; 1 s; *Style* - John Tyrwhitt Esq

TYRWHITT, Sir Reginald Thomas Newman; 3 Bt (UK 1919); s of Adm Sir St John Reginald Joseph Tyrwhitt, 2 Bt, KCB, DSO, DSC (d 1961); *b* 21 Feb 1947; *Educ* Downside; *m* 1972 (m dis 1980), Sheila Gail, da of William Alistair Crawford Nicoll, of Liphook, Hants; *Heir* bro, John Edward Charles Tyrwhitt; *Career* 2 Lt RA 1966, Lt 1969, RARO 1969; *Style* - Sir Reginald Tyrwhitt, Bt; c/o Lloyds Bank, 21 High st, Ascot, Berks SL5 7JE

TYSER, Hon Mrs (Susan Frances); *née* Remnant; da of 2 Baron Remnant, MBE; *b* 9 May 1938; *m* 1967, Alan Tyser, s of Granville Tyser, of Park Lane, London W1; 1 s; *Style* - The Hon Mrs Tyser; West

Hannay House, Wantage, Oxon

U

UDALL, David Victor; s of George Edward Udal; *b* 8 Nov 1937; *Educ* Hampton G S; *m* 1974, Ann, nee Ellwood; 2 c; *Career* chartered accountant, dir Estates Property Investment Co Ltd; *Recreations* tennis, landscape gardening, travelling; *Style* - David Udall Esq; Dukes Edge, Lunghurst rd, Woldingham, Surrey (☎ Woldingham 2340)

UDNY-HAMILTON, Hon Victoria Edith; da of 11 Lord Belhaven and Stenton, CIE (d 1950, assumed additional surname of Udny 1934); *b* 1941; *Style* - The Hon Victoria Udny-Hamilton; The Home Farm, Udny, Aberdeenshire (☎ 367)

UHLMAN, Hon Mrs (Nancy Diana Joyce); da of 1 Baron Croft, CMG, TD, PC (d 1947) and Hon Nancy, da of 1 Baron Borwick; *b* 1912; *m* 1936, Manfred Uhlman; 1 s, 1 da; *Style* - The Hon Mrs Uhlman; 47 Downshire Hill, NW3

ULLSWATER, 2 Viscount (UK 1921); Nicholas James Christopher Lowther; s of Lt John Arthur Lowther, MVO, RNVR (d 1942); suc ggf, 1 Viscount Ullswater, GCB (s of late Hon William Lowther, bro of late 3 Earl of Lonsdale), 1949; *b* 9 Jan 1942; *Educ* Eton, Trin Cambridge; *m* 1967, Susan, da of James Howard Weatherby, of Lemington Grange, Moreton-in-Marsh, by his w Mary (4 da of Sir Hereward Wake, 13 Bt, CB, CMG, DSO, JP, DL); 1 s, 2 da; *Heir* s, Hon Benjamin James Lowther; *Career* farmer; Capt Roy Wessex Yeo TAVR 1973-78; *Clubs* Cavalry & Guards; *Style* - The Rt Hon the Viscount Ullswater; Barrow Street House, nr Mere, Warminster, Wilts (☎ 0747 860621)

ULSTER, Earl of; Alexander Patrick Gregers Richard; s of HRH The Duke of Gloucester, GCVO; *b* 24 Oct 1974; *Style* - Earl of Ulster

ULYATT, Hon Mrs (Frances Margaret); da of 1 and last Baron Douglas of Barloch, KCMG by 1 w, Minnie, nee Smith; *b* 1920; *Educ* MB and BS London 1943; *m* 1943, Kenneth Ulyatt, PhD, MSc; 2 s, 1 da; *Career* Fell of Faculty of Anaesthetists 1957; *Style* - The Hon Mrs Ulyatt; 134 Knights Hill, SE27

UNDERHILL, Baron (Life Peer UK 1979); (Henry) Reg(inall) Underhill; CBE (1976); s of Henry James Underhill, of Walthamstow; *b* 8 May 1914; *Educ* Tom Hood Central Sch Leyton; *m* 1937, Flora Janet, da of Leonard Philbrick; 2 s (Hon Terry Leonard m 1959 Dorothy Askew; Hon Robert m 1970 Christine Vinson), 1 da (Hon Mrs (Joan Evelyn m Ian) Taylor); *Career* memb APEX 1931-; advr Home Sec 1980-, memb Parly Delegn to Zimbabwe 1980; Nat Agent of the Labour Party 1972-79, Propaganda Officer 1947, Regional Organiser W Midlands 1948, Assist Nat Agent 1960; *Style* - The Rt Hon the Lord Underhill, CBE; 94 Loughton Way, Buckhurst Hill, Essex 1G9 6AH (☎ 01 504 1910)

UNDERHILL, Hon Robert; s of Baron Underhill, CBE (Life Peer); *b* 1948; *m* 1970, Christine Ann, da of E Laurie Vinsen; *Style* - The Hon Robert Underhill; 12 Lyndhurst Close, Wilmslow, Cheshire

UNDERHILL, Hon Terry Leonard; s of Baron Underhill, CBE (Life Peer); *b* 1938; *m* 1960, Dorothy, da of late Edwin Askew; *Style* - The Hon Terry Underhill; Gardner's Cottage, Dartington Hall, Totnes, Devon

UNIACKE, Hon Mrs (Susan Geraldine); *née* Verney; da of 20 Baron Willoughby de Broke, MC, AFC, AE, JP; *b* 2 Dec 1942; *m* 1, 1964 (m dis 1969), Jeremy Wagg, gs of Sir James Horlick, 4 Bt, OBE; m 2, 1972, Robie Uniacke; 1 s; *Style* - The Hon Mrs Uniacke

UPJOHN, Baroness; Marjorie Dorothy Bertha; da of late Maj Ernest Murray Lucas; *m* 1947, Baron Upjohn (Life Peer d 1971); *Style* - The Rt Hon The Lady

Upjohn; Orpen's Hill House, Birch, Colchester

UPTON, John; s of Ernest Upton (d 1940); *b* 3 Dec 1905; *m* 1951, Kathleen Ruth; 2 s, 2 da; *Career* md The Liverpool Warehousing Co Ltd; chm The Br Public Warehousekeepers Cttee 1979-80; dir Lukwa Storage Ltd, North West Storage Co, Cheshire Storage; *Recreations* golf; *Clubs* Roy Birkdale Golf; *Style* - John Upton Esq; 5 Westbourne rd, Birkdale, Southport

UPTON, Philip Valentine; MBE (1943), TD (1944), JP (Essex 1953), DL (1954); s of the late Col E J Upton, DL; *b* 14 Nov 1902; *Educ* Harrow, Trinity Coll Cambridge; *m* 1930, Veronica Rosemary, da of late Lt-Col L H Thornton, CMG, DSO; 1 s; *Career* commissioned TA 1924; embodied 1/5 Essex Regt TA 1939; served 1939-45 UK, Egypt & Iraq; AQ MG GHQ PAIFORCE 1943-44; AH & QMG South Iraq Area 1944-45; County Commandant ACF Essex 1957-62, High Sheriff 1954; *Recreations* shooting, fishing, gardening; *Clubs* MCC; *Style* - Philip Upton Esq, MBE, TD, JP, DL; Park Lodge, Margaretting, Ingatestone, Essex (☎ 027 75 3199)

URE, Alan Willis; RD (1969); s of Colin McGregory Ure (d 1963); *b* 30 March 1916; *Educ* Kelvinside Academy, Merchiston Castle Sch, Pembroke Cambridge; *m* 1953, Mary Christine, nee Henry; 1 s, 2 da; *Career* Pres Nat Fedn of Building Trades Employers 1981, memb Roy Cmmn on Civil Liability and Compensation for Personal Injury 1974-78, md Trollope & Colls Management Ltd 1979-; *Recreations* vintage motoring, bell ringing, walking, reading; *Clubs* Naval; *Style* - Alan Ure Esq, RD; Preyste House, North st, Petworth, W Sussex (☎ 42848)

URQUHART, Alastair Hugh; CBE (1967); s of late Geoffrey Urquhart of Collaroy, NSW, Australia; *b* 3 Nov 1919; *Educ* Sydney C of E Grammar Sch; *m* 1947, Joyce Muriel, nee Oswald; 2 da; *Career* Capt N Africa (Tobruk, El Alamein), UK POW Rehabilitation Work 1944-45; stockbroker; sr ptnr Mullens & Co, memb Sydney Stock Exchange Ltd 1949-, chm 1959-66 (and former v-chm), resident Aust Assoc Stock Exchanges 1959, 1964-66, v-pres 1960-63, v-chm Aust Red Cross Soc (NSW Div) 1964, tstee Sydney Opera House 1969-, memb Dvpt Corpn of NSW 1967-75, chm Chubbs Australia Ltd, Hogg Robinsons CCL Gp Australia, NSW Permanent Bldg Soc, Oswalds Bonded & Freestores Pty Ltd, dir P & O Australia Ltd; *Recreations* swimming, golf, yachting; *Clubs* Union, Roy Sydney Golf, Elanora Golf, Roy Sydney Yacht Sqdn, Imperial Services, Rotary; *Style* - Alastair Urquhart Esq, CBE; 4 Wentworth pla, Point Pier, NSW, Australia 2027 (☎ home 364424, office 2336277)

URQUHART, Donald John; CBE (1970); s of the late Roderick Urquhart; *b* 27 Nov 1909; *Educ* Barnard Castle Sch, Sheffield U; *m* 1939, Beatrice Winifride, nee Parker; 2 s; *Career* dir National Lending Library for Science and Technology 1961-73, dir-gen British Library Lending Division 1973-74; *Clubs* Athenaeum; *Style* - Donald Urquhart Esq, CBE; Woodgarth, 15 First Avenue, Bardsey, Leeds (☎ Collingham Bridge 73228)

URQUHART, Hon Ronald Douglas Lauchlan; s of Baron Tayside (Life Peer, d 1975); *b* 1948; *Educ* Fettes Coll, Edinburgh U (LLB); *m* 1975, Dorothy May Jackson; *Career* chartered accountant; *Clubs* Caledonian; *Style* - The Hon Ronald Urquhart

URQUHART, Maj-Gen Robert Elliott; CB (1944), DSO and Bar (1943); s of late Alexander Urquhart MA, MD, DPH; *b* 28 Nov 1901; *Educ* St Paul's; *m* 1939, Pamela, da of Brig William Condon, OBE (d 1971); 1 s, 3 da (Elspeth m 1 (m dis) Sir Philip Grant Suttie, Bt, *qv*); *Career* GOC 1 Airborne Div 1944-45, dir TA & ACF 1945-46, GOC 16 Airborne Div 1947-48, Cdr Lowland Dist 1948-50, GOC Malaya 1950-52, GOCIC British Troops Austria 1952-55, dir Davy & United Engineering Co Ltd 1957-70; *Recreations* golf and bridge; *Style* - Maj-Gen Robert Urquhart CB, DSO*; Bigram, Port of Menteith, By Stirling, Scotland (☎ Port of Menteith 267)

URQUHART, Hon William James Lauchlan; s of Baron Tayside (Life Peer d 1975); *b* 1944; *Educ* Fettes Coll, Glasgow U; *m* 1967, Wendy Helen Cook; *Career* chartered accountant, memb Inst of Taxation; *Style* - The Hon William Urquhart; Thorngarth, 139 Strathern rd, Broughty Ferry, Dundee

URRY, John Arian Marshall; s of John Marshall Urry (d 1972); *b* 11 March 1938; *Educ* Solihull Sch, Aston U; *m* 1968, Carol Elizabeth, nee Blakely; 2 s; *Career* md Powell Piggott Ltd, Hudson Edmunds & Co Ltd, dir Econa Ltd, Hon Sec Warwicks GC; *Recreations* golf; *Clubs* St Paul's (Birmingham); *Style* - John Urry Esq; Dormers, Dickens Heath rd, Shirley, Solihull, W Midlands (☎ 0564 82 3114)

URWICK, Lt-Col Anthony Christopher Moore; DL (1971); s of Col Frank Davidson Urwick, DSO, TD, JP (d 1936); *b* 31 May 1913; *Educ* Malvern and RMC; *m* 1947, Jacqueline Denise, da of Judge John Doyle, ICS (d 1934); 2 da; *Career* Lt-Col Sudan Defence Force 1939-48, E African Campaign, N Africa, cmd 9 Bn 1944-45, Western Arab Corps 1945-48; Regular Offr Somerset Light Infantry 1933-53, Regimental Sec (ret Offr) 1955-79; *Style* - Lt-Col Anthony Urwick, DL; Ashfield House, 19 Mount st, Taunton, Somerset (☎ 0823 87399)

USHER, Andrew Michael; s of Francis George Usher; *b* 15 Oct 1938; *Educ* Cheltenham Coll; *m* 1964, Anne, nee Whittington; 3 s, 1 da; *Career* slr 1964, sec British Investment Trust Ltd 1979-, dir Fledgeling Investments Ltd 1978-; *Recreations* genealogy, family; *Clubs* New (Edinburgh), Hon Company of Edinburgh Golfers; *Style* - Andrew Usher Esq; 12 Blackford rd, Edinburgh

USHER, Lady; Gertrude Martha; da of Lionel Barnard Sampson, of Tresmontes, Villa Valira, Cordoba, Argentina; *m* 1930, Sir Robert Stuart Usher, 4 Bt (d 1962); *Style* - Lady Usher; Hallrule, Hawick, Roxburghshire

USHER, Sir Peter Lionel; 5 Bt (UK 1899), of Norton, Midlothian, and of Wells, Co Roxburgh; s of Sir (Robert) Stuart Usher, 4 Bt (d 1962); *b* 1 Oct 1931; *Educ* privately; *Heir* bro, Robert Edward Usher; *Style* - Sir Peter Usher, Bt; Hallrule, Hawick, Roxburghshire

USHER, Robert Edward; s of Sir Robert Stuart Usher, 4 Bt (d 1962), and hp of bro, Sir Peter Usher, 5 Bt; *b* 18 April 1934; *Style* - Robert Usher Esq

UTTLEY, Hon Mrs (Katherine Barbara); da (by 1 m) of late 18 Baron St John of Bletso; *b* 1907; *m* 1945, George William Uttley, MA, BSc, late Fl Lt RAF; 1 da; *Style* - The Hon Mrs Uttley

UVEDALE OF NORTH END, Baroness; Joyce Eleanor; JP (Middx 1951); da of late S H Holman, of Highgate, N6, and St Margaret's Bay, Kent, and widow of the Rt Hon Hastings Bertrand Lees-Smith, DSc, MP; *m* 1949, 1 Baron Uvedale of North End, MD, FRCS (d 1974, when the title became ext); *Style* - The Rt Hon the Lady Uvedale of North End, JP; 1 The Park, North End rd, NW11

UXBRIDGE, Earl of; Charles Alexander Vaughan Paget; s and h of 7 Marquess of Anglesey, DL; *b* 13 Nov 1950; *Educ* Eton, Exeter Coll Oxford; *Heir* bro, Lord Rupert Paget; *Style* - Earl of Uxbridge; Plâs Newydd, Llanfairpwll, Gwynedd

UZIELL-HAMILTON, Mario Reginald; s of Don Nino Uziell (d 1951); *b* 4 May 1922; *Educ* Brentwood, Sorbonne, St Catharine's Coll Cambridge; *m* 1952, Adrianne Pauline, da of Dr Marcus Grantham (d 1975); 1 s, 1 da; *Career* Lt (Acting Capt) Intelligence Corps, slr Hooper Holt & Co (formerly barr), chm: Fabian Properties Ltd, Fabian Properties (Surrey) Ltd, Hamilton Muller Ltd, dir: Clydetronic Ltd, Clydetronic Research & Dvpt Ltd, Euro-African Advisors Ltd; *Style* - Mario Uziell-Hamilton Esq; 12 Jeymer av, NW2

UZIELLI, William John; s of Herbert Rex Uzielli, CIE (d 1961); *b* 2 March 1937; *Educ* Marlborough, Oxford; *m* 1968, Angela Mary, nee Carrick; 1 s, 1 da; *Career* insurance broker and memb of Lloyds, md Hogg Robinson & Gardner Mountain (Marine) Ltd 1981-;

Recreations golf, gardening; *Clubs* Roy and Ancient GC, Berkshire GC; *Style* - William Uzielli Esq; Buckhurst Park Cottage, Cheapside, Ascot, Berks (☎ 22932)

V

VAIZEY, Baron (Life Peer UK 1976); John Ernest Vaizey; s of late Ernest Vernon Vaizey; *b* 1 Oct 1929; *Educ* Queen Mary's Hosp Sch, Queens' Cambridge; *m* 1961, Marina Alandra, *qv* (the art critic Marina Vaizey), da of Lyman Stansky; 2 s, 1 da; *Career* MA Oxford, DSc Brunel, DLitt Adelaide, Fell St Catharine's Coll Cambridge 1953-56, Lecturer Oxford U 1956-60 and 1962-67, dir of Research Unit London U 1960-62, Fell and Tutor Worcester Coll Oxford 1962-67, Prof of Economics 1966- and Head of Sch of Social Sciences Brunel U 1973-; *Clubs* Garrick; *Style* - The Rt Hon The Lord Vaizey; 24 Heathfield Terrace, W4 4JE (☎ 01 994 7994)

VAIZEY, Hon Edward; s of Baron Vaizey (Life Peer); *b* 1968; *Style* - The Hon Edward Vaizey

VAIZEY, Baroness; Marina Alandra; da of Lyman Stansky, of New York, USA; *b* 16 Jan 1938; *Educ* Brearley Sch New York, Putney Sch Putney Vermont, Radcliffe Coll Harvard U, Girton Cambridge; *m* 1961, Baron Vaizey; 2 s, 1 da; *Career* Art Critic Financial Times 1970-74, Art Critic Sunday Times 1974-, Dance Critic Now! 1979-81, broadcaster, occasional exhibition organiser and lecturer; *Style* - The Rt Hon The Lady Vaizey; 24 Heathfield Terrace, W4 4JE (☎ 01 994 7994)

VAIZEY, Hon Polly; da of Baron Vaizey (Life Peer); *b* 1962; *Style* - The Hon Polly Vaizey

VAIZEY, Hon Thomas; s of Baron Vaizey (Life Peer); *b* 1964; *Style* - The Hon Thomas Vaizey

VALËRE, Hon Mrs; Hon Gloria; da of Baron Constantine (Life Peer, d 1971); *b* 1928; *Educ* St Andrews U (MA), Inst of Education, London U; *m* 1954, André Valëre, barrister; children; *Style* - The Hon Mrs Valëre; 202A Terrace Vale rd, Point Cumana, Trinidad and Tobago

VALENTIA, 14 Viscount (I 1642 but with precedence 1622); Sir Francis Dighton Annesley; Bt (I 1620, Premier Baronet of Ireland), MC (1918); also Baron Mountnorris (I 1628); s of George Annesley, unc of 13 Viscount (d 1951); established succession 1959; *b* 12 Aug 1888; *Educ* St Lawrence Coll, Guy's Hosp; *m* 1925, Joan, da of John Curtis; 1 s, 3 da; *Heir* s, Hon Richard Annesley; *Career* Brig, served WW I & II and 1914-48 continuously in RAMC MRCS, LRCP; *Style* - The Rt Hon The Viscount Valentia, MC; St Michael's, Lea, Malmesbury, Wilts (☎ 2312)

VALENTIA, Gladys, Viscountess; Gladys May Kathleen; da of late Uriah Fowler; *m* 1938, 13 Viscount Valentia (d 1951); *Style* - The Rt Hon Gladys, Viscountess Valentia; Wassall House, Wincanton, Somerset

VALENTINE, Lady Freda; *née* Butler; CBE (1979); da of 8 Earl of Lanesborough (d 1950); *b* 8 Sept 1895; *m* 1931, Francis Cyril Oliphant Valentine, MRCP (d 1957); 2 s; *Career* V-Pres Butler Soc, Tibetan Breed (dog) Soc; memb Irish Georgian Soc, Westminster Con Assoc, Mayfair Soho Cttee, Cncl Guide Dogs For Blind Assoc, Soho Soc (housing and preservation); *Recreations* racing; *Clubs* Twenty Ghost (international rallying); *Style* - Lady Freda Valentine, CBE; A11, Albany, W1

VALENTINE, Hon Mrs (Janet Sibella); *née* Weir; da of 2 Viscount Weir, CBE; *b* 13 April 1947; *m* 1978, Francis Anthony, 2 s of Francis Valentine and Lady Freda, nee Butler, half-sis of 9 Earl of Lanesborough, TD, JP, DL; *Style* - The Hon Mrs Valentine; The Gate House, Astrop, Banbury, Oxon; 29 Cornwall gdns, SW7

VALENTINE, Michael Robert; s of Alfred Buyers Valentine (d 1971); *b* 16 Jan 1928; *Educ* Shrewsbury, CCC Cambridge; *m* 1957, Shirley Josephine, nee Hall; 1 s (James b 1964), 2 da (Josephine, Helen); *Career* Lt Roy Signals, FCA 1955, sr dir SG Warburg & Co Ltd (merchant bankers) 1966-, dir Mercury Securities Ltd 1973-; *Recreations* opera, vintage cars, social life; *Clubs* National Film Theatre, London Rowing, Vintage Sports Car, Lagonda; *Style* - Michael Valentine Esq; 30 Gresham st, EC2 (☎ 01 600 4555)

VALENTINI, Baroness - Princess Giovanna Ethel; da of late Prince Giambattista Pia Sigismondo Francesco Rospigliosi (s of Lady Elena Maria Concetta Isabella Gioacchina Giuseppa Giustiniani-Bandini, Princess Camillo Rospigliosi, 3 da of late 8 Earl of Newburgh) and sis of 11 Earl of Newburgh; *b* 1911; *m* 1937, Baron Umberto Duranti Valentini; *Style* - Princess Giovanna Valentini; Piazza Adriana, 10 Rome, Italy

VALLANCE, Col James Newton; OBE (1955), TD (1948) and Bar, DL (Notts 1966); s of C J Vallance (d 1939); *b* 23 Jan 1906; *Educ* Malvern; *m* 1, 1931, Edith Mary, nee Hart (d 1974); 2 da; m 2, 1976, Muriel Hattie, nee Prentice; *Career* solicitor of the Supreme Court; *Recreations* shooting; *Clubs* Army & Navy; *Style* - Col James Vallance, OBE, TD*, DL; The Hermitage, Hermitage Lane, Mansfield, Notts

VAN CUTSEM, Edward; s of Hugh van Cutsem, *qv*; *aet* 8 in 1981; Page to Lady Diana Spencer at her marriage to HRH The Prince of Wales 1981; *Style* - Edward van Cutsem

VAN CUTSEM, Hugh Bernard Edward; s of Bernard van Cutsem (d 1975) by his 1 w, Mary, da of Capt Edward Compton, JP, DL (himself s of Lord Alwyne Compton, who was in his turn 2 s of 4 Marquess of Northampton, KG), of Newby Hall, Ripon; *b* 21 July 1941; *Educ* Ampleforth; *m* 1971, Jonkvrouwe Emilie Elise Christine, da of Jonkheer Pieter Quarles van Ufford (Netherlands cr of Willem I 1814), of Ackworth House, E Bergholt, Suffolk; 4 s (*see* van Cutsem, Edward); *Career* Lt Life Gds; bloodstock breeder, farmer, co chm; *Clubs* White's; *Style* - Hugh van Cutsem Esq; Northmore, Exning, Newmarket, Suffolk (☎ Exning 332)

VAN DEN BOSCH, Baron Jean; Hon GCVO (1966); s of Baron Firmin van den Bosch and Anne de Volder; *b* 27 Jan 1910; *Educ* Ecole Abbatiale, Maredsous; Notre Dame de la Paix, Namur; Université Catholique de Louvain; *m* 1944, Hélène Cloquet; 2 da; *Career* Belgian Ambass to UK and Belgian Perm Rep to Cncl of WEU 1966-72, dir Lloyds Bank Internat 1972-; *Clubs* Beefsteak, White's; *Style* - Baron Jean van den Bosch, GCVO; 114 Ave Winston Churchill, B1, 1180 Brussels, Belgium (☎ 347 29 09)

VAN DER NOOT, Hon Mrs (Barbara Mary); *née* Cokayne; da of late 1 Baron Cullen of Ashbourne, and Grace, da of late Rev the Hon John Marsham (s of 3 Earl of Romney); *b* 1905; *m* 1929, Maj Gilbert Francis Van der Noot, late Irish Gds; 1 da; *Style* - The Hon Mrs Van der Noot; Oak Cottage, Hartley Wintney, Hants

VAN DER WOUDE, Lady (Anne) Penelope Marian; *née* Herbert; da (by 1 m) of 6 Earl of Carnarvon; *b* 1925; *m* 1945, Gerrit van der Woude, Gren Gds; 2 s, 1 da; *Style* - Lady Penelope van der Woude; Herondon, Eastry, Sandwich, Kent

VAN GEEST, Leonard Waling; s of Leonard van Geest; *b* 1 April 1950; *Educ* Spalding G S; *m* 1978, Gillian Denise, nee Fox; 1 s; *Career* dir Geest Holdings Ltd, dir L Van Geest Farms Ltd, md Geest Foods; *Recreations* rugby, tennis; *Style* - Leonard Van Geest Esq; Wool Hall, Cross Gate, Wykeham, Spalding (☎ 66256)

VAN MARLE, Johan Tyo; s of Tyo Henrik van Marle; *b* 20 Oct 1940; *Educ* Baarns Lyceum, Amsterdam U, Harvard Business Sch USA; *m* 1972, Isabella Christina, da of Rudolph Maximillian Crommelin; 2 children; *Career* man Pierson, Heldring and Pierson, (bankers) Amsterdam 1966-72; dir J Henry Schroder Wagg and Co Ltd (merchant bankers)

1972-; *Recreations* opera, golf, skiing; *Clubs* Sunningdale G C; *Style* - Johan van Marle Esq; 22 Pelham Crescent, SW7 (☎ 584 7369)

VAN RAALTE, Hon Mrs (Mary Anne); *née* Berry; da of 2 Viscount Kemsley; *b* 1934; *m* 1960, Charles Henry van Raalte; 1 s, 2 da; *Style* - The Hon Mrs van Raalte; Boreland House, Kilmarnock, Ayrshire

VAN STRAUBENZEE, Sir William Radcliffe; MBE (1954), MP (C) Wokingham 1959-; s of late Brig A B van Straubenzee, DSO, MC, and Margaret Joan, da of A N Radcliffe, of Bag Park Widecombe-in-the-Moor, Newton Abbot, South Devon; *b* 27 Jan 1924; *Educ* Westminster; *Career* served 1939-45 War; trustee of Lambeth Palace Library; Joint Parliamentary Under-Secretary of State Department of Education and Science 1970-72; kt 1981; *Style* - Sir William van Straubenzee, MBE, MP; 30 Rose Street, Wokingham, Berkshire (☎ Wokingham 784464)

VANCE, Hon Mrs (Imogen Anne Ierne); *née* Moynihan; da of 2 Baron Moynihan, OBE, TD (d 1965); *b* 1932; *m* 1, 1953 (m dis 1965), Michael Edward Peter Williams; m 2, 1965, Charles Ivan Vance; 1 da; *Style* - The Hon Mrs Vance; Quince Cottage, Bilsington, Ashford, Kent

VANDEN-BEMPDE-JOHNSTONE, *see* Johnstone

VANDER DUSSEN, Neil; s of Herman Vander Dussen; *b* 22 Sept 1931; *Educ* Kansas State U, Massachusetts Inst of Technology USA; *m* 1953, Gerie, nee McLaughlin; *Career* dir: RCA Jersey (CI), RCA Australia, RCA SpA (Italy), Random House Inc, and others; exec vice-president RCA Corporation USA, chm RCA Ltd UK 1979- (joined RCA 1957; manager Broadcast Systems: Central then Eastern Sales District 1962, Eastern Field Sales 1962-64, Scientific Instruments Sales, then Govt and Scientific Instruments Sales 1964-66, Scientific Instruments Marketing and Engrg 1967-70, Studio Equipment Engrg and Product Management 1970-71; div v-pres and gen man Broadcast Systems 1971-76 and Commercial Communications Systems 1977-79); *Recreations* golf; *Clubs* Tavistock Country USA, Les Ambassadeurs; *Style* - Neil Vander Dussen Esq; 21 Signal Hill Rd, Cherry Hill, New Jersey, 08003

VANE, Hon Carolyn Mary; da of 11 Baron Barnard, TD, JP, by his w, Lady Davina, nee Cecil, da of 6 Marq of Exeter; *b* 5 May 1954; *Style* - The Hon Carolyn Vane

VANE, Hon Elizabeth Anne; da of 11 Baron Barnard, TD, JP, by his w, Lady Davina, nee Cecil, da of 6 Marq of Exeter; *b* 17 May 1956; *Style* - The Hon Elizabeth Vane

VANE, Eric Digby Tempest; s of Harry Tempest Vane CBE (d 1942); *b* 27 Dec 1912; *Educ* Mill Hill Sch, London U; *m* 1936, Kathleen Doreen, nee Libby; 4 c; *Career* engrg & management consultant, dir of several family companies and trust co; *Recreations* administering the Island of Eilean Shona (owner); *Clubs* RAC; *Style* - Eric Vane Esq; Eilean Shona, Acharacle, Argyll, Scot (☎ 096785 249)

VANE, Hon Gerald Raby; s of 10 Baron Barnard, CMG, OBE, MC, TD (d 1964); *b* 2 Dec 1926; *Educ* Eton, Trin Cambridge; *Career* chm Watermill Theatre Bagnor 1975-, memb Southern Arts Assoc Exec; chm Western Area Planning Newbury DC 1979-; dir publishing co; late Durham Light Infantry, memb Newbury Dist Cncl; *Recreations* politics, local govt, architecture, gardens; *Style* - The Hon Gerald Vane; 20 Midgham Green, Reading, Berks (☎ Woolhampton 3376, office- Ascot 23377)

VANE, Hon Henry Francis Cecil; s and h of 11 Baron Barnard, TD, JP, by his w, Lady Davina, nee Cecil, da of 6 Marq of Exeter; *b* 11 March 1954; *Style* - The Hon Henry Vane

VANE, Hon Louise Cicely; da of 11 Baron Barnard, TD, JP, by his w, Lady Davina, nee Cecil, da of 6 Marq of Exeter;

b 30 May 1968; *Style* - The Hon Louise Vane

VANE, Hon Sophia Rosalind; da of 11 Baron Barnard, TD, JP, by his w, Lady Davina, nee Cecil, da of 6 Marq of Exeter; *b* 24 Jan 1962; *Educ* Cobham Hall, Westfield Coll London U; *Career* student; *Style* - The Hon Sophia Vane

VANE PERCY, Hon Mrs (Linda Denise); *née* Grosvenor; da of late 5 Baron Ebury, DSO, by 2 w, Hon Denise Yarde-Buller (da of 3 Baron Churston); *b* 1948; *m* 1973, Christopher D Vane Percy; 1 s; *Style* - The Hon Mrs Vane Percy

VANE-TEMPEST-STEWART, Lady Cosima Maria Gabriella; da of 9 Marq of Londonderry; *b* 1961; *Style* - Lady Cosima Vane-Tempest-Stewart

VANE-TEMPEST-STEWART, Lady Sophia Frances Anne; da of 9 Marq of Londonderry; *b* 1959; *Style* - Lady Sophia Vane-Tempest-Stewart

VANE-TEMPEST-STEWART, Lord Reginald Alexander; s of 9 Marquess of Londonderry; *b* 1977

VANNECK, Hon Mrs Andrew; Britta; da of Count Nils Bonde, of Stockholm; *m* 1939, as his 2 w, late Hon Andrew Nicholas Armstrong Vanneck, MC (bro of late 5 Baron Huntingfield, KCMG; raised to the rank of a Baron's son 1922, d 1965); 1 s, 1 da; *Style* - The Hon Mrs Andrew Vanneck; Sylchester, 2/4 Trahlee rd, Bellevue Hill, Sydney 2023, Australia

VANNECK, Hon Joshua Charles; s and h of 6 Baron Huntingfield; *b* 10 Aug 1954; *Educ* Eton; *Career* 2 Lt Scots Dragoon Gds; *Style* - The Hon Joshua Vanneck

VANNECK, Air Cdre Hon Sir Peter Beckford Rutgers; GBE (1977, OBE 1963), CB (1973), AFC (1955), AE (1954), MEP (C) Cleveland 1979-; s of 5 Baron Huntingfield, KCMG (d 1969); *b* 7 Jan 1922; *Educ* Geelong G S Australia, Stowe, Trin Cambridge, Harvard U USA; Hon DSc City U; *m* 1943, Cordelia, da of Capt Reginald Hugh Errington, RN (ret); 1 da (and 1 da decd); *Career* late Lt RN, late Air Cdre RAuxAF, OC No 3619 (Suffolk) Fighter Control Unit RAuxAF 1959-61, Inspector RAuxAF 1962-73, Hon Inspr-Gen RAuxAF 1974-, Hon Air Cdre No 1 MHU RAuxAF, ADC to HM 1963-73, a Gentleman Usher to HM 1967-79, Alderman of City of London 1969 (a Sheriff 1974-75), Lord Mayor of London 1978-79, High Sheriff Suffolk 1979, KStJ, DL Greater London 1970; *Clubs* White's, Pratt's, Royal Yacht Squadron, Royal London Yacht; *Style* - Air Commodore the Hon Sir Peter Vanneck, GBE, CB, AFC, AE, DL, MEP; White Lodge, Waldringfield, Woodbridge, Suffolk (☎ Waldringfield 244); 9 Pensioners Court, Charterhouse, EC1 (☎ 01 250 0555); Moulin de Tressange, Mercœur, 19 Corrèze, France

VANSITTART, Baroness; Sarita Enriqueta; da of late Herbert Ward, of 105 Avenue Malakoff, Paris, and widow of the Rt Hon Sir Colville Adrian de Rune Barclay, KCMG, CB, CBE, MVO; *m* 1931, as his 2 w, 1 and last Baron Vansittart (d 1957); *Style* - The Rt Hon the Lady Vansittart; 8 Hyde Park gdns, W2

VARDY, Peter Christian; s of Mark Vardy; *b* 29 July 1945; *Educ* Charterhouse, King's Coll London; *m* 1974, Anne Maree, da of Patrick Moore; 2 s, 2 da; *Career* CA; chm H Young Holdings Gp 1979-, dir of various cos; *Recreations* philosophy, forestry; *Clubs* East India, Sports & Public Schools; *Style* - Peter Vardy Esq; Rhode Cottage, Selborne, Alton, Hants

VARLEY, Hon Mrs (Elizabeth Susan); *née* Douglas-Scott-Montagu; da of 2 Baron Montagu of Beaulieu, KCIE, CSI (d 1929); *b* 1909; *m* 1962, Col Arthur Noel Claude Varley, CBE; *Style* - The Hon Mrs Varley; By the Mill, Beaulieu, Hants

VARNEY, Lady Mary Bethune; *née* Lindesay-Bethune; da of 14 Earl of Lindsay; *b* 1935; *m* 1956, Capt Owen Buckingham Varney; 2 s, 1 da; *Style* - Lady Mary Varney; Hill House, Dedham, nr Colchester, Essex

VARTAN, John Brian Robertson; s of Dr Ronald Hepworth Vartan; *b* 13 Sept 1937; *Educ* Uppingham Sch, Caius Cambridge; *m* 1963, Frances Margaret, nee Bowser; 2 c; *Career* stockbroker, memb Cncl The Stock Exchange 1976-, chm Provincial Unit of Stock Exchange 1980-, memb Central Exec Cttee NSPCC 1972-81; *Recreations* shooting, fishing, golf, tennis; *Clubs* Inst of Dirs; *Style* - John Vartan Esq; Castor Heights, Castor, Peterborough, Cambs (☎ 073 121 315)

VASSAR-SMITH, John Rathborne; s and h of Sir Richard Vassar-Smith, 3 Bt, TD; *b* 23 July 1936; *Educ* Eton; *m* 1971, Roberta Elaine, da of Wing Cdr N Williamson; 1 s; *Style* - John Vassar-Smith Esq; St Ronan's, Hawkhurst, Kent

VASSAR-SMITH, Sir Richard Rathborne; 3 Bt (UK 1917), of Charlton Park, Charlton Kings, TD (1950); s of late Maj Charles Martin Vassar-Smith (2 s of 1 Bt); suc unc, Sir John George Lawley Vassar-Smith (d 1942); *b* 24 Nov 1909; *Educ* Lancing Coll, Pembroke Coll Cambridge; *m* 1932, Dawn Mary, da of Sir Raymond Wybrow Woods CBE (d 1943); 1 s, 1 da (1 c decd); *Heir* s, John Rathborne Vassar-Smith; *Career* Maj RA 1939-45; Headmaster St Ronan's Prep Sch 1957- (at present a ptnr with son John Rathborne Vassar-Smith), ptnr St Ronan's Prep Sch 1946-57; *Recreations* golf; *Clubs* Hawks (Cambridge), Rye Golf; *Style* - Sir Richard Vassar-Smith, Bt, TD; Orchard House, St Ronan's, Hawkhurst, Kent (☎ Hawkhurst 2300)

VAUGHAN, Lady Auriel (Rosemary Malet); da of 7 Earl of Lisburne (d 1965); *b* 1923; *Style* Style - Lady Auriel Vaughan

VAUGHAN, Hon Digby Dylan; s and h of Viscount Vaughan; *b* 3 Jan 1973; *Style* - The Hon Digby Vaughan

VAUGHAN, Viscount; David John Francis Malet Vaughan; s and h of 8 Earl of Lisburne; *b* 15 June 1945; *Educ* Ampleforth; *m* 1973, Jennifer Jane, da of late James Desiré John William Fraser Campbell, of Glengarry, Inverness-shire; 1 s, 1 da; *Heir* s, Hon Digby Vaughan; *Style* - Viscount Vaughan; The Old Church House, Cross, Isle of Lewis

VAUGHAN, Hon John Edward Malet; s of 8 Earl of Lisburne; *b* 1952; *Educ* Ampleforth; *m* 1977, Catherine Euphan, da of J P Waterer, of Norton Canon, Hereford; *Style* - The Hon John Vaughan

VAUGHAN, Hon Lucy Bronwyn; da of Viscount Vaughan; *b* 1971; *Style* - The Hon Lucy Vaughan

VAUGHAN, Hon Michael John Wilmot Malet; s of 8 Earl of Lisburne; *b* 1948; *Educ* Ampleforth; *m* 1978, Lucinda Mary Louisa, da of Hon John Francis Harcourt Baring, s of 6 Baron Ashburton, KG, KCVO; *Style* - The Hon Michael Vaughan

VAUGHAN, Lady Rose Mary Sydney; *née* Yorke; da of 9 Earl of Hardwicke; *b* 1951; *Educ* St Mary's Convent Ascot; *m* (m dis); resumed maiden name of Yorke; m 2, 1981, Herbert Richard Vaughan (b 25 Dec 1919, publisher); *Style* - Lady Rose Vaughan; Pigeon House Meadow, Grove rd, Beaconsfield, Bucks (☎ 00446 3008)

VAUX OF HARROWDEN, 10 Baron (E 1523); John Hugh Philip Gilbey; s of William Gordon Gilbey (d 1965), and Grace Mary Eleanor, Baroness Vaux of Harrowden (d 1958); suc bro, 9 Baron, 1977; *b* 4 Aug 1915; *Educ* Ampleforth, Ch Ch Oxford; *m* 1939, his 1 cous Maureen Pamela, da of late Hugh Gilbey, of Shellwood Bend, Leigh, Reigate, Surrey; 3 s, 1 da; *Heir* s, Hon Anthony William Gilbey; *Career* formerly Maj, Duke of Wellington's Regt; served War of 1939-45; *Style* - The Rt Hon the Lord Vaux of Harrowden; Cholmondeley Cottage, 2 Cholmondeley Walk, Richmond, Surrey

VAVASOUR, Sir Geoffrey William; 5 Bt (UK 1828), DSC (1943); s of Capt Sir Leonard Pius Vavasour, 4 Bt (d 1961, himself ggs of Hon Sir Edward Vavasour, 1 Bt, né Stourton and 2 surviving s of 17 Baron Stourton, but who changed his name to Vavasour on inheriting the estates of his mother's 1 cous, Sir Thomas Vavasour, 7 & last Bt of the 1628 cr; the 1 Bt of this previous cr was Knight Marshal of the King's Household and ggs through his mother of the 1 Earl of Rutland, while his w Ursula was one of the Giffards of Chillington); *b* 5 Sept 1914; *Educ* RNC Dartmouth; *m* 1, 1940 (m dis 1947), Joan Millicent Kirkland, da of Arthur John Robb; 2 da; m 2, 1971, Marcia Christine, da of Marshall Shaw Lodge, of Batley, Yorks; *Heir* kinsman, Hugh Bernard Moore Vavasour; *Career* dir W M Still & Sons; RN (ret); *Clubs* Hurlingham, MCC, Royal Wimbledon Golf, All England Lawn Tennis; *Style* - Sir Geoffrey Vavasour, Bt, DSC; 8 Bede House, Manor Fields, Putney, SW15 (☎ 01 788 0707)

VAVASOUR, Hugh Bernard Moore; s of Oswald Joseph Stanislaus Vavasour (d 1973, himself n of Sir William Vavasour, 3 Bt), and hp of 2 cous, Sir Geoffrey Vavasour, 5 Bt, DSC; *b* 4 July 1918; *Educ* Stonyhurst; *m* 1952, Monique Pauline Marie Madeleine, da of Maurice Erick Beck, of St Aubin sur Scie, Seine Maritime, France; 1 s, 1 da; *Career* 1939-45 War as Capt RA served UK & S & SE Asia; dep md Blythe Colours Ltd, Pres Blythe-Karel Italy; dir: Colores Blythe SA Spain, Blythe Vidrados de Portugal; *Recreations* golf; *Style* - Hugh Vavasour Esq; Blakeley House, Draycott, Stoke-on-Trent

VEALE, Alan John Ralph; s of Leslie Henry Veale, (d 1971); *b* 2 Feb 1920; *Educ* Exeter School, Manchester College of Technology; *m* 1946, Muriel, da of John William Edwards; 2 c; *Career* CA; dir and gen man AEI Motor & Control Gp 1966-68; man dir GEC Diesels Ltd 1968-70; man dir GEC Power Eng Ltd 1970-; dir GEC 1973-; *Recreations* sailing, walking; *Style* - Alan Veale Esq; Leamington Spa, Warwickshire CV32 6HF (☎ Leamington Spa 24349)

VELISSAROPOULOS, Hon Mrs (Penelope Jane); *née* Allsopp; da of 4 Baron Hindlip (d 1966); *b* 1940; *m* 1965, Theodore D Velissaropoulos; *Style* - The Hon Mrs Velissaropoulos; c/o First National City Bank, Athens 118, Greece

VENABLES-VERNON, Hon Georgina Frances; da of 10 Baron Vernon; *b* 1963; *Style* - The Hon Georgina Venables-Vernon

VENABLES-VERNON, Hon Joanna Elizabeth; da of 10 Baron Vernon; *b* 1965; *Style* - The Hon Joanna Venables-Vernon

VENTRY, 7 Baron (I 1800); Sir Arthur Frederick Daubeney Olav Eveleigh-de-Moleyns; 7 Bt (I 1797); s of 6 Baron Ventry (d 1936); *b* 28 July 1898; *Educ* Wellington Coll; *Heir* n, Andrew Wesley Daubeny de Moleyns; *Career* 1914-18 War as Lt Irish Gds, and RAF (wounded) 1939-45 War as Fl Lt RAFVR, late Hon Air Cdre No 902 (Co London) (Balloon) Squadron AAF; Freedom Medal of Norway; *Style* - The Rt Hon The Lord Ventry; 29 Lindsay rd, Branksome, Dorset

VERDON-SMITH, Sir (William) Reginald; DL (Avon 1974); s of Sir William George Verdon-Smith CBE (d 1957); *b* 5 Nov 1912; *Educ* Repton, BNC Oxford; *m* 1946, Jane Margaret, nee Hobbs; 1 s, 1 da; *Career* kt 1953, dir Lloyds Bank Ltd 1952-, chm Lloyds Bristol Regnl Bd 1977-, dir Lloyds Bank Int 1973-, ptnr George White Evans Tribe & Co Stockbrokers 1952-, Vice Lord Lieutenant of Avon 1980; *Recreations* sailing, golf, travel; *Clubs* Roy Yacht Sqdn, Roy Cruising, Athenaeum, Roy Lymington Yacht; owner yacht 'Dulcimer of Dart'; *Style* - Sir Reginald Verdon-Smith, HM Vice Lord-Lieutenant for Avon; Redcliffe Parade West, Bristol (☎ 0272 292220); Saltings, Bath rd, Lymington, Hants (☎05907 3048)

VERE OF HANWORTH, Lord; Charles Francis Topham de Vere Beauclerk; s of Earl of Burford, *qv*; *b* 22 Feb 1965; *Educ* Eton; *Style* - Lord Vere of Hanworth

VEREY, David Cecil Wynter; s of Rev C H Verey (d 1958); *b* 9 Sept 1913; *Educ* St Aubyn's Rottingdean, Eton, Trin Coll Cambridge; *m* 1939, Rosemary Isabel Baird, da of Lt-Col P Sandilands DSO (d 1956); 2 s, 2 da; *Career* sr investigator Historic Bldgs Miny Housing and Local Govt 1946-65 (ret), chm Alan Sutton Publishing 1979, chm Gloucester Diocesan Advsy Ctee 1967-, High Sheriff Glos 1966; *Recreations* private museum (Arlington Mill, Bibury); *Style* - David Verey Esq; Barnsley House, Barnsley, Cirencester, Glos (☎ Bibury 281)

VERNEY, Hon (Leopold) David; s and h of 20 Baron Willoughby de Broke; *b* 14 Sept 1938; *Educ* Le Rosey, New Coll Oxford; *m* 1965, his kinswoman Petra, 2 da of Col Sir John Aird, 3 Bt, MVO, MC, and Lady Priscilla Heathcote-Drummond-Willoughby (yr da of 2 Earl of Ancaster); 2 s; *Style* - The Hon David Verney; Ditchford Friary, Shipston on Stour, Warwicks

VERNEY, Lt-Cdr David; 2 s of Sir Ralph Verney, 1 Bt, and bro of Sir John Verney, 2 Bt, MC; *b* 31 May 1918; *Educ* Eton; *m* 1948, Hon Mary Boscawen, JP, da of 8 Viscount Falmouth; 1 s, 2 da (including Mrs Peter Bickford-Smith); *Career* High Sheriff Cornwall 1964; served WW II RN (ret); *Style* - Lt-Cdr David Verney, RN; Trevella, St Erme, Truro, Cornwall

VERNEY, Hon Mrs (Dorothy Cecily); *née* Tollemache; da of 3 Baron Tollemache (d 1955); *b* 1907; *m* 1942, Air Cdre Reynell Henry Verney, CBE, RAF (d 1974); *Style* - The Hon Mrs Verney; Stone House, Bishop's Hill, Lighthorne, Warwick

VERNEY, Edmund Ralph; s and h of Sir Ralph Verney, 5 Bt; *b* 28 June 1950; *Educ* Harrow and York U (ARICS); *Clubs* Brooks's; *Style* - Edmund Verney Esq

VERNEY, Sir John; 2 Bt (UK 1946), of Eaton Square, City of Westminster, MC (1944), TD (1970); s of Lt-Col Sir Ralph Verney, 1 Bt, CB, CIE, CVO (d 1959); Sir Ralph's f, Frederick, was 4 s of Sir Harry Verney, 2 Bt, of Claydon (*see* Sir Ralph Bruce Verney, 5 Bt); *b* 30 Sept 1913; *Educ* Eton, Ch Ch Oxford; *m* 1939, Jeanie Lucinda, da of late Maj Herbert Musgrave, DSO, RE; 1 s, 5 da (and 1 s decd); *Heir* s, John Sebastian Verney; *Career* painter, illustrator and author; 1939-45 War as Maj RAC (MC); Légion d'Honneur 1945; *Style* - Sir John Verney, Bt, MC, TD; The White House, Clare, Suffolk (☎ Clare 494)

VERNEY, Janette, Lady; Janette Cheveria Hamilton; da of late Hon J T Walker (Senator 1901-13), of Sydney, NSW; *m* 1909, Lt-Col Sir Ralph Verney, 1 Bt, CB, CIE, CVO (d 1959); 2 s (Sir John V, 2 Bt; David Verney, *qqv*), 1 da (Mrs Andrew Thorne); *Style* - Janette, Lady Verney

VERNEY, John Sebastian; s and h of Sir John Verney, 2 Bt, MC; *b* 30 Aug 1945; *Style* - John Verney Esq

VERNEY, His Hon Judge (Lawrence) John; TD (1955), DL (Bucks 1967); s of younger s of Sir Harry Verney, 4 Bt (d 1974) by his w Lady Rachel Bruce, da of g Earl of Elgin and Kincardine, KG; *b* 19 July 1924; *Educ* Harrow, Oriel Oxford; *m* 1972, Zoë Auriel, da of Lt-Col P G Goodeve-Docker, of Ireland; *Career* Capt Gren Gds 1943-46, Lt-Col Roy Bucks Yeomanry TA 1947-68, Hon Col Bucks Army Cadet Force 1975-80; barr 1952, dep chm Quarter Sessions Bucks 1962-71, Middlesex 1971, Circuit Judge 1972-, Govr Harrow Sch 1972-; *Style* - His Hon Judge Verney, TD, DL; Windmill House, Church Lane, Oving, Aylesbury, Bucks

VERNEY, Hon Mrs (Mary Kathleen); *née* Boscawen; JP (Cornwall 1960); da of 8 Viscount Falmouth; *b* 11 June 1926; *Educ* Heathfield Ascot; *m* 1948, David (*qv*), yr s of Sir Ralph Verney, 1 Bt; 1 s, 2 da; *Style* - The Hon Mrs Verney, JP; Trevella, St Erme, Truro, Cornwall

VERNEY, Sir Ralph Bruce; 5 Bt (UK 1818), of Claydon House, Buckinghamshire, KBE (1974), JP (Bucks 1954); s of Sir Harry Calvert Williams Verney, 4 Bt, DSO (d 1974, whose stepmother was sister of Florence Nightingale, relics of whom may be seen at Claydon; more noteworthy is the rococo plaster work, than which there is arguably no finer in the kingdom) and Lady Rachel Bruce (da of 9 Earl of Elgin and Kincardine, KG); Sir Ralph's ggf, Rt Hon Sir Harry Verney, 2 Bt, PC, DL, sometime MP for Buckingham then Bedford, changed his name from Calvert on inheriting the estates of his 3 cous twice removed, Catherine; the latter had in turn inherited the estates of her half-sis Mary, Lady Fermanagh - Catherine's mother (before espousing Catherine's f Richard Calvert) having been m 1 to the Hon John Verney, s of 1 Earl Verney); *b* 18 Jan 1915; *Educ* Canford, Balliol Oxford (BA); *m* 1948, Mary (LRAM), da of late Percy Charles Vestey (3 s of Sir Edmund Vestey, 1 Bt) and 2 cous of the present Lord Vestey; 1 s, 3 da; *Heir* s, Edmund Ralph

Verney; *Career* Java 1945 as Maj RA, Vice Ld-Lt for Bucks 1965-, High Sheriff 1957, CC 1952-73, Co Alderman 1961-73, Chm Nat Ctee for England of Forestry Cmmn 1968-80, Pres Country Landowners' Assoc 1961-63, member Royal Cmmn on Environmental Pollution 1973-79, Trustee of Radcliffe, Ernest Cook and Chequers Trusts, Chm Nature Conservancy Council 1980-; *Clubs* Brooks's, Cavalry and Guards; *Style* - Sir Ralph Verney, Bt, KBE, JP, HM Vice-Lieut for Bucks; Claydon House, Middle Claydon, Buckingham MK18 2EX (☎ Steeple Claydon 297); Plas Rhôscolyn, Holyhead LL65 2NZ (☎ Trearddur Bay 860288)

VERNEY, Rt Rev Stephen Edmund; MBE (1945); 2 s of Sir Harry Verney, 4 Bt, DSO, by Lady Rachel Bruce (da of 9 Earl of Elgin and Kincardine); *b* 17 April 1919; *Educ* Harrow, Balliol Oxford; *m* 1, 1947, Priscilla (d 1974), da of George Schwerdt, of Alresford; 1 s, 3 da; m 2, 1981, Sandra Bailey, of Llandeilo; *Career* late Lt & Temp Capt Intelligence Corps; Canon St George's Chapel Windsor 1970-77; Suffragan Bp Repton 1977-; *Style* - The Rt Rev Stephen Verney MBE; Repton House, Lea, Matlock, Derbys

VERNEY-CAVE, Hon Ambrose Jordan; s of Cdr 6 Baron Braye; *b* 23 Oct 1906; *Educ* Ampleforth; *Career* former Fl Lt RAF Vol Reserve; *Style* - The Hon Ambrose Verney-Cave; The Cottage, Lodge Park, Aldsworth, Glos

VERNON, 10 Baron (GB 1762); John Lawrance Venables-Vernon; s of 9 Baron (d 1963); *b* 1 Feb 1923; *Educ* Eton, Magdalen Oxford; *m* 1955, Sheila Jean, da of W Marshall Clark, OBE, of Johannesburg, S Africa; 2 da; *Heir* kinsman, Robert Vernon-Harcourt; *Career* 1939-45 War as Capt Scots Gds, barr Lincoln's Inn 1949, served in Cabinet Office 1953-57, Colonial Office Kenya 1957-58, and Foreign Office 1958-60; JP Derbys 1965-77; *Style* - The Rt Hon The Lord Vernon; Sudbury House, Sudbury, Derbyshire DE6 5HT

VERNON, Anthony John; s of John Bloor Vernon; *b* 21 May 1937; *Educ* Abbotsholme Sch Rocester Derbys; *m* 1962, Beatrice Jane, nee Murray; 2 s; *Career* chm and md Murray Vernon Ltd, chm Sandfield Securities Ltd, Leyfos Plastics Ltd, Greenfield Dairies Ltd, dir Castle Dairies (Caerphilly) Ltd, Fastnet Fish Ltd, Govr Ellesmere Coll Salop, Pres Haslington Conservative Association; *Recreations* shooting, sailing; *Clubs* Roy Ocean Racing; *Style* - Anthony Vernon Esq; Haslington Hall, Haslington, Crewe, Ches (☎ 582662)

VERNON, Hon Grant; s of 6 Baron Lyveden; *b* 1952; *Style* - The Hon Grant Vernon

VERNON, John Humphrey; s of the late Major Humphrey Bagnall Vernon, MC; *b* 7 Dec 1940; *Educ* Charterhouse, Madgalen Coll Oxford; *m* 1973, Alison Margaret, nee Watt; 1 da; *Career* exec with Babcock International Ltd 1977-80, md: Dynamo & Electrical Services Ltd, Secundalux Emergency Lighting Ltd, Piranha Ignition Ltd; present dep chm Piranha Ignition Ltd 1980-; *Recreations* fishing, photography; *Style* - John Vernon Esq; Ribblesdale, 23 Priorslee Village, Telford, Shropshire (☎ Telford 615381)

VERNON, Hon Jack Leslie; s and h of 6 Baron Lyveden; *b* 10 Nov 1938; *m* 1961, Lynette June, da of William Herbert Lilley; 1 s, 2 da; *Style* - The Hon Jack Vernon; 17 Carlton st, Te Aroha, New Zealand

VERNON, James Loudon; s of Capt Reginald Thornycroft Vernon RFC (d 1977); *b* 27 Oct 1940; *Educ* Eton, Trin Coll Dublin; *m* 1971, Elspeth Mary Stewart, da of Rev Cyril R Thomson; 2 s, 2 da; *Career* dir Constantine Holdings Ltd 1977, underwriting memb Lloyd's 1980, memb Baltic Exchange 1966, liveryman Skinners' Co 1977; *Recreations* sailing, shooting; *Clubs* Roy Yacht Sqdn, RAC, Roy St George; owner of yacht 'Minx'; *Style* - James Vernon Esq; 45 Egerton Cresc, Brompton, SW3 (☎ 589 0858)

VERNON, James William; s and h of Sir Nigel Vernon, 4 Bt; *b* 2 April 1949; *Educ* Shrewsbury; *m* 1981, Davina, da of Christopher David Howard, of Ryton

Corner, Ryton, Shrewsbury; *Career* FCA; *Style* - James Vernon Esq

VERNON, Sir Nigel John Douglas; 4 Bt (UK 1914), of Shotwick Park, Co Chester; s of Sir (William) Norman Vernon, 3 Bt (d 1967); *b* 2 May 1924; *Educ* Charterhouse; *m* 1947, Margaret Ellen, da of late Robert Lyle Dobell, of The Mount, Waverton, Chester; 2 s, 1 da; *Heir* s, James William Vernon; *Career* Lt RNVR 1942-45, dir Robert Barron (Insurance Services) Ltd 1977-, dir Travel Finance Ltd 1971-; *Recreations* gardening, shooting, golf; *Clubs* Naval; *Style* - Sir Nigel Vernon Bt; Top-y-Fron Hall, Kelsterton, nr Flint, Clwyd

VERNON, Hon Robert Howard; s of 6 Baron Lyveden; *b* 1942; *m* 1968, Louise Smith; 1 s; *Style* - The Hon Robert Vernon

VERNON, Hon Mrs; Hon Victoria; *née* Arthur; da of 3 Baron Glenarthur, OBE, DL, by his 2 w; *b* 20 June 1946; *m* 1976, Hugh Vernon, 2 s of Mervyn Vernon, MVO (2 s of Rupert Vernon, DSO, JP, 5 s of Hon Greville Vernon, JP, DL, sometime MP Ayrshire and 4 s of 1 Baron Lyveden), by his w, Lady Violet Baring, yr da of 2 Earl of Cromer; *Style* - The Hon Mrs Vernon; Rodinghead Cottage, Mauchline, Ayrshire

VERNON-HARCOURT, Robert; s of late Simon Evelyn Vernon-Harcourt (himself ggs of Most Rev & Hon Edward Vernon-Venables, DD, sometime Archbp of York and in his turn s of 1 Baron Vernon by his 3 w Martha, who was sis of 1 Earl of Harcourt); hp of 4 cous twice removed, 10 Baron Vernon; *b* 26 Dec 1918; *Educ* Marlborough, Ch Ch Oxford (MA); *m* 1948, Sylvia Jeanette, da of late Lt-Col Charles Henry Kitching, DSO; *Career* 1939-45 War as Capt RTR; *Style* - Robert Vernon-Harcourt Esq; Theydon Mount, Epping, Essex

VERTUE, Beryl Frances; *née* Johnson; da of Frank Edward Johnson (d 1973); *b* 8 April 1931; *Educ* Mitcham County Sch for Girls; *m* 1951, Clement George Vertue; 2 da; *Career* film/TV producer; co-dep chm Robert Stigwood Group; *Clubs* Landsdowne, White Elephant, Burke's; *Style* - Mrs George Vertue; Hartswood Manor, Doversgreen rd, Reigate, Surrey (☎ Reigate 44227)

VERULAM, 7 Earl of (UK 1815); Sir John Duncan Grimston; 14 Bt (E 1629); also Lord Forrester (S 1633), Baron Dunboyne and Viscount Grimston (I 1719), Baron Verulam (GB 1790), Viscount Grimston (UK 1815); s of 6 Earl of Verulam (d 1973); *b* 21 April 1951; *Educ* Eton, Ch Ch Oxford; *m* 1976, Dione Angela, da of Jeremy Smith, of Balcombe House, Balcombe, Sussex; 2 s; *Heir* s, Viscount Grimston; *Career* engrg cos dir; a patron of six livings; *Recreations* marbles; *Clubs* Beefsteak, White's, Turf; *Style* - The Rt Hon the Earl of Verulam; Gorhambury, St Albans, Herts AL3 6AH (☎ St Albans 55000)

VERULAM, Dowager Countess of; Marjorie Ray; da of late Walter Atholl Duncan; *m* 1938, 6 Earl of Verulam (d 1973); *Style* - The Rt Hon the Dowager Countess of Verulam; Pré Mill House, Redbourn rd, St Albans, Herts

VESEY, Hon Catherine Anne; da of 6 Viscount de Vesci; *b* 1953; *Style* - The Hon Catherine Vesey

VESEY, Hon Emma Francis; da of 6 Viscount de Vesci; *b* 1951; *Style* - The Hon Emma Vesey

VESEY, Hon Thomas Eustace; s and h of 6 Viscount de Vesci; *b* 8 Oct 1955; *Educ* Oxford U; *Style* - The Hon Thomas Vesey

VESTEY, 3 Baron (UK 1922); Sir Samuel George Armstrong Vestey; 3 Bt (UK 1913); s of late Capt the Hon William Howarth Vestey (ka Italy 1944, only s of 2 Baron Vestey); suc gf 1954; *b* 19 March 1941; *Educ* Eton; *m* 1970, Kathryn Mary, da of John Eccles, of Moor Park, Herts; 2 da; *Heir* bro, Hon Mark William Vestey; *Career* Lt Scots Gds, dir Union Int Co Ltd and associated cos, Pres London Meat Trade and Drovers Benevolent Assoc 1973, Inst of Meat 1978-, Glos Assoc of Boys' Clubs, County Pres St John Ambulance Bde (Glos), Liveryman Butchers' Co; patron of one living; *Clubs* White's, Jockey (Newmarket), Melbourne (Melbourne);

Style - The Rt Hon the Lord Vestey; Stowell Park, Northleach, Glos

VESTEY, Sir (John) Derek; 2 Bt (UK 1921); s of late John Joseph Vestey (eldest s of Sir Edmund Vestey, 1 Bt, the latter being bro of 1 Baron Vestey); suc gf 1953 & is 2 cous of Lord Vestey; *b* 4 June 1914; *Educ* Leys Sch Cambridge; *m* 1938, Phyllis Irene, da of H Brewer, of Banstead; 1 s, 1 da; *Heir* s, Paul Edmund Vestey; *Career* Fl Lt RAFVR 1940-45; *Clubs* MCC, Farmers', Royal Automobile; *Style* - Sir Derek Vestey, Bt; 5 Carlton gdns, SW1 (☎ 01 930 1610); Harcombe House, Ropley, Hants (☎ Ropley 2394)

VESTEY, Hon Flora Grace; da of 3 Baron Vestey; *b* 1978; *Style* - The Hon Flora Vestey

VESTEY, Hon Mark William; s of Capt the Hon William Howarth Vestey (ka 1944), and hp of bro, 3 Baron Vestey; *b* 16 April 1943; *Educ* Eton; *m* 1975, Rose Amelia, da of Lt-Col Peter Thomas Clifton, DSO; 1 s, 1 da; *Career* 2 Lt Scots Gds; raised to rank of a Baron's younger son 1955; *Style* - The Hon Mark Vestey; 20 Eaton Mews S, SW1 (☎ 01 235 8932); Stowell Park, Glos

VESTEY, Paul Edmund; s and h of Sir (John) Derek Vestey, 2 Bt; *b* 15 Feb 1944; *Educ* Radley; *m* 1971, Victoria Anne Scudamore, da of John Salter, of Old Ford House, Tiverton, Devon; 3 da; *Clubs* British Racing Drivers; *Style* - Paul Vestey Esq; 53 Cheval Place, SW7 (☎ 01 589 0562); Manor House Farm, Bishops Sutton, Hants

VESTEY, Pamela, Baroness; (Helen) Pamela Fullerton (Melba); da of late George Nesbitt Armstrong; *m* 1939, Capt the Hon William Howarth Vestey, Scots Gds (ka 1944, eld s of 2 Baron Vestey); raised to the rank of a Baron's widow 1955; *Style* - The Rt Hon Pamela, Lady Vestey; Coombe Cottage, Coldstream, Victoria, Australia

VESTEY, Ronald Arthur; DL (1970); s of Sir Edmund Hoyle Vestey, 1 Bt (d 1953); *b* 10 May 1898; *Educ* Malvern; *m* 1923, Florence Ellen McLean (d 1966), da of late Col T G Luis; 1 s, 3 da; *Career* landowner, company director, High Sheriff Suffolk 1961; *Recreations* shooting, fishing; *Clubs* Carlton, MCC; *Style* - Ronald Vestey Esq, DL; Great Thurlow Hall, Great Thurlow, Suffolk

VESTEY, Hon Saffron Alexandra; da of 3 Baron Vestey; *b* 1971; *Style* - The Hon Saffron Vestey

VICARS-HARRIS, Noël Hedley; CMG (1953); s of Charles Frederick Harris (d 1953); *b* 22 Nov 1901; *Educ* Charterhouse, St John's Coll Cambridge; *m* 1, 1926, Maria Guimaraes (m dis 1939); 2 s; m 2, 1940, Joan M, da of Col C A Francis (d 1924); 1 s; *Career* Colonial Serv 1927-55, assist dir Tsetse Research 1930-36, sec Lands and Mines 1937-45, dir of Establishments 1946-50, memb Lands and Mines Tanganyika 1950-55; *Recreations* gardening; *Style* - Noël Vicars-Harris Esq, CMG; Bampfylde Cottage, Sparkford, Yeovil (☎ 0963 40454)

VICK, Sir (Francis) Arthur; OBE (1945); s of Wallace Devenport Vick (d 1952); *b* 5 June 1911; *Educ* Birmingham U; *m* 1943, Elizabeth Dorothy, nee Story; 1 da; *Career* kt 1973; physicist; assist dir Scientific Res Miny of Supply 1939-44, lecturer & sr lecturer Manchester U 1944-50, Physics Prof Univ Coll N Staffs (now Keele U) 1950-59, memb for research UKAEA 1964-66 (former dir); Pres & V-Chllr Queen's U Belfast 1966-76, Pro-Chllr & Ch of Cncl Warwick U 1977-; *Recreations* music, gardening, DIY; *Clubs* Athenaeum, Savile; *Style* - Sir Arthur Vick OBE; Fieldhead Cottage, Fieldhead Lane, Myton rd, Warwick (☎ 0926 41822)

VICK, Arnold Oughtred Russell; QC (1980); s of His Hon Judge Sir Godfrey Russell Vick, QC, of Seal, Kent; *b* 14 Sept 1933; *Educ* The Leys School, Jesus Coll Camb (MA); *m* 1959, Zinnia Mary, nee Yates; 2 s, 1 da; *Career* barrister, a Recorder of the Crown Court 1972-; *Recreations* golf, cricket and bridge; *Clubs* MCC, Hawks (Cambridge), Wildernesse G C; *Style* - Arnold Vick Esq, QC; 2 Harcourt Buildings, Temple, EC4 (☎ 01 353 4746)

VICKERS, Baroness (Life Peeress UK 1974); Joan Helen Vickers; DBE (1964, MBE 1946); da of late Horace Cecil

Vickers; *b* 1907; *Educ* St Monica's Coll Burgh Heath Surrey; *Career* BRCS in SE Asia (MBE), memb LCC 1937-45, with Colonial Office 1946-50, Chm Anglo-Indonesian Soc 1958-; Pres Int Ctee for Suppression of Traffic in Persons, Inst of Qualified Private Secretaries 1969-, Int Friendship League 1972-, Status of Women Ctee, Europe China Assoc; chm: London Centre for Homeless Young Persons 1977-, MP (C) Devonport 1955-74; Netherlands Red Cross Medal 1946, and Polish Medal 1972; *Style* - The Rt Hon The Lady Vickers; The Manor House, East Chisenbury, Pewsey, Wilts

VICKERS, Angus Douglas; TD; s of Douglas Vickers (d 1937); *b* 15 Feb 1904; *Educ* Eton, Magdalen Coll Oxford; *m* 1937, Phyllis Maud, da of Norton Francis CMG (d 1939); *Career* Feudal Baron of Tulloch; underwriter Lloyd's, member Roy Co of Archers (Queen's Bodyguard for Scotland), JP (1946-68) & DL (1950-68) Ross and Cromarty, Hon Sheriff Substitute Inverness, Moray, Nairn, Ross and Cromarty from 1949-; *Recreations* photography; *Clubs* New (Edinburgh); *Style* - Angus Vickers Esq, TD; Casa Sta Catarina, Parque Da Praia, Luz-8600 Lagos, Algarve, Portugal (☎ Portimao 62660)

VICKERS, Hugo Ralph; s of Ralph Cecil Vickers; *b* 12 Nov 1951; *Educ* Eton, Strasbourg U; *Career* author; worked with London Celebrations Committee for Queen's Silver Jubilee 1977, administrator Great Children's Pty 1979; Books: *We Want the Queen* (1977), *Gladys, Duchess of Marlborough* (1979), *Debrett's Book of The Royal Wedding* (1981); reviewer, broadcaster; *Recreations* reading, music, travel; *Style* - Hugo Vickers Esq; 62 Lexham Gardens, W8

VICKERS, Thomas Douglas; CMG (1956); *b* 25 Sept 1916; *Educ* Eton, King's Cambridge; *m* 1951, Margaret Headley; 1 s, 1 da; *Career* HM Overseas Civil Serv 1938-40 & 1945-68, Colonial Sec British Honduras 1953-60, Chief Sec Mauritius 1960-67, Dep Govr Mauritius 1968, Head of Personnel Servs Imp Cancer Res Fund 1969-81; *Clubs* Army & Navy; *Style* - Thomas Vickers Esq, CMG; Wood End, Worplesdon, Surrey (☎ Worplesdon 233468)

VILLIERS, Sir Charles Hyde; MC (1945); s of Algernon Hyde Villiers (ka 1917); *b* 14 Aug 1912; *Educ* Eton, New Coll Oxford; *m* 1946, Marie José, da of Count Henri de la Barre d'Erquelinnes, of Belgium (d 1961); 1 s, 2 da; *Career* kt 1975; chm BSC (Industry) Ltd 1976-, chm Br Steel Corpn 1976-80, chm Guinness Mahon & Co 1971-76, md Industrial Reorganisation Corpn 1967-71, md Helbert Wagg (Schroder Wagg) 1947-67, Glyn Mills & Co Bankers 1931-46; *Recreations* gardening; *Clubs* Anglo Belgian; *Style* - Sir Charles Villiers MC; Blacknest House, Sunninghill, Berks (☎ Ascot 22137)

VILLIERS, Viscount; George Henry Child-Villiers; s and h of 9 Earl of Jersey; *b* 29 Aug 1948; *Educ* Eton, Millfield; *m* 1, 1969 (m dis 1973), Verna, da of K A Stott, of St Mary, Jersey; 1 da (Hon Sophia b 1971); m 2, 1974, Sacha Jane Hooper, da of Peter Hooper Valpy, and formerly wife of K F Lauder; 1 s (Hon George b 1976), 2 da (Hon Helen b 1978, Hon Luciana b 1981); *Career* late 2 Lt 11 Hussars and the Roy Hussars; *Clubs* Brooks's, Royal Automobile; *Style* - Viscount Villiers; Bel Respiro, Mont au Prêtre, St Helier, Jersey, CI

VILLIERS, Sir (John) Michael; KCB (1962, CB 1960), OBE (1943); s of Rear-Adm E C Villiers CMG (d 1939); *b* 22 June 1907; *Educ* Oundle; *m* 1936, Rosemary, da of Lt-Col B S Grissell DSO (ka 1917); 2 da; *Career* served RN, cmd HMS Bulwark 1954-57, Ch of Naval Staff New Zealand 1958-60, Vice-Adm 4 Sea Lord 1960-63, Lt-Govr & C-in-C Jersey 1964-69; *Clubs* Army and Navy; *Style* - Sir Michael Villiers KCB OBE; Decoy House, Melton, Woodbridge, Suffolk

VILLIERS, Hon (William) Nicholas Somers Laurence Hyde; JP (Hants); s of late 6 Earl of Clarendon; *b* 1916; *Educ* Eton, New Coll Oxford; *m* 1939, Mary Cecilia Georgina, da of Maj the Hon Edric Weld-Forester, CVO (6 s of 5 Baron Forester); 3 da; *Career* Maj Grenadier Gds (Supp Res), served 1937-47 Middle

East, N Africa, Italy ; OStJ; memb Lloyd's; dir & sec Anderson Finch Villiers (Agencies) Ltd; *Recreations* all field sports, cricket, golf; *Clubs* White's; *Style* - Maj The Hon Nicholas Villiers, JP; Firs Farm, Milbourne, Malmesbury, Wilts

VILLIERS, Lady Sarah Katherine; da of 7 Earl of Clarendon; *b* 1977; *Style* - Lady Sarah Villiers

VINCENT, Edward Mark William; s and h of Sir William Vincent, 3 Bt; *b* 6 March 1978; *Style* - Edward Vincent

VINCENT, Helen, Lady; Helen Millicent; da of Field Marshal Sir William Robertson, 1 Bt, GCB, GCMG, GCVO, DSO; sis of 1 Baron Robertson of Oakridge, GCB, GBE, KCMG, KCVO, DSO, MC; *b* 17 Dec 1905; *m* 1938, Sir Lacey Vincent, 2 Bt (d 1963); 1 s (Sir William Vincent, 3 Bt), 1 da; *Style* - Helen, Lady Vincent; 17 Eresby House, Rutland Gate, SW7 (☎ 01 589 4217)

VINCENT, John Anthony; s of Frederick John Vincent (d 1957); *b* 28 Sept 1936; *Educ* Wandsworth Technical G S, Hammersmith Coll of Building; *m* 1956, Frances Ruth, nee Protopapa; 3 da; *Career* sales & marketing director Hy-Ten Reinforcement Co Ltd 1974-; sales man Pioneer Concrete Ltd 1967-74; chief buyer Pitchers Ltd (Contractors) 1962-67; *Recreations* swimming, riding; *Clubs* The Lighthouse and The Eccentric; *Style* - John Vincent Esq; Silverdell, Golf Drive, Camberley, Surrey

VINCENT, Paul Howard; s of Stanley Howard Vincent (d 1975); *b* 9 April 1924; *Educ* Bishop's Stortford Coll, St John's Cambridge; *m* 1957, Jean, nee Ford; 1 s, 2 da; *Career* dir: Vincents of Yeovil Ltd, Vincent Fin Co (Yeovil) Ltd, Binding and Payne Ltd, H and E Services Ltd, Bridgewater Motor Co Ltd, Yeovil Sheet Metal Co Ltd, C B Morgan (Shaftesbury) Ltd; *Style* - Paul Vincent Esq; Watermeadows, Turners Barn Lane, Yeovil, Somerset (☎ 23201)

VINCENT, Sir William Percy Maxwell; 3 Bt (UK 1936); s of Sir Lacey Vincent, 2 Bt (d 1963), and Helen, Lady Vincent, *qv*; *b* 1 Feb 1945; *Educ* Eton, New York Institute of Finance; *m* 1976, Christine, da of Rev Edward Walton, of Hendon; 2 s; *Heir* s, Edward Vincent; *Career* late 2 Lt Irish Gds, served Malaya; dir Save & Prosper Investment Tst 1980-; *Recreations* sailing (yacht: Westerly GK 29 'Got Knotted'), skiing; *Clubs* Household Division Yacht, Chichester Cruiser Racing; *Style* - Sir William Vincent, Bt; Whistlers, Buriton, Petersfield, Hants (☎ 0730 3532)

VINER, Ruben; OBE; s of Adolf Viner (d 1953); *b* 21 Aug 1907; *Educ* King Edward VII Sheffield; *m* 1932, Elaine Rhoda, nee Aubrey; 2 children; *Career* pres Viners Ltd, pres and treasurer Sheffield Chamber of Commerce 1965-, pres Sheffield Sheffield Cutlery Mfrs' Assoc 1958-61, freeman Cutlers' Co, Guardian of the Assay, underwriting member of Lloyd's, chm Talbot Trusts; *Recreations* sailing, gardening, walking; *Clubs* Constitutional, Sheffield; *Style* - Ruben Viner Esq, OBE; 4 Ivy Park Ct, Ivy Park rd, Sheffield, S10 3LA (☎ home 306036; work 21391)

VINEY, Hon Mrs (Anne Margaret); *née* Morton; da of Baron Morton of Henryton (Life Peer) (d 1973); *b* 1926; *m* 1947, Peter Andrew Hopwood Viney, DFC; 1 s, 2 da; *Style* - The Hon Mrs Viney; 4 Lansdowne rd, W11 (☎ 01 727 4884); Worth House, Worth Matravers, Dorset

VINEY, Elliott Merriam; DSO (1945), MBE (1946), TD, DL (Bucks 1952); s of Col Oscar Viney, of Green End House, Aylesbury, (d 1976); *b* 21 August 1913; *Educ* Oundle, Univ Coll Oxford (MA); *m* 1950, Rosamund Ann, da of the late E P L Pelly; 2 da; *Career* dir Hazell Watson & Viney, Printers 1947-78 & British Printing Corpn 1964-75 Pres British Fed Master Printers 1972-3, Master Grocers' Co 1970-71, High Sheriff 1964; *Style* - Elliott Viney Esq DSO MBE TD DL; Cross Farmhouse, Quainton, Aylesbury, Bucks (☎ Quainton 537)

VIVIAN, 5 Baron (UK 1841); Sir Anthony Crespigny Claud Vivian; 5 Bt (UK 1828); s of 4 Baron Vivian, DSO (d

1940); *b* 4 March 1906; *Educ* Eton; *m* 1930, Victoria, da of late Capt Henry Gerard Laurence Oliphant, DSO, MVO, RN; 2 s, 1 da; *Heir* s, Hon Nicholas Crespigny Laurence Vivian; *Career* European War 1939-40 in RA; Special Constabulary and War Correspondent; *Style* - The Rt Hon The Lord Vivian; 154 Coleherne Court, SW5; Boskenna Ros, St Buryan, nr Penzance, Cornwall

VIVIAN, Hon Amanda Ursula Georgina; da of 4 Baron Swansea; *b* 1958; *Style* - The Hon Amanda Vivian

VIVIAN, Hon Mrs Douglas - Mary Alice; da of late Francis John Gordon Borthwick; *m* 1943, Lt-Cdr the Hon Douglas David Edward Vivian, DSC, RN (d 1973, s of late 4 Baron Vivian); *Style* - The Hon Mrs Douglas Vivian; Monastery Garden, Edington, Westbury, Wilts

VIVIAN, Hon Louisa Caroline Sarah; da of 4 Baron Swansea; *b* 1963; *Style* - The Hon Louisa Vivian

VIVIAN, Hon Nicholas Crespigny Laurence; s and h of 5 Baron Vivian; *b* 11 Dec 1935; *Educ* Eton, Madrid U; *m* 1, 1960 (m dis 1972), Catherine Joyce, da of James Kenneth Hope, CBE, DL; 1 s, 1 da; m 2, 1972, Carol, da of F Alan Martineau, MBE, JP, of Valley End House, Chobham, Surrey; 1 s, 1 da; *Career* Lt-Col 16/5 The Queen's Royal Lancers; *Clubs* Cavalry and Guards'; *Style* - The Hon Nicholas Vivian; 5 Edith ter, SW10

VIVIAN, Hon Richard Anthony Hussey; s and h of 4 Baron Swansea; *b* 24 Jan 1957; *Style* - The Hon Richard Vivian

VIVIAN, Hon Victor Anthony Brabazon Ralph; s of 5 Baron Vivian; *b* 1940; *m* 1966, Inger Johanne, da of Advokat Per Gulliksen, of Sandeford, Norway; 1 s, 1 da; *Career* late Merchant Navy; *Style* - The Hon Victor Vivian; 43 Frewin rd, SW18

VON BÜLTZINGSLÖWEN, Baroness Fritz; Hon Elizabeth Alexandra Sophia; *née* Waldegrave; 3 da of 5 and last Baron Radstock (ggs of Hon Sir William Waldegrave, GCB, Adm of the Red and 2 s of 3 Earl Waldegrave, cr Baron Radstock 1800); *b* 22 Sept 1902; *m* 1940, Baron Fritz von Bültzingslöwen (d 1943), Maj 7 Cuirassiers and son of Wulff von Bültzingslöwen; 1 s; *Style* - Baroness Fritz von Bültzingslöwen; 9494 Planken, Liechtenstein

VON BEBENBURG, Baroness Margaret; da of Baron Hans Karg von Bebenburg, s of Baron Georg von Bebenburg, and Hon Vivien (d 1980), da of 2 Viscount Ridley, JP, DL, by Hon Rosamond Guest, DBE, 4 da of 1 Baron Wimborne; *b* 1 June 1937; *Style* - Baroness Margaret von Bebenburg; 10 Habsburgergasse, Wien, Austria

VON BERGEN, Hon Mrs; Hon Sheila; da of Baron Thomas, DFC (Life Peer d 1980); *b* 1925; *m* 1948, Julian von Bergen; *Style* - The Hon Mrs von Bergen; Ellicombe, Minehead, Som

VON HOYNINGEN-HUENE, Baroness Nancy; *née* Oakes; da of Sir Harry Oakes, 1 Bt; *b* 17 May 1925; *m* 1, 1942 (m annulled 1949), Marie-Alfred Fouquerreaux de Marigny, of Mauritius; m 2, 1952 (m dis 1961), Baron Ernst von Hoyningen-Huene, 2 s of Baron Hermann von Hoyningen-Huene, of Munich; 1 s (Baron Alexander George Lyssardt, b 17 Feb 1955); m 3, 1962 (m dis), Patrick Tritton, *qv*; resumed surname of 2 husb; *Style* - Baroness Nancy von Hoyningen-Huene; Marsella 44, Colonìa Juaroz, Mexico 6, D F Mexico

VON PREUSSEN, Princess Nicholas - Hon Victoria Lucinda; *née* Mancroft; da of 2 Baron Mancroft, KBE, TD; *b* 1952; *m* 1980, HRH Prince (Frederick) Nicholas von Preussen; 1 da; *Style* - Princess Nicholas von Preussen; Patmore Hall, Hadham, Herts

VON VERSERGH, Hon Mrs (Pelline Margot); *née* Lyon-Dalberg-Acton; da of 3 Baron Acton, CMG, MBE, TD, and Hon Daphne Strutt, da of 4 Baron Rayleigh; *b* 24 Dec 1932; *m* 1953, Laszlo de Marffy von Versergh; 6 s, 1 da; *Style* - The Hon Mrs von Versegh; Ealing Farm, PO Box 29, Umvukwes, Zimbabwe

VON WESTENHOLZ, Lady Mary (Marianella Anne); *née* Kerr; da of 12 Marquess of Lothian; *b* 1944; *m* 1970, Charles von Westenholz; 3 s; *Style* - Lady Mary von Westenholz; Little Blakesware, Widford, Ware, Herts

VON WESTENHOLZ, Piers Patrick Frederick; s of Baron Henry Frederick Everard von Westenholz, of Crackney, Widford, Herts; *b* 10 Dec 1943; *Educ* Downside; *m* 1, 1964 (m dis 1969), Sarah, da of Raimund von Hofmannstahl (s of the poet Hugo von Hofmannstahl) by his 2 w, Lady Elizabeth Paget (da of 6 Marquess of Anglesey, GCVO); m 2, 1979, Jane, da of Arthur Leveson, of Hall Place, Ropley, Hants; 1 s; *Career* antique dealer and decorator; *Recreations* shooting, fishing, skiing; *Clubs* Turf; *Style* - Piers von Westenholz Esq; Letterellan, by Aberfeldy, Perthshire (☎ Kenmore 221); Barrow Farm, Widford, Herts (☎ 027 984 2146)

VYNER, Lady Doris Hilda; *née* Gordon-Lennox; da of 8 Duke of Richmond and (3 of) Gordon, DSO, MVO; *b* 6 Sept 1896; *m* 1923, Lt-Cdr Clare George Vyner, DL, RN (s of Lord Alwyne Compton, DSO, MP, DL, 3 s of 4 Marquess of Northampton, by Lord Alwyne's w Mary, da of Robert Vyner, DL, of Gautby Hall, Lincs, and Newby Hall, W Yorks), who assumed the surname Vyner by Roy Licence; 1 s (and 1 s, 1 da decd); *Style* - Lady Doris Vyner; Fountains Hall, Ripon, Yorks

VYVYAN, Sir John Stanley; 12 Bt (E 1645); s of late Maj-Gen Ralph Ernest Vyvyan, CBE, MC (himself only s of late Capt Herbert Reginald Vyvyan, OBE, who was in turn 2 s of Rev Herbert Francis Vyvyan, while the Rev Herbert was 3 s of Rev Vyell Francis Vyvyan, the latter being 2 s of Sir Vyell Vyvyan, 7 Bt); suc cous Sir Richard Philip Vyvyan, 11 Bt, 1978; *b* 20 Jan 1916; *Educ* Charterhouse, London Sch of Oriental Studies; *m* 1, 1940 (m dis 1946), Joyce Lilia, da of late Frederick Marsh, of Kailan Mining Admin, Peking; 1 da; m 2 1948 (m dis 1958), Marie, da of late Dr O'Shea, of Hamilton, Ont; m 3, 1958, Jonet Noël, da of Lt-Col Alexander Hubert Barclay, DSO, MC; 1 s, 1 da; *Heir* s, Ralph Ferrers Alexander Vyvyan; *Career* 1939-45 War as Maj Roy Signals, in India and Arakan; owner and manager of Trelowarren Estate 1950-; *Clubs* Army and Navy, Royal Cornwall Yacht (Falmouth); *Style* - Sir John Vyvyan, Bt; Trelowarren, Mawgan, Helston, Cornwall (☎ Mawgan 224)

VYVYAN, Ralph Ferrers Alexander; s and h of Sir John Vyvyan, 12 Bt; *b* 21 Aug 1960; *Style* - Ralph Vyvyan Esq

W

WÄBER, Hon Mrs; Hon Jill; da of Baron Taylor of Gryfe (Life Peer); *b* 1945; *m* 1, 1969, Dr Thomas Egli; m 2, 1976, Hans Wäber; *Style* - The Hon Mrs Wäber; Herzbodenweg 80, Basel 4052, Switzerland

WADDS, Her Excellency Mrs Jean Casselman; da of Hon Earl Rowe and Treva Rowe; *b* 16 Sept 1920; *Educ* Toronto U, Weller Business Coll; *m* 1, 1946, Clair Casselman; 1 s, 1 da; m 2, 1964 (m dis 1977), Robert Wadds; *Career* Canadian High Commissioner to UK 1980-; Freedom City of London 1981; MP Canada 1958-68, Parly Sec Min Health & Welfare 1962, Nat Sec Progressive Con Pty 1970-75; *Style* - HE Mrs Jean Casselman Wadds; 1 Grosvenor sq, London W1 (☎ 01 629 9492) (office); 12 Upper Brook st, London W1

WADE, Baron (Life Peer UK 1964); Donald William Wade; DL (N Yorks 1974); s of William Wade, of Ilkley; *b* 16 June 1904; *Educ* Mill Hill and Trinity Hall Cambridge; *m* 1932, Ellenora Beatrice, da of F H Bentham, of Bradford; 2 s, 2 da; *Career* solicitor 1929; MP (Lib) Huddersfield West 1950-64, Lib Whip 1956-62, Dep Leader Liberal Party 1962-64; Dep Lib Whip House of Lords 1965-67 Pres Lib Pty 1967-68; *Style* - The Rt Hon The Lord Wade, DL; High Houses

Wath-in-Nidderdale, Pateley Bridge, Yorks

WADE, Maj-Gen (Douglas) Ashton (Lofft); CB (1945), OBE (1940), MC (1918); s of the late C S D Wade; *b* 13 March 1898; *Educ* St Lawrence Coll, RMA Woolwich, Clare Coll Cambridge; *m* 1, 1926, Heather, nee Bulmer; 1 da; m 2, 1972, Cynthia, nee Allen; *Career* commissioned RA 1916; served 1914-18 War France and Italy, 1919 South Russia; 1939-45 France, 1948 Malaya; British Member of Indian Armed Forces Nationalisation Committee 1947, Special Appointments War Office 1948-50, ret 1950; Telecommunications Attaché Br Embassy Washington DC 1951-54, ITA 1954-64, HQ WRVS 1970-75, chm SE Forum for Closed Circuit TV in Higher Education 1967-73; National Chm Dunkirk Veterans Assoc 1967-74, v-chm 1962-67, v-pres 1962-; *Recreations* gardening, writing; *Style* - Maj-Gen Ashton Wade, CB, OBE, MC; Phoenix Cottage, 6 Church Street, Old Catton, Norwich (☎ 0603 45755)

WADE, Charles Gordon Campbell; OBE (1947), DL (1957); s of Arthur Campbell Wade (d 1933); *b* 25 Sept 1900; *Educ* Wellington Coll; *m* 1932, Katherine Emily, nee Watson; 2 s; *Career* Brig 1944 (India, NW Europe, Italy, SEAC), Royal Fusiliers Staff 1922-52; *Recreations* skiing, hunting, charitable work; *Clubs* Army and Navy; *Style* - Charles Wade Esq, OBE, DL; Matching Green, Harlow, Essex

WADE, Derwent Malcolm Mercer; s of Roland Henry Wade, CBE, JP; *b* 26 June 1939; *Educ* Marlborough, Selwyn Coll Cambridge; *m* 1967, Rosemary, nee Whiteley; 1 s, 1 da; *Career* slr 1965, dir Wades Departmental Stores Ltd 1972-80, BNL Holdings 1979, FTL Co Ltd 1974; *Recreations* hunting; *Clubs* Leeds; *Style* - Derwent Wade Esq; Walnut Cottage, Gt Ouseburn, York (☎ Green Hammerton 30487)

WADE, Hon Donald William Mercer; s of Baron Wade, DL; *b* 1941; *Educ* Silcoates Sch, Trin Hall Cambridge; *Style* - The Hon Donald Wade; 18 Pinewood Grove, W5

WADE, Hon Robert Alexander Mercer; s of Baron Wade, DL; *b* 1943; *Educ* Mill Hill, Trin Cambridge; *m* 1, 1967, Jennifer, da of Leslie Elliott, of Grantley Grange, Ripon; m 2, 1978, Elizabeth, da of James Lobban, of Dundee; *Career* slr 1968; *Style* - The Hon Robert Wade; The Old Rectory, Barwick-in-Elmet, Leeds, W Yorks

WAECHTER, Sir (Harry Leonard) d'Arcy; 2 Bt (UK 1911), of Ramsnest, Chiddingfold, Surrey; s of Sir Harry Waechter, 1 Bt, CMG (d 1929); *b* 22 May 1912; *Educ* Nautical Coll Pangbourne; *m* 1939, Philippa Margaret (m dis 1957), da of James Twinberrow; *Career* Lt E Yorks Regt 1930-35, Lt RASC 1942, Capt Worcs Regt (TA) 1947, Capt TA Res of Offrs 1948; *Style* - Sir D'Arcy Waechter, Bt

WAGNER, Sir Anthony Richard; KCB (1978), KCVO (1961); s of Orlando Wagner; *b* 6 Sept 1908; *Educ* Eton, Balliol Oxford; *m* 1953, Gillian, OBE, da of Maj Henry Graham; 2 s, 1 da; *Career* Garter King of Arms 1961-78, ed *Dictionary of British Arms* 1940-, Clarenceux King of Arms & Dir Heralds' Museum Tower of London 1978-, Jt Register Ct of Chivalry 1954-; *Style* - Sir Anthony Wagner, KCB, KCVO; College of Arms, Queen Victoria st, EC4

WAGSTAFF, Col Henry Wynter; MC, CSI; s of Edward Wynter Wagstaff (d 1939); *b* 19 July 1890; *Educ* Woodbridge Sch, RMA Sandhurst; *m* 1, 1918, Jean Everil, nee Mathieson; 2 s; m 2, 1967, Margaret Annie, nee Marshall; *Career* RE 1910, Col WW I Mesopotamia, WW II India; memb Railway Bd Govt of India 1939-46, Fell Chartered Inst of Transport; *Recreations* reading, writing; *Style* - Col Henry Wagstaff, MC, CSI; 15 Ockfields, Milford, Godalming, Surrey

WAINWRIGHT, John; CBE (1961); s of John Arthur Wainwright (d 1926); *b* 23 Oct 1894; *Educ* St Mark's Newtown Wigan, Wigan Mining Coll; *m* 1923, Gwyneth Mary, nee Ritson; 2 s, 1 da; *Career* Lt Tank Corps 1918, mining engineer, chm SW Lancs Coal Owners' Assoc 1940-46, chm Central Lancs Coal

Owners' Assoc Ltd 1946-76, consultant Lancs Assoc Collieries 1934-48, chm Fedn of Small Mines of GB 1946-; *Recreations* mining history; *Style* - John Wainwright Esq, CBE; Ty Draw, Winchester rd, Billinge, Wigan, Lancs

WAINWRIGHT, Rear-Adm Rupert Charles Purchas; CB (1966), DSC (1943); s of Lt-Cdr Oswald Johnson Wainwright, RN (ka 1918); *b* 16 Oct 1913; *Educ* RNC Dartmouth; *m* 1937, Patricia Mary Helen, da of Col Frederick Herbert Blackwood DSO (d 1926); 2 s (Rupert Michael Blackwood, Richard John Peter Blackwood), 2 da (Rosemary Patricia Nora Pockley, Sara Elisabeth Sybella); *Career* Naval appointments: 1965 ADC to HM The Queen, 1952-57 cmd HM ships and establishments (Actaeon, Tintagel Castle, Zephyr, Cambridge), 1958-60 Ch of Staff S Atlantic & S America Station, 1960-62 Dir of Naval Recruiting, 1962-64 Cdre Naval Drafting, 1965-67 V-Naval Dep to Supreme Allied Command Europe, 1967 ret; 1968-77 Redditch Dvpt Corpn, 1973- Stratford-upon-Avon Dist Cncl, 1976- Assoc of Dist Cncls, 1976- Keep Britain Tidy Gp; *Recreations* hockey (v-pres Eng Hockey Assoc), swimming (RN), tennis; *Clubs* Naval and Military, Royal Navy; *Style* - Rear-Adm Rupert Wainwright CB, DSC; Regency Cottage, Maidenhead rd, Stratford-upon-Avon, Warwickshire (☎ 293574)

WAIT, Lady Rosemary Ann; *née* FitzGerald; da of 8 Duke of Leinster by his 1 w Joane; *b* 4 Aug 1939; *Educ* LMH Oxford; *m* 1963 (m dis 1967), Mark Killigrew Wait; *Style* - Lady Rosemary Wait

WAKE, Lady Doune Mabell; *née* Ogilvy; da of 13 Earl of Airlie, DL; *b* 13 Aug 1953; *m* 1977, Hereward Charles, s and h of Sir Hereward Wake, 14 Bt; 1 s; *Style* - Lady Doune Wake

WAKE, Sir Hereward; 14 Bt (E 1621), of Clevedon, Somerset, MC (1942), DL (Northants 1955); s of Maj-Gen Sir Hereward Wake, 13 Bt, CB, CMG, DSO, JP, DL (d 1963, himself tenth in descent from the 1 Bt; the latter was in turn fifteenth in descent from Hugh Wac or Wake, feudal Baron by tenure of Bourne and Deeping *temp* King Stephen; this family's descent from Hereward the Wake, albeit in the female line, seems probable although not proven); *b* 7 Oct 1916. *Educ* Eton, RMC; *m* 1952, Julia Rosemary, JP, da of Capt Geoffrey W M Lees, of Falcutt House, nr Brackley, Northants; 1 s, 3 da; *Heir* s, Hereward Charles, b 22 Nov 1952; *Career* served 1937-46 with 1, 2, 7 and 9 Bns 60 Rifles (Burma Egypt, N Africa, NW Europe and Greece), Maj, ret 1947; High Sheriff Northants 1955; *Style* - Sir Hereward Wake, Bt, MC, DL; Courteenhall, Northampton (☎ Roade 204)

WAKE, Hereward Baldwin Lawrence; s of Rev Prebendary Hereward Eyre Wake (d 1934, 5 in descent from Sir William Wake, 7 Bt); *b* 26 Aug 1900; *Educ* Marlborough, Keble Oxford; *m* 1926, Sheila Winifred Lilian, nee Harris; 2 s; *Career* WW II Glos Regt, GSOI Lt-Col (War Office); headmaster St John's Sch Leatherhead 1948-60; *Style* - Hereward Wake Esq; High Ridge, Knoll Wood, Knoll rd, Godalming, Surrey (☎ 22622)

WAKE-WALKER, Lady Anne; *née* Spencer; da of 7 Earl Spencer and aunt of HRH The Princess of Wales; *b* 1920; *m* 1944, Capt Christopher Wake-Walker, RN, gn of Sir Francis Wake Walker, 3 Bt; 3 s, 1 da; *Style* - Lady Anne Wake-Walker; East Bergholt Lodge, Suffolk

WAKE-WALKER, David Christopher; s of Capt Christopher Baldwin Hughes Wake-Walker, RN and Lady Anne (nee Spencer, da of 7 Earl Spencer, making David 1 cous to HRH the Princess of Wales); *b* 11 Mar 1947; *Educ* Winchester, St Andrews U; *m* 1979, Jennifer Rosemary, nee Vaulkhard; *Career* banker; Kleinwort Benson Ltd 1969-, dir 1980-; *Clubs* Wanderers; *Style* - David Wake-Walker Esq; 4 Lanfrey pla, W14 (☎ 01 385 7368); 4 The Terrace, Snape, Saxmundham, Suffolk (☎ Snape 376)

WAKEFIELD, 9 Bishop of 1977-; Rt Rev Colin Clement Walter James; s of Rev Canon Charles James; *b* 20 Sept 1926; *Educ* Aldenham, King's Cambridge, Cuddesdon Theological Coll; *m* 1962, Margaret, da of Maj William Henshaw; 1 s, 2 da; *Career* Bp Basingstoke 1973-77, chm Church Info Cttee 1976-, Pres Woodard Corpn 1977-; patron of 74 livings and the Archdeaconries & Canonries in his cathedral; *Recreations* broadcasting, theatre, walking, travel; *Style* - The Rt Rev the Bishop of Wakefield; Bishop's Lodge, Woodthorpe Lane, Wakefield, W Yorks (☎ 255349)

WAKEFIELD OF KENDAL, 1 Baron (UK 1963); (William) Wavell Wakefield; s of Roger Wakefield, JP; *b* 10 March 1898; *Educ* Sedbergh, Pembroke Cambridge; *m* 1919, Rowena (d 1981), da of Dr Llewellyn Lewis, OBE, JP, of Neath; 3 da; *Heir* none; *Career* served WW I and to 1923 RAF; MP (Nat C) Swindon 1935-45, St Marylebone (C) 1945-63; dir Lake Dist Estates, Shapland & Petter, Portman Bldg Soc; past Capt England XV RFU; *Clubs* Carlton, MCC; *Style* - Rt Hon Lord Wakefield of Kendal; The Old Park House, Kendal, Cumbria (☎ 20861); 71 Park st, W1

WAKEFIELD, Dowager Lady; Constance Lalage; da of Sir John Perronet Thompson, KCSI, KCIE; *m* 1929, Sir Edward Wakefield, 1 Bt, CIE (d 1969); *Style* - Dowager Lady Wakefield; 13 St Mary Abbot's Terrace, W14 (☎ 01 602 3042)

WAKEFIELD, Sir (Edward) Humphry Tyrrell; 2 Bt (UK 1962), of Kendal, Co Westmorland; s of Sir Edward Birkbeck Wakefield, 1 Bt, CIE (d 1969, himself yr bro of 1 Baron Wakefield of Kendal); *b* 11 July 1936; *Educ* Gordonstoun and Trin Cambridge; *m* 1, 1960, Priscilla (m dis 1964), da of (Oliver) Robin Bagot; m 2, 1966, Hon Elizabeth Sophia Sidney (m dis 1971), da of 1 Viscount De L'Isle, KG, VC, GCMG, GCVO, PC (d 1973); 1 s; m 3, 1974, Hon Katherine Mary Alice Baring, da of 1 Baron Howick of Glendale, GCMG, KCVO (d 1973); 2 s, (1 decd), 1 da; *Heir* s, Maximilian Edward Vereker Wakefield, b 1977; *Career* Lt 10 Roy Hussars; exec vice-pres Mallett America Ltd 1970-75; formerly dir Mallett & Son (Antiques) Ltd, chm Tyrrell & Moore Ltd, Nicolai Patricia Co Ltd; dir F William Free Advertising (UK), Internat Finance Co Madrid, Save Piccadilly Fndn; dir Spoleto Festival; memb Standing Cncl Baronetage; pres 'Enterprise', Republic of Ireland; *Style* - Sir Humphry Wakefield, Bt; 53 Campden Hill rd, W8 (☎ 01 937 7829); c/o Barclays Bank, St James' st, Derby

WAKEFIELD, Hon Lady; Hon Katherine Mary; *née* Baring; da of 1 Baron Howick of Glendale, KG, GCMG, KCVO (d 1973); *b* 1936; *m* 1974, as his 3 wife, Sir (Edward) Humphry Tyrrell Wakefield, 2 Bt; *Style* - The Hon Lady Wakefield

WAKEHURST, 3 Baron (UK 1934); (John) Christopher Loder; s of 2 Baron Wakehurst (d 1970, s of 1 Baron by Lady Louise de Vere Beauclerk, da of 10 Duke of St Albans) and Margaret, Baroness Wakehurst, *qv*; *b* 23 Sept 1925; *Educ* Eton, King's Sch Sydney, Trin Cambridge; *m* 1956, Ingeborg (d 1977), da of Walter Krumbholz-Hess; 1 s, 1 da; *Heir* s, Hon Timothy Loder; *Career* chm Continental Illinois Ltd 1973-, Anglo-American Securities Corpn 1980-, N Atlantic Securities Corpn, Oil & Gas Enterprises (NS); dep chm London & Manchester Assur Co; CStJ; barr 1950; served WW II RANVR & RNVR; dir & chm Hampton Gold Mining Areas 1981-; *Style* - The Rt Hon Lord Wakehurst; c/o Continental Bank House, 162 Queen Victoria st, EC4 (☎ 01 236 5292)

WAKEHURST, Margaret, Baroness; Dame Margaret; DBE (1965); 6 da of Sir Charles Tennant, 1 Bt, MP, JP, DL, by his 2 w Marguerite; half sis of Margot Asquith and 1 Baron Glenconner; *b* 4 Nov 1899; *m* 1920, 2 Baron Wakehurst, KG, KCMG (d 1970); 3 s, 1 da; *Career* GStJ; Hon LLD Belfast; *Style* - Rt Hon Margaret, Lady Wakehurst DBE; 31 Lennox gdns, SW1 (☎ 01 589 0956)

WAKELEY, Elizabeth, Lady; Elizabeth Muriel; da of James Nicolson-Smith, of Blackheath; *m* 1925, Sir Cecil Wakeley, 1 Bt, KBE, CB (d 1979); *Career* MB, BS; CStJ; *Style* - Elizabeth, Lady Wakeley; 240 Maidstone rd, Chatham, Kent

WAKELEY, Sir John Cecil Nicholson; 2 Bt (UK 1952), of Liss, Co

Southampton; s of Sir Cecil Pembrey Grey Wakeley, 1 Bt, KBE, CB, FRCS (d 1979); *b* 27 Aug 1926; *Educ* Canford Sch London; *m* 1954, June Leney; 2 s, 1 da; *Heir* s, Nicholas Jeremy Wakeley, b 17 Oct 1957; *Career* formerly ch inspector City of London Special Constabulary; consulting surgeon W Cheshire Gp of Hosps; memb of Liverpool Regional Hosp Bd, Mersey Regional Health Authority; *Style* - Sir John Wakeley, Bt; Mickle Lodge, Mickle Trafford, Chester (☎ Mickle Trafford 300316)

WAKELY, Leonard John Dean; CMG (1965), OBE (1945); s of Sir Leonard Wakely, KCIE, CB (d 1961); *b* 18 June 1909; *Educ* Westminster Sch, Ch Ch Oxford, Sch of Oriental Studies London; *m* 1938, Margaret Houssemayne, da of Lt-Cdr C W Tinson, OBE, RN; 2 s; *Career* ICS 1932-47, Commonwealth Relations Office 1947, Dep UK High Cmmr in Ghana 1957-60, Dep British High Cmmr in Canada 1962-65, Br Ambass Burma 1965-67; *Style* - Leonard Wakely Esq, CMG, OBE; Long Meadow, Forest Row, E Horsley, Surrey (☎ E Horsley 3152)

WAKEMAN, Sir (Offley) David; 5 Bt (UK 1828), of Perdiswell Hall, Worcestershire; s of Sir Offley Wakeman, 4 Bt, CBE (d 1975); *b* 6 March 1922; *Educ* Canford Sch; *m* 1946, Pamela Rose Arabella, da of late Lt-Col C Hunter Little, DSO, MBE; *Heir* half-bro Edward Offley Bertram Wakeman, b 31 July 1934; *Career* formerly employed by Herefordshire War Agricultural Exec Ctee; *Clubs* Lansdowne, Shropshire; *Style* - Sir David Wakeman, Bt; Peverey House, Bomere Heath, Shrewsbury, Salop (☎ Shrewsbury 850561)

WAKLEY, His Hon Judge; Bertram Joseph Wakley; MBE (1945); s of late Joseph Wakley; *b* 7 July 1917; *Educ* Wellington, Ch Ch Oxford; *m* 1953, Alice Margaret, nee Lorimer; *Career* barr 1948, Circuit Judge 1973-; *Style* - His Hon Judge Wakley, MBE; Hamilton House, Kingston Hill, Surrey

WALDEGRAVE, 12 Earl (GB 1729); Sir Geoffrey Noel Waldegrave; 16 Bt (E 1643), KG (1971), GCVO (1976), TD, DL (Somerset 1951); also Baron Waldegrave (E 1686) and Viscount Chewton (GB 1729); s of 11 Earl Waldegrave (d 1936, descended from Sir Richard Walgrave, Speaker of the House of Commons *temp* Richard II) and Anne, da of Rev William Bastard (of one of the oldest families in Devon), of Buckland Court, Ashburton; *b* 21 Nov 1905; *Educ* Winchester, Trin Cambridge; *m* 1930, Mary, da of Lt-Col Arthur Grenfell, DSO (n of 1 Baron Grenfell); 2 s, 5 da; *Heir* s, Viscount Chewton; *Career* memb Prince's Cncl Duchy of Cornwall 1951-58 & 1965-76, Lord Warden Stannaries 1965-76; Jt Parly Sec Miny Ag & Fish 1958-62; chm Forestry Cmmn 1963-65, Friends of Wells Cathedral; Vice-Lt Somerset 1955-60; *Clubs* Travellers', Farmers'; *Style* - Rt Hon Earl Waldegrave KG GCVO TD DL; Chewton House, Chewton Mendip, Bath (☎ Chewton Mendip 264)

WALDEGRAVE, Hon William Arthur; MP (C) Bristol W 1979-; 2 s of 12 Earl Waldegrave (whose ancestor, 1 Baron Waldegrave, m Henrietta FitzJames, love child of Arabella Churchill by James II, making William 8 cous once removed to Sir Winston Churchill and 9 cous to HRH The Princess of Wales); through the 4 Earl Waldegrave's m with his cous Lady Elizabeth Waldegrave (whose mother was another love child, this time of Hon Sir Edward Walpole, 2 s of 1 Earl of Orford), William is ggggggs of Great Britain's First Prime Minister, that fellow Old Etonian Sir Robert Walpole; his ancestor the 2 Earl Waldegrave (f of Lady Elizabeth) was also briefly PM (in "the two days ministry" of 1746, whose short life prevented Lord W doing more than recruit colleagues); *b* 15 Aug 1946; *Educ* Eton, CCC Oxford, Harvard; *m* 1977, Caroline Burrows; 1 da; *Career* Fellow All Souls 1971-78 and 1979-; late Central Policy Review Staff, Political Staff 10 Downing st, Head Leader Opposition's Office 1974-75; memb IBA Advsy Cncl 1980-; *Style* - The Hon William Waldegrave MP; 18 Wellington ter, Bristol 8 (☎ 34817)

WALDRON, Lady Olivia Elsie June; *née* Taylour; da of 5 Marquess of Headfort, TD (d 1960); *b* 1929; *m* 1955, Victor Echevarri Waldron; 2 da; *Style* - Lady Olivia Waldron; Ascot Cottage, Winkfield, Berks

WALDY, Hon Mrs (Helen Patricia); *née* Roche; da of Baron Roche, PC (Life Peer, d 1956); *b* 1906; *m* 1931, Sqdn Ldr Edward Waldy, RAFVR; 1 da; *Style* - The Hon Mrs Waldy; Ashcroft House, Chadlington, Oxford (☎ 421)

WALERAN, Baroness; Valentine; da of Eric Anderson, CBE; *m* 1954, as his 3 w, 2 and last Baron Waleran (d 1966); *Style* - The Rt Hon The Lady Waleran; 29 Elvaston Place, SW7

WALES, Hon Mrs (Susan Clare); *née* Richardson; da of Baron Richardson, MVO; *b* 25 March 1940; *m* 1970, Robert Wales; 1 s; *Style* - The Hon Mrs Wales; 2 Thorne st, SW13

WALEY-COHEN, Sir Bernard Nathaniel; 1 Bt (UK 1961), of Honeymead, Co Somerset; s of late Sir Robert Waley Cohen, KBE (1 cous of Sir Herbert Cohen, 2 & last Bt, OBE); assumed by deed poll 1950 his f's final forename as an additional surname; 2 cous of late Baron Cohen (Life Peer d 1973), and 4 (half) cous of both 3 Baron Rothschild and 7 Earl of Rosebery (through the m of Hannah Rothschild, the heiress of Mentmore, with the 5 Earl in 1850); *b* 29 March 1914; *Educ* HMS Britannia (RNC Dartmouth), Clifton Coll, Magdalene Cambridge; *m* Hon Joyce Nathan (*see* Hon Lady Waley-Cohen); 2 s, 2 da; *Heir* s, Stephen Harry Waley-Cohen; *Career* Pres Trades Advsy Cncl 1981-; Lloyd's underwriter 1939-, chm Simo Securities Tst Ltd 1955-70, dir Matthews Wrightson Pulbrook Ltd, Central London Region Lloyds Bank Ltd, Kleeman Industrial Holdings Ltd, Bagworthy Land, Bray Gibb Agencies, Habick Ltd, Ramteazle Ltd; liveryman Clothworkers' Co, Lord Mayor of London 1960-61 (Sheriff 1955-56, Alderman 1949, HM Lieut 1977); Assoc KStJ 1961, kt 1957; former chm Coll Cncl Univ Coll London, former memb Senate and Court London U, memb Fin and Gen Purposes Ctee British Field Sports Soc 1957, pres Devon Cattle Breeders' Soc 1963, W of England Hound Show (Honiton) 1974, Govr Hon Irish Soc 1973-76, v-pres Anglo-Jewish Assoc 1962; *Style* - Sir Bernard Waley-Cohen, Bt, HM Lieut for City of London; 11 Little St James's st, SW1 (☎ 01 629 1615); Honeymead, Simonsbath, Minehead, Somerset (☎ Exford 242)

WALEY-COHEN, Hon Mrs (Felicity Ann); *née* Samuel; da of 3 Viscount Bearsted, TD, DL; *b* 3 April 1948; *m* 1975, Robert, 2 s of Sir Bernard Waley-Cohen, 1 Bt, and Hon Joyce, JP, da of 1 Baron Nathan; 1 s; *Style* - The Hon Mrs Waley-Cohen; 18 Gilston rd, SW10 (☎ 01 373 4212)

WALEY-COHEN, Hon Lady - Hon Joyce Constance Ina; *née* Nathan; JP (Somerset 1959-); da of 1 Baron Nathan, TD, PC (d 1963); *b* 20 Jan 1920; *Educ* St Felix Sch and Girton, Camb; *m* 1943, Sir Bernard Nathaniel Waley-Cohen, 1 Bt, *qv*; *Career* memb Bd of Governors Westminster Hosp Group 1952-68; chm of Westminster Children's Hosp 1952-68, chm Gordon Hosp 1961-68, chm Governing Bodies of Girls Schs Assocn 1974-79 (memb 1963-), memb Ind Schs Information Serv Council and Managing Ctee 1972-, vice-chm Ind Schs Joint Ctee 1974-, (chm 1977-), Governor Taunton Sch 1978-, Wellington Coll 1979-; JP Middx 1949-59; *Style* - Hon Lady Waley-Cohen, JP; 11 Little St James's st, SW1; Honeymead, Simonsbath, Minehead, Somerset (☎ Exford 242)

WALEY-COHEN, Robert Bernard; 2 s of Sir Bernard Waley-Cohen, 1 Bt, and Hon Joyce Nathan, da of 1 Baron Nathan; *b* 10 Nov 1948; *Educ* Eton; *m* 1975, Hon Felicity Anne, da of 3 Viscount Bearsted, TD; 1 s (Marcus Richard b 1977), 1 da (Jessica Suzanna b 1979); *Career* exec Christie's 1969, gen man USA 1970-73; dir Samuel Properties 1977-, Sec Amateur Riders Assoc 1978-; fndr memb Horseracing Advsy Cncl 1979-; Steward Cheltenham 1980-, Plumpton 1978-; *Recreations* the arts, opera, hunting, racing (racehorses: 'Sun Lion', 'Givus Justice', 'Foxbank'); *Clubs* Boodle's, Queen's; *Style* - Robert Waley-Cohen Esq; 18 Gilston rd, SW10 (☎ 01 373 4212)

WALEY-COHEN, Stephen Harry; s and h of Sir Bernard Waley-Cohen, 1 Bt; *b* 22 June 1946; *Educ* Eton, Magdalene Cambridge; *m* 1972, Pamela Elizabeth, da of J E Doniger; 2 s, 1 da; *Career* financial journalist Daily Mail 1968-73, ed Money Mail Handbook, publisher Euromoney 1977-, govr Wellesley House Sch; *Style* - Stephen Waley-Cohen Esq; 31 Chelsea Park gdns, SW3

WALFORD, John Howard; s of Henry Howard Walford (d 1928); *b* 16 May 1927; *Educ* Cheltenham, Gonville and Caius Cambridge; *m* 1953, Peggy Ann, da of Richard Frederick Jessel, DSO, OBE, DSC; 2 s, 2 da; *Career* Cdr Order of Bernardo O'Higgins (Chile) 1972; slr 1950, sr ptnr Bischoff & Co 1979-, pres Slrs Disciplinary Tribunal 1979-, govr College of Law 1967-, memb Cncl of the Law Soc 1961-69, govr St John's Hospital for Diseases of the Skin 1967-, master of the City of London Slrs Co 1981, chm Appeal Ctee of the Skin Disease Research Fund; *Recreations* being in the country, travelling abroad; *Clubs* Garrick, City U, City Law; *Style* - John Walford Esq; 8 Essex Villas, W8 (☎ 01 937 6845)

WALKDEN, Hon Margaret; da of 1 Baron Walkden; *b* 1914; *Style* - The Hon Margaret Walkden; 7 Priory av, Hastings, Sussex

WALKER, Lady Bettie Mary; *née* Feilding; da of late 9 Earl of Denbigh; *b* 1899; *m* 1926, Eric George Sherbrooke Walker, MC, formerly RAF (d 1976); 2 da; *Style* - Lady Bettie Walker; Ca's Fidave, Calle Isabel II, 108 Soller, Majorca

WALKER, Sir Baldwin Patrick; 4 Bt (UK 1856), of Oakley House, Suffolk; also hereditary Pasha of the Ottoman Empire; s of late Cdr Baldwin Charles Walker, himself s of Sir Francis Walker, 3 Bt (d 1928, in his turn 2 surviving s of Adm Sir Baldwin Wake Walker, 1 Bt, KCB, who was Comptroller of the (Royal) Navy and sometime Adm in the Turkish service, whereby he was cr a Pasha); *b* 10 Sept 1924; *Educ* Abberley Hall, Gordonstoun; *m* 1, 1948, Joy Yvonne (m dis 1954), da of Sir Arrol Moir, 2 Bt (d 1957); m 2, 1954, Sandra Stewart; m 3, 1966, Rosemary Ann, da of Henry Hollingdrake; 1 s, 1 da; *Heir* s, Christopher Robert Baldwin Walker, b 25 Oct 1969; *Career* formerly London regnl man Planned Music Ltd, Planned Equipment Ltd, Planned Communications Ltd; *Style* - Sir Baldwin Walker, Bt; Eikerus, Bo Daljosaphat, nr Paarl, CP, S Africa

WALKER, Maj Sir Hugh Ronald Walker; 4 Bt (UK 1906), of Pembroke House, City of Dublin; s of Maj Sir Cecil Edward Walker, 3 Bt , DSO, MC (d 1964); *b* 13 Dec 1925; *Educ* Wellington Coll; *m* 1971, Norna, da of Lt-Cdr R D Baird; 1 s; *Heir* s, Robert Cecil Walker, b 26 Sept 1974; *Career* Maj RA, ret; memb Assoc of Supervisory and Exec Engineers; *Style* - Maj Sir Hugh Walker, Bt; c/o Lloyds Bank Ltd, Somerton, Somerset

WALKER, Ian Royaards; s of Alexander Walker (d 1971); *b* 22 April 1927; *Educ* Bryanston Sch, Ch Ch Cambridge, Bristol U; *m* 1956, Margaret Elizabeth, nee Bardsley; 3 s; *Career* ch exec and md BP Oil Ltd 1981- (dep md from 1976); *Recreations* music; *Style* - Ian Walker Esq; The Old Vicarage, Elsenham, nr Bishop's Stortford, Herts (☎ Bishop's Stortford 81 3222)

WALKER, Hon Mrs; Hon Julia; da of Baron Cross of Chelsea (Life Peer); *b* 1953; *m* 1973, Barney Walker; *Style* - The Hon Mrs Walker

WALKER, Prof James; CBE (1974); s of James Walker (d 1952); *b* 8 Mar 1916; *Educ* H S Stirling, Glasgow U; *m* 1940, Catherine Clark, nee Johnston; 2 s, 1 da; *Career* Wing Cdr RAF; Prof Obstetrics/Gynaecology Dundee U 1967-, St Andrews 1956-67, Reader London U 1954-56, Visiting Prof Florida U, New York State, McGill, Pennsylvania; chm Nat Medical Consultative Ctee (Scotland); *Clubs* RAF; *Style* - Prof James Walker, CBE; 1 Ellieslea rd, Broughty Ferry, Dundee, DD5 1JC (☎ 79238)

WALKER, Sir James Heron; 5 Bt (UK 1868), of Sand Hutton, Co York, and of Beachampton, Bucks; s of Sir Robert Milo Walker, 4 Bt (d 1930), by his 1 w, Synolda (da of James Augustine Harvey Thursby-Pelham, JP, DL); *b* 7 April 1914; *Educ* Eton, Magdalene Cambridge; *m* 1, 1939, Angela Margaret (m dis 1972), da of V A Beaufort; 1 s, (1 da decd); m 2, 1972,

Sharrone, da of David Read; 1 s; *Heir* s, Victor Stewart Heron Walker, b 8 Oct 1942; *Style* - Sir James Walker, Bt; Ringdale Manor, Faringdon, Oxon

WALKER, Kenneth Lane; s of Herbert Arthur Walker (d 1961); *b* 26 Feb 1936; *Educ* Moseley G S, U Coll Oxford; *m* 1964, Isabella Mary, nee Moffat; *Career* CA, dir of Mono Containers Ltd 1967-77, v-chm Mono Containers Int Ltd 1975-77 (dir 1971-77), Pontneau Mono & Cie SA France 1970-77, Monoplast SA Spain 1972-77, Thurbaform Ltd 1975-77, md Mono Containers GmbH W Germany 1975-77, md Mono Containers (Holdings) AG Switzerland 1975-77, dir Kode Int Ltd, Kode Investments Ltd and Kode Europe SA Belgium 1977-; *Recreations* gliding, reading; *Style* - Kenneth Walker Esq; Whitley Grange, Whitley, Melksham, Wilts (☎ 702242)

WALKER, Lady Margaret Gwendolen Mary; *née* Drummond; da of 16 Earl of Perth, GCMG, CB, PC (d 1951); *b* 1905; *m* 1937, John Walker; 1 s, 1 da; *Style* - Lady Margaret Walker; 2806, N st, Washington DC, USA

WALKER, Sir (Edward) Ronald; CBE (1956); s of Frederick Thomas Walker (d 1928); *b* 26 Jan 1907; *Educ* Fort St H S Sydney, Sydney U, Cambridge U; *m* 1933, Louise Clementine, nee Donckers; 2 c; *Career* kt 1956; economist, diplomat, lectr in Economics Sydney U 1927-31 and 1933-39, prof Tasmania U 1939-46, dep dir gen Australian Dept of War Orgn of Industry 1942-45, counsellor Australian Embassy Paris 1945-50, PM's Dept 1951-52, HM Australian Ambass to Japan 1952-55, United Nations 1955-59 (rep Security Cncl 1956-57), France 1959-68, Federal Repub Germany 1968-71, Org for Economic Cooperation & Development 1971-73; *Style* - Sir Ronald Walker, CBE; 1 Rue de Longchamp, 75116 Paris, France (☎ 553 0300)

WALKER, Victor Stewart Heron; s & h of Sir James Walker, 5 Bt, by his 1 w Angela; *b* 8 Oct 1942; *Educ* Eton; *m* 1969, Caroline, da of Lt-Col Frederick Wignall by his w Anne, herself da of Maj Herbert Acland Troyte, MC (ggs of Sir Thomas Acland, 10 Bt), and formerly w of (1) 5 Baron Ebury, (2) Henry Peregrine Hoare, and who m subsequently Anthony Marreco; Mrs Victor Walker is therefore half-sis of 6 Baron Ebury and Hon Victor Grosvenor; 2 s (James b 1970, Andrew b 1973), 1 da (Rosanna Celia b 1979); *Career* late 2 Lt Gren Gds & Lt Roy Wilts Yeo & Roy Yeo; *Clubs* Roy Yacht Sqdn; *Style* - Victor Walker Esq; Villa Josephine, Madliena, Malta

WALKER, Hon Mrs (Yvonne Marie); *née* Wall; da of Baron Wall, OBE (Life Peer d 1980); *b* 1942; *m* 1970, Hugh Walker; *Style* - The Hon Mrs Walker; Fairfield, Sevenhills Close, Walton, Surrey

WALKER-OKEOVER, Col Sir Ian Peter Andrew Monro; 3 Bt (UK 1886), of Gateacre Grange, Co Lancaster and Osmaston Manor, Co Derby, DSO and Bar (1945), TD, JP (Derbyshire 1932); s of Sir Peter Walker, 2 Bt (d 1915); *b* 30 Nov 1902; *m* 1938, Dorothy Elizabeth, da of Capt Josceline Heber-Percy; 1 s, 2 da; *Heir* s, Peter Ralph Leopold Walker-Okeover; *Career* formerly Lt-Col Commanding 1 (Derby Yeo) RAC (TA); High Sheriff 1934, Ld-Lt 1951-77; a memb of Queen's Body Guard for Scotland; KStJ; Hon Attaché at Brussels 1925-26; appointed Hon Col Derbyshire Yeo 1951; assumed by Roy Licence 1956 the additional surname of Okeover after his patronymic, and the Arms of Okeover quarterly with those of Walker; *Style* - Col Sir Ian Walker-Okeover, Bt, DSO* TD, JP; House of Glenmuick, Ballater, Aberdeenshire; Okeover Hall, Ashbourne, Derbyshire

WALKER-OKEOVER, Peter Ralph Leopold; s and h of Sir Ian Peter Andrew Monro Walker-Okeover, 3 Bt, DSO, TD; *b* 22 July 1947; *m* 1972, Catherine Mary Maule, da of Col George Patrick Maule Ramsay; 1 s, 1 da; *Career* Capt Blues and Royals; *Style* - Peter Walker-Okeover Esq; Park Cottage, Osmaston, Ashbourne, Derbys

WALKER-SMITH, Rt Hon Sir Derek Colclough; 1 Bt (UK 1960), of Broxbourne, Co Herts, TD, PC (1957), QC (1955), MP (C) Herts 1955-; s of late Sir Jonah Walker-Smith; *b* 13 April 1910;

Educ Rossall, Ch Ch Oxford; *m* 1938, Dorothy, da of L J W Etherton, of Rowlands Castle, Hants; 1 s, 2 da; *Heir* s, John Jonah Walker-Smith, b 6 Sept 1939; *Career* barr Middle Temple 1934, bencher 1963, chm Conservative Members (1922) Ctee 1951-55, chm Conservative Advisory Committee on Local Govt 1954-55, Parliamentary Sec to Bd of Trade 1955-56, Economic Sec to the Treasury 1956-57, Min of State Board of Trade Jan to Sept 1957, Min of Health Sept 1957, and Min of Health Sept 1957 to July 1960; European War 1939-45 as Lt-Col RA (TA); MP (C) Herts 1945-55; *Style* - Rt Hon Sir Derek Walker-Smith, Bt, TD, PC, QC, MP; 25 Cavendish Close, NW8 (☎ 01 286 1441)

WALL, Baroness; Gladys Evelyn; da of William Wright; *m* 1939, Baron Wall, OBE (Life Peer, d 1980); 2 s, 1 da; *Style* - The Rt Hon Lady Wall; Wychwood, Coombe End, Coombe Hill, Kingston, Surrey

WALL, Hon Martin John; twin s of Baron Wall, OBE (Life Peer d 1980); *b* 1948; *m* 1976, Margaret, da of J Scott; *Style* - The Hon Martin Wall

WALL, Maj Sir Patrick Henry Bligh; MC (1945), VRD (1957), MP (C) Haltemprice E Yorks 1955-; s of Henry Benedict Wall; *b* 19 Oct 1916; *Educ* Downside; *m* 1953, Sheila Elizabeth Putnam; 1 da; *Career* 1935-50 with RM, Maj 1949, Jt Services Staff Coll 1947; memb Westminster City Cncl 1953-63; MP (C) Kingston-upon-Hull 1954-55; delegate to UN Gen Assembly 1962; kt 1981; *Style* - Maj Sir Patrick Wall, MC, VRD, MP; Brantinghamthorp, Brantingham, nr Brough, North Humberside; 8 Westminster gdns, Marsham st, SW1 (☎ 01 828 1803)

WALL, Hon Robin John; twin s of Baron Wall, OBE (Life Peer d 1980); *b* 1948; *Style* - The Hon Robin Wall

WALLACE OF COSLANY, Baron (Life Peer UK 1974); George Douglas Wallace; s of George Wallace; *b* 18 April 1906; *Educ* Centl Sch Cheltenham; *m* 1932, Vera, da of William Randall; 1 s, 1 da; *Career* MP (L) Chislehurst 1945-50, Norwich N 1964-74, Govt Whip 1947-50; Lord in Waiting 1977-79, Oppn Whip 1979-; Pres Radio Soc GB 1977; *Recreations* gardening, amateur radio; *Style* - The Rt Hon Lord Wallace of Coslany; 44 Shuttle Close, Sidcup, Kent (☎ 01 300 3634)

WALLACE OF CAMPSIE, Baron (Life Peer UK 1974); George Wallace; JP (1968), DL (Glasgow 1971); s of John Wallace; *b* 13 Feb 1915; *Educ* Glasgow U; *m* 1977, Irene Phipps; *Career* KStJ 1976; Pres Wallace Cameron Hldgs 1977-; slr Supreme Courts 1950-, Hon Sheriff Hamilton 1971-; FRSA, FInstM, MBIM; *Style* - The Rt Hon Lord Wallace of Campsie JP DL; 14 Fernleigh rd, Newlands, Glasgow (☎ 041 637 3337)

WALLACE, Wing Cdr Alen; DL (Stirlings 1956); s of William Morgan Wallace (d 1946); *b* 18 Apr 1906; *Educ* Strathallan Sch, Edinburgh U; *m* 1937, Elfrida, nee Pearson; 1 s, 1 da; *Career* wing-cdr RAF 1941, v-chm T and AF Assoc Co of Stirling 1953-; md Carron Grove Paper Co Ltd and John Collins Ltd 1964-71, memb Roy Co of Archers (Queens Bodyguard for Scotland) 1954-; *Clubs* Roy Scottish Automobile; *Style* - Wing Cdr Alen Wallace Esq, DL; Endrick Lodge, Stirling (☎ 4077)

WALLACE, Albert Frederick; CBE (1963, OBE 1955), DFC (1943); s of Maj Frederick Wallace (d 1951); *b* 22 Aug 1921; *Educ* Roan Sch Blackheath; *m* 1940, Evelyn, nee White; 1 s, 1 da; *Career* Gp Capt RAF (ret 1969); controller of Manpower GLC 1978-, county personnel officer W Midlands CC 1973-78, assist clerk Warwicks CC 1969-73; *Recreations* golf, bridge; *Clubs* RAF; *Style* - Albert Wallace Esq, CBE, DFC; 25 Purley Rise, Purley, Surrey, CR2 3AW

WALLACE, Hon Elizabeth Anne; da of Baron Wallace of Coslany; *b* 21 Jan 1933; *Educ* Chislehurst G S, Avery Hill Training Coll Eltham; *Career* sr mistress St Mary's C of E Jr Sch Swanley; *Style* - The Hon Elizabeth Wallace; 44 Shuttle Close, Sidcup, Kent

WALLACE, Hon Mrs (Elizabeth Anne Hoyer); *née* Millar; da of 1 Baron Inchyra,

GCMG, CVO; *b* 1933; *m* 1965, William Euan Wallace (d 1977); *Style* - The Hon Mrs Wallace; Egbury House, St Mary Bourne, Andover, Hants

WALLACE, Hon Jim Anthony Hill; s of Baroness Dudley and late Guy Wallace and h to Barony; *b* 9 Nov 1930; *Educ* Lancing; *m* 1962, Nicola Jane, nee Dunsterville; 2 s; *Style* - The Hon Jim Wallace; Little Grange, Kempsey, Worcs

WALLACE, John Malcolm Agnew; JP, (Wigtownshire), DL (1971); s of Maj John Alexander Agnew Wallace, MC (d 1956); *b* 30 Jan 1928; *Educ* Brooks Sch Andover Mass USA, Harrow; *m* 1955, Louise Arden, nee Haworth-Booth; 1 s, 2 da; *Career* farmer; *Style* - John Wallace Esq, JP, DL; Lochryan, Stranraer, Wigtownshire (☎ 05812284)

WALLACE, Hon Mrs (Karis Valerie Violet); *née* Mond; da of 2 Baron Melchett (d 1949); *b* 1927; *m* 1, 1949 (m dis 1956), John Hackman Sumner; 1 s; m 2, 1956, Brian Wallace; 2 da; *Style* - The Hon Mrs Wallace; Coppington Stud, Lambourne, Berks

WALLACE, Hon Michael George; s of Baron Wallace of Coslany; *b* 1944; *m* 1974, Susan, da of Henry Price; has issue; *Style* - The Hon Michael Wallace; 35 Winchelsea av, Bexley Heath, Kent

WALLACE, Robert; TD (1956); s of Joseph Duncan Wallace (decd); *b* 4 July 1915; *Educ* Glasgow Academy; *m* 1949, Jeanne Houlden, da of Thomas Beswick; 2 children; *Career* memb Inst of CA of Scotland 1946-; dir Brookhurst Switchgear Ltd 1954-58, chm The Automatic Sprinkler Co Ltd 1958-79, chm The Atlas and Automatic Sprinkler Co Ltd 1977-1979; *Recreations* golf, gardening; *Style* - Robert Wallace Esq TD; Tirley End, Cotebrook, nr Tarporley, Ches (☎ 082 921 205)

WALLACE, Hon Robin Guy Hill; s of Baroness Dudley and late Guy Wallace; *b* 1936; *Educ* Malvern; *m* 1959, Jill Alexandra, nee Williams; 2 s; *Style* - The Hon Robin Wallace

WALLACE, Richard Lindsay; CBE (1946), AFC (1941); s of William James Lindsay Wallace (d 1937); *b* 28 Feb 1909; *Educ* Sedbergh Sch, RAF Coll Cranwell; *m* 1, 1940, Lorna (d 1960), da of Martin Comrie, of Bittering Hall, Norfolk; 1 s, 1 da; m 2, 1912, Mary, da of Percy Marsden, of Sutton Waldron House, Dorset; *Career* Gp Capt RAF Singapore 1938-39, Flying Instructor 1939-42, Leuchars (Coastal Command) 1943-44, OC 298 Wing (gen Reconnaissance) W Africa 1944-45; assist admin London Hosp 1953-57, Nuffield Orthopaedic Centre & Utd Oxford Hosps 1957-1975; *Recreations* painting; *Style* - Gp Capt Richard Wallace CBE AFC; 6 Abberbury Rd, Iffley, Oxford (☎ 777056)

WALLACE, Hon William John Sutton; s of Baroness Dudley and late Guy Wallace; *b* 1938; *Educ* Malvern; *m* 1962, Jean Carol Ann, nee Shipton; 2 s; *Style* - The Hon William Wallace; Beechmont House, Hallow, Worcs

WALLACE-TURNER, Robert John Aufrère Carr; s of Alfred Wallace Wallace-Turner (d 1968); *b* 22 July 1931; *Educ* Eton, Trin Oxford; *m* 1966, Sabine Marie Madeleine Alexandrine, da of Godefroy de Falguerolles, of Château de La Devèze, Puylaurens, Tarn, France; 3 da; *Career* Lt Gren Gds (Nat Serv); FCA, banker; *Recreations* gardening, carpentry; *Clubs* Berkshire Golf, Gresham; *Style* - Robert Wallace-Turner Esq; 39 Marryat rd, SW19 (☎ 01 946 6418); Cayenne, par St Germain-des-Prés, Tarn, France

WALLER, Hon Lady (Elizabeth Margery); JP; da of 1 Baron Hacking; *b* 1916; *m* 1936, Rt Hon Lord Justice Waller; 2 s, 1 da; *Style* The Hon Lady Waller JP; Hatchway, Kingsley Green, Surrey

WALLER, Helen, Lady; Helen Madeline; da of Joseph Radl, of NJ, USA; *m* 1919, Sir Roland Waller, 8 Bt (d 1958); 1 s (9 Bt), 2 da (Mrs Arthur Warshauer, Mrs Howard Schier); *Style* - Helen, Lady Waller; 11200 86th Ave N, Bldg 1, Apartment 104, Seminole Gardens, Seminole, Fla, USA

WALLER, Herbert Robert; MBE (1949, OBE 1972), DL (Beds 1953); s of Robert George Waller (d 1929); *b* 19 March 1899;

Educ Luton G S; *m* 1920, Edith Jane, nee Meachem; 2 s; *Career* Fl Lt RAFVR; co dir 1955-; High Sheriff Beds 1953-54; former Master Worshipful Co of Feltmakers 1957; *Recreations* swimming, golf, walking, theatre; *Clubs* St Stephen's Constitutional, City Livery, Lansdowne (Beds); *Style* - Herbert Waller Esq, MBE, DL; 53 Hexton rd, Barton le Clay, Bedford (☎ Luton (0582) 881213)

WALLER, Sir John Stanier Waller; 7 Bt (UK 1815), of Braywick Lodge, Berkshire; s of late Capt Stanier Waller, gs of late Rev Ernest Waller, 2 s of 1 Bt; suc kinsman, Sir Edmund Waller, 6 Bt, 1954; *b* 27 July 1917; *Educ* Weymouth Coll, Worcester Oxford; *Heir* none; *Career* served WW II Capt RASC M East; information & editorial work for Br Miny Info & Br Embassy in M East, later teacher and with COI London; dir Export Trade Ships Ltd 1956, Bristol Stone & Concrete Ltd 1974; author, poet, journalist; *Style* - Sir John Waller, Bt; 99 The Grove, Isleworth, Middx (☎ 01 560 8142)

WALLER, Hon Mrs (Margery Edith); *née* Sugden; da of late Hon Henry Frank Sugden, bro of 2 Baron St Leonards, & ggda of 1 Baron St Leonards; raised to rank of a Baron's da 1912; *b* 1885; *m* 1918, Maj Robert Jocelyn Rowan Waller DSO (d 1968); 2 da; *Style* - The Hon Mrs Waller; Ickford House, Little Ickford, nr Aylesbury, Bucks

WALLER, Sir Robert William; 9 Bt (I 1780), of Newport, Tipperary; s of 8 Bt (d 1958); *b* 16 June 1934; *Educ* St Peter's Prep Sch, Newark Coll of Engineering, Farleigh Dickinson U; *m* 1960, Carol Anne, da of John Edward Hines, of Hampton, New Hampshire and Lynn, Mass, USA; 3 s, (1 decd), 1 da; *Heir* s, John Michael Waller, b 14 May 1962; *Career* engineer General Electric Co; *Style* - Sir Robert Waller, Bt; 5 Lookout ter, Lynnfield, Mass 01940, USA

WALLIS, Arthur Hammond; CBE (1952); s of Harold Tom Wallis (decd); *b* 16 Sept 1903; *Educ* Wixenford, RNCs Osborne, Dartmouth, Greenwich; *m* 1940, Lucy Joyce, nee Becher; 1 s, 1 da; *Career* RN, Staff of RA Destroyers (1936-38), HMS Nelson (1938-41), HMS Illustrious (1941-43), Underwater Detection Establishment Portland (1948-50); Cdre 1951, NATO 1952-53, Dir Underwater Weapons 1953-56, Ch Naval Info 1957-1964; *Recreations* now onlooker; *Clubs* Naval & Military, Worplesdon G C; *Style* - Cdre Arthur Wallis CBE; Compton's Barn, Woodstreet, nr Guildford, Surrey

WALLIS-JONES, His Hon Judge; Ewan Perrins Wallis-Jones; s of William Wallis-Jones MBE (d 1944); *b* 22 June 1913; *Educ* Mill Hill Sch, U Coll of Wales Aberystwyth, Balliol Oxford; *m* 1940, Veronica Mary, nee Fowler; 1 s, 2 da; *Career* barr, county court judge 1964-72, circuit judge 1972, chm (dep chm 1965-66) Carmarthenshire Quarter Sessions 1966-71; *Recreations* music, photography; *Style* - His Hon Judge Wallis-Jones; 25 Cotham Grove, Bristol, BS6 6AN (☎ 48908); 28 Quay st, Carmarthen (☎ 5106)

WALLOP, Lady Jane Alianora Borlase; da of 9 Earl of Portsmouth; *b* 1939; *Style* - Lady Jane Wallop

WALLOP, Hon Lucinda Ruth; da of Viscount Lymington; *b* 1956; *Style* - The Hon Lucinda Wallop; c/o The Old Rectory, Aldon Lane, Offham, Maidstone, Kent

WALLOP, Hon Nicholas Valoynes Bermingham; s of 9 Earl of Portsmouth; *b* 1946; *Educ* Stowe; *m* 1969, Lavinia, da of David Karmel, CBE, QC; 1 s, 1 da; *Style* - The Hon Nicholas Wallop; 15 Tregunter rd, SW10

WALLOP, Hon Oliver Malcolm; s of 8 Earl of Portsmouth (d 1943); *b* 1905; *m* 1, 1929, Jean (d 1943), da of Edward Small Moore, of New York; 2 s, 2 da; m 2, 1944 (m dis 1954), Mrs Alberta J Hines; m 3, 1954, Mrs Carolyn Towle Russell (d 1972); *Career* rancher; served with US Army Air Corps 1942; *Style* - The Hon Oliver Wallop; Box 928, Big Horn, Sheridan Co, Wyoming, USA 82833

WALLOP, Hon Quentin Gerard Carew; s and h of Viscount Lymington; *b* 1954; *m* 1981, Candia Howard, adopted da of 4 Baron Strathcona and Mount Royal; *Style* - The Hon Quentin

Wallop; c/o The Old Rectory, Aldon Lane, Offham, Maidstone, Kent

WALLROCK, John; s of Samuel Wallrock (d 1955); *b* 14 Nov 1922; *Educ* Bradfield; *m* 1967, Audrey, da of Edward Arion, of New York; 1 s, 2 da; *Career* Lloyd's underwriter; master mariner; dir J H Minet & Co 1955, chm J H Minet & Co 1972-79, chm Minet Hldgs 1972-; Lt RNR, FCIB; *Recreations* yachting, shooting; *Clubs* Boodle's, Roy London Yacht, Roy Southern Yacht, Lloyd's Yacht; *Style* - John Wallrock Esq; Cleeve Lodge, 42 Hyde Park Gate, SW7

WALPOLE, 9 Baron (GB 1723); Robert Henry Montgomerie Walpole; TD; also 7 Baron Walpole of Wolterton (GB 1756); s of Lt Horatio Walpolee (ggs of Thomas Walpole, sometime Min Plenipotentiary to Court of Munich, by Margaret, da of 2 Earl of Egmont and his 2 w Catherine Compton, Baroness Arden (gda of 4 Earl of Northampton through her father and, through her mother (Mary Lucy), fifth in descent from Sir Thomas Lucy, whose portrayal as Justice Shallow may well have made him rue the day he prosecuted Shakespeare for deer stealing); Thomas Walpole, whose seat was - in view of his w's antecedents - appropriately named Stagbury Park, was gn of Sir Robert Walpole, Britain's first Prime Minister; his w was sis of Spencer Perceval, Britain's only PM to be assassinated); suc kinsman, 5 Earl of Orford (d 1931), in the Baronies above mentioned only; *b* 25 April 1913; *Educ* Eton, SE Ag Coll Wye, RAC Cirencester; *m* 1937, Nancy, OBE, da of Frank Jones; 1 s, 1 da (1 s and 1 da decd); *Heir* s, Hon Robert Walpole; *Career* Capt RA; patron of 6 livings; *Clubs* Bath, Norfolk (Norwich); *Style* - The Rt Hon Lord Walpole TD; Wolterton Hall, Erpingham, Norfolk (☎ Hanworth 210, Matlaske 274)

WALPOLE, Hon Pamela Frances; OBE (1960, MBE 1954); da of Lt Horatio Walpole and sis of 9 Baron Walpole TD; *b* 1908; *Career* raised to rank of Baron's da 1939; *Style* - The Hon Pamela Walpole; Greystones, Sir Lowry's Pass, Cape Province, S Africa

WALPOLE, Hon Robert Horatio; s and h of 9 Baron Walpole TD; *b* 8 Dec 1938; *Educ* Eton, King's Cambridge; *m* 1962 (m dis 1979), Judith, yr da of Theodore Schofield; 2 s, 2 da; m 2, Laurel, da of S Ball, of Swindon; 1 s; *Style* - The Hon Robert Walpole; Mannington Hall, Norwich

WALSH, Hon Jane Emily Mary; da of 5 Baron Ormathwaite MVO (d 1944); *b* 1910; *m* a Lady-in-Waiting to HRH Princess Alice Duchess of Gloucester 1969-75; *Style* - The Hon Jane Walsh; 13 Mount st, W1

WALSH, Hon Mrs (Sarah Louise); *née* Wedderburn; da of Baron Wedderburn of Charlton by his 1 w, Nina; *b* 1954; *m* 1975, Michael Walsh; *Style* - The Hon Mrs Walsh; 76 Cromwell av, N6

WALSHAM, Rear-Adm Sir John Scarlett Warren; 4 Bt (UK 1831), of Knill Court, Herefordshire, CB (1963), OBE (1944); s of Sir John Walsham, 3 Bt (d 1940), by his w Bessie (gda of Sir John Warren, 4 Bt); *b* 29 Nov 1910; *Educ* Rugby; *m* 1936, Sheila Christina, da of late Cdr Bertrand Bannerman, DSO, RN, and herself 2 cous of Sir Donald Bannerman, 13 Bt; 1 s, 2 da; *Heir* s, Timothy John Walsham, b 26 April 1939; *Career* Lt RN 1933, Cdr 1944, Capt 1953, Ch Engineer Singapore Dockyard 1956, Commanding Offr RN Engineering Coll Plymouth, Rear-Adm 1961, ret 1965; *Style* - Rear-Adm Sir John Walsham, Bt, CB, OBE; Ash Beacon, Churchill, Axminster, Devon

WALSINGHAM, 9 Baron (GB 1780); John de Grey; MC (1951); s of 8 Baron Walsingham, DSO, OBE, JP, DL (d 1965, himself half-nephew of the 8 Baron, considered by some the best game shot of his generation, also a noted cricketer (Cambridge blue) and lepidopterist); *b* 21 Feb 1925; *Educ* Wellington, Aberdeen U, Magdalen Oxford; *m* 1963, Wendy, da of Edward Hoare; 1 s, 2 da; *Heir* s, Hon Robert de Grey; *Career* Lt-Col RA ret; patron of 3 livings; landowner & farmer; co dir; *Recreations* etymology; *Clubs* Army & Navy, Special Forces, Farmers', Norfolk; *Style* - The Rt Hon Lord Walsingham MC; Merton Hall, nr Watton, Thetford,

Norfolk (☎ 0953 881226 home, 883370 office)

WALSTON, Baron (Life Peer UK 1961); Henry David Leonard George Walston; CVO (1976), JP (Cambridge 1944); s of Sir Charles Walston (né Waldstein), an archaeologist, by Florence, da of David Einstein, of New York; *b* 16 June 1912; *Educ* Eton, King's Cambridge; *m* 1, Catherine Macdonald (d 1978); 3 s, 2 da (and 1 s decd); m 2, 1979, Elizabeth, da of late John Bissett-Robinson and formerly w of Nicholas Scott, MP; *Career* farmer; agriculturist; Cnsllr Duchy of Lancaster 1948-54; contested: Hunts 1945 (Lib), Cambs 1951 & 55 and Gainsborough 1957 & 59 (all L); Parly Sec BOT 1967; MEP 1975-77; memb C'wlth Devpt Corpn 1975-; *Style* - The Rt Hon Lord Walston CVO JP; Town's End Springs, Thriplow, Royston, Herts; Marquis Estates, St Lucia, WI; A14 Albany, Piccadilly, W1 (☎ 01 734 0781)

WALSTON, Hon James Patrick Francis; 3 surviving s of Baron Walston, CVO, JP; *b* 28 July 1950; *Educ* Ampleforth, Eton, Jesus Cambridge; *Style* - The Hon James Walston

WALSTON, Hon Oliver; s of Baron Walston, CVO, JP; *b* 1941; *Educ* Eton, King's Cambridge; *m* 1, 1966, Leslie, da of Milton Gordon, of New York (m dis); m 2, 1969, Anne Dunbar, of Washington DC; has issue; *Style* - The Hon Oliver Walston; Thriplow Farm, Thriplow, Royston, Herts

WALSTON, Hon Susan; da of (twin with Hon William) Baron Walston, CVO, JP; *b* 18 Nov 1942; *Style* - The Hon Susan Walston

WALSTON, Hon William; 2 surviving s of Baron Walston, CVO, JP; *b* 18 Nov 1942; *Educ* Eton, Downside, King's Cambridge; *m* 1963, Hilary, da of William Galbraith, of Malaga; has issue; *Style* - The Hon William Walston

WALTER, Hon Mrs (Deborah Hamar); *née* Greenwood; JP (Inner London); da of 1 Viscount Greenwood, PC, KC; *b* 9 May 1917; *m* 1, 1940 (m dis 1970), Patrick de Laszlo (who d 1980, having m 2, Baroness Sharples), s of Philip de Laszlo MVO, the portrait painter; 1 s (Damon, who m 1972 Hon Sandra Hacking, *see* de Laszlo, Hon Mrs), 4 da; m 2, 1975, Roderick Walter; *Style* - The Hon Mrs Walter JP; 12 Stanford Court, Cornwall gdns, SW7

WALTER, Lady Mary-Jill; *née* Fitz-Clarence; da of 6 Earl of Munster by his 1 w Monica; *b* 6 Feb 1928; *m* 1, 1953 (m annulled 1960), Melvin Flyer; resumed surname of Fitz-Clarence 1959; m 2, 1968, as his 2 w, John Walter (d 1980, whose f, also John, made over the presentation to the livings of Barkham, Finchampstead, St Paul's Wokingham and St Catherine Bearwood to the ecclesiastical authorities when he went over to Rome in 1960; John Sr was fourth in descent from John Walter, founder & proprietor of The Times); *Style* - Lady Mary-Jill Walter; Casa Merlot, 6911 Vico Morcote, Ticino, Switzerland

WALTER, Lady Sarah (Marion); *née* Coke; da of 5 Earl of Leicester (d 1976); *b* 1944; *m* 1970, Maj David Finlayson Wylie Hill Walter; 2 s ; *Style* - Lady Sarah Walter; 14 Hyde Park st, W2; Westwood, Balthayock, by Perth

WALTERS, Hon Mrs (Alice Elizabeth); da of Baron Carver (Life Peer); *b* 1954; *m* 1976, Capt Claude Walters, Gren Gds; *Style* - The Hon Mrs Walters; 71 Knightsbridge, SW1

WALTERS, Peter Ingram; s of Stephen Walters (d 1945); *b* 11 March 1931; *Educ* King Edward's Sch Birmingham, Birmingham U; *m* 1960, Patricia Anne, nee Tulloch; 2 s, 1 da; *Career* Lt RASC; md British Petroleum Co Ltd 1973, dep chm 1980-81, chm 1981-; *Recreations* golf; *Style* - Peter Walters Esq; British Petroleum Co Ltd, Britannic House, Moore lane, EC2 (☎ 920 6091)

WALTON, Dennis; CBE (1967), MC, TD; s of Harry Walton (d 1966); *b* 7 Feb 1920; *Educ* Bury G S, Emmanuel Cambridge; *m* 1949, Barbara Shirley, nee Jones; 2 da; *Career* WW II N Africa, Italy, Austria, Col RA (TA), Dep Cdr 42 Div 1962-67; md Dalkeith Knitwear Ltd 1963-78, md Branded Knitwear Div of Coats Patons Ltd 1976-78, pres Nottingham &

District Hosiery Mfrs Assoc 1967-69, dir Kitchin Thompson Assocs Ltd 1980-, counselling adviser E Midlands Small Firms Counselling Serv 1978-; *Clubs* Roy Overseas League; *Style* - Dennis Walton Esq, CBE, MC, TD; Riber Manor, Matlock, Derbys (☎ 3864)

WARBURTON, Col Alfred Arthur; CBE (1960), DSO (1946), JP (Notts 1968), DL (1966); s of Alfred Victor Warburton; *b* 12 April 1913; *Educ* Sedbergh; *Career* served with RA 1939-45, Lt Col cmd S Notts Hussars Yeomanry 1953-58, Col DCRA 1958-60, Hon Col S Notts Hussars Yeomanry 1966-76, ADC to HM 1961-66; High Sheriff Notts 1968; chm Notts County TA Assoc 1973-78, pres Notts County Br Legion 1979-; *Recreations* shooting, fishing, gardening; *Clubs* Cavalry & Guards; *Style* - Col Alfred Warburton, CBE, DSO, JP, DL; Wigthorpe House, Wigthorpe, Worksop, Notts (☎ 0909 730357)

WARBURTON, Hon Mrs (Belinda Anne); *née* Hewitt; da of 8 Viscount Lifford; *b* 1939; *m* 1963, the Rev Piers Eliot de Dutton Warburton; 1 s, 1 da; *Style* - The Hon Mrs Warburton; The Rectory, Sherborne St John, Basingstoke

WARD OF WITLEY, 1 Viscount (UK 1960); Hon George Reginald Ward; PC (1957); 4 (twin) s of 2 Earl of Dudley by Rachel, nee Gurney, CBE, of the extensive Norfolk banking family; 2 cous by m of the celebrated Mrs Dudley Ward (*see* Marquesa de Casa Maury), friend of Edward VIII as Prince of Wales; *b* 20 Nov 1907; *Educ* Eton, Ch Ch Oxford; *m* 1, 1940, Ann Ayesha (m dis 1951), da of Capt Arthur Capel, CBE, and Diana, Countess of Westmorland, *qv*, and great niece of 1 Baron Glenconner and Margot Asquith; 1 s, 1 da; m 2, 1962, Barbara (d 1980), da of Capt Ronald McNeill and formerly w of Hon Michael Astor; *Heir* s, Hon Anthony Ward; *Career* served RAF 1932-37 & 1939-45; MP (C) Worcester 1945-60, Sec of State Air 1957-60; *Clubs* White's, Pratt's; *Style* - Rt Hon Viscount Ward of Whitley PC; Friars Well, Aynho, Banbury, Oxon; 3/23 Queens Gate gdns, SW7 (☎ 01 589 2028)

WARD, Hon Mrs (Alathea Gwendoline Alys Mary); *née* Fitzalan-Howard; da of late 2 Viscount Fitzalan of Derwent; *b* 1923; *m* 1953, Hon Edward Frederick Ward; *Style* - The Hon Mrs Ward; 34 Ave des Mousquines, Lausanne, Switzerland

WARD, Hon Anthony Giles Humble; s and h of 1 Viscount Ward of Witley PC, by his 1 w, Ann; *b* 10 June 1943; *Educ* Eton; *Style* - The Hon Anthony Ward

WARD, Lady Amelia Maureen Erica; da (by 2 m) of 4 Earl of Dudley; *b* 1967; *Style* - Lady Amelia Ward

WARD, Hon Bethany Rowena; da (by 2 m) of 4 Earl of Dudley; *b* 1977

WARD, Gen Sir Dudley; GCB (1959, KCB 1967, CB 1945), KBE (1953, CBE 1945), DSO (1944); s of Lionel Howell Ward; *b* 27 Jan 1905; *Educ* Queen Elizabeth's G S Wimborne, Sandhurst; *m* 1, 1933, Beatrice Constance (d 1962), da of Rev T F Griffith (d 1950); 1 da; m 2, 1963, Joan Elspeth de Pechell, da of late Col D C Scott; *Career* Gen Central Mediterranean Theatre (Italy & Greece), Cdr: 4 Div 1944-45, Staff Coll 1948-51, 1 Corps 1951-52; Dep CIGS 1952-56, Cdr N Army Gp 1957-59, C in C Br Forces Nr East 1960-62, Govr Gibraltar 1962-65; *Recreations* golf; *Clubs* Army & Navy; *Style* - Gen Sir Dudley Ward, GCB, KBE, DSO; Wynneys Farmhouse, Dennington, Woodbridge, Suffolk (☎ Badingham 663)

WARD, Hon Edward Frederick; s of late 2 Earl of Dudley, GCB, GCMG, GCVO, PC; *b* 1907; *Educ* Eton; *m* 1, 1940 (m dis 1947), Pauline, da of Hon Charles Winn (himself 2 s of 2 Baron St Oswald); m 2, 1953, Hon Alathea Fitzalan-Howard, *see* Hon Mrs Ward; *Career* sometime 2 Lt 10 Roy Hussars, Gp Capt (ret) RAF, served War (despatches) 1939-45; *Clubs* White's; *Style* - The Hon Edward Ward; 34 Ave des Mousquines, Lausanne, Switzerland

WARD, Ven Edwin James Greenfield; MVO (1963); s of Canon Frederick Greenfield Ward MC (d 1963); *b* 26 Oct 1919; *Educ* St John's Leatherhead, Christ's Coll Cambridge; *m* 1946, Grizell

Evelyn, da of Capt Harry Gurney Buxton; 1 s, 2 da; *Career* Lt King's Guards 1940-46, ordained 1948, Vicar North Elmham 1950-55, Chaplain to HM 1955-, Chaplain Windsor Great Park 1955-67, Archdeacon of Sherborne and Rector of W Stafford 1967-; *Recreations* fishing; *Style* - The Ven the Archdeacon of Sherborne; West Stafford Rectory, Dorchester, Dorset

WARD, Lady Emma Sophia Cressida; da (by 2 m) of 4 Earl of Dudley; *b* 1970

WARD, Gerald John; s of Col Edward Ward MVO MC; *b* 31 May 1938; *Educ* Eton, Sandhurst, RAC Cirencester; *m* 1967, Rosalind, da of Hon Richard Lygon (3 s of 7 Earl Beauchamp); 2 c; *Career* Capt Roy Horse Guards; industrialist: chm UK Solenoid Ltd, dep chm Energy Capital Ltd, dir NCC Energy Ltd; farmer, chm Chilton Farms Ltd; *Clubs* White's, Portland; *Style* -Gerald Ward Esq; Chilton Park Farm, Hungerford, Berks (☎ 04886 2329); 34 Bryanston Square, London W1 (☎ 01 262 4966)

WARD, Sir Joseph James Laffey; 4 Bt (UK 1911), of Wellington, New Zealand; s of 3 Bt (d 1970); *b* 11 Nov 1946; *m* 1968, Robyn Allison, da of William Maitland Martin, of Rotorua NZ; *Heir* bro, Roderic Anthony Ward, b 23 April 1948; *Style* - Sir Joseph Ward, Bt

WARD, Joan, Lady; Joan Mary Haden; da of Maj Thames Patrick Laffey, of Auckland NZ; *m* 1944, Sir Joseph Ward, 3 Bt, LLM (d 1970); 3 s (including 4 Bt), 3 da; *Style* - Joan, Lady Ward; Westbrook, 75 Harakeke Street, Christchurch 1, New Zealand

WARD, Keith John; s of Thomas B Ward; *b* 10 Sept 1933; *Educ* St Christopher's Herts; *m* 1960, Susan Jean Robson; 2 s; *Career* builder's merchant, timber merchant, timber importer; dir The Graham Group 1974; devpt dir The Graham Group 1981; md Graham-Reeves Ltd 1974-81; *Recreations* sailing, fishing, shooting, horticulture; *Clubs* Reform; *Style* - Keith Ward Esq; The Malthouse, Frogmore, Kingsbridge, Devon (☎ 0548 153 306)

WARD, Hon Leander Grenville Dudley; s (by 2 m) of 4 Earl of Dudley; *b* 1971; *Style* - The Hon Leander Ward

WARD, Lady; Margaret Mary; da of Anthony Davis, of New York; *m* 1, Capt Ralph Risley, USN (decd); m 2, 1965, as his 3 w, Cdr Sir Melvill Ward, 3 & last Bt, DSC, RN (d 1973); *Style* - Lady Ward; Box 276, Southport, Conn, USA

WARD, Lady Melissa Patricia Eileen; da (by 2 m) of 4 Earl of Dudley; *b* 1964; *Style* - Lady Melissa Ward

WARD, Hon Peter Alistair; s of late 3 Earl of Dudley, MC, TD; *b* 1926; *Educ* Eton, British Columbia U, Ch Ch Oxford; *m* 1, 1956 (m dis 1974), Claire Leonora, nee Baring; 1 s, 2 da; m 2, 1974, Elizabeth Rose, da of Richard Westmacott, of Ascona, Switzerland; 2 s; *Career* Roy Canadian Air Force 1943-45 and Fleet Air Army; *Clubs* White's, Pratt's, Royal Yacht Sqdn; *Style* - The Hon Peter Ward; Cornwall Manor, Kingham, Oxon; 29 Egerton ter, SW3

WARD, Gen Sir Richard Erskine; GBE (1975), KCB (1971), DSO and Bar (1943), MC (1942); s of John Petty Ward (d 1956); *b* 15 Oct 1917; *Educ* Marlborough, Sandhurst; *m* 1948, Stella Elizabeth, da of Brig Philip Neville Ellis (d 1948); 2 s, 2 d; *Career* Cmd 3 Roy Tank Regt 1957-59, 20 Armoured Bde 1963-66, 1 Div 1966-68, Cdr Br Forces Hong Kong 1970-73, Ch of Personnel and Logistics 1974-76; *Recreations* shooting, golf; *Clubs* Army & Navy, North Hants Golf; *Style* - Gen Sir Richard Ward, GBE, KCB DSO*, MC; Little Sheldons, Hook, Hants (☎ Hook 2221)

WARD, Lady Susanna Louise; da (by 2 m) of 4 Earl of Dudley; *b* 1963; *Style* - Lady Susanna Ward

WARD, Lady Victoria Cecilia Larissa; da (by 2 m) of of 4 Earl of Dudley; *b* 1966; *Style* - Lady Victoria Ward

WARD, Hon William Maxwell David; s (by 3 m) and h of 7 Viscount Bangor; *b* 9 Aug 1948; *Educ* St Edward's Sch Oxford;

m 1976, Mrs Sarah Bradford; *Style* - The Hon William Ward

WARD-BOOTH, Maj-Gen John Antony; OBE (1969); s of Rev John Vernon William Ward-Booth (d 1973); *b* 18 July 1927; *Educ* Worksop Coll; *m* 1952, Margaret Joan, da of Rev Aubrey Hooper MC; 4 c; *Career* joined army 1945, Maj-Gen Parachute Regt 1963-, National Defence Coll Canada 1973-74, DAG HQ BAOR 1974-75, Dir Army Air Corps 1976-79; *Recreations* sports; *Clubs* Army & Navy; *Style* - Maj-Gen John Ward-Booth OBE; Hurstbourne Priors, nr Whitchurch, Hants (☎ Whitchurch 2461)

WARDE, Millicent Anne; CBE (1953); da of Ralph Montagu Cook JP (d 1946); *b* 12 May 1902; *m* 1933, John Roberts O'Brien Warde, TD, JP, DL; 1 s, 2 da; *Career* chm National Union of Conservative Assocs 1953, Br Delegate Status of Women Cmmn at UN 1953 & 1954; *Style* - Mrs John Warde CBE; Squerryes Court, Westerham, Kent (☎ Westerham 634885)

WARDE-ALDAM, Maj William; JP (W Yorks 1972), DL (S Yorks 1979); s of Lt-Col John Patientius Warde-Aldam; *b* 14 June 1925; *Educ* Eton; *m* 1960, Gillian, da of Malcolm Scott, of Lyons Hall, Essex; 2 s, 1 da; *Career* Coldstream Gds 1943-64, High Sheriff Hallamshire 1971; *Clubs* Cavalry & Guards', MCC, Pratt's; *Style* - Maj William Warde-Aldam JP DL; Frickley Hall, Doncaster (☎ S Elmsall 42854); Ederline, Ford, Lochgilphead, Argyll (☎ Ford 284)

WARDELL, Lady Antonia Pamela Mary; *née* Crichton; da of late 5 Earl of Erne and Lady Davidema, da of 2 Earl of Lytton; *b* 1934; *m* 1953, Timothy William Wardell, Sub-Lt (ret) RN, gs of Sir Kenneth Crossley, 2 Bt; 3 s, 1 da; *Style* - Lady Antonia Wardell; Garryard, Naas, Co Kildare

WARDINGTON, 2 Baron (UK 1936); Christopher Henry Beaumont Pease; s of 1 Baron Wardington (d 1950) and Dorothy, Baroness Wardington, *qv*; *b* 22 Jan 1924; *Educ* Eton; *m* 1964, Audrey, da of John White; 1 s, 2 da (all adopted); *Heir* bro, Hon William Pease; *Career* Capt Scots Gds 1942-47; stockbroker Hoare Govett & Co, memb Cncl Stock Exchange 1963-; *Recreations* books, gardening, golf; *Clubs* RAC; *Style* - The Rt Hon Lord Wardington; 29 Moore st, SW3 (☎ 01 584 5245); Wardington Manor, Banbury, Oxon (☎ 029 575 202)

WARDINGTON, Dorothy, Baroness; Hon Dorothy Charlotte; da of late 1 Baron Forster; *b* 1891; *m* 1, 1914, Capt Hon Harold Lubbock, Grenadier Gds (ka 1918, 4 s of 1 Baron Avebury); m 2, 1923, 1 Baron Wardington (d 1950); 2 s; *Style* - The Rt Hon Dorothy, Lady Wardington; Lepe House, Exbury, Southampton

WARDLAW, Sir Henry; 20 Bt (NS 1631), of Pitreavie, Fifeshire; s of Sir Henry Wardlaw, 19 Bt (d 1954, himself ninth in descent from Sir Henry Wardlaw, 1 Bt, who was Chamberlain to James I's Queen, Anne of Denmark); *b* 30 Aug 1894; *m* 1929, Ellen, da of late John Francis Brady, of Hawthorn, Victoria, Australia; 4 s, 1 da; *Heir* s, Henry John Wardlaw, b 30 Nov 1930; *Style* - Sir Henry Wardlaw, Bt; Wamba, 57 Kinkora rd, Hawthorn, Melbourne, Victoria, Australia

WARDLAW, Henry John; s & h of Sir Henry Wardlaw, 20 Bt; *b* 30 Nov 1930; *Educ* Melbourne U; *m* 1962, Julie-Ann, da of Edward Kirwan; 5 s (Henry b 1963, Edward b 1964, Simon b 1965, Anthony b 1970, Adrian b 1971), 1 da (Janet b 1969); *Career* MB, BS; *Style* - Henry Wardlaw Esq; 82 Vincent st, Sandringham, Melbourne, Victoria, Australia

WARE, Peter Morrell; s of the late Arthur Coates Ware; *b* 14 Sept 1922; *Educ* Malvern Coll; *m* 1955, Elizabeth Ann, nee Farrell; 1 s, 2 da; *Career* Warrant Officer UK; md CPC (UK) Ltd 1975-, gen man CPC Benelux and Scandinavia 1966-70, chm British Maize Refiners Assoc 1976-77, pres Assoc des Amidonneries de Mais de la CEE 1978-79; *Recreations* cricket, tennis; *Clubs* MCC; *Style* - Peter Ware Esq; 1 Fairacres, Roehampton Lane, SW15 (☎ 01 878 1979)

WARING, Sir Alfred Holburt; 3 Bt (UK 1935); s of Sir Alfred Waring, 2 Bt (d

1981), and Winifred, Lady Waring; *b* 2 Aug 1933; *Educ* Rossall Sch; *m* 1958, Ana, da of Señor Valentine Medinilla; 1 s, 2 da; *Heir* s, Michael Holburt Waring, b 3 Jan 1964; *Career* dir: SRM Plastics, Waring Investments, Rotaprint Ltd, Property Realisation Co Ltd, Moor Park (1958) Ltd, Moor Park Golf Club Ltd; *Recreations* tennis, golf, squash, swimming; *Clubs* Moor Park Golf, Northwood Squash; *Style* - Sir Alfred Waring, Bt; 30 Russell rd, Moor Park, Northwood, Middx (☎ 24570)

WARING, Winifred, Lady; Winifred; da of Albert Boston, of Stockton-on-Tees; *m* 1930, Sir Harold Waring, 2 Bt (d 1981); 1 s (Sir Alfred W, 3 Bt), 2 da (Mrs Michael Mark, Mrs John Holderness); *Style* - Winifred, Lady Waring; Pen Moel, Tidenham, Glos

WARMINGTON, Sir Marshall George Clitheroe; 3 Bt (UK 1908), JP (1935); s of Sir Marshall Denham Warmington, 2 Bt, JP (d 1935), by his 1 w Alice; *b* 26 May 1910; *Educ* Charterhouse; *m* 1, 1933, Mollie (m dis 1941), da of late Capt Malcolm Alfred Kennard RN; 1 s, 1 da; m 2, 1942, Eileen Mary (d 1969), da of late P J Howes; 2 s; m 3, 1972, Sheila (m dis 1977), da of Stanley Brotherhood JP, of Thornhaugh Hall, Peterborough, and widow of Adm the Hon Sir Cyril Eustace Douglas-Pennant, KCB, CBE, DSO, DSC (s of 5 Baron Penrhyn); *Heir* son, Marshall Denham Malcolm Warmington; *Career* Lt Cdr RN 1928-54; co sec Securicor 1963-69; *Recreations* fishing, golf; *Clubs* MCC, Army & Navy; *Style* - Sir Marshall Warmington, Bt, JP; Swallowfield Park, Reading

WARNER, Sir Fred(erick) Archibald; GCVO (1975), KCMG (1972, CMG 1963), MEP (C) Somerset 1979-; s of Lt-Col Frederick Archibald Warner RN (d 1918); *b* 2 May 1918; *Educ* Wixenford Berks, RNC Dartmouth, Magdalen Oxford; *m* 1971, Simone Georgina de Ferranti, da of Lt-Col Hubert Jocelyn Nangle (d 1968); 2 s, 1 step da; *Career* Lt-Cdr RNVR; Ambassador: Laos 1965-67, UN 1969-71, Japan 1972-75; dir Guinness Peat Gp & Chloride Gp, dir Loraz Int, chm National Trust Wessex Region 1976-78, farmer; *Clubs* Beefsteak, Turf; *Style* - Sir Fred Warner, GCVO, KCMG, MEP; Laverstock, Bridport, Dorset (☎ 0308 68543); 113 Fulham rd, SW3 (☎ 01 589 4253)

WARNER, Sir (Edward Courtenay) Henry; 3 Bt (UK 1910), of Brettenham, Suffolk; s of 2 Bt, DSO, MC (d 1955); *b* 3 Aug 1922; *Educ* Eton, Ch Ch Oxford; *m* 1949, Jocelyn Mary, da of Cdr Sir Thomas Lubbock Beevor, 6 Bt, RN (ka 1943); 3 s; *Heir* s, Philip Courtenay Thomas Warner, b 3 April 1951; *Career* served 1939-45 with Scots Gds; chm Law Land Co Ltd 1975-; *Style* - Sir Henry Warner, Bt; The Grove, Great Baddow, Essex

WARREN, Alastair Kennedy; TD (1952); s of Maj John Russell Warren JP (d 1941); *b* 17 July 1922; *Educ* Glasgow Acad, Loretto, Glasgow U; *m* 1952, Ann Lindsay, nee Maclean; 2 c; *Career* Maj served with HLI 1939-45; journalist, editor Glasgow Herald 1965-74, editor Dumfries & Galloway Standard 1976-, Provost Roy Borough of New Galloway and Kells Community Cncl 1978-; *Recreations* writing poetry, hill walking, swimming; *Clubs* Glasgow Academicals; *Style* - Alastair Warren Esq TD; Rathan, New Galloway, Kirkcudbrightshire (☎ New Galloway 257)

WARREN, Rt Rev Alwyn Keith; CMG (1967), MC; s of Thomas John Cory Warren (d 1942); *b* 23 Sept 1900; *Educ* Huntly Sch Marton NZ, Marlborough, Magdalen Oxford; *m* 1928, Doreen Eda, nee Laws; 1 s, 2 da; *Career* chaplain NZ Div Cavalry 1944-45, ordained 1925, Archdeacon Christchurch 1934-44, Dean Christchurch 1944-51, Bishop of Christchurch 1951-66, sub prelate Order of St John's, chancellor Canterbury U 1965-69, trustee NA National Library; *Recreations* rowing, music, people, reading; *Clubs* Univ of Canterbury, Univ Staff; *Style* - The Rt Rev Alwyn Warren CMG MC; Little Court, 193 Memorial ave, Christchurch, New Zealand

WARREN, Hon Mrs (Anne Philippa); *née* Russell; da of 2 Baron Russell of Liverpool, CBE, MC, by his 1 w, Constance, nee Gordon; *b* 13 Feb 1924; *m* 1947, Gershom Warren, late Maj Canadian Army; *Style* - The Hon Mrs

Warren; 1611 McTavish rd, RR2 Sidney, Vancouver, BC, Canada

WARREN, Alec Stephen; CMG (1950); s of James Herbert Warren (d 1926); *b* 27 June 1894; *Educ* Aldenham; *m* 1958, Beryl May, nee Cheese; *Career* Coronation Medal 1953; dir Warren Sons & Co Ltd 1920, chm Warren & Reynolds 1935, Ministry of Food 1939-56, memb Potato Marketing Bd 1956-59, chm Albers Ark Investment Co Ltd 1960-; *Recreations* billiards; *Style* - Alec Warren Esq CMG; Maison Pommier, Sark, Channel Islands (☎ Sark 2035)

WARREN, Sir (Brian) Charles Pennefather; 9 Bt (I 1784), of Warren's Court, Co Cork; s of Sir Thomas Warren, 8 Bt, CBE, DL (d 1961); *b* 23 June 1923; *Educ* Bilton Grange, Wellington; *m* 1976, Nicola, da of Capt Edward Cazenove (4 cous of Christopher Cazenove the actor), of Great Dalby, Leics, by his w Grania (ggda of Sir John Kennedy, 1 Bt); *Heir* 1 cous, Maj Patrick Vaughton Warren RA; *Career* served with 2 (Armoured) Bn Irish Gds 1941-45; *Style* - Sir Charles Warren, Bt; The Wilderness, Castle Oliver, Kilmallock, Co Limerick, Ireland

WARREN, Charles Wyatt; JP (1968), DL (1969); s of Charles Wyatt Warren (d 1931); *b* 15 Aug 1908; *Educ* Caernarvon G S, London U; *m* 1938, Margaret Mary, nee Lewis; 2 da; *Career* landscape painter; *Recreations* hill walking, reading, music, poetry, foreign travel; *Style* - Charles Warren Esq, JP, DL; High Meadows, Caernarvon, Gwynedd (☎ Caernarvon 3108); Pen Towyn, Llangadwaladr, Bodorgan, Anglesey (☎ Bodorgan 472)

WARREN, Sir Freddie (Alfred Henry); CBE (1970, MBE 1957); s of William Warren (d 1917); *b* 19 Dec 1915; *Educ* Sir Walter St John's Sch; *m* 1940, Margaret, nee Murphy; 1 s, 1 da; *Career* kt 1976, Capt RAPC 1939-47; assist to Sec of the Cabinet 1951-58, assist to Government Chief Whip 1958-79; *Recreations* the press; *Clubs* Institute of Directors; *Style* - Sir Freddie Warren CBE; 93 South Eden pk rd, Beckenham, Kent (☎ 658 6951)

WARREN, Patrick Vaughton; s of Lt-Col William Warren, OBE, MC, RASC (d 1981, himself yr bro of Sir Thomas Warren, 8 Bt), by his 1 w Marjorie; hp to Btcy of 1 cous, Sir Charles Warren, 9 Bt; *b* 11 Jan 1917; *Career* Maj RA; *Style* - Maj Patrick Warren; c/o Executors of late Lt-Col William Warren, c/o Barclays Bank, Tavistock, Devon

WARRENDER, Col Hon John Robert; OBE (1963), MC (1943), TD (1967), DL (Somerset 1965); s (by 1 m) and h of 1 Baron Bruntisfield MC; *b* 7 Feb 1921; *Educ* Eton, Sandhurst; *m* 1, 1948, Ann Moireen, da of Lt-Col Sir Walter Fendall Campbell KCIE; 2 s, 2 da; m 2, 1977, Mrs Shirley Crawley, da of Sqdn Ldr Edward Ross RAF ret; *Career* Col RARO; memb (Brig) Roy Co of Archers (Queen's Body-guard for Scotland), late Capt 2 Dragoons, Roy Scots Greys; ADC to Govr of Madras 1946-48 and cmdg N Som Yeo 44 Roy Tank Regt 1957-62; chm Thistle Industl Hldgs Edinburgh; Kt of Sov Mil Order of Malta; *Style* - Col The Hon John Warrender OBE MC TD DL; 97 Cadogan gdns, SW3; Whitelaws, Garvald, Haddington, E Lothian (☎ Garvald 246)

WARWICK, 7 Earl of (GB 1746); Charles Guy Fulke Greville; JP (1952), DL (Warwicks 1952); also Baron Brooke (E 1621) and Earl Brooke (GB 1759); s of 6 Earl of Warwick, CMG, MVO (d 1928, whose mother (Daisy) Countess of Warwick was the *bonne amie* of Edward VII), by Elfrida, da of Sir William Eden, 7 Bt, and sis of Sir Anthony Eden (cr Earl of Avon); *b* 4 March 1911; *Educ* Eton; *m* 1, 1933 (m dis 1938), Rose, da of David Bingham (nephew of 5 Earl of Lucan and ggs of the Crimean War Commander, the 3 Earl); 1 s; m 2, 1942 (m dis 1949), Mary, da of Percy Hopkinson and formerly w of Harold Bell; m 3, 1963, Mme Janine Detry de Marès; *Heir* s, Lord Brooke; *Career* patron of 2 livings; Lt Reserve of Offrs Gren Gds; Govr Birmingham U; Alderman Warwick 1952-; *Clubs* Roy Yacht Sqdn; *Style* - The Rt Hon Earl of Warwick JP DL

WARWICK, Frederick Richard; MC (1942), TD (1946), JP (Notts 1960); s of Col Philip H Warwick DSO TD (d 1954); *b* 22 May 1919; *Educ* Eton; *m* 1955, Kathleen, nee Walker; 1 s, 1 da; *Career*

Maj, served with Sherwood Rangers Yeomanry 1939-45; dir John Smith's Tadcaster Brewery Ltd 1962, md 1966-75, chm 1975-80; dir Courage Ltd 1971-80; *Style* - Maj Frederick Warwick MC TD JP; Willow Green, Boston Spa, Wetherby, W Yorks (☎ Wetherby 843112)

WARWICK-SMITH, Myles Humphrey; s of Reginald Warwick-Smith (d 1944); *b* 26 Dec 1929; *Educ* Nautical Coll Worcester; *m* 1952, Diana Mary Stella, nee Freeman; 2 s, 2 da; *Career* Capt (Leicesters) TA; dir LRC Int Ltd, md LRC Industrial Holdings Ltd, md LRC Overseas Ltd, chm United Photographic Laboratories and others; *Recreations* riding, tennis; *Clubs* IOD; owns racehorses 'Cornish Tess', 'Kelly Bright Hope'; *Style* - Myles Warwick-Smith Esq; Shorehill Farm, Otford Hills, Sevenoaks, Kent (☎ Otford 2868)

WASS, Francis Harry; s of Frank Wass, of Burton Coggles, Lincolnshire (d 1955); *b* 6 August 1927; *Educ* King's Sch, Grantham, London University, Newark Technical Coll; *m* 1951, Phyllis May; 1 s, 1 da; *Career* chartered engr; dir Goodwin Barsby Ltd since 1977, formerly assist ch engr Aveling Barford Ltd 1966-77; *Style* - Francis Wass Esq; 20 Bleakmoor Close, Rearsby, Leicester (☎ Rearsby 526)

WASS, Lawrence Farbon; CBE (1963), JP (1957); s of William Henry Wass (d 1963); *b* 19 Feb 1912; *Educ* Southend H S, McGill U, Queen's U Canada; *m* 1938, Margaret Kate, nee Wilson; 1 s, 1 da; *Career* chm Wass Pritchard Ltd 1964-78, chm Enfield Conservative Assoc 1964-68, memb Enfield Borough Cncl 1949-60, dep chm Edmonton Div Mddx Petty Sessions; *Recreations* music, garden; *Clubs* St Stephen's Constitutional; *Style* - Lawrence Wass Esq, CBE, JP; 141 Green Dragon Lane, Southgate, N14 (☎ 360 3870)

WASSALL, Graham Wainwright; s of William Wainwright Wassall, of Meadow Farm, Brownmills, Staffs; *b* 12 Dec 1950; *Educ* Queen Mary's G S; *m* 1978, Anne, da of Maj William Frederick Martin Hunt MBE, of Green Lodge, Newport Pagnell, Bucks (d 1979); 1 s; *Career* dir J W Wassall Ltd; *Recreations* golf, shooting, squash, gardening; *Style* - Graham Wassall Esq; Millstone Cottage, Abbots Bromley, Staffs (☎ 0283 840389)

WASSERMAN, Hon Mrs; Hon Cressida; da of Rt Hon Hugh Gaitskell, CBE, MP (d 1963), and Baroness Gaitskell; *b* 1942; *Educ* Somerville Oxford; *m* 1964, Gordon Wasserman, Assist Sec Home Off; 2 da; *Style* - The Hon Mrs Wasserman; 18 Frognal gdns, NW3 (☎ 01 435 3671)

WATERFORD, 8 Marquess of (I 1789); Sir John Hubert de la Poer Beresford; 12 Bt (I 1665); also Baron of Le Power and Coroghmore (I 1535; the 8 Baron's da Katherine claimed 1763 an alleged Barony of La Poer, said to have been cr by writ of summons 1375, but leading authorities dismiss any such right, though George III (1767) confirmed the I House of Lords's ruling that her claim was valid), Viscount Tyrone, Baron Beresford (both I 1720), Earl of Tyrone (I 1746), and Baron Tyrone (GB 1786, which sits in House of Lords as); s of 7 Marquess of Waterford (d 1934) and ggn of Lord Charles Beresford, whose opposition to what he saw as Lord ('Jackie') Fisher's cheeseparing ways imperilling the RN did so much to prepare the UK for WW I; also 1 cous of Mark Girouard, *qv*, the architectural writer; the 3, 5 & 6 Marquesses and the eldest s & h of the 1 Marquess all died violent deaths, the latter after a riding accident, the two former by, or as a result of, hunting accidents (the 5 Marquess shot himself, but in a bout of temporary insanity, to which, however, a crippling fall in the hunting field is thought to have contributed), while the 6 Marquess was drowned in a river near the Curraghmore kennels; in such circumstances, Jorrocks's claim, that hunting has 'only' five & twenty percent of war's dangers, perhaps says more about war than the chase; *b* 14 July 1933; *Educ* Eton; *m* 1957, Lady Caroline Wyndham-Quin, da of 6 Earl of Dunraven and Mount-Earl; 3 s, 1 da; *Heir* s, Earl of Tyrone; *Career* Lt RHG Supp Res; *Style* - The Most Hon Marquess of Waterford; Curraghmore, Portlaw, Co Waterford, Eire (☎ 87102)

WATERFORD, Marchioness of; Lady Caroline Olein Geraldine; *née* Wyndham-Quin; da of late 6 Earl of Dunraven and Mount-Earl, CB, CBE, MC; *b* 1936; *m* 1957, 8 Marq of Waterford; *Style* - The Most Hon the Marchioness of Waterford

WATERHOUSE, Lady Caroline; *née* Spencer-Churchill; da of 10 Duke of Marlborough (d 1972); *b* 1923; *m* 1946, Maj (Charles) Hugo Waterhouse; 2 s, 1 da; *Career* appointed an Extra Lady in Waiting to HRH Princess Alexandra, the Hon Mrs Angus Ogilvy 1970; *Style* - Lady Caroline Waterhouse; Middleton Hall, Bakewell, Derbys

WATERHOUSE, Maj (Charles) Hugo; s of Capt Rt Hon Charles Waterhouse, MC, JP, DL, sometime Parly Sec BOT; *b* 11 June 1918; *Educ* Eton, Trin Cambridge; *m* 1946, Lady Caroline Spencer-Churchill (b 1923, Extra Lady in Waiting to HRH Princess Alexandra The Hon Mrs Angus Ogilvy 1970-), da of 10 Duke of Marlborough; 2 s, 1 da; *Career* late Maj served Europe; *Recreations* shooting; *Clubs* Pratt's, White's; *Style* - Maj Hugo Waterhouse; 36 St George's dve, SW1 (☎ 01 834 3950); Middleton Hall, Bakewell, Derbys (☎ Youlgreave 224)

WATERLOW, Sir Christopher Rupert; 5 Bt (UK 1873), of London; s of (Peter) Rupert Waterlow (d 1969), of Knightsbridge, London, & gs of Sir Philip Alexander Waterlow, 4 Bt (d 1973); Sir Christopher is 3 cous twice removed of Sir Thomas Waterlow, 3 Bt, CBE, of Harrow Weald; *b* 12 Aug 1959; *Educ* Stonyhurst; *Heir* great unc, Derek Vaudrey Waterlow, b 19 Feb 1902; *Recreations* archery; *Style* - Sir Christopher Waterlow, Bt; Grenville Manor, Haddenham, Bucks (☎ 0844 291 496)

WATERLOW, (James) Gerard; s and h of Sir Thomas Waterlow, 3 Bt, CBE; *b* 3 Sept 1939; *Educ* Marlborough, Trin Cambridge; *m* 1965, Diana, da of Sir Thomas Skyrme, KCVO, CB, CBE, TD, JP, chm Magistrates' Assoc Eng & Wales 1979-, by his 1 w, Hon Barbara Lyle, herself da of 1 Baron Lyle of Westbourne ; 1 s (Thomas b 1970), 1 da (Amanda b 1968); *Style* - Gerard Waterlow Esq; 12 Cliveden Place, SW1 (☎ 01 730 6595)

WATERLOW, Lady; Gwendoline Florence Elizabeth; da of Léon Balanché; *m* 1, Baden Murch; m 2, 1972, as his 3 w, Sir Philip Waterlow, 4 Bt (d 1973); *Style* - Lady Waterlow; 11 Elmwood av, Hawkwell, Essex

WATERLOW, Sir Thomas Gordon; 3 Bt (UK 1930), of Harrow Weald, Middx; s of Sir William A Waterlow, 1 Bt, KBE (d 1931), and bro of Sir (William) James Waterlow, 2 Bt, CBE, TD (d 1969); *see also* Waterlow, 5 Bt, Sir Christopher; *b* 2 Jan 1911; *Educ* Marlborough, Trin Cambridge; *m* 1938, Helen Elizabeth (d 1970), da of Gerard A H Robinson, of Bix, Henley-on-Thames; 3 s; *Heir* s, (James) Gerard Waterlow, b 3 Sept 1939; *Career* dep chm Royal Bank of Scotland, Edinburgh, 1966-75; dir Scottish cos; pres Edinburgh Chamber of Commerce 1963-65; *Style* - Sir Thomas Waterlow, Bt; 1 Lennox st, Edinburgh EH4 1QB (☎ 031 332 2621)

WATERPARK, 7 Baron (I 1729); Sir Frederick Caryll Philip Cavendish; 8 Bt (GB 1755); s of Brig-Gen Frederick Cavendish, bro of 6 Baron and 6 in descent from William Cavendish, love child of 3 Duke of Devonshire; suc unc 1948; *b* 6 Oct 1926; *Educ* Eton; *m* 1951, Danièle, da of Roger Guirche, of Paris; 1 s, 2 da; *Heir* s, Hon Roderick Cavendish; *Career* served Gren Gds, Kenya Police Reserve; sales dir CSE Aviation Ltd 1962-; *Clubs* Cavalry & Guards; *Style* - The Rt Hon Lord Waterpark; 2/74 Elm Park rd, SW3 (☎ 01 351 3663)

WATERS, Kenneth; *Career* dir Yule Catto & Co Ltd, chm: Cobb's Quay Ltd, Hartford Marina Ltd, Thomas Bell & Co Ltd, William Cox Ltd; *Style* - Kenneth Waters Esq; Yule Catto & Co Ltd, New Bond Street House, New Bond st, W1

WATERTON, John Brian; s of Laurence Maude Waterton (d 1976); *b* 10 March 1934; *Educ* Giggleswick Sch Yorks; *m* 1959, Jane Pollack, da of Harry Anthony Pitt Wilkinson (d 1966); 2 s, 2 da; *Career*

co dir; gp marketing dir Dawson Int Ltd; *Recreations* golf; *Style* - John Waterton Esq; 4 Royal Terrace, Falkland, Fife, (☎ 03375 358)

WATES, Sir Ronald Wallace; JP (Inner London 1947), DL (Surrey 1981); s of Edward Wates; *b* 4 June 1907; *Educ* Emanuel Sch; *m* 1931, Phyllis Trace; 4 da; *Career* Pres Wates Ltd 1973- (chm 1969-73); FRICS, FIOB; chm Roy Soc for the Blind, Tstee Historic Churches Preservation Tst, kt 1975; *Style* - Sir Ronald Wates JP DL; Manor House, Headley, Epsom, Surrey (☎ Leatherhead 77346)

WATHEN, Mark William Gerard; TD (1946); s of Gerard Anstruther Wathen CIE (d 1958); *b* 18 Sept 1912; *Educ* Gresham's Sch Holt; *m* 1940, Rosemary, nee Hartridge; 2 s, 2 da; *Career* dir Barclays Bank (City, Ipswich, Norwich) 1948-72, High Sheriff Norfolk 1968, Master Mercers Co 1963, Church Cmmnr 1973-78, memb Gen Synod C of E 1970-80, Fellow Roy Soc of Art; *Recreations* shooting, fishing, writing; *Clubs* Brooks's, MCC; *Style* - Mark Wathen Esq TD; Talisker House, Isle of Skye (☎ Carbost 245); Bolwick Hall Farm, Marsham, Norwich (☎ Aylsham 3130)

WATHERSTON, John Michael; s of John Robert Watherston; *b* 30 June 1932; *Educ* Sedbergh; *m* 1960, Lorna Kathryn, da of George Warren Enniskillen (d 1956); 1 s, 1 da; *Career* memb Inst of CA (Scotland), exec dir Murray Johnstone Ltd; *Recreations* golf, shooting, skiing; *Clubs* Honourable Co of Edinburgh Golfers, Western (Glasgow); *Style* - John Watherston Esq; 22 Murrayfield Drive, Edinburgh (☎ 031 337 2948)

WATHERSTON, Maj John Robert; TD (1942 and 3 bars), DL (Edinburgh 1958); s of John Watherston (d 1949); *b* 4 July 1903; *Educ* Edinburgh Academy, Sedbergh; *m* 1929, Jean Kathleen, nee Muirhead; 3 s; *Career* served RA (TA) 1939-45, High Constable and Guard of Honour Palace of Holyroodhouse 1953-, moderator 1968, Master Edinburgh Merchant Co 1959-60, Lord Dean of Guild Edinburgh 1954-56, govr Fettes Coll 1948-; *Clubs* New (Edinburgh), Hon Co Edinburgh Golfers; *Style* - Maj John Watherston, TD***, DL; Beechwood Mains, Murrayfield, Edinburgh (☎ 031 337 4080)

WATKINS, Baron (UK 1872); Tudor Elwyn Watkins; s of Howell Watkins JP; *b* 9 May 1903; *Educ* Harlech Coll; *m* 1936, Bronwen Richards, da of Thomas Stather, of Talgarth; *Career* MP (L) Brecon & Radnor 1945-70, PPS to Sec State Wales 1964-68; formerly miner and political agent; chm Brecon Beacons Nat Park Ctee 1974-78; *Style* - Rt Hon Lord Watkins; Bronafon, Penyfan rd, Powys (☎ 2961)

WATKINS, Stephen Desmond; s of Stephen Christopher Watkins; *b* 29 June 1933; *Educ* Newport High Sch, Keble Oxford; *m* 1957, Mervee Parry, da of David Parry Williams (d 1974); 1 s; *Career* Appointments with the Roy Dutch/Shell Gp Thailand, Phillippines, Cyprus, Australia, Venezuela, S America, and UK 1957-78; dir UK Oil Pipelines, v pres Oil Industl Club 1981-, pres UK Petroleum Industl Assoc 1981-; *Recreations* music, golf; *Clubs* Oxford Union Soc (past pres); *Style* - Stephen Watkins Esq; Castle Court, Cyprus; 50 Sheffield ter, W8

WATKINSON, 1 Viscount (UK 1964); Harold Arthur Watkinson; CH (1962), PC (1955); s of Arthur Watkinson; *b* 25 Jan 1910; *Educ* Queen's Coll Taunton, King's London; *m* 1939, Vera, da of John Langmead; 2 da; *Heir* none; *Career* MP (C) Woking 1950-64, Min T'port & Civil Aviation 1955-59, Min Def 1959-62; dir Midland Bank; Pres CBI 1976-77, chm Cadbury Schweppes 1969-74; *Style* - The Rt Hon Viscount Watkinson CH PC; Tyma House, Bosham, Chichester, Sussex

WATKINSON, Leonard James; s of Leonard Watkinson (d 1966); *b* 27 June 1928; *Educ* W Leeds H S, Leeds U; *m* 1957, Norma, nee Schofield; 1 s, 2 da; *Career* tech dir Universal Ink Co Ltd 1960-64, dir of Research WH Howson Ltd 1964-70, tech dir Howson-Algraphy Gp of Vickers Ltd 1970-; *Recreations* fell walking, photography, botany, choral music; *Style* - Leonard Watkinson Esq; 95 Cookridge Lane, Leeds, LS16 7NE (☎ 673853)

WATLING, His Honour Judge; (David) Brian Watling; QC (1979); s of Vernon Watling and Edith, nee Ridley; *b* 18 June 1935; *Educ* Charterhouse, King's Coll London; *m* 1964, Noelle Bugden, WRNS; *Career* barr 1957, Crown Court Recorder 1979-81, Circuit Judge (SE) 1981-, Visiting Prof Law U Coll Buckingham 1980; *Style* - His Hon Judge Watling QC; Queen Elizabeth Building, Temple, EC4 (☎ 01 353 6453)

WATNEY, Lady Katherine Felicity; *née* Courtenay; da of 17 Earl of Devon; *b* 1940; *m* 1966, Anthony Stephen Pope Watney; 1 s; *Style* - Lady Katherine Watney; Yule Cottage, Wargrave, Berks

WATSON, Hon Mrs Alastair - Joan; da of late Capt Philip Wyndham Cobbold; *m* 1925, Hon Alastair Joseph Watson (d 1955 - s of 1 Baron Manton); 2 s; *Style* - The Hon Mrs Alastair Watson; Newton Farm, Orford, Suffolk

WATSON, Maj-Gen Andrew Linton; s of Col W L Watson OBE (d 1961); *b* 9 April 1927; *Educ* Wellington; *m* 1952, Mary Elizabeth (Ginty), nee Rigby; 2 s, 1 da; *Career* cmd 1 Bn Black Watch 1969-71, GSO 17 Div Malaya 1967-68, Cdr 19 Airportable Bde 1972-73, Cdr Br Army Staff, Mil Attachée Washington 1975-77, Gen Offr Eastern District 1977-80; Ch of Staff Allied Forces N Europe 1980-; *Recreations* shooting, tennis, walking, classical music; *Clubs* Army & Navy, Puffin's (Edinburgh); *Style* - Maj-Gen Andrew Watson; Royal Bank of Scotland, 18 South Methven st, Perth

WATSON, Alexander Stuart; s of William Stuart Alexander Watson, of China (d 1960); *b* 16 July 1920; *Educ* Worksop Coll, Coll of Aeronautical Engineering; *m* 1949, Jean Patricia, nee Kerswell; 1 s, 2 da; *Career* marketing dir British Aerospace 1977-, sales dir Hawker Siddeley Aviation 1972, sales dir Dowty Rotol Gp 1962; *Recreations* sailing (yacht Kit IV: 'Christchurch'); *Style* - Alexander Watson Esq; Saxon Hill, South Cadbury, Somerset

WATSON, Hon Mrs (Bridget Doreen); *née* de Courcy; da of 29 Baron Kingsale, DSO (d 1969); *b* 1915; *m* 1, 1938 (m dis 1951), Rev George Ian Falconer Thomson; 1 da; m 2, 19--, Stephen Watson; 1 s; *Style* - The Hon Mrs Watson; North Blagdon Farm, Ashbury, Okehampton

WATSON, Brig Bruce Edmeston; s of Prof Herbert Edmeston Watson (d 1980); *b* 5 April 1918; *Educ* Marlborough, Univ Coll London; *m* 1941, Joan Elizabeth, da of Maj William Moore (d 1950); 2 da; *Career* served RA 1939-73 (ret); Dep Dir Inspectorate of Armaments 1967-70, Dir Heavy Weapons Projects 1970-73; MBIM 1969, FBIM 1980; dir FN (England) Ltd 1973-; *Recreations* walking, touring, photography, gardening; *Clubs* Army & Navy; *Style* - Brig Bruce Watson; Chestnut Cottage, 12 Longdon Wood, Keston pk, Kent (☎ Farnborough 52619)

WATSON, Hon Mrs; Hon Catriona Mary Antonia; da of Baron Swann (Life Peer); *b* 15 March 1953; *Educ* St George's Sch for Girls Edinburgh, N of Scotland Coll of Ag; *m* 1976, Robert Noble, s of Robert John Watson; 1 da; *Career* farmer; *Recreations* riding, sailing, skiing, gardening; *Style* - The Hon Mrs Watson; Ballingall Farm, Leslie, Fife (☎ Glenrothes 742963)

WATSON, Daniel Stewart; CB (1967), OBE (1958); s of William Watson DD DLitt (d 1972); *b* 30 Dec 1911; *Educ* Robert Gordon's Coll Aberdeen, Aberdeen U; *m* 1939, Isabel, nee Gibson; 1 s; *Career* Scientific Offr Admiralty 1938, Dir Admlty Surface Weapons Establishment 1961-68, Head RN Scientific Serv 1968-72; *Recreations* caravanning, vintage cars; *Style* - Daniel Watson Esq, CB, OBE; The Cedars, Jumps rd, Churt, Farnham, Surrey (☎ Frensham 2374)

WATSON, Edward Howsley; CB (1968); s of Ernest Watson (d 1945); *b* 16 June 1910; *Educ* Harrogate G S, Leeds U; *m* 1951, Alice Mary, nee Atkinson; 1 s; *Career* solicitor Ministry of Health 1946-68, solicitor & legal advsr Ministry of Housing and Local Govt 1965-70; *Clubs* Civil Service; *Style* - Edward Watson Esq CB; Iddons, Henley's Down, Catsfield, Battle, E Sussex (☎ Crowhurst 226)

WATSON, Ella, Lady; Ella Marguerite; da of Sir George Farrar, 1 & last Bt; *m* 1935, Sir Thomas Watson, 4 Bt (ka 1941); 1 s (5 Bt); *Style* - Ella, Lady Watson; Talton Lodge, Newbold-on-Stour, Stratford-on-Avon, Warwicks

WATSON, George Menzies; s of William George Watson; *b* 15 July, 1941; *Educ* Barnard Castle Sch; *m* 1969, Irene, da of Albert Johnson; 1 s, 1 da; *Career* FCA 1965, fin dir and co sec Wailes Dove Bitumastic Ltd, co sec Barford Chemicals Ltd, ptnr C and G Model Railways; *Recreations* golf, photography, railways; *Style* - George Watson Esq; 'Craigroyal', Well Bank, Aycliffe Village, Durham (☎ 0632 314677)

WATSON, Sir James Andrew; 5 Bt (UK 1866), of Henrietta Street, Cavendish Sq, St Marylebone, Co Middx; s of Sir Thomas Watson, 4 Bt (d 1941), and Ella, Lady Watson, *qv*; *b* 30 Dec 1937; *Educ* Eton; *m* 1965, Christabel Mary, da of Kenneth Ralph Malcolm Carlisle; 2 s, 1 da; *Heir* s, Roland Victor Watson; *Career* Lt Life Gds; barr; *Style* - Sir James Watson, Bt; Talton House, Newbold-on-Stour, Stratford-on-Avon, Warwicks

WATSON, John Forbes; s and h of Sir Derrick William Inglefield-Watson; *b* 16 May 1926; *Educ* Eton; *Career* Lt-Col RE; *Style* - John Watson Esq

WATSON, Rear-Adm John Garth; CB (1965); s of Alexander Henry St Croix Watson (d 1963); *b* 20 Feb 1914; *Educ* Univ Coll London, Northampton Engrg Coll London U; *m* 1943, Barbara Elizabeth, nee Falloon; 2 s, 1 da; *Career* Admiralty RN 1939-66; chartered engr, sec The Institution of Civil Engrs 1967-79; *Recreations* sailing, gardening; *Clubs* Athenaeum, Roy Thames Yacht, Roy Naval & Roy Albert Yacht; owner of yacht 'Icemaid'; *Style* - Rear-Adm John Watson CB; Little Hall Court, Shedfield nr Southampton (☎ 0329 833216); 58 Iverna Court, Kensington, W8 (☎ 937 2508)

WATSON, John Henry; s of Henry William Watson (d 1963); *b* 25 Jan 1944; *Educ* Wolverhampton G S; *m* 1966, Marigold Anne, nee Milne; 1 s, 2 da; *Career* CA 1966, articled with Worcester Country Practise 1960-66, man consultant Touche Ross 1968-71, fin dir H J Green & Co Ltd 1975-; *Recreations* home, family, music; *Style* - John Watson Esq; Killarney, Holt Pound, Farnham, Surrey (☎ Bentley 3108)

WATSON, J Jordan; CMG (1972); s of John Henry Watson (d 1928); *b* 15 Dec 1912; *Educ* Gosforth G S; *m* 1940, Marjorie, nee Lumb; 1 s, 1 da; *Career* Dept of Employment 1930, Foreign Serv 1945-53; Cnsllr (Labour) Br Embassy Washington DC 1966-72; *Recreations* angling, golf; *Style* - Jordan Watson Esq CMG; West Cottage, 19 Riverside rd, Alnmouth, Alnwick, Northumberland (☎ 066 066 573)

WATSON, Kenneth Tomalin; CBE (1965); s of John William Watson (d 1959); *b* 14 Aug 1922; *Educ* Henry Mellish Sch Nottingham, Nottingham U; *m* 1948, Gwendoline, nee Park; *Career* chartered civil engr, joined Air Ministry 1943-67 (ret ch engr), civil engr Br Airport Authority 1967-73, sr civil engr 1973-; *Style* - Kenneth Watson Esq CBE; 1 Mandeville rd, Shepperton, Middlesex, (☎ Walton-on-Thames 24898)

WATSON, Hon Miles Ronald Marcus; s and h of 3 Baron Manton; *b* 7 May 1958; *Educ* Eton; *Career* 2 Lt Life Gds; BAOR; *Recreations* shooting, skiing; *Style* - Lt The Hon Miles Watson

WATSON, Martin Yorke; CBE (1948); s of Arthur Herbert Watson, Archdeacon of Richmond, Yorks (d 1952); *b* 10 Nov 1905; *Educ* Lancing, Ch Ch Oxford; *m* 1936, Ursula Catherine, da of Maj Harold Hunter Grotrian (d 1951); 3 s, 1 da; *Career* HM Consular Serv 1928, principal 1939-42 & assist sec 1942-45 Miny Economic Warfare, dep dir Jt Intelligence Bureau 1945-58, dir economic Intelligence MOD 1958-65; *Recreations* gardening, woodworking, shooting, fishing; *Style* - Martin Watson Esq CBE; The Old Vicarage, 7 May st, Great Chishill, Royston, Herts

WATSON, Sir Norman James; 2 Bt (UK 1912), of Sulhamstead, Sulhamstead Abbots, Berks; s of 1 Bt (d 1930); *b* 17

March 1897; *Educ* Eton; *m* 1974, Beryl, da of Alfred Norris, and widow of Sqdn Ldr Basil Montefiore Davis RAF, and formerly w of Sir Francis Cyril Rose, 4 Bt; *Heir* none; *Career* served in 1914-18 War, Lt with KRRC and RAF, Pilot Offr RAFVR 1940, Flying Offr 1942, ret 1942; High Sheriff Berkshire 1940; *Style* - Sir Norman Watson, Bt; Flat 132, 55 Park Lane, W1 (☎ 01 499 5621)

WATSON, Vice-Adm Sir Philip Alexander; KBE (1976), MVO (1960); s of Alexander Henry St Croix Watson (d 1963); *b* 7 Oct 1919; *Educ* St Albans Sch; *m* 1948, Jennifer Beatrice, nee Tanner; 1 s, 2 da; *Career* joined RNVR 1940, Vice-Adm 1974, Ch Naval Engr Offr 1974-76 (ret 1976); dir Marconi Int Marine Co Ltd and Naval Consultant to GEC Marconi Electronics Ltd 1977-; *Clubs* Army & Navy; *Style* - Vice-Adm Sir Philip Alexander KBE MVO; Finchingfield, Braintree, Essex (☎ Great Dunmow 810289)

WATSON, Hon Mrs Robert - Enid Agnes Maud; da of late Arthur Levita, and formerly wife of Ewen Donald Cameron; *m* 1961, as his 2 wife, the Hon Robert Fraser Watson (decd - 2 s of 1 Baron Manton); *Style* - The Hon Mrs Robert Watson; 11 Cadogan sq, SW1

WATSON, Richard James Lea; s of Col William Linton Watson OBE IMS (d 1961); *b* 11 Dec 1928; *Educ* Charterhouse, Cambridge; *m* 1961, Daphne Christian, da of Capt H S Bowlby RN (d 1977); 2 c; *Career* Lt Malaya; md Cuttall Windows Ltd 1974-, dir: Darlington & Simpson Rolling Mills Ltd 1979-, Cuttall-McKinney Ltd 1980-; *Recreations* fishing, shooting, local affairs; *Clubs* United Oxford & Cambridge; *Style* - Richard Watson Esq; Stocks, Castle Hedingham, Halstead, Essex

WATSON, Lady Susan Diana; *née* Wood; da of 2 Earl of Halifax (d 1980); *b* 1938; *m* 1959, Brig Ian Watson CBE TD; 2 s; *Style* Lady Susan Watson; Bossall, Barton-le-Willows, York

WATSON, Hon Thomas Philip; 2 s (triplet with Hon Miles W and Hon Mrs Cottrell) of 3 Baron Manton; *b* 7 May 1958; *Educ* Eton; *Career* Lt QOH TAVR 1981 (seniority 1980-); *Style* - Lt The Hon Thomas Watson

WATSON, Hon Victoria Monica; da of 3 Baron Manton; *b* 1958; *Style* - The Hon Victoria Watson

WATSON, Hon Mrs William - Enid Agnes; da of late Colin Balantyne, of Kirna, Walkerburn; *m* 1934, Hon William Watson TD WS (d 1971, s of Baron Thankerton, Life Peer); *Style* - The Hon Mrs William Watson; Rock Cottage, 12 Walkerburn, Peeblesshire EH43 6AZ

WATT, Arthur Alexander; *b* 22 May 1940; *Educ* George Heriot's Sch Edinburgh, Falkirk H S; *m* 1, 1965 (m dis 1977), Judith Mary, nee Mangles; 2 s, 1 da; m 2, 1979; *Career* CA; gp md Aurora Holdings Ltd 1974-, gp fin dir Cooper & Turner Ltd 1971-74, consultant PA Management Consultants Ltd 1968-71; *Recreations* running, climbing, squash; *Clubs* Oriental; *Style* - Arthur Watt Esq; Priory Farmhouse, S Leverton, Notts (☎ 0427 880250)

WATT, Hon Mrs - Hon Mary; *née* Mackintosh; da of 1 Viscount Mackintosh of Halifax (d 1964); *b* 1927; *m* 1949, (Charles) Michael Watt; 2 s, 1 da; *Career* JP Norfolk; *Style* - The Hon Mrs Watt; Wychwood House, Hethersett, Nr Norwich, Norfolk NR9 3AT

WATTS, Arthur Desmond; CMG (1977); s of Col Arthur Edward Watts (d 1958); *b* 14 Nov 1931; *Educ* Haileybury & ISC, Sandhurst, Downing College Cambridge; *m* 1957, Iris Ann, nee Collier; 1 s, 1 da; *Career* barr 1957, legal assist Br Embassy 1957-; legal cnsllr: FCO 1970-73 & 1977-, Office of UK Permanent Rep to European Communities 1973-77; *Recreations* cricket; *Style* - Arthur Watts Esq CMG; 2 Manor Lodge, Manor pk, Chislehurst, Kent

WAUGH, Auberon Alexander; s of Evelyn Waugh, the novelist, by his 2 w Laura (da of Hon Aubrey Herbert and Hon Mary Vesey, herself da of 4 Viscount de Vesci); Aubrey was in his turn 2 s of 4 Earl of Carnarvon by his 2 Countess,

Elizabeth (sis of 1 Baron Howard of Penrith & great niece of 12 Duke of Norfolk, the latter being the 'Barney' of Creevey's memoirs); Mr Waugh is 5 cous of the present (17) Duke of Norfolk and 1 cous four times removed of the 13 Duke, who reversed the fashionable trend of the mid-nineteenth century by 'going over' from Rome to Lambeth in religion. He was, besides, a disciple of Marie-Antoinette in political economy, recommending the Irish to counteract the effects of their potato famine by consuming curry powder dissolved in water. That the Howards did not perhaps quite understand the Irish may be inferred from the bankruptcy of the 13 Duke's gf (and Mr Waugh's gggggf) as a Dublin wine merchant, which the minor essayist Leo Larch-Symes likened to failing as an undertaker during the Black Death); *b* 17 Nov 1939; *Educ* Downside, Ch Ch Oxford; *m* 1961, Lady Teresa Onslow, *see below*; 2 s, 2 da; *Career* journalist and novelist;currently columnist with Private Eye and The Spectator, also main fiction reviewer for Evening Standard to 1980; served with RHG 1957-58, Daily Telegraph 1960-63, Catholic Herald, Mirror Group, New Statesman, The Times, Books and Bookmen; stood for N Devon 1979 as Dog Lovers Party candidate; *Style* - Auberon Waugh Esq; Combe Florey House, Combe Florey, Taunton, Somerset (☎ 0823 432297)

WAUGH, Lady Teresa (Lorraine); *née* Onslow; da of 6 Earl of Onslow, KBE, MC, TD (d 1971); *b* 1940; *m* 1961, Auberon Alexander Waugh; 2 s, 2 da; *Style* - Lady Teresa Waugh; Combe Florey House, Taunton, Somerset

WAVELL, Countess; Eugénie Marie; da of Col John Quirk, CB, DSO; *m* 1915, 1 Earl Wavell (d 1950); 3 da; *Style* - The Rt Hon Countess Wavell; Marston Meysey Grange, Cricklade, Wilts

WAVERLEY, 2 Viscount (UK 1952); David Alastair Pearson Anderson; s of 1 Viscount Waverley, GCB, OM, GCSI, GCIE, PC, FRS, Chllr of Exchequer 1943-45 (d 1958), by his 1 w, Christina; *b* 18 Feb 1911; *Educ* Malvern, Pembroke Cambridge, Frankfurt U; *m* 1948, Lorna, da of Lt-Col Frederick Ledgerwood; 1 s, 1 da (and 1 da decd); *Heir* s, Hon John Anderson; *Career* consultant Reading Gp of Hosps 1951-; *Style* - The Rt Hon Viscount Waverley; Path Hill House, Whitchurch, Oxon (☎ Pangbourne 2417)

WAY, Rt Rev Wilfrid Lewis Mark; s of late Charles Cecil Lewis Way; *b* 12 May 1905; *Educ* Rossall Sch, Trin Cambridge; *m* 1960, Marion Crosbie, da of Sir Robert Robinson OM; 1 s (adopted), 1 da (adopted); *Career* ordained 1928, Bishop of Masasi 1952-59, Rector of Averham-with-Kelham and Assist Bishop Southwell 1960 (ret 1971); *Recreations* bridge, walking; *Style* - The Rt Rev Wilfrid Way; 5 Redhills Lane, Durham (☎ Durham 43885)

WAYMOUTH, Lady Victoria Mary Verenia Braganza; *née* Yorke; da of 9 Earl of Hardwicke (d 1974); *b* 22 Feb 1947; *Educ* St Mary's Convent, Ascot; *m* 1976, Nigel Norman de Glanville, s of Wing Cdr T G Waymouth, of Bideford; 2 s; *Career* interior designer; *Style* - Lady Victoria Waymouth; 36 Elms rd, SW4 (☎ 01 622 2985)

WEARING, Hon Mrs (Caroline Ruth); *née* Addison; da of 3 Viscount Addison; *b* 30 July 1942; *m* 1965, John Wearing; 1 s, 1 da; *Style* - The Hon Mrs Wearing; 12 Hill Street North, Richmond, Nelson, New Zealand

WEATHERALL, Hon Mrs (Jean Stewart); *née* Macpherson; da of 1 Baron Drumalbyn, KBE, PC; *b* 1938; *m* 1962, Cdr James L Weatherall RN; 1 s (twin), 2 da; *Style* - The Hon Mrs Weatherall; Craig House, Bishop's Waltham, Hants

WEAVER, Leonard John; s of Alfred Wallace Weaver; *b* 10 June 1936; *Educ* St Mary's Sch, Surrey U; *m* 1963, Penelope Ann, nee Sturge-Young; 5 s, 1 da; *Career* md P-E International 1980-, AEI Ltd 1962-64; works manager PYE-TMC 1964-66; dir P-E Consulting Gp 1975- (joined 1966), dir BIM Foundation Ltd 1977-; memb BIM Cncl 1978-, IMC Cncl 1978- (v-pres 1981-), Inst Production Engineering Cncl 1980-; *Recreations* cricket, book-collecting, shooting; *Clubs* Reform, MCC; *Style* - Leonard Weaver Esq; Crab Apple

Court, Oxshott rd, Leatherhead, Surrey (☎ Oxshott 3647)

WEBB, Anthony David; s of Thomas James Webb, of Birmingham; *b* 16 Oct 1941; *Educ* West Bromwich G S; University of Aston (BSc Metallurgy); *m* 1963, Joyce, da of Arthur Furnival; 2 c; *Career* md Blackheath Stamping Co 1978-; *Recreations* coastal cruising (boating); *Clubs* Rotary; *Style* - Anthony Webb Esq; 11 Boscobel rd, Great Barr, Birmingham B43 (☎ 021 358 1288)

WEBB, James; CB 1978; s of James Webb (d 1930); *b* 11 Nov 1918; *Educ* St Francis Xavier's Liverpool, King's London U; *m* 1957, Kathleen Veronica, nee Downey; *Career* civil servant, principal establishment officer and dir of personnel Inland Revenue 1971-75, cmmr Inland Revenue 1968-78; *Style* - James Webb Esq CB; 'Ailsa', 3 Avondale ave, Esher, Surrey (☎ 398 6330)

WEBB, Hon Mrs (Janet Diana); *née* Allanson-Winn; da of 7 Baron Headley; *b* 1932; *m* 1, 1955 (m dis 1969), Antony John Vlassopulos; 2 s; m 2, 1975, David Walter Webb; *Style* - The Hon Mrs Webb; Springs, Rookery Drive, Westcott, Surrey

WEBB, Jeremy Richard; s of C R Webb OBE MC (d 1976); *b* 25 March 1931; *Educ* Radley Coll, Hertford Coll Oxford; *m* 1956, Clover Margaret, da of Maj J Suckling (d 1981); 3 c; *Career* 2 Lt Roy Sussex Regt; advertising (creative dir): Foote, Cone & Beldins 1956-61, Lintas Ltd 1961-65, Wasey-Campbell-Ewald 1966-71, Ferrero & Co spa Turin 1971-74, Wasey-Campbell-Ewald 1974-75, Everetts Ltd 1975-; *Recreations* bridge, swimming; *Style* - Jeremy Webb Esq; 107 Woodwarde rd, Dulwich, SE22 (☎ 01 693 7297)

WEBB, Lawrence Desmond; s of Maj George Lawrence Webb; *b* 18 April 1939; *Educ* Harrow & Neuchâtel, Switzerland; *Career* slr; dir of PLC (investment co) since 1965; *Recreations* squash, sailing/sailboarding, golf; *Clubs* Carlton, Lansdowne; *Style* - Lawrence Webb Esq; c/o Barclays Bank, 6 Clarence st, Kinsgton-upon-Thames, Surrey; c/o Credit Suisse, Paradeplatz, Zurich

WEBB, Hon Mrs (Marigold Elizabeth Cassandra); *née* Neave; da of Baroness Airey of Abingdon and Airey Neave, DSO, OBE, MC, TD, MP (assassinated 1979); *b* 5 May 1944; *m* 1966, William, s of Lt-Cdr William Broughton Webb, DSC, RN (ret), of Caulin Court, Droitwich; children; *Style* - The Hon Mrs Webb; Barbers, Martley, Worcs

WEBB, Hon Mrs (Ruth Isabel); *née* Wakefield; da of 1 Baron Wakefield of Kendal; *b* 1932; *m* 1955, Maj Nigel Webb; 1 s, 2 da; *Style* - The Hon Mrs Webb; Buckstone House, Carnforth, Lancs

WEBB-CARTER, Hon Mrs (Anne Celia); *née* Wigram; da of 2 Baron Wigram, MC, JP, DL; *b* 23 April 1945; *m* 1973, Maj Evelyn Webb-Carter, Gren Gds, s of Brig Brian Webb-Carter, DSO, OBE (s of Maj-Gen Sir John Carter, KCMG, of Ixworth Court, Bedford), by Evelyn Hood, great niece of 4 Viscount Hood; 1 s, 1 da; *Style* - The Hon Mrs Webb-Carter; Ashton Cottage, Bishop's Waltham, Hants

WEBBER, Norman George; s of James William Webber (d 1967); *b* 9 Dec 1916; *Educ* St Edward's Sch, Oxford; *m* 1940, Katherine Redfern; 1 s, 1 da; *Career* Capt Royal Signals; Brigade Signal Officer in the Middle East in the 1939-45 war; chartered acountant, appointed partner Ware Ward & Co October 1949-, partner Ernst & Whinney January 1979-, ret 1980; *Recreations* golf, mountain walking in the the Lake District; *Clubs* Exeter Golf & Country; Exeter & County; *Style* - Norman Webber Esq; Beulah, 14 Rydon Lane, Exeter, Devon EX2 7AW (☎ 039287 4155)

WEBSTER, Michael George Thomas; DL (Berks 1975); s of James Alexander Webster, CB, DSO (d 1965); *b* 27 May 1920; *Educ* Stowe, Magdalen Oxford; *m* 1947, Isabel, da of Major J L Dent DSO MC (ka 1918); 3 da; *Career* Maj NW Europe 1944-45; High Sheriff Berks 1971; Master Brewer's Co 1964-65; chm Aldenham Sch Governors 1977-, dir Grand Metropolitan Ltd 1972-74, chm Fitch Lovell Ltd 1977-; *Recreations* fishing, shooting, golf, listening to music; *Clubs*

Cavalry and Guards, White's, MCC; *Style* - Michael Webster Esq; The Vale, Woodside, Windsor Forest, Berks (☎ Winkfield Row 2658)

WEBSTER, Richard Joseph; s of Peter Joseph Webster; *b* 7 July 1953; *Educ* William Penn Sch Dulwich; *m* 1980, Patricia Catherine, nee Edwards; *Career* Lloyd's insurance broker; dir Howden Cross Ltd 1977-, Alexander Howden Insur Brokers 1978-; *Recreations* riding, squash, swimming, judo; *Clubs* Lloyd's of London and others; *Style* - Richard Webster Esq; 27 Tylney av, Dulwich Wood Park, SE19 (☎ 01 670 9129)

WEDDERBURN OF CHARLTON, Baron (Life Peer UK 1977); Kenneth William Wedderburn; s of Herbert Wedderburn; *b* 13 April 1927; *Educ* Whitgift Sch, Queens' Cambridge; *m* 1, 1951 (m dis 1962), Nina, da of Dr Myer Salaman; 1 s, 2 da; m 2, 1962 (m dis 1969), Dorothy, da of Frederick Barnard and formerly w of William Cole; m 3, 1969, Frances, da of Basil Knight; 1 s; *Career* Cassel Prof Commercial Law LSE 1964-; barr 1953; chm Independent Review Cttee 1976-; *Style* - Rt Hon Lord Wedderburn of Charlton; LSE, Aldwych, WC2 (☎ 01 405 7686)

WEDDERBURN, Hon David Roland; s of Baron Wedderburn of Charlton by his 1 w, Nina; *b* 1956; *Style* - The Hon David Wedderburn; 76 Cromwell av, N6

WEDDERBURN, Hon Jonathan Michael; s of Baron Wedderburn of Charlton by his 3 w, Frances; *b* 1972; *Style* - The Hon Jonathan Wedderburn

WEDDERBURN, Hon Lucy Rachel; da of Baron Wedderburn of Charlton; *b* 1960; *Style* - The Hon Lucy Wedderburn

WEDDERBURN OF THAT ILK, Hon Marina Patricia; da of Lord Scrymgeour, *qv*; *b* 1980

WEDDERBURN-MAXWELL, Hon Mrs (Ann Madeline); *née* Cunliffe; da of late 1 Baron Cunliffe GBE; *b* 1901; *m* 1922, Brig John Wedderburn-Maxwell, DSO, MC, s of late Maj James Andrew Colville Wedderburn-Maxwell; *Style* - The Hon Mrs Wedderburn-Maxwell; The Granary, St George's Hill, Weybridge, Surrey

WEDDERBURN-OGILVY, Caryl Eustace; s (by 1 m) of late Donald Wedderburn-Ogilvy; hp of cous, Sir Andrew Ogilvy-Wedderburn, 7 Bt; *b* 10 Dec 1925; *m* 1953, Katharine Mary, da of William Steele, of Dundee; 1 s, 2 da; *Career* ARIBA; *Style* - Caryl Wedderburn-Ogilvy Esq; Pucklepeggies, 3A Glassford st, Milngavie, Glasgow

WEDGWOOD, 4 Baron (UK 1942); Piers Anthony Weymouth Wedgwood; s of 3 Baron Wedgwood (d 1970, 5 in descent from Josiah Wedgwood, 1 MP for the newly enfranchised Stoke-on-Trent 1832-34 and s of Josiah Wedgwood, who founded the eponymous pottery at Etruria), by his 2 w, Jane; *b* 20 Sept 1954; *Educ* Marlborough; *Heir* 1 cous once removed, John Wedgwood; *Career* late Lt Roy Scots; *Style* - The Rt Hon Lord Wedgwood; Harewood Cottage, Chicksgrove, Tisbury, Wilts (☎ Fovant 325)

WEDGWOOD, Hugo Martin; s & h of Sir John Wedgwood, 2 Bt, TD; *b* 27 Dec 1933; *Educ* Eton, Trin Oxford; *m* 1963, Alexandra, da of late Judge Gordon Clark by his w Mary (herself da of Sir William Lawrence, 3 Bt, JP); 1 s (Ralph b 1964), 2 da (Julia b 1966, Frances b 1969); *Style* - Hugo Wedgwood Esq; Pixham Mill, Pixham Lane, Dorking, Surrey

WEDGWOOD, Iris, Lady; Iris Veronica; da of Albert Pawson; *m* 1906, Brig-Gen Sir Ralph Wedgwood, 1 Bt, CB, CMG, TD (d 1956); 1 s (2 Bt), 1 da (Dame Veronica Wedgwood, OM, DBE); *Style* - Iris, Lady Wedgwood

WEDGWOOD, Dr John; s of Hon Josiah Wedgwood (yr s of 1 Baron Wedgwood); hp to 1 cous once removed, 4 Baron Wedgwood; *b* 28 Sept 1919; *Educ* Abbotsholme, Trin Cambridge; *m* 1, 1943 (m dis 1971), Margaret, da of Alfred Mason, of Bury St Edmunds; 3 s, 2 da; m 2, 1972, Jo, da of Harold Ripsher; *Career* consultant Middx Hosp 1968-80, med dir

Roy Hosp for Incurables 1980-, hon sr lectr Middx Hosp Med Sch 1980-; dir Wedgwood Ltd 1967; ACA, FRCP; served WW II as Surgn-Lt RNVR; *Recreations* ceramics, history; *Clubs* Savile, Roy Soc Medicine, Lansdowne; *Style* - The Hon Dr John Wedgwood; 227 Ashley gdns, SW1; 9 Upper Wimpole st, W1 (☎ 01 486 6478/794 3311)

WEDGWOOD, Sir John Hamilton; 2 Bt (UK 1942), of Etruria, Co Stafford, TD (1948); s of Sir Ralph Wedgwood, 1 Bt, CB, CMG, TD (d 1956, himself yr bro of 1 Baron Wedgwood); bro of (Dame) C(icely) V(eronica) Wedgwood, OM, DBE, the historian; *b* 16 Nov 1907; *Educ* Winchester, Trin Cambridge; *m* 1933, Diana Mildred (d 1976), da of Col Oliver Hawkshaw (d 1949); 4 s, 1 da; *Heir* s, (Hugo) Martin Wedgwood, b 27 Dec 1933; *Career* 2 Lt 1938, Capt 1940, Maj 1942; formerly JP (Stone); formerly dep chm Josiah Wdgwood & Sons Ltd; memb British Nat Export Council 1964-66; chm Artistic Framing Ltd 1970-; *Style* - Sir John Wedgwood, Bt, TD; c/o Artistic Framing, Dobles Lane, Holsworthy, N Devon

WEDGWOOD, Baroness; Jane Weymouth; da of William Poulton, of Kenya; *m* 1949, as his 2 w, 3 Baron Wedgwood (d 1970); 1 s (4 Baron), 2 da (Hon Susan, Hon Sarah Wedgwood); *Style* - The Rt Hon Lady Wedgwood; Harewood Cottage, Chicksgrove, Tisbury, Wilts

WEDGWOOD, Hon Sarah Jane Edith; da of 3 Baron Wedgwood by his 2 w Jane; *b* 11 July 1958; *Style* - The Hon Sarah Wedgwood

WEDGWOOD, Hon Susan Margaret; da of 3 Baron Wedgwood by his 2 w Jane; *b* 22 July 1950; *Style* - The Hon Susan Wedgwood

WEDGWOOD, Dame (Cicely) Veronica; OM (1969), DBE (1968, CBE 1956); da of Sir Ralph Wedgwood, 1 Bt, sis of Sir John Wedgwood, 2 Bt, and 1 cous twice removed of 4 Baron Wedgwood; *b* 20 July 1910; *Educ* privately, LMH Oxford; *Career* historian, particularly of the sixteenth and seventeenth centuries; FRHistS, FBA; formerly memb Arts Cncl, Advsy Cncl V & A; books include *The King's Peace* 1955, *The King's War* 1958; *Style* - Dame Veronica Wedgwood OM DBE; c/o Messrs Collins, 14 St James's Place, SW1 (☎ 01 493 7070)

WEEKS, Baroness; Cynthia Mary; da of John Wood Irvine; *m* 1931, as his 2 w, Lt-Gen 1 and last Baron Weeks (d 1960), KCB, CBE, DSO, MC, TD; 2 da (Hon Mrs Plunkett-Ernle-Erle-Drax and Hon Lady Troubridge); *Style* - The Rt Hon Lady Weeks; The Manor House, Elsted, Sussex

WEIDEMANN, Hon Mrs (Hilary Mary); da of Baron Carron (Life Peer, d 1969); *b* 1933; *m* 1959, John Simon Weidemann; c; *Style* - The Hon Mrs Weidemann; The Gables, 27 Bromley rd, SE6

WEIDENFELD, Baron (Life Peer UK 1976); (Arthur) George Weidenfeld; s of Max and Rosa Weidenfeld; *b* 13 Sept 1919; *Educ* Piaristen Gymnasium Vienna, Vienna U, Konsular Akademie; *m* 1, 1952, Jane, da of J Edward Sieff; 1 da; m 2, 1956 (m dis 1961), Mrs Barbara Connolly, da of Maj George Skelton; m 3 (m dis 1973), Sandra, da of Charles Payson; *Career* kt 1969; chm Weidenfeld & Nicolson 1948- & assoc cos, served during WW II in BBC Monitoring Serv, journalist with BBC & News Chronicle 1942-46 and 1943-44; fndr Contact Magazine and Books 1945; spent 1 year as political advsr and Ch of Cabinet to Pres Weizmann of Israel; memb Roy Opera House Tst; *Style* - The Rt Hon Lord Weidenfeld; 9 Chelsea Embankment, SW3 (☎ 01 351 0042)

WEINBERG, Mark Aubrey; s of Philip Weinberg (d 1933); *b* 9 Aug 1931; *Educ* King Edward's School Johannesburg, Witwatersrand U, LSE; *m* 1980, Anouska, da of Albert Geissler (d 1980); *Career* md Abbey Life Assurance 1961-70, dep chm Hambro Life Assurance 1971-; *Recreations* riding, tennis, skiing; *Style* - Mark Weinberg Esq

WEINSTOCK, Baron (Life Peer UK 1980); Arnold Weinstock; s of Simon and Golda Weinstock; *b* 29 July 1924; *Educ*

London U; *m* 1949, Netta, da of Sir Michael Sobell, chm GEC; 1 s, 1 da; *Career* md GEC 1963-, late financier & property developer; FSS, kt 1970; *Style* - The Rt Hon Lord Weinstock; 7 Grosvenor sq, W1 (☎ 01 493 7676)

WEINSTOCK, Hon Simon Andrew; s of Baron Weinstock; *b* 1952; *Educ* Winchester, Magdalen Oxford; *m* 1979, Laura, da of Maj Hon Sir Francis Legh, KCVO (3 s of 3 Baron Newton, TD, JP, DL); *Style* - The Hon Simon Weinstock

WEIR, 3 Viscount (UK 1938); William Kenneth James Weir; also Baron Weir (UK 1918); s of 2 Viscount Weir, CBE (d 1975), by his 1 w, Lucy; *b* 9 Nov 1933; *Educ* Eton, Trin Cambridge; *m* 1, 1964 (m dis 1974), Diana, da of Peter MacDougall, of Ontario; 1 s, 1 da; m 2, 1976, Baroness Jacqueline, da of Baron Louis de Chollet, of Fribourg, Switzerland; *Heir* s, Hon James Weir; *Career* chm & ch exec Weir Gp 1972-, chm Gt Northern Investment Tst 1975-; dir BICC 1977-, Br Bank of M East 1977-79; memb London Advsy Cttee Br Bank of M East 1980-; memb Court of Bank of England 1972-, Scottish Ec Cncl 1972, Engrg Industries Cncl 1975; *Recreations* shooting, golf, fishing; *Clubs* White's; *Style* - The Rt Hon Viscount Weir; Rodinghead, Mauchline, Ayrshire (☎ Fiveways 233); 32 Abbotsbury Close, W14 (☎ 01 603 9622)

WEIR, Hon Andrew Peter; s and h of 3 Baron Inverforth; *b* 16 Nov 1966; *Style* - The Hon Andrew Weir

WEIR, Hon Clarinda Jane; da of 3 Baron Inverforth; *b* 1968; *Style* - The Hon Clarinda Weir

WEIR, Dorothy, Viscountess; Dorothy; da of William Yerrington Dear; *m* 1, Edward Hutton (decd); m 2, 1973, as his 2 w, 2 Viscount Weir CBE (d 1975); *Style* - The Rt Hon Dorothy, Viscountess Weir; Montgreenan, Kilwinning, Ayrshire

WEIR, Hon Douglas Nigel; s of 2 Viscount Weir, CBE; *b* 6 Oct 1935; *Educ* Eton, Trin Cambridge; *m* 1964, Penelope, da of Gp Capt John Whitehead; 3 da; *Style* - The Hon Douglas Weir; Creagdubh Lodge, Newtonmore, Inverness-shire

WEIR, Hon George Anthony; s of 2 Viscount Weir, CBE; *b* 27 April 1940; *Educ* Winchester, Trin Cambridge, MIT; *m* 1962, Hon Jane Anstruther-Gray, da of Baron Kilmany; 2 s, 1 da; *Style* - The Hon George Weir; Fiunary House, Newton Mearns, Renfrewshire; 20 Royal Avenue House, Royal Avenue, SW3

WEIR, Hon Mrs (Grania Rachel); *née* O'Brien; da of 16 Baron Inchiquin (d 1968); *b* 1928; *m* 1973, Hugh William Lindsay Weir; *Career* was social sec to British Ambassador to Peru 1958-60; *Style* - The Hon Mrs Weir; Ballinakella Lodge, Whitegate, co Clare

WEIR, Hon Mrs John (Irene Marguerite Robertson); da of James McKechnie, JP, of Glasgow; *m* 1950, Hon John Weir (d 1953), 2 s of 1 Viscount Weir, GCB, PC, JP, DL; *Style* - The Hon Mrs John Weir; Dunderdave Castle, Inveraray, Argyll

WEIR, Hon Mrs (Jane Caroline); *née* Anstruther-Gray; da of Baron Kilmany, MC, PC (Life Peer); *b* 1943; *m* 1962, Hon George Anthony Weir, s of 2 Viscount Weir (d 1975); 2 s, 1 da; *Style* - The Hon Mrs Weir; Fiunary House, Newton Mearns, Renfrewshire; 20 Royal Avenue House, Royal av, SW3

WEIR, Hon James Richard Canning; 4 s of 2 Viscount Weir CBE; *b* 1 May 1949; *Educ* Winchester, Strathclyde U; *m* 1977, Haude Chantal Gabrielle, da of Marc Charpentier, of Paris; 2 da; *Career* business; *Recreations* shooting, fishing, golf; *Clubs* Prestwick Golf, Gatineau Fish and Game; *Style* - The Hon James Weir; 13 Place des Vosges, 75004 Paris, France (☎ 271 9444)

WEIR, Hon James William Hartland; s and h of 3 Viscount Weir; *b* 6 June 1965; *Style* - The Hon James Weir

WEIR, Kenneth George; s of Thomas Weir, of Annan, Dumfriesshire; *b* 30 Oct 1921; *Educ* Alloa Acad; *m* 1950, Mary Whittingham, da of John Stewart Heugh; 2 c; *Career* Fellow of Faculty of Actuaries past president of the Society of Pension Consultants 1972-74; past president of the Pensions Management Institute 1979-80; dep chm Hogg Robinson Europe Ltd and Hogg Robinson (Benefit Consultants) Ltd; *Recreations* bridge, tennis, swimming; *Style* - Kenneth Weir Esq; Castle Point, 11 Harebell Hill, Cobham, Surrey (☎ Cobham 4604)

WEIR, Hon Lorna Elizabeth; da of 3 Viscount Weir; *b* 17 May 1967; *Style* - The Hon Lorna Weir

WEIR, (John) Vincent; yr s of 2 Baron Inverforth (d 1975); *b* 8 Feb 1935; *Educ* Malvern; *Career* chm: Andrew Weir Agencies Ltd 1965-, Andrew Weir London Ltd 1964-, Bank Line Airways Ltd 1964-, Inver Tankers Ltd 1964-, Spink & Son Ltd 1980-; dir of Andrew Weir Management Servs Ltd 1979-, Dunita Holdings Ltd 1956, Forestdale Trust Ltd 1976 and others; *Recreations* natural history, wildlife conservation; *Clubs* Bath; *Style* - The Hon Vincent Weir; Brock House, Manor Lane, Gt Chesterford, Saffron Walden, Essex (☎ 30222)

WEISS, Charles; CBE (1974); s of Frank Weiss (d 1944); *b* 29 Jan 1914; *Educ* Bolyai G S Budapest, Florence U; *m* 1, 1935, Isabel Katherine; m 2, 1964, Lesley Anne, nee Ryan; 4 da; *Career* Maj RE (India, Assam, Burma), consulting engineer; *Recreations* cinephotography, history, music; *Clubs* White Elephant; *Style* - Charles Weiss Esq CBE; 21 Coombe Lane West, Kingston-upon Thames, Surrey (☎ 949 2513)

WEISS, Sir Eric; s of late Siegfried Soloman Weiss; *b* 30 Dec 1908; *Educ* Augustinius Gymnasium Weiden Germany, Neues Gymnasium Nürnberg Germany; *m* 1934, Maria Margarete Gertrud (Greta), da of Jean Kobaltzky (d 1953); 4 c; *Career* founded Foundry Services Ltd (original co of Foseco Minsep Gp) 1932, chm Minerals Separation Ltd 1964, chm Foseco Minsep Ltd 1969 (pres 1979); Lloyd's underwriter 1976-79; dep presiding member UK Commission of United World Colleges 1973-76, member International Council 1969-76, dir 1970-76, governor Atlantic College; trustee Oakham School; memb Inst British Foundrymen; kt 1980; *Recreations* golf, travel; *Clubs* Garrick; *Style* - Sir Eric Weiss; 33 Chester sq, London SW1; 36 Queen Anne's Gate, SW1 (☎ 01 222 7030); The Manor House, Little Marlow, Bucks

WELBY, Barbara, Lady; Barbara Angela Mary Lind; da of John Gregory, CB, CMG (himself s of Sir Philip Gregory) by his w Gwendolen (gda of Hon Capt Francis Maude RN, who in turn was 6 s of 1 Viscount Hawarden by his 3 w Anne - she being sis of 1 Viscount Monck); *m* 1927, Sir Oliver Welby, 6 Bt, TD, JP (d 1977); 2 s (including 7 Bt); *Style* - Barbara, Lady Welby; Denton Manor, Grantham, Lincs

WELBY, Sir (Richard) Bruno Gregory Welby; 7 Bt (UK 1801), of Denton Manor, Lincolnshire; s of Sir Oliver Welby, 6 Bt, TD (d 1977, whose mother was Lady Maria Hervey, sis of 4 Marquess of Bristol); n of Dowager Lady Saltoun & Viscountess Portal of Hungerford; *b* 11 March 1928; *Educ* Eton, Ch Ch Oxford; *m* 1952, Jane Biddulph, da of the late Ralph Hodder-Williams; 3 s, 1 da; *Heir* s, Charles William Hodder Welby, b May 6 1953; *Style* - Sir Bruno Welby, Bt; 24 Ilchester pla, W14 (☎ 01 602 2572)

WELBY, Charles William Hodder; s & h of Sir Bruno Welby, 7 B; *b* 6 May 1953; *m* 1978, Suzanna, da of Maj Ian Stuart-Routledge, of Harston Hall, Grantham; *Style* - Charles Welby Esq

WELBY-EVERARD, Capt Philip Herbert Earle; OBE (1980), DSC (1944), JP (Lincs 1956), DL (1957); s of Edward Everard Earle Welby-Everard (d 1951); *b* 7 May 1902; *Educ* Selwyn House Broadstairs, RNCs Osborne and Dartmouth; *m* 1928, Lilla Anna Florence Maree, nee Spence; 2 s, 1 da (1 da decd); *Career* KStJ 1972; Capt RN 1944, served 1939-55, ret; High Sheriff Lincs 1972-73, Cdr St John Ambulance 1963-76; memb Deeping Fen Internal Drainage Bd 1955-69, pres Lincoln SCC 1962-80, EMEB Consultative Cncl 1960-70; memb CLA; *Recreations* gardening, shooting, fishing; *Clubs* Naval & Mil; *Style* - Capt Philip Welby-Everard OBE DSC JP DL RN;

Frieston Old Place, Caythorpe, Grantham, Lincs (☎ 0400 72459)

WELCH, Irene, Lady; Irene Avril; da of John Foster OBE; *m* 1969, as his 2 w, Sir Cullum Welch, 1 Bt, OBE, MC (d 1980); *Style* - Irene, Lady Welch; 43 St Margarets, Rottingdean, Sussex

WELCH, Sir John Reader; 2 Bt (UK 1957), of Chard, Co Somerset; s of Sir Cullum Welch, 1 Bt, OBE, MC (d 1980); *b* 26 July 1933; *Educ* Marlborough, Hertford Oxford; *m* 1962, Margaret Kerry, da of Kenneth Douglass; 1 s, 2 da; *Heir* s, James Douglass Cullum Welch, b 10 Nov 1973; *Career* OStJ; *Style* - Sir John Welch, Bt; Killara, The Glade, Kingswood, Surrey

WELD-FORESTER, Hon Alice Sophie; da of 8 Baron Forester; *b* 1969; *Style* - The Hon Alice Weld-Forester

WELD-FORESTER, Hon Charles Richard George; s and h of 8 Baron Forester; *b* 8 July 1975

WELD-FORESTER, Hon Kythe Priscilla; da of late 7 Baron Forester; *b* 1941; *Style* - The Hon Kythe Weld-Forester

WELD-FORESTER, Hon Selina Lucy; da of 8 Baron Forester; *b* 1968; *Style* - The Hon Selina Weld-Forester

WELDON, Anthony Henry David; s of Max Weldon (d 1979); *b* 23 Dec 1945; *Educ* Uppingham; *m* 1970, Claire Ellen, nee Gessler; 2 s, 1 da; *Career* dir Cocoa Merchants Gp Ltd; *Recreations* sport; *Clubs* RAC, Roy Tennis, MCC; *Style* - Anthony Weldon Esq; 19 Cumberland ter, Regents Park, NW1 (☎ 01 935 9055)

WELDON, Sir Anthony William; 9 Bt (I 1723), of Dunmore, Co Carlow; s of Sir Thomas Weldon, 8 Bt (d 1979), by his w Meribel, Lady Weldon, *qv*; *b* 11 May 1947; *Educ* Sherborne; *m* 1980, Amanda, formerly w of Anthony Wigan & da of Maj Geoffrey North MC, by his w, Hon Margaret de Grey (2 da of 8 Baron Walsingham, DSO, OBE, JP, DL); *Heir* 1 cous once removed, Brig Hamilton Weldon CBE; *Career* late Lt Irish Gds, holder of Gen Serv Medal S Arabia; *Style* - Sir Anthony Weldon, Bt; c/o Meribel, Lady Weldon (*see below*)

WELDON, Brig Hamilton Edward Crosdill; CBE (1960, OBE 1950), DL (Gter London 1967); s of Lt-Col Henry Weldon, DSO (himself 5 s of Sir Anthony Weldon, 5 Bt), by his w Helen (da of Sir Edward Cowan); hp of 1 cous once removed, Sir Anthony Weldon, 9 Bt; *b* 14 Sept 1910; *Educ* Charterhouse, RMA Woolwich; *m* 1, 1935 (m dis 1946), Margaret, da of Maj Frederic Passy; 1 da (Mrs Ian Grant); m 2, 1948, Elwyne, 2 da of Harold Chaldecott OBE; 2 s (Kevin b 1951, Mark b 1953), 1 da (Mrs Richard Evetts); *Career* late RA; ADC to HM; Sec County of London & Gter London TA 1962-74; E Regimental Organiser Army Benevolent Fund 1975-; DCllr Waverley Surrey; served WW II; *Style* - Brig Hamilton Weldon CBE DL; Loaders, Echo Barn Lane, Wrecclesham, Farnham, Surrey

WELDON, Meribel, Lady; Marie Isobel; da of Hon William French (2 s of 4 Baron de Freyne by his 2 w Marie, nee Lamb); *m* 1942, Sir Thomas Weldon, 8 Bt; 1 s (9 Bt), 1 da (Mrs Alan Elliot); *Style* - Meribel, Lady Weldon; The Fighting Cocks, W Amesbury, Salisbury, Wilts

WELFARE, Bertran Alfred; s of Alfred Welfare; *b* 14 April 1907; *m* 1938, Winifred Grace, nee Truman; 1 c; *Career* jt chm Precision Engrg Co (ROG) Ltd, Precision Reinforced Fibres Ltd, Precision Weighers, chm Precision Aircraft (Reading) Ltd; *Style* - Bertran Welfare Esq; 254 Peppard rd, Caversham, Reading, Berks (☎ Reading 477976)

WELLBELOVED, James; MP (L but resigned Whip and joined SDP July 1981) Bexley, Erith & Crayford 1974-; s of Wilfred Wellbeloved; *b* 29 July 1926; *Educ* SE London Tech; *m* 1948, Mavis Ratcliff; 2 s, 1 da; *Career* MP (L) Erith & Crayford 1965-74, PPS Min Def 1967-69, Sec State For & C'wlth Affrs 1969-70, Oppn Whip 1972-74, Parly Under Sec Def (RAF) 1976-79; dep chm London MPs Parly Gp 1970-; commercial consultant; writer & broadcaster on for & def matters; *Style* -

James Wellbeloved Esq MP; House of Commons, SW1 (☎ 01 219 4563/4077)

WELLESLEY, Lady Alexia Anne Elizabeth; da of 6 Earl Cowley (d 1975) and Maria, da of Enrique Buenaño, of Buenos Aires; *b* 1973; *Style* - Lady Alexia Wellesley

WELLESLEY, Hon Brian Timothy; s (by 1 m) of 7 Earl Cowley; *b* 1938; *Educ* Arizona State Coll, Denver U, Colorado and Nevada U (BS); *m* 1, 1961 (m dis 1964), Patricia Tribbey; m 2, 1966, Karen Elizabeth Bradbury, of Reno, Nevada, USA; *Career* Ch of Intelligence Div US Tres Dept Alaska; *Style* - The Hon Brian Wellesley; PO Box 974, Anchorage, Alaska, 99510 USA

WELLESLEY, Lady Caroline; da of 6 Earl Cowley (d 1975) and Maria, da of Enrique Buenaño, of Buenos Aires; *b* 1976

WELLESLEY, Hon (Henry) Gerald Valerian Francis; s of late 3 Earl Cowley by his 2 w, Hon Millicent, da of 1 Baron Nunburnholme and former w of Sir Charles Cradock-Hartopp, 5 Bt; *b* 1907; *Educ* Harrow; *m* 1, 1929 (m dis 1953), Sabia, da of late Edward Robert Kennedy (gs of 1 Bt); m 2, 1954 (m annulled 1955), Nancy Joan, da of B C Hilliam; *Style* - The Hon Gerald Wellesley

WELLESLEY, Lady Honor Victoria; da of Marquess of Douro; *b* 1979; *Style* - Lady Honor Wellesley

WELLESLEY, Lady (Caroline) Jane; da of 8 Duke of Wellington; *b* 6 July 1951; *Career* works for BBC; *Style* - Lady Jane Wellesley

WELLESLEY, Lady George; Jane; da of John McGillivray, of The Braes of Glenlivet, Banffshire; *m* 1955, as his 2 w, Lt-Col Lord George Wellesley (d 1967), 4 s of 4 Duke of Wellington and bro of 5 & 7 Dukes; *Style* - Lady George Wellesley; Flat 5, Woodsford, 14 Melbury rd, W14 (☎ 01 602 3031)

WELLESLEY, Lord James Christopher Douglas; 4 s of 8 Duke of Wellington; *b* 16 Dec 1964; *Style* - Lord James Wellesley

WELLESLEY, Lord John Henry; 3 s of 8 Duke of Wellington; *b* 20 April 1954; *Educ* Eton; *m* 1977, Corinne, da of HE Robert Vaes, Belgian Ambass; *Style* - Lord John Wellesley

WELLESLEY, Julian Valerian; s of Gerald Wellesley MC, of Highfield Park, Sussex (gn of 1 Earl Cowley, KG, GCB, PC, and ggs of 1 Baron Cowley, bro of 1 Duke of Wellington), by Elizabeth, da of Otho Ball, of Chicago, and formerly w of Quintin Gilbey, the racing correspondent; *b* 9 Aug 1933; *Educ* RNCs Dartmouth & Greenwich; *m* 1965, Elizabeth, da of Cyril Stocken and formerly w of Mr Hall; 1 s, 3 step da; *Career* late Lt RN; jt md Ayer Barker 1971-, chm Charles Barker ABH 1978-; *Recreations* reading, music, family, gardening, tennis, watching cricket; *Clubs* Brooks's, Sussex; *Style* - Julian Wellesley Esq; Tidebrook Manor, Wadhurst, Sussex (☎ 01 236 3011)

WELLESLEY, Robin Alfred; s of Gerald Wellesley, of Withyham, Sussex; *b* 23 July 1928; *Educ* Eton; *m* 1953, Marianne, da of John McDonald, of Chicago; 1 s, 2 da (Kate; Laura E C, m 1981 Jonathan, er s of Rt Hon Francis Pym, MC, PC, DL, MP, Chllr Duchy of Lancaster); *Career* dir Prestige Gp 1965-; *Recreations* gardening, cricket, travel; *Style* - Robin Wellesley; Shingle Barn, Dwelly Lane, Edenbridge, Kent; 36 Edge st, W8 (☎ 01 727 4503)

WELLESLEY, Lord Richard Gerald; 2 s of 8 Duke of Wellington; *b* 20 June 1949; *Educ* Eton, RAC Cirencester; *m* 1973, Joanna, da of John Sumner; 2 da; *Style* - Lord Richard Wellesley

WELLESLEY, Lady Tara Lennon; da (by 1 m) of 7 Earl Cowley; *b* 1962; *Style* - Lady Tara Wellesley

WELLESLEY, Hon Mrs Youla Edithe; *née* Littleton; da of 4 Baron Hatherton (d 1944); *b* 13 March 1904; *m* 1927, John Elvine Harris (m dis 1938, adopted name Wellesley 1939); 3 s; *Style* - The Hon Mrs Youla Wellesley; Cliffways, Hay Lane, Farley, Oakamoor, Stoke-on-Trent (☎ (Oakamoor 702359)

WELLINGS, Trevor Frederick; s of

Harry Bunch Wellings; *b* 14 April 1929; *Educ* King Edward's G S Birmingham; *m* Jacqueline, nee Barker; 5 c; *Career* NCO RAF; accountant, dep fndr chm Richards & Wallington Industries 1961-81, chm J Thomas Edwards & Sons 1970- (builders & plumbers merchants); *Recreations* freemasonry, gardening; *Style* - Trevor Wellings Esq; Alcester, Warwicks

WELLINGS, Victor Gordon; QC (1973); s of Gordon Wellings; *b* 19 July 1919; *Educ* Reading Sch, Exeter Coll Oxford; *m* 1948, Helen Margaret Jill, nee Lovell; 3 s; *Career* barr 1949-73; memb Lands Tribunal 1973-; *Recreations* golf, fishing; *Clubs* United Oxford and Cambridge; *Style* - Victor Wellings Esq QC; Cherry Tree Cottage, Whitchurch Hill, Pangbourne, Berks

WELLINGTON, 8 Duke of (UK 1814); Arthur Valerian Wellesley; MVO (1952), OBE (1957), MC (1941), DL (Hants 1975); also Baron of Mornington (I 1746), Earl of Mornington, Viscount Wellesley (both I 1760), Viscount Wellington of Talavera and of Wellington, Baron Douro (both UK 1809), Conde do Vimeiro (Portugal 1811), Earl of Wellington (UK 1812), Marquess of Wellington (UK 1812), Duque de Ciudad Rodrigo and a Grandee of the 1 Class (Spain 1812), Duque da Vittoria, Marques de Torres Vedras (both Portugal 1812), Marquess of Douro (UK 1814), and Prince of Waterloo (Netherlands 1815); s of 7 Duke of Wellington, KG (d 1972, but ceded Sp Dukedom and Grandeeship to present Duke 1966); His Grace is gggs of the (1) Great Duke, whose choice of title has been thought to derive from a medieval holding of land near Wellington in Somerset; the 1 Duke's gf changed his name from Colley to Wesley as a condition of inheriting lands from a relative, Garret Wesley (His Grace appeared as Arthur Wesley in the Army List as late as 1800); Garret had previously proposed to adopt another kinsman, Charles Wesley, bro of John the founder of Methodism and unc of the hymn writer S S Wesley; the Wellesleys and Wesleys are hence, albeit remotely, connected; whether the Great Duke was born on 29 April or 1 May matters only in relation to the irony of a man, whose windows the mob smashed in 1831 for opposing the Reform Bill, first seeing the light on a day sacred to labour; *b* 2 July 1915; *Educ* Eton; *m* 1944, Diana, da of Maj-Gen Douglas McConnel, CB, CBE, DSO, of Ayrshire; 4 s, 1 da; *Heir* s, Marquess of Douro; *Career* patron of 4 livings, Brig (ret) RHG; Silver Stick in Waiting, Lt-Col Cmdg Household Cavalry 1959-60, OC 22 Armoured Bde 1960-61; Defence Attaché Madrid 1964-67; Col-in-Chief The Duke of Wellington's Regt 1974-; Pres SE Roy Br Legion, memb Cncl RASE & Zoological Soc; dir: Massey Ferguson Hldgs 1967, Massey Ferguson 1973, Bodegas Internacionales Madrid; Pres Game Conservancy 1976; OStJ; Noble Friend of the Grand Order of the Friends of English Country Cheeses 1981; *Clubs* Turf, White's, Buck's; (Although His Grace inhabits Apsley House, it is now administered as a national repository of Wellingtoniana by the Victoria & Albert Museum. Designed by Robert Adam, it was long known as Number 1 London. Stratfield Saye House, considered modest for a ducal establishment, is a rare example of Caroline architecture in England. Some eponymous memorials to the Great Duke are: the public school in Berkshire, the capital of NZ, the mountain overlooking Hobart, the (demolished) barracks near Buckingham Palace, the boot, the apple and the colossal Californian redwood tree.) *Style* - His Grace The Duke of Wellington, MVO, OBE, MC, DL; Stratfield Saye House, Reading, Berks (☎ 0256 882882/ Turgis Green 602); Apsley House, Piccadilly, W1 (☎ 01 499 1953)

WELLS, Christopher Charles; s & h of Sir Charles Wells, 2 Bt, TD; *b* 12 Aug 1936; *Educ* McGill & Toronto Us; *m* 1960, Elizabeth, da of I Griffiths, of Outrement, Quebec; 2 s (Michael b 1966, Geoffrey b 1970), 2 da (Felicity b 1964, Megan b 1969); *Career* MD in family practice; *Style* - Christopher Wells Esq; St Michael's Family Practice, 30 Bond st, Toronto M5B 1W8, Canada

WELLS, Sir Charles Maltby; 2 Bt (UK 1944), of Felmersham, Co Bedford, TD; s of 1 Bt (d 1956); *b* 24 July 1908; *Educ* Bedford Sch, Pembroke Cambridge; *m* 1935, Katharine Boulton, da of Frank B

Kenrick, of Toronto, Canada; 2 s; *Heir* s, Christopher Charles Wells, b 12 Aug 1936; *Career* joined RE (TA) 1933, Capt 1939, Lt-Col 1941, Acting Col 1945, served in 54 Div 1939-41, and 76 Div 1941-43, British Army Staff Washington 1943-45; *Style* - Sir Charles Wells, Bt, TD; 37 Duggan Avenue, Toronto, Canada

WELLS, Hon Mrs (Gillian Hermione Christian); *née* Turton; da of Baron Tranmire (Life Peer); *b* 1930; *m* 1960, David Poulett Wells, BM, BCh; *Style* - The Hon Mrs Wells; Hilperton House, Hilperton, Trowbridge, Wilts

WELLS, Lt-Col Herbert James; CBE (1958), MC (1918), JP (Surrey 1952), DL (1962); s of late James J Wells, of New South Wales, Australia; *b* 27 March 1897; *Educ* Newcastle, NSW; *m* 1926, Rose Hamilton, da of late H D Brown, of Bournemouth; *Career* AIF and Australian Flying Corps WW I, 55 Surrey Bn Home Gd WW II, Lt-Col 1954; chartered accountant (FCA); v-chm Surrey CC 1959-62, chm 1962-65, High Sheriff Surrey 1965, Freeman of City of London; gen cmmr Income Tax, former memb Surrey TA & FA, chm Queen Mary's Hosp Carshalton 1958-60; *Style* - Lt-Col Herbert Wells, CBE, MC, JP, DL; 17 Oakhurst Rise, Carshalton Beeches, Surrey (☎ 01 643 4125)

WELLS, Capt John Gerard; CBE (1964), DSC (1940); s of Vice-Adm Sir Gerard Aylmer Wells KBE (d 1943); *b* 22 Sept 1915; *Educ* Summer Fields Prep Sch Oxford, Britannia RNC Darmouth; *m* 1947, Diana, da of Lt-Gen Sir Edmond Schreiber, KCB, DSO; 2 s; *Career* Capt RN 1939-64 (ret); Management Business Services (London) 1980; gen man Gulfspan 1977-78, consultant Wakeman Trower & Ptnrs 1975-76, dir Clarksons Holidays 1970-74, gen man Aviemore Centre Inverness-shire 1965-70; *Recreations* sailing, skiing, shooting, stalking, naval historical research; *Clubs* Army & Navy, Roy Cruising; *Style* - Capt John Wells, CBE, DSC; High Firs House, Hatch Lane, Liss, Hants (☎ Liss 3343)

WELLS, Wing Cdr Oliver John; DL (Beds 1964); s of Sir Richard Wells, 1 Bt, of Felmersham Grange, nr Bedford (d 1956); *b* 10 March 1922; *Educ* Uppingham Sch, RAF Staff Coll; *m* 1949, Felicity Anne, da of Brig M E Mascall DSO OBE (d 1958); 2 s, 1 da; *Career* served RAF 1941-56, High Sheriff of Bedfordshire 1970, chm & ch exec of brewery co; *Recreations* flying, sailing; *Clubs* RAF; *Style* - Wing Cdr Oliver Wells DL; Ickwell Grange, nr Biggleswade, Beds

WELLS-PESTELL, Baron (Life Peer UK 1965); Reginald Alfred Wells-Pestell; JP (London); s of Robert Pestell; *b* 27 Jan 1910; *Educ* London U, diploma Ec & Soc Sci Geneva Coll, NC, USA; *m* 1935, Irene Mabel, da of Arthur Wells; 2 s; *Career* Capt KRRC; sociologist, memb Inner London Probation Cttee, fndr memb Nat Marriage Guidance Cncl; Lord in Waiting (Govt Whip) 1974-79, Parly Under Sec DHSS 1979; *Recreations* music, opera; assumed additional surname Wells by deed poll; *Style* - The Rt Hon Lord Wells-Pestell; 22 Vicarage Close, Oxford (☎ 0865 771142)

WELLS-PESTELL, Hon Philip Anthony; s of Baron Wells-Pestell, JP; *b* 31 July 1941; *Educ* City of London School, London University; *m* 1965, Holly, da of Lorne Hopkins, of Connecticut, USA; children; *Style* - The Hon Philip Wells-Pestell; 7 Woodberry Avenue, Winchmore Hill, London N21 (☎ 01 886 7958)

WELLS-PESTELL, Hon Richard Quentin; s of Baron Wells-Pestell, JP; *b* 10 March 1945; *Educ* City of London School, Keble College Oxford (MA, BPhil), University of California at Berkeley, London University; *m* 1973 (m dis 1977), Claudia Marseille, step da of Professor John Gerhart, of Berkeley, California; *Style* - The Hon Richard Wells-Pestell; 2 Queen's Mansions, Queen's Avenue, Muswell Hill, London N10

WELMAN, Douglas Pole; CBE (1966); engr; late chm S Gas Bd, co dir; CStJ 1968; *Club* Roy Thames Yacht; *Style* - Douglas Welman Esq CBE; 11 St Michael's gdns, St Cross, Winchester (☎ 68091)

WELSH, Brig David; CBE (1959), DSO (1944); s of Capt Tom Welsh (ka 1915); *b*

10 April 1908; *Educ* Winchester, RMA; *m* 1947, Maud Elinor Mitchell (d 1977), da of Maj M Campbell MC (ka 1918); 1 s; *Career* cmd 2 Lt RA 1928, served with Roy Horse Artillery & Roy Artillery 1939-45 (France, N Africa, Italy), Brigadier 1958 (ret 1961); *Clubs* Army & Navy; *Style* - Brig David Welsh, CBE, DSO; 27 Manor House Lane, Walkington, Beverley, N Humberside (☎ 0482 867876)

WELTER, Lady Gilean Frances; *née* Blunt-Mackenzie; da (by 1 m) of 4 Earl of Cromartie, *qv*; *b* 1936; *m* 1959 (m dis 1973), René Eugène Welter; 1 s, 1 da; *Style* - Lady Gilean Welter; 52 South Edwardes sq, W8 (☎ 01 602 6058)

WEMYSS, Lady Jean Christian; *née* Bruce; da of late 10 Earl of Elgin and (14 of) Kincardine, KT, CMG, TD, CD, and Hon Dame Katherine Cochrane, DBE (da of late 1 Baron Cochrane of Cults and Lady Gertrude Boyle, OBE, da of 6 Earl of Glasgow); *b* 1923; *m* 1945, Capt David Wemyss, late Roy Corps of Signals; *Career* formerly in WAAF; *Style* - Lady Jean Wemyss; Invermay, Forteviot, Perthshire

WEMYSS, Lady Victoria Alexandrina Violet; *née* Cavendish-Bentinck; CVO (1953); da of 6 Duke of Portland, KG, GCVO, TD, PC (d 1943); *b* 1890; *m* 1918, Capt Michael John Wemyss, late Household Cavalry; *Career* appointed an Extra Woman of the Bedchamber to HM Queen Elizabeth the Queen Mother 1937; *Style* - Lady Victoria Wemyss CVO; Wemyss Castle, East Wemyss, Fife

WEMYSS AND MARCH, 12 (and 8) Earl of (S 1633 & 1697); Francis David Charteris; KT (1966), JP (E Lothian); also Lord Wemyss of Elcho (S 1628), Lord Elcho and Methel (S 1633), Viscount of Peebles, Lord Douglas of Neidpath, Lyne, and Munard (both S 1697), and Baron Wemyss of Wemyss (UK 1821); s of Lord Elcho (s and h of 11 Earl, but predeceased him) and Lady Violet Manners, 2 da of 8 Duke of Rutland; suc gf 1937; *b* 19 Jan 1912; *Educ* Eton, Balliol Oxford, Trin Cambridge; *m* 1940, Mavis, da of Edwin Murray, of Cape Province, SA; 1 s, 1 da (and 1 s, 1 da decd); *Heir* s, Lord Neidpath; *Career* landowner; Lord High Commissioner to Gen Assembly Church of Scotland 1959, 1960 & 1977; Pres Nat Bible Soc Scotland 1960; Ld-Lt E Lothian 1976-; Pres Nat Tst for Scotland; chm Roy Commission on Ancient & Historical Monuments & Constructions of Scotland; Ld Clerk Register of Scotland & Keeper of the Signet 1974-; Ensign Roy Co of Archers (Queen's Bodyguard for Scotland); Pres The Thistle Fndn; dir: Wemyss & March Estates Management Co, Standard Life Assur, STV; *Clubs* New (Edinburgh); *Style* - Rt Hon Earl of Wemyss and March KT JP, HM Lord-Lieut for E Lothian; Gosford House, Longniddry, E Lothian (☎ Aberlady 200/389)

WENTWORTH-STANLEY, Geoffrey David; s of the late Charles Sidney Bowen Wentworth-Stanley CBE; *b* 28 May 1924; *Educ* Eton; *m* 1951, Bridget, da of the late Maj Philip Pease; 4 s; *Career* memb Stock Exchange 1948, ptnr Cazenove & Co; High Sheriff Herts 1972; *Clubs* White's, Buck's; *Style* - Geoffrey Wentworth-Stanley Esq; Great Munden House, Ware, Herts (☎ Dane End (092084) 244)

WERNICK, Lionel Rufus; s of Samuel Wernick (d 1967); *b* 6 Nov 1928; *Educ* Wolverhampton G S, London U *m* 1955, Sheila, da of Jack Lambert; 4 c; *Career* late Lt RSC; chm & md Wernick Gp; chm Prefabricated Bldg Mfrs Assoc of GB; *Recreations* bridge, travel, spectator sport; *Clubs* IOD; *Style* - Lionel Wernick Esq; 'The Lyches', Greenway, Hutton, Brentwood, Essex (☎ 220535)

WESSON, Willam Simpson; *b* 5 June 1929; *Educ* Cornell (BA, MBA); chm & md Bowater-Scott Corpn 1976-; *Style* - William Wesson Esq; Broad Acres, Old Place, Lindfield, Sussex

WEST, Kenneth; s of Albert West; *b* 1 Sept 1930; *Educ* Archbishop Holgate's GS, Univ Oxford; *m* 1957, Doreen, da of Joseph Adamson; 3 da; *Career* chemist; dep chm ICI Fibres 1978-; dir: Fiber Industries Inc USA 1977-, South African Nylon Spinners 1976-; chairman Harrogate WEA 1960-67, Granby High School PTA 1973-81; *Recreations* flying (pilot), sailing, theatre (producing), violin playing; *Clubs* Yorkshire Aeroplane Club; *Style* -

Kenneth West Esq; 16 Beech Grove, Harrogate (☎ 0428 69980)

WESTBROOK, Hon Mrs (Mary Joan); *née* Fraser; da of late 1 Baron Strathalmond CBE; *b* 1922; *m* 1945, Neil Gowanloch Westbrook; 1 s, 1 da; *Style* - The Hon Mrs Westbrook; White Gables, Prestbury, Cheshire

WESTBURY, 5 Baron (UK 1861); David Alan Bethell; MC (1942), DL (N Yorks 1973); s of Capt Hon Richard Bethell (s of 3 Baron, who he predecesased, and Lady Agatha Tollemache, sis of 9 Earl of Dysart); suc bro, 4 Baron, 1961; *b* 16 July 1922; *Educ* Harrow; *m* 1947, Ursula, da of Hon Robert James (3 s of 2 Baron Northbourne) by his 2 w, Lady Serena Lumley (da of 10 Earl of Scarbrough); 2 s, 1 da; *Heir* s, Hon Richard Bethell; *Career* Equerry to HRH Duke of Gloucester 1947-49; KStJ 1977; served WW II N Africa & Italy; *Style* - The Rt Hon Lord Westbury, MC, DL; Barton Cottage, Malton, N Yorks (☎ 2293)

WESTENRA, Hon Mrs Brigid Mary; da of 6 Baron Rossmore; *b* 23 Sept 1928; *m* 1956 (m dis 1969), Hon Jonathan Howard, s of 3 Baron Strathcona and Mountroyal; 2 da; *Career* reverted to maiden name; *Style* - The Hon Mrs Brigid Westenra; Pratolino, Radda-in-Chianti, Siena, Italy

WESTHEAD, John Michael; s of Percy Westhead (d 1961); *b* 13 Nov 1928; *Educ* St John's Coll & St Antony's Coll Oxford; *m* 1958, Portia Joan Peters, da of Capt John Wentworth Rooke OBE; 2 s; *Career* group managing director of Bowthorpe Holdings Ltd; *Recreations* squash, music, reading; *Clubs* United Oxford and Cambridge, Roy Soc of Arts; *Style* - John Westhead Esq; 'Hapstead Green Cottage', 63 High st, Ardingly, W Sussex (☎ Ardingly 892 362); Garden Flat, 33 Coleherne rd, SW10 (☎ 01 373 1395)

WESTLAKE, Peter Alan Grant; CMG (1972), MC (1943); s of Alan Robert Cecil Westlake CSI CIE (d 1978); *b* 2 Feb 1919; *Educ* Sherborne, Corpus Christi Oxford; *m* 1943, Katherine Gertrude, nee Spackman; 2 s; *Career* Order of the Rising Sun (Japan) 1975; HM Foreign Serv 1946-75: Head of Chancery Tel Aviv 1955-57, Min Br Embassy Toyko 1971-75, Cmmr Gen Int Ocean Expo Okinawa 1975; *Recreations* sailing, oceanography; *Clubs* RAYC; *Style* - Peter Westlake Esq, CMG, MC; 53 Church st, Beaumaris, Gwynedd (☎ Beaumaris 810114)

WESTMEATH, 13 Earl of (I 1621); William Anthony Nugent; also Baron Delvin (I before 1489, evolved from a feudal Barony, the date of whose origin is uncertain); s of 12 Earl of Westmeath (d 1971); *b* 21 Nov 1928; *Educ* Marlborough, Sandhurst; *m* 1963, Susanna, da of Judge (James) Leonard, of Sutton Courtenay; 2 s; *Heir* s, Lord Delvin; *Career* sr master St Andrew's Sch Pangbourne; *Style* - The Rt Hon The Earl of Westmeath; Farthings, Tutts Clump, Reading (☎ 0734 744426)

WESTMINSTER, 6 Duke of (UK 1874); Sir Gerald Cavendish Grosvenor; 15 Bt (E 1622); also Baron Grosvenor (GB 1761), Earl Grosvenor, Viscount Belgrave (both GB 1784), and Marquess of Westminster (UK 1831); s of 5 Duke of Westminster, TD (d 1979), and Hon Viola Lyttelton (*see* Viola, Duchess of Westminster), da of 9 Viscount Cobham; bro of Countess of Lichfield and Duchess of Roxburghe; *b* 22 Dec 1951; *Educ* Harrow; *m* 1978, Natalia, yst da of Lt-Col Harold Phillips FRGS, and Georgina (da of Sir Harold Wernher, 3 Bt, GCVO, TD, and Lady Zia CBE, nee Countess Anastasia Mikhailovna, da of HIH Grand Duke Michael of Russia by his morganatic m with Countess de Torby; the Grand Duke was 2 s of another HIH Grand Duke Michael, 4 s of Tsar Nicholas I), also sis of Duchess of Abercorn; 1 da; *Heir* to Duchy none, to Marquessate and all inferior honours: 7 Earl of Wilton, *qv*; *Career* landowner (of some of the choicest tracts of London); Pres NW Industl Cncl, London Tourist Bd 1980-, Chester Con Assoc, Chester YCs Freeman- Chester, England, City of London; V-Pres Inc Liverpool Sch of Tropical Medicine 1981-; dir Claridge's 1981-, Sun Alliance Insur West End Branch 1981-, Stuart Devlin 1979-, Hennell Ltd 1978-, Chester Grosvenor Hotel Co; Tstee

Grosvenor Estate 1981-; commissioned Queen's Own Yeo 1973; *Recreations* shooting, fishing; *Clubs* Roy Yacht Sqdn, Brooks's, Cavalry, MCC; *Style* - His Grace The Duke of Westminster; Eaton Hall, Chester, Cheshire

WESTMINSTER, Anne, Duchess of; Anne Winifred; da of Brig-Gen Edward Sullivan, CB, CMG, of Glanmire House, Co Cork; *m* 1947, as his 4 w, 2 Duke of Westminster, GCVO, DSO (d 1953); *Style* - Her Grace Anne, Duchess of Westminster; Lochmore, Lairg, Sutherland; Eaton Lodge, Eccleston, Chester

WESTMINSTER, Sally, Duchess of; Sally; twin da of George Perry; *m* 1945, 4 Duke of Westminster, DSO, PC, DL (d 1967); *Style* - Her Grace Sally, Duchess of Westminster; Hill House, Wickwar, Glos

WESTMINSTER, Viola, Dowager Duchess of - Hon Viola Maud; *née* Lyttelton; da of late 9 Viscount Cobham; *b* 1912; *m* 1946, 5 Duke of Westminster (d 1979); 1 s, 2 da; *Career* late Sqdn Offr WAAF, Dist Pres Order of St John of Jerusalem Commandery of Ards 1939-45 War (despatches); *Style* - Her Grace Viola, Dowager Duchess of Westminster; Ely Lodge, Enniskillen, Co Fermanagh

WESTMORLAND, 15 Earl of (E 1624); David Anthony Thomas Fane; KCVO (1970); also Baron Burghersh (E 1624); s of 14 Earl of Westmorland (d 1948) and Diana Countess of Westmorland, *qv*; *b* 31 March 1924; *Educ* Eton; *m* 1950, Barbara, da of Lt-Col Sir Roland Lewis Findlay, 3 Bt; 2 s, 1 da; *Heir* s, Lord Burghersh; *Career* late RHG; Master of the Horse 1978-, Lord in Waiting to HM 1955-78; OStJ 1981; *Clubs* White's, Buck's; *Style* - The Rt Hon Earl of Westmorland KCVO; Kingsmead, Didmarton, Glos; 23 Chester Row, SW1 (01 730 3389)

WESTMORLAND, Diana, Countess of; Hon Diana; *née* Lister; da of 4 and last Baron Ribblesdale (d 1925); *b* 1893; *m* 1, 1913, Lt Percy Wyndham, Coldstream Gds (ka 1914; gn of 2 Baron Leconfield); m 2, 1918, Capt Arthur Capel CBE (d 1919); 2 da; m 3, 1923, 14 Earl of Westmorland (d 1948); 2 s (15 Earl and Hon Julian Fane), 1 da (Lady Rose Bardsley) *qqv*; *Style* - Rt Hon Diana, Countess of Westmorland; Lyegrove, Badminton, Glos (☎ 213)

WESTMORLAND AND FURNESS, Archdeacon of; Ven Arthur Henry; s of late Henry John Attwell; *b* 5 Aug 1920; *Educ* Leeds U, London U; *Career* Clerk in Holy Orders, Dean of Kimberley S Africa 1952-59, Rector of Workington 1960-72, Canon Residentiary Carlisle 1972-78, Archdeacon of Westmorland and Furness 1978-; *Recreations* travel; *Style* - The Ven the Archdeacon of Westmorland and Furness; St John's Vicarage, Brock rd, Windermere, Cumbria (☎ 3447)

WESTOLL, James; DL (Cumbria); s of James Westoll (d 1969); *b* 26 July 1918; *Educ* Eton, Trin Cambridge; *m* 1946, Sylvia Jane MBE, da of Lord Justice Luxmoore (d 1944); 2 s, 2 da; *Career* OStJ, barr 1952; farmer; chm Cumberland CC 1958-74, Cumbria CC 1973-76, High Sheriff Cumberland 1964, dep chm Quarter Sessions 1960-71, memb NW Electricity Bd 1959-66; *Recreations* gardening, shooting; *Clubs* Boodle's, Farmer's; owner of racehorse 'Soldan'; *Style* - James Westoll Esq DL; Dykeside, Longtown, Cumbria (☎ Longtown 791235)

WESTON, Rear-Adm Charles Arthur Winfield; CB (1978); s of the late C W Weston; *b* 12 July 1922; *Educ* Merchant Taylors' Sch; *m* 1946, Jeanie Findlay, nee Miller; 1 s, 1 da; *Career* war service in Mediterranean, Indian Ocean, Atlantic, joined Navy as Cadet 1940, Admiral; president RN Coll Greenwich 1976-78; appeals secretary King Edward V11's Hospital for Officers 1979, ADC to HM the Queen 1976; *Recreations* cricket, golf, gardening; *Clubs* MCC, Army & Navy; *Style* - Rear-Adm Charles Weston CB; Westacre, Liphook, Hants (☎ 0428 723337)

WESTON, Hon Mrs (Caroline Cecily); *née* Douglas-Scott-Montagu; da of 2 Baron Montagu of Beaulieu; *b* 1925; *m* 1950 (George) Grainger Weston; 3 s, 1 da; *Style* - The Hon Mrs Weston; Santa Clara

Ranch, Marion, Texas, USA; 301 Wiltshire, San Antonio, Texas, USA

WESTON, Rev Canon Frank Valentine; s of Rev William Valentine Weston (d 1937); *b* 16 Sept 1935; *Educ* Christ's Hosp, Queen's Oxford; *m* 1963, Penelope Brighid, nee Athorpe; 1 s, 2 da; *Career* curate St John Baptist Atherton 1961-65, Chaplin Coll of the Ascension Selly Oak 1965-69, Princ 1969-76, Princ and Pantonian Prof of Theology Edinburgh Theological Coll 1976-; *Recreations* music, books, stamps, exploring the countryside; *Style* - Rev Canon Frank Weston; The Theological Coll, Rosebery Crescent, Edinburgh; 5 Birnam Terrace, Birnam, by Dunkeld, Perthshire

WESTON, Lady Moyra (Elizabeth); *née* Butler; da of 7 Earl of Lanesborough (d 1929); *b* 22 May 1899; *m* 1944, as his 2 w, Brigadier John Leslie Weston, CBE, DSO (d 1963); *Style* - Lady Moyra Weston; Kingsthorpe, South Hamilton rd, N Berwick

WESTON SMITH, John Harry; s of Cdr E Weston Smith OBE RN (ret); *b* 3 Feb 1932; *Educ* Fettes Coll Edinburgh, St John's Coll Cambridge; *m* 1955, Margaret Fraser, da of Prof E A Milne FRS (d 1954), 1 s (Hugh b 1961), 2 da (Elizabeth m 1980 Prof Horace Barlow FRS, Lucinda b 1964); *Career* Capt Roy Signals, jt gen man Abbey Nat Bldg Soc 1968-69, dir British Land Co 1973-; *Style* - John Weston Smith Esq; 10 Eldon Grove, NW3 (☎ 01 435 5069)

WESTROPP, Anthony Henry; s of Col Westropp; *b* 22 Dec 1944; *Educ* Sherborne, Kings' College, Univ of London; *m* 1977, Zoe Rosaleen, da of Charles Douglas Walker, of Paris; *Career* with Lazard Bros 1967-72; dir Trafalgar House Investment Mgmnt 1972-75, md Bardsey Investments & subsids 1975-; *Recreations* hunting, fishing, tennis; *Clubs* Boodle's; *Style* - Anthony Westropp Esq; 12 Onslow ct, Drayton gdns, London SW10 (☎ 01 373 8644); Ludwell Farm, Glympton, Woodstock, Oxon (☎ 812726)

WESTWOOD, 2 Baron (UK 1944); William Westwood; JP (Newcastle 1949); s of 1 Baron Westwood (d 1953) by his 1 w, Margaret; *b* 25 Dec 1907; *Educ* Glasgow; *m* 1937, Marjorie, da of Arthur Bonwick; 2 s; *Heir* s, Hon William Westwood; *Career* Pres Football League & V-Pres FA 1974-; FRSA, FCIS; *Style* - The Rt Hon Lord Westwood JP; 12 Westfield dve, Newcastle on Tyne NE3 4XU

WESTWOOD, Hon James Young Shaw; 2 s of 1 Baron Westwood OBE; *b* 1915; *m* 1941 (m dis 1969), Joan, da of Raymond Potts; 1 s; *Career* late Capt Roy Fleet Aux; *Style* - The Hon James Westwood

WESTWOOD, Hon Mrs Douglas (Mary Katherine); da of John Carter; *m* 1939, Hon Douglas Westwood (d 1968, s of 1 Baron Westwood); 1 da; *Style* - The Hon Mrs Douglas Westwood; 70 Granville Court, Newcastle-on-Tyne NE2 1TR

WESTWOOD, Hon Nigel Alistair; 2 s of 2 Baron Westwood JP; *b* 1950; *Educ* Fettes; *m* 1977, Joan Ibison; *Style* - The Hon Nigel Westwood

WESTWOOD, Hon William Gavin; s and h of 2 Baron Westwood JP; *b* 30 Jan 1944; *Educ* Fettes; *m* 1969, Penelope, da of Charles Shafto, VRD, MB; 2 s; *Career* ACA; *Style* - The Hon William Westwood

WEYMOUTH, Viscount; Alexander George Thynn (*sic*, reverted to this spelling); s and h of 6 Marquess of Bath, ED; *b* 6 May 1932; *Educ* Eton, Ch Ch Oxford; *m* 1969, Anna, da of Laszlo Gyarmarthy, of Los Angeles (Anna Gael, the actress); 1 s, 1 da; *Heir* s, Hon Ceawlin Thynn; *Career* late Lt Life Gds & Roy Wilts Yeo; contested Westbury (Feb 1974) & Wells (1979) in Wessex Regional Pty's interest, Wessex (Euro elections 1979) Wessex Regional and European Fed Pty; painter, author; *Style* - Viscount Weymouth; Longleat, Warminster, Wilts (☎ Maiden Bradley 300)

WHADDON, Baron (Life Peer UK 1978); John Derek Page; s of John Page; *b* 14 Aug 1927; *Educ* St Bede's Coll Manchester; *m* 1, 1948, Catherine (d

1979), da of John Halls; 1 s, 1 da; m 2, 1981, Angela, da of Luigi della Bella, of Treviso; *Career* dir Cambridge Chemicals 1962-; MP (L) King's Lynn 1964-70; memb Cncl Management COSIRA; *Recreations* flying; *Clubs* Reform; *Style* - The Rt Hon Lord Whaddon; The Old Vicarage, Whaddon, Royston, Herts (☎ Arrington 209)

WHARNCLIFFE, 4 Earl of (UK 1876); Alan James Montagu-Stuart-Wortley-Mackenzie; also Baron Wharncliffe (UK 1826) and Viscount Carlton (UK 1876); s of 3 Earl of Wharncliffe (d 1953) and Lady Maud Wentworth-Fitzwilliam, da of 7 Earl Fitzwilliam; *b* 23 March 1935; *Educ* Eton, RAC Cirencester; *m* 1957, Aline, da of Robert Dunlop Bruce, of Dyson Holmes House, nr Sheffield; 1 da (and 1 da decd); *Heir* kinsman, Alan Montagu-Stuart-Wortley; *Career* self-employed in Wharncliffe Estates, Wortley Arms, Wharncliffe Engrg; Master of the Ecclesfield Beagles; patron of 1 living; RNVR; *Recreations* shooting, fishing; *Clubs* Lansdowne; *Style* - The Rt Hon The Earl of Wharncliffe; Wharncliffe House, Wortley, Sheffield, S30 4DG (☎ 882331)

WHARTON, Hon Mrs (Frances Mary); *née* Edmondson; da of 2 Baron Sandford DSC; *b* 1953; *Educ* Down House Sch, Bristol U; *m* 1, 1977, Simon Holland; m 2, 1979, Geoffrey Wharton; *Career* research scientist; *Style* - The Hon Mrs Wharton

WHEADON, Richard Anthony; s of Ivor Cecil Newman Wheadon; *b* 31 Aug 1933; *Educ* Cranleigh Sch, Balliol Oxford; *m* 1961, Ann Mary, da of Frederick Charles Richardson CBE; 2 s; *Career* Sword of Honour RAF 1955, Air Radar Offr 1956-57; assist master Eton 1957-66, dep headmaster & head of Science Dept Dauntsey's Sch 1966-71; principal Elizabeth Coll Guernsey 1972-; rowed for Oxford 100th Boat Race, capt & coach RAF Eight 1956-57, rowed Bow British VIII European Championships 1956 & Olympic Games 1956, coach of Oxford crew for Boat Race 1957, Nat coach and Olympic selector 1965-66; *Recreations* French horn, photography, sailing, electronics, rowing, swimming; *Clubs* E India, Devonshire Sports and Public Schs; *Style* - Richard Wheadon Esq; Elizabeth Coll, Guernsey (☎ 25544); L'Enclos Galliennes, Rue du Court Laurent, Torteval, Guernsey, CI

WHEATLEY, Baron (Life Peer UK 1970); John Wheatley; PC (1947); s of Patrick Wheatley; *b* 17 Jan 1908; *Educ* St Aloysius College Glasgow, Mount St Mary's College Sheffield, Glasgow University, Stirling University; *m* 1935, Agnes, da of Samuel Nichol, of Tollcross, Glasgow (d 1929); 4 s, 1 da (Hon Mrs Tam Dalyell); *Career* Scottish Lord of Session 1954-, Lord Justice-Clerk 1972-, advocate 1932; MP (L) E Edinburgh 1947-54, Solicitor-General Scotland 1947, QC (Scotland) 1947, Lord Advocate 1947-51; chm Scottish Nurses' Salaries Committee 1945-47, Ctee on Teaching Profession (Scotland) 1961-63; memb Royal Commission on Penal Reform (England and Wales) 1964-66; chm executive committee Royal Scottish Society for the Prevention of Cruelty to Children 1956-79, chm Royal Commission on Local Government in Scotland 1966-69; *Recreations* golf; *Clubs* KSC (London); *Style* - The Rt Hon The Lord Wheatley PC; 3 Greenhill Gardens, Edinburgh EH10 4BN (☎ 031 229 4783)

WHEATLEY, Hon Anthony; s of Baron Wheatley PC; *b* 1945; *Educ* Fordham U New York; *Style* - The Hon Anthony Wheatley

WHEATLEY, John Edward Clive; MC, JP; s of Edward Pearce Wheatley, alderman, sheriff of Exeter (d 1968); *b* 7 March 1921; *Educ* The Leys Sch Cambridge, Exeter U; *m* 1945, Rosemarie Joy Malet, da of Captain Victor Samuel Rowbotham, RFC; 2 s, 2 da; *Career* Staff Capt N Africa, Italy; metal merchant; chm E Pearse & Co Ltd, South Western Industrial Gases Ltd, C Philipp & Son Ltd, Pearse Complex Alloys Ltd, Exeter Housing Soc; pres British Scrap Fedn 1978-79; dir Parks & Co Ltd; *Recreations* travel, photography, collecting old books; *Clubs* Army and Navy; *Style* - John Wheatley Esq, MC, JP; Pipers Chantry, Rosebarn Lane, Exeter (☎ 56087)

WHEATLEY, Hon John Francis; s of Baron Wheatley; *b* 9 May 1941; *Educ* Mount St Mary's College Derbyshire, Edinburgh U; *m* 1970, Bronwen Catherine, da of Alastair Fraser; 2 s; *Career* advocate, advocate depute 1974; Sheriff Tayside Central & Fife at Perth 1980; *Recreations* gardening, music, farming; *Style* - Sheriff The Hon John Wheatley; Braefoot Farmhouse, Fossoway, Kinross-shire (☎ 212)

WHEATLEY, Hon Michael; s of Baron Wheatley PC; *b* 1949; *m* 1971, Anne, da of Thomas Barry; *Style* - The Hon Michael Wheatley; Millburn, Old Philipstoun, W Lothian

WHEATLEY, Hon Patrick; 2 s of Baron Wheatley PC; *b* 1943; *m* 1968, Sheena, da of Douglas Lawrie; *Style* - The Hon Patrick Wheatley

WHEATLEY-HUBBARD, Evelyn Raymond; s of Eric Wyndham Hubbard (d 1946); assumed additional name of Wheatley by Deed Poll 1949; *b* 22 Feb 1921; *Educ* Eton; *m* 1949, Ann Christobel, OBE, da of late Col Charles Joshua Hirst Wheatley, TD, JP, DL; 1 s, 1 da; *Career* Coldstream Gds 1940-46; *Clubs* Guards and Cavalry; *Style* - Evelyn Wheatley-Hubbard Esq; Broadleaze, Boyton, Warminster, Wilts (☎ 098 55 214)

WHEATON, The Rev David Harry; s of Harry Wheaton, MBE; *b* 2 June 1930; *Educ* Abingdon Sch, St John's Oxford, London Bible Coll; *m* 1956, Helen Joy, nee Forrer; 1 s, 2 da; *Career* hon canon of St Albans 1976, princ Oak Hill Coll 1971, vicar St Paul's Onslow sq SW7 1966-71, chaplain Brompton Hospital 1969-71, rector Ludgershall Bucks 1962-66, tutor Oak Hill Coll 1954-62; *Recreations* walking, DIY; *Style* - The Rev David Wheaton; Oak Hill Coll, Southgate, N14 (☎ 01 441 5996); Dalegarth, Hare Lane, Buckland St Mary, Chard, Somerset (☎ Buckland 377)

WHEELDON, The Right Rev Philip William; OBE (1946); s of Alfred Leonard Wheeldon (d 1936); *b* 20 May 1913; *Educ* Clifton Coll Bristol, Downing Cambridge; *m* 1966, Margaret, nee Redfearn; *Career* dep assist Chaplain-General BAOR, Farnham Parish Church 1937-39, chaplain to the Forces 1939-46, chaplain 1 Bn Coldstream Gds 1939-42, hon chaplain to the Forces 1946-, domestic chaplain to Archbishop York 1946-49, hon chaplain 1949-54, gen sec CACTM 1949-54, prebendary of Wedmore II in Wells Cathedral 1952-54, suffragan Bishop of Whitby 1954-61, Bishop of Kimberley and Kuruman 1961-65 and 1968-76, assist Bishop Diocese Worcester 1965-68, hon assist Bishop in Diocese Wakefield 1977-; *Recreations* music, gardens; *Clubs* Brooks's; *Style* - The Right Rev Philip Wheeldon OBE; Westgate Close, Clifton, Brighouse, W Yorks

WHEELER, Alice, Lady; Alice Webster; da of George Stones; *m* 1938, Sir Arthur Wheeler, 2 Bt (d 1964); 1 s (3 Bt), 1 da (Nancie); *Style* - Alice, Lady Wheeler; E12, Marine Gate, Marine Parade, Brighton 7, Sussex

WHEELER, Arthur William Edge; CBE (1979, OBE 1967); s of Arthur William Wheeler, of Dublin (d 1969); *b* 1 Aug 1930; *Educ* Mountjoy Sch, Trin Coll Dublin; *m* 1956, Gay, nee Brady; 2 s, 1 da; *Career* barr, Crown Cncl Nigeria 1955, acting legal sec Southern Cameroons and memb exec Cncl and House of Assembly 1958, princ Crown Cncl Fedn of Nigeria 1961, dir of Public Prosecutions N Nigeria 1966, High Ct Judge N Nigeria 1967, Ch Justice Kaduna State of Nigeria 1975, Cmmr for the Revision of the Laws of Bauchi, Benue, Borno, Kano, Gongola, Kaduna, Kwara, Niger, Plateau and Sokoto States of Nigeria 1980; *Recreations* squash, tennis, golf, formerly cricket and hockey (Nigerian Hockey Int); *Clubs* Roy Commonwealth Soc, Kildare Street and University Club (Dublin); *Style* - Arthur Wheeler Esq CBE; c/o Barclays Bank International Ltd, 16/18 Brompton rd, SW1; Miny of Justice, PMB 2072, Kaduna, Nigeria

WHEELER, Air Chief Marshal Sir Henry Neil George; GCB (1975, KCB 1969, CB 1967), CBE (1957, OBE 1949), DSO (1943), DFC (1941) and Bar (1943), AFC (1954); s of Thomas Wheeler; *b* 8 July 1917; *Educ* St Helens Coll Southsea; *m* 1942, Alice Elizabeth, da of William Henry

Weightman CMG; 3 c; *Career* RAF 1935-76, Air Ch Marshal Europe and Far East; dir Rolls Royce Ltd 1977-, dir Flight Refuelling Ltd 1977-; *Recreations* flyfishing, painting, gardening; *Clubs* Flyfishers, RAF, Hurlingham; *Style* - Air Chief Marshal Sir Henry Wheeler, GCB, CBE, DSO, DFC*, AFC; Boundary Hall, Cooksbridge, Lewes, Sussex (☎ Barcombe 400207)

WHEELER, John Frederick; s & h of Sir John Wheeler, 3 Bt; *b* 3 May 1933; *m* 1963, Barbara, da of Raymond Flint, of Leicester; 2 s (John b 1965, Andrew b 1969), 1 da (Jane b 1964); *Style* - John Wheeler Esq; Frostenden Hall, Frostenden, Suffolk

WHEELER, Sir John Hieron; 3 Bt (UK 1920), of Woodhouse Eaves, Co Leicester; s of Sir Arthur Wheeler, 1 Bt, JP, DL (d 1943) and bro of 2 Bt (d 1964); *b* 22 July 1905; *Educ* Charterhouse; *m* 1929, Gwendolen Alice, da of late Alfred Ernest Oram, of Kirby Muxloe, Leics; 2 s; *Heir* s, John Wheeler; chm & md printing cos, ret 1973; *Style* - Sir John Wheeler, Bt; 39 Morland ave, Stoneygate, Leicester

WHEELER, John Vashon Tyrwhitt; s of Wing-Cdr Vashon James Wheeler MC DFC (ka 1944); *b* 24 Oct 1931; *Educ* Eton, Trin Coll Cambridge; *m* 1; 3 s (James b 1960, Nicholas b 1965, Justin b 1970), 1 da (Susan); m 2, Mrs Caroline Susan Chance, da of Patrick Holmes MBE; 2 step s (Timothy, Henry), 1 step da (Lucy); *Career* Flying Offr, Nat Serv; dir Wolseley-Hughes Ltd 1970-; chm and md: F W McConnell Ltd 1970-, Nu-Way Benson Ltd 1970-; chm Bruff Mfg Co Ltd 1970-; *Recreations* land management; *Clubs* RAF; *Style* - John Wheeler Esq; Bitterley Court, Ludlow, Shropshire (☎ Ludlow 890 265)

WHEELER, Russell Phillip; s of John Harrold Wheeler, of USA (d 1934); *b* 16 March 1927; *Educ* University of Tulsa (Oklahoma), Washington U; *m* 1951, Dorothy Ann, da of Judge Albert Hampton Thomas, of USA (d 1966); 2 s (Russell Phillip Jr, Mark Thomas), 1 da (Melissa Ann b 1963); *Career* 1945 US Naval Aviation V5 program; 1962-63 US Govt petroleum consultant, 1963- US Govt petroleum exec reservist, currently petroleum exec, former pres of Continental Oil Co Far East (Tokyo), md of Continental Oil Co Ltd London, dir Conch Int Methane Ltd & Benzene Marketing Co Ltd; *Recreations* golf, skiing, tennis, swimming; *Clubs* Hurlingham, Highgate G C, Les Ambassadeurs; *Style* - Russell Wheeler Esq; 43 Wilton cres, SW1 (☎ 01 235 6920); 30 Rapids Lane, Greenwich, Connecticut, USA

WHEEN, Rear-Adm Charles Kerr Thorneycroft; CB (1966); s of Francis Thorneycroft; *b* 28 Sept 1912; *Educ* RN Coll Dartmouth; *m* 1940, Veryan Rosamond, nee Acworth; 3 s, 1 da; *Career* Rear-Adm 1964, Naval Attaché Beirut, Amman and Addis Ababa 1958-60; Admiralty 1960-63, Flag Offr Admiralty Interview Bd 1964-66, ret 1966; dir Cement Makers Fedn 1967-79; chm govrs Gordon Boys' Sch 1971-; *Recreations* golf, fishing; *Clubs* Army and Navy, MCC; *Style* - Rear-Adm Charles Wheen CB; Donnystone, Chobham, Surrey (☎ 8118)

WHELAN, Prof Robert Ford; s of the late R H Whelan; *b* 22 Dec 1922; *Educ* Queen's U Belfast; *m* 1951, Helen Elizabeth Macdonald, nee Hepburn; 2 s, 1 da; *Career* Prof of Human Physiology & Pharmacology Adelaide University 1957-71, V-Chancellor U of Western Australia 1971-76, V-Chancellor U of Liverpool 1977-; *Clubs* Athenaeum; *Style* - Prof Robert Whelan; Vice-Chancellor's Lodge, Sefton Park rd, Liverpool (☎ 051 727 2264); Drumber Castle Cottage, Tiverton, Cheshire (☎ 082 93 2851); 22 Conway Street, London W1 (☎ 01 387 3143)

WHELER, Edward Woodford; s & h of Sir Trevor Wheler, 13 Bt; *b* 13 June 1920; *Educ* Radley; *m* 1945, Molly, da of Thomas Lever; 1 s (Trevor), 1 da (Mrs Clive Knight); *Career* late Capt; Overseas Audit Dept 1948-58, Capt Roy Sussex Regt & IA during WW II; *Style* - Edward Wheler Esq; 25 Cavendish rd, Chesham, Bucks

WHELER, Sir Trevor Wood; 13 Bt (E 1660), of City of Westminster, Co London; s of 12 Bt (d 1903) by Mary Leontine, da of late Sir Richard Wood, GCMG, CB; *b* 20 Sept 1889; *Educ* Radley; *m* 1915, Margaret Idris, da of Sir Ernest W Birch KCMG (d 1929); 1 s, 2 da; *Heir* s, Capt Edward Woodford Wheler, b 13 June 1920; *Career* Capt The Roy Sussex Regt 1914-20; served on NW Frontier Waziristan, Capt RE 1940-47; control commission for Germany 1947-59; Kenya Police Reserve throughout Mau Mau Emergency; *Style* - Sir Trevor Wheler, Bt; 5A Motcombe Court, Bedford ave, Bexhill-on-Sea, Sussex

WHETHERLY, Hon Mrs (Rosemary Gertrude Alexandra); *née* Lever; da of 2 Viscount Leverhulme (d 1949); *b* 1919; *m* 1938, Lt-Col William Erskine Stobart Whetherly; 2 s, 1 da; *Style* - The Hon Mrs Whetherly; Hallam, Ogbourne St George, Marlborough, Wilts

WHIDBORNE, Hon Mrs (Elaine Barbara Julia); da of late Lt-Col the Hon Rowland Tudor St John DLI, s of 16 Baron St John of Bletso, and sis of late 20 Baron; raised to the rank of a Baron's da 1977; *b* 1921; *m* 1939, Lt-Col John Francis Whidborne, (ret) RA; 1 s, 1 da; *Style* - The Hon Mrs Whidborne; Hannaford Old House, nr Ashburton, S Devon

WHIFFING, Kenneth Arthur; s of Duke Wellington Whiffing (d 1964); *b* 28 June 1925; *Educ* White Hart Lane Elementary Sch; *m* 1954, Muriel Rose, nee Cotton; 2 s (Paul, Kenneth), 1 da (Karen b 1961); *Career* md Hahn & Co Ltd 1977- (sales dir 1970-77, rep 1950-70), chm Nast Hyde Conservatives & Conservative Club; *Clubs* Hatfield Conservative, Institute of Directors; *Style* - Kenneth Whiffing Esq; Khaya, 2 Ashbury Close, Hatfield, Herts

WHILEY, Reginald Raymond; JP (1979); s of Harry Hewitt Whiley (d 1957); *b* 7 July 1924; *Educ* Kilburn G S; *Career* insurance; dir CT Bowring (London) 1974-, memb of Lloyd's, chm Shipton Insurance Services 1976-; hon tres Nat Fund for Research into Crippling Diseases 1979-; govr Southlands Coll and Luton Indust Coll 1981-; *Recreations* walking, watching sport; *Clubs* City of London, Royal Automobile, MCC; *Style* - Reginald Whiley Esq JP; 21 Francis Rd, Pinner, HA5 2ST (☎ 01 866 6147)

WHITAKER, Alan Arthur; s of Sir Arthur Whitaker KCB; *b* 21 March 1925; *Educ* Aldenham Sch, Ch Ch Oxford; *m* 1957, Beulah, nee Hatcher; *Career* CA, fin dir S Pearson & Son Ltd 1969-, dir Lazard Bros & Co Ltd 1973-, Doulton & Co Ltd 1978-; *Recreations* gardening; *Style* - Alan Whitaker Esq; Hartfield, Martinsend Lane, Gt Missenden, Bucks (☎ 5124)

WHITAKER, Sir James Herbert Ingham Whitaker; 3 Bt (UK 1936), of Babworth, Nottinghamshire; s of Maj-Gen Sir John Whitaker, 2 Bt, CB, CBE (d 1957); *b* 27 July 1925; *Educ* Eton; *m* 1948, Mary Elisabeth Lander JP (who m 1940, Capt David Urling Clark MC, d 1942), da of Ernest Johnston; 1 s, 1 da; *Heir* s, John James Ingham Whitaker, b 23 Oct 1952, m 1981, Janey, da of L Starke, of NZ; *Career* 2 Lt Coldstream Gds 1944, served in N W Europe, Egypt and Palestine 1945, ret 1947; dep chm Halifax Bldg Soc and chm of London Bd; dir NCC and Moorside Trust; dep chm Bd of Govrs Atlantic Coll; dir Economic Forestry Gp; dir Updown Investment Trust; High Sheriff Notts 1969; *Style* - Sir James Whitaker, Bt; Auchnafree, Dunkeld, Perthshire (☎ Amulree 233); Babworth Hall, Retford, Notts (☎ 3454)

WHITBREAD, Hugh William; s of Col William Henry Whitbread, TA, by his 2 w Betty, nee Russell; *b* 11 Feb 1942; *Educ* Eton, Cambridge U, Harvard U; *m* 1972, Katherine Elizabeth, nee Hall; 3 c; *Career* brewing industry exec, dir Whitbread & Co, md Thomas Wethereds of Marlow 1976-81; HM Diplomatic Serv 1966-71, 3 Sec Vientiane 1966-68, 2 Sec Vientiane 1968-70; *Recreations* fishing, shooting, private flying; *Clubs* Brooks's, RAC; *Style* - Hugh Whitbread Esq; Englefield, Cookham, Maidenhead, Berks; Kinlochewe Lodge, Achnasheen, Ross-shire

WHITBREAD, Michael William; 2 s of Col William Whitbread and half bro of Hugh William Whitbread, *qv*; *b* 25 June 1930; *Educ* Stowe; *m* 1965, Helen Mary, nee Aikenhead; 1 s, 1 da; *Career* brewery dir, pres Licenced Victualler's Nat Homes 1981-82; *Recreations* shooting, fishing, rugby; *Style* - Michael Whitbread Esq; The Grey House, Turkdean, Northleach, Glos (☎ 045 16 389)

WHITCOMBE, Hon Mrs (Rosemary Anne Heather); *née* Colville; da of late 1 Baron Clydesmuir, GCIE, TD, PC; *b* 1927; *m* 1954, Philip Arthur Whitcombe; 1 s, 1 da; *Style* - The Hon Mrs Whitcombe; Green Cross Farm, Churt, Farnham, Surrey

WHITE, Baroness (Life Peeress UK 1970); Eirene Lloyd White; da of Thomas Jones, CH, of Aberystwyth; *b* 7 Nov 1909; *Educ* St Paul's Girls' Sch, Somerville Oxford; *m* 1948, John White (d 1968); *Career* former journalist & civil servant; MP (L) Flint E 1950-70, Min State For Affrs 1966-67, Welsh Off 1967-70; chm Lab NEC 1968-69; chm Select Cttee EEC & pncpl dep chm Ctees House of Lds 1979; *Style* - The Rt Hon Lady White; Panteg, Ceinws, Machynlleth, Powys (☎ Corris 679); 36 Westminster gdns, Marsham st, SW1 (☎ 01 828 3320)

WHITE, Bernard Henry; s of John Henry White (d 1970); *b* 17 July 1932; *Educ* Cardiff H S, Queens' Cambridge; *m* 1957, (Elizabeth) Jane, nee Evans; 2 s, 1 da; *Career* marketing dir Laporte Industries Ltd 1978-; *Recreations* golf, the arts, music; *Clubs* Oriental; *Style* - Bernard White Esq; Westgate, Millfield Lane, St Ippolyts, Hitchin, Herts

WHITE, Hon Caroline Davina; da of 5 Baron Annaly by his 2 w; *b* 8 Feb 1963; *Style* - The Hon Caroline White

WHITE, Sir Christopher Robert Meadows White; 3 Bt (UK 1937), of Boulge Hall, Co Suffolk; s of Sir (Eric) Richard Meadows White, 2 Bt (d 1972); *b* 26 Aug 1940; *Educ* Bradfield Coll; *m* 1962, Anne Marie Ghislaine (m dis 1968), da of late Maj Tom Brown, OBE, MC; m 2, 1968 Dinah Mary Sutton (m dis 1972); m 3, 1976, Ingrid Carolyn, da of Eric Jowett, of Gt Baddow, Essex; *Heir* none; *Career* formerly schoolmaster; housemaster St Michael's Sch, Ingoldisthorpe, Norfolk 1963-69; *Style* - Sir Christopher White, Bt

WHITE, David Julian; s of Arthur John Stanley White, CMG, OBE; *b* 17 July 1942; *Educ* Marlborough; *m* 1967, Claire Rosemary, nee Emett; 3 da; *Career* md Cater Ryder & Co Ltd 1980-; *Style* - David White Esq; Flint House, Penn st, Amersham, Bucks (☎ High Wycombe 713262)

WHITE, Hon Doone Patricia; da of 5 Baron Annaly by his 2 w; *b* 16 June 1961; *Style* - The Hon Doone White

WHITE, Lady; Elizabeth Victoria Mary; da of Wilfrid Wrightson JP (3 s of Sir Thomas Wrightson, 1 Bt, JP, DL, sometime MP Stockton also St Pancras E); *m* 1943, Sir Headley White, 3 Bt (d 1971); 1 s (4 Bt), 2 da (Morna b 1944, Isabelle b 1948); *Style* - Lady White; Salle Park, Reepham, Norfolk

WHITE, Hon Mrs (Frances Alice); da (by 1 m) of 3 Baron Fisher; *b* 1951; *m* 1981, Angus J White; *Style* - The Hon Mrs White

WHITE, Sir George (Stanley Midelton); 3 Bt (UK 1904), of Cotham House, Bristol; s of 2 Bt (d 1964); *b* 11 April 1913; *Educ* Harrow; *m* 1939, Diane Eleanor, da of late Mrs B Abdy Collins; 1 s, 1 da; *Heir* s, George Stanley James White, b 4 Nov 1948; *Career* chm Bristol Cars Ltd; memb George White Evans and Co, stockbrokers, of Bristol; *Style* - Sir George White, Bt; Pypers, Rudgeway, nr Bristol (☎ Thornbury 412312)

WHITE, Geoffrey Ian; s of George White (1970); *b* 16 Nov 1928; *Educ* Dulwich Coll, CCC Oxford; *m* 1956, Hazel, nee Allenby; 2 s, 1 da; *Career* FRSA; memb Beckenham Borough Cncl 1955-65, dep sr ptnr Montagu Loebl Stanley & Co 1978 (ptnr 1959, fin ptnr 1974); *Recreations* theatre, opera, gardening, watching rugby, cricket, wine; *Clubs* City of London; *Style* - Geoffrey White Esq; Pilgrim Cottage, Godstone, Surrey (☎ 842232)

WHITE, George Stanley James; s & h of Sir George White, 3 Bt; *b* 4 Nov 1948; *Educ* Harrow; *m* 1974 (m dis 1979), Susan, da of John Ford; m 2, Elizabeth, da of Sir William Reginald Verdon-Smith, and formerly w of Robert Clinton; *Style* - George White Esq; Hawkesbury Stoke, Hawkesbury, Badminton, Avon

WHITE, Dowager Lady; Isabelle Stuart; da of James MacGowan, of Paris; *m* 1912, Sir Dymoke White, 2 Bt (d 1968); 2 s (3 Bt, Lt-Col Lynton White, *qv*), 1 da (Lady Martell); *Style* - Dowager Lady White; 2 Swan Close, Emsworth, Hants

WHITE, Hon Mrs (Jessica Jane Vronwy); *née* Scott-Ellis; da of 9 Baron Howard de Walden and 5 Baron Seaford; *b* 6 Aug 1941; *m* 1966, Adrian Tancred White; 4 s; *Career* co-heiress to Barony of Howard de Walden; *Style* - The Hon Mrs White; 17 Pelham Place, SW7 (☎ 01 589 0728); Farnborough Downs Farm, Wantage, Oxon

WHITE, Sir John Woolmer; 4 Bt (UK 1922), of Salle Park, Norfolk; s of Sir Headley Dymoke White, 3 Bt (d 1971); *b* 4 Feb 1947; *Educ* Cheltenham Coll; *Heir* uncle, Lt-Col Lynton Stuart White, MBE, TD, b 11 Aug 1916; *Style* - Sir John White, Bt; Salle Park, Reepham, Norfolk

WHITE, Hon Luke Richard; s and h of 5 Baron Annaly by his 1 w, Lady Marye Pepys, da of 7 Earl of Cottenham; *b* 29 June 1954; *Educ* Eton; *Career* Lt Roy Hussars; *Style* - The Hon Luke White

WHITE, Lt-Col Lynton Stuart; MBE (1943), TD, DL (Hants); s of Sir Dymoke White, 2 Bt, JP, DL (d 1968); hp of nephew, Sir John White, 4 Bt; *b* 11 Aug 1916; *Educ* Harrow, Trin Cambridge; *m* 1945, Phyllis, da of Sir Newham Worley; 4 s (Anthony b 1946, Richard b 1953, Robert b 1956, Philip b 1958), 1 da (Mrs Christopher Wernham); *Career* chm Hants CC 1977-; served WW II RA; *Style* - Lt-Col Lynton White MBE TD DL; Oxenbourne House, East Meon, Petersfield, Hants

WHITE, Hon Mrs (Pamela Anne); *née* Moncreiff; da of 4 Baron Moncreiff (d 1942); *b* 1927; *Educ* MB, ChB Edinburgh 1949; *m* 1951, Edward James White; 2 s, 1 da; *Style* - The Hon Mrs White; 13 Barntongate ave, Edinburgh 4

WHITE, Richard Taylor; DSO (1940) and 2 Bars (1941, 1942); s of Sir Archibald Woolaston White, 4 Bt (d 1954), and hp of bro, 5 Bt; *b* 29 Jan 1908; *Educ* RNC Dartmouth; *m* 1936, Gabrielle Ursula, yr da of Capt Robert Style JP (n of Sir William Style, 9 Bt); 3 s, 2 da; *Career* Capt RN WW II: Atlantic, Mediterranean, Far East, Capt RN Coll Dartmouth 1951-53; *Style* - Richard White Esq, DSO**; Tilts House, Boughton Monchelsea, Maidstone, Kent (☎ 43465)

WHITE, Sir Thomas Astley Wollaston; 5 Bt (UK 1802), of Wallingwells, Nottinghamshire; JP (Wigtownshire 1952); s of Lt-Col Sir Archibald White, 4 Bt, TD (d 1945); *b* 13 May 1904; *Educ* Wellington; *m* 1935, Daphne Margaret, da of Lt-Col Francis Remi Imbert Athill, CMG, OBE, DL, of Harbottle Castle, Morpeth, Northumberland (d 1958); 1 da; *Heir* bro, Capt Richard Taylor White, DSO, RN (ret), b 29 Jan 1908; *Career* FRICS, Hon Sheriff Substitute Wigtownshire; *Style* - Sir Thomas White, Bt, JP; Torhousemuir, Wigtown (☎ Wigtown 2138)

WHITE-THOMSON, The Rev Ian Hugh; s of The Right Rev Leonard Jauncey White-Thomson, Bishop of Ely (d 1933); *b* 18 Dec 1904; *Educ* Harrow, Oxford U; *m* 1954, Wendy Ernesta, nee Woolliams; 2 s, 2 da; *Career* ordained 1929, rector St Martin with St Paul Canterbury 1934-39, chaplain to Archbishop of Canterbury, vicar of Folkestone 1947-55, chaplain to HM King George VI 1947-52, to HM the Queen 1952-63, archdeacon of Northumberland 1955-63, dean of Canterbury 1963-76; *Recreations* walking, painting; *Style* - The Rev Ian White-Thomson; Camphill, Wye, Kent (☎ 812210)

WHITEHEAD, Hon Mrs (Annabel Alice Hoyer); *née* Millar; da of 1 Baron Inchyra, GCMG, CVO; *b* 1943; *m* 1973, Christopher James Bovill Whitehead; 1 s, 1 da; *Career* a Lady in Waiting to HRH The Princess Margaret, Countess of Snowdon 1971-75, Extra Lady in Waiting 1975-; *Style* - The Hon Mrs Whitehead; 5

Vicarage gdns, W8

WHITEHEAD, Hon Mrs (Lucia Edith); *née* Lawson; da of Maj-Gen 4 Baron Burnham, CB, DSO, MC, TD (d 1963); *b* 29 Aug 1922; *m* 1, 1946, Flight Lt Hon Roger Marquis (later 2 Earl of Woolton; m dis 1953, he d 1969); m 2, 1966, John Whitehead; *Career* served WW II 1941-46 as CSM ATS (despatches); *Style* - The Hon Mrs Whitehead; The Hill, Gilsland, Carlisle

WHITEHEAD, Sir Rowland John Rathbone; 5 Bt (UK 1889), of Highfield House, Catford Bridge, Kent; s of Maj Sir Philip Henry Rathbone Whitehead, 4 Bt (d 1953); *b* 24 June 1930; *Educ* Radley, Trin Hall Cambridge; *m* 1954, Marie-Louise, da of Arnold Christian Gausel, of Stavanger, Norway; 1 s, 1 da; *Heir* s, Philip Henry Rathbone Whitehead, b 13 Oct 1957; *Career* fell Roy Statistical Soc; memb British Operational Research Soc; memb Inst of Public Relations; *Style* - Sir Rowland Whitehead, Bt; Sutton House, Chiswick Mall, W4 (☎ 01 994 2710)

WHITEHORN, John Roland Malcolm; CMG (1974); s of Alan Whitehorn; *b* 19 May 1924; *Educ* Rugby, Trin Cambridge; *m* 1, 1951 (m dis 1973), Josephine Plummer; m 2, 1973, Marion, nee Gutmann; *Career* Flying Offr RAFVR 1943-46; dir Industry Affairs Lilly Industries Ltd, dir Mitchell Cotts Gp Ltd; memb Gen Advisory Ctee BBC 1966-78, dep dir-gen CBI; *Clubs* Reform, MCC; *Style* - John Whitehorn Esq CMG; 2 Ordnance Hill, NW8 (☎ 01 722 4665); New Cottage, Park Farm, Lurgashall, Petworth, W Sussex (☎ N Chapel 413)

WHITEHOUSE, Brian Paul; s of Rev Sydney Paul Whitehouse (d 1978); *b* 24 May 1933; *Educ* Manchester G S, CCC Oxford; *m* 1958, Jane Margaret, da of Lt Cdr John Roberts-West (d 1942); 4 c; *Career* 2 Lt Northamptonshire Regt; dir Hambro's Bank 1970-; *Recreations* croquet, bridge, racing; *Style* - Brian Whitehouse Esq; Hambro's Bank, 41 Bishopsgate, EC2

WHITELEY, Lady Anne Patricia; *née* Nevill; da of 5 Marquess of Abergavenny, KG, OBE, JP; *b* 25 Oct 1938; *m* 1971, Martin Whiteley; 1 da; *Style* - Lady Anne Whiteley; Dalmar House, Culworth, Banbury, Oxon

WHITELEY, Hon William Francis; s and h of 3 Baron Marchamley; *b* 27 July 1968; *Style* - The Hon William Whiteley

WHITFELD, Hon Mrs (Deborah Mary); *née* Vaughan-Morgan; da of Baron Reigate PC; *b* 1944; *m* 1966, Michael Whitfeld; 2 s, 1 da; *Style* - The Hon Mrs Whitfeld; Querns, Goring Heath, Reading, Berks

WHITFIELD, Hon Anthony John; s of 2 Baron Kenswood; *b* 1957; *Style* - The Hon Anthony Whitfield

WHITFIELD, Hon Anna Louise; da of 2 Baron Kenswood; *b* 1964; *Style* - The Hon Anna Whitfield

WHITFIELD, Hon Benjamin Matthew; s of 2 Baron Kenswood; *b* 1961; *Style* - The Hon Benjamin Whitfield

WHITFIELD, Lady Fiona Catharine; da (by 1 m) of late 19 Earl of Caithness; *b* 1941; *m* 1969, Capt Michael Stephen Whitfield; 1 s, 1 da; *Style* Lady Fiona Whitfield

WHITFIELD, The Rev George Joshua Newbold; s of Joshua Newbold Whitfield; *b* 2 June 1909; *Educ* Bede G S Sunderland, King's Coll London, Bishops' Coll Cheshunt; *m* 1937, Audrey Priscilla, nee Dence; 2 s, 2 da; *Career* headmaster Tavistock G S 1943-46, Stockport Sch 1946-50, Hampton Sch 1950-68; pres Headmasters' Assoc 1967, gen sec of Bd of Educn Gen Synod of Church of England 1968-74, memb Corpn Church House Westminster 1974-; *Recreations* gardening, photography; *Clubs* Athenaeum; *Style* - The Rev George Whitfield; 31 Foxholes Hill, Exmouth, Devon (☎ 74162)

WHITFIELD, Prof John Humphreys; s of late John Allen Whitfield; *b* 2 Nov 1906; *Educ* Handsworth G S, Magdalen Oxford; *m* 1936, Joan Herrin ARCA; 2 s; *Career* assistant master King Edward VII Sch

Sheffield 1930-36, lectr in Italian Oxford U 1936-46, Serena Prof of Italian Language and Literature Birmingham U 1946-74, Serena Prof Emeritus 1974-, chm Soc for Italian Studies 1962-74, sr ed 'Italian Studies' 1967-74; author *Petrarch and the Renascence* 1943, *Machiavelli* 1947, *Dante and Virgil* 1949, *Giacomo Leopardi* 1954, *A Short History of Italian Literature* 1960, *Discourses on Machiavelli* 1969; Commendatore Ordine al Merito della Repubblica Italiana (Cavaliere Ufficiale 1960); *Style* - Prof John Whitfield; 2 Woodbourne rd, Edgbaston, Birmingham 15 (☎ 021 454 1035)

WHITFIELD, John Robert; s of Wesley Simpson Whitfield (d 1976); *b* 6 May 1930; *Educ* Consett G S, Coll of Technology Leeds; *m* 1960, May, da of Robert Hindhaugh; 2 c; *Career* dir Brims & Co 1976- (bldg contractors); *Recreations* golf, caravanning, sailing; *Style* - John Whitfield Esq; 31 Earnshaw Way, Beaumont Park, Whitley Bay, Tyne & Wear (☎ 534591)

WHITFIELD, Hon Michael Christopher; s and h of 2 Baron Kenswood; *b* 3 July 1955; *Style* - The Hon Michael Whitfield

WHITFIELD, Paul Martin; s of Christopher Gilbert FSA (d 1967); *b* 9 Dec 1942; *Educ* Stowe School, The Middle Temple; *m* 1965, Rowan Janet Gordon, da of Norman Fleming (d 1968); 1 s, 1 da; *Career* dir Christie Manson & Woods 1972; joint md Christie's South Kensington 1974-77; md Christie Manson Woods 1977-; dir Christie's International 1978-; Govr Stowe 1980-; *Recreations* music, reading, sleeping; owns narrow-boat 'Bohemia'; *Clubs* Brooks's, Travellers'; *Style* - Paul Whitfield Esq; Lloyds Bank, 16 St James's st, SW1

WHITFIELD, Hon Steven James; s of 2 Baron Kenswood; *b* 1958; *Style* - The Hon Steven Whitfield

WHITLEY, Charles Francis Peter; s of Peter Whitley and Lady Mary Whitley, *qv*, through the latter of whom he is ggggs of George III and 5 cous of HM The Queen; *b* 10 Sept 1961; *Style* - Charles Whitley Esq

WHITLEY, Air Marshal Sir John René; KBE (1956, CBE 1945), CB (1946), DSO (1943), AFC (1937) and Bar (1956); *b* 7 Sept 1905; *Educ* Haileybury; *m* 1, 1932, Barbara Alice Patricia (d 1965), nee Liscombe; 3 s (and 1 d 1978); m 2, Alison, da of late Sir Nigel Campbell; *Career* RAF 1926-62: Director of Organisation (Establishments) Air Miny 1948-49, Imperial Defence College 1950, Air Offr Adminstration 1951-52, Air Memb for Personnel 1957-59, Inspector Gen RAF 1959-62, Controller RAF Benevolent Fund 1962-68; *Recreations* sailing, fishing, skiing; *Clubs* RAF, Royal Lymington Yacht; *Style* - Air Marshal Sir John Whitley KBE CB DSO AFC*; 2 Woodside Close, Woodside av, Lymington, Hants (☎ 76920)

WHITLEY, Lady Mary Ilona Margaret; da of 2 and last Marquess of Cambridge (and last Prince of Teck to 1917), GCVO (d 1981, s of 1 Marquess of Cambridge and last Duke of Teck, which latter title was resigned 1917, by the 1 Marquess's w Lady Margaret Grosvenor, da of 1 Duke of Westminster; the 1 Marquess was eldest s of HH The Prince and Duke of Teck, GCB, GCVO, and bro of late Queen Mary; the 1 Marquess's m was HRH Princess Mary, da of HRH 1 Duke of Cambridge, KG, GCB, GCMG, GCH, 7 s of George III) and Marchioness of Cambridge, *qv*; *b* 24 Sept 1924; *m* 1950, Peter Whitley, s of Sir Norman Henry Pownall Whitley, MC; 1 s, 1 da; *Career* bridesmaid to HM The Queen when as HRH Princess Elizabeth she m 1947; *Recreations* bird watching, beagling, gardening, sailing; *Clubs* ladies' side Boodle's; *Style* - Lady Mary Whitley; Penharbour, Hurstpierpoint, Sussex (☎ 832264)

WHITLEY, Sarah Elizabeth; da of Peter Whitley and Lady Mary Whitley, *qv*, through the latter of whom she is ggggda of George III and 5 cous of HM The Queen; *b* 30 Nov 1954; *Style* - Miss Sarah Whitley

WHITMORE, Sir John Henry Douglas; 2 Bt (UK 1954), of Orsett, Co Essex; s of Col Sir Francis Henry

Douglas Charlton Whitmore, 1 Bt, KCB, CMG, DSO, TD (d 1962, maternal gs of Sir William Cradock-Hartopp, 3 Bt, while his grandmother on his f's side was Lady Louisa Douglas, eldest da of 5 Marquess of Queensberry); *b* 16 Oct 1937; *Educ* Eton; *m* 1, 1962, Ella Gunilla, (m dis 1969), da of Sven A Hansson, of Danderyd, Sweden; 1 da; m 2, 1977, Diana Elaine, da of Fred A Becchetti, of California USA; *Heir* none; *Clubs* British Racing Drivers; *Style* - Sir John Whitmore, Bt; 200a West End Lane, NW6

WHITTAKER, George Anthony; s of George Whittaker (d 1980); *b* 10 May 1930; *Educ* McGill U Montreal, Inst of Technol, Charlottesville, Virginia, USA; *m* 1964, Elizabeth Anne, nee Smyth; 1 s, 2 da; *Career* 2 Lt REME; dir Guinness Peat Group Ltd 1968-, non-exec dir Spillers Ltd 1979-80; *Recreations* cricket, walking, fishing; *Clubs* Institute of Directors; *Style* - George Whittaker Esq; Craigie Lea, Church lane, Stoke Poges, Bucks (☎ Slough 20123)

WHITTAKER, John Macnaghten; s of Sir Edmund Taylor Whittaker (d 1956); *b* 7 March 1905; *Educ* Fettes, Trin Cambridge; *m* 1933, Iona, da of Lt Cdr J S Elliot; 2 s; *Career* FRS 1949; Lt-Col RA N Africa WW II; Fellow Pembroke Coll Cambridge 1929-33, Prof of Pure Mathematics Liverpool U 1933-52, V-Chancellor Sheffield U 1952-65; *Style* - John Whittaker Esq; 11b Endcliffe cres, Sheffield (☎ 663712)

WHITTALL, Michael; s of Dr Geoffrey Whittall (of a family resident in the Levant, where they were merchants, for upwards of two centuries), of Phillimore Gardens, Kensington, and Vava, da of Ivan Pouschine (a leading Liberal in the first Duma summoned by Tsar Nicholas II) by his w, *nee* Narishkin; through the latter Mr Whittall is related to the mother (Natalia Kirillovna Narishkin) of Tsar Peter The Great; *b* 18 July 1943; *Educ* Highgate Sch, St John's Oxford; *Career* FCO 1966-70, with BP 1970-; *Recreations* music, art, tennis; *Style* - Michael Whittall Esq; 1 Gloucester Mews West, Cleveland sq, W2 (☎ 01 262 0820; office 01 628 4090)

WHITTAM, Ronald; s of Edward Whittam (d 1966); *b* 21 March 1925; *Educ* cncl and tech schs Oldham and Manchester, Sheffield U, Cambridge U; *m* 1957, Christinia Patricia Margaret, nee Lamb; 1 s, 1 da; *Career* FRS 1973, prof of Physiology 1965-, formerly lectr in Biochemistry Oxford U 1955-58, dean of the Faculty of Science Leicester U 1979-; *Recreations* walking, bridge, gardening; *Style* - Ronald Whittam Esq; 9 Guildford rd, Stoneygate, Leicester (☎ 0533 707132)

WHITTEMORE, Hon Mrs (Ivy Lorna); *née* Jervis; da of late 6 Viscount St Vincent and Marion, nee Brown; *b* 1895; *m* 1920, W Laurence Whittemore, MC; 1 s, 1 da; *Style* - The Hon Mrs Whittemore; St James, Long Island, Harbour House, New York, USA

WHITTET, Dr Thomas Douglas; CBE (1977); s of Thomas Douglas Whittet (d 1967); *b* 4 Jan 1980; *Educ* Rosebank Sch Hartlepool, Sunderland Poly, Univ Coll London; *m* 1942, Doreen Mary, nee Bowes; 3 s (1 decd); *Career* memb Roy Spanish Academy of Pharmacy 1956, chief pharmacist Department of Health & Social Security 1965-78, chief pharmacist & lecturer in Pharmacy Charing Cross Hospital 1943-47, University College Hospital London 1947-65; *Recreations* medical and pharmaceutical history, travel, music, sport; *Clubs* Roy Commonwealth Soc, MCC; *Style* - Dr Thomas Whittet CBE; 8 Lyndhurst dve, Harpenden, Herts, AL5 5QN (☎ 4376)

WHITTICK, Richard James; s of Ernest George Whittick (d 1947); *b* 21 Aug 1912; *Educ* George Heriot's Sch, Edinburgh U; *m* 1938, Violet Enid Elizabeth, nee Mason; 2 s; *Career* assist keeper British Museum (Natural History) 1936, Home Office 1940, Princ Private Sec to Home Sec 1952-53, Assist Sec 1953, Assist Under-Sec of State 1967-72; *Recreations* gardening, photography; *Style* - Richard Whittick Esq; Coombe Cottage, Coombe, Sherborne, Dorset (☎ 4488)

WHITTON, Cuthbert; s of Henry McManus Whitton (d 1951); *b* 18 Feb

1905; *Educ* St Andrew's Coll Dublin, Dublin U; *m* 1938, Iris Elva, nee Moody; 1 da (and 1 s decd); *Career* Coronation Medal 1953; High Ct Judge Federation of Malaya 1951-53, Singapore 1953-57; *Recreations* gardening; *Clubs* Roy Commonwealth Soc, Kildare Street & University Dublin; *Style* - Cuthbert Whitton Esq; Far End, Hill Waye, Gerrards Cross, Bucks

WHITWORTH, Anthony Elliott; s of Geoffrey Maden Whitworth; *b* 12 Feb 1935; *Educ* Bromsgrove; *m*; 1 s, 1 da; *Career* CA; chm & ch exec Leigh & Sillavan Gp; *Recreations* sailing (yachts: 'Blue Magic of Alderley', 'Cobaltina'), squash, business; *Clubs* Army & Navy; *Style* - Anthony Whitworth Esq; Rose Cottage, Snelson Lane, Marthall, Knutsford, Cheshire (☎ 861236)

WHITWORTH, Gp Capt Frank; QC (1965); s of Daniel Arthur Whitworth (d 1958); *b* 13 May 1910; *Educ* Shrewsbury, Trin Hall Cambridge; *m* 1, 1939, Mary Lucy (d 1979), da of late Sir John Holdsworth Robinson; m 2, 1980, Irene Violet, da of late William Davidson, of S Africa; *Career* Gp Capt special duties RAFVR 1940-45; barr 1934, Recorder of Crown Ct 1972-, Judge of Cts of Appeal of Jersey & Guernsey 1971-80; *Recreations* reading, writing; *Clubs* Oxford & Cambridge; *Style* - Gp Capt Frank Whitworth QC; Little Manor House, Westcott, Dorking, Surrey (☎ 5888)

WHITWORTH, John Leslie; DFC (1945); s of Frank Sunderland Whitworth (d 1959); *b* 9 Jan 1921; *Educ* Bishop Vesey G S Sutton Coldfield; *m* 1950, Audrey Beatrice, nee Girling; 2 s; *Career* RAF, Acting Sqdn Ldr (pilot) Bomber Cmd RAF (Middle East) 1942-43, Bomber Cmd Pathfinder Force (Europe) 1944-45, RAF Transport Cmd (Burma) 1945-46; engr and dir Heaton Ward Ltd 1951, (managing director 1971-, acting chm & md 1978-); *Recreations* golf (Warwicks Co champion 1959); *Clubs* Pathfinder, Walmsley GC; *Style* - John Whitworth Esq DFC; Brelade, 4 Upper Clifton rd, Sutton Coldfield, W Midlands

WHITWORTH, Maj-Gen Reginald Henry; CB (1969), CBE (1963); s of Aymer William Whitworth (d 1974); *b* 27 Aug 1916; *Educ* Eton, Balliol and Queen's Oxford; *m* 1946, June Rachel, da of late Sir Bartle Mordaunt Edwards, CVO, DL; 2 s (and 1 decd), 1 da; *Career* Gren Gds 1940, GSO 1944, Brigade Maj 1945-46, Staff Coll Camberley 1953-55, cmdg 1 Bn 1955-57, SHAPE 1958-59, Sr Army Instructor Jt Servs Staff Coll 1959-61, Cdr Berlin Infantry Brigade Gp 1961-63, DMS Army Dept MOD 1961-66, GOC Yorks District Catterick 1966, Northumberland Dist 1967-68, Ch of Staff Southern Command 1968-70; bursar & fell Exeter Oxford 1970-, govr St Marys Wantage; books include *Famous Regiments: Grenadier Guards*; *Club* Army & Navy; *Style* - Maj-Gen Reginald Whitworth CB CBE; Old Manor, Letcombe Regis, Wantage, Oxon

WICKHAM, Hon Mrs (Helen Mary); *née* Wade; da of Baron Wade DL; *b* 1933; *m* 1963, Rev Lionel Wickham; *Style* - The Hon Mrs Wickham; 18 Furzedown rd, Southampton

WICKLOW, Countess of; Eleanor; da of Prof Rudolph Butler, of Dublin; *m* 1959, 8 and last Earl of Wicklow (d 1978); *Career* memb Irish Senate 1948-51; *Style* - The Rt Hon Countess of Wicklow; Sea Grange, Sandycove av East, Dun Laoghaire, Co Dublin, Eire

WIDDECOMBE, James Muray; CB (1968), OBE (1959); s of Charles Frederick Widdecombe (d 1944); *b* 7 Jan 1910; *Educ* Devonport H S; *m* 1936, Rita Noreen, nee Plummer; 1 s, 1 da; *Career* Capt RNVR: entered Admiralty as Exec Offr 1929, Dep Dir Armament Supply Admiralty 1959-61, Dir Victualling Admiralty 1961-66, Head RN Supply & Transport Serv MOD 1966-68, Dir Gen of Supplies & Transport (Naval) MOD 1968-70, Gen Sec Civil Serv Retirement Fellowship 1973-79; *Recreations* golf, gardening, amateur dramatics; *Clubs* Hindhead G C, Navy Dept Golfing Soc; *Style* - Dr James Widdecombe, CB, OBE; Keng Hua, 1 Manor Close, Haslemere, Surrey (☎ 2899)

WIDDOWS, Air Cdre (Stanley) Charles; CB (1959), DFC (1941); s of Percy Lionel Widdows; *b* 4 Oct 1909; *Educ*

St Bartholemew's Sch Newbury, Tech Training Sch RAF Halton, RAF Coll Cranwell; *m* 1939, Irene Ethel, da of Sydney Rawlings; 2 s; *Career* RAF: Middle East, Sudan, Palestine 1933-37, Aeroplane and Armament Experimental Establishment 1937-37, CO RAF W Malling 1941-42, OC RAF Wahn Germany 1944-46, Instructor Sr Offrs' War Course RN Coll Greenwich 1946-48, Fighter Cmd 1948-54, Ch Instructor Air Defence Wing Sch of Land/Air Warfare, Sector Cdr Eastern Sector Imperial Defence Coll 1955, Dir of Operations (Air Defence) Air Ministry 1956-58; *Style* - Air Cdre Charles Widdows, CB, DFC; Les Granges de Beauvoir, Rohais, St Peter Port, Guernsey (☎ 20219)

WIDGERY, Baron (Life Peer UK 1971); John Passmore Widgery; OBE (1945), TD, PC (1968), DL (London 1951); s of Samuel Widgery, of S Molton Devon; *b* 24 July 1911; *Educ* Queen's Coll Taunton; *m* 1948, Ann, da of William Kermode, of Peel, IOM; *Career* slr 1933; served WW II RA, Brig (TA) 1952; barr 1946, QC 1958; High Court Judge (Queen's Bench) 1961-68, Ld Justice of Appeal 1968-71, Ld Ch Justice 1971-80, kt 1961; *Style* - The Rt Hon Lord Widgery OBE TD PC DL; 8 New sq, Lincoln's Inn, WC2

WIEN, Lady; Anita, formerly Hermer; *m* 1947, Phillip (later Hon Mr Justice) Wien, sometime High Court Judge (Queen's Bench, d 1981); 2 da; *Style* - Lady Wien

WIGAN, Sir Alan Lewis; 5 Bt (UK 1898), of Clare Lawn, Mortlake, Surrey, and Purland Chase, Ross, Herefordshire; s of Sir Roderick Grey Wigan, 3 Bt (d 1954), and bro of Sir Frederick Adair Wigan, 4 Bt (d 1979); *b* 19 Nov 1913; *Educ* Eton, Magdalen Oxford; *m* 1950, Robina, sis of Countess of Arran (w of 8 Earl), aunt of Duchess of Argyll (w of 12 Duke) and da of Lt-Col Sir Iain Colquhoun of Luss, 7 Bt, KT, DSO; 1 s, 1 da (Rebecca, b 1953, m 1976 John Spearman, fourth in descent from Rt Hon Sir Alexander Spearman, 1 Bt, PC); *Heir* s, Michael Iain, b 3 Oct 1951, educ Eton; *Career* served 1939-45 War; formerly dir Charrington & Co (Brewers); *Style* - Sir Alan Wigan, Bt; Badingham House, Woodbridge, Suffolk (☎ 072875 664); Moorburn, The Lake, Kirkcudbright

WIGAN, Christophher; s of Maj A D Wigan; *b* 2 Jan 1947; *Educ* Eton; *m* 1970, Hon Caroline, da of 13 Lord Kinnaird; 2 c; *Career* FCA 1979, dir Samuel Montagu & Co; *Recreations* tennis, cinema, theatre; *Clubs* Brooks's; *Style* - Christopher Wigan Esq; 14 Zetland House, Marloes rd, W8

WIGAN, Hon Mrs; Hon Caroline; da of 13 Lord Kinnaird; *b* 1949; *m* 1970, Christopher Wigan, s of Algernon Wigan; 1 s, 1 da; *Style* - The Hon Mrs Wigan; 14 Zetland House, Marloes rd, W8

WIGG, Baron (Life Peer UK 1967); George Edward Cecil Wigg; PC (1964); s of Edward Wigg; *b* 28 Nov 1900; *Educ* Queen Mary's G S Basingstoke; *m* 1930, Florence, da of William Veal; 3 da; *Career* MP (L) Dudley 1945-67, Paymaster Gen 1964-67, Chm Horse Race Betting Levy Bd 1967-72; Served WW I & II and regular army 1918-37, Col Roy Army Educnl Corps 1945-46; Pres Betting Off Licensees' Assoc 1973-; *Style* - The Rt Hon Lord Wigg PC; 117 Newcastle rd, Trent Vale, Stoke-on-Trent

WIGGIN, Charles Rupert John; s & h of Sir John Wiggin, 4 Bt, MC, by his 1 w, Lady Cecilia, nee Anson, whereby Charles is 1 cous of 5 Earl of Lichfield and Lady Elizabeth Shakerley; *b* 2 July 1949; *Educ* Eton; *m* 1979, Mrs Mary Burnett-Hitchcock; 1 s (b 1 July 1980); *Career* Capt Gren Gds; *Style* - Charles Wiggin Esq; 10 Ovington st, SW3

WIGGIN, Fergus Frederick Francis; s of Clarence Ethelred Wiggin MBE (1975); *b* 2 Nov 1930; *Educ* Queen's Coll Taunton, Faraday House Electrical Engineering Coll London; *m* 1952, Jennifer Phillis, da of Maj Frederick Burbidge; 3 c; *Career* chartered engineer in field of power utilities: sr engineer Central Electricity Generating Bd 1964-68, sr engineer and man Greater London Cncl 1968-75, dir and generation man Slough Industrial Estates Ltd 1975-; *Recreations* sailing, fishing; *Style* - Fergus Wiggin Esq; 24

Clarefield Drive, Pinkneys Green, Maidenhead, Berks

WIGGIN, Sir John Henry; 4 Bt (UK 1892), of Metchley Grange, Harborne, Staffordshire, MC (1946), JP (Berks 1966); s of Col Sir Charles Richard Henry Wiggin, 3 Bt, TD, JP, DL (d 1972), by his w Mabel (da of Sir William Jaffray, 2 Bt); *b* 3 March 1921; *Educ* Eton, Trin Cambridge; *m* 1, 1947, Lady Cecilia Evelyn Anson, (m dis 1961 and who d 1963), da of 4 Earl of Lichfield; 2 s; m 2, 1963, Sarah, da of Brig Stewart A Forster; 2 s; *Heir* s, Capt Charles Wiggin; *Career* served 1940-45 WW II Europe & Middle East (POW); High Sheriff Warwickshire 1976-77; Maj Gren Gds Reserve; *Clubs* Guards'; *Style* - Sir John Wiggin, Bt, MC, JP; Honington Hall, Shipston-on Stour, Warwickshire (☎ 61434)

WIGGIN, Hon Mrs Julia Redmond; *née* Vaughan-Morgan; da of Baron Reigate PC; *b* 1943; *Educ* London U; *m* 1962 (m dis 1978), Henry, 2 s of Sir William Wiggin, KCB, DSO and Bar, TD, JP, DL (gs of Sir Henry Wiggin, 1 Bt); 2 da; *Style* - The Hon Mrs Julia Wiggin; 31 Abberbury rd, Iffley, Oxford (☎ 778825)

WIGGINS, Barclay William; s of John Wiggins (d 1964); *b* 26 March 1918; *Educ* Albert Road Academy Glasgow; *m* 1942, Isobel, nee Draper; 1 s, 3 da; *Career* F/O RAF; company director; *Recreations* sport, music, art; *Style* - Barclay Wiggins Esq; 'Rarc-An-Ilan', Coliemore rd, Dalkey, Co Dublin, Eire (☎ 859612)

WIGHTMAN, Gerald; s of John Wightman (d 1972); *b* 18 June 1926; *Educ* Balshaws Leyland, Downing Cambridge; *m* 1950, Margaret Audrey, nee Shorrock; 3 s; *Career* chm and ch exec Sketchley Ltd; *Recreations* opera, golf, foreign travel; *Clubs* RAC; *Style* - Gerald Wightman Esq; Alms Court, Church Brampton, Northampton

WIGODER, Baron (Life Peer UK 1974); Basil Thomas Wigoder; QC (1966); s of Phillip Wigoder, LRCPI, LRCSI, of Manchester; *b* 12 Feb 1921; *Educ* Manchester G S, Oriel Oxford; *m* 1948, Yoland, da of Ben Levinson; 3 s, 1 da; *Career* served WW II Lt RA N Africa, Italy, Greece; chm Health Servs Bd 1977-80, BUPA 1981-, dir BUPA Hospitals 1981-; barr 1946, Crown Court Recorder 1972-; V-Pres Lib Pty 1966-, Lib Ch Whip House of Lords 1977- (Dep Whip 1976-77); contested (Lib) Bournemouth 1945 & Westbury 1959 & 1964; memb Crown Court Rules Cttee 1971-, Cncl on Tbnls 1980-; *Recreations* cricket; *Clubs* Nat Liberal, MCC; *Style* - The Rt Hon Lord Wigoder QC; 3 Temple gdns, EC4 (☎ 01 353 1662)

WIGODER, Hon Charles; s of Baron Wigoder QC; *b* 2 March 1960; *Style* - The Hon Charles Wigoder

WIGODER, Hon Carolyn; da of Baron Wigoder QC (twin with Giles, *qv*); *b* 17 Aug 1963; *Style* - The Hon Carolyn Wigoder

WIGODER, Hon Giles; twin (with Carolyn) s of Baron Wigoder QC; *b* 17 Aug 1963; *Style* - The Hon Giles Wigoder

WIGODER, Hon Justin; s of Baron Wigoder QC; *b* 11 May 1951; *Style* - The Hon Justin Wigoder

WIGRAM, 2 Baron (UK 1935); (George) Neville Clive Wigram; MC (1945), JP (Glos 1959), DL (1969); s of 1 Baron Wigram, GCB, GCVO, CSI, PC, Equerry to George V both as Prince of Wales and King (d 1960, himself ggs of Sir Robert Wigram, 1 Bt), by his w Nora, da of Sir Neville Chamberlain (gs of Sir Henry Chamberlain, 1 Bt, and 1 cous of Houston Stewart Chamberlain, the son-in-law of Wagner and, in Dr Schollesmayer's words, "member, with the Comte de Gobineau and Oswald Spengler, of that unholy trinity of mages whose adoration at the cradle of National Socialism proved baneful to, rather than beneficiary of, the Star of David") by his w Mary (da of Gen Alexander Hay, ggs of Hon William Hay, 2 s by his 2 w of 1 Earl of Tweeddale and half-bro of 1 Marquess of Tweeddale); *b* 2 Aug 1915; *Educ* Winchester, Magdalen Oxford; *m* 1941, Margaret, da of Gen Sir Andrew Thorne, KCB, CMG, DSO, by his w Hon Margaret Douglas-Pennant, 10 da (by his 2 w Gertrude) of 2 Baron Penrhyn, JP, DL; 1 s, 2 da; *Heir* s, Hon Andrew

Wigram; *Career* late Lt-Col Gren Gds, Page of Honour to HM 1925-32; Mil Sec & Comptroller to Govr-Gen NZ 1946-49; *Clubs* Cavalry & Guards; *Style* - The Rt Hon Lord Wigram, MC, JP, DL; Poulton Fields, Cirencester, Glos (☎ Poulton 250)

WIGRAM, Hon Andrew Francis Clive; s and h of 2 Baron Wigram, MC, JP, DL; *b* 18 March 1949; *Educ* Winchester, RMA Sandhurst; *m* 1974, Gabrielle, yst da of R Moore, of NZ; 2 s (Harry Richard Clive b 20 May 1977, Robert Christopher Clive b 29 Feb 1980); *Career* Maj Gren Gds, served M East LF, London Dist, HKLF, Berlin; *Clubs* Cavalry and Guards, Leander; *Style* - Maj The Hon Andrew Wigram; Garden House, Poulton, Cirencester, Glos (☎ Poulton 388)

WIGRAM, Rev Canon Sir Clifford Woolmore; 7 Bt (UK 1805), of Walthamstow, Essex; s of late Robert Ainger Wigram; suc unc, Sir Edgar Thomas Ainger Wigram, 6 Bt (d 1935); *b* 24 Jan 1911; *Educ* Winchester, Trin Cambridge; *m* 1948, Christobel Joan (who m 1, Eric Llewellyn Marriott CIE d 1945), da of late William Winter Goode, of Curry Rivel, Somerset; *Heir* bro, Edward Robert Woolmore Wigram, b 19 July 1913; *Career* ordained 1934; vicar of Marston St Lawrence with Warkworth and Thenford; non-residentiary Canon of Peterborough Cathedral 1973; *Style* - The Rev Canon Sir Clifford Wigram, Bt; Marston St Lawrence Vicarage, nr Banbury, Oxon

WIGRAM, Edward Robert Woolmore; s of Robert Wigram; hp of bro, Rev Sir Clifford Wigram, 7 Bt; *b* 19 July 1913; *Educ* Winchester, Trin Cambridge; *m* 1944, Viva, da of Douglas Bailey, of Laughton Lodge, nr Lewes; 1 da (Mrs Frederick Procope); *Career* late Maj IA; late master Westminster Sch; *Style* - Edward Wigram Esq; Hilliers Lodge, St Mary Bourne, Andover, Hants

WIGRAM, Hon Mrs (Sally Ann); *née* Bethell; da of Hon William Gladstone Bethell (3 s of 1 Baron) and sis of 4 Baron Bethell MEP; *b* 1943; *m* 1965, Anthony Francis Wigram; 1 s, 2 twin da; *Style* - The Hon Mrs Wigram; 7 Gloucester sq, W2 (☎ 01 262 8419)

WILBERFORCE, Baron (Life Peer UK 1964); Richard Orme Wilberforce; CMG (1965), OBE (1944), PC (1964); s of Samuel Wilberforce, of Lavington House, Petworth, Sussex (4 s of Reginald Wilberforce, JP, DL, by Anna Maria, da of Hon Richard Denman, 3 s of 1 Baron Denman; Reginald was 2 s of the celebrated Bp of Oxford 'Soapey Sam', later translated to Winchester and sometime Sub-Almoner to Queen Victoria, also founder of Cuddesdon Theological Coll; tho' High Church, he was no friend to Tractarians; his brothers, his bro-in-law (CardinaL Manning), his only daughter, and his son-in-law, all went over to Rome - possibly a record in any one family circle in the 19th century; the Bp was 3 s of William Wilberforce, the philanthropical foe of slavery); the family name derives from a Yorkshire village, Wilberfoss, formed by the elision of Wild-Boar-Foss (ie the forest rich in wild boar); *b* 11 March 1907; *Educ* Winchester, New Coll Oxford; *m* 1947, Yvette, da of Roger Lenoan, of Paris; 1 s, 1 da; *Career* served WW II Norway & Germany as Brig; barr 1932, QC 1954; High Court Judge (Chancery) 1961-64, Lord of Appeal in Ordinary 1964-; High Steward Oxford U 1967-, Chllr Hull U 1978-; kt 1961; *Clubs* Athenaeum; *Style* - Rt Hon Lord Wilberforce CMG OBE PC; c/o House of Lords, SW1

WILBERFORCE, Hon Samuel Herbert; s of Baron Wilberforce, CMG, OBE, PC; *b* 15 Dec 1951; *Educ* Eton; *m* 1978, Mrs Sarah Scorer, da of Arthur Allen, of Northampton; *Style* - The Hon Samuel Wilberforce

WILBRAHAM, Hon Mrs (Catherine Mary); *née* Sidney; da (by 1 m) of 1 Visc De L'Isle, VC, KG, GCMG, GCVO, PC; *b* 1942; *m* 1964, (Martin) John Wilbraham; 3 s; *Style* - The Hon Mrs Wilbraham; Kermincham House, Holmes Chapel, Cheshire

WILCOX, Malcolm George; CBE (1979, MBE 1943 mil); s of George Harrison Wilcox (d 1979); *b* 3 June 1921; *Educ* Wallasey G S; *m* 1958, Sheila Mary, nee Hewitt; 1 s, 1 da; *Career* Maj Far East 1944; dep chm Thomas Cook Gp Ltd 1980, dir Midland Montague Leasing

1979-, Forward Trust Gp Ltd 1979-, Forward Trust Ltd 1979-, Midland & Int Banks Ltd 1974-, and others; pres Inst of Bankers 1977-79, chm Export Guarantees Advisory Cncl and others; govr Royal Shakespeare Co 1979-; *Recreations* travel, theatre, gardening, reading, golf; *Clubs* Wildernesse (Seal, Kent); *Style* - Malcolm Wilcox Esq CBE; Woodland Chase, Blackhall, Sevenoaks (☎ 61215)

WILDMAN, Hon Mrs - Hon Corinna; da of late 2 Baron Cunliffe; *b* 1929; *m* 1957, Frederick Starr Wildman; 1 s; *Style* - The Hon Mrs Wildman; 100 Milton pk, Highgate, N6

WILEY, Lady Jane Lily Serena; *née* Lumley; da of late 11 Earl of Scarbrough, KG, GCSI, GCIE, GCVO, TD, PC, by Katharine, nee McEwen, DCVO; *b* 1935; *m* 1963, Hugh Wiley; 3 s; *Style* - Lady Jane Wiley; Oak Hill, Palmyra, Virginia, USA

WILKINSON, Hon Mrs (Anthea Mary); *née* Roberthall; da of Baron Roberthall, KCMG, CB; *b* 3 June 1939; *Educ* Oxford H S for Girls, LMH Oxford; *m* David Wilkinson; 1 s, 1 da; *Style* - The Hon Mrs Wilkinson; 112 Hemingford rd, N1

WILKINSON, Hon Mrs (Elizabeth Jane Molyneux); da of Baron Fletcher, PC (Life Peer); *b* 1938; *m* 1962, David Blair Wilkinson; *Style* - The Hon Mrs Wilkinson; The Orchard, Repton, Derbys

WILKINSON, Freda, Lady; Freda Dorothy; da of Robert Volland; *m* 1912, Sir George Wilkinson, 1 Bt, KCVO (d 1967); (1 s, the 2 Bt, now decd), 1 da (Mrs John Sidey); *Career* CStJ; *Style* - Freda, Lady Wilkinson; 50 Eresby House, Rutland Gate, SW7

WILKINSON, Sir (David) Graham Brook; 3 Bt (UK 1941), of Brook, Witley, Co Surrey; s of Sir David Wilkinson, 2 Bt, DSC (d 1972); *b* 18 May 1947; *Educ* Millfield, Ch Ch Oxford; *m* 1977, Sandra Caroline, da of Dr Richard Rossdale; 1 da (Louise Caroline Sylvia b 1980); *Heir* none; *Career* OStJ; *Style* - Sir Graham Wilkinson, Bt; 126 Marsham Court, SW1

WILKINSON, Hon Mrs Muriel May; *née* French; da of late 4 Baron De Freyne; *b* 1891; *m* 1920 (m dis 1947), Major William Alexander (Alex) Camc Wilkinson, MC, Coldstream Gds; *Style* - The Hon Mrs Muriel Wilkinson

WILLIAM-POWLETT, Hon Mrs (Katherine Elizabeth); da of Adm of the Fleet 1 Baron Keyes, GCB, KCVO, CMG, DSO (d 1945); *b* 1911; *m* 1935, Major Peter de Barton Vernon Wallop William-Powlett MC; 1 s, 1 da; *Style* - The Hon Mrs William-Powlett; 22 St Leonard's Terrace, SW3

WILLIAMS, Betty, Lady; Betty Kathleen; da of John Taylor, of Hitchin; *m* 1950, Sir William Williams, 8 Bt, of Tregullow (d 1960); *Style* - Betty, Lady Williams; The Flat, St Brannocks House, Braunton, N Devon

WILLIAMS, Hon Mrs (Diana Gillian Amanda); *née* Pritchard; da of Baron Pritchard (Life Peer); *b* 1948; *m* 1969, David Huntingdon Williams; *Style* - The Hon Mrs Williams; 4118 Woodbine st, Chevy Chase, Maryland 20015, USA

WILLIAMS, Sir Donald Mark; 10 Bt (UK 1866), of Tregullow, Cornwall; s of Sir Robert Ernest Williams, 9 Bt (d 1976); *b* 7 Nov 1954; *Educ* W Buckland Sch; *Heir* bro, Barton Matthew Williams, b 21 Nov 1956; *Style* - Sir Donald Williams, Bt; Kamsack, Saskatchewan, Canada; Upcott House, Barnstaple, N Devon

WILLIAMS, Elizabeth, Lady; Elizabeth Mary Garneys; JP (Dorset 1959); da of William Bond, whose mother was da of Sir Harry Meysey-Thompson, 1 Bt, also sis of 1 & last Baron Knaresborough and the late Countess of Iddesleigh (w of 2 Earl); *b* 1 May 1921; *m* 1948, as his 2 w, Sir David Williams, 3 Bt (d 1970); 2 s (including 4 Bt), 1 da (Mrs Michael Widen); *Career* High Sheriff Dorset 1979; *Style* - Elizabeth, Lady Williams JP; Bridehead, Dorchester, Dorset

WILLIAMS, Sir Francis John Watkin; 8 Bt (GB 1798), of Bodelwyddan, Flintshire, QC (1952), JP (Denbighshire 1951); s of Col Lawrence Williams OBE,

JP, DL (d 1958, himself gs of Sir John Williams, 1 Bt, whose gggf was Speaker of the House of Commons); suc bro, Sir Reginald Williams, 7 Bt, MBE, TD (d 1971); *b* 24 Jan 1905; *Educ* Malvern, Trin Hall Cambridge; *m* 1932, Brenda, JP, da of Sir (Joseph) John Jervis, 1 Bt (d 1950); 4 da; *Heir* half-bro Lawrence Hugh Williams, b 25 Aug 1929; *Career* barr Middle Temple 1928; Cdr RAFVR; High Sheriff Denbighshire 1957 and Anglesey 1963; a recorder of Crown Court 1972-75; chm Medical Appeal Tribunal, N Wales area 1954-57; *Clubs* United Oxford and Cambridge University club; *Style* - Sir Francis Williams, Bt, QC, JP; Llys Meirchion, Denbigh

WILLIAMS, George; OBE (1968); s of Charles Henry Williams (d 1971); *b* 6 Aug 1917; *Educ* Truro Sch, St John's Cambridge; *m* 1941, Margaret Jean, nee Hoyle; 1 da; *Career* Cmmr of the Most Hon Order of Crown of Brunei 1965; Wing Cdr RAF Europe and Middle East; ch exec Shell's Cos British Borneo 1963-64, md Shell UK Exploration & Production 1964-73, md Trafalgar Offshore Ltd 1973-74, dir gen UK Offshore Operators' Assoc 1975-; *Recreations* golf; *Clubs* Berkshire, Roy and Ancient, RAF; *Style* - George Williams Esq OBE; Sarum House, Hancocks Mount, Sunningdale, Berks (☎ Ascot 23549)

WILLIAMS, George Mervyn; CBE (1977), MC (1944), DL (Glamorgan 1967); s of Owain Lloyd Joseph Williams (d 1928); *b* 30 Oct 1918; *Educ* Radley; *m* 1950, Grizel Cochrane, da of late Maj Walter Stewart DSO; 1 s; *Career* Maj Roy Fusiliers N Africa, Italy, Greece; chm Christie-Tyler Ltd 1950-, dir Lloyds Bank UK Management Ltd, chm S Wales Region Lloyds Bank Ltd; High Sheriff Glamorgan 1966; *Clubs* Brooks's, Bath, Cardiff and County; *Style* - George Williams Esq, CBE, MC, DL; Llanharan House, Llanharan, Mid Glamorgan (☎ Llantrisant 226253); Craig y Bwla, Crickhowell, Powys (☎ 810413)

WILLIAMS, Sir Gwilym Tecwyn; CBE (1966); s of late David Williams; *b* 9 Aug 1913; *Educ* Llanfyllin CSS, Harper Adams Ag College; *m* 1936, Kathleen Isobel, nee Edwards; 2 s (Rev John Roger, David Edward), 1 da (Bridget Anne Kemp); *Career* kt 1970; farmer (ret); v-pres and dep pres NFU 1952-55 and 1960-66, chm Potato Marketing Bd 1955-59, pres NFU 1966-70; dir Dalgety (UK) 1976-, Dalgety Spillers 1980-; chm govrs Harper Adams Coll; *Recreations* golf, shooting, fishing; *Clubs* Farmers'; *Style* - Sir Gwilym Williams CBE; Red Gables, Longford, Newport, Shropshire (☎ Newport 810439)

WILLIAMS, Lt-Cdr Gerald Wellington; JP (Tunbridge Wells); s of Wellington Archbold Williams JP, of Shernfold Park, Frant; *b* 9 Aug 1903; *Educ* Eton, Ch Ch Oxford; *m* 1930, Mary, da of Capt Josceline Heber-Percy JP DL; 1 s, 2 da; *Career* Lt-Cdr RNVR WW II; High Sheriff Kent 1968-69; MP (C) Tonbridge 1945-56; *Clubs* Carlton, MCC; *Style* - Lt-Cdr Gerald Williams, JP; Crockham House, Westerham, Kent (☎ Crockham Hill 215)

WILLIAMS, Hon Horace; s of Baron Williams of Barnburgh (Life Peer, d 1967); *b* 1914; *m* 1, 1941 (m dis 1948), Hon Mary Morrison, da of Baron Morrison of Lambeth; m 2, Margaret Chisholm, da of William Green; *Style* - The Hon Horace Williams; 11 Lombardy dve, Berkhamsted, Herts

WILLIAMS, Hubert Glyn; s of John Christmas Williams (d 1944); *b* 18 Dec 1912; *Educ* Ruthin Sch; *m* 1952, Audrey Elizabeth, nee Righton; 1 s, 1 da; *Career* AE (1944), RAFVR 1939-45; solicitor 1934, sr ptnr Blake Lapthorn Rea & Williams, Portsmouth; pres Hampshire Inc Law Society 1977-78;, Recorder Crown Court 1977; *Recreations* cricket; *Clubs* MCC, Fareham and County; *Style* - Hubert Williams Esq; 29 The Avenue, Alverstoke, Gosport, Hants (☎ Gosport 83058)

WILLIAMS, Hon Mrs (Katharine Lucy); *née* Roskill; da of Baron Roskill, PC, QC, JP, DL; *b* 1953; *m* 1977, Nicholas Williams; has issue; *Style* - The Hon Mrs Williams

WILLIAMS, Baroness; Lavinia; da of Charles Northam, of Plumstead; *m* 1921, 1

and last Baron Williams (d 1966); 1 da; *Style* - The Rt Hon Lady Williams; 4 The Hallgate, Blackheath Park, SE3

WILLIAMS, Sir Leonard; KBE (1981), CB (1975); *b* 19 Sept 1919; *Educ* St Olave's G S; King's Coll London; *m* Anne Taylor Witherley; 3 da; *Career* Director Gen for Energy Commission of the European Communities 1976-; *Style* - Sir Leonard Williams, KBE, CB; 200 rue de la Loi, 1049 Brussels, Belgium

WILLIAMS, Lawrence Hugh; s of Col Lawrence Williams, OBE, JP, DL, by his 2 w and 1 cous once removed, Elinor (da of Sir William Williams, 4 Bt, JP, DL); hp of half-bro Sir Francis Williams, 8 Bt, QC, JP; *b* 25 Aug 1929; *m* 1952, Sara, 3 da of Prof Sir Harry Platt, 1 Bt, MD, MS, FRCS; 2 da (Emma b 1961, Antonia b 1963); *Career* High Sheriff Anglesey 1970; Capt RM ret; *Style* - Lawrence Williams Esq

WILLIAMS, Meriol, Lady; (Elinor) Meriol Enriqueta; da of Frederic Trevor, of Anglesey; *m* 1936, Sir Reginald Williams, 7 Bt, MBE, TD (d 1971); *Style* - Meriol, Lady Williams; Trewyn, Beaumaris, Anglesey

WILLIAMS, Sir (Michael) Osmond; 2 Bt (UK 1909), of Castell Deudraeth, and Borthwen, Co Merioneth, MC (1944); s of Capt Osmond Trahairn Deudraeth Williams, DSO (d 1915), by his w Lady Gladys Finch-Hatton (da of 13 Earl of Winchilsea); suc gf, Sir Arthur Osmond Williams, 1 Bt, JP, sometime Ld-Lieut & MP Merionethshire, 1927; *b* 22 April 1914; *Educ* Eton, Freiburg U; *m* 1947, Benita Mary, da of the late G Henry Booker; 2 da; *Heir* none; *Career* 2 Lt The Greys 1933-37 and 1939, Capt 1940, Maj 1945; *Style* - Sir Osmond Williams, Bt, MC; Borthwen, Minffordd, Penrhyndeudraeth, Gwynedd

WILLIAMS, Sir (Robert) Philip Nathaniel; 4 Bt (UK 1915), of Bridehead, Co Dorset; s of Sir David Philip Williams, 3 Bt, DL (d 1970), by his 2 w, Elizabeth, Lady Williams, *qv*; *b* 3 May 1950; *Educ* Marlborough, St Andrews U; *m* 1979, Catherine, da of Canon C Pouncey, of Abbey House, Tewkesbury; 1 s; *Heir* s, b 31 Oct 1980; *Clubs* MCC; *Style* - Sir Philip Williams, Bt; Bridehead, nr Dorchester, Dorset (☎ Long Bredy 232)

WILLIAMS, Hon Mrs (Ruth Margaret); *née* Cokayne; da of late 1 Baron Cullen of Ashbourne and Grace, da of the late Rev the Hon John Marsham (s of 3 Earl of Romney); *b* 1909; *m* 1, 1939, Capt Robert William Alfred Moore, RA (ka 1940); 1 da; m 2, 1949, Rev David Henry Aitcheson Williams (d 1955); *Style* - The Hon Mrs Williams; Ivy Cottage, Chirton, Wilts

WILLIAMS, Lady; Ruth Margaret; da of Charles Butcher, of Hudson Bay; *m* 1948, Sir Robert Williams, 9 Bt, of Tregullow (d 1976); 3 s (1 decd, 10 Bt, Barton), 1 da (Phyllis); *Style* - Lady Williams; Kamsack, Saskatchewan, Canada; Upcott House, Barnstaple, N Devon

WILLIAMS, Sir Robin Philip; 2 Bt (UK 1953), of Cilgeraint, Co Caernarvon; s of Sir Herbert Geraint Williams, 1 Bt, sometime MP Reading, also Croydon S, & Parly Sec BOT 1928-29 (d 1954); Sir Robin's sis is Lady (2 w of 13 Lord) Belhaven and Stenton; *b* 27 May 1928; *Educ* Eton, St John's Cambridge; *m* 1955, Wendy Adele Marguerite, da of the late Felix Joseph Alexander, of Hong Kong; 2 s; *Heir* s, Anthony Geraint Williams, b 22 Dec 1958; *Career* chm Bow Gp 1954 & Anti-Common Mkt League 1969; Borough Cllr Haringay 1968-74; Lt RA 1947; barr Middle Temple 1954; insurance broker 1952-; memb Lloyd's 1961-; *Style* - Sir Robin Williams, Bt; 1 Broadlands Close, Broadlands rd, Highgate N6

WILLIAMS, Col Richard Thomas Meurig; OBE, MC, TD, DL (S Glam 1981); *Style* - Col Richard Williams OBE MC TD DL; Ty-Newydd, Castleton, Cardiff (☎ Castleton 680342)

WILLIAMS, Susan Eva; MBE (1958), JP (Glam 1961); da of Robert Henry Williams (d 1963), of Bonvilston House, Glam; *b* 17 Aug 1915; *Educ* St James's W Malvern; *m* 1950, Charles Crofts Llewellyn Williams, of Llanrumney Hall, St Mellons, Mon; *Career* WAAF Offr WW

II; HM Ld-Lt S Glam 1981- (DL 1973), High Sheriff Glam 1968; *Style* - Mrs Robert Williams MBE JP, HM Lord-Lieut for S Glamorgan; Caercady, Welsh St Donat's, Cowbridge, S Glam (☎ 2346)

WILLIAMS, His Honour Judge Sir (William) Thomas; QC (1964); s of David Williams, of Aberdare; *b* 22 Sept 1915; *Educ* U Coll Cardiff, St Cat's Oxford, London U; *m* 1942, Gwyneth, da of Rev D Harries, of Aberdare; 1 s, 1 da; *Career* kt 1976; Circuit Judge (SE) 1981-, Crown Court Recorder 1972-81; MP (L & Co-op) Warrington 1961-81 (Hammersmith S 1949-55, Barons Court 1955-59), PPS to Attorney-Gen 1965-67; chm Select Ctee Parly Procedure 1974-81; *Style* - His Hon Judge Sir Thomas Williams QC; 20 Alleyn Park, Dulwich, SE 21 (☎ 01 670 4554)

WILLIAMS-BULKELEY, Sir Richard Harry David; 13 Bt (E 1661), JP (1934); s of late Maj Richard Gerard Wellesley Williams-Bulkeley MC (himself the only s of the 12 Bt); suc gf, Sir Richard Williams-Bulkeley, 12 Bt, KCB, 1942; *b* 5 Oct 1911; *Educ* Eton; *m* 1938, Renée Arundell, da of Sir Thomas Lewis Hughes Neave, 5 Bt; 2 s; *Heir* s, Richard Williams-Bulkeley; *Career* Maj Roy Welch Fusiliers WW II; former Lt-Col Cmdt of Caernarvonshire and Anglesey Army Cadet Force; CStJ; Lord-Lt of Anglesey 1947-74, Gwynedd 1974-; *Style* - Sir Richard Williams-Bulkeley, Bt, JP, HM Lord-Lieut for Gwynedd; Plâs Meigan, Beaumaris, Gwynedd

WILLIAMS-BULKELEY, Richard Thomas; s and h of Sir Richard Willliams-Bulkeley, 13 Bt; *b* 25 May 1939; *Educ* Eton; *m* 1964, Susan Sarah, da of late Rt Hon Lord Justice (Sir Henry Josceline) Phillimore, OBE; 2 s (twins), 1 da; *Career* Capt Welsh Gds 1963; *Style* - Richard Williams-Bulkeley Esq; Glan Aber, Pentraeth, Anglesey, Gwynedd

WILLIAMS-FREEMAN, Lady Jean Elizabeth; da (by his 1 w) of late 19 Earl of Caithness; *b* 1936; *m* 1961, David Peere Williams-Freeman; 1 s , 3 da; *Style* - Lady Jean Williams-Freeman; Glendean Trout Hatcheries, Nottingham rd, Natal, SA

WILLIAMS-WYNN, David Watkin; s & h of Sir Watkin Williams-Wynn, 10 Bt, CBE, JP; *b* 18 Feb 1940; *Educ* Eton; *m* 1968, Harriet, da of Gen Sir Norman Tailyour, KCB, DSO; 2 s (Charles b 1970, Robert b 1977), twin da (Henrietta & Lucinda both b 1971); *Career* late Lt Roy Dragoons; *Style* - David Williams-Wynn Esq; Twining Hill, Erbistock, Wrexham, Clwyd

WILLIAMS-WYNN, Sir (Owen) Watkin; 10 Bt (E 1688), of Gray's Inn, Co Middx, CBE (1969), JP (Denbighshire 1937), DL (1947); s of Sir Robert Williams-Wynn, 9 Bt, KCB, DSO, TD, JP (d 1951, whose paternal grandmother was Lady Henrietta Clive, eldest da of 1 Earl of Powis), by his w Elizabeth, MBE (gda of Sir Charles Lowther, 3 Bt); *b* 30 Nov 1904; *Educ* Eton, RMA Woolwich; *m* 1, 1939, Margaret Jean (d 1961), da of late Col William Alleyne Macbean, RA, by his w Margaret (sis of Lt-Gen Sir Thomas Humphreys, KCB, CMG, DSO; she later m Maj-Gen Hon Gerald Scarlett, CB, MC, DL, bro of 5 & 6 Barons Abinger); 2 s (1 decd); m 2, 1968, Mrs Gabrielle Haden Matheson, da of late Herbert Alexander Caffin; *Heir* s, Maj David Watkin Williams-Wynn, b 18 Feb 1940; *Career* joined RA, Lt RHA 1930, Capt 1937, served 1939-45 War, Maj 1940, Lt-Col (TA) 1947; Hon Col 361 Medium Regt RA 1953-57; Vice-Lt 1957, High Sheriff Denbighshire 1954, Ld-Lt 1966-74; Lt of Clwyd 1974, Ld Lt 1976-; *Style* - Sir Watkin Williams-Wynn, Bt, CBE, JP, HM Lord-Lieut for Clwyd; Llangedwyn, Oswestry, Salop (☎ Llanrhaiadr 269)

WILLIAMS-WYNNE, Hon Mrs (Veronica Frances); *née* Buxton; 3 da of Baron Buxton of Alsa; *b* 24 March 1953; *m* 1975, William, s of John Williams-Wynne, DSO, JP (himself gs of Charles Williams-Wynn and Lady Annora, yr da of 2 Earl Manvers; Charles was in turn gs of Sir Watkin Williams-Wynn, 4 Bt, by his w Lady Henrietta Somerset, da of 4 Duke of Beaufort); 1 da; *Style* - The Hon Mrs Williams-Wynne; Bryngwyn, Llanegrin, Tywyn, Gwynnedd

WILLIAMSON, Baron (Life Peer UK 1962); Thomas Williamson; CBE (1950), JP (Liverpool 1933); s of James

Williamson, of St Helens; *b* 2 Sept 1897; *Educ* Knowsley rd Sch St Helens; WEA; *m* 1925, Hilda, da of John Hartley, of St Helens; 1 da; *Career* Gen Sec GMWU 1946-61, MP (L) Lincoln & Rutland (Brigg) 1945-48; chm TUC 1956-57; dir Securicor 1964-; served WW I as NCO Flanders; kt 1956; *Style* - The Rt Hon Lord Williamson CBE JP; 13 Hurst Lea Court, Alderley Edge, Cheshire

WILLIAMSON, Sir Nicholas (Frederick Hedworth); 11 Bt (E 1642), of East Markham, Nottinghamshire; s of Maj William Hedworth Williamson (ka 1942) and Diana (who m 2, 1 & last Baron Hailes, and d 1980; she was only da of Brig-Gen Hon Charles Lambton, DSO, himself 4 s of 2 Earl of Durham); suc unc, Sir Charles Williamson, 10 Bt (d 1946); through his mother, Sir Nicholas is 2 cous of (1) 6 Duke of Sutherland, (2) Baron Home of the Hirsel, (3) 4 Baron Joicey and (4) Antony Lambton; he is also 3 cous of the 5 Duke of Abercorn and 1 cous twice removed of 11 Baron Middleton; *b* 26 Oct 1937; *Educ* Eton; *Heir* none; *Career* commissioned Roy Dragoon Gds 1957 (Nat Service); *Style* - Sir Nicholas Williamson, Bt; Lane House, Mortimer, Reading, Berks (☎ Mortimer 324)

WILLINGDON, Marchioness of; Daphne; da of Seymour Caldwell; *m* 1943, as his 3 w, 2 and last Marquess of Willingdon (d 1979); *Style* - The Most Hon The Marchioness of Willingdon; Kilbees Farm, Winkfield, Windsor Forest

WILLINK, Sir Charles William; 2 Bt (UK 1957), of Dingle Bank, City of Liverpool; s of The Rt Hon Sir Henry Urmston Willink, 1 Bt, MC, QC (d 1973, himself ggs of Daniel Willink, sometime Dutch Consul in Liverpool), by his 1 w, Cynthia (da of Herbert Morley Fletcher, MD, FRCP, of Harley Street); *b* 10 Sept 1929; *Educ* Eton, Trin Cambridge; *m* 1954, Elizabeth, da of Humfrey Andrewes, of North Grove, Highgate, N6; 1s, 1 da; *Heir* s, Edward Daniel Willink, b 17 Feb 1957; *Career* housemaster Eton 1964-77; *Style* - Sir Charles Willink, Bt; 22 High st, Eton, Windsor, Berks

WILLIS, Baron (Life Peer UK 1963); Ted (Edward) Henry Willis; s of Alfred Willis, of Tottenham; *b* 13 Jan 1918; *Educ* Downhills Centl Sch Tottenham; *m* 1944, Audrey, da of Alfred Hale; 1 s, 1 da; *Career* FRTS, FRSA; dir World Wide Pictures 1967-, Capital Radio; writer (scripts include *Dixon of Dock Green* series, books *The Churchill Commando*); Govr Nat Film Sch; *Style* - The Rt Hon Lord Willis; 5 Shepherds Green, Chislehurst, Kent

WILLIS, Hector Ford; CB (1960); s of William Frank Willis (d 1941); *b* 3 March 1909; *Educ* U Coll Cardiff; *m* 1936, Maria Iddon, nee Renwick; *Career* scientist British Cotton Industry Research Assoc 1935-38, joined Admiralty 1938, ch of Roy Naval Scientific Serv 1954-62, scientific adviser MOD 1962-70, ret 1970; *Recreations* chess; *Style* - Hector Willis Esq, CB; Fulwood, Eaton Park, Cobham, Surrey

WILLIS, Hon John Edward; s of Baron Willis; *b* 4 April 1946; *Educ* Eltham Coll, Fitzwilliam Cambridge, Bristol U; *m* 1971, Janet, da of Kenneth Sperrin; 1 s (Thomas Edward b 1975), 1 da (Beth Anna b 1978); *Career* researcher ATV to 1970, dir Yorkshire TV 1971-; *Recreations* tennis, football; *Clubs* BAFTA; *Style* - The Hon John Willis; 52 Lady Somerset rd, NW5 (☎ 01 485 2461)

WILLIS, Rear-Adm K H G; *Career* Ch of Staff to CIC Naval Home Cmd to Sept 1981; *Style* - Rear-Adm K H G Willis; c/o MOD, SW1

WILLIS-FLEMING, Hon Mrs (Elizabeth Sarah); *née* James; da of 4 Baron Northbourne; *b* 1933; *m* 1960, Michael Edward Willis-Fleming; 1 s, 1 da; *Style* - The Hon Mrs Willis-Fleming; Updown Farm, Eastry, Kent

WILLOUGHBY, Hon (Henry Ernest) Christopher; s of 11 Baron Middleton, KG, MC, TD (d 1970); *b* 1932; *Educ* Eton; *m* 1955, Jean Adini, da of Lt-Col John David Hills, MC; 1 s, 2 da; *Clubs* Cavalry and Guards; *Style* - The Hon Christopher Willoughby; Buckhold Farm, Pangbourne, Berks

WILLOUGHBY, Hon John Hugh

Francis; s of 12 Baron Middleton, MC; *b* 1951; *Educ* Eton; *Career* Capt Coldstream Gds; *Style* - The Hon John Willoughby; c/o Birdsall House, Malton, N Yorks

WILLOUGHBY, Hon Mrs (Lucy Corinna Agneta); *née* Sidney; da (by 1 m) of 1 Viscount De L'Isle, VC, KG, GCMG, GCVO, PC; *b* 1953; *m* 1974, Hon Michael Charles Willoughby, *qv*; 1 s, 1 da; *Style* - The Hon Mrs Willoughby; North Grimsto House, Malton, N Yorks

WILLOUGHBY, Hon Michael Charles James; s and h of 12 Baron Middleton, MC; *b* 14 July 1948; *Educ* Eton; *m* 1974, the Hon Lucy Corinna Agneta Sidney, da of 1 Viscount de L'Isle; 1 s, 1 da; *Career* late Lt Coldstream Gds; *Style* - The Hon Michael Willoughby; North Grimston House, Malton, N Yorks

WILLOUGHBY, Hon Thomas Henry Richard; s of 12 Baron Middleton, MC; *b* 1955; *Educ* Harrow; *Style* - The Hon Thomas Willoughby

WILLOUGHBY DE BROKE, 20 Baron (E 1491); John Henry Peyto Verney; MC (1918), AFC (1940), AE, JP (Warwicks); s of 19 Baron (d 1923, descended from the 1 Baron, who was so cr after being on the winning side at Bosworth, and was fourth in descent from 4 Baron Willoughby de Eresby, which dignity is at present held by 3 Earl of Ancaster; both Lords Ancaster and Willoughby de Broke are coheirs to the Barony of Beke, abeyant since 1303-04) and Marie, OBE, da of Charles Addington Hanbury, JP, DL, by his w Christina (gda of Sir Hector Mackenzie, 4 Bt); *b* 21 May 1896; *Educ* Eton, Sandhurst; *m* 1933, Rachel, da of Sir Bourchier Wrey, 11 Bt; 1 s, 1 da; *Heir* s, Hon David Verney; *Career* Ld-Lt Warwicks 1939-67; KStJ; patron of 2 livings; memb Jockey Club (Steward 1944-47 & 1954-56) & Nat Hunt Cttee (Steward 1942-44, 1950-53 & 1964-67); Cdr 605 (Co Warwick) Sqdn AAF 1936-39; served WW I & II; Jt Master Warwicks Hounds 1929-35; *Clubs* Cavalry & Guards; *Style* - The Rt Hon Lord Willoughby de Broke MC, AFC, AE, JP; Fox Cottage, Kineton, Warwicks; 2 Upper Phillimore gdns, W8 (☎ 01 937 8548)

WILLS, David Seton; s of Maj George Wills by his 1 w, Lilah (da of Capt Percy Hare, himself gs of 2 Earl of Listowel, by his w Matilda, nee Tiarks) - his 2 w was Lilah's er sis Victoria; hp of unc, Sir Edward Wills, 4 Bt, of Hazelwood; through his mother David is 2 cous of Marchioness of Tavistock and 3 cous once removed of Capt Mark Phillips, CVO; *b* 29 Dec 1939; *Educ* Eton; *m* 1968, Gillian, twin da of Albert Eastoe; 1 s, 3 da; *Career* FRICS; *Style* - David Wills Esq; Littlecote, Hungerford, Berks

WILLS, Hon Mrs (Elizabeth Anne); *née* Cecil; da of 2 Baron Rockley; *b* 6 July 1939; *m* 1961, Capt Andrew Wills, late Life Gds, s of Maj John Wills, of Allanbay Park, Binfield, Berks (gs of Sir Edward Wills, 1 Bt, KCB, of the West Country tobacco family), by Hon Jean, 2 da of 16 Lord Elphinstone, KT, by Lady Mary Bowes-Lyon, DCVO (da of 14 Earl of Strathmore and sis of HM Queen Elizabeth the Queen Mother), in consequence of which the Capt is 2 cous of HRH The Prince of Wales; 2 s, 1 da; *Style* - The Hon Mrs Wills; Middleton House, Longparish, Andover, Hants

WILLS, Hon Edward Robert Hamilton; s of late 1 Baron Dulverton, OBE; *b* 1918; *Educ* Eton; *Career* Maj late Grenadier Gds (wounded) 1939-45; *Style* - The Hon Edward Wills; Farmington Lodge, Northleach, Glos

WILLS, Sir (Ernest) Edward (de Winton); 4 Bt (UK 1904), of Hazelwood, Stoke Bishop, Westbury-on-Trym, Gloucestershire, and Clapton-in-Gordano, Somerset; s of Sir Ernest Wills, 3 Bt, JP, Ld-Lt Wilts 1930-42 (d 1958, himself 1 cous of Sir George Wills, 1 Bt, of Blagdon, so that Sir Edward is 2 cous of 2 Baron Dulverton and 2 cous once removed of Sir John Wills, 4 Bt, of Blagdon); *b* 8 Dec 1903; *Educ* Eton; *m* 1, 1926, Sylvia Margaret (d 1946), da of late William B Ogden and late Mrs Gordon Moore; 2 da (Mrs Alan Hopkins, whose husb is chm Wellman Engrg Corpn; Mrs Christopher Bonn, by whose 1 m to the present (8) Marquess of Ailesbury Sir Edward is gf of Earl of Cardigan); m 2, 1949, Juliet, da of Capt John E H Graham-Clarke (d 1961), of Frocester Manor, Glos; *Heir* n, David Seton Wills; *Career* late Scots Gds, served WW II, late Lt-Col cmdg 5 Bn Manchester Regt; memb of Lloyd's; *Clubs* Cavalry & Guards', Household Division Yacht clubs; *Style* - Sir Edward Wills, Bt; Mount Prosperous, Hungerford, Berks (☎ 2624)

WILLS, Hon Gilbert Michael Hamilton; s (by 1 m) and h of 2 Baron Dulverton, CBE, TD; *b* 2 May 1944; *Educ* Gordonstoun; *m* 1980, Rosalind J M, da of J van der Velde; *Style* - The Hon Gilbert Wills

WILLS, Hon Mrs (Jean Constance); *née* Buller-Fullerton-Elphinstone; da of late 16 Lord Elphinstone, KT and Lady Mary Bowes-Lyon, DCVO, da of 14 Earl of Strathmore; *b* 1915; *m* 1936, Maj John Lycett Wills, Life Gds (ret), gs of Sir Edward Wills, 1 Bt, KCB; 1 s (*see* Hon Mrs (Elizabeth) Wills), 1 da; *Career* Extra Lady-in-Waiting to HRH The Princess Margaret 1970; *Style* - The Hon Mrs Wills; Allanbay Park, Binfield, Berks

WILLS, Sir John Vernon; 4 Bt (UK 1923), of Blagdon, Co Somerset, TD, JP (Somerset 1962), DL (1968); s of 2 Bt (d 1931) and bro of 3 Bt (ka 1945); *see also* Wills, Bt, Sir Edward; *b* 3 July 1928; *Educ* Eton; *m* 1953, Diana Veronica Cecil (Jane), da of Douglas R M Baker, of Thiery House, Litton, nr Bath; 4 s; *Heir* s, David James Vernon Wills, b 2 Jan 1955; *Career* Lt-Col (TA) 1965-67, Bt Col 1967; dir Bristol & West Bldg Soc; High Sheriff 1968 Somerset, Co Alderman (1970); Ld-Lt & Custos Rotulorum of Avon 1974-; chm Wessex Water Authority and memb Nat Water Council; dep chm (dir 1973-) Bristol Evening Post 1978-; *Style* - Sir John Wills, Bt, TD, JP, HM Lord-Lieut for Avon; Langford Court, Langford, Bristol (☎ Wrington 862338)

WILLS, Hon Robert Ian Hamilton; s (by 1 m) of 2 Baron Dulverton, CBE, TD; *b* 1948; *Educ* Harrow; *m* 1979, Elizabeth Jane, nee Downes; *Style* - The Hon Robert Wills

WILLS, Hon Sarah May Hamilton; da (by 1 m) of 2 Baron Dulverton, CBE, TD; *b* 1942; *Style* - The Hon Sarah Wills

WILLS, Hon Victor Patrick Hamilton; DL (Hants); s of late 1 Baron Dulverton, OBE; *b* 1926; *Educ* Eton; *m* 1, 1948 (m dis 1962), Felicity Betty, da of late Maj Aubrey Jonsson, Roy Irish Rifles; 2 s, 1 da; m 2, 1963, Jean Felicity Strutt, da of late Hon Francis Erskine (s of 12 Earl of Mar and Kellie); *Career* late Grenadier Gds and Parachute Regt, FRICS, Fellow of Chartered Land Agents' Soc, former CC Hants, former V-Chm Internat Students Trust; *Style* - The Hon Victor Wills, DL; Litchfield Down, Whitchurch, Hants

WILLSON, Hon Mrs Anne Mildred; *née* Curzon; da of late 2 Viscount Scarsdale; *b* 1923; *m* 1942 (m dis 1960), Maj Walter James Latimer Willson, DSO, Gren Gds, s of Sir Walter Willson; 1 s, 1 da; *Career* ATS 1942-44; *Style* - The Hon Mrs Anne Willson; Hill Farm, Garsdale, Sedbergh, Cumbria

WILLSON, Stanley William; s of Stephen Willson (decd); *b* 17 May 1927; *Educ* George Dixon G S; *m* 1957, Rachel, nee Nickerson; 3 c; *Career* CA 1955, in practise 1957-65; chm Birmingham Building Soc (dir 1977-80) 1980-, Company Dvpts Ltd 1965-, Kean & Scott Ltd 1971-79, Aston Martin Lagonda Ltd 1972-75; dir Guardian Roy Exchange Gp (B'ham) 1960-; councillor Warwick Rural District Cncl 1971-74, chm Tapster Valley Preservation Soc 1971, pres Birmingham Sporting Club 1979-, v-pres B'ham Assoc Youth Clubs (hon tres 1962-70) 1970-; *Recreations* preservation of wild life and countryside; *Style* - Stanley Willson Esq; Pound House, Lapworth, Warwicks (☎ 3224/2994)

WILMOT, Sir Henry Robert; 9 Bt (GB 1759), of Chaddesden, Derbyshire; s of Capt Sir Robert Arthur Wilmot, 8 Bt, sometime Equerry to HRH The (1) Duke of Gloucester (d 1974); *b* 10 April 1967; *Heir* bro, Charles Sacheverel Wilmot, b 13 Feb 1969; *Style* - Sir Henry Wilmot, Bt; Pitters Farmhouse, Sandy Lane, Chippenham, Wilts

WILMOT, Robert; *aet* 36 in June 1981; *Educ* Nottingham U (electrical engrg graduate 1966); *Career* with Texas Instruments 1966-81, tech dir Nice, divnl man (professional calculators) Lubbock Texas, md Texas Instruments Ltd 1978-80, Assist V-Pres Texas Instruments Inc 1980-81; md ICL 1981-; *Style* - Robert Wilmot Esq; ICL House, Putney High st, SW 15 (☎ 01 788 7272)

WILSON OF RADCLIFFE, Baron (Life Peer UK 1974); Alfred Wilson; s of William Wilson; *b* 10 June 1909; *Educ* Newcastle Tech; *m* 1, 1932, Elsie (d 1974), da of Arthur Hulton; 1 da (and 1 s decd); m 2, 1976, Freda Mather; *Career* chm Co-Op Bank, FC Finance Ltd; CWS ch exec offr 1969-74; dir Estate & Gen Investments Ltd 1975-; FCIS; *Recreations* walking; *Style* - Rt Hon Lord Wilson of Radcliffe; 58 Ringley rd, Whitefield, Manchester

WILSON OF LANGSIDE, Baron (Life Peer UK 1967); Henry Stephen Wilson; PC (1967), QC (Scot 1965); s of James Wilson, slr, of Glasgow; *b* 21 March 1916; *Educ* Glasgow H S & U; *m* 1942, Jessie, da of William Waters, of Paisley; *Career* served WW II HLI & RAC; barr 1946, Slr-Gen Scotland 1965-67, Ld-Advocate 1967-70, Sheriff Pncpl Glasgow & Strathkelvin 1975-77; contested (L) Dumfriesshire 1950 & 1955, Edinburgh W 1951; joined SDP 1981; *Style* - Rt Hon Lord Wilson of Langside PC QC; Dunallan, Kippen, Stirlingshire (☎ 210)

WILSON, 2 Baron (UK 1946); Patrick Maitland Wilson; s of 1 Baron Wilson, GCB, GBE, DSO, Supreme Allied Mil Cdr Mediterranean 1944 (d 1964); *b* 14 Sept 1915; *Educ* Eton, King's Cambridge; *m* 1945, Violet, da of Maj James Douglas-Campbell, OBE, and Hon Anna, nee Massey, 4 da (by his 2 w Sophia, nee Butler) of 5 Baron Clarina; through her mother, Lady Wilson is 1 cous of Baron Nugent, *qv*; *Heir* none; *Career* served WW II, Lt-Col Rifle Bde; *Style* - The Rt Hon Lord Wilson; c/o Barclays Bank, Cambridge

WILSON, Andrew Norman; s of Lt-Col Norman Wilson; *b* 27 Oct 1950; *Educ* Rugby, New Coll Oxford; *m* 1971, Katherine Dorothea, da of the late Prof Austin Ernest Duncan-Jones; 2 da; *Career* author; Chancellor's Essay Prize 1971, Ellerton Theological Prize 1975, FRSL 1981; Books: *The Sweets of Pimlico* (John Llewellyn Rhys Memorial Prize 1978), *Unguarded Hours* 1978, *Kindly Light* 1979, *The Laird of Abbotsford* 1980, *The Healing Art* (Somerset Maugham Prize, Arts Cncl Nat Book Award, Southern Arts Prizes 1981), *Who Was Oswald Fish?* 1981; *Recreations* church-going, gossip, literary journalism; *Style* - Andrew Wilson Esq; c/o A D Peters Ltd, 10 Buckingham street, WC2 (☎ 01 839 2556)

WILSON, Lady Alexandra Patricia Gwendoline; da of 2 Earl Jellicoe, DSO, MC, PC; *b* 1944; *m* 1970, (Edward) Philip Wilson, s of Peter Wilson, CBE; *Style* - Lady Alexandra Wilson; 58 Gibson sq, N1 (☎ 01 359 2267)

WILSON, Anthony Thomas; 2 s of Sir Mathew Wilson, 4 Bt, CSI, DSO; hp of bro, Sir Martin Wilson, 5 Bt; *b* 15 Nov 1908; *Educ* Eton; *m* 1, 1934 (m dis 1938), Margaret, da of Alfred Holden and formerly w of Vernon Motion; 1 s (Lt-Col Mathew W, MBE, MC, who m Janet Mowll; 1 s Mathew, 1 da Victoria); m 2, 1939, Emily, da of John T Milliken, of St Louis, Mo; *Career* served WW II Wing Cdr RAF; *Style* - Anthony Wilson Esq; 1406 34th Street NW, Washington DC, USA

WILSON, Christopher David; CBE (1968), MC (1945); s of James Anthony Wilson (d 1921); *b* 17 Dec 1916; *Educ* St George's Sch Windsor, Aldenham Sch; *m* 1947, Jean Barbara, nee Smith; *Career* late Capt RA; FCA; business manager Associated Newpapers Ltd 1955-57, dir Associated Rediffusion 1956-57; chm Southern TV (dir & gen manager 1957-59, md 1956-76) 1976-; *Recreations* sailing, music; *Clubs* MCC, Roy Southern Yacht; *Style* - Christopher Wilson Esq CBE MC; Little Croft, Upham, Southampton, Hants (☎ Durley 204); Hill House, Jesus Pobre, Javea, Alecante, Spain

WILSON, Hon Charles Thomas; s of 3 Baron Nunburnholme (d 1974) and hp of bro, 4 Baron; *b* 27 May 1935; *Educ* Eton; *m* 1969, Linda Kay, da of Cyril James Stephens; 1 s, 1 da; *Career* was a Page of

Honour to HM King George VI 1950-52; *Style* - The Hon Charles Wilson; Grassthorpe Mill, Sutton-on-Trent, Newark, Notts

WILSON, Sir David; 3 Bt (UK 1920), of Carbeth, Killearn, Co Stirling; s of Sir John Mitchell Harvey Wilson, 2 Bt, KCVO (d 1975); *b* 30 Oct 1928; *Educ* Harrow, Oriel Oxford; *m* 1955, Eva Margareta, da of Tore Lindell, of Malmö, Sweden; 2 s, 1 da; *Heir* s, Thomas David Wilson, b 6 Jan 1959; *Career* ptnr Simmons & Simmons 1963-; barr Lincoln's Inn 1953, slr 1962; *Style* - Sir David Wilson, Bt; Tandem House, Queen's dve, Oxshott, Surrey

WILSON, Hon David Mark; s of 3 Baron Nunburnholme (d 1974); *b* 1954; *Style* - The Hon David Wilson

WILSON, Hon Mrs Guy - Avery; da of Geoffrey Fowell Buxton CB; *m* 1911, as his 2 w, Col Hon Guy Wilson CMG DSO TD (d 1943, s of 1 Baron Nunburnholme); 2 s, 2 da; *Style* - The Hon Mrs Guy Wilson; 29 Campden Hill Gate, W8

WILSON, Rear-Adm Guy Austen Moore; CB (1958); s of Ernest Moore Wilson (d 1951); *b* 7 June 1906; *Educ* RN Colls Osborne, Dartmouth, Keyham; *m* 1932, Dorothy, da of late Sir Arthur Watson CBE; 2 s, 3 da; *Career* Capt RN 1952-55, superintendent of RN aircraft yard Fleetlands, dep dir of Aircraft Maintenance and Repair, Rear-Adm, Admiralty SW1 in charge of Dvpt of Nuclear Propulsion for the RN, Dep Engineer-in-Ch of the Fleet, ret; ch exec Dracone Developments Ltd 1960-63; *Recreations* breeding Guide Dogs for the Blind, swimming, gardening; *Style* - Rear-Adm Guy Wilson, CB; Barn Acre, Saxstead Green, Woodbridge, Suffolk (☎ Earl Soham 365)

WILSON, Hon Geoffrey Hazlitt; s of 1 Baron Moran, MC, MD, FRCP (d 1977); *b* 28 Dec 1929; *Educ* Eton, King's Cambridge; FCA; *m* 1955, (Barbara) Jane, da of W E H Hebblethwaite, of Itchen Stoke, Alresford, Hants; 2 s, 2 da; *Career* late Roy Horse Guards; dep ch exec The Delta Metal Group; memb Council of Inst of Cost and Management Accountants, of Accounting Standards Ctee, and of 100 Group of London CAs; Hon Treasurer, Roy Jubilee Trusts; memb management bd Engineering Employers Fedn; *Recreations* family, reading, collecting vintage cars; *Clubs* Boodle's, City Livery and RAC; *Style* - The Hon Geoffrey Wilson; The Manor House, Newton Valence, nr Alton, Hants (☎ 042 058 336); Cliff Lodge, Nefyn, Gwynedd

WILSON, Hon Ines; twin da of 4 Baron Nunburnholme; *b* 1962; *Style* - The Hon Ines Wilson

WILSON, Lt-Gen Sir (Alexander) James; KBE (1974, CBE 1966, MBE 1948), MC (1945); s of Maj-Gen Bevil Wilson, CB, DSO, and Florence, da of Sir John Starkey, 1 Bt, JP, DL (by Emily, da of Sir Charles Seely, 1 Bt, and aunt of 1 Baron Sherwood); *b* 13 April 1921; *Educ* Winchester, New Coll Oxford; *m* 1958, Hon Jean, nee Hope, da of 2 Baron Rankeillour (she was b 7 Jan 1923, m 1, 1942 (m dis 1955), Capt Anthony Paul, adopted s of F Paul; 1 s, 2 da); 2 s; *Career* chm Tobacco Advsy Cncl 1977-; Dir Army Recruiting 1967-70, Vice Adj-Gen 1972-74, GOC SE Dist 1974-77; Col Cmdt Roy Green Jackets 1977-; memb Sports Cncl 1973-; Hon V-Pres FA 1976-; Sunday Times football correspondent 1957-; *Style* - Lt-Gen Sir James Wilson KBE MC; Goldhill Farm House, Edingley, Newark, Notts (☎ Southwell 813308); Flat 4, 33 Wilton Place, SW1

WILSON, Sir John Foster; CBE (1965, OBE 1955); s of Rev George Henry Wilson (d 1959); *b* 20 Jan 1919; *Educ* Worcester Coll for the Blind 1932-37, Oxford U; *m* 1944, Chloe Jean, nee McDermid; 2 da; *Career* kt 1975, Int health administrator, dir Roy Commonwealth Soc for the Blind 1950-, pres Int Agency for the Prevention of Blindness 1975-; *Style* - Sir John Wilson, CBE; 22 the Cliff, Roedean, Brighton, E Sussex (☎ 607667)

WILSON, Sir John Martindale; KCB (1974, CB 1960); s of John Wilson (d 1920); *b* 3 Sept 1915; *Educ* Bradfield, Gonville and Caius Cambridge; *m* 1941, Penelope Beatrice, nee Bolton; 1 s, 1 da; *Career* late Maj RA; civil servant 1938-75, private sec to Min of Supply 1947-50,

Under-Sec Miny Supply 1954-55, Cabinet Office 1955-58, Dep Sec Miny Aviation 1960-65, Dep Under-Sec State MOD 1965-72, 2 Permanent Under-Sec State 1972-75; chm Crown Leasing 1975-78, chm Civil Serv Appeal Bd 1978-, chm Civil Serv Retirement Fellowship 1978-; *Clubs* Army and Navy; *Style* - Sir John Wilson, KCB; Bourne Close, Bourne Lane, Twyford, Winchester, Hants (☎ Twyford 713488)

WILSON, Hon James McMoran; s and h of 2 Baron Moran, CMG; *b* 6 Aug 1952; *Educ* Eton and Trin Cambridge; *m* 1980, Hon (Mary) Jane Hepburne-Scott, da of 10 Lord Polwarth, TD; *Style* - The Hon James Wilson

WILSON, Hon Lorraine Mary Charmiane Nicole; da of 4 Baron Nunburnholme; *b* 1959; *Style* - The Hon Lorraine Wilson

WILSON, Sir (Mathew) Martin; 5 Bt (UK 1874), of Eshton Hall, Co York; s of Sir Mathew Richard Henry Wilson, 4 Bt, CSI, DSO (d 1958), by his w Hon Barbara Lister (da of 4 & last Baron Ribblesdale); *b* 2 July 1906; *Educ* Eton; *Heir* bro, Anthony Thomas Wilson, b 15 Nov 1909; *Career* patron of four livings; *Style* - Sir Martin Wilson, Bt; 1 Sandgate Esplanade, Folkestone, Kent

WILSON, Hon Mrs (Margaret Eleanor); *née* Maybray-King; da of Baron Maybray-King, PC (Life Peer); *b* 1926; *m* 1945, Roy Wilson; *Career* JP, Havant; *Style* - The Hon Mrs Wilson JP; 105 Silvester rd, Cowplain, Portsmouth

WILSON, Hon Mrs (Mary Jane); *née* Hepburne-Scott; da of 10 Lord Polwarth, TD; *b* 1955; *m* 1980, Hon James McMoran Wilson, s of 2 Baron Moran, CMG; *Style* - The Hon Mrs Wilson

WILSON, Hon Maud Maitland; da of 1 Baron Wilson; *b* 19 Nov 1917; *Style* - The Hon Maud Wilson; Hampton Court Palace, E Molesey, Surrey

WILSON, Hon Mrs (Mary Stewart); *née* Macpherson; da of 1 Baron Drumalbyn, KBE, PC; *b* 1942; *m* 1967, Philip D Wilson; *Style* - The Hon Mrs Wilson; 5 Clancarty rd, SW6

WILSON, Peter Cecil; CBE (1970); 3 s of Sir Mathew Wilson, 4 Bt, CSI, DSO; *b* 8 March 1913; *Educ* Eton, New Coll Oxford; *m* 1935 (m dis), Grace Helen, nee Ranken; 2 c; *Career* chm Sotheby & Co 1958-80, chm SPB Gp 1977-80, dir SPB Gp 1980; *Recreations* gardening; *Style* - Peter Wilson Esq, CBE; Château de Clavary, Auribeau sur Siagne, 06810 France

WILSON, Phillip John Maurice; s of Col Maurice James Hartley Wilson (decd); *b* 5 Nov 1927; *Educ* Trin Coll Glenalmond; *m* 1956, June Valerie Fairburn, da of late Arthur Bibby, of Ziwa, Kenya; 1 s, 1 da; *Career* pres Chevron Serv Co 1975-, md Chevron Oil (UK) Ltd 1975-, md Chevron Int Oil Co 1967-75, assist Marine Man Caltex in Europe 1965-67; *Recreations* farming, shooting, fishing; *Clubs* Roy Thames Yacht, Naval and Military; *Style* - Phillip Wilson Esq; Merstham Lodge, Harps Oak Lane, Merstham, Surrey (☎ 01 649 2160)

WILSON, Peter Thomas Matthew; s of Joseph Charles Wilson (d 1941); *b* 1 Aug 1903; *Educ* Bridlington Yorks; *m* 1941, Edith Mary, da of Frank Edwards; 1 s; *Career* solicitor & notary public; *Recreations* sports commensurate with age; *Clubs* County (Northampton), Farmers'; *Style* - Peter Wilson Esq; 35 Westhill dve, Kettering, Northants

WILSON, Robert William; s of the late Alfred Wilson; *b* 18 Sept 1926; *Educ* Retford G S; *m* 1951, Pamela Marjorie, nee Dixon; 2 da; *Career* solicitor 1951, HM Coroner East Berks 1970; *Recreations* yachting (yacht 'Josephine'); *Clubs* Arun Yacht; *Style* - Robert Wilson Esq; Oak Trees, Plough Lane, Waltham St Lawrence, Berks (☎ Shurlock Row 406)

WILSON, Hon Mrs (Sally Ann Marie Gabrielle); da of 5 Baron Vivian; *b* 1930; *m* 1, 1954 (m dis 1962), (William) Robin Charles Edward Cecil Lowe; m 2, 1963, Charles William Munro Wilson; 1 s; *Style* - The Hon Mrs Wilson; 12 Wellington sq, SW3

WILSON, Hon Mrs (Shirley Cynthia); da of late 2 Baron Cunliffe; *b* 1926; *m* 1959, Alan Desmond Wilson; 1 s, 1 da; *Style* -

The Hon Mrs Wilson; 40 Sutherland pla, W2

WILSON, Hon Tatiana; da of 4 Baron Nunburnholme; *b* 1960; *Style* - The Hon Tatiana Wilson

WILSON, Sir Thomas Douglas; 4 Bt (UK 1906), of Airdrie, New Monkland, Co Lanark, MC (1940); s of Thomas Douglas Wilson (ka 1917), and nephew of Sir John Menzies Wilson, 3 Bt (d 1968); *b* posthumously 10 June 1917; *Educ* Marlborough, RMC Sandhurst; *m* 1947, Pamela Aileen, da of Sir Griffin Wyndham Edward Hanmer, 7 Bt; 1 s, 3 da; *Heir* s, James William Wilson, b 8 Oct 1960; *Career* commissioned 15/19 Hussars 1937, served France 1939-40, M East 1941-45, ret 1947; *Club* Cavalry; *Style* - Sir Thomas Wilson, Bt, MC; Lillingstone Lovell Manor, Buckingham (☎ 028 06 237)

WILSON OF HIGH WRAY, Baroness; Valerie Frances Elizabeth; da of William Baron Fletcher, of Cape Town; *m* 1935, Baron Wilson of High Wray, OBE, DSC (d 1980); *Style* - The Rt Hon Lady Wilson of High Wray; Gillingate House, Kendal, Cumbria

WILSON, Hon William Edward Alexander; s of 2 Baron Moran, CMG; *b* 1956; *Educ* Eton; *Career* barr; *Style* - The Hon William Wilson

WILSON, Hon Ysabelle; da of 4 Baron Nunburnholme; *b* 1962; *Style* - The Hon Ysabelle Wilson

WILSON, Hon Mrs (Yvette Latham); da of 1 Baron Baillieu, KBE, CMG (d 1967); *b* 1922; *m* 1946, Robert Ruttan Wilson (gggs of Rev George Wilson, bro of 9 and 10 Barons Berners), of San Francisco; 4 da; *Style* - The Hon Mrs Wilson; Durford Knoll, Upper Durford Wood, Petersfield, Hants

WILTON, 7 Earl of (UK 1801); Seymour William Arthur John Egerton; also Viscount Grey de Wilton (UK 1801); s of 6 Earl of Wilton (d 1927, gs of 2 Earl, himself yr bro of 2 Marquess of Westminster and er bro of 1 Baron Ebury; hence Lord Wilton is hp to Marquessate of W, and all lesser attendant honours, at present held by 6 Duke of Westminster (tho' not the Dukedom itself), while his kinsman, Lord Ebury, is in turn hp to Lord Wilton) and Brenda, da of Sir William Petersen, KBE; *b* 29 May 1921; *Educ* Eton; *m* 1962, Diana, da of Roy Galway and formerly w of David Naylor-Leyland, MVO, 3 s of Sir Albert Naylor-Leyland, 2 Bt; *Heir* 4 cous, 6 Baron Ebury; *Clubs* White's; *Style* - The Rt Hon The Earl of Wilton; 27 Egerton ter, SW3 (☎ 01 584 4750)

WILTON, Sir (Arthur) John; KCMG (1979, CMG 1967), KCVO (1979), MC (1945); s of Walter Wilton (d 1944); *b* 21 Oct 1921; *Educ* Wanstead H S, St John's Oxford; *m* 1950, Maureen Elizabeth Alison, nee Meaker; 4 s, 1 da; *Career* Roy Ulster Rifles 1942, despatches 1944, Maj; HM Diplomatic Serv 1947-79, dir Middle East Centre for Arabic Studies Shemlan 1960-65, Dep High Cmmr Aden 1966-67, Ambass Kuwait 1970-74, Under-Sec FCO 1974-75, Ambass Jedda 1976-79; dir London House for Overseas Graduates 1979-; *Recreations* have changed with age and environment, reading, current affairs persist; *Clubs* Athenaeum; *Style* - Sir John Wilton, KCMG, KCVO, MC; London House, Mecklenburgh sq, WC1 (☎ 01 837 8888); Wilmere Lodge, Middleton Park, Middleton Stoney, Oxon (☎ 363)

WILTSHIRE, Earl of; Christopher John Hilton Paulet; s and h of 18 Marquess of Winchester; *b* 30 July 1969; *Style* - Earl of Wiltshire

WIMBERLEY, Maj Gen Douglas (Neil); CB (1943), DSO (1942), MC (1918), DL (Dundee 1947-75, Perths 1975); s of Col C Neil Campbell Wimberley, CMG (d 1949); *b* 15 Aug 1896; *Educ* Wellington, Emmanuel Cambridge; *m* 1925, Myrtle Livington, nee Campbell; 1 s, 1 da; *Career* Maj-Gen cmdg 51 Highland Div in 8 Army N Africa and Sicily in Battles of Alamein 1941-43, Cmdt Army Staff Coll Camberley 1943-44, Dir of Infantry War Office 1944-46, ret; Princ of Univ Coll Dundee 1946-54, Scarlet Rod of Order of the Bath 1948-54, Registrar and Sec Order of the Bath 1954-64, Col Queen's Own Cameron

Highlanders 1951-61, memb Roy Co of Archers (Queen's Body Gd for Scotland 1941); *Recreations* genealogy; *Clubs* Naval and Military; *Style* - Maj-Gen Douglas Wimberley Esq, CB, DSO, MC, DL; Foxhall, Coupar Angus, Perthshire (☎ 082 82 384)

WIMBORNE, 3 Viscount (UK 1918); Sir Ivor Fox-Strangways Guest; 5 Bt (UK 1838); also Baron Wimborne (UK 1880) and Baron Ashby St Legers (UK 1910); s of 2 Viscount Wimborne, OBE (d 1967), and Lady Mabel Fox-Strangways, da of 6 Earl of Ilchester; *b* 2 Dec 1939; *Educ* Eton; *m* 1966, Victoria, da of Col Mervyn Vigors, DSO, MC, by his 2 w Margaret (da of Maj-Gen Sir George Aston, KCB); 1 s; *Heir* s, Hon Ivor Guest; *Career* chm Harris & Dixon 1972-76, Jt Master Pytchley 1968-76; *Clubs* Travellers'; *Style* - The Rt Hon Viscount Wimborne; c/o Travellers' Club, 25 Champs Elysées, 75008 Paris, France

WIMBORNE, Dowager Viscountess; Lady Mabel Edith; *née* Fox-Strangways; da of 6 Earl of Ilchester, GBE, and Lady Helen Mary Theresa Vane-Tempest-Stewart, da of 6 Marquess of Londonderry; *b* 17 Feb 1918; *m* 1938, 2 Viscount Wimborne; 3 s (3 Viscount, Hon Julian & Hon Charles Guest), 1 da (Hon Mrs Johnson), *qqv*; *Style* - Rt Hon Dowager Viscountess Wimborne; Rozel, Mt Durand, St Peter Port, Guernsey

WINCH, Hon Mrs (Jean Rosemary Vera); *née* Cary; da of 14 Viscount Falkland by his 1 w Joan; *b* 30 Oct 1928; *Educ* Lady Walsingham's Sch; *m* 1950, Henry Herman Montagu, s of late Henry Louis Winch (d 1903) and Vera, Lady Newborough (1 w of 5 Baron); *Recreations* country pursuits, flat racing (race horse: 'Mysolitaire' by 'Sparkler'); *Style* - The Hon Mrs Winch; Castle Barn, Penrhyndeudraeth, Gwynedd

WINCHESTER, 18 Marquess of (Premier Marquess of England, cr 1551); Nigel George Paulet; also Baron St John of Basing (E 1539) and Earl of Wiltshire (E 1550); s of George Paulet (1 cous of 17 Marquess, who d 1968; also eighth in descent from 5 Marquess, a Roman Catholic who held Basing House for the King in the Great Rebellion at a personal cost in destroyed plate, jewels etc of some £200,000; treasure is still held to be hidden somewhere in or around the ruins; the 5 Marquess's gggf, the 1 Marquess, was noted for his attention to prevailing orthodoxies in successfully remaining Lord Treasurer of England continuously throughout Edward VI's, Mary's, and Elizabeth I's reigns; only death prised loose his hold on office); *b* 23 Dec 1941; *m* 1967, Rosemary, da of Maj Aubrey Hilton, of Salisbury, Zimbabwe; 2 s, 1 da; *Heir* s, Earl of Wiltshire; *Career* dir Rhodesia Mineral Ventures Ltd, Sani-Dan Servs Ltd, Rhodesia Prospectors Ltd; *Style* - The Most Hon Marquess of Winchester; Lydford Cottage, 35 Whyteladies Lane, Borrowdale, Salisbury, Zimbabwe

WINCHESTER, Bapsy, Marchioness of; Bapsy; da of Most Rev Khurshedji Pavry, High Priest of Parsees in India; *Educ* Columbia U, New York; *m* 1952, as his 3 w, 16 Marquess of Winchester (d 1962); *Career* authoress (*Heroines of Ancient Iran*); *Style* - The Most Hon Bapsy, Marchioness of Winchester

WINCHESTER, 94 Bishop of (AD 636) 1975-; Rt Rev John Vernon Taylor; s of Rt Rev John Taylor, sometime Bp of Sodor & Man; *b* 11 Sept 1914; *Educ* St Lawrence Coll Ramsgate, Trin Cambridge, St Cat's Soc Oxford, Wycliffe Hall Oxford, Inst of Educn London; *m* 1940, Margaret, da of Walter Wright; 1 s, 2 da; *Career* DD; patron of 89 livings and 23 alternately, the Canonries in his Cathedral, and the Archdeaconries of Winchester & Basingstoke; *Style* - The Rt Rev Bishop of Winchester; Wolvesey, Winchester, Hants

WINCHILSEA & NOTTINGHAM, 16 & 11 Earl of (E 1628 & 1681); Sir Christopher Denys Stormont Finch Hatton; 17 & 11 Bt (E 1611 & 1660), of Eastwell & Raunston respectively; also Viscount Maidstone (E 1623) and Baron Finch (E 1673); s of 15 & 10 Earl of Winchilsea & Nottingham (d 1950) by his 1 w, Countess Gladys Széchényi, 3 da of Count László Széchényi (sometime Hungarian Min in London, also Imperial & Roy Chamberlain 1905) and Gladys, da of Cornelius Vanderbilt Jr (s of 'The Commodore') and great aunt of Gloria, also 1 cous of Consuelo, who m 9 Duke of Marlborough; Lord Winchilsea is therefore 3 cous of 11 Duke of Marlborough as well as the Vanderbilts and (through marriage) Whitneys; *b* 17 Nov 1936; *Educ* Eton, Gordonstoun; *m* 1962, Shirley, da of Bernard Hatfield; 1 s, 1 da; *Heir* s, Viscount Maidstone; *Career* Hereditary Lord of Roy Manor of Wye; *Style* - The Rt Hon The Earl of Winchilsea and Nottingham; South Cadbury House, Yeovil, Somerset (☎ 0963 40361/40777)

WINDHAM, John Jeremy; s of Sir Ralph Windham, of Tetbury (d 1980); kinsman and hp of Sir Thomas Bowyer-Smyth, 15 Bt; *b* 1948; *Educ* Wellington; *m* 1976, Rachel, da of late Lt-Col Walter Finney, TD; *Career* Capt Irish Gds; *Style* - John Windham Esq; 81 Broxash rd, SW11

WINDHAM, Lady - Kathleen Mary; da of Capt Cecil Henry FitzHerbert, DSC, of Latimerstown, Wexford; *m* 1946, Sir Ralph Windham (d 1980); 2 s, 2 da; er s is John Windham, hp to Btcy of Bowyer-Smyth; *Style* - Lady Windham; Hook's Cottage, Kingscote, nr Tetbury, Glos

WINDLESHAM, 3 Baron (UK 1937); Sir David James George Hennessy; 3 Bt (UK 1927), CVO, PC (1973); s of 2 Baron Windlesham (d 1962) by his 1 w Angela (d 1956, da of Julian Duggan, of Buenos Aires and Lowther gdns); *b* 28 Jan 1932; *Educ* Ampleforth, Trin Oxford; *m* 1965, Prudence Glynn, *qv*, yr da of Lt-Col Rupert Glynn, MC; *Heir* s, Hon James Hennessy; *Career* dir Assoc Communications Corpn 1975-, md ATV 1975-81, V-Pres Roy TV Soc 1977-; Min State Home Off 1970-72, NI 1972-73, Ld Privy Seal & Ldr Ho of Lds 1973-74; chm Oxford Preservn Tst 1979-; late Lt Gren Gds; Tstee Br Museum 1981-; *Clubs* Beefsteak; *Style* - The Rt Hon Lord Windlesham CVO PC; c/o House of Lords, SW1

WINDSOR, Viscount; Ivor Edward Other Windsor-Clive; s and h of 3 Earl of Plymouth, DL, by his w Caroline, nee Rice; through her Lord Windsor is 1 cous twice removed of Lord Kilbracken and the economist (Hon) Wynne Godley; *b* 19 Nov 1951; *Educ* Harrow; *m* 1979, Caroline, da of Frederick Nettlefold and Hon Mrs Juliana Roberts (da of 2 Viscount Scarsdale, hence great niece of Lord (Marquess) Curzon (of Kedleston) and 2 cous of Lord Ravensdale); 1 s; *Heir* s, Hon Robert Windsor-Clive; *Career* co-fndr & dir Centre for Study of Modern Art 1973; *Style* - Viscount Windsor; The Stables, Oakly Park, Ludlow, Shropshire (☎ Bromfield 393)

WINDSOR-CLIVE, Hon Mrs; Hon (Mary) Alice; *née* Jolliffe; da of 4 Baron Hylton (d 1967); *b* 1937; *m* 1, 1959 (m dis 1969), John Paget Chancellor; 1 s, 3 da; m 2, 1969, the Hon Richard Archer Alan Windsor-Clive, s of 2 Earl of Plymouth, PC (d 1943); *Style* - The Hon Mrs Windsor-Clive; Combe, Nettlecombe, Taunton, Som

WINDSOR-CLIVE, Hon David Justin; s of 3 Earl of Plymouth; *b* 1960; *Educ* Harrow; *Style* - The Hon David Windsor-Clive; c/o Oakly Park, Ludlow

WINDSOR-CLIVE, Hon Richard Archer Alan; s of 2 Earl of Plymouth, PC (d 1943); *b* 1928; *Educ* Eton and Trin, Cambridge; *m* 1, 1955 (m dis 1968) Joanna Mary, da of Edward Corbet Woodall, OBE; 1 s, 2 da; m 2, 1968, Hon (Mary) Alice Chancellor, da of 4 Baron Hylton; *Career* late Lt RA; *Style* - The Hon Richard Windsor-Clive; Combe, Netlecombe, Taunton

WINDSOR-CLIVE, Hon Robert Other Ivor; s and h of Viscount Windsor and gs of 3 Earl of Plymouth, DL; *b* 25 March 1981; godparents include James Mayor and Lady Celestria Noel; *Style* - The Hon Robert Windsor-Clive

WINDSOR-CLIVE, Hon Simon Percy; s of 3 Earl of Plymouth; *b* 1956; *Educ* Harrow; *Style* - The Hon Simon Windsor-Clive; c/o Oakly Park, Ludlow

WINGATE, Lady; Mary; da of late John Harpoth, of Copenhagen, and step-da of late Sir Paul Vinogradoff; *m* 1916, Sir Ronald Wingate, 2 & last Bt, CB, CMG, CIE, OBE (d 1978, 2 cous of Maj-Gen

Orde Wingate, DSO**, the legendary 'Chindit' (the word refers to the mythical beasts, akin to gryphons, that guard Burmese temples) leader in Japanese-occupied Burma during WW II); *Style* - Lady Wingate; Barford Manor, Barford St Martin, Salisbury, Wilts

WINGATE, His Honour Judge; William Granville; QC (1963); s of Col George Wingate, CIE (d 1936); *b* 28 May 1911; *Educ* Brighton Coll, Lincoln Oxford; *m* 1960, Judith Rosemary, da of Lt-Col J H B Evatt, RA (decd); 1 s, 1 da (twins); *Career* barr 1933, memb Bar Council 1961-65 and 1966-67, Circuit Judge (E Sussex) 1967-, Dep Chm Essex Quarter Sessions 1965-71, memb County Court Rule Ctee and Lord Chancellor's Legal Aid Advisory Ctee 1971, Lord Chancellor's Law Reform Ctee 1976-; chm of Governors of Brighton Coll 1978-; *Clubs* Bar Yacht, Roy Corinthian Yacht; *Style* - His Honour Judge Wingate, QC; Cox's Mill, Dallington, Heathfield, Sussex (☎ Rushlake Green 217); 2 Garden Court, Temple EC4 (☎ 01 236 4741)

WINGFIELD, Hon Mrs (Cynthia Meriel); *née* Hill; da of 6 Baron Sandys; *b* 1929; *m* 1954, Charles Talbot Rhys Wingfield; 1 s, 3 da; *Style* - The Hon Mrs Wingfield; Barrington Park, Burford, Oxon

WINGFIELD, Hon Guy Claude Patrick; s of 9 Viscount Powerscourt (d 1973); *b* 1940; *Educ* Millfield; *Style* - The Hon Guy Wingfield; 3045, Jackson st, Apt 103, San Francisco, Calif, USA

WINGFIELD, Hon Julia; da of 10 Viscount Powerscourt; *b* 1965; *Style* - The Hon Julia Wingfield

WINGFIELD, Hon Mervyn Anthony; s and h of 10 Viscount Powerscourt; *b* 21 Aug 1963; *Style* - The Hon Mervyn Wingfield

WINGFIELD, Lady Norah Beryl Cayzer; *née* Jellicoe; da of Adm of the Fleet, 1 Earl Jellicoe, GCB, OM, GCVO (d 1935); *b* 1910; *m* 1935, Maj Edward William Rhys Wingfield, late King's Roy Rifle Corps; 1 s, 2 da; *Style* - Lady Norah Wingfield; Salterbridge, Cappoquin, Co Waterford

WINGFIELD DIGBY, Rev Richard Shuttleworth; s of George Everard Wingfield Digby (d 1915), gt nephew through his paternal g-mother of 1st Viscount Portman, by his 2 w; *b* 19 Aug 1911; *Educ* Nautical Coll Pangbourne, Christ's Cambridge; *m* 1936, Rosamond Frances, da of Lt-Col William Trench Digby; 2 s, 1 da; *Career* RN 1928-30; ordained deacon C of E 1936, vicar of All Saints Newmarket 1946-53, rector of Bury Lancs 1953-66, dean of Peterborough Cathedral 1966-80, dean emeritus 1980; *Recreations* golf, walking; *Clubs* Army and Navy; *Style* - Rev Richard Wingfield Digby; Byways, Higher Holton, Wincanton, Somerset (☎ 32137)

WINGFIELD DIGBY, Maj (Kenelm) Simon; s of Col F J B Wingfield Digby, TD, JP, DL of Sherborne Castle Dorset, whose mother was Hon Georgina, da of 4 Viscount Lifford; *b* 13 Feb 1910; *Educ* Harrow, Trin Cambridge; *m* 1936, Kathleen Elizabeth, da of late Hon Justice Courtney Kingstone, of Canada; 1 s, 1 da; *Career* Maj NW Europe; barr, MP 1941-74, C Whip 1948-51, Civil Ld of the Admiralty 1951-57, del Cncl of Europe 1968-74, leader 1972-74; *Recreations* fishing, bloodstock breeding; *Clubs* Carlton; *Style* - Maj Simon Wingfield Digby; Compton Cottage, Sandley, Gillingham, Dorset (☎ 2650); Coleshill House, Coleshill, Birmingham

WINN, Hon Derek Edward Anthony; s of 3 Baron St Oswald (d 1976); hp of bro, 4 Baron, MC; *b* 9 July 1919; *Educ* Stowe; *m* 1954, Charlotte Denise Eileen, da of Wilfrid Haig Loyd; 1 s, 1 da; *Career* formerly Lt King's Roy Rifle Corps (Supp Reserve), Capt Army Air Corps (Regular Army Reserve) 1939-45; Assist Supt Malayan Police Force 1948-51; *Clubs* Lansdowne, White's; *Style* - The Hon Derek Winn; White Lodge, 12 Gilston rd, SW10

WINN, Hon Reginald Henry; s of late 2 Baron St Oswald, and Mabel, da of Sir Charles Forbes, 4 Bt; *b* 1899; *Educ* Eton, Ch Ch Oxford; *m* 1924, Alice, da of late

Moncure Perkins, of Virginia USA; 2 da (*see* Hon Mark Wyndham, MC); *Career* formerly Major Gren Gds; *Clubs* White's, Buck's; *Style* - The Hon Reginald Winn

WINNINGTON, Lady Betty (Marjorie); *née* Anson; da of 4 Earl of Lichfield (d 1960); *b* 1917; *m* 1944, Col Thomas Foley Churchill Winnington, MBE; *Style* - Lady Betty Winnington; 9 Westminster gdns, SW1

WINNINGTON, Sir Francis Salwey William; 6 Bt (GB 1755), of Stanford Court, Worcestershire; s of Francis Salwey Winnington (d 1913), and gs of Sir Francis Winnington, 5 Bt, JP, DL (d 1931), by Sir Francis's w Jane (da of Lord Alfred Spencer-Churchill, himself 2 s of 6 Duke of Marlborough); the present Sir Francis is thus 3 cous once removed to the 11 Duke of Marlborough and 2 cous once removed to the late Sir Winston Churchill; *b* 24 June 1907; *Educ* Eton; *m* 1944, Anne Beryl Jane, da of late Capt Lawrence Drury-Lowe, Scots Gds; 1 da; *Heir* bro, Col Thomas Foley Churchill Winnington, MBE, b 16 Aug 1910; *Career* landed proprietor (4,700 acres); Lt Welsh Gds 1928-32; re-employed 1939 (despatches); patron of three livings; *Clubs* Cavalry and Guards; *Style* - Sir Francis Winnington, Bt; Brockhill Court, Shelsley Beauchamp, Worcs

WINNINGTON, Thomas Foley Churchill; MBE (1948); s of Francis Winnington; hp to bro, Sir Francis Winnington, 6 Bt; *b* 16 Aug 1910; *Educ* Eton, Balliol Oxford; *m* 1944, Lady Betty Anson, da of 4 Earl of Lichfield; 2 s (Anthony b 1948, m 1978 Karyn Kettles, 1 da; Henry b 1961), 2 da (Viscountess Campden, da-in-law of 5 Earl of Gainsborough; Emma b 1956); *Career* Col Gren Gds; *Style* - Col Thomas Winnington MBE; 9 Westminster gdns, SW1 (☎ 01 834 4080)

WINSTANLEY, Baron (Life Peer UK 1975); Michael Platt Winstanley; s of Dr Sydney Winstanley; *b* 27 Aug 1918; *Educ* Manchester G S & U; *m* 1, 1945 (m dis 1952), Nancey Penney; 1 s; m 2, 1955, Joyce, da of Arthur Woodhouse; 1 s, 1 da; *Career* MP (Lib) Cheadle 1966-70, Hazel Grove Feb-Oct 1974; chm Lib Pty Health Cttee 1965-66, Lib Spokesman Health, PO & Broadcasting; memb Water Space Amenity Commission 1980-; MRCS, LRCP; GP Urmston Manchester 1948-66; broadcaster; *Style* - The Rt Hon Lord Winstanley; 30 Broad Lane, Hale, Cheshire

WINSTANLEY, Hon Diana Christine; da of Baron Winstanley by his 2 w, Joyce; *b* 1960; *Style* - The Hon Diana Winstanley

WINSTANLEY, Hon Nicholas Clayton Platt; s of Baron Winstanley by his 1 w, Nancey; *b* 1945; *Style* - The Hon Nicholas Winstanley

WINSTANLEY, Hon Stephen Woodhouse; s of Baron Winstanley by his 2 w, Joyce; *b* 1957; *Style* - The Hon Stephen Winstanley

WINTERBOTTOM, Baron (Life Peer UK 1965); Ian Winterbottom; s of George Harold Winterbottom, JP, High Sheriff Northants 1908, Ld of the Manor and patron of livings of Horton, Hackleton and Piddington, by his 2 w, Georgina, da of Rev Ian McLeod, of Skye; *b* 13 April 1913; *Educ* Charterhouse and Clare Cambridge; *m* 1944, Ira (Irene Eva), da of Dr Walter Munk, of Haifa; 3 s, 1 da; *Career* MP (L) Nottingham Centl 1950-55, Under-Sec MOD (RN) 1966-67, Parly Sec Min Pub Bldg & Works 1967-68, Under-Secretary of State MOD 1968-70; Lord in Waiting to HM 1974-78; chm Venesta Internat 1972-74; *Style* - The Rt Hon Lord Winterbottom; Woodland Place, St Briavels, Lydney, Glos

WINTERBOTTOM, Hon Caroline Margaret Alyson; da of Baron Winterbottom; *b* Dec 1950; *Style* - The Hon Caroline Winterbottom

WINTERBOTTOM, Hon Dudley Walter Gordon; s of Baron Winterbottom; *b* 25 June 1946; *Educ* Charterhouse, U of Kent at Canterbury, Wolfson Oxford; *m* 1978, Mirjana; *Career* co dir; sec Chelsea Arts Club; *Recreations* piano playing, reading, sleeping; *Style* - The Hon Dudley Winterbottom; 18 Norham rd, Oxford

WINTERBOTTOM, Hon Graham Anthony; 3 s of Baron Winterbottom; *b* 23 June 1948; *Educ* Charterhouse, RNC; *Style* - The Hon Graham Winterbottom

WINTERBOTTOM, Hon John; s of Baron Winterbottom; *b* Sept 1940; *Educ* Charterhouse, Clare Cambridge; *Style* - The Hon John Winterbottom

WINTERTON, 7 Earl (I 1766); Robert Chad Turnour; also Baron Winterton (I 1761) and Viscount Turnour (I 1766); s of Cecil Turnour (gs of Rev Hon Augustus Turnour, 3 s of 2 Earl Winterton); suc 3 cous once removed, 6 Earl, 1962, but has not yet established his right of his Peerages; *b* 13 Sept 1915; *Educ* Nutana Coll; *m* 1, 1941, Kathleen (d 1969), da of D Whyte, of Saskatoon; m 2, 1971, Marion, da of Arthur Phillips; *Heir* bro, Noel Turnour; *Career* Fl Sgt Roy Canadian AF, served WW II & Sardinia 1957-58; *Style* - The Rt Hon Earl Winterton; 1326 55th st, Delta, BC, Canada

WISE, 2 Baron (UK 1951); John Clayton Wise; s of 1 Baron Wise, DL (d 1968); *b* 11 June 1923; *m* 1946, Margaret, da of Frederick Snead; 2 s; *Heir* s, Hon Christopher Wise; *Career* farmer; *Style* - The Rt Hon Lord Wise; Ramsley Farm, N Elmham, Norfolk

WISE, Hon Christopher John Clayton; s and h of 2 Baron Wise; *b* 19 March 1949; *Educ* Norwich Sch, Southampton U; *Style* - The Hon Christopher Wise

WISE, Kate, Baroness; Kate Elizabeth; da of John Sturgeon, of Bury St Edmunds; *m* 1911, 1 Baron Wise, DL (d 1968); 1 s, 3 da; *Style* - Rt Hon Kate, Lady Wise; The Great Wood Cottage, N Elmham, Norfolk

WISE, Hon Martin Highfield; 2 s of 2 Baron Wise; *b* 18 April 1950; *Educ* Norwich Sch, Bristol U; *Style* - The Hon Martin Wise

WISEMAN, Joan, Lady; Joan Mary Lesureur; da of Arthur Phelps, of Harrow; *m* 1944, as his 3 w, Sir William Wiseman, 10 Bt, CB; 1 s (11 Bt); *Style* - Joan, Lady Wiseman; 32 Victoria rd, W8 (☎ 01 937 1558)

WISEMAN, Sir John William; 11 Bt (E 1628), of Canfield Hall, Essex; s of Sir William Wiseman, 10 Bt, CB, CMG (d 1962), by his 3 w, Joan, Lady Wiseman, *qv*; *b* 16 March 1957; *Educ* Millfield, Hartford U (Conn, USA); *m* 1980, Nancy, da of Casimer Zylu, of New Britain, Conn, USA; *Heir* fifth cous, Thomas Alan Wiseman, b 8 July 1921; *Style* - Sir John Wiseman, Bt; 32 Victoria rd, W8 (☎ 01 937 1558)

WISEMAN, Thomas Alan; s of Thomas Edward Wiseman (himself fifth in descent from Sir Thomas Wiseman, 6 Bt); hp to fifth cous, Sir John Wiseman, 11 Bt; *b* 8 July 1921; *m* 1946, Hildemarie, da of Gustav Domnik, of Allstein, formerly E Prussia; *Career* formerly Staff Sgt RAOC; *Style* - Thomas Wiseman Esq; 14 Havisham rd, Chalk, Gravesend, Kent

WITHERINGTON, Giles Somerville Gwynne; *Career* memb IOD; dep chm Reed Internat Ltd, memb exec cttee; dir Beaubush Ltd, Keatfold Ltd, Reed Bldg Products, Reed Finance Pty Ltd SA, Reed Overseas Corpn, Save The Children (Sales) Ltd, The Wallpaper Mfrs Ltd; *Style* - Giles Witherington Esq; c/o Reed International Ltd, Reed House, 83 Piccadilly, W1 (☎ 01 499 4020)

WITHERS, Roy Joseph; s of Joseph Withers (d 1973); *b* 18 June 1924; *Educ* Tiffin Sch Kingston on Thames, Trin Cambridge; *m* 1947, Pauline Mary Gillian, nee Johnston; 4 s; *Career* md Davy Corp Ltd 1974-, non exec dir Transmark, memb Overseas Project Bd and ECGD Advisory Panel; *Recreations* golf, squash, painting; *Clubs* Carlton; *Style* - Roy Withers Esq; Spaniards Court, 41 Ingram av, Hampstead, NW11

WITTON-DAVIES, The Ven Carlyle; s of Prof Thomas Witton Davies (d 1923); *b* 10 June 1913; *Educ* Friars Sch Bangor, Exeter Coll Oxford; *m* 1941, Mary, nee Rees; 3 s, 4 da; *Career* ChapStJ 1954; clerk in Holy Orders, subwarden of St Michael's Coll Llandaff 1940-44, canon of St George's Cathedral Jerusalem 1944-49, dean of St David's Cathedral 1950-57, archdeacon of

Oxford and Canon of Ch Ch Oxford 1957-; *Recreations* lawn tennis, swimming, music; *Style* - The Ven the Archdeacon of Oxford; Archdeacon's Lodging, Christ Church, Oxford (☎ 43847)

WODEHOUSE, Hon Charles James; s of 4 Earl of Kimberley (by his 4 w); *b* 1963; *Style* - The Hon Charles Wodehouse

WODEHOUSE, Lady - Hon Carol Lylie; *née* Palmer; da of 3 Baron Palmer, OBE; *b* 1951; *see* Lord Wodehouse; *Style* - Lady Wodehouse

WODEHOUSE, Hon David Simon John; s and h of Lord Wodehouse; *b* 10 Oct 1978; *Style* - The Hon David Wodehouse

WODEHOUSE, Hon Edward Abdy; s of 4 Earl of Kimberley (by his 3 w); *b* 1954; *Educ* Eton; *Style* - The Hon Edward Wodehouse

WODEHOUSE, Hon Henry Wyndham; s of 4 Earl of Kimberley (by his 3 w); *b* 1956; *Educ* Millfield; *Style* - The Hon Henry Wodehouse

WODEHOUSE, Lord; John Armine Wodehouse; s and h of 4 Earl of Kimberley by his 2 w, Carmel; *b* 15 Jan 1951; *Educ* Eton, E Anglia U; *m* 1973, Hon Carol, da of 3 Baron Palmer; 1 s, 1 da; *Heir* s, Hon David Wodehouse; *Career* scientist 1979-, now systems programmer with Glaxo Gp Research Ltd; FRSA; *Recreations* photography, computing; *Clubs* Br Interplanetary Soc; *Style* - Lord Wodehouse; Derry House, North End, Henley-on-Thames, Oxon

WODEHOUSE, Hon Katherine Frances; da of Lord Wodehouse; *b* 1976; *Style* - The Hon Katherine Wodehouse

WOLF, Prof Peter Otto; s of Richard Wolf (d 1967); *b* 9 May 1918; *Educ* St Polten, London U; *m* 1, 1944, Jennie, nee Robinson; 2 s, 1 da; m 2, 1977, Janet Elizabeth, da of T R Robertson OBE; *Career* chartered civil engr, Prof and Head Civil Engrg Dept City U London 1966-, Imperial Coll of Science and Tech London U 1949-66 (Reader in Hydrology 1955-); *Recreations* classical music, reading, skiing, sailing, walking; *Clubs* Athenaeum; *Style* - Prof Peter Wolf; 69 Shepherd's Hill, N6

WOLFE MURRAY, James Archibald; s of Lt-Col Malcolm Wolfe Murray, DL (ggs of James Murray, who as a Lord of Session took the title Lord Cringletie; he was gggs of Sir Alexander Murray, 2 Bt, of Blackbarony), by his 1 w, Lady Grizel Boyle, da of 8 Earl of Glasgow; *b* 25 April 1936; *Educ* Eton, Worcester Coll Oxford; *m* 1, 1963, Hon (Lady until 1963) Diana Douglas-Home, (b 1940) 3 da of Baron Home of the Hirsel (14 Earl of Home to 1963); 1 s, 2 da; m 2, 1978, Amanda, da of A F Street; 1 s; *Career* v-chm & md Macdonald Greenlees Ltd 1975-; export dir James Buchanan & Co 1969-75; *Recreations* golf, fishing, shooting, cricket; *Clubs* White's, Naval & Military, Roy St George's Golf, MCC, Hon Co Edinburgh Golfers; *Style* - James Wolf Murray Esq; 73 Murrayfield gdns, Edinburgh EH 12 6DL (☎ 031 337 2884)

WOLFE-PARRY, Hon Mrs (Juno Odette Denisa Palma); *née* Wynn; da of 5 Baron Newborough (d 1957); *b* 1940; *m* 1963, Philip Wolfe-Parry, LDS, RCS; 1 s; *Style* - The Hon Mrs Wolfe-Parry; 54 Hans Place, Knightsbridge, SW1

WOLFENDEN, Baron (Life Peer UK 1974); John Frederick Wolfenden; CBE (1942); s of George Wolfenden, of Bournemouth; *b* 26 June 1906; *Educ* Wakefield Sch, Queen's Oxford; *m* 1932, Eileen, da of A J Spilsbury; 1 s, 2 da; *Career* kt 1956; philosophy tutor Magdalen Oxford, Headmaster Uppingham then Shrewsbury, V-Chllr Reading U 1950-63; chm Departmental Cttee Homosexual Offences & Prostitution 1954-57; Pres Chelsea Coll London U 1972-, Metropolitan Assoc Bldg Socs 1978-, Chelsea Bldg Soc 1978-; *Style* - The Rt Hon Lord Wolfenden, CBE; The White House, Westcott, Dorking, Surrey (☎ 5475)

WOLFENDEN, Hon Daniel Mark; s of Baron Wolfenden, CBE; *b* 1942; *m* 1972, Sally Frankel; *Style* - The Hon Daniel Wolfenden; 44 Mortimer st, W1

WOLFF, Hon Mrs - Hon Mary; *née* Clifford; da of late 14 Baron Clifford of Chudleigh; *b* 1919; *m* 1943, Major Jack Philip Albert Galvin Clifford Wolff, MBE; 2 da; *Style* - The Hon Mrs Wolff; Barkham Manor, Barkham, Wokingham, Berks

WOLFFER, Hon Mrs (Naomi Anne); *née* Marks; da of 2 Baron Marks of Broughton; *b* 1952; *m* 1980, Martin Christian Wolffer; *Style* - The Hon Mrs Wolffer

WOLFSON, Geoffrey Mark; MP (C) Sevenoaks 1979-; s of Capt Vladimir Wolfson RNVR (d 1954); *b* 7 April 1934; *Educ* Eton, Cambridge; *m* 1965, Edna Webb, nee Hardman; 2 s; *Career* personnel dir Hambros Bank 1973-, head of Youth Servs Industrial Soc, warden Brathay Hall Centre Westmorland 1962-66; *Recreations* rowing, gardening; *Style* - Geoffrey Wolfson Esq, MP; The Manor House, Heverham, Sevenoaks, Kent (☎ 0732 61008)

WOLFSON, Sir Isaac; 1 Bt (UK 1962), of St Marylebone, Co London; s of late Solomon Wolfson, of Glasgow; *b* 17 Sept 1897; *Educ* Queen's Park Sch Glasgow; *m* 1926, Edith (d 1981), da of Ralph Specterman; 1 s; *Heir* s, Sir Leonard Gordon Wolfson, *qv*; *Career* (Hon) FRCP, (Hon) FRCS; joined The Great Universal Stores Ltd 1932, chm 1946-; member of Worshipful Company of Pattenmakers; hon pres Weizmann Institute of Science Israel; trustee of Religious Centre Jerusalem; hon fell St Edmund's Coll Oxford 1961; founder pres and trustee Wolfson Foundation cr 1955 for the advancement of health education and youth activities in the UK and Commonwealth; *Style* - Sir Isaac Wolfson, Bt; 74 Portland pla, W1

WOLFSON, Sir Leonard Gordon; s & h of Sir Isaac Wolfson, 1 Bt; *b* 11 Nov 1927; *Educ* King's Sch Worcester; *m* 1949, Ruth, da of E Sterling; 4 da; *Career* kt 1977; chm & fndr tstee Wolfson Fndn; md Great Universal Stores 1962- (dir 1952-), chm Gt Universal Stores Merchandise Corpn 1966-; Pres Jewish Welfare Bd; *Clubs* Carlton, MCC; *Style* - Sir Leonard Wolfson; Universal House, 251 Tottenham Court rd, W1 (☎ 01 636 4080)

WOLLASTON, Henry Woods; s of Sir Gerald Woods Wollaston, KCB, KCVO (d 1957); *b* 14 Nov 1916; *Educ* Harrow, Cambridge; *m* 1944, Daphne Margaret, nee Clark; 1 s, 2 da; *Career* barr, standing counsel Gen Synod 1981-, Princ Assist Legal Advr Home Off 1978-80 (joined 1946), Master of the Haberdasher's Co 1974-75; *Recreations* real tennis, lawn tennis; *Style* - Henry Wollaston Esq; 2 Ashtead House, Ashtead, Surrey (☎ Ashtead 73869)

WOLMER, Viscount; William Lewis Palmer; s and h of 4 Earl of Selborne, *qv*; *b* 1 Sept 1971; *Style* - Viscount Wolmer

WOLSELEY, Sir Charles Garnet Richard Mark; 11 Bt (E 1628), of Wolseley, Staffs; s of Capt Stephen Wolseley (ka 1944, s of Sir Edric Wolseley, 10 Bt, JP, who d 1954); the family (of which the Wolseleys of Mt Wolseley, Co Carlow, who produced Sir Garnet, the Victorian general cr Viscount Wolseley, are a junior branch) probably descends from Eadricht de Wulsellegh, who flourished *temp* William Rufus; *b* 16 June 1944; *Educ* Ampleforth, RAC Cirencester; *m* 1968, Anita, da of Hugo Fried, of Epsom; 1 s, 3 da; *Heir* s, Stephen Garnet Hugo Charles, b 1980; *Career* FRICS; ptnr Smiths Gore Chartered Surveyors 1979-; *Recreations* shooting, fishing, water-colour painting; *Clubs* Farmers'; *Style* - Sir Charles Wolseley, Bt; Wolseley Park, Rugeley, Staffs (☎ 2346); Hilliers, Petworth, W Sussex (☎ 42414)

WOLSELEY, Sir Garnet; 12 Bt (I 1745), of Mount Wolseley, Co Carlow; s of Richard Bingham Wolseley (d 1938) and kinsman of 11 Bt (d 1950); *b* 27 May 1915; *Educ* Wallasey Central Sch; *m* 1950, Lillian Mary, da of William Bertram Ellison; *Career* served 1939-45 with Northants Regt (Madagascar, Sicily, Italy and Germany); *Style* - Sir Garnet Wolseley, Bt; 73 Dorothy st, Brantford, Ontario, Canada (☎ Plaza 37957)

WOLSELEY, Pamela, Lady; Pamela Violette; da of Capt F Barry, of Co Cork and latterly Old Court, Whitchurch, Herefs, and Mrs W N Power, of Wolseley Park; *m* 1942, Capt Stephen Wolseley, RA (ka 1944); 1 s (Sir Charles Wolseley, 11 Bt), 1 da; granted the rank of Baronet's wife 1955; *Style* - Pamela, Lady Wolseley; Wolsely Park, Rugeley, Staffs

WOLVERTON, 5 Baron (UK 1869); Nigel Reginald Victor Glyn; s of 4 Baron Wolverton, JP, DL (d 1932, of the Glyn Mills bank family), and Lady Edith Ward, da of 1 Earl of Dudley; *b* 23 June 1904; *Educ* Eton; *Heir* 2 cous once removed, Jeremy Glyn; *Career* patron of one living, Capt RA (TA); *Style* - The Rt Hon The Lord Wolverton; Queensberry House, Newmarket, Suffolk

WOMBWELL, Sir George Philip Frederick; 7 Bt (GB 1778), of Wombwell, Yorkshire; s of Maj Sir Philip Wombwell, 6 Bt, MBE (d 1977); *b* 21 May 1949; *Educ* Repton; *m* 1974, Jane, da of Thomas Wrightson, of Ulshaw Grange, Leyburn, N Yorks; 1 s, 1 da; *Heir* s, Stephen Wombwell, b 12 May 1977; *Career* farmer; *Style* - Sir George Wombwell, Bt; Oulston Hall, Oulston, York (☎ Coxwold 435)

WOMERSLEY, Sir Peter John Walter; 2 Bt (UK 1945), of Grimsby, Co Lincoln; s of late Capt John Walter Womersley (ka 1944) and gs of Rt Hon Sir Walter Womersley, 1 Bt, PC (d 1961); *b* 10 Nov 1941; *Educ* Charterhouse and RMA Sandhurst; *m* 1968, Janet Margaret, da of Alastair Grant; 2 s; *Heir* s, John Gavin Grant Womersley, b 7 Dec 1971; *Career* served Regular Army, offr cadet at Sandhurst to 1962, 2 Lt King's Own Roy Border Regt 1962, Lt 1964, ret 1968; *Style* - Sir Peter Womersley, Bt; Sunnycroft, The Street, Bramber, Steyning, Sussex

WOOD, Lady; Betty (Dorothy Elizabeth Emory); da of Harry Chubb, CBE; *m* 1936, Sir Ian Wood, 3 & last Bt (d 1946); *Style* - Lady Wood; Highcroft Cottage, Milford, Godalming, Surrey

WOOD, Hon Edward Orlando Charles; s of Baron Holderness, PC, DL (Life Peer); *b* 1951; *m* 1977, Joan H, da of John Pinches; *Style* - The Hon Edward Wood

WOOD, Ian Clark; s of John Wood; *b* 21 July 1942; *Educ* Robert Gordon's Coll Aberdeen, Aberdeen U; *m*, Helen, nee Macrae; 3 s; *Career* md John Wood Gp (Aberdeen) Ltd; *Style* - Ian Wood Esq; Marchmont, 42 Rubislaw Den South, Aberdeen (☎ 33625)

WOOD, Hon Mrs (Joan Mary); *née* Wise; da of 1 Baron Wise, DL; *b* 27 Sept 1912; *m* 1938, John Wood; 3 s, 1 da; *Style* - The Hon Mrs Wood; Ham Farm, Berrow, Burnham-on-Sea, Somerset

WOOD, Joseph Neville; CBE (1978); s of Robert Hind Wood (d 1973); *b* 25 Oct 1916; *Educ* Johnston Sch Durham, LSE; *m* 1, 1944, Elizabeth, nee May (d 1959); 3 da; m 2, 1965, Josephine, nee Dane; *Career* civil servant 1935, Assist Sec Miny of Transport & Civil Aviation 1951, Far East Rep 1952-55, Under- Sec 1961, Ch Highway Admin Miny of Transport 1967-68, Chamber of Shipping 1968 (dir 1972-75), Dir-Gen Gen Cncl Br Shipping 1974-78 (ret), memb Chichester DC 1979; *Recreations* gardening; *Style* - Joseph Wood Esq, CBE; Barbers Cottage, Heyshott, Midhurst, W Sussex (☎ Midhurst 4282)

WOOD, Lady Joanna Victoria; da of 3 Earl of Halifax; *b* 1980; *Style* - Lady Joanna Wood

WOOD, Robert Eric; CBE (1972); s of Robert Wood (d 1959); *b* 6 May 1909; *Educ* Birkenhead Inst, Liverpool U; *m* 1935, Beatrice May, nee Skinner; 1 s, 1 da; *Career* dir Leicester Polytech 1969-73, princ Leicester Tech Coll 1953-69, v-chm Nat Advsy Cncl Education for Industry & Commerce 1967-72; memb: Cncl Tech Education and Training in Overseas Countries 1962-66, Cncl Nat Academic Awards 1964-70; *Recreations* voluntary service; *Style* - Robert Wood Esq, CBE; Gapler, Peppers Lane, Burton Lazars, Melton Mowbray, Leics (☎ Melton Mowbray 4576)

WOOD, René Victor; s of Frederick Wood (d 1973); *b* 4 Oct 1925; *Educ* Jesus Coll Oxford; *m* 1950, Helen Morag, nee Stewart; *Career* actuary; chm Lifeguard Assurance Gp Ltd, chm Peter Merrick Assoc Ltd, dir Haslemere Estates Ltd, dir

Coalite Gp Ltd, dir Chandos Insurance Co Ltd, dir Colbourne Insurance Co Ltd, dir Welbeck Finance Ltd, dir Wenham & Wemyss Ltd; *Style* - René Wood Esq; Little Woodbury, Newchapel, nr Lingfield, Surrey (☎ 0342 832054)

WOODBINE PARISH, Sir David Elmer; CBE (1964); s of Walter Woodbine Parish (d 1952); *b* 29 June 1911; *Educ* Eton; *m* 1939, Mona Blair McGarel, nee Johnston; 2 da; *Career* kt 1980; industrial consultant; dep chm Marine & Gen Mutual Life Assurance Soc, chm St Thomas's Hosp Medical Sch 1971-81, chm City & Guilds of London Institute 1967-78, chm Bovis Ltd 1959-66; *Recreations* travel, music; *Clubs* Boodle's; *Style* - Sir David Woodbine Parish CBE; The Glebe Barn, Pulborough, Sussex (☎ 07982 2613)

WOODFIELD, Philip John; CB (1974), CBE (1963); s of Ralph Woodfield; *b* 30 Aug 1923; *Educ* Alleyn's Sch Dulwich, King's Coll London; *m* 1958, Diana, da of Sydney Herington; 3 da; *Career* PUS NI Off 1981-, Dep Sec Home Off 1974-81, served WW II RA, subsequently NI & Home Offs; *Style* - Philip Woodfield Esq CB CBE; 5 Erskine Hill, NW11 (☎ 01 458 4655)

WOODHOUSE, Lady Davidema Katharine Cynthia Mary Millicent; *née* Bulwer-Lytton; da of late 2 Earl of Lytton; *b* 1909; *m* 1, 1931, 5 Earl of Erne (d 1940); 1 s (*see* 6 Earl), 2 da (*see* Lady Rosanagh Raben-Levetzau and Lady Antonia Wardell); m 2, 1945, Col the Hon (Christopher) Montague Woodhouse, DSO, OBE, *qv*; *Style* - Lady Davidema Woodhouse; Willow Cottage, Latimer, Bucks (☎ Little Chalfont 2627)

WOODHOUSE, Hon Davina Mary; (now Countess Alexander of Tunis); da of 4 Baron Terrington; *b* 12 April 1955; *m*, 1981, 2 Earl Alexander of Tunis, *qv*; *Career* Lady in Waiting to HRH The Princess Margaret, Countess of Snowdon 1975-79; Extra Lady in Waiting 1979-; *Style* - The Rt Hon Countess Alexander of Tunis; Flat 5, 171 Sussex gdns, W2 (☎ 01 262 9844)

WOODHOUSE, Hon Georgina Caroline; da of 4 Baron Terrington; *b* 1946; *Style* - The Hon Georgina Woodhouse; 171 Sussex gdns, W2 (☎ 01 723 2836)

WOODHOUSE, James Stephen; s of Rt Rev John Walker Woodhouse (d 1956); *b* 21 May 1933; *Educ* St Edward's Sch Oxford, St Cat's Cambridge; *m* 1957, Sarah Maud, da of Col Hubert Blount MC (d 1979); 3 s, 1 da; *Career* headmaster Lancing Coll 1981-, headmaster Rugby Sch 1967-81, undermaster and master of The Queen's Scholars Westminster Sch 1963-67, assist master Westminster Sch 1957-63; *Recreations* sailing, music, hill walking, natural history; *Clubs* East India, Sports and Public Schools; *Style* - James Woodhouse Esq; The Old Farmhouse, Lancing College, Sussex

WOODHOUSE, Hon (Christopher) Montague; DSO (1943), OBE (1944); s of 3 Baron Terrington, KBE (d 1961), and hp of bro, 4 Baron Terrington; *b* 11 May 1917; *Educ* Winchester, New Coll Oxford (MA); *m* 1945, Lady Davidema, da of 2 Earl of Lytton, KG, PC, GCSI, GCIE (d 1947), and widow of 5 Earl of Erne; 2 s, 1 da; *Career* Dir-Gen Roy Inst of Int Affairs, and Dir of Studies 1955-59, MP (C) Oxford 1959-66, and 1970-74, Parly Sec Miny of Aviation 1961-62, Joint Under-Sec of State Home Office 1962-64, Dir Educ and Training CBI 1966-70, Fell Trin Hall Cambridge 1950; FRSL 1951, Special Memb Acad of Athens 1980; dir IDC Gp; *Style* - The Hon Christopher Woodhouse DSO, OBE; Willow Cottage, Latimer, Bucks (☎ Little Chalfont 2627)

WOODHOUSE, The Rt Hon Mr Justice; Rt Hon Sir (Arthur) Owen; KBE (1981), DSC (1944), PC (1974); s of A J Woodhouse; *b* 18 July 1916; *Educ* Napier Boys' H S, Auckland U; *m* 1940, Margaret Leah Thorp; 4 s, 2 da; *Career* served 1939-45 War; assist to naval attaché HM Embassy Belgrade 1945; a judge of the Supreme Court New Zealand 1961-; *Style* - The Rt Hon Mr Justice Woodhouse KBE DSC PC; Judge's Chambers, Box 1606, Wellington, New Zealand

WOODROW, Maj-Gen Albert John; MBE (1949); s of Frederick Henry Woodrow (d 1940); *b* 3 June 1919; *Educ*

Nunthorpe, Sheffield U; *m* 1944, Elizabeth, da of Maj Sir J T Prestige (d 1962); 2 s, 1 da; *Career* Roy Signals 1940, CO 1 Div Signals 1961-63, Br Army Staff Washington DC 1963-65, Cdr Training Bde Roy Signals 1965-68, Dir Public Relations (Army) 1968-70, Maj-Gen 1970, Col Cmdt RS 1970-78 (ret); dir Security (Army) 1973-78; *Clubs* Army & Navy; *Style* - Maj-Gen Albert Woodrow MBE; Hookers Green, Bishopsbourne, nr Canterbury, Kent (☎ Bridge 830264)

WOODRUFF, Hon Mrs (Marie Immaculée Antoinette); *née* Lyon-Dalberg-Acton; da of 2 Baron Acton, KCVO (d 1924); *b* 1905; *m* 1933, John Douglas Woodruff, CBE (d 1978); *Career* Dame of Honour and Devotion of Sovereign Order of Malta; has Cross Pro Ecclesia et Pontifice; *Style* - The Hon Mrs Woodruff; Marcham Priory, Abingdon, Oxon

WOODS, Alan Thomas De-Lima; s of Herbert De-Lima Woods (d 1970); *b* 19 Oct 1924; *Educ* Epsom Coll; *m* 1956, Sylvia Rose, nee Read; 1 s, 1 da; *Career* slr; sr ptnr Bird & Bird, chm Society for Computers & Law 1973-78, trustee of Nat Law Library; *Recreations* walking; *Style* - Alan Woods Esq; 2 Grays Inn sq, WC1 (☎ 01 242 6681)

WOODS, Basil Joseph Pontifex; *Career* chm Allied Steel and Wire (specialist co involving merger of GKN and BSC elements) 1981-, dir corporate planning and ec affairs GKN; MA Cantab, BEcon; *Style* - Basil Woods Esq; c/o GKN, Group Head Office, Smethwick, Warley, W Midlands B66 2R2

WOODS, Rex Salisbury; s of Henry Thomas Woods (d 1916); *b* 15 Feb 1891; *Educ* Dulwich Coll, Cambridge U, St George's Hosp London U; *m* 1918, Irene Charlotte CBE, TD, nee Pickering; 2 da (1 s decd); *Career* GP/surgeon, Médaille d'Argent d'Honneur de l'Education Physique et des Sports, République Française 1947, hon life memb Br Assoc Sport and Medicine; surgical specialist to insurance cos; Maj RAMC WW II; *Recreations* golf, rugby; *Clubs* Br Sportsman's, Cambridge County, Hawks, Pitt, Achilles, Oxford and Cambridge Golfing Soc; *Style* - Rex Woods Esq; 4 Manor ct, Grange rd, Cambridge; 40 Green st, Cambridge

WOODS, Maj-Gen Thomas Frederic Mackie; CB (1960), OBE (1945); s of Dr A A Woods (d 1948); *b* 14 July 1904; *Educ* St Paul's Sch, Trin Coll Dublin U; *m* 1930, Juliet Frances, nee Rogers; 2 da; *Career* RAMC 1927, served WW II, seconded to Miny of Food 1946-48, Cmdt RAMC Depot 1951-54, Admin HQ London Dist 1954-56, DDMS HQ 1 (BR) Corps 1956, Maj-Gen 1957, Queen's Hon Physician 1959-61; *Recreations* sailing, fishing; *Style* - Maj-Gen Thomas Woods CB OBE; White Lodge, Berwick St James, Salisbury, Wilts (☎ Stapleford 389)

WOODS, Hon Mrs; Hon Victoria Venetia; da of late 5 Baron Stanley of Alderley, KCMG; *b* 1917; *m* 1942, Lt-Cdr James Douglas Woods, Roy Canadian Naval Vol Res; 2 da; *Style* - The Hon Mrs Woods; 31 Boswell av, Toronto 180, Ontario, Canada

WOOKEY, Eric Edgar; MC (1916); s of Edgar Wookey (d 1930); *b* 11 Jan 1892; *Educ* Haverford West G S, Clevedon Coll Bristol U, Roy Dental Hosp London; *m* 1927, Doris Kathleen, nee Fenner (d 1976); 1 s, 2 da; *Career* dental surgeon of Wimpole St 1933-68 (ret); sr dental surgeon Roy Free Hosp 1936-58, hon consultant Dental Surgeon 1958-68, fndr memb Br Soc of Medical and Dental Hypnosis (past-pres & chairman of cncl); *Recreations* piano, numismatics, philately, horology; *Style* - Eric Wookey Esq MC; 51 Lake View, Edgware, Middx (☎ 958 6029)

WOOLFORD, Harry Russell Halkerston; OBE (1970); s of Henry Woolford (d 1941); *b* 23 May 1905; *Educ* Roy Scottish Acad, Edinburgh Coll of Art; *m* 1932, Agnes Henderson, nee Philip; 1 da; *Career* freelance consultant on the conservation of pictures, ch restorer The National Galleries of Scotland until 1970 (ret), supervisor of the evacuation and conservation of the National Galleries of Scotland 1940; *Clubs* Scottish Arts; *Style* - Harry Woolford Esq, OBE; Dean Park House, Golf Course rd, Bonnyrigg, Midlothian (☎ 031 663 7949)

WOOLLAM, John Victor; s of Thomas Alfred Woollam; *b* 14 Aug 1927; *Educ* Liverpool U; *m* 1964, Lavinia Rosamund Ela, nee Snow; 2 s; *Career* barr; MP (C) W Derby Division of Liverpool 1954-64, Parly Private Sec to Min of Labour 1960-62; *Recreations* philately; *Style* - John Woollam Esq; 3 South Hill Grove, Oxton, Birkenhead, Merseyside (☎ 051 652 0885)

WOOLLCOMBE, Victor Rupert De Ambrosis; s of Frank Rupert Woollcombe, MC (d 1968); *b* 9 July 1921; *Educ* Sherborne Sch; Magdalene Cambridge; *m* 1947, Elisabeth Hume, nee Harvey; 1 s, 3 da; *Career* Captain Royal Artillery, Tunisia, Italy; solicitor (Walker Martineau & Co); *Style* - Victor Woollcombe Esq; Berryfield, Much Hadham, Herts

WOOLLETT, Maj-Gen John Castle; CBE (1957, OBE 1955), MC (1945), RE (ret); s of John Castle Woollett (d 1921); *b* 5 Nov 1915; *Educ* St Benedict's Sch, RMA Woolwich, St John's Coll Cambridge; *m* 1, 1941, Joan Eileen, nee Stranks (m dis 1957); 2 s (1 s decd); m 2, 1959, Helen Wendy, nee Braithwaite; 2 step s; *Career* cmmnd RE 1935, served 1939-45 and Korea; Maj-Gen; Ch Engr BAOR 1967-70 (ret), Col Cmdt RE 1973-78, Princ Planning Inspector DOE 1975-; *Recreations* cruising, shooting; *Clubs* Army & Navy, Roy Cruising, Roy Ocean Cruising, Roy Lymington Yacht; owner of yacht: 'Cymbeline'; *Style* - Maj-Gen John Woollett, CBE, MC; 42 Rhinefield Close, Brockenhurst, Hants (☎ Brockenhurst 2417)

WOOLLEY, Baron (Life Peer UK 1967); Harold Woolley; CBE (1958), DL (Cheshire 1969); s of William Woolley, JP, of Blackburn; *b* 6 Feb 1905; *Educ* Blackburn G S, Lancs Sch of Ag; *m* 1, 1926, Martha (d 1936), da of William Jeffs, of Cheshire; 4 s; m 2, 1937, Hazel (d 1975), da of Thomas Archer Jones, of Denbighshire; 2 da; *Career* kt 1964; Pres NFU 1960-66; *Style* - The Rt Hon Lord Woolley CBE DL; Hatton House Farm, Hatton Heath, Chester (☎ Tattenhall 356)

WOOLLEY, Hon David Jeffs; 3 s of Baron Woolley, CBE, DL; *b* 11 Jan 1934; *Educ* Dauntsey's Sch, Seale Hayne Ag Coll; *m* 1958, Freda, da of Alfred Smith Walker, of Barrow-in-Furness; 2 s, 1 da; *Style* - The Hon David Woolley; 3050 Spencer dve, W Vancouver, BC, Canada

WOOLLEY, Hon Harold Ewart; 2 s of Baron Woolley, CBE, DL; *b* 10 July 1929; *Educ* Woodhouse Grove Sch Yorks. BC U; *m* 1954, Margaret, da of Alderman Thomas Bennett, JP, of Worcester; 1 s, 2 da; *Career* MD, FRCS; *Style* - The Hon Harold Woolley; 1350 Laurier av, Vancouver, BC, Canada

WOOLLEY, Hon Peter Jeffs; 4 s of Baron Woolley, CBE, DL; *b* 11 Jan 1934; *Educ* Dauntsey's Sch, Trin Hall Cambridge; *m* 1960, Lois, da of Edward Chanter; 3 da; *Career* CA; *Style* - The Hon Peter Woolley; 2660 Queen's av, W Vancouver, BC, Canada

WOOLLEY, Rev (Alfred) Russell; s of Alfred Walter Woolley (d 1934); *b* 10 Sept 1899; *Educ* King Edward VI Camp Hill G S, Wadham Coll Oxford, Trin Coll Cambridge, Westcott House Cambridge; *m* 1933, Lina Mariana, da of Col B Hopkinson CMG FRS (d 1918); 4 s, 3 da; *Career* headmaster Scarborough Coll 1933-37 and Wellingborough G S 1937-45, Educn Sec Oxford U Appts Ctee 1945-62, ordained 1960; memb: Oxon Educn Ctee 1955-62, governing body Milton Abbey Sch 1955-74 & Lindisfarne Coll 1961-77; *Recreations* reading, walking, travel; *Style* - The Rev Russell Woolley; Gestingthorpe Hall, nr Halstead, Essex (☎ 0787 60638)

WOOLLEY, Hon William Graham; s of Baron Woolley, CBE, JP; *b* 27 Oct 1927; *Educ* Wrekin Coll; *m* 1955, Joan (d 1974), da of Ralph Rowlands, of Flintshire; 2 s, 1 da; *Style* - The Hon William Woolley; Hatton Hall, Hatton Heath, Cheshire

WOOLMER, Kenneth John; MP (L) Batley and Morley 1979-; s of Joseph William Woolmer (d 1979); *b* 25 April 1940; *Educ* Kettering G S, Leeds U; *m* 1961, Janice, nee Chambers; 3 s; *Career* Cnclr Leeds CC 1970-78, W Yorks MCC 1973-80, Leader of Opposition 1977-79; lecturer of economics: Leeds U 1963-66 & 1968-79, Ahmadu Bello U Nigeria 1966-

68; *Recreations* football, cricket, walking; *Style* - Kenneth Woolmer Esq, MP; House of Commons, Westminster, SW1

WOOLTON, 3 Earl of (UK 1956); Simon Frederick Marquis; also Baron Woolton (UK 1939), Viscount Woolton (UK 1953), and Viscount Walberton (UK 1956); s of 2 Earl of Woolton (d 1969, s of 1 Earl of Woolton, CH, PC, JP, DL, sometime Controller of Civilian Boots and Min of Food, who gave the world the eponymous pie) by his 2 w Cecily, Baroness Forres, *qv*; *b* 24 May 1958; *Clubs* Royal & Ancient (St Andrews), New (Edinburgh), Brooks's; *Style* - The Rt Hon Earl of Woolton; Glenogil, by Forfar, Angus (☎ 03565 224); 31 Tite st, SW3 (☎ 01 352 1333)

WOOLTON, Countess of; Margaret Eluned; da of Richard Thomas, of N Wales; *m* 1962, as his 2 w, 1 Earl of Woolton, CH, PC, JP, DL (d 1964); *Career* MB, ChB; *Style* - The Rt Hon The Countess of Woolton; The Old Vicarage, Walberton, Arundel, Sussex

WOOTTON OF ABINGER, Baroness (Life Peeress UK 1958); Barbara Frances Wootton (continues to be known by last name despite 2 marriage); CH (1977); s of Dr James Adam, Fellow and Sr Tutor Emmanuel Coll Cambridge, by Adela, da of Arthur Kensington; *b* 14 April 1897; *Educ* Perse H S for Girls Cambridge, Girton Cambridge; *m* 1, 1917, John Wootton (d of wounds 1917); m 2, 1935, George Wright (d 1964); *Career* Prof Soc Studies London U 1948-52, Govr BBC 1950-56; chm Nat Parks Commission 1966-68, Dep Spkr Ho Lds 1967-; late JP London; *Style* - The Rt Hon Baroness Wootton of Abinger CH; High Barn, Abinger Common, Dorking, Surrey (☎ 730180)

WORDEN, Prof Alastair Norman; s of Dr C N G J Worden (d 1959); *b* 23 April 1916; *Educ* Queen Elizabeth's Sch Barnet, St John's Cambridge, London U, Zürich U; *m* 1, Agnes Marshall, nee Murray; 2 s; m 2, Dorothy Mary, nee Peel; 1 s, 1 da; *Career* Veterinary Medicine, Prof of Toxicology Bath U 1973-, Fellow of Univ College Cambridge 1971-, chairman Huntingdon Research Centre 1951-78, Milford Research Prof Wales U 1945-50; *Recreations* history, natural history, sport, travel; *Clubs* Athenaeum, United Oxford and Cambridge U; *Style* - Prof Alastair Worden; Cross Keys Orchard, Hemingford Abbots, Cambridge (☎ 0480 62434); Wolfson Coll, Cambridge (☎ 0223 354096)

WORLOCK, Hon Mrs; Hon Ann; da of Baron Edmund-Davies, PC (Life Peer); *b* 1936; *m* 1959, Frederick Cecil Worlock, MB, BChir, MRCS, LRCP; *Style* - The Hon Mrs Worlock; The Monastery, Fladbury, Pershore, Worcs

WORRALL, Air Vice-Marshal John; CB (1963), DFC (1940); s of John Ridley Slowe Worrall (d 1937); *b* 9 April 1911; *Educ* Cranleigh, RAF Coll Cranwell, London U; *m* 1967, Barbara Jocelyne, nee Robb; 2 s, 1 step s, 1 step da; *Career* RAF 1931-63 (ret): Air Vice-Marshal 1958, Air Offr Adminve HQs Flying Training Cmd 1956-58, Assist Ch Air Staff Training Air Miny 1958-60, Sr Air Staff Offr Middle East Air Force 1960-63; first md Advertising Agency Poster Bureau London 1964-65; *Recreations* sailing, surf sailing; *Style* - Air Vice-Marshal John Worrall, CB, DFC; Calle Ramon Llull 49, Alqueria, Blanca (Santanyi), Mallorca, Spain (☎ Mallorca 653873)

WORSLEY, Hon Lady - Hon Bridget; *née* Assheton; da of 1 Baron Clitheroe; *b* 1926; *m* 1955, Sir (William) Marcus John Worsley, 5 Bt; *Career* late WRNS; *Style* - The Hon Lady Worsley; 25 Flood st, SW3; Hovingham Hall, York

WORSLEY, Lord; Charles John Pelham; s and h of 7 Earl of Yarborough, JP; *b* 5 Nov 1963; *Style* - Lord Worsley

WORSLEY, Hon Mrs (Carolyn Wynyard); da of 4 Viscount Hardinge (d 1979); *b* 1932; *m* 1954, John Arthington, s of Col Sir William Worsley, 4 Bt (d 1973), of Hovingham Hall, York, and bro of HRH Duchess of Kent and Sir Marcus Worsley, 5 Bt, JP; 3 s, 2 da; *Style* - The Hon Mrs Worsley; RRZ, Uxbridge, Ontario (☎ 852 6220)

WORSLEY, Sir (William) Marcus John; 5 Bt (UK 1838), of Hovingham, Yorkshire, JP (N Yorks 1957), DL (1978); s of Col Sir William Worsley, 4 Bt (d 1973, gggggs of Thomas Worsley, whose wife's maternal great-grandfather was Oliver Cromwell, so that the marriage of the present Bt's sis Katharine to HRH the Duke of Kent in 1961 was a beautiful instance of historical reconciliation between the family of the regicide and that of his victim); *b* 6 April 1925; *Educ* Eton, New Coll Oxford; *m* 1955, Hon Bridget Assheton, da of 1 Baron Clitheroe; 3 s, 1 da; *Heir* s, William Ralph (b 12 Sept 1956, educ Harrow; 2 Lt QOY TAVR); *Career* MP (C) for Keighley 1959-64, MP (C) for Chelsea 1966-75; Church Commissioner 1976-; chm Nat Trust Properties Cttee 1980-; Pres Royal Forestry Soc of England Wales & NI 1980-; served WW II India & W Africa Green Howards; *Recreations* reading, walking, travel; *Clubs* Yorkshire (York); *Style* - Sir Marcus Worsley, Bt, JP, DL; Hovingham Hall, York (☎ Hovingham 206)

WORSLEY, Gen Sir Richard Edward; KCB (1976), OBE (1964); s of H Worsley, of Grey Abbey, Co Down; *b* 29 May 1923; *Educ* Radley; *m* 1, 1959, Sarah Mitchell; 1 s, 1 da; m 2, 1980, Caroline, Duchess of Fife (Hon Caroline Dewar, da of 3 Baron Forteviot); *Career* QMG 1979-; served WW II & Malaya Rifle Bde; GOC 1 Corps 1976-78; *Clubs* Cavalry & Guards; *Style* - Gen Sir Richard Worsley, KCB, OBE; c/o Barclays Bank, 27 Regent st, W1

WORSTHORNE, Peregrine Gerard; s of Col Alexander Koch de Gooreynd, OBE, late Irish Gds (assumed by deed poll surname of Worsthorne 1923, but reassumed original one 1937; the Col's mother, who was also his f's cous, was Manuela, da of Alexandre de Laski by Joaquima, Marquesa de Souza Lisboa, herself da of José Marques Lisboa, sometime Min Plenipotentiary of Emperor of Brazil to Court of St James), and Baroness Norman, *qv* (whose mother was Lady Alice Bertie, 2 da of 7 Earl of Abingdon, JP, DL); is bro of Simon Towneley, JP, *qv*; it is from the Worsthorne portion of the estates of the old recusant Towneley family that the subject of this entry derives his surname; *b* 22 Dec 1923; *Educ* Stowe, Peterhouse Cambridge, Magdalen Oxford; *m* 1950, Claudia, da of Victor Bertrand de Colasse, of Paris, and former w of Geoffrey Baynham; 1 da; *Career* journalist and writer; assoc ed Sunday Telegraph 1976-; at various times has worked on the Glasgow Herald, The Times, Daily Telegraph; *Clubs* Beefsteak, Garrick; *Style* - Peregrine Worsthorne Esq; Westerlies, Wivenhoe, Essex (☎ 2886); 6 Kempson rd, SW6 (☎ 01 736 0572)

WORTLEY, Prof Ben (Benjamin) Atkinson Wortley; CMG (1978), OBE (1946), QC (1969); s of John Edward Wortley; *b* 16 Nov 1907; *Educ* King James's G S, Leeds U; *m* 1935, Kathleen Mary, da of Augustus Prynne; 2 s, 1 da; *Career* Prof Jurisprudence and International Law Manchester U 1946-75 (now Emeritus); barr 1947, Min of Home Security 1939-43, Instructor Cdr RN (temp) 1943-46, memb Inst Advanced Legal Studies 1947-77, Cncl UNIDROIT 1950-, Rep HM Govt at Int Conferences; *Recreations* literature, gardening, languages; *Clubs* Athenaeum; *Style* - Prof Ben Wortley CMG OBE QC; 24 Gravel Lane, Wilmslow, Cheshire

WRAIGHT, Sir John Richard; KBE (1976), CMG (1962); s of Richard George Wraight (d 1964); *b* 4 June 1916; *Educ* Selhurst G S, London U; *m* 1947, Marquita, nee Elliott; *Career* Maj HAC and RHA 1939-45; FO 1945, Diplomatic Serv 1947, 2 Sec Athens 1948, First Sec Tel Aviv 1950, Washington 1953; Cnsllr Cairo 1959, Brussels and Luxembourg 1962; Min and HM Consul-Gen Milan 1968-73, Ambassador Switzerland 1973-76; *Recreations* music, gardening; *Style* - Sir John Wraight KBE CMG; 35 Jameson st, W8 (☎ 229 1566)

WRAXALL, 2 Baron (UK 1928); George Richard Lawley Gibbs; DL (Avon 1974); s of 1 Baron Wraxall, TD, PC (d 1931, s of Anthony Gibbs, of the extensive banking family and 1 cous of 1 Baron Aldenham) by his 2 w, Hon Ursula Lawley (d 1979), da of 6 & last Baron Wenlock, GCSI, GCIE, KCMG; *b* 16 May 1928; *Educ* Eton, Sandhurst; *Heir* bro,

Hon Eustace Gibbs; *Career* landowner; late Maj N Somerset & Bristol Yeo, also late Lt Coldstream Gds; chm N Somerset Con Assoc 1970-74, Avon County Scout Assoc 1976-; *Recreations* shooting; *Clubs* RAC, Cavalry & Guards; *Style* - The Rt Hon Lord Wraxall, DL; Tyntesfield, Bristol (☎ Flax Bourton 2923)

WRAXALL, Sir Charles Frederick Lascelles; 9 Bt (UK 1813), of Wraxall, Somersetshire; s of Sir Morville Wraxall, 8 Bt (d 1978); *b* 17 Sept 1961; *Educ* ArchBp Tenison's G S Croydon; *Heir* bro, Peter Wraxall; *Career* management t'ning (Woolworth's); *Recreations* football, stamps; *Style* - Sir Charles Wraxall, Bt

WRAXALL, Lady; Irmgard Wilhelmina Maria; da of Alois Larry Schnidrig, of Switzerland; *m* 1956, Sir Morville Wraxall, 8 Bt (d 1978); 2 s, 1 da; *Style* - Lady Wraxall; 10 Orchard Rise, Shirley, Surrey

WRAXALL, Peter Edward Lascelles; s of Sir Morville Wraxall, 8 Bt; *b* 30 March 1967; *Style* - Peter Wraxall Esq

WRENBURY, 3 Baron (UK 1915); John Burton Buckley; s of 2 Baron Wrenbury (d 1940) and Helen, Baroness Wrenbury, *qv*; *b* 18 June 1927; *Educ* Eton, King's Cambridge; *m* 1, 1956 (m dis 1961), Carolyn, da of Col Ian Burn-Murdoch, OBE; m 2, 1961, Penelope, da of Edward Fort, of Dorset; 1 s, 2 da; *Heir* s, Hon William Buckley; *Career* slr 1952, ptnr Thomson Snell & Passmore 1974-; assist legal advsr Nat Tst 1955-56; *Clubs* Oriental; *Style* - The Rt Hon Lord Wrenbury; Oldcastle, Dallington, Heathfield, Sussex (☎ Rushlake Green 400)

WRENBURY, Helen, Baroness; Helen Malise; da of His Hon John Cameron Graham, of Stirlingshire; *m* 1925, 2 Baron Wrenbury (d 1940); 1 s (3 Baron), 1 da (Hon Mrs Homan); *Style* - The Rt Hon Helen, Lady Wrenbury; Church End, Dallington, Heathfield, Sussex

WREY, Sir (Castel) Richard Bourchier; 14 Bt (E 1628), of Trebitch, Cornwall; s of late Edward Castel Wrey, and nephew of 13 Bt (d 1948); *b* 27 March 1903; *Educ* Oundle; *m* 1947, Sybil Mabel Alice, da of Dr George Lubke, of Durban, S Africa; 2 s; *Heir* s, George Richard Bourchier Wrey, 2 Oct 1948; *Career* served 1939-40 in France 2 Lt RASC; joined RN 1940, Lt RNVR 1942; *Style* - Sir Richard Wrey, Bt; Hollamoor, Barnstaple, N Devon

WRIGHT, Hon Mrs (Doreen Julia); *née* Wingfield; da of 8 Viscount Powerscourt, KP, MVO (d 1946); *b* 1904; *m* 1928, FitzHerbert Wright, formerly 15/19 Hussars; 1 s, 3 da; *Style* - The Hon Mrs Wright; Grove End, Pudding Lane, Bright Walton, Newbury, Berks

WRIGHT, Hon Mrs (Emily Ann); *née* Hughes; da of Baron Cledwyn of Penrhos (Life Peer); *b* 1950; *m* 1976, Peter Wright; children; *Style* - The Hon Mrs Wright; Genallt, Bryngwran, Anglesey

WRIGHT, Ernest George; GM (1952), QPM (1957); s of Thomas Bennet Wright (d 1966); *b* 25 Feb 1923; *Educ* Dame Allen's Sch Newcastle; *m* 1955, Lady Sarah Caroline, da of 12 Earl Waldegrave; 2 s (Thomas Geoffrey, David James); *Career* Fl Lt Bomber Command RAF 1942-46, Sr-Supt Colonial Police Service (Kenya) 1947-63, fisheries & recreation man Bristol Water Works Co 1963-, Mendip Dist Cncl 1976-, Wells City Cncl 1976- (Mayor 1979-80); *Recreations* fishing, shooting; *Clubs* Flyfishers', Kenya Flyfishers', and Nairobi and Mombasa; *Style* - Ernest Wright Esq, GM, QPM; Beaumont House, Wells, Somerset (☎ Wells 73983)

WRIGHT, Gerald; s of William Arthur Reginald Wright (d 1967); *b* 9 Sept 1935; *Educ* Monmouth Sch, Cambridge U; *m* 1959, Elizabeth Ann, da of William Harris (d 1974); 3 children; *Career* dir Lintas London 1972-73, chm Lintas Scandinavia 1973-74, dep chm and md Lintas London 1975-80, md Thresher and Co Ltd 1980-; *Recreations* squash, opera, walking, cricket; *Clubs* Reform; *Style* - Gerald Wright Esq; Brambledown, Clarendon Way, Cheslehurst, Kent

WRIGHT, Hon Glyn David; s of Baron Wright of Ashton Under Lyne, CBE (d

1974); *b* 22 May 1940; *Educ* Ashton Tech; *m* 1965, May, da of Frederick Alldridge; 1 da; *Style* - The Hon Glyn Wright; 12 Brookfield Grove, Ashton under Lyne, Lancs

WRIGHT, Hon Mrs - Hon (Jane Anne Caroline); da of 5 Baron Hatherton (d 1969); *b* 1929; *m* 1967, Rev Charles Piachaud Wright; *Style* - The Hon Mrs Wright; 12 St Swithun st, Winchester, Hants

WRIGHT, John Keith; s of James Henry Wright (d 1965); *b* 30 May 1928; *Educ* Tiffins', King's Coll Cambridge; *m* 1958, Thérèse Marie-Claire, nee Aubenas; *Career* under-sec Overseas Dvpt Admin FCO 1971-, FCO 1966-71, MOD 1961-66, UKAEA 1956-61, Economics and Statistics Directorate subsequently Food and Agriculture Directorate 1951-56; *Recreations* economic and mil history, music, radio; *Clubs* Athenaeum, Beefsteak; *Style* - John Wright Esq; 47 Brunswick Gardens, W8; Bowling Corner, Sandwich, Kent

WRIGHT, Malcolm Carter; s of Edward Wright (d 1977); *b* 11 Apr 1938; *Educ* King's Sch Macclesfield; *m* 1964, Susan Helen, nee Winter; 2 s; *Career* jt md R Bailey & Son Ltd, chm Surgical Dressings Manufacturers Association; *Recreations* yachting ('Sunchase'); *Clubs* South Caernarvon Yacht; *Style* - Malcolm Wright Esq; 6 Woodside Mews, Ladybrook rd, Bramhall, Cheshire (☎ 061 485 8308)

WRIGHT, Hon Owen Mortimer; s of Baron Wright of Ashton Under Lyne, CBE (d 1974); *b* 18 Nov 1934; *m* 1960, Barbara, da of Arthur Hudson, of Stalybridge; 1 s, 1 da; *Style* - The Hon Owen Wright; Wingthorne, Scade rd, Newton, Swansea

WRIGHT, Lady Sarah Caroline; *née* Waldegrave; da of 12 Earl Waldegrave; *b* 23 Oct 1931; *m* 1955, Ernest Wright, GM, *qv*; 2 s; *Style* - Lady Sarah Wright; Beaumont House, Wells, Somerset (☎ 73983)

WRIGHT, Stanley Harris; s of John Charles Wright (d 1965); *b* 9 Apr 1930; *Educ* Bolton Sch, Merton Oxford; *m* 1973, Alison Elizabeth, da of Baron Franks, OM, GCMG, KCB, CBE; 1 s; *Career* Bd of Trade 1952, HM Foreign Serv 1955-57, HM Treasury 1958, first sec (financial) British Embassy Washington 1964-66, HM Treasury 1972-, und-sec 1970-72, dir Lazard Bros & Co Ltd 1972-, non exec dir Wilkinson Match Ltd 1974, Law Land Co Ltd 1979 and others; *Recreations* various; *Clubs* Reform, MCC; *Style* - Stanley Wright Esq; 6 Holly pla, NW3 (☎ 01 435 0237)

WRIGHTSON, Charles Mark Garmondsway; s & h of Sir John Wrightson, 3 Bt, TD, DL; *b* 18 Feb 1951; *m* 1975, Stella, da of late George Dean; 1 s (Barnaby Thomas Garmondsway, b 5 Aug 1979); *Style* - Charles Wrightson Esq

WRIGHTSON, Sir John Garmondsway; 3 Bt (UK 1900), of Neasham Hall, Co Durham, TD (1953), DL (Co Durham 1961); s of Col Sir Thomas Wrightson, 2 Bt, TD, JP, DL (d 1950); *b* 18 June 1911; *Educ* Eton; *m* 1939, Hon Rosemary, da of 1 Viscount Dawson of Penn, GCVO, KCB, KCMG, PC (d 1945); 1 s, 3 da; *Heir* s, Charles Mark Garmondsway Wrightson; *Career* served 1939-45 War, Maj 1943; Hon Col 7 LI 1975; High Sheriff Co Durham 1959; Hon DCL Durham 1971; *Style* - Sir John Wrightson, Bt, TD, DL; Neasham Hall, nr Darlington, Co Durham

WRIGHTSON, Hon Lady; Rosemary Monica; *née* Dawson; da of late 1 Visc Dawson of Penn; *b* 1913; *m* 1939, Maj Sir John Garmondsay Wrightson, 3 Bt, *qv*; *Style* - The Hon Lady Wrightson; Neasham Hall, nr Darlington

WRIXON-BECHER, John William Michael; s (by 1 m) and h of Sir William Wrixon-Becher, 5 Bt, MC; *b* 29 Sept 1950; *Educ* Harrow; *Style* - John Wrixon-Becher Esq

WRIXON-BECHER, Maj Sir William Fane; 5 Bt (UK 1831), MC; s of Sir Eustace William Windham Wrixon-Becher, 4 Bt (d 1934); *b* 7 Sept 1915; *Educ* Harrow, Magdalene Cambridge; *m* 1, 1946 (m dis 1960), Hon Mrs (Ursula

Vanda Maud) Bridgewater (now Countess of Glasgow, *qv*); 1 s, 1 da; m 2, 1960, Hon Mrs Yvonne Margaret Mostyn (former w of Hon Roger Lloyd-Mostyn, now 5 Baron Mostyn, *qv*), da of A Stuart Johnson, of Henshall Hall, Congleton, Cheshire; *Heir* s, John Wrixon-Becher; *Career* temp Maj Rifle Bde (Supp Reserve), MC WW II; *Style* - Maj Sir William Wrixon-Becher, Bt, MC; 16 Wilton pla, SW1

WROTH, Hon Mrs (Mary Octavia); *née* Addington; da of late 6 Viscount Sidmouth; *b* 1927; *m* 1, 1953, David Christopher Leeming; 1 s; m 2, 1959, David Tilling Wroth; *Style* - The Hon Mrs Wroth; Morleigh Cottage, Savernake Forest, Marlborough, Wilts

WROTTESLEY, 6 Baron (UK 1838); Sir Clifton Hugh Lancelot de Verdon Wrottesley; 14 Bt (E 1642); s of Hon Richard Wrottesley (d 1970) and Hon Mrs Richard Wrottesley, *qv*; suc gf (5 Baron, sixteenth in descent from Sir Walter Wrottesley, a Chamberlain of the Exchequer under Edward IV and himself third in descent from Sir Hugh de Wrottesley, KG (one of the original members of the Order), who fought in the Black Prince's division at Crécy) 1977; *b* 10 Aug 1968; *Heir* half unc, Hon Mark Wrottesley; *Career* patron of three livings; *Style* - The Rt Hon Lord Wrottesley; Dummer House, Basingstoke, Hants

WROTTESLEY, Hon Mrs Richard; Georgina Anna; da of Lt-Col Peter Clifton, DSO, JP, DL (s of Percy Clifton, CMG, DSO, TD, who was bro of Sir Hervey Bruce, 5 Bt, but changed his name; Peter was his s by his 2 m with Evelyn, er da of Maj Thomas Leith, DL, nephew of 5 Baron Burgh) by his 2 w Patricia, da of Maj James Gibson-Watt and sis of Baron Gibson-Watt, MC, PC; *b* 1 Sept 1949; *m* 1967, Hon Richard Wrottesley (d 1970), eldest s of 5 Baron Wrottesley (d 1977); 1 s (6 Baron); *Style* - The Hon Mrs Richard Wrottesley; Dummer House, Basingstoke, Hants

WROTTESLEY, Hon Mark; s of 5 Baron Wrottesley, MC (d 1977), by his 2 w Marion; hp to half-n 6 Baron; *b* 21 June 1951; *Educ* St Andrew's Grahamstown (S Africa); *Style* - The Hon Mark Wrottesley

WROTTESLEY, Baroness; Mary Ada Van Echten; da of Edgar Tudhope; *m* 1955, as his 3 w, 5 Baron Wrottesley (d 1977); 2 s; *Style* - The Rt Hon Lady Wrottesley; De Verdon House, Josephine rd, Rondebosch, Cape Province, S Africa

WROTTESLEY, Hon Nicholas Charles; s of 5 Baron Wrottesley, MC, by his 3 w, Mary; *b* 24 Sept 1963; *Style* - The Hon Nicholas Wrottesley

WROTTESLEY, Hon Stephen John; s of 5 Baron Wrottesley, MC, by his 3 w, Mary; *b* 21 Dec 1955; *Educ* Harrow; *Style* - The Hon Stephen Wrottesley

WYATT, Gavin Edward; CMG (1965); s of Edward Adolphus Wyatt (d 1947); *b* 12 Jan 1914; *Educ* Newton Abbot G S; *m* 1950, Mary Mackinnon, nee MacDonald; 1 s, 1 da; *Career* engineer and man, now consultant, ch exec offr and gen man Electricity Corp of Nigeria 1957-62, md E African Power & Lighting Co Ltd 1962-64, dir Projects Dept Europe, Middle East and N Africa Region World Bank 1965-76 (formerly senior engineer); *Recreations* gardening, sailing; *Style* - Gavin Wyatt Esq, CMG; Holne Bridge Lodge, Ashburton, Devon (☎ 52597)

WYATT, Vice-Adm Sir (Arthur) Guy Norris; KBE (1949), CB (1948); s of Arthur Wyatt (ggs of Benjamin, er bro of James the architect, *see* Woodrow Wyatt); is 4 cous once removed of Woodrow Wyatt, *qv*; *b* 8 March 1893; *Educ* RNCs Dartmouth & Osborne; *m* 1922, Anne, da of Hon James Hogue, MLA, of Sydney; *Career* served WW I & II RN, surveys 1918-39; Hydrographer of the Navy 1945-50, ret 1948; *Style* - Vice-Adm Sir Guy Wyatt, KBE, CB; Holly Tree Orchard, Woodbridge, Tasmania 7162, Australia

WYATT, Hon Mrs (Margaret Agnes); *née* Blades; da (twin) of late 1 Baron Ebbisham, GBE; *b* 1908; *m* 1933, Brig Richard John Penfold Wyatt, MC, TD, DL, JP, late Roy Sussex Regt (TA) (d 1954); 2 s; *Style* - The Hon Mrs Wyatt; Cissbury, nr Worthing, Sussex

WYATT, Woodrow Lyle; s of Robert Wyatt (fourth in descent from William Wyatt, er bro of James, the celebrated architect who gave the world the Gothick glories of Fonthill and Ashridge, though the justice of his sobriquet 'The Destroyer' may be gauged by a one time plan of his to demolish the medieval quadrangle and cloisters at Magdalen), fourth cous of Vice-Adm Sir Guy Wyatt, *qv*; *b* 4 July 1918; *Educ* Eastbourne Coll, Worcester Coll Oxford; *m* 1 (m dis), Susan; m 2, 1948 (m dis 1956), Nora Robins; m 3, 1957 (m dis 1966), Lady Moorea Hastings (now Black), da of 15 Earl of Huntingdon by his 1 w, Cristina; 1 s (Pericles); m 4, 1966, Verushka (Veronica), nee Racz, widow of Dr Laszlo Banszky; 1 da; *Career* chm Horserace Totalisator Bd 1976-; Maj WW II; MP (L) Birmingham Aston 1945-55, Leicester Bosworth 1959-70, Parly Under Sec State & Fin Sec War Off 1951; journalist New Statesman, Daily Mirror, Panorama (which started); dir Woodrow Wyatt Hldgs; *Style* - Woodrow Wyatt Esq; Conock Old Manor, Devizes, Wilts (☎ Chirton 214); 19 Cavendish av, NW8 (☎ 01 286 9020)

WYBREW, John Leonard; s of Leonard Percival Wybrew; *b* 27 Jan 1943; *Educ* Bushey G S, Sir John Cass Coll; *m* 1967, Linda Gillian, da of John Frederick Long; 1 s, 2 da; *Career* life man and actuary Time Assurance Soc 1971-2, gen man and dir Windsor Life Assurance Co Ltd and World Wide Assurance Co Ltd 1972-76, md Windsor Life Assurance Co Ltd 1976-; *Recreations* horses, sailing; *Clubs* East India, Public Schools Club, 59 Club; *Style* - John Wybrew Esq; The Firs, Potter Row, Great Missenden, Bucks (☎ GM 4297)

WYFOLD, 3 Baron (UK 1919); Sir Hermon Robert Fleming Hermon-Hodge; 3 Bt (UK 1902); s of 2 Baron Wyfold, DSO, MVO (d 1942), by Dorothy, da of Robert Fleming and aunt of Peter Fleming the travel writer and Ian Fleming, the creator of James Bond; *b* 26 June 1915; *Educ* Eton, Le Rosey Switzerland; *Heir* none; *Career* Capt Gren Gds (reserve); dir Robert Fleming Hldgs & other cos; *Recreations* gardening; *Clubs* Carlton, Pratt's, Metropolitan (New York); *Style* - The Rt Hon Lord Wyfold; Sarsden House, Churchill, Oxon (☎ Kingham 226)

WYLDBORE-SMITH, Maj-Gen Sir (Francis) Brian; CB (1964), OBE (1944), DSO (1943); s of William Reginald Wyldbore-Smith (d 1943); *b* 10 July 1913; *Educ* Wellington Coll; *m* 1944, Molly Angela Cayzer, yr da of 1 Baron Rotherwick; 5 children; *Career* Maj-Gen Middle East, Far E, France, Italy, Germany; dep Constable of Dover Castle 1965-68, ret 1968; dir Con Pty Bd of Finance 1970; kt 1980; *Recreations* shooting, hunting; *Clubs* Bucks, Naval and Military; *Style* - Maj-Gen Sir Brian Wyldbore-Smith, CB, OBE, DSO; Grantham House, Grantham, Lincs (☎ 4705)

WYLDBORE-SMITH, Hon Lady (Molly Angela); *née* Cayzer; da of 1 Baron Rotherwick; *b* 1917; *m* 1944, Maj-Gen Sir Brian Wyldbore-Smith, CB, DSO, OBE (gggs of Sir John Smith, 2 Bt); 1 s, 4 da; *Style* - The Hon Lady Wyldbore-Smith; Grantham House, Grantham, Lincs

WYNDHAM, Hon Constance Rose; da of 7 Baron Leconfield and (2) Egremont; *b* Dec 1980

WYNDHAM, Hon Mrs Everard - Ruth Constance; da of late Hubert Delaval Astley; *b* 5 March 1900; *m* 1920, Col the Hon Everard Humphrey Wyndham, MC (s of 2 Baron Leconfield); 1 s, 1 da; *Style* - The Hon Mrs Wyndham; Caversfield, Bicester, Oxon

WYNDHAM, Hon Harry Hugh Patrick; s of late 6 Baron Leconfield and (1) Egremont, and Pamela Wyndham, gda of 5 Earl of Dunraven and Mount-Earl; hp to bro, 7 and 2 Baron; *b* 28 Sept 1957; *Style* - The Hon Harry Wyndham

WYNDHAM, Hon Jessica Mary; da of 7 Baron Leconfield and (2) Egremont; *b* 1979

WYNDHAM, Hon Mark Hugh; MC; s of late 5 Baron Leconfield, DSO and Gladys, da of late Fitzroy Farquhar, OBE (s of 3 Bt); *b* 1921; *m* 1947, Anne, da of Hon Reginald Winn (s of 2 Baron St Oswald); 1 s, 2 da (*see* Lord Charles

Spencer-Churchill); *Career* late Capt 12 R Lancers, chm C of E Children's Soc; wounded twice War M East and Italy 1939-45; *Style* - The Hon Mark Wyndham, MC; Yew Tree Farm, Ascott, Shipston-on-Stour, Warwicks

WYNDHAM, Hon Ursula Constance; da of late 5 Baron Leconfield, DSO, and Gladys, da of late Fitzroy Farquhar (s of 3 Bt); *b* 1913; *Style* - The Hon Ursula Wyndham; Laundry Cottage, Petworth, Sussex

WYNDHAM-QUIN, Lady Ana; da of 7 Earl of Dunraven and Mount-Earl; *b* 1972; *Style* - Lady Ana Wyndham-Quin

WYNDHAM-QUIN, Hon Valentine Maurice; s of late 5 Earl of Dunraven and Mount-Earl, CB, DSO, and Lady Eva Bourke, da of 6 Earl of Mayo; hp of nephew, 7 Earl; *b* 22 May 1890; *Educ* Eton; *m* 1919, Marjorie Elizabeth (d 1969), da of late Rt Hon Ernest George Pretyman; 3 da (*see* Lord Roderic Pratt, Marchioness of Salisbury, Dowager Baroness Egremont); *Career* Capt RN (ret) 1914-18 War (despatches four times), Naval Attaché Buenos Aires 1945; *Clubs* White's and Roy Yacht Squadron; *Style* - The Hon Valentine Wyndham-Quin; 66 Cadogan sq, SW1

WYNFORD, 8 Baron (UK 1829); Robert Samuel Best; MBE (Mil 1952), DL (Dorset 1970); s of 7 Baron Wynford (d 1942) and Evelyn (d 1929), da of Maj-Gen Sir Edward Sinclair May, KCB, CMG; *b* 5 Jan 1917; *Educ* Eton, Sandhurst; *m* 1941, Anne, da of Maj-Gen John Minshull-Ford, CB, DSO, MC (d 1948); 1 s, 2 da; *Heir* s, Hon John Best; *Career* landowner and farmer, former Instructor Jt Servs Staff Coll 1957-60; *Recreations* shooting, skiing, tennis; *Clubs* Army & Navy; *Style* - The Rt Hon The Lord Wynford, MBE, DL; Wynford House, Wynford Eagle, Dorchester, Dorset (☎ Maiden Newton 20241)

WYNN, Hon Mrs Arthur - Gladys Catherine; da of late Richard Hanbury Joseph Gurney; *m* 1915, Hon Arthur Romer Wynn (d 1964, s of Hon Charles Wynn (s of 3 Baron Newborough) and unc of 7 Baron); 2 s, 1 da; *Style* - The Hon Mrs Arthur Wynn

WYNN, Hon Mrs (Angela Hermione Ida); *née* Willoughby; da of 11 Baron Middleton, KG, MC, TD (d 1970); *b* 1924; *m* 1947, Lt-Cdr the Hon Charles Henry Romer Wynn, s of 6 Baron Newborough, OBE (d 1965); 2 s; *Style* - The Hon Mrs Wynn; Bunkersland, Withleigh, Tiverton, Devon

WYNN, Hon Charles Henry Romer; s of 6 Baron Newborough, OBE (d 1965); *b* 1923; *m* 1947, Hon Angela Hermione Ida Willoughby, da of late 11 Baron Middleton; 2 s; *Career* Lt-Cdr RN (ret); *Style* - Lt-Cdr The Hon Charles Wynn; Bunkersland, Withleigh, Tiverton, Devon

WYNN, Hon Mrs Rowland - Eleanor Mary Tydfil; da of late Arthur Edmund Smith-Thomas; *m* 1943, Hon Rowland Tempest Beresford Wynn, CBE (d 1977, s of Hon Charles Wynn (s of 3 Baron Newborough) and unc of 7 Baron); *Style* - The Hon Mrs Rowland Wynn; Sunningdale, The Heights, Worthing

WYNN, Hon Robert Vaughan; s and h of 7 Baron Newborough, DSC; *b* 11 Aug 1949; *Educ* Milton Abbey; *Style* - The Hon Robert Wynn

WYNN-WILLIAMS, Lady Penelope; da of 1 Earl Jowitt (ext 1957); *b* 1923; *m* 1943, George Wynn-Williams, FRCS, FRCOG; 2 s, 1 da; *Style* - Lady Penelope Wynn-Williams; 39 Hurlingham Court, SW6; The Hall, Isle of Oxney, Wittersham, Kent

WYNNE, Hon Mrs (Nancy Clare); *née* Eden; da of 6 Baron Henley (d 1962); *b* 1918; *m* 1941, Edmund Ernest Wynne, Lt Reconnaissance Corps; 1 s, 5 da; *Style* - The Hon Mrs Wynne; 580 Lytham rd, Blackpool

WYNNE-JONES, Baron (Life Peer UK 1964); William Francis Kenrick Wynne-Jones; s of Rev T Jones, of India; *b* 8 May 1903; *Educ* Monkton Combe Sch Bath, U Coll Wales, Balliol Oxford; *m* 1, 1928, Ann (d 1969), da of Duncan Drummond, of Perths; 2 da; m 2, 1972, Rusheen, da of Neville Preston; *Career* Chllr Newcastle on Tyne Poly 1976-, late Pro-V-Chllr & Chemistry Prof Newcastle U; *Style* - The Rt Hon Lord Wynne-Jones; Carlyle House, 16 Chelsea Embankment,

SW3 (☎ 01 352 8511)

WYNNE-PARKER, Michael; s of David Boothby Wynne-Parker (d 1955); *b* 20 Nov 1945; *Educ* Lady Manners Sch; *m* 1975, Jennifer, nee Lubbock; 1 s; *Career* chairman Wynne-Parker Financial Management, English-Speaking Union (E Region UK), Cncl for Advancement of Arab-British Understanding in E Anglia, editorial bd of The Monarchist, v-pres Norfolk Ag Assoc, Muscular Dystrophy Soc, memb of Monday Club, Roy Stuart Soc, CLA, Norfolk Soc, Prayer Bk Soc, Richard III Soc, Norfolk & Suffolk Flyfishers' Soc, Clan Hay Soc, Keats Shelley Soc; Papal Medal (Pope Paul VI, Rome 1971); Knight Military & Hospitaller Order of St Lazarus of Jerusalem 1980; *Recreations* antique collecting, fishing, gardening, hunting, travelling, politics; *Clubs* English Speaking Union; *Style* - Michael Wynne-Parker Esq; The Lodge, Saxlingham Thorpe, Norfolk (☎ 0508 470018); 15 Unthank rd, Norwich, Norfolk (☎ 612769)

WYVILL, Marmaduke Charles Asty; s of Marmaduke Wyvill (seventh in descent from D'Arcy Wyvill, yr bro of Sir Marmaduke Wyvill, 5 Bt, unc of 6 Bt and great unc of 7 Bt, since whose death in 1774 the Btcy has been dormant; probable heirs have been traced to a branch of the family settled in Virginia, but terminating, as far as one can see, in the male line with the death (1971) of Newlon D'Arcy Wyvill, probably *de jure* 17 Bt; D'Arcy was himself 11th in descent from Richard Wyvill, one of the 25,000 supporters of Henry VI killed at the rout of Towton 1461; the Wyvills claim descent from Sir Humphrey de Wyvill, of Slingsby Castle, a follower of William the Conqueror); *b* 30 Aug 1945; *Educ* Stowe, RAC Cirencester; *m* 1972, Margaret Ann, da of Maj Sydney Hardcastle, RA; 2 s; *Career* ARICS; lord of the manor of Constable Burton; patron of three livings; *Recreations* shooting, fishing; *Clubs* Brooks's; *Style* - Marmaduke Wyvill Esq; Constable Burton Hall, Leyburn, N Yorks (☎ Bedale 50361)

Y

YARBOROUGH, 7 Earl of (UK 1837); John Edward Pelham; JP (Parts of Lindsey 1965); also Baron Yarborough (GB 1794) and Baron Worsley (UK 1837); s of 6 Earl of Yarborough, DL (d 1966, ggs of 2 Earl, Ld-Lt & custos rotulorum of Lincs, who did something to recoup the outlay involved in his father's munificent hospitality as Commodore of the Roy Yacht Sqdn by offering odds of 1,000 to 1 against a 'Yarborough' turning up in a Whist hand, whereas the actual odds are 1,827 to 1; the term 'Yarborough', meaning an honourless hand, is now standard in Bridge, tho' unhappy the player who often comes across one), and Hon Pamela Douglas-Pennant, da of 3 Baron Penrhyn; *b* 2 June 1920; *Educ* Eton, Trin Cambridge; *m* 1957, Florence Ann Petronel, da of John Upton, JP, of Ingmire Hall, Yorks, by his 2 w (Petronel, nee Fursdon, whose mother was da of Sir William Salusbury-Trelawny, 10 Bt, sometime Capt Roy Cornwall Rangers); 1 s, 3 da; *Heir* s, Lord Worsley; *Career* late Maj Gren Gds, High Sheriff Lincs 1964, V Ld-Lt (formerly V-Lt) 1964-; served WW II France & NW Europe; contested (C) Grimsby 1955; Patron E Midlands Br Legion 1974-; *Clubs* Roy Yacht Sqdn, Cavalry & Guards, Boodle's; *Style* - The Rt Hon Earl of Yarborough JP, HM Vice Lord-Lieut for Lincolnshire; Brocklesby Park, Habrough, S Humberside (☎ Roxton 60242)

YARDE-BULLER, Hon John Francis; s (by 1 m) and h of 4 Baron Churston, VRD; *b* 29 Dec 1934; *Educ* Eton; *m* 1973, Alexandra, da of Anthony Contomichalos; 1 s, 2 da; *Career* late 2 Lt RHG; *Style* - The Hon John Yarde-Buller; Yowlestone House, Puddington, Tiverton, S Devon

YARDE-BULLER, Hon Mrs John - Guendolen; da of late Rev Charles Roots; *m* 1939, Hon Reginald Henry Yarde-Buller (d 1962); 2 s; *Style* - The Hon Mrs

John Yarde-Buller; Le Vallon, Mont Felard, Jersey

YARMOUTH, Earl of; Henry Jocelyn; s and h of 8 Marquess of Hertford; *b* 6 July 1958; *Style* - Earl of Yarmouth

YARROW, Sir Eric Grant; 3 Bt (UK 1916), of Homestead, Hindhead, Frensham, Co Surrey, MBE (1946), DL (Renfrewshire 1970); s of Sir Harold Yarrow, 2 Bt, GBE (d 1962), by his 1 w, Eleanor; *b* 23 April 1920; *Educ* Marlborough, Glasgow U; *m* 1, 1951, Rosemary Ann (d 1957), da of H T Young, of Roehampton SW15; 1 s; m 2, 1959, Annette Elizabeth Françoise (m dis 1975), da of A J E Steven; 3 s (2 twin); *Heir* s, Richard Grant Yarrow, b 21 March 1953; *Career* served 1939-45 War with RE, Maj 1944; chm Yarrow & Co and Yarrow (Shipbuilders) Ltd; chm Yarrow Engineers (Glasgow) Ltd, Y-ARD Ltd, Yarrow Africa Maritime Consultancy (Pty) Ltd and Y-ARD (Australia) (Pty) Ltd; memb exec council of Shipbuilders and Repairers Nat Assoc; hon v-pres Council of Roy Inst of Naval Architects; deacon of Incorporation of Hammermen of Glasgow 1961-62; dir Standard Life Assurance Co; dir Yarrow (Africa) (Pty) Ltd and jt dep chm Clydesdale Bank; OStJ; *Style* - Sir Eric Yarrow, Bt, MBE, DL; Cloak, Kilmacolm, Renfrewshire (☎ 2067)

YARROW, Rosalynde, Lady; Rosalynde; da of Sir Oliver Lodge, LLD, DSc, FRS; *m* 1935, as his 2 w, Sir Harold Yarrow, 2 Bt, GBE (d 1962); 1 da (Mrs Clive Griffiths); *Style* - Rosalynde, Lady Yarrow; 8 Glensanda Court, Montpelier Spa rd, Cheltenham, Glos

YEATS, William Michael Butler; s of William Butler Yeats, the poet, and Bertha, da of William Hyde-Lees, of Pickham Hall, Wroxham Norfolk; *b* 22 Aug 1921; *Educ* St Columba's, Trin Coll Dublin; *m* 1949, Grainne Ni Eigeartaigh, da of late Patrick O'Hegarty, sometime Sec Posts & Telegraphs; 1 s, 3 da; *Career* memb Irish Senate 1951-54 & 1961- (chm 1969-73); V-Pres Euro Parl 1973; dir Cuala Press Ltd; *Style* - William Yeats Esq; Cliff House, Coliemore rd, Dalkey, Co Dublin, Eire

YELVERTON, Barry Goring; s of Barry Yelverton (d 1960, gs of Augustus Yelverton, himself gs of 2 Viscount Avonmore through the 2 Viscount's 3 s, Hon Augustus); *b* 1923; *m* 1950, Frances, da of William Battersby, of Feilding, NZ; 2 s (Ian Foster b 1950, Avon Barry b 1954); *Career* served WW II NZ Forces; if sr male descendant of Hon Augustus Yelverton, is presumably h to Viscountcy of Avonmore (dormant since 1910); *Style* - Barry Yelverton Esq; c/o Bank of New Zealand, Woodville, New Zealand

YERBURGH, Hon Robert Richard Guy; s and h of 2 Baron Alvingham, CBE; *b* 10 Dec 1956; *Style* - The Hon Robert Yerburgh

YORK, 94 Archbishop of (AD 625) 1975-; Most Rev & Rt Hon Stuart Yarworth Blanch; PC (1975); Primate of England and Metropolitan; s of William Blanch; *b* 2 Feb 1918; *Educ* Alleyns Sch Dulwich, St Cat's & Wycliffe Hall Oxford; *m* 1943, Brenda, da of William Coyte; 1 s, 4 da; *Career* DD; Vicar of Eynsham (a village noted for witchcraft), Oxon, 1952-57, Tutor & V-Princ Wycliffe Hall 1957-60 (chm Cncl 1967-); Pro-Chllr Hull U 1975, York U 1977; Bp Liverpool 1966-75; patron of 129 livings, six alternately with others and one conjointly, the Archdeaconries of York, Cleveland and E Riding, and the Canonries in York Minster; the province comprises 14 sees; *Style* - The Most Rev and Rt Hon Archbishop of York, PC; Bishopthorpe, York (☎ 0904 70721)

YORKE, David John Napier Edward; JP (W Sussex); s of Hon Claud Yorke (d 1940); gs of 7 Earl of Hardwicke; *b* 1919; *Educ* Eton, Jesus Cambridge; *m* 1950, Anne Margaret, da of Denis George Mackail; 2 s; *Career* barr 1949, Lloyd's underwriter; *Style* - David Yorke Esq, JP; Gatewick, Steyning, Sussex

YORKE, Lady Jemima Rose; da of Visc Royston (d 1973), gda of 9 Earl of Hardwicke (d 1974) and sis of 10 Earl; *b* 17 May 1969

YORKE, Richard Charles John; s of Hon Claud John Yorke (d 1940); gs of 7

Earl of Hardwicke and hp of 10 Earl; *b* 25 July 1916; *Style* - Richard Yorke Esq

YOUENS, Sir Peter William; CMG (1962), OBE (1960); s of Rev Canon F A C Youens (d 1968); *b* 29 April 1916; *Educ* King Edward VII Sch Sheffield, Wadham Coll Oxford; *m* 1943, Diana Stephanie, nee Hawkins; 2 da; *Career* kt 1965; Colonial Serv 1939, dep ch sec Nyasaland 1953-63, sec to Prime Min and Cabinet Malawi 1964-66 (ret); exec dir Lonrho Ltd 1966-69 (dir 1980-), ptnr Tyzack and Ptnrs Ltd 1969-81, dir Oxford Playhouse Co (Anvil Prods Ltd) 1978; *Recreations* walking, theatre; *Clubs* East India and Sports, Vincent's; *Style* - Sir Peter Youens CMG OBE; The Old Parsonage, Hurstbourne Priors, Whitchurch, Hants

YOUNG, Baroness (Life Peeress UK 1971); Janet Mary Young; da of John Baker and Phyllis, nee Hancock; *b* 23 Oct 1926; *Educ* Dragon Sch Oxford, St Anne's Oxford; *m* 1950, Geoffrey Tyndale Young; 3 da; *Career* memb Oxford City Cncl 1957-72 (Alderman 1967-72); Baroness-in-Waiting to HM 1972-73, Parly Under Sec State Environment 1973-74, V-Chm Con Pty Orgn 1975, dep chm 1977; Min State DES 1979-81, Leader of House of Lords 1981, Chllr of Duchy of Lancaster 1981, Min in charge of Civil Serv 1981; *Style* - The Rt Hon Lady Young; House of Lords, SW1

YOUNG OF DARTINGTON, Baron (Life Peer UK 1978); Michael Young; s of Gibson Young (musician); *b* 9 Aug 1915; *Educ* Dartington Hall, London U; *m* 1, 1945, Joan Lawson; 2 s, 1 da; m 2, 1960, Sasha, da of Raisley Moorsom; 1 s, 1 da; *Career* barr 1939; Sec Res Dept Labour Pty 1945-51; Dir Inst Community Studies 1953-, Tstee Dartington Hall 1942-; memb NEDC 1975-; Pres Consumers' Assoc 1965-, Nat Extension Coll 1971-, ACE 1976-; Dep Chm Dartington Hall 1980-; *Style* - Rt Hon Lord Young of Dartington; 18 Victoria pk sq, E2

YOUNG, Hon Alexandra Janet; da of Baroness Young; *b* 1951; *Style* - The Hon Alexandra Young

YOUNG, Hon Audrey Louise; da of 2 Baron Kennet; *b* 1959; *Style* - The Hon Audrey Young

YOUNG, Hon Alice Matelda Zoë; da of 2 Baron Kennet; *b* 1969; *Style* - The Hon Alice Young

YOUNG, Air Vice-Marshal Brian Pashley; CB (1972), CBE (1960, OBE 1944); s of Kenneth Young of Durban, Natal, South Africa (d 1971); *b* 5 May 1918; *Educ* Michael House, Natal, South Africa and RAF Coll Cranwell; *m* 1942, Patricia, da of late Thomas Cole; 3 s 2 da; *Career* Air V-Marshal; Fighter Command UK and France, Coastal Command Atlantic, Aden, Palestine and Egypt; post War: Air Miny, Bomber Command, NATO (France), Cmdt Gen RAF Regiment to 1973, now Planning Inspector DOE; *Clubs* RAF; *Style* - Air Vice-Marshal Brian Young, CB, CBE; Chapel Walk House, Didmarton, Gloucestershire (☎ Didmarton 661)

YOUNG, His Hon Judge (Christopher Godfrey); s of Dr H G Young MB (d 1949); *b* 9 Sept 1932; *Educ* Bedford Sch, King's Coll London U; *m* 1969, Jeanetta Margaret, nee Vaughan; 1 s; *Career* barr 1957, Circuit Judge 1980-, Liaison Judge with Magistrates for Peterborough Huntingdon and Toseland 1980, Recorder 1975-79, Midland and Oxford Circuit 1959-75; *Recreations* music, natural history, gardening, foreign travel; *Clubs* County (Northampton); *Style* - His Hon Judge Young; School Farm House, Maidwell, Northamptonshire (☎ 0601 28682)

YOUNG, Hon Christopher Ivan; s of Baron Young of Dartington by 1 w Joan; *b* 1946; *Style* - The Hon Christopher Young

YOUNG, Hon David; s of Baron Young of Dartington by 1 w Joan; *b* 1948; *Style* - The Hon David Young

YOUNG, Hon Emma Dorothy; da of Baron Young of Dartington by 1 w Joan; *b* 1956; *Style* - The Hon Emma Young

YOUNG, Hon Emily Tacita; da of 2 Baron Kennet; *b* 1951; *Style* - The Hon Emily Young

YOUNG, Sir Frank George; s of Frank Edgar Young (d 1948); *b* 25 March 1908;

Educ Alleyn's Sch Dulwich, Univ Coll London U (PhD, DSc), Cambridge U (MA); *m* 1933, Ruth Eleanor, da of late Thomas Turner; 3 s, 1 da; *Career* kt 1973, Prof of Biochemistry London U 1942-49, Sir William Dunn Prof of Biochemistry Cambridge U 1949-75, Emeritus 1975-, Master of Darwin Coll Cambridge 1964-76; *Clubs* Athenaeum; *Style* - Sir Frank Young; 11 Bentley rd, Cambridge (☎ 0223 352650)

YOUNG, Gertrude, Lady; Gertrude Annie; da of John Elliott, of Braunton, N Devon; *m* 1912, Sir Cyril Young, 4 Bt; 3 s (1 - late 5 Bt - decd, also Patrick Young, *qv*), 1 da (Mrs Stanley Claremont); *Style* - Gertrude, Lady Young; Le Copacabana, Jardin des Hesperides, Palm Beach, Cannes, Alpes Maritimes, France; 66 Kensington Mans, Trebovir rd, SW5

YOUNG, Hon Mrs (Gillian Margaret); da of late 2 Baron Colgrain; *b* 1925; *m* 1951, Peter Scott Young; 2 s, 2 da; *Style* - The Hon Mrs Young; Stumble Hill, Shipbourne, Tonbridge, Kent

YOUNG, Sir George Samuel Knatchbull; 6 Bt (UK 1813), of Formosa Place, Berkshire, MP (C) Ealing (Acton) 1974-; s of Sir George Young, 5 Bt, CMG (d 1960), by his w Elisabeth (herself er da of Sir Hugh Knatchbull-Hugessen, KCMG, who was in turn n of 1 Baron Brabourne); *b* 16 July 1941; *Educ* Eton, Ch Ch Oxford; *m* 1964, Aurelia, da of Oscar Nemon and Mrs Nemon-Stuart, of Boars Hill, Oxford; 2 s, 2 da; *Heir* s, George Horatio Young, b 11 Oct 1966; *Career* Oppn Whip 1976-79, Under-Sec State DHSS 1979-; economist Nat Economic Development Office 1966-67; Kobler Res Fell U of Surrey 1967-69; memb Lambeth Borough Council 1968-71; economic adviser Post Office Corpn 1969-74; memb GLC 1970-73; *Style* - Sir George Young, Bt, MP; Formosa Place, Cookham, Berks (☎ Bourne End 25519)

YOUNG, Dowager Lady; Joan; da of Rev Frank Bullock-Webster, of Sonning, Berks; *m* 1948, as his 2 w, Sir George Young, 4 Bt, MVO (d 1952); *Style* - Dowager Lady Young; Grove Cottage, Sonning, Berks

YOUNG, Sir John Kenyon Roe; 6 Bt (UK 1821), of Bailieborough Castle, Co Cavan; s of Sir John William Roe Young, 5 Bt (d 1981), by his 1 w, Joan; *b* 23 April 1947; *Educ* Harncourt Sch, Christchurch, Hants; *Heir* unc, Patrick Young; *Style* - Sir John Young, Bt; c/o Mrs Robertson, The Thatched Cottage, Honor End Lane, Gt Missenden, Bucks

YOUNG, Hon Juliet Marguerite; 3 da of Baroness Young; *b* 1962; *Style* - The Hon Juliet Young

YOUNG, Lady; Joy Maureen Agnes; da of A G Clarke, of Southsea, Hants; *m* 1960, as his 2 w, Sir John Young, 5 Bt (d 1981); *Style* - Lady Young

YOUNG, Hon Mr Justice; Hon Sir John McIntosh; KCMG (1975); s of George David Young (d 1956); *b* 17 Dec 1919; *Educ* Geelong G S , BNC Oxford; *m* 1951, Elisabeth Mary, da of Dr E Twining; 1 s, 2 da; *Career* KStJ 1977; barr 1949-74, QC 1961, Lt-Govr Victoria & Ch Justice Supreme Ct of Victoria 1974-, pres Victoria Scout Assoc 1974-, pres St John Cncl Victoria 1975-, Hon Col 4/19 Prince of Wales Light Horse 1978-; *Recreations* riding, golf; *Clubs* Cavalry and Guards (London), Melbourne and Australian; *Style* - The Hon Mr Justice Young KCMG; 17 Jorrett ave, Malvern, Victoria, Australia (☎ 03 206259); Tyrone, Flinders, Victoria, 3929 Australia (☎ 059 89 0212)

YOUNG, Hon Mrs (Lilian Vida Lechmere); *née* Moncreiff; da of 4 Baron Moncreiff (d 1942); *b* 1912; *m* 1942, David Robert Young; 1 s, 1 da; *Style* - The Hon Mrs Young; Tanworth, Fossoway, Kinross-shire

YOUNG, Hon Mopsa Mary; da of 2 Baron Kennet; *b* 1953; *Style* - The Hon Mopsa Young

YOUNG, Patrick Elliott; 2 s of Sir Cyril Young, 4 Bt; hp of n, Sir John Young, 6 Bt; *b* 6 March 1917; *m* 1946, Sadie, da of Laurence Beattie, of Prestwick, Ayrshire; 1 s (Christopher b 1965), 3 da (Patricia b 1947, Veronica b 1949, Nancy b 1952); *Career* late Sub-Lt Hong Kong RNVR,

Japanese POW during WW II; *Style* - Patrick Young Esq; 3625 Lombardy rd, Pasadena, Calif, USA

YOUNG, Hon Rosalind Ann; 2 da of Baroness Young; *b* 1954; *Style* - The Hon Rosalind Young

YOUNG, Hon Sophie Ann; da of Baron Young of Dartington by his 2 w Sasha; *b* 1961; *Style* - The Hon Sophie Young

YOUNG, Sir Stephen Stewart Templeton; 3 Bt (UK 1945), of Partick, Co City of Glasgow; s of Sir Alastair Spencer Templeton Young, 2 Bt, DL (d 1963); *b* 24 May 1947; *Educ* Rugby, Trin Oxford, Edinburgh U; *m* 1974, Viola Margaret, da of Prof Patrick Horace Nowell-Smith (whose mother was Cecil, ggda of Most Rev Hon Edward Vernon-Harcourt, DD, sometime Archbp of York and yr bro of 3 Baron Vernon) by his 1 w, Perilla (da of Sir Richard Southwell & who m subsequently, as his 2 w, Baron Roberthall); 1 s; *Heir* s, Charles Alastair Stephen Young, b 21 July 1979; *Career* slr (Scotland); *Style* - Sir Stephen Young, Bt; 18 Moray pla, Edinburgh 3

YOUNG, Hon (William Aldus) Thoby; s and h of 2 Baron Kennet; *b* 1957; *Style* - The Hon Thoby Young

YOUNG, Hon Toby Daniel Moorsom; s of Baron Young of Dartington by his 2 w Sasha; *b* 1963; *Style* - The Hon Toby Young

YOUNG, Sir William Neil; 10 Bt (GB 1769), of North Dean, Buckinghamshire; s of Capt William Elliot Young (ka 1942), and gs of Sir Charles Young, 9 Bt, KCMG, MVO (d 1944); Sir Charles's w was Clara, da of Sir Francis Elliot, GCMG, GCVO (gs of 2 Earl of Minto, also Envoy Extraordinary & Min Plenipotentiary to the King of the Hellenes 1903-17); *b* 22 Jan 1941; *Educ* Wellington Coll, RMA Sandhurst; *m* 1965, Christine Veronica, da of R B Morley, of Buenos Aires; 1 s, 1 da; *Heir* s, William Lawrence Elliot Young, b 26 May 1970; *Career* formerly Capt 16/5 Queen's Roy Lancers; stockbroker with Phillips & Drew; *Style* - Sir William Young, Bt; 22 Elm Park rd, SW3

YOUNGER OF LECKIE, 3 Viscount (UK 1923); Sir Edward George Younger; 3 Bt (UK 1911), OBE (1940), TD; s of 2 Viscount Younger of Leckie, DSO, TD, JP, DL (d 1946, himself s of 1 Viscount and nephew of 1 & last Baron Blanesburgh, GBE, PC; the 1 Viscount was gggs of George, the founder of the brewing empire), and Maud, er da of Sir John Gilmour, 1 Bt; *b* 21 Nov 1906; *Educ* Winchester, New Coll Oxford; *m* 1930, Evelyn, MBE, da of Alexander McClure, KC, sometime Sheriff of Aberdeen, Kincardine and Banff; 3 s, 1 da; *Heir* s, Rt Hon George Younger, TD, PC, DL, MP; *Career* Lt-Col (ret) Argyll & Sutherland Highlanders (TA); Ld-Lt Stirling & Falkirk 1964-79; served WW II Col Gen Staff; *Style* - Rt Hon Viscount Younger of Leckie OBE TD; Leckie, Gargunnock, Stirling (☎ 281)

YOUNGER, Hon Alexander James; 2 s of 3 Viscount Younger of Leckie, OBE, TD; *b* 5 May 1933; *Educ* Winchester, Worcester Coll Oxford; *m* 1959, Annabelle Christine, da of late Gerald Furnivall, of Bishop's Waltham, Hants; 2 s, 2 da; *Career* late Capt Argyll & Sutherland Highlanders (served Korea 1952); dir Sir J Causton & Sons 1963-68; md Robert Maclehose & Co; *Style* - The Hon Alexander Younger; Wester Leckie, Kippen, Stirlingshire

YOUNGER, Hon Lady (Elizabeth Kirsteen); da of William Duncan Stewart, JP, of Achara, Duror, Argyll; *m* 1934, Rt Hon Sir Kenneth Younger, KBE, PC, MP (L) Grimsby 1945-59, Min State Foreign Affrs 1950-51 (d 1976, 2 s of 2 Viscount Younger of Leckie, DSO, TD, JP, DL); 1 s, 2 da; *Style* - The Hon Lady Younger; 3 Clareville Grove, SW7 (☎ 01 373 2766)

YOUNGER, Rt Hon George Kenneth Hotson; TD (1964), PC (1979), DL (Stirlingshire 1968), MP (C) Ayr 1964-; s and h of 3 Viscount Younger of Leckie, OBE, TD; *b* 22 Sept 1931; *Educ* Winchester, New Coll Oxford; *m* 1954, Diana, da of Capt Gerald Tuck, DSO, RN (ret); 3 s, 1 da; *Career* Sec State Scotland

1979-; Hon Col 154 T'port Regt RCT TAVR 1977- (served BAOR & Korea with Argyll & Sutherland Highlanders); dir Tennant Caledonian Breweries 1977-, memb Roy Co Archers (Queen's Bodyguard for Scotland); stood as U candidate N Lanarks 1959 & Kinross & W Perths 1963 till stood down in favour of Lord Home of the Hirsel (then Sir Alec Douglas-Home, Bt); Scot Con Whip 1965-67, Parly Under-Sec State Devpt Scot Off 1970-74, Min State Def 1974; *Style* - The Rt Hon George Younger TD PC DL MP; Easter Leckie, Gargunnock, Stirlingshire (☎ 274)

YOUNGER, Maj-Gen Sir John William; 3 Bt (UK 1911), of Auchen Castle, Kirkpatrick-Juxta, Co Dumfries, CBE (1969); s of Sir William Robert Younger, 2 Bt (d 1973), by his 1 w, Joan (da of Hon Louis Vanden-Bempde-Johnstone, himself 5 s of 1 Baron Derwent) who m (2) Capt Hubert Pelham-Burn (d 1927) and (3) Dennis Wheatley, the writer; *b* 18 Nov 1920; *Educ* Canford Sch, RMC Sandhurst; *m* 1, 1948, Mrs Stella Jane Dodd (m dis 1952), da of Rev John George Lister; 1 s, 1 da; m 2, 1953, Marcella Granito, Princess Pignatelli di Belmonte, da of Prof Avvocato Roberto Scheggi; *Heir* s, Julian William Richard Younger, b 10 Feb 1950, educ Eton and Grinnell (University, USA); *Career* served 1939-45 War (Middle East POW), late Coldstream Gds, Maj-Gen 1971; dir Management and Support Intelligence, MOD 1973-76, ret 1976, C-in-C St John Ambulance 1980; CStJ; *Style* - Maj-Gen Sir John Younger, Bt, CBE; 23 Cadogan Sq, SW1

YOUNGER, Hon Robert Edward Gilmour; 3 s of 3 Viscount Younger of Leckie, OBE, TD; *b* 25 Sept 1940; *Educ* Winchester, New Coll Oxford; *m* 1972, Helen, da of Eric Hayes (d 1958) and Margaret (sis of Sir John Muir, 3 Bt, TD) and 2 cous of Sir Iain Moncreiffe of that Ilk, 11 Bt; 1 s, 1 da; *Style* - The Hon Robert Younger; Old Leckie, Gargunnock, Stirling (☎ 281)

YOUNGER, Sir William McEwan; 1 Bt (UK 1964), of Fountainbridge, Co and City of Edinburgh, DSO (1942), DL (Midlothian 1956); s of late William Younger (yr bro of 1 Viscount Younger, and er bro of 1 & last Baron Blanesburgh, GBE, PC), of Ravenswood, Melrose; *b* 6 Sept 1905; *Educ* Winchester, Balliol Oxford; *m* 1963, Nora Elizabeth (m dis 1967), da of Brig Edward Balfour, CVO, DSO, OBE, MC (d 1955), and Lady Ruth Balfour (eldest da of 2 Earl of Balfour - himself s of the Con PM 1902-05 - by his w Lady Elizabeth Lytton, da of 1 Earl of Lytton), of Balbirnie, Markinch, Fife; 1 da; *Heir* none; *Career* served 1939-45 War (RA), Lt-Col 1944; memb Roy Co of Archers (Queen's Bodyguard for Scotland) 1955-; formerly chm and md Scottish Investment Trust Co Ltd 1965-; chairman Highland Tourist (Cairngorm Development) Ltd 1966-; chairman Conservative Party in Scotland 1971-74; *Style* - Sir William Younger, Bt, DSO, DL; 29 Moray pla, Edinburgh (☎ 031 225 8173)

YOUNSON, Maj-Gen Eric John; OBE (1952); s of Ernest Younson, B Com, M Litt, (d 1974); *b* 1 March 1919; *Educ* Jarrow G S, Durham U, BSc (Hons Chem), RMC of Science; *m* 1946, Jean Beaumont, da of William Henry Carter (d 1970); *Career* Royal Artillery & Staff Dir Staff RMCS 1952-54; Attaché British Embassy 1958-61; Head Def Science 3, MOD 1961-64; Dep Dir Artillery 1964-67; Dir-Gen Weapons Trials Miny of Technol 1967-70; v-pres and Pres Ordnance Board 1970-73; Depy Dir SIMA 1974-78; clerk Scientific Instrument Makers' Co 1976-; *Recreations* photography; *Clubs* Army & Navy; *Style* - Maj-Gen Eric Younson, OBE; 7 Pondwick rd, Harpenden, Herts (☎ 5892); Worshipful Co of Scientific Instrument Makers, 9 Montague Close, London SE1 (01 403 3300)

YPRES, 3 Earl of (UK 1922); John Richard Charles Lambart French; also Viscount French of Ypres (UK 1916); s of 2 Earl of Ypres (d 1958, s of Sir John French, the WW I Cdr (who started his career in the Navy, however) cr Earl of Ypres; the 1 Earl was fifth in descent from a yr bro of the Arthur French from whom the Barons de Freyne descend; both these branches share an ancestor with the

Barons ffrench in Walter ffrench, Ch Magistrate of Galway 1444-45) by his 1 w Olivia (da of Maj-Gen Thomas John and Edith Lambart, sis of Countess of Charlemont (3 Earl's w), 1 cous of Sir Gustavus Lambart, 1 Bt, and sixth in descent from Hon Oliver Lambart, 2 s of 1 Earl of Cavan); *b* 30 Dec 1921; *Educ* Winchester, Trin Coll Dublin; *m* 1, 1943 (m dis 1972), Maureen, da of H John Kelly, late of US Foreign Serv, resident at Stow Bedon Hall, Attleborough, Norfolk; 3 da; m 2, 1972, Deborah, da of R Roberts, of Liverpool; 1 da; *Heir* none; *Career* served WW II Capt KRRC; *Style* - The Rt Hon The Earl of Ypres

Z

ZAMOYSKA, Countess Betka Marya; da of Count Andrzej Zamoyski (yr bro of Count Stefan, whose children are Counts Zdzisz, *chef de famille* in UK, and Adam and Countess Marilena, *qqv*) by Priscilla, 2 da of Sir Hugh Stucley, 4 Bt, JP, DL; *b* 12 March 1948; *Educ* Cranborne Chase, LMH Oxford; *Career* freelance journalist; *Recreations* reading, theatre, films; *Style* - Countess Betke Zamoyska; 136 Hurlingham rd, SW6

ZAMOYSKI, Count Andrzej; 2 s of Count Moritz or Maurice Zamoyski, sometime Polish Ambass to France and Polish Foreign Min, also 2 cous of gf of Count Adam Zamoyski, *qv*; Maurice's gf was the eldest of the children of Count Stanislaus, himself the surviving s of Count Andreas Zamoyski, the recipient of the title of nobility from Empress Maria Teresa of Austria; *b* 10 Jan 1914; *Educ* U of Political Sci Warsaw, Nancy U (France); *m* 1950, Irena Dabrowska; 4 da (Barbara b 28 Jan 1951, Rosa Maria b 12 May 1955, Christina b 4 Jan 1959, Helena b 1960); *Career* formerly Capt Polish Army, later CA, now ret; *Recreations* shooting, fishing; *Style* - Count Andrzej Zamoyski; 16 Cleveland Mansions, Mowll st, SW9 (☎ 01 735 3728)

ZAMOYSKI, Count Adam Stefan; s of Lt-Col Count Stefan Zamoyski, OBE, VM, LLD, Order of Polonia Restituta (d 1976, fifth in descent from Andreas Zamoyski, cr Count 1778 (confirmed 1780) by Empress Maria Teresa of Austria at the time of the Partitions of Poland) by his w Princess Elizabeth Czartoryska; the Princess's gf was Prince Wladyslaw Czartoryski (s of Tsar Alexander I's For Minister Prince Adam, who was also briefly head of Independent Poland 1830), while her grand mother (Wladyslaw's w) was HRH Princess Marguerite d'Orléans (da of HRH The Duc de Nemours, 2 s of Louis Philippe, King of the French); *b* 11 Jan 1949 in New York; *Educ* Downside, Queen's Oxford; *Career* Knight of Honour & Devotion Sov Mil Order of Malta 1977, Kt of Justice Constantinian Order of St George (House of Bourbon Sicily) 1978; author; *Clubs* Pratt's, Polish Hearth; *Style* - Count Adam Zamoyski; 33 Ennismore gdns, SW7 (☎ 01 584 9053)

ZAMOYSKI, Tomasz Józef Tadeusz Rózyc; s of Tadeusz Kazimierz Juljan Rózyc Zamoyski, Kt Cdr Order of Polonia Restituta (d 1980, of a different clan to that of the Counts Zamoyski; Tadeusz's ancestors were involved in defence of Czestochowa during the Polish Swedish War of the 1660s); *b* 22 May 1935; *Educ* Malvern, Sidney Sussex Cambridge, Johann Wolfgang Goethe U Frankfurt, Florence U; *m* 1959, Nicole, da of Marcel Tranier, of Paris; 1 s (Matthew Tadeusz Tomasz Rózyc b 1972), 1 da (Arabella Halina Suzanne Rózyc Zamoyska b 1974); *Career* dir HZI International Ltd; *Recreations* hunting; *Clubs* Lansdowne; *Style* - Tomasz Zamoyski Esq; 132 Kensington Park rd, W11 (☎ 01 229 8040)

ZAMOYSKI, Count Wojciech Michal; s of Count Michal Zamoyski (himself 2 s of Count Adam Z, sometime ADC to Tsar Nicholas II, by his marriage with Countess Marie Potocka; Adam the ADC was the youngest bro of Count Adam Zamoyski's (*qv*) ggf Count Stefan); *b* 12 Sept 1927; *Educ* Poland, Angola, S Africa; *m* 1955, Isobel, da of William Forbes-Robertson Mutch, of Aberdeenshire; 2 s (Paul b 1957, Alexander b 1962), 1 da (Anna Isabella b 1960); *Career* formerly official at

Rhodesian High Commission, now at Miny Overseas Devpt; *Recreations* Poland, the Third World; *Style* - Count Wojciech Zamoyski; 7 Bradford House, Springvale Terrace, W14 (☎ 01 602 6723)

ZAMOYSKI, Count Zdzisz; s of late Count (Stefan) Zamoyski, *chef de famille* in UK; er bro of Count Adam Zamoyski, *qv*; *Style* - Count Zdzisz Zamoyski; Ashfield House, The Horns, Hawkhurst, Kent

ZAMOYSKI, Count Zygmunt Ignacy Stukely; s of Count Andrzej Zamoyski (s of Count Wladislaw Zamoyski and yr bro of late Count Stefan, f of Counts Zdzisz and Adam and Countess Marilena, *qqv*) by Priscilla, 2 da of Sir Hugh Stucley, 4 Bt, JP, DL; *b* 23 Nov 1937; *Educ* Stowe, Ch Ch Oxford; *Style* - Count Zygmunt Zamoyski

ZANKEL, Hon Mrs (Alison Victoria); *née* Poole; da of 1 Baron Poole, CBE, TD, PC; *b* 1936; *m* 1961, Dr Fritz Zankel; 2 s; *Style* - The Hon Mrs Zankel; Staudgasse 75, Vienna, Austria

ZETLAND, 3 Marquess of (UK 1892); Sir Lawrence Aldred Mervyn Dundas; 7 Bt (GB 1762), ED, DL (N Yorks 1965); also Baron Dundas (GB 1794), Earl of Zetland (UK 1838), and Earl of Ronaldshay (UK 1892); s of 2 Marquess of Zetland, KG, GCSI, GCIE, PC (d 1961); *b* 12 Nov 1908; *Educ* Harrow, Trin Cambridge; *m* 1936, Katherine Mary Penelope, CStJ, da of Col Ebenezer Lecky Pike, CBE, MC; 3 s, 1 da; *Heir* s, Earl of Ronaldshay; *Career* ret co dir & farmer; late Maj M East WW II; patron one living; *Recreations* tennis, racing (race horse: 'Irishman'); *Clubs* Jockey, All England Lawn Tennis; *Style* - The Most Hon Marquess of Zetland ED DL; Aske, Richmond, N Yorks (☎ 0748 3222); 59 Cadogan Place, SW1 (☎ 01 235 6542)

ZIEGLER, Paul Oliver; s of Maj Colin Louis Ziegler DSO DL (d 1977); *b* 9 Dec 1925; *Educ* Eton; *m* 1950, Margaret Sybil, da of Sir Lionel Cust, CBE (d 1963, s of Sir Lionel Cust, KCVO, and Hon Sybil Lyttelton; Sybil was da of 4 Baron Lyttelton and sis of Hester, who m the Rev Cyril Alington, sometime Headmaster of Eton and f-in-law of Lord Home of the Hirsel; Sir Lionel sr was gs of 1 Baron Brownlow); 2 s (Adam b 1952; William b 1956, m 1979 Sarah, maternal gda of Lt Robert Harcourt, whose half bro was cr Viscount Harcourt, by Margorie Cunard, 1 cous of Sir Bache Cunard, 3 Bt, husb of Emerald and f of Nancy); *Career* slr, sr ptnr Moore & Blatch, of Lymington; *Recreations* reading, gardening, theatre; *Style* - Paul Ziegler Esq; Hightown Farm, Ringwood, Hants (☎ 4278)

ZIEGLER, Philip Sandeman; s of Maj C L Ziegler DSO, DL (d 1977); *b* 24 Dec 1928; *Educ* Eton, New Coll Oxford; *m* 1, 1960, Sarah, da of late Sir William Collins; 1 s, 1 da; m 2, 1971, Mary Clare, nee Charrington; 1 s; *Career* editorial dir Collins 1972, ed-in-ch 1979-80 (joined 1967); HM Diplomatic Serv 1952-67; author, official biographer of Earl Mountbatten of Burma; *Clubs* Travellers'; *Style* - Philip Ziegler Esq; 22 Cottesmore Gardens, W8 (☎ 01 937 1903); Picket Orchard, Ringwood, Hants (☎ 3258)

ZIELENKIEWICZ, Hon Mrs; Hon Catherine; *née* Sinclair; da of 1 Viscount Thurso, KT, CMG, PC (d 1970); *b* 25 Oct 1919; *m* 1957, Kazimier Zielenkiewicz; 1 da (Clementina b 1958); *Career* memb Soc Scottish Women Artists; *Style* - The Hon Mrs Zielenkiewicz; The Mill House, Isle Brewers, Taunton

ZIFF, Robert Paul; *b* 20 Dec 1935; *Educ* Giggleswick Sch; *Career* memb Livery Co Worshipful Co of Pattenmakers 1979, dir Stylo Shoes Ltd, chm of Stylo Matchmakers Int Ltd, Public Eye Enterprises Ltd, Whitham & Schofield Ltd; *Recreations* golf, tennis, skiing; *Clubs* St James's, Annabel's, White Elephant; *Style* - Robert Ziff Esq; Gallogate House, Weeton, Leeds

ZILKHA, Selim Khedoury; s of Khedoury Aboodi Zilkha; *b* 7 April 1927; *Educ* English Sch Heliopolis Egypt, Horace Mann Sch for Boys USA, Williams Coll USA; *m* 1953, Diane (m dis); 1 s, 1 da; *Career* chm and md Mothercare Ltd and assoc cos 1961-, chm Amerfin Co Ltd GB 1955-68, Sirella Co of GB Ltd 1957-62, chm/jt md Lewis and Burrows Ltd 1961-64, dir Zilkha and Sons Inc 1947-; *Recreations* bridge, backgammon, golf, tennis, horse racing; *Clubs* Portland, Brooks's, Sunningdale Golf, Roy St George's, Travellers'; owner of racehorses: Prince Thatch, Safarik, Un Grenadier, Set In His Ways (Sire: Habitat), Princesse Steel, Prince Blakeney (Sire: Blakeney), Six Shooter, Royal Feast, Prince Rheingold (Sire: Rheingold), Prince Bustino (Sire: Bustino), Prince Nonoalco, Prince Northfields, Prince Spruce, Prince Fandango, Prince Reviewer, Prince Bless, Prince Moulton, Princess Galicia, Prince Judger, Princess Gayle, Princess Majestic, Prince Maj, Prince Nono, Prince Mississipi; *Style* - Selim Zilkha Esq; 74 Portland Place, W1 (☎ 01 580 3563)

ZINNEMANN, Fred; s of Dr Oskar Zinnemann (d 1941); *b* 29 April 1907; *Educ* Vienna U, Ecole Technique de Cinématographie Paris; *m* 1936, Renée, nee Bartlett; 1 s; *Career* film director: *High Noon* 1951, *From Here To Eternity* 1953, *Oklahoma* 1955, *The Nun's Story* 1958, *A Man For All Seasons* 1967, *The Day Of The Jackal* 1973, *Julia* 1977; motion picture Academy Awards (Oscars) for directing 1951, 1954, 1967; Br Film Academy Award (BAFTA) 1979; *Recreations* mountaineering, chamber music; *Clubs* Sierra (San Francisco); *Style* - Fred Zinnemann Esq; 128 Mount st, W1 (☎ 629 4335)

ZOLLINGER, Fred Edward; s of Alfred Edward Zollinger (d 1957); *b* 6 July 1922; *Educ* Queens' Cambridge; *m* 1953, Flora, da of late Brig-Gen Wallace Wright, VC; *Career* chm of Imperial Continental Gas Assoc 1974-, chm Century Power & Light Ltd 1974-, dir of Calor Gas Holding Co Ltd 1974-, Pirelli Gen Cable Works Ltd 1971-, Lazard Bros & Co Ltd 1966-; *Recreations* skiing; *Style* - Fred Zollinger Esq; The House of Barns, Chobham, Woking, Surrey (☎ Chobham 8815)

ZOUCHE, 18 Baron (E 1308); Sir James Assheton Frankland; 12 Bt (E 1660); s of Hon Sir Thomas Frankland, 11 Bt (d 1944, s of Sir Frederick Frankland, 10 Bt, by his w Baroness Zouche (d 1965), 17 holder of the Peerage and descendant of Eudes La Zouche, yr bro of Sir Roger La Zouche of Ashby after whose family Ashby-de-la-Zouch is named); Lord Zouche is coheir to Baronies of St Maur and Grey of Codnor (abeyant since 1628 & 1496 respectively); *b* 23 Feb 1943; *Educ* Lycée Jacard Lausanne; *m* 1978, Sally, da of Roderic Barton; *Heir* unc, Hon Roger Frankland; *Career* Capt 15/19 King's Roy Hussars (ret 1968), ADC to Govr Tasmania 1965-68, Hon ADC to Govr Victoria 1975-; V-Pres Multiple Sclerosis Soc Victoria 1973-; co dir; *Recreations* shooting; *Clubs* Cavalry & Guards, Melbourne; *Style* - The Rt Hon Lord Zouche; 25 Erin st, Richmond, Victoria 3121, Australia (☎ 03 429 1405)

ZU LÖWENSTEIN-WERTHEIM-FREUDENBERG, HSH Prince Rupert Ludwig Ferdinand; also Count von Loewenstein-Scharffeneck; s of Prince Leopold zu Löwenstein-Wertheim-Freudenberg (of the family of mediatised Princes, title of Bavarian Prince conferred 1812, stemming from the morganatic marriage of Elector Palatine Friedrich I, who d 1476, with Klara Tott, of Augsburg; Counts of HRE 1494, recreated 1875); *b* 24 Aug 1933; *Educ* St Christopher's Letchworth, Magdalen Oxford; *m* 1957, Josephine Clare, da of Capt Montagu Lowry-Corry (d 1977, gggs of 2 Earl Belmore) by his 1 w, Hon Mary Biddulph, yr da of 2 Baron Biddulph; 2 s (Prince Rudolf Amadeus, b 1957; Prince Konrad Friedrich Ferdinand Johannes Ottokar Sylvester, b 1958), 1 da (Princess Maria Theodora Marjorie, b 1966); *Career* fin advsr, formerly merchant banker; Kt of Honour & Devotion Sov Mil Order Malta 1980, Kt of Justice Constantine Order of St George 1981; *Recreations* music; *Clubs* Beefsteak, Boodle's, Buck's, Portland, White's; *Style* - HSH Prince Rupert zu Löwenstein-Wertheim-Freudenberg; Biddestone Manor, Chippenham, Wilts (☎ 0249 714520); 63 Campden Hill Court, W8 (☎ 01 937 3591)

ZUCCOLILLO, His Excellency Señor Antonio R; *m*; *Career* Paraguayan Ambass to UK 1981-; *Style* - HE Señor Antonio R Zuccolillo; The Paraguayan Embassy, Braemar Lodge, Cornwall gdns, SW7 (☎ 01 937 1253)

ZUCKERMAN, Baron (Life Peer UK 1971); Solly Zuckerman; OM (1968), KCB (1964, CB 1946); s of Moses Zuckerman; *b* 30 May 1904; *Educ* Cape Town U; *m* 1939, Lady Joan Rufus Isaacs, da of 2 Marquess of Reading; 1 s, 1 da; *Career* FRS, MRCS, FRCP; kt 1956; pres: Fauna Preservation Soc 1974-, Br Industrial Biological Res Assoc 1974, Zoological Preservation Soc 1974-; Prof Emeritus E Anglia and Birmingham Us; ch scientific advr to Def Sec 1960-66, to HM Govt 1964-71; *Style* The Rt Hon The Lord Zuckerman, OM, KCB; The Shooting Box, Burnham Thorpe, King's Lynn, Norfolk; East Anglia University, Norwich

ZUCKERMAN, Baroness; Lady Joan Alice Violet Rufus; *née* Isaacs; JP (Birmingham 1961, Norfolk 1967); da of 2 Marquess of Reading, GCMG, CBE, TD, QC, and Hon Eva Mond, CBE, JP (da of 1 Baron Melchett); *b* 19 July 1918; *m* 1939, Baron Zuckerman, *qv*; 1 s, 1 da; *Style* - The Rt Hon The Lady Zuckerman, JP; The Shooting Box, Burnham Thorpe, King's Lynn, Norfolk

ZUCKERMAN, Hon Paul Sebastian; s of Baron Zuckerman and Lady Joan Rufus Isaacs, da of 2 Marquess of Reading; *b* 1945; *Educ* Rugby, Trin Cambridge; *m* 1972, Mrs Janette Hampel, da of R R Mather, of Stoke-by-Clare, Suffolk; *Style* The Hon Paul Zuckerman, 3526 Edmund's st NW, Washington DC, USA

ZUZE, His Excellency Lt-Gen Peter Dingiswayo; *Career* High Cmmr Republic of Zambia to UK 1981-; *Style* His Excellency Lt-Gen Peter Dingiswayo Zuze, Zambian High Commission, Zambia House, 7 Cavendish Place, W1 (☎ 01 580 0691)